THE
CIA
WORLD
FACTBOOK
2018-2019

THE CIA WORLD FACTBOOK 2018-2019

CENTRAL INTELLIGENCE AGENCY

Skyhorse Publishing

Skyhorse Publishing books may be purchased in bulk at special discounts for sales promotion, corporate gifts, fund-raising, or educational purposes. Special editions can also be created to specifications. For details, contact the Special Sales Department, Skyhorse Publishing, 307 West 36th Street, 11th Floor, New York, NY 10018 or info@skyhorsepublishing.com.

Skyhorse® and Skyhorse Publishing® are registered trademarks of Skyhorse Publishing, Inc.®, a Delaware corporation.

Visit our website at www.skyhorsepublishing.com.

10 9 8 7 6 5 4 3 2 1

Library of Congress Cataloging-in-Publication Data is available on file.

Cover design by Rain Saukas

Print ISBN: 978-1-5107-4027-3
Ebook ISBN: 978-1-5107-4028-0

Printed in Canada

CONTENTS

INTRODUCTION

The *World Factbook* is prepared by the Central Intelligence Agency for the use of US Government officials, and the style, format, coverage, and content are designed to meet their specific requirements. Information is provided by Antarctic Information Program (National Science Foundation), Armed Forces Medical Intelligence Center (Department of Defense), Bureau of the Census (Department of Commerce), Bureau of Labor Statistics (Department of Labor), Central Intelligence Agency, Council of Managers of National Antarctic Programs, Defense Intelligence Agency (Department of Defense), Department of Energy, Department of State, Fish and Wildlife Service (Department of the Interior), Maritime Administration (Department of Transportation), National Geospatial-Intelligence Agency (Department of Defense), Naval Facilities Engineering Command (Department of Defense), Office of Insular Affairs (Department of the Interior), Office of Naval Intelligence (Department of Defense), US Board on Geographic Names (Department of the Interior), US Transportation Command (Department of Defense), Oil & Gas Journal, and other public and private sources.

The *Factbook* is in the public domain. Accordingly, it may be copied freely without permission of the Central Intelligence Agency (CIA). The official seal of the CIA, however, may **NOT** be copied without permission as required by the CIA Act of 1949 (50 U.S.C. section 403m). Misuse of the official seal of the CIA could result in civil and criminal penalties.

Citation model:
The World Factbook 2013-14. Washington, DC: Central Intelligence Agency, 2013.
https://www.cia.gov/library/publications/the-world-factbook/index.html

Comments and queries are welcome and may be addressed to:

Central Intelligence Agency
Attn: Office of Public Affairs
Washington, DC 20505
Hours: Monday-Friday 8:00 AM-4:30 PM Eastern Standard Time
Telephone: [1] (703) 482-0623
FAX: [1] (703) 482-17

A BRIEF HISTORY OF BASIC INTELLIGENCE AND *THE WORLD FACTBOOK*

The Intelligence Cycle is the process by which information is acquired, converted into intelligence, and made available to policymakers. Information is raw data from any source, data that may be fragmentary, contradictory, unreliable, ambiguous, deceptive, or wrong. Intelligence is information that has been collected, integrated, evaluated, analyzed, and interpreted. Finished intelligence is the final product of the Intelligence Cycle ready to be delivered to the policymaker.

The three types of finished intelligence are: basic, current, and estimative. Basic intelligence provides the fundamental and factual reference material on a country or issue. Current intelligence reports on new developments. Estimative intelligence judges probable outcomes. The three are mutually supportive: basic intelligence is the foundation on which the other two are constructed; current intelligence continually updates the inventory of knowledge; and estimative intelligence revises overall interpretations of country and issue prospects for guidance of basic and current intelligence. *The World Factbook, The President's Daily Brief*, and the *National Intelligence Estimates* are examples of the three types of finished intelligence.

The United States has carried on foreign intelligence activities since the days of George Washington but only since World War II have they been coordinated on a government-wide basis. Three programs have highlighted the development of coordinated basic intelligence since that time: (1) *the Joint Army Navy Intelligence Studies* (JANIS), (2) *the National Intelligence Survey* (NIS), and (3) *The World Factbook*.

During World War II, intelligence consumers realized that the production of basic intelligence by different components of the US Government resulted in a great duplication of effort and conflicting information. The Japanese attack on Pearl Harbor in 1941 brought home to leaders in Congress and the executive branch the need for integrating departmental reports to national policymakers. Detailed and coordinated information was needed not only on such major powers as Germany and Japan, but also on places of little previous interest. In the Pacific Theater, for example, the Navy and Marines

had to launch amphibious operations against many islands about which information was unconfirmed or nonexistent. Intelligence authorities resolved that the United States should never again be caught unprepared.

In 1943, Gen. George B. Strong (G-2), Adm. H. C. Train (Office of Naval Intelligence—ONI), and Gen. William J. Donovan (Director of the Office of Strategic Services—OSS) decided that a joint effort should be initiated. A steering committee was appointed on 27 April 1943 that recommended the formation of a Joint Intelligence Study Publishing Board to assemble, edit, coordinate, and publish the *Joint Army Navy Intelligence Studies* (JANIS). JANIS was the first interdepartmental basic intelligence program to fulfill the needs of the US Government for an authoritative and coordinated appraisal of strategic basic intelligence. Between April 1943 and July 1947, the board published 34 JANIS studies. JANIS performed well in the war effort, and numerous letters of commendation were received, including a statement from Adm. Forrest Sherman, Chief of Staff, Pacific Ocean Areas, which said, "JANIS has become the indispensable reference work for the shore-based planners."

The need for more comprehensive basic intelligence in the postwar world was well expressed in 1946 by George S. Pettee, a noted author on national security. He wrote in *The Future of American Secret Intelligence* (Infantry Journal Press, 1946, page 46) that world leadership in peace requires even more elaborate intelligence than in war. "The conduct of peace involves all countries, all human activities—not just the enemy and his war production."

The Central Intelligence Agency was established on 26 July 1947 and officially began operating on 18 September 1947. Effective 1 October 1947, the Director of Central Intelligence assumed operational responsibility for JANIS. On 13 January 1948, the National Security Council issued Intelligence Directive (NSCID) No. 3, which authorized the *National Intelligence Survey* (NIS) program as a peacetime replacement for the wartime JANIS program. Before adequate NIS country sections could be produced, government agencies had to develop more comprehensive gazetteers and better maps. The US Board on Geographic Names (BGN) compiled the names; the Department of the Interior produced the gazetteers; and CIA produced the maps.

The Hoover Commission's Clark Committee, set up in 1954 to study the structure and administration of the CIA, reported to Congress in 1955 that: "The National Intelligence Survey is an invaluable publication which provides the essential elements of basic intelligence on all areas of the world. There will always be a continuing requirement for keeping the Survey up-to-date." The *Factbook* was created as an annual summary and update to the encyclopedic NIS studies. The first classified *Factbook* was published in August 1962, and the first unclassified version was published in June 1971. The NIS program was terminated in 1973 except for the *Factbook*, map, and gazetteer components. The 1975 *Factbook* was the first to be made available to the public with sales through the US Government Printing Office (GPO). The *Factbook* was first made available on the Internet in June 1997. The year 2010 marks the 63th anniversary of the establishment of the Central Intelligence Agency and the 67th year of continuous basic intelligence support to the US Government by *The World Factbook* and its two predecessor programs.

The Evolution of The World Factbook

National Basic Intelligence Factbook produced semiannually until 1980. Country entries include sections on Land, Water, People, Government, Economy, Communications, and Defense Forces.

1981—Publication becomes an annual product and is renamed *The World Factbook*. A total of 165 nations are covered on 225 pages.

1983—Appendices (Conversion Factors, International Organizations) first introduced.

1984—Appendices expanded; now include: A. The United Nations, B. Selected United Nations Organizations, C. Selected International Organizations, D. Country Membership in Selected Organizations, E. Conversion Factors.

1987—A new Geography section replaces the former separate Land and Water sections. UN Organizations and Selected International Organizations appendices merged into a new International Organizations appendix. First multi-color-cover *Factbook*.

1988—More than 40 new geographic entities added to provide complete world coverage without overlap or omission. Among the new entities are Antarctica, oceans (Arctic, Atlantic, Indian, Pacific), and the World. The front-of-the-book explanatory introduction expanded and retitled to Notes, Definitions, and Abbreviations. Two new Appendices added: Weights and Measures (in place of Conversion Factors) and a Cross-Reference List of Geographic Names. *Factbook* size reaches 300 pages.

1989—Economy section completely revised and now includes an Overview briefly describing a country's economy. New entries added under People, Government, and Communications.

1990—The Government section revised and considerably expanded with new entries.

1991—A new International Organizations and Groups appendix added. *Factbook* size reaches 405 pages.

1992—Twenty new successor state entries replace those of the Soviet Union and Yugoslavia. New countries are respectively: Armenia, Azerbaijan, Belarus, Estonia, Georgia, Kazakhstan, Kyrgyzstan, Latvia, Lithuania, Moldova, Russia, Tajikistan, Turkmenistan, Ukraine, Uzbekistan; and Bosnia and Hercegovina, Croatia, Macedonia, Serbia and Montenegro, Slovenia. Number of nations in the *Factbook* rises to 188.

1993—Czechoslovakia's split necessitates new Czech Republic and Slovakia entries. New Eritrea entry added after it secedes from Ethiopia. Substantial enhancements made to Geography section.

1994—Two new appendices address Selected International Environmental Agreements. The gross domestic product (GDP) of most developing countries changed to a purchasing power parity (PPP) basis rather than an exchange rate basis. *Factbook* size up to 512 pages.

1995—The GDP of all countries now presented on a PPP basis. New appendix lists estimates of GDP on an exchange rate basis. Communications category split; Railroads, Highways, Inland waterways, Pipelines, Merchant marine, and Airports entries now make up a new Transportation category. *The World Factbook* is first produced on CD-ROM.

1996—Maps accompanying each entry now present more detail. Flags also introduced for nearly all entities. Various new entries appear under Geography and Communications. *Factbook* abbreviations consolidated into a new Appendix A. Two new appendices present a Cross-Reference List of Country Data Codes and a Cross-Reference List of Hydrogeographic Data Codes. Geographic coordinates added to Appendix H, Cross-Reference List of Geographic Names. *Factbook* size expands by 95 pages in one year to reach 652.

1997—*The World Factbook* introduced onto the Internet. A special printed edition prepared for the CIA's 50th anniversary. A schema or Guide to Country Profiles introduced. New color maps and flags now accompany each country profile. Category headings distinguished by shaded backgrounds. Number of categories expanded to nine with the addition of an Introduction (for only a few countries) and Transnational Issues (which includes Disputes-international and Illicit drugs).

1998—The Introduction category with two entries, Current issues and Historical perspective, expanded to more countries. Last year for the production of CD-ROM versions of the *Factbook*.

1999—Historical perspective and Current issues entries in the Introduction category combined into a new Background statement. Several new Economy entries introduced. A new physical map of the world added to the back-of-the-book reference maps.

2000—A new "country profile" added on the Southern Ocean. The Background statements dramatically expanded to over 200 countries and possessions. A number of new Communications entries added.

2001—Background entries completed for all 267 entities in the *Factbook*. Several new HIV/AIDS entries introduced under the People category. Revision begun on individual country maps to include elevation extremes and a partial geographic grid. Weights and Measures appendix deleted.

2002—New entry on Distribution of Family income—Gini index added. Revision of individual country maps continued (process still ongoing).

2003—In the Economy category, petroleum entries added for oil production, consumption, exports, imports, and proved reserves, as well as natural gas proved reserves.

2004—Bi-weekly updates launched on *The World Factbook* website. Additional petroleum entries included for natural gas production, consumption, exports, and imports. In the Transportation category, under Merchant marine, subfields added for foreign-owned vessels and those registered in other countries. Descriptions of the many forms of government mentioned in the Factbook incorporated into the Definitions and Notes.

2005—In the People category, a Major infectious diseases field added for countries deemed to pose a higher risk for travelers. In the Economy category, entries included for Current account balance, Investment, Public debt, and Reserves of foreign exchange and gold. The Transnational issues category expanded to include Refugees and internally displaced persons. Size of the printed *Factbook* reaches 702 pages.

2006—In the Economy category, national GDP figures now presented at Official Exchange Rates (OER) in addition to GDP at purchasing power parity (PPP). Entries in the Transportation section reordered; Highways changed to Roadways, and Ports and harbors to Ports and terminals.

2007—In the Government category, the Capital entry significantly expanded with up to four subfields, including new information having to do with time. The subfields consist of the name of the capital itself, its geographic coordinates, the time difference at the capital from coordinated universal time (UTC), and, if applicable, information on daylight saving time (DST). Where appropriate, a special note is added to highlight those countries with multiple time zones. A Trafficking in persons entry added to the Transnational issues category. A new appendix, Weights and Measures, (re)introduced to the online version of the *Factbook*.

2008—In the Geography category, two fields focus on the increasingly vital resource of water: Total renewable water resources and Freshwater withdrawal. In the Economy category, three fields added for: Stock of direct foreign investment—at home, Stock of direct foreign investment—abroad, and Market value of publicly traded shares. Concise descriptions of all major religions included in the Definitions and Notes. Responsibility for printing of *The World Factbook* turned over to the Government Printing Office.

2009—The online *Factbook* site completely redesigned with many new features. In the People category, two new fields provide information on education in terms of opportunity and resources: School Life Expectancy and Education expenditures. Additionally, the Urbanization entry expanded to include all countries. In the Economy category, five fields added: Central bank discount rate, Commercial bank prime lending rate, Stock of narrow money, Stock of broad money, and Stock of domestic credit.

2010—Weekly updates inaugurated on the *The World Factbook* website. The dissolution of the Netherlands Antilles results in two new listings: Curacao and Sint Maarten. In the Communications category, a Broadcast media field replaces the former Radio broadcast stations and TV broadcast stations entries. In the Geography section, under Natural hazards, a Volcanism subfield added for countries with historically active volcanoes. In the Government category, a new National anthems field introduced. Concise descriptions of all major Legal systems incorporated into the Definitions and Notes. In order to facilitate comparisons over time, dozens of the entries in the Economy category expanded to include two (and in some cases three) years' worth of data.

2011—The People section expanded to People and Society, incorporating ten new fields. The Economy category added Taxes and other revenues and Budget surplus (+) or deficit (–), while the Government section introduced International law organization participation and National symbols. A new African nation, South Sudan, brings the total number of countries in *The World Factbook* to 195.

2012—A new Energy category introduced with 23 energy-related fields. Several distinctive features added to *The World Factbook* website: 1) playable audio files in the Government section for the National Anthems entry, 2) online graphics in the form of a Population Pyramid feature in the People and Society category's Age Structure field, and 3) a Users Guide enabling visitors to navigate the *Factbook* more easily and efficiently. A new and distinctive Map of the World Oceans highlights an expanded array of regional and country maps. Size of the printed *Factbook*'s 50th anniversary edition reaches 847 pages.

2013—In the People and Society section five fields introduced: Demographic profile, Mother's mean age at first birth, Contraceptive prevalence rate, Dependency ratios, and Child labor—children ages 5–14. In the Transnational Issues category, a new *stateless persons* subfield embedded under the Refugees and internally displaced persons entry. In the Economy section two fields added: GDP—composition by end use and Gross national saving. In the Government category the Judicial branch entry revised and expanded to include three new subfields: *highest court(s)*, *judge selection and term of office*, and *subordinate courts*.

2014—In the Transportation category, the Ports and terminals field substantially expanded with subfields for major seaport(s), river port(s), lake port(s), oil/gas terminal(s), LNG terminal(s), dry bulk cargo port(s), container port(s), and cruise/ferry port(s). In the Geography section, the Land boundaries entry revised for all countries, including the total country border length as well as the border lengths for all neighboring countries.

2015—In the Government category, the first part of the Legislative Branch field thoroughly revised, expanded, and updated for all countries under a new description heading. This sub-entry includes the legislative structure, the formal name(s), the number of legislative seats, the types of voting constituencies and voting systems, and the member term of office. Area Comparison Maps introduced online for about half of the world's countries. (More to follow when they become available.)

2016—In the Government section for all countries, a new Citizenship field added to describe policies related to the acquisition of citizenship and to the recognition of dual citizenship. Also, under the Country Name entry, etymologies (historical origins) added to explain how countries acquired their names. A new Electricity Access field added to introduce the Energy category. A Population Distribution field included in both the People and Society and the Geography sections. A major addition to the Transportation category is National Air Transport system with subfields on a country's registered air carriers, inventory of registered aircraft, annual passenger traffic, and annual freight traffic.

2017—In the Government category the Constitution entry revised and expanded with new subfields for history and amendments. Information on piracy moved from the Transportation category to a new Maritime threats field in the Military and Security category. In the Transportation section, the Merchant marine entry revised to not only include the total number of ships, but also the major types: bulk carrier, container ship, general cargo, oil tanker, and other.

Abbreviations This information is included in **Appendix A: Abbreviations**, which includes all abbreviations and acronyms used in the *Factbook*, with their expansions.

Acronyms An acronym is an abbreviation coined from the initial letter of each successive word in a term or phrase. In general, an acronym made up solely from the first letter of the major words in the expanded form is rendered in all capital letters (NATO from North Atlantic Treaty Organization; an exception would be ASEAN for Association of Southeast Asian Nations). In general, an acronym made up of more than the first letter of the major words in the expanded form is rendered with only an initial capital letter (Comsat from Communications Satellite Corporation; an exception would be NAM from Nonaligned Movement). Hybrid forms are sometimes used to distinguish between initially identical terms (ICC for International Chamber of Commerce and ICCt for International Criminal Court).

Administrative divisions This entry generally gives the numbers, designatory terms, and first-order administrative divisions as approved by the US Board on Geographic Names (BGN). Changes that have been reported but not yet acted on by the BGN are noted.

Age structure This entry provides the distribution of the population according to age. Information is included by sex and age group as follows: *0-14 years (children), 15-24 years (early working age), 25-54 years (prime working age), 55-64 years (mature working age), 65 years and over (elderly)*. The age structure of a population affects a nation's key socioeconomic issues. Countries with young populations (high percentage under age 15) need to invest more in schools, while countries with older populations (high percentage ages 65 and over) need to invest more in the health sector. The age structure can also be used to help predict potential political issues. For example, the rapid growth of a young adult population unable to find employment can lead to unrest.

Agriculture—products This entry is an ordered listing of major crops and products starting with the most important.

Airports This entry gives the total number of airports or airfields recognizable from the air. The runway(s) may be paved (concrete or asphalt surfaces) or unpaved (grass, earth, sand, or gravel surfaces) and may include closed or abandoned installations. Airports or airfields that are no longer recognizable (overgrown, no facilities, etc.) are not included. Note that not all airports have accommodations for refueling, maintenance, or air traffic control.

Airports—with paved runways This entry gives the total number of airports with paved runways (concrete or asphalt surfaces) by length. For airports with more than one runway, only the longest runway is included according to the following five groups—(1) *over 3,047 m* (over 10,000 ft), (2) *2,438 to 3,047 m* (8,000 to 10,000 ft), (3) *1,524 to 2,437 m* (5,000 to 8,000 ft), (4) *914 to 1,523 m* (3,000 to 5,000 ft), and (5) *under 914 m* (under 3,000 ft). Only airports with usable runways are included in this listing. Not all airports have facilities for refueling, maintenance, or air traffic control. The type aircraft capable of operating from a runway of a given length is dependent upon a number of factors including elevation of the runway, runway gradient, average maximum daily temperature at the airport, engine types, flap settings, and take-off weight of the aircraft.

Airports—with unpaved runways This entry gives the total number of airports with unpaved runways (grass, dirt, sand, or gravel surfaces) by length. For airports with more than one runway, only the longest runway is included according to the following five groups—(1) *over 3,047 m* (over 10,000 ft), (2) *2,438 to 3,047 m* (8,000 to 10,000 ft), (3) *1,524 to 2,437 m* (5,000 to 8,000 ft), (4) *914 to 1,523 m* (3,000 to 5,000 ft), and (5) *under 914 m* (under 3,000 ft). Only airports with usable runways are included in this listing. Not all airports have facilities for refueling, maintenance, or air traffic control. The type aircraft capable of operating from a runway of a given length is dependent upon a number of factors including elevation of the runway, runway gradient, average maximum daily temperature at the airport, engine types, flap settings, and take-off weight of the aircraft.

Appendixes This section includes *Factbook*-related material by topic.

Area This entry includes three subfields. *Total area* is the sum of all land and water areas delimited by international boundaries and/or coastlines. *Land area* is the aggregate of all surfaces delimited by international boundaries and/or coastlines, excluding inland water bodies (lakes, reservoirs, rivers). *Water area* is the sum of the surfaces of all inland water bodies, such as lakes, reservoirs, or rivers, as delimited by international boundaries and/or coastlines.

Area—comparative This entry provides an area comparison based on total area equivalents. Most entities are compared with the entire US or one of the 50 states based on area measurements (1990 revised) provided by the US Bureau of the Census. The smaller entities are compared with Washington, DC (178 sq km, 69 sq mi) or The Mall in Washington, DC (0.59 sq km, 0.23 sq mi, 146 acres).

Background This entry usually highlights major historic events and current issues and may include a statement about one or two key future trends.

Birth rate This entry gives the average annual number of births during a year per 1,000 persons in the population at midyear; also known as crude birth rate. The birth rate is usually the dominant factor in determining the rate of population growth. It depends on both the level of fertility and the age structure of the population.

Broadcast media This entry provides information on the approximate number of public and private TV and radio stations in a country, as well as basic information on the availability of satellite and cable TV services.

Budget This entry includes *revenues, expenditures,* and capital expenditures. These figures are calculated on an exchange rate basis, i.e., not in purchasing power parity (PPP) terms.

Budget surplus (+) or deficit (−) This entry records the difference between national government revenues and expenditures, expressed as a percent of GDP. A positive (+) number indicates that revenues exceeded expenditures (a budget surplus), while a negative (−) number indicates the reverse (a budget deficit). Normalizing the data, by dividing the budget balance by GDP, enables easy comparisons across countries and indicates whether a national government saves or borrows money. Countries with high budget deficits (relative to their GDPs) generally have more difficulty raising funds to finance expenditures, than those with lower deficits.

Capital This entry gives the *name* of the seat of government, its *geographic coordinates,* the *time difference* relative to **Coordinated Universal Time (UTC)** and the time observed in Washington, DC, and, if applicable, information on *daylight saving time* (DST). Where appropriate, a special note has been added to highlight those countries that have multiple time zones.

Carbon dioxide emissions from consumption of energy This entry is the total amount of carbon dioxide, measured in metric tons, released by burning fossil fuels in the process of producing and consuming energy.

Central bank discount rate This entry provides the annualized interest rate a country's central bank charges commercial, depository banks for loans to meet temporary shortages of funds.

Child labor—children ages 5-14 This entry gives the percent of children aged 5-14 (or the age range specified) engaged in child labor. We define "child labor" as work that deprives children of their childhood, their potential, and their dignity, and that is harmful to physical and mental development. It refers to work that is mentally, physically, socially, or morally dangerous and harmful to children. Such labor may deprive them of the opportunity to attend school, oblige them to leave school prematurely, or require them to combine school attendance with excessively long and heavy work. In its most extreme forms, child labor involves children being enslaved, separated from their families, exposed to serious hazards and illnesses, and/or left to fend for themselves on the streets of large cities—often a very early age.

Children under the age of 5 years underweight This entry gives the percent of children under five considered to be underweight. Underweight means weight-for-age is approximately 2 kg below for standard at age one, 3 kg below standard for ages two and three, and 4 kg below standard for ages four and five. This statistic is an indicator of the nutritional status of a community. Children who suffer from growth retardation as a result of poor diets and/or recurrent infections tend to have a greater risk of suffering illness and death.

Climate This entry includes a brief description of typical weather regimes throughout the year.

Coastline This entry gives the total length of the boundary between the land area (including islands) and the sea.

Commercial bank prime lending rate This entry provides a simple average of annualized interest rates commercial banks charge on new loans, denominated in the national currency, to their most credit-worthy customers.

Communications This category deals with the means of exchanging information and includes the telephone, radio, television, and Internet host entries.

Communications—note This entry includes miscellaneous communications information of significance not included elsewhere.

Constitution This entry provides information on a country's constitution. It includes the dates of previous constitutions, the dates of the main steps in making and implementing the latest constitution, and the dates of amendments. For countries with 1-3 previous constitutions, the years are listed; for those with 4-9 previous, the entry is listed as "several previous," and for those with 10 or more, the entry is "many previous." Amendment entries are treated in the same manner, and include the date(s) of the last amendment(s).

The main steps in creating a constitution and amending it usually include drafting, legislative and/or executive branch review and approval, public referendum, and entry into law. In many countries this process is lengthy. Terms commonly used to describe constitutional changes are "amended," "revised," or "reformed." In countries such as South Korea and Turkmenistan, sources differ as to whether changes are stated as new constitutions or are amendments/ revisions to existing ones.

A few countries including Canada, Israel, and UK have no single constitution document, but have various written and unwritten acts, statutes, common laws, and practices that, when taken together, describe a body of fundamental principles or established precedents as to how their countries are governed. Countries including Hong Kong, Macau, Oman, and Saudi Arabia use the term "basic law" instead of constitution.

A number of self-governing dependencies and territories such as the Cayman Islands, Bermuda, and Gibraltar (UK), Greenland and Faroe Islands (Denmark), Aruba, Curacao, and Sint Maarten (Netherlands), and Puerto Rico and the Virgin Islands (US) have their own country-level constitutions.

Contraceptive prevalence rate This field gives the percent of women of reproductive age (15-49) who are married or in union and are using, or whose sexual partner is using, a method of contraception according to the date of the most recent available data. The contraceptive prevalence rate is an indicator of health services, development, and women's empowerment. It is also useful in understanding, past, present, and future fertility trends, especially in developing countries.

Coordinated Universal Time (UTC) UTC is the international atomic time scale that serves as the basis of timekeeping for most of the world. The hours, minutes, and seconds expressed by UTC represent the time of day at the Prime Meridian (0° longitude) located near Greenwich, England as reckoned from midnight. UTC is calculated by the Bureau International des Poids et Mesures (BIPM) in Sevres, France. The BIPM averages data collected from more than 200 atomic time and frequency standards located at about 50 laboratories worldwide. UTC is the basis for all civil time with the Earth divided into time zones expressed as positive or negative differences from UTC. UTC is also referred to as "Zulu time." See the Standard Time Zones of the World map included with the **Reference Maps**.

Country data codes See **Data codes**.

Country map Most versions of the *Factbook* provide a country map in color. The maps were produced from the best information available at the time of preparation. Names and/or boundaries may have changed subsequently.

Country name This entry includes all forms of the country's name approved by the US Board on Geographic Names (Italy is used as an example): *conventional long form* (Italian Republic), *conventional short form* (Italy), *local long form* (Repubblica Italiana), *local short form* (Italia), *former* (Kingdom of Italy), as well as the *abbreviation*. Also see the **Terminology** note.

Crude oil—exports This entry is the total amount of crude oil exported, in barrels per day (bbl/day).

Crude oil—imports This entry is the total amount of crude oil imported, in barrels per day (bbl/day).

Crude oil—production This entry is the total amount of crude oil produced, in barrels per day (bbl/day).

Crude oil—proved reserves This entry is the stock of proved reserves of crude oil, in barrels (bbl). Proved reserves are those quantities of petroleum which, by analysis of geological and engineering data, can be estimated with a high degree of confidence to be commercially recoverable from a given date forward, from known reservoirs and under current economic conditions.

Current account balance This entry records a country's net trade in goods and services, plus net earnings from rents, interest, profits, and dividends, and net transfer payments (such as pension funds and worker remittances) to and from the rest of the world during the period specified. These figures are calculated on an exchange rate basis, i.e., not in purchasing power parity (PPP) terms.

Data codes This information is presented in **Appendix D: Cross-Reference List of Country Data Codes** and **Appendix E: Cross-Reference List of Hydrographic Data Codes.**

Date of information In general, information available as of January in a given year is used in the preparation of the printed edition.

Daylight Saving Time (DST) This entry is included for those entities that have adopted a policy of adjusting the official local time forward, usually one hour, from Standard Time during summer months. Such policies are most common in mid-latitude regions.

Death rate This entry gives the average annual number of deaths during a year per 1,000 population at midyear; also known as crude death rate. The death rate, while only a rough indicator of the mortality situation in a country, accurately indicates the current mortality impact on population growth. This indicator is significantly affected by age distribution, and most countries will eventually show a rise in the overall death rate, in spite of continued decline in mortality at all ages, as declining fertility results in an aging population.

Debt—external This entry gives the total public and private debt owed to nonresidents repayable in internationally accepted currencies, goods, or services. These figures are calculated on an exchange rate basis, i.e., not in purchasing power parity (PPP) terms.

Demographic profile This entry describes a country's key demographic features and trends and how they vary among regional, ethnic, and socioeconomic sub-populations. Some of the topics addressed are population age structure, fertility, health, mortality, poverty, education, and migration.

Dependency ratios Dependency ratios are a measure of the age structure of a population. They relate the number of individuals that are likely to be economically "dependent" on the support of others. Dependency ratios contrast the ratio of youths (ages 0-14) and the elderly (ages 65+) to the number of those in the working-age group (ages 15-64).Changes in the dependency ratio provide an indication of potential social support requirements resulting from changes in population age structures. As fertility levels decline, the dependency ratio initially falls because the proportion of youths decreases while the proportion of the population of working age increases. As fertility levels continue to decline, dependency ratios eventually increase because the proportion of the population of working age starts to decline and the proportion of elderly persons continues to increase.

total dependency ratio—The total dependency ratio is the ratio of combined youth population (ages 0-14) and elderly population (ages 65+) per 100 of working age (ages 15-64). A high total dependency ratio indicates that the working-age population and the overall economy face a greater burden to support and provide social services for youth and elderly persons, who are often economically dependent.

youth dependency ratio—The youth dependency ratio is the ratio of the youth population (ages 0-14) per 100 people of working age (ages 15-64). A high youth dependency ratio indicates that a greater investment needs to be made in schooling and other services for children.

elderly dependency ratio—The elderly dependency ratio is the ratio of the elderly population (ages 65+) per 100 people of working age (ages 15-64). Increases in the elderly dependency ratio put added pressure on governments to fund pensions and healthcare.

potential support ratio—The potential support ratio is the number of working-age people (ages 15-64) per one elderly person (ages 65+). As a population ages, the potential support ratio tends to fall, meaning there are fewer potential workers to support the elderly.

Dependency status This entry describes the formal relationship between a particular nonindependent entity and an independent state.

Dependent areas This entry contains an alphabetical listing of all nonindependent entities associated in some way with a particular independent state.

Diplomatic representation The US Government has diplomatic relations with 190 independent states, including 188 of the 193 UN members (excluded UN members are Bhutan, Cuba, Iran, North Korea, and the US itself). In addition, the US has diplomatic relations with 2 independent states that are not in the UN, the Holy See and Kosovo, as well as with the EU.

Diplomatic representation from the US This entry includes the *chief of mission*, *embassy* address, *mailing* address, *telephone* number, *FAX* number, *branch office* locations, *consulate general* locations, and *consulate* locations.

Diplomatic representation in the US This entry includes the *chief of mission*, *chancery address*, *telephone*, *FAX*, *consulate general locations*, and *consulate locations*. The use of the annotated title Appointed Ambassador refers to a new ambassador who has presented his/her credentials to the secretary of state but not the US president. Such ambassadors fulfill all diplomatic functions except meeting with or appearing at functions attended by the president until such time as they formally present their credentials at a White House ceremony.

Disputes—international This entry includes a wide variety of situations that range from traditional bilateral boundary disputes to unilateral claims of one sort or another. Information regarding disputes over international terrestrial and maritime boundaries has been reviewed by the US Department of State. References to other situations involving borders or frontiers may also be included, such as resource disputes, geopolitical questions, or irredentist issues; however, inclusion does not necessarily constitute official acceptance or recognition by the US Government.

Distribution of family income—Gini index This index measures the degree of inequality in the distribution of family income in a country. The index is calculated from the Lorenz curve, in which cumulative family income is plotted against the number of families arranged from the poorest to the richest. The index is the ratio of (a) the area between a country's Lorenz curve and the 45 degree helping line to (b) the entire triangular area under the 45 degree line. The more nearly equal a country's income distribution, the closer its Lorenz curve to the 45 degree line and the lower its Gini index, e.g., a Scandinavian country with an index of 25. The more unequal a country's income distribution, the farther its Lorenz curve from the 45 degree line and the higher its Gini index, e.g., a Sub-Saharan country with an index of 50. If income were distributed with perfect equality, the Lorenz curve would coincide with the 45 degree line and the index would be zero; if income were distributed with perfect inequality, the Lorenz curve would coincide with the horizontal axis and the right vertical axis and the index would be 100.

Drinking water source This entry provides information about access to improved or unimproved drinking water sources available to segments of the population of a country. *improved* drinking water—use of any of the following sources: piped water into dwelling, yard, or plot; public tap or standpipe; tubewell or borehole; protected dug well; protected spring; or rainwater collection. *Unimproved* drinking water—use of any of the following sources: unprotected dug well; unprotected spring; cart with small tank or drum; tanker truck; surface water, which includes rivers, dams, lakes, ponds, streams, canals or irrigation channels; or bottled water.

Economy This category includes the entries dealing with the size, development, and management of productive resources, i.e., land, labor, and capital.

Economy—overview This entry briefly describes the type of economy, including the degree of market orientation, the level of economic development, the most important natural resources, and the unique areas of specialization. It also characterizes major economic events and policy changes in the most recent 12 months and may include a statement about one or two key future macroeconomic trends.

Education expenditures This entry provides the public expenditure on education as a percent of GDP.

Electricity—consumption This entry consists of total electricity generated annually plus imports and minus exports, expressed in kilowatt-hours. The discrepancy between the amount of electricity generated and/or imported and the amount consumed and/or exported is accounted for as loss in transmission and distribution.

Electricity—exports This entry is the total exported electricity in kilowatt-hours.

Electricity—from fossil fuels This entry measures the capacity of plants that generate electricity by burning fossil fuels (such as coal, petroleum products, and natural gas), expressed as a share of the country's total generating capacity.

Electricity—from hydroelectric plants This entry measures the capacity of plants that generate electricity by water-driven turbines, expressed as a share of the country's total generating capacity.

Electricity—from nuclear fuels This entry measures the capacity of plants that generate electricity through radioactive decay of nuclear fuel, expressed as a share of the country's total generating capacity.

Electricity—from other renewable sources This entry measures the capacity of plants that generate electricity by using renewable energy sources other than hydroelectric (including, for example, wind, waves, solar, and geothermal), expressed as a share of the country's total generating capacity.

Electricity—imports This entry is the total imported electricity in kilowatt-hours.

Electricity—installed generating capacity This entry is the total capacity of currently installed generators, expressed in kilowatts (kW), to produce electricity. A 10-kilowatt (kW) generator will produce 10 kilowatt hours (kWh) of electricity, if it runs continuously for one hour.

Electricity—production This entry is the annual electricity generated expressed in kilowatt-hours. The discrepancy between the amount of electricity generated and/or imported and the amount consumed and/or exported is accounted for as loss in transmission and distribution.

Elevation extremes This entry includes both the highest point and the lowest point.

Energy This category includes entries dealing with the production, consumption, import, and export of various forms of energy including electricity, crude oil, refined petroleum products, and natural gas.

Entities Some of the independent states, dependencies, areas of special sovereignty, and governments included in this publication

are not independent, and others are not officially recognized by the US Government. "Independent state" refers to a people politically organized into a sovereign state with a definite territory. "Dependencies" and "areas of special sovereignty" refer to a broad category of political entities that are associated in some way with an independent state. "Country" names used in the table of contents or for page headings are usually the short-form names as approved by the US Board on Geographic Names and may include independent states, dependencies, and areas of special sovereignty, or other geographic entities. There are a total of 267 separate geographic entities in The World Factbook that may be categorized as follows:

INDEPENDENT STATES

195 Afghanistan, Albania, Algeria, Andorra, Angola, Antigua and Barbuda, Argentina, Armenia, Australia, Austria, Azerbaijan, The Bahamas, Bahrain, Bangladesh, Barbados, Belarus, Belgium, Belize, Benin, Bhutan, Bolivia, Bosnia and Herzegovina, Botswana, Brazil, Brunei, Bulgaria, Burkina Faso, Burma, Burundi, Cambodia, Cameroon, Canada, Cape Verde, Central African Republic, Chad, Chile, China, Colombia, Comoros, Democratic Republic of the Congo, Republic of the Congo, Costa Rica, Cote d'Ivoire, Croatia, Cuba, Cyprus, Czech Republic, Denmark, Djibouti, Dominica, Dominican Republic, Ecuador, Egypt, El Salvador, Equatorial Guinea, Eritrea, Estonia, Ethiopia, Fiji, Finland, France, Gabon, The Gambia, Georgia, Germany, Ghana, Greece, Grenada, Guatemala, Guinea, Guinea-Bissau, Guyana, Haiti, Holy See, Honduras, Hungary, Iceland, India, Indonesia, Iran, Iraq, Ireland, Israel, Italy, Jamaica, Japan, Jordan, Kazakhstan, Kenya, Kiribati, North Korea, South Korea, Kosovo, Kuwait, Kyrgyzstan, Laos, Latvia, Lebanon, Lesotho, Liberia, Libya, Liechtenstein, Lithuania, Luxembourg, Macedonia, Madagascar, Malawi, Malaysia, Maldives, Mali, Malta, Marshall Islands, Mauritania, Mauritius, Mexico, Federated States of Micronesia, Moldova, Monaco, Mongolia, Montenegro, Morocco, Mozambique, Namibia, Nauru, Nepal, Netherlands, NZ, Nicaragua, Niger, Nigeria, Norway, Oman, Pakistan, Palau, Panama, Papua New Guinea, Paraguay, Peru, Philippines, Poland, Portugal, Qatar, Romania, Russia, Rwanda, Saint Kitts and Nevis, Saint Lucia, Saint Vincent and the Grenadines, Samoa, San Marino, Sao Tome and Principe, Saudi Arabia, Senegal, Serbia, Seychelles, Sierra Leone, Singapore, Slovakia, Slovenia, Solomon Islands, Somalia, South Africa, South Sudan, Spain, Sri Lanka, Sudan, Suriname, Swaziland, Sweden, Switzerland, Syria, Tajikistan, Tanzania, Thailand, Timor-Leste, Togo, Tonga, Trinidad and Tobago, Tunisia, Turkey, Turkmenistan, Tuvalu, Uganda, Ukraine, UAE, UK, US, Uruguay, Uzbekistan, Vanuatu, Venezuela, Vietnam, Yemen, Zambia, Zimbabwe

OTHER

2 Taiwan, European Union

DEPENDENCIES AND AREAS OF SPECIAL SOVEREIGNTY

6 Australia—Ashmore and Cartier Islands, Christmas Island, Cocos (Keeling) Islands, Coral Sea Islands, Heard Island and McDonald Islands, Norfolk Island

2 China—Hong Kong, Macau

2 Denmark—Faroe Islands, Greenland

8 France—Clipperton Island, French Polynesia, French Southern and Antarctic Lands, New Caledonia, Saint Barthelemy, Saint Martin, Saint Pierre and Miquelon, Wallis and Futuna

3 Netherlands—Aruba, Curacao, Sint Maarten

3 New Zealand—Cook Islands, Niue, Tokelau

3 Norway—Bouvet Island, Jan Mayen, Svalbard

17 UK—Akrotiri, Anguilla, Bermuda, British Indian Ocean Territory, British Virgin Islands, Cayman Islands, Dhekelia, Falkland Islands, Gibraltar, Guernsey, Jersey, Isle of Man, Montserrat, Pitcairn Islands, Saint Helena, South Georgia and the South Sandwich Islands, Turks and Caicos Islands

14 US—American Samoa, Baker Island*, Guam, Howland Island*, Jarvis Island*, Johnston Atoll*, Kingman Reef*, Midway Islands*, Navassa Island, Northern Mariana Islands, Palmyra Atoll*, Puerto Rico, Virgin Islands, Wake Island (* consolidated in United States Pacific Island Wildlife Refuges entry)

MISCELLANEOUS
6 Antarctica, Gaza Strip, Paracel Islands, Spratly Islands, West Bank, Western Sahara

OTHER ENTITIES
5 oceans—Arctic Ocean, Atlantic Ocean, Indian Ocean, Pacific Ocean, Southern Ocean
1 World

267 total

Environment—current issues This entry lists the most pressing and important environmental problems. The following terms and abbreviations are used throughout the entry:

Acidification—the lowering of soil and water pH due to acid precipitation and deposition usually through precipitation; this process disrupts ecosystem nutrient flows and may kill freshwater fish and plants dependent on more neutral or alkaline conditions (see acid rain).

Acid rain—characterized as containing harmful levels of sulfur dioxide or nitrogen oxide; acid rain is damaging and potentially deadly to the earth's fragile ecosystems; acidity is measured using the pH scale where 7 is neutral, values greater than 7 are considered alkaline, and values below 5.6 are considered acid precipitation; note—a pH of 2.4 (the acidity of vinegar) has been measured in rainfall in New England.

Aerosol—a collection of airborne particles dispersed in a gas, smoke, or fog.

Afforestation—converting a bare or agricultural space by planting trees and plants; reforestation involves replanting trees on areas that have been cut or destroyed by fire.

Asbestos—a naturally occurring soft fibrous mineral commonly used in fireproofing materials and considered to be highly carcinogenic in particulate form.

Biodiversity—also biological diversity; the relative number of species, diverse in form and function, at the genetic, organism, community, and ecosystem level; loss of biodiversity reduces an ecosystem's ability to recover from natural or man-induced disruption.

Bio-indicators—a plant or animal species whose presence, abundance, and health reveal the general condition of its habitat.

Biomass—the total weight or volume of living matter in a given area or volume.

Carbon cycle—the term used to describe the exchange of carbon (in various forms, e.g., as carbon dioxide) between the atmosphere, ocean, terrestrial biosphere, and geological deposits.

Catchments—assemblages used to capture and retain rainwater and runoff; an important water management technique in areas with limited freshwater resources, such as Gibraltar.

DDT (dichloro-diphenyl-trichloro-ethane)—a colorless, odorless insecticide that has toxic effects on most animals; the use of DDT was banned in the US in 1972.

Defoliants—chemicals which cause plants to lose their leaves artificially; often used in agricultural practices for weed control, and may have detrimental impacts on human and ecosystem health.

Deforestation—the destruction of vast areas of forest (e.g., unsustainable forestry practices, agricultural and range land clearing, and the over exploitation of wood products for use as fuel) without planting new growth.

Desertification—the spread of desert-like conditions in arid or semi-arid areas, due to overgrazing, loss of agriculturally productive soils, or climate change.

Dredging—the practice of deepening an existing waterway; also, a technique used for collecting bottom-dwelling marine organisms (e.g., shellfish) or harvesting coral, often causing significant destruction of reef and ocean-floor ecosystems.

Drift-net fishing—done with a net, miles in extent, that is generally anchored to a boat and left to float with the tide; often results in an over harvesting and waste of large populations of non-commercial marine species (by-catch) by its effect of "sweeping the ocean clean."

Ecosystems—ecological units comprised of complex communities of organisms and their specific environments.

Effluents—waste materials, such as smoke, sewage, or industrial waste which are released into the environment, subsequently polluting it.

Endangered species—a species that is threatened with extinction either by direct hunting or habitat destruction.

Freshwater—water with very low soluble mineral content; sources include lakes, streams, rivers, glaciers, and underground aquifers.

Greenhouse gas—a gas that "traps" infrared radiation in the lower atmosphere causing surface warming; water vapor, carbon dioxide, nitrous oxide, methane, hydrofluorocarbons, and ozone are the primary greenhouse gases in the Earth's atmosphere.

Groundwater—water sources found below the surface of the earth often in naturally occurring reservoirs in permeable rock strata; the source for wells and natural springs.

Highlands Water Project—a series of dams constructed jointly by Lesotho and South Africa to redirect Lesotho's abundant water supply into a rapidly growing area in South Africa; while it is the largest infrastructure project in southern Africa, it is also the most costly and controversial; objections to the project include claims that it forces people from their homes, submerges farmlands, and squanders economic resources.

Inuit Circumpolar Conference (ICC)—represents the roughly 150,000 Inuits of Alaska, Canada, Greenland, and Russia in international environmental issues; a General Assembly convenes every three years to determine the focus of the ICC; the most current concerns are long-range transport of pollutants, sustainable development, and climate change.

Metallurgical plants—industries which specialize in the science, technology, and processing of metals; these plants produce highly concentrated and toxic wastes which can contribute to pollution of ground water and air when not properly disposed.

Noxious substances—injurious, very harmful to living beings.

Overgrazing—the grazing of animals on plant material faster than it can naturally regrow leading to the permanent loss of plant cover, a common effect of too many animals grazing limited range land.

Ozone shield—a layer of the atmosphere composed of ozone gas (O3) that resides approximately 25 miles above the Earth's surface and absorbs solar ultraviolet radiation that can be harmful to living organisms.

Poaching—the illegal killing of animals or fish, a great concern with respect to endangered or threatened species.

Pollution—the contamination of a healthy environment by man-made waste.

Potable water—water that is drinkable, safe to be consumed.

Salination—the process through which fresh (drinkable) water becomes salt (undrinkable) water; hence, desalination is the reverse process; also involves the accumulation of salts in topsoil caused by evaporation of excessive irrigation water, a process that can eventually render soil incapable of supporting crops.

Siltation—occurs when water channels and reservoirs become clotted with silt and mud, a side effect of deforestation and soil erosion.

Slash-and-burn agriculture—a rotating cultivation technique in which trees are cut down and burned in order to clear land for temporary agriculture; the land is used until its productivity declines at which point a new plot is selected and the process repeats; this practice is sustainable while population levels are low and time is permitted for regrowth of natural vegetation; conversely, where these conditions do not exist, the practice can have disastrous consequences for the environment.

Soil degradation—damage to the land's productive capacity because of poor agricultural practices such as the excessive use of pesticides or fertilizers, soil compaction from heavy equipment, or erosion of topsoil, eventually resulting in reduced ability to produce agricultural products.

Soil erosion—the removal of soil by the action of water or wind, compounded by poor agricultural practices, deforestation, overgrazing, and desertification.

Ultraviolet (UV) radiation—a portion of the electromagnetic energy emitted by the sun and naturally filtered in the upper atmosphere by the ozone layer; UV radiation can be harmful to living organisms and has been linked to increasing rates of skin cancer in humans.

Waterborne diseases—those in which bacteria survive in, and are transmitted through, water; always a serious threat in areas with an untreated water supply.

Environment—international agreements This entry separates country participation in international environmental agreements into two levels—*party to* and *signed, but not ratified*. Agreements are listed in alphabetical order by the abbreviated form of the full name.

Environmental agreements This information is presented in **Appendix C: Selected International Environmental Agreements**, which includes the name, abbreviation, date opened for signature, date entered into force, objective, and parties by category.

Ethnic groups This entry provides an ordered listing of ethnic groups starting with the largest and normally includes the percent of total population.

Exchange rates This entry provides the average annual price of a country's monetary unit for the time period specified, expressed in units of local currency per US dollar, as determined by international market forces or by official fiat. The International Organization for Standardization (ISO) 4217 alphabetic currency code for the national medium of exchange is presented in parenthesis. Closing daily exchange rates are not presented in *The World Factbook*, but are used to convert stock values—e.g., the market value of publicly traded shares—to US dollars as of the specified date.

Executive branch This entry includes several subfields. *Chief of state* includes the name and title of the titular leader of the country who represents the state at official and ceremonial functions but may not be involved with the day-to-day activities of the government. *Head of government* includes the name and title of the top administrative leader who is designated to manage the day-to-day activities of the government. For example, in the UK, the monarch is the chief of state, and the prime minister is the head of government. In the US, the president is both the chief of state and the head of government. *Cabinet* includes the official name for this body of high-ranking advisers and the method for selection of members. *Elections* includes the nature of election process or accession to power, date of the last election, and date of the next election. *Election results* includes the percent of vote for each candidate in the last election.

Exports This entry provides the total US dollar amount of merchandise exports on an f.o.b. (free on board) basis. These figures are calculated on an exchange rate basis, i.e., not in purchasing power parity (PPP) terms.

Exports—commodities This entry provides a listing of the highest-valued exported products; it sometimes includes the percent of total dollar value.

Exports—partners This entry provides a rank ordering of trading partners starting with the most important; it sometimes includes the percent of total dollar value.

Fiscal year This entry identifies the beginning and ending months for a country's accounting period of 12 months, which often is the calendar year but which may begin in any month. All yearly references are for the calendar year (CY) unless indicated as a non-calendar fiscal year (FY).

Flag description This entry provides a written flag description produced from actual flags or the best information available at the time the entry was written. The flags of independent states are used by their dependencies unless there is an officially recognized local flag. Some disputed and other areas do not have flags.

Flag graphic Most versions of the *Factbook* include a color flag at the beginning of the country profile. The flag graphics were produced from actual flags or the best information available at the time of preparation. The flags of independent states are used by their dependencies unless there is an officially recognized local flag. Some disputed and other areas do not have flags.

Freshwater withdrawal (domestic/industrial/agricultural) This entry provides the annual quantity of water in cubic kilometers removed from available sources for use in any purpose. Water drawn-off is not necessarily entirely consumed and some portion may be returned for further use downstream. Domestic sector use refers to water supplied by public distribution systems. Note that some of this total may be used for small industrial and/or limited agricultural purposes. Industrial sector use is the quantity of water used by self-supplied industries not connected to a public distribution system. Agricultural sector use includes water used for irrigation and livestock watering, and does not account for agriculture directly dependent on rainfall. Included are figures for *total* annual water withdrawal and *per capita* water withdrawal.

GDP (official exchange rate) This entry gives the gross domestic product (GDP) or value of all final goods and services produced within a nation in a given year. A nation's GDP at official exchange rates (OER) is the home-currency-denominated annual GDP figure divided by the bilateral average US exchange rate with that country in that year. The measure is simple to compute and gives a precise measure of the value of output. Many economists prefer this measure when gauging the economic power an economy maintains vis-à-vis its neighbors, judging that an exchange rate captures the purchasing power a nation enjoys in the international marketplace. Official exchange rates, however, can be artificially fixed and/or subject to manipulation—resulting in claims of the country having an under- or over-valued currency—and are not necessarily the equivalent of a market-determined exchange rate. Moreover, even if the official exchange rate is market-determined, market exchange rates are frequently established by a relatively small set of goods and services (the ones the country trades) and may not capture the value of the larger set of goods the country produces. Furthermore, OER-converted GDP is not well suited to comparing domestic GDP over time, since appreciation/depreciation from one year to the next will make the OER GDP value rise/fall regardless of whether home-currency-denominated GDP changed.

GDP (purchasing power parity) This entry gives the gross domestic product (GDP) or value of all final goods and services produced within a nation in a given year. A nation's GDP at purchasing power parity (PPP) exchange rates is the sum value of all goods and services produced in the country valued at prices prevailing in the United States in the year noted. This is the measure most economists prefer when looking at per-capita welfare and when comparing living conditions or use of resources across countries. The measure is difficult to compute, as a US dollar value has to be assigned to all goods and services in the country regardless of whether these goods and services have a direct equivalent in the United States (for example, the value of an ox-cart or non-US military equipment); as a result, PPP estimates for some countries are based on a small and sometimes different set of goods and services. In addition, many countries do not formally participate in the World Bank's PPP project that calculates these measures, so the resulting GDP estimates for these countries may lack precision. For many developing countries, PPP-based GDP measures are multiples of the official exchange rate (OER) measure. The differences between the OER- and PPP-denominated GDP values for most of the wealthy industrialized countries are generally much smaller.

GDP—composition, by end use This entry shows who does the spending in an economy: consumers, businesses, government, and foreigners. The distribution gives the percentage contribution to total GDP of *household consumption, government consumption, investment in fixed capital, investment in inventories, exports of goods and services*, and *imports of goods and services*, and will total 100 percent of GDP if the data are complete.

  household consumption—consists of expenditures by resident households, and by nonprofit institutions that serve households, on goods and services that are consumed by individuals. This includes consumption of both domestically produced and foreign goods and services.

  government consumption—consists of government expenditures on goods and services. These figures exclude government transfer payments, such as interest on debt, unemployment, and social security, since such payments are not made in exchange for goods and services supplied.

  investment in fixed capital—consists of total business spending on fixed assets, such as factories, machinery, equipment, dwellings, and inventories of raw materials, which provide the basis for future production. It is measured gross of the depreciation of the assets, i.e., it includes investment that merely replaces worn-out or scrapped capital. Earlier editions of *The World Factbook* referred to this concept as Investment (gross fixed) and that data now have been moved to this new field.

  investment in inventories—consists of net changes to the stock of outputs that are still held by the units that produce them, awaiting further sale to an end user, such as automobiles sitting on a dealer's lot or groceries on the store shelves. This figure may be positive or negative. If the stock of unsold output increases during the relevant time period, *investment in inventories* is positive, but, if the stock of unsold goods declines, it will be negative. *Investment in inventories* normally is an early indicator of the state of the economy. If the stock of unsold items increases unexpectedly—because people stop buying—the economy may be entering a recession;but if the stock of unsold items falls—and goods "go flying off the shelves"—businesses normally try to replace those stocks, and the economy is likely to accelerate.

  exports of goods and services—consist of sales, barter, gifts, or grants of goods and services from residents to nonresidents.

  imports of goods and services—consist of purchases, barter, or receipts of gifts, or grants of goods and services by residents from nonresidents. *Exports* are treated as a positive item, while imports are treated as a negative item. In a purely accounting sense, *imports* have no direct impact on GDP, which only measures output of the domestic economy. Imports are entered

as a negative item to offset the fact that the expenditure figures for consumption, investment, government, and exports also include expenditures on imports. These imports contribute directly to foreign GDP but only indirectly to domestic GDP. Because of this negative offset for imports of goods and services, the sum of the other five items, excluding imports, will always total more than 100 percent of GDP. A surplus of exports of goods and services over imports indicates an economy is investing abroad, while a deficit indicates an economy is borrowing from abroad.

GDP—composition, by sector of origin This entry shows where production takes place in an economy. The distribution gives the percentage contribution of *agriculture, industry*, and *services* to total GDP, and will total 100 percent of GDP if the data are complete. Agriculture includes farming, fishing, and forestry. Industry includes mining, manufacturing, energy production, and construction. Services cover government activities, communications, transportation, finance, and all other private economic activities that do not produce material goods.

GDP—per capita (PPP) This entry shows GDP on a purchasing power parity basis divided by population as of 1 July for the same year.

GDP—real growth rate This entry gives GDP growth on an annual basis adjusted for inflation and expressed as a percent. The growth rates are year-over-year, and not compounded.

GDP methodology In the **Economy** category, GDP dollar estimates for countries are reported both on an official exchange rate (OER) and a purchasing power parity (PPP) basis. Both measures contain information that is useful to the reader. The PPP method involves the use of standardized international dollar price weights, which are applied to the quantities of final goods and services produced in a given economy. The data derived from the PPP method probably provide the best available starting point for comparisons of economic strength and well-being between countries. In contrast, the currency exchange rate method involves a variety of international and domestic financial forces that may not capture the value of domestic output. Whereas PPP estimates for OECD countries are quite reliable, PPP estimates for developing countries are often rough approximations. In developing countries with weak currencies, the exchange rate estimate of GDP in dollars is typically one-fourth to one-half the PPP estimate. Most of the GDP estimates for developing countries are based on extrapolation of PPP numbers published by the UN International Comparison Program (UNICP) and by Professors Robert Summers and Alan Heston of the University of Pennsylvania and their colleagues. GDP derived using the OER method should be used for the purpose of calculating the share of items such as exports, imports, military expenditures, external debt, or the current account balance, because the dollar values presented in the *Factbook* for these items have been converted at official exchange rates, not at PPP. One should use the OER GDP figure to calculate the proportion of, say, Chinese defense expenditures in GDP, because that share will be the same as one calculated in local currency units. Comparison of OER GDP with PPP GDP may also indicate whether a currency is over- or under-valued. If OER GDP is smaller than PPP GDP, the official exchange rate may be undervalued, and vice versa. However, there is no strong historical evidence that market exchange rates move in the direction implied by the PPP rate, at least not in the short- or medium-term. Note: the numbers for GDP and other economic data should not be chained together from successive volumes of the *Factbook* because of changes in the US dollar measuring rod, revisions of data by statistical agencies, use of new or different sources of information, and changes in national statistical methods and practices.

Geographic coordinates This entry includes rounded latitude and longitude figures for the centroid or center point of a country expressed in degrees and minutes; it is based on the locations provided in the Geographic Names Server (GNS), maintained by the National Geospatial-Intelligence Agency on behalf of the US Board on Geographic Names.

Geographic names This information is presented in **Appendix F: Cross Reference List of Geographic Names.** It includes a listing of various alternate names, former names, local names, and regional names referenced to one or more related *Factbook* entries. Spellings are normally, but not always, those approved by the US Board on Geographic Names (BGN). Alternate names and additional information are included in parentheses.

Geography This category includes the entries dealing with the natural environment and the effects of human activity.

Geography—note This entry includes miscellaneous geographic information of significance not included elsewhere.

Gini index See entry for **Distribution of family income—Gini index**

GNP Gross national product (GNP) is the value of all final goods and services produced within a nation in a given year, plus income earned by its citizens abroad, minus income earned by foreigners from domestic production. The *Factbook*, following current practice, uses GDP rather than GNP to measure national production. However, the user must realize that in certain countries net remittances from citizens working abroad may be important to national well-being.

Government This category includes the entries dealing with the system for the adoption and administration of public policy.

Government—note This entry includes miscellaneous government information of significance not included elsewhere.

Government type This entry gives the basic form of government. Definitions of the major governmental terms are as follows. (Note that for some countries more than one definition applies.):

   Absolute monarchy—a form of government where the monarch rules unhindered, i.e., without any laws, constitution, or legally organized opposition.

   Anarchy—a condition of lawlessness or political disorder brought about by the absence of governmental authority.

   Authoritarian—a form of government in which state authority is imposed onto many aspects of citizens' lives.

   Commonwealth—a nation, state, or other political entity founded on law and united by a compact of the people for the common good.

   Communist—a system of government in which the state plans and controls the economy and a single—often authoritarian—party holds power; state controls are imposed with the elimination of private ownership of property or capital while claiming to make progress toward a higher social order in which all goods are equally shared by the people (i.e., a classless society).

   Confederacy (Confederation)—a union by compact or treaty between states, provinces, or territories, that creates a central government with limited powers; the constituent entities retain supreme authority over all matters except those delegated to the central government.

   Constitutional—a government by or operating under an authoritative document (constitution) that sets forth the system of fundamental laws and principles that determines the nature, functions, and limits of that government.

   Constitutional democracy—a form of government in which the sovereign power of the people is spelled out in a governing constitution.

   Constitutional monarchy—a system of government in which a monarch is guided by a constitution whereby his/her rights, duties, and responsibilities are spelled out in written law or by custom.

   Democracy—a form of government in which the supreme power is retained by the people, but which is usually exercised indirectly through a system of representation and delegated authority periodically renewed.

   Democratic republic—a state in which the supreme power rests in the body of citizens entitled to vote for officers and representatives responsible to them.

   Dictatorship—a form of government in which a ruler or small clique wield absolute power (not restricted by a constitution or laws).

   Ecclesiastical—a government administrated by a church.

   Emirate—similar to a monarchy or sultanate, but a government in which the supreme power is in the hands of an emir (the ruler of a Muslim state); the emir may be an absolute overlord or a sovereign with constitutionally limited authority.

   Federal (Federation)—a form of government in which sovereign power is formally divided—usually by means of a constitution—between a central authority and a number of constituent regions (states, colonies, or provinces) so that each region retains some management of its internal affairs; differs from a confederacy in that the central government exerts influence directly upon both individuals as well as upon the regional units.

   Federal republic—a state in which the powers of the central government are restricted and in which the component parts (states, colonies, or provinces) retain a degree of self-government; ultimate sovereign power rests with the voters who chose their governmental representatives.

   Islamic republic—a particular form of government adopted by some Muslim states; although such a state is, in theory, a theocracy, it remains a republic, but its laws are required to be compatible with the laws of Islam.

   Maoism—the theory and practice of Marxism-Leninism developed in China by Mao Zedong (Mao Tse-tung), which states that a continuous revolution is necessary if the leaders of a communist state are to keep in touch with the people.

   Marxism—the political, economic, and social principles espoused by 19th century economist Karl Marx; he viewed the struggle of workers as a progression of historical forces that would proceed from a class struggle of the proletariat (workers) exploited by capitalists (business owners), to a socialist "dictatorship of the proletariat," to, finally, a classless society—Communism.

   Marxism-Leninism—an expanded form of communism developed by Lenin from doctrines of Karl Marx; Lenin saw imperialism as the final stage of capitalism and shifted the focus of workers' struggle from developed to underdeveloped countries.

   Monarchy—a government in which the supreme power is lodged in the hands of a monarch who reigns over a state or territory, usually for life and by hereditary right; the monarch may be either a sole absolute ruler or a sovereign—such as a king, queen, or prince—with constitutionally limited authority.

   Oligarchy—a government in which control is exercised by a small group of individuals whose authority generally is based on wealth or power.

   Parliamentary democracy—a political system in which the legislature (parliament) selects the government—a prime minister, premier, or chancellor along with the cabinet ministers—according to party strength as expressed in elections; by this system, the government acquires a dual responsibility: to the people as well as to the parliament.

   Parliamentary government (Cabinet-Parliamentary government)—a government in which members of an executive branch (the cabinet and its leader—a prime minister, premier, or chancellor) are nominated to their positions by a legislature or parliament, and are directly responsible to it; this type of government can be dissolved at will by the parliament (legislature) by means of a no confidence vote or the leader of the cabinet may dissolve the parliament if it can no longer function.

Parliamentary monarchy—a state headed by a monarch who is not actively involved in policy formation or implementation (i.e., the exercise of sovereign powers by a monarch in a ceremonial capacity); true governmental leadership is carried out by a cabinet and its head—a prime minister, premier, or chancellor—who are drawn from a legislature (parliament).

Presidential—a system of government where the executive branch exists separately from a legislature (to which it is generally not accountable).

Republic—a representative democracy in which the people's elected deputies (representatives), not the people themselves, vote on legislation.

Socialism—a government in which the means of planning, producing, and distributing goods is controlled by a central government that theoretically seeks a more just and equitable distribution of property and labor; in actuality, most socialist governments have ended up being no more than dictatorships over workers by a ruling elite.

Sultanate—similar to a monarchy, but a government in which the supreme power is in the hands of a sultan (the head of a Muslim state); the sultan may be an absolute ruler or a sovereign with constitutionally limited authority.

Theocracy—a form of government in which a Deity is recognized as the supreme civil ruler, but the Deity's laws are interpreted by ecclesiastical authorities (bishops, mullahs, etc.); a government subject to religious authority.

Totalitarian—a government that seeks to subordinate the individual to the state by controlling not only all political and economic matters, but also the attitudes, values, and beliefs of its population.

Greenwich Mean Time (GMT)
The mean solar time at the Greenwich Meridian, Greenwich, England, with the hours and days, since 1925, reckoned from midnight. GMT is now a historical term having been replaced by UTC on 1 January 1972. See **Coordinated Universal Time.**

Gross domestic product
See GDP

Gross national product
See GNP

Gross national saving
Gross national saving is derived by deducting final consumption expenditure (household plus government) from Gross national disposable income, and consists of personal saving, plus business saving (the sum of the capital consumption allowance and retained business profits), plus government saving (the excess of tax revenues over expenditures), but excludes foreign saving (the excess of imports of goods and services over exports). The figures are presented as a percent of GDP. A negative number indicates that the economy as a whole is spending more income than it produces, thus drawing down national wealth (dissaving).

Gross world product
See GWP

GWP
This entry gives the gross world product (GWP) or aggregate value of all final goods and services produced worldwide in a given year.

Health expenditures
This entry provides the total expenditure on health as a percentage of GDP. Health expenditures are broadly defined as activities performed either by institutions or individuals through the application of medical, paramedical, and/or nursing knowledge and technology, the primary purpose of which is to promote, restore, or maintain health.

Heliports
This entry gives the total number of heliports with hard-surface runways, helipads, or landing areas that support routine sustained helicopter operations exclusively and have support facilities including one or more of the following facilities: lighting, fuel, passenger handling, or maintenance. It includes former airports used exclusively for helicopter operations but excludes heliports limited to day operations and natural clearings that could support helicopter landings and takeoffs.

HIV/AIDS—adult prevalence rate
This entry gives an estimate of the percentage of adults (aged 15-49) living with HIV/AIDS. The adult prevalence rate is calculated by dividing the estimated number of adults living with HIV/AIDS at yearend by the total adult population at yearend.

HIV/AIDS—deaths
This entry gives an estimate of the number of adults and children who died of AIDS during a given calendar year.

HIV/AIDS—people living with HIV/AIDS
This entry gives an estimate of all people (adults and children) alive at yearend with HIV infection, whether or not they have developed symptoms of AIDS.

Hospital bed density
This entry provides the number of hospital beds per 1,000 people; it serves as a general measure of inpatient service availability. Hospital beds include inpatient beds available in public, private, general, and specialized hospitals and rehabilitation centers. In most cases, beds for both acute and chronic care are included. Because the level of inpatient services required for individual countries depends on several factors—such as demographic issues and the burden of disease—there is no global target for the number of hospital beds per country. So, while 2 beds per 1,000 in one country may be sufficient, 2 beds per 1,000 in another may be woefully inadequate because of the number of people hospitalized by disease.

Household income or consumption by percentage share
Data on household income or consumption come from household surveys, the results adjusted for household size. Nations use different standards and procedures in collecting and adjusting the data. Surveys based on income will normally show a more unequal distribution than surveys based on consumption. The quality of surveys is improving with time, yet caution is still necessary in making inter-country comparisons.

Hydrographic data codes
See **Data codes**

Illicit drugs
This entry gives information on the five categories of illicit drugs—narcotics, stimulants, depressants (sedatives), hallucinogens, and cannabis. These categories include many drugs legally produced and prescribed by doctors as well as those illegally produced and sold outside of medical channels.

> **Cannabis** (*Cannabis sativa*) is the common hemp plant, which provides hallucinogens with some sedative properties, and includes marijuana (pot, Acapulco gold, grass, reefer), tetrahydrocannabinol (THC, Marinol), hashish (hash), and hashish oil (hash oil).
>
> **Coca** (mostly *Erythroxylum* coca) is a bush with leaves that contain the stimulant used to make cocaine. Coca is not to be confused with cocoa, which comes from cacao seeds and is used in making chocolate, cocoa, and cocoa butter.
>
> **Cocaine** is a stimulant derived from the leaves of the coca bush.
>
> **Depressants** (sedatives) are drugs that reduce tension and anxiety and include chloral hydrate, barbiturates (Amytal, Nembutal, Seconal, phenobarbital), benzodiazepines (Librium,

Valium), methaqualone (Quaalude), glutethimide (Doriden), and others (Equanil, Placidyl, Valmid).

Drugs are any chemical substances that effect a physical, mental, emotional, or behavioral change in an individual.

Drug abuse is the use of any licit or illicit chemical substance that results in physical, mental, emotional, or behavioral impairment in an individual.

Hallucinogens are drugs that affect sensation, thinking, self-awareness, and emotion. Hallucinogens include LSD (acid, microdot), mescaline and peyote (mexc, buttons, cactus), amphetamine variants (PMA, STP, DOB), phencyclidine (PCP, angel dust, hog), phencyclidine analogues (PCE, PCPy, TCP), and others (psilocybin, psilocyn).

Hashish is the resinous exudate of the cannabis or hemp plant (Cannabis sativa).

Heroin is a semisynthetic derivative of morphine.

Mandrax is a trade name for methaqualone, a pharmaceutical depressant.

Marijuana is the dried leaf of the cannabis or hemp plant (*Cannabis sativa*).

Methaqualone is a pharmaceutical depressant, referred to as mandrax in Southwest Asia and Africa.

Narcotics are drugs that relieve pain, often induce sleep, and refer to opium, opium derivatives, and synthetic substitutes. Natural narcotics include opium (paregoric, parepectolin), morphine (MS-Contin, Roxanol), codeine (Tylenol with codeine, Empirin with codeine, Robitussin AC), and thebaine. Semisynthetic narcotics include heroin (horse, smack), and hydromorphone (Dilaudid). Synthetic narcotics include meperidine or Pethidine (Demerol, Mepergan), methadone (Dolophine, Methadose), and others (Darvon, Lomotil).

Opium is the brown, gummy exudate of the incised, unripe seedpod of the opium poppy.

Opium poppy (*Papaver somniferum*) is the source for the natural and semisynthetic narcotics.

Poppy straw is the entire cut and dried opium poppy-plant material, other than the seeds. Opium is extracted from poppy straw in commercial operations that produce the drug for medical use.

Qat (kat, khat) is a stimulant from the buds or leaves of *Catha edulis* that is chewed or drunk as tea.

Quaaludes is the North American slang term for methaqualone, a pharmaceutical depressant.

Stimulants are drugs that relieve mild depression, increase energy and activity, and include cocaine (coke, snow, crack), amphetamines (Desoxyn, Dexedrine), ephedrine, ecstasy (clarity, essence, doctor, Adam), phenmetrazine (Preludin), methylphenidate (Ritalin), and others (Cylert, Sanorex, Tenuate).

Imports This entry provides the total US dollar amount of merchandise imports on a c.i.f. (cost, insurance, and freight) or f.o.b. (free on board) basis. These figures are calculated on an exchange rate basis, i.e., not in purchasing power parity (PPP) terms.

Imports—commodities This entry provides a listing of the highest-valued imported products; it sometimes includes the percent of total dollar value.

Imports—partners This entry provides a rank ordering of trading partners starting with the most important; it sometimes includes the percent of total dollar value.

Independence For most countries, this entry gives the date that sovereignty was achieved and from which nation, empire, or trusteeship. For the other countries, the date given may not represent "independence" in the strict sense, but rather some significant nationhood event such as the traditional founding date or the date of unification, federation, confederation, establishment, fundamental change in the form of government, or state succession. For a number of countries, the establishment of statehood was a lengthy evolutionary process occurring over decades or even centuries. In such cases, several significant dates are cited. Dependent areas include the notation "none" followed by the nature of their dependency status. Also see the **Terminology** note.

Industrial production growth rate This entry gives the annual percentage increase in industrial production (includes manufacturing, mining, and construction).

Industries This entry provides a rank ordering of industries starting with the largest by value of annual output.

Infant mortality rate This entry gives the number of deaths of infants under one year old in a given year per 1,000 live births in the same year. This rate is often used as an indicator of the level of health in a country.

Inflation rate (consumer prices) This entry furnishes the annual percent change in consumer prices compared with the previous year's consumer prices.

International disputes See Disputes—international

International law organization participation This entry includes information on a country's acceptance of jurisdiction of the International Court of Justice (ICJ) and of the International Criminal Court (ICCt); 55 countries have accepted ICJ jurisdiction with reservations and 11 have accepted ICJ jurisdiction without reservations; 114 countries have accepted ICCt jurisdiction. **Appendix B: International Organizations and Groups** explains the differing mandates of the ICJ and ICCt.

International organization participation This entry lists in alphabetical order by abbreviation those international organizations in which the subject country is a member or participates in some other way.

International organizations This information is presented in **Appendix B: International Organizations and Groups** which includes the name, abbreviation, date established, aim, and members by category.

Internet country code This entry includes the two-letter codes maintained by the International Organization for Standardization (ISO) in the ISO 3166 Alpha-2 list and used by the Internet Assigned Numbers Authority (IANA) to establish country-coded top-level domains (ccTLDs).

Internet hosts This entry lists the number of Internet hosts available within a country. An Internet host is a computer connected directly to the Internet; normally an Internet Service Provider's (ISP) computer is a host. Internet users may use either a hard-wired terminal, at an institution with a mainframe computer connected directly to the Internet, or may connect remotely by way of a modem via telephone line, cable, or satellite to the Internet Service Provider's host computer. The number of hosts is one indicator of the extent of Internet connectivity.

Internet users This entry gives the number of users within a country that access the Internet. Statistics vary from country to country and may include users who access the Internet at least several times a week to those who access it only once within a period of several months.

Introduction This category includes one entry, **Background**.

Investment (gross fixed) This entry records total business spending on fixed assets, such as factories, machinery, equipment, dwellings, and inventories of raw materials, which provide the basis for future production. It is measured gross of the depreciation of the assets, i.e., it includes investment that merely replaces worn-out or scrapped capital.

Irrigated land This entry gives the number of square kilometers of land area that is artificially supplied with water.

Judicial branch This entry includes three subfields. *The highest court(s)* subfield includes the name(s) of a country's highest level court(s), the number and titles of the judges, and the types of cases heard by the court, which commonly are based on civil, criminal, administrative, and constitutional law. A number of countries have separate constitutional courts. The *judge selection and term of office* subfield includes the organizations and associated officials responsible for nominating and appointing judges, and a brief description of the process. The selection process can be indicative of the independence of a country's court system from other branches of its government. Also included in this subfield are judges' tenures, which can range from a few years, to a specified retirement age, to lifelong appointments. *The subordinate courts* subfield lists the courts lower in the hierarchy of a country's court system. A few countries with federal-style governments, such as Brazil, Canada, and the US, in addition to their federal court, have separate state - or province-level court systems, though generally the two systems interact.

Labor force This entry contains the total labor force figure.

Labor force—by occupation This entry lists the percentage distribution of the labor force by sector of occupation. *Agriculture* includes farming, fishing, and forestry. *Industry* includes mining, manufacturing, energy production, and construction. *Services* cover government activities, communications, transportation, finance, and all other economic activities that do not produce material goods. The distribution will total less than 100 percent if the data are incomplete and may range from 99-101 percent due to rounding.

Land boundaries This entry contains the *total* length of all land boundaries and the individual lengths for each of the contiguous *border countries*. When available, official lengths published by national statistical agencies are used. Because surveying methods may differ, country border lengths reported by contiguous countries may differ.

Land use This entry contains the percentage shares of total land area for three different types of land use: *arable land*—land cultivated for crops like wheat, maize, and rice that are replanted after each harvest; *permanent crops*—land cultivated for crops like citrus, coffee, and rubber that are not replanted after each harvest; includes land under flowering shrubs, fruit trees, nut trees, and vines, but excludes land under trees grown for wood or timber; *other*—any land not arable or under permanent crops; includes permanent meadows and pastures, forests and woodlands, built-on areas, roads, barren land, etc.

Languages This entry provides a rank ordering of languages starting with the largest and sometimes includes the percent of total population speaking that language.

Legal system This entry provides the description of a country's legal system. A statement on judicial review of legislative acts is also included for a number of countries. The legal systems of nearly all countries are generally modeled upon elements of five main types: civil law (including French law, the Napoleonic Code, Roman law, Roman-Dutch law, and Spanish law); common law (including United State law); customary law; mixed or pluralistic law; and religious law (including Islamic law). An additional type of legal system—international law, which governs the conduct of independent nations in their relationships with one another—is also addressed below. The following list describes these legal systems, the countries or world regions where these systems are enforced, and a brief statement on the origins and major features of each.

Civil Law—The most widespread type of legal system in the world, applied in various forms in approximately 150 countries. Also referred to as European continental law, the civil law system is derived mainly from the Roman *Corpus Juris Civilus*, (Body of Civil Law), a collection of laws and legal interpretations compiled under the East Roman (Byzantine) Emperor Justinian I between A.D. 528 and 565. The major feature of civil law systems is that the laws are organized into systematic written codes. In civil law the sources recognized as authoritative are principally legislation—especially codifications in constitutions or statutes enacted by governments—and secondarily, custom. The civil law systems in some countries are based on more than one code.

Common Law—A type of legal system, often synonymous with "English common law," which is the system of England and Wales in the UK, and is also in force in approximately 80 countries formerly part of or influenced by the former British Empire. English common law reflects Biblical influences as well as remnants of law systems imposed by early conquerors including the Romans, Anglo-Saxons, and Normans. Some legal scholars attribute the formation of the English common law system to King Henry II (r. 1154-1189). Until the time of his reign, laws customary among England's various manorial and ecclesiastical (church) jurisdictions were administered locally. Henry II established the king's court and designated that laws were "common" to the entire English realm. The foundation of English common law is "legal precedent"—referred to as *stare decisis*, meaning "to stand by things decided." In the English common law system, court judges are bound in their decisions in large part by the rules and other doctrines developed—and supplemented over time—by the judges of earlier English courts.

Customary Law—A type of legal system that serves as the basis of, or has influenced, the present-day laws in approximately 40 countries—mostly in Africa, but some in the Pacific islands, Europe, and the Near East. Customary law is also referred to as "primitive law," "unwritten law," "indigenous law," and "folk law." There is no single history of customary law such as that found in Roman civil law, English common law, Islamic law, or the Napoleonic Civil Code. The earliest systems of law in human society were customary, and usually developed in small agrarian and hunter-gatherer communities. As the term implies, customary law is based upon the customs of a community. Common attributes of customary legal systems are that they are seldom written down, they embody an organized set of rules regulating social relations, and they are agreed upon by members of the community. Although such law systems include sanctions for law infractions, resolution tends to be reconciliatory rather than punitive. A number of African states practiced customary law many centuries prior to colonial influences. Following colonization, such laws were written down and incorporated to varying extents into the legal systems imposed by their colonial powers.

European Union Law—A sub-discipline of international law known as "supranational law" in which the rights of sovereign nations are limited in relation to one another. Also referred to as the Law of the European Union or Community Law, it is the unique and complex legal system that operates in tandem with the laws of the 27 member states of the European Union (EU). Similar to federal states, the EU legal system ensures compliance from the member states because of the Union's decentralized political nature. The

European Court of Justice (ECJ), established in 1952 by the Treaty of Paris, has been largely responsible for the development of EU law. Fundamental principles of European Union law include: *subsidiarity*—the notion that issues be handled by the smallest, lowest, or least centralized competent authority; *proportionality*—the EU may only act to the extent needed to achieve its objectives; *conferral*—the EU is a union of member states, and all its authorities are voluntarily granted by its members; *legal certainty*—requires that legal rules be clear and precise; and *precautionary principle*—a moral and political principle stating that if an action or policy might cause severe or irreversible harm to the public or to the environment, in the absence of a scientific consensus that harm would not ensue, the burden of proof falls on those who would advocate taking the action.

French Law—A type of civil law that is the legal system of France. The French system also serves as the basis for, or is mixed with, other legal systems in approximately 50 countries, notably in North Africa, the Near East, and the French territories and dependencies. French law is primarily codified or systematic written civil law. Prior to the French Revolution (1789-1799), France had no single national legal system. Laws in the northern areas of present-day France were mostly local customs based on privileges and exemptions granted by kings and feudal lords, while in the southern areas Roman law predominated. The introduction of the Napoleonic Civil Code during the reign of Napoleon I in the first decade of the 19th century brought major reforms to the French legal system, many of which remain part of France's current legal structure, though all have been extensively amended or redrafted to address a modern nation. French law distinguishes between "public law" and "private law." Public law relates to government, the French Constitution, public administration, and criminal law. Private law covers issues between private citizens or corporations. The most recent changes to the French legal system—introduced in the 1980s—were the decentralization laws, which transferred authority from centrally appointed government representatives to locally elected representatives of the people.

International Law—The law of the international community, or the body of customary rules and treaty rules accepted as legally binding by states in their relations with each other. International law differs from other legal systems in that it primarily concerns sovereign political entities. There are three separate disciplines of international law: public international law, which governs the relationship between provinces and international entities and includes treaty law, law of the sea, international criminal law, and international humanitarian law; private international law, which addresses legal jurisdiction; and supranational law—a legal framework wherein countries are bound by regional agreements in which the laws of the member countries are held inapplicable when in conflict with supranational laws. At present the European Union is the only entity under a supranational legal system. The term "international law" was coined by Jeremy Bentham in 1780 in his *Principles of Morals and Legislation*, though laws governing relations between states have been recognized from very early times (many centuries B.C.). Modern international law developed alongside the emergence and growth of the European nation-states beginning in the early 16th century. Other factors that influenced the development of international law included the revival of legal studies, the growth of international trade, and the practice of exchanging emissaries and establishing legations. The sources of International law are set out in Article 38-1 of the Statute of the International Court of Justice within the UN Charter.

Islamic Law—The most widespread type of religious law, it is the legal system enforced in over 30 countries, particularly in the Near East, but also in Central and South Asia, Africa, and Indonesia. In many countries Islamic law operates in tandem with a civil law system. Islamic law is embodied in the sharia, an Arabic word meaning "the right path." Sharia covers all aspects of public and private life and organizes them into five categories: obligatory, recommended, permitted, disliked, and forbidden. The primary sources of sharia law are the Qur'an, believed by Muslims to be the word of God revealed to the Prophet Muhammad by the angel Gabriel, and the Sunnah, the teachings of the Prophet and his work. In addition to these two primary sources, traditional Sunni Muslims recognize the consensus of Muhammad's companions and Islamic jurists on certain issues, called ijmas, and various forms of reasoning, including analogy by legal scholars, referred to as qiyas. Shia Muslims reject ijmas and qiyas as sources of sharia law.

Mixed Law—Also referred to as pluralistic law, mixed law consists of elements of some or all of the other main types of legal systems—civil, common, customary, and religious. The mixed legal systems of a number of countries came about when colonial powers overlaid their own legal systems upon colonized regions but retained elements of the colonies' existing legal systems.

Napoleonic Civil Code—A type of civil law, referred to as the Civil Code or *Code Civil des Francais,* forms part of the legal system of France, and underpins the legal systems of Bolivia, Egypt, Lebanon, Poland, and the US state of Louisiana. The Civil Code was established under Napoleon I, enacted in 1804, and officially designated the *Code Napoleon* in 1807. This legal system combined the Teutonic civil law tradition of the northern provinces of France with the Roman law tradition of the southern and eastern regions of the country. The Civil Code bears similarities in its arrangement to the Roman *Body of Civil Law* (see Civil Law above). As enacted in 1804, the Code addressed personal status, property, and the acquisition of property. Codes added over the following six years included civil procedures, commercial law, criminal law and procedures, and a penal code.

Religious Law—A legal system which stems from the sacred texts of religious traditions and in most cases professes to cover all aspects of life as a seamless part of devotional obligations to a transcendent, imminent, or deep philosophical reality. Implied as the basis of religious law is the concept of unalterability, because the word of God cannot be amended or legislated against by judges or governments. However, a detailed legal system generally requires human elaboration. The main types of religious law are sharia in Islam, halakha in Judaism, and canon law in some Christian groups. Sharia is the most widespread religious legal system (see Islamic Law), and is the sole system of law for countries including Iran, the Maldives, and Saudi Arabia. No country is fully governed by halakha, but Jewish people may decide to settle disputes through Jewish courts and be bound by their rulings. Canon law is not a divine law as such because it is not found in revelation. It is viewed instead as human law inspired by the word of God and applying the demands of that revelation to the actual situation of the church. Canon law regulates the internal ordering of the Roman Catholic Church, the Eastern Orthodox Church, and the Anglican Communion.

Roman Law—A type of civil law developed in ancient Rome and practiced from the time of the city's founding (traditionally 753 B.C.) until the fall of the Western Empire in the 5th century A.D. Roman law remained the legal system of the Byzantine (Eastern Empire) until the fall of Constantinople in 1453. Preserved fragments of the first legal text, known as the Law of the Twelve Tables, dating from the 5th century B.C., contained specific provisions designed to change the prevailing customary law. Early Roman law was drawn from custom and statutes; later, during the time of the empire, emperors asserted their authority as the ultimate source of law. The basis for Roman laws was the idea that the exact form—not the intention—of words or of actions produced legal consequences. It was only in the late 6th century A.D. that a comprehensive Roman code of laws was published (see Civil Law above). Roman law served as the basis of law systems developed in a number of continental European countries.

Roman-Dutch Law—A type of civil law based on Roman law as applied in the Netherlands. Roman-Dutch law serves as the basis for legal systems in seven African countries, as well as Guyana, Indonesia, and Sri Lanka. This law system, which originated in the province of Holland and expanded throughout the Netherlands (to be replaced by the French Civil Code in 1809), was instituted in a number of sub-Saharan African countries during the Dutch colonial period. The Dutch jurist/philosopher Hugo Grotius was the first to attempt to reduce Roman-Dutch civil law into a system in his *Jurisprudence of Holland* (written 1619-20, commentary published 1621). The Dutch historian/lawyer Simon van Leeuwen coined the term "Roman-Dutch law" in 1652.

Spanish Law—A type of civil law, often referred to as the Spanish Civil Code, it is the present legal system of Spain and is the basis of legal systems in 12 countries mostly in Central and South America, but also in southwestern Europe, northern and western Africa, and southeastern Asia. The Spanish Civil Code reflects a complex mixture of customary, Roman, Napoleonic, local, and modern codified law. The laws of the Visigoth invaders of Spain in the 5th to 7th centuries had the earliest major influence on Spanish legal system development. The Christian Reconquest of Spain in the 11th through 15th centuries witnessed the development of customary law, which combined canon (religious) and Roman law. During several centuries of Hapsburg and Bourbon rule, systematic recompilations of the existing national legal system were attempted, but these often conflicted with local and regional customary civil laws. Legal system development for most of the 19th century concentrated on formulating a national civil law system, which was finally enacted in 1889 as the Spanish Civil Code. Several sections of the code have been revised, the most recent of which are the penal code in 1989 and the judiciary code in 2001. The Spanish Civil Code separates public and private law. Public law includes constitutional law, administrative law, criminal law, process law, financial and tax law, and international public law. Private law includes civil law, commercial law, labor law, and international private law.

United States Law—A type of common law, which is the basis of the legal system of the United States and that of its island possessions in the Caribbean and the Pacific. This legal system has several layers, more possibly than in most other countries, and is due in part to the division between federal and state law. The United States was founded not as one nation but as a union of 13 colonies, each claiming independence from the British Crown. The US Constitution, implemented in 1789, began shifting power away from the states and toward the federal government, though the states today retain substantial legal authority. US law draws its authority from four sources: *constitutional law*, *statutory law*, *administrative regulations*, and *case law*. Constitutional law is based on the US Constitution and serves as the supreme federal law. Taken together with those of the state constitutions, these documents outline the general structure of the federal and state governments and provide the rules and limits of power. US statutory law is legislation enacted by the US Congress and is codified in the United States Code.

The 50 state legislatures have similar authority to enact state statutes. Administrative law is the authority delegated to federal and state executive agencies. Case law, also referred to as common law, covers areas where constitutional or statutory law is lacking. Case law is a collection of judicial decisions, customs, and general principles that began in England centuries ago, that were adopted in America at the time of the Revolution, and that continue to develop today.

Legislative branch This entry contains information on the structure (unicameral, bicameral, tricameral), formal name, number of seats, and term of office. *Elections* includes the nature of the election process or accession to power, date of the last election, and date of the next election. *Election results* includes the percent of vote and/or number of seats held by each party in the last election.

Life expectancy at birth This entry contains the average number of years to be lived by a group of people born in the same year, if mortality at each age remains constant in the future. Life expectancy at birth is also a measure of overall quality of life in a country and summarizes the mortality at all ages. It can also be thought of as indicating the potential return on investment in human capital and is necessary for the calculation of various actuarial measures.

Literacy This entry includes a *definition* of literacy and Census Bureau percentages for the *total population*, *males*, and *females*. There are no universal definitions and standards of literacy. Unless otherwise specified, all rates are based on the most common definition—the ability to read and write at a specified age. Detailing the standards that individual countries use to assess the ability to read and write is beyond the scope of the *Factbook*. Information on literacy, while not a perfect measure of educational results, is probably the most easily available and valid for international comparisons. Low levels of literacy, and education in general, can impede the economic development of a country in the current rapidly changing, technology-driven world.

Location This entry identifies the country's regional location, neighboring countries, and adjacent bodies of water.

Major infectious diseases This entry lists major infectious diseases likely to be encountered in countries where the risk of such diseases is assessed to be very high as compared to the United States. These infectious diseases represent risks to US government personnel traveling to the specified country for a period of less than three years. The **degree of risk** is assessed by considering the foreign nature of these infectious diseases, their severity, and the probability of being affected by the diseases present. The diseases listed do not necessarily represent the total disease burden experienced by the local population.

The risk to an individual traveler varies considerably by the specific location, visit duration, type of activities, type of accommodations, time of year, and other factors. Consultation with a travel medicine physician is needed to evaluate individual risk and recommend appropriate preventive measures such as vaccines.

Diseases are organized into the following six exposure categories shown in italics *and listed in typical descending order of risk*. Note: The sequence of exposure categories listed in individual country entries may vary according to local conditions.

food or waterborne diseases acquired through eating or drinking on the local economy:

Hepatitis A—viral disease that interferes with the functioning of the liver; spread through consumption of food or water contaminated with fecal matter, principally in areas of poor sanitation; victims exhibit fever, jaundice, and diarrhea; 15% of victims will experience prolonged symptoms over 6-9 months; vaccine available.

Hepatitis E—water-borne viral disease that interferes with the functioning of the liver; most commonly spread through fecal contamination of drinking water; victims exhibit jaundice, fatigue, abdominal pain, and dark colored urine.

Typhoid fever—bacterial disease spread through contact with food or water contaminated by fecal matter or sewage; victims exhibit sustained high fevers; left untreated, mortality rates can reach 20%.

vectorborne diseases acquired through the bite of an infected arthropod:

Malaria—caused by single-cell parasitic protozoa *Plasmodium*; transmitted to humans via the bite of the female Anopheles mosquito; parasites multiply in the liver attacking red blood cells resulting in cycles of fever, chills, and sweats accompanied by anemia; death due to damage to vital organs and interruption of blood supply to the brain; endemic in 100, mostly tropical, countries with 90% of cases and the majority of 1.5-2.5 million estimated annual deaths occurring in sub-Saharan Africa.

Dengue fever—mosquito-borne (*Aedes aegypti*) viral disease associated with urban environments; manifests as sudden onset of fever and severe headache; occasionally produces shock and hemorrhage leading to death in 5% of cases.

Yellow fever—mosquito-borne viral disease; severity ranges from influenza-like symptoms to severe hepatitis and hemorrhagic fever; occurs only in tropical South America and sub-Saharan Africa, where most cases are reported; fatality rate is less than 20%.

Japanese Encephalitis—mosquito-borne (*Culex tritaeniorhynchus*) viral disease associated with rural areas in Asia; acute encephalitis can progress to paralysis, coma, and death; fatality rates 30%.

African Trypanosomiasis—caused by the parasitic protozoa *Trypanosoma*; transmitted to humans via the bite of bloodsucking Tsetse flies; infection leads to malaise and irregular fevers and, in advanced cases when the parasites invade the central nervous system, coma and death; endemic in 36 countries of sub-Saharan Africa; cattle and wild animals act as reservoir hosts for the parasites.

Cutaneous Leishmaniasis—caused by the parasitic protozoa *leishmania*; transmitted to humans via the bite of sandflies; results in skin lesions that may become chronic; endemic in 88 countries; 90% of cases occur in Iran, Afghanistan, Syria, Saudi Arabia, Brazil, and Peru; wild and domesticated animals as well as humans can act as reservoirs of infection.

Plague—bacterial disease transmitted by fleas normally associated with rats; person-to-person airborne transmission also possible; recent plague epidemics occurred in areas of Asia, Africa, and South America associated with rural areas or small towns and villages; manifests as fever, headache, and painfully swollen lymph nodes; disease progresses rapidly and without antibiotic treatment leads to pneumonic form with a death rate in excess of 50%.

Crimean-Congo hemorrhagic fever—tick-borne viral disease; infection may also result from exposure to infected animal blood or tissue; geographic distribution includes Africa, Asia, the Middle East, and Eastern Europe; sudden onset of fever, headache, and muscle aches followed by hemorrhaging in the bowels, urine, nose, and gums; mortality rate is approximately 30%.

Rift Valley fever—viral disease affecting domesticated animals and humans; transmission is by mosquito and other biting insects; infection may also occur through handling of infected meat or contact with blood; geographic distribution includes eastern and southern Africa where cattle and sheep are raised; symptoms are generally mild with fever and some liver abnormalities, but the disease may progress to hemorrhagic fever, encephalitis, or ocular disease; fatality rates are low at about 1% of cases.

Chikungunya—mosquito-borne (*Aedes aegypti*) viral disease associated with urban environments, similar to Dengue Fever; characterized by sudden onset of fever, rash, and severe joint pain usually lasting 3-7 days, some cases result in persistent arthritis.

water contact diseases acquired through swimming or wading in freshwater lakes, streams, and rivers:

Leptospirosis—bacterial disease that affects animals and humans; infection occurs through contact with water, food, or soil contaminated by animal urine; symptoms include high fever, severe headache, vomiting, jaundice, and diarrhea; untreated, the disease can result in kidney damage, liver failure, meningitis, or respiratory distress; fatality rates are low but left untreated recovery can take months.

Schistosomiasis—caused by parasitic trematode flatworm *Schistosoma*; fresh water snails act as intermediate host and release larval form of parasite that penetrates the skin of people exposed to contaminated water; worms mature and reproduce in the blood vessels, liver, kidneys, and intestines releasing eggs, which become trapped in tissues triggering an immune response; may manifest as either urinary or intestinal disease resulting in decreased work or learning capacity; mortality, while generally low, may occur in advanced cases usually due to bladder cancer; endemic in 74 developing countries with 80% of infected people living in sub-Saharan Africa; humans act as the reservoir for this parasite.

aerosolized dust or soil contact disease acquired through inhalation of aerosols contaminated with rodent urine:

Lassa fever—viral disease carried by rats of the genus *Mastomys*; endemic in portions of West Africa; infection occurs through direct contact with or consumption of food contaminated by rodent urine or fecal matter containing virus particles; fatality rate can reach 50% in epidemic outbreaks.

respiratory disease acquired through close contact with an infectious person:

Meningococcal meningitis—bacterial disease causing an inflammation of the lining of the brain and spinal cord; one of the most important bacterial pathogens is *Neisseria meningitidis* because of its potential to cause epidemics; symptoms include stiff neck, high fever, headaches, and vomiting; bacteria are transmitted from person to person by respiratory droplets and facilitated by close and prolonged contact resulting from crowded living conditions, often with a seasonal distribution; death occurs in 5-15% of cases, typically within 24-48 hours of onset of symptoms; highest burden of meningococcal disease occurs in the hyperendemic region of sub-Saharan Africa known as the "Meningitis Belt" which stretches from Senegal east to Ethiopia.

animal contact disease acquired through direct contact with local animals:

Rabies—viral disease of mammals usually transmitted through the bite of an infected animal, most commonly dogs; virus affects the central nervous system causing brain alteration and death; symptoms initially are non-specific fever and headache progressing to neurological symptoms; death occurs within days of the onset of symptoms.

Major urban areas—population This entry provides the population of the capital and up to five major cities defined as urban agglomerations with populations of at least 750,000 people. An *urban agglomeration* is defined as comprising the city or town proper and also the suburban fringe or thickly settled territory lying outside of, but adjacent to, the boundaries of the city. For smaller countries, lacking urban centers of 750,000 or more, only the population of the capital is presented.

Manpower available for military service This entry gives the number of males and females falling in the military age range for a country (defined as being ages 16-49) and assumes that every individual is fit to serve.

Manpower fit for military service This entry gives the number of males and females falling in the military age range for a country (defined as being ages 16-49) and who are not otherwise disqualified for health reasons; accounts for the health situation in the country and provides a more realistic estimate of the actual number fit to serve.

Manpower reaching militarily significant age annually This entry gives the number of males and females entering the military manpower pool (i.e., reaching age 16) in any given year and is a measure of the availability of military-age young adults.

Map references This entry includes the name of the *Factbook* reference map on which a country may be found. Note that boundary representations on these maps are not necessarily authoritative. The entry on **Geographic coordinates** may be helpful in finding some smaller countries.

Maritime claims This entry includes the following claims, the definitions of which are excerpted from the United Nations Convention on the Law of the Sea (UNCLOS), which alone contains the full and definitive descriptions:

territorial sea—the sovereignty of a coastal state extends beyond its land territory and internal waters to an adjacent belt of sea, described as the territorial sea in the UNCLOS (Part II); this sovereignty extends to the air space over the territorial sea as well as its underlying seabed and subsoil; every state has the right to establish the breadth of its territorial sea up to a limit not exceeding 12 nautical miles; the normal baseline for measuring the breadth of the territorial sea is the mean low-water line along the coast as marked on large-scale charts officially recognized by the coastal state; where the coasts of two states are opposite or adjacent to each other, neither state is entitled to extend its territorial sea beyond the median line, every point of which is equidistant from the nearest points on the baseline from which the territorial seas of both states are measured; the UNCLOS describes specific rules for archipelagic states.

contiguous zone—according to the UNCLOS (Article 33), this is a zone contiguous to a coastal state's territorial sea, over which it may exercise the control necessary to: prevent infringement of its customs, fiscal, immigration, or sanitary laws and regulations within its territory or territorial sea; punish infringement of the above laws and regulations committed within its territory or territorial sea; the contiguous zone may not extend beyond 24 nautical miles from the baselines from which the breadth of the territorial sea is measured (e.g., the US has claimed a 12-nautical mile contiguous zone in addition to its 12-nautical mile territorial sea); where the coasts of two states are opposite or adjacent to each other, neither state is entitled to extend its contiguous zone beyond the median line, every point of which is equidistant from the nearest points on the baseline from which the contiguous zone of both states are measured.

exclusive economic zone (EEZ)—the UNCLOS (Part V) defines the EEZ as a zone beyond and adjacent to the territorial sea in which a coastal state has: sovereign rights for the purpose of exploring and exploiting, conserving and managing the natural resources, whether living or non-living, of the waters superjacent to the seabed and of the seabed and its subsoil, and with regard to other activities for the economic exploitation and exploration of the zone, such as the production of energy from the water, currents, and winds; jurisdiction with regard to the establishment and use of artificial islands, installations, and structures; marine scientific research; the protection and preservation of the marine environment; the outer limit of the exclusive economic zone shall not exceed 200 nautical miles from the baselines from which the breadth of the territorial sea is measured.

continental shelf—the UNCLOS (Article 76) defines the continental shelf of a coastal state as comprising the seabed and subsoil of the submarine areas that extend beyond its territorial sea throughout the natural prolongation of its land territory to the outer edge of the continental margin, or to a distance of 200 nautical miles from the baselines from which the breadth of the territorial sea is measured where the outer edge of the continental margin does not extend up to that distance; the continental margin comprises the submerged prolongation of the landmass of the coastal state, and consists of the seabed and subsoil of the shelf, the slope and the rise; wherever the continental margin extends beyond 200 nautical miles from the baseline, coastal states may extend their claim to a distance not to exceed 350 nautical miles from the baseline or 100 nautical miles from the 2,500-meter isobath, which is a line connecting points of 2,500 meters in depth; it does not include the deep ocean floor with its oceanic ridges or the subsoil thereof.

exclusive fishing zone—while this term is not used in the UNCLOS, some states (e.g., the United Kingdom) have chosen not to claim an EEZ, but rather to claim jurisdiction over the living resources off their coast; in such cases, the term exclusive fishing zone is often used; the breadth of this zone is normally the same as the EEZ or 200 nautical miles.

Market value of publicly traded shares This entry gives the value of shares issued by publicly traded companies at a price determined in the national stock markets on the final day of the period indicated. It is simply the latest price per share multiplied by the total number of outstanding shares, cumulated over all companies listed on the particular exchange.

Maternal mortality rate The maternal mortality rate (MMR) is the annual number of female deaths per 100,000 live births from any cause related to or aggravated by pregnancy or its management (excluding accidental or incidental causes). The MMR includes deaths during pregnancy, childbirth, or within 42 days of termination of pregnancy, irrespective of the duration and site of the pregnancy, for a specified year.

Median age This entry is the age that divides a population into two numerically equal groups; that is, half the people are younger than this age and half are older. It is a single index that summarizes the age distribution of a population. Currently, the median age ranges from a low of about 15 in Uganda and Gaza Strip to 40 or more in several European countries and Japan. See the entry for "Age structure" for the importance of a young versus an older age structure and, by implication, a low versus a higher median age.

Merchant marine Merchant marine may be defined as all ships engaged in the carriage of goods; or all commercial vessels (as opposed to all nonmilitary ships), which excludes tugs, fishing vessels, offshore oil rigs, etc. This entry contains information in four fields—*total, ships by type, foreign-owned, and registered in other countries.*

Total includes the number of ships (1,000 GRT or over), total DWT for those ships, and total GRT for those ships. DWT or dead weight tonnage is the total weight of cargo, plus bunkers, stores, etc., that a ship can carry when immersed to the appropriate load line. GRT or gross register tonnage is a figure obtained by measuring the entire sheltered volume of a ship available for cargo and passengers and converting it to tons on the basis of 100 cubic feet per ton; there is no stable relationship between GRT and DWT.

Ships *by type* includes a listing of barge carriers, bulk cargo ships, cargo ships, chemical tankers, combination bulk carriers, combination ore/oil carriers, container ships, liquefied gas tankers, livestock carriers, multifunctional large-load carriers, petroleum tankers, passenger ships, passenger/cargo ships, railcar carriers, refrigerated cargo ships, roll-on/roll-off cargo ships, short-sea passenger ships, specialized tankers, and vehicle carriers.

Foreign-owned are ships that fly the flag of one country but belong to owners in another.

Registered in other countries are ships that belong to owners in one country but fly the flag of another.

Military This category includes the entries dealing with a country's military structure, manpower, and expenditures.

Military—note This entry includes miscellaneous military information of significance not included elsewhere.

Military branches This entry lists the service branches subordinate to defense ministries or the equivalent (typically ground, naval, air, and marine forces).

Military expenditures This entry gives spending on defense programs for the most recent year available as a percent of gross domestic product (GDP); the GDP is calculated on an exchange rate basis, i.e., not in terms of purchasing power parity (PPP). For countries with no military forces, this figure can include expenditures on public security and police.

Military service age and obligation This entry gives the required ages for voluntary or conscript military service and the length of service obligation.

Money figures All money figures are expressed in contemporaneous US dollars unless otherwise indicated.

Mother's mean age at first birth This entry provides the mean (average) age of mothers at the birth of their first child. It is a useful indicator for gauging the success of family planning programs aiming to reduce maternal mortality, increase contraceptive use—particularly among married and unmarried adolescents, delay age at first marriage, and improve the health of newborns.

National anthem A generally patriotic musical composition—usually in the form of a song or hymn of praise—that evokes and eulogizes the history, traditions, or struggles of a nation or its people. National anthems can be officially recognized as a national song by a country's constitution or by an enacted law, or simply by tradition. Although most anthems contain lyrics, some do not.

National holiday This entry gives the primary national day of celebration—usually independence day.

National symbol(s) A national symbol is a faunal, floral, or other abstract representation—or some distinctive object—that over time has come to be closely identified with a country or entity. Not all countries have national symbols; a few countries have more than one.

Nationality This entry provides the identifying terms for citizens—*noun* and *adjective.*

Natural gas—consumption This entry is the total natural gas consumed in cubic meters (cu m). The discrepancy between the amount of natural gas produced and/or imported and the amount consumed and/or exported is due to the omission of stock changes and other complicating factors.

Natural gas—exports This entry is the total natural gas exported in cubic meters (cu m).

Natural gas—imports This entry is the total natural gas imported in cubic meters (cu m).

Natural gas—production This entry is the total natural gas produced in cubic meters (cu m). The discrepancy between the amount of natural gas produced and/or imported and the amount consumed and/or exported is due to the omission of stock changes and other complicating factors.

Natural gas—proved reserves This entry is the stock of proved reserves of natural gas in cubic meters (cu m). Proved reserves are those quantities of natural gas, which, by analysis of geological and engineering data, can be estimated with a high degree of confidence to be commercially recoverable from a given date forward, from known reservoirs and under current economic conditions.

Natural hazards This entry lists potential natural disasters. For countries where volcanic activity is common, a *volcanism* subfield highlights historically active volcanoes.

Natural resources This entry lists a country's mineral, petroleum, hydropower, and other resources of commercial importance, such as rare earth elements (REEs). In general, products appear only if they make a significant contribution to the economy, or are likely to do so in the future.

Net migration rate This entry includes the figure for the difference between the number of persons entering and leaving a country during the year per 1,000 persons (based on midyear population). An excess of persons entering the country is referred to as net immigration (e.g., 3.56 migrants/1,000 population); an excess of persons leaving the country as net emigration (e.g., -9.26 migrants/1,000 population). The net migration rate indicates the contribution of migration to the overall level of population change. The net migration rate does not distinguish between economic migrants, refugees, and other types of migrants nor does it distinguish between lawful migrants and undocumented migrants.

Obesity—adult prevalence rate This entry gives the percent of a country's population considered to be obese. Obesity is defined as an adult having a Body Mass Index (BMI) greater to or equal to 30.0. BMI is calculated by taking a person's weight in kg and dividing it by the person's squared height in meters.

People—note This entry includes miscellaneous demographic information of significance not included elsewhere.

People and Society This category includes entries dealing with national identity (including ethnicities, languages, and religions), demography (a variety of population statistics) and societal characteristics (health and education indicators).

Personal Names—Capitalization The *Factbook* capitalizes the surname or family name of individuals for the convenience of our users who are faced with a world of different cultures and naming conventions. The need for capitalization, bold type, underlining, italics, or some other indicator of the individual's surname is apparent in the following examples: MAO Zedong, Fidel CASTRO Ruz, George W. BUSH, and TUNKU SALAHUDDIN Abdul Aziz Shah ibni Al-Marhum Sultan Hisammuddin Alam Shah. By knowing the surname, a short form without all capital letters can be used with confidence as in President Castro, Chairman Mao, President Bush, or Sultan Tunku Salahuddin. The same system of capitalization is extended to the names of leaders with surnames that are not commonly used such as Queen ELIZABETH II. For Vietnamese names, the given name is capitalized because officials are referred to by their given name rather than by their surname. For example, the president of Vietnam is Tran Duc LUONG. His surname is Tran, but he is referred to by his given name—President LUONG.

Personal Names—Spelling The romanization of personal names in the *Factbook* normally follows the same transliteration system used by the US Board on Geographic Names for spelling place names. At times, however, a foreign leader expressly indicates a preference for, or the media or official documents regularly use, a romanized spelling that differs from the transliteration derived from the US Government standard. In such cases, the Factbook uses the alternative spelling.

Personal Names—Titles The *Factbook* capitalizes any valid title (or short form of it) immediately preceding a person's name. A title standing alone is not capitalized. Examples: President PUTIN and President OBAMA are chiefs of state. In Russia, the president is chief of state and the premier is the head of the government, while in the US, the president is both chief of state and head of government.

Petroleum See entries under **Refined petroleum products.**

Petroleum products See entries under **Refined petroleum products.**

Physicians density This entry gives the number of medical doctors (physicians), including generalist and specialist medical practitioners, per 1,000 of the population. Medical doctors are defined as doctors that study, diagnose, treat, and prevent illness, disease, injury, and other physical and mental impairments in humans through the application of modern medicine. They also plan, supervise, and evaluate care and treatment plans by other health care providers. The World Health Organization estimates that fewer than 2.3 health workers (physicians, nurses, and midwives only) per 1,000 would be insufficient to achieve coverage of primary healthcare needs.

Pipelines This entry gives the lengths and types of pipelines for transporting products like natural gas, crude oil, or petroleum products.

Piracy Piracy is defined by the 1982 United Nations Convention on the Law of the Sea as any illegal act of violence, detention, or depredation directed against a ship, aircraft, persons, or property in a place outside the jurisdiction of any State. Such criminal acts committed in the territorial waters of a littoral state are generally considered to be armed robbery against ships. Information on piracy may be found, where applicable, in the **Transportation—note.**

Political parties and leaders This entry includes a listing of significant political parties, coalitions, and electoral lists as of each country's last legislative election, unless otherwise noted.

Political pressure groups and leaders This entry includes a listing of a country's political, social, labor, or religious organizations that are involved in politics, or that exert political pressure, but whose leaders do not stand for legislative election. International movements or organizations are generally not listed.

Population This entry gives an estimate from the US Bureau of the Census based on statistics from population censuses, vital statistics registration systems, or sample surveys pertaining to the recent past and on assumptions about future trends. The total population presents one overall measure of the potential impact of the country on the world and within its region. Note: Starting with the 1993 *Factbook*, demographic estimates for some countries (mostly African) have explicitly taken into account the effects of the growing impact of the HIV/AIDS epidemic. These countries are currently: The Bahamas, Benin, Botswana, Brazil, Burkina Faso, Burma, Burundi, Cambodia, Cameroon, Central African Republic, Democratic Republic of the Congo, Republic of the Congo, Cote d'Ivoire, Ethiopia, Gabon, Ghana, Guyana, Haiti, Honduras, Kenya, Lesotho, Malawi, Mozambique, Namibia, Nigeria, Rwanda, South Africa, Swaziland, Tanzania, Thailand, Togo, Uganda, Zambia, and Zimbabwe.

Population below poverty line National estimates of the percentage of the population falling below the poverty line are based on surveys of sub-groups, with the results weighted by the number of people in each group. Definitions of poverty vary considerably

among nations. For example, rich nations generally employ more generous standards of poverty than poor nations.

Population growth rate The average annual percent change in the population, resulting from a surplus (or deficit) of births over deaths and the balance of migrants entering and leaving a country. The rate may be positive or negative. The growth rate is a factor in determining how great a burden would be imposed on a country by the changing needs of its people for infrastructure (e.g., schools, hospitals, housing, roads), resources (e.g., food, water, electricity), and jobs. Rapid population growth can be seen as threatening by neighboring countries.

Population pyramid A population pyramid illustrates the age and sex structure of a country's population and may provide insights about political and social stability, as well as economic development. The population is distributed along the horizontal axis, with males shown on the left and females on the right. The male and female populations are broken down into 5-year age groups represented as horizontal bars along the vertical axis, with the youngest age groups at the bottom and the oldest at the top. The shape of the population pyramid gradually evolves over time based on fertility, mortality, and international migration trends.
Some distinctive types of population pyramids are:

- A **youthful distribution** has a broad base and narrow peak and is characterized by a high proportion of children and low proportion of the elderly. This population distribution results from high fertility, high mortality, low life expectancy, and high population growth. It is typical of developing countries where female education and contraceptive use are low and health care and sanitation are poor.

- A **transitional distribution** is caused by declining fertility and mortality rates, increasing life expectancy, and slowing population growth. The population has a larger proportion of working-age people relative to children and the elderly and produces a barrel-shaped pyramid, where the mid-section bulges and the base and top are narrower. The large proportion of working-age people can create a "demographic bonus" if it is educated and productively employed.

- A **mature distribution** has fairly balanced proportions of the population in the child, working-age, and elderly age groups and will gradually form an inverted triangle population pyramid as population growth continues to fall or ceases and the proportion of older people increases. Low fertility, low mortality, and high life expectancy—made possible by the availability of advanced healthcare, family planning, sanitation, and education—lead to aging populations in industrialized countries.

Ports and terminals This entry lists major ports and terminals primarily on the basis of the amount of cargo tonnage shipped through the facilities on an annual basis. In some instances, the number of containers handled or ship visits were also considered. Most ports service multiple classes of vessels including bulk carriers (dry and liquid), break bulk cargoes (goods loaded individually in bags, boxes, crates, or drums; sometimes palletized), containers,roll-on/roll-off, and passenger ships. The listing leads off with *major seaports* handling all types of cargo. Inland *river and lake ports* are listed separately along with the river or lake name. Ports configured specifically to handle bulk cargoes are designated as *oil/gas terminals* or *dry bulk cargo ports.* As break bulk cargoes are largely transported by containers today, the entry also includes a listing of major *container ports* with the corresponding throughput measured in twenty-foot equivalent units (TEUs). Some ports are significant for handling passenger traffic and are listed as *cruise/ferry ports.* In addition to commercial traffic, many seaports also provide important military infrastructure as naval bases or dockyards.

Public debt This entry records the cumulative total of all government borrowings less repayments that are denominated in a country's home currency. Public debt should not be confused with external debt, which reflects the foreign currency liabilities of both the private and public sector and must be financed out of foreign exchange earnings.

Railways This entry states the *total* route length of the railway network and of its component parts by gauge, which is the measure of the distance between the inner sides of the load-bearing rails. The four typical types of gauges are: *broad, standard, narrow,* and *dual.* Other gauges are listed under *note.* Some 60% of the world's railways use the standard gauge of 1.4 m (4.7 ft). Gauges vary by country and sometimes within countries. The choice of gauge during initial construction was mainly in response to local conditions and the intent of the builder. Narrow-gauge railways were cheaper to build and could negotiate sharper curves, broad-gauge railways gave greater stability and permitted higher speeds. Standard-gauge railways were a compromise between narrow and broad gauges.

Rare earth elements Rare earth elements or REEs are 17 chemical elements that are critical in many of today's high-tech industries. They include lanthanum, cerium, praseodymium, neodymium, promethium, samarium, europium, gadolinium, terbium, dysprosium, holmium, erbium, thulium, ytterbium, lutetium, scandium, and yttrium. Typical applications for REEs include batteries in hybrid cars, fiber optic cables, flat panel displays, and permanent magnets, as well as some defense and medical products.

Reference maps This section includes world and regional maps.

Refined petroleum products—consumption This entry is the country's total consumption of refined petroleum products, in barrels per day (bbl/day). The discrepancy between the amount of refined petroleum products produced and/or imported and the amount consumed and/or exported is due to the omission of stock changes, refinery gains, and other complicating factors.

Refined petroleum products—exports This entry is the country's total exports of refined petroleum products, in barrels per day (bbl/day).

Refined petroleum products—imports This entry is the country's total imports of refined petroleum products, in barrels per day (bbl/day).

Refined petroleum products—production This entry is the country's total output of refined petroleum products, in barrels per day (bbl/day). The discrepancy between the amount of refined petroleum products produced and/or imported and the amount consumed and/or exported is due to the omission of stock changes, refinery gains, and other complicating factors.

Refugees and internally displaced persons This entry includes those persons residing in a country as *refugees* or internally displaced persons (*IDPs*). Each country's refugee entry includes only countries of origin that are the source of refugee populations of 5,000 or more. The definition of a refugee according to a United Nations Convention is "a person who is outside his/her country of nationality or habitual residence; has a well-founded fear of persecution because of his/her race, religion, nationality, membership in a particular social group or political opinion; and is unable or unwilling to avail himself/herself of the protection of that country, or to return there, for fear of persecution." The UN established the Office of the UN High Commissioner for Refugees (UNHCR) in 1950 to handle refugee matters worldwide. The UN Relief and Works Agency for Palestine Refugees in the Near East (UNRWA) has a different operational definition for a Palestinian refugee: "a person whose normal place of residence was Palestine

during the period 1 June 1946 to 15 May 1948 and who lost both home and means of livelihood as a result of the 1948 conflict." However, UNHCR also assists some 400,000 Palestinian refugees not covered under the UNRWA definition. The term "internally displaced person" is not specifically covered in the UN Convention; it is used to describe people who have fled their homes for reasons similar to refugees, but who remain within their own national territory and are subject to the laws of that state.

Religions This entry is an ordered listing of religions by adherents starting with the largest group and sometimes includes the percent of total population. The core characteristics and beliefs of the world's major religions are described below.

Baha'i—Founded by Mirza Husayn-Ali (known as Baha'u'llah) in Iran in 1852, Baha'i faith emphasizes monotheism and believes in one eternal transcendent God. Its guiding focus is to encourage the unity of all peoples on the earth so that justice and peace may be achieved on earth. Baha'i revelation contends the prophets of major world religions reflect some truth or element of the divine, believes all were manifestations of God given to specific communities in specific times, and that Baha'u'llah is an additional prophet meant to call all humankind. Bahais are an open community, located worldwide, with the greatest concentration of believers in South Asia.

Buddhism—Religion or philosophy inspired by the 5th century B.C. teachings of Siddhartha Gautama (also known as Gautama Buddha "the enlightened one"). Buddhism focuses on the goal of spiritual enlightenment centered on an understanding of Gautama Buddha's Four Noble Truths on the nature of suffering, and on the Eightfold Path of spiritual and moral practice, to break the cycle of suffering of which we are a part. Buddhism ascribes to a karmic system of rebirth. Several schools and sects of Buddhism exist, differing often on the nature of the Buddha, the extent to which enlightenment can be achieved—for one or for all, and by whom—religious orders or laity.

Basic Groupings

Theravada Buddhism: The oldest Buddhist school, Theravada is practiced mostly in Sri Lanka, Cambodia, Laos, Burma, and Thailand, with minority representation elsewhere in Asia and the West. Theravadans follow the Pali Canon of Buddha's teachings, and believe that one may escape the cycle of rebirth, worldly attachment, and suffering for oneself; this process may take one or several lifetimes.

Mahayana Buddhism, including subsets Zen and Tibetan (Lamaistic) Buddhism: Forms of Mahayana Buddhism are common in East Asia and Tibet, and parts of the West. Mahayanas have additional scriptures beyond the Pali Canon and believe the Buddha is eternal and still teaching. Unlike Theravada Buddhism, Mahayana schools maintain the Buddha-nature is present in all beings and all will ultimately achieve enlightenment. Hoa Hao: a minority tradition of Buddhism practiced in Vietnam that stresses lay participation, primarily by peasant farmers; it eschews expensive ceremonies and temples and relocates the primary practices into the home.

Christianity—Descending from Judaism, Christianity's central belief maintains Jesus of Nazareth is the promised messiah of the Hebrew Scriptures, and that his life, death, and resurrection are salvific for the world. Christianity is one of the three monotheistic Abrahamic faiths, along with Islam and Judaism, which traces its spiritual lineage to Abraham of the Hebrew Scriptures. Its sacred texts include the Hebrew Bible and the New Testament (or the Christian Gospels).

Basic Groupings

Catholicism (or Roman Catholicism): This is the oldest established western Christian church and the world's largest single religious body. It is supranational, and recognizes a hierarchical structure with the Pope, or Bishop of Rome, as its head, located at the Vatican. Catholics believe the Pope is the divinely ordered head of the Church from a direct spiritual legacy of Jesus' apostle Peter. Catholicism is comprised of 23 particular Churches, or Rites—one Western (Roman or Latin-Rite) and 22 Eastern. The Latin Rite is by far the largest, making up about 98% of Catholic membership. Eastern-Rite Churches, such as the Maronite Church and the Ukrainian Catholic Church, are in communion with Rome although they preserve their own worship traditions and their immediate hierarchy consists of clergy within their own rite. The Catholic Church has a comprehensive theological and moral doctrine specified for believers in its catechism, which makes it unique among most forms of Christianity.

Mormonism (including the Church of Jesus Christ of Latter-Day Saints): Originating in 1830 in the United States under Joseph Smith, Mormonism is not characterized as a form of Protestant Christianity because it claims additional revealed Christian scriptures after the Hebrew Bible and New Testament. The Book of Mormon maintains there was an appearance of Jesus in the New World following the Christian account of his resurrection, and that the Americas are uniquely blessed continents. Mormonism believes earlier Christian traditions, such as the Roman Catholic, Orthodox, and Protestant reform faiths, are apostasies and that Joseph Smith's revelation of the Book of Mormon is a restoration of true Christianity. Mormons have a hierarchical religious leadership structure, and actively proselytize their faith; they are located primarily in the Americas and in a number of other Western countries.

Jehovah's Witnesses structure their faith on the Christian Bible, but their rejection of the Trinity is distinct from mainstream Christianity. They believe that a Kingdom of God, the Theocracy, will emerge following Armageddon and usher in a new earthly society. Adherents are required to evangelize and to follow a strict moral code.

Orthodox Christianity: The oldest established eastern form of Christianity, the Holy Orthodox Church, has a ceremonial head in the Bishop of Constantinople (Istanbul), also known as a Patriarch, but its various regional forms (e.g., Greek Orthodox, Russian Orthodox, Serbian Orthodox, Ukrainian Orthodox) are autocephalous (independent of Constantinople's authority, and have their own Patriarchs). Orthodox churches are highly nationalist and ethnic. The Orthodox Christian faith shares many theological tenets with the Roman Catholic Church, but diverges on some key premises and does not recognize the governing authority of the Pope.

Protestant Christianity: Protestant Christianity originated in the 16th century as an attempt to reform Roman Catholicism's practices, dogma, and theology. It encompasses several forms or denominations which are extremely varied in structure, beliefs, relationship to state, clergy, and governance. Many protestant theologies emphasize the primary role of scripture in their faith, advocating individual interpretation of Christian texts without the mediation of a final religious authority such as the Roman Pope. The oldest Protestant Christianities include Lutheranism, Calvinism (Presbyterians), and Anglican Christianity (Episcopalians), which have established liturgies, governing structure, and formal clergy. Other variants on Protestant Christianity, including Pentecostal movements and independent churches, may lack one or more of these elements, and their leadership and beliefs are individualized and dynamic.

Hinduism—Originating in the Vedic civilization of India (second and first millennium B.C.), Hinduism is an extremely diverse set of beliefs and practices with no single founder or religious authority. Hinduism has many scriptures; the Vedas, the Upanishads, and the Bhagavad-Gita are among some of the most important. Hindus may worship one or many deities, usually with prayer rituals within their own home. The most common figures of devotion are the gods Vishnu, Shiva, and a mother goddess, Devi. Most Hindus believe the soul, or *atman*, is eternal, and goes through a cycle of birth, death, and rebirth (*samsara*) determined by one's positive or negative karma, or the consequences of one's actions. The goal of religious life is to learn to act so as to finally achieve liberation (*moksha*) of one's soul, escaping the rebirth cycle.

Islam—The third of the monotheistic Abrahamic faiths, Islam originated with the teachings of Muhammad in the 7th century. Muslims believe Muhammad is the final of all religious prophets (beginning with Abraham) and that the Qu'ran, which is the Islamic scripture, was revealed to him by God. Islam derives from the word submission, and obedience to God is a primary theme in this religion. In order to live an Islamic life, believers must follow the five pillars, or tenets, of Islam, which are the testimony of faith (*shahada*), daily prayer (*salah*), giving alms (*zakah*), fasting during Ramadan (*sawm*), and the pilgrimage to Mecca (*hajj*).

Basic Groupings

The two primary branches of Islam are Sunni and Shia, which split from each other over a religio-political leadership dispute about the rightful successor to Muhammad. The Shia believe Muhammad's cousin and son-in-law, Ali, was the only divinely ordained Imam (religious leader), while the Sunni maintain the first three caliphs after Muhammad were also legitimate authorities. In modern Islam, Sunnis and Shia continue to have different views of acceptable schools of Islamic jurisprudence, and who is a proper Islamic religious authority. Islam also has an active mystical branch, Sufism, with various Sunni and Shia subsets.

Sunni Islam accounts for over 75% of the world's Muslim population. It recognizes the Abu Bakr as the first caliph after Muhammad. Sunni has four schools of Islamic doctrine and law—Hanafi, Maliki, Shafi'i, and Hanbali—which uniquely interpret the *Hadith*, or recorded oral traditions of Muhammad. A Sunni Muslim may elect to follow any one of these schools, as all are considered equally valid.

Shia Islam represents 10-20% of Muslims worldwide, and its distinguishing feature is its reverence for Ali as an infallible, divinely inspired leader, and as the first Imam of the Muslim community after Muhammad. A majority of Shia are known as "Twelvers," because they believe that the 11 familial successor imams after Muhammad culminate in a 12th Imam (al-Mahdi) who is hidden in the world and will reappear at its end to redeem the righteous.

Variants

Ismaili faith: A sect of Shia Islam, its adherents are also known as "Seveners," because they believe that the rightful seventh Imam in Islamic leadership was Isma'il, the elder son of Imam Jafar al-Sadiq. Ismaili tradition awaits the return of the seventh Imam as the Mahdi, or Islamic messianic figure. Ismailis are located in various parts of the world, particularly South Asia and the Levant.

Alawi faith: Another Shia sect of Islam, the name reflects followers' devotion to the religious authority of Ali. Alawites are a closed, secretive religious group who assert they are Shia Muslims, although outside scholars speculate their beliefs may have a syncretic mix with other faiths originating in the Middle East. Alawis live mostly in Syria, Lebanon, and Turkey.

Druze faith: A highly secretive tradition and a closed community that derives from the Ismaili sect of Islam; its core beliefs are thought to emphasize a combination of Gnostic principles believing that the Fatimid caliph, al-Hakin, is the one who embodies the key aspects of goodness of the universe, which are, the intellect, the word, the soul, the preceder, and the follower. The Druze have a key presence in Syria, Lebanon, and Israel.

Jainism—Originating in India, Jain spiritual philosophy believes in an eternal human soul, the eternal universe, and a principle of "the own nature of things." It emphasizes compassion for all living things, seeks liberation of the human soul from reincarnation through enlightenment, and values personal responsibility due to the belief in the immediate consequences of one's behavior. Jain philosophy teaches non-violence and prescribes vegetarianism for monks and laity alike; its adherents are a highly influential religious minority in Indian society.

Judaism—One of the first known monotheistic religions, likely dating to between 2000-1500 B.C., Judaism is the native faith of the Jewish people, based upon the belief in a covenant of responsibility between a sole omnipotent creator God and Abraham, the patriarch of Judaism's Hebrew Bible, or *Tanakh*. Divine revelation of principles and prohibitions in the Hebrew Scriptures form the basis of Jewish law, or *halakhah*, which is a key component of the faith. While there are extensive traditions of Jewish halakhic and theological discourse, there is no final dogmatic authority in the tradition. Local communities have their own religious leadership. Modern Judaism has three basic categories of faith: Orthodox, Conservative, and Reform/Liberal. These differ in their views and observance of Jewish law, with the Orthodox representing the most traditional practice, and Reform/Liberal communities the most accommodating of individualized interpretations of Jewish identity and faith.

Shintoism—A native animist tradition of Japan, Shinto practice is based upon the premise that every being and object has its own spirit or *kami*. Shinto practitioners worship several particular *kamis*, including the *kamis* of nature, and families often have shrines to their ancestors' *kamis*. Shintoism has no fixed tradition of prayers or prescribed dogma, but is characterized by individual ritual. Respect for the *kamis* in nature is a key Shinto value. Prior to the end of World War II, Shinto was the state religion of Japan, and bolstered the cult of the Japanese emperor.

Sikhism—Founded by the Guru Nanak (born 1469), Sikhism believes in a non-anthropomorphic, supreme, eternal, creator God; centering one's devotion to God is seen as a means of escaping the cycle of rebirth. Sikhs follow the teachings of Nanak and nine subsequent gurus. Their scripture, the Guru Granth Sahib—also known as the Adi Granth—is considered the living Guru, or final authority of Sikh faith and theology. Sikhism emphasizes equality of humankind and disavows caste, class, or gender discrimination.

Taoism—Chinese philosophy or religion based upon Lao Tzu's Tao Te Ching, which centers on belief in the Tao, or the way, as the flow of the universe and the nature of things. Taoism encourages a principle of non-force, or wu-wei, as the means to live harmoniously with the Tao. Taoists believe the esoteric world is made up of a perfect harmonious balance and nature, while in the manifest world—particularly in the body—balance is distorted. The Three Jewels of the Tao—compassion, simplicity, and humility—serve as the basis for Taoist ethics. **Zoroastrianism**—Originating from the teachings of Zoroaster in about the 9th or 10th century B.C., Zoroastrianism may be the oldest continuing creedal religion. Its key beliefs center on a transcendent creator God, Ahura Mazda, and the concept of free will. The key ethical tenets of Zoroastrianism expressed in its scripture, the Avesta, are based on a dualistic worldview where one may prevent chaos if one chooses to serve God and exercises good thoughts, good words, and good deeds. Zoroastrianism is generally a closed religion and members are almost always born to Zoroastrian parents. Prior to the spread of Islam, Zoroastrianism dominated greater Iran. Today, though a minority, Zoroastrians remain primarily in Iran, India (where they are known as Parsi), and Pakistan.

Traditional beliefs

Animism: the belief that non-human entities contain souls or spirits.

Badimo: a form of ancestor worship of the Tswana people of Botswana.

Confucianism: an ideology that humans are perfectible through self-cultivation and self-creation; developed from teachings of the Chinese philosopher Confucius. Confucianism has strongly influenced the culture and beliefs of East Asian countries, including China, Japan, Korea, Singapore, Taiwan, and Vietnam.

Inuit beliefs are a form of shamanism (see below) based on animistic principles of the Inuit or Eskimo peoples.

Kirant: the belief system of the Kirat, a people who live mainly in the Himalayas of Nepal. It is primarily a form of polytheistic shamanism, but includes elements of animism and ancestor worship.

Pagan is a blanket term used to describe many unconnected belief practices throughout history, usually in reference to religions outside of the Abrahamic category (monotheistic faiths like Judaism, Christianity, and Islam).

Shamanism: beliefs and practices promoting communication with the spiritual world. Shamanistic beliefs are organized around a shaman or medicine man who—as an intermediary between the human and spirit world—is believed to be able to heal the sick (by healing their souls), communicate with the spirit world, and help souls into the afterlife through the practice of entering a trance. In shaman-based religions, the shaman is also responsible for leading sacred rites.

Spiritualism: the belief that souls and spirits communicate with the living usually through intermediaries called mediums.

Syncretic (fusion of diverse religious beliefs and practices)

Cao Dai: a nationalistic Vietnamese sect, officially established in 1926, that draws practices and precepts from Confucianism, Taoism, Buddhism, and Catholicism.

Chondogyo: or the religion of the Heavenly Way, is based on Korean shamanism, Buddhism, and Korean folk traditions, with some elements drawn from Christianity. Formulated in the 1860s, it holds that God lives in all of us and strives to convert society into a paradise on earth, populated by believers transformed into intelligent moral beings with a high social conscience.

Kimbanguist: a puritan form of the Baptist denomination founded by Simon Kimbangu in the 1920s in what is now the Democratic Republic of Congo. Adherents believe that salvation comes through Jesus' death and resurrection, like Christianity, but additionally that living a spiritually pure life following strict codes of conduct is required for salvation.

Modekngei: a hybrid of Christianity and ancient Palauan culture and oral traditions founded around 1915 on the island of Babeldaob. Adherents simultaneously worship Jesus Christ and Palauan goddesses.

Rastafarian: an afro-centrist ideology and movement based on Christianity that arose in Jamaica in the 1930s; it believes that Haile Selassie I, Emperor of Ethiopia from 1930-74, was the incarnation of the second coming of Jesus.

Santeria: practiced in Cuba, the merging of the Yoruba religion of Nigeria with Roman Catholicism and native Indian traditions. Its practitioners believe that each person has a destiny and eventually transcends to merge with the divine creator and source of all energy, Olorun.

Voodoo/Vodun: a form of spirit and ancestor worship combined with some Christian faiths, especially Catholicism. Haitian and

Louisiana Voodoo, which have included more Catholic practices, are separate from West African Vodun, which has retained a focus on spirit worship.

Non-religious

Agnosticism: the belief that most things are unknowable. In regard to religion it is usually characterized as neither a belief nor non belief in a deity.

Atheism: the belief that there are no deities of any kind.

Reserves of foreign exchange and gold This entry gives the dollar value for the stock of all financial assets that are available to the central monetary authority for use in meeting a country's balance of payments needs as of the end-date of the period specified. This category includes not only foreign currency and gold, but also a country's holdings of Special Drawing Rights in the International Monetary Fund, and its reserve position in the Fund.

Roadways This entry gives the *total* length of the road network and includes the length of the *paved* and *unpaved* portions.

Sanitation facility access This entry provides information about access to improved or unimproved sanitation facilities available to segments of the population of a country. *Improved* sanitation—use of any of the following facilities: flush or pour-flush to a piped sewer system, septic tank or pit latrine; ventilated improved pit (VIP) latrine; pit latrine with slab; or a composting toilet, *unimproved* sanitation—use of any of the following facilities: flush or pour-flush not piped to a sewer system, septic tank or pit latrine; pit latrine without a slab or open pit; bucket; hanging toilet or hanging latrine; shared facilities of any type; no facilities; or bush or field.

School life expectancy (primary to tertiary education) School life expectancy (SLE) is the total number of years of schooling (primary to tertiary) that a child can expect to receive, assuming that the probability of his or her being enrolled in school at any particular future age is equal to the current enrollment ratio at that age. Caution must be maintained when utilizing this indicator in international comparisons. For example, a year or grade completed in one country is not necessarily the same in terms of educational content or quality as a year or grade completed in another country. SLE represents the expected number of years of schooling that will be completed, including years spent repeating one or more grades.

Sex ratio This entry includes the number of males for each female in five age groups—*at birth, under 15 years, 15-64 years, 65 years and over,* and for the *total population*. Sex ratio at birth has recently emerged as an indicator of certain kinds of sex discrimination in some countries. For instance, high sex ratios at birth in some Asian countries are now attributed to sex-selective abortion and infanticide due to a strong preference for sons. This will affect future marriage patterns and fertility patterns. Eventually, it could cause unrest among young adult males who are unable to find partners.

Stateless person Statelessness is the condition whereby an individual is not considered a national by any country. Stateless people are denied basic rights, such as access to employment, housing, education, healthcare, and pensions, and they may be unable to vote, own property, open a bank account, or legally register a marriage or birth. They may also be vulnerable to arbitrary treatment and human trafficking. In at least 30 states, women cannot pass their nationality on to their children. In these countries, if a child's father is foreign, stateless, or absent, the child usually becomes stateless. Estimates of the number of stateless people are inherently imprecise because few countries have procedures to identify them; the UN approximates that there are 12 million stateless people worldwide. Stateless people are counted in a country's overall population figure if they have lived there for a year.

Stock of broad money This entry covers all of "Narrow money," plus the total quantity of time and savings deposits, credit union deposits, institutional money market funds, short-term repurchase agreements between the central bank and commercial deposit banks, and other large liquid assets held by nonbank financial institutions, state and local governments, nonfinancial public enterprises, and the private sector of the economy. National currency units have been converted to US dollars at the closing exchange rate for the date of the information. Because of exchange rate movements, changes in money stocks measured in national currency units may vary significantly from those shown in US dollars, and caution is urged when making comparisons over time in US dollars. In addition to serving as a medium of exchange, broad money includes assets that are slightly less liquid than narrow money and the assets tend to function as a "store of value"—a means of holding wealth.

Stock of direct foreign investment—abroad This entry gives the cumulative US dollar value of all investments in foreign countries made directly by residents—primarily companies—of the home country, as of the end of the time period indicated. Direct investment excludes investment through purchase of shares.

Stock of direct foreign investment—at home This entry gives the cumulative US dollar value of all investments in the home country made directly by residents—primarily companies—of other countries as of the end of the time period indicated. Direct investment excludes investment through purchase of shares.

Stock of domestic credit This entry is the total quantity of credit, denominated in the domestic currency, provided by financial institutions to the central bank, state and local governments, public non-financial corporations, and the private sector. The national currency units have been converted to US dollars at the closing exchange rate on the date of the information.

Stock of narrow money This entry, also known as "M1," comprises the total quantity of currency in circulation (notes and coins) plus demand deposits denominated in the national currency held by nonbank financial institutions, state and local governments, nonfinancial public enterprises, and the private sector of the economy, measured at a specific point in time. National currency units have been converted to US dollars at the closing exchange rate for the date of the information. Because of exchange rate movements, changes in money stocks measured in national currency units may vary significantly from those shown in US dollars, and caution is urged when making comparisons over time in US dollars. Narrow money consists of more liquid assets than broad money and the assets generally function as a "medium of exchange" for an economy.

Suffrage This entry gives the age at enfranchisement and whether the right to vote is universal or restricted.

Taxes and other revenues This entry records total taxes and other revenues received by the national government during the time period indicated, expressed as a percent of GDP. Taxes include personal and corporate income taxes, value added taxes, excise taxes, and tariffs. Other revenues include social contributions—such as payments for social security and hospital insurance—grants, and net revenues from public enterprises. Normalizing the data, by dividing total revenues by GDP, enables easy comparisons across countries, and provides an average rate at which all income (GDP) is paid to the national level government for the supply of public goods and services.

Telephone numbers All telephone numbers in *The World Factbook* consist of the country code in brackets, the city or area code (where required) in parentheses, and the local number. The one component that is not presented is the international access code, which varies from country to country. For example, an international direct dial telephone call placed from the US to Madrid, Spain, would be as follows: 011 [34] (1) 577-xxxx, where 011 is the international access code for station-to-station calls; 01 is for calls other than station-to-station calls, [34] is the country code for Spain, (1) is the city code for Madrid, 577 is the local exchange, and xxxx is the local telephone number. An international direct dial telephone call placed from another country to the US would be as follows: international access code +[1] (202) 939-xxxx, where [1] is the country code for the US, (202) is the area code for Washington, DC, 939 is the local exchange, and xxxx is the local telephone number.

Telephone system This entry includes a brief general assessment of the system with details on the domestic and international components. The following terms and abbreviations are used throughout the entry:

Arabsat—Arab Satellite Communications Organization (Riyadh, Saudi Arabia).

Autodin—Automatic Digital Network (US Department of Defense).

CB—citizen's band mobile radio communications.

Cellular telephone system—the telephones in this system are radio transceivers, with each instrument having its own private radio frequency and sufficient radiated power to reach the booster station in its area (cell), from which the telephone signal is fed to a telephone exchange.

Central American Microwave System—a trunk microwave radio relay system that links the countries of Central America and Mexico with each other.

Coaxial cable—a multichannel communication cable consisting of a central conducting wire, surrounded by and insulated from a cylindrical conducting shell; a large number of telephone channels can be made available within the insulated space by the use of a large number of carrier frequencies.

Comsat—Communications Satellite Corporation (US).

DSN—Defense Switched Network (formerly Automatic Voice Network or Autovon); basic general-purpose, switched voice network of the Defense Communications System (US Department of Defense).

Eutelsat—European Telecommunications Satellite Organization (Paris).

Fiber-optic cable—a multichannel communications cable using a thread of optical glass fibers as a transmission medium in which the signal (voice, video, etc.) is in the form of a coded pulse of light.

GSM—a global system for mobile (cellular) communications devised by the Groupe Special Mobile of the pan-European standardization organization, Conference Europeanne des Posts et Telecommunications (CEPT) in 1982.

HF—high frequency; any radio frequency in the 3,000-to 30,000-kHz range.

Inmarsat—International Maritime Satellite Organization (London); provider of global mobile satellite communications for commercial, distress, and safety applications at sea, in the air, and on land.

Intelsat—International Telecommunications Satellite Organization (Washington, DC).

Intersputnik—International Organization of Space Communications (Moscow); first established in the former Soviet Union and the East European countries, it is now marketing its services worldwide with earth stations in North America, Africa, and East Asia.

Landline—communication wire or cable of any sort that is installed on poles or buried in the ground.

Marecs—Maritime European Communications Satellite used in the Inmarsat system on lease from the European Space Agency.

Marisat—satellites of the Comsat Corporation that participate in the Inmarsat system.

Medarabtel—the Middle East Telecommunications Project of the International Telecommunications Union (ITU) providing a modern telecommunications network, primarily by microwave radio relay, linking Algeria, Djibouti, Egypt, Jordan, Libya, Morocco, Saudi Arabia, Somalia, Sudan, Syria, Tunisia, and Yemen; it was initially started in Morocco in 1970 by the Arab Telecommunications Union (ATU) and was known at that time as the Middle East Mediterranean Telecommunications Network.

Microwave radio relay—transmission of long distance telephone calls and television programs by highly directional radio microwaves that are received and sent on from one booster station to another on an optical path.

NMT—Nordic Mobile Telephone; an analog cellular telephone system that was developed jointly by the national telecommunications authorities of the Nordic countries (Denmark, Finland, Iceland, Norway, and Sweden).

Orbita—a Russian television service; also the trade name of a packet-switched digital telephone network.

Radiotelephone communications—the two-way transmission and reception of sounds by broadcast radio on authorized frequencies using telephone handsets.

PanAmSat—PanAmSat Corporation (Greenwich, CT).

SAFE—South African Far East Cable

Satellite communication system—a communication system consisting of two or more earth stations and at least one satellite that provide long distance transmission of voice, data, and television; the system usually serves as a trunk connection between telephone exchanges; if the earth stations are in the same country, it is a domestic system.

Satellite earth station—a communications facility with a microwave radio transmitting and receiving antenna and required receiving and transmitting equipment for communicating with satellites.

Satellite link—a radio connection between a satellite and an earth station permitting communication between them, either one-way (down link from satellite to earth station—television receive-only transmission) or two-way (telephone channels).

SHF—super high frequency; any radio frequency in the 3,000-to 30,000-MHz range.

Shortwave—radio frequencies (from 1.605 to 30 MHz) that fall above the commercial broadcast band and are used for communication over long distances.

Solidaridad—geosynchronous satellites in Mexico's system of international telecommunications in the Western Hemisphere.

Statsionar—Russia's geostationary system for satellite telecommunications.

Submarine cable—a cable designed for service under water.

TAT—Trans-Atlantic Telephone; any of a number of high-capacity submarine coaxial telephone cables linking Europe with North America.

Telefax—facsimile service between subscriber stations via the public switched telephone network or the international Datel network.

Telegraph—a telecommunications system designed for unmodulated electric impulse transmission.

Telex—a communication service involving teletypewriters connected by wire through automatic exchanges.

Tropospheric scatter—a form of microwave radio transmission in which the troposphere is used to scatter and reflect a fraction of the incident radio waves back to earth; powerful, highly directional antennas are used to transmit and receive the microwave signals; reliable over-the-horizon communications are

realized for distances up to 600 miles in a single hop; additional hops can extend the range of this system for very long distances. **Trunk network**—a network of switching centers, connected by multichannel trunk lines.
UHF—ultra high frequency; any radio frequency in the 300-to 3,000-MHz range.
VHF—very high frequency; any radio frequency in the 30-to 300-MHz range.

Telephones—main lines in use This entry gives the total number of main telephone lines in use.

Telephones—mobile cellular This entry gives the total number of mobile cellular telephone subscribers.

Terminology Due to the highly structured nature of the *Factbook* database, some collective generic terms have to be used. For example, the word **Country** in the **Country name** entry refers to a wide variety of dependencies, areas of special sovereignty, uninhabited islands, and other entities in addition to the traditional countries or independent states. **Military** is also used as an umbrella term for various civil defense, security, and defense activities in many entries. The **Independence** entry includes the usual colonial independence dates and former ruling states as well as other significant nationhood dates such as the traditional founding date or the date of unification, federation, confederation, establishment, or state succession that are not strictly independence dates. Dependent areas have the nature of their dependency status noted in this same entry.

Terrain This entry contains a brief description of the topography.

Time difference This entry is expressed in *The World Factbook* in two ways. First, it is stated as the difference in hours between the capital of an entity and **Coordinated Universal Time (UTC)** during Standard Time. Additionally, the difference in time between the capital of an entity and that observed in Washington, D.C. is also provided. Note that the time difference assumes both locations are simultaneously observing Standard Time or Daylight Saving Time.

Time zones Ten countries (Australia, Brazil, Canada, Indonesia, Kazakhstan, Mexico, New Zealand, Russia, Spain, and the United States) and the island of Greenland observe more than one official time depending on the number of designated time zones within their boundaries. An illustration of time zones throughout the world and within countries can be seen in the Standard Time Zones of the World map included in the **Reference Maps** section of *The World Factbook*.

Total fertility rate This entry gives a figure for the average number of children that would be born per woman if all women lived to the end of their childbearing years and bore children according to a given fertility rate at each age. The total fertility rate (TFR) is a more direct measure of the level of fertility than the crude birth rate, since it refers to births per woman. This indicator shows the potential for population change in the country. A rate of two children per woman is considered the replacement rate for a population, resulting in relative stability in terms of total numbers. Rates above two children indicate populations growing in size and whose median age is declining. Higher rates may also indicate difficulties for families, in some situations, to feed and educate their children and for women to enter the labor force. Rates below two children indicate populations decreasing in size and growing older. Global fertility rates are in general decline and this trend is most pronounced in industrialized countries, especially Western Europe, where populations are projected to decline dramatically over the next 50 years.

Total renewable water resources This entry provides the long-term average water availability for a country in cubic kilo-meters of precipitation, recharged ground water, and surface inflows from surrounding countries. The values have been adjusted to account for overlap resulting from surface flow recharge of groundwater sources. Total renewable water resources provides the water total available to a country but does not include water resource totals that have been reserved for upstream or downstream countries through international agreements. Note that these values are averages and do not accurately reflect the total available in any given year. Annual available resources can vary greatly due to short-term and long-term climatic and weather variations.

Trafficking in persons Trafficking in persons is modern-day slavery, involving victims who are forced, defrauded, or coerced into labor or sexual exploitation. The International Labor Organization (ILO), the UN agency charged with addressing labor standards, employment, and social protection issues, estimates that 12.3 million people worldwide are enslaved in forced labor, bonded labor, forced child labor, sexual servitude, and involuntary servitude at any given time. Human trafficking is a multi-dimensional threat, depriving people of their human rights and freedoms, risking global health, promoting social breakdown, inhibiting development by depriving countries of their human capital, and helping fuel the growth of organized crime. In 2000, the US Congress passed the Trafficking Victims Protection Act (TVPA), reauthorized in 2003 and 2005, which provides tools for the US to combat trafficking in persons, both domestically and abroad. One of the law's key components is the creation of the US Department of State's annual *Trafficking in Persons Report*, which assesses the government response (i.e., the *current situation*) in some 150 countries with a significant number of victims trafficked across their borders who are recruited, harbored, transported, provided, or obtained for forced labor or sexual exploitation. Countries in the annual report are rated in three tiers, based on government efforts to combat trafficking. The countries identified in this entry are those listed in the *2010 Trafficking in Persons Report as Tier 2 Watch List or Tier 3* based on the following *tier rating* definitions:

> **Tier 2 Watch List** *countries do not fully comply with the minimum standards for the elimination of trafficking but are making significant efforts to do so, and meet one of the following criteria:*
> *1. they display high or significantly increasing number of victims,*
> *2. they have failed to provide evidence of increasing efforts to combat trafficking in persons, or,*
> *3. they have committed to take action over the next year.*
> **Tier 3** *countries neither satisfy the minimum standards for the elimination of trafficking nor demonstrate a significant effort to do so. Countries in this tier are subject to potential non-humanitarian and non-trade sanctions.*

Transnational issues This category includes four entries—**Disputes—international, Refugees and internally displaced persons, Trafficking in persons,** and **Illicit drugs**—that deal with current issues going beyond national boundaries.

Transportation This category includes the entries dealing with the means for movement of people and goods.

Transportation—note This entry includes miscellaneous transportation information of significance not included elsewhere.

Unemployment rate This entry contains the percent of the labor force that is without jobs. Substantial underemployment might be noted.

Unemployment, youth ages 15-24 This entry gives the percent of the total labor force ages 15-24 unemployed during a specified year.

Urbanization This entry provides two measures of the degree of urbanization of a population. The first, *urban population*, describes the percentage of the total population living in urban areas, as defined by the country. The second, *rate of urbanization*, describes the projected average rate of change of the size of the urban population over the given period of time. Additionally, the World entry includes a list of the *ten largest urban agglomerations*. An *urban agglomeration* is defined as comprising the city or town proper and also the suburban fringe or thickly settled territory lying outside of, but adjacent to, the boundaries of the city.

UTC (Coordinated Universal Time) See entry for Coordinated Universal Time.

Waterways This entry gives the total length of navigable rivers, canals, and other inland bodies of water.

Weights and Measures This information is presented in **Appendix G: Weights and Measures** and includes mathematical notations (mathematical powers and names), metric interrelationships (prefix; symbol; length, weight, or capacity; area; volume), and standard conversion factors.

Years All year references are for the calendar year (CY) unless indicated as fiscal year (FY). The calendar year is an accounting period of 12 months from 1 January to 31 December. The fiscal year is an accounting period of 12 months other than 1 January to 31 December.

GUIDE TO COUNTRY PROFILES

INTRODUCTION

Background

GEOGRAPHY

Location
Geographic coordinates
Map references
Area
total
land
water
Area—comparative
Land boundaries
total
border countries
Coastline
Maritime claims
territorial sea
contiguous zone
exclusive economic zone
continental shelf
exclusive fishing zone
Climate
Terrain
Elevation extremes
lowest point
highest point
Natural resources
Land use
arable land
permanent crops
other
Irrigated land
Total renewable water resources
**Freshwater withdrawal (domestic/
industrial/agricultural)**
total
per capita
Natural hazards
volcanism
Environment—current issues
Environment—international agreements
party to
signed, but not ratified
Geography—note

PEOPLE AND SOCIETY

Nationality
noun
adjective
Ethnic groups
Languages
Religions
Demographic profile

Population
Age structure
0-14 years
15-24 years
25-54 years
55-64 years
65 years and over
Median Age
total
male
female
Population growth rate
Birth rate
Death rate
Net migration rate
Urbanization
urban population
rate of urbanization
Major cities—population
Sex ratio
at birth
under 15 years
15-64 years
65 years and over
total population
Maternal mortality rate
Infant mortality rate
total
male
female
Life expectancy at birth
total population
male
female
Total fertility rate
Health expenditures
Physicians density
Hospital bed density
Drinking water source
improved
unimproved
Sanitation facility access
improved
unimproved
HIV/AIDS—adult prevalence rate
HIV/AIDS—people living with HIV/AIDS
HIV/AIDS—deaths
Major infectious diseases
degree of risk
food or waterborne diseases
vectorborne diseases
water contact diseases
aerosolized dust or soil contact disease
respiratory disease
animal contact disease
Obesity—adult prevalence rate

**Children under the age of 5 years
underweight**
Education expenditures
Literacy
definition
total population
male
female
**School life expectancy (primary to
tertiary)**
Unemployment, youth ages 15-24
People—note

GOVERNMENT

Country name
conventional long form
conventional short form
local long form
local short form
former
abbreviation
Dependency status
Government type
Capital
name
geographic coordinates
time difference
daylight saving time
Administrative divisions
Dependent areas
Independence
National holiday
Constitution
Legal system
**International law organization
participation**
Suffrage
Executive branch
chief of state
head of government
cabinet
elections
election results
Legislative branch
elections
election results
Judicial branch
Political parties and leaders
Political pressure groups and leaders
International organization participation
Diplomatic representation in the US
chief of mission
chancery
telephone
FAX
consulate(s) general

Background: Ahmad Shah DURRANI unified the Pashtun tribes and founded Afghanistan in 1747. The country served as a buffer between the British and Russian Empires until it won independence from notional British control in 1919. A brief experiment in democracy ended in a 1973 coup and a 1978 communist countercoup. The Soviet Union invaded in 1979 to support the tottering Afghan communist regime, touching off a long and destructive war. The USSR withdrew in 1989 under relentless pressure by internationally supported anti-communist mujahidin rebels. A series of subsequent civil wars saw Kabul finally fall in 1996 to the Taliban, a hardline Pakistani-sponsored movement that emerged in 1994 to end the country's civil war and anarchy. Following the 11 September 2001 terrorist attacks, a US, Allied, and anti-Taliban Northern Alliance military action toppled the Taliban for sheltering Usama BIN LADIN.

A UN-sponsored Bonn Conference in 2001 established a process for political reconstruction that included the adoption of a new constitution, a presidential election in 2004, and National Assembly elections in 2005. In December 2004, Hamid KARZAI became the first democratically elected president of Afghanistan, and the National Assembly was inaugurated the following December. KARZAI was reelected in August 2009 for a second term. The 2014 presidential election was the country's first to include a runoff, which featured the top two vote-getters from the first round, Abdullah ABDULLAH and Ashraf GHANI. Throughout the summer of 2014, their campaigns disputed the results and traded accusations of fraud, leading to a US-led diplomatic intervention that included a full vote audit as well as political negotiations between the two camps. In September 2014, GHANI and ABDULLAH agreed to form the Government of National Unity, with GHANI inaugurated as president and ABDULLAH elevated to the newly-created position of chief executive officer. The day after the inauguration, the GHANI administration signed the US-Afghan Bilateral Security Agreement and NATO Status of Forces Agreement, which provide the legal basis for the post-2014 international military presence in Afghanistan.

Despite gains toward building a stable central government, the Taliban remains a serious challenge for the Afghan Government in almost every province. The Taliban still considers itself the rightful government of Afghanistan, and it remains a capable and confident insurgent force despite its last two spiritual leaders being killed; it continues to declare that it will pursue a peace deal with Kabul only after foreign military forces depart.

GEOGRAPHY

Location: Southern Asia, north and west of Pakistan, east of Iran

Geographic coordinates: 33 00 N, 65 00 E

Map references: Asia

Area: *total:* 652,230 sq km
land: 652,230 sq km
water: 0 sq km
country comparison to the world: 42

Area—comparative: almost six times the size of Virginia; slightly smaller than Texas

Land boundaries: *total:* 5,987 km
border countries (6): China 91 km, Iran 921 km, Pakistan 2,670 km, Tajikistan 1,357 km, Turkmenistan 804 km, Uzbekistan 144 km

Coastline: 0 km (landlocked)

Maritime claims: none (landlocked)

Climate: arid to semiarid; cold winters and hot summers

Terrain: mostly rugged mountains; plains in north and southwest

Elevation: *mean elevation:* 1,884 m

elevation extremes: *lowest point:* Amu Darya 258 m
highest point: Noshak 7,492 m

Natural resources: natural gas, petroleum, coal, copper, chromite, talc, barites, sulfur, lead, zinc, iron ore, salt, precious and semiprecious stones, arable land

Land use: *agricultural land:* 58.07%
arable land 20.5%;
permanent crops 0.37%;
permanent pasture 79%
forest: 2.07%
other: 39.86% (2014 est.)
Irrigated land: 32,080 sq km (2012)

Population—distribution: populations tend to cluster in the foothills and periphery of the rugged Hindu Kush range; smaller groups are found in many of the country's interior valleys; in general, the east is more densely settled while the south is sparsely populated

Natural hazards: damaging earthquakes occur in Hindu Kush mountains; flooding; droughts

Environment—current issues: limited natural freshwater resources; inadequate supplies of potable water; soil degradation; overgrazing; deforestation (much of the remaining forests are being cut down for fuel and building materials); desertification; air and water pollution

Environment—international agreements: party to: Biodiversity, Climate Change, Desertification, Endangered Species, Environmental Modification, Marine Dumping, Ozone Layer Protection
signed, but not ratified: Hazardous Wastes, Law of the Sea, Marine Life Conservation

Geography—note: landlocked; the Hindu Kush mountains that run northeast to southwest divide the northern provinces from the rest of the country; the highest peaks are in the northern Vakhan (Wakhan Corridor)

PEOPLE AND SOCIETY

Population: 34,124,811 (July 2017 est.)
country comparison to the world: 39

Nationality: *noun:* Afghan(s)
adjective: Afghan

Ethnic groups: Pashtun, Tajik, Hazara, Uzbek, other (includes smaller numbers of Baloch, Turkmen, Nuristani, Pamiri, Arab, Gujar, Brahui, Qizilbash, Aimaq, Pashai, and Kyrghyz)
note: current statistical data on the sensitive subject of ethnicity in Afghanistan are not available, and ethnicity data from small samples of respondents to opinion polls are not a reliable alternative; Afghanistan's 2004 constitution recognizes 14 ethnic groups: Pashtun, Tajik, Hazara, Uzbek, Baloch, Turkmen, Nuristani, Pamiri, Arab, Gujar, Brahui, Qizilbash, Aimaq, and Pashai (2015)

Languages: Afghan Persian or Dari (official) 80% (Dari functions as the lingua franca), Pashto (official) 47%, Uzbek 11%, English 5%, Turkmen 2%, Urdu 2%, Pashayi 1%, Nuristani 1%, Arabic 1%, Balochi, Shughni, Pamiri, Hindi, Russian, German, French <.5% each, don't know/refused <1%
note 1: data represent most widely spoken languages; shares sum to more than 100% because there is much bilingualism in the country and because respondents were allowed to select more than one language
note 2: the Turkic languages Uzbek and Turkmen, as well as Balochi, Pashayi, Nuristani, and Pamiri are the third official languages in areas where the majority speaks them (2017 est.)

Religions: Muslim 99.7% (Sunni 84.7—89.7%, Shia 10—15%), other 0.3% (2009 est.)

Age structure: *0-14 years:* 40.92% (male 7,093,980/female 6,869,737)
15-24 years: 22.22% (male 3,859,696/female 3,723,679)
25-54 years: 30.35% (male 5,273,969/female 5,082,972)
55-64 years: 3.92% (male 659,635/female 678,942)
65 years and over: 2.59% (male 407,437/female 474,764) (2017 est.)

Dependency ratios: *total dependency ratio:* 88.8

youth dependency ratio: 84.1
elderly dependency ratio: 4.7
potential support ratio: 21.2 (2015 est.)

Median age: total: 18.8 years
male: 18.8 years
female: 18.9 years (2017 est.)
country comparison to the world: 208

Population growth rate: 2.36% (2017 est.)
country comparison to the world: 29

Birth rate: 37.9 births/1,000 population (2017 est.)
country comparison to the world: 12

Death rate: 13.4 deaths/1,000 population (2017 est.)
country comparison to the world: 10

Net migration rate: -0.9 migrant(s)/1,000 population (2017 est.)
country comparison to the world: 134

Population distribution: populations tend to cluster in the foothills and periphery of the rugged Hindu Kush range; smaller groups are found in many of the country's interior valleys; in general, the east is more densely settled while the south is sparsely populated

Urbanization: *urban population:* 27.6% of total population (2017)
rate of urbanization: 3.77% annual rate of change (2015-20 est.)

Major urban areas—population: KABUL (capital) 4.635 million (2015)

Sex ratio: *at birth:* 1.05 male(s)/female
0-14 years: 1.03 male(s)/female
15-24 years: 1.04 male(s)/female
25-54 years: 1.04 male(s)/female
55-64 years: 0.97 male(s)/female
65 years and over: 0.86 male(s)/female
total population: 1.03 male(s)/female (2016 est.)

Mother's mean age at first birth: 19.9 years
note: median age at first birth among women 25-29 (2015 est.)

Maternal mortality ratio: 396 deaths/100,000 live births (2015 est.)
country comparison to the world: 28

Infant mortality rate: total: 110.6 deaths/1,000 live births
male: 118 deaths/1,000 live births
female: 102.9 deaths/1,000 live births (2017 est.)
country comparison to the world: 1

Life expectancy at birth: total population: 51.7 years
male: 50.3 years
female: 53.2 years (2017 est.)
country comparison to the world: 222

Total fertility rate: 5.12 children born/woman (2017 est.)
country comparison to the world: 10

Contraceptive prevalence rate: 22.5% (2015/16)

Health expenditures: 8.2% of GDP (2014)
country comparison to the world: 52

Physicians density: 0.3 physicians/1,000 population (2014)

Hospital bed density: 0.5 beds/1,000 population (2012)

Drinking water source:
improved:
urban: 78.2% of population
rural: 47% of population
total: 55.3% of population
unimproved:
urban: 21.8% of population
rural: 53% of population
total: 44.7% of population (2015 est.)

Sanitation facility access:
improved:
urban: 45.1% of population
rural: 27% of population
total: 31.9% of population
unimproved:
urban: 54.9% of population
rural: 73% of population
total: 68.1% of population (2015 est.)

HIV/AIDS—adult prevalence rate: <.1% (2016 est.)

HIV/AIDS—people living with HIV/AIDS: 7,500 (2016 est.)
country comparison to the world: 103

HIV/AIDS—deaths: <500 (2016 est.)

Major infectious diseases: *degree of risk:* intermediate
food or waterborne diseases: bacterial diarrhea, hepatitis A, and typhoid fever
vectorborne disease: malaria (2016)
Obesity—adult prevalence rate: 5.5% (2016)
country comparison to the world: 177

Children under the age of 5 years underweight: 25% (2013)
country comparison to the world: 8

Education expenditures: 3.4% of GDP (2015)

Literacy: *definition:* age 15 and over can read and write
total population: 38.2%
male: 52%
female: 24.2% (2015 est.)

School life expectancy (primary to tertiary education): *total:* 11 years
male: 13 years
female: 8 years (2014)

GOVERNMENT

Country name: *conventional long form:* Islamic Republic of Afghanistan
conventional short form: Afghanistan
local long form: Jamhuri-ye Islami-ye Afghanistan
local short form: Afghanistan
former: Republic of Afghanistan
etymology: the name "Afghan" originally referred to the Pashtun people (today it is understood to include all the country's ethnic groups), while the suffix "-stan" means "place of" or "country"; so Afghanistan literally means the "Land of the Afghans"

Government type: presidential Islamic republic

Capital: *name:* Kabul

geographic coordinates: 34 31 N, 69 11 E
time difference: UTC+4.5 (9.5 hours ahead of Washington, DC, during Standard Time)

Administrative divisions: 34 provinces (welayat, singular—welayat); Badakhshan, Badghis, Baghlan, Balkh, Bamyan, Daykundi, Farah, Faryab, Ghazni, Ghor, Helmand, Herat, Jowzjan, Kabul, Kandahar, Kapisa, Khost, Kunar, Kunduz, Laghman, Logar, Nangarhar, Nimroz, Nuristan, Paktika, Paktiya, Panjshir, Parwan, Samangan, Sar-e Pul, Takhar, Uruzgan, Wardak, Zabul

Independence: 19 August 1919 (from UK control over Afghan foreign affairs)

National holiday: Independence Day, 19 August (1919)

Constitution: *history:* several previous; latest drafted 14 December 2003—4 January 2004, signed 16 January 2004, ratified 26 January 2004
amendments: proposed by a commission formed by presidential decree followed by the convention of a Grand Council (Loya Jirga) decreed by the president; passage requires at least two-thirds majority vote of the Loya Jirga membership and endorsement by the president (2017)

Legal system: mixed legal system of civil, customary, and Islamic law

International law organization participation: has not submitted an ICJ jurisdiction declaration; accepts ICCt jurisdiction

Citizenship: *citizenship by birth:* no
citizenship by descent only: at least one parent must have been born in—and continuously lived in—Afghanistan
dual citizenship recognized: no
residency requirement for naturalization: 5 years

Suffrage: 18 years of age; universal

Executive branch: *chief of state:* President of the Islamic Republic of Afghanistan Ashraf GHANI Ahmadzai (since 29 September 2014); CEO Abdullah ABDULLAH, Dr. (since 29 September 2014); First Vice President Abdul Rashid DOSTAM (since 29 September 2014); Second Vice President Sarwar DANESH (since 29 September 2014); First Deputy CEO Khyal Mohammad KHAN; Second Deputy CEO Mohammad MOHAQQEQ; note—the president is both chief of state and head of government

head of government: President of the Islamic Republic of Afghanistan Ashraf GHANI Ahmadzai (since 29 September 2014); CEO Abdullah ABDULLAH, Dr. (since 29 September 2014); First Vice President Abdul Rashid DOSTAM (since 29 September 2014); Second Vice President Sarwar DANESH (since 29 September 2014); First Deputy CEO Khyal Mohammad KHAN; Second Deputy CEO Mohammad MOHAQQEQ
cabinet: Cabinet consists of 27 ministers appointed by the president, approved by the National Assembly
elections/appointments: president directly elected by absolute majority popular vote in 2 rounds if needed for a 5-year term (eligible for a second term); election last held in 2 rounds on 5 April and 14 June 2014 (next to be held in 2018)

election results: Ashraf GHANI elected president in the second round; percent of vote in first round—Abdullah ABDULLAH (National Coalition of Afghanistan) 45%, Ashraf GHANI (independent) 31.6%, Zalmai RASSOUL 11.4%, other 12%; percent of vote in second round—Ashraf GHANI 56.4%, Abdullah ABDULLAH 43.6%

Legislative branch: *description:* bicameral National Assembly consists of the Meshrano Jirga or House of Elders (102 seats; 34 members indirectly elected by district councils to serve 3-year terms, 34 indirectly elected by provincial councils to serve 4-year terms, and 34 nominated by the president of which 17 must be women, 2 must represent the disabled, and 2 must be Kuchi nomads; members serve 5-year terms) and the Wolesi Jirga or House of People (249 seats; members directly elected in multi-seat constituencies by proportional representation vote to serve 5-year terms)
note: the constitution allows the government to convene a constitutional Loya Jirga (Grand Council) on issues of independence, national sovereignty, and territorial integrity; it can amend the provisions of the constitution and prosecute the president; it consists of members of the National Assembly and chairpersons of the provincial and district councils; no constitutional Loya Jirga has ever been held, and district councils have never been elected; the president appointed 34 members of the Meshrano Jirga that the district councils should have indirectly elected
elections: Meshrano Jirga—last held 10 January 2015 (next to be held in 2018); Wolesi Jirga—last held on 18 September 2010 (next originally scheduled on 15 October 2016 but postponed to 7 July 2018)
election results: Meshrano Jirga—percent of vote by party—NA; seats by party—NA; Meshrano Jirga—percent of vote by party NA; seats by party—NA

Judicial branch: *highest court(s):* Supreme Court or Stera Mahkama (consists of the supreme court chief and 8 justices organized into criminal, public security, civil, and commercial divisions or dewans)
judge selection and term of office: court chief and justices appointed by the president with the approval of the Wolesi Jirga; court chief and justices serve single 10-year terms
subordinate courts: Appeals Courts; Primary Courts; Special Courts for issues including narcotics, security, property, family, and juveniles

Political parties and leaders: note—the Ministry of Justice licensed 57 political parties as of September 2016

Political pressure groups and leaders: religious groups, tribal leaders, ethnically based groups, Taliban

International organization participation: ADB, CICA, CP, ECO, EITI (candidate country), FAO, G-77, IAEA, IBRD, ICAO, ICC (NGOs), ICCt, ICRM, IDA, IDB, IFAD, IFC, IFRCS, ILO, IMF, Interpol, IOC, IOM, IPU, ISO (correspondent), ITSO, ITU, ITUC (NGOs), MIGA, NAM, OIC, OPCW, OSCE (partner), SAARC, SACEP, SCO (dialogue member), UN, UNAMA, UNCTAD, UNESCO, UNHCR, UNIDO, UNWTO, UPU, WCO, WFTU (NGOs), WHO, WIPO, WMO, WTO

Diplomatic representation in the US: *chief of mission:* Ambassador Kare AAS
chancery: 2341 Wyoming Avenue NW, Washington, DC 20008
telephone: [1] (202) 483-6410
FAX: [1] (202) 483-6488
consulate(s) general: Los Angeles, New York, Washington, DC

Diplomatic representation from the US: *chief of mission:* Ambassador (vacant); Special Charge d'Affaires Hugo LLORENS (since December 2016)
embassy: Bibi Mahru, Kabul
mailing address: U.S. Embassy Kabul, APO, AE 09806
telephone: [00 93] 0700 108 001
FAX: [00 93] 0700 108 564

Flag description: three equal vertical bands of black (hoist side), red, and green, with the national emblem in white centered on the red band and slightly overlapping the other 2 bands; the center of the emblem features a mosque with pulpit and flags on either side, below the mosque are numerals for the solar year 1298 (1919 in the Gregorian calendar, the year of Afghan independence from the UK); this central image is circled by a border consisting of sheaves of wheat on the left and right, in the upper-center is an Arabic inscription of the Shahada (Muslim creed) below which are rays of the rising sun over the Takbir (Arabic expression meaning "God is great"), and at bottom center is a scroll bearing the name Afghanistan; black signifies the past, red is for the blood shed for independence, and green can represent either hope for the future, agricultural prosperity, or Islam
note: Afghanistan had more changes to its national flag in the 20th century—19 by one count—than any other country; the colors black, red, and green appeared on most of them

National symbol(s): lion; national colors: red, green, black

National anthem: *name:* "Milli Surood" (National Anthem)
lyrics/music: Abdul Bari JAHANI/Babrak WASA
note: adopted 2006; the 2004 constitution of the post-Taliban government mandated that a new national anthem should be written containing the phrase "Allahu Akbar" (God is Greatest) and mentioning the names of Afghanistan's ethnic groups

ECONOMY

Economy—overview: Afghanistan is gradually recovering from decades of conflict. Before 2014, the economy had sustained nearly a decade of strong growth, largely because of international assistance. Since 2014, however, the economy has slowed, in large part because of the withdrawal of nearly 100,000 foreign troops that had artificially inflated the country's economic growth. Despite improvements in life expectancy, incomes, and literacy since 2001, Afghanistan is extremely poor, landlocked, and highly dependent on foreign aid. Much of the population continues to suffer from shortages of housing, clean water, electricity, medical care, and jobs. Corruption, insecurity, weak governance, lack of infrastructure, and the Afghan Government's difficulty in extending rule of law to all parts of the country pose challenges to future economic growth. Afghanistan's living standards are among the lowest in the world.

The international community remains committed to Afghanistan's development, pledging over $83 billion at ten donors' conferences between 2003 and 2016. In October 2016, the donors at the Brussels conference pledged an additional $3.8 billion in development aid annually from 2017 to 2020. Despite this help, the Government of Afghanistan will need to overcome a number of challenges, including low revenue collection, anemic job creation, high levels of corruption, weak government capacity, and poor public infrastructure.

In 2017 Afghanistan's growth rate was only marginally above that of the 2014-2016 average. The drawdown of international security forces that started in 2012 has negatively affected economic growth, as a substantial portion of commerce, especially in the services sector, has catered to the ongoing international troop presence in the country. Afghan President Ashraf GHANI Ahmadzai is dedicated to instituting economic reforms to include improving revenue collection and fighting corruption. However, the reforms will take time to implement and Afghanistan will remain dependent on international donor support over the next several years.

GDP (purchasing power parity):
$69.51 billion (2017 est.)
$67.81 billion (2016 est.)
$66.25 billion (2015 est.)
note: data are in 2017 dollars
country comparison to the world: 100

GDP (official exchange rate): $21.06 billion (2016 est.)

GDP—real growth rate:
2.5% (2017 est.)
2.4% (2016 est.)
1.3% (2015 est.)
country comparison to the world: 129

GDP—per capita (PPP):
$1,900 (2017 est.)
$2,000 (2016 est.)
$2,100 (2015 est.)
note: data are in 2017 dollars
country comparison to the world: 211

Gross national saving:
22.7% of GDP (2017 est.)
25.5% of GDP (2016 est.)
21.4% of GDP (2015 est.)
country comparison to the world: 68

GDP—composition, by end use:
household consumption: 108.6%
government consumption: 12.8%
investment in fixed capital: 18.2%

investment in inventories: 0%
exports of goods and services: 6.6%
imports of goods and services: -46.2% (2014 est.)

GDP—composition, by sector of origin:
agriculture: 22%
industry: 22%
services: 56%
note: data exclude opium production (2015 est.)

Agriculture—products: opium, wheat, fruits, nuts; wool, mutton, sheepskins, lambskins, poppies

Industries: small-scale production of bricks, textiles, soap, furniture, shoes, fertilizer, apparel, food products, non-alcoholic beverages, mineral water, cement; handwoven carpets; natural gas, coal, copper

Industrial production growth rate: 2.4% (2014 est.)
country comparison to the world: 116

Labor force: 7.983 million (2013 est.)
country comparison to the world: 62

Labor force—by occupation: *agriculture:* 78.6%
industry: 5.7%
services: 15.7% (FY08/09 est.)

Unemployment rate: 35% (2008 est.)
40% (2005 est.)
country comparison to the world: 208

Population below poverty line: 35.8% (2011 est.)

Household income or consumption by percentage share: *lowest 10%:* 3.8%
highest 10%: 24% (2008)

Budget: *revenues:* $1.992 billion
expenditures: $6.636 billion (2016 est.)
Taxes and other revenues: 9.5% of GDP (2016 est.)
country comparison to the world: 214

Budget surplus (+) or deficit (-): -22.1% of GDP (2016 est.)
country comparison to the world: 218

Public debt: 8.3% of GDP (2016 est.)
9.3% of GDP (2015 est.)
country comparison to the world: 199

Fiscal year: 21 December—20 December

Inflation rate (consumer prices):
6% (2017 est.)
4.4% (2016 est.)
country comparison to the world: 183

Commercial bank prime lending rate: 15% (31 December 2016 est.)
15% (31 December 2015 est.)
country comparison to the world: 45

Stock of narrow money: $6.644 billion (31 December 2014 est.)
$6.192 billion (31 December 2013 est.)
country comparison to the world: 93

Stock of broad money: $6.945 billion (31 December 2014 est.)
$6.544 billion (31 December 2013 est.)
country comparison to the world: 118

Stock of domestic credit: $-240.6 million (31 December 2016 est.)
$-240.6 million (31 December 2016 est.)
country comparison to the world: 192

Market value of publicly traded shares: $NA

Current account balance: $999 million (2017 est.)
$1.372 billion (2016 est.)
country comparison to the world: 38

Exports: $619.2 million (2016 est.)
$580 million (2015 est.)
note: not including illicit exports or reexports
country comparison to the world: 171

Exports—commodities: opium, fruits and nuts, handwoven carpets, wool, cotton, hides and pelts, precious and semi-precious gems

Exports—partners: Pakistan 46.3%, India 37.6% (2016)

Imports: $6.16 billion (2016 est.)
$7.034 billion (2015 est.)
country comparison to the world: 114

Imports—commodities: machinery and other capital goods, food, textiles, petroleum products

Imports—partners: Iran 19.3%, Pakistan 18.3%, China 16.7%, Kazakhstan 9.5%, Uzbekistan 6.1%, Turkmenistan 5.4%, Malaysia 4% (2016)

Reserves of foreign exchange and gold: $6.477 billion (31 December 2016 est.)
$6.232 billion (31 December 2015 est.)
country comparison to the world: 87

Debt—external:
$1.28 billion (FY10/11)
$2.7 billion (FY08/09)
country comparison to the world: 163

Exchange rates: afghanis (AFA) per US dollar—
67.87 (2016 est.)
67.87 (2016 est.)
67.87 (2015)
61.14 (2014 est.)
57.25 (2013 est.)

ENERGY

Electricity access: population without electricity: 18,999,254
electrification—*total population:* 43%
electrification—urban areas: 83%
electrification—rural areas: 32% (2012)

Electricity—production: 1.034 billion kWh (2015 est.)
country comparison to the world: 149

Electricity—consumption: 4.741 billion kWh (2015 est.)
country comparison to the world: 124

Electricity—exports: 0 kWh (2016 est.)
country comparison to the world: 99

Electricity—imports: 3.779 billion kWh (2015 est.)
country comparison to the world: 48

Electricity—installed generating capacity: 599,100 kW (2015 est.)
country comparison to the world: 139

Electricity—from fossil fuels: 44.7% of total installed capacity (2015 est.)
country comparison to the world: 161

Electricity—from nuclear fuels: 0% of total installed capacity (2015 est.)
country comparison to the world: 36

Electricity—from hydroelectric plants: 55.1% of total installed capacity (2015 est.)
country comparison to the world: 33

Electricity—from other renewable sources: 0.2% of total installed capacity (2015 est.)
country comparison to the world: 160

Crude oil—production: 0 bbl/day (2016 est.)
country comparison to the world: 102

Crude oil—exports: 0 bbl/day (2014 est.)
country comparison to the world: 86

Crude oil—imports: 0 bbl/day (2014 est.)
country comparison to the world: 89

Crude oil—proved reserves: 0 bbl (1 January 2017 es)
country comparison to the world: 102

Refined petroleum products—production: 0 bbl/day (2014 est.)
country comparison to the world: 111

Refined petroleum products—consumption: 130,000 bbl/day (2015 est.)
country comparison to the world: 76

Refined petroleum products—exports: 0 bbl/day (2014 est.)
country comparison to the world: 129

Refined petroleum products—imports: 127,200 bbl/day (2014 est.)
country comparison to the world: 52

Natural gas—production: 189 million cu m (2015 est.)
country comparison to the world: 77

Natural gas—consumption: 816 million cu m (2015 est.)
country comparison to the world: 104

Natural gas—exports: 0 cu m (2013 est.)
country comparison to the world: 59

Natural gas—imports: 0 cu m (2013 est.)
country comparison to the world: 81

Natural gas—proved reserves: 49.55 billion cu m (1 January 2017 es)
country comparison to the world: 64

Carbon dioxide emissions from consumption of energy: 7.4 million Mt (2013 est.)
country comparison to the world: 115

COMMUNICATIONS

Telephones—fixed lines: *total subscriptions:* 114,192
subscriptions per 100 inhabitants: less than 1 (July 2016 est.)
country comparison to the world: 145

Telephones—mobile cellular: *total:* 21,602,982
subscriptions per 100 inhabitants: 65 (July 2016 est.)
country comparison to the world: 51

Telephone system: *general assessment:* limited fixed-line telephone service; an increasing number of Afghans utilize mobile-cellular phone networks *domestic:* aided by the presence of multiple providers, mobile-cellular telephone service continues to improve rapidly; the Afghan Ministry of Communications and Information claims that

more than 90 percent of the population live in areas with access to mobile-cellular services
international: country code—93; multiple VSAT's provide international and domestic voice and data connectivity (2016)

Broadcast media: state-owned broadcaster, Radio Television Afghanistan (RTA), operates a series of radio and television stations in Kabul and the provinces; an estimated 150 private radio stations, 50 TV stations, and about a dozen international broadcasters are available (2007)

Internet country code: .af

Internet users: *total:* 3,531,770
percent of population: 10.6% (July 2016 est.)
country comparison to the world: 100

TRANSPORTATION

National air transport system: *number of registered air carriers:* 4
inventory of registered aircraft operated by air carriers: 20
annual passenger traffic on registered air carriers: 1,929,907
annual freight traffic on registered air carriers: 33,102,038 mt-km (2015)
Civil aircraft registration country code prefix: YA (2016)

Airports: 43 (2016)
country comparison to the world: 91

Airports—with paved runways: *total:* 25
over 3,047 m: 4
2,438 to 3,047 m: 4
1,524 to 2,437 m: 14
914 to 1,523 m: 2
under 914 m: 1 (2017)

Airports—with unpaved runways: *total:* 18
2,438 to 3,047 m: 1
1,524 to 2,437 m: 8
914 to 1,523 m: 4
under 914 m: 5 (2016)

Heliports: 9 (2013)

Pipelines: gas 466 km (2013)

Roadways: *total:* 42,150 km
paved: 12,350 km
unpaved: 29,800 km (2006)
country comparison to the world: 86

Waterways: 1,200 km; (chiefly Amu Darya, which handles vessels up to 500 DWT) (2011)
country comparison to the world: 60

Ports and terminals: *river port(s):* Kheyrabad, Shir Khan

MILITARY AND SECURITY

Military expenditures: 0.89% of GDP (2016)
0.99% of GDP (2015)
1.33% of GDP (2014)
1.06% of GDP (2013)
1.14% of GDP (2012)

Military branches: Afghan National Defense and Security Forces (ANDSF): Afghan National Army (includes Afghan Air Force), Afghan National Police, Afghan Local Police (2016)

Military service age and obligation: 18 is the legal minimum age for voluntary military service; no conscription (2016)

TERRORISM

Terrorist groups—home based: *Islamic State of Iraq and the Levant-Khorasan (ISIL-K):*
aim(s): overthrow the Afghanistan Government and, ultimately, establish an Islamic caliphate in the Afghanistan-Pakistan region
area(s) of operation: ISIL-K's last three leaders were killed within 12 months: ABU SAYED in Kunar Province on 11 July 2017, Abdul HASIB Logari in Nangarhar Province on 27 April 2017, and Hafiz Saeed KHAN Orakzai on 26 July 2016 in the Achin District of eastern Nangarhar Province; headquartered in Kunar Province near the Afghanistan-Pakistan border; operatives have launched attacks against Shia Muslims, Taliban members, and Afghan National Security and Defense Forces primarily in neighboring Nangarhar Province and Kabul since the summer of 2015; recruits, trains, and equips fighters mainly in Nangarhar Province, who are deployed to fight throughout the country; responsible for the deadliest attack in Kabul in over 10 years, when a suicide bomber targeted a Shia Muslim ethnic Hazara demonstration on 23 July 2016 in Kabul, killing more than 80 demonstrators and injuring 260; assessed in mid-2017 to have 1,000 fighters, with most of them operating in Afghanistan; recruits heavily in prisons; operates a radio station; core ISIL refers to Afghanistan and Pakistan as its Wilayat al-Khorasan

Lashkar i Jhangvi (LJ): *aim(s):* enhance its networks and paramilitary training in Afghanistan
area(s) of operation: headquartered in the east; operates paramilitary training camps near the Afghanistan-Pakistan border across from the central area of Pakistan's Federally Administered Tribal Areas (FATA) region; Pakistani recruits travel to Afghanistan from Pakistan's central FATA borders to attend LJ's paramilitary training; beyond staging attacks to conduct inside Pakistan, operatives conduct limited operations inside Afghanistan

Tehrik-e-Taliban Pakistan (TTP): *aim(s):* drive foreign troops from Afghanistan; remove Pakistani forces from Pakistan's Federally Administered Tribal Areas (FATA) and, ultimately, overthrow the Pakistan Government to install TTP's strict interpretation of Sharia throughout the country
area(s) of operation: headquartered in several eastern Afghanistan provinces near the Afghanistan-Pakistan border; operates primarily along the northeastern Afghanistan-Pakistan border, especially in Kunar Province where TTP has established sanctuaries; seeks regions out of the country's government's control; trains and deploys fighters in the tribal belt in the Pashtun areas; commanders based in Afghanistan continue to orchestrate attacks inside Pakistan; launches attacks inside Afghanistan against foreign troops and US personnel and interests; on 30 December 2009, a TTP suicide bomber described as a double agent for the US Government detonated

explosives inside the US's Camp Chapman in eastern Khost Province, killing seven US Government personnel and injuring six other people

Terrorist groups—foreign based: *al-Qa'ida:*
aim(s): overthrow the Afghanistan Government and, ultimately, establish a pan-Islamic caliphate under a strict Salafi Muslim interpretation of Sharia
area(s) of operation: maintains established networks and a longtime operational presence, especially in the northwest and in the northeast near the Afghanistan-Pakistan border; headquartered in Taliban-controlled Afghanistan between 1996 and November 2001, when US-led Coalition Forces toppled the Taliban Government

al-Qa'ida in the Indian Subcontinent (AQIS):
aim(s): establish an Islamic caliphate in the Indian subcontinent
area(s) of operation: heaviest presence is in Afghanistan, especially in the eastern and southern regions, where most of the Afghan-based leaders are based and recruits train for fighting; targets primarily Afghan military and security personnel and US interest

Haqqani Network (HQN): *aim(s):* eradicate Western influence and replace the Afghan Government with a strict Salafi Muslim interpretation of Sharia
area(s) of operation: stages attacks from Pakistan's North Waziristan Agency in the Federally Administered Tribal Areas across from Afghanistan's southeastern border; operational throughout the country, especially in Kabul and the provinces of Paktiya and Khost, targeting Afghan, US, and NATO forces and other Afghan Government personnel and Westerners for attack or kidnappings for ransom; deemed to be the most lethal group striking Afghan personnel and NATO's International Security Assistance Force; operatives used explosives, rocket-propelled grenades, and sprayed bullets on 13 September 2011 during a 19-hour attack on the US Embassy in Kabul and NATO's nearby International Security Assistance Force's headquarters, killing 16 Afghans, including six children and police officers; continues to hold Americans and other Westerners hostage for the stated purpose of demanding senior leader Anas HAQQANI's release from Afghan custody, where he has been sentenced to death

Harakat ul-Jihad-i-Islami (HUJI): *aim(s):* enhance its networks and drive foreign troops from Afghanistan and, unltimately, install Sharia in Afghanistan
area(s) of operation: operations throughout Afghanistan, targeting primarily Afghan Government personnel and Coalition forces

Harakat ul-Mujahidin (HUM): *aim(s):* enhance its networks and paramilitary training in Afghanistan and, ultimately, annex Kashmir into Pakistan and establish an Islamic state in Kashmir
area(s) of operation: maintains paramilitary training camps in the east

Islamic Jihad Union (IJU): *aim(s):* drive NATO forces out of Afghanistan and destablize the country *area(s) of operation:* conducts attacks in collaboration with other armed groups, including the Taliban, against NATO and Afghan forces across the country, especially in the northern and eastern provinces of Paktika, Paktia, and Nangarhar; played a key role in the Taliban's recapture of Kunduz Province in September 2015; uploads propaganda videos showcasing attacks on Afghan forces

Islamic Movement of Uzbekistan (IMU): *aim(s):* enhance its networks and secure its territory in Afghanistan to meet its historic goal of establishing an Islamic state in the Fergana Valley, a fertile valley spread across eastern Uzbekistan, southern Kyrgyzstan, and northern Tajikistan
area(s) of operation: operates mostly in the north along the Afghanistan-Pakistan border, with its heaviest presence in Badakhshan Province, where IMU operates paramilitary training camps and bases; has historically fought alongside al-Qa'ida and the Taliban and their affiliate groups; IMU's attack tempo has diminished since 2015

Jaish-e-Mohammed (JEM): *aim(s):* enhance operational and logistic networks in Afghanistan and, ultimately, drive foreign forces from the country
area(s) of operation: maintains a limited training and operational presence, primarily along the border with Pakistan

Jundallah: *aim(s):* enhance its operational networks and capabilities for staging cross-border attacks into Pakistan and Iran

area(s) of operation: operational in the greater Balochistan area, where fighters stage attacks targeting Shia Muslims in Iran and Pakistan

Lashkar-e Tayyiba (LeT): *aim(s):* enhances its recruitment networks and paramilitary training in Afghanistan
area(s) of operation: targets Coalition forces and Western interests throughout the country; maintains several facilities such as paramilitary training camps, medical clinics serving locals, and schools for thousands of youth; targets Pushtun youth for recruitment; LeT changed its name to Kashmir Tehrik Azadi in early 2017

TRANSNATIONAL ISSUES

Disputes—international: Afghan, Coalition, and Pakistan military meet periodically to clarify the alignment of the boundary on the ground and on maps and since 2014 have met to discuss collaboration on the Taliban insurgency and counterterrorism efforts; Afghan and Iranian commissioners have discussed boundary monument densification and resurvey; Iran protests Afghanistan's restricting flow of dammed Helmand River tributaries during drought; Pakistan has sent troops across and built fences along some remote tribal areas of its treaty-defined Durand Line border with Afghanistan which serve as bases for foreign terrorists and other illegal activities; Russia remains concerned about the smuggling of poppy

derivatives from Afghanistan through Central Asian countries

Refugees and internally displaced persons:
refugees (country of origin): 59,737 (Pakistan) (2016)
IDPs: 1.553 million (mostly Pashtuns and Kuchis displaced in the south and west due to natural disasters and political instability) (2016)

Illicit drugs: world's largest producer of opium; poppy cultivation increased 10 percent, to 201,000 hectares in 2016, while eradication declined significantly; the 2016 crop yielded an estimated 4,800 mt of raw opium, a 43% increase over 2015; the Taliban and other antigovernment groups participate in and profit from the opiate trade, which is a key source of revenue for the Taliban inside Afghanistan; widespread corruption and instability impede counterdrug efforts; most of the heroin consumed in Europe and Eurasia is derived from Afghan opium; Afghanistan is also struggling to respond to a burgeoning domestic opiate addiction problem; a 2015 national drug use survey found that roughly 11% of the population tested positive for one or more illicit drugs; vulnerable to drug money laundering through informal financial networks; illicit cultivation of cannabis and regional source of hashish

AKROTIRI

CYPRUS
Area controlled by
Cyprus Government
(Greek Cypriot area)

Limassol

Episkopi
Cantonment

Akrotiri
airfield
Cape
Gata
Cape
Zevgari

Mediterranean Sea

INTRODUCTION

Background: By terms of the 1960 Treaty of Establishment that created the independent Republic of Cyprus, the UK retained full sovereignty and jurisdiction over two areas of almost 254 square kilometers—Akrotiri and Dhekelia. The southernmost and smallest of these is the Akrotiri Sovereign Base Area, which is also referred to as the Western Sovereign Base Area.

GEOGRAPHY

Location: Eastern Mediterranean, peninsula on the southwest coast of Cyprus
Geographic coordinates: 34 37 N, 32 58 E
Map references: Middle East
Area: *total:* 123 sq km
note: includes a salt lake and wetlands
country comparison to the world: 224
Area—comparative: about 0.7 times the size of Washington, DC
Land boundaries: *total:* 48 km
border countries (1): Cyprus 48 km
Coastline: 56.3 km
Climate: temperate; Mediterranean with hot, dry summers and cool winters
Environment—current issues: hunting around the salt lake; note—breeding place for loggerhead and green turtles; only remaining colony of griffon vultures is on the base
Geography—note: British extraterritorial rights also extended to several small off-post sites scattered across Cyprus; of the Sovereign Base Area (SBA) land, 60% is privately owned and farmed, 20% is owned by the Ministry of Defense, and 20% is SBA Crown land

PEOPLE AND SOCIETY

Population: approximately 15,700 on the Sovereign Base Areas of Akrotiri and Dhekelia including 7,700 Cypriots, 3,600 Service and UK-based contract personnel, and 4,400 dependents
Languages: English, Greek

GOVERNMENT:: AKROTIRI

Country name: *conventional long form:* none
conventional short form: Akrotiri
etymology: named for the village that lies within the Western Sovereign Base Area on Cyprus

Dependency status: a special form of UK overseas territory; administered by an administrator who is also the Commander, British Forces Cyprus

Capital: *name:* Episkopi Cantonment (base administrative center for Akrotiri and Dhekelia)
geographic coordinates: 34 40 N, 32 51 E
time difference: UTC+2 (7 hours ahead of Washington, DC, during Standard Time)
daylight saving time: +1hr, begins last Sunday in March; ends last Sunday in October

Constitution: presented 3 August 1960, effective 16 August 1960 (The Sovereign Base Areas of Akrotiri and Dhekelia Order in Council 1960 serves as a basic legal document); amended 1966 (2016)

Legal system: laws applicable to the Cypriot population are, as far as possible, the same as the laws of the Republic of Cyprus; note—the Sovereign Base Area Administration has its own court system to deal with civil and criminal matters

Executive branch: *chief of state:* Queen ELIZABETH II (since 6 February 1952)

head of government: Administrator Major General James ILLINGWORTH (since 14 March 2017); note—administrator reports to the British Ministry of Defense; the chief officer is responsible for the day-to-day running of the civil government of the Sovereign Bases

elections/appointments: the monarchy is hereditary; administrator appointed by the monarch on the advice of the Ministry of Defense

Judicial branch: *highest court(s):* Senior Judges' Court (consists of several visiting judges from England and Wales)

judge selection and term of office: see entry for United Kingdom

subordinate courts: Resident Judges' Court; Courts Martial

Diplomatic representation in the US: none (overseas territory of the UK)

Diplomatic representation from the US: none (overseas territory of the UK)

Flag description: the flag of the UK is used
National anthem: note: as a UK area of special sovereignty, "God Save the Queen" is official (see United Kingdom)

ECONOMY

Economy—overview: Economic activity is limited to providing services to the military and their families located in Akrotiri. All food and manufactured goods must be imported.

Exchange rates: note: uses the euro

COMMUNICATIONS

Broadcast media: British Forces Broadcast Service (BFBS) provides multi-channel satellite TV service as well as BFBS radio broadcasts to the Akrotiri Sovereign Base Area (2009)

TRANSPORTATION

Airports: 1 (2017)

Airports—with paved runways: 2,438 to 3,047 m: 1 (2017)

MILITARY AND SECURITY:: AKROTIRI

Military—note: defense is the responsibility of the UK; Akrotiri has a full RAF base, headquarters for British Forces Cyprus, and Episkopi Support Unit

ALBANIA

INTRODUCTION

Background: Albania declared its independence from the Ottoman Empire in 1912, but was conquered by Italy in 1939 and occupied by Germany in 1943. Communist partisans took over the country in 1944. Albania allied itself first with the USSR (until 1960), and then with China (to 1978). In the early 1990s, Albania ended 46 years of xenophobic communist rule and established a multiparty democracy. The transition has proven challenging as successive governments have tried to deal with high unemployment, widespread corruption, dilapidated infrastructure, powerful organized crime networks, and combative political opponents.

Albania has made progress in its democratic development since first holding multiparty elections in 1991, but deficiencies remain. Most of Albania's post-communist elections were marred by claims of electoral fraud; however, international observers judged elections to be largely free and fair since the restoration of political stability

following the collapse of pyramid schemes in 1997. Albania joined NATO in April 2009 and in June 2014 became a candidate for EU accession. Albania in November 2016 received a European Commission recommendation to open EU accession negotiations conditioned upon implementation of a judicial reform package passed earlier the same year. Although Albania's economy continues to grow, it has slowed, and the country is still one of the poorest in Europe. A large informal economy and a weak energy and transportation infrastructure remain obstacles.

GEOGRAPHY

Location: Southeastern Europe, bordering the Adriatic Sea and Ionian Sea, between Greece to the south and Montenegro and Kosovo to the north

Geographic coordinates: 41 00 N, 20 00 E

Map references: Europe

Area: *total:* 28,748 sq km
land: 27,398 sq km
water: 1,350 sq km
country comparison to the world: 145

Area—comparative: slightly smaller than Maryland

Land boundaries: *total:* 691 km
border countries (4): Greece 212 km, Kosovo 112 km, Macedonia 181 km, Montenegro 186 km

Coastline: 362 km

Maritime claims: *territorial sea:* 12 nm
continental shelf: 200-m depth or to the depth of exploitation

Climate: mild temperate; cool, cloudy, wet winters; hot, clear, dry summers; interior is cooler and wetter

Terrain: mostly mountains and hills; small plains along coast

Elevation: *mean elevation:* 708 m

elevation extremes: *lowest point:* Adriatic Sea 0 m
highest point: Maja e Korabit (Golem Korab) 2,764 m

Natural resources: petroleum, natural gas, coal, bauxite, chromite, copper, iron ore, nickel, salt, timber, hydropower, arable land

Land use: *agricultural land:* 42.86%
arable land 52.42%;
permanent crops 6.84%;
permanent pasture 40.73%
forest: 28.19%
other: 28.95% (2014 est.)
Irrigated land: 3,537 sq km (2014)

Population—distribution: a fairly even distribution, with somewhat higher concentrations of people in the western and central parts of the country

Natural hazards: destructive earthquakes; tsunamis occur along southwestern coast; floods; drought

Environment—current issues: deforestation; soil erosion; water pollution from industrial and domestic effluents

Environment—international agreements: *party to:* Air Pollution, Biodiversity, Climate Change, Climate Change-Kyoto Protocol, Desertification, Endangered Species, Hazardous Wastes, Law of the Sea, Ozone Layer Protection, Wetlands
signed, but not ratified: none of the selected agreements

Geography—note: strategic location along Strait of Otranto (links Adriatic Sea to Ionian Sea and Mediterranean Sea)

PEOPLE AND SOCIETY

Population: 3,047,987 (July 2017 est.)
country comparison to the world: 136

Nationality: *noun:* Albanian(s)
adjective: Albanian

Ethnic groups: Albanian 82.6%, Greek 0.9%, other 1% (including Vlach, Romani, Macedonian, Montenegrin, and Egyptian), unspecified 15.5% (2011 est.)

Languages: Albanian 98.8% (official—derived from Tosk dialect), Greek 0.5%, other 0.6% (including Macedonian, Romani, Vlach, Turkish, Italian, and Serbo-Croatian), unspecified 0.1% (2011 est.)

Religions: Muslim 56.7%, Roman Catholic 10%, Orthodox 6.8%, atheist 2.5%, Bektashi (a Sufi order) 2.1%, other 5.7%, unspecified 16.2%
note: all mosques and churches were closed in 1967 and religious observances prohibited; in November 1990, Albania began allowing private religious practice (2011 est.)

Age structure: 0-14 years: 18.05% (male 290,572/ female 259,544)
15-24 years: 17.47% (male 275,969/female 256,416)
25-54 years: 41.06% (male 597,421/female 653,965)
55-64 years: 11.54% (male 173,105/female 178,575)
65 years and over: 11.89% (male 169,681/female 192,739) (2017 est.)

Dependency ratios: *total dependency ratio:* 44
youth dependency ratio: 26
elderly dependency ratio: 18.1
potential support ratio: 5.5 (2015 est.)

Median age: *total:* 32.9 years
male: 31.6 years
female: 34.3 years (2017 est.)
country comparison to the world: 96

Population growth rate: 0.31% (2017 est.)
country comparison to the world: 170

Birth rate: 13.2 births/1,000 population (2017 est.)
country comparison to the world: 149

Death rate: 6.8 deaths/1,000 population (2017 est.)
country comparison to the world: 136

Net migration rate: -3.3 migrant(s)/1,000 population (2017 est.)
country comparison to the world: 178

Population distribution: a fairly even distribution, with somewhat higher concentrations of people in the western and central parts of the country

Urbanization: *urban population:* 59.3% of total population (2017)
rate of urbanization: 1.81% annual rate of change (2015-20 est.)

Major urban areas—population: TIRANA (capital) 454,000 (2015)
Sex ratio: at birth: 1.1 male(s)/female
0-14 years: 1.12 male(s)/female
15-24 years: 1.07 male(s)/female
25-54 years: 0.91 male(s)/female
55-64 years: 0.98 male(s)/female
65 years and over: 0.89 male(s)/female
total population: 0.98 male(s)/female (2016 est.)

Mother's mean age at first birth: 24.5 years (2014 est.)

Maternal mortality ratio: 29 deaths/100,000 live births (2015 est.)
country comparison to the world: 115

Infant mortality rate: *total:* 11.9 deaths/1,000 live births
male: 13.3 deaths/1,000 live births
female: 10.5 deaths/1,000 live births (2017 est.)
country comparison to the world: 124

Life expectancy at birth: *total population:* 78.5 years
male: 75.8 years
female: 81.4 years (2017 est.)
country comparison to the world: 59

Total fertility rate: 1.51 children born/woman (2017 est.)
country comparison to the world: 195

Contraceptive prevalence rate: 69.3% (2008/09)

Health expenditures: 5.9% of GDP (2014)
country comparison to the world: 105

Physicians density: 1.29 physicians/1,000 population (2013)

Hospital bed density: 2.6 beds/1,000 population (2012)

Drinking water source:
improved:
urban: 84.3% of population
rural: 81.8% of population
total: 83.6% of population
unimproved:
urban: 15.7% of population
rural: 18.2% of population
total: 16.4% of population (2015 est.)

Sanitation facility access:
improved:
urban: 95.5% of population
rural: 90.2% of population
total: 93.2% of population
unimproved:
urban: 4.5% of population
rural: 9.8% of population
total: 6.8% of population (2015 est.)

HIV/AIDS—adult prevalence rate: 0.1% (2016 est.)
country comparison to the world: 99

HIV/AIDS—people living with HIV/AIDS: 1,700 (2016 est.)
country comparison to the world: 118

HIV/AIDS—deaths: <100 (2016 est.)

Obesity—adult prevalence rate: 21.7% (2016)
country comparison to the world: 85

Children under the age of 5 years underweight: 6.3% (2009)
country comparison to the world: 80

Education expenditures: 3.5% of GDP (2013)
country comparison to the world: 130

Literacy: *definition:* age 15 and over can read and write
total population: 97.6%
male: 98.4%
female: 96.9% (2015 est.)

School life expectancy (primary to tertiary education): *total:* 16 years
male: 15 years
female: 16 years (2015)

Unemployment, youth ages 15-24: *total:* 39.8%
male: 39.3%
female: 40.8% (2015 est.)
country comparison to the world: 46

GOVERNMENT

Country name: *conventional long form:* Republic of Albania
conventional short form: Albania
local long form: Republika e Shqiperise
local short form: Shqiperia
former: People's Socialist Republic of Albania
etymology: the English-language country name seems to be derived from the ancient Illyrian tribe of the Albani; the native name "Shqiperia" is derived from the Albanian word "Shqiponje" ("Eagle") and is popularly interpreted to mean "Land of the Eagles"

Government type: parliamentary republic

Capital: *name:* Tirana (Tirane)
geographic coordinates: 41 19 N, 19 49 E
time difference: UTC+1 (6 hours ahead of Washington, DC, during Standard Time)
daylight saving time: +1hr, begins last Sunday in March; ends last Sunday in October

Administrative divisions: 12 counties (qarqe, singular—qark); Berat, Diber, Durres, Elbasan, Fier, Gjirokaster, Korce, Kukes, Lezhe, Shkoder, Tirane, Vlore

Independence: 28 November 1912 (from the Ottoman Empire)

National holiday: Independence Day, 28 November (1912) also known as Flag Day

Constitution: *history:* several previous; latest approved by the Assembly 21 October 1998, adopted by referendum 22 November 1998, promulgated 28 November 1998
amendments: proposed by at least one-fifth of the Assembly membership; passage requires at least a two-thirds majority vote by the Assembly; referendum required only if approved by two-thirds of the Assembly; amendments approved by referendum effective upon declaration by the president of the republic; amended several times, last in 2016 (2017)

Legal system: civil law system except in the northern rural areas where customary law known as the "Code of Leke" prevails

International law organization participation: has not submitted an ICJ jurisdiction declaration; accepts ICCt jurisdiction

Citizenship: *citizenship by birth:* no
citizenship by descent only: at least one parent must be a citizen of Albania
dual citizenship recognized: yes
residency requirement for naturalization: 5 years

Suffrage: 18 years of age; universal

Executive branch: *chief of state:* President of the Republic Ilir META (since 24 July 2017)

head of government: Prime Minister Edi RAMA (since 10 September 2013); Deputy Prime Minister Niko PELESHI

cabinet: Council of Ministers proposed by the prime minister, nominated by the president, and approved by the Assembly

elections/appointments: president indirectly elected by the Assembly for a 5-year term (eligible for a second term); a candidate needs three-fifths majority vote of the Assembly in 1 of 3 rounds or a simple majority in 2 additional rounds to become president; election last held in 4 rounds on 19, 20, 27, and 28 April 2017 (next election to be held in 2022); prime minister appointed by the president on the proposal of the majority party or coalition of parties in the Assembly

election results: Ilir META elected president; Assembly vote—87—2 in fourth round

Legislative branch: *description:* unicameral Assembly or Kuvendi (140 seats; members directly elected in multi-seat constituencies by proportional representation vote to serve 4-year terms)

elections: last held on 25 June 2017 (next to be held in 2021)

election results: percent of vote by party—PS 48.3%, PD 28.9%, LSI 14.3%, PDIU 4.8%, PSD 1%, other 2.7%; seats by party—PS 74, PD 43, LSI 19, PDIU 3, PSD 1

Judicial branch: *highest court(s):* Supreme Court (consists of 17 judges, including the chief justice); Constitutional Court (consists of 9 judges, including the chairman)

judge selection and term of office: Supreme Court judges, including the chairman, appointed by the president with the consent of the Assembly to serve single 9-year terms; Constitutional Court judges appointed by the president with the consent of the Assembly to serve single 9-year terms with one-third of the membership renewed every 3 years; chairman elected by the People's Assembly for a single 3-year term

subordinate courts: Courts of Appeal; Courts of First Instance

Political parties and leaders: Democratic Party or PD [Lulzim BASHA]
Party for Justice, Integration and Unity or PDIU [Shpetim IDRIZI] (formerly part of APMI)
Social Democratic Party or PSD [Skender GJINUSHI]
Socialist Movement for Integration or LSI [Monika KRYEMADHI]
Socialist Party or PS [Edi RAMA]

Political pressure groups and leaders: Confederation of Trade Unions of Albania or KSSH [Kol NIKOLLAJ]
Omonia [Leonidha PAPA]
Union of Independent Trade Unions of Albania or BSPSH [Gezim KALAJA]

International organization participation: BSEC, CD, CE, CEI, EAPC, EBRD, EITI (compliant country), FAO, IAEA, IBRD, ICAO, ICC (national committees), ICCt, ICRM, IDA, IDB, IFAD, IFC, IFRCS, ILO, IMF, IMO, Interpol, IOC, IOM, IPU, ISO (correspondent), ITU, ITUC (NGOs), MIGA, NATO, OAS (observer), OIC, OIF, OPCW, OSCE, PCA, SELEC, UN, UNCTAD, UNESCO, UNIDO, UNWTO, UPU, WCO, WFTU (NGOs), WHO, WIPO, WMO, WTO

Diplomatic representation in the US: *chief of mission:* Ambassador Floreta FABER (since 18 May 2015)

chancery: 2100 S Street NW, Washington, DC 20008

telephone: [1] (202) 223-4942

FAX: [1] (202) 628-7342

consulate(s) general: New York

Diplomatic representation from the US: *chief of mission:* Ambassador Donald LU (since 13 January 2015)

embassy: Rruga e Elbasanit, 103, Tirana

mailing address: US Department of State, 9510 Tirana Place, Dulles, VA 20189-9510

telephone: [355] (4) 2247-285

FAX: [355] (4) 2232-222

Flag description: red with a black two-headed eagle in the center; the design is claimed to be that of 15th-century hero George Kastrioti SKANDERBEG, who led a successful uprising against the Ottoman Turks that resulted in a short-lived independence for some Albanian regions (1443-78); an unsubstantiated explanation for the eagle symbol is the tradition that Albanians see themselves as descendants of the eagle; they refer to themselves as "Shqiptare," which translates as "sons of the eagle"

National symbol(s): black double-headed eagle; national colors: red, black

National anthem: name: "Hymni i Flamurit" (Hymn to the Flag)

lyrics/music: Aleksander Stavre DRENOVA/Ciprian PORUMBESCU

note: adopted 1912

ECONOMY

Economy—overview: Albania, a formerly closed, centrally-planned state, is a developing country with a modern open-market economy. Albania managed to weather the first waves of the global financial crisis but, the negative effects of the crisis caused a significant economic slowdown. Since 2014, Albania's economy has steadily improved and economic growth reached 3.8% in 2017. However, close trade, remittance, and banking sector ties with Greece and Italy make Albania vulnerable to spillover effects of possible debt crises and weak growth in the euro zone.

Remittances, a significant catalyst for economic growth, declined from 12-15% of GDP before the 2008 financial crisis to 5.8% of GDP in 2015, mostly from Albanians residing in Greece and Italy. The agricultural sector, which accounts for more than 40% of employment but less than one quarter of GDP, is limited primarily to small family operations and subsistence farming, because of a lack of modern equipment, unclear property rights, and the prevalence of small, inefficient plots of land. Complex tax codes and licensing requirements, a weak judicial system, endemic corruption, poor enforcement of contracts and property issues, and antiquated infrastructure contribute to Albania's poor business environment making attracting foreign investment difficult. Since 2015, Albania has launched an ambitious program to increase tax compliance and bring more businesses into the formal economy. In July 2016, Albania passed constitutional amendments reforming the judicial system in order to strengthen the rule of law and to reduce deeply entrenched corruption.

Albania's electricity supply is uneven despite upgraded transmission capacities with neighboring countries. However, the government has recently taken steps to stem non-technical losses and has begun to upgrade the distribution grid. Better enforcement of electricity contracts has improved the financial viability of the sector, decreasing its reliance on budget support. Also, with help from international donors, the government is taking steps to improve the poor road and rail networks, a long standing barrier to sustained economic growth.

Inward FDI has increased significantly in recent years as the government has embarked on an ambitious program to improve the business climate through fiscal and legislative reforms. The government is focused on the simplification of licensing requirements and tax codes, and it entered into a new arrangement with the IMF for additional financial and technical support. Albania's three-year IMF program, an extended fund facility arrangement, was successfully concluded in February 2017. The Albanian Government has strengthened tax collection amid moderate public wage and pension increases in an effort to reduce its budget deficit. The country continues to face high public debt, exceeding its former statutory limit of 60% of GDP in 2013 and reaching 72% in 2016.

GDP (purchasing power parity):
$35.87 billion (2017 est.)
$34.59 billion (2016 est.)
$33.46 billion (2015 est.)
note: data are in 2017 dollars
unreported output may be as large as 50% of official GDP
country comparison to the world: 126

GDP (official exchange rate): $13 billion (2016 est.)

GDP—real growth rate:
3.7% (2017 est.)
3.4% (2016 est.)
2.2% (2015 est.)
country comparison to the world: 83

GDP—per capita (PPP):
$12,500 (2017 est.)
$12,000 (2016 est.)
$11,600 (2015 est.)
note: data are in 2017 dollars
country comparison to the world: 124

Gross national saving:
15.6% of GDP (2017 est.)
15.9% of GDP (2016 est.)

16.3% of GDP (2015 est.)
country comparison to the world: 122

GDP—composition, by end use:
household consumption: 77.6%
government consumption: 10.9%
investment in fixed capital: 27%
investment in inventories: 0%
exports of goods and services: 29.7%
imports of goods and services: -45.2% (2017 est.)

GDP—composition, by sector of origin:
agriculture: 22.6%
industry: 23.8%
services: 53.7% (2017 est.)

Agriculture—products: wheat, corn, potatoes, vegetables, fruits, olives and olive oil, grapes; meat, dairy products; sheep and goats

Industries: food; footwear, apparel and clothing; lumber, oil, cement, chemicals, mining, basic metals, hydropower

Industrial production growth rate: 3.5% (2017 est.)
country comparison to the world: 82

Labor force: 1.407 million (2017 est.)
country comparison to the world: 135

Labor force—by occupation: *agriculture:* 41.8%
industry: 11.4%
services: 46.8% (December 2014 est)

Unemployment rate: 14% (2017 est.)
15.2% (2016 est.)
note: these official rates may not include those working at near-subsistence farming
country comparison to the world: 168

Population below poverty line: 14.3% (2012 est.)

Household income or consumption by percentage share: *lowest 10%:* 4.1%
highest 10%: 19.6% (2015 est.)

Distribution of family income—Gini index: 29 (2012 est.)
30 (2008 est.)
country comparison to the world: 131

Budget: *revenues:* $3.486 billion
expenditures: $3.765 billion (2017 est.)
Taxes and other revenues: 26.8% of GDP (2017 est.)
country comparison to the world: 105

Budget surplus (+) or deficit (-): -2.1% of GDP (2017 est.)
country comparison to the world: 87

Public debt: 71.3% of GDP (2017 est.)
72% of GDP (2016 est.)
country comparison to the world: 49

Fiscal year: calendar year

Inflation rate (consumer prices): 2.1% (2017 est.)
1.3% (2016 est.)
country comparison to the world: 97

Central bank discount rate: 1.25% (31 December 2016)
1.75% (31 December 2015)
country comparison to the world: 124

Commercial bank prime lending rate: 7.2% (31 December 2017 est.)
9.65% (31 December 2016 est.)

country comparison to the world: 117

Stock of narrow money:
$3.979 billion (31 December 2017 est.)
$3.397 billion (31 December 2016 est.)
country comparison to the world: 112

Stock of broad money: $6.665 billion (31 December 2017 est.)
$5.75 billion (31 December 2016 est.)
country comparison to the world: 122

Stock of domestic credit: $8.147 billion (31 December 2017 est.)
$7.065 billion (31 December 2016 est.)
country comparison to the world: 117

Market value of publicly traded shares: $NA

Current account balance: -$1.201 billion (2017 est.)
-$899 million (2016 est.)
country comparison to the world: 139

Exports: $960.9 million (2017 est.)
$789.1 million (2016 est.)
country comparison to the world: 160

Exports—commodities: apparel and clothing, footwear; asphalt, metals and metallic ores, crude oil; cement and construction materials, vegetables, fruits, tobacco

Exports—partners: Italy 50.5%, Serbia 8.1%, Kosovo 7.5%, Greece 4.2% (2016)

Imports: $4.084 billion (2017 est.)
$3.671 billion (2016 est.)
country comparison to the world: 132

Imports—commodities: machinery and equipment, foodstuffs, textiles, chemicals

Imports—partners: Italy 29%, Germany 9.4%, China 8.7%, Greece 7.8%, Turkey 7.8%, Serbia 4.1% (2016)

Reserves of foreign exchange and gold: $3.274 billion (31 December 2017 est.)
$3.109 billion (31 December 2016 est.)
country comparison to the world: 102

Debt—external:
$8.579 billion (31 December 2017 est.)
$8.421 billion (31 December 2016 est.)
country comparison to the world: 120

Stock of direct foreign investment—at home:
$6.056 billion (31 December 2014)
$5.459 billion (31 December 2013)
country comparison to the world: 102

Exchange rates: leke (ALL) per US dollar—
121.9 (2017 est.)
124.14 (2016 est.)
124.14 (2015 est.)
125.96 (2014 est.)
105.48 (2013 est.)

ENERGY

Electricity access: electrification—*total population:* 100% (2016)

Electricity—production: 7.135 billion kWh (2016 est.)
country comparison to the world: 113

Electricity—consumption: 7.094 billion kWh (2016 est.)
country comparison to the world: 110

Electricity—exports: 1.869 billion kWh (2016 est.)
country comparison to the world: 45

Electricity—imports: 1.827 billion kWh (2016 est.)
country comparison to the world: 56

Electricity—installed generating capacity: 1.897 million kW (2015 est.)
country comparison to the world: 115

Electricity—from fossil fuels: 5.2% of total installed capacity (2015 est.)
country comparison to the world: 205

Electricity—from nuclear fuels: 0% of total installed capacity (2015 est.)
country comparison to the world: 39

Electricity—from hydroelectric plants: 94.8% of total installed capacity (2015 est.)
country comparison to the world: 7

Electricity—from other renewable sources: 0.1% of total installed capacity (2015 est.)
country comparison to the world: 164

Crude oil—production: 22,750 bbl/day (2016 est.)
country comparison to the world: 66

Crude oil—exports: 19,100 bbl/day (2014 est.)
country comparison to the world: 52

Crude oil—imports: 1,000 bbl/day (2014 est.)
country comparison to the world: 79

Crude oil—proved reserves: 168.3 million bbl (1 January 2017 es)
country comparison to the world: 61

Refined petroleum products—production: 290 bbl/day (2016 est.)
country comparison to the world: 108

Refined petroleum products—consumption: 27,000 bbl/day (2014 est.)
country comparison to the world: 126

Refined petroleum products—exports: 16,250 bbl/day (2016 est.)
country comparison to the world: 75

Refined petroleum products—imports: 13,250 bbl/day (2016 est.)
country comparison to the world: 135

Natural gas—production: 35 million cu m (2015 est.)
country comparison to the world: 87

Natural gas—consumption: 200 million cu m (2015 est.)
country comparison to the world: 110

Natural gas—exports: 0 cu m (2013 est.)
country comparison to the world: 60

Natural gas—imports: 0 cu m (2013 est.)
country comparison to the world: 83

Natural gas—proved reserves: 821.2 million cu m (1 January 2017 es)
country comparison to the world: 106

Carbon dioxide emissions from consumption of energy: 4.3 million Mt (2013 est.)
country comparison to the world: 130

COMMUNICATIONS

Telephones—fixed lines: *total subscriptions:* 245,336
subscriptions per 100 inhabitants: 8 (July 2016 est.)
country comparison to the world: 123

Telephones—mobile cellular: *total:* 3,369,756
subscriptions per 100 inhabitants: 111 (July 2016 est.)
country comparison to the world: 133

Telephone system: *general assessment:* fixed line, teledensity continues to decline due to heavy use of mobile-cellular telephone services; mobile-cellular telephone use is widespread and generally effective; of 3.4 million active mobile telephone users, 1.3 million use mobile broadband services (3G/4G)
domestic: offsetting the shortage of fixed-line capacity, mobile-cellular phone service has been available since 1996; by 2015, four companies were providing mobile services and mobile teledensity had reached 110 per 100 persons; Internet broadband services initiated in 2005, and the penetration rate rose to over 65% by 2016; Internet cafes are popular in major urban areas
international: country code—355; submarine cable provides connectivity to Italy, Croatia, and Greece; the Trans-Balkan Line, a combination submarine cable and land fiber-optic system, provides additional connectivity to Bulgaria, Macedonia, and Turkey; international traffic carried by fiber-optic cable and, when necessary, by microwave radio relay from the Tirana exchange to Italy and Greece (2016)

Broadcast media: Albania has more than 65 TV stations, including several that broadcast nationally; Albanian TV broadcasts are also available to Albanian-speaking populations in neighboring countries; many viewers have access to Italian and Greek TV broadcasts via terrestrial reception; Albania's TV stations have begun a government-mandated conversion from analog to digital broadcast; the government has pledged to provide analog-to-digital converters to low-income families affected by this decision; cable TV service is available; 2 public radio networks and roughly 78 private radio stations; several international broadcasters are available (2017)

Internet country code: .al

Internet users: *total:* 2,016,516
percent of population: 66.4% (July 2016 est.)
country comparison to the world: 104

TRANSPORTATION

National air transport system: *number of registered air carriers:* 1
inventory of registered aircraft operated by air carriers: 1
annual passenger traffic on registered air carriers: 151,632
annual freight traffic on registered air carriers: 0 mt-km (2015)
Civil aircraft registration country code prefix: ZA (2016)

Airports: 4 (2016)
country comparison to the world: 183

Airports—with paved runways: *total:* 4
2,438 to 3,047 m: 3
1,524 to 2,437 m: 1 (2017)

Airports—with unpaved runways: total: 1
914 to 1,523 m: 1 (2012)

Heliports: 1 (2013)

Pipelines: gas 498 km (a majority of the network is in disrepair and parts of it are missing); oil 249 km (2015)

Railways: *total:* 677 km (447 km of major railway lines and 230 km of secondary lines)
standard gauge: 677 km 1.435-m gauge (2015)
country comparison to the world: 104

Roadways: *total:* 18,000 km
paved: 7,020 km
unpaved: 10,980 km (2002)
country comparison to the world: 116

Waterways: 41 km (on the Bojana River) (2011)
country comparison to the world: 103

Merchant marine: *total:* 57
by type: bulk carrier 1, general cargo 49, other 7 (2017)

Ports and terminals: *major seaport(s):* Durres, Sarande, Shengjin, Vlore

MILITARY AND SECURITY

Military expenditures:
1.22% of GDP (2017)
1.23% of GDP (2016)
1.16% of GDP (2015)
1.35% of GDP (2014)
1.41% of GDP (2013)
country comparison to the world: 112

Military branches: Land Forces Command, Navy Force Command, Air Forces Command (2013)

Military service age and obligation: 19 is the legal minimum age for voluntary military service; 18 is the legal minimum age in case of general/partial compulsory mobilization (2012)

TRANSNATIONAL ISSUES

Disputes—international: none
Refugees and internally displaced persons: stateless persons: 4,921 (2016)

Illicit drugs: active transshipment point for Southwest Asian opiates, hashish, and cannabis transiting the Balkan route and—to a lesser extent—cocaine from South America destined for Western Europe; significant source country for cannabis production; ethnic Albanian narcotrafficking organizations active and expanding in Europe; vulnerable to money laundering associated with regional trafficking in narcotics, arms, contraband, and illegal aliens

ALGERIA

INTRODUCTION

Background: After more than a century of rule by France, Algerians fought through much of the 1950s to achieve independence in 1962. Algeria's primary political party, the National Liberation Front (FLN), was established in 1954 as part of the struggle for independence and has since largely dominated politics. The Government of Algeria in 1988 instituted a multi-party system in response to public unrest, but the surprising first round success of the Islamic Salvation Front (FIS) in the December 1991 balloting led the Algerian army to intervene and postpone the second round of elections to prevent what the secular elite feared would be an extremist-led government from assuming power. The army began a crackdown on the FIS that spurred FIS supporters to begin attacking government targets. Fighting escalated into an insurgency, which saw intense violence from 1992-98, resulting in over 100,000 deaths—many attributed to indiscriminate massacres of villagers by extremists. The government gained the upper hand by the late-1990s, and FIS's armed wing, the Islamic Salvation Army, disbanded in January 2000.

Abdelaziz BOUTEFLIKA, with the backing of the military, won the presidency in 1999 in an election widely viewed as fraudulent and won subsequent elections in 2004, 2009, and 2014. The government in 2011 introduced some political reforms in response to the Arab Spring, including lifting the 19-year-old state of emergency restrictions and increasing women's quotas for elected assemblies, while also increasing subsidies to the populace. Since 2014, Algeria's reliance on hydrocarbon revenues to fund the government and finance the large subsidies for the population has fallen under stress because of declining oil prices.

GEOGRAPHY

Location: Northern Africa, bordering the Mediterranean Sea, between Morocco and Tunisia

Geographic coordinates: 28 00 N, 3 00 E

Map references: Africa

Area: *total:* 2,381,741 sq km
land: 2,381,741 sq km
water: 0 sq km
country comparison to the world: 11

Area—comparative: slightly less than 3.5 times the size of Texas

Land boundaries: *total:* 6,734 km
border countries (7): Libya 989 km, Mali 1,359 km, Mauritania 460 km, Morocco 1,900 km, Niger 951 km, Tunisia 1,034 km, Western Sahara 41 km

Coastline: 998 km

Maritime claims:
territorial sea: 12 nm
exclusive fishing zone: 32-52 nm

Climate: arid to semiarid; mild, wet winters with hot, dry summers along coast; drier with cold winters and hot summers on high plateau; sirocco is a hot, dust/sand-laden wind especially common in summer

Terrain: mostly high plateau and desert; some mountains; narrow, discontinuous coastal plain

Elevation: mean elevation: 800 m

elevation extremes: *lowest point:* Chott Melrhir -40 m
highest point: Tahat 2,908 m

Natural resources: petroleum, natural gas, iron ore, phosphates, uranium, lead, zinc

Land use: *agricultural land:* 17.4%
arable land 18.02%;
permanent crops 2.34%;
permanent pasture 79.63%
forest: 0.82%
other: 81.8% (2014 est.)
Irrigated land: 13,600 sq km (2014)

Population—distribution: the vast majority of the populace is found in the extreme northern part of the country along the Mediterranean Coast
Natural hazards: mountainous areas subject to severe earthquakes; mudslides and floods in rainy season; droughts

Environment—current issues: soil erosion from overgrazing and other poor farming practices; desertification; dumping of raw sewage, petroleum refining wastes, and other industrial effluents is leading to the pollution of rivers and coastal waters; Mediterranean Sea, in particular, becoming polluted from oil wastes, soil erosion, and fertilizer runoff; inadequate supplies of potable water

Environment—international agreements:
party to: Biodiversity, Climate Change, Climate Change-Kyoto Protocol, Desertification, Endangered Species, Environmental Modification, Hazardous Wastes, Law of the Sea, Ozone Layer Protection, Ship Pollution, Wetlands
signed, but not ratified: none of the selected agreements

Geography—note: largest country in Africa

PEOPLE AND SOCIETY

Population: 40,969,443 (July 2017 est.)
country comparison to the world: 33

Nationality: *noun:* Algerian(s)
adjective: Algerian Ethnic groups: Arab-Berber 99%, European less than 1% note: although almost all Algerians are Berber in origin (not Arab), only a minority identify themselves as Berber, about 15% of the total population; these people live mostly in the mountainous region of Kabylie east of Algiers; the Berbers are also Muslim but identify with their Berber rather than Arab cultural heritage; Berbers have long agitated, sometimes violently, for autonomy; the government is unlikely to grant autonomy but has offered to begin sponsoring teaching Berber language in schools

Languages: Arabic (official), French (lingua franca), Berber or Tamazight (official); dialects include Kabyle Berber (Taqbaylit), Shawiya Berber (Tacawit), Mzab Berber, Tuareg Berber (Tamahaq)

Religions: Muslim (official; predominantly Sunni) 99%, other (includes Christian and Jewish) <1% (2012 est.)

Demographic profile: For the first two-thirds of the 20th century, Algeria's high fertility rate caused its population to grow rapidly. However, about a decade after independence from France in 1962 the total fertility rate fell dramatically from 7 children per woman in the 1970s to about 2.4 in 2000, slowing Algeria's population growth rate by the late 1980s. The lower fertility rate was mainly the result of women's rising age at first marriage (virtually all Algerian children being born in wedlock) and to a lesser extent the wider use of contraceptives. Later marriages and a preference for smaller families are attributed to increases in women's education and participation in the labor market; higher unemployment; and a shortage of housing forcing multiple generations to live together. The average woman's age at first marriage increased from about 19 in the mid-1950s to 24 in the mid-1970s to 30.5 in the late 1990s.

Algeria's fertility rate experienced an unexpected upturn in the early 2000s, as the average woman's age at first marriage dropped slightly. The reversal in fertility could represent a temporary fluctuation in marriage age or, less likely, a decrease in the steady rate of contraceptive use.

Thousands of Algerian peasants—mainly Berber men from the Kabylia region—faced with land dispossession and economic hardship under French rule migrated temporarily to France to work in manufacturing and mining during the first half of the 20th century. This movement accelerated during World War I, when Algerians filled in for French factory workers or served as soldiers. In the years following independence, low-skilled Algerian workers and Algerians who had supported the French (harkis) emigrated en masse to France. Tighter French immigration rules and Algiers' decision to cease managing labor migration to France in the 1970s limited legal emigration largely to family reunification.

Not until Algeria's civil war in the 1990s did the country again experience substantial outmigration. Many Algerians legally entered Tunisia without visas claiming to be tourists and then stayed as workers. Other Algerians headed to Europe seeking asylum, although France imposed restrictions. Sub-Saharan African migrants came to Algeria after its civil war to work in agriculture and mining. In the 2000s, a wave of educated Algerians went abroad seeking skilled jobs in a wider range of destinations, increasing their presence in North America and Spain. At the same time, legal foreign workers principally from China and Egypt came to work in Algeria's construction and oil sectors. Illegal migrants from sub-Saharan Africa, particularly Malians, Nigeriens, and Gambians, continue to come to Algeria in search of work or to use it as a stepping stone to Libya and Europe. Since 1975, Algeria also has been the main recipient of Sahrawi refugees from the ongoing conflict in Western Sahara. An estimated 90,000 Sahrawis live in five refugee camps in southwestern Algeria near Tindouf.

Age structure: *0-14 years:* 29.31% (male 6,148,568/female 5,858,922)
15-24 years: 15.3% (male 3,208,185/female 3,061,179)
25-54 years: 42.93% (male 8,906,160/female 8,682,894)
55-64 years: 6.81% (male 1,410,298/female 1,378,282)
65 years and over: 5.65% (male 1,079,218/female 1,235,737) (2017 est.)

Dependency ratios:
total dependency ratio: 52.7
youth dependency ratio: 43.8
elderly dependency ratio: 9
potential support ratio: 11.2 (2015 est.)

Median age: *total:* 28.1 years
male: 27.8 years
female: 28.4 years (2017 est.)
country comparison to the world: 137

Population growth rate: 1.7% (2017 est.)
country comparison to the world: 62

Birth rate: 22.2 births/1,000 population (2017 est.)
country comparison to the world: 69

Death rate: 4.3 deaths/1,000 population (2017 est.)
country comparison to the world: 206

Net migration rate: -0.9 migrant(s)/1,000 population (2017 est.)
country comparison to the world: 135

Population distribution: the vast majority of the populace is found in the extreme northern part of the country along the Mediterranean Coast

Urbanization: *urban population:* 71.9% of total population (2017)
rate of urbanization: 2.26% annual rate of change (2015-20 est.)

Major urban areas—population: ALGIERS (capital) 2.594 million; Oran 858,000 (2015)

Sex ratio: *at birth:* 1.05 male(s)/female
0-14 years: 1.05 male(s)/female
15-24 years: 1.05 male(s)/female
25-54 years: 1.02 male(s)/female
55-64 years: 1.03 male(s)/female
65 years and over: 0.86 male(s)/female
total population: 1.03 male(s)/female (2016 est.)

Maternal mortality ratio: 140 deaths/100,000 live births (2015 est.)
country comparison to the world: 62

Infant mortality rate: *total:* 19.6 deaths/1,000 live births
male: 21.2 deaths/1,000 live births
female: 17.9 deaths/1,000 live births (2017 est.)
country comparison to the world: 81

Life expectancy at birth: *total population:* 77 years
male: 75.6 years
female: 78.4 years (2017 est.)
country comparison to the world: 78

Total fertility rate: 2.7 children born/woman (2017 est.)
country comparison to the world: 66

Contraceptive prevalence rate: 57.1% (2012/13)

Health expenditures: 7.2% of GDP (2014)
country comparison to the world: 74

Physicians density: 1.19 physicians/1,000 population (2007)

Drinking water source:
improved:
urban: 84.3% of population
rural: 81.8% of population
total: 83.6% of population
unimproved:
urban: 15.7% of population
rural: 18.2% of population
total: 16.4% of population (2015 est.)

Sanitation facility access: *improved:* urban: 89.8% of population
rural: 82.2% of population
total: 87.6% of population
unimproved:
urban: 10.2% of population
rural: 17.8% of population
total: 12.4% of population (2015 est.)

HIV/AIDS—adult prevalence rate: <.01% (2016 est.)

HIV/AIDS—people living with HIV/AIDS: 13,000 (2016 est.)
country comparison to the world: 85

HIV/AIDS—deaths: <200 (2016 est.)

Obesity—adult prevalence rate: 27.4% (2016)
country comparison to the world: 38

Children under the age of 5 years underweight: 3% (2012)
country comparison to the world: 102

Education expenditures: 4.3% of GDP (2008)
country comparison to the world: 97

Literacy: *definition:* age 15 and over can read and write

total population: 80.2%
male: 87.2%
female: 73.1% (2015 est.)

School life expectancy (primary to tertiary education): *total:* 14 years
male: 14 years
female: 15 years (2011)

Unemployment, youth ages 15-24: *total:* 25.2%
male: 22.1%
female: 41.5% (2014 est.)
country comparison to the world: 47

GOVERNMENT

Country name: *conventional long form:* People's Democratic Republic of Algeria
conventional short form: Algeria
local long form: Al Jumhuriyah al Jaza'iriyah ad Dimuqratiyah ash Sha'biyah
local short form: Al Jaza'ir
etymology: the country name derives from the capital city of Algiers

Government type: presidential republic

Capital: *name:* Algiers

geographic coordinates: 36 45 N, 3 03 E
time difference: UTC+1 (6 hours ahead of Washington, DC, during Standard Time)

Administrative divisions: 48 provinces (wilayas, singular—wilaya); Adrar, Ain Defla, Ain Temouchent, Alger, Annaba, Batna, Bechar, Bejaia, Biskra, Blida, Bordj Bou Arreridj, Bouira, Boumerdes, Chlef, Constantine, Djelfa, El Bayadh, El Oued, El Tarf, Ghardaia, Guelma, Illizi, Jijel, Khenchela, Laghouat, Mascara, Medea, Mila, Mostaganem, M'Sila, Naama, Oran, Ouargla, Oum el Bouaghi, Relizane, Saida, Setif, Sidi Bel Abbes, Skikda, Souk Ahras, Tamanrasset, Tebessa, Tiaret, Tindouf, Tipaza, Tissemsilt, Tizi Ouzou, Tlemcen

Independence: 5 July 1962 (from France)

National holiday: Revolution Day, 1 November (1954)

Constitution: *history:* several previous; latest approved by referendum 23 February 1989
amendments: proposed by the president of the republic or through the president with the support of three-fourths of the members of both houses of Parliament in joint session; passage requires approval by both houses, approval by referendum, and promulgation by the president; the president can forego a referendum if the Constitutional Council determines the proposed amendment does not conflict with basic constitutional principles; articles including the republican form of government, the integrity and unity of the country, and fundamental citizens' liberties and rights cannot be amended; amended several times, last in 2016 (2016)

Legal system: mixed legal system of French civil law and Islamic law; judicial review of legislative acts in ad hoc Constitutional Council composed of various public officials including several Supreme Court justices

International law organization participation: has not submitted an ICJ jurisdiction declaration; non-party state to the ICCt

Citizenship: citizenship by birth: no
citizenship by descent only: the mother must be a citizen of Algeria
dual citizenship recognized: no
residency requirement for naturalization: 7 years

Suffrage: 18 years of age; universal

Executive branch: *chief of state:* President Abdelaziz BOUTEFLIKA (since 28 April 1999)

head of government: Prime Minister Ahmed OUYAHIA (since 16 August 2017)
cabinet: Cabinet of Ministers appointed by the president
elections/appointments: president directly elected by absolute majority popular vote in two rounds if needed for a 5-year term (2-term limit reinstated by constitutional amendment in February 2016); election last held on 17 April 2014 (next to be held in April 2019); prime minister nominated by the president from the majority party in Parliament
election results: Abdelaziz BOUTEFLIKA reelected president for a fourth term; percent of vote—Abdelaziz BOUTEFLIKA (FLN) 81.5%, Ali BENFLIS (FLN) 12.2%, Abdelaziz BELAID (Future Front) 3.4%, other 2.9%

Legislative branch: *description:* bicameral Parliament consists of the Council of the Nation (upper house with 144 seats; one-third of members appointed by the president, two-thirds indirectly elected by simple majority vote by an electoral college composed of local council members; members serve 6-year terms with one-half of the membership renewed every 3 years) and the National People's Assembly (lower house with 462 seats including 8 seats for Algerians living abroad); members directly elected in multi-seat constituencies by proportional representation vote to serve 5-year terms)
elections: Council of the Nation—last held on 29 December 2015 (next to be held in December 2018); National People's Assembly—last held on 4 May 2017 (next to be held in 2022)
election results: Council of the Nation—percent of vote by party—NA; seats by party—NA; National People's Assembly—percent of vote by party—NA; seats by party—FLN 164, RND 97, MSP-FC 33, TAJ 19, Ennahda-FJD 15, FFS 14, El Mostakbel 14, MPA 13, PT 11, RCD 9, ANR 8, MEN 4, other 33, independent 28

Judicial branch: *highest court(s):* Supreme Court or Cour Supreme (consists of 150 judges organized into 4 divisions: civil and commercial; social security and labor; criminal; and administrative; Constitutional Council (consists of 12 members including the court chairman and deputy chairman); note—Algeria's judicial system does not include sharia courts
judge selection and term of office: Supreme Court judges appointed by the High Council of Magistracy, an administrative body presided over by the president of the republic, and includes

the republic vice-president and several members; judges appointed for life; Constitutional Council members—4 appointed by the president of the republic, 2 each by the 2 houses of Parliament, 2 by the Supreme Court, and 2 by the Council of State; Council president and members appointed for single 6-year terms with half the membership renewed every 3 years

subordinate courts: appellate or wilaya courts; first instance or daira tribunals

Political parties and leaders: Algerian National Front or FNA [Moussa TOUATI]

Algerian Popular Movement or MPA [Amara BENYOUNES]

Algerian Rally or RA [Ali ZAGHDOUD]

Algeria's Hope Rally or TAJ [Amar GHOUL]

Dignity or El Karama [Mohamed BENHAMOU]

Ennour El Djazairi Party (Algerian Radiance Party) or PED [Badreddine BELBAZ]

Front for Change or FC [Abdelmadjid MENASRA]

Front for Justice and Development or El Adala [Abdallah DJABALLAH]

Future Front or El Mostakbel [Abdelaziz BELAID]

Green Algeria Alliance or AAV [Bouguerra SOLTANI] (includes Islah, Ennahda Movement, and MSP)

Islamic Renaissance Movement or Ennahda Movement [Mohamed DOUIBI]

Justice and Development Front or FJD

Movement of National Understanding or MEN

Movement for National Reform or Islah [Djilali GHOUINI]

Movement of Society for Peace or MSP [Abderrazak MOKRI]

National Democratic Rally (Rassemblement National Democratique) or RND [Ahmed OUYAHIA]

National Front for Social Justice or FNJS [Khaled BOUNEDJEMA]

National Liberation Front or FLN [Djamel OULD ABBES]

National Party for Solidarity and Development or PNSD [Dalila YALAQUI]

National Reform Movement or Islah [Djahid YOUNSI]

National Republican Alliance or ANR [Redha MALEK]

New Dawn Party or PFJ [Tahar BENBAIBECHE]

New Generation or Jil Jadid [Soufiane DJILALI]

Oath of 1954 or Ahd 54 [Ali Fawzi REBAINE]

Party of Justice and Liberty [Mohammed SAID]

Rally for Culture and Democracy or RCD [Mohcine BELABBAS]

Rally for Hope in Algeria or TAJ

Socialist Forces Front or FFS [Mustafa BOUCHACHI]

Union of Democratic and Social Forces or UFDS [Noureddine BAHBOUH]

Vanguard of Freedoms [Ali BENFLIS]

Youth Party or PJ [Hamana BOUCHARMA]

Workers Party or PT [Louisa HANOUNE]

note: a law banning political parties based on religion was enacted in March 1997

Political pressure groups and leaders: Algerian League for the Defense of Human Rights or LADDH [Noureddine BENISSAD]

SOS Disparus [Nacera DUTOUR] Youth Action Rally or RAJ

International organization participation: ABEDA, AfDB, AFESD, AMF, AMU, AU, BIS, CAEU, CD, FAO, G-15, G-24, G-77, IAEA, IBRD, ICAO, ICC (national committees), ICRM, IDA, IDB, IFAD, IFC, IFRCS, IHO, ILO, IMF, IMO, IMSO, Interpol, IOC, IOM, IPU, ISO, ITSO, ITU, ITUC (NGOs), LAS, MIGA, MONUSCO, NAM, OAPEC, OAS (observer), OIC, OPCW, OPEC, OSCE (partner), UN, UNCTAD, UNESCO, UNHCR, UNIDO, UNITAR, UNWTO, UPU, WCO, WHO, WIPO, WMO, WTO (observer)

Diplomatic representation in the US: *chief of mission:* Ambassador Madjid BOUGUERRA (since 23 February 2015)

chancery: 2118 Kalorama Road NW, Washington, DC 20008

telephone: [1] (202) 265-2800

FAX: [1] (202) 986-5906

consulate(s) general: New York

Diplomatic representation from the US: *chief of mission:* Ambassador John P. DESROCHER (since 5 September 2017)

embassy: 05 Chemin Cheikh Bachir, El Ibrahimi, El-Biar 16030 Algieria

mailing address: B. P. 408, Alger-Gare, 16030 Algiers

telephone: [213] (0) 770-08-2000

FAX: [213] (0) 770-08-2064

Flag description: two equal vertical bands of green (hoist side) and white; a red, 5-pointed star within a red crescent centered over the two-color boundary; the colors represent Islam (green), purity and peace (white), and liberty (red); the crescent and star are also Islamic symbols, but the crescent is more closed than those of other Muslim countries because Algerians believe the long crescent horns bring happiness

National symbol(s): star and crescent, fennec fox; national colors: green, white, red

National anthem: *name:* "Kassaman" (We Pledge)

lyrics/music: Mufdi ZAKARIAH/Mohamed FAWZI

note: adopted 1962; ZAKARIAH wrote "Kassaman" as a poem while imprisoned in Algiers by French colonial forces

ECONOMY

Economy—overview: Algeria's economy remains dominated by the state, a legacy of the country's socialist post-independence development model. In recent years the Algerian Government has halted the privatization of state-owned industries and imposed restrictions on imports and foreign involvement in its economy. Hydrocarbons have long been the backbone of the economy, accounting for roughly 30% of GDP, 60% of budget revenues, and nearly 95% of export earnings. Algeria has the 10th-largest reserves of natural gas in the world and is the sixth-largest gas exporter. It ranks 16th in oil reserves. Hydrocarbon exports enabled Algeria to maintain macroeconomic stability and amass large foreign currency reserves while oil prices were high. In addition, Algeria's external debt is extremely low at about 2% of GDP. However, Algeria has struggled to develop non-hydrocarbon industries because of heavy regulation and an emphasis on state-driven growth. Declining oil prices since 2014 have reduced the government's ability to use state-driven growth to distribute rents and fund generous public subsidies. Algeria's foreign exchange reserves have declined by more than 40% since late 2013 and its oil stabilization fund has decreased from about $75 billion at the end of 2013 to about $7 billion in 2017, which is the statutory minimum. Algiers has strengthened protectionist measures since 2015 to limit its import bill and encourage domestic production of non-oil and gas industries. Since 2015, the government has imposed additional regulatory requirements on access to foreign exchange for imports and import quotas for specific products, such as cars, to limit their importation. Meanwhile, Algeria has not increased non-hydrocarbon exports, and hydrocarbon exports have declined because of field depletion and increased domestic demand.

With declining revenues caused by falling oil prices, the government has been under pressure to reduce spending. A wave of economic protests in February and March 2011 prompted Algiers to offer more than $23 billion in public grants and retroactive salary and benefit increases, moves which continue to weigh on public finances. In 2016, the government increased taxes on electricity and fuel, resulting in a modest increase in gasoline prices, and in 2017 raised by 2% the value-added tax on nearly all products, but has refrained from directly reducing subsidies, particularly for education, healthcare, and housing programs. Long-term economic challenges include diversifying the economy away from its reliance on hydrocarbon exports, bolstering the private sector, attracting foreign investment, and providing adequate jobs for younger Algerians.

GDP (purchasing power parity):
$629.3 billion (2017 est.)
$620.2 billion (2016 est.)
$600.4 billion (2015 est.)
note: data are in 2017 dollars
country comparison to the world: 37

GDP (official exchange rate):
$175.5 billion (2016 est.)

GDP—real growth rate:
1.5% (2017 est.)
3.3% (2016 est.)
3.7% (2015 est.)
country comparison to the world: 176

GDP—per capita (PPP):
$15,100 (2017 est.)
$15,200 (2016 est.)
$15,000 (2015 est.)

note: data are in 2017 dollars
country comparison to the world: 110

Gross national saving:
34.9% of GDP (2017 est.)
37.2% of GDP (2016 est.)
36.3% of GDP (2015 est.)
country comparison to the world: 13

GDP—composition, by end use:
household consumption: 42.7%
government consumption: 21.4%
investment in fixed capital: 42.7%
investment in inventories: 7.6%
exports of goods and services: 21%
imports of goods and services: -35.5% (2017 est.)

GDP—composition, by sector of origin:
agriculture: 13.2%
industry: 36.1%
services: 50.7% (2017 est.)

Agriculture—products: wheat, barley, oats, grapes, olives, citrus, fruits; sheep, cattle

Industries: petroleum, natural gas, light industries, mining, electrical, petrochemical, food processing

Industrial production growth rate: 0.9% (2017 est.)
country comparison to the world: 171

Labor force: 11.82 million (2017 est.)
country comparison to the world: 51

Labor force—by occupation: *agriculture:* 30.9%
industry: 30.9%
services: 58.4% (2011 est.) (2011 est.)

Unemployment rate: 11.7% (2017 est.)
10.5% (2016 est.)
country comparison to the world: 150

Population below poverty line: 23% (2006 est.)

Household income or consumption by percentage share: *lowest 10%:* 2.8%
highest 10%: 26.8% (1995)

Distribution of family income—Gini index: 35.3 (1995)
country comparison to the world: 92

Budget: *revenues:* $52.08 billion
expenditures: $70.74 billion (2017 est.)
Taxes and other revenues: 29.7% of GDP (2017 est.)
country comparison to the world: 84

Budget surplus (+) or deficit (-): -10.6% of GDP (2017 est.)
country comparison to the world: 210

Public debt: 19.9% of GDP (2017 est.)
18% of GDP (2016 est.)
note: data cover central government debt, as well as debt issued by subnational entities and intra-governmental debt
country comparison to the world: 187

Fiscal year: calendar year

Inflation rate (consumer prices):
5.5% (2017 est.)
6.4% (2016 est.)
country comparison to the world: 177

Central bank discount rate: 4% (31 December 2010)

4% (31 December 2009)
country comparison to the world: 97

Commercial bank prime lending rate: 8% (31 December 2017 est.)
8% (31 December 2016 est.)
country comparison to the world: 111

Stock of narrow money:
$86.45 billion (31 December 2017 est.)
$85.11 billion (31 December 2016 est.)
country comparison to the world: 43

Stock of broad money: $126.5 billion (31 December 2017 est.)
$125 billion (31 December 2016 est.)
country comparison to the world: 54

Stock of domestic credit: $105.8 billion (31 December 2017 est.)
$86.53 billion (31 December 2016 est.)
country comparison to the world: 58

Market value of publicly traded shares: $NA

Current account balance: -$22.87 billion (2017 est.)
-$26.31 billion (2016 est.)
country comparison to the world: 194

Exports: $33.15 billion (2017 est.)
$29.06 billion (2016 est.)
country comparison to the world: 60

Exports—commodities: petroleum, natural gas, and petroleum products 97% (2009 est.)

Exports—partners: Italy 17.4%, Spain 12.9%, US 12.9%, France 11.4%, Brazil 5.4%, Netherlands 4.9%, Turkey 4.5%, Canada 4.3% (2016)

Imports: $49.99 billion (2017 est.)
$49.43 billion (2016 est.)
country comparison to the world: 50

Imports—commodities: capital goods, foodstuffs, consumer goods

Imports—partners: China 17.8%, France 10.1%, Italy 9.8%, Spain 7.6%, Germany 6.4%, US 4.9%, Turkey 4.1% (2016)

Reserves of foreign exchange and gold: $97.67 billion (31 December 2017 est.)
$114.7 billion (31 December 2016 est.)
country comparison to the world: 26

Debt—external:
$8.163 billion (31 December 2017 est.)
$5.088 billion (31 December 2016 est.)
country comparison to the world: 122

Stock of direct foreign investment—at home: $26.24 billion (31 December 2017 est.)
$25.74 billion (31 December 2016 est.)
country comparison to the world: 72

Stock of direct foreign investment—abroad: $2.123 billion (31 December 2017 est.)
$2.025 billion (31 December 2016 est.)
country comparison to the world: 81

Exchange rates: Algerian dinars (DZD) per US dollar—
108.9 (2017 est.)
109.443 (2016 est.)
109.443 (2015 est.)
100.691 (2014 est.)

80.579 (2013 est.)

ENERGY

Electricity access: population without electricity: 400,000
electrification—*total population:* 99%
electrification—*urban areas:* 100%
electrification—*rural areas:* 97% (2016)

Electricity—production: 64.67 billion kWh (2015 est.)
country comparison to the world: 44

Electricity—consumption: 53.44 billion kWh (2015 est.)
country comparison to the world: 47

Electricity—exports: 641 million kWh (2015 est.)
country comparison to the world: 63

Electricity—imports: 610 million kWh (2015 est.)
country comparison to the world: 77

Electricity—installed generating capacity: 17.12 million kW (2015 est.)
country comparison to the world: 48

Electricity—from fossil fuels: 97.9% of total installed capacity (2015 est.)
country comparison to the world: 39

Electricity—from nuclear fuels: 0% of total installed capacity (2015 est.)
country comparison to the world: 37

Electricity—from hydroelectric plants: 1.6% of total installed capacity (2015 est.)
country comparison to the world: 143

Electricity—from other renewable sources: 1.5% of total installed capacity (2015 est.)
country comparison to the world: 132

Crude oil—production: 1.348 million bbl/day (2016 est.)
country comparison to the world: 19

Crude oil—exports: 798,900 bbl/day (2014 est.)
country comparison to the world: 16

Crude oil—imports: 5,880 bbl/day (2014 est.)
country comparison to the world: 78

Crude oil—proved reserves: 12.2 billion bbl (1 January 2017 es)
country comparison to the world: 16

Refined petroleum products—production: 657,600 bbl/day (2014 est.)
country comparison to the world: 27

Refined petroleum products—consumption: 428,000 bbl/day (2015 est.)
country comparison to the world: 36

Refined petroleum products—exports: 575,800 bbl/day (2014 est.)
country comparison to the world: 13

Refined petroleum products—imports: 62,480 bbl/day (2014 est.)
country comparison to the world: 73

Natural gas—production: 83.04 billion cu m (2015 est.)
country comparison to the world: 11

Natural gas—consumption: 44.32 billion cu m (2015 est.)
country comparison to the world: 25

Natural gas—exports: 43.42 billion cu m (2015 est.)
country comparison to the world: 8

Natural gas—imports: 0 cu m (2013 est.)
country comparison to the world: 82

Natural gas—proved reserves: 4.504 trillion cu m (1 January 2017 es)
country comparison to the world: 11

Carbon dioxide emissions from consumption of energy: 128 million Mt (2013 est.)
country comparison to the world: 36

COMMUNICATIONS

Telephones—fixed lines: total subscriptions: 3,404,709
subscriptions per 100 inhabitants: 8 (July 2016 est.)
country comparison to the world: 46

Telephones—mobile cellular: total: 48,348,505
subscriptions per 100 inhabitants: 120 (July 2016 est.)
country comparison to the world: 33

Telephone system: *general assessment:* privatization of Algeria's telecommunications sector began in 2000; three mobile cellular licenses have been issued and, in 2005, a consortium led by Egypt's Orascom Telecom won a 15-year license to build and operate a fixed-line network in Algeria
domestic: a limited network of fixed lines with a teledensity of less than 10 telephones per 100 persons has been offset by the rapid increase in mobile-cellular subscribership; in 2016, mobile-cellular teledensity was roughly 120 telephones per 100 persons
international: country code—213; landing point for the SEA-ME-WE-4 fiber-optic submarine cable system that provides links to Europe, the Middle East, and Asia; microwave radio relay to Italy, France, Spain, Morocco, and Tunisia; coaxial cable to Morocco and Tunisia (2016)

Broadcast media: state-run Radio-Television Algerienne operates the broadcast media and carries programming in Arabic, Berber dialects, and French; use of satellite dishes is widespread, providing easy access to European and Arab satellite stations; state-run radio operates several national networks and roughly 40 regional radio stations (2009)

Internet country code: .dz

Internet users: total: 17,291,463
percent of population: 42.9% (July 2016 est.)
country comparison to the world: 55

TRANSPORTATION

National air transport system: *number of registered air carriers:* 4
inventory of registered aircraft operated by air carriers: 74
annual passenger traffic on registered air carriers: 5,910,835
annual freight traffic on registered air carriers: 24,723,377 mt-km (2015)

Civil aircraft registration country code prefix: 7T (2016)

Airports: 157 (2016)
country comparison to the world: 36

Airports—with paved runways: total: 64
over 3,047 m: 12
2,438 to 3,047 m: 29
1,524 to 2,437 m: 17
914 to 1,523 m: 5
under 914 m: 1 (2017)

Airports—with unpaved runways: total: 93
2,438 to 3,047 m: 2
1,524 to 2,437 m: 18
914 to 1,523 m: 39
under 914 m: 34 (2013)
Heliports: 3 (2013)

Pipelines: condensate 2,600 km; gas 16,415 km; liquid petroleum gas 3,447 km; oil 7,036 km; refined products 144 km (2013)

Railways: total: 3,973 km
standard gauge: 2,888 km 1.432-m gauge (283 km electrified)
narrow gauge: 1,085 km 1.055-m gauge (2014)
country comparison to the world: 45

Roadways: total: 113,655 km
paved: 87,605 km (includes 645 km of expressways)
unpaved: 26,050 km (2010)
country comparison to the world: 43

Merchant marine: total: 110
by type: bulk carrier 3, general cargo 13, oil tanker 9, other 85 (2017)
country comparison to the world: 80

Ports and terminals: *major seaport(s):* Algiers, Annaba, Arzew, Bejaia, Djendjene, Jijel, Mostaganem, Oran, Skikda
LNG terminal(s) (export): Arzew, Bethioua, Skikda

MILITARY AND SECURITY

Military expenditures:
6.55% of GDP (2016)
6.32% of GDP (2015)
5.54% of GDP (2014)
4.84% of GDP (2013)
4.46% of GDP (2012)
country comparison to the world: 8

Military branches: People's National Army (Armee Nationale Populaire, ANP): Land Forces (Forces Terrestres, FT), Navy of the Republic of Algeria (Marine de la Republique Algerienne, MRA), Air Force (Al-Quwwat al-Jawwiya al-Jaza'eriya, QJJ), Territorial Air Defense Force (2016)

Military service age and obligation: 17 is the legal minimum age for voluntary military service; 19-30 years of age for compulsory service; conscript service obligation is 18 months (6 months basic training, 12 months civil projects) (2012)

TERRORISM

Terrorist groups—home based: *al-Qaida in the Islamic Maghreb (AQIM):* aim(s): replace the Algerian Government with Sharia and, ultimately, create a regional Islamic caliphate across all of North and West Africa
area(s) of operation: a core al-Qa'ida affiliate headquartered in Algeria; most active in the southwestern, southeastern, and upper northern regions; engages heavily in kidnappings for ransom—its primary income source

Terrorist groups—foreign based: *al-Mulathamun Battalion:* aim(s): replace regional governments, including Algeria's Government, with an Islamic state
area(s) of operation: conducts kidnappings for ransom

HAMAS: aim(s): enhance its networks in Algeria
area(s) of operation: has maintained an unofficial political bureau in Algeria for several years, which received the Algerian Government's official approval circa August 2016

Islamic State of Iraq and the Levant (ISIL): aim(s): replace the Algerian Government with an Islamic state and implement ISIL's strict interpretation of Sharia
area(s) of operation: maintains an operational and recruitment presence mostly in the northeast, targeting local security forces and US and Western interests; since circa September 2014 under its former leader Abdelmalek GOURI in Algeria, ISIL has referred to Algeria as its Wilayat al-Jazair; as an official branch of core ISIL, it is also known as Islamic State of Iraq and the Levant-Algeria (ISIL-Algeria) and Islamic State of Iraq and al-Sham—Algeria (ISIS-Algeria), formerly known as Jund al-Khilafa—Algeria (JAK-A); ISIL-Algeria's leader as of 2017 is unknown; hundreds of ISIL's fighters now in Syria are from Algeria

TRANSNATIONAL ISSUES

Disputes—international: Algeria and many other states reject Moroccan administration of Western Sahara; the Polisario Front, exiled in Algeria, represents the Sahrawi Arab Democratic Republic; Algeria's border with Morocco remains an irritant to bilateral relations, each nation accusing the other of harboring militants and arms smuggling; dormant disputes include Libyan claims of about 32,000 sq km still reflected on its maps of southeastern Algeria and the National Liberation Front's (FLN) assertions of a claim to Chirac Pastures in southeastern Morocco

Refugees and internally displaced persons: *refugees (country of origin):* 90,000 (Western Saharan Sahrawi, mostly living in Algerian-sponsored camps in the southwestern Algerian town of Tindouf) (2016)

Trafficking in persons: current situation: Algeria is a transit and, to a lesser extent, a destination and source country for women subjected to forced labor and sex trafficking and, to a lesser extent, men subjected to forced labor; criminal networks, sometimes extending to sub-Saharan Africa and to Europe, are involved in human smuggling and trafficking in Algeria; sub-Saharan adults enter Algeria voluntarily but illegally, often with the aid of smugglers, for onward travel to Europe, but some of the women are forced into prostitution, domestic service, and begging; some sub-Saharan men, mostly from Mali, are forced into domestic servitude; some Algerian women and children are also forced into prostitution domestically

tier rating: Tier 3—Algeria does not fully comply with the minimum standards for the elimination of trafficking and is not making significant efforts to do so: some officials denied the existence of human trafficking, hindering law enforcement efforts; the government reported its first conviction under its anti-trafficking law; one potential trafficking case was investigated in 2014, but no suspected offenders were arrested; no progress was made in identifying victims among vulnerable groups or referring them to NGO-run protection service, which left trafficking victims subject to arrest and detention; no anti-trafficking public awareness or educational campaigns were conducted (2015)

AMERICAN SAMOA

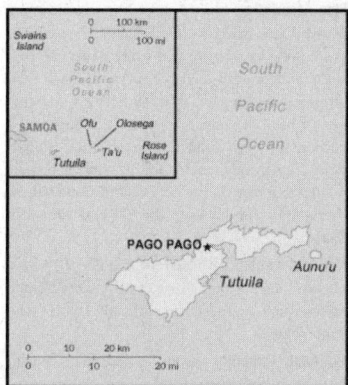

INTRODUCTION

Background: Settled as early as 1000 B.C., Samoa was not reached by European explorers until the 18th century. International rivalries in the latter half of the 19th century were settled by an 1899 treaty in which Germany and the US divided the Samoan archipelago. The US formally occupied its portion—a smaller group of eastern islands with the excellent harbor of Pago Pago—the following year.

GEOGRAPHY

Location: Oceania, group of islands in the South Pacific Ocean, about halfway between Hawaii and New Zealand

Geographic coordinates: 14 20 S, 170 00 W

Map references: Oceania

Area: *total:* 199 sq km
land: 199 sq km
water: 0 sq km
note: includes Rose Island and Swains Island
country comparison to the world: 216

Area—comparative: slightly larger than Washington, DC

Land boundaries: 0 km

Coastline: 116 km

Maritime claims: *territorial sea:* 12 nm
exclusive economic zone: 200 nm

Climate: tropical marine, moderated by southeast trade winds; annual rainfall averages about 3 m; rainy season (November to April), dry season (May to October); little seasonal temperature variation

Terrain: five volcanic islands with rugged peaks and limited coastal plains, two coral atolls (Rose Island, Swains Island)

Elevation:

mean elevation: NA

elevation extremes: *lowest point:* Pacific Ocean 0 m
highest point: Lata Mountain 964 m

Natural resources: pumice, pumicite

Land use: *agricultural land:* 24.5%
arable land 61.22%;
permanent crops 38.78%;
permanent pasture 0%
forest: 87.9%
other: 0% (2014 est.)
Irrigated land: 0 sq km (2012)

Natural hazards: cyclones common from December to March
volcanism: limited volcanic activity on the Ofu and Olosega Islands; neither has erupted since the 19th century

Environment—current issues: limited natural freshwater resources; the water division of the government has spent substantial funds in the past few years to improve water catchments and pipelines

Geography—note: Pago Pago has one of the best natural deepwater harbors in the South Pacific Ocean, sheltered by shape from rough seas and protected by peripheral mountains from high winds; strategic location in the South Pacific Ocean

PEOPLE AND SOCIETY

Population: 51,504 (July 2017 est.)
country comparison to the world: 210

Nationality: *noun:* American Samoan(s) (US nationals)
adjective: American Samoan

Ethnic groups: Pacific Islander 92.6% (includes Samoan 88.9%, Tongan 2.9%, other .8%), Asian 3.6% (includes Filipino 2.2%, other 1.4%), mixed 2.7%, other 1.2% (2010 est.)

Languages: Samoan 88.6% (closely related to Hawaiian and other Polynesian languages), English 3.9%, Tongan 2.7%, other Pacific islander 3%, other 1.8%
note: most people are bilingual (2010 est.)
Religions: Christian 98.3%, other 1%, unaffiliated 0.7% (2010 est.)

Age structure: *0-14 years:* 30.28% (male 8,017/female 7,580)
15-24 years: 18.79% (male 4,846/female 4,831)
25-54 years: 36.38% (male 9,274/female 9,463)
55-64 years: 8.58% (male 2,186/female 2,232)
65 years and over: 5.97% (male 1,452/female 1,623) (2017 est.)

Median age: *total:* 25.5 years
male: 25.1 years
female: 26 years (2017 est.)
country comparison to the world: 121

Population growth rate: -1.3% (2017 est.)
country comparison to the world: 232

Birth rate: 19.6 births/1,000 population (2017 est.)
country comparison to the world: 82

Death rate: 5.9 deaths/1,000 population (2017 est.)
country comparison to the world: 168

Net migration rate: -26.7 migrant(s)/1,000 population (2017 est.)
country comparison to the world: 221

Urbanization: *urban population:* 87.1% of total population (2017)
rate of urbanization: 0.63% annual rate of change (2015-20 est.)

Major urban areas—population: PAGO PAGO (capital) 48,000 (2014)

Sex ratio: *at birth:* 1.06 male(s)/female
0-14 years: 0.96 male(s)/female
15-24 years: 0.96 male(s)/female
25-54 years: 1.06 male(s)/female
55-64 years: 0.96 male(s)/female
65 years and over: 0.85 male(s)/female
total population: 1 male(s)/female (2016 est.)

Infant mortality rate: *total:* 11.3 deaths/1,000 live births
male: 13.2 deaths/1,000 live births
female: 9.3 deaths/1,000 live births (2017 est.)
country comparison to the world: 128

Life expectancy at birth: *total population:* 73.4 years
male: 71.3 years
female: 75.6 years (2017 est.)
country comparison to the world: 134

Total fertility rate: 2.68 children born/woman (2017 est.)
country comparison to the world: 69

Drinking water source:
improved:
urban: 100% of population
rural: 100% of population
total: 100% of population

unimproved:
urban: 0% of population
rural: 0% of population
total: 0% of population (2015 est.)

Sanitation facility access:
improved:
urban: 62.5% of population
rural: 62.5% of population
total: 62.5% of population
unimproved: urban: 37.5% of population
rural: 37.5% of population
total: 37.5% of population (2015 est.)

HIV/AIDS—adult prevalence rate: NA

HIV/AIDS—people living with HIV/AIDS: NA

HIV/AIDS—deaths: NA

Major infectious diseases: *note:* active local transmission of Zika virus by Aedes species mosquitoes has been identified in this country (as of August 2016); it poses an important risk (a large number of cases possible) among US citizens if bitten by an infective mosquito; other less common ways to get Zika are through sex, via blood transfusion, or during pregnancy, in which the pregnant woman passes Zika virus to her fetus (2016)

Education expenditures: NA

GOVERNMENT

Country name: *conventional long form:* Territory of American Samoa
conventional short form: American Samoa
abbreviation: AS
etymology: the name Samoa is composed of two parts, "sa" meaning "sacred" and "moa" meaning "center," so the name can mean Holy Center; alternatively, it can mean "place of the sacred moa bird" of Polynesian mythology

Dependency status: unincorporated and unorganized territory of the US; administered by the Office of Insular Affairs, US Department of the Interior

Government type: presidential democracy; a self-governing territory of the US

Capital: *name:* Pago Pago

geographic coordinates: 14 16 S, 170 42 W
time difference: UTC-11 (6 hours behind Washington, DC, during Standard Time)

Administrative divisions:
none (territory of the US); there are no first-order administrative divisions as defined by the US Government, but there are 3 districts and 2 islands* at the second order; Eastern, Manu'a, Rose Island*, Swains Island*, Western

Independence: none (territory of the US)

National holiday: Flag Day, 17 April (1900)

Constitution: adopted 17 October 1960; revised 1 July 1967; amended several times, last in 2013 (2016)

Legal system: mixed legal system of US common law and customary law

Citizenship: see United States

Suffrage: 18 years of age; universal

Executive branch: *chief of state:* President Donald J. TRUMP (since 20 January 2017); Vice President Michael R. PENCE (since 20 January 2017)

head of government: Governor Lolo Matalasi MOLIGA (since 3 January 2013)
cabinet: Cabinet consists of 12 department directors appointed by the governor with the consent of the Legislative Assembly
elections/appointments: president and vice president indirectly elected on the same ballot by an Electoral College of 'electors' chosen from each state to serve a 4-year term (eligible for a second term); under the US Constitution, residents of unincorporated territories, such as American Samoa, do not vote in elections for US president and vice president; however, they may vote in Democratic and Republican presidential primary elections; governor and lieutenant governor directly elected on the same ballot by absolute majority popular vote in 2 rounds if needed for a 4-year term (eligible for a second term); election last held on 8 November 2016 (next to be held in November 2020)
election results: Lolo Matalasi MOLIGA reelected governor in first round; percent of vote—Lolo Matalasi MOLIGA (independent) 60.2%, Faoa Aitofele SUNIA (Democratic Party) 35.8%, Tuika TUIKA (independent) 4%

Legislative branch: *description:* bicameral Fono or Legislative Assembly consists of the Senate (18 seats; members indirectly selected by regional governing councils to serve 4-year terms) and the House of Representatives (21 seats; 20 members directly elected by simple majority vote and 1 decided by public meeting on Swains Island; members serve 2-year terms)
elections: Senate—last held on 8 November 2016 (next to be held in November 2020); House of Representatives—last held on 8 November 2016 (next to be held in November 2018)
election results: Senate—percent of vote by party—NA; seats by party—independent 18; House of Representatives—percent of vote by party—NA; seats by party—independent 20
note: American Samoa elects 1 member by simple majority vote to serve a 2-year term as a delegate to the US House of Representatives; the delegate can vote when serving on a committee and when the House meets as the Committee of the Whole House, but not when legislation is submitted for a "full floor" House vote; election of delegate last held on 8 November 2016 (next to be held in November 2018)

Judicial branch: *highest court(s):* High Court of American Samoa (consists of the chief justice, associate chief justice, and 6 Samoan associate judges and organized into trial, family, drug, and appellate divisions); note—American Samoa has no US federal courts
judge selection and term of office: chief justice and associate chief justice appointed by the US Secretary of the Interior to serve for life; Samoan associate judges appointed by the governor to serve for life
subordinate courts: district and village courts

Political parties and leaders: Democratic Party [Fagafaga Daniel LANGKILDE]
Republican Party [Utu Abe MALAE, chairman]

International organization participation: AOSIS (observer), Interpol (subbureau), IOC, PIF (observer), SPC

Diplomatic representation in the US: none (territory of the US)

Diplomatic representation from the US: none (territory of the US)

Flag description: blue, with a white triangle edged in red that is based on the fly side and extends to the hoist side; a brown and white American bald eagle flying toward the hoist side is carrying 2 traditional Samoan symbols of authority, a war club known as a "fa'alaufa'i" (upper; left talon), and a coconut-fiber fly whisk known as a "fue" (lower; right talon); the combination of symbols broadly mimics that seen on the US Great Seal and reflects the relationship between the US and American Samoa

National symbol(s): a fue (coconut fiber fly whisk; representing wisdom) crossed with a to'oto'o (staff; representing authority); national colors: red, white, blue

National anthem: *name:* "Amerika Samoa" (American Samoa)
lyrics/music: Mariota Tiumalu TUIASOSOPO/ Napoleon Andrew TUITELELEAPAGA
note: local anthem adopted 1950; as a territory of the United States, "The Star-Spangled Banner" is official (see United States)

ECONOMY

Economy—overview: American Samoa has a traditional Polynesian economy in which more than 90% of the land is communally owned. Economic activity is strongly linked to the US with which American Samoa conducts most of its commerce. Tuna fishing and tuna processing plants are the backbone of the private sector with canned tuna the primary export. The two tuna canneries accounted for 13.1% of employment in 2013.
In late September 2009, an earthquake and the resulting tsunami devastated American Samoa and nearby Samoa, disrupting transportation and power generation, and resulting in about 200 deaths. The US Federal Emergency Management Agency oversaw a relief program of nearly $25 million. Transfers from the US Government add substantially to American Samoa's economic well-being. Attempts by the government to develop a larger and broader economy are restrained by Samoa's remote location, its limited transportation, and its devastating hurricanes. Tourism is a promising developing sector. In 2015, a new fish processing company completed refurbishing the processing facilities left behind by one of the two canneries that closed in 2009 and opened a new cannery. With two operating canneries once again, fish processing and exports will rise in the coming years.

GDP (purchasing power parity):
$711 million (2013 est.)

$718 million (2012 est.)
$647 million (2012 est.)
country comparison to the world: 208

GDP (official exchange rate): $748.6 million (2005)

GDP—real growth rate:
-2.4% (2013 est.)
-2.7% (2012 est.)
0.6% (2012 est.)
country comparison to the world: 213

GDP—per capita (PPP):
$13,000 (2013 est.)
$13,100 (2012 est.)
$11,700 (2011 est.)
country comparison to the world: 120

GDP—composition, by end use:
household consumption: 54.6%
government consumption: 52.8%
investment if fixed capital: 2.7%
investment in inventories: 2.3%
exports of goods and services: 54.4%
imports of goods and services: -66.8% (2013)

GDP—composition, by sector of origin:
agriculture: 27.4%
industry: 12.4%
services: 60.2% (2012)

Agriculture—products: bananas, coconuts, vegetables, taro, breadfruit, yams, copra, pineapples, papayas; dairy products, livestock

Industries: tuna canneries (largely supplied by foreign fishing vessels), handicrafts

Industrial production growth rate: NA%

Labor force: 16,090 (2013)
country comparison to the world: 215

Labor force—by occupation: *agriculture:* NA
industry: 13.1%
services: 86.9% (2013)

Unemployment rate: 29.8% (2005)
country comparison to the world: 203

Population below poverty line: NA%

Household income or consumption by percentage share: *lowest 10%:* NA%
highest 10%: NA%

Budget: *revenues:* $241.2 million
expenditures: $243.7 million (2013 est.)
Taxes and other revenues: 32.2% of GDP (2013 est.)
country comparison to the world: 73

Budget surplus (+) or deficit (-): -0.3% of GDP (2013 est.)
country comparison to the world: 40

Fiscal year: 1 October—30 September

Inflation rate (consumer prices):
2.1% (2013)
3.5% (2012)
country comparison to the world: 100

Exports: $459 million (2013 est.)
$489 million (2012)
country comparison to the world: 177

Exports—commodities: canned tuna 93%

Exports—partners: Australia 21.6%, Ghana 16.1%, Netherlands 11.5%, Burma 8.1%, South

Korea 7.9%, Colombia 4.7%, Indonesia 4.3% (2016)

Imports: $564 million (2013 est.)
$508 million (2012)
country comparison to the world: 187

Imports—commodities: raw materials for canneries, food, petroleum products, machinery and parts

Imports—partners: Singapore 22.6%, NZ 19.1%, Samoa 8.7%, Malaysia 8.2%, Fiji 7.6%, South Korea 7.4%, Australia 4.6% (2016)

Debt—external: $NA

Exchange rates: the US dollar is used

ENERGY

Electricity access: *population without electricity:* 22,219
electrification—*total population:* 59%
electrification—urban areas: 60%
electrification—rural areas: 45% (2012)

Electricity—production: 163 million kWh (2015 est.)
country comparison to the world: 194

Electricity—consumption: 151.6 million kWh (2015 est.)
country comparison to the world: 196

Electricity—exports: 0 kWh (2016 est.)
country comparison to the world: 101

Electricity—imports: 0 kWh (2016 est.)
country comparison to the world: 120

Electricity—installed generating capacity: 41,000 kW (2015 est.)
country comparison to the world: 198

Electricity—from fossil fuels: 100% of total installed capacity (2015 est.)
country comparison to the world: 21

Electricity—from nuclear fuels: 0% of total installed capacity (2015 est.)
country comparison to the world: 42

Electricity—from hydroelectric plants: 0% of total installed capacity (2015 est.)
country comparison to the world: 159

Electricity—from other renewable sources: 0% of total installed capacity (2015 est.)
country comparison to the world: 170

Crude oil—production: 0 bbl/day (2016 est.)
country comparison to the world: 103

Crude oil—exports: 0 bbl/day (2014 est.)
country comparison to the world: 89

Crude oil—imports: 0 bbl/day (2014 est.)
country comparison to the world: 94

Crude oil—proved reserves: 0 bbl (1 January 2017 es)
country comparison to the world: 103

Refined petroleum products—production: 0 bbl/day (2014 est.)
country comparison to the world: 112

Refined petroleum products—consumption: 2,375 bbl/day (2015 est.)
country comparison to the world: 191

Refined petroleum products—exports: 0.09 bbl/day (2014 est.)
country comparison to the world: 127

Refined petroleum products—imports: 2,346 bbl/day (2014 est.)
country comparison to the world: 185

Natural gas—production: 0 cu m (2013 est.)
country comparison to the world: 105

Natural gas—consumption: 0 cu m (2013 est.)
country comparison to the world: 155

Natural gas—exports: 0 cu m (2013 est.)
country comparison to the world: 63

Natural gas—imports: 0 cu m (2013 est.)
country comparison to the world: 86

Natural gas—proved reserves: 0 cu m (1 January 2014 es)
country comparison to the world: 112

Carbon dioxide emissions from consumption of energy: 600,000 Mt (2013 est.)
country comparison to the world: 177

COMMUNICATIONS

Telephones—fixed lines: *total subscriptions:* 10,000 subscriptions per 100 inhabitants: 18 (July 2016 est.)
country comparison to the world: 199

Telephone system: *general assessment:* good telex, telegraph, facsimile, and cellular telephone services
domestic: domestic satellite system with 1 Comsat earth station
international: country code—1-684; satellite earth station—1 (Intelsat-Pacific Ocean)

Broadcast media: 3 TV stations; multi-channel pay TV services are available; about a dozen radio stations, some of which are repeater stations (2009)

Internet country code: .as

Internet users: *total:* 17,000
percent of population: 31.3% (July 2016 est.)

TRANSPORTATION

Airports: 3 (2016)
country comparison to the world: 192

Airports—with paved runways: *total:* 3
over 3,047 m: 1
914 to 1,523 m: 1
under 914 m: 1 (2017)

Roadways: *total:* 241 km (2008)
country comparison to the world: 208

Ports and terminals: *major seaport(s):* Pago Pago

MILITARY AND SECURITY

Military—note: defense is the responsibility of the US

TRANSNATIONAL ISSUES

Disputes—international: Tokelau included American Samoa's Swains Island (Olosega) in its 2006 draft independence constitution

ANDORRA

INTRODUCTION

Background: The landlocked Principality of Andorra is one of the smallest states in Europe, nestled high in the Pyrenees between the French and Spanish borders. For 715 years, from 1278 to 1993, Andorrans lived under a unique coprincipality, ruled by French and Spanish leaders (from 1607 onward, the French chief of state and the Bishop of Urgell). In 1993, this feudal system was modified with the introduction of a modern, constitution; the co-princes remained as titular heads of state, but the government transformed into a parliamentary democracy. Andorra has become a popular tourist destination visited by approximately 8 million people each year drawn by the winter sports, summer climate, and duty-free shopping. Andorra has also become a wealthy international commercial center because of its mature banking sector and low taxes. As part of its effort to modernize its economy, Andorra has opened to foreign investment, and engaged in other reforms, such as advancing tax initiatives aimed at supporting a broader infrastructure. Although not a member of the EU, Andorra enjoys a special relationship with the bloc that is governed by various customs and cooperation agreements and uses the euro as its national currency.

GEOGRAPHY

Location: Southwestern Europe, Pyrenees mountains, on the border between France and Spain

Geographic coordinates: 42 30 N, 1 30 E

Map references: Europe

Area: *total:* 468 sq km
land: 468 sq km
water: 0 sq km
country comparison to the world: 196

Area—comparative: 2.5 times the size of Washington, DC

Land boundaries: *total:* 118 km
border countries (2): France 55 km, Spain 63 km

Coastline: 0 km (landlocked)

Maritime claims: none (landlocked)

Climate: temperate; snowy, cold winters and warm, dry summers

Terrain: rugged mountains dissected by narrow valleys

Elevation: mean elevation: 1,996 m

elevation extremes: *lowest point:* Riu Runer 840 m
highest point: Pic de Coma Pedrosa 2,946 m

Natural resources: hydropower, mineral water, timber, iron ore, lead

Land use: *agricultural land:* 44.47%
arable land 13.4%;
permanent crops 0%;
permanent pasture 86.6%
forest: 34%
other: 21.5% (2014 est.)
Irrigated land: 0 sq km (2012)

Population—distribution: population is unevenly distributed and is concentrated in the 7 urbanized valleys that make up the country's parishes (political administrative divisions)

Natural hazards: avalanches

Environment—current issues: deforestation; overgrazing of mountain meadows contributes to soil erosion; air pollution; wastewater treatment and solid waste disposal

Environment—international agreements:
party to: Biodiversity, Desertification, Hazardous Wastes, Ozone Layer Protection
signed, but not ratified: none of the selected agreements

Geography—note: landlocked; straddles a number of important crossroads in the Pyrenees

PEOPLE AND SOCIETY

Population: 76,965 (July 2017 est.)
country comparison to the world: 200

Nationality: *noun:* Andorran(s)
adjective: Andorran

Ethnic groups: Andorran 46.2%, Spanish 26.4%, Portuguese 12.8%, French 5%, other 9.6% (2016 est.)

Languages: Catalan (official), French, Castilian, Portuguese

Religions: Roman Catholic (predominant)

Age structure: *0-14 years:* 14.4% (male 6,340/female 6,003)
15-24 years: 9.64% (male 4,289/female 3,976)
25-54 years: 46.18% (male 20,233/female 19,348)
55-64 years: 14.16% (male 6,458/female 5,677)
65 years and over: 15.61% (male 6,788/female 6,590) (2017 est.)

Median age: *total:* 44.3 years
male: 44.4 years
female: 44.1 years (2017 est.)
country comparison to the world: 13

Population growth rate: 0.03% (2017 est.)
country comparison to the world: 190

Birth rate: 7.5 births/1,000 population (2017 est.)
country comparison to the world: 224

Death rate: 7.3 deaths/1,000 population (2017 est.)
country comparison to the world: 120

Net migration rate: 0 migrant(s)/1,000 population (2017 est.)
country comparison to the world: 70

Population distribution: population is unevenly distributed and is concentrated in the 7 urbanized valleys that make up the country's parishes (political administrative divisions)

Urbanization: *urban population:* 84.1% of total population (2017)
rate of urbanization: 0.09% annual rate of change (2015-20 est.)

Major urban areas—population: ANDORRA LA VELLA (capital) 23,000 (2014)

Sex ratio: *at birth:* 1.07 male(s)/female
0-14 years: 1.05 male(s)/female
15-24 years: 1.08 male(s)/female
25-54 years: 1.05 male(s)/female
55-64 years: 1.15 male(s)/female
65 years and over: 1.02 male(s)/female
total population: 1.06 male(s)/female (2016 est.)

Infant mortality rate: *total:* 3.6 deaths/1,000 live births
male: 3.6 deaths/1,000 live births
female: 3.6 deaths/1,000 live births (2017 est.)
country comparison to the world: 199

Life expectancy at birth: *total population:* 82.9 years
male: 80.7 years
female: 85.2 years (2017 est.)
country comparison to the world: 8

Total fertility rate: 1.4 children born/woman (2017 est.)
country comparison to the world: 212

Health expenditures: 8.1% of GDP (2014)
country comparison to the world: 55

Physicians density: 3.69 physicians/1,000 population (2015)

Hospital bed density: 2.5 beds/1,000 population (2009)

Drinking water source: *improved:*
urban: 100% of population
rural: 100% of population
total: 100% of population
unimproved:
urban: 0% of population
rural: 0% of population
total: 0% of population (2015 est.)

Sanitation facility access: *improved:*
urban: 100% of population
rural: 100% of population
total: 100% of population
unimproved:

urban: 0% of population
rural: 0% of population
total: 0% of population (2015 est.)

HIV/AIDS—adult prevalence rate: NA

HIV/AIDS—people living with HIV/AIDS: NA

HIV/AIDS—deaths: NA

Obesity—adult prevalence rate: 25.6% (2016)
country comparison to the world: 49

Education expenditures: 3.1% of GDP (2014)

Literacy: *definition:* age 15 and over can read and write
total population: 100%
male: 100%
female: 100% (2016 est.)

GOVERNMENT

Country name: *conventional long form:* Principality of Andorra
conventional short form: Andorra
local long form: Principat d'Andorra
local short form: Andorra
etymology: the origin of the country's name is obscure; the name may derive from the Arabic "ad-darra" meaning "the forest," a reference to its location as part of the Spanish March (defensive buffer zone) against the invading Moors in the 8th century

Government type: parliamentary democracy (since March 1993) that retains its chiefs of state in the form of a co-principality; the two princes are the President of France and Bishop of Seu d'Urgell, Spain, who delegate responsibility to other officials

Capital: *name:* Andorra la Vella
geographic coordinates: 42 30 N, 1 31 E
time difference: UTC+1 (6 hours ahead of Washington, DC during Standard Time)
daylight saving time: +1hr, begins last Sunday in March; ends last Sunday in October

Administrative divisions: 7 parishes (parroquies, singular—parroquia); Andorra la Vella, Canillo, Encamp, Escaldes-Engordany, La Massana, Ordino, Sant Julia de Loria

Independence: 1278 (formed under the joint sovereignty of the French Count of Foix and the Spanish Bishop of Urgell)

National holiday: Our Lady of Meritxell Day, 8 September (1278)

Constitution: *history:* drafted 1991, approved by referendum 14 March 1993, effective 28 April 1993
amendments: proposed by the coprinces jointly or by the General Council; passage requires at least a two-thirds majority vote by the General Council, ratification in a referendum, and sanctioning by the coprinces (2017)

Legal system: mixed legal system of civil and customary law with the influence of canon law

International law organization participation: has not submitted an ICJ jurisdiction declaration; accepts ICCt jurisdiction

Citizenship: *citizenship by birth:* no

citizenship by descent only: the mother must be an Andorran citizen or the father must have been born in Andorra and both parents maintain permanent residence in Andorra
dual citizenship recognized: no
residency requirement for naturalization: 25 years

Suffrage: 18 years of age; universal

Executive branch: *chief of state:* Co-prince Emmanuel MACRON (since 14 May 2017); represented by Patrick STROZDA (since 14 May 2017); and Co-prince Archbishop Joan-Enric VIVES i Sicilia (since 12 May 2003); represented by Josep Maria MAURI (since 20 July 2012)

head of government: Head of Government (or Cap de Govern) Antoni MARTI PETIT (since 1 April 2015)
cabinet: Executive Council of ten ministers designated by the head of government
elections/appointments: head of government indirectly elected by the General Council (Andorran parliament), formally appointed by the coprinces for a 4-year term; election last held on 31 March 2015 (next to be held in March 2019); the leader of the majority party in the General Council is usually elected head of government
election results: Antoni MARTI Petit (DA) elected head of government; percent of General Council vote—79%

Legislative branch: *description:* unicameral General Council of the Valleys or Consell General de les Valls (a minimum of 28 seats; 14 members directly elected in multi-seat constituencies (parishes) by simple majority vote and 14 directly elected in a single national constituency by proportional representation vote; members serve 4-year terms); note—each voter casts two separate ballots—one for a national list and one for a parish list
elections: last held on 1 March 2015 (next to be held in March 2019)
election results: percent of vote by party—DA 37.03%, PLA 27.68%, PS-VA-IC-independent coalition 23.53%, SDP 11.74%; seats by party—DA 15, PLA 8, PS-VA-IC-independent coalition 3, SDP 2

Judicial branch: *highest court(s):* Supreme Court of Justice of Andorra or Tribunal Superior de la Justicia d'Andorra (consists of the court president and 8 judges organized into civil, criminal, and administrative chambers); Constitutional Court or Tribunal Constitucional (consists of 4 magistrates)
judge selection and term of office: Supreme Court president and judges appointed by the Supreme Council of Justice, a 5-member judicial policy and administrative body appointed 1 each by the coprinces, 1 by the General Council, 1 by the executive council president, and 1 by the courts; judges serve 6-year renewable terms; Constitutional magistrates appointed 2 by the coprinces and 2 by the General Council; magistrates' appointments limited to 2 consecutive 8-year terms
subordinate courts: Tribunal of Judges or Tribunal de Batlles; Tribunal of the Courts or Tribunal de Corts

Political parties and leaders: Citizens' Initiative or IC [Sergi RICART] (including PS, VA, IC, and independents)
Democrats for Andorra or DA [Antoni MARTI PETIT]
Greens of Andorra or VA [Isabel LOZANO MUNOZ, Juli FERNANDEZ BLASI]
Liberal Party or PLA [Jordi GALLARDO]
Social Democratic Party or PS [Vincenc ALAY FERRER]
Social Democratic Progress Party or SDP [Victor NAUDI ZAMORA]
note: Andorra has several smaller parties at the parish level (one is Lauredian Union)

International organization participation: CE, FAO, ICAO, ICC (NGOs), ICCt, ICRM, IFRCS, Interpol, IOC, IPU, ITU, OIF, OPCW, OSCE, UN, UNCTAD, UNESCO, Union Latina, UNWTO, WCO, WHO, WIPO, WTO (observer)

Diplomatic representation in the US: *chief of mission:* Ambassador Elisenda VIVES BALMANA (since 2 March 2016)
chancery: 2 United Nations Plaza, 27th Floor, New York, NY 10017
telephone: [1] (212) 750-8064
FAX: [1] (212) 750-6630

Diplomatic representation from the US: the US does not have an embassy in Andorra; the US ambassador to Spain is accredited to Andorra; US interests in Andorra are represented by the US Consulate General's office in Barcelona (Spain); mailing address: Paseo Reina Elisenda de Montcada, 23, 08034 Barcelona, Spain;
telephone: [34] (93) 280-2227;
FAX: [34] (93) 280-6175

Flag description: three vertical bands of blue (hoist side), yellow, and red, with the national coat of arms centered in the yellow band; the latter band is slightly wider than the other 2 so that the ratio of band widths is 8:9:8; the coat of arms features a quartered shield with the emblems of (starting in the upper left and proceeding clockwise): Urgell, Foix, Bearn, and Catalonia; the motto reads VIRTUS UNITA FORTIOR (Strength United is Stronger); the flag combines the blue and red French colors with the red and yellow of Spain to show Franco-Spanish protection
note: similar to the flags of Chad and Romania, which do not have a national coat of arms in the center, and the flag of Moldova, which does bear a national emblem

National symbol(s): red cow (breed unspecified); national colors: blue, yellow, red

National anthem: *name:* "El Gran Carlemany" (The Great Charlemagne)
lyrics/music: Joan BENLLOCH i VIVO/Enric MARFANY BONS
note: adopted 1921; the anthem provides a brief history of Andorra in a first person narrative

ECONOMY

Economy—overview: Andorra has a developed economy and a free market, with per capita income above the European average and above the level of its neighbors, Spain and France. The country has developed a sophisticated infrastructure including a one-of-a-kind micro-fiber-optic network for the entire country. Tourism, retail sales, and finance comprise more than three-quarters of GDP. Duty-free shopping for some products and the country's summer and winter resorts attract millions of visitors annually. Andorra uses the euro and is effectively subject to the monetary policy of the European Central Bank. Andorra's comparative advantage as a tax haven eroded when the borders of neighboring France and Spain opened and the government eased bank secrecy laws under pressure from the EU and OECD. Agricultural production is limited—only about 5% of the land is arable—and most food has to be imported, making the economy vulnerable to changes in fuel and food prices. The principal livestock is sheep. Manufacturing output and exports consist mainly of perfumes and cosmetic products, products of the printing industry, electrical machinery and equipment, clothing, tobacco products, and furniture. Andorra is a member of the EU Customs Union and is treated as an EU member for trade in manufactured goods (no tariffs) and as a non-EU member for agricultural products. Andorra is open to, and actively seeking to attract, foreign investment. The Andorran economy is undergoing a process of diversification centered largely on the sectors of tourism, trade, property, and finance. To provide incentives for growth and diversification in the economy, the Andorran government began sweeping economic reforms in 2006. The Parliament approved three laws to complement the first phase of economic openness: on companies (October 2007), on business accounting (December 2007), and on foreign investment (April 2008 and June 2012). From 2011 to 2015, the Parliament also approved direct taxes in the form of taxes on corporations, on individual incomes of residents and non-residents, and on capital gains, savings, and economic activities. These regulations aim to establish a transparent, modern, and internationally comparable regulatory framework. The economic reforms aim to attract investment and businesses that can contribute most to Andorra's economic development and offer greater diversification and higher value added. Prior to 2008, Andorra offered limited foreign investment opportunities largely because of concerns about the impact of foreign firms on such a small economy.

GDP (purchasing power parity):
$3.327 billion (2015 est.)
$3.363 billion (2014 est.)
$3.273 billion (2013 est.)
note: data are in 2012 US dollars
country comparison to the world: 186

GDP (official exchange rate):
$2.712 billion (2012 est.)

GDP—real growth rate:
-1.1% (2015 est.)
1.4% (2014 est.)
-0.1% (2013 est.)
country comparison to the world: 208

GDP—per capita (PPP):
$49,900 (2015 est.)
$51,300 (2014 est.)
$50,300 (2013 est.)
country comparison to the world: 29

GDP—composition, by sector of origin:
agriculture: 11.9%
industry: 33.6%
services: 54.5% (2015 est.)

Agriculture—products: small quantities of rye, wheat, barley, oats, vegetables, tobacco; sheep, cattle

Industries: tourism (particularly skiing), banking, timber, furniture

Industrial production growth rate: NA%

Labor force: 39,750 (2016)
country comparison to the world: 196

Labor force—by occupation: *agriculture:* 0.5%
industry: 4.4%
services: 95.1% (2015)

Unemployment rate: 3.7% (2016 est.)
4.1% (2015 est.)
country comparison to the world: 41

Population below poverty line: NA%

Household income or consumption by percentage share: *lowest 10%:* NA%
highest 10%: NA%

Budget: *revenues:* $1.872 billion
expenditures: $2.06 billion (2016)
Taxes and other revenues: 69% of GDP (2016)
country comparison to the world: 4

Budget surplus (+) or deficit (-): -6.9% of GDP (2016)
country comparison to the world: 186

Public debt: 41% of GDP (2014 est.)
41.4% of GDP (2013 est.)
country comparison to the world: 134

Fiscal year: calendar year

Inflation rate (consumer prices):
-0.9% (2015 est.)
-0.1% (2014 est.)
country comparison to the world: 2

Exports: $78.71 million (2015 est.)
$79.57 million (2014 est.)
country comparison to the world: 199

Exports—commodities: tobacco products, furniture

Imports: $1.257 billion (2015 est.)
$1.264 billion (2014 est.)
country comparison to the world: 172

Imports—commodities: consumer goods, food, fuel, electricity

Debt—external: $0 (2016)
country comparison to the world: 207

Exchange rates: euros (EUR) per US dollar—
0.906 (2017 est.)
0.9214 (2016 est.)
0.9214 (2015 est.)
0.885 (2014 est.)
0.7634 (2013 est.)

ENERGY

Electricity access: electrification—*total population:* 100% (2016)

Electricity—production: 99.48 million kWh (2015)
country comparison to the world: 198

Electricity—consumption: 221.6 million kWh (2015)
country comparison to the world: 187

Electricity—exports: 6,000 kWh (2015 est.)
country comparison to the world: 95

Electricity—imports: 471.3 million kWh (2015 est.)
country comparison to the world: 82

Electricity—installed generating capacity: 520,000 kW (2010 est.)
country comparison to the world: 145

Electricity—from fossil fuels: 61.3% of total installed capacity (2010 est.)
country comparison to the world: 126

Electricity—from nuclear fuels: 0% of total installed capacity (2016 est.)
country comparison to the world: 40

Electricity—from hydroelectric plants: 23.3% of total installed capacity (2010 est.)
country comparison to the world: 83

Crude oil—production: 0 bbl/day (2016)
country comparison to the world: 104

Crude oil—exports: 0 bbl/day (2016) (2016)
country comparison to the world: 88

Crude oil—imports: 0 bbl/day (2016) (2016)
country comparison to the world: 92

Crude oil—proved reserves: 0 bbl (2016) (2016)
country comparison to the world: 104

Refined petroleum products—production: 0 bbl/day (2016)
country comparison to the world: 113

Natural gas—production: 0 cu m (2016) (2016)
country comparison to the world: 104

Natural gas—consumption: 0 cu m (2016) (2016)
country comparison to the world: 154

Natural gas—exports: 0 cu m (2016) (2016)
country comparison to the world: 62

Natural gas—imports: 0 cu m (2016) (2016)
country comparison to the world: 84

Natural gas—proved reserves: 0 cu m (2016)
country comparison to the world: 111

COMMUNICATIONS

Telephones—fixed lines: *total subscriptions:* 38,694
subscriptions per 100 inhabitants: 45 (July 2016 est.)
country comparison to the world: 168

Telephones—mobile cellular: total: 71,132
subscriptions per 100 inhabitants: 83 (July 2016 est.)
country comparison to the world: 198

Telephone system: *general assessment:* modern automatic telephone system
domestic: modern system with microwave radio relay connections between exchanges
international: country code—376; landline circuits to France and Spain (2016)

Broadcast media: 1 public TV station and 2 public radio stations; about 10 commercial radio stations; good reception of radio and TV broadcasts from stations in France and Spain; upgraded to terrestrial digital TV broadcasting in 2007; roughly 25 international TV channels available (2016)

Internet country code: .ad

Internet users: *total:* 83,887
percent of population: 97.9% (July 2016 est.)
country comparison to the world: 176

TRANSPORTATION

Civil aircraft registration country code prefix: C3 (2016)

Roadways: *total:* 320 km (2015)
country comparison to the world: 205

MILITARY AND SECURITY

Military branches: no regular military forces; Police Corps of Andorra (2017)

Military—note: defense is the responsibility of France and Spain

TRANSNATIONAL ISSUES

Disputes—international: none

ANGOLA

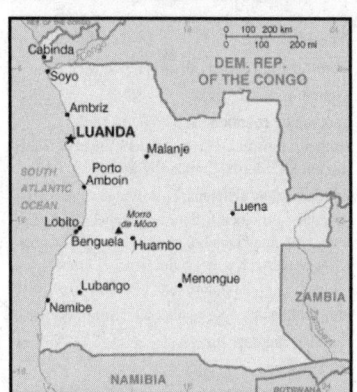

INTRODUCTION

Background: Angola scores low on human development indexes despite using its large oil reserves to rebuild since the end of a 27-year civil war in 2002. Fighting between the Popular Movement for the Liberation of Angola (MPLA), led by Jose Eduardo DOS SANTOS, and the National Union for the Total Independence of Angola (UNITA), led by Jonas SAVIMBI, followed independence from Portugal in 1975. Peace seemed imminent in 1992 when Angola held national elections, but fighting picked up again in 1993. Up to 1.5 million lives may have been lost—and 4 million people displaced—during the more than a quarter century of fighting. SAVIMBI's death in 2002 ended UNITA's insurgency and cemented the MPLA's hold on power. President DOS SANTOS pushed through a new constitution in 2010 and was elected to a five year term as president in 2012.

GEOGRAPHY

Location: Southern Africa, bordering the South Atlantic Ocean, between Namibia and Democratic Republic of the Congo

Geographic coordinates: 12 30 S, 18 30 E

Map references: Africa

Area: *total:* 1,246,700 sq km

land: 1,246,700 sq km
water: 0 sq km
country comparison to the world: 24

Area—comparative: about eight times the size of Georgia; slightly less than twice the size of Texas

Land boundaries: *total:* 5,369 km
border countries (4): Democratic Republic of the Congo 2,646 km (of which 225 km is the boundary of discontiguous Cabinda Province), Republic of the Congo 231 km, Namibia 1,427 km, Zambia 1,065 km

Coastline: 1,600 km

Maritime claims: *territorial sea:* 12 nm
contiguous zone: 24 nm
exclusive economic zone: 200 nm

Climate: semiarid in south and along coast to Luanda; north has cool, dry season (May to October) and hot, rainy season (November to April)

Terrain: narrow coastal plain rises abruptly to vast interior plateau

Elevation: *mean elevation:* 1,112 m

elevation extremes: *lowest point:* Atlantic Ocean 0 m
highest point: Moca 2,620 m

Natural resources: petroleum, diamonds, iron ore, phosphates, copper, feldspar, gold, bauxite, uranium

Land use: *agricultural land:* 47.5%
arable land 8.3%;
permanent crops 0.5%;
permanent pasture 91.23%
forest: 46.5%
other: 6% (2014 est.)
Irrigated land: 860 sq km (2014)

Population—distribution: most people live in the western half of the country; urban areas account for the highest concentrations of people, particularly Luanda

Natural hazards: locally heavy rainfall causes periodic flooding on the plateau

Environment—current issues: overuse of pastures and subsequent soil erosion attributable to population pressures; desertification; deforestation of tropical rain forest, in response to both international demand for tropical timber and to domestic use as fuel, resulting in loss of biodiversity; soil erosion contributing to water pollution and siltation of rivers and dams; inadequate supplies of potable water

Environment—international agreements: *party to:* Biodiversity, Climate Change, Climate Change-Kyoto Protocol, Desertification, Law of the Sea, Marine Dumping, Ozone Layer Protection, Ship Pollution
signed, but not ratified: none of the selected agreements

Geography—note: the province of Cabinda is an exclave, separated from the rest of the country by the Democratic Republic of the Congo

PEOPLE AND SOCIETY

Population: 29,310,273 (July 2017 est.)
note: Angola's national statistical agency projects the country's 2017 population to be 28.4 million
country comparison to the world: 46

Nationality: *noun:* Angolan(s)
adjective: Angolan

Ethnic groups: Ovimbundu 37%, Kimbundu 25%, Bakongo 13%, mestico (mixed European and native African) 2%, European 1%, other 22%

Languages: Portuguese 71.2% (official), Umbundu 23%, Kikongo 8.2%, Kimbundu 7.8%, Chokwe 6.5%, Nhaneca 3.4%, Nganguela 3.1%, Fiote 2.4%, Kwanhama 2.3%, Muhumbi 2.1%, Luvale 1%, other 3.6%
note: most widely spoken languages; shares sum to more than 100% because some respondents gave more than one answer on the census (2014 est.)

Religions: Roman Catholic 41.1%, Protestant 38.1%, other 8.6%, none 12.3% (2014 est.)

Demographic profile: More than a decade after the end of Angola's 27-year civil war, the country still faces a variety of socioeconomic problems, including poverty, high maternal and child mortality, and illiteracy. Despite the country's rapid post-war economic growth based on oil production, more than 40 percent of Angolans live below the poverty line and unemployment is widespread, especially among the large young-adult population. Only about 70% of the population is literate, and the rate drops to around 60% for women. The youthful

23

population—about 45% are under the age of 15—is expected to continue growing rapidly with a fertility rate of more 5 children per woman and a low rate of contraceptive use. Fewer than half of women deliver their babies with the assistance of trained health care personnel, which contributes to Angola's high maternal mortality rate.

Of the estimated 550,000 Angolans who fled their homeland during its civil war, most have returned home since 2002. In 2012, the UN assessed that conditions in Angola had been stable for several years and invoked a cessation of refugee status for Angolans. Following the cessation clause, some of those still in exile returned home voluntarily through UN repatriation programs, and others integrated into host countries.

Age structure: *0-14 years:* 48.12% (male 7,005,891/female 7,097,392)
15-24 years: 18.25% (male 2,593,355/female 2,756,367)
25-54 years: 28.03% (male 3,921,046/female 4,293,307)
55-64 years: 3.26% (male 438,268/female 517,690)
65 years and over: 2.34% (male 290,247/female 396,710) (2017 est.)

Dependency ratios:
total dependency ratio: 97.6
youth dependency ratio: 93
elderly dependency ratio: 4.6
potential support ratio: 21.9 (2015 est.)

Median age: *total:* 15.9 years
male: 15.4 years
female: 16.3 years (2017 est.)
country comparison to the world: 213

Population growth rate: 3.52% (2017 est.)
country comparison to the world: 2

Birth rate: 44.2 births/1,000 population (2017 est.)
country comparison to the world: 1

Death rate: 9.2 deaths/1,000 population (2017 est.)
country comparison to the world: 62

Net migration rate: 0.2 migrant(s)/1,000 population (2017 est.)
country comparison to the world: 67

Population distribution: most people live in the western half of the country; urban areas account for the highest concentrations of people, particularly Luanda

Urbanization: *urban population:* 45.6% of total population (2017)
rate of urbanization: 4.6% annual rate of change (2015-20 est.)

Major urban areas—population: LUANDA (capital) 5.506 million; Huambo 1.269 million (2015)

Sex ratio: *at birth:* 1.05 male(s)/female
0-14 years: 1.04 male(s)/female
15-24 years: 1.04 male(s)/female
25-54 years: 1.02 male(s)/female
55-64 years: 0.94 male(s)/female
65 years and over: 0.86 male(s)/female
total population: 1.02 male(s)/female (2016 est.)

Mother's mean age at first birth: 19.4 years

note: median age at first birth among women 25-29 (2015/16 est.)

Maternal mortality ratio: 477 deaths/100,000 live births (2015 est.)
country comparison to the world: 23

Infant mortality rate: *total:* 67.6 deaths/1,000 live births
male: 73.3 deaths/1,000 live births
female: 61.8 deaths/1,000 live births (2017 est.)
country comparison to the world: 12

Life expectancy at birth: *total population:* 60.2 years
male: 58.2 years
female: 62.3 years (2017 est.)
country comparison to the world: 205

Total fertility rate: 6.16 children born/woman (2017 est.)
country comparison to the world: 2

Contraceptive prevalence rate: 13.7% (2015/16)

Health expenditures: 3.3% of GDP (2014)
country comparison to the world: 178

Physicians density: 0.14 physicians/1,000 population (2009)

Drinking water source: *improved:*
urban: 75.4% of population
rural: 28.2% of population
total: 49% of population
unimproved:
urban: 24.6% of population
rural: 71.8% of population
total: 51% of population (2015 est.)

Sanitation facility access: *improved:*
urban: 88.6% of population
rural: 22.5% of population
total: 51.6% of population
unimproved:
urban: 11.4% of population
rural: 77.5% of population
total: 48.4% of population (2015 est.)

HIV/AIDS—adult prevalence rate: 1.9% (2016 est.)
country comparison to the world: 26

HIV/AIDS—people living with HIV/AIDS: 280,000 (2016 est.)
country comparison to the world: 21

HIV/AIDS—deaths: 11,000 (2016 est.)
country comparison to the world: 20

Major infectious diseases: degree of risk: very high
food or waterborne diseases: bacterial and protozoal diarrhea, hepatitis A, typhoid fever
vectorborne diseases: dengue fever, malaria
water contact disease: schistosomiasis
animal contact disease: rabies (2016)

Obesity—adult prevalence rate: 8.2% (2016)
country comparison to the world: 154

Children under the age of 5 years underweight: 19% (2016)
country comparison to the world: 45

Education expenditures: 3.5% of GDP (2010)
country comparison to the world: 127

Literacy: *definition:* age 15 and over can read and write

total population: 71.1%
male: 82%
female: 60.7% (2015 est.)

School life expectancy (primary to tertiary education): *total:* 10 years
male: 13 years
female: 8 years (2011)

GOVERNMENT

Country name: *conventional long form:* Republic of Angola
conventional short form: Angola
local long form: Republica de Angola
local short form: Angola
former: People's Republic of Angola
etymology: name derived by the Portuguese from the title "ngola" held by kings of the Ndongo (Ndongo was a kingdom in what is now northern Angola)

Government type: presidential republic

Capital: *name:* Luanda
geographic coordinates: 8 50 S, 13 13 E
time difference: UTC+1 (6 hours ahead of Washington, DC, during Standard Time)

Administrative divisions: 18 provinces (provincias, singular—provincia); Bengo, Benguela, Bie, Cabinda, Cunene, Huambo, Huila, Kwando Kubango, Kwanza Norte, Kwanza Sul, Luanda, Lunda Norte, Lunda Sul, Malanje, Moxico, Namibe, Uige, Zaire

Independence: 11 November 1975 (from Portugal)

National holiday: Independence Day, 11 November (1975)

Constitution: *history:* previous 1975, 1992; latest passed by National Assembly 21 January 2010, adopted 5 February 2010
amendments: proposed by the president of the republic or supported by at least one-third of the National Assembly membership; passage requires at least two-thirds majority vote of the Assembly subject to prior Constitutional Court review if requested by the president of the republic

Legal system: civil legal system based on Portuguese civil law; no judicial review of legislation

International law organization participation: has not submitted an ICJ jurisdiction declaration; non-party state to the ICCt

Citizenship: *citizenship by birth:* no
citizenship by descent only: at least one parent must be a citizen of Angola
dual citizenship recognized: no
residency requirement for naturalization: 10 years

Suffrage: 18 years of age; universal

Executive branch: *chief of state:* President Joao Manuel Goncalves LOURENCO (since 26 September 2017); Vice President Bornito De Sousa Baltazar DIOGO (since 26 September 2017); note—the president is both chief of state and head of government

head of government: President Joao Manuel Goncalves LOURENCO (since 26 September 2017);

Vice President Bornito De Sousa Baltazar DIOGO (since 26 September 2017)
cabinet: Council of Ministers appointed by the president
elections/appointments: president indirectly elected by the National Assembly for a 5-year term (eligible for a second consecutive or discontinuous term); last held on 23 August 2017 (next to be held in 2022) election results: Joao Manuel Goncalves LOURENCO (MPLA) elected president by the National Assembly

Legislative branch: *description:* unicameral National Assembly or Assembleia Nacional (220 seats; members directly elected in a single national constituency and in multi-seat constituencies by proportional representation vote; members serve 5-year terms)
elections: last held on 23 August 2017 (next to be held in August 2022)
election results: percent of vote by party—MPLA 61.1%, UNITA 26.7%, CASA-CE 9.5%, PRS 1.4%, FNLA .9%, other 0.5%; seats by party—MPLA 150, UNITA 51, CASA-CE 16, PRS 2, FNLA 1

Judicial branch: *highest court(s):* Supreme Court or Supremo Tribunal de Justica (consists of the court president, vice president, and a minimum of 16 judges); Constitutional Court or Tribunal Constitucional (consists of 11 judges)
judge selection and term of office: Supreme Court judges appointed by the president upon recommendation of the Supreme Judicial Council, an 18-member body chaired by the president; judge tenure NA; Constitutional Court judges—4 nominated by the president, 4 elected by National Assembly, 2 elected by Supreme National Council, 1 elected by competitive submission of curricula; judges serve single 7-year terms
subordinate courts: provincial and municipal courts

Political parties and leaders: Broad Convergence for the Salvation of Angola Electoral Coalition or CASA-CE [Abel CHIVUKUVUKU]
National Front for the Liberation of Angola or FNLA; note—party has two factions; one led by Lucas NGONDA; the other by Ngola KABANGU
National Union for the Total Independence of Angola or UNITA [Isaias SAMAKUVA] (largest opposition party)
Popular Movement for the Liberation of Angola or MPLA [Jose Eduardo DOS SANTOS] (ruling party in power since 1975)
Social Renewal Party or PRS [Benedito DANIEL]
Political pressure groups and leaders: Angolan Revolutionary Movement or ARM
Front for the Liberation of the Enclave of Cabinda—Armed Forces of Cabinda or FLEC-FAC [Emmanuel NZITA]
note: FLEC's small-scale armed struggle for the independence of Cabinda Province persists despite the signing of a peace accord with the government in August 2006; several factions of FLEC have broken off over the past 30 years, including the FLEC-PM [Rodrigues MINGAS], which was responsible for a deadly attack on the Togolese national soccer team in 2010

International organization participation: ACP, AfDB, AU, CEMAC, CPLP, FAO, G-77, IAEA, IBRD, ICAO, ICRM, IDA, IF AD, IFC, IFRCS, ILO, IMF, IMO, Interpol, IOC, IOM, IPU, ISO (correspondent), ITSO, ITU, ITUC (NGOs), MIGA, NAM, OAS (observer), OPEC, SADC, UN, UNCTAD, UNESCO, UNIDO, Union Latina, UNWTO, UPU, WCO, WFTU (NGOs), WHO, WIPO, WMO, WTO

Diplomatic representation in the US: *chief of mission:* Ambassador Agostinho Tavares da Silva NETO (since 18 November 2014)
chancery: 2100-2108 16th Street NW, Washington, DC 20009
telephone: [1] (202) 785-1156
FAX: [1] (202) 822-9049
consulate(s) general: Houston, Los Angeles, New York

Diplomatic representation from the US: *chief of mission:* Ambassador Helen Meagher LA LIME (15 May 2014)
embassy: number 32 Rua Houari Boumedienne (in the Miramar area of Luanda), Luanda, C.P. 6468
mailing address: international mail: Caixa Postal 6468, Luanda; pouch: US Embassy Luanda, US Department of State, 2550 Luanda Place, Washington, DC 20521-2550
telephone: [244] 946440977
FAX: [244] (222) 64-1000

Flag description: two equal horizontal bands of red (top) and black with a centered yellow emblem consisting of a 5-pointed star within half a cogwheel crossed by a machete (in the style of a hammer and sickle); red represents liberty; black the African continent; the symbols characterize workers and peasants

National symbol(s): Palanca Negra Gigante (giant black sable antelope); national colors: red, black, yellow

National anthem: *name:* "Angola Avante" (Forward Angola)
lyrics/music: Manuel Rui Alves MONTEIRO/Rui Alberto Vieira Dias MINGAO
note: adopted 1975

ECONOMY

Economy—overview: Angola's economy is overwhelmingly driven by its oil sector. Oil production and its supporting activities contribute about 50% of GDP, more than 70% of government revenue, and more than 90% of the country's exports; Angola is an OPEC member and subject to its direction regarding oil production levels. Diamonds contribute an additional 5% to exports. Subsistence agriculture provides the main livelihood for most of the people, but half of the country's food is still imported.

Increased oil production supported growth averaging more than 17% per year from 2004 to 2008. A postwar reconstruction boom and resettlement of displaced persons led to high rates of growth in construction and agriculture as well.

Some of the country's infrastructure is still damaged or undeveloped from the 27-year-long civil war. However, the government since 2005 has used billions of dollars in credit from China, Brazil, Portugal, Germany, Spain, and the EU to help rebuild Angola's public infrastructure. Land mines left from the war still mar the countryside, and as a result, the national military, international partners, and private Angolan firms all continue to remove them.

The global recession that started in 2008 stalled Angola's economic growth and many construction projects stopped because Luanda accrued billions in arrears to foreign construction companies when government revenue fell. Lower prices for oil and diamonds also resulted in GDP falling 0.7% in 2016. Angola formally abandoned its currency peg in 2009 but reinstituted it in April 2016 and maintains an overvalued exchange rate. In late 2016, Angola lost the last of its dollar-clearing international correspondent banking relationships, further exacerbating hard currency problems. Since 2013 the central bank has consistently spent down reserves to defend the kwanza, gradually allowing a 40% depreciation since late 2014. Consumer inflation declined from 325% in 2000 to less than 9% in 2014, before rising again to above 30% from 2015-2017.

Continued low oil prices, the depreciation of the kwanza, and slower than expected growth in non-oil GDP have reduced growth prospects, although several major international oil companies remain in Angola. Corruption, especially in the extractive sectors, is a major long-term challenge that poses an additional threat to the economy.

GDP (purchasing power parity):
$192 billion (2017 est.)
$189.2 billion (2016 est.)
$190.5 billion (2015 est.)
note: data are in 2017 dollars
country comparison to the world: 66

GDP (official exchange rate): $124 billion (2016 est.)

GDP—real growth rate: 1.5% (2017 est.)
-0.7% (2016 est.)
3% (2015 est.)
country comparison to the world: 177

GDP—per capita (PPP):
$6,800 (2017 est.)
$6,900 (2016 est.)
$7,200 (2015 est.)
note: data are in 2017 dollars
country comparison to the world: 161

Gross national saving:
3.1% of GDP (2017 est.)
3.3% of GDP (2016 est.)
-0.4% of GDP (2015 est.)
country comparison to the world: 172

GDP—composition, by end use:
household consumption: 75.6%
government consumption: 15.4%
investment in fixed capital: 9.8%
investment in inventories: 0.1%
exports of goods and services: 28.4%

imports of goods and services: -29.3% (2017 est.)

GDP—composition, by sector of origin:
agriculture: 10.2%
industry: 61.4%
services: 28.4% (2011 est.)

Agriculture—products: bananas, sugarcane, coffee, sisal, corn, cotton, cassava (manioc, tapioca), tobacco, vegetables, plantains; livestock; forest products; fish

Industries: petroleum; diamonds, iron ore, phosphates, feldspar, bauxite, uranium, and gold; cement; basic metal products; fish processing; food processing, brewing, tobacco products, sugar; textiles; ship repair

Industrial production growth rate: 1.9% (2017 est.)
country comparison to the world: 141

Labor force: 12.51 million (2017 est.)
country comparison to the world: 46

Labor force—by occupation: *agriculture:* 85%
industry and services: 15% (2003 est.)

Unemployment rate: NA%

Population below poverty line: 40.5% (2006 est.)

Household income or consumption by percentage share: *lowest 10%:* 0.6%
highest 10%: 44.7% (2000)

Budget: *revenues:* $35.59 billion
expenditures: $44.64 billion (2017 est.)
Taxes and other revenues: 28.7% of GDP (2017 est.)
country comparison to the world: 90

Budget surplus (+) or deficit (-): -7.3% of GDP (2017 est.)
country comparison to the world: 193

Public debt: 87.8% of GDP (2017 est.)
77.2% of GDP (2016 est.)
country comparison to the world: 29

Fiscal year: calendar year

Inflation rate (consumer prices): 30.9% (2017 est.)
32.4% (2016 est.)
country comparison to the world: 223

Central bank discount rate: 9% (31 December 2014)
25% (31 December 2010)
country comparison to the world: 35

Commercial bank prime lending rate: 20% (31 December 2017 est.)
15.71% (31 December 2016 est.)
country comparison to the world: 16

Stock of narrow money:
$30.04 billion (31 December 2017 est.)
$23.17 billion (31 December 2016 est.)
country comparison to the world: 63

Stock of broad money: $48.82 billion (31 December 2017 est.)
$39.28 billion (31 December 2016 est.)
country comparison to the world: 69

Stock of domestic credit: $14.51 billion (31 December 2017 est.)
$14.25 billion (31 December 2016 est.)
country comparison to the world: 95

Current account balance: -$5.922 billion (2017 est.)
-$4.904 billion (2016 est.)
country comparison to the world: 176

Exports: $33.82 billion (2017 est.)
$31.03 billion (2016 est.)
country comparison to the world: 59

Exports—commodities: crude oil, diamonds, refined petroleum products, coffee, sisal, fish and fish products, timber, cotton

Exports—partners: China 53.7%, India 7.6%, US 5.6%, South Africa 5.3%, France 4.4% (2016)

Imports: $23 billion (2017 est.)
$19.25 billion (2016 est.)
country comparison to the world: 68

Imports—commodities: machinery and electrical equipment, vehicles and spare parts; medicines, food, textiles, military goods

Imports—partners: Portugal 15.9%, US 12.5%, China 12.2%, South Africa 6.8%, Belgium 6.3%, Brazil 5.5%, UK 4.3% (2016)

Reserves of foreign exchange and gold: $18.1 billion (31 December 2017 est.)
$23.74 billion (31 December 2016 est.)
country comparison to the world: 64

Debt—external: $27.34 billion (31 December 2017 est.)
$27.14 billion (31 December 2016 est.)
country comparison to the world: 85

Stock of direct foreign investment—at home: $15.8 billion (31 December 2017 est.)
$9.16 billion (31 December 2016 est.)
country comparison to the world: 89

Stock of direct foreign investment—abroad: $23.66 billion (31 December 2017 est.)
$23.02 billion (31 December 2016 est.)
country comparison to the world: 51

Exchange rates: kwanza (AOA) per US dollar—
172.6 (2017 est.)
163.656 (2016 est.)
163.656 (2015 est.)
120.061 (2014 est.)
98.303 (2013 est.)

ENERGY

Electricity access: *population without electricity:* 15,000,000
electrification—*total population:* 30%
electrification—*urban areas:* 46%
electrification—*rural areas:* 18% (2013)

Electricity—production: 9.438 billion kWh (2015 est.)
country comparison to the world: 105

Electricity—consumption: 8.338 billion kWh (2015 est.)
country comparison to the world: 100

Electricity—exports: 0 kWh (2016 est.)
country comparison to the world: 100

Electricity—imports: 0 kWh (2016 est.)
country comparison to the world: 119

Electricity—installed generating capacity: 1.704 million kW (2015 est.)
country comparison to the world: 118

Electricity—from fossil fuels: 45.2% of total installed capacity (2015 est.)
country comparison to the world: 158

Electricity—from nuclear fuels: 0% of total installed capacity (2015 est.)
country comparison to the world: 41

Electricity—from hydroelectric plants: 54% of total installed capacity (2015 est.)
country comparison to the world: 36

Electricity—from other renewable sources: 0.9% of total installed capacity (2015 est.)
country comparison to the world: 145

Crude oil—production: 1.77 million bbl/day (2016 est.)
country comparison to the world: 14

Crude oil—exports: 1.7 million bbl/day (2014 est.)
country comparison to the world: 8

Crude oil—imports: 0 bbl/day (2014 est.)
country comparison to the world: 93

Crude oil—proved reserves: 8.273 billion bbl (1 January 2017 es)
country comparison to the world: 17

Refined petroleum products—production: 46,680 bbl/day (2014 est.)
country comparison to the world: 83

Refined petroleum products—consumption: 142,000 bbl/day (2015 est.)
country comparison to the world: 72

Refined petroleum products—exports: 23,980 bbl/day (2014 est.)
country comparison to the world: 68

Refined petroleum products—imports: 118,000 bbl/day (2014 est.)
country comparison to the world: 55

Natural gas—production: 773 million cu m (2015 est.)
country comparison to the world: 69

Natural gas—consumption: 1.094 billion cu m (2015 est.)
country comparison to the world: 97

Natural gas—exports: 500 million cu m (2014 est.)
country comparison to the world: 43

Natural gas—imports: 0 cu m (2013 est.)
country comparison to the world: 85

Natural gas—proved reserves: 308.1 billion cu m (1 January 2017 es)
country comparison to the world: 39

Carbon dioxide emissions from consumption of energy: 33 million Mt (2013 est.)
country comparison to the world: 75

COMMUNICATIONS

Telephones—fixed lines: *total subscriptions:* 304,493
subscriptions per 100 inhabitants: 2 (July 2016 est.)
country comparison to the world: 117

Telephones—mobile cellular: *total:* 13,001,124 *subscriptions per 100 inhabitants:* 64 (July 2016 est.)
country comparison to the world: 69

Telephone system: *general assessment:* limited system; state-owned telecom had monopoly for fixed lines until 2005; demand outstripped capacity, prices were high, and services poor; Telecom Namibia, through an Angolan company, became the first private licensed operator in Angola's fixed-line telephone network; by 2010, the number of fixed-line providers had expanded to five; Angola Telecom established mobile-cellular service in Luanda in 1993 and the network has been extended to larger towns; a privately owned, mobile-cellular service provider began operations in 2001
domestic: only about one fixed line per 100 persons; mobile-cellular teledensity about 64 telephones per 100 persons in 2016
international: country code—244; landing point for the SAT-3/WASC fiber-optic submarine cable that provides connectivity to Europe and Asia; satellite earth stations—29 (2016)

Broadcast media: state controls all broadcast media with nationwide reach; state-owned Televisao Popular de Angola (TPA) provides terrestrial TV service on 2 channels; a third TPA channel is available via cable and satellite; TV subscription services are available; state-owned Radio Nacional de Angola (RNA) broadcasts on 5 stations; about a half-dozen private radio stations broadcast locally (2009)

Internet country code: .ao

Internet users: *total:* 2,622,403
percent of population: 13.0% (July 2016 est.)
country comparison to the world: 81

TRANSPORTATION

National air transport system: *number of registered air carriers:* 10

inventory of registered aircraft operated by air carriers: 55
annual passenger traffic on registered air carriers: 1,244,491
annual freight traffic on registered air carriers: 46.043 million mt-km (2015)
Civil aircraft registration country code prefix: D2 (2016)

Airports: 176 (2013)
country comparison to the world: 32

Airports—with paved runways: *total:* 31
over 3,047 m: 7
2,438 to 3,047 m: 8
1,524 to 2,437 m: 12
914 to 1,523 m: 4 (2017)

Airports—with unpaved runways: *total:* 145
over 3,047 m: 2
2,438 to 3,047 m: 3
1,524 to 2,437 m: 31
914 to 1,523 m: 66
under 914 m: 43 (2013)

Heliports: 1 (2013)

Pipelines: gas 352 km; liquid petroleum gas 85 km; oil 1,065 km; oil/gas/water 5 km (2013)

Railways: *total:* 2,852 km
narrow gauge: 2,729 km 1.067-m gauge; 123 km 0.600-m gauge (2014)
country comparison to the world: 60
Roadways: total: 51,429 km
paved: 5,349 km
unpaved: 46,080 km (2001)
country comparison to the world: 77

Waterways: 1,300 km (2011)
country comparison to the world: 54

Merchant marine: *total:* 55
by type: general cargo 14, oil tanker 9, other 32 (2017)
country comparison to the world: 110

Ports and terminals: *major seaport(s):* Cabinda, Lobito, Luanda, Namibe

LNG terminal(s) (export): Angola Soyo

MILITARY AND SECURITY

Military expenditures:
2.95% of GDP (2016)
3.52% of GDP (2015)
5.4% of GDP (2014)
4.88% of GDP (2013)
3.59% of GDP (2012)
country comparison to the world: 13

Military branches: Angolan Armed Forces (Forcas Armadas Angolanas, FAA): Army, Navy (Marinha de Guerra Angola, MGA), Angolan National Air Force (Forca Aerea Nacional Angolana, FANA; under operational control of the Army) (2012)

Military service age and obligation: 20-45 years of age for compulsory male and 18-45 years for voluntary male military service (registration at age 18 is mandatory); 20-45 years of age for voluntary female service; 2-year conscript service obligation; Angolan citizenship required; the Navy (MGA) is entirely staffed with volunteers (2013)

TRANSNATIONAL ISSUES

Disputes—international: Democratic Republic of Congo accuses Angola of shifting monuments

Refugees and internally displaced persons: *refugees (country of origin):* 48,000 (Democratic Republic of the Congo) (2017)

Illicit drugs: used as a transshipment point for cocaine destined for Western Europe and other African states, particularly South Africa

ANGUILLA

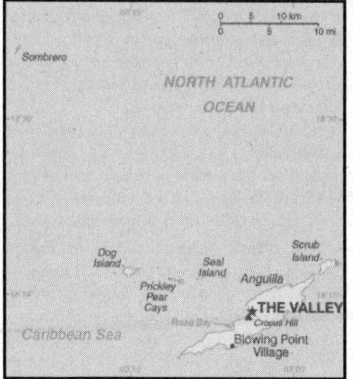

INTRODUCTION

Background: Colonized by English settlers from Saint Kitts in 1650, Anguilla was administered by Great Britain until the early 19th century, when the island—against the wishes of the inhabitants—was incorporated into a single British dependency along with Saint Kitts and Nevis. Several attempts at separation failed. In 1971, two years after a revolt, Anguilla was finally allowed to secede; this arrangement was formally recognized in 1980, with Anguilla becoming a separate British dependency. On 7 September 2017, the island suffered extensive damage from Hurricane Irma, particularly to communications and residential and business infrastructure.

GEOGRAPHY

Location: Caribbean, islands between the Caribbean Sea and North Atlantic Ocean, east of Puerto Rico

Geographic coordinates: 18 15 N, 63 10 W

Map references: Central America and the Caribbean

Area: *total:* 91 sq km
land: 91 sq km
water: 0 sq km
country comparison to the world: 227

Area—comparative: about one-half the size of Washington, DC

Land boundaries: 0 km

Coastline: 61 km

Maritime claims:
territorial sea: 3 nm
exclusive fishing zone: 200 nm

Climate: tropical; moderated by northeast trade winds

Terrain: flat and low-lying island of coral and limestone

Elevation: mean elevation: NA

elevation extremes: lowest point: Caribbean Sea 0 m
highest point: Crocus Hill 73 m

Natural resources: salt, fish, lobster

Land use: *agricultural land:* 0%
arable land 0%;
permanent crops 0%;
permanent pasture 0%
forest: 61.1%
other: 38.9% (mostly rock with some commercial salt ponds) (2011 est.)
Irrigated land: 0 sq km (2012)

Population—distribution: most of the population is concentrated in The Valley in the center of the island; settlement is fairly uniform in the southwest, but rather sparse in the northeast

Natural hazards: frequent hurricanes and other tropical storms (July to October)

Environment—current issues: supplies of potable water sometimes cannot meet increasing demand largely because of poor distribution system

Geography—note: the most northerly of the Leeward Islands in the Lesser Antilles

PEOPLE AND SOCIETY

Population: 17,087 (July 2017 est.)
country comparison to the world: 220

Nationality: *noun:* Anguillan(s)
adjective: Anguillan

Ethnic groups: African/black 85.3%, hispanic 4.9%, mixed 3.8%, white 3.2%, East Indian/Indian 1%, other 1.6%, unspecified 0.3% (2011 est.)

Languages: English (official)

Religions: Protestant 73.2% (includes Anglican 22.7%, Methodist 19.4%, Pentecostal 10.5%, Seventh Day Adventist 8.3%, Baptist 7.1%, Church of God 4.9%, Presbytarian 0.2%, Brethren 0.1%), Roman Catholic 6.8%, Jehovah's Witness 1.1%, other Christian 10.9%, other 3.2%, unspecified 0.3%, none 4.5% (2011 est.)

Age structure: *0-14 years:* 22.21% (male 1,936/female 1,859)
15-24 years: 14.08% (male 1,205/female 1,200)
25-54 years: 43.82% (male 3,363/female 4,124)
55-64 years: 11.06% (male 880/female 1,010)
65 years and over: 8.84% (male 750/female 760) (2017 est.)

Median age: *total:* 34.8 years
male: 32.9 years
female: 36.7 years (2017 est.)
country comparison to the world: 80

Population growth rate: 1.97% (2017 est.)
country comparison to the world: 48

Birth rate: 12.5 births/1,000 population (2017 est.)
country comparison to the world: 157

Death rate: 4.6 deaths/1,000 population (2017 est.)
country comparison to the world: 204

Net migration rate: 11.7 migrant(s)/1,000 population (2017 est.)
country comparison to the world: 7

Population distribution: most of the population is concentrated in The Valley in the center of the island; settlmeement is fairly uniform in the southwest, but rather sparce in the northeast

Urbanization: *urban population:* 100% of total population (2017)
rate of urbanization: 0.88% annual rate of change (2015-20 est.)

Major urban areas—population: THE VALLEY (capital) 1,000 (2014)

Sex ratio: *at birth:* 1.04 male(s)/female
0-14 years: 1.04 male(s)/female
15-24 years: 1 male(s)/female
25-54 years: 0.82 male(s)/female
55-64 years: 0.9 male(s)/female
65 years and over: 0.98 male(s)/female
total population: 0.91 male(s)/female (2016 est.)

Infant mortality rate: *total:* 3.3 deaths/1,000 live births
male: 3.7 deaths/1,000 live births
female: 2.9 deaths/1,000 live births (2017 est.)
country comparison to the world: 211

Life expectancy at birth: *total population:* 81.5 years
male: 78.9 years
female: 84.2 years (2017 est.)
country comparison to the world: 24

Total fertility rate: 1.74 children born/woman (2017 est.)
country comparison to the world: 165

Drinking water source: *improved:*
urban: 94.6% of population
rural: NA
total: 94.6% of population
unimproved:
urban: 5.4% of population
rural: NA
total: 5.4% of population (2015 est.)

Sanitation facility access: *improved:*
urban: 97.9% of population
rural: NA
total: 97.9% of population
unimproved:
urban: 2.1% of population
rural: NA
total: 2.1% of population (2015 est.)

HIV/AIDS—adult prevalence rate: NA

HIV/AIDS—people living with HIV/AIDS: NA

HIV/AIDS—deaths: NA

Major infectious diseases: *note:* active local transmission of Zika virus by Aedes species mosquitoes has been identified in this country (as of August 2016); it poses an important risk (a large number of cases possible) among US citizens if bitten by an infective mosquito; other less common ways to get Zika are through sex, via blood transfusion, or during pregnancy, in which the pregnant woman passes Zika virus to her fetus (2016)

Education expenditures: 2.8% of GDP (2008)
country comparison to the world: 146

GOVERNMENT

Country name: *conventional long form:* none
conventional short form: Anguilla
etymology: the name Anguilla means "eel" in various Romance languages (Spanish, Italian, Portuguese, French) and likely derives from the island's lengthy shape

Dependency status: overseas territory of the UK

Government type: parliamentary democracy (House of Assembly); self-governing overseas territory of the UK

Capital: *name:* The Valley
geographic coordinates: 18 13 N, 63 03 W
time difference: UTC-4 (1 hour ahead of Washington, DC, during Standard Time)

Administrative divisions: none (overseas territory of the UK)

Independence: none (overseas territory of the UK)

National holiday: Anguilla Day, 30 May (1967)

Constitution: several previous; latest 1 April 1982; amended 1990 (2016)

Legal system: common law based on the English model

Citizenship: see United Kingdom

Suffrage: 18 years of age; universal

Executive branch: *chief of state:* Queen ELIZABETH II (since 6 February 1952); represented by Governor Christina SCOTT (since 23 July 2013)

head of government: Chief Minister Hubert HUGHES (since 16 February 2010)
cabinet: Executive Council appointed by the governor from among elected members of the House of Assembly
elections/appointments: the monarchy is hereditary; governor appointed by the monarch; following legislative elections, the leader of the majority party or majority coalition usually appointed chief minister by the governor

Legislative branch: *description:* unicameral House of Assembly (11 seats; 7 members directly elected in single-seat constituencies by simple majority vote, 2 appointed by the governor, and 2 ex officio members—the attorney general and deputy governor; members serve five-year terms)
elections: last held on 22 April 2015 (next to be held in 2020)
election results: percent of vote by party—AUF 54.4%, AUM 38.3%, DOVE 1.4%, independent 5.9%; seats by party—AUF 6, independent 1

Judicial branch: *highest court(s):* the Eastern Caribbean Supreme Court (ECSC) is the superior court of the Organization of Eastern Caribbean States; the ECSC—headquartered on St. Lucia—consists of the Court of Appeal—headed by the chief justice and 4 judges—and the High Court with 18 judges; the Court of Appeal is itinerant,

travelling to member states on a schedule to hear appeals from the High Court and subordinate courts; High Court judges reside in the member states, though none on Anguilla
judge selection and term of office: Eastern Caribbean Supreme Court chief justice appointed by Her Majesty, Queen ELIZABETH II; other justices and judges appointed by the Judicial and Legal Services Commission; Court of Appeal justices appointed for life with mandatory retirement at age 65; High Court judges appointed for life with mandatory retirement at age 62
subordinate courts: Magistrate's Court; Juvenile Court

Political parties and leaders: Anguilla Democratic Party or ADP
Anguilla National Alliance or ANA
Anguilla United Front or AUF [Victor BANKS] (an alliance ADP and ANA)
Anguilla United Movement or AUM [Dr. Ellis WEBSTER]
Democracy, Opportunity, Vision, and Empowerment Party or DOVE [Sutcliffe HODGE]

International organization participation: Caricom (associate), CDB, Interpol (subbureau), OECS, UNESCO (associate), UPU

Diplomatic representation in the US: none (overseas territory of the UK)

Diplomatic representation from the US: none (overseas territory of the UK)

Flag description: blue, with the flag of the UK in the upper hoist-side quadrant and the Anguillan coat of arms centered in the outer half of the flag; the coat of arms depicts three orange dolphins in an interlocking circular design on a white background with a turquoise-blue field below; the white in the background represents peace; the blue base symbolizes the surrounding sea, as well as faith, youth, and hope; the three dolphins stand for endurance, unity, and strength

National symbol(s): dolphin

National anthem: name: "God Bless Anguilla"
lyrics/music: Alex RICHARDSON
note: local anthem adopted 1981; as a territory of the United Kingdom, "God Save the Queen" is official (see United Kingdom)

ECONOMY

Economy—overview: Anguilla has few natural resources, and the economy depends heavily on luxury tourism, offshore banking, lobster fishing, and remittances from emigrants. Increased activity in the tourism industry has spurred the growth of the construction sector contributing to economic growth. Anguillan officials have put substantial effort into developing the offshore financial sector, which is small but growing. In the medium term, prospects for the economy will depend largely on the tourism sector and, therefore, on revived income growth in the industrialized nations as well as on favorable weather conditions.

GDP (purchasing power parity):
$175.4 million (2009 est.)
$191.7 million (2008 est.)

$108.9 million (2004 est.)
country comparison to the world: 223

GDP (official exchange rate): $175.4 million (2009 est.)

GDP—real growth rate: -8.5% (2009 est.)
country comparison to the world: 221

GDP—per capita (PPP): $12,200 (2008 est.)
country comparison to the world: 129

GDP—composition, by end use:
household consumption: 71.3%
government consumption: 14.5%
investment in fixed capital: 19.5%
investment in inventories: 0%
exports of goods and services: 42.5%
imports of goods and services: -47.9% (2017 est.)

GDP—composition, by sector of origin:
agriculture: 2.4%
industry: 21.3%
services: 76.3% (2017 est.)

Agriculture—products: small quantities of tobacco, vegetables; cattle raising

Industries: tourism, boat building, offshore financial services

Industrial production growth rate: 2% (2017 est.)
country comparison to the world: 138

Labor force: 6,049 (2001)
country comparison to the world: 220

Labor force—by occupation: *agriculture/fishing/forestry/mining:* 4%
manufacturing: 3%
construction: 18%
transportation and utilities: 10%
commerce: 36%
services: 29% (2000 est.)

Unemployment rate: 8% (2002)
country comparison to the world: 106

Population below poverty line: 23% (2002 est.)

Household income or consumption by percentage share: lowest 10%: NA%
highest 10%: NA%

Budget: *revenues:* $91.15 million
expenditures: $90.96 million (2017 est.)
Taxes and other revenues: 52% of GDP (2017 est.)
country comparison to the world: 12

Budget surplus (+) or deficit (-): 0.1% of GDP (2017 est.)
country comparison to the world: 31

Public debt: 20.1% of GDP (2015 est.)
20.8% of GDP (2014 est.)
country comparison to the world: 186

Fiscal year: 1 April–31 March

Inflation rate (consumer prices):
2.1% (2017 est.)
-0.6% (2016 est.)
country comparison to the world: 101

Central bank discount rate: 6.5% (31 December 2010)
6.5% (31 December 2009)
country comparison to the world: 55

Commercial bank prime lending rate: 9.1% (31 December 2017 est.)
9.2% (31 December 2016 est.)
country comparison to the world: 91

Stock of narrow money:
$25.06 million (31 December 2017 est.)
$23.74 million (31 December 2016 est.)
country comparison to the world: 192

Stock of broad money: $378.1 million (31 December 2017 est.)
$374.4 million (31 December 2016 est.)
country comparison to the world: 189

Stock of domestic credit: $207.5 million (31 December 2017 est.)
$209.1 million (31 December 2016 est.)
country comparison to the world: 183

Current account balance: -$23.2 million (2017 est.)
-$25.3 million (2016 est.)
country comparison to the world: 66

Exports: $4.2 million (2017 est.)
$3.9 million (2016 est.)
country comparison to the world: 218

Exports—commodities: lobster, fish, livestock, salt, concrete blocks, rum

Imports: $111.1 million (2017 est.)
$104 million (2016 est.)
country comparison to the world: 211

Imports—commodities: fuels, foodstuffs, manufactures, chemicals, trucks, textiles

Debt—external:
$41.04 million (31 December 2013)
$8.8 million (1998)
country comparison to the world: 196

Exchange rates: East Caribbean dollars (XCD) per US dollar—
2.7 (2017 est.)
2.7 (2016 est.)
2.7 (2015 est.)
2.7 (2014 est.)
2.7 (2013 est.)

COMMUNICATIONS

Telephones—fixed lines: *total subscriptions:* 6,000
subscriptions per 100 inhabitants: 37 (July 2016 est.)
country comparison to the world: 206

Telephones—mobile cellular: *total:* 26,000
subscriptions per 100 inhabitants: 158 (July 2016 est.)
country comparison to the world: 209

Telephone system: *general assessment:* modern internal telephone system
domestic: fixed-line teledensity is about 35 per 100 persons; mobile-cellular teledensity is roughly 160 per 100 persons
international: country code—1-264; landing point for the East Caribbean Fiber System submarine cable with links to 13 other islands in the eastern Caribbean extending from the British Virgin Islands to Trinidad; microwave radio relay to island of Saint Martin/Sint Maarten (2015)

Broadcast media: 1 private TV station; multi-channel cable TV subscription services are available; about 10 radio stations, one of which is government-owned (2009)

Internet country code: .ai

Internet users: *total:* 13,665
percent of population: 81.6% (July 2016 est.)
country comparison to the world: 208

TRANSPORTATION

National air transport system: *number of registered air carriers:* 2 inventory of registered aircraft operated by air carriers: 3 (2015)

Civil aircraft registration country code prefix: VP-A (2016)

Airports: 2 (2013)
country comparison to the world: 197

Airports—with paved runways: *total:* 1
1,524 to 2,437 m: 1 (2017)

Airports—with unpaved runways: *total:* 1
under 914 m: 1 (2013)

Roadways: *total:* 175 km
paved: 82 km
unpaved: 93 km (2004)
country comparison to the world: 211

Merchant marine: *total:* 1

by type: other 1 (2017)
country comparison to the world: 169

Ports and terminals: *major seaport(s):* Blowing Point, Road Bay

MILITARY AND SECURITY

Military—note: defense is the responsibility of the UK

TRANSNATIONAL ISSUES

Disputes—international: none

Illicit drugs: transshipment point for South American narcotics destined for the US and Europe

ANTARCTICA

INTRODUCTION

Background: Speculation over the existence of a "southern land" was not confirmed until the early 1820s when British and American commercial operators and British and Russian national expeditions began exploring the Antarctic Peninsula region and other areas south of the Antarctic Circle. Not until 1840 was it established that Antarctica was indeed a continent and not merely a group of islands or an area of ocean. Several exploration "firsts" were achieved in the early 20th century, but generally the area saw little human activity. Following World War II, however, the continent experienced an upsurge in scientific research. A number of countries have set up a range of year-round and seasonal stations, camps, and refuges to support scientific research in Antarctica. Seven have made territorial claims, but not all countries recognize these claims. In order to form a legal framework for the activities of nations on the continent, an Antarctic Treaty was negotiated that neither denies nor gives recognition to existing territorial claims; signed in 1959, it entered into force in 1961.

GEOGRAPHY

Location: continent mostly south of the Antarctic Circle

Geographic coordinates: 90 00 S, 0 00 E

Map references: Antarctic Region

Area: *total:* 14 million sq km
land: 14 million sq km (280,000 sq km ice-free, 13.72 million sq km ice-covered) (est.)
note: fifth-largest continent, following Asia, Africa, North America, and South America, but larger than Australia and the subcontinent of Europe
country comparison to the world: 2

Area—comparative: slightly less than 1.5 times the size of the US

Land boundaries: 0 km
note: see entry on Disputes—international

Coastline: 17,968 km

Maritime claims: Australia, Chile, and Argentina claim Exclusive Economic Zone (EEZ) rights or similar over 200 nm extensions seaward from their continental claims, but like the claims themselves, these zones are not accepted by other countries; 22 of 29 Antarctic consultative nations have made no claims to Antarctic territory (although Russia and the US have reserved the right to do so) and do not recognize the claims of the other nations; also see the Disputes—international entry

Climate: the coldest, windiest, and driest continent on Earth; severe low temperatures vary with latitude, elevation, and distance from the ocean; East Antarctica is colder than West Antarctica because of its higher elevation; Antarctic Peninsula has the most moderate climate; higher temperatures occur in January along the coast and average slightly below freezing; summers characterized by continuous daylight, while winters bring continous darkness; persistent high pressure over the interior brings dry, subsiding air that results in very little cloud cover

Terrain: about 98% thick continental ice sheet and 2% barren rock, with average elevations between 2,000 and 4,000 m; mountain ranges up to nearly 5,000 m; ice-free coastal areas include parts of southern Victoria Land, Wilkes Land, the Antarctic Peninsula area, and parts of Ross Island on McMurdo Sound; glaciers form ice shelves along

about half of the coastline, and floating ice shelves constitute 11% of the area of the continent

Elevation: *mean elevation:* 2,300 m

elevation extremes: *lowest point:* Bentley Subglacial Trench -2,540 m
highest point: Vinson Massif 4,892 m
note: the lowest known land point in Antarctica is hidden in the Bentley Subglacial Trench; at its surface is the deepest ice yet discovered and the world's lowest elevation not under seawater

Natural resources: iron ore, chromium, copper, gold, nickel, platinum and other minerals, and coal and hydrocarbons have been found in small noncommercial quantities; none presently exploited; krill, finfish, and crab have been taken by commercial fisheries

Land use: *agricultural land:* 0%
forest: 0%
other: 100% (ice 98%, barren rock 2%) (2015 est.)

Natural hazards: katabatic (gravity-driven) winds blow coastward from the high interior; frequent blizzards form near the foot of the plateau; cyclonic storms form over the ocean and move clockwise along the coast; volcanism on Deception Island and isolated areas of West Antarctica; other seismic activity rare and weak; large icebergs may calve from ice shelf

Environment—current issues: the discovery of a large Antarctic ozone hole in the earth's stratosphere (the ozone layer)—first announced in 1985—spurred the signing of the Montreal Protocol in 1987, an international agreement phasing out the use of ozone-depleting chemicals; the ozone layer prevents most harmful wavelengths of ultra-violet (UV) light from passing through the earth's atmosphere; ozone depletion has been shown to harm a variety of Antarctic marine plants and animals (plankton); in 2002, significant areas of ice shelves disintegrated in response to regional warming; in 2016, a gradual trend toward "healing" of the ozone hole was reported

Geography—note: the coldest, windiest, highest (on average), and driest continent; during summer, more solar radiation reaches the surface at the South Pole than is received at the Equator in an equivalent period; mostly uninhabitable, 98% of the land area is covered by the Antarctic ice sheet, the largest single mass of ice on earth

PEOPLE AND SOCIETY

Population: no indigenous inhabitants, but there are both permanent and summer-only staffed research stations
note: 53 countries have signed the 1959 Antarctic Treaty; 30 of those operate through their National Antarctic Program a number of seasonal-only (summer) and year-round research stations on the continent and its nearby islands south of 60 degrees south latitude (the region covered by the Antarctic Treaty); the population engaging in and supporting science or managing and protecting the Antarctic region varies from approximately 4,400 in summer to 1,100 in winter; in addition, approximately 1,000 personnel, including ship's crew and scientists doing onboard research, are present in the waters of the treaty region peak summer (December-February) population—4,490 total; Argentina 667, Australia 200, Australia and Romania jointly 13, Belgium 20, Brazil 40, Bulgaria 18, Chile 359, China 90, Czech Republic 20, Ecuador 26, Finland 20, France 125, France and Italy jointly 60, Germany 90, India 65, Italy 102, Japan 125, South Korea 70, NZ 85, Norway 44, Peru 28, Poland 40, Russia 429, South Africa 80, Spain 50, Sweden 20, Ukraine 24, UK 217, US 1,293, Uruguay 70 (2008-09) winter (June-August) station population—1,106 total; Argentina 176, Australia 62, Brazil 12, Chile 114, China 29, France 26, France and Italy jointly 13, Germany 9, India 25, Japan 40, South Korea 18, NZ 10, Norway 7, Poland 12, Russia 148, South Africa 10, Ukraine 12, UK 37, US 337, Uruguay 9 (2009); research stations operated within the Antarctic Treaty area (south of 60 degrees south latitude) by National Antarctic Programs year-round stations—approximately 40 total; Argentina 6, Australia 3, Brazil 1, Chile 6, China 2, France 1, France and Italy jointly 1, Germany 1, India 1, Japan 1, South Korea 1, NZ 1, Norway 1, Poland 1, Russia 5, South Africa 1, Ukraine 1, UK 2, US 3, Uruguay 1 (2009) a range of seasonal-only (summer) stations, camps, and refuges—Argentina, Australia, Belarus, Belgium, Bulgaria, Brazil, Chile, China, Czech Republic, Ecuador, Finland, France, Germany, India, Italy, Japan, South Korea, New Zealand, Norway, Peru, Poland, Russia, South Africa, Spain, Sweden, Ukraine, UK, US, and Uruguay (2008-09) in addition, during the austral summer some nations have numerous occupied locations such as tent camps, summer-long temporary facilities, and mobile traverses in support of research (May 2009 est.)

GOVERNMENT

Country name: *conventional long form:* none
conventional short form: Antarctica
etymology: name derived from two Greek words meaning "opposite to the Arctic" or "opposite to the north"

Government type: Antarctic Treaty Summary—the Antarctic region is governed by a system

known as the Antarctic Treaty System; the system includes: 1. the Antarctic Treaty, signed on 1 December 1959 and entered into force on 23 June 1961, which establishes the legal framework for the management of Antarctica, 2. Recommendations and Measures adopted at meetings of Antarctic Treaty countries, 3. The Convention for the Conservation of Antarctic Seals (1972), 4. The Convention for the Conservation of Antarctic Marine Living Resources (1980), and 5. The Protocol on Environmental Protection to the Antarctic Treaty (1991); the 40th Antarctic Treaty Consultative Meeting was held 22 May-1 June 2017 in Beijing, China; at these annual meetings, decisions are made by consensus (not by vote) of all consultative member nations; by January 2016 there were 53 treaty member nations: 29 consultative and 24 non-consultative; consultative (decision-making) members include the seven nations that claim portions of Antarctica as national territory (some claims overlap) and 46 non-claimant nations; the US and Russia have reserved the right to make claims; the US does not recognize the claims of others; Antarctica is administered through meetings of the consultative member nations; decisions from these meetings are carried out by these member nations (with respect to their own nationals and operations) in accordance with their own national laws; the years in parentheses indicate when a consultative member-nation acceded to the Treaty and when it was accepted as a consultative member, while no date indicates the country was an original 1959 treaty signatory; claimant nations are—Argentina, Australia, Chile, France, NZ, Norway, and the UK; nonclaimant consultative nations are—Belgium, Brazil (1975/1983), Bulgaria (1978/1998), China (1983/1985), Czech Republic (1962/2017), Ecuador (1987/1990), Finland (1984/1989), Germany (1979/1981), India (1983/1983), Italy (1981/1987), Japan, South Korea (1986/1989), Netherlands (1967/1990), Peru (1981/1989), Poland (1961/1977), Russia, South Africa, Spain (1982/1988), Sweden (1984/1988), Ukraine (1992/2004), Uruguay (1980/1985), and the US; non-consultative members, with year of accession in parentheses, are—Austria (1987), Belarus (2006), Canada (1988), Colombia (1989), Cuba (1984), Denmark (1965), Estonia (2001), Greece (1987), Guatemala (1991), Hungary (1984), Iceland (2015), Kazakhstan (2015), North Korea (1987), Malaysia (2011), Monaco (2008), Mongolia (2015), Pakistan (2012), Papua New Guinea (1981), Portugal (2010), Romania (1971), Slovakia (1962/1993), Switzerland (1990), Turkey (1996), and Venezuela (1999); note—Czechoslovakia acceded to the Treaty in 1962 and separated into the Czech Republic and Slovakia in 1993; Article 1—area to be used for peaceful purposes only; military activity, such as weapons testing, is prohibited, but military personnel and equipment may be used for scientific research or any other peaceful purpose; Article 2—freedom of scientific investigation and cooperation shall continue; Article 3—free exchange of information and personnel, cooperation with the UN and other international

agencies; Article 4—does not recognize, dispute, or establish territorial claims and no new claims shall be asserted while the treaty is in force; Article 5—prohibits nuclear explosions or disposal of radioactive wastes; Article 6—includes under the treaty all land and ice shelves south of 60 degrees 00 minutes south and reserves high seas rights; Article 7—treaty-state observers have free access, including aerial observation, to any area and may inspect all stations, installations, and equipment; advance notice of all expeditions and of the introduction of military personnel must be given; Article 8—allows for jurisdiction over observers and scientists by their own states; Article 9—frequent consultative meetings take place among member nations; Article 10—treaty states will discourage activities by any country in Antarctica that are contrary to the treaty; Article 11—disputes to be settled peacefully by the parties concerned or, ultimately, by the ICJ; Articles 12, 13, 14—deal with upholding, interpreting, and amending the treaty among involved nations; other agreements—some 200 recommendations adopted at treaty consultative meetings and ratified by governments; a mineral resources agreement was signed in 1988 but remains unratified; the Protocol on Environmental Protection to the Antarctic Treaty was signed 4 October 1991 and entered into force 14 January 1998; this agreement provides for the protection of the Antarctic environment through six specific annexes: 1) environmental impact assessment, 2) conservation of Antarctic fauna and flora, 3) waste disposal and waste management, 4) prevention of marine pollution, 5) area protection and management and 6) liability arising from environmental emergencies; it prohibits all activities relating to mineral resources except scientific research; a permanent Antarctic Treaty Secretariat was established in 2004 in Buenos Aires, Argentina

Legal system: Antarctica is administered through annual meetings—known as Antarctic Treaty Consultative Meetings—which include consultative member nations, non-consultative member nations, observer organizations, and expert organizations; decisions from these meetings are carried out by these member nations (with respect to their own nationals and operations) in accordance with their own national laws; more generally, access to the Antarctic Treaty area, that is to all areas between 60 and 90 degrees south latitude, is subject to a number of relevant legal instruments and authorization procedures adopted by the states party to the Antarctic Treaty; note—US law, including certain criminal offenses by or against US nationals, such as murder, may apply extraterritorially; some US laws directly apply to Antarctica; for example, the Antarctic Conservation Act, 16 U.S.C. section 2401 et seq., provides civil and criminal penalties for the following activities unless authorized by regulation of statute: the taking of native mammals or birds; the introduction of nonindigenous plants and animals; entry into specially protected areas; the discharge or disposal of pollutants; and the importation into the US of certain items from Antarctica; violation of the Antarctic Conservation Act carries penalties of up to $10,000 in fines and one year in prison; the National Science Foundation and Department of Justice share enforcement responsibilities; Public Law 95-541, the US Antarctic Conservation Act of 1978, as amended in 1996, requires expeditions from the US to Antarctica to notify, in advance, the Office of Oceans, Room 5805, Department of State, Washington, DC 20520, which reports such plans to other nations as required by the Antarctic Treaty; for more information, contact Permit Office, Office of Polar Programs, National Science Foundation, Arlington, Virginia 22230; telephone: (703) 292-8030, or visit its website at www.nsf.gov

ECONOMY

Economy—overview: Scientific undertakings rather than commercial pursuits are the predominant human activity in Antarctica. Offshore fishing and tourism, both based abroad, account for Antarctica's limited economic activity. Antarctic fisheries, targeting three main species—Patagonian and Antarctic toothfish (Dissostichus eleginoides and D. mawsoni), mackerel icefish (Champsocephalus gunnari), and krill (Euphausia superba)—reported landing 295,000 metric tons in 2013-14 (estimated fishing is from the area covered by the Convention on the Conservation of Antarctic Marine Living Resources (CCAMLR), which extends slightly beyond the Antarctic Treaty area). Unregulated fishing, particularly of Patagonian toothfish (also known as Chilean sea bass), is an ongoing problem. The CCAMLR determines the recommended catch limits for marine species. A total of 36,702 tourists visited the Antarctic Treaty area in the 2014-15 Antarctic summer, slightly lower than the 37,405 visitors in 2013-14. These estimates were provided to the Antarctic Treaty by the International Association of Antarctica Tour Operators (IAATO) and do not include passengers on overflights. Nearly all of them were passengers on commercial

(nongovernmental) ships and several yachts that make trips during the summer.

COMMUNICATIONS

Telephone system: *general assessment:* local systems at some research stations
domestic: commercial cellular networks operating in a small number of locations
international: country code—none allocated; via satellite (including mobile Inmarsat and Iridium systems) to and from all research stations, ships, aircraft, and most field parties (2015)

Internet country code: .aq

Internet users: *total:* 4,400
percent of population: 100% (July 2016 est.)

TRANSPORTATION

Airports: 23 (2013)
country comparison to the world: 134

Airports—with unpaved runways: *total:* 23
over 3,047 m: 3
2,438 to 3,047 m: 5
1,524 to 2,437 m: 1
914 to 1,523 m: 8
under 914 m: 6 (2013)

Heliports: 53

note: all year-round and seasonal stations operated by National Antarctic Programs stations have some kind of helicopter landing facilities, prepared (helipads) or unprepared (2012)

Ports and terminals: McMurdo Station; most coastal stations have sparse and intermittent offshore anchorages; a few stations have basic wharf facilities

Transportation—note: US coastal stations include McMurdo (77 51 S, 166 40 E) and Palmer (64 43 S, 64 03 W); government use only except by permit (see Permit Office under "Legal System"); all ships at port are subject to inspection in accordance with Article 7, Antarctic Treaty; relevant legal instruments and authorization procedures

adopted by the states parties to the Antarctic Treaty regulating access to the Antarctic Treaty area to all areas between 60 and 90 degrees of latitude south have to be complied with (see "Legal System"); The Hydrographic Commission on Antarctica (HCA), a commission of the International Hydrographic Organization (IHO), is responsible for hydrographic surveying and nautical charting matters in Antarctic Treaty area; it coordinates and facilitates provision of accurate and appropriate charts and other aids to navigation in support of safety of navigation in region; membership of HCA is open to any IHO Member State whose government has acceded to the Antarctic Treaty and which contributes resources or data to IHO Chart coverage of the area

MILITARY AND SECURITY

Military—note: the Antarctic Treaty prohibits any measures of a military nature, such as the establishment of military bases and fortifications, the carrying out of military maneuvers, or the testing of any type of weapon; it permits the use of military personnel or equipment for scientific research or for any other peaceful purposes

TRANSNATIONAL ISSUES

Disputes—international: the Antarctic Treaty freezes, and most states do not recognize, the land and maritime territorial claims made by Argentina, Australia, Chile, France, New Zealand, Norway, and the UK (some overlapping) for three-fourths of the continent; the US and Russia reserve the right to make claims; no formal claims have been made in the sector between 90 degrees west and 150 degrees west; the International Whaling Commission created a sanctuary around the entire continent to deter catches by countries claiming to conduct scientific whaling; Australia has established a similar preserve in the waters around its territorial claim.

ANTIGUA AND BARBUDA

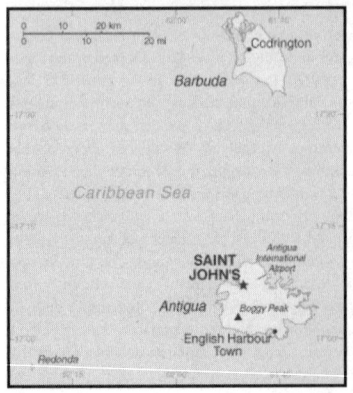

INTRODUCTION

Background: The Siboney were the first people to inhabit the islands of Antigua and Barbuda in 2400 B.C., but Arawak Indians populated the islands when COLUMBUS landed on his second voyage in 1493. Early Spanish and French settlements were succeeded by an English colony in 1667. Slavery, established to run the sugar plantations on Antigua, was abolished in 1834. The islands became an independent state within the British Commonwealth of Nations in 1981. On 6 September 2017, Hurricane Irma passed over the island of Barbuda devastating the island and forcing the evacuation of the population to Antigua. Almost all the structures on Barbuda were

destroyed and the vegetation stripped, but Antigua was spared the worst.

GEOGRAPHY

Location: Caribbean, islands between the Caribbean Sea and the North Atlantic Ocean, east-southeast of Puerto Rico

Geographic coordinates: 17 03 N, 61 48 W

Map references: Central America and the Caribbean

Area: *total:* 442.6 sq km (Antigua 280 sq km; Barbuda 161 sq km)
land: 442.6 sq km
water: 0 sq km
note: includes Redonda, 1.6 sq km
country comparison to the world: 201

Area—comparative: 2.5 times the size of Washington, DC

Land boundaries: 0 km

Coastline: 153 km

Maritime claims:
territorial sea: 12 nm
contiguous zone: 24 nm
exclusive economic zone: 200 nm
continental shelf: 200 nm or to the edge of the continental margin

Climate: tropical maritime; little seasonal temperature variation

Terrain: mostly low-lying limestone and coral islands, with some higher volcanic areas

Elevation: *mean elevation:* NA
elevation extremes: lowest point: Caribbean Sea 0 m
highest point: Mount Obama 402 m

Natural resources: NEGL; pleasant climate fosters tourism

Land use: *agricultural land:* 20.5%
arable land 9.1%;
permanent crops 2.3%;
permanent pasture 9.1%
forest: 22.3%
other: 57.2% (2011 est.)
Irrigated land: 1.3 sq km (2012)

Population—distribution: the island of Antigua is home to approximately 97% of the population; nearly the entire population of Barbuda lives in Codrington

Natural hazards: hurricanes and tropical storms (July to October); periodic droughts

Environment—current issues: water management—a major concern because of limited natural freshwater resources—is further hampered by the clearing of trees to increase crop production, causing rainfall to run off quickly

Environment—international agreements: *party to:* Biodiversity, Climate Change, Climate Change-Kyoto Protocol, Desertification, Endangered Species, Environmental Modification, Hazardous Wastes, Law of the Sea, Marine Dumping, Ozone Layer Protection, Ship Pollution, Wetlands, Whaling
signed, but not ratified: none of the selected agreements

Geography—note: Antigua has a deeply indented shoreline with many natural harbors and beaches; Barbuda has a large western harbor

PEOPLE AND SOCIETY

Population: 94,731 (July 2017 est.)
country comparison to the world: 197

Nationality: *noun:* Antiguan(s), Barbudan(s)
adjective: Antiguan, Barbudan

Ethnic groups: black 87.3%, mixed 4.7%, hispanic 2.7%, white 1.6%, other 2.7%, unspecified 0.9% (2011 est.)

Languages: English (official), Antiguan creole

Religions: Protestant 68.3% (Anglican 17.6%, Seventh Day Adventist 12.4%, Pentecostal

12.2%, Moravian 8.3%, Methodist 5.6%, Wesleyan Holiness 4.5%, Church of God 4.1%, Baptist 3.6%), Roman Catholic 8.2%, other 12.2%, unspecified 5.5%, none 5.9% (2011 est.)

Age structure: *0-14 years:* 23.09% (male 11,116/female 10,760)
15-24 years: 16.83% (male 7,939/female 8,008)
25-54 years: 42.19% (male 18,268/female 21,695)
55-64 years: 9.83% (male 4,179/female 5,130)
65 years and over: 8.06% (male 3,279/female 4,357) (2017 est.)

Dependency ratios:
total dependency ratio: 45.2
youth dependency ratio: 35.7
elderly dependency ratio: 9.6
potential support ratio: 10.5 (2015 est.)

Median age: *total:* 31.9 years
male: 30 years
female: 33.5 years (2017 est.)
country comparison to the world: 103

Population growth rate: 1.21% (2017 est.)
country comparison to the world: 92

Birth rate: 15.7 births/1,000 population (2017 est.)
country comparison to the world: 118

Death rate: 5.7 deaths/1,000 population (2017 est.)
country comparison to the world: 175

Net migration rate: 2.2 migrant(s)/1,000 population (2017 est.)
country comparison to the world: 42

Population distribution: the island of Antigua is home to approximately 97% of the population; nearly the entire population of Barbuda lives in Codrington

Urbanization: *urban population:* 23% of total population (2017)
rate of urbanization: -0.38% annual rate of change (2015-20 est.)

Major urban areas—population: SAINT JOHN'S (capital) 22,000 (2014)

Sex ratio: *at birth:* 1.05 male(s)/female
0-14 years: 1.03 male(s)/female
15-24 years: 0.99 male(s)/female
25-54 years: 0.84 male(s)/female
55-64 years: 0.82 male(s)/female
65 years and over: 0.76 male(s)/female
total population: 0.9 male(s)/female (2016 est.)

Infant mortality rate: *total:* 12.1 deaths/1,000 live births
male: 13.9 deaths/1,000 live births
female: 10.2 deaths/1,000 live births (2017 est.)
country comparison to the world: 118

Life expectancy at birth: *total population:* 76.7 years
male: 74.6 years
female: 79 years (2017 est.)
country comparison to the world: 84

Total fertility rate: 2 children born/woman (2017 est.)
country comparison to the world: 119

Health expenditures: 5.5% of GDP (2014)
country comparison to the world: 127

Hospital bed density: 2.1 beds/1,000 population (2011)

Drinking water source:
improved:
urban: 97.9% of population
rural: 97.9% of population
total: 97.9% of population
unimproved:
urban: 2.1% of population
rural: 2.1% of population
total: 2.1% of population (2015 est.)

Sanitation facility access:
improved:
urban: 91.4% of population
rural: 91.4% of population
total: 91.4% of population
unimproved:
urban: 8.6% of population
rural: 8.6% of population
total: 8.6% of population (2011 est.)

HIV/AIDS—adult prevalence rate: NA

HIV/AIDS—people living with HIV/AIDS: NA

HIV/AIDS—deaths: NA

Major infectious diseases: *note:* active local transmission of Zika virus by Aedes species mosquitoes has been identified in this country (as of August 2016); it poses an important risk (a large number of cases possible) among US citizens if bitten by an infective mosquito; other less common ways to get Zika are through sex, via blood transfusion, or during pregnancy, in which the pregnant woman passes Zika virus to her fetus (2016)

Obesity—adult prevalence rate: 18.9% (2016)
country comparison to the world: 113

Education expenditures: 2.6% of GDP (2009)
country comparison to the world: 159

Literacy: *definition:* age 15 and over has completed five or more years of schooling
total population: 99%
male: 98.4%
female: 99.4% (2012 est.)

School life expectancy (primary to tertiary education): *total:* 14 years
male: 13 years
female: 15 years (2012)

GOVERNMENT

Country name: *conventional long form:* none
conventional short form: Antigua and Barbuda
etymology: "antiguo" is Spanish for "ancient" or "old"; the island was discovered by Christopher COLUMBUS in 1493 and, according to tradition, named by him after the church of Santa Maria la Antigua (Old Saint Mary's) in Seville; "barbuda" is Spanish for "bearded" and the adjective may refer to the alleged beards of the indigenous people or to the island's bearded fig trees

Government type: parliamentary democracy (Parliament) under a constitutional monarchy; a Commonwealth realm

Capital: *name:* Saint John's
geographic coordinates: 17 07 N, 61 51 W

33

time difference: UTC-4 (1 hour ahead of Washington, DC, during Standard Time)

Administrative divisions: 6 parishes and 2 dependencies*; Barbuda*, Redonda*, Saint George, Saint John, Saint Mary, Saint Paul, Saint Peter, Saint Philip

Independence: 1 November 1981 (from the UK)

National holiday: Independence Day, 1 November (1981)

Constitution: several previous; latest presented 31 July 1981, effective 31 October 1981 (Antigua and Barbuda Constitutional Order 1981); amended 2009, 2011 (2016)

Legal system: common law based on the English model

International law organization participation: has not submitted an ICJ jurisdiction declaration; accepts ICCt jurisdiction

Citizenship: *citizenship by birth:* yes
citizenship by descent: yes
dual citizenship recognized: yes
residency requirement for naturalization: 7 years

Suffrage: 18 years of age; universal

Executive branch: *chief of state:* Queen ELIZABETH II (since 6 February 1952); represented by Governor General Rodney WILLIAMS (since 14 August 2014)

head of government: Prime Minister Gaston BROWNE (since 13 June 2014)
cabinet: Council of Ministers appointed by the governor general on the advice of the prime minister
elections/appointments: the monarchy is hereditary; governor general appointed by the monarch on the advice of the prime minister; following legislative elections, the leader of the majority party or majority coalition usually appointed prime minister by the governor general

Legislative branch: *description:* bicameral Parliament consists of the Senate (17 seats; members appointed by the governor general) and the House of Representatives (17 seats; members directly elected in single-seat constituencies by simple majority vote to serve 5-year terms)
elections: House of Representatives—last held on 12 June 2014 (next to be held in 2019)
election results: percent of vote by party—ALP 56.5%, UPP 42%, other 1.5%; seats by party—ALP 14, UPP 3

Judicial branch: *highest court(s):* the Eastern Caribbean Supreme Court (ECSC) is the superior court of the Organization of Eastern Caribbean States; the ECSC—headquartered on St. Lucia—consists of the Court of Appeal—headed by the chief justice and 4 judges—and the High Court with 18 judges; the Court of Appeal is itinerant, travelling to member states on a schedule to hear appeals from the High Court and subordinate courts; High Court judges reside at the member states with 2 assigned to Antigua and Barbuda
judge selection and term of office: chief justice of Eastern Caribbean Supreme Court appointed by the Her Majesty, Queen ELIZABETH II; other justices and judges appointed by the Judicial and Legal Services Commission; Court of Appeal justices appointed for life with mandatory retirement at age 65; High Court judges appointed for life with mandatory retirement at age 62
subordinate courts: Industrial Court; Magistrates' Courts

Political parties and leaders: Antigua Caribbean Liberation Movement or ACLM
Antigua Labor Party or ALP [Gaston BROWNE]
Barbuda People's Movement or BPM [Trevor WALKER]
Barbuda People's Movement for Change [Arthur NIBBS]
Barbudans for a Better Barbuda [Ordrick SAMUEL]
Progressive Labor Movement or PLM
United National Democratic Party or UNDP
United Progressive Party or UPP [W. Baldwin SPENCER] (a coalition of ACLM, PLM, UNDP)

Political pressure groups and leaders: Antigua Trades and Labor Union or ATLU [Wigley GEORGE] People's Democratic Movement or PDM [Hugh MARSHALL]

International organization participation: ACP, AOSIS, C, Caricom, CDB, CELAC, FAO, G-77, IBRD, ICAO, ICC (NGOs), ICCt, ICRM, IDA, IFAD, IFC, IFRCS, ILO, IMF, IMO, IMSO, Interpol, IOC, IOM, ISO (subscriber), ITU, ITUC (NGOs), MIGA, NAM (observer), OAS, OECS, OPANAL, OPCW, Petrocaribe, UN, UNCTAD, UNESCO, UPU, WFTU (NGOs), WHO, WIPO, WMO, WTO

Diplomatic representation in the US: *chief of mission:* Ambassador Sir Ronald SANDERS (since 17 September 2015)
chancery: 3216 New Mexico Avenue NW, Washington, DC 20016
telephone: [1] (202) 362-5122
FAX: [1] (202) 362-5525
consulate(s) general: Miami, New York

Diplomatic representation from the US: the US does not have an embassy in Antigua and Barbuda; the US Ambassador to Barbados is accredited to Antigua and Barbuda

Flag description: red, with an inverted isosceles triangle based on the top edge of the flag; the triangle contains three horizontal bands of black (top), light blue, and white, with a yellow rising sun in the black band; the sun symbolizes the dawn of a new era, black represents the African heritage of most of the population, blue is for hope, and red is for the dynamism of the people; the "V" stands for victory; the successive yellow, blue, and white coloring is also meant to evoke the country's tourist attractions of sun, sea, and sand

National symbol(s): fallow deer; national colors: red, white, blue, black, yellow

National anthem: *name:* "Fair Antigua, We Salute Thee"
lyrics/music: Novelle Hamilton RICHARDS/ Walter Garnet Picart CHAMBERS

note: adopted 1967; as a Commonwealth country, in addition to the national anthem, "God Save the Queen" serves as the royal anthem (see United Kingdom)

ECONOMY

Economy—overview: Tourism continues to dominate Antigua and Barbuda's economy, accounting for nearly 60% of GDP and 40% of investment. The dual-island nation's agricultural production is focused on the domestic market and constrained by a limited water supply and a labor shortage stemming from the lure of higher wages in tourism and construction. Manufacturing comprises enclave-type assembly for export with major products being bedding, handicrafts, and electronic components. Like other countries in the region, Antigua's economy was severely hit by effects of the global economic recession in 2009. The country suffered from the collapse of its largest private sector employer, a steep decline in tourism, a rise in debt, and a sharp economic contraction between 2009 and 2011. Antigua has not yet returned to its pre-crisis growth levels. Prospects for economic growth in the medium term will continue to depend on tourist arrivals from the US, Canada, and Europe and could be disrupted by potential damage from natural disasters. The new government, elected in 2014 and led by Prime Minister Gaston Browne, continues to face significant fiscal challenges. The government places some hope in a new Citizenship by Investment Program to both reduce public debt levels and spur growth.

GDP (purchasing power parity):
$2.39 billion (2017 est.)
$2.328 billion (2016 est.)
$2.209 billion (2015 est.)
note: data are in 2017 dollars
country comparison to the world: 193

GDP (official exchange rate):
$1.535 billion (2016 est.)

GDP—real growth rate:
2.7% (2017 est.)
5.3% (2016 est.)
4.1% (2015 est.)
country comparison to the world: 127

GDP—per capita (PPP):
$26,300 (2017 est.)
$25,900 (2016 est.)
$24,800 (2015 est.)
note: data are in 2017 dollars
country comparison to the world: 76

Gross national saving:
26% of GDP (2017 est.)
24.5% of GDP (2016 est.)
30.7% of GDP (2015 est.)
country comparison to the world: 46

GDP—composition, by end use:
household consumption: 68%
government consumption: 16%
investment in fixed capital: 21.7%
investment in inventories: 0.1%
exports of goods and services: 34%
imports of goods and services: -39.7% (2017 est.)

GDP—composition, by sector of origin:
agriculture: 2.3%
industry: 20.2%
services: 77.5% (2017 est.)

Agriculture—products: cotton, fruits, vegetables, bananas, coconuts, cucumbers, mangoes, sugarcane; livestock

Industries: tourism, construction, light manufacturing (clothing, alcohol, household appliances)

Industrial production growth rate: 3% (2017 est.)
country comparison to the world: 96

Labor force: 30,000 (1991)
country comparison to the world: 205

Labor force—by occupation: agriculture: 7%
industry: 11%
services: 82% (1983)

Unemployment rate: 11% (2014 est.)
country comparison to the world: 141

Population below poverty line: NA%

Household income or consumption by percentage share: *lowest 10%:* NA%
highest 10%: NA%

Budget: *revenues:* $295.9 million
expenditures: $322.9 million (2017 est.)
Taxes and other revenues: 19.3% of GDP (2017 est.)
country comparison to the world: 158

Budget surplus (+) or deficit (-): -1.8% of GDP (2017 est.)
country comparison to the world: 78

Public debt: 92.7% of GDP (2016 est.)
99.1% of GDP (2015 est.)
country comparison to the world: 22

Fiscal year: 1 April—31 March

Inflation rate (consumer prices):
2.4% (2017 est.)
-0.5% (2016 est.)
country comparison to the world: 111

Central bank discount rate: 6.5% (31 December 2010)
6.5% (31 December 2009)
country comparison to the world: 60

Commercial bank prime lending rate: 9.6% (31 December 2017 est.)
9.61% (31 December 2016 est.)
country comparison to the world: 86

Stock of narrow money:
$307.7 million (31 December 2017 est.)
$293 million (31 December 2016 est.)
country comparison to the world: 178

Stock of broad money: $1.229 billion (31 December 2017 est.)
$1.194 billion (31 December 2016 est.)
country comparison to the world: 169

Stock of domestic credit: $925.9 million (31 December 2017 est.)
$913 million (31 December 2016 est.)
country comparison to the world: 168

Current account balance: $22 million (2017 est.)
$2 million (2016 est.)
country comparison to the world: 57

Exports: $61.3 million (2017 est.)
$56.5 million (2016 est.)
country comparison to the world: 200

Exports—commodities: petroleum products, bedding, handicrafts, electronic components, transport equipment, food and live animals

Exports—partners: Poland 53.2%, UK 12.7%, Cameroon 7.2%, Germany 5.5%, US 4.5% (2016)

Imports: $420.7 million (2017 est.)
$407.3 million (2016 est.)
country comparison to the world: 192

Imports—commodities: food and live animals, machinery and transport equipment, manufactures, chemicals, oil

Imports—partners: US 44.3%, Japan 4.7%, China 4.1% (2016)

Debt—external:
$441.2 million (31 December 2012)
$458 million (June 2010)
country comparison to the world: 182

Exchange rates: East Caribbean dollars (XCD) per US dollar—
2.7 (2017 est.)
2.7 (2016 est.)
2.7 (2015 est.)
2.7 (2014 est.)
2.7 (2013 est.)

ENERGY

Electricity access: *population without electricity:* 9,358
electrification—*total population:* 91%
electrification—urban areas: 100%
electrification—rural areas: 80% (2012)

Electricity—production: 330 million kWh (2015 est.)
country comparison to the world: 178

Electricity—consumption: 306.9 million kWh (2015 est.)
country comparison to the world: 183

Electricity—exports: 0 kWh (2016 est.)
country comparison to the world: 97

Electricity—imports: 0 kWh (2016 est.)
country comparison to the world: 117

Electricity—installed generating capacity: 87,000 kW (2015 est.)
country comparison to the world: 180

Electricity—from fossil fuels: 96.6% of total installed capacity (2015 est.)
country comparison to the world: 45

Electricity—from nuclear fuels: 0% of total installed capacity (2015 est.)
country comparison to the world: 34

Electricity—from hydroelectric plants: 0% of total installed capacity (2015 est.)
country comparison to the world: 215

Electricity—from other renewable sources: 4.6% of total installed capacity (2015 est.)
country comparison to the world: 100

Crude oil—production: 0 bbl/day (2016 est.)
country comparison to the world: 105

Crude oil—exports: 0 bbl/day (2014 est.)
country comparison to the world: 85

Crude oil—imports: 0 bbl/day (2014 est.)
country comparison to the world: 87

Crude oil—proved reserves: 0 bbl (1 January 2017 es)
country comparison to the world: 105

Refined petroleum products—production: 0 bbl/day (2014 est.)
country comparison to the world: 114

Refined petroleum products—consumption: 5,000 bbl/day (2015 est.)
country comparison to the world: 177

Refined petroleum products—exports: 90.55 bbl/day (2014 est.)
country comparison to the world: 122

Refined petroleum products—imports: 4,884 bbl/day (2014 est.)
country comparison to the world: 168

Natural gas—production: 0 cu m (2013 est.)
country comparison to the world: 102

Natural gas—consumption: 0 cu m (2013 est.)
country comparison to the world: 153

Natural gas—exports: 0 cu m (2013 est.)
country comparison to the world: 58

Natural gas—imports: 0 cu m (2013 est.)
country comparison to the world: 80

Natural gas—proved reserves: 0 cu m (1 January 2014 es)
country comparison to the world: 109

Carbon dioxide emissions from consumption of energy: 600,000 Mt (2013 est.)
country comparison to the world: 178

COMMUNICATIONS

Telephones—fixed lines: *total subscriptions:* 22,504
subscriptions per 100 inhabitants: 24 (July 2016 est.)
country comparison to the world: 172

Telephones—mobile cellular: *total:* 126,000
subscriptions per 100 inhabitants: 136 (July 2016 est.)
country comparison to the world: 189

Telephone system: *general assessment:* good automatic telephone system
domestic: fixed-line teledensity roughly 24 per 100 persons (2016); mobile-cellular teledensity is about 135 per 100 persons (2015)
international: country code—1-268; landing points for the East Caribbean Fiber System (ECFS) and the Global Caribbean Network (GCN) submarine cable systems with links to other islands in the eastern Caribbean extending from the British Virgin Islands to Trinidad; satellite earth stations—2; tropospheric scatter to Saba (Netherlands) and Guadeloupe (France) (2016)

Broadcast media: state-controlled Antigua and Barbuda Broadcasting Service (ABS) operates 1 TV station; multi-channel cable TV subscription services are available; ABS operates 1 radio station; roughly 15 radio stations, some broadcasting on multiple frequencies (2009)

Internet country code: .ag

Internet users: total: 60,000
percent of population: 65.2% (July 2016 est.)
country comparison to the world: 174

TRANSPORTATION

National air transport system: *number of registered air carriers:* 1
inventory of registered aircraft operated by air carriers: 9
annual passenger traffic on registered air carriers: 1,039,809
annual freight traffic on registered air carriers: 526,545 mt-km (2015)
Civil aircraft registration country code prefix: V2 (2016)

Airports: 3 (2013)
country comparison to the world: 193

Airports—with paved runways: total: 2
2,438 to 3,047 m: 1
under 914 m: 1 (2017)

Airports—with unpaved runways: total: 1
under 914 m: 1 (2013)

Roadways: total: 1,170 km

paved: 386 km
unpaved: 784 km (2011)
country comparison to the world: 183

Merchant marine: *total:* 964
by type: bulk carrier 36, container ship 238, general cargo 615, oil tanker 2, other 73 (2017)
country comparison to the world: 25

Ports and terminals: *major seaport(s):* Saint John's

MILITARY AND SECURITY

Military branches: Ministry of National Security, Royal Antigua and Barbuda Defense Force (includes Antigua and Barbuda Coast Guard) (2012)

Military service age and obligation: 18 years of age for voluntary military service; no conscription; Governor-General has powers to call up men for national service and set the age at which they could be called up (2012)

TRANSNATIONAL ISSUES

Disputes—international: none

Trafficking in persons: *current situation:* Antigua and Barbuda is a destination and transit country for adults and children subjected to sex trafficking and

forced labor; forced prostitution has been reported in bars, taverns, and brothels, while forced labor occurs in domestic service and the retail sector

tier rating: Tier 2 Watch List—Antigua and Barbuda does not fully comply with the minimum standards for the elimination of trafficking; however, it is making significant efforts to do so; the government made no discernible progress in convicting traffickers in 2014 but charged two individuals in separate cases; efforts to convict traffickers have been impeded by a 2014 ruling that found the 2010 anti-trafficking act was unconstitutional because jurisdiction rests with the Magistrate's Court rather than the High Court; no new prosecutions, convictions, or punishments were recorded in 2014; credible sources have raised concerns about trafficking-related complicity among some off-duty police officers, which could hinder investigations or victims willingness to report offenses; prevention efforts were sustained, but progress in protecting victims was uneven; seven victims were assisted, which was an increase over 2013 (2015)

Illicit drugs: considered a minor transshipment point for narcotics bound for the US and Europe; more significant as an offshore financial center

ARCTIC OCEAN

GEOGRAPHY

Location: body of water between Europe, Asia, and North America, mostly north of the Arctic Circle

Geographic coordinates: 90 00 N, 0 00 E

Map references: Arctic Region

Area: *total:* 14.056 million sq km
note: includes Baffin Bay, Barents Sea, Beaufort Sea, Chukchi Sea, East Siberian Sea, Greenland Sea, Hudson Bay, Hudson Strait, Kara Sea, Laptev Sea, Northwest Passage, and other tributary water bodies

Area—comparative: slightly less than 1.5 times the size of the US

Coastline: 45,389 km

Climate: polar climate characterized by persistent cold and relatively narrow annual temperature range; winters characterized by continuous darkness, cold and stable weather conditions, and clear skies; summers characterized by continuous daylight, damp and foggy weather, and weak cyclones with rain or snow

Terrain: central surface covered by a perennial drifting polar icepack that, on average, is about 3 m thick, although pressure ridges may be three times that thickness; the icepack is surrounded by open seas during the summer, but more than doubles in size during the winter and extends to the encircling landmasses; the ocean floor is about 50% continental shelf (highest percentage of any

ocean) with the remainder a central basin interrupted by three submarine ridges (Alpha Cordillera, Nansen Cordillera, and Lomonosov Ridge)
major surface currents: two major, slow-moving, wind-driven currents (drift streams) dominate: a clockwise drift pattern in the Beaufort Gyre in the western part of the Arctic Ocean and a nearly straight line Transpolar Drift Stream that moves across the ocean from the New Siberian Islands (Russia) to the Fram Strait (between Greenland and Svalbard); sea ice that lies close to the center of the gyre can complete a 360 degree circle in about 2 years, while ice on the gyre periphery will complete the same circle in about 7-8 years; sea ice in the Transpolar Drift crosses the ocean in about 3 years

Elevation: *mean depth:* -1,205 m

elevation extremes: *lowest point:* Molloy Deep -5,607 m
highest point: sea level 0 m

Natural resources: sand and gravel aggregates, placer deposits, polymetallic nodules, oil and gas fields, fish, marine mammals (seals and whales)

Natural hazards: ice islands occasionally break away from northern Ellesmere Island; icebergs calved from glaciers in western Greenland and extreme northeastern Canada; permafrost in islands; virtually ice locked from October to June; ships subject to superstructure icing from October to May

INTRODUCTION

Background: The Arctic Ocean is the smallest of the world's five oceans (after the Pacific Ocean, Atlantic Ocean, Indian Ocean, and the Southern Ocean). The Northwest Passage (US and Canada) and Northern Sea Route (Norway and Russia) are two important seasonal waterways. In recent years the polar ice pack has receded in the summer allowing for increased navigation and raising the possibility of future sovereignty and shipping disputes among the six countries bordering the Arctic Ocean (Canada, Denmark (Greenland), Iceland, Norway, Russia, US).

Environment—current issues: endangered marine species include walruses and whales; fragile ecosystem slow to change and slow to recover from disruptions or damage; thinning polar icepack

Geography—note: major chokepoint is the southern Chukchi Sea (northern access to the Pacific Ocean via the Bering Strait); strategic location between North America and Russia; shortest marine link between the extremes of eastern and western Russia; floating research stations operated by the US and Russia; maximum snow cover in March or April about 20 to 50 centimeters over the frozen ocean; snow cover lasts about 10 months

GOVERNMENT

Country name: *etymology:* the name Arctic comes from the Greek word "arktikos" meaning "near the bear" or "northern," and that word derives from "arktos," meaning "bear"; the name refers either to the constellation Ursa Major, the "Great Bear," which is prominent in the northern celestial sphere, or to the constellation Ursa Minor, the "Little Bear," which contains Polaris, the North (Pole) Star

ECONOMY

Economy—overview: Economic activity is limited to the exploitation of natural resources, including petroleum, natural gas, fish, and seals.

TRANSPORTATION

Ports and terminals: *major seaport(s):* Churchill (Canada), Murmansk (Russia), Prudhoe Bay (US)

Transportation—note: sparse network of air, ocean, river, and land routes; the Northwest Passage (North America) and Northern Sea Route (Eurasia) are important seasonal waterways

TRANSNATIONAL ISSUES

Disputes—international: Canada and the US dispute how to divide the Beaufort Sea and the status of the Northwest Passage but continue to work cooperatively to survey the Arctic continental shelf; Denmark (Greenland) and Norway have made submissions to the Commission on the Limits of the Continental shelf (CLCS) and Russia is collecting additional data to augment its 2001 CLCS submission; record summer melting of sea ice in the Arctic has renewed interest in maritime shipping lanes and sea floor exploration; Norway and Russia signed a comprehensive maritime boundary agreement in 2010

ARGENTINA

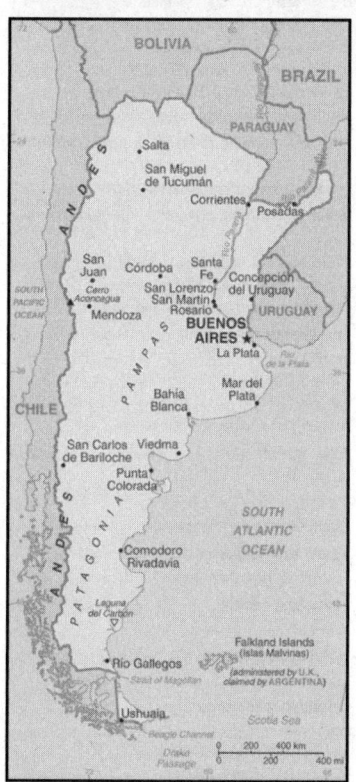

INTRODUCTION

Background: In 1816, the United Provinces of the Rio Plata declared their independence from Spain. After Bolivia, Paraguay, and Uruguay went their separate ways, the area that remained became Argentina. The country's population and culture were heavily shaped by immigrants from throughout Europe, with Italy and Spain providing the largest percentage of newcomers from 1860 to 1930. Up until about the mid-20th century, much of Argentina's history was dominated by periods of internal political conflict between Federalists and Unitarians and between civilian and military factions. After World War II, an era of Peronist populism and direct and indirect military interference in subsequent governments was followed by a military junta that took power in 1976. Democracy returned in 1983 after a failed bid to seize the Falkland Islands (Islas Malvinas) by force, and has persisted despite numerous challenges, the most formidable of which was a severe economic crisis in 2001-02 that led to violent public protests and the successive resignations of several presidents. The years 2003-15 saw Peronist rule by Nestor and Cristina FERNANDEZ de KIRCHNER, whose policies isolated Argentina and caused economic stagnation. With the election of Mauricio MACRI in November 2015, Argentina began a period of reform and international reintegration.

GEOGRAPHY

Location: Southern South America, bordering the South Atlantic Ocean, between Chile and Uruguay

Geographic coordinates: 34 00 S, 64 00 W

Map references: South America

Area: *total:* 2,780,400 sq km
land: 2,736,690 sq km
water: 43,710 sq km
country comparison to the world: 9

Area—comparative: slightly less than three-tenths the size of the US
Land boundaries: total: 11,968 km

border countries (5): Bolivia 942 km, Brazil 1,263 km, Chile 6,691 km, Paraguay 2,531 km, Uruguay 541 km

Coastline: 4,989 km

Maritime claims: *territorial sea:* 12 nm
contiguous zone: 24 nm
exclusive economic zone: 200 nm
continental shelf: 200 nm or to the edge of the continental margin

Climate: mostly temperate; arid in southeast; subantarctic in southwest

Terrain: rich plains of the Pampas in northern half, flat to rolling plateau of Patagonia in south, rugged Andes along western border

Elevation: *mean elevation:* 595 m

elevation extremes: *lowest point:* Laguna del Carbon -105 m (located between Puerto San Julian and Comandante Luis Piedra Buena in the province of Santa Cruz)
highest point: Cerro Aconcagua 6,962 m (located in the northwestern corner of the province of Mendoza; highest point in South America)

Natural resources: fertile plains of the pampas, lead, zinc, tin, copper, iron ore, manganese, petroleum, uranium, arable land

Land use: *agricultural land:* 53.9%
arable land 13.9%;
permanent crops 0.4%;
permanent pasture 39.6%
forest: 10.7%
other: 35.4% (2011 est.)
Irrigated land: 23,600 sq km (2012)

Population—distribution: one-third of the population lives in Buenos Aires; pockets of agglomeration occur throughout the northern and central parts of the country; Patagonia to the south remains sparsely populated

Natural hazards: San Miguel de Tucuman and Mendoza areas in the Andes subject to earthquakes; pamperos are violent windstorms that can strike the pampas and northeast; heavy flooding in some areas

volcanism: volcanic activity in the Andes Mountains along the Chilean border; Copahue (2,997 m) last erupted in 2000; other historically active volcanoes include Llullaillaco, Maipo, Planchon-Peteroa, San Jose, Tromen, Tupungatito, and Viedma

Environment—current issues: environmental problems (urban and rural) typical of an industrializing economy such as deforestation, soil degradation, desertification, air pollution, and water pollution

note: Argentina is a world leader in setting voluntary greenhouse gas targets

Environment—international agreements: *party to:* Antarctic-Environmental Protocol, Antarctic-Marine Living Resources, Antarctic Seals, Antarctic Treaty, Biodiversity, Climate Change, Climate Change-Kyoto Protocol, Desertification, Endangered Species, Environmental Modification, Hazardous Wastes, Law of the Sea, Marine Dumping, Ozone Layer Protection, Ship Pollution, Wetlands, Whaling

signed, but not ratified: Marine Life Conservation

Geography—note: second-largest country in South America (after Brazil); strategic location relative to sea lanes between the South Atlantic and the South Pacific Oceans (Strait of Magellan, Beagle Channel, Drake Passage); diverse geophysical landscapes range from tropical climates in the north to tundra in the far south; Cerro Aconcagua is the Western Hemisphere's tallest mountain, while Laguna del Carbon is the lowest point in the Western Hemisphere; shares Iguazu Falls, the world's largest waterfalls system, with Brazil

PEOPLE AND SOCIETY

Population: 44,293,293 (July 2017 est.)
country comparison to the world: 31

Nationality: *noun:* Argentine(s)
adjective: Argentine

Ethnic groups: European (mostly Spanish and Italian descent) and mestizo (mixed European and Amerindian ancestry) 97.2%, Amerindian 2.4%, African 0.4% (2010 est.)

Languages: Spanish (official), Italian, English, German, French, indigenous (Mapudungun, Quechua)

Religions: nominally Roman Catholic 92% (less than 20% practicing), Protestant 2%, Jewish 2%, other 4%

Demographic profile: Argentina's population continues to grow but at a slower rate because of its steadily declining birth rate. Argentina's fertility decline began earlier than in the rest of Latin America, occurring most rapidly between the early 20th century and the 1950s and then becoming more gradual. Life expectancy has been improving, most notably among the young and the poor. While the population under age 15 is shrinking, the youth cohort—ages 15-24—is the largest in Argentina's history and will continue to

bolster the working-age population. If this large working-age population is well-educated and gainfully employed, Argentina is likely to experience an economic boost and possibly higher per capita savings and investment. Although literacy and primary school enrollment are nearly universal, grade repetition is problematic and secondary school completion is low. Both of these issues vary widely by region and socioeconomic group. Argentina has been primarily a country of immigration for most of its history, welcoming European immigrants (often providing needed low-skilled labor) after its independence in the 19th century and attracting especially large numbers from Spain and Italy. More than 7 million European immigrants are estimated to have arrived in Argentina between 1880 and 1930, when it adopted a more restrictive immigration policy. European immigration also began to wane in the 1930s because of the global depression. The inflow rebounded temporarily following WWII and resumed its decline in the 1950s when Argentina's military dictators tightened immigration rules and European economies rebounded. Regional migration increased, however, supplying low-skilled workers escaping economic and political instability in their home countries. As of 2015, immigrants made up almost 5% of Argentina's population, the largest share in South America. Migration from neighboring countries accounted for approximately 80% of Argentina's immigrant population in 2015. The first waves of highly skilled Argentine emigrant workers headed mainly to the United States and Spain in the 1960s and 1970s, driven by economic decline and repressive military dictatorships. The 2008 European economic crisis drove the return migration of some Argentinean and other Latin American nationals, as well as the immigration of Europeans to South America, where Argentina was a key recipient. In 2015, Argentina received the highest number of legal migrants in Latin America and the Caribbean. The majority of its migrant inflow came from Paraguay and Bolivia.

Age structure: *0-14 years:* 24.59% (male 5,612,766/female 5,278,857)
15-24 years: 15.28% (male 3,460,276/female 3,307,227)
25-54 years: 39.38% (male 8,707,818/female 8,733,370)
55-64 years: 9.13% (male 1,963,923/female 2,081,796)
65 years and over: 11.62% (male 2,159,811/female 2,987,449) (2017 est.)

Dependency ratios:
total dependency ratio: 56.5
youth dependency ratio: 39.4
elderly dependency ratio: 17.1
potential support ratio: 5.8 (2015 est.)

Median age: *total:* 31.7 years
male: 30.5 years
female: 32.9 years (2017 est.)
country comparison to the world: 105

Population growth rate: 0.91% (2017 est.)
country comparison to the world: 121

Birth rate: 16.7 births/1,000 population (2017 est.)

country comparison to the world: 110

Death rate: 7.5 deaths/1,000 population (2017 est.)
country comparison to the world: 110

Net migration rate: -0.1 migrant(s)/1,000 population (2017 est.)
country comparison to the world: 102

Population distribution: one-third of the population lives in Buenos Aires; pockets of agglomeration occur throughout the northern and central parts of the country; Patagonia to the south remains sparsely populated

Urbanization: *urban population:* 92% of total population (2017)
rate of urbanization: 0.93% annual rate of change (2015-20 est.)

Major urban areas—population: BUENOS AIRES (capital) 15.18 million; Cordoba 1.511 million; Rosario 1.381 million; Mendoza 1.009 million; San Miguel de Tucuman 910,000; La Plata 846,000 (2015)

Sex ratio: *at birth:* 1.05 male(s)/female
0-14 years: 1.06 male(s)/female
15-24 years: 1.05 male(s)/female
25-54 years: 1 male(s)/female
55-64 years: 0.94 male(s)/female
65 years and over: 0.71 male(s)/female
total population: 0.98 male(s)/female (2016 est.)

Maternal mortality ratio: 52 deaths/100,000 live births (2015 est.)
country comparison to the world: 94

Infant mortality rate: *total:* 9.8 deaths/1,000 live births
male: 10.7 deaths/1,000 live births
female: 8.8 deaths/1,000 live births (2017 est.)
country comparison to the world: 139

Life expectancy at birth: *total population:* 77.3 years
male: 74.2 years
female: 80.6 years (2017 est.)
country comparison to the world: 74

Total fertility rate: 2.26 children born/woman (2017 est.)
country comparison to the world: 93

Contraceptive prevalence rate: 81.3% (2013)

Health expenditures: 4.8% of GDP (2014)
country comparison to the world: 146

Physicians density: 3.76 physicians/1,000 population (2013)

Hospital bed density: 4.7 beds/1,000 population (2012)

Drinking water source:
improved:
urban: 99% of population
rural: 100% of population
total: 99.1% of population
unimproved:
urban: 1% of population
rural: 0% of population
total: 0.9% of population (2015 est.)

Sanitation facility access:
improved:

urban: 96.2% of population
rural: 98.3% of population
total: 96.4% of population
unimproved:
urban: 3.8% of population
rural: 1.7% of population
total: 3.6% of population (2015 est.)

HIV/AIDS—adult prevalence rate: 0.4% (2016 est.)
country comparison to the world: 75

HIV/AIDS—people living with HIV/AIDS: 120,000 (2016 est.)
country comparison to the world: 38

HIV/AIDS—deaths: 2,400 (2016 est.)
country comparison to the world: 48

Major infectious diseases: *note:* active local transmission of Zika virus by Aedes species mosquitoes has been identified in this country (as of August 2016); it poses an important risk (a large number of cases possible) among US citizens if bitten by an infective mosquito; other less common ways to get Zika are through sex, via blood transfusion, or during pregnancy, in which the pregnant woman passes Zika virus to her fetus (2016)

Obesity—adult prevalence rate: 28.3% (2016)
country comparison to the world: 31

Children under the age of 5 years underweight: 2.3% (2005)
country comparison to the world: 119

Education expenditures: 5.5% of GDP (2014)
country comparison to the world: 32

Literacy: *definition:* age 15 and over can read and write
total population: 98.1%
male: 98%
female: 98.1% (2015 est.)

School life expectancy (primary to tertiary education): *total:* 17 years
male: 16 years
female: 18 years (2014)

Unemployment, youth ages 15-24: *total:* 18.3%
male: 15.6%
female: 22.8% (2014 est.)
country comparison to the world: 63

GOVERNMENT

Country name: *conventional long form:* Argentine Republic
conventional short form: Argentina
local long form: Republica Argentina
local short form: Argentina
etymology: originally the area was referred to as Tierra Argentina, i.e., "Land beside the Silvery River" or "silvery land," which referred to the massive estuary in the east of the country, the Rio de la Plata (River of Silver); over time the name shortened to simply Argentina or "silvery"

Government type: presidential republic

Capital: *name:* Buenos Aires

geographic coordinates: 34 36 S, 58 22 W
time difference: UTC-3 (2 hours ahead of Washington, DC, during Standard Time)

Administrative divisions: 23 provinces (provincias, singular—provincia) and 1 autonomous city*; Buenos Aires, Catamarca, Chaco, Chubut, Ciudad Autonoma de Buenos Aires*, Cordoba, Corrientes, Entre Rios, Formosa, Jujuy, La Pampa, La Rioja, Mendoza, Misiones, Neuquen, Rio Negro, Salta, San Juan, San Luis, Santa Cruz, Santa Fe, Santiago del Estero, Tierra del Fuego—Antartida e Islas del Atlantico Sur (Tierra del Fuego), Tucuman
note: the US does not recognize any claims to Antarctica

Independence: 9 July 1816 (from Spain)

National holiday: Revolution Day (May Revolution Day), 25 May (1810)

Constitution: several previous; latest effective 11 May 1853; amended many times, last in 1994 (2016)

Legal system: civil law system based on West European legal systems; note—in mid-2015, Argentina adopted a new civil code, replacing the old one in force since 1871

International law organization participation: has not submitted an ICJ jurisdiction declaration; accepts ICCt jurisdiction

Citizenship: *citizenship by birth:* yes
citizenship by descent: yes
dual citizenship recognized: yes
residency requirement for naturalization: 2 years

Suffrage: 18-70 years of age; universal and compulsory; 16-17 years of age—optional for national elections

Executive branch: *chief of state:* President Mauricio MACRI (since 10 December 2015); Vice President Gabriela MICHETTI (since 10 December 2015); note—the president is both chief of state and head of government

head of government: President Mauricio MACRI (since 10 December 2015); Vice President Gabriela MICHETTI (since 10 December 2015)
cabinet: Cabinet appointed by the president
elections/appointments: president and vice president directly elected on the same ballot by qualified majority popular vote for a 4-year term (eligible for a second consecutive term); election last held in 2 rounds on 25 October and 22 November 2015 (next to be held in October 2019)
election results: Mauricio MACRI elected president in second round; percent of vote in first round—Daniel SCIOLI (PJ) 37.1%, Mauricio MACRI (PRO) 34.2%, Sergio MASSA (FR/PJ) 21.4%, other 7.3%; percent of vote in second round—Mauricio MACRI (PRO) 51.4%, Daniel SCIOLI (PJ) 48.6%

Legislative branch: *description:* bicameral National Congress or Congreso Nacional consists of the Senate (72 seats; members directly elected in multi-seat constituencies by simple majority vote to serve 6-year terms with one-third of the membership elected every 2 years) and the Chamber of Deputies (257 seats; members directly elected in multi-seat constituencies by proportional representation vote; members serve 4-year

terms with one-half of the membership renewed every 2 years)
elections: Senate—last held on 22 October 2017 (next to be held in October 2019); Chamber of Deputies—last held on 22 October 2017 (next to be held in October 2019)
election results: Senate—percent of vote by bloc or party—NA; seats by bloc or party—Cambiemos 12, UC 6, PJ 4, FRC 2; Chamber of Deputies—percent of vote by bloc or party—NA; seats by bloc or party—Cambiemos 61, UC 28, PJ 18, FR 7, FCS 3, FRC 2, other 8

Judicial branch: *highest court(s):* Supreme Court or Corte Suprema (consists of the court president, vice-president, and 5 judges)
judge selection and term of office: judges nominated by the president and approved by the Senate; judges can serve until mandatory retirement at age 75
subordinate courts: federal level appellate, district, and territorial courts; provincial level supreme, appellate, and first instance courts

Political parties and leaders: Cambiemos [Mauricio MACRI] (coalition of CC-ARI, PRO, and UCR)
Citizen's Unity or UC [Cristina FERNANDEZ DE KIRCHNER]
Civic Coalition ARI or CC-ARI [Elisa CARRIO]
Civic Front for Santiago or FCS [Gerardo ZAMORA]
Dissident Peronists (PJ Disidente) or Federal Peronism (a right-wing faction of PJ which is opposed to the Kirchners) [Eduardo DUHALDE]
Front for the Renewal of Concord or FRC
Front for Victory or FpV (left-wing faction of PJ) [Cristina FERNANDEZ DE KIRCHNER]
Justicialist Party or PJ [Jose Luis GIOJA]
Progresistas [Margarita STOLBIZER]
Radical Civic Union or UCR [Lilia PUIG DE STUBRIN]
Renewal Front (Frente Renovador) or FR [Sergio MASSA]
Republican Proposal or PRO [Mauricio MACRI]
Socialist Party or PS [Antonio BONFATTI]
United for a New Alternative or UNA (includes FR)
numerous provincial parties

Political pressure groups and leaders: Argentine Association of Pharmaceutical Labs or CILFA
Argentine Industrial Union (manufacturers' association)
Argentine Rural Confederation or CRA (small to medium landowners' association)
Argentine Rural Society (large landowners' association)
Blue and White CGT (dissident CGT labor confederation)
Central of Argentine Workers or CTA (a union for employed and unemployed workers)
General Confederation of Labor or CGT (Peronist-leaning umbrella labor organization)
Roman Catholic Church
other: business organizations; Peronist-dominated labor movement; Piquetero groups (popular protest organizations that can be either pro- or anti-government); students

International organization participation: AfDB (nonregional member), Australia Group, BCIE, BIS, CAN (associate), CD, CELAC, FAO, FATF, G-15, G-20, G-24, G-77, IADB, IAEA, IBRD, ICAO, ICC (national committees), ICCt, ICRM, IDA, IFAD, IFC, IFRCS, IHO, ILO, IMF, IMO, IMSO, Interpol, IOC, IOM, IPU, ISO, ITSO, ITU, ITUC (NGOs), LAES, LAIA, Mercosur, MIGA, MINURSO, MINUSTAH, NAM (observer), NSG, OAS, OPANAL, OPCW, Paris Club (associate), PCA, SICA (observer), UN, UNASUR, UNCTAD, UNESCO, UNFICYP, UNHCR, UNIDO, Union Latina (observer), UNTSO, UNWTO, UPU, WCO, WFTU (NGOs), WHO, WIPO, WMO, WTO, ZC

Diplomatic representation in the US: *chief of mission:* Ambassador Fernando ORIS DE ROA (since 24 January 2018)
chancery: 1600 New Hampshire Avenue NW, Washington, DC 20009
telephone: [1] (202) 238-6400
FAX: [1] (202) 332-3171
consulate(s) general: Atlanta, Chicago, Houston, Los Angeles, Miami, New York, Washington, DC

Diplomatic representation from the US: *chief of mission:* Ambassador (vacant); Charge d'Affaires Tom COONEY (since 20 January 2017)
embassy: Avenida Colombia 4300, C1425GMN Buenos Aires
mailing address: international mail: use embassy street address; APO address: US Embassy Buenos Aires, Unit 4334, APO AA 34034
telephone: [54] (11) 5777-4533
FAX: [54] (11) 5777-4240

Flag description: three equal horizontal bands of sky blue (top), white, and sky blue; centered in the white band is a radiant yellow sun with a human face (delineated in brown) known as the Sun of May; the colors represent the clear skies and snow of the Andes; the sun symbol commemorates the appearance of the sun through cloudy skies on 25 May 1810 during the first mass demonstration in favor of independence; the sun features are those of Inti, the Inca god of the sun

National symbol(s): Sun of May (a sun-with-face symbol); national colors: sky blue, white

National anthem: name: "Himno Nacional Argentino" (Argentine National Anthem)
lyrics/music: Vicente LOPEZ y PLANES/Jose Blas PARERA
note: adopted 1813; Vicente LOPEZ was inspired to write the anthem after watching a play about the 1810 May Revolution against Spain

ECONOMY

Economy—overview: Argentina benefits from rich natural resources, a highly literate population, an export-oriented agricultural sector, and a diversified industrial base. Although one of the world's wealthiest countries 100 years ago, Argentina suffered during most of the 20th century from recurring economic crises, persistent fiscal and current account deficits, high inflation, mounting external debt, and capital flight. In 2016, the World Bank downgraded Argentina from a high-income to upper-middle-income economy, on par with Columbia. A severe depression, growing public and external indebtedness, and an unprecedented bank run culminated in 2001 in the most serious economic, social, and political crisis in the country's turbulent history. Interim President Adolfo RODRIGUEZ SAA declared a default—at the time the largest ever—on the government's foreign debt in December of that year, and abruptly resigned only a few days after taking office. His successor, Eduardo DUHALDE, announced an end to the peso's decade-long 1-to-1 peg to the US dollar in early 2002. The economy bottomed out that year, with real GDP 18% smaller than in 1998 and almost 60% of Argentines below the poverty line. Real GDP rebounded to grow by an average 8.5% annually over the subsequent six years, taking advantage of previously idled industrial capacity and labor, and expansionary monetary and fiscal policies. Inflation also increased, however, during the administration of President Nestor KIRCHNER, which responded with price restraints on businesses, as well as export taxes and restraints, and beginning in 2007, with understating inflation data.

Cristina FERNANDEZ DE KIRCHNER succeeded her husband as president in late 2007, and the rapid economic growth of previous years began to slow sharply the following year as government policies held back exports and the world economy fell into recession. The economy in 2010 rebounded strongly from the 2009 recession, but slowed in late 2011 even as the government continued to rely on expansionary fiscal and monetary policies, which kept inflation in the double digits. In order to deal with these problems, the government expanded state intervention in the economy: it nationalized the oil company YPF from Spain's Repsol, expanded measures to restrict imports, and further tightened currency controls in an effort to bolster foreign reserves and stem capital flight. Between 2011 and 2013, Central Bank foreign reserves dropped $21.3 billion from a high of $52.7 billion. In July 2014, Argentina and China agreed on an $11 billion currency swap; the Argentine Central Bank has received the equivalent of $3.2 billion in Chinese yuan, which it counts as international reserves. With the election of President Mauricio MACRI in November 2015, Argentina began a historic political and economic transformation, as his administration took steps to liberalize the Argentine economy, lifting capital controls, floating the peso, removing export controls on some commodities, cutting some energy subsidies, and reforming the country's official statistics. Argentina negotiated debt payments with holdout bond creditors and returned to international capital markets in April 2016. In September 2016, Argentina completed its first IMF Article IV Consultation since 2006.

After years of international isolation, Argentina took on several international leadership roles in 2017, including hosting the World Economic Forum on Latin America and the World Trade Organization Ministerial Conference, and is set to assume the presidency of the G-20 in 2018.

GDP (purchasing power parity):
$911.5 billion (2017 est.)
$889.5 billion (2016 est.)
$910 billion (2015 est.)
note: data are in 2017 dollars
country comparison to the world: 29

GDP (official exchange rate):
$619.9 billion (2016 est.)

GDP—real growth rate:
2.5% (2017 est.)
-2.2% (2016 est.)
2.6% (2015 est.)
country comparison to the world: 130

GDP—per capita (PPP):
$20,700 (2017 est.)
$20,400 (2016 est.)
$21,100 (2015 est.)
note: data are in 2017 dollars
country comparison to the world: 87

Gross national saving:
12.8% of GDP (2017 est.)
13.6% of GDP (2016 est.)
14.2% of GDP (2015 est.)
country comparison to the world: 141

GDP—composition, by end use:
household consumption: 66.5%
government consumption: 18%
investment in fixed capital: 15.3%
investment in inventories: 1.5%
exports of goods and services: 12%
imports of goods and services: -13.4% (2017 est.)

GDP—composition, by sector of origin:
agriculture: 10.9%
industry: 28.2%
services: 60.9% (2017 est.)

Agriculture—products: sunflower seeds, lemons, soybeans, grapes, corn, tobacco, peanuts, tea, wheat; livestock

Industries: food processing, motor vehicles, consumer durables, textiles, chemicals and petrochemicals, printing, metallurgy, steel

Industrial production growth rate: 2.4%
note: based on private sector estimates (2017 est.)
country comparison to the world: 117

Labor force: 18 million
note: urban areas only (2017 est.)
country comparison to the world: 35

Labor force—by occupation: *agriculture:* 0.5%
industry: 24.8%
services: 74.7% (2014 est.)

Unemployment rate: 8.1% (2017 est.)
8.5% (2016 est.)
country comparison to the world: 112

Population below poverty line: 32.2%
note: data are based on private estimates (2016 est.)

Household income or consumption by percentage share: *lowest 10%:* 1.6%
highest 10%: 30.8% (2014 est.)

Distribution of family income—Gini index: 42.7 (2014)
45.8 (2009)
country comparison to the world: 48

Budget: *revenues:* $123.2 billion
expenditures: $161.1 billion (2017 est.)
Taxes and other revenues: 19.9% of GDP (2017 est.)
country comparison to the world: 154

Budget surplus (+) or deficit (-):
-6.1% of GDP (2017 est.)
country comparison to the world: 176

Public debt: 53.7% of GDP (2017 est.)
54.5% of GDP (2016 est.)
country comparison to the world: 89

Fiscal year: calendar year

Inflation rate (consumer prices):
26.9% (2017 est.)
26.5% (2015 est.)
note: data are derived from private estimates
country comparison to the world: 221

Central bank discount rate: NA%

Commercial bank prime lending rate: 24.5% (31 December 2017 est.)
31.23% (31 December 2016 est.)
country comparison to the world: 11

Stock of narrow money:
$62.95 billion (31 December 2017 est.)
$59 billion (31 December 2016 est.)
country comparison to the world: 49

Stock of broad money: $166.9 billion (31 December 2017 est.)
$146.5 billion (31 December 2016 est.)
country comparison to the world: 48

Stock of domestic credit: $216.7 billion (31 December 2017 est.)
$194 billion (31 December 2016 est.)
country comparison to the world: 46

Market value of publicly traded shares:
$56.13 billion (31 December 2015 est.)
$60.14 billion (31 December 2014 est.)
$53.1 billion (31 December 2013 est.)
country comparison to the world: 48

Current account balance: -$22.13 billion (2017 est.)
-$14.9 billion (2016 est.)
country comparison to the world: 193

Exports: $59.69 billion (2017 est.)
$57.78 billion (2016 est.)
country comparison to the world: 47

Exports—commodities: soybeans and derivatives, petroleum and gas, vehicles, corn, wheat

Exports—partners: Brazil 15.5%, US 7.7%, China 7.6%, Vietnam 4.4% (2016)

Imports: $60.78 billion (2017 est.)
$53.24 billion (2016 est.)
country comparison to the world: 46

Imports—commodities: machinery, motor vehicles, petroleum and natural gas, organic chemicals, plastics

Imports—partners: Brazil 24.3%, China 18.7%, US 12.5%, Germany 5.5% (2016)

Reserves of foreign exchange and gold: $52.97 billion (31 December 2017 est.)
$38.43 billion (31 December 2016 est.)
country comparison to the world: 39

Debt—external:
$208.6 billion (31 December 2017 est.)
$190.2 billion (31 December 2016 est.)
country comparison to the world: 37

Stock of direct foreign investment—at home: $84.14 billion (31 December 2017 est.)
$72.11 billion (31 December 2016 est.)
country comparison to the world: 49

Stock of direct foreign investment—abroad: $40.94 billion (31 December 2017 est.)
$39.74 billion (31 December 2016 est.)
country comparison to the world: 47

Exchange rates: Argentine pesos (ARS) per US dollar—
16.92 (2017 est.)
14.7582 (2016 est.)
14.7582 (2015 est.)
9.2332 (2014 est.)
8.0753 (2013 est.)

ENERGY

Electricity access: *population without electricity:* 1,500,000
electrification—total population: 96.4%
electrification—urban areas: 99.2%
electrification—rural areas: 96% (2013)

Electricity—production: 133.8 billion kWh (2015 est.)
country comparison to the world: 31

Electricity—consumption: 122.5 billion kWh (2015 est.)
country comparison to the world: 31

Electricity—exports: 55 million kWh (2015 est.)
country comparison to the world: 84

Electricity—imports: 9.018 billion kWh (2015 est.)
country comparison to the world: 28

Electricity—installed generating capacity: 38.19 million kW (2015 est.)
country comparison to the world: 28

Electricity—from fossil fuels: 66.9% of total installed capacity (2015 est.)
country comparison to the world: 111

Electricity—from nuclear fuels: 4.3% of total installed capacity (2015 est.)
country comparison to the world: 24

Electricity—from hydroelectric plants: 23.8% of total installed capacity (2015 est.)
country comparison to the world: 81

Electricity—from other renewable sources: 2.5% of total installed capacity (2015 est.)
country comparison to the world: 115

Crude oil—production: 510,600 bbl/day (2016 est.)
country comparison to the world: 28

Crude oil—exports: 38,600 bbl/day (2014 est.)
country comparison to the world: 44

Crude oil—imports: 10,180 bbl/day (2014 est.)
country comparison to the world: 75

Crude oil—proved reserves: 2.185 billion bbl (1 January 2017 es)
country comparison to the world: 36

Refined petroleum products—production: 687,100 bbl/day (2014 est.)
country comparison to the world: 26

Refined petroleum products—consumption: 803,000 bbl/day (2015 est.)
country comparison to the world: 27

Refined petroleum products—exports: 52,500 bbl/day (2014 est.)
country comparison to the world: 52

Refined petroleum products—imports: 145,000 bbl/day (2014 est.)
country comparison to the world: 48

Natural gas—production: 36.4 billion cu m (2015 est.)
country comparison to the world: 24

Natural gas—consumption: 72.03 billion cu m (2015 est.)
country comparison to the world: 17

Natural gas—exports: 80 million cu m (2015 est.)
country comparison to the world: 49

Natural gas—imports: 10.67 billion cu m (2015 est.)
country comparison to the world: 27

Natural gas—proved reserves: 316.4 billion cu m (1 January 2017 es)
country comparison to the world: 37

Carbon dioxide emissions from consumption of energy: 202 million Mt (2013 est.)
country comparison to the world: 30

COMMUNICATIONS

Telephones—fixed lines: *total subscriptions:* 9,938,630
subscriptions per 100 inhabitants: 23 (July 2016 est.)
country comparison to the world: 21

Telephones—mobile cellular: *total:* 64,033,692
subscriptions per 100 inhabitants: 146 (July 2016 est.)
country comparison to the world: 23

Telephone system: *general assessment:* in 1998 Argentina opened its telecommunications market to competition and foreign investment encouraging the growth of modern telecommunications technology; fiber-optic cable trunk lines are being installed between all major cities; major networks are entirely digital and the availability of telephone service continues to improve to rural areas *domestic:* microwave radio relay, fiber-optic cable, and a domestic satellite system with 40 earth stations serve the trunk network; fixed-line teledensity is increasing gradually and mobile-cellular subscribership is increasing rapidly; broadband Internet services are gaining ground
international: country code—54; landing point for the Atlantis-2, UNISUR, South America-1, and South American Crossing/Latin American

Nautilus submarine cable systems that provide links to Europe, Africa, South and Central America, and US; satellite earth stations—112; 2 international gateways near Buenos Aires (2016)

Broadcast media: government owns a TV station and radio network; more than 2 dozen TV stations and hundreds of privately owned radio stations; high rate of cable TV subscription usage (2009)

Internet country code: .ar

Internet users: total: 30,786,889
percent of population: 70.2% (July 2016 est.)
country comparison to the world: 23

TRANSPORTATION

National air transport system: number of registered air carriers: 6
inventory of registered aircraft operated by air carriers: 107
annual passenger traffic on registered air carriers: 14,245,183
annual freight traffic on registered air carriers: 243,772,567 mt-km (2015)
Civil aircraft registration country code prefix: LV (2016)

Airports: 1,138 (2013)
country comparison to the world: 6

Airports—with paved runways: total: 161
over 3,047 m: 4
2,438 to 3,047 m: 29
1,524 to 2,437 m: 65
914 to 1,523 m: 53
under 914 m: 10 (2017)

Airports—with unpaved runways: total: 977
over 3,047 m: 1
2,438 to 3,047 m: 1
1,524 to 2,437 m: 43
914 to 1,523 m: 484
under 914 m: 448 (2013)

Heliports: 2 (2013)

Pipelines: gas 29,930 km; liquid petroleum gas 41 km; oil 6,248 km; refined products 3,631 km (2013)

Railways: total: 36,917.4 km
broad gauge: 26,391 km 1.676-m gauge (149 km electrified)
standard gauge: 2,745.1 km 1.435-m gauge (41.1 km electrified)
narrow gauge: 7,523.3 km 1.000-m gauge; 258 km 0.750-m gauge (2014)
country comparison to the world: 8

Roadways: total: 231,374 km
paved: 69,412 km (includes 734 km of expressways)
unpaved: 161,962 km (2004)
country comparison to the world: 22

Waterways: 11,000 km (2012)
country comparison to the world: 12

Merchant marine: total: 161
by type: container ship 1, general cargo 9, oil tanker 27, other 124 (2017)
country comparison to the world: 69

Ports and terminals: major seaport(s): Bahia Blanca, Buenos Aires, La Plata, Punta Colorada, Ushuaia
river port(s): Arroyo Seco, Rosario, San Lorenzo-San Martin (Parana)
container port(s) (TEUs): Buenos Aires (1,851,701)
LNG terminal(s) (import): Bahia Blanca

MILITARY AND SECURITY

Military expenditures:
0.95% of GDP (2016)
0.86% of GDP (2015)
0.88% of GDP (2014)
0.84% of GDP (2013)
0.78% of GDP (2012)
country comparison to the world: 106

Military branches: Argentine Army (Ejercito Argentino), Navy of the Argentine Republic (Armada Republica; includes naval aviation and naval infantry), Argentine Air Force (Fuerza Aerea Argentina, FAA) (2013)

Military service age and obligation: 18-24 years of age for voluntary military service (18-21 requires parental consent); no conscription; if the number of volunteers fails to meet the quota of recruits for a particular year, Congress can authorize the conscription of citizens turning 18 that year for a period not exceeding one year (2012)

Military—note: the Argentine military is a well-organized force constrained by the country's prolonged economic hardship; the country has recently experienced a strong recovery, and the military is implementing a modernization plan aimed at making the ground forces lighter and more responsive (2008)

TERRORISM

Terrorist groups—foreign based: Hizballah: aim(s): disrupt Israel's security in Argentina and, ultimately, destroy the state of Israel

area(s) of operation: maintains a limited presence; on 18 July 1994, an operative drove a bomb-laden car into the Argentine Israelite Mutual Association building in Buenos Aires, killing 85 civilians and injuring 300 more; on 17 March 1992, operatives detonated a vehicle-borne improvised explosive device in front of the Israeli Embassy in Buenos Aires, killing 29 people and injuring at least 270 others; Hizballah's leadership stated that the bombing was in retaliation for Israel killing its secretary general, Abbas al-MUSAWI on 16 February 1992

TRANSNATIONAL ISSUES

Disputes—international: Argentina continues to assert its claims to the UK-administered Falkland Islands (Islas Malvinas), South Georgia, and the South Sandwich Islands in its constitution, forcibly occupying the Falklands in 1982, but in 1995 agreed to no longer seek settlement by force; UK continues to reject Argentine requests for sovereignty talks; territorial claim in Antarctica partially overlaps UK and Chilean claims; uncontested dispute between Brazil and Uruguay over Braziliera/Brasiliera Island in the Quarai/Cuareim River leaves the tripoint with Argentina in question; in 2010, the ICJ ruled in favor of Uruguay's operation of two paper mills on the Uruguay River, which forms the border with Argentina; the two countries formed a joint pollution monitoring regime; the joint boundary commission, established by Chile and Argentina in 2001 has yet to map and demarcate the delimited boundary in the inhospitable Andean Southern Ice Field (Campo de Hielo Sur); contraband smuggling, human trafficking, and illegal narcotic trafficking are problems in the porous areas of the border with Bolivia

Illicit drugs: a transshipment country for cocaine headed for Europe, heroin headed for the US, and ephedrine and pseudoephedrine headed for Mexico; some money-laundering activity, especially in the Tri-Border Area; law enforcement corruption; a source for precursor chemicals; increasing domestic consumption of drugs in urban centers, especially cocaine base and synthetic drugs

ARMENIA

INTRODUCTION

Background: Armenia prides itself on being the first nation to formally adopt Christianity (early 4th century). Despite periods of autonomy, over the centuries Armenia came under the sway of various empires including the Roman, Byzantine, Arab, Persian, and Ottoman. During World War I in the western portion of Armenia, the Ottoman

Empire instituted a policy of forced resettlement coupled with other harsh practices that resulted in at least 1 million Armenian deaths. The eastern area of Armenia was ceded by the Ottomans to Russia in 1828; this portion declared its independence in 1918, but was conquered by the Soviet Red Army in 1920.

Armenian leaders remain preoccupied by the long conflict with Azerbaijan over Nagorno-Karabakh,

a primarily Armenian-populated region, assigned to Soviet Azerbaijan in the 1920s by Moscow. Armenia and Azerbaijan began fighting over the area in 1988; the struggle escalated after both countries attained independence from the Soviet Union in 1991. By May 1994, when a trilateral cease-fire between Armenia, Azerbaijan, and Nagorno-Karabakh took hold, ethnic Armenian forces held not only Nagorno-Karabakh but also seven surrounding regions—approximately 14 percent of Azerbaijan's territory. The economies of both sides have been hurt by their inability to make substantial progress toward a peaceful resolution.

Turkey closed the common border with Armenia in 1993 in support of Azerbaijan in its conflict with Armenia over control of Nagorno-Karabakh and surrounding areas, further hampering Armenian economic growth. In 2009, senior Armenian leaders began pursuing rapprochement with Turkey, aiming to secure an opening of the border, but Turkey has not yet ratified the Protocols normalizing relations between the two countries. In January 2015, Armenia joined Russia, Belarus, and Kazakhstan as a member of the Eurasian Economic Union.

GEOGRAPHY

Location: Southwestern Asia, between Turkey (to the west) and Azerbaijan; note—Armenia views itself as part of Europe; geopolitically, it can be classified as falling within Europe, the Middle East, or both

Geographic coordinates: 40 00 N, 45 00 E

Map references: Asia

Area: *total:* 29,743 sq km
land: 28,203 sq km
water: 1,540 sq km
country comparison to the world: 143

Area—comparative: slightly smaller than Maryland

Land boundaries: *total:* 1,570 km
border countries (4): Azerbaijan 996 km, Georgia 219 km, Iran 44 km, Turkey 311 km

Coastline: 0 km (landlocked)

Maritime claims: none (landlocked)

Climate: highland continental, hot summers, cold winters

Terrain: Armenian Highland with mountains; little forest land; fast flowing rivers; good soil in Aras River valley

Elevation: *mean elevation:* 1,792 m

elevation extremes: *lowest point:* Debed River 400 m

highest point: Aragats Lerrnagagat' 4,090 m

Natural resources: small deposits of gold, copper, molybdenum, zinc, bauxite

Land use: *agricultural land:* 59.7%
arable land 15.8%;
permanent crops 1.9%;
permanent pasture 42%
forest: 9.1%
other: 31.2% (2011 est.)
Irrigated land: 2,740 sq km (2012)

Population—distribution: most of the population is located in the northern half of the country; the capital of Yerevan is home to more than five times as many people as Gyumri, the second largest city in the country

Natural hazards: occasionally severe earthquakes; droughts

Environment—current issues: soil pollution from toxic chemicals such as DDT; deforestation; pollution of Hrazdan (Razdan) and Aras Rivers; the draining of Sevana Lich (Lake Sevan), a result of its use as a source for hydropower, threatens drinking water supplies; restart of Metsamor nuclear power plant in spite of its location in a seismically active zone

Environment—international agreements: party to: Air Pollution, Biodiversity, Climate Change, Climate Change-Kyoto Protocol, Desertification, Environmental Modification, Hazardous Wastes, Law of the Sea, Ozone Layer Protection, Wetlands
signed, but not ratified: Air Pollution-Persistent Organic Pollutants

Geography—note: landlocked in the Lesser Caucasus Mountains; Sevana Lich (Lake Sevan) is the largest lake in this mountain range

PEOPLE AND SOCIETY

Population: 3,045,191 (July 2017 est.)
country comparison to the world: 137

Nationality: *noun:* Armenian(s)
adjective: Armenian

Ethnic groups: Armenian 98.1%, Yezidi (Kurd) 1.1%, other 0.7% (2011 est.)

Languages: Armenian (official) 97.9%, Kurdish (spoken by Yezidi minority) 1%, other 1% (2011 est.)

Religions: Armenian Apostolic 92.6%, Evangelical 1%, other 2.4%, none 1.1%, unspecified 2.9% (2011 est.)

Age structure: *0-14 years:* 18.94% (male 306,322/female 270,388)

15-24 years: 12.89% (male 203,358/female 189,092)

25-54 years: 43.43% (male 640,881/female 681,784)

55-64 years: 13.41% (male 187,178/female 221,071)

65 years and over: 11.33% (male 138,458/female 206,659) (2017 est.)

Dependency ratios:
total dependency ratio: 44.4
youth dependency ratio: 28.7

elderly dependency ratio: 15.8
potential support ratio: 6.3 (2015 est.)

Median age: *total:* 35.1 years
male: 33.3 years
female: 36.9 years (2017 est.)
country comparison to the world: 79

Population growth rate: -0.21% (2017 est.)
country comparison to the world: 210

Birth rate: 12.9 births/1,000 population (2017 est.)
country comparison to the world: 154

Death rate: 9.4 deaths/1,000 population (2017 est.)
country comparison to the world: 54

Net migration rate: -5.7 migrant(s)/1,000 population (2017 est.)
country comparison to the world: 195

Population distribution: most of the population is located in the northern half of the country; the capital of Yerevan is home to more than five times as many people as Gyumri, the second largest city in the country

Urbanization: *urban population:* 62.5% of total population (2017)
rate of urbanization: -0.1% annual rate of change (2015-20 est.)

Major urban areas—population: YEREVAN (capital) 1,044 (2015)

Sex ratio: *at birth:* 1.13 male(s)/female
0-14 years: 1.14 male(s)/female
15-24 years: 1.06 male(s)/female
25-54 years: 0.93 male(s)/female
55-64 years: 0.84 male(s)/female
65 years and over: 0.67 male(s)/female
total population: 0.94 male(s)/female (2016 est.)

Mother's mean age at first birth: 24.4 years (2015/16 est.)

Maternal mortality ratio: 25 deaths/100,000 live births (2015 est.)
country comparison to the world: 121

Infant mortality rate: *total:* 12.7 deaths/1,000 live births
male: 14.1 deaths/1,000 live births
female: 11.1 deaths/1,000 live births (2017 est.)
country comparison to the world: 113

Life expectancy at birth: *total population:* 74.9 years
male: 71.6 years
female: 78.5 years (2017 est.)
country comparison to the world: 114

Total fertility rate: 1.64 children born/woman (2017 est.)
country comparison to the world: 177

Contraceptive prevalence rate: 57.1% (2015/16)

Health expenditures: 4.5% of GDP (2014)
country comparison to the world: 155

Physicians density: 2.8 physicians/1,000 population (2014)

Hospital bed density: 3.9 beds/1,000 population (2012)

Drinking water source:
improved:
urban: 100% of population

rural: 100% of population
total: 100% of population
unimproved:
urban: 0% of population
rural: 0% of population
total: 0% of population (2015 est.)

Sanitation facility access:
improved:
urban: 96.2% of population
rural: 78.2% of population
total: 89.5% of population
unimproved:
urban: 3.8% of population
rural: 21.8% of population
total: 10.5% of population (2015 est.)

HIV/AIDS—adult prevalence rate: 0.2% (2016 est.)
country comparison to the world: 88

HIV/AIDS—people living with HIV/AIDS: 3,300 (2016 est.)
country comparison to the world: 111

HIV/AIDS—deaths: <200 (2016 est.)

Obesity—adult prevalence rate: 20.2% (2016)
country comparison to the world: 103

Children under the age of 5 years underweight: 2.6% (2016)
country comparison to the world: 89

Education expenditures: 2.8% of GDP (2015)
country comparison to the world: 132

Literacy: *definition:* age 15 and over can read and write
total population: 99.7%
male: 99.7%
female: 99.6% (2015 est.)

School life expectancy (primary to tertiary education): *total:* 13 years
male: 13 years
female: 13 years (2015)

Unemployment, youth ages 15-24: *total:* 32.5%
male: 28.6%
female: 37.2% (2013 est.)
country comparison to the world: 13

GOVERNMENT

Country name: *conventional long form:* Republic of Armenia
conventional short form: Armenia
local long form: Hayastani Hanrapetut'yun
local short form: Hayastan
former: Armenian Soviet Socialist Republic, Armenian Republic
etymology: the etymology of the country's name remains obscure; according to tradition, the country is named after Hayk, the legendary patriarch of the Armenians and the great-great-grandson of Noah; Hayk's descendant, Aram, purportedly is the source of the name Armenia

Government type: parliamentary democracy

Capital: *name:* Yerevan

geographic coordinates: 40 10 N, 44 30 E
time difference: UTC+4 (9 hours ahead of Washington, DC, during Standard Time)

Administrative divisions: 11 provinces (marzer, singular—marz); Aragatsotn, Ararat, Armavir, Geghark'unik', Kotayk', Lorri, Shirak, Syunik', Tavush, Vayots' Dzor, Yerevan

Independence: 21 September 1991 (from the Soviet Union)

National holiday: Independence Day, 21 September (1991)

Constitution: *history:* previous 1915, 1978; latest adopted 5 July 1995
amendments: proposed by the president of the republic or by the National Assembly; passage requires approval by the president, by the National Assembly, and by a referendum with at least 25% registered voter participation and more than 50% of votes; constitutional articles on the form of government and democratic procedures are not amendable; amended 2005, 2007, 2008, last in 2015
note: a 2015 amendment, approved in December 2015 by a public referendum and effective for the 2017-18 electoral cycle, changes the government type from the current semi-presidential system to a parliamentary system (2017)

Legal system: civil law system

International law organization participation: has not submitted an ICJ jurisdiction declaration; non-party state to the ICCt

Citizenship: *citizenship by birth:* no
citizenship by descent only: at least one parent must be a citizen of Armenia
dual citizenship recognized: yes
residency requirement for naturalization: 3 years

Suffrage: 18 years of age; universal

Executive branch: *chief of state:* President Serzh SARGSIAN (since 9 April 2008)
head of government: Prime Minister Karen KARAPETYAN (since 13 September 2016)
cabinet: Council of Ministers appointed by the prime minister
elections/appointments: president directly elected by absolute majority popular vote in 2 rounds if needed for a 5-year term (eligible for a second term); election last held on 18 February 2013 (next to be held in February 2018); prime minister appointed by the president based on majority support in the National Congress; the prime minister and Council of Ministers must resign if the National Congress refuses to accept their program
election results: Serzh SARGSIAN reelected president in first round; percent of vote—Serzh SARGSIAN (RPA) 58.6%, Raffi HOVHANNI-SIAN (Heritage Party) 36.7%, Hrant BAGRA-TIAN (ANM) 2.2%, other 2.5%
note: constitutional changes adopted in December 2015 will transform the government to a parliamentary system by 2018; for the scheduled February 2018 election, the president will be indirectly elected by parliament and will serve a single 7-year term; following the 2018 election, the prime minister will be elected based on majority support of the National Assembly

Legislative branch: *description:* unicameral National Assembly (Parliament) or Azgayin Zhoghov (minimum 101 seats, currently 105; members directly elected in single-seat constituencies by proportional representation vote; members serve 5-year terms)
elections: last held on 2 April 2017 (next to be held in spring of 2022)
election results: percent of vote by party—RPA 49.2%, Tsarukyan Alliance 27.4%, Yelk (Way Out) 7.8%, ARF (Dashnak) 6.6%, other 9%; seats by party—RPA 58, Tsarukyan Alliance 31, Yelk (Way Out) 9, ARF (Dashnak) 7

Judicial branch: *highest court(s):* Court of Cassation (consists of the court chairman and organized into the criminal chamber and a civil and administrative chamber, each with a chamber chairman and 2 judges); Constitutional Court (consists of 9 judges)
judge selection and term of office: Court of Cassation judges nominated by the Judicial Council, a 9-member body of selected judges and legal scholars; judges appointed by the president; Constitutional Court judges—4 appointed by the president, and 5 elected by National Assembly; judges of both courts can serve until retirement at age 65
subordinate courts: 2 Courts of Appeal (for civil cases and for criminal and military cases); district courts; Administrative Court

Political parties and leaders: Armenian National Congress or ANC (bloc of independent and opposition parties) [Levon TER-PETROSSIAN]
Armenian National Movement or ANM [Ararat ZURABIAN]
Armenian Revolutionary Federation or ARF ("Dashnak" Party) [Hrant MARKARIAN]
Heritage Party [Raffi HOVHANNISIAN]
People's Party of Armenia [Stepan DEMIRCHIAN]
Prosperous Armenia [Gagik TSARUKYAN]
Republican Party of Armenia or RPA [Serzh SARGSIAN]
Rule of Law Party (Orinats Yerkir) [Artur BAGHDASARIAN]
Tsarukyan Alliance [Gagik TSARUKYAN]
Yelk (Way Out) Alliance [Edmon Marukyan]

Political pressure groups and leaders: Aylentrank (Impeachment Alliance) [Nikol PASHINIAN]
Yerkrapah Union [Manvel GRIGORIAN]

International organization participation: ADB, BSEC, CD, CE, CIS, CSTO, EAEC (observer), EAEU, EAPC, EBRD, FAO, GCTU, IAEA, IBRD, ICAO, ICC (NGOs), ICRM, IDA, IFAD, IFC, IFRCS, ILO, IMF, Interpol, IOC, IOM, IPU, ISO, ITSO, ITU, MIGA, NAM (observer), OAS (observer), OIF, OPCW, OSCE, PFP, UN, UNC-TAD, UNESCO, UNIDO, UNIFIL, UNWTO, UPU, WCO, WFTU (NGOs), WHO, WIPO, WMO, WTO

Diplomatic representation in the US: *chief of mission:* Ambassador Grigor HOVHANNISSIAN (since 28 January 2016)
chancery: 2225 R Street NW, Washington, DC 20008
telephone: [1] (202) 319-1976
FAX: [1] (202) 319-2982

consulate(s) general: Glendale (CA)

Diplomatic representation from the US: *chief of mission:* Ambassador Richard MILLS (since 13 February 2015)

embassy: 1 American Ave., Yerevan 0082

mailing address: American Embassy Yerevan, US Department of State, 7020 Yerevan Place, Washington, DC 20521-7020

telephone: [374](10) 464-700

FAX: [374](10) 464-742

Flag description: three equal horizontal bands of red (top), blue, and orange; the color red recalls the blood shed for liberty, blue the Armenian skies as well as hope, and orange the land and the courage of the workers who farm it

National symbol(s): Mount Ararat, eagle, lion; national colors: red, blue, orange

National anthem: name: "Mer Hayrenik" (Our Fatherland)

lyrics/music: Mikael NALBANDIAN/Barsegh KANACHYAN

note: adopted 1991; based on the anthem of the Democratic Republic of Armenia (1918-1922) but with different lyrics

ECONOMY

Economy—overview: Under the old Soviet central planning system, Armenia developed a modern industrial sector, supplying machine tools, textiles, and other manufactured goods to sister republics, in exchange for raw materials and energy. Armenia has since switched to small-scale agriculture and away from the large agro industrial complexes of the Soviet era. Armenia has only two open trade borders—Iran and Georgia—because its borders with Azerbaijan and Turkey have been closed since 1991 and 1993, respectively, as a result of Armenia's ongoing conflict with Azerbaijan over the separatist Nagorno-Karabakh region.

Armenia joined the World Trade Organization in January 2003. The government has made some improvements in tax and customs administration in recent years, but anti-corruption measures have been largely ineffective. Armenia will need to pursue additional economic reforms and strengthen the rule of law in order to raise its economic growth and improve economic competitiveness and employment opportunities, especially given its economic isolation from Turkey and Azerbaijan.

Armenia's geographic isolation, a narrow export base, and pervasive monopolies in important business sectors have made it particularly vulnerable to volatility in the global commodity markets and the economic challenges in Russia. Armenia is particularly dependent on Russian commercial and governmental support, as most key Armenian infrastructure is Russian-owned and/or managed, especially in the energy sector. Remittances from expatriates working in Russia are equivalent to about 12-14% of GDP. Armenia joined the Russia-led Eurasian Economic Union in January 2015, but has remained interested in pursuing closer ties with the EU as well, signing Comprehensive and Enhanced Partnership Agreement with the EU in November 2017. Armenia's rising government debt is leading Yerevan to tighten its fiscal policies—the amount is approaching the debt to GDP ratio threshold set by national legislation.

GDP (purchasing power parity):
$27.21 billion (2017 est.)
$26.28 billion (2016 est.)
$26.23 billion (2015 est.)
note: data are in 2017 dollars
country comparison to the world: 138

GDP (official exchange rate):
$11.04 billion (2017 est.)

GDP—real growth rate:
3.5% (2017 est.)
0.2% (2016 est.)
3.3% (2015 est.)
country comparison to the world: 94

GDP—per capita (PPP):
$9,100 (2017 est.)
$8,800 (2016 est.)
$8,800 (2015 est.)
note: data are in 2017 dollars
country comparison to the world: 144

Gross national saving:
17.4% of GDP (2017 est.)
17% of GDP (2016 est.)
18.4% of GDP (2015 est.)
country comparison to the world: 106

GDP—composition, by end use:
household consumption: 76.6%
government consumption: 13.1%
investment in fixed capital: 17.9%
investment in inventories: 3%
exports of goods and services: 37.3%
imports of goods and services: -47.9% (2017 est.)

GDP—composition, by sector of origin:
agriculture: 17.7%
industry: 27.8%
services: 54.5% (2017 est.)

Agriculture—products: fruit (especially grapes and apricots), vegetables; livestock

Industries: brandy, mining, diamond processing, metal-cutting machine tools, forging and pressing machines, electric motors, knitted wear, hosiery, shoes, silk fabric, chemicals, trucks, instruments, microelectronics, jewelry, software, food processing

Industrial production growth rate: 5% (2017 est.)
country comparison to the world: 46

Labor force: 1.507 million (2017 est.)
country comparison to the world: 132

Labor force—by occupation: agriculture: 36.3%
industry: 17%
services: 46.7% (2013 est.)

Unemployment rate: 18.9% (2017 est.)
18.8% (2016 est.)
country comparison to the world: 181

Population below poverty line: 32% (2013 est.)

Household income or consumption by percentage share: *lowest 10%:* 3.5%
highest 10%: 25.7% (2014)

Distribution of family income—Gini index: 31.5 (2014)
31.5 (2013 est.)
country comparison to the world: 118

Budget: *revenues:* $2.536 billion
expenditures: $2.91 billion (2017 est.)
Taxes and other revenues: 23% of GDP (2017 est.)
country comparison to the world: 129

Budget surplus (+) or deficit (-): -3.4% of GDP (2017 est.)
country comparison to the world: 128

Public debt: 56.7% of GDP (2017 est.)
56.5% of GDP (2016 est.)
country comparison to the world: 83

Fiscal year: calendar year

Inflation rate (consumer prices):
1.9% (2017 est.)
-1.4% (2016 est.)
country comparison to the world: 85

Central bank discount rate: 6.5% (14 December 2016)
10.5% (10 February 2015)
note: this is the Refinancing Rate, the key monetary policy instrument of the Armenian National Bank
country comparison to the world: 61

Commercial bank prime lending rate: 16% (31 December 2017 est.)
17.36% (31 December 2016 est.)
note: average lending rate on loans up to one year
country comparison to the world: 34

Stock of narrow money:
$1.514 billion (31 December 2017 est.)
$1.355 billion (31 December 2016 est.)
country comparison to the world: 143

Stock of broad money: $2.563 billion (31 December 2017 est.)
$2.219 billion (31 December 2016 est.)
country comparison to the world: 145

Stock of domestic credit: $6.616 billion (31 December 2017 est.)
$5.689 billion (31 December 2016 est.)
country comparison to the world: 123

Market value of publicly traded shares:
$132.1 million (31 December 2012 est.)
$139.6 million (31 December 2011 est.)
$144.8 million (31 December 2010 est.)
country comparison to the world: 121

Current account balance: -$398 million (2017 est.)
-$238 million (2016 est.)
country comparison to the world: 100

Exports: $2.233 billion (2017 est.)
$1.891 billion (2016 est.)
country comparison to the world: 137

Exports—commodities: unwrought copper, pig iron, nonferrous metals, gold, diamonds, mineral products, foodstuffs, brandy, cigarettes, energy

Exports—partners: Russia 21%, Bulgaria 8.7%, Georgia 8.1%, Canada 7.9%, Germany 7.9%, Iraq 7.8%, China 5.7%, Iran 4.2%, Switzerland 4.2% (2016)

Imports: $3.361 billion (2017 est.)
$2.835 billion (2016 est.)
country comparison to the world: 139

Imports—commodities: natural gas, petroleum, tobacco products, foodstuffs, diamonds, pharmaceuticals, cars

Imports—partners: Russia 30.7%, China 11%, Iran 5.1%, Turkey 5%, Germany 5% (2016)

Reserves of foreign exchange and gold: $2.242 billion (31 December 2017 est.)
$2.204 billion (31 December 2016 est.)
country comparison to the world: 116

Debt—external:
$9.17 billion (31 December 2017 est.)
$8.987 billion (31 December 2016 est.)
country comparison to the world: 117

Stock of direct foreign investment—at home:
$4.169 billion (2015 est.)
$4.087 billion (2014 est.)
country comparison to the world: 107

Stock of direct foreign investment—abroad: $228 million (2015 est.)
$215 million (2014 est.)
country comparison to the world: 99

Exchange rates: drams (AMD) per US dollar—
487.9 (2017 est.)
480.49 (2016 est.)
480.49 (2015 est.)
477.92 (2014 est.)
415.92 (2013 est.)

ENERGY

Electricity access: electrification—*total population:* 100% (2016)

Electricity—production: 7.393 billion kWh (2015 est.)
country comparison to the world: 112

Electricity—consumption: 5.331 billion kWh (2015 est.)
country comparison to the world: 119

Electricity—exports: 1.424 billion kWh (2015 est.)
country comparison to the world: 50

Electricity—imports: 174 million kWh (2015 est.)
country comparison to the world: 95

Electricity—installed generating capacity: 4.068 million kW (2015 est.)
country comparison to the world: 87

Electricity—from fossil fuels: 58.8% of total installed capacity (2015 est.)
country comparison to the world: 133

Electricity—from nuclear fuels: 9.2% of total installed capacity (2015 est.)
country comparison to the world: 19

Electricity—from hydroelectric plants: 31.9% of total installed capacity (2015 est.)
country comparison to the world: 67

Electricity—from other renewable sources: 0.1% of total installed capacity (2015 est.)
country comparison to the world: 166

Crude oil—production: 0 bbl/day (2016 est.)
country comparison to the world: 106

Crude oil—exports: 0 bbl/day (2014 est.)
country comparison to the world: 87

Crude oil—imports: 0 bbl/day (2014 est.)
country comparison to the world: 91

Crude oil—proved reserves: 0 bbl (1 January 2017 es)
country comparison to the world: 106

Refined petroleum products—production: 0 bbl/day (2014 est.)
country comparison to the world: 115

Refined petroleum products—consumption: 8,000 bbl/day (2015 est.)
country comparison to the world: 161

Refined petroleum products—exports: 0 bbl/day (2014 est.)
country comparison to the world: 130

Refined petroleum products—imports: 7,736 bbl/day (2014 est.)
country comparison to the world: 148

Natural gas—production: 0 cu m (2013 est.)
country comparison to the world: 103

Natural gas—consumption: 2.73 billion cu m (2015 est.)
country comparison to the world: 80

Natural gas—exports: 0 cu m (2013 est.)
country comparison to the world: 61

Natural gas—imports: 2.05 billion cu m (2015 est.)
country comparison to the world: 51

Natural gas—proved reserves: 0 cu m (1 January 2014 es)
country comparison to the world: 110

Carbon dioxide emissions from consumption of energy: 12 million Mt (2013 est.)
country comparison to the world: 98

COMMUNICATIONS

Telephones—fixed lines: *total subscriptions:* 531,624
subscriptions per 100 inhabitants: 17 (July 2016 est.)
country comparison to the world: 94

Telephones—mobile cellular: *total:* 3,434,567
subscriptions per 100 inhabitants: 113 (July 2016 est.)
country comparison to the world: 130

Telephone system: *general assessment:* telecommunications investments have made major inroads in modernizing and upgrading the outdated telecommunications network inherited from the Soviet era; now 100% privately owned and undergoing modernization and expansion; mobile-cellular services monopoly terminated in late 2004, and a second and third provider began operations in 2005 and 2009 respectively
domestic: reliable modern fixed-line and mobile-cellular services are available across Yerevan and

in major cities and towns; mobile-cellular coverage available in most rural areas
international: country code—374; Yerevan is connected to the Trans-Asia-Europe fiber-optic cable through Iran; additional international service is available by microwave radio relay and landline connections to the other countries of the Commonwealth of Independent States, through the Moscow international switch, and by satellite to the rest of the world; satellite earth stations—3 (2015)

Broadcast media: 2 public TV networks operating alongside about 40 privately owned TV stations that provide local to near nationwide coverage; major Russian broadcast stations are widely available; subscription cable TV services are available in most regions; Armenian TV completed conversion from analog to digital broadcasting in late 2016; Public Radio of Armenia is a national, state-run broadcast network that operates alongside 21 privately owned radio stations; several major international broadcasters are available (2017)

Internet country code: .am

Internet users: *total:* 1,891,775
percent of population: 62.0% (July 2016 est.)
country comparison to the world: 117

TRANSPORTATION

National air transport system: *number of registered air carriers:* 3
inventory of registered aircraft operated by air carriers: 5 (2015)
Civil aircraft registration country code prefix: EK (2016)

Airports: 11 (2013)
country comparison to the world: 154

Airports—with paved runways: *total:* 10
over 3,047 m: 2
2,438 to 3,047 m: 2
1,524 to 2,437 m: 4
914 to 1,523 m: 2 (2017)

Airports—with unpaved runways: *total:* 1
914 to 1,523 m: 1 (2013)

Pipelines: gas (high and medium pressure) 3,838 km (2017)

Railways: *total:* 780 km
broad gauge: 780 km 1.520-m gauge (780 km electrified)
note: 726 km operational (2014)
country comparison to the world: 97

Roadways: total: 7,792 km (2013)
country comparison to the world: 142

MILITARY AND SECURITY

Military expenditures: 4.09% of GDP (2016)
4.25% of GDP (2015)
3.94% of GDP (2014)
4% of GDP (2013)
3.58% of GDP (2012)
country comparison to the world: 10

Military branches: *Armenian Armed Forces:* Ground Forces, Air Force and Air Defense; "Nagorno-Karabakh Republic": Nagorno-Karabakh Self-Defense Force (NKSDF) (2011)

Military service age and obligation: 18-27 years of age for voluntary or compulsory military service; 2-year conscript service obligation; 17 year olds are eligible to become cadets at military higher education institutes, where they are classified as military personnel (2012)

TRANSNATIONAL ISSUES

Disputes—international: the dispute over the break-away Nagorno-Karabakh region and the Armenian military occupation of surrounding lands in Azerbaijan remains the primary focus of regional instability; residents have evacuated the former Soviet-era small ethnic enclaves in Armenia and Azerbaijan; Turkish authorities have complained that blasting from quarries in Armenia might be damaging the medieval ruins of Ani, on the other side of the Arpacay valley; in 2009, Swiss mediators facilitated an accord reestablishing diplomatic ties between Armenia and Turkey, but neither side has ratified the agreement and the rapprochement effort has faltered; local border forces struggle to control the illegal transit of goods and people across the porous, undemarcated Armenian, Azerbaijani, and Georgian borders; ethnic Armenian groups in the Javakheti region of Georgia seek greater autonomy from the Georgian Government

Refugees and internally displaced persons: *refugees (country of origin):* 14,626 (Syria—ethnic Armenians) (2016)
IDPs: 8,400 (conflict with Azerbaijan over Nagorno-Karabakh) (2016)
stateless persons: 512 (2016)

Illicit drugs: illicit cultivation of small amount of cannabis for domestic consumption; minor transit point for illicit drugs—mostly opium and hashish—moving from Southwest Asia to Russia and to a lesser extent the rest of Europe

ARUBA

INTRODUCTION

Background: Discovered and claimed for Spain in 1499, Aruba was acquired by the Dutch in 1636. The island's economy has been dominated by three main industries. A 19th century gold rush was followed by prosperity brought on by the opening in 1924 of an oil refinery. The last decades of the 20th century saw a boom in the tourism industry. Aruba seceded from the Netherlands Antilles in 1986 and became a separate, autonomous member of the Kingdom of the Netherlands. Movement toward full independence was halted at Aruba's request in 1990.

GEOGRAPHY

Location: Caribbean, island in the Caribbean Sea, north of Venezuela

Geographic coordinates: 12 30 N, 69 58 W

Map references: Central America and the Caribbean

Area: *total:* 180 sq km
land: 180 sq km
water: 0 sq km
country comparison to the world: 218

Area—comparative: slightly larger than Washington, DC

Land boundaries: 0 km

Coastline: 68.5 km

Maritime claims: *territorial sea:* 12 nm
exclusive economic zone: 200 nm

Climate: tropical marine; little seasonal temperature variation

Terrain: flat with a few hills; scant vegetation

Elevation: *mean elevation:* NA

elevation extremes: *lowest point:* Caribbean Sea 0 m
highest point: Ceru Jamanota 188 m

Natural resources: NEGL; white sandy beaches foster tourism

Land use: *agricultural land:* 11.1%
arable land 11.1%;
permanent crops 0%;
permanent pasture 0%
forest: 2.3%
other: 86.6% (2011 est.)
Irrigated land: NA

Population—distribution: most residents live in or around Oranjestad and San Nicolaas; most settlements tend to be located on the less mountainous western side of the island

Natural hazards: hurricanes; lies outside the Caribbean hurricane belt and is rarely threatened

Environment—current issues: difficulty in properly disposing of waste produced by large numbers of tourists

Geography—note: a flat, riverless island renowned for its white sand beaches; its tropical climate is moderated by constant trade winds from the Atlantic Ocean; the temperature is almost constant at about 27 degrees Celsius (81 degrees Fahrenheit)

PEOPLE AND SOCIETY

Population: 115,120 (July 2017 est.)
country comparison to the world: 189

Nationality: *noun:* Aruban(s)
adjective: Aruban; Dutch

Ethnic groups: Dutch 82.1%, Colombian 6.6%, Venezuelan 2.2%, Dominican 2.2%, Haitian 1.2%, other 5.5%, unspecified 0.1% (2010 est.)

Languages: Papiamento (official) (a creole language that is a mixture of Portuguese, Spanish, Dutch, English, and, to a lesser extent, French, as well as elements of African languages and the language of the Arawak) 69.4%, Spanish 13.7%, English (widely spoken) 7.1%, Dutch (official) 6.1%, Chinese 1.5%, other 1.7%, unspecified 0.4% (2010 est.)

Religions: Roman Catholic 75.3%, Protestant 4.9% (includes Methodist 0.9%, Adventist 0.9%, Anglican 0.4%, other Protestant 2.7%), Jehovah's Witness 1.7%, other 12%, none 5.5%, unspecified 0.5% (2010 est.)

Age structure: *0-14 years:* 17.64% (male 10,189/female 10,115)
15-24 years: 12.78% (male 7,405/female 7,307)
25-54 years: 41.72% (male 23,117/female 24,906)
55-64 years: 14.28% (male 7,664/female 8,773)
65 years and over: 13.59% (male 6,132/female 9,512) (2017 est.)

Dependency ratios:
total dependency ratio: 44.6
youth dependency ratio: 27
elderly dependency ratio: 17.5
potential support ratio: 5.7 (2015 est.)

Median age: *total:* 39.3 years
male: 37.5 years
female: 41.1 years (2017 est.)
country comparison to the world: 56

Population growth rate: 1.27% (2017 est.)
country comparison to the world: 88

Birth rate: 12.4 births/1,000 population (2017 est.)
country comparison to the world: 159

Death rate: 8.4 deaths/1,000 population (2017 est.)
country comparison to the world: 82

Net migration rate: 8.7 migrant(s)/1,000 population (2017 est.)
country comparison to the world: 11

Population distribution: most residents live in or around Oranjestad and San Nicolaas; most settlments tend to be located on the less mountainous western side of the island

Urbanization: *urban population:* 41.1% of total population (2017)

rate of urbanization: -0.1% annual rate of change (2015-20 est.)

Major urban areas—population: ORANJESTAD (capital) 29,000 (2014)

Sex ratio: at birth: 1.02 male(s)/female
0-14 years: 1.01 male(s)/female
15-24 years: 1.01 male(s)/female
25-54 years: 0.93 male(s)/female
55-64 years: 0.87 male(s)/female
65 years and over: 0.64 male(s)/female
total population: 0.9 male(s)/female (2016 est.)

Infant mortality rate: *total:* 10.7 deaths/1,000 live births
male: 14 deaths/1,000 live births
female: 7.4 deaths/1,000 live births (2017 est.)
country comparison to the world: 131

Life expectancy at birth: *total population:* 76.9 years
male: 73.9 years
female: 80.1 years (2017 est.)
country comparison to the world: 80

Total fertility rate: 1.83 children born/woman (2017 est.)
country comparison to the world: 148

Drinking water source:
improved:
urban: 98.1% of population
rural: 98.1% of population
total: 98.1% of population
unimproved:
urban: 1.9% of population
rural: 1.9% of population
total: 1.9% of population (2015 est.)

Sanitation facility access:
improved:
urban: 97.7% of population
rural: 97.7% of population
total: 97.7% of population
unimproved:
urban: 2.3% of population
rural: 2.3% of population
total: 2.3% of population (2015 est.)

HIV/AIDS—adult prevalence rate: NA

HIV/AIDS—people living with HIV/AIDS: NA

HIV/AIDS—deaths: NA

Major infectious diseases: *note:* active local transmission of Zika virus by Aedes species mosquitoes has been identified in this country (as of August 2016); it poses an important risk (a large number of cases possible) among US citizens if bitten by an infective mosquito; other less common ways to get Zika are through sex, via blood transfusion, or during pregnancy, in which the pregnant woman passes Zika virus to her fetus (2016)

Education expenditures: 6.1% of GDP (2014)
country comparison to the world: 41

Literacy: *definition:* age 15 and over can read and write
total population: 97.5%
male: 97.5%
female: 97.5% (2015 est.)

School life expectancy (primary to tertiary education): *total:* 14 years

male: 13 years
female: 14 years (2012)

Unemployment, youth ages 15-24:
total: 28.9%
male: 29.9%
female: 27.5% (2010 est.)
country comparison to the world: 43

GOVERNMENT

Country name: *conventional long form:* none
conventional short form: Aruba
etymology: the origin of the island's name is unclear; according to tradition, the name comes from the Spanish phrase "oro huba" (there was gold), but in fact no gold was ever found on the island; another possibility is the native word "oruba," which means "well-situated"

Dependency status: constituent country of the Kingdom of the Netherlands; full autonomy in internal affairs obtained in 1986 upon separation from the Netherlands Antilles; Dutch Government responsible for defense and foreign affairs

Government type: parliamentary democracy (Legislature); part of the Kingdom of the Netherlands

Capital: *name:* Oranjestad

geographic coordinates: 12 31 N, 70 02 W
time difference: UTC-4 (1 hour ahead of Washington, DC, during Standard Time)

Administrative divisions: none (part of the Kingdom of the Netherlands)
note: Aruba is one of four constituent countries of the Kingdom of the Netherlands; the other three are the Netherlands, Curacao, and Sint Maarten

Independence: none (part of the Kingdom of the Netherlands)

National holiday: National Anthem and Flag Day, 18 March (1976)

Constitution: previous 1947, 1955; latest drafted and approved August 1985, enacted 1 January 1986 (regulates governance of Aruba but is subordinate to the Charter for the Kingdom of the Netherlands); note—in October 2010, following dissolution of the Netherlands Antilles, Aruba became a constituent country within the Kingdom of the Netherlands (2016)

Legal system: civil law system based on the Dutch civil code

Citizenship: see the Netherlands

Suffrage: 18 years of age; universal

Executive branch: *chief of state:* King WILLEM-ALEXANDER of the Netherlands (since 30 April 2013); represented by Governor General Alfonso BOEKHOUDT (since 1 January 2017)

head of government: Prime Minister Evelyn WEVER-CROES (since 17 November 2017)
cabinet: Council of Ministers elected by the Legislature (Staten) elections/appointments: the monarchy is hereditary; governor general appointed by the monarch for a 6-year term; prime minister and deputy prime minister indirectly elected by the Staten for 4-year term; election last held on 27 September 2013 (next to be held by September 2017)

election results: Evelyn WEVER-CROES (MEP) elected prime minister; percent of legislative vote—NA

Legislative branch: *description:* unicameral Legislature or Staten (21 seats; members directly elected in a single nationwide constituency by proportional representation vote; members serve 4-year terms)
elections: last held on 22 September 2017 (next to be held in September 2021)
election results: percent of vote by party AVP 39.8%, MEP 37.6%, POR 9.4%, RED 7.1%; seats by party—AVP 9, MEP 9, POR 2, RED 1

Judicial branch: *highest court(s):* Joint Court of Justice of Aruba, Curacao, Sint Maarten, and of Bonaire, Sint Eustatitus and Saba or "Joint Court of Justice" (sits as a 3-judge panel); final appeals heard by the Supreme Court, in The Hague, Netherlands
judge selection and term of office: Joint Court judges appointed by the monarch for life
subordinate courts: Courts in First Instance

Political parties and leaders: Aruban People's Party or AVP [Michiel "Mike" EMAN]
Democratic Electoral Network or RED [L.R. CROES]
People's Electoral Movement Party or MEP [Evelyn WEVER-CROES]
Pueblo Orguyoso y Respeta or POR [O.E. ODUBER]
Real Democracy or PDR [Andin BIKKER]

Political pressure groups and leaders: environmental groups

International organization participation: Caricom (observer), FATF, ILO, IMF, Interpol, IOC, ITUC (NGOs), UNESCO (associate), UNWTO (associate), UPU

Diplomatic representation in the US: none (represented by the Kingdom of the Netherlands); note—there is a Minister Plenipotentiary for Aruba at the Embassy of the Kingdom of the Netherlands

Diplomatic representation from the US: the US does not have an embassy in Aruba; the Consul General to Curacao is accredited to Aruba

Flag description: blue, with two narrow, horizontal, yellow stripes across the lower portion and a red, four-pointed star outlined in white in the upper hoist-side corner; the star represents Aruba and its red soil and white beaches, its four points the four major languages (Papiamento, Dutch, Spanish, English) as well as the four points of a compass, to indicate that its inhabitants come from all over the world; the blue symbolizes Caribbean waters and skies; the stripes represent the island's two main "industries": the flow of tourists to the sun-drenched beaches and the flow of minerals from the earth

National symbol(s): Hooiberg (Haystack) Hill; national colors: blue, yellow, red, white

National anthem: *name:* "Aruba Deshi Tera" (Aruba Precious Country)
lyrics/music: Juan Chabaya 'Padu' LAMPE/Rufo Inocencio WEVER

note: local anthem adopted 1986; as part of the Kingdom of the Netherlands, "Het Wilhelmus" is official (see Netherlands)

ECONOMY

Economy—overview: Tourism, petroleum bunkering, hospitality, and financial and business services are the mainstays of the small open Aruban economy.

Tourism accounts for a majority of economic activity; as of 2014, over 1.7 million tourists visited Aruba annually, with the large majority of those from the US. The rapid growth of the tourism sector has resulted in a substantial expansion of other activities. Construction continues to boom, especially in the hotel sector.

Aruba is heavily dependent on imports and is making efforts to expand exports to improve its trade balance. Almost all consumer and capital goods are imported, with the US, the Netherlands, and Panama being the major suppliers.

In 2016, Citgo Petroleum Corporation, an indirect wholly owned subsidiary of Petroleos de Venezuela SA, and the Government of Aruba signed an agreement to restart Valero Energy Corp.'s former 235,000-b/d refinery . Tourism and related industries have continued to grow, and the Aruban government is working to attract more diverse industries. Aruba's banking sector continues to be a strong sector; unemployment has significantly decreased.

GDP (purchasing power parity):
$2.516 billion (2009 est.)
$2.258 billion (2005 est.)
$2.205 billion (2004 est.)
country comparison to the world: 191

GDP (official exchange rate):
$2.516 billion (2009 est.)

GDP—real growth rate: 2.4% (2005 est.)
country comparison to the world: 139

GDP—per capita (PPP): $25,300 (2011 est.)
country comparison to the world: 78

GDP—composition, by end use:
household consumption: 60.3%
government consumption: 26.2%
investment in fixed capital: 22.3%
investment in inventories: 0%
exports of goods and services: 70.2%
imports of goods and services: -79% (2014 est.)

GDP—composition, by sector of origin:
agriculture: 0.4%
industry: 33.3%
services: 66.3% (2002 est.)

Agriculture—products: aloes; livestock; fish

Industries: tourism, petroleum transshipment facilities, banking

Industrial production growth rate: NA%

Labor force: 51,610
note: of the 51,610 workers aged 15 and over in the labor force, 32,252 were born in Aruba and 19,353 came from abroad; foreign workers are 38% of the employed population (2007 est.)
country comparison to the world: 192

Labor force—by occupation: *agriculture:* NA%
industry: NA%
services: NA%
note: most employment is in wholesale and retail trade, followed by hotels and restaurants

Unemployment rate: 6.9% (2005 est.)
country comparison to the world: 98

Population below poverty line: NA%

Household income or consumption by percentage share: *lowest 10%:* NA%
highest 10%: NA%

Budget: *revenues:* $695.4 million
expenditures: $794 million (2017 est.)
Taxes and other revenues: 27.6% of GDP (2017 est.)
country comparison to the world: 101

Budget surplus (+) or deficit (-): -3.9% of GDP (2017 est.)
country comparison to the world: 141
Public debt: 67% of GDP (2013)
55% of GDP (2012)
country comparison to the world: 55

Fiscal year: calendar year

Inflation rate (consumer prices): -0.1% (2017 est.)
-0.9% (2016 est.)
country comparison to the world: 9

Central bank discount rate: 1% (31 December 2010)
3% (31 December 2009)
country comparison to the world: 127

Commercial bank prime lending rate: 8.5% (31 December 2017 est.)
7.83% (31 December 2016 est.)
country comparison to the world: 98

Stock of narrow money:
$1.257 billion (31 December 2016 est.)
$1.257 billion (31 December 2016 est.)
country comparison to the world: 151

Stock of broad money: $2.328 billion (31 December 2016 est.)
$2.126 billion (31 December 2015 est.)
country comparison to the world: 150

Stock of domestic credit: $1.848 billion (31 December 2016 est.)
country comparison to the world: 150

Exports: $246.3 million (2017 est.)
$283.1 million (2016 est.)
country comparison to the world: 185

Exports—commodities: live animals and animal products, art and collectibles, machinery and electrical equipment, transport equipment

Exports—partners: Colombia 23.4%, US 19.8%, Netherlands 16.9%, Venezuela 13.9% (2016)

Imports: $1.165 billion (2017 est.)
$1.142 billion (2016 est.)
country comparison to the world: 175

Imports—commodities: machinery and electrical equipment, refined oil for bunkering and reexport, chemicals; foodstuffs

Imports—partners: US 55.4%, Netherlands 12.6% (2016)

Debt—external:
$693.2 million (31 December 2014 est.)
$666.4 million (31 December 2013 est.)
country comparison to the world: 173

Exchange rates: Aruban guilders/florins per US dollar—
1.79 (2017 est.)
1.79 (2016 est.)
1.79 (2015 est.)
1.79 (2014 est.)
1.79 (2013 est.)

ENERGY

Electricity access: *population without electricity:* 11,364
electrification—*total population:* 91%
electrification—*urban areas:* 100%
electrification—*rural areas:* 80% (2012)

Electricity—production: 959 million kWh (2015 est.)
country comparison to the world: 153

Electricity—consumption: 891.9 million kWh (2015 est.)
country comparison to the world: 159

Electricity—exports: 0 kWh (2016 est.)
country comparison to the world: 96

Electricity—imports: 0 kWh (2016 est.)
country comparison to the world: 116

Electricity—installed generating capacity: 296,000 kW (2015 est.)
country comparison to the world: 158

Electricity—from fossil fuels: 87.2% of total installed capacity (2015 est.)
country comparison to the world: 69

Electricity—from nuclear fuels: 0% of total installed capacity (2015 est.)
country comparison to the world: 33

Electricity—from hydroelectric plants: 0% of total installed capacity (2015 est.)
country comparison to the world: 156

Electricity—from other renewable sources: 12.8% of total installed capacity (2015 est.)
country comparison to the world: 57

Crude oil—production: 0 bbl/day (2016 est.)
country comparison to the world: 107

Crude oil—exports: 0 bbl/day (2014 est.)
country comparison to the world: 84

Crude oil—imports: 0 bbl/day (2014 est.)
country comparison to the world: 86

Crude oil—proved reserves: 0 bbl (1 January 2017 es)
country comparison to the world: 107

Refined petroleum products—production: 0 bbl/day (2014 est.)
country comparison to the world: 116

Refined petroleum products—consumption: 7,500 bbl/day (2015 est.)
country comparison to the world: 164

Refined petroleum products—exports: 0 bbl/day (2014 est.)
country comparison to the world: 128

Refined petroleum products—imports: 7,661 bbl/day (2014 est.)
country comparison to the world: 149

Natural gas—production: 1 cu m (2013 est.)
country comparison to the world: 101

Natural gas—consumption: 1 cu m (2013 est.)
country comparison to the world: 116

Natural gas—exports: 1 cu m (2013 est.)
country comparison to the world: 57

Natural gas—imports: 1 cu m (2013 est.)
country comparison to the world: 79

Natural gas—proved reserves: 0 cu m (1 January 2014 es)
country comparison to the world: 108

Carbon dioxide emissions from consumption of energy: 900,000 Mt (2013 est.)
country comparison to the world: 165

COMMUNICATIONS

Telephones—fixed lines: total subscriptions: 35,000
subscriptions per 100 inhabitants: 31 (July 2016 est.)
country comparison to the world: 169

Telephones—mobile cellular: total: 141,000
subscriptions per 100 inhabitants: 126 (July 2016 est.)
country comparison to the world: 185

Telephone system: *general assessment:* modern fully automatic telecommunications system

domestic: increased competition through privatization has increased mobile-cellular teledensity to over 125 per 100 persons; three mobile-cellular service providers are now licensed
international: country code—297; landing site for the PAN-AM submarine telecommunications cable system that extends from the US Virgin Islands through Aruba to Venezuela, Colombia, Panama, and the west coast of South America; extensive interisland microwave radio relay links (2016)

Broadcast media: 2 commercial TV stations; cable TV subscription service provides access to foreign channels; about 19 commercial radio stations broadcast (2014)

Internet country code: .aw

Internet users: *total:* 106,309
percent of population: 93.5% (July 2016 est.)
country comparison to the world: 172

TRANSPORTATION

National air transport system: *number of registered air carriers:* 3
inventory of registered aircraft operated by air carriers: 19
annual passenger traffic on registered air carriers: 2,120,578
annual freight traffic on registered air carriers: 0 mt-km (2015)

Civil aircraft registration country code prefix: P4 (2016)

Airports: 1 (2013)
country comparison to the world: 210

Airports—with paved runways: total: 1
2,438 to 3,047 m: 1 (2017)

Ports and terminals: *major seaport(s):* Barcadera, Oranjestad
oil terminal(s): Sint Nicolaas
cruise port(s): Oranjestad

MILITARY AND SECURITY

Military branches: no regular military forces (2011)

Military—note: defense is the responsibility of the Netherlands; the Aruba security services focus on organized crime and terrorism

TRANSNATIONAL ISSUES

Disputes—international: none

Illicit drugs: transit point for US- and Europe-bound narcotics with some accompanying money-laundering activity; relatively high percentage of population consumes cocaine

ASHMORE AND CARTIER ISLANDS

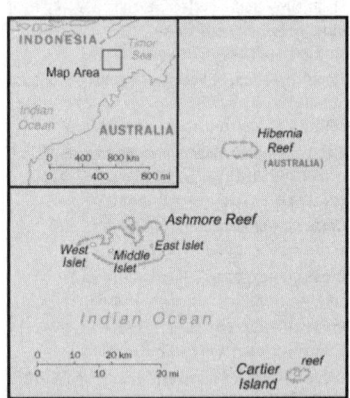

INTRODUCTION

Background: These uninhabited islands came under Australian authority in 1931; formal administration began two years later. Ashmore Reef supports a rich and diverse avian and marine habitat; in 1983, it became a National Nature Reserve.

Cartier Island, a former bombing range, became a marine reserve in 2000.

GEOGRAPHY

Location: Southeastern Asia, islands in the Indian Ocean, midway between northwestern Australia and Timor island

Geographic coordinates: 12 14 S, 123 05 E

Map references: Southeast Asia

Area: *total:* 5 sq km
land: 5 sq km
water: 0 sq km
note: includes Ashmore Reef (West, Middle, and East Islets) and Cartier Island
country comparison to the world: 251

Area—comparative: about eight times the size of the National Mall in Washington, DC

Land boundaries: 0 km

Coastline: 74.1 km

Maritime claims: *territorial sea:* 12 nm
contiguous zone: 12 nm
exclusive fishing zone: 200 nm
continental shelf: 200-m depth or to the depth of exploitation

Climate: tropical

Terrain: low with sand and coral

Elevation: *mean elevation:* NA

elevation extremes: *lowest point:* Indian Ocean 0 m
highest point: Cartier Island 5 m

Natural resources: fish

Land use: *agricultural land:* 0%
forest: 0%
other: 100% (all grass and sand) (2011 est.)

Natural hazards: surrounded by shoals and reefs that can pose maritime hazards

Environment—current issues: illegal killing of protected wildlife by traditional Indonesian fisherman, as well as fishing by non-traditional Indonesian vessels, are ongoing problems

Geography—note: Ashmore Reef National Nature Reserve established in August 1983; Cartier Island Marine Reserve established in 2000

PEOPLE AND SOCIETY

Population: no indigenous inhabitants
note: Indonesian fishermen are allowed access to the lagoon and fresh water at Ashmore Reef's

West Island; access to East and Middle Islands is by permit only

GOVERNMENT

Country name: *conventional long form:* Territory of Ashmore and Cartier Islands
conventional short form: Ashmore and Cartier Islands
etymology: named after British Captain Samuel ASHMORE, who first sighted his namesake island in 1811, and after the ship Cartier, from which the second island was discovered in 1800

Dependency status: territory of Australia; administered from Canberra by the Department of Regional Australia, Local Government, Arts and Sport

Legal system: the laws of the Commonwealth of Australia and the laws of the Northern Territory of Australia, where applicable, apply

Citizenship: see Australia

Diplomatic representation in the US: none (territory of Australia)

Diplomatic representation from the US: none (territory of Australia)

Flag description: the flag of Australia is used

ECONOMY

Economy—overview: no economic activity

TRANSPORTATION

Ports and terminals: *none; offshore anchorage only*

MILITARY AND SECURITY

Military—note: defense is the responsibility of Australia; periodic visits by the Royal Australian Navy and Royal Australian Air Force

TRANSNATIONAL ISSUES

Disputes—international: Australia has closed parts of the Ashmore and Cartier reserve to Indonesian traditional fishing; Indonesian groups challenge Australia's claim to Ashmore Reef

ATLANTIC OCEAN

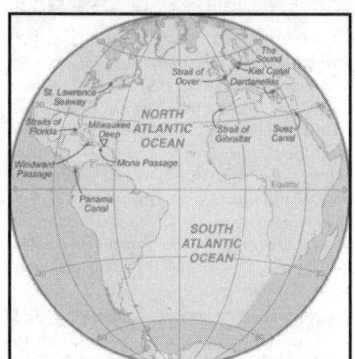

INTRODUCTION

Background: The Atlantic Ocean is the second largest of the world's five oceans (after the Pacific Ocean, but larger than the Indian Ocean, Southern Ocean, and Arctic Ocean). The Kiel Canal (Germany), Oresund (Denmark-Sweden), Bosporus (Turkey), Strait of Gibraltar (Morocco-Spain), and the Saint Lawrence Seaway (Canada-US) are important strategic access waterways. The decision by the International Hydrographic Organization in the spring of 2000 to delimit a fifth world ocean, the Southern Ocean, removed the portion of the Atlantic Ocean south of 60 degrees south latitude.

GEOGRAPHY

Location: body of water between Africa, Europe, the Arctic Ocean, the Americas, and the Southern Ocean

Geographic coordinates: 0 00 N, 25 00 W

Map references: Political Map of the World

Area: *total:* 76.762 million sq km
note: includes Baltic Sea, Black Sea, Caribbean Sea, Davis Strait, Denmark Strait, part of the Drake Passage, Gulf of Mexico, Labrador Sea, Mediterranean Sea, North Sea, Norwegian Sea, almost all of the Scotia Sea, and other tributary water bodies

Area—comparative: about 7.5 times the size of the US

Coastline: 111,866 km

Climate: tropical cyclones (hurricanes) develop off the coast of Africa near Cabo Verde and move westward into the Caribbean Sea; hurricanes can occur from May to December but are most frequent from August to November

Terrain: surface usually covered with sea ice in Labrador Sea, Denmark Strait, and coastal portions of the Baltic Sea from October to June; surface dominated by two large gyres (broad, circular systems of currents), one in the northern Atlantic and another in the southern Atlantic; the ocean floor is dominated by the Mid-Atlantic Ridge, a rugged north-south centerline for the entire Atlantic basin

major surface currents: clockwise North Atlantic Gyre consists of the warm Gulf Stream in the west, the North Atlantic Current in the north, the cold Canary Current in the east, and the North Equatorial Current in the south; the counterclockwise South Atlantic Gyre composed of the warm Brazil Current in the west, the South Atlantic Current in the south, the cold Benguela Current in the east, and the South Equatorial Current in the north

Elevation: mean depth: -3,646 m

elevation extremes: *lowest point:* Milwaukee Deep in the Puerto Rico Trench -8,605 m
highest point: sea level 0 m

Natural resources: oil and gas fields, fish, marine mammals (seals and whales), sand and gravel aggregates, placer deposits, polymetallic nodules, precious stones

Natural hazards: icebergs common in Davis Strait, Denmark Strait, and the northwestern Atlantic Ocean from February to August and have been spotted as far south as Bermuda and the Madeira Islands; ships subject to superstructure icing in extreme northern Atlantic from October to May; persistent fog can be a maritime hazard from May to September; hurricanes (May to December)

Environment—current issues: endangered marine species include the manatee, seals, sea lions, turtles, and whales; drift net fishing is hastening the decline of fish stocks and contributing to international disputes; municipal sludge pollution off eastern US, southern Brazil, and eastern Argentina; oil pollution in Caribbean Sea, Gulf of Mexico, Lake Maracaibo, Mediterranean Sea, and North Sea; industrial waste and municipal sewage pollution in Baltic Sea, North Sea, and Mediterranean Sea

Geography—note: major chokepoints include the Dardanelles, Strait of Gibraltar, access to the Panama and Suez Canals; strategic straits include the Strait of Dover, Straits of Florida, Mona Passage, The Sound (Oresund), and Windward Passage; the Equator divides the Atlantic Ocean into the North Atlantic Ocean and South Atlantic Ocean

GOVERNMENT

Country name: *etymology:* name derives from the Greek description of the waters beyond the Strait of Gibraltar, Atlantis thalassa, meaning "Sea of Atlas"

ECONOMY

Economy—overview: The Atlantic Ocean provides some of the world's most heavily trafficked sea routes, between and within the Eastern and Western Hemispheres. Other economic activity includes the exploitation of natural resources, e.g., fishing, dredging of aragonite sands (The Bahamas), and production of crude oil and natural gas (Caribbean Sea, Gulf of Mexico, and North Sea).

TRANSPORTATION

Ports and terminals: *major seaport(s):* Alexandria (Egypt), Algiers (Algeria), Antwerp (Belgium), Barcelona (Spain), Buenos Aires (Argentina), Casablanca (Morocco), Colon (Panama),

51

Copenhagen (Denmark), Dakar (Senegal), Gdansk (Poland), Hamburg (Germany), Helsinki (Finland), Las Palmas (Canary Islands, Spain), Le Havre (France), Lisbon (Portugal), London (UK), Marseille (France), Montevideo (Uruguay), Montreal (Canada), Naples (Italy), New Orleans (US), New York (US), Oran (Algeria), Oslo (Norway), Peiraiefs or Piraeus (Greece), Rio de Janeiro (Brazil), Rotterdam (Netherlands), Saint Petersburg (Russia), Stockholm (Sweden)

Transportation—note: Kiel Canal and Saint Lawrence Seaway are two important waterways; significant domestic commercial and recreational use of Intracoastal Waterway on central and south Atlantic seaboard and Gulf of Mexico coast of US; the International Maritime Bureau reports the territorial waters of littoral states and offshore Atlantic waters as high risk for piracy and armed robbery against ships, particularly in the Gulf of Guinea off West Africa; in 2014, 41 commercial vessels were attacked in the Gulf of Guinea with 5 hijacked and 144 crew members taken hostage; hijacked vessels are often disguised and cargoes stolen; crews have been robbed and stores or cargoes stolen

TRANSNATIONAL ISSUES

Disputes—international: some maritime disputes (see littoral states)

AUSTRALIA

INTRODUCTION

Background: Prehistoric settlers arrived on the continent from Southeast Asia at least 40,000 years before the first Europeans began exploration in the 17th century. No formal territorial claims were made until 1770, when Capt. James COOK took possession of the east coast in the name of Great Britain (all of Australia was claimed as British territory in 1829 with the creation of the colony of Western Australia). Six colonies were created in the late 18th and 19th centuries; they federated and became the Commonwealth of Australia in 1901. The new country took advantage of its natural resources to rapidly develop agricultural and manufacturing industries and to make a major contribution to the Allied effort in World Wars I and II.

In recent decades, Australia has become an internationally competitive, advanced market economy due in large part to economic reforms adopted in the 1980s and its location in one of the fastest growing regions of the world economy. Long-term concerns include an aging population, pressure on infrastructure, and environmental issues such as floods, droughts, and bushfires. Australia is the driest inhabited continent on earth, making it particularly vulnerable to the challenges of climate change. Australia is home to 10 per cent of the world's biodiversity, and a great number of its flora and fauna exist nowhere else in the world.

GEOGRAPHY

Location: Oceania, continent between the Indian Ocean and the South Pacific Ocean

Geographic coordinates: 27 00 S, 133 00 E

Map references: Oceania

Area: *total:* 7,741,220 sq km
land: 7,682,300 sq km
water: 58,920 sq km
note: includes Lord Howe Island and Macquarie Island
country comparison to the world: 7

Area—comparative: slightly smaller than the US contiguous 48 states

Land boundaries: 0 km

Coastline: 25,760 km

Maritime claims: *territorial sea:* 12 nm
contiguous zone: 24 nm
exclusive economic zone: 200 nm
continental shelf: 200 nm or to the edge of the continental margin

Climate: generally arid to semiarid; temperate in south and east; tropical in north

Terrain: mostly low plateau with deserts; fertile plain in southeast

Elevation: *mean elevation:* 330 m

elevation extremes: *lowest point:* Lake Eyre -15 m
highest point: Mount Kosciuszko 2,228 m

Natural resources: bauxite, coal, iron ore, copper, tin, gold, silver, uranium, nickel, tungsten, rare earth elements, mineral sands, lead, zinc, diamonds, natural gas, petroleum
note: Australia is the world's largest net exporter of coal accounting for 29% of global coal exports

Land use: *agricultural land:* 53.4%
arable land 6.2%; *permanent crops* 0.1%; *permanent pasture* 47.1%
forest: 19.3%
other: 27.3% (2011 est.)
Irrigated land: 25,500 sq km (2012)

Population—distribution: population is primarily located on the periphery, with the highest concentration of people residing in the southeast; a secondary population center is located in and around Perth in the west; of the States and Territories, New South Wales has, by far, the largest population; the interior, or "outback", has a very sparse population

Natural hazards: cyclones along the coast; severe droughts; forest fires
volcanism: volcanic activity on Heard and McDonald Islands

Environment—current issues: soil erosion from overgrazing, industrial development, urbanization, and poor farming practices; soil salinity rising due to the use of poor quality water; desertification; clearing for agricultural purposes threatens the natural habitat of many unique animal and plant species; the Great Barrier Reef off the northeast coast, the largest coral reef in the world, is threatened by increased shipping and its popularity as a tourist site; limited natural freshwater resources

Environment—international agreements: party to: Antarctic-Environmental Protocol, Antarctic-Marine Living Resources, Antarctic Seals, Antarctic Treaty, Biodiversity, Climate Change, Climate Change-Kyoto Protocol, Desertification, Endangered Species, Environmental Modification, Hazardous Wastes, Law of the Sea, Marine Dumping, Marine Life Conservation, Ozone Layer Protection, Ship Pollution, Tropical Timber 83, Tropical Timber 94, Wetlands, Whaling
signed, but not ratified: none of the selected agreements

Geography—note: world's smallest continent but sixth-largest country; the largest country in Oceania, the largest country entirely in the Southern Hemisphere, and the largest country without land borders; the only continent without glaciers; population concentrated along the eastern and southeastern coasts; the invigorating sea breeze known as the "Fremantle Doctor" affects the city of Perth on the west coast and is one of the most consistent winds in the world

PEOPLE AND SOCIETY

Population: 23,232,413 (July 2017 est.)
country comparison to the world: 56

Nationality: *noun:* Australian(s)
adjective: Australian

Ethnic groups: English 25.9%, Australian 25.4%, Irish 7.5%, Scottish 6.4%, Italian 3.3%, German 3.2%, Chinese 3.1%, Indian 1.4%, Greek 1.4%, Dutch 1.2%, other 15.8% (includes Australian aboriginal .5%), unspecified 5.4%
note: data represent self-identified ancestry, over a third of respondents reported two ancestries (2011 est.)

Languages: English 76.8%, Mandarin 1.6%, Italian 1.4%, Arabic 1.3%, Greek 1.2%, Cantonese 1.2%, Vietnamese 1.1%, other 10.4%, unspecified 5% (2011 est.)

Religions: Protestant 23.1% (Anglican 13.3%, Uniting Church 3.7%, Presbyterian and Reformed 2.3%, Baptist 1.5%, Pentecostal 1.1%, Lutheran .7%, other Protestant .5%), Roman Catholic 22.6%, other Christian 4.2%, Muslim 2.6%, Buddhist 2.4%, Orthodox 2.3% (Eastern Orthodox 2.1%, Oriental Orthodox .2%), Hindu 1.9%, other 1.3%, none 30.1%, unspecified 9.6% (2016 est.)

Age structure: *0-14 years:* 17.8% (male 2,122,139/female 2,012,670)
15-24 years: 12.79% (male 1,524,368/female 1,446,663)
25-54 years: 41.45% (male 4,903,130/female 4,725,976)
55-64 years: 11.83% (male 1,363,331/female 1,384,036)
65 years and over: 16.14% (male 1,736,951/female 2,013,149) (2017 est.)

Dependency ratios: *total dependency ratio:* 51.1
youth dependency ratio: 28.5
elderly dependency ratio: 22.6
potential support ratio: 4.4 (2015 est.)

Median age: *total:* 38.7 years
male: 37.9 years
female: 39.5 years (2017 est.)
country comparison to the world: 58

Population growth rate: 1.03% (2017 est.)
country comparison to the world: 110

Birth rate: 12.1 births/1,000 population (2017 est.)
country comparison to the world: 165

Death rate: 7.3 deaths/1,000 population (2017 est.)
country comparison to the world: 119

Net migration rate: 5.5 migrant(s)/1,000 population (2017 est.)
country comparison to the world: 21

Population distribution: population is primarily located on the periphery, with the highest concentration of people residing in the southeast; a secondary population center is located in and around Perth in the west; of the States and Territories, New South Wales has, by far, the largest population; the interior, or "outback", has a very sparse population

Urbanization: *urban population:* 89.7% of total population (2017)
rate of urbanization: 1.37% annual rate of change (2015-20 est.)
note: data include Christmas Island, Cocos Islands, and Norfolk Island

Major urban areas—population: Sydney 4.505 million; Melbourne 4.203 million; Brisbane 2.202 million; Perth 1.861 million; Adelaide 1.256 million; CANBERRA (capital) 423,000 (2015)

Sex ratio: *at birth:* 1.06 male(s)/female
0-14 years: 1.05 male(s)/female
15-24 years: 1.05 male(s)/female
25-54 years: 1.04 male(s)/female
55-64 years: 0.98 male(s)/female
65 years and over: 0.86 male(s)/female
total population: 1.01 male(s)/female (2016 est.)

Mother's mean age at first birth: 28.7 years (2014 est.)

Maternal mortality ratio: 6 deaths/100,000 live births (2015 est.)
country comparison to the world: 166

Infant mortality rate: *total:* 4.3 deaths/1,000 live births
male: 4.6 deaths/1,000 live births
female: 3.9 deaths/1,000 live births (2017 est.)
country comparison to the world: 184

Life expectancy at birth: *total population:* 82.3 years
male: 79.8 years
female: 84.9 years (2017 est.)
country comparison to the world: 14

Total fertility rate: 1.77 children born/woman (2017 est.)
country comparison to the world: 156

Contraceptive prevalence rate: 67.8%
note: percent of women aged 18-45 (2011)

Health expenditures: 9.4% of GDP (2014)
country comparison to the world: 32

Physicians density: 3.37 physicians/1,000 population (2013)

Hospital bed density: 3.9 beds/1,000 population (2010)

Drinking water source:
improved:
urban: 100% of population
rural: 100% of population
total: 100% of population
unimproved:
urban: 0% of population
rural: 0% of population
total: 0% of population (2015 est.)

Sanitation facility access:
improved:
urban: 100% of population
rural: 100% of population
total: 100% of population
unimproved:
urban: 0% of population
rural: 0% of population
total: 0% of population (2015 est.)

HIV/AIDS—adult prevalence rate: 0.1% (2016 est.)
country comparison to the world: 100

HIV/AIDS—people living with HIV/AIDS: 25,000 (2016 est.)
country comparison to the world: 69

HIV/AIDS—deaths: <500 (2016 est.)

Obesity—adult prevalence rate: 29% (2016)
country comparison to the world: 27

Children under the age of 5 years underweight: 0.2% (2007)
country comparison to the world: 138

Education expenditures: 5.3% of GDP (2013)
country comparison to the world: 56

School life expectancy (primary to tertiary education): *total:* 20 years
male: 20 years
female: 21 years (2014)

Unemployment, youth ages 15-24:
total: 12.7%
male: 13.9%
female: 11.4% (2016 est.)
country comparison to the world: 93

GOVERNMENT

Country name: *conventional long form:* Commonwealth of Australia
conventional short form: Australia
etymology: the name Australia derives from the Latin "australis" meaning "southern"; the Australian landmass was long referred to as "Terra Australis" or the Southern Land

Government type: parliamentary democracy (Federal Parliament) under a constitutional monarchy; a Commonwealth realm

Capital: *name:* Canberra
geographic coordinates: 35 16 S, 149 08 E
time difference: UTC+10 (15 hours ahead of Washington, DC, during Standard Time)
daylight saving time: +1hr, begins first Sunday in October; ends first Sunday in April
note: Australia has three time zones

Administrative divisions: 6 states and 2 territories*; Australian Capital Territory*, New South Wales, Northern Territory*, Queensland, South Australia, Tasmania, Victoria, Western Australia
Dependent areas: Ashmore and Cartier Islands, Christmas Island, Cocos (Keeling) Islands, Coral Sea Islands, Heard Island and McDonald Islands, Norfolk Island

Independence: 1 January 1901 (from the federation of UK colonies)

National holiday: Australia Day (commemorates the arrival of the First Fleet of Australian settlers), 26 January (1788); ANZAC Day (commemorates the anniversary of the landing of troops of the Australian and New Zealand Army Corps during World War I at Gallipoli, Turkey), 25 April (1915)

Constitution: 9 July 1900; effective 1 January 1901; amended several times, last in 1977; note—a referendum to amend the constitution to reflect the Aboriginal and Torres Strait Islander Peoples Recognition Act 2013 held in 2017 was rejected (2017)

Legal system: common law system based on the English model

International law organization participation: accepts compulsory ICJ jurisdiction with reservations; accepts ICCt jurisdiction

Citizenship: *citizenship by birth:* no
citizenship by descent only: at least one parent must be a citizen or permanent resident of Australia
dual citizenship recognized: yes
residency requirement for naturalization: 4 years

Suffrage: 18 years of age; universal and compulsory

Executive branch: *chief of state:* Queen of Australia ELIZABETH II (since 6 February 1952); represented by Governor Gen. Sir Peter COSGROVE (since 28 March 2014)
head of government: Prime Minister Malcolm TURNBULL (since 15 September 2015)
cabinet: Cabinet nominated by the prime minister from among members of Parliament and sworn in by the governor general
elections/appointments: the monarchy is hereditary; governor general appointed by the monarch on the recommendation of the prime minister; following legislative elections, the leader of the majority party or majority coalition is sworn in as prime minister by the governor general

Legislative branch: *description:* bicameral Federal Parliament consists of the Senate (76 seats; 12 members from each of the 6 states and 2 each from the 2 mainland territories; members directly elected in multi-seat constituencies by proportional representation vote; members serve 6-year terms with one-half of state membership renewed every 3 years and territory membership renewed every 3 years) and the House of Representatives (150 seats; members directly elected in single-seat constituencies by majority preferential vote; members serve terms of up to 3 years)
elections: Senate—last held on 2 July 2016 (next to be held in 2019); House of Representatives—last held on 2 July 2016; this election represents a rare double dissolution where all 226 seats in both the Senate and House of Representatives are up for reelection
election results: Senate—percent of vote by party—Liberal/National Coalition 35.2%, ALP 29.8%, the Greens 8.7%, Pauline Hanson's One Nation 4.3%, Nick Xenophon Team 3.3%, other 18.7%; seats by party—Liberal/National Coalition 30, ALP 26, The Greens 9, Pauline Hanson's One Nation 4, Nick Xenophon Team 3, other 4; House of Representatives—percent of vote by party—Liberal/National Coalition 42%, ALP 34.7%, The Greens 10.2%, Nick Xenophon Team 1.9%, Katter's Australian Party 0.5%, independent 2.8%, other 7.8%; seats by party—Liberal/National Coalition 76, ALP 69, The Greens 1, Katter's Australian Party 1, Nick Xenophon Team 1, independent 2

Judicial branch: *highest court(s):* High Court of Australia (consists of 7 justices, including the chief justice); note—each of the 6 states, 2 territories, and Norfolk Island has a Supreme Court; the High Court is the final appellate court beyond the state and territory supreme courts
judge selection and term of office: justices appointed by the governor-general in council for life with mandatory retirement at age 70

subordinate courts: subordinate courts: subordinate courts at the federal level: Federal Court; Federal Magistrates' Courts of Australia; Family Court; subordinate courts at the state and territory level: Local Court—New South Wales; Magistrates' Courts—Victoria, Queensland, South Australia, Western Australia, Tasmania, Northern Territory, Australian Capital Territory; District Courts—New South Wales, Queensland, South Australia, Western Australia; County Court—Victoria; Family Court—Western Australia; Court of Petty Sessions—Norfolk Island

Political parties and leaders: Australian Greens Party [Richard DI NATALE]
Australian Labor Party [Bill SHORTEN]
Country Liberal Party or CLP [Gary HIGGINS]
Family First Party [Bob DAY]
Katter's Australian Party [Bob KATTER]
Liberal National Party of Queensland or LNP [Deb FRECKLINGTON]
Liberal Party [Malcolm TURNBULL]
National Party of Australia [Barnaby JOYCE]
Palmer United Party or PUP [Clive PALMER]

Political pressure groups and leaders: business groups, environmental groups, social groups, trade unions

International organization participation: ADB, ANZUS, APEC, ARF, ASEAN (dialogue partner), Australia Group, BIS, C, CD, CP, EAS, EBRD, EITI (implementing country), FAO, FATF, G-20, IAEA, IBRD, ICAO, ICC (national committees), ICCt, ICRM, IDA, IEA, IFC, IFRCS, IHO, ILO, IMF, IMO, IMSO, Interpol, IOC, IOM, IPU, ISO, ITSO, ITU, ITUC (NGOs), MIGA, NEA, NSG, OECD, OPCW, OSCE (partner), Pacific Alliance (observer), Paris Club, PCA, PIF, SAARC (observer), SICA (observer), Sparteca, SPC, UN, UNCTAD, UNESCO, UNHCR, UNMISS, UNMIT, UNRWA, UNTSO, UNWTO, UPU, WCO, WFTU (NGOs), WHO, WIPO, WMO, WTO, ZC

Diplomatic representation in the US: *chief of mission:* Ambassador Joseph Benedict HOCKEY (since 28 January 2016)
chancery: 1601 Massachusetts Avenue NW, Washington, DC 20036
telephone: [1] (202) 797-3000
FAX: [1] (202) 797-3168
consulate(s) general: Atlanta, Chicago, Honolulu, Houston, Los Angeles, New York, San Francisco

Diplomatic representation from the US: *chief of mission:* Ambassador (vacant); Charge d'Affaires James CAROUSO (since September 2016)
embassy: Moonah Place, Yarralumla, Canberra, Australian Capital Territory 2600
mailing address: APO AP 96549
telephone: [61] (02) 6214-5600
FAX: [61] (02) 6214-5970
consulate(s) general: Melbourne, Perth, Sydney

Flag description: blue with the flag of the UK in the upper hoist-side quadrant and a large seven-pointed star in the lower hoist-side quadrant known as the Commonwealth or Federation Star, representing the federation of the colonies of

Australia in 1901; the star depicts one point for each of the six original states and one representing all of Australia's internal and external territories; on the fly half is a representation of the Southern Cross constellation in white with one small, five-pointed star and four larger, seven-pointed stars

National symbol(s): Southern Cross constellation (composed of five stars: four large seven-pointed stars, one small five-pointed star), kangaroo, emu; national colors: green, gold

National anthem: *name:* "Advance Australia Fair"
lyrics/music: Peter Dodds McCORMICK
note: adopted 1984; although originally written in the late 19th century, the anthem was not used for all official occasions until 1984; as a Commonwealth country, in addition to the national anthem, "God Save the Queen" is also played at Royal functions (see United Kingdom)

ECONOMY

Economy—overview: Following two decades of continuous growth, low unemployment, contained inflation, very low public debt, and a strong and stable financial system, Australia enters 2018 facing a range of growth constraints, principally driven by the sharp fall in global prices of key export commodities. Demand for resources and energy from Asia and especially China has stalled and sharp drops in current prices have impacted growth.

The services sector is the largest part of the Australian economy, accounting for about 70% of GDP and 75% of jobs. Australia was comparatively unaffected by the global financial crisis as the banking system has remained strong and inflation is under control.

Australia benefited from a dramatic surge in its terms of trade in recent years, although this trend has reversed due to falling global commodity prices. Australia is a significant exporter of natural resources, energy, and food. Australia's abundant and diverse natural resources attract high levels of foreign investment and include extensive reserves of coal, iron, copper, gold, natural gas, uranium, and renewable energy sources. A series of major investments, such as the US$40 billion Gorgon Liquid Natural Gas Project, will significantly expand the resources sector.

Australia is an open market with minimal restrictions on imports of goods and services. The process of opening up has increased productivity, stimulated growth, and made the economy more flexible and dynamic. Australia plays an active role in the WTO, APEC, the G20, and other trade forums. Australia's free trade agreement (FTA) with China entered into force in 2015, adding to existing FTAs with the Republic of Korea, Japan, Chile, Malaysia, New Zealand, Singapore, Thailand, and the US, and a regional FTA with ASEAN and New Zealand. Australia continues to negotiate bilateral agreements with India and Indonesia, as well as larger agreements with its Pacific neighbors and the Gulf Cooperation Council countries, and an Asia-wide Regional Comprehensive Economic Partnership that includes the

10 ASEAN countries and China, Japan, Korea, New Zealand and India.

GDP (purchasing power parity):
$1.235 trillion (2017 est.)
$1.209 trillion (2016 est.)
$1.179 trillion (2015 est.)
note: data are in 2017 dollars
country comparison to the world: 20

GDP (official exchange rate): $1.39 trillion (2016 est.)

GDP—real growth rate:
2.2% (2017 est.)
2.5% (2016 est.)
2.4% (2015 est.)
country comparison to the world: 148

GDP—per capita (PPP):
$49,900 (2017 est.)
$49,600 (2016 est.)
$49,100 (2015 est.)
note: data are in 2017 dollars
country comparison to the world: 28

Gross national saving:
22.3% of GDP (2017 est.)
21.9% of GDP (2016 est.)
22.1% of GDP (2015 est.)
country comparison to the world: 72

GDP—composition, by end use:
household consumption: 57.1%
government consumption: 19%
investment in fixed capital: 24.2%
investment in inventories: 0%
exports of goods and services: 20.5%
imports of goods and services: -20.8% (2017 est.)

GDP—composition, by sector of origin:
agriculture: 3.6%
industry: 26.1%
services: 70.3% (2017 est.)

Agriculture—products: wheat, barley, sugarcane, fruits; cattle, sheep, poultry

Industries: mining, industrial and transportation equipment, food processing, chemicals, steel

Industrial production growth rate: 1% (2017 est.)
country comparison to the world: 166

Labor force: 12.91 million (2017 est.)
country comparison to the world: 45

Labor force—by occupation: *agriculture:* 3.6%
industry: 21.1%
services: 75.3% (2009 est.)

Unemployment rate: 5.6% (2017 est.)
5.7% (2016 est.)
country comparison to the world: 78

Population below poverty line: NA%

Household income or consumption by percentage share: *lowest 10%:* 2%
highest 10%: 25.4% (1994)

Distribution of family income—Gini index: 30.3 (2008)
35.2 (1994)
country comparison to the world: 126

Budget: *revenues:* $461 billion
expenditures: $484.9 billion (2017 est.)

Taxes and other revenues: 33.2% of GDP (2017 est.)
country comparison to the world: 67

Budget surplus (+) or deficit (-): -1.7% of GDP (2017 est.)
country comparison to the world: 73

Public debt: 47.1% of GDP (2017 est.)
46.6% of GDP (2016 est.)
country comparison to the world: 110

Fiscal year: 1 July—30 June

Inflation rate (consumer prices):
2% (2017 est.)
1.3% (2016 est.)
country comparison to the world: 88

Central bank discount rate: 3% (28 February 2013)
4.35% (31 December 2010)
note: this is the Reserve Bank of Australia's "cash rate target," or policy rate
country comparison to the world: 106

Commercial bank prime lending rate: 5.3% (31 December 2017 est.)
5.42% (31 December 2016 est.)
country comparison to the world: 140

Stock of narrow money:
$271.9 billion (31 December 2017 est.)
$243.1 billion (31 December 2016 est.)
country comparison to the world: 19

Stock of broad money: $1.586 trillion (31 December 2017 est.)
$1.415 trillion (31 December 2016 est.)
country comparison to the world: 12

Stock of domestic credit: $2.336 trillion (31 December 2017 est.)
$2.098 trillion (31 December 2016 est.)
country comparison to the world: 13

Market value of publicly traded shares:
$1.187 trillion (31 December 2015 est.)
$1.289 trillion (31 December 2014 est.)
$1.366 trillion (31 December 2013 est.)
country comparison to the world: 13

Current account balance: -$21.68 billion (2017 est.)
-$33.31 billion (2016 est.)
country comparison to the world: 192

Exports: $224.5 billion (2017 est.)
$191.7 billion (2016 est.)
country comparison to the world: 25

Exports—commodities: coal, iron ore, gold, meat, wool, alumina, wheat, machinery and transport equipment

Exports—partners: China 30.5%, Japan 12.4%, US 6.5%, South Korea 6.1% (2016)

Imports: $215.4 billion (2017 est.)
$198.5 billion (2016 est.)
country comparison to the world: 22

Imports—commodities: machinery and transport equipment, computers and office machines, telecommunication equipment and parts; crude oil and petroleum products

Imports—partners: China 23.4%, US 11.5%, Japan 7.8%, Thailand 5.6%, Germany 5.3%, South Korea 4.3% (2016)

Reserves of foreign exchange and gold: $60.3 billion (31 December 2017 est.)
$55.07 billion (31 December 2016 est.)
country comparison to the world: 36

Debt—external:
$1.67 trillion (31 December 2017 est.)
$1.547 trillion (31 December 2016 est.)
country comparison to the world: 12

Stock of direct foreign investment—at home:
$647.7 billion (31 December 2017 est.)
$617.7 billion (31 December 2016 est.)
country comparison to the world: 16

Stock of direct foreign investment—abroad:
$443.4 billion (31 December 2017 est.)
$441.4 billion (31 December 2016 est.)
country comparison to the world: 18

Exchange rates: Australian dollars (AUD) per US dollar—
1.311 (2017 est.)
1.3442 (2016 est.)
1.3442 (2015 est.)
1.3291 (2014 est.)
1.1094 (2013 est.)

ENERGY

Electricity access: electrification—*total population:* 100% (2016)

Electricity—production: 237.9 billion kWh (2015 est.)
country comparison to the world: 20

Electricity—consumption: 223.6 billion kWh (2015 est.)
country comparison to the world: 18

Electricity—exports: 0 kWh (2016 est.)
country comparison to the world: 102

Electricity—imports: 0 kWh (2016 est.)
country comparison to the world: 121

Electricity—installed generating capacity: 67.03 million kW (2015 est.)
country comparison to the world: 18

Electricity—from fossil fuels: 72.9% of total installed capacity (2015 est.)
country comparison to the world: 98

Electricity—from nuclear fuels: 0% of total installed capacity (2015 est.)
country comparison to the world: 43

Electricity—from hydroelectric plants: 10.9% of total installed capacity (2015 est.)
country comparison to the world: 116

Electricity—from other renewable sources: 16.1% of total installed capacity (2015 est.)
country comparison to the world: 43

Crude oil—production: 289,700 bbl/day (2016 est.)
country comparison to the world: 33

Crude oil—exports: 213,600 bbl/day (2016 est.)
country comparison to the world: 29

Crude oil—imports: 339,500 bbl/day (2016 est.)
country comparison to the world: 25

Crude oil—proved reserves: 1.821 billion bbl (1 January 2017 es)
country comparison to the world: 39

Refined petroleum products—production: 472,100 bbl/day (2016 est.)
country comparison to the world: 34

Refined petroleum products—consumption: 1.1 million bbl/day (2016 est.)
country comparison to the world: 21

Refined petroleum products—exports: 60,290 bbl/day (2016 est.)
country comparison to the world: 50

Refined petroleum products—imports: 564,300 bbl/day (2016 est.)
country comparison to the world: 14

Natural gas—production: 67.2 billion cu m (2015 est.)
country comparison to the world: 13

Natural gas—consumption: 46.99 billion cu m (2015 est.)
country comparison to the world: 24

Natural gas—exports: 34.06 billion cu m (2015 est.)
country comparison to the world: 11

Natural gas—imports: 6.373 billion cu m (2015 est.)
country comparison to the world: 32

Natural gas—proved reserves: 1.989 trillion cu m (1 January 2017 es)
country comparison to the world: 18

Carbon dioxide emissions from consumption of energy: 385 million Mt (2013 est.)
country comparison to the world: 18

COMMUNICATIONS

Telephones—fixed lines: *total subscriptions:* 8.18 million
subscriptions per 100 inhabitants: 36 (July 2016 est.)
country comparison to the world: 22

Telephones—mobile cellular: *total:* 26.55 million
subscriptions per 100 inhabitants: 115 (July 2016 est.)
country comparison to the world: 39

Telephone system: *general assessment:* excellent domestic and international service
domestic: domestic satellite system; significant use of radiotelephone in areas of low population density; rapid growth of mobile telephones
international: country code—61; landing point for the SEA-ME-WE-3 optical telecommunications submarine cable with links to Asia, the Middle East, and Europe; the Southern Cross fiber-optic submarine cable provides links to NZ and the US; satellite earth stations—10 Intelsat (4 Indian Ocean and 6 Pacific Ocean), 2 Inmarsat, 2 Globalstar, 5 other (2015)

Broadcast media: the Australian Broadcasting Corporation (ABC) runs multiple national and local radio networks and TV stations, as well as Australia Network, a TV service that broadcasts throughout the Asia-Pacific region and is the main public broadcaster; Special Broadcasting Service

(SBS), a second large public broadcaster, operates radio and TV networks broadcasting in multiple languages; several large national commercial TV networks, a large number of local commercial TV stations, and hundreds of commercial radio stations are accessible; cable and satellite systems are available (2009)

Internet country code: .au

Internet users: total: 20,288,409
percent of population: 88.2% (July 2016 est.)
country comparison to the world: 28

TRANSPORTATION

National air transport system: *number of registered air carriers:* 11
inventory of registered aircraft operated by air carriers: 175
annual passenger traffic on registered air carriers: 69,294,187
annual freight traffic on registered air carriers: 1,887,295,820 mt-km (2015)
Civil aircraft registration country code prefix: VH (2016)

Airports: 480 (2013)
country comparison to the world: 16

Airports—with paved runways: *total:* 349
over 3,047 m: 11
2,438 to 3,047 m: 14
1,524 to 2,437 m: 155
914 to 1,523 m: 155
under 914 m: 14 (2017)

Airports—with unpaved runways: *total:* 131
1,524 to 2,437 m: 16
914 to 1,523 m: 101
under 914 m: 14 (2013)

Heliports: 1 (2013)

Pipelines: condensate/gas 637 km; gas 30,054 km; liquid petroleum gas 240 km; oil 3,609 km; oil/gas/water 110 km; refined products 72 km (2013)

Railways: *total:* 36,967.5 km
broad gauge: 3,727 km 1.600-m gauge (372 km electrified)
standard gauge: 18,727 km 1.435-m gauge (650 km electrified)
narrow gauge: 14,513.5 km 1.067-m gauge (2,075.5 km electrified) (2014)
country comparison to the world: 7

Roadways: *total:* 823,217 km
paved: 356,343 km
unpaved: 466,874 km (2011)
country comparison to the world: 9

Waterways: 2,000 km (mainly used for recreation on Murray and Murray-Darling River systems) (2011)
country comparison to the world: 42

Merchant marine: *total:* 549
by type: bulk carrier 4, general cargo 83, oil tanker 10, other 452 (2017)
country comparison to the world: 39

Ports and terminals: *major seaport(s):* Brisbane, Cairns, Darwin, Fremantle, Geelong, Gladstone, Hobart, Melbourne, Newcastle, Port Adelaide, Port Kembla, Sydney
dry bulk cargo port(s): Dampier (iron ore), Dalrymple Bay (coal), Hay Point (coal), Port Hedland (iron ore), Port Walcott (iron ore)
container port(s) (TEUs): Brisbane (1,152,000), Melbourne (2,638,000), Sydney (2,330,000) (2015)
LNG terminal(s) (export): Darwin, Karratha, Burrup, Curtis Island

MILITARY AND SECURITY

Military expenditures:
2% of GDP (2016)
1.98% of GDP (2015)
1.8% of GDP (2014)
1.68% of GDP (2013)
1.7% of GDP (2012)
country comparison to the world: 50

Military branches: Australian Defense Force (ADF): Australian Army, Royal Australian Navy (includes Naval Aviation Force), Royal Australian Air Force, Joint Operations Command (JOC) (2013)

Military service age and obligation: 17 years of age for voluntary military service (with parental consent); no conscription; women allowed to serve in most combat roles, except the Army special forces (2013)

TRANSNATIONAL ISSUES

Disputes—international: In 2007, Australia and Timor-Leste agreed to a 50-year development zone and revenue sharing arrangement and deferred a maritime boundary; Australia asserts land and maritime claims to Antarctica; Australia's 2004 submission to the Commission on the Limits of the Continental Shelf extends its continental margins over 3.37 million square kilometers, expanding its seabed roughly 30 percent beyond its claimed EEZ; all borders between Indonesia and Australia have been agreed upon bilaterally, but a 1997 treaty that would settle the last of their maritime and EEZ boundary has yet to be ratified by Indonesia's legislature; Indonesian groups challenge Australia's claim to Ashmore Reef; Australia closed parts of the Ashmore and Cartier reserve to Indonesian traditional fishing

Refugees and internally displaced persons: *refugees (country of origin):* 9,217 (Afghanistan); 6,128 (Iran) (2016)

Illicit drugs: Tasmania is one of the world's major suppliers of licit opiate products; government maintains strict controls over areas of opium poppy cultivation and output of poppy straw concentrate; major consumer of cocaine and amphetamines

AUSTRIA

INTRODUCTION

Background: Once the center of power for the large Austro-Hungarian Empire, Austria was reduced to a small republic after its defeat in World War I. Following annexation by Nazi Germany in 1938 and subsequent occupation by the victorious Allies in 1945, Austria's status remained unclear for a decade. A State Treaty signed in 1955 ended the occupation, recognized Austria's independence, and forbade unification with Germany. A constitutional law that same year declared the country's "perpetual neutrality" as a condition for Soviet military withdrawal. The Soviet Union's collapse in 1991 and Austria's entry into the EU in 1995 have altered the meaning of this neutrality. A prosperous, democratic country, Austria entered the EU Economic and Monetary Union in 1999.

GEOGRAPHY

Location: Central Europe, north of Italy and Slovenia

Geographic coordinates: 47 20 N, 13 20 E

Map references: Europe

Area: *total:* 83,871 sq km
land: 82,445 sq km
water: 1,426 sq km
country comparison to the world: 115

Area—comparative: about the size of South Carolina; slightly more than two-thirds the size of Pennsylvania

Land boundaries: *total:* 2,524 km
border countries (8): Czech Republic 402 km, Germany 801 km, Hungary 321 km, Italy 404 km, Liechtenstein 34 km, Slovakia 105 km, Slovenia 299 km, Switzerland 158 km

Coastline: 0 km (landlocked)

Maritime claims: none (landlocked)

Climate: temperate; continental, cloudy; cold winters with frequent rain and some snow in lowlands and snow in mountains; moderate summers with occasional showers

Terrain: mostly mountains (Alps) in the west and south; mostly flat or gently sloping along the eastern and northern margins

Elevation: *mean elevation:* 910 m

elevation extremes: *lowest point:* Neusiedler See 115 m
highest point: Grossglockner 3,798 m

Natural resources: oil, coal, lignite, timber, iron ore, copper, zinc, antimony, magnesite, tungsten, graphite, salt, hydropower

Land use: *agricultural land:* 38.4%
arable land 16.5%; *permanent crops* 0.8%; *permanent pasture* 21.1%
forest: 47.2%
other: 14.4% (2011 est.)
Irrigated land: 1,170 sq km (2012)

Population—distribution: the northern and eastern portions of the country are more densely populated; nearly two-thirds of the populace lives in urban areas

Natural hazards: landslides; avalanches; earthquakes

Environment—current issues: some forest degradation caused by air and soil pollution; soil pollution results from the use of agricultural chemicals; air pollution results from emissions by coal- and oil-fired power stations and industrial plants and from trucks transiting Austria between northern and southern Europe

Environment—international agreements: *party to:* Air Pollution, Air Pollution-Nitrogen Oxides, Air Pollution-Persistent Organic Pollutants, Air Pollution-Sulfur 85, Air Pollution-Sulphur 94, Air Pollution-Volatile Organic Compounds, Antarctic Treaty, Biodiversity, Climate Change, Climate Change-Kyoto Protocol, Desertification, Endangered Species, Environmental Modification, Hazardous Wastes, Law of the Sea, Ozone Layer Protection, Ship Pollution, Tropical Timber 83, Tropical Timber 94, Wetlands, Whaling
signed, but not ratified: none of the selected agreements

Geography—note: landlocked; strategic location at the crossroads of central Europe with many easily traversable Alpine passes and valleys; major river is the Danube; population is concentrated on eastern lowlands because of steep slopes, poor soils, and low temperatures elsewhere

PEOPLE AND SOCIETY

Population: 8,754,413 (July 2017 est.)
country comparison to the world: 95

Nationality: *noun:* Austrian(s)
adjective: Austrian

Ethnic groups: Austrians 91.1%, former Yugoslavs 4% (includes Croatians, Slovenes, Serbs, and Bosniaks), Turks 1.6%, Germans 0.9%, other or unspecified 2.4% (2001 census)

Languages: German (official nationwide) 88.6%, Turkish 2.3%, Serbian 2.2%, Croatian (official in Burgenland) 1.6%, other (includes Slovene, official in South Carinthia, and Hungarian, official in Burgenland) 5.3% (2001 est.)

Religions: Catholic 73.8% (includes Roman Catholic 73.6%, other Catholic 0.2%), Protestant 4.9%, Muslim 4.2%, Orthodox 2.2%, other 0.8% (includes other Christian), none 12%, unspecified 2% (2001 est.)

Age structure: *0-14 years:* 14.01% (male 628,205/female 598,519)
15-24 years: 11.07% (male 494,016/female 475,500)
25-54 years: 42.42% (male 1,856,532/female 1,856,937)
55-64 years: 13.23% (male 574,570/female 584,022)
65 years and over: 19.26% (male 731,126/female 954,986) (2017 est.)

Dependency ratios:
total dependency ratio: 49.2
youth dependency ratio: 21.1
elderly dependency ratio: 28.1
potential support ratio: 3.6 (2015 est.)

Median age: *total:* 44 years
male: 42.8 years
female: 45.1 years (2017 est.)
country comparison to the world: 12

Population growth rate: 0.47% (2017 est.)
country comparison to the world: 156

Birth rate: 9.5 births/1,000 population (2017 est.)
country comparison to the world: 201

Death rate: 9.6 deaths/1,000 population (2017 est.)
country comparison to the world: 50

Net migration rate: 4.8 migrant(s)/1,000 population (2017 est.)
country comparison to the world: 25
Population distribution: the northern and eastern portions of the country are more densely populated; nearly two-thirds of the populace lives in urban areas

Urbanization: *urban population:* 66.1% of total population (2017)
rate of urbanization: 0.51% annual rate of change (2015-20 est.)

Major urban areas—population: VIENNA (capital) 1.753 million (2015)

Sex ratio: *at birth:* 1.05 male(s)/female
0-14 years: 1.05 male(s)/female
15-24 years: 1.04 male(s)/female
25-54 years: 1 male(s)/female
55-64 years: 0.98 male(s)/female
65 years and over: 0.76 male(s)/female
total population: 0.96 male(s)/female (2016 est.)

Mother's mean age at first birth: 29 years (2014 est.)

Maternal mortality ratio: 4 deaths/100,000 live births (2015 est.)
country comparison to the world: 175

Infant mortality rate: *total:* 3.4 deaths/1,000 live births
male: 3.8 deaths/1,000 live births
female: 3 deaths/1,000 live births (2017 est.)
country comparison to the world: 208

Life expectancy at birth: *total population:* 81.6 years
male: 78.9 years
female: 84.4 years (2017 est.)
country comparison to the world: 23

Total fertility rate: 1.47 children born/woman (2017 est.)
country comparison to the world: 201

Contraceptive prevalence rate: 65.7%
note: percent of women aged 18-49 (2012/13)

Health expenditures: 11.2% of GDP (2014)
country comparison to the world: 11

Physicians density: 5.15 physicians/1,000 population (2015)

Hospital bed density: 7.6 beds/1,000 population (2011)

Drinking water source:
improved:
urban: 100% of population
rural: 100% of population
total: 100% of population
unimproved:
urban: 0% of population
rural: 0% of population
total: 0% of population (2015 est.)

Sanitation facility access:
improved:
urban: 100% of population
rural: 100% of population
total: 100% of population
unimproved:
urban: 0% of population
rural: 0% of population
total: 0% of population (2015 est.)

HIV/AIDS—adult prevalence rate: NA

HIV/AIDS—people living with HIV/AIDS: NA

HIV/AIDS—deaths: NA

Obesity—adult prevalence rate: 20.1% (2016)
country comparison to the world: 105

Education expenditures: 5.6% of GDP (2013)
country comparison to the world: 44

School life expectancy (primary to tertiary education): *total:* 16 years
male: 16 years
female: 16 years (2015)

Unemployment, youth ages 15-24: *total:* 10.6%
male: 11.1%
female: 10% (2015 est.)
country comparison to the world: 108

GOVERNMENT

Country name: *conventional long form:* Republic of Austria
conventional short form: Austria
local long form: Republik Oesterreich
local short form: Oesterreich

etymology: the name Oesterreich means "eastern realm" or "eastern march" and dates to the 10th century; the designation refers to the fact that Austria was the easternmost extension of Bavaria, and, in fact, of all the Germans; the word Austria is a Latinization of the German name

Government type: federal parliamentary republic

Capital: *name:* Vienna

geographic coordinates: 48 12 N, 16 22 E
time difference: UTC+1 (6 hours ahead of Washington, DC, during Standard Time)
daylight saving time: +1hr, begins last Sunday in March; ends last Sunday in October

Administrative divisions: 9 states (Bundeslaender, singular—Bundesland); Burgenland, Kaernten (Carinthia), Niederoesterreich (Lower Austria), Oberoesterreich (Upper Austria), Salzburg, Steiermark (Styria), Tirol (Tyrol), Vorarlberg, Wien (Vienna)

Independence: 12 November 1918 (republic proclaimed); notable earlier dates: 976 (Margravate of Austria established); 17 September 1156 (Duchy of Austria founded); 11 August 1804 (Austrian Empire proclaimed)

National holiday: National Day (commemorates passage of the law on permanent neutrality), 26 October (1955)

Constitution: *history:* several previous; latest adopted 1 October 1920, revised 1929, replaced May 1934 (authoritarian corporate state), replaced by German Weimar constitution in 1938 following German annexation, reinstated 1 May 1945
amendments: proposed through laws designated "constitutional laws" or through the constitutional process if the amendment is part of another law; approval required by at least a two-thirds majority vote by the National Assembly if one-half of the members are present; a referendum is required only if requested by one-third of the National Council or Federal Council membership; passage by referendum requires absolute majority vote; amended many times, last in 2014 (2016)

Legal system: civil law system; judicial review of legislative acts by the Constitutional Court

International law organization participation: accepts compulsory ICJ jurisdiction; accepts ICCt jurisdiction

Citizenship: *citizenship by birth:* no
citizenship by descent only: at least one parent must be a citizen of Austria
dual citizenship recognized: no
residency requirement for naturalization: 10 years

Suffrage: 16 years of age; universal

Executive branch: *chief of state:* Alexander VAN DER BELLEN (since 26 January 2017)

head of government: Chancellor Sebastian KURZ (since 18 December 2017); Vice Chancellor Heinz-Christian STRACHE (since 18 December 2017)
cabinet: Council of Ministers chosen by the president on the advice of the chancellor

elections/appointments: president directly elected by absolute majority popular vote in 2 rounds if needed for a 6-year term (eligible for a second term); elections last held on 24 April 2016 (first round), 22 May 2016 (second round, which was annulled), and 4 December 2016 (second round re-vote); next election to be held in April 2022; chancellor appointed by the president but determined by the majority coalition parties in the Federal Assembly; vice chancellor appointed by the president on the advice of the chancellor
election results: Alexander VAN DER BELLEN elected in second round; percent of vote in first round—Norbet HOFER (FPOe) 35.1%, Alexander VAN DER BELLEN (independent, allied with the Greens) 21.3%, Irmgard GRISS (independent) 18.9%, Rudolf HUNDSTORFER (SPOe) 11.3%, Andreas KHOL (OeVP) 11.1%, Richard LUGNER (independent) 2.3%; percent of vote in second round—Alexander VAN DER BELLEN 53.8%, Norbet HOFER 46.2%

Legislative branch: *description:* bicameral Federal Assembly or Bundesversammlung consists of the Federal Council or Bundesrat (62 seats; members appointed by state parliaments with each state receiving 3 to 12 seats in proportion to its population; members serve 5- or 6-year terms) and the National Council or Nationalrat (183 seats; members directly elected in single-seat constituencies by proportional representation vote; members serve 5-year terms)
elections: National Council—last held on 15 October 2017 (next to be held in 2022); note—an early election was called after the coalition government collapsed
election results: National Council—percent of vote by party—OeVP 31.5%, SPOe 26.9%, FPOe 26%, NEOS 5.3%, PILZ 4.4%, other 5.9%; seats by party—OeVP 62, SPOe 62, FPOe 51, NEOS 10, PILZ 8

Judicial branch: *highest court(s):* Supreme Court of Justice or Oberster Gerichtshof (consists of 85 judges organized into 17 senates or panels of 5 judges each); Constitutional Court or Verfassungsgerichtshof (consists of 20 judges including 6 substitutes; Administrative Court or Verwaltungsgerichtshof—2 judges plus other members depending on the importance of the case)
judge selection and term of office: Supreme Court judges nominated by executive branch departments and appointed by the president; judges serve for life; Constitutional Court judges nominated by several executive branch departments and approved by the president; judges serve for life; Administrative Court judges recommended by executive branch departments and appointed by the president; terms of judges and members determined by the president
subordinate courts: Courts of Appeal (4); Regional Courts (20); district courts (120); county courts

Political parties and leaders: Austrian People's Party or OeVP [Sebastian KURZ]
Communist Party of Austria or KPOe [Mirko MESSNER]

Freedom Party of Austria or FPOe [Heinz Christian STRACHE]
The Greens [Werner KOGLER]
NEOS—The New Austria [Matthias STROLZ]
Pilz List or PILZ [Peter KOLBA]
Social Democratic Party of Austria or SPOe [Christian KERN]

Political pressure groups and leaders: Austrian Trade Union Federation or OeGB (nominally independent but primarily Social Democratic)
Federal Agriculture Chamber (OeVP-dominated)
Federal Economic Chamber (OeVP-dominated)
Labor Chamber or AK (Social Democratic-leaning think tank)
OeVP-oriented Association of Austrian Industrialists or IV
Roman Catholic Church, including its chief lay organization, Catholic Action
other: 3 composite leagues of the Austrian People's Party or OeVP representing business, labor, farmers, and other nongovernment organizations in the areas of environment and human rights

International organization participation: ADB (nonregional member), AfDB (nonregional member), Australia Group, BIS, BSEC (observer), CD, CE, CEI, CERN, EAPC, EBRD, ECB, EIB, EMU, ESA, EU, FAO, FATF, G-9, IADB, IAEA, IBRD, ICAO, ICC (national committees), ICCt, ICRM, IDA, IEA, IFAD, IFC, IFRCS, IGAD (partners), ILO, IMF, IMO, Interpol, IOC, IOM, IPU, ISO, ITSO, ITU, ITUC (NGOs), MIGA, MINURSO, NEA, NSG, OAS (observer), OECD, OIF (observer), OPCW, OSCE, Paris Club, PCA, PFP, Schengen Convention, SELEC (observer), UN, UNCTAD, UNESCO, UNFICYP, UNHCR, UNIDO, UNIFIL, UNTSO, UNWTO, UPU, WCO, WFTU (NGOs), WHO, WIPO, WMO, WTO, ZC

Diplomatic representation in the US: *chief of mission:* Ambassador Wolfgang WALDNER (since 28 January 2016)
chancery: 3524 International Court NW, Washington, DC 20008-3035
telephone: [1] (202) 895-6700
FAX: [1] (202) 895-6750
consulate(s) general: Los Angeles, New York
consulate(s): Chicago

Diplomatic representation from the US: *chief of mission:* Ambassador (vacant); Charge d'Affaires Eugene YOUNG (since 20 January 2017)
embassy: Boltzmanngasse 16, A-1090, Vienna
mailing address: use embassy street address
telephone: [43] (1) 31339-0
FAX: [43] (1) 3100682

Flag description: three equal horizontal bands of red (top), white, and red; the flag design is certainly one of the oldest—if not the oldest—national banners in the world; according to tradition, in 1191, following a fierce battle in the Third Crusade, Duke Leopold V of Austria's white tunic became completely blood-spattered; upon removal of his wide belt or sash, a white band was revealed; the red-white-red color combination was subsequently adopted as his banner

National symbol(s): eagle, edelweiss, Alpine gentian; national colors: red, white

National anthem: *name:* "Bundeshymne" (Federal Hymn)
lyrics/music: Paula von PRERADOVIC/Wolfgang Amadeus MOZART or Johann HOLZER (disputed)
note: adopted 1947; the anthem is also known as "Land der Berge, Land am Strome" (Land of the Mountains, Land by the River); Austria adopted a new national anthem after World War II to replace the former imperial anthem composed by Franz Josef HAYDN, which had been appropriated by Germany in 1922 and was thereafter associated with the Nazi regime; a gendered version of the lyrics was adopted by the Austrian Federal Assembly in fall 2011 and became effective 1 January 2012

ECONOMY

Economy—overview: Austria, with its well-developed market economy, skilled labor force, and high standard of living, is closely tied to other EU economies, especially Germany's. Its economy features a large service sector, a relatively sound industrial sector, and a small, but highly developed agricultural sector.

Economic growth has been relatively weak in recent years, approaching 1% in 2015, but rising to 2.3% in 2017. Austria's 5.8% unemployment rate, while low by European standards, is at its highest rate since the end of World War II, driven by an increased number of refugees and EU migrants entering the labor market. Without extensive vocational training programs and generous early retirement, the unemployment rate would be even higher.

Although Austria's fiscal position compares favorably with other euro-zone countries, it faces several external risks, such as unexpectedly weak world economic growth threatening the export market, Austrian banks' continued exposure to Central and Eastern Europe, repercussions from the Hypo Alpe Adria bank collapse, political and economic uncertainties caused by the European sovereign debt crisis, the current refugee crisis, and continued unrest in Russia/Ukraine. The budget deficit stood at 1% of GDP in 2016 and public debt reached a post-war high of 84.6% of the GDP in 2016.

GDP (purchasing power parity):
$434.1 billion (2017 est.)
$424.4 billion (2016 est.)
$418.2 billion (2015 est.)
note: data are in 2017 dollars
country comparison to the world: 46

GDP (official exchange rate):
$409.3 billion (2016 est.)

GDP—real growth rate:
2.3% (2017 est.)
1.5% (2016 est.)
1% (2015 est.)
country comparison to the world: 144

GDP—per capita (PPP):
$49,200 (2017 est.)

$48,600 (2016 est.)
$48,500 (2015 est.)
note: data are in 2017 dollars
country comparison to the world: 33

Gross national saving: 26.2% of GDP (2017 est.)
25.5% of GDP (2016 est.)
25.4% of GDP (2015 est.)
country comparison to the world: 44

GDP—composition, by end use:
household consumption: 52.1%
government consumption: 19.8%
investment in fixed capital: 23.1%
investment in inventories: 1.1%
exports of goods and services: 54.2%
imports of goods and services: -50.3% (2017 est.)

GDP—composition, by sector of origin:
agriculture: 1.2%
industry: 28.2%
services: 70.5% (2017 est.)

Agriculture—products: grains, potatoes, wine, fruit; dairy products, cattle, pigs, poultry; lumber and other forestry products

Industries: construction, machinery, vehicles and parts, food, metals, chemicals, lumber, paper and paperboard, communications equipment, tourism

Industrial production growth rate: 3.8% (2017 est.)
country comparison to the world: 75

Labor force: 3.997 million (2017 est.)
country comparison to the world: 94

Labor force—by occupation: agriculture: 0.7%
industry: 25.3%
services: 74% (2015 est.)

Unemployment rate: 5.4% (2017 est.)
6% (2016 est.)
country comparison to the world: 73

Population below poverty line: 4% (2014 est.)

Household income or consumption by percentage share: *lowest 10%:* 2.8%
highest 10%: 23.5% (2012 est.)

Distribution of family income—Gini index: 29.2 (2013)
26.3 (2007)
country comparison to the world: 129

Budget: *revenues:* $197.8 billion
expenditures: $201.9 billion (2017 est.)
Taxes and other revenues: 48.3% of GDP (2017 est.)
country comparison to the world: 17

Budget surplus (+) or deficit (-): -1% of GDP (2017 est.)
country comparison to the world: 60

Public debt: 81.7% of GDP (2017 est.)
84.6% of GDP (2016 est.)
note: this is general government gross debt, defined in the Maastricht Treaty as consolidated general government gross debt at nominal value, outstanding at the end of the year; it covers the following categories of government liabilities (as defined in ESA95): currency and deposits (AF.2), securities other than shares excluding financial derivatives (AF.3, excluding AF.34), and loans (AF.4); the general government sector comprises the sub-sectors of central government, state

government, local government and social security funds; as a percentage of GDP, the GDP used as a denominator is the gross domestic product in current year prices
country comparison to the world: 35

Fiscal year: calendar year

Inflation rate (consumer prices):
1.6% (2017 est.)
1% (2016 est.)
country comparison to the world: 71

Commercial bank prime lending rate: 1.7% (31 December 2017 est.)
1.86% (31 December 2016 est.)
country comparison to the world: 180

Stock of narrow money: $258.6 billion (31 December 2017 est.)
$214 billion (31 December 2016 est.)
note: see entry for the European Union for money supply for the entire euro area; the European Central Bank (ECB) controls monetary policy for the 18 members of the Economic and Monetary Union (EMU); individual members of the EMU do not control the quantity of money circulating within their own borders
country comparison to the world: 20

Stock of broad money: $371.1 billion (31 December 2017 est.)
$326.2 billion (31 December 2016 est.)
country comparison to the world: 31

Stock of domestic credit: $556.7 billion (31 December 2017 est.)
$489.3 billion (31 December 2016 est.)
country comparison to the world: 26

Market value of publicly traded shares:
$96.08 billion (31 December 2015 est.)
$96.79 billion (31 December 2014 est.)
$117.7 billion (31 December 2013 est.)
country comparison to the world: 40

Current account balance:
$8.546 billion (2017 est.)
$6.642 billion (2016 est.)
country comparison to the world: 22

Exports: $157.5 billion (2017 est.)
$142.8 billion (2016 est.)
country comparison to the world: 32

Exports—commodities: machinery and equipment, motor vehicles and parts, paper and paperboard, metal goods, chemicals, iron and steel, textiles, foodstuffs

Exports—partners: Germany 29.9%, US 6.3%, Italy 6.2%, Switzerland 5.7%, Slovakia 4.4% (2016)

Imports: $157.6 billion (2017 est.)
$143 billion (2016 est.)
country comparison to the world: 28

Imports—commodities: machinery and equipment, motor vehicles, chemicals, metal goods, oil and oil products, natural gas; foodstuffs

Imports—partners: Germany 42.5%, Italy 6%, Switzerland 5.6%, Czech Republic 4.4%, Netherlands 4% (2016)

Reserves of foreign exchange and gold: $23.36 billion (31 December 2016 est.)

$22.24 billion (31 December 2015 est.)
country comparison to the world: 56

Debt—external:
$689.1 billion (31 March 2016 est.)
$679.3 billion (31 March 2015 est.)
country comparison to the world: 18

Stock of direct foreign investment—at home:
$245.8 billion (31 December 2017 est.)
$242.8 billion (31 December 2016 est.)
country comparison to the world: 26

Stock of direct foreign investment—abroad:
$309.8 billion (31 December 2017 est.)
$300.5 billion (31 December 2016 est.)
country comparison to the world: 23

Exchange rates: euros (EUR) per US dollar—
0.906 (2017 est.)
0.9214 (2016 est.)
0.9214 (2015 est.)
0.885 (2014 est.)
0.7634 (2013 est.)

ENERGY

Electricity access: electrification—*total population:* 100% (2016)

Electricity—production: 56.05 billion kWh (2015 est.)
country comparison to the world: 50

Electricity—consumption: 62.78 billion kWh (2015 est.)
country comparison to the world: 42

Electricity—exports: 19.19 billion kWh (2016 est.)
country comparison to the world: 10

Electricity—imports: 26.34 billion kWh (2016 est.)
country comparison to the world: 7

Electricity—installed generating capacity: 24.44 million kW (2015 est.)
country comparison to the world: 36

Electricity—from fossil fuels: 22.2% of total installed capacity (2015 est.)
country comparison to the world: 193

Electricity—from nuclear fuels: 0% of total installed capacity (2015 est.)
country comparison to the world: 44

Electricity—from hydroelectric plants: 33.2% of total installed capacity (2015 est.)
country comparison to the world: 63

Electricity—from other renewable sources: 24.3% of total installed capacity (2015 est.)
country comparison to the world: 23

Crude oil—production: 15,160 bbl/day (2016 est.)
country comparison to the world: 75

Crude oil—exports: 0 bbl/day (2016 est.)
country comparison to the world: 90

Crude oil—imports: 148,400 bbl/day (2016 est.)
country comparison to the world: 35

Crude oil—proved reserves: 43 million bbl (1 January 2017 es)
country comparison to the world: 81

Refined petroleum products—production: 188,000 bbl/day (2016 est.)
country comparison to the world: 52

Refined petroleum products—consumption: 267,500 bbl/day (2016 est.)
country comparison to the world: 48

Refined petroleum products—exports: 49,230 bbl/day (2016 est.)
country comparison to the world: 54

Refined petroleum products—imports: 132,100 bbl/day (2016 est.)
country comparison to the world: 49

Natural gas—production: 1.263 billion cu m (2015 est.)
country comparison to the world: 63

Natural gas—consumption: 12.12 billion cu m (2015 est.)
country comparison to the world: 51

Natural gas—exports: 5.407 billion cu m (2015 est.)
country comparison to the world: 30

Natural gas—imports: 11.48 billion cu m (2015 est.)
country comparison to the world: 26

Natural gas—proved reserves: 6.994 billion cu m (1 January 2017 es)
country comparison to the world: 89

Carbon dioxide emissions from consumption of energy: 78.9 million Mt (2015 est.)
country comparison to the world: 45

COMMUNICATIONS

Telephones—fixed lines: *total subscriptions:* 3,567,200
subscriptions per 100 inhabitants: 41 (July 2016 est.)
country comparison to the world: 45

Telephones—mobile cellular: *total:* 14.27 million
subscriptions per 100 inhabitants: 164 (July 2016 est.)
country comparison to the world: 71

Telephone system: *general assessment:* highly developed and efficient
domestic: mobile-cellular subscribership is ubiquitous; cable networks are very extensive, the fiber-optic net is being developed; all telephone applications and Internet services are available; broadband is available in all large municipalities
international: country code—43; earth stations available in the Astra, Intelsat, Eutelsat satellite systems (2016)

Broadcast media: worldwide cable and satellite TV are available; the public incumbent ORF competes with three other major, several regional domestic, and up to 400 international TV stations; TV coverage is in principle 100%, but only 90% use broadcast media; Internet streaming not only complements, but increasingly replaces regular TV stations (2016)

Internet country code: .at

Internet users: *total:* 7,346,055
percent of population: 84.3% (July 2016 est.)

country comparison to the world: 53

TRANSPORTATION

National air transport system: *number of registered air carriers:* 11
inventory of registered aircraft operated by air carriers: 130
annual passenger traffic on registered air carriers: 14,718,641
annual freight traffic on registered air carriers: 351.379 million mt-km (2015)
Civil aircraft registration country code prefix: OE (2016)

Airports: 52 (2013)
country comparison to the world: 90

Airports—with paved runways: *total:* 24
over 3,047 m: 1
2,438 to 3,047 m: 5
1,524 to 2,437 m: 1
914 to 1,523 m: 4
under 914 m: 13 (2017)

Airports—with unpaved runways: *total:* 28
1,524 to 2,437 m: 1
914 to 1,523 m: 3
under 914 m: 24 (2013)

Heliports: 1 (2013)

Pipelines: gas 1,888 km; oil 594 km; refined products 157 km (2017)

Railways: *total:* 5,800 km (2016)
standard gauge: 5,267.7 km 1.435-m gauge (3,556.4 km electrified) (2014)
country comparison to the world: 35

Roadways: *total:* 138,696 km
paved: 138,696 km (includes 2,208 km of expressways) (2016)
country comparison to the world: 39

Waterways: 358 km (2011)
country comparison to the world: 89

Merchant marine: *total:* 1
by type: other 1 (2017)

Ports and terminals: river port(s): Enns, Krems, Linz, Vienna (Danube)

MILITARY AND SECURITY

Military expenditures:
0.68% of GDP (2016 est.)
0.67% of GDP (2015)
0.75% of GDP (2014)
0.75% of GDP (2013)
0.78% of GDP (2012)
country comparison to the world: 115

Military branches: Land Forces (KdoLdSK), Air Forces (KdoLuSK) (2014)

Military service age and obligation: registration requirement at age 17, the legal minimum age for voluntary military service; 18 is the legal minimum age for compulsory military service (6 months), or optionally, alternative civil/community service (9 months); males 18 to 50 years old in the militia or inactive reserve are subject to compulsory service; in a January 2012 referendum, a majority of Austrians voted in favor of retaining the system of compulsory military service (with the option of alternative/non-military service) instead of switching to a professional army system (2015)

TRANSNATIONAL ISSUES

Disputes—international: *none*

Refugees and internally displaced persons: *refugees (country of origin):* 30,958 (Syria); 20,220 (Afghanistan); 13,773 (Russia); 5,555 (Iraq) (2016)
stateless persons: 937 (2016)

Illicit drugs: transshipment point for Southwest Asian heroin and South American cocaine destined for Western Europe; increasing consumption of European-produced synthetic drugs

AZERBAIJAN

INTRODUCTION

Background: Azerbaijan—a nation with a majority-Turkic and majority-Shia Muslim population—was briefly independent (from 1918 to 1920) following the collapse of the Russian Empire; it was subsequently incorporated into the Soviet Union for seven decades. Azerbaijan has yet to resolve its conflict with Armenia over Nagorno-Karabakh, a primarily ethnic Armenian-populated region that Moscow recognized in 1923 as an autonomous republic within Soviet Azerbaijan after Armenia and Azerbaijan disputed the territory's status. Armenia and Azerbaijan reignited their dispute over the area in 1988; the struggle escalated

militarily after both countries attained independence from the Soviet Union in 1991. By May 1994, when a cease-fire took hold, ethnic Armenian forces held not only Nagorno-Karabakh but also seven surrounding provinces in the territory of Azerbaijan. The OSCE Minsk Group, co-chaired by the US, France, and Russia, is the framework established to mediate a peaceful resolution of the conflict.

Corruption in the country is widespread, and the government, which eliminated presidential term limits in a 2009 referendum and approved extending presidential terms from 5 to 7 years in 2016, has been accused of authoritarianism. Although the poverty rate has been reduced and infrastructure investment has increased substantially in recent years due to revenue from oil and gas production, reforms have not adequately addressed weaknesses in most government institutions, particularly in the education and health sectors, as well as the court system.

GEOGRAPHY

Location: Southwestern Asia, bordering the Caspian Sea, between Iran and Russia, with a small European portion north of the Caucasus range

Geographic coordinates: 40 30 N, 47 30 E

Map references: Asia

Area: *total:* 86,600 sq km
land: 82,629 sq km
water: 3,971 sq km

note: includes the exclave of Naxcivan Autonomous Republic and the Nagorno-Karabakh region; the region's autonomy was abolished by Azerbaijani Supreme Soviet on 26 November 1991
country comparison to the world: 114

Area—comparative: about three-quarters the size of Pennsylvania; slightly smaller than Maine

Land boundaries: *total:* 2,468 km
border countries (5): Armenia 996 km, Georgia 428 km, Iran 689 km, Russia 338 km, Turkey 17 km

Coastline: 0 km (landlocked); note—Azerbaijan borders the Caspian Sea (713 km)

Maritime claims: none (landlocked)

Climate: dry, semiarid steppe

Terrain: large, flat Kur-Araz Ovaligi (Kura-Araks Lowland, much of it below sea level) with Great Caucasus Mountains to the north, Qarabag Yaylasi (Karabakh Upland) to the west; Baku lies on Abseron Yasaqligi (Apsheron Peninsula) that juts into Caspian Sea

Elevation: *mean elevation:* 384 m

elevation extremes: *lowest point:* Caspian Sea -28 m
highest point: Bazarduzu Dagi 4,466 m

Natural resources: petroleum, natural gas, iron ore, nonferrous metals, bauxite

Land use: *agricultural land:* 57.6%
arable land 22.8%;
permanent crops 2.7%;
permanent pasture 32.1%

forest: 11.3%
other: 31.1% (2011 est.)
Irrigated land: 14,277 sq km (2012)

Population—distribution: highest population density is found in the far eastern area of the county, in and around Baku; apart from smaller urbanized areas, the rest of the country has a fairly light and evenly distributed population

Natural hazards: droughts

Environment—current issues: local scientists consider the Abseron Yasaqligi (Apsheron Peninsula) (including Baku and Sumqayit) and the Caspian Sea to be the ecologically most devastated area in the world because of severe air, soil, and water pollution; soil pollution results from oil spills, from the use of DDT pesticide, and from toxic defoliants used in the production of cotton

Environment—international agreements: *party to:* Air Pollution, Biodiversity, Climate Change, Climate Change-Kyoto Protocol, Desertification, Endangered Species, Hazardous Wastes, Marine Dumping, Ozone Layer Protection, Ship Pollution, Wetlands
signed, but not ratified: none of the selected agreements

Geography—note: both the main area of the country and the Naxcivan exclave are landlocked

PEOPLE AND SOCIETY

Population: 9,961,396 (July 2017 est.)
country comparison to the world: 90

Nationality: *noun:* Azerbaijani(s)
adjective: Azerbaijani

Ethnic groups: Azerbaijani 91.6%, Lezghin 2%, Russian 1.3%, Armenian 1.3%, Talysh 1.3%, other 2.4%
note: the separatist Nagorno-Karabakh region is populated almost entirely by ethnic Armenians (2009 est.)

Languages: Azerbaijani (Azeri) (official) 92.5%, Russian 1.4%, Armenian 1.4%, other 4.7% (2009 est.)

Religions: Muslim 96.9% (predominantly Shia), Christian 3%, other <0.1, unaffiliated <0.1 (2010 est.)
note: religious affiliation is still nominal in Azerbaijan; percentages for actual practicing adherents are much lower

Age structure: *0-14 years:* 22.95% (male 1,220,356/female 1,065,514)
15-24 years: 14.84% (male 775,422/female 703,027)
25-54 years: 45.39% (male 2,219,613/female 2,302,356)
55-64 years: 10.17% (male 467,830/female 545,505)
65 years and over: 6.64% (male 253,679/female 408,094) (2017 est.)

Dependency ratios: *total dependency ratio:* 40.2
youth dependency ratio: 32.1
elderly dependency ratio: 8
potential support ratio: 12.4 (2015 est.)

Median age: *total:* 31.3 years

male: 29.8 years
female: 33 years (2017 est.)
country comparison to the world: 107

Population growth rate: 0.87% (2017 est.)
country comparison to the world: 124

Birth rate: 15.8 births/1,000 population (2017 est.)
country comparison to the world: 116

Death rate: 7.1 deaths/1,000 population (2017 est.)
country comparison to the world: 128

Net migration rate: 0 migrant(s)/1,000 population (2017 est.)
country comparison to the world: 101

Population distribution: highest population density is found in the far eastern area of the county, in and around Baku; apart from smaller urbanized areas, the rest of the country has a fairly light and evenly distributed population

Urbanization: *urban population:* 55.2% of total population (2017)
rate of urbanization: 1.38% annual rate of change (2015-20 est.)

Major urban areas—population: BAKU (capital) 2.374 million (2015)

Sex ratio: *at birth:* 1.11 male(s)/female
0-14 years: 1.15 male(s)/female
15-24 years: 1.09 male(s)/female
25-54 years: 0.96 male(s)/female
55-64 years: 0.86 male(s)/female
65 years and over: 0.62 male(s)/female
total population: 0.98 male(s)/female (2016 est.)

Mother's mean age at first birth: 23.2 years (2014 est.)

Maternal mortality ratio: 25 deaths/100,000 live births (2015 est.)
country comparison to the world: 120

Infant mortality rate: *total:* 23.8 deaths/1,000 live births
male: 24.7 deaths/1,000 live births
female: 22.9 deaths/1,000 live births (2017 est.)
country comparison to the world: 70

Life expectancy at birth: *total population:* 72.8 years
male: 69.7 years
female: 76.1 years (2017 est.)
country comparison to the world: 144

Total fertility rate: 1.89 children born/woman (2017 est.)
country comparison to the world: 137

Health expenditures: 6% of GDP (2014)
country comparison to the world: 104

Physicians density: 3.4 physicians/1,000 population (2014)

Hospital bed density: 4.7 beds/1,000 population (2012)

Drinking water source:
improved:
urban: 94.7% of population
rural: 77.8% of population
total: 87% of population
unimproved: urban: 5.3% of population
rural: 22.2% of population

total: 13% of population (2015 est.)

Sanitation facility access:
improved:
urban: 91.6% of population
rural: 86.6% of population
total: 89.3% of population
unimproved: urban: 8.4% of population
rural: 13.4% of population
total: 10.7% of population (2015 est.)

HIV/AIDS—adult prevalence rate: 0.1% (2016 est.)
country comparison to the world: 101

HIV/AIDS—people living with HIV/AIDS: 9,200 (2016 est.)
country comparison to the world: 96

HIV/AIDS—deaths: <500 (2016 est.)

Obesity—adult prevalence rate: 19.9% (2016)
country comparison to the world: 106

Children under the age of 5 years underweight: 4.9% (2013)
country comparison to the world: 75

Education expenditures: 2.6% of GDP (2014)
country comparison to the world: 158

Literacy: *definition:* age 15 and over can read and write
total population: 99.8%
male: 99.9%
female: 99.7% (2016 est.)

School life expectancy (primary to tertiary education): *total:* 13 years
male: 13 years
female: 13 years (2014)

Unemployment, youth ages 15-24: *total:* 13.4%
male: 11.4%
female: 15.8% (2015 est.)
country comparison to the world: 83

GOVERNMENT

Country name: *conventional long form:* Republic of Azerbaijan
conventional short form: Azerbaijan
local long form: Azarbaycan Respublikasi
local short form: Azarbaycan
former: Azerbaijan Soviet Socialist Republic
etymology: the name translates as "Land of Fire" and refers to naturally occurring surface fires on ancient oil pools or from natural gas discharges

Government type: presidential republic

Capital: *name:* Baku (Baki, Baky)
geographic coordinates: 40 23 N, 49 52 E
time difference: UTC+4 (9 hours ahead of Washington, DC, during Standard Time)

Administrative divisions: 66 rayons (rayonlar; rayon—singular), 11 cities (saharlar; sahar—singular);
rayons: Abseron, Agcabadi, Agdam, Agdas, Agstafa, Agsu, Astara, Babak, Balakan, Barda, Beylaqan, Bilasuvar, Cabrayil, Calilabad, Culfa, Daskasan, Fuzuli, Gadabay, Goranboy, Goycay, Goygol, Haciqabul, Imisli, Ismayilli, Kalbacar, Kangarli, Kurdamir, Lacin, Lankaran, Lerik, Masalli, Neftcala, Oguz, Ordubad, Qabala, Qax,

Qazax, Qobustan, Quba, Qubadli, Qusar, Saatli, Sabirabad, Sabran, Sadarak, Sahbuz, Saki, Salyan, Samaxi, Samkir, Samux, Sarur, Siyazan, Susa, Tartar, Tovuz, Ucar, Xacmaz, Xizi, Xocali, Xocavand, Yardimli, Yevlax, Zangilan, Zaqatala, Zardab

cities: Baku, Ganca, Lankaran, Mingacevir, Naftalan, Naxcivan (Nakhichevan), Saki, Sirvan, Sumqayit, Xankandi, Yevlax

Independence: 30 August 1991 (declared from the Soviet Union); 18 October 1991 (adopted by the Supreme Council of Azerbaijan)

National holiday: Republic Day (founding of the Democratic Republic of Azerbaijan), 28 May (1918)

Constitution: *history:* several previous; latest adopted 12 November 1995
amendments: proposed by the president of the republic or by at least 63 members of the National Assembly; passage requires at least 95 votes of Assembly members in two separate readings of the draft amendment six months apart and requires presidential approval after each of the two Assembly votes, followed by presidential signature; constitutional articles on the authority, sovereignty, and unity of the people cannot be amended; amended 2002, 2009, 2016 (2017)

Legal system: civil law system

International law organization participation: has not submitted an ICJ jurisdiction declaration; non-party state to the ICCt

Citizenship: *citizenship by birth:* yes
citizenship by descent: yes
dual citizenship recognized: no
residency requirement for naturalization: 5 years

Suffrage: 18 years of age; universal

Executive branch: *chief of state:* President Ilham ALIYEV (since 31 October 2003); First Vice President Mehriban ALIYEVA (since 21 February 2017)

head of government: Prime Minister Artur RASI-ZADE (since 4 November 2003); First Deputy Prime Minister Yaqub EYYUBOV (since June 2006); note—RASIZADE was previously prime minister from 20 July 1996 to 4 August 2003
cabinet: Council of Ministers appointed by the president and confirmed by the National Assembly
elections/appointments: president directly elected by absolute majority popular vote in 2 rounds if needed for a 5-year term (eligible for unlimited terms); election last held on 9 October 2013 (next to be held in October 2018); prime minister and first deputy prime minister appointed by the president and confirmed by the National Assembly; note—a constitutional amendment approved in a September 2016 referendum will expand presidential terms from 5 to 7 years when it formally takes effect; a separate constitutional amendment approved in the September 2016 referendum also introduced the post of first vice-president and additional vice-presidents, who are directly appointed by the
election results: Ilham ALIYEV reelected president in first round; percent of vote—Ilham

ALIYEV (YAP) 84.5%, Jamil HASANLI (National Council of Democratic Forces) 5.5%, other 10%
note: OSCE observers concluded that the election did not meet international standards

Legislative branch: *description:* unicameral National Assembly or Milli Mejlis (125 seats; members directly elected in single-seat constituencies by simple majority vote to serve 5-year terms)
elections: last held on 1 November 2015 (next to be held in November 2020)
election results: percent of vote by party—NA; seats by party—YAP 69, CSP 2, Democratic Reforms 1, Social Democratic Party 1, Social Prosperity 1, Unity Party 1, Democratic Enlightenment 1, Whole Azerbaijan Popular Front 1, Motherland 1, Civil Unity 1, Great Undertaking Party 1, National Renaissance Party 1, independent 43, invalid 1

Judicial branch: *highest court(s):* Supreme Court (consists of the chairman, vice chairman, and 23 judges in plenum sessions and organized into civil, economic affairs, criminal, and rights violations chambers); Constitutional Court (consists of 9 judges)
judge selection and term of office: Supreme Court judges nominated by the president and appointed by the Milli Majlis; judges appointed for 10 years; Constitutional Court chairman and deputy chairman appointed by the president; other court judges nominated by the president and appointed by the Milli Majlis to serve single 15-year terms
subordinate courts: Courts of Appeal (replaced the Economic Court in 2002); district and municipal courts;

Political parties and leaders: Civil Solidarity Party or CSP [Sabir RUSTAMKHANLI]
Civil Unity Party or CUP [Sabir HAJIYEV]
Democratic Enlightenment [Elshan MUSAYEV]
Democratic Reforms Party [Asim MOLLAZADE]
Great Undertaking [Fazil MUSTAFA]
Musavat [Arif HAJILI]
Popular Front Party [Ali KARIMLI]
Motherland Party or AVP [Fazail AGAMALI]
Social Democratic Party [Ayaz MUTALIBOV]
Social Prosperity Party [Khanhusein KAZIMLI]
Unity Party [Tahir KARIMLI]
Whole Azerbaijan Popular Front Party [Gudrat HASANGULIYEV]
Yeni (New) Azerbaijan Party or YAP [President Ilham ALIYEV]

Political pressure groups and leaders: D18 [Ruslan IZZETLI]]
Ireli Public Union or Ireli PU [MirHasan SEYIDOV]
National Council of Democratic Forces [Jamil HASANLI]
N!DA Civic Movement [Turgut GAMBAR, Ulvi HASANLI] (youth movement)
Republican Alternative or REAL [Ilgar MAM-MADOV (in prison since 2013)]

International organization participation: ADB, BSEC, CD, CE, CICA, CIS, EAPC, EBRD, ECO, EITI (compliant country), FAO, GCTU, GUAM, IAEA, IBRD, ICAO, ICC (NGOs),

ICRM, IDA, IDB, IFAD, IFC, IFRCS, ILO, IMF, IMO, Interpol, IOC, IOM, IPU, ISO, ITSO, ITU, ITUC (NGOs), MIGA, NAM, OAS (observer), OIC, OPCW, OSCE, PFP, SELEC (observer), UN, UNCTAD, UNESCO, UNHCR, UNIDO, UNWTO, UPU, WCO, WFTU (NGOs), WHO, WIPO, WMO, WTO (observer)

Diplomatic representation in the US: *chief of mission:* Ambassador Elin SULEYMANOV (since 5 December 2011)
chancery: 2741 34th Street NW, Washington, DC 20008
telephone: [1] (202) 337-3500
FAX: [1] (202) 337-5911
consulate(s) general: Los Angeles

Diplomatic representation from the US: *chief of mission:* Ambassador Robert CEKUTA (since 19 February 2015)
embassy: 111 Azadlig Prospekti, Baku AZ1007
mailing address: American Embassy Baku, US Department of State, 7050 Baku Place, Washington, DC 20521-7050
telephone: [994] (12) 488-3300
FAX: [994] (12) 488-3330

Flag description: three equal horizontal bands of sky blue (top), red, and green; a crescent and eight-pointed star in white are centered in the red band; the blue band recalls Azerbaijan's Turkic heritage, red stands for modernization and progress, and green refers to Islam; the crescent moon and star are a Turkic insignia; the eight star points represent the eight Turkic peoples of the world

National symbol(s): flames of fire; national colors: blue, red, green

National anthem: *name:* "Azerbaijan Marsi" (March of Azerbaijan)
lyrics/music: Ahmed JAVAD/Uzeyir HAJIBEYOV
note: adopted 1992; although originally written in 1919 during a brief period of independence, "Azerbaijan Marsi" did not become the official anthem until after the dissolution of the Soviet Union

AZERBAIJAN

Economy—overview: Prior to the decline in global oil prices since 2014, Azerbaijan's high economic growth was attributable to rising energy exports, and some non-export sectors also featured double-digit growth. Oil exports through the Baku-Tbilisi-Ceyhan Pipeline, the Baku-Novorossiysk, and the Baku-Supsa Pipelines remain the main economic driver, but efforts to boost Azerbaijan's gas production are underway. The expected completion of the geopolitically important Southern Gas Corridor between Azerbaijan and Europe will open up another source of revenue from gas exports. Declining oil prices caused a 3.1% contraction in GDP in 2016, and a 0.8% decline in 2017, highlighted by a sharp reduction in the construction sector. The economic decline has been accompanied by higher inflation and a weakened banking sector in the aftermath of the two sharp currency devaluations since 2015. Azerbaijan's financial sector continued to struggle in 2017. In May 2017, Baku allowed the state-owned International Bank of Azerbaijan (IBA), the nation's largest bank, to default on some of its outstanding debt and file for bankruptcy in the US.

Azerbaijan has made limited progress with market-based economic reforms. Pervasive public and private sector corruption and structural economic inefficiencies remain a drag on long-term growth, particularly in non-energy sectors, but the government has made efforts to combat corruption, particularly in customs and with the "ASAN" one-stop window concept for government services. Several other obstacles impede Azerbaijan's economic progress, including the need for more foreign investment in the non-energy sector and the continuing conflict with Armenia over the Nagorno-Karabakh region. While trade with Russia and the other former Soviet republics remains important, Azerbaijan has expanded trade with Turkey and Europe and is seeking new markets for non-oil/gas exports, mainly from the agricultural sector, for example with Gulf Cooperation Council member countries, the US, and others.

Long-term prospects depend on world oil prices, Azerbaijan's ability to implement export routes for its growing gas production, and its ability to improve the business environment and diversify the economy. In late 2016, the President approved a strategic roadmap that identified key non-energy segments of the economy for development, such as agriculture, logistics, and tourism. In October, the long-awaited Baku-Tbilisi-Kars railway, stretching from the Azerbaijani capital to Kars in north-eastern Turkey, began limited service.

GDP (purchasing power parity):
$166.8 billion (2017 est.)
$168.6 billion (2016 est.)
$173.9 billion (2015 est.)
note: data are in 2017 dollars
country comparison to the world: 74

GDP (official exchange rate): $39.21 billion (2016 est.)

GDP—real growth rate:
-1% (2017 est.)
-3.1% (2016 est.)
0.6% (2015 est.)
country comparison to the world: 206

GDP—per capita (PPP):
$17,400 (2017 est.)
$17,800 (2016 est.)
$18,500 (2015 est.)
note: data are in 2017 dollars
country comparison to the world: 99

Gross national saving:
25% of GDP (2017 est.)
18% of GDP (2016 est.)
22.2% of GDP (2015 est.)
country comparison to the world: 51

GDP—composition, by end use:
household consumption: 53.9%
government consumption: 12.1%
investment in fixed capital: 26.3%
investment in inventories: 0.1%
exports of goods and services: 45.9%
imports of goods and services: -38.2% (2017 est.)

GDP—composition, by sector of origin: agriculture: 6.2%
industry: 49.1%
services: 44.7% (2017 est.)

Agriculture—products: fruit, vegetables, grain, rice, grapes, tea, cotton, tobacco; cattle, pigs, sheep, goats

Industries: petroleum and petroleum products, natural gas, oilfield equipment; steel, iron ore; cement; chemicals and petrochemicals; textiles

Industrial production growth rate: -6% (2017 est.)
country comparison to the world: 200

Labor force: 5.118 million (2017 est.)
country comparison to the world: 82

Labor force—by occupation: agriculture: 37%
industry: 14.3%
services: 48.9% (2015)

Unemployment rate: 6% (2017 est.)
6% (2016 est.)
country comparison to the world: 83

Population below poverty line: 4.9% (2015 est.)

Household income or consumption by percentage share: lowest 10%: 3.4%
highest 10%: 27.4% (2008)

Distribution of family income—Gini index: 33.7 (2008)
36.5 (2001)
country comparison to the world: 104

Budget: revenues: $9.852 billion
expenditures: $10.4 billion (2017 est.)
Taxes and other revenues: 25.1% of GDP (2017 est.)
country comparison to the world: 112

Budget surplus (+) or deficit (-): -1.4% of GDP (2017 est.)
country comparison to the world: 67

Public debt: 48.8% of GDP (2017 est.)
39.2% of GDP (2016 est.)
country comparison to the world: 104

Fiscal year: calendar year

Inflation rate (consumer prices): 12% (2017 est.)
12.4% (2016 est.)
country comparison to the world: 207

Central bank discount rate: 15% (10 March 2017)
15% (14 September 2016)
note: this is the Refinancing Rate, the key policy rate for the National Bank of Azerbaijan
country comparison to the world: 10

Commercial bank prime lending rate: 12.4% (31 December 2017 est.)
12.56% (31 December 2016 est.)
country comparison to the world: 64

Stock of narrow money: $6.044 billion (31 December 2017 est.)
$5.06 billion (31 December 2016 est.)
country comparison to the world: 97

Stock of broad money: $7.86 billion (31 December 2017 est.)
$6.521 billion (31 December 2016 est.)
country comparison to the world: 114

Stock of domestic credit: $13.79 billion (31 December 2017 est.)
$13.65 billion (31 December 2016 est.)

country comparison to the world: 100

Market value of publicly traded shares: $NA

Current account balance: $732 million (2017 est.)
-$1.363 billion (2016 est.)
country comparison to the world: 43

Exports: $15.69 billion (2017 est.)
$13.21 billion (2016 est.)
country comparison to the world: 74

Exports—commodities: oil and gas roughly 90%, machinery, foodstuffs, cotton

Exports—partners: Italy 19.9%, Germany 10.5%, France 8%, Indonesia 5.8%, Czech Republic 5.2% (2016)

Imports: $8.734 billion (2017 est.)
$9.004 billion (2016 est.)
country comparison to the world: 103

Imports—commodities: machinery and equipment, foodstuffs, metals, chemicals

Imports—partners: Russia 15.7%, Turkey 12.5%, US 9.6%, Germany 7.5%, Italy 6.7%, Japan 6.2%, China 5.4%, UK 5.4% (2016)

Reserves of foreign exchange and gold: $8.886 billion (31 December 2017 est.)
$7.142 billion (31 December 2016 est.)
country comparison to the world: 75

Debt—external: $16.62 billion (31 December 2017 est.)
$13.83 billion (31 December 2016 est.)
country comparison to the world: 99

Stock of direct foreign investment—at home: $80.63 billion (31 December 2017 est.)
$73.83 billion (31 December 2016 est.)
country comparison to the world: 51

Stock of direct foreign investment—abroad: $19.05 billion (31 December 2017 est.)
$17.05 billion (31 December 2016 est.)
country comparison to the world: 54

Exchange rates: Azerbaijani manats (AZN) per US dollar—
1.723 (2017 est.)
1.5957 (2016 est.)
1.5957 (2015 est.)
1.0246 (2014 est.)
0.7844 (2013 est.)

ENERGY

Electricity access: electrification—total population: 100% (2016)

Electricity—production: 23.3 billion kWh (2015 est.)
country comparison to the world: 73

Electricity—consumption: 20.27 billion kWh (2015 est.)
country comparison to the world: 71

Electricity—exports: 265 million kWh (2015 est.)
country comparison to the world: 72

Electricity—imports: 108 million kWh (2015 est.)
country comparison to the world: 97

Electricity—installed generating capacity: 7.417 million kW (2015 est.)
country comparison to the world: 72

Electricity—from fossil fuels: 84.5% of total installed capacity (2015 est.)
country comparison to the world: 77

Electricity—from nuclear fuels: 0% of total installed capacity (2015 est.)
country comparison to the world: 38

Electricity—from hydroelectric plants: 14.6% of total installed capacity (2015 est.)
country comparison to the world: 102

Electricity—from other renewable sources: 1% of total installed capacity (2015 est.)
country comparison to the world: 139

Crude oil—production: 833,500 bbl/day (2016 est.)
country comparison to the world: 23

Crude oil—exports: 721,600 bbl/day (2014 est.)
country comparison to the world: 18

Crude oil—imports: 0 bbl/day (2014 est.)
country comparison to the world: 90

Crude oil—proved reserves: 7 billion bbl (1 January 2017 es)
country comparison to the world: 20

Refined petroleum products—production: 142,100 bbl/day (2014 est.)
country comparison to the world: 60

Refined petroleum products—consumption: 101,000 bbl/day (2015 est.)
country comparison to the world: 81

Refined petroleum products—exports: 46,770 bbl/day (2014 est.)
country comparison to the world: 56

Refined petroleum products—imports: 6,171 bbl/day (2014 est.)
country comparison to the world: 158

Natural gas—production: 29.37 billion cu m (2016 est.)
country comparison to the world: 27

Natural gas—consumption: 18.2 billion cu m (2015 est.)
country comparison to the world: 45

Natural gas—exports: 7.32 billion cu m (2015 est.)
country comparison to the world: 27

Natural gas—imports: 200 million cu m (2015 est.)
country comparison to the world: 71

Natural gas—proved reserves: 991.1 billion cu m (1 January 2017 es)
country comparison to the world: 27

Carbon dioxide emissions from consumption of energy: 35 million Mt (2013 est.)
country comparison to the world: 73

COMMUNICATIONS

Telephones—fixed lines: *total subscriptions:* 1,700,233
subscriptions per 100 inhabitants: 17 (July 2016 est.)
country comparison to the world: 63

Telephones—mobile cellular: total: 10,315,993
subscriptions per 100 inhabitants: 104 (July 2016 est.)

country comparison to the world: 83

Telephone system: *general assessment:* requires considerable expansion and modernization; fixed-line telephone and a broad range of other telecom services are controlled by a state-owned telecommunications monopoly and growth has been stagnant; more competition exists in the mobile-cellular market with three providers in 2017
domestic: teledensity of some 17 fixed lines per 100 persons; mobile-cellular teledensity has increased to 104 telephones per 100 persons; satellite service connects Baku to a modern switch in its exclave of Naxcivan (Nakhchivan)
international: country code—994; the Trans-Asia-Europe (TAE) fiber-optic link transits Azerbaijan providing international connectivity to neighboring countries; the old Soviet system of cable and microwave is still serviceable; satellite earth stations—2 (2017)

Broadcast media: 3 state-run and 1 public TV channels; 4 domestic commercial TV stations and about 15 regional TV stations; cable TV services are available in Baku; 1 state-run and 1 public radio network operating; a small number of private commercial radio stations broadcasting; local FM relays of Baku commercial stations are available in many localities; local relays of several international broadcasters had been available until late 2008 when their broadcasts were banned from FM frequencies (2010)

Internet country code: .az

Internet users: total: 7,720,502
percent of population: 78.2% (July 2016 est.)
country comparison to the world: 60

TRANSPORTATION

National air transport system: *number of registered air carriers:* 2
inventory of registered aircraft operated by air carriers: 35
annual passenger traffic on registered air carriers: 1,803,112
annual freight traffic on registered air carriers: 41,954,600 mt-km (2015)
Civil aircraft registration country code prefix: 4K (2016)

Airports: 37 (2013)
country comparison to the world: 108

Airports—with paved runways: total: 30
over 3,047 m: 5
2,438 to 3,047 m: 5
1,524 to 2,437 m: 13
914 to 1,523 m: 4
under 914 m: 3 (2017)

Airports—with unpaved runways: total: 7
under 914 m: 7 (2013)

Heliports: 1 (2012)

Pipelines: condensate 89 km; gas 3,890 km; oil 2,446 km (2013)

Railways: total: 2,944.3 km
broad gauge: 2,944.3 km 1.520-m gauge (approx. 1,767 km electrified) (2017)
country comparison to the world: 71

Roadways: *total:* 52,942 km
paved: 26,789 km
unpaved: 26,153 km (2006)
country comparison to the world: 76

Merchant marine: total: 311
by type: general cargo 48, oil tanker 48, other 215 (2017)
country comparison to the world: 50

Ports and terminals: *major seaport(s):* Baku (Baki) located on the Caspian Sea

MILITARY AND SECURITY

Military expenditures: 3.64% of GDP (2016)
5.61% of GDP (2015)
4.56% of GDP (2014)
4.54% of GDP (2013)
4.66% of GDP (2012)
country comparison to the world: 6

Military branches: Army, Navy, Air, and Air Defense Forces (2010)

Military service age and obligation: 18-35 years of age for compulsory military service; service obligation 18 months or 12 months for university graduates; 17 years of age for voluntary service; 17 year olds are considered to be on active service at cadet military schools (2012)

TRANSNATIONAL ISSUES

Disputes—international: Azerbaijan, Kazakhstan, and Russia ratified the Caspian seabed delimitation treaties based on equidistance, while Iran continues to insist on a one-fifth slice of the sea; the dispute over the break-away Nagorno-Karabakh region and the Armenian military occupation of surrounding lands in Azerbaijan remains the primary focus of regional instability; residents have evacuated the former Soviet-era small ethnic enclaves in Armenia and Azerbaijan; local border forces struggle to control the illegal transit of goods and people across the porous, undemarcated Armenian, Azerbaijani, and Georgian borders; bilateral talks continue with Turkmenistan on dividing the seabed and contested oilfields in the middle of the Caspian

Refugees and internally displaced persons: IDPs: 582,000 (conflict with Armenia over Nagorno-Karabakh; IDPs are mainly ethnic Azerbaijanis but also include ethnic Kurds, Russians, and Turks predominantly from occupied territories around Nagorno-Karabakh; includes IDPs' descendants, returned IDPs, and people living in insecure areas and excludes people displaced by natural disasters; around half the IDPs live in the capital Baku) (2016)
stateless persons: 3,585 (2016)

Illicit drugs: limited illicit cultivation of cannabis and opium poppy, mostly for CIS consumption; small government eradication program; transit point for Southwest Asian opiates bound for Russia and to a lesser extent the rest of Europe

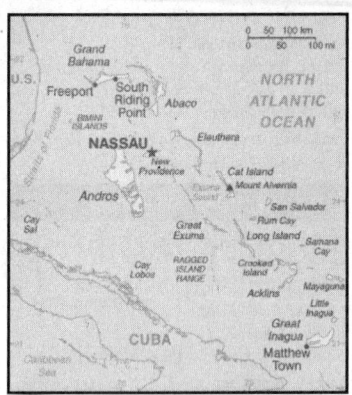

INTRODUCTION

Background: Lucayan Indians inhabited the islands when Christopher COLUMBUS first set foot in the New World on San Salvador in 1492. British settlement of the islands began in 1647; the islands became a colony in 1783. Piracy thrived in the 17th and 18th centuries because of The Bahamas close proximity to shipping lanes. Since attaining independence from the UK in 1973, The Bahamas has prospered through tourism, international banking, and investment management. Because of its location, the country is a major transshipment point for illegal drugs, particularly shipments to the US and Europe, and its territory is used for smuggling illegal migrants into the US.

GEOGRAPHY

Location: chain of islands in the North Atlantic Ocean, southeast of Florida, northeast of Cuba

Geographic coordinates: 24 15 N, 76 00 W

Map references: Central America and the Caribbean

Area: *total:* 13,880 sq km
land: 10,010 sq km
water: 3,870 sq km
country comparison to the world: 161

Area—comparative: slightly smaller than Connecticut

Land boundaries: 0 km

Coastline: 3,542 km

Maritime claims: *territorial sea:* 12 nm
exclusive economic zone: 200 nm

Climate: tropical marine; moderated by warm waters of Gulf Stream

Terrain: long, flat coral formations with some low rounded hills

Elevation: *mean elevation:* NA

elevation extremes: *lowest point:* Atlantic Ocean 0 m
highest point: Mount Alvernia on Cat Island 64 m

Natural resources: salt, aragonite, timber, arable land

Land use: *agricultural land:* 1.4%
arable land: 0.8%;
permanent crops: 0.4%;
permanent pasture: 0.2%
forest: 51.4%
other: 47.2% (2011 est.)
Irrigated land: 10 sq km (2012)

Population—distribution: most of the population lives in urban areas, with two-thirds living on New Providence Island where Nassau is located

Natural hazards: hurricanes and other tropical storms cause extensive flood and wind damage

Environment—current issues: coral reef decay; solid waste disposal

Environment—international agreements: party to: Biodiversity, Climate Change, Climate Change-Kyoto Protocol, Desertification, Endangered Species, Hazardous Wastes, Law of the Sea, Ozone Layer Protection, Ship Pollution, Wetlands
signed, but not ratified: none of the selected agreements

Geography—note: strategic location adjacent to US and Cuba; extensive island chain of which 30 are inhabited

PEOPLE AND SOCIETY

Population: 329,988
note: estimates for this country explicitly take into account the effects of excess mortality due to AIDS; this can result in lower life expectancy, higher infant mortality, higher death rates, lower population growth rates, and changes in the distribution of population by age and sex than would otherwise be expected (July 2017 est.)
country comparison to the world: 179

Nationality: *noun:* Bahamian(s)
adjective: Bahamian

Ethnic groups: black 90.6%, white 4.7%, black and white 2.1%, other 1.9%, unspecified 0.7% (2010 est.)

Languages: English (official), Creole (among Haitian immigrants)

Religions: Protestant 69.9% (includes Baptist 34.9%, Anglican 13.7%, Pentecostal 8.9% Seventh Day Adventist 4.4%, Methodist 3.6%, Church of God 1.9%, Brethren 1.6%), Roman Catholic 12%, other Christian 13% (includes Jehovah's Witness 1.1%), other 0.6%, none 1.9%, unspecified 2.6% (2010 est.)

Age structure: *0-14 years:* 22.55% (male 37,760/female 36,667)
15-24 years: 16.4% (male 27,415/female 26,703)
25-54 years: 44.14% (male 73,016/female 72,626)
55-64 years: 9.16% (male 13,647/female 16,567)
65 years and over: 7.75% (male 9,843/female 15,744) (2017 est.)

Dependency ratios: *total dependency ratio:* 40.8
youth dependency ratio: 29.1

elderly dependency ratio: 11.7
potential support ratio: 8.5 (2015 est.)

Median age: *total:* 32 years
male: 30.9 years
female: 33.2 years (2017 est.)
country comparison to the world: 100

Population growth rate: 0.81% (2017 est.)
country comparison to the world: 130

Birth rate: 15.3 births/1,000 population (2017 est.)
country comparison to the world: 125

Death rate: 7.2 deaths/1,000 population (2017 est.)
country comparison to the world: 125

Net migration rate: 0 migrant(s)/1,000 population (2017 est.)
country comparison to the world: 72

Population distribution: most of the population lives in urban areas, with two-thirds living on New Providence Island where Nassau is located

Urbanization: *urban population:* 83% of total population (2017)
rate of urbanization: 1.21% annual rate of change (2015-20 est.)

Major urban areas—population: NASSAU (capital) 267,000 (2014)

Sex ratio: *at birth:* 1.03 male(s)/female
0-14 years: 1.03 male(s)/female
15-24 years: 1.03 male(s)/female
25-54 years: 1 male(s)/female
55-64 years: 0.81 male(s)/female
65 years and over: 0.62 male(s)/female
total population: 0.96 male(s)/female (2016 est.)

Maternal mortality ratio: 80 deaths/100,000 live births (2015 est.)
country comparison to the world: 80

Infant mortality rate: *total:* 11.3 deaths/1,000 live births
male: 11.4 deaths/1,000 live births
female: 11.3 deaths/1,000 live births (2017 est.)
country comparison to the world: 127

Life expectancy at birth: *total population:* 72.6 years
male: 70.2 years
female: 75.1 years (2017 est.)
country comparison to the world: 145

Total fertility rate: 1.94 children born/woman (2017 est.)
country comparison to the world: 128
Health expenditures: 7.7% of GDP (2014)
country comparison to the world: 61

Physicians density: 2.72 physicians/1,000 population (2008)

Hospital bed density: 2.9 beds/1,000 population (2011)

Drinking water source:
improved:
urban: 98.4% of population
rural: 98.4% of population
total: 98.4% of population

unimproved:
urban: 1.6% of population
rural: 1.6% of population
total: 1.6% of population (2015 est.)

Sanitation facility access:
improved:
urban: 92% of population
rural: 92% of population
total: 92% of population
unimproved:
urban: 8% of population
rural: 8% of population
total: 8% of population (2015 est.)

HIV/AIDS—adult prevalence rate: 3.3% (2016 est.)
country comparison to the world: 17

HIV/AIDS—people living with HIV/AIDS: 8,200 (2016 est.)
country comparison to the world: 101

HIV/AIDS—deaths: NA

Obesity—adult prevalence rate: 31.6% (2016)
country comparison to the world: 21

Education expenditures: NA

Unemployment, youth ages 15-24: *total:* 30.8%
male: 29.6%
female: 32.2% (2012 est.)
country comparison to the world: 24

GOVERNMENT

Country name: *conventional long form:* Commonwealth of The Bahamas
conventional short form: The Bahamas
etymology: name derives from the Spanish "baha mar," meaning "shallow sea," which describes the shallow waters of the Bahama Banks

Government type: parliamentary democracy (Parliament) under a constitutional monarchy; a Commonwealth realm

Capital: *name:* Nassau

geographic coordinates: 25 05 N, 77 21 W

time difference: UTC-5 (same time as Washington, DC, during Standard Time)
daylight saving time: +1hr, begins second Sunday in March; ends first Sunday in November

Administrative divisions: 31 districts; Acklins Islands, Berry Islands, Bimini, Black Point, Cat Island, Central Abaco, Central Andros, Central Eleuthera, City of Freeport, Crooked Island and Long Cay, East Grand Bahama, Exuma, Grand Cay, Harbour Island, Hope Town, Inagua, Long Island, Mangrove Cay, Mayaguana, Moore's Island, North Abaco, North Andros, North Eleuthera, Ragged Island, Rum Cay, San Salvador, South Abaco, South Andros, South Eleuthera, Spanish Wells, West Grand Bahama

Independence: 10 July 1973 (from the UK)

National holiday: Independence Day, 10 July (1973)

Constitution: previous 1964 (preindependence); latest adopted 20 June 1973, effective 10 July 1973; amended many times, last in 2016 (2016)

Legal system: common law system based on the English model

International law organization participation: has not submitted an ICJ jurisdiction declaration; non-party state to the ICCt

Citizenship: *citizenship by birth:* no
citizenship by descent only: at least one parent must be a citizen of The Bahamas
dual citizenship recognized: no
residency requirement for naturalization: 6-9 years

Suffrage: 18 years of age; universal

Executive branch: *chief of state:* Queen ELIZABETH II (since 6 February 1952); represented by Governor General Dame Marguerite PINDLING (since 8 July 2014)
head of government: Prime Minister Hubert MINNIS (since 11 May 2017)
cabinet: Cabinet appointed by governor general on recommendation of prime minister
elections/appointments: the monarchy is hereditary; governor general appointed by the monarch; following legislative elections, the leader of the majority party or majority coalition usually appointed prime minister by the governor general; the prime minister recommends the deputy prime minister

Legislative branch: *description:* bicameral Parliament consists of the Senate (16 seats; members appointed by the governor general upon the advice of the prime minister and the opposition leader to serve 5-year terms) and the House of Assembly (39 seats; members directly elected in single-seat constituencies by simple majority vote to serve 5-year terms); note—the government may dissolve the parliament and call elections at any time
elections: last held on 10 May 2017 (next to be held by May 2022)
election results: percent of vote by party—FNM 57%, PLP 36.9%, other 6.1%; seats by party—FNM 35, PLP 4

Judicial branch: highest resident court(s): Court of Appeal (consists of the court president and 4 justices, organized in 3-member panels); Supreme Court (consists of the chief justice and a maximum of 11 and a minimum of 2 justices)
note: as of 2008, the Bahamas was not a party to the agreement establishing the Caribbean Court of Justice as the highest appellate court for the 15-member Caribbean Community (CARICOM); the Judicial Committee of the Privy Council (in London) serves as the final court of appeal for The Bahamas
judge selection and term of office: Court of Appeal president and Supreme Court chief justice appointed by the governor-general on the advice of the prime minister after consultation with the leader of the opposition party; other Court of Appeal and Supreme Court justices appointed by the governor general upon recommendation of the Judicial and Legal Services Commission, a 5-member body headed by the chief justice; Court of Appeal justices appointed for life with mandatory retirement normally at age 68 but can be extended

until age 70; Supreme Court justices appointed for life with mandatory retirement normally at age 65 but can be extended until age 67
subordinate courts: Industrial Tribunal; Stipendiary and Magistrates' Courts; Family Island Administrators

Political parties and leaders: Democratic National Alliance or DNA [Branville MCCARTNEY]
Free National Movement or FNM [Hubert MINNIS]
Progressive Liberal Party or PLP [Philip "Brave" DAVIS]

Political pressure groups and leaders: Friends of the Environment [Wynsome FERGUSON]
other: trade unions

International organization participation: ACP, AOSIS, C, Caricom, CDB, CELAC, FAO, G-77, IADB, IAEA, IBRD, ICAO, ICC (NGOs), ICRM, IDA, IFAD, IFC, IFRCS, ILO, IMF, IMO, IMSO, Interpol, IOC, IOM, ISO (correspondent), ITSO, ITU, LAES, MIGA, NAM, OAS, OPANAL, OPCW, Petrocaribe, UN, UNCTAD, UNESCO, UNIDO, UNWTO, UPU, WCO, WHO, WIPO, WMO, WTO (observer)

Diplomatic representation in the US: *chief of mission:* Ambassador Sidney Stanley COLLIE (since 20 November 2017)
chancery: 2220 Massachusetts Avenue NW, Washington, DC 20008
telephone: [1] (202) 319-2660
FAX: [1] (202) 319-2668
consulate(s) general: Atlanta, Miami, New York

Diplomatic representation from the US: *chief of mission:* Ambassador (vacant); Charge d' Affaires Lisa A. JOHNSON (since 9 July 2014)
embassy: 42 Queen Street, Nassau, New Providence
mailing address: local or express mail address: P. O. Box N-8197, Nassau; US Department of State, 3370 Nassau Place, Washington, DC 20521-3370
telephone: [1] (242) 322-1181, 328-2206 (after hours)
FAX: [1] (242) 356-7174

Flag description: three equal horizontal bands of aquamarine (top), gold, and aquamarine, with a black equilateral triangle based on the hoist side; the band colors represent the golden beaches of the islands surrounded by the aquamarine sea; black represents the vigor and force of a united people, while the pointing triangle indicates the enterprise and determination of the Bahamian people to develop the rich resources of land and sea

National symbol(s): blue marlin, flamingo, Yellow Elder flower; national colors: aquamarine, yellow, black

National anthem: *name:* "March On, Bahamaland!"
lyrics/music: Timothy GIBSON
note: adopted 1973; as a Commonwealth country, in addition to the national anthem, "God Save the Queen" serves as the royal anthem (see United Kingdom)

ECONOMY

Economy—overview: The Bahamas has the second highest per capital GDP in the English-speaking Caribbean with an economy heavily dependent on tourism and international banking. Tourism accounts for approximately 75-80% of GDP and directly or indirectly employs half of the archipelago's labor force. Financial services constitute the second-most important sector of the Bahamian economy, accounting for about 15% of GDP. Manufacturing and agriculture combined contribute less than 7% of GDP and show little growth, despite government incentives aimed at those sectors. On January 1, 2015, the Government introduced a 7.5% Value Added Tax (VAT) on most goods and services, a measure designed to strengthen the fiscal balance sheet. In August 2016, Moody's downgraded the Bahamas' bond and issue ratings to Baa3 from Baa2 with a stable outlook, maintaining that rating in its February 2017 review. In December 2016, S&P downgraded the country to BB+ (speculative grade) from BBB- (investment grade) with a stable outlook based on projections of slow economic growth and the pace of debt accumulation. The Bahamas is the only country in the Western Hemisphere that is not a member of the World Trade Organization.

GDP (purchasing power parity): $9.339 billion (2017 est.)
$9.174 billion (2016 est.)
$9.197 billion (2015 est.)
note: data are in 2017 dollars
country comparison to the world: 162

GDP (official exchange rate): $9.127 billion (2016 est.)

GDP—real growth rate: 1.8% (2017 est.)
-0.3% (2016 est.)
-1.7% (2015 est.)
country comparison to the world: 164

GDP—per capita (PPP): $25,100 (2017 est.)
$24,900 (2016 est.)
$25,300 (2015 est.)
note: data are in 2017 dollars
country comparison to the world: 79

Gross national saving: 8.6% of GDP (2017 est.)
13.4% of GDP (2016 est.)
13.6% of GDP (2015 est.)
country comparison to the world: 164

GDP—composition, by end use:
household consumption: 66.4%
government consumption: 16.9%
investment in fixed capital: 28.3%
investment in inventories: 1%
exports of goods and services: 38.3%
imports of goods and services: -50.8% (2017 est.)

GDP—composition, by sector of origin:
agriculture: 2.3%
industry: 7.7%
services: 90% (2017 est.)

Agriculture—products: citrus, vegetables; poultry

Industries: tourism, banking, oil bunkering, maritime industries, transshipment and logistics, salt, aragonite, pharmaceuticals

Industrial production growth rate: 1.5% (2017 est.)
country comparison to the world: 152

Labor force: 196,900 (2013 est.)
country comparison to the world: 173

Labor force—by occupation: *agriculture:* 3%
industry: 11%
tourism: 49%
other services: 37% (2011 est.)

Unemployment rate: 10% (2017 est.)
12.2% (2016 est.)
country comparison to the world: 137

Population below poverty line: 9.3% (2010 est.)

Household income or consumption by percentage share: *lowest 10%:* 1%
highest 10%: 22% (2007)

Budget: *revenues:* $2.1 billion
expenditures: $2.6 billion (2017 est.)
Taxes and other revenues: 23% of GDP (2017 est.)
country comparison to the world: 128

Budget surplus (+) or deficit (-): -5.5% of GDP (2017 est.)
country comparison to the world: 170

Public debt: 66.9% of GDP (2016 est.)
64.5% of GDP (2015 est.)
country comparison to the world: 56

Fiscal year: 1 July—30 June

Inflation rate (consumer prices): 2.4% (2017 est.)
0.8% (2016 est.)
country comparison to the world: 110

Central bank discount rate: 4.5% (1 January 2014)
4.5% (31 December 2012)
country comparison to the world: 83

Commercial bank prime lending rate: 4.3% (31 December 2017 est.)
4.8% (31 December 2016 est.)
country comparison to the world: 157

Stock of narrow money: $2.576 billion (31 December 2017 est.)
$2.461 billion (31 December 2016 est.)
country comparison to the world: 125

Stock of broad money: $7.033 billion (31 December 2017 est.)
$6.622 billion (31 December 2016 est.)
country comparison to the world: 117

Stock of domestic credit: $9.7 billion (31 December 2017 est.)
$9.1 billion (31 December 2016 est.)
country comparison to the world: 110

Market value of publicly traded shares: $2.78 billion (31 December 2012 est.)
country comparison to the world: 97

Current account balance: -$1.626 billion (2017 est.)
-$1.126 billion (2016 est.)
country comparison to the world: 150

Exports: $934.7 million (2017 est.)
$444.3 million (2016 est.)
country comparison to the world: 162

Exports—commodities: Rock lobster, aragonite, crude salt, polystyrene products

Exports—partners: US 53.4%, Namibia 31.4% (2016)

Imports: $3.105 billion (2017 est.)
$2.594 billion (2016 est.)
country comparison to the world: 143

Imports—commodities: machinery and transport equipment, manufactures, chemicals, mineral fuels; food and live animals

Imports—partners: US 81.8% (2016)

Reserves of foreign exchange and gold: $922.1 million (31 December 2017 est.)
$1.002 billion (31 December 2016 est.)
country comparison to the world: 128

Debt—external: $17.56 billion (31 December 2013 est.)
$16.35 billion (31 December 2012 est.)
country comparison to the world: 95

Exchange rates: Bahamian dollars (BSD) per US dollar—
1 (2017 est.)
1 (2016 est.)
1 (2015 est.)
1 (2014 est.)
1 (2013 est.)

ENERGY

Electricity access: electrification—*total population:* 100% (2016)

Electricity—production: 1.807 billion kWh (2015 est.)
country comparison to the world: 141

Electricity—consumption: 1.681 billion kWh (2015 est.)
country comparison to the world: 147

Electricity—exports: 0 kWh (2016 est.)
country comparison to the world: 106

Electricity—imports: 0 kWh (2016 est.)
country comparison to the world: 124

Electricity—installed generating capacity: 577,000 kW (2015 est.)
country comparison to the world: 141

Electricity—from fossil fuels: 99.8% of total installed capacity (2015 est.)
country comparison to the world: 26

Electricity—from nuclear fuels: 0% of total installed capacity (2015 est.)
country comparison to the world: 49

Electricity—from hydroelectric plants: 0% of total installed capacity (2015 est.)
country comparison to the world: 164

Electricity—from other renewable sources: 0.2% of total installed capacity (2015 est.)
country comparison to the world: 162

Crude oil—production: 0 bbl/day (2016 est.)
country comparison to the world: 108

Crude oil—exports: 0 bbl/day (2014 est.)
country comparison to the world: 95

Crude oil—imports: 0 bbl/day (2014 est.)
country comparison to the world: 98

Crude oil—proved reserves: 0 bbl (1 January 2017 es)
country comparison to the world: 108

Refined petroleum products—production: 0 bbl/day (2014 est.)
country comparison to the world: 117

Refined petroleum products—consumption: 24,000 bbl/day (2015 est.)
country comparison to the world: 130

Refined petroleum products—exports: 922.7 bbl/day (2014 est.)
country comparison to the world: 108

Refined petroleum products—imports: 26,330 bbl/day (2014 est.)
country comparison to the world: 105

Natural gas—production: 0 cu m (2013 est.)
country comparison to the world: 109

Natural gas—consumption: 0 cu m (2013 est.)
country comparison to the world: 158

Natural gas—exports: 0 cu m (2013 est.)
country comparison to the world: 68

Natural gas—imports: 0 cu m (2013 est.)
country comparison to the world: 91

Natural gas—proved reserves: 0 cu m (1 January 2009 es)
country comparison to the world: 116

Carbon dioxide emissions from consumption of energy: 4.1 million Mt (2013 est.)
country comparison to the world: 132

COMMUNICATIONS

Telephones—fixed lines: *total subscriptions:* 121,088
subscriptions per 100 inhabitants: 37 (July 2016 est.)
country comparison to the world: 140

Telephones—mobile cellular: *total:* 360,200
subscriptions per 100 inhabitants: 110 (July 2016 est.)

country comparison to the world: 178

Telephone system: *general assessment:* modern facilities
domestic: totally automatic system; highly developed; the Bahamas Domestic Submarine Network links all of the major islands; Bahamas Telecommunications Company (BTC) privatized in 2011, but the government reacquired 51% share in 2014
international: country code—1-242; landing point for the Americas Region Caribbean Ring System (ARCOS-1) and two additional fiber-optic submarine cables that provide links to South and Central America, parts of the Caribbean, and the US; satellite earth stations—2 (2017)

Broadcast media: The Bahamas has 4 major TV providers that provide service to all major islands in the archipelago; 1 TV station is operated by government-owned, commercially run Broadcasting Corporation of the Bahamas (BCB) and competes freely with 3 privately owned TV stations; multi-channel cable TV subscription service is widely available; there are 31 licensed broadcast (radio) service providers, 28 are privately owned FM radio stations operating on New Providence, Grand Bahama Island, Abaco Island, and on smaller islands in the country; the BCB operates a multi-channel radio broadcasting network that has national coverage; the sector is regulated by the Utilities Regulation and Competition Authority (2017)

Internet country code: .bs

Internet users: *total:* 261,853
percent of population: 80.0% (July 2016 est.)
country comparison to the world: 151

TRANSPORTATION

National air transport system: *number of registered air carriers:* 4
inventory of registered aircraft operated by air carriers: 16
annual passenger traffic on registered air carriers: 587,516
annual freight traffic on registered air carriers: 172,730 mt-km (2015)

Civil aircraft registration country code prefix: C6 (2016)

Airports: 61 (2013)
country comparison to the world: 80

Airports—with paved runways: *total:* 24
over 3,047 m: 2
2,438 to 3,047 m: 2
1,524 to 2,437 m: 13
914 to 1,523 m: 7 (2017)

Airports—with unpaved runways: *total:* 37
1,524 to 2,437 m: 4
914 to 1,523 m: 16
under 914 m: 17 (2013)

Heliports: 1 (2013)

Roadways: *total:* 2,700 km
paved: 1,620 km
unpaved: 1,080 km (2011)
country comparison to the world: 170

Merchant marine: *total:* 1,440
by type: bulk carrier 335, container ship 53, general cargo 98, oil tanker 284, other 670 (2017)
country comparison to the world: 19

Ports and terminals: *major seaport(s):* Freeport, Nassau, South Riding Point
container port(s) (TEUs): Freeport (1,116,272) (2011)
cruise port(s): Nassau

MILITARY AND SECURITY

Military branches: *Royal Bahamas Defense Force:* Land Force, Navy, Air Wing (2011)

Military service age and obligation: 18 years of age for voluntary male and female service; no conscription (2012)

TRANSNATIONAL ISSUES

Disputes—international: disagrees with the US on the alignment of the northern axis of a potential maritime boundary
Refugees and internally displaced persons: stateless persons: 11 (2016)

Illicit drugs: transshipment point for cocaine and marijuana bound for US and Europe; offshore financial center

BAHRAIN

INTRODUCTION

Background: In 1783, the Sunni Al-Khalifa family took power in Bahrain. In order to secure these holdings, it entered into a series of treaties with the UK during the 19th century that made Bahrain a British protectorate. The archipelago attained its independence in 1971. A steady decline in oil production and reserves since 1970 prompted Bahrain to take steps to diversify its economy, in the process developing petroleum processing and refining, aluminum production, and hospitality and retail sectors. It has also endeavored to become a leading regional banking center, especially with respect to

Islamic finance. Bahrain's small size, central location among Gulf countries, economic dependence on Saudi Arabia, and proximity to Iran require it to play a delicate balancing act in foreign affairs among its larger neighbors. Its foreign policy activities usually fall in line with Saudi Arabia and the UAE.

The Sunni royal family has long struggled to manage relations with its large Shia-majority population. In early 2011, amid Arab uprisings elsewhere in the region, the Bahraini Government confronted similar pro-democracy and reform protests at home with police and military action, including deploying Gulf Cooperation Council

security forces to Bahrain. Political talks throughout 2014 between the government and opposition and loyalist political groups failed to reach an agreement, prompting opposition political societies to boycott legislative and municipal council elections in late 2014. Ongoing dissatisfaction with the political status quo continues to factor into sporadic clashes between demonstrators and security forces.

GEOGRAPHY

Location: Middle East, archipelago in the Persian Gulf, east of Saudi Arabia

Geographic coordinates: 26 00 N, 50 33 E

Map references: Middle East

Area: *total:* 760 sq km
land: 760 sq km
water: 0 sq km
country comparison to the world: 188

Area—comparative: 3.5 times the size of Washington, DC

Land boundaries: 0 km

Coastline: 161 km

Maritime claims: *territorial sea:* 12 nm
contiguous zone: 24 nm
continental shelf: extending to boundaries to be determined

Climate: arid; mild, pleasant winters; very hot, humid summers

Terrain: mostly low desert plain rising gently to low central escarpment

Elevation: *mean elevation:* NA

elevation extremes: *lowest point:* Persian Gulf 0 m
highest point: Jabal ad Dukhan 135 m

Natural resources: oil, associated and nonassociated natural gas, fish, pearls

Land use: *agricultural land:* 11.3%
arable land: 2.1%;
permanent crops: 3.9%;
permanent pasture: 5.3%
forest: 0.7%
other: 88% (2011 est.)
Irrigated land: 40 sq km (2012)

Population—distribution: smallest population of the Gulf States, but urbanization rate exceeds 90%; largest settlement concentration is found on the far northern end of the island in and around Manamah and Al Muharraq

Natural hazards: periodic droughts; dust storms

Environment—current issues: desertification resulting from the degradation of limited arable land, periods of drought, and dust storms; coastal degradation (damage to coastlines, coral reefs, and sea vegetation) resulting from oil spills and other discharges from large tankers, oil refineries, and distribution stations; lack of freshwater resources (groundwater and seawater are the only sources for all water needs)

Environment—international agreements: party to: Biodiversity, Climate Change, Climate Change-Kyoto Protocol, Desertification, Hazardous Wastes, Law of the Sea, Ozone Layer Protection, Wetlands
signed, but not ratified: none of the selected agreements

Geography—note: close to primary Middle Eastern petroleum sources; strategic location in Persian Gulf, through which much of the Western world's petroleum must transit to reach open ocean

PEOPLE AND SOCIETY

Population: 1,410,942 (July 2017 est.)
note: immigrants make up approximately 48% of the total population, according to UN data (2017)
country comparison to the world: 155

Nationality: *noun:* Bahraini(s)
adjective: Bahraini

Ethnic groups: Bahraini 46%, Asian 45.5%, other Arab 4.7%, African 1.6%, European 1%, other 1.2% (includes Gulf Co-operative country nationals, North and South Americans, and Oceanians) (2010 est.)

Languages: Arabic (official), English, Farsi, Urdu

Religions: Muslim 70.3%, Christian 14.5%, Hindu 9.8%, Buddhist 2.5%, Jewish 0.6%, folk religion <.1, unaffiliated 1.9%, other 0.2% (2010 est.)

Age structure: *0-14 years:* 19.08% (male 136,669/female 132,493)
15-24 years: 15.65% (male 124,906/female 95,881)
25-54 years: 56.04% (male 516,064/female 274,604)
55-64 years: 6.28% (male 56,671/female 31,983)
65 years and over: 2.95% (male 20,656/female 21,015) (2017 est.)

Dependency ratios: *total dependency ratio:* 30.2
youth dependency ratio: 27.1
elderly dependency ratio: 3
potential support ratio: 33.1 (2015 est.)

Median age: *total:* 32.3 years
male: 33.8 years
female: 29.5 years (2017 est.)
country comparison to the world: 99

Population growth rate: 2.26% (2017 est.)
country comparison to the world: 34

Birth rate: 13.3 births/1,000 population (2017 est.)
country comparison to the world: 145

Death rate: 2.8 deaths/1,000 population (2017 est.)
country comparison to the world: 223

Net migration rate: 12.1 migrant(s)/1,000 population (2017 est.)
country comparison to the world: 6

Population distribution: smallest population of the Gulf States, but urbanization rate exceeds 90%; largest settlement concentration is found on the far northern end of the island in and around Manamah and Al Muharraq

Urbanization: *urban population:* 88.9% of total population (2017)
rate of urbanization: 1.77% annual rate of change (2015-20 est.)

Major urban areas—population: MANAMA (capital) 411,000 (2015)

Sex ratio: *at birth:* 1.03 male(s)/female
0-14 years: 1.03 male(s)/female
15-24 years: 1.3 male(s)/female
25-54 years: 1.88 male(s)/female
55-64 years: 1.81 male(s)/female
65 years and over: 0.95 male(s)/female
total population: 1.54 male(s)/female (2016 est.)

Maternal mortality ratio: 15 deaths/100,000 live births (2015 est.)
country comparison to the world: 135

Infant mortality rate: *total:* 8.9 deaths/1,000 live births
male: 9.9 deaths/1,000 live births
female: 7.9 deaths/1,000 live births (2017 est.)
country comparison to the world: 147

Life expectancy at birth: *total population:* 79 years
male: 76.8 years
female: 81.3 years (2017 est.)
country comparison to the world: 50

Total fertility rate: 1.75 children born/woman (2017 est.)
country comparison to the world: 164
Health expenditures: 5% of GDP (2014)
country comparison to the world: 142

Physicians density: 0.94 physicians/1,000 population (2014)

Hospital bed density: 2.1 beds/1,000 population (2012)

Drinking water source:
improved:
urban: 100% of population
rural: 100% of population
total: 100% of population
unimproved:
urban: 0% of population
rural: 0% of population
total: 0% of population (2015 est.)

Sanitation facility access:
improved:
urban: 99.2% of population
rural: 99.2% of population
total: 99.2% of population
unimproved:
urban: 0.8% of population
rural: 0.8% of population
total: 0.8% of population (2015 est.)

HIV/AIDS—adult prevalence rate: <.01% (2016 est.)

HIV/AIDS—people living with HIV/AIDS: <500 (2016 est.)

HIV/AIDS—deaths: <100 (2016 est.)

Obesity—adult prevalence rate: 29.8% (2016)
country comparison to the world: 25

Education expenditures: 2.6% of GDP (2012)
country comparison to the world: 153

Literacy: *definition:* age 15 and over can read and write
total population: 95.7%
male: 96.9%
female: 93.5% (2015 est.)

Unemployment, youth ages 15-24: *total:* 5.3%
male: 2.6%
female: 12.2% (2012 est.)
country comparison to the world: 127

GOVERNMENT

Country name: *conventional long form:* Kingdom of Bahrain
conventional short form: Bahrain
local long form: Mamlakat al Bahrayn
local short form: Al Bahrayn
former: Dilmun, State of Bahrain
etymology: the name means "the two seas" in Arabic and refers to the water bodies surrounding the archipelago

Government type: constitutional monarchy

Capital: *name:* Manama

geographic coordinates: 26 14 N, 50 34 E

time difference: UTC+3 (8 hours ahead of Washington, DC, during Standard Time)

Administrative divisions: 4 governorates (muhafazat, singular—muhafazah); Asimah (Capital), Janubiyah (Southern), Muharraq, Shamaliyah (Northern)
note: each governorate administered by an appointed governor

Independence: 15 August 1971 (from the UK)

National holiday: National Day, 16 December (1971); note—15 August 1971 was the date of independence from the UK, 16 December 1971 was the date of independence from British protection

Constitution: *history:* adopted 14 February 2002
amendments: proposed by the king or by at least 15 members of either chamber of the National Assembly followed by submission to an Assembly committee for review and, if approved, submitted to the government for restatement as drafts; passage requires a two-thirds majority vote by the membership of both chambers and validation by the king; constitutional articles on the state religion (Islam), state language (Arabic), and the monarchy and "inherited rule" cannot be amended; amended 2012, 2017 (2017)

Legal system: mixed legal system of Islamic law, English common law, Egyptian civil, criminal, and commercial codes; customary law

International law organization participation: has not submitted an ICJ jurisdiction declaration; non-party state to the ICCt

Citizenship: *citizenship by birth:* no
citizenship by descent only: the father must be a citizen of Bahrain
dual citizenship recognized: no
residency requirement for naturalization: 25 years; 15 years for Arab nationals

Suffrage: 20 years of age; universal; note—Bahraini Cabinet in May 2011 endorsed a draft law lowering eligibility to 18 years

Executive branch: *chief of state:* King HAMAD bin Isa Al-Khalifa (since 6 March 1999); Crown Prince SALMAN bin Hamad Al-Khalifa (son of the monarch, born 21 October 1969)

head of government: Prime Minister KHALIFA bin Salman Al-Khalifa (since 1971); First Deputy Prime Minister SALMAN bin Hamad Al Khalifa (since 11 March 2013); Deputy Prime Ministers MUHAMMAD bin Mubarak Al-Khalifa (since September 2005), Jawad bin Salim al-ARAIDH, ALI bin Khalifa bin Salman Al-Khalifa (since 11 December 2006), KHALID bin Abdallah Al Khalifa (since November 2010)
cabinet: Cabinet appointed by the monarch
elections/appointments: the monarchy is hereditary; prime minister appointed by the monarch

Legislative branch: *description:* bicameral National Assembly consists of the Consultative Council or Majlis al Shura (40 seats; members appointed by the king) and the Council of Representatives or Majlis al Nuwab (40 seats; members directly elected in single-seat constituencies by absolute majority vote in 2 rounds if needed; members serve 4-year renewable terms)
elections: Council of Representatives—last held in two rounds on 23 and 29 November 2014 (next to be held in late 2018)
election results: Council of Representatives—percent of vote by society—NA; seats by society—Al-Asalah (Sunni Salafi) 2, Islamic Minbar (Sunni Muslim Brotherhood) 1, independent 37; note—Bahrain has societies rather than parties

Judicial branch: *highest court(s):* Court of Cassation or Supreme Court of Appeal (consists of the chairman and 3 judges); Constitutional Court (consists of the president and 6 members); High Sharia Court of Appeal (court sittings include the president and at least one judge); appeals beyond the High Sharia Court of Appeal are heard by the Supreme Court of Appeal
note: the judiciary of Bahrain is divided into civil law courts and sharia law courts; sharia courts(involving personal status and family law) are further divided into Sunni Muslim and Shia Muslim
judge selection and term of office: Court of Cassation judges appointed by royal decree and serve for a specified tenure; Constitutional Court president and members appointed by the Higher Judicial Council, a body chaired by the monarch and includes judges from the Court of Cassation, sharia law courts, and Civil High Courts of Appeal; members serve 9-year terms; High Sharia Court of Appeal member appointment and tenure NA
subordinate courts: Civil High Courts of Appeal; middle and lower civil courts; High Sharia Court of Appeal; Senior Sharia Court; Administrative Courts of Appeal; military courts

Political parties and leaders: *note:* political parties are prohibited, but political societies were legalized under a July 2005 law

Arab Islamic Center Society [Abdulrahman AL-BAKER]
Constitutional Gathering Society [Abdulrahman AL-BAKER]
Islamic Asalah [Abd al-Halim MURAD]
Islamic Saff Society [Abdullah Khalil BU GHAMAR]
Islamic Shura Society
Movement of National Justice Society [Muhi al-Din KHAN]
National Action Charter Society [Muhammad AL-BUAYNAYN]
National Democratic Assembly [Hasan AL-ALI]
National Dialogue Society
National Fraternity Society [Musa AL-ANSARI]
National Islamic Minbar [Ali AHMAD]
National Progressive Tribune [Abd al-Nabi SALMAN]
National Unity Gathering [Abdullatif AL-MAHMOOD]
Unitary National Democratic Assemblage [Fadhil ABBAS]

Political pressure groups and leaders: none

International organization participation: ABEDA, AFESD, AMF, CAEU, CICA, FAO, G-77, GCC, IAEA, IBRD, ICAO, ICC (national committees), ICRM, IDA, IDB, IFC, IFRCS, IHO, ILO, IMF, IMO, IMSO, Interpol, IOC, IOM (observer), IPU, ISO, ITSO, ITU, ITUC (NGOs), LAS, MIGA, NAM, OAPEC, OIC, OPCW, PCA, UN, UNCTAD, UNESCO, UNIDO, UNWTO, UPU, WCO, WFTU (NGOs), WHO, WIPO, WMO, WTO

Diplomatic representation in the US: *chief of mission:* Ambassador Abdulla bin Rashid AL KHALIFA (since 21 July 2017)
chancery: 3502 International Drive NW, Washington, DC 20008
telephone: [1] (202) 342-1111
FAX: [1] (202) 362-2192
consulate(s) general: New York

Diplomatic representation from the US: *chief of mission:* Ambassador Justin H. SIBERELL (since November 2017)
embassy: Building
mailing address: PSC 451, Box 660, FPO AE 09834-5100; international mail: American Embassy, Box 26431, Manama
telephone: [973] 1724-2700
FAX: [973] 1727-2594

Flag description: red, the traditional color for flags of Persian Gulf states, with a white serrated band (five white points) on the hoist side; the five points represent the five pillars of Islam
note: until 2002 the flag had eight white points, but this was reduced to five to avoid confusion with the Qatari flag

National symbol(s): a red field surmounted by a white serrated band with five white points; national colors: red, white

National anthem: *name:* "Bahrainona" (Our Bahrain)
lyrics/music: unknown

note: adopted 1971; although Mohamed Sudqi AYYASH wrote the original lyrics, they were changed in 2002 following the transformation of Bahrain from an emirate to a kingdom

ECONOMY

Economy—overview: Low oil prices have generated a budget deficit of at least a $4 billion deficit in 2016, nearly 14% of GDP. Bahrain has few options for covering this deficit, with meager foreign assets and fewer oil resources compared to its GCC neighbors. In 2016 the three major US credit agencies downgraded Bahrain's sovereign debt rating to "junk" status, citing persistently low oil prices and the government's inability to more effectively cut spending. Nevertheless, Bahrain in 2017 was able to raise about $3 billion by issuing international debt.

Oil comprises 86% of Bahraini budget revenues, despite past efforts to diversify its economy and to build communication and transport facilities for multinational firms with business in the Gulf. As part of its diversification plans, Bahrain implemented a Free Trade Agreement (FTA) with the US in August 2006, the first FTA between the US and a Gulf state.

Other major economic activities are production of aluminum—Bahrain's second biggest export after oil—finance, and construction. Bahrain continues to seek new natural gas supplies as feedstock to support its expanding petrochemical and aluminum industries.

In 2011, Bahrain experienced economic setbacks as a result of domestic unrest driven by the majority Shia population; however, the economy recovered in 2012-15, partly as a result of improved tourism. In addition to addressing its current fiscal woes, Bahraini authorities face the long-term challenge of boosting Bahrain's regional competitiveness—especially regarding industry, finance, and tourism —and reconciling revenue constraints with popular pressure to maintain generous state subsidies and a large public sector. Since 2015, the government lifted subsidies on meat, diesel, kerosene, and gasoline and announced new higher prices for electricity and water, although it plans to roll these increases out more gradually than previous subsidy cuts.

GDP (purchasing power parity): $69.77 billion (2017 est.)
$68.08 billion (2016 est.)
$66.12 billion (2015 est.)
note: data are in 2017 dollars
country comparison to the world: 99

GDP (official exchange rate): $33.87 billion (2016 est.)

GDP—real growth rate: 2.5% (2017 est.)
3% (2016 est.)
2.9% (2015 est.)
country comparison to the world: 131

GDP—per capita (PPP): $51,800 (2017 est.)
$51,600 (2016 est.)
$51,100 (2015 est.)
note: data are in 2017 dollars
country comparison to the world: 25

Gross national saving: 19% of GDP (2017 est.)
21% of GDP (2016 est.)
22% of GDP (2015 est.)
country comparison to the world: 97

GDP—composition, by end use:
household consumption: 45.8%
government consumption: 15.5%
investment in fixed capital: 26.1%
investment in inventories: 0.4%
exports of goods and services: 80.2%
imports of goods and services: -67.9% (2017 est.)

GDP—composition, by sector of origin:
agriculture: 0.3%
industry: 38.2%
services: 61.5% (2017 est.)

Agriculture—products: fruit, vegetables; poultry, dairy products; shrimp, fish

Industries: petroleum processing and refining, aluminum smelting, iron pelletization, fertilizers, Islamic and offshore banking, insurance, ship repairing, tourism

Industrial production growth rate: 0% (2017 est.)
country comparison to the world: 187

Labor force: 831,600
note: excludes unemployed; 44% of the population in the 15-64 age group is non-national (2017 est.)
country comparison to the world: 150

Labor force—by occupation: *agriculture:* 1%
industry: 32%
services: 67% (2004 est.)

Unemployment rate: 3.8% (2017 est.)
3.7% (2016 est.)
note: official estimate; actual rate is higher
country comparison to the world: 42

Population below poverty line: NA%

Household income or consumption by percentage share: *lowest 10%:* NA%
highest 10%: NA%

Budget: *revenues:* $5.463 billion
expenditures: $9.281 billion (2017 est.)
Taxes and other revenues: 16.1% of GDP (2017 est.)
country comparison to the world: 183

Budget surplus (+) or deficit (-): -11.3% of GDP (2017 est.)
country comparison to the world: 211

Public debt: 82.7% of GDP (2017 est.)
72% of GDP (2016 est.)
country comparison to the world: 34

Fiscal year: calendar year

Inflation rate (consumer prices): 0.9% (2017 est.)
2.8% (2016 est.)
country comparison to the world: 33

Commercial bank prime lending rate: 5.7% (31 December 2017 est.)
5.2% (31 December 2016 est.)
country comparison to the world: 131

Stock of narrow money: $9.239 billion (31 December 2017 est.)
$9.157 billion (31 December 2016 est.)
country comparison to the world: 86

Stock of broad money: $27.72 billion (31 December 2017 est.)
$27.36 billion (31 December 2016 est.)
country comparison to the world: 83

Stock of domestic credit: $29.72 billion (31 December 2017 est.)
$29.08 billion (31 December 2016 est.)
country comparison to the world: 79

Market value of publicly traded shares: $19.25 billion (31 December 2015 est.)
$22.07 billion (31 December 2014 est.)
$18.57 billion (31 December 2013 est.)
country comparison to the world: 67

Current account balance: -$1.556 billion (2017 est.)
-$1.493 billion (2016 est.)
country comparison to the world: 148

Exports: $14.33 billion (2017 est.)
$12.78 billion (2016 est.)
country comparison to the world: 77

Exports—commodities: petroleum and petroleum products, aluminum, textiles

Exports—partners: Saudi Arabia 18.3%, UAE 17.5%, US 11.1%, Japan 8.7%, Qatar 4.8%, China 4.2% (2016)

Imports: $13.96 billion (2017 est.)
$13.59 billion (2016 est.)
country comparison to the world: 89

Imports—commodities: crude oil, machinery, chemicals

Imports—partners: China 9.7%, US 8.6%, UAE 7.4%, Japan 6.1%, Saudi Arabia 5.5% (2016)

Reserves of foreign exchange and gold: $2.166 billion (31 December 2017 est.)
$3.094 billion (31 December 2016 est.)
country comparison to the world: 118

Debt—external: $42.39 billion (31 December 2017 est.)
$42.55 billion (31 December 2016 est.)
country comparison to the world: 70

Stock of direct foreign investment—at home: $22.11 billion (31 December 2017 est.)
$21.56 billion (31 December 2016 est.)
country comparison to the world: 76

Stock of direct foreign investment—abroad: $10.66 billion (31 December 2017 est.)
$10.5 billion (31 December 2016 est.)
country comparison to the world: 61

Exchange rates: Bahraini dinars (BHD) per US dollar—
0.376 (2017 est.)
0.376 (2016 est.)
0.376 (2015 est.)
0.376 (2014 est.)
0.376 (2013 est.)

ENERGY

Electricity access: *population without electricity:* 41,317
electrification—*total population:* 98%
electrification—urban areas: 98%
electrification—rural areas: 93% (2012)

Electricity—production: 26.78 billion kWh (2015 est.)
country comparison to the world: 69

Electricity—consumption: 26.09 billion kWh (2015 est.)
country comparison to the world: 66

Electricity—exports: 213 million kWh (2015 est.)
country comparison to the world: 75

Electricity—imports: 205 million kWh (2015 est.)
country comparison to the world: 93

Electricity—installed generating capacity: 3.928 million kW (2015 est.)
country comparison to the world: 90

Electricity—from fossil fuels: 99.8% of total installed capacity (2015 est.)
country comparison to the world: 27

Electricity—from nuclear fuels: 0% of total installed capacity (2015 est.)
country comparison to the world: 45

Electricity—from hydroelectric plants: 0% of total installed capacity (2015 est.)
country comparison to the world: 160

Electricity—from other renewable sources: 0.2% of total installed capacity (2015 est.)
country comparison to the world: 159

Crude oil—production: 50,000 bbl/day (2016 est.)
country comparison to the world: 53

Crude oil—exports: 0 bbl/day (2014 est.)
country comparison to the world: 91

Crude oil—imports: 223,900 bbl/day (2014 est.)
country comparison to the world: 27

Crude oil—proved reserves: 124.6 million bbl (1 January 2017 es)
country comparison to the world: 70

Refined petroleum products—production: 270,100 bbl/day (2014 est.)
country comparison to the world: 45

Refined petroleum products—consumption: 58,000 bbl/day (2015 est.)
country comparison to the world: 98

Refined petroleum products—exports: 244,500 bbl/day (2014 est.)
country comparison to the world: 30

Refined petroleum products—imports: 13,320 bbl/day (2014 est.)
country comparison to the world: 133

Natural gas—production: 15.5 billion cu m (2015 est.)

country comparison to the world: 36

Natural gas—consumption: 21.92 billion cu m (2015 est.)
country comparison to the world: 42

Natural gas—exports: 0 cu m (2013 est.)
country comparison to the world: 64

Natural gas—imports: 0 cu m (2013 est.)
country comparison to the world: 87

Natural gas—proved reserves: 92.03 billion cu m (1 January 2017 es)
country comparison to the world: 55

Carbon dioxide emissions from consumption of energy: 37 million Mt (2013 est.)
country comparison to the world: 71

COMMUNICATIONS

Telephones—fixed lines: *total subscriptions:* 287,203
subscriptions per 100 inhabitants: 21 (July 2016 est.)
country comparison to the world: 118

Telephones—mobile cellular: *total:* 2,994,865
subscriptions per 100 inhabitants: 217 (July 2016 est.)
country comparison to the world: 148

Telephone system: *general assessment: modern system*
domestic: modern fiber-optic integrated services; digital network with rapidly growing use of mobile-cellular telephones
international: country code—973; landing point for the Fiber-Optic Link Around the Globe (FLAG) submarine cable network that provides links to Asia, Middle East, Europe, and US; tropospheric scatter to Qatar and UAE; microwave radio relay to Saudi Arabia; satellite earth station—1 (2016)

Broadcast media: state-run Bahrain Radio and Television Corporation (BRTC) operates 5 terrestrial TV networks and several radio stations; satellite TV systems provide access to international broadcasts; 1 private FM station directs broadcasts to Indian listeners; radio and TV broadcasts from countries in the region are available (2009)

Internet country code: .bh

Internet users: *total:* 1,351,326
percent of population: 98.0% (July 2016 est.)
country comparison to the world: 116

TRANSPORTATION

National air transport system: *number of registered air carriers:* 6
inventory of registered aircraft operated by air carriers: 42
annual passenger traffic on registered air carriers: 5,313,756
annual freight traffic on registered air carriers: 240,107,004 mt-km (2015)
Civil aircraft registration country code prefix: A9C (2016)

Airports: 4 (2013)
country comparison to the world: 184

Airports—with paved runways: *total:* 4
over 3,047 m: 3
914 to 1,523 m: 1 (2017)

Heliports: 1 (2013)

Pipelines: gas 20 km; oil 54 km (2013)

Roadways: *total:* 4,122 km
paved: 3,392 km
unpaved: 730 km (2010)
country comparison to the world: 156

Merchant marine: *total:* 260
by type: container ship 3, general cargo 11, oil tanker 4, other 242 (2017)
country comparison to the world: 59

Ports and terminals: *major seaport(s):* Mina' Salman, Sitrah

MILITARY AND SECURITY

Military expenditures: 4.59% of GDP (2015)
4.42% of GDP (2014)
4.14% of GDP (2013)
3.84% of GDP (2012)
3.59% of GDP (2011)
country comparison to the world: 19

Military branches: Bahrain Defense Force (BDF): Royal Bahraini Army (RBA), Royal Bahraini Navy (RBN), Royal Bahraini Air Force (RBAF), Royal Bahraini Air Defense Force (RBADF) (2013)

Military service age and obligation: 18 years of age for voluntary military service; 15 years of age for NCOs, technicians, and cadets; no conscription (2012)

TRANSNATIONAL ISSUES

Disputes—international: none

BANGLADESH

INTRODUCTION

Background: The huge delta region formed at the confluence of the Ganges and Brahmaputra River systems—now referred to as Bangladesh—was a loosely incorporated outpost of various empires centered on the Gangetic plain for much of the first millennium A.D. Muslim conversions and settlement in the region began in the 10th century, primarily from Arab and Persian traders and preachers. Europeans established trading posts in the area in the 16th century. Eventually the area known as Bengal, primarily Hindu in the western section and mostly Muslim in the eastern half, became part of British India. Partition in 1947 resulted in an eastern wing of Pakistan in the Muslim-majority area, which became East Pakistan. Calls for greater autonomy and animosity between the eastern and western wings of Pakistan led to a Bengali independence movement. That movement, led by the Awami League (AL) and *border countries (2):* Burma 271 km, India 4,142 km

Coastline: 580 km

Maritime claims: *territorial sea:* 12 nm
contiguous zone: 18 nm
exclusive economic zone: 200 nm
continental shelf: to the outer limits of the continental margin

Climate: tropical; mild winter (October to March); hot, humid summer (March to June); humid, warm rainy monsoon (June to October)

Terrain: mostly flat alluvial plain; hilly in southeast

Elevation: *mean elevation:* 85 m

elevation extremes: *lowest point:* Indian Ocean 0 m
highest point: Keokradong 1,230 m

Natural resources: natural gas, arable land, timber, coal

Land use: *agricultural land:* 70.1%
arable land: 59%;
permanent crops: 6.5%;
permanent pasture: 4.6%
forest: 11.1%
other: 18.8% (2011 est.)
Irrigated land: 53,000 sq km (2012)

Natural hazards: droughts; cyclones; much of the country routinely inundated during the summer monsoon season

Environment—current issues: many people are landless and forced to live on and cultivate flood-prone land; waterborne diseases prevalent in surface water; water pollution, especially of fishing areas, results from the use of commercial pesticides; ground water contaminated by naturally occurring arsenic; intermittent water shortages because of falling water tables in the northern and central parts of the country; soil degradation and erosion; deforestation; severe overpopulation

Environment—international agreements: party to: Biodiversity, Climate Change, Climate Change-Kyoto Protocol, Desertification, Endangered Species, Environmental Modification, Hazardous Wastes, Law of the Sea, Ozone Layer Protection, Ship Pollution, Wetlands
signed, but not ratified: none of the selected agreements

Geography—note: most of the country is situated on deltas of large rivers flowing from the Himalayas: the Ganges unites with the Jamuna (main channel of the Brahmaputra) and later joins the Meghna to eventually empty into the Bay of Bengal

PEOPLE AND SOCIETY

Population: 157,826,578 (July 2017 est.)
country comparison to the world: 8

Nationality: *noun:* Bangladeshi(s)
adjective: Bangladeshi

Ethnic groups: Bengali at least 98%, ethnic groups 1.1%
note: Bangladesh's government recognizes 27 ethnic groups under the 2010 Cultural Institution for

Small Anthropological Groups Act; other sources estimate there are about 75 ethnic groups; critics of the 2011 census claim that it underestimates the size of Bangladesh's ethnic population (2011 est.)

Languages: Bangla 98.8% (official, also known as Bengali), other 1.2% (2011 est.)

Religions: Muslim 89.1%, Hindu 10%, other 0.9% (includes Buddhist, Christian) (2013 est.)

Age structure: *0-14 years:* 27.76% (male 22,283,780/female 21,521,977)
15-24 years: 19.36% (male 15,309,543/female 15,241,971)
25-54 years: 39.73% (male 30,094,014/female 32,614,286)
55-64 years: 6.93% (male 5,405,900/female 5,527,330)
65 years and over: 6.23% (male 4,666,033/female 5,161,744) (2017 est.)

Dependency ratios: *total dependency ratio:* 52.6
youth dependency ratio: 44.9
elderly dependency ratio: 7.7
potential support ratio: 13 (2015 est.)

Median age: *total:* 26.7 years
male: 26 years
female: 27.3 years (2017 est.)
country comparison to the world: 147

Population growth rate: 1.04% (2017 est.)
country comparison to the world: 108

Birth rate: 18.8 births/1,000 population (2017 est.)
country comparison to the world: 89

Death rate: 5.4 deaths/1,000 population (2017 est.)
country comparison to the world: 178

Net migration rate: -3.1 migrant(s)/1,000 population (2017 est.)
country comparison to the world: 174

Urbanization: *urban population:* 35.8% of total population (2017)
rate of urbanization: 3.19% annual rate of change (2015-20 est.)

Major urban areas—population: DHAKA (capital) 17.598 million; Chittagong 4.539 million; Khulna 1.022 million; Rajshahi 844,000 (2015)

Sex ratio: *at birth:* 1.04 male(s)/female
0-14 years: 1.04 male(s)/female
15-24 years: 1 male(s)/female
25-54 years: 0.93 male(s)/female
55-64 years: 0.98 male(s)/female
65 years and over: 0.97 male(s)/female
total population: 0.97 male(s)/female (2016 est.)

Mother's mean age at first birth: 18.5 years
note: median age at first birth among women 25-29 (2014 est.)

Maternal mortality ratio: 176 deaths/100,000 live births (2015 est.)
country comparison to the world: 55

Infant mortality rate: *total:* 31.7 deaths/1,000 live births
male: 34 deaths/1,000 live births
female: 29.2 deaths/1,000 live births (2017 est.)
country comparison to the world: 61

supported by India, won the independence war for Bangladesh in 1971.

The post-independence AL government faced daunting challenges and in 1975 was overthrown by the military, triggering a series of military coups that resulted in a military-backed government and subsequent creation of the Bangladesh Nationalist Party (BNP) in 1978. That government also ended in a coup in 1981, followed by military-backed rule until democratic elections occurred in 1991. The BNP and AL alternated in power between 1991 and 2013, with the exception of a military-backed, emergency caretaker regime that suspended parliamentary elections planned for January 2007 in an effort to reform the political system and root out corruption. That government returned the country to fully democratic rule in December 2008 with the election of the AL and Prime Minister Sheikh HASINA. In January 2014, the incumbent AL won the national election by an overwhelming majority after the BNP boycotted, extending HASINA's term as prime minister. With the help of international development assistance, Bangladesh has reduced the poverty rate from over half of the population to less than a third, achieved Millennium Development Goals for maternal and child health, and made great progress in food security since independence. The economy has grown at an annual average of about 6% over the last two decades and the country reached World Bank lower-middle income status in 2015.

GEOGRAPHY

Location: Southern Asia, bordering the Bay of Bengal, between Burma and India

Geographic coordinates: 24 00 N, 90 00 E

Map references: Asia

Area: *total:* 148,460 sq km
land: 130,170 sq km
water: 18,290 sq km
country comparison to the world: 95

Area—comparative: slightly larger than Pennsylvania and New Jersey combined; slightly smaller than Iowa

Land boundaries: *total:* 4,413 km

Life expectancy at birth: *total population:* 73.4 years
male: 71.3 years
female: 75.6 years (2017 est.)
country comparison to the world: 136

Total fertility rate: 2.17 children born/woman (2017 est.)
country comparison to the world: 100

Contraceptive prevalence rate: 62.3% (2014)
Health expenditures: 2.8% of GDP (2014)
country comparison to the world: 183

Physicians density: 0.39 physicians/1,000 population (2012)

Hospital bed density: 0.6 beds/1,000 population (2011)

Drinking water source:
improved:
urban: 86.5% of population
rural: 87% of population
total: 86.9% of population
unimproved:
urban: 13.5% of population
rural: 13% of population
total: 13.1% of population (2015 est.)

Sanitation facility access:
improved:
urban: 57.7% of population
rural: 62.1% of population
total: 60.6% of population
unimproved:
urban: 42.3% of population
rural: 37.9% of population
total: 39.4% of population (2015 est.)

HIV/AIDS—adult prevalence rate: <.01% (2016 est.)

HIV/AIDS—people living with HIV/AIDS: 12,000 (2016 est.)
country comparison to the world: 87

HIV/AIDS—deaths: 1,000 (2016 est.)
country comparison to the world: 63

Major infectious diseases: *degree of risk:* high
food or waterborne diseases: bacterial and protozoal diarrhea, hepatitis A and E, and typhoid fever
vectorborne diseases: dengue fever and malaria are high risks in some locations
water contact disease: leptospirosis
animal contact disease: rabies (2016)

Obesity—adult prevalence rate: 3.6% (2016)
country comparison to the world: 191

Children under the age of 5 years underweight: 32.6% (2014)
country comparison to the world: 5

Education expenditures: 2.2% of GDP (2015)
country comparison to the world: 161

Literacy: *definition:* age 15 and over can read and write
total population: 72.8%
male: 75.6%
female: 69.9% (2016 est.)

School life expectancy (primary to tertiary education): *total:* 10 years
male: 10 years
female: 10 years (2011)

Unemployment, youth ages 15-24: *total:* 9.4%
male: 9.5%
female: 9.4% (2013 est.)
country comparison to the world: 105

GOVERNMENT

Country name: *conventional long form:* People's Republic of Bangladesh
conventional short form: Bangladesh
local long form: Gana Prajatantri Bangladesh
local short form: Bangladesh
former: East Bengal, East Pakistan
etymology: the name—a compound of the Bengali words "Bangla" (Bengal) and "desh" (country)—means "Country of Bengal"

Government type: parliamentary republic

Capital: *name:* Dhaka

geographic coordinates: 23 43 N, 90 24 E

time difference: UTC+6 (11 hours ahead of Washington, DC, during Standard Time)

Administrative divisions: 8 divisions; Barisal, Chittagong, Dhaka, Khulna, Mymensingh, Rajshahi, Rangpur, Sylhet

Independence: 16 December 1971 (from West Pakistan)

National holiday: Independence Day, 26 March (1971); Victory Day, 16 December (1971); note—26 March 1971 is the date of the Awami League's declaration of an independent Bangladesh, and 16 December (Victory Day) memorializes the military victory over Pakistan and the official creation of the state of Bangladesh

Constitution: *history:* previous 1935, 1956, 1962 (pre-independence); latest enacted 4 November 1972, effective 16 December 1972, suspended March 1982, restored November 1986
amendments: proposed by the House of the Nation; approval requires at least a two-thirds majority vote by the House membership, assented to by the president of the republic, and approved in a referendum by a majority of voters; amended many times, last in 2014 (2017)

Legal system: mixed legal system of mostly English common law and Islamic law

International law organization participation: has not submitted an ICJ jurisdiction declaration; accepts ICCt jurisdiction

Citizenship: *citizenship by birth:* no
citizenship by descent only: at least one parent must be a citizen of Bangladesh
dual citizenship recognized: yes, but limited to select countries
residency requirement for naturalization: 5 years

Suffrage: 18 years of age; universal

Executive branch: *chief of state:* President Abdul HAMID (since 24 April 2013); note—Abdul HAMID served as acting president following the death of Zillur RAHMAN in March 2013; HAMID was subsequently indirectly elected by the National Parliament and sworn in 24 April 2013

head of government: Prime Minister Sheikh HASINA (since 6 January 2009)
cabinet: Cabinet selected by the prime minister, appointed by the president
elections/appointments: president indirectly elected by the National Parliament for a 5-year term (eligible for a second term); election last held on 7 February 2018 (next to be held by 2023); the president appoints as prime minister the majority party leader in the National Parliament
election results: President Abdul HAMID (AL) reelected by the National Parliament unopposed; Sheikh HASINA reappointed prime minister as leader of the majority AL party

Legislative branch: *description:* unicameral House of the Nation or Jatiya Sangsad (350 seats; 300 members in single-seat territorial constituencies directly elected by simple majority popular vote; 50 members—reserved for women only—indirectly elected by the elected members by proportional representation vote using the single transferable vote method; all members serve 5-year terms)
elections: last held on 5 January 2014 (next to be held by January 2019); note—the 5 January 2014 poll was marred by widespread violence, boycotts, general strikes, and low voter turnout
election results: percent of vote by party—AL 79.1%, JP (Ershad) 11.3%, WP 2.1%, JSD 1.8%, other 1%, independent 4.8%; seats by party—AL 234, JP 34, WP 6, JSD 5, other 5, independent 15; 1 seat repolled

Judicial branch: *highest court(s):* Supreme Court of Bangladesh (organized into the Appellate Division with 7 justices and the High Court Division with 99 justices)
judge selection and term of office: chief justice and justices appointed by the president; justices serve until retirement at age 67
subordinate courts: subordinate courts: civil courts include: Assistant Judge's Court; Joint District Judge's Court; Additional District Judge's Court; District Judge's Court; criminal courts include: Court of Sessions; Court of Metropolitan Sessions; Metropolitan Magistrate Courts; Magistrate Court; special courts/tribunals

Political parties and leaders: Awami League or AL [Sheikh HASINA]
Bangladesh Nationalist Front or BNF [Abdul Kalam AZADI]
Bangladesh Nationalist Party or BNP [Khaleda ZIA]
Bangladesh Tariqat Federation or BTF [Syed Nozibul Bashar MAIZBHANDARI]
Jamaat-i-Islami Bangladesh or JIB (Mujibur RAHMAN)
Jatiya Party or JP (Ershad faction) [Hussain Mohammad ERSHAD]
Jatiya Party or JP (Manju faction) [Anwar Hossain MANJU]
Liberal Democratic Party or LDP [Oli AHMED]
National Socialist Party or JSD [KHALEQUZZAMAN]
Workers Party or WP [Rashed Khan MENON]

Political pressure groups and leaders: Ain o Salish Kendro (Centre for Law and Mediation) or ASK (legal aid and civil rights)

Bangladesh Center for Worker Solidarity or BCWS

Bangladesh Rural Advancement Committee or BRAC [Sir Fasel Hasan ABED]

Federation of Bangladesh Chambers of Commerce and Industry or FBCCI [Md. Shafiul Islam (Mohiuddin)]

Ministry of Women's and Children's Affairs or MoWCA [Meher Afroze CHUMKI] (advocacy group to end gender-based violence)

Odikhar [Dr. C.R. ABRAR (human rights group)

other: associations of madrassa teachers; business associations, including those intended to promote international trade; development and advocacy NGOs associated with the Grameen Bank; environmentalists; Islamist groups; labor rights advocacy groups; NGOs focused on poverty alleviation, and international trade; religious leaders; tribal groups and advocacy organizations; union leaders

International organization participation: ADB, ARF, BIMSTEC, C, CD, CICA (observer), CP, D-8, FAO, G-77, IAEA, IBRD, ICAO, ICC (national committees), ICRM, IDA, IDB, IFAD, IFC, IFRCS, IHO, ILO, IMF, IMO, IMSO, Interpol, IOC, IOM, IPU, ISO, ITSO, ITU, ITUC (NGOs), MIGA, MINURSO, MINUSMA, MONUSCO, NAM, OIC, OPCW, PCA, SAARC, SACEP, UN, UNAMID, UNCTAD, UNESCO, UNHCR, UNIDO, UNIFIL, UNMIL, UNMISS, UNOCI, UNWTO, UPU, WCO, WFTU (NGOs), WHO, WIPO, WMO, WTO

Diplomatic representation in the US: *chief of mission:* Ambassador Mohammad ZIAUDDIN (since 18 September 2014)

chancery: 3510 International Drive NW, Washington, DC 20008

telephone: [1] (202) 244-0183

FAX: [1] (202) 244-2771

consulate(s) general: Los Angeles, New York

Diplomatic representation from the US: *chief of mission:* Ambassador Marcia BERNICAT (since 4 February 2015)

embassy: Madani Avenue, Baridhara, Dhaka 1212

mailing address: G. P. O. Box 323, Dhaka 1000

telephone: [880] (2) 5566-2000

FAX: [880] (2) 5566-2915

Flag description: green field with a large red disk shifted slightly to the hoist side of center; the red disk represents the rising sun and the sacrifice to achieve independence; the green field symbolizes the lush vegetation of Bangladesh

National symbol(s): Bengal tiger, water lily; national colors: green, red

National anthem: *name:* "Amar Shonar Bangla" (My Golden Bengal)

lyrics/music: Rabindranath TAGORE

note: adopted 1971; Rabindranath TAGORE, a Nobel laureate, also wrote India's national anthem

ECONOMY

Economy—overview: Bangladesh's economy has grown roughly 6% per year since 1996 despite prolonged periods of political instability, poor infrastructure, endemic corruption, insufficient power supplies, and slow implementation of economic reforms. Although more than half of GDP is generated through the services sector, almost half of Bangladeshis are employed in the agriculture sector, with rice as the single-most-important product.

Garment exports, the backbone of Bangladesh's industrial sector, accounted for more than 80% of total exports and were on track to again surpass $25 billion in 2017. The sector continues to grow, despite the need for improvements in factory working conditions to avert further high-profile accidents that have killed more than 1,000 workers in recent years. Steady export growth in the garment sector combined with remittances from overseas Bangladeshis—which totaled about $13 billion and 6% of GDP in 2016—are key contributors to Bangladesh's sustained economic growth and rising foreign exchange reserves.

The recent influx of hundreds of millions of additional refugees from Burma will place pressure on the Bangladeshi government's budget and the country's rice supplies, which declined in 2017 in part because of adverse weather.

GDP (purchasing power parity): $686.5 billion (2017 est.)

$640.7 billion (2016 est.)

$597.8 billion (2015 est.)

note: data are in 2017 dollars

country comparison to the world: 34

GDP (official exchange rate): $250 billion (2016 est.)

GDP—real growth rate: 7.1% (2017 est.)

7.2% (2016 est.)

6.8% (2015 est.)

country comparison to the world: 8

GDP—per capita (PPP): $4,200 (2017 est.)

$4,000 (2016 est.)

$3,700 (2015 est.)

note: data are in 2017 dollars

country comparison to the world: 177

Gross national saving: 29.7% of GDP (2017 est.)

30.9% of GDP (2016 est.)

30.3% of GDP (2015 est.)

country comparison to the world: 25

GDP—composition, by end use:

household consumption: 67.5%

government consumption: 6.4%

investment in fixed capital: 30.3%

investment in inventories: 1%

exports of goods and services: 15.5%

imports of goods and services: -20.7% (2017 est.)

GDP—composition, by sector of origin:

agriculture: 14.2%

industry: 29.2%

services: 56.5% (2017 est.)

Agriculture—products: rice, jute, tea, wheat, sugarcane, potatoes, tobacco, pulses, oilseeds, spices, fruit; beef, milk, poultry

Industries: jute, cotton, garments, paper, leather, fertilizer, iron and steel, cement, petroleum products, tobacco, pharmaceuticals, ceramics, tea, salt, sugar, edible oils, soap and detergent, fabricated metal products, electricity, natural gas

Industrial production growth rate: 8.2% (2017 est.)

country comparison to the world: 16

Labor force: 73.41 million

note: extensive migration of labor to Saudi Arabia, Kuwait, UAE, Oman, Qatar, and Malaysia (2017 est.)

country comparison to the world: 8

Labor force—by occupation: *agriculture:* 47%

industry: 13%

services: 40% (2010 est.)

Unemployment rate: 4.1% (2017 est.)

4.1% (2016 est.)

note: about 40% of the population is underemployed; many persons counted as employed work only a few hours a week and at low wages

country comparison to the world: 55

Population below poverty line: 31.5% (2010 est.)

Household income or consumption by percentage share: *lowest 10%:* 4%

highest 10%: 27% (2010 est.)

Distribution of family income—Gini index: 32.1 (2010)

33.6 (1996)

country comparison to the world: 113

Budget: *revenues:* $27.08 billion

expenditures: $39.31 billion (2017 est.)

Taxes and other revenues: 10.8% of GDP (2017 est.)

country comparison to the world: 211

Budget surplus (+) or deficit (-): -4.9% of GDP (2017 est.)

country comparison to the world: 160

Public debt: 28.1% of GDP (2017 est.)

26.9% of GDP (2016 est.)

country comparison to the world: 167

Fiscal year: 1 July—30 June

Inflation rate (consumer prices): 5.7% (2017 est.)

5.7% (2016 est.)

country comparison to the world: 178

Central bank discount rate: 5% (30 October 2016)

5% (30 October 2015)

country comparison to the world: 80

Commercial bank prime lending rate: 10.2% (31 December 2017 est.)

10.41% (31 December 2016 est.)

country comparison to the world: 81

Stock of narrow money: $28.37 billion (31 December 2017 est.)

$25.94 billion (31 December 2016 est.)

country comparison to the world: 64

Stock of broad money: $132.1 billion (31 December 2017 est.)

$121.1 billion (31 December 2016 est.)

country comparison to the world: 53

Stock of domestic credit: $144.9 billion (31 December 2017 est.)

$133.3 billion (31 December 2016 est.)

country comparison to the world: 51

Market value of publicly traded shares: $50.98 billion (31 December 2015 est.)

$41.73 billion (31 December 2014 est.)

$23.55 billion (31 December 2011 est.)

country comparison to the world: 52

Current account balance: -$1.751 billion (2017 est.)
$1.381 billion (2016 est.)
country comparison to the world: 152

Exports: $35.91 billion (2017 est.)
$34.14 billion (2016 est.)
country comparison to the world: 58

Exports—commodities: garments, knitwear, agricultural products, frozen food (fish and seafood), jute and jute goods, leather

Exports—partners: US 16.4%, Germany 15.3%, UK 10.9%, France 6.1%, Spain 5% (2016)

Imports: $42.38 billion (2017 est.)
$40.37 billion (2016 est.)
country comparison to the world: 55

Imports—commodities: cotton, machinery and equipment, chemicals, iron and steel, foodstuffs

Imports—partners: China 26.3%, India 14.8%, Singapore 5.2%, Japan 4.5% (2016)

Reserves of foreign exchange and gold: $33.66 billion (31 December 2017 est.)
$32.28 billion (31 December 2016 est.)
country comparison to the world: 48

Debt—external: $45.07 billion (31 December 2017 est.)
$41.85 billion (31 December 2016 est.)
country comparison to the world: 68

Stock of direct foreign investment—at home: $14.62 billion (31 December 2017 est.)
$13.24 billion (31 December 2016 est.)
country comparison to the world: 91

Stock of direct foreign investment—abroad: $389.5 million (31 December 2017 est.)
$228.5 million (31 December 2016 est.)
country comparison to the world: 94

Exchange rates: taka (BDT) per US dollar—
80.69 (2017 est.)
78.468 (2016 est.)
78.468 (2015 est.)
77.947 (2014 est.)
77.614 (2013 est.)

ENERGY

Electricity access: *population without electricity:* 60,300,000
electrification—total population: 60%
electrification—urban areas: 90%
electrification—rural areas: 49% (2013)

Electricity—production: 55.5 billion kWh (2015 est.)
country comparison to the world: 51

Electricity—consumption: 48.98 billion kWh (2015 est.)
country comparison to the world: 50

Electricity—exports: 0 kWh (2016 est.)
country comparison to the world: 107

Electricity—imports: 0 kWh (2016 est.)
country comparison to the world: 125

Electricity—installed generating capacity: 11.7 million kW (2015 est.)

country comparison to the world: 57

Electricity—from fossil fuels: 96.6% of total installed capacity (2015 est.)
country comparison to the world: 44

Electricity—from nuclear fuels: 0% of total installed capacity (2015 est.)
country comparison to the world: 50

Electricity—from hydroelectric plants: 2% of total installed capacity (2015 est.)
country comparison to the world: 137

Electricity—from other renewable sources: 1.6% of total installed capacity (2015 est.)
country comparison to the world: 130

Crude oil—production: 4,000 bbl/day (2016 est.)
country comparison to the world: 83

Crude oil—exports: 313 bbl/day (2014 est.)
country comparison to the world: 78

Crude oil—imports: 26,160 bbl/day (2014 est.)
country comparison to the world: 61

Crude oil—proved reserves: 28 million bbl (1 January 2017 es)
country comparison to the world: 84

Refined petroleum products—production: 25,720 bbl/day (2014 est.)
country comparison to the world: 89

Refined petroleum products—consumption: 107,000 bbl/day (2015 est.)
country comparison to the world: 79

Refined petroleum products—exports: 1,802 bbl/day (2014 est.)
country comparison to the world: 106

Refined petroleum products—imports: 85,990 bbl/day (2014 est.)
country comparison to the world: 62

Natural gas—production: 26.86 billion cu m (2015 est.)
country comparison to the world: 28

Natural gas—consumption: 39.88 billion cu m (2015 est.)
country comparison to the world: 31

Natural gas—exports: 0 cu m (2013 est.)
country comparison to the world: 69

Natural gas—imports: 0 cu m (2013 est.)
country comparison to the world: 92

Natural gas—proved reserves: 205.4 billion cu m (1 January 2017 es)
country comparison to the world: 45

Carbon dioxide emissions from consumption of energy: 66 million Mt (2013 est.)
country comparison to the world: 53

COMMUNICATIONS

Telephones—fixed lines: *total subscriptions:* 772,369
subscriptions per 100 inhabitants: less than 1 (July 2016 est.)
country comparison to the world: 74

Telephones—mobile cellular: *total:* 126,391,269
subscriptions per 100 inhabitants: 81 (July 2016 est.)
country comparison to the world: 12

Telephone system: *general assessment:* inadequate for a modern country; introducing digital systems; trunk systems include VHF and UHF microwave radio relay links, and some fiber-optic cable in cities
domestic: fixed-line teledensity remains less than 1 per 100 persons; mobile-cellular telephone subscribership has been increasing rapidly and now exceeds 80 telephones per 100 persons
international: country code—880; landing point for the SEA-ME-WE-4 fiber-optic submarine cable system that provides links to Europe, the Middle East, and Asia; satellite earth stations—6; international radiotelephone communications and landline service to neighboring countries (2016)

Broadcast media: state-owned Bangladesh Television (BTV) operates 1 terrestrial TV station, 3 radio networks, and about 10 local stations; 8 private satellite TV stations and 3 private radio stations also broadcasting; foreign satellite TV stations are gaining audience share in the large cities; several international radio broadcasters are available (2009)

Internet country code: .bd

Internet users: *total:* 28,499,324
percent of population: 18.2% (July 2016 est.)
country comparison to the world: 42

TRANSPORTATION

National air transport system: *number of registered air carriers:* 6
inventory of registered aircraft operated by air carriers: 30
annual passenger traffic on registered air carriers: 2,906,799
annual freight traffic on registered air carriers: 182,692,553 mt-km (2015)
Civil aircraft registration country code prefix: S2 (2016)

Airports: 18 (2013)
country comparison to the world: 139

Airports—with paved runways: *total:* 16
over 3,047 m: 2
2,438 to 3,047 m: 2
1,524 to 2,437 m: 6
914 to 1,523 m: 1
under 914 m: 5 (2017)

Airports—with unpaved runways: *total:* 2
1,524 to 2,437 m: 1
under 914 m: 1 (2013)

Heliports: 3 (2013)

Pipelines: gas 2,950 km (2013)

Railways: *total:* 2,460 km
broad gauge: 659 km 1.676-m gauge
narrow gauge: 1,801 km 1.000-m gauge (2014)
country comparison to the world: 66

Roadways: *total:* 21,269 km
paved: 2,021 km
unpaved: 19,248 km (2010)
country comparison to the world: 106

Waterways: 8,370 km (includes up to 3,060 km of main cargo routes; network reduced to 5,200 km in the dry season) (2011)

country comparison to the world: 16

Merchant marine: *total:* 306
by type: bulk carrier 28, container ship 4, general cargo 75, oil tanker 110, other 89 (2017)
country comparison to the world: 52

Ports and terminals: *major seaport(s):* Chittagong
river port(s): Mongla Port (Sela River)
container port(s): Chittagong (1,392,104) (2011)

MILITARY AND SECURITY

Military expenditures: 1.44% of GDP (2016)
1.46% of GDP (2015)
1.36% of GDP (2014)
1.33% of GDP (2013)
1.41% of GDP (2012)
country comparison to the world: 86

Military branches: Bangladesh Defense Force: Bangladesh Army (Sena Bahini), Bangladesh Navy (Noh Bahini, BN), Bangladesh Air Force (Biman Bahini, BAF) (2013)

Military service age and obligation: 16-19 years of age for voluntary military service; Bangladeshi birth and 10th grade education required; initial obligation 15 years (2012)

Maritime threats: the International Maritime Bureau reports the territorial waters of Bangladesh remain a risk for armed robbery against ships; in 2016, the number of attacks against commercial vessels decreased to three over 11 such incidents in 2015

TERRORISM

Terrorist groups—home based: *Harakat ul-Jihad-i-Islami/Bangladesh (HUJI-B):* aim(s): install an Islamic state in Bangladesh
area(s) of operation: headquartered in Bangladesh and mostly active in the southeast; conducts occasional low-level bombing attacks against Bangladeshi officials and Westerners, especially

US citizens; operations have waned in recent years due to aggressive counterterrorism measures; continues to train fighters and maintain a network of madrassas in Bangladesh; on 21 August 2004, operatives lobbed handgrenades at Sheikh HASINA during an anti-terrorism rally in Dhaka, where approximately 20,000 protesters attended a rally that HASINA's party, the Awami League, had organized; HASINA survived, but 24 Awami League leaders and workers were killed and over 300 people were injured; this was the HUJI-B's most lethal attack since its inception in 1992

Terrorist groups—foreign based: *al-Qa'ida (AQ):* aim(s): overthrow the Bangladesh Government and, ultimately, establish a pan-Islamic caliphate under a strict Salafi Muslim interpretation of Sharia
area(s) of operation: operates in collaboration with its al-Qa'ida in the Indian Subcontinent affiliate

al-Qa'ida in the Indian Subcontinent (AQIS): *aim(s):* protect Muslims in Bangladesh from perceived injustices and, ultimately, establish an Islamic caliphate in the Indian subcontinent
area(s) of operation: active throughout the country, targeting primarily military and security personnel, US interests, and using machetes to attack university professors, bloggers, and others who oppose AQIS's ideology; spokesman Abdullah ASHRAF is based in Bangladesh

Islamic State of Iraq and the Levant (ISIL): aim(s): replace the Bangladesh Government with an Islamic state and implement ISIL's strict interpretation of Sharia; ISIL operates in Bangladesh under the name Islamic State in Bangladesh (ISB)
area(s) of operation: operates primarily in Dhaka under Shaykh Abu Ibrahim al-HANAFI under the name Islamic State in Bangladesh; targets foreigners, foreign aid workers, university professors, and secular bloggers and students for assassination;

conducted Bangladesh's deadliest terrorist attack on 1-2 July 2016 during a 12-hour standoff in Dhaka, when gunmen overran the Holey Artisan Bakery and its restaurant, O'Kitchen, killing 20 civilian hostages and two police officers; majority of members are Bangladeshi; affiliate Jamaatul Mujahideen Bangladesh is a prominent Bangladeshi armed group known for attacking religious minorities such as Hindu clerics and minority Muslims from the Shia Muslim, Ahmadiyya, and Sufi communities; core ISIL refers to its Bangladesh branch as Bengal

TRANSNATIONAL ISSUES

Disputes—international: Bangladesh referred its maritime boundary claims with Burma and India to the International Tribunal on the Law of the Sea; Indian Prime Minister Singh's September 2011 visit to Bangladesh resulted in the signing of a Protocol to the 1974 Land Boundary Agreement between India and Bangladesh, which had called for the settlement of longstanding boundary disputes over undemarcated areas and the exchange of territorial enclaves, but which had never been implemented; Bangladesh struggles to accommodate 32,000 Rohingya, Burmese Muslim minority from Arakan State, living as refugees in Cox's Bazar; Burmese border authorities are constructing a 200 km (124 mi) wire fence designed to deter illegal cross-border transit and tensions from the military build-up along border

Refugees and internally displaced persons: *refugees (country of origin):* 900,500 (Burma) (2018) (includes an estimated 688,000 Rohingya refugees who have fled conflict since 25 August 2017)
IDPs: 426,000 (conflict, development, human rights violations, religious persecution, natural disasters) (2016)

Illicit drugs: transit country for illegal drugs produced in neighboring countries

BARBADOS

INTRODUCTION

Background: The island was uninhabited when first settled by the British in 1627. African slaves worked the sugar plantations established on the island until 1834 when slavery was abolished. The economy remained heavily dependent on sugar, rum, and molasses production through most of the 20th century. The gradual introduction of social and political reforms in the 1940s and 1950s led to complete independence from the UK in 1966. In the 1990s, tourism and manufacturing surpassed the sugar industry in economic importance.

GEOGRAPHY

Location: Caribbean, island in the North Atlantic Ocean, northeast of Venezuela

Geographic coordinates: 13 10 N, 59 32 W

Map references: Central America and the Caribbean

Area: *total:* 430 sq km
land: 430 sq km
water: 0 sq km
country comparison to the world: 202

Area—comparative: 2.5 times the size of Washington, DC

Land boundaries: 0 km

Coastline: 97 km

Maritime claims: *territorial sea:* 12 nm
exclusive economic zone: 200 nm

Climate: tropical; rainy season (June to October)

Terrain: relatively flat; rises gently to central highland region

Elevation: *mean elevation:* NA

elevation extremes: *lowest point:* Atlantic Ocean 0 m
highest point: Mount Hillaby 336 m

Natural resources: petroleum, fish, natural gas

Land use: *agricultural land:* 32.6%
arable land: 25.6%;
permanent crops: 2.3%;
permanent pasture: 4.7%
forest: 19.4%
other: 48% (2011 est.)
Irrigated land: 50 sq km (2012)

Population—distribution: most densely populated country in the eastern Caribbean; approximately one-third live in urban areas

Natural hazards: infrequent hurricanes; periodic landslides

Environment—current issues: pollution of coastal waters from waste disposal by ships; soil erosion; illegal solid waste disposal threatens contamination of aquifers

Environment—international agreements: party to: Biodiversity, Climate Change, Climate Change-Kyoto Protocol, Desertification, Endangered Species, Hazardous Wastes, Law of the Sea, Marine Dumping, Ozone Layer Protection, Ship Pollution, Wetlands
signed, but not ratified: none of the selected agreements

Geography—note: easternmost Caribbean island

PEOPLE AND SOCIETY

Population: 292,336 (July 2017 est.)
country comparison to the world: 180

Nationality: *noun:* Barbadian(s) or Bajan (colloquial)
adjective: Barbadian or Bajan (colloquial)

Ethnic groups: black 92.4%, white 2.7%, mixed 3.1%, East Indian 1.3%, other 0.2%, unspecified 0.2% (2010 est.)

Languages: English (official), Bajan (English-based creole language, widely spoken in informal settings)

Religions: Protestant 66.4% (includes Anglican 23.9%, other Pentecostal 19.5%, Adventist 5.9%, Methodist 4.2%, Wesleyan 3.4%, Nazarene 3.2%, Church of God 2.4%, Baptist 1.8%, Moravian 1.2%, other Protestant 0.9%), Roman Catholic 3.8%, other Christian 5.4% (includes Jehovah's Witness 2.0%, other 3.4%), Rastafarian 1%, other 1.5%, none 20.6%, unspecified 1.2% (2010 est.)

Age structure: *0-14 years:* 17.97% (male 26,256/ female 26,266)
15-24 years: 12.74% (male 18,504/female 18,732)
25-54 years: 44.06% (male 64,198/female 64,594)
55-64 years: 13.43% (male 18,497/female 20,770)
65 years and over: 11.81% (male 13,927/female 20,592) (2017 est.)

Dependency ratios: *total dependency ratio:* 50.4
youth dependency ratio: 29.1
elderly dependency ratio: 21.3
potential support ratio: 4.7 (2015 est.)

Median age: *total:* 38.6 years

male: 37.5 years
female: 39.8 years (2017 est.)
country comparison to the world: 60

Population growth rate: 0.28% (2017 est.)
country comparison to the world: 174

Birth rate: 11.7 births/1,000 population (2017 est.)
country comparison to the world: 169

Death rate: 8.6 deaths/1,000 population (2017 est.)
country comparison to the world: 77

Net migration rate: -0.3 migrant(s)/1,000 population (2017 est.)
country comparison to the world: 116

Population distribution: most densely populated country in the eastern Caribbean; approximately one-third live in urban areas

Urbanization: *urban population:* 31.4% of total population (2017)
rate of urbanization: 0.4% annual rate of change (2015-20 est.)

Major urban areas—population: BRIDGETOWN (capital) 90,000 (2014)

Sex ratio: *at birth:* 1.01 male(s)/female
0-14 years: 1 male(s)/female
15-24 years: 0.99 male(s)/female
25-54 years: 0.99 male(s)/female
55-64 years: 0.88 male(s)/female
65 years and over: 0.66 male(s)/female
total population: 0.94 male(s)/female (2016 est.)

Maternal mortality ratio: 27 deaths/100,000 live births (2015 est.)
country comparison to the world: 117

Infant mortality rate: *total:* 10.2 deaths/1,000 live births
male: 11.7 deaths/1,000 live births
female: 8.8 deaths/1,000 live births (2017 est.)
country comparison to the world: 134

Life expectancy at birth: *total population:* 75.5 years
male: 73.2 years
female: 77.9 years (2017 est.)
country comparison to the world: 106

Total fertility rate: 1.68 children born/woman (2017 est.)
country comparison to the world: 175

Contraceptive prevalence rate: 59.2% (2012)
Health expenditures: 7.5% of GDP (2014)
country comparison to the world: 64

Hospital bed density: 6.2 beds/1,000 population (2012)

Drinking water source:
improved:
urban: 99.7% of population
rural: 99.7% of population
total: 99.7% of population
unimproved:
urban: 0.3% of population
rural: 0.3% of population
total: 0.3% of population (2015 est.)

Sanitation facility access:
improved:
urban: 96.2% of population

rural: 96.2% of population
total: 96.2% of population
unimproved:
urban: 3.8% of population
rural: 3.8% of population
total: 3.8% of population (2015 est.)

HIV/AIDS—adult prevalence rate: 1.3% (2016 est.)
country comparison to the world: 36

HIV/AIDS—people living with HIV/AIDS: 2,600 (2016 est.)
country comparison to the world: 116

HIV/AIDS—deaths: <100 (2016 est.)
Major infectious diseases: note: active local transmission of Zika virus by Aedes species mosquitoes has been identified in this country (as of August 2016); it poses an important risk (a large number of cases possible) among US citizens if bitten by an infective mosquito; other less common ways to get Zika are through sex, via blood transfusion, or during pregnancy, in which the pregnant woman passes Zika virus to her fetus (2016)

Obesity—adult prevalence rate: 23.1% (2016)
country comparison to the world: 68

Children under the age of 5 years underweight: 3.5% (2012)

Education expenditures: 6.7% of GDP (2014)
country comparison to the world: 54

School life expectancy (primary to tertiary education): *total:* 15 years
male: 14 years
female: 17 years (2011)

Unemployment, youth ages 15-24: *total:* 32.4%
male: 31.8%
female: 33.3% (2015 est.)

GOVERNMENT

Country name: *conventional long form:* none
conventional short form: Barbados
etymology: the name derives from the Portuguese "as barbadas," which means "the bearded ones" and can refer either to the long, hanging roots of the island's bearded fig trees or to the alleged beards of the native Carib inhabitants

Government type: parliamentary democracy (Parliament) under a constitutional monarchy; a Commonwealth realm

Capital: *name:* Bridgetown
geographic coordinates: 13 06 N, 59 37 W
time difference: UTC-4 (1 hour ahead of Washington, DC, during Standard Time)

Administrative divisions: 11 parishes and 1 city*; Bridgetown*, Christ Church, Saint Andrew, Saint George, Saint James, Saint John, Saint Joseph, Saint Lucy, Saint Michael, Saint Peter, Saint Philip, Saint Thomas

Independence: 30 November 1966 (from the UK)

National holiday: Independence Day, 30 November (1966)

Constitution: adopted 22 November 1966, effective 30 November 1966; amended several times, last in 2007 (2016)

Legal system: English common law; no judicial review of legislative acts

International law organization participation: accepts compulsory ICJ jurisdiction with reservations; accepts ICCt jurisdiction

Citizenship: *citizenship by birth:* yes
citizenship by descent: yes
dual citizenship recognized: yes
residency requirement for naturalization: 5 years

Suffrage: 18 years of age; universal

Executive branch: *chief of state:* Queen ELIZABETH II (since 6 February 1952); represented by Governor General Sandra MASON (since 8 January 2018)

head of government: Prime Minister Freundel STUART (since 23 October 2010)
cabinet: Cabinet appointed by the governor general on the advice of the prime minister
elections/appointments: the monarchy is hereditary; governor general appointed by the monarch; following legislative elections, the leader of the majority party or leader of the majority coalition usually appointed prime minister by the governor general; the prime minister recommends the deputy prime minister

Legislative branch: *description:* bicameral Parliament consists of the Senate (21 seats; members appointed by the governor general—12 on the advice of the Prime Minister, 2 on the advice of the opposition leader, and 7 at the discretion of the governor general) and the House of Assembly (30 seats; members directly elected in single-seat constituencies by simple majority vote to serve 5-year terms)
elections: House of Assembly—last held on 21 February 2013 (next to be held in 2018)
election results: House of Assembly—percent of vote by party—DLP 51.3%, BLP 48.3%, other 0.4%; seats by party—DLP 16, BLP 14

Judicial branch: *highest court(s):* Supreme Court (consists of the High Court with 8 justices) and the Court of Appeal (consists of the High Court chief justice and president of the court and 4 justices; note—in 2010, Barbados, a member of the Caribbean Court of Justice, replaced the Judicial Committee of the Privy Council in London as the final court of appeal
judge selection and term of office: Supreme Court chief justice appointed by the governor-general on the recommendation of the prime minister and opposition leader of Parliament; other justices appointed by the governor-general on the recommendation of the Judicial and Legal Service Commission, a 5-member independent body consisting of the Supreme Court chief justice, the commission head, and governor-general appointees recommended by the prime minister; justices serve until mandatory retirement at age 65
subordinate courts: Magistrates' Courts

Political parties and leaders: Barbados Labor Party or BLP [Mia MOTTLEY]
Democratic Labor Party or DLP [Freundel STUART]
People's Empowerment Party or PEP [David COMISSIONG]

Political pressure groups and leaders: Barbados Secondary Teachers' Union or BSTU [Mary REDMAN]
Barbados Union of Teachers or BUT [Pedro SHEPHERD]
Barbados Workers Union or BWU [Linda BROOKS]
Clement Payne Labor Union [David COMISSIONG]
Congress of Trade Unions and Staff Associations of Barbados or CTUSAB, (includes the BWU, NUPW, BUT, and BSTU) [Cedric MURRELL]
National Union of Public Workers or NUPW [Akanni MCDOWALL]

International organization participation: ACP, AOSIS, C, Caricom, CDB, CELAC, FAO, G-77, IADB, IBRD, ICAO, ICCt, ICRM, IDA, IFAD, IFC, IFRCS, ILO, IMF, IMO, Interpol, IOC, ISO, ITSO, ITU, ITUC (NGOs), LAES, MIGA, NAM, OAS, OPANAL, OPCW, UN, UNCTAD, UNESCO, UNHCR, UNIDO, UPU, WCO, WFTU (NGOs), WHO, WIPO, WMO, WTO

Diplomatic representation in the US: *chief of mission:* Ambassador Selwin Charles HART (since 18 January 2017)
chancery: 2144 Wyoming Avenue NW, Washington, DC 20008
telephone: [1] (202) 939-9200
FAX: [1] (202) 332-7467
consulate(s) general: Miami, New York
consulate(s): Los Angeles

Diplomatic representation from the US: *chief of mission:* Ambassador Linda S. TAGLIALATELA (since 1 February 2016) note—also accredited to Antigua and Barbuda, Dominica, Grenada, Saint Kitts and Nevis, Saint Lucia, and Saint Vincent and the Grenadines
embassy: Wildey Business Park, Wildey, St. Michael BB 14006, Barbados
mailing address: P. O. Box 302, Bridgetown BB 11000; (Department Name) Unit 3120, DPO AA 34055
telephone: [1] (246) 227-4000
FAX: [1] (246) 431-0179

Flag description: three equal vertical bands of ultramarine blue (hoist side), gold, and ultramarine blue with the head of a black trident centered on the gold band; the band colors represent the blue of the sea and sky and the gold of the beaches; the trident head represents independence and a break with the past (the colonial coat of arms contained a complete trident)

National symbol(s): Neptune's trident, pelican, Red Bird of Paradise flower (also known as Pride of Barbados); national colors: blue, yellow, black

National anthem: *name:* "The National Anthem of Barbados"
lyrics/music: Irving BURGIE/C. Van Roland EDWARDS
note: adopted 1966; the anthem is also known as "In Plenty and In Time of Need"

ECONOMY

Economy—overview: Barbados is the wealthiest and one of the most developed countries in the Eastern Caribbean and enjoys one of the highest per capita incomes in the region. Historically, the Barbadian economy was dependent on sugarcane cultivation and related activities. However, in recent years the economy has diversified into light industry and tourism. Offshore finance and information services are important foreign exchange earners, boosted by being in the same time zone as eastern US financial centers and by a relatively highly educated workforce. Following the 2008-09 recession, the economy has grown due to increases in tourist arrivals, construction, financial services and exports. However, Barbados' high public debt to GDP ratio and falling international reserves remain areas of concern. Growth prospects are limited because of a weak economic outlook.

GDP (purchasing power parity): $4.919 billion (2017 est.)
$4.876 billion (2016 est.)
$4.799 billion (2015 est.)
note: data are in 2017 dollars
country comparison to the world: 177

GDP (official exchange rate): $4.821 billion (2016 est.)

GDP—real growth rate: 0.9% (2017 est.)
1.6% (2016 est.)
0.9% (2015 est.)
country comparison to the world: 189

GDP—per capita (PPP): $17,500 (2017 est.)
$17,400 (2016 est.)
$17,100 (2015 est.)
note: data are in 2017 dollars
country comparison to the world: 98

Gross national saving: 10.4% of GDP (2017 est.)
8.6% of GDP (2016 est.)
8.8% of GDP (2015 est.)
country comparison to the world: 157

GDP—composition, by end use:
household consumption: 82.1%
government consumption: 13.6%
investment in fixed capital: 14.5%
investment in inventories: 0.8%
exports of goods and services: 35.3%
imports of goods and services: -46.3% (2017 est.)

GDP—composition, by sector of origin:
agriculture: 1.6%
industry: 11.2%
services: 87.1% (2017 est.)

Agriculture—products: sugarcane, vegetables, cotton

Industries: tourism, sugar, light manufacturing, component assembly for export

Industrial production growth rate: 1.6% (2017 est.)
country comparison to the world: 148

Labor force: 142,900 (2017 est.)
country comparison to the world: 179

Labor force—by occupation: *agriculture:* 10%
industry: 15%
services: 75% (1996 est.)

Unemployment rate: 9.8% (2017 est.)
9.9% (2016 est.)
country comparison to the world: 135

Population below poverty line: NA%

Household income or consumption by percentage share: *lowest 10%:* NA%
highest 10%: NA%

Budget: *revenues:* $1.35 billion (2013 est.)
expenditures: $1.65 billion (2017 est.)
Taxes and other revenues: 28% of GDP (2017 est.)
country comparison to the world: 95

Budget surplus (+) or deficit (-): -6.2% of GDP (2017 est.)
country comparison to the world: 178

Public debt: 108.3% of GDP (2017 est.)
107.9% of GDP (2016 est.)
country comparison to the world: 13

Fiscal year: 1 April—31 March

Inflation rate (consumer prices): 5% (2017 est.)
1.3% (2016 est.)
country comparison to the world: 173

Central bank discount rate: 7% (31 December 2010)
7% (31 December 2009)
country comparison to the world: 51

Commercial bank prime lending rate: 8.1% (31 December 2017 est.)
8.05% (31 December 2016 est.)
country comparison to the world: 109

Stock of narrow money: $2.17 billion (31 December 2017 est.)
$2.143 billion (31 December 2016 est.)
country comparison to the world: 131

Stock of broad money: $4.581 billion (31 December 2017 est.)
$4.55 billion (31 December 2016 est.)
country comparison to the world: 133

Stock of domestic credit: $5.963 billion (31 December 2017 est.)
$5.798 billion (31 December 2016 est.)
country comparison to the world: 121

Market value of publicly traded shares: $4.495 billion (31 December 2012 est.)
$4.571 billion (31 December 2011 est.)
$4.366 billion (31 December 2010 est.)
country comparison to the world: 89

Current account balance: -$160 million (2017 est.)
-$208 million (2016 est.)
country comparison to the world: 87

Exports: $531.4 million (2017 est.)
$517 million (2016 est.)
country comparison to the world: 173

Exports—commodities: manufactures, sugar, molasses, rum, other foodstuffs and beverages, chemicals, electrical components

Exports—partners: US 39.6%, Trinidad and Tobago 8.9%, Guyana 5.2%, China 4.9%, Jamaica 4.8%, St. Lucia 4.3% (2016)

Imports: $1.618 billion (2017 est.)
$1.541 billion (2016 est.)
country comparison to the world: 166

Imports—commodities: consumer goods, machinery, foodstuffs, construction materials, chemicals, fuel, electrical components

Imports—partners: US 39%, Trinidad and Tobago 13.4%, China 7.3%, UK 4.8% (2016)

Reserves of foreign exchange and gold: $407.6 million (31 December 2017 est.)
$431.8 million (31 December 2016 est.)
country comparison to the world: 146

Debt—external: $4.49 billion (2010 est.)
$668 million (2003 est.)
country comparison to the world: 137

Exchange rates: Barbadian dollars (BBD) per US dollar—
2 (2017 est.)
2 (2016 est.)
2 (2015 est.)
2 (2014 est.)
2 (2013 est.)
note: the Barbadian dollar is pegged to the US dollar

ENERGY

Electricity access: *population without electricity:* 29,149
electrification—*total population:* 91%
electrification—urban areas: 100%
electrification—rural areas: 80% (2012)

Electricity—production: 915 million kWh (2015 est.)
country comparison to the world: 155

Electricity—consumption: 865 million kWh (2015 est.)
country comparison to the world: 160

Electricity—exports: 0 kWh (2016 est.)
country comparison to the world: 103

Electricity—imports: 0 kWh (2016 est.)
country comparison to the world: 122

Electricity—installed generating capacity: 248,000 kW (2015 est.)
country comparison to the world: 161

Electricity—from fossil fuels: 96.4% of total installed capacity (2015 est.)
country comparison to the world: 46

Electricity—from nuclear fuels: 0% of total installed capacity (2015 est.)
country comparison to the world: 46

Electricity—from hydroelectric plants: 0% of total installed capacity (2015 est.)
country comparison to the world: 161

Electricity—from other renewable sources: 8.1% of total installed capacity (2015 est.)
country comparison to the world: 78

Crude oil—production: 1,000 bbl/day (2016 est.)
country comparison to the world: 92

Crude oil—exports: 764.5 bbl/day (2014 est.)
country comparison to the world: 74

Crude oil—imports: 0 bbl/day (2014 est.)
country comparison to the world: 95

Crude oil—proved reserves: 2.082 million bbl (1 January 2017 es)
country comparison to the world: 98

Refined petroleum products—production: 0 bbl/day (2014 est.)
country comparison to the world: 118

Refined petroleum products—consumption: 12,000 bbl/day (2015 est.)

country comparison to the world: 158

Refined petroleum products—exports: 0 bbl/day (2014 est.)
country comparison to the world: 131

Refined petroleum products—imports: 11,490 bbl/day (2014 est.)
country comparison to the world: 138

Natural gas—production: 20 million cu m (2014 est.)
country comparison to the world: 93

Natural gas—consumption: 20 million cu m (2014 est.)
country comparison to the world: 113

Natural gas—exports: 0 cu m (2013 est.)
country comparison to the world: 65

Natural gas—imports: 0 cu m (2013 est.)
country comparison to the world: 88

Natural gas—proved reserves: 113.3 million cu m (1 January 2017 es)
country comparison to the world: 107

Carbon dioxide emissions from consumption of energy: 1.3 million Mt (2013 est.)
country comparison to the world: 162

COMMUNICATIONS

Telephones—fixed lines: *total subscriptions:* 139,948
subscriptions per 100 inhabitants: 48 (July 2016 est.)
country comparison to the world: 138

Telephones—mobile cellular: *total:* 332,208
subscriptions per 100 inhabitants: 114 (July 2016 est.)
country comparison to the world: 176

Telephone system: *general assessment:* island-wide automatic telephone system
domestic: fixed-line teledensity of roughly 50 per 100 persons; mobile-cellular telephone density about 115 per 100 persons
international: country code—1-246; landing point for the East Caribbean Fiber System (ECFS) submarine cable with links to 13 other islands in the eastern Caribbean extending from the British Virgin Islands to Trinidad; satellite earth stations—1 (Intelsat—Atlantic Ocean); tropospheric scatter to Trinidad and Saint Lucia (2016)

Broadcast media: government-owned Caribbean Broadcasting Corporation (CBC) operates the lone terrestrial TV station; CBC also operates a multi-channel cable TV subscription service; roughly a dozen radio stations, consisting of a CBC-operated network operating alongside privately owned radio stations (2009)

Internet country code: .bb

Internet users: *total:* 231,883
percent of population: 79.5% (July 2016 est.)
country comparison to the world: 152

TRANSPORTATION

Civil aircraft registration country code prefix: 8P (2016)

Airports: 1 (2013)
country comparison to the world: 236

Airports—with paved runways: *total:* 1
over 3,047 m: 1 (2017)

Pipelines: gas 33 km; oil 64 km; refined products
6 km (2013)

Roadways: *total:* 1,700 km
paved: 1,700 km (2015)
country comparison to the world: 177

Merchant marine: *total:* 112
by type: bulk carrier 18, general cargo 71, oil
tanker 2, other 21 (2017)
country comparison to the world: 79

Ports and terminals: *major seaport(s):* Bridgetown

MILITARY AND SECURITY

Military branches: Royal Barbados Defense Force:
Troops Command, Barbados Coast Guard (2011)

Military service age and obligation: 18 years of
age for voluntary military service, or earlier with
parental consent; no conscription (2013)

Military—note: the Royal Barbados Defense Force
includes a land-based Troop Command and a small
Coast Guard; the primary role of the land element
is island defense against external aggression; the
Command consists of a single, part-time battalion
with a small regular cadre deployed throughout the
island; the cadre increasingly supports the police
in patrolling the coastline for smuggling and other
illicit activities

TRANSNATIONAL ISSUES

Disputes—international: Barbados and Trinidad
and Tobago abide by the April 2006 Permanent
Court of Arbitration decision delimiting a maritime boundary and limiting catches of flying fish
in Trinidad and Tobago's exclusive economic zone;
joins other Caribbean states to counter Venezuela's
claim that Aves Island sustains human habitation,
a criterion under the UN Convention on the Law
of the Sea, which permits Venezuela to extend its
Economic Exclusion Zone/continental shelf over a
large portion of the eastern Caribbean Sea

Illicit drugs: one of many Caribbean transshipment points for narcotics bound for Europe and
the US; offshore financial center

BELARUS

Geographic coordinates: 53 00 N, 28 00 E

Map references: Europe

Area: *total:* 207,600 sq km
land: 202,900 sq km
water: 4,700 sq km
country comparison to the world: 87

Area—comparative: slightly less than twice the
size of Kentucky; slightly smaller than Kansas

Land boundaries: *total:* 3,642 km
border countries (5): Latvia 161 km, Lithuania
640 km, Poland 418 km, Russia 1,312 km, Ukraine
1,111 km

Coastline: 0 km (landlocked)

Maritime claims: none (landlocked)

Climate: cold winters, cool and moist summers;
transitional between continental and maritime

Terrain: generally flat with much marshland

Elevation: *mean elevation:* 160 m

elevation extremes: *lowest point:* Nyoman River
90 m
highest point: Dzyarzhynskaya Hara 346 m

Natural resources: timber, peat deposits, small
quantities of oil and natural gas, granite, dolomitic
limestone, marl, chalk, sand, gravel, clay

Land use: *agricultural land:* 43.7%
arable land: 27.2%;
permanent crops: 0.6%;
permanent pasture: 15.9%
forest: 42.7%
other: 13.6% (2011 est.)
Irrigated land: 1,140 sq km (2012)

Population—distribution: a fairly even distribution
throughout most of the country, with urban areas
attracting larger and denser populations

Natural hazards: large tracts of marshy land

Environment—current issues: soil pollution
from pesticide use; southern part of the country
contaminated with fallout from 1986 nuclear reac-
tor accident at Chornobyl' in northern Ukraine

Environment—international agreements: party
to: Air Pollution, Air Pollution-Nitrogen Oxides,
Air Pollution-Sulfur 85, Biodiversity, Climate
Change, Climate Change-Kyoto Protocol, Deser-
tification, Endangered Species, Environmental
Modification, Hazardous Wastes, Law of the Sea,
Marine Dumping, Ozone Layer Protection, Ship
Pollution, Wetlands
signed, but not ratified: none of the selected
agreements

Geography—note: landlocked; glacial scouring
accounts for the flatness of Belarusian terrain and
for its 11,000 lakes

PEOPLE AND SOCIETY

Population: 9,549,747 (July 2017 est.)
country comparison to the world: 93

Nationality: *noun:* Belarusian(s)
adjective: Belarusian

Ethnic groups: Belarusian 83.7%, Russian 8.3%,
Polish 3.1%, Ukrainian 1.7%, other 2.4%, unspecified 0.9% (2009 est.)

Languages: Russian (official) 70.2%, Belarusian
(official) 23.4%, other 3.1% (includes small Pol-
ish- and Ukrainian-speaking minorities), unspecified 3.3% (2009 est.)

Religions: Orthodox 48.3%, Catholic 7.1%, other
3.5%, non-believers 41.1% (2011 est.)

Age structure: *0-14 years:* 15.78% (male 774,995/
female 732,191)
15-24 years: 10.29% (male 505,420/female
477,123)
25-54 years: 44.76% (male 2,104,170/female
2,170,515)
55-64 years: 14.21% (male 599,630/female
757,744)

INTRODUCTION

Background: After seven decades as a constituent
republic of the USSR, Belarus attained its independence in 1991. It has retained closer political and economic ties to Russia than have any
of the other former Soviet republics. Belarus and
Russia signed a treaty on a two-state union on 8
December 1999 envisioning greater political and
economic integration. Although Belarus agreed to
a framework to carry out the accord, serious implementation has yet to take place. Since his election
in July 1994 as the country's first and only directly
elected president, Aleksandr LUKASHENKO has
steadily consolidated his power through authoritarian means and a centralized economic system.
Government restrictions on political and civil
freedoms, freedom of speech and the press, peaceful assembly, and religion have remained in place.

GEOGRAPHY

Location: Eastern Europe, east of Poland

65 years and over: 14.95% (male 457,766/female 970,193) (2017 est.)

Dependency ratios: *total dependency ratio:* 43.8
youth dependency ratio: 23.2
elderly dependency ratio: 20.6
potential support ratio: 4.9 (2015 est.)

Median age: *total:* 40 years
male: 37.1 years
female: 43.1 years (2017 est.)
country comparison to the world: 51

Population growth rate: -0.22% (2017 est.)
country comparison to the world: 212

Birth rate: 10.3 births/1,000 population (2017 est.)
country comparison to the world: 191

Death rate: 13.2 deaths/1,000 population (2017 est.)
country comparison to the world: 12

Net migration rate: 0.7 migrant(s)/1,000 population (2017 est.)
country comparison to the world: 61

Population distribution: a fairly even distribution throughout most of the country, with urban areas attracting larger and denser populations

Urbanization: *urban population:* 77.4% of total population (2017)
rate of urbanization: -0.04% annual rate of change (2015-20 est.)

Major urban areas—population: MINSK (capital) 1.915 million (2015)

Sex ratio: *at birth:* 1.06 male(s)/female
0-14 years: 1.06 male(s)/female
15-24 years: 1.06 male(s)/female
25-54 years: 0.97 male(s)/female
55-64 years: 0.79 male(s)/female
65 years and over: 0.46 male(s)/female
total population: 0.87 male(s)/female (2016 est.)

Mother's mean age at first birth: 25.7 years (2014 est.)

Maternal mortality ratio: 4 deaths/100,000 live births (2015 est.)
country comparison to the world: 176

Infant mortality rate: *total:* 3.6 deaths/1,000 live births
male: 4 deaths/1,000 live births
female: 3.1 deaths/1,000 live births (2017 est.)
country comparison to the world: 200

Life expectancy at birth: *total population:* 73 years
male: 67.5 years
female: 78.8 years (2017 est.)
country comparison to the world: 141

Total fertility rate: 1.48 children born/woman (2017 est.)
country comparison to the world: 199

Contraceptive prevalence rate: 63.1% (2012)
Health expenditures: 5.7% of GDP (2014)
country comparison to the world: 117

Physicians density: 4.07 physicians/1,000 population (2014)

Hospital bed density: 11.3 beds/1,000 population (2011)

Drinking water source:

improved:
urban: 99.9% of population
rural: 99.1% of population
total: 99.7% of population
unimproved:
urban: 0.1% of population
rural: 0.9% of population
total: 0.3% of population (2015 est.)

Sanitation facility access:
improved:
urban: 94.1% of population
rural: 95.2% of population
total: 94.3% of population
unimproved:
urban: 5.9% of population
rural: 4.8% of population
total: 5.7% of population (2015 est.)

HIV/AIDS—adult prevalence rate: 0.4% (2016 est.)
country comparison to the world: 76

HIV/AIDS—people living with HIV/AIDS: 19,000 (2016 est.)
country comparison to the world: 80

HIV/AIDS—deaths: <200 (2016 est.)

Obesity—adult prevalence rate: 24.5% (2016)
country comparison to the world: 58

Education expenditures: 4.9% of GDP (2015)
country comparison to the world: 71

Literacy: *definition:* age 15 and over can read and write
total population: 99.7%
male: 99.8%
female: 99.7% (2015 est.)

School life expectancy (primary to tertiary education): *total:* 16 years
male: 15 years
female: 16 years (2015)

Unemployment, youth ages 15-24: *total:* 12.5%
male: 12.4%
female: 12.6% (2009 est.)
country comparison to the world: 88

GOVERNMENT

Country name: *conventional long form:* Republic of Belarus
conventional short form: Belarus
local long form: Respublika Byelarus'/Respublika Belarus'
local short form: Byelarus'/Belarus'
former: Belorussian (Byelorussian) Soviet Socialist Republic
etymology: the name is a compound of the Belarusian words "bel" (white) and "Rus" (the Old East Slavic ethnic designation) to form the meaning White Rusian or White Ruthenian

Government type: presidential republic in name, although in fact a dictatorship

Capital: *name:* Minsk

geographic coordinates: 53 54 N, 27 34 E

time difference: UTC+2 (7 hours ahead of Washington, DC, during Standard Time)

Administrative divisions: 6 provinces (voblastsi, singular—voblasts') and 1 municipality* (horad); Brest, Homyel' (Gomel'), Horad Minsk* (Minsk City), Hrodna (Grodno), Mahilyow (Mogilev), Minsk, Vitsyebsk (Vitebsk)
note: administrative divisions have the same names as their administrative centers; Russian spelling provided for reference when different from Belarusian

Independence: 25 August 1991 (from the Soviet Union)

National holiday: Independence Day, 3 July (1944); note—3 July 1944 was the date Minsk was liberated from German troops, 25 August 1991 was the date of independence from the Soviet Union

Constitution: *history:* several previous; latest drafted between late 1991 and early 1994, signed 15 March 1994
amendments: proposed by the president of the republic through petition to the National Assembly or by petition of least 150,000 eligible voters; approval required by at least two-thirds majority vote in both chambers or by simple majority of votes cast in a referendum (2016)

Legal system: civil law system; note—nearly all major codes (civil, civil procedure, criminal, criminal procedure, family, and labor) were revised and came into force in 1999 and 2000

International law organization participation: has not submitted an ICJ jurisdiction declaration; non-party state to the ICCt

Citizenship: *citizenship by birth:* no
citizenship by descent only: at least one parent must be a citizen of Belarus
dual citizenship recognized: no
residency requirement for naturalization: 7 years

Suffrage: 18 years of age; universal

Executive branch: *chief of state:* president Aleksandr LUKASHENKO (since 20 July 1994)

head of government: prime minister Andrey KOBYAKOV (since 27 December 2014); first deputy prime minister Vasiliy MATYUSHEVSKIY (since 27 December 2014)
cabinet: Council of Ministers appointed by the president
elections/appointments: president directly elected by absolute majority popular vote in 2 rounds if needed for a 5-year term (no term limits); first election took place on 23 June and 10 July 1994; according to the 1994 constitution, the next election should have been held in 1999; however, Aleksandr LUKASHENKO extended his term to 2001 via a November 1996 referendum; subsequent election held on 9 September 2001; an October 2004 referendum ended presidential term limits and allowed the president to run and win in a third (19 March 2006), fourth (19 December 2010), and fifth election (11 October 2015); next election in 2020; prime minister and deputy prime ministers appointed by the president and approved by the National Assembly
election results: Aleksandr LUKASHENKO reelected president; percent of vote—Aleksandr

LUKASHENKO (independent) 83.5%, Tatstyana KARATKEVICH (Tell the Truth) 4.4%, Sergey GAYDUKEVICH (LDP) 3.3%, other 8.8%; note—election marred by electoral fraud

Legislative branch: *description:* bicameral National Assembly or Natsionalnoye Sobraniye consists of the Council of the Republic or Sovet Respubliki (64 seats; 56 members indirectly elected by regional and Minsk city councils and 8 members appointed by the president; members serve 4-year terms) and the House of Representatives or Palata Predstaviteley (110 seats; members directly elected in single-seat constituencies by absolute majority vote in 2 rounds if needed; members serve 4-year terms); note—the US does not recognize the legitimacy of the National Assembly *elections:* House of Representatives—last held on 11 September 2016 (next to be held in 2020); OSCE observers determined that the election was neither free nor impartial and that vote counting was problematic in a number of polling stations; pro-LUKASHENKO candidates won virtually every seat, with only the UCP member and one independent forming alternative representation in the House; international observers determined that the previous elections, on 28 September 2008 and 23 September 2012, also fell short of democratic standards, with pro-LUKASHENKO candidates winning every seat *election results:* Council of the Republic—percent of vote by party—NA; seats by party—NA; House of Representatives—percent of vote by party—NA; seats by party—KPB 8, Belarusian Patriotic Party 3, Republican Party of Labor and Justice 3, LDP 1, UCP 1, independent 94

Judicial branch: *highest court(s):* Supreme Court (consists of the chairman and deputy chairman and organized into several specialized panels, including economic and military; number of judges set by the president of the republic and the court chairman); Constitutional Court (consists of 12 judges including a chairman and deputy chairman) *judge selection and term of office:* Supreme Court judges appointed by the president with the consent of the Council of the Republic; judges initially appointed for 5 years and evaluated for life appointment; Constitutional Court judges—6 appointed by the president and 6 elected by the Council of the Republic; the presiding judge directly elected by the president and approved by the Council of the Republic; judges can serve for 11 years with an age limit of 70 *subordinate courts:* provincial (including Minsk city) courts; first instance (district) courts; economic courts; military courts

Political parties and leaders: pro-government parties: Belarusian Agrarian Party or AP [Mikhail SHIMANSKIY]
Belarusian Patriotic Party [Nikolai ULAKHOVICH]
Belarusian Social Sport Party [Vladimir ALEKSANDROVICH]
Communist Party of Belarus or KPB [Igor KARPENKO]

Liberal Democratic Party or LDP [Sergey GAYDUKEVICH]
Republican Party [Vladimir BELOZOR]
Republican Party of Labor and Justice [Vasiliy ZADNEPRYANIY]
opposition parties: Belarusian Christian Democracy Party [Paval SEVIARYNETS] (unregistered)
Belarusian Party of the Green [Anastasiya DOROFEYEVA]
Belarusian Party of the Left "Just World" [Sergey KALYAKIN]
Belarusian Popular Front or BPF [Alyaksey YANUKEVICH]
Belarusian Social-Democratic Assembly [Stanislav SHUSHKEVICH]
Belarusian Social Democratic Party ("Assembly") or BSDPH [Irina VESHTARD]
Belarusian Social Democratic Party (People's Assembly) [Mikalay STATKEVICH] (unregistered)
Christian Conservative Party or BPF [Zyanon PAZNYAK]
United Civic Party or UCP [Anatoliy LEBEDKO]

Political pressure groups and leaders: Assembly of Pro-Democratic NGOs [Sergey MATSKEVICH] (unregistered)
Belarusian Association of Journalists [Andrei BASTUNETS]
Belarusian Congress of Democratic Trade Unions or BRDP [Aleksandr YAROSHUK]
Belarusian Helsinki Committee or BHC [Aleh HULAK]
Belarusian Language Society [Aleh TRUSAU, Alena ANISIM]
Center-Right Coalition [Vital RYMASHEUSKI, ANATOLY LEBEDKO, YURAS HUBAREVICH]
Congress of Democratic Forces [Mikalay STATKEVICH]
For Freedom Movement [Yuras HUBAREVICH]
Malady Front (Young Front) [Zmitser DASHKEVICH] (unregistered)
Perspektiva [Anatoliy SHUMCHENKO] (small business association)
"Tell the Truth" Movement [Tatsyana KARATKEVICH] (unregistered)
Vyasna (Spring) human rights center [Ales BELYATSKIY] (unregistered)
Women's Independent Democratic Movement [Ludmila PETINA]

International organization participation: BSEC (observer), CBSS (observer), CEI, CIS, CSTO, EAEC, EAEU, EAPC, EBRD, FAO, GCTU, IAEA, IBRD, ICAO, ICC (NGOs), ICRM, IDA, IFC, IFRCS, ILO, IMF, IMSO, Interpol, IOC, IOM, IPU, ISO, ITU, ITUC (NGOs), MIGA, NAM, NSG, OPCW, OSCE, PCA, PFP, SCO (dialogue member), UN, UNCTAD, UNESCO, UNIDO, UNIFIL, UNWTO, UPU, WCO, WFTU (NGOs), WHO, WIPO, WMO, WTO (observer), ZC

Diplomatic representation in the US: *chief of mission:* Ambassador (vacant; recalled by Belarus in 2008); Charge d'Affaires Pavel SHIDLOVSKIY (since 23 April 2014)

chancery: 1619 New Hampshire Avenue NW, Washington, DC 20009
telephone: [1] (202) 986-1606
FAX: [1] (202) 986-1805
consulate(s) general: New York

Diplomatic representation from the US: *chief of mission:* Ambassador (vacant; left in 2008 upon insistence of Belarusian Government); Charge d'Affaires Robert RILEY (since 22 August 2016) *embassy:* 46 Starovilenskaya Street, Minsk 220002 *mailing address:* Unit 7010 Box 100, DPO AE 09769
telephone: [375] (17) 210-1283
FAX: [375] (17) 234-7853

Flag description: red horizontal band (top) and green horizontal band one-half the width of the red band; a white vertical stripe on the hoist side bears Belarusian national ornamentation in red; the red band color recalls past struggles from oppression, the green band represents hope and the many forests of the country

National symbol(s): no clearly defined current national symbol, the mounted knight known as Pahonia (the Chaser) is the traditional Belarusian symbol; national colors: green, red, white

National anthem: *name:* "My, Bielarusy" (We Belarusians)
lyrics/music: Mikhas KLIMKOVICH and Uladzimir KARYZNA/Nester SAKALOUSKI
note: music adopted 1955, lyrics adopted 2002; after the fall of the Soviet Union, Belarus kept the music of its Soviet-era anthem but adopted new lyrics; also known as "Dziarzauny himn Respubliki Bielarus" (State Anthem of the Republic of Belarus)

ECONOMY

Economy—overview: As part of the former Soviet Union, Belarus had a relatively well-developed, though aging industrial base; it retained this industrial base—which is now outdated, energy inefficient, and dependent on subsidized Russian energy and preferential access to Russian markets—following the breakup of the USSR. The country also has a broad agricultural base which is largely inefficient and dependent on government subsidies. After an initial burst of capitalist reform between 1991 and 1994, including privatization of smaller state enterprises and some service sector businesses, creation of institutions of private property, and development of entrepreneurship, Belarus' economic development greatly slowed. About 80% of all industry remains in state hands, and non-Russian foreign investment has been hindered by a reluctance to welcome private investment absent joint ownership or affiliation with the state. A few businesses, which had been privatized after independence, were renationalized. State banks account for 75% of the banking sector.

Economic output declined for several years following the collapse of the Soviet Union, but revived in the mid-2000s due to the boom in oil prices. Belarus has only small reserves of crude oil, though it imports most of its crude oil and natural gas from Russia at prices substantially below world market prices. Belarus then derives export revenue by refining Russian crude and selling it at market prices. In late 2006, Russia began a process of rolling back its subsidies on oil and gas exports to Belarus. Several times since, Russia and Belarus have had serious disagreements over the level and price of Russian energy supplies. At one point in 2010, Russia stopped the export of all subsidized oil to Belarus save for domestic needs before the two countries reached a deal to restart the export of discounted oil to Belarus. Beginning in early 2016, Russia claimed Belarus began accumulating debt—reaching $740 million by April 2017—for paying below an agreed price for Russian natural gas. Russia decided to reduce its export of crude oil as a result of the debt. In April 2017, Belarus agreed to pay its gas debt and Russia restored the flow of crude. The agreement paved the way for resumption of cheap energy imports and financial assistance from the Eurasian Fund for Stabilization and Development.

New non-Russian foreign investment has been limited in recent years. In 2011, a financial crisis began, triggered by government-directed salary hikes, compounded by an increased cost in Russian energy inputs and an overvalued Belarusian ruble that lead to a nearly three-fold devaluation of the Belarusian ruble. In November 2011, Belarus agreed to sell to Russia its remaining shares of Beltransgaz, the Belarusian natural gas pipeline operator, in exchange for reduced prices for Russian natural gas. The situation stabilized in 2012, after Belarus received part of a $3 billion loan from the Russian-dominated Eurasian Economic Community Bailout Fund, a $1 billion loan from the Russian state-owned bank Sberbank, and $2.5 billion from the sale of Beltransgaz to Russian state-owned Gazprom; nevertheless, the Belarusian currency lost more than 60% of its value, as inflation reached new highs in 2011 and 2012, before calming in 2013. In December 2013, Russia announced a new loan for Belarus of up to $2 billion for 2014. Notwithstanding foreign assistance, the Belarusian economy continued to struggle under the weight of high external debt servicing payments and trade deficit. In mid-December 2014, structural economic shortcomings were aggravated by the devaluation of the Russian ruble, which triggered a near 40% devaluation of the Belarusian ruble.

Belarus's economy stagnated between 2012 and 2016, which led to widening productivity and income gaps between Belarus and neighboring countries. Since 2015, the Belarusian government has tightened its macro-economic policies, allowed more flexibility to its exchange rate, taken steps towards price liberalization, and reduced subsidized government lending to state-owned industrial and agricultural enterprises, amid a drop in state budget revenues that resulted from falling global prices on key Belarusian export commodities—petroleum products and potash fertilizer. Belarus returned to weak growth in 2017, largely driven by improvement of external conditions that allowed for growth in its manufacturing sector. Belarus also issued sovereign debt for the first time

since 2011 for $1.4 billion in June 2017, which provided the country with badly-needed liquidity.

GDP (purchasing power parity): $175.9 billion (2017 est.)
$174.6 billion (2016 est.)
$179.4 billion (2015 est.)
note: data are in 2017 dollars
country comparison to the world: 72

GDP (official exchange rate): $52.78 billion (2016 est.)

GDP—real growth rate: 0.7% (2017 est.)
-2.6% (2016 est.)
-3.8% (2015 est.)
country comparison to the world: 192

GDP—per capita (PPP): $18,600 (2017 est.)
$18,400 (2016 est.)
$18,900 (2015 est.)
note: data are in 2017 dollars
country comparison to the world: 95

Gross national saving: 19.4% of GDP (2017 est.)
21.7% of GDP (2016 est.)
25.8% of GDP (2015 est.)
country comparison to the world: 95

GDP—composition, by end use:
household consumption: 54.8%
government consumption: 16.8%
investment in fixed capital: 24.1%
investment in inventories: -1.1%
exports of goods and services: 65%
imports of goods and services: -59.6% (2017 est.)

GDP—composition, by sector of origin:
agriculture: 8.3%
industry: 40.6%
services: 51.1% (2017 est.)

Agriculture—products: grain, potatoes, vegetables, sugar beets, flax; beef, milk

Industries: metal-cutting machine tools, tractors, trucks, earthmovers, motorcycles, synthetic fibers, fertilizer, textiles, refrigerators, washing machines and other household appliances

Industrial production growth rate: 3.5% (2017 est.)
country comparison to the world: 86

Labor force: 4.381 million (2016 est.)
country comparison to the world: 90

Labor force—by occupation: *agriculture:* 9.7%
industry: 23.4%
services: 66.8% (2015 est.)

Unemployment rate: 1% (2017 est.)
1% (2016 est.)
note: official registered unemployed; large number of underemployed workers
country comparison to the world: 6

Population below poverty line: 5.7% (2016 est.)

Household income or consumption by percentage share: *lowest 10%:* 3.8%
highest 10%: 21.9% (2008)

Distribution of family income—Gini index: 26.5 (2011)
21.7 (1998)
country comparison to the world: 140

Budget: *revenues:* $22.8 billion
expenditures: $22.54 billion (2017 est.)

Taxes and other revenues: 43.2% of GDP (2017 est.)
country comparison to the world: 28

Budget surplus (+) or deficit (-): 0.5% of GDP (2017 est.)
country comparison to the world: 23

Public debt: 46.2% of GDP (2017 est.)
47.5% of GDP (2016 est.)
country comparison to the world: 113

Fiscal year: calendar year

Inflation rate (consumer prices): 8% (2017 est.)
11.8% (2016 est.)
country comparison to the world: 197

Central bank discount rate: 14% (19 April 2017)
15% (15 March 2017)
country comparison to the world: 11

Commercial bank prime lending rate: 14% (31 December 2017 est.)
14.4% (31 December 2016 est.)
country comparison to the world: 52

Stock of narrow money: $2.881 billion (31 December 2017 est.)
$2.718 billion (31 December 2016 est.)
country comparison to the world: 121

Stock of broad money: $6.03 billion (31 December 2017 est.)
$5.431 billion (31 December 2016 est.)
country comparison to the world: 125

Stock of domestic credit: $21.45 billion (31 December 2017 est.)
$20.64 billion (31 December 2016 est.)
country comparison to the world: 88

Market value of publicly traded shares: $NA

Current account balance: -$2.801 billion (2017 est.)
-$1.703 billion (2016 est.)
country comparison to the world: 164

Exports: $24.2 billion (2017 est.)
$22.98 billion (2016 est.)
country comparison to the world: 67

Exports—commodities: machinery and equipment, mineral products, chemicals, metals, textiles, foodstuffs

Exports—partners: Russia 46.3%, Ukraine 12.2%, UK 4.6%, Germany 4% (2016)

Imports: $26.2 billion (2017 est.)
$25.57 billion (2016 est.)
country comparison to the world: 67

Imports—commodities: mineral products, machinery and equipment, chemicals, foodstuffs, metals

Imports—partners: Russia 55.5%, China 7.8%, Germany 4.9%, Poland 4.4% (2016)

Reserves of foreign exchange and gold: $5.059 billion (31 December 2017 est.)
$4.927 billion (31 December 2016 est.)
country comparison to the world: 93

Debt—external: $38.75 billion (31 December 2017 est.)
$37.74 billion (31 December 2016 est.)
country comparison to the world: 75

Stock of direct foreign investment—at home:
$6.929 billion (31 December 2016 est.)
$7.241 billion (31 December 2015)
country comparison to the world: 99

Stock of direct foreign investment—abroad:
$3.547 billion (31 December 2016 est.)
$4.649 billion (31 December 2015)
country comparison to the world: 77

Exchange rates: Belarusian rubles (BYB/BYR) per
US dollar—
1.9 (2017 est.)
2 (2016 est.)
2 (2015 est.)
15,926 (2014 est.)
10,224.1 (2013 est.)

ENERGY

Electricity access: electrification—*total popula-*
tion: 100% (2016)

Electricity—production: 32.04 billion kWh (2015
est.)
country comparison to the world: 63

Electricity—consumption: 31.75 billion kWh
(2015 est.)
country comparison to the world: 61

Electricity—exports: 3.482 billion kWh (2015
est.)
country comparison to the world: 40

Electricity—imports: 6.104 billion kWh (2015
est.)
country comparison to the world: 35

Electricity—installed generating capacity: 10.08
million kW (2015 est.)
country comparison to the world: 60

Electricity—from fossil fuels: 99.2% of total
installed capacity (2015 est.)
country comparison to the world: 31

Electricity—from nuclear fuels: 0% of total
installed capacity (2015 est.)
country comparison to the world: 56

Electricity—from hydroelectric plants: 0.4% of
total installed capacity (2015 est.)
country comparison to the world: 151

Electricity—from other renewable sources: 0.9%
of total installed capacity (2015 est.)
country comparison to the world: 143

Crude oil—production: 32,670 bbl/day (2016 est.)
country comparison to the world: 61

Crude oil—exports: 31,770 bbl/day (2014 est.)
country comparison to the world: 48

Crude oil—imports: 450,200 bbl/day (2014 est.)
country comparison to the world: 21

Crude oil—proved reserves: 198 million bbl (1
January 2017 es)
country comparison to the world: 59

Refined petroleum products—production: 471,600
bbl/day (2014 est.)
country comparison to the world: 36

Refined petroleum products—consumption:
172,000 bbl/day (2015 est.)
country comparison to the world: 62

Refined petroleum products—exports: 290,300
bbl/day (2014 est.)
country comparison to the world: 27

Refined petroleum products—imports: 2,387 bbl/
day (2014 est.)
country comparison to the world: 184

Natural gas—production: 30 million cu m (2015
est.)
country comparison to the world: 88

Natural gas—consumption: 26.5 billion cu m
(2015 est.)
country comparison to the world: 40

Natural gas—exports: 0 cu m (2016 est.)
country comparison to the world: 73

Natural gas—imports: 17.3 billion cu m (2015
est.)
country comparison to the world: 21

Natural gas—proved reserves: 2.832 billion cu m
(1 January 2017 es)
country comparison to the world: 99

Carbon dioxide emissions from consumption of
energy: 70 million Mt (2013 est.)
country comparison to the world: 50

COMMUNICATIONS

Telephones—fixed lines: *total subscriptions:*
4,515,382
subscriptions per 100 inhabitants: 47 (July 2016
est.)
country comparison to the world: 35

Telephones—mobile cellular: *total:* 11,439,866
subscriptions per 100 inhabitants: 120 (July 2016
est.)
country comparison to the world: 80

Telephone system: *general assessment:* Belarus
lags behind its neighbors in upgrading telecommunications infrastructure; modernization of the network progressing with over two-thirds of switching
equipment now digital
domestic: state-owned Beltelcom is the sole provider of fixed-line local and long distance service;
fixed-line teledensity is improving although rural
areas continue to be underserved; the country
has three major GSM mobile-cellular networks;
mobile-cellular teledensity now approaches 120
telephones per 100 persons
international: country code—375; Belarus is a
member of the Trans-European Line (TEL), Trans-
Asia-Europe (TAE) fiber-optic line, and has access
to the Trans-Siberia Line (TSL); 3 fiber-optic
segments provide connectivity to Latvia, Poland,
Russia, and Ukraine; worldwide service is available
to Belarus through this infrastructure; additional
analog lines to Russia; Intelsat, Eutelsat, and Intersputnik earth stations (2017)

Broadcast media: 7 state-controlled national TV
channels; Polish and Russian TV broadcasts are
available in some areas; state-run Belarusian Radio
operates 5 national networks and an external service; Russian and Polish radio broadcasts are available (2017)

Internet country code: .by

Internet users: *total:* 6,805,786

percent of population: 71.1% (July 2016 est.)
country comparison to the world: 66

TRANSPORTATION

National air transport system: *number of regis-*
tered air carriers: 2
inventory of registered aircraft operated by air
carriers: 30
annual passenger traffic on registered air carri-
ers: 1,489,035
annual freight traffic on registered air carriers:
1.807 million mt-km (2015)
Civil aircraft registration country code prefix:
EW (2016)

Airports: 65 (2013)
country comparison to the world: 75

Airports—with paved runways: *total:* 33
over 3,047 m: 1
2,438 to 3,047 m: 20
1,524 to 2,437 m: 4
914 to 1,523 m: 1
under 914 m: 7 (2017)

Airports—with unpaved runways: *total:* 32
over 3,047 m: 1
1,524 to 2,437 m: 1
914 to 1,523 m: 2
under 914 m: 28 (2013)

Heliports: 1 (2013)

Pipelines: gas 5,386 km; oil 1,589 km; refined
products 1,730 km (2013)

Railways: *total:* 5,528 km
broad gauge: 5,503 km 1.520-m gauge (874 km
electrified)
standard gauge: 25 km 1.435-m gauge (2014)
country comparison to the world: 34

Roadways: *total:* 86,392 km
paved: 74,651 km
unpaved: 11,741 km (2010)
country comparison to the world: 56

Waterways: 2,500 km (major rivers are the west-
flowing Western Dvina and Neman Rivers and the
south-flowing Dnepr River and its tributaries, the
Berezina, Sozh, and Pripyat Rivers) (2011)
country comparison to the world: 35

Merchant marine: *total:* 4
by type: other 4 (2017)
country comparison to the world: 158

Ports and terminals: *river port(s):* Mazyr
(Prypyats')

MILITARY AND SECURITY

Military expenditures: 1.2% of GDP (2016)
1.33% of GDP (2015)
1.33% of GDP (2014)
1.33% of GDP (2013)
1.28% of GDP (2012)
country comparison to the world: 82

Military branches: *Belarus Armed Forces:* Land
Force, Air and Air Defense Force, Special Operations Force (2013)

Military service age and obligation: 18-27 years of
age for compulsory military or alternative service;

conscript service obligation is 12-18 months, depending on academic qualifications, and 24-36 months for alternative service, depending on academic qualifications; 17 year olds are eligible to become cadets at military higher education institutes, where they are classified as military personnel (2016)

TRANSNATIONAL ISSUES

Disputes—international: boundary demarcated with Latvia and Lithuania; as a member state that forms part of the EU's external border, Poland has implemented strict Schengen border rules to restrict illegal immigration and trade along its border with Belarus

Refugees and internally displaced persons: *refugees (country of origin):* 244,621 applicants for forms of legal stay other than asylum (Ukraine) (2017)
stateless persons: 6,182 (2016)

Trafficking in persons: current situation: Belarus is a source, transit, and destination country for women, men, and children subjected to sex trafficking and forced labor; more victims are exploited within Belarus than abroad; Belarusians exploited abroad are primarily trafficked to Germany, Poland, Russian, and Turkey but also other European countries, the Middle East, Japan, Kazakhstan, and Mexico; Moldovans, Russians, Ukrainians, and Vietnamese are exploited in Belarus; state-sponsored forced labor is a continuing problem; students are forced to do farm labor without pay and military conscripts are forced to perform unpaid non-military work; the government has retained a decree forbidding workers in state-owned wood processing factories from leaving their jobs without their employers' permission

tier rating: Tier 3—Belarus does not fully comply with the minimum standards for the elimination of trafficking and was placed on Tier 3 after being on the Tier 2 Watch List for two consecutive years

without making progress; government efforts to repeal state-sponsored forced labor policies and domestic trafficking were inadequate; no trafficking offenders were convicted in 2014, and the number of investigations progressively declined from 2005-14; efforts to protect trafficking victims remain insufficient, with no identification and referral mechanism in place; care facilities were not trafficking-specific and were poorly equipped, leading most victims to seek assistance from private shelters (2015)

Illicit drugs: limited cultivation of opium poppy and cannabis, mostly for the domestic market; transshipment point for illicit drugs to and via Russia, and to the Baltics and Western Europe; a small and lightly regulated financial center; anti-money-laundering legislation does not meet international standards and was weakened further when know-your-customer requirements were curtailed in 2008; few investigations or prosecutions of money-laundering activities

BELGIUM

INTRODUCTION

Background: Belgium became independent from the Netherlands in 1830; it was occupied by Germany during World Wars I and II. The country prospered in the past half century as a modern, technologically advanced European state and member of NATO and the EU. In recent years, political divisions between the Dutch-speaking Flemish of the north and the French-speaking Walloons of the south have led to constitutional amendments granting these regions formal recognition and autonomy. The capital city of Brussels is home to numerous international organizations including the EU and NATO.

GEOGRAPHY

Location: Western Europe, bordering the North Sea, between France and the Netherlands

Geographic coordinates: 50 50 N, 4 00 E

Map references: Europe

Area: *total:* 30,528 sq km
land: 30,278 sq km
water: 250 sq km
country comparison to the world: 141

Area—comparative: about the size of Maryland

Land boundaries: *total:* 1,297 km
border countries (4): France 556 km, Germany 133 km, Luxembourg 130 km, Netherlands 478 km

Coastline: 66.5 km

Maritime claims: *territorial sea:* 12 nm
contiguous zone: 24 nm
exclusive economic zone: geographic coordinates define outer limit
continental shelf: median line with neighbors

Climate: temperate; mild winters, cool summers; rainy, humid, cloudy

Terrain: flat coastal plains in northwest, central rolling hills, rugged mountains of Ardennes Forest in southeast

Elevation: *mean elevation:* 181 m

elevation extremes: *lowest point:* North Sea 0 m
highest point: Botrange 694 m

Natural resources: construction materials, silica sand, carbonates, arable land

Land use: *agricultural land:* 44.1%
arable land: 27.2%;
permanent crops: 0.8%;
permanent pasture: 16.1%
forest: 22.4%
other: 33.5% (2011 est.)
Irrigated land: 230 sq km (2012)

Population—distribution: most of the population concentrated in the northern two-thirds of the

country; the southeast is more thinly populated; considered to have one of the highest population densities in the world; approximately 97% live in urban areas

Natural hazards: flooding is a threat along rivers and in areas of reclaimed coastal land, protected from the sea by concrete dikes

Environment—current issues: intense pressures from human activities: urbanization, dense transportation network, industry, extensive animal breeding and crop cultivation; air and water pollution also have repercussions for neighboring countries

Environment—international agreements: party to: Air Pollution, Air Pollution-Nitrogen Oxides, Air Pollution-Persistent Organic Pollutants, Air Pollution-Sulfur 85, Air Pollution-Sulfur 94, Air Pollution-Volatile Organic Compounds, Antarctic-Environmental Protocol, Antarctic-Marine Living Resources, Antarctic Seals, Antarctic Treaty, Biodiversity, Climate Change, Climate Change-Kyoto Protocol, Desertification, Endangered Species, Environmental Modification, Hazardous Wastes, Law of the Sea, Marine Dumping, Marine Life Conservation, Ozone Layer Protection, Ship Pollution, Tropical Timber 83, Tropical Timber 94, Wetlands, Whaling
signed, but not ratified: none of the selected agreements

Geography—note: crossroads of Western Europe; most West European capitals are within 1,000 km of Brussels, the seat of both the European Union and NATO

PEOPLE AND SOCIETY

Population: 11,491,346 (July 2017 est.)
country comparison to the world: 77

Nationality: *noun:* Belgian(s)
adjective: Belgian

Ethnic groups: Belgian 75%, Italian 4.1%, Moroccan 3.7%, French 2.4%, Turkish 2%, Dutch 2%, other 12.8% (2011 est.)

Languages: Dutch (official) 60%, French (official) 40%, German (official) less than 1%

Religions: Roman Catholic 50%, Protestant and other Christian 2.5%, Muslim 5%, Jewish 0.4%, Buddhist 0.3%, atheist 9.2%, none 32.6% (2009 est.)

Age structure: *0-14 years:* 17.16% (male 1,010,201/female 961,994)
15-24 years: 11.34% (male 665,483/female 637,700)
25-54 years: 40.05% (male 2,320,845/female 2,281,411)
55-64 years: 12.86% (male 732,062/female 746,212)
65 years and over: 18.58% (male 929,594/female 1,205,844) (2017 est.)

Dependency ratios: *total dependency ratio:* 54.2
youth dependency ratio: 26.2
elderly dependency ratio: 28
potential support ratio: 3.6 (2015 est.)

Median age: *total:* 41.4 years
male: 40.2 years
female: 42.7 years (2017 est.)
country comparison to the world: 37

Population growth rate: 0.7% (2017 est.)
country comparison to the world: 143

Birth rate: 11.3 births/1,000 population (2017 est.)
country comparison to the world: 175

Death rate: 9.7 deaths/1,000 population (2017 est.)
country comparison to the world: 46

Net migration rate: 5.4 migrant(s)/1,000 population (2017 est.)
country comparison to the world: 22

Population distribution: most of the population concentrated in the northern two-thirds of the country; the southeast is more thinly populated; considered to have one of the highest population densities in the world; approximately 97% live in urban areas

Urbanization: *urban population:* 97.9% of total population (2017)
rate of urbanization: 0.36% annual rate of change (2015-20 est.)

Major urban areas—population: BRUSSELS (capital) 2.045 million; Antwerp 994,000 (2015)

Sex ratio: *at birth:* 1.05 male(s)/female
0-14 years: 1.05 male(s)/female
15-24 years: 1.04 male(s)/female
25-54 years: 1.02 male(s)/female
55-64 years: 0.98 male(s)/female
65 years and over: 0.76 male(s)/female
total population: 0.97 male(s)/female (2016 est.)

Mother's mean age at first birth: 28.6 years (2013 est.)

Maternal mortality ratio: 7 deaths/100,000 live births (2015 est.)

country comparison to the world: 160

Infant mortality rate: *total:* 3.4 deaths/1,000 live births
male: 3.8 deaths/1,000 live births
female: 3 deaths/1,000 live births (2017 est.)
country comparison to the world: 207

Life expectancy at birth: *total population:* 81.1 years
male: 78.5 years
female: 83.8 years (2017 est.)
country comparison to the world: 30

Total fertility rate: 1.78 children born/woman (2017 est.)
country comparison to the world: 155

Contraceptive prevalence rate: 66.8%
note: percent of women aged 15-54 (2013)
Health expenditures: 10.6% of GDP (2014)
country comparison to the world: 18

Physicians density: 2.97 physicians/1,000 population (2014)

Hospital bed density: 6.5 beds/1,000 population (2012)

Drinking water source:
improved:
urban: 100% of population
rural: 100% of population
total: 100% of population
unimproved:
urban: 0% of population
rural: 0% of population
total: 0% of population (2015 est.)

Sanitation facility access:
improved:
urban: 99.5% of population
rural: 99.4% of population
total: 99.5% of population
unimproved:
urban: 0.5% of population
rural: 0.6% of population
total: 0.5% of population (2015 est.)

HIV/AIDS—adult prevalence rate: NA

HIV/AIDS—people living with HIV/AIDS: NA

HIV/AIDS—deaths: NA

Obesity—adult prevalence rate: 22.1% (2016)
country comparison to the world: 81

Education expenditures: 6.4% of GDP (2011)
country comparison to the world: 30

School life expectancy (primary to tertiary education): *total:* 20 years
male: 19 years
female: 21 years (2014)

Unemployment, youth ages 15-24: *total:* 22.1%
male: 23.8%
female: 20% (2015 est.)
country comparison to the world: 55

GOVERNMENT

Country name: *conventional long form:* Kingdom of Belgium
conventional short form: Belgium

local long form: Royaume de Belgique (French)/ Koninkrijk Belgie (Dutch)/Koenigreich Belgien (German)
local short form: Belgique/Belgie/Belgien
etymology: the name derives from the Belgae, an ancient Celtic tribal confederation that inhabited an area between the English Channel and the west bank of the Rhine in the first centuries B.C.

Government type: federal parliamentary democracy under a constitutional monarchy

Capital: *name:* Brussels

geographic coordinates: 50 50 N, 4 20 E

time difference: UTC+1 (6 hours ahead of Washington, DC, during Standard Time)
daylight saving time: +1hr, begins last Sunday in March; ends last Sunday in October

Administrative divisions: 3 regions (French: regions, singular—region; Dutch: gewesten, singular—gewest); Brussels-Capital Region, also known as Brussels Hoofdstedelijk Gewest (Dutch), Region de Bruxelles-Capitale (French long form), Bruxelles-Capitale (French short form); Flemish Region (Flanders), also known as Vlaams Gewest (Dutch long form), Vlaanderen (Dutch short form), Region Flamande (French long form), Flandre (French short form); Walloon Region (Wallonia), also known as Region Wallone (French long form), Wallonie (French short form), Waals Gewest (Dutch long form), Wallonie (Dutch short form)
note: as a result of the 1993 constitutional revision that furthered devolution into a federal state, there are now three levels of government (federal, regional, and linguistic community) with a complex division of responsibilities; the 2012 sixth state reform transferred additional competencies from the federal state to the regions and linguistic communities

Independence: 4 October 1830 (a provisional government declared independence from the Netherlands); 21 July 1831 (King LEOPOLD I ascended to the throne)

National holiday: Belgian National Day (ascension to the throne of King LEOPOLD I), 21 July (1831)

Constitution: *history:* drafted 25 November 1830, approved 7 February 1831, entered into force 26 July 1831, revised 14 July 1993 (creating a federal state)
amendments: "revisions" proposed as declarations by the federal government in accord with the king or by Parliament followed by dissolution of Parliament and new elections; adoption requires two-thirds majority vote of a two-thirds quorum in both houses of the next elected Parliament; amended many times, last in 2014 (2016)

Legal system: civil law system based on the French Civil Code; note—Belgian law continues to be modified in conformance with the legislative norms mandated by the European Union; judicial review of legislative acts

International law organization participation: accepts compulsory ICJ jurisdiction with reservations; accepts ICCt jurisdiction

Citizenship: *citizenship by birth:* no
citizenship by descent only: at least one parent must be a citizen of Belgium
dual citizenship recognized: yes
residency requirement for naturalization: 5 years

Suffrage: 18 years of age; universal and compulsory

Executive branch: *chief of state:* King PHILIPPE (since 21 July 2013); Heir Apparent Princess ELISABETH, daughter of the monarch

head of government: Prime Minister Charles MICHEL (since 11 October 2014); Deputy Prime Ministers Alexander DE CROO (since 22 October 2012), Jan JAMBON (since 11 October 2014), Kris PEETERS, Didier REYNDERS (since 30 December 2008)
cabinet: Council of Ministers formally appointed by the monarch
elections/appointments: the monarchy is hereditary and constitutional; following legislative elections, the leader of the majority party or majority coalition usually appointed prime minister by the monarch and approved by Parliament

Legislative branch: *description:* bicameral Parliament consists of the Senate or Senaat (in Dutch), Senat (in French) (60 seats; 50 members indirectly elected by the community and regional parliaments based on their election results, and 10 elected by the 50 other senators; members serve 5-year terms) and the Chamber of Representatives or Kamer van Volksvertegenwoordigers (in Dutch), Chambre des Representants (in French) (150 seats; members directly elected in multi-seat constituencies by proportional representation vote; members serve 5-year terms)
note: the 1993 constitutional revision that further devolved Belgium into a federal state created three levels of government (federal, regional, and linguistic community) with a complex division of responsibilities; this reality leaves six governments, each with its own legislative assembly; changes above occurred since the sixth state reform
elections: Chamber of Representatives—last held on 25 May 2014 (next to be held in May 2019); note—elections will coincide with the EU's elections
election results: Chamber of Representatives—percent of vote by party—N-VA 20.3%, PS 11.7%, CD&V 11.6%, Open VLD 9.8%, MR 9.6%, SP.A 8.8%, Groen! 5.3%, CDH 5.0% Workers' Party 3.7%, VB 3.7%, Ecolo 3.3%, Defi 1.8%, PP 1.5%, other 3.9%; seats by party—N-VA 33, PS 23, MR 20, CD&V 18, Open VLD 14, SP.A 13, Groen! 6, CDH 9, Workers' Party 2, VB 3, Ecolo 6, Defi 2, PP 1

Judicial branch: *highest court(s):* Constitutional Court or Grondwettelijk Hof in Dutch and Cour constitutionelle in French (consists of 12 judges—6 Dutch-speaking and 6 French-speaking); Supreme Court of Justice or Hof van Cassatie in Dutch and Cour de Cassation in French (court organized into 3 chambers: civil and commercial; criminal; social, fiscal, and armed forces; each chamber includes a Dutch division and a French division, each with a chairperson and 5-6 judges)

judge selection and term of office: Constitutional Court judges appointed by the monarch from candidates submitted by Parliament; judges appointed for life with mandatory retirement at age 70; Supreme Court judges appointed by the monarch from candidates submitted by the High Council of Justice, a 44-member independent body of judicial and non-judicial members; judges appointed for life
subordinate courts: Courts of Appeal; regional courts; specialized courts for administrative, commercial, labor, immigration, and audit issues; magistrate's courts; justices of the peace

Political parties and leaders: Flemish parties: Christian Democratic and Flemish or CD&V [Wouter BEKE]
Flemish Liberals and Democrats or Open VLD [Gwendolyn RUTTEN]
Groen [Meyrem ALMACI] (formerly AGALEV, Flemish Greens)
New Flemish Alliance or N-VA [Bart DE WEVER]
Social Progressive Alternative or SP.A [John CROMBEZ and Stephanie VAN HOUTVEN]
Vlaams Belang (Flemish Interest) or VB [Tom VAN GRIEKEN]
Francophone parties: Ecolo (Francophone Greens) [Patrick DUPRIEZ and Zakia KHATTABI]
Francophone Federalist Democrats or Defi [Olivier MAINGAIN]
Humanist and Democratic Center or CDH [Benoit LUTGEN]
People's Party or PP [Mischael MODRIKAMEN]
Reform Movement or MR [Olivier CHASTEL]
Socialist Party or PS [Elio DI RUPO]
Workers' Party or PTB [Peter MERTENS]
other minor parties

Political pressure groups and leaders: Belgian General Federation of Labor or ABVV or FGTB [Rudy DE LEEUW, Marc GOBLET]
Confederation of Christian Trade Unions or ACV or CSC [Marc LEEMANS, Marie-Helene SKA]
Federation of Enterprises in Belgium or VBO or FEB [Pieter TIMMERMANS, Bernard GILLIOT]
other: numerous other associations representing bankers, manufacturers, middle-class artisans, and the legal and medical professions; trade unions; various organizations representing the cultural interests of Flanders and Wallonia; various peace groups such as BEPax and groups representing immigrants

International organization participation: ADB (nonregional members), AfDB (nonregional members), Australia Group, Benelux, BIS, CD, CE, CERN, EAPC, EBRD, ECB, EIB, EITI (implementing country), EMU, ESA, EU, FAO, FATF, G-9, G-10, IADB, IAEA, IBRD, ICAO, ICC (national committees), ICCt, ICRM, IDA, IEA, IFAD, IFC, IFRCS, IGAD (partners), IHO, ILO, IMF, IMO, IMSO, Interpol, IOC, IOM, IPU, ISO, ITSO, ITU, ITUC (NGOs), MIGA, MONUSCO, NATO, NEA, NSG, OAS (observer), OECD, OIF, OPCW, OSCE, Pacific Alliance (observer), Paris Club, PCA, Schengen Convention, SELEC (observer), UN, UNCTAD, UNESCO, UNHCR, UNIDO, UNIFIL,

UNRWA, UNTSO, UPU, WCO, WHO, WIPO, WMO, WTO, ZC

Diplomatic representation in the US: *chief of mission:* Ambassador Dirk Jozef M. WOUTERS (since 16 September 2016)
chancery: 3330 Garfield Street NW, Washington, DC 20008
telephone: [1] (202) 333-6900
FAX: [1] (202) 333-3079
consulate(s) general: Atlanta, Los Angeles, New York

Diplomatic representation from the US: *chief of mission:* Ambassador (vacant); Charge d'Affaires Matthew LUSSENHOP (since 21 January 2017)
embassy: 27 Boulevard du Regent [Regentlaan], B-1000 Brussels
mailing address: PSC 82, Box 002, APO AE 09710
telephone: [32] (2) 811-4000
FAX: [32] (2) 811-4500

Flag description: three equal vertical bands of black (hoist side), yellow, and red; the vertical design was based on the flag of France; the colors are those of the arms of the duchy of Brabant (yellow lion with red claws and tongue on a black field)

National symbol(s): golden rampant lion; national colors: red, black, yellow

National anthem: *name:* "La Brabanconne" (The Song of Brabant)
lyrics/music: Louis-Alexandre DECHET[French] Victor CEULEMANS [Dutch]/Francois VAN CAMPENHOUT
note: adopted 1830; according to legend, Louis-Alexandre DECHET, an actor at the theater in which the revolution against the Netherlands began, wrote the lyrics with a group of young people in a Brussels cafe

ECONOMY

Economy—overview: Belgium's central geographic location and highly developed transport network have helped develop a well-diversified economy, with a broad mix of transport, services, manufacturing, and high tech. Service and high-tech industries are concentrated in the northern Flanders region while the southern region of Wallonia is home to industries like coal and steel manufacturing. Belgium is completely reliant on foreign sources of fossil fuels, and the planned closure of its seven nuclear plants by 2025 should increase its dependence on foreign energy. Its role as a regional logistical hub makes its economy vulnerable to shifts in foreign demand, particularly with EU trading partners. Roughly three-quarters of Belgium's trade is with other EU countries, and the port of Zeebrugge conducts almost half its trade with the United Kingdom alone, leaving Belgium's economy vulnerable to the outcome of negotiations on the UK's exit from the EU.

Belgium's GDP grew by 1.7% in 2017 and the budget deficit was 1.5% of GDP. Unemployment stood at 7.3%, however the unemployment rate is lower in Flanders than Wallonia, 4.4% compared to 9.4%, because of industrial differences between the regions. The economy largely recovered from the March 2016 terrorist attacks that mainly impacted the Brussels region tourist and hospitality industry. Prime Minister Charles MICHEL's center-right government has pledged to further reduce the deficit in response to EU pressure to decrease Belgium's high public debt of about 104% of GDP, but such efforts could also dampen economic growth. In addition to restrained public spending, low wage growth and higher inflation promise to curtail a more robust recovery in private consumption.

The government has pledged to pursue a reform program to improve Belgium's competitiveness, including changes to labor market rules and welfare benefits. These changes have generally made Belgian wages more competitive regionally, but risk worsening tensions with trade unions and triggering extended strikes. In 2017, Belgium approved a tax reform plan to ease corporate rates from 33% to 29% by 2018 and down to 25% by 2020. The tax plan also included benefits for innovation and SMEs, intended to spur competitiveness and private investment.

GDP (purchasing power parity): $526.4 billion (2017 est.)
$517.9 billion (2016 est.)
$511.8 billion (2015 est.)
note: data are in 2017 dollars
country comparison to the world: 38

GDP (official exchange rate): $491.7 billion (2016 est.)

GDP—real growth rate: 1.6% (2017 est.)
1.2% (2016 est.)
1.5% (2015 est.)
country comparison to the world: 170

GDP—per capita (PPP): $46,300 (2017 est.)
$45,800 (2016 est.)
$45,500 (2015 est.)
note: data are in 2017 dollars
country comparison to the world: 35

Gross national saving: 23.2% of GDP (2017 est.)
22.3% of GDP (2016 est.)
23.6% of GDP (2015 est.)
country comparison to the world: 64

GDP—composition, by end use:
household consumption: 50.8%
government consumption: 23.3%
investment in fixed capital: 23%
investment in inventories: 0.5%
exports of goods and services: 87.7%
imports of goods and services: -85.3% (2017 est.)

GDP—composition, by sector of origin:
agriculture: 0.7%
industry: 21.8%
services: 77.5% (2017 est.)

Agriculture—products: sugar beets, fresh vegetables, fruits, grain, tobacco; beef, veal, pork, milk

Industries: engineering and metal products, motor vehicle assembly, transportation equipment, scientific instruments, processed food and beverages, chemicals, pharmaceuticals, base metals, textiles, glass, petroleum

Industrial production growth rate: 1.5% (2017 est.)
country comparison to the world: 150

Labor force: 5.324 million (2017 est.)
country comparison to the world: 79

Labor force—by occupation: *agriculture:* 1.3%
industry: 18.6%
services: 80.1% (2013 est.)

Unemployment rate: 7.5% (2017 est.)
7.9% (2016 est.)
country comparison to the world: 105

Population below poverty line: 15.1% (2013 est.)

Household income or consumption by percentage share: *lowest 10%:* 3.4%
highest 10%: 28.4% (2006)

Distribution of family income—Gini index: 25.9 (2013 est.)
28.7 (1996)
country comparison to the world: 143

Budget: *revenues:* $249.7 billion
expenditures: $260 billion (2017 est.)
Taxes and other revenues: 50.8% of GDP (2017 est.)
country comparison to the world: 14

Budget surplus (+) or deficit (-): -2.1% of GDP (2017 est.)
country comparison to the world: 88

Public debt: 104.3% of GDP (2017 est.)
106% of GDP (2016 est.)
note: data cover general government debt, and includes debt instruments issued (or owned) by government entities other than the treasury; the data include treasury debt held by foreign entities; the data include debt issued by subnational entities, as well as intra-governmental debt; intra-governmental debt consists of treasury borrowings from surpluses in the social funds, such as for retirement, medical care, and unemployment; debt instruments for the social funds are not sold at public auctions; general government debt is defined by the Maastricht definition and calculated by the National Bank of Belgium as consolidated gross debt; the debt is defined in European Regulation EC479/2009 concerning the implementation of the protocol on the excessive deficit procedure annexed to the Treaty on European Union (Treaty of Maastricht) of 7 February 1992; the sub-sectors of consolidated gross debt are: federal government, communities and regions, local government, and social security funds
country comparison to the world: 16

Fiscal year: calendar year

Inflation rate (consumer prices): 2.2% (2017 est.)
1.8% (2016 est.)
country comparison to the world: 104

Central bank discount rate: 0.25% (31 December 2016)
0.3% (31 December 2010)
note: this is the European Central Bank's rate on the marginal lending facility, which offers overnight credit to banks in the euro area
country comparison to the world: 142

Commercial bank prime lending rate: 2% (31 December 2017 est.)

2.01% (31 December 2016 est.)
country comparison to the world: 178

Stock of narrow money: $238 billion (31 December 2017 est.)
$198 billion (31 December 2016 est.)
note: see entry for the European Union for money supply for the entire euro area; the European Central Bank (ECB) controls monetary policy for the 18 members of the Economic and Monetary Union (EMU); individual members of the EMU do not control the quantity of money circulating within their own borders
country comparison to the world: 22

Stock of broad money: $601.3 billion (31 December 2017 est.)
$525.8 billion (31 December 2016 est.)
country comparison to the world: 21

Stock of domestic credit: $783.2 billion (31 December 2017 est.)
$684.8 billion (31 December 2016 est.)
country comparison to the world: 20

Market value of publicly traded shares: $414.6 billion (31 December 2015 est.)
$378.5 billion (31 December 2014 est.)
$374.3 billion (31 December 2013 est.)
country comparison to the world: 25

Current account balance: -$1.47 billion (2017 est.)
-$1.849 billion (2016 est.)
country comparison to the world: 145

Exports: $309.1 billion (2017 est.)
$277.7 billion (2016 est.)
country comparison to the world: 19

Exports—commodities: chemicals, machinery and equipment, finished diamonds, metals and metal products, foodstuffs

Exports—partners: Germany 16.7%, France 15.4%, Netherlands 11.2%, UK 8.9%, US 5.8%, Italy 5.2% (2016)

Imports: $306.1 billion (2017 est.)
$271.2 billion (2016 est.)
country comparison to the world: 17

Imports—commodities: raw materials, machinery and equipment, chemicals, raw diamonds, pharmaceuticals, foodstuffs, transportation equipment, oil products

Imports—partners: Netherlands 16.1%, Germany 13.6%, France 9.5%, US 8.1%, UK 4.8%, Ireland 4.5%, China 4.3% (2016)

Reserves of foreign exchange and gold: $23.57 billion (31 December 2016 est.)
$24.1 billion (31 December 2015 est.)
country comparison to the world: 55

Debt—external: $1.281 trillion (31 March 2016 est.)
$1.214 trillion (31 March 2015 est.)
country comparison to the world: 16

Stock of direct foreign investment—at home: $1.093 trillion (31 December 2017 est.)
$1.054 trillion (31 December 2016 est.)
country comparison to the world: 11

Stock of direct foreign investment—abroad: $1.035 trillion (31 December 2017 est.)

$1.016 trillion (31 December 2016 est.)
country comparison to the world: 13

Exchange rates: euros (EUR) per US dollar—
0.906 (2017 est.)
0.9214 (2016 est.)
0.9214 (2015 est.)
0.885 (2014 est.)
0.7634 (2013 est.)

ENERGY

Electricity access: electrification—*total population:* 100% (2016)

Electricity—production: 64.78 billion kWh (2015 est.)
country comparison to the world: 43

Electricity—consumption: 81.96 billion kWh (2015 est.)
country comparison to the world: 36

Electricity—exports: 8.465 billion kWh (2016 est.)
country comparison to the world: 27

Electricity—imports: 14.65 billion kWh (2016 est.)
country comparison to the world: 15

Electricity—installed generating capacity: 21.15 million kW (2015 est.)
country comparison to the world: 43

Electricity—from fossil fuels: 34.8% of total installed capacity (2015 est.)
country comparison to the world: 178

Electricity—from nuclear fuels: 28% of total installed capacity (2015 est.)
country comparison to the world: 3

Electricity—from hydroelectric plants: 0.5% of total installed capacity (2015 est.)
country comparison to the world: 150

Electricity—from other renewable sources: 32.1% of total installed capacity (2015 est.)
country comparison to the world: 11

Crude oil—production: 0 bbl/day (2016 est.)
country comparison to the world: 109

Crude oil—exports: 0 bbl/day (2016 est.)
country comparison to the world: 94

Crude oil—imports: 639,500 bbl/day (2016 est.)
country comparison to the world: 16

Crude oil—proved reserves: 0 bbl (1 January 2017 es)
country comparison to the world: 109

Refined petroleum products—production: 701,700 bbl/day (2016 est.)
country comparison to the world: 25

Refined petroleum products—consumption: 662,400 bbl/day (2016 est.)
country comparison to the world: 31

Refined petroleum products—exports: 597,000 bbl/day (2016 est.)
country comparison to the world: 12

Refined petroleum products—imports: 585,700 bbl/day (2016 est.)
country comparison to the world: 13

Natural gas—production: 0 cu m (2014 est.)

country comparison to the world: 108

Natural gas—consumption: 23.01 billion cu m (2015 est.)
country comparison to the world: 41

Natural gas—exports: 1.694 billion cu m (2015 est.)
country comparison to the world: 39

Natural gas—imports: 18.81 billion cu m (2015 est.)
country comparison to the world: 18

Natural gas—proved reserves: 0 cu m (1 January 2014 es)
country comparison to the world: 115

Carbon dioxide emissions from consumption of energy: 93.62 million Mt (2013 est.)
country comparison to the world: 41

COMMUNICATIONS

Telephones—fixed lines: *total subscriptions:* 4,371,055
subscriptions per 100 inhabitants: 38 (July 2016 est.)
country comparison to the world: 32

Telephones—mobile cellular: *total:* 12,457,820
subscriptions per 100 inhabitants: 109 (July 2016 est.)
country comparison to the world: 73

Telephone system: *general assessment:* highly developed, technologically advanced, and completely automated domestic and international telephone and telegraph facilities
domestic: nationwide mobile-cellular telephone system; extensive cable network; limited microwave radio relay network
international: country code—32; landing point for a number of submarine cables that provide links to Europe, the Middle East, and Asia; satellite earth stations—7 (Intelsat—3) (2015)

Broadcast media: a segmented market with the three major communities (Flemish, French, and German-speaking) each having responsibility for their own broadcast media; multiple TV channels exist for each community; additionally, in excess of 90% of households are connected to cable and can access broadcasts of TV stations from neighboring countries; each community has a public radio network coexisting with private broadcasters (2009)

Internet country code: .be

Internet users: *total:* 9,870,734
percent of population: 86.5% (July 2016 est.)
country comparison to the world: 46

TRANSPORTATION

National air transport system: *number of registered air carriers:* 7
inventory of registered aircraft operated by air carriers: 117
annual passenger traffic on registered air carriers: 11,193,023
annual freight traffic on registered air carriers: 1,464,316,900 mt-km (2015)
Civil aircraft registration country code prefix: OO (2016)

Airports: 41 (2013)
country comparison to the world: 102

Airports—with paved runways: *total:* 26
over 3,047 m: 6
2,438 to 3,047 m: 9
1,524 to 2,437 m: 2
914 to 1,523 m: 1
under 914 m: 8 (2017)

Airports—with unpaved runways: *total:* 15
under 914 m: 15 (2013)

Heliports: 1 (2013)

Pipelines: gas 3,139 km; oil 154 km; refined products 535 km (2013)

Railways: *total:* 3,592 km
standard gauge: 3,592 km 1.435-m gauge (2,960 km electrified) (2014)
country comparison to the world: 50

Roadways: *total:* 154,012 km
paved: 120,514 km (includes 1,756 km of expressways)
unpaved: 33,498 km (2010)
country comparison to the world: 33

Waterways: 2,043 km (1,528 km in regular commercial use) (2012)
country comparison to the world: 41

Merchant marine: *total:* 185
by type: bulk carrier 15, general cargo 15, oil tanker 20, other 135 (2017)
country comparison to the world: 65

Ports and terminals: *major seaport(s):* Oostende, Zeebrugge
river port(s): Antwerp, Gent (Schelde River); Brussels (Senne River); Liege (Meuse River)
container port(s) (TEUs): Antwerp (9,654,000), Zeebrugge (1,569,000) (2015)
LNG terminal(s) (import): Zeebrugge

MILITARY AND SECURITY

Military expenditures: 0.87% of GDP (2016)
0.93% of GDP (2015)
0.97% of GDP (2014)
1.01% of GDP (2013)
1.04% of GDP (2012)
country comparison to the world: 97

Military branches: Belgian Armed Forces: Land Operations Command, Naval Operations Command, Air Operations Command (2012)

Military service age and obligation: 18 years of age for male and female voluntary military service; conscription abolished in 1994 (2012)

TERRORISM

Terrorist groups—foreign based: *Islamic State of Iraq and the Levant (ISIL): aim(s):* destabilize Belgium's economy and government
area(s) of operation: remains operational; responsible for twin bombings in Belgium at the Brussels Airport and Maelbeek metro station near the European Union headquarters on 22 March 2016, killing 32 civilians and injuring at least 200; In Europe, Belgium is a top source country for ISIL recruits, where recruiters target youth; as of early

2017, approximately 450 Belgian citizens were fighting in Syria or Iraq alongside ISIL, planning to go to fight, or had returned from the fight

TRANSNATIONAL ISSUES

Disputes—international: none

Refugees and internally displaced persons: *refugees (country of origin):* 9,080 (Syria) (2016) *stateless persons:* 2,630 (2016)

Illicit drugs: growing producer of synthetic drugs and cannabis; transit point for US-bound ecstasy; source of precursor chemicals for South American

cocaine processors; transshipment point for cocaine, heroin, hashish, and marijuana entering Western Europe; despite a strengthening of legislation, the country remains vulnerable to money laundering related to narcotics, automobiles, alcohol, and tobacco; significant domestic consumption of ecstasy

BELIZE

border countries (2): Guatemala 266 km, Mexico 276 km

Coastline: 386 km

Maritime claims: *territorial sea:* 12 nm in the north, 3 nm in the south; note—from the mouth of the Sarstoon River to Ranguana Cay, Belize's territorial sea is 3 nm; according to Belize's Maritime Areas Act, 1992, the purpose of this limitation is to provide a framework for negotiating a definitive agreement on territorial differences with Guatemala

exclusive economic zone: 200 nm

Climate: tropical; very hot and humid; rainy season (May to November); dry season (February to May)

Terrain: flat, swampy coastal plain; low mountains in south

Elevation: *mean elevation:* 173 m

elevation extremes: lowest point: Caribbean Sea 0 m

highest point: Doyle's Delight 1,124 m

Natural resources: arable land: potential, timber, fish, hydropower

Land use: *agricultural land:* 6.9%

arable land: 3.3%;

permanent crops: 1.4%;

permanent pasture: 2.2%

forest: 60.6%

other: 32.5% (2011 est.)

Irrigated land: 35 sq km (2012)

Population—distribution: approximately 25% to 30% of the population lives in the former capital, Belize City; over half of the overall population is rural; population density is slightly higher in the north and east

Natural hazards: frequent, devastating hurricanes (June to November) and coastal flooding (especially in south)

Environment—current issues: deforestation; water pollution from sewage, industrial effluents, agricultural runoff; solid and sewage waste disposal

Environment—international agreements: party to: Biodiversity, Climate Change, Climate Change-Kyoto Protocol, Desertification, Endangered Species, Hazardous Wastes, Law of the Sea, Ozone Layer Protection, Ship Pollution, Wetlands, Whaling

signed, but not ratified: none of the selected agreements

Geography—note: only country in Central America without a coastline on the North Pacific Ocean

PEOPLE AND SOCIETY

Population: 360,346 (July 2017 est.) *country comparison to the world:* 177

Nationality: *noun:* Belizean(s) *adjective:* Belizean

Ethnic groups: mestizo 52.9%, Creole 25.9%, Maya 11.3%, Garifuna 6.1%, East Indian 3.9%, Mennonite 3.6%, white 1.2%, Asian 1%, other 1.2%, unknown 0.3%

note: percentages add up to more than 100% because respondents were able to identify more than one ethnic origin (2010 est.)

Languages: English 62.9% (official), Spanish 56.6%, Creole 44.6%, Maya 10.5%, German 3.2%, Garifuna 2.9%, other 1.8%, unknown 0.3%, none 0.2% (cannot speak)

note: shares sum to more than 100% because some respondents gave more than one answer on the census (2010 est.)

Religions: Roman Catholic 40.1%, Protestant 31.5% (includes Pentecostal 8.4%, Seventh Day Adventist 5.4%, Anglican 4.7%, Mennonite 3.7%, Baptist 3.6%, Methodist 2.9%, Nazarene 2.8%), Jehovah's Witness 1.7%, other 10.5% (includes Baha'i, Buddhist, Hindu, Mormon, Muslim, Rastafarian, Salvation Army), unspecified 0.6%, none 15.5% (2010 est.)

Demographic profile: Migration continues to transform Belize's population. About 16% of Belizeans live abroad, while immigrants constitute approximately 15% of Belize's population. Belizeans seeking job and educational opportunities have preferred to emigrate to the United States rather than former colonizer Great Britain because of the United States' closer proximity and stronger trade ties with Belize. Belizeans also emigrate to Canada, Mexico, and English-speaking Caribbean countries. The emigration of a large share of Creoles (Afro-Belizeans) and the influx of Central American immigrants, mainly Guatemalans, Salvadorans, and Hondurans, has changed Belize's ethnic composition. Mestizos have become the largest ethnic group, and Belize now has more native Spanish speakers than English or Creole speakers, despite English being the official language. In addition, Central American immigrants are establishing new communities in rural areas, which contrasts with the urbanization trend seen

INTRODUCTION

Background: Belize was the site of several Mayan city states until their decline at the end of the first millennium A.D. The British and Spanish disputed the region in the 17th and 18th centuries; it formally became the colony of British Honduras in 1862. Territorial disputes between the UK and Guatemala delayed the independence of Belize until 1981. Guatemala refused to recognize the new nation until 1992 and the two countries are involved in an ongoing border dispute. Tourism has become the mainstay of the economy. Current concerns include the country's heavy foreign debt burden, high unemployment, growing involvement in the Mexican and South American drug trade, high crime rates, and one of the highest HIV/AIDS prevalence rates in Central America.

GEOGRAPHY

Location: Central America, bordering the Caribbean Sea, between Guatemala and Mexico

Geographic coordinates: 17 15 N, 88 45 W

Map references: Central America and the Caribbean

Area: *total:* 22,966 sq km

land: 22,806 sq km

water: 160 sq km

country comparison to the world: 152

Area—comparative: slightly smaller than Massachusetts

Land boundaries: *total:* 542 km

in neighboring countries. Recently, Chinese, European, and North American immigrants have become more frequent.

Immigration accounts for an increasing share of Belize's population growth rate, which is steadily falling due to fertility decline. Belize's declining birth rate and its increased life expectancy are creating an aging population. As the elderly population grows and nuclear families replace extended households, Belize's government will be challenged to balance a rising demand for pensions, social services, and healthcare for its senior citizens with the need to reduce poverty and social inequality and to improve sanitation.

Age structure: *0-14 years:* 33.95% (male 62,454/female 59,896)
15-24 years: 20.55% (male 37,730/female 36,339)
25-54 years: 36.62% (male 66,880/female 65,082)
55-64 years: 4.99% (male 8,834/female 9,130)
65 years and over: 3.89% (male 6,562/female 7,439) (2017 est.)

Dependency ratios: *total dependency ratio:* 56.8
youth dependency ratio: 50.9
elderly dependency ratio: 5.9
potential support ratio: 17 (2015 est.)

Median age: *total:* 22.7 years
male: 22.5 years
female: 22.9 years (2017 est.)
country comparison to the world: 176

Population growth rate: 1.8% (2017 est.)
country comparison to the world: 58

Birth rate: 24 births/1,000 population (2017 est.)
country comparison to the world: 53

Death rate: 6 deaths/1,000 population (2017 est.)
country comparison to the world: 164

Net migration rate: 0 migrant(s)/1,000 population (2017 est.)
country comparison to the world: 73

Population distribution: approximately 25% to 30% of the population lives in the former capital, Belize City; over half of the overall population is rural; population density is slightly higher in the north and east

Urbanization: *urban population:* 43.7% of total population (2017)
rate of urbanization: 1.93% annual rate of change (2015-20 est.)

Major urban areas—population: BELMOPAN (capital) 17,000 (2014)

Sex ratio: *at birth:* 1.05 male(s)/female
0-14 years: 1.04 male(s)/female
15-24 years: 1.04 male(s)/female
25-54 years: 1.03 male(s)/female
55-64 years: 0.97 male(s)/female
65 years and over: 0.89 male(s)/female
total population: 1.03 male(s)/female (2016 est.)

Maternal mortality ratio: 28 deaths/100,000 live births (2015 est.)
country comparison to the world: 116

Infant mortality rate: *total:* 18.9 deaths/1,000 live births
male: 21.3 deaths/1,000 live births
female: 16.4 deaths/1,000 live births (2017 est.)

country comparison to the world: 85

Life expectancy at birth: *total population:* 68.9 years
male: 67.3 years
female: 70.6 years (2017 est.)
country comparison to the world: 163

Total fertility rate: 2.85 children born/woman (2017 est.)
country comparison to the world: 59

Contraceptive prevalence rate: 51.4% (2015)
Health expenditures: 5.8% of GDP (2014)
country comparison to the world: 109

Physicians density: 0.77 physicians/1,000 population (2009)

Hospital bed density: 1.1 beds/1,000 population (2012)

Drinking water source:
improved:
urban: 98.9% of population
rural: 100% of population
total: 99.5% of population
unimproved:
urban: 1.1% of population
rural: 0% of population
total: 0.5% of population (2015 est.)

Sanitation facility access:
improved:
urban: 93.5% of population
rural: 88.2% of population
total: 90.5% of population
unimproved:
urban: 6.5% of population
rural: 11.8% of population
total: 9.5% of population (2015 est.)

HIV/AIDS—adult prevalence rate: 1.8% (2016 est.)
country comparison to the world: 27

HIV/AIDS—people living with HIV/AIDS: 4,300 (2016 est.)
country comparison to the world: 107

HIV/AIDS—deaths: <200 (2016 est.)

Major infectious diseases: *degree of risk:* high
food or waterborne diseases: bacterial diarrhea, hepatitis A, and typhoid fever
vectorborne diseases: dengue fever and malaria
note: active local transmission of Zika virus by Aedes species mosquitoes has been identified in this country (as of August 2016); it poses an important risk (a large number of cases possible) among US citizens if bitten by an infective mosquito; other less common ways to get Zika are through sex, via blood transfusion, or during pregnancy, in which the pregnant woman passes Zika virus to her fetus (2016)

Obesity—adult prevalence rate: 24.1% (2016)
country comparison to the world: 60

Children under the age of 5 years underweight: 4.6% (2015)
country comparison to the world: 81

Education expenditures: 6.2% of GDP (2013)
country comparison to the world: 29

School life expectancy (primary to tertiary education): *total:* 13 years
male: 13 years
female: 13 years (2015)

Unemployment, youth ages 15-24: *total:* 18.9%
male: 12.1%
female: 29.6% (2015 est.)
country comparison to the world: 56

GOVERNMENT

Country name: *conventional long form:* none
conventional short form: Belize
former: British Honduras
etymology: may be named for the Belize River, whose name possibly derives from the Maya word "belix," meaning "muddy-watered"

Government type: parliamentary democracy (National Assembly) under a constitutional monarchy; a Commonwealth realm

Capital: *name:* Belmopan

geographic coordinates: 17 15 N, 88 46 W

time difference: UTC-6 (1 hour behind Washington, DC, during Standard Time)

Administrative divisions: 6 districts; Belize, Cayo, Corozal, Orange Walk, Stann Creek, Toledo

Independence: 21 September 1981 (from the UK)

National holiday: Battle of St. George's Caye Day (National Day), 10 September (1798); Independence Day, 21 September (1981)

Constitution: previous 1954, 1963 (preindependence); latest signed and entered into force 21 September 1981; amended several times, last in 2012 (2016)

Legal system: English common law

International law organization participation: has not submitted an ICJ jurisdiction declaration; accepts ICCt jurisdiction

Citizenship: *citizenship by birth:* yes
citizenship by descent: yes
dual citizenship recognized: yes
residency requirement for naturalization: 5 years

Suffrage: 18 years of age; universal

Executive branch: *chief of state:* Queen ELIZABETH II (since 6 February 1952); represented by Governor General Sir Colville Norbert YOUNG, Sr. (since 17 November 1993)

head of government: Prime Minister Dean Oliver BARROW (since 8 February 2008); Deputy Prime Minister Patrick FABER (since 7 June 2016)
cabinet: Cabinet appointed by the governor general on the advice of the prime minister from among members of the National Assembly
elections/appointments: the monarchy is hereditary; governor general appointed by the monarch; following legislative elections, the leader of the majority party or majority coalition usually appointed prime minister by the governor general; prime minister recommends the deputy prime minister

Legislative branch: *description:* bicameral National Assembly consists of the Senate (12 seats; members appointed by the governor general—6 on the advice of the prime minister, 3 on the advice of the leader of the opposition, and 1 each on the advice of the Belize Council of Churches and Evangelical Association of Churches, the Belize Chamber of Commerce and Industry and the Belize Better Business Bureau, and the National Trade Union Congress and the Civil Society Steering Committee; members serve 5-year terms) and the House of Representatives (31 seats; members directly elected in single-seat constituencies by simple majority vote to serve 5-year terms)

elections: House of Representatives—last held on 4 November 2015 (next to be held in November 2020)

election results: percent of vote by party—UDP 50%, PUP 47.3%, other 2.7%; seats by party—UDP 19, PUP 12

Judicial branch: *highest court(s):* Supreme Court of Judicature (consists of the Court of Appeal with the court president and 3 justices, and the Supreme Court with the chief justice and 2 judges); note—in 2010, Belize ceased final appeals in civil and criminal cases to the Judicial Committee of the Privy Council (in London) and acceded to the Caribbean Court of Justice

judge selection and term of office: Court of Appeal president and justices appointed by the governor general upon advice of the prime minister after consultation with the National Assembly opposition leader; justices' tenures vary by terms of appointment; Supreme Court chief justice appointed by the governor-general upon the advice of the prime minister and the National Assembly opposition leader; other judges appointed by the governor-general upon the advice of the Judicial and Legal Services Section of the Public Services Commission and with the concurrence of the prime minister after consultation with the National Assembly opposition leader; judges can be appointed beyond age 65 but must retire by age 75; in 2013, the Supreme Court chief justice overturned a constitutional amendment that had restricted Court of Appeal judge appointments to as short as 1 year

subordinate courts: Magistrate Courts; Family Court

Political parties and leaders: Belize Progressive Party or BPP [Patrick ROGERS] (formed in 2015 from a merger of the People's National Party, elements of the Vision Inspired by the People, and other smaller political groups)
People's United Party or PUP [Johnny BRICENO]
United Democratic Party or UDP [Dean Oliver BARROW]

Political pressure groups and leaders: National Trade Union Congress of Belize or NTUCB [Floyd NEAL]

International organization participation: ACP, AOSIS, C, Caricom, CD, CDB, CELAC, FAO, G-77, IADB, IAEA, IBRD, ICAO, ICC (NGOs), ICRM, IDA, IFAD, IFC, IFRCS, ILO, IMF, IMO, Interpol, IOC, IOM, ITU, LAES, MIGA, NAM, OAS, OPANAL, OPCW, PCA, Petrocaribe,

SICA, UN, UNCTAD, UNESCO, UNIDO, UPU, WCO, WHO, WIPO, WMO, WTO

Diplomatic representation in the US: *chief of mission:* Ambassador Francisco Daniel GUTIERREZ (since 21 July 2017)
chancery: 2535 Massachusetts Avenue NW, Washington, DC 20008
telephone: [1] (202) 332-9636
FAX: [1] (202) 332-6888
consulate(s) general: Los Angeles

Diplomatic representation from the US: *chief of mission:* Ambassador (vacant); Charge d'Affaires Adrienne GALANEK (since 20 January 2017)
embassy: Floral Park Road, Belmopan City, Cayo District
mailing address: P.O. Box 497, Belmopan City, Cayo District, Belize
telephone: [011] (501) 822-4011
FAX: [011] (501) 822-4012

Flag description: royal blue with a narrow red stripe along the top and the bottom edges; centered is a large white disk bearing the coat of arms; the coat of arms features a shield flanked by two workers in front of a mahogany tree with the related motto SUB UMBRA FLOREO (I Flourish in the Shade) on a scroll at the bottom, all encircled by a green garland of 50 mahogany leaves; the colors are those of the two main political parties: blue for the PUP and red for the UDP; various elements of the coat of arms—the figures, the tools, the mahogany tree, and the garland of leaves—recall the logging industry that led to British settlement of Belize
note: Belize's flag is the only national flag that depicts human beings; two British overseas territories, Montserrat and the British Virgin Islands, also depict humans

National symbol(s): Baird's tapir (a large, browsing, forest-dwelling mammal), keel-billed toucan, Black Orchid; national colors: red, blue

National anthem: *name:* "Land of the Free"
lyrics/music: Samuel Alfred HAYNES/Selwyn Walford YOUNG
note: adopted 1981; as a Commonwealth country, in addition to the national anthem, "God Save the Queen" serves as the royal anthem (see United Kingdom)

ECONOMY

Economy—overview: Tourism is the number one foreign exchange earner in this small economy, followed by exports of sugar, bananas, citrus, marine products, and crude oil.

The government's expansionary monetary and fiscal policies, initiated in September 1998, led to GDP growth averaging nearly 4% in 1999-2007, however GDP growth slowed to 1% in 2015, and 0% in 2016. Oil discoveries in 2006 bolstered this growth and oil exploration continues, but production has fallen in recent years and future oil revenues remain uncertain and are offset by Belize's growing imports of refined oil.

Although Belize has the third highest per capita income in Central America, the average income

figure masks a huge income disparity between rich and poor, and a key government objective remains reducing poverty and inequality with the help of international donors. High unemployment, a growing trade deficit and heavy foreign debt burden continue to be major concerns. Belize faces continued pressure from rising sovereign debt, and a growing trade imbalance.

GDP (purchasing power parity): $3.23 billion (2017 est.)
$3.151 billion (2016 est.)
$3.176 billion (2015 est.)
note: data are in 2017 dollars
country comparison to the world: 187

GDP (official exchange rate): $1.819 billion (2016 est.)

GDP—real growth rate: 2.5% (2017 est.)
-0.8% (2016 est.)
2.9% (2015 est.)
country comparison to the world: 132

GDP—per capita (PPP): $8,300 (2017 est.)
$8,400 (2016 est.)
$8,700 (2015 est.)
note: data are in 2017 dollars
country comparison to the world: 151

Gross national saving: 11% of GDP (2017 est.)
11.3% of GDP (2016 est.)
12.1% of GDP (2015 est.)
country comparison to the world: 152

GDP—composition, by end use:
household consumption: 75.6%
government consumption: 14.1%
investment in fixed capital: 23%
investment in inventories: 1%
exports of goods and services: 57.8%
imports of goods and services: -71.5% (2017 est.)

GDP—composition, by sector of origin:
agriculture: 9.7%
industry: 13.8%
services: 62.2% (2017 est.)

Agriculture—products: bananas, cacao, citrus, sugar; fish, cultured shrimp; lumber

Industries: garment production, food processing, tourism, construction, oil

Industrial production growth rate: -2% (2017 est.)
country comparison to the world: 193

Labor force: 120,500
note: shortage of skilled labor and all types of technical personnel (2008 est.)
country comparison to the world: 181

Labor force—by occupation: *agriculture:* 10.2%
industry: 18.1%
services: 71.7% (2007 est.)

Unemployment rate: 10.1% (2017 est.)
11.1% (2016 est.)
country comparison to the world: 139

Population below poverty line: 41% (2013 est.)

Household income or consumption by percentage share: *lowest 10%:* NA%
highest 10%: NA%

Budget: *revenues:* $500 million
expenditures: $550 million (2017 est.)

Taxes and other revenues: 27.5% of GDP (2017 est.)
country comparison to the world: 102

Budget surplus (+) or deficit (-): -2.7% of GDP (2017 est.)
country comparison to the world: 105

Public debt: 88.5% of GDP (2017 est.)
91.4% of GDP (2016 est.)
country comparison to the world: 28

Fiscal year: 1 April—31 March

Inflation rate (consumer prices): 1.8% (2017 est.)
0.6% (2016 est.)
country comparison to the world: 78

Central bank discount rate: 9.86% (1 September 2016)
10.01% (31 December 2015)
country comparison to the world: 24

Commercial bank prime lending rate: 9.6% (31 December 2017 est.)
9.84% (31 December 2016 est.)
country comparison to the world: 87

Stock of narrow money: $737.5 million (31 December 2017 est.)
$735.9 million (31 December 2016 est.)
country comparison to the world: 162

Stock of broad money: $1.311 billion (31 December 2017 est.)
$1.475 billion (31 December 2016 est.)
country comparison to the world: 168

Stock of domestic credit: $1.1 billion (31 December 2017 est.)
$1.278 billion (31 December 2016 est.)
country comparison to the world: 163

Market value of publicly traded shares: $NA

Current account balance: -$145 million (2017 est.)
-$163 million (2016 est.)
country comparison to the world: 85

Exports: $483.4 million (2017 est.)
$442.7 million (2016 est.)
country comparison to the world: 176

Exports—commodities: sugar, bananas, citrus, clothing, fish products, molasses, wood, crude oil

Exports—partners: Burma 30.7%, US 22.6%, UK 19.3% (2016)

Imports: $944.4 million (2017 est.)
$916.2 million (2016 est.)
country comparison to the world: 181

Imports—commodities: machinery and transport equipment, manufactured goods; fuels, chemicals, pharmaceuticals; food, beverages, tobacco

Imports—partners: US 37.2%, China 11.6%, Mexico 10.8%, Guatemala 7% (2016)

Reserves of foreign exchange and gold: $368.3 million (31 December 2017 est.)
$376.7 million (31 December 2016 est.)
country comparison to the world: 152

Debt—external: $1.326 billion (31 December 2017 est.)
$1.338 billion (31 December 2016 est.)
country comparison to the world: 162

Exchange rates: Belizean dollars (BZD) per US dollar—
2 (2017 est.)
2 (2016 est.)
2 (2015 est.)
2 (2014 est.)
2 (2013 est.)

ENERGY

Electricity access: electrification—*total population:* 100% (2016)

Electricity—production: 248 million kWh (2015 est.)
country comparison to the world: 183

Electricity—consumption: 413 million kWh (2015 est.)
country comparison to the world: 173

Electricity—exports: 0 kWh (2016 est.)
country comparison to the world: 108

Electricity—imports: 230 million kWh (2015 est.)
country comparison to the world: 90

Electricity—installed generating capacity: 191,000 kW (2015 est.)
country comparison to the world: 164

Electricity—from fossil fuels: 52.4% of total installed capacity (2015 est.)
country comparison to the world: 147

Electricity—from nuclear fuels: 0% of total installed capacity (2015 est.)
country comparison to the world: 51

Electricity—from hydroelectric plants: 28.3% of total installed capacity (2015 est.)
country comparison to the world: 74

Electricity—from other renewable sources: 19.4% of total installed capacity (2015 est.)
country comparison to the world: 32

Crude oil—production: 2,000 bbl/day (2016 est.)
country comparison to the world: 89

Crude oil—exports: 3,000 bbl/day (2014 est.)
country comparison to the world: 66

Crude oil—imports: 0 bbl/day (2014 est.)
country comparison to the world: 99

Crude oil—proved reserves: 6.7 million bbl (1 January 2017 es)
country comparison to the world: 96

Refined petroleum products—production: 33.05 bbl/day (2014 est.)
country comparison to the world: 110

Refined petroleum products—consumption: 3,700 bbl/day (2015 est.)
country comparison to the world: 181

Refined petroleum products—exports: 0 bbl/day (2014 est.)
country comparison to the world: 134

Refined petroleum products—imports: 3,638 bbl/day (2014 est.)
country comparison to the world: 172

Natural gas—production: 0 cu m (2013 est.)
country comparison to the world: 110

Natural gas—consumption: 0 cu m (2013 est.)
country comparison to the world: 159

Natural gas—exports: 0 cu m (2013 est.)
country comparison to the world: 70

Natural gas—imports: 0 cu m (2013 est.)
country comparison to the world: 93

Natural gas—proved reserves: 0 cu m (1 January 2014 es)
country comparison to the world: 117

Carbon dioxide emissions from consumption of energy: 700,000 Mt (2013 est.)
country comparison to the world: 173

COMMUNICATIONS

Telephones—fixed lines: *total subscriptions:* 23,000
subscriptions per 100 inhabitants: 6 (July 2016 est.)
country comparison to the world: 180

Telephones—mobile cellular: *total:* 227,000
subscriptions per 100 inhabitants: 64 (July 2016 est.)
country comparison to the world: 182

Telephone system: *general assessment:* above-average system; trunk network depends primarily on microwave radio relay
domestic: fixed-line teledensity of only about 6 per 100 persons; mobile-cellular teledensity approaching 65 per 100 persons
international: country code—501; landing point for the Americas Region Caribbean Ring System (ARCOS-1) fiber-optic telecommunications submarine cable that provides links to South and Central America, parts of the Caribbean, and the US; satellite earth station—8 (Intelsat—2, unknown—6) (2016)

Broadcast media: 8 privately owned TV stations; multi-channel cable TV provides access to foreign stations; about 25 radio stations broadcasting on roughly 50 different frequencies; state-run radio was privatized in 1998 (2009)

Internet country code: .bz

Internet users: *total:* 157,735
percent of population: 44.6% (July 2016 est.)
country comparison to the world: 170

TRANSPORTATION

National air transport system: *number of registered air carriers:* 2
inventory of registered aircraft operated by air carriers: 28
annual passenger traffic on registered air carriers: 935,603
annual freight traffic on registered air carriers: 2,463,420 mt-km (2015)
Civil aircraft registration country code prefix: V3 (2016)

Airports: 47 (2013)
country comparison to the world: 92

Airports—with paved runways: *total:* 6
2,438 to 3,047 m: 1
914 to 1,523 m: 2
under 914 m: 3 (2017)

Airports—with unpaved runways: *total:* 41

2,438 to 3,047 m: 1
914 to 1,523 m: 11
under 914 m: 29 (2013)

Roadways: *total:* 2,870 km
paved: 488 km
unpaved: 2,382 km (2011)
country comparison to the world: 169

Waterways: 825 km (navigable only by small craft) (2011)
country comparison to the world: 70

Merchant marine: *total:* 756
by type: bulk carrier 53, container ship 3, general cargo 373, oil tanker 55, other 272 (2017)
country comparison to the world: 29

Ports and terminals: *major seaport(s):* Belize City, Big Creek

MILITARY AND SECURITY

Military expenditures: 1.17% of GDP (2016)
1.09% of GDP (2015)
1.06% of GDP (2014)
1.1% of GDP (2013)
0.97% of GDP (2012)

Military branches: *Belize Defense Force (BDF):* Army, BDF Air Wing; Belize Coast Guard; Belize Police Department (2017)

Military service age and obligation: 18 years of age for voluntary military service; laws allow for conscription only if volunteers are insufficient; conscription has never been implemented; volunteers typically outnumber available positions by 3:1; initial service obligation 12 years (2012)

TRANSNATIONAL ISSUES

Disputes—international: Guatemala persists in its territorial claim to approximately half of Belize, but agrees to the Line of Adjacency to keep Guatemalan squatters out of Belize's forested interior; both countries agreed in April 2012 to hold simultaneous referenda, scheduled for 6 October 2013, to decide whether to refer the dispute to the ICJ for binding resolution, but this vote was suspended indefinitely; Belize and Mexico are working to solve minor border demarcation discrepancies arising from inaccuracies in the 1898 border treaty

Trafficking in persons: current situation: Belize is a source, destination, and transit country for men, women, and children subjected to forced labor and sex trafficking; the coerced prostitution of women and children by family members has not led to arrests; child sex tourism, involving primarily US citizens, is on the rise; sex trafficking and forced labor of Belizean and foreign women and LGBT individuals occurs in bars, nightclubs, brothels, and domestic service; workers from Central America, Mexico, and Asia may fall victim to forced labor in restaurants, shops, agriculture, and fishing

tier rating: Tier 3—Belize does not comply fully with the minimum standards for the elimination of human trafficking and is not making significant efforts to do so; authorities did not initiate any new trafficking investigations of prosecutions, and cases from previous years remain pending; law enforcement efforts to use informal means to identify and refer victims were ineffective and draft procedures for referring victims to services are still not finalized; trafficking victims were more commonly arrested, detained, or deported based on immigration violations than provided with assistance; the government did not make progress in implementing the 2012-14 anti-trafficking national strategic plan (2015)

Illicit drugs: major transshipment point for cocaine; small-scale illicit producer of cannabis, primarily for local consumption; offshore sector money-laundering activity related to narcotics trafficking and other crimes

BENIN

INTRODUCTION

Background: Present day Benin was the site of Dahomey, a West African kingdom that rose to prominence in about 1600 and over the next two and a half centuries became a regional power, largely based on its slave trade. Coastal areas of Dahomey began to be controlled by the French in the second half of the 19th century; the entire kingdom was conquered by 1894. French Dahomey achieved independence in 1960; it changed its name to the Republic of Benin in 1975.

A succession of military governments ended in 1972 with the rise to power of Mathieu KEREKOU and the establishment of a government based on Marxist-Leninist principles. A move to representative government began in 1989. Two years later, free elections ushered in former Prime Minister Nicephore SOGLO as president, marking the first successful transfer of power in Africa from a dictatorship to a democracy. KEREKOU was returned to power by elections held in 1996 and 2001, though some irregularities were alleged. KEREKOU stepped down at the end of his second term in 2006 and was succeeded by Thomas YAYI Boni, a political outsider and independent, who won a second five-year term in March 2011. Patrice TALON, a wealthy businessman, took office in 2016 after campaigning to restore public confidence in the government.

GEOGRAPHY

Location: Western Africa, bordering the Bight of Benin, between Nigeria and Togo

Geographic coordinates: 9 30 N, 2 15 E

Map references: Africa

Area: *total:* 112,622 sq km
land: 110,622 sq km
water: 2,000 sq km
country comparison to the world: 103

Area—comparative: slightly smaller than Pennsylvania

Land boundaries: *total:* 2,123 km
border countries (4): Burkina Faso 386 km, Niger 277 km, Nigeria 809 km, Togo 651 km

Coastline: 121 km

Maritime claims: *territorial sea:* 200 nm
exclusive fishing zone: 200 nm
continental shelf: 200 nm

Climate: tropical; hot, humid in south; semiarid in north

Terrain: mostly flat to undulating plain; some hills and low mountains

Elevation: *mean elevation:* 273 m

elevation extremes: *lowest point:* Atlantic Ocean 0 m
highest point: Mont Sokbaro 658 m

Natural resources: small offshore oil deposits, limestone, marble, timber

Land use: *agricultural land:* 31.3%
arable land: 22.9%;
permanent crops: 3.5%;
permanent pasture: 4.9%
forest: 40%
other: 28.7% (2011 est.)
Irrigated land: 230 sq km (2012)

Population—distribution: the population is primarily located in the south, with the highest concentration of people residing in and around the cities on the Atlantic coast; most of the north remains sparsely populated with higher concentrations of residents in the west

Natural hazards: hot, dry, dusty harmattan wind may affect north from December to March

Environment—current issues: inadequate supplies of potable water; poaching threatens wildlife populations; deforestation; desertification

Environment—international agreements: party to: Biodiversity, Climate Change, Climate Change-Kyoto Protocol, Desertification, Endangered Species, Environmental Modification, Hazardous Wastes, Law of the Sea, Ozone Layer Protection, Ship Pollution, Wetlands, Whaling
signed, but not ratified: none of the selected agreements

Geography—note: sandbanks create difficult access to a coast with no natural harbors, river mouths, or islands

PEOPLE AND SOCIETY

Population: 11,038,805
note: estimates for this country explicitly take into account the effects of excess mortality due to AIDS; this can result in lower life expectancy, higher infant mortality, higher death rates, lower population growth rates, and changes in the distribution of population by age and sex than would otherwise be expected (July 2017 est.)
country comparison to the world: 82

Nationality: *noun:* Beninese (singular and plural)
adjective: Beninese

Ethnic groups: Fon and related 38.4%, Adja and related 15.1%, Yoruba and related 12%, Bariba and related 9.6%, Fulani and related 8.6%, Ottamari and related 6.1%, Yoa-Lokpa and related 4.3%, Dendi and related 2.9%, other 0.9%, foreigner 1.9% (2013 est.)

Languages: French (official), Fon and Yoruba (most common vernaculars in south), tribal languages (at least six major ones in north)

Religions: Muslim 27.7%, Roman Catholic 25.5%, Protestant 13.5% (Celestial 6.7%, Methodist 3.4%, other Protestant 3.4%), Vodoun 11.6%, other Christian 9.5%, other traditional religions 2.6%, other 2.6%, none 5.8% (2013 est.)

Demographic profile: Benin has a youthful age structure—almost 65% of the population is under the age of 25—which is bolstered by high fertility and population growth rates. Benin's total fertility has been falling over time but remains high, declining from almost 7 children per women in 1990 to 4.8 in 2016. Benin's low contraceptive use and high unmet need for contraception contribute to the sustained high fertility rate. Although the majority of Beninese women use skilled health care personnel for antenatal care and delivery, the high rate of maternal mortality indicates the need for more access to high quality obstetric care.

Poverty, unemployment, increased living costs, and dwindling resources increasingly drive the Beninese to migrate. An estimated 4.4 million, more than 40%, of Beninese live abroad. Virtually all Beninese emigrants move to West African countries, particularly Nigeria and Cote d'Ivoire. Of the less than 1% of Beninese emigrants who settle in Europe, the vast majority live in France, Benin's former colonial ruler.

With about 40% of the population living below the poverty line, many desperate parents resort to sending their children to work in wealthy households as domestic servants (a common practice known as vidomegon), mines, quarries, or agriculture domestically or in Nigeria and other neighboring countries, often under brutal conditions. Unlike in other West African countries, where rural people move to the coast, farmers from Benin's densely populated southern and northwestern regions move to the historically sparsely populated central region to pursue agriculture. Immigrants from West African countries came to Benin in increasing numbers between 1992 and 2002 because of its political stability and porous borders.

Age structure: *0-14 years:* 42.65% (male 2,402,029/female 2,305,622)
15-24 years: 20.44% (male 1,148,204/female 1,108,342)
25-54 years: 30.44% (male 1,699,623/female 1,660,517)
55-64 years: 3.61% (male 174,633/female 223,398)
65 years and over: 2.87% (male 124,708/female 191,729) (2017 est.)

Dependency ratios: *total dependency ratio:* 86.1
youth dependency ratio: 80.1
elderly dependency ratio: 6
potential support ratio: 16.6 (2015 est.)

Median age: *total:* 18.2 years
male: 17.9 years
female: 18.6 years (2017 est.)
country comparison to the world: 215

Population growth rate: 2.71% (2017 est.)
country comparison to the world: 12

Birth rate: 35 births/1,000 population (2017 est.)
country comparison to the world: 21

Death rate: 7.9 deaths/1,000 population (2017 est.)
country comparison to the world: 92

Net migration rate: 0 migrant(s)/1,000 population (2017 est.)
country comparison to the world: 74

Population distribution: the population is primarily located in the south, with the highest concentration of people residing in and around the cities on the Atlantic coast; most of the north remains sparsely populated with higher concentrations of residents in the west

Urbanization: *urban population:* 44.8% of total population (2017)
rate of urbanization: 3.55% annual rate of change (2015-20 est.)

Major urban areas—population: PORTO-NOVO (capital) 268,000 (2014); COTONOU (seat of government) 682,000; Abomey-Calavi 757,000 (2015)

Sex ratio: *at birth:* 1.05 male(s)/female
0-14 years: 1.04 male(s)/female
15-24 years: 1.04 male(s)/female
25-54 years: 1.02 male(s)/female
55-64 years: 0.76 male(s)/female
65 years and over: 0.66 male(s)/female
total population: 1.01 male(s)/female (2016 est.)

Mother's mean age at first birth: 20.3 years
note: median age at first birth among women 25-29 (2011/12 est.)

Maternal mortality ratio: 405 deaths/100,000 live births (2015 est.)
country comparison to the world: 26

Infant mortality rate: *total:* 52.8 deaths/1,000 live births
male: 55.9 deaths/1,000 live births
female: 49.6 deaths/1,000 live births (2017 est.)
country comparison to the world: 23

Life expectancy at birth: *total population:* 62.3 years
male: 60.9 years
female: 63.8 years (2017 est.)
country comparison to the world: 198

Total fertility rate: 4.77 children born/woman (2017 est.)
country comparison to the world: 17

Contraceptive prevalence rate: 17.9% (2014)
Health expenditures: 4.6% of GDP (2014)
country comparison to the world: 154

Physicians density: 0.15 physicians/1,000 population (2013)

Hospital bed density: 0.5 beds/1,000 population (2010)

Drinking water source:
improved:
urban: 85.2% of population
rural: 72.1% of population
total: 77.9% of population
unimproved:
urban: 14.8% of population
rural: 27.9% of population
total: 22.1% of population (2015 est.)

Sanitation facility access:
improved:
urban: 35.6% of population
rural: 7.3% of population
total: 19.7% of population
unimproved:
urban: 64.4% of population
rural: 92.7% of population
total: 80.3% of population (2015 est.)

HIV/AIDS—adult prevalence rate: 1% (2016 est.)

country comparison to the world: 43

HIV/AIDS—people living with HIV/AIDS: 67,000 (2016 est.)
country comparison to the world: 50

HIV/AIDS—deaths: 2,400 (2016 est.)
country comparison to the world: 49

Major infectious diseases: *degree of risk:* very high
food or waterborne diseases: bacterial and protozoal diarrhea, hepatitis A, and typhoid fever
vectorborne diseases: dengue fever, malaria, and yellow fever
respiratory disease: meningococcal meningitis
animal contact disease: rabies (2016)

Obesity—adult prevalence rate: 9.6% (2016)
country comparison to the world: 142

Children under the age of 5 years underweight: 18% (2014)
country comparison to the world: 30

Education expenditures: 4.3% of GDP (2014)
country comparison to the world: 64

Literacy: *definition:* age 15 and over can read and write
total population: 38.4%
male: 49.9%
female: 27.3% (2015 est.)

School life expectancy (primary to tertiary education): *total:* 12 years
male: 14 years
female: 11 years (2013)

Unemployment, youth ages 15-24: *total:* 2.4%
male: 1.5%
female: 3.1% (2010 est.)

GOVERNMENT

Country name: *conventional long form:* Republic of Benin
conventional short form: Benin
local long form: Republique du Benin
local short form: Benin
former: Dahomey
etymology: named for the Bight of Benin, the body of water on which the country lies

Government type: presidential republic

Capital: *name:* Porto-Novo (constitutional capital); Cotonou (seat of government)
geographic coordinates: 6 29 N, 2 37 E
time difference: UTC+1 (6 hours ahead of Washington, DC, during Standard Time)

Administrative divisions: 12 departments; Alibori, Atacora, Atlantique, Borgou, Collines, Couffo, Donga, Littoral, Mono, Oueme, Plateau, Zou

Independence: 1 August 1960 (from France)

National holiday: Independence Day, 1 August (1960)

Constitution: *history:* previous 1946, 1958 (preindependence); latest adopted by referendum 2 December 1990, promulgated 11 December 1990
amendments: proposed concurrently by the president of the republic (after a decision in the Council of Ministers) and the National Assembly;

consideration of drafts or proposals requires at least three-fourths majority vote of the Assembly membership; passage requires approval in a referendum unless approved by at least four-fifths majority vote of the Assembly membership; constitutional articles affecting territorial sovereignty, the republican form of government, and secularity of Benin cannot be amended (2017)

Legal system: civil law system modeled largely on the French system and some customary law

International law organization participation: has not submitted an ICJ jurisdiction declaration; accepts ICCt jurisdiction

Citizenship: *citizenship by birth:* no
citizenship by descent only: at least one parent must be a citizen of Benin
dual citizenship recognized: yes
residency requirement for naturalization: 10 years

Suffrage: 18 years of age; universal

Executive branch: *chief of state:* President Patrice TALON (since 6 April 2016); note—the president is both chief of state and head of government

head of government: President Patrice TALON (since 6 April 2016); prime minister position abolished
cabinet: Council of Ministers appointed by the president
elections/appointments: president directly elected by absolute majority popular vote in 2 rounds if needed for a 5-year term (eligible for a second term); last held on 6 March and 20 March 2016 (next to be held in 2021)
election results: Patrice TALON elected president in second round; percent of vote in first round—Lionel ZINSOU (FCBE) 28.4%, Patrice TALON (independent) 24.8%, Sebastien AJAVON (independent) 23.0%, Abdoulaye Bio TCHANE (ABT) 8.8%, Pascal KOUPAKI (NC) 5.9%, other 9.1%; percent of vote in second round—Patrice TALON 65.4%, Lionel ZINSOU 34.6%

Legislative branch: *description:* unicameral National Assembly or Assemblee Nationale (83 seats; members directly elected in multi-seat constituencies by proportional representation vote; members serve 4-year terms)
elections: last held on 26 April 2015 (next to be held in April 2019)
election results: percent of vote by party—FCBE 30.2%, UN 14.4%, PRD 10.6%, AND 7.6%, RB-RP 7.1%, other 30.1%; seats by party—FCBE 33, UN 13, PRD 10, AND 5, RB-RP 7, other 15

Judicial branch: *highest court(s):* Supreme Court or Cour Supreme (consists of the court president and 3 chamber presidents organized into an administrative division, judicial chamber, and chamber of accounts); Constitutional Court or Cour Constitutionnelle (consists of 7 members including the court president); High Court of Justice (consists of the Constitutional Court members, 6 members appointed by the National Assembly, and the Supreme Court president); note—jurisdiction of the High Court of Justice is limited to cases of high

treason by the national president or members of the government while in office
judge selection and term of office: Supreme Court president and judges appointed by the national president upon the advice of the National Assembly; judges appointed for single renewable 5-year terms; Constitutional Court members—4 appointed by the National Assembly and 3 by the national president; members appointed for single renewable 5-year terms; High Court of Justice "other" members elected by the National Assembly; member tenure NA
subordinate courts: Court of Appeal or Cour d'Appel; district courts; village courts; Assize courts

Political parties and leaders: Alliance for a Triumphant Benin or ABT [Abdoulaye BIO TCHANE]
African Movement for Development and Progress or MADEP [Sefou FAGBOHOUN]
Benin Renaissance or RB [Lehady SOGLO]
Cowrie Force for an Emerging Benin or FCBE [Yayi BONI]
Democratic Renewal Party or PRD [Adrien HOUNGBEDJI]
New Consciousness Rally or NC [Pascal KOUPAKI]
Patriotic Awakening or RP [Janvier YAHOUEDEOU]
Social Democrat Party or PSD [Emmanuel GOLOU]
Sun Alliance or AS [Sacca LAFIA]
Union Makes the Nation or UN [Adrien HOUNGBEDJI] (includes PRD, MADEP)
United Democratic Forces or FDU [Mathurin NAGO]
note: approximately 20 additional minor parties

Political pressure groups and leaders: economic groups; environmentalists; political groups; teachers' unions and other educational groups

International organization participation: ACP, AfDB, AU, CD, ECOWAS, Entente, FAO, FZ, G-77, IAEA, IBRD, ICAO, ICCt, ICRM, IDA, IDB, IFAD, IFC, IFRCS, ILO, IMF, IMO, Interpol, IOC, IOM, IPU, ISO, ITSO, ITU, ITUC (NGOs), MIGA, MINUSMA, MONUSCO, NAM, OAS (observer), OIC, OIF, OPCW, PCA, UN, UNAMID, UNCTAD, UNESCO, UNHCR, UNIDO, UNMIL, UNMISS, UNOCI, UNWTO, UPU, WADB (regional), WAEMU, WCO, WFTU (NGOs), WHO, WIPO, WMO, WTO

Diplomatic representation in the US: *chief of mission:* Ambassador Hector POSSET (since 18 January 2017)
chancery: 2124 Kalorama Road NW, Washington, DC 20008
telephone: [1] (202) 232-6656
FAX: [1] (202) 265-1996

Diplomatic representation from the US: *chief of mission:* Ambassador Lucy TAMLYN (since 8 November 2015)
embassy: Caporal Bernard Anani, 01 BP 2012, Cotonou
mailing address: 01 B. P. 2012, Cotonou
telephone: [229] 21-30-06-50
FAX: [229] 21-30-03-84

Flag description: two equal horizontal bands of yellow (top) and red (bottom) with a vertical green band on the hoist side; green symbolizes hope and revival, yellow wealth, and red courage
note: uses the popular Pan-African colors of Ethiopia

National symbol(s): leopard; national colors: green, yellow, red

National anthem: *name:* "L'Aube Nouvelle" (The Dawn of a New Day)
lyrics/music: Gilbert Jean DAGNON
note: adopted 1960

ECONOMY

Economy—overview: The free market economy of Benin has grown consecutively for three years, averaging about 5% annually since 2014, but its close trade links to Nigeria expose Benin to risks from volatile commodity prices. Cotton is a key export commodity; high prices supported export earnings, but prices have fallen. Inflation had subsided, but probably accelerated in 2017.

During the first 6 months of President TALON's administration, electrical supply, which has hampered Benin's economic growth, increased and blackouts have been reduced. Private foreign direct investment is small, and foreign aid accounts for the majority of investment in infrastructure projects.

Benin's 2001 privatization policy continues in telecommunications, water, electricity, and agriculture. Benin has appealed for international assistance to mitigate piracy against commercial shipping in its territory. Pilferage has significantly dropped as the Port of Cotonou is still making progress towards implementing the International Ship and Port Facility Security (ISPS) Code in an effort to remain competitive. Projects included in Benin's $307 million Millennium Challenge Corporation (MCC) compact (2006-11) were designed to increase investment and private sector activity by improving key institutional and physical infrastructure. The four projects focused on access to land, access to financial services, access to justice, and access to markets (including modernization of the port). The Port of Cotonou is the largest component of Benin's economy with revenues projected to account for more than 40% of Benin's national budget.

Realizing its economic potential requires further efforts to infrastructure upgrades, stemming corruption, and expanding access to foreign markets in Nigeria and neighboring landlocked countries. In September 2015, Benin signed a MCC second Compact for $375 million that is designed to strengthen the national utility service provider, attract private sector investment, fund infrastructure investments in electricity generation and distribution, and develop off-grid electrification for poor and unserved households. In order to raise growth, Benin plans to attract more foreign investment, place more emphasis on tourism, facilitate the development of new food processing systems and agricultural products, encourage new information and communication technology, and

establish Independent Power Producers (IPP). In April 2017, the IMF approved a three year $150.4 million Extended Credit Facility agreement to maintain debt sustainability and boost donor confidence.

GDP (purchasing power parity): $25.29 billion (2017 est.)
$23.99 billion (2016 est.)
$23.06 billion (2015 est.)
note: data are in 2017 dollars
country comparison to the world: 142

GDP (official exchange rate): $9.41 billion (2016 est.)

GDP—real growth rate: 5.4% (2017 est.)
4% (2016 est.)
2.1% (2015 est.)
country comparison to the world: 30

GDP—per capita (PPP): $2,200 (2017 est.)
$2,200 (2016 est.)
$2,100 (2015 est.)
note: data are in 2017 dollars
country comparison to the world: 204

Gross national saving: 20% of GDP (2017 est.)
17.4% of GDP (2016 est.)
17.6% of GDP (2015 est.)
country comparison to the world: 89

GDP—composition, by end use:
household consumption: 69%
government consumption: 17%
investment in fixed capital: 26.5%
investment in inventories: -0.1%
exports of goods and services: 27.1%
imports of goods and services: -39.6% (2017 est.)

GDP—composition, by sector of origin:
agriculture: 25.6%
industry: 23.1%
services: 51.3% (2017 est.)

Agriculture—products: cotton, corn, cassava (manioc, tapioca), yams, beans, palm oil, peanuts, cashews; livestock

Industries: textiles, food processing, construction materials, cement

Industrial production growth rate: 5% (2017 est.)
country comparison to the world: 47

Labor force: 3.662 million (2007 est.)
country comparison to the world: 100

Unemployment rate: 1% (2014 est.)
country comparison to the world: 7

Population below poverty line: 36.2% (2011 est.)

Household income or consumption by percentage share: *lowest 10%:* 3.1%
highest 10%: 29% (2003)

Distribution of family income—Gini index: 36.5 (2003)
country comparison to the world: 86

Budget: *revenues:* $1.372 billion
expenditures: $2.261 billion (2017 est.)
Taxes and other revenues: 14.6% of GDP (2017 est.)
country comparison to the world: 195

Budget surplus (+) or deficit (-): -9.4% of GDP (2017 est.)

country comparison to the world: 203

Public debt: 56.4% of GDP (2017 est.)
50.4% of GDP (2016 est.)
country comparison to the world: 84

Fiscal year: calendar year

Inflation rate (consumer prices): 2% (2017 est.)
-0.8% (2016 est.)
country comparison to the world: 87

Central bank discount rate: 4.25% (31 December 2010)
4.25% (31 December 2009)
country comparison to the world: 90

Commercial bank prime lending rate: 5.3% (31 December 2015)
country comparison to the world: 141

Stock of narrow money: $2.41 billion (31 December 2017 est.)
$2.182 billion (31 December 2016 est.)
country comparison to the world: 127

Stock of broad money: $3.958 billion (31 December 2017 est.)
$3.609 billion (31 December 2016 est.)
country comparison to the world: 136

Stock of domestic credit: $1.822 billion (31 December 2017 est.)
$1.661 billion (31 December 2016 est.)
country comparison to the world: 155

Market value of publicly traded shares: $NA

Current account balance: -$822 million (2017 est.)
-$615 million (2016 est.)
country comparison to the world: 126

Exports: $1.76 billion (2017 est.)
$1.588 billion (2016 est.)
country comparison to the world: 146

Exports—commodities: cotton, cashews, shea butter, textiles, palm products, seafood

Exports—partners: India 14.3%, Malaysia 12.2%, Bangladesh 9.5%, Belarus 7.4%, China 6.2%, Nigeria 6.1%, Niger 5.6% (2016)

Imports: $2.448 billion (2017 est.)
$2.209 billion (2016 est.)
country comparison to the world: 153

Imports—commodities: foodstuffs, capital goods, petroleum products

Imports—partners: India 14.9%, Thailand 12.4%, France 10.1%, China 8.4%, Togo 7.3%, Netherlands 4.8%, Belgium 4.7% (2016)

Reserves of foreign exchange and gold: $60.2 million (31 December 2017 est.)
$57.5 million (31 December 2016 est.)
country comparison to the world: 170

Debt—external: $2.716 billion (31 December 2017 est.)
$2.476 billion (31 December 2016 est.)
country comparison to the world: 146

Exchange rates: Communaute Financiere Africaine francs (XOF) per US dollar—
605.3 (2017 est.)
593.01 (2016 est.)
593.01 (2015 est.)
591.45 (2014 est.)

494.42 (2013 est.)

ENERGY

Electricity access: *population without electricity:* 7,300,000
electrification—*total population:* 29%
electrification—urban areas: 57%
electrification—rural areas: 9% (2013)

Electricity—production: 311.6 million kWh (2015 est.)
country comparison to the world: 180

Electricity—consumption: 1.121 billion kWh (2015 est.)
country comparison to the world: 153

Electricity—exports: 0 kWh (2016 est.)
country comparison to the world: 111

Electricity—imports: 1.078 billion kWh (2015 est.)
country comparison to the world: 66

Electricity—installed generating capacity: 213,000 kW (2015 est.)
country comparison to the world: 163

Electricity—from fossil fuels: 97.2% of total installed capacity (2015 est.)
country comparison to the world: 42

Electricity—from nuclear fuels: 0% of total installed capacity (2015 est.)
country comparison to the world: 55

Electricity—from hydroelectric plants: 0.5% of total installed capacity (2015 est.)
country comparison to the world: 149

Electricity—from other renewable sources: 2.3% of total installed capacity (2015 est.)
country comparison to the world: 116

Crude oil—production: 0 bbl/day (2016 est.)
country comparison to the world: 110

Crude oil—exports: 0 bbl/day (2014 est.)
country comparison to the world: 98

Crude oil—imports: 0 bbl/day (2014 est.)
country comparison to the world: 101

Crude oil—proved reserves: 8 million bbl (1 January 2017 es)
country comparison to the world: 95

Refined petroleum products—production: 0 bbl/day (2014 est.)
country comparison to the world: 119

Refined petroleum products—consumption: 44,000 bbl/day (2015 est.)
country comparison to the world: 110

Refined petroleum products—exports: 5,152 bbl/day (2014 est.)
country comparison to the world: 94

Refined petroleum products—imports: 47,940 bbl/day (2014 est.)
country comparison to the world: 83

Natural gas—production: 0 cu m (2013 est.)
country comparison to the world: 112

Natural gas—consumption: 0 cu m (2013 est.)
country comparison to the world: 160

Natural gas—exports: 0 cu m (2013 est.)
country comparison to the world: 72

Natural gas—imports: 0 cu m (2013 est.)
country comparison to the world: 96

Natural gas—proved reserves: 1.133 billion cu m (1 January 2017 es)
country comparison to the world: 103

Carbon dioxide emissions from consumption of energy: 5 million Mt (2013 est.)
country comparison to the world: 126

COMMUNICATIONS

Telephones—fixed lines: *total subscriptions:* 124,883
subscriptions per 100 inhabitants: 1 (July 2016 est.)
country comparison to the world: 127

Telephones—mobile cellular: *total:* 8,892,490
subscriptions per 100 inhabitants: 83 (July 2016 est.)
country comparison to the world: 82

Telephone system: *general assessment:* inadequate system of open-wire, microwave radio relay, and cellular connections; fixed-line network characterized by aging, deteriorating equipment
domestic: fixed-line teledensity only about 1 per 100 persons; spurred by the presence of multiple mobile-cellular providers, cellular telephone subscribership has increased rapidly, exceeding 80 per 100 persons in 2016
international: country code—229; landing point for the SAT-3/WASC fiber-optic submarine cable that provides connectivity to Europe and Asia; long distance fiber-optic links with Togo, Burkina Faso, Niger, and Nigeria; satellite earth stations—7 (Intelsat-Atlantic Ocean) (2016)

Broadcast media: state-run Office de Radiodiffusion et de Television du Benin (ORTB) operates a TV station providing a wide broadcast reach; several privately owned TV stations broadcast from Cotonou; satellite TV subscription service is available; state-owned radio, under ORTB control, includes a national station supplemented by a number of regional stations; substantial number of privately owned radio broadcast stations; transmissions of a few international broadcasters are available on FM in Cotonou (2016)

Internet country code: .bj

Internet users: *total:* 1,288,336
percent of population: 12.0% (July 2016 est.)
country comparison to the world: 132

TRANSPORTATION

National air transport system: *number of registered air carriers:* 1
inventory of registered aircraft operated by air carriers: 1
annual passenger traffic on registered air carriers: 112,392
annual freight traffic on registered air carriers: 805,347 mt-km (2015)
Civil aircraft registration country code prefix: TY (2016)

Airports: 6 (2013)
country comparison to the world: 171

Airports—with paved runways: *total:* 1
1,524 to 2,437 m: 1 (2017)

Airports—with unpaved runways: *total:* 5
2,438 to 3,047 m: 2
1,524 to 2,437 m: 1
914 to 1,523 m: 2 (2013)

Railways: *total:* 438 km
narrow gauge: 438 km 1.000-m gauge (2014)
country comparison to the world: 118

Roadways: *total:* 16,000 km
paved: 1,400 km
unpaved: 14,600 km (2006)
country comparison to the world: 120

Waterways: 150 km (seasonal navigation on River Niger along northern border) (2011)
country comparison to the world: 101

Merchant marine: *total:* 6
by type: other 6 (2017)
country comparison to the world: 155

Ports and terminals: *major seaport(s):* Cotonou
LNG terminal(s) (import): Cotonou

MILITARY AND SECURITY

Military expenditures: 1.14% of GDP (2016)
1.1% of GDP (2015)
0.96% of GDP (2014)
0.94% of GDP (2013)
0.96% of GDP (2012)
country comparison to the world: 99

Military branches: Benin Armed Forces (Forces Armees Beninoises, FAB): Army (l'Arme de Terre), Benin Navy (Forces Navales Beninois, FNB), Benin Air Force (Force Aerienne du Benin, FAB) (2013)

Military service age and obligation: 18-35 years of age for selective compulsory and voluntary military service; a higher education diploma is required; both sexes are eligible for military service; conscript tour of duty—18 months (2013)

TERRORISM

Terrorist groups—foreign based: *Boko Haram:* aim(s): replace the Benin Government with an Islamic state and, ultimately, establish an Islamic caliphate across Africa; violently opposes any political or social activity associated with Western society, including voting, attending secular schools, and wearing shirts and trousers
area(s) of operation: maintains an operational presence, especially in the west along the Benin-Nigeria border; Benin continues in 2017 to participate in the Joint Multinational Force's military offensives combating Boko Haram

TRANSNATIONAL ISSUES

Disputes—international: talks continue between Benin and Togo on funding the Adjrala hydroelectric dam on the Mona River; Benin retains a border dispute with Burkina Faso near the town of Koualou; location of Benin-Niger-Nigeria tripoint is unresolved

Illicit drugs: transshipment point used by traffickers for cocaine destined for Western Europe; vulnerable to money laundering due to poorly enforced financial regulations

BERMUDA

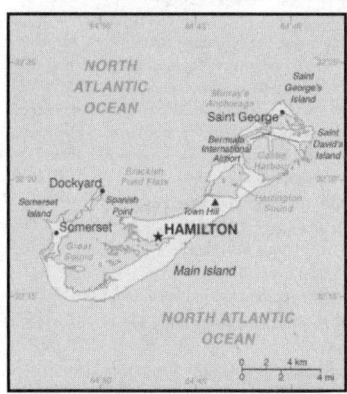

INTRODUCTION

Background: Bermuda was first settled in 1609 by shipwrecked English colonists heading for Virginia. Self-governing since 1620, Bermuda is the oldest and most populous of the British overseas territories. Vacationing to the island to escape North American winters first developed in Victorian times. Tourism continues to be important to the island's economy, although international business has overtaken it in recent years. Bermuda has also developed into a highly successful offshore financial center. A referendum on independence from the UK was soundly defeated in 1995.

GEOGRAPHY

Location: North America, group of islands in the North Atlantic Ocean, east of South Carolina (US)

Geographic coordinates: 32 20 N, 64 45 W

Map references: North America

Area: *total:* 54 sq km
land: 54 sq km
water: 0 sq km
country comparison to the world: 233

Area—comparative: about one-third the size of Washington, DC

Land boundaries: 0 km

Coastline: 103 km

Maritime claims: *territorial sea:* 12 nm
exclusive fishing zone: 200 nm

Climate: subtropical; mild, humid; gales, strong winds common in winter

Terrain: low hills separated by fertile depressions

Elevation: *mean elevation:* NA

elevation extremes: *lowest point:* Atlantic Ocean 0 m
highest point: Town Hill 79 m

Natural resources: limestone, pleasant climate fostering tourism

Land use: *agricultural land:* 14.8%
arable land: 14.8%;
permanent crops: 0%;
permanent pasture: 0%
forest: 20%
other: 65.2% (2011 est.)
Irrigated land: NA

Population—distribution: relatively even population distribution throughout

Natural hazards: hurricanes (June to November)

Environment—current issues: dense population and heavy vehicle traffic create serious pollution problems; water resources scarce (most obtained as rainwater or from wells); there is no sewage treatment on the island

Geography—note: consists of about 138 coral islands and islets with ample rainfall, but no rivers or freshwater lakes; some land was leased by the US Government from 1941 to 1995

PEOPLE AND SOCIETY

Population: 70,864 (July 2017 est.)
country comparison to the world: 203

Nationality: *noun:* Bermudian(s)
adjective: Bermudian

Ethnic groups: black 53.8%, white 31%, mixed 7.5%, other 7.1%, unspecified 0.6% (2010 est.)

Languages: English (official), Portuguese

Religions: Protestant 46.2% (includes Anglican 15.8%, African Methodist Episcopal 8.6%, Seventh Day Adventist 6.7, Pentecostal 3.5%, Methodist 2.7%, Presbyterian 2.0%, Church of God 1.6%, Baptist 1.2%, Salvation Army 1.1%, Brethren 1.0%, other Protestant 2.0%), Roman Catholic 14.5%, Jehovah's Witness 1.3%, other Christian 9.1%, Muslim 1%, other 3.9%, none 17.8%, unspecified 6.2% (2010 est.)

Age structure: *0-14 years:* 17.04% (male 6,104/female 5,974)
15-24 years: 12% (male 4,300/female 4,207)
25-54 years: 37.24% (male 13,230/female 13,163)
55-64 years: 15.73% (male 5,244/female 5,902)
65 years and over: 17.98% (male 5,395/female 7,345) (2017 est.)

Median age: *total:* 43.4 years
male: 41.5 years
female: 45.3 years (2017 est.)
country comparison to the world: 18

Population growth rate: 0.45% (2017 est.)
country comparison to the world: 157

Birth rate: 11.3 births/1,000 population (2017 est.)
country comparison to the world: 173

Death rate: 8.6 deaths/1,000 population (2017 est.)
country comparison to the world: 75

Net migration rate: 1.8 migrant(s)/1,000 population (2017 est.)
country comparison to the world: 50

Population distribution: relatively even population distribution throughout

Urbanization: *urban population:* 100% of total population (2017)
rate of urbanization: 0.16% annual rate of change (2015-20 est.)

Major urban areas—population: HAMILTON (capital) 10,000 (2014)

Sex ratio: *at birth:* 1.02 male(s)/female
0-14 years: 1.02 male(s)/female
15-24 years: 1.01 male(s)/female
25-54 years: 1 male(s)/female
55-64 years: 0.89 male(s)/female
65 years and over: 0.73 male(s)/female
total population: 0.94 male(s)/female (2016 est.)

Infant mortality rate: *total:* 2.5 deaths/1,000 live births
male: 2.6 deaths/1,000 live births
female: 2.4 deaths/1,000 live births (2017 est.)
country comparison to the world: 219

Life expectancy at birth: *total population:* 81.4 years
male: 78.2 years
female: 84.6 years (2017 est.)
country comparison to the world: 26

Total fertility rate: 1.93 children born/woman (2017 est.)
country comparison to the world: 129

HIV/AIDS—adult prevalence rate: NA

HIV/AIDS—people living with HIV/AIDS: NA

HIV/AIDS—deaths: NA

Education expenditures: 1.7% of GDP (2015)
country comparison to the world: 151

School life expectancy (primary to tertiary education): *total:* 12 years
male: 11 years
female: 12 years (2015)

Unemployment, youth ages 15-24: *total:* 29.3%
male: 29.7%
female: 29% (2014 est.)

GOVERNMENT

Country name: *conventional long form:* none
conventional short form: Bermuda
former: Somers Islands
etymology: the islands making up Bermuda are named after Juan de BERMUDEZ, an early 16th century Spanish sea captain and the first European explorer of the archipelago

Dependency status: overseas territory of the UK

Government type: parliamentary democracy (Parliament); self-governing overseas territory of the UK

Capital: *name:* Hamilton

geographic coordinates: 32 17 N, 64 47 W

time difference: UTC-4 (1 hour ahead of Washington, DC, during Standard Time) *daylight saving time:* +1hr, begins second Sunday in March; ends first Sunday in November

Administrative divisions: 9 parishes and 2 municipalities*; Devonshire, Hamilton, Hamilton*, Paget, Pembroke, Saint George*, Saint George's, Sandys, Smith's, Southampton, Warwick

Independence: none (overseas territory of the UK)

National holiday: Bermuda Day, 24 May; note—formerly known as Victoria Day, Empire Day, and Commonwealth Day

Constitution: several previous (dating to 1684); latest entered into force 8 June 1968; amended several times, last in 2012 (2017)

Legal system: English common law

International law organization participation: has not submitted an ICJ jurisdiction declaration; non-party state to the ICCt

Citizenship: *citizenship by birth:* no
citizenship by descent only: at least one parent must be a citizen of the UK
dual citizenship recognized: yes
residency requirement for naturalization: 10 years

Suffrage: 18 years of age; universal

Executive branch: *chief of state:* Queen ELIZABETH II (since 6 February 1952); represented by Governor John RANKIN (since 5 December 2016)

head of government: Premier David BURT (since 19 July 2017)
cabinet: Cabinet nominated by the premier, appointed by the governor
elections/appointments: the monarchy is hereditary; governor appointed by the monarch; following legislative elections, the leader of the majority party or majority coalition usually appointed premier by the governor

Legislative branch: *description:* bicameral Parliament consists of the Senate (11 seats; 3 members appointed by the governor, 5 by the premier, and 3 by the opposition party; members serve 5-year terms) and the House of Assembly (36 seats; members directly elected in single-seat constituencies by simple majority vote to serve up to 5-year terms)
elections: last held on 18 July 2017 (next to be held not later than 2022)
election results: percent of vote by party—PLP 58.9%, OBA 40.6%, other 0.5%; seats by party—PLP 24, OBA 12

Judicial branch: highest resident court(s): Court of Appeal (consists of the court president and at least 2 justices); Supreme Court (consists of the chief justice, 4 puisne judges, and 1 associate justice); note—the Judicial Committee of the Privy Council in London is the court of final appeal
judge selection and term of office: Court of Appeal justice appointed by the governor; justice tenure by individual appointment; Supreme Court judges nominated by the Judicial and Legal Services Commission and appointed by the governor; judge tenure based on terms of appointment
subordinate courts: commercial court (began in 2006); magistrates' courts

Political parties and leaders: One Bermuda Alliance or OBA [Jeanne ATHERDEN]
Progressive Labor Party or PLP [David BURT]

Political pressure groups and leaders: Association of Bermuda Insurers and Reinsurers or ABIR [Bradley KADING]
Association of Bermuda International Companies or ABIC [Patrick TANNOCK]
Bermuda Employers' Council [Keith JENSEN]
Bermuda Industrial Union or BIU [Chris FURBERT]
Bermuda Public Services Union or BPSU [Kevin GRANT, Edward G. BALL, Jr.]
Bermuda Union of Teachers [Michael CHARLES]

International organization participation: Caricom (associate), ICC (NGOs), Interpol (subbureau), IOC, ITUC (NGOs), UPU, WCO

Diplomatic representation in the US: none (overseas territory of the UK)

Diplomatic representation from the US: *chief of mission:* Consul General Mary Ellen KOENIG (since 28 November 2015)
consulate(s) general: Crown Hill, 16 Middle Road, Devonshire DVO3
mailing address: P. O. Box HM325, Hamilton HMBX; American Consulate General Hamilton, US Department of State, 5300 Hamilton Place, Washington, DC 20520-5300
telephone: [1] (441) 295-1342
FAX: [1] (441) 295-1592, 296-9233

Flag description: red, with the flag of the UK in the upper hoist-side quadrant and the Bermudian coat of arms (a white shield with a red lion standing on a green grassy field holding a scrolled shield showing the sinking of the ship Sea Venture off Bermuda in 1609) centered on the outer half of the flag; it was the shipwreck of the vessel, filled with English colonists originally bound for Virginia, that led to the settling of Bermuda
note: the flag is unusual in that it is only British overseas territory that uses a red ensign, all others use blue

National symbol(s): red lion

National anthem: *name:* "Hail to Bermuda"
lyrics/music: Bette JOHNS
note: serves as a local anthem; as a territory of the United Kingdom, "God Save the Queen" is official (see United Kingdom)

ECONOMY

Economy—overview: Tourism accounts for about 5% of Bermuda's GDP, but a much larger share of employment. Over 80% of its visitors come from the US. The sector struggled in the wake of the global recession of 2008-09. International business, which consists primarily of reinsurance and other financial services, is the real bedrock of Bermuda's economy, consistently accounting for about 85% of the island's GDP. Even this sector, however, has lost roughly 5,000 high-paying expatriate jobs since 2008, weighing heavily on household consumption and retail sales. Bermuda must import almost everything. Agriculture and industry are limited due to the small size of the island.

Bermuda's economy entered its seventh straight year of recession in 2015. Unemployment is 9%, public debt is growing and exceeds $2.3 billion, the government pension fund faces a $2.4 billion shortfall, and the economy has not attracted significant new foreign investment. Bermuda's FY15/16 budget projects a 12% larger deficit than FY14/15. The government announced it would borrow $125 million in 2015 to meet current operating expenses. Still, Bermuda enjoys the fourth highest per capita income in the world, about 70% higher than that of the US.

GDP (purchasing power parity): $5.198 billion (2013 est.)
$5.331 billion (2012 est.)
$5.6 billion (2011 est.)
country comparison to the world: 174

GDP (official exchange rate): $5.198 billion (2013 est.)

GDP—real growth rate: -2.5% (2013 est.)
-4.8% (2012)
-3.5% (2011 est.)
country comparison to the world: 214

GDP—per capita (PPP): $85,700 (2013 est.)
$85,400 (2012 est.)
$86,000 (2011 est.)
country comparison to the world: 8

GDP—composition, by end use:
household consumption: 54.2%
government consumption: 16.3%
investment in fixed capital: 13.1%
investment in inventories: 0%
exports of goods and services: 50.4%
imports of goods and services: -34% (2017 est.)

GDP—composition, by sector of origin:
agriculture: 0.8%
industry: 5.8%
services: 93.3% (2017 est.)

Agriculture—products: bananas, vegetables, citrus, flowers; dairy products, honey

Industries: international business, tourism, light manufacturing

Industrial production growth rate: 2.3% (2017 est.)
country comparison to the world: 120

Labor force: 33,490 (2014 est.)
country comparison to the world: 203

Labor force—by occupation: *agriculture:* 2%
industry: 15%
services: 83% (2013 est.)

Unemployment rate: 9% (2014 est.)
7% (2013)
country comparison to the world: 121

Population below poverty line: 11% (2008 est.)

Household income or consumption by percentage share: *lowest 10%:* NA%
highest 10%: NA%

Budget: *revenues:* $1.013 billion
expenditures: $1.16 billion (2017 est.)
Taxes and other revenues: 19.5% of GDP (2017 est.)
country comparison to the world: 157

Budget surplus (+) or deficit (-): -2.8% of GDP (2017 est.)
country comparison to the world: 106

Public debt: 43% of GDP (FY14/15)
country comparison to the world: 126

Fiscal year: 1 April—31 March

Inflation rate (consumer prices): 1.6% (2017 est.)
1.4% (2016 est.)
country comparison to the world: 70

Stock of narrow money: $3.374 billion (30 September 2014 est.)
$3.422 billion (31 December 2013 est.)
note: figures do not include US dollars, which also circulate freely
country comparison to the world: 114

Stock of broad money: $22.1 billion (30 September 2014 est.)
$25.1 billion (31 December 2013 est.)
country comparison to the world: 87

Stock of domestic credit: $NA

Market value of publicly traded shares: $1.85 billion (31 December 2015 est.)
$1.601 billion (31 December 2014 est.)
$1.467 billion (31 December 2013 est.)
country comparison to the world: 101

Exports: $20 million (2017 est.)
$19 million (2016 est.)
country comparison to the world: 211

Exports—commodities: reexports of pharmaceuticals

Exports—partners: Latvia 33.4%, Jamaica 16.6%, US 13.7%, Nigeria 11.7%, Israel 4.7% (2016)

Imports: $979.5 million (2017 est.)
$951 million (2016 est.)
country comparison to the world: 179

Imports—commodities: clothing, fuels, machinery and transport equipment, construction materials, chemicals, food and live animals

Imports—partners: US 54.2%, Japan 17.9%, South Korea 13.7%, Canada 4.9% (2016)

Debt—external: $2.435 billion (2015 est.)
$1.4 billion (2012 est.)
country comparison to the world: 150

Stock of direct foreign investment—at home: $2.641 billion (2014 est.)
$2.664 billion (2013 est.)
country comparison to the world: 112

Stock of direct foreign investment—abroad: $889 million (2014 est.)
$835 million (2013 est.)
country comparison to the world: 87

Exchange rates: Bermudian dollars (BMD) per US dollar—
1 (2017 est.)
1 (2016 est.)
1 (2015 est.)
1 (2014 est.)
1 (2013 est.)

ENERGY

Electricity access: electrification—*total population:* 100% (2016)

Electricity—production: 662 million kWh (2015 est.)
country comparison to the world: 160

Electricity—consumption: 615.7 million kWh (2015 est.)
country comparison to the world: 167

Electricity—exports: 0 kWh (2016 est.)
country comparison to the world: 105

Electricity—imports: 0 kWh (2016 est.)
country comparison to the world: 123

Electricity—installed generating capacity: 171,000 kW (2015 est.)
country comparison to the world: 167

Electricity—from fossil fuels: 100% of total installed capacity (2015 est.)
country comparison to the world: 22

Electricity—from nuclear fuels: 0% of total installed capacity (2015 est.)
country comparison to the world: 48

Electricity—from hydroelectric plants: 0% of total installed capacity (2015 est.)
country comparison to the world: 163

Electricity—from other renewable sources: 0% of total installed capacity
note: the Tynes Bay Waste Treatment Facility turns waste to electric energy (2015 est.)
country comparison to the world: 213

Crude oil—production: 0 bbl/day (2016 est.)
country comparison to the world: 111

Crude oil—exports: 0 bbl/day (2014 est.)
country comparison to the world: 93

Crude oil—imports: 0 bbl/day (2014 est.)
country comparison to the world: 97

Crude oil—proved reserves: 0 bbl (1 January 2017 es)
country comparison to the world: 110

Refined petroleum products—production: 0 bbl/day (2014 est.)
country comparison to the world: 120

Refined petroleum products—consumption: 3,300 bbl/day (2015 est.)
country comparison to the world: 185

Refined petroleum products—exports: 0 bbl/day (2014 est.)
country comparison to the world: 133

Refined petroleum products—imports: 2,968 bbl/day (2014 est.)
country comparison to the world: 180

Natural gas—production: 0 cu m (2014 est.)
country comparison to the world: 107

Natural gas—consumption: 0 cu m (2013 est.)
country comparison to the world: 157

Natural gas—exports: 0 cu m (2013 est.)
country comparison to the world: 67

Natural gas—imports: 0 cu m (2014 est.)
country comparison to the world: 90

Natural gas—proved reserves: 0 cu m (1 January 2014 es)
country comparison to the world: 114

Carbon dioxide emissions from consumption of energy: 600,000 Mt (2013 est.)

country comparison to the world: 175

COMMUNICATIONS

Telephones—fixed lines: *total subscriptions:* 29,200
subscriptions per 100 inhabitants: 42 (July 2016 est.)
country comparison to the world: 173

Telephones—mobile cellular: *total:* 59,500
subscriptions per 100 inhabitants: 85 (July 2016 est.)
country comparison to the world: 201

Telephone system: *general assessment:* a good, fully automatic digital telephone system with fiber-optic trunk lines
domestic: the system has a high fixed-line teledensity coupled with a mobile-cellular teledensity of roughly 125 per 100 persons
international: country code—1-441; landing points for the GlobeNet, Gemini Bermuda, CBUS, and the Challenger Bermuda-1 (CB-1) submarine cables; satellite earth stations—3 (2015)

Broadcast media: 3 TV stations; cable and satellite TV subscription services are available; roughly 13 radio stations operating (2012)

Internet country code: .bm

Internet users: *total:* 69,126
percent of population: 98.0% (July 2016 est.)
country comparison to the world: 179

TRANSPORTATION

Civil aircraft registration country code prefix: VP-B (2016)

Airports: 1 (2013)
country comparison to the world: 212

Airports—with paved runways: *total:* 1
2,438 to 3,047 m: 1 (2017)

Roadways: *total:* 447 km
paved: 447 km
note: 225 km public roads; 222 km private roads (2010)
country comparison to the world: 198

Merchant marine: *total:* 160
by type: bulk carrier 10, container ship 8, general cargo 1, oil tanker 18, other 123 (2017)
country comparison to the world: 71

Ports and terminals: *major seaport(s):* Hamilton, Ireland Island, Saint George

MILITARY AND SECURITY

Military branches: Bermuda Regiment (2012)

Military service age and obligation: 18-45 years of age for voluntary male or female enlistment in the Bermuda Regiment; males must register at age 18 and may be subject to conscription; term of service is 38 months for volunteers or conscripts (2012)

Military—note: defense is the responsibility of the UK

TRANSNATIONAL ISSUES

Disputes—international: none

BHUTAN

INTRODUCTION

Background: Following Britain's victory in the 1865 Duar War, Britain and Bhutan signed the Treaty of Sinchulu, under which Bhutan would receive an annual subsidy in exchange for ceding land to British India. Ugyen WANGCHUCK—who had served as the de facto ruler of an increasingly unified Bhutan and had improved relations with the British toward the end of the 19th century—was named king in 1907. Three years later, a treaty was signed whereby the British agreed not to interfere in Bhutanese internal affairs, and Bhutan allowed Britain to direct its foreign affairs. Bhutan negotiated a similar arrangement with independent India after 1947. Two years later, a formal Indo-Bhutanese accord returned to Bhutan a small piece of the territory annexed by the British, formalized the annual subsidies the country received, and defined India's responsibilities in defense and foreign relations. Under a succession of modernizing monarchs beginning in the 1950s, Bhutan joined the UN in 1971 and slowly continued its engagement beyond its borders.

In March 2005, King Jigme Singye WANGCHUCK unveiled the government's draft constitution—which introduced major democratic reforms—and held a national referendum for its approval. In December 2006, the King abdicated the throne in favor of his son, Jigme Khesar Namgyel WANGCHUCK. In early 2007, India and Bhutan renegotiated their treaty, eliminating the clause that stated that Bhutan would be "guided by" India in conducting its foreign policy, although Thimphu continues to coordinate closely with New Delhi. Elections for seating the country's first parliament were completed in March 2008; the king ratified the country's first constitution in July 2008. Bhutan experienced a peaceful turnover of power following parliamentary elections in 2013, which resulted in the defeat of the incumbent party. The disposition of some 8,500 refugees of the more than 100,000 who fled or were forced out of

Bhutan in the 1990s—and who are housed in two UN refugee camps in Nepal—remains unresolved.

GEOGRAPHY

Location: Southern Asia, between China and India

Geographic coordinates: 27 30 N, 90 30 E

Map references: Asia

Area: *total:* 38,394 sq km
land: 38,394 sq km
water: 0 sq km
country comparison to the world: 137

Area—comparative: slightly larger than Maryland; about one-half the size of Indiana

Land boundaries: *total:* 1,136 km
border countries (2): China 477 km, India 659 km

Coastline: 0 km (landlocked)

Maritime claims: none (landlocked)

Climate: varies; tropical in southern plains; cool winters and hot summers in central valleys; severe winters and cool summers in Himalayas

Terrain: mostly mountainous with some fertile valleys and savanna

Elevation: *mean elevation:* 2,220 m

elevation extremes: *lowest point:* Drangeme Chhu 97 m
highest point: Gangkar Puensum 7,570 m

Natural resources: timber, hydropower, gypsum, calcium carbonate

Land use: *agricultural land:* 13.6%
arable land: 2.6%;
permanent crops: 0.3%;
permanent pasture: 10.7%
forest: 85.5%
other: 0.9% (2011 est.)
Irrigated land: 320 sq km (2012)

Natural hazards: violent storms from the Himalayas are the source of the country's Bhutanese name, which translates as Land of the Thunder Dragon; frequent landslides during the rainy season

Environment—current issues: soil erosion; limited access to potable water

Environment—international agreements: party to: Biodiversity, Climate Change, Climate Change-Kyoto Protocol, Desertification, Endangered Species, Hazardous Wastes, Ozone Layer Protection
signed, but not ratified: Law of the Sea

Geography—note: landlocked; strategic location between China and India; controls several key Himalayan mountain passes

PEOPLE AND SOCIETY

Population: 758,288 (July 2017 est.)
country comparison to the world: 165

Nationality: *noun:* Bhutanese (singular and plural)
adjective: Bhutanese

Ethnic groups: Ngalop (also known as Bhote) 50%, ethnic Nepalese 35% (includes Lhotsampas—one of several Nepalese ethnic groups), indigenous or migrant tribes 15%

Languages: Sharchhopka 28%, Dzongkha (official) 24%, Lhotshamkha 22%, other 26% (includes foreign languages) (2005 est.)

Religions: Lamaistic Buddhist 75.3%, Indian- and Nepalese-influenced Hinduism 22.1%, other 2.6% (2005 est.)

Age structure: *0-14 years:* 25.8% (male 99,977/female 95,652)
15-24 years: 18.81% (male 72,634/female 70,018)
25-54 years: 43.07% (male 173,310/female 153,314)
55-64 years: 6.03% (male 24,482/female 21,206)
65 years and over: 6.29% (male 24,874/female 22,821) (2017 est.)

Dependency ratios: *total dependency ratio:* 47.3
youth dependency ratio: 40.4
elderly dependency ratio: 6.9
potential support ratio: 14.5 (2015 est.)

Median age: *total:* 27.6 years
male: 28.2 years
female: 27.1 years (2017 est.)
country comparison to the world: 143

Population growth rate: 1.07% (2017 est.)
country comparison to the world: 106

Birth rate: 17.3 births/1,000 population (2017 est.)
country comparison to the world: 107

Death rate: 6.5 deaths/1,000 population (2017 est.)
country comparison to the world: 144

Net migration rate: 0 migrant(s)/1,000 population (2017 est.)
country comparison to the world: 75

Urbanization: *urban population:* 40.1% of total population (2017)
rate of urbanization: 2.89% annual rate of change (2015-20 est.)

Major urban areas—population: THIMPHU (capital) 152,000 (2014)

Sex ratio: *at birth:* 1.05 male(s)/female
0-14 years: 1.04 male(s)/female
15-24 years: 1.04 male(s)/female
25-54 years: 1.14 male(s)/female
55-64 years: 1.16 male(s)/female
65 years and over: 1.1 male(s)/female
total population: 1.09 male(s)/female (2016 est.)

Maternal mortality ratio: 148 deaths/100,000 live births (2015 est.)
country comparison to the world: 61

Infant mortality rate: *total:* 32.1 deaths/1,000 live births
male: 32.3 deaths/1,000 live births
female: 31.8 deaths/1,000 live births (2017 est.)
country comparison to the world: 59

Life expectancy at birth: *total population:* 70.6 years
male: 69.6 years
female: 71.7 years (2017 est.)
country comparison to the world: 158

Total fertility rate: 1.9 children born/woman (2017 est.)
country comparison to the world: 135

Contraceptive prevalence rate: 65.6% (2010)
Health expenditures: 3.6% of GDP (2014)
country comparison to the world: 168

Physicians density: 0.26 physicians/1,000 population (2014)

Hospital bed density: 1.8 beds/1,000 population (2012)

Drinking water source:
improved:
urban: 100% of population
rural: 100% of population
total: 100% of population
unimproved:
urban: 0% of population
rural: 0% of population
total: 0% of population (2015 est.)

Sanitation facility access:
improved:
urban: 77.9% of population
rural: 33.1% of population
total: 50.4% of population
unimproved:
urban: 22.1% of population
rural: 66.9% of population
total: 49.6% of population (2015 est.)

HIV/AIDS—adult prevalence rate: NA

HIV/AIDS—people living with HIV/AIDS: NA

HIV/AIDS—deaths: NA

Major infectious diseases: *degree of risk:* high
food or waterborne diseases: bacterial and protozoal diarrhea, hepatitis A, and typhoid fever
vectorborne diseases: dengue fever (2016)

Obesity—adult prevalence rate: 6.4% (2016)
country comparison to the world: 167

Children under the age of 5 years underweight: 12.8% (2010)
country comparison to the world: 59

Education expenditures: 7.4% of GDP (2015)
country comparison to the world: 86

Literacy: *definition:* age 15 and over can read and write
total population: 64.9%
male: 73.1%
female: 55% (2015 est.)

School life expectancy (primary to tertiary education): *total:* 13 years
male: 12 years
female: 13 years (2013)

Unemployment, youth ages 15-24: *total:* 10.7%
male: 8.2%
female: 12.7% (2015 est.)
country comparison to the world: 119

GOVERNMENT

Country name: *conventional long form:* Kingdom of Bhutan
conventional short form: Bhutan

local long form: Druk Gyalkhap
local short form: Druk Yul
etymology: named after the Bhotia, the ethnic Tibetans who migrated from Tibet to Bhutan; "Bod" is the Tibetan name for their land; the Bhutanese name "Druk Yul" means "Land of the Thunder Dragon"

Government type: constitutional monarchy

Capital: *name:* Thimphu

geographic coordinates: 27 28 N, 89 38 E

time difference: UTC+6 (11 hours ahead of Washington, DC, during Standard Time)

Administrative divisions: 20 districts (dzongkhag, singular and plural); Bumthang, Chhukha, Chirang, Daga, Gasa, Geylegphug, Ha, Lhuntshi, Mongar, Paro, Pemagatsel, Punakha, Samchi, Samdrup Jongkhar, Shemgang, Tashigang, Tashi Yangtse, Thimphu, Tongsa, Wangdi Phodrang

Independence: 17 December 1907 (became a unified kingdom under its first hereditary king)

National holiday: National Day (Ugyen WANGCHUCK became first hereditary king), 17 December (1907)

Constitution: *history:* previous governing documents were various royal decrees; first constitution drafted November 2001—March 2005, ratified 18 July 2008
amendments: proposed as a motion by simple majority vote in a joint session of Parliament; passage requires at least a three-fourths majority vote in a joint session of the next Parliament and assented to by the king; amended 2011 (2017)

Legal system: civil law based on Buddhist religious law

International law organization participation: has not submitted an ICJ jurisdiction declaration; non-party state to the ICCt

Citizenship: *citizenship by birth:* no
citizenship by descent only: the father must be a citizen of Bhutan
dual citizenship recognized: no
residency requirement for naturalization: 10 years

Suffrage: 18 years of age; universal

Executive branch: *chief of state:* King Jigme Khesar Namgyel WANGCHUCK (since 14 December 2006); note—King Jigme Singye WANGCHUCK abdicated the throne on 14 December 2006 to his son

head of government: Prime Minister Tshering TOBGAY (since 27 July 2013)
cabinet: Council of Ministers or Lhengye Zhungtshog members nominated by the monarch in consultation with the prime minister and approved by the National Assembly; members serve 5-year terms
elections/appointments: the monarchy is hereditary but can be removed by a two-third vote of Parliament; leader of the majority party in Parliament is nominated as the prime minister, appointed by the monarch

Legislative branch: *description:* bicameral Parliament or Chi Tshog consists of the non-partisan National Council or Gyelyong Tshogde (25 seats; 20 members directly elected in single-seat constituencies by simple majority vote and 5 members appointed by the king; members serve 5-year terms) and the National Assembly or Tshogdu (47 seats; members directly elected in single-seat constituencies by proportional representation vote to serve 5-year terms)
elections: National Council election last held on 23 April 2013 (next to be held in 2018); National Assembly election first round held on 31 May 2013 and second round on 13 July 2013 ((next to be held in 2018)
election results: National Council—seats by party—independent 20 (all candidates required to run as independents); National Assembly—percent of vote by party in first round—DPT 44.5%; PDP 32.5%; DNT 17.0%; DCT 5.9%; percent of vote in second round—PDP 54.9%, DPT 45.1%; seats by party—PDP 32, DPT 15

Judicial branch: *highest court(s):* Supreme Court (consists of 5 justices including the chief justice); note—the Supreme Court has sole jurisdiction in constitutional matters
judge selection and term of office: Supreme Court chief justice appointed by the monarch upon the advice of the National Judicial Commission, a 4-member body to include the Legislative Committee of the National Assembly, the attorney general, the Chief Justice of Bhutan and the senior Associate Justice of the Supreme Court; other judges (drangpons) appointed by the monarch from among the High Court judges selected by the National Judicial Commission; chief justice serves a 5-year term or until reaching age 65 years, whichever is earlier; the 4 other judges serve 10-year terms or until age 65, whichever is earlier
subordinate courts: High Court (first appellate court); District or Dzongkhag Courts; sub-district or Dungkhag Courts

Political parties and leaders: Bhutan Kuen-Nyam Party or BKP [Dasho Neten ZANGMO]
Bhutan Peace and Prosperity Party (Druk Phuensum Tshogpa) or DPT [Pema GYAMTSHO]
Druk Chirwang Tshogpa or DCT [Lily WANGCHUK]
Druk Nymarup Tshogpa or DNT [Tandin DORJI]
People's Democratic Party or PDP [Tshering TOBGAY]

Political pressure groups and leaders: Druk National Congress or DNC [Gedun CHOEPHEL] (group in exile)
United Front for Democracy or UFD (group in exile)
United Front for Democracy Against Dictatorship or UDD [Jatuporn PROMPAN, chairman]
other: Buddhist clergy; ethnic Nepali-Bhutanese organizations (exiled)

International organization participation: ADB, BIMSTEC, CP, FAO, G-77, IBRD, ICAO, IDA, IFAD, IFC, IMF, Interpol, IOC, IOM (observer), IPU, ISO (correspondent), ITSO, ITU, MIGA, NAM, OPCW, SAARC, SACEP, UN, UNCTAD,

UNESCO, UNIDO, UNTSO, UNWTO, UPU, WCO, WHO, WIPO, WMO, WTO (observer)

Diplomatic representation in the US: none; note—the Permanent Mission to the UN for Bhutan has consular jurisdiction in the US; the permanent representative to the UN is Kunzang C. NAM-GYEL (since February 2014); address: 343 East 43rd Street, New York, NY 10017; telephone [1] (212) 682-2268; FAX [1] (212) 661-0551

consulate(s) general: New York

Diplomatic representation from the US: the US and Bhutan have no formal diplomatic relations, although frequent informal contact is maintained via the US embassy in New Delhi (India) and Bhutan's Permanent Mission to the UN

Flag description: divided diagonally from the lower hoist-side corner; the upper triangle is yellow and the lower triangle is orange; centered along the dividing line is a large black and white dragon facing away from the hoist side; the dragon, called the Druk (Thunder Dragon), is the emblem of the nation; its white color stands for purity and the jewels in its claws symbolize wealth; the background colors represent spiritual and secular powers within Bhutan: the orange is associated with Buddhism, while the yellow denotes the ruling dynasty

National symbol(s): thunder dragon known as Druk Gyalpo; national colors: orange, yellow

National anthem: *name:* "Druk tsendhen" (The Thunder Dragon Kingdom)

lyrics/music: Gyaldun Dasho Thinley DORJI/Aku TONGMI

note: adopted 1953

ECONOMY

Economy—overview: Bhutan's small economy is based largely on hydropower, agriculture, and forestry, which provide the main livelihood for more than half of the population. Because rugged mountains dominate the terrain and make the building of roads and other infrastructure difficult and expensive, industrial production is primarily of the cottage industry type. The economy is closely aligned with India's through strong trade and monetary links and is dependent on India for financial assistance and migrant laborers for development projects, especially for road construction. Bhutan also inked a pact in December 2014 to expand duty-free trade with Bangladesh.

Multilateral development organizations administer most educational, social, and environment programs, and take into account the government's desire to protect the country's environment and cultural traditions. For example, the government, in its cautious expansion of the tourist sector, encourages visits by upscale, environmentally conscientious tourists. Complicated controls and uncertain policies in areas such as industrial licensing, trade, labor, and finance continue to hamper foreign investment.

Bhutan's largest export—hydropower to India—could spur sustainable growth in the coming years if Bhutan resolves chronic delays in construction. Bhutan's hydropower exports comprise 40% of total exports and 25% of the government's total revenue. Bhutan currently taps only 6.5% of its 24,000-megawatt hydropower potential and is behind schedule in building 12 new hydropower dams with a combined capacity of 10,000 megawatts by 2020 in accordance with a deal signed in 2008 with India. The high volume of imported materials to build hydropower plants has expanded Bhutan's trade and current account deficits. Bhutan also signed a memorandum of understanding with Bangladesh and India in July 2017 to jointly construct a new hydropower plant for exporting electricity to Bangladesh.

GDP (purchasing power parity): $7.011 billion (2017 est.)

$6.621 billion (2016 est.)

$6.232 billion (2015 est.)

note: data are in 2017 dollars

country comparison to the world: 169

GDP (official exchange rate): $2.321 billion (2016 est.)

GDP—real growth rate: 5.9% (2017 est.)

6.2% (2016 est.)

6.1% (2015 est.)

country comparison to the world: 25

GDP—per capita (PPP): $8,700 (2017 est.)

$8,400 (2016 est.)

$8,000 (2015 est.)

note: data are in 2017 dollars

country comparison to the world: 147

Gross national saving: 34.4% of GDP (2017 est.)

33.4% of GDP (2016 est.)

32% of GDP (2015 est.)

country comparison to the world: 15

GDP—composition, by end use:

household consumption: 50.1%

government consumption: 15.9%

investment in fixed capital: 49.4%

investment in inventories: 0%

exports of goods and services: 25.9%

imports of goods and services: -41.4% (2017 est.)

GDP—composition, by sector of origin:

agriculture: 15.7%

industry: 42.6%

services: 41.7% (2017 est.)

Agriculture—products: rice, corn, root crops, citrus; dairy products, eggs

Industries: cement, wood products, processed fruits, alcoholic beverages, calcium carbide, tourism

Industrial production growth rate: 8.9% (2017 est.)

country comparison to the world: 12

Labor force: 353,000

note: major shortage of skilled labor (2015 est.)

country comparison to the world: 162

Labor force—by occupation: *agriculture:* 58%

industry: 20%

services: 22% (2015 est.)

Unemployment rate: 3.2% (2017 est.)

3.2% (2016 est.)

country comparison to the world: 36

Population below poverty line: 13.3% (2012 est.)

Household income or consumption by percentage share: *lowest 10%:* 2.8%

highest 10%: 30.6% (2012)

Distribution of family income—Gini index: 38.8 (2012)

38.1 (2007)

country comparison to the world: 69

Budget: *revenues:* $692.6 million

expenditures: $818.8 million

note: the government of India finances nearly one-quarter of Bhutan's budget expenditures (2017 est.)

Taxes and other revenues: 29.8% of GDP (2017 est.)

country comparison to the world: 82

Budget surplus (+) or deficit (-): -5.4% of GDP (2017 est.)

country comparison to the world: 167

Public debt: 93.7% of GDP (2017 est.)

106.8% of GDP (2016 est.)

country comparison to the world: 21

Fiscal year: 1 July—30 June

Inflation rate (consumer prices): 3.5% (2017 est.)

3.9% (2016 est.)

country comparison to the world: 141

Central bank discount rate: 6%

note: this is the policy rate of Bhutan's central bank

Commercial bank prime lending rate: 13.6% (31 December 2017 est.)

14.15% (31 December 2016 est.)

country comparison to the world: 56

Stock of narrow money: $963.9 million (31 December 2017 est.)

$769 million (31 December 2016 est.)

country comparison to the world: 157

Stock of broad money: $1.69 billion (31 December 2017 est.)

$1.379 billion (31 December 2016 est.)

country comparison to the world: 164

Stock of domestic credit: $1.434 billion (31 December 2017 est.)

$1.17 billion (31 December 2016 est.)

country comparison to the world: 165

Market value of publicly traded shares: $355.3 million (31 December 2015)

$283.4 million (31 December 2012)

country comparison to the world: 115

Current account balance: -$682 million (2017 est.)

-$618 million (2016 est.)

country comparison to the world: 111

Exports: $580 million (2017 est.)

$495.3 million (2016 est.)

country comparison to the world: 172

Exports—commodities: electricity (to India), ferrosilicon, cement, cardamom, calcium carbide, steel rods/bars, dolomite, gypsum

Exports—partners: India 95.7% (2016)

Imports: $1.1 billion (2017 est.)

$1.033 billion (2016 est.)

country comparison to the world: 177

Imports—commodities: fuel and lubricants, airplanes, machinery and parts, rice, motor vehicles

Imports—partners: India 91.1% (2016)

Debt—external: $2.71 billion (31 December 2017 est.)
$2.355 billion (31 December 2016 est.)
country comparison to the world: 147

Stock of direct foreign investment—at home:
$185.5 million (31 December 2017 est.)
$168.4 million (31 December 2016 est.)
country comparison to the world: 128

Exchange rates: ngultrum (BTN) per US dollar—
64.97 (2017 est.)
67.2 (2016 est.)
67.2 (2015 est.)
64.15 (2014 est.)
61.03 (2013 est.)

ENERGY

Electricity access: *population without electricity:* 187,531

electrification—*total population:* 76%
electrification—urban areas: 100%
electrification—rural areas: 53% (2012)

Electricity—production: 7.732 billion kWh (2015 est.)
country comparison to the world: 111

Electricity—consumption: 2.6 billion kWh (2015 est.)
country comparison to the world: 141

Electricity—exports: 5.308 billion kWh (2015 est.)
country comparison to the world: 34

Electricity—imports: 200 million kWh (2015 est.)
country comparison to the world: 94

Electricity—installed generating capacity: 1.631 million kW (2015 est.)
country comparison to the world: 119

Electricity—from fossil fuels: 1% of total installed capacity (2015 est.)
country comparison to the world: 211

Electricity—from nuclear fuels: 0% of total installed capacity (2015 est.)
country comparison to the world: 58

Electricity—from hydroelectric plants: 99% of total installed capacity (2015 est.)
country comparison to the world: 3

Electricity—from other renewable sources: 0% of total installed capacity (2015 est.)
country comparison to the world: 172

Crude oil—production: 0 bbl/day (2016 est.)
country comparison to the world: 112

Crude oil—exports: 0 bbl/day (2014 est.)

country comparison to the world: 100

Crude oil—imports: 0 bbl/day (2014 est.)
country comparison to the world: 103

Crude oil—proved reserves: 0 bbl (1 January 2017 es)
country comparison to the world: 111

Refined petroleum products—production: 0 bbl/day (2014 est.)
country comparison to the world: 121

Refined petroleum products—consumption: 3,000 bbl/day (2015 est.)
country comparison to the world: 189

Refined petroleum products—exports: 0 bbl/day (2014 est.)
country comparison to the world: 137

Refined petroleum products—imports: 3,135 bbl/day (2014 est.)
country comparison to the world: 177

Natural gas—production: 0 cu m (2016 est.)
country comparison to the world: 114

Natural gas—consumption: 0 cu m (2016 est.)
country comparison to the world: 162

Natural gas—exports: 0 cu m (2016 est.)
country comparison to the world: 75

Natural gas—imports: 0 cu m (2016 est.)
country comparison to the world: 98

Natural gas—proved reserves: 0 cu m (2016 est.)
country comparison to the world: 120

Carbon dioxide emissions from consumption of energy: 260,300 Mt (2015 est.)
country comparison to the world: 197

COMMUNICATIONS

Telephones—fixed lines: *total subscriptions:* 21,081
subscriptions per 100 inhabitants: 3 (July 2016 est.)
country comparison to the world: 176

Telephones—mobile cellular: *total:* 698,373
subscriptions per 100 inhabitants: 93 (July 2016 est.)
country comparison to the world: 165

Telephone system: *general assessment:* urban towns and district headquarters have telecommunications services
domestic: domestic service inadequate, especially in rural areas; mobile-cellular service, begun in 2003, is now widely available; Internet services widely available
international: country code—975; international telephone and telegraph service via landline and microwave relay through India; satellite earth station—1 Intelsat (2016)

Broadcast media: state-owned TV station established in 1999; cable TV service offers dozens of Indian and other international channels; first radio station, privately launched in 1973, is now state-owned; 5 private radio stations are currently broadcasting (2012)

Internet country code: .bt

Internet users: *total:* 313,347
percent of population: 41.8% (July 2016 est.)
country comparison to the world: 155

TRANSPORTATION

National air transport system: *number of registered air carriers:* 2
inventory of registered aircraft operated by air carriers: 6
annual passenger traffic on registered air carriers: 162,864
annual freight traffic on registered air carriers: 538,041 mt-km (2015)
Civil aircraft registration country code prefix: A5 (2016)

Airports: 2 (2013)
country comparison to the world: 198

Airports—with paved runways: *total:* 2
1,524 to 2,437 m: 1
914 to 1,523 m: 1 (2017)

Airports—with unpaved runways: *total:* 1
914 to 1,523 m: 1 (2012)

Roadways: *total:* 10,578 km
paved: 2,975 km (includes 2,180 km of national highways)
unpaved: 7,603 km (2013)
note: a more recent figure for 2015 lists 11,177 km for total roadway length, but no breakdown of paved or unpaved
country comparison to the world: 135

MILITARY AND SECURITY

Military branches: Royal Bhutan Army (includes Royal Bodyguard and Royal Bhutan Police) (2009)

Military service age and obligation: 18 years of age for voluntary military service; no conscription; militia training is compulsory for males aged 20-25, over a 3-year period (2012)

TRANSNATIONAL ISSUES

Disputes—international: lacking any treaty describing the boundary, Bhutan and China continue negotiations to establish a common boundary alignment to resolve territorial disputes arising from substantial cartographic discrepancies, the most contentious of which lie in Bhutan's west along China's Chumbi salient

BOLIVIA

INTRODUCTION

Background: Bolivia, named after independence fighter Simon BOLIVAR, broke away from Spanish rule in 1825; much of its subsequent history has consisted of a series of coups and countercoups, with the last coup occurring in 1978. Democratic civilian rule was established in 1982, but leaders have faced difficult problems of deep-seated poverty, social unrest, and illegal drug production.

In December 2005, Bolivians elected Movement Toward Socialism leader Evo MORALES president—by the widest margin of any leader since the restoration of civilian rule in 1982—after he ran on a promise to change the country's traditional political class and empower the nation's poor, indigenous majority. In December 2009 and October 2014, President MORALES easily won reelection. His party maintained control of the legislative branch of the government, which has allowed him to continue his process of change. In February 2016, MORALES narrowly lost a referendum to approve a constitutional amendment that would have allowed him to compete in the 2019 presidential election. Despite the loss, MORALES has already been chosen by his party to run again in 2019, via a still-undetermined method for him to appear on the ballot.

GEOGRAPHY

Location: Central South America, southwest of Brazil

Geographic coordinates: 17 00 S, 65 00 W

Map references: South America

Area: total: 1,098,581 sq km
land: 1,083,301 sq km
water: 15,280 sq km
country comparison to the world: 29

Area—comparative: slightly less than three times the size of Montana

Land boundaries: total: 7,252 km

border countries (5): Argentina 942 km, Brazil 3,403 km, Chile 942 km, Paraguay 753 km, Peru 1,212 km

Coastline: 0 km (landlocked)

Maritime claims: none (landlocked)

Climate: varies with altitude; humid and tropical to cold and semiarid

Terrain: rugged Andes Mountains with a highland plateau (Altiplano), hills, lowland plains of the Amazon Basin

Elevation: *mean elevation:* 1,192 m

elevation extremes: lowest point: Rio Paraguay 90 m

highest point: Nevado Sajama 6,542 m

Natural resources: tin, natural gas, petroleum, zinc, tungsten, antimony, silver, iron, lead, gold, timber, hydropower

Land use: *agricultural land:* 34.3%
arable land: 3.6%;
permanent crops: 0.2%;
permanent pasture: 30.5%
forest: 52.5%
other: 13.2% (2011 est.)
Irrigated land: 3,000 sq km (2012)

Population—distribution: a high altitude plain in the west between two cordillera of the Andes, known as the Altiplano, is the focal area for most of the population; a dense settlement pattern is also found in and around the city of Santa Cruz, located on the eastern side of the Andes

Natural hazards: flooding in the northeast (March to April)
volcanism: volcanic activity in Andes Mountains on the border with Chile; historically active volcanoes in this region are Irruputuncu (5,163 m), which last erupted in 1995, and the Olca-Paruma volcanic complex (5,762 m to 5,167 m)

Environment—current issues: the clearing of land for agricultural purposes and the international demand for tropical timber are contributing to deforestation; soil erosion from overgrazing and poor cultivation methods (including slash-and-burn agriculture); desertification; loss of biodiversity; industrial pollution of water supplies used for drinking and irrigation

Environment—international agreements: party to: Biodiversity, Climate Change, Climate Change-Kyoto Protocol, Desertification, Endangered Species, Hazardous Wastes, Law of the Sea, Marine Dumping, Ozone Layer Protection, Ship Pollution, Tropical Timber 83, Tropical Timber 94, Wetlands *signed, but not ratified:* Environmental Modification, Marine Life Conservation

Geography—note: landlocked; shares control of Lago Titicaca, world's highest navigable lake (elevation 3,805 m), with Peru

PEOPLE AND SOCIETY

Population: 11,138,234 (July 2017 est.)
country comparison to the world: 81

Nationality: *noun:* Bolivian(s)

adjective: Bolivian

Ethnic groups: mestizo (mixed white and Amerindian ancestry) 68%, indigenous 20%, white 5%, cholo/chola 2%, black 1%, other 1%, unspecified 3% ; 44% of respondents indicated feeling part of some indigenous group, predominantly Quechua or Aymara
note: results among surveys vary based on the wording of the ethnicity question and the available response choices; the 2001 national census did not provide "mestizo" as a response choice, resulting in a much higher proportion of respondents identifying themselves as belonging to one of the available indigenous ethnicity choices; the use of "mestizo" and "cholo" varies among response choices in surveys, with surveys using the terms interchangeably, providing one or the other as a response choice, or providing the two as separate response choices (2009 est.)

Languages: Spanish (official) 60.7%, Quechua (official) 21.2%, Aymara (official) 14.6%, foreign languages 2.4%, Guarani (official) 0.6%, other native languages 0.4%, none 0.1%
note: Bolivia's 2009 constitution designates Spanish and all indigenous languages as official; 36 indigenous languages are specified, including a few that are extinct (2001 est.)

Religions: Roman Catholic 76.8%, Evangelical and Pentecostal 8.1%, Protestant 7.9%, other 1.7%, none 5.5% (2012 est.)

Demographic profile: Bolivia ranks at or near the bottom among Latin American countries in several areas of health and development, including poverty, education, fertility, malnutrition, mortality, and life expectancy. On the positive side, more children are being vaccinated and more pregnant women are getting prenatal care and having skilled health practitioners attend their births. Bolivia's income inequality is the highest in Latin America and one of the highest in the world. Public education is of poor quality, and educational opportunities are among the most unevenly distributed in Latin America, with girls and indigenous and rural children less likely to be literate or to complete primary school. The lack of access to education and family planning services helps to sustain Bolivia's high fertility rate—approximately three children per woman. Bolivia's lack of clean water and basic sanitation, especially in rural areas, contributes to health problems.

Bolivia's income inequality is the highest in Latin America and one of the highest in the world. Public education is of poor quality, and educational opportunities are among the most unevenly distributed in Latin America, with girls and indigenous and rural children less likely to be literate or to complete primary school. The lack of access to education and family planning services helps to sustain Bolivia's high fertility rate—approximately three children per woman. Bolivia's lack of clean water and basic sanitation, especially in rural areas, contributes to health problems.

Between 7% and 16% of Bolivia's population lives abroad (estimates vary in part because of illegal migration). Emigrants primarily seek jobs and better wages in Argentina (the principal destination), the US, and Spain. In recent years, more restrictive immigration policies in Europe and the US have increased the flow of Bolivian emigrants to neighboring countries. Fewer Bolivians migrated to Brazil in 2015 and 2016 because of its recession; increasing numbers have been going to Chile, mainly to work as miners.

Age structure: *0-14 years:* 31.85% (male 1,807,735/female 1,739,763)
15-24 years: 19.46% (male 1,098,097/female 1,069,950)
25-54 years: 37.48% (male 2,041,866/female 2,133,065)
55-64 years: 5.9% (male 303,409/female 353,598)
65 years and over: 5.3% (male 260,424/female 330,327) (2017 est.)

Dependency ratios: *total dependency ratio:* 63.7
youth dependency ratio: 53.1
elderly dependency ratio: 10.6
potential support ratio: 9.4 (2015 est.)

Median age: *total:* 24.3 years
male: 23.6 years
female: 25 years (2017 est.)
country comparison to the world: 162

Population growth rate: 1.51% (2017 est.)
country comparison to the world: 75

Birth rate: 22 births/1,000 population (2017 est.)
country comparison to the world: 73

Death rate: 6.4 deaths/1,000 population (2017 est.)
country comparison to the world: 147

Net migration rate: -0.5 migrant(s)/1,000 population (2017 est.)
country comparison to the world: 126

Population distribution: a high altitude plain in the west between two cordillera of the Andes, known as the Altiplano, is the focal area for most of the population; a dense settlement pattern is also found in and around the city of Santa Cruz, located on the eastern side of the Andes

Urbanization: *urban population:* 69.3% of total population (2017)
rate of urbanization: 2.11% annual rate of change (2015-20 est.)

Major urban areas—population: Santa Cruz 2.107 million; LA PAZ (capital) 1.816 million; Cochabamba 1.24 million; Sucre (constitutional capital) 372,000 (2015)

Sex ratio: *at birth:* 1.05 male(s)/female
0-14 years: 1.04 male(s)/female
15-24 years: 1.03 male(s)/female
25-54 years: 0.95 male(s)/female
55-64 years: 0.86 male(s)/female
65 years and over: 0.79 male(s)/female
total population: 0.98 male(s)/female (2016 est.)

Mother's mean age at first birth: 21.2 years

note: median age at first birth among women 25-29 (2008 est.)

Maternal mortality ratio: 206 deaths/100,000 live births (2015 est.)
country comparison to the world: 51

Infant mortality rate: *total:* 35.3 deaths/1,000 live births
male: 38.7 deaths/1,000 live births
female: 31.7 deaths/1,000 live births (2017 est.)
country comparison to the world: 52

Life expectancy at birth: *total population:* 69.5 years
male: 66.7 years
female: 72.4 years (2017 est.)
country comparison to the world: 161

Total fertility rate: 2.63 children born/woman (2017 est.)
country comparison to the world: 73

Contraceptive prevalence rate: 60.5% (2008)
Health expenditures: 6.3% of GDP (2014)
country comparison to the world: 99

Physicians density: 0.47 physicians/1,000 population (2011)

Hospital bed density: 1.1 beds/1,000 population (2012)

Drinking water source:
improved:
urban: 96.7% of population
rural: 75.6% of population
total: 90% of population
unimproved:
urban: 3.3% of population
rural: 24.4% of population
total: 10% of population (2015 est.)

Sanitation facility access:
improved:
urban: 60.8% of population
rural: 27.5% of population
total: 50.3% of population
unimproved:
urban: 39.2% of population
rural: 72.5% of population
total: 49.7% of population (2015 est.)

HIV/AIDS—adult prevalence rate: 0.3% (2016 est.)
country comparison to the world: 82

HIV/AIDS—people living with HIV/AIDS: 19,000 (2016 est.)
country comparison to the world: 78

HIV/AIDS—deaths: <1000 (2016 est.)

Major infectious diseases: *degree of risk:* very high
food or waterborne diseases: bacterial diarrhea and hepatitis A
vectorborne diseases: dengue fever, malaria, and yellow fever
note: active local transmission of Zika virus by Aedes species mosquitoes has been identified in this country (as of August 2016); it poses an important risk (a large number of cases possible) among US citizens if bitten by an infective mosquito; other less common ways to get Zika are through sex, via blood transfusion, or during

pregnancy, in which the pregnant woman passes Zika virus to her fetus (2016)

Obesity—adult prevalence rate: 20.2% (2016)
country comparison to the world: 104

Children under the age of 5 years underweight: 3.6% (2012)
country comparison to the world: 95

Education expenditures: 7.3% of GDP (2014)
country comparison to the world: 24

Literacy: *definition:* age 15 and over can read and write
total population: 92.5%
male: 96.5%
female: 88.6% (2015 est.)

School life expectancy (primary to tertiary education): *total:* 14 years
male: 14 years
female: 14 years (2007)

Unemployment, youth ages 15-24: *total:* 6.9%
male: 6.4%
female: 7.6% (2013 est.)
country comparison to the world: 122

GOVERNMENT

Country name: *conventional long form:* Plurinational State of Bolivia
conventional short form: Bolivia
local long form: Estado Plurinacional de Bolivia
local short form: Bolivia
etymology: the country is named after Simon BOLIVAR, a 19th-century leader in the South American wars for independence

Government type: presidential republic

Capital: *name:* La Paz (administrative capital); Sucre (constitutional [legislative and judicial] capital)

geographic coordinates: 16 30 S, 68 09 W

time difference: UTC-4 (1 hour ahead of Washington, DC, during Standard Time)

Administrative divisions: 9 departments (departamentos, singular—departamento); Beni, Chuquisaca, Cochabamba, La Paz, Oruro, Pando, Potosi, Santa Cruz, Tarija

Independence: 6 August 1825 (from Spain)

National holiday: Independence Day, 6 August (1825)

Constitution: many previous; latest drafted 6 August 2006—9 December 2008, approved by referendum 25 January 2009, effective 7 February 2009; amended 2013; note—in late 2017, the Constitutional Court changed the presidential two consecutive term limit to no term limits (2017)

Legal system: civil law system with influences from Roman, Spanish, canon (religious), French, and indigenous law

International law organization participation: has not submitted an ICJ jurisdiction declaration; accepts ICCt jurisdiction

Citizenship: *citizenship by birth:* yes
citizenship by descent: yes
dual citizenship recognized: yes

residency requirement for naturalization: 3 years

Suffrage: 18 years of age, universal and compulsory

Executive branch: *chief of state:* President Juan Evo MORALES Ayma (since 22 January 2006); Vice President Alvaro GARCIA Linera (since 22 January 2006); note—the president is both chief of state and head of government

head of government: President Juan Evo MORALES Ayma (since 22 January 2006); Vice President Alvaro GARCIA Linera (since 22 January 2006)

cabinet: Cabinet appointed by the president

elections/appointments: president and vice president directly elected on the same ballot one of 3 ways: candidate wins at least 50% of the vote, or at least 40% of the vote and 10% more than the next highest candidate; otherwise a second round is held and the winner determined by simple majority vote ; no term limits (changed from two consecutive term limit by Constitutional Court in late 2017); election last held on 12 October 2014 (next to be held in 2019)

election results: Juan Evo MORALES Ayma reelected president; percent of vote—Juan Evo MORALES Ayma (MAS) 61%; Samuel DORIA MEDINA Arana (UN) 24.5%; Jorge QUIROGA Ramirez (POC) 9.1%; other 5.4%

Legislative branch: *description:* bicameral Plurinational Legislative Assembly or Asamblea Legislativa Plurinacional consists of the Chamber of Senators or Camara de Senadores (36 seats; members directly elected in multi-seat constituencies by proportional representation vote; members serve 5-year terms) and the Chamber of Deputies or Camara de Diputados (130 seats; 70 members directly elected in single-seat constituencies by simple majority vote, 53 indirectly elected in single-seat constituencies by proportional representation vote, and 7—apportioned to non-contiguous, rural areas in 7 of the 9 states—directly elected in single-seat constituencies by simple majority vote; members serve 5-year terms)

elections: Chamber of Senators and Chamber of Deputies—last held on 12 October 2014 (next to be held in 2019)

election results: Chamber of Senators—percent of vote by party—NA; seats by party—MAS 25, UD 9, PDC 2; Chamber of Deputies—percent of vote by party—NA; seats by party—MAS 88, UD 32, PDC 10

Judicial branch: *highest court(s):* Supreme Court or Tribunal Supremo de Justicia (consists of 12 judges or ministros organized into civil, penal, social, and administrative chambers); Plurinational Constitutional Tribunal (consists of 7 primary and 7 alternate magistrates); Plurinational Electoral Organ (consists of 7 members and 6 alternates); National Agro-Environment Court (consists of 5 primary and 5 alternate judges; Council of the Judiciary (consists of 3 primary and 3 alternate judges)

judge selection and term of office: Supreme Court, Plurinational Constitutional Tribunal, National Agro-Environmental Court, and Council of the Judiciary candidates pre-selected by the Plurinational Legislative Assembly and elected by direct popular vote; judges elected for 6-year terms; Plurinational Electoral Organ judges appointed—6 by the Legislative Assembly and 1 by the president of the republic; members serve single 6-year terms

subordinate courts: National Electoral Court; District Courts (in each of the 9 administrative departments); Agro-Environmental lower courts

Political parties and leaders: Christian Democratic Party or PDC [Jorge Fernando QUIROGA Ramirez]
Movement Toward Socialism or MAS [Juan Evo MORALES Ayma]
National Unity or UN [Samuel DORIA MEDINA Arana]

Political pressure groups and leaders: Bolivian Workers Central or COB
Central Bolivian Workers' Union or COB
Confederation of Indigenous Peoples of Eastern Bolivia or CIDOB
Federation of Neighborhood Councils of El Alto or FEJUVE-El Alto
Landless Movement or MST
National Confederation of Native Rural Indigenous Women of Bolivia or Bartolina Sisa
National Coordination for Change or CONALCAM
National Council of Ayullus and Markas of Quollasuyu or CONAMAQ
Sole Confederation of Campesino Workers of Bolivia or CSUTCB [Jacinto HERRARA]
other: Cocalero unions
Interculturales union or CSCIB
various federations of neighborhood councils or FEJUVEs (including the national organization)

International organization participation: CAN, CD, CELAC, FAO, G-77, IADB, IAEA, IBRD, ICAO, ICC (national committees), ICCt, ICRM, IDA, IFAD, IFC, IFRCS, ILO, IMF, IMO, Interpol, IOC, IOM, IPU, ISO (correspondent), ITSO, ITU, LAES, LAIA, Mercosur (associate), MIGA, MINUSTAH, MONUSCO, NAM, OAS, OPANAL, OPCW, PCA, UN, UN Security Council (temporary), UNAMID, UNASUR, UNCTAD, UNESCO, UNIDO, Union Latina, UNMIL, UNMISS, UNOCI, UNWTO, UPU, WCO, WFTU (NGOs), WHO, WIPO, WMO, WTO

Diplomatic representation in the US: *chief of mission:* Ambassador (vacant); Charge d'Affaires Rafael Pablo CANEDO Daroca (since July 2017)
chancery: 3014 Massachusetts Avenue NW, Washington, DC 20008
telephone: [1] (202) 328-4155
FAX: [1] (202) 328-3712
consulate(s) general: Houston, Los Angeles, Miami, New York, Washington, DC
note: in September 2008, the US expelled the Bolivian ambassador to the US in reciprocity for Bolivia expelling the US ambassador to Bolivia

Diplomatic representation from the US: *chief of mission:* Ambassador (vacant); Charge d'Affaires Bruce WILLIAMSON (since December 2017)
embassy: Avenida Arce 2780, Casilla 425, La Paz

mailing address: 3220 La Paz Place, Dulles, VA, 20189-3220
telephone: [591] (2) 216-8000
FAX: [591] (2) 216-8111
note: in September 2008, the Bolivian Government expelled the US Ambassador to Bolivia, Philip GOLDBERG, and both countries have yet to reinstate their ambassadors

Flag description: three equal horizontal bands of red (top), yellow, and green with the coat of arms centered on the yellow band; red stands for bravery and the blood of national heroes, yellow for the nation's mineral resources, and green for the fertility of the land
note: similar to the flag of Ghana, which has a large black five-pointed star centered in the yellow band; in 2009, a presidential decree made it mandatory for a so-called wiphala—a square, multi-colored flag representing the country's indigenous peoples—to be used alongside the traditional flag

National symbol(s): llama, Andean condor; national colors: red, yellow, green

National anthem: *name:* "Cancion Patriotica" (Patriotic Song)
lyrics/music: Jose Ignacio de SANJINES/Leopoldo Benedetto VINCENTI
note: adopted 1852

ECONOMY

Economy—overview: Bolivia is a resource rich country with strong growth attributed to captive markets for natural gas exports to Brazil and Argentina. However, the country remains one of the least developed countries in Latin America because of state-oriented policies that deter investment and growth.

Following a disastrous economic crisis during the early 1980s, reforms spurred private investment, stimulated economic growth, and cut poverty rates in the 1990s. The period 2003-05 was characterized by political instability, racial tensions, and violent protests against plans—subsequently abandoned—to export Bolivia's newly discovered natural gas reserves to large Northern Hemisphere markets. In 2005, the government passed a controversial hydrocarbons law that imposed significantly higher royalties and required foreign firms then operating under risk-sharing contracts to surrender all production to the state energy company in exchange for a predetermined service fee. High commodity prices between 2010 and 2014 sustained rapid growth and large trade surpluses. The global decline in oil prices that began in late 2014 exerted downward pressure on the price Bolivia receives for exported gas and resulted in lower GDP growth rates—declining from 4.9% in 2015 to 4.2% in 2017—and losses in government revenue as well as fiscal and trade deficits.

A lack of foreign investment in the key sectors of mining and hydrocarbons, along with conflict among social groups, pose challenges for the Bolivian economy. In 2015, in an attempt to improve the investment climate, President Evo MORALES expanded efforts to court international investment and boost Bolivia's energy production capacity, passing an investment law and promising not to nationalize additional industries. In early 2016, the Government of Bolivia approved the 2016-20 National Economic and Social Development Plan aimed at maintaining growth of 5% and reducing poverty.

GDP (purchasing power parity): $83.5 billion (2017 est.)
$80.14 billion (2016 est.)
$76.86 billion (2015 est.)
note: data are in 2017 dollars
country comparison to the world: 93

GDP (official exchange rate): $37.78 billion (2016 est.)

GDP—real growth rate: 4.2% (2017 est.)
4.3% (2016 est.)
4.9% (2015 est.)
country comparison to the world: 59

GDP—per capita (PPP): $7,500 (2017 est.)
$7,400 (2016 est.)
$7,200 (2015 est.)
note: data are in 2017 dollars
country comparison to the world: 155

Gross national saving: 15.6% of GDP (2017 est.)
15.1% of GDP (2016 est.)
14.2% of GDP (2015 est.)
country comparison to the world: 123

GDP—composition, by end use:
household consumption: 69%
government consumption: 17.6%
investment in fixed capital: 20.3%
investment in inventories: 0.5%
exports of goods and services: 24.2%
imports of goods and services: -31.6% (2017 est.)

GDP—composition, by sector of origin:
agriculture: 13%
industry: 37.4%
services: 54.1% (2017 est.)

Agriculture—products: soybeans, quinoa, Brazil nuts, sugarcane, coffee, corn, rice, potatoes, chia, coca

Industries: mining, smelting, petroleum, food and beverages, tobacco, handicrafts, clothing, jewelry

Industrial production growth rate: 3.5% (2017 est.)
country comparison to the world: 81

Labor force: 5.07 million (2017 est.)
country comparison to the world: 83

Labor force—by occupation: agriculture: 29.4%
industry: 22%
services: 48.6% (2015 est.)

Unemployment rate: 4% (2017 est.)
4% (2016 est.)
note: data are for urban areas; widespread underemployment
country comparison to the world: 48

Population below poverty line: 38.6%
note: based on percent of population living on less than the international standard of $2/day (2011 est.)

Household income or consumption by percentage share: lowest 10%: 0.9%
highest 10%: 36.1% (2014 est.)

Distribution of family income—Gini index: 47 (2016 est.)
57.9 (1999)

country comparison to the world: 28

Budget: revenues: $15.01 billion
expenditures: $17.35 billion (2017 est.)
Taxes and other revenues: 39.7% of GDP (2017 est.)
country comparison to the world: 36

Budget surplus (+) or deficit (-): -6.2% of GDP (2017 est.)
country comparison to the world: 179

Public debt: 51.5% of GDP (2017 est.)
44.8% of GDP (2016 est.)
note: data cover general government debt, and includes debt instruments issued by government entities other than the treasury; the data include treasury debt held by foreign entities; the data include debt issued by subnational entities
country comparison to the world: 99

Fiscal year: calendar year

Inflation rate (consumer prices): 3.2% (2017 est.)
3.6% (2016 est.)
country comparison to the world: 133

Central bank discount rate: 1.5% (31 December 2016 est.)
2.5% (31 December 2015 est.)
country comparison to the world: 120

Commercial bank prime lending rate: 9.9% (31 December 2017 est.)
7.95% (31 December 2016 est.)
country comparison to the world: 85

Stock of narrow money: $10.41 billion (31 December 2017 est.)
$9.09 billion (31 December 2016 est.)
country comparison to the world: 84

Stock of broad money: $17.08 billion (31 December 2017 est.)
$14.85 billion (31 December 2016 est.)
country comparison to the world: 93

Stock of domestic credit: $26.42 billion (31 December 2017 est.)
$22.39 billion (31 December 2016 est.)
country comparison to the world: 84

Market value of publicly traded shares: $12.3 billion (31 December 2016 est.)
$11.11 billion (31 December 2015 est.)
$9.833 billion (31 December 2014 est.)
country comparison to the world: 72

Current account balance: -$1.791 billion (2017 est.)
-$1.928 billion (2016 est.)
country comparison to the world: 153

Exports: $7.541 billion (2017 est.)
$7 billion (2016 est.)
country comparison to the world: 100

Exports—commodities: natural gas, silver, zinc, lead, tin, gold, quinoa, soybeans and soy products

Exports—partners: Brazil 19.3%, US 13.6%, Argentina 11.4%, Colombia 8.8%, China 6.8%, Japan 5.9%, South Korea 5.4%, Peru 4.8%, Belgium 4.6% (2016)

Imports: $8.239 billion (2017 est.)
$7.888 billion (2016 est.)
country comparison to the world: 106

Imports—commodities: machinery, petroleum products, vehicles, iron and steel, plastics

Imports—partners: China 19.9%, Brazil 17.5%, Argentina 10.5%, US 9.8%, Peru 6.9%, Japan 4.9%, Chile 4.1% (2016)

Reserves of foreign exchange and gold: $8.287 billion (31 December 2017 est.)
$10.08 billion (31 December 2016 est.)
country comparison to the world: 78

Debt—external: $14.81 billion (31 December 2017 est.)
$11.65 billion (31 December 2016 est.)
country comparison to the world: 103

Stock of direct foreign investment—at home: $1.059 billion (31 December 2016 est.)
$1.084 billion (31 December 2015 est.)
country comparison to the world: 118

Stock of direct foreign investment—abroad: $0 (31 December 2016 est.)
$0 (31 December 2015 est.)
country comparison to the world: 112

Exchange rates: bolivianos (BOB) per US dollar—
6.91 (2017 est.)
6.91 (2016 est.)
6.91 (2015 est.)
6.91 (2014 est.)
6.91 (2013 est.)

ENERGY

Electricity access: population without electricity: 1,200,000
electrification—total population: 90%
electrification—urban areas: 99%
electrification—rural areas: 72% (2013)

Electricity—production: 8.147 billion kWh (2015 est.)
country comparison to the world: 110

Electricity—consumption: 7.332 billion kWh (2015 est.)
country comparison to the world: 107

Electricity—exports: 0 kWh (2016 est.)
country comparison to the world: 109

Electricity—imports: 0 kWh (2016 est.)
country comparison to the world: 126

Electricity—installed generating capacity: 2.362 million kW (2015 est.)
country comparison to the world: 107

Electricity—from fossil fuels: 71.9% of total installed capacity (2015 est.)
country comparison to the world: 100

Electricity—from nuclear fuels: 0% of total installed capacity (2015 est.)
country comparison to the world: 53

Electricity—from hydroelectric plants: 21% of total installed capacity (2015 est.)
country comparison to the world: 86

Electricity—from other renewable sources: 8% of total installed capacity (2015 est.)
country comparison to the world: 79

Crude oil—production: 59,330 bbl/day (2016 est.)
country comparison to the world: 50

Crude oil—exports: 0 bbl/day (2014 est.)
country comparison to the world: 97

Crude oil—imports: 0 bbl/day (2014 est.)
country comparison to the world: 100

Crude oil—proved reserves: 211.5 million bbl (1 January 2017 es)

country comparison to the world: 57

Refined petroleum products—production: 59,050 bbl/day (2014 est.)
country comparison to the world: 80

Refined petroleum products—consumption: 86,000 bbl/day (2015 est.)
country comparison to the world: 87

Refined petroleum products—exports: 8,642 bbl/day (2014 est.)
country comparison to the world: 86

Refined petroleum products—imports: 22,340 bbl/day (2014 est.)
country comparison to the world: 113

Natural gas—production: 21.1 billion cu m (2016 est.)
country comparison to the world: 31

Natural gas—consumption: 5.366 billion cu m (2016 est.)
country comparison to the world: 62

Natural gas—exports: 15.73 billion cu m (2016 est.)
country comparison to the world: 16

Natural gas—imports: 0 cu m (2015 est.)
country comparison to the world: 94

Natural gas—proved reserves: 295.9 billion cu m (1 January 2017 es)
country comparison to the world: 41

Carbon dioxide emissions from consumption of energy: 16 million Mt (2013 est.)
country comparison to the world: 90

COMMUNICATIONS

Telephones—fixed lines: *total subscriptions:* 867,302
subscriptions per 100 inhabitants: 8 (July 2016 est.)
country comparison to the world: 83

Telephones—mobile cellular: *total:* 10,165,308
subscriptions per 100 inhabitants: 93 (July 2016 est.)
country comparison to the world: 84

Telephone system: *general assessment:* Bolivian National Telecommunications Company was privatized in 1995 but re-nationalized in 2007; the primary trunk system is being expanded and employs digital microwave radio relay; some areas are served by fiber-optic cable; system operations, reliability, and coverage have steadily improved
domestic: most telephones are concentrated in La Paz, Santa Cruz, and other capital cities; mobile-cellular telephone use expanding rapidly and, in 2016, teledensity stood at 93 per 100 persons
international: country code—591; satellite earth station—1 Intelsat (Atlantic Ocean) (2016)

Broadcast media: large number of radio and TV stations broadcasting with private media outlets dominating; state-owned and private radio and TV stations generally operating freely, although both pro-government and anti-government groups have attacked media outlets in response to their reporting (2010)

Internet country code: .bo

Internet users: *total:* 4,354,678

percent of population: 39.7% (July 2016 est.)
country comparison to the world: 78

TRANSPORTATION

National air transport system: *number of registered air carriers:* 7
inventory of registered aircraft operated by air carriers: 39
annual passenger traffic on registered air carriers: 2,578,959
annual freight traffic on registered air carriers: 9,456,548 mt-km (2015)
Civil aircraft registration country code prefix: CP (2016)

Airports: 855 (2013)
country comparison to the world: 7

Airports—with paved runways: *total:* 21
over 3,047 m: 5
2,438 to 3,047 m: 4
1,524 to 2,437 m: 6
914 to 1,523 m: 6 (2017)

Airports—with unpaved runways: *total:* 834
over 3,047 m: 1
2,438 to 3,047 m: 4
1,524 to 2,437 m: 47
914 to 1,523 m: 151
under 914 m: 631 (2013)

Pipelines: gas 5,457 km; liquid petroleum gas 51 km; oil 2,511 km; refined products 1,627 km (2013)

Railways: *total:* 3,504 km
narrow gauge: 3,504 km 1.000-m gauge (2014)
country comparison to the world: 51

Roadways: *total:* 90,568 km
paved: 9,792 km
unpaved: 80,776 km (2017)
country comparison to the world: 61

Waterways: 10,000 km (commercially navigable almost exclusively in the northern and eastern parts of the country) (2012)
country comparison to the world: 13

Merchant marine: *total:* 55
by type: general cargo 41, oil tanker 3, other 11 (2017)
country comparison to the world: 108

Ports and terminals: *river port(s):* Puerto Aguirre (Paraguay/Parana)
note: Bolivia has free port privileges in maritime ports in Argentina, Brazil, Chile, and Paraguay

MILITARY AND SECURITY

Military expenditures: 1.5% of GDP (2017 est.)
1.68% of GDP (2016)
1.74% of GDP (2015)
1.9% of GDP (2014)
1.84% of GDP (2013)
1.85% of GDP (2012)
country comparison to the world: 64

Military branches: Bolivian Armed Forces: Bolivian Army (Ejercito Boliviano, EB), Bolivian Naval Force (Fuerza Naval Boliviana, FNB, includes Marines), Bolivian Air Force (Fuerza Aerea Boliviana, FAB) (2017)

Military service age and obligation: 16-49 years of age for 12-month voluntary male and female

military service; Bolivian citizenship required; minimum age of combat is 18; when annual number of volunteers falls short of goal, compulsory recruitment is effected, including conscription of boys as young as 14; 15-19 years of age for voluntary premilitary service, provides exemption from further military service (2017)

TRANSNATIONAL ISSUES

Disputes—international: Chile and Peru rebuff Bolivia's reactivated claim to restore the Atacama corridor, ceded to Chile in 1884, but Chile offers instead unrestricted but not sovereign maritime access through Chile for Bolivian products; contraband smuggling, human trafficking, and illegal narcotic trafficking are problems in the porous areas of its border regions with all of its neighbors (Argentina, Brazil, Chile, Paraguay, and Peru)

Trafficking in persons: current situation: Bolivia is a source country for men, women, and children subjected to forced labor and sex trafficking domestically and abroad; indigenous children are particularly vulnerable; Bolivia is a source country for men, women, and children subjected to forced labor and sex trafficking domestically and abroad; rural and poor Bolivians, most of whom are indigenous, and LGBT youth are particularly vulnerable; Bolivians perform forced labor domestically in mining, ranching, agriculture, and domestic service, and a significant number are in forced labor abroad in sweatshops, agriculture, domestic service, and the informal sector; women and girls are sex trafficked within Bolivia and in neighboring countries, such as Argentina, Peru, and Chile; a limited number of women from nearby countries are sex trafficked in Bolivia

tier rating: Tier 2 Watch List—Bolivia does not comply fully with the minimum standards for the elimination of human trafficking; however, it is making significant efforts to do so; the government did not demonstrate overall increasing anti-trafficking efforts, and poor data collection made it difficult to assess the number of investigations, prosecutions, and victim identifications and referrals to care services; authorities did not adequately differentiate between human trafficking and other crimes, such as domestic violence and child abuse; law enforcement failed to implement an early detection protocol for identifying trafficking cases and lacked a formal process for identifying trafficking victims among vulnerable populations; specialized victim services were inadequately funded and virtually non-existent for adult women and male victims (2015)

Illicit drugs: world's third-largest cultivator of coca (after Colombia and Peru) with an estimated 36,500 hectares under cultivation in 2015, a 3 percent increase over 2014; third largest producer of cocaine, estimated at 255 metric tons potential pure cocaine in 2015; transit country for Peruvian and Colombian cocaine destined for Brazil, Argentina, Chile, Paraguay, and Europe; weak border controls; some money-laundering activity related to narcotics trade; major cocaine consumption

BOSNIA AND HERZEGOVINA

INTRODUCTION

Background: Bosnia and Herzegovina declared sovereignty in October 1991 and independence from the former Yugoslavia on 3 March 1992 after a referendum boycotted by ethnic Serbs. The Bosnian Serbs—supported by neighboring Serbia and Montenegro—responded with armed resistance aimed at partitioning the republic along ethnic lines and joining Serb-held areas to form a "Greater Serbia." In March 1994, Bosniaks and Croats reduced the number of warring factions from three to two by signing an agreement creating a joint Bosniak-Croat Federation of Bosnia and Herzegovina. On 21 November 1995, in Dayton, Ohio, the warring parties initialed a peace agreement that ended three years of interethnic civil strife (the final agreement was signed in Paris on 14 December 1995).

The Dayton Peace Accords retained Bosnia and Herzegovina's international boundaries and created a multiethnic and democratic government charged with conducting foreign, diplomatic, and fiscal policy. Also recognized was a second tier of government composed of two entities roughly equal in size: the predominantly Bosniak-Bosnian Croat Federation of Bosnia and Herzegovina and the predominantly Bosnian Serb-led Republika Srpska (RS). The Federation and RS governments are responsible for overseeing most government functions. Additionally, the Dayton Accords established the Office of the High Representative to oversee the implementation of the civilian aspects of the agreement. The Peace Implementation Council at its conference in Bonn in 1997 also gave the High Representative the authority to impose legislation and remove officials, the so-called "Bonn Powers." An original NATO-led international peacekeeping force (IFOR) of 60,000 troops assembled in 1995 was succeeded over time by a smaller, NATO-led Stabilization Force (SFOR). In 2004, European Union peacekeeping troops (EUFOR) replaced SFOR. Currently,

EUFOR deploys around 600 troops in theater in a security assistance and training capacity.

GEOGRAPHY

Location: Southeastern Europe, bordering the Adriatic Sea and Croatia

Geographic coordinates: 44 00 N, 18 00 E

Map references: Europe

Area: *total:* 51,197 sq km
land: 51,187 sq km
water: 10 sq km
country comparison to the world: 129

Area—comparative: slightly smaller than West Virginia

Land boundaries: *total:* 1,543 km
border countries (3): Croatia 956 km, Montenegro 242 km, Serbia 345 km

Coastline: 20 km

Maritime claims: NA

Climate: hot summers and cold winters; areas of high elevation have short, cool summers and long, severe winters; mild, rainy winters along coast

Terrain: mountains and valleys

Elevation: *mean elevation:* 500 m

elevation extremes: *lowest point:* Adriatic Sea 0 m
highest point: Maglic 2,386 m

Natural resources: coal, iron ore, bauxite, copper, lead, zinc, chromite, cobalt, manganese, nickel, clay, gypsum, salt, sand, timber, hydropower

Land use: *agricultural land:* 42.2%
arable land: 19.7%;
permanent crops: 2%;
permanent pasture: 20.5%
forest: 42.8%
other: 15% (2011 est.)
Irrigated land: 30 sq km (2012)

Population—distribution: the northern and central areas of the country are the most densely populated

Natural hazards: destructive earthquakes

Environment—current issues: air pollution; deforestation and illegal logging; inadequate wastewater treatment and flood management facilities; sites for disposing of urban waste are limited; land mines left over from the 1992-95 civil strife are a hazard in some areas

Environment—international agreements: party to: Air Pollution, Biodiversity, Climate Change, Climate Change-Kyoto Protocol, Desertification, Hazardous Wastes, Law of the Sea, Marine Life Conservation, Ozone Layer Protection, Wetlands *signed, but not ratified:* none of the selected agreements

Geography—note: within Bosnia and Herzegovina's recognized borders, the country is divided into a joint Bosniak/Croat Federation (about 51%

of the territory) and the Bosnian Serb-led Republika Srpska or RS (about 49% of the territory); the region called Herzegovina is contiguous to Croatia and Montenegro, and traditionally has been settled by an ethnic Croat majority in the west and an ethnic Serb majority in the east

PEOPLE AND SOCIETY

Population: 3,856,181 (July 2017 est.)
country comparison to the world: 128

Nationality: *noun:* Bosnian(s), Herzegovinian(s)
adjective: Bosnian, Herzegovinian

Ethnic groups: Bosniak 50.1%, Serb 30.8%, Croat 15.4%, other 2.7%, not declared/no answer 1%
note: the methodology remains disputed and Republika Srpska authorities refuse to recognize the results; Bosniak has replaced Muslim as an ethnic term in part to avoid confusion with the religious term Muslim—an adherent of Islam (2013 est.)

Languages: Bosnian (official) 52.9%, Serbian (official) 30.8%, Croatian (official) 14.6%, other 1.6%, no answer 0.2% (2013 est.)

Religions: Muslim 50.7%, Orthodox 30.7%, Roman Catholic 15.2%, atheist 0.8%, agnostic 0.3%, other 1.2%, undeclared/no answer 1.1% (2013 est.)

Age structure: *0-14 years:* 13.29% (male 264,718/female 247,587)
15-24 years: 11.58% (male 230,495/female 216,107)
25-54 years: 45.88% (male 889,686/female 879,514)
55-64 years: 14.83% (male 275,550/female 296,236)
65 years and over: 14.43% (male 218,823/female 337,465) (2017 est.)

Dependency ratios: *total dependency ratio:* 43.3
youth dependency ratio: 20.7
elderly dependency ratio: 22.5
potential support ratio: 4.4 (2015 est.)

Median age: *total:* 42.1 years
male: 40.5 years
female: 43.5 years (2017 est.)
country comparison to the world: 34

Population growth rate: -0.16% (2017 est.)
country comparison to the world: 207

Birth rate: 8.8 births/1,000 population (2017 est.)
country comparison to the world: 211

Death rate: 10 deaths/1,000 population (2017 est.)
country comparison to the world: 39

Net migration rate: -0.4 migrant(s)/1,000 population (2017 est.)
country comparison to the world: 119

Population distribution: the northern and central areas of the country are the most densely populated

Urbanization: *urban population:* 40.1% of total population (2017)

rate of urbanization: 0.38% annual rate of change (2015-20 est.)

Major urban areas—population: SARAJEVO (capital) 318,000 (2015)

Sex ratio: *at birth:* 1.07 male(s)/female
0-14 years: 1.07 male(s)/female
15-24 years: 1.07 male(s)/female
25-54 years: 1.01 male(s)/female
55-64 years: 0.92 male(s)/female
65 years and over: 0.64 male(s)/female
total population: 0.95 male(s)/female (2016 est.)

Mother's mean age at first birth: 27 years (2014 est.)

Maternal mortality ratio: 11 deaths/100,000 live births (2015 est.)
country comparison to the world: 143

Infant mortality rate: *total:* 5.5 deaths/1,000 live births
male: 5.6 deaths/1,000 live births
female: 5.4 deaths/1,000 live births (2017 est.)
country comparison to the world: 172

Life expectancy at birth: *total population:* 76.9 years
male: 73.9 years
female: 80.2 years (2017 est.)
country comparison to the world: 81

Total fertility rate: 1.3 children born/woman (2017 est.)
country comparison to the world: 217

Contraceptive prevalence rate: 45.8% (2011/12)
Health expenditures: 9.6% of GDP (2014)
country comparison to the world: 30

Physicians density: 1.89 physicians/1,000 population (2013)

Hospital bed density: 3.5 beds/1,000 population (2010)

Drinking water source:
improved:
urban: 99.7% of population
rural: 100% of population
total: 99.9% of population
unimproved:
urban: 0.3% of population
rural: 0% of population
total: 0.1% of population (2015 est.)

Sanitation facility access:
improved:
urban: 98.9% of population
rural: 92% of population
total: 94.8% of population
unimproved:
urban: 1.1% of population
rural: 8% of population
total: 5.2% of population (2015 est.)

HIV/AIDS—adult prevalence rate: NA

HIV/AIDS—people living with HIV/AIDS: NA

HIV/AIDS—deaths: NA

Obesity—adult prevalence rate: 17.9% (2016)
country comparison to the world: 118

Children under the age of 5 years underweight: 1.5% (2012)
country comparison to the world: 127

Education expenditures: NA

Literacy: *definition:* age 15 and over can read and write
total population: 98.5%
male: 99.5%
female: 97.5% (2015 est.)

School life expectancy (primary to tertiary education): *total:* 14 years
male: 14 years
female: 15 years (2014)

Unemployment, youth ages 15-24: *total:* 62.3%
male: 43.5%
female: 62.3% (2015 est.)
country comparison to the world: 1

GOVERNMENT

Country name: *conventional long form:* none
conventional short form: Bosnia and Herzegovina
local long form: none
local short form: Bosna i Hercegovina
former: People's Republic of Bosnia and Herzegovina, Socialist Republic of Bosnia and Herzegovina
abbreviation: BiH
etymology: the larger northern territory is named for the Bosna River; the smaller southern section takes its name from the German word "herzog," meaning "duke," and the ending "-ovina," meaning "land," forming the combination denoting "dukedom"

Government type: parliamentary republic

Capital: *name:* Sarajevo

geographic coordinates: 43 52 N, 18 25 E

time difference: UTC+1 (6 hours ahead of Washington, DC, during Standard Time)
daylight saving time: +1hr, begins last Sunday in March; ends last Sunday in October

Administrative divisions: 3 first-order administrative divisions—Brcko District (Brcko Distrikt) (ethnically mixed), the Federation of Bosnia and Herzegovina (Federacija Bosne i Hercegovine) (predominantly Bosniak-Croat), the Republic of Srpska (Republika Srpska) (predominantly Serb)

Independence: 1 March 1992 (from Yugoslavia); note—referendum for independence completed on 1 March 1992; independence declared on 3 March 1992

National holiday: Independence Day, 1 March (1992) and Statehood Day, 25 November (1943)—both observed in the Federation of Bosnia and Herzegovina entity; Victory Day, 9 May (1945) and Dayton Agreement Day, 21 November (1995)—both observed in the Republika Srpska entity
note: there is no national-level holiday

Constitution: *history:* 14 December 1995 (constitution included as part of the Dayton Peace Accords); note—each of the political entities has its own constitution
amendments: decided by the Parliamentary Assembly, including a two-thirds majority vote of members present in the House of Representatives; the constitutional article on human rights

and fundamental freedoms cannot be amended; amended several times, last in 2009 (2016)

Legal system: civil law system; Constitutional Court review of legislative acts

International law organization participation: has not submitted an ICJ jurisdiction declaration; accepts ICCt jurisdiction

Citizenship: *citizenship by birth:* no
citizenship by descent only: at least one parent must be a citizen of Bosnia and Herzegovina
dual citizenship recognized: yes, provided there is a bilateral agreement with the other state
residency requirement for naturalization: 8 years

Suffrage: 18 years of age, 16 if employed; universal

Executive branch: *chief of state:* Chairman of the Presidency Dragan COVIC (chairman since 17 July 2017, presidency member since 17 November 2014—Croat), Mladen IVANIC (presidency member since 17 November 2014—Serb); Bakir IZETBEGOVIC (presidency member since 10 November 2010—Bosniak)

head of government: Chairman of the Council of Ministers Denis ZVIZDIC (since 11 February 2015)
cabinet: Council of Ministers nominated by the council chairman, approved by the state-level House of Representatives
elections/appointments: 3-member presidency (1 Bosniak and 1 Croat elected from the Federation of Bosnia and Herzegovina and 1 Serb elected from the Republika Srpska) directly elected by simple majority popular vote for a 4-year term (eligible for a second term, but then ineligible for 4 years); the presidency chairpersonship rotates every 8 months and resumes where it left off following each general election; election last held on 12 October 2014 (next to be held in October 2018); the chairman of the Council of Ministers appointed by the presidency and confirmed by the state-level House of Representatives
election results: percent of vote—Mladen IVANIC (PDP) 48.7%—Serb seat; Dragan COVIC (HDZ-BiH) 52.2%—Croat seat; Bakir IZETBEGOVIC (SDA) 32.9%—Bosniak seat
note: President of the Federation of Bosnia and Herzegovina Marinko CAVARA (since 11 February 2015); Vice Presidents Melika MAHMUT-BEGOVIC (since 11 February 2015), Milan DUNOVIC (since 11 February 2015); President of the Republika Srpska Milorad DODIK (since 15 November 2010); Vice Presidents Ramiz SAL-KIC (since 24 November 2014), Josip JERKOVIC (since 24 November 2014)

Legislative branch: *description:* bicameral Parliamentary Assembly or Skupstina consists of the House of Peoples or Dom Naroda (15 seats—5 Bosniak, 5 Croat, 5 Serb; members designated by the Federation of Bosnia and Herzegovina's House of Peoples and the Republika Srpska's National Assembly to serve 4-year terms) and the state-level House of Representatives or Predstavnicki Dom (42 seats to include 28 seats allocated to the Federation of Bosnia and Herzegovina and 14 to the Republika Srpska; members directly elected by proportional representation vote to serve 4-year terms); note—the Federation of Bosnia and Herzegovina has a bicameral legislature that consists of the House of Peoples (58 seats—17 Bosniak, 17 Croat, 17 Serb, 7 other) and the House of Representatives (98 seats; members directly elected by proportional representation vote to serve 4-year terms); Republika Srpska's unicameral legislature is the National Assembly (83 directly elected delegates serve 4-year terms)

elections: House of Peoples—last constituted in 11 February 2015 (next likely to be constituted in 2019); state-level House of Representatives—election last held on 12 October 2014 (next to be held in October 2018)

election results: House of Peoples—percent of vote by party/coalition—NA; seats by party/coalition—NA; state-level House of Representatives—percent of vote by party/coalition—Federation votes: SDA 27.9%, DF 15.3%, SBB BiH 14.4%, Croat People's Assembly coalition or HNS (HDZ BiH-HSS-NHI-HKDU-HSP BiH-HSP HB) 12.2%, SDP 9.5%, HDZ-1990 4.1%, BPS-Sefer Halilovic 3.7%, A-SDA 2.3%, other 10.6%; Republika Srpska votes: SNSD 38.5%, SDS 32.6%, PDP-NDP 7.8%, DNS 5.7%, SDA 4.9%, other 10.5%; seats by party/coalition—SDA 10, SNSD 6, SDS 5, DF 5, SBB BiH 4, Croat People's Assembly coalition or HNS (HDZ BiH-HSS-NHI-HKDU-HSP BiH-HSP HB) 4, SDP 3, PDP-NDP 1, HDZ-1990 1, BPS-Sefer Halilovic 1, DNS 1, A-SDA 1

Judicial branch: *highest court(s):* Bosnia and Herzegovina (BiH) Constitutional Court (consists of 9 members); Court of BiH (consists of 44 national judges and 7 international judges organized into 3 divisions—Administrative, Appellate, and Criminal, which includes a War Crimes Chamber)

judge selection and term of office: BiH Constitutional Court judges—4 selected by the Federation of Bosnia and Herzegovina House of Representatives, 2 selected by the Republika Srpska's National Assembly, and 3 non-Bosnian judges selected by the president of the European Court of Human Rights; Court of BiH president and national judges appointed by the High Judicial and Prosecutorial Council; Court of BiH president appointed for renewable 6-year term; other national judges appointed to serve until age 70; international judges recommended by the president of the Court of BiH and appointed by the High Representative for Bosnia and Herzegovina; international judges appointed to serve until age 70

subordinate courts: the Federation has 10 cantonal courts plus a number of municipal courts; the Republika Srpska has a supreme court, 5 district courts, and a number of municipal courts

Political parties and leaders: Alliance for a Better Future of BiH or SBB BiH [Fahrudin RADONCIC]
Alliance of Independent Social Democrats or SNSD [Milorad DODIK]
Alternative Party for Democratic Activity or A-SDA [Nermin OGRESEVIC]
Bosnian-Herzegovinian Patriotic Party-Sefer Halilovic or BPS-Sefer Halilovic [Sefer HALILOVIC]

Croat Peasants' Party or HSS [Mario KARAMATIC]
Croatian Christian Democratic Union of Bosnia and Herzegovina or HKDU [Ivan MUSA]
Croatian Democratic Union of Bosnia and Herzegovina or HDZ-BiH [Dragan COVIC]
Croatian Democratic Union 1990 or HDZ-1990 [Ilija CVITANOVIC]
Croatian Party of Rights or HSP BiH [Stanko PRIMORAC]
Croatian Party of Rights of Herceg-Bosne or HSP HB [Vesna PINJUH]
Croatian People's Party-Liberal Democrats or HNS [Ivan VRDOLJAK]
Democratic Front of DF [Zeljko KOMSIC]
Democratic Peoples' Alliance or DNS [Marko PAVIC]
Party for Democratic Action or SDA [Bakir IZETBEGOVIC]
Party of Democratic Progress or PDP [Branislav BORENOVIC]
People's Democratic Movement or NDP [Dragan CAVIC]
Serb Democratic Party or SDS [Vukota GOVEDARICA]
Social Democratic Party or SDP [Nermin NIKSIC]

Political pressure groups and leaders: war veterans; displaced persons associations; family associations of missing persons; private media

International organization participation: BIS, CD, CE, CEI, EAPC, EBRD, FAO, G-77, IAEA, IBRD, ICAO, ICC (NGOs), ICCt, ICRM, IDA, IFAD, IFC, IFRCS, ILO, IMF, IMO, IMSO, Interpol, IOC, IOM, IPU, ISO, ITSO, ITU, ITUC (NGOs), MIGA, MINUSMA, MONUSCO, NAM (observer), OAS (observer), OIC (observer), OIF (observer), OPCW, OSCE, PFP, SELEC, UN, UNCTAD, UNESCO, UNIDO, UNWTO, UPU, WCO, WHO, WIPO, WMO, WTO (observer)

Diplomatic representation in the US: *chief of mission:* Ambassador Haris HRLE (since 23 October 2015)
chancery: 2109 E Street NW, Washington, DC 20037
telephone: [1] (202) 337-1500
FAX: [1] (202) 337-1502
consulate(s) general: Chicago, New York

Diplomatic representation from the US: *chief of mission:* Ambassador Maureen CORMACK (since 16 January 2015)
embassy: 1 Robert C. Frasure Street, 71000 Sarajevo
mailing address: use embassy street address
telephone: [387] (33) 704-000
FAX: [387] (33) 659-722
branch office(s): Banja Luka, Mostar

Flag description: a wide blue vertical band on the fly side with a yellow isosceles triangle abutting the band and the top of the flag; the remainder of the flag is blue with seven full five-pointed white stars and two half stars top and bottom along the hypotenuse of the triangle; the triangle approximates the shape of the country and its three points stand for the constituent peoples—Bosniaks, Croats, and

Serbs; the stars represent Europe and are meant to be continuous (thus the half stars at top and bottom); the colors (white, blue, and yellow) are often associated with neutrality and peace, and traditionally are linked with Bosnia

note: one of several flags where a prominent component of the design reflects the shape of the country; other such flags are those of Brazil, Eritrea, and Vanuatu

National symbol(s): golden lily; national colors: blue, yellow, white

National anthem: *name:* "Drzavna himna Bosne i Hercegovine" (The National Anthem of Bosnia and Herzegovina)
lyrics/music: none officially; Dusan SESTIC and Benjamin ISOVIC/Dusan SESTIC
note: music adopted 1999; lyrics accepted 2009 but not yet approved

ECONOMY

Economy—overview: Bosnia and Herzegovina has a transitional economy with limited market reforms. The economy relies heavily on the export of metals, energy, textiles, and furniture as well as on remittances and foreign aid. A highly decentralized government hampers economic policy coordination and reform, while excessive bureaucracy and a segmented market discourage foreign investment. The economy is among the least competitive in the region. Foreign banks, primarily from Austria and Italy, control much of the banking sector, though the largest bank in the Republika Srpska entity is a private domestic one. The konvertibilna marka (convertible mark)—the national currency introduced in 1998—is pegged to the euro through a currency board arrangement, which has maintained confidence in the currency and has facilitated reliable trade links with European partners. In 2016, Bosnia began a three-year IMF loan program, but it has struggled to meet the economic reform benchmarks required to receive all funding installments.

Interethnic warfare in Bosnia and Herzegovina caused production to plummet by 80% from 1992 to 1995 and unemployment to soar, but the economy made progress until 2008, when the global economic crisis caused a downturn. Since 2013, Bosnia and Herzegovina has posted positive economic growth, though severe flooding hampered recovery in 2014. Bosnia and Herzegovina became a full member of the Central European Free Trade Agreement in September 2007.

Bosnia and Herzegovina's private sector is growing slowly, but foreign investment dropped sharply after 2007 and remains low. High unemployment remains the most serious macroeconomic problem. Successful implementation of a value-added tax in 2006 provided a steady source of revenue for the government and helped rein in gray-market activity, though public perceptions of government corruption and misuse of taxpayer money has encouraged a large informal economy to persist. National-level statistics have improved over time, but a large share of economic activity remains unofficial and unrecorded.

Bosnia and Herzegovina's top economic priorities are: acceleration of integration into the EU; strengthening the fiscal system; public administration reform; World Trade Organization membership; and securing economic growth by fostering a dynamic, competitive private sector.

GDP (purchasing power parity): $43.85 billion (2017 est.)
$42.78 billion (2016 est.)
$41.94 billion (2015 est.)
note: data are in 2017 dollars
country comparison to the world: 113

GDP (official exchange rate): $17.46 billion (2016 est.)

GDP—real growth rate: 2.5% (2017 est.)
2% (2016 est.)
3% (2015 est.)
country comparison to the world: 133

GDP—per capita (PPP): $11,400 (2017 est.)
$11,100 (2016 est.)
$10,900 (2015 est.)
note: data are in 2017 dollars
country comparison to the world: 135

Gross national saving: 12.9% of GDP (2017 est.)
11.9% of GDP (2016 est.)
10.5% of GDP (2015 est.)
country comparison to the world: 140

GDP—composition, by end use:
household consumption: 78.8%
government consumption: 19.5%
investment in fixed capital: 17%
investment in inventories: 1.5%
exports of goods and services: 36.3%
imports of goods and services: -53.2% (2017 est.)

GDP—composition, by sector of origin:
agriculture: 7.8%
industry: 26.8%
services: 65.4% (2017 est.)

Agriculture—products: wheat, corn, fruits, vegetables; livestock

Industries: steel, coal, iron ore, lead, zinc, manganese, bauxite, aluminum, motor vehicle assembly, textiles, tobacco products, wooden furniture, ammunition, domestic appliances, oil refining

Industrial production growth rate: 3% (2017 est.)
country comparison to the world: 97

Labor force: 1.51 million (2017 est.)
country comparison to the world: 131

Labor force—by occupation: *agriculture:* 19%
industry: 30%
services: 51% (2013)

Unemployment rate: 20.5% (2017 est.)
25.4% (2016 est.)
note: official rate; actual rate is lower as many technically unemployed persons work in the gray economy
country comparison to the world: 186

Population below poverty line: 17.2% (2011 est.)

Household income or consumption by percentage share: *lowest 10%:* 2.7%
highest 10%: 27.3% (2007)

Distribution of family income—Gini index: 36.2 (2007)
country comparison to the world: 88

Budget: *revenues:* $7.798 billion
expenditures: $7.996 billion (2017 est.)
Taxes and other revenues: 44.7% of GDP (2017 est.)
country comparison to the world: 23

Budget surplus (+) or deficit (-): -1.1% of GDP (2017 est.)
country comparison to the world: 63

Public debt: 43.2% of GDP (2017 est.)
44.2% of GDP (2016 est.)
note: data cover general government debt, and includes debt instruments issued (or owned) by government entities other than the treasury; the data include treasury debt held by foreign entities; the data include debt issued by subnational entities, as well as intra-governmental debt; intra-governmental debt consists of treasury borrowings from surpluses in the social funds, such as for retirement, medical care, and unemployment; debt instruments for the social funds are not sold at public auctions.
country comparison to the world: 124

Fiscal year: calendar year

Inflation rate (consumer prices): 1.8% (2017 est.)
-1.1% (2016 est.)
country comparison to the world: 80

Commercial bank prime lending rate: 4.5% (31 December 2017 est.)
5.24% (31 December 2016 est.)
country comparison to the world: 152

Stock of narrow money: $6.424 billion (31 December 2017 est.)
$5.013 billion (31 December 2016 est.)
country comparison to the world: 95

Stock of broad money: $13.34 billion (31 December 2017 est.)
$10.89 billion (31 December 2016 est.)
country comparison to the world: 101

Stock of domestic credit: $10.68 billion (31 December 2017 est.)
$9.271 billion (31 December 2016 est.)
country comparison to the world: 109

Market value of publicly traded shares: $NA

Current account balance: -$752 million (2017 est.)
-$741 million (2016 est.)
country comparison to the world: 119

Exports: $4.803 billion (2017 est.)
$4.288 billion (2016 est.)
country comparison to the world: 110

Exports—commodities: metals, clothing, wood products

Exports—partners: Germany 16.6%, Italy 12.7%, Croatia 11%, Serbia 9.2%, Slovenia 9.1%, Austria 8.2%, Turkey 4.5% (2016)

Imports: $9.113 billion (2017 est.)
$8.361 billion (2016 est.)
country comparison to the world: 99

Imports—commodities: machinery and equipment, chemicals, fuels, foodstuffs

Imports—partners: Germany 12.3%, Italy 11.7%, Serbia 11.2%, Croatia 9.9%, China 6.8%, Slovenia 5%, Russia 4.4%, Turkey 4.3% (2016)

Reserves of foreign exchange and gold: $5.37 billion (31 December 2017 est.)
$5.137 billion (31 December 2016 est.)
country comparison to the world: 91

Debt—external: $10.45 billion (31 December 2017 est.)
$10.64 billion (31 December 2016 est.)
country comparison to the world: 113

Stock of direct foreign investment—at home: $7.92 billion (2014 est.)
$7.721 billion (2013 est.)
country comparison to the world: 97

Stock of direct foreign investment—abroad: $0 (2014)
country comparison to the world: 113

Exchange rates: konvertibilna markas (BAM) per US dollar—
1.729 (2017 est.)
1.7674 (2016 est.)
1.7674 (2015 est.)
1.7626 (2014 est.)
1.4718 (2013 est.)

ENERGY

Electricity access: *electrification—total population:* 100% (2016)

Electricity—production: 14.97 billion kWh (2015 est.)
country comparison to the world: 87

Electricity—consumption: 11.44 billion kWh (2015 est.)
country comparison to the world: 89

Electricity—exports: 6.007 billion kWh (2015 est.)
country comparison to the world: 32

Electricity—imports: 3.872 billion kWh (2015 est.)
country comparison to the world: 47

Electricity—installed generating capacity: 4.243 million kW (2015 est.)
country comparison to the world: 85

Electricity—from fossil fuels: 41.6% of total installed capacity (2015 est.)
country comparison to the world: 168

Electricity—from nuclear fuels: 0% of total installed capacity (2015 est.)
country comparison to the world: 52

Electricity—from hydroelectric plants: 48.3% of total installed capacity (2015 est.)
country comparison to the world: 42

Electricity—from other renewable sources: 0.3% of total installed capacity (2015 est.)
country comparison to the world: 157

Crude oil—production: 0 bbl/day (2016 est.)
country comparison to the world: 113

Crude oil—exports: 0 bbl/day (2014 est.)
country comparison to the world: 96

Crude oil—imports: 18,940 bbl/day (2014 est.)
country comparison to the world: 64

Crude oil—proved reserves: 0 bbl (1 January 2017 es)
country comparison to the world: 112

Refined petroleum products—production: 20,700 bbl/day (2014 est.)
country comparison to the world: 90

Refined petroleum products—consumption: 31,000 bbl/day (2015 est.)
country comparison to the world: 120

Refined petroleum products—exports: 5,910 bbl/day (2014 est.)
country comparison to the world: 93

Refined petroleum products—imports: 15,700 bbl/day (2014 est.)
country comparison to the world: 129

Natural gas—production: 0 cu m (2014 est.)
country comparison to the world: 111

Natural gas—consumption: 881 million cu m (2015 est.)
country comparison to the world: 102

Natural gas—exports: 0 cu m (2014 est.)
country comparison to the world: 71

Natural gas—imports: 200 million cu m (2015 est.)
country comparison to the world: 72

Natural gas—proved reserves: 0 cu m (1 January 2014 es)
country comparison to the world: 118

Carbon dioxide emissions from consumption of energy: 17 million Mt (2013 est.)
country comparison to the world: 86

COMMUNICATIONS

Telephones—fixed lines: *total subscriptions:* 744,991
subscriptions per 100 inhabitants: 19 (July 2016 est.)
country comparison to the world: 84

Telephones—mobile cellular: *total:* 3,404,043
subscriptions per 100 inhabitants: 88 (July 2016 est.)
country comparison to the world: 129

Telephone system: *general assessment:* postwar reconstruction of the telecommunications network, aided by an internationally sponsored program, resulted in sharp increases in fixed-line telephone availability
domestic: fixed-line teledensity roughly 20 per 100 persons; mobile-cellular subscribership has been increasing rapidly and stands at roughly 90 telephones per 100 persons
international: country code—387; no satellite earth stations (2016)

Broadcast media: 3 public TV broadcasters: Radio and TV of Bosnia and Herzegovina, Federation TV (operating 2 networks), and Republika Srpska Radio-TV; a local commercial network of 5 TV stations; 3 private, near-national TV stations and dozens of small independent TV broadcasting stations; 3 large public radio broadcasters and many private radio stations (2010)

Internet country code: .ba

Internet users: *total:* 2,677,502
percent of population: 69.3% (July 2016 est.)
country comparison to the world: 89

TRANSPORTATION

National air transport system: *number of registered air carriers:* 1
inventory of registered aircraft operated by air carriers: 1
annual passenger traffic on registered air carriers: 7,070
annual freight traffic on registered air carriers: 87 mt-km (2015)
Civil aircraft registration country code prefix: T9 (2016)

Airports: 24 (2013)
country comparison to the world: 130

Airports—with paved runways: *total:* 7
2,438 to 3,047 m: 4
1,524 to 2,437 m: 1
under 914 m: 2 (2017)

Airports—with unpaved runways: *total:* 17
1,524 to 2,437 m: 1
914 to 1,523 m: 5
under 914 m: 11 (2013)

Heliports: 6 (2013)

Pipelines: gas 147 km; oil 9 km (2013)

Railways: *total:* 965 km
standard gauge: 965 km 1.435-m gauge (565 km electrified) (2014)
country comparison to the world: 91

Roadways: *total:* 22,926 km

paved: 19,426 km (4,652 km of interurban roads)
unpaved: 3,500 km (2010)
country comparison to the world: 102

Waterways: (Sava River on northern border; open to shipping but use limited) (2011)

Ports and terminals: *river port(s):* Bosanska Gradiska, Bosanski Brod, Bosanski Samac, Brcko, Orasje (Sava River)

MILITARY AND SECURITY

Military expenditures: 0.99% of GDP (2016)
1% of GDP (2015)
1.03% of GDP (2014)
1.09% of GDP (2013)
1.15% of GDP (2012)
country comparison to the world: 75

Military branches: Armed Forces of Bosnia and Herzegovina (Oruzanih Snaga Bosne i Hercegovine, OSBiH): Army of Bosnia and Herzegovina, Air Force and Air Defense (Brigada Zracnih Snaga i Protuzracne Odbrane, br ZSiPZO), Tactical Support Brigade (Brigada Takticke Podrske, br TP) (2015)

Military service age and obligation: 18 years of age for voluntary military service; mandatory retirement at age 35 or after 15 years of service for E-1 through E-4, mandatory retirement at age 50 and 30 years of service for E-5 through E-9, mandatory retirement at age 55 and 30 years of service for all officers (2014)

TRANSNATIONAL ISSUES

Disputes—international: Serbia delimited about half of the boundary with Bosnia and Herzegovina, but sections along the Drina River remain in dispute

Refugees and internally displaced persons: *refugees (country of origin):* 5,164 (Croatia) (2016)
IDPs: 98,000 (Bosnian Croats, Serbs, and Bosniaks displaced by inter-ethnic violence, human rights violations, and armed conflict during the 1992-95 war) (2016)
stateless persons: 49 (2016)

Illicit drugs: increasingly a transit point for heroin being trafficked to Western Europe; minor transit point for marijuana; remains highly vulnerable to money-laundering activity given a primarily cash-based and unregulated economy, weak law enforcement, and instances of corruption

BOTSWANA

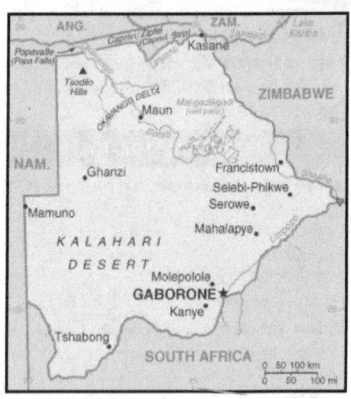

INTRODUCTION

Background: Formerly the British protectorate of Bechuanaland, Botswana adopted its new name at independence in 1966. More than four decades of uninterrupted civilian leadership, progressive social policies, and significant capital investment have created one of the most stable economies in Africa. The ruling Botswana Democratic Party has won every election since independence; President Ian KHAMA was reelected for a second term in 2014. Mineral extraction, principally diamond mining, dominates economic activity, though tourism is a growing sector due to the country's conservation practices and extensive nature preserves. Botswana has one of the world's highest known rates of HIV/AIDS infection, but also one of Africa's most progressive and comprehensive programs for dealing with the disease.

GEOGRAPHY

Location: Southern Africa, north of South Africa

Geographic coordinates: 22 00 S, 24 00 E

Map references: Africa

Area: *total:* 581,730 sq km
land: 566,730 sq km
water: 15,000 sq km
country comparison to the world: 49

Area—comparative: slightly smaller than Texas

Land boundaries: *total:* 4,347.15 km
border countries (4): Namibia 1,544 km, South Africa 1,969 km, Zambia 0.15 km, Zimbabwe 834 km

Coastline: 0 km (landlocked)

Maritime claims: none (landlocked)

Climate: semiarid; warm winters and hot summers

Terrain: predominantly flat to gently rolling tableland; Kalahari Desert in southwest

Elevation: *mean elevation:* 1,013 m

elevation extremes: *lowest point:* junction of the Limpopo and Shashe Rivers 513 m
highest point: Tsodilo Hills 1,489 m

Natural resources: diamonds, copper, nickel, salt, soda ash, potash, coal, iron ore, silver

Land use: *agricultural land:* 45.8%
arable land: 0.6%;
permanent crops: 0%;
permanent pasture: 45.2%
forest: 19.8%
other: 34.4% (2011 est.)
Irrigated land: 20 sq km (2012)

Population—distribution: the population is primarily concentrated in the east with a focus in and around the captial of Gaborone, and the far central-eastern city of Francistown; population density remains low in other areas in the country, especially in the Kalahari to the west

Natural hazards: periodic droughts; seasonal August winds blow from the west, carrying sand and dust across the country, which can obscure visibility

Environment—current issues: overgrazing; desertification; limited freshwater resources

Environment—international agreements: party to: Biodiversity, Climate Change, Climate Change-Kyoto Protocol, Desertification, Endangered Species, Hazardous Wastes, Law of the Sea, Ozone Layer Protection, Wetlands
signed, but not ratified: none of the selected agreements

Geography—note: landlocked; population concentrated in eastern part of the country

PEOPLE AND SOCIETY

Population: 2,214,858
note: estimates for this country explicitly take into account the effects of excess mortality due to AIDS; this can result in lower life expectancy, higher infant mortality, higher death rates, lower population growth rates, and changes in the distribution of population by age and sex than would otherwise be expected (July 2017 est.)
country comparison to the world: 144

Nationality: *noun:* Motswana (singular), Batswana (plural)
adjective: Motswana (singular), Batswana (plural)

Ethnic groups: Tswana (or Setswana) 79%, Kalanga 11%, Basarwa 3%, other, including Kgalagadi and white 7%

Languages: Setswana 77.3%, Sekalanga 7.4%, Shekgalagadi 3.4%, English (official) 2.8%, Zezuru/Shona 2%, Sesarwa 1.7%, Sembukushu 1.6%, Ndebele 1%, other 2.8% (2011 est.)

Religions: Christian 79.1%, Badimo 4.1%, other 1.4% (includes Baha'i, Hindu, Muslim, Rastafarian), none 15.2%, unspecified 0.3% (2011 est.)

Demographic profile: Botswana has experienced one of the most rapid declines in fertility in sub-Saharan Africa. The total fertility rate has fallen from more than 5 children per woman in the mid 1980s to approximately 2.4 in 2013. The fertility reduction has been attributed to a host of factors, including higher educational attainment among women, greater participation of women in the workforce, increased contraceptive use, later first births, and a strong national family planning program. Botswana was making significant progress in several health indicators, including life expectancy and infant and child mortality rates, until being devastated by the HIV/AIDs epidemic in the 1990s.

Today Botswana has the third highest HIV/AIDS prevalence rate in the world at approximately 22%, however comprehensive and effective treatment programs have reduced HIV/AIDS-related deaths. The combination of declining fertility and increasing mortality rates because of HIV/AIDS is slowing the population aging process, with a narrowing of the youngest age groups and little expansion of the oldest age groups. Nevertheless, having the bulk of its population (about 60%) of working age will only yield economic benefits if the labor force is healthy, educated, and productively employed.

Batswana have been working as contract miners in South Africa since the 19th century. Although Botswana's economy improved shortly after independence in 1966 with the discovery of diamonds and other minerals, its lingering high poverty rate and lack of job opportunities continued to push workers to seek mining work in southern African countries. In the early 1970s, about a third of Botswana's male labor force worked in South Africa (lesser numbers went to Namibia and Zimbabwe). Not until the 1980s and 1990s, when South African mining companies had reduced their recruitment of foreign workers and Botswana's economic prospects had improved, were Batswana increasingly able to find job opportunities at home.

Most Batswana prefer life in their home country and choose cross-border migration on a temporary basis only for work, shopping, visiting family, or tourism. Since the 1970s, Botswana has pursued an open migration policy enabling it to recruit thousands of foreign workers to fill skilled labor shortages. In the late 1990s, Botswana's prosperity and political stability attracted not only skilled workers but small numbers of refugees from neighboring Angola, Namibia, and Zimbabwe.

Age structure: *0-14 years:* 31.95% (male 357,003/female 350,657)
15-24 years: 18.91% (male 207,209/female 211,629)
25-54 years: 38.45% (male 401,082/female 450,437)
55-64 years: 5.46% (male 51,195/female 69,835)

65 years and over: 5.23% (male 50,206/female 65,605) (2017 est.)

Dependency ratios: *total dependency ratio:* 55.1
youth dependency ratio: 49.3
elderly dependency ratio: 5.8
potential support ratio: 17.3 (2015 est.)

Median age: *total:* 24.5 years
male: 23.5 years
female: 25.6 years (2017 est.)
country comparison to the world: 169

Population growth rate: 1.55% (2017 est.)
country comparison to the world: 72

Birth rate: 22.1 births/1,000 population (2017 est.)
country comparison to the world: 71

Death rate: 9.6 deaths/1,000 population (2017 est.)
country comparison to the world: 49

Net migration rate: 3 migrant(s)/1,000 population (2017 est.)
country comparison to the world: 34

Population distribution: the population is primarily concentrated in the east with a focus in and around the captial of Gaborone, and the far central-eastern city of Francistown; population density remains low in other areas in the country, especially in the Kalahari to the west

Urbanization: *urban population:* 58% of total population (2017)
rate of urbanization: 1.38% annual rate of change (2015-20 est.)

Major urban areas—population: GABORONE (capital) 247,000 (2014)

Sex ratio: *at birth:* 1.03 male(s)/female
0-14 years: 1.04 male(s)/female
15-24 years: 0.99 male(s)/female
25-54 years: 1.15 male(s)/female
55-64 years: 0.82 male(s)/female
65 years and over: 0.66 male(s)/female
total population: 1.04 male(s)/female (2016 est.)

Mother's mean age at first birth: 19 years (2007 est.)

Maternal mortality ratio: 129 deaths/100,000 live births (2015 est.)
country comparison to the world: 66

Infant mortality rate: *total:* 29.6 deaths/1,000 live births
male: 32.2 deaths/1,000 live births
female: 26.9 deaths/1,000 live births (2017 est.)
country comparison to the world: 65

Life expectancy at birth: *total population:* 63.3 years
male: 61.2 years
female: 65.5 years (2017 est.)
country comparison to the world: 194

Total fertility rate: 2.56 children born/woman (2017 est.)
country comparison to the world: 77

Contraceptive prevalence rate: 52.8%
note: percent of women aged 12-49 (2007/08)
Health expenditures: 5.4% of GDP (2014)
country comparison to the world: 129

Physicians density: 0.38 physicians/1,000 population (2012)

Hospital bed density: 1.8 beds/1,000 population (2010)

Drinking water source:
improved:
urban: 99.2% of population
rural: 92.3% of population
total: 96.2% of population
unimproved:
urban: 0.8% of population
rural: 7.7% of population
total: 3.8% of population (2015 est.)

Sanitation facility access:
improved:
urban: 78.5% of population
rural: 43.1% of population
total: 63.4% of population
unimproved:
urban: 21.5% of population
rural: 56.9% of population
total: 36.6% of population (2015 est.)

HIV/AIDS—adult prevalence rate: 21.9% (2016 est.)
country comparison to the world: 3

HIV/AIDS—people living with HIV/AIDS: 360,000 (2016 est.)
country comparison to the world: 18

HIV/AIDS—deaths: 3,900 (2016 est.)
country comparison to the world: 36

Major infectious diseases: *degree of risk:* high
food or waterborne diseases: bacterial diarrhea, hepatitis A, and typhoid fever
vectorborne disease: malaria (2016)

Obesity—adult prevalence rate: 18.9% (2016)
country comparison to the world: 114

Children under the age of 5 years underweight: 11.2% (2007)
country comparison to the world: 66

Education expenditures: 9.6% of GDP (2009)
country comparison to the world: 5

Literacy: *definition:* age 15 and over can read and write
total population: 88.5%
male: 88%
female: 88.9% (2015 est.)

School life expectancy (primary to tertiary education): *total:* 13 years
male: 13 years
female: 13 years (2013)

Unemployment, youth ages 15-24: *total:* 36%
male: 29.6%
female: 43.5% (2010 est.)

GOVERNMENT

Country name: *conventional long form:* Republic of Botswana
conventional short form: Botswana
local long form: Republic of Botswana
local short form: Botswana
former: Bechuanaland

etymology: the name Botswana means "Land of the Tswana"—referring to the country's major ethnic group

Government type: parliamentary republic

Capital: *name:* Gaborone

geographic coordinates: 24 38 S, 25 54 E

time difference: UTC+2 (7 hours ahead of Washington, DC, during Standard Time)

Administrative divisions: 10 districts and 6 town councils*; Central, Chobe, Francistown*, Gaborone*, Ghanzi, Jwaneng*, Kgalagadi, Kgatleng, Kweneng, Lobatse*, North East, North West, Selebi-Phikwe*, South East, Southern, Sowa Town*

Independence: 30 September 1966 (from the UK)

National holiday: Independence Day (Botswana Day), 30 September (1966)

Constitution: *history:* previous 1960 (preindependence); latest adopted March 1965, effective 30 September 1966
amendments: proposed by the National Assembly; passage requires approval in two successive Assembly votes with at least two-thirds majority in the final vote; proposals to amend constitutional provisions on fundamental rights and freedoms, the structure and branches of government, and public services also requires approval by majority vote in a referendum and assent by the president of the republic; amended several times, last in 2006 (2017)

Legal system: mixed legal system of civil law influenced by the Roman-Dutch model and also customary and common law

International law organization participation: accepts compulsory ICJ jurisdiction with reservations; accepts ICCt jurisdiction

Citizenship: *citizenship by birth:* no
citizenship by descent only: at least one parent must be a citizen of Botswana
dual citizenship recognized: no
residency requirement for naturalization: 10 years

Suffrage: 18 years of age; universal

Executive branch: *chief of state:* President Seretse Khama Ian KHAMA (since 1 April 2008); Vice President Mokgweetsi Eric MASISI (since 12 November 2014); President KHAMA is anticipated to hand over the presidency to MASSI in April 2018, in keeping with Botswanan political tradition; note—the president is both chief of state and head of government

head of government: President Seretse Khama Ian KHAMA (since 1 April 2008); Vice President Mokgweetsi Eric MASISI (since 12 November 2014); President KHAMA is anticipated to hand over the preidency to MASISI in April 2018, in keeping with Botswanan political tradition
cabinet: Cabinet appointed by the president
elections/appointments: president indirectly elected by the National Assembly for a 5-year term (eligible for a second term); election last held on 24 October 2014 (next to be held in October 2019); vice president appointed by the president
election results: Seretse Khama Ian KHAMA elected president; percent of National Assembly vote—NA

Legislative branch: *description:* unicameral Parliament consists of the National Assembly (65 seats; 57 members directly elected in single-seat constituencies by simple majority vote, 6 nominated by the president and indirectly elected by simple majority vote by the rest of the National Assembly, and 2 ex-officio members—the president and attorney general; elected members serve 5-year terms); note—the House of Chiefs (Ntlo ya Dikgosi), an advisory body to the National Assembly, consists of 35 members—8 hereditary chiefs from Botswana's principal tribes, 22 indirectly elected by the chiefs, and 5 appointed by the president; the House of Chiefs consults on issues including powers of chiefs, customary courts, customary law, tribal property, and constitutional amendments
elections: last held on 24 October 2014 (next to be held in October 2019)
election results: percent of vote by party—BDP 46.5%, UDC 30.0%, BCP 20.4%, independent 3.1%; seats by party—BDP 37, UDC 17, BCP 3

Judicial branch: *highest court(s):* Court of Appeal, High Court (each consists of a chief justice and a number of other judges as prescribed by the Parliament)
judge selection and term of office: Court of Appeal and High Court chief justices appointed by the president and other judges appointed by the president upon the advice of the Judicial Service Commission; all judges appointed to serve until age 70
subordinate courts: Industrial Court (with circuits scheduled monthly in the capital city and in 3 districts); Magistrates Courts (1 in each district); Customary Court of Appeal; Paramount Chief's Court/Urban Customary Court; Senior Chief's Representative Court; Chief's Representative's Court; Headman's Court

Political parties and leaders: Botswana Alliance Movement or BAM [Ephraim Lepetu SETSHWAELO]
Botswana Congress Party or BCP [Dumelang SALESHANDO]
Botswana Democratic Party or BDP [Ian KHAMA]
Botswana Movement for Democracy or BMD [Ndaba GAOLATHE]
Botswana National Front or BNF [Duma BOKO]
Botswana Peoples Party or BPP [Motlatsi MOLAPISI]
Umbrella for Democratic Change or UDC [Duma BOKO] (coalition includes BMD, BPP, BCP and BNF)

International organization participation: ACP, AfDB, AU, C, CD, FAO, G-77, IAEA, IBRD, ICAO, ICCt, ICRM, IDA, IFAD, IFC, IFRCS, ILO, IMF, Interpol, IOC, IOM, IPU, ISO, ITSO, ITU, ITUC (NGOs), MIGA, NAM, OPCW, SACU, SADC, UN, UNCTAD, UNESCO, UNIDO, UNWTO, UPU, WCO, WFTU (NGOs), WHO, WIPO, WMO, WTO

Diplomatic representation in the US: *chief of mission:* Ambassador David John NEWMAN (since 3 August 2015)
chancery: 1531-1533 New Hampshire Avenue NW, Washington, DC 20036
telephone: [1] (202) 244-4990
FAX: [1] (202) 244-4164
consulate(s) general: Atlanta

Diplomatic representation from the US: *chief of mission:* Ambassador Earl R. MILLER (since 30 January 2015)
embassy: Embassy Drive, Government Enclave (off Khama Crescent), Gaborone
mailing address: Embassy Enclave, P. O. Box 90, Gaborone
telephone: [267] 395-3982
FAX: [267] 318-0232

Flag description: light blue with a horizontal white-edged black stripe in the center; the blue symbolizes water in the form of rain, while the black and white bands represent racial harmony

National symbol(s): zebra; national colors: blue, white, black

National anthem: *name:* "Fatshe leno la rona" (Our Land)
lyrics/music: Kgalemang Tumedisco MOTSETE
note: adopted 1966

ECONOMY

Economy—overview: Until the global recession, Botswana maintained one of the world's highest economic growth rates since independence in 1966. Diamond mining fueled much of the economic expansion and currently accounts for one-quarter of GDP, approximately 85% of export earnings, and about one-third of the government's revenues. Tourism is the secondary earner of foreign exchange and many Batswana engage in tourism-related services, subsistence farming, and cattle rearing. Through fiscal discipline and sound management, Botswana transformed itself from one of the poorest countries in the world to a middle-income country with a per capita GDP of approximately $18,100 in 2017. Botswana also ranks as one of the least corrupt and best places to do business in sub-Saharan Africa.

Botswana's economy closely follows global economic trends because of its heavy reliance on a single luxury export. According to official government statistics, unemployment is around 20%, but unofficial estimates run much higher. De Beers, a major international diamond company, signed a 10-year deal with Botswana in 2012 and moved its rough stone sorting and trading division from London to Gaborone in 2013. The move was geared to support the development of Botswana's nascent downstream diamond industry.

Botswana's economy recovered from the 2008 global recession in 2010, but has only grown modestly since then, primarily due to the downturn in the global diamond market, though water and power shortages also played a role. The prevalence of HIV/AIDS is second highest in the world and threatens the country's impressive economic gains. Diamond exports increased again in 2017 to the highest levels since 2013 at about 22 million carats of output, driving Botswana's economic growth of about 4.5% in 2017 and increasing foreign reserves to about 45% of GDP.

GDP (purchasing power parity): $39.55 billion (2017 est.)
$37.86 billion (2016 est.)
$36.3 billion (2015 est.)
note: data are in 2017 dollars
country comparison to the world: 120

GDP (official exchange rate): $16.73 billion (2016 est.)

GDP—real growth rate: 4.5% (2017 est.)
4.3% (2016 est.)
-1.7% (2015 est.)
country comparison to the world: 51

GDP—per capita (PPP): $18,100 (2017 est.)
$17,600 (2016 est.)
$17,000 (2015 est.)
note: data are in 2017 dollars
country comparison to the world: 96

Gross national saving: 29.5% of GDP (2017 est.)
42.1% of GDP (2016 est.)
40.5% of GDP (2015 est.)
country comparison to the world: 26

GDP—composition, by end use:
household consumption: 46.8%
government consumption: 17.7%
investment in fixed capital: 30.7%
investment in inventories: -10%
exports of goods and services: 54.1%
imports of goods and services: -39.3% (2017 est.)

GDP—composition, by sector of origin:
agriculture: 1.7%
industry: 29.2%
services: 69.1% (2017 est.)

Agriculture—products: livestock, sorghum, maize, millet, beans, sunflowers, groundnuts

Industries: diamonds, copper, nickel, salt, soda ash, potash, coal, iron ore, silver; beef processing; textiles

Industrial production growth rate: 3% (2017 est.)
country comparison to the world: 98

Labor force: 1.177 million (2017 est.)
country comparison to the world: 141

Labor force—by occupation: *agriculture:* NA%
industry: NA%
services: NA%

Unemployment rate: 20% (2013 est.)
17.8% (2009 est.)
country comparison to the world: 183

Population below poverty line: 30.3% (2003 est.)

Household income or consumption by percentage share: *lowest 10%:* NA%
highest 10%: NA%

Distribution of family income—Gini index: 60.5 (2009)
63 (1993)
country comparison to the world: 6

Budget: *revenues:* $5.609 billion
expenditures: $6.072 billion (2017 est.)
Taxes and other revenues: 33.5% of GDP (2017 est.)
country comparison to the world: 64

Budget surplus (+) or deficit (-): -2.8% of GDP (2017 est.)
country comparison to the world: 108

Public debt: 18.5% of GDP (2017 est.)
18.1% of GDP (2016 est.)
country comparison to the world: 190

Fiscal year: 1 April—31 March

Inflation rate (consumer prices): 3.7% (2017 est.)
2.8% (2016 est.)
country comparison to the world: 145

Central bank discount rate: 5.5% (31 December 2016)
6% (31 December 2015)
country comparison to the world: 75

Commercial bank prime lending rate: 6.5% (31 December 2017 est.)
7.3% (31 December 2016 est.)
country comparison to the world: 123

Stock of narrow money: $1.574 billion (31 December 2017 est.)
$1.505 billion (31 December 2016 est.)
country comparison to the world: 141

Stock of broad money: $6.893 billion (31 December 2017 est.)
$6.689 billion (31 December 2016 est.)
country comparison to the world: 119

Stock of domestic credit: $2.859 billion (31 December 2017 est.)
$2.597 billion (31 December 2016 est.)
country comparison to the world: 141

Market value of publicly traded shares: $4.588 billion (31 December 2012 est.)
$4.107 billion (31 December 2011 est.)
$4.076 billion (31 December 2010 est.)
country comparison to the world: 88

Current account balance: $746 million (2017 est.)
$1.824 billion (2016 est.)
country comparison to the world: 42

Exports: $7.58 billion (2017 est.)
$7.226 billion (2016 est.)
country comparison to the world: 99

Exports—commodities: diamonds, copper, nickel, soda ash, beef, textiles

Exports—partners: Belgium 18.9%, India 15.1%, South Africa 13.6%, Namibia 11.6%, UAE 9.7%, Israel 6.1%, Singapore 5.6%, Canada 5% (2016)

Imports: $5.998 billion (2017 est.)
$5.906 billion (2016 est.)
country comparison to the world: 115

Imports—commodities: foodstuffs, machinery, electrical goods, transport equipment, textiles, fuel and petroleum products, wood and paper products, metal and metal products

Imports—partners: South Africa 64.5%, Namibia 10.5%, Canada 5.6% (2016)

Reserves of foreign exchange and gold: $7.476 billion (31 December 2017 est.)
$7.189 billion (31 December 2016 est.)
country comparison to the world: 82

Debt—external: $2.461 billion (31 December 2017 est.)
$2.421 billion (31 December 2016 est.)
country comparison to the world: 149

Exchange rates: pulas (BWP) per US dollar—
10.19 (2017 est.)
10.9022 (2016 est.)
10.9022 (2015 est.)
10.1263 (2014 est.)
8.9761 (2013 est.)

ENERGY

Electricity access: *population without electricity:* 700,000
electrification—*total population:* 66%
electrification—urban areas: 75%

electrification—rural areas: 54% (2013)

Electricity—production: 2.789 billion kWh (2015 est.)
country comparison to the world: 136

Electricity—consumption: 3.722 billion kWh (2015 est.)
country comparison to the world: 130

Electricity—exports: 0 kWh (2016 est.)
country comparison to the world: 104

Electricity—imports: 1.468 billion kWh (2015 est.)
country comparison to the world: 60

Electricity—installed generating capacity: 134,000 kW (2015 est.)
country comparison to the world: 172

Electricity—from fossil fuels: 98.5% of total installed capacity (2015 est.)
country comparison to the world: 37

Electricity—from nuclear fuels: 0% of total installed capacity (2015 est.)
country comparison to the world: 47

Electricity—from hydroelectric plants: 0% of total installed capacity (2015 est.)
country comparison to the world: 162

Electricity—from other renewable sources: 1.5% of total installed capacity (2015 est.)
country comparison to the world: 131

Crude oil—production: 0 bbl/day (2016 est.)
country comparison to the world: 114

Crude oil—exports: 0 bbl/day (2014 est.)
country comparison to the world: 92

Crude oil—imports: 0 bbl/day (2014 est.)
country comparison to the world: 96

Crude oil—proved reserves: 0 bbl (1 January 2017 es)
country comparison to the world: 113

Refined petroleum products—production: 0 bbl/day (2014 est.)
country comparison to the world: 122

Refined petroleum products—consumption: 23,000 bbl/day (2015 est.)
country comparison to the world: 134

Refined petroleum products—exports: 0 bbl/day (2014 est.)
country comparison to the world: 132

Refined petroleum products—imports: 21,290 bbl/day (2014 est.)
country comparison to the world: 116

Natural gas—production: 0 cu m (2013 est.)
country comparison to the world: 106

Natural gas—consumption: 0 cu m (2013 est.)
country comparison to the world: 156

Natural gas—exports: 0 cu m (2013 est.)
country comparison to the world: 66

Natural gas—imports: 0 cu m (2013 est.)
country comparison to the world: 89

Natural gas—proved reserves: 0 cu m (1 January 2014 es)
country comparison to the world: 113

Carbon dioxide emissions from consumption of energy: 4.4 million Mt (2013 est.)

country comparison to the world: 128

COMMUNICATIONS

Telephones—fixed lines: *total subscriptions:* 142,122
subscriptions per 100 inhabitants: 6 (July 2016 est.)
country comparison to the world: 132

Telephones—mobile cellular: *total:* 3,288,986
subscriptions per 100 inhabitants: 149 (July 2016 est.)
country comparison to the world: 131

Telephone system: *general assessment:* Botswana is participating in regional development efforts; expanding fully digital system with fiber-optic cables linking the major population centers in the east as well as a system of open-wire lines, microwave radio relays links, and radiotelephone communication stations; the Botswana Telecommunications Corporation is rolling out 4G service to over 95 sites in the country that will improve network connectivity
domestic: fixed-line teledensity has declined in recent years and now stands at roughly 6 telephones per 100 persons; mobile-cellular teledensity now pushing 150 telephones per 100 persons
international: country code—267; international calls are made via satellite, using international direct dialing; 2 international exchanges; digital microwave radio relay links to Namibia, Zambia, Zimbabwe, and South Africa; satellite earth station—1 Intelsat (Indian Ocean) (2016)

Broadcast media: 2 TV stations—1 state-owned and 1 privately owned; privately owned satellite TV subscription service is available; 2 state-owned national radio stations; 3 privately owned radio stations broadcast locally (2007)

Internet country code: .bw

Internet users: *total:* 869,610
percent of population: 39.4% (July 2016 est.)
country comparison to the world: 144

TRANSPORTATION

National air transport system: *number of registered air carriers:* 1
inventory of registered aircraft operated by air carriers: 6
annual passenger traffic on registered air carriers: 194,005
annual freight traffic on registered air carriers: 94,729 mt-km (2015)
Civil aircraft registration country code prefix: A2 (2016)

Airports: 74 (2013)
country comparison to the world: 70

Airports—with paved runways: *total:* 10
over 3,047 m: 2
2,438 to 3,047 m: 1
1,524 to 2,437 m: 6
914 to 1,523 m: 1 (2017)

Airports—with unpaved runways: *total:* 64
1,524 to 2,437 m: 5
914 to 1,523 m: 46

under 914 m: 13 (2013)

Railways: *total:* 888 km
narrow gauge: 888 km 1.067-m gauge (2014)
country comparison to the world: 94

Roadways: *total:* 17,916 km
note: includes 8,916 km of Public Highway Network roads (6,116 km paved and 2,800 km unpaved) and 9,000 km of District Council roads (2011)
country comparison to the world: 117

MILITARY AND SECURITY

Military expenditures: 3.37% of GDP (2016)
2.66% of GDP (2015)
2.13% of GDP (2014)
2.06% of GDP (2013)
2.23% of GDP (2012)

country comparison to the world: 34

Military branches: Botswana Defence Force (BDF): Ground Forces Command, Air Arm Command, Defense Logistics Command (2017)

Military service age and obligation: 18 is the legal minimum age for voluntary military service; no conscription (2012)

TRANSNATIONAL ISSUES

Disputes—international: none

Trafficking in persons: current situation: Botswana is a source, transit, and destination country for women and children subjected to sex trafficking and forced labor; young Batswana serving as domestic workers, sometimes sent by their parents, may be denied education and basic necessities or experience confinement and abuse indicative of forced labor; Batswana girls and women also are forced into prostitution domestically; adults and children of San ethnicity were reported to be in forced labor on farms and at cattle posts in the country's rural west

tier rating: Tier 2 Watch List—Botswana does not fully comply with the minimum standards for the elimination of trafficking; however, it is making significant efforts to do so; an anti-trafficking act was passed at the beginning of 2014, but authorities did not investigate, prosecute, or convict any offenders or government officials complicit in trafficking or operationalize victim identification and referral procedures based on the new law; the government sponsored a radio campaign to familiarize the public with the issue of human trafficking (2015)

BOUVET ISLAND

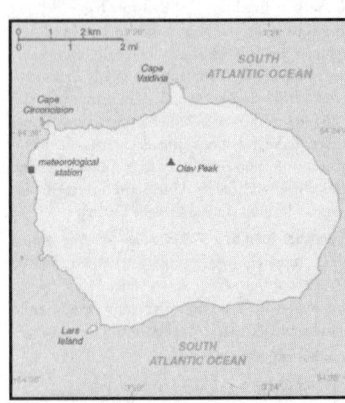

INTRODUCTION

Background: This uninhabited, volcanic, Antarctic island is almost entirely covered by glaciers making it difficult to approach; it is recognized as the most remote island on Earth. Bouvet Island was discovered in 1739 by a French naval officer after whom it is named. No claim was made until 1825, when the British flag was raised. A few expeditions visited the island in the late 19th century. In 1928, the UK waived its claim in favor of Norway, which had occupied the island the previous year. In 1971, Norway designated Bouvet Island and the adjacent territorial waters a nature reserve. Since 1977, Norway has run an automated meteorological station and studied foraging strategies and distribution of fur seals and penguins on the island. In February 2006, an earthquake weakened the station's foundation causing it to be blown out to sea in a winter storm. Norway erected a new research station in 2014 that can hold six people for periods of two to four months.

GEOGRAPHY

Location: island in the South Atlantic Ocean, southwest of the Cape of Good Hope (South Africa)

Geographic coordinates: 54 26 S, 3 24 E

Map references: Antarctic Region

Area: *total:* 49 sq km
land: 49 sq km
water: 0 sq km
country comparison to the world: 234

Area—comparative: about 0.3 times the size of Washington, DC

Land boundaries: 0 km

Coastline: 29.6 km

Maritime claims: *territorial sea:* 4 nm

Climate: antarctic

Terrain: volcanic; coast is mostly inaccessible

Elevation: *mean elevation:* NA

elevation extremes: *lowest point:* South Atlantic Ocean 0 m
highest point: Olavtoppen (Olav Peak) 780 m

Natural resources: none

Land use: *agricultural land:* 0%
arable land: 0%;
permanent crops: 0%;
permanent pasture: 0%
forest: 0%
other: 100% (93% ice) (2011 est.)

Natural hazards: occasional volcanism, rock slides; harsh climate, surrounded by pack ice in winter

Environment—current issues: none; almost entirely ice covered

Geography—note: covered by glacial ice; declared a nature reserve by Norway

PEOPLE AND SOCIETY

Population: uninhabited

GOVERNMENT

Country name: *conventional long form:* none
conventional short form: Bouvet Island
etymology: named after the French naval officer Jean-Baptiste Charles BOUVET who discovered the island in 1739

Dependency status: territory of Norway; administered by the Polar Department of the Ministry of Justice and Oslo Police

Legal system: the laws of Norway, where applicable, apply

Flag description: the flag of Norway is used

ECONOMY

Economy—overview: no economic activity; declared a nature reserve

COMMUNICATIONS

Internet country code: .bv
Communications—note: has an automated meteorological station

TRANSPORTATION

Ports and terminals: none; offshore anchorage only

MILITARY AND SECURITY

Military—note: defense is the responsibility of Norway

TRANSNATIONAL ISSUES

Disputes—international: none

BRAZIL

INTRODUCTION

Background: Following more than three centuries under Portuguese rule, Brazil gained its independence in 1822, maintaining a monarchical system of government until the abolition of slavery in 1888 and the subsequent proclamation of a republic by the military in 1889. Brazilian coffee exporters politically dominated the country until populist leader Getulio VARGAS rose to power in 1930. By far the largest and most populous country in South America, Brazil underwent more than a half century of populist and military government until 1985, when the military regime peacefully ceded power to civilian rulers. Brazil continues to pursue industrial and agricultural growth and development of its interior. Having successfully weathered a period of global financial difficulty in the late 20th century, Brazil was seen as one of the world's strongest emerging markets and a contributor to global growth. The awarding of the 2014 FIFA World Cup and 2016 Summer Olympic Games, the first ever to be held in South America, was seen as symbolic of the country's rise. However, from about 2013 to 2016, Brazil was plagued by a sagging economy, high unemployment, and high inflation, only emerging from recession in 2017. Political scandal resulted in the impeachment of President Dilma ROUSSEFF in May 2016, a conviction that was upheld by the Senate in August 2016; her vice president, Michel TEMER, will serve as president until 1 January 2019, completing her second term.

GEOGRAPHY

Location: Eastern South America, bordering the Atlantic Ocean

Geographic coordinates: 10 00 S, 55 00 W

Map references: South America

Area: *total:* 8,515,770 sq km
land: 8,358,140 sq km
water: 157,630 sq km

note: includes Arquipelago de Fernando de Noronha, Atol das Rocas, Ilha da Trindade, Ilhas Martin Vaz, and Penedos de Sao Pedro e Sao Paulo
country comparison to the world: 6

Area—comparative: slightly smaller than the US

Land boundaries: *total:* 16,145 km
border countries (10): Argentina 1,263 km, Bolivia 3,403 km, Colombia 1,790 km, French Guiana 649 km, Guyana 1,308 km, Paraguay 1,371 km, Peru 2,659 km, Suriname 515 km, Uruguay 1,050 km, Venezuela 2,137 km

Coastline: 7,491 km

Maritime claims: *territorial sea:* 12 nm
contiguous zone: 24 nm
exclusive economic zone: 200 nm
continental shelf: 200 nm or to edge of the continental margin

Climate: mostly tropical, but temperate in south

Terrain: mostly flat to rolling lowlands in north; some plains, hills, mountains, and narrow coastal belt

Elevation: *mean elevation:* 320 m
elevation extremes: lowest point: Atlantic Ocean 0 m
highest point: Pico da Neblina 2,994 m

Natural resources: bauxite, gold, iron ore, manganese, nickel, phosphates, platinum, tin, rare earth elements, uranium, petroleum, hydropower, timber

Land use: *agricultural land:* 32.9%
arable land: 8.6%;
permanent crops: 0.8%;
permanent pasture: 23.5%
forest: 61.9%
other: 5.2% (2011 est.)
Irrigated land: 54,000 sq km (2012)

Population—distribution: the vast majority of people live along, or relatively near, the Atlantic coast in the east; the population core is in the southeast, anchored by the cities of Sao Paolo, Brasilia, and Rio de Janeiro

Natural hazards: recurring droughts in northeast; floods and occasional frost in south

Environment—current issues: deforestation in Amazon Basin destroys the habitat and endangers a multitude of plant and animal species indigenous to the area; there is a lucrative illegal wildlife trade; air and water pollution in Rio de Janeiro, Sao Paulo, and several other large cities; land degradation and water pollution caused by improper mining activities; wetland degradation; severe oil spills

Environment—international agreements: party to: Antarctic-Environmental Protocol, Antarctic-Marine Living Resources, Antarctic Seals, Antarctic Treaty, Biodiversity, Climate Change, Climate Change-Kyoto Protocol, Desertification, Endangered Species, Environmental Modification, Hazardous Wastes, Law of the Sea, Marine

Dumping, Ozone Layer Protection, Ship Pollution, Tropical Timber 83, Tropical Timber 94, Wetlands, Whaling
signed, but not ratified: none of the selected agreements

Geography—note: largest country in South America and in the Southern Hemisphere; shares common boundaries with every South American country except Chile and Ecuador; most of the Pantanal, the world's largest tropical wetland, extends through the west central part of the country; shares Iguazu Falls, the world's largest waterfalls system, with Argentina

PEOPLE AND SOCIETY

Population: 207,353,391 (July 2017 est.)
country comparison to the world: 5

Nationality: *noun:* Brazilian(s)
adjective: Brazilian

Ethnic groups: white 47.7%, mulatto (mixed white and black) 43.1%, black 7.6%, Asian 1.1%, indigenous 0.4% (2010 est.)

Languages: Portuguese (official and most widely spoken language)
note: less common languages include Spanish (border areas and schools), German, Italian, Japanese, English, and a large number of minor Amerindian languages

Religions: Roman Catholic 64.6%, other Catholic 0.4%, Protestant 22.2% (includes Adventist 6.5%, Assembly of God 2.0%, Christian Congregation of Brazil 1.2%, Universal Kingdom of God 1.0%, other Protestant 11.5%), other Christian 0.7%, Spiritist 2.2%, other 1.4%, none 8%, unspecified 0.4% (2010 est.)

Demographic profile: Brazil's rapid fertility decline since the 1960s is the main factor behind the country's slowing population growth rate, aging population, and fast-paced demographic transition. Brasilia has not taken full advantage of its large working-age population to develop its human capital and strengthen its social and economic institutions but is funding a study abroad program to bring advanced skills back to the country. The current favorable age structure will begin to shift around 2025, with the labor force shrinking and the elderly starting to compose an increasing share of the total population. Well-funded public pensions have nearly wiped out poverty among the elderly, and Bolsa Familia and other social programs have lifted tens of millions out of poverty. More than half of Brazil's population is considered middle class, but poverty and income inequality levels remain high; the Northeast, North, and Center-West, women, and black, mixed race, and indigenous populations are disproportionately affected. Disparities in opportunities foster social exclusion and contribute to Brazil's high crime rate, particularly violent crime in cities and favelas (slums).

Brazil has traditionally been a net recipient of immigrants, with its southeast being the prime destination. After the importation of African slaves was outlawed in the mid-19th century, Brazil sought Europeans (Italians, Portuguese, Spaniards, and Germans) and later Asians (Japanese) to work in agriculture, especially coffee cultivation. Recent immigrants come mainly from Argentina, Chile, and Andean countries (many are unskilled illegal migrants) or are returning Brazilian nationals. Since Brazil's economic downturn in the 1980s, emigration to the United States, Europe, and Japan has been rising but is negligible relative to Brazil's total population. The majority of these emigrants are well-educated and middle-class. Fewer Brazilian peasants are emigrating to neighboring countries to take up agricultural work.

Age structure: *0-14 years:* 22.33% (male 23,599,867/female 22,696,756)
15-24 years: 16.36% (male 17,212,048/female 16,721,295)
25-54 years: 43.86% (male 45,114,076/female 45,836,147)
55-64 years: 9.12% (male 8,931,065/female 9,974,723)
65 years and over: 8.33% (male 7,356,838/female 9,910,576) (2017 est.)

Dependency ratios: *total dependency ratio:* 43.8
youth dependency ratio: 32.4
elderly dependency ratio: 11.4
potential support ratio: 8.7 (2015 est.)

Median age: *total:* 32 years
male: 31.1 years
female: 32.8 years (2017 est.)
country comparison to the world: 104

Population growth rate: 0.73% (2017 est.)
country comparison to the world: 140

Birth rate: 14.1 births/1,000 population (2017 est.)
country comparison to the world: 136

Death rate: 6.7 deaths/1,000 population (2017 est.)
country comparison to the world: 139

Net migration rate: -0.1 migrant(s)/1,000 population (2017 est.)
country comparison to the world: 104

Population distribution: the vast majority of people live along, or relatively near, the Atlantic coast in the east; the population core is in the southeast, anchored by the cities of Sao Paolo, Brasilia, and Rio de Janeiro

Urbanization: *urban population:* 86.2% of total population (2017)
rate of urbanization: 0.99% annual rate of change (2015-20 est.)

Major urban areas—population: Sao Paulo 21.066 million; Rio de Janeiro 12.902 million; Belo Horizonte 5.716 million; BRASILIA (capital) 4.155 million; Fortaleza 3.88 million; Recife 3.739 million (2015)

Sex ratio: *at birth:* 1.05 male(s)/female
0-14 years: 1.04 male(s)/female
15-24 years: 1.03 male(s)/female
25-54 years: 0.98 male(s)/female

55-64 years: 0.89 male(s)/female
65 years and over: 0.74 male(s)/female
total population: 0.97 male(s)/female (2016 est.)

Maternal mortality ratio: 44 deaths/100,000 live births (2015 est.)
country comparison to the world: 102

Infant mortality rate: *total:* 17.5 deaths/1,000 live births
male: 20.5 deaths/1,000 live births
female: 14.2 deaths/1,000 live births (2017 est.)
country comparison to the world: 92

Life expectancy at birth: *total population:* 74 years
male: 70.5 years
female: 77.7 years (2017 est.)
country comparison to the world: 128

Total fertility rate: 1.75 children born/woman (2017 est.)
country comparison to the world: 163

Contraceptive prevalence rate: 80.2% (2013)
Health expenditures: 8.3% of GDP (2014)
country comparison to the world: 51

Physicians density: 1.85 physicians/1,000 population (2013)

Hospital bed density: 2.3 beds/1,000 population (2012)

Drinking water source:
improved:
urban: 100% of population
rural: 87% of population
total: 98.1% of population
unimproved:
urban: 0% of population
rural: 13% of population
total: 1.9% of population (2015 est.)

Sanitation facility access:
improved:
urban: 88% of population
rural: 51.5% of population
total: 82.8% of population
unimproved:
urban: 12% of population
rural: 48.5% of population
total: 17.2% of population (2015 est.)

HIV/AIDS—adult prevalence rate: 0.6% (2016 est.)
country comparison to the world: 60

HIV/AIDS—people living with HIV/AIDS: 830,000 (2016 est.)
country comparison to the world: 11

HIV/AIDS—deaths: 14,000 (2016 est.)
country comparison to the world: 18

Major infectious diseases: *degree of risk:* very high
food or waterborne diseases: bacterial diarrhea and hepatitis A
vectorborne diseases: dengue fever and malaria
water contact disease: schistosomiasis
note: active local transmission of Zika virus by Aedes species mosquitoes has been identified in this country (as of August 2016); it poses an important risk (a large number of cases possible) among US citizens if bitten by an infective

mosquito; other less common ways to get Zika are through sex, via blood transfusion, or during pregnancy, in which the pregnant woman passes Zika virus to her fetus (2016)

Obesity—adult prevalence rate: 22.1% (2016)
country comparison to the world: 82

Children under the age of 5 years underweight: 2.2% (2007)
country comparison to the world: 121

Education expenditures: 6% of GDP (2013)
country comparison to the world: 49

Literacy: *definition:* age 15 and over can read and write
total population: 92.6%
male: 92.2%
female: 92.9% (2015 est.)

School life expectancy (primary to tertiary education): *total:* 15 years
male: 15 years
female: 16 years (2014)

Unemployment, youth ages 15-24: *total:* 16.1%
male: 13.8%
female: 21.2% (2014 est.)
country comparison to the world: 76

GOVERNMENT

Country name: *conventional long form:* Federative Republic of Brazil
conventional short form: Brazil
local long form: Republica Federativa do Brasil
local short form: Brasil
etymology: the country name derives from the brazilwood tree that used to grow plentifully along the coast of Brazil and that was used to produce a deep red dye

Government type: federal presidential republic

Capital: *name:* Brasilia
geographic coordinates: 15 47 S, 47 55 W
time difference: UTC-3 (2 hours ahead of Washington, DC, during Standard Time)
daylight saving time: +1hr, begins third Sunday in October; ends third Sunday in February
note: Brazil has three time zones, including one for the Fernando de Noronha Islands

Administrative divisions: 26 states (estados, singular—estado) and 1 federal district* (distrito federal); Acre, Alagoas, Amapa, Amazonas, Bahia, Ceara, Distrito Federal*, Espirito Santo, Goias, Maranhao, Mato Grosso, Mato Grosso do Sul, Minas Gerais, Para, Paraiba, Parana, Pernambuco, Piaui, Rio de Janeiro, Rio Grande do Norte, Rio Grande do Sul, Rondonia, Roraima, Santa Catarina, Sao Paulo, Sergipe, Tocantins

Independence: 7 September 1822 (from Portugal)
National holiday: Independence Day, 7 September (1822)
Constitution: several previous; latest ratified 5 October 1988; amended many times, last in 2016 (2016)

Legal system: civil law; note—a new civil law code was enacted in 2002 replacing the 1916 code

International law organization participation: has not submitted an ICJ jurisdiction declaration; accepts ICCt jurisdiction

Citizenship: *citizenship by birth:* yes
citizenship by descent: yes
dual citizenship recognized: yes
residency requirement for naturalization: 4 years

Suffrage: voluntary between 16 to 18 years of age, over 70, and the illiterate; compulsory between 18 to 70 years of age; note—military conscripts by law cannot vote

Executive branch: *chief of state:* President Michel Miguel Elias TEMER Lulia (since 31 August 2016); Vice President (vacant); note—the president is both chief of state and head of government

head of government: President Michel Miguel Elias TEMER Lulia (since 31 August 2016); Vice President (vacant)
cabinet: Cabinet appointed by the president
elections/appointments: president and vice president directly elected on the same ballot by absolute majority popular vote in 2 rounds if needed for a single 4-year term (eligible for a second term); election last held on 5 October 2014 with runoff on 26 October 2014 (next to be held in October 2018)
election results: Dilma ROUSSEFF reelected president in second round; percent of vote—Dilma ROUSSEFF (PT) 51.6%, Aecio NEVES (PSDB) 48.4%
note: on 12 May 2016, Brazil's Senate voted to hold an impeachment trial of President Dilma ROUSSEFF, who was then suspended from her executive duties; Vice President Michel TEMER took over as acting president; on 31 August 2016 the Senate voted 61-20 in favor of conviction and her removal from office; TEMER is serving as president for the remainder of ROUSSEFF's term, which ends 1 January 2019

Legislative branch: *description:* bicameral National Congress or Congresso Nacional consists of the Federal Senate or Senado Federal (81 seats; 3 members each from 26 states and 3 from the federal district directly elected in multi-seat constituencies by simple majority vote to serve 8-year terms, with one-third and two-thirds of the membership elected alternately every 4 years) and the Chamber of Deputies or Camara dos Deputados (513 seats; members directly elected in multi-seat constituencies by proportional representation vote to serve 4-year terms)
elections: Federal Senate—last held on 5 October 2014 for one-third of the Senate (next to be held in October 2018 for two-thirds of the Senate); Chamber of Deputies—last held on 5 October 2014 (next to be held in October 2018)
election results: Federal Senate—percent of vote by party—NA; seats by party—PMDB 5, PSDB 4, PDT 4, PSB 3, DEM (formerly PFL) 3, PT 2, PSD 2, PTB 2, PP 1, PR 1; Chamber of Deputies—percent of vote by party—NA; seats by party—PT 70, PMDB 66, PSDB 54, PSD 37, PP 36, PR 34, PSB 34, PTB 25, DEM (formerly PFL) 22, PRB 21, PDT 19, SD 15, PSC 12, PROS 11, PCdoB 10,

PPS 10, PV 8, PHS 5, PSOL 5, PTN 4, PMN 3, PRP 3, PEN 2, PTC 2, PSDC 2, PTdoB 1, PSL 1, PRTB 1

Judicial branch: *highest court(s):* Supreme Federal Court or Supremo Tribunal Federal (consists of 11 justices)
judge selection and term of office: justices appointed by the president and approved by the Federal Senate; justices appointed to serve until mandatory retirement at age 75
subordinate courts: Tribunal of the Union, Federal Appeals Court, Superior Court of Justice, Superior Electoral Court, regional federal courts; state court system

Political parties and leaders: Brazilian Communist Party or PCB [Ivan Martins PINHEIRO]
Brazilian Democratic Movement Party or PMDB [Michel TEMER]
Brazilian Labor Party or PTB [Cristiane BRASIL]
Brazilian Renewal Labor Party or PRTB [Jose Levy FIDELIX da Cruz]
Brazilian Republican Party or PRB [Marcos Antonio PEREIRA]
Brazilian Social Democracy Party or PSDB [Aecio NEVES]
Brazilian Socialist Party or PSB [Carlos Roberto SIQUEIRA de Barros]
Christian Labor Party or PTC [Daniel TOURINHO]
Christian Social Democratic Party or PSDC [Jose Maria EYMAEL]
Communist Party of Brazil or PCdoB [Jose Renato RABELO]
Democratic Labor Party or PDT [Carlos Roberto LUPI]
The Democrats or DEM [Jose AGRIPINO] (formerly Liberal Front Party or PFL)
Free Homeland Party or PPL [Sergio RUBENS]
Green Party or PV [Jose Luiz PENNA]
Humanist Party of Solidarity or PHS [Eduardo MACHADO]
Labor Party of Brazil or PTdoB [Luis Henrique de Oliveira RESENDE]
National Ecologic Party or PEN [Adilson Barroso OLIVEIRA]
National Labor Party or PTN [Jose Masci de ABREU]
National Mobilization Party or PMN [Telma RIBEIRO dos Santos]
Party of the Republic or PR [Alfredo NASCIMENTO]
Popular Socialist Party or PPS [Roberto Joao Pereira FREIRE]
Progressive Party or PP [Ciro NOGUEIRA]
Progressive Republican Party or PRP [Ovasco Roma Altimari RESENDE]
Republican Social Order Party or PROS [Euripedes JUNIOR]
Social Christian Party or PSC [Vitor Jorge Abdala NOSSEIS]
Social Democratic Party or PSD [Guilherme CAMPOS]
Social Liberal Party or PSL [Luciano Caldas BIVAR]
Socialism and Freedom Party or PSOL [Luiz ARAUJO]

Solidarity or SD [Paulo PEREIRA DA SILVA]
United Socialist Workers' Party or PSTU [Jose Maria DE ALMEIDA]
Workers' Cause Party or PCO [Rui Costa PIMENTA]
Workers' Party or PT [Rui FALCAO]

Political pressure groups and leaders: Landless Workers' Movement or MST [Joao Pedro STEDILE]
other: industrial federations; labor unions and federations; large farmers' associations; religious groups including evangelical Christian churches and the Catholic Church

International organization participation: AfDB (nonregional member), BIS, BRICS, CAN (associate), CD, CELAC, CPLP, FAO, FATF, G-15, G-20, G-24, G-5, G-77, IADB, IAEA, IBRD, ICAO, ICC (national committees), ICCt, ICRM, IDA, IFAD, IFC, IFRCS, IHO, ILO, IMF, IMO, IMSO, Interpol, IOC, IOM, IPU, ISO, ITSO, ITU, ITUC (NGOs), LAES, LAIA, LAS (observer), Mercosur, MIGA, MINURSO, MINUSTAH, MONUSCO, NAM (observer), NSG, OAS, OECD (enhanced engagement), OPANAL, OPCW, Paris Club (associate), PCA, SICA (observer), UN, UNASUR, UNCTAD, UNESCO, UNFICYP, UNHCR, UNIDO, UNIFIL, Union Latina, UNISFA, UNITAR, UNMIL, UNMISS, UNOCI, UNRWA, UNWTO, UPU, WCO, WFTU (NGOs), WHO, WIPO, WMO, WTO

Diplomatic representation in the US: *chief of mission:* Ambassador Sergio Silva do AMARAL (since 16 September 2016)
chancery: 3006 Massachusetts Avenue NW, Washington, DC 20008
telephone: [1] (202) 238-2700
FAX: [1] (202) 238-2827
consulate(s) general: Atlanta, Boston, Chicago, Hartford (CT), Houston, Los Angeles, Miami, New York, San Francisco, Washington, DC

Diplomatic representation from the US: *chief of mission:* Ambassador Michael MCKINLEY (since 19 December 2016)
embassy: Avenida das Nacoes, Quadra 801, Lote 3, Distrito Federal Cep 70403-900, Brasilia
mailing address: Unit 7500, DPO, AA 34030
telephone: [55] (61) 3312-7000
FAX: [55] (61) 3225-9136
consulate(s) general: Recife, Rio de Janeiro, Sao Paulo

Flag description: green with a large yellow diamond in the center bearing a blue celestial globe with 27 white five-pointed stars; the globe has a white equatorial band with the motto ORDEM E PROGRESSO (Order and Progress); the current flag was inspired by the banner of the former Empire of Brazil (1822-1889); on the imperial flag, the green represented the House of Braganza of Pedro I, the first Emperor of Brazil, while the yellow stood for the Habsburg Family of his wife; on the modern flag the green represents the forests of the country and the yellow rhombus its mineral wealth (the diamond shape roughly mirrors that of the country); the blue circle and stars, which replaced the coat of arms of the original flag, depict the sky over Rio de Janeiro on the morning of 15 November 1889—the day the Republic of Brazil was declared; the number of stars has changed with the creation of new states and has risen from an original 21 to the current 27 (one for each state and the Federal District)

note: one of several flags where a prominent component of the design reflects the shape of the country; other such flags are those of Bosnia and Herzegovina, Eritrea, and Vanuatu

National symbol(s): Southern Cross constellation; national colors: green, yellow, blue

National anthem: *name:* "Hino Nacional Brasileiro" (Brazilian National Anthem)
lyrics/music: Joaquim Osorio Duque ESTRADA/ Francisco Manoel DA SILVA
note: music adopted 1890, lyrics adopted 1922; the anthem's music, composed in 1822, was used unofficially for many years before it was adopted

ECONOMY

Economy—overview: Brazil is the eighth-largest economy in the world, but is recovering from a recession in 2015 and 2016 that ranks as the worst in the country's history. Falling commodity prices reduced export revenues and investment, which weakened the Brazilian real and cut tax revenues. The weaker real made existing public debt, which was largely denominated in foreign currency, more expensive. Lower tax revenues strained the government budget.

Economic reforms, proposed in 2016, aim to slow the growth of government spending and reduce barriers to foreign investment. Government spending helped to push public debt to 78% of GDP at the end of 2017, up from 50% in 2012. Policies to strengthen Brazil's workforce and industrial sector, such as local content requirements, may have boosted employment at the expense of investment.

Former President Dilma ROUSSEFF was impeached and convicted in August 2016 for moving funds among government budgets; the economy has also been affected by multiple corruption scandals involving private companies and government officials. Sanctions against the firms involved —some of the largest in Brazil —has limited their business opportunities, producing a ripple effect on associated businesses and contractors. In addition, investment in these companies has declined because of the scandals.

Brazil is a member of the Common Market of the South (Mercosur), a trade bloc including Argentina, Paraguay, Uruguay, and Venezuela. After the Asian and Russian financial crises, Mercosur adopted a protectionist stance to guard against exposure to the volatility of foreign markets. Brazil and its Mercosur partners have pledged to open the bloc to more trade and investment, but changes require approval of all five members, which makes policy adjustments too difficult to enact.

GDP (purchasing power parity): $3.219 trillion (2017 est.)

$3.195 trillion (2016 est.)
$3.314 trillion (2015 est.)
note: data are in 2017 dollars
country comparison to the world: 9

GDP (official exchange rate): $2.081 trillion (2016 est.)

GDP—real growth rate: 0.7% (2017 est.)
-3.6% (2016 est.)
-3.8% (2015 est.)
country comparison to the world: 193

GDP—per capita (PPP): $15,500 (2017 est.)
$15,500 (2016 est.)
$16,200 (2015 est.)
note: data are in 2017 dollars
country comparison to the world: 107

Gross national saving: 16.2% of GDP (2017 est.)
16.2% of GDP (2016 est.)
15.8% of GDP (2015 est.)
country comparison to the world: 119

GDP—composition, by end use:
household consumption: 63.5%
government consumption: 19.9%
investment in fixed capital: 16.6%
investment in inventories: 0%
exports of goods and services: 11.8%
imports of goods and services: -11.7% (2017 est.)

GDP—composition, by sector of origin:
agriculture: 6.2%
industry: 21%
services: 72.8%
(2017 est.)

Agriculture—products: coffee, soybeans, wheat, rice, corn, sugarcane, cocoa, citrus; beef

Industries: textiles, shoes, chemicals, cement, lumber, iron ore, tin, steel, aircraft, motor vehicles and parts, other machinery and equipment

Industrial production growth rate: 1% (2017 est.)
country comparison to the world: 165

Labor force: 111.6 million (2017 est.)
country comparison to the world: 6

Labor force—by occupation: *agriculture:* 10%
industry: 39.8%
services: 50.2%
(2016 est.)

Unemployment rate: 13.1% (2017 est.)
11.3% (2016 est.)
country comparison to the world: 164

Population below poverty line: 3.7%
note: approximately 4% of the population are below the "extreme" poverty line (2016 est.)

Household income or consumption by percentage share: *lowest 10%:* 1.2%
highest 10%: 41.6% (2014 est.)

Distribution of family income—Gini index: 49.7 (2014)
55.3 (2001)
country comparison to the world: 19

Budget: *revenues:* $726.6 billion
expenditures: $749 billion (2017 est.)
Taxes and other revenues: 34.9% of GDP (2017 est.)
country comparison to the world: 55

Budget surplus (+) or deficit (-): -1.1% of GDP (2017 est.)
country comparison to the world: 62

Public debt: 78.4% of GDP (2017 est.)
69.9% of GDP (2016 est.)
country comparison to the world: 42

Fiscal year: calendar year

Inflation rate (consumer prices): 3.7% (2017 est.)
8.7% (2016 est.)
country comparison to the world: 144

Central bank discount rate: 13.75% (31 December 2016 est.)
14.25% (31 December 2015)
country comparison to the world: 14

Commercial bank prime lending rate: 48.7% (31 December 2017 est.)
52.1% (31 December 2016 est.)
country comparison to the world: 2

Stock of narrow money: $106.9 billion (31 December 2017 est.)
$106.7 billion (31 December 2016 est.)
country comparison to the world: 37

Stock of broad money: $761.2 billion (31 December 2017 est.)
$727.7 billion (31 December 2016 est.)
country comparison to the world: 19

Stock of domestic credit: $2.237 trillion (31 December 2017 est.)
$2.138 trillion (31 December 2016 est.)
country comparison to the world: 12

Market value of publicly traded shares: $490.5 billion (31 December 2015 est.)
$843.9 billion (31 December 2014 est.)
$1.02 trillion (31 December 2013 est.)
country comparison to the world: 22

Current account balance: -$28.99 billion (2017 est.)
-$23.53 billion (2016 est.)
country comparison to the world: 196

Exports: $215.4 billion (2017 est.)
$184.5 billion (2016 est.)
country comparison to the world: 27

Exports—commodities: transport equipment, iron ore, soybeans, footwear, coffee, automobiles

Exports—partners: China 19%, US 12.6%, Argentina 7.3%, Netherlands 5.6% (2016)

Imports: $151.9 billion (2017 est.)
$139.4 billion (2016 est.)
country comparison to the world: 30

Imports—commodities: machinery, electrical and transport equipment, chemical products, oil, automotive parts, electronics

Imports—partners: US 17.6%, China 16.9%, Argentina 6.7%, Germany 6.6%, South Korea 4.4% (2016)

Reserves of foreign exchange and gold: $377.1 billion (31 December 2017 est.)
$365 billion (31 December 2016 est.)
country comparison to the world: 10

Debt—external: $554.5 billion (31 December 2017 est.)
$551.3 billion (31 December 2016 est.)

country comparison to the world: 20

Stock of direct foreign investment—at home:
$828.7 billion (31 December 2017 est.)
$763.7 billion (31 December 2016 est.)
country comparison to the world: 14

Stock of direct foreign investment—abroad:
$327.3 billion (31 December 2017 est.)
$319.1 billion (31 December 2016 est.)
country comparison to the world: 22

Exchange rates: reals (BRL) per US dollar—
3.214 (2017 est.)
3.4901 (2016 est.)
3.4901 (2015 est.)
3.3315 (2014 est.)
2.3535 (2013 est.)

ENERGY

Electricity access: *population without electricity:* 800,000
electrification—*total population:* 99.5%
electrification—urban areas: 100%
electrification—rural areas: 97% (2013)

Electricity—production: 559.2 billion kWh (2015 est.)
country comparison to the world: 9

Electricity—consumption: 500.6 billion kWh (2015 est.)
country comparison to the world: 9

Electricity—exports: 219 million kWh (2015 est.)
country comparison to the world: 74

Electricity—imports: 34.64 billion kWh (2015 est.)
country comparison to the world: 4

Electricity—installed generating capacity: 155.6 million kW (2015 est.)
country comparison to the world: 8

Electricity—from fossil fuels: 25.4% of total installed capacity (2015 est.)
country comparison to the world: 189

Electricity—from nuclear fuels: 1.2% of total installed capacity (2015 est.)
country comparison to the world: 32

Electricity—from hydroelectric plants: 59.2% of total installed capacity (2015 est.)
country comparison to the world: 29

Electricity—from other renewable sources: 16% of total installed capacity (2015 est.)
country comparison to the world: 45

Crude oil—production: 2.515 million bbl/day (2016 est.)
country comparison to the world: 10

Crude oil—exports: 518,800 bbl/day (2014 est.)
country comparison to the world: 22

Crude oil—imports: 350,100 bbl/day (2014 est.)
country comparison to the world: 24

Crude oil—proved reserves: 13 billion bbl (1 January 2017 es)
country comparison to the world: 15

Refined petroleum products—production: 2.899 million bbl/day (2014 est.)
country comparison to the world: 8

Refined petroleum products—consumption: 3.102 million bbl/day (2015 est.)
country comparison to the world: 8

Refined petroleum products—exports: 269,400 bbl/day (2014 est.)
country comparison to the world: 29

Refined petroleum products—imports: 559,000 bbl/day (2014 est.)
country comparison to the world: 15

Natural gas—production: 20.41 billion cu m (2015 est.)
country comparison to the world: 32

Natural gas—consumption: 43.4 billion cu m (2015 est.)
country comparison to the world: 26

Natural gas—exports: 100 million cu m (2014 est.)
country comparison to the world: 48

Natural gas—imports: 18.98 billion cu m (2015 est.)
country comparison to the world: 17

Natural gas—proved reserves: 429.9 billion cu m (1 January 2017 es)
country comparison to the world: 34

Carbon dioxide emissions from consumption of energy: 535 million Mt (2013 est.)
country comparison to the world: 13

COMMUNICATIONS

Telephones—fixed lines: *total subscriptions:* 41,846,846
subscriptions per 100 inhabitants: 20 (July 2016 est.)
country comparison to the world: 6

Telephones—mobile cellular: *total:* 244,066,759
subscriptions per 100 inhabitants: 119 (July 2016 est.)
country comparison to the world: 6

Telephone system: *general assessment:* good working system including an extensive microwave radio relay system and a domestic satellite system with 64 earth stations
domestic: fixed-line connections have remained relatively stable in recent years and stand at about 20 per 100 persons; less-expensive mobile-cellular technology has been a major driver in expanding telephone service to the lower-income segments of the population with mobile-cellular teledensity roughly 120 per 100 persons
international: country code—55; landing point for a number of submarine cables, including Americas-1, Americas-2, Atlantis-2, GlobeNet, South America-1, South American Crossing/Latin American Nautilus, and UNISUR that provide direct connectivity to South and Central America, the Caribbean, the US, Africa, and Europe; satellite earth stations—3 Intelsat (Atlantic Ocean), 1 Inmarsat (Atlantic Ocean region east), connected by microwave relay system to Mercosur Brazilsat B3 satellite earth station (2016)

Broadcast media: state-run Radiobras operates a radio and a TV network; more than 1,000 radio stations and more than 100 TV channels

operating—mostly privately owned; private media ownership highly concentrated (2007)

Internet country code: .br

Internet users: *total:* 122,841,218
percent of population: 59.7% (July 2016 est.)
country comparison to the world: 6

TRANSPORTATION

National air transport system: *number of registered air carriers:* 9
inventory of registered aircraft operated by air carriers: 443
annual passenger traffic on registered air carriers: 102,039,359
annual freight traffic on registered air carriers: 149.393 million mt-km (2015)
Civil aircraft registration country code prefix: PP (2016)

Airports: 4,093 (2013)
country comparison to the world: 2

Airports—with paved runways: *total:* 698
over 3,047 m: 7
2,438 to 3,047 m: 27
1,524 to 2,437 m: 179
914 to 1,523 m: 436
under 914 m: 49 (2017)

Airports—with unpaved runways: *total:* 3,395
1,524 to 2,437 m: 92
914 to 1,523 m: 1,619
under 914 m: 1,684 (2013)

Heliports: 13 (2013)

Pipelines: condensate/gas 251 km; gas 17,312 km; liquid petroleum gas 352 km; oil 4,831 km; refined products 4,722 km (2013)

Railways: *total:* 29,849.9 km
broad gauge: 5,822.3 km 1.600-m gauge (498.3 km electrified)
dual gauge: 492 km 1.600-1.000-m gauge
standard gauge: 194 km 1.435-m gauge
narrow gauge: 23,341.6 km 1.000-m gauge (24 km electrified) (2014)
country comparison to the world: 10

Roadways: *total:* 1,580,964 km
paved: 212,798 km
unpaved: 1,368,166 km
note: does not include urban roads (2010)
country comparison to the world: 4

Waterways: 50,000 km (most in areas remote from industry and population) (2012)
country comparison to the world: 3

Merchant marine: *total:* 766
by type: bulk carrier 14, container ship 16, general cargo 48, oil tanker 37, other 651 (2017)
country comparison to the world: 28

Ports and terminals: *major seaport(s):* Belem, Paranagua, Rio Grande, Rio de Janeiro, Santos, Sao Sebastiao, Tubarao
river port(s): Manaus (Amazon)
dry bulk cargo port(s): Sepetiba ore terminal, Tubarao
container port(s) (TEUs): Santos (3,780,000) (2015)

127

oil terminal(s): DTSE/Gegua oil terminal, Ilha Grande (Gebig), Guaiba Island terminal, Guamare oil terminal

LNG terminal(s) (import): Pecem, Rio de Janiero

MILITARY AND SECURITY

Military expenditures: 1.32% of GDP (2016)
1.36% of GDP (2015)
1.33% of GDP (2014)
1.33% of GDP (2013)
1.38% of GDP (2012)
country comparison to the world: 65

Military branches: Brazilian Army (Exercito Brasileiro, EB), Brazilian Navy (Marinha do Brasil, MB, includes Naval Air and Marine Corps (Corpo de Fuzileiros Navais)), Brazilian Air Force (Forca Aerea Brasileira, FAB) (2011)

Military service age and obligation: 18-45 years of age for compulsory military service; conscript service obligation is 10-12 months; 17-45 years of age for voluntary service; an increasing percentage of the ranks are "long-service" volunteer professionals; women were allowed to serve in the armed forces beginning in early 1980s, when the Brazilian Army became the first army in South America to accept women into career ranks; women serve in Navy and Air Force only in Women's Reserve Corps (2012)

TRANSNATIONAL ISSUES

Disputes—international: uncontested boundary dispute between Brazil and Uruguay over Brazilera/Brasilera Island in the Quarai/Cuareim River leaves the tripoint with Argentina in question; smuggling of firearms and narcotics continues to be an issue along the Uruguay-Brazil border; Colombian-organized illegal narcotics and paramilitary activities penetrate Brazil's border region with Venezuela

Refugees and internally displaced persons: refugees (country of origin): 20,372 (Venezuela) (economic and political crisis; only includes Venezuelans who have claimed asylum) (2017)

Illicit drugs: second-largest consumer of cocaine in the world; illicit producer of cannabis; trace amounts of coca cultivation in the Amazon region, used for domestic consumption; government has a large-scale eradication program to control cannabis; important transshipment country for Bolivian, Colombian, and Peruvian cocaine headed for Europe; also used by traffickers as a way station for narcotics air transshipments between Peru and Colombia; upsurge in drug-related violence and weapons smuggling; important market for Colombian, Bolivian, and Peruvian cocaine; illicit narcotics proceeds are often laundered through the financial system; significant illicit financial activity in the Tri-Border Area

BRITISH INDIAN OCEAN TERRITORY

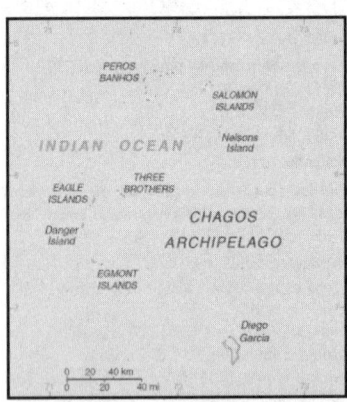

INTRODUCTION

Background: Formerly administered as part of the British Crown Colony of Mauritius, the British Indian Ocean Territory (BIOT) was established as an overseas territory of the UK in 1965. A number of the islands of the territory were later transferred to the Seychelles when it attained independence in 1976. Subsequently, BIOT has consisted only of the six main island groups comprising the Chagos Archipelago. Only Diego Garcia, the largest and most southerly of the islands, is inhabited. It contains a joint UK-US naval support facility and hosts one of four dedicated ground antennas (the others are on Ascension (Saint Helena, Ascension, and Tristan da Cunha), Kwajalein (Marshall Islands), and at Cape Canaveral, Florida (US)) that assist in the operation of the Global Positioning System (GPS) navigation system. The US Air Force also operates a telescope array on Diego Garcia as part of the Ground-Based Electro-Optical Deep Space Surveillance System (GEODSS) for tracking orbital debris, which can be a hazard to spacecraft and astronauts.

Between 1967 and 1973, former agricultural workers, earlier residents in the islands, were relocated primarily to Mauritius, but also to the Seychelles. Negotiations between 1971 and 1982 resulted in the establishment of a trust fund by the British Government as compensation for the displaced islanders, known as Chagossians. Beginning in 1998, the islanders pursued a series of lawsuits against the British Government seeking further compensation and the right to return to the territory. In 2006 and 2007, British court rulings invalidated the immigration policies contained in the 2004 BIOT Constitution Order that had excluded the islanders from the archipelago, but upheld the special military status of Diego Garcia. In 2008, the House of Lords, as the final court of appeal in the UK, ruled in favor of the British Government by overturning the lower court rulings and finding no right of return for the Chagossians. In March 2015, the Permanent Court of Arbitration unanimously held that the marine protected area (MPA) that the UK declared around the Chagos Archipelago in April 2010 was in violation of the UN Convention on the Law of the Sea.

GEOGRAPHY

Location: archipelago in the Indian Ocean, south of India, about halfway between Africa and Indonesia

Geographic coordinates: 6 00 S, 71 30 E; note—Diego Garcia 7 20 S, 72 25 E

Map references: Political Map of the World

Area: total: 60 sq km
land: 60 sq km; Diego Garcia 44 sq km
water: 54,340 sq km
note: includes the entire Chagos Archipelago of 55 islands

country comparison to the world: 230

Area—comparative: land area is about one-third the size of Washington, DC

Land boundaries: 0 km

Coastline: 698 km

Maritime claims: territorial sea: 12 nm
Environment (Protection and Preservation) Zone: 200 nm

Climate: tropical marine; hot, humid, moderated by trade winds

Terrain: flat and low (most areas do not exceed two m in elevation)

Elevation: mean elevation: NA

elevation extremes: lowest point: Indian Ocean 0 m
highest point: ocean-side dunes on Diego Garcia 9 m

Natural resources: coconuts, fish, sugarcane

Land use: agricultural land: 0%
arable land: 0%;
permanent crops: 0%;
permanent pasture: 0%;
forest: 0%
other: 100% (2011 est.)

Natural hazards: none; located outside routes of Indian Ocean cyclones

Environment—current issues: wastewater discharge into the lagoon on Diego Garcia

Geography—note: note 1: archipelago of 55 islands; Diego Garcia, the largest and southernmost island, occupies a strategic location in the central Indian Ocean; the island is the site of a joint US-UK military facility

note 2: Diego Garcia is the only inhabited island of the BIOT and one of only two British territories where traffic drives on the right, the other being Gibraltar

PEOPLE AND SOCIETY

Population: no indigenous inhabitants
note: approximately 1,200 former agricultural workers resident in the Chagos Archipelago, often referred to as Chagossians or Ilois, were relocated to Mauritius and the Seychelles in the 1960s and 1970s; approximately 3,000 UK and US military personnel and civilian contractors were living on the island of Diego Garcia

GOVERNMENT

Country name: *conventional long form:* British Indian Ocean Territory
conventional short form: none
abbreviation: BIOT
etymology: self-descriptive name specifying the territory's affiliation and location

Dependency status: overseas territory of the UK; administered by a commissioner, resident in the Foreign and Commonwealth Office in London

Legal system: the laws of the UK, where applicable, apply

Executive branch: *chief of state:* Queen ELIZABETH II (since 6 February 1952)

head of government: Commissioner Dr. Peter HAYES (since 17 October 2012); Administrator John MCMANUS (since April 2011); note—both reside in the UK and are represented by the officer commanding British Forces on Diego Garcia
cabinet: NA
elections/appointments: the monarchy is hereditary; commissioner and administrator appointed by the monarch

Diplomatic representation in the US: none (overseas territory of the UK)

Diplomatic representation from the US: none (overseas territory of the UK)

Flag description: white with six blue wavy horizontal stripes; the flag of the UK is in the upper hoist-side quadrant; the striped section bears a palm tree and yellow crown (the symbols of the territory) centered on the outer half of the flag; the wavy stripes represent the Indian Ocean; although not officially described, the six blue stripes may stand for the six main atolls of the archipelago

ECONOMY

Economy—overview: All economic activity is concentrated on the largest island of Diego Garcia, where a joint UK-US military facility is located. Construction projects and various services needed to support the military installation are performed by military and contract employees from the UK, Mauritius, the Philippines, and the US. Some of the natural resources found in this territory include coconuts, fish, and sugarcane. Sugarcane is still a major export for this territory. There are no industrial or agricultural activities on the islands. The territory earns foreign exchange by selling fishing licenses and postage stamps.

Exchange rates: the US dollar is used

COMMUNICATIONS

Telephone system: *general assessment:* separate facilities for military and public needs are available
domestic: all commercial telephone services are available, including connection to the Internet
international: country code (Diego Garcia)—246; international telephone service is carried by satellite (2015)

Broadcast media: Armed Forces Radio and Television Service (AFRTS) broadcasts over 3 separate frequencies for US and UK military personnel stationed on the islands (2009)

Internet country code: .io

TRANSPORTATION

Airports: 1 (2013)
country comparison to the world: 213
Airports—with paved runways: *total:* 1
over 3,047 m: 1 (2017)
Roadways: note: short section of paved road between port and airfield on Diego Garcia
Ports and terminals: *major seaport(s):* Diego Garcia

MILITARY AND SECURITY

Military branches: no regular military forces (2014)
Military—note: defense is the responsibility of the UK; the US lease on Diego Garcia expires in December 2016

TRANSNATIONAL ISSUES

Disputes—international: Mauritius and Seychelles claim the Chagos Islands; negotiations between 1971 and 1982 resulted in the establishment of a trust fund by the British Government as compensation for the displaced islanders, known as Chagossians, who were evicted between 1967-73; in 2001, the former inhabitants of the archipelago were granted UK citizenship and the right of return; in 2006 and 2007, British court rulings invalidated the immigration policies contained in the 2004 BIOT Constitution Order that had excluded the islanders from the archipelago; in 2008 a House of Lords' decision overturned lower court rulings, once again denying the right of return to Chagossians; in addition, the UK created the world's largest marine protection area around the Chagos islands prohibiting the extraction of any natural resources therein

BRITISH VIRGIN ISLANDS

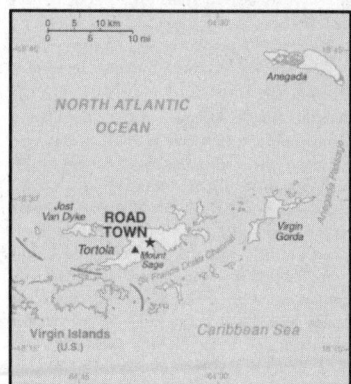

INTRODUCTION

Background: First inhabited by Arawak and later by Carib Indians, the Virgin Islands were settled by the Dutch in 1648 and then annexed by the English in 1672. The islands were part of the British colony of the Leeward Islands from 1872-1960; they were granted autonomy in 1967. The economy is closely tied to the larger and more populous US Virgin Islands to the west; the US dollar is the legal currency. On 6 September 2017, Hurricane Irma devastated the island of Tortola. An estimated 80% of residential and business structures were destroyed or damaged, communications disrupted, and local roads rendered impassable.

GEOGRAPHY

Location: Caribbean, between the Caribbean Sea and the North Atlantic Ocean, east of Puerto Rico

Geographic coordinates: 18 30 N, 64 30 W

Map references: Central America and the Caribbean

Area: *total:* 151 sq km
land: 151 sq km
water: 0 sq km
note: comprised of 16 inhabited and more than 20 uninhabited islands; includes the islands of Tortola, Anegada, Virgin Gorda, Jost van Dyke
country comparison to the world: 220

Area—comparative: about 0.9 times the size of Washington, DC

Land boundaries: 0 km

Coastline: 80 km

Maritime claims: *territorial sea:* 3 nm
exclusive fishing zone: 200 nm

Climate: subtropical; humid; temperatures moderated by trade winds

Terrain: coral islands relatively flat; volcanic islands steep, hilly

Elevation: *mean elevation:* NA

elevation extremes: *lowest point:* Caribbean Sea 0 m

highest point: Mount Sage 521 m

Natural resources: NEGL; pleasant climate, beaches foster tourism

Land use: *agricultural land:* 46.7%

arable land: 6.7%;

permanent crops: 6.7%;

permanent pasture: 33.3%

forest: 24.3%

other: 29% (2011 est.)

Irrigated land: NA

Population—distribution: a fairly even distribution throughout the inhabited islands, with the largest islands of Tortola, Anegada, Virgin Gorda, and Jost Van Dyke having the largest populations

Natural hazards: hurricanes and tropical storms (July to October)

Environment—current issues: limited natural freshwater resources except for a few seasonal streams and springs on Tortola; most of the islands' water supply comes from desalination plants

Geography—note: strong ties to nearby US Virgin Islands and Puerto Rico

PEOPLE AND SOCIETY

Population: 35,015 (July 2017 est.)
country comparison to the world: 214

Nationality: *noun:* British Virgin Islander(s)
adjective: British Virgin Islander

Ethnic groups: African/black 76.3%, Latino 5.5%, white 5.4%, mixed 5.3%, Indian 2.1%, East Indian 1.6%, other 3%, unspecified 0.8% (2010 est.)

Languages: English (official)

Religions: Protestant 70.2% (Methodist 17.6%, Church of God 10.4%, Anglican 9.5%, Seventh Day Adventist 9.0%, Pentecostal 8.2%, Baptist 7.4%, New Testament Church of God 6.9%, other Protestant 1.2%), Roman Catholic 8.9%, Jehovah's Witness 2.5%, Hindu 1.9%, other 6.2%, none 7.9%, unspecified 2.4% (2010 est.)

Age structure: *0-14 years:* 16.7% (male 2,877/female 2,971)
15-24 years: 13.37% (male 2,243/female 2,437)
25-54 years: 49.37% (male 8,116/female 9,170)
55-64 years: 11.6% (male 1,975/female 2,086)
65 years and over: 8.97% (male 1,522/female 1,618) (2017 est.)

Median age: *total:* 36.5 years
male: 36.3 years
female: 36.6 years (2017 est.)
country comparison to the world: 72

Population growth rate: 2.25% (2017 est.)
country comparison to the world: 35

Birth rate: 11.1 births/1,000 population (2017 est.)
country comparison to the world: 177

Death rate: 5.1 deaths/1,000 population (2017 est.)
country comparison to the world: 190

Net migration rate: 16.5 migrant(s)/1,000 population (2017 est.)
country comparison to the world: 1

Population distribution: a fairly even distribution throughout the inhabited islands, with the largest islands of Tortola, Anegada, Virgin Gorda, and Jost Van Dyke having the largest populations

Urbanization: *urban population:* 46.8% of total population (2017)
rate of urbanization: 1.63% annual rate of change (2015-20 est.)

Major urban areas—population: ROAD TOWN (capital) 13,000 (2014)

Sex ratio: *at birth:* 1.05 male(s)/female
0-14 years: 0.97 male(s)/female
15-24 years: 0.92 male(s)/female
25-54 years: 0.89 male(s)/female
55-64 years: 0.95 male(s)/female
65 years and over: 0.95 male(s)/female
total population: 0.92 male(s)/female (2016 est.)

Infant mortality rate: *total:* 12.1 deaths/1,000 live births
male: 13.8 deaths/1,000 live births
female: 10.4 deaths/1,000 live births (2017 est.)
country comparison to the world: 120

Life expectancy at birth: *total population:* 78.8 years
male: 77.4 years
female: 80.3 years (2017 est.)
country comparison to the world: 53

Total fertility rate: 1.29 children born/woman (2017 est.)
country comparison to the world: 218

Drinking water source:
improved:
urban: 98% of population
rural: 98% of population
total: 98% of population
unimproved:
urban: 2% of population
rural: 2% of population
total: 2% of population (2010 est.)

Sanitation facility access:
improved:
urban: 97.5% of population
rural: 97.5% of population
total: 97.5% of population
unimproved:
urban: 2.5% of population
rural: 2.5% of population
total: 2.5% of population (2015 est.)

HIV/AIDS—adult prevalence rate: NA

HIV/AIDS—people living with HIV/AIDS: NA

HIV/AIDS—deaths: NA

Education expenditures: 4.4% of GDP (2010)
country comparison to the world: 96

School life expectancy (primary to tertiary education): *total:* 14 years
male: NA
female: NA (2015)

GOVERNMENT

Country name: *conventional long form:* none
conventional short form: British Virgin Islands
abbreviation: BVI

etymology: the myriad islets, cays, and rocks surrounding the major islands reminded explorer Christopher COLUMBUS in 1493 of Saint Ursula and her 11,000 virgin followers (Santa Ursula y las Once Mil Virgenes), which over time shortened to the Virgins (las Virgenes)

Dependency status: overseas territory of the UK; internal self-governing

Government type: parliamentary democracy (House of Assembly); self-governing overseas territory of the UK

Capital: *name:* Road Town

geographic coordinates: 18 25 N, 64 37 W

time difference: UTC-4 (1 hour ahead of Washington, DC, during Standard Time)

Administrative divisions: none (overseas territory of the UK)

Independence: none (overseas territory of the UK)

National holiday: Territory Day, 1 July (1956)

Constitution: several previous; latest effective 15 June 2007 (2016)

Legal system: English common law

Citizenship: see United Kingdom

Suffrage: 18 years of age; universal

Executive branch: *chief of state:* Queen ELIZABETH II (since 6 February 1952); represented by Governor Gus JASPERT (since 22 August 2017)

head of government: Premier Orlando SMITH (since 9 November 2011)

cabinet: Executive Council appointed by the governor from members of the House of Assembly

elections/appointments: the monarchy is hereditary; governor appointed by the monarch; following legislative elections, the leader of the majority party or majority coalition usually appointed premier by the governor

Legislative branch: *description:* unicameral House of Assembly (13 seats; 9 members directly elected in single-seat constituencies and 4 at-large seats by simple majority vote to serve 4-year terms); note—the Assembly includes the attorney general, a non-voting ex officio member

elections: last held on 8 June 2015 (next to be held in 2019)

election results: percent of vote by party—NDP 60.2%, VIP 30.2%, other 9.6%; seats by party—NDP 11, VIP 2

Judicial branch: *highest court(s):* the Eastern Caribbean Supreme Court (ECSC) is the superior court of the Organization of Eastern Caribbean States; the ECSC—headquartered on St. Lucia—consists of the Court of Appeal—headed by the chief justice and 4 judges—and the High Court with 18 judges; the Court of Appeal is itinerant, travelling to member states on a schedule to hear appeals from the High Court and subordinate courts; High Court judges reside at the member states with 3 on the British Virgin Islands

judge selection and term of office: Eastern Caribbean Supreme Court chief justice appointed by Her Majesty, Queen ELIZABETH II; other justices and judges appointed by the Judicial and Legal

Services Commission; Court of Appeal justices appointed for life with mandatory retirement at age 65; High Court judges appointed for life with mandatory retirement at age 62
subordinate courts: Magistrates' Courts

Political parties and leaders: National Democratic Party or NDP [Orlando SMITH]

Virgin Islands Party or VIP [Julian FRASER]

Political pressure groups and leaders: Family Support Network or FSN
Office of Gender Affairs or ODA (formerly Woman's Desk)
other: environmentalists

International organization participation: Caricom (associate), CDB, Interpol (subbureau), IOC, OECS, UNESCO (associate), UPU

Diplomatic representation in the US: none (overseas territory of the UK)

Diplomatic representation from the US: none (overseas territory of the UK)

Flag description: blue with the flag of the UK in the upper hoist-side quadrant and the Virgin Islander coat of arms centered in the outer half of the flag; the coat of arms depicts a woman flanked on either side by a vertical column of six oil lamps above a scroll bearing the Latin word VIGILATE (Be Watchful); the islands were named by COLUMBUS in 1493 in honor of Saint Ursula and her 11 virgin followers (some sources say 11,000) who reputedly were martyred by the Huns in the 4th or 5th century; the figure on the banner holding a lamp represents the saint; the other lamps symbolize her followers

National symbol(s): zenaida dove, white cedar flower; national colors: yellow, green, red, white, blue
National anthem: note: as a territory of the United Kingdom, "God Save the Queen" is official (see United Kingdom)

ECONOMY

Economy—overview: The economy, one of the most stable and prosperous in the Caribbean, is highly dependent on tourism, which generates an estimated 45% of the national income. More than 934,000 tourists, mainly from the US, visited the islands in 2008. Because of traditionally close links with the US Virgin Islands, the British Virgin Islands has used the US dollar as its currency since 1959.

Livestock raising is the most important agricultural activity; poor soils limit the islands' ability to meet domestic food requirements.

In the mid-1980s, the government began offering offshore registration to companies wishing to incorporate in the islands, and incorporation fees now generate substantial revenues. Roughly 400,000 companies were on the offshore registry by yearend 2000. The adoption of a comprehensive insurance law in late 1994, which provides a blanket of confidentiality with regulated statutory gateways for investigation of criminal offenses, made the British Virgin Islands even more attractive to international business.

GDP (purchasing power parity): $500 million (2010 est.)
country comparison to the world: 214

GDP (official exchange rate): $1.095 billion (2008)

GDP—real growth rate: 1.3% (2010 est.)
-0.6% (2008 est.)
country comparison to the world: 181

GDP—per capita (PPP): $42,300 (2010 est.)
country comparison to the world: 43

GDP—composition, by end use:
household consumption: 25.1%
government consumption: 7.5%
investment in fixed capital: 21.7%
investment in inventories: 20.4%
exports of goods and services: 94.7%
imports of goods and services: -69.4% (2017 est.)

GDP—composition, by sector of origin:
agriculture: 1%
industry: 11.2%
services: 87.8% (2017 est.)

Agriculture—products: fruits, vegetables; livestock, poultry; fish

Industries: tourism, light industry, construction, rum, concrete block, offshore banking center

Industrial production growth rate: 2.2% (2017 est.)
country comparison to the world: 121

Labor force: 12,770 (2004)
country comparison to the world: 216

Labor force—by occupation: *agriculture:* 0.6%
industry: 40%
services: 59.4% (2005)

Unemployment rate: 8.7% (2010 est.)
country comparison to the world: 118

Population below poverty line: NA%

Household income or consumption by percentage share: *lowest 10%:* NA%
highest 10%: NA%

Budget: *revenues:* $400 million
expenditures: $400 million (2017 est.)
Taxes and other revenues: 36.5% of GDP (2017 est.)
country comparison to the world: 48

Budget surplus (+) or deficit (-): 0% of GDP (2017 est.)
country comparison to the world: 34

Fiscal year: 1 April–31 March

Inflation rate (consumer prices): 2.5% (2017 est.)
1.1% (2016 est.)
country comparison to the world: 117

Current account balance: $362.6 million (2011 est.)
$279.8 million (2010 est.)
country comparison to the world: 49

Exports: $23 million (2015 est.)
country comparison to the world: 209

Exports—commodities: rum, fresh fish, fruits, animals; gravel, sand

Imports: $NA (2016 est.)
$200 million (2015 est.)

Imports—commodities: building materials, automobiles, foodstuffs, machinery

Debt—external: $36.1 million (1997)
country comparison to the world: 198

Exchange rates: the US dollar is used

ENERGY

Electricity—production: 126 million kWh (2015 est.)
country comparison to the world: 197

Electricity—consumption: 631.5 million kWh (2015 est.)
country comparison to the world: 165

Electricity—exports: 0 kWh (2016 est.)
country comparison to the world: 213

Electricity—imports: 0 kWh (2016 est.)
country comparison to the world: 216

Electricity—installed generating capacity: 48,000 kW (2015 est.)
country comparison to the world: 193

Electricity—from fossil fuels: 658.3% of total installed capacity (2015 est.)
country comparison to the world: 1

Electricity—from nuclear fuels: 0% of total installed capacity (2015 est.)
country comparison to the world: 205

Electricity—from hydroelectric plants: 0% of total installed capacity (2015 est.)
country comparison to the world: 212

Electricity—from other renewable sources: 0% of total installed capacity (2015 est.)
country comparison to the world: 212

Crude oil—production: 0 bbl/day (2016 est.)
country comparison to the world: 115

Crude oil—exports: 0 bbl/day (2014 est.)
country comparison to the world: 208

Crude oil—imports: 0 bbl/day (2014 est.)
country comparison to the world: 207

Crude oil—proved reserves: 0 bbl (1 January 2017 es)
country comparison to the world: 114

Refined petroleum products—production: 0 bbl/day (2014 est.)
country comparison to the world: 123

Refined petroleum products—consumption: 1,200 bbl/day (2015 est.)
country comparison to the world: 203

Refined petroleum products—exports: 0 bbl/day (2014 est.)
country comparison to the world: 211

Refined petroleum products—imports: 1,209 bbl/day (2014 est.)
country comparison to the world: 199

Natural gas—production: 0 cu m (2013 est.)
country comparison to the world: 209

Natural gas—consumption: 0 cu m (2013 est.)
country comparison to the world: 144

Natural gas—exports: 0 cu m (2013 est.)
country comparison to the world: 206

Natural gas—imports: 0 cu m (2013 est.)

country comparison to the world: 205

Natural gas—proved reserves: 0 cu m (1 January 2014 es)
country comparison to the world: 205

Carbon dioxide emissions from consumption of energy: 200,000 Mt (2013 est.)
country comparison to the world: 203

COMMUNICATIONS

Telephones—fixed lines: *total subscriptions:* 12,000
subscriptions per 100 inhabitants: 36 (July 2016 est.)
country comparison to the world: 197

Telephones—mobile cellular: *total:* 42,000
subscriptions per 100 inhabitants: 126 (July 2016 est.)
country comparison to the world: 202

Telephone system: *general assessment:* good overall telephone service
domestic: fixed-line connections exceed 35 per 100 persons and mobile cellular subscribership is roughly 125 per 100 persons

international: country code—1-284; connected via submarine cable to Bermuda; the East Caribbean Fiber System (ECFS) submarine cable provides connectivity to 13 other islands in the eastern Caribbean (2015)

Broadcast media: 1 private TV station; multichannel TV is available from cable and satellite subscription services; about a half-dozen private radio stations (2007)

Internet country code: .vg

Internet users: *total:* 14,600
percent of population: 43.6% (July 2016 est.)
country comparison to the world: 207

TRANSPORTATION

National air transport system: *number of registered air carriers:* 1
inventory of registered aircraft operated by air carriers: 3 (2015)
Civil aircraft registration country code prefix: VP-L (2016)

Airports: 4 (2013)
country comparison to the world: 185

Airports—with paved runways: *total:* 2

914 to 1,523 m: 1
under 914 m: 1 (2017)

Airports—with unpaved runways: *total:* 2
914 to 1,523 m: 2 (2013)

Roadways: *total:* 200 km
paved: 200 km (2007)
country comparison to the world: 209

Merchant marine: *total:* 20
by type: general cargo 4, other 16 (2017)
country comparison to the world: 135

Ports and terminals: *major seaport(s):* Road Harbor

MILITARY AND SECURITY

Military—note: defense is the responsibility of the UK

TRANSNATIONAL ISSUES

Disputes—international: none

Illicit drugs: transshipment point for South American narcotics destined for the US and Europe; large offshore financial center makes it vulnerable to money laundering

BRUNEI

50th anniversary of the Sultan Hassanal BOLKIAH's accession to the throne.

GEOGRAPHY

Location: Southeastern Asia, along the northern coast of the island of Borneo, bordering the South China Sea and Malaysia

Geographic coordinates: 4 30 N, 114 40 E

Map references: Southeast Asia

Area: *total:* 5,765 sq km
land: 5,265 sq km
water: 500 sq km
country comparison to the world: 173

Area—comparative: slightly smaller than Delaware

Land boundaries: *total:* 266 km
border countries (1): Malaysia 266 km

Coastline: 161 km

Maritime claims: *territorial sea:* 12 nm
exclusive economic zone: 200 nm or to median line

Climate: tropical; hot, humid, rainy

Terrain: flat coastal plain rises to mountains in east; hilly lowland in west

Elevation: *mean elevation:* 478 m

elevation extremes: *lowest point:* South China Sea 0 m
highest point: Bukit Pagon 1,850 m

Natural resources: petroleum, natural gas, timber

Land use: *agricultural land:* 2.5%

arable land: 0.8%;
permanent crops: 1.1%;
permanent pasture: 0.6%
forest: 71.8%
other: 25.7% (2011 est.)
Irrigated land: 10 sq km (2012)

Natural hazards: typhoons, earthquakes, and severe flooding are rare

Environment—current issues: seasonal smoke/haze resulting from forest fires in Indonesia

Environment—international agreements: party to: Biodiversity, Climate Change, Desertification, Endangered Species, Hazardous Wastes, Law of the Sea, Ozone Layer Protection, Ship Pollution
signed, but not ratified: none of the selected agreements

Geography—note: close to vital sea lanes through South China Sea linking Indian and Pacific Oceans; two parts physically separated by Malaysia; almost an enclave within Malaysia

PEOPLE AND SOCIETY

Population: 443,593 (July 2017 est.)
country comparison to the world: 174

Nationality: *noun:* Bruneian(s)
adjective: Bruneian

Ethnic groups: Malay 65.7%, Chinese 10.3%, other 24% (2016 est.)

Languages: Malay (Bahasa Melayu) (official), English, Chinese dialects

INTRODUCTION

Background: The Sultanate of Brunei's influence peaked between the 15th and 17th centuries when its control extended over coastal areas of northwest Borneo and the southern Philippines. Brunei subsequently entered a period of decline brought on by internal strife over royal succession, colonial expansion of European powers, and piracy. In 1888, Brunei became a British protectorate; independence was achieved in 1984. The same family has ruled Brunei for over six centuries. Brunei benefits from extensive petroleum and natural gas fields, the source of one of the highest per capita GDPs in the world. In 2017, Brunei celebrated the

Religions: Muslim (official) 78.8%, Christian 8.7%, Buddhist 7.8%, other (includes indigenous beliefs) 4.7% (2011 est.)

Age structure: *0-14 years:* 23.12% (male 52,862/female 49,717)
15-24 years: 17.05% (male 37,637/female 38,005)
25-54 years: 46.75% (male 99,203/female 108,198)
55-64 years: 8.23% (male 18,537/female 17,974)
65 years and over: 4.84% (male 10,440/female 11,020) (2017 est.)

Dependency ratios: *total dependency ratio:* 38.4
youth dependency ratio: 32.8
elderly dependency ratio: 5.7
potential support ratio: 17.6 (2015 est.)

Median age: *total:* 30.2 years
male: 29.7 years
female: 30.7 years (2017 est.)
country comparison to the world: 116

Population growth rate: 1.57% (2017 est.)
country comparison to the world: 69

Birth rate: 17 births/1,000 population (2017 est.)
country comparison to the world: 108

Death rate: 3.6 deaths/1,000 population (2017 est.)
country comparison to the world: 214

Net migration rate: 2.4 migrant(s)/1,000 population (2017 est.)
country comparison to the world: 39

Urbanization: *urban population:* 77.8% of total population (2017)
rate of urbanization: 1.52% annual rate of change (2015-20 est.)

Major urban areas—population: BANDAR SERI BEGAWAN (capital) 241,000
note: the boundaries of the capital city were expanded in 2007, greatly increasing the city area; the population of the capital increased tenfold (2011)

Sex ratio: *at birth:* 1.05 male(s)/female
0-14 years: 1.06 male(s)/female
15-24 years: 0.99 male(s)/female
25-54 years: 0.92 male(s)/female
55-64 years: 1.04 male(s)/female
65 years and over: 0.95 male(s)/female
total population: 0.98 male(s)/female (2016 est.)

Maternal mortality ratio: 23 deaths/100,000 live births (2015 est.)
country comparison to the world: 127

Infant mortality rate: *total:* 9.6 deaths/1,000 live births
male: 11.4 deaths/1,000 live births
female: 7.7 deaths/1,000 live births (2017 est.)
country comparison to the world: 142

Life expectancy at birth: *total population:* 77.3 years
male: 75 years
female: 79.8 years (2017 est.)
country comparison to the world: 73

Total fertility rate: 1.78 children born/woman (2017 est.)
country comparison to the world: 154
Health expenditures: 2.6% of GDP (2014)

country comparison to the world: 186

Physicians density: 1.47 physicians/1,000 population (2012)

Hospital bed density: 2.8 beds/1,000 population (2012)

HIV/AIDS—adult prevalence rate: NA

HIV/AIDS—people living with HIV/AIDS: NA

HIV/AIDS—deaths: NA

Obesity—adult prevalence rate: 14.1% (2016)
country comparison to the world: 129

Children under the age of 5 years underweight: 9.6% (2009)

Education expenditures: 3.7% of GDP (2016)
country comparison to the world: 126

Literacy: *definition:* age 15 and over can read and write
total population: 96%
male: 97.5%
female: 94.5% (2015 est.)

School life expectancy (primary to tertiary education): *total:* 15 years
male: 14 years
female: 15 years (2015)

GOVERNMENT

Country name: *conventional long form:* Brunei Darussalam
conventional short form: Brunei
local long form: Negara Brunei Darussalam
local short form: Brunei
etymology: derivation of the name is unclear; according to legend, MUHAMMAD SHAH, who would become the first sultan of Brunei, upon discovering what would become Brunei exclaimed "Baru nah," which roughly translates as "there" or "that's it"

Government type: absolute monarchy or sultanate

Capital: *name:* Bandar Seri Begawan
geographic coordinates: 4 53 N, 114 56 E
time difference: UTC+8 (13 hours ahead of Washington, DC, during Standard Time)

Administrative divisions: 4 districts (daerah-daerah, singular—daerah); Belait, Brunei-Muara, Temburong, Tutong

Independence: 1 January 1984 (from the UK)

National holiday: National Day, 23 February (1984); note—1 January 1984 was the date of independence from the UK, 23 February 1984 was the date of independence from British protection

Constitution: drafted 1954 to 1959, signed 29 September 1959; amended 1984, 2004, 2011; note—some constitutional provisions suspended since 1962 under a state of emergency, others suspended since independence in 1984 (2016)

Legal system: mixed legal system based on English common law and Islamic law; note—in May 2014, the first of three phases of sharia-based penal codes was instituted, which applies to Muslims and non-Muslims and exists in parallel to the existing common law-based code

International law organization participation: has not submitted an ICJ jurisdiction declaration; non-party state to the ICCt

Citizenship: *citizenship by birth:* no
citizenship by descent only: the father must be a citizen of Brunei
dual citizenship recognized: no
residency requirement for naturalization: 12 years

Suffrage: 18 years of age for village elections; universal

Executive branch: *chief of state:* Sultan and Prime Minister Sir HASSANAL Bolkiah (since 5 October 1967); note—the monarch is both chief of state and head of government

head of government: Sultan and Prime Minister Sir HASSANAL Bolkiah (since 5 October 1967)
cabinet: Council of Ministers appointed and presided over by the monarch; note—4 additional advisory councils appointed by the monarch are the Religious Council, Privy Council for constitutional issues, Council of Succession, and Legislative Council
elections/appointments: none; the monarchy is hereditary

Legislative branch: *description:* Legislative Council or Majlis Mesyuarat Negara Brunei (36 seats; members appointed by the sultan including 3 ex-officio members—the speaker and first and second secretaries; members appointed for 5-year terms)
elections/appointments: appointed by the sultan

Judicial branch: *highest resident court(s):* Supreme Court (consists of Court of Appeal and High Court, each with a chief justice and 2 judges); Sharia Court of Appeal (consists of judges appointed by the monarch); note—Brunei has a dual judicial system of secular and sharia (religious) courts; the Judicial Committee of Privy Council in London serves as the final appellate court for civil cases only
judge selection and term of office: Supreme Court judges appointed by the monarch to serve until age 65, and older if approved by the monarch; Sharia Court of Appeal judges appointed by the monarch for life
subordinate courts: Intermediate Court; Magistrate's Courts; Juvenile Court; small claims courts; lower sharia courts

Political parties and leaders: National Development Party or NDP [YASSIN Affendi]
note: Brunei National Solidarity Party or PPKB [Abdul LATIF bin Chuchu] and People's Awareness Party or PAKAR [Awang Haji MAIDIN bin Haji Ahmad] were deregistered in 2007; parties are small and have limited activity

Political pressure groups and leaders: NA

International organization participation: ADB, APEC, ARF, ASEAN, C, CP, EAS, FAO, G-77, IAEA, IBRD, ICAO, ICC (NGOs), ICRM, IDA, IFRCS, ILO, IMF, IMO, IMSO, Interpol, IOC, ISO (correspondent), ITSO, ITU, NAM, OIC, OPCW, UN, UNCTAD, UNESCO, UNIFIL, UNWTO, UPU, WCO, WHO, WIPO, WMO, WTO

Diplomatic representation in the US: *chief of mission:* Ambassador Serbini ALI (since 28 January 2016)
chancery: 3520 International Court NW, Washington, DC 20008
telephone: [1] (202) 237-1838
FAX: [1] (202) 885-0560
consulate(s): New York

Diplomatic representation from the US: *chief of mission:* Ambassador Craig B. ALLEN (since 9 March 2015)
embassy: Simpang 336-52-16-9, Jalan Datu, Bandar Seri Begawan, BC4115
mailing address: Unit 4280, Box 40, FPO AP 96507; P.O. Box 2991, Bandar Seri Begawan BS8675, Negara Brunei Darussalam
telephone: [673] 238-4616
FAX: [673] 238-4604

Flag description: yellow with two diagonal bands of white (top, almost double width) and black starting from the upper hoist side; the national emblem in red is superimposed at the center; yellow is the color of royalty and symbolizes the sultanate; the white and black bands denote Brunei's chief ministers; the emblem includes five main components: a swallow-tailed flag, the royal umbrella representing the monarchy, the wings of four feathers symbolizing justice, tranquility, prosperity, and peace, the two upraised hands signifying the government's pledge to preserve and promote the welfare of the people, and the crescent moon denoting Islam, the state religion; the state motto "Always render service with God's guidance" appears in yellow Arabic script on the crescent; a ribbon below the crescent reads "Brunei, the Abode of Peace"

National symbol(s): royal parasol; national colors: yellow, white, black

National anthem: *name:* "Allah Peliharakan Sultan" (God Bless His Majesty)
lyrics/music: Pengiran Haji Mohamed YUSUF bin Pengiran Abdul Rahim/Awang Haji BESAR bin Sagap
note: adopted 1951

ECONOMY

Economy—overview: Brunei is an energy-rich sultanate on the northern coast of Borneo in Southeast Asia. Brunei boasts a well-educated, largely English-speaking population; excellent infrastructure; and a stable government intent on attracting foreign investment. Crude oil and natural gas production account for approximately 65% of GDP and 95% of exports, with Japan as the primary export market.

Per capita GDP is among the highest in the world, and substantial income from overseas investment supplements income from domestic hydrocarbon production. Bruneian citizens pay no personal income taxes, and the government provides free medical services and free education through the university level.

The Bruneian Government wants to diversify its economy away from hydrocarbon exports to other industries such as information and communications technology and halal manufacturing, permissible under Islamic law. Brunei's trade increased in 2016 and 2017, following its regional economic integration in the ASEAN Economic Community, and the expected ratification of the Trans-Pacific Partnership trade agreement.

GDP (purchasing power parity): $32.91 billion (2017 est.)
$33.33 billion (2016 est.)
$34.18 billion (2015 est.)
note: data are in 2017 dollars
country comparison to the world: 129

GDP (official exchange rate): $11.96 billion (2016 est.)

GDP—real growth rate: -1.3% (2017 est.)
-2.5% (2016 est.)
-0.4% (2015 est.)
country comparison to the world: 210

GDP—per capita (PPP): $76,700 (2017 est.)
$78,800 (2016 est.)
$82,000 (2015 est.)
note: data are in 2017 dollars
country comparison to the world: 10

Gross national saving: 48.8% of GDP (2017 est.)
43.5% of GDP (2016 est.)
51.3% of GDP (2015 est.)
country comparison to the world: 3

GDP—composition, by end use:
household consumption: 23%
government consumption: 26.7%
investment in fixed capital: 36.1%
investment in inventories: 0%
exports of goods and services: 54.9%
imports of goods and services: -40.7% (2017 est.)

GDP—composition, by sector of origin:
agriculture: 1.2%
industry: 56.5%
services: 42.3% (2017 est.)

Agriculture—products: rice, vegetables, fruits; chickens, water buffalo, cattle, goats, eggs

Industries: petroleum, petroleum refining, liquefied natural gas, construction, agriculture, transportation

Industrial production growth rate: 0.5% (2017 est.)
country comparison to the world: 181

Labor force: 203,600 (2014 est.)
country comparison to the world: 170

Labor force—by occupation: *agriculture:* 4.2%
industry: 62.8%
services: 33% (2008 est.)

Unemployment rate: 6.9% (2017 est.)
6.9% (2016 est.)
country comparison to the world: 97

Population below poverty line: NA%

Household income or consumption by percentage share: *lowest 10%:* NA%
highest 10%: NA%

Budget: *revenues:* $1.435 billion
expenditures: $4.017 billion (2017 est.)
Taxes and other revenues: 12% of GDP (2017 est.)

country comparison to the world: 206

Budget surplus (+) or deficit (-): -21.6% of GDP (2017 est.)
country comparison to the world: 217

Public debt: 3.1% of GDP (2016 est.)
3% of GDP (2015 est.)
country comparison to the world: 204

Fiscal year: 1 April—31 March

Inflation rate (consumer prices): -0.2% (2017 est.)
-0.7% (2016 est.)
country comparison to the world: 8

Commercial bank prime lending rate: 5.5% (31 December 2017 est.)
5.5% (31 December 2016 est.)
country comparison to the world: 133

Stock of narrow money: $3.359 billion (31 December 2017 est.)
$3.232 billion (31 December 2016 est.)
country comparison to the world: 115

Stock of broad money: $10.49 billion (31 December 2017 est.)
$10.08 billion (31 December 2016 est.)
country comparison to the world: 104

Stock of domestic credit: $4.701 billion (31 December 2017 est.)
$4.066 billion (31 December 2016 est.)
country comparison to the world: 131

Market value of publicly traded shares: $NA

Current account balance: $580 million (2017 est.)
$1.091 billion (2016 est.)
country comparison to the world: 46

Exports: $5.776 billion (2017 est.)
$5.023 billion (2016 est.)
country comparison to the world: 103

Exports—commodities: mineral fuels, organic chemicals

Exports—partners: Japan 36.5%, South Korea 16.8%, Thailand 10.6%, India 9.8%, Malaysia 6.6%, China 4.6% (2016)

Imports: $3.275 billion (2017 est.)
$3.119 billion (2016 est.)
country comparison to the world: 140

Imports—commodities: machinery and mechanical appliance parts, mineral fuels, motor vehicles, electric machinery

Imports—partners: US 28.4%, Malaysia 24%, Singapore 7.1%, Indonesia 5.7%, Japan 5.3%, China 4.9%, Australia 4.3% (2016)

Debt—external: $0 (2014)
$0 (2013)
note: public external debt only; private external debt unavailable
country comparison to the world: 204

Exchange rates: Bruneian dollars (BND) per US dollar—
1.394 (2017 est.)
1.3814 (2016 est.)
1.3814 (2015 est.)
1.3749 (2014 est.)
1.267 (2013 est.)

ENERGY

Electricity access: *population without electricity:* 104,788
electrification—*total population:* 76%
electrification—urban areas: 79%
electrification—rural areas: 67% (2012)

Electricity—production: 3.948 billion kWh (2015 est.)
country comparison to the world: 125

Electricity—consumption: 3.679 billion kWh (2015 est.)
country comparison to the world: 131

Electricity—exports: 0 kWh (2016 est.)
country comparison to the world: 113

Electricity—imports: 0 kWh (2016 est.)
country comparison to the world: 129

Electricity—installed generating capacity: 841,000 kW (2015 est.)
country comparison to the world: 133

Electricity—from fossil fuels: 99.9% of total installed capacity (2015 est.)
country comparison to the world: 24

Electricity—from nuclear fuels: 0% of total installed capacity (2015 est.)
country comparison to the world: 59

Electricity—from hydroelectric plants: 0% of total installed capacity (2015 est.)
country comparison to the world: 166

Electricity—from other renewable sources: 0.1% of total installed capacity (2015 est.)
country comparison to the world: 167

Crude oil—production: 109,100 bbl/day (2016 est.)
country comparison to the world: 42

Crude oil—exports: 119,500 bbl/day (2014 est.)
country comparison to the world: 35

Crude oil—imports: 160 bbl/day (2014 est.)
country comparison to the world: 82

Crude oil—proved reserves: 1.1 billion bbl (1 January 2017 es)
country comparison to the world: 43

Refined petroleum products—production: 8,345 bbl/day (2014 est.)
country comparison to the world: 101

Refined petroleum products—consumption: 18,000 bbl/day (2015 est.)
country comparison to the world: 143

Refined petroleum products—exports: 314.3 bbl/day (2014 est.)
country comparison to the world: 115

Refined petroleum products—imports: 8,313 bbl/day (2014 est.)
country comparison to the world: 146

Natural gas—production: 12 billion cu m (2015 est.)
country comparison to the world: 38

Natural gas—consumption: 4.545 billion cu m (2015 est.)
country comparison to the world: 68

Natural gas—exports: 8.52 billion cu m (2015 est.)
country comparison to the world: 24

Natural gas—imports: 0 cu m (2014 est.)
country comparison to the world: 99

Natural gas—proved reserves: 311.5 billion cu m (1 January 2017 es)
country comparison to the world: 38

Carbon dioxide emissions from consumption of energy: 8.4 million Mt (2013 est.)
country comparison to the world: 110

COMMUNICATIONS

Telephones—fixed lines: *total subscriptions:* 74,213
subscriptions per 100 inhabitants: 17 (July 2016 est.)
country comparison to the world: 164

Telephones—mobile cellular: *total:* 463,000
subscriptions per 100 inhabitants: 108 (July 2016 est.)
country comparison to the world: 171

Telephone system: *general assessment:* service throughout the country is good; international service is good to Southeast Asia, Middle East, Western Europe, and the US
domestic: every service available
international: country code—673; landing point for the SEA-ME-WE-3 optical telecommunications submarine cable that provides links to Asia, the Middle East, and Europe; the Asia-America Gateway submarine cable network provides new links to Asia and the US; satellite earth stations—2 Intelsat (1 Indian Ocean and 1 Pacific Ocean) (2015)

Broadcast media: state-controlled Radio Television Brunei (RTB) operates 5 channels; 3 Malaysian TV stations are available; foreign TV broadcasts are available via satellite systems; RTB operates 5 radio networks and broadcasts on multiple frequencies; British Forces Broadcast Service (BFBS) provides radio broadcasts on 2 FM stations; some radio broadcast stations from Malaysia are available via repeaters (2017)

Internet country code: .bn

Internet users: *total:* 306,000
percent of population: 71.2% (July 2016 est.)
country comparison to the world: 146

TRANSPORTATION

National air transport system: *number of registered air carriers:* 1
inventory of registered aircraft operated by air carriers: 10
annual passenger traffic on registered air carriers: 1,150,003
annual freight traffic on registered air carriers: 115.147 million mt-km (2015)
Civil aircraft registration country code prefix: V8 (2016)

Airports: 1 (2013)
country comparison to the world: 214

Airports—with paved runways: *total:* 1
over 3,047 m: 1 (2017)

Heliports: 3 (2013)

Pipelines: condensate 33 km; condensate/gas 86 km; gas 628 km; oil 492 km (2013)

Roadways: *total:* 3,029 km
paved: 2,425 km
unpaved: 604 km (2010)
country comparison to the world: 166

Waterways: 209 km (navigable by craft drawing less than 1.2 m; the Belait, Brunei, and Tutong Rivers are major transport links) (2012)
country comparison to the world: 96

Merchant marine: *total:* 102
by type: general cargo 20, oil tanker 2, other 80 (2017)
country comparison to the world: 84

Ports and terminals: *major seaport(s):* Muara
oil terminal(s): Lumut, Seria
LNG terminal(s) (export): Lumut

MILITARY AND SECURITY

Military expenditures: 3.54% of GDP (2016)
3.28% of GDP (2015)
3.08% of GDP (2014)
2.28% of GDP (2013)
2.16% of GDP (2012)
country comparison to the world: 30

Military branches: *Royal Brunei Armed Forces:* Royal Brunei Land Forces, Royal Brunei Navy, Royal Brunei Air Force (Tentera Udara Diraja Brunei) (2013)

Military service age and obligation: 17 years of age for voluntary military service; non-Malays are ineligible to serve; recruits from the army, navy, and air force all undergo 43-week initial training (2013)

TRANSNATIONAL ISSUES

Disputes—international: per Letters of Exchange signed in 2009, Malaysia in 2010 ceded two hydrocarbon concession blocks to Brunei in exchange for Brunei's sultan dropping claims to the Limbang corridor, which divides Brunei; nonetheless, Brunei claims a maritime boundary extending as far as a median with Vietnam, thus asserting an implicit claim to Louisa Reef

Refugees and internally displaced persons: *stateless persons:* 20,524 (2016); *note*—thousands of stateless persons, often ethnic Chinese, are permanent residents and their families have lived in Brunei for generations; obtaining citizenship is difficult and requires individuals to pass rigorous tests on Malay culture, customs, and language; stateless residents receive an International Certificate of Identity, which enables them to travel overseas; the government is considering changing the law prohibiting non-Bruneians, including stateless permanent residents, from owning land

Illicit drugs: drug trafficking and illegally importing controlled substances are serious offenses in Brunei and carry a mandatory death penalty

BULGARIA

Climate: temperate; cold, damp winters; hot, dry summers

Terrain: mostly mountains with lowlands in north and southeast

Elevation: *mean elevation:* 472 m

elevation extremes: *lowest point:* Black Sea 0 m
highest point: Musala 2,925 m

Natural resources: bauxite, copper, lead, zinc, coal, timber, arable land

Land use: *agricultural land:* 46.9%
arable land: 29.9%;
permanent crops: 1.5%;
permanent pasture: 15.5%
forest: 36.7%
other: 16.4% (2011 est.)
Irrigated land: 1,020 sq km (2012)

Population—distribution: a fairly even distribution throughout most of the country, with urban areas attracting larger populations

Natural hazards: earthquakes; landslides

Environment—current issues: air pollution from industrial emissions; rivers polluted from raw sewage, heavy metals, detergents; deforestation; forest damage from air pollution and resulting acid rain; soil contamination from heavy metals from metallurgical plants and industrial wastes

Environment—international agreements: party to: Air Pollution, Air Pollution-Nitrogen Oxides, Air Pollution-Persistent Organic Pollutants, Air Pollution-Sulfur 85, Air Pollution-Sulfur 94, Air Pollution-Volatile Organic Compounds, Antarctic-Environmental Protocol, Antarctic-Marine Living Resources, Antarctic Treaty, Biodiversity, Climate Change, Climate Change-Kyoto Protocol, Desertification, Endangered Species, Environmental Modification, Hazardous Wastes, Law of the Sea, Marine Dumping, Ozone Layer Protection, Ship Pollution, Wetlands
signed, but not ratified: none of the selected agreements

Geography—note: strategic location near Turkish Straits; controls key land routes from Europe to Middle East and Asia

PEOPLE AND SOCIETY

Population: 7,101,510 (July 2017 est.)
country comparison to the world: 103

Nationality: *noun:* Bulgarian(s)
adjective: Bulgarian

Ethnic groups: Bulgarian 76.9%, Turkish 8%, Romani 4.4%, other 0.7% (including Russian, Armenian, and Vlach), other (unknown) 10% (2011 est.)
note: Romani populations are usually underestimated in official statistics and may represent 9–11% of Bulgaria's population

Languages: Bulgarian (official) 76.8%, Turkish 8.2%, Romani 3.8%, other 0.7%, unspecified 10.5% (2011 est.)

Religions: Eastern Orthodox 59.4%, Muslim 7.8%, other (including Catholic, Protestant, Armenian Apostolic Orthodox, and Jewish) 1.7%, none 3.7%, unspecified 27.4% (2011 est.)

Age structure: *0-14 years:* 14.58% (male 532,924/ female 502,277)
15-24 years: 9.58% (male 354,872/female 325,538)
25-54 years: 43.21% (male 1,576,980/female 1,491,489)
55-64 years: 13.35% (male 445,412/female 502,924)
65 years and over: 19.28% (male 554,486/female 814,608) (2017 est.)

Dependency ratios: *total dependency ratio:* 51.7
youth dependency ratio: 21.2
elderly dependency ratio: 30.5
potential support ratio: 3.3 (2015 est.)

Median age: *total:* 42.7 years
male: 40.9 years
female: 44.7 years (2017 est.)
country comparison to the world: 24

Population growth rate: -0.61% (2017 est.)
country comparison to the world: 226

Birth rate: 8.7 births/1,000 population (2017 est.)
country comparison to the world: 212

Death rate: 14.5 deaths/1,000 population (2017 est.)
country comparison to the world: 3

Net migration rate: -0.3 migrant(s)/1,000 population (2017 est.)
country comparison to the world: 114

Population distribution: a fairly even distribution throughout most of the country, with urban areas attracting larger populations

Urbanization: *urban population:* 74.6% of total population (2017)
rate of urbanization: -0.4% annual rate of change (2015-20 est.)

Major urban areas—population: SOFIA (capital) 1.226 million (2015)

Sex ratio: *at birth:* 1.06 male(s)/female
0-14 years: 1.06 male(s)/female
15-24 years: 1.09 male(s)/female
25-54 years: 1.06 male(s)/female
55-64 years: 0.88 male(s)/female
65 years and over: 0.69 male(s)/female
total population: 0.95 male(s)/female (2016 est.)

Mother's mean age at first birth: 26.7 years (2014 est.)

Maternal mortality ratio: 11 deaths/100,000 live births (2015 est.)
country comparison to the world: 146

Infant mortality rate: *total:* 8.4 deaths/1,000 live births
male: 9.5 deaths/1,000 live births

INTRODUCTION

Background: The Bulgars, a Central Asian Turkic tribe, merged with the local Slavic inhabitants in the late 7th century to form the first Bulgarian state. In succeeding centuries, Bulgaria struggled with the Byzantine Empire to assert its place in the Balkans, but by the end of the 14th century the country was overrun by the Ottoman Turks. Northern Bulgaria attained autonomy in 1878 and all of Bulgaria became independent from the Ottoman Empire in 1908. Having fought on the losing side in both World Wars, Bulgaria fell within the Soviet sphere of influence and became a People's Republic in 1946. Communist domination ended in 1990, when Bulgaria held its first multiparty election since World War II and began the contentious process of moving toward political democracy and a market economy while combating inflation, unemployment, corruption, and crime. The country joined NATO in 2004 and the EU in 2007.

GEOGRAPHY

Location: Southeastern Europe, bordering the Black Sea, between Romania and Turkey

Geographic coordinates: 43 00 N, 25 00 E

Map references: Europe

Area: *total:* 110,879 sq km
land: 108,489 sq km
water: 2,390 sq km
country comparison to the world: 106

Area—comparative: almost identical in size to Virginia; slightly larger than Tennessee

Land boundaries: *total:* 1,806 km
border countries (5): Greece 472 km, Macedonia 162 km, Romania 605 km, Serbia 344 km, Turkey 223 km

Coastline: 354 km

Maritime claims: *territorial sea:* 12 nm
contiguous zone: 24 nm
exclusive economic zone: 200 nm

female: 7.3 deaths/1,000 live births (2017 est.)
country comparison to the world: 149

Life expectancy at birth: *total population:* 74.7 years
male: 71.4 years
female: 78.2 years (2017 est.)
country comparison to the world: 120

Total fertility rate: 1.46 children born/woman (2017 est.)
country comparison to the world: 202

Contraceptive prevalence rate: 69.2%
note: percent of women age 20-49 (2007)
Health expenditures: 8.4% of GDP (2014)
country comparison to the world: 50

Physicians density: 4 physicians/1,000 population (2014)

Hospital bed density: 6.4 beds/1,000 population (2011)

Drinking water source:
improved:
urban: 99.6% of population
rural: 99% of population
total: 99.4% of population
unimproved:
urban: 0.4% of population
rural: 1% of population
total: 0.6% of population (2015 est.)

Sanitation facility access:
improved:
urban: 86.8% of population
rural: 83.7% of population
total: 86% of population
unimproved:
urban: 13.2% of population
rural: 16.3% of population
total: 14% of population (2015 est.)

HIV/AIDS—adult prevalence rate: <.1% (2016 est.)

HIV/AIDS—people living with HIV/AIDS: 3,500 (2016 est.)
country comparison to the world: 109

HIV/AIDS—deaths: <200 (2016 est.)

Obesity—adult prevalence rate: 25% (2016)
country comparison to the world: 53

Education expenditures: 4.1% of GDP (2013)
country comparison to the world: 108

Literacy: *definition:* age 15 and over can read and write
total population: 98.4%
male: 98.7%
female: 98.1% (2015 est.)

School life expectancy (primary to tertiary education): *total:* 15 years
male: 15 years
female: 15 years (2015)

Unemployment, youth ages 15-24: *total:* 21.6%
male: 21.2%
female: 22.3% (2015 est.)
country comparison to the world: 30

GOVERNMENT

Country name: *conventional long form:* Republic of Bulgaria
conventional short form: Bulgaria
local long form: Republika Bulgaria
local short form: Bulgaria
etymology: named after the Bulgar tribes who settled the lower Balkan region in the 7th century A.D.

Government type: parliamentary republic

Capital: *name:* Sofia

geographic coordinates: 42 41 N, 23 19 E

time difference: UTC+2 (7 hours ahead of Washington, DC, during Standard Time)
daylight saving time: +1hr, begins last Sunday in March; ends last Sunday in October

Administrative divisions: 28 provinces (oblasti, singular—oblast): Blagoevgrad, Burgas, Dobrich, Gabrovo, Haskovo, Kardzhali, Kyustendil, Lovech, Montana, Pazardzhik, Pernik, Pleven, Plovdiv, Razgrad, Ruse, Shumen, Silistra, Sliven, Smolyan, Sofia, Sofia-Grad (Sofia City), Stara Zagora, Targovishte, Varna, Veliko Tarnovo, Vidin, Vratsa, Yambol

Independence: 3 March 1878 (as an autonomous principality within the Ottoman Empire); 22 September 1908 (complete independence from the Ottoman Empire)

National holiday: Liberation Day, 3 March (1878)

Constitution: *history:* several previous; latest drafted between late 1990 and early 1991, adopted 13 July 1991
amendments: proposed by the National Assembly or by the president of the republic; passage requires three-fourths majority vote of National Assembly members in three ballots; signed by the National Assembly chairperson; note—under special circumstances, a "Grand National Assembly" is elected with the authority to write a new constitution and amend certain articles of the constitution, including those affecting basic civil rights and national sovereignty; passage requires at least two-thirds majority vote in each of several readings; amended several times, last in 2015 (2016)

Legal system: civil law

International law organization participation: accepts compulsory ICJ jurisdiction with reservations; accepts ICCt jurisdiction

Citizenship: *citizenship by birth:* no
citizenship by descent only: at least one parent must be a citizen of Bulgaria
dual citizenship recognized: yes
residency requirement for naturalization: 5 years

Suffrage: 18 years of age; universal

Executive branch: *chief of state:* President Rumen RADEV (since 22 January 2017); Vice President Iliana YOTOVA (since 22 January 2017)

head of government: Prime Minister Boyko BORISSOV (since 4 May 2017); note—BORISSOV served 2 previous terms as prime minister (27 July 2009-13 March 2013 and 7 November 2014-27 January 2017)
cabinet: Council of Ministers nominated by the prime minister, elected by the National Assembly
elections/appointments: president and vice president elected on the same ballot by absolute majority popular vote in 2 rounds if needed for a 5-year term (eligible for a second term); election last held on 6 and 13 November 2016 (next to be held in fall 2021); chairman of the Council of Ministers (prime minister) elected by the National Assembly; deputy prime ministers nominated by the prime minister, elected by the National Assembly
election results: Rumen RADEV elected president in second round; percent of vote—Rumen RADEV (independent, supported by Bulgarian Socialist Party) 59.4%, Tsetska TSACHEVA (GERB) 36.2%, neither 4.5%; Boyko BORISSOV (GERB) elected prime minister; National Assembly vote—133 to 100

Legislative branch: *description:* unicameral National Assembly or Narodno Sabranie (240 seats; members directly elected in multi-seat constituencies by proportional representation vote to serve 4-year terms)
elections: last held on 26 March 2017 (next to be held spring 2021)
election results: percent of vote by party/coalition—GERB 32.7%, BSP 27.2%, United Patriots 9.1%, DPS 9%, Volya 4.2%, other 17.8%; seats by party/coalition—GERB 95, BSP 80, United Patriots 27, DPS 26, Volya 12

Judicial branch: *highest court(s):* Supreme Court of Cassation (consists of a chairman and approximately 72 judges organized into penal, civil, and commercial colleges); Supreme Administrative Court (organized in 2 colleges with various panels of 5 judges each); Constitutional Court (consists of 12 justices); note—Constitutional Court resides outside the judiciary
judge selection and term of office: Supreme Court of Cassation and Supreme Administrative judges elected by the Supreme Judicial Council or SJC (consists of 25 members with extensive legal experience) and appointed by the president; judges can serve until mandatory retirement at age 65; Constitutional Court justices elected by the National Assembly and appointed by the president and the SJC; justices appointed for 9-year terms with renewal of 4 justices every 3 years
subordinate courts: appeals courts; regional and district courts; administrative courts; courts martial

Political parties and leaders: Alternative for Bulgarian Revival or ABV [Konstantin PRODANOV]
Attack (Ataka) [Volen Nikolov SIDEROV]
Bulgarian Agrarian People's Union [Nikolay NENCHEV]
Bulgarian Socialist Party or BSP [Korneliya NINOVA]
Bulgaria of the Citizens or DBG [Meglena KUNEVA]
Citizens for the European Development of Bulgaria or GERB [Boyko BORISSOV]
Democrats for a Strong Bulgaria or DSB [Atanas ATANOSOV]
Democrats for Responsibility, Solidarity, and Tolerance or DOST [Lyutvi MESTAN]
IMRO—Bulgarian National Movement or IMRO-BNM [Krasimir KARAKACHANOV]
Movement for Rights and Freedoms or DPS [Mustafa KARADAYA]
National Front for the Salvation of Bulgaria or NFSB [Valeri SIMEONOV]
New Republic (alliance of DSB and other center-right parties) [Radan KANEV]
Reformist Bloc or RB (a four-party alliance including DBG and SDS)

United Patriots (alliance of IMRO-BNM, NFSB, and Attack)

Union of Democratic Forces or SDS [Bozhidar LUKARSKI]

Yes! Bulgaria [Hristo IVANOV]

Volya [Veselin MARESHKI]

Political pressure groups and leaders: Confederation of Independent Trade Unions of Bulgaria or CITUB [Plamen DIMITROV]

Podkrepa Labor Confederation [Dimitar MANOLOV]

other: numerous regional, ethnic, and national interest groups with various agendas

International organization participation: Australia Group, BIS, BSEC, CD, CE, CEI, CERN, EAPC, EBRD, ECB, EIB, EU, FAO, G- 9, IAEA, IBRD, ICAO, ICC (national committees), ICCt, ICRM, IDA, IFC, IFRCS, IHO (pending member), ILO, IMF, IMO, IMSO, Interpol, IOC, IOM, IPU, ISO, ITU, ITUC (NGOs), MIGA, NATO, NSG, OAS (observer), OIF, OPCW, OSCE, PCA, SELEC, UN, UNCTAD, UNESCO, UNHCR, UNIDO, UNMIL, UNWTO, UPU, WCO, WFTU (NGOs), WHO, WIPO, WMO, WTO, ZC

Diplomatic representation in the US: *chief of mission:* Ambassador Tihomir Anguelov STOYTCHEV (since 27 June 2016)

chancery: 1621 22nd Street NW, Washington, DC 20008

telephone: [1] (202) 387-0174

FAX: [1] (202) 234-7973

consulate(s) general: Chicago, Los Angeles, New York

Diplomatic representation from the US: *chief of mission:* Ambassador Eric Seth RUBIN (since 24 February 2016)

embassy: 16 Kozyak Street, Sofia 1408

mailing address: American Embassy Sofia, US Department of State, 5740 Sofia Place, Washington, DC 20521-5740

telephone: [359] (2) 937-5100

FAX: [359] (2) 937-5320

Flag description: three equal horizontal bands of white (top), green, and red; the pan-Slavic white-blue-red colors were modified by substituting a green band (representing freedom) for the blue

note: the national emblem, formerly on the hoist side of the white stripe, has been removed

National symbol(s): lion; national colors: white, green, red

National anthem: *name:* "Mila Rodino" (Dear Homeland)

lyrics/music: Tsvetan Tsvetkov RADOSLAVOV

note: adopted 1964; composed in 1885 by a student en route to fight in the Serbo-Bulgarian War

ECONOMY

Economy—overview: Bulgaria, a former communist country that entered the EU in 2007, has an open economy that historically has demonstrated strong growth, but its per-capita income remains the lowest among EU members and its reliance on energy imports and foreign demand for its exports makes its growth sensitive to external market conditions.

The government undertook significant structural economic reforms in the 1990s to move the economy from a centralized, planned economy to a more liberal, market-driven economy. These reforms included privatization of state-owned enterprises, liberalization of trade, and strengthening of the tax system—changes that initially caused some economic hardships but later helped to attract investment, spur growth, and make gradual improvements to living conditions. From 2000 through 2008, Bulgaria maintained robust, average annual real GDP growth in excess of 6%, which was followed by a deep recession in 2009 as the financial crisis caused domestic demand, exports, capital inflows and industrial production to contract, prompting the government to rein in spending. Real GDP growth remained slow—less than 2% annually—until 2015, when demand from EU countries for Bulgarian exports, plus an inflow of EU development funds, boosted growth to more than 3%. In recent years, strong domestic demand combined with low international energy prices have contributed to Bulgaria's economic growth approaching 4% and have also helped to ease inflation which turned positive in 2017. Bulgaria's prudent public financial management contributed to a balanced budget in 2016 and a near-balanced budget for 2017.

Bulgaria is heavily reliant on energy imports from Russia, a potential vulnerability, and is a participant in EU-backed efforts to diversify regional natural gas supplies. In late 2016, the Bulgarian Government provided funding to Bulgaria's National Electric Company to cover the $695 million compensation owed to Russian nuclear equipment manufacturer Atomstroyexport for the cancellation of the Belene Nuclear Power Plant project, which the Bulgarian Government terminated in 2012. The natural gas market, however, continues to be dominated by state-owned Bulgargaz, which is almost entirely supplied by Russia. Infrastructure projects such as the Inter-Connector Greece-Bulgaria and Inter-Connector Bulgaria-Serbia, which would enable Bulgaria to have access to non-Russian gas, have either stalled or made limited progress. In 2016, the Bulgarian Government established the State eGovernment Agency. This new agency is responsible for the implementation of projects related to electronic governance as well as coordination of national policies in this area with the EU requirements and practices, as well as to strengthen cybersecurity.

Despite a favorable investment regime, including low, flat corporate income taxes, significant challenges remain. Corruption in public administration, a weak judiciary, low productivity, and the presence of organized crime continue to hamper the country's investment climate and economic prospects.

GDP (purchasing power parity): $152.4 billion (2017 est.)

$147.1 billion (2016 est.)

$142.2 billion (2015 est.)

note: data are in 2017 dollars

country comparison to the world: 77

GDP (official exchange rate): $55.95 billion (2016 est.)

GDP—real growth rate: 3.6% (2017 est.)

3.4% (2016 est.)

3.6% (2015 est.)

country comparison to the world: 86

GDP—per capita (PPP): $21,600 (2017 est.)

$20,700 (2016 est.)

$19,900 (2015 est.)

note: data are in 2017 dollars

country comparison to the world: 85

Gross national saving: 22.5% of GDP (2017 est.)

24.5% of GDP (2016 est.)

21.1% of GDP (2015 est.)

country comparison to the world: 70

GDP—composition, by end use:

household consumption: 61.7%

government consumption: 15.6%

investment in fixed capital: 19%

investment in inventories: 0.5%

exports of goods and services: 65.5%

imports of goods and services: -62.3% (2017 est.)

GDP—composition, by sector of origin:

agriculture: 4.3%

industry: 28%

services: 67.7% (2017 est.)

Agriculture—products: vegetables, fruits, tobacco, wine, wheat, barley, sunflowers, sugar beets; livestock

Industries: electricity, gas, water; food, beverages, tobacco; machinery and equipment, automotive parts, base metals, chemical products, coke, refined petroleum, nuclear fuel; outsourcing centers

Industrial production growth rate: 4.2% (2017 est.)

country comparison to the world: 63

Labor force: 2.581 million

note: number of employed persons (2017 est.)

country comparison to the world: 116

Labor force—by occupation: *agriculture:* 6.8%

industry: 26.6%

services: 66.6% (2015 est.)

Unemployment rate: 6.6% (2017 est.)

7.7% (2016 est.)

country comparison to the world: 92

Population below poverty line: 22% (2015 est.)

Household income or consumption by percentage share: *lowest 10%:* 2.2%

highest 10%: 28.4% (2015)

Distribution of family income—Gini index: 37 (2015)

35.4 (2014)

country comparison to the world: 78

Budget: *revenues:* $19.53 billion

expenditures: $20.31 billion (2017 est.)

Taxes and other revenues: 34.9% of GDP (2017 est.)

country comparison to the world: 56

Budget surplus (+) or deficit (-): -1.4% of GDP (2017 est.)

country comparison to the world: 65

Public debt: 28.6% of GDP (2017 est.)

29.5% of GDP (2016 est.)

note:: defined by the EU's Maastricht Treaty as consolidated general government gross debt at nominal value, outstanding at the end of the year in the following categories of government liabilities: currency and deposits, securities other than shares excluding financial derivatives, and loans; general government sector comprises the subsectors: central government, state government, local government, and social security funds
country comparison to the world: 165

Fiscal year: calendar year

Inflation rate (consumer prices): 1.1% (2017 est.)
-1.3% (2016 est.)
country comparison to the world: 45

Central bank discount rate: 0% (31 December 2016)
0.01% (31 December 2015)
note: Bulgarian National Bank (BNB) has had no independent monetary policy since the introduction of the Currency Board regime in 1997; this is BNB's base interest rate
country comparison to the world: 150

Commercial bank prime lending rate: 5.8% (31 December 2017 est.)
6.41% (31 December 2016 est.)
country comparison to the world: 129

Stock of narrow money: $26.71 billion (31 December 2017 est.)
$22 billion (31 December 2016 est.)
country comparison to the world: 65

Stock of broad money: $50.98 billion (31 December 2017 est.)
$42.84 billion (31 December 2016 est.)
country comparison to the world: 66

Stock of domestic credit: $31.6 billion (31 December 2017 est.)
$27.56 billion (31 December 2016 est.)
country comparison to the world: 82

Market value of publicly traded shares: $5.205 billion (31 December 2016 est.)
$4.797 billion (31 December 2015 est.)
$5.45 billion (31 December 2014 est.)
country comparison to the world: 85

Current account balance: $1.371 billion (2017 est.)
$2.201 billion (2016 est.)
country comparison to the world: 35

Exports: $28.05 billion (2017 est.)
$24.96 billion (2016 est.)
country comparison to the world: 65

Exports—commodities: clothing, footwear, iron and steel, machinery and equipment, fuels, agriculture, tobacco, IT components

Exports—partners: Germany 13.7%, Italy 9.3%, Romania 8.8%, Turkey 7.9%, Greece 7%, France 4.5% (2016)

Imports: $30.78 billion (2017 est.)
$27 billion (2016 est.)
country comparison to the world: 62

Imports—commodities: machinery and equipment; metals and ores; chemicals and plastics; fuels, minerals, and raw materials

Imports—partners: Germany 13.1%, Russia 8.9%, Italy 7.9%, Romania 7%, Turkey 6.2%, Greece 4.8%, Poland 4.1% (2016)

Reserves of foreign exchange and gold: $27.52 billion (31 December 2017 est.)
$25.19 billion (31 December 2016 est.)
country comparison to the world: 52

Debt—external: $39.51 billion (31 December 2017 est.)
$37.99 billion (31 December 2016 est.)
country comparison to the world: 72

Stock of direct foreign investment—at home: $47.16 billion (31 December 2017 est.)
$45.26 billion (31 December 2016 est.)
country comparison to the world: 59

Stock of direct foreign investment—abroad: $5.338 billion (31 December 2017 est.)
$4.988 billion (31 December 2016 est.)
country comparison to the world: 70

Exchange rates: leva (BGN) per US dollar—
1.729 (2017 est.)
1.768 (2016 est.)
1.768 (2015 est.)
1.7644 (2014 est.)
1.4742 (2013 est.)

ENERGY

Electricity access: electrification—*total population:* 100% (2016)

Electricity—production: 46.15 billion kWh (2015 est.)
country comparison to the world: 57

Electricity—consumption: 31.79 billion kWh (2015 est.)
country comparison to the world: 60

Electricity—exports: 14.83 billion kWh (2015 est.)
country comparison to the world: 14

Electricity—imports: 4.25 billion kWh (2015 est.)
country comparison to the world: 45

Electricity—installed generating capacity: 10.91 million kW (2015 est.)
country comparison to the world: 58

Electricity—from fossil fuels: 36.3% of total installed capacity (2016 est.)
country comparison to the world: 172

Electricity—from nuclear fuels: 17.3% of total installed capacity (2016 est.)
country comparison to the world: 11

Electricity—from hydroelectric plants: 30% of total installed capacity (2016 est.)
country comparison to the world: 72

Electricity—from other renewable sources: 16.4% of total installed capacity (2016 est.)
country comparison to the world: 42

Crude oil—production: 1,000 bbl/day (2016 est.)
country comparison to the world: 93

Crude oil—exports: 0 bbl/day (2014 est.)
country comparison to the world: 101

Crude oil—imports: 122,800 bbl/day (2014 est.)
country comparison to the world: 39

Crude oil—proved reserves: 15 million bbl (1 January 2017 es)
country comparison to the world: 89

Refined petroleum products—production: 132,000 bbl/day (2014 est.)
country comparison to the world: 63

Refined petroleum products—consumption: 89,000 bbl/day (2015 est.)
country comparison to the world: 86

Refined petroleum products—exports: 83,450 bbl/day (2014 est.)
country comparison to the world: 45

Refined petroleum products—imports: 44,600 bbl/day (2014 est.)
country comparison to the world: 88

Natural gas—production: 94 million cu m (2016 est.)
country comparison to the world: 83

Natural gas—consumption: 3.209 billion cu m (2016 est.)
country comparison to the world: 76

Natural gas—exports: 0 cu m (2016 est.)
country comparison to the world: 76

Natural gas—imports: 3.093 billion cu m (2016 est.)
country comparison to the world: 44

Natural gas—proved reserves: 5.663 billion cu m (1 January 2017 es)
country comparison to the world: 93

Carbon dioxide emissions from consumption of energy: 49.92 million Mt (2016 est.)
country comparison to the world: 60

COMMUNICATIONS

Telephones—fixed lines: *total subscriptions:* 1,478,975
subscriptions per 100 inhabitants: 21 (July 2016 est.)
country comparison to the world: 64

Telephones—mobile cellular: *total:* 8,978,202
subscriptions per 100 inhabitants: 126 (July 2016 est.)
country comparison to the world: 87

Telephone system: *general assessment:* inherited an extensive but antiquated telecommunications network from the Soviet era; quality has improved with a modern digital trunk line now connecting switching centers in most of the regions; remaining areas are connected by digital microwave radio relay
domestic: the Bulgaria Telecommunications Company's fixed-line monopoly terminated in 2005 in an effort to upgrade fixed-line services; mobile-cellular teledensity, fostered by multiple service providers, is over 125 telephones per 100 persons
international: country code—359; submarine cable provides connectivity to Ukraine and Russia; a combination submarine cable and land fiber-optic system provides connectivity to Italy, Albania, and Macedonia; satellite earth stations—3 (1 Intersputnik in the Atlantic Ocean region, 2 Intelsat in the Atlantic and Indian Ocean regions) (2016)

Broadcast media: 4 national terrestrial TV stations with 1 state-owned and 3 privately owned; a vast array of TV stations are available from cable and satellite TV providers; state-owned national radio broadcasts over 3 networks; large number of private radio stations broadcasting, especially in urban areas (2010)

Internet country code: .bg

Internet users: *total:* 4,274,328
percent of population: 59.8% (July 2016 est.)
country comparison to the world: 75

TRANSPORTATION

National air transport system: *number of registered air carriers:* 8
inventory of registered aircraft operated by air carriers: 44
annual passenger traffic on registered air carriers: 1,118,689
annual freight traffic on registered air carriers: 1,583,340 mt-km (2015)
Civil aircraft registration country code prefix: LZ (2016)

Airports: 68 (2013)
country comparison to the world: 73

Airports—with paved runways: *total:* 57
over 3,047 m: 2
2,438 to 3,047 m: 17
1,524 to 2,437 m: 12
under 914 m: 26 (2017)

Airports—with unpaved runways: *total:* 11
914 to 1,523 m: 2
under 914 m: 9 (2013)

Heliports: 1 (2013)

Pipelines: gas 2,765 km; oil 346 km; refined products 378 km (2017)

Railways: *total:* 5,114 km

standard gauge: 4,989 km 1.435-m gauge (2,880 km electrified)
narrow gauge: 125 km 0.760-m gauge (2014)
country comparison to the world: 36

Roadways: *total:* 19,512 km
paved: 19,235 km (includes 458 km of expressways)
unpaved: 277 km
note: does not include Category IV local roads (2011)
country comparison to the world: 111

Waterways: 470 km (2009)
country comparison to the world: 83

Merchant marine: *total:* 80
by type: bulk carrier 2, general cargo 18, oil tanker 8, other 52 (2017)
country comparison to the world: 95

Ports and terminals: *major seaport(s):* Burgas, Varna (Black Sea)

MILITARY AND SECURITY

Military expenditures: 1.44% of GDP (2016)
1.32% of GDP (2015)
1.47% of GDP (2014)
1.61% of GDP (2013)
1.5% of GDP (2012)
country comparison to the world: 66

Military branches: *Bulgarian Armed Forces:* Land Forces (aka Army), Naval Forces, Bulgarian Air Forces (Voennovazdyshni Sily, VVS) (2017)

Military service age and obligation: 18-27 years of age for voluntary military service; conscription ended in January 2008; service obligation 6-9 months (2012)

TRANSNATIONAL ISSUES

Disputes—international: none

Refugees and internally displaced persons: *refugees (country of origin):* 15,027 (Syria) (2016)

stateless persons: 67 (2016)
note: 47,819 estimated refugee and migrant arrivals (January 2015—January 2018); Bulgaria is predominantly a transit country and hosts approximately 1,800 migrants and asylum seekers as of September 2017

Trafficking in persons: current situation: Bulgaria is a source and, to a lesser extent, a transit and destination country for men, women, and children subjected to sex trafficking and forced labor; Bulgaria is one of the main sources of human trafficking in the EU; women and children are increasingly sex trafficked domestically, as well as in Europe, Russia, the Middle East, and the US; adults and children become forced laborers in agriculture, construction, and the service sector in Europe, Israel, and Zambia; Romanian girls are also subjected to sex trafficking in Bulgaria

tier rating: Tier 2 Watch List—Bulgaria does not fully comply with the minimum standards for the elimination of trafficking; however, it is making significant efforts to do so; in 2014, authorities prosecuted and convicted fewer traffickers and issued suspended sentences for the majority of those convicted; victim protection efforts declined and were minimal relative to the number of victims identified; funding for the state's two NGO-operated shelters was significantly cut, forcing them to close; specialized services for child and adult male victims were non-existent; the government took action to combat trafficking-related complicity among public officials and police officers (2015)

Illicit drugs: major European transshipment point for Southwest Asian heroin and, to a lesser degree, South American cocaine for the European market; limited producer of precursor chemicals; vulnerable to money laundering because of corruption, organized crime; some money laundering of drug-related proceeds through financial institutions

BURKINA FASO

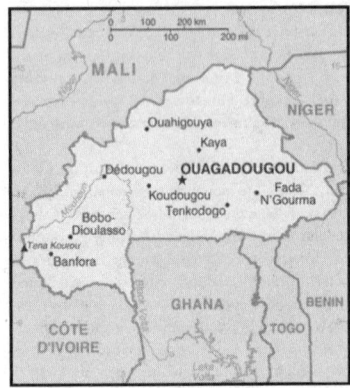

INTRODUCTION

Background: Burkina Faso (formerly Upper Volta) achieved independence from France in 1960. Repeated military coups during the 1970s and 1980s were followed by multiparty elections in the early 1990s. Former President Blaise COMPAORE (1987-2014) resigned in late October 2014 following popular protests against his efforts to amend the Constitution's two-term presidential limit. By mid-November, a framework for an interim government was adopted under the terms of the National Transition Charter. An interim administration, led by President Michel KAFANDO and Prime Minister Yacouba Isaac ZIDA, began organizing presidential and legislative elections planned for October 2015, but these were postponed during a weeklong failed coup in September. The rescheduled elections were held on 29 November, and Roch Marc Christian KABORE was elected

president in the first round. Burkina Faso's high population growth and limited natural resources result in poor economic prospects for the majority of its citizens.

GEOGRAPHY

Location: Western Africa, north of Ghana

Geographic coordinates: 13 00 N, 2 00 W

Map references: Africa

Area: *total:* 274,200 sq km
land: 273,800 sq km
water: 400 sq km
country comparison to the world: 76

Area—comparative: slightly larger than Colorado

Land boundaries: *total:* 3,611 km
border countries (6): Benin 386 km, Cote d'Ivoire 545 km, Ghana 602 km, Mali 1,325 km, Niger 622 km, Togo 131 km

Coastline: 0 km (landlocked)

Maritime claims: none (landlocked)

Climate: tropical; warm, dry winters; hot, wet summers

Terrain: mostly flat to dissected, undulating plains; hills in west and southeast

Elevation: *mean elevation:* 297 m

elevation extremes: *lowest point:* Mouhoun (Black Volta) River 200 m
highest point: Tena Kourou 749 m

Natural resources: manganese, limestone, marble; small deposits of gold, phosphates, pumice, salt

Land use: *agricultural land:* 43%
arable land: 20.8%;
permanent crops: 0.3%;
permanent pasture: 21.9%
forest: 20.4%
other: 36.6% (2011 est.)
Irrigated land: 550 sq km (2012)

Population—distribution: the population is concentrated in the central and southern parts of the country; the east, north, and southwest are less populated

Natural hazards: recurring droughts

Environment—current issues: recent droughts and desertification severely affecting agricultural activities, population distribution, and the economy; overgrazing; soil degradation; deforestation

Environment—international agreements: party to: Biodiversity, Climate Change, Climate Change-Kyoto Protocol, Desertification, Endangered Species, Hazardous Wastes, Law of the Sea, Marine Life Conservation, Ozone Layer Protection, Wetlands
signed, but not ratified: none of the selected agreements

Geography—note: landlocked savanna cut by the three principal rivers of the Black, Red, and White Voltas

PEOPLE AND SOCIETY

Population: 20,107,509
note: estimates for this country explicitly take into account the effects of excess mortality due to AIDS; this can result in lower life expectancy, higher infant mortality, higher death rates, lower population growth rates, and changes in the distribution of population by age and sex than would otherwise be expected (July 2017 est.)
country comparison to the world: 59

Nationality: *noun:* Burkinabe (singular and plural)
adjective: Burkinabe

Ethnic groups: Mossi 52%, Fulani 8.4%, Gurma 7%, Bobo 4.9%, Gurunsi 4.6%, Senufo 4.5%, Bissa 3.7%, Lobi 2.4%, Dagara 2.4%, Tuareg/Bella 1.9%, Dioula 0.8%, unspecified/no answer 0.3%, other 7.2% (2010 est.)

Languages: French (official), native African languages belonging to Sudanic family spoken by 90% of the population

Religions: Muslim 61.5%, Roman Catholic 23.3%, traditional/animist 7.8%, Protestant 6.5%, other/no answer 0.2%, none 0.7% (2010 est.)

Demographic profile: Burkina Faso has a young age structure—the result of declining mortality combined with steady high fertility—and continues to experience rapid population growth, which is putting increasing pressure on the country's limited arable land. More than 65% of the population is under the age of 25, and the population is growing at 3% annually. Mortality rates, especially those of infants and children, have decreased because of improved health care, hygiene, and sanitation, but women continue to have an average of almost 6 children. Even if fertility were substantially reduced, today's large cohort entering their reproductive years would sustain high population growth for the foreseeable future. Only about a third of the population is literate and unemployment is widespread, dampening the economic prospects of Burkina Faso's large working-age population.

Migration has traditionally been a way of life for Burkinabe, with seasonal migration being replaced by stints of up to two years abroad. Cote d'Ivoire remains the top destination, although it has experienced periods of internal conflict. Under French colonization, Burkina Faso became a main labor source for agricultural and factory work in Cote d'Ivoire. Burkinabe also migrated to Ghana, Mali, and Senegal for work between the world wars. Burkina Faso attracts migrants from Cote d'Ivoire, Ghana, and Mali, who often share common ethnic backgrounds with the Burkinabe. Despite its food shortages and high poverty rate, Burkina Faso has become a destination for refugees in recent years and hosts about 33,500 Malians as of May 2017.

Age structure: *0-14 years:* 44.88% (male 4,519,960/female 4,503,937)
15-24 years: 20.07% (male 2,024,501/female 2,012,053)
25-54 years: 29.42% (male 2,999,941/female 2,915,264)
55-64 years: 3.2% (male 284,374/female 359,159)
65 years and over: 2.43% (male 181,996/female 306,324) (2017 est.)

Dependency ratios: *total dependency ratio:* 92.2
youth dependency ratio: 87.6
elderly dependency ratio: 4.6
potential support ratio: 21.6 (2015 est.)

Median age: *total:* 17.3 years
male: 17.1 years
female: 17.4 years (2017 est.)
country comparison to the world: 220

Population growth rate: 3% (2017 est.)
country comparison to the world: 8

Birth rate: 41.2 births/1,000 population (2017 est.)
country comparison to the world: 7

Death rate: 11.2 deaths/1,000 population (2017 est.)
country comparison to the world: 28

Net migration rate: 0 migrant(s)/1,000 population (2017 est.)

country comparison to the world: 76

Population distribution: the population is concentrated in the central and southern parts of the country; the east, north, and southwest are less populated

Urbanization: *urban population:* 31.5% of total population (2017)
rate of urbanization: 5.29% annual rate of change (2015-20 est.)

Major urban areas—population: OUAGADOUGOU (capital) 2.741 million (2015)

Sex ratio: *at birth:* 1.03 male(s)/female
0-14 years: 1 male(s)/female
15-24 years: 1.01 male(s)/female
25-54 years: 1.03 male(s)/female
55-64 years: 0.77 male(s)/female
65 years and over: 0.6 male(s)/female
total population: 0.99 male(s)/female (2016 est.)

Mother's mean age at first birth: 19.4 years
note: median age at first birth among women 25-29 (2010 est.)

Maternal mortality ratio: 371 deaths/100,000 live births (2015 est.)
country comparison to the world: 31

Infant mortality rate: *total:* 72.2 deaths/1,000 live births
male: 79.3 deaths/1,000 live births
female: 64.9 deaths/1,000 live births (2017 est.)
country comparison to the world: 7

Life expectancy at birth: *total population:* 55.9 years
male: 53.8 years
female: 58 years (2017 est.)
country comparison to the world: 211

Total fertility rate: 5.71 children born/woman (2017 est.)
country comparison to the world: 6

Contraceptive prevalence rate: 25.5% (2016)
Health expenditures: 5% of GDP (2014)
country comparison to the world: 140

Physicians density: 0.05 physicians/1,000 population (2012)

Hospital bed density: 0.4 beds/1,000 population (2010)

Drinking water source:
improved:
urban: 97.5% of population
rural: 75.8% of population
total: 82.3% of population
unimproved:
urban: 2.5% of population
rural: 24.2% of population
total: 17.7% of population (2015 est.)

Sanitation facility access:
improved:
urban: 50.4% of population
rural: 6.7% of population
total: 19.7% of population
unimproved:
urban: 49.6% of population
rural: 93.3% of population
total: 80.3% of population (2015 est.)

HIV/AIDS—adult prevalence rate: 0.8% (2016 est.)
country comparison to the world: 51

HIV/AIDS—people living with HIV/AIDS: 95,000 (2016 est.)
country comparison to the world: 44

HIV/AIDS—deaths: 3,100 (2016 est.)
country comparison to the world: 40

Major infectious diseases: *degree of risk:* very high
food or waterborne diseases: bacterial and protozoal diarrhea, hepatitis A, and typhoid fever
vectorborne disease: dengue fever, malaria, and yellow fever
water contact disease: schistosomiasis
respiratory disease: meningococcal meningitis
animal contact disease: rabies (2016)

Obesity—adult prevalence rate: 5.6% (2016)
country comparison to the world: 175

Children under the age of 5 years underweight: 19.2% (2016)
country comparison to the world: 24

Education expenditures: 3.9% of GDP (2015)
country comparison to the world: 128

Literacy: *definition:* age 15 and over can read and write
total population: 36%
male: 43%
female: 29.3% (2015 est.)

School life expectancy (primary to tertiary education): *total:* 8 years
male: 8 years
female: 7 years (2013)

GOVERNMENT

Country name: *conventional long form:* none
conventional short form: Burkina Faso
local long form: none
local short form: Burkina Faso
former: Upper Volta, Republic of Upper Volta
etymology: name translates as "Land of the Honest (Incorruptible) Men"

Government type: presidential republic

Capital: *name:* Ouagadougou

geographic coordinates: 12 22 N, 1 31 W

time difference: UTC 0 (5 hours ahead of Washington, DC, during Standard Time)

Administrative divisions: 13 regions; Boucle du Mouhoun, Cascades, Centre, Centre-Est, Centre-Nord, Centre-Ouest, Centre-Sud, Est, Hauts-Bassins, Nord, Plateau-Central, Sahel, Sud-Ouest

Independence: 5 August 1960 (from France)

National holiday: Republic Day, 11 December (1958); note—commemorates the day that Upper Volta became an autonomous republic in the French Community

Constitution: *history:* several previous; latest approved by referendum 2 June 1991, adopted 11 June 1991, temporarily suspended late October to mid-November 2014
amendments: proposed by the president, by a majority of National Assembly membership, or

by petition of at least 30,000 eligible voters submitted to the Assembly; passage requires at least three-fourths majority vote in the Assembly; failure to meet that threshold requires majority voter approval in a referendum; constitutional provisions on the form of government, the multiparty system, and national sovereignty cannot be amended; amended several times, last in 2012 (2017)

Legal system: civil law based on the French model and customary law

International law organization participation: has not submitted an ICJ jurisdiction declaration; accepts ICCt jurisdiction

Citizenship: *citizenship by birth:* no
citizenship by descent only: at least one parent must be a citizen of Burkina Faso
dual citizenship recognized: yes
residency requirement for naturalization: 10 years

Suffrage: 18 years of age; universal

Executive branch: *chief of state:* President Roch Marc Christian KABORE (since 29 December 2015)

head of government: Prime Minister Paul Kaba THIEBA (since 6 January 2016)
cabinet: Council of Ministers appointed by the president on the recommendation of the prime minister
elections/appointments: president elected by absolute majority popular vote in two rounds if needed for a 5-year term (eligible for a second); election last held on 29 November 2015 (next scheduled for November 2020); prime minister appointed by the president with consent of the National Assembly
election results: Roch Marc Christian KABORE elected president in first round; percent of vote—Roch Marc Christian KABORE (MPP) 53.5%, Zephirin DIABRE (UPC) 29.6%, Tahirou BARRY (PAREN) 3.1%. Benewende Stanislas SANKARA (UNIR-MS) 2.8%, other 10.9%

Legislative branch: *description:* unicameral National Assembly (127 seats; members directly elected in multi-seat constituencies by proportional representation vote to serve 5-year terms)
elections: last held on 29 November 2015 (next to be held in 2020)
election results: percent of vote by party—NA; seats by party—MPP 55, UPC 33, CDP 18, Union for Rebirth/Sankarist Party 5, ADF/RDA 3, NTD 3, other 10

Judicial branch: *highest court(s):* Supreme Court of Appeals or Cour de Cassation (consists of NA judges); Council of State (consists of NA judges); Constitutional Council or Conseil Constitutionnel (consists of the council president and 9 members)
judge selection and term of office: Supreme Court judge appointments mostly controlled by the president of Burkina Faso; judges have no term limits; Council of State judge appointment and tenure NA; Constitutional Council judges appointed by the president of Burkina Faso upon the proposal

of the minister of justice and the president of the National Assembly; judges appointed for 9-year terms with one-third of membership renewed every 3 years
subordinate courts: Appeals Court; High Court; first instance tribunals; district courts; specialized courts relating to issues of labor, children, and juveniles; village (customary) courts

Political parties and leaders: African Democratic Rally/Alliance for Democracy and Federation or ADF/RDA [Gilbert Noel OUEDRAOGO]
African People's Movement or MAP [Victorien TOUGOUMA]
Congress for Democracy and Progress or CDP [Achille TAPSOBA]
Le Faso Autrement [Ablasse OUEDRAOGO]
New Alliance of the Faso or NAFA [Rasmane OUEDRAOGO]
New Time for Democracy or NTD [Vincent DABILGOU]
Organization for Democracy and Work or ODT [Mahamoudou SAWADOGO]
Party for Development and Change or PDC [Saran SEREME]
Party for Democracy and Progress-Socialist Party or PDP-PS [Francois O. KABORE]
Party for Democracy and Socialism/Metba or PDS/Metba [Philippe OUEDRAOGO]
Party for National Renaissance or PAREN [Tahirou BARRY]
People's Movement for Progress or MPP [Roch March Christian KABORE]
Rally for Democracy and Socialism or RDS [Francois OUEDRAOGO]
Rally for the Development of Burkina or RDB [Celestin Saidou COMPAORE]
Rally of Ecologists of Burkina Faso or RDEB [Adama SERE]
Union for a New Burkina or UBN [Yacouba OUEDRAOGO]
Union for Progress and Change or UPC [Zephirin DIABRE]
Union for Rebirth—Sankarist Movement or UNIR-MS [Benewende Stanislas SANKARA]
Union for the Republic or UPR [Toussaint Abel COULIBALY]
Youth Alliance for the Republic and Independence or AJIR [Adama KANAZOE]

Political pressure groups and leaders: Balai Citoyen [Guy Herve KAM]
Burkinabe General Confederation of Labor or CGTB [Bassolma BAZIE]
Burkinabe Movement for Human Rights or MBDHP [Chrysigone ZOUGMORE]
Burkinabe Society for Constitutional Law or SBDC [Abdoulaye SOMA]
Center for Democratic Governance or CGD [Thomas OUEDRAOGO]
Coalition for African Renaissance or CAR [Herve OUATTARA]
National Independent Union of Burkinabe Magistrates or SAMAB [Augustin LOADA]
National Union for Health Workers or SYNTSHA
National Union for Primary Education Teachers or SYNATEB

other: watchdog/political action groups throughout the country

International organization participation: ACP, AfDB, AU, CD, ECOWAS, EITI (compliant country), Entente, FAO, FZ, G-77, IAEA, IBRD, ICAO, ICC (NGOs), ICCt, ICRM, IDA, IDB, IFAD, IFC, IFRCS, ILO, IMF, Interpol, IOC, IOM, IPU, ISO, ITSO, ITU, ITUC (NGOs), MIGA, MINUSMA, MONUSCO, NAM, OIC, OIF, OPCW, PCA, UN, UNAMID, UNCTAD, UNESCO, UNIDO, UNISFA, UNITAR, UNWTO, UPU, WADB (regional), WAEMU, WCO, WFTU (NGOs), WHO, WIPO, WMO, WTO

Diplomatic representation in the US: *chief of mission:* Ambassador Seydou KABORE (since 18 January 2017)
chancery: 2340 Massachusetts Avenue NW, Washington, DC 20008
telephone: [1] (202) 332-5577
FAX: [1] (202) 667-1882

Diplomatic representation from the US: *chief of mission:* Ambassador Andrew YOUNG (since 1 December 2016)
embassy: Rue 15.873, Avenue Sembene Ousmane, Ouaga 2000, Secteur 15
mailing address: 01 B. P. 35, Ouagadougou 01; pouch mail—US Department of State, 2440 Ouagadougou Place, Washington, DC 20521-2440
telephone: [226] 25-49-53-00
FAX: [226] 25-49-56-28

Flag description: two equal horizontal bands of red (top) and green with a yellow five-pointed star in the center; red recalls the country's struggle for independence, green is for hope and abundance, and yellow represents the country's mineral wealth
note: uses the popular Pan-African colors of Ethiopia

National symbol(s): white stallion; national colors: red, yellow, green

National anthem: *name:* "Le Ditanye" (Anthem of Victory)
lyrics/music: Thomas SANKARA
note: adopted 1974; also known as "Une Seule Nuit" (One Single Night); written by the country's president, an avid guitar player

ECONOMY

Economy—overview: Burkina Faso is a poor, landlocked country that depends on adequate rainfall. About 90% of the population is engaged in subsistence farming and cotton is the main cash crop. The country has few natural resources and a weak industrial base.

Cotton and gold are Burkina Faso's key exports—gold has accounted for about three-quarters of the country's total export revenues. Burkina Faso's economic growth and revenue depends largely on production levels and global prices for the two commodities. The Burkinabe economy experienced high levels of growth over the last few years, and the country has seen an upswing in gold exploration, production, and exports.

Burkina Faso experienced a number of public protests over the high cost of living, corruption, and other socioeconomic issues in 2013, while the fall of the COMPAORE government in 2014 and failed coup in September 2015 disrupted economic activity and strained government finances. A new three-year IMF program, approved in 2013, was recently completed. Discussions are currently underway on a new program. Political insecurity in neighboring Mali, unreliable energy supplies, and poor transportation links pose long-term challenges.

GDP (purchasing power parity): $35.68 billion (2017 est.)
$33.54 billion (2016 est.)
$31.68 billion (2015 est.)
note: data are in 2017 dollars
country comparison to the world: 127

GDP (official exchange rate): $13.19 billion (2016 est.)

GDP—real growth rate: 6.4% (2017 est.)
5.9% (2016 est.)
4% (2015 est.)
country comparison to the world: 19

GDP—per capita (PPP): $1,900 (2017 est.)
$1,800 (2016 est.)
$1,700 (2015 est.)
note: data are in 2017 dollars
country comparison to the world: 209

Gross national saving: 9.2% of GDP (2017 est.)
7.7% of GDP (2016 est.)
5.3% of GDP (2015 est.)
country comparison to the world: 162

GDP—composition, by end use:
household consumption: 56.7%
government consumption: 26.2%
investment in fixed capital: 29.4%
investment in inventories: 2.4%
exports of goods and services: 20.9%
imports of goods and services: -35.7% (2017 est.)

GDP—composition, by sector of origin:
agriculture: 31.9%
industry: 22%
services: 46.1% (2017 est.)

Agriculture—products: cotton, peanuts, shea nuts, sesame, sorghum, millet, corn, rice; livestock

Industries: cotton lint, beverages, agricultural processing, soap, cigarettes, textiles, gold

Industrial production growth rate: 5.1% (2017 est.)
country comparison to the world: 42

Labor force: 8.501 million
note: a large part of the male labor force migrates annually to neighboring countries for seasonal employment (2016 est.)
country comparison to the world: 60

Labor force—by occupation: *agriculture:* 90%
industry and services: 10% (2000 est.)

Unemployment rate: 77% (2004)
country comparison to the world: 216

Population below poverty line: 40.1% (2009 est.)

Household income or consumption by percentage share: *lowest 10%:* 2.9%
highest 10%: 32.2% (2009 est.)

Distribution of family income—Gini index: 39.5 (2007)
48.2 (1994)
country comparison to the world: 66

Budget: *revenues:* $2.635 billion
expenditures: $3.332 billion (2017 est.)
Taxes and other revenues: 20% of GDP (2017 est.)
country comparison to the world: 152

Budget surplus (+) or deficit (-): -5.3% of GDP (2017 est.)
country comparison to the world: 166

Public debt: 32.5% of GDP (2016 est.)
32.5% of GDP (2015 est.)
country comparison to the world: 154

Fiscal year: calendar year

Inflation rate (consumer prices): 1.5% (2017 est.)
-0.2% (2016 est.)
country comparison to the world: 62

Central bank discount rate: 4.25% (31 December 2010)
4.25% (31 December 2009)
country comparison to the world: 87

Commercial bank prime lending rate: 5.3% (31 December 2017 est.)
5.3% (31 December 2016 est.)
country comparison to the world: 142

Stock of narrow money: $2.606 billion (31 December 2017 est.)
$2.274 billion (31 December 2016 est.)
country comparison to the world: 124

Stock of broad money: $4.904 billion (31 December 2017 est.)
$4.228 billion (31 December 2016 est.)
country comparison to the world: 130

Stock of domestic credit: $3.804 billion (31 December 2017 est.)
$3.205 billion (31 December 2016 est.)
country comparison to the world: 135

Market value of publicly traded shares: $NA

Current account balance: -$947 million (2017 est.)
-$828 million (2016 est.)
country comparison to the world: 132

Exports: $2.797 billion (2017 est.)
$2.641 billion (2016 est.)
country comparison to the world: 130

Exports—commodities: gold, cotton, livestock

Exports—partners: Switzerland 65.7%, India 6.3%, South Africa 5.2%, Singapore 4.6% (2016)

Imports: $2.923 billion (2017 est.)
$2.802 billion (2016 est.)
country comparison to the world: 145

Imports—commodities: capital goods, foodstuffs, petroleum

Imports—partners: China 12.2%, Cote dIvoire 8.2%, Japan 7.8%, France 7.1%, Netherlands 4.5%, Spain 4.2%, India 4.1%, Russia 4% (2016)

Reserves of foreign exchange and gold: $45.3 million (31 December 2017 est.)

$50.9 million (31 December 2016 est.)

country comparison to the world: 172

Debt—external: $3.075 billion (31 December 2017 est.)
$2.88 billion (31 December 2016 est.)
country comparison to the world: 142

Exchange rates: Communaute Financiere Africaine francs (XOF) per US dollar—
605.3 (2017 est.)
593.01 (2016 est.)
593.01 (2015 est.)
591.45 (2014 est.)
494.42 (2013 est.)

ENERGY

Electricity access: *population without electricity:* 14,100,000
electrification—*total population:* 17%
electrification—urban areas: 56%
electrification—rural areas: 1% (2013)

Electricity—production: 944 million kWh (2015 est.)
country comparison to the world: 154

Electricity—consumption: 1.321 billion kWh (2015 est.)
country comparison to the world: 151

Electricity—exports: 0 kWh (2016 est.)
country comparison to the world: 210

Electricity—imports: 443 million kWh (2015 est.)
country comparison to the world: 84

Electricity—installed generating capacity: 306,000 kW (2015 est.)
country comparison to the world: 157

Electricity—from fossil fuels: 86.9% of total installed capacity (2015 est.)
country comparison to the world: 70

Electricity—from nuclear fuels: 0% of total installed capacity (2015 est.)
country comparison to the world: 200

Electricity—from hydroelectric plants: 10.5% of total installed capacity (2015 est.)
country comparison to the world: 118

Electricity—from other renewable sources: 3.3% of total installed capacity (2015 est.)
country comparison to the world: 110

Crude oil—production: 0 bbl/day (2016 est.)
country comparison to the world: 116

Crude oil—exports: 0 bbl/day (2014 est.)
country comparison to the world: 205

Crude oil—imports: 0 bbl/day (2014 est.)
country comparison to the world: 204

Crude oil—proved reserves: 0 bbl (1 January 2017 es)
country comparison to the world: 115

Refined petroleum products—production: 0 bbl/day (2014 est.)
country comparison to the world: 124

Refined petroleum products—consumption: 22,000 bbl/day (2015 est.)
country comparison to the world: 137

Refined petroleum products—exports: 0 bbl/day (2014 est.)

country comparison to the world: 209

Refined petroleum products—imports: 20,890 bbl/day (2014 est.)
country comparison to the world: 118

Natural gas—production: 0 cu m (2013 est.)
country comparison to the world: 206

Natural gas—consumption: 0 cu m (2013 est.)
country comparison to the world: 142

Natural gas—exports: 0 cu m (2013 est.)
country comparison to the world: 202

Natural gas—imports: 0 cu m (2013 est.)
country comparison to the world: 202

Natural gas—proved reserves: 0 cu m (1 January 2014 es)
country comparison to the world: 202

Carbon dioxide emissions from consumption of energy: 1.4 million Mt (2013 est.)
country comparison to the world: 160

COMMUNICATIONS

Telephones—fixed lines: *total subscriptions:* 64,000
subscriptions per 100 inhabitants: less than 1 (July 2016 est.)
country comparison to the world: 141

Telephones—mobile cellular: *total:* 15,404,040
subscriptions per 100 inhabitants: 79 (July 2016 est.)
country comparison to the world: 74

Telephone system: *general assessment:* system includes microwave radio relay, open-wire, and radiotelephone communication stations
domestic: fixed-line connections stand at less than 1 per 100 persons; mobile-cellular usage, fostered by multiple providers, is increasing steadily from a low base
international: country code—226; satellite earth station—1 Intelsat (Atlantic Ocean) (2016)

Broadcast media: 2 TV stations—1 state-owned and 1 privately owned; state-owned radio runs a national and regional network; substantial number of privately owned radio stations; transmissions of several international broadcasters available in Ouagadougou (2007)

Internet country code: .bf

Internet users: *total:* 2,723,950
percent of population: 14.0% (July 2016 est.)
country comparison to the world: 125

TRANSPORTATION

National air transport system: *number of registered air carriers:* 1
inventory of registered aircraft operated by air carriers: 3
annual passenger traffic on registered air carriers: 122,589
annual freight traffic on registered air carriers: 55,868 mt-km (2015)
Civil aircraft registration country code prefix: XT (2016)

Airports: 23 (2013)
country comparison to the world: 133

Airports—with paved runways: *total:* 2
over 3,047 m: 1
2,438 to 3,047 m: 1 (2017)

Airports—with unpaved runways: *total:* 21
1,524 to 2,437 m: 3
914 to 1,523 m: 13
under 914 m: 5 (2013)

Railways: *total:* 622 km
narrow gauge: 622 km 1.000-m gauge
note: another 660 km of this railway extends into Cote d'Ivoire (2014)
country comparison to the world: 109

Roadways: *total:* 15,272 km
note: does not include urban roads (2010)
country comparison to the world: 122

MILITARY AND SECURITY

Military expenditures: 1.23% of GDP (2016)
1.33% of GDP (2015)
1.43% of GDP (2014)
1.39% of GDP (2013)
1.32% of GDP (2012)
country comparison to the world: 73

Military branches: Army, Air Force of Burkina Faso (Force Aerienne de Burkina Faso, FABF), National Gendarmerie (2011)

Military service age and obligation: 18 years of age for voluntary military service; no conscription; women may serve in supporting roles (2013)

TERRORISM

Terrorist groups—foreign based: *al-Mulathamun Battalion: aim(s):* replace regional governments, including Burkina Faso's government, with an Islamic state
area(s) of operation: engages in kidnappings for ransom and other violent activities across the country, including Ouagadougou; al-Mulathamun Battalion and AQIM operatives used gunfire and explosives on 15 January 2016 that killed 30 civilians from 18 countries and wounded approximately 70 people, resulting in operatives taking over 156 hostages in Ouagadougou at the Splendid Hotel and Cappuccino Restaurant, popular sites for Westerners and French soldiers based in the region; marked the first major attack in a country that had been largely spared extremist violence; security forces rescued 156 of the hostages

al-Qaida in the Islamic Maghreb (AQIM): *aim(s):* replace the Burkina Faso Government with Sharia and, ultimately, create a regional Islamic caliphate across all of North and West Africa
area(s) of operation: engages heavily in kidnappings for ransom and other violent activities across the country, primarily in the north; AQIM and al-Mulathamun Battalion operatives used gunfire and explosives on 15 January 2016 that killed 30 civilians from 18 countries and wounded approximately 70 people, resulting in operatives taking over 156 hostages in Ouagadougou at the Splendid Hotel and Cappuccino Restaurant, popular sites for Westerners and French soldiers based in the region; marked the first major attack in a country

that had been largely spared extremist violence; security forces rescued 156 of the hostages

TRANSNATIONAL ISSUES

Disputes—international: adding to illicit cross-border activities, Burkina Faso has issues concerning unresolved boundary alignments with its neighbors; demarcation is currently underway with Mali; the dispute with Niger was referred to the ICJ in 2010, and a dispute over several villages with Benin persists; Benin retains a border dispute with Burkina Faso around the town of Koualou

Refugees and internally displaced persons: *refugees (country of origin):* 24,083 (Mali) (2017)

Trafficking in persons: current situation: Burkina Faso is a source, transit, and destination country for women and children subjected to forced labor and sex trafficking; Burkinabe children are forced to work as farm hands, gold panners and washers, street vendors, domestic servants, and beggars or in the commercial sex trade, with some transported to nearby countries; to a lesser extent, Burkinabe women are recruited for legitimate jobs in the Middle East or Europe and subsequently forced into prostitution; women from other West African countries are also lured to Burkina Faso for work and subjected to forced prostitution, forced labor in restaurants, or domestic servitude

tier rating: Tier 2 Watch List—Burkina Faso does not fully comply with the minimum standards for the elimination of trafficking; however, it is making significant efforts to do so; law enforcement efforts decreased in 2014, with a significant decline in trafficking prosecutions (none for forced begging involving Koranic school teachers—a prevalent form of trafficking) and no convictions; a 2014 law criminalizing the sale of children, child prostitution, and child pornography is undermined by a provision allowing offenders to pay a fine in lieu of serving prison time proportionate to the crime; the government sustained efforts to identify and protect a large number of child victims, relying on support from NGOs and international organizations; nationwide awareness-raising activities were sustained, but little was done to stop forced begging (2015)

BURMA

INTRODUCTION

Background: Various ethnic Burmese and ethnic minority city-states or kingdoms occupied the present borders through the 19th century. Over a period of 62 years (1824-1886), Britain conquered Burma and incorporated the country into its Indian Empire. Burma was administered as a province of India until 1937 when it became a separate, self-governing colony; in 1948, Burma attained independence from the British Commonwealth. Gen. NE WIN dominated the government from 1962 to 1988, first as military ruler, then as self-appointed president, and later as political kingpin. In response to widespread civil unrest, NE WIN resigned in 1988, but within months the military crushed student-led protests and took power.

Multiparty legislative elections in 1990 resulted in the main opposition party—the National League for Democracy (NLD)—winning a landslide victory. Instead of handing over power, the junta placed NLD leader (and 1991 Nobel Peace Prize recipient) AUNG SAN SUU KYI under house arrest from 1989 to 1995, 2000 to 2002, and from May 2003 to November 2010. In late September 2007, the ruling junta brutally suppressed protests over increased fuel prices led by prodemocracy activists and Buddhist monks, killing an unknown number of people and arresting thousands for participating in the demonstrations. In early May 2008, Burma was struck by Cyclone Nargis, which left over 138,000 dead and tens of thousands injured and homeless. Despite this tragedy, the junta proceeded with its May constitutional referendum, the first vote in Burma since 1990. Legislative elections held in November 2010, which the NLD boycotted and were considered flawed by many in the international community, saw the ruling Union Solidarity and Development Party garner over 75% of the contested seats.

The national legislature convened in January 2011 and selected former Prime Minister THEIN SEIN as president. Although the vast majority of national-level appointees named by THEIN SEIN were former or current military officers, the government initiated a series of political and economic reforms leading to a substantial opening of the long-isolated country. These reforms included releasing hundreds of political prisoners, signing a nationwide cease-fire with several of the country's ethnic armed groups, pursuing legal reform, and gradually reducing restrictions on freedom of the press, association, and civil society. At least due in part to these reforms, AUNG SAN SUU KYI was elected to the national legislature in April 2012 and became chair of the Committee for Rule of Law and Tranquility. Burma served as chair of the Association of Southeast Asian Nations (ASEAN) for 2014. In a flawed but largely credible national legislative election in November 2015 featuring more than 90 political parties, the NLD again won a landslide victory. Using its overwhelming majority in both houses of parliament, the NLD elected HTIN KYAW, AUNG SAN SUU KYI's confidant and long-time NLD supporter, as president. Burma's first credibly elected civilian government after more than five decades of military dictatorship was sworn into office on 30 March 2016.

GEOGRAPHY

Location: Southeastern Asia, bordering the Andaman Sea and the Bay of Bengal, between Bangladesh and Thailand

Geographic coordinates: 22 00 N, 98 00 E

Map references: Southeast Asia

Area: *total:* 676,578 sq km
land: 653,508 sq km
water: 23,070 sq km
country comparison to the world: 41

Area—comparative: *slightly smaller than Texas*

Land boundaries: *total:* 6,522 km
border countries (5): Bangladesh 271 km, China 2,129 km, India 1,468 km, Laos 238 km, Thailand 2,416 km

Coastline: 1,930 km

Maritime claims: *territorial sea:* 12 nm
contiguous zone: 24 nm
exclusive economic zone: 200 nm
continental shelf: 200 nm or to the edge of the continental margin

Climate: tropical monsoon; cloudy, rainy, hot, humid summers (southwest monsoon, June to September); less cloudy, scant rainfall, mild temperatures, lower humidity during winter (northeast monsoon, December to April)

Terrain: central lowlands ringed by steep, rugged highlands

Elevation: *mean elevation:* 702 m

elevation extremes: *lowest point:* Andaman Sea/ Bay of Bengal 0 m
highest point: Gamlang Razi 5,870 m

Natural resources: petroleum, timber, tin, antimony, zinc, copper, tungsten, lead, coal, marble, limestone, precious stones, natural gas, hydropower, arable land

Land use: *agricultural land:* 19.2%
arable land: 16.5%;
permanent crops: 2.2%;
permanent pasture: 0.5%
forest: 48.2%
other: 32.6% (2011 est.)
Irrigated land: 22,950 sq km (2012)

Population—distribution: population concentrated along coastal areas and in general proximity to the shores of the Irrawaddy River; the extreme north is relatively underpopulated

Natural hazards: destructive earthquakes and cyclones; flooding and landslides common during rainy season (June to September); periodic droughts

Environment—current issues: deforestation; industrial pollution of air, soil, and water; inadequate sanitation and water treatment contribute to disease

Environment—international agreements: party to: Biodiversity, Climate Change, Climate Change-Kyoto Protocol, Desertification, Endangered Species, Law of the Sea, Ozone Layer Protection, Ship Pollution, Tropical Timber 83, Tropical Timber 94 *signed, but not ratified:* none of the selected agreements

Geography—note: strategic location near major Indian Ocean shipping lanes; the north-south flowing Irrawaddy River is the country's largest and most important commercial waterway

PEOPLE AND SOCIETY

Population: 55,123,814
note: estimates for this country take into account the effects of excess mortality due to AIDS; this can result in lower life expectancy, higher infant mortality, higher death rates, lower population growth rates, and changes in the distribution of population by age and sex than would otherwise be expected (July 2017 est.)
country comparison to the world: 24

Nationality: *noun:* Burmese (singular and plural)
adjective: Burmese

Ethnic groups: Burman (Bamar) 68%, Shan 9%, Karen 7%, Rakhine 4%, Chinese 3%, Indian 2%, Mon 2%, other 5%
note: government recognizes 135 indigenous ethnic groups

Languages: Burmese (official)

note: minority ethnic groups have their own languages

Religions: Buddhist 87.9%, Christian 6.2%, Muslim 4.3%, Animist 0.8%, Hindu 0.5%, other 0.2%, none 0.1%
note: religion estimate is based on the 2014 national census, including an estimate for the non-enumerated population of Rakhine State, which is assumed to mainly affiliate with the Islamic faith (2014 est.)

Age structure: *0-14 years:* 26.85% (male 7,567,976/female 7,233,577)
15-24 years: 17.75% (male 4,917,290/female 4,865,264)
25-54 years: 42.36% (male 11,426,913/female 11,922,728)
55-64 years: 7.52% (male 1,930,253/female 2,213,263)
65 years and over: 5.53% (male 1,327,811/female 1,718,739) (2017 est.)

Dependency ratios: *total dependency ratio:* 49.7
youth dependency ratio: 41.7
elderly dependency ratio: 8
potential support ratio: 12.6 (2015 est.)

Median age: *total:* 28.2 years
male: 27.4 years
female: 29 years (2017 est.)
country comparison to the world: 128

Population growth rate: 0.91% (2017 est.)
country comparison to the world: 122

Birth rate: 18.1 births/1,000 population (2017 est.)
country comparison to the world: 97

Death rate: 7.4 deaths/1,000 population (2017 est.)
country comparison to the world: 114

Net migration rate: -1.5 migrant(s)/1,000 population (2017 est.)
country comparison to the world: 148

Population distribution: population concentrated along coastal areas and in general proximity to the shores of the Irrawaddy River; the extreme north is relatively underpopulated

Urbanization: *urban population:* 35.2% of total population (2017)
rate of urbanization: 2.29% annual rate of change (2015-20 est.)

Major urban areas—population: RANGOON (Yangon) (capital) 4.802 million; Mandalay 1.167 million; Nay Pyi Taw 1.03 million (2015)

Sex ratio: *at birth:* 1.06 male(s)/female
0-14 years: 1.04 male(s)/female
15-24 years: 1.03 male(s)/female
25-54 years: 0.99 male(s)/female
55-64 years: 0.89 male(s)/female
65 years and over: 0.77 male(s)/female
total population: 0.99 male(s)/female (2016 est.)

Mother's mean age at first birth: 25 years
note: median age at first birth among women 25-29 (2015/16 est.)

Maternal mortality ratio: 178 deaths/100,000 live births (2015 est.)
country comparison to the world: 54

Infant mortality rate: *total:* 35.8 deaths/1,000 live births
male: 38.8 deaths/1,000 live births
female: 32.6 deaths/1,000 live births (2017 est.)
country comparison to the world: 51

Life expectancy at birth: *total population:* 68.2 years
male: 66.6 years
female: 69.9 years (2017 est.)
country comparison to the world: 167

Total fertility rate: 2.17 children born/woman (2017 est.)
country comparison to the world: 101

Contraceptive prevalence rate: 52.2% (2015/16)
Health expenditures: 2.3% of GDP (2014)
country comparison to the world: 188

Physicians density: 0.57 physicians/1,000 population (2012)

Hospital bed density: 0.6 beds/1,000 population (2006)

Drinking water source:
improved:
urban: 92.7% of population
rural: 74.4% of population
total: 80.6% of population
unimproved:
urban: 7.3% of population
rural: 25.6% of population
total: 19.4% of population (2015 est.)

Sanitation facility access:
improved:
urban: 84.3% of population
rural: 73.9% of population
total: 77.4% of population
unimproved:
urban: 15.7% of population
rural: 26.1% of population
total: 22.6% of population (2012 est.)

HIV/AIDS—adult prevalence rate: 0.8% (2016 est.)
country comparison to the world: 50

HIV/AIDS—people living with HIV/AIDS: 230,000 (2016 est.)
country comparison to the world: 25

HIV/AIDS—deaths: 7,800 (2016 est.)
country comparison to the world: 24

Major infectious diseases: *degree of risk:* very high
food or waterborne diseases: bacterial and protozoal diarrhea, hepatitis A, and typhoid fever
vectorborne diseases: dengue fever, malaria, and Japanese encephalitis
water contact disease: leptospirosis
animal contact disease: rabies (2016)

Obesity—adult prevalence rate: 5.8% (2016)
country comparison to the world: 173

Children under the age of 5 years underweight: 18.9% (2016)
country comparison to the world: 27

Literacy: *definition:* age 15 and over can read and write
total population: 75.6%
male: 80%

female: 71.8% (2016 est.)

School life expectancy (primary to tertiary education): *total:* 8 years
male: NA
female: NA (2007)

GOVERNMENT

Country name: *conventional long form:* Union of Burma
conventional short form: Burma
local long form: Pyidaungzu Thammada Myanma Naingngandaw (translated as the Republic of the Union of Myanmar)
local short form: Myanma Naingngandaw
former: Socialist Republic of the Union of Burma, Union of Myanmar
note: since 1989 the military authorities in Burma and the current parliamentary government have promoted the name Myanmar as a conventional name for their state; the US Government has not adopted the name
etymology: both "Burma" and "Myanmar" derive from the name of the majority Burmese Bamar ethnic group

Government type: parliamentary republic

Capital: *name:* Rangoon (Yangon); note—Nay Pyi Taw is the administrative capital

geographic coordinates: 16 48 N, 96 09 E

time difference: UTC+6.5 (11.5 hours ahead of Washington, DC, during Standard Time)

Administrative divisions: 7 regions (taing-myar, singular—taing), 7 states (pyi ne-myar, singular—pyi ne), 1 union territory
regions: Ayeyawady (Irrawaddy), Bago, Magway, Mandalay, Sagaing, Taninthayi, Yangon (Rangoon)
states: Chin, Kachin, Kayah, Kayin, Mon, Rakhine, Shan
union territory: Nay Pyi Taw

Independence: 4 January 1948 (from the UK)

National holiday: Independence Day, 4 January (1948); Union Day, 12 February (1947)

Constitution: *history:* previous 1947, 1974 (suspended until 2008); latest drafted 9 April 2008, approved by referendum 29 May 2008; amended 2015
amendments: proposals require at least 20% approval by the Assembly of the Union membership; passage of amendments to sections of the constitution on basic principles, government structure, branches of government, state emergencies, and amendment procedures requires 75% approval by the Assembly and approval in a referendum by absolute majority of registered voters; passage of amendments to other sections requires only 75% Assembly approval (2017)

Legal system: mixed legal system of English common law (as introduced in codifications designed for colonial India) and customary law

International law organization participation: has not submitted an ICJ jurisdiction declaration; non-party state to the ICCt

Citizenship: *citizenship by birth:* no

citizenship by descent only: both parents must be citizens of Burma
dual citizenship recognized: no
residency requirement for naturalization: none
note: an applicant for naturalization must be the child or spouse of a citizen

Suffrage: 18 years of age; universal

Executive branch: *chief of state:* President HTIN KYAW (since 30 March 2016); Vice Presidents MYINT SWE (since 30 March 2016) and HENRY VAN THIO (since 30 March 2016); note—the president is both chief of state and head of government

head of government: President HTIN KYAW (since 30 March 2016); Vice Presidents MYINT SWE (since 30 March 2016) and HENRY VAN THIO (since 30 March 2016)
note: a parliamentary bill creating the position of "state counsellor" was signed into law by President HTIN KYAW on 6 April 2016; a state counsellor serves the equivalent term of the president and is similar to a prime minister in that the holder acts as a link between the parliament and the executive branch
state counsellor: State Counselor AUNG SAN SUU KYI (since 6 April 2016); she concurrently serves as minister of foreign affairs and minister for the office of the president
cabinet: Cabinet appointments shared by the president and the commander-in-chief
elections/appointments: president indirectly elected by simple majority vote by the full Assembly of the Union from among 3 vice-presidential candidates nominated by the Presidential Electoral College (consists of members of the lower and upper houses and military members); the other 2 candidates become vice-presidents (president elected for a 5-year term); election last held on 15 March 2016 (next to be held in 2021)
election results: HTIN KYAW elected president; Assembly of the Union vote—HTIN KYAW (NLD) 360, MYINT SWE (USDP) 213, HENRY VAN THIO (NLD) 79 (652 votes cast)

Legislative branch: *description:* bicameral Assembly of the Union or Pyidaungsu consists of an upper house—the House of Nationalities or Amyotha Hluttaw, (224 seats; 168 members directly elected in single-seat constituencies by absolute majority vote with a second round if needed and 56 appointed by the military; members serve 5-year terms) and a lower house—the House of Representatives or Pyithu Hluttaw, (440 seats; 330 members directly elected in single-seat constituencies by simple majority vote and 110 appointed by the military; members serve 5-year terms)
elections: last held on 8 November 2015 (next to be held in 2020)
election results: Upper House—percent of vote by party—NLD 60.3%, USDP 4.9%, ANP 4.5%, SNLD 1.3%, military 25%, other 4%, ; seats by party—NLD 135, USDP 11, ANP 10, SNLD 3, ZCD 2, TNP 2, independent 2, other 3, military appointees 56; Lower House—percent of vote by party—NLD 58%, USDP 6.8%, ANP 2.7%, SNLD 2.7%, military 25%, other 4.8%; seats by

party—NLD 255, USDP 30, ANP 12, SNLD 12, PNO 3, TNP 3, ZCD 2, LNDP 2, independent 1, other 3, canceled due to insurgence 7, military appointees 110

Judicial branch: highest court(s): Supreme Court of the Union (consists of the chief justice and 7-11 judges)
judge selection and term of office: chief justice and judges nominated by the president, with approval of the Lower House, and appointed by the president; judges normally serve until mandatory retirement at age 70
subordinate courts: High Courts of the Region; High Courts of the State; Court of the Self-Administered Division; Court of the Self-Administered Zone; district and township courts; special courts (for juvenile, municipal, and traffic offenses); courts martial

Political parties and leaders: All Mon Region Democracy Party or AMRDP (vacant)
Arakan National Party or ANP (vacant) (formed from the 2013 merger of the Rakhine Nationalities Development Party and the Arakan League for Democracy)
National Democratic Force or NDF [KHIN MAUNG SWE]
National League for Democracy or NLD [AUNG SAN SUU KYI]
National Unity Party or NUP [THAN TIN]
Pa-O National Organization or PNO [AUNG KHAM HTI]
Shan Nationalities Democratic Party or SNDP [SAI AIK PAUNG]
Shan Nationalities League for Democracy or SNLD [KHUN HTUN OO]
Ta'ang National Party or TNP [AIK MONE]
Union Solidarity and Development Party or USDP [THAN HTAY]
Zomi Congress for Democracy or ZCD [PU CIN SIAN THANG]
numerous smaller parties

Political pressure groups and leaders: Thai border: Ethnic Nationalities Council or ENC
Federation of Trade Unions-Burma or FTUB (exiled trade union and labor advocates)
United Nationalities Federal Council or UNFC [NAI HONG SAR]
inside Burma: Kachin Independence Organization or KIO [Gen. LANYAW ZAWNG HRA]
Karen National Union or KNU [Gen. SAW MUTU SAY POE]
Karenni National People's Party or KNPP [KHUN ABEL TWEED]
United Wa State Army or UWSA [BAO YOU-XIANG]
88 Generation Students Group [collective leadership] (pro-democracy movement)
several other Chin, Karen, Mon, and Shan factions
note: many restrictions on freedom of expression have been relaxed by the government; a limited number of political groups, other than parties, are approved by the government

International organization participation: ADB, ARF, ASEAN, BIMSTEC, CP, EAS, EITI (candidate country), FAO, G-77, IAEA, IBRD, ICAO,

ICRM, IDA, IFAD, IFC, IFRCS, IHO, ILO, IMF, IMO, Interpol, IOC, IOM, IPU, ISO (correspondent), ITU, ITUC (NGOs), NAM, OPCW (signatory), SAARC (observer), UN, UNCTAD, UNESCO, UNIDO, UNWTO, UPU, WCO, WHO, WIPO, WMO, WTO

Diplomatic representation in the US: *chief of mission:* Ambassador AUNG LYNN (since 16 September 2016)

chancery: 2300 S Street NW, Washington, DC 20008

telephone: [1] (202) 332-3344

FAX: [1] (202) 332-4351

consulate(s) general: Los Angeles, New York

Diplomatic representation from the US: *chief of mission:* Ambassador Scot MARCIEL (since 27 April 2016)

embassy: 110 University Avenue, Kamayut Township, Rangoon

mailing address: Box B, APO AP 96546

telephone: [95] (1) 536-509, 535-756, 538-038

FAX: [95] (1) 511-069

Flag description: design consists of three equal horizontal stripes of yellow (top), green, and red; centered on the green band is a large white five-pointed star that partially overlaps onto the adjacent colored stripes; the design revives the triband colors used by Burma from 1943-45, during the Japanese occupation

National symbol(s): chinthe (mythical lion); national colors: yellow, green, red, white

National anthem: *name:* "Kaba Ma Kyei" (Till the End of the World, Myanmar)

lyrics/music: SAYA TIN

note: adopted 1948; Burma is among a handful of non-European nations that have anthems rooted in indigenous traditions; the beginning portion of the anthem is a traditional Burmese anthem before transitioning into a Western-style orchestrated work

ECONOMY

Economy—overview: Since Burma began the transition to a civilian-led government in 2011, the country initiated economic reforms aimed at attracting foreign investment and reintegrating into the global economy. Burma established a managed float of the Burmese kyat in 2012, granted the Central Bank operational independence in July 2013, enacted a new anti-corruption law in September 2013, and granted licenses to nine foreign banks in 2014 and four more foreign banks in 2016. State Counselor AUNG SAN SUU KYI and the ruling National League for Democracy, who took power in March 2016, are seeking to improve Burma's investment climate, following the US sanctions lift in October 2016 and reinstatement of Generalized System of Preferences trade benefits in November 2016. In October 2016, Burma passed a revised foreign investment law that consolidates investment regulations and eases the investment approval process and in 2017 passed a law on companies that eases rules on foreign ownership of businesses.

Burma's economic growth rate recovered from a low growth under 6% in 2011 but has been volatile between 6% and 7.2% during the past few years.. Burma's abundant natural resources and young labor force have the potential to attract foreign investment in the energy, garment, information technology, and food and beverage sectors.

Despite these improvements, living standards have not improved for the majority of the people residing in rural areas. Burma remains one of the poorest countries in Asia—approximately 26% of the country's 51 million people live in poverty. The isolationist policies and economic mismanagement of previous governments have left Burma with poor infrastructure, endemic corruption, underdeveloped human resources, and inadequate access to capital, which will require a major commitment to reverse. The Burmese Government has been slow to address impediments to economic development such as unclear land rights, a restrictive trade licensing system, an opaque revenue collection system, and an antiquated banking system. AUNG SAN SUU KYI's government is focusing on accelerating agricultural productivity and land reforms, modernizing and opening the financial sector, and developing transportation and electricity infrastructure.

GDP (purchasing power parity): $330.9 billion (2017 est.)

$308.6 billion (2016 est.)

$290.8 billion (2015 est.)

note: data are in 2017 dollars

country comparison to the world: 54

GDP (official exchange rate): $66.97 billion (2016 est.)

GDP—real growth rate: 7.2% (2017 est.)

6.1% (2016 est.)

7% (2015 est.)

country comparison to the world: 7

GDP—per capita (PPP): $6,300 (2017 est.)

$5,900 (2016 est.)

$5,600 (2015 est.)

note: data are in 2017 dollars

country comparison to the world: 163

Gross national saving: 16.2% of GDP (2017 est.)

16.5% of GDP (2016 est.)

19.3% of GDP (2015 est.)

country comparison to the world: 117

GDP—composition, by end use:

household consumption: 50.6%

government consumption: 15.2%

investment in fixed capital: 37.9%

investment in inventories: 2.6%

exports of goods and services: 20.6%

imports of goods and services: -26.9% (2017 est.)

GDP—composition, by sector of origin:

agriculture: 24.8%

industry: 35.4%

services: 39.9% (2017 est.)

Agriculture—products: rice, pulses, beans, sesame, groundnuts; sugarcane; fish and fish products; hardwood

Industries: agricultural processing; wood and wood products; copper, tin, tungsten, iron; cement;

construction materials; pharmaceuticals; fertilizer; oil and natural gas; garments; jade and gems

Industrial production growth rate: 9.6% (2017 est.)

country comparison to the world: 10

Labor force: 22.3 million (2017 est.)

country comparison to the world: 29

Labor force—by occupation: *agriculture:* 70%

industry: 7%

services: 23% (2001 est.)

Unemployment rate: 4% (2017 est.)

4% (2016 est.)

country comparison to the world: 49

Population below poverty line: 25.6% (2016 est.)

Household income or consumption by percentage share: *lowest 10%:* 2.8%

highest 10%: 32.4% (1998)

Budget: *revenues:* $9.211 billion

expenditures: $11.45 billion (2017 est.)

Taxes and other revenues: 13.8% of GDP (2017 est.)

country comparison to the world: 199

Budget surplus (+) or deficit (-): -3.3% of GDP (2017 est.)

country comparison to the world: 124

Fiscal year: 1 April—31 March

Inflation rate (consumer prices): 6.5% (2017 est.)

6.8% (2016 est.)

country comparison to the world: 188

Central bank discount rate: 9.95% (31 December 2010)

12% (31 December 2009)

country comparison to the world: 23

Commercial bank prime lending rate: 14% (31 December 2017 est.)

13% (31 December 2016 est.)

country comparison to the world: 53

Stock of narrow money: $18.53 billion (31 December 2017 est.)

$15.84 billion (31 December 2016 est.)

country comparison to the world: 70

Stock of domestic credit: $28.48 billion (31 December 2017 est.)

$23.08 billion (31 December 2016 est.)

country comparison to the world: 83

Market value of publicly traded shares: $NA

Current account balance: -$4.393 billion (2017 est.)

-$3.789 billion (2016 est.)

country comparison to the world: 172

Exports: $10.07 billion (2017 est.)

$9.085 billion (2016 est.)

note: official export figures are grossly underestimated due to the value of timber, gems, narcotics, rice, and other products smuggled to Thailand, China, and Bangladesh

country comparison to the world: 91

Exports—commodities: natural gas; wood products; pulses and beans; fish; rice; clothing; minerals, including jade and gems

Exports—partners: China 40.6%, Thailand 19.1%, India 8.8%, Singapore 7.6%, Japan 5.7% (2016)

Imports: $15.33 billion (2017 est.)
$12.8 billion (2016 est.)
note: import figures are grossly underestimated due to the value of consumer goods, diesel fuel, and other products smuggled in from Thailand, China, Malaysia, and India
country comparison to the world: 84

Imports—commodities: fabric; petroleum products; fertilizer; plastics; machinery; transport equipment; cement, construction materials; food products; edible oil

Imports—partners: China 33.9%, Singapore 14.3%, Thailand 12.5%, Japan 7.9%, India 6.9%, Malaysia 4.3% (2016)

Reserves of foreign exchange and gold: $5.032 billion (31 December 2017 est.)
$4.63 billion (31 December 2016 est.)
country comparison to the world: 94

Debt—external: $9.713 billion (31 December 2017 est.)
$8.2 billion (31 December 2016 est.)
country comparison to the world: 116

Exchange rates: kyats (MMK) per US dollar—
1,361.9 (2017 est.)
1,234.87 (2016 est.)
1,234.87 (2015 est.)
1,162.62 (2014 est.)
984.35 (2013 est.)

ENERGY

Electricity access: *population without electricity:* 36,300,000
electrification—*total population:* 52%
electrification—urban areas: 95%
electrification—rural areas: 31% (2013)

Electricity—production: 15.48 billion kWh (2015 est.)
country comparison to the world: 86

Electricity—consumption: 12.91 billion kWh (2015 est.)
country comparison to the world: 85

Electricity—exports: 0 kWh (2016 est.)
country comparison to the world: 110

Electricity—imports: 0 kWh (2016 est.)
country comparison to the world: 127

Electricity—installed generating capacity: 4.783 million kW (2015 est.)
country comparison to the world: 80

Electricity—from fossil fuels: 33.9% of total installed capacity (2015 est.)
country comparison to the world: 181

Electricity—from nuclear fuels: 0% of total installed capacity (2015 est.)
country comparison to the world: 54

Electricity—from hydroelectric plants: 65.9% of total installed capacity (2015 est.)
country comparison to the world: 21

Electricity—from other renewable sources: 0.3% of total installed capacity (2015 est.)
country comparison to the world: 156

Crude oil—production: 15,000 bbl/day (2016 est.)
country comparison to the world: 76

Crude oil—exports: 2,814 bbl/day (2014 est.)
country comparison to the world: 67

Crude oil—imports: 28.5 bbl/day (2014 est.)
country comparison to the world: 84

Crude oil—proved reserves: 139 million bbl (1 January 2017 es)
country comparison to the world: 67

Refined petroleum products—production: 15,870 bbl/day (2014 est.)
country comparison to the world: 96

Refined petroleum products—consumption: 91,000 bbl/day (2015 est.)
country comparison to the world: 85

Refined petroleum products—exports: 0 bbl/day (2014 est.)
country comparison to the world: 135

Refined petroleum products—imports: 73,260 bbl/day (2014 est.)
country comparison to the world: 67

Natural gas—production: 17.5 billion cu m (2015 est.)
country comparison to the world: 34

Natural gas—consumption: 4.766 billion cu m (2015 est.)
country comparison to the world: 66

Natural gas—exports: 13.91 billion cu m (2015 est.)
country comparison to the world: 19

Natural gas—imports: 0 cu m (2013 est.)
country comparison to the world: 95

Natural gas—proved reserves: 637.1 billion cu m (1 January 2017 es)
country comparison to the world: 31

Carbon dioxide emissions from consumption of energy: 15 million Mt (2013 est.)
country comparison to the world: 91

COMMUNICATIONS

Telephones—fixed lines: *total subscriptions:* 514,385
subscriptions per 100 inhabitants: 1 (July 2016 est.)
country comparison to the world: 96

Telephones—mobile cellular: *total:* 48,728,399
subscriptions per 100 inhabitants: 86 (July 2016 est.)
country comparison to the world: 47

Telephone system: *general assessment:* meets minimum requirements for local and intercity service for business and government
domestic: the government eased its monopoly on communications in 2013 and granted telecom licenses to three new operators, which has resulted in a dramatic expansion of the wireless network
international: country code—95; landing point for the SEA-ME-WE-3 optical telecommunications submarine cable that provides links to Asia, the Middle East, and Europe; satellite earth stations—2, Intelsat (Indian Ocean) and ShinSat (2016)

Broadcast media: government controls all domestic broadcast media; 2 state-controlled TV stations with 1 of the stations controlled by the armed forces; 2 pay-TV stations are joint state-private ventures; access to satellite TV is limited; 1 state-controlled domestic radio station and 9 FM stations that are joint state-private ventures; transmissions of several international broadcasters are available in parts of Burma; the Voice of America (VOA), Radio Free Asia (RFA), BBC Burmese service, the Democratic Voice of Burma (DVB), and Radio Australia use shortwave to broadcast in Burma; VOA, RFA, and DVB produce daily TV news programs that are transmitted by satellite to audiences in Burma; in March 2017, the government granted licenses to 5 private broadcasters, allowing them digital free-to-air TV channels to be operated in partnership with government-owned Myanmar Radio and Television (MRTV) and will rely upon MRTV's transmission infrastructure; the new channels are expected to begin airing programming early in 2018 (2017)

Internet country code: .mm

Internet users: *total:* 14,264,308
percent of population: 25.1% (July 2016 est.)
country comparison to the world: 128

TRANSPORTATION

National air transport system: *number of registered air carriers:* 11
inventory of registered aircraft operated by air carriers: 45
annual passenger traffic on registered air carriers: 2,029,139
annual freight traffic on registered air carriers: 3,365,967 mt-km (2015)
Civil aircraft registration country code prefix: XY (2016)

Airports: 64 (2013)
country comparison to the world: 76

Airports—with paved runways: *total:* 36
over 3,047 m: 12
2,438 to 3,047 m: 11
1,524 to 2,437 m: 12
under 914 m: 1 (2017)

Airports—with unpaved runways: *total:* 28
over 3,047 m: 1
1,524 to 2,437 m: 4
914 to 1,523 m: 10
under 914 m: 13 (2013)

Heliports: 11 (2013)

Pipelines: gas 3,739 km; oil 1,321 km (2017)

Railways: *total:* 5,031 km
narrow gauge: 5,031 km 1.000-m gauge (2008)
country comparison to the world: 38

Roadways: *total:* 34,377 km (includes 358 km of expressways) (2010)
country comparison to the world: 93

Waterways: 12,800 km (2011)
country comparison to the world: 10

Merchant marine: *total:* 97
by type: bulk carrier 1, general cargo 43, oil tanker 5, other 48 (2017)
country comparison to the world: 86

Ports and terminals: *major seaport(s):* Mawlamyine (Moulmein), Sittwe
river port(s): Rangoon (Yangon) (Rangoon River)

Military expenditures: 4.08% of GDP (2015)
3.58% of GDP (2014)
3.81% of GDP (2013)
3.71% of GDP (2012)

Military branches: Burmese Defense Service (Tatmadaw): Army (Tatmadaw Kyi), Navy (Tatmadaw Yay), Air Force (Tatmadaw Lay) (2013)

Military service age and obligation: 18-35 years of age (men) and 18-27 years of age (women) for voluntary military service; no conscription (a 2010 law reintroducing conscription has not yet entered into force); 2-year service obligation; male (ages 18-45) and female (ages 18-35) professionals (including doctors, engineers, mechanics) serve up to 3 years; service terms may be stretched to 5 years in an officially declared emergency; Burma signed the Convention on the Rights of the Child (CRC) on 15 August 1991; on 27 June 2012, the regime signed a Joint Action Plan on prevention of child recruitment; in February 2013, the military formed a new task force to address forced child conscription; approximately 600 children have been released from military service since the signing of the joint action plan (2015)

TERRORISM

Terrorist groups—foreign based: *al-Qa'ida (AQ):*
aim(s): overthrow the Burmese Government and, ultimately, establish a pan-Islamic caliphate under a strict Salafi Muslim interpretation of Sharia
area(s) of operation: operates in collaboration with its al-Qa'ida in the Indian Subcontinent affiliate

TRANSNATIONAL ISSUES

Disputes—international: over half of Burma's population consists of diverse ethnic groups who have substantial numbers of kin in neighboring countries; the Naf River on the border with Bangladesh serves as a smuggling and illegal transit route; Bangladesh struggles to accommodate 29,000 Rohingya, Burmese Muslim minority from Arakan

State, living as refugees in Cox's Bazar; Burmese border authorities are constructing a 200 km (124 mi) wire fence designed to deter illegal cross-border transit and tensions from the military build-up along border with Bangladesh in 2010; Bangladesh referred its maritime boundary claims with Burma and India to the International Tribunal on the Law of the Sea; Burmese forces attempting to dig in to the largely autonomous Shan State to rout local militias tied to the drug trade, prompts local residents to periodically flee into neighboring Yunnan Province in China; fencing along the India-Burma international border at Manipur's Moreh town is in progress to check illegal drug trafficking and movement of militants; over 100,000 mostly Karen refugees and asylum seekers fleeing civil strife, political upheaval, and economic stagnation in Burma were living in remote camps in Thailand near the border as of May 2017

Refugees and internally displaced persons: IDPs: 644,000 (government offensives against armed ethnic minority groups near its borders with China and Thailand, natural disasters, forced land evictions) (2016)

stateless persons: 925,939 (2016); note—Rohingya Muslims, living predominantly in Rakhine State, are Burma's main group of stateless people; the Burmese Government does not recognize the Rohingya as a "national race" and stripped them of their citizenship under the 1982 Citizenship Law, categorizing them as "non-nationals" or "foreign residents"; under the Rakhine State Action Plan drafted in October 2014, the Rohingya must demonstrate their family has lived in Burma for at least 60 years to qualify for a lesser naturalized citizenship and the classification of Bengali or be put in detention camps and face deportation; native-born but non-indigenous people, such as Indians, are also stateless; the Burmese Government does not grant citizenship to children born outside of the country to Burmese parents who left the country illegally or fled persecution, such as those born in Thailand
note: estimate does not include stateless IDPs or stateless persons in IDP-like situations because they are included in estimates of IDPs (2016)

Trafficking in persons: current situation: Burma is a source country for men, women, and children

trafficked for the purpose of forced labor and for women and children subjected to sex trafficking; Burmese adult and child labor migrants travel to East Asia, the Middle East, South Asia, and the US, where men are forced to work in the fishing, manufacturing, forestry, and construction industries and women and girls are forced into prostitution, domestic servitude, or forced labor in the garment sector; some Burmese economic migrants and Rohingya asylum seekers have become forced laborers on Thai fishing boats; some military personnel and armed ethnic groups unlawfully conscript child soldiers or coerce adults and children into forced labor; domestically, adults and children from ethnic areas are vulnerable to forced labor on plantations and in mines, while children may also be subject to forced prostitution, domestic service, and begging

tier rating: Tier 2 Watch List—Burma does not fully comply with the minimum standards for the elimination of trafficking, but it is making significant efforts to do so; the government has a written plan that, if implemented, would constitute making a significant effort toward meeting the minimum standard for eliminating human trafficking; in 2014, law enforcement continued to investigate and prosecute cross-border trafficking offenses but did little to address domestic trafficking; no civilians or government officials were prosecuted or convicted for the recruitment of child soldiers, a serious problem that is hampered by corruption and the influence of the military; victim referral and protection services remained inadequate, especially for men, and left victims vulnerable to being re-trafficked; the government coordinated anti-trafficking programs as part of its five-year national action plan (2015)

Illicit drugs: world's second largest producer of illicit opium with an estimated poppy cultivation totaling 55,500 hectares in 2015 and an estimated potential production of 647 mt of raw opium; Shan state is the source of 91% of Burma's poppy cultivation; lack of government will to take on major narcotrafficking groups and lack of serious commitment against money laundering continues to hinder the overall antidrug effort; major source of methamphetamine and heroin for regional consumption

BURUNDI

INTRODUCTION

Background: Burundi is a small country in East Africa bordered by Tanzania, Rwanda, and Lake Tanganyika. Burundi gained its independence from Belgium in 1962. Much of its history has been turbulent, and Burundi's first democratically elected president was assassinated in October 1993 after only 100 days in office. The internationally brokered Arusha Agreement ended the 1993-2005 civil war, paving the way for a new constitution

and 2005 elections. Pierre NKURUNZIZA was elected president in 2005 and 2010 and again in a controversial election in 2015. Burundi continues to face many political and economic challenges.

GEOGRAPHY

Location: Central Africa, east of the Democratic Republic of the Congo, west of Tanzania
Geographic coordinates: 3 30 S, 30 00 E

Map references: Africa
Area: *total:* 27,830 sq km
land: 25,680 sq km
water: 2,150 sq km
country comparison to the world: 147
Area—comparative: slightly smaller than Maryland
Land boundaries: *total:* 1,140 km
border countries (3): Democratic Republic of the Congo 236 km, Rwanda 315 km, Tanzania 589 km

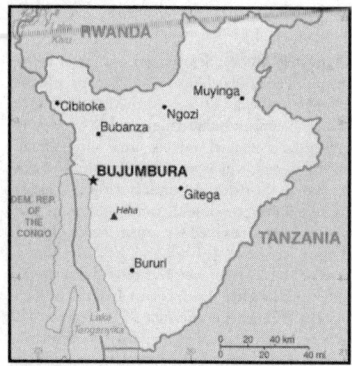

Coastline: 0 km (landlocked)

Maritime claims: none (landlocked)

Climate: equatorial; high plateau with considerable altitude variation (772 m to 2,670 m above sea level); average annual temperature varies with altitude from 23 to 17 degrees Celsius but is generally moderate as the average altitude is about 1,700 m; average annual rainfall is about 150 cm; two wet seasons (February to May and September to November), and two dry seasons (June to August and December to January)

Terrain: hilly and mountainous, dropping to a plateau in east, some plains

Elevation: *mean elevation:* 1,504 m

elevation extremes: *lowest point:* Lake Tanganyika 772 m
highest point: Heha 2,670 m

Natural resources: nickel, uranium, rare earth oxides, peat, cobalt, copper, platinum, vanadium, arable land, hydropower, niobium, tantalum, gold, tin, tungsten, kaolin, limestone

Land use: *agricultural land:* 73.3%
arable land: 38.9%;
permanent crops: 15.6%;
permanent pasture: 18.8%;
forest: 6.6%
other: 20.1% (2011 est.)
Irrigated land: 230 sq km (2012)

Population—distribution: one of Africa's most densely populated countries; concentrations tend to be in the north and along the northern shore of Lake Tanganyika in the west; most people live on farms near areas of fertile volcanic soil

Natural hazards: flooding; landslides; drought

Environment—current issues: soil erosion as a result of overgrazing and the expansion of agriculture into marginal lands; deforestation (little forested land remains because of uncontrolled cutting of trees for fuel); habitat loss threatens wildlife populations

Environment—international agreements: party to: Biodiversity, Climate Change, Climate Change-Kyoto Protocol, Desertification, Endangered Species, Hazardous Wastes, Ozone Layer Protection, Wetlands
signed, but not ratified: Law of the Sea

Geography—note: landlocked; straddles crest of the Nile-Congo watershed; the Kagera, which drains into Lake Victoria, is the most remote headstream of the White Nile

PEOPLE AND SOCIETY

Population: 11,466,756
note: estimates for this country explicitly take into account the effects of excess mortality due to AIDS; this can result in lower life expectancy, higher infant mortality, higher death rates, lower population growth rates, and changes in the distribution of population by age and sex than would otherwise be expected (July 2017 est.)
country comparison to the world: 78

Nationality: *noun:* Burundian(s)
adjective: Burundian

Ethnic groups: Hutu (Bantu) 85%, Tutsi (Hamitic) 14%, Twa (Pygmy) 1%, Europeans 3,000, South Asians 2,000

Languages: Kirundi 29.7% (official), Kirundi and other language 9.1%, French (official) and French and other language 0.3%, Swahili and Swahili and other language 0.2% (along Lake Tanganyika and in the Bujumbura area), English (official) and English and other language 0.06%, more than 2 languages 3.7%, unspecified 56.9%
note: data represent language read and written by people 10 years of age or older; spoken Kirundi is widespread (2008 est.)

Religions: Roman Catholic 62.1%, Protestant 23.9% (includes Adventist 2.3% and other Protestant 21.6%), Muslim 2.5%, other 3.6%, unspecified 7.9% (2008 est.)

Demographic profile: Burundi is a densely populated country with a high population growth rate, factors that combined with land scarcity and poverty place a large share of its population at risk of food insecurity. About 90% of the population relies on subsistence agriculture. Subdivision of land to sons, and redistribution to returning refugees, results in smaller, overworked, and less productive plots. Food shortages, poverty, and a lack of clean water contribute to a 60% chronic malnutrition rate among children. A lack of reproductive health services has prevented a significant reduction in Burundi's maternal mortality and fertility rates, which are both among the world's highest. With two-thirds of its population under the age of 25 and a birth rate of about 6 children per woman, Burundi's population will continue to expand rapidly for decades to come, putting additional strain on a poor country.

Historically, migration flows into and out of Burundi have consisted overwhelmingly of refugees from violent conflicts. In the last decade, more than a half million Burundian refugees returned home from neighboring countries, mainly Tanzania. Reintegrating the returnees has been problematic due to their prolonged time in exile, land scarcity, poor infrastructure, poverty, and unemployment. Repatriates and existing residents (including internally displaced persons) compete for limited land and other resources. To further complicate matters, international aid organizations reduced their assistance because they no longer classified Burundi as a post-conflict country. Conditions have deteriorated since renewed violence erupted in April 2015, causing another outpouring of refugees. In addition to refugee out-migration, Burundi has hosted thousands of refugees from neighboring countries, mostly from the Democratic Republic of the Congo and lesser numbers from Rwanda.

Age structure: *0-14 years:* 45.57% (male 2,628,767/female 2,596,719)
15-24 years: 19.15% (male 1,095,213/female 1,100,314)
25-54 years: 28.74% (male 1,643,319/female 1,651,679)
55-64 years: 3.92% (male 212,074/female 237,324)
65 years and over: 2.63% (male 129,482/female 171,865) (2017 est.)

Dependency ratios: *total dependency ratio:* 89.6
youth dependency ratio: 84.8
elderly dependency ratio: 4.7
potential support ratio: 21.1 (2015 est.)

Median age: *total:* 17 years
male: 16.8 years
female: 17.3 years (2017 est.)
country comparison to the world: 223

Population growth rate: 3.25% (2017 est.)
country comparison to the world: 4

Birth rate: 41.3 births/1,000 population (2017 est.)
country comparison to the world: 6

Death rate: 8.8 deaths/1,000 population (2017 est.)
country comparison to the world: 69

Net migration rate: 0 migrant(s)/1,000 population (2017 est.)
country comparison to the world: 77

Population distribution: one of Africa's most densely populated countries; concentrations tend to be in the north and along the northern shore of Lake Tanganyika in the west; most people live on farms near areas of fertile volcanic soil

Urbanization: *urban population:* 12.7% of total population (2017)
rate of urbanization: 5.48% annual rate of change (2015-20 est.)

Major urban areas—population: BUJUMBURA (capital) 751,000 (2015)

Sex ratio: *at birth:* 1.03 male(s)/female
0-14 years: 1.01 male(s)/female
15-24 years: 1 male(s)/female
25-54 years: 1 male(s)/female
55-64 years: 0.89 male(s)/female
65 years and over: 0.74 male(s)/female
total population: 0.99 male(s)/female (2016 est.)

Mother's mean age at first birth: 21.3 years
note: median age at first birth among women 25-29 (2010 est.)

Maternal mortality ratio: 712 deaths/100,000 live births (2015 est.)
country comparison to the world: 8

Infant mortality rate: *total:* 58.8 deaths/1,000 live births
male: 65.3 deaths/1,000 live births
female: 52.2 deaths/1,000 live births (2017 est.)
country comparison to the world: 19

Life expectancy at birth: *total population:* 60.9 years
male: 59.2 years

female: 62.7 years (2017 est.)
country comparison to the world: 202

Total fertility rate: 5.99 children born/woman (2017 est.)
country comparison to the world: 4

Contraceptive prevalence rate: 31.7% (2012)
Health expenditures: 7.5% of GDP (2014)
country comparison to the world: 63

Hospital bed density: 1.9 beds/1,000 population (2011)

Drinking water source:
improved:
urban: 91.1% of population
rural: 73.8% of population
total: 75.9% of population
unimproved:
urban: 8.9% of population
rural: 26.2% of population
total: 24.1% of population (2015 est.)

Sanitation facility access:
improved:
urban: 43.8% of population
rural: 48.6% of population
total: 48% of population
unimproved:
urban: 56.2% of population
rural: 51.4% of population
total: 52% of population (2015 est.)

HIV/AIDS—adult prevalence rate: 1.1% (2016 est.)
country comparison to the world: 42

HIV/AIDS—people living with HIV/AIDS: 84,000 (2016 est.)
country comparison to the world: 46

HIV/AIDS—deaths: 2,900 (2016 est.)
country comparison to the world: 42

Major infectious diseases: *degree of risk:* very high
food or waterborne diseases: bacterial and protozoal diarrhea, hepatitis A, and typhoid fever
vectorborne diseases: malaria and dengue fever
water contact disease: schistosomiasis
animal contact disease: rabies (2016)

Obesity—adult prevalence rate: 5.4% (2016)
country comparison to the world: 178

Children under the age of 5 years underweight: 29.1% (2010)
country comparison to the world: 16

Education expenditures: 5.4% of GDP (2013)
country comparison to the world: 50

Literacy: *definition:* age 15 and over can read and write
total population: 85.6%
male: 88.2%
female: 83.1% (2015 est.)

School life expectancy (primary to tertiary education): *total:* 11 years
male: 11 years
female: 10 years (2013)

GOVERNMENT

Country name: *conventional long form:* Republic of Burundi
conventional short form: Burundi
local long form: Republique du Burundi/Republika y'u Burundi

local short form: Burundi
former: Urundi
etymology: name derived from the pre-colonial Kingdom of Burundi (17th-19th century)

Government type: presidential republic

Capital: *name:* Bujumbura

geographic coordinates: 3 22 S, 29 21 E

time difference: UTC+2 (7 hours ahead of Washington, DC, during Standard Time)

Administrative divisions: 18 provinces; Bubanza, Bujumbura Mairie, Bujumbura Rural, Bururi, Cankuzo, Cibitoke, Gitega, Karuzi, Kayanza, Kirundo, Makamba, Muramvya, Muyinga, Mwaro, Ngozi, Rumonge, Rutana, Ruyigi

Independence: 1 July 1962 (from UN trusteeship under Belgian administration)

National holiday: Independence Day, 1 July (1962)

Constitution: *history:* several previous; latest ratified by referendum 28 February 2005
amendments: proposed by the president of the republic after consultation with the government or by absolute majority support of the membership in both houses of Parliament; passage requires at least two-thirds majority vote by the Senate membership and at least four-fifths majority vote by the National Assembly; the president can opt to submit amendment bills to a referendum; constitutional articles including those on national unity, the secularity of Burundi, its democratic form of government, and its sovereignty cannot be amended; note—in December 2017, the president began promoting a campaign for a referendum to amend the constitution (2017)

Legal system: mixed legal system of Belgian civil law and customary law

International law organization participation: has not submitted an ICJ jurisdiction declaration; accepts ICCt jurisdiction

Citizenship: *citizenship by birth:* no
citizenship by descent only: the father must be a citizen of Burundi
dual citizenship recognized: no
residency requirement for naturalization: 10 years

Suffrage: 18 years of age; universal

Executive branch: *chief of state:* President Pierre NKURUNZIZA (since 26 August 2005); First Vice President Gaston SINDIMWO (since 20 August 2015); Second Vice President Joseph BUTORE (since 20 August 2015); note—the president is both chief of state and head of government

head of government: President Pierre NKURUNZIZA (since 26 August 2005); First Vice President Gaston SINDIMWO (since 20 August 2015); Second Vice President Joseph BUTORE (since 20 August 2015)
cabinet: Council of Ministers appointed by president
elections/appointments: president directly elected by absolute majority popular vote in 2 rounds if needed for a 5-year term (eligible for a second term); election last held on 21 July 2015(next to be held in 2020); vice presidents nominated by the president, endorsed by Parliament
election results: Pierre NKURUNZIZA reelected president; percent of vote—Pierre NKURUNZIZA (CNDD-FDD) 69.4%, Agathon RWASA

(Independents of Hope—Amizerio y'Abarundi) 19%, other 11.6%

Legislative branch: *description:* bicameral Parliament or Parlement consists of the Senate or Inama Nkenguzamateka (43 seats in the July 2015 election; 36 members indirectly elected by an electoral college of provincial councils using a three-round voting system, which requires a two-thirds majority vote in the first two rounds and a simple majority vote for the two leading candidates in the final round; 4 seats reserved for former heads of state, 3 seats reserved for Twas, and 30% of all votes reserved for women; members serve 5-year terms) and the National Assembly or Inama Nshingamateka (121 seats in the June 2015 election; 100 members directly elected in multi-seat constituencies by proportional representation vote and 21 co-opted members—3 seats reserved for Twas and 30% of total seats reserved for women; members serve 5-year terms)
elections: Senate—last held on 24 July 2015 (next to be held in 2019); National Assembly—last held on 29 June 2015 (next to be held in 2020)
election results: Senate—percent of vote by party—NA; seats by party—CNDD-FDD 33, FRODEBU 2, CNDD 1, former heads of state 4, Twas 3, women 8; National Assembly—percent of vote by party (provisional results)—CNDD-FDD 60.3%, Independents of Hope 11.2%, UPRONA 2.5%, other 26%; seats by party—CNDD-FDD 77, Independents of Hope 21, UPRONA 2, women 18, Twas 3

Judicial branch: *highest court(s):* Supreme Court (consists of 9 judges and organized into judicial, administrative, and cassation chambers); Constitutional Court (consists of 7 members)
judge selection and term of office: Supreme Court judges nominated by the Judicial Service Commission, a 15-member independent body of judicial and legal profession officials), appointed by the president and confirmed by the Senate; judge tenure NA; Constitutional Court judges appointed by the president and confirmed by the Senate and serve 6-year nonrenewable terms
subordinate courts: Courts of Appeal; County Courts; Courts of Residence; Martial Court; Court Against Corruption; Commercial Court; Commerce Court

Political parties and leaders: Front for Democracy in Burundi or FRODEBU [Keffa NIBIZI]
Independents of Hope (Amizero y'Abarundi) [Agathon RWASA and Charles NDITIJE]
Movement for Solidarity and Development or MSD [Alexis SINDUHIJE]
National Council for the Defense of Democracy—Front for the Defense of Democracy or CNDD-FDD [Evariste NDAYISHIMIYE]
National Liberation Forces or FNL [Jacques BIGITIMANA]
Union for National Progress (Union pour le Progress Nationale) or UPRONA [Abel GASHATSI]

Political pressure groups and leaders: Forum for the Strengthening of Civil Society or FORSC (civil society umbrella organization) [Vital NSHIMIRIMANA]

International organization participation: ACP, AfDB, AU, CEMAC, CEPGL, CICA, COMESA, EAC, FAO, G-77, IBRD, ICAO, ICCt, ICRM,

IDA, IFAD, IFC, IFRC3, ILO, IMF, Interpol, IOC, IOM, IPU, ISO (correspondent), ITU, ITUC (NGOs), MIGA, NAM, OIF, OPCW, UN, UNAMID, UNCTAD, UNESCO, UNIDO, UNISFA, UNWTO, UPU, WCO, WHO, WIPO, WMO, WTO

Diplomatic representation in the US: *chief of mission:* Ambassador (vacant); Charge D'Affaires Benjamin MANIRAKIZA (since 7 December 2017)
chancery: 2233 Wisconsin Avenue NW, Suite 408, Washington, DC 20007
telephone: [1] (202) 342-2574
FAX: [1] (202) 342-2578

Diplomatic representation from the US: *chief of mission:* Ambassador Anne S. CASPER (since 20 October 2016)
embassy: Avenue Des Etats-Unis, Bujumbura
mailing address: B.P. 1720, Bujumbura
telephone: [257] 22-207-000
FAX: [257] 22-222-926

Flag description: divided by a white diagonal cross into red panels (top and bottom) and green panels (hoist side and fly side) with a white disk superimposed at the center bearing three red six-pointed stars outlined in green arranged in a triangular design (one star above, two stars below); green symbolizes hope and optimism, white purity and peace, and red the blood shed in the struggle for independence; the three stars in the disk represent the three major ethnic groups: Hutu, Twa, Tutsi, as well as the three elements in the national motto: unity, work, progress

National symbol(s): lion; national colors: red, white, green

National anthem: *name:* "Burundi Bwacu" (Our Beloved Burundi)
lyrics/music: Jean-Baptiste NTAHOKAJA/Marc BARENGAYABO
note: adopted 1962

ECONOMY

Economy—overview: Burundi is a landlocked, resource-poor country with an underdeveloped manufacturing sector. Agriculture accounts for over 40% of GDP and employs more than 90% of the population. Burundi's primary exports are coffee and tea, which account for more than 60% of foreign exchange earnings. Thus, Burundi's export earnings—and its ability to pay for imports—rest primarily on favorable weather conditions and international coffee and tea prices, although exports are a relatively small share of GDP. Burundi is heavily dependent on aid from bilateral and multilateral donors. Foreign aid represented 48% of Burundi's national income in 2015, one of the highest percentages in Sub-Saharan Africa, but decreased to 33.5% in 2016. Burundi joined the East African Community (EAC) in 2009.

The 1993-2005 civil war resulted in more than 200,000 deaths, forced more than 48,000 refugees into Tanzania, and displaced 140,000 others internally. Political stability, aid flows, and economic activity improved following the war's end, but underlying weaknesses—low governmental capacity, a high poverty rate, poor educational levels, a weak legal system, a poor transportation network, and overburdened utilities—have prevented the

implementation of planned economic reforms. Government corruption has also hindered the development of a private sector. The purchasing power of most Burundians has decreased as wage increases have not kept pace with inflation.

In 2015, Burundi's economy suffered from political turmoil, including street protests and an attempted coup, following President NKURUN-ZIZA's controversial announcement that he would run for a third term. Insecurity and refugee flows to neighboring countries slowed down economic activity and donors withdrew aid, increasing Burundi's budget deficit and decreasing hard currency reserves. Real GDP growth dropped precipitously and has yet to recover to pre-conflict levels.

GDP (purchasing power parity): $7.985 billion (2017 est.)
$7.985 billion (2016 est.)
$8.069 billion (2015 est.)
note: data are in 2017 dollars
country comparison to the world: 164

GDP (official exchange rate): $3.393 billion (2016 est.)

GDP—real growth rate: 0% (2017 est.)
-1% (2016 est.)
-4% (2015 est.)
country comparison to the world: 203

GDP—per capita (PPP): $800 (2017 est.)
$800 (2016 est.)
$900 (2015 est.)
note: data are in 2017 dollars
country comparison to the world: 228

Gross national saving: -5.4% of GDP (2017 est.)
-4.1% of GDP (2016 est.)
-6.7% of GDP (2015 est.)
country comparison to the world: 181

GDP—composition, by end use:
household consumption: 80.5%
government consumption: 21.3%
investment in fixed capital: 15.6%
investment in inventories: 0%
exports of goods and services: 5.5%
imports of goods and services: -22.9% (2017 est.)

GDP—composition, by sector of origin:
agriculture: 40%
industry: 16%
services: 44.1% (2017 est.)

Agriculture—products: coffee, cotton, tea, corn, beans, sorghum, sweet potatoes, bananas, cassava (manioc, tapioca); beef, milk, hides

Industries: light consumer goods (sugar, shoes, soap, beer); cement, assembly of imported components; public works construction; food processing (fruits)

Industrial production growth rate: -5% (2017 est.)
country comparison to the world: 198

Labor force: 5.012 million (2017 est.)
country comparison to the world: 84

Labor force—by occupation: *agriculture:* 93.6%
industry: 2.3%
services: 4.1% (2002 est.)

Unemployment rate: NA%

Population below poverty line: 64.6% (2014 est.)

Household income or consumption by percentage share: *lowest 10%:* 4.1%
highest 10%: 28% (2006)

Distribution of family income—Gini index: 42.4 (1998)
country comparison to the world: 50

Budget: *revenues:* $607.6 million
expenditures: $748.9 million (2017 est.)
Taxes and other revenues: 17.9% of GDP (2017 est.)
country comparison to the world: 169

Budget surplus (+) or deficit (-): -4.2% of GDP (2017 est.)
country comparison to the world: 145

Public debt: 40.9% of GDP (2017 est.)
43.4% of GDP (2016 est.)
country comparison to the world: 135

Fiscal year: calendar year

Inflation rate (consumer prices): 18% (2017 est.)
5.5% (2016 est.)
country comparison to the world: 216

Central bank discount rate: 11.25% (31 December 2010)
10% (31 December 2009)
country comparison to the world: 17

Commercial bank prime lending rate: 15.9% (31 December 2017 est.)
14.24% (31 December 2016 est.)
country comparison to the world: 35

Stock of narrow money: $498.1 million (31 December 2017 est.)
$456.3 million (31 December 2016 est.)
country comparison to the world: 169

Stock of broad money: $663.4 million (31 December 2017 est.)
$612.8 million (31 December 2016 est.)
country comparison to the world: 181

Stock of domestic credit: $1.05 billion (31 December 2017 est.)
$955.1 million (31 December 2016 est.)
country comparison to the world: 167

Market value of publicly traded shares: $NA

Current account balance: -$422 million (2017 est.)
-$411 million (2016 est.)
country comparison to the world: 101

Exports: $100.3 million (2017 est.)
$109.7 million (2016 est.)
country comparison to the world: 196

Exports—commodities: coffee, tea, sugar, cotton, hides

Exports—partners: Democratic Republic of the Congo 30.6%, UAE 15.7%, Kenya 14.5%, Rwanda 7.2% (2016)

Imports: $442.1 million (2017 est.)
$509.4 million (2016 est.)
country comparison to the world: 189

Imports—commodities: capital goods, petroleum products, foodstuffs

Imports—partners: China 13.3%, India 13%, Tanzania 8.6%, Saudi Arabia 7.9%, Kenya 7.5%, UAE 5.2%, Uganda 5% (2016)

Reserves of foreign exchange and gold: $79.3 million (31 December 2017 est.)
$95.17 million (31 December 2016 est.)
country comparison to the world: 167

Debt—external: $619.8 million (31 December 2017 est.)

$622.4 million (31 December 2016 est.)
country comparison to the world: 175

Exchange rates: Burundi francs (BIF) per US dollar—
1,731 (2017 est.)
1,654.63 (2016 est.)
1,654.63 (2015 est.)
1,571.9 (2014 est.)
1,546.7 (2013 est.)

ENERGY

Electricity access: *population without electricity:* 9,700,000
electrification—*total population:* 5%
electrification—urban areas: 28%
electrification—rural areas: 2% (2013)

Electricity—production: 230 million kWh (2015 est.)
country comparison to the world: 185

Electricity—consumption: 303.9 million kWh (2015 est.)
country comparison to the world: 184

Electricity—exports: 0 kWh (2016 est.)
country comparison to the world: 114

Electricity—imports: 90 million kWh (2015 est.)
country comparison to the world: 98

Electricity—installed generating capacity: 68,000 kW (2015 est.)
country comparison to the world: 187

Electricity—from fossil fuels: 13.2% of total installed capacity (2015 est.)
country comparison to the world: 200

Electricity—from nuclear fuels: 0% of total installed capacity (2015 est.)
country comparison to the world: 60

Electricity—from hydroelectric plants: 83.8% of total installed capacity (2015 est.)
country comparison to the world: 13

Electricity—from other renewable sources: 4.4% of total installed capacity (2015 est.)
country comparison to the world: 102

Crude oil—production: 0 bbl/day (2016 est.)
country comparison to the world: 117

Crude oil—exports: 0 bbl/day (2014 est.)
country comparison to the world: 102

Crude oil—imports: 0 bbl/day (2014 est.)
country comparison to the world: 104

Crude oil—proved reserves: 0 bbl (1 January 2017 es)
country comparison to the world: 116

Refined petroleum products—production: 0 bbl/day (2014 est.)
country comparison to the world: 125

Refined petroleum products—consumption: 1,500 bbl/day (2015 est.)
country comparison to the world: 200

Refined petroleum products—exports: 0 bbl/day (2014 est.)
country comparison to the world: 138

Refined petroleum products—imports: 1,636 bbl/day (2014 est.)
country comparison to the world: 192

Natural gas—production: 0 cu m (2013 est.)
country comparison to the world: 115

Natural gas—consumption: 0 cu m (2013 est.)
country comparison to the world: 163

Natural gas—exports: 0 cu m (2013 est.)
country comparison to the world: 77

Natural gas—imports: 0 cu m (2013 est.)
country comparison to the world: 100

Natural gas—proved reserves: 0 cu m (1 January 2014 es)
country comparison to the world: 121

Carbon dioxide emissions from consumption of energy: 300,000 Mt (2013 est.)
country comparison to the world: 192

COMMUNICATIONS

Telephones—fixed lines: *total subscriptions:* 19,540
subscriptions per 100 inhabitants: less than 1 (July 2016 est.)
country comparison to the world: 182

Telephones—mobile cellular: *total:* 5,357,816
subscriptions per 100 inhabitants: 48 (July 2016 est.)
country comparison to the world: 138

Telephone system: *general assessment:* sparse system of open-wire, radiotelephone communications, and low-capacity microwave radio relays
domestic: telephone density one of the lowest in the world; fixed-line connections stand at well less than 1 per 100 persons; mobile-cellular usage is approaching 50 per 100 persons
international: country code—257; satellite earth station—1 Intelsat (Indian Ocean) (2016)

Broadcast media: state-controlled Radio Television Nationale de Burundi (RTNB) operates a TV station and a national radio network; 3 private TV stations and about 10 privately owned radio stations; transmissions of several international broadcasters are available in Bujumbura (2017)

Internet country code: .bi

Internet users: *total:* 574,236
percent of population: 5.2% (July 2016 est.)
country comparison to the world: 165

TRANSPORTATION

Civil aircraft registration country code prefix: 9U (2016)

Airports: 7 (2013)
country comparison to the world: 165

Airports—with paved runways: *total:* 1
over 3,047 m: 1 (2017)

Airports—with unpaved runways: *total:* 6
914 to 1,523 m: 4
under 914 m: 2 (2013)

Heliports: 1 (2012)

Roadways: *total:* 12,322 km
paved: 1,500 km
unpaved: 10,822 km (2016)
country comparison to the world: 128

Waterways: (mainly on Lake Tanganyika between Bujumbura, Burundi's principal port, and lake ports in Tanzania, Zambia, and the Democratic Republic of the Congo) (2011)

Ports and terminals: *lake port(s):* Bujumbura (Lake Tanganyika)

MILITARY AND SECURITY

Military expenditures: 2.21% of GDP (2016)
2.14% of GDP (2015)
2.01% of GDP (2014)
2.24% of GDP (2013)
2.39% of GDP (2012)
country comparison to the world: 32

Military branches: National Defense Forces (Forces de Defense Nationale, FDN): Army (includes maritime wing, Air Wing), National Police (2017)

Military service age and obligation: 18 years of age for voluntary military service; the armed forces law of 31 December 2004 did not specify a minimum age for enlistment, but the government claimed that no one younger than 18 was being recruited; mandatory retirement ages: 45 (enlisted), 50 (NCOs), 55 (officers), and 60 (officers with the rank of general) (2017)

TRANSNATIONAL ISSUES

Disputes—international: Burundi and Rwanda dispute two sq km (0.8 sq mi) of Sabanerwa, a farmed area in the Rukurazi Valley where the Akanyaru/Kanyaru River shifted its course southward after heavy rains in 1965; cross-border conflicts persist among Tutsi, Hutu, other ethnic groups, associated political rebels, armed gangs, and various government forces in the Great Lakes region

Refugees and internally displaced persons: *refugees (country of origin):* 61,427 (Democratic Republic of the Congo) (2017)
IDPs: 175,936 (some ethnic Tutsis remain displaced from intercommunal violence that broke out after the 1993 coup and fighting between government forces and rebel groups; violence since April 2015) (2018)
stateless persons: 974 (2016)

Trafficking in persons: current situation: Burundi is a source country for children and possibly women subjected to forced labor and sex trafficking; business people recruit Burundian girls for prostitution domestically, as well as in Rwanda, Kenya, Uganda, and the Middle East, and recruit boys and girls for forced labor in Burundi and Tanzania; children and young adults are coerced into forced labor in farming, mining, informal commerce, fishing, or collecting river stones for construction; sometimes family, friends, and neighbors are complicit in exploiting children, at times luring them in with offers of educational or job opportunities

tier rating: Tier 3—Burundi does not comply fully with the minimum standards for the elimination of human trafficking and is not making significant efforts to do so; corruption, a lack of political will, and limited resources continue to hamper efforts to combat human trafficking; in 2014, the government did not inform judicial and law enforcement officials of the enactment of an anti-trafficking law or how to implement it and approved—but did not fund—its national anti-trafficking action plan; authorities again failed to identify trafficking victims or to provide them with adequate protective services; the government has focused on transnational child trafficking but gave little attention to its domestic child trafficking problem and adult trafficking victims (2015)

CABO VERDE

INTRODUCTION

Background: The uninhabited islands were discovered and colonized by the Portuguese in the 15th century; Cabo Verde subsequently became a trading center for African slaves and later an important coaling and resupply stop for whaling and transatlantic shipping. The fusing of European and various African cultural traditions is reflected in Cabo Verde's Crioulo language, music, and pano textiles. Following independence in 1975, and a tentative interest in unification with Guinea-Bissau, a one-party system was established and maintained until multi-party elections were held in 1990. Cabo Verde continues to sustain one of Africa's most stable democratic governments. Repeated droughts during the second half of the 20th century caused significant hardship and prompted heavy emigration. As a result, Cabo Verde's expatriate population is greater than its domestic one. Most Cabo Verdeans have both African and Portuguese antecedents. Cabo Verde's population descends from its first permanent inhabitants in the late 15th-century–a preponderance of West African slaves, a small share of Portuguese colonists, and even fewer Italians, Spaniards, and Portuguese Jews. Among the nine inhabited islands, population distribution is variable. Islands in the east are very dry and are only sparsely settled to exploit their extensive salt deposits. The more southerly islands receive more precipitation and support larger populations, but agriculture and livestock grazing have damaged their soil fertility and vegetation. For centuries, the country's overall population size has fluctuated significantly, as recurring periods of famine and epidemics have caused high death tolls and emigration.

GEOGRAPHY

Location: Western Africa, group of islands in the North Atlantic Ocean, west of Senegal

Geographic coordinates: 16 00 N, 24 00 W

Map references: Africa

Area: *total:* 4,033 sq km

land: 4,033 sq km

water: 0 sq km

country comparison to the world: 176

Area—comparative: slightly larger than Rhode Island

Land boundaries: 0 km

Coastline: 965 km

Maritime claims: measured from claimed archipelagic baselines

territorial sea: 12 nm

contiguous zone: 24 nm

exclusive economic zone: 200 nm

Climate: temperate; warm, dry summer; precipitation meager and erratic

Terrain: steep, rugged, rocky, volcanic

Elevation: *mean elevation:* NA

elevation extremes: lowest point: Atlantic Ocean 0 m

highest point: Mt. Fogo 2,829 m (a volcano on Fogo Island)

Natural resources: salt, basalt rock, limestone, kaolin, fish, clay, gypsum

Land use: *agricultural land:* 18.6%

arable land: 11.7%;

permanent crops: 0.7%;

permanent pasture: 6.2%

forest: 21%

other: 60.4% (2011 est.)

Irrigated land: 35 sq km (2012)

Population—distribution: among the nine inhabited islands, population distribution is variable; islands in the east are very dry and are only sparsely settled to exploit their extensive salt deposits; the more southerly islands receive more precipitation and support larger populations, but agriculture and livestock grazing have damaged the soil fertility and vegetation; approximately half of the population lives on Sao Tiago Island, which is the location of the capital of Praia; Mindelo, on the northern island of Sao Vicente, also has a large urban population

Natural hazards: prolonged droughts; seasonal harmattan wind produces obscuring dust; volcanically and seismically active

volcanism: Fogo (2,829 m), which last erupted in 1995, is Cabo Verde's only active volcano

Environment—current issues: soil erosion; deforestation due to demand for firewood; water shortages; desertification; environmental damage has threatened several species of birds and reptiles; illegal beach sand extraction; overfishing

Environment—international agreements: *party to:* Biodiversity, Climate Change, Climate Change-Kyoto Protocol, Desertification, Endangered Species, Environmental Modification, Hazardous Wastes, Law of the Sea, Marine Dumping, Ozone Layer Protection, Ship Pollution, Wetlands

signed, but not ratified: none of the selected agreements

Geography—note: strategic location 500 km from west coast of Africa near major north-south sea routes; important communications station; important sea and air refueling site

PEOPLE AND SOCIETY

Population: 560,899 (July 2017 est.)

country comparison to the world: 173

Nationality: *noun:* Cabo Verdean(s)

adjective: Cabo Verdean

Ethnic groups: Creole (mulatto) 71%, African 28%, European 1%

Languages: Portuguese (official), Crioulo (a blend of Portuguese and West African words)

Religions: Roman Catholic 77.3%, Protestant 4.6% (includes Church of the Nazarene 1.7%, Adventist 1.5%, Assembly of God 0.9%, Universal Kingdom of God 0.4%, and God and Love 0.1%), other Christian 3.4% (includes Christian Rationalism 1.9%, Jehovah's Witness 1%, and New Apostolic 0.5%), Muslim 1.8%, other 1.3%, none 10.8%, unspecified 0.7% (2010 est.)

Demographic profile: Cabo Verde's population descends from its first permanent inhabitants in the late 15th-century–a preponderance of West African slaves, a small share of Portuguese colonists, and even fewer Italians, Spaniards, and Portuguese Jews. Over the centuries, the country's overall population size has fluctuated significantly, as recurring periods of famine and epidemics have caused high death tolls and emigration.

Labor migration historically reduced Cabo Verde's population growth and still provides a key source of income through remittances. Expatriates probably outnumber Cabo Verde's resident population, with most families having a member abroad. Cabo Verdeans have settled in the US, Europe, Africa, and South America. The largest diaspora community in New Bedford, Massachusetts, dating to the early 1800s, is a byproduct of the transatlantic whaling industry. Cabo Verdean men fleeing poverty at home joined the crews of US whaling ships that stopped in the islands. Many settled in New Bedford and stayed in the whaling or shipping trade, worked in the textile or cranberry industries, or operated their own transatlantic packet ships that transported compatriots to the US. Increased Cabo Verdean emigration to the US coincided with the gradual and eventually complete abolition of slavery in the archipelago in 1878.

During the same period, Portuguese authorities coerced Cabo Verdeans to go to Sao Tome and Principe and other Portuguese colonies in Africa to work as indentured laborers on plantations. In the 1920s, when the US implemented immigration quotas, Cabo Verdean emigration shifted toward Portugal, West Africa (Senegal), and South America (Argentina). Growing numbers of Cabo Verdean labor migrants headed to Western Europe in the 1960s and 1970s. They filled unskilled jobs in Portugal, as many Portuguese sought out work opportunities in the more prosperous economies of northwest Europe. Cabo Verdeans eventually expanded their emigration to the Netherlands, where they worked in the shipping industry. Migration to the US resumed under relaxed migration laws. Cabo Verdean women also began migrating to southern Europe to become domestic workers, a trend that continues today and has shifted the gender balance of Cabo Verdean emigration.

Emigration has declined in more recent decades due to the adoption of more restrictive migration policies in destination countries. Reduced emigration along with a large youth population, decreased mortality rates, and increased life expectancies, has boosted population growth, putting further pressure on domestic employment and resources. In addition, Cabo Verde has attracted increasing numbers of migrants in recent decades, consisting primarily of people from West Africa, Portuguese-speaking African countries, Portugal, and China. Since the 1990s, some West African migrants have used Cabo Verde as a stepping stone for illegal migration to Europe.

Age structure: 0-14 years: 29.13% (male 82,157/ female 81,227)
15-24 years: 20.11% (male 56,401/female 56,391)
25-54 years: 39.64% (male 108,081/female 114,234)
55-64 years: 5.94% (male 14,547/female 18,761)
65 years and over: 5.19% (male 11,012/female 18,088) (2017 est.)

Dependency ratios: total dependency ratio: 55.4
youth dependency ratio: 48.4
elderly dependency ratio: 6.9
potential support ratio: 14.4 (2015 est.)

Median age: total: 25.4 years
male: 24.6 years
female: 26.2 years (2017 est.)
country comparison to the world: 155

Population growth rate: 1.33% (2017 est.)
country comparison to the world: 84

Birth rate: 20 births/1,000 population (2017 est.)
country comparison to the world: 79

Death rate: 6 deaths/1,000 population (2017 est.)
country comparison to the world: 163

Net migration rate: -0.6 migrant(s)/1,000 population (2017 est.)
country comparison to the world: 128

Population distribution: among the nine inhabited islands, population distribution is variable; islands in the east are very dry and are only sparsely settled to exploit their extensive salt deposits; the more southerly islands receive more precipitation and support larger populations, but agriculture and livestock grazing have damaged the soil fertility and vegetation; approximately half of the population lives on Sao Tiago Island, which is the location of the capital of Praia; Mindelo, on the northern island of Sao Vicente, also has a large urban population

Urbanization: urban population: 66.8% of total population (2017)

rate of urbanization: 1.8% annual rate of change (2015-20 est.)

Major urban areas—population: PRAIA (capital) 145,000 (2014)

Sex ratio: at birth: 1.03 male(s)/female
0-14 years: 1.01 male(s)/female
15-24 years: 1 male(s)/female
25-54 years: 0.94 male(s)/female
55-64 years: 0.75 male(s)/female
65 years and over: 0.61 male(s)/female
total population: 0.94 male(s)/female (2016 est.)

Maternal mortality ratio: 42 deaths/100,000 live births (2015 est.)
country comparison to the world: 103

Infant mortality rate: total: 21.9 deaths/1,000 live births
male: 25.1 deaths/1,000 live births
female: 18.6 deaths/1,000 live births (2017 est.)
country comparison to the world: 75

Life expectancy at birth: total population: 72.4 years
male: 70.1 years
female: 74.8 years (2017 est.)
country comparison to the world: 149

Total fertility rate: 2.24 children born/woman (2017 est.)
country comparison to the world: 96

Health expenditures: 4.8% of GDP (2014)
country comparison to the world: 147

Physicians density: 0.31 physicians/1,000 population (2011)

Hospital bed density: 2.1 beds/1,000 population (2010)

Drinking water source:
improved:
urban: 94% of population
rural: 87.3% of population
total: 91.7% of population
unimproved:
urban: 6% of population
rural: 12.7% of population
total: 8.3% of population (2015 est.)

Sanitation facility access:
improved:
urban: 81.6% of population
rural: 54.3% of population
total: 72.2% of population
unimproved:
urban: 1.4% of population
rural: 45.7% of population
total: 27.8% of population (2015 est.)

HIV/AIDS—adult prevalence rate: 0.8% (2016 est.)
country comparison to the world: 48

HIV/AIDS—people living with HIV/AIDS: 2,800 (2016 est.)
country comparison to the world: 114

HIV/AIDS—deaths: <100 (2016 est.)

Major infectious diseases: note: active local transmission of Zika virus by Aedes species mosquitoes has been identified in this country (as of August 2016); it poses an important risk (a large number

of cases possible) among US citizens if bitten by an infective mosquito; other less common ways to get Zika are through sex, via blood transfusion, or during pregnancy, in which the pregnant woman passes Zika virus to her fetus (2016)

Obesity—adult prevalence rate: 11.8% (2016)
country comparison to the world: 134

Education expenditures: 5% of GDP (2013)
country comparison to the world: 76

Literacy: definition: age 15 and over can read and write
total population: 86.8%
male: 91.7%
female: 82% (2015 est.)

School life expectancy (primary to tertiary education): total: 13 years
male: 13 years
female: 13 years (2015)

GOVERNMENT

Country name: conventional long form: Republic of Cabo Verde
conventional short form: Cabo Verde
local long form: Republica de Cabo Verde
local short form: Cabo Verde
etymology: the name derives from Cap-Vert (Green Cape) on the Senegalese coast, the westernmost point of Africa and the nearest mainland to the islands

Government type: parliamentary republic

Capital: name: Praia
geographic coordinates: 14 55 N, 23 31 W
time difference: UTC-1 (4 hours ahead of Washington, DC, during Standard Time)

Administrative divisions: 22 municipalities (concelhos, singular—concelho); Boa Vista, Brava, Maio, Mosteiros, Paul, Porto Novo, Praia, Ribeira Brava, Ribeira Grande, Ribeira Grande de Santiago, Sal, Santa Catarina, Santa Catarina do Fogo, Santa Cruz, Sao Domingos, Sao Filipe, Sao Lourenco dos Orgaos, Sao Miguel, Sao Salvador do Mundo, Sao Vicente, Tarrafal, Tarrafal de Sao Nicolau

Independence: 5 July 1975 (from Portugal)

National holiday: Independence Day, 5 July (1975)

Constitution: history: previous 1981; latest effective 25 September 1992
amendments: proposals require support of at least four-fifths of the active National Assembly membership; amendment drafts require sponsorship of at least one-third of the active Assembly membership; passage requires at least two-thirds majority vote by the Assembly membership; constitutional sections including those on national independence, form of government, political pluralism, suffrage, and human rights and liberties cannot be amended; revised 1995, 1999, 2010 (2017)

Legal system: civil law system of Portugal

International law organization participation: has not submitted an ICJ jurisdiction declaration; accepts ICCt jurisdiction

Citizenship: citizenship by birth: no

citizenship by descent only: at least one parent must be a citizen of Cabo Verde

dual citizenship recognized: yes

residency requirement for naturalization: 5 years

Suffrage: 18 years of age; universal

Executive branch: *chief of state:* President Jorge Carlos FONSECA (since 9 September 2011)

head of government: Prime Minister Ulisses CORREIA E. SILVA (since 22 April 2016)

cabinet: Council of Ministers appointed by the president on the recommendation of the prime minister

elections/appointments: president directly elected by absolute majority popular vote in 2 rounds if needed for a 5-year term (eligible for a second term); election last held on 2 October 2016 (next to be held in 2021); prime minister nominated by the National Assembly and appointed by the president

election results: Jorge Carlos FONSECA reelected president; percent of vote—Jorge Carlos FONSECA (MPD) 74%, Albertino GRACA (independent) 23%, other 3%

Legislative branch: *description:* unicameral National Assembly or Assembleia Nacional (72 seats; members directly elected in multi-seat constituencies by proportional representation vote; members serve 5-year terms)

elections: last held on 20 March 2016 (next to be held in 2021)

election results: percent of vote by party MPD 54.5%, PAICV 38.2%, UCID 6.96%, Other 0.4%; seats by party—MPD 40, PAICV 29, UCID 3

Judicial branch: *highest court(s):* Supreme Court of Justice (consists of the chief justice and at least 7 judges and organized into civil, criminal, and administrative sections)

judge selection and term of office: judge appointments—1 by the president of the republic, 1 elected by the National Assembly, and 3 by the Superior Judicial Council (SJC), a 16-member independent body chaired by the chief justice and includes the attorney general, 8 private citizens, 2 judges, 2 prosecutors, the senior legal inspector of the Attorney General's office, and a representative of the Ministry of Justice; chief justice appointed by the president of the republic from among peers of the Supreme Court of Justice and in consultation with the SJC; judges appointed for life

subordinate courts: appeals courts, first instance (municipal) courts; audit, military, and fiscal and customs courts

Political parties and leaders: African Party for Independence of Cabo Verde or PAICV [Janira Hopffer ALMADA]

Democratic and Independent Cabo Verdean Union or UCID [Antonio MONTEIRO]

Democratic Christian Party or PDC [Manuel RODRIGUES]

Democratic Renovation Party or PRD [Victor FIDALGO]

Movement for Democracy or MPD [Ulisses CORREIA E SILVA]

Party for Democratic Convergence or PCD [Dr. Eurico MONTEIRO]

Party of Work and Solidarity or PTS [Anibal MEDINA]

Social Democratic Party or PSD [Joao ALEM]

Political pressure groups and leaders: *other:* environmentalists; political pressure groups

International organization participation: ACP, AfDB, AOSIS, AU, CD, CPLP, ECOWAS, FAO, G-77, IAEA, IBRD, ICAO, ICCt (signatory), ICRM, IDA, IFAD, IFC, IFRCS, ILO, IMF, IMO, Interpol, IOC, IOM, IPU, ITSO, ITU, ITUC (NGOs), MIGA, NAM, OIF, OPCW, UN, UNCTAD, UNESCO, UNIDO, Union Latina, UNWTO, UPU, WCO, WHO, WIPO, WMO, WTO

Diplomatic representation in the US: *chief of mission:* Ambassador Carlos VEIGA (since 18 January 2017)

chancery: 3415 Massachusetts Avenue NW, Washington, DC 20007

telephone: [1] (202) 965-6820

FAX: [1] (202) 965-1207

consulate(s) general: Boston

Diplomatic representation from the US: *chief of mission:* Ambassador Donald L. HEFLIN (since 5 February 2015)

embassy: Rua Abilio Macedo 6, Praia

mailing address: C. P. 201, Praia

telephone: [238] 2-60-89-00

FAX: [238] 2-61-13-55

Flag description: five unequal horizontal bands; the top-most band of blue—equal to one half the width of the flag—is followed by three bands of white, red, and white, each equal to 1/12 of the width, and a bottom stripe of blue equal to one quarter of the flag width; a circle of 10 yellow, five-pointed stars is centered on the red stripe and positioned 3/8 of the length of the flag from the hoist side; blue stands for the sea and the sky, the circle of stars represents the 10 major islands united into a nation, the stripes symbolize the road to formation of the country through peace (white) and effort (red)

National symbol(s): ten, five-pointed, yellow stars; national colors: blue, white, red, yellow

National anthem: *name:* "Cantico da Liberdade" (Song of Freedom)

lyrics/music: Amilcar Spencer LOPES/Adalberto Higino Tavares SILVA

note: adopted 1996

ECONOMY

Economy—overview: Cabo Verde's economy is vulnerable to external shocks and depends on development aid, foreign investment, remittances, and tourism. The economy is service-oriented with commerce, transport, tourism, and public services accounting for about three-fourths of GDP. Tourism is the mainstay of the economy and depends on conditions in the euro-zone countries. Cabo Verde annually runs a high trade deficit financed by foreign aid and remittances from its large pool of emigrants; remittances as a share of GDP are one of the highest in Sub-Saharan Africa.

Although about 40% of the population lives in rural areas, the share of food production in GDP is low. The island economy suffers from a poor natural resource base, including serious water shortages, exacerbated by cycles of long-term drought, and poor soil for growing food on several of the islands, requiring it to import most of what it consumes. The fishing potential, mostly lobster and tuna, is not fully exploited.

Economic reforms are aimed at developing the private sector and attracting foreign investment to diversify the economy and mitigate high unemployment. The government's elevated debt levels have limited its capacity to finance any shortfalls.

GDP (purchasing power parity): $3.734 billion (2017 est.)

$3.591 billion (2016 est.)

$3.459 billion (2015 est.)

note: data are in 2017 dollars

country comparison to the world: 181

GDP (official exchange rate): $1.728 billion (2016 est.)

GDP—real growth rate: 4% (2017 est.)

3.8% (2016 est.)

1% (2015 est.)

country comparison to the world: 70

GDP—per capita (PPP): $6,900 (2017 est.)

$6,800 (2016 est.)

$6,600 (2015 est.)

note: data are in 2017 dollars

country comparison to the world: 160

Gross national saving: 33.8% of GDP (2017 est.)

33.3% of GDP (2016 est.)

33.8% of GDP (2015 est.)

country comparison to the world: 17

GDP—composition, by end use:

household consumption: 53.9%

government consumption: 17.1%

investment in fixed capital: 34.5%

investment in inventories: 2%

exports of goods and services: 45.1%

imports of goods and services: -52.6% (2017 est.)

GDP—composition, by sector of origin:

agriculture: 7.9%

industry: 17.9%

services: 74.2% (2017 est.)

Agriculture—products: bananas, corn, beans, sweet potatoes, sugarcane, coffee, peanuts; fish

Industries: food and beverages, fish processing, shoes and garments, salt mining, ship repair

Industrial production growth rate: 1.7% (2017 est.)

country comparison to the world: 146

Labor force: 196,100 (2007 est.)

country comparison to the world: 174

Unemployment rate: 9% (2017 est.)

9% (2016 est.)

country comparison to the world: 122

Population below poverty line: 30% (2000 est.)

Household income or consumption by percentage share: *lowest 10%:* 1.9%

highest 10%: 40.6% (2001)

Budget: *revenues:* $437.1 million
expenditures: $463.7 million (2017 est.)
Taxes and other revenues: 25.3% of GDP (2017 est.)
country comparison to the world: 110

Budget surplus (+) or deficit (-): -1.5% of GDP (2017 est.)
country comparison to the world: 68

Public debt: 127% of GDP (2017 est.)
123.9% of GDP (2016 est.)
country comparison to the world: 7

Fiscal year: calendar year

Inflation rate (consumer prices): 1% (2017 est.)
-1.4% (2016 est.)
country comparison to the world: 42

Central bank discount rate: 7.5% (31 December 2010)
7.5% (31 December 2009)
country comparison to the world: 43

Commercial bank prime lending rate: 10% (31 December 2017 est.)
9.61% (31 December 2016 est.)
country comparison to the world: 83

Stock of narrow money: $670.5 million (31 December 2017 est.)
$607.2 million (31 December 2016 est.)
country comparison to the world: 163

Stock of broad money: $1.743 billion (31 December 2017 est.)
$1.601 billion (31 December 2016 est.)
country comparison to the world: 162

Stock of domestic credit: $1.395 billion (31 December 2017 est.)
$1.327 billion (31 December 2016 est.)
country comparison to the world: 162

Current account balance: -$105 million (2017 est.)
-$61 million (2016 est.)
country comparison to the world: 81

Exports: $158.6 million (2017 est.)
$148.4 million (2016 est.)
country comparison to the world: 190

Exports—commodities: fuel (re-exports), shoes, garments, fish, hides

Exports—partners: Australia 48.6%, Spain 20.2%, Portugal 18.9% (2016)

Imports: $724.8 million (2017 est.)
$691 million (2016 est.)
country comparison to the world: 183

Imports—commodities: foodstuffs, industrial products, transport equipment, fuels

Imports—partners: Portugal 43%, Spain 12.8%, France 5.9%, China 5%, Russia 4.4% (2016)

Reserves of foreign exchange and gold: $589.1 million (31 December 2017 est.)
$572.7 million (31 December 2016 est.)
country comparison to the world: 138

Debt—external: $1.808 billion (31 December 2017 est.)
$1.688 billion (31 December 2016 est.)
country comparison to the world: 152

Exchange rates: Cabo Verdean escudos (CVE) per US dollar—
101.8 (2017 est.)
99.688 (2016 est.)
99.688 (2015 est.)
99.426 (2014 est.)
83.114 (2013 est.)

ENERGY

Electricity access: *population without electricity:* 153,027
electrification—total population: 70.6%
electrification—urban areas: 84.4%
electrification—rural areas: 46.8% (2012)

Electricity—production: 469 million kWh (2015 est.)
country comparison to the world: 169

Electricity—consumption: 436.2 million kWh (2015 est.)
country comparison to the world: 172

Electricity—exports: 0 kWh (2016 est.)
country comparison to the world: 126

Electricity—imports: 0 kWh (2016 est.)
country comparison to the world: 139

Electricity—installed generating capacity: 157,500 kW (2015 est.)
country comparison to the world: 168

Electricity—from fossil fuels: 76.8% of total installed capacity (2015 est.)
country comparison to the world: 93

Electricity—from nuclear fuels: 0% of total installed capacity (2015 est.)
country comparison to the world: 74

Electricity—from hydroelectric plants: 0% of total installed capacity (2015 est.)
country comparison to the world: 169

Electricity—from other renewable sources: 23.2% of total installed capacity (2015 est.)
country comparison to the world: 26

Crude oil—production: 0 bbl/day (2016 est.)
country comparison to the world: 118

Crude oil—exports: 0 bbl/day (2014 est.)
country comparison to the world: 111

Crude oil—imports: 0 bbl/day (2014 est.)
country comparison to the world: 114

Crude oil—proved reserves: 0 bbl (1 January 2017 es)
country comparison to the world: 117

Refined petroleum products—production: 0 bbl/day (2014 est.)
country comparison to the world: 126

Refined petroleum products—consumption: 6,000 bbl/day (2015 est.)
country comparison to the world: 173

Refined petroleum products—exports: 0 bbl/day (2014 est.)
country comparison to the world: 146

Refined petroleum products—imports: 5,328 bbl/day (2014 est.)
country comparison to the world: 164

Natural gas—production: 0 cu m (2016 est.)

country comparison to the world: 124

Natural gas—consumption: 0 cu m (2016 est.)
country comparison to the world: 172

Natural gas—exports: 0 cu m (2016 est.)
country comparison to the world: 90

Natural gas—imports: 0 cu m (2016 est.)
country comparison to the world: 114

Natural gas—proved reserves: 0 cu m (1 January 2016 es)
country comparison to the world: 130

Carbon dioxide emissions from consumption of energy: 400,000 Mt (2013 est.)
country comparison to the world: 188

COMMUNICATIONS

Telephones—fixed lines: *total subscriptions:* 59,730
subscriptions per 100 inhabitants: 11 (July 2016 est.)
country comparison to the world: 156

Telephones—mobile cellular: *total:* 625,851
subscriptions per 100 inhabitants: 113 (July 2016 est.)
country comparison to the world: 166

Telephone system: *general assessment:* effective system, extensive modernization from 1996-2000 following partial privatization in 1995
domestic: major service provider is Cabo Verde Telecom; fiber-optic ring, completed in 2001, links all islands providing Internet access and ISDN services; cellular service introduced in 1998; broadband services launched in 2004
international: country code—238; landing point for the Atlantis-2 fiber-optic transatlantic telephone cable that provides links to South America, Senegal, and Europe; HF radiotelephone to Senegal and Guinea-Bissau; satellite earth station—1 Intelsat (Atlantic Ocean) (2015)

Broadcast media: state-run TV and radio broadcast network plus a growing number of private broadcasters; Portuguese public TV and radio services for Africa are available; transmissions of a few international broadcasters are available (2007)

Internet country code: .cv
Internet users: total: 266,562

percent of population: 48.2% (July 2016 est.)
country comparison to the world: 153

TRANSPORTATION

National air transport system: *number of registered air carriers:* 2
inventory of registered aircraft operated by air carriers: 5
annual passenger traffic on registered air carriers: 567,182
annual freight traffic on registered air carriers: 1,728,152 mt-km (2015)
Civil aircraft registration country code prefix: D4 (2016)

Airports: 9 (2013)
country comparison to the world: 157

Airports—with paved runways: *total:* 9

over 3,047 m: 1
1,524 to 2,437 m: 3
914 to 1,523 m: 3
under 914 m: 2 (2017)

Roadways: total: 1,350 km
paved: 932 km
unpaved: 418 km (2013)
country comparison to the world: 180

Merchant marine: total: 42
by type: general cargo 19, oil tanker 2, other 21 (2017)

Ports and terminals: major seaport(s): Porto Grande

Military expenditures: 0.63% of GDP (2016)

0.57% of GDP (2015)
0.54% of GDP (2014)
0.53% of GDP (2013)
0.56% of GDP (2012)

Military branches: Armed Forces: Army (also called the National Guard, GN), Cabo Verde Coast Guard (Guardia Costeira de Cabo Verde, GCCV, includes naval infantry) (2013)

Military service age and obligation: 18-35 years of age for male and female selective compulsory military service; 2-years conscript service obligation; 17 years of age for voluntary service (with parental consent) (2013)

Disputes—international: none

Refugees and internally displaced persons: stateless persons: 115 (2016)

Illicit drugs: used as a transshipment point for Latin American cocaine destined for Western Europe, particularly because of Lusophone links to Brazil, Portugal, and Guinea-Bissau; has taken steps to deter drug money laundering, including a 2002 anti-money laundering reform that criminalizes laundering the proceeds of narcotics trafficking and other crimes and the establishment in 2008 of a Financial Intelligence Unit

CAMBODIA

Background: Most Cambodians consider themselves to be Khmers, descendants of the Angkor Empire that extended over much of Southeast Asia and reached its zenith between the 10th and 13th centuries. Attacks by the Thai and Cham (from present-day Vietnam) weakened the empire, ushering in a long period of decline. The king placed the country under French protection in 1863, and it became part of French Indochina in 1887. Following Japanese occupation in World War II, Cambodia gained full independence from France in 1953. In April 1975, after a seven-year struggle, communist Khmer Rouge forces captured Phnom Penh and evacuated all cities and towns. At least 1.5 million Cambodians died from execution, forced hardships, or starvation during the Khmer Rouge regime under POL POT. A December 1978 Vietnamese invasion drove the Khmer Rouge into the countryside, began a 10-year Vietnamese occupation, and touched off almost 13 years of civil war.

The 1991 Paris Peace Accords mandated democratic elections and a cease-fire, which was not fully respected by the Khmer Rouge. UN-sponsored elections in 1993 helped restore some semblance of normalcy under a coalition government. Factional fighting in 1997 ended the first coalition government, but a second round of national elections in 1998 led to the formation of another coalition government and renewed political stability. The remaining elements of the Khmer Rouge surrendered in early 1999. Some of the surviving Khmer Rouge leaders have been tried or are awaiting trial for crimes against humanity by a hybrid UN-Cambodian tribunal supported by international assistance. Elections in July 2003 were relatively peaceful, but it took one year of negotiations between contending political parties before a coalition government was formed. In October 2004, King Norodom SIHANOUK abdicated the throne and his son, Prince Norodom SIHAMONI, was selected to succeed him. The most recent local (Commune Council) elections were held in Cambodia in 2012, with little of the preelection violence that preceded prior elections. National elections in July 2013 were disputed, with the opposition—the Cambodian National Rescue Party (CNRP)—boycotting the National Assembly. The political impasse was ended nearly a year later, with the CNRP agreeing to enter parliament in exchange for ruling party commitments to electoral and legislative reforms. The CNRP made further gains in local commune elections in June 2017, accelerating sitting Prime Minister Hun SEN's efforts to marginalize the CNRP before national elections in 2018. Hun Sen arrested CNRP's President Kem Sokha in September 2017 and subsequently dissolved the CNRP in November 2017 and banned its leaders from participating in politics for at least five years. CNRP's seats in the National Assembly were redistributed to smaller, more pliant opposition parties.

Location: Southeastern Asia, bordering the Gulf of Thailand, between Thailand, Vietnam, and Laos

Geographic coordinates: 13 00 N, 105 00 E

Map references: Southeast Asia

Area: total: 181,035 sq km
land: 176,515 sq km
water: 4,520 sq km
country comparison to the world: 91

Area—comparative: one and a half times the size of Pennsylvania; slightly smaller than Oklahoma

Land boundaries: total: 2,530 km
border countries (3): Laos 555 km, Thailand 817 km, Vietnam 1,158 km

Coastline: 443 km

Maritime claims: territorial sea: 12 nm
contiguous zone: 24 nm
exclusive economic zone: 200 nm
continental shelf: 200 nm

Climate: tropical; rainy, monsoon season (May to November); dry season (December to April); little seasonal temperature variation

Terrain: mostly low, flat plains; mountains in southwest and north

Elevation: mean elevation: 126 m

elevation extremes: lowest point: Gulf of Thailand 0 m
highest point: Phnum Aoral 1,810 m

Natural resources: oil and gas, timber, gemstones, iron ore, manganese, phosphates, hydropower potential, arable land

Land use: agricultural land: 32.1%
arable land: 22.7%;
permanent crops: 0.9%;
permanent pasture: 8.5%
forest: 56.5%
other: 11.4% (2011 est.)
Irrigated land: 3,540 sq km (2012)

Population—distribution: population concentrated in the southeast, particularly in and around the capital of Phnom Penh; further distribution is linked closely to the Tonle Sap and Mekong Rivers

Natural hazards: monsoonal rains (June to November); flooding; occasional droughts

Environment—current issues: illegal logging activities throughout the country and strip mining for gems in the western region along the border with Thailand have resulted in habitat loss and declining biodiversity (in particular, destruction of mangrove swamps threatens natural fisheries); soil erosion; in rural areas, most of the population does not have access to potable water; declining fish stocks because of illegal fishing and overfishing

Environment—international agreements: *party to:* Biodiversity, Climate Change, Climate Change-Kyoto Protocol, Desertification, Endangered Species, Hazardous Wastes, Marine Life Conservation, Ozone Layer Protection, Ship Pollution, Tropical Timber 94, Wetlands, Whaling
signed, but not ratified: Law of the Sea

Geography—note: a land of paddies and forests dominated by the Mekong River and Tonle Sap (Southeast Asia's largest freshwater lake)

PEOPLE AND SOCIETY

Population: 16,204,486
note: estimates for this country take into account the effects of excess mortality due to AIDS; this can result in lower life expectancy, higher infant mortality, higher death rates, lower population growth rates, and changes in the distribution of population by age and sex than would otherwise be expected (July 2017 est.)
country comparison to the world: 68

Nationality: *noun:* Cambodian(s)
adjective: Cambodian

Ethnic groups: Khmer 97.6%, Cham 1.2%, Chinese 0.1%, Vietnamese 0.1%, other 0.9% (2013 est.)

Languages: Khmer (official) 96.3%, other 3.7% (2008 est.)

Religions: Buddhist (official) 96.9%, Muslim 1.9%, Christian 0.4%, other 0.8% (2008 est.)

Age structure: *0-14 years:* 31.01% (male 2,537,753/female 2,487,633)
15-24 years: 18.36% (male 1,471,965/female 1,503,977)
25-54 years: 40.68% (male 3,229,901/female 3,361,475)
55-64 years: 5.69% (male 374,663/female 547,971)
65 years and over: 4.25% (male 258,584/female 430,564) (2017 est.)

Dependency ratios: *total dependency ratio:* 55.6
youth dependency ratio: 49.2
elderly dependency ratio: 6.4
potential support ratio: 15.6 (2015 est.)

Median age: *total:* 25.3 years
male: 24.6 years
female: 26 years (2017 est.)
country comparison to the world: 156

Population growth rate: 1.52% (2017 est.)
country comparison to the world: 74

Birth rate: 23 births/1,000 population (2017 est.)
country comparison to the world: 67

Death rate: 7.5 deaths/1,000 population (2017 est.)
country comparison to the world: 109

Net migration rate: -0.3 migrant(s)/1,000 population (2017 est.)
country comparison to the world: 113

Population distribution: population concentrated in the southeast, particularly in and around the capital of Phnom Penh; further distribution is linked closely to the Tonle Sap and Mekong Rivers

Urbanization: *urban population:* 21.2% of total population (2017)
rate of urbanization: 2.73% annual rate of change (2015-20 est.)

Major urban areas—population: PHNOM PENH (capital) 1.731 million (2015)

Sex ratio: *at birth:* 1.05 male(s)/female
0-14 years: 1.02 male(s)/female
15-24 years: 0.98 male(s)/female
25-54 years: 0.96 male(s)/female
55-64 years: 0.65 male(s)/female
65 years and over: 0.6 male(s)/female
total population: 0.94 male(s)/female (2016 est.)

Mother's mean age at first birth: 22.9 years
note: median age at first birth among women 25-29 (2014 est.)

Maternal mortality ratio: 161 deaths/100,000 live births (2015 est.)
country comparison to the world: 57

Infant mortality rate: *total:* 47.4 deaths/1,000 live births
male: 53.8 deaths/1,000 live births
female: 40.7 deaths/1,000 live births (2017 est.)
country comparison to the world: 35

Life expectancy at birth: *total population:* 64.9 years
male: 62.4 years
female: 67.5 years (2017 est.)
country comparison to the world: 181

Total fertility rate: 2.52 children born/woman (2017 est.)
country comparison to the world: 78

Contraceptive prevalence rate: 56.3% (2014)

Health expenditures: 5.7% of GDP (2014)
country comparison to the world: 115

Physicians density: 0.17 physicians/1,000 population (2013)

Hospital bed density: 0.7 beds/1,000 population (2011)

Drinking water source:
improved:
urban: 100% of population
rural: 69.1% of population
total: 75.5% of population
unimproved:
urban: 0% of population
rural: 30.9% of population
total: 24.5% of population (2015 est.)

Sanitation facility access:
improved:
urban: 88.1% of population
rural: 30.5% of population

total: 42.4% of population
unimproved:
urban: 11.9% of population
rural: 69.5% of population
total: 57.6% of population (2015 est.)

HIV/AIDS—adult prevalence rate: 0.6% (2016 est.)
country comparison to the world: 54

HIV/AIDS—people living with HIV/AIDS: 71,000 (2016 est.)
country comparison to the world: 47

HIV/AIDS—deaths: 1,800 (2016 est.)
country comparison to the world: 54

Major infectious diseases: *degree of risk:* very high
food or waterborne diseases: bacterial diarrhea, hepatitis A, and typhoid fever
vectorborne diseases: dengue fever, Japanese encephalitis, and malaria (2016)

Obesity—adult prevalence rate: 3.9% (2016)
country comparison to the world: 188

Children under the age of 5 years underweight: 23.9% (2014)
country comparison to the world: 18

Education expenditures: 1.9% of GDP (2014)
country comparison to the world: 152

Literacy: *definition:* age 15 and over can read and write
total population: 77.2%
male: 84.5%
female: 70.5% (2015 est.)

School life expectancy (primary to tertiary education): *total:* 11 years
male: 11 years
female: 10 years (2008)

Unemployment, youth ages 15-24: *total:* 0.5%
male: 0.7%
female: 0.4%
note: according to official statistics (2010 est.)
country comparison to the world: 130

GOVERNMENT

Country name: *conventional long form:* Kingdom of Cambodia
conventional short form: Cambodia
local long form: Preahreacheanachakr Kampuchea (phonetic transliteration)
local short form: Kampuchea
former: Khmer Republic, Democratic Kampuchea, People's Republic of Kampuchea, State of Cambodia
etymology: the English name Cambodia is an anglicization of the French Cambodge, which is the French transliteration of the native name Kampuchea

Government type: parliamentary constitutional monarchy

Capital: *name:* Phnom Penh
geographic coordinates: 11 33 N, 104 55 E
time difference: UTC+7 (12 hours ahead of Washington, DC, during Standard Time)

Administrative divisions: 24 provinces (khett, singular and plural) and 1 municipality (krong, singular and plural)
provinces: Banteay Meanchey, Battambang, Kampong Cham, Kampong Chhnang, Kampong Speu, Kampong Thom, Kampot, Kandal, Kep, Koh Kong, Kratie, Mondolkiri, Oddar Meanchey, Pailin, Preah Vihear, Prey Veng, Pursat, Ratanakiri, Siem Reap, Sihanoukville, Stung Treng, Svay Rieng, Takeo, Tbong Khmum
municipalities: Phnom Penh (Phnum Penh)

Independence: 9 November 1953 (from France)

National holiday: Independence Day, 9 November (1953)

Constitution: previous 1947; latest promulgated 21 September 1993; amended 1999, 2008, 2014 (2016)

Legal system: civil law system (influenced by the UN Transitional Authority in Cambodia) customary law, Communist legal theory, and common law

International law organization participation: accepts compulsory ICJ jurisdiction with reservations; accepts ICCt jurisdiction

Citizenship: *citizenship by birth:* no
citizenship by descent only: at least one parent must be a citizen of Cambodia
dual citizenship recognized: yes
residency requirement for naturalization: 7 years

Suffrage: 18 years of age; universal

Executive branch: *chief of state:* King Norodom SIHAMONI (since 29 October 2004)

head of government: Prime Minister HUN SEN (since 14 January 1985); Permanent Deputy Prime Minister MEN SAM AN (since 25 September 2008); Deputy Prime Ministers SAR KHENG (since 3 February 1992), TEA BANH, Gen., HOR NAMHONG, NHEK BUNCHHAY (all since 16 July 2004), BIN CHHIN (since 5 September 2007), KEAT CHHON, YIM CHHAI LY (since 24 September 2008), KE KIMYAN (since 12 March 2009)
cabinet: Council of Ministers named by the prime minister and appointed by the monarch
elections/appointments: monarch chosen by the 9-member Royal Council of the Throne from among all eligible males of royal descent; following legislative elections, a member of the majority party or majority coalition named prime minister by the Chairman of the National Assembly and appointed by the monarch

Legislative branch: description: bicameral Parliament of Cambodia consists of the Senate (61 seats; 57 indirectly elected by parliamentarians and commune councils, 2 indirectly elected by the National Assembly, and 2 appointed by the monarch; members serve 6-year terms) and the National Assembly (123 seats; members directly elected in multi-seat constituencies by proportional representation vote; members serve 5-year terms)
note: two seats will be added to the National Assembly in 2018, for a total of 125

elections: Senate—last held on 4 February 2012 (next to be held on 25 February 2018); National Assembly—last held on 28 July 2013 (next to be held in July 2018)
election results: Senate—percent of vote by party—CPP 77.8%, SRP 22.2%; seats by party—CPP 46, SRP 11; National Assembly—percent of vote by party—CPP 48.8%, CNRP 44.5%, other 6.7%; seats by party—CPP 68, CNRP 55
note: as of November 2017, National Assembly seats by party—CPP 79, FUNCINPEC 41, CNP 2, KEDP 1; CNRP's National Assembly seats were redistributed following its dissolution on 16 November 2017

Judicial branch: *highest court(s):* Supreme Council (organized into 5- and 9-judge panels and includes a court chief and deputy chief); Constitutional Court (consists of 9 members); note—in 1997, the Cambodian Government requested UN assistance in establishing trials to prosecute former Khmer Rouge senior leaders for crimes against humanity committed during the 1975-1979 Khmer Rouge regime; the Extraordinary Chambers of the Courts in Cambodia (also called the Khmer Rouge Tribunal) were established and began hearings for the first case in 2009; court proceeding were ongoing in 2016
judge selection and term of office: Supreme Court and Constitutional Council judge candidates recommended by the Supreme Council of Magistracy, a 17-member body chaired by the monarch and includes other high-level judicial officers; judges of both courts appointed by the monarch; Supreme Court judges appointed for life; Constitutional Council judges appointed for 9-year terms with one-third of the court renewed every 3 years
subordinate courts: Appellate Court; provincial and municipal courts; Military Court

Political parties and leaders: Cambodian National Rescue Party or CNRP [KHEM SOKHA] (dissolved by the government in November 2017; formed from a 2012 merger of the Sam Rangsi Party or SRP and the former Human Rights Party or HRP [KHEM SOKHA, also spelled KEM SOKHA])
Cambodian Nationality Party or CNP [SENG SOKHENG]
Cambodian People's Party or CPP [HUN SEN]
Khmer Economic Development Party or KEDP [HUON REACH CHAMROEUN]
National United Front for an Independent, Neutral, Peaceful, and Cooperative Cambodia or FUNCINPEC [Prince NORODOM RANARIDDH]

Political pressure groups and leaders: Partnership for Transparency Fund or PTF [John CLARK] (anti-corruption organization)
Students Movement for Democracy
The Committee for Free and Fair Elections or Comfrel [Koul PANHA]
other: human rights organizations; labor unions; youth groups

International organization participation: ADB, ARF, ASEAN, CICA, CICA (observer), EAS, FAO, G-77, IAEA, IBRD, ICAO, ICRM, IDA,

IFAD, IFC, IFRCS, ILO, IMF, IMO, Interpol, IOC, IOM, IPU, ISO (correspondent), ITU, MINUSMA, MIGA, NAM, OIF, OPCW, PCA, UN, UNAMID, UNCTAD, UNESCO, UNIDO, UNIFIL, UNISFA, UNMISS, UNWTO, UPU, WCO, WFTU (NGOs), WHO, WIPO, WMO, WTO

Diplomatic representation in the US: *chief of mission:* Ambassador CHUM BUN RONG (since 3 August 2015)
chancery: 4530 16th Street NW, Washington, DC 20011
telephone: [1] (202) 726-7742
FAX: [1] (202) 726-8381

Diplomatic representation from the US: *chief of mission:* Ambassador William A. HEIDT (since 2 December 2015)
embassy: mailing address: Unit 8166, Box P, APO AP 96546
telephone: [855] (23) 728-000
FAX: [855] (23) 728-600

Flag description: three horizontal bands of blue (top), red (double width), and blue with a white, three-towered temple representing Angkor Wat outlined in black in the center of the red band; red and blue are traditional Cambodian colors
note: only national flag to incorporate an actual building into its design

National symbol(s): Angkor Wat temple, kouprey (wild ox); national colors: red, blue

National anthem: name: "Nokoreach" (Royal Kingdom)
lyrics/music: CHUON NAT/F. PERRUCHOT and J. JEKYLL
note: adopted 1941, restored 1993; the anthem, based on a Cambodian folk tune, was restored after the defeat of the Communist regime

ECONOMY

Economy—overview: Cambodia has experienced strong economic growth over the last decade; GDP grew at an average annual rate of over 8% between 2000 and 2010 and about 7% since 2011. The tourism, garment, construction and real estate, and agriculture sectors accounted for the bulk of growth. Around 700,000 people, the majority of whom are women, are employed in the garment and footwear sector. An additional 500,000 Cambodians are employed in the tourism sector, and a further 50,000 people in construction. Tourism has continued to grow rapidly with foreign arrivals exceeding 2 million per year since 2007 and reaching around 4.5 million visitors in 2014. Mining also is attracting some investor interest and the government has touted opportunities for mining bauxite, gold, iron and gems.

Cambodia remains one of the poorest countries in Asia and long-term economic development remains a daunting challenge, inhibited by endemic corruption, limited human resources, high income inequality, and poor job prospects. As of 2012, approximately 2.66 million people live on less than $1.20 per day, and 37% of Cambodian children under the age of 5 suffer from chronic malnutrition. More than 50% of the population is less than 25 years old. The population lacks education and productive skills, particularly in the impoverished countryside, which also lacks basic infrastructure.

The World Bank in 2016 formally reclassified Cambodia as a lower middle-income country as a result of continued rapid economic growth over the past several years. Cambodia's graduation from a low-income country will reduce its eligibility for foreign assistance and will challenge the government to seek new sources of financing. The Cambodian Government has been working with bilateral and multilateral donors, including the Asian Development Bank, the World Bank and IMF, to address the country's many pressing needs; more than 30% of the government budget comes from donor assistance. A major economic challenge for Cambodia over the next decade will be fashioning an economic environment in which the private sector can create enough jobs to handle Cambodia's demographic imbalance.

Textile exports, which accounted for 68% of total exports in 2017, have driven much of Cambodia's growth over the past several years. The textile sector relies on exports to the United States and European Union, and Cambodia's dependence on its comparative advantage in textile production is a key vulnerability for the economy, especially because Cambodia has continued to run a current account deficit of about 9% of GDP since 2011.

GDP (purchasing power parity): $64.21 billion (2017 est.)
$60.04 billion (2016 est.)
$56.09 billion (2015 est.)
note: data are in 2017 dollars
country comparison to the world: 106

GDP (official exchange rate): $22.25 billion (2016 est.)

GDP—real growth rate: 6.9% (2017 est.)
7% (2016 est.)
7.2% (2015 est.)
country comparison to the world: 10

GDP—per capita (PPP): $4,000 (2017 est.)
$3,800 (2016 est.)
$3,600 (2015 est.)
note: data are in 2017 dollars
country comparison to the world: 178

Gross national saving: 13.6% of GDP (2017 est.)
14.1% of GDP (2016 est.)
13.1% of GDP (2015 est.)
country comparison to the world: 132

GDP—composition, by end use:
household consumption: 76.4%
government consumption: 5.4%
investment in fixed capital: 22%
investment in inventories: 0.9%
exports of goods and services: 62.8%
imports of goods and services: -67.4% (2017 est.)

GDP—composition, by sector of origin:
agriculture: 25.3%
industry: 32.8%
services: 41.9% (2017 est.)

Agriculture—products: rice, rubber, corn, vegetables, cashews, cassava (manioc, tapioca), silk

Industries: tourism, garments, construction, rice milling, fishing, wood and wood products, rubber, cement, gem mining, textiles

Industrial production growth rate: 10.6% (2017 est.)
country comparison to the world: 7

Labor force: 7.897 million (2017 est.)
country comparison to the world: 65

Labor force—by occupation: *agriculture:* 48.7%
industry: 19.9%
services: 31.5% (2013 est.)

Unemployment rate: 0.3% (2017 est.)
0.2% (2012 est.)
note: according to official statistics; underemployment is high
country comparison to the world: 2

Population below poverty line: 17.7% (2012 est.)

Household income or consumption by percentage share: *lowest 10%:* 2%
highest 10%: 28% (2013 est.)

Distribution of family income—Gini index: 37.9 (2008 est.)
41.9 (2004 est.)
country comparison to the world: 72

Budget: *revenues:* $4.268 billion
expenditures: $4.69 billion (2017 est.)
Taxes and other revenues: 19.2% of GDP (2017 est.)
country comparison to the world: 160

Budget surplus (+) or deficit (-): -1.9% of GDP (2017 est.)
country comparison to the world: 81

Public debt: 28.2% of GDP (2017 est.)
29.1% of GDP (2016 est.)
country comparison to the world: 166

Fiscal year: calendar year

Inflation rate (consumer prices): 3.7% (2017 est.)
3% (2016 est.)
country comparison to the world: 146

Central bank discount rate: NA% (31 December 2012)
5.25% (31 December 2007)

Commercial bank prime lending rate: 11.1% (31 December 2017 est.)
11.36% (31 December 2016 est.)
country comparison to the world: 74

Stock of narrow money: $1.999 billion (31 December 2017 est.)
$1.748 billion (31 December 2016 est.)
country comparison to the world: 134

Stock of broad money: $16.82 billion (31 December 2017 est.)
$14.5 billion (31 December 2016 est.)
country comparison to the world: 94

Stock of domestic credit: $13.71 billion (31 December 2017 est.)
$11.82 billion (31 December 2016 est.)
country comparison to the world: 103

Market value of publicly traded shares: $NA

Current account balance: -$1.904 billion (2017 est.)
-$1.776 billion (2016 est.)
country comparison to the world: 157

Exports: $10.45 billion (2017 est.)
$9.233 billion (2016 est.)
country comparison to the world: 89

Exports—commodities: clothing, timber, rubber, rice, fish, tobacco, footwear

Exports—partners: US 21.3%, UK 9.4%, Germany 9%, Japan 8.2%, Canada 6.5%, China 6%, Thailand 4.2%, Spain 4% (2016)

Imports: $14.34 billion (2017 est.)
$12.65 billion (2016 est.)
country comparison to the world: 88

Imports—commodities: petroleum products, cigarettes, gold, construction materials, machinery, motor vehicles, pharmaceutical products

Imports—partners: China 35.3%, Thailand 14.8%, Vietnam 11%, Singapore 4.4%, Japan 4.1%, Hong Kong 4% (2016)

Reserves of foreign exchange and gold: $11.29 billion (31 December 2017 est.)
$9.122 billion (31 December 2016 est.)
country comparison to the world: 71

Debt—external: $11.34 billion (31 December 2017 est.)
$10.3 billion (31 December 2016 est.)
country comparison to the world: 109

Stock of direct foreign investment—at home: $29.17 billion (2014 est.)
country comparison to the world: 70

Exchange rates: riels (KHR) per US dollar—
4,055 (2017 est.)
4,058.7 (2016 est.)
4,058.7 (2015 est.)
4,067.8 (2014 est.)
4,037.5 (2013 est.)

ENERGY

Electricity access: *population without electricity:* 9,900,000
electrification—total population: 34%
electrification—urban areas: 97%
electrification—rural areas: 18% (2013)

Electricity—production: 4.236 billion kWh (2015 est.)
country comparison to the world: 124

Electricity—consumption: 4.952 billion kWh (2015 est.)
country comparison to the world: 121

Electricity—exports: 0 kWh (2016 est.)
country comparison to the world: 115

Electricity—imports: 1.526 billion kWh (2015 est.)
country comparison to the world: 59

Electricity—installed generating capacity: 1.542 million kW (2015 est.)
country comparison to the world: 122

Electricity—from fossil fuels: 37.6% of total installed capacity (2015 est.)
country comparison to the world: 171

Electricity—from nuclear fuels: 0% of total installed capacity (2015 est.)
country comparison to the world: 61

Electricity—from hydroelectric plants: 60.3% of total installed capacity (2015 est.)
country comparison to the world: 27

Electricity—from other renewable sources: 2.1% of total installed capacity (2015 est.)
country comparison to the world: 120

Crude oil—production: 0 bbl/day (2016 est.)
country comparison to the world: 119

Crude oil—exports: 0 bbl/day (2014 est.)
country comparison to the world: 103

Crude oil—imports: 0 bbl/day (2014 est.)
country comparison to the world: 105

Crude oil—proved reserves: 0 bbl (1 January 2017 es)
country comparison to the world: 118

Refined petroleum products—production: 0 bbl/day (2014 est.)
country comparison to the world: 127

Refined petroleum products—consumption: 39,000 bbl/day (2015 est.)
country comparison to the world: 115

Refined petroleum products—exports: 0 bbl/day (2014 est.)
country comparison to the world: 139

Refined petroleum products—imports: 37,930 bbl/day (2014 est.)
country comparison to the world: 93

Natural gas—production: 0 cu m (2013 est.)
country comparison to the world: 116

Natural gas—consumption: 0 cu m (2013 est.)
country comparison to the world: 164

Natural gas—exports: 0 cu m (2013 est.)
country comparison to the world: 78

Natural gas—imports: 0 cu m (2013 est.)
country comparison to the world: 101

Natural gas—proved reserves: 0 cu m (1 January 2014 es)
country comparison to the world: 122

Carbon dioxide emissions from consumption of energy: 6.5 million Mt (2013 est.)
country comparison to the world: 119

COMMUNICATIONS

Telephones—fixed lines: *total subscriptions:* 227,261
subscriptions per 100 inhabitants: 1.5 (July 2016 est.)
country comparison to the world: 99

Telephones—mobile cellular: *total:* 19,915,503
subscriptions per 100 inhabitants: 125 (July 2016 est.)
country comparison to the world: 48

Telephone system: *general assessment:* adequate fixed-line and/or cellular service in Phnom Penh and other provincial cities; mobile-cellular phone systems are widely used in urban areas to bypass deficiencies in the fixed-line network; mobile-phone coverage is rapidly expanding in rural areas *domestic:* fixed-line connections stand at about 1.5 per 100 persons; mobile-cellular usage, aided by competition among service providers, has increased to about 125 per 100 persons
international: country code—855; adequate but expensive landline and cellular service available to all countries from Phnom Penh and major provincial cities; satellite earth station—1 Intersputnik (Indian Ocean region) (2016)

Broadcast media: mixture of state-owned, joint public-private, and privately owned broadcast media; 9 TV broadcast stations with most operating on multiple channels, including 1 state-operated station broadcasting from multiple locations, 6 stations either jointly operated or privately owned with some broadcasting from several locations, and 2 TV relay stations—one relaying a French TV station and the other relaying a Vietnamese TV station; multi-channel cable and satellite systems are available; roughly 50 radio broadcast stations—1 state-owned broadcaster with multiple stations and a large mixture of public and private broadcasters; several international broadcasters are available (2009)

Internet country code: .kh
Internet users: total: 4,080,372

percent of population: 25.6% (July 2016 est.)
country comparison to the world: 124

TRANSPORTATION

National air transport system: *number of registered air carriers:* 4
inventory of registered aircraft operated by air carriers: 10
annual passenger traffic on registered air carriers: 1,103,880
annual freight traffic on registered air carriers: 2,301,260 mt-km (2015)
Civil aircraft registration country code prefix: XU (2016)

Airports: 16 (2013)
country comparison to the world: 142

Airports—with paved runways: *total:* 6
2,438 to 3,047 m: 3
1,524 to 2,437 m: 2
914 to 1,523 m: 1 (2017)

Airports—with unpaved runways: *total:* 10
1,524 to 2,437 m: 2
914 to 1,523 m: 7
under 914 m: 1 (2013)

Heliports: 1 (2013)

Railways: *total:* 642 km
narrow gauge: 642 km 1.000-m gauge
note: under restoration (2014)
country comparison to the world: 108

Roadways: *total:* 44,709 km
paved: 3,607 km
unpaved: 41,102 km (2010)
country comparison to the world: 80

Waterways: 3,700 km (mainly on Mekong River) (2012)
country comparison to the world: 28

Merchant marine: *total:* 442
by type: container ship 3, general cargo 328, oil tanker 26, other 85 (2017)
country comparison to the world: 43

Ports and terminals: *major seaport(s):* Sihanoukville (Kampong Saom)
river port(s): Phnom Penh (Mekong)

MILITARY AND SECURITY

Military expenditures: 1.85% of GDP (2016)
2.11% of GDP (2015)
1.66% of GDP (2014)
1.58% of GDP (2013)
1.55% of GDP (2012)
country comparison to the world: 60

Military branches: Royal Cambodian Armed Forces: Royal Cambodian Army, Royal Khmer Navy, Royal Cambodian Air Force; the Royal Cambodian Gendarmerie is the military police force responsible for internal security; the National Committee for Maritime Security performs Coast Guard functions and has representation from military and civilian agencies (2016)

Military service age and obligation: 18 is the legal minimum age for compulsory and voluntary military service (2012)

TRANSNATIONAL ISSUES

Disputes—international: Cambodia is concerned about Laos' extensive upstream dam construction; Cambodia and Thailand dispute sections of boundary; in 2011 Thailand and Cambodia resorted to arms in the dispute over the location of the boundary on the precipice surmounted by Preah Vihear Temple ruins, awarded to Cambodia by ICJ decision in 1962 and part of a UN World Heritage site; Cambodia accuses Vietnam of a wide variety of illicit cross-border activities; progress on a joint development area with Vietnam is hampered by an unresolved dispute over sovereignty of offshore islands

Trafficking in persons: *current situation:* Cambodia is a source, transit, and destination country for men, women, and children subjected to forced labor and sex trafficking; Cambodian men, women, and children migrate to countries within the region and, increasingly, the Middle East for legitimate work but are subjected to sex trafficking, domestic servitude, or forced labor in fishing, agriculture, construction, and factories; Cambodian men recruited to work on Thai-owned fishing vessels are subsequently subjected to forced labor in international waters and are kept at sea for years; poor Cambodian children are vulnerable and, often with the families' complicity, are subject to forced labor, including domestic servitude and forced begging, in Thailand and Vietnam; Cambodian and ethnic Vietnamese women and girls are trafficked from rural areas to urban centers and tourist spots for sexual exploitation; Cambodian men are the main exploiters of child prostitutes, but men from other Asian countries, and the West travel to Cambodia for child sex tourism

tier rating: Tier 2 Watch List–Cambodia does not fully comply with the minimum standards for the elimination of trafficking; however, it is making significant efforts to do so; the government has a written plan that, if implemented, would constitute making significant efforts to meet the minimum standards for the elimination of trafficking; authorities made modest progress in prosecutions and convictions of traffickers in 2014 but did not provide comprehensive data; endemic

corruption continued to impede law enforcement efforts, and no complicit officials were prosecuted or convicted; the government sustained efforts to identify victims and refer them to NGOs for care, but victim protection remained inadequate, particularly for assisting male victims and victims identified abroad; a new national action plan was adopted, but guidelines for victim identification

and guidance on undercover investigation techniques are still pending after several years (2015)

Illicit drugs: narcotics-related corruption reportedly involving some in the government, military, and police; limited methamphetamine production; vulnerable to money laundering due to its cash-based economy and porous borders

CAMEROON

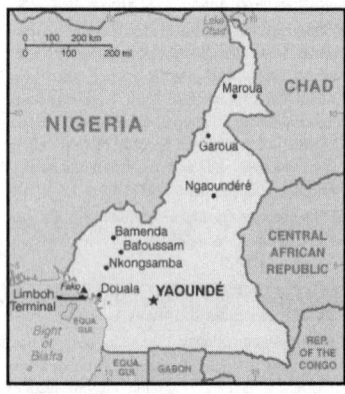

INTRODUCTION

Background: French Cameroon became independent in 1960 as the Republic of Cameroon. The following year the southern portion of neighboring British Cameroon voted to merge with the new country to form the Federal Republic of Cameroon. In 1972, a new constitution replaced the federation with a unitary state, the United Republic of Cameroon. The country has generally enjoyed stability, which has enabled the development of agriculture, roads, and railways, as well as a petroleum industry. Despite slow movement toward democratic reform, political power remains firmly in the hands of President Paul BIYA.

GEOGRAPHY

Location: Central Africa, bordering the Bight of Biafra, between Equatorial Guinea and Nigeria

Geographic coordinates: 6 00 N, 12 00 E

Map references: Africa

Area: *total:* 475,440 sq km
land: 472,710 sq km
water: 2,730 sq km
country comparison to the world: 55

Area—comparative: slightly larger than California

Land boundaries: *total:* 5,018 km
border countries (6): Central African Republic 901 km, Chad 1,116 km, Republic of the Congo 494 km, Equatorial Guinea 183 km, Gabon 349 km, Nigeria 1,975 km

Coastline: 402 km

Maritime claims: *territorial sea:* 12 nm
contiguous zone: 24 nm

Climate: varies with terrain, from tropical along coast to semiarid and hot in north

Terrain: diverse, with coastal plain in southwest, dissected plateau in center, mountains in west, plains in north

Elevation: *mean elevation:* 667 m

elevation extremes: *lowest point:* Atlantic Ocean 0 m
highest point: Fako on Mont Cameroun 4,045 m

Natural resources: petroleum, bauxite, iron ore, timber, hydropower

Land use: *agricultural land:* 20.6%
arable land: 13.1%;
permanent crops: 3.3%;
permanent pasture: 4.2%
forest: 41.7%
other: 37.7% (2011 est.)
Irrigated land: 290 sq km (2012)

Population—distribution: population concentrated in the west and north, with the interior of the country sparsely populated

Natural hazards: volcanic activity with periodic releases of poisonous gases from Lake Nyos and Lake Monoun volcanoes
volcanism: Mt. Cameroon (4,095 m), which last erupted in 2000, is the most frequently active volcano in West Africa; lakes in Oku volcanic field have released fatal levels of gas on occasion, killing some 1,700 people in 1986

Environment—current issues: waterborne diseases are prevalent; deforestation; overgrazing; desertification; poaching; overfishing

Environment—international agreements: *party to:* Biodiversity, Climate Change, Climate Change-Kyoto Protocol, Desertification, Endangered Species, Hazardous Wastes, Law of the Sea, Ozone Layer Protection, Tropical Timber 83, Tropical Timber 94, Wetlands, Whaling
signed, but not ratified: none of the selected agreements

Geography—note: sometimes referred to as the hinge of Africa because of its central location on the continent and its position at the west-south juncture of the Gulf of Guinea; throughout the country there are areas of thermal springs and indications of current or prior volcanic activity;

Mount Cameroon, the highest mountain in Sub-Saharan west Africa, is an active volcano

PEOPLE AND SOCIETY

Population: 24,994,885
note: estimates for this country explicitly take into account the effects of excess mortality due to AIDS; this can result in lower life expectancy, higher infant mortality, higher death rates, lower population growth rates, and changes in the distribution of population by age and sex than would otherwise be expected (July 2017 est.)
country comparison to the world: 53

Nationality: *noun:* Cameroonian(s)
adjective: Cameroonian

Ethnic groups: Cameroon Highlanders 31%, Equatorial Bantu 19%, Kirdi 11%, Fulani 10%, Northwestern Bantu 8%, Eastern Nigritic 7%, other African 13%, non-African less than 1%

Languages: 24 major African language groups, English (official), French (official)

Religions: Roman Catholic 38.4%, Protestant 26.3%, other Christian 4.5%, Muslim 20.9%, animist 5.6%, other 1%, non-believer 3.2% (2005 est.)

Demographic profile: Cameroon has a large youth population, with more than 60% of the populace under the age of 25. Fertility is falling but remains at a high level, especially among poor, rural, and uneducated women, in part because of inadequate access to contraception. Life expectancy remains low at about 55 years due to the prevalence of HIV and AIDs and an elevated maternal mortality rate, which has remained high since 1990. Cameroon, particularly the northern region, is vulnerable to food insecurity largely because of government mismanagement, corruption, high production costs, inadequate infrastructure, and natural disasters. Despite economic growth in some regions, poverty is on the rise, and is most prevalent in rural areas, which are especially affected by a shortage of jobs, declining incomes, poor school and health care infrastructure, and a lack of clean water and sanitation. Underinvestment in social safety nets and ineffective public financial management also contribute to Cameroon's high rate of poverty.

International migration has been driven by unemployment (including fewer government jobs), poverty, the search for educational opportunities, and corruption. The US and Europe are preferred destinations, but, with tighter immigration restrictions in these countries, young Cameroonians are increasingly turning to neighboring states, such as Gabon and Nigeria, South Africa, other parts of Africa, and the Near and Far East. Cameroon's limited resources make it dependent on UN support to host more than 320,000 refugees and asylum seekers as of September 2017. These refugees and asylum seekers are primarily from the Central African Republic and more recently Nigeria.

Age structure: *0-14 years:* 42.39% (male 5,337,879/female 5,257,026)
15-24 years: 19.56% (male 2,456,061/female 2,432,500)
25-54 years: 30.87% (male 3,880,906/female 3,835,107)
55-64 years: 3.98% (male 485,059/female 509,649)
65 years and over: 3.2% (male 372,415/female 428,283) (2017 est.)

Dependency ratios: *total dependency ratio:* 85.9
youth dependency ratio: 80
elderly dependency ratio: 5.9
potential support ratio: 17 (2015 est.)

Median age: *total:* 18.5 years
male: 18.4 years
female: 18.7 years (2017 est.)
country comparison to the world: 209

Population growth rate: 2.56% (2017 est.)
country comparison to the world: 16

Birth rate: 35.4 births/1,000 population (2017 est.)
country comparison to the world: 19

Death rate: 9.6 deaths/1,000 population (2017 est.)
country comparison to the world: 48

Net migration rate: -0.1 migrant(s)/1,000 population (2017 est.)
country comparison to the world: 103

Population distribution: population concentrated in the west and north, with the interior of the country sparsely populated

Urbanization: *urban population:* 55.5% of total population (2017)
rate of urbanization: 3.4% annual rate of change (2015-20 est.)

Major urban areas—population: YAOUNDE (capital) 3.066 million; Douala 2.943 million (2015)

Sex ratio: *at birth:* 1.03 male(s)/female
0-14 years: 1.02 male(s)/female
15-24 years: 1.01 male(s)/female
25-54 years: 1.01 male(s)/female
55-64 years: 0.95 male(s)/female
65 years and over: 0.87 male(s)/female
total population: 1.01 male(s)/female (2016 est.)

Mother's mean age at first birth: 19.7 years
note: median age at first birth among women 25-29 (2011 est.)

Maternal mortality ratio: 596 deaths/100,000 live births (2015 est.)
country comparison to the world: 15

Infant mortality rate: *total:* 51 deaths/1,000 live births
male: 54.6 deaths/1,000 live births
female: 47.3 deaths/1,000 live births (2017 est.)
country comparison to the world: 28

Life expectancy at birth: *total population:* 59 years
male: 57.6 years
female: 60.4 years (2017 est.)
country comparison to the world: 208

Total fertility rate: 4.64 children born/woman (2017 est.)
country comparison to the world: 21

Contraceptive prevalence rate: 34.4% (2014)

Health expenditures: 4.1% of GDP (2014)
country comparison to the world: 164

Physicians density: 0.08 physicians/1,000 population (2010)

Hospital bed density: 1.3 beds/1,000 population (2010)

Drinking water source:
improved:
urban: 94.8% of population
rural: 52.7% of population
total: 75.6% of population
unimproved:
urban: 5.2% of population
rural: 47.3% of population
total: 24.4% of population (2015 est.)

Sanitation facility access:
improved:
urban: 61.8% of population
rural: 26.8% of population
total: 45.8% of population
unimproved:
urban: 38.2% of population
rural: 73.2% of population
total: 54.2% of population (2015 est.)

HIV/AIDS—adult prevalence rate: 3.8% (2016 est.)
country comparison to the world: 15

HIV/AIDS—people living with HIV/AIDS: 560,000 (2016 est.)
country comparison to the world: 14

HIV/AIDS—deaths: 29,000 (2016 est.)
country comparison to the world: 9

Major infectious diseases: *degree of risk:* very high
food or waterborne diseases: bacterial and protozoal diarrhea, hepatitis A, and typhoid fever
vectorborne diseases: malaria, dengue fever, and yellow fever
water contact disease: schistosomiasis
respiratory disease: meningococcal meningitis
animal contact disease: rabies (2016)

Obesity—adult prevalence rate: 11.4% (2016)
country comparison to the world: 135

Children under the age of 5 years underweight: 14.8% (2014)
country comparison to the world: 47

Education expenditures: 3% of GDP (2013)
country comparison to the world: 133

Literacy: *definition:* age 15 and over can read and write
total population: 75%
male: 81.2%
female: 68.9% (2015 est.)

School life expectancy (primary to tertiary education): *total:* 12 years
male: 13 years
female: 11 years (2015)

Unemployment, youth ages 15-24: *total:* 6.4%
male: 5.3%
female: 7.5% (2010 est.)

GOVERNMENT

Country name: *conventional long form:* Republic of Cameroon
conventional short form: Cameroon
local long form: Republique du Cameroun/Republic of Cameroon
local short form: Cameroun/Cameroon
former: French Cameroon, British Cameroon, Federal Republic of Cameroon, United Republic of Cameroon
etymology: in the 15th century, Portuguese explorers named the area near the mouth of the Wouri River the Rio dos Camaroes (River of Prawns) after the abundant shrimp in the water; over time the designation became Cameroon in English; this is the only instance where a country is named after a crustacean

Government type: presidential republic

Capital: *name:* Yaounde
geographic coordinates: 3 52 N, 11 31 E
time difference: UTC+1 (6 hours ahead of Washington, DC, during Standard Time)

Administrative divisions: 10 regions (regions, singular—region); Adamaoua, Centre, East (Est), Far North (Extreme-Nord), Littoral, North (Nord), North-West (Nord-Ouest), West (Ouest), South (Sud), South-West (Sud-Ouest)

Independence: 1 January 1960 (from French-administered UN trusteeship)

National holiday: State Unification Day (National Day), 20 May (1972)

Constitution: history: several previous; latest effective 18 January 1996
amendments: proposed by the president of the republic or by Parliament; amendment drafts require approval of at least one-third of the membership in either house of Parliament; passage requires absolute majority vote of the Parliament membership; passage of drafts requested by the president for a second reading in Parliament requires two-thirds majority vote of its membership; the president can opt to submit drafts to a referendum, in which case passage requires a simple majority; constitutional articles on Cameroon's unity and territorial integrity and its democratic principles cannot be amended; amended 2008 (2017)

Legal system: mixed legal system of English common law, French civil law, and customary law

International law organization participation: accepts compulsory ICJ jurisdiction; non-party state to the ICCt

Citizenship: *citizenship by birth:* no
citizenship by descent only: at least one parent must be a citizen of Cameroon
dual citizenship recognized: no
residency requirement for naturalization: 5 years

Suffrage: 20 years of age; universal

Executive branch: *chief of state:* President Paul BIYA (since 6 November 1982)

head of government: Prime Minister Philemon YANG (since 30 June 2009)
cabinet: Cabinet proposed by the prime minister, appointed by the president
elections/appointments: president directly elected by simple majority popular vote for a 7-year term (no term limits); election last held on 9 October 2011 (next to be held in October 2018); prime minister appointed by the president
election results: Paul BIYA reelected president; percent of vote—Paul BIYA (CPDM) 78.0%, John FRU NDI (SDF) 10.7%, Garga Haman ADJI 3.2%, other 8.1%

Legislative branch: description: bicameral Parliament or Parlement consists of the Senate or Senat (100 seats; 70 members indirectly elected by regional councils and 30 appointed by the president; members serve 5-year terms) and the National Assembly or Assemblee Nationale (180 seats; members directly elected in multi-seat constituencies by simple majority vote to serve 5-year terms; note—the 100-member Senate was formed at the time of the April 2013 election
elections: Senate last held on 14 April 2013 (next to be held in 2018); National Assembly last held on 30 September 2013 (next to be held in 2018)
election results: Senate—percent of vote by party—NA; seats by party—CPDM 56, SDF 14; National Assembly—percent of vote by party—NA; seats by party—CPDM 148, SDF 18, UNDP 5, UDC 4, UPC 3, other 2

Judicial branch: *highest court(s):* Supreme Court of Cameroon (consists of 9 titular and 6 surrogate judges and organized into judicial, administrative, and audit chambers); Constitutional Council (consists of 11 members)
judge selection and term of office: Supreme Court judges appointed by the president with the advice of the Higher Judicial Council of Cameroon, a body chaired by the president and includes the minister of justice, selected magistrates, and representatives of the National Assembly; judge term NA; Constitutional Council members appointed by the president for single 9-year terms
subordinate courts: Parliamentary Court of Justice (jurisdiction limited to cases involving the president and prime minister); appellate and first instance courts; circuit and magistrate's courts

Political parties and leaders: Alliance for Democracy and Development
Cameroon People's Democratic Movement or CPDM [Paul BIYA]

Cameroon People's Party or CPP [Edith Kah WALLA]
Cameroon Renaissance Movement or MRC [Maurice KAMTO]
Cameroonian Democratic Union or UDC [Adamou Ndam NJOYA]
Movement for the Defense of the Republic or MDR [Dakole DAISSALA]
Movement for the Liberation and Development of Cameroon or MLDC [Marcel YONDO]
National Union for Democracy and Progress or UNDP [Maigari BELLO BOUBA]
Progressive Movement or MP [Jean-Jacques EKINDI]
Social Democratic Front or SDF [John FRU NDI]
Union of Peoples of Cameroon or UPC [Provisionary Management Bureau]

Political pressure groups and leaders: Network of Human Rights Defenders in Central Africa or REDHAC [Maximilliene Ngo MBE]
Tribunal 53 Articles [Patrice NGANANG]

International organization participation: ACP, AfDB, AU, BDEAC, C, CEMAC, EITI (compliant country), FAO, FZ, G-77, IAEA, IBRD, ICAO, ICRM, IDA, IDB, IFAD, IFC, IFRCS, IHO, ILO, IMF, IMO, IMSO, Interpol, IOC, IOM, IPU, ISO, ITSO, ITU, ITUC (NGOs), MIGA, MONUSCO, NAM, OIC, OIF, OPCW, PCA, UN, UNCTAD, UNESCO, UNHCR, UNIDO, UNOCI, UNWTO, UPU, WCO, WFTU (NGOs), WHO, WIPO, WMO, WTO

Diplomatic representation in the US: *chief of mission:* Ambassador Essomba ETOUNDI (since 27 June 2016)
chancery: 2349 Massachusetts Avenue NW, Washington, DC 20008; current temporary address—3400 International Drive NW, Washington, DC 20008
telephone: [1] (202) 265-8790
FAX: [1] (202) 387-3826

Diplomatic representation from the US: *chief of mission:* Ambassador (vacant); Charge d'Affaires Matthew SMITH (since 7 September 2017)
embassy: Avenue Rosa Parks, Yaounde
mailing address: P.O. Box 817, Yaounde; pouch: American Embassy, US Department of State, Washington, DC 20521-2520
telephone: [237] 22220 1500; Consular: [237] 22220 1603
FAX: [237] 22220 1500 Ext. 4531; Consular FAX: [237] 22220 1752
branch office(s): Douala

Flag description: three equal vertical bands of green (hoist side), red, and yellow, with a yellow five-pointed star centered in the red band; the vertical tricolor recalls the flag of France; red symbolizes unity, yellow the sun, happiness, and the savannahs in the north, and green hope and the forests in the south; the star is referred to as the "star of unity"
note: uses the popular Pan-African colors of Ethiopia

National symbol(s): lion; national colors: green, red, yellow

National anthem: name: "O Cameroun, Berceau de nos Ancetres" (O Cameroon, Cradle of Our Forefathers)

lyrics/music: Rene Djam AFAME, Samuel Minkio BAMBA, Moise Nyatte NKO'O [French], Benard Nsokika FONLON [English]/Rene Djam AFAME
note: adopted 1957; Cameroon's anthem, also known as "Chant de Ralliement" (The Rallying Song), has been used unofficially since 1948 and officially adopted in 1957; the anthem has French and English versions whose lyrics differ

ECONOMY

Economy—overview: Cameroon's market-based, diversified economy features oil and gas, timber, aluminum, agriculture, mining and the service sector. Oil remains Cameroon's main export commodity, and despite falling global oil prices, still accounts for nearly 40% of exports. Cameroon's economy suffers from factors that often impact underdeveloped countries, such as stagnant per capita income, a relatively inequitable distribution of income, a top-heavy civil service, endemic corruption, continuing inefficiencies of a large parastatal system in key sectors, and a generally unfavorable climate for business enterprise.

Since 1990, the government has embarked on various IMF and World Bank programs designed to spur business investment, increase efficiency in agriculture, improve trade, and recapitalize the nation's banks. The IMF continues to press for economic reforms, including increased budget transparency, privatization, and poverty reduction programs. The Government of Cameroon provides subsidies for electricity, food, and fuel that have strained the federal budget and diverted funds from education, healthcare, and infrastructure projects, as low oil prices have led to lower revenues.

Cameroon devotes significant resources to several large infrastructure projects currently under construction, including a deep seaport in Kribi and the Lom Pangar Hydropower Project. Cameroon's energy sector continues to diversify, recently opening a natural gas-powered electricity generating plant. Cameroon continues to seek foreign investment to improve its inadequate infrastructure, create jobs, and improve its economic footprint, but its unfavorable business environment remains a significant deterrent to foreign investment.

GDP (purchasing power parity): $81.55 billion (2017 est.)
$78.44 billion (2016 est.)
$74.94 billion (2015 est.)
note: data are in 2017 dollars
country comparison to the world: 94

GDP (official exchange rate): $30.65 billion (2016 est.)

GDP—real growth rate: 4% (2017 est.)
4.7% (2016 est.)
5.8% (2015 est.)
country comparison to the world: 73

GDP—per capita (PPP): $3,400 (2017 est.)
$3,300 (2016 est.)
$3,200 (2015 est.)
note: data are in 2017 dollars
country comparison to the world: 188

Gross national saving: 16.5% of GDP (2017 est.)
16.5% of GDP (2016 est.)

17.2% of GDP (2015 est.)
country comparison to the world: 114

GDP—composition, by end use:
household consumption: 71.3%
government consumption: 12.2%
investment in fixed capital: 20.3%
investment in inventories: 0.5%
exports of goods and services: 19.5%
imports of goods and services: -23.8% (2017 est.)

GDP—composition, by sector of origin:
agriculture: 23.1%
industry: 28%
services: 48.9% (2017 est.)

Agriculture—products: coffee, cocoa, cotton, rubber, bananas, oilseed, grains, cassava (manioc, tapioca); livestock; timber

Industries: petroleum production and refining, aluminum production, food processing, light consumer goods, textiles, lumber, ship repair

Industrial production growth rate: 4% (2017 est.)
country comparison to the world: 65

Labor force: 9.912 million (2017 est.)
country comparison to the world: 53

Labor force—by occupation: *agriculture:* 70%
industry: 13%
services: 17% (2001 est.)

Unemployment rate: 4.3% (2014 est.)
30% (2001 est.)
country comparison to the world: 58

Population below poverty line: 30% (2001 est.)

Household income or consumption by percentage share: *lowest 10%:* 37.5%
highest 10%: 35.4% (2014 est.)

Distribution of family income—Gini index: 44.6 (2001)
46.5 (2014 est.)
country comparison to the world: 41

Budget: *revenues:* $5.154 billion
expenditures: $6.964 billion (2017 est.)
Taxes and other revenues: 16.8% of GDP (2017 est.)
country comparison to the world: 178

Budget surplus (+) or deficit (-): -5.9% of GDP (2017 est.)
country comparison to the world: 173

Public debt: 32.3% of GDP (2017 est.)
30.5% of GDP (2016 est.)
country comparison to the world: 155

Fiscal year: 1 July—30 June

Inflation rate (consumer prices): 0.7% (2017 est.)
0.9% (2016 est.)
country comparison to the world: 24

Central bank discount rate: 4.25% (31 December 2009)
country comparison to the world: 85

Commercial bank prime lending rate: 13% (31 December 2017 est.)
12.5% (31 December 2016 est.)
country comparison to the world: 61

Stock of narrow money: $4.374 billion (31 December 2017 est.)
$3.86 billion (31 December 2016 est.)

country comparison to the world: 109

Stock of broad money: $7.102 billion (31 December 2017 est.)
$6.33 billion (31 December 2016 est.)
country comparison to the world: 116

Stock of domestic credit: $6.427 billion (31 December 2017 est.)
$5.714 billion (31 December 2016 est.)
country comparison to the world: 122

Market value of publicly traded shares: $230 million (31 December 2012 est.)
country comparison to the world: 117

Current account balance: -$1.095 billion (2017 est.)
-$1.065 billion (2016 est.)
country comparison to the world: 135

Exports: $5.158 billion (2017 est.)
$4.561 billion (2016 est.)
country comparison to the world: 108

Exports—commodities: crude oil and petroleum products, lumber, cocoa beans, aluminum, coffee, cotton

Exports—partners: Netherlands 21%, India 11.3%, Italy 11%, China 8%, Spain 6.7%, France 5.9% (2016)

Imports: $5.334 billion (2017 est.)
$4.784 billion (2016 est.)
country comparison to the world: 120

Imports—commodities: machinery, electrical equipment, transport equipment, fuel, food

Imports—partners: China 17.8%, Nigeria 12%, France 11%, Thailand 4.6%, Togo 4.5% (2016)

Reserves of foreign exchange and gold: $2.357 billion (31 December 2017 est.)
$2.26 billion (31 December 2016 est.)
country comparison to the world: 114

Debt—external: $8.238 billion (31 December 2017 est.)
$7.364 billion (31 December 2016 est.)
country comparison to the world: 121

Exchange rates: Cooperation Financiere en Afrique Centrale francs (XAF) per US dollar—
605.3 (2017 est.)
593.01 (2016 est.)
593.01 (2015 est.)
591.45 (2014 est.)
494.42 (2013 est.)

ENERGY

Electricity access: *population without electricity:* 10,100,000
electrification—*total population:* 55%
electrification—urban areas: 88%
electrification—rural areas: 17% (2013)

Electricity—production: 6.61 billion kWh (2015 est.)
country comparison to the world: 114

Electricity—consumption: 5.702 billion kWh (2015 est.)
country comparison to the world: 117

Electricity—exports: 0 kWh (2016 est.)
country comparison to the world: 121

Electricity—imports: 1.414 billion kWh (2015 est.)
country comparison to the world: 62

Electricity—installed generating capacity: 1.545 million kW (2015 est.)
country comparison to the world: 121

Electricity—from fossil fuels: 52.9% of total installed capacity (2015 est.)
country comparison to the world: 144

Electricity—from nuclear fuels: 0% of total installed capacity (2015 est.)
country comparison to the world: 68

Electricity—from hydroelectric plants: 46.7% of total installed capacity (2015 est.)
country comparison to the world: 45

Electricity—from other renewable sources: 0.6% of total installed capacity (2015 est.)
country comparison to the world: 149

Crude oil—production: 93,200 bbl/day (2016 est.)
country comparison to the world: 45

Crude oil—exports: 64,290 bbl/day (2014 est.)
country comparison to the world: 40

Crude oil—imports: 39,120 bbl/day (2014 est.)
country comparison to the world: 56

Crude oil—proved reserves: 200 million bbl (1 January 2017 es)
country comparison to the world: 58

Refined petroleum products—production: 54,740 bbl/day (2014 est.)
country comparison to the world: 82

Refined petroleum products—consumption: 42,000 bbl/day (2015 est.)
country comparison to the world: 114

Refined petroleum products—exports: 17,560 bbl/day (2014 est.)
country comparison to the world: 72

Refined petroleum products—imports: 3,320 bbl/day (2014 est.)
country comparison to the world: 176

Natural gas—production: 680 million cu m (2015 est.)
country comparison to the world: 70

Natural gas—consumption: 1.08 billion cu m (2015 est.)
country comparison to the world: 98

Natural gas—exports: 0 cu m (2013 est.)
country comparison to the world: 85

Natural gas—imports: 0 cu m (2013 est.)
country comparison to the world: 108

Natural gas—proved reserves: 135.1 billion cu m (1 January 2017 es)
country comparison to the world: 50

Carbon dioxide emissions from consumption of energy: 6.5 million Mt (2013 est.)
country comparison to the world: 120

COMMUNICATIONS

Telephones—fixed lines: *total subscriptions:* 1,051,073
subscriptions per 100 inhabitants: 4 (July 2016 est.)

country comparison to the world: 76

Telephones—mobile cellular: *total:* 16,331,852
subscriptions per 100 inhabitants: 67 (July 2016 est.)
country comparison to the world: 61

Telephone system: *general assessment:* system includes cable, microwave radio relay, and tropospheric scatter; Camtel, the monopoly provider of fixed-line service, provides connections for only about 4 per 100 persons; equipment is old and outdated, and connections with many parts of the country are unreliable
domestic: mobile-cellular usage, in part a reflection of the poor condition and general inadequacy of the fixed-line network, has increased sharply, reaching a subscribership base of over 65 per 100 persons
international: country code—237; landing point for the SAT-3/WASC fiber-optic submarine cable that provides connectivity to Europe and Asia; satellite earth stations—2 Intelsat (Atlantic Ocean) (2016)

Broadcast media: government maintains tight control over broadcast media; state-owned Cameroon Radio Television (CRTV), broadcasting on both a TV and radio network, was the only officially recognized and fully licensed broadcaster until August 2007, when the government finally issued licenses to 2 private TV broadcasters and 1 private radio broadcaster; about 70 privately owned, unlicensed radio stations operating but are subject to closure at any time; foreign news services required to partner with state-owned national station (2007)

Internet country code: .cm
Internet users: total: 6,090,201

percent of population: 25.0% (July 2016 est.)
country comparison to the world: 108

TRANSPORTATION

National air transport system: *number of registered air carriers:* 1
inventory of registered aircraft operated by air carriers: 3
annual passenger traffic on registered air carriers: 267,208
annual freight traffic on registered air carriers: 0 mt-km (2015)
Civil aircraft registration country code prefix: TJ (2016)

Airports: 33 (2013)
country comparison to the world: 112
Airports—with paved runways: *total:* 11
over 3,047 m: 2
2,438 to 3,047 m: 5
1,524 to 2,437 m: 3
914 to 1,523 m: 1 (2017)
Airports—with unpaved runways: *total:* 22
1,524 to 2,437 m: 4
914 to 1,523 m: 10
under 914 m: 8 (2013)

Pipelines: gas 53 km; liquid petroleum gas 5 km; oil 1,107 km; water 35 km (2013)

Railways: *total:* 987 km
narrow gauge: 987 km 1.000-m gauge
note: railway connections generally efficient but limited; rail lines connect major cities of Douala, Yaounde, Ngaoundere, and Garoua; passenger and freight service provided by CAMRAIL (2014)
country comparison to the world: 89

Roadways: *total:* 51,350 km
paved: 4,108 km
unpaved: 47,242 km
note: there are 28,857 km of national roads (2011)
country comparison to the world: 78

Waterways: (major rivers in the south, such as the Wouri and the Sanaga, are largely non-navigable; in the north, the Benue, which connects through Nigeria to the Niger River, is navigable in the rainy season only to the port of Garoua) (2010)

Merchant marine: *total:* 19
by type: general cargo 4, other 15 (2017)

Ports and terminals: *river port(s):* Douala (Wouri); Garoua (Benoue)
oil terminal(s): Limboh Terminal

MILITARY AND SECURITY

Military expenditures: 1.6% of GDP (2016)
1.25% of GDP (2015)
1.25% of GDP (2014)
1.33% of GDP (2013)
1.34% of GDP (2012)
country comparison to the world: 70

Military branches: Cameroon Armed Forces (Forces Armees Camerounaises, FAC): Army (L'Armee de Terre), Navy (Marine Nationale Republique, MNR, includes naval infantry), Air Force (Armee de l'Air du Cameroun, AAC),

Rapid Intervention Brigade, Fire Fighter Corps, Gendarmerie (2015)

Military service age and obligation: 18-23 years of age for male and female voluntary military service; no conscription; high school graduation required; service obligation 4 years; periodic government calls for volunteers (2012)

TERRORISM

Terrorist groups—foreign based: *Boko Haram:*
aim(s): replace the Cameroon Government with an Islamic state and, ultimately, establish an Islamic caliphate across Africa; violently opposes any polical or social activity associated with Western society, including voting, attending secular schools, and wearing Western dress
area(s) of operation: conducts lethal bombing attacks and assaults, displacing thousands of people, and contributing to food insecurity, especially in the Far North Region; one of the group's most high-profile operations in Cameroon occurred on 27 July 2014, when operatives killed three people and kidnapped Cameroon Deputy Prime Minister Amadou ALI's wife, Akaoua BABIANA, during a raid in Kolofata in the north; BABIANA and 27 other abductees were rescued in October 2014; Cameroon continued in 2017 to participate in the Joint Multinational Force's military offensives against Boko Haram

TRANSNATIONAL ISSUES

Disputes—international: Joint Border Commission with Nigeria reviewed 2002 ICJ ruling on the entire boundary and bilaterally resolved differences, including June 2006 Greentree Agreement that immediately ceded sovereignty of the Bakassi Peninsula to Cameroon with a full phase-out of Nigerian control and patriation of residents in 2008; Cameroon and Nigeria agreed on maritime delimitation in March 2008; sovereignty dispute between Equatorial Guinea and Cameroon over an island at the mouth of the Ntem River; only Nigeria and Cameroon have heeded the Lake Chad Commission's admonition to ratify the delimitation treaty, which also includes the Chad-Niger and Niger-Nigeria boundaries

Refugees and internally displaced persons: refugees (country of origin): 247,777 (Central African Republic); 90,728 (Nigeria) (2017)
IDPs: 241,030 (2017)

CANADA

INTRODUCTION

Background: A land of vast distances and rich natural resources, Canada became a self-governing dominion in 1867, while retaining ties to the British crown. Canada repatriated its constitution from the UK in 1982, severing a final colonial tie. Economically and technologically, the nation has developed in parallel with the US, its neighbor to the south across the world's longest international border. Canada faces the political challenges of meeting public demands for quality improvements in health care, education, social services, and economic competitiveness, as well as responding to the particular concerns of predominantly francophone Quebec. Canada also aims to develop its diverse energy resources while maintaining its commitment to the environment.

GEOGRAPHY

Location: Northern North America, bordering the North Atlantic Ocean on the east, North Pacific Ocean on the west, and the Arctic Ocean on the north, north of the conterminous US

Geographic coordinates: 60 00 N, 95 00 W

Map references: North America

Area: *total:* 9,984,670 sq km
land: 9,093,507 sq km
water: 891,163 sq km
country comparison to the world: 3

Area—comparative: slightly larger than the US

Land boundaries: *total:* 8,893 km
border countries (1): US 8,893 km (includes 2,477 km with Alaska)
note: Canada is the world's largest country that borders only one country

Coastline: 202,080 km
note: the Canadian Arctic Archipelago—consisting of 36,563 islands, several of them some of the world's largest—contributes to Canada easily having the longest coastline in the world

Maritime claims: *territorial sea:* 12 nm
contiguous zone: 24 nm
exclusive economic zone: 200 nm
continental shelf: 200 nm or to the edge of the continental margin

Climate: varies from temperate in south to subarctic and arctic in north

Terrain: mostly plains with mountains in west, lowlands in southeast

Elevation: *mean elevation:* 487 m

elevation extremes: *lowest point:* Atlantic Ocean 0 m
highest point: Mount Logan 5,959 m

Natural resources: iron ore, nickel, zinc, copper, gold, lead, rare earth elements, molybdenum, potash, diamonds, silver, fish, timber, wildlife, coal, petroleum, natural gas, hydropower

Land use: *agricultural land:* 6.8%
arable land: 4.7%;
permanent crops: 0.5%;
permanent pasture: 1.6%
forest: 34.1%
other: 59.1% (2011 est.)
Irrigated land: 8,700 sq km (2012)

Population—distribution: vast majority of Canadians are positioned in a discontinuous band within approximately 300 km (180 mi) of the southern border with the United States; the most populated province is Ontario, followed by Quebec and British Columbia

Natural hazards: continuous permafrost in north is a serious obstacle to development; cyclonic storms form east of the Rocky Mountains, a result of the mixing of air masses from the Arctic, Pacific, and North American interior, and produce most of the country's rain and snow east of the mountains
volcanism: the vast majority of volcanoes in Western Canada's Coast Mountains remain dormant

Environment—current issues: metal smelting, coal-burning utilities, and vehicle emissions impacting agricultural and forest productivity; air pollution and resulting acid rain severely affecting lakes and damaging forests; ocean waters becoming contaminated due to agricultural, industrial, mining, and forestry activities

Environment—international agreements: *party to:* Air Pollution, Air Pollution-Nitrogen Oxides, Air Pollution-Persistent Organic Pollutants, Air Pollution-Sulfur 85, Air Pollution-Sulfur 94, Antarctic-Environmental Protocol, Antarctic-Marine Living Resources, Antarctic Seals, Antarctic Treaty, Biodiversity, Climate Change, Desertification, Endangered Species, Environmental Modification, Hazardous Wastes, Law of the Sea, Marine Dumping, Ozone Layer Protection, Ship Pollution, Tropical Timber 83, Tropical Timber 94, Wetlands
signed, but not ratified: Air Pollution-Volatile Organic Compounds, Marine Life Conservation

Geography—note: second-largest country in world (after Russia) and largest in the Americas; strategic location between Russia and US via north polar route; approximately 90% of the population is concentrated within 160 km (100 mi) of the US border; Canada has more fresh water than any other country and almost 9% of Canadian territory is water; Canada has at least 2 million and possibly over 3 million lakes—that is more than all other countries combined

PEOPLE AND SOCIETY

Population: 35,623,680 (July 2017 est.)
country comparison to the world: 38

Nationality: *noun:* Canadian(s)
adjective: Canadian

Ethnic groups: Canadian 32.2%, English 19.8%, French 15.5%, Scottish 14.4%, Irish 13.8%, German 9.8%, Italian 4.5%, Chinese 4.5%, North American Indian 4.2%, other 50.9%
note: percentages add up to more than 100% because respondents were able to identify more than one ethnic origin (2011 est.)

Languages: English (official) 58.7%, French (official) 22%, Punjabi 1.4%, Italian 1.3%, Spanish 1.3%, German 1.3%, Cantonese 1.2%, Tagalog 1.2%, Arabic 1.1%, other 10.5% (2011 est.)

Religions: Catholic 39% (includes Roman Catholic 38.8%, other Catholic .2%), Protestant 20.3% (includes United Church 6.1%, Anglican 5%, Baptist 1.9%, Lutheran 1.5%, Pentecostal 1.5%, Presbyterian 1.4%, other Protestant 2.9%), Orthodox 1.6%, other Christian 6.3%, Muslim 3.2%, Hindu 1.5%, Sikh 1.4%, Buddhist 1.1%, Jewish 1%, other 0.6%, none 23.9% (2011 est.)

Age structure: *0-14 years:* 15.44% (male 2,819,279/female 2,680,024)
15-24 years: 11.85% (male 2,171,703/female 2,048,546)
25-54 years: 39.99% (male 7,227,145/female 7,020,156)
55-64 years: 14.1% (male 2,492,120/female 2,529,652)
65 years and over: 18.63% (male 2,958,721/female 3,676,334) (2017 est.)

Dependency ratios: *total dependency ratio:* 47.3
youth dependency ratio: 23.5
elderly dependency ratio: 23.8
potential support ratio: 4.2 (2015 est.)

Median age: *total:* 42.2 years
male: 40.9 years
female: 43.5 years (2017 est.)
country comparison to the world: 30

Population growth rate: 0.73% (2017 est.)
country comparison to the world: 141

Birth rate: 10.3 births/1,000 population (2017 est.)
country comparison to the world: 190

Death rate: 8.7 deaths/1,000 population (2017 est.)
country comparison to the world: 73

Net migration rate: 5.7 migrant(s)/1,000 population (2017 est.)
country comparison to the world: 18

Population distribution: vast majority of Canadians are positioned in a discontinuous band within approximately 300 km of the southern border with the United States; the most populated province is Ontario, followed by Quebec and British Columbia

Urbanization: *urban population:* 82.2% of total population (2017)
rate of urbanization: 1.16% annual rate of change (2015-20 est.)

Major urban areas—population: Toronto 5.993 million; Montreal 3.981 million; Vancouver 2.485 million; Calgary 1.337 million; OTTAWA (capital) 1.326 million; Edmonton 1.272 million (2015)

Sex ratio: *at birth:* 1.06 male(s)/female
0-14 years: 1.05 male(s)/female
15-24 years: 1.06 male(s)/female
25-54 years: 1.03 male(s)/female
55-64 years: 0.98 male(s)/female
65 years and over: 0.8 male(s)/female
total population: 0.98 male(s)/female (2016 est.)

Mother's mean age at first birth: 28.1 years (2012 est.)

Maternal mortality ratio: 7 deaths/100,000 live births (2015 est.)
country comparison to the world: 161

Infant mortality rate: *total:* 4.5 deaths/1,000 live births
male: 4.8 deaths/1,000 live births
female: 4.2 deaths/1,000 live births (2017 est.)
country comparison to the world: 180

Life expectancy at birth: *total population:* 81.9 years
male: 79.3 years
female: 84.7 years (2017 est.)
country comparison to the world: 21

Total fertility rate: 1.6 children born/woman (2017 est.)
country comparison to the world: 183

Health expenditures: 10.4% of GDP (2014)
country comparison to the world: 20

Physicians density: 2.48 physicians/1,000 population (2012)

Hospital bed density: 2.7 beds/1,000 population (2010)

Drinking water source:
improved:
urban: 100% of population
rural: 99% of population
total: 99.8% of population
unimproved:
urban: 0% of population
rural: 1% of population
total: 0.2% of population (2015 est.)

Sanitation facility access:
improved:
urban: 100% of population
rural: 99% of population
total: 99.8% of population
unimproved:
urban: 0% of population
rural: 1% of population
total: 0.2% of population (2015 est.)

HIV/AIDS—adult prevalence rate: NA

HIV/AIDS—people living with HIV/AIDS: NA

HIV/AIDS—deaths: NA

Obesity—adult prevalence rate: 29.4% (2016)

country comparison to the world: 26

Education expenditures: 5.3% of GDP (2011)
country comparison to the world: 62

Unemployment, youth ages 15-24: *total:* 13.1%
male: 14.8%
female: 11.3% (2016 est.)
country comparison to the world: 81

GOVERNMENT

Country name: *conventional long form:* none
conventional short form: Canada
etymology: the country name derives from the St. Lawrence Iroquoian word "kanata" meaning village or settlement

Government type: federal parliamentary democracy (Parliament of Canada) under a constitutional monarchy; a Commonwealth realm

Capital: *name:* Ottawa

geographic coordinates: 45 25 N, 75 42 W
time difference: UTC-5 (same time as Washington, DC, during Standard Time)
daylight saving time: +1hr, begins second Sunday in March; ends first Sunday in November
note: Canada has six time zones

Administrative divisions: 10 provinces and 3 territories*; Alberta, British Columbia, Manitoba, New Brunswick, Newfoundland and Labrador, Northwest Territories*, Nova Scotia, Nunavut*, Ontario, Prince Edward Island, Quebec, Saskatchewan, Yukon*

Independence: 1 July 1867 (union of British North American colonies); 11 December 1931 (recognized by UK per Statute of Westminster)

National holiday: Canada Day, 1 July (1867)

Constitution: made up of unwritten and written acts, customs, judicial decisions, and traditions dating from 1763; the written part of the constitution consists of the Constitution Act of 29 March 1867, which created a federation of four provinces, and the Constitution Act of 17 April 1982; several amendments to the 1982 Constitution Act, last in 2011 (2016)

Legal system: common law system except in Quebec, where civil law based on the French civil code prevails

International law organization participation: accepts compulsory ICJ jurisdiction with reservations; accepts ICCt jurisdiction

Citizenship: *citizenship by birth:* yes
citizenship by descent: yes
dual citizenship recognized: yes
residency requirement for naturalization: 3 years

Suffrage: 18 years of age; universal

Executive branch: head of state: Queen ELIZABETH II (since 6 February 1952); represented by Governor General Julie PAYETTE (since 2 October 2017)

head of government: Prime Minister Justin Pierre James TRUDEAU (Liberal Party) (since 4 November 2015)

cabinet: Federal Ministry chosen by the prime minister usually from among members of his/her own party sitting in Parliament
elections/appointments: the monarchy is hereditary; governor general appointed by the monarch on the advice of the prime minister for a 5-year term; following legislative elections, the leader of the majority party or majority coalition in the House of Commons generally designated prime minister by the governor general
note: Julie PAYETTE, a former space shuttle astronaut, is Canada's fourth female governor general but the first to have flown in space

Legislative branch: description: bicameral Parliament or Parlement consists of the Senate or Senat (105 seats; members appointed by the governor general on the advice of the prime minister and can serve until age 75) and the House of Commons or Chambre des Communes (338 seats; members directly elected in single-seat constituencies by simple majority vote with terms up to 4 years)
elections: House of Commons—last held on 19 October 2015 (next to be held in 2019)
election results: House of Commons—percent of vote by party—Liberal Party 39.5%, CPC 31.9%, NDP 19.7%, Bloc Quebecois 4.7%, Greens 3.4%, other .8%; seats by party—Liberal Party 184, CPC 99, NDP 44, Bloc Quebecois 10, Greens 1

Judicial branch: *highest court(s):* Supreme Court of Canada (consists of the chief justice and 8 judges); note—in 1949, Canada abolished all appeals beyond its Supreme Court, which prior to that time, were heard by the Judicial Committee of the Privy Council (in London)
judge selection and term of office: chief justice and judges appointed by the prime minister in council; all judges appointed for life with mandatory retirement at age 75
subordinate courts: federal level: Federal Court of Appeal; Federal Court; Tax Court; federal administrative tribunals; Courts Martial; provincial/territorial level: provincial superior, appeals, first instance, and specialized courts; in 1999, the Nunavut Court—a circuit court with the power of a provincial superior court, as well as a territorial court—was established to serve isolated settlements

Political parties and leaders: Bloc Quebecois [Martine OUELLET]
Conservative Party of Canada or CPC [Andrew SCHEER]
Green Party [Elizabeth MAY]
Liberal Party [Justin TRUDEAU]
New Democratic Party or NDP [Jagmeet SINGH]

Political pressure groups and leaders: other: agricultural sector; automobile industry; business groups; chemical industry; commercial banks; communications sector; energy industry; environmentalists; First Nations organizations; public administration groups; steel industry; trade unions

International organization participation: ADB (nonregional member), AfDB (nonregional member), APEC, Arctic Council, ARF, ASEAN (dialogue partner), Australia Group, BIS, C, CD, CDB, CE (observer), EAPC, EBRD, EITI (implementing country), FAO, FATF, G-7, G-8, G-10, G-20, IADB, IAEA, IBRD, ICAO, ICC (national committees), ICCt, ICRM, IDA, IEA, IFAD, IFC, IFRCS, IGAD (partners), IHO, ILO, IMF, IMO, IMSO, Interpol, IOC, IOM, IPU, ISO, ITSO, ITU, ITUC (NGOs), MIGA, MINUSTAH, MONUSCO, NAFTA, NATO, NEA, NSG, OAS, OECD, OIF, OPCW, OSCE, Pacific Alliance (observer), Paris Club, PCA, PIF (partner), UN, UNCTAD, UNESCO, UNFICYP, UNHCR, UNMISS, UNRWA, UNTSO, UPU, WCO, WFTU (NGOs), WHO, WIPO, WMO, WTO, ZC

Diplomatic representation in the US: *chief of mission:* Ambassador David Brookes MAC-NAUGHTON (since 2 March 2016)
chancery: 501 Pennsylvania Avenue NW, Washington, DC 20001
telephone: [1] (202) 682-1740
FAX: [1] (202) 682-7726
consulate(s) general: Atlanta, Boston, Chicago, Dallas, Denver, Detroit, Los Angeles, Miami, Minneapolis, New York, San Francisco/Silicon Valley, Seattle
trade office(s): Houston, Palo Alto (CA), San Diego; note—there are trade offices in the Consulates General

Diplomatic representation from the US: *chief of mission:* Ambassador Kelly CRAFT (since 23 October 2017)
embassy: 490 Sussex Drive, Ottawa, Ontario K1N 1G8
mailing address: P. O. Box 5000, Ogdensburg, NY 13669-0430; P.O. Box 866, Station B, Ottawa, Ontario K1P 5T1
telephone: [1] (613) 688-5335
FAX: [1] (613) 688-3082
consulate(s) general: Calgary, Halifax, Montreal, Quebec City, Toronto, Vancouver
consulate(s): Winnipeg

Flag description: two vertical bands of red (hoist and fly side, half width) with white square between them; an 11-pointed red maple leaf is centered in the white square; the maple leaf has long been a Canadian symbol

National symbol(s): maple leaf, beaver; national colors: red, white

National anthem: name: "O Canada"
lyrics/music: Adolphe-Basile ROUTHIER [French], Robert Stanley WEIR [English]/Calixa LAVALLEE
note: adopted 1980; originally written in 1880, "O Canada" served as an unofficial anthem many years before its official adoption; the anthem has French and English versions whose lyrics differ; as a Commonwealth realm, in addition to the national anthem, "God Save the Queen" serves as the royal anthem (see United Kingdom)

ECONOMY

Economy—overview: Canada resembles the US in its market-oriented economic system, pattern of production, and high living standards. Since World War II, the impressive growth of the manufacturing, mining, and service sectors has transformed the nation from a largely rural economy into one primarily industrial and urban. Canada has a large oil and natural gas sector with the majority of crude oil production derived from oil sands in the western provinces, especially Alberta. Canada now ranks third in the world in proved oil reserves behind Venezuela and Saudi Arabia and is the world's sixth-largest oil producer.

The 1989 Canada-US Free Trade Agreement and the 1994 North American Free Trade Agreement (which includes Mexico) dramatically increased trade and economic integration between the US and Canada. Canada and the US enjoy the world's most comprehensive and highly balanced bilateral trade and investment relationship, with merchandise trade of $544 billion in 2016, services trade of over $80 billion, and two-way investment stocks of nearly $700 billion. Over three-fourths of Canada's exports are destined for the US each year. Canada is the largest foreign supplier of energy to the US, including oil, natural gas, and electric power, and a top source of US uranium imports.

Given its abundant natural resources, highly skilled labor force, and modern capital stock, Canada enjoyed solid economic growth from 1993 through 2007. The global economic crisis of 2007-08 moved the Canadian economy into sharp recession by late 2008, and Ottawa posted its first fiscal deficit in 2009 after 12 years of surplus. Canada's major banks emerged from the financial crisis of 2008-09 among the strongest in the world, owing to the financial sector's tradition of conservative lending practices and strong capitalization. Since the fall in world oil prices in 2014, Canada has achieved modest economic growth.

GDP (purchasing power parity): $1.764 trillion (2017 est.)
$1.712 trillion (2016 est.)
$1.687 trillion (2015 est.)
note: data are in 2017 dollars
country comparison to the world: 18

GDP (official exchange rate): $1.64 trillion (2016 est.)

GDP—real growth rate: 3% (2017 est.)
1.5% (2016 est.)
0.9% (2015 est.)
country comparison to the world: 118

GDP—per capita (PPP): $48,100 (2017 est.)
$47,200 (2016 est.)
$47,100 (2015 est.)
note: data are in 2017 dollars
country comparison to the world: 34

Gross national saving: 19.9% of GDP (2017 est.)
19.6% of GDP (2016 est.)
20.4% of GDP (2015 est.)
country comparison to the world: 90

GDP—composition, by end use:
household consumption: 58.1%
government consumption: 20.9%
investment in fixed capital: 22.8%
investment in inventories: 0.3%
exports of goods and services: 31.4%
imports of goods and services: -33.6% (2017 est.)

GDP—composition, by sector of origin:
agriculture: 1.7%
industry: 28.1%
services: 70.2% (2017 est.)

Agriculture—products: wheat, barley, oilseed, tobacco, fruits, vegetables; dairy products; fish; forest products

Industries: transportation equipment, chemicals, processed and unprocessed minerals, food products, wood and paper products, fish products, petroleum, natural gas

Industrial production growth rate: 4.8% (2017 est.)
country comparison to the world: 52

Labor force: 19.52 million (2017 est.)
country comparison to the world: 33

Labor force—by occupation: *agriculture:* 2%
manufacturing: 13%
construction: 6%
services: 76%
other: 3% (2006 est.)

Unemployment rate: 6.5% (2017 est.)
7% (2016 est.)
country comparison to the world: 91

Population below poverty line: 9.4%
note: this figure is the Low Income Cut-Off, a calculation that results in higher figures than found in many comparable economies; Canada does not have an official poverty line (2008 est.)

Household income or consumption by percentage share: *lowest 10%:* 2.6%
highest 10%: 24.8% (2000)

Distribution of family income—Gini index: 32.1 (2005)
31.5 (1994)
country comparison to the world: 112

Budget: *revenues:* $623.7 billion
expenditures: $657.3 billion (2017 est.)
Taxes and other revenues: 38% of GDP (2017 est.)
country comparison to the world: 44

Budget surplus (+) or deficit (-): -2% of GDP (2017 est.)
country comparison to the world: 86

Public debt: 98.2% of GDP (2017 est.)
99.4% of GDP (2016 est.)
note: figures are for gross general government debt, as opposed to net federal debt; gross general government debt includes both intragovernmental debt and the debt of public entities at the subnational level
country comparison to the world: 18

Fiscal year: 1 April—31 March

Inflation rate (consumer prices): 1.6% (2017 est.)
1.4% (2016 est.)
country comparison to the world: 67

Central bank discount rate: 1% (31 December 2010)
0.25% (31 December 2009)
country comparison to the world: 128

Commercial bank prime lending rate: 2.9% (31 December 2017 est.)
2.7% (31 December 2016 est.)

country comparison to the world: 170

Stock of narrow money: $715.3 billion (31 December 2017 est.)
$637.3 billion (31 December 2016 est.)
country comparison to the world: 10

Stock of broad money: $1.554 trillion (31 December 2017 est.)
$1.362 trillion (31 December 2016 est.)
country comparison to the world: 13

Stock of domestic credit: $3.173 trillion (31 December 2017 est.)
$2.794 trillion (31 December 2016 est.)
country comparison to the world: 8

Market value of publicly traded shares: $1.593 trillion (31 December 2015 est.)
$2.095 trillion (31 December 2014 est.)
$2.114 trillion (31 December 2013 est.)
country comparison to the world: 8

Current account balance: -$55.57 billion (2017 est.)
-$50.53 billion (2016 est.)
country comparison to the world: 199

Exports: $433 billion (2017 est.)
$393.5 billion (2016 est.)
country comparison to the world: 12

Exports—commodities: motor vehicles and parts, industrial machinery, aircraft, telecommunications equipment; chemicals, plastics, fertilizers; wood pulp, timber, crude petroleum, natural gas, electricity, aluminum

Exports—partners: US 76.4%, China 4.1% (2016)

Imports: $443.7 billion (2017 est.)
$413.4 billion (2016 est.)
country comparison to the world: 10

Imports—commodities: machinery and equipment, motor vehicles and parts, crude oil, chemicals, electricity, durable consumer goods

Imports—partners: US 52.2%, China 12.1%, Mexico 6.2% (2016)

Reserves of foreign exchange and gold: $85.6 billion (31 December 2017 est.)
$82.72 billion (31 December 2016 est.)
country comparison to the world: 29

Debt—external: $1.608 trillion (31 March 2016 est.)
$1.55 trillion (31 March 2015 est.)
country comparison to the world: 15

Stock of direct foreign investment—at home: $1.045 trillion (31 December 2017 est.)
$1.004 trillion (31 December 2016 est.)
country comparison to the world: 12

Stock of direct foreign investment—abroad: $1.366 trillion (31 December 2017 est.)
$1.277 trillion (31 December 2016 est.)
country comparison to the world: 11

Exchange rates: Canadian dollars (CAD) per US dollar—
1.308 (2017 est.)
1.3256 (2016 est.)
1.3256 (2015 est.)
1.2788 (2014 est.)
1.0298 (2013 est.)

ENERGY

Electricity access: electrification—*total population:* 100% (2016)

Electricity—production: 643.2 billion kWh (2015 est.)
country comparison to the world: 7

Electricity—consumption: 516.6 billion kWh (2015 est.)
country comparison to the world: 7

Electricity—exports: 73.35 billion kWh (2016 est.)
country comparison to the world: 3

Electricity—imports: 9.303 billion kWh (2016 est.)
country comparison to the world: 27

Electricity—installed generating capacity: 147.6 million kW (2015 est.)
country comparison to the world: 9

Electricity—from fossil fuels: 26.3% of total installed capacity (2015 est.)
country comparison to the world: 188

Electricity—from nuclear fuels: 9.2% of total installed capacity (2015 est.)
country comparison to the world: 20

Electricity—from hydroelectric plants: 53.7% of total installed capacity (2015 est.)
country comparison to the world: 38

Electricity—from other renewable sources: 11.4% of total installed capacity (2015 est.)
country comparison to the world: 65

Crude oil—production: 3.679 million bbl/day (2016 est.)
country comparison to the world: 7

Crude oil—exports: 2.671 million bbl/day (2016 est.)
country comparison to the world: 5

Crude oil—imports: 892,500 bbl/day (2016 est.)
country comparison to the world: 11

Crude oil—proved reserves: 169.7 billion bbl (1 January 2017 es)
country comparison to the world: 3

Refined petroleum products—production: 1.883 million bbl/day (2016 est.)
country comparison to the world: 11

Refined petroleum products—consumption: 2.379 million bbl/day (2016 est.)
country comparison to the world: 11

Refined petroleum products—exports: 991,600 bbl/day (2016 est.)
country comparison to the world: 9

Refined petroleum products—imports: 381,200 bbl/day (2016 est.)
country comparison to the world: 24

Natural gas—production: 149.9 billion cu m (2015 est.)
country comparison to the world: 5

Natural gas—consumption: 114.8 billion cu m (2015 est.)
country comparison to the world: 12

Natural gas—exports: 78.25 billion cu m (2015 est.)
country comparison to the world: 5

Natural gas—imports: 19.63 billion cu m (2015 est.)
country comparison to the world: 15

Natural gas—proved reserves: 2.182 trillion cu m (1 January 2017 es)
country comparison to the world: 17

Carbon dioxide emissions from consumption of energy: 564 million Mt (2013 est.)
country comparison to the world: 12

COMMUNICATIONS

Telephones—fixed lines: *total subscriptions:* 14,987,520
subscriptions per 100 inhabitants: 42 (July 2016 est.)
country comparison to the world: 17

Telephones—mobile cellular: *total.* 30.45 million
subscriptions per 100 inhabitants: 86 (July 2016 est.)
country comparison to the world: 44

Telephone system: *general assessment:* excellent service provided by modern technology
domestic: comparatively low mobile penetration provides further room for growth; domestic satellite system with about 300 earth stations
international: country code—1; submarine cables provide links to the US and Europe; satellite earth stations—7 (5 Intelsat—4 Atlantic Ocean and 1 Pacific Ocean, and 2 Intersputnik—Atlantic Ocean region) (2016)

Broadcast media: 2 public TV broadcasting networks, 1 in English and 1 in French, each with a large number of network affiliates; several private-commercial networks also with multiple network affiliates; overall, about 150 TV stations; multi-channel satellite and cable systems provide access to a wide range of stations including US stations; mix of public and commercial radio broadcasters with the Canadian Broadcasting Corporation (CBC), the public radio broadcaster, operating 4 radio networks, Radio Canada International, and radio services to indigenous populations in the north; roughly 1,119 licensed radio stations (2016)

Internet country code: .ca
Internet users: total: 31,770,034

percent of population: 89.8% (July 2016 est.)
country comparison to the world: 21

TRANSPORTATION

National air transport system: *number of registered air carriers:* 51
inventory of registered aircraft operated by air carriers: 879
annual passenger traffic on registered air carriers: 80,228,301
annual freight traffic on registered air carriers: 2,074,830,881 mt-km (2015)
Civil aircraft registration country code prefix: C (2016)

Airports: 1,467 (2013)

country comparison to the world: 4

Airports—with paved runways: *total:* 523
over 3,047 m: 21
2,438 to 3,047 m: 19
1,524 to 2,437 m: 147
914 to 1,523 m: 257
under 914 m: 79 (2017)

Airports—with unpaved runways: *total:* 944
1,524 to 2,437 m: 75
914 to 1,523 m: 385
under 914 m: 484 (2013)

Heliports: 26 (2013)

Pipelines: gas and liquid petroleum 110,000 km (2017)

Railways: *total:* 77,932 km
standard gauge: 77,932 km 1.435-m gauge (2014)
country comparison to the world: 4

Roadways: *total:* 1,042,300 km
paved: 415,600 km (includes 17,000 km of expressways)
unpaved: 626,700 km (2011)
country comparison to the world: 7

Waterways: 636 km (Saint Lawrence Seaway of 3,769 km, including the Saint Lawrence River of 3,058 km, shared with United States) (2011)
country comparison to the world: 77

Merchant marine: *total:* 639
by type: bulk carrier 16, container ship 1, general cargo 88, oil tanker 15, other 519 (2017)

Ports and terminals: *major seaport(s):* Halifax, Saint John (New Brunswick), Vancouver

river and lake port(s): Montreal, Quebec City, Sept-Isles (St. Lawrence); Fraser River Port (Fraser); Hamilton (Lake Ontario)
oil terminal(s): Lower Lakes terminal
dry bulk cargo port(s): Port-Cartier (iron ore and grain),
container port(s): Montreal (1,446,000), Vancouver (3,054,000)(2015)
LNG terminal(s) (import): Saint John

MILITARY AND SECURITY

Military expenditures: 0.99% of GDP (2016)
0.99% of GDP (2015)
1% of GDP (2014)
1% of GDP (2013)
1.12% of GDP (2012)
country comparison to the world: 80

Military branches: *Canadian Forces:* Canadian Army, Royal Canadian Navy; Royal Canadian Air Force, Canadian Joint Operations Command (2015)

Military service age and obligation: 17 years of age for voluntary male and female military service (with parental consent); 16 years of age for Reserve and Military College applicants; Canadian citizenship or permanent residence status required; maximum 34 years of age; service obligation 3-9 years (2012)

TRANSNATIONAL ISSUES

Disputes—international: managed maritime boundary disputes with the US at Dixon Entrance,

Beaufort Sea, Strait of Juan de Fuca, and the Gulf of Maine, including the disputed Machias Seal Island and North Rock; Canada and the United States dispute how to divide the Beaufort Sea and the status of the Northwest Passage but continue to work cooperatively to survey the Arctic continental shelf; US works closely with Canada to intensify security measures for monitoring and controlling legal and illegal movement of people, transport, and commodities across the international border; sovereignty dispute with Denmark over Hans Island in the Kennedy Channel between Ellesmere Island and Greenland; commencing the collection of technical evidence for submission to the Commission on the Limits of the Continental Shelf in support of claims for continental shelf beyond 200 nm from its declared baselines in the Arctic, as stipulated in Article 76, paragraph 8, of the UN Convention on the Law of the Sea

Refugees and internally displaced persons: refugees (country of origin): 8,228 (Colombia); 7,356 (China); 6,774 (Haiti) (2016)

Illicit drugs: illicit producer of cannabis for the domestic drug market and export to US; use of hydroponics technology permits growers to plant large quantities of high-quality marijuana indoors; increasing ecstasy production, some of which is destined for the US; vulnerable to narcotics money laundering because of its mature financial services sector

CAYMAN ISLANDS

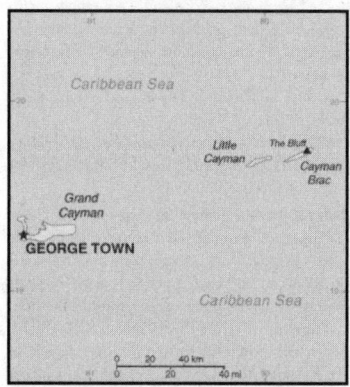

INTRODUCTION

Background: The Cayman Islands were colonized from Jamaica by the British during the 18th and 19th centuries and were administered by Jamaica after 1863. In 1959, the islands became a territory within the Federation of the West Indies. When

the Federation dissolved in 1962, the Cayman Islands chose to remain a British dependency. The territory has transformed itself into a significant offshore financial center.

GEOGRAPHY

Location: Caribbean, three-island group (Grand Cayman, Cayman Brac, Little Cayman) in Caribbean Sea, 240 km south of Cuba and 268 km northwest of Jamaica

Geographic coordinates: 19 30 N, 80 30 W

Map references: Central America and the Caribbean

Area: *total:* 264 sq km
land: 264 sq km
water: 0 sq km
country comparison to the world: 211

Area—comparative: 1.5 times the size of Washington, DC

Land boundaries: 0 km

Coastline: 160 km

Maritime claims: *territorial sea:* 12 nm
exclusive fishing zone: 200 nm

Climate: tropical marine; warm, rainy summers (May to October) and cool, relatively dry winters (November to April)

Terrain: low-lying limestone base surrounded by coral reefs

Elevation: *mean elevation:* NA

elevation extremes: *lowest point:* Caribbean Sea 0 m
highest point: 1 km SW of The Bluff on Cayman Brac 50 m

Natural resources: fish, climate and beaches that foster tourism

Land use: *agricultural land:* 11.2%
arable land: 0.8%;
permanent crops: 2.1%;
permanent pasture: 8.3%
forest: 52.9%
other: 35.9% (2011 est.)
Irrigated land: NA

Population—distribution: majority of the population resides on Grand Cayman

Natural hazards: hurricanes (July to November)

Environment—current issues: no natural freshwater resources; drinking water supplies are met by reverse osmosis desalination plants

Geography—note: important location between Cuba and Central America

PEOPLE AND SOCIETY

Population: 58,441
note: most of the population lives on Grand Cayman (July 2017 est.)
country comparison to the world: 205

Nationality: noun: Caymanian(s)
adjective: Caymanian

Ethnic groups: mixed 40%, white 20%, black 20%, expatriates of various ethnic groups 20%

Languages: English (official) 90.9%, Spanish 4%, Filipino 3.3%, other 1.7%, unspecified 0.1% (2010 est.)

Religions: Protestant 67.8% (includes Church of God 22.6%, Seventh Day Adventist 9.4%, Presbyterian/United Church 8.6%, Baptist 8.3%, Pentecostal 7.1%, non-denominational 5.3%, Anglican 4.1%, Wesleyan Holiness 2.4%), Roman Catholic 14.1%, Jehovah's Witness 1.1%, other 7%, none 9.3%, unspecified 0.7% (2010 est.)

Age structure: 0-14 years: 18% (male 5,298/female 5,224)
15-24 years: 12.41% (male 3,601/female 3,654)
25-54 years: 42.52% (male 12,123/female 12,727)
55-64 years: 14.47% (male 4,030/female 4,427)
65 years and over: 12.59% (male 3,425/female 3,932) (2017 est.)

Median age: total: 40 years
male: 39.3 years
female: 40.7 years (2017 est.)
country comparison to the world: 50

Population growth rate: 2.01% (2017 est.)
country comparison to the world: 45

Birth rate: 12 births/1,000 population (2017 est.)
country comparison to the world: 168

Death rate: 5.8 deaths/1,000 population (2017 est.)
country comparison to the world: 172

Net migration rate: 13.8 migrant(s)/1,000 population
note: major destination for Cubans trying to migrate to the US (2017 est.)
country comparison to the world: 4

Population distribution: majority of the population resides on Grand Cayman

Urbanization: urban population: 100% of total population (2017)
rate of urbanization: 0.98% annual rate of change (2015-20 est.)

Major urban areas—population: GEORGE TOWN (capital) 31,000 (2014)

Sex ratio: at birth: 1.02 male(s)/female
0-14 years: 1.01 male(s)/female
15-24 years: 0.98 male(s)/female
25-54 years: 0.95 male(s)/female
55-64 years: 0.91 male(s)/female
65 years and over: 0.89 male(s)/female

total population: 0.95 male(s)/female (2016 est.)

Infant mortality rate: total: 5.9 deaths/1,000 live births
male: 6.7 deaths/1,000 live births
female: 5 deaths/1,000 live births (2017 est.)
country comparison to the world: 168

Life expectancy at birth: total population: 81.3 years
male: 78.6 years
female: 84.1 years (2017 est.)
country comparison to the world: 28

Total fertility rate: 1.85 children born/woman (2017 est.)
country comparison to the world: 147

Drinking water source:
improved:
urban: 97.4% of population
rural: NA
total: 97.4% of population
unimproved:
urban: 2.6% of population
rural: NA
total: 2.6% of population (2015 est.)

Sanitation facility access:
improved:
urban: 95.6% of population
total: 95.6% of population
unimproved:
urban: 4.4% of population
total: 4.4% of population (2015 est.)

HIV/AIDS—adult prevalence rate: NA

HIV/AIDS—people living with HIV/AIDS: NA

HIV/AIDS—deaths: NA

Major infectious diseases: note: active local transmission of Zika virus by Aedes species mosquitoes has been identified in this country (as of August 2016); it poses an important risk (a large number of cases possible) among US citizens if bitten by an infective mosquito; other less common ways to get Zika are through sex, via blood transfusion, or during pregnancy, in which the pregnant woman passes Zika virus to her fetus (2016)

Education expenditures: NA

Literacy: definition: age 15 and over has ever attended school
total population: 98.9%
male: 98.7%
female: 99% (2007 est.)

Unemployment, youth ages 15-24: total: 13.8%
male: 16.4%
female: 11.4% (2015 est.)
country comparison to the world: 86

GOVERNMENT

Country name: conventional long form: none
conventional short form: Cayman Islands
etymology: the islands' name comes from the native Carib word "caiman," describing the marine crocodiles living there

Dependency status: overseas territory of the UK

Government type: parliamentary democracy (Legislative Assembly); self-governing overseas territory of the UK

Capital: name: George Town (on Grand Cayman)
geographic coordinates: 19 18 N, 81 23 W
time difference: UTC-5 (same time as Washington, DC, during Standard Time)

Administrative divisions: 6 districts; Bodden Town, Cayman Brac and Little Cayman, East End, George Town, North Side, West Bay

Independence: none (overseas territory of the UK)

National holiday: Constitution Day, first Monday in July (1959)

Constitution: several previous; latest approved 10 June 2009, entered into force 6 November 2009 (The Cayman Islands Constitution Order 2009) (2016)

Legal system: English common law and local statutes

Citizenship: see United Kingdom

Suffrage: 18 years of age; universal

Executive branch: chief of state: Queen ELIZABETH II (since 6 February 1952); represented by Governor Helen KILPATRICK (since 6 September 2013)

head of government: Premier Alden MCLAUGHLIN (since 29 May 2013)
cabinet: Cabinet selected from the Legislative Assembly and appointed by the governor on the advice of the premier
elections/appointments: the monarchy is hereditary; governor appointed by the monarch; following legislative elections, the leader of the majority party or majority coalition appointed premier by the governor

Legislative branch: description: unicameral Legislative Assembly (21 seats; 19 members directly elected by majority vote and 2 ex officio members—the deputy governor and attorney general—appointed by the governor; members serve 4-year terms)
elections: last held on 24 May 2017 (next to be held in 2021)
election results: percent of vote by party—independent 44.7%, PPM 31.2%, CDP 24.1%; seats by party—independent 9, PPM 7, CDP 3

Judicial branch: highest resident court(s): Court of Appeal (consists of the court president and at least 2 judges); Grand Court (consists of the court president and at least 2 judges); note—appeals beyond the Court of Appeal are heard by the Judicial Committee of the Privy Council (in London)
judge selection and term of office: Court of Appeal and Grand Court judges appointed by the governor on the advice of the Judicial and Legal Services Commission, an 8-member independent body consisting of governor appointees, Court of Appeal president, and attorneys; Court of Appeal judges' tenure based on their individual instruments of appointment; Grand Court judges normally appointed until retirement at age 65 but can be extended until age 70
subordinate courts: Summary Court

Political parties and leaders: People's Progressive Movement or PPM [Alden MCLAUGHLIN] Cayman Democratic Party or CDP [McKeeva BUSH]

Political pressure groups and leaders: Coalition for Cayman or C4C
People's National Alliance or PNA
National Trust
other: environmentalists

International organization participation: Caricom (associate), CDB, Interpol (subbureau), IOC, UNESCO (associate), UPU

Diplomatic representation in the US: none (overseas territory of the UK)

Diplomatic representation from the US: none (overseas territory of the UK); consular services provided through the US Embassy in Jamaica

Flag description: a blue field with the flag of the UK in the upper hoist-side quadrant and the Caymanian coat of arms centered on the outer half of the flag; the coat of arms includes a crest with a pineapple, representing the connection with Jamaica, and a turtle, representing Cayman's seafaring tradition, above a shield bearing a golden lion, symbolizing Great Britain, below which are three green stars (representing the three islands) surmounting white and blue wavy lines representing the sea and a scroll at the bottom bearing the motto HE HATH FOUNDED IT UPON THE SEAS

National symbol(s): green sea turtle

National anthem: name: "Beloved Isle Cayman"
lyrics/music: Leila E. ROSS
note: adopted 1993; served as an unofficial anthem since 1930; as a territory of the United Kingdom, in addition to the local anthem, "God Save the Queen" is official (see United Kingdom)

ECONOMY

Economy—overview: With no direct taxation, the islands are a thriving offshore financial center. More than 93,000 companies were registered in the Cayman Islands as of 2008, including almost 300 banks, 800 insurers, and 10,000 mutual funds. A stock exchange was opened in 1997. Nearly 90% of the islands' food and consumer goods must be imported. The Caymanians enjoy a standard of living comparable to that of Switzerland.

Tourism is also a mainstay, accounting for about 70% of GDP and 75% of foreign currency earnings. The tourist industry is aimed at the luxury market and caters mainly to visitors from North America. Total tourist arrivals exceeded 1.9 million in 2008, with about half from the US.

GDP (purchasing power parity): $2.507 billion (2014 est.)
$2.465 billion (2013 est.)
$2.435 billion (2012 est.)
country comparison to the world: 192

GDP (official exchange rate): $2.25 billion (2008 est.)

GDP—real growth rate: 1.7% (2014 est.)
1.2% (2013 est.)

1.6% (2012 est.)
country comparison to the world: 167

GDP—per capita (PPP): $43,800 (2004 est.)
country comparison to the world: 38

GDP—composition, by end use:
household consumption: 62.4%
government consumption: 14.7%
investment in fixed capital: 22.3%
investment in inventories: 0.1%
exports of goods and services: 62.1%
imports of goods and services: -61.5% (2017 est.)

GDP—composition, by sector of origin:
agriculture: 0.3%
industry: 7.5%
services: 91.3% (2017 est.)

Agriculture—products: vegetables, fruit; livestock; turtle farming

Industries: tourism, banking, insurance and finance, construction, construction materials, furniture

Industrial production growth rate: 2.2% (2017 est.)
country comparison to the world: 125

Labor force: 39,000
note: nearly 55% are non-nationals (2007 est.)
country comparison to the world: 198

Labor force—by occupation: *agriculture:* 1.9%
industry: 19.1%
services: 79% (2008 est.)

Unemployment rate: 4% (2008)
4.4% (2004)
country comparison to the world: 51

Population below poverty line: NA%

Household income or consumption by percentage share: *lowest 10%:* NA%
highest 10%: NA%

Budget: *revenues:* $870.2 million
expenditures: $732.2 million
Taxes and other revenues: 38.7% of GDP (2017 est.)
country comparison to the world: 41

Budget surplus (+) or deficit (-): 6.1% of GDP (2017 est.)
country comparison to the world: 6

Fiscal year: 1 April—31 March

Inflation rate (consumer prices): 1% (2017 est.)
-0.6% (2016 est.)
country comparison to the world: 41

Stock of narrow money: $334.3 million (31 December 2008)
country comparison to the world: 176

Stock of broad money: $5.564 billion (31 December 2008 est.)
country comparison to the world: 127

Market value of publicly traded shares: $315.6 million (31 December 2015 est.)
$183.5 million (31 December 2007)
$188.4 million (31 December 2006)
country comparison to the world: 116

Exports: $55.3 million (2017 est.)
$47.6 million (2016 est.)
country comparison to the world: 202

Exports—commodities: turtle products, manufactured consumer goods

Imports: $588.7 million (2017 est.)
$585.2 million (2016 est.)
country comparison to the world: 186

Imports—commodities: foodstuffs, manufactured goods, fuels

Stock of direct foreign investment—at home: $NA

Stock of direct foreign investment—abroad: $NA

Exchange rates: Caymanian dollars (KYD) per US dollar—
0.82 (2017 est.)
0.82 (2016 est.)
0.82 (2015 est.)
0.82 (2014 est.)
0.83 (2013 est.)

ENERGY

Electricity access: *population without electricity:* 5,726
electrification—*total population:* 91%
electrification—urban areas: 91%
electrification—rural areas: 80% (2012)

Electricity—production: 624 million kWh (2015 est.)
country comparison to the world: 163

Electricity—consumption: 587 million kWh (2015 est.)
country comparison to the world: 168

Electricity—exports: 0 kWh (2016 est.)
country comparison to the world: 120

Electricity—imports: 0 kWh (2016 est.)
country comparison to the world: 134

Electricity—installed generating capacity: 132,000 kW (2015 est.)
country comparison to the world: 173

Electricity—from fossil fuels: 100% of total installed capacity (2015 est.)
country comparison to the world: 4

Electricity—from nuclear fuels: 0% of total installed capacity (2015 est.)
country comparison to the world: 67

Electricity—from hydroelectric plants: 0% of total installed capacity (2015 est.)
country comparison to the world: 168

Electricity—from other renewable sources: 0% of total installed capacity (2015 est.)
country comparison to the world: 176

Crude oil—production: 0 bbl/day (2016 est.)
country comparison to the world: 120

Crude oil—exports: 0 bbl/day (2014 est.)
country comparison to the world: 106

Crude oil—imports: 0 bbl/day (2014 est.)
country comparison to the world: 109

Crude oil—proved reserves: 0 bbl (1 January 2017 es)
country comparison to the world: 119

Refined petroleum products—production: 0 bbl/day (2014 est.)
country comparison to the world: 128

175

Refined petroleum products—consumption: 4,000 bbl/day (2015 est.)
country comparison to the world: 179

Refined petroleum products—exports: 0 bbl/day (2014 est.)
country comparison to the world: 142

Refined petroleum products—imports: 3,984 bbl/day (2014 est.)
country comparison to the world: 170

Natural gas—production: 0 cu m (2013 est.)
country comparison to the world: 120

Natural gas—consumption: 0 cu m (2013 est.)
country comparison to the world: 168

Natural gas—exports: 0 cu m (2013 est.)
country comparison to the world: 84

Natural gas—imports: 0 cu m (2013 est.)
country comparison to the world: 107

Natural gas—proved reserves: 0 cu m (1 January 2014 es)
country comparison to the world: 126

Carbon dioxide emissions from consumption of energy: 500,000 Mt (2013 est.)
country comparison to the world: 181

COMMUNICATIONS

Telephones—fixed lines: *total subscriptions:* 34,116
subscriptions per 100 inhabitants: 60 (July 2016 est.)
country comparison to the world: 170

Telephones—mobile cellular: *total:* 95,656

subscriptions per 100 inhabitants: 167 (July 2016 est.)
country comparison to the world: 193

Telephone system: *general assessment:* reasonably good overall telephone system with a high fixed-line teledensity
domestic: liberalization of telecom market in 2003; introduction of competition in the mobile-cellular market in 2004 boosted subscriptions dramatically
international: country code—1-345; landing points for the Maya-1, Eastern Caribbean Fiber System (ECFS), and the Cayman-Jamaica Fiber System submarine cables that provide links to the US and parts of Central and South America; satellite earth station—1 Intelsat (Atlantic Ocean) (2015)

Broadcast media: 4 TV stations; cable and satellite subscription services offer a variety of international programming; government-owned Radio Cayman operates 2 networks broadcasting on 5 stations; 10 privately owned radio stations operate alongside Radio Cayman (2007)

Internet country code: .ky
Internet users: total: 45,242
percent of population: 79.0% (July 2016 est.)
country comparison to the world: 189

TRANSPORTATION

National air transport system: *number of registered air carriers:* 1
inventory of registered aircraft operated by air carriers: 6 (2015)

Civil aircraft registration country code prefix: VP-C (2016)

Airports: 3 (2013)
country comparison to the world: 196

Airports—with paved runways: *total:* 3
1,524 to 2,437 m: 2
914 to 1,523 m: 1 (2017)

Airports—with unpaved runways: *total:* 1
914 to 1,523 m: 1 (2012)

Roadways: *total:* 785 km
paved: 785 km (2007)
country comparison to the world: 190

Merchant marine: *total:* 161
by type: bulk carrier 29, general cargo 4, oil tanker 16, other 112 (2017)

Ports and terminals: *major seaport(s):* Cayman Brac, George Town

MILITARY AND SECURITY

Military branches: no regular military forces; Royal Cayman Islands Police Force (2012)

Military—note: defense is the responsibility of the UK

TRANSNATIONAL ISSUES

Disputes—international: none

Illicit drugs: major offshore financial center; vulnerable to drug transshipment to the US and Europe

CENTRAL AFRICAN REPUBLIC

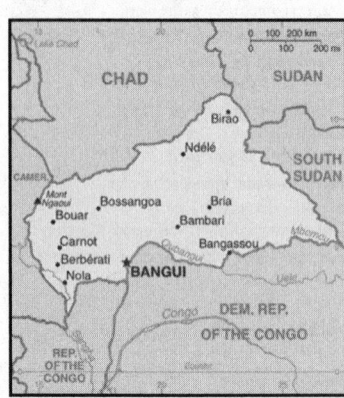

INTRODUCTION

Background: The former French colony of Ubangi-Shari became the Central African Republic upon independence in 1960. After three tumultuous decades of misrule—mostly by military governments—civilian rule was established in 1993 but lasted only a decade. In March 2003, President

Ange-Felix PATASSE was deposed in a military coup led by General Francois BOZIZE, who established a transitional government. Elections held in 2005 affirmed General BOZIZE as president; he was reelected in 2011 in voting widely viewed as flawed. The government still lacks full control of the countryside, where lawlessness persists. Several rebel groups joined together in early December 2012 to launch a series of attacks that left them in control of numerous towns in the northern and central parts of the country. The rebels—unhappy with BOZIZE's government—participated in peace talks in early January 2013 which resulted in a coalition government including the rebellion's leadership. In March 2013, the coalition government dissolved, rebels seized the capital, and President BOZIZE fled the country. Rebel leader Michel DJOTODIA assumed the presidency and the following month established a National Transitional Council (CNT). In January 2014, the CNT elected Catherine SAMBA-PANZA as interim president. Elections completed in March 2016 installed independent candidate Faustin-Archange TOUADERA as president; he continues to work towards peace between the government and armed groups, and is developing

a disarmament, demobilization, reintegration, and repatriation (DDRR) program to reintegrate the armed groups into society.

GEOGRAPHY

Location: Central Africa, north of Democratic Republic of the Congo

Geographic coordinates: 7 00 N, 21 00 E

Map references: Africa

Area: *total:* 622,984 sq km
land: 622,984 sq km
water: 0 sq km
country comparison to the world: 46

Area—comparative: slightly smaller than Texas

Land boundaries: *total:* 5,920 km
border countries (6): Cameroon 901 km, Chad 1,556 km, Democratic Republic of the Congo 1,747 km, Republic of the Congo 487 km, South Sudan 1,055 km, Sudan 174 km

Coastline: 0 km (landlocked)

Maritime claims: none (landlocked)

Climate: tropical; hot, dry winters; mild to hot, wet summers

Terrain: vast, flat to rolling plateau; scattered hills in northeast and southwest

Elevation: *mean elevation:* 635 m

elevation extremes: *lowest point:* Oubangui River 335 m

highest point: Mont Ngaoui 1,410 m

Natural resources: diamonds, uranium, timber, gold, oil, hydropower

Land use: *agricultural land:* 8.1%
arable land: 2.9%;
permanent crops: 0.1%;
permanent pasture: 5.1%
forest: 36.2%
other: 55.7% (2011 est.)
Irrigated land: 10 sq km (2012)

Population—distribution: majority of residents live in the western and central areas of the country, especially in and around the capital of Bangui

Natural hazards: hot, dry, dusty harmattan winds affect northern areas; floods are common

Environment—current issues: tap water is not potable; poaching has diminished the country's reputation as one of the last great wildlife refuges; desertification; deforestation

Environment—international agreements: *party to:* Biodiversity, Climate Change, Climate Change-Kyoto Protocol, Desertification, Endangered Species, Hazardous Wastes, Ozone Layer Protection, Tropical Timber 94, Wetlands
signed, but not ratified: Law of the Sea

Geography—note: landlocked; almost the precise center of Africa

PEOPLE AND SOCIETY

Population: 5,625,118

note: estimates for this country explicitly take into account the effects of excess mortality due to AIDS; this can result in lower life expectancy, higher infant mortality, higher death rates, lower population growth rates, and changes in the distribution of population by age and sex than would otherwise be expected (July 2017 est.)
country comparison to the world: 115

Nationality: *noun:* Central African(s)
adjective: Central African

Ethnic groups: Baya 33%, Banda 27%, Mandjia 13%, Sara 10%, Mboum 7%, M'Baka 4%, Yakoma 4%, other 2%

Languages: French (official), Sangho (lingua franca and national language), tribal languages

Religions: indigenous beliefs 35%, Protestant 25%, Roman Catholic 25%, Muslim 15%
note: animistic beliefs and practices strongly influence the Christian majority

Demographic profile: The Central African Republic's (CAR) humanitarian crisis has worsened since a coup in March 2013. CAR's high mortality rate and low life expectancy are attributed to elevated rates of preventable and treatable diseases (including malaria and malnutrition), an inadequate health care system, precarious food security, and armed conflict. Some of the worst

mortality rates are in western CAR's diamond mining region, which is impoverished because of government attempts to control the diamond trade and the fall in industrial diamond prices. To make matters worse, the government and international donors have reduced health funding in recent years. The CAR's weak educational system and low literacy rate have also suffered as a result of the country's ongoing conflict. Schools are closed, qualified teachers are scarce, infrastructure, funding, and supplies are lacking and subject to looting, and many students and teachers are displaced by violence.

Rampant poverty, human rights violations, unemployment, poor infrastructure, and a lack of security and stability have led to forced displacement internally and externally. Since the political crisis that resulted in CAR's March 2013 coup began in December 2012, approximately 370,000 people have fled to Chad, the Democratic Republic of the Congo (DRC), and other neighboring countries, while more than an estimated 600,000 are displaced internally as of October 2017. The UN has urged countries to refrain from repatriating CAR refugees amid the heightened lawlessness.

Age structure: *0-14 years:* 40.09% (male 1,133,361/female 1,121,640)
15-24 years: 19.94% (male 563,730/female 557,676)
25-54 years: 32.45% (male 913,363/female 912,096)
55-64 years: 4.1% (male 106,651/female 123,839)
65 years and over: 3.43% (male 74,834/female 117,928) (2017 est.)

Dependency ratios: *total dependency ratio:* 90
youth dependency ratio: 83.1
elderly dependency ratio: 7
potential support ratio: 14.4 (2015 est.)

Median age: *total:* 19.7 years
male: 19.4 years
female: 20 years (2017 est.)
country comparison to the world: 195

Population growth rate: 2.12% (2017 est.)
country comparison to the world: 40

Birth rate: 34.3 births/1,000 population (2017 est.)
country comparison to the world: 23

Death rate: 13.2 deaths/1,000 population (2017 est.)
country comparison to the world: 11

Net migration rate: 0 migrant(s)/1,000 population (2017 est.)
country comparison to the world: 78

Population distribution: majority of residents live in the western and central areas of the country, especially in and around the capital of Bangui

Urbanization: *urban population:* 40.6% of total population (2017)
rate of urbanization: 2.73% annual rate of change (2015-20 est.)

Major urban areas—population: BANGUI (capital) 794,000 (2015)

Sex ratio: *at birth:* 1.03 male(s)/female
0-14 years: 1.01 male(s)/female

15-24 years: 1.01 male(s)/female
25-54 years: 1 male(s)/female
55-64 years: 0.84 male(s)/female
65 years and over: 0.64 male(s)/female
total population: 0.98 male(s)/female (2016 est.)

Maternal mortality ratio: 882 deaths/100,000 live births (2015 est.)
country comparison to the world: 2

Infant mortality rate: *total:* 86.3 deaths/1,000 live births
male: 93.7 deaths/1,000 live births
female: 78.7 deaths/1,000 live births (2017 est.)
country comparison to the world: 3

Life expectancy at birth: *total population:* 52.8 years
male: 51.4 years
female: 54.2 years (2017 est.)
country comparison to the world: 217

Total fertility rate: 4.3 children born/woman (2017 est.)
country comparison to the world: 28

Contraceptive prevalence rate: 15.2% (2010/11)

Health expenditures: 4.2% of GDP (2014)
country comparison to the world: 162

Physicians density: 0.05 physicians/1,000 population (2009)

Hospital bed density: 1 beds/1,000 population (2011)

Drinking water source:
improved:
urban: 89.6% of population
rural: 54.4% of population
total: 68.5% of population
unimproved:
urban: 10.4% of population
rural: 45.6% of population
total: 31.5% of population (2015 est.)

Sanitation facility access:
improved:
urban: 43.6% of population
rural: 7.2% of population
total: 21.8% of population
unimproved:
urban: 56.4% of population
rural: 92.8% of population
total: 78.2% of population (2015 est.)

HIV/AIDS—adult prevalence rate: 4% (2016 est.)
country comparison to the world: 14

HIV/AIDS—people living with HIV/AIDS: 130,000 (2016 est.)
country comparison to the world: 33

HIV/AIDS—deaths: 7,300 (2016 est.)
country comparison to the world: 25

Major infectious diseases: *degree of risk:* very high
food or waterborne diseases: bacterial and protozoal diarrhea, hepatitis A and E, and typhoid fever
vectorborne diseases: malaria and dengue fever
respiratory disease: meningococcal meningitis
water contact disease: schistosomiasis
animal contact disease: rabies (2016)

Obesity—adult prevalence rate: 7.5% (2016)

177

country comparison to the world: 159

Children under the age of 5 years underweight: 23.5% (2010)
country comparison to the world: 26

Education expenditures: 1.2% of GDP (2011)
country comparison to the world: 171

Literacy: *definition:* age 15 and over can read and write
total population: 36.8%
male: 50.7%
female: 24.4% (2015 est.)

School life expectancy (primary to tertiary education): *total:* 7 years
male: 8 years
female: 6 years (2012)

GOVERNMENT

Country name: *conventional long form:* Central African Republic
conventional short form: none
local long form: Republique Centrafricaine
local short form: none
former: Ubangi-Shari, Central African Empire
abbreviation: CAR
etymology: self-descriptive name specifying the country's location on the continent; "Africa" is derived from the Roman designation of the area corresponding to present-day Tunisia "Africa terra," which meant "Land of the Afri" (the tribe resident in that area), but which eventually came to mean the entire continent

Government type: presidential republic

Capital: *name:* Bangui

geographic coordinates: 4 22 N, 18 35 E
time difference: UTC+1 (6 hours ahead of Washington, DC, during Standard Time)

Administrative divisions: 14 prefectures (prefectures, singular—prefecture), 2 economic prefectures* (prefectures economiques, singular—prefecture economique), and 1 commune**; Bamingui-Bangoran, Bangui**, Basse-Kotto, Haute-Kotto, Haut-Mbomou, Kemo, Lobaye, Mambere-Kadei, Mbomou, Nana-Grebizi*, Nana-Mambere, Ombella-Mpoko, Ouaka, Ouham, Ouham-Pende, Sangha-Mbaere*, Vakaga

Independence: 13 August 1960 (from France)

National holiday: Republic Day, 1 December (1958)

Constitution: history: several previous; latest (interim constitution) approved by the Transitional Council 30 August 2015, adopted by referendum 13-14 December 2015, ratified 27 March 2016
amendments: proposals require support of the government, two-thirds of the National Council of Transition, and assent by the "Mediator of the Central African" crisis; passage requires at least three-fourths majority vote by the National Council membership; non-amendable constitutional provisions include those on the secular and republican form of government, fundamental rights and freedoms, amendment procedures, or changes to

the authorities of various high-level executive, parliamentary, and judicial officials (2017)

Legal system: civil law system based on the French model

International law organization participation: has not submitted an ICJ jurisdiction declaration; accepts ICCt jurisdiction

Citizenship: *citizenship by birth:* no
citizenship by descent only: least one parent must be a citizen of the Central African Republic
dual citizenship recognized: yes
residency requirement for naturalization: 35 years

Suffrage: 18 years of age; universal

Executive branch: *chief of state:* President Faustin-Archange TOUADERA (since 30 March 2016)

head of government: Prime Minister Simplice SARANDJI (since 2 April 2016)
cabinet: Council of Ministers appointed by the president
elections/appointments: under the new constitution, the president is elected by universal direct suffrage for a period of 5 years (eligible for a second term); election last held 30 December 2015 with a runoff 20 February 2016 (next to be held in 2020)
election results: Faustin-Archange TOUADERA elected president in the second round; percent of vote in first round—Anicet-Georges DOLOGUELE (URCA) 23.7%, Faustin-Archange TOUADERA (independent) 19.1%, Desire KOLINGBA (RDC) 12.0%, Martin ZIGUELE (MLPC) 11.4%, other 33.8%; percent of vote in second round—Faustin-Archange TOUADERA 62.7%, Anicet-Georges DOLOGUELE 37.3%
note: rebel forces seized the capital in March 2013, forcing former President BOZIZE to flee the country; Interim President Michel DJOTODIA assumed the presidency, reinstated the prime minister, and established a National Transitional Council (CNT) in April 2013; the NTC elected Catherine SAMBA-PANZA interim president in January 2014 to serve until February 2015 when new elections were to be held; her term was extended because instability delayed new elections and the transition did not take place until the end of March 2016

Legislative branch: description: unicameral National Assembly or Assemblee Nationale (131 seats; members directly elected in single-seat constituencies by absolute majority vote with a second round if needed; members serve 5-year terms)
elections: last held 30 December 2015 (results annulled), 14 February 2016—first round and 31 March 2016—second round (next election to be held in 2021)
election results: percent of vote by party—NA; seats by party—UNDP 16, URCA 11, RDC 8, MLPC 10, KNK 7, other 19, independent 60

Judicial branch: *highest court(s):* Supreme Court or Cour Supreme (consists of NA judges); Constitutional Court (consists of 9 judges, at least 3 of whom are women)
judge selection and term of office: Supreme Court judges appointed by the president; Constitutional

Court judge appointments—2 by the president, 1 by the speaker of the National Assembly, 2 elected by their peers, 2 are advocates elected by their peers, and 2 are law professors elected by their peers; judges serve 7-year non-renewable terms
subordinate courts: high courts; magistrates' courts

Political parties and leaders: Action Party for Development or PAD
Alliance for Democracy and Progress or ADP [Clement BELIBANGA]
Central African Democratic Rally or RDC [Desire Nzanga KOLINGBA]
Movement for Democracy and Development or MDD [Louis PAPENIAH]
Movement for the Liberation of the Central African People or MLPC [Martin ZIGUELE]
National Convergence (also known as Kwa Na Kwa) or KNK [Francois BOZIZE]
National Union for Democracy and Progress or UNDP [Amine MICHEL]
New Alliance for Progress or NAP [Jean-Jacques DEMAFOUTH]
Social Democratic Party or PSD [Enoch LAKOUE]
Union for Central African Renewal or URCA [Anicet-Georges DOLOGUELE]

International organization participation: ACP, AfDB, AU, BDEAC, CEMAC, EITI (compliant country) (suspended), FAO, FZ, G-77, IAEA, IBRD, ICAO, ICCt, ICRM, IDA, IFAD, IFC, IFRCS, ILO, IMF, Interpol, IOC, IOM, ITSO, ITU, ITUC (NGOs), MIGA, NAM, OIC (observer), OIF, OPCW, UN, UNCTAD, UNESCO, UNIDO, UNWTO, UPU, WCO, WHO, WIPO, WMO, WTO

Diplomatic representation in the US: *chief of mission:* Ambassador Stanislas MOUSSA-KEMBE (since 24 August 2009)
chancery: 2704 Ontario Road NW, Washington, DC 20009
telephone: [1] (202) 483-7800
FAX: [1] (202) 332-9893

Diplomatic representation from the US: *chief of mission:* Ambassador (vacant); Charge d'Affaires David P. BROWNSTEIN (since September 2017)
embassy: Avenue David Dacko, Bangui
mailing address: P.O. Box 924, Bangui
telephone: [236] 21 61 0200
FAX: [236] 21 61 4494

Flag description: four equal horizontal bands of blue (top), white, green, and yellow with a vertical red band in center; a yellow five-pointed star to the hoist side of the blue band; banner combines the Pan-African and French flag colors; red symbolizes the blood spilled in the struggle for independence, blue represents the sky and freedom, white peace and dignity, green hope and faith, and yellow tolerance; the star represents aspiration towards a vibrant future

National symbol(s): elephant; national colors: blue, white, green, yellow, red

National anthem: name: "Le Renaissance" (The Renaissance)

lyrics/music: Barthelemy BOGANDA/Herbert PEPPER
note: adopted 1960; Barthelemy BOGANDA wrote the anthem's lyrics and was the first prime minister of the autonomous French territory

ECONOMY

Economy—overview: Subsistence agriculture, together with forestry and mining, remains the backbone of the economy of the Central African Republic (CAR), with about 60% of the population living in outlying areas. The agricultural sector generates more than half of estimated GDP, although reliable statistics are difficult to determine in the conflict-prone country. Timber and diamonds account for most export earnings, followed by cotton. Important constraints to economic development include the CAR's landlocked geography, poor transportation system, largely unskilled work force, and legacy of misdirected macroeconomic policies. Factional fighting between the government and its opponents remains a drag on economic revitalization. Distribution of income is extraordinarily unequal and grants from the international community can only partially meet humanitarian needs. CAR shares a common currency, which is pegged to the Euro, with the Central African Monetary Union.

Since 2009, the IMF has worked closely with the government to institute reforms that have resulted in some improvement in budget transparency, but other problems remain. The government's additional spending in the run-up to the 2011 election worsened CAR's fiscal situation. In 2012, the World Bank approved $125 million in funding for transport infrastructure and regional trade, focused on the route between CAR's capital and the port of Douala in Cameroon. In July 2016, the IMF approved a three-year extended credit facility valued at $116 million; in mid-2017, the IMF completed a review of CAR's fiscal performance and broadly approved of the government's management, although issues with revenue collection, weak government capacity, and transparency remain. The World Bank in late 2016 approved a $20 million grant to restore basic fiscal management, improve transparency, and assist with economic recovery.

Participation in the Kimberley Process, a commitment to remove conflict diamonds from the global supply chain, led to a partially lifted the ban on diamond exports from CAR in 2015, but persistent insecurity is likely to constrain real GDP growth.

GDP (purchasing power parity): $3.395 billion (2017 est.)
$3.241 billion (2016 est.)
$3.101 billion (2015 est.)
note: data are in 2017 dollars
country comparison to the world: 185

GDP (official exchange rate): $1.992 billion (2016 est.)

GDP—real growth rate: 4.7% (2017 est.)
4.5% (2016 est.)
4.8% (2015 est.)

country comparison to the world: 48

GDP—per capita (PPP): $700 (2017 est.)
$700 (2016 est.)
$600 (2015 est.)
note: data are in 2017 dollars
country comparison to the world: 229

Gross national saving: 5.6% of GDP (2017 est.)
4.6% of GDP (2016 est.)
4.9% of GDP (2015 est.)
country comparison to the world: 169

GDP—composition, by end use:
household consumption: 96.3%
government consumption: 7.8%
investment in fixed capital: 13.6%
investment in inventories: 0%
exports of goods and services: 11.8%
imports of goods and services: -29.5% (2017 est.)

GDP—composition, by sector of origin:
agriculture: 42.9%
industry: 15.9%
services: 41.2% (2017 est.)

Agriculture—products: cotton, coffee, tobacco, cassava (manioc, tapioca), yams, millet, corn, bananas; timber

Industries: gold and diamond mining, logging, brewing, sugar refining

Industrial production growth rate: 3.9% (2017 est.)
country comparison to the world: 73

Labor force: 2.242 million (2017 est.)
country comparison to the world: 120

Unemployment rate: 8% (2001 est.)
note: 23% unemployment in the capital, Bangui
country comparison to the world: 107

Population below poverty line: NA%

Household income or consumption by percentage share: lowest 10%: 2.1%
highest 10%: 33% (2003)

Distribution of family income—Gini index: 61.3 (1993)
country comparison to the world: 3

Budget: revenues: $230.6 million
expenditures: $271.1 million (2017 est.)
Taxes and other revenues: 11.6% of GDP (2017 est.)
country comparison to the world: 208

Budget surplus (+) or deficit (-): -2% of GDP (2017 est.)
country comparison to the world: 85

Public debt: 42.5% of GDP (2016 est.)
48.5% of GDP (2015 est.)
country comparison to the world: 128

Fiscal year: calendar year

Inflation rate (consumer prices): 3.8% (2017 est.)
4.6% (2016 est.)
country comparison to the world: 152

Central bank discount rate: 4.25% (31 December 2009)
4.75% (31 December 2008)
country comparison to the world: 86

Commercial bank prime lending rate: 15.5% (31 December 2017 est.)
15.5% (31 December 2016 est.)

country comparison to the world: 37

Stock of narrow money: $415.5 million (31 December 2017 est.)
$342.9 million (31 December 2016 est.)
country comparison to the world: 172

Stock of broad money: $534.1 million (31 December 2017 est.)
$432.4 million (31 December 2016 est.)
country comparison to the world: 185

Stock of domestic credit: $566.2 million (31 December 2017 est.)
$458.5 million (31 December 2016 est.)
country comparison to the world: 178

Market value of publicly traded shares: $NA

Current account balance: -$194 million (2017 est.)
-$161 million (2016 est.)
country comparison to the world: 89

Exports: $118.5 million (2017 est.)
$101.5 million (2016 est.)
country comparison to the world: 193

Exports—commodities: diamonds, timber, cotton, coffee

Exports—partners: Belarus 33.5%, Germany 15.3%, France 14.2%, Chad 12.6%, Cameroon 9.7%, China 8.1% (2016)

Imports: $380.5 million (2017 est.)
$340.8 million (2016 est.)
country comparison to the world: 193

Imports—commodities: food, textiles, petroleum products, machinery, electrical equipment, motor vehicles, chemicals, pharmaceuticals

Imports—partners: Egypt 29.8%, France 18.6%, China 6.8%, Belgium 5.7%, Cameroon 5.4% (2016)

Debt—external: $767.1 million (31 December 2017 est.)
$691.5 million (31 December 2016 est.)
country comparison to the world: 170

Exchange rates: Cooperation Financiere en Afrique Centrale francs (XAF) per US dollar—605.3 (2017 est.)
593.01 (2016 est.)
593.01 (2015 est.)
591.45 (2014 est.)
494.42 (2013 est.)

ENERGY

Electricity access: population without electricity: 4,500,000
electrification—total population: 3%
electrification—urban areas: 5%
electrification—rural areas: 1% (2013)

Electricity—production: 174 million kWh (2015 est.)
country comparison to the world: 193

Electricity—consumption: 161.8 million kWh (2015 est.)
country comparison to the world: 195

Electricity—exports: 0 kWh (2016 est.)
country comparison to the world: 124

Electricity—imports: 0 kWh (2016 est.)
country comparison to the world: 137

Electricity—installed generating capacity: 44,000 kW (2015 est.)
country comparison to the world: 196

Electricity—from fossil fuels: 43.2% of total installed capacity (2015 est.)
country comparison to the world: 165

Electricity—from nuclear fuels: 0% of total installed capacity (2015 est.)
country comparison to the world: 72

Electricity—from hydroelectric plants: 56.8% of total installed capacity (2015 est.)
country comparison to the world: 30

Electricity—from other renewable sources: 0% of total installed capacity (2015 est.)
country comparison to the world: 178

Crude oil—production: 0 bbl/day (2016 est.)
country comparison to the world: 121

Crude oil—exports: 0 bbl/day (2014 est.)
country comparison to the world: 109

Crude oil—imports: 0 bbl/day (2014 est.)
country comparison to the world: 113

Crude oil—proved reserves: 0 bbl (1 January 2017 es)
country comparison to the world: 120

Refined petroleum products—production: 0 bbl/day (2014 est.)
country comparison to the world: 129

Refined petroleum products—consumption: 3,000 bbl/day (2015 est.)
country comparison to the world: 188

Refined petroleum products—exports: 0 bbl/day (2014 est.)
country comparison to the world: 145

Refined petroleum products—imports: 2,828 bbl/day (2014 est.)
country comparison to the world: 181

Natural gas—production: 0 cu m (2013 est.)
country comparison to the world: 123

Natural gas—consumption: 0 cu m (2013 est.)
country comparison to the world: 171

Natural gas—exports: 0 cu m (2013 est.)
country comparison to the world: 88

Natural gas—imports: 0 cu m (2013 est.)
country comparison to the world: 112

Natural gas—proved reserves: 0 cu m (1 January 2014 es)
country comparison to the world: 129

Carbon dioxide emissions from consumption of energy: 400,000 Mt (2013 est.)
country comparison to the world: 186

COMMUNICATIONS

Telephones—fixed lines: *total subscriptions:* 1,964
subscriptions per 100 inhabitants: less than 1 (July 2016 est.)
country comparison to the world: 216

Telephones—mobile cellular: *total:* 982,000

subscriptions per 100 inhabitants: 18 (July 2016 est.)
country comparison to the world: 155

Telephone system: *general assessment:* network consists principally of microwave radio relay and low-capacity, low-powered radiotelephone communication
domestic: very limited telephone service with less than 1 fixed-line connection per 100 persons; spurred by the presence of multiple mobile-cellular service providers, cellular usage is increasing from a low base; most fixed-line and mobile-cellular telephone services are concentrated in Bangui
international: country code—236; satellite earth station—1 Intelsat (Atlantic Ocean) (2015)

Broadcast media: government-owned network, Radiodiffusion Television Centrafricaine, provides limited domestic TV broadcasting; state-owned radio network is supplemented by a small number of privately owned broadcast stations as well as a few community radio stations; transmissions of at least 2 international broadcasters are available (2017)

Internet country code: .cf
Internet users: total: 246,000

percent of population: 4.6% (July 2016 est.)
country comparison to the world: 157

TRANSPORTATION

National air transport system: *number of registered air carriers:* 2
inventory of registered aircraft operated by air carriers: 2
annual passenger traffic on registered air carriers: 46,364
annual freight traffic on registered air carriers: 0 mt-km (2015)
Civil aircraft registration country code prefix: TL (2016)

Airports: 39 (2013)
country comparison to the world: 106

Airports—with paved runways: *total:* 2
2,438 to 3,047 m: 1
1,524 to 2,437 m: 1 (2017)

Airports—with unpaved runways: *total:* 37
2,438 to 3,047 m: 1
1,524 to 2,437 m: 11
914 to 1,523 m: 19
under 914 m: 6 (2013)

Roadways: *total:* 20,278 km
paved: 1,385 km
unpaved: 18,893 km (2010)
country comparison to the world: 107

Waterways: 2,800 km (the primary navigable river is the Ubangi, which joins the River Congo; it was the traditional route for the export of products because it connected with the Congo-Ocean railway at Brazzaville; because of the warfare on both sides of the River Congo from 1997, importers and exporters preferred routes through Cameroon) (2011)
country comparison to the world: 34

Merchant marine: *total:* by type: (2017)

country comparison to the world: 106

Ports and terminals: *river port(s):* Bangui (Oubangui); Nola (Sangha)

MILITARY AND SECURITY

Military branches: Central African Armed Forces (Forces Armees Centrafricaines, FACA): Ground Forces (includes Military Air Service), General Directorate of Gendarmerie Inspection (DGIG), National Police (2017)

Military service age and obligation: 18 years of age for military service; no conscription (2017)

TRANSNATIONAL ISSUES

Disputes—international: periodic skirmishes persist over water and grazing rights among related pastoral populations along the border with southern Sudan

Refugees and internally displaced persons: *IDPs:* 688,700 (clashes between army and rebel groups since 2005; tensions between ethnic groups) (2017)

Trafficking in persons: *current situation:* Central African Republic (CAR) is a source, transit, and destination country for children subjected to forced labor and sex trafficking, women subjected to forced prostitution, and adults subjected to forced labor; most victims appear to be CAR citizens exploited within the country, with a smaller number transported back and forth between the CAR and nearby countries; armed groups operating in the CAR, including those aligned with the former SELEKA Government and the Lord's Resistance Army, continue to recruit and re-recruit children for militia activities and labor; children are also subject to domestic servitude, commercial sexual exploitation, and forced labor in agriculture, mines, shops, and street vending; women and girls are subject to domestic servitude, sexual slavery, commercial sexual exploitation, and forced marriage

tier rating: Tier 3–the Central African Republic does not fully comply with the minimum standards for the elimination of trafficking and is not making significant efforts to do so; the government conducted a limited number of investigations and prosecutions of cases of suspected human trafficking in 2014 but did not identify, provide protection to, or refer to care providers any trafficking victims; the government did not directly provide reintegration programs for demobilized child soldiers, leaving victims vulnerable to further exploitation or retrafficking by armed groups, including those affiliated with the government; in 2014, an NGO and the government began drafting a national action plan against trafficking but no efforts were reported to establish a policy against child soldiering or to raise awareness about existing laws prohibiting the use of children in the armed forces (2015)

CHAD

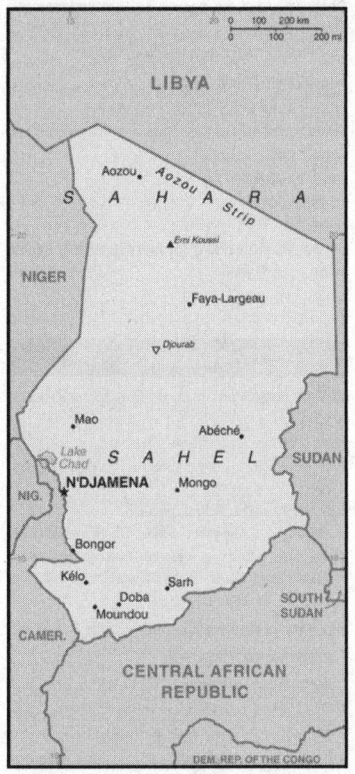

LIBYA

SAHARA

Aozou Aozou Strip

Emi Koussi

NIGER

Faya-Largeau

Djourab

Mao

Abéché

Lake Chad

SAHEL

SUDAN

N'DJAMENA Mongo

NIG.

Bongor

Kélo

Doba Sarh

Moundou

CAMER.

SOUTH SUDAN

CENTRAL AFRICAN REPUBLIC

DEM. REP. OF THE CONGO

INTRODUCTION

Background: Chad, part of France's African holdings until 1960, endured three decades of civil warfare, as well as invasions by Libya, before peace was restored in 1990. The government eventually drafted a democratic constitution and held flawed presidential elections in 1996 and 2001. In 1998, a rebellion broke out in northern Chad, which has sporadically flared up despite several peace agreements between the government and insurgents. In June 2005, President Idriss DEBY held a referendum successfully removing constitutional term limits and won another controversial election in 2006. Sporadic rebel campaigns continued throughout 2006 and 2007. The capital experienced a significant insurrection in early 2008, but has had no significant rebel threats since then, in part due to Chad's 2010 rapprochement with Sudan, which previously used Chadian rebels as proxies. In late 2015, the government imposed a state of emergency in the Lake Chad region following multiple attacks by the terrorist group Boko Haram throughout the year; Boko Haram also launched several bombings in N'Djamena in mid-2015. DEBY in 2016 was reelected to his fifth

term in an election that was peaceful but flawed. In December 2015, Chad completed a two-year rotation on the UN Security Council. In January 2017, DEBY completed a one-year term as President of the African Union.

GEOGRAPHY

Location: Central Africa, south of Libya

Geographic coordinates: 15 00 N, 19 00 E

Map references: Africa

Area: *total:* 1.284 million sq km
land: 1,259,200 sq km
water: 24,800 sq km
country comparison to the world: 22

Area—comparative: almost nine times the size of New York state; slightly more than three times the size of California

Land boundaries: *total:* 6,406 km
border countries (6): Cameroon 1,116 km, Central African Republic 1,556 km, Libya 1,050 km, Niger 1,196 km, Nigeria 85 km, Sudan 1,403 km

Coastline: 0 km (landlocked)

Maritime claims: none (landlocked)

Climate: tropical in south, desert in north

Terrain: broad, arid plains in center, desert in north, mountains in northwest, lowlands in south

Elevation: *mean elevation:* 543 m

elevation extremes: *lowest point:* Djourab 160 m
highest point: Emi Koussi 3,445 m

Natural resources: petroleum, uranium, natron, kaolin, fish (Lake Chad), gold, limestone, sand and gravel, salt

Land use: *agricultural land:* 39.6%
arable land: 3.9%;
permanent crops: 0%;
permanent pasture: 35.7%
forest: 9.1%
other: 51.3% (2011 est.)
Irrigated land: 300 sq km (2012)

Population—distribution: the population is unevenly distributed due to contrasts in climate and physical geography; the highest density is found in the southwest, particularly around Lake Chad and points south; the dry Saharan zone to the north is the least densely populated

Natural hazards: hot, dry, dusty harmattan winds occur in north; periodic droughts; locust plagues

Environment—current issues: inadequate supplies of potable water; improper waste disposal in rural areas contributes to soil and water pollution; desertification

Environment—international agreements: *party to:* Biodiversity, Climate Change, Desertification, Endangered Species, Hazardous Wastes, Ozone Layer Protection, Wetlands
signed, but not ratified: Law of the Sea, Marine Dumping

Geography—note: note 1: Chad is the largest of Africa's 16 landlocked countries

note 2: not long ago—geologically speaking—what is today the Sahara was green savannah teeming with wildlife; during the African Humid Period, roughly 11,000 to 5,000 years ago, a vibrant animal community, including elephants, giraffes, hippos, and antelope lived there; the last remnant of the "Green Sahara" exists in the Lakes of Ounianga (oo-nee-ahn-ga) in northern Chad, a series of 18 interconnected freshwater, saline, and hypersaline lakes now protected as a World Heritage site

note 3: Lake Chad, the most significant water body in the Sahel, is a remnant of a former inland sea, paleolake Mega-Chad; at its greatest extent, sometime before 5000 B.C., Lake Mega-Chad was the largest of four Saharan paleolakes that existed during the African Humid Period; it covered an area of about 400,000 sq km (150,000 sq mi), roughly the size of today's Caspian Sea

PEOPLE AND SOCIETY

Population: 12,075,985 (July 2017 est.)
country comparison to the world: 75

Nationality: *noun:* Chadian(s)
adjective: Chadian

Ethnic groups: Sara (Ngambaye/Sara/Madjingaye/Mbaye) 30.5%, Kanembu/Bornu/Buduma 9.8%, Arab 9.7%, Wadai/Maba/Masalit/Mimi 7%, Gorane 5.8%, Masa/Musseye/Musgum 4.9%, Bulala/Medogo/Kuka 3.7%, Marba/Lele/Mesme 3.5%, Mundang 2.7%, Bidiyo/Migaama/Kenga/ Dangleat 2.5%, Dadjo/Kibet/Muro 2.4%, Tupuri/ Kera 2%, Gabri/Kabalaye/Nanchere/Somrai 2%, Fulani/Fulbe/Bodore 1.8%, Karo/Zime/Peve 1.3%, Baguirmi/Barma 1.2%, Zaghawa/Bideyat/Kobe 1.1%, Tama/Assongori/Mararit 1.1%, Mesmedje/ Massalat/Kadjakse 0.8%, other Chadian ethnicities 3.4%, Chadians of foreign ethnicities 0.9%, foreign nationals 0.3%, unspecified 1.7% (2014-15 est.)

Languages: French (official), Arabic (official), Sara (in south), more than 120 different languages and dialects

Religions: Muslim 52.1%, Protestant 23.9%, Roman Catholic 20%, animist 0.3%, other Christian 0.2%, none 2.8%, unspecified 0.7% (2014-15 est.)

Demographic profile: Despite the start of oil production in 2003, 40% of Chad's population lives below the poverty line. The population will continue to grow rapidly because of the country's very high fertility rate and large youth cohort-more than 65% of the populace is under the age of 25– although the mortality rate is high and life expectancy is low. Chad has the world's third highest maternal mortality rate. Among the primary risk factors are poverty, anemia, rural habitation, high fertility, poor education, and a lack of access to family planning and obstetric care. Impoverished, uneducated adolescents living in rural areas are most affected. To improve women's reproductive health and reduce fertility, Chad will need to increase women's educational attainment, job participation, and knowledge of and access to family planning. Only about a quarter of women are literate, less than 5% use contraceptives, and more than 40% undergo genital cutting.

As of October 2017, more than 320,000 refugees from Sudan and more than 75,000 from the Central African Republic strain Chad's limited resources and create tensions in host communities. Thousands of new refugees fled to Chad in 2013 to escape worsening violence in the Darfur region of Sudan. The large refugee populations are hesitant to return to their home countries because of continued instability. Chad was relatively stable in 2012 in comparison to other states in the region, but past fighting between government forces and opposition groups and inter-communal violence have left nearly 60,000 of its citizens displaced in the eastern part of the country.

Age structure: *0-14 years:* 43.02% (male 2,634,817/female 2,560,790)
15-24 years: 21.46% (male 1,267,944/female 1,324,115)
25-54 years: 28.62% (male 1,574,782/female 1,881,183)
55-64 years: 3.88% (male 206,627/female 261,586)
65 years and over: 3.02% (male 150,364/female 213,777) (2017 est.)

Dependency ratios: *total dependency ratio:* 100.2
youth dependency ratio: 95.2
elderly dependency ratio: 4.9
potential support ratio: 20.3 (2015 est.)

Median age: *total:* 17.8 years
male: 16.8 years
female: 18.8 years (2017 est.)
country comparison to the world: 218

Population growth rate: 1.86% (2017 est.)
country comparison to the world: 52

Birth rate: 35.6 births/1,000 population (2017 est.)
country comparison to the world: 17

Death rate: 13.8 deaths/1,000 population (2017 est.)
country comparison to the world: 7

Net migration rate: -3.2 migrant(s)/1,000 population (2017 est.)
country comparison to the world: 176

Population distribution: the population is unevenly distributed due to contrasts in climate and physical geography; the highest density is found in the southwest, particularly around Lake Chad and points south; the dry Saharan zone to the north is the least densely populated

Urbanization: *urban population:* 22.8% of total population (2017)
rate of urbanization: 3.7% annual rate of change (2015-20 est.)

Major urban areas—population: N'DJAMENA (capital) 1.26 million (2015)

Sex ratio: *at birth:* 1.04 male(s)/female

0-14 years: 1.03 male(s)/female
15-24 years: 0.95 male(s)/female
25-54 years: 0.83 male(s)/female
55-64 years: 0.79 male(s)/female
65 years and over: 0.71 male(s)/female
total population: 0.93 male(s)/female (2016 est.)

Mother's mean age at first birth: 17.9 years
note: median age at first birth among women 25-29 (2014/15 est.)

Maternal mortality ratio: 856 deaths/100,000 live births (2015 est.)
country comparison to the world: 3

Infant mortality rate: *total:* 85.4 deaths/1,000 live births
male: 90.7 deaths/1,000 live births
female: 79.8 deaths/1,000 live births (2017 est.)
country comparison to the world: 5

Life expectancy at birth: *total population:* 50.6 years
male: 49.4 years
female: 51.9 years (2017 est.)
country comparison to the world: 224

Total fertility rate: 4.34 children born/woman (2017 est.)
country comparison to the world: 27

Contraceptive prevalence rate: 5.7% (2014/15)

Health expenditures: 3.6% of GDP (2014)
country comparison to the world: 169

Physicians density: 0.04 physicians/1,000 population (2013)

Drinking water source:
improved:
urban: 71.8% of population
rural: 44.8% of population
total: 50.8% of population
unimproved:
urban: 28.2% of population
rural: 55.2% of population
total: 49.2% of population (2015 est.)

Sanitation facility access:
improved:
urban: 31.4% of population
rural: 6.5% of population
total: 12.1% of population
unimproved:
urban: 68.6% of population
rural: 93.5% of population
total: 87.9% of population (2015 est.)

HIV/AIDS—adult prevalence rate: 1.3% (2016 est.)
country comparison to the world: 38

HIV/AIDS—people living with HIV/AIDS: 110,000 (2016 est.)
country comparison to the world: 41

HIV/AIDS—deaths: 2,800 (2016 est.)
country comparison to the world: 43

Major infectious diseases: *degree of risk:* very high
food or waterborne diseases: bacterial and protozoal diarrhea, hepatitis A and E, and typhoid fever
vectorborne diseases: malaria and dengue fever
water contact disease: schistosomiasis
respiratory disease: meningococcal meningitis

animal contact disease: rabies (2016)

Obesity—adult prevalence rate: 6.1% (2016)
country comparison to the world: 171

Children under the age of 5 years underweight: 28.8% (2015)
country comparison to the world: 13

Education expenditures: 2.9% of GDP (2013)
country comparison to the world: 160

Literacy: *definition:* age 15 and over can read and write French or Arabic
total population: 22.3%
male: 31.3%
female: 14% (2016 est.)

School life expectancy (primary to tertiary education): *total:* 7 years
male: 9 years
female: 6 years (2011)

GOVERNMENT

Country name: *conventional long form:* Republic of Chad
conventional short form: Chad
local long form: Republique du Tchad/Jumhuriyat Tshad
local short form: Tchad/Tshad
etymology: named for Lake Chad, which lies along the country's western border; the word "tsade" means "large body of water" or "lake" in several local native languages

Government type: presidential republic

Capital: *name:* N'Djamena
geographic coordinates: 12 06 N, 15 02 E
time difference: UTC+1 (6 hours ahead of Washington, DC, during Standard Time)

Administrative divisions: 23 regions (regions, singular—region); Barh el Gazel, Batha, Borkou, Chari-Baguirmi, Ennedi-Est, Ennedi-Ouest, Guera, Hadjer-Lamis, Kanem, Lac, Logone Occidental, Logone Oriental, Mandoul, Mayo-Kebbi Est, Mayo-Kebbi Ouest, Moyen-Chari, Ouaddai, Salamat, Sila, Tandjile, Tibesti, Ville de N'Djamena, Wadi Fira

Independence: 11 August 1960 (from France)

National holiday: Independence Day, 11 August (1960)

Constitution: history: several previous; latest approved by referendum 31 March 1996, entered into force 8 April 1996
amendments: proposed as a revision by the president of the republic after a Council of Ministers (cabinet) decision or by the National Assembly; approval for consideration of a revision requires at least three-fifths majority vote by the Assembly; passage requires approval by referendum or at least two-thirds majority vote by the Assembly; amended 2005, 2013 (2017)

Legal system: mixed legal system of civil and customary law

International law organization participation: has not submitted an ICJ jurisdiction declaration; accepts ICCt jurisdiction

Citizenship: *citizenship by birth:* no

citizenship by descent only: both parents must be citizens of Chad

dual citizenship recognized: Chadian law does not address dual citizenship

residency requirement for naturalization: 15 years

Suffrage: 18 years of age; universal

Executive branch: *chief of state:* President Idriss DEBY Itno, Lt. Gen. (since 4 December 1990)

head of government: Prime Minister Albert Pahimi PADACKE (since 15 February 2016)

cabinet: Council of Ministers; members appointed by the president on the recommendation of the prime minister

elections/appointments: president directly elected by absolute majority popular vote in 2 rounds if needed for a 5-year term (no term limits); election last held on 10 April 2016 (next to be held in April 2021); prime minister appointed by the president

election results: Lt. Gen. Idriss DEBY Itno reelected president in first round; percent of vote— Lt. Gen. Idriss DEBY (MPS) 61.6%, Saleh KEBZABO (UNDR) 12.8%, Laokein Kourayo MEDAR (CTPD) 10.7%, Djimrangar DADNADJI (CAP-SUR) 5.1%, other 9.8%

Legislative branch: description: unicameral National Assembly (188 seats; 118 directly elected in multi-seat constituencies by proportional representation vote and 70 directly elected in single-seat constituencies by absolute majority vote with a second round if needed; members serve 4-year terms)

elections: National Assembly—last held on 13 February and 6 May 2011 (next to be held in 2019)

election results: percent of vote by party—NA; seats by party—MPS 117, UNDR 10, RDP 9, URD 8, RNDT/Le Reveil 8, Viva-RNDP 5, FAR 4, PUR 2, UDR 2, PDSA 2, CTPD 2, other minor parties 19

note: the National Assembly mandate was extended, reportedly due to a lack of funding for the scheduled 2015 election

Judicial branch: *highest court(s):* Supreme Court (consists of the chief justice, 3 chamber presidents, and 12 judges or councilors and divided into 3 chambers); Constitutional Council (consists of 3 judges and 6 jurists)

judge selection and term of office: Supreme Court chief justice selected by the president; councilors—8 designated by the president and 7 by the speaker of the National Assembly; chief justice and councilors appointed for life; Constitutional Council judges—2 appointed by the president and 1 by the speaker of the National Assembly; jurists—3 each by the president and by the speaker of the National Assembly; judges appointed for 9-year terms

subordinate courts: High Court of Justice; Courts of Appeal; tribunals; justices of the peace

Political parties and leaders: Chadian Convention for Peace and Development or CTPD [Laoukein Kourayo MEDAR]

Federation Action for the Republic or FAR [Ngarledjy YORONGAR]

Framework of Popular Action for Solidarity and Unity of the Republic or CAP-SUR [Joseph Djimrangar DADNADJI]

National Rally for Development and Progress or Viva-RNDP [Dr. Nouradine Delwa Kassire COUMAKOYE]

National Union for Democracy and Renewal or UNDR [Saleh KEBZABO]

Party for Liberty and Development or PLD [Mahamat Allahou TAHER]

Party for Unity and Reconciliation

Patriotic Salvation Movement or MPS [Idriss DEBY]

Rally for Democracy and Progress or RDP [Mahamat Allahou TAHER]

RNDT/Le Reveil

Social Democratic Party for a Change-over of Power or PDSA

Union for Renewal and Democracy or URD [Sande NGARYIMBE]

Political pressure groups and leaders: NA

International organization participation: ACP, AfDB, AU, BDEAC, CEMAC, EITI (compliant country), FAO, FZ, G-77, IAEA, IBRD, ICAO, ICCt, ICRM, IDA, IDB, IFAD, IFC, IFRCS, ILO, IMF, Interpol, IOC, IOM, IPU, ITSO, ITU, ITUC (NGOs), MIGA, MINUSMA, NAM, OIC, OIF, OPCW, UN, UN Security Council (temporary), UNCTAD, UNESCO, UNIDO, UNOCI, UNWTO, UPU, WCO, WHO, WIPO, WMO, WTO

Diplomatic representation in the US: *hief of mission:* Ambassador (vacant)

chancery: 2401 Massachusetts Avenue NW, Washington, DC 20008

telephone: [1] (202) 652-1312

FAX: [1] (202) 758-0431

Diplomatic representation from the US: *chief of mission:* Ambassador Geeta PASI (since September 2016)

embassy: Avenue Felix Eboue, N'Djamena

mailing address: B. P. 413, N'Djamena

telephone: [235] 2251-70-09

FAX: [235] 2251-56-54

Flag description: three equal vertical bands of blue (hoist side), gold, and red; the flag combines the blue and red French (former colonial) colors with the red and yellow (gold) of the Pan-African colors; blue symbolizes the sky, hope, and the south of the country, which is relatively well-watered; gold represents the sun, as well as the desert in the north of the country; red stands for progress, unity, and sacrifice

note: almost identical to the flag of Romania but with a darker shade of blue; also similar to the flags of Andorra and Moldova, both of which have a national coat of arms centered in the yellow band; design based on the flag of France

National symbol(s): goat (north), lion (south); national colors: blue, yellow, red

National anthem: name: "La Tchadienne" (The Chadian)

lyrics/music: Louis GIDROL and his students/ Paul VILLARD

note: adopted 1960

ECONOMY

Economy—overview: Chad's landlocked location results in high transportation costs for imported goods and dependence on neighboring countries. Oil and agriculture are mainstays of Chad's economy. Oil provides about 60% of export revenues, while cotton, cattle, livestock, and gum arabic provide the bulk of Chad's non-oil export earnings. The services sector contributes less than one-third of GDP and has attracted foreign investment mostly through telecommunications and banking.

Nearly all of Chad's fuel is provided by one domestic refinery, and unanticipated shutdowns occasionally result in shortages. The country regulates the price of domestic fuel, providing an incentive for black market sales.

Although high oil prices and strong local harvests supported the economy in the past, low oil prices now stress Chad's fiscal position. Chad relies on foreign assistance and foreign capital for most of its public and private sector investment. Investment in Chad is difficult due to its limited infrastructure, lack of trained workers, extensive government bureaucracy, and corruption. Chad obtained a three-year extended credit facility from the IMF in 2014 and was granted debt relief under the Heavily Indebted Poor Countries Initiative in April 2015.

In 2018, economic policy will be driven by efforts that started in 2016 to reverse the recession and to repair damage to public finances and exports. The government is implementing an emergency action plan to counterbalance the drop in oil revenue and to diversify the economy. Multinational partners, such as the African Development Bank, the EU, and the World Bank are likely to continue budget support in 2018, but Chad will remain at high debt risk, given its dependence on oil revenue and pressure to spend on subsidies and security.

GDP (purchasing power parity): $29.64 billion (2017 est.)

$29.47 billion (2016 est.)

$31.49 billion (2015 est.)

note: data are in 2017 dollars

country comparison to the world: 133

GDP (official exchange rate): $9.74 billion (2016 est.)

GDP—real growth rate: 0.6% (2017 est.)

-6.4% (2016 est.)

1.8% (2015 est.)

country comparison to the world: 195

GDP—per capita (PPP): $2,400 (2017 est.)

$2,500 (2016 est.)

$2,700 (2015 est.)

note: data are in 2017 dollars

country comparison to the world: 199

Gross national saving: 17.8% of GDP (2017 est.)

7.5% of GDP (2016 est.)

14.6% of GDP (2015 est.)

country comparison to the world: 102

GDP—composition, by end use:

household consumption: 74.7%
government consumption: 4.6%
investment in fixed capital: 29.2%
investment in inventories: 0.4%
exports of goods and services: 33.5%
imports of goods and services: -42.5% (2017 est.)

GDP—composition, by sector of origin:
agriculture: 59%
industry: 14.1%
services: 27% (2017 est.)

Agriculture—products: cotton, sorghum, millet, peanuts, sesame, corn, rice, potatoes, onions, cassava (manioc, tapioca), cattle, sheep, goats, camels

Industries: oil, cotton textiles, brewing, natron (sodium carbonate), soap, cigarettes, construction materials

Industrial production growth rate: 0.5% (2017 est.)
country comparison to the world: 180

Labor force: 5.654 million (2017 est.)
country comparison to the world: 74

Labor force—by occupation: *agriculture:* 80%
industry and services: 20% (2006 est.)

Unemployment rate: NA%

Population below poverty line: 46.7% (2011 est.)

Household income or consumption by percentage share: *lowest 10%:* 2.6%
highest 10%: 30.8% (2003)

Distribution of family income—Gini index: 43.3 (2011 est.)
country comparison to the world: 46

Budget: *revenues:* $1.178 billion
expenditures: $1.522 billion (2017 est.)
Taxes and other revenues: 12.1% of GDP (2017 est.)
country comparison to the world: 205

Budget surplus (+) or deficit (-): -3.5% of GDP (2017 est.)
country comparison to the world: 132

Public debt: 60.8% of GDP (2017 est.)
59% of GDP (2016 est.)
country comparison to the world: 71

Fiscal year: calendar year

Inflation rate (consumer prices): 0.2% (2017 est.)
-1.1% (2016 est.)
country comparison to the world: 12

Central bank discount rate: 4.25% (31 December 2009)
4.75% (31 December 2008)
country comparison to the world: 89

Commercial bank prime lending rate: 15.5% (31 December 2017 est.)
15.5% (31 December 2016 est.)
country comparison to the world: 38

Stock of narrow money: $1.375 billion (31 December 2017 est.)
$1.241 billion (31 December 2016 est.)
country comparison to the world: 146

Stock of broad money: $1.826 billion (31 December 2017 est.)
$1.418 billion (31 December 2016 est.)
country comparison to the world: 160

Stock of domestic credit: $3.173 billion (31 December 2017 est.)
$2.387 billion (31 December 2016 est.)
country comparison to the world: 142

Market value of publicly traded shares: $NA

Current account balance: -$191 million (2017 est.)
-$927 million (2016 est.)
country comparison to the world: 88

Exports: $2.438 billion (2017 est.)
$2.187 billion (2016 est.)
country comparison to the world: 134

Exports—commodities: oil, livestock, cotton, sesame, gum arabic, shea butter

Exports—partners: US 57%, India 8.9%, China 6.7%, France 6.4%, UAE 4.3%, Japan 4.1% (2016)

Imports: $2.124 billion (2017 est.)
$1.988 billion (2016 est.)
country comparison to the world: 156

Imports—commodities: machinery and transportation equipment, industrial goods, foodstuffs, textiles

Imports—partners: France 19.8%, China 15.7%, Cameroon 15.1%, India 6.1%, US 5.4%, Belgium 4.4% (2016)

Reserves of foreign exchange and gold: $74.2 million (31 December 2017 est.)
$20.92 million (31 December 2016 est.)
country comparison to the world: 168

Debt—external: $1.268 billion (31 December 2017 est.)
$1.281 billion (31 December 2016 est.)
country comparison to the world: 164

Stock of direct foreign investment—at home: $4.5 billion (2006 est.)
country comparison to the world: 105

Stock of direct foreign investment—abroad: $NA

Exchange rates: Cooperation Financiere en Afrique Centrale francs (XAF) per US dollar—
605.3 (2017 est.)
593.01 (2016 est.)
593.01 (2015 est.)
591.45 (2014 est.)
494.42 (2013 est.)

ENERGY

Electricity access: *population without electricity:* 10,477,071
electrification—*total population:* 4%
electrification—urban areas: 14%
electrification—rural areas: 1% (2013)

Electricity—production: 215 million kWh (2015 est.)
country comparison to the world: 187

Electricity—consumption: 200 million kWh (2015 est.)
country comparison to the world: 189

Electricity—exports: 0 kWh (2016 est.)
country comparison to the world: 117

Electricity—imports: 0 kWh (2016 est.)
country comparison to the world: 131

Electricity—installed generating capacity: 47,000 kW (2015 est.)
country comparison to the world: 194

Electricity—from fossil fuels: 100% of total installed capacity (2015 est.)
country comparison to the world: 3

Electricity—from nuclear fuels: 0% of total installed capacity (2015 est.)
country comparison to the world: 62

Electricity—from hydroelectric plants: 0% of total installed capacity (2015 est.)
country comparison to the world: 167

Electricity—from other renewable sources: 0% of total installed capacity (2015 est.)
country comparison to the world: 173

Crude oil—production: 110,200 bbl/day (2016 est.)
country comparison to the world: 41

Crude oil—exports: 105,000 bbl/day (2014 est.)
country comparison to the world: 36

Crude oil—imports: 0 bbl/day (2014 est.)
country comparison to the world: 106

Crude oil—proved reserves: 1.5 billion bbl (1 January 2017 es)
country comparison to the world: 41

Refined petroleum products—production: 0 bbl/day (2014 est.)
country comparison to the world: 130

Refined petroleum products—consumption: 2,200 bbl/day (2015 est.)
country comparison to the world: 193

Refined petroleum products—exports: 0 bbl/day (2014 est.)
country comparison to the world: 140

Refined petroleum products—imports: 2,215 bbl/day (2014 est.)
country comparison to the world: 187

Natural gas—production: 0 cu m (2013 est.)
country comparison to the world: 118

Natural gas—consumption: 0 cu m (2013 est.)
country comparison to the world: 166

Natural gas—exports: 0 cu m (2013 est.)
country comparison to the world: 80

Natural gas—imports: 0 cu m (2013 est.)
country comparison to the world: 103

Natural gas—proved reserves: 0 cu m (1 January 2014 es)
country comparison to the world: 124

Carbon dioxide emissions from consumption of energy: 300,000 Mt (2013 est.)
country comparison to the world: 196

COMMUNICATIONS

Telephones—fixed lines: *total subscriptions:* 14,000
subscriptions per 100 inhabitants: less than 1 (July 2016 est.)
country comparison to the world: 177

Telephones—mobile cellular: *total:* 6,231,009
subscriptions per 100 inhabitants: 53 (July 2016 est.)

country comparison to the world: 115

Telephone system: *general assessment:* inadequate system of radiotelephone communication stations with high maintenance costs and low telephone density
domestic: fixed-line connections for less than 1 per 100 persons coupled with mobile-cellular subscribership base of about 40 per 100 persons
international: country code—235; satellite earth station—1 Intelsat (Atlantic Ocean) (2016)

Broadcast media: 1 state-owned TV station; 2 privately-owned TV stations; state-owned radio network, Radiodiffusion Nationale Tchadienne (RNT), operates national and regional stations; over 10 private radio stations; some stations rebroadcast programs from international broadcasters (2017)

Internet country code: .td
Internet users: total: 592,623
percent of population: 5.0% (July 2016 est.)
country comparison to the world: 148

TRANSPORTATION

National air transport system: *number of registered air carriers:* 1
inventory of registered aircraft operated by air carriers: 1
annual passenger traffic on registered air carriers: 28,332
annual freight traffic on registered air carriers: mt-km (2015)

Airports: 59 (2013)
country comparison to the world: 82

Airports—with paved runways: *total:* 9
over 3,047 m: 2
2,438 to 3,047 m: 4
1,524 to 2,437 m: 2
under 914 m: 1 (2017)

Airports—with unpaved runways: *total:* 50
over 3,047 m: 1
2,438 to 3,047 m: 2
1,524 to 2,437 m: 14

914 to 1,523 m: 22
under 914 m: 11 (2013)
Pipelines: oil 582 km (2013)
Roadways: *total:* 40,000 km
note: consists of 25,000 km of national and regional roads and 15,000 km of local roads; 206 km of urban roads are paved (2011)
country comparison to the world: 88
Waterways: (Chari and Legone Rivers are navigable only in wet season) (2012)

MILITARY AND SECURITY

Military expenditures: 2.79% of GDP (2016)
2.03% of GDP (2015)
2.82% of GDP (2014)
5.61% of GDP (2013)
Military branches: Chadian National Army (Armee Nationale du Tchad, ANT): Ground Forces (l'Armee de Terre, AdT), Chadian Air Force (l'Armee de l'Air Tchadienne, AAT), National Gendarmerie, National and Nomadic Guard of Chad (GNNT) (2013)
Military service age and obligation: 20 is the legal minimum age for compulsory military service, with a 3-year service obligation; 18 is the legal minimum age for voluntary service; no minimum age restriction for volunteers with consent from a parent or guardian; women are subject to 1 year of compulsory military or civic service at age 21; while provisions for military service have not been repealed, they have never been fully implemented (2015)

TERRORISM

Terrorist groups—foreign based: *al-Qaida in the Islamic Maghreb (AQIM):* aim(s): replace the Chadian Government with Sharia and, ultimately, create a regional Islamic caliphate across all of North and West Africa
area(s) of operation: members transit the country smuggling weapons and contraband in the northwestern regions, primarily near the Chad-Niger

border; clashes with Nigerien military and security forces patrolling the border

Boko Haram: *aim(s):* replace the Chadian Government with an Islamic state and, ultimately, establish an Islamic caliphate across Africa; violently opposes any political or social activity associated with Western society, including voting, attending secular schools, and wearing Western dress
area(s) of operation: conducts kidnappings, bombings, and assaults, including in the capital, N'Djamena; targets military and security personnel and civilians; responsible for displacing thousands of people and contributing to food insecurity, especially in the country's Lake Chad Basin region, where the Chadian Government has imposed a state of emergency since 2015 because of Boko Haram's frequent attacks; conducted its first lethal attack in Chad on 13 February 2015, when operatives crossed Lake Chad by boat to attack Ngouboua, a fishing village on the shores of Lake Chad in Chad, killing approximately 10 civilians and burning two thirds of the homes in the village; Chad continued in 2017 to participate in the Joint Multinational Force's military offensives against Boko Haram

TRANSNATIONAL ISSUES

Disputes—international: since 2003, ad hoc armed militia groups and the Sudanese military have driven hundreds of thousands of Darfur residents into Chad; Chad wishes to be a helpful mediator in resolving the Darfur conflict, and in 2010 established a joint border monitoring force with Sudan, which has helped to reduce cross-border banditry and violence; only Nigeria and Cameroon have heeded the Lake Chad Commission's admonition to ratify the delimitation treaty, which also includes the Chad-Niger and Niger-Nigeria boundaries

Refugees and internally displaced persons: refugees (country of origin): 324,327 (Sudan); 76,653 (Central African Republic) (2018); 9,541 (Nigeria) (2018)
IDPs: 147,032 (majority are in the east) (2017)

CHILE

INTRODUCTION

Background: Prior to the arrival of the Spanish in the 16th century, the Inca ruled northern Chile while an indigenous people, the Mapuche, inhabited central and southern Chile. Although Chile declared its independence in 1810, it did not achieve decisive victory over the Spanish until 1818. In the War of the Pacific (1879-83), Chile defeated Peru and Bolivia to win its present northern regions. In the 1880s, the Chilean central government gained control over the central and southern regions inhabited by the Mapuche. After a series of elected governments, the three-year-old Marxist government of Salvador ALLENDE was overthrown in 1973 by a military coup led by

General Augusto PINOCHET, who ruled until a democratically-elected president was inaugurated in 1990. Sound economic policies, maintained consistently since the 1980s, contributed to steady growth, reduced poverty rates by over half, and helped secure the country's commitment to democratic and representative government. Chile has increasingly assumed regional and international leadership roles befitting its status as a stable, democratic nation.

GEOGRAPHY

Location: Southern South America, bordering the South Pacific Ocean, between Argentina and Peru
Geographic coordinates: 30 00 S, 71 00 W

Map references: South America
Area: *total:* 756,102 sq km
land: 743,812 sq km
water: 12,290 sq km
note: includes Easter Island (Isla de Pascua) and Isla Sala y Gomez
country comparison to the world: 39
Area—comparative: slightly smaller than twice the size of Montana
Land boundaries: *total:* 7,801 km
border countries (3): Argentina 6,691 km, Bolivia 942 km, Peru 168 km
Coastline: 6,435 km
Maritime claims: *territorial sea:* 12 nm

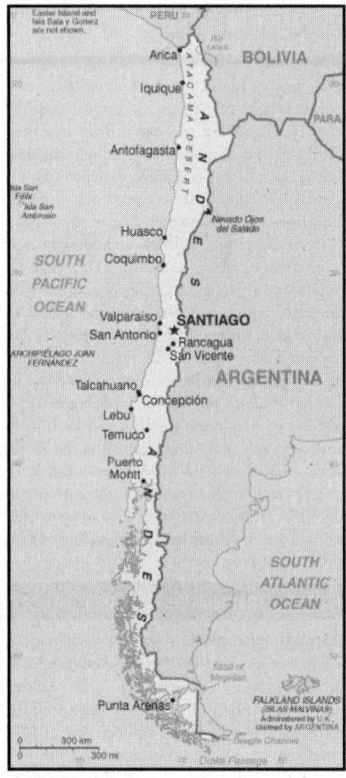

contiguous zone: 24 nm
exclusive economic zone: 200 nm
continental shelf: 200/350 nm

Climate: temperate; desert in north; Mediterranean in central region; cool and damp in south

Terrain: low coastal mountains, fertile central valley, rugged Andes in east

Elevation: mean elevation: 1,871 m

elevation extremes: lowest point: Pacific Ocean 0 m
highest point: Nevado Ojos del Salado 6,880 m

Natural resources: copper, timber, iron ore, nitrates, precious metals, molybdenum, hydropower

Land use: agricultural land: 21.1%
arable land: 1.7%;
permanent crops: 0.6%;
permanent pasture: 18.8%
forest: 21.9%
other: 57% (2011 est.)
Irrigated land: 11,100 sq km (2012)

Population—distribution: 90% of the population is located in the middle third of the country around the capital of Santiago; the far north (anchored by the Atacama Desert) and the extreme south are relatively underpopulated

Natural hazards: severe earthquakes; active volcanism; tsunamis

volcanism: significant volcanic activity due to more than three-dozen active volcanoes along the Andes Mountains; Lascar (5,592 m), which last erupted in 2007, is the most active volcano in the northern Chilean Andes; Llaima (3,125 m) in central Chile, which last erupted in 2009, is another of the country's most active; Chaiten's 2008 eruption forced major evacuations; other notable historically active volcanoes include Cerro Hudson, Calbuco, Copahue, Guallatiri, Llullaillaco, Nevados de Chillan, Puyehue, San Pedro, and Villarrica

Environment—current issues: widespread deforestation and mining threaten natural resources; air pollution from industrial and vehicle emissions; water pollution from raw sewage

Environment—international agreements: party to: Antarctic-Environmental Protocol, Antarctic-Marine Living Resources, Antarctic Seals, Antarctic Treaty, Biodiversity, Climate Change, Climate Change-Kyoto Protocol, Desertification, Endangered Species, Environmental Modification, Hazardous Wastes, Law of the Sea, Marine Dumping, Ozone Layer Protection, Ship Pollution, Wetlands, Whaling
signed, but not ratified: none of the selected agreements

Geography—note: the longest north-south trending country in the world, extending across 39 degrees of latitude; strategic location relative to sea lanes between the Atlantic and Pacific Oceans (Strait of Magellan, Beagle Channel, Drake Passage); Atacama Desert—the driest desert in the world—spreads across the northern part of the country; the small crater lake of Ojos del Salado is the world's highest lake (at 6,390 m)

PEOPLE AND SOCIETY

Population: 17,789,267 (July 2017 est.)
country comparison to the world: 65

Nationality: noun: Chilean(s)
adjective: Chilean

Ethnic groups: white and non-indigenous 88.9%, Mapuche 9.1%, Aymara 0.7%, other indigenous groups 1% (includes Rapa Nui, Likan Antai, Quechua, Colla, Diaguita, Kawesqar, Yagan or Yamana), unspecified 0.3% (2012 est.)

Languages: Spanish 99.5% (official), English 10.2%, indigenous 1% (includes Mapudungun, Aymara, Quechua, Rapa Nui), other 2.3%, unspecified 0.2%
note: shares sum to more than 100% because some respondents gave more than one answer on the census (2012 est.)

Religions: Roman Catholic 66.7%, Evangelical or Protestant 16.4%, Jehovah's Witness 1%, other 3.4%, none 11.5%, unspecified 1.1% (2012 est.)

Demographic profile: Chile is in the advanced stages of demographic transition and is becoming an aging society—with fertility below replacement level, low mortality rates, and life expectancy on par with developed countries. Nevertheless, with its dependency ratio nearing its low point, Chile could benefit from its favorable age structure. It

will need to keep its large working-age population productively employed, while preparing to provide for the needs of its growing proportion of elderly people, especially as women—the traditional caregivers—increasingly enter the workforce. Over the last two decades, Chile has made great strides in reducing its poverty rate, which is now lower than most Latin American countries. However, its severe income inequality ranks as the worst among members of the Organization for Economic Cooperation and Development. Unequal access to quality education perpetuates this uneven income distribution.

Chile has historically been a country of emigration but has slowly become more attractive to immigrants since transitioning to democracy in 1990 and improving its economic stability (other regional destinations have concurrently experienced deteriorating economic and political conditions). Most of Chile's small but growing foreign-born population consists of transplants from other Latin American countries, especially Peru.

Age structure: 0-14 years: 20.11% (male 1,825,254/female 1,751,735)
15-24 years: 15.04% (male 1,364,831/female 1,311,216)
25-54 years: 43.08% (male 3,830,538/female 3,832,989)
55-64 years: 10.96% (male 918,559/female 1,031,153)
65 years and over: 10.81% (male 805,880/female 1,117,112) (2017 est.)

Dependency ratios: total dependency ratio: 45.5
youth dependency ratio: 30.3
elderly dependency ratio: 15.2
potential support ratio: 6.6 (2015 est.)

Median age: total: 34.4 years
male: 33.2 years
female: 35.6 years (2017 est.)
country comparison to the world: 85

Population growth rate: 0.77% (2017 est.)
country comparison to the world: 135

Birth rate: 13.6 births/1,000 population (2017 est.)
country comparison to the world: 143

Death rate: 6.2 deaths/1,000 population (2017 est.)
country comparison to the world: 155

Net migration rate: 0.3 migrant(s)/1,000 population (2017 est.)
country comparison to the world: 66

Population distribution: 90% of the population is located in the middle third of the country around the capital of Santiago; the far north (anchored by the Atacama Desert) and the extreme south are relatively underpopulated

Urbanization: urban population: 89.9% of total population (2017)
rate of urbanization: 0.96% annual rate of change (2015-20 est.)

Major urban areas—population: SANTIAGO (capital) 6.507 million; Valparaiso 907,000; Concepcion 816,000 (2015)

Sex ratio: at birth: 1.04 male(s)/female

0-14 years: 1.04 male(s)/female
15-24 years: 1.04 male(s)/female
25-54 years: 1 male(s)/female
55-64 years: 0.89 male(s)/female
65 years and over: 0.72 male(s)/female
total population: 0.97 male(s)/female (2016 est.)

Maternal mortality ratio: 22 deaths/100,000 live births (2015 est.)
country comparison to the world: 128

Infant mortality rate: *total:* 6.6 deaths/1,000 live births
male: 7.1 deaths/1,000 live births
female: 6.1 deaths/1,000 live births (2017 est.)
country comparison to the world: 164

Life expectancy at birth: *total population:* 78.9 years
male: 75.9 years
female: 82.1 years (2017 est.)
country comparison to the world: 51

Total fertility rate: 1.8 children born/woman (2017 est.)
country comparison to the world: 152

Health expenditures: 7.8% of GDP (2014)
country comparison to the world: 60

Physicians density: 1.03 physicians/1,000 population (2009)

Hospital bed density: 2.1 beds/1,000 population (2011)

Drinking water source:
improved:
urban: 99.7% of population
rural: 93.3% of population
total: 99% of population
unimproved:
urban: 0.3% of population
rural: 6.7% of population
total: 1% of population (2015 est.)

Sanitation facility access:
improved:
urban: 100% of population
rural: 90.9% of population
total: 99.1% of population
unimproved:
urban: 0% of population
rural: 9.1% of population
total: 0.9% of population (2015 est.)

HIV/AIDS—adult prevalence rate: 0.5% (2016 est.)
country comparison to the world: 63

HIV/AIDS—people living with HIV/AIDS: 61,000 (2016 est.)
country comparison to the world: 53

HIV/AIDS—deaths: NA

Obesity—adult prevalence rate: 28% (2016)
country comparison to the world: 32

Children under the age of 5 years underweight: 0.5% (2014)
country comparison to the world: 137

Education expenditures: 4.8% of GDP (2014)
country comparison to the world: 90

Literacy: *definition:* age 15 and over can read and write

total population: 97.5%
male: 97.6%
female: 97.4% (2015 est.)

School life expectancy (primary to tertiary education): *total:* 16 years
male: 16 years
female: 17 years (2015)

Unemployment, youth ages 15-24: *total:* 15.4%
male: 14.3%
female: 17% (2015 est.)
country comparison to the world: 73

GOVERNMENT

Country name: *conventional long form:* Republic of Chile
conventional short form: Chile
local long form: Republica de Chile
local short form: Chile
etymology: derivation of the name is unclear, but it may come from the Mapuche word "chilli" meaning "limit of the earth" or from the Quechua "chiri" meaning "cold"

Government type: presidential republic

Capital: *name:* Santiago; note—Valparaiso is the seat of the national legislature
geographic coordinates: 33 27 S, 70 40 W
time difference: UTC-3 (2 hours ahead of Washington, DC, during Standard Time)
daylight saving time: +1hr, begins second Sunday in August; ends second Sunday in May; note—Punta Arenas observes DST throughout the year

Administrative divisions: 15 regions (regiones, singular—region); Aysen, Antofagasta, Araucania, Arica y Parinacota, Atacama, Biobio, Coquimbo, Libertador General Bernardo O'Higgins, Los Lagos, Los Rios, Magallanes y de la Antartica Chilena, Maule, Region Metropolitana (Santiago), Tarapaca, Valparaiso
note: the US does not recognize claims to Antarctica

Independence: 18 September 1810 (from Spain)

National holiday: Independence Day, 18 September (1810)

Constitution: many previous; latest adopted 11 September 1980, effective 11 March 1981; amended many times, last in 2011; note—in late 2015, the Chilean Government initiated a process to reform its constitution (2016)

Legal system: civil law system influenced by several West European civil legal systems; judicial review of legislative acts by the Constitutional Tribunal

International law organization participation: has not submitted an ICJ jurisdiction declaration; accepts ICCt jurisdiction

Citizenship: *citizenship by birth:* yes
citizenship by descent: yes
dual citizenship recognized: yes
residency requirement for naturalization: 5 years

Suffrage: 18 years of age; universal

Executive branch: *chief of state:* President Michelle BACHELET Jeria (since 11 March 2014); note—the president is both chief of state and head of government

head of government: President Michelle BACHELET Jeria (since 11 March 2014)
cabinet: Cabinet appointed by the president
elections/appointments: president directly elected by absolute majority popular vote in 2 rounds if needed for a single 4-year term; election last held on 19 November 2017 with a runoff held 17 December 2017 (next to be held in November 2021)
election results: Sebastian PINERA Echenique elected president in second round; percent of vote in first round—Sebastian PINERA Echenique (independent) 36.6%; Alejandro GUILLIER (independent) 22.7%; Beatriz SANCHEZ (independent) 20.3%; Jose Antonio KAST (independent) 7.9%; Carolina GOIC (PDC) 5.9%; Marco ENRIQUEZ-OMINAMI (PRO) 5.7%; other 0.9%; percent of second round vote—Sebastian PINERA Echenique 54.6%, Alejandro GUILLIER 45.4%; PINERA will take office 11 March 2018

Legislative branch: *description:* bicameral National Congress or Congreso Nacional consists of the Senate or Senado (38 seats; to increase to 43 on 11 March 2018 and 50 in 2022); members directly elected in multi-seat constituencies by simple majority vote to serve 8-year terms with one-half of the membership renewed every 4 years) and the Chamber of Deputies or Camara de Diputados (120 seats; to increase to 155 on 11 March 2018; members directly elected in multi-seat constituencies by simple majority vote to serve 4-year terms)
elections: Senate—last held on 19 November 2017 (next to be held in 2021); Chamber of Deputies—last held on 19 November 2017 (next to be held in 2021)
election results: Senate—percent of vote by party—NA; seats by party—New Majority Coalition (formerly known as Concertacion) 19 (PDC 6, PS 6, PPD 6, MAS 1), Let's Go Chile Coalition (formerly known as the Coalition for Change and the Alianza coalition) 15 (RN 6, UDI 8, Amplitude Party 1), independent 4; Chamber of Deputies—percent of vote by party—NA; seats by party—New Majority 68 (PDC 21, PS 16, PPD 14, PC 6, PRSD 6, Citizen Left 1, independent 4), Coalition for Change 47 (UDI 29, RN 14, independent 3, EP 1), Liberal Party 1, independent 4
note: in January 2015, the Chilean Congress voted to end the binomial system that was put in place under Gen. Augusto PINOCHET; the Congress also voted to expand its size (155 seats in the chamber of Deputies and 50 seats in the Senate) and establish rules to ensure that there is equitable gender representation; the new electoral system will be put in place in the November 2017 elections

Judicial branch: *highest court(s):* Supreme Court or Corte Suprema (consists of a court president and 20 members or ministros); Constitutional

Court (consists of 10 members); Elections Qualifying Court (consists of 5 members)

judge selection and term of office: Supreme Court president and judges (ministers) appointed by the president of the republic and ratified by the Senate from lists of candidates provided by the court itself; judges appointed for life with mandatory retirement at age 70; Constitutional Court members appointed—3 by the Supreme Court, 3 by the president of the republic, 2 by the Chamber of Deputies, and 2 by the Senate; members serve 9-year terms with partial membership replacement every 3 years (the court reviews constitutionality of legislation); Elections Qualifying Court members appointed by lottery—1 by the former president or vice-president of the Senate and 1 by the former president or vice-president of the Chamber of Deputies, 2 by the Supreme Court, and 1 by the Appellate Court of Valparasio; members appointed for 4-year terms

subordinate courts: Courts of Appeal; oral criminal tribunals; military tribunals; local police courts; specialized tribunals and courts in matters such as family, labor, customs, taxes, and electoral affairs

Political parties and leaders: Amplitude (Amplitud) [Lily PEREZ]

Broad Social Movement or MAS [Cristian TAPIA Ramos]

Democratic Revolution or RD [Rodrigo ECHECOPAR]

Let's Go Chile Coalition (Chile Vamos) (formerly the Alliance for Chile, includes Political Evolution or EVOPOLI [Jorge SAINT JEAN], Independent Regionalist Party or PRI [Alejandra BRAVO Hidalgo], National Renewal or RN [Cristian MONCKEBERG Bruner], and Independent Democratic Union or UDI [Jacqueline VAN RYS-SELBERGHE Herrera])

Liberal Party (Partido Liberal de Chile) [Vlado MIROSEVIC]

New Majority Coalition (Nueva Mayoria) (includes Christian Democratic Party or PDC [Carolina GOIC Boroevic], Communist Party of Chile or PC [Guillermo TEILLIER del Valle], Party for Democracy or PPD [Gonzalo NAVAR-RETE], Radical Social Democratic Party or PRSD [Ernesto VELASCO Rodriguez], and Socialist Party or PS [Alvaro ELIZALDE Soto])

Progressive Party or PRO [Patricia MORALES]

Political pressure groups and leaders: Roman Catholic Church, particularly conservative groups such as Opus Dei

United Labor Central or CUT (includes trade unionists from the country's 5 largest labor confederations)

other: university student federations at all major universities

International organization participation: APEC, BIS, CAN (associate), CD, CELAC, FAO, G-15, G-77, IADB, IAEA, IBRD, ICAO, ICC (national committees), ICCt, ICRM, IDA, IFAD, IFC, IFRCS, IHO, ILO, IMF, IMO, IMSO, Interpol, IOC, IOM, IPU, ISO, ITSO, ITU, ITUC (NGOs), LAES, LAIA, Mercosur (associate), MIGA, MINUSTAH, NAM, OAS, OECD (enhanced engagement), OPANAL, OPCW, Pacific Alliance, PCA, SICA (observer), UN, UNASUR, UNCTAD, UNESCO, UNFICYP, UNHCR, UNIDO, Union Latina, UNMOGIP, UNTSO, UNWTO, UPU, WCO, WFTU (NGOs), WHO, WIPO, WMO, WTO

Diplomatic representation in the US: *chief of mission:* Ambassador Juan Gabriel VALDES Soublette (since 21 May 2014)

chancery: 1732 Massachusetts Avenue NW, Washington, DC 20036

telephone: [1] (202) 785-1746

FAX: [1] (202) 887-5579

consulate(s) general: Chicago, Houston, Los Angeles, Miami, New York, San Francisco

Diplomatic representation from the US: *chief of mission:* Ambassador Carol PEREZ (since 14 November 2016)

embassy: Avenida Andres Bello 2800, Las Condes, Santiago

mailing address: APO AA 34033

telephone: [56] (2) 2330-3000

FAX: [56] (2) 2330-3710, 2330-3160

Flag description: two equal horizontal bands of white (top) and red; a blue square the same height as the white band at the hoist-side end of the white band; the square bears a white five-pointed star in the center representing a guide to progress and honor; blue symbolizes the sky, white is for the snow-covered Andes, and red represents the blood spilled to achieve independence

note: design influenced by the US flag

National symbol(s): huemul (mountain deer), Andean condor; national colors: red, white, blue

National anthem: *name:* "Himno Nacional de Chile" (National Anthem of Chile)

lyrics/music: Eusebio LILLO Robles and Bernardo DE VERA y Pintado/Ramon CARNICER y Battle

note: music adopted 1828, original lyrics adopted 1818, adapted lyrics adopted 1847; under Augusto PINOCHET"s military rule, a verse glorifying the army was added; however, as a protest, some citizens refused to sing this verse; it was removed when democracy was restored in 1990

ECONOMY

Economy—overview: Chile has a market-oriented economy characterized by a high level of foreign trade and a reputation for strong financial institutions and sound policy that have given it the strongest sovereign bond rating in South America. Exports of goods and services account for approximately one-third of GDP, with commodities making up some 60% of total exports. Copper is Chile's top export and provides 20% of government revenue.

From 2003 through 2013, real growth averaged almost 5% per year, despite a slight contraction in 2009 that resulted from the global financial crisis. Growth slowed to an estimated 1.4% in 2017. A continued drop in copper prices prompted Chile to experience its third consecutive year of slow growth.

Chile deepened its longstanding commitment to trade liberalization with the signing of a free trade agreement with the US, effective 1 January 2004. Chile has 22 trade agreements covering 60 countries including agreements with the EU, Mercosur, China, India, South Korea, and Mexico. In May 2010, Chile signed the OECD Convention, becoming the first South American country to join the OECD. In October 2015, Chile signed the Trans-Pacific Partnership trade agreement.

The Chilean Government has generally followed a countercyclical fiscal policy, accumulating surpluses in sovereign wealth funds during periods of high copper prices and economic growth, and generally allowing deficit spending only during periods of low copper prices and growth. As of 31 October 2016, those sovereign wealth funds—kept mostly outside the country and separate from Central Bank reserves—amounted to more than $23.5 billion. Chile used these funds to finance fiscal stimulus packages during the 2009 economic downturn.

In 2014, President Michelle BACHELET introduced tax reforms aimed at delivering her campaign promise to fight inequality and to provide access to education and health care. The reforms are expected to generate additional tax revenues equal to 3% of Chile's GDP, mostly by increasing corporate tax rates to OECD averages.

GDP (purchasing power parity): $452.1 billion (2017 est.)

$446 billion (2016 est.)

$439 billion (2015 est.)

note: data are in 2017 dollars

country comparison to the world: 45

GDP (official exchange rate): $263.2 billion (2016 est.)

GDP—real growth rate: 1.4% (2017 est.)

1.6% (2016 est.)

2.3% (2015 est.)

country comparison to the world: 178

GDP—per capita (PPP): $24,600 (2017 est.)

$24,500 (2016 est.)

$24,400 (2015 est.)

note: data are in 2017 dollars

country comparison to the world: 80

Gross national saving: 20% of GDP (2017 est.)

20.2% of GDP (2016 est.)

21.3% of GDP (2015 est.)

country comparison to the world: 88

GDP—composition, by end use:

household consumption: 63.9%

government consumption: 13.6%

investment in fixed capital: 22.2%

investment in inventories: -0.2%

exports of goods and services: 28.2%

imports of goods and services: -27.6% (2017 est.)

GDP—composition, by sector of origin:

agriculture: 4.4%

industry: 31.4%

services: 64.3% (2017 est.)

Agriculture—products: grapes, apples, pears, onions, wheat, corn, oats, peaches, garlic, asparagus, beans; beef, poultry, wool; fish; timber

Industries: copper, lithium, other minerals, foodstuffs, fish processing, iron and steel, wood and wood products, transport equipment, cement, textiles

Industrial production growth rate: 1.4% (2017 est.)
country comparison to the world: 154

Labor force: 8.881 million (2017 est.)
country comparison to the world: 58

Labor force—by occupation: *agriculture:* 9.2%
industry: 23.7%
services: 67.1% (2013)

Unemployment rate: 7% (2017 est.)
6.5% (2016 est.)
country comparison to the world: 100

Population below poverty line: 14.4% (2013)

Household income or consumption by percentage share: *lowest 10%:* 1.7%
highest 10%: 41.5% (2013 est.)

Distribution of family income—Gini index: 50.5 (2013)
57.1 (2000)
country comparison to the world: 15

Budget: *revenues:* $56.73 billion
expenditures: $64.89 billion (2017 est.)
Taxes and other revenues: 21.6% of GDP (2017 est.)
country comparison to the world: 139

Budget surplus (+) or deficit (-): -3.1% of GDP (2017 est.)
country comparison to the world: 115

Public debt: 25.2% of GDP (2017 est.)
21.3% of GDP (2016 est.)
country comparison to the world: 177

Fiscal year: calendar year

Inflation rate (consumer prices): 2.3% (2017 est.)
3.8% (2016 est.)
country comparison to the world: 106

Central bank discount rate: 3.35% (31 December 2015)
3% (31 December 2014)
country comparison to the world: 103

Commercial bank prime lending rate: 4.6% (31 December 2017 est.)
5.59% (31 December 2016 est.)
country comparison to the world: 150

Stock of narrow money: $51.77 billion (31 December 2017 est.)
$44.01 billion (31 December 2016 est.)
country comparison to the world: 54

Stock of broad money: $174.7 billion (31 December 2017 est.)
$158.3 billion (31 December 2016 est.)
country comparison to the world: 46

Stock of domestic credit: $233.3 billion (31 December 2017 est.)
$211.6 billion (31 December 2016 est.)
country comparison to the world: 45

Market value of publicly traded shares: $190.4 billion (31 December 2015 est.)
$233.2 billion (31 December 2014 est.)
$265.2 billion (31 December 2013 est.)
country comparison to the world: 35

Current account balance: -$5.94 billion (2017 est.)
-$3.528 billion (2016 est.)
country comparison to the world: 177

Exports: $64.51 billion (2017 est.)
$60.6 billion (2016 est.)
country comparison to the world: 44

Exports—commodities: copper, fruit, fish products, paper and pulp, chemicals, wine

Exports—partners: China 28.6%, US 14.1%, Japan 8.6%, South Korea 6.9%, Brazil 5% (2016)

Imports: $59.92 billion (2017 est.)
$55.34 billion (2016 est.)
country comparison to the world: 47

Imports—commodities: petroleum and petroleum products, chemicals, electrical and telecommunications equipment, industrial machinery, vehicles, natural gas

Imports—partners: China 24.3%, US 14.7%, Brazil 9.3%, Argentina 4.4%, France 4.2% (2016)

Reserves of foreign exchange and gold: $39.11 billion (31 December 2017 est.)
$40.49 billion (31 December 2016 est.)
country comparison to the world: 44

Debt—external: $167.9 billion (31 December 2017 est.)
$158.1 billion (31 December 2016 est.)
country comparison to the world: 40

Stock of direct foreign investment—at home: $208.8 billion (31 December 2017 est.)
$199.8 billion (31 December 2016 est.)
country comparison to the world: 29

Stock of direct foreign investment—abroad: $97.59 billion (31 December 2017 est.)
$90.54 billion (31 December 2016 est.)
country comparison to the world: 36

Exchange rates: Chilean pesos (CLP) per US dollar—
653.9 (2017 est.)
676.94 (2016 est.)
676.94 (2015 est.)
658.93 (2014 est.)
570.37 (2013 est.)

ENERGY

Electricity access: *population without electricity:* 70,600
electrification—total population: 99.6%
electrification—urban areas: 100%
electrification—rural areas: 98% (2012)

Electricity—production: 71.66 billion kWh (2015 est.)
country comparison to the world: 40

Electricity—consumption: 67.95 billion kWh (2015 est.)
country comparison to the world: 40

Electricity—exports: 0 kWh (2016 est.)
country comparison to the world: 119

Electricity—imports: 0 kWh (2016 est.)
country comparison to the world: 133

Electricity—installed generating capacity: 21.64 million kW (2015 est.)

country comparison to the world: 40

Electricity—from fossil fuels: 60.8% of total installed capacity (2015 est.)
country comparison to the world: 127

Electricity—from nuclear fuels: 0% of total installed capacity (2015 est.)
country comparison to the world: 66

Electricity—from hydroelectric plants: 30% of total installed capacity (2015 est.)
country comparison to the world: 71

Electricity—from other renewable sources: 16.1% of total installed capacity (2015 est.)
country comparison to the world: 44

Crude oil—production: 4,423 bbl/day (2016 est.)
country comparison to the world: 82

Crude oil—exports: 0 bbl/day (2016 est.)
country comparison to the world: 105

Crude oil—imports: 163,000 bbl/day (2016 est.)
country comparison to the world: 33

Crude oil—proved reserves: 150 million bbl (1 January 2017 es)
country comparison to the world: 64

Refined petroleum products—production: 215,300 bbl/day (2016 est.)
country comparison to the world: 50

Refined petroleum products—consumption: 337,400 bbl/day (2016 est.)
country comparison to the world: 41

Refined petroleum products—exports: 4,500 bbl/day (2016 est.)
country comparison to the world: 96

Refined petroleum products—imports: 160,900 bbl/day (2016 est.)
country comparison to the world: 43

Natural gas—production: 1.008 billion cu m (2015 est.)
country comparison to the world: 67

Natural gas—consumption: 5.23 billion cu m (2015 est.)
country comparison to the world: 63

Natural gas—exports: 0 cu m (2014 est.)
country comparison to the world: 83

Natural gas—imports: 3.727 billion cu m (2015 est.)
country comparison to the world: 39

Natural gas—proved reserves: 97.97 billion cu m (1 January 2017 es)
country comparison to the world: 54

Carbon dioxide emissions from consumption of energy: 76 million Mt (2013 est.)
country comparison to the world: 47

COMMUNICATIONS

Telephones—fixed lines: *total subscriptions:* 3,464,107
subscriptions per 100 inhabitants: 20 (July 2016 est.)
country comparison to the world: 44

Telephones—mobile cellular: *total:* 22,974,289
subscriptions per 100 inhabitants: 130 (July 2016 est.)

country comparison to the world: 49

Telephone system: *general assessment:* privatization began in 1988; most advanced telecommunications infrastructure in South America; modern system based on extensive microwave radio relay facilities; domestic satellite system with 3 earth stations
domestic: number of fixed-line connections have stagnated in recent years as mobile-cellular usage continues to increase, reaching 130 telephones per 100 persons
international: country code—56; landing points for the Pan American, South America-1, and South American Crossing/Latin America Nautilus submarine cables providing links to the US and to Central and South America; satellite earth stations—2 Intelsat (Atlantic Ocean) (2016)

Broadcast media: national and local terrestrial TV channels, coupled with extensive cable TV networks; the state-owned Television Nacional de Chile (TVN) network is self-financed through commercial advertising revenues and is not under direct government control; large number of privately owned TV stations; about 250 radio stations (2007)

Internet country code: .cl
Internet users: total: 11,650,840
percent of population: 66.0% (July 2016 est.)
country comparison to the world: 43

TRANSPORTATION

National air transport system: *number of registered air carriers:* 9
inventory of registered aircraft operated by air carriers: 173
annual passenger traffic on registered air carriers: 15,006,762
annual freight traffic on registered air carriers: 1,392.236 million mt-km (2015)

Civil aircraft registration country code prefix: CC (2016)

Airports: 481 (2013)
country comparison to the world: 15

Airports—with paved runways: *total:* 90
over 3,047 m: 5
2,438 to 3,047 m: 7
1,524 to 2,437 m: 23
914 to 1,523 m: 31
under 914 m: 24 (2017)

Airports—with unpaved runways: *total:* 391
2,438 to 3,047 m: 5
1,524 to 2,437 m: 11
914 to 1,523 m: 56
under 914 m: 319 (2013)

Heliports: 1 (2013)

Pipelines: gas 3,160 km; liquid petroleum gas 781 km; oil 985 km; refined products 722 km (2013)

Railways: *total:* 7,281.5 km
broad gauge: 3,428 km 1.676-m gauge (1,691 km electrified)
narrow gauge: 3,853.5 km 1.000-m gauge (2014)
country comparison to the world: 30

Roadways: *total:* 77,764 km
paved: 18,119 km (includes 2,387 km of expressways)
unpaved: 59,645 km (2010)
country comparison to the world: 62

Merchant marine: *total:* 211
by type: bulk carrier 10, container ship 5, general cargo 54, oil tanker 12, other 130 (2017)

Ports and terminals: *major seaport(s):* Coronel, Huasco, Lirquen, Puerto Ventanas, San Antonio, San Vicente, Valparaiso
LNG terminal(s) (import): Mejillones, Quintero

MILITARY AND SECURITY

Military expenditures: 1.87% of GDP (2016)

1.91% of GDP (2015)
1.96% of GDP (2014)
1.99% of GDP (2013)
2.05% of GDP (2012)
country comparison to the world: 38

Military branches: Chilean Army, Chilean Navy (Armada de Chile, includes Naval Aviation, Marine Corps, and Maritime Territory and Merchant Marine Directorate (Directemar)), Chilean Air Force (Fuerza Aerea de Chile, FACh) (2015)

Military service age and obligation: 18-45 years of age for voluntary male and female military service, although the right to compulsory recruitment of males 18-45 is retained; service obligation is 12 months for Army and 22 months for Navy and Air Force (2015)

TRANSNATIONAL ISSUES

Disputes—international: Chile and Peru rebuff Bolivia's reactivated claim to restore the Atacama corridor, ceded to Chile in 1884, but Chile has offered instead unrestricted but not sovereign maritime access through Chile to Bolivian natural gas; Chile rejects Peru's unilateral legislation to change its latitudinal maritime boundary with Chile to an equidistant line with a southwestern axis favoring Peru; in October 2007, Peru took its maritime complaint with Chile to the ICJ; territorial claim in Antarctica (Chilean Antarctic Territory) partially overlaps Argentine and British claims; the joint boundary commission, established by Chile and Argentina in 2001, has yet to map and demarcate the delimited boundary in the inhospitable Andean Southern Ice Field (Campo de Hielo Sur)

Illicit drugs: transshipment country for cocaine destined for Europe and the region; some money laundering activity, especially through the Iquique Free Trade Zone; imported precursors passed on to Bolivia; domestic cocaine consumption is rising, making Chile a significant consumer of cocaine

CHINA

INTRODUCTION

Background: For centuries China stood as a leading civilization, outpacing the rest of the world in the arts and sciences, but in the 19th and early 20th centuries, the country was beset by civil unrest, major famines, military defeats, and foreign occupation. After World War II, the Communist Party of China under MAO Zedong established

an autocratic socialist system that, while ensuring China's sovereignty, imposed strict controls over everyday life and cost the lives of tens of millions of people. After 1978, MAO's successor DENG Xiaoping and other leaders focused on market-oriented economic development and by 2000 output had quadrupled. For much of the population, living standards have improved dramatically but political controls remain tight. Since the early 1990s, China has increased its global outreach and participation in international organizations.

GEOGRAPHY

Location: Eastern Asia, bordering the East China Sea, Korea Bay, Yellow Sea, and South China Sea, between North Korea and Vietnam

Geographic coordinates: 35 00 N, 105 00 E

Map references: Asia

Area: *total:* 9,596,960 sq km
land: 9,326,410 sq km
water: 270,550 sq km
country comparison to the world: 5

Area—comparative: slightly smaller than the US

Land boundaries: *total:* 22,457 km
border countries (14): Afghanistan 91 km, Bhutan 477 km, Burma 2,129 km, India 2,659 km, Kazakhstan 1,765 km, North Korea 1,352 km, Kyrgyzstan 1,063 km, Laos 475 km, Mongolia 4,630 km, Nepal 1,389 km, Pakistan 438 km, Russia (northeast) 4,133 km, Russia (northwest) 46 km, Tajikistan 477 km, Vietnam 1,297 km
regional border(s) (2): Hong Kong 33 km, Macau 3 km

Coastline: 14,500 km

Maritime claims: *territorial sea:* 12 nm
contiguous zone: 24 nm

exclusive economic zone: 200 nm
continental shelf: 200 nm or to the edge of the continental margin

Climate: extremely diverse; tropical in south to subarctic in north

Terrain: mostly mountains, high plateaus, deserts in west; plains, deltas, and hills in east

Elevation: *mean elevation:* 1,840 m

elevation extremes: *lowest point:* Turpan Pendi -154 m
highest point: Mount Everest 8,848 m (highest peak in Asia and highest point on earth above sea level)

Natural resources: coal, iron ore, petroleum, natural gas, mercury, tin, tungsten, antimony, manganese, molybdenum, vanadium, magnetite, aluminum, lead, zinc, rare earth elements, uranium, hydropower potential (world's largest), arable land

Land use: *agricultural land:* 54.7%
arable land: 11.3%;
permanent crops: 1.6%;
permanent pasture: 41.8%
forest: 22.3%
other: 23% (2011 est.)
Irrigated land: 690,070 sq km (2012)

Population—distribution: overwhelming majority of the population is found in the eastern half of the country; the west, with its vast mountainous and desert areas, remains sparsely populated; though ranked first in the world in total population, overall density is less than that of many other countries in Asia and Europe; high population density is found along the Yangtze and Yellow River valleys, the Xi Jiang River delta, the Sichuan Basin (around Chengdu), in and around Beijing, and the industrial area around Shenyang

Natural hazards: frequent typhoons (about five per year along southern and eastern coasts); damaging floods; tsunamis; earthquakes; droughts; land subsidence
volcanism: China contains some historically active volcanoes including Changbaishan (also known as Baitoushan, Baegdu, or P'aektu-san), Hainan Dao, and Kunlun although most have been relatively inactive in recent centuries

Environment—current issues: air pollution (greenhouse gases, sulfur dioxide particulates) from reliance on coal produces acid rain; China is the world's largest single emitter of carbon dioxide from the burning of fossil fuels; water shortages, particularly in the north; water pollution from untreated wastes; coastal destruction due to land reclamation, industrial development, and aquaculture; deforestation and habitat destruction; poor land management leads to soil erosion, landslides, floods, droughts, dust storms and desertification; trade in endangered species

Environment—international agreements: *party to:* Antarctic-Environmental Protocol, Antarctic Treaty, Biodiversity, Climate Change, Climate Change-Kyoto Protocol, Desertification, Endangered Species, Environmental Modification, Hazardous Wastes, Law of the Sea, Marine Dumping, Ozone Layer Protection, Ship Pollution, Tropical Timber 83, Tropical Timber 94, Wetlands, Whaling
signed, but not ratified: none of the selected agreements

Geography—note: world's fourth largest country (after Russia, Canada, and US) and largest country situated entirely in Asia; Mount Everest on the border with Nepal is the world's tallest peak above sea level

PEOPLE AND SOCIETY

Population: 1,379,302,771 (July 2017 est.)
country comparison to the world: 1

Nationality: *noun:* Chinese (singular and plural)
adjective: Chinese

Ethnic groups: Han Chinese 91.6%, Zhuang 1.3%, other (includes Hui, Manchu, Uighur, Miao, Yi, Tujia, Tibetan, Mongol, Dong, Buyei, Yao, Bai, Korean, Hani, Li, Kazakh, Dai, and other nationalities) 7.1%
note: the Chinese Government officially recognizes 56 ethnic groups (2010 est.)

Languages: Standard Chinese or Mandarin (official; Putonghua, based on the Beijing dialect), Yue (Cantonese), Wu (Shanghainese), Minbei (Fuzhou), Minnan (Hokkien-Taiwanese), Xiang, Gan, Hakka dialects, minority languages (see Ethnic groups entry)
note: Zhuang is official in Guangxi Zhuang, Yue is official in Guangdong, Mongolian is official in Nei Mongol, Uighur is official in Xinjiang Uygur, Kyrgyz is official in Xinjiang Uygur, and Tibetan is official in Xizang (Tibet)

Religions: Buddhist 18.2%, Christian 5.1%, Muslim 1.8%, folk religion 21.9%, Hindu < 0.1%, Jewish < 0.1%, other 0.7% (includes Daoist (Taoist)), unaffiliated 52.2%
note: officially atheist (2010 est.)

Age structure: *0-14 years:* 17.15% (male 127,484,177/female 109,113,241)
15-24 years: 12.78% (male 94,215,607/female 82,050,623)
25-54 years: 48.51% (male 341,466,438/female 327,661,460)
55-64 years: 10.75% (male 74,771,050/female 73,441,177)
65 years and over: 10.81% (male 71,103,029/female 77,995,969) (2017 est.)

Dependency ratios: *total dependency ratio:* 37.7
youth dependency ratio: 24.3
elderly dependency ratio: 13.3
potential support ratio: 7.5
data do not include Hong Kong, Macau, and Taiwan (2015 est.)

Median age: *total:* 37.4 years
male: 36.5 years
female: 38.4 years (2017 est.)
country comparison to the world: 67

Population growth rate: 0.41% (2017 est.)
country comparison to the world: 160

Birth rate: 12.3 births/1,000 population (2017 est.)
country comparison to the world: 161

Death rate: 7.8 deaths/1,000 population (2017 est.)
country comparison to the world: 101

Net migration rate: -0.4 migrant(s)/1,000 population (2017 est.)
country comparison to the world: 121

Population distribution: overwhelming majority of the population is found in the eastern half of the country; the west, with its vast mountainous and desert areas, remains sparsely populated; though ranked first in the world in total population, overall density is less than that of many other countries in Asia and Europe; high population density is found along the Yangtze and Yellow River valleys, the Xi Jiang River delta, the Sichuan Basin (around Chengdu), in and around Beijing, and the industrial area around Shenyang

Urbanization: *urban population:* 57.9% of total population (2017)
rate of urbanization: 2.3% annual rate of change (2015-20 est.)
note: data do not include Hong Kong and Macau

Major urban areas—population: Shanghai 23.741 million; BEIJING (capital) 20.384 million; Chongqing 13.332 million; Guangdong 12.458 million; Tianjin 11.21 million; Shenzhen 10.749 million (2015)

Sex ratio: *at birth:* 1.15 male(s)/female
0-14 years: 1.17 male(s)/female
15-24 years: 1.14 male(s)/female
25-54 years: 1.04 male(s)/female
55-64 years: 1.02 male(s)/female
65 years and over: 0.92 male(s)/female
total population: 1.06 male(s)/female (2016 est.)

Maternal mortality ratio: 27 deaths/100,000 live births (2015 est.)
country comparison to the world: 119

Infant mortality rate: *total:* 12 deaths/1,000 live births
male: 12.3 deaths/1,000 live births
female: 11.7 deaths/1,000 live births (2017 est.)
country comparison to the world: 122

Life expectancy at birth: *total population:* 75.7 years
male: 73.6 years
female: 78 years (2017 est.)
country comparison to the world: 102

Total fertility rate: 1.6 children born/woman (2017 est.)
country comparison to the world: 182

Health expenditures: 5.5% of GDP (2014)
country comparison to the world: 125

Physicians density: 1.49 physicians/1,000 population (2011)

Hospital bed density: 3.8 beds/1,000 population (2011)

Drinking water source:
improved:
urban: 97.5% of population
rural: 93% of population
total: 95.5% of population
unimproved:
urban: 2.5% of population

rural: 7% of population
total: 4.5% of population (2015 est.)

Sanitation facility access:
improved:
urban: 86.6% of population
rural: 63.7% of population
total: 76.5% of population
unimproved:
urban: 13.4% of population
rural: 36.3% of population
total: 23.5% of population (2015 est.)

HIV/AIDS—adult prevalence rate: NA

HIV/AIDS—people living with HIV/AIDS: NA

HIV/AIDS—deaths: NA

Major infectious diseases: *degree of risk:*
intermediate
food or waterborne diseases: bacterial diarrhea,
hepatitis A, and typhoid fever
vectorborne disease: Japanese encephalitis
soil contact disease: hantaviral hemorrhagic fever
with renal syndrome (HFRS) (2016)

Obesity—adult prevalence rate: 6.2% (2016)
country comparison to the world: 169

Children under the age of 5 years underweight:
3.4% (2010)
country comparison to the world: 109

Education expenditures: NA

Literacy: *definition:* age 15 and over can read and
write
total population: 96.4%
male: 98.2%
female: 94.5% (2015 est.)

**School life expectancy (primary to tertiary educa-
tion):** *total:* 14 years
male: 14 years
female: 14 years (2015)

People—note: in October 2015, the Chinese Government announced that it would change its rules
to allow all couples to have two children, loosening a 1979 mandate that restricted many couples
to one child; the new policy was implemented on
1 January 2016 to address China's rapidly aging
population and economic needs

GOVERNMENT

Country name: *conventional long form:* People's
Republic of China
conventional short form: China
local long form: Zhonghua Renmin Gongheguo
local short form: Zhongguo
abbreviation: PRC
etymology: English name derives from the Qin
(Chin) rulers of the 3rd century B.C., who comprised the first imperial dynasty of ancient China;
the Chinese name Zhongguo translates as "Central
Nation"

Government type: communist party-led state

Capital: *name:* Beijing

geographic coordinates: 39 55 N, 116 23 E
time difference: UTC+8 (13 hours ahead of
Washington, DC, during Standard Time)

note: despite its size, all of China falls within one
time zone; many people in Xinjiang Province
observe an unofficial "Xinjiang time zone" of
UTC+6, two hours behind Beijing

Administrative divisions: 23 provinces (sheng, sin-
gular and plural), 5 autonomous regions (zizhiqu,
singular and plural), and 4 municipalities (shi,
singular and plural)
provinces: Anhui, Fujian, Gansu, Guangdong,
Guizhou, Hainan, Hebei, Heilongjiang, Henan,
Hubei, Hunan, Jiangsu, Jiangxi, Jilin, Liaoning,
Qinghai, Shaanxi, Shandong, Shanxi, Sichuan,
Yunnan, Zhejiang; (see note on Taiwan)
autonomous regions: Guangxi, Nei Mongol
(Inner Mongolia), Ningxia, Xinjiang Uygur,
Xizang (Tibet)
municipalities: Beijing, Chongqing, Shanghai,
Tianjin
note: China considers Taiwan its 23rd province;
see separate entries for the special administrative
regions of Hong Kong and Macau

Independence: 1 October 1949 (People's Republic
of China established); notable earlier dates: 221
B.C. (unification under the Qin Dynasty); 1 January 1912 (Qing Dynasty replaced by the Republic
of China)

National holiday: National Day (anniversary of
the founding of the People's Republic of China),
1 October (1949)

Constitution: several previous; latest promulgated
4 December 1982; amended several times, last in
2004 (2016)

Legal system: civil law influenced by Soviet and
continental European civil law systems; legislature
retains power to interpret statutes; note—in early
2017, the National People's Congress took the first
step in adopting a new civil code by passing the
General Provisions of the Civil Law

International law organization participation: has
not submitted an ICJ jurisdiction declaration;
non-party state to the ICCt

Citizenship: *citizenship by birth:* no
citizenship by descent only: least one parent must
be a citizen of China
dual citizenship recognized: no
residency requirement for naturalization: while
naturalization is theoretically possible, in practical
terms it is extremely difficult; residency is required
but not specified

Suffrage: 18 years of age; universal

Executive branch: *chief of state:* President XI Jinping (since 14 March 2013); Vice President LI
Yuanchao (since 14 March 2013)

head of government: Premier LI Keqiang (since 16
March 2013); Executive Vice Premiers ZHANG
Gaoli (since 16 March 2013), LIU Yandong (since
16 March 2013), MA Kai (since 16 March 2013),
WANG Yang (since 16 March 2013)
cabinet: State Council appointed by National
People's Congress
elections/appointments: president and vice president indirectly elected by National People's Congress for a 5-year term (eligible for a second term);
election last held on 5-17 March 2013 (next to be

held in March 2018); premier nominated by president, confirmed by National People's Congress
election results: XI Jinping elected president;
National People's Congress vote—2,952 ; LI Yuanchao elected vice president with 2,940 votes

Legislative branch: description: unicameral
National People's Congress or Quanguo Renmin
Daibiao Dahui (2,987 seats; members indirectly
elected by municipal, regional, and provincial people's congresses, and the People's Liberation Army;
members serve 5-year terms); note—in practice,
only members of the Chinese Communist Party
(CCP), its 8 allied parties, and CCP-approved
independent candidates are elected
elections: last held in December 2012-February
2013 (next to be held in late 2017 to early 2018)
election results: percent of vote—NA; seats by
party—2,987

Judicial branch: *highest court(s):* Supreme People's Court (consists of over 340 judges including
the chief justice, 13 grand justices organized into a
civil committee and tribunals for civil, economic,
administrative, complaint and appeal, and communication and transportation cases); note—in
late December 2016, the third, fourth, fifth, and
sixth circuit courts of the Supreme People's Court
began operation
judge selection and term of office: chief justice
appointed by the People's National Congress
(NPC); limited to 2 consecutive 5-year-terms;
other justices and judges nominated by the chief
justice and appointed by the Standing Committee of the NPC; term of other justices and judges
determined by the NPC
subordinate courts: Higher People's Courts;
Intermediate People's Courts; District and County
People's Courts; Autonomous Region People's
Courts; Special People's Courts for military, maritime, transportation, and forestry issues
note: in late 2014, China unveiled planned judicial reforms

Political parties and leaders: Chinese Communist
Party or CCP [XI Jinping]
note: China has 8 nominally independent small
parties ultimately controlled by the CCP

Political pressure groups and leaders: no substantial political opposition groups exist

International organization participation: ADB,
AfDB (nonregional member), APEC, Arctic
Council (observer), ARF, ASEAN (dialogue
partner), BIS, BRICS, CDB, CICA, EAS, FAO,
FATF, G-20, G-24 (observer), G-5, G-77, IADB,
IAEA, IBRD, ICAO, ICC (national committees),
ICRM, IDA, IFAD, IFC, IFRCS, IHO, ILO, IMF,
IMO, IMSO, Interpol, IOC, IOM (observer),
IPU, ISO, ITSO, ITU, LAIA (observer), MIGA,
MINURSO, MINUSMA, MONUSCO, NAM
(observer), NSG, OAS (observer), OPCW, Pacific
Alliance (observer), PCA, PIF (partner), SAARC
(observer), SCO, SICA (observer), UN, UNA-
MID, UNCTAD, UNESCO, UNFICYP, UNHCR,
UNIDO, UNIFIL, UNMIL, UNMISS, UNOCI,
UNSC (permanent), UNTSO, UNWTO, UPU,
WCO, WHO, WIPO, WMO, WTO, ZC

Diplomatic representation in the US: *chief of mission:* Ambassador CUI Tiankai (since 3 April 2013)
chancery: 3505 International Place NW, Washington, DC 20008
telephone: [1] (202) 495-2266
FAX: [1] (202) 495-2138
consulate(s) general: Chicago, Houston, Los Angeles, New York, San Francisco

Diplomatic representation from the US: *chief of mission:* Ambassador Terry BRANSTAD (since 12 July 2017)Charge d"Affaires Johnathan FRITZ (acting)(since 5 June 2017)
embassy: 55 An Jia Lou Lu, 100600 Beijing
mailing address: PSC 461, Box 50, FPO AP 96521-0002
telephone: [86] (10) 8531-3000
FAX: [86] (10) 8531-3300
consulate(s) general: Chengdu, Guangzhou, Shanghai, Shenyang, Wuhan

Flag description: red with a large yellow five-pointed star and four smaller yellow five-pointed stars (arranged in a vertical arc toward the middle of the flag) in the upper hoist-side corner; the color red represents revolution, while the stars symbolize the four social classes—the working class, the peasantry, the urban petty bourgeoisie, and the national bourgeoisie (capitalists)—united under the Communist Party of China

National symbol(s): dragon, giant panda; national colors: red, yellow

National anthem: name: "Yiyongjun Jinxingqu" (The March of the Volunteers)
lyrics/music: TIAN Han/NIE Er
note: adopted 1949; the anthem, though banned during the Cultural Revolution, is more commonly known as "Zhongguo Guoge" (Chinese National Song); it was originally the theme song to the 1935 Chinese movie, "Sons and Daughters in a Time of Storm"

ECONOMY

Economy—overview: Since the late 1970s, China has moved from a closed, centrally planned system to a more market-oriented one that plays a major global role. China has implemented reforms in a gradualist fashion, resulting in efficiency gains that have contributed to a more than tenfold increase in GDP since 1978. Reforms began with the phaseout of collectivized agriculture, and expanded to include the gradual liberalization of prices, fiscal decentralization, increased autonomy for state enterprises, growth of the private sector, development of stock markets and a modern banking system, and opening to foreign trade and investment. China continues to pursue an industrial policy, state support of key sectors, and a restrictive investment regime. Measured on a purchasing power parity (PPP) basis that adjusts for price differences, China in 2016 stood as the largest economy in the world, surpassing the US in 2014 for the first time in modern history. China became the world's largest exporter in 2010, and the largest trading nation in 2013. Still, China's per capita income is below the world average.

After keeping its currency tightly linked to the US dollar for years, China in July 2005 moved to an exchange rate system that references a basket of currencies. From mid-2005 to late 2008, the renminbi appreciated more than 20% against the US dollar, but the exchange rate remained virtually pegged to the dollar from the onset of the global financial crisis until June 2010, when Beijing announced it would allow a resumption of gradual liberalization. From 2013 until early2015, the renminbi (RMB) appreciated roughly 2% against the dollar, but the exchange rate fell 13% from mid-2015 until end-2016 amid strong capital outflows in part stemming from the August 2015 official devaluation; in 2017 the RMB resumed appreciating against the dollar–roughly 7% from end-of-2016 to end-of-2017. From 2013 to 2017, China had one of the fastest growing economies in the world, averaging slightly more than 7% real growth per year. In 2015, the People's Bank of China announced it would continue to carefully push for full convertibility of the renminbi, after the currency was accepted as part of the IMF's special drawing rights basket. However, since late 2015 the Chinese Government has strengthened capital controls and oversight of overseas investments to better manage the exchange rate and maintain financial stability.

The Chinese Government faces numerous economic challenges including: (a) reducing its high domestic savings rate and correspondingly low domestic household consumption; (b) managing its high corporate debt burden to maintain financial stability; (c) controlling off-balance sheet local government debt used to finance infrastructure stimulus; (d) facilitating higher-wage job opportunities for the aspiring middle class, including rural migrants and college graduates, while maintaining competitiveness; (e) dampening speculative investment in the real estate sector without sharply slowing the economy; (f) reducing industrial overcapacity; and (g) raising productivity growth rates through the more efficient allocation of capital and state-support for innovation. Economic development has progressed further in coastal provinces than in the interior, and by 2016 more than 169.3 million migrant workers and their dependents had relocated to urban areas to find work. One consequence of China's population control policy known as the "one-child policy"—which was relaxed in 2016 to permit all families to have two children—is that China is now one of the most rapidly aging countries in the world. Deterioration in the environment—notably air pollution, soil erosion, and the steady fall of the water table, especially in the North—is another long-term problem. China continues to lose arable land: because of erosion and urbanization. The Chinese Government is seeking to add energy production capacity from sources other than coal and oil, focusing on natural gas, nuclear, and clean energy development. In 2016, China ratified the Paris Agreement, a multilateral agreement to combat climate change, and committed to peak its carbon dioxide emissions between 2025 and 2030.

The government's 13th Five-Year Plan, unveiled in March 2016, emphasizes the need to increase innovation and boost domestic consumption to make the economy less dependent on government investment, exports, and heavy industry. However, China has made more progress on subsidizing innovation than rebalancing the economy. Beijing has committed to giving the market a more decisive role in allocating resources, but the Chinese Government's policies continue to favor state-owned enterprises and emphasize stability. Chinese leaders in 2010 pledged to double China's GDP by 2020, and the 13th Five Year Plan includes annual economic growth targets of at least 6.5% through 2020 to achieve that goal. In recent years, China has renewed its support for state-owned enterprises in sectors considered important to "economic security," explicitly looking to foster globally competitive industries. Chinese leaders also have undermined some market-oriented reforms by reaffirming the "dominant" role of the state in the economy, a stance that threatens to discourage private initiative and make the economy less efficient over time. The slight acceleration in economic growth in 2017—the first such uptick since 2010—gives Beijing more latitude to pursue its economic reforms, focusing on financial sector deleveraging and its Supply-Side Structural Reform agenda, first announced in late 2015.

GDP (purchasing power parity): $23.12 trillion (2017 est.)
$21.66 trillion (2016 est.)
$20.3 trillion (2015 est.)
note: data are in 2017 dollars
country comparison to the world: 1

GDP (official exchange rate): $11.94 trillion (2016 est.)
note: because China's exchange rate is determined by fiat rather than by market forces, the official exchange rate measure of GDP is not an accurate measure of China's output; GDP at the official exchange rate substantially understates the actual level of China's output vis-a-vis the rest of the world; in China's situation, GDP at purchasing power parity provides the best measure for comparing output across countries

GDP—real growth rate: 6.8% (2017 est.)
6.7% (2016 est.)
6.9% (2015 est.)
country comparison to the world: 13

GDP—per capita (PPP): $16,600 (2017 est.)
$15,700 (2016 est.)
$14,800 (2015 est.)
note: data are in 2017 dollars
country comparison to the world: 106

Gross national saving: 45.4% of GDP (2017 est.)
45.9% of GDP (2016 est.)
47.5% of GDP (2015 est.)
country comparison to the world: 4

GDP—composition, by end use:
household consumption: 39.1%
government consumption: 14.6%
investment in fixed capital: 43.3%
investment in inventories: 1.1%
exports of goods and services: 19.6%

imports of goods and services: -17.7% (2017 est.)

GDP—composition, by sector of origin:
agriculture: 8.2%
industry: 39.5%
services: 52.2%
(2017 est.)

Agriculture—products: world leader in gross value of agricultural output; rice, wheat, potatoes, corn, tobacco, peanuts, tea, apples, cotton, pork, mutton, eggs; fish, shrimp

Industries: world leader in gross value of industrial output; mining and ore processing, iron, steel, aluminum, and other metals, coal; machine building; armaments; textiles and apparel; petroleum; cement; chemicals; fertilizer; consumer products (including footwear, toys, and electronics); food processing; transportation equipment, including automobiles, railcars and locomotives, ships, aircraft; telecommunications equipment, commercial space launch vehicles, satellites

Industrial production growth rate: 6.2% (2017 est.)
country comparison to the world: 32

Labor force: 806.7 million
note: by the end of 2012, China's population at working age (15-64 years) was 1.004 billion (2017 est.)
country comparison to the world: 1

Labor force—by occupation: *agriculture:* 28.3%
industry: 29.3%
services: 42.4%
(2015 est.)

Unemployment rate: 4% (2017 est.)
4% (2016 est.)
note: data are for registered urban unemployment, which excludes private enterprises and migrants
country comparison to the world: 46

Population below poverty line: 3.3%
note: in 2011, China set a new poverty line at RMB 2300 (approximately US $400) (2016 est.)

Household income or consumption by percentage share: *lowest 10%:* 2.1%
highest 10%: 31.4%
note: data are for urban households only (2012)

Distribution of family income—Gini index: 46.5 (2016 est.)
46.2 (2015 est.)
country comparison to the world: 30

Budget: *revenues:* $2.672 trillion
expenditures: $3.146 trillion (2017 est.)
Taxes and other revenues: 22.4% of GDP (2017 est.)
country comparison to the world: 134

Budget surplus (+) or deficit (-): -4% of GDP (2017 est.)
country comparison to the world: 143

Public debt: 18.6% of GDP (2017 est.)
16.1% of GDP (2016 est.)
note: official data; data cover both central government debt and local government debt, including debt officially recognized by China's National Audit Office report in 2011; data exclude policy

bank bonds, Ministry of Railway debt, and China Asset Management Company debt
country comparison to the world: 189

Fiscal year: calendar year

Inflation rate (consumer prices): 1.8% (2017 est.)
2% (2016 est.)
country comparison to the world: 81

Central bank discount rate: 2.25% (31 December 2016 est.)
2.25% (31 December 2015 est.)
country comparison to the world: 114

Commercial bank prime lending rate: 4.4% (31 December 2017 est.)
4.35% (31 December 2016 est.)
country comparison to the world: 153

Stock of narrow money: $8.16 trillion (31 December 2017 est.)
$7.001 trillion (31 December 2016 est.)
country comparison to the world: 1

Stock of broad money: $25.24 trillion (31 December 2017 est.)
$22.3 trillion (31 December 2016 est.)
country comparison to the world: 1

Stock of domestic credit: $26.87 trillion (31 December 2017 est.)
$23.02 trillion (31 December 2016 est.)
country comparison to the world: 1

Market value of publicly traded shares: $7.321 trillion (31 December 2016 est.)
$8.188 trillion (31 December 2015 est.)
$6.005 trillion (31 December 2014 est.)
country comparison to the world: 2

Current account balance: $162.5 billion (2017 est.)
$196.4 billion (2016 est.)
country comparison to the world: 4

Exports: $2.157 trillion (2017 est.)
$1.99 trillion (2016 est.)
country comparison to the world: 1

Exports—commodities: electrical and other machinery, including computers and telecommunications equipment, apparel, furniture, textiles

Exports—partners: US 18.2%, Hong Kong 13.8%, Japan 6.1%, South Korea 4.5% (2016)

Imports: $1.731 trillion (2017 est.)
$1.495 trillion (2016 est.)
country comparison to the world: 2

Imports—commodities: electrical and other machinery, including integrated circuits and other computer components, oil and mineral fuels; optical and medical equipment, metal ores, motor vehicles; soybeans

Imports—partners: South Korea 10%, Japan 9.2%, US 8.5%, Germany 5.4%, Australia 4.4% (2016)

Reserves of foreign exchange and gold: $3.194 trillion (31 December 2017 est.)
$3.098 trillion (31 December 2016 est.)
country comparison to the world: 1

Debt—external: $1.649 trillion (31 December 2017 est.)
$1.467 trillion (31 December 2016 est.)
country comparison to the world: 14

Stock of direct foreign investment—at home: $1.514 trillion (31 December 2017 est.)
$1.391 trillion (31 December 2016 est.)
country comparison to the world: 6

Stock of direct foreign investment—abroad: $1.342 trillion (31 December 2017 est.)
$1.227 trillion (31 December 2016 est.)
country comparison to the world: 12

Exchange rates: Renminbi yuan (RMB) per US dollar—
6.7588 (2017 est.)
6.6445 (2016 est.)
6.2275 (2015 est.)
6.1434 (2014 est.)
6.1958 (2013 est.)

ENERGY

Electricity access: *population without electricity:* 1,200,000
electrification—*total population:* 99.9%
electrification—urban areas: 100%
electrification—rural areas: 99.8% (2016)

Electricity—production: 6.142 trillion kWh (2016 est.)
country comparison to the world: 1

Electricity—consumption: 5.92 trillion kWh (2016 est.)
country comparison to the world: 1

Electricity—exports: 18.91 billion kWh (2016 est.)
country comparison to the world: 11

Electricity—imports: 6.185 billion kWh (2016 est.)
country comparison to the world: 34

Electricity—installed generating capacity: 1.646 billion kW (2016 est.)
country comparison to the world: 2

Electricity—from fossil fuels: 64% of total installed capacity (2016 est.)
country comparison to the world: 117

Electricity—from nuclear fuels: 2% of total installed capacity (2016 est.)
country comparison to the world: 28

Electricity—from hydroelectric plants: 20.2% of total installed capacity (2016 est.)
country comparison to the world: 88

Electricity—from other renewable sources: 13.7% of total installed capacity (2016 est.)
country comparison to the world: 53

Crude oil—production: 3.981 million bbl/day (2016 est.)
country comparison to the world: 6

Crude oil—exports: 32,000 bbl/day (2014 est.)
country comparison to the world: 47

Crude oil—imports: 6.167 million bbl/day (2014 est.)
country comparison to the world: 2

Crude oil—proved reserves: 25.62 billion bbl (1 January 2017 es)
country comparison to the world: 13

Refined petroleum products—production: 10.85 million bbl/day (2014 est.)

country comparison to the world: 3

Refined petroleum products—consumption: 11.75 million bbl/day (2015 est.)
country comparison to the world: 3

Refined petroleum products—exports: 709,900 bbl/day (2014 est.)
country comparison to the world: 10

Refined petroleum products—imports: 971,900 bbl/day (2014 est.)
country comparison to the world: 6

Natural gas—production: 138.4 billion cu m (2016 est.)
country comparison to the world: 6

Natural gas—consumption: 210.3 billion cu m (2016 est.)
country comparison to the world: 6

Natural gas—exports: 3.243 billion cu m (2015 est.)
country comparison to the world: 35

Natural gas—imports: 75.1 billion cu m (2016 est.)
country comparison to the world: 5

Natural gas—proved reserves: 5.194 trillion cu m (1 January 2017 es)
country comparison to the world: 10

Carbon dioxide emissions from consumption of energy: 9.135 billion Mt (2014 est.)
country comparison to the world: 1

COMMUNICATIONS

Telephones—fixed lines: *total subscriptions:* 206.624 million
subscriptions per 100 inhabitants: 15 (July 2016 est.)
country comparison to the world: 1

Telephones—mobile cellular: *total:* 1,364.934 million
subscriptions per 100 inhabitants: 99 (July 2016 est.)
country comparison to the world: 1

Telephone system: *general assessment:* domestic and international services are available for private use; unevenly distributed domestic system serves principal cities, industrial centers, and many towns; China continues to develop its telecommunications infrastructure; China in the summer of 2008 began a major restructuring of its telecommunications industry, resulting in the consolidation of its six telecom service operators to three, China Telecom, China Mobile, and China Unicom, each providing both fixed-line and mobile services (2016)
domestic: interprovincial fiber-optic trunk lines and cellular telephone systems have been installed; mobile-cellular subscribership is increasing rapidly; the number of Internet users now over 50% of the population; a domestic satellite system with several earth stations is in place (2016)
international: country code—86; a number of submarine cables provide connectivity to Asia, the Middle East, Europe, and the US; satellite earth stations—7 (5 Intelsat—4 Pacific Ocean and 1 Indian Ocean; 1 Intersputnik—Indian Ocean region; and 1 Inmarsat—Pacific and Indian Ocean regions) (2012)

Broadcast media: all broadcast media are owned by, or affiliated with, the Communist Party of China or a government agency; no privately owned TV or radio stations; state-run Chinese Central TV, provincial, and municipal stations offer more than 2,000 channels; the Central Propaganda Department lists subjects that are off limits to domestic broadcast media with the government maintaining authority to approve all programming; foreign-made TV programs must be approved prior to broadcast; increasingly, Chinese turn to online television to access Chinese and international films and television shows (2017)

Internet country code: .cn
Internet users: total: 730,723,960
percent of population: 53.2% (July 2016 est.)
country comparison to the world: 1

TRANSPORTATION

National air transport system: *number of registered air carriers:* 56
inventory of registered aircraft operated by air carriers: 2,890
annual passenger traffic on registered air carriers: 436,183,969
annual freight traffic on registered air carriers: 19.806 billion mt-km (2015)
Civil aircraft registration country code prefix: B (2016)

Airports: 507 (2013)
country comparison to the world: 14

Airports—with paved runways: *total:* 463
over 3,047 m: 71
2,438 to 3,047 m: 158
1,524 to 2,437 m: 123
914 to 1,523 m: 25
under 914 m: 86 (2017)

Airports—with unpaved runways: *total:* 44
over 3,047 m: 4
2,438 to 3,047 m: 7
1,524 to 2,437 m: 6
914 to 1,523 m: 9
under 914 m: 18 (2013)

Heliports: 47 (2013)

Pipelines: gas 70,000 km; crude oil 22,900 km; refined petroleum products 25,500 km; water 710,206 km (2015)

Railways: *total:* 124,000 km
standard gauge: 124,000 km 1.435-m gauge (80,000 km electrified); 102,000 traditional, 22,000 high-speed (2017)
country comparison to the world: 2

Roadways: *total:* 4,577,300 km
paved: 4,046,300 km (includes 123,500 km of expressways)
unpaved: 531,000 km (2015)
country comparison to the world: 3

Waterways: 110,000 km (navigable waterways) (2011)
country comparison to the world: 1

Merchant marine: *total:* 4,287

by type: bulk carrier 1,069, container ship 198, general cargo 697, oil tanker 480, other 1,843 (2017)

Ports and terminals: *major seaport(s):* Dalian, Ningbo, Qingdao, Qinhuangdao, Shanghai, Shenzhen, Tianjin
river port(s): Guangzhou (Pearl)
container port(s) (TEUs): Dalian (9,591,000), Guangzhou (17,097,000), Ningbo (20,636,000), Qingdao (17,323,000), Shanghai (36,516,000), Shenzhen (24,142,000), Tianjin (13,881,000) (2015)
LNG terminal(s) (import): Fujian, Guangdong, Jiangsu, Shandong, Shanghai, Tangshan, Zhejiang
Transportation—note: seven of the world's ten largest container ports are in China

MILITARY AND SECURITY

Military expenditures: 1.9% of GDP (2016)
1.95% of GDP (2015)
1.9% of GDP (2014)
1.85% of GDP (2013)
1.84% of GDP (2012)
country comparison to the world: 40

Military branches: People's Liberation Army (PLA): Army, Navy (PLAN, includes marines and naval aviation), Air Force (Zhongguo Renmin Jiefangjun Kongjun, PLAAF, includes airborne forces), Rocket Force (strategic missile force), and Strategic Support Force (space and cyber forces); People's Armed Police (Renmin Wuzhuang Jingcha Budui, PAP); PLA Reserve Force (2016)

Military service age and obligation: 18-24 years of age for selective compulsory military service, with a 2-year service obligation; no minimum age for voluntary service (all officers are volunteers); 18-19 years of age for women high school graduates who meet requirements for specific military jobs; a recent military decision allows women in combat roles; the first class of women warship commanders was in 2011 (2012)

TRANSNATIONAL ISSUES

Disputes—international: continuing talks and confidence-building measures work toward reducing tensions over Kashmir that nonetheless remains militarized with portions under the de facto administration of China (Aksai Chin), India (Jammu and Kashmir), and Pakistan (Azad Kashmir and Northern Areas); India does not recognize Pakistan's ceding historic Kashmir lands to China in 1964; China and India continue their security and foreign policy dialogue started in 2005 related to the dispute over most of their rugged, militarized boundary, regional nuclear proliferation, and other matters; China claims most of India's Arunachal Pradesh to the base of the Himalayas; lacking any treaty describing the boundary, Bhutan and China continue negotiations to establish a common boundary alignment to resolve territorial disputes arising from substantial cartographic discrepancies, the most contentious of which lie in Bhutan's west along China's Chumbi salient; Burmese forces attempting to dig in to the largely autonomous

Shan State to rout local militias tied to the drug trade, prompts local residents to periodically flee into neighboring Yunnan Province in China; Chinese maps show an international boundary symbol off the coasts of the littoral states of the South China Seas, where China has interrupted Vietnamese hydrocarbon exploration; China asserts sovereignty over Scarborough Reef along with the Philippines and Taiwan, and over the Spratly Islands together with Malaysia, the Philippines, Taiwan, Vietnam, and Brunei; the 2002 Declaration on the Conduct of Parties in the South China Sea eased tensions in the Spratlys but is not the legally binding code of conduct sought by some parties; Vietnam and China continue to expand construction of facilities in the Spratlys and in March 2005, the national oil companies of China, the Philippines, and Vietnam signed a joint accord on marine seismic activities in the Spratly Islands;

China occupies some of the Paracel Islands also claimed by Vietnam and Taiwan; the Japanese-administered Senkaku Islands are also claimed by China and Taiwan; certain islands in the Yalu and Tumen Rivers are in dispute with North Korea; North Korea and China seek to stem illegal migration to China by North Koreans, fleeing privations and oppression, by building a fence along portions of the border and imprisoning North Koreans deported by China; China and Russia have demarcated the once disputed islands at the Amur and Ussuri confluence and in the Argun River in accordance with their 2004 Agreement; China and Tajikistan have begun demarcating the revised boundary agreed to in the delimitation of 2002; the decade-long demarcation of the

China-Vietnam land boundary was completed in 2009; citing environmental, cultural, and social concerns, China has reconsidered construction of 13 dams on the Salween River, but energy-starved Burma, with backing from Thailand, remains intent on building five hydro-electric dams downstream despite regional and international protests

Chinese and Hong Kong authorities met in March 2008 to resolve ownership and use of lands recovered in Shenzhen River channelization, including 96-hectare Lok Ma Chau Loop

Refugees and internally displaced persons: refugees (country of origin): 317,098 (Vietnam); undetermined (North Korea) (2016)
IDPs: undetermined (2014)

Trafficking in persons: *current situation:* China is a source, transit, and destination country for men, women, and children subjected to sex trafficking and forced labor; Chinese adults and children are forced into prostitution and various forms of forced labor, including begging and working in brick kilns, coal mines, and factories; women and children are recruited from rural areas and taken to urban centers for sexual exploitation, often lured by criminal syndicates or gangs with fraudulent job offers; state-sponsored forced labor, where detainees work for up to four years often with no remuneration, continues to be a serious concern; Chinese men, women, and children also may be subjected to conditions of sex trafficking and forced labor worldwide, particularly in overseas Chinese communities; women and children are trafficked to China from neighboring countries, as well as Africa and the Americas, for forced labor and prostitution

tier rating: Tier 2 Watch List—China does not fully comply with the minimum standards for the elimination of trafficking; however, it is making significant efforts to do so; official data for 2014 states that 194 alleged traffickers were arrested and at least 35 were convicted, but the government's conflation of human trafficking with other crimes makes it difficult to assess law enforcement efforts to investigate and to prosecute trafficking offenses according to international law; despite reports of complicity, no government officials were investigated, prosecuted, or convicted for their roles in trafficking offenses; authorities did not adequately protect victims and did not provide the data needed to ascertain the number of victims identified or assisted or the services provided; the National People's Congress ratified a decision to abolish "reform through labor" in 2013, but some continued to operate as state-sponsored drug detention or "custody and education" centers that force inmates to perform manual labor; some North Korean refugees continued to be forcibly repatriated as illegal economic migrants, despite reports that some were trafficking victims (2015)

Illicit drugs: major transshipment point for heroin produced in the Golden Triangle region of Southeast Asia; growing domestic consumption of synthetic drugs, and heroin from Southeast and Southwest Asia; source country for methamphetamine and heroin chemical precursors, despite new regulations on its large chemical industry; more people believed to be convicted and executed for drug offences than anywhere else in the world, according to NGOs

CHRISTMAS ISLAND

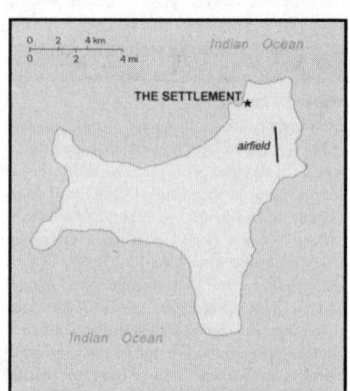

INTRODUCTION

Background: Named in 1643 for the day of its discovery, the island was annexed and settlement began by the UK in 1888 with the discovery of the island's phosphate deposits. Following the Second World War, Christmas Island came under the

jurisdiction of the new British Colony of Singapore. The island existed as a separate Crown colony from 1 January 1958 to 1 October 1958 when its transfer to Australian jurisdiction was finalized. That date is still celebrated on the first Monday in October as Territory Day. Almost two-thirds of the island has been declared a national park.

GEOGRAPHY

Location: Southeastern Asia, island in the Indian Ocean, south of Indonesia

Geographic coordinates: 10 30 S, 105 40 E

Map references: Southeast Asia

Area: *total:* 135 sq km
land: 135 sq km
water: 0 sq km
country comparison to the world: 222

Area—comparative: about three-quarters the size of Washington, DC

Land boundaries: 0 km

Coastline: 138.9 km

Maritime claims: *territorial sea:* 12 nm

contiguous zone: 12 nm
exclusive fishing zone: 200 nm

Climate: tropical with a wet season (December to April) and dry season; heat and humidity moderated by trade winds

Terrain: steep cliffs along coast rise abruptly to central plateau

Elevation: *mean elevation:* NA

elevation extremes: *lowest point:* Indian Ocean 0 m
highest point: Murray Hill 361 m

Natural resources: phosphate, beaches

Land use: *agricultural land:* 0%
arable land: 0%;
permanent crops: 0%;
permanent pasture: 0%
other: 100% (mainly tropical rainforest; 63% of the island is a national park) (2011 est.)
Irrigated land: NA

Population—distribution: majority of the population lives on the northern tip of the island

Natural hazards: the narrow fringing reef surrounding the island can be a maritime hazard

Environment—current issues: loss of rainforest; impact of phosphate mining

Geography—note: located along major sea lanes of Indian Ocean

PEOPLE AND SOCIETY

Population: 2,205 (July 2016 est.)
country comparison to the world: 232

Nationality: *noun:* Christmas Islander(s)
adjective: Christmas Island

Ethnic groups: Chinese 70%, European 20%, Malay 10%
note: no indigenous population (2001)

Languages: English (official), Mandarin, Cantonese, Malay, Tagalog

Religions: Buddhist 16.9%, Christian 16.4%, Muslim 14.8%, other 1.3%, none 9.2%, unspecified 41.5% (2011 est.)

Age structure: *0-14 years:* 12.79% (male 147/female 135)
15-24 years: 12.2% (male 202/female 67)
25-54 years: 57.91% (male 955/female 322)
55-64 years: 11.66% (male 172/female 85)
65 years and over: 5.44% (male 84/female 36) (2017 est.)

Population growth rate: 1.11% (2014 est.)
country comparison to the world: 104

Population distribution: majority of the population lives on the northern tip of the island

Sex ratio: NA

Infant mortality rate: *total:* NA
male: NA
female: NA

Life expectancy at birth: *total population:* NA
male: NA
female: NA (2017 est.)

Total fertility rate: NA

HIV/AIDS—adult prevalence rate: NA

HIV/AIDS—people living with HIV/AIDS: NA

HIV/AIDS—deaths: NA

GOVERNMENT

Country name: *conventional long form:* Territory of Christmas Island
conventional short form: Christmas Island
etymology: named by English Captain William MYNORS for the day of its discovery, Christmas Day (25 December 1643)

Dependency status: non-self governing territory of Australia; administered from Canberra by the Department of Regional Australia, Local Government, Arts and Sport

Government type: non-self-governing overseas territory of Australia

Capital: *name:* The Settlement
geographic coordinates: 10 25 S, 105 43 E
time difference: UTC+7 (12 hours ahead of Washington, DC, during Standard Time)

Administrative divisions: none (territory of Australia)

Independence: none (territory of Australia)

National holiday: Australia Day (commemorates the arrival of the First Fleet of Australian settlers), 26 January (1788)

Constitution: 1 October 1958 (Christmas Island Act 1958); amended many times, last in 2010 (Territories Law Reform Act 2010) (2016)

Legal system: legal system is under the authority of the governor general of Australia and Australian law

Citizenship: see Australia

Suffrage: 18 years of age

Executive branch: *chief of state:* Queen ELIZABETH II (since 6 February 1952); represented by Governor General of the Commonwealth of Australia General Sir Peter COSGROVE (since 28 March 2014)

head of government: Administrator Natasha GRIGGS (since 5 October 2018)

elections/appointments: the monarchy is hereditary; governor general appointed by the monarch on the recommendation of the Australian prime minister; administrator appointed by the governor general of Australia for a 2-year term and represents the monarch and Australia

Legislative branch: description: unicameral Christmas Island Shire Council (9 seats; members directly elected by simple majority vote to serve 4-year terms with a portion of the membership renewed every 2 years)
elections: held every 2 years with half the members standing for election; last held on 17 October 2015 (next to be held on 21 October 2017)
election results: percent of vote—NA; seats by party—independent 9

Judicial branch: *highest court(s):* under the terms of the Territorial Law Reform Act 1992, Western Australia provides court services as needed for the island, including the Supreme Court and subordinate courts (District Court, Magistrate Court, Family Court, Children's Court, and Coroners' Court)

Political parties and leaders: none

Political pressure groups and leaders: none

International organization participation: none

Diplomatic representation in the US: none (territory of Australia)

Diplomatic representation from the US: none (territory of Australia)

Flag description: territorial flag; divided diagonally from upper hoist to lower fly; the upper triangle is green with a yellow image of the Golden Bosun Bird superimposed; the lower triangle is blue with the Southern Cross constellation, representing Australia, superimposed; a centered yellow disk displays a green map of the island
note: the flag of Australia is used for official purposes

National symbol(s): golden bosun bird

National anthem: *note:* as a territory of Australia, "Advance Australia Fair" remains official as the national anthem, while "God Save the Queen" serves as the royal anthem (see Australia)

ECONOMY

Economy—overview: The main economic activities on Christmas Island are the mining of low grade phosphate, limited tourism, the provision of government services and, since 2005, the construction and operation of the Immigration Detention Center. The government sector includes administration, health, education, policing, customs, quarantine, and defense.

GDP (purchasing power parity): $NA

Agriculture—products: NA

Industries: tourism, phosphate extraction (near depletion)

Labor force: NA

Budget: *revenues:* $NA
expenditures: $NA

Fiscal year: 1 July–30 June

Exports: $NA

Exports—commodities: phosphate

Imports: $NA

Imports—commodities: consumer goods

Exchange rates: Australian dollars (AUD) per US dollar—
1.311 (2017)
1.3442 (2016)
1.3442 (2015)
1.3291 (2014 est.)
1.1094 (2013 est.)

COMMUNICATIONS

Telephone system: *general assessment:* service provided by the Australian network
domestic: local area code—08; GSM mobile-cellular telephone service is provided by Telstra as part of the Australian network
international: international code—61 8; satellite earth station—1 (Intelsat provides telephone and telex service) (2017)

Broadcast media: 1 community radio station; satellite broadcasts of several Australian radio and TV stations (2017)

Internet country code: .cx
Internet users: total: 790
percent of population: 35.8% (July 2016 est.)
country comparison to the world: 217

TRANSPORTATION

Airports: 1 (2013)
country comparison to the world: 215

Airports—with paved runways: *total:* 1
1,524 to 2,437 m: 1 (2017)

Railways: *total:* 18 km
standard gauge: 18 km 1.435-m (not in operation)

note: the 18-km Christmas Island Phosphate Company Railway between Flying Fish Cove and South Point was decommissioned in 1987; some tracks and scrap remain in place (2017)
country comparison to the world: 134

Roadways: *total:* 140 km
paved: 30 km
unpaved: 110 km (2011)

country comparison to the world: 212
Ports and terminals: *major seaport(s):* Flying Fish Cove

MILITARY AND SECURITY

Military—note: defense is the responsibility of Australia

TRANSNATIONAL ISSUES

Disputes—international: None

CLIPPERTON ISLAND

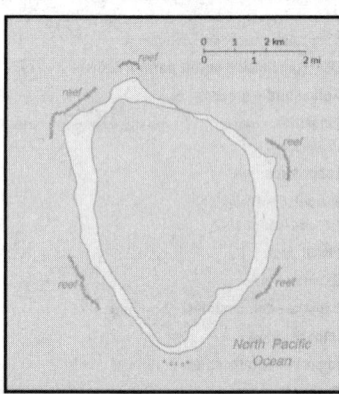

INTRODUCTION

Background: This isolated atoll was named for John CLIPPERTON, an English pirate who was rumored to have made it his hideout early in the 18th century. Annexed by France in 1855 and claimed by the US, it was seized by Mexico in 1897. Arbitration eventually awarded the island to France in 1931, which took possession in 1935.

GEOGRAPHY

Location: Middle America, atoll in the North Pacific Ocean, 1,120 km southwest of Mexico
Geographic coordinates: 10 17 N, 109 13 W
Map references: Political Map of the World
Area: *total:* 6 sq km
land: 6 sq km
water: 0 sq km
country comparison to the world: 248

Area—comparative: about 12 times the size of The Mall in Washington, DC
Land boundaries: 0 km
Coastline: 11.1 km
Maritime claims: *territorial sea:* 12 nm
exclusive economic zone: 200 nm
Climate: tropical; humid, average temperature 20-32 degrees Celsius, wet season (May to October)
Terrain: coral atoll
Elevation: *mean elevation:* NA
elevation extremes: lowest point: Pacific Ocean 0 m
highest point: Rocher Clipperton 29 m
Natural resources: fish
Land use: *agricultural land:* 0%
arable land: 0%;
permanent crops: 0%;
permanent pasture: 0%
forest: 0%
other: 100% (all coral) (2011 est.)
Natural hazards: subject to tropical storms and hurricanes from May to October
Environment—current issues: no natural resources, guano deposits depleted; the ring-shaped atoll encloses a stagnant fresh-water lagoon
Geography—note: the atoll reef is approximately 12 km (7.5 mi) in circumference; an attempt to colonize the atoll in the early 20th century ended in disaster and was abandoned in 1917

PEOPLE AND SOCIETY

Population: uninhabited

GOVERNMENT

Country name: *conventional long form:* none

conventional short form: Clipperton Island
local long form: none
local short form: Ile Clipperton
former: sometimes referred to as Ile de la Passion or Atoll Clipperton
etymology: named after an 18th-century English pirate who supposedly used the island as a base
Dependency status: possession of France; administered directly by the Minister of Overseas France
Legal system: the laws of France apply
Flag description: the flag of France is used

ECONOMY

Economy—overview: Although 115 species of fish have been identified in the territorial waters of Clipperton Island, the only economic activity is tuna fishing.

TRANSPORTATION

Ports and terminals: none; offshore anchorage only

MILITARY AND SECURITY

Military—note: defense is the responsibility of France

TRANSNATIONAL ISSUES

Disputes—international: none

COCOS (KEELING) ISLANDS

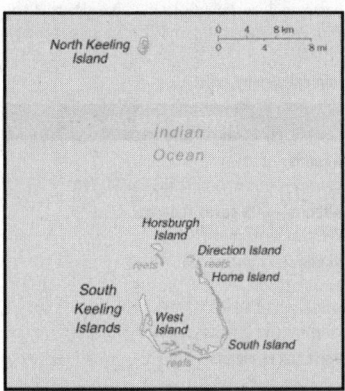

INTRODUCTION

Background: There are 27 coral islands in the group. Captain William KEELING discovered the islands in 1609, but they remained uninhabited until the 19th century. From the 1820s to 1978, members of the CLUNIES-ROSS family controlled the islands and the copra produced from local coconuts. Annexed by the UK in 1857, the Cocos Islands were transferred to the Australian Government in 1955. Apart from North Keeling Island, which lies 30 kilometers north of the main group, the islands form a horseshoe-shaped atoll surrounding a lagoon. North Keeling Island was declared a national park in 1995 and is administered by Parks Australia. The population on the two inhabited islands generally is split between the ethnic Europeans on West Island and the ethnic Malays on Home Island.

GEOGRAPHY

Location: Southeastern Asia, group of islands in the Indian Ocean, southwest of Indonesia, about halfway between Australia and Sri Lanka

Geographic coordinates: 12 30 S, 96 50 E

Map references: Southeast Asia

Area: *total:* 14 sq km
land: 14 sq km
water: 0 sq km
note: includes the two main islands of West Island and Home Island
country comparison to the world: 243

Area—comparative: about 24 times the size of The Mall in Washington, DC

Land boundaries: 0 km

Coastline: 26 km

Maritime claims: *territorial sea:* 12 nm
exclusive fishing zone: 200 nm

Climate: tropical with high humidity, moderated by the southeast trade winds for about nine months of the year

Terrain: flat, low-lying coral atolls

Elevation: *mean elevation:* NA

elevation extremes: *lowest point:* Indian Ocean 0 m
highest point: South Point on South Island 9 m

Natural resources: fish

Land use: *agricultural land:* 0%
arable land: 0%;
permanent crops: 0%;
permanent pasture: 0%
forest: 0%
other: 100% (2011 est.)
Irrigated land: NA

Population—distribution: only Home Island and West Island are populated

Natural hazards: cyclone season is October to April

Environment—current issues: freshwater resources are limited to rainwater accumulations in natural underground reservoirs

Geography—note: islands are thickly covered with coconut palms and other vegetation; site of a World War I naval battle in November 1914 between the Australian light cruiser HMAS Sydney and the German raider SMS Emden; after being heavily damaged in the engagement, the Emden was beached by her captain on North Keeling Island

PEOPLE AND SOCIETY

Population: 596 (July 2014 est.)
country comparison to the world: 236

Nationality: *noun:* Cocos Islander(s)
adjective: Cocos Islander

Ethnic groups: Europeans, Cocos Malays

Languages: Malay (Cocos dialect), English

Religions: Sunni Muslim 80%, other 20% (2002 est.)

Population growth rate: 0% (2014 est.)
country comparison to the world: 195

Population distribution: only Home Island and West Island are populated

Infant mortality rate: *total:* NA
male: NA
female: NA

Life expectancy at birth: *total population:* NA
male: NA
female: NA (2017 est.)

Total fertility rate: NA

HIV/AIDS—adult prevalence rate: NA

HIV/AIDS—people living with HIV/AIDS: NA

HIV/AIDS—deaths: NA

GOVERNMENT

Country name: *conventional long form:* Territory of Cocos (Keeling) Islands
conventional short form: Cocos (Keeling) Islands

etymology: the name refers to the abundant coconut trees on the islands and to English Captain William KEELING, the first European to sight the islands in 1609

Dependency status: non-self governing territory of Australia; administered from Canberra by the Department of Regional Australia, Local Government, Arts and Sport

Government type: non-self-governing overseas territory of Australia

Capital: *name:* West Island

geographic coordinates: 12 10 S, 96 50 E
time difference: UTC+6.5 (11.5 hours ahead of Washington, DC, during Standard Time)

Administrative divisions: none (territory of Australia)

Independence: none (territory of Australia)

National holiday: Australia Day (commemorates the arrival of the First Fleet of Australian settlers), 26 January (1788)

Constitution: 23 November 1955 (Cocos (Keeling) Islands Act 1955); amended many times, last in 2010 (2016)

Legal system: common law based on the Australian model

Citizenship: see Australia

Suffrage: 18 years of age

Executive branch: *chief of state:* Queen ELIZABETH II (since 6 February 1952); represented by Governor General of the Commonwealth of Australia General Sir Peter COSGROVE (since 28 March 2014)

head of government: Administrator Natasha GRIGGS (since 5 October 2018)
cabinet: NA
elections/appointments: the monarchy is hereditary; governor general appointed by the monarch on the recommendation of the Australian prime minister; administrator appointed by the governor general for a 2-year term and represents the monarch and Australia

Legislative branch: description: unicameral Cocos (Keeling) Islands Shire Council (7 seats; members directly elected by simple majority vote to serve 4-year terms with half the membership renewed every 2 years)
elections: last held in October 2015 (next to be held in October 2017)

Judicial branch: *highest court(s):* under the terms of the Territorial Law Reform Act 1992, Western Australia provides court services as needed for the island including the Supreme Court and subordinate courts (District Court, Magistrate Court, Family Court, Children's Court, and Coroners' Court)

Political parties and leaders: none

Political pressure groups and leaders: The Cocos Islands Youth Support Centre

International organization participation: none

Diplomatic representation in the US: none (territory of Australia)

Diplomatic representation from the US: none (territory of Australia)

Flag description: the flag of Australia is used

National anthem: *note:* as a territory of Australia, "Advance Australia Fair" remains official as the national anthem, while "God Save the Queen" serves as the royal anthem (see Australia)

ECONOMY

Economy—overview: Coconuts, grown throughout the islands, are the sole cash crop. Small local gardens and fishing contribute to the food supply, but additional food and most other necessities must be imported from Australia. There is a small tourist industry.

GDP (purchasing power parity): $NA

GDP—real growth rate: 1% (2003)
country comparison to the world: 184

Agriculture—products: vegetables, bananas, paw-paws, coconuts

Industries: copra products, tourism

Labor force: NA

Labor force—by occupation: *note:* the Cocos Islands Cooperative Society Ltd. employs

construction workers, stevedores, and lighter-age workers; tourism is the other main source of employment

Unemployment rate: 0.1% (2011)
    60% (2000 est.)
country comparison to the world: 1

Budget: *revenues:* $NA
expenditures: $NA

Fiscal year: 1 July—30 June

Exports: $NA

Exports—commodities: copra

Imports: $NA

Imports—commodities: foodstuffs

Exchange rates: Australian dollars (AUD) per US dollar—
1.311 (2017)
1.3442 (2016)
1.3442 (2015)
1.3291 (2014)
1.1094 (2013)

COMMUNICATIONS

Telephone system: *general assessment:* telephone service is part of the Australian network; an operational local mobile-cellular network available; wireless Internet connectivity available
domestic: local area code—08
international: international code—61 8; telephone, telex, and facsimile communications with

Australia and elsewhere via satellite; satellite earth station—1 (Intelsat) (2017)

Broadcast media: 1 local radio station staffed by community volunteers; satellite broadcasts of several Australian radio and TV stations available (2017)

Internet country code: .cc

TRANSPORTATION

Airports: 1 (2013)
country comparison to the world: 216

Airports—with paved runways: *total:* 1
2,438 to 3,047 m: 1 (2017)

Roadways: *total:* 22 km
paved: 10 km
unpaved: 12 km (2007)
country comparison to the world: 222

Ports and terminals: *major seaport(s):* Port Refuge

MILITARY AND SECURITY

Military—note: defense is the responsibility of Australia; the territory has a five-person police force

TRANSNATIONAL ISSUES

Disputes—international: none

COLOMBIA

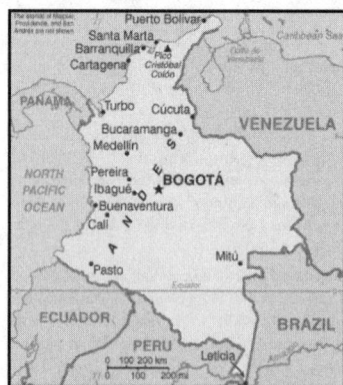

INTRODUCTION

Background: Colombia was one of the three countries that emerged after the dissolution of Gran Colombia in 1830 (the others are Ecuador and Venezuela). A decades-long conflict between government forces and antigovernment insurgent groups, principally the Revolutionary Armed Forces of Colombia (FARC) heavily funded by the drug trade, escalated during the 1990s. More than 31,000 former paramilitaries demobilized

by the end of 2006 and the United Self Defense Forces of Colombia as a formal organization ceased to operate. In the wake of the paramilitary demobilization, organized criminal groups arose, whose members include some former paramilitaries. After four years of formal peace negotiations, the Colombian Government signed a revised final peace accord with the FARC in November 2016, which was subsequently ratified by the Colombian Congress. The accord calls for members of the FARC to demobilize, disarm, and reincorporate into society and politics, and it creates an alternative system for transitional justice that includes a "Special Jurisdiction for Peace" to address accountability for conflict-related crimes and established truth-telling mechanisms. The Colombian Government has stepped up efforts to reassert government control throughout the country, and now has a presence in every one of its administrative departments. Despite decades of internal conflict and drug related security challenges, Colombia maintains relatively strong democratic institutions characterized by peaceful, transparent elections and the protection of civil liberties.

GEOGRAPHY

Location: Northern South America, bordering the Caribbean Sea, between Panama and Venezuela,

and bordering the North Pacific Ocean, between Ecuador and Panama

Geographic coordinates: 4 00 N, 72 00 W

Map references: South America

Area: *total:* 1,138,910 sq km
land: 1,038,700 sq km
water: 100,210 sq km
note: includes Isla de Malpelo, Roncador Cay, and Serrana Bank
country comparison to the world: 27

Area—comparative: slightly less than twice the size of Texas

Land boundaries: *total:* 6,672 km
border countries (5): Brazil 1,790 km, Ecuador 708 km, Panama 339 km, Peru 1,494 km, Venezuela 2,341 km

Coastline: 3,208 km (Caribbean Sea 1,760 km, North Pacific Ocean 1,448 km)

Maritime claims: *territorial sea:* 12 nm
exclusive economic zone: 200 nm
continental shelf: 200-m depth or to the depth of exploitation

Climate: tropical along coast and eastern plains; cooler in highlands

Terrain: flat coastal lowlands, central highlands, high Andes Mountains, eastern lowland plains (Llanos)

Elevation: *mean elevation:* 593 m

elevation extremes: *lowest point:* Pacific Ocean 0 m

highest point: Pico Cristobal Colon 5,730 m

note: nearby Pico Simon Bolivar also has the same elevation

Natural resources: petroleum, natural gas, coal, iron ore, nickel, gold, copper, emeralds, hydropower

Land use: *agricultural land:* 37.5%

arable land: 1.4%;

permanent crops: 1.6%;

permanent pasture: 34.5%

forest: 54.4%

other: 8.1% (2011 est.)

Irrigated land: 10,900 sq km (2012)

Population—distribution: the majority of people live in the north and west where agricultural opportunities and natural resources are found; the vast grasslands of the llanos to the south and east, which make up approximately 60% of the country, are sparsely populated

Natural hazards: highlands subject to volcanic eruptions; occasional earthquakes; periodic droughts

volcanism: Galeras (4,276 m) is one of Colombia's most active volcanoes, having erupted in 2009 and 2010 causing major evacuations; it has been deemed a Decade Volcano by the International Association of Volcanology and Chemistry of the Earth's Interior, worthy of study due to its explosive history and close proximity to human populations; Nevado del Ruiz (5,321 m), 129 km (80 mi) west of Bogota, erupted in 1985 producing lahars (mudflows) that killed 23,000 people; the volcano last erupted in 1991; additionally, after 500 years of dormancy, Nevado del Huila reawakened in 2007 and has experienced frequent eruptions since then; other historically active volcanoes include Cumbal, Dona Juana, Nevado del Tolima, and Purace

Environment—current issues: deforestation; soil and water quality damage from overuse of pesticides; air pollution, especially in Bogota, from vehicle emissions

Environment—international agreements: *party to:* Antarctic Treaty, Biodiversity, Climate Change, Climate Change-Kyoto Protocol, Desertification, Endangered Species, Hazardous Wastes, Marine Life Conservation, Ozone Layer Protection, Ship Pollution, Tropical Timber 83, Tropical Timber 94, Wetlands

signed, but not ratified: Law of the Sea

Geography—note: only South American country with coastlines on both the North Pacific Ocean and Caribbean Sea

PEOPLE AND SOCIETY

Population: 47,698,524 (July 2017 est.)
country comparison to the world: 29

Nationality: *noun:* Colombian(s)
adjective: Colombian

Ethnic groups: mestizo and white 84.2%, Afro-Colombian (includes mulatto, Raizal, and Palenquero) 10.4%, Amerindian 3.4%, Romani <.01, unspecified 2.1% (2005 est.)

Languages: Spanish (official)

Religions: Roman Catholic 79%, Protestant 14% (includes Pentecostal 6%, mainline Protestant 2%, other 6%), other 2%, unspecified 5% (2014 est.)

Demographic profile: Colombia is in the midst of a demographic transition resulting from steady declines in its fertility, mortality, and population growth rates. The birth rate has fallen from more than 6 children per woman in the 1960s to just above replacement level today as a result of increased literacy, family planning services, and urbanization. However, income inequality is among the worst in the world, and more than a third of the population lives below the poverty line.

Colombia experiences significant legal and illegal economic emigration and refugee outflows. Large-scale labor emigration dates to the 1960s; the United States and, until recently, Venezuela have been the main host countries. Emigration to Spain picked up in the 1990s because of its economic growth, but this flow has since diminished because of Spain's ailing economy and high unemployment. Colombia has been the largest source of Latin American refugees in Latin America, nearly 400,000 of whom live primarily in Venezuela and Ecuador. Venezuela's political and economic crisis since 2015, however, has created a reverse flow, consisting largely of Colombians returning home.

Forced displacement continues to be prevalent because of violence among guerrillas, paramilitary groups, and Colombian security forces. Afro-Colombian and indigenous populations are disproportionately affected. Even with the Colombian Government's December 2016 peace agreement with the Revolutionary Armed Forces of Colombia (FARC), the risk of displacement remains as other rebel groups fill the void left by the FARC. Between 1985 and September 2017, nearly 7.6 million persons have been internally displaced, the highest total in the world. These estimates may undercount actual numbers because many internally displaced persons are not registered. Historically, Colombia also has one of the world's highest levels of forced disappearances. About 30,000 cases have been recorded over the last four decades—although the number is likely to be much higher—including human rights activists, trade unionists, Afro-Colombians, indigenous people, and farmers in rural conflict zones.

Because of political violence and economic problems, Colombia received limited numbers of immigrants during the 19th and 20th centuries, mostly from the Middle East, Europe, and Japan. More recently, growth in the oil, mining, and manufacturing sectors has attracted increased labor migration; the primary source countries are Venezuela, the US, Mexico, and Argentina. Colombia has also become a transit area for illegal migrants from Africa, Asia, and the Caribbean -- especially Haiti and Cuba -- who are en route to the US or Canada.

Age structure: *0-14 years:* 24.22% (male 5,917,425/female 5,634,516)

15-24 years: 17.25% (male 4,191,033/female 4,038,314)

25-54 years: 41.91% (male 9,918,698/female 10,071,419)

55-64 years: 9.18% (male 2,059,712/female 2,318,320)

65 years and over: 7.44% (male 1,480,966/female 2,068,121) (2017 est.)

Dependency ratios: *total dependency ratio:* 45.6
youth dependency ratio: 35.4
elderly dependency ratio: 10.2
potential support ratio: 9.8 (2015 est.)

Median age: *total:* 30 years
male: 29 years
female: 31 years (2017 est.)
country comparison to the world: 119

Population growth rate: 0.99% (2017 est.)
country comparison to the world: 115

Birth rate: 16.1 births/1,000 population (2017 est.)
country comparison to the world: 114

Death rate: 5.5 deaths/1,000 population (2017 est.)
country comparison to the world: 177

Net migration rate: -0.6 migrant(s)/1,000 population (2017 est.)
country comparison to the world: 129

Population distribution: the majority of people live in the north and west where agricultural opportunities and natural resources are found; the vast grasslands of the llanos to the south and east, which make up approximately 60% of the country, are sparsely populated

Urbanization: *urban population:* 77% of total population (2017)
rate of urbanization: 1.47% annual rate of change (2015-20 est.)

Major urban areas—population: BOGOTA (capital) 9.765 million; Medellin 3.911 million; Cali 2.646 million; Barranquilla 1.991 million; Bucaramanga 1.215 million; Cartagena 1.092 million (2015)

Sex ratio: *at birth:* 1.06 male(s)/female
0-14 years: 1.05 male(s)/female
15-24 years: 1.04 male(s)/female
25-54 years: 0.98 male(s)/female
55-64 years: 0.88 male(s)/female
65 years and over: 0.72 male(s)/female
total population: 0.98 male(s)/female (2016 est.)

Mother's mean age at first birth: 21.7 years
note: median age at first birth among women 25-29 (2015 est.)

Maternal mortality ratio: 64 deaths/100,000 live births (2015 est.)
country comparison to the world: 87

Infant mortality rate: *total:* 13.6 deaths/1,000 live births
male: 16.5 deaths/1,000 live births
female: 10.6 deaths/1,000 live births (2017 est.)
country comparison to the world: 106

Life expectancy at birth: *total population:* 75.9 years

male: 72.8 years
female: 79.3 years (2017 est.)
country comparison to the world: 96

Total fertility rate: 2 children born/woman (2017 est.)
country comparison to the world: 122

Contraceptive prevalence rate: 79.1% (2009/10)

Health expenditures: 7.2% of GDP (2014)
country comparison to the world: 76

Physicians density: 1.57 physicians/1,000 population (2010)

Hospital bed density: 1.5 beds/1,000 population (2012)

Drinking water source:
improved:
urban: 96.8% of population
rural: 73.8% of population
total: 91.4% of population
unimproved:
urban: 3.2% of population
rural: 26.2% of population
total: 8.6% of population (2015 est.)

Sanitation facility access:
improved:
urban: 85.2% of population
rural: 67.9% of population
total: 81.1% of population
unimproved:
urban: 14.8% of population
rural: 32.1% of population
total: 18.9% of population (2015 est.)

HIV/AIDS—adult prevalence rate: 0.4% (2016 est.)
country comparison to the world: 73

HIV/AIDS—people living with HIV/AIDS: 120,000 (2016 est.)
country comparison to the world: 37

HIV/AIDS—deaths: 2,800 (2016 est.)
country comparison to the world: 44

Major infectious diseases: *degree of risk:* high
food or waterborne diseases: bacterial diarrhea
vectorborne diseases: dengue fever, malaria, and yellow fever
note: active local transmission of Zika virus by Aedes species mosquitoes has been identified in this country (as of August 2016); it poses an important risk (a large number of cases possible) among US citizens if bitten by an infective mosquito; other less common ways to get Zika are through sex, via blood transfusion, or during pregnancy, in which the pregnant woman passes Zika virus to her fetus (2016)

Obesity—adult prevalence rate: 22.3% (2016)
country comparison to the world: 78

Children under the age of 5 years underweight: 3.4% (2010)
country comparison to the world: 108

Education expenditures: 4.5% of GDP (2015)
country comparison to the world: 95

Literacy: *definition:* age 15 and over can read and write
total population: 94.2%

male: 94.1%
female: 94.4% (2015 est.)

School life expectancy (primary to tertiary education): *total:* 14 years
male: 14 years
female: 15 years (2015)

Unemployment, youth ages 15-24: *total:* 16.6%
male: 12.6%
female: 22.2% (2015 est.)
country comparison to the world: 50

GOVERNMENT

Country name: *conventional long form:* Republic of Colombia
conventional short form: Colombia
local long form: Republica de Colombia
local short form: Colombia
etymology: the country is named after explorer Christopher COLUMBUS

Government type: presidential republic

Capital: *name:* Bogota
geographic coordinates: 4 36 N, 74 05 W
time difference: UTC-5 (same time as Washington, DC, during Standard Time)

Administrative divisions: 32 departments (departamentos, singular—departamento) and 1 capital district* (distrito capital); Amazonas, Antioquia, Arauca, Atlantico, Bogota*, Bolivar, Boyaca, Caldas, Caqueta, Casanare, Cauca, Cesar, Choco, Cordoba, Cundinamarca, Guainia, Guaviare, Huila, La Guajira, Magdalena, Meta, Narino, Norte de Santander, Putumayo, Quindio, Risaralda, Archipielago de San Andres, Providencia y Santa Catalina (colloquially San Andres y Providencia), Santander, Sucre, Tolima, Valle del Cauca, Vaupes, Vichada

Independence: 20 July 1810 (from Spain)

National holiday: Independence Day, 20 July (1810)

Constitution: several previous; latest promulgated 5 July 1991; amended many times, last in 2015 (2016)

Legal system: civil law system influenced by the Spanish and French civil codes

International law organization participation: has not submitted an ICJ jurisdiction declaration; accepts ICCt jurisdiction

Citizenship: *citizenship by birth:* no
citizenship by descent only: least one parent must be a citizen or permanent resident of Colombia
dual citizenship recognized: yes
residency requirement for naturalization: 5 years

Suffrage: 18 years of age; universal

Executive branch: *chief of state:* President Juan Manuel SANTOS Calderon (since 7 August 2010); Vice President Ret. Gen. Oscar Adolfo NARANJO Trujillo (since 30 March 2017); note—Vice President German VARGAS Lleras' resignation on 15 March 2017 became effective on 21 March 2017; the president is both chief of state and head of government

head of government: President Juan Manuel SANTOS Calderon (since 7 August 2010); Vice President Ret. Gen. Oscar Adolfo NARANJO Trujillo (since 30 March 2017)
cabinet: Cabinet appointed by the president
elections/appointments: president directly elected by absolute majority vote in 2 rounds if needed for a single 4-year term (beginning in 2018); election last held on 25 May 2014 with a runoff held on 15 June 2014 (next to be held on 27 May 2018); note—political reform in 2015 eliminated presidential reelection; beginning in 2018, presidents can serve only one 4-year term
election results: Juan Manuel SANTOS Calderon reelected president in second round; percent of vote—Juan Manuel SANTOS Calderon (U Party) 51.0%, Oscar Ivan ZULUAGA (CD) 45.0%, other 4.0%

Legislative branch: description: bicameral Congress or Congreso consists of the Senate or Senado (102 seats; 100 members elected in a single nationwide constituency by party-list proportional representation popular vote and 2 members elected in a special nationwide for indigenous communities to serve 4-year terms) and the Chamber of Representatives or Camara de Representantes (166 seats; members elected in multi-seat constituencies by party-list proportional representation constituency popular vote to serve 4-year terms)
elections: Senate—last held on 9 March 2014 (next to be held on 11 March 2018); Chamber of Representatives—last held on 9 March 2014 (next to be held on 11 March 2018)
election results: Senate—percent of vote by party—NA; seats by party—U Party 21, CD 20, PC 18, PL 17, CR 9, PDA 5, Green Party 5, other 7; Chamber of Representatives—percent of vote by party—NA; seats by party—PL 39, U Party 37, PC 27, CD 19, CR 16, Green Party 6, PDA 3, other 19

Judicial branch: *highest court(s):* Supreme Court of Justice or Corte Suprema de Justicia (consists of the Civil-Agrarian and Labor Chambers each with 7 judges, and the Penal Chamber with 9 judges); Constitutional Court (consists of 9 magistrates); Council of State (consists of 31 members); Superior Judiciary Council (consists of 13 magistrates)
judge selection and term of office: Supreme Court judges appointed by the Supreme Court members from candidates submitted by the Superior Judiciary Council; judges elected for individual 8-year terms; Constitutional Court magistrates—nominated by the president, by the Supreme Court, and elected by the Senate; judges elected for individual 8-year terms; Council of State members appointed by the State Council plenary from lists nominated by the Superior Judiciary Council
subordinate courts: Superior Tribunals (appellate courts for each of the judicial districts); regional courts; civil municipal courts; Superior Military Tribunal; first instance administrative courts

Political parties and leaders: Alternative Democratic Pole or PDA [Clara LOPEZ]
Conservative Party or PC [David BARGUIL]

Democratic Center Party or CD [Alvaro URIBE Velez, Oscar Ivan ZULUAGA, Carlos HOLMES TRUJILLO, Ivan DUQUE]

Green Alliance [Jorge LONDONO, Antonio SANGUINO, Luis AVELLANEDA, Camilo ROMERO]

Liberal Party or PL [Horacio SERPA]

Citizens Option (Opcion Ciudadana) or OC [Angel ALIRIO Moreno] (formerly known as the National Integration Party or PIN)

Radical Change or CR [Carlos Fernando GALAN]

Social National Unity Party or U Party [Roy BAR-RERAS, Jose David NAME]

note: Colombia has numerous smaller movements

Political pressure groups and leaders: Central Union of Workers or CUT

Colombian Confederation of Workers or CTC

General Confederation of Workers or CGT

National Liberation Army or ELN

International organization participation: BCIE, BIS, CAN, Caricom (observer), CD, CDB, CELAC, EITI (candidate country), FAO, G-3, G-24, G-77, IADB, IAEA, IBRD, ICAO, ICC (national committees), ICCt, ICRM, IDA, IFAD, IFC, IFRCS, IHO, ILO, IMF, IMO, IMSO, Interpol, IOC, IOM, IPU, ISO, ITSO, ITU, ITUC (NGOs), LAES, LAIA, Mercosur (associate), MIGA, NAM, OAS, OPANAL, OPCW, Pacific Alliance, PCA, UN, UNASUR, UNCTAD, UNESCO, UNHCR, UNIDO, Union Latina, UNWTO, UPU, WCO, WFTU (NGOs), WHO, WIPO, WMO, WTO

Diplomatic representation in the US: chief of mission: Ambassador Camilo REYES Rodriguez (since 21 July 2017)

chancery: 2118 Leroy Place NW, Washington, DC 20008

telephone: [1] (202) 387-8338

FAX: [1] (202) 232-8643

consulate(s) general: Atlanta, Houston, Los Angeles, Miami, New York, Newark (NJ), Orlando, San Juan (Puerto Rico)

consulate(s): Boston, Chicago, San Francisco

Diplomatic representation from the US: chief of mission: Ambassador Kevin WHITAKER (since 11 June 2014)

embassy: Calle 24 Bis No. 48-50, Bogota, D.C.

mailing address: Carrera 45 No. 24B-27, Bogota, D.C.

telephone: [57] (1) 275-2000

FAX: [57] (1) 275-4600

Flag description: three horizontal bands of yellow (top, double-width), blue, and red; the flag retains the three main colors of the banner of Gran Colombia, the short-lived South American republic that broke up in 1830; various interpretations of the colors exist and include: yellow for the gold in Colombia's land, blue for the seas on its shores, and red for the blood spilled in attaining freedom; alternatively, the colors have been described as representing more elemental concepts such as sovereignty and justice (yellow), loyalty and vigilance (blue), and valor and generosity (red); or simply the principles of liberty, equality, and fraternity

note: similar to the flag of Ecuador, which is longer and bears the Ecuadorian coat of arms superimposed in the center

National symbol(s): Andean condor; national colors: yellow, blue, red

National anthem: name: "Himno Nacional de la Republica de Colombia" (National Anthem of the Republic of Colombia)

lyrics/music: Rafael Nunez/Oreste Sindici

note: adopted 1920; the anthem was created from an inspirational poem written by President Rafael Nunez

ECONOMY

Economy—overview: Colombia heavily depends on energy and mining exports, making it vulnerable to fluctuations in commodity prices. Colombia is Latin America's fourth largest oil producer and the world's fourth largest coal producer, third largest coffee exporter, and second largest cut flowers exporter. Colombia's economic development is hampered by inadequate infrastructure, poverty, narcotrafficking, and an uncertain security situation, in addition to dependence on primary commodities.

Colombia's economy slowed in 2017 because of falling global oil prices and lower oil production due to insurgent attacks on pipeline infrastructure. Although real GDP growth averaged 4.7% during the past decade, it fell to an estimated 1.8% in 2017. Declining oil prices also have contributed to reduced government revenues. In 2016, oil revenue dropped below 4% of the federal budget and likely remained below 4% in 2017. A Western credit rating agency in December 2017 downgraded Colombia's sovereign credit rating to BBB-, because of weaker-than-expected growth and increasing external debt. Colombia has struggled to address local referendums against foreign investment, which have slowed its expansion, especially in the oil and mining sectors. Colombia's FDI declined by 3% to $10.2 billion between January and September 2017.

Colombia has signed or is negotiating Free Trade Agreements (FTA) with more than a dozen countries; the US-Colombia FTA went into effect in May 2012. Colombia is a founding member of the Pacific Alliance—a regional trade block formed in 2012 by Chile, Colombia, Mexico, and Peru to promote regional trade and economic integration. The Colombian government took steps in 2017 to address several bilateral trade irritants with the US, including those on truck scrappage, distilled spirits, pharmaceuticals, ethanol imports, and labor rights. Colombia hopes to accede to the Organization for Economic Cooperation and Development.

GDP (purchasing power parity): $712.5 billion (2017 est.)

$700.6 billion (2016 est.)

$687.2 billion (2015 est.)

note: data are in 2017 dollars

country comparison to the world: 32

GDP (official exchange rate): $307.5 billion (2016 est.)

GDP—real growth rate: 1.7% (2017 est.)

2% (2016 est.)

3.1% (2015 est.)

country comparison to the world: 165

GDP—per capita (PPP): $14,500 (2017 est.)

$14,400 (2016 est.)

$14,300 (2015 est.)

note: data are in 2017 dollars

country comparison to the world: 113

Gross national saving: 21.7% of GDP (2017 est.)

21% of GDP (2016 est.)

20.3% of GDP (2015 est.)

country comparison to the world: 78

GDP—composition, by end use:

household consumption: 62.1%

government consumption: 18.2%

investment in fixed capital: 24.8%

investment in inventories: 0.2%

exports of goods and services: 14.2%

imports of goods and services: -19.4% (2017 est.)

GDP—composition, by sector of origin:

agriculture: 7.4%

industry: 31.3%

services: 61.4% (2017 est.)

Agriculture—products: coffee, cut flowers, bananas, rice, tobacco, corn, sugarcane, cocoa beans, oilseed, vegetables; shrimp; forest products

Industries: textiles, food processing, oil, clothing and footwear, beverages, chemicals, cement; gold, coal, emeralds

Industrial production growth rate: -2.5% (2017 est.)

country comparison to the world: 196

Labor force: 24.67 million (2017 est.)

country comparison to the world: 27

Labor force—by occupation: agriculture: 17%

industry: 21%

services: 62% (2011 est.)

Unemployment rate: 9.3% (2017 est.)

9.2% (2016 est.)

country comparison to the world: 127

Population below poverty line: 27.8% (2015 est.)

Household income or consumption by percentage share: lowest 10%: 1.1%

highest 10%: 42.2% (2014 est.)

Distribution of family income—Gini index: 53.5 (2014)

56.9 (1996)

country comparison to the world: 10

Budget: revenues: $85.14 billion

expenditures: $95.28 billion (2017 est.)

Taxes and other revenues: 27.7% of GDP (2017 est.)

country comparison to the world: 99

Budget surplus (+) or deficit (-): -3.3% of GDP (2017 est.)

country comparison to the world: 126

Public debt: 53% of GDP (2017 est.)

52% of GDP (2016 est.)

note: data cover general government debt, and includes debt instruments issued (or owned) by government entities other than the treasury; the

data include treasury debt held by foreign entities; the data include debt issued by subnational entities
country comparison to the world: 90

Fiscal year: calendar year

Inflation rate (consumer prices): 4.3% (2017 est.)
7.5% (2016 est.)
country comparison to the world: 163

Central bank discount rate: 7.5% (31 December 2016)
6.5% (31 December 2014)
country comparison to the world: 44

Commercial bank prime lending rate: 13.8% (31 December 2017 est.)
14.65% (31 December 2016 est.)
country comparison to the world: 55

Stock of narrow money: $36.63 billion (31 December 2017 est.)
$34.01 billion (31 December 2016 est.)
country comparison to the world: 58

Stock of broad money: $167.8 billion (31 December 2017 est.)
$136 billion (31 December 2016 est.)
country comparison to the world: 47

Stock of domestic credit: $162.5 billion (31 December 2017 est.)
$153.1 billion (31 December 2016 est.)
country comparison to the world: 49

Market value of publicly traded shares: $85.96 billion (31 December 2015 est.)
$146.7 billion (31 December 2014 est.)
$202.7 billion (31 December 2013 est.)
country comparison to the world: 42

Current account balance: -$11.7 billion (2017 est.)
-$12.24 billion (2016 est.)
country comparison to the world: 187

Exports: $36.79 billion (2017 est.)
$33.38 billion (2016 est.)
country comparison to the world: 57

Exports—commodities: petroleum, coal, emeralds, coffee, nickel, cut flowers, bananas, apparel

Exports—partners: US 33.5%, Panama 6.3% (2016)

Imports: $44.68 billion (2017 est.)
$43.24 billion (2016 est.)
country comparison to the world: 53

Imports—commodities: industrial equipment, transportation equipment, consumer goods, chemicals, paper products, fuels, electricity

Imports—partners: US 26.4%, China 19.1%, Mexico 7.5%, Brazil 4.7% (2016)

Reserves of foreign exchange and gold: $46.4 billion (31 December 2017 est.)
$46.18 billion (31 December 2016 est.)
country comparison to the world: 42

Debt—external: $120.4 billion (31 December 2017 est.)
$115 billion (31 December 2016 est.)
country comparison to the world: 47

Stock of direct foreign investment—at home: $178.4 billion (31 December 2017 est.)
$164.3 billion (31 December 2016 est.)

country comparison to the world: 32

Stock of direct foreign investment—abroad: $55.32 billion (31 December 2017 est.)
$51.82 billion (31 December 2016 est.)
country comparison to the world: 43

Exchange rates: Colombian pesos (COP) per US dollar—
2,975.5 (2017 est.)
3,055.3 (2016 est.)
3,055.3 (2015 est.)
2,001 (2014 est.)
2,001.1 (2013 est.)

ENERGY

Electricity access: *population without electricity:* 1,200,000
electrification—total population: 97%
electrification—urban areas: 100%
electrification—rural areas: 88% (2013)

Electricity—production: 67.26 billion kWh (2015 est.)
country comparison to the world: 41

Electricity—consumption: 57.6 billion kWh (2015 est.)
country comparison to the world: 45

Electricity—exports: 460 million kWh (2015 est.)
country comparison to the world: 70

Electricity—imports: 45 million kWh (2015 est.)
country comparison to the world: 105

Electricity—installed generating capacity: 16.66 million kW (2015 est.)
country comparison to the world: 49

Electricity—from fossil fuels: 29.4% of total installed capacity (2015 est.)
country comparison to the world: 186

Electricity—from nuclear fuels: 0% of total installed capacity (2015 est.)
country comparison to the world: 70

Electricity—from hydroelectric plants: 69% of total installed capacity (2015 est.)
country comparison to the world: 19

Electricity—from other renewable sources: 1.6% of total installed capacity (2015 est.)
country comparison to the world: 129

Crude oil—production: 886,000 bbl/day (2016 est.)
country comparison to the world: 22

Crude oil—exports: 681,900 bbl/day (2014 est.)
country comparison to the world: 19

Crude oil—imports: 0 bbl/day (2014 est.)
country comparison to the world: 111

Crude oil—proved reserves: 2.002 billion bbl (1 January 2017 es)
country comparison to the world: 37

Refined petroleum products—production: 362,100 bbl/day (2014 est.)
country comparison to the world: 39

Refined petroleum products—consumption: 345,000 bbl/day (2015 est.)
country comparison to the world: 40

Refined petroleum products—exports: 83,920 bbl/day (2014 est.)
country comparison to the world: 44

Refined petroleum products—imports: 95,790 bbl/day (2014 est.)

country comparison to the world: 59

Natural gas—production: 11.91 billion cu m (2015 est.)
country comparison to the world: 39

Natural gas—consumption: 18.82 billion cu m (2015 est.)
country comparison to the world: 44

Natural gas—exports: 400 million cu m (2015 est.)
country comparison to the world: 45

Natural gas—imports: 0 cu m (2013 est.)
country comparison to the world: 110

Natural gas—proved reserves: 123.5 billion cu m (1 January 2017 es)
country comparison to the world: 51

Carbon dioxide emissions from consumption of energy: 74 million Mt (2013 est.)
country comparison to the world: 49

COMMUNICATIONS

Telephones—fixed lines: *total subscriptions:* 7,115,984
subscriptions per 100 inhabitants: 15 (July 2016 est.)
country comparison to the world: 24

Telephones—mobile cellular: *total:* 58,684,924
subscriptions per 100 inhabitants: 124 (July 2016 est.)
country comparison to the world: 28

Telephone system: *general assessment:* modern system in many respects with a nationwide microwave radio relay system, a domestic satellite system with 41 earth stations, and a fiber-optic network linking 50 cities; multiple providers of both fixed-line and mobile-cellular services, but infrastructure remains poor in small urban centers and rural areas
domestic: fixed-line connections stand at about 15 per 100 persons; mobile cellular telephone subscribership is about 120 per 100 persons; competition among cellular service providers is resulting in falling local and international calling rates and contributing to the steep decline in the market share of fixed-line services
international: country code—57; multiple submarine cable systems provide links to the US, parts of the Caribbean, and Central and South America; satellite earth stations—10 (6 Intelsat, 1 Inmarsat, 3 fully digitalized international switching centers) (2016)

Broadcast media: combination of state-owned and privately owned broadcast media provide service; more than 500 radio stations and many national, regional, and local TV stations (2007)

Internet country code: .co
Internet users: total: 27,452,550

percent of population: 58.1% (July 2016 est.)
country comparison to the world: 25

TRANSPORTATION

National air transport system: *number of registered air carriers:* 12
inventory of registered aircraft operated by air carriers: 157

annual passenger traffic on registered air carriers: 30,742,928

annual freight traffic on registered air carriers: 1,317,562,271 mt-km (2015)

Civil aircraft registration country code prefix: HJ, HK (2016)

Airports: 836 (2013)
country comparison to the world: 8

Airports—with paved runways: *total:* 121
over 3,047 m: 2
2,438 to 3,047 m: 9
1,524 to 2,437 m: 39
914 to 1,523 m: 53
under 914 m: 18 (2017)

Airports—with unpaved runways: *total:* 715
over 3,047 m: 1
1,524 to 2,437 m: 25
914 to 1,523 m: 201
under 914 m: 488 (2013)

Heliports: 3 (2013)

Pipelines: gas 4,991 km; oil 6,796 km; refined products 3,429 km (2013)

Railways: *total:* 2,141 km
standard gauge: 150 km 1.435-m gauge
narrow gauge: 1,991 km 0.914-m gauge (2015)
country comparison to the world: 70

Roadways: *total:* 206,500 km (2016)
country comparison to the world: 25

Waterways: 24,725 km (18,300 km navigable; the most important waterway, the River Magdalena, of which 1,488 km is navigable, is dredged regularly to ensure safe passage of cargo vessels and container barges) (2012)
country comparison to the world: 6

Merchant marine: *total:* 103
by type: general cargo 17, oil tanker 9, other 77 (2017)
country comparison to the world: 82

Ports and terminals: *major seaport(s):* Atlantic Ocean (Caribbean)—Cartagena, Santa Marta, Turbo; Pacific Ocean—Buenaventura
river port(s): Barranquilla (Rio Magdalena)
oil terminal(s): Covenas offshore terminal
dry bulk cargo port(s): Puerto Bolivar (coal)
container port(s) (TEUs): Cartagena (1,853,342)

MILITARY AND SECURITY

Military expenditures: 3.39% of GDP (2016)
3.13% of GDP (2015)
3.13% of GDP (2014)
3.29% of GDP (2013)
3.17% of GDP (2012)
country comparison to the world: 17

Military branches: National Army (Ejercito Nacional), Republic of Colombia Navy (Armada Republica de Colombia, ARC, includes Naval Aviation, Naval Infantry (Infanteria de Marina, IM), and Coast Guard), Colombian Air Force (Fuerza Aerea de Colombia, FAC) (2012)

Military service age and obligation: 18-24 years of age for compulsory and voluntary military service; service obligation is 18 months (2012)

TERRORISM

Terrorist groups—home based: *National Liberation Army (Ejercito de Liberacion Nacional, ELN): aim(s):* represent the rural poor against the nation's wealthy and block the privatization of national resources
area(s) of operation: the nation's second-largest insurgent group operates mainly in the rural and mountainous areas in the northeast, especially Arauca Province, and is active in the northern and southwestern regions and along the borders with Venezuela and Ecuador; after lengthy behind-the-scenes discussions, peace talks with the Colombian Government officially began on 7 February 2017 in Quito, Ecuador, with Colombia releasing imprisoned members to serve as peace negotiators and ELN releasing former congressman Odin Sanchez, who ELN has held since April 2016; as of June 2017, negotiators on both sides remained committed to moving toward a bilateral ceasefire, on the condition that ELN cease and desist engaging in kidnappings, extortion, and other illegal practices; claimed responsibility for the 19 February 2017 bombing near the Santamaria Bullring in Bogota that killed one police officer and injured 26 police officers and at least four civilians; on 25 January 2017, an international narcotics investigation in Colombia led to the seizure of just under 4 metric tons of cocaine, the largest drug seizure ever involving the ELN; the group has a long history of engaging in narcotics production and trafficking, extortion, and kidnappings for ransom to fund operations; has increased its revenue from the narcotics trade in 2017; Colombian forces continue to pursue leaders and members, especially those who oppose peace talks and are conducting lethal attacks on military and security personnel or civilians; historically, group leaders directed attacks against primarily Colombian political, military, security, and economic figures and targeted foreign citizens for kidnappings for ransom; assessed in 2017 to have 1,500-2,500 members

Revolutionary Armed Forces of Colombia (Fuerzas Armadas Revolucionarias de Colombia, FARC): *aim(s):* enter the political arena to change Colombia's economic model, nationalize industries like oil and mining, and renegotiate free trade deals; historically, FARC's aim has been to install a Marxist-Leninist regime in Colombia through a violent revolution
area(s) of operation: headquartered in Uribe, Narino Department, in the southwest on the border with Ecuador and the Pacific Ocean shores; recognized as the nation's largest insurgent group, with less than 10,000 members in recent years; active mostly in Colombia's center, northeast, and mountainous southwest; historically, operatives have targeted Colombian political, military, and economic figures and structures for attack and foreign citizens for kidnappings for ransom; on 29 August 2016, a bilateral ceasefire went into effect between FARC leaders and the Colombian Government, followed by peace talks between FARC leader Rodrigo LONDONO and Colombia's President Juan Manuel SANTOS; on 30 November 2016, the Colombian Congress approved a peace accord between the FARC and Colombian Government; both sides remain committed to peace; FARC has commenced disarming

in UN-monitored zones, with an estimated 7,000 members turning in their weapons by mid-March 2017 and preparing to reintegrate into civilian life; in exchange for disarmament, the government will allow FARC to form an official political party and integrate fighters into society through measures such as funding education and providing housing and jobs; FARC is striving to be ready to participate in 2018 elections as a political party; an estimated 300 FARC members remain resistant to demobilization, including the Armando Rios First Front's estimated 200 fighters; the five-decade conflict resulted in tens of thousands missing persons, massive land seizures, an estimated 5.7 million people displaced from their homes—primarily peasants, and at least 220,000 Colombian lives lost, including thousands of soldiers and police personnel; FARC leaders have vowed to cease participating in the narcotics trade, which has been the group's principal source of revenue for the past several years; an increasing number of members have defected recently to use their heavy-weapons skills to serve South American drug traffickers

TRANSNATIONAL ISSUES

Disputes—international: in December 2007, ICJ allocated San Andres, Providencia, and Santa Catalina islands to Colombia under 1928 Treaty but did not rule on 82 degrees W meridian as maritime boundary with Nicaragua; managed dispute with Venezuela over maritime boundary and Venezuelan-administered Los Monjes Islands near the Gulf of Venezuela; Colombian-organized illegal narcotics, guerrilla, and paramilitary activities penetrate all neighboring borders and have caused Colombian citizens to flee mostly into neighboring countries; Colombia, Honduras, Nicaragua, Jamaica, and the US assert various claims to Bajo Nuevo and Serranilla Bank

Refugees and internally displaced persons: *IDPs:* 7,582,085 (conflict between government and illegal armed groups and drug traffickers since 1985; about 300,000 new IDPs each year since 2000) (2017)
stateless persons: 11 (2016)

Illicit drugs: illicit producer of coca, opium poppy, and cannabis; world's leading coca cultivator with 159,000 hectares in coca cultivation in 2015, a 42% increase over 2014, producing a potential of 495 mt of pure cocaine; the world's largest producer of coca derivatives; supplies cocaine to nearly all of the US market and the great majority of other international drug markets; in 2016, the Colombian government reported manual eradication of 17,642 hectares; Colombia suspended aerial eradication in October 2015 making 2016 the first full year without aerial eradication; a significant portion of narcotics proceeds are either laundered or invested in Colombia through the black market peso exchange; Colombia probably remains the second largest supplier of heroin to the US market; opium poppy cultivation was estimated to be 1,100 hectares in 2015, sufficient to potentially produce three metric tons of pure heroin

COMOROS

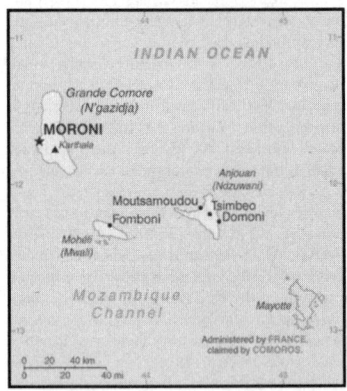

INTRODUCTION

Background: The archipelago of the Comoros in the Indian Ocean, composed of the islands of Mayotte, Anjouan, Moheli, and Grand Comore declared independence from France on 6 July 1975. France did not recognize the independence of Mayotte, which remains under French administration. Since independence, Comoros has endured political instability through realized and attempted coups. In 1997, the islands of Anjouan and Moheli declared independence from Comoros. In 1999, military chief Col. AZALI Assoumani seized power of the entire government in a bloodless coup; he initiated the 2000 Fomboni Accords, a power-sharing agreement in which the federal presidency rotates among the three islands, and each island maintains its local government. AZALI won the 2002 federal presidential election as president of the Union of the Comoros from Grand Comore Island, which held the first five-year term. AZALI stepped down in 2006 and President Ahmed Abdallah Mohamed SAMBI was elected to office as president from Anjouan. In 2007, Mohamed BACAR effected Anjouan's de-facto secession from the Union of the Comoros, refusing to step down when Comoros' other islands held legitimate elections in July. The African Union (AU) initially attempted to resolve the political crisis by applying sanctions and a naval blockade to Anjouan, but in March 2008 the AU and Comoran soldiers seized the island. The island's inhabitants generally welcomed the move. In May 2011, Ikililou DHOININE won the presidency in peaceful elections widely deemed to be free and fair. In closely contested elections in 2016, former President AZALI Assoumani won a second term, when the rotating presidency returned to Grande Comore.

GEOGRAPHY

Location: Southern Africa, group of islands at the northern mouth of the Mozambique Channel, about two-thirds of the way between northern Madagascar and northern Mozambique

Geographic coordinates: 12 10 S, 44 15 E

Map references: Africa

Area: *total:* 2,235 sq km
land: 2,235 sq km
water: 0 sq km
country comparison to the world: 180

Area—comparative: slightly more than 12 times the size of Washington, DC

Land boundaries: 0 km

Coastline: 340 km

Maritime claims: *territorial sea:* 12 nm
exclusive economic zone: 200 nm

Climate: tropical marine; rainy season (November to May)

Terrain: volcanic islands, interiors vary from steep mountains to low hills

Elevation: *mean elevation:* NA

elevation extremes: *lowest point:* Indian Ocean 0 m
highest point: Karthala 2,360 m

Natural resources: fish

Land use: *agricultural land:* 84.4%
arable land: 46.7%;
permanent crops: 29.6%;
permanent pasture: 8.1%
forest: 1.4%
other: 14.2% (2011 est.)
Irrigated land: 1.3 sq km (2012)

Population—distribution: the capital city of Maroni, located on the western side of the island of Grande Comore, is the country's largest city; however, of the three islands that comprise Comoros, it is Anjouan that is the most densely populated

Natural hazards: cyclones possible during rainy season (December to April); volcanic activity on Grand Comore
volcanism: Karthala (2,361 m) on Grand Comore Island last erupted in 2007; a 2005 eruption forced thousands of people to be evacuated and produced a large ash cloud

Environment—current issues: soil degradation and erosion results from crop cultivation on slopes without proper terracing; deforestation

Environment—international agreements: *party to:* Biodiversity, Climate Change, Climate Change-Kyoto Protocol, Desertification, Endangered Species, Hazardous Wastes, Law of the Sea, Ozone Layer Protection, Ship Pollution, Wetlands
signed, but not ratified: none of the selected agreements

Geography—note: important location at northern end of Mozambique Channel

PEOPLE AND SOCIETY

Population: 808,080 (July 2017 est.)

country comparison to the world: 163

Nationality: *noun:* Comoran(s)
adjective: Comoran

Ethnic groups: Antalote, Cafre, Makoa, Oimatsaha, Sakalava

Languages: Arabic (official), French (official), Shikomoro (official; a blend of Swahili and Arabic) (Comorian)

Religions: Sunni Muslim 98%, other (including Shia Muslim, Roman Catholic, Jehovah's Witness, Protestant) 2%
note: Islam is the state religion

Demographic profile: Comoros' population is a melange of Arabs, Persians, Indonesians, Africans, and Indians, and the much smaller number of Europeans that settled on the islands between the 8th and 19th centuries, when they served as a regional trade hub. The Arab and Persian influence is most evident in the islands' overwhelmingly Muslim majority–about 98% of Comorans are Sunni Muslims. The country is densely populated, averaging nearly 350 people per square mile, although this varies widely among the islands, with Anjouan being the most densely populated.

Given the large share of land dedicated to agriculture and Comoros' growing population, habitable land is becoming increasingly crowded. The combination of increasing population pressure on limited land and resources, widespread poverty, and poor job prospects motivates thousands of Comorans each year to attempt to illegally migrate using small fishing boats to the neighboring island of Mayotte, which is a French territory. The majority of legal Comoran migration to France came after Comoros' independence from France in 1975, with the flow peaking in the mid-1980s.

At least 150,000 to 200,000 people of Comoran citizenship or descent live abroad, mainly in France, where they have gone seeking a better quality of life, job opportunities, higher education (Comoros has no universities), advanced health care, and to finance elaborate traditional wedding ceremonies (aada). Remittances from the diaspora are an economic mainstay, in 2013 representing approximately 25% of Comoros' GDP and significantly more than the value of its exports of goods and services (only 15% of GDP). Grand Comore, Comoros' most populous island, is both the primary source of emigrants and the main recipient of remittances. Most remittances are spent on private consumption, but this often goes toward luxury goods and the aada and does not contribute to economic development or poverty reduction. Although the majority of the diaspora is now French-born with more distant ties to Comoros, it is unclear whether they will sustain the current level of remittances.

Age structure: *0-14 years:* 39.35% (male 158,516/female 159,491)
15-24 years: 19.53% (male 76,425/female 81,393)

25-54 years: 32.91% (male 126,279/female 139,659)
55-64 years: 4.27% (male 15,375/female 19,133)
65 years and over: 3.94% (male 14,605/female 17,204) (2017 est.)

Dependency ratios: *total dependency ratio:* 75.5
youth dependency ratio: 70.5
elderly dependency ratio: 5.1
potential support ratio: 19.7 (2015 est.)

Median age: *total:* 19.9 years
male: 19.2 years
female: 20.5 years (2017 est.)
country comparison to the world: 194

Population growth rate: 1.64% (2017 est.)
country comparison to the world: 64

Birth rate: 26.1 births/1,000 population (2017 est.)
country comparison to the world: 48

Death rate: 7.2 deaths/1,000 population (2017 est.)
country comparison to the world: 124

Net migration rate: -2.4 migrant(s)/1,000 population (2017 est.)
country comparison to the world: 169

Population distribution: the capital city of Maroni, located on the western side of the island of Grande Comore, is the country's largest city; however, of the three islands that comprise Comoros, it is Anjouan that is the most densely populated

Urbanization: *urban population:* 28.5% of total population (2017)
rate of urbanization: 2.71% annual rate of change (2015-20 est.)

Major urban areas—population: MORONI (capital) 56,000 (2014)

Sex ratio: *at birth:* 1.03 male(s)/female
0-14 years: 0.99 male(s)/female
15-24 years: 0.94 male(s)/female
25-54 years: 0.9 male(s)/female
55-64 years: 0.8 male(s)/female
65 years and over: 0.88 male(s)/female
total population: 0.94 male(s)/female (2016 est.)

Mother's mean age at first birth: 24.6 years
note: median age at first birth among women 25-29 (2012 est.)

Maternal mortality ratio: 335 deaths/100,000 live births (2015 est.)
country comparison to the world: 38

Infant mortality rate: *total:* 60 deaths/1,000 live births
male: 70.3 deaths/1,000 live births
female: 49.4 deaths/1,000 live births (2017 est.)
country comparison to the world: 18

Life expectancy at birth: *total population:* 64.6 years
male: 62.3 years
female: 67 years (2017 est.)
country comparison to the world: 182

Total fertility rate: 3.34 children born/woman (2017 est.)
country comparison to the world: 46

Contraceptive prevalence rate: 19.4% (2012)

Health expenditures: 6.7% of GDP (2014)

country comparison to the world: 88

Hospital bed density: 2.2 beds/1,000 population (2006)

Drinking water source:
improved:
urban: 92.6% of population
rural: 89.1% of population
total: 90.1% of population
unimproved:
urban: 7.4% of population
rural: 10.9% of population
total: 9.9% of population (2015 est.)

Sanitation facility access:
improved:
urban: 48.3% of population
rural: 30.9% of population
total: 35.8% of population
unimproved:
urban: 51.7% of population
rural: 69.1% of population
total: 64.2% of population (2015 est.)

HIV/AIDS—adult prevalence rate: <.1% (2016 est.)

HIV/AIDS—people living with HIV/AIDS: <200 (2016 est.)

HIV/AIDS—deaths: <100 (2016 est.)

Obesity—adult prevalence rate: 7.8% (2016)
country comparison to the world: 157

Children under the age of 5 years underweight: 16.9% (2012)
country comparison to the world: 39

Education expenditures: 5.1% of GDP (2014)
country comparison to the world: 15

Literacy: *definition:* age 15 and over can read and write
total population: 77.8%
male: 81.8%
female: 73.7% (2015 est.)

School life expectancy (primary to tertiary education): *total:* 11 years
male: 11 years
female: 11 years (2014)

GOVERNMENT

Country name: *conventional long form:* Union of the Comoros
conventional short form: Comoros
local long form: Udzima wa Komori (Comorian); Union des Comores (French); Jumhuriyat al Qamar al Muttahidah (Arabic)
local short form: Komori (Comorian); Comores (French); Juzur al Qamar (Arabic)
etymology: name derives from the Arabic designation "Juzur al Qamar" meaning "Islands of the Moon"

Government type: federal presidential republic

Capital: *name:* Moroni

geographic coordinates: 11 42 S, 43 14 E
time difference: UTC+3 (8 hours ahead of Washington, DC, during Standard Time)

Administrative divisions: 3 islands and 4 municipalities*; Anjouan (Ndzuwani), Domoni*,

Fomboni*, Grande Comore (N'gazidja), Moheli (Mwali), Moroni*, Moutsamoudou*

Independence: 6 July 1975 (from France)

National holiday: Independence Day, 6 July (1975)

Constitution: history: previous 1996; latest ratified 23 December 2001
amendments: proposed by the president of the union or supported by at least one-third of the Assembly of the Union membership; passage requires approval by at least two-thirds majority of the total Assembly membership and approval by at least two-thirds of the membership of the Island Councils, or approval in a referendum; amended 2009, 2014 (2017)

Legal system: mixed legal system of Islamic religious law, the French civil code of 1975, and customary law

International law organization participation: has not submitted an ICJ jurisdiction declaration; accepts ICCt jurisdiction

Citizenship: *citizenship by birth:* no
citizenship by descent only: at least one parent must be a citizen of the Comoros
dual citizenship recognized: no
residency requirement for naturalization: 10 years

Suffrage: 18 years of age; universal

Executive branch: *chief of state:* President AZALI Assoumani(since 26 May 2016); note—the president is both chief of state and head of government

head of government: President AZALI Assoumani (since 26 May 2016)
cabinet: Council of Ministers appointed by the president
elections/appointments: the Union presidency rotates among the 3 islands; president directly elected by simple majority popular vote in 2 rounds for a single nonrenewable 5-year term (in the first round or primary, 3 candidates with the highest vote count by voters on the island concerned compete in the second round; second round winner determined by simple majority vote by voters on all 3 islands; election last held on 21 February 2016 and second round held 10 April 2016 (next to be held in 2021); note—in addition to the Union president, each island elects its own president
election results: AZALI Assoumani elected president in the second round of voting by a plurality; percent of vote in first round—Mohamed Ali SOILIHI 17.6%, Mouigni BARAKA 15.1%, AZALI Assoumani 15.0%, Fahmi Said IBRAHIM 14.5%; percent of vote in second round—AZALI Assoumani 41.0%, Mohamed Ali SOILIHI 39.9%; Mouigni BARAKA 19.1%

Legislative branch: description: unicameral Assembly of the Union (33 seats; 24 members directly elected by absolute majority vote in 2 rounds if needed and 9 members indirectly elected by the 3 island assemblies; members serve 5-year terms)
elections: last held on 25 January 2015 with a run-off on 22 February 2015 (next to be held in 2020)

election results: percent of vote by party—UPDC 29.1%, PJ 20.5%, RDC 21.3%, other 29.1%; seats by party—UPDC 8, PJ 7, RDC 2, CRC 2, RADHI 1, PEC 1, independents 3; note—in addition 9 seats will be filled by nominations from the 3 island assemblies

Judicial branch: *highest court(s):* Supreme Court or Cour Supreme (consists of 7 judges); Constitutional Court (consists of 8 members)

judge selection and term of office: Supreme Court judges—2 selected by the president of the Union, 2 by the Assembly of the Union, and 1 each by the 3 island councils; judges appointed for life; Constitutional Court members appointed—1 by the president, 1 each by the 3 vice presidents, 1 by the Assembly, and 1 each by the island executives; all members serve 6-year renewable terms

subordinate courts: Court of Appeals (in Moroni); Tribunal de premiere instance; island village (community) courts; religious courts

Political parties and leaders: Convention for the Renewal of the Comoros or CRC [AZALI Assoumani]

Democratic Rally of the Comoros or RDC [Mouigni BARAKA]

Juwa Party or PJ [Ahmed Abdallah SAMBI]

Party for the Comorian Agreement (Partie Pour l'Entente Commorienne) or PEC [Fahmi Said IBRAHIM]

Rally for an Alternative of Harmonious and Integrated Development or RADHI [Abdou SOEFO]

Rally with a Development Intiiative for Enlightened Youth or RIDJA [Said LARIFOU]

Union for the Development of the Comoros or UPDC [Mohamed HALIFA]

Political pressure groups and leaders: Federation Comorienne des Consommateurs or FCC [Mohamed Said Abdallah MCHANGAMA]

Mouvement des Entreprises comorienne or MODEC [Faharate HOUSSEIN]

Union des Chambres de Commerce et de l'Industrie et de l'Agriculture or UCCIA [Ahmed Ali BAZI]

Confederation des Travailleurs Comoriens or CTC [Salim SOULAIMANA]

other: environmentalists

International organization participation: ACP, AfDB, AMF, AOSIS, AU, CAEU (candidates), COMESA, FAO, FZ, G-77, IBRD, ICAO, ICCt, ICRM, IDA, IDB, IFAD, IFC, IFRCS, ILO, IMF, IMO, IMSO, InOC, Interpol, IOC, IOM, ITSO, ITU, ITUC (NGOs), LAS, MIGA, NAM, OIC, OIF, OPCW, UN, UNCTAD, UNESCO, UNIDO, UPU, WCO, WHO, WIPO, WMO, WTO (observer)

Diplomatic representation in the US: *chief of mission:* Ambassador Soilihi Mohamed SOILIHI (since 18 November 2014)

chancery: Mission to the US, 866 United Nations Plaza, Suite 418, New York, NY 10017

telephone: [1] (212) 750-1637

FAX: [1] (212) 750-1657

Diplomatic representation from the US: the US does not have an embassy in Comoros; the

US Ambassador to Madagascar is accredited to Comoros

Flag description: four equal horizontal bands of yellow (top), white, red, and blue, with a green isosceles triangle based on the hoist; centered within the triangle is a white crescent with the convex side facing the hoist and four white, five-pointed stars placed vertically in a line between the points of the crescent; the horizontal bands and the four stars represent the four main islands of the archipelago—Mwali, N'gazidja, Ndzuwani, and Mahore (Mayotte—department of France, but claimed by Comoros)

note: the crescent, stars, and color green are traditional symbols of Islam

National symbol(s): four stars and crescent; national colors: green, white

National anthem: *name:* "Udzima wa ya Masiwa" (The Union of the Great Islands)

lyrics/music: Said Hachim SIDI ABDEREMANE/ Said Hachim SIDI ABDEREMANE and Kamildine ABDALLAH

note: adopted 1978

ECONOMY

Economy—overview: One of the world's poorest countries, the Comoros is made up of three islands that are hampered by inadequate transportation links, a young and rapidly increasing population, and few natural resources. The low educational level of the labor force contributes to a subsistence level of economic activity and a heavy dependence on foreign grants and technical assistance. Agriculture, including fishing, hunting, and forestry, accounts for 50% of GDP, employs 80% of the labor force, and provides most of the exports. Export income is heavily reliant on the three main crops of vanilla, cloves, and ylang ylang (perfume essence); and the Comoros' export earnings are easily disrupted by disasters such as fires and extreme weather. Despite agriculture's importance to the economy, the country imports roughly 70% of its food; rice, the main staple, accounts for the bulk of imports. Remittances from about 300,000 Comorans contribute about 25% of the country's GDP.

The new government, elected in mid-2016, will be challenged to provide basic services, upgrade education and technical training, privatize commercial and industrial enterprises, improve health services, diversify exports, promote tourism, and reduce the high population growth rate. Recurring political instability, sometimes initiated from outside the country, has inhibited growth. In late 2015, Saudi Arabia provided a large budget grant to the Comorian Government, allowing arrears to be cleared and resulting in an overall fiscal surplus for 2016. The government has moved to improve revenue mobilization, reduce expenditures, and improve electricity access.

GDP (purchasing power parity): $1.323 billion (2017 est.)

$1.281 billion (2016 est.)

$1.254 billion (2015 est.)

note: data are in 2017 dollars

country comparison to the world: 201

GDP (official exchange rate): $659 million (2016 est.)

GDP—real growth rate: 3.3% (2017 est.)

2.2% (2016 est.)

1% (2015 est.)

country comparison to the world: 102

GDP—per capita (PPP): $1,600 (2017 est.)

$1,600 (2016 est.)

$1,600 (2015 est.)

note: data are in 2017 dollars

country comparison to the world: 219

Gross national saving: 12.2% of GDP (2017 est.)

10.9% of GDP (2016 est.)

18.9% of GDP (2015 est.)

country comparison to the world: 144

GDP—composition, by end use:

household consumption: 104%

government consumption: 19.3%

investment in fixed capital: 4.6%

investment in inventories: 5.7%

exports of goods and services: 19.2%

imports of goods and services: -52.8% (2017 est.)

GDP—composition, by sector of origin:

agriculture: 49.5%

industry: 11.8%

services: 38.7% (2017 est.)

Agriculture—products: vanilla, cloves, ylang-ylang (perfume essence), coconuts, bananas, cassava (manioc)

Industries: fishing, tourism, perfume distillation

Industrial production growth rate: 0.8% (2017 est.)

country comparison to the world: 173

Labor force: 278,500 (2016 est.)

country comparison to the world: 167

Labor force—by occupation: *agriculture:* 80%

industry and services: 20% (1996 est.)

Unemployment rate: 6.5% (2014 est.)

country comparison to the world: 88

Population below poverty line: 44.8% (2004 est.)

Household income or consumption by percentage share: *lowest 10%:* 0.9%

highest 10%: 55.2% (2004)

Budget: *revenues:* $148.6 million

expenditures: $183.1 million (2017 est.)

Taxes and other revenues: 22.6% of GDP (2017 est.)

country comparison to the world: 132

Budget surplus (+) or deficit (-): -5.2% of GDP (2017 est.)

country comparison to the world: 164

Public debt: 26.3% of GDP (2016 est.)

25.2% of GDP (2015 est.)

country comparison to the world: 173

Fiscal year: calendar year

Inflation rate (consumer prices): 2% (2017 est.)

1.8% (2016 est.)

country comparison to the world: 90

Central bank discount rate: 1.93% (31 December 2010)

2.21% (31 December 2009)

country comparison to the world: 117

Commercial bank prime lending rate: 10.5% (31 December 2017 est.)
10.5% (31 December 2016 est.)
country comparison to the world: 77

Stock of narrow money: $193.8 million (31 December 2017 est.)
$180.5 million (31 December 2016 est.)
country comparison to the world: 185

Stock of broad money: $295.5 million (31 December 2017 est.)
$268.8 million (31 December 2016 est.)
country comparison to the world: 190

Stock of domestic credit: $204.3 million (31 December 2017 est.)
$183.9 million (31 December 2016 est.)
country comparison to the world: 185

Current account balance: -$63 million (2017 est.)
-$62 million (2016 est.)
country comparison to the world: 73

Exports: $18.4 million (2017 est.)
$17.9 million (2016 est.)
country comparison to the world: 213

Exports—commodities: vanilla, ylang-ylang (perfume essence), cloves

Exports—partners: France 25.6%, South Korea 15%, Germany 11.8%, India 10.4%, Singapore 4.4%, Russia 4.2%, Mauritius 4.1% (2016)

Imports: $194.8 million (2017 est.)
$189 million (2016 est.)
country comparison to the world: 204

Imports—commodities: rice and other foodstuffs, consumer goods, petroleum products, cement and construction materials, transport equipment

Imports—partners: UAE 29.5%, France 21.2%, China 11.3%, Pakistan 7.3%, Madagascar 6.2%, India 4.7% (2016)

Debt—external: $131.1 million (31 December 2017 est.)
$132 million (31 December 2016 est.)
country comparison to the world: 192

Exchange rates: Comoran francs (KMF) per US dollar—
458.2 (2017 est.)
444.76 (2016 est.)
444.76 (2015 est.)
443.6 (2014 est.)
370.81 (2013 est.)

ENERGY

Electricity access: population without electricity: 200,000
electrification—total population: 69%
electrification—urban areas: 89%
electrification—rural areas: 62% (2013)

Electricity—production: 54 million kWh (2015 est.)
country comparison to the world: 206

Electricity—consumption: 50.22 million kWh (2015 est.)
country comparison to the world: 204

Electricity—exports: 0 kWh (2016 est.)

country comparison to the world: 122

Electricity—imports: 0 kWh (2016 est.)
country comparison to the world: 135

Electricity—installed generating capacity: 26,000 kW (2015 est.)
country comparison to the world: 204

Electricity—from fossil fuels: 96.2% of total installed capacity (2015 est.)
country comparison to the world: 49

Electricity—from nuclear fuels: 0% of total installed capacity (2015 est.)
country comparison to the world: 69

Electricity—from hydroelectric plants: 3.8% of total installed capacity (2015 est.)
country comparison to the world: 131

Electricity—from other renewable sources: 0% of total installed capacity (2015 est.)
country comparison to the world: 177

Crude oil—production: 0 bbl/day (2016 est.)
country comparison to the world: 122

Crude oil—exports: 0 bbl/day (2014 est.)
country comparison to the world: 107

Crude oil—imports: 0 bbl/day (2014 est.)
country comparison to the world: 110

Crude oil—proved reserves: 0 bbl (1 January 2017 es)
country comparison to the world: 121

Refined petroleum products—production: 0 bbl/day (2014 est.)
country comparison to the world: 131

Refined petroleum products—consumption: 1,300 bbl/day (2015 est.)
country comparison to the world: 202

Refined petroleum products—exports: 0 bbl/day (2014 est.)
country comparison to the world: 143

Refined petroleum products—imports: 1,350 bbl/day (2014 est.)
country comparison to the world: 197

Natural gas—production: 0 cu m (2013 est.)
country comparison to the world: 121

Natural gas—consumption: 0 cu m (2013 est.)
country comparison to the world: 169

Natural gas—exports: 0 cu m (2013 est.)
country comparison to the world: 86

Natural gas—imports: 0 cu m (2013 est.)
country comparison to the world: 109

Natural gas—proved reserves: 0 cu m (1 January 2014 es)
country comparison to the world: 127

Carbon dioxide emissions from consumption of energy: 200,000 Mt (2013 est.)
country comparison to the world: 202

COMMUNICATIONS

Telephones—fixed lines: total subscriptions: 13,049
subscriptions per 100 inhabitants: 2 (July 2016 est.)
country comparison to the world: 178

Telephones—mobile cellular: total: 454,213

subscriptions per 100 inhabitants: 57 (July 2016 est.)
country comparison to the world: 173

Telephone system: general assessment: sparse system of microwave radio relay and HF radiotelephone communication stations
domestic: fixed-line connections only about 2 per 100 persons; mobile cellular usage over 55 per 100 persons; two companies, Comoros Telecom and Telma, provide domestic and international mobile service and wireless data.
international: country code—269; landing point for the EASSy fiber-optic submarine cable system connecting East Africa with Europe and North America; HF radiotelephone communications to Madagascar and Reunion (2017)

Broadcast media: national state-owned TV station and a TV station run by Anjouan regional government; national state-owned radio; regional governments on the islands of Grande Comore and Anjouan each operate a radio station; a few independent and small community radio stations operate on the islands of Grande Comore and Moheli, and these two islands have access to Mayotte Radio and French TV (2007)

Internet country code: .km
Internet users: total: 63,084

percent of population: 7.9% (July 2016 est.)
country comparison to the world: 182

TRANSPORTATION

National air transport system: number of registered air carriers: 2
inventory of registered aircraft operated by air carriers: 9 (2015)
Civil aircraft registration country code prefix: D6 (2016)

Airports: 4 (2013)
country comparison to the world: 186

Airports—with paved runways: total: 4
2,438 to 3,047 m: 1
914 to 1,523 m: 3 (2017)

Roadways: total: 880 km
paved: 673 km
unpaved: 207 km (2002)
country comparison to the world: 188

Merchant marine: total: 203
by type: bulk carrier 4, container ship 1, general cargo 86, oil tanker 26, other 86 (2017)
country comparison to the world: 64

Ports and terminals: major seaport(s): Moroni, Mutsamudu

MILITARY AND SECURITY

Military branches: National Army for Development (l'Armee Nationale de Developpement, AND): Comoran Security Force (also called Comoran Defense Force (Force Comorienne de Defense, FCD), includes Gendarmerie), Comoran Coast Guard, Comoran Federal Police (2015)

Military service age and obligation: 18 years of age for 2-year voluntary male and female military service; no conscription (2015)

TRANSNATIONAL ISSUES

Disputes—international: claims French-administered Mayotte and challenges France's and Madagascar's claims to Banc du Geyser, a drying reef in the Mozambique Channel; in May 2008, African Union forces assisted the Comoros military recapture Anjouan Island from rebels who seized it in 2001

Trafficking in persons: *current situation:* Comoros is a source country for children subjected to forced labor and, reportedly, sex trafficking domestically, and women and children are subjected to forced labor in Mayotte; it is possibly a transit and destination country for Malagasy women and girls and a transit country for East African women and girls exploited in domestic service in the Middle East; Comoran children are forced to labor in domestic service, roadside and street vending, baking, fishing, and agriculture; some Comoran students at Koranic schools are exploited for forced agricultural or domestic labor, sometimes being subjected to physical and sexual abuse; Comoros may be particularly vulnerable to transnational trafficking because of inadequate border controls, government corruption, and the presence of international criminal networks

tier rating: Tier 3–Comoros does not fully comply with the minimum standards for the elimination of trafficking and was placed on Tier 3 after being on the Tier 2 Watch List for two consecutive years without making progress; Parliament passed revisions to the penal code in 2014, including anti-trafficking provisions and enforcement guidelines, but these amendments have not yet been passed approved by the President and put into effect; a new child labor law was passed in 2015 prohibiting child trafficking, but existing laws do not criminalize the forced prostitution of adults; authorities did not investigate, prosecute, or convict alleged trafficking offenders, including complicit officials; the government lacked victim identification and care referral procedures, did not assist any victims during 2014, and provided minimal support to NGOs offering victims psychosocial services (2015)

CONGO, DEMOCRATIC REPUBLIC OF THE

INTRODUCTION

Background: Established as an official Belgian colony in 1908, the then-Republic of the Congo gained its independence in 1960, but its early years were marred by political and social instability. Col. Joseph MOBUTU seized power and declared himself president in a November 1965 coup. He subsequently changed his name—to MOBUTU Sese Seko—as well as that of the country—to Zaire. MOBUTU retained his position for 32 years through several sham elections, as well as through brutal force. Ethnic strife and civil war, touched off by a massive inflow of refugees in 1994 from fighting in Rwanda and Burundi, led in May 1997 to the toppling of the MOBUTU regime by a rebellion backed by Rwanda and Uganda and fronted by Laurent KABILA. KABILA renamed the country the Democratic Republic of the Congo (DRC), but in August 1998 his regime was itself challenged by a second insurrection again backed by Rwanda and Uganda. Troops from Angola, Chad, Namibia, Sudan, and Zimbabwe intervened to support KABILA's regime. In January 2001, KABILA was assassinated and his son, Joseph KABILA, was named head of state. In October 2002, the new president was successful in negotiating the withdrawal of Rwandan forces occupying the eastern DRC; two months later, the Pretoria Accord was signed by all remaining warring parties to end the fighting and establish a government of national unity. A transitional government was set up in July 2003; it held a successful constitutional referendum in December 2005 and elections for the presidency, National Assembly, and provincial legislatures took place in 2006.

In 2009, following a resurgence of conflict in the eastern DRC, the government signed a peace agreement with the National Congress for the Defense of the People (CNDP), a primarily Tutsi rebel group. An attempt to integrate CNDP members into the Congolese military failed, prompting their defection in 2012 and the formation of the M23 armed group—named after the 23 March 2009 peace agreements. Renewed conflict led to large population displacements and significant human rights abuses before the M23 was pushed out of DRC to Uganda and Rwanda in late 2013 by a joint DRC and UN offensive. In addition, the DRC continues to experience violence committed by other armed groups including the Democratic Forces for the Liberation of Rwanda, the Allied Democratic Forces, and assorted Mai Mai militias. In the most recent national elections, held in November 2011, disputed results allowed Joseph KABILA to be reelected to the presidency. The DRC Constitution bars President KABILA from running for a third term, but the DRC Government has delayed national elections, originally slated for November 2016, to December 2018. The failure to hold elections as scheduled has fueled sporadic street protests by KABILA's opponents.

GEOGRAPHY

Location: Central Africa, northeast of Angola

Geographic coordinates: 0 00 N, 25 00 E

Map references: Africa

Area: *total:* 2,344,858 sq km
land: 2,267,048 sq km
water: 77,810 sq km
country comparison to the world: 12

Area—comparative: slightly less than one-fourth the size of the US

Land boundaries: *total:* 10,481 km
border countries (9): Angola 2,646 km (of which 225 km is the boundary of Angola's discontiguous Cabinda Province), Burundi 236 km, Central African Republic 1,747 km, Republic of the Congo 1,229 km, Rwanda 221 km, South Sudan 714 km, Tanzania 479 km, Uganda 877 km, Zambia 2,332 km

Coastline: 37 km

Maritime claims: *territorial sea:* 12 nm
exclusive economic zone: since 2011 the DRC has a Common Interest Zone agreement with Angola for the mutual development of off-shore resources

Climate: tropical; hot and humid in equatorial river basin; cooler and drier in southern highlands; cooler and wetter in eastern highlands; north of Equator—wet season (April to October), dry season (December to February); south of Equator—wet season (November to March), dry season (April to October)

Terrain: vast central basin is a low-lying plateau; mountains in east

Elevation: *mean elevation:* 726 m

elevation extremes: *lowest point:* Atlantic Ocean 0 m
highest point: Pic Marguerite on Mont Ngaliema (Mount Stanley) 5,110 m

Natural resources: cobalt, copper, niobium, tantalum, petroleum, industrial and gem diamonds, gold, silver, zinc, manganese, tin, uranium, coal, hydropower, timber

Land use: *agricultural land:* 11.4%
arable land: 3.1%;
permanent crops: 0.3%;
permanent pasture: 8%
forest: 67.9%
other: 20.7% (2011 est.)
Irrigated land: 110 sq km (2012)

Population—distribution: urban clusters are spread throughout the country, particularly in the northeast along the boarder with Uganda, Rwanda, and Burundi; the largest city is the capital, Kinshasha, located in the west along the Congo River; the south is least densely populated

Natural hazards: periodic droughts in south; Congo River floods (seasonal); active volcanoes in the east along the Great Rift Valley

volcanism: Nyiragongo (3,470 m), which erupted in 2002 and is experiencing ongoing activity, poses a major threat to the city of Goma, home to a quarter million people; the volcano produces unusually fast-moving lava, known to travel up to 100 km /hr; Nyiragongo has been deemed a Decade Volcano by the International Association of Volcanology and Chemistry of the Earth's Interior, worthy of study due to its explosive history and close proximity to human populations; its neighbor, Nyamuragira, which erupted in 2010, is Africa's most active volcano; Visoke is the only other historically active volcano

Environment—current issues: poaching threatens wildlife populations; water pollution; deforestation; soil erosion; mining (diamonds, gold, coltan—a mineral used in creating capacitors for electronic devices) causing environmental damage

Environment—international agreements: *party to:* Biodiversity, Climate Change, Climate Change-Kyoto Protocol, Desertification, Endangered Species, Hazardous Wastes, Law of the Sea, Marine Dumping, Ozone Layer Protection, Tropical Timber 83, Tropical Timber 94, Wetlands
signed, but not ratified: Environmental Modification

Geography—note: note 1: second largest country in Africa (after Algeria) and largest country in Sub-Saharan Africa; straddles the equator; dense tropical rain forest in central river basin and eastern highlands; the narrow strip of land that controls the lower Congo River is the DRC's only outlet to the South Atlantic Ocean
note 2: because of its speed, cataracts, rapids, and turbulence the Congo River, most of which flows through the DRC, has never been accurately measured along much of its length; nonetheless, it is conceded to be the deepest river in the world; estimates of its greatest depth vary between 220 and 250 meters

PEOPLE AND SOCIETY

Population: 83,301,151
note: estimates for this country explicitly take into account the effects of excess mortality due to AIDS; this can result in lower life expectancy, higher infant mortality, higher death rates, lower population growth rates, and changes in the distribution of population by age and sex than would otherwise be expected (July 2017 est.)
country comparison to the world: 16

Nationality: *noun:* Congolese (singular and plural)
adjective: Congolese or Congo

Ethnic groups: over 200 African ethnic groups of which the majority are Bantu; the four largest tribes—Mongo, Luba, Kongo (all Bantu), and the Mangbetu-Azande (Hamitic) make up about 45% of the population

Languages: French (official), Lingala (a lingua franca trade language), Kingwana (a dialect of Kiswahili or Swahili), Kikongo, Tshiluba

Religions: Roman Catholic 50%, Protestant 20%, Kimbanguist 10%, Muslim 10%, other (includes syncretic sects and indigenous beliefs) 10%

Demographic profile: Despite a wealth of fertile soil, hydroelectric power potential, and mineral resources, the Democratic Republic of the Congo (DRC) struggles with many socioeconomic problems, including high infant and maternal mortality rates, malnutrition, poor vaccination coverage, lack of access to improved water sources and sanitation, and frequent and early fertility. Ongoing conflict, mismanagement of resources, and a lack of investment have resulted in food insecurity; almost 30 percent of children under the age of 5 are malnourished. The overall coverage of basic public services–education, health, sanitation, and potable water–is very limited and piecemeal, with substantial regional and rural/urban disparities. Fertility remains high at almost 5 children per woman and is likely to remain high because of the low use of contraception and the cultural preference for larger families.

The DRC is a source and host country for refugees. Between 2012 and 2014, more than 119,000 Congolese refugees returned from the Republic of Congo to the relative stability of northwest DRC, but more than 540,000 Congolese refugees remained abroad as of year-end 2015. In addition, an estimated 3.9 million Congolese were internally displaced as of October 2017, the vast majority fleeing violence between rebel group and Congolese armed forces. Thousands of refugees have come to the DRC from neighboring countries, including Rwanda, the Central African Republic, and Burundi.

Age structure: *0-14 years:* 41.74% (male 17,525,063/female 17,241,929)
15-24 years: 21.46% (male 8,969,922/female 8,909,903)
25-54 years: 30.53% (male 12,691,612/female 12,738,316)
55-64 years: 3.6% (male 1,421,619/female 1,579,034)
65 years and over: 2.67% (male 941,926/female 1,281,827) (2017 est.)

Dependency ratios: *total dependency ratio:* 97.5
youth dependency ratio: 91.5
elderly dependency ratio: 6
potential support ratio: 16.8 (2015 est.)

Median age: *total:* 18.6 years
male: 18.3 years
female: 18.8 years (2017 est.)
country comparison to the world: 210

Population growth rate: 2.37% (2017 est.)
country comparison to the world: 27

Birth rate: 33.5 births/1,000 population (2017 est.)
country comparison to the world: 26

Death rate: 9.6 deaths/1,000 population (2017 est.)
country comparison to the world: 51

Net migration rate: -0.2 migrant(s)/1,000 population (2017 est.)
country comparison to the world: 110

Population distribution: urban clusters are spread throughout the country, particularly in the northeast along the boarder with Uganda, Rwanda, and Burundi; the largest city is the capital, Kinshasha, located in the west along the Congo River; the south is least densely populated

Urbanization: *urban population:* 43.5% of total population (2017)
rate of urbanization: 3.83% annual rate of change (2015-20 est.)

Major urban areas—population: KINSHASA (capital) 11.587 million; Lubumbashi 2.015 million; Mbuji-Mayi 2.007 million; Kananga 1.169 million; Kisangani 1.04 million; Bukavu 832,000 (2015)

Sex ratio: *at birth:* 1.03 male(s)/female
0-14 years: 1.02 male(s)/female
15-24 years: 1.01 male(s)/female
25-54 years: 1 male(s)/female
55-64 years: 0.89 male(s)/female
65 years and over: 0.73 male(s)/female
total population: 1 male(s)/female (2016 est.)

Mother's mean age at first birth: 19.9 years
note: median age at first birth among women 25-29 (2013/14 est.)

Maternal mortality ratio: 693 deaths/100,000 live births (2015 est.)
country comparison to the world: 10

Infant mortality rate: *total:* 68.2 deaths/1,000 live births
male: 71.7 deaths/1,000 live births
female: 64.6 deaths/1,000 live births (2017 est.)
country comparison to the world: 11

Life expectancy at birth: *total population:* 57.7 years
male: 56.1 years
female: 59.3 years (2017 est.)
country comparison to the world: 210

Total fertility rate: 4.39 children born/woman (2017 est.)
country comparison to the world: 24

Contraceptive prevalence rate: 20.4% (2013/14)

Health expenditures: 4.3% of GDP (2014)
country comparison to the world: 161

Physicians density: 9 physicians/1,000 population (2009)

Hospital bed density: 0.8 beds/1,000 population (2006)

Drinking water source:
improved:
urban: 81.1% of population
rural: 31.2% of population
total: 52.4% of population
unimproved:
urban: 18.9% of population
rural: 68.8% of population
total: 47.6% of population (2015 est.)

Sanitation facility access:
improved:
urban: 28.5% of population
rural: 28.7% of population
total: 28.7% of population
unimproved:
urban: 71.5% of population
rural: 71.3% of population
total: 71.3% of population (2015 est.)

HIV/AIDS—adult prevalence rate: 0.7% (2016 est.)
country comparison to the world: 53

HIV/AIDS—people living with HIV/AIDS: 370,000 (2016 est.)
country comparison to the world: 17

HIV/AIDS—deaths: 19,000 (2016 est.)
country comparison to the world: 15

Major infectious diseases: *degree of risk:* very high
food or waterborne diseases: bacterial and protozoal diarrhea, hepatitis A, and typhoid fever
vectorborne diseases: malaria, dengue fever, and trypanosomiasis-gambiense (African sleeping sickness)
water contact disease: schistosomiasis
animal contact disease: rabies (2016)

Obesity—adult prevalence rate: 6.7% (2016)
country comparison to the world: 164

Children under the age of 5 years underweight: 23.4% (2013)
country comparison to the world: 25

Education expenditures: 2.2% of GDP (2013)
country comparison to the world: 157

Literacy: *definition:* age 15 and over can read and write French, Lingala, Kingwana, or Tshiluba
total population: 77%
male: 88.5%
female: 66.5% (2016 est.)

School life expectancy (primary to tertiary education): *total:* 9 years
male: 10 years
female: 8 years (2013)

GOVERNMENT

Country name: *conventional long form:* Democratic Republic of the Congo
conventional short form: DRC
local long form: Republique Democratique du Congo
local short form: RDC
former: Congo Free State, Belgian Congo, Congo/Leopoldville, Congo/Kinshasa, Zaire
abbreviation: DRC (or DROC)
etymology: named for the Congo River, most of which lies within the DRC; the river name derives from Kongo, a Bantu kingdom that occupied its mouth at the time of Portuguese discovery in the late 15th century and whose name stems from its people the Bakongo, meaning "hunters"

Government type: semi-presidential republic

Capital: *name:* Kinshasa

geographic coordinates: 4 19 S, 15 18 E

time difference: UTC+1 (6 hours ahead of Washington, DC, during Standard Time)

Administrative divisions: 26 provinces (provinces, singular—province); Bas-Uele (Lower Uele), Equateur, Haut-Katanga (Upper Katanga), Haut-Lomami (Upper Lomami), Haut-Uele (Upper Uele), Ituri, Kasai, Kasai-Central, Kasai-Oriental (East Kasai), Kinshasa, Kongo Central, Kwango, Kwilu, Lomami, Lualaba, Mai-Ndombe, Maniema, Mongala, Nord-Kivu (North Kivu), Nord-Ubangi (North Ubangi), Sankuru, Sud-Kivu (South Kivu), Sud-Ubangi (South Ubangi), Tanganyika, Tshopo, Tshuapa

Independence: 30 June 1960 (from Belgium)

National holiday: Independence Day, 30 June (1960)

Constitution: history: several previous; latest adopted 13 May 2005, approved by referendum 18-19 December 2005, promulgated 18 February 2006
amendments: proposed by the president of the republic, by the government, by either house of Parliament, or by public petition; agreement on the substance of a proposed bill requires absolute majority vote in both houses; passage requires a referendum only if both houses in joint meeting fail to achieve three-fifths majority vote; constitutional articles including the form of government, universal suffrage, judicial independence, political pluralism, and personal freedoms cannot be amended; amended 2011 (2017)

Legal system: civil law system primarily based on Belgian law, but also customary, and tribal law

International law organization participation: accepts compulsory ICJ jurisdiction with reservations; accepts ICCt jurisdiction

Citizenship: *citizenship by birth:* no
citizenship by descent only: at least one parent must be a citizen of the Democratic Republic of the Congo
dual citizenship recognized: no
residency requirement for naturalization: 5 years

Suffrage: 18 years of age; universal and compulsory

Executive branch: *chief of state:* President Joseph KABILA (since 17 January 2001)

head of government: Prime Minister Bruno TSHIBALA (since 7 April 2017); Deputy Prime Ministers Jose MAKILA, Leonard She OKITUNDU, Emmanuel RAMAZANI Shadary (since December 2016)
cabinet: Ministers of State appointed by the president
elections/appointments: president directly elected by simple majority vote for a 5-year term (eligible for a second term); election last held on 28 November 2011 (next originally scheduled for 27 November 2016 but now scheduled for 23 December 2018); prime minister appointed by the president
election results: Joseph KABILA reelected president; percent of vote—Joseph KABILA (PPRD) 49%, Etienne TSHISEKEDI (UDPS) 32.3%,

other 18.7%; note—election marred by serious voting irregularities

Legislative branch: description: bicameral Parliament or Parlament consists of the Senate (108 seats; members indirectly elected by provincial assemblies by proportional representation vote; members serve 5-year terms) and the National Assembly (500 seats; 439 members directly elected in multi-seat constituencies by proportional representation vote and 61 directly elected in single-seat constituencies by simple majority vote; members serve 5-year terms)
elections: Senate—last held on 19 January 2007 (follow-on elections have been delayed); National Assembly—last held on 28 November 2011 (next originally scheduled for 27 November 2016, postponed until April 2018)
election results: Senate—percent of vote by party—NA; seats by party—PPRD 22, MLC 14, FR 7, RCD 7, PDC 6, CDC 3, MSR 3, PALU 2, independent 26, other 18; National Assembly—percent of vote by party—NA; seats by party—PPRD 62, UDPS 41, PPPD 29, MSR 27, MLC 22, PALU 19, UNC 17, ARC 16, AFDC 15, ECT 11, RRC 11, independent 16, other 214 (includes numerous political parties that won 10 or fewer seats and 2 constituencies where voting was halted); note—the November 2011 election was marred by violence including the destruction of ballots in 2 constituencies resulting in the closure of polling sites; election results were delayed 3 months, strongly contested, and continue to be unresolved

Judicial branch: *highest court(s):* Court of Cassation or Cour de Cassation (consists of 26 justices and organized into legislative and judiciary sections); Constitutional Court (consists of 9 judges)
judge selection and term of office: Court of Cassation judges nominated by the Judicial Service Council, an independent body of public prosecutors and selected judges of the lower courts; judge tenure NA; Constitutional Court judges—3 nominated by the president, 3 by the Judicial Service Council, and 3 by the legislature; judges appointed by the president to serve 9-year non-renewable terms with one-third of the membership renewed every 3 years
subordinate courts: State Security Court; Court of Appeals (organized into administrative and judiciary sections); Tribunal de Grande; magistrates' courts; customary courts

Political parties and leaders: Christian Democrat Party or PDC [Jose ENDUNDO]
Congolese Rally for Democracy or RCD [Azarias RUBERWA]
Convention of Christian Democrats or CDC
Forces of Renewal or FR [Mbusa NYAMWISI]
Movement for the Liberation of the Congo or MLC [Jean-Pierre BEMBA]
People's Party for Reconstruction and Democracy or PPRD [Henri MOVA]
Social Movement for Renewal or MSR [Pierre LUMBI]
Unified Lumumbist Party or PALU [Antoine GIZENGA]

Union for the Congolese Nation or UNC [Vital KAMERHE]

Union for Democracy and Social Progress or UDPS [Felix TSHISEKEDI]

Political pressure groups and leaders: Allied Democratic Forces or ADF (anti-Ugandan Government rebel groups)

Army of the Democratic Republic of the Congo (Forces Armies de la Republique Democratique du Congo) or FARDC

Forces Democratiques de Liberation du Rwanda or FDLR (Rwandan militia group made up of some of the perpetrators of Rwanda's genocide in 1994)

Le Rassemblement (established in 2016 as a coalition of members from several political parties)

International organization participation: ACP, AfDB, AU, CEMAC, CEPGL, COMESA, EITI (compliant country), FAO, G-24, G-77, IAEA, IBRD, ICAO, ICC (NGOs), ICCt, ICRM, IDA, IFAD, IFC, IFRCS, IHO, ILO, IMF, IMO, Interpol, IOC, IOM, IPU, ISO, ITSO, ITU, ITUC (NGOs), MIGA, NAM, OIF, OPCW, PCA, SADC, UN, UNCTAD, UNESCO, UNHCR, UNIDO, UNWTO, UPU, WCO, WFTU (NGOs), WHO, WIPO, WMO, WTO

Diplomatic representation in the US: *chief of mission:* Ambassador Francois Nkuna BALUMUENE (since 23 September 2015)

chancery: 1726 M Street, NW, Suite 601, Washington, DC, 20036

telephone: [1] (202) 234-7690 through 7691

FAX: [1] (202) 234-2609

representative office: New York New York

Diplomatic representation from the US: *chief of mission:* Ambassador (vacant); Charge d'Affaires Robert WHITEHEAD (since January 2016)

embassy: 310 Avenue des Aviateurs, Kinshasa, Gombe

mailing address: Unit 2220, DPO AE 09828

telephone: [243] (081) 556-0151

FAX: [243] (081) 556-0175

Flag description: sky blue field divided diagonally from the lower hoist corner to upper fly corner by a red stripe bordered by two narrow yellow stripes; a yellow, five-pointed star appears in the upper hoist corner; blue represents peace and hope, red the blood of the country's martyrs, and yellow the country's wealth and prosperity; the star symbolizes unity and the brilliant future for the country

National symbol(s): leopard; national colors: sky blue, red, yellow

National anthem: *name:* "Debout Congolaise" (Arise Congolese)

lyrics/music: Joseph LUTUMBA/Simon-Pierre BOKA di Mpasi Londi

note: adopted 1960; replaced when the country was known as Zaire; but readopted in 1997

ECONOMY

Economy—overview: The economy of the Democratic Republic of the Congo—a nation endowed with vast natural resource wealth—continues to perform poorly. Systemic corruption since independence in 1960, combined with countrywide instability and intermittent conflict that began in the early-90s, has reduced national output and government revenue, and increased external debt. With the installation of a transitional government in 2003 after peace accords, economic conditions slowly began to improve as the government reopened relations with international financial institutions and international donors, and President KABILA began implementing reforms. Progress on implementing substantive economic reforms remains slow because of political instability, bureaucratic inefficiency, corruption, and patronage, which also dampen international investment prospects.

Renewed activity in the mining sector, the source of most export income, boosted Kinshasa's fiscal position and GDP growth until 2015, but low commodity prices have led to slower growth, volatile inflation, currency depreciation, and a growing fiscal deficit. An uncertain legal framework, corruption, and a lack of transparency in government policy are long-term problems for the large mining sector and for the economy as a whole. Much economic activity still occurs in the informal sector and is not reflected in GDP data.

Poverty remains widespread in DRC, and the country failed to meet any Millennium Development Goals by 2015. DRC also concluded its program with the IMF in 2015. The price of copper—the DRC's primary export—plummeted in 2015 and remained at record lows during 2016-17, reducing government revenues, expenditures, and foreign exchange reserves, while inflation reached nearly 50% in mid-2017—its highest level since the early 2000s.

GDP (purchasing power parity): $67.99 billion (2017 est.)

$66.15 billion (2016 est.)

$64.6 billion (2015 est.)

note: data are in 2017 dollars

country comparison to the world: 104

GDP (official exchange rate): $40.42 billion (2016 est.)

GDP—real growth rate: 2.8% (2017 est.)

2.4% (2016 est.)

6.9% (2015 est.)

country comparison to the world: 121

GDP—per capita (PPP): $800 (2017 est.)

$800 (2016 est.)

$800 (2015 est.)

note: data are in 2017 dollars

country comparison to the world: 227

Gross national saving: 7.9% of GDP (2017 est.)

8.4% of GDP (2016 est.)

16.3% of GDP (2015 est.)

country comparison to the world: 165

GDP—composition, by end use:

household consumption: 76.4%

government consumption: 11.8%

investment in fixed capital: 13.8%

investment in inventories: 0%

exports of goods and services: 30.5%

imports of goods and services: -32.5% (2017 est.)

GDP—composition, by sector of origin:

agriculture: 21.1%

industry: 33%

services: 45.9% (2017 est.)

Agriculture—products: coffee, sugar, palm oil, rubber, tea, cotton, cocoa, quinine, cassava (manioc, tapioca), bananas, plantains, peanuts, root crops, corn, fruits; wood products

Industries: mining (copper, cobalt, gold, diamonds, coltan, zinc, tin, tungsten), mineral processing, consumer products (textiles, plastics, footwear, cigarettes), metal products, processed foods and beverages, timber, cement, commercial ship repair

Industrial production growth rate: 1.6% (2017 est.)

country comparison to the world: 147

Labor force: 31.36 million (2017 est.)

country comparison to the world: 19

Labor force—by occupation: *agriculture:* NA%

industry: NA%

services: NA%

Unemployment rate: NA%

Population below poverty line: 63% (2012 est.)

Household income or consumption by percentage share: *lowest 10%:* 2.3%

highest 10%: 34.7% (2006)

Budget: *revenues:* $3.238 billion

expenditures: $3.366 billion (2017 est.)

Taxes and other revenues: 8% of GDP (2017 est.)

country comparison to the world: 216

Budget surplus (+) or deficit (-): -0.3% of GDP (2017 est.)

country comparison to the world: 41

Public debt: 14.6% of GDP (2017 est.)

17.6% of GDP (2016 est.)

country comparison to the world: 193

Fiscal year: calendar year

Inflation rate (consumer prices): 41.7% (2017 est.)

18.2% (2016 est.)

country comparison to the world: 225

Central bank discount rate: 4% (31 December 2012)

20% (31 December 2011)

country comparison to the world: 98

Commercial bank prime lending rate: 35.9% (31 December 2017 est.)

18.76% (31 December 2016 est.)

country comparison to the world: 4

Stock of narrow money: $1.386 billion (31 December 2017 est.)

$1.192 billion (31 December 2016 est.)

country comparison to the world: 145

Stock of broad money: $3.863 billion (31 December 2017 est.)

$4.272 billion (31 December 2016 est.)

country comparison to the world: 137

Stock of domestic credit: $3.492 billion (31 December 2017 est.)

$3.523 billion (31 December 2016 est.)

country comparison to the world: 133

Market value of publicly traded shares: $NA

Current account balance: -$1.849 billion (2017 est.)
-$1.334 billion (2016 est.)
country comparison to the world: 156

Exports: $8.598 billion (2017 est.)
$8.228 billion (2016 est.)
country comparison to the world: 95

Exports—commodities: diamonds, copper, gold, cobalt, wood products, crude oil, coffee

Exports—partners: China 35.3%, Zambia 15.8%, South Korea 8.7%, Saudi Arabia 8%, Belgium 5.2% (2016)

Imports: $8.845 billion (2017 est.)
$8.671 billion (2016 est.)
country comparison to the world: 100

Imports—commodities: foodstuffs, mining and other machinery, transport equipment, fuels

Imports—partners: China 20.2%, South Africa 15.7%, Zambia 8.6%, Belgium 7.6%, Tanzania 5.8%, France 5.2%, India 4.6%, Kenya 4.2% (2016)

Reserves of foreign exchange and gold: $444.6 million (31 December 2017 est.)
$708.2 million (31 December 2016 est.)
country comparison to the world: 144

Debt—external: $5.324 billion (31 December 2017 est.)
$5.35 billion (31 December 2016 est.)
country comparison to the world: 133

Exchange rates: Congolese francs (CDF) per US dollar—
1,546.8 (2017 est.)
1,010.3 (2016 est.)
1,010.3 (2015 est.)
925.99 (2014 est.)
925.23 (2013 est.)

ENERGY

Electricity access: *population without electricity:* 61,400,000
electrification—*total population:* 9%
electrification—urban areas: 19%
electrification—rural areas: 2% (2013)

Electricity—production: 8.852 billion kWh (2015 est.)
country comparison to the world: 107

Electricity—consumption: 7.19 billion kWh (2015 est.)
country comparison to the world: 109

Electricity—exports: 422 million kWh (2015 est.)
country comparison to the world: 71

Electricity—imports: 20 million kWh (2015 est.)
country comparison to the world: 108

Electricity—installed generating capacity: 2.624 million kW (2015 est.)
country comparison to the world: 103

Electricity—from fossil fuels: 1.3% of total installed capacity (2015 est.)
country comparison to the world: 209

Electricity—from nuclear fuels: 0% of total installed capacity (2015 est.)
country comparison to the world: 65

Electricity—from hydroelectric plants: 98.7% of total installed capacity (2015 est.)
country comparison to the world: 4

Electricity—from other renewable sources: 0% of total installed capacity (2015 est.)
country comparison to the world: 175

Crude oil—production: 20,000 bbl/day (2016 est.)
country comparison to the world: 71

Crude oil—exports: 20,000 bbl/day (2014 est.)
country comparison to the world: 51

Crude oil—imports: 0 bbl/day (2014 est.)
country comparison to the world: 108

Crude oil—proved reserves: 180 million bbl (1 January 2017 es)
country comparison to the world: 60

Refined petroleum products—production: 0 bbl/day (2014 est.)
country comparison to the world: 132

Refined petroleum products—consumption: 30,000 bbl/day (2015 est.)
country comparison to the world: 122

Refined petroleum products—exports: 0 bbl/day (2014 est.)
country comparison to the world: 141

Refined petroleum products—imports: 36,410 bbl/day (2014 est.)
country comparison to the world: 96

Natural gas—production: 8.495 million cu m (2011 est.)
country comparison to the world: 96

Natural gas—consumption: 8.495 million cu m (2011 est.)
country comparison to the world: 114

Natural gas—exports: 0 cu m (2013 est.)
country comparison to the world: 82

Natural gas—imports: 0 cu m (2013 est.)
country comparison to the world: 106

Natural gas—proved reserves: 991.1 million cu m (1 January 2017 es)
country comparison to the world: 105

Carbon dioxide emissions from consumption of energy: 1.4 million Mt (2013 est.)
country comparison to the world: 159

COMMUNICATIONS

Telephones—fixed lines: *total subscriptions:* 0
subscriptions per 100 inhabitants: 8 (July 2016 est.)
country comparison to the world: 217

Telephones—mobile cellular: *total:* 37.753 million
subscriptions per 100 inhabitants: 48 (July 2016 est.)
country comparison to the world: 34

Telephone system: *general assessment:* barely adequate wire and microwave radio relay service in and between urban areas; domestic satellite system with 14 earth stations; inadequate fixed-line infrastructure
domestic: fixed-line connections only about 8 per 100 persons; given the backdrop of a wholly inadequate fixed-line infrastructure, the use of

mobile-cellular services has surged and mobile tel-edensity is over 45 per 100 persons
international: country code—243; satellite earth station—1 Intelsat (Atlantic Ocean) (2015)

Broadcast media: state-owned TV broadcast station with near national coverage; more than a dozen privately owned TV stations—2 with near national coverage; 2 state-owned radio stations are supplemented by more than 100 private radio stations; transmissions of at least 2 international broadcasters are available (2007)

Internet country code: .cd
Internet users: total: 3.016 million

percent of population: 3.8% (July 2016 est.)
country comparison to the world: 143

TRANSPORTATION

National air transport system: *number of registered air carriers:* 8
inventory of registered aircraft operated by air carriers: 13
annual passenger traffic on registered air carriers: 476,352
annual freight traffic on registered air carriers: 85,839 mt-km (2015)
Civil aircraft registration country code prefix: 9Q (2016)

Airports: 198 (2013)
country comparison to the world: 27

Airports—with paved runways: *total:* 26
over 3,047 m: 3
2,438 to 3,047 m: 3
1,524 to 2,437 m: 17
914 to 1,523 m: 2
under 914 m: 1 (2017)

Airports—with unpaved runways: *total:* 172
1,524 to 2,437 m: 20
914 to 1,523 m: 87
under 914 m: 65 (2013)

Heliports: 1 (2013)

Pipelines: gas 62 km; oil 77 km; refined products 756 km (2013)

Railways: *total:* 4,007 km
narrow gauge: 3,882 km 1.067-m gauge (858 km electrified); 125 km 1.000-m gauge (2014)
country comparison to the world: 44

Roadways: *total:* 153,497 km
paved: 2,794 km
unpaved: 150,703 km (2004)
country comparison to the world: 34

Waterways: 15,000 km (including the Congo River, its tributaries, and unconnected lakes) (2011)
country comparison to the world: 8

Merchant marine: *total:* 33
by type: general cargo 18, oil tanker 1, other 14 (2017)
country comparison to the world: 119

Ports and terminals: *major seaport(s):* Banana
river or lake port(s): Boma, Bumba, Kinshasa, Kisangani, Matadi, Mbandaka (Congo); Kindu

(Lualaba); Bukavu, Goma (Lake Kivu); Kalemie (Lake Tanganyika)

MILITARY AND SECURITY

Military expenditures: 1.34% of GDP (2016)
1.36% of GDP (2015)
1% of GDP (2014)
1.25% of GDP (2013)
1.21% of GDP (2012)
country comparison to the world: 49

Military branches: Armed Forces of the Democratic Republic of the Congo (Forces d'Armees de la Republique Democratique du Congo, FARDC): Army, National Navy (La Marine Nationale), Congolese Air Force (Force Aerienne Congolaise, FAC) (2011)

Military service age and obligation: 18-45 years of age for voluntary and compulsory military service (2012)

TRANSNATIONAL ISSUES

Disputes—international: heads of the Great Lakes states and UN pledged in 2004 to abate tribal, rebel, and militia fighting in the region, including northeast Congo, where the UN Organization Mission in the Democratic Republic of the Congo (MONUC), organized in 1999, maintains over 16,500 uniformed peacekeepers; members of Uganda's Lord's Resistance Army forces continue to seek refuge in Congo's Garamba National Park as peace talks with the Uganda Government evolve; the location of the boundary in the broad Congo River with the Republic of the Congo is indefinite except in the Pool Malebo/Stanley Pool area; Uganda and DRC dispute Rukwanzi Island in

Lake Albert and other areas on the Semliki River with hydrocarbon potential; boundary commission continues discussions over Congolese-administered triangle of land on the right bank of the Lunkinda River claimed by Zambia near the DRC village of Pweto; DRC accuses Angola of shifting monuments

Refugees and internally displaced persons: refugees (country of origin): 220,377 (Rwanda); 181,917 (Central African Republic); 88,970 (South Sudan) (refugees and asylum seekers); 44,450 (Burundi) (2017)
IDPs: 4.1 million (fighting between government forces and rebels since mid-1990s; conflict in Kasai region since 2016) (2017)

Trafficking in persons: *current situation:* The Democratic Republic of the Congo is a source, destination, and possibly a transit country for men, women, and children subjected to forced labor and sex trafficking; the majority of this trafficking is internal, and much of it is perpetrated by armed groups and rogue government forces outside official control in the country's unstable eastern provinces; Congolese adults are subjected to forced labor, including debt bondage, in unlicensed mines, and women may be forced into prostitution; Congolese women and girls are subjected to forced marriages where they are vulnerable to domestic servitude or sex trafficking, while children are forced to work in agriculture, mining, mineral smuggling, vending, portering, and begging; Congolese women and children migrate to countries in Africa, the Middle East, and Europe where some are subjected to forced prostitution, domestic servitude, and forced labor in agriculture and diamond mining; indigenous and foreign armed groups, including

the Lord's Resistance Army, abduct and forcibly recruit Congolese adults and children to serve as laborers, porters, domestics, combatants, and sex slaves; some elements of the Congolese national army (FARDC) also forced adults to carry supplies, equipment, and looted goods, but no cases of the FARDC recruiting child soldiers were reported in 2014—a significant change

tier rating: Tier 2 Watch List—The Democratic Republic of the Congo does not fully comply with the minimum standards for the elimination of trafficking; however, it is making significant efforts to do so; the government took significant steps to hold military and police officials complicit in human trafficking accountable with convictions for sex slavery and arrests of armed group commanders for the recruitment and use of child soldiers; the government appears to have ceased the recruitment of child soldiers through the implementation of a UN-backed action plan; little effort was made to address labor and sex trafficking crimes committed by persons other than officials, or to identify the victims, or to provide or refer the victims to care services; awareness of various forms of trafficking is limited among law enforcement personnel and training and resources are inadequate to conduct investigations (2015)

Illicit drugs: traffickers exploit lax shipping controls to transit pseudoephedrine through the capital; while rampant corruption and inadequate supervision leave the banking system vulnerable to money laundering, the lack of a well-developed financial system limits the country's utility as a money-laundering center

CONGO, REPUBLIC OF THE

INTRODUCTION

Background: Upon independence in 1960, the former French region of Middle Congo became the Republic of the Congo. A quarter century of experimentation with Marxism was abandoned

in 1990 and a democratically elected government took office in 1992. A brief civil war in 1997 restored former Marxist President Denis SASSOU-Nguesso, and ushered in a period of ethnic and political unrest. Southern-based rebel groups agreed to a final peace accord in March 2003. The Republic of Congo is one of Africa's largest petroleum producers, but with declining production it will need new offshore oil finds to sustain its oil earnings over the long term.

GEOGRAPHY

Location: Central Africa, bordering the South Atlantic Ocean, between Angola and Gabon

Geographic coordinates: 1 00 S, 15 00 E

Map references: Africa

Area: *total:* 342,000 sq km
land: 341,500 sq km
water: 500 sq km
country comparison to the world: 65

Area—comparative: slightly smaller than Montana

Land boundaries: *total:* 5,008 km
border countries (5): Angola 231 km, Cameroon 494 km, Central African Republic 487 km, Democratic Republic of the Congo 1,229 km, Gabon 2,567 km

Coastline: 169 km

Maritime claims: *territorial sea:* 12 nm
contiguous zone: 24 nm
exclusive economic zone: 200 nm

Climate: tropical; rainy season (March to June); dry season (June to October); persistent high temperatures and humidity; particularly enervating climate astride the Equator

Terrain: coastal plain, southern basin, central plateau, northern basin

Elevation: *mean elevation:* 430 m

elevation extremes: *lowest point:* Atlantic Ocean 0 m
highest point: Mount Berongou 903 m

Natural resources: petroleum, timber, potash, lead, zinc, uranium, copper, phosphates, gold, magnesium, natural gas, hydropower

Land use: *agricultural land:* 31.1%
arable land: 1.6%;
permanent crops: 0.2%;
permanent pasture: 29.3%
forest: 65.6%
other: 3.3% (2011 est.)
Irrigated land: 20 sq km (2012)

Population—distribution: the population is primarily located in the south, in and around the capital of Brazzaville

Natural hazards: seasonal flooding

Environment—current issues: air pollution from vehicle emissions; water pollution from raw sewage; tap water is not potable; deforestation

Environment—international agreements: *party to:* Biodiversity, Climate Change, Climate Change-Kyoto Protocol, Desertification, Endangered Species, Hazardous Wastes, Law of the Sea, Ozone Layer Protection, Ship Pollution, Tropical Timber 83, Tropical Timber 94, Wetlands
signed, but not ratified: none of the selected agreements

Geography—note: about 70% of the population lives in Brazzaville, Pointe-Noire, or along the railroad between them

PEOPLE AND SOCIETY

Population: 4,954,674
note: estimates for this country explicitly take into account the effects of excess mortality due to AIDS; this can result in lower life expectancy, higher infant mortality, higher death rates, lower population growth rates, and changes in the distribution of population by age and sex than would otherwise be expected (July 2017 est.)
country comparison to the world: 122

Nationality: *noun:* Congolese (singular and plural)
adjective: Congolese or Congo

Ethnic groups: Kongo 48%, Sangha 20%, M'Bochi 12%, Teke 17%, Europeans and other 3%

Languages: French (official), Lingala and Monokutuba (lingua franca trade languages), many local languages and dialects (of which Kikongo is the most widespread)

Religions: Roman Catholic 33.1%, Awakening Churches/Christian Revival 22.3%, Protestant 19.9%, Salutiste 2.2%, Muslim 1.6%, Kimbanguiste 1.5%, other 8.1%, none 11.3% (2010 est.)

Age structure: *0-14 years:* 41.67% (male 1,041,761/female 1,022,763)
15-24 years: 17.1% (male 424,521/female 422,755)
25-54 years: 33.89% (male 843,856/female 835,041)
55-64 years: 4.29% (male 106,776/female 105,573)
65 years and over: 3.06% (male 66,962/female 84,666) (2017 est.)

Dependency ratios: *total dependency ratio:* 84.5
youth dependency ratio: 78.3
elderly dependency ratio: 6.2
potential support ratio: 16.1 (2015 est.)

Median age: *total:* 19.7 years
male: 19.5 years

female: 19.8 years (2017 est.)
country comparison to the world: 192

Population growth rate: 2.11% (2017 est.)
country comparison to the world: 41

Birth rate: 34.4 births/1,000 population (2017 est.)
country comparison to the world: 22

Death rate: 9.5 deaths/1,000 population (2017 est.)
country comparison to the world: 52

Net migration rate: -3.8 migrant(s)/1,000 population (2017 est.)
country comparison to the world: 180

Population distribution: the population is primarily located in the south, in and around the capital of Brazzaville

Urbanization: *urban population:* 66.2% of total population (2017)
rate of urbanization: 3.02% annual rate of change (2015-20 est.)

Major urban areas—population: BRAZZAVILLE (capital) 1.888 million; Pointe-Noire 969,000 (2015)

Sex ratio: *at birth:* 1.03 male(s)/female
0-14 years: 1.02 male(s)/female
15-24 years: 1 male(s)/female
25-54 years: 1.01 male(s)/female
55-64 years: 0.99 male(s)/female
65 years and over: 0.78 male(s)/female
total population: 1.01 male(s)/female (2016 est.)

Mother's mean age at first birth: 19.8 years
note: median age at first birth among women 25-29 (2011/12 est.)

Maternal mortality ratio: 442 deaths/100,000 live births (2015 est.)
country comparison to the world: 25

Infant mortality rate: *total:* 54.9 deaths/1,000 live births
male: 59.8 deaths/1,000 live births
female: 49.9 deaths/1,000 live births (2017 est.)
country comparison to the world: 22

Life expectancy at birth: *total population:* 59.8 years
male: 58.6 years
female: 61.1 years (2017 est.)
country comparison to the world: 206

Total fertility rate: 4.59 children born/woman (2017 est.)
country comparison to the world: 22

Contraceptive prevalence rate: 30.1% (2014/15)

Health expenditures: 5.2% of GDP (2014)
country comparison to the world: 135

Physicians density: 0.11 physicians/1,000 population (2007)

Drinking water source:
improved:
urban: 95.8% of population
rural: 40% of population
total: 76.5% of population
unimproved:
urban: 4.2% of population
rural: 60% of population
total: 23.5% of population (2015 est.)

Sanitation facility access:
improved:
urban: 20% of population
rural: 5.6% of population
total: 15% of population
unimproved:
urban: 80% of population
rural: 94.4% of population
total: 85% of population (2015 est.)

HIV/AIDS—adult prevalence rate: 3.1% (2016 est.)
country comparison to the world: 19

HIV/AIDS—people living with HIV/AIDS: 91,000 (2016 est.)
country comparison to the world: 45

HIV/AIDS—deaths: 3,800 (2016 est.)
country comparison to the world: 37

Major infectious diseases: *degree of risk:* very high
food or waterborne diseases: bacterial and protozoal diarrhea, hepatitis A, and typhoid fever
vectorborne disease: malaria and dengue fever
animal contact disease: rabies
water contact disease: schistosomiasis (2016)

Obesity—adult prevalence rate: 9.6% (2016)
country comparison to the world: 143

Children under the age of 5 years underweight: 12.3% (2015)
country comparison to the world: 61

Education expenditures: 6.2% of GDP (2010)
country comparison to the world: 39

Literacy: *definition:* age 15 and over can read and write
total population: 79.3%
male: 86.4%
female: 72.9% (2015 est.)

School life expectancy (primary to tertiary education): *total:* 11 years
male: 11 years
female: 11 years (2012)

GOVERNMENT

Country name: *conventional long form:* Republic of the Congo
conventional short form: Congo (Brazzaville)
local long form: Republique du Congo
local short form: Congo
former: French Congo, Middle Congo, People's Republic of the Congo, Congo/Brazzaville
etymology: named for the Congo River, which makes up much of the country's eastern border; the river name derives from Kongo, a Bantu kingdom that occupied its mouth at the time of Portuguese discovery in the late 15th century and whose name stems from its people the Bakongo, meaning "hunters"

Government type: presidential republic

Capital: *name:* Brazzaville

geographic coordinates: 4 15 S, 15 17 E
time difference: UTC+1 (6 hours ahead of Washington, DC, during Standard Time)

Administrative divisions: 12 departments (departments, singular—department); Bouenza, Brazzaville, Cuvette, Cuvette-Ouest, Kouilou, Lekoumou, Likouala, Niari, Plateaux, Pointe-Noire, Pool, Sangha

Independence: 15 August 1960 (from France)

National holiday: Independence Day, 15 August (1960)

Constitution: history: several previous; latest approved by referendum 25 October 2015
amendments: proposed by the president of the republic or by Parliament; passage of presidential proposals requires Supreme Court review followed by approval in a referendum; such proposals may also be submitted directly to Parliament, in which case passage requires at least three-quarters majority vote of both houses in joint session; proposals by Parliament require three-fourths majority vote of both houses in joint session; constitutional articles including those affecting the country's territory, republican form of government, and secularity of the state are not amendable (2017)

Legal system: mixed legal system of French civil law and customary law

International law organization participation: has not submitted an ICJ jurisdiction declaration; accepts ICCt jurisdiction

Citizenship: *citizenship by birth:* no
citizenship by descent only: at least one parent must be a citizen of the Republic of the Congo
dual citizenship recognized: no
residency requirement for naturalization: 10 years

Suffrage: 18 years of age; universal

Executive branch: *chief of state:* President Denis SASSOU-Nguesso (since 25 October 1997)
head of government: Prime Minister (vacant); Prime Minister Clement MOUAMBA (since 23 April 2016) resigned on 18 August 2017; note—a constitutional referendum held in 2015 approved the change of the head of government from the president to the prime minister
cabinet: Council of Ministers appointed by the president
elections/appointments: president directly elected by absolute majority popular vote in 2 rounds if needed for a 5-year term (eligible for 2 additional terms); election last held on 20 March 2016 (next to be held in 2021)
election results: Denis SASSOU-Nguesso reelected president; percent of vote—Denis SASSOU-Nguesso (PCT) 60.4%, Guy Price Parfait KOLELAS (MCDDI) 15.1%, Jean-Marie MOKOKO (independent) 13.9%, Pascal Tsaty MABIALA (UPADS) 4.4%, other 6.2%

Legislative branch: description: bicameral Parliament or Parlement consists of the Senate (72 seats; members indirectly elected by regional councils by simple majority vote to serve 6-year terms with one-half of membership renewed every 3 years) and the National Assembly (151 seats; members directly elected in single-seat constituencies by absolute majority popular vote in 2 rounds if needed; members serve 5-year terms)

elections: Senate—last held on 12 October 2014 for expiry of half the seats (next to be held in 2020); National Assembly—last held on 16 and 30 July 2017 (next to be held in July 2022)
election results: Senate—percent of vote by party—NA; seats by party—RMP 33, FDU 23, UPADS 2, other 7, independent 7; National Assembly—percent of vote by party—NA; seats by party—PCT 89, MCDDI 7, UPADS 7, RDPS 5, MAR 4, RC 3, MUST 2, UPDP 2, CPR 1, PRL 1, PUR 1, UFD 1, UR 1, independent 12, vacant 3

Judicial branch: *highest court(s):* Supreme Court or Cour Supreme (consists of NA judges); Constitutional Court (consists of 9 members); note—a High Court of Justice, outside the judicial authority, tries cases involving treason by the president of the republic
judge selection and term of office: Supreme Court judges elected by Parliament and serve until age 65; Constitutional Court members appointed by the president of the republic—3 directly by the president and 6 nominated by Parliament; members appointed for renewable 9-year terms with one-third of the membership renewed every 3 years
subordinate courts: Court of Audit and Budgetary Discipline; courts of appeal; regional and district courts; employment tribunals; juvenile courts

Political parties and leaders: Action Movement for Renewal or MAR [Roland BOUITI-VIAUDO]
Citizen's Rally or RC [Claude Alphonse NSILOU]
Congolese Labour Party or PCT [Denis SASSOU-NGUESSO]
Congolese Movement for Democracy and Integral Development or MCDDI [Guy Price Parfait KOLELAS]
Movement for Unity, Solidarity, and Work or MUST [Claudine MUNARI]
Pan-African Union for Social Development or UPADS [Pascal Tsaty MABIALA]
Party for the Unity of the Republic or PUR
Patriotic Union for Democracy and Progress or UPDP [Auguste-Celestin GONGARD NKOUA]
Prospects and Realities Club or CPR
Rally for Democracy and Social Progress or RDPS [Bernard BATCHI]
Rally of the Presidential Majority or RMP
Republican and Liberal Party or PRL [Bonaventure MIZIDY]
Union for the Republic or UR
Union of Democratic Forces or UDF
Union for Democracy and Republic or UDR
many smaller parties

Political pressure groups and leaders: Congolese Trade Union Conferenation or CSC
General Union of Congolese Pupils and Students or UGEEC
Revolutionary Union of Congolese Women or URFC
Congolese Socialist Youth Union or UJSC

International organization participation: ACP, AfDB, AU, BDEAC, CEMAC, EITI (compliant country), FAO, FZ, G-77, IAEA, IBRD, ICAO, ICCt, ICRM, IDA, IFAD, IFC, IFRCS, ILO, IMF, IMO, Interpol, IOC, IOM, IPU, ISO

(correspondent), ITSO, ITU, ITUC (NGOs), MIGA, NAM, OIF, OPCW, UN, UNCTAD, UNESCO, UNHCR, UNIDO, UNITAR, UNWTO, UPU, WCO, WFTU (NGOs), WHO, WIPO, WMO, WTO

Diplomatic representation in the US: *chief of mission:* Ambassador Serge MOMBOULI (since 31 July 2001)
chancery: 1720 16th Street NW, Washington, DC 20009
telephone: [1] (202) 726-5500
FAX: [1] (202) 726-1860

Diplomatic representation from the US: *chief of mission:* Ambassador (vacant); Charge d'Affaires Mary DASCHBACH (since January 2015)
embassy: 70-83 Section D, Maya-Maya Boulevard, Brazzaville
mailing address: B.P. 1015, Brazzaville
telephone: [242] 06 612-2000

Flag description: divided diagonally from the lower hoist side by a yellow band; the upper triangle (hoist side) is green and the lower triangle is red; green symbolizes agriculture and forests, yellow the friendship and nobility of the people, red is unexplained but has been associated with the struggle for independence
note: uses the popular Pan-African colors of Ethiopia

National symbol(s): lion, elephant; national colors: green, yellow, red

National anthem: name: "La Congolaise" (The Congolese)
lyrics/music: Jacques TONDRA and Georges KIBANGHI/Jean ROYER and Joseph SPADILIERE
note: originally adopted 1959, restored 1991

ECONOMY

Economy—overview: The Republic of the Congo's economy is a mixture of subsistence farming, an industrial sector based largely on oil and support services, and government spending. Oil has supplanted forestry as the mainstay of the economy, providing a major share of government revenues and exports. Natural gas is increasingly being converted to electricity rather than being flared, greatly improving energy prospects. New mining projects, particularly iron ore, which entered production in late 2013, may add as much as $1 billion to annual government revenue. The Republic of the Congo is a member of the Central African Economic and Monetary Community (CEMAC) and shares a common currency–the Central African Franc–with five other member states in the region.

The current administration faces difficult economic challenges of stimulating recovery and reducing poverty. The recent drop in oil prices has constrained government spending; lower oil prices forced the government to cut more than $1 billion in planned spending. In 2017, in the wake of a multi-year recession, the country reached out to the IMF for a new program; the IMF noted that low oil prices, unsustainable debt, and significant governance weakness are key impediments to the country's economy. The fiscal deficit exceeded 18% of GDP in 2015, but had subsided to about 11% of GDP by 2017. The government's inability to pay civil servant salaries has resulted in multiple rounds of protests by many groups, including doctors, nurses, and teachers.

GDP (purchasing power parity): $29.16 billion (2017 est.)
$30.26 billion (2016 est.)
$31.13 billion (2015 est.)
note: data are in 2017 dollars
country comparison to the world: 135

GDP (official exchange rate): $7.799 billion (2016 est.)

GDP—real growth rate: -3.6% (2017 est.)
-2.8% (2016 est.)
2.6% (2015 est.)
country comparison to the world: 217

GDP—per capita (PPP): $6,700 (2017 est.)
$7,100 (2016 est.)
$7,500 (2015 est.)
note: data are in 2017 dollars
country comparison to the world: 162

Gross national saving: 13.5% of GDP (2017 est.)
-26.3% of GDP (2016 est.)
-2.2% of GDP (2015 est.)
country comparison to the world: 133

GDP—composition, by end use:
household consumption: 54.8%
government consumption: 12.8%
investment in fixed capital: 46.5%
investment in inventories: 0.1%
exports of goods and services: 58.2%
imports of goods and services: -72.4% (2017 est.)

GDP—composition, by sector of origin:
agriculture: 8.9%
industry: 50.8%
services: 40.3% (2017 est.)

Agriculture—products: cassava (manioc, tapioca), sugar, rice, corn, peanuts, vegetables, coffee, cocoa; forest products

Industries: petroleum extraction, cement, lumber, brewing, sugar, palm oil, soap, flour, cigarettes

Industrial production growth rate: 2% (2017 est.)
country comparison to the world: 136

Labor force: 2.055 million (2016 est.)
country comparison to the world: 124

Labor force—by occupation: agriculture: 35.4%
industry: 20.6%
services: 44% (2005 est.)

Unemployment rate: 36% (2014 est.)
country comparison to the world: 209

Population below poverty line: 46.5% (2011 est.)

Household income or consumption by percentage share: lowest 10%: 2.1%
highest 10%: 37.1% (2005)

Budget: revenues: $2.516 billion
expenditures: $3.336 billion (2017 est.)
Taxes and other revenues: 32.3% of GDP (2017 est.)
country comparison to the world: 72

Budget surplus (+) or deficit (-): -10.5% of GDP (2017 est.)
country comparison to the world: 209

Public debt: 92.2% of GDP (2017 est.)
83.1% of GDP (2016 est.)
country comparison to the world: 23

Fiscal year: calendar year

Inflation rate (consumer prices): -0.4% (2017 est.)
3.6% (2016 est.)
country comparison to the world: 5

Central bank discount rate: 4.25% (31 December 2009)
4.75% (31 December 2008)
country comparison to the world: 88

Commercial bank prime lending rate: 14% (31 December 2017 est.)
14% (31 December 2016 est.)
country comparison to the world: 51

Stock of narrow money: $2.955 billion (31 December 2017 est.)
$2.456 billion (31 December 2016 est.)
country comparison to the world: 120

Stock of broad money: $3.581 billion (31 December 2017 est.)
$3.037 billion (31 December 2016 est.)
country comparison to the world: 141

Stock of domestic credit: $2.703 billion (31 December 2017 est.)
$2.901 billion (31 December 2016 est.)
country comparison to the world: 139

Market value of publicly traded shares: $NA

Current account balance: -$1.243 billion (2017 est.)
-$5.514 billion (2016 est.)
country comparison to the world: 140

Exports: $5.238 billion (2017 est.)
$4.116 billion (2016 est.)
country comparison to the world: 106

Exports—commodities: petroleum, lumber, plywood, sugar, cocoa, coffee, diamonds

Exports—partners: China 39.8%, Italy 10.2%, Australia 7%, Gabon 6.6%, Angola 6%, Singapore 4.2% (2016)

Imports: $3.519 billion (2017 est.)
$3.498 billion (2016 est.)
country comparison to the world: 137

Imports—commodities: capital equipment, construction materials, foodstuffs

Imports—partners: South Korea 18.2%, France 12.8%, China 12.2%, Norway 11.2%, Belgium 6.9% (2016)

Reserves of foreign exchange and gold: $813.4 million (31 December 2017 est.)
$727.1 million (31 December 2016 est.)
country comparison to the world: 132

Debt—external: $5.197 billion (31 December 2017 est.)
$4.721 billion (31 December 2016 est.)
country comparison to the world: 135

Exchange rates: Cooperation Financiere en Afrique Centrale francs (XAF) per US dollar—

579.8 (2017 est.)
593.01 (2016 est.)
593.01 (2015 est.)
591.45 (2014 est.)
494.42 (2013 est.)

ENERGY

Electricity access: population without electricity: 2,600,000
electrification—total population: 42%
electrification—urban areas: 62%
electrification—rural areas: 5% (2013)

Electricity—production: 1.676 billion kWh (2015 est.)
country comparison to the world: 143

Electricity—consumption: 900.5 million kWh (2015 est.)
country comparison to the world: 158

Electricity—exports: 22 million kWh (2015 est.)
country comparison to the world: 90

Electricity—imports: 18 million kWh (2015 est.)
country comparison to the world: 109

Electricity—installed generating capacity: 545,000 kW (2015 est.)
country comparison to the world: 144

Electricity—from fossil fuels: 61.7% of total installed capacity (2015 est.)
country comparison to the world: 125

Electricity—from nuclear fuels: 0% of total installed capacity (2015 est.)
country comparison to the world: 64

Electricity—from hydroelectric plants: 38.3% of total installed capacity (2015 est.)
country comparison to the world: 55

Electricity—from other renewable sources: 0% of total installed capacity (2015 est.)
country comparison to the world: 174

Crude oil—production: 308,400 bbl/day (2016 est.)
country comparison to the world: 31

Crude oil—exports: 254,400 bbl/day (2014 est.)
country comparison to the world: 28

Crude oil—imports: 0 bbl/day (2014 est.)
country comparison to the world: 107

Crude oil—proved reserves: 1.6 billion bbl (1 January 2017 es)
country comparison to the world: 40

Refined petroleum products—production: 16,530 bbl/day (2014 est.)
country comparison to the world: 95

Refined petroleum products—consumption: 18,000 bbl/day (2015 est.)
country comparison to the world: 142

Refined petroleum products—exports: 6,058 bbl/day (2014 est.)
country comparison to the world: 92

Refined petroleum products—imports: 6,821 bbl/day (2014 est.)
country comparison to the world: 153

Natural gas—production: 1.5 billion cu m (2015 est.)

country comparison to the world: 62

Natural gas—consumption: 2.6 billion cu m (2015 est.)
country comparison to the world: 82

Natural gas—exports: 39 million cu m (2012 est.)
country comparison to the world: 51

Natural gas—imports: 0 cu m (2013 est.)
country comparison to the world: 105

Natural gas—proved reserves: 90.61 billion cu m (1 January 2017 es)
country comparison to the world: 56

Carbon dioxide emissions from consumption of energy: 6.5 million Mt (2013 est.)
country comparison to the world: 121

COMMUNICATIONS

Telephones—fixed lines: *total subscriptions:* 17,000
subscriptions per 100 inhabitants: less than 1 (July 2016 est.)
country comparison to the world: 193

Telephones—mobile cellular: *total:* 5.216 million
subscriptions per 100 inhabitants: 110 (July 2016 est.)
country comparison to the world: 118

Telephone system: *general assessment:* primary network consists of microwave radio relay and coaxial cable with services barely adequate for government use; key exchanges are in Brazzaville, Pointe-Noire, and Loubomo; intercity lines frequently out of order
domestic: fixed-line infrastructure inadequate, providing less than 1 connection per 100 persons; in the absence of an adequate fixed-line infrastructure, mobile-cellular subscribership has surged to 110 per 100 persons
international: country code—242; satellite earth station—1 Intelsat (Atlantic Ocean) (2015)

Broadcast media: 1 state-owned TV and 3 state-owned radio stations; several privately owned TV and radio stations; satellite TV service is available; rebroadcasts of several international broadcasters are available (2007)

Internet country code: .cg
Internet users: total: 362,000

percent of population: 7.6% (July 2016 est.)
country comparison to the world: 171

TRANSPORTATION

National air transport system: *number of registered air carriers:* 3

inventory of registered aircraft operated by air carriers: 12
annual passenger traffic on registered air carriers: 657,926
annual freight traffic on registered air carriers: 2,987,493 mt-km (2015)
Civil aircraft registration country code prefix: TN (2016)

Airports: 27 (2013)
country comparison to the world: 125

Airports—with paved runways: *total:* 8
over 3,047 m: 2
2,438 to 3,047 m: 1
1,524 to 2,437 m: 5 (2017)

Airports—with unpaved runways: *total:* 19
1,524 to 2,437 m: 8
914 to 1,523 m: 9
under 914 m: 2 (2013)

Pipelines: gas 232 km; liquid petroleum gas 4 km; oil 982 km (2013)

Railways: *total:* 510 km
narrow gauge: 510 km 1.067-m gauge (2014)
country comparison to the world: 113

Roadways: *total:* 17,000 km
paved: 1,212 km
unpaved: 15,788 km (2006)
country comparison to the world: 119

Waterways: 1,120 km (commercially navigable on Congo and Oubanqui Rivers above Brazzaville; there are many ferries across the river to Kinshasa; the Congo south of Brazzaville-Kinshasa to the coast is not navigable because of rapids, necessitating a rail connection to Pointe Noire; other rivers are used for local traffic only) (2011)
country comparison to the world: 61

Merchant marine: *total:* 40
by type: general cargo 27, oil tanker 2, other 11 (2017)
country comparison to the world: 121

Ports and terminals: *major seaport(s):* Pointe-Noire
river port(s): Brazzaville (Congo); Impfondo (Oubangi); Ouesso (Sangha); Oyo (Alima)
oil terminal(s): Djeno

MILITARY AND SECURITY

Military expenditures: 7.17% of GDP (2016)
4.97% of GDP (2014)
2.61% of GDP (2013)

Military branches: Congolese Armed Forces (Forces Armees Congolaises, FAC): Army (Armee de Terre), Navy, Congolese Air Force (Armee de

l'Air Congolaise); Gendarmerie; Special Presidential Security Guard (GSSP) (2013)

Military service age and obligation: 18 years of age for voluntary military service; women may serve in the Armed Forces (2012)

TRANSNATIONAL ISSUES

Disputes—international: the location of the boundary in the broad Congo River with the Democratic Republic of the Congo is undefined except in the Pool Malebo/Stanley Pool area

Refugees and internally displaced persons: refugees (country of origin): 9,202 (Rwanda) (2016); 31,688 (Central African Republic); 12,280 (Democratic Republic of the Congo) (2017)
IDPs: 33,000 (multiple civil wars since 1992) (2016)

Trafficking in persons: *current situation:* the Republic of the Congo is a source and destination country for children, men, and women, subjected to forced labor and sex trafficking; most trafficking victims are from Benin, the Democratic Republic of the Congo (DRC) and, to a lesser extent, other neighboring countries and are subjected to domestic servitude and market vending by West African and Congolese nationals; adults and children, the majority from the DRC, are also sex trafficked in Congo, mainly Brazzaville; internal trafficking victims, often from rural areas, are exploited as domestic servants or forced to work in quarries, bakeries, fishing, and agriculture
tier rating: Tier 2 Watch List—the Republic of the Congo does not fully comply with the minimum standards for the elimination of trafficking; however, it is making significant efforts to do so; the country drafted an action plan based on anti-trafficking legislation, which remains pending in the Supreme Court; the government made minimal anti-trafficking law enforcement efforts in 2014, failing to prosecute or convict suspected traffickers from cases dating back to 2010; serious allegations of official complicity continue to be reported; the government lacks a systematic means of identifying victims and relies on NGOs and international organizations to identify victims and NGOs and foster families to provide care to victims; the quality of care varied widely because the foster care system was allegedly undermined by inadequate security and official complicity (2015)

COOK ISLANDS

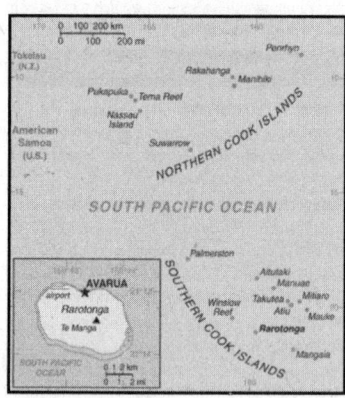

INTRODUCTION

Background: Named after Captain COOK, who sighted them in 1770, the islands became a British protectorate in 1888. By 1900, administrative control was transferred to New Zealand; in 1965, residents chose self-government in free association with New Zealand. The emigration of skilled workers to New Zealand, government deficits, and limited natural resources are of continuing concern.

GEOGRAPHY

Location: Oceania, group of islands in the South Pacific Ocean, about halfway between Hawaii and New Zealand

Geographic coordinates: 21 14 S, 159 46 W

Map references: Oceania

Area: *total:* 236 sq km
land: 236 sq km
water: 0 sq km
country comparison to the world: 215

Area—comparative: 1.3 times the size of Washington, DC

Land boundaries: 0 km

Coastline: 120 km

Maritime claims: *territorial sea:* 12 nm
exclusive economic zone: 200 nm
continental shelf: 200 nm or to the edge of the continental margin

Climate: tropical oceanic; moderated by trade winds; a dry season from April to November and a more humid season from December to March

Terrain: low coral atolls in north; volcanic, hilly islands in south

Elevation: *mean elevation:* NA

elevation extremes: *lowest point:* Pacific Ocean 0 m
highest point: Te Manga 652 m

Natural resources: coconuts (copra)

Land use: *agricultural land:* 8.4%

arable land: 4.2%;
permanent crops: 4.2%;
permanent pasture: 0%
forest: 64.6%
other: 27% (2011 est.)
Irrigated land: NA

Population—distribution: most of the population is found on the island of Rarotonga

Natural hazards: tropical cyclones (November to March)

Environment—current issues: limited land presents solid and liquid waste disposal problems; environmental degradation due to unregulated building

Environment—international agreements: *party to:* Biodiversity, Climate Change, Climate Change-Kyoto Protocol, Desertification, Hazardous Wastes, Law of the Sea, Ozone Layer Protection

Geography—note: the northern Cook Islands are seven low-lying, sparsely populated, coral atolls; the southern Cook Islands, where most of the population lives, consist of eight elevated, fertile, volcanic isles, including the largest, Rarotonga, at 67 sq km

PEOPLE AND SOCIETY

Population: 9,290 (July 2017 est.)
note: the Cook Islands' Ministry of Finance & Economic Management estimated the resident population to have been 11,700 in September 2016
country comparison to the world: 224

Nationality: *noun:* Cook Islander(s)
adjective: Cook Islander

Ethnic groups: Cook Island Maori (Polynesian) 81.3%, part Cook Island Maori 6.7%, other 11.9% (2011 est.)

Languages: English (official) 86.4%, Cook Islands Maori (Rarotongan) (official) 76.2%, other 8.3%
note: shares sum to more than 100% because some respondents gave more than one answer on the census (2011 est.)

Religions: Protestant 62.8% (Cook Islands Christian Church 49.1%, Seventh Day Adventist 7.9%, Assemblies of God 3.7%, Apostolic Church 2.1%), Roman Catholic 17%, Mormon 4.4%, other 8%, none 5.6%, no response 2.2% (2011 est.)

Age structure: *0-14 years:* 21.12% (male 1,036/female 926)
15-24 years: 16.63% (male 826/female 719)
25-54 years: 38.09% (male 1,767/female 1,772)
55-64 years: 11.99% (male 603/female 511)
65 years and over: 12.16% (male 557/female 573) (2017 est.)

Median age: *total:* 36.6 years
male: 36 years
female: 37 years (2017 est.)
country comparison to the world: 74

Population growth rate: -2.79% (2017 est.)
country comparison to the world: 234

Birth rate: 14 births/1,000 population (2017 est.)
country comparison to the world: 138

Death rate: 8.4 deaths/1,000 population (2017 est.)
country comparison to the world: 80

Population distribution: most of the population is found on the island of Rarotonga

Urbanization: *urban population:* 75% of total population (2017)
rate of urbanization: 0.8% annual rate of change (2015-20 est.)

Sex ratio: *at birth:* 1.04 male(s)/female
0-14 years: 1.12 male(s)/female
15-24 years: 1.14 male(s)/female
25-54 years: 1 male(s)/female
55-64 years: 1.17 male(s)/female
65 years and over: 0.97 male(s)/female
total population: 1.07 male(s)/female (2016 est.)

Infant mortality rate: *total:* 13 deaths/1,000 live births
male: 15.8 deaths/1,000 live births
female: 10.1 deaths/1,000 live births (2017 est.)
country comparison to the world: 109

Life expectancy at birth: *total population:* 76 years
male: 73.2 years
female: 79 years (2017 est.)
country comparison to the world: 93

Total fertility rate: 2.19 children born/woman (2017 est.)
country comparison to the world: 98

Health expenditures: 3.4% of GDP (2014)
country comparison to the world: 174

Physicians density: 1.19 physicians/1,000 population (2009)

Drinking water source:
improved:
urban: 99.9% of population
rural: 99.9% of population
total: 99.9% of population
unimproved:
urban: 0.1% of population
rural: 0.1% of population
total: 0.1% of population (2015 est.)

Sanitation facility access:
improved:
urban: 97.6% of population
rural: 97.6% of population
total: 97.6% of population
unimproved:
urban: 2.4% of population
rural: 2.4% of population
total: 2.4% of population (2015 est.)

HIV/AIDS—adult prevalence rate: NA

HIV/AIDS—people living with HIV/AIDS: NA

HIV/AIDS—deaths: NA

Obesity—adult prevalence rate: 55.9% (2016)
country comparison to the world: 2

Education expenditures: 4% of GDP (2015)
country comparison to the world: 137

School life expectancy (primary to tertiary education): *total:* 15 years
male: 15 years
female: 16 years (2015)

GOVERNMENT

Country name: *conventional long form:* none
conventional short form: Cook Islands
etymology: named after Captain James COOK, the British explorer who visited the islands in 1773 and 1777

Dependency status: self-governing in free association with New Zealand; Cook Islands is fully responsible for internal affairs; New Zealand retains responsibility for external affairs and defense in consultation with the Cook Islands

Government type: self-governing parliamentary democracy (Parliament of the Cook Islands) in free association with New Zealand

Capital: *name:* Avarua
geographic coordinates: 21 12 S, 159 46 W
time difference: UTC-10 (5 hours behind Washington, DC, during Standard Time)

Administrative divisions: none

Independence: none (became self-governing in free association with New Zealand on 4 August 1965 and has the right at any time to move to full independence by unilateral action)

National holiday: Constitution Day, first Monday in August (1965)

Constitution: 4 August 1965 (Cook Islands Constitution Act 1964); amended many times, last in 2004 (2016)

Legal system: common law similar to New Zealand common law

International law organization participation: has not submitted an ICJ jurisdiction declaration (New Zealand normally retains responsibility for external affairs); accepts ICCt jurisdiction

Suffrage: 18 years of age; universal

Executive branch: *chief of state:* Queen ELIZABETH II (since 6 February 1952); represented by Tom J. MARSTERS (since 9 August 2013); New Zealand High Commissioner Peter MARSHALL (since 10 January 2017)

head of government: Prime Minister Henry PUNA (since 30 November 2010)
cabinet: Cabinet chosen by the prime minister
elections/appointments: the monarchy is hereditary; UK representative appointed by the monarch; New Zealand high commissioner appointed by the New Zealand Government; following legislative elections, the leader of the majority party or majority coalition usually becomes prime minister

Legislative branch: description: unicameral Parliament, formerly the Legislative Assembly (24 seats; members directly elected in single-seat constituencies by simple majority vote to serve 4-year terms);

note—the House of Ariki, a 24-member parliamentary body of traditional leaders appointed by the Queen's representative serves as a consultative body to the Parliament
elections: last held on 9 July 2014 (next to be held by 2018)
election results: percent of vote by party—CIP 46.1%, Demo 42.3%, One Cook Islands 9.6%, other 2.0%; seats by party—CIP 13, Demo 9, One Cook Islands Movement 2

Judicial branch: highest resident court(s): Court of Appeal (consists of the chief justice and 3 judges of the High Court); High Court (consists of the chief justice and at least 4 judges and organized into civil, criminal, and land divisions); note—appeals beyond the Cook Islands Court of Appeal are heard by the Judicial Committee of the Privy Council (in London)
judge selection and term of office: High Court chief justice appointed by the Queen's Representative on the advice of the Executive Council tendered by the prime minister; other judges appointed by the Queen's Representative, on the advice of the Executive Council tendered by the chief justice, High Court chief justice, and the minister of justice; chief justice and judges appointed for 3-year renewable terms
subordinate courts: justices of the peace

Political parties and leaders: Cook Islands Party or CIP [Henry PUNA]
Democratic Party or Demo [William HEATHER]
One Cook Islands Movement [Teina BISHOP]

Political pressure groups and leaders: Political Reform Conference (lobby for political system changes)
other: various political change lobbyist groups

International organization participation: ACP, ADB, AOSIS, FAO, ICAO, ICCt, ICRM, IFAD, IFRCS, IMO, IMSO, IOC, ITUC (NGOs), OPCW, PIF, Sparteca, SPC, UNESCO, UPU, WHO, WMO

Diplomatic representation in the US: none (self-governing in free association with New Zealand)

Diplomatic representation from the US: none (self-governing in free association with New Zealand)

Flag description: blue with the flag of the UK in the upper hoist-side quadrant and a large circle of 15 white five-pointed stars (one for every island) centered in the outer half of the flag

National symbol(s): a circle of 15, five-pointed, white stars on a blue field, Tiare maori (Gardenia taitensis) flower; national colors: blue, white

National anthem: name: "Te Atua Mou E" (To God Almighty)
lyrics/music: Tepaeru Te RITO/Thomas DAVIS
note: adopted 1982; as prime minister, Sir Thomas DAVIS composed the anthem; his wife, a tribal chief, wrote the lyrics

ECONOMY

Economy—overview: Like many other South Pacific island nations, the Cook Islands' economic development is hindered by the isolation

of the country from foreign markets, the limited size of domestic markets, lack of natural resources, periodic devastation from natural disasters, and inadequate infrastructure. Agriculture, employing more than one-quarter of the working population, provides the economic base with major exports of copra and citrus fruit. Black pearls are the Cook Islands' leading export. Manufacturing activities are limited to fruit processing, clothing, and handicrafts. Trade deficits are offset by remittances from emigrants and by foreign aid overwhelmingly from New Zealand. In the 1980s and 1990s, the country became overextended, maintaining a bloated public service and accumulating a large foreign debt. Subsequent reforms, including the sale of state assets, the strengthening of economic management, the encouragement of tourism, and a debt restructuring agreement, have rekindled investment and growth.

GDP (purchasing power parity): $244.1 million (2010 est.)
$183.2 million (2005 est.)
country comparison to the world: 219

GDP (official exchange rate): $244.1 million (2010 est.)

GDP—real growth rate: 0.1% (2005 est.)
country comparison to the world: 201

GDP—per capita (PPP): $12,300 (2010 est.)
$9,100 (2005 est.)
country comparison to the world: 127

GDP—composition, by sector of origin:
agriculture: 5.1%
industry: 12.7%
services: 82.1% (2010 est.)

Agriculture—products: copra, citrus, pineapples, tomatoes, beans, pawpaws, bananas, yams, taro, coffee; pigs, poultry

Industries: fruit processing, tourism, fishing, clothing, handicrafts

Industrial production growth rate: 1% (2002)
country comparison to the world: 164

Labor force: 6,820 (2001)
country comparison to the world: 219

Labor force—by occupation: *agriculture:* 29%
industry: 15%
services: 56% (1995)

Unemployment rate: 13.1% (2005)
country comparison to the world: 165

Population below poverty line: NA%

Household income or consumption by percentage share: *lowest 10%:* NA%
highest 10%: NA%

Budget: *revenues:* $86.9 million
expenditures: $77.9 million (2010)
Taxes and other revenues: 35.6% of GDP (2010 est.)
country comparison to the world: 53

Budget surplus (+) or deficit (-): 3.7% of GDP (2010 est.)
country comparison to the world: 9

Fiscal year: 1 April—31 March

Inflation rate (consumer prices): 2.2% (2011 est.)

country comparison to the world: 103

Stock of narrow money: $38.99 million (31 December 2011 est.)
country comparison to the world: 191

Stock of broad money: $148.2 million (31 December 2011 est.)
$170.9 million (31 December 2010 est.)
country comparison to the world: 193

Current account balance: $26.67 million (2005)
country comparison to the world: 56

Exports: $3.125 million (2011 est.)
$5.163 million (2010 est.)
country comparison to the world: 219

Exports—commodities: copra, papayas, fresh and canned citrus fruit, coffee; fish; pearls and pearl shells; clothing

Imports: $109.3 million (2011 est.)
$90.62 million (2010 est.)
country comparison to the world: 212

Imports—commodities: foodstuffs, textiles, fuels, timber, capital goods

Debt—external: $141 million (1996 est.)
country comparison to the world: 191

Exchange rates: NZ dollars (NZD) per US dollar—
1.416 (2017 est.)
1.4341 (2016 est.)
1.4341 (2015 est.)
1.441 (2014 est.)
1.4279 (2013 est.)

ENERGY

Electricity—production: 32 million kWh (2015 est.)
country comparison to the world: 210

Electricity—consumption: 29.76 million kWh (2015 est.)
country comparison to the world: 209

Electricity—exports: 0 kWh (2016 est.)
country comparison to the world: 127

Electricity—imports: 0 kWh (2016 est.)
country comparison to the world: 140

Electricity—installed generating capacity: 10,000 kW (2015 est.)
country comparison to the world: 208

Electricity—from fossil fuels: 80% of total installed capacity (2015 est.)
country comparison to the world: 89

Electricity—from nuclear fuels: 0% of total installed capacity (2015 est.)
country comparison to the world: 75

Electricity—from hydroelectric plants: 0% of total installed capacity (2015 est.)
country comparison to the world: 170

Electricity—from other renewable sources: 30% of total installed capacity (2015 est.)
country comparison to the world: 14

Crude oil—production: 0 bbl/day (2016 est.)
country comparison to the world: 123

Crude oil—exports: 0 bbl/day (2014 est.)
country comparison to the world: 112

Crude oil—imports: 0 bbl/day (2014 est.)
country comparison to the world: 115

Crude oil—proved reserves: 0 bbl (1 January 2017 es)
country comparison to the world: 122

Refined petroleum products—production: 0 bbl/day (2014 est.)
country comparison to the world: 133

Refined petroleum products—consumption: 530 bbl/day (2015 est.)
country comparison to the world: 210

Refined petroleum products—exports: 0 bbl/day (2014 est.)
country comparison to the world: 147

Refined petroleum products—imports: 528.2 bbl/day (2014 est.)
country comparison to the world: 205

Natural gas—production: 0 cu m (2013 est.)
country comparison to the world: 125

Natural gas—consumption: 0 cu m (2013 est.)
country comparison to the world: 173

Natural gas—exports: 0 cu m (2013 est.)
country comparison to the world: 91

Natural gas—imports: 0 cu m (2013 est.)
country comparison to the world: 115

Natural gas—proved reserves: 0 cu m (1 January 2014 es)
country comparison to the world: 131

Carbon dioxide emissions from consumption of energy: 200,000 Mt (2013 est.)
country comparison to the world: 201

COMMUNICATIONS

Telephones—fixed lines: *total:* 7,800
subscriptions per 100 inhabitants: 75 (July 2016 est.)
country comparison to the world: 202

Telephones—mobile cellular: *total:* 11,000
subscriptions per 100 inhabitants: 105 (July 2016 est.)
country comparison to the world: 213

Telephone system: *general assessment:* Telecom Cook Islands offers international direct dialing, Internet, email, fax, and Telex
domestic: individual islands are connected by a combination of satellite earth stations, microwave systems, and VHF and HF radiotelephone; within the islands, service is provided by small exchanges connected to subscribers by open-wire, cable, and fiber-optic cable
international: country code—682; satellite earth station—1 Intelsat (Pacific Ocean) (2015)

Broadcast media: 1 privately owned TV station broadcasts from Rarotonga providing a mix of local news and overseas-sourced programs (2016)

Internet country code: .ck
Internet users: total: 5,160

percent of population: 54.0% (July 2016 est.)
country comparison to the world: 216

TRANSPORTATION

National air transport system: *number of registered air carriers:* 1
inventory of registered aircraft operated by air carriers: 1 (2015)
Civil aircraft registration country code prefix: E5 (2016)

Airports: 11 (2013)
country comparison to the world: 153

Airports—with paved runways: *total:* 1
1,524 to 2,437 m: 1 (2017)

Airports—with unpaved runways: *total:* 10
1,524 to 2,437 m: 2
914 to 1,523 m: 7
under 914 m: 1 (2013)

Roadways: *total:* 320 km
paved: 33 km
unpaved: 287 km (2003)
country comparison to the world: 204

Merchant marine: *total:* 218
by type: bulk carrier 27, container ship 5, general cargo 102, oil tanker 17, other 67 (2017)
country comparison to the world: 62

Ports and terminals: *major seaport(s):* Avatiu

MILITARY AND SECURITY

Military branches: no regular military forces; National Police Department

Military—note: defense is the responsibility of New Zealand in consultation with the Cook Islands and at its request

TRANSNATIONAL ISSUES

Disputes—international: none

CORAL SEA ISLANDS

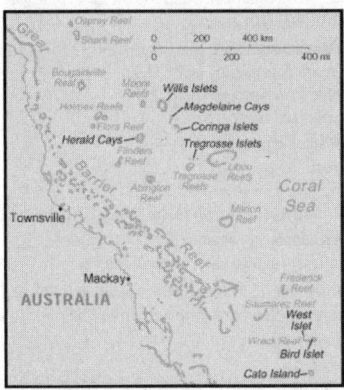

INTRODUCTION

Background: Scattered over more than three-quarters of a million square kilometers of ocean, the Coral Sea Islands were declared a territory of Australia in 1969. They are uninhabited except for a small meteorological staff on the Willis Islets. Automated weather stations, beacons, and a lighthouse occupy many other islands and reefs. The Coral Sea Islands Act 1969 was amended in 1997 to extend the boundaries of the Coral Sea Islands Territory around Elizabeth and Middleton Reefs.

GEOGRAPHY

Location: Oceania, islands in the Coral Sea, northeast of Australia

Geographic coordinates: 18 00 S, 152 00 E

Map references: Oceania

Area: *total:* less than 3 sq km
land: less than 3 sq km
water: 0 sq km
note: includes numerous small islands and reefs scattered over a sea area of about 780,000 sq km

(300,000 sq mi) with the Willis Islets the most important
country comparison to the world: 252

Area—comparative: about four times the size of the National Mall in Washington, DC

Land boundaries: 0 km

Coastline: 3,095 km

Maritime claims: *territorial sea:* 3 nm
exclusive fishing zone: 200 nm

Climate: tropical

Terrain: sand and coral reefs and islands (cays)

Elevation: *mean elevation:* NA

elevation extremes: *lowest point:* Pacific Ocean 0 m
highest point: unnamed location on Cato Island 9 m

Natural resources: fish

Land use: *agricultural land:* 0%
arable land: 0%;
permanent crops: 0%;
permanent crops: 0%
forest: 0%
other: 100% (mostly grass or scrub cover) (2011 est.)

Natural hazards: occasional tropical cyclones

Environment—current issues: no permanent freshwater resources

Geography—note: important nesting area for birds and turtles

PEOPLE AND SOCIETY

Population: no indigenous inhabitants
note: there is a staff of four at the meteorological station on Willis Island (2017 est.)

GOVERNMENT

Country name: *conventional long form:* Coral Sea Islands Territory

conventional short form: Coral Sea Islands
etymology: self-descriptive name to reflect the islands' position in the Coral Sea off the northeastern coast of Australia

Dependency status: territory of Australia; administered from Canberra by the Department of Regional Australia, Local Government, Arts and Sport

Legal system: the common law legal system of Australia, where applicable, applies

Citizenship: see Australia

Diplomatic representation in the US: none (territory of Australia)

Diplomatic representation from the US: none (territory of Australia)

Flag description: the flag of Australia is used

ECONOMY

Economy—overview: no economic activity

COMMUNICATIONS

Communications—note: automatic weather stations on many of the isles and reefs relay data to the mainland

TRANSPORTATION

Ports and terminals: none; offshore anchorage only

MILITARY AND SECURITY

Military—note: defense is the responsibility of Australia

TRANSNATIONAL ISSUES

Disputes—international: none

COSTA RICA

INTRODUCTION

Background: Although explored by the Spanish early in the 16th century, initial attempts at colonizing Costa Rica proved unsuccessful due to a combination of factors, including disease from mosquito-infested swamps, brutal heat, resistance by natives, and pirate raids. It was not until 1563 that a permanent settlement of Cartago was established in the cooler, fertile central highlands. The area remained a colony for some two and a half centuries. In 1821, Costa Rica became one of several Central American provinces that

jointly declared their independence from Spain. Two years later it joined the United Provinces of Central America, but this federation disintegrated in 1838, at which time Costa Rica proclaimed its sovereignty and independence. Since the late 19th century, only two brief periods of violence have marred the country's democratic development. In 1949, Costa Rica dissolved its armed forces. Although it still maintains a large agricultural sector, Costa Rica has expanded its economy to include strong technology and tourism industries. The standard of living is relatively high. Land ownership is widespread.

GEOGRAPHY

Location: Central America, bordering both the Caribbean Sea and the North Pacific Ocean, between Nicaragua and Panama

Geographic coordinates: 10 00 N, 84 00 W

Map references: Central America and the Caribbean

Area: *total:* 51,100 sq km
land: 51,060 sq km
water: 40 sq km
note: includes Isla del Coco
country comparison to the world: 130

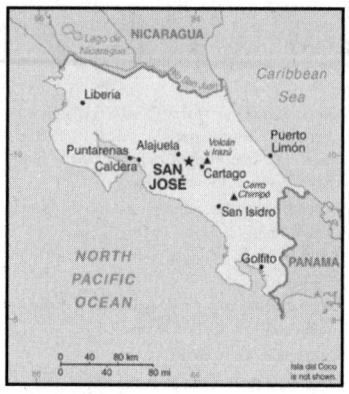

Area—comparative: slightly smaller than West Virginia

Land boundaries: *total:* 661 km
border countries (2): Nicaragua 313 km, Panama 348 km

Coastline: 1,290 km

Maritime claims: *territorial sea:* 12 nm
exclusive economic zone: 200 nm
continental shelf: 200 nm

Climate: tropical and subtropical; dry season (December to April); rainy season (May to November); cooler in highlands

Terrain: coastal plains separated by rugged mountains including over 100 volcanic cones, of which several are major active volcanoes

Elevation: *mean elevation:* 746 m

elevation extremes: *lowest point:* Pacific Ocean 0 m
highest point: Cerro Chirripo 3,819 m

Natural resources: hydropower

Land use: *agricultural land:* 37.1%
arable land: 4.9%
permanent crops: 6.7%
permanent pasture: 25.5%
forest: 51.5%
other: 11.4% (2011 est.)
Irrigated land: 1,015 sq km (2012)

Population—distribution: roughly half of the nation's population resides in urban areas; the capital of San Jose is the largest city and home to approximately one-fifth of the population

Natural hazards: occasional earthquakes, hurricanes along Atlantic coast; frequent flooding of lowlands at onset of rainy season and landslides; active volcanoes
volcanism: Arenal (1,670 m), which erupted in 2010, is the most active volcano in Costa Rica; a 1968 eruption destroyed the town of Tabacon; Irazu (3,432 m), situated just east of San Jose, has the potential to spew ash over the capital city as it did between 1963 and 1965; other historically active volcanoes include Miravalles, Poas, Rincon de la Vieja, and Turrialba

Environment—current issues: deforestation and land use change, largely a result of the clearing of land for cattle ranching and agriculture; soil erosion; coastal marine pollution; fisheries protection; solid waste management; air pollution

Environment—international agreements: *party to:* Biodiversity, Climate Change, Climate Change-Kyoto Protocol, Desertification, Endangered Species, Environmental Modification, Hazardous Wastes, Law of the Sea, Marine Dumping, Ozone Layer Protection, Wetlands, Whaling
signed, but not ratified: Marine Life Conservation

Geography—note: four volcanoes, two of them active, rise near the capital of San Jose in the center of the country; one of the volcanoes, Irazu, erupted destructively in 1963-65

PEOPLE AND SOCIETY

Population: 4,930,258 (July 2017 est.)
country comparison to the world: 123

Nationality: *noun:* Costa Rican(s)
adjective: Costa Rican

Ethnic groups: white or mestizo 83.6%, mulato 6.7%, indigenous 2.4%, black of African descent 1.1%, other 1.1%, none 2.9%, unspecified 2.2% (2011 est.)

Languages: Spanish (official), English

Religions: Roman Catholic 76.3%, Evangelical 13.7%, Jehovah's Witness 1.3%, other Protestant 0.7%, other 4.8%, none 3.2%

Demographic profile: Costa Rica's political stability, high standard of living, and well-developed social benefits system set it apart from its Central American neighbors. Through the government's sustained social spending—almost 20% of GDP annually—Costa Rica has made tremendous progress toward achieving its goal of providing universal access to education, healthcare, clean water, sanitation, and electricity. Since the 1970s, expansion of these services has led to a rapid decline in infant mortality, an increase in life expectancy at birth, and a sharp decrease in the birth rate. The average number of children born per women has fallen from about 7 in the 1960s to 3.5 in the early 1980s to below replacement level today. Costa Rica's poverty rate is lower than in most Latin American countries, but it has stalled at around 20% for almost two decades.

Costa Rica is a popular regional immigration destination because of its job opportunities and social programs. Almost 9% of the population is foreign-born, with Nicaraguans comprising nearly three-quarters of the foreign population. Many Nicaraguans who perform unskilled seasonal labor enter Costa Rica illegally or overstay their visas, which continues to be a source of tension. Less than 3% of Costa Rica's population lives abroad. The overwhelming majority of expatriates have settled in the United States after completing a university degree or in order to work in a highly skilled field.

Age structure: *0-14 years:* 22.61% (male 570,063/female 544,502)
15-24 years: 16.35% (male 410,993/female 394,865)

25-54 years: 44.03% (male 1,092,504/female 1,078,458)
55-64 years: 9.2% (male 220,879/female 232,530)
65 years and over: 7.82% (male 177,882/female 207,582) (2017 est.)

Dependency ratios: *total dependency ratio:* 45.4
youth dependency ratio: 32.4
elderly dependency ratio: 12.9
potential support ratio: 7.7 (2015 est.)

Median age: *total:* 31.3 years
male: 30.8 years
female: 31.8 years (2017 est.)
country comparison to the world: 108

Population growth rate: 1.16% (2017 est.)
country comparison to the world: 98

Birth rate: 15.5 births/1,000 population (2017 est.)
country comparison to the world: 120

Death rate: 4.7 deaths/1,000 population (2017 est.)
country comparison to the world: 201

Net migration rate: 0.8 migrant(s)/1,000 population (2017 est.)
country comparison to the world: 60

Population distribution: roughly half of the nation's population resides in urban areas; the capital of San Jose is the largest city and home to approximately one-fifth of the population

Urbanization: *urban population:* 78.5% of total population (2017)
rate of urbanization: 2.1% annual rate of change (2015-20 est.)

Major urban areas—population: SAN JOSE (capital) 1.17 million (2015)

Sex ratio: *at birth:* 1.05 male(s)/female
0-14 years: 1.05 male(s)/female
15-24 years: 1.04 male(s)/female
25-54 years: 1.01 male(s)/female
55-64 years: 0.95 male(s)/female
65 years and over: 0.86 male(s)/female
total population: 1.01 male(s)/female (2016 est.)

Maternal mortality ratio: 25 deaths/100,000 live births (2015 est.)
country comparison to the world: 124

Infant mortality rate: *total:* 8 deaths/1,000 live births
male: 8.8 deaths/1,000 live births
female: 7.3 deaths/1,000 live births (2017 est.)
country comparison to the world: 154

Life expectancy at birth: *total population:* 78.7 years
male: 76.1 years
female: 81.5 years (2017 est.)
country comparison to the world: 58

Total fertility rate: 1.89 children born/woman (2017 est.)
country comparison to the world: 139

Contraceptive prevalence rate: 76.2% (2011)

Health expenditures: 9.3% of GDP (2014)
country comparison to the world: 33

Physicians density: 1.15 physicians/1,000 population (2013)

Hospital bed density: 1.2 beds/1,000 population (2012)

Drinking water source:
improved:
urban: 99.6% of population
rural: 91.9% of population
total: 97.8% of population
unimproved:
urban: 0.4% of population
rural: 8.1% of population
total: 2.2% of population (2015 est.)

Sanitation facility access:
improved:
urban: 95.2% of population
rural: 92.3% of population
total: 94.5% of population
unimproved:
urban: 4.8% of population
rural: 7.7% of population
total: 5.5% of population (2015 est.)

HIV/AIDS—adult prevalence rate: 0.4% (2016 est.)
country comparison to the world: 72

HIV/AIDS—people living with HIV/AIDS: 13,000 (2016 est.)
country comparison to the world: 86

HIV/AIDS—deaths: <500 (2016 est.)

Major infectious diseases: *degree of risk:* intermediate
food or waterborne diseases: bacterial diarrhea
vectorborne diseases: dengue fever
note: active local transmission of Zika virus by Aedes species mosquitoes has been identified in this country (as of August 2016); it poses an important risk (a large number of cases possible) among US citizens if bitten by an infective mosquito; other less common ways to get Zika are through sex, via blood transfusion, or during pregnancy, in which the pregnant woman passes Zika virus to her fetus (2016)

Obesity—adult prevalence rate: 25.7% (2016)
country comparison to the world: 48

Children under the age of 5 years underweight: 1.1% (2008)
country comparison to the world: 130

Education expenditures: 7.6% of GDP (2015)
country comparison to the world: 34

Literacy: *definition:* age 15 and over can read and write
total population: 97.8%
male: 97.7%
female: 97.8% (2015 est.)

School life expectancy (primary to tertiary education): *total:* 15 years
male: 15 years
female: 16 years (2015)

Unemployment, youth ages 15-24: *total:* 23.3%
male: 18.8%
female: 31.7% (2016 est.)
country comparison to the world: 62

GOVERNMENT

Country name: *conventional long form:* Republic of Costa Rica
conventional short form: Costa Rica
local long form: Republica de Costa Rica

local short form: Costa Rica
etymology: the name means "rich coast" in Spanish and was first applied in the early colonial period of the 16th century

Government type: presidential republic

Capital: *name:* San Jose
geographic coordinates: 9 56 N, 84 05 W
time difference: UTC-6 (1 hour behind Washington, DC, during Standard Time)

Administrative divisions: 7 provinces (provincias, singular—provincia); Alajuela, Cartago, Guanacaste, Heredia, Limon, Puntarenas, San Jose

Independence: 15 September 1821 (from Spain)

National holiday: Independence Day, 15 September (1821)

Constitution: previous 1825; latest effective 8 November 1949; amended many times, last in 2015 (2016)

Legal system: civil law system based on Spanish civil code; judicial review of legislative acts in the Supreme Court

International law organization participation: accepts compulsory ICJ jurisdiction; accepts ICCt jurisdiction

Citizenship: *citizenship by birth:* yes
citizenship by descent: yes
dual citizenship recognized: yes
residency requirement for naturalization: 7 years

Suffrage: 18 years of age; universal and compulsory

Executive branch: *chief of state:* President Luis Guillermo SOLIS Rivera (since 8 May 2014); First Vice President Helio FALLAS Venega (since 8 May 2014); Second Vice President Ana Helena CHACON Echeverria (since 8 May 2014); note—the president is both chief of state and head of government

head of government: President Luis Guillermo SOLIS Rivera (since 8 May 2014); First Vice President Helio FALLAS Venegas (since 8 May 2014); Second Vice President Ana Helena CHACON Echeverria (since 8 May 2014)
cabinet: Cabinet selected by the president
elections/appointments: president and vice presidents directly elected on the same ballot by modified majority popular vote (40% threshold) for a 4-year term (eligible for non-consecutive terms); election last held on 2 February 2014 with a runoff on 6 April 2014 (next to be held in February 2018)
election results: Luis Guillermo SOLIS Rivera elected president; percent of vote—Luis Guillermo SOLIS Rivera (PAC) 77.8%; Johnny ARAYA (PLN) 22.2%

Legislative branch: description: unicameral Legislative Assembly or Asamblea Legislativa (57 seats; members directly elected in multi-seat constituencies—corresponding to the country's 7 provinces—by proportional representation vote; members serve 4-year terms)
elections: last held on 2 February 2014 (next to be held in February 2018)
election results: percent of vote by party—PLN 25.5%, PAC 23.8%, FA 13.1%, PUSC 10.0%,

PML 7.9%, other 19.7% ; seats by party—PLN 18, PAC 13, FA 9, PUSC 8, PML 4, other 5

Judicial branch: *highest court(s):* Supreme Court of Justice (consists of 22 judges organized into 3 cassation chambers each with 5 judges and the Constitutional Chamber with 7 judges)
judge selection and term of office: Supreme Court of Justice judges elected by the National Assembly for 8-year terms with renewal decided by the National Assembly
subordinate courts: appellate courts; trial courts; first instance and justice of the peace courts; Superior Electoral Tribunal

Political parties and leaders: Accessibility Without Exclusion or PASE [Oscar Andres LOPEZ Arias]
Broad Front (Frente Amplio) or PFA [Ana Patricia MORA]
Citizen Action Party or PAC [Olivier PEREZ Gonzalez]
Costa Rican Renovation Party or PRC [Gerardo Justo OROZCO Alvarez]
Libertarian Movement Party or ML [Victor Danilo CUBERO Corrales]
National Integration Party or PIN [Walter MUNOZ Cespedes]
National Liberation Party or PLN [Bernal JIMENEZ]
National Restoration Party or PRN [Carlos AVENDANO]
Patriotic Alliance [Jorge ARAYA Westover]
Popular Vanguard [Humberto VARGAS]
Social Christian Unity Party or PUSC [Gerardo VARGAS]

Political pressure groups and leaders: Authentic Confederation of Democratic Workers or CATD (Communist Party affiliate)
National Chamber of Coffee Growers
Confederated Union of Workers or CUT (Communist Party affiliate)
Confederation of Workers Rerum Novarum or CTRN (National Libertion Party affiliate)
Costa Rican Confederation of Democratic Workers or CCTD (National Libertion Party affiliate)
Costa Rican Exporter's Chamber or CADEXCO
Costa Rican Solidarity Movement
Costa Rican Union of Private Sector Enterprises or UCCAEP
Federation of Public Service Workers or FTSP
National Association for Economic Development or ANFE
National Association of Educators or ANDE
National Association of Public and Private Employees or ANEP

International organization participation: BCIE, CACM, CD, CELAC, FAO, G-77, IADB, IAEA, IBRD, ICAO, ICC (national committees), ICCt, ICRM, IDA, IFAD, IFC, IFRCS, ILO, IMF, IMO, IMSO, Interpol, IOC, IOM, IPU, ISO, ITSO, ITU, ITUC (NGOs), LAES, LAIA (observer), MIGA, NAM (observer), OAS, OIF (observer), OPANAL, OPCW, Pacific Alliance (observer), PCA, SICA, UN, UNCTAD, UNESCO, UNHCR, UNIDO, Union Latina, UNWTO,

UPU, WCO, WFTU (NGOs), WHO, WIPO, WMO, WTO

Diplomatic representation in the US: *chief of mission:* Ambassador Roman MACAYA Hayes (since 18 September 2014)
chancery: 2114 S Street NW, Washington, DC 20008
telephone: [1] (202) 480-2200
FAX: [1] (202) 265-4795
consulate(s) general: Atlanta, Chicago, Houston, Los Angeles, Miami, New Orleans, New York, San Juan (Puerto Rico), Tampa (FL), Washington DC
consulate(s): San Francisco

Diplomatic representation from the US: *chief of mission:* Ambassador Sharon DAY (since 5 October 2017)
embassy: Calle 98 Via 104, Pavas, San Jose
mailing address: APO AA 34020
telephone: [506] 2519-2000
FAX: [506] 2519-2305

Flag description: five horizontal bands of blue (top), white, red (double width), white, and blue, with the coat of arms in a white elliptical disk placed toward the hoist side of the red band; Costa Rica retained the earlier blue-white-blue flag of Central America until 1848 when, in response to revolutionary activity in Europe, it was decided to incorporate the French colors into the national flag and a central red stripe was added; today the blue color is said to stand for the sky, opportunity, and perseverance, white denotes peace, happiness, and wisdom, while red represents the blood shed for freedom, as well as the generosity and vibrancy of the people
note: somewhat resembles the flag of North Korea; similar to the flag of Thailand but with the blue and red colors reversed

National symbol(s): yiguirro (clay-colored robin); national colors: blue, white, red

National anthem: name: "Himno Nacional de Costa Rica" (National Anthem of Costa Rica)
lyrics/music: Jose Maria ZELEDON Brenes/ Manuel Maria GUTIERREZ
note: adopted 1949; the anthem's music was originally written for an 1853 welcome ceremony for diplomatic missions from the US and UK; the lyrics were added in 1903

ECONOMY

Economy—overview: Since 2010, Costa Rica has enjoyed strong and stable economic growth—4.3% in 2016. Exports of bananas, coffee, sugar, and beef are the backbone of its commodity exports. Various industrial and processed agricultural products have broadened exports in recent years, as have high value-added goods, including medical devices. Costa Rica's impressive biodiversity also makes it a key destination for ecotourism.

Foreign investors remain attracted by the country's political stability and relatively high education levels, as well as the incentives offered in the free-trade zones; Costa Rica has attracted one of the highest levels of foreign direct investment per capita in Latin America. The US-Central American-Dominican Republic Free Trade Agreement (CAFTA-DR), which became effective for Costa Rica in 2009, helped increase foreign direct investment in key sectors of the economy, including insurance and telecommunication. However, poor infrastructure, high energy costs, a complex bureaucracy, weak investor protection, and uncertainty of contract enforcement impede greater investment.

Costa Rica's economy also faces challenges due to a rising fiscal deficit, rising public debt, and relatively low levels of domestic revenue. Poverty has remained around 20-25% for nearly 20 years, and the government's strong social safety net has eroded due to increased constraints on its expenditures. Costa Rica's credit rating was downgraded from stable to negative in 2015, upping pressure on lending rates—which could hurt small business, on the budget deficit—which could hurt infrastructure development, and on the rate of return on investment—which could soften foreign direct investment (FDI). Unlike the rest of Central America, Costa Rica is not highly dependent on remittances—which represented just 0.7% of GDP in 2015, but instead relies on FDI—which accounted for 4% of GDP.

GDP (purchasing power parity): $85.2 billion (2017 est.)
$82.08 billion (2016 est.)
$78.68 billion (2015 est.)
note: data are in 2017 dollars
country comparison to the world: 92

GDP (official exchange rate): $58.91 billion (2016 est.)

GDP—real growth rate: 3.8% (2017 est.)
4.3% (2016 est.)
4.7% (2015 est.)
country comparison to the world: 82

GDP—per capita (PPP): $17,200 (2017 est.)
$16,700 (2016 est.)
$16,200 (2015 est.)
note: data are in 2017 dollars
country comparison to the world: 101

Gross national saving: 16.2% of GDP (2017 est.)
16.5% of GDP (2016 est.)
15.9% of GDP (2015 est.)
country comparison to the world: 118

GDP—composition, by end use:
household consumption: 63.6%
government consumption: 17.2%
investment in fixed capital: 19.3%
investment in inventories: 0.4%
exports of goods and services: 32.9%
imports of goods and services: -33.3% (2017 est.)

GDP—composition, by sector of origin:
agriculture: 5.5%
industry: 21%
services: 73.5% (2017 est.)

Agriculture—products: bananas, pineapples, coffee, melons, ornamental plants, sugar, corn, rice, beans, potatoes; beef, poultry, dairy; timber

Industries: medical equipment, food processing, textiles and clothing, construction materials, fertilizer, plastic products

Industrial production growth rate: 4.4% (2017 est.)
country comparison to the world: 61

Labor force: 2.229 million
note: official estimate; excludes Nicaraguans living in Costa Rica (2017 est.)
country comparison to the world: 121

Labor force—by occupation: *agriculture:* 14%
industry: 22%
services: 64% (2006 est.)

Unemployment rate: 8.1% (2017 est.)
9.3% (2016 est.)
country comparison to the world: 111

Population below poverty line: 21.7% (2014 est.)

Household income or consumption by percentage share: *lowest 10%:* 1.5%
highest 10%: 36.9% (2014 est.)

Distribution of family income—Gini index: 48.5 (2014)
49.2 (2013)
country comparison to the world: 22

Budget: *revenues:* $8.262 billion
expenditures: $11.34 billion (2017 est.)
Taxes and other revenues: 14% of GDP (2017 est.)
country comparison to the world: 197

Budget surplus (+) or deficit (-): -5.2% of GDP (2017 est.)
country comparison to the world: 165

Public debt: 66.2% of GDP (2017 est.)
62.7% of GDP (2016 est.)
country comparison to the world: 58

Fiscal year: calendar year

Inflation rate (consumer prices): 1.7% (2017 est.)
0% (2016 est.)
country comparison to the world: 75

Central bank discount rate: 3.5% (31 December 2016 est.)
21.5% (31 December 2010)
country comparison to the world: 101

Commercial bank prime lending rate: 11.8% (31 December 2017 est.)
11.64% (31 December 2016 est.)
country comparison to the world: 69

Stock of narrow money: $5.765 billion (31 December 2017 est.)
$5.536 billion (31 December 2016 est.)
country comparison to the world: 100

Stock of broad money: $22.52 billion (31 December 2017 est.)
$21.85 billion (31 December 2016 est.)
country comparison to the world: 86

Stock of domestic credit: $34.3 billion (31 December 2017 est.)
$33.43 billion (31 December 2016 est.)
country comparison to the world: 75

Market value of publicly traded shares: $2.015 billion (31 December 2012 est.)
$1.443 billion (31 December 2011 est.)
$1.445 billion (31 December 2010 est.)
country comparison to the world: 100

Current account balance: -$2.291 billion (2017 est.)

-$1.88 billion (2016 est.)
country comparison to the world: 160

Exports: $10.55 billion (2017 est.)
$10.15 billion (2016 est.)
country comparison to the world: 87

Exports—commodities: bananas, pineapples, coffee, melons, ornamental plants, sugar; beef; seafood; electronic components, medical equipment

Exports—partners: US 41%, Netherlands 5.8%, Panama 5.7%, Belgium 5.4%, Nicaragua 5.2%, Guatemala 5.2% (2016)

Imports: $15.55 billion (2017 est.)
$14.66 billion (2016 est.)
country comparison to the world: 83

Imports—commodities: raw materials, consumer goods, capital equipment, petroleum, construction materials

Imports—partners: US 37.1%, China 13.5%, Mexico 6.9% (2016)

Reserves of foreign exchange and gold: $7.523 billion (31 December 2017 est.)
$7.574 billion (31 December 2016 est.)
country comparison to the world: 80

Debt—external: $25.83 billion (31 December 2017 est.)
$24.3 billion (31 December 2016 est.)
country comparison to the world: 87

Stock of direct foreign investment—at home: $35.01 billion (31 December 2017 est.)
$31.84 billion (31 December 2016 est.)
country comparison to the world: 67

Stock of direct foreign investment—abroad: $4.327 billion (31 December 2017 est.)
$3.781 billion (31 December 2016 est.)
country comparison to the world: 75

Exchange rates: Costa Rican colones (CRC) per US dollar—
573.5 (2017 est.)
544.74 (2016 est.)
544.74 (2015 est.)
534.57 (2014 est.)
538.32 (2013 est.)

ENERGY

Electricity access: *population without electricity:* 24,362
electrification—*total population:* 99.5%
electrification—urban areas: 99.9%
electrification—rural areas: 98.3% (2013)

Electricity—production: 10.38 billion kWh (2015 est.)
country comparison to the world: 99

Electricity—consumption: 9.113 billion kWh (2015 est.)
country comparison to the world: 98

Electricity—exports: 643 million kWh (2015 est.)
country comparison to the world: 62

Electricity—imports: 537 million kWh (2015 est.)
country comparison to the world: 79

Electricity—installed generating capacity: 3.127 million kW (2015 est.)
country comparison to the world: 97

Electricity—from fossil fuels: 21% of total installed capacity (2015 est.)
country comparison to the world: 194

Electricity—from nuclear fuels: 0% of total installed capacity (2015 est.)
country comparison to the world: 71

Electricity—from hydroelectric plants: 62% of total installed capacity (2015 est.)
country comparison to the world: 25

Electricity—from other renewable sources: 17.6% of total installed capacity (2015 est.)
country comparison to the world: 38

Crude oil—production: 0 bbl/day (2016 est.)
country comparison to the world: 124

Crude oil—exports: 0 bbl/day (2014 est.)
country comparison to the world: 108

Crude oil—imports: 0 bbl/day (2014 est.)
country comparison to the world: 112

Crude oil—proved reserves: 0 bbl (1 January 2017 es)
country comparison to the world: 123

Refined petroleum products—production: 0 bbl/day (2014 est.)
country comparison to the world: 134

Refined petroleum products—consumption: 54,000 bbl/day (2015 est.)
country comparison to the world: 101

Refined petroleum products—exports: 0 bbl/day (2014 est.)
country comparison to the world: 144

Refined petroleum products—imports: 53,140 bbl/day (2014 est.)
country comparison to the world: 80

Natural gas—production: 0 cu m (2013 est.)
country comparison to the world: 122

Natural gas—consumption: 0 cu m (2013 est.)
country comparison to the world: 170

Natural gas—exports: 0 cu m (2013 est.)
country comparison to the world: 87

Natural gas—imports: 0 cu m (2013 est.)
country comparison to the world: 111

Natural gas—proved reserves: 0 cu m (1 January 2014 es)
country comparison to the world: 128

Carbon dioxide emissions from consumption of energy: 7.616 million Mt (2013 est.)
country comparison to the world: 112

COMMUNICATIONS

Telephones—fixed lines: *total subscriptions:* 827,000
subscriptions per 100 inhabitants: 17 (July 2016 est.)
country comparison to the world: 82

Telephones—mobile cellular: *total:* 8,063,091
subscriptions per 100 inhabitants: 165 (July 2016 est.)
country comparison to the world: 104

Telephone system: *general assessment:* good domestic telephone service in terms of breadth of coverage

domestic: point-to-point and point-to-multi-point microwave, fiber-optic, and coaxial cable link rural areas; Internet service is available
international: country code—506; landing points for the Americas Region Caribbean Ring System (ARCOS-1), MAYA-1, and the Pan American Crossing submarine cables that provide links to South and Central America, parts of the Caribbean, and the US; connected to Central American Microwave System; satellite earth stations—2 Intelsat (Atlantic Ocean) (2015)

Broadcast media: multiple privately owned TV stations and 1 publicly owned TV station; cable network services are widely available; more than 100 privately owned radio stations and a public radio network (2017)

Internet country code: .cr
Internet users: total: 3,217,277
percent of population: 66.0% (July 2016 est.)
country comparison to the world: 92

TRANSPORTATION

National air transport system: *number of registered air carriers:* 1
inventory of registered aircraft operated by air carriers: 39
annual passenger traffic on registered air carriers: 1,617,075
annual freight traffic on registered air carriers: 9,284,160 mt-km (2015)
Civil aircraft registration country code prefix: TI (2016)

Airports: 161 (2013)
country comparison to the world: 35

Airports—with paved runways: *total:* 47
2,438 to 3,047 m: 2
1,524 to 2,437 m: 2
914 to 1,523 m: 27
under 914 m: 16 (2017)

Airports—with unpaved runways: *total:* 114
914 to 1,523 m: 18
under 914 m: 96 (2013)

Pipelines: refined products 662 km (2013)

Railways: *total:* 278 km
narrow gauge: 278 km 1.067-m gauge
note: the entire rail network fell into disrepair and out of use at the end of the 20th century; since 2005, certain sections of rail have been rehabilitated (2014)
country comparison to the world: 124

Roadways: *total:* 39,018 km
paved: 10,133 km
unpaved: 28,885 km (2010)
country comparison to the world: 90

Waterways: 730 km (seasonally navigable by small craft) (2011)
country comparison to the world: 74

Merchant marine: *total:* 10
by type: general cargo 2, other 8 (2017)
country comparison to the world: 144

Ports and terminals: *major seaport(s):* Atlantic Ocean (Caribbean)—Puerto Limon; Pacific Ocean—Caldera

MILITARY AND SECURITY

Military branches: no regular military forces; Ministry of Public Security, Government, and Police (2011)

TRANSNATIONAL ISSUES

Disputes—international: Costa Rica and Nicaragua regularly file border dispute cases over the delimitations of the San Juan River and the northern tip of Calero Island to the International Court of Justice (ICJ); in 2009, the ICJ ruled that Costa Rican vessels carrying out police activities could not use the river, but official Costa Rican vessels providing essential services to riverside inhabitants and Costa Rican tourists could travel freely on the river; in 2011, the ICJ provisionally ruled that both countries must remove personnel from the disputed area; in 2013, the ICJ rejected Nicaragua's 2012 suit to halt Costa Rica's construction of a highway paralleling the river on the grounds of irreparable environmental damage; in 2013, the ICJ, regarding the disputed territory, ordered that Nicaragua should refrain from dredging or canal construction and refill and repair damage caused by trenches connecting the river to the Caribbean and upheld its 2010 ruling that Nicaragua must remove all personnel; in early 2014, Costa Rica brought Nicaragua to the ICJ over offshore oil concessions in the disputed region

Refugees and internally displaced persons: *stateless persons:* 127 (2016)

Trafficking in persons: *current situation:* Costa Rica is a source, transit, and destination country for men, women, and children subjected to sex trafficking and forced labor; Costa Rican women and children, as well as those from Nicaragua, the Dominican Republic, and other Latin American countries, are sex trafficked in Costa Rica; child sex tourism is a particular problem with offenders coming from the US and Europe; men and children from Central America, including indigenous Panamanians, and Asia are exploited in agriculture, construction, fishing, and commerce; Nicaraguans transit Costa Rica to reach Panama, where some are subjected to forced labor or sex trafficking

tier rating: Tier 2 Watch List–Costa Rica does not fully comply with the minimum standards for the elimination of trafficking; however, it is making significant efforts to do so; anti-trafficking law enforcement efforts declined in 2014, with fewer prosecutions and no convictions and no actions taken against complicit government personnel; some officials conflated trafficking with smuggling, and authorities reported the diversion of funds to combat smuggling hindered anti-trafficking efforts; the government identified more victims than the previous year but did not make progress in ensuring that victims received adequate protective services; specialized services were limited and mostly provided by NGOs without government support, even from a dedicated fund for anti-trafficking efforts; victims services were virtually non-existent outside of the capital (2015)

Illicit drugs: transshipment country for cocaine and heroin from South America; illicit production of cannabis in remote areas; domestic cocaine consumption, particularly crack cocaine, is rising; significant consumption of amphetamines; seizures of smuggled cash in Costa Rica and at the main border crossing to enter Costa Rica from Nicaragua have risen in recent years

COTE D'IVOIRE

INTRODUCTION

Background: Close ties to France following independence in 1960, the development of cocoa production for export, and foreign investment all made Cote d'Ivoire one of the most prosperous of the West African states but did not protect it from political turmoil. In December 1999, a military coup—the first ever in Cote d'Ivoire's history—overthrew the government. Junta leader Robert GUEI blatantly rigged elections held in late 2000 and declared himself the winner. Popular protest forced him to step aside and an election brought Laurent GBAGBO into power. Ivoirian dissidents and disaffected members of the military launched a failed coup attempt in September 2002 that developed into a rebellion and then a civil war. In 2003, a cease-fire resulted in the country being divided with the rebels holding the north, the government the south, and peacekeeping forces a buffer zone between the two. In March 2007, President GBAGBO and former New Forces rebel leader Guillaume SORO signed an agreement in which SORO joined GBAGBO's government as prime minister and the two agreed to reunite the country by dismantling the buffer zone, integrating rebel forces into the national armed forces, and holding elections. Difficulties in preparing electoral registers delayed balloting until 2010. In November 2010, Alassane Dramane OUATTARA won the presidential election over GBAGBO, but GBAGBO refused to hand over power, resulting in a five-month resumption of violent conflict. In April 2011, after widespread fighting, GBAGBO was formally forced from office by armed OUATTARA supporters with the help of UN and French forces. The UN peacekeeping mission departed in June 2017. OUATTARA is focused on rebuilding the country's economy and infrastructure while rebuilding the security forces. GBAGBO is in The Hague on trial for crimes against humanity.

GEOGRAPHY

Location: Western Africa, bordering the North Atlantic Ocean, between Ghana and Liberia

Geographic coordinates: 8 00 N, 5 00 W

Map references: Africa

Area: *total:* 322,463 sq km
land: 318,003 sq km
water: 4,460 sq km
country comparison to the world: 70

Area—comparative: slightly larger than New Mexico

Land boundaries: *total:* 3,458 km
border countries (5): Burkina Faso 545 km, Ghana 720 km, Guinea 816 km, Liberia 778 km, Mali 599 km

Coastline: 515 km

Maritime claims: *territorial sea:* 12 nm
exclusive economic zone: 200 nm
continental shelf: 200 nm

Climate: tropical along coast, semiarid in far north; three seasons—warm and dry (November to March), hot and dry (March to May), hot and wet (June to October)

Terrain: mostly flat to undulating plains; mountains in northwest

Elevation: *mean elevation:* 250 m

elevation extremes: *lowest point:* Gulf of Guinea 0 m
highest point: Monts Nimba 1,752 m

Natural resources: petroleum, natural gas, diamonds, manganese, iron ore, cobalt, bauxite, copper, gold, nickel, tantalum, silica sand, clay, cocoa beans, coffee, palm oil, hydropower

Land use: *agricultural land:* 64.8%
arable land: 9.1%;
permanent crops: 14.2%;
permanent pasture: 41.5%
forest: 32.7%
other: 2.5% (2011 est.)

Irrigated land: 730 sq km (2012)

Population—distribution: the population is primarily located in the forested south, with the highest concentration of people residing in and around the cities on the Atlantic coast; most of the northern savanna remains sparsely populated with higher concentrations located along transportation corridors

Natural hazards: coast has heavy surf and no natural harbors; during the rainy season torrential flooding is possible

Environment—current issues: deforestation (most of the country's forests—once the largest in West Africa—have been heavily logged); water pollution from sewage and industrial and agricultural effluents

Environment—international agreements: *party to:* Biodiversity, Climate Change, Climate Change-Kyoto Protocol, Desertification, Endangered Species, Hazardous Wastes, Law of the Sea, Marine Dumping, Ozone Layer Protection, Ship Pollution, Tropical Timber 83, Tropical Timber 94, Wetlands, Whaling
signed, but not ratified: none of the selected agreements

Geography—note: most of the inhabitants live along the sandy coastal region; apart from the capital area, the forested interior is sparsely populated

PEOPLE AND SOCIETY

Population: 24,184,810
note: estimates for this country explicitly take into account the effects of excess mortality due to AIDS; this can result in lower life expectancy, higher infant mortality, higher death rates, lower population growth rates, and changes in the distribution of population by age and sex than would otherwise be expected (July 2017 est.)
country comparison to the world: 54

Nationality: *noun:* Ivoirian(s)
adjective: Ivoirian

Ethnic groups: Akan 28.8%, Voltaique or Gur 16.1%, Northern Mande 14.5%, Kru 8.5%, Southern Mande 6.9%, unspecified 0.9%, non-Ivoirian 42.3% (2014 est.)

Languages: French (official), 60 native dialects of which Dioula is the most widely spoken

Religions: Muslim 42.9%, Catholic 17.2%, Evangelical 11.8%, Methodist 1.7%, other Christian 3.2%, animist 3.6%, other religion 0.5%, none 19.1%
note: the majority of foreign migrant workers are Muslim (72.7%) and Christian (17.7%) (2014 est.)

Demographic profile: Cote d'Ivoire's population is likely to continue growing for the foreseeable future because almost 60% of the populace is younger than 25, the total fertility rate is holding steady at about 3.5 children per woman, and contraceptive use is under 20%. The country will need to improve education, health care, and gender equality in order to turn its large and growing youth cohort into human capital. Even

prior to 2010 unrest that shuttered schools for months, access to education was poor, especially for women. As of 2015, only 53% of men and 33% of women were literate. The lack of educational attainment contributes to Cote d'Ivoire's high rates of unskilled labor, adolescent pregnancy, and HIV/AIDS prevalence.

Following its independence in 1960, Cote d'Ivoire's stability and the blossoming of its labor-intensive cocoa and coffee industries in the southwest made it an attractive destination for migrants from other parts of the country and its neighbors, particularly Burkina Faso. The HOUPHOUET-BOIGNY administration continued the French colonial policy of encouraging labor immigration by offering liberal land ownership laws. Foreigners from West Africa, Europe (mainly France), and Lebanon composed about 25% of the population by 1998.

Ongoing economic decline since the 1980s and the power struggle after HOUPHOUET-BOIGNY's death in 1993 ushered in the politics of "Ivoirite," institutionalizing an Ivoirian identity that further marginalized northern Ivoirians and scapegoated immigrants. The hostile Muslim north-Christian south divide snowballed into a 2002 civil war, pushing tens of thousands of foreign migrants, Liberian refugees, and Ivoirians to flee to war-torn Liberia or other regional countries and more than a million people to be internally displaced. Subsequently, violence following the contested 2010 presidential election prompted some 250,000 people to seek refuge in Liberia and other neighboring countries and again internally displaced as many as a million people. By July 2012, the majority had returned home, but ongoing inter-communal tension and armed conflict continue to force people from their homes.

Age structure: *0-14 years:* 36.97% (male 4,508,541/female 4,431,979)
15-24 years: 20.91% (male 2,549,588/female 2,508,317)
25-54 years: 34.58% (male 4,272,294/female 4,090,997)
55-64 years: 4.04% (male 490,918/female 486,702)
65 years and over: 3.5% (male 403,757/female 441,717) (2017 est.)

Dependency ratios: *total dependency ratio:* 83.8
youth dependency ratio: 78.5
elderly dependency ratio: 5.3
potential support ratio: 18.9 (2015 est.)

Median age: *total:* 20.9 years
male: 21 years
female: 20.9 years (2017 est.)
country comparison to the world: 187

Population growth rate: 1.84% (2017 est.)
country comparison to the world: 55

Birth rate: 27.7 births/1,000 population (2017 est.)
country comparison to the world: 45

Death rate: 9.4 deaths/1,000 population (2017 est.)
country comparison to the world: 53

Net migration rate: 0 migrant(s)/1,000 population (2017 est.)
country comparison to the world: 79

Population distribution: the population is primarily located in the forested south, with the highest concentration of people residing in and around the cities on the Atlantic coast; most of the northern savanna remains sparsely populated with higher concentrations located along transportation corridors

Urbanization: *urban population:* 55.5% of total population (2017)
rate of urbanization: 3.39% annual rate of change (2015-20 est.)

Major urban areas—population: YAMOUS-SOUKRO (capital) 259,000 (2014); ABIDJAN (seat of government) 4.86 million; Bouake 762,000 (2015)

Sex ratio: *at birth:* 1.03 male(s)/female
0-14 years: 1.02 male(s)/female
15-24 years: 1.02 male(s)/female
25-54 years: 1.05 male(s)/female
55-64 years: 1.01 male(s)/female
65 years and over: 0.93 male(s)/female
total population: 1.02 male(s)/female (2016 est.)

Mother's mean age at first birth: 19.8 years
note: median age at first birth among women 25-29 (2011/12 est.)

Maternal mortality ratio: 645 deaths/100,000 live births (2015 est.)
country comparison to the world: 12

Infant mortality rate: *total:* 55.8 deaths/1,000 live births
male: 61.5 deaths/1,000 live births
female: 49.8 deaths/1,000 live births (2017 est.)
country comparison to the world: 21

Life expectancy at birth: *total population:* 59 years
male: 57.8 years
female: 60.2 years (2017 est.)
country comparison to the world: 207

Total fertility rate: 3.38 children born/woman (2017 est.)
country comparison to the world: 45

Contraceptive prevalence rate: 18.2% (2011/12)

Health expenditures: 5.7% of GDP (2014)
country comparison to the world: 113

Physicians density: 0.14 physicians/1,000 population (2008)

Hospital bed density: 0.4 beds/1,000 population (2006)

Drinking water source:
improved:
urban: 93.1% of population
rural: 68.8% of population
total: 81.9% of population
unimproved:
urban: 6.9% of population
rural: 31.2% of population
total: 18.1% of population (2015 est.)

Sanitation facility access:
improved:
urban: 32.8% of population

rural: 10.3% of population
total: 22.5% of population
unimproved:
urban: 67.2% of population
rural: 89.7% of population
total: 77.5% of population (2015 est.)

HIV/AIDS—adult prevalence rate: 2.7% (2016 est.)
country comparison to the world: 22

HIV/AIDS—people living with HIV/AIDS: 460,000 (2016 est.)
country comparison to the world: 15

HIV/AIDS—deaths: 25,000 (2016 est.)
country comparison to the world: 11

Major infectious diseases: *degree of risk:* very high
food or waterborne diseases: bacterial diarrhea, hepatitis A, and typhoid fever
vectorborne diseases: malaria, dengue fever, and yellow fever
water contact disease: schistosomiasis
animal contact disease: rabies
respiratory disease: meningococcal meningitis (2016)

Obesity—adult prevalence rate: 10.3% (2016)
country comparison to the world: 139

Children under the age of 5 years underweight: 15.7% (2012)
country comparison to the world: 43

Education expenditures: 4.7% of GDP (2014)
country comparison to the world: 89

Literacy: *definition:* age 15 and over can read and write
total population: 43.1%
male: 53.1%
female: 32.5% (2015 est.)

School life expectancy (primary to tertiary education): *total:* 9 years
male: 10 years
female: 8 years (2015)

GOVERNMENT

Country name: *conventional long form:* Republic of Cote d'Ivoire
conventional short form: Cote d'Ivoire
local long form: Republique de Cote d'Ivoire
local short form: Cote d'Ivoire
note: pronounced coat-div-whar
former: Ivory Coast
etymology: name reflects the intense ivory trade that took place in the region from the 15th to 17th centuries

Government type: presidential republic

Capital: *name:* Yamoussoukro (legislative capital), Abidjan (administrative capital); note—although Yamoussoukro has been the official capital since 1983, Abidjan remains the administrative capital as well as the officially designated commercial capital; the US, like other countries, maintains its Embassy in Abidjan
geographic coordinates: 6 49 N, 5 16 W
time difference: UTC 0 (5 hours ahead of Washington, DC, during Standard Time)

Administrative divisions: 12 districts and 2 autonomous districts*; Abidjan*, Bas-Sassandra, Comoe, Denguele, Goh-Djiboua, Lacs, Lagunes, Montagnes, Sassandra-Marahoue, Savanes, Vallee du Bandama, Woroba, Yamoussoukro*, Zanzan

Independence: 7 August 1960 (from France)

National holiday: Independence Day, 7 August (1960)

Constitution: history: previous 1960, 2000; latest draft completed 24 September 2016, approved by the National Assembly 11 October 2016, approved by referendum 30 October 2016, promulgated 8 November 2016
amendments: proposed by the president of the republic or by Parliament; consideration of drafts or proposals requires an absolute majority vote by the parliamentary membership; passage of amendments affecting presidential elections, presidential term of office and vacancies, and amendment procedures requires approval by absolute majority in a referendum; passage of other proposals by the president requires at least four-fifths majority vote by Parliament; constitutional articles on the sovereignty of the state and its republican and secular form of government cannot be amended (2017)

Legal system: civil law system based on the French civil code; judicial review of legislation held in the Constitutional Chamber of the Supreme Court

International law organization participation: accepts compulsory ICJ jurisdiction with reservations; accepts ICCt jurisdiction

Citizenship: *citizenship by birth:* no
citizenship by descent only: at least one parent must be a citizen of Cote d'Ivoire
dual citizenship recognized: no
residency requirement for naturalization: 5 years

Suffrage: 18 years of age; universal

Executive branch: *chief of state:* President Alassane Dramane OUATTARA (since 4 December 2010); Vice President Daniel Kablan DUNCAN (since 16 January 2017); note—the constitution of 2016 calls for the position of a vice-president

head of government: Prime Minister Amadou Gon COULIBALY (since 11 January 2017)
cabinet: Council of Ministers appointed by the president
elections/appointments: president directly elected by absolute majority popular vote in 2 rounds if needed for a 5-year term (no term limits); election last held on 25 October 2015 (next to be held in 2020); prime minister appointed by the president; note—the 2016 constitution limits the presidential tenure to 2 terms beginning with the 2020 election; the vice president is named by the president
election results: Alassane OUATTARA reelected president; percent of vote—Alassane OUATTARA (RDR) 83.7%, Pascal Affi N'GUESSAN (FPI) 9.3%, Konan Bertin KOUADIO (independent) 3.9%, other 3.1%

Legislative branch: description: unicameral Parliament consists of the National Assembly (255 seats; members directly elected in single- and multi-seat constituencies by simple majority vote to serve 5-year terms); note—the new constitution of November 2016 calls for a bicameral legislature with the addition of a Senate, with one-third of members appointed by the president and two-thirds indirectly appointed by municipal and regional councils
elections: last held on 18 December 2016 (next to be held on December 2021)
election results: percent of vote by party—RHDP 50.3%, FPI 5.8%, UDPCI 3.0%, UPCI 1.0%, independent 38.5%, other 1.39%; seats by party—RHDP 167, UDPCI 6, FPI 3, UPCI 3, independent 76

Judicial branch: *highest court(s):* Supreme Court or Cour Supreme (organized into Judicial, Audit, Constitutional, and Administrative Chambers; consists of the court president, 3 vice-presidents for the Judicial, Audit, and Administrative chambers, and 9 associate justices or magistrates)
judge selection and term of office: judges nominated by the Superior Council of the Magistrature, a 7-member body consisting of the national president (chairman), 3 "bench" judges, and 3 public prosecutors; judges appointed for life
subordinate courts: Courts of Appeal (organized into civil, criminal, and social chambers); first instance courts; peace courts

Political parties and leaders: Democratic Party of Cote d'Ivoire or PDCI [Henri Konan BEDIE]
Ivorian Popular Front or FPI [Pascal Affi N'GUESSAN]
Liberty and Democracy for the Republic or LIDER [Mamadou KOULIBALY]
Movement of the Future Forces or MFA [Innocent Augustin ANAKY KOBENA]
Rally of the Republicans or RDR [Henriette DIABATE]
Union for Cote d'Ivoire or UPCI [Gnamien KONAN]
Union for Democracy and Peace in Cote d'Ivoire or UDPCI [Albert Toikeusse MABRI]
other: more than 144 smaller registered parties

Political pressure groups and leaders: Federation of University and High School Students of Cote d'Ivoire or FESCI [Fulgene ASSI]
National Congress for the Resistance and Democracy or CNRD [Bernard DADIE]
Panafrican Congress for Justice and Peoples Equality or COJEP [Roselin BLY]

International organization participation: ACP, AfDB, AU, ECOWAS, EITI (compliant country), Entente, FAO, FZ, G-24, G-77, IAEA, IBRD, ICAO, ICC, ICCt, ICRM, IDA, IDB, IFAD, IFC, IFRCS, ILO, IMF, IMO, Interpol, IOC, IOM, IPU, ISO, ITSO, ITU, ITUC (NGOs), MIGA, MINUSMA, MONUSCO, NAM, OIC, OIF, OPCW, UN, UNCTAD, UNESCO, UNHCR, UNIDO, Union Latina, UNWTO, UPU, WADB (regional), WAEMU, WCO, WFTU (NGOs), WHO, WIPO, WMO, WTO

Diplomatic representation in the US: *chief of mission:* Ambassador Daouda DIABATE (since 11 February 2011)

chancery: 2424 Massachusetts Avenue NW, Washington, DC 20008
telephone: [1] (202) 797-0300
FAX: [1] (202) 462-9444

Diplomatic representation from the US: *chief of mission:* Ambassador (vacant); Charge d'Affaires Katherine BRUCKER (since 28 August 2017)
embassy: Cocody Riviera Golf 01, Abidjan
mailing address: B. P. 1712, Abidjan 01
telephone: [225] 22 49 40 00
FAX: [225] 22 49 43 23

Flag description: three equal vertical bands of orange (hoist side), white, and green; orange symbolizes the land (savannah) of the north and fertility, white stands for peace and unity, green represents the forests of the south and the hope for a bright future
note: similar to the flag of Ireland, which is longer and has the colors reversed—green (hoist side), white, and orange; also similar to the flag of Italy, which is green (hoist side), white, and red; design was based on the flag of France

National symbol(s): elephant; national colors: orange, white, green

National anthem: *name:* "L'Abidjanaise" (Song of Abidjan)
lyrics/music: Mathieu EKRA, Joachim BONY, and Pierre Marie COTY/Pierre Marie COTY and Pierre Michel PANGO
note: adopted 1960; although the nation's capital city moved from Abidjan to Yamoussoukro in 1983, the anthem still owes its name to the former capital

ECONOMY

Economy—overview: Cote d'Ivoire is heavily dependent on agriculture and related activities, which engage roughly two-thirds of the population. Cote d'Ivoire is the world's largest producer and exporter of cocoa beans and a significant producer and exporter of coffee and palm oil. Consequently, the economy is highly sensitive to fluctuations in international prices for these products and to climatic conditions. Cocoa, oil, and coffee are the country's top export revenue earners, but the country has targeted agricultural processing of cocoa, cashews, mangoes, and other commodities as a high priority. Mining gold and exporting electricity are growing industries outside agriculture.

Following the end of more than a decade of civil conflict in 2011, Cote d'Ivoire has experienced a boom in foreign investment and economic growth. In June 2012, the IMF and the World Bank announced $4.4 billion in debt relief for Cote d'Ivoire under the Highly Indebted Poor Countries Initiative. For the last 5 years Cote d'Ivoire's growth rate has been among the highest in the world.

GDP (purchasing power parity): $96.27 billion (2017 est.)
$89.44 billion (2016 est.)
$83.04 billion (2015 est.)
note: data are in 2017 dollars
country comparison to the world: 87

GDP (official exchange rate): $39.91 billion (2016 est.)

GDP—real growth rate: 7.6% (2017 est.)
7.7% (2016 est.)
8.9% (2015 est.)
country comparison to the world: 5

GDP—per capita (PPP): $3,900 (2017 est.)
$3,700 (2016 est.)
$3,500 (2015 est.)
note: data are in 2017 dollars
country comparison to the world: 181

Gross national saving: 16.5% of GDP (2017 est.)
18.5% of GDP (2016 est.)
17.5% of GDP (2015 est.)
country comparison to the world: 115

GDP—composition, by end use:
household consumption: 61.7%
government consumption: 14.9%
investment in fixed capital: 22.4%
investment in inventories: 0.3%
exports of goods and services: 30.8%
imports of goods and services: -30.1% (2017 est.)

GDP—composition, by sector of origin:
agriculture: 17.4%
industry: 28.8%
services: 53.8% (2017 est.)

Agriculture—products: coffee, cocoa beans, bananas, palm kernels, corn, rice, cassava (manioc, tapioca), sweet potatoes, sugar, cotton, rubber; timber

Industries: foodstuffs, beverages; wood products, oil refining, gold mining, truck and bus assembly, textiles, fertilizer, building materials, electricity

Industrial production growth rate: 7% (2017 est.)
country comparison to the world: 26

Labor force: 8.747 million (2017 est.)
country comparison to the world: 59

Labor force—by occupation: *agriculture:* 68%
industry and services: NA% (2007 est.)

Unemployment rate: 9.4% (2013 est.)
country comparison to the world: 129

Population below poverty line: 46.3% (2015 est.)

Household income or consumption by percentage share: *lowest 10%:* 2.2%
highest 10%: 31.8% (2008)

Distribution of family income—Gini index: 41.5 (2008)
36.7 (1995)
country comparison to the world: 53

Budget: *revenues:* $7.121 billion
expenditures: $8.886 billion (2017 est.)
Taxes and other revenues: 17.8% of GDP (2017 est.)
country comparison to the world: 170

Budget surplus (+) or deficit (-): -4.4% of GDP (2017 est.)
country comparison to the world: 148

Public debt: 51.4% of GDP (2017 est.)
47.4% of GDP (2016 est.)
country comparison to the world: 100

Fiscal year: calendar year

Inflation rate (consumer prices): 1% (2017 est.)

0.7% (2016 est.)
country comparison to the world: 38

Central bank discount rate: 4.25% (31 December 2010)
4.25% (31 December 2009)
country comparison to the world: 91

Commercial bank prime lending rate: 5.4% (31 December 2017 est.)
5.3% (31 December 2016 est.)
country comparison to the world: 137

Stock of narrow money: $11.36 billion (31 December 2017 est.)
$9.438 billion (31 December 2016 est.)
country comparison to the world: 83

Stock of broad money: $16.66 billion (31 December 2017 est.)
$13.88 billion (31 December 2016 est.)
country comparison to the world: 95

Stock of domestic credit: $13.72 billion (31 December 2017 est.)
$10.9 billion (31 December 2016 est.)
country comparison to the world: 105

Market value of publicly traded shares: $12.49 billion (31 December 2015 est.)
$11.71 billion (31 December 2014 est.)
$11.82 billion (31 December 2013 est.)
country comparison to the world: 71

Current account balance: -$1.161 billion (2017 est.)
-$397 million (2016 est.)
country comparison to the world: 137

Exports: $11.08 billion (2017 est.)
$11.77 billion (2016 est.)
country comparison to the world: 85

Exports—commodities: cocoa, coffee, timber, petroleum, cotton, bananas, pineapples, palm oil, fish

Exports—partners: Netherlands 11.3%, US 7.4%, France 6.8%, Belgium 6.1%, Germany 5.2%, India 5.1%, Burkina Faso 4.6%, Mali 4.5%, Switzerland 4.1% (2016)

Imports: $8.789 billion (2017 est.)
$8.524 billion (2016 est.)
country comparison to the world: 101

Imports—commodities: fuel, capital equipment, foodstuffs

Imports—partners: France 13.5%, Nigeria 13.3%, China 11.8%, US 4.2% (2016)

Reserves of foreign exchange and gold: $4.688 billion (31 December 2017 est.)
$4.935 billion (31 December 2016 est.)
country comparison to the world: 95

Debt—external: $12.38 billion (31 December 2017 est.)
$11.02 billion (31 December 2016 est.)
country comparison to the world: 107

Stock of direct foreign investment—at home: $NA

Stock of direct foreign investment—abroad: $NA

Exchange rates: Communaute Financiere Africaine francs (XOF) per US dollar—
594.3 (2017 est.)

231

593.01 (2016 est.)
593.01 (2015 est.)
591.45 (2014 est.)
494.42 (2013 est.)

ENERGY

Electricity access: *population without electricity:* 15,000,000
electrification—*total population:* 26%
electrification—urban areas: 42%
electrification—rural areas: 8% (2013)

Electricity—production: 8.262 billion kWh (2015 est.)
country comparison to the world: 109

Electricity—consumption: 5.669 billion kWh (2015 est.)
country comparison to the world: 118

Electricity—exports: 872 million kWh (2015 est.)
country comparison to the world: 59

Electricity—imports: 23 million kWh (2015 est.)
country comparison to the world: 107

Electricity—installed generating capacity: 1.9 million kW (2016 est.)
country comparison to the world: 114

Electricity—from fossil fuels: 66.9% of total installed capacity (2015 est.)
country comparison to the world: 112

Electricity—from nuclear fuels: 0% of total installed capacity (2015 est.)
country comparison to the world: 114

Electricity—from hydroelectric plants: 33.1% of total installed capacity (2015 est.)
country comparison to the world: 64

Electricity—from other renewable sources: 0% of total installed capacity (2015 est.)
country comparison to the world: 188

Crude oil—production: 30,000 bbl/day (2016 est.)
country comparison to the world: 63

Crude oil—exports: 34,720 bbl/day (2014 est.)
country comparison to the world: 45

Crude oil—imports: 65,540 bbl/day (2014 est.)
country comparison to the world: 48

Crude oil—proved reserves: 100 million bbl (1 January 2017 es)
country comparison to the world: 73

Refined petroleum products—production: 67,260 bbl/day (2014 est.)
country comparison to the world: 74

Refined petroleum products—consumption: 43,000 bbl/day (2015 est.)
country comparison to the world: 111

Refined petroleum products—exports: 31,550 bbl/day (2014 est.)
country comparison to the world: 60

Refined petroleum products—imports: 5,975 bbl/day (2014 est.)
country comparison to the world: 161

Natural gas—production: 2.063 billion cu m (2015 est.)
country comparison to the world: 58

Natural gas—consumption: 2.897 billion cu m (2015 est.)
country comparison to the world: 79

Natural gas—exports: 0 cu m (2013 est.)
country comparison to the world: 123

Natural gas—imports: 0 cu m (2013 est.)
country comparison to the world: 140

Natural gas—proved reserves: 28.32 billion cu m (1 January 2017 es)
country comparison to the world: 71

Carbon dioxide emissions from consumption of energy: 8.995 million Mt (2013 est.)
country comparison to the world: 109

COMMUNICATIONS

Telephones—fixed lines: *total subscriptions:* 289,108
subscriptions per 100 inhabitants: 1 (July 2016 est.)
country comparison to the world: 124

Telephones—mobile cellular: *total:* 27,451,250
subscriptions per 100 inhabitants: 116 (July 2016 est.)
country comparison to the world: 54

Telephone system: *general assessment:* well-developed by African standards; telecommunications sector privatized in late 1990s and operational fixed lines have increased since that time with 2 fixed-line providers operating over open-wire lines, microwave radio relay, and fiber-optics; 90% digitalized
domestic: with multiple mobile-cellular service providers competing in the market, usage has increased sharply to about 115 per 100 persons
international: country code—225; landing point for the SAT-3/WASC fiber-optic submarine cable that provides connectivity to Europe and Asia; satellite earth stations—2 Intelsat (1 Atlantic Ocean and 1 Indian Ocean) (2016)

Broadcast media: 2 state-owned TV stations; no private terrestrial TV stations, but satellite TV subscription service is available; 2 state-owned radio stations; some private radio stations; transmissions of several international broadcasters are available (2007)

Internet country code: .ci
Internet users: total: 6,297,676
percent of population: 26.5% (July 2016 est.)
country comparison to the world: 129

TRANSPORTATION

National air transport system: *number of registered air carriers:* 1
inventory of registered aircraft operated by air carriers: 10
annual passenger traffic on registered air carriers: 359,260
annual freight traffic on registered air carriers: 4,719,120 mt-km (2015)
Civil aircraft registration country code prefix: TU (2016)

Airports: 27 (2013)
country comparison to the world: 124

Airports—with paved runways: *total:* 7
over 3,047 m: 1
2,438 to 3,047 m: 2
1,524 to 2,437 m: 4 (2017)

Airports—with unpaved runways: *total:* 20
1,524 to 2,437 m: 6
914 to 1,523 m: 11
under 914 m: 3 (2013)

Heliports: 1 (2013)

Pipelines: condensate 101 km; gas 256 km; oil 118 km; oil/gas/water 5 km; water 7 km (2013)

Railways: *total:* 660 km
narrow gauge: 660 km 1.000-m gauge
note: an additional 622 km of this railroad extends into Burkina Faso (2008)
country comparison to the world: 106

Roadways: *total:* 81,996 km
paved: 6,502 km
unpaved: 75,494 km
note: includes intercity and urban roads; another 20,000 km of dirt roads are in poor condition and 150,000 km of dirt roads are impassable (2007)
country comparison to the world: 60

Waterways: 980 km (navigable rivers, canals, and numerous coastal lagoons) (2011)
country comparison to the world: 66

Merchant marine: *total:* 9
by type: oil tanker 2, other 7 (2017)
country comparison to the world: 149

Ports and terminals: *major seaport(s):* Abidjan, San-Pedro
oil terminal(s): Espoir Offshore Terminal

MILITARY AND SECURITY

Military expenditures: 1.18% of GDP (2016)
1.74% of GDP (2015)
1.48% of GDP (2014)
1.38% of GDP (2013)
1.51% of GDP (2012)
country comparison to the world: 55

Military branches: Armed Forces of Cote d'Ivoire (Force Armee de Cote d'Ivoire, FACI): Army, Navy, Cote d'Ivoire Air Force (Force Aerienne de la Cote d'Ivoire) (2017)

Military service age and obligation: 18-25 years of age for compulsory and voluntary male and female military service; conscription is not enforced; voluntary recruitment of former rebels into the new national army is restricted to ages 22-29 (2012)

TERRORISM

Terrorist groups—foreign based: *al-Qaida in the Islamic Maghreb (AQIM): aim(s):* replace the Cote d'Ivoire Government with Sharia and, ultimately, create a regional Islamic caliphate across all of North and West Africa
area(s) of operation: maintains an operational presence; gunmen killed 15 civilians and three special force members and wounded approximately 33 people, when they attacked a beach resort on 13 March 2016 at the L'Etoile du Sud hotel in Grand Bassam

Disputes—international: disputed maritime border between Cote d'Ivoire and Ghana

Refugees and internally displaced persons: IDPs: 301,000 (post-election conflict in 2010-11, as well as civil war from 2002-04; most pronounced in western and southwestern regions) (2016)
stateless persons: 692,800 (2017); note—many Ivoirians lack documentation proving their nationality, which prevent them from accessing education and healthcare; birth on Ivorian soil does not automatically result in citizenship; disputes over citizenship and the associated rights of the large population descended from migrants from neighboring countries is an ongoing source of tension and contributed to the country's 2002 civil war; some observers believe the government's mass naturalizations of thousands of people over the last couple of years is intended to boost its electoral support base; the government in October 2013 acceded to international conventions on statelessness and in August 2013 reformed its nationality law, key steps to clarify the nationality of thousands of residents; since the adoption of the Abidjan Declaration to eradicate statelessness in West Africa in February 2015, 6,400 people have received nationality papers

Illicit drugs: illicit producer of cannabis, mostly for local consumption; utility as a narcotic transshipment point to Europe reduced by ongoing political instability; while rampant corruption and inadequate supervision leave the banking system vulnerable to money laundering, the lack of a developed financial system limits the country's utility as a major money-laundering center

CROATIA

INTRODUCTION

Background: The lands that today comprise Croatia were part of the Austro-Hungarian Empire until the close of World War I. In 1918, the Croats, Serbs, and Slovenes formed a kingdom known after 1929 as Yugoslavia. Following World War II, Yugoslavia became a federal independent communist state under the strong hand of Marshal Josip Broz, aka TITO. Although Croatia declared its independence from Yugoslavia in 1991, it took four years of sporadic, but often bitter, fighting before occupying Serb armies were mostly cleared from Croatian lands, along with a majority of Croatia's ethnic Serb population. Under UN supervision, the last Serb-held enclave in eastern Slavonia was returned to Croatia in 1998. The country joined NATO in April 2009 and the EU in July 2013.

GEOGRAPHY

Location: Southeastern Europe, bordering the Adriatic Sea, between Bosnia and Herzegovina and Slovenia

Geographic coordinates: 45 10 N, 15 30 E

Map references: Europe

Area: *total:* 56,594 sq km
land: 55,974 sq km
water: 620 sq km

country comparison to the world: 128
Area—comparative: slightly smaller than West Virginia

Land boundaries: *total:* 2,237 km
border countries (5): Bosnia and Herzegovina 956 km, Hungary 348 km, Montenegro 19 km, Serbia 314 km, Slovenia 600 km

Coastline: 5,835 km (mainland 1,777 km, islands 4,058 km)

Maritime claims: *territorial sea:* 12 nm
continental shelf: 200-m depth or to the depth of exploitation

Climate: Mediterranean and continental; continental climate predominant with hot summers and cold winters; mild winters, dry summers along coast

Terrain: geographically diverse; flat plains along Hungarian border, low mountains and highlands near Adriatic coastline and islands

Elevation: *mean elevation:* 331 m

elevation extremes: *lowest point:* Adriatic Sea 0 m
highest point: Dinara 1,831 m

Natural resources: oil, some coal, bauxite, low-grade iron ore, calcium, gypsum, natural asphalt, silica, mica, clays, salt, hydropower

Land use: *agricultural land:* 23.7%
arable land: 16%;
permanent crops: 1.5%;
permanent pasture: 6.2%
forest: 34.4%
other: 41.9% (2011 est.)
Irrigated land: 240 sq km (2012)

Population—distribution: more of the population lives in the northern half of the country, with approximately a quarter of the populace residing in and around the capital of Zagreb; many of the islands are sparsely populated

Natural hazards: destructive earthquakes

Environment—current issues: air pollution improving but still a concern in urban settings and in emissions arriving from neighboring countries; surface water pollution in the Danube River Basin

Environment—international agreements: *party to:* Air Pollution, Air Pollution-Nitrogen Oxides, Air Pollution-Persistent Organic Pollutants, Air Pollution-Sulfur 94, Air Pollution-Volatile Organic Compounds, Biodiversity, Climate Change, Climate Change-Kyoto Protocol, Desertification, Endangered Species, Hazardous Wastes, Law of the Sea, Marine Dumping, Ozone Layer Protection, Ship Pollution, Wetlands, Whaling
signed, but not ratified: none of the selected agreements

Geography—note: controls most land routes from Western Europe to Aegean Sea and Turkish Straits; most Adriatic Sea islands lie off the coast of Croatia—some 1,200 islands, islets, ridges, and rocks

PEOPLE AND SOCIETY

Population: 4,292,095 (July 2017 est.)
country comparison to the world: 127

Nationality: *noun:* Croat(s), Croatian(s)
adjective: Croatian

Ethnic groups: Croat 90.4%, Serb 4.4%, other 4.4% (including Bosniak, Hungarian, Slovene, Czech, and Romani), unspecified 0.8% (2011 est.)

Languages: Croatian (official) 95.6%, Serbian 1.2%, other 3% (including Hungarian, Czech, Slovak, and Albanian), unspecified 0.2% (2011 est.)

Religions: Roman Catholic 86.3%, Orthodox 4.4%, Muslim 1.5%, other 1.5%, unspecified 2.5%, not religious or atheist 3.8% (2011 est.)

Age structure: *0-14 years:* 14.21% (male 314,287/female 295,520)
15-24 years: 11.24% (male 247,394/female 235,166)
25-54 years: 40.43% (male 867,978/female 867,125)
55-64 years: 14.82% (male 309,794/female 326,102)
65 years and over: 19.31% (male 330,406/female 498,323) (2017 est.)

Dependency ratios: *total dependency ratio:* 50.9
youth dependency ratio: 22.4
elderly dependency ratio: 28.5
potential support ratio: 3.5 (2015 est.)

233

Median age: *total:* 43 years
male: 41.1 years
female: 45 years (2017 est.)
country comparison to the world: 20

Population growth rate: -0.5% (2017 est.)
country comparison to the world: 222

Birth rate: 8.9 births/1,000 population (2017 est.)
country comparison to the world: 210

Death rate: 12.2 deaths/1,000 population (2017 est.)
country comparison to the world: 21

Net migration rate: -1.7 migrant(s)/1,000 population (2017 est.)
country comparison to the world: 151

Population distribution: more of the population lives in the northern half of the country, with approximately a quarter of the populace residing in and around the capital of Zagreb; many of the islands are sparsely populated

Urbanization: *urban population:* 59.6% of total population (2017)
rate of urbanization: 0.22% annual rate of change (2015-20 est.)

Major urban areas—population: ZAGREB (capital) 687,000 (2015)

Sex ratio: *at birth:* 1.06 male(s)/female
0-14 years: 1.06 male(s)/female
15-24 years: 1.05 male(s)/female
25-54 years: 1 male(s)/female
55-64 years: 0.96 male(s)/female
65 years and over: 0.69 male(s)/female
total population: 0.93 male(s)/female (2016 est.)

Mother's mean age at first birth: 28 years (2014 est.)

Maternal mortality ratio: 8 deaths/100,000 live births (2015 est.)
country comparison to the world: 158

Infant mortality rate: *total:* 9.3 deaths/1,000 live births
male: 9 deaths/1,000 live births
female: 9.6 deaths/1,000 live births (2017 est.)
country comparison to the world: 145

Life expectancy at birth: *total population:* 76.1 years
male: 72.9 years
female: 79.4 years (2017 est.)
country comparison to the world: 89

Total fertility rate: 1.4 children born/woman (2017 est.)
country comparison to the world: 211

Health expenditures: 7.8% of GDP (2014)
country comparison to the world: 58

Physicians density: 3.13 physicians/1,000 population (2014)

Hospital bed density: 5.9 beds/1,000 population (2014)

Drinking water source:
improved:
urban: 99.6% of population
rural: 99.7% of population
total: 99.6% of population
unimproved:
urban: 0.4% of population
rural: 0.3% of population
total: 0.4% of population (2015 est.)

Sanitation facility access:
improved:
urban: 97.8% of population
rural: 95.8% of population
total: 97% of population
unimproved:
urban: 2.2% of population
rural: 4.2% of population
total: 3% of population (2015 est.)

HIV/AIDS—adult prevalence rate: <.1% (2016 est.)

HIV/AIDS—people living with HIV/AIDS: 1,500 (2016 est.)
country comparison to the world: 119

HIV/AIDS—deaths: <100 (2016 est.)

Major infectious diseases: *degree of risk:* intermediate
vectorborne diseases: tickborne encephalitis (2016)

Obesity—adult prevalence rate: 24.4% (2016)
country comparison to the world: 59

Education expenditures: 4.6% of GDP (2013)
country comparison to the world: 99

Literacy: *definition:* age 15 and over can read and write
total population: 99.3%
male: 99.7%
female: 98.9% (2015 est.)

School life expectancy (primary to tertiary education): *total:* 15 years
male: 15 years
female: 16 years (2014)

Unemployment, youth ages 15-24: *total:* 43%
male: 41.9%
female: 44.5% (2015 est.)
country comparison to the world: 9

GOVERNMENT

Country name: *conventional long form:* Republic of Croatia
conventional short form: Croatia
local long form: Republika Hrvatska
local short form: Hrvatska
former: People's Republic of Croatia, Socialist Republic of Croatia
etymology: name derives from the Croats, a Slavic tribe who migrated to the Balkans in the 7th century A.D.

Government type: parliamentary republic

Capital: *name:* Zagreb

geographic coordinates: 45 48 N, 16 00 E
time difference: UTC+1 (6 hours ahead of Washington, DC, during Standard Time)
daylight saving time: +1hr, begins last Sunday in March; ends last Sunday in October

Administrative divisions: 20 counties (zupanije, zupanija—singular) and 1 city* (grad—singular) with special county status; Bjelovarsko-Bilogorska(Bjelovar-Bilogora), Brodsko-Posavska (Brod-Posavina), Dubrovacko-Neretvanska (Dubrovnik-Neretva), Istarska (Istria), Karlovacka (Karlovac), Koprivnicko-Krizevacka (Koprivnica-Krizevci), Krapinsko-Zagorska (Krapina-Zagorje), Licko-Senjska (Lika-Senj), Medimurska (Medimurje), Osjecko-Baranjska (Osijek-Baranja), Pozesko-Slavonska (Pozega-Slavonia), Primorsko-Goranska (Primorje-Gorski Kotar), Sibensko-Kninska (Sibenik-Knin), Sisacko-Moslavacka (Sisak-Moslavina), Splitsko-Dalmatinska (Split-Dalmatia), Varazdinska (Varazdin), Viroviticko-Podravska (Virovitica-Podravina), Vukovarsko-Srijemska (Vukovar-Syrmia), Zadarska (Zadar), Zagreb*, Zagrebacka (Zagreb county)

Independence: 25 June 1991 (from Yugoslavia)

National holiday: Independence Day, 8 October (1991) and Statehood Day, 25 June (1991); note—25 June 1991 was the day the Croatian parliament voted for independence; following a three-month moratorium to allow the European Community to solve the Yugoslav crisis peacefully, parliament adopted a decision on 8 October 1991 to sever constitutional relations with Yugoslavia

Constitution: *history:* several previous; latest adopted 22 December 1990
amendments: proposed by at least one-fifth of the Assembly membership, by the president of the republic, by the Government of Croatia, or through petition by at least 10% of the total electorate; proceedings to amend require majority vote by the Assembly; passage requires two-thirds majority vote by the Assembly; passage by petition requires a majority vote in a referendum, and promulgation by the Assembly; amended several times, last in 2014 (2016)

Legal system: civil law system influenced by legal heritage of Austria-Hungary; note—Croatian law was fully harmonized with the European Community acquis as of the June 2010 completion of EU accession negotiations

International law organization participation: has not submitted an ICJ jurisdiction declaration; accepts ICCt jurisdiction

Citizenship: *citizenship by birth:* no
citizenship by descent only: at least one parent must be a citizen of Croatia
dual citizenship recognized: yes
residency requirement for naturalization: 5 years

Suffrage: 18 years of age; universal

Executive branch: *chief of state:* President Kolinda GRABAR-KITAROVIC (since 19 February 2015)

head of government: Prime Minister Andrej PLENKOVIC (since 19 October 2016); Deputy Prime Ministers Damir KRSTICEVIC (since 19 October 2016), Martina DALIC (since 19 October 2016), Predrag STROMAR (since 9 June 2017), and Marija Pejcinovic BURIC (since 19 June 2017)
cabinet: Council of Ministers named by the prime minister and approved by the Assembly
elections/appointments: president directly elected by absolute majority popular vote in 2 rounds if needed for a 5-year term (eligible for a

second term); election last held on 28 December 2014 and 11 January 2015 (next to be held in 2019); the leader of the majority party or majority coalition usually appointed prime minister by the president and approved by the Assembly
election results: Kolinda GRABAR-KITAROVIC elected president in second round; percent of vote—Kolinda GRABAR-KITAROVIC (HDZ) 50.7%, Ivo JOSIPOVIC (Forward Croatia Progressive Alliance) 49.3%

Legislative branch: description: unicameral Assembly or Hrvatski Sabor (151 seats; 140 members in 10 multi-seat constituencies and 3 members in a single constituency for Croatian diaspora directly elected by proportional representation vote using the D'Hondt method with a 5% threshold; an additional 8 members elected from a nationwide constituency by simple majority by voters belonging to minorities recognized by Croatia; the Serb minority elects 3 Assembly members, the Hungarian and Italian minorities elect 1 each, the Czech and Slovak minorities elect 1 jointly, and all other minorities elect 2; all members serve 4-year terms
elections: last held on 11 September 2016 (next to be held by December 2020)—Assembly voted on 20 June 2016 to dissolve on 15 July 2016, resulting in snap elections
election results: percent of vote by party/coalition—NA; number of seats by party/coalition—HDZ coalition 61, People's Coalition 54, Most-NL 13, Only Option 8, minorities 8 (includes SDSS 3), other 7
note: as of August 2017, seats by party—HDZ 55, SDP 37, MOST-NL 12, HNS 5, HSS 5, GLAS 4, IDS 3, SDSS 3, Human Blockade 3, HDS 2, PH 2, other 7, independent 13

Judicial branch: *highest court(s):* Supreme Court (consists of the court president and vice president, 25 civil department justices, and 16 criminal department justices)
judge selection and term of office: president of Supreme Court nominated by president of Croatia and elected by Croatian Sabor for a 4-year term; other Supreme Court justices appointed by National Judicial Council; all judges serve until age 70
subordinate courts: Administrative Court; county, municipal, and specialized courts; note—there is an 11-member Constitutional Court with jurisdiction limited to constitutional issues but is outside Croatia's judicial system

Political parties and leaders: Bloc of Pensioners Together or BUZ [Milivoj SPIKA]
Bridge of Independent Lists or Most-NL [Bozo PETROV]
Civic Liberal Alliance or GLAS [Ankar Mrak TARITAS]
Croatian Christian Democratic Party or HDS [Goran DODIG]
Croatian Democratic Congress of Slavonia and Baranja or HDSSB [Branimir GLAVAS]
Croatian Democratic Union or HDZ [Andrej PLENKOVIC]

Croatian Laborists—Labor Party or HL [David BREGOVAC]
Croatian Party of Rights—dr. Ante Starcevic or HSP AS [Hrvoje NICE]
Croatian Peasant Party or HSS [Kreso BELJAK]
Croatian Pensioner Party or HSU [Silvano HRELJA]
Croatian People's Party—Liberal Democrats or HNS [Ivan VRDOLJAK]
Croatian Social Liberal Party or HSLS [Darinko KOSOR]
Forward Croatia Progressive Alliance [Ivo JOSIPOVIC]
Human Blockade ("Living Wall") [Ivan SINCIC]
Independent Democratic Serb Party or SDSS [Milorad PUPOVAC]
Istrian Democratic Assembly or IDS [Boris MILETIC]
Let's Change Croatia or PH [Ivan LOVRINOVIC]
Milan Bandic 365—Party of Labor and Solidarity or BM365-SRS [Milan BANDIC]
Movement for Successful Croatia or HRAST [Ladislav ILCIC]
People's Party—Reformists Party [Radimir CACIC]
Smart Party or PAMETNO [Marijana PULJAK]
Social Democratic Party of Croatia or SDP [Davor BERNARDIC]

Political pressure groups and leaders: human rights groups

International organization participation: Australia Group, BIS, BSEC (observer), CD, CE, CEI, EAPC, EBRD, ECB, EMU, EU, FAO, G-11, IADB, IAEA, IBRD, ICAO, ICC (national committees), ICCt, ICRM, IDA, IFAD, IFC, IFRCS, IHO, ILO, IMF, IMO, IMSO, Interpol, IOC, IOM, IPU, ISO, ITSO, ITU, ITUC (NGOs), MIGA, MINURSO, NAM (observer), NATO, NSG, OAS (observer), OIF (observer), OPCW, OSCE, PCA, SELEC, UN, UNCTAD, UNESCO, UNFICYP, UNHCR, UNIDO, UNIFIL, UNMIL, UNMOGIP, UNWTO, UPU, WCO, WHO, WIPO, WMO, WTO, ZC

Diplomatic representation in the US: *chief of mission:* Ambassador Pjer SIMUNOVIC (since 8 September 2017)
chancery: 2343 Massachusetts Avenue NW, Washington, DC 20008
telephone: [1] (202) 588-5899
FAX: [1] (202) 588-8936
consulate(s) general: Chicago, Los Angeles, New York

Diplomatic representation from the US: *chief of mission:* Ambassador Julieta Valls NOYES (since 5 October 2015)
embassy: 2 Thomas Jefferson Street, 10010 Zagreb
mailing address: use embassy street address
telephone: [385] (1) 661-2200
FAX: [385] (1) 661-2373

Flag description: three equal horizontal bands of red (top), white, and blue—the Pan-Slav colors—superimposed by the Croatian coat of arms; the coat of arms consists of one main shield (a checkerboard of 13 red and 12 silver (white) fields) surmounted by five smaller shields that form a

crown over the main shield; the five small shields represent five historic regions (from left to right): Croatia, Dubrovnik, Dalmatia, Istria, and Slavonia
note: the Pan-Slav colors were inspired by the 19th-century flag of Russia

National symbol(s): red-white checkerboard; national colors: red, white, blue

National anthem: name: "Lijepa nasa domovino" (Our Beautiful Homeland)
lyrics/music: Antun MIHANOVIC/Josip RUNJANIN
note: adopted 1972; "Lijepa nasa domovino," whose lyrics were written in 1835, served as an unofficial anthem beginning in 1891

ECONOMY

Economy—overview: Though still one of the wealthiest of the former Yugoslav republics, Croatia's economy suffered badly during the 1991-95 war. The country's output during that time collapsed, and Croatia missed the early waves of investment in Central and Eastern Europe that followed the fall of the Berlin Wall. Between 2000 and 2007, however, Croatia's economic fortunes began to improve with moderate but steady GDP growth between 4% and 6%, led by a rebound in tourism and credit-driven consumer spending. Inflation over the same period remained tame and the currency, the kuna, stable.

Croatia experienced an abrupt slowdown in the economy in 2008 and is slowly recovering; economic growth was stagnant or negative in each year between 2009 and 2014, but has picked up since 2015. Difficult problems still remain including a stubbornly high unemployment rate, uneven regional development, and a challenging investment climate. Its stubbornly high unemployment rate is slowly coming down. In 2016 Croatia demonstrated a commitment to improving the business climate, simplifying its tax code to stimulate growth from domestic consumption and foreign investment. Even before 2016, Croatia has worked to become a regional energy player and plans to import liquefied natural gas through a prospective import terminal and re-export it to European consumers.

On 1 July 2013, Croatia joined the EU, following a decade-long application process. Croatia will be a member of the European Exchange Rate Mechanism, with its currency effectively pegged to the euro, until it meets the criteria for joining the Economic and Monetary Union and adopts the euro as its currency. EU accession has increased pressure on the government to reduce Croatia's relatively high public debt and as a result Zagreb has cut spending and has raised additional revenues through more stringent tax collection and by raising the value-added tax. The government has also sought to accelerate privatization of nonstrategic assets, with mixed success. Croatia's economic recovery is still somewhat fragile, though, as one of the country's largest companies almost collapsed in 2017.

GDP (purchasing power parity): $100.2 billion (2017 est.)

$97.32 billion (2016 est.)
$94.5 billion (2015 est.)
note: data are in 2017 dollars
country comparison to the world: 85

GDP (official exchange rate): $53.48 billion (2016 est.)

GDP—real growth rate: 2.9% (2017 est.)
3% (2016 est.)
2.2% (2015 est.)
country comparison to the world: 120

GDP—per capita (PPP): $24,100 (2017 est.)
$23,300 (2016 est.)
$22,500 (2015 est.)
note: data are in 2017 dollars
country comparison to the world: 82

Gross national saving: 24.4% of GDP (2017 est.)
22.4% of GDP (2016 est.)
24.6% of GDP (2015 est.)
country comparison to the world: 56

GDP—composition, by end use:
household consumption: 58.1%
government consumption: 19.1%
investment in fixed capital: 20.7%
investment in inventories: -0.4%
exports of goods and services: 50.9%
imports of goods and services: -48.3% (2017 est.)

GDP—composition, by sector of origin:
agriculture: 4%
industry: 26.5%
services: 69.5% (2017 est.)

Agriculture—products: arable crops (wheat, corn, barley, sugar beet, sunflower, rapeseed, alfalfa, clover); vegetables (potatoes, cabbage, onion, tomato, pepper); fruits (apples, plum, mandarins, olives), grapes for wine; livestock (cattle, cows, pigs); dairy products

Industries: chemicals and plastics, machine tools, fabricated metal, electronics, pig iron and rolled steel products, aluminum, paper, wood products, construction materials, textiles, shipbuilding, petroleum and petroleum refining, food and beverages, tourism

Industrial production growth rate: 3% (2017 est.)
country comparison to the world: 99

Labor force: 1.552 million (2017 est.)
country comparison to the world: 130

Labor force—by occupation: agriculture: 1.9%
industry: 27.6%
services: 70.4% (2014)

Unemployment rate: 13.9% (2017 est.)
15% (2016 est.)
country comparison to the world: 167

Population below poverty line: 19.5% (2014 est.)

Household income or consumption by percentage share: lowest 10%: 3.3%
highest 10%: 27.5% (2008 est.)

Distribution of family income—Gini index: 32 (2010)
29 (1998)
country comparison to the world: 114

Budget: revenues: $25.79 billion
expenditures: $26.92 billion (2017 est.)

Taxes and other revenues: 48.2% of GDP (2017 est.)
country comparison to the world: 18

Budget surplus (+) or deficit (-): -2.1% of GDP (2017 est.)
country comparison to the world: 90

Public debt: 81.5% of GDP (2017 est.)
83.8% of GDP (2016 est.)
country comparison to the world: 36

Fiscal year: calendar year

Inflation rate (consumer prices): 1.1% (2017 est.)
-1.1% (2016 est.)
country comparison to the world: 49

Central bank discount rate: 7% (31 December 2013)
7% (31 December 2012)
country comparison to the world: 52

Commercial bank prime lending rate: 4.4% (31 December 2017 est.)
4.85% (31 December 2016 est.)
country comparison to the world: 154

Stock of narrow money: $14.75 billion (31 December 2017 est.)
$11.64 billion (31 December 2016 est.)
country comparison to the world: 74

Stock of broad money: $50.54 billion (31 December 2017 est.)
$41.97 billion (31 December 2016 est.)
country comparison to the world: 67

Stock of domestic credit: $46.95 billion (31 December 2017 est.)
$41.38 billion (31 December 2016 est.)
country comparison to the world: 70

Market value of publicly traded shares: $36.29 billion (31 December 2014 est.)
$33.75 billion (31 December 2013 est.)
$33.44 billion (31 December 2012 est.)
country comparison to the world: 60

Current account balance: $2.038 billion (2017 est.)
$1.326 billion (2016 est.)
country comparison to the world: 33

Exports: $12.35 billion (2017 est.)
$11.63 billion (2016 est.)
country comparison to the world: 80

Exports—commodities: transport equipment, machinery, textiles, chemicals, foodstuffs, fuels

Exports—partners: Italy 13.5%, Slovenia 12.3%, Germany 11.6%, Bosnia and Herzegovina 9.2%, Austria 6.3%, Serbia 4.2% (2016)

Imports: $21.2 billion (2017 est.)
$19.76 billion (2016 est.)
country comparison to the world: 72

Imports—commodities: machinery, transport and electrical equipment; chemicals, fuels and lubricants; foodstuffs

Imports—partners: Germany 16.1%, Italy 12.6%, Slovenia 10.9%, Austria 7.9%, Hungary 7.1% (2016)

Reserves of foreign exchange and gold: $15.53 billion (31 December 2017 est.)
$14.24 billion (31 December 2016 est.)

country comparison to the world: 68

Debt—external: $44.53 billion (31 December 2017 est.)
$45.1 billion (31 December 2016 est.)
country comparison to the world: 69

Stock of direct foreign investment—at home: $43.25 billion (31 December 2017 est.)
$41.63 billion (31 December 2016 est.)
country comparison to the world: 60

Stock of direct foreign investment—abroad: $8.204 billion (31 December 2017 est.)
$7.757 billion (31 December 2016 est.)
country comparison to the world: 64

Exchange rates: kuna (HRK) per US dollar—
6.568 (2017 est.)
6.806 (2016 est.)
6.806 (2015 est.)
6.8583 (2014 est.)
5.7482 (2013 est.)

ENERGY

Electricity access: electrification—total population: 100% (2016)

Electricity—production: 10.82 billion kWh (2015 est.)
country comparison to the world: 98

Electricity—consumption: 15.8 billion kWh (2015 est.)
country comparison to the world: 76

Electricity—exports: 1.858 billion kWh (2015 est.)
country comparison to the world: 46

Electricity—imports: 8.64 billion kWh (2015 est.)
country comparison to the world: 29

Electricity—installed generating capacity: 4.915 million kW (2015 est.)
country comparison to the world: 79

Electricity—from fossil fuels: 43.8% of total installed capacity (2015 est.)
country comparison to the world: 164

Electricity—from nuclear fuels: 0% of total installed capacity (2015 est.)
country comparison to the world: 109

Electricity—from hydroelectric plants: 39% of total installed capacity (2015 est.)
country comparison to the world: 53

Electricity—from other renewable sources: 12% of total installed capacity (2015 est.)
country comparison to the world: 62

Crude oil—production: 13,580 bbl/day (2016 est.)
country comparison to the world: 78

Crude oil—exports: 0 bbl/day (2014 est.)
country comparison to the world: 138

Crude oil—imports: 47,200 bbl/day (2014 est.)
country comparison to the world: 54

Crude oil—proved reserves: 71 million bbl (1 January 2017 es)
country comparison to the world: 78

Refined petroleum products—production: 65,860 bbl/day (2014 est.)
country comparison to the world: 75

Refined petroleum products—consumption: 69,000 bbl/day (2015 est.)
country comparison to the world: 93

Refined petroleum products—exports: 33,660 bbl/day (2014 est.)
country comparison to the world: 58

Refined petroleum products—imports: 31,840 bbl/day (2014 est.)
country comparison to the world: 100

Natural gas—production: 1.829 billion cu m (2015 est.)
country comparison to the world: 59

Natural gas—consumption: 3.59 billion cu m (2015 est.)
country comparison to the world: 72

Natural gas—exports: 422 million cu m (2014 est.)
country comparison to the world: 44

Natural gas—imports: 1.072 billion cu m (2015 est.)
country comparison to the world: 59

Natural gas—proved reserves: 24.92 billion cu m (1 January 2017 es)
country comparison to the world: 73

Carbon dioxide emissions from consumption of energy: 19 million Mt (2013 est.)
country comparison to the world: 84

COMMUNICATIONS

Telephones—fixed lines: *total subscriptions:* 1,435,977
subscriptions per 100 inhabitants: 33 (July 2016 est.)
country comparison to the world: 66

Telephones—mobile cellular: *total:* 4,414,347
subscriptions per 100 inhabitants: 102 (July 2016 est.)
country comparison to the world: 123

Telephone system: *general assessment:* the telecommunications network has improved steadily since the mid-1990s, covering much of what were once inaccessible areas; local lines are digital
domestic: fixed-line teledensity has dropped somewhat to about 33 per 100 persons; mobile-cellular telephone subscriptions now even with the population
international: country code—385; digital international service is provided through the main switch in Zagreb; Croatia participates in the Trans-Asia-Europe fiber-optic project, which consists of 2 fiber-optic trunk connections with Slovenia and a fiber-optic trunk line from Rijeka to Split and Dubrovnik; the ADRIA-1 submarine cable provides connectivity to Albania and Greece (2016)

Broadcast media: the national state-owned public broadcaster, Croatian Radiotelevision, operates 4 terrestrial TV networks, a satellite channel that rebroadcasts programs for Croatians living abroad, and 6 regional TV centers; 2 private broadcasters operate national terrestrial networks; roughly 25 privately owned regional TV stations; multi-channel cable and satellite TV subscription services are available; state-owned public broadcaster operates 3 national radio networks and 9 regional radio stations; 2 privately owned national radio networks and more than 170 regional, county, city, and community radio stations (2012)

Internet country code: .hr
Internet users: total: 3,135,949

percent of population: 72.7% (July 2016 est.)
country comparison to the world: 86

TRANSPORTATION

National air transport system: *number of registered air carriers:* 3
inventory of registered aircraft operated by air carriers: 46
annual passenger traffic on registered air carriers: 1,782,666
annual freight traffic on registered air carriers: 775,320 mt-km (2015)
Civil aircraft registration country code prefix: 9A (2016)

Airports: 69 (2013)
country comparison to the world: 72

Airports—with paved runways: *total:* 24
over 3,047 m: 2
2,438 to 3,047 m: 6
1,524 to 2,437 m: 3
914 to 1,523 m: 3
under 914 m: 10 (2017)

Airports—with unpaved runways: *total:* 45
1,524 to 2,437 m: 1
914 to 1,523 m: 6
under 914 m: 38 (2013)

Heliports: 1 (2013)

Pipelines: gas 2,410 km; oil 610 km (2011)

Railways: *total:* 2,722 km
standard gauge: 2,722 km 1.435-m gauge (985 km electrified) (2014)
country comparison to the world: 61

Roadways: *total:* 26,958 km (includes 1,416 km of expressways) (2015)
country comparison to the world: 98

Waterways: 785 km (2009)
country comparison to the world: 73

Merchant marine: *total:* 288
by type: bulk carrier 17, general cargo 39, oil tanker 18, other 214 (2017)
country comparison to the world: 53

Ports and terminals: *major seaport(s):* Ploce, Rijeka, Sibernik, Split

river port(s): Vukovar (Danube)
oil terminal(s): Omisalj

MILITARY AND SECURITY

Military expenditures: 1.27% of GDP (2017)
1.38% of GDP (2016)
1.55% of GDP (2015)
1.59% of GDP (2014)
1.66% of GDP (2013)
country comparison to the world: 51

Military branches: Armed Forces of the Republic of Croatia (Oruzane Snage Republike Hrvatske, OSRH) consists of five major commands directly subordinate to a General Staff: Ground Forces (Hrvatska Kopnena Vojska, HKoV), Naval Forces (Hrvatska Ratna Mornarica, HRM, includes coast guard), Air Force and Air Defense Command (Hrvatsko Ratno Zrakoplovstvo I Protuzracna Obrana), Joint Education and Training Command, Logistics Command; Military Police Force supports each of the three Croatian military forces (2017)

Military service age and obligation: 18-27 years of age for voluntary military service; conscription abolished in 2008 (2017)

TRANSNATIONAL ISSUES

Disputes—international: dispute remains with Bosnia and Herzegovina over several small sections of the boundary related to maritime access that hinders ratification of the 1999 border agreement; since the breakup of Yugoslavia in the early 1990s, Croatia and Slovenia have each claimed sovereignty over Piranski Bay and four villages, and Slovenia has objected to Croatia's claim of an exclusive economic zone in the Adriatic Sea; in 2009, however Croatia and Slovenia signed a binding international arbitration agreement to define their disputed land and maritime borders, which led to Slovenia lifting its objections to Croatia joining the EU; Slovenia continues to impose a hard border Schengen regime with Croatia, which joined the EU in 2013 but has not yet fulfilled Schengen requirements

Refugees and internally displaced persons: *stateless persons:* 2,873 (2016)
note: 659,105 estimated refugee and migrant arrivals (January 2015—December 2016); flows have slowed considerably in 2017; Croatia is predominantly a transit country and hosts fewer than 600 asylum seekers as of September 2017

Illicit drugs: primarily a transit country along the Balkan route for maritime shipments of South American cocaine bound for Western Europe and other illicit drugs and chemical precursors to and from Western Europe; no significant domestic production of illicit drugs

CUBA

INTRODUCTION

Background: The native Amerindian population of Cuba began to decline after the European discovery of the island by Christopher COLUMBUS in 1492 and following its development as a Spanish colony during the next several centuries. Large numbers of African slaves were imported to work the coffee and sugar plantations, and Havana became the launching point for the annual treasure fleets bound for Spain from Mexico and Peru. Spanish rule eventually provoked an independence movement and occasional rebellions that were harshly suppressed. US intervention during the Spanish-American War in 1898 assisted the Cubans in overthrowing Spanish rule. The Treaty of Paris established Cuban independence from Spain in 1898 and, following three-and-a-half years of subsequent US military rule, Cuba became an independent republic in 1902 after which the island experienced a string of governments mostly dominated by the military and corrupt politicians. Fidel CASTRO led a rebel army to victory in 1959; his authoritarian rule held the subsequent regime together for nearly five decades. He stepped down as president in February 2008 in favor of his younger brother Raul CASTRO. Cuba's communist revolution, with Soviet support, was exported throughout Latin America and Africa during the 1960s, 1970s, and 1980s. On 8-9 September 2017, Hurricane Irma passed along the north coast of Cuba causing extensive damage to structures, roads, and power supplies.

The country faced a severe economic downturn in 1990 following the withdrawal of former Soviet subsidies worth $4-6 billion annually. Cuba at times portrays the US embargo, in place since 1961, as the source of its difficulties. Over the past decade, there has been growing communication with the Cuban Government to address national interests. As a result of efforts begun in December 2014 to re-establish diplomatic relations with the Cuban Government, which were severed in January 1961, the US and Cuba reopened embassies in their respective countries on 20 July 2015. However, the embargo remains in place.

Illicit migration of Cuban nationals to the US via maritime and overland routes has been a longstanding challenge. In FY 2016, the US Coast Guard interdicted 5,228 Cuban nationals at sea. Also in FY 2016, 44,553 Cuban migrants presented themselves at various land border ports of entry throughout the US. On 12 January 2017, the US and Cuba signed a Joint Statement ending the so-called "wet-foot, dry-foot" policy–by which Cuban nationals who reached US soil were permitted to stay–facilitating the repatriation of Cuban migrants. Illicit Cuban migration has since dropped significantly.

GEOGRAPHY

Location: Caribbean, island between the Caribbean Sea and the North Atlantic Ocean, 150 km south of Key West, Florida

Geographic coordinates: 21 30 N, 80 00 W

Map references: Central America and the Caribbean

Area: *total:* 110,860 sq km
land: 109,820 sq km
water: 1,040 sq km
country comparison to the world: 107

Area—comparative: slightly smaller than Pennsylvania

Land boundaries: *total:* 28.5 km
border countries: US Naval Base at Guantanamo Bay 28.5 km
note: Guantanamo Naval Base is leased by the US and remains part of Cuba

Coastline: 3,735 km

Maritime claims: *territorial sea:* 12 nm
contiguous zone: 24 nm
exclusive economic zone: 200 nm

Climate: tropical; moderated by trade winds; dry season (November to April); rainy season (May to October)

Terrain: mostly flat to rolling plains, with rugged hills and mountains in the southeast

Elevation: *mean elevation:* 108 m

elevation extremes: *lowest point:* Caribbean Sea 0 m
highest point: Pico Turquino 1,974 m

Natural resources: cobalt, nickel, iron ore, chromium, copper, salt, timber, silica, petroleum, arable land

Land use: *agricultural land:* 60.3%
arable land: 33.8%;
permanent crops: 3.6%;
permanent pasture: 22.9%
forest: 27.3%
other: 12.4% (2011 est.)
Irrigated land: 8,700 sq km (2012)

Population—distribution: large population clusters found throughout the country, the more significant ones being in the larger towns and cities, particularly the capital of Havana

Natural hazards: the east coast is subject to hurricanes from August to November (in general, the country averages about one hurricane every other year); droughts are common

Environment—current issues: air and water pollution; biodiversity loss; deforestation

Environment—international agreements: *party to:* Antarctic Treaty, Biodiversity, Climate Change, Climate Change-Kyoto Protocol, Desertification, Endangered Species, Environmental Modification, Hazardous Wastes, Law of the Sea, Marine Dumping, Ozone Layer Protection, Ship Pollution, Wetlands
signed, but not ratified: Marine Life Conservation

Geography—note: largest country in Caribbean and westernmost island of the Greater Antilles

PEOPLE AND SOCIETY

Population: 11,147,407 (July 2017 est.)
country comparison to the world: 80

Nationality: *noun:* Cuban(s)
adjective: Cuban

Ethnic groups: white 64.1%, mulatto or mixed 26.6%, black 9.3%
note: data represent racial self-identification from Cuba's 2012 national census (2012 est.)

Languages: Spanish (official)

Religions: nominally Roman Catholic 85%, Protestant, Jehovah's Witnesses, Jewish, Santeria
note: prior to CASTRO assuming power

Age structure: *0-14 years:* 16.57% (male 950,870/female 896,476)
15-24 years: 12.22% (male 706,882/female 655,446)
25-54 years: 44.43% (male 2,490,483/female 2,462,250)
55-64 years: 11.84% (male 640,150/female 679,603)
65 years and over: 14.94% (male 763,058/female 902,189) (2017 est.)

Dependency ratios: *total dependency ratio:* 43.3
youth dependency ratio: 23.3
elderly dependency ratio: 19.9
potential support ratio: 5 (2015 est.)

Median age: *total:* 41.5 years
male: 40.1 years
female: 42.6 years (2017 est.)
country comparison to the world: 41

Population growth rate: -0.29% (2017 est.)
country comparison to the world: 217

Birth rate: 10.7 births/1,000 population (2017 est.)
country comparison to the world: 184

Death rate: 8.7 deaths/1,000 population (2017 est.)
country comparison to the world: 74

Net migration rate: -4.9 migrant(s)/1,000 population (2017 est.)
country comparison to the world: 190

Population distribution: large population clusters found throughout the country, the more significant ones being in the larger towns and cities, particularly the capital of Havana

Urbanization: *urban population:* 77.3% of total population (2017)
rate of urbanization: 0% annual rate of change (2015-20 est.)

Major urban areas—population: HAVANA (capital) 2.137 million (2015)

Sex ratio: *at birth:* 1.06 male(s)/female
0-14 years: 1.06 male(s)/female
15-24 years: 1.08 male(s)/female
25-54 years: 1.01 male(s)/female
55-64 years: 0.94 male(s)/female
65 years and over: 0.81 male(s)/female
total population: 0.99 male(s)/female (2016 est.)

Maternal mortality ratio: 39 deaths/100,000 live births (2015 est.)
country comparison to the world: 106

Infant mortality rate: *total:* 4.4 deaths/1,000 live births
male: 4.9 deaths/1,000 live births
female: 3.9 deaths/1,000 live births (2017 est.)
country comparison to the world: 181

Life expectancy at birth: *total population:* 78.8 years
male: 76.5 years
female: 81.3 years (2017 est.)
country comparison to the world: 57

Total fertility rate: 1.71 children born/woman (2017 est.)
country comparison to the world: 171

Contraceptive prevalence rate: 73.7% (2014)

Health expenditures: 11.1% of GDP (2014)
country comparison to the world: 12

Physicians density: 7.52 physicians/1,000 population (2014)

Hospital bed density: 5.3 beds/1,000 population (2012)

Drinking water source:
improved:
urban: 96.4% of population
rural: 89.8% of population
total: 94.9% of population
unimproved:
urban: 3.6% of population
rural: 10.2% of population
total: 5.1% of population (2015 est.)

Sanitation facility access:
improved:
urban: 94.4% of population
rural: 89.1% of population
total: 93.2% of population
unimproved:
urban: 5.6% of population
rural: 10.9% of population
total: 6.8% of population (2015 est.)

HIV/AIDS—adult prevalence rate: 0.4% (2016 est.)
country comparison to the world: 71

HIV/AIDS—people living with HIV/AIDS: 25,000 (2016 est.)
country comparison to the world: 70

HIV/AIDS—deaths: <200 (2016 est.)

Major infectious diseases: *degree of risk:* intermediate
food or waterborne diseases: bacterial diarrhea and hepatitis A
vectorborne diseases: dengue fever
note: active local transmission of Zika virus by Aedes species mosquitoes has been identified in this country (as of August 2016); it poses an important risk (a large number of cases possible) among US citizens if bitten by an infective mosquito; other less common ways to get Zika are through sex, via blood transfusion, or during pregnancy, in which the pregnant woman passes Zika virus to her fetus (2016)

Obesity—adult prevalence rate: 24.6% (2016)
country comparison to the world: 56

Education expenditures: 12.8% of GDP (2010)
country comparison to the world: 2

Literacy: *definition:* age 15 and over can read and write
total population: 99.8%
male: 99.9%
female: 99.8% (2015 est.)

School life expectancy (primary to tertiary education): *total:* 14 years
male: 13 years
female: 14 years (2015)

Unemployment, youth ages 15-24: *total:* 6.1%
male: 6.4%
female: 5.6% (2010 est.)
country comparison to the world: 131

People—note: illicit emigration is a continuing problem; Cubans attempt to depart the island and enter the US using homemade rafts, alien smugglers, direct flights, or falsified visas; Cubans also use non-maritime routes to enter the US including direct flights to Miami and overland via the southwest border; the number of Cubans migrating to the US surged after the announcement of normalization of US-Cuban relations in late December 2014 but has decreased since the end of the so-called "wet-foot, dry-foot" policy on 12 January 2017

GOVERNMENT

Country name: *conventional long form:* Republic of Cuba
conventional short form: Cuba
local long form: Republica de Cuba
local short form: Cuba
etymology: name derives from the Taino Indian designation for the island "coabana" meaning "great place"

Government type: communist state

Capital: *name:* Havana
geographic coordinates: 23 07 N, 82 21 W
time difference: UTC-5 (same time as Washington, DC, during Standard Time)
daylight saving time: +1hr, begins second Sunday in March; ends first Sunday in November; note—Cuba has been known to alter the schedule of DST on short notice in an attempt to conserve electricity for lighting

Administrative divisions: 15 provinces (provincias, singular—provincia) and 1 special municipality* (municipio especial); Artemisa, Camaguey, Ciego de Avila, Cienfuegos, Granma, Guantanamo, Holguin, Isla de la Juventud*, La Habana, Las Tunas, Matanzas, Mayabeque, Pinar del Rio, Sancti Spiritus, Santiago de Cuba, Villa Clara

Independence: 20 May 1902 (from Spain 10 December 1898; administered by the US from 1898 to 1902); not acknowledged by the Cuban Government as a day of independence

National holiday: Triumph of the Revolution (Liberation Day), 1 January (1959)

Constitution: several previous; latest adopted by referendum 15 February 1976, effective 24 February 1976; amended 1978, 1992, 2002 (2016)

Legal system: civil law system based on Spanish civil code

International law organization participation: has not submitted an ICJ jurisdiction declaration; non-party state to the ICCt

Citizenship: *citizenship by birth:* yes
citizenship by descent: yes
dual citizenship recognized: no
residency requirement for naturalization: unknown

Suffrage: 16 years of age; universal

Executive branch: *chief of state:* President of the Council of State and President of the Council of Ministers Gen. Raul CASTRO Ruz (president since 24 February 2008); First Vice President of the Council of State and First Vice President of the Council of Ministers Miguel DIAZ-CANEL Bermudez (since 24 February 2013); note—the president is both chief of state and head of government

head of government: President of the Council of State and President of the Council of Ministers Gen. Raul CASTRO Ruz (president since 24 February 2008); First Vice President of the Council of State and First Vice President of the Council of Ministers Miguel DIAZ-CANEL Bermudez (since 24 February 2013)

cabinet: Council of Ministers proposed by the president of the Council of State and appointed by the National Assembly; it is subordinate to the 31-member Council of State, which is elected by the Assembly to act on its behalf when it is not in session

elections/appointments: president and vice presidents indirectly elected by the National Assembly for a 5-year term (may be reelected for another 5-year term); election last held on 24 February 2013 (next to be held in April 2018)

election results: Gen. Raul CASTRO Ruz (PCC) reelected president; percent of National Assembly vote—100%; Miguel DIAZ-CANEL Bermudez (PCC) elected vice president; percent of National Assembly vote—100%

Legislative branch: *description:* unicameral National Assembly of People's Power or Asamblea Nacional del Poder Popular (614 seats; members directly elected by absolute majority vote; members serve 5-year terms); note—the National Candidature Commission submits a slate of approved candidates; to be elected, candidates must receive more than 50% of valid votes otherwise the seat remains vacant or the Council of State can declare another election

elections: last held on 3 February 2013 (next to be held on 11 March 2018)

election results: Cuba's Communist Party is the only legal party, and officially sanctioned candidates run unopposed

Judicial branch: *highest court(s):* People's Supreme Court (consists of court president, vice president, 41 professional justices, and NA lay judges); organization includes the State Council, criminal, civil, administrative, labor, crimes against the state, and military courts)

judge selection and term of office: professional judges elected by the National Assembly are not subject to a specific term; lay judges nominated by workplace collectives and neighborhood associations and elected by municipal or provincial assemblies; lay judges appointed for 5-year terms and serve up to 30 days per year

subordinate courts: People's Provincial Courts; People's Regional Courts; People's Courts

Political parties and leaders: Cuban Communist Party or PCC [Raul CASTRO Ruz]

Political pressure groups and leaders: Cuban Commission for Human Rights and National Reconciliation (CCDHRN)
Ladies in White (Damas de Blanco)
Patriotic Union of Cuba or UNPACU
other: political dissidents and bloggers

International organization participation: ACP, ALBA, AOSIS, CELAC, FAO, G-77, IAEA, ICAO, ICC (national committees), ICRM, IFAD, IFRCS, IHO, ILO, IMO, IMSO, Interpol, IOC, IOM (observer), IPU, ISO, ITSO, ITU, LAES, LAIA, NAM, OAS (excluded from formal participation since 1962), OPANAL, OPCW, PCA, Petrocaribe, PIF (partner), UN, UNCTAD, UNESCO, UNIDO, Union Latina, UNWTO, UPU, WCO, WFTU (NGOs), WHO, WIPO, WMO, WTO

Diplomatic representation in the US: *chief of mission:* Ambassador Jose Ramon CABANAS Rodriguez (since 17 September 2015)
chancery: 2630 16th Street NW, Washington, DC 20009
telephone: [1] (202) 797-8518
FAX: NA
consulate(s) general: NA

Diplomatic representation from the US: *chief of mission:* Ambassador (vacant); Charge d'Affaires Scott HAMILTON (since 13 July 2017)
embassy: Calzada between L & M Streets, Vedado, Havana
mailing address: use embassy street address
telephone: [53] (7) 839-4100
FAX: NA

Flag description: five equal horizontal bands of blue (top, center, and bottom) alternating with white; a red equilateral triangle based on the hoist side bears a white, five-pointed star in the center; the blue bands refer to the three old divisions of the island: central, occidental, and oriental; the white bands describe the purity of the independence ideal; the triangle symbolizes liberty, equality, and fraternity, while the red color stands for the blood shed in the independence struggle; the white star, called La Estrella Solitaria (the Lone Star) lights the way to freedom and was taken from the flag of Texas

note: design similar to the Puerto Rican flag, with the colors of the bands and triangle reversed

National symbol(s): royal palm; national colors: red, white, blue

National anthem: *name:* "La Bayamesa" (The Bayamo Song)
lyrics/music: Pedro FIGUEREDO
note: adopted 1940; Pedro FIGUEREDO first performed "La Bayamesa" in 1868 during the Ten Years War against the Spanish; a leading figure in the uprising, FIGUEREDO was captured in 1870 and executed by a firing squad; just prior to the fusillade he is reputed to have shouted, "Morir por la Patria es vivir" (To die for the country is to live), a line from the anthem

ECONOMY

Economy—overview: The government continues to balance the need for loosening its socialist economic system against a desire for firm political control. In April 2011, the government held the first Cuban Communist Party Congress in almost 13 years, during which leaders approved a plan for wide-ranging economic changes. Since then, the government has slowly and incrementally implemented limited economic reforms, including allowing Cubans to buy electronic appliances and cell phones, stay in hotels, and buy and sell used cars. The government has cut state sector jobs as part of the reform process, and it has opened up some retail services to "self-employment," leading to the rise of so-called "cuentapropistas" or entrepreneurs. More than 500,000 Cuban workers are currently registered as self-employed.

The Cuban regime has updated its economic model to include permitting the private ownership and sale of real estate and new vehicles, allowing private farmers to sell agricultural goods directly to hotels, allowing the creation of non-agricultural cooperatives, adopting a new foreign investment law, and launching a "Special Development Zone" around the Mariel port.

Since 2016, Cuba has attributed slowed economic growth in part to problems with petroleum product deliveries from Venezuela. Since late 2000, Venezuela provided petroleum products to Cuba on preferential terms, supplying at times nearly 100,000 barrels per day. Cuba paid for the oil, in part, with the services of Cuban personnel in Venezuela, including some 30,000 medical professionals.

GDP (purchasing power parity): $132.9 billion (2016 est.)
$134.2 billion (2015 est.)
$128.5 billion (2014 est.)
note: data are in 2016 US dollars
country comparison to the world: 80

GDP (official exchange rate): $81.56 billion (2013 est.)
note: data are in Cuban Pesos at 1 CUP = 1 US$; official exchange rate

GDP—real growth rate: -0.9% (2016 est.)
4.4% (2015 est.)
1% (2014 est.)
country comparison to the world: 205

GDP—per capita (PPP): $11,900 (2016 est.)
$12,200 (2015 est.)
$11,600 (2014 est.)
note: data are in 2016 US dollars
country comparison to the world: 132

Gross national saving: 10.1% of GDP (2017 est.)
11% of GDP (2016 est.)
12.1% of GDP (2015 est.)
country comparison to the world: 158

GDP—composition, by end use:
household consumption: 58.2%
government consumption: 31.7%
investment in fixed capital: 9.9%
investment in inventories: 0%
exports of goods and services: 13.6%
imports of goods and services: -13.5% (2017 est.)

GDP—composition, by sector of origin:
agriculture: 3.9%
industry: 21.5%
services: 74.2% (2017 est.)

Agriculture—products: sugar, tobacco, citrus, coffee, rice, potatoes, beans; livestock

Industries: petroleum, nickel, cobalt, pharmaceuticals, tobacco, construction, steel, cement, agricultural machinery, sugar

Industrial production growth rate: 0.6% (2017 est.)
country comparison to the world: 179

Labor force: 4.691 million
note: state sector 72.3%, non-state sector 27.7% (2017 est.)
country comparison to the world: 87

Labor force—by occupation: *agriculture:* 18%
industry: 10%
services: 72% (2013 est.)

Unemployment rate: 2.2% (2017 est.)
2% (2016 est.)
note: data are official rates; unofficial estimates are about double the official figures
country comparison to the world: 18

Population below poverty line: NA%

Household income or consumption by percentage share: *lowest 10%:* NA%
highest 10%: NA%

Budget: *revenues:* $52.36 billion
expenditures: $60.57 billion (2017 est.)
Taxes and other revenues: 64.2% of GDP (2017 est.)
country comparison to the world: 7

Budget surplus (+) or deficit (-): -10.1% of GDP (2017 est.)
country comparison to the world: 208

Public debt: 35.8% of GDP (2017 est.)
32.1% of GDP (2016 est.)
country comparison to the world: 144

Fiscal year: calendar year

Inflation rate (consumer prices): 4.8% (2017 est.) 4.5% (2016 est.)

country comparison to the world: 171

Central bank discount rate: NA%

Commercial bank prime lending rate: NA%

Stock of narrow money: $23.49 billion (31 December 2017 est.) $21.92 billion (31 December 2016 est.)

country comparison to the world: 67

Stock of broad money: $50.2 billion (31 December 2017 est.) $48.19 billion (31 December 2016 est.)

country comparison to the world: 68

Stock of domestic credit: $NA

Current account balance: $985.4 million (2017 est.) $2.008 billion (2016 est.)

country comparison to the world: 39

Exports: $2.885 billion (2017 est.) $2.535 billion (2016 est.)

country comparison to the world: 128

Exports—commodities: petroleum, nickel, medical products, sugar, tobacco, fish, citrus, coffee

Exports—partners: Russia 22.9%, Venezuela 15.4%, Spain 10.3% (2016)

Imports: $10.84 billion (2017 est.) $10.28 billion (2016 est.)

country comparison to the world: 95

Imports—commodities: petroleum, food, machinery and equipment, chemicals

Imports—partners: China 29.2%, Spain 14%, Italy 5.1%, Brazil 4.7%, Mexico 4.4%, Russia 4.3%, Canada 4.1%, US 4% (2016)

Reserves of foreign exchange and gold: $12.8 billion (31 December 2017 est.) $12.3 billion (31 December 2016 est.)

country comparison to the world: 70

Debt—external: $20.55 billion (31 December 2017 est.) $20.59 billion (31 December 2016 est.)

country comparison to the world: 92

Stock of direct foreign investment—at home: $NA

Stock of direct foreign investment—abroad: $4.138 billion (2006 est.)

country comparison to the world: 76

Exchange rates: Cuban pesos (CUP) per US dollar—
1 (2017 est.)
1 (2016 est.)
1 (2015 est.)
1 (2014 est.)
22.7 (2013 est.)

ENERGY

Electricity access: *population without electricity:* 200,000

electrification—*total population:* 99.9%
electrification—urban areas: 100%
electrification—rural areas: 95% (2013)

Electricity—production: 19.12 billion kWh (2015 est.)

country comparison to the world: 77

Electricity—consumption: 15.98 billion kWh (2015 est.)

country comparison to the world: 75

Electricity—exports: 0 kWh (2016 est.)
country comparison to the world: 125

Electricity—imports: 0 kWh (2016 est.)
country comparison to the world: 138

Electricity—installed generating capacity: 6.711 million kW (2015 est.)

country comparison to the world: 74

Electricity—from fossil fuels: 90.7% of total installed capacity (2015 est.)

country comparison to the world: 60

Electricity—from nuclear fuels: 0% of total installed capacity (2015 est.)

country comparison to the world: 73

Electricity—from hydroelectric plants: 0.9% of total installed capacity (2015 est.)

country comparison to the world: 147

Electricity—from other renewable sources: 8.5% of total installed capacity (2015 est.)

country comparison to the world: 75

Crude oil—production: 49,830 bbl/day (2016 est.)
country comparison to the world: 54

Crude oil—exports: 0 bbl/day (2014 est.)
country comparison to the world: 110

Crude oil—imports: 101,500 bbl/day (2014 est.)
country comparison to the world: 44

Crude oil—proved reserves: 124 million bbl (1 January 2017 es)

country comparison to the world: 71

Refined petroleum products—production: 102,800 bbl/day (2014 est.)

country comparison to the world: 68

Refined petroleum products—consumption: 180,000 bbl/day (2015 est.)

country comparison to the world: 60

Refined petroleum products—exports: 25,540 bbl/day (2014 est.)

country comparison to the world: 66

Refined petroleum products—imports: 51,970 bbl/day (2014 est.)

country comparison to the world: 82

Natural gas—production: 1.25 billion cu m (2015 est.)

country comparison to the world: 64

Natural gas—consumption: 2.063 billion cu m (2015 est.)

country comparison to the world: 87

Natural gas—exports: 0 cu m (2016 est.)
country comparison to the world: 89

Natural gas—imports: 0 cu m (2016 est.)
country comparison to the world: 113

Natural gas—proved reserves: 70.79 billion cu m (1 January 2017 es)

country comparison to the world: 59

Carbon dioxide emissions from consumption of energy: 26 million Mt (2013 est.)

country comparison to the world: 77

COMMUNICATIONS

Telephones—fixed lines: *total subscriptions:* 1,322,002

subscriptions per 100 inhabitants: 12 (July 2016 est.)

country comparison to the world: 67

Telephones—mobile cellular: *total:* 3,987,900

subscriptions per 100 inhabitants: 36 (July 2016 est.)

country comparison to the world: 144

Telephone system: *general assessment:* fixed-line and mobile services run by the state-run ETESCA; mobile-cellular telephone service is expensive and must be paid in convertible pesos; Cuban Government has opened several hundred Wi-Fi hotspots around the island, which are expensive, and launched a new residential Internet pilot in Havana

domestic: fixed-line density remains low at about 10 per 100 inhabitants; mobile-cellular service expanding but remains only about 35 per 100 persons

international: country code—53; the ALBA-1 fiber-optic submarine cable links Cuba, Jamaica, and Venezuela; fiber-optic cable laid to but not linked to US network; satellite earth station—1 Intersputnik (Atlantic Ocean region); several US telecommunication companies have signed voice and data deals to serve their customers while in Cuba (2017)

Broadcast media: government owns and controls all broadcast media with private ownership of electronic media prohibited; however, several online independent news sites exist and those that are not openly critical of the government are often tolerated; government operates 5 national TV networks and many local TV stations; government operates 6 national radio networks, an international station, and many local radio stations; Radio-TV Marti is beamed from the US (2017)

Internet country code: .cu
Internet users: total: 4,334,022

percent of population: 38.8%

note: private citizens are prohibited from buying computers or accessing the Internet without special authorization; foreigners may access the Internet in large hotels but are subject to firewalls; some Cubans buy illegal passwords on the black market or take advantage of public outlets to access limited email and the government-controlled "intranet" (July 2016 est.)

country comparison to the world: 85

TRANSPORTATION

National air transport system: *number of registered air carriers:* 3
inventory of registered aircraft operated by air carriers: 18
annual passenger traffic on registered air carriers: 1,294,458
annual freight traffic on registered air carriers: 20,919,645 mt-km (2015)

Civil aircraft registration country code prefix: CU (2016)

Airports: 133 (2017)
country comparison to the world: 43

Airports—with paved runways: *total:* 64
over 3,047 m: 7
2,438 to 3,047 m: 10
1,524 to 2,437 m: 16
914 to 1,523 m: 4
under 914 m: 27 (2017)

Airports—with unpaved runways: *total:* 69
914 to 1,523 m: 11
under 914 m: 58 (2013)

Pipelines: gas 41 km; oil 230 km (2013)

Railways: *total:* 8,367 km
standard gauge: 8,195 km 1.435-m gauge (105 km electrified)
narrow gauge: 172 km 1.000-m gauge
note: 70 km of standard gauge track is not for public use (2015)
country comparison to the world: 26

Roadways: *total:* 60,858 km
paved: 29,820 km (includes 639 km of expressways)
unpaved: 31,038 km (2001)
country comparison to the world: 69

Waterways: 240 km (almost all navigable inland waterways are near the mouths of rivers) (2011)
country comparison to the world: 94

Merchant marine: *total:* 43
by type: general cargo 11, oil tanker 3, other 29 (2017)
country comparison to the world: 115

Ports and terminals: *major seaport(s):* Antilla, Cienfuegos, Guantanamo, Havana, Matanzas, Mariel, Nuevitas Bay, Santiago de Cuba

MILITARY AND SECURITY

Military expenditures: 3.08% of GDP (2015)
3.54% of GDP (2014)
3.51% of GDP (2013)
3.94% of GDP (2012)
3.08% of GDP (2011)

Military branches: Revolutionary Armed Forces (Fuerzas Armadas Revolucionarias, FAR): Revolutionary Army (Ejercito Revolucionario, ER, includes Territorial Militia Troops (Milicia de Tropas de Territoriales, MTT)), Revolutionary Navy (Marina de Guerra Revolucionaria, MGR, includes Marine Corps), Revolutionary Air and Air Defense Forces (Defensas Anti-Aereas y Fuerza Aerea Revolucionaria, DAAFAR); Youth Labor Army (Ejercito Juvenil del Trabajo, EJT) (2013)

Military service age and obligation: 17-28 years of age for compulsory military service; 2-year service obligation for males, optional for females (2017)

Military—note: the collapse of the Soviet Union deprived the Cuban military of its major economic and logistic support and had a significant impact on the state of Cuban equipment; the army remains well trained and professional in nature; the lack of replacement parts for its existing equipment has increasingly affected operational capabilities (2013)

TRANSNATIONAL ISSUES

Disputes—international: US Naval Base at Guantanamo Bay is leased to US and only mutual agreement or US abandonment of the facility can terminate the lease

Trafficking in persons: *current situation:* Cuba is a source country for adults and children subjected to sex trafficking and forced labor; child sex trafficking and child sex tourism occur in Cuba, while some Cubans are forced into prostitution in South America and the Caribbean; allegations have been made that some Cubans have been forced or coerced to work at Cuban medical missions abroad; assessing the scope of trafficking within Cuba is difficult because of the lack of information

tier rating: Tier 2 Watch List—Cuba does not fully comply with the minimum standards for the elimination of trafficking; however, it is making significant efforts to do so; Cuba's penal code does not criminalize all forms of human trafficking, but the government reported that it is in the process of amending its criminal code to comply with the 2000 UN TIP Protocol, to which it acceded in 2013; the government in 2014 prosecuted and convicted 13 sex traffickers and provided services to the victims in those cases but does not have shelters specifically for trafficking victims; the government did not recognize forced labor as a problem and took no action to address it; state media produced newspaper articles and TV and radio programs to raise public awareness about sex trafficking (2015)

Illicit drugs: territorial waters and air space serve as transshipment zone for US- and European-bound drugs; established the death penalty for certain drug-related crimes in 1999

CURACAO

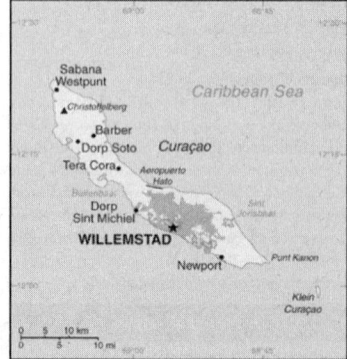

hard hit economically by the abolition of slavery in 1863. Its prosperity (and that of neighboring Aruba) was restored in the early 20th century with the construction of the Isla Refineria to service the newly discovered Venezuelan oil fields. In 1954, Curacao and several other Dutch Caribbean possessions were reorganized as the Netherlands Antilles, part of the Kingdom of the Netherlands. In referenda in 2005 and 2009, the citizens of Curacao voted to become a self-governing country within the Kingdom of the Netherlands. The change in status became effective in October 2010 with the dissolution of the Netherlands Antilles.

GEOGRAPHY

Location: Caribbean, an island in the Caribbean Sea, 55 km off the coast of Venezuela

Geographic coordinates: 12 10 N, 69 00 W

Map references: Central America and the Caribbean

Area: *total:* 444 sq km
land: 444 sq km

water: 0 sq km
country comparison to the world: 200

Area—comparative: more than twice the size of Washington, DC

Land boundaries: 0 km

Coastline: 364 km

Maritime claims: *territorial sea:* 12 nm
exclusive economic zone: 200 nm

Climate: tropical marine climate, ameliorated by northeast trade winds, results in mild temperatures; semiarid with average rainfall of 60 cm/year

Terrain: generally low, hilly terrain

Elevation: *mean elevation:* NA

elevation extremes: *lowest point:* Caribbean Sea 0 m
highest point: Mt. Christoffel 372 m

Natural resources: calcium phosphates, aloes, sorghum, peanuts, vegetables, tropical fruit

Land use: *agricultural land:* 10%
arable land: 10%;
permanent crops: 0%;

INTRODUCTION

Background: Originally settled by Arawak Indians, Curacao was seized by the Dutch in 1634 along with the neighboring island of Bonaire. Once the center of the Caribbean slave trade, Curacao was

permanent pasture: 0%
forest: 0%
other: 90% (2011 est.)
Irrigated land: NA

Population—distribution: largest concentration on the island is Willemstad; smaller settlements near the coast can be found throughout the island, particularly in the northwest

Natural hazards: Curacao is south of the Caribbean hurricane belt and is rarely threatened

Environment—current issues: problems in waste management that threaten environmental sustainability on the island include pollution of marine areas from domestic sewage, inadequate sewage treatment facilities, industrial effluents and agricultural runoff, the management of toxic substances, and ineffective regulations

Geography—note: Curacao is a part of the Windward Islands (southern) group in the Lesser Antilles

PEOPLE AND SOCIETY

Population: 149,648 (July 2017 est.)
country comparison to the world: 188

Nationality: *noun:* Curacaoan
adjective: Curacaoan; Dutch

Ethnic groups: Afro-Caribbean majority; Dutch, French, Latin American, East Asian, South Asian, Jewish minorities

Languages: Papiamento (official) (a creole language that is a mixture of Portuguese, Spanish, Dutch, English, and, to a lesser extent, French, as well as elements of African languages and the language of the Arawak) 81.2%, Dutch (official) 8%, Spanish 4%, English (official) 2.9%, other 3.9% (2001 census)

Religions: Roman Catholic 72.8%, Pentecostal 6.6%, Protestant 3.2%, Adventist 3%, Jehovah's Witness 2%, Evangelical 1.9%, other 3.8%, none 6%, unspecified 0.6% (2011 est.)

Age structure: *0-14 years:* 20% (male 15,274/female 14,661)
15-24 years: 14.33% (male 11,170/female 10,280)
25-54 years: 36.87% (male 27,152/female 28,029)
55-64 years: 13.69% (male 8,862/female 11,620)
65 years and over: 15.1% (male 9,270/female 13,330) (2017 est.)

Dependency ratios: *total dependency ratio:* 52.4
youth dependency ratio: 28.7
elderly dependency ratio: 23.6
potential support ratio: 4.2 (2015 est.)

Median age: *total:* 36.1 years
male: 33.5 years
female: 39.7 years (2017 est.)
country comparison to the world: 73

Population growth rate: 0.4% (2017 est.)
country comparison to the world: 161

Birth rate: 13.7 births/1,000 population (2017 est.)
country comparison to the world: 140

Death rate: 8.4 deaths/1,000 population (2017 est.)
country comparison to the world: 81

Net migration rate: -1.3 migrant(s)/1,000 population (2017 est.)
country comparison to the world: 146

Population distribution: largest concentration on the island is Willemstad; smaller settlements near the coast can be found throughout the island, particularly in the northwest

Urbanization: *urban population:* 89.2% of total population (2017)
rate of urbanization: 0.73% annual rate of change (2015-20 est.)

Major urban areas—population: WILLEMSTAD (capital) 145,000 (2014)

Sex ratio: *at birth:* 1.05 male(s)/female
0-14 years: 1.04 male(s)/female
15-24 years: 1.09 male(s)/female
25-54 years: 0.96 male(s)/female
55-64 years: 0.76 male(s)/female
65 years and over: 0.7 male(s)/female
total population: 0.92 male(s)/female (2016 est.)

Infant mortality rate: *total:* 7.5 deaths/1,000 live births
male: 8.1 deaths/1,000 live births
female: 7 deaths/1,000 live births (2017 est.)
country comparison to the world: 159

Life expectancy at birth: *total population:* 78.5 years
male: 76.2 years
female: 80.9 years (2017 est.)
country comparison to the world: 60

Total fertility rate: 2.04 children born/woman (2017 est.)
country comparison to the world: 113

HIV/AIDS—adult prevalence rate: NA

HIV/AIDS—people living with HIV/AIDS: NA

HIV/AIDS—deaths: NA

Major infectious diseases: *note:* active local transmission of Zika virus by Aedes species mosquitoes has been identified in this country (as of August 2016); it poses an important risk (a large number of cases possible) among US citizens if bitten by an infective mosquito; other less common ways to get Zika are through sex, via blood transfusion, or during pregnancy, in which the pregnant woman passes Zika virus to her fetus (2016)

Education expenditures: 4.9% of GDP (2013)

School life expectancy (primary to tertiary education): *total:* 18 years
male: 18 years
female: 19 years (2013)

Unemployment, youth ages 15-24: *total:* 29.7%
male: NA
female: NA (2015 est.)

GOVERNMENT

Country name: *conventional long form:* none
conventional short form: Curacao
local long form: Land Curacao (Dutch); Pais Korsou (Papiamento)
local short form: Curacao (Dutch); Korsou (Papiamento)

former: Netherlands Antilles; Curacao and Dependencies
etymology: the most plausible name derivation is that the island was designated Isla de la Curacion (Spanish meaning "Island of the Cure" or "Island of Healing") or Ilha da Curacao (Portuguese meaning the same) to reflect the locale's function as a recovery stop for sick crewmen

Dependency status: constituent country within the Kingdom of the Netherlands; full autonomy in internal affairs granted in 2010; Dutch Government responsible for defense and foreign affairs

Government type: parliamentary democracy

Capital: *name:* Willemstad
geographic coordinates: 12 06 N, 68 55 W
time difference: UTC-4 (1 hour ahead of Washington, DC, during Standard Time)

Administrative divisions: none (part of the Kingdom of the Netherlands)
note: Curacao is one of four constituent countries of the Kingdom of the Netherlands; the other three are the Netherlands, Aruba, and Sint Maarten

Independence: none (part of the Kingdom of the Netherlands)

National holiday: King's Day (birthday of King WILLEM-ALEXANDER), 27 April (1967); note—King's or Queen's Day are observed on the ruling monarch's birthday; celebrated on 26 April if 27 April is a Sunday

Constitution: previous 1947, 1955; latest adopted 5 September 2010, entered into force 10 October 2010 (regulates governance of Curacao but is subordinate to the Charter for the Kingdom of the Netherlands); note—in October 2010, with the dissolution of the Netherlands Antilles, Curacao became a constituent country within the Kingdom of the Netherlands (2017)

Legal system: based on Dutch civil law system with some English common law influence

Citizenship: see the Netherlands

Suffrage: 18 years of age; universal

Executive branch: *chief of state:* King WILLEM-ALEXANDER of the Netherlands (since 30 April 2013); represented by Governor Lucille A. GEORGE-WOUT (since 4 November 2013)

head of government: Prime Minister Eugene RHUGGENAATH (since 29 May 2017)
cabinet: Cabinet appointed by the governor
elections: the monarch is hereditary; governor general appointed by the monarch; following legislative elections, the leader of the majority party is usually elected prime minister by the parliament

Legislative branch: description: unicameral Estates of Curacao or Staten van Curacao (21 seats; members directly elected by proportional representation vote to serve 4-year terms)
elections: last held 28 April 2017 (next to be held on 2021); early elections are being held after Prime Minister Hensley KOEIMAN resigned on 12 February 2017, when the coalition government lost its majority

election results: percent of vote by party—PAR 23.3%, MAN 20.4%, MFK 19.9%, KdnT 9.4%, PIN 5.3%, PS 5.1%, MP 4.9%, other 11.7%; seats by party—PAR 6, MAN 5, MFK 5, KdnT 2, PIN 1, PS 1, MP 1

Judicial branch: *highest court(s):* Joint Court of Justice of Aruba, Curacao, Sint Maarten, and of Bonaire, Sint Eustatitus and Saba or "Joint Court of Justice" (sits as a 3-judge panel); final appeals heard by the Supreme Court, in The Hague, Netherlands
judge selection and term of office: Joint Court judges appointed by the monarch for life
subordinate courts: first instance courts, appeals court; specialized courts

Political parties and leaders: Korsou di Nos Tur or KdnT [Amparo dos SANTOS]
Movementu Futuro Korsou or MFK [Gerrit SCHOTTE]
Movementu Progresivo or MP [Marylin MOSES]
Movishon Antia Nobo or MAN [Hensley KOEIMAN]
Partido Antia Restruktura or PAR [Eugene RHUGGENAATH]
Partido Inovashon Nashonal or PIN [Suzanne CAMELIA-ROMER]
Partido pa Adelanto I Inovashon Soshal or PAIS [Alex ROSARIA]
Partido Nashonal di Pueblo or PNP [Humphrey DAVELAAR]
Pueblo Soberano or PS (vacant)
Un Korsou Hustu [Omayra LEEFLANG]

Diplomatic representation in the US: none (represented by the Kingdom of the Netherlands)

Diplomatic representation from the US: *chief of mission:* Consul General Margaret HAWTHORNE (since April 2016); note—also accredited to Aruba and Sint Maarten
consulate(s) general: J. B. Gorsiraweg
mailing address: P. O. Box 158, Willemstad, Curacao
telephone: [599] (9) 4613066
FAX: [599] (9) 4616489

Flag description: on a blue field a horizontal yellow band somewhat below the center divides the flag into proportions of 5:1:2; two five-pointed white stars—the smaller above and to the left of the larger—appear in the canton; the blue of the upper and lower sections symbolizes the sky and sea respectively; yellow represents the sun; the stars symbolize Curacao and its uninhabited smaller sister island of Klein Curacao; the five star points signify the five continents from which Curacao's people derive

National symbol(s): laraha (citrus tree); national colors: blue, yellow, white

National anthem: name: Himmo di Korsou (Anthem of Curacao)
lyrics/music: Guillermo ROSARIO, Mae HENRIQUEZ, Enrique MULLER, Betty DORAN/Frater Candidus NOWENS, Errol "El Toro" COLINA

note: adapted 1978; the lyrics, originally written in 1899, were rewritten in 1978 to make them less colonial in nature

ECONOMY

Economy—overview: Most of Curacao's GDP results from services. Tourism, petroleum refining and bunkering, offshore finance, and transportation and communications are the mainstays of this small island economy, which is closely tied to the outside world. Curacao has limited natural resources, poor soil, and inadequate water supplies, and budgetary problems complicate reform of the health and education systems. Although GDP grew only slightly during the past decade, Curacao enjoys a high per capita income and a well-developed infrastructure compared to other countries in the region.

Curacao has an excellent natural harbor that can accommodate large oil tankers, and the port of Willemstad hosts a free trade zone and a dry dock. Venezuelan state-owned oil company PdVSA, under a contract in effect until 2019, leases the single refinery on the island from the government, directly employing some 1,000 people. Most of the oil for the refinery is imported from Venezuela and most of the refined products are exported to the US and Asia. Almost all consumer and capital goods are imported, with the US, the Netherlands, and Venezuela being the major suppliers.

The government is attempting to diversify its industry and trade. Curacao is an Overseas Countries and Territories (OCT) of the European Union. Nationals of Curacao are citizens of the European Union, even though it is not a member. Based on its OCT status, products that originate in Curacao have preferential access to the EU and are exempt from import duties. Curacao is a beneficiary of the Caribbean Basin Initiative and, as a result, products originating in Curacao can be imported tax free into the US if at least 35% has been added to the value of these products in Curacao. The island has state-of-the-art information and communication technology connectivity with the rest of the world, including a Tier IV datacenter. With several direct satellite and submarine optic fiber cables, Curacao has one of the best Internet speeds and reliability in the Western Hemisphere.

GDP (purchasing power parity): $3.128 billion (2012 est.)
$3.02 billion (2011 est.)
$2.96 billion (2010 est.)
note: data are in 2012 US dollars
country comparison to the world: 188

GDP (official exchange rate): $5.6 billion (2012 est.)

GDP—real growth rate: 3.6% (2012 est.)
2% (2011 est.)
0.1% (2010 est.)
country comparison to the world: 88

GDP—per capita (PPP): $15,000 (2004 est.)
country comparison to the world: 111

GDP—composition, by end use:

household consumption: 66.9%
government consumption: 33.6%
investment in fixed capital: 19.4%
investment in inventories: 0%
exports of goods and services: 17.5%
imports of goods and services: -37.5% (2016 est.)

GDP—composition, by sector of origin:
agriculture: 0.7%
industry: 15.5%
services: 83.8% (2012 est.)

Agriculture—products: aloe, sorghum, peanuts, vegetables, tropical fruit

Industries: tourism, petroleum refining, petroleum transshipment, light manufacturing, financial and business services

Industrial production growth rate: NA%

Labor force: 73,010 (2013)
country comparison to the world: 185

Labor force—by occupation: *agriculture:* 1.2%
industry: 16.9%
services: 81.8% (2008 est.)

Unemployment rate: 13% (2013 est.)
9.8% (2011 est.)
country comparison to the world: 161
Taxes and other revenues: 16.6% of GDP (2012 est.)
country comparison to the world: 180

Budget surplus (+) or deficit (-): -0.4% of GDP (2012 est.)
country comparison to the world: 43

Public debt: 33.2% of GDP (2012 est.)
40.6% of GDP (2011 est.)
country comparison to the world: 150

Inflation rate (consumer prices): 2.6% (2013 est.)
2.8% (2012 est.)
country comparison to the world: 121

Exports: $1.607 billion (2011 est.)
$1.44 billion (2010 est.)
country comparison to the world: 148

Exports—commodities: petroleum products

Imports: $1.285 billion (2011 est.)
$1.275 billion (2010 est.)
country comparison to the world: 171

Imports—commodities: crude petroleum, food, manufactures

Exchange rates: Netherlands Antillean guilders (ANG) per US dollar—
1.79 (2014 est.)
1.79 (2013 est.)

ENERGY

Electricity access: *population without electricity:* 14,903
electrification—*total population:* 91%
electrification—*urban areas:* 91%
electrification—*rural areas:* 80% (2012)

Electricity—production: 1.785 billion kWh (2012 est.)
country comparison to the world: 142

Electricity—consumption: 968 million kWh (2008 est.)

country comparison to the world: 156

Electricity—exports: 0 kWh (2009 est.)
country comparison to the world: 116

Electricity—imports: 0 kWh (2009 est.)
country comparison to the world: 130

Crude oil—proved reserves: 0 bbl (1 January 2011 es)
country comparison to the world: 124

Refined petroleum products—production: 531.1 bbl/day (2010 est.)
country comparison to the world: 106

Refined petroleum products—consumption: 72,000 bbl/day (2010 est.)
country comparison to the world: 91

Refined petroleum products—exports: 211,100 bbl/day (2009 est.)
country comparison to the world: 33

Refined petroleum products—imports: 291,700 bbl/day (2009 est.)
country comparison to the world: 27

Natural gas—production: 0 cu m (2009 est.)
country comparison to the world: 117

Natural gas—consumption: 0 cu m (2009 est.)

country comparison to the world: 165

Natural gas—exports: 0 cu m (2009 est.)
country comparison to the world: 79

Natural gas—imports: 0 cu m (2009 est.)
country comparison to the world: 102

Natural gas—proved reserves: 0 cu m (1 January 2011 es)
country comparison to the world: 123

COMMUNICATIONS

Telephone system: *international:* country code—599

Broadcast media: government-run TeleCuracao operates a TV station and a radio station; 3 other privately owned TV stations and several privately owned radio stations (2017)

Internet country code: .cw
Internet users: total: 138,750

percent of population: 93.9% (July 2016 est.)

TRANSPORTATION

National air transport system: *number of registered air carriers:* 2

inventory of registered aircraft operated by air carriers: 11 (2015)
Civil aircraft registration country code prefix: PJ (2016)

Airports: 1 (2017)
Airports—with paved runways: over 3,047 m: 1 (2017)

Roadways: *total:* 550 km
country comparison to the world: 194

Merchant marine: *total:* 92
by type: general cargo 18, oil tanker 1, other 73 (2017)

Ports and terminals: *major seaport(s):* Willemstad
oil terminal(s): Bullen Baai (Curacao Terminal)
bulk cargo port(s): Fuik Bay (phosphate rock)

MILITARY AND SECURITY

Military branches: no regular military forces; the Dutch Government controls foreign and defense policy (2012)

Military service age and obligation: no conscription (2010)

Military—note: defense is the responsibility of the Kingdom of the Netherlands

CYPRUS

INTRODUCTION

Background: A former British colony, Cyprus became independent in 1960 following years of resistance to British rule. Tensions between the Greek Cypriot majority and Turkish Cypriot minority came to a head in December 1963, when violence broke out in the capital of Nicosia. Despite the deployment of UN peacekeepers in 1964, sporadic intercommunal violence continued, forcing most Turkish Cypriots into enclaves throughout the island. In 1974, a Greek Government-sponsored attempt to overthrow the elected president of Cyprus was met by military intervention from Turkey, which soon controlled more than a third of the island. In 1983, the Turkish Cypriot administered area declared itself the "Turkish Republic of Northern Cyprus" ("TRNC"), but it is recognized only by Turkey. A UN-mediated agreement, the Annan Plan, failed to win approval by both communities in 2004. In February 2014, after a hiatus of nearly two years, the leaders of the two communities resumed formal discussions under UN auspices aimed at reuniting the divided island. Talks were suspended in

October 2014, but resumed in earnest in May 2015 following the election of a new Turkish Cypriot "president." The entire island entered the EU on 1 May 2004, although the EU acquis—the body of common rights and obligations—applies only to the areas under the internationally recognized government, and is suspended in the area administered by Turkish Cypriots. However, individual Turkish Cypriots able to document their eligibility for Republic of Cyprus citizenship legally enjoy the same rights accorded to other citizens of EU states.

GEOGRAPHY

Location: Middle East, island in the Mediterranean Sea, south of Turkey; note—Cyprus views itself as part of Europe; geopolitically, it can be classified as falling within Europe, the Middle East, or both

Geographic coordinates: 35 00 N, 33 00 E

Map references: Middle East

Area: *total:* 9,251 sq km (of which 3,355 sq km are in north Cyprus)
land: 9,241 sq km
water: 10 sq km
country comparison to the world: 170

Area—comparative: about 0.6 times the size of Connecticut

Land boundaries: *total:* 156 km
border sovereign base areas: Akrotiri 48 km, Dhekelia 108 km

Coastline: 648 km

Maritime claims: *territorial sea:* 12 nm
contiguous zone: 24 nm

continental shelf: 200-m depth or to the depth of exploitation

Climate: temperate; Mediterranean with hot, dry summers and cool winters

Terrain: central plain with mountains to north and south; scattered but significant plains along southern coast

Elevation: *mean elevation:* 91 m
elevation extremes: *lowest point:* Mediterranean Sea 0 m
highest point: Mount Olympus 1,951 m

Natural resources: copper, pyrites, asbestos, gypsum, timber, salt, marble, clay earth pigment

Land use: *agricultural land:* 13.4%
arable land: 9.8%;
permanent crops: 3.2%;
permanent pasture: 0.4%
forest: 18.8%
other: 67.8% (2011 est.)
Irrigated land: 460 sq km (2012)

Population—distribution: population concentrated in central Nicosia and in the major cities of the south: Paphos, Limassol, and Larnaca

Natural hazards: moderate earthquake activity; droughts

Environment—current issues: water resource problems (no natural reservoir catchments, seasonal disparity in rainfall, sea water intrusion to island's largest aquifer, increased salination in the north); water pollution from sewage and industrial wastes; coastal degradation; loss of wildlife habitats from urbanization

Environment—international agreements: *party to:* Air Pollution, Air Pollution-Nitrogen Oxides, Air Pollution-Persistent Organic Pollutants, Air Pollution-Sulfur 94, Biodiversity, Climate Change, Climate Change-Kyoto Protocol, Desertification, Endangered Species, Environmental Modification, Hazardous Wastes, Law of the Sea, Marine Dumping, Ozone Layer Protection, Ship Pollution, Wetlands
signed, but not ratified: none of the selected agreements

Geography—note: the third largest island in the Mediterranean Sea (after Sicily and Sardinia)

PEOPLE AND SOCIETY

Population: 1,221,549 (July 2017 est.)
country comparison to the world: 159

Nationality: *noun:* Cypriot(s)
adjective: Cypriot

Ethnic groups: Greek 98.8%, other 1% (includes Maronite, Armenian, Turkish-Cypriot), unspecified 0.2%
note: data represent only the government-controlled area of Cyprus (2011 est.)

Languages: Greek (official) 80.9%, Turkish (official) 0.2%, English 4.1%, Romanian 2.9%, Russian 2.5%, Bulgarian 2.2%, Arabic 1.2%, Filipino 1.1%, other 4.3%, unspecified 0.6%
note: data represent only the government-controlled area of Cyprus (2011 est.)

Religions: Orthodox Christian 89.1%, Roman Catholic 2.9%, Protestant/Anglican 2%, Muslim 1.8%, Buddhist 1% other (includes Maronite, Armenian Church, Hindu) 1.4%, unknown 1.1%, none/atheist 0.6%
note: data represent only the government-controlled area of Cyprus (2011 est.)

Age structure: *0-14 years:* 15.6% (male 97,955/female 92,648)
15-24 years: 13.81% (male 91,846/female 76,853)
25-54 years: 47.04% (male 303,297/female 271,364)
55-64 years: 11.45% (male 67,053/female 72,854)
65 years and over: 12.09% (male 63,870/female 83,809) (2017 est.)

Dependency ratios: *total dependency ratio:* 42.3
youth dependency ratio: 24
elderly dependency ratio: 18.3
potential support ratio: 5.5
note: data represent the whole country (2015 est.)

Median age: *total:* 36.8 years
male: 35.5 years
female: 38.3 years (2017 est.)
country comparison to the world: 69

Population growth rate: 1.32% (2017 est.)
country comparison to the world: 86

Birth rate: 11.3 births/1,000 population (2017 est.)
country comparison to the world: 176

Death rate: 6.8 deaths/1,000 population (2017 est.)
country comparison to the world: 137

Net migration rate: 8.7 migrant(s)/1,000 population (2017 est.)

country comparison to the world: 12

Population distribution: population concentrated in central Nicosia and in the major cities of the south: Paphos, Limassol, and Larnaca

Urbanization: *urban population:* 66.8% of total population (2017)
rate of urbanization: 0.84% annual rate of change (2015-20 est.)

Major urban areas—population: NICOSIA (capital) 251,000 (2014)

Sex ratio: *at birth:* 1.05 male(s)/female
0-14 years: 1.06 male(s)/female
15-24 years: 1.19 male(s)/female
25-54 years: 1.11 male(s)/female
55-64 years: 0.92 male(s)/female
65 years and over: 0.77 male(s)/female
total population: 1.04 male(s)/female (2016 est.)

Mother's mean age at first birth: 28.8 years
note: data represent only government-controlled areas (2014 est.)

Maternal mortality ratio: 7 deaths/100,000 live births (2015 est.)
country comparison to the world: 164

Infant mortality rate: *total:* 7.9 deaths/1,000 live births
male: 9.2 deaths/1,000 live births
female: 6.4 deaths/1,000 live births (2017 est.)
country comparison to the world: 155

Life expectancy at birth: *total population:* 78.8 years
male: 76 years
female: 81.8 years (2017 est.)
country comparison to the world: 54

Total fertility rate: 1.47 children born/woman (2017 est.)
country comparison to the world: 200

Health expenditures: 7.4% of GDP (2014)
country comparison to the world: 67

Physicians density: 2.5 physicians/1,000 population (2014)

Hospital bed density: 3.5 beds/1,000 population (2011)

Drinking water source:
improved:
urban: 100% of population
rural: 100% of population
total: 100% of population
unimproved:
urban: 0% of population
rural: 0% of population
total: 0% of population (2015 est.)

Sanitation facility access:
improved:
urban: 100% of population
rural: 100% of population
total: 100% of population
unimproved:
urban: 0% of population
rural: 0% of population
total: 0% of population (2015 est.)

HIV/AIDS—adult prevalence rate: NA

HIV/AIDS—people living with HIV/AIDS: NA

HIV/AIDS—deaths: NA

Obesity—adult prevalence rate: 21.8% (2016)
country comparison to the world: 84

Education expenditures: 6.4% of GDP (2013)
country comparison to the world: 19

Literacy: *definition:* age 15 and over can read and write
total population: 99.1%
male: 99.5%
female: 98.7% (2015 est.)

School life expectancy (primary to tertiary education): *total:* 15 years
male: 14 years
female: 15 years (2015)

Unemployment, youth ages 15-24: *total:* 32.8%
male: 34.7%
female: 31.1% (2015 est.)
country comparison to the world: 32

People—note: demographic data for Cyprus represent the population of the government-controlled area and the area administered by Turkish Cypriots, unless otherwise indicated

GOVERNMENT

Country name: *conventional long form:* Republic of Cyprus
conventional short form: Cyprus
local long form: Kypriaki Dimokratia/Kibris Cumhuriyeti
local short form: Kypros/Kibris
note: the Turkish Cypriot community, which administers the northern part of the island, refers to itself as the "Turkish Republic of Northern Cyprus" or "TRNC" ("Kuzey Kibris Turk Cumhuriyeti" or "KKTC")
etymology: the derivation of the name "Cyprus" is unknown, but the extensive mining of copper metal on the island in antiquity gave rise to the Latin word "cuprum" for copper

Government type: Republic of Cyprus—presidential democracy; Turkish Republic of Northern Cyprus (self-declared)—semi-presidential democracy
note: a separation of the two main ethnic communities inhabiting the island began following the outbreak of communal strife in 1963; this separation was further solidified when a Greek military-junta-supported coup attempt prompted the Turkish intervention in July 1974 that gave the Turkish Cypriots de facto control in the north; Greek Cypriots control the only internationally recognized government on the island; on 15 November 1983, then Turkish Cypriot "President" Rauf DENKTAS declared independence and the formation of a "Turkish Republic of Northern Cyprus" ("TRNC"), which is recognized only by Turkey

Capital: *name:* Nicosia (Lefkosia/Lefkosa)

geographic coordinates: 35 10 N, 33 22 E
time difference: UTC+2 (7 hours ahead of Washington, DC, during Standard Time)

daylight saving time: +1hr, begins last Sunday in March; ends last Sunday in October

Administrative divisions: 6 districts; Ammochostos (Famagusta); (all but a small part located in the Turkish Cypriot community), Keryneia (Kyrenia; the only district located entirely in the Turkish Cypriot community), Larnaka (Larnaca; with a small part located in the Turkish Cypriot community), Lefkosia (Nicosia; a small part administered by Turkish Cypriots), Lemesos (Limassol), Pafos (Paphos); note—the 5 "districts" of the "TRNC" are Gazimagusa (Famagusta), Girne (Kyrenia), Guzelyurt (Morphou), Iskele (Trikomo), Lefkosa (Nicosia)

Independence: 16 August 1960 (from the UK); note—Turkish Cypriots proclaimed self-rule on 13 February 1975 and independence in 1983, but these proclamations are recognized only by Turkey

National holiday: Independence Day, 1 October (1960); note—Turkish Cypriots celebrate 15 November (1983) as "Republic Day"

Constitution: history: ratified 16 August 1960; note—in 1963, the constitution was partly suspended as Turkish Cypriots withdrew from the government; Turkish-held territory in 1983 was declared the "Turkish Republic of Northern Cyprus" ("TRNC"); in 1985, the "TRNC" approved its own constitution

amendments: constitution of the Republic of Cyprus—proposed by the House of Representatives; passage requires at least two-thirds majority vote of the total membership of the "Greek Community" and the "Turkish Community"; however, all seats of Turkish Cypriot members have remained vacant since 1964; amended several times, last in 2016 constitution of the "Turkish Republic of Northern Cyprus"—proposed by at least 10 members of the Assembly of the Republic; passage requires at least two-thirds majority vote of the total Assembly membership and approval by referendum; amended 2014

Legal system: mixed legal system of English common law and civil law with European law supremacy

International law organization participation: accepts compulsory ICJ jurisdiction with reservations; accepts ICCt jurisdiction

Citizenship: *citizenship by birth:* no
citizenship by descent only: at least one parent must be a citizen of Cyprus
dual citizenship recognized: yes
residency requirement for naturalization: 7 years

Suffrage: 18 years of age; universal

Executive branch: chief of state: President Nikos ANASTASIADIS (since 28 February 2013); the president is both chief of state and head of government; note—vice presidency reserved for a Turkish Cypriot, but vacant since 1974 because Turkish Cypriots do not participate in the Cyprus Government

head of government: President Nikos ANASTASIADIS (since 28 February 2013)
cabinet: Council of Ministers appointed by the president; note—under the 1960 constitution, 3 of the ministerial posts reserved for Turkish Cypriots,

appointed by the vice president; positions currently filled by Greek Cypriots
elections/appointments: president directly elected by absolute majority popular vote in 2 rounds if needed for a 5-year term; election last held on 28 January 2018 with a runoff on 4 February 2018 (next to be held in February 2023)
election results: Nikos ANASTASIADIS reelected president in second round; percent of vote in first round—Nikos ANASTASIADIS (DISY) 35.5%, Stavros MALAS (AKEL) 30.2%, Niolas PAPADOPOULOS (DIKO) 25.7%, other 8.6%; percent of vote in second round—Nikos ANASTASIADIS 56%, Savros MALAS 44%
note: Mustafa AKINCI assumed office as "president" of the "TRNC" on 30 April 2015; percent of vote in first round (19 April 2015)—Dervis EROGLU (UBP) 28.2%, Mustafa AKINCI (TDP) 26.9%, other 44.9%; percent of vote in runoff (26 April 2015)—AKINCI 60.5%, EROGLU 39.5%; Huseyin OZGURGUN is "TRNC prime minister" since 8 April 2016

Legislative branch: description: area under government control: unicameral House of Representatives or Vouli Antiprosopon (80 seats; 56 assigned to Greek Cypriots, 24 to Turkish Cypriots, but only those assigned to Greek Cypriots are filled; members directly elected by both proportional representation and preferential vote; members serve 5-year terms); area administered by Turkish Cypriots: unicameral Assembly of the Republic or Cumhuriyet Meclisi (50 seats; members directly elected by proportional representation vote to serve 5-year terms)
elections: area under government control: last held on 22 May 2016 (next to be held in May 2021); area administered by Turkish Cypriots: last held on 11 February 2018 (next to be held in 2023)
election results: area under government control: House of Representatives—percent of vote by party—DISY 30.7%, AKEL 25.7%, DIKO 14.5%, KS-EDEK 6.2%, Citizen's Alliance 6.0% Solidarity Movement 5.2%, other 11.7%; seats by party—DISY 18, AKEL 16, DIKO 9, KS-EDEK 3, Citizen's Alliance 3, Solidarity Movement 3, other 4; area administered by Turkish Cypriots: "Assembly of the Republic"—percent of vote by party—UBP 35.6%, CTP 20.9%, HP 17.1%, TDP 8.6%, DP 7.8%, YDP 7.0%; seats by party—UBP 21, CTP 12, HP 9, TDP 3, DP 3, YDP2

Judicial branch: highest court(s): Supreme Court of Cyprus (consists of 13 judges including the court president); note—the highest court in the "Turkish Republic of Northern Cyprus (TRNC)" is the "Supreme Court" (consists of 8 "judges" including the "court president")
judge selection and term of office: Republic of Cyprus Supreme Court judges appointed by the president of the republic upon the recommendation of the Supreme Court judges; judges can serve until age 68; "TRNC Supreme Court" judges appointed by the "Supreme Council of Judicature," a 12-member body of judges, the attorney general, appointees—1 each by the president of the "TRNC" and by the "Legislative Assembly"—and

1 member elected by the bar association; judge tenure NA
subordinate courts: Republic of Cyprus district courts; Assize Courts; Administrative Court; specialized courts for issues relating to family, industrial disputes, military, and rent control; "TRNC Assize Courts"; "district and family courts"

Political parties and leaders: area under government control: Citizens' Alliance or SP [Giorgos LILLIKAS]
Democratic Party or DIKO [Nikolas PAPADOPOULOS]
Democratic Rally or DISY [Averof NEOPHYTOU]
Ecological and Environmental Movement or KOP (Green party) [Giorgos PERDIKIS]
Movement of Social Democrats-United Democratic Center Union or KS-EDEK [Marinos SIZOPOULOS]
National Popular Front or ELAM [Christos CHRISTOU]
Progressive Party of the Working People or AKEL (Communist party) [Andros KYPRIANOU]
Solidarity Movement [Eleni THEOCHAROUS]
United Democrats or EDI [Praxoula ANTONIADOU]
area administered by Turkish Cypriots: Communal Democracy Party or TDP [Cemal OZYIGIT]
Cyprus Socialist Party or KSP [Mehmet BIRINCI]
Democrat Party-National Forces or DP-UG [Serdar DENKTAS]
National Justice Party or UAP [Fatma SOLMAZ]
National Unity Party or UBP [Huseyin OZGURGUN]
New Cyprus Party or YKP [Murat KANATLI]
People's Party or HP [Kudret OZERSAY]
Rebirth Party or YDP [Erhan ARIKLI]
Republican Turkish Party-United Forces or CTP-BG [Tufan ERHURMAN]
Social Democratic Party or SDP [Tozun TUNALI]
United Cyprus Party or BKP [Izzet IZCAN]

Political pressure groups and leaders: Confederation of Cypriot Workers or SEK [Andreas MATSAS] (pro-West)
Pan-Cyprian Labor Federation or PEO [Pambis KYRITSIS] (communist-controlled)
area administered by Turkish Cypriots: Federation of Revolutionary Labor Unions or Dev-Is
Federation of Turkish Cypriot Labor Unions or Turk-Sen [Arslan BICAKLI]

International organization participation: Australia Group, C, CD, CE, EBRD, ECB, EIB, EMU, EU, FAO, IAEA, IBRD, ICAO, ICC (national committees), ICCt, ICRM, IDA, IFAD, IFC, IFRCS, IHO, ILO, IMF, IMO, IMSO, Interpol, IOC, IOM, IPU, ISO, ITSO, ITU, ITUC (NGOs), MIGA, NAM, NSG, OAS (observer), OIF, OPCW, OSCE, PCA, UN, UNCTAD, UNESCO, UNHCR, UNIDO, UNIFIL, UNWTO, UPU, WCO, WFTU (NGOs), WHO, WIPO, WMO, WTO

Diplomatic representation in the US: *chief of mission:* Ambassador Leonidas PANTELIDIS (since 27 June 2016)
chancery: 2211 R Street NW, Washington, DC 20008

telephone: [1] (202) 462-5772, 462-0873
FAX: [1] (202) 483-6710
consulate(s) general: New York
note: representative of the Turkish Cypriot community in the US is Ismet KORUKOGLU; office at 1667 K Street NW, Washington, DC; telephone [1] (202) 887-6198

Diplomatic representation from the US: *chief of mission:* Ambassador Kathleen Ann DOHERTY (since 7 October 2015)
embassy: corner of Metochiou and Ploutarchou Streets, 2407 Engomi, Nicosia
mailing address: P. O. Box 24536, 1385 Nicosia
telephone: [357] (22) 393939
FAX: [357] (22) 393344

Flag description: centered on a white field is a copper-colored silhouette of the island (the island has long been famous for its copper deposits) above two olive-green-colored, crossed olive branches; the branches symbolize the hope for peace and reconciliation between the Greek and Turkish communities
note 1: one of only two national flags that uses a map as a design element; the flag of Kosovo is the other
note 2: the "Turkish Republic of Northern Cyprus" flag retains the white field of the Cyprus national flag but displays narrow horizontal red stripes positioned a small distance from the top and bottom edges between which are centered a red crescent and a red five-pointed star; the banner is modeled after the Turkish national flag but with the colors reversed

National symbol(s): Cypriot mouflon (wild sheep), white dove; national colors: blue, white

National anthem: *name:* "Ymnos eis tin Eleftherian" (Hymn to Liberty)
lyrics/music: Dionysios SOLOMOS/Nikolaos MANTZAROS
note: adopted 1960; Cyprus adopted the Greek national anthem as its own; the Turkish Cypriot community in Cyprus uses the anthem of Turkey

ECONOMY

Economy—overview: The area of the Republic of Cyprus under government control has a market economy dominated by a services sector that accounts for more than four-fifths of GDP. Tourism, finance, shipping, and real estate have traditionally been the most important services. Cyprus has been a member of the EU since May 2004 and adopted the euro as its national currency in January 2008.

During the first five years of EU membership, the Cyprus economy grew at an average rate of about 4%, with unemployment between 2004 and 2008 averaging about 4%. However, the economy tipped into recession in 2009 as the ongoing global financial crisis and resulting low demand hit the tourism and construction sectors. An overextended banking sector with excessive exposure to Greek debt added to the contraction. Cyprus' biggest two banks were among the largest holders of Greek bonds in Europe and had a substantial presence in Greece through bank branches and

subsidiaries. Following numerous downgrades of its credit rating, Cyprus lost access to international capital markets in May 2011. In July 2012, Cyprus became the fifth euro-zone government to request an economic bailout program from the European Commission, European Central Bank and the International Monetary Fund—known collectively as the "Troika."

Shortly after the election of President Nikos ANASTASIADES in February 2013, Cyprus reached an agreement with the Troika on a $13 billion bailout that triggered a two-week bank closure and the imposition of capital controls that remained partially in place until April 2015. Cyprus' two largest banks merged and the combined entity was recapitalized through conversion of some large bank deposits to shares and imposition of losses on bank bondholders. As with other EU countries, the Troika conditioned the bailout on passing financial and structural reforms and privatizing state-owned enterprises. Despite downsizing and restructuring, the Cypriot financial sector remains burdened by the largest stock of non-performing loans in the euro zone, equal to nearly half of all loans. Since the bailout, Cyprus has received positive appraisals by the Troika and outperformed fiscal targets but has struggled to overcome political opposition to bailout-mandated legislation, particularly regarding privatizations. Cyprus emerged from recession in 2015 and its economy grew an estimated 1.5% for the year, setting a positive tone for the scheduled end of the bailout program in March 2016. Growth recovered to 2.8% in 2016 and 3.4% in 2017, while unemployment dropped to 11.8%. The rate of non-performing loans (NPLs) is still very high at around 49%, and growth would accelerate if Cypriot banks would increase the pace of resolution of the NPLs.

In October 2013, a US-Israeli consortium completed preliminary appraisals of hydrocarbon deposits in Cyprus' exclusive economic zone (EEZ), which estimated gross mean reserves of about 130 billion cubic meters. Though exploration continues in Cyprus' EEZ, no additional commercially exploitable reserves have been identified. Developing offshore hydrocarbon resources remains a critical component of the government's economic recovery efforts, but development has been delayed as a result of regional developments and disagreements about exploitation methods.

Economy—overview: Even though the whole of the island is part of the EU, implementation of the EU "acquis communautaire" has been suspended in the area administered by Turkish Cypriots, known locally as the "Turkish Republic of Northern Cyprus" ("TRNC"), until political conditions permit the reunification of the island. The market-based economy of the "TRNC" is roughly one-fifth the size of its southern neighbor and is likewise dominated by the service sector with a large portion of the population employed by the government. In 2012—the latest year for which data are available—the services sector, which includes the public sector, trade, tourism, and education, contributed 58.7% to economic output. In the same year, light manufacturing and

agriculture contributed 2.7% and 6.2%, respectively. Manufacturing is limited mainly to food and beverages, furniture and fixtures, construction materials, metal and non-metal products, textiles and clothing. The "TRNC" maintains few economic ties with the Republic of Cyprus outside of trade in construction materials. Since its creation, the "TRNC" has heavily relied on financial assistance from Turkey, which supports the "TRNC" defense, telecommunications, water and postal services. The Turkish Lira is the preferred currency, though foreign currencies are widely accepted in business transactions. The "TRNC" remains vulnerable to the Turkish market and monetary policy because of its use of the Turkish Lira. The "TRNC" weathered the European financial crisis relatively unscathed—compared to the Republic of Cyprus—because of the lack of financial sector development, the health of the Turkish economy, and its separation from the rest of the island. The "TRNC" economy experienced growth estimated at 2.8% in 2013 and 2.3% in 2014 and is projected to grow 3.8% in 2015.

GDP (purchasing power parity): $31.19 billion (2017 est.)
$30.18 billion (2016 est.)
$29.34 billion (2015 est.)
note: data are in 2017 dollars

GDP (purchasing power parity): $1.829 billion (2007 est.)
country comparison to the world: 131

GDP (official exchange rate): $21.11 billion (2016 est.)

GDP—real growth rate: 3.4% (2017 est.)
2.8% (2016 est.)
1.7% (2015 est.)

GDP—real growth rate: 2.3% (2014 est.)
country comparison to the world: 100

GDP—per capita (PPP): $36,600 (2017 est.)
$35,600 (2016 est.)
$34,600 (2015 est.)
note: data are in 2017 dollars
country comparison to the world: 52

Gross national saving: 11.9% of GDP (2017 est.)
10.3% of GDP (2016 est.)
11.6% of GDP (2015 est.)
country comparison to the world: 146

GDP—composition, by end use:
household consumption: 69.4%
government consumption: 15%
investment in fixed capital: 17.7%
investment in inventories: 0.8%
exports of goods and services: 63.5%
imports of goods and services: -66.4% (2017 est.)

GDP—composition, by sector of origin:
agriculture: 2.3%
industry: 11%
services: 86.8% (2017 est.)

Agriculture—products: citrus, vegetables, barley, grapes, olives, vegetables; poultry, pork, lamb; dairy, cheese

Agriculture—products: citrus fruit, dairy, potatoes, grapes, olives, poultry, lamb

Industries: tourism, food and beverage processing, cement and gypsum, ship repair and refurbishment, textiles, light chemicals, metal products, wood, paper, stone and clay products

Industries: foodstuffs, textiles, clothing, ship repair, clay, gypsum, copper, furniture

Industrial production growth rate: 2.5% (2017 est.)

Industrial production growth rate: -0.3% (2007 est.)

country comparison to the world: 115

Labor force: 426,600 (2017 est.)

Labor force: 95,030 (2007 est.)

country comparison to the world: 159

Labor force—by occupation: *agriculture:* 3.8% *industry:* 15.2%

services: 81% (2014 est.)

Labor force—by occupation: *agriculture:* 14.5%, industry: 29%, services: 56.5% (2004)

Unemployment rate: 11.8% (2017 est.) 13% (2016 est.)

Unemployment rate: 9.4% (2005 est.)

country comparison to the world: 152

Population below poverty line: NA%

Population below poverty line: %NA

Household income or consumption by percentage share: *lowest 10%:* 3.3% *highest 10%:* 28.8% (2014)

Distribution of family income—Gini index: 34.8 (2014 est.)

32.4 (2013 est.)

country comparison to the world: 95

Budget: revenues:: $7.677 billion

expenditures:: $7.875 billion (2017 est.)

Budget: revenues: $2.5 billion, expenditures: $2.5 billion (2006)

Taxes and other revenues: 36.4% of GDP (2017 est.)

country comparison to the world: 50

Budget surplus (+) or deficit (-): -0.9% of GDP (2017 est.)

country comparison to the world: 54

Public debt: 104.5% of GDP (2017 est.)

107.8% of GDP (2016 est.)

note: data cover general government debt, and includes debt instruments issued (or owned) by government entities other than the treasury; the data include treasury debt held by foreign entities; the data exclude debt issued by subnational entities, as well as intra-governmental debt; intragovernmental debt consists of treasury borrowings from surpluses in the social funds, such as for retirement, medical care, and unemployment

country comparison to the world: 14

Fiscal year: calendar year

Inflation rate (consumer prices): 0.8% (2017 est.) -1.2% (2016 est.)

country comparison to the world: 27

Central bank discount rate: 0.25% (31 December 2016)

0.3% (31 December 2010)

note: this is the European Central Bank's rate on the marginal lending facility, which offers overnight credit to banks in the euro area

country comparison to the world: 136

Commercial bank prime lending rate: 4.2% (31 December 2017 est.)

4.33% (31 December 2016 est.)

country comparison to the world: 158

Stock of narrow money: $4.245 billion (31 December 2017 est.)

$3.978 billion (31 December 2016 est.)

note: see entry for the European Union for money supply for the entire euro area; the European Central Bank (ECB) controls monetary policy for the 18 members of the Economic and Monetary Union (EMU); individual members of the EMU do not control the quantity of money circulating within their own borders

country comparison to the world: 111

Stock of broad money: $37.21 billion (31 December 2017 est.)

$34.8 billion (31 December 2016 est.)

country comparison to the world: 75

Stock of domestic credit: $51.81 billion (31 December 2017 est.)

$50.82 billion (31 December 2016 est.)

country comparison to the world: 65

Market value of publicly traded shares: $2.692 billion (31 December 2015 est.)

$4.031 billion (31 December 2014 est.)

$2.105 billion (31 December 2013 est.)

country comparison to the world: 98

Current account balance: -$798 million (2017 est.)

-$1.042 billion (2016 est.)

country comparison to the world: 121

Exports: $2.905 billion (2017 est.)

$2.7 billion (2016 est.)

Exports: $68.1 million, f.o.b. (2007 est.)

country comparison to the world: 127

Exports—commodities: citrus, potatoes, pharmaceuticals, cement, clothing

Exports—partners: UK 12%, Greece 10.2%, Sweden 6.9%, Liberia 5.8%, Libya 4.9% (2016)

Imports: $7.884 billion (2017 est.)

$6.96 billion (2016 est.)

Imports: $1.2 billion, f.o.b. (2007 est.)

country comparison to the world: 107

Imports—commodities: consumer goods, petroleum and lubricants, machinery, transport equipment

Imports—partners: Greece 18%, Germany 16.9%, China 7.7%, Italy 5.7%, UK 5.5%, South Korea 4.4%, France 4% (2016)

Reserves of foreign exchange and gold: $879.1 million (31 December 2017 est.)

$817.7 million (31 December 2016 est.)

Reserves of foreign exchange and gold: $NA

country comparison to the world: 130

Debt—external: $95.28 billion (31 December 2013 est.)

$103.5 billion (31 December 2012 est.)

Debt—external: $NA

country comparison to the world: 49

Stock of direct foreign investment—at home: $178 billion (31 December 2017 est.)

$174.5 billion (31 December 2016 est.)

country comparison to the world: 33

Stock of direct foreign investment—abroad: $179.8 billion (31 December 2017 est.)

$175.3 billion (31 December 2016 est.)

country comparison to the world: 27

Exchange rates: euros (EUR) per US dollar— 0.906 (2017 est.)

0.9214 (2016 est.)

0.9214 (2015 est.)

0.885 (2014 est.)

0.7634 (2013 est.)

Exchange rates: Turkish new lira per US dollar: 1.9 (2013) 1.8 (2012) 1.67 (2011) 1.5 (2010) 1.55 (2009)

Economy of the area administered by Turkish Cypriots: Economy—*overview:* Even though the whole of the island is part of the EU, implementation of the EU "acquis communautaire" has been suspended in the area administered by Turkish Cypriots, known locally as the "Turkish Republic of Northern Cyprus" ("TRNC"), until political conditions permit the reunification of the island. The market-based economy of the "TRNC" is roughly one-fifth the size of its southern neighbor and is likewise dominated by the service sector with a large portion of the population employed by the government. In 2012—the latest year for which data are available—the services sector, which includes the public sector, trade, tourism, and education, contributed 58.7% to economic output. In the same year, light manufacturing and agriculture contributed 2.7% and 6.2%, respectively. Manufacturing is limited mainly to food and beverages, furniture and fixtures, construction materials, metal and non-metal products, textiles and clothing. The "TRNC" maintains few economic ties with the Republic of Cyprus outside of trade in construction materials. Since its creation, the "TRNC" has heavily relied on financial assistance from Turkey, which supports the "TRNC" defense, telecommunications, water and postal services. The Turkish Lira is the preferred currency, though foreign currencies are widely accepted in business transactions. The "TRNC" remains vulnerable to the Turkish market and monetary policy because of its use of the Turkish Lira. The "TRNC" weathered the European financial crisis relatively unscathed—compared to the Republic of Cyprus—because of the lack of financial sector development, the health of the Turkish economy, and its separation from the rest of the island. The "TRNC" economy experienced growth estimated at 2.8% in 2013 and 2.3% in 2014 and is projected to grow 3.8% in 2015.

GDP (purchasing power parity): $1.829 billion (2007 est.)

GDP—real growth rate: 2.3% (2014 est.) 2.8% (2013 est.)

GDP—per capita: $11,700 (2007 est.)

GDP—composition by sector: agriculture: 6.2%, industry: 35.1%, services: 58.7% (2012 est.)

Labor force: 95,030 (2007 est.)

Labor force—by occupation: *agriculture:* 14.5%, industry: 29%, services: 56.5% (2004)

Unemployment rate: 9.4% (2005 est.)

Population below poverty line: %NA

Inflation rate: 11.4% (2006)

Budget: revenues: $2.5 billion, expenditures: $2.5 billion (2006)

Agriculture—products: citrus fruit, dairy, potatoes, grapes, olives, poultry, lamb

Industries: foodstuffs, textiles, clothing, ship repair, clay, gypsum, copper, furniture

Industrial production growth rate: -0.3% (2007 est.)

Electricity production: 998.9 million kWh (2005)

Electricity consumption: 797.9 million kWh (2005)

Exports: $68.1 million, f.o.b. (2007 est.)

Export—commodities: citrus, dairy, potatoes, textiles

Export—partners: Turkey 40%; direct trade between the area administered by Turkish Cypriots and the area under government control remains limited

Imports: $1.2 billion, f.o.b. (2007 est.)

Import—commodities: vehicles, fuel, cigarettes, food, minerals, chemicals, machinery

Import—partners: Turkey 60%; direct trade between the area administered by Turkish Cypriots and the area under government control remains limited

Reserves of foreign exchange and gold: $NA

Debt—external: $NA

Currency (code): Turkish new lira (YTL)

Exchange rates: Turkish new lira per US dollar: 1.9 (2013) 1.8 (2012) 1.67 (2011) 1.5 (2010) 1.55 (2009)

ENERGY

Electricity access: electrification—*total population:* 100% (2016)

Electricity—production: 4.243 billion kWh (2015 est.)
country comparison to the world: 123

Electricity—consumption: 4.028 billion kWh (2015 est.)
country comparison to the world: 127

Electricity—exports: 0 kWh (2016 est.)
country comparison to the world: 128

Electricity—imports: 0 kWh (2016 est.)
country comparison to the world: 141

Electricity—installed generating capacity: 1.742 million kW (2015 est.)
country comparison to the world: 117

Electricity—from fossil fuels: 87.4% of total installed capacity (2015 est.)
country comparison to the world: 66

Electricity—from nuclear fuels: 0% of total installed capacity (2015 est.)
country comparison to the world: 76

Electricity—from hydroelectric plants: 0% of total installed capacity (2015 est.)
country comparison to the world: 171

Electricity—from other renewable sources: 12.8% of total installed capacity (2015 est.)
country comparison to the world: 58

Crude oil—production: 0 bbl/day (2016 est.)
country comparison to the world: 125

Crude oil—exports: 0 bbl/day (2014 est.)
country comparison to the world: 113

Crude oil—imports: 0 bbl/day (2014 est.)
country comparison to the world: 116

Crude oil—proved reserves: 0 bbl (1 January 2017 es)
country comparison to the world: 125

Refined petroleum products—production: 0 bbl/day (2014 est.)
country comparison to the world: 135

Refined petroleum products—consumption: 46,000 bbl/day (2015 est.)
country comparison to the world: 106

Refined petroleum products—exports: 0 bbl/day (2014 est.)
country comparison to the world: 148

Refined petroleum products—imports: 45,740 bbl/day (2014 est.)
country comparison to the world: 86

Natural gas—production: 0 cu m (2013 est.)
country comparison to the world: 126

Natural gas—consumption: 0 cu m (2013 est.)
country comparison to the world: 174

Natural gas—exports: 0 cu m (2013 est.)
country comparison to the world: 92

Natural gas—imports: 0 cu m (2013 est.)
country comparison to the world: 116

Natural gas—proved reserves: 141.6 billion cu m (1 January 2014 es)
country comparison to the world: 48

Carbon dioxide emissions from consumption of energy: 9.1 million Mt (2013 est.)
country comparison to the world: 108

COMMUNICATIONS

Telephones—fixed lines: *total subscriptions:* 320,573
subscriptions per 100 inhabitants: 27 (July 2016 est.)
country comparison to the world: 112

Telephones—mobile cellular: *total:* 1,133,780
subscriptions per 100 inhabitants: 94 (July 2016 est.)
country comparison to the world: 157

Telephone system: *general assessment:* excellent in both area under government control and area administered by Turkish Cypriots
domestic: open-wire, fiber-optic cable, and micro-wave radio relay

international: country code—357 (area administered by Turkish Cypriots uses the country code of Turkey—90); a number of submarine cables, including the SEA-ME-WE-3, combine to provide connectivity to Western Europe, the Middle East, and Asia; tropospheric scatter; satellite earth stations—8 (3 Intelsat—1 Atlantic Ocean and 2 Indian Ocean, 2 Eutelsat, 2 Intersputnik, and 1 Arabsat) (2015)

Broadcast media: mixture of state and privately run TV and radio services; the public broadcaster operates 2 TV channels and 4 radio stations; 6 private TV broadcasters, satellite and cable TV services including telecasts from Greece and Turkey, and a number of private radio stations are available; in areas administered by Turkish Cypriots, there are 2 public TV stations, 4 public radio stations, and 7 privately owned TV and 21 radio broadcast stations plus 6 radio and 4 TV channels of local universities, plus 1 radio station of military, security forces and 1 radio station of civil defense cooperation, as well as relay stations from Turkey (2017)

Internet country code: .cy
Internet users: total: 915,036

percent of population: 75.9% (July 2016 est.)
country comparison to the world: 127

TRANSPORTATION

National air transport system: *number of registered air carriers:* 2
inventory of registered aircraft operated by air carriers: 6
annual passenger traffic on registered air carriers: 23,404
annual freight traffic on registered air carriers: 230,600 mt-km (2015)
Civil aircraft registration country code prefix: 5B (2016)

Airports: 15 (2013)
country comparison to the world: 145

Airports—with paved runways: *total:* 13
2,438 to 3,047 m: 7
1,524 to 2,437 m: 2
914 to 1,523 m: 3
under 914 m: 1 (2017)

Airports—with unpaved runways: *total:* 2
under 914 m: 2 (2013)

Heliports: 9 (2013)

Roadways: *total:* 20,006 km
government control: 13,006 km (includes 2,277 km of expressways)
paved: 8,564 km
unpaved: 4,442 km
Turkish Cypriot control: 7,000 km (2011)
country comparison to the world: 108

Merchant marine: *total:* 1,022
by type: bulk carrier 307, container ship 183, general cargo 164, oil tanker 57, other 311 (2017)
country comparison to the world: 24

Ports and terminals: *major seaport(s):* area under government control: Larnaca, Limassol, Vasilikos;

area administered by Turkish Cypriots: Famagusta, Kyrenia

MILITARY AND SECURITY

Military expenditures: 1.78% of GDP (2016)
1.68% of GDP (2015)
1.54% of GDP (2014)
1.6% of GDP (2013)
1.66% of GDP (2012)
country comparison to the world: 37

Military branches: Republic of Cyprus: Cypriot National Guard (Ethniki Froura, EF, includes naval and air elements); Northern Cyprus: Turkish Cypriot Security Force (GKK) (2014)

Military service age and obligation: Cypriot National Guard (CNG): 18-50 years of age for compulsory military service for all Greek Cypriot males; 17 years of age for voluntary service; 14-month service obligation (2016)

TRANSNATIONAL ISSUES

Disputes—international: hostilities in 1974 divided the island into two de facto autonomous entities, the internationally recognized Cypriot Government and a Turkish-Cypriot community (north Cyprus); the 1,000-strong UN Peacekeeping Force in Cyprus (UNFICYP) has served in Cyprus since 1964 and maintains the buffer zone between north and south; on 1 May 2004, Cyprus

entered the EU still divided, with the EU's body of legislation and standards (acquis communitaire) suspended in the north; Turkey protests Cypriot Government creating hydrocarbon blocks and maritime boundary with Lebanon in March 2007

Refugees and internally displaced persons: *IDPs:* 272,000 (both Turkish and Greek Cypriots; many displaced since 1974) (2016)

Illicit drugs: minor transit point for heroin and hashish via air routes and container traffic to Europe, especially from Lebanon and Turkey; some cocaine transits as well; despite a strengthening of anti-money-laundering legislation, remains vulnerable to money laundering; reporting of suspicious transactions in offshore sector remains weak

CZECHIA

INTRODUCTION

Background: At the close of World War I, the Czechs and Slovaks of the former Austro-Hungarian Empire merged to form Czechoslovakia. During the interwar years, having rejected a federal system, the new country's predominantly Czech leaders were frequently preoccupied with meeting the increasingly strident demands of other ethnic minorities within the republic, most notably the Slovaks, the Sudeten Germans, and the Ruthenians (Ukrainians). On the eve of World War II, Nazi Germany occupied the territory that today comprises Czechia, and Slovakia became an independent state allied with Germany. After the war, a reunited but truncated Czechoslovakia (less Ruthenia) fell within the Soviet sphere of influence. In 1968, an invasion by Warsaw Pact troops ended the efforts of the country's leaders to liberalize communist rule and create "socialism with a human face," ushering in a period of repression known as "normalization." The peaceful "Velvet Revolution" swept the Communist Party from power at the end of 1989 and inaugurated a return to democratic rule and a market economy. On 1 January 1993, the country underwent a nonviolent "velvet divorce" into its two national components,

the Czech Republic and Slovakia. The Czech Republic joined NATO in 1999 and the European Union in 2004. The country changed its short-form name to Czechia in 2016.

GEOGRAPHY

Location: Central Europe, between Germany, Poland, Slovakia, and Austria

Geographic coordinates: 49 45 N, 15 30 E

Map references: Europe

Area: *total:* 78,867 sq km
land: 77,247 sq km
water: 1,620 sq km
country comparison to the world: 117

Area—comparative: about two-thirds the size of Pennsylvania; slightly smaller than South Carolina

Land boundaries: *total:* 2,143 km
border countries (4): Austria 402 km, Germany 704 km, Poland 796 km, Slovakia 241 km

Coastline: 0 km (landlocked)

Maritime claims: none (landlocked)

Climate: temperate; cool summers; cold, cloudy, humid winters

Terrain: Bohemia in the west consists of rolling plains, hills, and plateaus surrounded by low mountains; Moravia in the east consists of very hilly country

Elevation: *mean elevation:* 433 m

elevation extremes: *lowest point:* Labe (Elbe) River 115 m
highest point: Snezka 1,602 m

Natural resources: hard coal, soft coal, kaolin, clay, graphite, timber, arable land

Land use: *agricultural land:* 54.8%
arable land: 41%;
permanent crops: 1%;
permanent pasture: 12.8%
forest: 34.4%
other: 10.8% (2011 est.)
Irrigated land: 320 sq km (2012)

Population—distribution: a fairly even distribution throughout most of the country, but the northern and eastern regions tend to have larger urban concentrations

Natural hazards: flooding

Environment—current issues: air and water pollution in areas of northwest Bohemia and in northern Moravia around Ostrava present health risks; acid rain damaging forests; efforts to bring industry up to EU code should improve domestic pollution

Environment—international agreements: *party to:* Air Pollution, Air Pollution-Nitrogen Oxides, Air Pollution-Persistent Organic Pollutants, Air Pollution-Sulfur 85, Air Pollution-Sulfur 94, Air Pollution-Volatile Organic Compounds, Antarctic-Environmental Protocol, Antarctic Treaty, Biodiversity, Climate Change, Climate Change-Kyoto Protocol, Desertification, Endangered Species, Environmental Modification, Hazardous Wastes, Law of the Sea, Ozone Layer Protection, Ship Pollution, Wetlands, Whaling
signed, but not ratified: none of the selected agreements

Geography—note: landlocked; strategically located astride some of oldest and most significant land routes in Europe; Moravian Gate is a traditional military corridor between the North European Plain and the Danube in central Europe

PEOPLE AND SOCIETY

Population: 10,674,723 (July 2017 est.)
country comparison to the world: 87

Nationality: *noun:* Czech(s)
adjective: Czech

Ethnic groups: Czech 64.3%, Moravian 5%, Slovak 1.4%, other 1.8%, unspecified 27.5% (2011 est.)

Languages: Czech (official) 95.4%, Slovak 1.6%, other 3% (2011 census)

Religions: Roman Catholic 10.4%, Protestant (includes Czech Brethren and Hussite) 1.1%, other and unspecified 54%, none 34.5% (2011 est.)

Age structure: *0-14 years:* 15.16% (male 831,150/female 786,984)

15-24 years: 9.59% (male 527,232/female 496,530)

25-54 years: 43.84% (male 2,403,333/female 2,276,261)

55-64 years: 12.44% (male 646,106/female 681,541)

65 years and over: 18.98% (male 842,384/female 1,183,202) (2017 est.)

Dependency ratios: *total dependency ratio:* 49.5
youth dependency ratio: 22.6
elderly dependency ratio: 26.9
potential support ratio: 3.7 (2015 est.)

Median age: *total:* 42.1 years
male: 40.8 years
female: 43.4 years (2017 est.)
country comparison to the world: 33

Population growth rate: 0.12% (2017 est.)
country comparison to the world: 188

Birth rate: 9.3 births/1,000 population (2017 est.)
country comparison to the world: 203

Death rate: 10.5 deaths/1,000 population (2017 est.)
country comparison to the world: 31

Net migration rate: 2.3 migrant(s)/1,000 population (2017 est.)
country comparison to the world: 41

Population distribution: a fairly even distribution throughout most of the country, but the northern and eastern regions tend to have larger urban concentrations

Urbanization: *urban population:* 73% of total population (2017)
rate of urbanization: 0.3% annual rate of change (2015-20 est.)

Major urban areas—population: PRAGUE (capital) 1.314 million (2015)

Sex ratio: *at birth:* 1.06 male(s)/female
0-14 years: 1.06 male(s)/female
15-24 years: 1.06 male(s)/female
25-54 years: 1.05 male(s)/female
55-64 years: 0.94 male(s)/female
65 years and over: 0.7 male(s)/female
total population: 0.97 male(s)/female (2016 est.)

Mother's mean age at first birth: 28.1 years (2014 est.)

Maternal mortality ratio: 4 deaths/100,000 live births (2015 est.)
country comparison to the world: 180

Infant mortality rate: *total:* 2.6 deaths/1,000 live births
male: 2.8 deaths/1,000 live births
female: 2.5 deaths/1,000 live births (2017 est.)
country comparison to the world: 217

Life expectancy at birth: *total population:* 78.8 years
male: 75.8 years
female: 81.9 years (2017 est.)
country comparison to the world: 56

Total fertility rate: 1.45 children born/woman (2017 est.)
country comparison to the world: 203

Contraceptive prevalence rate: 86.3%
note: percent of women aged 18-44 (2008)

Health expenditures: 7.4% of GDP (2014)
country comparison to the world: 71

Physicians density: 3.68 physicians/1,000 population (2013)

Hospital bed density: 6.8 beds/1,000 population (2011)

Drinking water source:
improved:
urban: 100% of population
rural: 100% of population
total: 100% of population
unimproved:
urban: 0% of population
rural: 0% of population
total: 0% of population (2015 est.)

Sanitation facility access:
improved:
urban: 99.1% of population
rural: 99.2% of population
total: 99.1% of population
unimproved:
urban: 0.9% of population
rural: 0.8% of population
total: 0.9% of population (2015 est.)

HIV/AIDS—adult prevalence rate: <.1% (2016 est.)

HIV/AIDS—people living with HIV/AIDS: 3,400 (2016 est.)
country comparison to the world: 110

HIV/AIDS—deaths: <100 (2016 est.)

Obesity—adult prevalence rate: 26% (2016)
country comparison to the world: 46

Education expenditures: 4.1% of GDP (2013)
country comparison to the world: 106

Literacy: *definition:* NA
total population: 99%
male: 99%
female: 99% (2011 est.)

School life expectancy (primary to tertiary education): *total:* 17 years
male: 16 years
female: 18 years (2014)

Unemployment, youth ages 15-24: *total:* 12.6%
male: 11.3%
female: 14.4% (2015 est.)
country comparison to the world: 57

GOVERNMENT

Country name: *conventional long form:* Czech Republic
conventional short form: Czechia
local long form: Ceska republika
local short form: Cesko
etymology: name derives from the Czechs, a West Slavic tribe who rose to prominence in the late 9th century A.D.

Government type: parliamentary republic

Capital: *name:* Prague
geographic coordinates: 50 05 N, 14 28 E
time difference: UTC+1 (6 hours ahead of Washington, DC, during Standard Time)
daylight saving time: +1hr, begins last Sunday in March; ends last Sunday in October

Administrative divisions: 13 regions (kraje, singular—kraj) and 1 capital city* (hlavni mesto); Jihocesky (South Bohemia), Jihomoravsky (South Moravia), Karlovarsky (Karlovy Vary), Kralovehradecky (Hradec Kralove), Liberecky (Liberec), Moravskoslezsky (Moravia-Silesia), Olomoucky (Olomouc), Pardubicky (Pardubice), Plzensky (Pilsen), Praha (Prague)*, Stredocesky (Central Bohemia), Ustecky (Usti), Vysocina (Highlands), Zlinsky (Zlin)

Independence: 1 January 1993 (Czechoslovakia split into the Czech Republic and Slovakia); note—although 1 January is the day the Czech Republic came into being, the Czechs commemorate 28 October 1918, the day the former Czechoslovakia declared its independence from the Austro-Hungarian Empire, as their independence day

National holiday: Czechoslovak Founding Day, 28 October (1918)

Constitution: history: previous 1960; latest ratified 16 December 1992, effective 1 January 1993
amendments: passage requires at least three-fifths concurrence by members present in both houses of Parliament; amended several times, last in 2013 (2016)

Legal system: new civil code enacted in 2014, replacing civil code of 1964—based on former Austro-Hungarian civil codes and socialist theory—and reintroducing former Czech legal terminology

International law organization participation: has not submitted an ICJ jurisdiction declaration; accepts ICCt jurisdiction

Citizenship: *citizenship by birth:* no
citizenship by descent only: at least one parent must be a citizen of Czechia
dual citizenship recognized: no
residency requirement for naturalization: 5 years

Suffrage: 18 years of age; universal

Executive branch: *chief of state:* President Milos ZEMAN (since 8 March 2013)

head of government: Prime Minister Designate Andrej BABIS (since 6 December 2017); First Deputy Prime Minister Richard BRABEC (since 24 May 2017); Second Deputy Prime Minister Martin STROPNICKY (since 13 December 2017); note—the government of Prime Minister Bohuslav SOBOTKA (since 17 January 2014) resigned on 29 November 2017; BABIS' government was sworn in on 13 December but lost a confidence vote on 16 January 2018 and resigned the next day; President Milos ZEMAN accepted the resignation on 24 January 2018
cabinet: Cabinet appointed by the president on the recommendation of the prime minister

elections/appointments: president directly elected by absolute majority popular vote in 2 rounds if needed for a 5-year term (limited to 2 consecutive terms); elections last held on 12-13 January 2018 with a runoff on 26-27 January 2018 (next to be held in January 2023); prime minister appointed by the president for a 4-year term

election results: Milos ZEMAN reelected president in the second round; percent of vote—Milos ZEMAN (SPO) 51.4%, Jiri DRAHOS (independent) 48.6%

Legislative branch: description: bicameral Parliament or Parlament consists of the Senate or Senat (81 seats; members directly elected in single-seat constituencies by absolute majority vote in 2 rounds if needed; members serve 6-year terms with one-third of the membership renewed every 2 years) and the Chamber of Deputies or Poslanecka Snemovna (200 seats; members directly elected in 14 multi-seat constituencies by proportional representation vote with a 5% threshold required to fill a seat; members serve 4-year terms)

elections: Senate—last held in 2 rounds on 7-8 and 14-15 October 2016 (next to be held in October 2018); Chamber of Deputies—last held on 20-21 October 2017 (next to be held by October 2021)

election results: Senate—percent of vote by party—NA; CSSD 25, KDU-CSL 14, ODS 9, ANO 7, STAN 5, SZ 4, TOP 09 2, SLK 2, SZ 2, SPO 1, Movement for Prague 1, S.cz. 1, KSCM 1, other 5, independent 2; Chamber of Deputies—percent of vote by party—ANO 29.6%, ODS 11.3%, Pirates 10.8%, SPD 10.6%, KSCM 7.8%, CSSD 7.3%, KDU-CSL 5.8%, TOP 09 5.3%, STAN 5.2%, other 6.3%; seats by party—ANO 78, ODS 25, Pirates 22, SPD 22, KSCM 15, CSSD 15, KDU-CSL 10, TOP 09 7, STAN 6

note: Senate seats by party as of 20 May 2017—CSSD 25, KDU-CSL 16, STAN and TOP 09 11, ODS 10, ANO 7, SPO 2, SZ 2, S.cz. 1, KSCM 1, Movement for Prague 1, independent 5

Judicial branch: *highest court(s):* Supreme Court (organized into Civil Law and Commercial Division, and Criminal Division each with a court chief justice, vice justice, and several judges); Constitutional Court (consists of 15 justices); Supreme Administrative Court (consists of 28 judges)

judge selection and term of office: Supreme Court judges proposed by the Chamber of Deputies and appointed by the president; judges appointed for life; Constitutional Court judges appointed by the president and confirmed by the Senate; judges appointed for 10-year, renewable terms; Supreme Administrative Court judges selected by the president of the Court; unlimited terms

subordinate courts: High Court; superior, regional, and district courts

Political parties and leaders: Christian Democratic Union-Czechoslovak People's Party or KDU-CSL [Pavel BELOBRADEK]
Civic Democratic Party or ODS [Petr FIALA]
Communist Party of Bohemia and Moravia or KSCM [Vojtech FILIP]

Czech Social Democratic Party or CSSD [Milan CHOVANEC]
Dawn—National Coalition or Usvit-NK [Miroslav LIDINSKY]
Free Citizens Party or Svobodni [Petr MACH]
Freedom and Direct Democracy or SPD [Tomio OKAMURA]
Green Party or SZ [Matej STROPNICKY]
Mayors and Independents or STAN [Petr GAZDIK]
Movement for Prague
Movement of Dissatisfied Citizens or ANO [Andrej BABIS]
Nestranici (Non-Partisans) or NK [Vera RYBOVA]
North Bohemians or S.cz [Bronislav SCHWARZ]
Party of Civic Rights or SPO [Jan VELEBA]
Pirate Party or Pirates [Ivan BARTOS]
Tradition Responsibility Prosperity 09 or TOP 09 [Jiri POSPISIL]

Political pressure groups and leaders: Czech-Moravian Confederation of Trade Unions or CMKOS [Josef STREDULA]

International organization participation: Australia Group, BIS, BSEC (observer), CD, CE, CEI, CERN, EAPC, EBRD, ECB, EIB, ESA, EU, FAO, IAEA, IBRD, ICAO, ICC (national committees), ICCt, ICRM, IDA, IEA, IFC, IFRCS, ILO, IMF, IMO, IMSO, Interpol, IOC, IOM, IPU, ISO, ITSO, ITU, ITUC (NGOs), MIGA, MONUSCO, NATO, NEA, NSG, OAS (observer), OECD, OIF (observer), OPCW, OSCE, PCA, Schengen Convention, SELEC, UN, UNCTAD, UNESCO, UNHCR, UNIDO, UNWTO, UPU, WCO, WFTU (NGOs), WHO, WIPO, WMO, WTO, ZC

Diplomatic representation in the US: *chief of mission:* Ambassador Hynek KMONICEK (since 24 April 2017)

chancery: 3900 Spring of Freedom Street NW, Washington, DC 20008

telephone: [1] (202) 274-9100

FAX: [1] (202) 966-8540

consulate(s) general: Chicago, Los Angeles, New York

Diplomatic representation from the US: *chief of mission:* Ambassador Stephen B. KING (since 6 December 2017)

embassy: Trziste 15, 118 01 Prague 1—Mala Strana

mailing address: use embassy street address

telephone: [420] 257 022 000

FAX: [420] 257 022 809

Flag description: two equal horizontal bands of white (top) and red with a blue isosceles triangle based on the hoist side

note: combines the white and red colors of Bohemia with blue from the arms of Moravia; is identical to the flag of the former Czechoslovakia

National symbol(s): silver (or white), double-tailed, rampant lion; national colors: white, red, blue

National anthem: name: "Kde domov muj?" (Where is My Home?)

lyrics/music: Josef Kajetan TYL/Frantisek Jan SKROUP

note: adopted 1993; the anthem was originally written as incidental music to the play "Fidlovacka" (1834), it soon became very popular as an unofficial anthem of the Czech nation; its first verse served as the official Czechoslovak anthem beginning in 1918, while the second verse (Slovak) was dropped after the split of Czechoslovakia in 1993

ECONOMY

Economy—overview: Czechia is a prosperous market economy that boasts one of the highest GDP growth rates and lowest unemployment levels in the EU, but its dependence on exports makes economic growth vulnerable to contractions in external demand. Czechia's exports comprise some 80% of GDP and largely consist of automobiles, the country's single largest industry. Czechia acceded to the EU in 2004 but has yet to join the euro-zone. While the flexible koruna helps Czechia weather external shocks, it was one of the world's strongest performing currencies in 2017, appreciating approximately 16% relative to the US dollar after the central bank (Czech National Bank—CNB) in early April ended its cap on the currency's value, which it had maintained since November 2013. The CNB hiked rates in August and November 2017—the first rate changes in nine years—to address rising inflationary pressures brought by strong economic growth and a tight labor market.

After slowly recovering from a steep recession in 2009, the Czech economy again fell into recession in 2012 and 2013 because of a slump in demand within the EU and government austerity measures. Inflows of EU development funds underpinned a rebound in 2014-15, with GDP growth reaching 4.5% in 2015, followed by a slowdown in 2016 largely due to a cyclical lag in EU funding in connection with a new EU budget cycle. The Czech economy was one of the EU's best performers in 2017, with broad-based growth of nearly 4.5% and an unemployment rate of 2.8%, one of the lowest rates in the EU.

Since coming to power in 2014, the new government has undertaken some reforms to try to reduce corruption, attract investment, and improve social welfare programs, which could help increase the government's revenues and improve living conditions for Czechs. The government introduced in December 2016 an online tax reporting system intended to reduce tax evasion and increase revenues. The government also plans to remove labor market rigidities to improve the business climate, bring procurement procedures in line with EU best practices, and boost wages. The country's low unemployment rate has led to steady increases in salaries, and the government is facing pressure from businesses to allow greater migration of qualified workers, at least from Ukraine and neighboring Central European countries.

Long-term challenges include dealing with a rapidly aging population, a shortage of skilled workers, a lagging education system, funding an unsustainable pension and health care system, and diversifying away from manufacturing and toward a more high-tech, services-based, knowledge economy.

GDP (purchasing power parity): $372.6 billion (2017 est.)
$360 billion (2016 est.)
$350.9 billion (2015 est.)
note: data are in 2017 dollars
country comparison to the world: 50

GDP (official exchange rate): $209.7 billion (2016 est.)

GDP—real growth rate: 3.5% (2017 est.)
2.6% (2016 est.)
5.3% (2015 est.)
country comparison to the world: 92

GDP—per capita (PPP): $35,200 (2017 est.)
$34,100 (2016 est.)
$33,300 (2015 est.)
note: data are in 2017 dollars
country comparison to the world: 55

Gross national saving: 27.2% of GDP (2017 est.)
27.4% of GDP (2016 est.)
28.2% of GDP (2015 est.)
country comparison to the world: 40

GDP—composition, by end use:
household consumption: 47.7%
government consumption: 19.2%
investment in fixed capital: 25.2%
investment in inventories: 1.2%
exports of goods and services: 79.1%
imports of goods and services: -72.4% (2017 est.)

GDP—composition, by sector of origin:
agriculture: 2.5%
industry: 37.8%
services: 59.7% (2017 est.)

Agriculture—products: wheat, potatoes, sugar beets, hops, fruit; pigs, poultry

Industries: motor vehicles, metallurgy, machinery and equipment, glass, armaments

Industrial production growth rate: 5.3% (2017 est.)
country comparison to the world: 41

Labor force: 5.427 million (2017 est.)
country comparison to the world: 76

Labor force—by occupation: *agriculture:* 2.8%
industry: 38%
services: 59.2% (2015)

Unemployment rate: 2.8% (2017 est.)
4% (2016 est.)
country comparison to the world: 28

Population below poverty line: 9.7% (2015 est.)

Household income or consumption by percentage share: *lowest 10%:* 4.1%
highest 10%: 21.7% (2015 est.)

Distribution of family income—Gini index: 25 (2015)
25.1 (2014)
country comparison to the world: 144

Budget: *revenues:* $83.62 billion
expenditures: $83.93 billion (2017 est.)

Taxes and other revenues: 39.9% of GDP (2017 est.)
country comparison to the world: 35

Budget surplus (+) or deficit (-): -0.1% of GDP (2017 est.)
country comparison to the world: 39

Public debt: 35.1% of GDP (2017 est.)
36.8% of GDP (2016 est.)
country comparison to the world: 147

Fiscal year: calendar year

Inflation rate (consumer prices): 2.3% (2017 est.)
0.7% (2016 est.)
country comparison to the world: 107

Central bank discount rate: 0.05% (31 December 2016)
0.05% (31 December 2015)
note: this is the two-week repo, the main rate CNB uses
country comparison to the world: 149

Commercial bank prime lending rate: 3.9% (31 December 2017 est.)
3.91% (31 December 2016 est.)
country comparison to the world: 161

Stock of narrow money: $172.7 billion (31 December 2017 est.)
$133.5 billion (31 December 2016 est.)
country comparison to the world: 28

Stock of broad money: $190 billion (31 December 2017 est.)
$148.7 billion (31 December 2016 est.)
country comparison to the world: 43

Stock of domestic credit: $142.8 billion (31 December 2017 est.)
$124.3 billion (31 December 2016 est.)
country comparison to the world: 52

Market value of publicly traded shares: $44.5 billion (31 December 2016 est.)
$39.91 billion (31 December 2015 est.)
$45.63 billion (31 December 2014 est.)
country comparison to the world: 55

Current account balance: $1.192 billion (2017 est.)
$2.154 billion (2016 est.)
country comparison to the world: 36

Exports: $157.4 billion (2017 est.)
$131.1 billion (2016 est.)
country comparison to the world: 33

Exports—commodities: machinery and transport equipment, raw materials, fuel, chemicals

Exports—partners: Germany 32.4%, Slovakia 8.4%, Poland 5.8%, UK 5.2%, France 5.2%, Italy 4.3%, Austria 4.2% (2016)

Imports: $147.4 billion (2017 est.)
$120.8 billion (2016 est.)
country comparison to the world: 31

Imports—commodities: machinery and transport equipment, raw materials and fuels, chemicals

Imports—partners: Germany 30.6%, Poland 9.6%, China 7.5%, Slovakia 6.3%, Netherlands 5.3%, Italy 4.1% (2016)

Reserves of foreign exchange and gold: $161 billion (31 December 2017 est.)

$85.73 billion (31 December 2016 est.)
country comparison to the world: 16

Debt—external: $145.8 billion (31 December 2017 est.)
$138 billion (31 December 2016 est.)
country comparison to the world: 42

Stock of direct foreign investment—at home: $146.5 billion (31 December 2017 est.)
$139.6 billion (31 December 2016 est.)
country comparison to the world: 36

Stock of direct foreign investment—abroad: $45.79 billion (31 December 2017 est.)
$43.09 billion (31 December 2016 est.)
country comparison to the world: 45

Exchange rates: koruny (CZK) per US dollar—
23.34 (2017 est.)
24.44 (2016 est.)
24.44 (2015 est.)
24.599 (2014 est.)
20.758 (2013 est.)

ENERGY

Electricity access: electrification—*total population:* 100% (2016)

Electricity—production: 77.74 billion kWh (2015 est.)
country comparison to the world: 39

Electricity—consumption: 61.16 billion kWh (2015 est.)
country comparison to the world: 43

Electricity—exports: 24.79 billion kWh (2016 est.)
country comparison to the world: 8

Electricity—imports: 13.82 billion kWh (2016 est.)
country comparison to the world: 19

Electricity—installed generating capacity: 21.51 million kW (2015 est.)
country comparison to the world: 41

Electricity—from fossil fuels: 56.6% of total installed capacity (2015 est.)
country comparison to the world: 139

Electricity—from nuclear fuels: 18.3% of total installed capacity (2015 est.)
country comparison to the world: 9

Electricity—from hydroelectric plants: 5.1% of total installed capacity (2015 est.)
country comparison to the world: 129

Electricity—from other renewable sources: 14.5% of total installed capacity (2015 est.)
country comparison to the world: 50

Crude oil—production: 2,333 bbl/day (2016 est.)
country comparison to the world: 87

Crude oil—exports: 518.7 bbl/day (2016 est.)
country comparison to the world: 75

Crude oil—imports: 105,800 bbl/day (2016 est.)
country comparison to the world: 43

Crude oil—proved reserves: 15 million bbl (1 January 2017 es)
country comparison to the world: 87

Refined petroleum products—production: 121,000 bbl/day (2016 est.)
country comparison to the world: 64

Refined petroleum products—consumption: 180,400 bbl/day (2016 est.)
country comparison to the world: 59

Refined petroleum products—exports: 49,000 bbl/day (2016 est.)
country comparison to the world: 55

Refined petroleum products—imports: 103,200 bbl/day (2016 est.)
country comparison to the world: 57

Natural gas—production: 247 million cu m (2015 est.)
country comparison to the world: 76

Natural gas—consumption: 11.51 billion cu m (2015 est.)
country comparison to the world: 52

Natural gas—exports: 1 million cu m (2014 est.)
country comparison to the world: 56

Natural gas—imports: 7.474 billion cu m (2015 est.)
country comparison to the world: 30

Natural gas—proved reserves: 3.964 billion cu m (1 January 2017 es)
country comparison to the world: 97

Carbon dioxide emissions from consumption of energy: 103 million Mt (2013 est.)
country comparison to the world: 39

COMMUNICATIONS

Telephones—fixed lines: *total subscriptions:* 1,682,194
subscriptions per 100 inhabitants: 16 (July 2016 est.)
country comparison to the world: 60

Telephones—mobile cellular: *total:* 12,484,885
subscriptions per 100 inhabitants: 117 (July 2016 est.)
country comparison to the world: 70

Telephone system: *general assessment:* good telephone and Internet service; there are three major mobile phone providers, though the government is facing criticism for failing to promote sufficient competition, with critics complaining that Czech mobile phone and data prices are among the highest in the EU

domestic: access to the fixed-line telephone network expanded throughout the 1990s, but the number of fixed-line connections has been dropping since then; mobile telephone usage increased sharply beginning in the mid-1990s, and the number of cellular telephone subscriptions now greatly exceeds the population
international: country code—420; satellite earth stations—6 (2 Intersputnik—Atlantic and Indian Ocean regions, 1 Intelsat, 1 Eutelsat, 1 Inmarsat, 1 Globalstar) (2017)

Broadcast media: roughly 130 TV broadcasters operating some 350 channels with 4 publicly operated and the remainder in private hands; 16 TV stations have national coverage with 4 being publicly operated; cable and satellite TV subscription services are available; 63 radio broadcasters are registered operating roughly 80 radio stations with 15 stations publicly operated; 10 radio stations provide national coverage with the remainder local or regional (2008)

Internet country code: .cz
Internet users: total: 8,141,303

percent of population: 76.5% (July 2016 est.)
country comparison to the world: 49

TRANSPORTATION

National air transport system: *number of registered air carriers:* 4
inventory of registered aircraft operated by air carriers: 48
annual passenger traffic on registered air carriers: 4,971,616
annual freight traffic on registered air carriers: 26,619,650 mt-km (2015)
Civil aircraft registration country code prefix: OK (2016)

Airports: 128 (2013)
country comparison to the world: 46

Airports—with paved runways: *total:* 41
over 3,047 m: 2
2,438 to 3,047 m: 9
1,524 to 2,437 m: 12
914 to 1,523 m: 2
under 914 m: 16 (2017)

Airports—with unpaved runways: *total:* 87
1,524 to 2,437 m: 1
914 to 1,523 m: 25

under 914 m: 61 (2013)

Heliports: 1 (2013)

Pipelines: gas 7,160 km; oil 536 km; refined products 94 km (2013)

Railways: *total:* 9,621.5 km
standard gauge: 9,519.5 km 1.435-m gauge (3,240.5 km electrified)
narrow gauge: 102 km 0.760-m gauge (2014)
country comparison to the world: 24

Roadways: *total:* 130,661 km (includes urban roads)
paved: 130,661 km (includes 730 km of expressways) (2011)
country comparison to the world: 40

Waterways: 664 km (principally on Elbe, Vltava, Oder, and other navigable rivers, lakes, and canals) (2010)
country comparison to the world: 76

Ports and terminals: *river port(s):* Prague (Vltava); Decin, Usti nad Labem (Elbe)

MILITARY AND SECURITY

Military expenditures: 0.98% of GDP (2016)
0.96% of GDP (2015)
0.97% of GDP (2014)
0.99% of GDP (2013)
1.03% of GDP (2012)
country comparison to the world: 94

Military branches: Army of the Czech Republic (Armada Ceske Republiky): General Staff (Generalni Stab, includes Land Forces (Pozemni Sily) and Air Forces (Vzdusne Sily)) (2015)

Military service age and obligation: 18-28 years of age for male and female voluntary military service; no conscription (2012)

TRANSNATIONAL ISSUES

Disputes—international: none

Refugees and internally displaced persons: *stateless persons:* 1,502 (2016)

Illicit drugs: transshipment point for Southwest Asian heroin and minor transit point for Latin American cocaine to Western Europe; producer of synthetic drugs for local and regional markets; susceptible to money laundering related to drug trafficking, organized crime; significant consumer of ecstasy

D

INTRODUCTION

Background: Once the seat of Viking raiders and later a major north European power, Denmark has evolved into a modern, prosperous nation that is participating in the general political and economic integration of Europe. It joined NATO in 1949 and the EEC (now the EU) in 1973. However, the country has opted out of certain elements of the EU's Maastricht Treaty, including the European Economic and Monetary Union, European defense cooperation, and issues concerning certain justice and home affairs.

GEOGRAPHY

Location: Northern Europe, bordering the Baltic Sea and the North Sea, on a peninsula north of Germany (Jutland); also includes several major islands (Sjaelland, Fyn, and Bornholm)

Geographic coordinates: 56 00 N, 10 00 E

Map references: Europe

Area: *total:* 43,094 sq km
land: 42,434 sq km
water: 660 sq km
note: includes the island of Bornholm in the Baltic Sea and the rest of metropolitan Denmark (the Jutland Peninsula, and the major islands of Sjaelland and Fyn), but excludes the Faroe Islands and Greenland
country comparison to the world: 134

Area—comparative: slightly less than twice the size of Massachusetts
Land boundaries: total: 140 km
border countries (1): Germany 140 km

Coastline: 7,314 km
Maritime claims: territorial sea: 12 nm
contiguous zone: 24 nm
exclusive economic zone: 200 nm
continental shelf: 200-m depth or to the depth of exploitation

Climate: temperate; humid and overcast; mild, windy winters and cool summers

Terrain: low and flat to gently rolling plains

Elevation: *mean elevation:* 34 m
elevation extremes: *lowest point:* Lammefjord -7 m
highest point: Mollehoj/Ejer Bavnehoj 171 m

Natural resources: petroleum, natural gas, fish, arable land, salt, limestone, chalk, stone, gravel and sand

Land use: *agricultural land:* 63.4%
arable land: 58.9%;
permanent crops: 0.1%;
permanent pasture: 4.4%
forest: 12.9%
other: 23.7%
note: highest percentage of arable land: for any country in the world (2011 est.)

Irrigated land: 4,350 sq km (2012)

Population—distribution: with excellent access to the North Sea, Skagerrak, Kattegat, and the Baltic Sea, population centers tend to be along coastal areas, particularly in Copenhagen and the eastern side of the country's mainland

Natural hazards: flooding is a threat in some areas of the country (e.g., parts of Jutland, along the southern coast of the island of Lolland) that are protected from the sea by a system of dikes

Environment—current issues: air pollution, principally from vehicle and power plant emissions; nitrogen and phosphorus pollution of the North Sea; drinking and surface water becoming polluted from animal wastes and pesticides

Environment—international agreements: *party to:* Air Pollution, Air Pollution-Nitrogen Oxides, Air Pollution-Persistent Organic Pollutants, Air Pollution-Sulfur 85, Air Pollution-Sulfur 94, Air Pollution-Volatile Organic Compounds, Antarctic Treaty, Biodiversity, Climate Change, Climate Change-Kyoto Protocol, Desertification, Endangered Species, Environmental Modification, Hazardous Wastes, Law of the Sea, Marine Dumping, Marine Life Conservation, Ozone Layer Protection, Ship Pollution, Tropical Timber 83, Tropical Timber 94, Wetlands, Whaling
signed, but not ratified: none of the selected agreements

Geography—note: controls Danish Straits (Skagerrak and Kattegat) linking Baltic and North Seas; about one-quarter of the population lives in greater Copenhagen

PEOPLE AND SOCIETY

Population: 5,605,948 (July 2017 est.)
country comparison to the world: 116

Nationality: *noun:* Dane(s)
adjective: Danish

Ethnic groups: Danish (includes Greenlandic (who are predominantly Inuit) and Faroese) 86.7%, Turkish 1.1%, other 12.2% (largest groups are Polish, Syrian, German, Iraqi, and Romanian)
note: data represent population by ancestry (2017 est.)

Languages: Danish, Faroese, Greenlandic (an Inuit dialect), German (small minority)
note: English is the predominant second language

Religions: Evangelical Lutheran (official) 76%, Muslim 4%, other (denominations of less than 1% each, includes Roman Catholic, Jehovah's Witness, Serbian Orthodox Christian, Jewish, Baptist, and Buddhist) 20% (2017 est.)

Age structure: 0-14 years: 16.41% (male 472,106/female 447,997)
15-24 years: 13.08% (male 374,379/female 358,927)
25-54 years: 38.76% (male 1,080,118/female 1,092,503)
55-64 years: 12.52% (male 349,091/female 352,903)
65 years and over: 19.23% (male 483,519/female 594,405) (2017 est.)

Dependency ratios: *total dependency ratio:* 56
youth dependency ratio: 26.3
elderly dependency ratio: 29.7
potential support ratio: 3.4 (2015 est.)

Median age: *total:* 42.2 years
male: 41.2 years
female: 43.2 years (2017 est.)
country comparison to the world: 29

Population growth rate: 0.22% (2017 est.)
country comparison to the world: 182

Birth rate: 10.5 births/1,000 population (2017 est.)
country comparison to the world: 186

Death rate: 10.3 deaths/1,000 population (2017 est.)
country comparison to the world: 35

Net migration rate: 2.1 migrant(s)/1,000 population (2017 est.)
country comparison to the world: 46

Population distribution: with excellent access to the North Sea, Skagerrak, Kattegat, and the Baltic Sea, population centers tend to be along coastal areas, particularly in Copenhagen and the eastern side of the country's mainland

Urbanization: *urban population:* 88% of total population (2017)
rate of urbanization: 0.58% annual rate of change (2015-20 est.)

Major urban areas—population: COPENHAGEN (capital) 1.268 million (2015)

Sex ratio: *at birth:* 1.06 male(s)/female
0-14 years: 1.05 male(s)/female
15-24 years: 1.04 male(s)/female
25-54 years: 0.99 male(s)/female
55-64 years: 0.99 male(s)/female
65 years and over: 0.81 male(s)/female
total population: 0.97 male(s)/female (2016 est.)

Mother's mean age at first birth: 29.1 years (2015 est.)

Maternal mortality ratio: 6 deaths/100,000 live births (2015 est.)
country comparison to the world: 169

Infant mortality rate: *total:* 4 deaths/1,000 live births
male: 4.1 deaths/1,000 live births
female: 3.9 deaths/1,000 live births (2017 est.)
country comparison to the world: 191

Life expectancy at birth: *total population:* 79.5 years
male: 77.1 years
female: 82.1 years (2017 est.)
country comparison to the world: 47

Total fertility rate: 1.73 children born/woman (2017 est.)
country comparison to the world: 167
Health expenditures: 10.8% of GDP (2014)
country comparison to the world: 16

Physicians density: 3.65 physicians/1,000 population (2013)

Hospital bed density: 3.5 beds/1,000 population (2010)

Drinking water source:
improved:
urban: 100% of population
rural: 100% of population
total: 100% of population
unimproved:
urban: 0% of population
rural: 0% of population
total: 0% of population (2015 est.)

Sanitation facility access:
improved:
urban: 99.6% of population
rural: 99.6% of population
total: 99.6% of population
unimproved:
urban: 0.4% of population
rural: 0.4% of population
total: 0.4% of population (2015 est.)

HIV/AIDS—adult prevalence rate: NA

HIV/AIDS—people living with HIV/AIDS: NA

HIV/AIDS—deaths: NA

Obesity—adult prevalence rate: 19.7% (2016)
country comparison to the world: 111
Education expenditures: 8.6% of GDP (2013)
country comparison to the world: 8

School life expectancy (primary to tertiary education): *total:* 19 years
male: 18 years
female: 20 years (2014)

Unemployment, youth ages 15-24: *total:* 12%
male: 13.1%
female: 10.9% (2016 est.)
country comparison to the world: 84

GOVERNMENT

Country name: *conventional long form:* Kingdom of Denmark
conventional short form: Denmark
local long form: Kongeriget Danmark
local short form: Danmark
etymology: the name derives from the words "Dane(s)" and "mark"; the latter referring to a march (borderland) or forest

Government type: parliamentary constitutional monarchy

Capital: *name:* Copenhagen
geographic coordinates: 55 40 N, 12 35 E
time difference: UTC+1 (6 hours ahead of Washington, DC, during Standard Time)
daylight saving time: +1hr, begins last Sunday in March; ends last Sunday in October
note: applies to continental Denmark only, not to its North Atlantic components

Administrative divisions: metropolitan Denmark—5 regions (regioner, singular—region); Hovedstaden (Capital), Midtjylland (Central Jutland), Nordjylland (North Jutland), Sjaelland (Zealand), Syddanmark (Southern Denmark)
note: an extensive local government reform merged 271 municipalities into 98 and 13 counties into five regions, effective 1 January 2007

Independence: ca. 965 (unified and Christianized under HARALD I Gormson); 5 June 1849 (became a parliamentary constitutional monarchy)

National holiday: Constitution Day, 5 June (1849); note—closest equivalent to a national holiday

Constitution: history: several previous; latest adopted 5 June 1953
amendments: proposed by the Folketing with consent of the government; passage requires approval by the next Folketing following a general election, approval by simple majority vote of at least 40% of voters in a referendum, and assent by the chief of state; changed several times, last in 2009 (Danish Act of Succession) (2016)

Legal system: civil law; judicial review of legislative acts

International law organization participation: accepts compulsory ICJ jurisdiction with reservations; accepts ICCt jurisdiction

Citizenship: *citizenship by birth:* no
citizenship by descent only: at least one parent must be a citizen of Denmark
dual citizenship recognized: yes
residency requirement for naturalization: 7 years

Suffrage: 18 years of age; universal

Executive branch: *chief of state:* Queen MARGRETHE II (since 14 January 1972); Heir Apparent Crown Prince FREDERIK, elder son of the monarch (born on 26 May 1968)

head of government: Prime Minister Lars LOKKE RASMUSSEN (since 28 June 2015)
cabinet: Council of State appointed by the monarch
elections/appointments: the monarchy is hereditary; following legislative elections, the leader of the majority party or majority coalition usually appointed prime minister by the monarch

Legislative branch: description: unicameral People's Assembly or Folketing (179 seats, including 2 representing Greenland and 2 representing the Faroe Islands; members directly elected in multi-seat constituencies by proportional representation vote; members serve 4-year terms unless the Folketing is dissolved earlier)

elections: last held on 18 June 2015 (next to be held by June 2019)
election results: percent of vote by party—SDP 26.3%, DF 21.1%, V 19.5%, EL 7.8%, LA 7.5%, AP 4.8%, SLP 4.6%, SF 4.2%, C 3.4%, other 0.9%; seats by party—SDP 47, DF 37, V 34, EL 14, LA 13, AP 9, SLP 8, SF 7, C 6; note—does not include each of the 2 seats from Greenland and the Faroe Islands

Judicial branch: *highest court(s):* Supreme Court (consists of the court president and 18 judges)
judge selection and term of office: judges appointed by the monarch upon the recommendation of the Minister of Justice with the advice of the Judicial Appointments Council, a 6-member independent body of judges and lawyers; judges appointed for life with retirement at age 70
subordinate courts: Special Court of Indictment and Revision; 2 High Courts; Maritime and Commercial Court; county courts

Political parties and leaders: The Alternative A or AP [Uffe ELBAEK]
Conservative People's Party or DKF or C [Soren PAPE POULSEN]
Danish People's Party or DF or O [Kristian THULESEN DAHL]
Liberal Alliance or LA [Anders SAMUELSEN]
Liberal Party (Venstre) or V [Lars LOKKE RASMUSSEN]
Red-Green Alliance (Unity List) or EL [collective leadership, spokesperson Pernille SKIPPER]
Social Democrats or A [Mette FREDERIKSEN]
Social Liberal Party or B [Morten OSTERGAARD]
Socialist People's Party or SF [Pia OLSEN DYHR]

Political pressure groups and leaders: Confederation of Danish Employers or DA [Jacob HOLBRAAD]
Confederation of Danish Industries or DI [Karsten DYBVAD]
Confederation of Danish Labor Unions or LO [Lizette RISGAARD]
DaneAge Association [Bjarne HASTRUP]
Danish Shipowners' Association [Anne STEFFENSEN]
Danish Bankers Association [Ulrik NODGAARD]
Danish Society for Nature Conservation or DN [Ella Maria BISSCHOP-LARSEN]
other: environmental groups; humanitarian relief; development assistance; human rights NGOs

International organization participation: ADB (nonregional member), AfDB (nonregional member), Arctic Council, Australia Group, BIS, CBSS, CD, CE, CERN, EAPC, EBRD, ECB, EIB, EITI (implementing country), ESA, EU, FAO, FATF, G-9, IADB, IAEA, IBRD, ICAO, ICC (national committees), ICCt, ICRM, IDA, IEA, IFAD, IFC, IFRCS, IGAD (partners), IHO, ILO, IMF, IMO, IMSO, Interpol, IOC, IOM, IPU, ISO, ITSO, ITU, ITUC (NGOs), MIGA, MINUSMA, NATO, NC, NEA, NIB, NSG, OAS (observer), OECD, OPCW, OSCE, Paris Club, PCA, Schengen Convention, UN, UNCTAD, UNESCO, UNHCR, UNIDO, UNMIL, UNMISS, UNRWA, UNTSO, UPU, WCO, WHO, WIPO, WMO, WTO, ZC

Diplomatic representation in the US: *chief of mission:* Ambassador Lars Gert LOSE (since 17 September 2015)
chancery: 3200 Whitehaven Street NW, Washington, DC 20008
telephone: [1] (202) 234-4300
FAX: [1] (202) 328-1470
consulate(s) general: Chicago, New York

Diplomatic representation from the US: *chief of mission:* Ambassador (vacant); Charge d'Affaires Laura LOCHMAN (since 2 January 2017)
embassy: Dag Hammarskjolds Alle 24, 2100 Copenhagen 0
mailing address: Unit 5280, DPO, AE 09716
telephone: [45] 33 41 71 00
FAX: [45] 35 43 02 23

Flag description: red with a white cross that extends to the edges of the flag; the vertical part of the cross is shifted to the hoist side; the banner is referred to as the Dannebrog (Danish flag) and is one of the oldest national flags in the world; traditions as to the origin of the flag design vary, but the best known is a legend that the banner fell from the sky during an early-13th century battle; caught up by the Danish king before it ever touched the earth, this heavenly talisman inspired the royal army to victory; in actuality, the flag may derive from a crusade banner or ensign
note: the shifted cross design element was subsequently adopted by the other Nordic countries of Finland, Iceland, Norway, and Sweden

National symbol(s): lion, mute swan; national colors: red, white

National anthem: *name:* "Der er et yndigt land" (There is a Lovely Land); "Kong Christian" (King Christian)
lyrics/music: Adam Gottlob OEHLENSCHLAGER/Hans Ernst KROYER; Johannes EWALD/unknown
note: Denmark has two national anthems with equal status; "Der er et yndigt land," adopted 1844, is a national anthem, while "Kong Christian," adopted 1780, serves as both a national and royal anthem; "Kong Christian" is also known as "Kong Christian stod ved hojen mast" (King Christian Stood by the Lofty Mast) and "Kongesangen" (The King's Anthem); within Denmark, the royal anthem is played only when royalty is present and is usually followed by the national anthem; when royalty is not present, only the national anthem is performed; outside Denmark, the royal anthem is played, unless the national anthem is requested

ECONOMY

Economy—overview: This thoroughly modern market economy features a high-tech agricultural sector, advanced industry with world-leading firms in pharmaceuticals, maritime shipping, and in renewable energy, and a high dependence on foreign trade. Denmark is a net exporter of food, oil, and gas and enjoys a comfortable balance of payments surplus, but depends on imports of raw materials for the manufacturing sector. Danes enjoy a high standard of living, and the Danish economy is characterized by extensive government

welfare measures and an equitable distribution of income. An aging population will be a long-term issue.

Denmark is a member of the EU; Danish legislation and regulations conform to EU standards on almost all issues. Despite previously meeting the criteria to join the European Economic and Monetary Union, Denmark has negotiated an opt-out with the EU and is not required to adopt the euro. Within the EU, Denmark is among the strongest supporters of trade liberalization.

Denmark is experiencing a modest economic expansion. The economy grew by 1.7% in 2016 and an estimated 1.9% in 2017. The expansion is expected to continue at similar rates in 2018. The labor market has strengthened since 2013, and unemployment stood at 5.8% in 2017, based on the national measure. Productivity growth was significantly below the OECD average from the mid-1990s until 2011, but has increased in recent years. Improvement in productivity is needed to ensure continued growth.

Denmark maintained a healthy budget surplus for many years up to 2008, but the global financial crisis swung the budget balance into deficit. The 2017 deficit was 0.6%. The government projects a lower deficit in 2018, and public debt (EMU debt) as a share of GDP is expected to decline. In 2015, household indebtedness remained relatively high at more than 292% of net disposable income, while household net worth—from private pension schemes and other assets—amounted to 497% of net disposable income.

GDP (purchasing power parity): $285.5 billion (2017 est.)
$280.1 billion (2016 est.)
$275.4 billion (2015 est.)
note: data are in 2017 dollars
country comparison to the world: 60

GDP (official exchange rate): $324.1 billion (2016 est.)

GDP—real growth rate: 1.9% (2017 est.)
1.7% (2016 est.)
1.6% (2015 est.)
country comparison to the world: 159

GDP—per capita (PPP): $49,600 (2017 est.)
$49,100 (2016 est.)
$48,700 (2015 est.)
note: data are in 2017 dollars
country comparison to the world: 31

Gross national saving: 27.9% of GDP (2017 est.)
28.2% of GDP (2016 est.)
28.9% of GDP (2015 est.)
country comparison to the world: 38

GDP—composition, by end use:
household consumption: 48%
government consumption: 25.2%
investment in fixed capital: 20%
investment in inventories: -0.2%
exports of goods and services: 54.5%
imports of goods and services: -47.5% (2017 est.)

GDP—composition, by sector of origin:
agriculture: 1.1%
industry: 23.7%

services: 75.2% (2017 est.)

Agriculture—products: barley, wheat, potatoes, sugar beets; pork, dairy products; fish

Industries: iron, steel, nonferrous metals, chemicals, food processing, machinery and transportation equipment, textiles and clothing, electronics, construction, furniture and other wood products, shipbuilding and refurbishment, windmills, pharmaceuticals, medical equipment

Industrial production growth rate: 2% (2017 est.)
country comparison to the world: 139

Labor force: 2.998 million (2017 est.)
country comparison to the world: 104

Labor force—by occupation: *agriculture:* 2.4%
industry: 18.3%
services: 79.3% (2016 est.)

Unemployment rate: 5.8% (2017 est.)
6.2% (2016 est.)
country comparison to the world: 80

Population below poverty line: 13.4% (2011 est.)

Household income or consumption by percentage share: *lowest 10%:* 1.9%
highest 10%: 28.7% (2007)

Distribution of family income—Gini index: 28.8 (2015 est.)
25.7 (2005 est.)
country comparison to the world: 132

Budget: *revenues:* $173.5 billion
expenditures: $175.5 billion (2017 est.)
Taxes and other revenues: 53.5% of GDP (2017 est.)
country comparison to the world: 11

Budget surplus (+) or deficit (-): -0.6% of GDP (2017 est.)
country comparison to the world: 51

Public debt: 35.1% of GDP (2017 est.)
37.7% of GDP (2016 est.)
note: data cover general government debt, and includes debt instruments issued (or owned) by government entities other than the treasury; the data include treasury debt held by foreign entities; the data include debt issued by subnational entities, as well as intra-governmental debt; intra-governmental debt consists of treasury borrowings from surpluses in the social funds, such as for retirement, medical care, and unemployment; debt instruments for the social funds are not sold at public auctions
country comparison to the world: 146

Fiscal year: calendar year

Inflation rate (consumer prices): 1% (2017 est.)
0.3% (2016 est.)
country comparison to the world: 43

Central bank discount rate: 0.05% (2016)
0.05% (2015)
country comparison to the world: 148

Commercial bank prime lending rate: 2.9% (31 December 2017 est.)
3.25% (31 December 2016 est.)
country comparison to the world: 169

Stock of narrow money: $191.5 billion (31 December 2017 est.)

$159.3 billion (31 December 2016 est.)
country comparison to the world: 26

Stock of broad money: $201.8 billion (31 December 2017 est.)
$173.4 billion (31 December 2016 est.)
country comparison to the world: 39

Stock of domestic credit: $739.9 billion (31 December 2017 est.)
$637.3 billion (31 December 2016 est.)
country comparison to the world: 22

Market value of publicly traded shares: $224.9 billion (31 December 2012 est.)
$179.5 billion (31 December 2011 est.)
$231.7 billion (31 December 2010 est.)
country comparison to the world: 32

Current account balance: $23.61 billion (2017 est.)
$24.09 billion (2016 est.)
country comparison to the world: 14

Exports: $113.2 billion (2017 est.)
$103.6 billion (2016 est.)
country comparison to the world: 35

Exports—commodities: machinery and instruments, meat and meat products, dairy products, fish, pharmaceuticals, furniture and design, windmills

Exports—partners: Germany 16.3%, Sweden 11.9%, US 8.2%, UK 6.5%, Norway 6.1%, Netherlands 5.1%, China 4.4% (2016)

Imports: $94.61 billion (2017 est.)
$86.39 billion (2016 est.)
country comparison to the world: 35

Imports—commodities: machinery and equipment, raw materials and semimanufactures for industry, chemicals, grain and foodstuffs, consumer goods

Imports—partners: Germany 21.4%, Sweden 12.2%, Netherlands 8%, China 7.3%, Norway 5.5%, UK 4.2% (2016)

Reserves of foreign exchange and gold: $68.8 billion (31 December 2017 est.)
$64.25 billion (31 December 2016 est.)
country comparison to the world: 32

Debt—external: $484.8 billion (31 March 2016 est.)
$519.8 billion (31 March 2015 est.)
country comparison to the world: 24

Stock of direct foreign investment—at home: $145.9 billion (31 December 2017 est.)
$147.9 billion (31 December 2016 est.)
country comparison to the world: 37

Stock of direct foreign investment—abroad: $248 billion (31 December 2017 est.)
$235.4 billion (31 December 2016 est.)
country comparison to the world: 24

Exchange rates: Danish kroner (DKK) per US dollar—
6.586 (2017 est.)
6.7309 (2016 est.)
6.7309 (2015 est.)
6.7236 (2014 est.)
5.6125 (2013 est.)

ENERGY

Electricity access: *electrification—total population:* 100% (2016)

Electricity—production: 27.34 billion kWh (2015 est.)
country comparison to the world: 68

Electricity—consumption: 31.41 billion kWh (2015 est.)
country comparison to the world: 62

Electricity—exports: 9.919 billion kWh (2016 est.)
country comparison to the world: 23

Electricity—imports: 14.98 billion kWh (2016 est.)
country comparison to the world: 14

Electricity—installed generating capacity: 14.01 million kW (2015 est.)
country comparison to the world: 52

Electricity—from fossil fuels: 48.1% of total installed capacity (2015 est.)
country comparison to the world: 154

Electricity—from nuclear fuels: 0% of total installed capacity (2015 est.)
country comparison to the world: 77

Electricity—from hydroelectric plants: 0% of total installed capacity (2015 est.)
country comparison to the world: 172

Electricity—from other renewable sources: 53.6% of total installed capacity (2015 est.)
country comparison to the world: 2

Crude oil—production: 140,600 bbl/day (2016 est.)
country comparison to the world: 40

Crude oil—exports: 78,370 bbl/day (2016 est.)
country comparison to the world: 38

Crude oil—imports: 77,950 bbl/day (2016 est.)
country comparison to the world: 47

Crude oil—proved reserves: 490.6 million bbl (1 January 2017 es)
country comparison to the world: 49

Refined petroleum products—production: 187,700 bbl/day (2016 est.)
country comparison to the world: 53

Refined petroleum products—consumption: 158,200 bbl/day (2016 est.)
country comparison to the world: 65

Refined petroleum products—exports: 171,600 bbl/day (2016 est.)
country comparison to the world: 35

Refined petroleum products—imports: 165,400 bbl/day (2016 est.)
country comparison to the world: 40

Natural gas—production: 4.618 billion cu m (2015 est.)
country comparison to the world: 52

Natural gas—consumption: 4.392 billion cu m (2015 est.)
country comparison to the world: 70

Natural gas—exports: 2.192 billion cu m (2015 est.)

country comparison to the world: 37

Natural gas—imports: 658 million cu m (2015 est.)
country comparison to the world: 65

Natural gas—proved reserves: 16.88 billion cu m (1 January 2017 es)
country comparison to the world: 78

Carbon dioxide emissions from consumption of energy: 42 million Mt (2013 est.)
country comparison to the world: 67

COMMUNICATIONS

Telephones—fixed lines: *total subscriptions:* 1,557,101
subscriptions per 100 inhabitants: 28 (July 2016 est.)
country comparison to the world: 61

Telephones—mobile cellular: *total:* 6,985,035
subscriptions per 100 inhabitants: 125 (July 2016 est.)
country comparison to the world: 106

Telephone system: *general assessment:* excellent telephone and Internet services
domestic: buried and submarine cables and microwave radio relay form trunk network; multiple mobile-cellular communications systems
international: country code—45; a series of fiber-optic submarine cables link Denmark with Canada, Faroe Islands, Germany, Iceland, Netherlands, Norway, Poland, Russia, Sweden, and UK; satellite earth stations—18 (6 Intelsat, 10 Eutelsat, 1 Orion, 1 Inmarsat (Blaavand-Atlantic-East)); note—the Nordic countries (Denmark, Finland, Iceland, Norway, and Sweden) share the Danish earth station and the Eik, Norway, station for worldwide Inmarsat access (2015)

Broadcast media: strong public-sector TV presence with state-owned Danmarks Radio (DR) operating 6 channels and publicly owned TV2 operating roughly a half-dozen channels; broadcasts of privately owned stations are available via satellite and cable feed; DR operates 4 nationwide FM radio stations, 10 digital audio broadcasting stations, and 14 web-based radio stations; in 2010, there were 140 commercial and 187 community (non-commercial) radio stations (2012)

Internet country code: .dk
Internet users: total: 5,424,169

percent of population: 97.0% (July 2016 est.)
country comparison to the world: 62

TRANSPORTATION

National air transport system: *number of registered air carriers:* 10
inventory of registered aircraft operated by air carriers: 76
annual passenger traffic on registered air carriers: 582,011
annual freight traffic on registered air carriers: 0 mt-km (2015)
Civil aircraft registration country code prefix: OY (2016)

Airports: 80 (2013)

country comparison to the world: 68

Airports—with paved runways: total: 28
over 3,047 m: 2
2,438 to 3,047 m: 7
1,524 to 2,437 m: 5
914 to 1,523 m: 12
under 914 m: 2 (2017)

Airports—with unpaved runways: total: 52
914 to 1,523 m: 5
under 914 m: 47 (2013)
Pipelines: gas 1,536 km; oil 330 km (2015)

Railways: total: 3,476 km
standard gauge: 3,476 km 1.435-m gauge (1,756
km electrified) (2017)
country comparison to the world: 62

Roadways: total: 74,558 km
paved: 74,558 km (includes 1,205 km of expressways) (2017)
country comparison to the world: 64

Waterways: 400 km (2010)
country comparison to the world: 87

Merchant marine: total: 654
by type: bulk carrier 7, container ship 114, general
cargo 77, oil tanker 75, other 381 (2017)
country comparison to the world: 31

Ports and terminals: major seaport(s): Baltic
Sea—Aarhus, Copenhagen, Fredericia, Kalund-
borg; North Sea—Esbjerg,
river port(s): Aalborg (Langerak)
dry bulk cargo port(s): Ensted (coal)
cruise port(s): Copenhagen

MILITARY AND SECURITY

Military expenditures: 1.15% of GDP (2016)
1.12% of GDP (2015)
1.15% of GDP (2014)
1.23% of GDP (2013)
1.35% of GDP (2012)
country comparison to the world: 71

Military branches: Danish Army, Royal Danish
Navy, Royal Danish Air Force (2017)

Military service age and obligation: 18 years of
age for compulsory and voluntary military service;
conscripts serve an initial training period that varies from 4 to 12 months according to specialization; former conscripts are assigned to mobilization units; women eligible to volunteer for military
service; in addition to full time employment, the
Danish Military offers reserve contracts in all three
branches (2016)

TERRORISM

Terrorist groups—foreign based: Islamic State
of Iraq and the Levant (ISIL): aim(s): destabilize
Denmark's economy and government
area(s) of operation: maintains a limited operational presence, primarily Danish citizens returning to Denmark after fighting alongside ISIL in
Syria; a Danish-born gunman inspired by ISIL shot
and killed two civilians and wounded five police
officers in Copenhagen on 15 February 2015

TRANSNATIONAL ISSUES

Disputes—international: Iceland, the UK, and
Ireland dispute Denmark's claim that the Faroe
Islands' continental shelf extends beyond 200 nm;
sovereignty dispute with Canada over Hans Island
in the Kennedy Channel between Ellesmere Island
and Greenland; Denmark (Greenland) and Norway have made submissions to the Commission on
the Limits of the Continental Shelf (CLCS) and
Russia is collecting additional data to augment its
2001 CLCS submission

Refugees and internally displaced persons: refugees (country of origin): 18,215 (Syria) (2016)
stateless persons: 7,610 (2016)

DHEKELIA

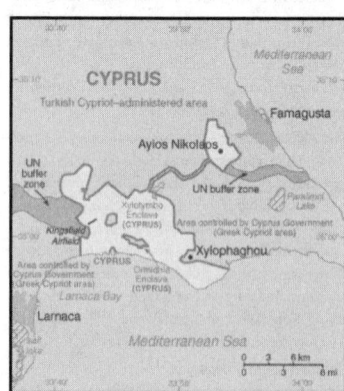

INTRODUCTION

Background: By terms of the 1960 Treaty of Establishment that created the independent Republic of
Cyprus, the UK retained full sovereignty and jurisdiction over two areas of almost 254 square kilometers—Akrotiri and Dhekelia. The larger of these
is the Dhekelia Sovereign Base Area, which is also
referred to as the Eastern Sovereign Base Area.

GEOGRAPHY

Location: Eastern Mediterranean, on the southeast
coast of Cyprus near Famagusta
Geographic coordinates: 34 59 N, 33 45 E

Map references: Middle East
Area: total: 130.8 sq km
note: area surrounds three Cypriot enclaves
country comparison to the world: 223
Area—comparative: about three-quarters the size
of Washington, DC
Land boundaries: total: 108 km
border countries (1): Cyprus 108 km

Coastline: 27.5 km

Climate: temperate; Mediterranean with hot, dry
summers and cool winters

Environment—current issues: netting and trap-
ping of small migrant songbirds in the spring and
autumn

Geography—note: British extraterritorial rights
also extended to several small off-post sites scattered across Cyprus; of the Sovereign Base Area
(SBA) land, 60% is privately owned and farmed,
20% is owned by the Ministry of Defense, and 20%
is SBA Crown land

PEOPLE AND SOCIETY

Population: approximately 15,700 live on the
Sovereign Base Areas of Akrotiri and Dhekelia
including 7,700 Cypriots, 3,600 service and UK
based contract personnel, and 4,400 dependents
Languages: English, Greek

GOVERNMENT

Country name: conventional long form: none
conventional short form: Dhekelia

Dependency status: a special form of UK overseas
territory; administered by an administrator who is
also the Commander, British Forces Cyprus

Capital: name: Episkopi Cantonment (base
administrative center for Akrotiri and Dhekelia);
located in Akrotiri

geographic coordinates: 34 40 N, 32 51 E
time difference: UTC+2 (7 hours ahead of Washington, DC, during Standard Time)
daylight saving time: +1hr, begins last Sunday in
March; ends last Sunday in October

Constitution: presented 3 August 1960, effective
16 August 1960 (The Sovereign Base Areas of
Akrotiri and Dhekelia Order in Council 1960,
serves as a basic legal document); amended 1966
(2016)

Legal system: laws applicable to the Cypriot population are, as far as possible, the same as the laws of
the Republic of Cyprus; note—the Sovereign Base
Area Administration has its own court system to
deal with civil and criminal matters

Executive branch: chief of state: Queen ELIZA-
BETH II (since 6 February 1952)

head of government: Administrator Major General James ILLINGWORTH (since 14 March
2017); note—reports to the British Ministry of
Defense
elections/appointments: the monarchy is hereditary; administrator appointed by the monarch on
the advice of the Ministry of Defense

Judicial branch: *highest court(s):* Senior Judges' Court (consists of several visiting judges from England and Wales)

judge selection and term of office: see entry for United Kingdom

subordinate courts: Resident Judges' Court; military courts

Diplomatic representation in the US: none (overseas territory of the UK)

Diplomatic representation from the US: none (overseas territory of the UK)

Flag description: the flag of the UK is used

National anthem: note: as a United Kingdom area of special sovereignty, "God Save the Queen" is official (see United Kingdom)

ECONOMY

Economy—overview: Economic activity is limited to providing services to the military and their families located in Dhekelia. All food and manufactured goods must be imported.

Industries: none

Exchange rates: note: uses the euro

COMMUNICATIONS

Broadcast media: British Forces Broadcast Service (BFBS) provides multi-channel satellite TV service as well as BFBS radio broadcasts to the Dhekelia Sovereign Base (2009)

MILITARY AND SECURITY

Military—note: defense is the responsibility of the UK; includes Dhekelia Garrison and Ayios Nikolaos Station connected by a roadway

DJIBOUTI

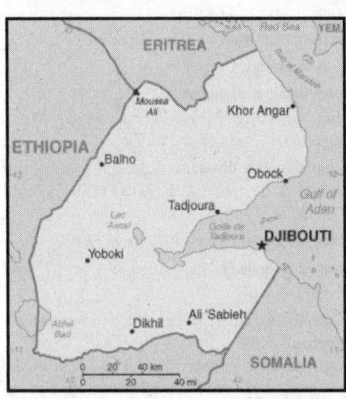

INTRODUCTION

Background: The French Territory of the Afars and the Issas became Djibouti in 1977. Hassan Gouled APTIDON installed an authoritarian one-party state and proceeded to serve as president until 1999. Unrest among the Afar minority during the 1990s led to a civil war that ended in 2001 with a peace accord between Afar rebels and the Somali Issa-dominated government. In 1999, Djibouti's first multiparty presidential election resulted in the election of Ismail Omar GUELLEH as president; he was reelected to a second term in 2005 and extended his tenure in office via a constitutional amendment, which allowed him to serve a third term in 2011 and begin a fourth term in 2016. Djibouti occupies a strategic geographic location at the intersection of the Red Sea and the Gulf of Aden and serves as an important shipping portal for goods entering and leaving the east African highlands and transshipments between Europe, the Middle East, and Asia. The government holds longstanding ties to France, which maintains a significant military presence in the country, and has strong ties with the US. Djibouti hosts several thousand members of US armed services at US-run Camp Lemonnier.

GEOGRAPHY

Location: Eastern Africa, bordering the Gulf of Aden and the Red Sea, between Eritrea and Somalia

Geographic coordinates: 11 30 N, 43 00 E

Map references: Africa

Area: *total:* 23,200 sq km
land: 23,180 sq km
water: 20 sq km
country comparison to the world: 151

Area—comparative: slightly smaller than New Jersey
Land boundaries: total: 528 km
border countries (3): Eritrea 125 km, Ethiopia 342 km, Somalia 61 km

Coastline: 314 km
Maritime claims: territorial sea: 12 nm
contiguous zone: 24 nm
exclusive economic zone: 200 nm

Climate: desert; torrid, dry

Terrain: coastal plain and plateau separated by central mountains

Elevation: *mean elevation:* 430 m

elevation extremes: *lowest point:* Lac Assal -155 m
highest point: Moussa Ali 2,021 m

Natural resources: potential geothermal power, gold, clay, granite, limestone, marble, salt, diatomite, gypsum, pumice, petroleum

Land use: *agricultural land:* 73.4%
arable land: 0.1%;
permanent crops: 0%;
permanent pasture: 73.3%
forest: 0.2%
other: 26.4% (2011 est.)

Irrigated land: 10 sq km (2012)

Population—distribution: most densely populated areas are in the east; the largest city is Djibouti, with a population over 600,000; no other city in the country has a total population over 50,000

Natural hazards: earthquakes; droughts; occasional cyclonic disturbances from the Indian Ocean bring heavy rains and flash floods

volcanism: experiences limited volcanic activity; Ardoukoba (298 m) last erupted in 1978; Manda-Inakir, located along the Ethiopian border, is also historically active

Environment—current issues: inadequate supplies of potable water; limited arable land; desertification; endangered species

Environment—international agreements: *party to:* Biodiversity, Climate Change, Climate Change-Kyoto Protocol, Desertification, Endangered Species, Hazardous Wastes, Law of the Sea, Ozone Layer Protection, Ship Pollution, Wetlands
signed, but not ratified: none of the selected agreements

Geography—note: strategic location near world's busiest shipping lanes and close to Arabian oilfields; terminus of rail traffic into Ethiopia; mostly wasteland; Lac Assal (Lake Assal) is the lowest point in Africa and the saltiest lake in the world

PEOPLE AND SOCIETY

Population: 865,267 (July 2017 est.)
country comparison to the world: 162

Nationality: *noun:* Djiboutian(s)
adjective: Djiboutian

Ethnic groups: Somali 60%, Afar 35%, other 5% (includes French, Arab, Ethiopian, and Italian)

Languages: French (official), Arabic (official), Somali, Afar

Religions: Muslim 94%, Christian 6%

Demographic profile: Djibouti is a poor, predominantly urban country, characterized by high rates of illiteracy, unemployment, and childhood malnutrition. More than 75% of the population lives in cities and towns (predominantly in the capital, Djibouti). The rural population subsists primarily on nomadic herding. Prone to droughts and floods, the country has few natural resources and must import more than 80% of its food from neighboring countries or Europe. Health care, particularly outside the capital, is limited by poor infrastructure, shortages of equipment and supplies, and a lack of qualified personnel. More than a third of health care recipients are migrants because the services are still better than those available in their neighboring home countries. The nearly universal practice of female genital cutting reflects Djibouti's lack of gender equality and is a major contributor to obstetrical complications and its high rates of maternal and infant mortality. A 1995 law prohibiting the practice has never been enforced.

Because of its political stability and its strategic location at the confluence of East Africa and the Gulf States along the Gulf of Aden and the Red Sea, Djibouti is a key transit point for migrants and asylum seekers heading for the Gulf States and beyond. Each year some hundred thousand people, mainly Ethiopians and some Somalis, journey through Djibouti, usually to the port of Obock, to attempt a dangerous sea crossing to Yemen. However, with the escalation of the ongoing Yemen conflict, Yemenis began fleeing to Djibouti in March 2015, with almost 20,000 arriving by August 2017. Most Yemenis remain unregistered and head for Djibouti City rather than seeking asylum at one of Djibouti's three spartan refugee camps. Djibouti has been hosting refugees and asylum seekers, predominantly Somalis and lesser numbers of Ethiopians and Eritreans, at camps for 20 years, despite lacking potable water, food shortages, and unemployment.

Age structure: *0-14 years:* 31.14% (male 135,151/female 134,312)
15-24 years: 21.32% (male 86,820/female 97,656)
25-54 years: 39.03% (male 140,242/female 197,484)
55-64 years: 4.75% (male 18,593/female 22,515)
65 years and over: 3.76% (male 14,559/female 17,935) (2017 est.)

Dependency ratios: *total dependency ratio:* 56.5
youth dependency ratio: 50.1
elderly dependency ratio: 6.4
potential support ratio: 15.6 (2015 est.)

Median age: *total:* 23.9 years
male: 22.1 years
female: 25.3 years (2017 est.)
country comparison to the world: 166

Population growth rate: 2.16% (2017 est.)
country comparison to the world: 39

Birth rate: 23.4 births/1,000 population (2017 est.)
country comparison to the world: 64

Death rate: 7.5 deaths/1,000 population (2017 est.)
country comparison to the world: 108

Net migration rate: 5.7 migrant(s)/1,000 population (2017 est.)
country comparison to the world: 20

Population distribution: most densely populated areas are in the east; the largest city is Djibouti, with a population over 600,000; no other city in the country has a total population over 50,000

Urbanization: *urban population:* 77.5% of total population (2017)
rate of urbanization: 1.52% annual rate of change (2015-20 est.)

Major urban areas—population: DJIBOUTI (capital) 529,000 (2015)

Sex ratio: *at birth:* 1.03 male(s)/female
0-14 years: 1.01 male(s)/female
15-24 years: 0.89 male(s)/female
25-54 years: 0.71 male(s)/female
55-64 years: 0.85 male(s)/female
65 years and over: 0.82 male(s)/female
total population: 0.84 male(s)/female (2016 est.)

Maternal mortality ratio: 229 deaths/100,000 live births (2015 est.)
country comparison to the world: 46

Infant mortality rate: *total:* 45.8 deaths/1,000 live births
male: 52.6 deaths/1,000 live births
female: 38.8 deaths/1,000 live births (2017 est.)
country comparison to the world: 39

Life expectancy at birth: *total population:* 63.6 years
male: 61 years
female: 66.2 years (2017 est.)
country comparison to the world: 191

Total fertility rate: 2.31 children born/woman (2017 est.)
country comparison to the world: 89

Contraceptive prevalence rate: 19% (2012)
Health expenditures: 10.6% of GDP (2014)
country comparison to the world: 17

Physicians density: 0.23 physicians/1,000 population (2014)

Hospital bed density: 1.4 beds/1,000 population (2012)

Drinking water source:
improved:
urban: 97.4% of population
rural: 64.7% of population
total: 90% of population
unimproved:
urban: 2.6% of population
rural: 35.3% of population
total: 10% of population (2015 est.)

Sanitation facility access:
improved:
urban: 59.8% of population
rural: 5.1% of population
total: 47.4% of population
unimproved:
urban: 40.2% of population
rural: 94.9% of population
total: 52.6% of population (2015 est.)

HIV/AIDS—adult prevalence rate: 1.3% (2016 est.)
country comparison to the world: 37

HIV/AIDS—people living with HIV/AIDS: 8,600 (2016 est.)
country comparison to the world: 98

HIV/AIDS—deaths: <1000 (2016 est.)

Major infectious diseases: *degree of risk:* high
food or waterborne diseases: bacterial and protozoal diarrhea, hepatitis A, and typhoid fever
vectorborne disease: dengue fever (2016)

Obesity—adult prevalence rate: 13.5% (2016)
country comparison to the world: 131

Children under the age of 5 years underweight: 29.8% (2012)

country comparison to the world: 14
Education expenditures: 4.5% of GDP (2010)
country comparison to the world: 11

School life expectancy (primary to tertiary education): *total:* 6 years
male: 7 years
female: 6 years (2011)

GOVERNMENT

Country name: *conventional long form:* Republic of Djibouti
conventional short form: Djibouti
local long form: Republique de Djibouti/Jumhuriyat Jibuti
local short form: Djibouti/Jibuti
former: French Territory of the Afars and Issas, French Somaliland
etymology: the country name derives from the capital city of Djibouti

Government type: semi-presidential republic

Capital: *name:* Djibouti

geographic coordinates: 11 35 N, 43 09 E
time difference: UTC+3 (8 hours ahead of Washington, DC, during Standard Time)

Administrative divisions: 6 districts (cercles, singular—cercle); Ali Sabieh, Arta, Dikhil, Djibouti, Obock, Tadjourah

Independence: 27 June 1977 (from France)

National holiday: Independence Day, 27 June (1977)

Constitution: history: approved by referendum 4 September 1992
amendments: proposed by the president of the republic or by the National Assembly; Assembly consideration of proposals requires assent by at least one-third of the membership; passage requires a simple majority vote by the Assembly and approval by simple majority vote in a referendum; the president can opt to bypass a referendum if adopted by at least two-thirds majority vote of the Assembly; constitutional articles on the sovereignty of Djibouti, its republican form of government, and its pluralist form of democracy cannot by amended; amended 2006, 2008, 2010 (2017)

Legal system: mixed legal system based primarily on the French civil code (as it existed in 1997), Islamic religious law (in matters of family law and successions), and customary law

International law organization participation: accepts compulsory ICJ jurisdiction with reservations; accepts ICCt jurisdiction

Citizenship: *citizenship by birth:* no
citizenship by descent only: the mother must be a citizen of Djibouti
dual citizenship recognized: no
residency requirement for naturalization: 10 years

Suffrage: 18 years of age; universal

Executive branch: *chief of state:* President Ismail Omar GUELLEH (since 8 May 1999)

head of government: Prime Minister Abdoulkader Kamil MOHAMED (since 1 April 2013) *cabinet:* Council of Ministers appointed by the prime minister

elections/appointments: president directly elected by absolute majority popular vote in 2 rounds if needed for a 5-year term; (constitution amended in 2010 to allow a third term); election last held on 8 April 2016 (next to be held by 2021); prime minister appointed by the president

election results: Ismail Omar GUELLEH reelected president for a fourth term; percent of vote—Ismail Omar GUELLEH (RPP) 87%, Omar Elmi KHAIREH (CDU) 7.3%, other 5.6%

Legislative branch: description: unicameral National Assembly or Assemblee Nationale, formerly the Chamber of Deputies (65 seats; 52 members directly elected in multi-seat constituencies by simple majority vote and 13 directly elected in multi-seat constituencies by proportional representation vote; members serve 5-year terms)

elections: last held on 22 February 2013 (next to be held in 2018)

election results: percent of vote by party—UMP 61.5%, USN 35.6%, CDU 3%; seats by party—UMP 43, USN 21, CDU 1

Judicial branch: *highest court(s):* Supreme Court or Cour Supreme (consists of NA magistrates); Constitutional Council (consists of 6 magistrates)

judge selection and term of office: Supreme Court magistrates appointed by the president with the advice of the Superior Council of the Magistracy or CSM, a 10-member body consisting of 4 judges, 3 members (non parliamentarians and judges) appointed by the president, and 3 appointed by the National Assembly president or speaker; magistrates appointed for life with retirement at age 65; Constitutional Council magistrate appointments—2 by the president of the republic, 2 by the president of the National Assembly, and 2 by the CSM; magistrates appointed for 8-year, non-renewable terms

subordinate courts: High Court of Appeal; 5 Courts of First Instance; customary courts; State Court (replaced sharia courts in 2003)

Political parties and leaders: Center for United Democrats or CDU [Omar Elmi KHAIREH, chairman]
Democratic Renewal Party or PRD [Abdillahi HAMARITEH]
Djibouti Development Party or PDD [Mohamed Daoud CHEHEM]
Front for Restoration of Unity and Democracy (Front pour la Restauration de l'Unite Democratique) or FRUD [Ali Mohamed DAOUD]
Movement for Democratic Renewal and Development [Daher Ahmed FARAH]
Movement for Development and Liberty or MODEL [Ismail Ahmed WABERI]
National Democratic Party or PND [Aden Robleh AWALEH]
People's Rally for Progress or RPP [Ismail Omar GUELLEH] (governing party)
Peoples Social Democratic Party or PPSD [Hasna Moumin BAHDON]
Republican Alliance for Democracy or ARD

Union for a Presidential Majority or UMP (a coalition of parties including RPP, FRUD, PND, and PPSD)
Union for Democracy and Justice or UDJ [Ilya Ismail GUEDI Hared]
Union for National Salvation or USN [Ahmed Youssouf HOUMED] (coalition includes ARD, MoDel, MRD, PDD, PND, UDJ)

International organization participation: ACP, AfDB, AFESD, AMF, AU, CAEU (candidates), COMESA, FAO, G-77, IBRD, ICAO, ICCt, ICRM, IDA, IDB, IFAD, IFC, IFRCS, IGAD, ILO, IMF, IMO, Interpol, IOC, IOM, IPU, ITU, ITUC (NGOs), LAS, MIGA, MINURSO, NAM, OIC, OIF, OPCW, UN, UNCTAD, UNESCO, UNHCR, UNIDO, UNWTO, UPU, WCO, WFTU (NGOs), WHO, WIPO, WMO, WTO

Diplomatic representation in the US: *chief of mission:* Ambassador (vacant); Charge D'Affaires Mark BOULWARE (since February 2017)

chancery: 1156 15th Street NW, Suite 515, Washington, DC 20005

telephone: [1] (202) 331-0270

FAX: [1] (202) 331-0302

Diplomatic representation from the US: *chief of mission:* Ambassador (vacant); Charge d'Affaires J. Alexander HAMILTON (since 23 June 2017)

embassy: Lot 350-B, Haramouss

mailing address: B.P. 185, Djibouti

telephone: [253] 21 45 30 00

FAX: [253] 21 45 31 29

Flag description: two equal horizontal bands of light blue (top) and light green with a white isosceles triangle based on the hoist side bearing a red five-pointed star in the center; blue stands for sea and sky and the Issa Somali people; green symbolizes earth and the Afar people; white represents peace; the red star recalls the struggle for independence and stands for unity

National symbol(s): red star; national colors: light blue, green, white, red

National anthem: name: "Jabuuti" (Djibouti)

lyrics/music: Aden ELMI/Abdi ROBLEH

note: adopted 1977

ECONOMY

Economy—overview: Djibouti's economy is based on service activities connected with the country's strategic location as a deepwater port on the Red Sea. Three-fourths of Djibouti's inhabitants live in the capital city; the remainder are mostly nomadic herders. Scant rainfall and less than 4% arable land: limits crop production to small quantities of fruits and vegetables, and most food must be imported.

Djibouti provides services as both a transit port for the region and an international transshipment and refueling center. Imports, exports, and reexports represent 70% of port activity at Djibouti's container terminal. Reexports consist primarily of coffee from landlocked neighbor Ethiopia. Djibouti has few natural resources and little industry. The nation is, therefore, heavily dependent on foreign assistance to support its balance of payments

and to finance development projects. An official unemployment rate of nearly 40%—with youth unemployment near 80%—continues to be a major problem. Inflation was a modest 3% in 2014-2017, due to low international food prices and a decline in electricity tariffs.

Djibouti's reliance on diesel-generated electricity and imported food and water leave average consumers vulnerable to global price shocks, though in mid-2015 Djibouti passed new legislation to liberalize the energy sector. The government has emphasized infrastructure development for transportation and energy and Djibouti – with the help of foreign partners, particularly China – has begun to increase and modernize its port capacity. In 2017, Djibouti opened two of the largest projects in its history, the Doraleh Port and Djibouti-Addis Ababa Railway, which will increase the country's ability to capitalize on its strategic location.

GDP (purchasing power parity): $3.64 billion (2017 est.)
$3.402 billion (2016 est.)
$3.194 billion (2015 est.)
note: data are in 2017 dollars
country comparison to the world: 182

GDP (official exchange rate): $2.082 billion (2016 est.)

GDP—real growth rate: 7% (2017 est.)
6.5% (2016 est.)
6.5% (2015 est.)
country comparison to the world: 9

GDP—per capita (PPP): $3,600 (2017 est.)
$3,400 (2016 est.)
$3,300 (2015 est.)
note: data are in 2017 dollars
country comparison to the world: 186

Gross national saving: 12.6% of GDP (2017 est.)
16.9% of GDP (2016 est.)
19% of GDP (2015 est.)
country comparison to the world: 142

GDP—composition, by end use:
household consumption: 56.5%
government consumption: 29.2%
investment in fixed capital: 41.8%
investment in inventories: 0.3%
exports of goods and services: 38.6%
imports of goods and services: -66.4% (2017 est.)

GDP—composition, by sector of origin:
agriculture: 2.8%
industry: 21%
services: 76.1% (2017 est.)

Agriculture—products: fruits, vegetables; goats, sheep, camels, animal hides

Industries: construction, agricultural processing, shipping

Industrial production growth rate: 8.3% (2017 est.)
country comparison to the world: 15

Labor force: 294,600 (2012)
country comparison to the world: 164

Labor force—by occupation: *agriculture:* NA%
industry: NA%
services: NA%

Unemployment rate: 60% (2014 est.)

263

48.4% (2012 est.)
country comparison to the world: 215

Population below poverty line: 23%
note: percent of population below $1.25 per day at
purchasing power parity (2015 est.)

**Household income or consumption by percentage
share:** *lowest 10%:* 2.4%
highest 10%: 30.9% (2002)

Distribution of family income—Gini index: 40.9
(2002)
country comparison to the world: 56

Budget: *revenues* $699.8 million
expenditures $865.4 million (2017 est.)
Taxes and other revenues 33.6% of GDP (2017
est.)
country comparison to the world: 62

Budget surplus (+) or deficit (-): -8% of GDP
(2017 est.)
country comparison to the world: 196

Public debt: 31.3% of GDP (2016 est.)
33.7% of GDP (2015 est.)
country comparison to the world: 159

Fiscal year: calendar year

Inflation rate (consumer prices): 3% (2017 est.)
2.7% (2016 est.)
country comparison to the world: 127

Commercial bank prime lending rate: 11.6% (31
December 2017 est.)
11.45% (31 December 2016 est.)
country comparison to the world: 71

Stock of narrow money: $1.493 billion (31 December 2017 est.)
$1.323 billion (31 December 2016 est.)
country comparison to the world: 144

Stock of broad money: $1.795 billion (31 December 2017 est.)
$1.652 billion (31 December 2016 est.)
country comparison to the world: 161

Stock of domestic credit: $680.3 million (31
December 2017 est.)
$639.9 million (31 December 2016 est.)
country comparison to the world: 172

Current account balance: -$437 million (2017
est.)
-$575 million (2016 est.)
country comparison to the world: 102

Exports: $155.5 million (2017 est.)
$139.9 million (2016 est.)
country comparison to the world: 191

Exports—commodities: reexports, hides and skins,
scrap metal

Exports—partners: Ethiopia 39%, Somalia 17.8%,
Qatar 9.4%, Brazil 9.1%, Yemen 5.1% (2016)

Imports: $1.172 billion (2017 est.)
$1.128 billion (2016 est.)
country comparison to the world: 174

Imports—commodities: foods, beverages, transport equipment, chemicals, petroleum products,
clothing

Imports—partners: UAE 25.8%, France 16.4%,
China 10.4%, Saudi Arabia 8.4%, Ethiopia 7%,
Yemen 4.8% (2016)

Debt—external: $1.554 billion (31 December
2017 est.)

$1.519 billion (31 December 2016 est.)
country comparison to the world: 158

Stock of direct foreign investment—at home:
$1.784 billion (31 December 2017 est.)
$1.483 billion (31 December 2016 est.)
country comparison to the world: 116

Exchange rates: Djiboutian francs (DJF) per US
dollar—
177.7 (2017 est.)
177.72 (2016 est.)
177.72 (2015 est.)
177.72 (2014 est.)
177.72 (2013 est.)

ENERGY

Electricity access: *population without electricity:* 400,000
electrification—*total population:* 50%
electrification—*urban areas:* 61%
electrification—*rural areas:* 14% (2013)

Electricity—production: 405 million kWh (2015
est.)
country comparison to the world: 172

Electricity—consumption: 376.7 million kWh
(2015 est.)
country comparison to the world: 176

Electricity—exports: 0 kWh (2016 est.)
country comparison to the world: 129

Electricity—imports: 0 kWh (2016 est.)
country comparison to the world: 142

Electricity—installed generating capacity:
130,000 kW (2015 est.)
country comparison to the world: 174

Electricity—from fossil fuels: 100% of total
installed capacity (2015 est.)
country comparison to the world: 5

Electricity—from nuclear fuels: 0% of total
installed capacity (2015 est.)
country comparison to the world: 78

Electricity—from hydroelectric plants: 0% of total
installed capacity (2015 est.)
country comparison to the world: 173

Electricity—from other renewable sources: 0% of
total installed capacity (2015 est.)
country comparison to the world: 179

Crude oil—production: 0 bbl/day (2016 est.)
country comparison to the world: 126

Crude oil—exports: 0 bbl/day (2014 est.)
country comparison to the world: 114

Crude oil—imports: 0 bbl/day (2014 est.)
country comparison to the world: 117

Crude oil—proved reserves: 0 bbl (1 January 2017
es)
country comparison to the world: 126

Refined petroleum products—production: 0 bbl/
day (2014 est.)
country comparison to the world: 136

Refined petroleum products—consumption: 6,000
bbl/day (2015 est.)
country comparison to the world: 171

Refined petroleum products—exports: 402.7 bbl/
day (2014 est.)
country comparison to the world: 113

Refined petroleum products—imports: 6,509 bbl/
day (2014 est.)
country comparison to the world: 156

Natural gas—production: 0 cu m (2013 est.)
country comparison to the world: 127

Natural gas—consumption: 0 cu m (2013 est.)
country comparison to the world: 175

Natural gas—exports: 0 cu m (2013 est.)
country comparison to the world: 93

Natural gas—imports: 0 cu m (2013 est.)
country comparison to the world: 117

Natural gas—proved reserves: 0 cu m (1 January
2014 es)
country comparison to the world: 132

**Carbon dioxide emissions from consumption of
energy:** 1.8 million Mt (2013 est.)
country comparison to the world: 151

COMMUNICATIONS

Telephones—fixed lines: *total subscriptions:*
24,925
subscriptions per 100 inhabitants: 3 (July 2016
est.)
country comparison to the world: 181

Telephones—mobile cellular: *total:* 345,246
subscriptions per 100 inhabitants: 41 (July 2016
est.)
country comparison to the world: 177

Telephone system: *general assessment:* telephone
facilities in the city of Djibouti are adequate, as are
the microwave radio relay connections to outlying
areas of the country
domestic: Djibouti Telecom is the sole provider of
telecommunications services and utilizes mostly a
microwave radio relay network; fiber-optic cable is
installed in the capital; rural areas connected via
wireless local loop radio systems; mobile cellular
coverage is primarily limited to the area in and
around Djibouti city
international: country code—253; landing point
for the SEA-ME-WE-3 and EASSy fiber-optic submarine cable systems providing links to Asia, the
Middle East, Europe and North America; satellite
earth stations—2 (1 Intelsat—Indian Ocean and
1 Arabsat); Medarabtel regional microwave radio
relay telephone network (2015)

Broadcast media: state-owned Radiodiffusion-
Television de Djibouti operates the sole terrestrial
TV station, as well as the only 2 domestic radio
networks; no private TV or radio stations; transmissions of several international broadcasters are
available (2007)

Internet country code: .dj
Internet users: total: 111,212

percent of population: 13.1% (July 2016 est.)
country comparison to the world: 178

TRANSPORTATION

National air transport system: *number of registered air carriers:* 2

inventory of registered aircraft operated by air carriers: 4 (2015)

Civil aircraft registration country code prefix: J2 (2016)

Airports: 13 (2013)

country comparison to the world: 152

Airports—with paved runways: *total:* 3

over 3,047 m: 1

2,438 to 3,047 m: 1

1,524 to 2,437 m: 1 (2017)

Airports—with unpaved runways: *total:* 10

1,524 to 2,437 m: 1

914 to 1,523 m: 7

under 914 m: 2 (2013)

Railways: *total:* 97 km (Djibouti segment of the 756 km Addis Ababa-Djibouti railway)

standard gauge: 97 km 1.435-m gauge (2017)

country comparison to the world: 128

Roadways: *total:* 3,065 km

paved: 1,379 km

unpaved: 1,686 km (2000)

country comparison to the world: 165

Merchant marine: *total:* 18

by type: oil tanker 2, other 16 (2017)

country comparison to the world: 136

Ports and terminals: *major seaport(s):* Djibouti

MILITARY AND SECURITY

Military branches: Djibouti Armed Forces (Forces Armees Djiboutiennes, FAD): Djibouti National Army (includes Navy, Djiboutian Air Force (Force Aerienne Djiboutienne, FAD), National Gendarmerie (GN)) (2013)

Military service age and obligation: 18 years of age for voluntary military service; 16-25 years of age for voluntary military training; no conscription (2012)

Maritime threats: while attacks continued to decrease, the International Maritime Bureau reports offshore waters in the Red Sea and Gulf of Aden remain a high risk for piracy; the presence of several naval task forces in the Gulf of Aden and additional anti-piracy measures on the part of ship operators, including the use of on-board armed security teams, contributed to the drop in incidents; there were no incidents in the Red Sea in 2016, however one ship was fired upon during the first half of 2017; Operation Ocean Shield, the NATO/EUNAVFOR naval task force established in 2009 to combat Somali piracy, concluded its operations in December 2016 as a result of the drop in reported incidents over the last few years

TERRORISM

Terrorist groups—foreign based: *al-Shabaab:* aim(s): avenge Djibouti's support for NATO and other forces combatting al-Shabaab

area(s) of operation: responsible for killing a Turkish national and injuring 11 international soldiers on 24 May 2014, when two suicide bombers detonated their explosives inside La Chaumiere, a restaurant in Djibouti's capital popular with tourists and Western military personnel; the suicide bombings were the first in the country's history; continues to conduct lethal attacks; leadership claims the attacks are in retaliation for Djibouti's support for NATO and the African Union Mission for Somalia, a regional peacekeeping force operated by the African Union with the approval of the UN

TRANSNATIONAL ISSUES

Disputes—international: Djibouti maintains economic ties and border accords with "Somaliland" leadership while maintaining some political ties to various factions in Somalia; Kuwait is chief investor in the 2008 restoration and upgrade of the Ethiopian-Djibouti rail link; in 2008, Eritrean troops moved across the border on Ras Doumera peninsula and occupied Doumera Island with undefined sovereignty in the Red Sea

Refugees and internally displaced persons: *refugees (country of origin):* 19,636 (Yemen); 13,043 (Somalia) (2017)

Trafficking in persons: current situation: Djibouti is a transit, source, and destination country for men, women, and children subjected to forced labor and sex trafficking; economic migrants from East Africa en route to Yemen and other Middle East locations are vulnerable to exploitation in Djibouti; some women and girls may be forced into domestic servitude or prostitution after reaching Djibouti City, the Ethiopia-Djibouti trucking corridor, or Obock – the main crossing point into Yemen; Djiboutian and foreign children may be forced to beg, to work as domestic servants, or to commit theft and other petty crimes

tier rating: Tier 2 Watch List – Djibouti does not fully comply with the minimum standards for the elimination of trafficking; however, it is making significant efforts to do so; in 2014, Djibouti was granted a waiver from an otherwise required downgrade to Tier 3 because its government has a written plan that, if implemented would constitute making significant efforts to bring itself into compliance with the minimum standards for the elimination of trafficking; one forced labor trafficker was convicted in 2014 but received a suspended sentence inadequate to deter trafficking; authorities did not investigate or prosecute any other forced labor crimes, any sex trafficking offenses, or any officials complicit in human trafficking, and remained limited in their ability to recognize or protect trafficking victims; official round-ups, detentions, and deportations of non-Djiboutian residents, including children without screening for trafficking victims remained routine; the government did not provide care to victims but supported local NGOs operating centers that assisted victims (2015)

DOMINICA

INTRODUCTION

Background: Dominica was the last of the Caribbean islands to be colonized by Europeans due chiefly to the fierce resistance of the native Caribs. France ceded possession to Great Britain in 1763, which colonized the island in 1805. In 1980, two years after independence, Dominica's fortunes improved when a corrupt and tyrannical administration was replaced by that of Mary Eugenia CHARLES, the first female prime minister in the Caribbean, who remained in office for 15 years. On 18 September 2017, Hurricane Maria passed over the island causing extensive damage to structures, roads, communications, and the power supply, and largely destroying critical agricultural areas.

GEOGRAPHY

Location: Caribbean, island between the Caribbean Sea and the North Atlantic Ocean, about halfway between Puerto Rico and Trinidad and Tobago

Geographic coordinates: 15 25 N, 61 20 W

Map references: Central America and the Caribbean

Area: *total:* 751 sq km

land: 751 sq km

water: 0 sq km

country comparison to the world: 189

Area—comparative: slightly more than four times the size of Washington, DC

Land boundaries: 0 km

Coastline: 148 km
Maritime claims: territorial sea: 12 nm
contiguous zone: 24 nm
exclusive economic zone: 200 nm

Climate: tropical; moderated by northeast trade winds; heavy rainfall

Terrain: rugged mountains of volcanic origin

Elevation: *mean elevation:* NA

elevation extremes: *lowest point:* Caribbean Sea 0 m
highest point: Morne Diablotins 1,447 m

Natural resources: timber, hydropower, arable land

Land use: *agricultural land:* 34.7%
arable land: 8%;
permanent crops: 24%;
permanent pasture: 2.7%
forest: 59.2%
other: 6.1% (2011 est.)

Irrigated land: NA

Population—distribution: population is mostly clustered along the coast, with roughly a third living in the parish of St. George, in or around the capital of Roseau; the volcanic interior is sparsely populated

Natural hazards: flash floods are a constant threat; destructive hurricanes can be expected during the late summer months
volcanism: Dominica was the last island to be formed in the Caribbean some 26 million years ago, it lies in the middle of the volcanic island arc of the Lesser Antilles that extends from the island of Saba in the north to Grenada in the south; of the 16 volcanoes that make up this arc, five are located on Dominica, more than any other island in the Caribbean: Morne aux Diables (861 m), Morne Diablotins (1,430 m), Morne Trois Pitons (1,387 m), Watt Mountain (1,224 m), which last erupted in 1997, and Morne Plat Pays (940 m); the two best known volcanic features on Dominica, the Valley of Desolation and the Boiling Lake thermal areas, lie on the flanks of Watt Mountain and both are popular tourist destinations

Environment—current issues: water shortages a continuing concern; pollution from chemicals used in farming and from untreated sewage; forests endangered by the expansion of farming activities

Environment—international agreements: *party to:* Biodiversity, Climate Change, Climate Change-Kyoto Protocol, Desertification, Endangered Species, Environmental Modification, Hazardous Wastes, Law of the Sea, Ozone Layer Protection, Ship Pollution, Whaling
signed, but not ratified: none of the selected agreements

Geography—note: known as "The Nature Island of the Caribbean" due to its spectacular, lush, and varied flora and fauna, which are protected by an extensive natural park system; the most mountainous of the Lesser Antilles, its volcanic peaks are cones of lava craters and include Boiling Lake, the second-largest, thermally active lake in the world

---

PEOPLE AND SOCIETY

Population: 73,897 (July 2017 est.)
country comparison to the world: 202

Nationality: *noun:* Dominican(s)
adjective: Dominican

Ethnic groups: black 86.6%, mixed 9.1%, indigenous 2.9%, other 1.3%, unspecified 0.2% (2001 est.)

Languages: English (official), French patois

Religions: Roman Catholic 61.4%, Protestant 28.6% (includes Evangelical 6.7%, Seventh Day Adventist 6.1%, Pentecostal 5.6%, Baptist 4.1%, Methodist 3.7%, Church of God 1.2%, other 1.2%), Rastafarian 1.3%, Jehovah's Witness 1.2%, other 0.3%, none 6.1%, unspecified 1.1% (2001 est.)

Age structure: *0-14 years:* 21.72% (male 8,210/female 7,843)
15-24 years: 15.14% (male 5,758/female 5,428)
25-54 years: 42.2% (male 15,809/female 15,372)
55-64 years: 9.81% (male 3,860/female 3,387)
65 years and over: 11.14% (male 3,679/female 4,551) (2017 est.)

Median age: *total:* 33.5 years
male: 33 years
female: 34 years (2017 est.)
country comparison to the world: 91

Population growth rate: 0.18% (2017 est.)
country comparison to the world: 184

Birth rate: 15.1 births/1,000 population (2017 est.)
country comparison to the world: 127

Death rate: 7.9 deaths/1,000 population (2017 est.)
country comparison to the world: 93

Net migration rate: -5.4 migrant(s)/1,000 population (2017 est.)
country comparison to the world: 193

Population distribution: population is mosly clustered along the coast, with roughly a third living in the parish of St. George, in or around the capital of Roseau; the volcanic interior is sparsely populated

Urbanization: *urban population:* 70.1% of total population (2017)
rate of urbanization: 0.85% annual rate of change (2015-20 est.)

Major urban areas—population: ROSEAU (capital) 15,000 (2014)

Sex ratio: *at birth:* 1.05 male(s)/female
0-14 years: 1.05 male(s)/female
15-24 years: 1.06 male(s)/female
25-54 years: 1.03 male(s)/female
55-64 years: 1.15 male(s)/female
65 years and over: 0.79 male(s)/female
total population: 1.02 male(s)/female (2016 est.)

Infant mortality rate: *total:* 10.6 deaths/1,000 live births
male: 14 deaths/1,000 live births
female: 7 deaths/1,000 live births (2017 est.)
country comparison to the world: 132

Life expectancy at birth: *total population:* 77.2 years
male: 74.2 years
female: 80.3 years (2017 est.)
country comparison to the world: 76

Total fertility rate: 2.03 children born/woman (2017 est.)
country comparison to the world: 115
Health expenditures: 5.5% of GDP (2014)
country comparison to the world: 126

Hospital bed density: 3.8 beds/1,000 population (2012)

Drinking water source:
improved:
urban: 95.7% of population
unimproved:
urban: 4.3% of population (2015 est.)

Sanitation facility access:
improved:
urban: 79.6% of population
rural: 84.3% of population
total: 81.1% of population
unimproved:
urban: 20.4% of population
rural: 15.7% of population
total: 18.9% of population (2007 est.)

HIV/AIDS—adult prevalence rate: NA

HIV/AIDS—people living with HIV/AIDS: NA

HIV/AIDS—deaths: NA

Major infectious diseases: *note:* active local transmission of Zika virus by Aedes species mosquitoes has been identified in this country (as of August 2016); it poses an important risk (a large number of cases possible) among US citizens if bitten by an infective mosquito; other less common ways to get Zika are through sex, via blood transfusion, or during pregnancy, in which the pregnant woman passes Zika virus to her fetus (2016)

Obesity—adult prevalence rate: 27.9% (2016)
country comparison to the world: 33

People—note: 3,000-3,500 Kalinago (Carib) still living on Dominica are the only pre-Columbian population remaining in the Caribbean; only 70-100 may be "pure" Kalinago because of years of integration into the broader population

---

GOVERNMENT

Country name: *conventional long form:* Commonwealth of Dominica
conventional short form: Dominica
etymology: the island was named by explorer Christopher COLUMBUS for the day of the week on which he spotted it, Sunday ("Domingo" in Latin), 3 November 1493

Government type: parliamentary republic

Capital: *name:* Roseau
geographic coordinates: 15 18 N, 61 24 W
time difference: UTC-4 (1 hour ahead of Washington, DC, during Standard Time)

Administrative divisions: 10 parishes; Saint Andrew, Saint David, Saint George, Saint John,

Saint Joseph, Saint Luke, Saint Mark, Saint Patrick, Saint Paul, Saint Peter

Independence: 3 November 1978 (from the UK)

National holiday: Independence Day, 3 November (1978)

Constitution: previous 1967 (preindependence); latest presented 25 July 1978, entered into force 3 November 1978; amended several times, last in 2015 (2016)

Legal system: common law based on the English model

International law organization participation: accepts compulsory ICJ jurisdiction; accepts ICCt jurisdiction

Citizenship: *citizenship by birth:* yes
citizenship by descent: yes
dual citizenship recognized: yes
residency requirement for naturalization: 5 years

Suffrage: 18 years of age; universal

Executive branch: *chief of state:* President Charles A. SAVARIN (since 2 October 2013)

head of government: Prime Minister Roosevelt SKERRIT (since 8 January 2004)
cabinet: Cabinet appointed by the president on the advice of the prime minister
elections/appointments: president nominated by the prime minister and leader of the opposition party and elected by the House of Assembly for a 5-year term (eligible for a second term); election last held on 30 September 2013 (next to be held in October 2018); prime minister appointed by the president
election results: Charles A. SAVARIN (DLP) elected president; House of Assembly vote—19-0

Legislative branch: description: unicameral House of Assembly (32 seats; 21 representatives directly elected in single-seat constituencies by simple majority vote, 9 senators appointed by the Assembly, and 2 ex-officio members—the House Speaker and the Clerk of the House; members serve 5-year terms)
elections: last held on 8 December 2014 (next to be held in 2019); note—tradition dictates that the election is held within 5 years of the last election, but technically it is 5 years from the first seating of parliament plus a 90-day grace period
election results: percent of vote by party—DLP 57.0%, UWP 42.9%, other 0.1%; seats by party—DLP 15, UWP 6

Judicial branch: *highest court(s):* the Eastern Caribbean Supreme Court (ECSC) is the superior court of the Organization of Eastern Caribbean States; the ECSC—headquartered on St. Lucia—consists of the Court of Appeal—headed by the chief justice and 4 judges—and the High Court with 18 judges; the Court of Appeal is itinerant, travelling to member states on a schedule to hear appeals from the High Court and subordinate courts; High Court judges reside at the member states with 2 in Dominica; note—Dominica is a member of the Caribbean Court of Justice

judge selection and term of office: chief justice of Eastern Caribbean Supreme Court appointed by the Her Majesty, Queen ELIZABETH II; other justices and judges appointed by the Judicial and Legal Services Commission, an independent body of judicial officials; Court of Appeal justices appointed for life with mandatory retirement at age 65; High Court judges appointed for life with mandatory retirement at age 62
subordinate courts: Court of Summary Jurisdiction; magistrates' courts

Political parties and leaders: Dominica Freedom Party or DFP [Judith PESTAINA]
Dominica Labor Party or DLP [Roosevelt SKERRIT]
Dominica United Workers Party or UWP [Lennox LINTON]

Political pressure groups and leaders: Dominica Trade Union [Harold SEALY]
Dominca Public Service Union [Mervin ANTHONY]

International organization participation: ACP, AOSIS, C, Caricom, CD, CDB, CELAC, Commonwealth of Nations, ECCU, FAO, G-77, IAEA, IBRD, ICCt, ICRM, IDA, IFAD, IFC, IFRCS, ILO, IMF, IMO, Interpol, IOC, ISO (correspondent), ITU, ITUC (NGOs), MIGA, NAM, OAS, OECS, OIF, OPANAL, OPCW, Petrocaribe, UN, UNCTAD, UNESCO, UNIDO, UPU, WFTU, WHO, WIPO, WMO, WTO

Diplomatic representation in the US: *chief of mission:* Ambassador Vince HENDERSON (since 18 January 2017)
chancery: 3216 New Mexico Avenue NW, Washington, DC 20016
telephone: [1] (202) 364-6781
FAX: [1] (202) 364-6791
consulate(s) general: New York

Diplomatic representation from the US: the US does not have an embassy in Dominica; the US Ambassador to Barbados is accredited to Dominica

Flag description: green with a centered cross of three equal bands—the vertical part is yellow (hoist side), black, and white and the horizontal part is yellow (top), black, and white; superimposed in the center of the cross is a red disk bearing a Sisserou parrot, unique to Dominica, encircled by 10 green, five-pointed stars edged in yellow; the 10 stars represent the 10 administrative divisions (parishes); green symbolizes the island's lush vegetation; the triple-colored cross represents the Christian Trinity; the yellow color denotes sunshine, the main agricultural products (citrus and bananas), and the native Carib Indians; black is for the rich soil and the African heritage of most citizens; white signifies rivers, waterfalls, and the purity of aspirations; the red disc stands for social justice

National symbol(s): Sisserou parrot, Carib Wood flower; national colors: green, yellow, black, white, red

National anthem: name: "Isle of Beauty"
lyrics/music: Wilfred Oscar Morgan POND/Lemuel McPherson CHRISTIAN

note: adopted 1967

ECONOMY

Economy—overview: The Dominican economy has been dependent on agriculture—primarily bananas—in years past, but increasingly has been driven by tourism as the government seeks to promote Dominica as an "ecotourism" destination. Moreover, Dominica has an offshore medical education sector. In order to diversify the island's economy, the government is also attempting to foster an offshore financial industry and plans to sign agreements with the private sector to develop geothermal energy resources. In 2003, the government began a comprehensive restructuring of the economy—including the elimination of price controls, privatization of the state banana company, and tax increases—to address an economic and financial crisis and to meet IMF requirements. In 2009 and 2013, the economy contracted as a result of the global recession; growth remains anemic. Although public debt levels continue to exceed pre-recession levels, the debt burden declined from 78% of GDP in 2011 to approximately 70% in 2012.

GDP (purchasing power parity): $851 million (2017 est.)
$818.8 million (2016 est.)
$797.7 million (2015 est.)
note: data are in 2017 dollars
country comparison to the world: 206

GDP (official exchange rate): $608 million (2016 est.)

GDP—real growth rate: 3.9% (2017 est.)
2.6% (2016 est.)
-2.5% (2015 est.)
country comparison to the world: 77

GDP—per capita (PPP): $12,000 (2017 est.)
$11,500 (2016 est.)
$11,200 (2015 est.)
note: data are in 2017 dollars
country comparison to the world: 130

Gross national saving: 16.7% of GDP (2017 est.)
20.4% of GDP (2016 est.)
14.6% of GDP (2015 est.)
country comparison to the world: 111

GDP—composition, by end use:
household consumption: 72.7%
government consumption: 23%
investment in fixed capital: 12.7%
investment in inventories: 0%
exports of goods and services: 40.9%
imports of goods and services: -49.4% (2017 est.)

GDP—composition, by sector of origin:
agriculture: 15.3%
industry: 13.6%
services: 71.1% (2017 est.)

Agriculture—products: bananas, citrus, mangos, root crops, coconuts, cocoa
note: forest and fishery potential not exploited

Industries: soap, coconut oil, tourism, copra, furniture, cement blocks, shoes

Industrial production growth rate: 3% (2017 est.)

country comparison to the world: 100

Labor force: 25,000 (2000 est.)
country comparison to the world: 209

Labor force—by occupation: *agriculture:* 40%
industry: 32%
services: 28% (2002 est.)

Unemployment rate: 23% (2000 est.)
country comparison to the world: 190

Population below poverty line: 29% (2009 est.)

Household income or consumption by percentage share: *lowest 10%:* NA%
highest 10%: NA%

Budget: *revenues:* $148.1 million
expenditures: $148.1 million (2017 est.)
Taxes and other revenues: 24.4% of GDP (2017 est.)
country comparison to the world: 118

Budget surplus (+) or deficit (-): 0% of GDP (2017 est.)
country comparison to the world: 32

Public debt: 81% of GDP (2016 est.)
83% of GDP (2015 est.)
country comparison to the world: 38

Fiscal year: 1 July—30 June

Inflation rate (consumer prices): 0.6% (2017 est.)
0% (2016 est.)
country comparison to the world: 21

Central bank discount rate: 6.5% (31 December 2010)
6.5% (31 December 2009)
country comparison to the world: 56

Commercial bank prime lending rate: 8.1% (31 December 2017 est.)
8.33% (31 December 2016 est.)
country comparison to the world: 108

Stock of narrow money: $116.2 million (31 December 2017 est.)
$112 million (31 December 2016 est.)
country comparison to the world: 189

Stock of broad money: $535.2 million (31 December 2017 est.)
$509.7 million (31 December 2016 est.)
country comparison to the world: 184

Stock of domestic credit: $222.2 million (31 December 2017 est.)
$195.9 million (31 December 2016 est.)
country comparison to the world: 184

Current account balance: -$38 million (2017 est.)
$5 million (2016 est.)
country comparison to the world: 67

Exports: $47.4 million (2017 est.)
$43.7 million (2016 est.)
country comparison to the world: 204

Exports—commodities: bananas, soap, bay oil, vegetables, grapefruit, oranges

Exports—partners: Trinidad and Tobago 15.4%, Jamaica 13.3%, Saudi Arabia 13%, St. Kitts and Nevis 11.8%, Guyana 9.3%, Barbados 5.1%, US 5.1%, Antigua and Barbuda 4.5%, Egypt 4.1% (2016)

Imports: $198 million (2017 est.)

$186.4 million (2016 est.)
country comparison to the world: 203

Imports—commodities: manufactured goods, machinery and equipment, food, chemicals

Imports—partners: US 23.4%, Trinidad and Tobago 18.1%, Italy 8.7%, UK 5.4% (2016)

Reserves of foreign exchange and gold: $150 million (31 December 2017 est.)
$221.9 million (31 December 2016 est.)
country comparison to the world: 163

Debt—external: $288.6 million (31 December 2016 est.)
$314.2 million (31 December 2015 est.)
country comparison to the world: 187

Exchange rates: East Caribbean dollars (XCD) per US dollar—
2.7 (2017 est.)
2.7 (2016 est.)
2.7 (2015 est.)
2.7 (2014 est.)
2.7 (2013 est.)

ENERGY

Electricity access: *population without electricity:* 5,900
electrification—total population: 93%
electrification—urban areas: 99%
electrification—rural areas: 80% (2012)

Electricity—production: 94 million kWh (2015 est.)
country comparison to the world: 199

Electricity—consumption: 87.42 million kWh (2015 est.)
country comparison to the world: 200

Electricity—exports: 0 kWh (2016 est.)
country comparison to the world: 130

Electricity—imports: 0 kWh (2016 est.)
country comparison to the world: 143

Electricity—installed generating capacity: 33,200 kW (2015 est.)
country comparison to the world: 200

Electricity—from fossil fuels: 60.2% of total installed capacity (2015 est.)
country comparison to the world: 128

Electricity—from nuclear fuels: 0% of total installed capacity (2015 est.)
country comparison to the world: 79

Electricity—from hydroelectric plants: 18.1% of total installed capacity (2015 est.)
country comparison to the world: 95

Electricity—from other renewable sources: 21.7% of total installed capacity (2015 est.)
country comparison to the world: 29

Crude oil—production: 0 bbl/day (2016 est.)
country comparison to the world: 127

Crude oil—exports: 0 bbl/day (2014 est.)
country comparison to the world: 115

Crude oil—imports: 0 bbl/day (2014 est.)
country comparison to the world: 118

Crude oil—proved reserves: 0 bbl (1 January 2017 es)

country comparison to the world: 127

Refined petroleum products—production: 0 bbl/day (2014 est.)
country comparison to the world: 137

Refined petroleum products—consumption: 1,000 bbl/day (2015 est.)
country comparison to the world: 206

Refined petroleum products—exports: 0 bbl/day (2014 est.)
country comparison to the world: 149

Refined petroleum products—imports: 978.2 bbl/day (2014 est.)
country comparison to the world: 202

Natural gas—production: 0 cu m (2013 est.)
country comparison to the world: 128

Natural gas—consumption: 0 cu m (2013 est.)
country comparison to the world: 176

Natural gas—exports: 0 cu m (2013 est.)
country comparison to the world: 94

Natural gas—imports: 0 cu m (2013 est.)
country comparison to the world: 118

Natural gas—proved reserves: 0 cu m (1 January 2014 es)
country comparison to the world: 133

Carbon dioxide emissions from consumption of energy: 100,000 Mt (2013 est.)
country comparison to the world: 207

COMMUNICATIONS

Telephones—fixed lines: *total subscriptions:* 13,328
subscriptions per 100 inhabitants: 18 (July 2016 est.)
country comparison to the world: 188

Telephones—mobile cellular: *total:* 78,444
subscriptions per 100 inhabitants: 106 (July 2016 est.)
country comparison to the world: 192

Telephone system: *general assessment:* fully automatic network
domestic: fixed-line connections continued to decline slowly with the two active operators providing about 18 fixed-line connections per 100 persons; subscribership among the three mobile-cellular providers is about 105 per 100 persons
international: country code—1-767; landing points for the East Caribbean Fiber Optic System (ECFS) and the Global Caribbean Network (GCN) submarine cables providing connectivity to other islands in the eastern Caribbean extending from the British Virgin Islands to Trinidad; microwave radio relay and SHF radiotelephone links to Martinique and Guadeloupe; VHF and UHF radiotelephone links to Saint Lucia (2016)

Broadcast media: no terrestrial TV service available; subscription cable TV provider offers some locally produced programming plus channels from the US, Latin America, and the Caribbean; state-operated radio broadcasts on 6 stations; privately owned radio broadcasts on about 15 stations (2007)

Internet country code: .dm

Internet users: total: 49,439

percent of population: 67.0% (July 2016 est.)
country comparison to the world: 190

TRANSPORTATION

National air transport system: *number of registered air carriers:* 0
inventory of registered aircraft operated by air carriers: 0
annual passenger traffic on registered air carriers: 0
annual freight traffic on registered air carriers: 0 mt-km (2015)
Civil aircraft registration country code prefix: J7 (2016)

Airports: 2 (2013)
country comparison to the world: 199

Airports—with paved runways: total: 2

1,524 to 2,437 m: 1
914 to 1,523 m: 1 (2017)

Roadways: *total:* 1,512 km
paved: 762 km
unpaved: 750 km (2010)
country comparison to the world: 178

Merchant marine: *total:* 76
by type: general cargo 24, oil tanker 15, other 37 (2017)
country comparison to the world: 99

Ports and terminals: *major seaport(s):* Portsmouth, Roseau

MILITARY AND SECURITY

Military branches: no regular military forces; Commonwealth of Dominica Police Force (includes Coast Guard) (2012)

TRANSNATIONAL ISSUES

Disputes—international: Dominica is the only Caribbean state to challenge Venezuela's sovereignty claim over Aves Island and joins the other island nations in challenging whether the feature sustains human habitation, a criterion under the UN Convention on the Law of the Sea, which permits Venezuela to extend its EEZ and continental shelf claims over a large portion of the eastern Caribbean Sea

Illicit drugs: transshipment point for narcotics bound for the US and Europe; minor cannabis producer

DOMINICAN REPUBLIC

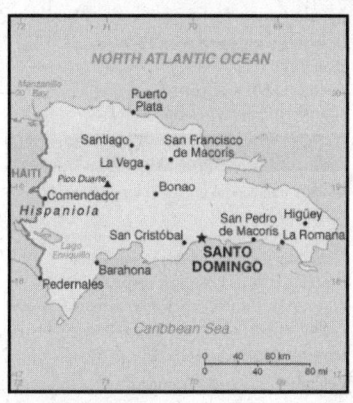

INTRODUCTION

Background: The Taino—indigenous inhabitants of Hispaniola prior to the arrival of the Europeans—divided the island into five chiefdoms and territories. Christopher COLUMBUS explored and claimed the island on his first voyage in 1492; it became a springboard for Spanish conquest of the Caribbean and the American mainland. In 1697, Spain recognized French dominion over the western third of the island, which in 1804 became Haiti. The remainder of the island, by then known as Santo Domingo, sought to gain its own independence in 1821 but was conquered and ruled by the Haitians for 22 years; it finally attained independence as the Dominican Republic in 1844. In 1861, the Dominicans voluntarily returned to the Spanish Empire, but two years later they launched a war that restored independence in 1865. A legacy of unsettled, mostly non-representative rule followed, capped by the dictatorship of Rafael Leonidas TRUJILLO from 1930 to 1961. Juan BOSCH

was elected president in 1962 but was deposed in a military coup in 1963. In 1965, the US led an intervention in the midst of a civil war sparked by an uprising to restore BOSCH. In 1966, Joaquin BALAGUER defeated BOSCH in the presidential election. BALAGUER maintained a tight grip on power for most of the next 30 years when international reaction to flawed elections forced him to curtail his term in 1996. Since then, regular competitive elections have been held in which opposition candidates have won the presidency. Former President Leonel FERNANDEZ Reyna (first term 1996-2000) won election to a new term in 2004 following a constitutional amendment allowing presidents to serve more than one term, and was later reelected to a second consecutive term. In 2012, Danilo MEDINA Sanchez became president; he was reelected in 2016.

GEOGRAPHY

Location: Caribbean, eastern two-thirds of the island of Hispaniola, between the Caribbean Sea and the North Atlantic Ocean, east of Haiti

Geographic coordinates: 19 00 N, 70 40 W

Map references: Central America and the Caribbean

Area: *total:* 48,670 sq km
land: 48,320 sq km
water: 350 sq km
country comparison to the world: 132

Area—comparative: slightly more than twice the size of New Jersey
Land boundaries: total: 376 km
border countries (1): Haiti 376 km

Coastline: 1,288 km

Maritime claims: measured from claimed archipelagic straight baselines
territorial sea: 12 nm

contiguous zone: 24 nm
exclusive economic zone: 200 nm
continental shelf: 200 nm or to the edge of the continental margin

Climate: tropical maritime; little seasonal temperature variation; seasonal variation in rainfall

Terrain: rugged highlands and mountains interspersed with fertile valleys

Elevation: *mean elevation:* 424 m

elevation extremes: *lowest point:* Lago Enriquillo -46 m
highest point: Pico Duarte 3,098 m

Natural resources: nickel, bauxite, gold, silver, arable land

Land use: *agricultural land:* 51.5%
arable land: 16.6%;
permanent crops: 10.1%;
permanent pasture: 24.8%
forest: 40.8%
other: 7.7% (2011 est.)

Irrigated land: 3,070 sq km (2012)

Population—distribution: coastal development is significant, especially in the southern coastal plains and the Cibao Valley, where population density is highest; smaller population clusters exist in the interior mountains (Cordillera Central)

Natural hazards: lies in the middle of the hurricane belt and subject to severe storms from June to October; occasional flooding; periodic droughts

Environment—current issues: water shortages; soil eroding into the sea damages coral reefs; deforestation

Environment—international agreements: party to: Biodiversity, Climate Change, Climate Change-Kyoto Protocol, Desertification, Endangered Species, Hazardous Wastes, Marine Dumping, Marine Life Conservation, Ozone Layer Protection, Ship Pollution, Wetlands

269

signed, but not ratified: Law of the Sea

Geography—note: shares island of Hispaniola with Haiti (eastern two-thirds makes up the Dominican Republic, western one-third is Haiti); the second largest country in the Antilles (after Cuba); geographically diverse with the Caribbean's tallest mountain, Pico Duarte, and lowest elevation and largest lake, Lago Enriquillo

PEOPLE AND SOCIETY

Population: 10,734,247 (July 2017 est.)
country comparison to the world: 86

Nationality: *noun:* Dominican(s)
adjective: Dominican

Ethnic groups: mixed 70.4% (mestizo/indio 58%, mulatto 12.4%), black 15.8%, white 13.5%, other 0.3%
note: respondents self-identified their race; the term "indio" in the Dominican Republic is not associated with people of indigenous ancestry but people of mixed ancestry or skin color between light and dark (2014 est.)

Languages: Spanish (official)

Religions: Roman Catholic 95%, other 5%

Age structure: *0-14 years:* 26.63% (male 1,454,527/female 1,404,538)
15-24 years: 18.18% (male 993,642/female 957,466)
25-54 years: 39.66% (male 2,178,477/female 2,078,371)
55-64 years: 7.9% (male 426,810/female 421,727)
65 years and over: 7.63% (male 378,226/female 440,463) (2017 est.)

Dependency ratios: *total dependency ratio:* 57.8
youth dependency ratio: 47.3
elderly dependency ratio: 10.5
potential support ratio: 9.5 (2015 est.)

Median age: *total:* 28.1 years
male: 27.9 years
female: 28.3 years (2017 est.)
country comparison to the world: 135

Population growth rate: 1.18% (2017 est.)
country comparison to the world: 95

Birth rate: 18.4 births/1,000 population (2017 est.)
country comparison to the world: 92

Death rate: 4.7 deaths/1,000 population (2017 est.)
country comparison to the world: 202

Net migration rate: -1.9 migrant(s)/1,000 population (2017 est.)
country comparison to the world: 158

Population distribution: coastal development is significant, especially in the southern coastal plains and the Cibao Valley, where population density is highest; smaller population clusters exist in the interior mountains (Cordillera Central)

Urbanization: *urban population:* 80.6% of total population (2017)
rate of urbanization: 2% annual rate of change (2015-20 est.)

Major urban areas—population: SANTO DOMINGO (capital) 2.945 million (2015)

Sex ratio: *at birth:* 1.04 male(s)/female
0-14 years: 1.04 male(s)/female
15-24 years: 1.04 male(s)/female
25-54 years: 1.05 male(s)/female
55-64 years: 1.01 male(s)/female
65 years and over: 0.86 male(s)/female
total population: 1.03 male(s)/female (2016 est.)

Mother's mean age at first birth: 21.3 years
note: median age at first birth among women 25-29 (2013 est.)

Maternal mortality ratio: 92 deaths/100,000 live births (2015 est.)
country comparison to the world: 75

Infant mortality rate: *total:* 17.5 deaths/1,000 live births
male: 19.3 deaths/1,000 live births
female: 15.5 deaths/1,000 live births (2017 est.)
country comparison to the world: 93

Life expectancy at birth: *total population:* 78.3 years
male: 76 years
female: 80.6 years (2017 est.)
country comparison to the world: 61

Total fertility rate: 2.29 children born/woman (2017 est.)
country comparison to the world: 92

Contraceptive prevalence rate: 69.5% (2014)
Health expenditures: 4.4% of GDP (2014)
country comparison to the world: 157

Physicians density: 1.49 physicians/1,000 population (2011)

Hospital bed density: 1.7 beds/1,000 population (2011)

Drinking water source:
improved:
urban: 85.4% of population
rural: 81.9% of population
total: 84.7% of population
unimproved:
urban: 14.6% of population
rural: 18.1% of population
total: 15.3% of population (2015 est.)

Sanitation facility access:
improved:
urban: 86.2% of population
rural: 75.7% of population
total: 84% of population
unimproved:
urban: 13.8% of population
rural: 24.3% of population
total: 16% of population (2015 est.)

HIV/AIDS—adult prevalence rate: 1% (2016 est.)
country comparison to the world: 45

HIV/AIDS—people living with HIV/AIDS: 67,000 (2016 est.)
country comparison to the world: 49

HIV/AIDS—deaths: 2,200 (2016 est.)
country comparison to the world: 50

Major infectious diseases: *degree of risk:* high
food or waterborne diseases: bacterial diarrhea, hepatitis A, and typhoid fever
vectorborne disease: dengue fever

note: active local transmission of Zika virus by Aedes species mosquitoes has been identified in this country (as of August 2016); it poses an important risk (a large number of cases possible) among US citizens if bitten by an infective mosquito; other less common ways to get Zika are through sex, via blood transfusion, or during pregnancy, in which the pregnant woman passes Zika virus to her fetus (2016)

Obesity—adult prevalence rate: 27.6% (2016)
country comparison to the world: 37

Children under the age of 5 years underweight: 4% (2013)
country comparison to the world: 106
Education expenditures: 2.1% of GDP (2007)
country comparison to the world: 163

Literacy: *definition:* age 15 and over can read and write
total population: 91.8%
male: 91.2%
female: 92.3% (2015 est.)

School life expectancy (primary to tertiary education): *total:* 13 years
male: 13 years
female: 14 years (2014)

Unemployment, youth ages 15-24: *total:* 10.8%
male: 7.7%
female: 15.8% (2015 est.)
country comparison to the world: 26

GOVERNMENT

Country name: *conventional long form:* Dominican Republic
conventional short form: The Dominican
local long form: Republica Dominicana
local short form: La Dominicana
etymology: the country name derives from the capital city of Santo Domingo (Saint Dominic)

Government type: presidential republic

Capital: *name:* Santo Domingo
geographic coordinates: 18 28 N, 69 54 W
time difference: UTC-4 (1 hour ahead of Washington, DC, during Standard Time)

Administrative divisions: 10 regions (regiones, singular—region); Cibao Nordeste, Cibao Noroeste, Cibao Norte, Cibao Sur, El Valle, Enriquillo, Higuamo, Ozama, Valdesia, Yuma

Independence: 27 February 1844 (from Haiti)

National holiday: Independence Day, 27 February (1844)

Constitution: many previous (38 total); latest proclaimed 26 January 2010; note—the Dominican Republic Government has a practice of promulgating a "new" constitution whenever an amendment is ratified (2016)

Legal system: civil law system based on the French civil code; Criminal Procedures Code modified in 2004 to include important elements of an accusatory system

International law organization participation: accepts compulsory ICJ jurisdiction; accepts ICCt jurisdiction

Citizenship: *citizenship by birth:* no
citizenship by descent only: at least one parent must be a citizen of the Dominican Republic
dual citizenship recognized: yes
residency requirement for naturalization: 2 years

Suffrage: 18 years of age, universal and compulsory; married persons regardless of age can vote; note—members of the armed forces and national police by law cannot vote

Executive branch: *chief of state:* President Danilo MEDINA Sanchez (since 16 August 2012); Vice President Margarita CEDENO DE FERNANDEZ (since 16 August 2012); note—the president is both chief of state and head of government

head of government: President Danilo MEDINA Sanchez (since 16 August 2012); Vice President Margarita CEDENO DE FERNANDEZ (since 16 August 2012)
cabinet: Cabinet nominated by the president
elections/appointments: president and vice president directly elected on the same ballot by absolute vote in 2 rounds if needed for a 4-year term (eligible for consecutive terms); election last held on 15 May 2016 (next to be held in 2020)
election results: Danilo MEDINA Sanchez reelected president; percent of vote—Danilo MEDINA Sanchez (PLD) 61.7%, Luis Rodolfo ABINADER Corona (PRM) 35%, other 3.3%; Margarita CEDENO DE FERNANDEZ (PLD) reelected vice president

Legislative branch: description: bicameral National Congress or Congreso Nacional consists of the Senate or Senado (32 seats; members directly elected in single-seat constituencies by simple majority vote to serve 4-year terms) and the House of Representatives or Camara de Diputados (190 seats; members directly elected in multi-seat constituencies by proportional representation vote; members serve 4-year terms)
elections: Senate—last held on 15 May 2016 (next to be held in May 2020); House of Representatives—last held on 15 May 2016 (next to be held in May 2020)
election results: Senate—percent of vote by party—NA; seats by party—PLD 26, PRM 2, BIS 1, PLRD 1, PRD 1, PRSC 1
House of Representatives—percent of vote by party—NA; seats by party—PLD 106, PRM 42, PRSC 18, PRD 16, PLRD 3, other 5

Judicial branch: *highest court(s):* Supreme Court of Justice or Suprema Corte de Justicia (consists of a minimum of 16 magistrates); Constitutional Court or Tribunal Constitucional (consists of 13 judges); note—the Constitutional Court was established in 2010 by constitutional amendment
judge selection and term of office: Supreme Court and Constitutional Court judges appointed by the National Council of the Judiciary comprised of the president, the leaders of both chambers of congress, the president of the Supreme Court, and a non-governing party congressional representative; Supreme Court judges appointed for 7-year terms; Constitutional Court judges appointed for 9-year terms

subordinate courts: courts of appeal; courts of first instance; justices of the peace; special courts for juvenile, labor, and land cases; Contentious Administrative Court for cases filed against the government

Political parties and leaders: Dominican Liberation Party or PLD [Leonel FERNANDEZ Reyna] Dominican Revolutionary Party or PRD [Miguel VARGAS Maldonado]
Institutional Social Democratic Bloc or BIS
Liberal Reformist Party or PRL
Modern Revolutionary Party or PRM [Andres BAUTISTA Garcia]
National Progressive Front or FNP [Vinicio CASTILLO, Pelegrin CASTILLO]
Social Christian Reformist Party or PRSC [Federico ANTUN]

Political pressure groups and leaders: Citizen Participation Group (Participacion Ciudadania)
Collective of Popular Organizations or COP
Foundation for Institution-Building and Justice or FINJUS

International organization participation: ACP, AOSIS, BCIE, Caricom (observer), CD, CELAC, FAO, G-77, IADB, IAEA, IBRD, ICAO, ICC (national committees), ICCt, ICRM, IDA, IFAD, IFC, IFRCS, IHO, ILO, IMF, IMO, Interpol, IOC, IOM, IPU, ISO (correspondent), ITSO, ITU, ITUC (NGOs), LAES, LAIA, MIGA, MINUSMA, NAM, OAS, OIF (observer), OPANAL, OPCW, Pacific Alliance (observer), PCA, Petrocaribe, SICA (associated member), UN, UNCTAD, UNESCO, UNIDO, Union Latina, UNWTO, UPU, WCO, WFTU (NGOs), WHO, WIPO, WMO, WTO

Diplomatic representation in the US: *chief of mission:* Ambassador Jose Tomas PEREZ Vazquez (since 23 February 2015)
chancery: 1715 22nd Street NW, Washington, DC 20008
telephone: [1] (202) 332-6280
FAX: [1] (202) 265-8057
consulate(s) general: Boston, Chicago, Los Angeles, Mayaguez (Puerto Rico), Miami, New Orleans, New York, San Juan (Puerto Rico)
consulate(s): San Francisco

Diplomatic representation from the US: *chief of mission:* Ambassador (vacant); Charge d'Affaires Robert COPLEY (since 21 July 2017)
embassy: Av. Republica de Colombia
mailing address: Unit 5500, APO AA 34041-5500
telephone: [1] (809) 567-7775
FAX: [1] (809) 686-7437

Flag description: a centered white cross that extends to the edges divides the flag into four rectangles—the top ones are ultramarine blue (hoist side) and vermilion red, and the bottom ones are vermilion red (hoist side) and ultramarine blue; a small coat of arms featuring a shield supported by a laurel branch (left) and a palm branch (right) is at the center of the cross; above the shield a blue ribbon displays the motto, DIOS, PATRIA, LIBERTAD (God, Fatherland, Liberty), and below the shield, REPUBLICA DOMINICANA appears on

a red ribbon; in the shield a bible is opened to a verse that reads "Y la verdad nos hara libre" (And the truth shall set you free); blue stands for liberty, white for salvation, and red for the blood of heroes

National symbol(s): palmchat (bird); national colors: red, white, blue

National anthem: name: "Himno Nacional" (National Anthem)
lyrics/music: Emilio PRUD'HOMME/Jose REYES
note: adopted 1934; also known as "Quisqueyanos valientes" (Valiant Sons of Quisqueye); the anthem never refers to the people as Dominican but rather calls them "Quisqueyanos," a reference to the indigenous name of the island

ECONOMY

Economy—overview: The Dominican Republic was for most of its history primarily an exporter of sugar, coffee, and tobacco, but in recent years the service sector has overtaken agriculture as the economy's largest employer, due to growth in construction, tourism, and free trade zones. The mining sector has also played a greater role in the export market since late 2012 with the commencement of the extraction phase of the Pueblo Viejo Gold and Silver mine, one of the largest gold mines in the world. The country suffers from marked income inequality; the poorest half of the population receives less than one-fifth of GDP, while the richest 10% enjoys nearly 40% of GDP. High unemployment, a large informal sector, and underemployment remain important long-term challenges.

The economy is highly dependent upon the US, the destination for approximately half of exports. Remittances from the US amount to about 7% of GDP, equivalent to about a third of exports and two-thirds of tourism receipts. The Central America-Dominican Republic Free Trade Agreement came into force in March 2007, boosting investment and manufacturing exports.

The Dominican Republic's economy rebounded from the global recession in 2010-16, and the fiscal situation is improving. A tax reform package passed in November 2012, a reduction in government spending, and lower energy costs helped to narrow the central government budget deficit from 6.6% of GDP in 2012 to 2.6% in 2016. A liability management operation in January 2015, in which the government paid down over $4 billion of the country's Petrocaribe debt at a discount of 52% with proceeds from the sale of $2.5 billion in global bonds, reduced the country's debt load by approximately by 4% of GDP. Since 2015 the Dominican Republic has posted the fastest economic growth in Latin America.

GDP (purchasing power parity): $172.6 billion (2017 est.)
$164.7 billion (2016 est.)
$154.5 billion (2015 est.)
note: data are in 2017 dollars
country comparison to the world: 73

GDP (official exchange rate): $74.87 billion (2016 est.)

GDP—real growth rate: 4.8% (2017 est.)
6.6% (2016 est.)
7% (2015 est.)
country comparison to the world: 45

GDP—per capita (PPP): $17,000 (2017 est.)
$16,400 (2016 est.)
$15,500 (2015 est.)
note: data are in 2017 dollars
country comparison to the world: 104

GDP—composition, by end use:
household consumption: 69.8%
government consumption: 10.9%
investment in fixed capital: 23.3%
investment in inventories: 0.6%
exports of goods and services: 25.8%
imports of goods and services: -30.4% (2017 est.)

GDP—composition, by sector of origin:
agriculture: 5.5%
industry: 33.8%
services: 60.8% (2017 est.)

Agriculture—products: cocoa, tobacco, sugarcane, coffee, cotton, rice, beans, potatoes, corn, bananas; cattle, pigs, dairy products, beef, eggs

Industries: tourism, sugar processing, gold mining, textiles, cement, tobacco, electrical components, medical devices

Industrial production growth rate: 6% (2017 est.)
country comparison to the world: 34

Labor force: 4.732 million (2017 est.)
country comparison to the world: 86

Labor force—by occupation: *agriculture:* 14.4%
industry: 20.8%
services: 64.7% (2014 est.)

Unemployment rate: 5.5% (2017 est.)
5.5% (2016 est.)
country comparison to the world: 75

Population below poverty line: 30.5% (2016 est.)

Household income or consumption by percentage share: *lowest 10%:* 1.9%
highest 10%: 37.4% (2013 est.)

Distribution of family income—Gini index: 47.1 (2013 est.)
45.7 (2012 est.)
country comparison to the world: 25

Budget: *revenues:* $11.18 billion
expenditures: $12.77 billion (2017 est.)
Taxes and other revenues: 14.9% of GDP (2017 est.)
country comparison to the world: 191

Budget surplus (+) or deficit (-): -2.1% of GDP (2017 est.)
country comparison to the world: 89

Public debt: 47.1% of GDP (2017 est.)
47.4% of GDP (2016 est.)
country comparison to the world: 109

Fiscal year: calendar year

Inflation rate (consumer prices): 3% (2017 est.)
1.6% (2016 est.)
country comparison to the world: 128

Commercial bank prime lending rate: 14.6% (31 December 2017 est.)
15.08% (31 December 2016 est.)

country comparison to the world: 47

Stock of narrow money: $6.921 billion (31 December 2017 est.)
$6.491 billion (31 December 2016 est.)
country comparison to the world: 91

Stock of broad money: $21.44 billion (31 December 2017 est.)
$19.81 billion (31 December 2016 est.)
country comparison to the world: 88

Stock of domestic credit: $35.64 billion (31 December 2017 est.)
$33.6 billion (31 December 2016 est.)
country comparison to the world: 74

Market value of publicly traded shares: $NA

Current account balance: -$1.192 billion (2017 est.)
-$1.066 billion (2016 est.)
country comparison to the world: 138

Exports: $10.33 billion (2017 est.)
$9.86 billion (2016 est.)
country comparison to the world: 90

Exports—commodities: gold, silver, cocoa, sugar, coffee, tobacco, meats, consumer goods

Exports—partners: US 47.3%, Haiti 12%, Canada 7.8%, India 6.2% (2016)

Imports: $19 billion (2017 est.)
$17.48 billion (2016 est.)
country comparison to the world: 76

Imports—commodities: petroleum, foodstuffs, cotton and fabrics, chemicals and pharmaceuticals

Imports—partners: US 40.4%, China 12.5%, Mexico 5.2% (2016)

Reserves of foreign exchange and gold: $6.233 billion (31 December 2017 est.)
$6.134 billion (31 December 2016 est.)
country comparison to the world: 88

Debt—external: $29.69 billion (31 December 2017 est.)
$27.7 billion (31 December 2016 est.)
country comparison to the world: 81

Stock of direct foreign investment—at home: $35.93 billion (31 December 2017 est.)
$33.56 billion (31 December 2016 est.)
country comparison to the world: 66

Stock of direct foreign investment—abroad: $487.8 million (31 December 2017 est.)
$387.8 million (31 December 2016 est.)
country comparison to the world: 92

Exchange rates: Dominican pesos (DOP) per US dollar—
47.42 (2017 est.)
46.078 (2016 est.)
46.078 (2015 est.)
45.052 (2014 est.)
43.556 (2013 est.)

ENERGY

Electricity access: *population without electricity:* 300,000
electrification—total population: 98%
electrification—urban areas: 99%
electrification—rural areas: 97% (2013)

Electricity—production: 15.53 billion kWh (2015 est.)
country comparison to the world: 85

Electricity—consumption: 13.25 billion kWh (2015 est.)
country comparison to the world: 83

Electricity—exports: 0 kWh (2016 est.)
country comparison to the world: 131

Electricity—imports: 0 kWh (2016 est.)
country comparison to the world: 144

Electricity—installed generating capacity: 3.732 million kW (2015 est.)
country comparison to the world: 93

Electricity—from fossil fuels: 80.8% of total installed capacity (2015 est.)
country comparison to the world: 85

Electricity—from nuclear fuels: 0% of total installed capacity (2015 est.)
country comparison to the world: 80

Electricity—from hydroelectric plants: 16.1% of total installed capacity (2015 est.)
country comparison to the world: 99

Electricity—from other renewable sources: 5.7% of total installed capacity (2015 est.)
country comparison to the world: 91

Crude oil—production: 0 bbl/day (2016 est.)
country comparison to the world: 128

Crude oil—exports: 0 bbl/day (2014 est.)
country comparison to the world: 116

Crude oil—imports: 27,440 bbl/day (2014 est.)
country comparison to the world: 60

Crude oil—proved reserves: 0 bbl (1 January 2017 es)
country comparison to the world: 128

Refined petroleum products—production: 27,060 bbl/day (2014 est.)
country comparison to the world: 88

Refined petroleum products—consumption: 114,000 bbl/day (2015 est.)
country comparison to the world: 77

Refined petroleum products—exports: 0 bbl/day (2014 est.)
country comparison to the world: 150

Refined petroleum products—imports: 84,370 bbl/day (2014 est.)
country comparison to the world: 63

Natural gas—production: 0 cu m (2013 est.)
country comparison to the world: 129

Natural gas—consumption: 1.895 billion cu m (2015 est.)
country comparison to the world: 89

Natural gas—exports: 0 cu m (2013 est.)
country comparison to the world: 95

Natural gas—imports: 1.108 billion cu m (2015 est.)
country comparison to the world: 58

Natural gas—proved reserves: 0 cu m (1 January 2014 es)
country comparison to the world: 134

Carbon dioxide emissions from consumption of energy: 22 million Mt (2013 est.)

country comparison to the world: 79

COMMUNICATIONS

Telephones—fixed lines: *total subscriptions:* 1,345,091
subscriptions per 100 inhabitants: 13 (July 2016 est.)
country comparison to the world: 68

Telephones—mobile cellular: *total:* 8,708,131
subscriptions per 100 inhabitants: 82 (July 2016 est.)
country comparison to the world: 94

Telephone system: *general assessment:* relatively efficient system based on island-wide microwave radio relay network
domestic: fixed-line teledensity is about 13 per 100 persons; multiple providers of mobile-cellular service with a subscribership of over 80 per 100 persons
international: country code—1-809; 1-829; 1-849; landing point for the Americas Region Caribbean Ring System (ARCOS-1), Antillas 1, AMX-1, and the Fibralink submarine cables that provide links to South and Central America, parts of the Caribbean, and US; satellite earth station—1 Intelsat (Atlantic Ocean) (2016)

Broadcast media: combination of state-owned and privately owned broadcast media; 1 state-owned TV network and a number of private TV networks; networks operate repeaters to extend signals throughout country; combination of state-owned and privately owned radio stations with more than 300 radio stations operating (2015)

Internet country code: .do
Internet users: total: 6,504,998

percent of population: 61.3% (July 2016 est.)
country comparison to the world: 69

TRANSPORTATION

National air transport system: *number of registered air carriers:* 1
inventory of registered aircraft operated by air carriers: 6
annual passenger traffic on registered air carriers: 14,463

annual freight traffic on registered air carriers: 0 mt-km (2015)
Civil aircraft registration country code prefix: HI (2016)

Airports: 36 (2013)
country comparison to the world: 110

Airports—with paved runways: *total:* 16
over 3,047 m: 3
2,438 to 3,047 m: 4
1,524 to 2,437 m: 4
914 to 1,523 m: 4
under 914 m: 1 (2017)

Airports—with unpaved runways: *total:* 20
1,524 to 2,437 m: 1
914 to 1,523 m: 1
under 914 m: 18 (2013)

Heliports: 1 (2013)

Pipelines: gas 27 km; oil 103 km (2013)

Railways: *total:* 496 km
standard gauge: 354 km 1.435-m gauge
narrow gauge: 142 km 0.762-m gauge (2014)
country comparison to the world: 115

Roadways: *total:* 19,705 km
paved: 9,872 km
unpaved: 9,833 km (2002)
country comparison to the world: 110

Merchant marine: *total:* 23
by type: general cargo 2, other 21 (2017)
country comparison to the world: 131

Ports and terminals: *major seaport(s):* Puerto Haina, Puerto Plata, Santo Domingo
oil terminal(s): Punta Nizao oil terminal
LNG terminal(s) (import): Andres LNG terminal (Boca Chica)

MILITARY AND SECURITY

Military expenditures: 0.64% of GDP (2016)
0.67% of GDP (2015)
0.67% of GDP (2014)
0.62% of GDP (2013)
0.65% of GDP (2012)
country comparison to the world: 121

Military branches: Army (Ejercito Nacional, EN), Navy (Marina de Guerra, MdG, includes naval infantry), Dominican Air Force (Fuerza Aerea Dominicana, FAD) (2017)

Military service age and obligation: 17-21 years of age for voluntary military service; recruits must have completed primary school and be Dominican Republic citizens; women may volunteer (2012)

TRANSNATIONAL ISSUES

Disputes—international: Haitian migrants cross the porous border into the Dominican Republic to find work; illegal migrants from the Dominican Republic cross the Mona Passage each year to Puerto Rico to find better work

Refugees and internally displaced persons: *stateless persons:* 133,770 (2016); note—a September 2013 Constitutional Court ruling revoked the citizenship of those born after 1929 to immigrants without proper documentation, even though the constitution at the time automatically granted citizenship to children born in the Dominican Republic and the 2010 constitution provides that constitutional provisions cannot be applied retroactively; the decision overwhelmingly affected people of Haitian descent whose relatives had come to the Dominican Republic since the 1890s as a cheap source of labor for sugar plantations; a May 2014 law passed by the Dominican Congress regularizes the status of those with birth certificates but will require those without them to prove they were born in the Dominican Republic and to apply for naturalization; the government has issued documents to thousands of individuals who may claim citizenship under this law, but no official estimate has been released
note: revised estimate includes only individuals born to parents who were both born abroad; it does not include individuals born in the country to one Dominican-born and one foreign-born parent or subsequent generations of individuals of foreign descent; the estimate, as such, does not include all stateless persons (2015)

Illicit drugs: transshipment point for South American drugs destined for the US and Europe; has become a transshipment point for ecstasy from the Netherlands and Belgium destined for US and Canada; substantial money laundering activity in particular by Colombian narcotics traffickers; significant amphetamine consumption

INTRODUCTION

Background: What is now Ecuador formed part of the northern Inca Empire until the Spanish conquest in 1533. Quito became a seat of Spanish colonial government in 1563 and part of the Vice-royalty of New Granada in 1717. The territories of the Viceroyalty—New Granada (Colombia), Venezuela, and Quito—gained their independence between 1819 and 1822 and formed a federation known as Gran Colombia. When Quito withdrew in 1830, the traditional name was changed in favor of the "Republic of the Equator." Between 1904 and 1942, Ecuador lost territories in a series of conflicts with its neighbors. A border war with Peru that flared in 1995 was resolved in 1999. Although Ecuador marked 30 years of civilian governance in 2004, the period was marred by political instability. Protests in Quito contributed to the mid-term ouster of three of Ecuador's last four democratically elected presidents. In late 2008, voters approved a new constitution, Ecuador's 20th since gaining independence. General elections were held in April 2017, and voters elected President Lenin MORENO.

GEOGRAPHY

Location: Western South America, bordering the Pacific Ocean at the Equator, between Colombia and Peru

Geographic coordinates: 2 00 S, 77 30 W

Map references: South America

Area: *total:* 283,561 sq km
land: 276,841 sq km
water: 6,720 sq km
note: includes Galapagos Islands
country comparison to the world: 75

Area—comparative: slightly smaller than Nevada

Land boundaries: *total:* 2,237 km
border countries (2): Colombia 708 km, Peru 1,529 km

Coastline: 2,237 km

Maritime claims: *territorial sea:* 200 nm

exclusive economic zone: 200 nm
continental shelf: 200 nm
note: Ecuador has declared its right to extend its continental shelf to 350nm measured from the baselines of the Galapagos Archipelago

Climate: tropical along coast, becoming cooler inland at higher elevations; tropical in Amazonian jungle lowlands

Terrain: coastal plain (costa), inter-Andean central highlands (sierra), and flat to rolling eastern jungle (oriente)

Elevation: *mean elevation:* 1,117 m

elevation extremes: *lowest point:* Pacific Ocean 0 m
highest point: Chimborazo 6,267 m
note: because the earth is not a perfect sphere and has an equatorial bulge, the highest point on the planet farthest from its center is Mount Chimborazo not Mount Everest, which is merely the highest peak above sea level

Natural resources: petroleum, fish, timber, hydropower

Land use: *agricultural land:* 29.7%
arable land: 4.7%;
permanent crops: 5.6%;
permanent pasture: 19.4%
forest: 38.9%
other: 31.4% (2011 est.)

Irrigated land: 15,000 sq km (2012)

Population—distribution: nearly half of the population is concentrated in the interior in the Andean intermontane basins and valleys, with large concentrations also found along the western coastal strip; the rainforests of the east remain sparsely populated

Natural hazards: frequent earthquakes; landslides; volcanic activity; floods; periodic droughts
volcanism: volcanic activity concentrated along the Andes Mountains; Sangay (5,230 m), which erupted in 2010, is mainland Ecuador's most active volcano; other historically active volcanoes in the Andes include Antisana, Cayambe, Chacana, Cotopaxi, Guagua Pichincha, Reventador, Sumaco, and Tungurahua; Fernandina (1,476 m), a shield volcano that last erupted in 2009, is the most active of the many Galapagos volcanoes; other historically active Galapagos volcanoes include Wolf, Sierra Negra, Cerro Azul, Pinta, Marchena, and Santiago

Environment—current issues: deforestation; soil erosion; desertification; water pollution; pollution from oil production wastes in ecologically sensitive areas of the Amazon Basin and Galapagos Islands

Environment—international agreements: *party to:* Antarctic-Environmental Protocol, Antarctic Treaty, Biodiversity, Climate Change, Climate Change-Kyoto Protocol, Desertification, Endangered Species, Hazardous Wastes, Ozone Layer Protection, Ship Pollution, Tropical Timber 83, Tropical Timber 94, Wetlands

signed, but not ratified: none of the selected agreements

Geography—note: Cotopaxi in Andes is highest active volcano in world

PEOPLE AND SOCIETY

Population: 16,290,913 (July 2017 est.)
country comparison to the world: 67

Nationality: *noun:* Ecuadorian(s)
adjective: Ecuadorian

Ethnic groups: mestizo (mixed Amerindian and white) 71.9%, Montubio 7.4%, Amerindian 7%, white 6.1%, Afroecuadorian 4.3%, mulatto 1.9%, black 1%, other 0.4% (2010 est.)

Languages: Spanish (Castilian) 93% (official), Quechua 4.1%, other indigenous 0.7%, foreign 2.2%
note: (Quechua and Shuar are official languages of intercultural relations; other indigenous languages are in official use by indigenous peoples in the areas they inhabit) (2010 est.)

Religions: Roman Catholic 74%, Evangelical 10.4%, Jehovah's Witness 1.2%, other 6.4% (includes Mormon Buddhist, Jewish, Spiritualist, Muslim, Hindu, indigenous religions, African American religions, Pentecostal), atheist 7.9%, agnostic 0.1%
note: data represent persons at least 16 years of age from five Ecuadoran cities (2012 est.)

Demographic profile: Ecuador's high poverty and income inequality most affect indigenous, mixed race, and rural populations. The government has increased its social spending to ameliorate these problems, but critics question the efficiency and implementation of its national development plan. Nevertheless, the conditional cash transfer program, which requires participants' children to attend school and have medical check-ups, has helped improve educational attainment and healthcare among poor children. Ecuador is stalled at above replacement level fertility and the population most likely will keep growing rather than stabilize.

An estimated 2 to 3 million Ecuadorians live abroad, but increased unemployment in key receiving countries—Spain, the United States, and Italy—is slowing emigration and increasing the likelihood of returnees to Ecuador. The first large-scale emigration of Ecuadorians occurred between 1980 and 2000, when an economic crisis drove Ecuadorians from southern provinces to New York City, where they had trade contacts. A second, nationwide wave of emigration in the late 1990s was caused by another economic downturn, political instability, and a currency crisis. Spain was the logical destination because of its shared language and the wide availability of low-skilled, informal jobs at a time when increased border surveillance made illegal migration to the US difficult. Ecuador has a small but growing immigrant population and is Latin America's top recipient of refugees; 98% are neighboring Colombians fleeing violence in their country.

Age structure: *0-14 years:* 27.08% (male 2,250,000/female 2,161,123)

15-24 years: 18.35% (male 1,519,255/female 1,469,372)

25-54 years: 39.59% (male 3,145,954/female 3,303,520)

55-64 years: 7.53% (male 599,032/female 628,477)

65 years and over: 7.45% (male 576,196/female 637,984) (2017 est.)

Dependency ratios: *total dependency ratio:* 55.6 *youth dependency ratio:* 45.1 *elderly dependency ratio:* 10.4 *potential support ratio:* 9.6 (2015 est.)

Median age: *total:* 27.7 years *male:* 27 years *female:* 28.4 years (2017 est.) *country comparison to the world:* 142

Population growth rate: 1.28% (2017 est.) *country comparison to the world:* 87

Birth rate: 17.9 births/1,000 population (2017 est.) *country comparison to the world:* 102

Death rate: 5.1 deaths/1,000 population (2017 est.) *country comparison to the world:* 191

Net migration rate: 0 migrant(s)/1,000 population (2017 est.) *country comparison to the world:* 80

Population distribution: nearly half of the population is concentrated in the interior in the Andean intermontane basins and valleys, with large concentrations also found along the western coastal strip; the rainforests of the east remain sparsely populated

Urbanization: *urban population:* 64.2% of total population (2017) *rate of urbanization:* 1.8% annual rate of change (2015-20 est.)

Major urban areas—population: Guayaquil 2.709 million; QUITO (capital) 1.726 million (2015)

Sex ratio: *at birth:* 1.05 male(s)/female *0-14 years:* 1.04 male(s)/female *15-24 years:* 1.03 male(s)/female *25-54 years:* 0.95 male(s)/female *55-64 years:* 0.96 male(s)/female *65 years and over:* 0.91 male(s)/female *total population:* 0.99 male(s)/female (2016 est.)

Maternal mortality ratio: 64 deaths/100,000 live births (2015 est.) *country comparison to the world:* 86

Infant mortality rate: *total:* 16.4 deaths/1,000 live births *male:* 19.4 deaths/1,000 live births *female:* 13.2 deaths/1,000 live births (2017 est.) *country comparison to the world:* 98

Life expectancy at birth: *total population:* 77 years *male:* 74 years *female:* 80.1 years (2017 est.) *country comparison to the world:* 79

Total fertility rate: 2.19 children born/woman (2017 est.) *country comparison to the world:* 99

Contraceptive prevalence rate: 80.1% (2007/12) *Health expenditures:* 9.2% of GDP (2014) *country comparison to the world:* 35

Physicians density: 1.67 physicians/1,000 population (2011)

Hospital bed density: 1.6 beds/1,000 population (2011)

Drinking water source: improved: *urban:* 93.4% of population *rural:* 75.5% of population *total:* 86.9% of population unimproved: *urban:* 6.6% of population *rural:* 24.5% of population *total:* 13.1% of population (2015 est.)

Sanitation facility access: improved: *urban:* 87% of population *rural:* 80.7% of population *total:* 84.7% of population unimproved: *urban:* 13% of population *rural:* 19.3% of population *total:* 15.3% of population (2015 est.)

HIV/AIDS—adult prevalence rate: 0.3% (2016 est.) *country comparison to the world:* 81

HIV/AIDS—people living with HIV/AIDS: 33,000 (2016 est.) *country comparison to the world:* 64

HIV/AIDS—deaths: <1000 (2016 est.)

Major infectious diseases: *degree of risk:* high *food or waterborne diseases:* bacterial diarrhea, hepatitis A, and typhoid fever *vectorborne diseases:* dengue fever and malaria *note:* active local transmission of Zika virus by Aedes species mosquitoes has been identified in this country (as of August 2016); it poses an important risk (a large number of cases possible) among US citizens if bitten by an infective mosquito; other less common ways to get Zika are through sex, via blood transfusion, or during pregnancy, in which the pregnant woman passes Zika virus to her fetus (2016)

Obesity—adult prevalence rate: 19.9% (2016) *country comparison to the world:* 108

Children under the age of 5 years underweight: 6.4% (2012) *country comparison to the world:* 82 *Education expenditures:* 4.9% of GDP (2015) *country comparison to the world:* 94

Literacy: *definition:* age 15 and over can read and write *total population:* 94.4% *male:* 95.4% *female:* 93.3% (2016 est.)

School life expectancy (primary to tertiary education): *total:* 15 years *male:* 15 years

female: 16 years (2012)

Unemployment, youth ages 15-24: *total:* 11.8% *male:* 9.4% *female:* 15.7% (2015 est.) *country comparison to the world:* 96

GOVERNMENT

Country name: *conventional long form:* Republic of Ecuador *conventional short form:* Ecuador *local long form:* Republica del Ecuador *local short form:* Ecuador *etymology:* the country's position on the globe, straddling the Equator, accounts for its Spanish name

Government type: presidential republic

Capital: *name:* Quito *geographic coordinates:* 0 13 S, 78 30 W *time difference:* UTC-5 (same time as Washington, DC, during Standard Time)

Administrative divisions: 24 provinces (provincias, singular—provincia); Azuay, Bolivar, Canar, Carchi, Chimborazo, Cotopaxi, El Oro, Esmeraldas, Galapagos, Guayas, Imbabura, Loja, Los Rios, Manabi, Morona-Santiago, Napo, Orellana, Pastaza, Pichincha, Santa Elena, Santo Domingo de los Tsachilas, Sucumbios, Tungurahua, Zamora-Chinchipe

Independence: 24 May 1822 (from Spain)

National holiday: Independence Day (independence of Quito), 10 August (1809)

Constitution: many previous; latest approved 20 October 2008; amended 2011, 2015; note—a 2015 constitutional amendment lifting presidential term limits became effective 2017 (2017)

Legal system: civil law based on the Chilean civil code with modifications; traditional law in indigenous communities

International law organization participation: has not submitted an ICJ jurisdiction declaration; accepts ICCt jurisdiction

Citizenship: *citizenship by birth:* yes *citizenship by descent:* yes *dual citizenship recognized:* no *residency requirement for naturalization:* 3 years

Suffrage: 18-65 years of age, universal and compulsory; 16-18, over 65, and other eligible voters, voluntary

Executive branch: *chief of state:* President Lenin MORENO Garces (since 24 May 2017); Vice President Maria Alejandra VICUNA Munoz (since 6 January 2018); note—Vice President Jorge GLAS Espinel (since 24 May 2013) has been jailed for corruption and absent from office for more than 3 months, causing him to be constitutionally stripped of his office; president is both chief of state and head of government

head of government: President Lenin MORENO Garces (since 24 May 2017); Vice President Maria Alejandra VICUNA Munoz (since 6 January 2018); note—Vice President Jorge GLAS Espinel (since 24 May 2013)has been jailed for corruption and absent from office for more than 3 months, causing him to be constitutionally stripped of his office; president is both chief of state and head of government

cabinet: Cabinet appointed by the president

elections/appointments: president and vice president directly elected on the same ballot by absolute majority popular vote in 2 rounds if needed for a 4-year term (eligible for a second term); election last held on 19 February 2017 with a runoff on 2 April 2017 (next to be held in 2021)

election results: Lenin MORENO Garces elected president in second round; percent of vote—Lenin MORENO Garces (Alianza PAIS Movement) 51.1%, Guillermo LASSO (CREO) 48.9%

Legislative branch: description: unicameral National Assembly or Asamblea Nacional (137 seats; 116 members directly elected in single-seat constituencies by simple majority vote, 15 members directly elected in a single nationwide constituency by proportional representation vote, and 6 directly elected in multi-seat constituencies for Ecuadorians living abroad by simple majority vote; members serve 4-year terms)

elections: last held on 19 February 2017 (next to be held in 2021)

election results: percent of vote by party—PAIS 39.1%, CREO-SUMA 20.1%, PSC 15.9%, ID 3.8%, MUPP 2.7%; seats by party—PAIS 74, CREO-SUMA 34, PSC 15, ID 4, MUPP 4, Independents 3, PSP 2, Fuerza Ecuador 1; note—defections by members of National Assembly are commonplace, resulting in frequent changes in the numbers of seats held by the various parties

Judicial branch: *highest court(s):* National Court of Justice or Corte Nacional de Justicia (consists of 21 judges including the chief justice and organized into 5 specialized chambers); Constitutional Court or Corte Constitucional (consists of 9 judges)

judge selection and term of office: justices of National Court of Justice elected by the Judiciary Council, a 9-member independent body of law professionals; judges elected for 9-year, non-renewable terms, with one-third of the membership renewed every 3 years; Constitutional Court judges appointed by the executive, legislative, and Citizen Participation branches of government; judges appointed for 9-year non-renewable terms with one-third of the membership renewed every 3 years

subordinate courts: Fiscal Tribunal; Election Dispute Settlement Courts, provincial courts (one for each province); cantonal courts

Political parties and leaders: Alianza PAIS movement [Lenin Voltaire MORENO Garces]
Avanza Party or AVANZA [Ramiro GONZALEZ]
Creating Opportunities Movement or CREO [Guillermo LASSO]
Democratic Left or ID
Forward Ecuador Movement [Alvaro NOBOA]
Fuerza Ecuador [Abdala BUCARAM] (successor to Roldosist Party)
Pachakutik Plurinational Unity Movement or MUPP [Marlon Rene SANTI Gualinga]

Patriotic Society Party or PSP [Gilmar GUTIER-REZ Borbua]
Popular Democracy Movement or MPD [Luis VILLACIS]
Social Christian Party or PSC [Pascual DEL CIOPPO]
Socialist Party [Patricio ZABRANO]
Society United for More Action or SUMA [Mauricio RODAS]

Political pressure groups and leaders: Confederation of Indigenous Nationalities of Ecuador or CONAIE [Humberto CHOLANGO]

Federation of Indigenous Evangelists of Ecuador or FEINE [Manuel CHUGCHILAN]

National Federation of Indigenous Afro-Ecuatorianos and Peasants or FENOCIN

International organization participation: CAN, CD, CELAC, FAO, G-11, G-77, IADB, IAEA, IBRD, ICAO, ICC (national committees), ICCt, ICRM, IDA, IFAD, IFC, IFRCS, IHO, ILO, IMF, IMO, Interpol, IOC, IOM, IPU, ISO, ITSO, ITU, ITUC (NGOs), LAES, LAIA, Mercosur (associate), MIGA, MINUSTAH, NAM, OAS, OPANAL, OPCW, OPEC, Pacific Alliance (observer), PCA, SICA (observer), UN, UNAMID, UNASUR, UNCTAD, UNESCO, UNHCR, UNIDO, Union Latina, UNISFA, UNMIL, UNMISS, UNOCI, UNWTO, UPU, WCO, WFTU (NGOs), WHO, WIPO, WMO, WTO

Diplomatic representation in the US: *chief of mission:* Ambassador Francisco Benjamin Esteban CARRION Mena(since 24 January 2018)

chancery: 2535 15th Street NW, Washington, DC 20009

telephone: [1] (202) 234-7200

FAX: [1] (202) 667-3482

consulate(s) general: Atlanta, Chicago, Houston, Los Angeles, Miami, Minneapolis, New Haven (CT), New Orleans, New York, Newark (NJ), Phoenix, San Francisco

Diplomatic representation from the US: *chief of mission:* Ambassador Todd C. CHAPMAN (since 14 April 2016)

embassy: Avenida Avigiras E12-170 y Avenida Eloy Alfaro, Quito

mailing address: Avenida Guayacanes N52-205 y Avenida Avigiras

telephone: [593] (2) 398-5000

FAX: [593] (2) 398-5100

consulate(s) general: Guayaquil

Flag description: three horizontal bands of yellow (top, double width), blue, and red with the coat of arms superimposed at the center of the flag; the flag retains the three main colors of the banner of Gran Colombia, the South American republic that broke up in 1830; the yellow color represents sunshine, grain, and mineral wealth, blue the sky, sea, and rivers, and red the blood of patriots spilled in the struggle for freedom and justice

note: similar to the flag of Colombia, which is shorter and does not bear a coat of arms

National symbol(s): Andean condor; national colors: yellow, blue, red

National anthem: name: "Salve, Oh Patria!" (We Salute You, Our Homeland)

lyrics/music: Juan Leon MERA/Antonio NEUMANE

note: adopted 1948; Juan Leon MERA wrote the lyrics in 1865; only the chorus and second verse are sung

ECONOMY

Economy—overview: Ecuador is substantially dependent on its petroleum resources, which have accounted for more than half of the country's export earnings and approximately 25% of public sector revenues in recent years.

In 1999/2000, Ecuador's economy suffered from a banking crisis, with GDP contracting by 5.3% and poverty increasing significantly. In March 2000, the Congress approved a series of structural reforms that also provided for the adoption of the US dollar as legal tender. Dollarization stabilized the economy, and positive growth returned in the years that followed, helped by high oil prices, remittances, and increased non-traditional exports. The economy grew an average of 4.3% per year from 2002 to 2006, the highest five-year average in 25 years. After moderate growth in 2007, the economy reached a growth rate of 6.4% in 2008, buoyed by high global petroleum prices and increased public sector investment. President Rafael CORREA Delgado, who took office in January 2007, defaulted in December 2008 on Ecuador's sovereign debt, which, with a total face value of approximately US$3.2 billion, represented about 30% of Ecuador's public external debt. In May 2009, Ecuador bought back 91% of its "defaulted" bonds via an international reverse auction.

Economic policies under the CORREA administration—for example, an announcement in late 2009 of its intention to terminate 13 bilateral investment treaties, including one with the US—generated economic uncertainty and discouraged private investment. China has become Ecuador's largest foreign lender since Quito defaulted in 2008, allowing the government to maintain a high rate of social spending; Ecuador contracted with the Chinese government for more than $9.9 billion in forward oil sales, project financing, and budget support loans as of December 2013.

The level of foreign investment in Ecuador continues to be one of the lowest in the region as a result of an unstable regulatory environment, weak rule of law, and the crowding-out effect of public investments. Faced with a 2013 trade deficit of $1.1 billion, Ecuador erected technical barriers to trade in December 2013, causing tensions with its largest trading partners. Ecuador also decriminalized intellectual property rights violations in February 2014. In March, 2015 Ecuador imposed tariff surcharges from 5% to 45% on an estimated 32% of imports. In 2014, oil output increased slightly and production remained steady in 2015 however the oil price decrease from 2014 onward affected government revenue. Ecuador's economy fell in to recession in 2015 and remained in recession in 2016. As a result, CORREA cut the budget twice in 2015, and reduced it further in 2016. Growth resumed in 2017.

GDP (purchasing power parity): $188.5 billion (2017 est.)
$188.1 billion (2016 est.)
$190.9 billion (2015 est.)
note: data are in 2017 dollars
country comparison to the world: 67

GDP (official exchange rate): $98.58 billion (2016 est.)

GDP—real growth rate: 0.2% (2017 est.)
-1.5% (2016 est.)
0.2% (2015 est.)
country comparison to the world: 199

GDP—per capita (PPP): $11,200 (2017 est.)
$11,400 (2016 est.)
$11,700 (2015 est.)
note: data are in 2017 dollars
country comparison to the world: 136

Gross national saving: 23.2% of GDP (2017 est.)
24.9% of GDP (2016 est.)
24.7% of GDP (2015 est.)
country comparison to the world: 63

GDP—composition, by end use:
household consumption: 64.3%
government consumption: 13.3%
investment in fixed capital: 22.8%
investment in inventories: 0.3%
exports of goods and services: 20.4%
imports of goods and services: -21.1% (2017 est.)

GDP—composition, by sector of origin:
agriculture: 6.5%
industry: 33.8%
services: 59.7% (2017 est.)

Agriculture—products: bananas, coffee, cocoa, rice, potatoes, cassava (manioc, tapioca), plantains, sugarcane; cattle, sheep, pigs, beef, pork, dairy products; fish, shrimp; balsa wood

Industries: petroleum, food processing, textiles, wood products, chemicals

Industrial production growth rate: -0.8%
note: excludes oil refining (2017 est.)
country comparison to the world: 190

Labor force: 8.011 million (2017 est.)
country comparison to the world: 61

Labor force—by occupation: agriculture: 27.8%
industry: 17.8%
services: 54.4% (2012 est.)

Unemployment rate: 5.1% (2017 est.)
5.2% (2016 est.)
country comparison to the world: 69

Population below poverty line: 25.6% (December 2013 est)

Household income or consumption by percentage share: lowest 10%: 1.4%
highest 10%: 35.4%
note: data are for urban households only (2012 est.)

Distribution of family income—Gini index: 48.5 (December 2013)
50.5 (December 2010)
note: data are for urban households
country comparison to the world: 23

Budget: revenues: $32.3 billion
expenditures: $37.7 billion (2017 est.)
Taxes and other revenues: 32.8% of GDP (2017 est.)
country comparison to the world: 68

Budget surplus (+) or deficit (-): -5.5% of GDP (2017 est.)
country comparison to the world: 169

Public debt: 41% of GDP (2017 est.)
36.4% of GDP (2016 est.)
country comparison to the world: 133

Fiscal year: calendar year

Inflation rate (consumer prices): 0.7% (2017 est.)
1.7% (2016 est.)
country comparison to the world: 23

Central bank discount rate: 8.17% (31 December 2011)
8.68% (31 December 2010)
country comparison to the world: 40

Commercial bank prime lending rate: 8% (31 December 2017 est.)
8.69% (31 December 2016 est.)
country comparison to the world: 110

Stock of narrow money: $10.17 billion (31 December 2017 est.)
$9.281 billion (31 December 2016 est.)
country comparison to the world: 85

Stock of broad money: $33.31 billion (31 December 2017 est.)
$32.84 billion (31 December 2016 est.)
country comparison to the world: 77

Stock of domestic credit: $36.3 billion (31 December 2017 est.)
$35.56 billion (31 December 2016 est.)
country comparison to the world: 72

Market value of publicly traded shares: $5.911 billion (31 December 2012 est.)
$5.779 billion (31 December 2011 est.)
$5.263 billion (31 December 2010 est.)
country comparison to the world: 83

Current account balance: -$706 million (2017 est.)
$1.414 billion (2016 est.)
country comparison to the world: 112

Exports: $18.34 billion (2017 est.)
$17.43 billion (2016 est.)
country comparison to the world: 73

Exports—commodities: petroleum, bananas, cut flowers, shrimp, cacao, coffee, wood, fish

Exports—partners: US 32.3%, Chile 6.8%, Vietnam 6.6%, Peru 5.6%, Colombia 4.8%, Russia 4.6% (2016)

Imports: $16.84 billion (2017 est.)
$15.86 billion (2016 est.)
country comparison to the world: 81

Imports—commodities: industrial materials, fuels and lubricants, nondurable consumer goods

Imports—partners: US 23%, China 19%, Colombia 8%, Brazil 4.2% (2016)

Reserves of foreign exchange and gold: $3.935 billion (31 December 2017 est.)
$4.178 billion (31 December 2016 est.)

country comparison to the world: 98

Debt—external: $37.75 billion (31 December 2017 est.)
$32.32 billion (31 December 2016 est.)
country comparison to the world: 76

Stock of direct foreign investment—at home: $17.33 billion (31 December 2017 est.)
$16.63 billion (31 December 2016 est.)
country comparison to the world: 82

Stock of direct foreign investment—abroad: $6.33 billion (31 December 2012 est.)
country comparison to the world: 68

Exchange rates: the US dollar became Ecuador's currency in 2001

ENERGY

Electricity access: population without electricity: 500,000
electrification—total population: 97%
electrification—urban areas: 100%
electrification—rural areas: 92% (2013)

Electricity—production: 24.95 billion kWh (2015 est.)
country comparison to the world: 71

Electricity—consumption: 22.14 billion kWh (2015 est.)
country comparison to the world: 70

Electricity—exports: 46 million kWh (2015 est.)
country comparison to the world: 88

Electricity—imports: 512 million kWh (2015 est.)
country comparison to the world: 80

Electricity—installed generating capacity: 5.986 million kW (2015 est.)
country comparison to the world: 76

Electricity—from fossil fuels: 56.9% of total installed capacity (2015 est.)
country comparison to the world: 136

Electricity—from nuclear fuels: 0% of total installed capacity (2015 est.)
country comparison to the world: 81

Electricity—from hydroelectric plants: 39.9% of total installed capacity (2015 est.)
country comparison to the world: 51

Electricity—from other renewable sources: 3.2% of total installed capacity (2015 est.)
country comparison to the world: 111

Crude oil—production: 548,400 bbl/day (2016 est.)
country comparison to the world: 27

Crude oil—exports: 400,700 bbl/day (2014 est.)
country comparison to the world: 23

Crude oil—imports: 0 bbl/day (2014 est.)
country comparison to the world: 119

Crude oil—proved reserves: 8.273 billion bbl (1 January 2017 es)
country comparison to the world: 18

Refined petroleum products—production: 146,500 bbl/day (2014 est.)
country comparison to the world: 59

Refined petroleum products—consumption: 274,000 bbl/day (2015 est.)

country comparison to the world: 47

Refined petroleum products—exports: 25,940 bbl/day (2014 est.)
country comparison to the world: 65

Refined petroleum products—imports: 155,700 bbl/day (2014 est.)
country comparison to the world: 45

Natural gas—production: 497 million cu m (2015 est.)
country comparison to the world: 72

Natural gas—consumption: 1.002 billion cu m (2015 est.)
country comparison to the world: 99

Natural gas—exports: 0 cu m (2015 est.)
country comparison to the world: 96

Natural gas—imports: 0 cu m (2013 est.)
country comparison to the world: 119

Natural gas—proved reserves: 10.9 billion cu m (1 January 2017 es)
country comparison to the world: 82

Carbon dioxide emissions from consumption of energy: 38 million Mt (2013 est.)
country comparison to the world: 70

COMMUNICATIONS

Telephones—fixed lines: *total subscriptions:* 2,441,173
subscriptions per 100 inhabitants: 15 (July 2016 est.)
country comparison to the world: 55

Telephones—mobile cellular: *total:* 13,882,280
subscriptions per 100 inhabitants: 86 (July 2016 est.)
country comparison to the world: 65

Telephone system: *general assessment:* elementary fixed-line service but increasingly sophisticated mobile-cellular network
domestic: fixed-line services provided by multiple telecommunications operators; fixed-line teledensity stands at about 15 per 100 persons; mobile-cellular use has surged and subscribership has reached 85 per 100 persons
international: country code—593; landing points for the PAN-AM and South America-1 submarine cables that provide links to the west coast of South America, Panama, Colombia, Venezuela, and extending onward to Aruba and the US Virgin Islands in the Caribbean; satellite earth station—1 Intelsat (Atlantic Ocean) (2016)

Broadcast media: multiple TV networks and many local channels, as well as more than 300 radio stations; many TV and radio stations are privately owned; the government owns or controls 5 national TV stations and multiple radio stations; broadcast media required by law to give the government free air time to broadcast programs produced by the state (2007)

Internet country code: .ec
Internet users: total: 8,693,739
percent of population: 54.1% (July 2016 est.)
country comparison to the world: 59

TRANSPORTATION

National air transport system: *number of registered air carriers:* 7
inventory of registered aircraft operated by air carriers: 35
annual passenger traffic on registered air carriers: 5,762,485
annual freight traffic on registered air carriers: 86,128,720 mt-km (2015)
Civil aircraft registration country code prefix: HC (2016)

Airports: 432 (2013)
country comparison to the world: 20

Airports—with paved runways: *total:* 104
over 3,047 m: 4
2,438 to 3,047 m: 5
1,524 to 2,437 m: 18
914 to 1,523 m: 26
under 914 m: 51 (2017)

Airports—with unpaved runways: *total:* 328
914 to 1,523 m: 37
under 914 m: 291 (2013)

Heliports: 2 (2013)

Pipelines: extra heavy crude 527 km; gas 71 km; oil 2,131 km; refined products 1,526 km (2013)

Railways: *total:* 965 km
narrow gauge: 965 km 1.067-m gauge (2014)
country comparison to the world: 90

Roadways: *total:* 43,670 km
paved: 6,472 km
unpaved: 37,198 km (2007)
country comparison to the world: 84

Waterways: 1,500 km (most inaccessible) (2012)
country comparison to the world: 52

Merchant marine: *total:* 138
by type: general cargo 6, oil tanker 37, other 95 (2017)
country comparison to the world: 75

Ports and terminals: *major seaport(s):* Esmeraldas, Manta, Puerto Bolivar
river port(s): Guayaquil (Guayas)
container port(s) (TEUs): Guayaquil (1,405,762)

MILITARY AND SECURITY

Military expenditures: 1.7% of GDP (2017)
2.21% of GDP (2016)
2.44% of GDP (2015)
2.72% of GDP (2014)
2.88% of GDP (2013)
2.95% of GDP (2012)
country comparison to the world: 24

Military branches: Ecuadorian Armed Forces: Ecuadorian Land Force (Fuerza Terrestre Ecuatoriana, FTE), Ecuadorian Navy (Fuerza Naval del Ecuador, FNE, includes Naval Infantry, Naval Aviation, Coast Guard), Ecuadorian Air Force (Fuerza Aerea Ecuatoriana, FAE) (2012)

Military service age and obligation: 18 years of age for selective conscript military service; conscription has been suspended; 18 years of age for voluntary military service; Air Force 18-22 years of age, Ecuadorian birth requirement; 1-year service obligation (2012)

Maritime threats: the International Maritime Bureau continues to report the territorial and offshore waters as at risk for piracy and armed robbery against ships; vessels, including commercial shipping and pleasure craft, have been attacked and hijacked both at anchor and while underway; crews have been robbed and stores or cargoes stolen; after several years with no incident, in January 2017 a ship anchored in the port of Quayaquil was boarded and robbed

TRANSNATIONAL ISSUES

Disputes—international: organized illegal narcotics operations in Colombia penetrate across Ecuador's shared border, which thousands of Colombians also cross to escape the violence in their home country

Refugees and internally displaced persons: *refugees (country of origin):* 101,161 (Colombia) (2016)
IDPs: 11,137 (earthquake April 2016) (2016)

Illicit drugs: significant transit country for cocaine originating in Colombia and Peru, with much of the US-bound cocaine passing through Ecuadorian Pacific waters; importer of precursor chemicals used in production of illicit narcotics; attractive location for cash-placement by drug traffickers laundering money because of dollarization and weak anti-money-laundering regime; increased activity on the northern frontier by trafficking groups and Colombian insurgents

EGYPT

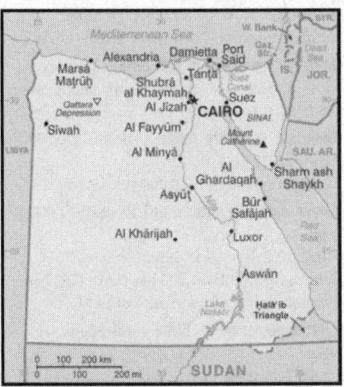

INTRODUCTION

Background: The regularity and richness of the annual Nile River flood, coupled with semi-isolation provided by deserts to the east and west, allowed for the development of one of the world's great civilizations. A unified kingdom arose circa 3200 B.C., and a series of dynasties ruled in Egypt for the next three millennia. The last native dynasty fell to the Persians in 341 B.C., who in turn were replaced by the Greeks, Romans, and Byzantines. It was the Arabs who introduced Islam and the Arabic language in the 7th century and who ruled for the next six centuries. A local military caste, the Mamluks took control about 1250 and continued to govern after the conquest of Egypt by the Ottoman Turks in 1517. Completion of the Suez Canal in 1869 elevated Egypt as an important world transportation hub. Ostensibly to protect its investments, Britain seized control of Egypt's government in 1882, but nominal allegiance to the Ottoman Empire continued until 1914. Partially independent from the UK in 1922, Egypt acquired full sovereignty from Britain in 1952. The completion of the Aswan High Dam in 1971 and the resultant Lake Nasser have altered the time-honored place of the Nile River in the agriculture and ecology of Egypt. A rapidly growing population (the largest in the Arab world), limited arable land, and dependence on the Nile all continue to overtax resources and stress society. The government has struggled to meet the demands of Egypt's population through economic reform and massive investment in communications and physical infrastructure.

Inspired by the 2010 Tunisian revolution, Egyptian opposition groups led demonstrations and labor strikes countrywide, culminating in President Hosni MUBARAK's ouster in 2011. Egypt's military assumed national leadership until a new parliament was in place in early 2012; later that same year, Mohammed MORSI won the presidential election. Following often violent protests throughout the spring of 2013 against MORSI's government and the Muslim Brotherhood, the Egyptian Armed Forces intervened and removed MORSI from power in July 2013 and replaced him with interim president Adly MANSOUR. In January 2014, voters approved a new constitution by referendum and in May 2014 elected Abdelfattah ELSISI president. Egypt elected a new legislature in December 2015, the first parliament since 2012.

GEOGRAPHY

Location: Northern Africa, bordering the Mediterranean Sea, between Libya and the Gaza Strip, and the Red Sea north of Sudan, and includes the Asian Sinai Peninsula

Geographic coordinates: 27 00 N, 30 00 E

Map references: Africa

Area: *total:* 1,001,450 sq km
land: 995,450 sq km
water: 6,000 sq km
country comparison to the world: 31

Area—comparative: more than eight times the size of Ohio; slightly more than three times the size of New Mexico

Land boundaries: *total:* 2,612 km
border countries (4): Gaza Strip 13 km, Israel 208 km, Libya 1,115 km, Sudan 1,276 km

Coastline: 2,450 km

Maritime claims: *territorial sea:* 12 nm
contiguous zone: 24 nm
exclusive economic zone: 200 nm or the equidistant median line with Cyprus
continental shelf: 200 nm

Climate: desert; hot, dry summers with moderate winters

Terrain: vast desert plateau interrupted by Nile valley and delta

Elevation: *mean elevation:* 321 m

elevation extremes: *lowest point:* Qattara Depression -133 m
highest point: Mount Catherine 2,629 m

Natural resources: petroleum, natural gas, iron ore, phosphates, manganese, limestone, gypsum, talc, asbestos, lead, rare earth elements, zinc

Land use: *agricultural land:* 3.6%
arable land: 2.8%;
permanent crops: 0.8%;
permanent pasture: 0%
forest: 0.1%
other: 96.3% (2011 est.)

Irrigated land: 36,500 sq km (2012)

Population—distribution: approximately 95% of the population lives within 20 km of the Nile River and its delta; vast areas of the country remain sparsely populated or uninhabited

Natural hazards: periodic droughts; frequent earthquakes; flash floods; landslides; hot, driving windstorms called khamsin occur in spring; dust storms; sandstorms

Environment—current issues: agricultural land being lost to urbanization and windblown sands; increasing soil salination below Aswan High Dam; desertification; oil pollution threatening coral reefs, beaches, and marine habitats; other water pollution from agricultural pesticides, raw sewage, and industrial effluents; limited natural freshwater resources away from the Nile, which is the only perennial water source; rapid growth in population overstraining the Nile and natural resources

Environment—international agreements: *party to:* Biodiversity, Climate Change, Climate Change-Kyoto Protocol, Desertification, Endangered Species, Environmental Modification, Hazardous Wastes, Law of the Sea, Marine Dumping, Ozone Layer Protection, Ship Pollution, Tropical Timber 83, Tropical Timber 94, Wetlands
signed, but not ratified: none of the selected agreements

Geography—note: controls Sinai Peninsula, only land bridge between Africa and remainder of Eastern Hemisphere; controls Suez Canal, a sea link between Indian Ocean and Mediterranean Sea; size, and juxtaposition to Israel, establish its major role in Middle Eastern geopolitics; dependence on upstream neighbors; dominance of Nile basin issues; prone to influxes of refugees from Sudan and the Palestinian territories

PEOPLE AND SOCIETY

Population: 97,041,072 (July 2017 est.)
country comparison to the world: 14

Nationality: *noun:* Egyptian(s)
adjective: Egyptian

Ethnic groups: Egyptian 99.6%, other 0.4% (2006 census)

Languages: Arabic (official), English and French widely understood by educated classes

Religions: Muslim (predominantly Sunni) 90%, Christian (majority Coptic Orthodox, other Christians include Armenian Apostolic, Catholic, Maronite, Orthodox, and Anglican) 10% (2015 est.)

Demographic profile: Egypt is the most populous country in the Arab world and the third most populous country in Africa, behind Nigeria and Ethiopia. Most of the country is desert, so about 95% of the population is concentrated in a narrow strip of fertile land along the Nile River, which represents only about 5% of Egypt's land area. Egypt's rapid population growth—46% between 1994 and 2014—stresses limited natural resources, jobs, housing, sanitation, education, and health care.

Although the country's total fertility rate (TFR) fell from roughly 5.5 children per woman in 1980 to just over 3 in the late 1990s, largely as a result of state-sponsored family planning programs, the population growth rate dropped more modestly because of decreased mortality rates and longer life expectancies. During the last decade, Egypt's TFR decline stalled for several years and then reversed, reaching 3.6 in 2011, and has plateaued the last few years. Contraceptive use has held steady at about 60%, while preferences for larger families and early marriage may have strengthened in the wake of the recent 2011 revolution. The large cohort of women of or nearing childbearing age will sustain high population growth for the foreseeable future (an effect called population momentum).

Nevertheless, post-MUBARAK governments have not made curbing population growth a priority. To increase contraceptive use and to prevent further overpopulation will require greater government commitment and substantial social change, including encouraging smaller families and better educating and empowering women. Currently, literacy, educational attainment, and labor force participation rates are much lower for women than men. In addition, the prevalence of violence against women, the lack of female political representation, and the perpetuation of the nearly universal practice of female genital cutting continue to keep women from playing a more significant role in Egypt's public sphere.

Population pressure, poverty, high unemployment, and the fragmentation of inherited land holdings have historically motivated Egyptians, primarily young men, to migrate internally from rural and smaller urban areas in the Nile Delta region and the poorer rural south to Cairo, Alexandria, and other urban centers in the north, while a much smaller number migrated to the Red Sea and Sinai areas. Waves of forced internal migration also resulted from the 1967 Arab-Israeli War and the floods caused by the completion of the Aswan High Dam in 1970. Limited numbers of students and professionals emigrated temporarily prior to the early 1970s, when economic problems and high unemployment pushed the Egyptian Government to lift restrictions on labor migration. At the same time, high oil revenues enabled Saudi Arabia, Iraq, and other Gulf states, as well as Libya and Jordan, to fund development projects, creating a demand for unskilled labor (mainly in construction), which attracted tens of thousands of young Egyptian men.

Between 1970 and 1974 alone, Egyptian migrants in the Gulf countries increased from approximately 70,000 to 370,000. Egyptian officials encouraged legal labor migration both to alleviate unemployment and to generate remittance income (remittances continue to be one of Egypt's largest sources of foreign currency and GDP). During the mid-1980s, however, depressed oil prices resulting from the Iran-Iraq War, decreased demand for low-skilled labor, competition from less costly South Asian workers, and efforts to replace foreign workers with locals significantly reduced Egyptian migration to the Gulf States. The number of Egyptian migrants dropped from a peak of almost 3.3 million in 1983 to about 2.2 million at the start of the 1990s, but numbers gradually recovered.

In the 2000s, Egypt began facilitating more labor migration through bilateral agreements, notably with Arab countries and Italy, but illegal migration to Europe through overstayed visas or maritime human smuggling via Libya also rose. The Egyptian Government estimated there were 6.5 million Egyptian migrants in 2009, with roughly 75% being temporary migrants in other Arab countries (Libya, Saudi Arabia, Jordan, Kuwait, and the United Arab Emirates) and 25% being predominantly permanent migrants in the West (US, UK, Italy, France, and Canada).

During the 2000s, Egypt became an increasingly important transit and destination country for economic migrants and asylum seekers, including Palestinians, East Africans, and South Asians and, more recently, Iraqis and Syrians. Egypt draws many refugees because of its resettlement programs with the West; Cairo has one of the largest urban refugee populations in the world. Many East African migrants are interned or live in temporary encampments along the Egypt-Israel border, and some have been shot and killed by Egyptian border guards.

Age structure: 0-14 years: 33.29% (male 16,720,307/female 15,583,019)
15-24 years: 18.94% (male 9,464,262/female 8,919,614)
25-54 years: 37.6% (male 18,545,422/female 17,944,582)
55-64 years: 5.95% (male 2,861,136/female 2,911,586)
65 years and over: 4.22% (male 1,993,248/female 2,097,896) (2017 est.)

Dependency ratios: total dependency ratio: 61.8
youth dependency ratio: 53.6
elderly dependency ratio: 8.2
potential support ratio: 12.2 (2015 est.)

Median age: total: 23.9 years
male: 23.6 years
female: 24.2 years (2017 est.)
country comparison to the world: 164

Population growth rate: 2.45% (2017 est.)
country comparison to the world: 22

Birth rate: 29.6 births/1,000 population (2017 est.)
country comparison to the world: 40

Death rate: 4.6 deaths/1,000 population (2017 est.)
country comparison to the world: 203

Net migration rate: -0.5 migrant(s)/1,000 population (2017 est.)
country comparison to the world: 123

Population distribution: approximately 95% of the population lives within 20 km of the Nile River and its delta; vast areas of the country remain sparsely populated or uninhabited

Urbanization: urban population: 43.3% of total population (2017)
rate of urbanization: 1.8% annual rate of change (2015-20 est.)

Major urban areas—population: CAIRO (capital) 18.772 million; Alexandria 4.778 million (2015)

Sex ratio: at birth: 1.05 male(s)/female

0-14 years: 1.07 male(s)/female
15-24 years: 1.06 male(s)/female
25-54 years: 1.03 male(s)/female
55-64 years: 0.98 male(s)/female
65 years and over: 0.82 male(s)/female
total population: 1.05 male(s)/female (2016 est.)

Mother's mean age at first birth: 22.7 years
note: median age at first birth among women 25-29 (2014 est.)

Maternal mortality ratio: 33 deaths/100,000 live births (2015 est.)
country comparison to the world: 110

Infant mortality rate: total: 19 deaths/1,000 live births
male: 20.2 deaths/1,000 live births
female: 17.7 deaths/1,000 live births (2017 est.)
country comparison to the world: 84

Life expectancy at birth: total population: 73 years
male: 71.6 years
female: 74.4 years (2017 est.)
country comparison to the world: 142

Total fertility rate: 3.47 children born/woman (2017 est.)
country comparison to the world: 44

Contraceptive prevalence rate: 58.5% (2014)
Health expenditures: 5.6% of GDP (2014)
country comparison to the world: 119

Physicians density: 0.81 physicians/1,000 population (2014)

Hospital bed density: 0.5 beds/1,000 population (2012)

Drinking water source:
improved:
urban: 100% of population
rural: 99% of population
total: 99.4% of population
unimproved:
urban: 0% of population
rural: 1% of population
total: 0.6% of population (2015 est.)

Sanitation facility access:
improved:
urban: 96.8% of population
rural: 93.1% of population
total: 94.7% of population
unimproved:
urban: 3.2% of population
rural: 6.9% of population
total: 5.3% of population (2015 est.)

HIV/AIDS—adult prevalence rate: <.1% (2016 est.)

HIV/AIDS—people living with HIV/AIDS: 11,000 (2016 est.)
country comparison to the world: 90

HIV/AIDS—deaths: <500 (2016 est.)

Major infectious diseases: degree of risk: intermediate
food or waterborne diseases: bacterial diarrhea, hepatitis A, and typhoid fever
water contact disease: schistosomiasis (2016)

Obesity—adult prevalence rate: 32% (2016)

country comparison to the world: 18

Children under the age of 5 years underweight: 7% (2014)

country comparison to the world: 77

Education expenditures: 3.8% of GDP (2008)

country comparison to the world: 117

Literacy: *definition:* age 15 and over can read and write

total population: 73.8%

male: 82.2%

female: 65.4% (2015 est.)

School life expectancy (primary to tertiary education): *total:* 13 years

male: 13 years

female: 13 years (2014)

Unemployment, youth ages 15-24: *total:* 31.3%

male: 28.4%

female: 37.6% (2015 est.)

country comparison to the world: 37

Government :: EGYPT

Country name: *conventional long form:* Arab Republic of Egypt

conventional short form: Egypt

local long form: Jumhuriyat Misr al-Arabiyah

local short form: Misr

former: United Arab Republic (with Syria)

etymology: the English name "Egypt" derives from the ancient Greek name for the country "Aigyptos"; the Arabic name "Misr" can be traced to the ancient Akkadian "misru" meaning border or frontier

Government type: presidential republic

Capital: *name:* Cairo

geographic coordinates: 30 03 N, 31 15 E

time difference: UTC+2 (7 hours ahead of Washington, DC, during Standard Time)

Administrative divisions: 27 governorates (muhafazat, singular—muhafazat); Ad Daqahliyah, Al Bahr al Ahmar (Red Sea), Al Buhayrah, Al Fayyum, Al Gharbiyah, Al Iskandariyah (Alexandria), Al Isma'iliyah (Ismailia), Al Jizah (Giza), Al Minufiyah, Al Minya, Al Qahirah (Cairo), Al Qalyubiyah, Al Uqsur (Luxor), Al Wadi al Jadid (New Valley), As Suways (Suez), Ash Sharqiyah, Aswan, Asyut, Bani Suwayf, Bur Sa'id (Port Said), Dumyat (Damietta), Janub Sina' (South Sinai), Kafr ash Shaykh, Matruh, Qina, Shamal Sina' (North Sinai), Suhaj

Independence: 28 February 1922 (from UK protectorate status; the revolution that began on 23 July 1952 led to a republic being declared on 18 June 1953 and all British troops withdrawn on 18 June 1956); note—it was ca. 3200 B.C. that the Two Lands of Upper (southern) and Lower (northern) Egypt were first united politically

National holiday: Revolution Day, 23 July (1952)

Constitution: history: several previous; latest approved by a constitutional committee in December 2013, approved by referendum held on 14-15 January 2014, ratified by interim president on 19 January 2014

amendments: proposed by the president of the republic or by one-fifth of the House of Representatives members; a decision to accept the proposal requires majority vote by House members; passage of amendment requires a two-thirds majority vote by House members and passage by majority vote in a referendum; articles of reelection of the president and principles of freedom not amendable unless the amendment "brings more guarantees"

note: in mid-2017, some members of the House of Representatives suggested revisions to the 2014 constitution that, if approved, would extend the term of the president and expand presidential powers (2017)

Legal system: mixed legal system based on Napoleonic civil and penal law, Islamic religious law, and vestiges of colonial-era laws; judicial review of the constitutionality of laws by the Supreme Constitutional Court

International law organization participation: accepts compulsory ICJ jurisdiction with reservations; non-party state to the ICCt

Citizenship: *citizenship by birth:* no

citizenship by descent only: if the father was born in Egypt

dual citizenship recognized: only with prior permission from the government

residency requirement for naturalization: 10 years

Suffrage: 18 years of age; universal and compulsory

Executive branch: Chief of state: President Abdelfattah Said ELSISI (since 8 June 2014)

head of government: Prime Minister Sherif ISMAIL (since 12 September 2015); note—Prime Minister Ibrahim MEHLAB resigned 12 September 2015

cabinet: Cabinet sworn in 19 September 2015

elections/appointments: president elected by absolute majority popular vote in 2 rounds if needed for a 4-year term (eligible for a second term); election last held on 26-28 May 2014 (next to be held in May 2018); prime minister appointed by the president, approved by the House of Representatives

election results: Abdelfattah Said ELSISI elected president in first round; percent of vote—Abdelfattah Said ELSISI (independent) 96.6%, Hamdeen SABAHI (Egyptian Current Party) 3.4%

Legislative branch: description: unicameral House of Representatives (Majlis Al-Nowaab); 596 seats; 448 members directly elected by individual candidacy system, 120 members—with quotas for women, youth, Christians and workers—elected in party-list constituencies by simple majority popular vote, and 28 members selected by the president; member term 5 years; note—inaugural session held on 10 January 2016

elections: multi-phase election completed on 16 December 2015 (next to be held in 2020)

election results: percent of vote by party—NA; seats by party — Free Egyptians Party 65, Nation's Future Party 53, New Wafd Party 36, Homeland's Protector Party 18, Republican People's Party 13, Congress Party 12, al-Nour Party 11, Conservative

Party 6, Democratic Peace Party 5, Egyptian Social Democratic Party 4, Egyptian National Movement 4, Modern Egypt Party 4, Reform and Development Party 3, Freedom Party 3, My Homeland Egypt Party 3, National Progressive Unionist Party 2, Arab Democratic Nasserist Party 1, Revolutionary Guards Party 1, Free Egyptian Building Party 1, independent 351

Judicial branch: *highest court(s):* Supreme Constitutional Court or SCC (consists of the court president and 10 justices); the SCC serves as the final court of arbitraton on the constitutionality of laws and conflicts between lower courts regarding jurisdiction and rulings; Court of Cassation (CC) (consists of the court president and 550 judges organized in circuits with cases heard by panels of 5 judges); the CC is the highest appeals body for civil and criminal cases, also known as "ordinary justices"; Supreme Administrative Court (SAC)—consists of the court president and organized in circuits with cases heard by panels of 5 judges); the SAC is the highest court of the State Council

judge selection and term of office: under the 2014 constitution, all judges and justices selected by the Supreme Judiciary Council and appointed by the president of the Republic; judges appointed for life

subordinate courts: Courts of Appeal; Courts of First Instance; courts of limited jurisdiction; Family Court (established in 2004)

Political parties and leaders: Al-Nour [Yunis MAKHYUN]

Arab Democratic Nasserist Party [Sameh ASHOUR]

Congress Party [Omar Mokhtar SEMEIDA]

Conservative Party [Akmal KOURTAM]

Democratic Peace Party [Ahmed FADALY]

Egyptian National Movement Party [Ibrahim DARWISH]

Egyptian Social Democratic Party [Mervat TALAWAY]

Freedom Party [Mamdouh HASSAN]

Free Egyptian Building Party

Free Egyptians Party [Essam KHALIL]

Homeland's Protector Party [Lt. Gen. (retired) Galal AL-HARIDI]

Modern Egypt Party [Nabil DEIBIS]

Mostaqbal Watan (Nation's Future) Party [Mohamed Ashraf RASHAD]

My Homeland Egypt Party [Qadry ABU HUSSEIN]

National Progressive Unionist (Tagammu) Party [Sayed Abdel AAL]

Nation's Future Party [Ashraf RASHAD, secretary general]

New Wafd Party [Sayed al-BADAWI]

Reform and Development Party [Mohamad Anwar al-SADAT]

Republican People's Party [Hazim AMR]

Revolutionary Guards Party [Magdy EL-SHARIF]

Political pressure groups and leaders: labor unions

student unions

teacher unions

International organization participation: ABEDA, AfDB, AFESD, AMF, AU, BSEC (observer),

CAEU, CD, CICA, COMESA, D-8, EBRD, FAO, G-15, G-24, G-77, IAEA, IBRD, ICAO, ICC (national committees), ICRM, IDA, IDB, IFAD, IFC, IFRCS, IHO, ILO, IMF, IMO, IMSO, Interpol, IOC, IOM, IPU, ISO, ITSO, ITU, LAS, MIGA, MINURSO, MINUSMA, MONUSCO, NAM, OAPEC, OAS (observer), OIC, OIF, OSCE (partner), PCA, UN, UN Security Council (temporary), UNAMID, UNCTAD, UNESCO, UNHCR, UNIDO, UNMISS, UNOCI, UNRWA, UNWTO, UPU, WCO, WFTU (NGOs), WHO, WIPO, WMO, WTO

Diplomatic representation in the US: *chief of mission:* Ambassador Yasser REDA (since 19 September 2015)
chancery: 3521 International Court NW, Washington, DC 20008
telephone: [1] (202) 895-5400
FAX: [1] (202) 244-5131
consulate(s) general: Chicago, Houston, Los Angeles, New York

Diplomatic representation from the US: *chief of mission:* Ambassador (vacant); Charge d'Affaires Thomas H. GOLDBERGER (since 30 June 2017)
embassy: 5 Tawfik Diab St., Garden City, Cairo
mailing address: Unit 64900, Box 15, APO AE 09839-4900; 5 Tawfik Diab Street, Garden City, Cairo
telephone: [20] (2) 2797-3300
FAX: [20] (2) 2797-3200

Flag description: three equal horizontal bands of red (top), white, and black; the national emblem (a gold Eagle of Saladin facing the hoist side with a shield superimposed on its chest above a scroll bearing the name of the country in Arabic) centered in the white band; the band colors derive from the Arab Liberation flag and represent oppression (black), overcome through bloody struggle (red), to be replaced by a bright future (white)
note: similar to the flag of Syria, which has two green stars in the white band, Iraq, which has an Arabic inscription centered in the white band, and Yemen, which has a plain white band

National symbol(s): golden eagle, white lotus; national colors: red, white, black

National anthem: *name:* "Bilady, Bilady, Bilady" (My Homeland, My Homeland, My Homeland)
lyrics/music: Younis-al QADI/Sayed DARWISH
note: adopted 1979; the current anthem, less militaristic than the previous one, was created after the signing of the 1979 peace treaty with Israel; Sayed DARWISH, commonly considered the father of modern Egyptian music, composed the anthem

ECONOMY

Economy—overview: Occupying the northeast corner of the African continent, Egypt is bisected by the highly fertile Nile valley where most economic activity takes place. Egypt's economy was highly centralized during the rule of former President Gamal Abdel NASSER but opened up considerably under former Presidents Anwar EL-SADAT and Mohamed Hosni MUBARAK.

Agriculture, hydrocarbons, manufacturing, tourism, and other service sectors drove the country's relatively diverse economic activity.

Despite Egypt's mixed record for attracting foreign investment over the past two decades, poor living conditions and limited job opportunities have contributed to public discontent. These socioeconomic pressures were a major factor leading to the January 2011 revolution that ousted MUBARAK. The uncertain political, security, and policy environment since 2011 has restricted economic growth and failed to alleviate persistent unemployment, especially among the young.

In late 2016, persistent dollar shortages and waning aid from its Gulf allies led Cairo to turn to the IMF for a 3-year, $12 billion loan program. To secure the deal, Cairo floated its currency, introduced new taxes, and cut energy subsidies—all of which pushed inflation above 30% for most of 2017, a high that had not been seen in a generation. Since the currency float, foreign investment in Egypt's high interest treasury bills has risen exponentially, boosting both dollar availability and central bank reserves. Cairo will need to make a sustained effort to implement a range of business reforms, however, to induce foreign and local investment in manufacturing and other labor-intensive sectors.

GDP (purchasing power parity): $1.199 trillion (2017 est.)
$1.152 trillion (2016 est.)
$1.104 trillion (2015 est.)
note: data are in 2017 dollars
country comparison to the world: 22

GDP (official exchange rate): $332.3 billion (2016 est.)

GDP—real growth rate: 4.1% (2017 est.)
4.3% (2016 est.)
4.4% (2015 est.)
country comparison to the world: 62

GDP—per capita (PPP): $13,000 (2017 est.)
$12,800 (2016 est.)
$12,400 (2015 est.)
note: data are in 2017 dollars
country comparison to the world: 119

Gross national saving: 9.7% of GDP (2017 est.)
9.1% of GDP (2016 est.)
10.7% of GDP (2015 est.)
country comparison to the world: 161

GDP—composition, by end use:
household consumption: 79.2%
government consumption: 12.2%
investment in fixed capital: 17.3%
investment in inventories: 1.3%
exports of goods and services: 13.5%
imports of goods and services: -23.5% (2017 est.)

GDP—composition, by sector of origin:
agriculture: 11.9%
industry: 33.1%
services: 55.7% (2017 est.)

Agriculture—products: cotton, rice, corn, wheat, beans, fruits, vegetables; cattle, water buffalo, sheep, goats

Industries: textiles, food processing, tourism, chemicals, pharmaceuticals, hydrocarbons, construction, cement, metals, light manufactures

Industrial production growth rate: 3.5% (2017 est.)
country comparison to the world: 80

Labor force: 29.95 million (2017 est.)
country comparison to the world: 23

Labor force—by occupation: *agriculture:* 29.2%
industry: 23.5%
services: 47.3% (2013 est.)

Unemployment rate: 12.2% (2017 est.)
12.7% (2016 est.)
country comparison to the world: 156

Population below poverty line: 25.2% (2011 est.)

Household income or consumption by percentage share: *lowest 10%:* 4%
highest 10%: 26.6% (2008)

Distribution of family income—Gini index: 30.8 (2008)
32.1 (2005)
country comparison to the world: 121

Budget: *revenues:* $35.54 billion
expenditures: $55.09 billion (2017 est.)
Taxes and other revenues: 14.7% of GDP (2016 est.)
country comparison to the world: 193

Budget surplus (+) or deficit (-): -9.8% of GDP (2016 est.)
country comparison to the world: 206

Public debt: 104.4% of GDP (2017 est.)
111.2% of GDP (2016 est.)
note: data cover central government debt and includes debt instruments issued (or owned) by government entities other than the treasury; the data include treasury debt held by foreign entities; the data include debt issued by subnational entities, as well as intra-governmental debt; intra-governmental debt consists of treasury borrowings from surpluses in the social funds, such as for retirement, medical care, and unemployment; debt instruments for the social funds are sold at public auctions
country comparison to the world: 15

Fiscal year: 1 July—30 June

Inflation rate (consumer prices): 23.5% (2017 est.)
10.2% (2016 est.)
country comparison to the world: 219

Central bank discount rate: 9.75% (30 October 2014)
8.75% (5 December 2013)
country comparison to the world: 25

Commercial bank prime lending rate: 19.5% (31 December 2017 est.)
13.6% (31 December 2016 est.)
country comparison to the world: 19

Stock of narrow money: $43.56 billion (31 December 2017 est.)
$34.51 billion (31 December 2016 est.)
country comparison to the world: 57

Stock of broad money: $196.6 billion (31 December 2017 est.)
$146.6 billion (31 December 2016 est.)

country comparison to the world: 42

Stock of domestic credit: $194.1 billion (31 December 2017 est.)
$178.7 billion (31 December 2016 est.)
country comparison to the world: 48

Market value of publicly traded shares: $55.19 billion (31 December 2015 est.)
$70.08 billion (31 December 2014 est.)
$61.63 billion (31 December 2013 est.)
country comparison to the world: 49

Current account balance: -$19.83 billion (2017 est.)
-$19.83 billion (2016 est.)
country comparison to the world: 191

Exports: $23.53 billion (2017 est.)
$20.02 billion (2016 est.)
country comparison to the world: 68

Exports—commodities: crude oil and petroleum products, fruits and vegetables, cotton, textiles, metal products, chemicals, processed food

Exports—partners: UAE 12.5%, Saudi Arabia 7.7%, Italy 6.5%, Turkey 6.3%, UK 4.6%, US 4.5% (2016)

Imports: $53.02 billion (2017 est.)
$56.71 billion (2016 est.)
country comparison to the world: 48

Imports—commodities: machinery and equipment, foodstuffs, chemicals, wood products, fuels

Imports—partners: China 12.9%, Germany 8.7%, US 5.3%, Italy 4.5%, Turkey 4.3%, Saudi Arabia 4.1% (2016)

Reserves of foreign exchange and gold: $34.02 billion (31 December 2017 est.)
$23.2 billion (31 December 2016 est.)
country comparison to the world: 47

Debt—external: $76.31 billion (31 December 2017 est.)
$62.38 billion (31 December 2016 est.)
country comparison to the world: 57

Stock of direct foreign investment—at home: $103.6 billion (31 December 2017 est.)
$97.14 billion (31 December 2016 est.)
country comparison to the world: 46

Stock of direct foreign investment—abroad: $7.547 billion (31 December 2017 est.)
$7.257 billion (31 December 2016 est.)
country comparison to the world: 67

Exchange rates: Egyptian pounds (EGP) per US dollar—
18.05 (2017 est.)
10.07 (2016 est.)
10.07 (2015 est.)
7.7133 (2014 est.)
7.08 (2013 est.)

ENERGY

Electricity access: *population without electricity:* 300,000
electrification—total population: 99.6%
electrification—urban areas: 100%
electrification—rural areas: 99.3% (2013)

Electricity—production: 171.9 billion kWh (2015 est.)
country comparison to the world: 23

Electricity—consumption: 150.4 billion kWh (2015 est.)
country comparison to the world: 24

Electricity—exports: 1.158 billion kWh (2015 est.)
country comparison to the world: 57

Electricity—imports: 43 million kWh (2015 est.)
country comparison to the world: 106

Electricity—installed generating capacity: 38.88 million kW (2015 est.)
country comparison to the world: 27

Electricity—from fossil fuels: 90.5% of total installed capacity (2015 est.)
country comparison to the world: 61

Electricity—from nuclear fuels: 0% of total installed capacity (2015 est.)
country comparison to the world: 82

Electricity—from hydroelectric plants: 7.3% of total installed capacity (2015 est.)
country comparison to the world: 125

Electricity—from other renewable sources: 2.2% of total installed capacity (2015 est.)
country comparison to the world: 117

Crude oil—production: 494,300 bbl/day (2016 est.)
country comparison to the world: 29

Crude oil—exports: 197,700 bbl/day (2014 est.)
country comparison to the world: 31

Crude oil—imports: 60,940 bbl/day (2014 est.)
country comparison to the world: 51

Crude oil—proved reserves: 4.4 billion bbl (1 January 2017 es)
country comparison to the world: 27

Refined petroleum products—production: 471,800 bbl/day (2014 est.)
country comparison to the world: 35

Refined petroleum products—consumption: 802,000 bbl/day (2015 est.)
country comparison to the world: 28

Refined petroleum products—exports: 39,220 bbl/day (2014 est.)
country comparison to the world: 57

Refined petroleum products—imports: 206,100 bbl/day (2014 est.)
country comparison to the world: 31

Natural gas—production: 3.61 billion cu m (2015 est.)
country comparison to the world: 55

Natural gas—consumption: 77.93 billion cu m (2015 est.)
country comparison to the world: 16

Natural gas—exports: 720 million cu m (2014 est.)
country comparison to the world: 40

Natural gas—imports: 2.832 billion cu m (2013 est.)
country comparison to the world: 46

Natural gas—proved reserves: 2.186 trillion cu m (1 January 2017 es)
country comparison to the world: 16

Carbon dioxide emissions from consumption of energy: 207 million Mt (2013 est.)
country comparison to the world: 28

COMMUNICATIONS

Telephones—fixed lines: *total subscriptions:* 6,118,250
subscriptions per 100 inhabitants: 6 (July 2016 est.)
country comparison to the world: 26

Telephones—mobile cellular: *total:* 97,791,441
subscriptions per 100 inhabitants: 103 (July 2016 est.)
country comparison to the world: 17

Telephone system: *general assessment:* Telecom Egypt remains largely state owned; principal centers at Alexandria, Cairo, Al Mansurah, Ismailia, Suez, and Tanta are connected by coaxial cable and microwave radio relay
domestic: largest fixed-line system in Africa and the Arab region; multiple mobile-cellular networks with a 100-percent penetration of the market
international: country code—20; landing point for Aletar, the SEA-ME-WE-3 and SEA-ME-WE-4 submarine cable networks, Link Around the Globe (FLAG) Falcon and FLAG FEA; satellite earth stations—4 (2 Intelsat—Atlantic Ocean and Indian Ocean, 1 Arabsat, and 1 Inmarsat); tropospheric scatter to Sudan; microwave radio relay to Israel; a participant in Medarabtel (2016)

Broadcast media: mix of state-run and private broadcast media; state-run TV operates 2 national and 6 regional terrestrial networks, as well as a few satellite channels; about 20 private satellite channels and a large number of Arabic satellite channels are available via subscription; state-run radio operates about 70 stations belonging to 8 networks; 2 privately owned radio stations operational (2008)

Internet country code: .eg
Internet users: total: 37,122,537

percent of population: 39.2% (July 2016 est.)
country comparison to the world: 15

TRANSPORTATION

National air transport system: *number of registered air carriers:* 14
inventory of registered aircraft operated by air carriers: 101
annual passenger traffic on registered air carriers: 10,159,464
annual freight traffic on registered air carriers: 397,531,535 mt-km (2015)
Civil aircraft registration country code prefix: SU (2016)

Airports: 83 (2013)
country comparison to the world: 66

Airports—with paved runways: *total:* 72
over 3,047 m: 15
2,438 to 3,047 m: 36

1,524 to 2,437 m: 15
under 914 m: 6 (2017)

Airports—with unpaved runways: *total:* 11
2,438 to 3,047 m: 1
1,524 to 2,437 m: 3
914 to 1,523 m: 4
under 914 m: 3 (2013)

Heliports: 7 (2013)

Pipelines: condensate 486 km; condensate/gas 74 km; gas 7,986 km; liquid petroleum gas 957 km; oil 5,225 km; oil/gas/water 37 km; refined products 895 km; water 65 km (2013)

Railways: *total:* 5,085 km
standard gauge: 5,085 km 1.435-m gauge (62 km electrified) (2014)
country comparison to the world: 37

Roadways: *total:* 137,430 km
paved: 126,742 km (includes 838 km of expressways)
unpaved: 10,688 km (2010)
country comparison to the world: 38

Waterways: 3,500 km (includes the Nile River, Lake Nasser, Alexandria-Cairo Waterway, and numerous smaller canals in Nile Delta; the Suez Canal (193.5 km including approaches) is navigable by oceangoing vessels drawing up to 17.68 m) (2011)
country comparison to the world: 29

Merchant marine: *total:* 399
by type: bulk carrier 14, container ship 8, general cargo 33, oil tanker 36, other 308 (2017)
country comparison to the world: 46

Ports and terminals: *major seaport(s):* Mediterranean Sea—Alexandria, Damietta, El Dekheila, Port Said; Gulf of Suez—Suez
oil terminal(s): Ain Sukhna terminal, Sidi Kerir terminal
container port(s) (TEUs): Alexandria (1,662,000), Port Said (East) (3,036,000) (2015)
LNG terminal(s) (export): Damietta, Idku (Abu Qir Bay)

MILITARY AND SECURITY

Military expenditures: 1.67% of GDP (2016)
1.72% of GDP (2015)
1.69% of GDP (2014)
1.61% of GDP (2013)
1.65% of GDP (2012)
country comparison to the world: 53

Military branches: Army, Navy, Air Force, Air Defense Forces (2015)

Military service age and obligation: 18-30 years of age for male conscript military service; service obligation—18-36 months, followed by a 9-year reserve obligation; voluntary enlistment possible from age 15 (2017)

TERRORISM

Terrorist groups—home based: *Gama'a al-Islamiyya (Islamic Group) (IG):* *aim(s):* replace the Egyptian Government with an Islamist state
area(s) of operation: headquartered in Egypt and has largely honored the 1999 ceasefire agreement

with the Egyptian Government by moving away from violence to meet its goal in favor of political and other non-violent means; on 20 June 2011, IG announced its political wing, Al-Banna' wa Al-Tanmiyya (The Construction and Development Party); Doha, Qatar-based Dr. Tariq al-ZUMUR, a fugitive in Egypt has chaired the party since he was elected in 2013 was reelected in May 2017; IG's political party secured 13 seats in Egypt's 2011 parliamentary elections; however, it did not win any seats in the 2015 parliamentary elections; during IG's violent era, on 17 November 1997, six gunmen fired on a group of foreign tourists visiting a temple in Luxor in southern Egypt, killing 65 tourists, who were mostly Swiss and Japanese, a local guide, and two policemen; the ambush coincided with a trial in Cairo accusing 65 alleged members of conspiracy to murder and resulted in the citizenry rallying in strong support behind the Egyptian Government's counterterrorism efforts; remains one of the deadliest terrorist attacks on Egyptian soil; IG remains outlawed in Egypt; founder and spiritual leader Shaykh Dr. Omar Abd al-RAHMAN (a.k.a. the blind Sheikh) was serving a life sentence in a US prison for his involvement in the 1993 World Trade Center bombing and other attacks, until his death on 18 February 2017

ISIL Sinai Province (formerly Ansar Bayt al-Maqdis): *aim(s):* establish an Islamic emirate in the Sinai
area(s) of operation: Ansar Bayt al-Maqdis joined ISIL in 2014; headquartered in the northeastern Sinai Peninsula under Abu Hajir al-HASHIMI; operational throughout Egypt, primarily in North Sinai, where operatives have killed hundreds of Egyptian policemen and soldiers; conducts attacks in Cairo, where operatives killed 28 people in a church in December 2016; continues to launch rockets from Egypt into southern Israeli's Eshkol region and to approach city of Eilat; on several occasions has sabotaged a Sinai pipeline that exports gas to Israel; core ISIL refers to Egypt as its Wilayat Sinai

Terrorist groups—foreign based: *al-Qa'ida (AQ):* *aim(s):* overthrow the Egyptian Government and, ultimately, establish a pan-Islamic caliphate under a strict Salafi Muslim interpretation of Sharia
area(s) of operation: maintains a longtime operational presence and established networks

Army of Islam (AOI): *aim(s):* disrupt the Egyptian Government's efforts to provide security and, ultimately, establish an Islamic caliphate
area(s) of operation: operational mainly in Cairo and the Sinai Peninsula; conducted bombing attacks in Cairo and Heliopolis in 2009 against Egyptian citizens, which resulted in casualities and deaths; associated with ISIL Sinai Province (formerly Ansar Bayt al-Maqdis); targets Israeli Government interests, sometimes in collaboration with the Mujahidin Shura Council in the Environs of Jerusalem, including launching rockets into southern Israel; rocket attacks launched from the Gaza Strip into Egyptian territory have ebbed in recent years

HAMAS: *aim(s):* bolster its relationship with the Egyptian Government to facilitate free movement in Egyptian territory
area(s) of operation: maintains a growing political presence, collaborating with the Egyptian Government to secure the border against ISIL fighters, who have killed hundreds of Egyptian policemen and soldiers in northern Sinai; in return, HAMAS is granted freer movement to take trucks of food and other goods into the Gaza Strip; has a history of using a few thousand tunnels at the Egypt-Gaza Strip border to smuggle weapons, fighters, and consumer goods into the Gaza Strip

Mujahidin Shura Council in the Environs of Jerusalem (MSC): *aim(s):* enhance its networks in Egypt and, ultimately, destroy the state of Israel
area(s) of operation: maintains a limited operational presence as of 2017; majority of veteran members have defected to join other groups; previously, operatives staged numerous attacks inside Israeli territory along the Egypt-Israel border, especially coordinated attacks with the Army of Islam, another US-designated foreign terrorist organization

TRANSNATIONAL ISSUES

Disputes—international: Sudan claims but Egypt de facto administers security and economic development of Halaib region north of the 22nd parallel boundary; Egypt no longer shows its administration of the Bir Tawil trapezoid in Sudan on its maps; Gazan breaches in the security wall with Egypt in January 2008 highlight difficulties in monitoring the Sinai border; Saudi Arabia claims Egyptian-administered islands of Tiran and Sanafir

Refugees and internally displaced persons:
refugees (country of origin): 70,027 (West Bank and Gaza Strip) (2016); 126,291 (Syria); 35,227 (Sudan) (refugees and asylum seekers); 14,009 (Erthiopia) (refugees and asylum seekers); 10,795 (Eritrea) (refugees and asylum seekers); 8,578 (South Sudan) (refugees and asylum seekers); 6,611 (Iraq) (refugees and asylum seekers); 6,561 (Somalia) (refugees and asylum seekers) (2017)
IDPs: 78,000 (2016)
stateless persons: 19 (2016)

Trafficking in persons: *current situation:* Egypt is a source, transit, and destination country for men, women, and children subjected to sex trafficking and forced labor; Egyptian children, including the large population of street children are vulnerable to forced labor in domestic service, begging and agriculture or may be victims of sex trafficking or child sex tourism, which occurs in Cairo, Alexandria, and Luxor; some Egyptian women and girls are sold into "temporary" or "summer" marriages with Gulf men, through the complicity of their parents or marriage brokers, and are exploited for prostitution or forced labor; Egyptian men are subject to forced labor in neighboring countries, while adults from South and Southeast Asia and East Africa—and increasingly Syrian refugees—are forced to work in domestic service, construction, cleaning, and begging in Egypt; women and girls, including migrants and refugees, from Asia, sub-Saharan Africa, and the Middle East are sex trafficked in Egypt; the Egyptian military cracked down on criminal group's smuggling, abducting, trafficking, and extorting African migrants in the Sinai Peninsula, but the practice has reemerged along Egypt's western border with Libya

tier rating: Tier 2 Watch List—Egypt does not fully comply with the minimum standards for the elimination of trafficking; however, it is making significant efforts to do so; the government gathered data nationwide on trafficking cases to better allocate and prioritize anti-trafficking efforts, but overall it did not demonstrate increased progress; prosecutions increased in 2014, but no offenders were convicted for the second consecutive year; fewer trafficking victims were identified in 2014, which represents a significant and ongoing decrease from the previous two reporting periods; the government relied on NGOs and international organizations to identify and refer victims to protective services, and focused on Egyptian victims and refused to provide some services to foreign victims, at times including shelter (2015)

Illicit drugs: transit point for cannabis, heroin, and opium moving to Europe, Israel, and North Africa; transit stop for Nigerian drug couriers; concern as money laundering site due to lax enforcement of financial regulations

EL SALVADOR

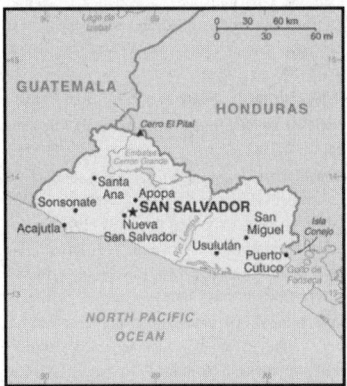

INTRODUCTION

Background: El Salvador achieved independence from Spain in 1821 and from the Central American Federation in 1839. A 12-year civil war, which cost about 75,000 lives, was brought to a close in 1992 when the government and leftist rebels signed a treaty that provided for military and political reforms. El Salvador is beset by one of the world's highest homicide rates and pervasive criminal gangs.

GEOGRAPHY

Location: Central America, bordering the North Pacific Ocean, between Guatemala and Honduras

Geographic coordinates: 13 50 N, 88 55 W

Map references: Central America and the Caribbean

Area: *total:* 21,041 sq km
land: 20,721 sq km
water: 320 sq km
country comparison to the world: 153

Area—comparative: about the same size as New Jersey

Land boundaries: *total:* 590 km
border countries (2): Guatemala 199 km, Honduras 391 km

Coastline: 307 km

Maritime claims: *territorial sea:* 12 nm
contiguous zone: 24 nm

exclusive economic zone: 200 nm

Climate: tropical; rainy season (May to October); dry season (November to April); tropical on coast; temperate in uplands

Terrain: mostly mountains with narrow coastal belt and central plateau

Elevation: *mean elevation:* 442 m

elevation extremes: *lowest point:* Pacific Ocean 0 m
highest point: Cerro El Pital 2,730 m

Natural resources: hydropower, geothermal power, petroleum, arable land

Land use: *agricultural land:* 74.7%
arable land: 33.1%;
permanent crops: 10.9%;
permanent pasture: 30.7%;
forest: 13.6%
other: 11.7% (2011 est.)

Irrigated land: 452 sq km (2012)

Natural hazards: known as the Land of Volcanoes; frequent and sometimes destructive earthquakes and volcanic activity; extremely susceptible to hurricanes

volcanism: significant volcanic activity; San Salvador (1,893 m), which last erupted in 1917, has the potential to cause major harm to the country's capital, which lies just below the volcano's slopes; San Miguel (2,130 m), which last erupted in 2002, is one of the most active volcanoes in the country; other historically active volcanoes include Conchagua, Ilopango, Izalco, and Santa Ana

Environment—current issues: deforestation; soil erosion; water pollution; contamination of soils from disposal of toxic wastes

Environment—international agreements: *party to:* Biodiversity, Climate Change, Climate Change-Kyoto Protocol, Desertification, Endangered Species, Hazardous Wastes, Ozone Layer Protection, Wetlands
signed, but not ratified: Law of the Sea

Geography—note: smallest Central American country and only one without a coastline on the Caribbean Sea

PEOPLE AND SOCIETY

Population: 6,172,011 (July 2017 est.)
country comparison to the world: 108

Nationality: *noun:* Salvadoran(s)
adjective: Salvadoran

Ethnic groups: mestizo 86.3%, white 12.7%, Amerindian 0.2% (includes Lenca, Kakawira, Nahua-Pipil), black 0.1%, other 0.6% (2007 est.)

Languages: Spanish (official), Nawat (among some Amerindians)

Religions: Roman Catholic 50%, Protestant 36%, other 2%, none 12% (2014 est.)

Demographic profile: El Salvador is the smallest and most densely populated country in Central America. It is well into its demographic transition, experiencing slower population growth, a decline in its number of youths, and the gradual aging of its population. The increased use of family planning has substantially lowered El Salvador's fertility rate, from approximately 6 children per woman in the 1970s to replacement level today. A 2008 national family planning survey showed that female sterilization remained the most common contraception method in El Salvador—its sterilization rate is among the highest in Latin America and the Caribbean—but that the use of injectable contraceptives is growing. Fertility differences between rich and poor and urban and rural women are narrowing.

Salvadorans fled during the 1979 to 1992 civil war mainly to the United States but also to Canada and to neighboring Mexico, Guatemala, Honduras, Nicaragua, and Costa Rica. Emigration to the United States increased again in the 1990s and 2000s as a result of deteriorating economic conditions, natural disasters (Hurricane Mitch in 1998 and earthquakes in 2001), and family reunification. At least 20% of El Salvador's population lives abroad. The remittances they send home account for close to 20% of GDP, are the second largest source of external income after exports, and have helped reduce poverty.

Age structure: *0-14 years:* 25.92% (male 820,255/female 779,306)
15-24 years: 20.23% (male 628,535/female 620,230)
25-54 years: 39.23% (male 1,120,705/female 1,300,771)
55-64 years: 7.14% (male 194,360/female 246,164)
65 years and over: 7.48% (male 203,320/female 258,365) (2017 est.)

Dependency ratios: *total dependency ratio:* 56.8
youth dependency ratio: 44.4
elderly dependency ratio: 12.4
potential support ratio: 8 (2015 est.)

Median age: *total:* 27.1 years
male: 25.6 years
female: 28.6 years (2017 est.)
country comparison to the world: 146

Population growth rate: 0.25% (2017 est.)
country comparison to the world: 178

Birth rate: 16.2 births/1,000 population (2017 est.)
country comparison to the world: 112

Death rate: 5.8 deaths/1,000 population (2017 est.)
country comparison to the world: 173

Net migration rate: -8 migrant(s)/1,000 population (2017 est.)
country comparison to the world: 205

Population distribution: athough it is the smallest country in land area in Central America, El Salvador has a population that is 18 times larger than Belize; at least 20% of the population lives abroad; high population density country-wide, with particular concentration around the capital of San Salvador

Urbanization: *urban population:* 67.6% of total population (2017)
rate of urbanization: 1.23% annual rate of change (2015-20 est.)

Major urban areas—population: SAN SALVADOR (capital) 1.098 million (2015)

Sex ratio: *at birth:* 1.05 male(s)/female
0-14 years: 1.05 male(s)/female
15-24 years: 1.01 male(s)/female
25-54 years: 0.86 male(s)/female
55-64 years: 0.8 male(s)/female
65 years and over: 0.8 male(s)/female
total population: 0.93 male(s)/female (2016 est.)

Mother's mean age at first birth: 20.8 years
note: median age at first birth among women 25-29 (2008 est.)

Maternal mortality ratio: 54 deaths/100,000 live births (2015 est.)
country comparison to the world: 92

Infant mortality rate: *total:* 16.8 deaths/1,000 live births
male: 18.8 deaths/1,000 live births
female: 14.6 deaths/1,000 live births (2017 est.)
country comparison to the world: 96

Life expectancy at birth: *total population:* 74.9 years
male: 71.6 years
female: 78.3 years (2017 est.)
country comparison to the world: 115

Total fertility rate: 1.87 children born/woman (2017 est.)
country comparison to the world: 144

Contraceptive prevalence rate: 72% (2014)
Health expenditures: 6.8% of GDP (2014)
country comparison to the world: 86

Physicians density: 1.92 physicians/1,000 population (2008)

Hospital bed density: 1.1 beds/1,000 population (2012)

Drinking water source:
improved:
urban: 97.5% of population
rural: 86.5% of population
total: 93.8% of population
unimproved:
urban: 2.5% of population
rural: 13.5% of population
total: 6.2% of population (2015 est.)

Sanitation facility access:
improved:
urban: 82.4% of population
rural: 60% of population
total: 75% of population
unimproved:
urban: 17.6% of population
rural: 40% of population
total: 25% of population (2015 est.)

HIV/AIDS—adult prevalence rate: 0.6% (2016 est.)
country comparison to the world: 58

HIV/AIDS—people living with HIV/AIDS: 24,000 (2016 est.)
country comparison to the world: 71

HIV/AIDS—deaths: <1000 (2016 est.)

Major infectious diseases: *degree of risk:* high
food or waterborne diseases: bacterial and protozoal diarrhea
vectorborne diseases: dengue fever
note: active local transmission of Zika virus by Aedes species mosquitoes has been identified in this country (as of August 2016); it poses an important risk (a large number of cases possible) among US citizens if bitten by an infective mosquito; other less common ways to get Zika are through sex, via blood transfusion, or during pregnancy, in which the pregnant woman passes Zika virus to her fetus (2016)

Obesity—adult prevalence rate: 24.6% (2016)
country comparison to the world: 57

Children under the age of 5 years underweight: 5% (2014)
country comparison to the world: 78
Education expenditures: 3.4% of GDP (2014)
country comparison to the world: 129

Literacy: *definition:* age 15 and over can read and write
total population: 88%
male: 90%
female: 86.2% (2015 est.)

School life expectancy (primary to tertiary education): *total:* 13 years
male: 13 years
female: 13 years (2014)

Unemployment, youth ages 15-24: *total:* 12.4%
male: 11.8%
female: 13.6% (2013 est.)
country comparison to the world: 89

GOVERNMENT

Country name: *conventional long form:* Republic of El Salvador
conventional short form: El Salvador
local long form: Republica de El Salvador

local short form: El Salvador
etymology: name is an abbreviation of the original Spanish conquistador designation for the area "Provincia de Nuestro Senor Jesus Cristo, el Salvador del Mundo" (Province of Our Lord Jesus Christ, the Saviour of the World), which became simply "El Salvador" (The Savior)

Government type: presidential republic

Capital: *name:* San Salvador
geographic coordinates: 13 42 N, 89 12 W
time difference: UTC-6 (1 hour behind Washington, DC, during Standard Time)

Administrative divisions: 14 departments (departamentos, singular—departamento); Ahuachapan, Cabanas, Chalatenango, Cuscatlan, La Libertad, La Paz, La Union, Morazan, San Miguel, San Salvador, San Vicente, Santa Ana, Sonsonate, Usulutan

Independence: 15 September 1821 (from Spain)

National holiday: Independence Day, 15 September (1821)

Constitution: many previous; latest drafted 16 December 1983, enacted 23 December 1983; amended many times, last in 2014 (2016)

Legal system: civil law system with minor common law influence; judicial review of legislative acts in the Supreme Court

International law organization participation: has not submitted an ICJ jurisdiction declaration; non-party state to the ICCt

Citizenship: *citizenship by birth:* yes
citizenship by descent: yes
dual citizenship recognized: yes
residency requirement for naturalization: 5 years

Suffrage: 18 years of age; universal

Executive branch: *chief of state:* President Salvador SANCHEZ CEREN (since 1 June 2014); Vice President Salvador Oscar ORTIZ (since 1 June 2014); note—the president is both chief of state and head of government

head of government: President Salvador SANCHEZ CEREN (since 1 June 2014); Vice President Salvador Oscar ORTIZ (since 1 June 2014)
cabinet: Council of Ministers selected by the president
elections/appointments: president and vice president directly elected on the same ballot by absolute majority popular vote in 2 rounds if needed for a single 5-year term; election last held on 2 February 2014 with a runoff on 9 March 2014 (next to be held in early 2019)
election results: Salvador SANCHEZ CEREN elected president in second round; percent of vote in first round—Salvador SANCHEZ CEREN (FMLN) 48.9%, Norman QUIJANO (ARENA) 39%, Antonio SACA (CN) 11.4%, other 0.7%; percent of vote in second round—Salvador SANCHEZ CEREN 50.1%, Norman QUIJANO 49.9%

Legislative branch: description: unicameral Legislative Assembly or Asamblea Legislativa (84 seats;

members directly elected in multi-seat constituencies and a single nationwide constituency by proportional representation vote to serve 3-year terms)

elections: last held on 1 March 2015 (next to be held in March 2018)

election results: percent of vote by party—ARENA 38.8%, FMLN 37.3%, GANA 9.3%, PCN 6.8%, PDC 2.5%, other 5.2%; seats by party—ARENA 32, FMLN 31, GANA 11, PCN 4, ARENA-PCN 3, PCN-DS 1, PCN-PDC 1, PDC 1

Judicial branch: *highest court(s):* Supreme Court or Corte Suprema de Justicia (consists of 15 judges assigned to constitutional, civil, penal, and administrative conflict divisions)

judge selection and term of office: judges elected by the Legislative Assembly on the recommendation of both the National Council of the Judicature, an independent body elected by the Legislative Assembly and the Bar Association; judges elected for 9-year terms, with renewal of one-third of membership every 3 years; consecutive reelection is allowed

subordinate courts: Appellate Courts; Courts of First Instance; Courts of Peace

Political parties and leaders: Christian Democratic Party or PDC [Rodolfo Antonio PARKER Soto]

Democratic Change (Cambio Democratico) or CD [Douglas AVILES] (formerly United Democratic Center or CDU)

Farabundo Marti National Liberation Front or FMLN [Medardo GONZALEZ]

Great Alliance for National Unity or GANA [Jose Andres ROVIRA Caneles]

National Coalition Party or PCN [Manuel RODRIGUEZ]

Nationalist Republican Alliance or ARENA [Mauricio INTERIANO]

Political pressure groups and leaders: labor organizations: Electrical Industry Union of El Salvador or SIES

Federation of the Construction Industry, Similar Transport, and other activities or FESINCONTRANS

National Confederation of Salvadoran Workers or CNTS

National Trade Union Federation of Salvadoran Workers or FENASTRAS

National Union of Salvadoran Workers or UNTS

Port Industry Union of El Salvador or SIPES

Salvadoran Workers Central or CTS

Union of Judiciary Workers or SITTOJ

Union of Workers of the Ministry of the Treasury or SITRAMI

Workers Union of Electrical Corporation or STCEL

business organizations: American Chamber of Commerce in El Salvador

National Association of Private Enterprise or ANEP

Salvadoran Chamber of Commerce or SACOC

Salvadoran Chamber of the Construction Industry or CASALCO

Salvadoran Industrial Association or ASI

International organization participation: BCIE, CACM, CD, CELAC, FAO, G-11, G-77, IADB, IAEA, IBRD, ICAO, ICC (national committees), ICRM, IDA, IFAD, IFC, IFRCS, ILO, IMF, IMO, Interpol, IOC, IOM, IPU, ISO (correspondent), ITSO, ITU, ITUC (NGOs), LAES, LAIA (observer), MIGA, MINURSO, MINUSTAH, NAM (observer), OAS, OPANAL, OPCW, Pacific Alliance (observer), PCA, Petrocaribe, SICA, UN, UNCTAD, UNESCO, UNIDO, UNIFIL, Union Latina, UNISFA, UNMISS, UNOCI, UNWTO, UPU, WCO, WFTU (NGOs), WHO, WIPO, WMO, WTO

Diplomatic representation in the US: *chief of mission:* Ambassador Claudia Ivette CANJURA de Centeno (since 17 June 2016)

chancery: 1400 16th Street NW, Suite 100, Washington, DC 20036

telephone: [1] (202) 595-7517

FAX: [1] (202) 232-1928

consulate(s) general: Atlanta, Boston, Brentwood (NY), Chicago, Coral Gables (FL), Dallas, Houston, Las Vegas (NV), Los Angeles, McAllen (TX), New York, Nogales (AZ), San Francisco, Seattle, Tucson (AZ), Washington, DC, Woodbridge (VA), Woodstock (GA)

consulate(s): Elizabeth (NJ), Newark (NJ)

Diplomatic representation from the US: *chief of mission:* Ambassador Jean Elizabeth MANES (since 29 March 2016)

embassy: Final Boulevard Santa Elena Sur, Antiguo Cuscatlan, La Libertad, San Salvador

mailing address: Unit 3450, APO AA 34023; 3450 San Salvador Place, Washington, DC 20521-3450

telephone: [503] 2501-2999

FAX: [503] 2501-2150

Flag description: three equal horizontal bands of cobalt blue (top), white, and cobalt blue with the national coat of arms centered in the white band; the coat of arms features a round emblem encircled by the words REPUBLICA DE EL SALVADOR EN LA AMERICA CENTRAL; the banner is based on the former blue-white-blue flag of the Federal Republic of Central America; the blue bands symbolize the Pacific Ocean and the Caribbean Sea, while the white band represents the land between the two bodies of water, as well as peace and prosperity

note: similar to the flag of Nicaragua, which has a different coat of arms centered in the white band; also similar to the flag of Honduras, which has five blue stars arranged in an X pattern centered in the white band

National symbol(s): turquoise-browed motmot (bird); national colors: blue, white

National anthem: name: "Himno Nacional de El Salvador" (National Anthem of El Salvador)

lyrics/music: Juan Jose CANAS/Juan ABERLE

note: officially adopted 1953, in use since 1879; at 4:20 minutes the anthem of El Salvador is one of the world's longest

ECONOMY

Economy—overview: The smallest country in Central America geographically, El Salvador has the fourth largest economy in the region. With the global recession, real GDP contracted in 2009 and economic growth has since remained low, averaging less than 2% from 2010 to 2014, but recovered somewhat in 2015-17 with an average annual growth rate of 2.4%. Remittances accounted for approximately 17.1% of GDP in 2016 and were received by about a third of all households.

In 2006, El Salvador was the first country to ratify the Dominican Republic-Central American Free Trade Agreement, which has bolstered the export of processed foods, sugar, and ethanol, and supported investment in the apparel sector amid increased Asian competition. In September 2015, El Salvador kicked off a five-year $277 million second compact with the Millennium Challenge Corporation—a US Government agency aimed at stimulating economic growth and reducing poverty—to improve El Salvador's competitiveness and productivity in international markets.

The Salvadoran Government maintained fiscal discipline during post-war reconstruction and rebuilding following earthquakes in 2001 and hurricanes in 1998 and 2005, but El Salvador's public debt, estimated at 68.1% of GDP in 2017, has been growing over the last several years. Total external debt was about 60% of GDP in 2017.

GDP (purchasing power parity): $56.9 billion (2017 est.)

$55.62 billion (2016 est.)

$54.34 billion (2015 est.)

note: data are in 2017 dollars

country comparison to the world: 108

GDP (official exchange rate): $27.41 billion (2016 est.)

GDP—real growth rate: 2.3% (2017 est.)

2.4% (2016 est.)

2.3% (2015 est.)

country comparison to the world: 141

GDP—per capita (PPP): $8,900 (2017 est.)

$8,800 (2016 est.)

$8,600 (2015 est.)

note: data are in 2017 dollars

country comparison to the world: 145

Gross national saving: 13% of GDP (2017 est.)

11.7% of GDP (2016 est.)

10.3% of GDP (2015 est.)

country comparison to the world: 138

GDP—composition, by end use:

household consumption: 88.5%

government consumption: 12.1%

investment in fixed capital: 13.7%

investment in inventories: 0%

exports of goods and services: 25.1%

imports of goods and services: -39.4% (2017 est.)

GDP—composition, by sector of origin:

agriculture: 10.6%

industry: 24.6%

services: 64.9% (2017 est.)

Agriculture—products: coffee, sugar, corn, rice, beans, oilseed, cotton, sorghum; beef, dairy products

Industries: food processing, beverages, petroleum, chemicals, fertilizer, textiles, furniture, light metals

Industrial production growth rate: 2% (2017 est.)
country comparison to the world: 140

Labor force: 2.774 million (2017 est.)
country comparison to the world: 109

Labor force—by occupation: *agriculture:* 21%
industry: 20%
services: 58% (2011 est.)

Unemployment rate: 7% (2017 est.)
7% (2016 est.)
note: data are official rates; but underemployment is high
country comparison to the world: 101

Population below poverty line: 34.9% (2015 est.)

Household income or consumption by percentage share: *lowest 10%:* 2.2%
highest 10%: 32.3% (2014 est.)

Distribution of family income—Gini index: 37 (2015 est.)
38 (2014)
country comparison to the world: 79

Budget: *revenues:* $5.756 billion
expenditures: $6.751 billion (2017 est.)
Taxes and other revenues: 21% of GDP (2017 est.)
country comparison to the world: 142

Budget surplus (+) or deficit (-): -3.6% of GDP (2017 est.)
country comparison to the world: 136

Public debt: 68.1% of GDP (2017 est.)
65.5% of GDP (2016 est.)
note: El Salvador's total public debt includes non-financial public sector debt, financial public sector debt, and central bank debt
country comparison to the world: 53

Fiscal year: calendar year

Inflation rate (consumer prices): 0.8% (2017 est.)
0.6% (2016 est.)
country comparison to the world: 28

Commercial bank prime lending rate: 6.6% (31 December 2017 est.)
6.37% (31 December 2016 est.)
country comparison to the world: 122

Stock of narrow money: $3.311 billion (31 December 2017 est.)
$3.129 billion (31 December 2016 est.)
country comparison to the world: 116

Stock of broad money: $12.55 billion (31 December 2017 est.)
$11.97 billion (31 December 2016 est.)
country comparison to the world: 102

Stock of domestic credit: $15.02 billion (31 December 2017 est.)
$13.71 billion (31 December 2016 est.)
country comparison to the world: 97

Market value of publicly traded shares: $4.4 billion (December 2016 est.)
$3.816 billion (December 2015 est.)
$3.535 billion (December 2014 est.)

country comparison to the world: 91

Current account balance: -$266 million (2017 est.)
-$531 million (2016 est.)
country comparison to the world: 94

Exports: $4.25 billion (2017 est.)
$4.186 billion (2016 est.)
country comparison to the world: 115

Exports—commodities: offshore assembly exports, coffee, sugar, textiles and apparel, ethanol, chemicals, electricity, iron and steel manufactures

Exports—partners: US 48.3%, Honduras 14.2%, Guatemala 13.5%, Nicaragua 6.5%, Costa Rica 4.7% (2016)

Imports: $9.503 billion (2017 est.)
$8.823 billion (2016 est.)
country comparison to the world: 98

Imports—commodities: raw materials, consumer goods, capital goods, fuels, foodstuffs, petroleum, electricity

Imports—partners: US 37.9%, Guatemala 10.2%, China 8.8%, Mexico 7.6%, Honduras 6.3% (2016)

Reserves of foreign exchange and gold: $3.067 billion (31 December 2017 est.)
$3.238 billion (31 December 2016 est.)
country comparison to the world: 106

Debt—external: $16.29 billion (31 December 2017 est.)
$15.2 billion (31 December 2016 est.)
country comparison to the world: 100

Stock of direct foreign investment—at home: $10.78 billion (31 December 2017 est.)
$10.31 billion (31 December 2016 est.)
country comparison to the world: 96

Stock of direct foreign investment—abroad: $961.4 million (31 December 2017 est.)
$1.111 billion (31 December 2016 est.)
country comparison to the world: 85

Exchange rates: *note:* the US dollar is used as a medium of exchange and circulates freely in the economy, 1 (2017 est.)

ENERGY

Electricity access: *population without electricity:* 400,000
electrification—*total population:* 94%
electrification—urban areas: 98%
electrification—rural areas: 86% (2013)

Electricity—production: 5.482 billion kWh (2016 est.)
country comparison to the world: 118

Electricity—consumption: 6.351 billion kWh (2016)
country comparison to the world: 113

Electricity—exports: 74.3 million kWh (2016 est.)
country comparison to the world: 82

Electricity—imports: 1.066 billion kWh (2016 est.)
country comparison to the world: 67

Electricity—installed generating capacity: 1.792 million kW (2016 est.)

country comparison to the world: 116

Electricity—from fossil fuels: 51.6% of total installed capacity (2015 est.)
country comparison to the world: 148

Electricity—from nuclear fuels: 0% of total installed capacity (2015 est.)
country comparison to the world: 87

Electricity—from hydroelectric plants: 25.6% of total installed capacity (2015 est.)
country comparison to the world: 78

Electricity—from other renewable sources: 25.7% of total installed capacity (2015 est.)
country comparison to the world: 20

Crude oil—production: 0 bbl/day (2016 est.)
country comparison to the world: 129

Crude oil—exports: 220 bbl/day (2014 est.)
country comparison to the world: 79

Crude oil—imports: 0 bbl/day (2014 est.)
country comparison to the world: 123

Crude oil—proved reserves: 0 bbl (1 January 2017 es)
country comparison to the world: 129

Refined petroleum products—production: 0 bbl/day (2014 est.)
country comparison to the world: 138

Refined petroleum products—consumption: 46,000 bbl/day (2015 est.)
country comparison to the world: 108

Refined petroleum products—exports: 224.8 bbl/day (2014 est.)
country comparison to the world: 120

Refined petroleum products—imports: 45,540 bbl/day (2014 est.)
country comparison to the world: 87

Natural gas—production: 0 cu m (2016 est.)
country comparison to the world: 132

Natural gas—consumption: 0 cu m (2016 est.)
country comparison to the world: 178

Natural gas—exports: 0 cu m (2016 est.)
country comparison to the world: 100

Natural gas—imports: 0 cu m (2016 est.)
country comparison to the world: 122

Natural gas—proved reserves: 0 cu m (1 January 2016 es)
country comparison to the world: 137

Carbon dioxide emissions from consumption of energy: 4.318 million Mt (2015 est.)
country comparison to the world: 129

COMMUNICATIONS

Telephones—fixed lines: *total subscriptions:* 933,377
subscriptions per 100 inhabitants: 15 (July 2016 est.)
country comparison to the world: 79

Telephones—mobile cellular: *total:* 9,101,868
subscriptions per 100 inhabitants: 148 (July 2016 est.)
country comparison to the world: 90

Telephone system: *general assessment:* multiple mobile-cellular began rolling out Long Term

Evolution (LTE) data services in late-2016; growth in fixed-line services has slowed in the face of mobile-cellular competition; Internet usage grew almost 400% between 2007 and 2015

domestic: nationwide microwave radio relay system

international: country code—503; satellite earth station—1 Intelsat (Atlantic Ocean); connected to Central American Microwave System (2017)

Broadcast media: multiple privately owned national terrestrial TV networks, supplemented by cable TV networks that carry international channels; hundreds of commercial radio broadcast stations and 1 government-owned radio broadcast station; transition to digital transmission to begin in 2018 along with adaptation of the Japanese-Brazilian Digital Standard (ISDB-T) (2017)

Internet country code: total: .sv
Internet users: total: 1,785,254

percent of population: 29.0% (July 2016 est.)
country comparison to the world: 102

TRANSPORTATION

National air transport system: *number of registered air carriers:* 2
inventory of registered aircraft operated by air carriers: 36
annual passenger traffic on registered air carriers: 2,597,649
annual freight traffic on registered air carriers: 13,873,884 mt-km (2015)
Civil aircraft registration country code prefix: YS (2016)

Airports: 68 (2013)
country comparison to the world: 74
Airports—with paved runways: *total:* 5
over 3,047 m: 1
1,524 to 2,437 m: 1
914 to 1,523 m: 2
under 914 m: 1 (2017)
Airports—with unpaved runways: *total:* 63
1,524 to 2,437 m: 1
914 to 1,523 m: 11
under 914 m: 51 (2013)
Heliports: 2 (2013)
Railways: *total:* 12.5 km
narrow gauge: 12.5 km 0.914-m gauge (2014)
country comparison to the world: 135
Roadways: *total:* 6,979 km
paved: 4,414 km (includes 341 km of expressways)
unpaved: 2,565 km (2016)
country comparison to the world: 147
Waterways: (Rio Lempa River is partially navigable by small craft) (2011)
Merchant marine: *total:* 2
by type: other 2 (2017)
country comparison to the world: 164
Ports and terminals: *major seaport(s):* Puerto Cutuco
oil terminal(s): Acajutla offshore terminal

MILITARY AND SECURITY

Military expenditures: 0.87% of GDP (2016)
0.95% of GDP (2015)
0.93% of GDP (2014)

0.98% of GDP (2013)
0.94% of GDP (2012)
country comparison to the world: 101

Military branches: Salvadoran Armed Forces (Fuerza Armada de El Salvador, FAES): Salvadoran Army (Ejercito de El Salvador, ES), Salvadoran Navy (Fuerza Naval de El Salvador, FNES), Salvadoran Air Force (Fuerza Aerea Salvadorena, FAS) (2017)

Military service age and obligation: 18 years of age for selective compulsory military service; 16-22 years of age for voluntary male or female service; service obligation is 12 months, with 11 months for officers and NCOs (2012)

TRANSNATIONAL ISSUES

Disputes—international: International Court of Justice (ICJ) ruled on the delimitation of "bolsones" (disputed areas) along the El Salvador-Honduras boundary, in 1992, with final agreement by the parties in 2006 after an Organization of American States survey and a further ICJ ruling in 2003; the 1992 ICJ ruling advised a tripartite resolution to a maritime boundary in the Gulf of Fonseca advocating Honduran access to the Pacific; El Salvador continues to claim tiny Conejo Island, not identified in the ICJ decision, off Honduras in the Gulf of Fonseca
Refugees and internally displaced persons: IDPs: 220,000 (2016)

Illicit drugs: transshipment point for cocaine; small amounts of marijuana produced for local consumption; significant use of cocaine

EQUATORIAL GUINEA

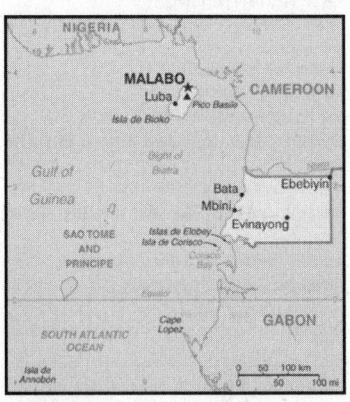

INTRODUCTION

Background: Equatorial Guinea gained independence in 1968 after 190 years of Spanish rule; it is one of the smallest countries in Africa consisting of a mainland territory and five inhabited islands. The capital of Malabo is located on the island of Bioko, approximately 25 km from the Cameroonian coastline in the Gulf of Guinea. Between 1968 and 1979, autocratic President Francisco MACIAS NGUEMA virtually destroyed all of the country's political, economic, and social institutions before being deposed by his nephew Teodoro OBIANG NGUEMA MBASOGO in a coup. President OBIANG has ruled since October 1979 and was reelected in 2016. Although nominally a constitutional democracy since 1991, presidential and legislative elections since 1996 have generally been labeled as flawed. The president exerts almost total control over the political system and has placed legal and bureaucratic barriers that prevent political opposition. Equatorial Guinea has experienced rapid economic growth due to the discovery of large offshore oil reserves, and in the last decade has become Sub-Saharan Africa's third largest oil exporter. Despite the country's economic windfall from oil production, resulting in a massive increase in government revenue in recent years, the drop in global oil prices has placed significant strain on the state budget. Equatorial Guinea continues to seek to diversify its economy and to increase foreign investment despite limited improvements in the population's living standards. Equatorial Guinea is the host of major regional and international conferences and continues to seek a greater role in regional affairs.

GEOGRAPHY

Location: Central Africa, bordering the Bight of Biafra, between Cameroon and Gabon

Geographic coordinates: 2 00 N, 10 00 E

Map references: Africa

Area: *total:* 28,051 sq km
land: 28,051 sq km
water: 0 sq km
country comparison to the world: 146

Area—comparative: slightly smaller than Maryland

Land boundaries: *total:* 528 km
border countries (2): Cameroon 183 km, Gabon 345 km

Coastline: 296 km

Maritime claims: *territorial sea:* 12 nm
exclusive economic zone: 200 nm

Climate: tropical; always hot, humid

Terrain: coastal plains rise to interior hills; islands are volcanic

Elevation: *mean elevation:* 577 m

elevation extremes: *lowest point:* Atlantic Ocean 0 m

highest point: Pico Basile 3,008 m

Natural resources: petroleum, natural gas, timber, gold, bauxite, diamonds, tantalum, sand and gravel, clay

Land use: *agricultural land:* 10.1%

arable land: 4.3%;

permanent crops: 2.1%;

permanent pasture: 3.7%

forest: 57.5%

other: 32.4% (2011 est.)

Irrigated land: NA

Population—distribution: only two large cities over 30,000 people (Bata on the mainland, and the capital Malabo on the island of Bioko); small communities are scattered throughout the mainland and the five inhabited islands

Natural hazards: violent windstorms; flash floods

volcanism: Santa Isabel (3,007 m), which last erupted in 1923, is the country's only historically active volcano; Santa Isabel, along with two dormant volcanoes, form Bioko Island in the Gulf of Guinea

Environment—current issues: tap water is nonpotable; deforestation

Environment—international agreements: *party to:* Biodiversity, Climate Change, Climate Change-Kyoto Protocol, Desertification, Endangered Species, Hazardous Wastes, Law of the Sea, Marine Dumping, Ozone Layer Protection, Ship Pollution, Wetlands

signed, but not ratified: none of the selected agreements

Geography—note: insular and continental regions widely separated

PEOPLE AND SOCIETY

Population: 778,358 (July 2017 est.)

country comparison to the world: 164

Nationality: *noun:* Equatorial Guinean(s) or Equatoguinean(s)

adjective: Equatorial Guinean or Equatoguinean

Ethnic groups: Fang 85.7%, Bubi 6.5%, Mdowe 3.6%, Annobon 1.6%, Bujeba 1.1%, other 1.4% (1994 census)

Languages: Spanish (official) 67.6%, other (includes French (official), Fang, Bubi) 32.4% (1994 census)

Religions: nominally Christian and predominantly Roman Catholic, pagan practices

Demographic profile: Equatorial Guinea is one of the smallest and least populated countries in continental Africa and is the only independent African country where Spanish is an official language. Despite a boom in oil production in the 1990s, authoritarianism, corruption, and resource mismanagement have concentrated the benefits among a small elite. These practices have perpetuated income inequality and unbalanced development, such as low public spending on education and health care. Unemployment remains problematic because the oil-dominated economy employs a small labor force dependent on skilled foreign workers. The agricultural sector, Equatorial Guinea's main employer, continues to deteriorate because of a lack of investment and the migration of rural workers to urban areas. About three-quarters of the population lives below the poverty line.

Equatorial Guinea's large and growing youth population—about 60% are under the age of 25—is particularly affected because job creation in the non-oil sectors is limited, and young people often do not have the skills needed in the labor market. Equatorial Guinean children frequently enter school late, have poor attendance, and have high dropout rates. Thousands of Equatorial Guineans fled across the border to Gabon in the 1970s to escape the dictatorship of MACIAS NGUEMA; smaller numbers have followed in the decades since. Continued inequitable economic growth and high youth unemployment increases the likelihood of ethnic and regional violence.

Age structure: *0-14 years:* 39.81% (male 157,388/female 152,469)

15-24 years: 19.72% (male 78,145/female 75,348)

25-54 years: 32.15% (male 125,108/female 125,096)

55-64 years: 4.37% (male 14,676/female 19,349)

65 years and over: 3.95% (male 12,808/female 17,971) (2017 est.)

Dependency ratios: *total dependency ratio:* 67.5

youth dependency ratio: 62.7

elderly dependency ratio: 4.8

potential support ratio: 20.6 (2015 est.)

Median age: *total:* 19.8 years

male: 19.3 years

female: 20.3 years (2017 est.)

country comparison to the world: 196

Population growth rate: 2.44% (2017 est.)

country comparison to the world: 23

Birth rate: 32.2 births/1,000 population (2017 est.)

country comparison to the world: 32

Death rate: 7.8 deaths/1,000 population (2017 est.)

country comparison to the world: 97

Net migration rate: 0 migrant(s)/1,000 population (2017 est.)

country comparison to the world: 81

Population distribution: only two large cities over 30,000 people (Bata on the mainland, and the capital Malabo on the island of Bioko); small communities are scattered throughout the mainland and the five inhabited islands

Urbanization: *urban population:* 40.3% of total population (2017)

rate of urbanization: 3.09% annual rate of change (2015-20 est.)

Major urban areas—population: MALABO (capital) 145,000 (2014)

Sex ratio: *at birth:* 1.03 male(s)/female

0-14 years: 1.03 male(s)/female

15-24 years: 1.04 male(s)/female

25-54 years: 1 male(s)/female

55-64 years: 0.76 male(s)/female

65 years and over: 0.72 male(s)/female

total population: 0.99 male(s)/female (2016 est.)

Maternal mortality ratio: 342 deaths/100,000 live births (2015 est.)

country comparison to the world: 37

Infant mortality rate: *total:* 65.2 deaths/1,000 live births

male: 66.3 deaths/1,000 live births

female: 64.1 deaths/1,000 live births (2017 est.)

country comparison to the world: 14

Life expectancy at birth: *total population:* 64.6 years

male: 63.4 years

female: 65.8 years (2017 est.)

country comparison to the world: 183

Total fertility rate: 4.39 children born/woman (2017 est.)

country comparison to the world: 25

Contraceptive prevalence rate: 12.6% (2011)

Health expenditures: 3.8% of GDP (2014)

country comparison to the world: 165

Hospital bed density: 2.1 beds/1,000 population (2010)

Drinking water source:

improved:

urban: 72.5% of population

rural: 31.5% of population

total: 47.9% of population

unimproved:

urban: 27.5% of population

rural: 68.5% of population

total: 52.1% of population (2015 est.)

Sanitation facility access:

improved:

urban: 79.9% of population

rural: 71% of population

total: 74.5% of population

unimproved:

urban: 20.1% of population

rural: 29% of population

total: 25.5% of population (2015 est.)

HIV/AIDS—adult prevalence rate: 6.2% (2016 est.)

country comparison to the world: 11

HIV/AIDS—people living with HIV/AIDS: 35,000 (2016 est.)

country comparison to the world: 63

HIV/AIDS—deaths: <1000 (2016 est.)

Major infectious diseases: *degree of risk:* very high

food or waterborne diseases: bacterial and protozoal diarrhea, hepatitis A, and typhoid fever

vectorborne disease: malaria and dengue fever

animal contact disease: rabies (2016)

Obesity—adult prevalence rate: 8% (2016)

country comparison to the world: 156

Children under the age of 5 years underweight: 5.6% (2010)

country comparison to the world: 87

Literacy: *definition:* age 15 and over can read and write
total population: 95.3%
male: 97.4%
female: 93% (2015 est.)

GOVERNMENT

Country name: *conventional long form:* Republic of Equatorial Guinea
conventional short form: Equatorial Guinea
local long form: Republica de Guinea Ecuatorial/Republique de Guinee Equatoriale
local short form: Guinea Ecuatorial/Guinee Equatoriale
former: Spanish Guinea
etymology: the country is named for the Guinea region of West Africa that lies along the Gulf of Guinea and stretches north to the Sahel; the "equatorial" refers to the fact that the country lies just north of the Equator

Government type: presidential republic

Capital: *name:* Malabo; note—a new capital of Oyala is being built on the mainland near Djibloho; Malabo is on the island of Bioko

geographic coordinates: 3 45 N, 8 47 E
time difference: UTC+1 (6 hours ahead of Washington, DC, during Standard Time)

Administrative divisions: 7 provinces (provincias, singular—provincia); Annobon, Bioko Norte, Bioko Sur, Centro Sur, Kie-Ntem, Litoral, Wele-Nzas

Independence: 12 October 1968 (from Spain)

National holiday: Independence Day, 12 October (1968)

Constitution: history: previous 1968, 1973, 1982; approved by referendum 17 November 1991
amendments: proposed by the president of the republic or supported by three-fourths of the membership in either house of the National Assembly; passage requires three-fourths majority vote by both houses of the Assembly and approval in a referendum if requested by the president; amended several times, last in 2012 (2017)

Legal system: mixed system of civil and customary law

International law organization participation: has not submitted an ICJ jurisdiction declaration; non-party state to the ICCt

Citizenship: *citizenship by birth:* no
citizenship by descent only: at least one parent must be a citizen of Equatorial Guinea
dual citizenship recognized: no
residency requirement for naturalization: 10 years

Suffrage: 18 years of age; universal

Executive branch: *chief of state:* President Brig. Gen. (Ret.) Teodoro OBIANG Nguema Mbasogo (since 3 August 1979 when he seized power in a military coup)

head of government: Prime Minister Francisco Pascual Eyegue OBAMA Asue (since 23 June 2016); First Deputy Prime Minister Clemente Engonga NGUEMA Onguene (since 23 June 2016); Second Deputy Prime Minister Andres Jorge Mbomio Nsem ABUA (since 23 June 2016); Third Deputy Prime Minister Alfonso Nsue MOKUY (since 23 June 2016)
cabinet: Council of Ministers appointed by the president
elections/appointments: president directly elected by simple majority popular vote for a 7-year term (eligible for a second term); election last held on 24 April 2016 (next to be held in 2023); prime minister and deputy prime ministers appointed by the president
election results: Teodoro OBIANG Nguema Mbasogo reelected president; percent of vote—Teodoro OBIANG Nguema Mbasogo (PDGE) 93.5%, other 6.5%

Legislative branch: description: bicameral National Assembly or Asemblea Nacional, formerly the unicameral Parliament, consists of the Senate or Senado (70 seats; 55 members directly elected by simple majority vote and 15 appointed by the president) and the Chamber of Deputies or Camara de los Deputados (100 seats; members directly elected in multi-seat constituencies by proportional representation vote to serve 5-year terms); note—the constitutional referendum of 2011 established the Senate and was implemented at the time of the May 2013 elections
elections: last held on 12 Novermber 2017 (next to be held in 2022)
election results: Senate—percent of vote by party—NA; seats by party—PDGE 75; Chamber of Deputies—percent of vote by party—NA; seats by party—PDGE 99, CI 1

Judicial branch: *highest court(s):* Supreme Court of Justice (consists of the chief justice—who is also chief of state—and 9 judges and organized into civil, criminal, commercial, labor, administrative, and customary sections); Constitutional Court (consists of the court president and 4 members)
judge selection and term of office: Supreme Court judges appointed by the president for 5-year terms; Constitutional Court members appointed by the president, 2 of which are nominated by the Chamber of Deputies
subordinate courts: Court of Guarantees; military courts; Courts of Appeal; first instance tribunals; district and county tribunals

Political parties and leaders: Convergence Party for Social Democracy or CPDS [Andres ESONO ONDO]
Democratic Party for Equatorial Guinea or PDGE [Teodoro OBIANG Nguema Mbasogo]
Electoral Coalition or EC
Front of Democratic Opposiiton or FOD (coalition includes CPDS, FDR, UP)
Popular Action of Equatorial Guinea or APGE [Carmelo MBA BACALE]
Popular Union or UP [Daniel MARTINEZ AYECABA]
not officially registered parties: Democratic Republican Force or FDR [Guillermo NGUEMA ELA]
Citizens for Innovation or CI

Party for Progress of Equatorial Guinea or PPGE [Severo MOTO]
Union for the Center Right or UDC [Avelino MOCACHE MEAENGA]

Political pressure groups and leaders: ASODEGUE (Madrid-based pressure group for democratic reform)
Coalicion CEIBA (group formed by diverse, exiled political parties)
C.O.R.E.D. [Raimundo Ela NSANG] (based in Paris)
EG Justice (US-based anti-corruption group)

International organization participation: ACP, AfDB, AU, BDEAC, CEMAC, CPLP (associate), FAO, FZ, G-77, IBRD, ICAO, ICRM, IDA, IFAD, IFC, IFRCS, ILO, IMF, IMO, Interpol, IOC, IPU, ITSO, ITU, MIGA, NAM, OAS (observer), OIF, OPCW, UN, UNCTAD, UNESCO, UNIDO, UNWTO, UPU, WHO, WIPO, WTO (observer)

Diplomatic representation in the US: *chief of mission:* Ambassador Miguel Ntutumu EVUNA ANDEME (since 23 February 2015)
chancery: 2020 16th Street NW, Washington, DC 20009
telephone: [1] (202) 518-5700
FAX: [1] (202) 518-5252
consulate(s) general: Houston

Diplomatic representation from the US: *chief of mission:* Ambassador Julie FURUTA-TOY (since January 2016)
embassy: Carretera Malabo II, Malabo, Guinea Ecuatorial
mailing address: US Embassy Malabo, US Department of State, Washington, DC 20521-2520
telephone: [240] 333 09 57 41

Flag description: three equal horizontal bands of green (top), white, and red, with a blue isosceles triangle based on the hoist side and the coat of arms centered in the white band; the coat of arms has six yellow six-pointed stars (representing the mainland and five offshore islands) above a gray shield bearing a silk-cotton tree and below which is a scroll with the motto UNIDAD, PAZ, JUSTICIA (Unity, Peace, Justice); green symbolizes the jungle and natural resources, blue represents the sea that connects the mainland to the islands, white stands for peace, and red recalls the fight for independence

National symbol(s): silk cotton tree; national colors: green, white, red, blue

National anthem: name: "Caminemos pisando la senda" (Let Us Tread the Path)
lyrics/music: Atanasio Ndongo MIYONO/Atanasio Ndongo MIYONO or Ramiro Sanchez LOPEZ (disputed)
note: adopted 1968

ECONOMY

Economy—overview: Exploitation of oil and gas deposits, beginning in the 1990s, has driven economic growth in Equatorial Guinea; a recent rebasing of GDP resulted in an upward revision of the size of the economy by approximately 30%. Forestry and farming are minor components of

GDP. Although preindependence Equatorial Guinea counted on cocoa production for hard currency earnings, the neglect of the rural economy since independence has diminished the potential for agriculture-led growth. Subsistence farming is the dominant form of livelihood. Declining revenue from hydrocarbon production, high levels of infrastructure expenditures, lack of economic diversification, and corruption have pushed the economy into decline in recent years and limited improvements in the general population's living conditions. Equatorial Guinea's real GDP growth has been weak in recent years, averaging -0.5% per year from 2010 to 2014, because of a declining hydrocarbon sector. Inflation remained very low in 2016, down from an average of 4% in 2014.

Foreign assistance programs by the World Bank and the IMF have been cut since 1993 because of corruption and mismanagement, and as a middle income country Equatorial Guinea is now ineligible for most low-income donor funding. The government has been widely criticized for its lack of transparency and misuse of oil revenues and has attempted to address this issue by working toward compliance with the Extractive Industries Transparency Initiative. US foreign assistance to Equatorial Guinea is limited in part because of US restrictions pursuant to the Trafficking Victims Protection Act.

Equatorial Guinea hosted two economic diversification symposia in 2014 that focused on attracting investment in five sectors: agriculture and animal ranching, fishing, mining and petrochemicals, tourism, and financial services. Undeveloped mineral resources include gold, zinc, diamonds, columbite-tantalite, and other base metals. In 2017 Equatorial Guinea signed a preliminary agreement with Ghana to sell liquefied natural gas (LNG); as oil production wanes, the government believes LNG could provide a boost to revenues, but it will require large investments and long lead times to develop.

GDP (purchasing power parity): $29.38 billion (2017 est.)
$31.73 billion (2016 est.)
$35.13 billion (2015 est.)
note: data are in 2017 dollars
country comparison to the world: 134

GDP (official exchange rate): $10.07 billion (2016 est.)

GDP—real growth rate: -7.4% (2017 est.)
-9.7% (2016 est.)
-9.1% (2015 est.)
country comparison to the world: 220

GDP—per capita (PPP): $34,900 (2017 est.)
$38,600 (2016 est.)
$44,000 (2015 est.)
note: data are in 2017 dollars
country comparison to the world: 56

Gross national saving: 0.9% of GDP (2017 est.)
0.5% of GDP (2016 est.)
17.6% of GDP (2015 est.)
country comparison to the world: 176

GDP—composition, by end use:
household consumption: 47.9%
government consumption: 22.8%
investment in fixed capital: 24.6%
investment in inventories: 0.2%
exports of goods and services: 58.5%
imports of goods and services: -54.1% (2017 est.)

GDP—composition, by sector of origin:
agriculture: 2.5%
industry: 56.5%
services: 41% (2017 est.)

Agriculture—products: coffee, cocoa, rice, yams, cassava (manioc, tapioca), bananas, palm oil nuts; livestock; timber

Industries: petroleum, natural gas, sawmilling

Industrial production growth rate: -5.6% (2017 est.)
country comparison to the world: 199

Labor force: 195,200 (2007 est.)
country comparison to the world: 175

Unemployment rate: 8.6% (2014 est.)
22.3% (2009 est.)
country comparison to the world: 116

Population below poverty line: 44% (2011 est.)

Household income or consumption by percentage share: lowest 10%: NA%
highest 10%: NA%

Budget: revenues: $3.186 billion
expenditures: $3.431 billion (2017 est.)
Taxes and other revenues: 31.6% of GDP (2017 est.)
country comparison to the world: 74

Budget surplus (+) or deficit (-): -2.4% of GDP (2017 est.)
country comparison to the world: 98

Public debt: 23.4% of GDP (2017 est.)
23.1% of GDP (2016 est.)
country comparison to the world: 182

Fiscal year: calendar year

Inflation rate (consumer prices): 1.7% (2017 est.)
1.4% (2016 est.)
country comparison to the world: 76

Central bank discount rate: 8.5% (31 December 2010)
4.25% (31 December 2009)
country comparison to the world: 37

Commercial bank prime lending rate: 14% (31 December 2017 est.)
14% (31 December 2016 est.)
country comparison to the world: 54

Stock of narrow money: $1.516 billion (31 December 2017 est.)
$1.467 billion (31 December 2016 est.)
country comparison to the world: 142

Stock of broad money: $1.959 billion (31 December 2017 est.)
$1.864 billion (31 December 2016 est.)
country comparison to the world: 158

Stock of domestic credit: $2.416 billion (31 December 2017 est.)
$2.254 billion (31 December 2016 est.)
country comparison to the world: 143

Current account balance: -$806 million (2017 est.)
-$1.067 billion (2016 est.)
country comparison to the world: 122

Exports: $5.412 billion (2017 est.)
$5.042 billion (2016 est.)
country comparison to the world: 105

Exports—commodities: petroleum products, timber

Exports—partners: India 19.4%, China 13.5%, South Korea 13.2%, Spain 12.3%, Italy 5.1%, Netherlands 5.1%, US 4.1% (2016)

Imports: $2.555 billion (2017 est.)
$2.862 billion (2016 est.)
country comparison to the world: 149

Imports—commodities: petroleum sector equipment, other equipment, construction materials, vehicles

Imports—partners: US 23.3%, Spain 21.8%, China 12.8% (2016)

Reserves of foreign exchange and gold: $140.9 million (31 December 2017 est.)
$62.31 million (31 December 2016 est.)
country comparison to the world: 164

Debt—external: $1.181 billion (31 December 2017 est.)
$1.074 billion (31 December 2016 est.)
country comparison to the world: 165

Exchange rates: Cooperation Financiere en Afrique Centrale francs (XAF) per US dollar—
605.3 (2017 est.)
593.01 (2016 est.)
593.01 (2015 est.)
591.45 (2014 est.)
494.42 (2013 est.)

ENERGY

Electricity access: population without electricity: 300,000
electrification—total population: 66%
electrification—urban areas: 93%
electrification—rural areas: 48% (2013)

Electricity—production: 425 million kWh (2015 est.)
country comparison to the world: 171

Electricity—consumption: 395.3 million kWh (2015 est.)
country comparison to the world: 174

Electricity—exports: 0 kWh (2016 est.)
country comparison to the world: 132

Electricity—imports: 0 kWh (2016 est.)
country comparison to the world: 145

Electricity—installed generating capacity: 334,000 kW (2015 est.)
country comparison to the world: 153

Electricity—from fossil fuels: 55.1% of total installed capacity (2015 est.)
country comparison to the world: 142

Electricity—from nuclear fuels: 0% of total installed capacity (2015 est.)
country comparison to the world: 84

Electricity—from hydroelectric plants: 44.9% of total installed capacity (2015 est.)
country comparison to the world: 46

Electricity—from other renewable sources: 0% of total installed capacity (2015 est.)
country comparison to the world: 180

Crude oil—production: 227,000 bbl/day (2016 est.)
country comparison to the world: 36

Crude oil—exports: 278,000 bbl/day (2014 est.)
country comparison to the world: 27

Crude oil—imports: 0 bbl/day (2014 est.)
country comparison to the world: 120

Crude oil—proved reserves: 1.1 billion bbl (1 January 2017 es)
country comparison to the world: 42

Refined petroleum products—production: 0 bbl/day (2014 est.)
country comparison to the world: 139

Refined petroleum products—consumption: 5,200 bbl/day (2015 est.)
country comparison to the world: 175

Refined petroleum products—exports: 0 bbl/day (2014 est.)
country comparison to the world: 151

Refined petroleum products—imports: 5,197 bbl/day (2014 est.)
country comparison to the world: 165

Natural gas—production: 6.2 billion cu m (2015 est.)
country comparison to the world: 47

Natural gas—consumption: 2.05 billion cu m (2015 est.)
country comparison to the world: 88

Natural gas—exports: 5.01 billion cu m (2015 est.)
country comparison to the world: 32

Natural gas—imports: 0 cu m (2013 est.)
country comparison to the world: 120

Natural gas—proved reserves: 36.81 billion cu m (1 January 2017 es)
country comparison to the world: 68

Carbon dioxide emissions from consumption of energy: 3.7 million Mt (2013 est.)
country comparison to the world: 136

COMMUNICATIONS

Telephones—fixed lines: *total subscriptions:* 10,000
subscriptions per 100 inhabitants: 1 (July 2016 est.)
country comparison to the world: 194

Telephones—mobile cellular: *total:* 541,000
subscriptions per 100 inhabitants: 71 (July 2016 est.)
country comparison to the world: 170

Telephone system: *general assessment:* digital fixed-line network in most major urban areas and decent mobile cellular coverage
domestic: fixed-line density is about 1 per 100 persons; mobile-cellular subscribership has been increasing and in 2016 stood at about 70 percent of the population
international: country code—240; international communications from Bata and Malabo to African and European countries; satellite earth station—1 Intelsat (Indian Ocean) (2016)

Broadcast media: state maintains control of broadcast media with domestic broadcast media limited to 1 state-owned TV station, 1 private TV station owned by the president's eldest son, 1 state-owned radio station, and 1 private radio station owned by the president's eldest son; satellite TV service is available; transmissions of multiple international broadcasters are accessible (2013)

Internet country code: .gq
Internet users: total: 180,597

percent of population: 23.8% (July 2016 est.)
country comparison to the world: 167

TRANSPORTATION

National air transport system: *number of registered air carriers:* 6
inventory of registered aircraft operated by air carriers: 15
annual passenger traffic on registered air carriers: 400,759
annual freight traffic on registered air carriers: 461,650 mt-km (2015)
Civil aircraft registration country code prefix: 3C (2016)

Airports: 7 (2013)
country comparison to the world: 166

Airports—with paved runways: *total:* 6
over 3,047 m: 1
2,438 to 3,047 m: 2
1,524 to 2,437 m: 1
under 914 m: 2 (2017)

Airports—with unpaved runways: *total:* 1
2,438 to 3,047 m: 1 (2013)

Pipelines: condensate 42 km; condensate/gas 5 km; gas 79 km; oil 71 km (2013)

Roadways: *total:* 2,880 km (2000)
country comparison to the world: 168

Merchant marine: *total:* 40
by type: container ship 1, general cargo 7, oil tanker 8, other 24 (2017)
country comparison to the world: 118

Ports and terminals: *major seaport(s):* Bata, Luba, Malabo
LNG terminal(s) (export): Bioko Island

MILITARY AND SECURITY

Military expenditures: 0.18% of GDP (2016)
0.78% of GDP (2014)

Military branches: Equatorial Guinea Armed Forces (FAGE): Equatorial Guinea National Guard (Guardia Nacional de Guinea Ecuatorial, GNGE (Army), Navy, Air Force (2013)

Military service age and obligation: 18 years of age for selective compulsory military service, although conscription is rare in practice; 2-year service obligation; women hold only administrative positions in the Navy (2013)

TRANSNATIONAL ISSUES

Disputes—international: in 2002, ICJ ruled on an equidistance settlement of Cameroon-Equatorial Guinea-Nigeria maritime boundary in the Gulf of Guinea, but a dispute between Equatorial Guinea and Cameroon over an island at the mouth of the Ntem River and imprecisely defined maritime coordinates in the ICJ decision delayed final delimitation; UN urged Equatorial Guinea and Gabon to resolve the sovereignty dispute over Gabon-occupied Mbane and lesser islands and to create a maritime boundary in the hydrocarbon-rich Corisco Bay

Trafficking in persons: current situation: Equatorial Guinea is a source country for children subjected to sex trafficking and destination country for men, women, and children subjected to forced labor; Equatorial Guinean girls may be encouraged by their parents to engage in the sex trade in urban centers to receive groceries, gifts, housing, and money; children are also trafficked from nearby countries for work as domestic servants, market laborers, ambulant vendors, and launderers; women are trafficked to Equatorial Guinea from Cameroon, Benin, other neighboring countries, and China for forced labor or prostitution

tier rating: Tier 3—Equatorial Guinea does not fully comply with the minimum standards on the elimination of trafficking and is not making significant efforts to do so; in 2014, the government made no efforts to investigate or prosecute any suspected trafficking offenders or to identify or protect victims, despite its 2004 law prohibiting all forms of trafficking and mandating the provision of services to victims; undocumented migrants continued to be deported without being screened to assess whether any were trafficking victims; authorities did not undertake any trafficking awareness campaigns, implement any programs to address forced child labor, or make any other efforts to prevent trafficking (2015)

ERITREA

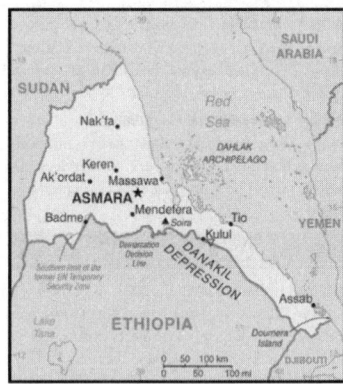

INTRODUCTION

Background: After independence from Italian colonial control in 1941 and 10 years of British administrative control, the UN established Eritrea as an autonomous region within the Ethiopian federation in 1952. Ethiopia's full annexation of Eritrea as a province 10 years later sparked a violent 30-year struggle for independence that ended in 1991 with Eritrean rebels defeating government forces. Eritreans overwhelmingly approved independence in a 1993 referendum. ISAIAS Afworki has been Eritrea's only president since independence; his rule, particularly since 2001, has been highly autocratic and repressive. His government has created a highly militarized society by pursuing an unpopular program of mandatory conscription into national service, sometimes of indefinite length. A two-and-a-half-year border war with Ethiopia that erupted in 1998 ended under UN auspices in December 2000. A UN peacekeeping operation was established that monitored a 25 km-wide Temporary Security Zone. The Eritrea-Ethiopia Boundary Commission (EEBC) created in April 2003 was tasked "to delimit and demarcate the colonial treaty border based on pertinent colonial treaties (1900, 1902, and 1908) and applicable international law." The EEBC on 30 November 2007 remotely demarcated the border, assigning the town of Badme to Eritrea, despite Ethiopia's maintaining forces there from the time of the 1998-2000 war. Eritrea insisted that the UN terminate its peacekeeping mission on 31 July 2008. Eritrea has accepted the EEBC's "virtual demarcation" decision and repeatedly called on Ethiopia to remove its troops. Ethiopia has not accepted the demarcation decision, and neither party has entered into meaningful dialogue to resolve the impasse. Eritrea is subject to several UN Security Council Resolutions (initially in 2009 and renewed annually) imposing an arms embargo and a travel ban and assets freeze on certain individuals, in view of evidence that it has supported armed opposition groups in the region.

GEOGRAPHY

Location: Eastern Africa, bordering the Red Sea, between Djibouti and Sudan

Geographic coordinates: 15 00 N, 39 00 E

Map references: Africa

Area: *total:* 117,600 sq km
land: 101,000 sq km
water: 16,600 sq km
country comparison to the world: 102

Area—comparative: slightly larger than Pennsylvania

Land boundaries: *total:* 1,840 km
border countries (3): Djibouti 125 km, Ethiopia 1,033 km, Sudan 682 km

Coastline: 2,234 km (mainland on Red Sea 1,151 km, islands in Red Sea 1,083 km)

Maritime claims: *territorial sea:* 12 nm

Climate: hot, dry desert strip along Red Sea coast; cooler and wetter in the central highlands (up to 61 cm of rainfall annually, heaviest June to September); semiarid in western hills and lowlands

Terrain: dominated by extension of Ethiopian north-south trending highlands, descending on the east to a coastal desert plain, on the northwest to hilly terrain and on the southwest to flat-to-rolling plains

Elevation: *mean elevation:* 853 m

elevation extremes: *lowest point:* near Kulul within the Danakil Depression -75 m
highest point: Soira 3,018 m

Natural resources: gold, potash, zinc, copper, salt, possibly oil and natural gas, fish

Land use: *agricultural land:* 75.1%
arable land: 6.8%;
permanent crops: 0%;
permanent pasture: 68.3%
forest: 15.1%
other: 9.8% (2011 est.)

Irrigated land: 210 sq km (2012)

Population—distribution: density is highest in the center of the country in and around the cities of Asmara (capital) and Keren; smaller settlements exist in the north and south

Natural hazards: frequent droughts, rare earthquakes and volcanoes; locust swarms
volcanism: Dubbi (1,625 m), which last erupted in 1861, was the country's only historically active volcano until Nabro (2,218 m) came to life on 12 June 2011

Environment—current issues: deforestation; desertification; soil erosion; overgrazing

Environment—international agreements: *party to:* Biodiversity, Climate Change, Climate Change-Kyoto Protocol, Desertification, Endangered Species, Hazardous Wastes, Ozone Layer Protection
signed, but not ratified: none of the selected agreements

Geography—note: strategic geopolitical position along world's busiest shipping lanes; Eritrea retained the entire coastline of Ethiopia along the Red Sea upon de jure independence from Ethiopia on 24 May 1993

PEOPLE AND SOCIETY

Population: 5,918,919 (July 2017 est.)
country comparison to the world: 112

Nationality: *noun:* Eritrean(s)
adjective: Eritrean

Ethnic groups: nine recognized ethnic groups: Tigrinya 55%, Tigre 30%, Saho 4%, Kunama 2%, Rashaida 2%, Bilen 2%, other (Afar, Beni Amir, Nera) 5% (2010 est.)

Languages: Tigrinya (official), Arabic (official), English (official), Tigre, Kunama, Afar, other Cushitic languages

Religions: Muslim, Coptic Christian, Roman Catholic, Protestant

Demographic profile: Eritrea is a persistently poor country that has made progress in some socioeconomic categories but not in others. Education and human capital formation are national priorities for facilitating economic development and eradicating poverty. To this end, Eritrea has made great strides in improving adult literacy—doubling the literacy rate over the last 20 years—in large part because of its successful adult education programs. The overall literacy rate was estimated to be almost 74% in 2015; more work needs to be done to raise female literacy and school attendance among nomadic and rural communities. Subsistence farming fails to meet the needs of Eritrea's growing population because of repeated droughts, dwindling arable land, overgrazing, soil erosion, and a shortage of farmers due to conscription and displacement. The government's emphasis on spending on defense over agriculture and its lack of foreign exchange to import food also contribute to food insecurity.

Eritrea has been a leading refugee source country since at least the 1960s, when its 30-year war for independence from Ethiopia began. Since gaining independence in 1993, Eritreans have continued migrating to Sudan, Ethiopia, Yemen, Egypt, or Israel because of a lack of basic human rights or political freedom, educational and job opportunities, or to seek asylum because of militarization. Eritrea's large diaspora has been a source of vital remittances, funding its war for independence and providing 30% of the country's GDP annually since it became independent.

In the last few years, Eritreans have increasingly been trafficked and held hostage by Bedouins in the Sinai Desert, where they are victims of organ harvesting, rape, extortion, and torture. Some Eritrean trafficking victims are kidnapped after being smuggled to Sudan or Ethiopia, while others are kidnapped from within or around refugee camps or crossing Eritrea's borders. Eritreans composed approximately 90% of the conservatively estimated 25,000-30,000 victims of Sinai trafficking from 2009-2013, according to a 2013 consultancy firm report.

Age structure: *0-14 years:* 40.17% (male 1,195,210/female 1,182,603)
15-24 years: 19.57% (male 576,315/female 582,143)
25-54 years: 32.63% (male 950,121/female 981,163)
55-64 years: 3.7% (male 94,767/female 124,528)
65 years and over: 3.92% (male 97,530/female 134,539) (2017 est.)

Dependency ratios: *total dependency ratio:* 85
youth dependency ratio: 78.3
elderly dependency ratio: 6.8
potential support ratio: 14.8 (2015 est.)

Median age: *total:* 19.7 years
male: 19.2 years
female: 20.1 years (2017 est.)
country comparison to the world: 200

Population growth rate: 0.85% (2017 est.)
country comparison to the world: 126

Birth rate: 29.6 births/1,000 population (2017 est.)
country comparison to the world: 39

Death rate: 7.2 deaths/1,000 population (2017 est.)
country comparison to the world: 126

Net migration rate: -13.9 migrant(s)/1,000 population (2017 est.)
country comparison to the world: 215

Population distribution: density is highest in the center of the country in and around the cities of Asmara (capital) and Keren; smaller settlements exist in the north and south

Urbanization: *urban population:* 23.6% of total population (2017)
rate of urbanization: 4.72% annual rate of change (2015-20 est.)

Major urban areas—population: ASMARA (capital) 804,000 (2015)

Sex ratio: *at birth:* 1.03 male(s)/female
0-14 years: 1.01 male(s)/female
15-24 years: 0.99 male(s)/female
25-54 years: 0.97 male(s)/female
55-64 years: 0.74 male(s)/female
65 years and over: 0.75 male(s)/female
total population: 0.97 male(s)/female (2016 est.)

Mother's mean age at first birth: 21.3 years
note: median age at first birth among women 25-29 (2010 est.)

Maternal mortality ratio: 501 deaths/100,000 live births (2015 est.)
country comparison to the world: 20

Infant mortality rate: *total:* 45 deaths/1,000 live births
male: 52 deaths/1,000 live births
female: 37.9 deaths/1,000 live births (2017 est.)
country comparison to the world: 41

Life expectancy at birth: *total population:* 65.2 years
male: 62.7 years
female: 67.8 years (2017 est.)

country comparison to the world: 179

Total fertility rate: 3.99 children born/woman (2017 est.)
country comparison to the world: 36

Contraceptive prevalence rate: 8.4% (2010)
Health expenditures: 3.3% of GDP (2014)
country comparison to the world: 177

Hospital bed density: 0.7 beds/1,000 population (2011)

Drinking water source:
improved:
urban: 73.2% of population
rural: 53.3% of population
total: 57.8% of population
unimproved:
urban: 26.8% of population
rural: 46.7% of population
total: 42.2% of population (2015 est.)

Sanitation facility access:
improved:
urban: 44.5% of population
rural: 7.3% of population
total: 15.7% of population
unimproved:
urban: 55.5% of population
rural: 92.7% of population
total: 84.3% of population (2015 est.)

HIV/AIDS—adult prevalence rate: 0.6% (2016 est.)
country comparison to the world: 57

HIV/AIDS—people living with HIV/AIDS: 15,000 (2016 est.)
country comparison to the world: 82

HIV/AIDS—deaths: <1000 (2016 est.)

Major infectious diseases: *degree of risk:* high
food or waterborne diseases: bacterial diarrhea, hepatitis A, and typhoid fever
vectorborne diseases: malaria and dengue fever (2016)

Obesity—adult prevalence rate: 5% (2016)
country comparison to the world: 183

Children under the age of 5 years underweight: 38.8% (2010)
country comparison to the world: 7

Literacy: *definition:* age 15 and over can read and write
total population: 73.8%
male: 82.4%
female: 65.5% (2015 est.)

School life expectancy (primary to tertiary education): *total:* 5 years
male: 6 years
female: 5 years (2014)

GOVERNMENT

Country name: *conventional long form:* State of Eritrea
conventional short form: Eritrea
local long form: Hagere Ertra
local short form: Ertra
former: Eritrea Autonomous Region in Ethiopia

etymology: the country name derives from the ancient Greek appellation "Erythra Thalassa" meaning Red Sea, which is the major water body bordering the country

Government type: presidential republic

Capital: *name:* Asmara (Asmera)
geographic coordinates: 15 20 N, 38 56 E
time difference: UTC+3 (8 hours ahead of Washington, DC, during Standard Time)

Administrative divisions: 6 regions (zobatat, singular—zoba); Anseba, Debub (South), Debubawi K'eyih Bahri (Southern Red Sea), Gash Barka, Ma'akel (Central), Semenawi Keyih Bahri (Northern Red Sea)

Independence: 24 May 1993 (from Ethiopia)

National holiday: Independence Day, 24 May (1991)

Constitution: history: ratified by the Constituent Assembly 23 May 1997 (not fully implemented); note—drafting of a new constitution, which began in 2014, continued into 2017
amendments: proposed by the president of Eritrea or by assent of at least one-half of the National Assembly membership; passage requires at least an initial three-quarters majority vote by the Assembly and, after one year, final passage by at least four-fifths majority vote by the Assembly (2017)

Legal system: mixed legal system of civil, customary, and Islamic religious law

International law organization participation: has not submitted an ICJ jurisdiction declaration; non-party state to the ICCt

Citizenship: *citizenship by birth:* no
citizenship by descent only: at least one parent must be a citizen of Eritrea
dual citizenship recognized: no
residency requirement for naturalization: 20 years

Suffrage: 18 years of age; universal

Executive branch: *chief of state:* President ISAIAS Afworki (since 8 June 1993); note—the president is both chief of state and head of government and is head of the State Council and National Assembly

head of government: President ISAIAS Afworki (since 8 June 1993)
cabinet: State Council appointed by the president
elections/appointments: president indirectly elected by the National Assembly for a 5-year term (eligible for a second term); the only election was held on 8 June 1993, following independence from Ethiopia (next election postponed indefinitely)
election results: ISAIAS Afworki elected president by the transitional National Assembly; percent of National Assembly vote—ISAIAS Afworki (PFDJ) 95%, other 5%

Legislative branch: description: unicameral National Assembly or Hagerawi Baito (150 seats; 75 members indirectly elected by the ruling party and 75 directly elected by simple majority vote; members serve 5-year terms)
elections: in May 1997, following the adoption of the new constitution, 75 members of the PFDJ

Central Committee (the old Central Committee of the EPLF), 60 members of the 527-member Constituent Assembly, which had been established in 1997 to discuss and ratify the new constitution, and 15 representatives of Eritreans living abroad were formed into a Transitional National Assembly to serve as the country's legislative body until countrywide elections to form a National Assembly were held; although only 75 of 150 members of the Transitional National Assembly were elected, the constitution stipulates that once past the transition stage, all members of the National Assembly will be elected by secret ballot of all eligible voters; National Assembly elections scheduled for December 2001 were postponed indefinitely due to the war with Ethiopia

Judicial branch: *highest court(s):* High Court (consists of 20 judges and organized into civil, commercial, criminal, labor, administrative, and customary sections)
judge selection and term of office: High Court judges appointed by the president
subordinate courts: regional/zonal courts; community courts; special courts; sharia courts (for issues dealing with Muslim marriage, inheritance, and family); military courts

Political parties and leaders: People's Front for Democracy and Justice or PFDJ [ISAIAS Afworki] (the only party recognized by the government)

Political pressure groups and leaders: Democratic Movement for the Liberation of Eritrean Kunama or DMLEK

Eritrean Democratic Alliance or EDA
Eritrean Islamic Party for Justice and Development or EIPJD (includes the Eritrean Islamic Jihad (EIJ), Eritrean Islamic Jihad Movement (EIJM), Eritrean Islamic Salvation, and the Eritrean Islamic Foundation)
Eritrean National Congress for Democratic Change or ENCDC
Eritrean National Salvation Front or ENSF
Eritrean People's Democratic Party or EPDP
Red Sea Afar Democratic Organization or RSADO

International organization participation: ACP, AfDB, AU, COMESA, FAO, G-77, IAEA, IBRD, ICAO, ICC (NGOs), IDA, IFAD, IFC, IFRCS (observer), ILO, IMF, IMO, Interpol, IOC, ISO (correspondent), ITU, ITUC (NGOs), LAS (observer), MIGA, NAM, OPCW, PCA, UN, UNCTAD, UNESCO, UNIDO, UNWTO, UPU, WCO, WFTU (NGOs), WHO, WIPO, WMO

Diplomatic representation in the US: *chief of mission:* Ambassador (vacant); Charge d'Affaires BERHANE Gebrehiwet Solomon (since 15 March 2011)
chancery: 1708 New Hampshire Avenue NW, Washington, DC 20009
telephone: [1] (202) 319-1991
FAX: [1] (202) 319-1304

Diplomatic representation from the US: *chief of mission:* Ambassador (vacant); Charge d'Affaires Natalie E. BROWN (since September 2016)
embassy: 179 Ala Street, Asmara
mailing address: P.O. Box 211, Asmara
telephone: [291] (1) 120004

FAX: [291] (1) 127584

Flag description: red isosceles triangle (based on the hoist side) dividing the flag into two right triangles; the upper triangle is green, the lower one is blue; a gold wreath encircling a gold olive branch is centered on the hoist side of the red triangle; green stands for the country's agriculture economy, red signifies the blood shed in the fight for freedom, and blue symbolizes the bounty of the sea; the wreath-olive branch symbol is similar to that on the first flag of Eritrea from 1952; the shape of the red triangle broadly mimics the shape of the country
note: one of several flags where a prominent component of the design reflects the shape of the country; other such flags are those of Bosnia and Herzegovina, Brazil, and Vanuatu

National symbol(s): camel; national colors: green, red, blue

National anthem: *name:* "Ertra, Ertra, Ertra" (Eritrea, Eritrea, Eritrea)
lyrics/music: SOLOMON Tsehaye Beraki/Isaac Abraham MEHAREZGI and ARON Tekle Tesfatsion
note: adopted 1993; upon independence from Ethiopia

ECONOMY

Economy—overview: Since formal independence from Ethiopia in 1993, Eritrea has faced many economic problems, including lack of financial resources and chronic drought, which have been exacerbated by restrictive economic policies. Eritrea has a command economy under the control of the sole political party, the People's Front for Democracy and Justice. Like the economies of many African nations, a large share of the population—nearly 80% in Eritrea—is engaged in subsistence agriculture, but the sector only produces a small share of the country's total output.

Since the conclusion of the Ethiopia-Eritrea war in 2000, the government has expanded military- and party-owned businesses to complete President ISAIAS's development agenda. The government has strictly controlled the use of foreign currency by limiting access and availability; new regulations in 2013 aimed at relaxing currency controls have had little economic effect. Few large private enterprises exist in Eritrea and most operate in conjunction with government partners, including a number of large international mining ventures, which began production in 2013. In late 2015, the Government of Eritrea introduced a new currency, retaining the name nakfa, and restricted the amount of hard currency individuals could withdraw from banks per month. The changeover has resulted in exchange fluctuations and the scarcity of hard currency available in the market.

While reliable statistics on Eritrea are difficult to obtain, erratic rainfall and the percentage of the labor force tied up in national service continue to interfere with agricultural production and economic development. Eritrea's harvests generally cannot meet the food needs of the country without supplemental grain purchases. Copper, potash,

and gold production are likely to continue to drive limited economic growth and government revenue over the next few years, but military spending will continue to compete with development and investment plans.

GDP (purchasing power parity): $9.631 billion (2017 est.)
$9.327 billion (2016 est.)
$8.997 billion (2015 est.)
note: data are in 2017 dollars
country comparison to the world: 161

GDP (official exchange rate): $6.05 billion (2016 est.)

GDP—real growth rate: 3.3% (2017 est.)
3.7% (2016 est.)
4.8% (2015 est.)
country comparison to the world: 101

GDP—per capita (PPP): $1,400 (2017 est.)
$1,400 (2016 est.)
$1,400 (2015 est.)
note: data are in 2017 dollars
country comparison to the world: 221

Gross national saving: 4.6% of GDP (2017 est.)
4% of GDP (2016 est.)
1.3% of GDP (2015 est.)
country comparison to the world: 170

GDP—composition, by end use:
household consumption: 80.8%
government consumption: 24.3%
investment in fixed capital: 6.4%
investment in inventories: 0.1%
exports of goods and services: 11%
imports of goods and services: -22.5% (2017 est.)

GDP—composition, by sector of origin:
agriculture: 11.7%
industry: 29.6%
services: 58.7% (2017 est.)

Agriculture—products: sorghum, lentils, vegetables, corn, cotton, tobacco, sisal; livestock, goats; fish

Industries: food processing, beverages, clothing and textiles, light manufacturing, salt, cement

Industrial production growth rate: 5.4% (2017 est.)
country comparison to the world: 39

Labor force: 2.71 million (2017 est.)
country comparison to the world: 111

Labor force—by occupation: *agriculture:* 80%
industry and services: 20% (2004 est.)

Unemployment rate: 8.6% (2013 est.)
10% (2012 est.)
country comparison to the world: 117

Population below poverty line: 50% (2004 est.)

Household income or consumption by percentage share: *lowest 10%:* NA%
highest 10%: NA%

Budget: *revenues:* $2.029 billion
expenditures: $2.601 billion (2017 est.)
Taxes and other revenues: 33.5% of GDP (2017 est.)
country comparison to the world: 65

Budget surplus (+) or deficit (-): -9.5% of GDP (2017 est.)

country comparison to the world: 204

Public debt: 113.7% of GDP (2017 est.)
120.9% of GDP (2016 est.)
country comparison to the world: 12

Fiscal year: calendar year

Inflation rate (consumer prices): 9% (2017 est.)
9% (2016 est.)
country comparison to the world: 203

Commercial bank prime lending rate: NA%

Stock of narrow money: $3.096 billion (31 December 2017 est.)
$2.74 billion (31 December 2016 est.)
country comparison to the world: 118

Stock of broad money: $6.671 billion (31 December 2017 est.)
$5.993 billion (31 December 2016 est.)
country comparison to the world: 121

Stock of domestic credit: $5.767 billion (31 December 2017 est.)
$5.236 billion (31 December 2016 est.)
country comparison to the world: 125

Current account balance: $40 million (2017 est.)
-$3 million (2016 est.)
country comparison to the world: 55

Exports: $635.7 million (2017 est.)
$485.4 million (2016 est.)
country comparison to the world: 170

Exports—commodities: gold and other minerals, livestock, sorghum, textiles, food, small industry manufactures

Exports—partners: China 57.7%, India 21.9%, South Korea 4.9%, Serbia 4.2% (2016)

Imports: $1.127 billion (2017 est.)
$1.049 billion (2016 est.)
country comparison to the world: 176

Imports—commodities: machinery, petroleum products, food, manufactured goods

Imports—partners: China 18.1%, UAE 15.4%, Saudi Arabia 13.7%, Italy 6.5%, Turkey 5.9%, Brazil 5.3%, Belgium 4.1% (2016)

Reserves of foreign exchange and gold: $236.6 million (31 December 2017 est.)
$218.4 million (31 December 2016 est.)
country comparison to the world: 157

Debt—external: $869.9 million (31 December 2017 est.)
$875.6 million (31 December 2016 est.)
country comparison to the world: 169

Exchange rates: nakfa (ERN) per US dollar—
15.38 (2017 est.)
15.375 (2016 est.)
15.375 (2015 est.)
15.375 (2014 est.)
15.375 (2013 est.)

ENERGY

Electricity access: *population without electricity:* 4,300,000
electrification—total population: 32%
electrification—urban areas: 86%
electrification—rural areas: 17% (2013)

Electricity—production: 383.8 million kWh (2015 est.)
country comparison to the world: 173

Electricity—consumption: 329.8 million kWh (2015 est.)
country comparison to the world: 179

Electricity—exports: 0 kWh (2016 est.)
country comparison to the world: 133

Electricity—imports: 0 kWh (2016 est.)
country comparison to the world: 146

Electricity—installed generating capacity: 141,000 kW (2015 est.)
country comparison to the world: 171

Electricity—from fossil fuels: 98.6% of total installed capacity (2015 est.)
country comparison to the world: 35

Electricity—from nuclear fuels: 0% of total installed capacity (2015 est.)
country comparison to the world: 86

Electricity—from hydroelectric plants: 0% of total installed capacity (2015 est.)
country comparison to the world: 174

Electricity—from other renewable sources: 1.4% of total installed capacity (2015 est.)
country comparison to the world: 133

Crude oil—production: 0 bbl/day (2016 est.)
country comparison to the world: 130

Crude oil—exports: 0 bbl/day (2014 est.)
country comparison to the world: 119

Crude oil—imports: 0 bbl/day (2014 est.)
country comparison to the world: 122

Crude oil—proved reserves: 0 bbl (1 January 2017 es)
country comparison to the world: 130

Refined petroleum products—production: 0 bbl/day (2014 est.)
country comparison to the world: 140

Refined petroleum products—consumption: 3,600 bbl/day (2015 est.)
country comparison to the world: 182

Refined petroleum products—exports: 0 bbl/day (2014 est.)
country comparison to the world: 152

Refined petroleum products—imports: 3,598 bbl/day (2014 est.)
country comparison to the world: 173

Natural gas—production: 0 cu m (2013 est.)
country comparison to the world: 131

Natural gas—consumption: 0 cu m (2013 est.)
country comparison to the world: 177

Natural gas—exports: 0 cu m (2013 est.)
country comparison to the world: 99

Natural gas—imports: 0 cu m (2013 est.)
country comparison to the world: 121

Natural gas—proved reserves: 0 cu m (1 January 2014 es)
country comparison to the world: 136

Carbon dioxide emissions from consumption of energy: 800,000 Mt (2013 est.)
country comparison to the world: 169

COMMUNICATIONS

Telephones—fixed lines: *total subscriptions:* 66,086
subscriptions per 100 inhabitants: 1 (July 2016 est.)
country comparison to the world: 154

Telephones—mobile cellular: *total:* 506,000
subscriptions per 100 inhabitants: 9 (July 2016 est.)
country comparison to the world: 172

Telephone system: *general assessment:* woefully inadequate service provided by state-owned telecom monopoly; most fixed-line telephones are in Asmara; cell phone use only slowly increasing throughout the country; no data service
domestic: combined fixed-line and mobile-cellular subscribership is less than 10 per 100 persons
international: country code—291 (2016)

Broadcast media: government controls broadcast media with private ownership prohibited; 1 state-owned TV station; state-owned radio operates 2 networks; purchases of satellite dishes and subscriptions to international broadcast media are permitted (2007)

Internet country code: .er
Internet users: total: 69,095

percent of population: 1.2% (July 2016 est.)
country comparison to the world: 180

TRANSPORTATION

National air transport system: *number of registered air carriers:* 1
inventory of registered aircraft operated by air carriers: 1 (2015)
Civil aircraft registration country code prefix: E3 (2016)

Airports: 13 (2013)
country comparison to the world: 151

Airports—with paved runways: *total:* 4
over 3,047 m: 2
2,438 to 3,047 m: 2 (2017)

Airports—with unpaved runways: *total:* 9
over 3,047 m: 1
2,438 to 3,047 m: 1
1,524 to 2,437 m: 5
914 to 1,523 m: 2 (2013)

Heliports: 1 (2013)

Railways: *total:* 306 km
narrow gauge: 306 km 0.950-m gauge (2014)
country comparison to the world: 122

Roadways: *total:* 4,010 km
paved: 874 km
unpaved: 3,136 km (2000)
country comparison to the world: 158

Merchant marine: *total:* 9
by type: general cargo 4, oil tanker 1, other 4 (2017)
country comparison to the world: 147

Ports and terminals: *major seaport(s):* Assab, Massawa

MILITARY AND SECURITY

Military branches: Eritrean Armed Forces: Eritrean Ground Forces, Eritrean Navy, Eritrean Air Force (includes Air Defense Force) (2011)

Military service age and obligation: 18-40 years of age for male and female voluntary and compulsory military service; 16-month conscript service obligation (2012)

TRANSNATIONAL ISSUES

Disputes—international: Eritrea and Ethiopia agreed to abide by 2002 Ethiopia-Eritrea Boundary Commission's (EEBC) delimitation decision, but neither party responded to the revised line detailed in the November 2006 EEBC Demarcation Statement; Sudan accuses Eritrea of supporting eastern Sudanese rebel groups; in 2008, Eritrean troops

moved across the border on Ras Doumera peninsula and occupied Doumera Island with undefined sovereignty in the Red Sea

Trafficking in persons: current situation: Eritrea is a source country for men, women, and children trafficked for the purposes of forced labor domestically and, to a lesser extent, sex and labor trafficking abroad; the country's national service program is often abused, with conscripts detained indefinitely and subjected to forced labor; Eritrean migrants, often fleeing national service, face strict exit control procedures and limited access to passports and visas, making them vulnerable to trafficking; Eritrean secondary school children are required to take part in public works projects during their summer breaks and must attend military and educational camp in their final year to obtain a high school graduation certificate and

to gain access to higher education and some jobs; some Eritreans living in or near refugee camps, particularly in Sudan, are kidnapped by criminal groups and held for ransom in the Sinai Peninsula and Libya, where they are subjected to forced labor and abuse

tier rating: Tier 3—Eritrea does not fully comply with the minimum standards for the elimination of trafficking and is not making significant efforts to do so; the government failed to investigate or prosecute any trafficking offenses or to identify or protect any victims; while the government continued to warn citizens of the dangers of human trafficking through awareness-raising events and poster campaigns, authorities lacked an understanding of the crime, conflating trafficking with transnational migration; Eritrea is not a party to the 2000 UN TIP Protocol (2015)

ESTONIA

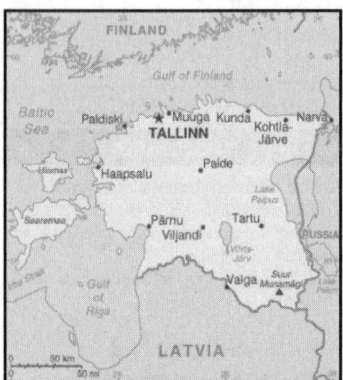

INTRODUCTION

Background: After centuries of Danish, Swedish, German, and Russian rule, Estonia attained independence in 1918. Forcibly incorporated into the USSR in 1940—an action never recognized by the US and many other countries—it regained its freedom in 1991 with the collapse of the Soviet Union. Since the last Russian troops left in 1994, Estonia has been free to promote economic and political ties with the West. It joined both NATO and the EU in the spring of 2004, formally joined the OECD in late 2010, and adopted the euro as its official currency on 1 January 2011.

GEOGRAPHY

Location: Eastern Europe, bordering the Baltic Sea and Gulf of Finland, between Latvia and Russia

Geographic coordinates: 59 00 N, 26 00 E

Map references: Europe

Area: *total:* 45,228 sq km

land: 42,388 sq km

water: 2,840 sq km

note: includes 1,520 islands in the Baltic Sea

country comparison to the world: 133

Area—comparative: about twice the size of New Jersey

Land boundaries: *total:* 657 km

border countries (2): Latvia 333 km, Russia 324 km

Coastline: 3,794 km

Maritime claims: *territorial sea:* 12 nm

exclusive economic zone: limits as agreed to by Estonia, Finland, Latvia, Sweden, and Russia

Climate: maritime; wet, moderate winters, cool summers

Terrain: marshy, lowlands; flat in the north, hilly in the south

Elevation: *mean elevation:* 61 m

elevation extremes: *lowest point:* Baltic Sea 0 m

highest point: Suur Munamagi 318 m

Natural resources: oil shale, peat, rare earth elements, phosphorite, clay, limestone, sand, dolomite, arable land, sea mud

Land use: *agricultural land:* 22.2%

arable land: 14.9%;

permanent crops: 0.1%;

permanent pasture: 7.2%

forest: 52.1%

other: 25.7% (2011 est.)

Irrigated land: 40 sq km (2012)

Population—distribution: a fairly even distribution throughout most of the country, with urban areas attracting larger and denser populations

Natural hazards: sometimes flooding occurs in the spring

Environment—current issues: air polluted with sulfur dioxide from oil-shale burning power plants

in northeast; however, the amounts of pollutants emitted to the air have fallen dramatically and the pollution load of wastewater at purification plants has decreased substantially due to improved technology and environmental monitoring; Estonia has more than 1,400 natural and manmade lakes, the smaller of which in agricultural areas need to be monitored; coastal seawater is polluted in certain locations

Environment—international agreements: *party to:* Air Pollution, Air Pollution-Nitrogen Oxides, Air Pollution-Persistent Organic Pollutants, Air Pollution-Sulfur 85, Air Pollution-Volatile Organic Compounds, Antarctic Treaty, Biodiversity, Climate Change, Climate Change-Kyoto Protocol, Endangered Species, Hazardous Wastes, Law of the Sea, Ozone Layer Protection, Ship Pollution, Wetlands

signed, but not ratified: none of the selected agreements

Geography—note: the mainland terrain is flat, boggy, and partly wooded; offshore lie more than 1,500 islands

PEOPLE AND SOCIETY

Population: 1,251,581 (July 2017 est.)

country comparison to the world: 158

Nationality: *noun:* Estonian(s)

adjective: Estonian

Ethnic groups: Estonian 68.7%, Russian 24.8%, Ukrainian 1.7%, Belarusian 1%, Finn 0.6%, other 1.6%, unspecified 1.6% (2011 est.)

Languages: Estonian (official) 68.5%, Russian 29.6%, Ukrainian 0.6%, other 1.2%, unspecified 0.1% (2011 est.)

Religions: Lutheran 9.9%, Orthodox 16.2%, other Christian (including Methodist, Seventh-Day Adventist, Roman Catholic, Pentecostal) 2.2%, other 0.9%, none 54.1%, unspecified 16.7% (2011 est.)

Age structure: *0-14 years:* 16.23% (male 104,130/female 98,941)
15-24 years: 8.99% (male 58,432/female 54,122)
25-54 years: 41.37% (male 261,366/female 256,383)
55-64 years: 13.57% (male 76,591/female 93,194)
65 years and over: 19.85% (male 84,466/female 163,956) (2017 est.)

Dependency ratios: *total dependency ratio:* 53.7
youth dependency ratio: 24.8
elderly dependency ratio: 28.9
potential support ratio: 3.5 (2015 est.)

Median age: *total:* 42.7 years
male: 39.4 years
female: 46.1 years (2017 est.)
country comparison to the world: 23

Population growth rate: -0.57% (2017 est.)
country comparison to the world: 225

Birth rate: 10.1 births/1,000 population (2017 est.)
country comparison to the world: 193

Death rate: 12.6 deaths/1,000 population (2017 est.)
country comparison to the world: 17

Net migration rate: -3.2 migrant(s)/1,000 population (2017 est.)
country comparison to the world: 175

Population distribution: a fairly even distribution throughout most of the country, with urban areas attracting larger and denser populations

Urbanization: *urban population:* 67.4% of total population (2017)
rate of urbanization: -0.37% annual rate of change (2015-20 est.)

Major urban areas—population: TALLINN (capital) 391,000 (2015)

Sex ratio: *at birth:* 1.05 male(s)/female
0-14 years: 1.05 male(s)/female
15-24 years: 1.08 male(s)/female
25-54 years: 1.01 male(s)/female
55-64 years: 0.81 male(s)/female
65 years and over: 0.51 male(s)/female
total population: 0.88 male(s)/female (2016 est.)

Mother's mean age at first birth: 26.6 years (2014 est.)

Maternal mortality ratio: 9 deaths/100,000 live births (2015 est.)
country comparison to the world: 151

Infant mortality rate: *total:* 3.8 deaths/1,000 live births
male: 3.7 deaths/1,000 live births
female: 3.9 deaths/1,000 live births (2017 est.)
country comparison to the world: 196

Life expectancy at birth: *total population:* 76.9 years
male: 72.1 years
female: 81.9 years (2017 est.)
country comparison to the world: 83

Total fertility rate: 1.6 children born/woman (2017 est.)
country comparison to the world: 181

Health expenditures: 6.4% of GDP (2014)
country comparison to the world: 94

Physicians density: 3.32 physicians/1,000 population (2014)

Hospital bed density: 5.3 beds/1,000 population (2011)

Drinking water source:
improved:
urban: 100% of population
rural: 99% of population
total: 99.6% of population
unimproved:
urban: 0% of population
rural: 1% of population
total: 0.4% of population (2015 est.)

Sanitation facility access:
improved:
urban: 97.5% of population
rural: 96.6% of population
total: 97.2% of population
unimproved:
urban: 2.5% of population
rural: 3.4% of population
total: 2.8% of population (2015 est.)

HIV/AIDS—adult prevalence rate: NA

HIV/AIDS—people living with HIV/AIDS: NA

HIV/AIDS—deaths: NA

Major infectious diseases: *degree of risk:* intermediate
vectorborne disease: tickborne encephalitis (2016)

Obesity—adult prevalence rate: 21.2% (2016)
country comparison to the world: 92
Education expenditures: 4.8% of GDP (2013)
country comparison to the world: 52

Literacy: *definition:* age 15 and over can read and write
total population: 99.8%
male: 99.8%
female: 99.8% (2015 est.)

School life expectancy (primary to tertiary education): *total:* 16 years
male: 16 years
female: 17 years (2015)

Unemployment, youth ages 15-24: *total:* 13.1%
male: 13.8%
female: 12.2% (2015 est.)
country comparison to the world: 53

GOVERNMENT

Country name: *conventional long form:* Republic of Estonia
conventional short form: Estonia
local long form: Eesti Vabariik
local short form: Eesti
former: Estonian Soviet Socialist Republic
etymology: the country name may be derived from the Aesti, an ancient people who lived along the eastern Baltic Sea in the first centuries A.D.

Government type: parliamentary republic

Capital: *name:* Tallinn
geographic coordinates: 59 26 N, 24 43 E

time difference: UTC+2 (7 hours ahead of Washington, DC, during Standard Time)
daylight saving time: +1hr, begins last Sunday in March; ends last Sunday in October

Administrative divisions: 15 counties (maakonnad, singular—maakond); Harjumaa (Tallinn), Hiiumaa (Kardla), Ida-Virumaa (Johvi), Jarvamaa (Paide), Jogevamaa (Jogeva), Laanemaa (Haapsalu), Laane-Virumaa (Rakvere), Parnumaa (Parnu), Polvamaa (Polva), Raplamaa (Rapla), Saaremaa (Kuressaare), Tartumaa (Tartu), Valgamaa (Valga), Viljandimaa (Viljandi), Vorumaa (Voru)
note: counties have the administrative center name following in parentheses

Independence: 20 August 1991 (declared); 6 September 1991 (recognized by the Soviet Union)

National holiday: Independence Day, 24 February (1918); note—24 February 1918 was the date Estonia declared its independence from Soviet Russia and established its statehood; 20 August 1991 was the date it declared its independence from the Soviet Union

Constitution: history: several previous; latest adopted 28 June 1992
amendments: proposed by at least one-fifth of Parliament members or by the president of the republic; passage requires three readings of the proposed amendment and a simple majority vote in two successive memberships of Parliament; passage of amendments to the "General Provisions" and "Amendment of the Constitution" chapters requires at least three-fifths majority vote by Parliament to conduct a referendum and majority vote in a referendum; amended several times, last in 2015 (2016)

Legal system: civil law system

International law organization participation: accepts compulsory ICJ jurisdiction with reservations; accepts ICCt jurisdiction

Citizenship: *citizenship by birth:* no
citizenship by descent only: at least one parent must be a citizen of Estonia
dual citizenship recognized: no
residency requirement for naturalization: 5 years

Suffrage: 18 years of age; universal; age 16 for local elections

Executive branch: *chief of state:* President Kersti KALJULAID (since 10 October 2016)

head of government: Juri RATAS (since 23 November 2016)
cabinet: Cabinet appointed by the prime minister, approved by Parliament
elections/appointments: president indirectly elected by Parliament for a 5-year term (eligible for a second term); if a candidate does not secure two-thirds of the votes after 3 rounds of balloting, then an electoral college consisting of Parliament members and local council members elects the president, choosing between the 2 candidates with the highest number of votes; election last held on 29-30 August 2016, but three rounds were inconclusive; two electoral college votes on 24

September 2016 were also indecisive, so the election passed back to Parliament; on 3 October the Parliament elected Kersti KALJULAID as president; prime minister nominated by the president and approved by Parliament

election results: Kersti KALJULAID elected president; Parliament vote—Kersti KALJULAID (independent) 81 of 98 votes; note—KALJULAID is Estonia's first female president

Legislative branch: description: unicameral Parliament or Riigikogu (101 seats; members directly elected in multi-seat constituencies by proportional representation vote to serve 4-year terms)
elections: last held on 1 March 2015 (next to be held in March 2019)
election results: percent of vote by party—RE 27.7%, K 24.8%, SDE 15.2%, IRL 13.7%, EV 8.7%, EKRE 8.1%, other 1.8%; seats by party—RE 30, K 27, SDE 15, IRL 14, EV 8, EKRE 7

Judicial branch: *highest court(s):* Supreme Court (consists of 19 justices including the chief justice and organized into civil, criminal, administrative, and constitutional review chambers)
judge selection and term of office: the chief justice is proposed by the president of the republic and appointed by the Riigikogu; other justices proposed by the chief justice and appointed by the Riigikogu; justices appointed for life
subordinate courts: circuit (appellate) courts; administrative, county, city, and specialized courts

Political parties and leaders: Center Party of Estonia (Keskerakond) or EK [Juri RATAS]
Estonian Conservative People's Party (Konservatiivne Rahvaerakond) or EKRE [Mart HELME]
Estonian Reform Party (Reformierakond) or RE [Hanno PEVKUR]
Free Party or EV [Andres HERKEL]
Social Democratic Party or SDE [Jevgeni OSSINOVSKI]
Union of Pro Patria and Res Publica (Isamaa je Res Publica Liit) or IRL [Margus TSAHKNA]

International organization participation: Australia Group, BA, BIS, CBSS, CD, CE, EAPC, EBRD, ECB, EIB, EMU, ESA (cooperating state), EU, FAO, IAEA, IBRD, ICAO, ICC (national committees), ICCt, ICRM, IDA, IEA, IFAD, IFC, IFRCS, IHO, ILO, IMF, IMO, Interpol, IOC, IOM, IPU, ISO, ITSO, ITU, ITUC (NGOs), MIGA, MINUSMA, NATO, NIB, NSG, OAS (observer), OECD, OIF (observer), OPCW, OSCE, PCA, Schengen Convention, UN, UNCTAD, UNESCO, UNHCR, UNTSO, UPU, WCO, WHO, WIPO, WMO, WTO

Diplomatic representation in the US: *chief of mission:* Ambassador Lauri LEPIK (since 8 September 2017)
chancery: 2131 Massachusetts Avenue NW, Washington, DC 20008
telephone: [1] (202) 588-0101
FAX: [1] (202) 588-0108
consulate(s) general: New York

Diplomatic representation from the US: *chief of mission:* Ambassador James D. MELVILLE Jr. (since 8 December 2015)
embassy: Kentmanni 20, 15099 Tallinn

mailing address: use embassy street address
telephone: [372] 668-8100
FAX: [372] 668-8265

Flag description: three equal horizontal bands of blue (top), black, and white; various interpretations are linked to the flag colors; blue represents faith, loyalty, and devotion, while also reminiscent of the sky, sea, and lakes of the country; black symbolizes the soil of the country and the dark past and suffering endured by the Estonian people; white refers to the striving towards enlightenment and virtue, and is the color of birch bark and snow, as well as summer nights illuminated by the midnight sun

National symbol(s): barn swallow, cornflower; national colors: blue, black, white

National anthem: name: "Mu isamaa, mu onn ja room" (My Native Land, My Pride and Joy)
lyrics/music: Johann Voldemar JANNSEN/Fredrik PACIUS
note: adopted 1920, though banned between 1940 and 1990 under Soviet occupation; the anthem, used in Estonia since 1869, shares the same melody as Finland's but has different lyrics

ECONOMY

Economy—overview: Estonia, a member of the EU since 2004 and the euro zone since 2011, has a modern market-based economy and one of the higher per capita income levels in Central Europe and the Baltic region, but its economy is highly dependent on trade, leaving it vulnerable to external shocks. Estonia's successive governments have pursued a free market, pro-business economic agenda, and sound fiscal policies that have resulted in balanced budgets and the lowest debt-to-GDP ratio in the EU.

The economy benefits from strong electronics and telecommunications sectors and strong trade ties with Finland, Sweden, Germany, and Russia. After two years of robust recovery in 2011 and 2012, the Estonian economy faltered in 2013 with only 1.6% GDP growth, mainly due to a continuing recession in much of the EU. GDP growth dropped below 2% in 2015 due to lower demand in key Scandinavian and Russian export markets. Rapid increases in investment, which includes EU development funding, and the recovery of export markets contributed to an estimated 4.2% GDP growth in 2017. Inflation also rose in 2017 alongside increased global prices for food and energy, which make up a large share of Estonia's consumption basket.

Estonia is challenged by a shortage of labor, both skilled and unskilled, although the government has amended its immigration law to allow easier hiring of highly qualified foreign workers, and wage growth that outpaces productivity gains. The government is also pursuing efforts to boost productivity growth with a focus on innovations that emphasize technology start-ups and e-commerce.

GDP (purchasing power parity): $41.2 billion (2017 est.)
$39.62 billion (2016 est.)

$38.82 billion (2015 est.)
note: data are in 2017 dollars
country comparison to the world: 116

GDP (official exchange rate): $25.68 billion (2016 est.)

GDP—real growth rate: 4% (2017 est.)
2.1% (2016 est.)
1.7% (2015 est.)
country comparison to the world: 72

GDP—per capita (PPP): $31,500 (2017 est.)
$30,200 (2016 est.)
$29,600 (2015 est.)
note: data are in 2017 dollars
country comparison to the world: 61

Gross national saving: 26.3% of GDP (2017 est.)
24.6% of GDP (2016 est.)
26% of GDP (2015 est.)
country comparison to the world: 43

GDP—composition, by end use:
household consumption: 52.2%
government consumption: 20.5%
investment in fixed capital: 24.7%
investment in inventories: -1.1%
exports of goods and services: 85.9%
imports of goods and services: -82.2% (2017 est.)

GDP—composition, by sector of origin:
agriculture: 3.4%
industry: 27.8%
services: 68.8% (2017 est.)

Agriculture—products: grain, potatoes, vegetables; livestock and dairy products; fish

Industries: food, engineering, electronics, wood and wood products, textiles; information technology, telecommunications

Industrial production growth rate: 3.8% (2017 est.)
country comparison to the world: 74

Labor force: 670,200 (2017 est.)
country comparison to the world: 153

Labor force—by occupation: *agriculture:* 3.1%
industry: 20.2%
services: 76.7% (2016 est.)

Unemployment rate: 8.4% (2017 est.)
6.8% (2016 est.)
country comparison to the world: 114

Population below poverty line: 21.3% (2015 est.)

Household income or consumption by percentage share: *lowest 10%:* 2.3%
highest 10%: 25.6% (2015)

Distribution of family income—Gini index: 34.8 (2015)
35.6 (2014)
country comparison to the world: 96

Budget: *revenues:* $9.772 billion
expenditures: $9.89 billion (2017 est.)
Taxes and other revenues: 38% of GDP (2017 est.)
country comparison to the world: 45

Budget surplus (+) or deficit (-): -0.5% of GDP (2017 est.)
country comparison to the world: 47

Public debt: 9.3% of GDP (2017 est.)
9.5% of GDP (2016 est.)

note: data cover general government debt, and includes debt instruments issued (or owned) by government entities, including sub-sectors of central government, state government, local government, and social security funds
country comparison to the world: 197

Fiscal year: calendar year

Inflation rate (consumer prices): 3.8% (2017 est.)
0.8% (2016 est.)
country comparison to the world: 151

Central bank discount rate: 0% (31 December 2016 est.)
0.05% (31 December 2015 est.)
country comparison to the world: 157

Commercial bank prime lending rate: 4.2% (31 December 2017 est.)
4.23% (31 December 2016 est.)
country comparison to the world: 159

Stock of narrow money: $13.42 billion (31 December 2017 est.)
$11.8 billion (31 December 2016 est.)
note: see entry for the European Union for money supply for the entire euro area; the European Central Bank (ECB) controls monetary policy for the 18 members of the Economic and Monetary Union (EMU); individual members of the EMU do not control the quantity of money circulating within their own borders
country comparison to the world: 77

Stock of broad money: $16.55 billion (31 December 2017 est.)
$14.66 billion (31 December 2016 est.)
country comparison to the world: 96

Stock of domestic credit: $23.2 billion (31 December 2017 est.)
$20.97 billion (31 December 2016 est.)
country comparison to the world: 87

Market value of publicly traded shares: $6.76 billion (31 December 2016 est.)
$6.799 billion (31 December 2015 est.)
$7.127 billion (31 December 2014 est.)
country comparison to the world: 80

Current account balance: $452 million (2017 est.)
$443 million (2016 est.)
country comparison to the world: 47

Exports: $14.02 billion (2017 est.)
$12.36 billion (2016 est.)
country comparison to the world: 79

Exports—commodities: machinery and electrical equipment 30%, food products and beverages 9%, mineral fuels 6%, wood and wood products 14%, articles of base metals 7%, furniture and bedding 11%, vehicles and parts 3%, chemicals 4% (2016 est.)

Exports—partners: Sweden 17.9%, Finland 16%, Latvia 9.2%, Russia 6.5%, Lithuania 6%, Germany 5.9%, Norway 4.1% (2016)

Imports: $15.31 billion (2017 est.)
$13.31 billion (2016 est.)
country comparison to the world: 85

Imports—commodities: machinery and electrical equipment 28%, mineral fuels 11%, food and food

products 10%, vehicles 9%, chemical products 8%, metals 8% (2015 est.)

Imports—partners: Finland 13%, Germany 11%, Lithuania 9%, Sweden 8.3%, Latvia 8.2%, Poland 7.2%, Netherlands 6.3%, Russia 5.7%, China 4.8% (2016)

Reserves of foreign exchange and gold: $389.8 million (31 December 2017 est.)
$352.2 million (31 December 2016 est.)
country comparison to the world: 149

Debt—external: $19.05 billion (31 December 2016 est.)
$18.3 billion (31 December 2015 est.)
country comparison to the world: 93

Stock of direct foreign investment—at home: $23.84 billion (31 December 2017 est.)
$22.19 billion (31 December 2016 est.)
country comparison to the world: 75

Stock of direct foreign investment—abroad: $9.771 billion (31 December 2017 est.)
$9.396 billion (31 December 2016 est.)
country comparison to the world: 62

Exchange rates: euros (EUR) per US dollar—
0.9228 (2017 est.)
0.9037 (2016 est.)
0.9037 (2015 est.)
0.885 (2014 est.)
0.7634 (2013 est.)

ENERGY

Electricity access: *electrification—total population:* 100% (2016)

Electricity—production: 9.779 billion kWh (2015 est.)
country comparison to the world: 101

Electricity—consumption: 8.158 billion kWh (2015 est.)
country comparison to the world: 102

Electricity—exports: 5.613 billion kWh (2016 est.)
country comparison to the world: 33

Electricity—imports: 3.573 billion kWh (2016 est.)
country comparison to the world: 49

Electricity—installed generating capacity: 2.864 million kW (2015 est.)
country comparison to the world: 99

Electricity—from fossil fuels: 75.6% of total installed capacity (2015 est.)
country comparison to the world: 95

Electricity—from nuclear fuels: 0% of total installed capacity (2015 est.)
country comparison to the world: 85

Electricity—from hydroelectric plants: 0.2% of total installed capacity (2015 est.)
country comparison to the world: 154

Electricity—from other renewable sources: 25.1% of total installed capacity (2015 est.)
country comparison to the world: 22

Crude oil—production: 0 bbl/day (2016 est.)
country comparison to the world: 131

Crude oil—exports: 0 bbl/day (2016 est.)

country comparison to the world: 118

Crude oil—imports: 0 bbl/day (2016 est.)
country comparison to the world: 121

Crude oil—proved reserves: 0 bbl (1 January 2017 es)
country comparison to the world: 131

Refined petroleum products—production: 0 bbl/day (2016 est.)
country comparison to the world: 141

Refined petroleum products—consumption: 29,140 bbl/day (2016 est.)
country comparison to the world: 123

Refined petroleum products—exports: 21,250 bbl/day (2016 est.)
country comparison to the world: 70

Refined petroleum products—imports: 34,410 bbl/day (2016 est.)
country comparison to the world: 97

Natural gas—production: 0 cu m (2015 est.)
country comparison to the world: 130

Natural gas—consumption: 964 million cu m (2015 est.)
country comparison to the world: 100

Natural gas—exports: 0 cu m (2015 est.)
country comparison to the world: 98

Natural gas—imports: 471 million cu m (2015 est.)
country comparison to the world: 68

Natural gas—proved reserves: 0 cu m (1 January 2014 es)
country comparison to the world: 135

Carbon dioxide emissions from consumption of energy: 5.8 million Mt (2013 est.)
country comparison to the world: 123

COMMUNICATIONS

Telephones—fixed lines: *total subscriptions:* 370,589
subscriptions per 100 inhabitants: 29 (July 2016 est.)
country comparison to the world: 103

Telephones—mobile cellular: *total:* 1,897,921
subscriptions per 100 inhabitants: 151 (July 2016 est.)
country comparison to the world: 150

Telephone system: *general assessment:* foreign investment in the form of joint business ventures greatly improved telephone service with a wide range of high-quality voice, data, and Internet services available
domestic: substantial fiber-optic cable systems carry telephone, TV, and radio traffic in the digital mode; Internet services are widely available; schools and libraries are connected to the Internet, a large percentage of the population files income tax returns online, and online voting—in local and parliamentary elections—has climbed steadily since first introduced in 2005; 85% of Estonian households have broadband access
international: country code—372; fiber-optic cables to Finland, Sweden, Latvia, and Russia provide worldwide packet-switched service;

2 international switches are located in Tallinn (2016)

Broadcast media: the publicly owned broadcaster, Eesti Rahvusringhaaling (ERR), operates 3 TV channels and 5 radio networks; growing number of private commercial radio stations broadcasting nationally, regionally, and locally; fully transitioned to digital television in 2010; national private TV channels expanding service; a range of channels are aimed at Russian-speaking viewers; in 2016, there were 42 on-demand services available in Estonia, including 19 pay TVOD and SVOD services; roughly 85% of households accessed digital television services (2016)

Internet country code: .ee
Internet users: total: 1,097,921

percent of population: 87.2% (July 2016 est.)
country comparison to the world: 122

TRANSPORTATION

National air transport system: *number of registered air carriers:* 3
inventory of registered aircraft operated by air carriers: 14
annual passenger traffic on registered air carriers: 512,388
annual freight traffic on registered air carriers: 870,362 mt-km (2015)
Civil aircraft registration country code prefix: ES (2016)

Airports: 18 (2013)
country comparison to the world: 141

Airports—with paved runways: *total:* 13
over 3,047 m: 2
2,438 to 3,047 m: 8
1,524 to 2,437 m: 2
914 to 1,523 m: 1 (2017)

Airports—with unpaved runways: *total:* 5
1,524 to 2,437 m: 1
914 to 1,523 m: 1

under 914 m: 3 (2013)

Heliports: 1 (2012)

Pipelines: gas 2,360 km (2016)

Railways: *total:* 2,146 km
broad gauge: 2,146 km 1.520-m and 1.524-m gauge (132 km electrified)
note: includes 1,510 km public and 636 km non-public railway (2016)
country comparison to the world: 86

Roadways: *total:* 58,412 km (includes urban roads)
paved: 10,427 km (includes 115 km of expressways)
unpaved: 47,985 km (2011)
country comparison to the world: 73

Waterways: 335 km (320 km are navigable year-round) (2011)
country comparison to the world: 90

Merchant marine: *total:* 78
by type: general cargo 7, oil tanker 5, other 66 (2017)
country comparison to the world: 97

Ports and terminals: *major seaport(s):* Kuivastu, Kunda, Muuga, Parnu Reid, Sillamae, Tallinn

MILITARY AND SECURITY

Military expenditures: 2.17% of GDP (2016)
2.09% of GDP (2015)
1.95% of GDP (2014)
1.91% of GDP (2013)
1.9% of GDP (2012)
country comparison to the world: 39

Military branches: Estonian Defense Forces (Eesti Kaitsevagi): Ground Forces (Maavagi), Navy (Merevagi), Air Force (Ohuvagi), Reserves (Kaitseliit) (2016)

Military service age and obligation: 18-27 for compulsory military or governmental service, conscript service requirement 8-11 months depending on education; NCOs, reserve officers, and specialists serve 11 months (2016)

TRANSNATIONAL ISSUES

Disputes—international: Russia and Estonia in May 2005 signed a technical border agreement, but Russia in June 2005 recalled its signature after the Estonian parliament added to its domestic ratification act a historical preamble referencing the Soviet occupation and Estonia's pre-war borders under the 1920 Treaty of Tartu; Russia contends that the preamble allows Estonia to make territorial claims on Russia in the future, while Estonian officials deny that the preamble has any legal impact on the treaty text; Russia demands better treatment of the Russian-speaking population in Estonia; as a member state that forms part of the EU's external border, Estonia implements strict Schengen border rules with Russia

Refugees and internally displaced persons: *stateless persons:* 82,585 (2016); note—following independence in 1991, automatic citizenship was restricted to those who were Estonian citizens prior to the 1940 Soviet occupation and their descendants; thousands of ethnic Russians remained stateless when forced to choose between passing Estonian language and citizenship tests or applying for Russian citizenship; one reason for demurring on Estonian citizenship was to retain the right of visa-free travel to Russia; stateless residents can vote in local elections but not general elections; stateless parents who have been lawful residents of Estonia for at least five years can apply for citizenship for their children before they turn 15 years old

Illicit drugs: growing producer of synthetic drugs; increasingly important transshipment zone for cannabis, cocaine, opiates, and synthetic drugs since joining the European Union and the Schengen Accord; potential money laundering related to organized crime and drug trafficking is a concern, as is possible use of the gambling sector to launder funds; major use of opiates and ecstasy

ETHIOPIA

INTRODUCTION

Background: Unique among African countries, the ancient Ethiopian monarchy maintained its freedom from colonial rule with the exception of a short-lived Italian occupation from 1936-41. In 1974, a military junta, the Derg, deposed Emperor Haile SELASSIE (who had ruled since 1930) and established a socialist state. Torn by bloody coups, uprisings, wide-scale drought, and massive refugee problems, the regime was finally toppled in 1991 by a coalition of rebel forces, the Ethiopian People's Revolutionary Democratic Front. A constitution was adopted in 1994, and Ethiopia's first multiparty elections were held in 1995. A border war with Eritrea in the late 1990s ended with a peace treaty in December 2000. In November 2007, the Eritrea-Ethiopia Border Commission (EEBC) issued specific coordinates as virtually demarcating the border and pronounced its work finished. Alleging that the EEBC acted beyond its mandate in issuing the coordinates, Ethiopia has not accepted them and has not withdrawn troops from previously contested areas pronounced by the EEBC as belonging to Eritrea. In August 2012, longtime leader Prime Minister MELES Zenawi died in office and was replaced by his Deputy Prime Minister HAILEMARIAM Desalegn, marking the first peaceful transition of power in decades.

GEOGRAPHY

Location: Eastern Africa, west of Somalia
Geographic coordinates: 8 00 N, 38 00 E

Mup references: Africa

Area: *total:* 1,104,300 sq km
land: 1 million sq km
water: 104,300 sq km
country comparison to the world: 28

Area—comparative: slightly less than twice the size of Texas

Land boundaries: *total:* 5,925 km
border countries (6): Djibouti 342 km, Eritrea 1,033 km, Kenya 867 km, Somalia 1,640 km, South Sudan 1,299 km, Sudan 744 km

Coastline: 0 km (landlocked)

Maritime claims: none (landlocked)

Climate: tropical monsoon with wide topographic-induced variation

Terrain: high plateau with central mountain range divided by Great Rift Valley

Elevation: *mean elevation:* 1,330 m
elevation extremes: *lowest point:* Danakil Depression -125 m
highest point: Ras Dejen 4,550 m

Natural resources: small reserves of gold, platinum, copper, potash, natural gas, hydropower

Land use: *agricultural land:* 36.3%
arable land: 15.2%;
permanent crops: 1.1%;
permanent pasture: 20%
forest: 12.2%
other: 51.5% (2011 est.)

Irrigated land: 2,900 sq km (2012)

Population—distribution: highest density is found in the highlands of the north and middle areas of the country, particularly around the centrally located capital city of Addis Ababa; the far east and southeast are sparsely populated

Natural hazards: geologically active Great Rift Valley susceptible to earthquakes, volcanic eruptions; frequent droughts
volcanism: volcanic activity in the Great Rift Valley; Erta Ale (613 m), which has caused frequent lava flows in recent years, is the country's most active volcano; Dabbahu became active in 2005, forcing evacuations; other historically active volcanoes include Alayta, Dalaffilla, Dallol, Dama Ali, Fentale, Kone, Manda Hararo, and Manda-Inakir

Environment—current issues: deforestation; overgrazing; soil erosion; desertification; water shortages in some areas from water-intensive farming and poor management

Environment—international agreements: *party to:* Biodiversity, Climate Change, Climate Change-Kyoto Protocol, Desertification, Endangered Species, Hazardous Wastes, Ozone Layer Protection
signed, but not ratified: Environmental Modification, Law of the Sea

Geography—note: landlocked—entire coastline along the Red Sea was lost with the de jure independence of Eritrea on 24 May 1993; Ethiopia is, therefore, the most populous landlocked country in the world; the Blue Nile, the chief headstream of the Nile by water volume, rises in T'ana Hayk

(Lake Tana) in northwest Ethiopia; three major crops are believed to have originated in Ethiopia: coffee, grain sorghum, and castor bean

PEOPLE AND SOCIETY

Population: 105,350,020
note: estimates for this country explicitly take into account the effects of excess mortality due to AIDS; this can result in lower life expectancy, higher infant mortality, higher death rates, lower population growth rates, and changes in the distribution of population by age and sex than would otherwise be expected (July 2017 est.)
country comparison to the world: 12

Nationality: *noun:* Ethiopian(s)
adjective: Ethiopian

Ethnic groups: Oromo 34.4%, Amhara (Amara) 27%, Somali (Somalie) 6.2%, Tigray (Tigrinya) 6.1%, Sidama 4%, Gurage 2.5%, Welaita 2.3%, Hadiya 1.7%, Afar (Affar) 1.7%, Gamo 1.5%, Gedeo 1.3%, Silte 1.3%, Kefficho 1.2%, other 8.8% (2007 est.)

Languages: Oromo (official working language in the State of Oromiya) 33.8%, Amharic (official national language) 29.3%, Somali (official working language of the State of Sumale) 6.2%, Tigrigna (Tigrinya) (official working language of the State of Tigray) 5.9%, Sidamo 4%, Wolaytta 2.2%, Gurage 2%, Afar (official working language of the State of Afar) 1.7%, Hadiyya 1.7%, Gamo 1.5%, Gedeo 1.3%, Opuuo 1.2%, Kafa 1.1%, other 8.1%, English (major foreign language taught in schools), Arabic (2007 est.)

Religions: Ethiopian Orthodox 43.5%, Muslim 33.9%, Protestant 18.5%, traditional 2.7%, Catholic 0.7%, other 0.6% (2007 est.)

Demographic profile: Ethiopia is a predominantly agricultural country—more than 80% of the population lives in rural areas—that is in the early stages of demographic transition. Infant, child, and maternal mortality have fallen sharply over the past decade, but the total fertility rate has declined more slowly and the population continues to grow. The rising age of marriage and the increasing proportion of women remaining single have contributed to fertility reduction. While the use of modern contraceptive methods among married women has increased significantly from 6 percent in 2000 to 27 percent in 2012, the overall rate is still quite low.

Ethiopia's rapid population growth is putting increasing pressure on land resources, expanding environmental degradation, and raising vulnerability to food shortages. With more than 40 percent of the population below the age of 15 and a fertility rate of over 5 children per woman (and even higher in rural areas), Ethiopia will have to make further progress in meeting its family planning needs if it is to achieve the age structure necessary for reaping a demographic dividend in the coming decades.

Poverty, drought, political repression, and forced government resettlement have driven Ethiopia's internal and external migration since

the 1960s. Before the 1974 revolution, only small numbers of the Ethiopian elite went abroad to study and then returned home, but under the brutal Derg regime thousands fled the country, primarily as refugees. Between 1982 and 1991 there was a new wave of migration to the West for family reunification. Since the defeat of the Derg in 1991, Ethiopians have migrated to escape violence among some of the country's myriad ethnic groups or to pursue economic opportunities. Internal and international trafficking of women and children for domestic work and prostitution is a growing problem.

Age structure: *0-14 years:* 43.47% (male 22,963,502/female 22,826,957)
15-24 years: 20.11% (male 10,516,591/female 10,669,695)
25-54 years: 29.58% (male 15,464,171/female 15,702,104)
55-64 years: 3.91% (male 1,998,711/female 2,115,210)
65 years and over: 2.94% (male 1,391,339/female 1,701,740) (2017 est.)

Dependency ratios: *total dependency ratio:* 82.1
youth dependency ratio: 75.8
elderly dependency ratio: 6.3
potential support ratio: 15.8 (2015 est.)

Median age: *total:* 17.9 years
male: 17.7 years
female: 18.1 years (2017 est.)
country comparison to the world: 217

Population growth rate: 2.85% (2017 est.)
country comparison to the world: 10

Birth rate: 36.5 births/1,000 population (2017 est.)
country comparison to the world: 14

Death rate: 7.7 deaths/1,000 population (2017 est.)
country comparison to the world: 102

Net migration rate: -0.2 migrant(s)/1,000 population (2017 est.)
country comparison to the world: 112

Population distribution: highest density is found in the highlands of the north and middle areas of the country, particularly around the centrally located capital city of Addis Ababa; the far east and southeast are sparsely populated

Urbanization: *urban population:* 20.4% of total population (2017)
rate of urbanization: 4.64% annual rate of change (2015-20 est.)

Major urban areas—population: ADDIS ABABA (capital) 3.238 million (2015)

Sex ratio: *at birth:* 1.03 male(s)/female
0-14 years: 1.01 male(s)/female
15-24 years: 0.99 male(s)/female
25-54 years: 0.99 male(s)/female
55-64 years: 0.95 male(s)/female
65 years and over: 0.82 male(s)/female
total population: 0.99 male(s)/female (2016 est.)

Mother's mean age at first birth: 20 years
note: median age at first birth among women 25-29 (2016 est.)

Maternal mortality ratio: 353 deaths/100,000 live births (2015 est.)
country comparison to the world: 35

Infant mortality rate: *total:* 49.6 deaths/1,000 live births
male: 56.9 deaths/1,000 live births
female: 42.2 deaths/1,000 live births (2017 est.)
country comparison to the world: 31

Life expectancy at birth: *total population:* 62.6 years
male: 60.1 years
female: 65.1 years (2017 est.)
country comparison to the world: 196

Total fertility rate: 4.99 children born/woman (2017 est.)
country comparison to the world: 15

Contraceptive prevalence rate: 39.2% (2016)
Health expenditures: 4.9% of GDP (2014)
country comparison to the world: 145

Physicians density: 0.03 physicians/1,000 population (2009)

Hospital bed density: 6.3 beds/1,000 population (2011)

Drinking water source:
improved:
urban: 93.1% of population
rural: 48.6% of population
total: 57.3% of population
unimproved:
urban: 6.9% of population
rural: 51.4% of population
total: 42.7% of population (2015 est.)

Sanitation facility access:
improved:
urban: 27.2% of population
rural: 28.2% of population
total: 28% of population
unimproved:
urban: 72.8% of population
rural: 71.8% of population
total: 72% of population (2015 est.)

HIV/AIDS—adult prevalence rate: 1.1% (2016 est.)
country comparison to the world: 41

HIV/AIDS—people living with HIV/AIDS: 710,000 (2016 est.)
country comparison to the world: 12

HIV/AIDS—deaths: 20,000 (2016 est.)
country comparison to the world: 14

Major infectious diseases: *degree of risk:* very high
food or waterborne diseases: bacterial and protozoal diarrhea, hepatitis A, and typhoid fever
vectorborne diseases: malaria and dengue fever
respiratory disease: meningococcal meningitis
animal contact disease: rabies
water contact disease: schistosomiasis (2016)

Obesity—adult prevalence rate: 4.5% (2016)
country comparison to the world: 185

Children under the age of 5 years underweight: 23.6% (2016)
country comparison to the world: 15
Education expenditures: 4.5% of GDP (2013)

country comparison to the world: 85
Literacy: *definition:* age 15 and over can read and write
total population: 49.1%
male: 57.2%
female: 41.1% (2015 est.)

School life expectancy (primary to tertiary education): *total:* 8 years
male: 9 years
female: 8 years (2012)

Unemployment, youth ages 15-24: *total:* 26.7%
male: 22%
female: 30.4% (2014 est.)
country comparison to the world: 36

GOVERNMENT

Country name: *conventional long form:* Federal Democratic Republic of Ethiopia
conventional short form: Ethiopia
local long form: Ityop'iya Federalawi Demokrasiyawi Ripeblik
local short form: Ityop'iya
former: Abyssinia, Italian East Africa
abbreviation: FDRE
etymology: the country name derives from the Greek word "Aethiopia," which in classical times referred to lands south of Egypt in the Upper Nile region

Government type: federal parliamentary republic

Capital: *name:* Addis Ababa
geographic coordinates: 9 02 N, 38 42 E
time difference: UTC+3 (8 hours ahead of Washington, DC, during Standard Time)

Administrative divisions: 9 ethnically based states (kililoch, singular—kilil) and 2 self-governing administrations* (astedaderoch, singular—astedader); Adis Abeba* (Addis Ababa), Afar, Amara (Amhara), Binshangul Gumuz, Dire Dawa*, Gambela Hizboch (Gambela Peoples), Hareri Hizb (Harari People), Oromiya (Oromia), Sumale (Somali), Tigray, Ye Debub Biheroch Bihereseboch na Hizboch (Southern Nations, Nationalities and Peoples)

Independence: oldest independent country in Africa and one of the oldest in the world—at least 2,000 years (may be traced to the Aksumite Kingdom, which coalesced in the first century B.C.)

National holiday: Derg Downfall Day (defeat of MENGISTU regime), 28 May (1991)

Constitution: history: several previous; latest drafted June 1994, adopted 8 December 1994, entered into force 21 August 1995
amendments: proposals submitted for discussion require two-thirds majority approval in either house of Parliament or majority approval of one-third of the State Councils; passage of amendments other than constitutional articles on fundamental rights and freedoms and the initiation and amendment of the constitution requires two-thirds majority vote in a joint session of Parliament and majority vote by two-thirds of the State Councils; passage of amendments affecting rights and freedoms and amendment procedures requires

two-thirds majority vote in each house of Parliament and majority vote by all the State Councils (2017)

Legal system: civil law system

International law organization participation: has not submitted an ICJ jurisdiction declaration; non-party state to the ICCt

Citizenship: *citizenship by birth:* no
citizenship by descent only: at least one parent must be a citizen of Ethiopia
dual citizenship recognized: no
residency requirement for naturalization: 4 years

Suffrage: 18 years of age; universal

Executive branch: *chief of state:* President MULATU Teshome Wirtu (since 7 October 2013)
head of government: Interim Prime Minister HAILEMARIAM Desalegn (since 15 February 2018); Deputy Prime Minister DEMEKE Mekonnen Hassen (since 29 November 2012); note—Prime Minister HAILEMARIAM Desalegn (since 21 September 2012) resigned on 15 February 2018
cabinet: Council of Ministers selected by the prime minister and approved by the House of People's Representatives
elections/appointments: president indirectly elected by both chambers of Parliament for a 6-year term (eligible for a second term); election last held on 7 October 2013 (next to be held in October 2019); prime minister designated by the majority party following legislative elections
election results: MULATU Teshome Wirtu (OPDO) elected president; Parliament vote—659 (unanimous)

Legislative branch: bicameral Parliament consists of the House of Federation or Yefedereshein Mikir Bete (153 seats; members indirectly elected by state assemblies to serve 5-year terms) and the House of People's Representatives or Yehizb Tewokayoch Mekir Bete (547 seats; members directly elected in single-seat constituencies by simple majority vote; 22 seats reserved for minorities; all members serve 5-year terms); note—the House of Federation is responsible for interpreting the constitution and federal-regional issues and the House of People's Representatives is responsible for passing legislation
elections: last held on 24 May 2015 (next to be held in 2020)
election results: House of Representatives percent of vote by party/coalition—NA; seats by party/coalition—EPRDF 501, SPDP 24, BGPDUP 9, ANDP 8, GPUDM 3, APDO 1, HNL 1

Judicial branch: *highest court(s):* Federal Supreme Court (consists of 11 judges); note—the House of Federation has jurisdiction for all constitutional issues
judge selection and term of office: president and vice president of Federal Supreme Court recommended by the prime minister and appointed by the House of People's Representatives; other Supreme Court judges nominated by the Federal Judicial Administrative Council (a 10-member body chaired by the president of the Federal

Supreme Court) and appointed by the House of People's Representatives; judges serve until retirement at age 60

subordinate courts: federal high courts and federal courts of first instance; state court systems (mirror structure of federal system); sharia courts and customary and traditional courts

Political parties and leaders: Afar National Democratic Party or ANDP [Taha AHMED]

Argoba People Democratic Organization or APDO

Benishangul Gumuz People's Democratic Unity Party or BGPDUP

Blue Party (Semayawi Party) [Solomon TESSEMA, spokesman]

Ethiopian Federal Democratic Unity Forum or MEDREK [Beyene PETROS] (a 4-party alliance)

Ethiopian People's Revolutionary Democratic Front or EPRDF [Hailemarian DESALEGN] (includes Amhara National Democratic Movement or ANDM; Oromo People's Democratic Organization or OPDO; Southern Ethiopian People's Democratic Movement or SEPDM; Tigray People's Liberation Front or TPLF)

Gambella Peoples Unity Democratic Movement or GPUDM

Harari National League or HNL [Murad ABDULHADI]

Somali People's Democratic Party or SPDP

Political pressure groups and leaders: Ginbot 7 Movement

Ogaden National Liberation Front or ONLF

Oromo Liberation Front or OLF [DAOUD Ibsa]

International organization participation: ACP, AfDB, AU, COMESA, EITI (candidate country), FAO, G-24, G-77, IAEA, IBRD, ICAO, ICRM, IDA, IFAD, IFC, IFRCS, IGAD, ILO, IMF, IMO, Interpol, IOC, IOM, IPU, ISO, ITSO, ITU, ITUC (NGOs), MIGA, NAM, OPCW, PCA, UN, UN Security Council (temporary), UNAMID, UNCTAD, UNESCO, UNHCR, UNIDO, UNISFA, UNMIL, UNOCI, UNWTO, UPU, WCO, WFTU (NGOs), WHO, WIPO, WMO, WTO (observer)

Diplomatic representation in the US: *chief of mission:* Ambassador Kassa TEKLEBERHAN Gebrehiwet (since 24 January 2018)

chancery: 3506 International Drive NW, Washington, DC 20008

telephone: [1] (202) 364-1200

FAX: [1] (202) 587-0195

consulate(s) general: Los Angeles, Seattle

consulate(s): Houston, New York

Diplomatic representation from the US: *chief of mission:* Ambassador Michael RAYNOR (since 3 October 2017)

embassy: Entoto Street, Addis Ababa

mailing address: P.O. Box 1014, Addis Ababa

telephone: [251] 11 130-6000

FAX: 124-2401 [251] 11 124 2401

Flag description: three equal horizontal bands of green (top), yellow, and red, with a yellow pentagram and single yellow rays emanating from the angles between the points on a light blue disk centered on the three bands; green represents hope and the fertility of the land, yellow symbolizes

justice and harmony, while red stands for sacrifice and heroism in the defense of the land; the blue of the disk symbolizes peace and the pentagram represents the unity and equality of the nationalities and peoples of Ethiopia

note: Ethiopia is the oldest independent country in Africa, and the three main colors of her flag (adopted ca. 1895) were so often appropriated by other African countries upon independence that they became known as the Pan-African colors; the emblem in the center of the current flag was added in 1996

National symbol(s): Abyssinian lion (traditional), yellow pentagram with five rays of light on a blue field (promoted by current government); national colors: green, yellow, red

National anthem: name: "Whedefit Gesgeshi Woud Enat Ethiopia" (March Forward, Dear Mother Ethiopia)

lyrics/music: DEREJE Melaku Mengesha/SOLOMON Lulu

note: adopted 1992

ECONOMY

Economy—overview: Ethiopia—the second most populous country in Africa—is a one-party state with a planned economy. For more than a decade before 2016, Ethiopia grew at a rate between 8% and 11% annually—one of the fastest growing states among the 188 IMF member countries. This growth was driven by government investment in infrastructure, as well as sustained progress in the agricultural and service sectors. More than 70% of Ethiopia's population is still employed in the agricultural sector, but services have surpassed agriculture as the principal source of GDP.

Ethiopia has the lowest level of income-inequality in Africa and one of the lowest in the world, with a Gini coefficient comparable to that of the Scandinavian countries. Yet despite progress toward eliminating extreme poverty, Ethiopia remains one of the poorest countries in the world, due both to rapid population growth and a low starting base. Changes in rainfall associated with world-wide weather patterns resulted in the worst drought in 30 years in 2015-16, creating food insecurity for millions of Ethiopians.

The state is heavily engaged in the economy. Ongoing infrastructure projects include power production and distribution, roads, rails, airports and industrial parks. Key sectors are state-owned, including telecommunications, banking and insurance, and power distribution. Under Ethiopia's constitution, the state owns all land and provides long-term leases to tenants. Title rights in urban areas, particularly Addis Ababa, are poorly regulated, and subject to corruption.

Ethiopia's foreign exchange earnings are led by the services sector—primarily the state-run Ethiopian Airlines—followed by exports of several commodities. While coffee remains the largest foreign exchange earner, Ethiopia is diversifying exports, and commodities such as gold, sesame, khat, livestock and horticulture products are becoming increasingly important. Manufacturing

represented less than 8% of total exports in 2016, but manufacturing exports should increase in future years due to a growing international presence.

The banking, insurance, telecommunications, and micro-credit industries are restricted to domestic investors, but Ethiopia has attracted roughly $8.5 billion in foreign direct investment, mostly from China, Turkey, India and the EU; US FDI is $567 million. Investment has been primarily in infrastructure, construction, agriculture/horticulture, agricultural processing, textiles, leather and leather products.

In the fall of 2015, the government finalized and published the current 2016-20 five-year plan, known as the Growth and Transformation Plan II, which emphasizes developing manufacturing in sectors where Ethiopia has a comparative advantage, such as textiles and garments, leather goods, and processed agricultural products. To support industrialization, Ethiopia plans to increase installed power generation capacity by 8,320 MW, up from a capacity of 2,000 MW, by building three more major dams and expanding to other sources of renewable energy. In 2017, the government devalued the birr by 15% to increase exports and alleviate a chronic foreign currency shortage in the country.

GDP (purchasing power parity): $195.8 billion (2017 est.)

$180.5 billion (2016 est.)

$167.2 billion (2015 est.)

note: data are in 2017 dollars

country comparison to the world: 65

GDP (official exchange rate): $79.74 billion (2016 est.)

GDP—real growth rate: 8.5% (2017 est.)

8% (2016 est.)

10.4% (2015 est.)

country comparison to the world: 4

GDP—per capita (PPP): $2,100 (2017 est.)

$2,000 (2016 est.)

$1,900 (2015 est.)

note: data are in 2017 dollars

country comparison to the world: 206

Gross national saving: 28.9% of GDP (2017 est.)

32% of GDP (2016 est.)

31.3% of GDP (2015 est.)

country comparison to the world: 30

GDP—composition, by end use:

household consumption: 70.5%

government consumption: 10.5%

investment in fixed capital: 41.9%

investment in inventories: -0.1%

exports of goods and services: 8.1%

imports of goods and services: -31% (2017 est.)

GDP—composition, by sector of origin:

agriculture: 35.8%

industry: 22.2%

services: 42% (2017 est.)

Agriculture—products: cereals, coffee, oilseed, cotton, sugarcane, vegetables, khat, cut flowers; hides, cattle, sheep, goats; fish

Industries: food processing, beverages, textiles, leather, garments, chemicals, metals processing, cement

Industrial production growth rate: 10.5% (2017 est.)
country comparison to the world: 9

Labor force: 52.82 million (2017 est.)
country comparison to the world: 14

Labor force—by occupation: *agriculture:* 72.7%
industry: 7.4%
services: 19.9% (2013 est.)

Unemployment rate: 17.5% (2012 est.)
18% (2011 est.)
country comparison to the world: 179

Population below poverty line: 29.6% (2014 est.)

Household income or consumption by percentage share: *lowest 10%:* 4.1%
highest 10%: 25.6% (2005)

Distribution of family income—Gini index: 33 (2011)
30 (2000)
country comparison to the world: 108

Budget: *revenues:* $12.11 billion
expenditures: $14.63 billion (2017 est.)
Taxes and other revenues: 15.2% of GDP (2017 est.)
country comparison to the world: 185

Budget surplus (+) or deficit (-): -3.2% of GDP (2017 est.)
country comparison to the world: 122

Public debt: 60.2% of GDP (2017 est.)
54.5% of GDP (2016 est.)
country comparison to the world: 74

Fiscal year: 8 July—7 July

Inflation rate (consumer prices): 8.1% (2017 est.)
7.3% (2016 est.)
country comparison to the world: 199

Central bank discount rate: NA%

Commercial bank prime lending rate: 13% (31 December 2017 est.)
12.2% (31 December 2016 est.)
country comparison to the world: 62

Stock of narrow money: $14.92 billion (31 December 2017 est.)
$14.56 billion (31 December 2016 est.)
country comparison to the world: 73

Stock of broad money: $28.53 billion (31 December 2017 est.)
$28.21 billion (31 December 2016 est.)
country comparison to the world: 79

Stock of domestic credit: $39.26 billion (31 December 2017 est.)
$36.37 billion (31 December 2016 est.)
country comparison to the world: 71

Market value of publicly traded shares: $NA

Current account balance: -$6.592 billion (2017 est.)
-$7.206 billion (2016 est.)
country comparison to the world: 180

Exports: $3.076 billion (2017 est.)
$2.814 billion (2016 est.)

country comparison to the world: 124

Exports—commodities: coffee (27%, by value), oilseeds (17%), edible vegetables including khat (17%), gold (13%), flowers (7%), live animals (7%), raw leather products (3%), meat products (3%)

Exports—partners: US 9.7%, Saudi Arabia 9.6%, Germany 8.5%, Switzerland 7.5%, China 5.1%, UAE 4.9%, Pakistan 4.4% (2016)

Imports: $16.76 billion (2017 est.)
$16.03 billion (2016 est.)
country comparison to the world: 82

Imports—commodities: machinery and aircraft (14%, by value), metal and metal products, (14%), electrical materials, (13%), petroleum products (12%), motor vehicles, (10%), chemicals and fertilizers (4%)

Imports—partners: China 28.8%, US 8%, India 6.7%, Kuwait 5% (2016)

Reserves of foreign exchange and gold: $3.147 billion (31 December 2017 est.)
$3.022 billion (31 December 2016 est.)
country comparison to the world: 103

Debt—external: $29.09 billion (31 December 2017 est.)
$24.82 billion (31 December 2016 est.)
country comparison to the world: 82

Exchange rates: birr (ETB) per US dollar—
23.6 (2017 est.)
21.732 (2016 est.)
21.732 (2015 est.)
21.55 (2014 est.)
19.8 (2013 est.)

ENERGY

Electricity access: *population without electricity:* 71,200,000
electrification—total population: 24%
electrification—urban areas: 85%
electrification—rural areas: 10% (2013)

Electricity—production: 10.08 billion kWh (2015 est.)
country comparison to the world: 100

Electricity—consumption: 8.143 billion kWh (2015 est.)
country comparison to the world: 103

Electricity—exports: 166 million kWh (2015 est.)
country comparison to the world: 77

Electricity—imports: 0 kWh (2016 est.)
country comparison to the world: 147

Electricity—installed generating capacity: 2.704 million kW (2015 est.)
country comparison to the world: 102

Electricity—from fossil fuels: 7.5% of total installed capacity (2015 est.)
country comparison to the world: 201

Electricity—from nuclear fuels: 0% of total installed capacity (2015 est.)
country comparison to the world: 88

Electricity—from hydroelectric plants: 79.5% of total installed capacity (2015 est.)
country comparison to the world: 14

Electricity—from other renewable sources: 13.4% of total installed capacity (2015 est.)
country comparison to the world: 54

Crude oil—production: 0 bbl/day (2016 est.)
country comparison to the world: 132

Crude oil—exports: 0 bbl/day (2014 est.)
country comparison to the world: 120

Crude oil—imports: 0 bbl/day (2014 est.)
country comparison to the world: 124

Crude oil—proved reserves: 428,000 bbl (1 January 2017 es)
country comparison to the world: 101

Refined petroleum products—production: 0 bbl/day (2014 est.)
country comparison to the world: 142

Refined petroleum products—consumption: 65,000 bbl/day (2015 est.)
country comparison to the world: 95

Refined petroleum products—exports: 0 bbl/day (2014 est.)
country comparison to the world: 153

Refined petroleum products—imports: 64,380 bbl/day (2014 est.)
country comparison to the world: 72

Natural gas—production: 0 cu m (2013 est.)
country comparison to the world: 133

Natural gas—consumption: 0 cu m (2013 est.)
country comparison to the world: 179

Natural gas—exports: 0 cu m (2013 est.)
country comparison to the world: 101

Natural gas—imports: 0 cu m (2013 est.)
country comparison to the world: 123

Natural gas—proved reserves: 24.92 billion cu m (1 January 2017 es)
country comparison to the world: 74

Carbon dioxide emissions from consumption of energy: 9.3 million Mt (2013 est.)
country comparison to the world: 107

COMMUNICATIONS

Telephones—fixed lines: *total subscriptions:* 1.147 million
subscriptions per 100 inhabitants: 1 (July 2016 est.)
country comparison to the world: 87

Telephones—mobile cellular: *total:* 51.224 million
subscriptions per 100 inhabitants: 50 (July 2016 est.)
country comparison to the world: 41

Telephone system: *general assessment:* Ethio Telecom maintains a monopoly over telecommunication services; open-wire, microwave radio relay; radio communication in the HF, VHF, and UHF frequencies; 2 domestic satellites provide the national trunk service
domestic: the number of mobile telephones is increasing steadily from a small base and now stands at over 50 per 100 persons
international: country code—251; open-wire to Sudan and Djibouti; microwave radio relay to Kenya and Djibouti; satellite earth stations—3

Intelsat (1 Atlantic Ocean and 2 Pacific Ocean) (2016)

Broadcast media: 6 public TV stations broadcasting nationally and 10 public radio broadcasters; 7 private radio stations and 19 community radio stations (2017)

Internet country code: .et
Internet users: total: 15,731,741

percent of population: 15.4% (July 2016 est.)
country comparison to the world: 107

National air transport system: *number of registered air carriers:* 1
inventory of registered aircraft operated by air carriers: 75
annual passenger traffic on registered air carriers: 7,074,779
annual freight traffic on registered air carriers: 1,228,738,320 mt-km (2015)
Civil aircraft registration country code prefix: ET (2016)

Airports: 57 (2013)
country comparison to the world: 83

Airports—with paved runways: *total:* 17
over 3,047 m: 3
2,438 to 3,047 m: 8
1,524 to 2,437 m: 4
under 914 m: 2 (2017)

Airports—with unpaved runways: *total:* 40
2,438 to 3,047 m: 3
1,524 to 2,437 m: 9
914 to 1,523 m: 20
under 914 m: 8 (2013)

Railways: *total:* 659 km (Ethiopian segment of the 756 km Addis Ababa-Djibouti railroad)

standard gauge: 659 km 1.435-m gauge
note: electric railway with redundant power supplies; under joint control of Djibouti and Ethiopia and managed by a Chinese contractor (2017)
country comparison to the world: 102

Roadways: *total:* 110,414 km
paved: 14,354 km
unpaved: 96,060 km (2015)
country comparison to the world: 44

Merchant marine: *total:* 11
by type: general cargo 9, oil tanker 2 (2017)
country comparison to the world: 141

Ports and terminals: Ethiopia is landlocked and uses the ports of Djibouti in Djibouti and Berbera in Somalia

Military expenditures: 0.67% of GDP (2016)
0.71% of GDP (2015)
0.77% of GDP (2014)
0.81% of GDP (2013)
0.87% of GDP (2012)
country comparison to the world: 107

Military branches: Ethiopian National Defense Force (ENDF): Ground Forces, Ethiopian Air Force (Ye Ityopya Ayer Hayl, ETAF) (2013)

Military service age and obligation: 18 years of age for voluntary military service; no compulsory military service, but the military can conduct callups when necessary and compliance is compulsory (2012)

Disputes—international: Eritrea and Ethiopia agreed to abide by the 2002 Eritrea-Ethiopia Boundary Commission's (EEBC) delimitation

decision, but neither party responded to the revised line detailed in the November 2006 EEBC Demarcation Statement; the undemarcated former British administrative line has little meaning as a political separation to rival clans within Ethiopia's Ogaden and southern Somalia's Oromo region; Ethiopian forces invaded southern Somalia and routed Islamist courts from Mogadishu in January 2007; "Somaliland" secessionists provide port facilities in Berbera and trade ties to landlocked Ethiopia; civil unrest in eastern Sudan has hampered efforts to demarcate the porous boundary with Ethiopia

Refugees and internally displaced persons: *refugees (country of origin):* 253,889 (Somalia) (refugees and asylum seekers); 164,668 (Eritrea) (refugees and asylum seekers); 44,386 (Sudan) (refugees and asylum seekers) (2017); 421,453 (South Sudan) (refugees and asylum seekers) (2018)
IDPs: 1,078,429 (border war with Eritrea from 1998-2000; ethnic clashes; and ongoing fighting between the Ethiopian military and separatist rebel groups in the Somali and Oromia regions; natural disasters; intercommunal violence; most IDPs live in Sumale state) (2017)

Illicit drugs: transit hub for heroin originating in Southwest and Southeast Asia and destined for Europe, as well as cocaine destined for markets in southern Africa; cultivates qat (khat) for local use and regional export, principally to Djibouti and Somalia (legal in all three countries); the lack of a well-developed financial system limits the country's utility as a money laundering center

EUROPEAN UNION

Legend: Member / Candidate

Preliminary statement: The evolution of what is today the European Union (EU) from a regional

economic agreement among six neighboring states in 1951 to today's hybrid intergovernmental and supranational organization of 28 countries across the European continent stands as an unprecedented phenomenon in the annals of history. Dynastic unions for territorial consolidation were long the norm in Europe; on a few occasions even country-level unions were arranged—the Polish-Lithuanian Commonwealth and the Austro-Hungarian Empire were examples. But for such a large number of nation-states to cede some of their sovereignty to an overarching entity is unique.

Although the EU is not a federation in the strict sense, it is far more than a free-trade association such as ASEAN, NAFTA, or Mercosur, and it has certain attributes associated with independent nations: its own flag, currency (for some members), and law-making abilities, as well as diplomatic representation and a common foreign and security policy in its dealings with external partners.

Thus, inclusion of basic intelligence on the EU has been deemed appropriate as a separate entity

in The World Factbook. However, because of the EU's special status, this description is placed after the regular country entries.

Background: Following the two devastating World Wars in the first half of the 20th century, a number of far-sighted European leaders in the late 1940s sought a response to the overwhelming desire for peace and reconciliation on the continent. In 1950, the French Foreign Minister Robert SCHUMAN proposed pooling the production of coal and steel in Western Europe and setting up an organization for that purpose that would bring France and the Federal Republic of Germany together and would be open to other countries as well. The following year, the European Coal and Steel Community (ECSC) was set up when six members—Belgium, France, West Germany, Italy, Luxembourg, and the Netherlands—signed the Treaty of Paris.

The ECSC was so successful that within a few years the decision was made to integrate other elements of the countries' economies. In 1957,

THE CIA WORLD FACTBOOK

envisioning an "ever closer union," the Treaties of Rome created the European Economic Community (EEC) and the European Atomic Energy Community (Euratom), and the six member states undertook to eliminate trade barriers among themselves by forming a common market. In 1967, the institutions of all three communities were formally merged into the European Community (EC), creating a single Commission, a single Council of Ministers, and the body known today as the European Parliament. Members of the European Parliament were initially selected by national parliaments, but in 1979 the first direct elections were undertaken and have been held every five years since.

In 1973, the first enlargement of the EC took place with the addition of Denmark, Ireland, and the UK. The 1980s saw further membership expansion with Greece joining in 1981 and Spain and Portugal in 1986. The 1992 Treaty of Maastricht laid the basis for further forms of cooperation in foreign and defense policy, in judicial and internal affairs, and in the creation of an economic and monetary union—including a common currency. This further integration created the European Union (EU), at the time standing alongside the EC. In 1995, Austria, Finland, and Sweden joined the EU/EC, raising the membership total to 15.

A new currency, the euro, was launched in world money markets on 1 January 1999; it became the unit of exchange for all EU member states except Denmark, Sweden, and the UK. In 2002, citizens of those 12 countries began using euro banknotes and coins. Ten new countries joined the EU in 2004—Cyprus, the Czech Republic, Estonia, Hungary, Latvia, Lithuania, Malta, Poland, Slovakia, and Slovenia. Bulgaria and Romania joined in 2007 and Croatia in 2013, bringing the current membership to 28. (Seven of these new countries—Cyprus, Estonia, Latvia, Lithuania, Malta, Slovakia, and Slovenia—have now adopted the euro, bringing total euro-zone membership to 19.)

In an effort to ensure that the EU could function efficiently with an expanded membership, the Treaty of Nice (concluded in 2000; entered into force in 2003) set forth rules to streamline the size and procedures of EU institutions. An effort to establish a "Constitution for Europe," growing out of a Convention held in 2002-2003, foundered when it was rejected in referenda in France and the Netherlands in 2005. A subsequent effort in 2007 incorporated many of the features of the rejected draft Constitutional Treaty while also making a number of substantive and symbolic changes. The new treaty, referred to as the Treaty of Lisbon, sought to amend existing treaties rather than replace them. The treaty was approved at the EU intergovernmental conference of the then 27 member states held in Lisbon in December 2007, after which the process of national ratifications began. In October 2009, an Irish referendum approved the Lisbon Treaty (overturning a previous rejection) and cleared the way for an ultimate unanimous endorsement. Poland and the Czech Republic ratified soon after. The Lisbon Treaty came into force on 1 December 2009 and the EU

officially replaced and succeeded the EC. The Treaty's provisions are part of the basic consolidated versions of the Treaty on European Union (TEU) and the Treaty on the Functioning of the European Union (TFEU) now governing what remains a very specific integration project.

Frustrated by a remote bureaucracy in Brussels and massive migration into the country, UK citizens on 23 June 2016 narrowly voted to leave the EU. The so-called "Brexit" will take years to carry out, but could embolden skeptics of EU membership in other member states.

GEOGRAPHY

Location: Europe between the North Atlantic Ocean in the west and Russia, Belarus, and Ukraine to the east

Map references: Europe

Area: *total:* 4,479,968 sq km
rank by area (sq km):
1. France (includes five overseas regions) 643,801
2. Spain 505,370
3. Sweden 450,295
4. Germany 357,022
5. Finland 338,145
6. Poland 312,685
7. Italy 301,340
8. United Kingdom (includes Gibraltar) 243,617
9. Romania 238,391
10. Greece 131,957
11. Bulgaria 110,879
12. Hungary 93,028
13. Portugal 92,090
14. Austria 83,871
15. Czechia 78,867
16. Ireland 70,273
17. Lithuania 65,300
18. Latvia 64,589
19. Croatia 56,594
20. Slovakia 49,035
21. Estonia 45,228
22. Denmark 43,094
23. Netherlands 41,543
24. Belgium 30,528
25. Slovenia 20,273
26. Cyprus 9,251
27. Luxembourg 2,586
28. Malta 316

Area—comparative: less than one-half the size of the US

Land boundaries: *total:* 13,271 km
border countries (17): Albania 212 km, Andorra 118 km, Belarus 1,176 km, Bosnia and Herzegovina 956 km, Holy See 3 km, Liechtenstein 34 km, Macedonia 396 km, Moldova 683 km, Monaco 6 km, Montenegro 19 km, Norway 2,375 km, Russia 2,435 km, San Marino 37 km, Serbia 1,353 km, Switzerland 1,729 km, Turkey 415 km, Ukraine 1,324 km
note: data for European continent only

Coastline: 65,992.9 km

Climate: cold temperate; potentially subarctic in the north to temperate; mild wet winters; hot dry summers in the south

Terrain: fairly flat along Baltic and Atlantic coasts; mountainous in the central and southern areas

Elevation: *mean elevation:* about 300 m

elevation extremes: *lowest point:* Lammefjord, Denmark -7 m; Zuidplaspolder, Netherlands -7 m *highest point:* Mont Blanc 4,810 m

Natural resources: iron ore, natural gas, petroleum, coal, copper, lead, zinc, bauxite, uranium, potash, salt, hydropower, arable land, timber, fish *Irrigated land:* 154,539.82 sq km (2011 est.)

Population—distribution: population distribution varies considerably from country to country, but tends to follow a pattern of coastal and river settlement, with urban agglomerations forming large hubs facilitating large scale housing, industry, and commerce; the area in and around the Netherlands, Belgium, and Luxembourg (known collectively as Benelux), is the most densely populated area in the EU

Natural hazards: flooding along coasts; avalanches in mountainous area; earthquakes in the south; volcanic eruptions in Italy; periodic droughts in Spain; ice floes in the Baltic

Environment—current issues: various forms of air, soil, and water pollution; see individual country entries

Environment—international agreements: *party to:* Air Pollution, Air Pollution-Nitrogen Oxides, Air Pollution-Persistent Organic Pollutants, Air Pollution-Sulphur 94, Antarctic-Marine Living Resources, Biodiversity, Climate Change, Climate Change-Kyoto Protocol, Desertification, Hazardous Wastes, Law of the Sea, Ozone Layer Protection, Tropical Timber 83, Tropical Timber 94 *signed but not ratified:* Air Pollution-Volatile Organic Compounds

PEOPLE AND SOCIETY

Population: *total:* 516,195,432
rank by population:
1. Germany 80,594,017
2. France 67,106,161
3. United Kingdom 64,769,452
4. Italy 62,137,802
5. Spain 48,958,159
6. Poland 38,476,269
7. Romania 21,529,967
8. Netherlands 17,084,719
9. Belgium 11,491,346
10. Portugal 10,839,514
11. Greece 10,768,477
12. Czechia 10,674,723
13. Sweden 9,960,487
14. Hungary 9,850,845
15. Austria 8,754,413
16. Bulgaria 7,101,510
17. Denmark 5,605,948
18. Finland 5,518,371
19. Slovakia 5,445,829
20. Ireland 5,011,102
21. Croatia 4,292,095
22. Lithuania 2,823,859
23. Slovenia 1,972,126
24. Latvia 1,944,643

25. Estonia 1,251,581
26. Cyprus 1,221,549
27. Luxembourg 594,130
28. Malta 416,338 (July 2017 est.)

Languages: Bulgarian, Croatian, Czech, Danish, Dutch, English, Estonian, Finnish, French, German, Greek, Hungarian, Irish, Italian, Latvian, Lithuanian, Maltese, Polish, Portuguese, Romanian, Slovak, Slovene, Spanish, Swedish
note: only the 24 official languages are listed; German, the major language of Germany, Austria, and Switzerland, is the most widely spoken mother tongue—about 16% of the EU population; English is the most widely spoken foreign language—about 38% of the EU population is conversant with it (2012)

Religions: Roman Catholic 48%, Protestant 12%, Orthodox 8%, other Christian 4%, Muslim 2%, other 1% (includes Jewish, Sikh, Buddhist, Hindu), atheist 7%, non-believer/agnostic 16%, unspecified 2% (2012 est.)

Age structure: *0-14 years:* 15.5% (male 40,853,366/female 38,783,889)
15-24 years: 10.9% (male 28,680,885/female 27,396,922)
25-54 years: 41.8% (male 108,312,731/female 106,407,509)
55-64 years: 12.9% (male 32,287,068/female 34,128,099)
65 years and over: 19.1% (male 42,074,448/female 56,127,861) (2017 est.)

Median age: *total:* 42.9 years
male: 41.5 years
female: 44.4 years (2017 est.)
country comparison to the world: 21

Population growth rate: 0.23% (2016 est.)
country comparison to the world: 180

Birth rate: 10.1 births/1,000 population (2016 est.)

Death rate: 10.2 deaths/1,000 population (2016 est.)

Net migration rate: 2.5 migrant(s)/1,000 population (2016 est.)

Population distribution: population distribution varies considerably from country to country, but tends to follow a pattern of coastal and river settlement, with urban agglomerations forming large hubs facilitating large scale housing, industry, and commerce; the area in and around the Netherlands, Belgium, and Luxembourg (known collectively as Benelux), is the most densely populated area in the EU

Sex ratio: *at birth:* 1.06 male(s)/female
0-14 years: 1.05 male(s)/female
15-24 years: 1.05 male(s)/female
25-54 years: 1.02 male(s)/female
55-64 years: 0.95 male(s)/female
65 years and over: 0.75 male(s)/female
total population: 0.96 male(s)/female (2016 est.)

Infant mortality rate: *total:* 4 deaths/1,000 live births
male: 4.4 deaths/1,000 live births
female: 3.6 deaths/1,000 live births (2016 est.)
country comparison to the world: 192

Life expectancy at birth: *total population:* 80.2 years
male: 77.4 years
female: 83.2 years (2017 est.)
country comparison to the world: 41

Total fertility rate: 1.61 children born/woman (2016 est.)

Hospital bed density: 5.4 beds/1,000 population (2011)

HIV/AIDS—adult prevalence rate: *note*—see individual entries of member states

HIV/AIDS—people living with HIV/AIDS: *note*—see individual entries of member states

HIV/AIDS—deaths: *note*—see individual entries of member states

Unemployment, youth ages 15-24: *total:* 22.7%
male: 22.9%
female: 22.5% (2015 est.)

GOVERNMENT

Union name: *conventional long form:* European Union
abbreviation: EU

Political structure: a hybrid and unique intergovernmental and supranational organization

Capital: *name:* Brussels (Belgium), Strasbourg (France), Luxembourg, Frankfurt (Germany); *note*—the European Council, a gathering of the EU heads of state and/or government, and the Council of the European Union, a ministerial-level body of ten formations, meet in Brussels, Belgium, except for Council meetings held in Luxembourg in April, June, and October; the European Parliament meets in Brussels and Strasbourg, France, and has administrative offices in Luxembourg; the Court of Justice of the European Union is located in Luxembourg; and the European Central Bank is located in Frankfurt, Germany

geographic coordinates: (Brussels) 50 50 N, 4 20 E
time difference: UTC+1 (6 hours ahead of Washington, DC, during Standard Time)
daylight saving time: +1hr, begins last Sunday in March; ends last Sunday in October

Member states: 28 countries: Austria, Belgium, Bulgaria, Croatia, Cyprus, Czech Republic, Denmark, Estonia, Finland, France, Germany, Greece, Hungary, Ireland, Italy, Latvia, Lithuania, Luxembourg, Malta, Netherlands, Poland, Portugal, Romania, Slovakia, Slovenia, Spain, Sweden, UK; *note*—candidate countries: Albania, Macedonia, Montenegro, Serbia, Turkey
note: there are non-European overseas countries and territories (OCTs) having special relations with Denmark, France, the Netherlands, and the UK (list is annexed to the Treaty on the Functioning of the European Union), that are associated with the Union to promote their economic and social development; member states apply to their trade with OCTs the same treatment as they accord each other pursuant to the treaties; OCT nationals are in principle EU citizens, but these countries are neither part of the EU, nor subject to the EU

there are 25 OCTs (1 with Denmark [Greenland], 6 with France [French Polynesia; French Southern and Antarctic Lands; New Caledonia; Saint Barthelemy; Saint Pierre and Miquelon; Wallis and Futuna], 6 with the Netherlands [Aruba, Bonaire, Curacao, Saba, Sint Eustatius, Sint Maarten], and 12 with the UK [Anguilla; Bermuda; British Antarctic Territory; British Indian Ocean Territory; British Virgin Islands; Cayman Islands; Falkland Islands; Montserrat; Pitcairn Islands; Saint Helena, Ascension, and Tristan da Cunha; South Georgia and the South Sandwich Islands; Turks and Caicos Islands]), of which 22 have joined the Overseas Countries and Territories Association (OCTA); the 3 OCTs that are not part of OCTA (British Antarctic Territory, British Indian Ocean Territory, South Georgia and the South Sandwich Islands) do not have a permanent population

Independence: 7 February 1992 (Maastricht Treaty signed establishing the European Union); 1 November 1993 (Maastricht Treaty entered into force)
note: the Treaties of Rome, signed on 25 March 1957 and subsequently entered into force on 1 January 1958, created the European Economic Community and the European Atomic Energy Community; a series of subsequent treaties have been adopted to increase efficiency and transparency, to prepare for new member states, and to introduce new areas of cooperation—such as a single currency; the Treaty of Lisbon, signed on 13 December 2007 and entered into force on 1 December 2009 is the most recent of these treaties and is intended to make the EU more democratic, more efficient, and better able to address global problems with one voice

National holiday: Europe Day (also known as Schuman Day), 9 May (1950); *note*—the day in 1950 that Robert SCHUMAN proposed the creation of what became the European Coal and Steel Community, the progenitor of today's European Union, with the aim of achieving a united Europe

Constitution: *history:* none; *note*—the EU legal order relies primarily on two consolidated texts encompassing all provisions as amended from a series of past treaties: the Treaty on European Union (TEU), as modified by the Lisbon Treaty states in Article 1 that "the HIGH CONTRACTING PARTIES establish among themselves a EUROPEAN UNION ... on which the Member States confer competences to attain objectives they have in common"; Article 1 of the TEU states further that the EU is "founded on the present Treaty and on the Treaty on the Functioning of the European Union (hereinafter referred to as 'the Treaties')", both possessing the same legal value; Article 6 of the TEU provides that a separately adopted Charter of Fundamental Rights of the European Union "shall have the same legal value as the Treaties"
amendments: European Union treaties can be amended in several ways: 1) Ordinary Revision Procedure (for key amendments to the treaties); initiated by an EU country's government, by the

EU Parliament, or by the EU Commission; following adoption of the proposal by the European Council, a convention is formed of national government representatives to review the proposal and subsequently a conference of government representatives also reviews the proposal; passage requires ratification by all EU countries; 2) Simplified Revision Procedure (for amendment of EU internal policies and actions); passage of a proposal requires unanimous European Council vote following European Council consultation with the EU Commission, the European Council, and the European Parliament, and requires ratification by all EU countries; 3) Passerelle Clause (allows the alteration of a legislative procedure without a formal amendment of the treaties); 4) Flexibility Clause (permits the EU to decide in subject areas not covered by the EU treaties); note—the Treaty of Lisbon (signed in December 2007 and effective in December 2009) amended the two treaties that formed the EU—the Maastricht Treaty (1993) and the Treaty of Rome (1958), known in updated form as the Treaty on the Functioning of the European Union (2007) (2016)

Legal system: unique supranational law system in which, according to an interpretive declaration of member-state governments appended to the Treaty of Lisbon, "the Treaties and the law adopted by the Union on the basis of the Treaties have primacy over the law of Member States" under conditions laid down in the case law of the Court of Justice; key principles of EU law include fundamental rights as guaranteed by the Charter of Fundamental Rights and as resulting from constitutional traditions common to the EU's 28-member states; EU law is divided into 'primary' and 'secondary' legislation; primary legislation is derived from the consolidated versions of the Treaty on European Union and the Treaty on the Functioning of the European Union and are the basis for all EU action; secondary legislation—which includes directives, regulations, and decisions—is derived from the principles and objectives set out in the treaties

Suffrage: 18 years of age (16 years in Austria); universal; voting for the European Parliament is permitted in each member state

Executive branch: under the EU treaties there are three distinct institutions, each of which conducts functions that may be regarded as executive in nature: the European Council: brings together heads of state and government, along with the president of the European Commission, and meets at least four times a year; its aim is to provide the impetus for the development of the Union and to issue general policy guidelines; the Treaty of Lisbon established the position of "permanent" (full-time) president of the European Council; leaders of the EU member states appoint the president for a 2 1/2 year term, renewable once; the president's responsibilities include chairing the EU summits and providing policy and organizational continuity; the current president is Donald TUSK (Poland), since 1 December 2014, succeeding Herman VAN ROMPUY (Belgian; 2009-14)

the Council of the European Union: consists of ministers of each EU member state and meets regularly in 10 different configurations depending on the subject matter; it conducts policymaking and coordinating functions as well as legislative functions; ministers of EU member states chair meetings of the Council of the EU based on a 6-month rotating presidency except for the meetings of EU Foreign Ministers in the Foreign Affairs Council that are chaired by the High Representative for Foreign Affairs and Security Policy

the European Commission: headed by a College of Commissioners comprised of 28 members (one from each member country) including the president; each commissioner is responsible for one or more policy areas; the Commission's main responsibilities include the sole right to initiate EU legislation (except for foreign and security/defense policy), promoting the general interest of the EU, acting as "guardian of the Treaties" by monitoring the application of EU law, implementing/executing the EU budget, managing programs, negotiating on the EU's behalf in core policy areas such as trade, and ensuring the Union's external representation in some policy areas; its current president is Jean-Claude JUNCKER (Luxembourg) elected on 15 July 2014 (took office on 1 November 2014); the president of the European Commission is nominated by the European Council and formally "elected" by the European Parliament; the Commission president allocates specific responsibilities among the members of the College (appointed by common accord of the member state governments in consultation with the president-elect); the European Parliament confirms the entire Commission for a 5-year term; President JUNCKER reorganized the structure of the College around clusters or project teams coordinated by 7 vice presidents in line with the current Commission's main political priorities and appointed Frans TIMMERMANS (Netherlands) to act as his first vice president; the confirmation process for the next Commission expected be held in the fall of 2019 note: for external representation and foreign policy making, leaders of the EU member states appointed Federica MOGHERINI (Italy) as the High Representative of the European Union for Foreign Affairs and Security Policy; MOGHERINI took office on 1 November 2014, succeeding Catherine ASHTON (UK) (2009-14); the High Representative's concurrent appointment as Vice President of the European Commission endows her position with the policymaking influence of the Council of the EU and the budgetary influence (subject to Council's approval) of the Council of the EU and the budgetary/management influence of the European Commission; the High Representative helps develop and implement the EU's Common Foreign and Security Policy and Common Security and Defense Policy component, chairs the Foreign Affairs Council, represents and acts for the Union in many international contexts, and oversees the European External Action Service, the diplomatic corps of the EU, established on 1 December 2010

Legislative branch: description: two legislative bodies consisting of the Council of the European Union (28 seats; ministers representing the 28 member states) and the European Parliament (751 seats; seats allocated among member states roughly in proportion to population size; members elected by proportional representation to serve 5-year terms); note—the European Parliament President, Antonio TAJANI (Italian center-right), was elected in January 2017 by a majority of fellow members of the European Parliament (MEPs) and represents the Parliament within the EU and internationally; the Council of the EU and the MEPs share responsibilities for adopting the bulk of EU legislation, normally acting in co-decision on Commission proposals (but not in the area of Common Foreign and Security Policy, which is governed by consensus of the EU member state governments)

elections: last held on 22-25 May 2014 (next to be held 23-26 May 2019)

election results: percent of vote—EPP 29.4%, S&D 25.4%, ECR 9.3%, ALDE 8.9%, GUE/NGL 6.9%, Greens/EFA 6.7%, EFD 6.4%, independent 6.9%; seats by party—EPP 221, S&D 191, ECR 70, ALDE 67, GUE/NGL 52, Greens/EFA 50, EFD 48, independent 52

Judicial branch: *highest court(s):* European Court of Justice or ECJ (consists of 28 judges—1 from each member state); the court may sit as a full court, in a "Grand Chamber" of 13 judges in special cases but usually in chambers of 3 to 5 judges *note:* the ECJ is the supreme judicial authority of the EU; ECJ ensures that EU law is interpreted and applied uniformly throughout the EU, resolves disputed issues among the EU institutions and with member states, issues opinions on questions of EU law referred by member state courts

judge selection and term of office: judges appointed by the common consent of the member states to serve 6-year renewable terms

subordinate courts: General Court; Civil Service Tribunal

Political parties and leaders: Alliance of Liberals and Democrats for Europe or ALDE [Guy VERHOFSTADT]
European United Left-Nordic Green Left or GUE/NGL [Gabriele ZIMMER]
Europe of Freedom and Direct Democracy or EFDD [Nigel FARAGE]
Europe of Nations and Freedom or ENF or ENL [Nicolas BAY and Marcel DE GRAAFF]
European Conservatives and Reformists or ECR [Syed KAMALL, Ryszard LEGUTKO]
European Greens/European Free Alliance or Greens/EFA [Ska KELLER and Philippe LAMBERTS]
European People's Party or EPP [Joseph DAUL]
Progressive Alliance of Socialists and Democrats or S&D [Gianni PITELLA]

International organization participation: ARF, ASEAN (dialogue member), Australian Group, BIS, BSEC (observer), CBSS, CERN, EBRD, FAO, FATF, G-8, G-10, G-20, IDA, IEA, IGAD (partners), LAIA (observer), NSG (observer),

OAS (observer), OECD, PIF (partner), SAARC (observer), SICA (observer), UN (observer), UNRWA (observer), WCO, WTO, ZC (observer)

Diplomatic representation in the US: *chief of mission:* Ambassador David O'SULLIVAN (since 18 November 2014)
chancery: 2175 K Street, NW, Suite 800, Washington, DC 20037
telephone: [1] (202) 862-9500
FAX: [1] (202) 429-1766

Diplomatic representation from the US: *chief of mission:* Ambassador (vacant); Charge d'affaires Adam SHUB (since 20 January 2017)
embassy: 13 Zinnerstraat/Rue Zinner, B-1000 Brussels
mailing address: use embassy street address
telephone: [32] (2) 811-4100
FAX: [32] (2) 811-5154

Flag description: a blue field with 12 five-pointed gold stars arranged in a circle in the center; blue represents the sky of the Western world, the stars are the peoples of Europe in a circle, a symbol of unity; the number of stars is fixed

National symbol(s): a circle of 12, five-pointed, golden yellow stars on a blue field; union colors: blue, yellow

National anthem: name: "Ode to Joy"
lyrics/music: no lyrics/Ludwig VAN BEETHOVEN, arranged by Herbert VON KARAJAN
note: official EU anthem since 1985; the anthem is meant to represent all of Europe rather than just the organization, conveying ideas of peace, freedom, and unity

ECONOMY

Economy—overview: The 28 member states that make up the EU have adopted an internal single market with free movement of goods, services, capital, and labor. The EU, which is also a customs union, aims to bolster Europe's trade position and its political and economic weight in international affairs.

Despite great differences in per capita income among member states (from $28,000 to $109,000) and in national attitudes toward issues like inflation, debt, and foreign trade, the EU has achieved a high degree of coordination of monetary and fiscal policies. A common currency—the euro—circulates among 19 of the member states that make up the European Economic and Monetary Union (EMU). Eleven member states introduced the euro as their common currency on 1 January 1999 (Greece did so two years later). Since 2004, 13 states acceded to the EU. Of the 13, Slovenia (2007), Cyprus and Malta (2008), Slovakia (2009), Estonia (2011), Latvia (2014), and Lithuania (2015) have adopted the euro; 7 other member states—not including the UK nor Denmark, which have formal opt-outs—are required by EU treaties to adopt the common currency upon meeting fiscal and monetary convergence criteria.

The EU economy posted moderate GDP growth for 2014 through 2017, capping 5 years of sustained growth since the 2008-09 global economic crisis and the ensuing sovereign debt crisis in the euro zone in 2011. However, the bloc's recovery has been uneven. Some EU member states (Czechia, Ireland, Malta, Romania, Sweden, and Spain) have recorded strong growth, others (Italy and the United Kingdom) are experiencing modest expansion and some (Greece) have only recently shaken off recession. Only Greece remains under an EU rescue program (due to end in August 2018), while Cyprus, Ireland, Portugal, and Spain have successfully concluded their agreements. Overall, the EU's recovery has been buoyed by lower commodities prices and accommodative monetary policy, which has lowered interest rates and stimulated demand. The euro-zone, which makes up about 70% of the total EU economy, is also performing well, achieving a growth rate not seen in a decade. In October 2017 the European Central Bank (ECB) announced it would extend its bond-buying program through September 2018, and possibly beyond that date, to keep the euro-zone recovery on track. The ECB's efforts to spur more lending and investment through its asset-buying program, negative interest rates, and long-term loan refinancing programs have not yet raised inflation in line with the ECB's statutory target of just under 2%.

Despite its performance, high unemployment in some member states, high levels of public and private debt, muted productivity, and an aging population remain sources of potential drag on the EU's future growth. Moreover, the EU economy remains vulnerable to a slowdown of global trade and bouts of political and financial turmoil. In June 2016, the UK voted to withdraw from the EU, the first member country ever to attempt to secede. Continued uncertainty about the implications of the UK's exit from the EU (set for March 2019) could hurt consumer and investor confidence and dampen EU growth, particularly if trade and cross-border investment significantly declines. Political disagreements between EU member states on reforms to fiscal and economic policy also may impair the EU's ability to bolster its crisis-prevention and resolution mechanisms. International investors' fears of a broad dissolution of the single currency area have largely dissipated, but these concerns could resurface if elected leaders implement policies that contravene euro-zone budget or banking rules. State interventions in ailing banks, including rescue of banks in Italy and resolution of banks in Spain, have eased financial vulnerabilities in the European banking sector even though some banks are struggling with low profitability and a large stock of bad loans, fragilities that could precipitate localized crises. Externally, the EU has continued to pursue comprehensive free trade agreements to expand EU external market share, particularly with Asian countries; EU and Japanese leaders reached a political-level agreement on a free trade agreement in July 2017.

GDP (purchasing power parity): $19.97 trillion (2016 est.)
$19.6 trillion (2015 est.)
$18.91 trillion (2014 est.)
note: data are in 2017 dollars

country comparison to the world: 2

GDP (official exchange rate): $16.52 trillion (2016 est.)

GDP—real growth rate: 1.9% (2016 est.)
2.3% (2015 est.)
1.6% (2014 est.)
country comparison to the world: 160

GDP—per capita (PPP): $39,200 (2016 est.)
$38,100 (2015 est.)
$37,000 (2014 est.)
note: data are in 2017 dollars
country comparison to the world: 46

Gross national saving: 22% of GDP (2016 est.)
21.8% of GDP (2015 est.)
21.3% of GDP (2014 est.)
country comparison to the world: 75

GDP—composition, by end use:
household consumption: 56.3%
government consumption: 20.5%
investment in fixed capital: 19.5%
investment in inventories: 0.1%
exports of goods and services: 43.9%
imports of goods and services: -40.5% (2015 est.)

GDP—composition, by sector of origin:
agriculture: 1.6%
industry: 25.6%
services: 74% (2017 est.)

Agriculture—products: wheat, barley, oilseeds, sugar beets, wine, grapes; dairy products, cattle, sheep, pigs, poultry; fish

Industries: among the world's largest and most technologically advanced regions, the EU industrial base includes: ferrous and non-ferrous metal production and processing, metal products, petroleum, coal, cement, chemicals, pharmaceuticals, aerospace, rail transportation equipment, passenger and commercial vehicles, construction equipment, industrial equipment, shipbuilding, electrical power equipment, machine tools and automated manufacturing systems, electronics and telecommunications equipment, fishing, food and beverages, furniture, paper, textiles

Industrial production growth rate: 1.8% (2017 est.)
country comparison to the world: 143

Labor force: 234.7 million (2017 est.)
country comparison to the world: 3
Labor force—by occupation: agriculture: 5%
industry: 21.9%
services: 73.1% (2014 est.)

Unemployment rate: 9.4% (2015 est.)
10.2% (2014 est.)
country comparison to the world: 130

Population below poverty line: 9.8%
note: see individual country entries of member states (2013 est.)

Household income or consumption by percentage share: *lowest 10%:* 2.8%
highest 10%: 24.1% (2015 est.)

Distribution of family income—Gini index: 31 (2015 est.)
30.9 (2014 est.)
country comparison to the world: 120

Taxes and other revenues: 45.2% of GDP (2014)
country comparison to the world: 22

Budget surplus (+) or deficit (-): -3% of GDP (2014)
country comparison to the world: 113

Public debt: 86.8% of GDP (2014)
85.5% of GDP (2013)
country comparison to the world: 30

Fiscal year: NA

Inflation rate (consumer prices): 0.1% (2015 est.)
0.5% (2014 est.)
country comparison to the world: 11

Central bank discount rate: 0.25% (31 December 2016 est.)
0.3% (31 December 2015 est.)
note: this is the European Central Bank's rate on the marginal lending facility, which offers overnight credit to banks in the euro area
country comparison to the world: 143

Commercial bank prime lending rate: 0.32% (31 December 2014 est.)
0.56% (31 December 2013 est.)
country comparison to the world: 187

Stock of narrow money: $6.613 trillion (31 December 2015 est.)
$5.947 trillion (31 December 2014 est.)
note: this is the quantity of money, M1, for the euro area, converted into US dollars at the exchange rate for the date indicated; it excludes the stock of money carried by non-euro-area members of the European Union, e.g., UK pounds, Danish kroner, and Czech koruny
country comparison to the world: 2

Stock of broad money: $10.84 trillion (31 December 2015 est.)
$10.33 trillion (31 December 2014 est.)
note: this is the quantity of broad money for the euro area, converted into US dollars at the exchange rate for the date indicated; it excludes the stock of broad money carried by non-euro-area members of the European Union
country comparison to the world: 3

Stock of domestic credit: $16.57 trillion (31 December 2015 est.)
$17.12 trillion (31 December 2014 est.)
note: this figure refers to the euro area only; it excludes credit data for non-euro-area members of the EU
country comparison to the world: 3

Market value of publicly traded shares: $7.185 trillion (31 December 2014 est.)
$7.932 trillion (31 December 2013 est.)
$10.4 trillion (31 December 2012 est.)
country comparison to the world: 3

Current account balance: $387.1 billion (2016 est.)
$365.5 billion (2015 est.)
country comparison to the world: 1

Exports: $1.9 trillion (2015 est.)
$1.808 trillion (2014 est.)
note: external exports, excluding intra-EU trade
country comparison to the world: 2

Exports—commodities: machinery, motor vehicles, pharmaceuticals and other chemicals, fuels, aircraft, plastics, iron and steel, wood pulp and paper products, alcoholic beverages, furniture

Exports—partners: United States 20.7%, China 9.6%, Switzerland 8.1%, Turkey 4.4%, Russia 4.1% (2016 est.)

Imports: $1.727 trillion (2015 est.)
$1.692 trillion (2014 est.)
note: external imports, excluding intra-EU trade
country comparison to the world: 3

Imports—commodities: fuels and crude oil, machinery, vehicles, pharmaceuticals and other chemicals, precious gemstones, textiles, aircraft, plastics, metals, ships

Imports—partners: China 20.1%, United States 14.5%, Switzerland 7.1%, Russia 6.3% (2016 est.)

Reserves of foreign exchange and gold: $740.9 billion (31 December 2014 est.)
$746.9 billion (31 December 2013)
note: data are for the European Central Bank
country comparison to the world: 3

Debt—external: $13.05 trillion (31 December 2014 est.)
$14.14 trillion (31 December 2013)
country comparison to the world: 2

Stock of direct foreign investment—at home: $5.148 trillion (2012)
$4.828 trillion (2011)
country comparison to the world: 1

Stock of direct foreign investment—abroad: $9.121 trillion (2012)
$8.721 trillion (2011)
country comparison to the world: 1

Exchange rates: euros per US dollar—
0.906 (2017 est.)
0.9214 (2016 est.)
0.9214 (2015 est.)
0.885 (2014 est.)
0.7634 (2013 est.)

ENERGY

Electricity—production: 3.166 trillion kWh (2014 est.)
country comparison to the world: 3

Electricity—consumption: 2.771 trillion kWh (2013 est.)
country comparison to the world: 3

Electricity—exports: 336.2 billion kWh (2013 est.)
country comparison to the world: 1

Electricity—imports: 349.5 billion kWh (2013 est.)
country comparison to the world: 1

Electricity—installed generating capacity: 9.47 billion kW (2012 est.)
country comparison to the world: 1

Electricity—from fossil fuels: 49% of total installed capacity (2012 est.)
country comparison to the world: 153

Electricity—from nuclear fuels: 12.9% of total installed capacity (2012 est.)

country comparison to the world: 13

Electricity—from hydroelectric plants: 10.7% of total installed capacity (2012 est.)
country comparison to the world: 117

Electricity—from other renewable sources: 22.9% of total installed capacity (2012 est.)
country comparison to the world: 27

Crude oil—production: 1.507 million bbl/day (2015 est.)
country comparison to the world: 18

Crude oil—proved reserves: 5.6 billion bbl (1 January 2015 es)
country comparison to the world: 22

Refined petroleum products—production: 11.12 million bbl/day (2014 est.)
country comparison to the world: 2

Refined petroleum products—consumption: 12.53 million bbl/day (2014 est.)
country comparison to the world: 2

Refined petroleum products—exports: 2.196 million bbl/day (2016 est.)
country comparison to the world: 4

Refined petroleum products—imports: 8.613 million bbl/day (2016 est.)
country comparison to the world: 1

Natural gas—production: 120 billion cu m (2015 est.)
country comparison to the world: 7

Natural gas—consumption: 402.1 billion cu m (2015 est.)
country comparison to the world: 5

Natural gas—exports: 93.75 billion cu m (2010 est.)
country comparison to the world: 4

Natural gas—imports: 420.6 billion cu m (2010 est.)
country comparison to the world: 1

Natural gas—proved reserves: 1.3 trillion cu m (1 January 2015 es)
country comparison to the world: 23

Carbon dioxide emissions from consumption of energy: 3.705 billion Mt (2014 est.)
country comparison to the world: 3

COMMUNICATIONS

Telephones—fixed lines: *total:* 213.8 million (July 2016 est.)
country comparison to the world: 2

Telephones—mobile cellular: *total:* 632.5 million (July 2016 est.)
country comparison to the world: 3

Telephone system: *note*—see individual country entries of member states

Internet country code: .eu; *note*—see country entries of member states for individual country codes

Internet users: *total:* 398.1 million (July 2016 est.)
country comparison to the world: 2

TRANSPORTATION

Airports: 3,102 (2013)

Airports—with paved runways: *total:* 1,882
over 3,047 m: 120
2,438 to 3,047 m: 341
1,524 to 2,437 m: 507
914 to 1,523 m: 425
under 914 m: 489 (2017)

Airports—with unpaved runways: *total:* 1,244
over 3,047 m: 1
2,437 to 3,047 m: 1
1,524 to 2,437 m: 15
914 to 1,523 m: 245
under 914 m: 982 (2013)

Heliports: 90 (2013)

Railways: *total:* 230,548 km (2013)

Roadways: *total:* 10,582,653 km (2013)

Waterways: 53,384 km (2013)

Ports and terminals: major port(s): Antwerp (Belgium), Barcelona (Spain), Braila (Romania), Bremen (Germany), Burgas (Bulgaria), Constanta (Romania), Copenhagen (Denmark), Galati (Romania), Gdansk (Poland), Hamburg (Germany), Helsinki (Finland), Las Palmas (Canary Islands, Spain), Le Havre (France), Lisbon (Portugal), London (UK), Marseille (France), Naples (Italy), Peiraiefs or Piraeus (Greece), Riga (Latvia), Rotterdam (Netherlands), Split (Croatia), Stockholm (Sweden), Talinn (Estonia), Tulcea (Romania), Varna (Bulgaria)

MILITARY AND SECURITY

Military expenditures: 1.52% of GDP (2016)
1.51% of GDP (2015)
1.52% of GDP (2014)
1.56% of GDP (2013)
1.63% of GDP (2012)
country comparison to the world: 56

Military—note: the five-nation Eurocorps—created in 1992 by France, Germany, Belgium, Spain, and Luxembourg—has deployed troops and police on peacekeeping missions to Bosnia-Herzegovina, Macedonia, and the Democratic Republic of the Congo and assumed command of the ISAF in Afghanistan in August 2004; Eurocorps directly commands the 5,000-man Franco-German Brigade, the Multinational Command Support Brigade, and EUFOR in Bosnia and Herzegovina; in November 2004, the EU Council of Ministers formally committed to creating 13 1,500-man battle groups by the end of 2007, to respond to international crises on a rotating basis; 22 of the EU's 28 nations have agreed to supply troops; France, Italy, and the UK formed the first of three battle groups in 2005; Norway, Sweden, Estonia, and Finland established the Nordic Battle Group effective 1 January 2008; nine other groups are to be formed; a rapid-reaction naval EU Maritime Task Group was stood up in March 2007 (2007)

TRANSNATIONAL ISSUES

Disputes—international: as a political union, the EU has no border disputes with neighboring countries, but Estonia has no land boundary agreements with Russia, Slovenia disputes its land and maritime boundaries with Croatia, and Spain has territorial and maritime disputes with Morocco and with the UK over Gibraltar; the EU has set up a Schengen area—consisting of 22 EU member states that have signed the convention implementing the Schengen agreements or "acquis" (1985 and 1990) on the free movement of persons and the harmonization of border controls in Europe; these agreements became incorporated into EU law with the implementation of the 1997 Treaty of Amsterdam on 1 May 1999; in addition, non-EU states Iceland and Norway (as part of the Nordic Union) have been included in the Schengen area since 1996 (full members in 2001), Switzerland since 2008, and Liechtenstein since 2011 bringing the total current membership to 26; the UK (since 2000) and Ireland (since 2002) take part in only some aspects of the Schengen area, especially with respect to police and criminal matters; nine of the 13 new member states that joined the EU since 2004 joined Schengen on 21 December 2007; of the four remaining EU states, Romania, Bulgaria, and Croatia are obligated to eventually join, while Cyprus' entry is held up by the ongoing Cyprus dispute

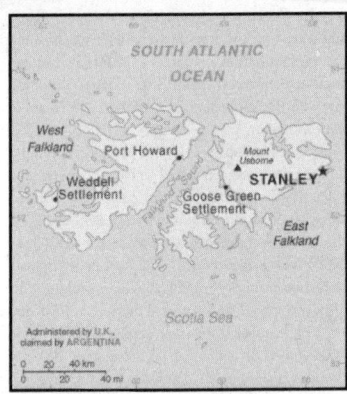

INTRODUCTION

Background: Although first sighted by an English navigator in 1592, the first landing (English) did not occur until almost a century later in 1690, and the first settlement (French) was not established until 1764. The colony was turned over to Spain two years later and the islands have since been the subject of a territorial dispute, first between Britain and Spain, then between Britain and Argentina. The UK asserted its claim to the islands by establishing a naval garrison there in 1833. Argentina invaded the islands on 2 April 1982. The British responded with an expeditionary force that landed seven weeks later and after fierce fighting forced an Argentine surrender on 14 June 1982. With hostilities ended and Argentine forces withdrawn, UK administration resumed. In response to renewed calls from Argentina for Britain to relinquish control of the islands, a referendum was held in March 2013, which resulted in 99.8% of the population voting to remain a part of the UK.

GEOGRAPHY

Location: Southern South America, islands in the South Atlantic Ocean, about 500 km east of southern Argentina

Geographic coordinates: 51 45 S, 59 00 W

Map references: South America

Area: *total:* 12,173 sq km
land: 12,173 sq km
water: 0 sq km
note: includes the two main islands of East and West Falkland and about 200 small islands
country comparison to the world: 164

Area—comparative: slightly smaller than Connecticut

Land boundaries: 0 km

Coastline: 1,288 km

Maritime claims: *territorial sea:* 12 nm
continental shelf: 200 nm
exclusive fishing zone: 200 nm

Climate: cold marine; strong westerly winds, cloudy, humid; rain occurs on more than half of days in year; average annual rainfall is 60 cm in Stanley; occasional snow all year, except in January and February, but typically does not accumulate

Terrain: rocky, hilly, mountainous with some boggy, undulating plains

Elevation: *mean elevation:* NA

elevation extremes: *lowest point:* Atlantic Ocean 0 m
highest point: Mount Usborne 705 m

Natural resources: fish, squid, wildlife, calcified seaweed, sphagnum moss

Land use: *agricultural land:* 92.4%
arable land: 0%;
permanent crops: 0%;
permanent pasture: 92.4%
forest: 0%
other: 7.6% (2011 est.)

Irrigated land: NA

Population—distribution: a very small population, with most residents living in and around Stanley

Natural hazards: strong winds persist throughout the year

Environment—current issues: overfishing by unlicensed vessels is a problem; reindeer—introduced to the islands in 2001 from South Georgia—are part of a farming effort to produce specialty meat and diversify the islands' economy; this is the only commercial reindeer herd in the world unaffected by the 1986 Chornobyl disaster

Geography—note: deeply indented coast provides good natural harbors; short growing season

PEOPLE AND SOCIETY

Population: 3,198
note: data include all persons usually resident in the islands at the time of the 2016 census (2016 est.)
country comparison to the world: 229

Nationality: *noun:* Falkland Islander(s)
adjective: Falkland Island

Ethnic groups: Falkland Islander 48.3%, British 23.1%, St. Helenian 7.5%, Chilean 4.6%, mixed 6%, other 8.5%, unspecified 2% (2016 est.)

Languages: English 89%, Spanish 7.7%, other 3.3% (2006 est.)

Religions: Christian 57.1%, other 1.6%, none 35.4%, unspecified 6% (2016 est.)

Population growth rate: 0.01% (2014 est.)
country comparison to the world: 191

Birth rate: 10.9 births/1,000 population (2012 est.)
country comparison to the world: 181

Death rate: 4.9 deaths/1,000 population (2012 est.)
country comparison to the world: 194

Net migration rate: NA

Population distribution: a very small population, with most residents living in and around Stanley

Urbanization: *urban population:* 77.2% of total population (2017)
rate of urbanization: 0.68% annual rate of change (2015-20 est.)

Major urban areas—population: STANLEY (capital) 2,000 (2014)

Sex ratio: *total population:* 1.11 male(s)/female
note: sex ratio is somewhat skewed by the high proportion of males at the Royal Air Force station, Mount Pleasant Airport (MPA); excluding MPA, the sex ratio of the total population would be 1.01 (2012 est.)

Infant mortality rate: *total:* NA
male: NA
female: NA

Life expectancy at birth: *total population:* 77.9
male: 75.6
female: 79.6 (2017 est.)

Total fertility rate: NA

HIV/AIDS—adult prevalence rate: NA

HIV/AIDS—people living with HIV/AIDS: NA

HIV/AIDS—deaths: NA

GOVERNMENT

Country name: *conventional long form:* none
conventional short form: Falkland Islands (Islas Malvinas)
etymology: the archipelago takes its name from the Falkland Sound, the strait separating the two main islands; the channel itself was named after the Viscount of Falkland who sponsored an expedition to the islands in 1690; the Spanish name for the archipelago derives from the French "Iles Malouines," the name applied to the islands by French explorer Louis-Antoine de BOUGAINVILLE in 1764

Dependency status: overseas territory of the UK; also claimed by Argentina

Government type: parliamentary democracy (Legislative Assembly); self-governing overseas territory of the UK

Capital: *name:* Stanley
geographic coordinates: 51 42 S, 57 51 W
time difference: UTC-4 (1 hour ahead of Washington, DC, during Standard Time)

Administrative divisions: none (overseas territory of the UK; also claimed by Argentina)

Independence: none (overseas territory of the UK; also claimed by Argentina)

National holiday: Liberation Day, 14 June (1982)

Constitution: previous 1985; latest entered into force 1 January 2009 (2016)

Legal system: English common law and local statutes

Citizenship: see United Kingdom

Suffrage: 18 years of age; universal

Executive branch. *chief of state:* Queen ELIZABETH II (since 6 February 1952); represented by Governor Nigel PHILLIPS (since 12 September 2017)

head of government: Chief Executive Barry ROWLAND (since 3 October 2016)

cabinet: Executive Council elected by the Legislative Council

elections/appointments: the monarchy is hereditary; governor appointed by the monarch; chief executive appointed by the governor

Legislative branch: description: unicameral Legislative Assembly, formerly the Legislative Council (10 seats; 8 members directly elected by majority vote and 2 appointed ex-officio members—the chief executive, appointed by the governor, and the financial secretary; members serve 4-year terms)

elections: last held on 9 November 2017 (next to be held in November 2021)

election results: percent of vote—NA; seats—independent 8

Judicial branch: highest resident court(s): Court of Appeal (consists of the court president, the chief justice as an ex officio, non-resident member, and 2 justices of appeal); Supreme Court (consists of the chief justice); note—appeals beyond the Court of Appeal are referred to the Judicial Committee of the Privy Council (in London)

judge selection and term of office: all justices appointed by the governor; tenure specified in each justice's instrument of appointment

subordinate courts: Magistrate's Court (senior magistrate presides over civil and criminal divisions); Court of Summary Jurisdiction

Political parties and leaders: none; all independents

Political pressure groups and leaders: Falkland Islands Association (supports freedom of the people from external causes)

International organization participation: UPU

Diplomatic representation in the US: none (overseas territory of the UK)

Diplomatic representation from the US: none (overseas territory of the UK; also claimed by Argentina)

Flag description: blue with the flag of the UK in the upper hoist-side quadrant and the Falkland Island coat of arms centered on the outer half of the flag; the coat of arms contains a white ram (sheep raising was once the major economic activity) above the sailing ship Desire (whose crew discovered the islands) with a scroll at the bottom bearing the motto DESIRE THE RIGHT

National symbol(s): ram

National anthem: name: "Song of the Falklands"" *lyrics/music:* Christopher LANHAM *note:* adopted 1930s; the song is the local unofficial anthem; as a territory of the United Kingdom, "God Save the Queen" is official (see United Kingdom)

ECONOMY

Economy—overview: The economy was formerly based on agriculture, mainly sheep farming, but fishing and tourism currently comprise the bulk of economic activity. In 1987, the government began selling fishing licenses to foreign trawlers operating within the Falkland Islands' exclusive fishing zone. These license fees net more than $40 million per year, which help support the island's health, education, and welfare system. The waters around the Falkland Islands are known for their squid, which account for around 75% of the annual 200,000-ton catch.

Dairy farming supports domestic consumption; crops furnish winter fodder. Foreign exchange earnings come from shipments of high-grade wool to the UK and from the sale of postage stamps and coins. In 2001, the government purchased 100 reindeer with the intent to increase the number to 10,000 over the following 20 years so that venison could be exported to Scandinavia and Chile.

Tourism, especially ecotourism, is increasing rapidly, with about 69,000 visitors in 2009. The British military presence also provides a sizable economic boost. The islands are now self-financing except for defense.

In 1993, the British Geological Survey announced a 200-mile oil exploration zone around the islands, and early seismic surveys suggest substantial reserves capable of producing 500,000 barrels per day. Political tensions between the UK and Argentina remain high following the start of oil drilling activities in the waters. Although production by a British exploration firm has yet to begin, the firm expects to be able to produce 60,000 barrels per day by 2020.

GDP (purchasing power parity): $281.8 million (2012 est.)
$164.5 million (2007 est.)
$105.1 million (2002 est.)
country comparison to the world: 218

GDP (official exchange rate): $164.5 million (2007 est.)

GDP—per capita (PPP): $96,200 (2012 est.)
$55,400 (2002 est.)
country comparison to the world: 6

GDP—composition, by sector of origin:
agriculture: 95%
industry: NA%
services: NA% (1996)

Agriculture—products: fodder and vegetable crops; venison, sheep, dairy products; fish, squid

Industries: fish and wool processing; tourism

Industrial production growth rate: NA%

Labor force: 1,944 (2012 est.)
country comparison to the world: 228

Labor force—by occupation: *agriculture:* 95% (mostly sheepherding and fishing)
industry and services: 5% (1996)

Unemployment rate: 4.1% (2010)
country comparison to the world: 54

Population below poverty line: NA%

Household income or consumption by percentage share: *lowest 10%:* NA%
highest 10%: NA%

Distribution of family income—Gini index: 36 (2015)
country comparison to the world: 89

Budget: *revenues:* $67.1 million
expenditures: $75.3 million (FY09/10)
Taxes and other revenues: 40.8% of GDP (FY09/10)
country comparison to the world: 33

Budget surplus (+) or deficit (-): -5% of GDP (FY09/10)
country comparison to the world: 161

Fiscal year: 1 April—31 March

Inflation rate (consumer prices): 1.4% (2014 est.)
country comparison to the world: 59

Exports: $257.3 million (2015 est.)
$125 million (2004 est.)
country comparison to the world: 184

Exports—commodities: wool, hides, meat, venison, fish, squid

Exports—partners: Spain 67.8%, UK 10%, Namibia 8.9%, US 7.2% (2016)

Imports: $90 million (2004 est.)
country comparison to the world: 214

Imports—commodities: fuel, food and drink, building materials, clothing

Imports—partners: UK 68.8%, Greece 8.8%, Cote dIvoire 6.7%, Spain 5.7%, Netherlands 4.8% (2016)

Debt—external: $NA

Exchange rates: Falkland pounds (FKP) per US dollar—
0.7836 (2017)
0.6542 (2016)
0.6542 (2015)
0.6542 (2014 est.)
0.6391 (2013 est.)

ENERGY

Electricity—production: 17 million kWh (2015 est.)
country comparison to the world: 214

Electricity—consumption: 15.81 million kWh (2015 est.)
country comparison to the world: 213

Electricity—exports: 0 kWh (2016 est.)
country comparison to the world: 135

Electricity—imports: 0 kWh (2016 est.)
country comparison to the world: 149

Electricity—installed generating capacity: 10,000 kW (2015 est.)
country comparison to the world: 209

Electricity—from fossil fuels: 90% of total installed capacity (2015 est.)
country comparison to the world: 62

Electricity—from nuclear fuels: 0% of total installed capacity (2015 est.)
country comparison to the world: 90

Electricity—from hydroelectric plants: 0% of total installed capacity (2015 est.)
country comparison to the world: 175

Electricity—from other renewable sources: 10% of total installed capacity (2015 est.)
country comparison to the world: 71

Crude oil—production: 0 bbl/day (2016 est.)
country comparison to the world: 133

Crude oil—exports: 0 bbl/day (2014 est.)
country comparison to the world: 123

Crude oil—imports: 0 bbl/day (2014 est.)
country comparison to the world: 126

Crude oil—proved reserves: 0 bbl (1 January 2017 es)
country comparison to the world: 132

Refined petroleum products—production: 0 bbl/day (2014 est.)
country comparison to the world: 143

Refined petroleum products—consumption: 300 bbl/day (2015 est.)
country comparison to the world: 213

Refined petroleum products—exports: 0 bbl/day (2014 est.)
country comparison to the world: 155

Refined petroleum products—imports: 292 bbl/day (2014 est.)
country comparison to the world: 209

Natural gas—production: 0 cu m (2013 est.)
country comparison to the world: 135

Natural gas—consumption: 0 cu m (2013 est.)
country comparison to the world: 181

Natural gas—exports: 0 cu m (2013 est.)
country comparison to the world: 104

Natural gas—imports: 0 cu m (2013 est.)
country comparison to the world: 125

Natural gas—proved reserves: 0 cu m (1 January 2014 es)
country comparison to the world: 139

Carbon dioxide emissions from consumption of energy: 45,570 Mt (2012 est.)
country comparison to the world: 211

COMMUNICATIONS

Telephones—fixed lines: *total subscriptions:* 2,255
subscriptions per 100 inhabitants: 77 (July 2016 est.)
country comparison to the world: 214

Telephones—mobile cellular: *total:* 5,000
subscriptions per 100 inhabitants: 171 (July 2016 est.)
country comparison to the world: 216

Telephone system: *domestic:* government-operated radiotelephone and private VHF/CB radio-telephone networks provide effective service to almost all points on both islands
international: country code—500; satellite earth station—1 Intelsat (Atlantic Ocean) with links through London to other countries (2015)

Broadcast media: TV service provided by a multichannel service provider; radio services provided by the public broadcaster, Falkland Islands Radio Service, broadcasting on both AM and FM frequencies, and by the British Forces Broadcasting Service (BFBS) (2007)

Internet country code: .fk
Internet users: total: 3,000
percent of population: 98.3% (July 2016 est.)
country comparison to the world: 209

TRANSPORTATION

National air transport system: *number of registered air carriers:* 1

inventory of registered aircraft operated by air carriers: 5 (2015)
Civil aircraft registration country code prefix: VP-F (2016)

Airports: 7 (2013)
country comparison to the world: 170

Airports—with paved runways: *total:* 2
2,438 to 3,047 m: 1
914 to 1,523 m: 1 (2017)

Airports—with unpaved runways: *total:* 5
under 914 m: 5 (2013)

Roadways: *total:* 440 km
paved: 50 km
unpaved: 390 km (2008)
country comparison to the world: 199

Merchant marine: *total:*
by type: general cargo 1, other 2 (2017)
country comparison to the world: 161

Ports and terminals: *major seaport(s):* Stanley

MILITARY AND SECURITY

Military branches: no regular military forces
Military—note: defense is the responsibility of the UK

TRANSNATIONAL ISSUES

Disputes—international: Argentina, which claims the islands in its constitution and briefly occupied them by force in 1982, agreed in 1995 to no longer seek settlement by force; UK continues to reject Argentine requests for sovereignty talks

FAROE ISLANDS

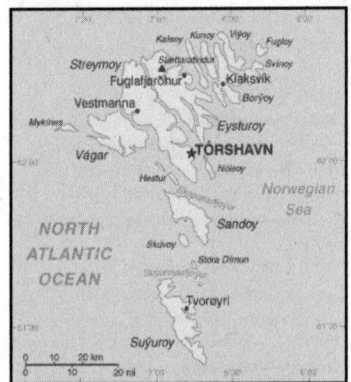

INTRODUCTION

Background: The population of the Faroe Islands is largely descended from Viking settlers who arrived

in the 9th century. The islands have been connected politically to Denmark since the 14th century. A high degree of self-government was granted the Faroese in 1948, who have autonomy over most internal affairs while Denmark is responsible for justice, defense, and foreign affairs. The Faroe Islands are not part of the European Union.

GEOGRAPHY

Location: Northern Europe, island group between the Norwegian Sea and the North Atlantic Ocean, about halfway between Iceland and Norway

Geographic coordinates: 62 00 N, 7 00 W

Map references: Europe

Area: *total:* 1,393 sq km
land: 1,393 sq km
water: 0 sq km (some lakes and streams)
country comparison to the world: 183

Area—comparative: eight times the size of Washington, DC

Land boundaries: 0 km

Coastline: 1,117 km

Maritime claims: *territorial sea:* 12 nm
continental shelf: 200 nm or agreed boundaries or median line
exclusive fishing zone: 200 nm or agreed boundaries or median line

Climate: mild winters, cool summers; usually overcast; foggy, windy

Terrain: rugged, rocky, some low peaks; cliffs along most of coast

Elevation: *mean elevation:* NA

elevation extremes: *lowest point:* Atlantic Ocean 0 m
highest point: Slaettaratindur 882 m

Natural resources: fish, whales, hydropower, possible oil and gas

Land use: *agricultural land:* 2.1%
arable land: 2.1%;
permanent crops: 0%;
permanent pasture: 0%
forest: 0.1%

other: 97.8% (2011 est.)

Population—distribution: the island of Streymoy is by far the most populous with over 40% of the population; it has approximately twice as many inhabitants as Eysturoy, the second most populous island; seven of the inhabited islands have fewer than 100 people

Natural hazards: strong winds and heavy rains can occur throughout the year

Environment—current issues: coastal erosion, landslides and rockfalls, flash flooding, wind storms; oil spills

Environment—international agreements: *party to:* Marine Dumping—associate member to the London Convention and Ship Pollution

Geography—note: archipelago of 17 inhabited islands and one uninhabited island, and a few uninhabited islets; strategically located along important sea lanes in northeastern Atlantic; precipitous terrain limits habitation to small coastal lowlands

PEOPLE AND SOCIETY

Population: 50,730 (July 2017 est.)
country comparison to the world: 211

Nationality: *noun:* Faroese (singular and plural)
adjective: Faroese

Ethnic groups: Faroese 88% (Scandinavian and Anglo-Saxon descent), Danish 7.6%, other 4.4% (includes Icelandic, Norwegian, Greenlandic, Filipino, Thai, British)
note: data represent respondents by country of birth (2017 est.)

Languages: Faroese 93.8% (derived from Old Norse), Danish 3.2%, other 3% (2011 est.)

Religions: Christian 89.3% (predominantly Evangelical Lutheran), other 0.7%, more than one religion 0.2%, none 3.8%, unspecified 6% (2011 est.)

Age structure: *0-14 years:* 19.89% (male 5,214/female 4,878)
15-24 years: 14.34% (male 3,738/female 3,538)
25-54 years: 37.31% (male 10,252/female 8,676)
55-64 years: 11.69% (male 3,054/female 2,878)
65 years and over: 16.76% (male 4,111/female 4,391) (2017 est.)

Median age: *total:* 37.6 years
male: 37.1 years
female: 38.3 years (2017 est.)
country comparison to the world: 64

Population growth rate: 0.55% (2017 est.)
country comparison to the world: 150

Birth rate: 14.3 births/1,000 population (2017 est.)
country comparison to the world: 134

Death rate: 8.8 deaths/1,000 population (2017 est.)
country comparison to the world: 68

Net migration rate: 0 migrant(s)/1,000 population (2017 est.)
country comparison to the world: 82

Population distribution: the island of Streymoy is by far the most populous with over 40% of the population; it has approximately twice as many

inhabitants as Eysturoy, the second most populous island; seven of the inhabited islands have fewer than 100 people

Urbanization: *urban population:* 42.4% of total population (2017)
rate of urbanization: 0.87% annual rate of change (2015-20 est.)

Major urban areas—population: TORSHAVN (capital) 21,000 (2014)

Sex ratio: *at birth:* 1.07 male(s)/female
0-14 years: 1.07 male(s)/female
15-24 years: 1.05 male(s)/female
25-54 years: 1.18 male(s)/female
55-64 years: 1.06 male(s)/female
65 years and over: 0.94 male(s)/female
total population: 1.08 male(s)/female (2016 est.)

Infant mortality rate: *total:* 5.4 deaths/1,000 live births
male: 5.7 deaths/1,000 live births
female: 5.1 deaths/1,000 live births (2017 est.)
country comparison to the world: 173

Life expectancy at birth: *total population:* 80.5 years
male: 78 years
female: 83.2 years (2017 est.)
country comparison to the world: 38

Total fertility rate: 2.35 children born/woman (2017 est.)
country comparison to the world: 86

Physicians density: 2.63 physicians/1,000 population (2014)

Hospital bed density: 5.14 beds/1,000 population (2014)

HIV/AIDS—adult prevalence rate: NA

HIV/AIDS—people living with HIV/AIDS: NA

HIV/AIDS—deaths: NA

GOVERNMENT

Country name: *conventional long form:* none
conventional short form: Faroe Islands
local long form: none
local short form: Foroyar
etymology: the archipelago's name may derive from the Old Norse word "faer," meaning sheep

Dependency status: part of the Kingdom of Denmark; self-governing overseas administrative division of Denmark since 1948

Government type: parliamentary democracy (Faroese Parliament); part of the Kingdom of Denmark

Capital: *name:* Torshavn

geographic coordinates: 62 00 N, 6 46 W
time difference: UTC 0 (5 hours ahead of Washington, DC, during Standard Time)
daylight saving time: +1hr, begins last Sunday in March; ends last Sunday in October

Administrative divisions: none (part of the Kingdom of Denmark; self-governing overseas administrative division of Denmark); there are no first-order administrative divisions as defined by the US Government, but there are 30 municipalities

Independence: none (part of the Kingdom of Denmark; self-governing overseas administrative division of Denmark)

National holiday: Olaifest (Olavsoka) (commemorates the death in battle of King Olaf II of Norway, later St. Olaf), 29 July (1030)

Constitution: *history:* 5 June 1953 (Danish Constitution), 23 March 1948 (Home Rule Act), and 24 June 2005 (Takeover Act) serve as the Faroe Islands constitutional position in the Unity of the Realm
amendments: see entry for Denmark (2016)

Legal system: the laws of Denmark, where applicable, apply

Citizenship: see Denmark

Suffrage: 18 years of age; universal

Executive branch: *chief of state:* Queen MARGRETHE II of Denmark (since 14 January 1972), represented by High Commissioner Dan Michael KNUDSEN, chief administrative officer (since 1 January 2008)
head of government: Prime Minister Aksel V. JOHANNESEN (since 15 September 2015)
cabinet: Landsstyri appointed by the prime minister
elections/appointments: the monarchy is hereditary; high commissioner appointed by the monarch; following legislative elections, the leader of the majority party or majority coalition usually elected prime minister by the Faroese Parliament; election last held on 1 September 2015 (next to be held in 2019)
election results: Aksel V. JOHANNESEN elected prime minister; Parliament vote—NA

Legislative branch: *description:* unicameral Faroese Parliament or Logting (33 seats; members directly elected in a single nationwide constituency by proportional representation vote; members serve 4-year terms)
elections: last held on 1 September 2015 (next to be held no later than October 2019)
election results: percent of vote by party—JF 25.1%, Republic 20.7%, People's Party, 18.9%, Union Party 18.7%, Progressive Party 7%, Center Party 5.5%, Self-Government Party 4.1%; seats by party—JF 8, Republic 7, People's Party 6, Union Party 6, Center Party 2, Progressive Party 2, Self-Government Party 2
note: election for 2 seats in the Danish Parliament was last held on 18 June 2015 (next to be held no later than June 2019); percent of vote by party—NA; seats by party—Social Democratic Party 1, Republican Party 1

Judicial branch: *highest court(s):* Faroese Court or Raett (Rett—Danish) decides both civil and criminal cases; the Court is part of the Danish legal system
subordinate courts: Court of the First Instance or Tribunal de Premiere Instance; Court of Administrative Law or Tribunal Administratif; Mixed Commercial Court; Land Court

Political parties and leaders: Center Party (Midflokkurin) [Jenis av RANA]

317

New Self-Government Party (Nytt Sjalvstyri) [Jogvan SKORHEIM] (formerly Self-Govenment Party) (Sjalvstyrisflokkurin)

People's Party (Folkaflokkurin) [Jorgen NICLASEN]

Progressive Party (Framsokn) [Poul MICHELSEN]

Republic (Tjodveldi) [Hogni HOYDAL] (formerly the Republican Party)

Social Democratic Party (Javnadarflokkurin) or JF [Aksel V. JOHANNESEN]

Union Party (Sambandsflokkurin) [Bardur a STEIG NIELSEN]

Political pressure groups and leaders: conservationists

International organization participation: Arctic Council, IMO (associate), NC, NIB, UNESCO (associate), UPU

Diplomatic representation in the US: none (self-governing overseas administrative division of Denmark)

Diplomatic representation from the US: none (self-governing overseas administrative division of Denmark)

Flag description: white with a red cross outlined in blue extending to the edges of the flag; the vertical part of the cross is shifted toward the hoist side in the style of the Dannebrog (Danish flag); referred to as Merkid, meaning "the banner" or "the mark," the flag resembles those of neighboring Iceland and Norway, and uses the same three colors—but in a different sequence; white represents the clear Faroese sky as well as the foam of the waves; red and blue are traditional Faroese colors

note: the blue on the flag is a lighter blue (azure) than that found on the flags of Iceland or Norway

National symbol(s): ram; national colors: red, white, blue

National anthem: name: "Mitt alfagra land" (My Fairest Land)

lyrics/music: Simun av SKAROI/Peter ALBERG

note: adopted 1948; the anthem is also known as "Tu alfagra land mitt" (Thou Fairest Land of Mine); as a self-governing overseas administrative division of Denmark, the Faroe Islands are permitted their own national anthem

ECONOMY

Economy—overview: The Faroese economy has experienced a period of significant growth since 2011, due to higher fish prices and increased salmon farming and catches in the pelagic fisheries. Nominal GDP, measured in current prices, grew 8.0% in 2015 and 7.8% in 2016. The fisheries sector accounts for about 97% of exports and half of GDP. Dependence on fishing makes the economy vulnerable to price fluctuations. Unemployment is low, estimated at 2.5% in early 2017. Aided by an annual subsidy from Denmark, which amounts to about 4% of Faroese GDP, Faroese have a standard of living equal to that of Denmark.

For the first time in 8 years, the Faroe Islands managed to generate a public budget surplus in 2016, a trend which is continuing in 2017. The local government intends to use this to reduce public debt, which reached 38% of GDP in 2015.

Increasing public infrastructure investments are likely to lead to continued growth in the short term, but could contribute to overheating the economy. Signs of overheating led the Danish Central Bank in fall of 2016 to advise the Faroese local government to initiate measures to cool the economy, including postponing spending on infrastructure spending. The local government is planning to allocate part of the expected public surplus to a business-cycle-equalization fund.

GDP (purchasing power parity): $2.001 billion (2014 est.)

$1.89 billion (2013 est.)

$1.608 billion (2013 est.)

country comparison to the world: 198

GDP (official exchange rate): $2.765 billion (2010 est.)

GDP—real growth rate: 5.9% (2014 est.)

7.5% (2013 est.)

2.4% (2013 est.)

country comparison to the world: 26

GDP—per capita (PPP): $40,000 (2014 est.)

country comparison to the world: 44

Gross national saving: 25.7% of GDP (2012 est.)

25.2% of GDP (2011 est.)

25.9% of GDP (2010 est.)

country comparison to the world: 48

GDP—composition, by sector of origin:

agriculture: 18%

industry: 39%

services: 43% (2013 est.)

Agriculture—products: milk, potatoes, vegetables, sheep, salmon, herring, mackerel and other fish

Industries: fishing, fish processing, tourism, small ship repair and refurbishment, handicrafts

Industrial production growth rate: 3.4% (2009 est.)

country comparison to the world: 88

Labor force: 28,900 (2015 est.)

country comparison to the world: 206

Labor force—by occupation: *agriculture:* 15%

industry: 15%

services: 70% (December 2016 est)

Unemployment rate: 2.8% (2016 est.)

2.9% (2015 est.)

country comparison to the world: 32

Population below poverty line: 4.2% (2012 est.)

Household income or consumption by percentage share: *lowest 10%:* NA%

highest 10%: NA%

Distribution of family income—Gini index: 22.7 (2013 est.)

21.6 (2011 est.)

country comparison to the world: 149

Budget: *revenues:* $835.6 million

expenditures: $883.8 million

note: Denmark supplies the Faroe Islands with almost one-third of their public funds (2014 est.)

Taxes and other revenues: 30.2% of GDP (2014 est.)

country comparison to the world: 81

Budget surplus (+) or deficit (-): -1.7% of GDP (2014 est.)

country comparison to the world: 76

Public debt: 35% of GDP (2014 est.)

country comparison to the world: 148

Fiscal year: calendar year

Inflation rate (consumer prices): -0.3% (2016) -1.7% (2015)

country comparison to the world: 6

Exports: $1.184 billion (2016 est.)

$1.019 billion (2015 est.)

country comparison to the world: 153

Exports—commodities: fish and fish products (97%) (2017 est.)

Exports—partners: UK 17.8%, Russia 17.3%, Germany 9.8%, China 9.2%, Denmark 6.5%, US 6%, Spain 4.8%, Poland 4.3% (2016)

Imports: $978.4 million (2016 est.)

$906.1 million (2015 est.)

country comparison to the world: 180

Imports—commodities: goods for household consumption, machinery and transport equipment, fuels, raw materials and semi-manufactures, cars

Imports—partners: Denmark 26.6%, Germany 10.7%, China 10.6%, Norway 10.2%, Poland 6.2%, Ireland 5%, Chile 4.2% (2016)

Debt—external: $387.6 million (2012)

$274.5 million (2010)

country comparison to the world: 183

Exchange rates: Danish kroner (DKK) per US dollar—

6.586 (2016)

6.7269 (2016)

6.7269 (2015)

6.7236 (2014 est.)

5.6125 (2013 est.)

ENERGY

Electricity access: electrification—*total population:* 100% (2016)

Electricity—production: 317.4 million kWh (2016 est.)

country comparison to the world: 179

Electricity—consumption: 291.4 million kWh (2016 est.)

country comparison to the world: 185

Electricity—exports: 0 kWh (2016 est.)

country comparison to the world: 137

Electricity—imports: 0 kWh (2016 est.)

country comparison to the world: 151

Electricity—installed generating capacity: 128,000 kW (2015 est.)

country comparison to the world: 175

Electricity—from fossil fuels: 50.1% of total installed capacity (2016 est.)

country comparison to the world: 151

Electricity—from nuclear fuels: 0% of total installed capacity (2016 est.)

country comparison to the world: 92

Electricity—from hydroelectric plants: 33.5% of total installed capacity (2016 est.)

country comparison to the world: 62

Electricity—from other renewable sources: 16.4% of total installed capacity (2016 est.)
country comparison to the world: 41

Crude oil—production: 0 bbl/day (2016 est.)
country comparison to the world: 134

Crude oil—exports: 0 bbl/day (2014 est.)
country comparison to the world: 125

Crude oil—imports: 0 bbl/day (2014 est.)
country comparison to the world: 128

Crude oil—proved reserves: 0 bbl (1 January 2017 es)
country comparison to the world: 133

Refined petroleum products—production: 0 bbl/day (2016 est.)
country comparison to the world: 144

Refined petroleum products—consumption: 3,947 bbl/day (2015 est.)
country comparison to the world: 180

Refined petroleum products—exports: 0 bbl/day (2015 est.)
country comparison to the world: 157

Refined petroleum products—imports: 3,947 bbl/day (2016 est.)
country comparison to the world: 171

Natural gas—production: 0 cu m (2016 est.)
country comparison to the world: 137

Natural gas—consumption: 0 cu m (2013 est.)
country comparison to the world: 182

Natural gas—exports: 0 cu m (2016 est.)
country comparison to the world: 105

Natural gas—imports: 0 cu m (2013 est.)
country comparison to the world: 126

Natural gas—proved reserves: 0 cu m (1 January 2014 es)
country comparison to the world: 141

Carbon dioxide emissions from consumption of energy: 800,000 Mt (2013 est.)
country comparison to the world: 171

COMMUNICATIONS

Telephones—fixed lines: *total subscriptions:* 23,139
subscriptions per 100 inhabitants: 46 (July 2016 est.)
country comparison to the world: 189

Telephones—mobile cellular: *total:* 54,487
subscriptions per 100 inhabitants: 108 (July 2016 est.)
country comparison to the world: 199

Telephone system: *general assessment:* good international communications; good domestic facilities
domestic: conversion to digital system completed in 1998; both NMT (analog) and GSM (digital) mobile telephone systems are installed
international: country code—298; satellite earth stations—1 Orion; 1 fiber-optic submarine cable to the Shetland Islands, linking the Faroe Islands with Denmark and Iceland; fiber-optic submarine cable connection to Canada-Europe cable (2015)

Broadcast media: 1 publicly owned TV station; the Faroese telecommunications company distributes local and international channels through its digital terrestrial network; publicly owned radio station supplemented by 3 privately owned stations broadcasting over multiple frequencies (2015)

Internet country code: .fo
Internet users: total: 47,988
percent of population: 95.1% (July 2016 est.)
country comparison to the world: 188

TRANSPORTATION

National air transport system: *number of registered air carriers:* 1 (registered in Denmark)
inventory of registered aircraft operated by air carriers: 3 (registered in Denmark) (2015)

Civil aircraft registration country code prefix: OY-H (2016)

Airports: 1 (2013)
country comparison to the world: 217

Airports—with paved runways: *total:* 1
1,524 to 2,437 m: 1 (2017)

Roadways: *total:* 960 km
note: those islands not commected by roads (bridges or tunnels) are connected by seven different ferry links operated by the nationally owned company SSL (2017)
country comparison to the world: 187

Merchant marine: *total:* 96
by type: container ship 2, general cargo 41, oil tanker 1, other 52 (2017)
country comparison to the world: 87

Ports and terminals: *major seaport(s):* Fuglafjordur, Torshavn, Vagur

MILITARY AND SECURITY

Military branches: no regular military forces or conscription; the Government of Denmark has responsibility for defense; as such, the Danish military's Joint Arctic Command in Nuuk, Greenland is responsible for territorial defense of the Faroe Islands; the Joint Arctic Command has a contact element in the capital of Torshavn (2017)

Military—note: defense is the responsibility of Denmark

TRANSNATIONAL ISSUES

Disputes—international: because anticipated offshore hydrocarbon resources have not been realized, earlier Faroese proposals for full independence have been deferred; Iceland, the UK, and Ireland dispute Denmark's claim to UNCLOS that the Faroe Islands' continental shelf extends beyond 200 nm

FIJI

INTRODUCTION

Background: Fiji became independent in 1970 after nearly a century as a British colony. Democratic rule was interrupted by two military coups in 1987 caused by concern over a government perceived as dominated by the Indian community (descendants of contract laborers brought to the islands by the British in the 19th century). The coups and a 1990 constitution that cemented native Melanesian control of Fiji led to heavy Indian emigration; the population loss resulted in economic difficulties, but ensured that Melanesians became the majority. A new constitution enacted in 1997 was more equitable. Free and peaceful elections in 1999 resulted in a government led by an Indo-Fijian, but a civilian-led coup in 2000 ushered in a prolonged period of political turmoil. Parliamentary elections held in 2001 provided Fiji with a democratically elected government led by Prime Minister Laisenia QARASE. Reelected in May 2006, QARASE was ousted in a December 2006 military coup led by Commodore Voreqe BAINIMARAMA, who initially appointed himself acting president but in January 2007 became interim prime minister. Following years of political turmoil, long-delayed legislative elections were held in September 2014 that were deemed "credible" by international observers and that resulted in BAINIMARAMA being reelected.

GEOGRAPHY

Location: Oceania, island group in the South Pacific Ocean, about two-thirds of the way from Hawaii to New Zealand

Geographic coordinates: 18 00 S, 175 00 E

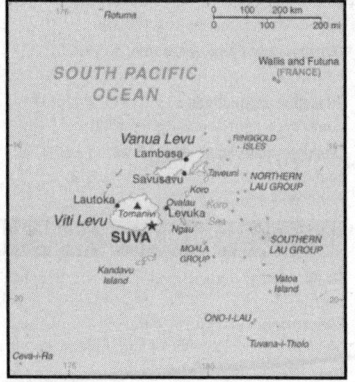

Map references: Oceania

Area: *total:* 18,274 sq km
land: 18,274 sq km
water: 0 sq km
country comparison to the world: 157

Area—comparative: slightly smaller than New Jersey

Land boundaries: 0 km

Coastline: 1,129 km

Maritime claims: measured from claimed archipelagic straight baselines
territorial sea: 12 nm
contiguous zone: 24 nm
exclusive economic zone: 200 nm
continental shelf: 200-m depth or to the depth of exploitation

Climate: tropical marine; only slight seasonal temperature variation

Terrain: mostly mountains of volcanic origin

Elevation: *mean elevation:* NA

elevation extremes: *lowest point:* Pacific Ocean 0 m
highest point: Tomanivi 1,324 m

Natural resources: timber, fish, gold, copper, offshore oil potential, hydropower

Land use: *agricultural land:* 23.3%
arable land: 9%;
permanent crops: 4.7%;
permanent pasture: 9.6%
forest: 55.7%
other: 21% (2011 est.)

Irrigated land: 40 sq km (2012)

Population—distribution: approximately 70% of the population lives on the island of Viti Levu; roughly half of the population lives in urban areas

Natural hazards: cyclonic storms can occur from November to January

Environment—current issues: deforestation; soil erosion

Environment—international agreements: *party to:* Biodiversity, Climate Change, Climate Change-Kyoto Protocol, Desertification, Endangered Species, Law of the Sea, Marine Life Conservation, Ozone Layer Protection, Tropical Timber 83, Tropical Timber 94, Wetlands
signed, but not ratified: none of the selected agreements

Geography—note: includes 332 islands; approximately 110 are inhabited

PEOPLE AND SOCIETY

Population: 920,938 (July 2017 est.)
country comparison to the world: 161

Nationality: *noun:* Fijian(s)
adjective: Fijian

Ethnic groups: iTaukei 56.8% (predominantly Melanesian with a Polynesian admixture), Indian 37.5%, Rotuman 1.2%, other 4.5% (European, part European, other Pacific Islanders, Chinese)

note: a 2010 law replaces 'Fijian' with 'iTuakei' when referring to the original and native settlers of Fiji (2007 est.)

Languages: English (official), Fijian (official), Hindustani

Religions: Protestant 45% (Methodist 34.6%, Assembly of God 5.7%, Seventh Day Adventist 3.9%, and Anglican 0.8%), Hindu 27.9%, other Christian 10.4%, Roman Catholic 9.1%, Muslim 6.3%, Sikh 0.3%, other 0.3%, none 0.8% (2007 est.)

Age structure: *0-14 years:* 27.7% (male 130,394/female 124,734)
15-24 years: 16.13% (male 75,803/female 72,774)
25-54 years: 41.08% (male 193,700/female 184,629)
55-64 years: 8.53% (male 39,853/female 38,748)
65 years and over: 6.55% (male 27,714/female 32,589) (2017 est.)

Dependency ratios: *total dependency ratio:* 52.8
youth dependency ratio: 43.9
elderly dependency ratio: 8.9
potential support ratio: 11.2 (2015 est.)

Median age: *total:* 28.9 years
male: 28.7 years
female: 29.1 years (2017 est.)
country comparison to the world: 127

Population growth rate: 0.6% (2017 est.)
country comparison to the world: 148

Birth rate: 18.6 births/1,000 population (2017 est.)
country comparison to the world: 91

Death rate: 6.1 deaths/1,000 population (2017 est.)
country comparison to the world: 159

Net migration rate: -6.5 migrant(s)/1,000 population (2017 est.)
country comparison to the world: 200

Population distribution: approximately 70% of the population lives on the island of Viti Levu; roughly half of the population lives in urban areas

Urbanization: *urban population:* 54.5% of total population (2017)
rate of urbanization: 1.18% annual rate of change (2015-20 est.)

Major urban areas—population: SUVA (capital) 176,000 (2014)

Sex ratio: *at birth:* 1.05 male(s)/female
0-14 years: 1.05 male(s)/female
15-24 years: 1.04 male(s)/female
25-54 years: 1.05 male(s)/female
55-64 years: 1.03 male(s)/female
65 years and over: 0.85 male(s)/female
total population: 1.03 male(s)/female (2016 est.)

Maternal mortality ratio: 30 deaths/100,000 live births (2015 est.)
country comparison to the world: 113

Infant mortality rate: *total:* 9.5 deaths/1,000 live births
male: 10.5 deaths/1,000 live births
female: 8.5 deaths/1,000 live births (2017 est.)
country comparison to the world: 143

Life expectancy at birth: *total population:* 73 years
male: 70.3 years
female: 75.8 years (2017 est.)
country comparison to the world: 140

Total fertility rate: 2.41 children born/woman (2017 est.)
country comparison to the world: 83
Health expenditures: 4.5% of GDP (2014)
country comparison to the world: 156

Physicians density: 0.44 physicians/1,000 population (2009)

Hospital bed density: 2 beds/1,000 population (2009)

Drinking water source:
improved:
urban: 99.5% of population
rural: 91.2% of population
total: 95.7% of population
unimproved:
urban: 0.5% of population
rural: 8.8% of population
total: 4.3% of population (2015 est.)

Sanitation facility access:
improved:
urban: 93.4% of population
rural: 88.4% of population
total: 91.1% of population
unimproved:
urban: 6.6% of population
rural: 11.6% of population
total: 8.9% of population (2015 est.)

HIV/AIDS—adult prevalence rate: 0.1% (2016 est.)
country comparison to the world: 102

HIV/AIDS—people living with HIV/AIDS: <1000 (2016 est.)

HIV/AIDS—deaths: <100 (2016 est.)

Major infectious diseases: *note:* active local transmission of Zika virus by Aedes species mosquitoes has been identified in this country (as of August 2016); it poses an important risk (a large number of cases possible) among US citizens if bitten by an infective mosquito; other less common ways to get Zika are through sex, via blood transfusion, or during pregnancy, in which the pregnant woman passes Zika virus to her fetus (2016)

Obesity—adult prevalence rate: 30.2% (2016)
country comparison to the world: 24

Education expenditures: 3.9% of GDP (2013)
country comparison to the world: 102

Unemployment, youth ages 15-24: *total:* 18.7%
male: 14.8%
female: 25.4% (2007 est.)

GOVERNMENT

Country name: *conventional long form:* Republic of Fiji
conventional short form: Fiji
local long form: Republic of Fiji/Matanitu ko Viti
local short form: Fiji/Viti
etymology: the Fijians called their home Viti, but the neighboring Tongans called it Fisi, and

in the Anglicized spelling of the Tongan pronunciation—promulgated by explorer Captain James COOK—the designation became Fiji

Government type: parliamentary republic

Capital: *name:* Suva (on Viti Levu)

geographic coordinates: 18 08 S, 178 25 E

time difference: UTC+12 (17 hours ahead of Washington, DC, during Standard Time)

daylight saving time: +1hr, begins first Sunday in November; ends second Sunday in January

Administrative divisions: 14 provinces and 1 dependency*; Ba, Bua, Cakaudrove, Kadavu, Lau, Lomaiviti, Macuata, Nadroga and Navosa, Naitasiri, Namosi, Ra, Rewa, Rotuma*, Serua, Tailevu

Independence: 10 October 1970 (from the UK)

National holiday: Fiji (Independence) Day, 10 October (1970)

Constitution: several previous; latest signed into law September 2013 (2016)

Legal system: common law system based on the English model

International law organization participation: has not submitted an ICJ jurisdiction declaration; accepts ICCt jurisdiction

Citizenship: *citizenship by birth:* no

citizenship by descent only: at least one parent must be a citizen of Fiji

dual citizenship recognized: yes

residency requirement for naturalization: 5 years

Suffrage: 18 years of age; universal

Executive branch: *chief of state:* President Jioji Konousi KONROTE (since 12 November 2015)

head of government: Prime Minister Voreqe "Frank" BAINIMARAMA (since 22 September 2014)

cabinet: Cabinet appointed by the prime minister from among members of Parliament and is responsible to Parliament

elections/appointments: president elected by Parliament for a 3-year term (eligible for a second term); election last held on 12 October 2015 (next to be held in 2018); prime minister appointed by the president

election results: Jioji Konousi KONROTE elected president; Parliament vote—Jioji Konousi KONROTE (Fiji First) 31, Ratu Epeli GANILAU (opposition) 14

Legislative branch: description: unicameral Parliament (50 seats—51 beginning in 2018; members directly elected in a nationwide, multi-seat constituency by open-list proportional representation vote to serve 4-year terms)

elections: last held on 17 September 2014 (next to be held in 2018)

election results: percent of vote by party—FijiFirst 59.2%, SODELPA 28.2%, NFP 5.5%, other 7.1%; seats by party—FijiFirst 32, SODELPA 15, NFP 3

Judicial branch: *highest court(s):* Supreme Court (consists of the chief justice, all justices of the Court of Appeal, and judges appointed specifically as Supreme Court judges); Court of Appeal (consists of the court president, all puisne judges of the High Court, and judges specifically appointed to the Court of Appeal); High Court (chaired by the chief justice and includes a minimum of 10 puisne judges; High Court organized into civil, criminal, family, employment, and tax divisions)

judge selection and term of office: chief justice appointed by the president of Fiji on the advice of the prime minister following consultation with the parliamentary leader of the opposition; judges of the Supreme Court, the president of the Court of Appeal, the justices of the Court of Appeal, and puisne judges of the High Court appointed by the president of Fiji upon the nomination of the Judicial Service Commission after consulting with the cabinet minister and the committee of the House of Representatives responsible for the administration of justice; the chief justice, Supreme Court judges and justices of Appeal generally required to retire at age 70 but may be waived for one or more sessions of the court; puisne judges appointed for not less than 4 years nor more than 7 years with mandatory retirement at age 65

subordinate courts: Magistrates' Court (organized into civil, criminal, juvenile, and small claims divisions)

Political parties and leaders: FijiFirst [Frank BAINIMARAMA]

Fiji Labor Party or FLP [Mahendra CHAUDHRY]

Fiji United Freedon Party or FUFP [Jagath KARUNARATNE]

National Federation Party or NFP [Biman PRASAD] (primarily Indian)

Peoples Democratic Party or PDP [Lynda TABUYA]

Social Democratic Liberal Party or SODELPA [Sitiveni RABUKA]

Political pressure groups and leaders: Group Against Racial Discrimination or GARD [Dr. Anirudk SINGH] (suports restoration of a democratic government)

Viti Landowners Association

International organization participation: ACP, ADB, AOSIS, C, CP, FAO, G-77, IAEA, IBRD, ICAO, ICCt, ICRM, IDA, IFAD, IFC, IFRCS, IHO, ILO, IMF, IMO, Interpol, IOC, IOM, ISO, ITSO, ITU, ITUC (NGOs), MIGA, OPCW, PCA, PIF, Sparteca (suspended), SPC, UN, UNCTAD, UNDOF, UNESCO, UNIDO, UNMISS, UNWTO, UPU, WCO, WFTU (NGOs), WHO, WIPO, WMO, WTO

Diplomatic representation in the US: *chief of mission:* Ambassador Solo MARA (since 28 January 2016)

chancery: 2000 M Street NW, Suite 710, Washington, DC 20036

telephone: [1] (202) 466-8320

FAX: [1] (202) 466-8325

Diplomatic representation from the US: *chief of mission:* Ambassador Judith CEFKIN (since 3 February 2015); note—also accredited to Kiribati, Nauru, Tonga, and Tuvalu

embassy: 158 Princes Rd, Tamavua

mailing address: P. O. Box 218, Suva

telephone: [679] 331-4466

FAX: [679] 330-8685

Flag description: light blue with the flag of the UK in the upper hoist-side quadrant and the Fijian shield centered on the outer half of the flag; the blue symbolizes the Pacific ocean and the Union Jack reflects the links with Great Britain; the shield—taken from Fiji's coat of arms—depicts a yellow lion, holding a coconut pod between its paws, above a white field quartered by the cross of Saint George; the four quarters depict stalks of sugarcane, a palm tree, a banana bunch, and a white dove of peace

National symbol(s): Fijian canoe; national color: light blue

National anthem: name: "God Bless Fiji"

lyrics/music: Michael Francis Alexander PRESCOTT/C. Austin MILES (adapted by Michael Francis Alexander PRESCOTT)

note: adopted 1970; known in Fijian as "Meda Dau Doka" (Let Us Show Pride); adapted from the hymn, "Dwelling in Beulah Land," the anthem's English lyrics are generally sung, although they differ in meaning from the official Fijian lyrics

ECONOMY

Economy—overview: Fiji, endowed with forest, mineral, and fish resources, is one of the most developed and connected of the Pacific island economies. Earnings from the tourism industry, with an estimated 792,300 tourists visiting in 2016, and remittances from Fijian's working abroad are the country's largest foreign exchange earners.

Fiji's sugar sector remains a significant industry and a major export, but crops and one of the sugar mills suffered damage during Cyclone Winston in 2016. The sector also faces the complete withdrawal of European Union preferential prices in 2017. Fiji's trade imbalance continues to widen with increased imports and sluggish performance of domestic exports.

The return to parliamentary democracy and successful elections in September 2014 improved investor confidence, but increasing bureaucratic regulation, new taxes and lack of consultation with relevant stakeholders brought four consecutive years of decline for Fiji on the World Bank Ease of Doing Business index. Private sector investment in 2017 approached 20% of GDP, compared to 13% in 2013.

GDP (purchasing power parity): $8.647 billion (2017 est.)

$8.33 billion (2016 est.)

$8.299 billion (2015 est.)

note: data are in 2017 dollars

country comparison to the world: 163

GDP (official exchange rate): $5.054 billion (2016 est.)

GDP—real growth rate: 3.8% (2017 est.)

0.4% (2016 est.)

3.8% (2015 est.)

country comparison to the world: 78

GDP—per capita (PPP): $9,900 (2017 est.)

$9,500 (2016 est.)

$9,500 (2015 est.)

note: data are in 2017 dollars
country comparison to the world: 139

Gross national saving: 10.6% of GDP (2017 est.)
9.7% of GDP (2016 est.)
16.9% of GDP (2015 est.)
country comparison to the world: 154

GDP—composition, by end use:
household consumption: 71.6%
government consumption: 16%
investment in fixed capital: 18.4%
investment in inventories: 0%
exports of goods and services: 44.2%
imports of goods and services: -50.3% (2017 est.)

GDP—composition, by sector of origin:
agriculture: 10.6%
industry: 17.9%
services: 71.5% (2017 est.)

Agriculture—products: sugarcane, coconuts, cassava (manioc, tapioca), rice, sweet potatoes, bananas; cattle, pigs, horses, goats; fish

Industries: tourism, sugar processing, clothing, copra, gold, silver, lumber, small cottage industries

Industrial production growth rate: 2.8% (2017 est.)
country comparison to the world: 105

Labor force: 353,100 (2017 est.)
country comparison to the world: 161

Labor force—by occupation: *agriculture:* 70%
industry and services: 30% (2001 est.)

Unemployment rate: 5.5% (2017 est.)
5.5% (2016 est.)
country comparison to the world: 77

Population below poverty line: 31% (2009 est.)

Household income or consumption by percentage share: *lowest 10%:* 2.6%
highest 10%: 34.9% (2009 est.)

Budget: *revenues:* $1.446 billion
expenditures: $1.687 billion (2017 est.)
Taxes and other revenues: 28.6% of GDP (2017 est.)
country comparison to the world: 91

Budget surplus (+) or deficit (-): -4.8% of GDP (2017 est.)
country comparison to the world: 158

Public debt: 50.4% of GDP (2017 est.)
49.6% of GDP (2016 est.)
country comparison to the world: 101

Fiscal year: calendar year

Inflation rate (consumer prices): 3.8% (2017 est.)
3.9% (2016 est.)
country comparison to the world: 150

Central bank discount rate: 1.75% (31 December 2010)
3% (31 December 2009)
country comparison to the world: 118

Commercial bank prime lending rate: 6% (31 December 2017 est.)
5.85% (31 December 2016 est.)
country comparison to the world: 126

Stock of narrow money: $2.138 billion (31 December 2017 est.)
$1.994 billion (31 December 2016 est.)
country comparison to the world: 133

Stock of broad money: $3.693 billion (31 December 2017 est.)
$3.486 billion (31 December 2016 est.)
country comparison to the world: 140

Stock of domestic credit: $3.663 billion (31 December 2017 est.)
$3.295 billion (31 December 2016 est.)
country comparison to the world: 134

Market value of publicly traded shares: $452.5 million (31 December 2012 est.)
$392.2 million (31 December 2011 est.)
$418.8 million (31 December 2010 est.)
country comparison to the world: 114

Current account balance: -$254 million (2017 est.)
-$236 million (2016 est.)
country comparison to the world: 92

Exports: $758.6 million (2017 est.)
$709 million (2016 est.)
country comparison to the world: 169

Exports—commodities: sugar, garments, gold, timber, fish, molasses, coconut oil, mineral water

Exports—partners: US 21.8%, Australia 18.1%, NZ 8.5%, China 6.2%, Tonga 5.1%, Vanuatu 5.1%, UK 4.5%, Kiribati 4.1% (2016)

Imports: $1.918 billion (2017 est.)
$1.844 billion (2016 est.)
country comparison to the world: 161

Imports—commodities: manufactured goods, machinery and transport equipment, petroleum products, food, chemicals

Imports—partners: NZ 17.1%, Australia 17%, Singapore 15.1%, China 15%, Japan 6.7% (2016)

Reserves of foreign exchange and gold: $966.8 million (31 December 2017 est.)
$908.6 million (31 December 2016 est.)
country comparison to the world: 127

Debt—external: $750.4 million (31 December 2017 est.)
$696.4 million (31 December 2016 est.)
country comparison to the world: 171

Stock of direct foreign investment—at home: $4.342 billion (31 December 2017 est.)
$4.022 billion (31 December 2016 est.)
country comparison to the world: 106

Stock of direct foreign investment—abroad: $117.1 million (31 December 2017 est.)
$115.1 million (31 December 2016 est.)
country comparison to the world: 103

Exchange rates: Fijian dollars (FJD) per US dollar—
2.075 (2017 est.)
2.0947 (2016 est.)
2.0947 (2015 est.)
2.0976 (2014 est.)
1.8874 (2013 est.)

ENERGY

Electricity access: *population without electricity:* 375,274
electrification—*total population:* 59%
electrification—urban areas: 72%

electrification—rural areas: 45% (2012)

Electricity—production: 890 million kWh (2015 est.)
country comparison to the world: 157

Electricity—consumption: 827.7 million kWh (2015 est.)
country comparison to the world: 161

Electricity—exports: 0 kWh (2016 est.)
country comparison to the world: 134

Electricity—imports: 0 kWh (2016 est.)
country comparison to the world: 148

Electricity—installed generating capacity: 333,000 kW (2015 est.)
country comparison to the world: 154

Electricity—from fossil fuels: 36% of total installed capacity (2015 est.)
country comparison to the world: 174

Electricity—from nuclear fuels: 0% of total installed capacity (2015 est.)
country comparison to the world: 89

Electricity—from hydroelectric plants: 39% of total installed capacity (2015 est.)
country comparison to the world: 52

Electricity—from other renewable sources: 25.2% of total installed capacity (2015 est.)
country comparison to the world: 21

Crude oil—production: 0 bbl/day (2016 est.)
country comparison to the world: 135

Crude oil—exports: 0 bbl/day (2014 est.)
country comparison to the world: 122

Crude oil—imports: 0 bbl/day (2014 est.)
country comparison to the world: 125

Crude oil—proved reserves: 0 bbl (1 January 2017 es)
country comparison to the world: 134

Refined petroleum products—production: 0 bbl/day (2014 est.)
country comparison to the world: 145

Refined petroleum products—consumption: 16,000 bbl/day (2015 est.)
country comparison to the world: 146

Refined petroleum products—exports: 0 bbl/day (2014 est.)
country comparison to the world: 154

Refined petroleum products—imports: 15,970 bbl/day (2014 est.)
country comparison to the world: 128

Natural gas—production: 0 cu m (2013 est.)
country comparison to the world: 134

Natural gas—consumption: 0 cu m (2013 est.)
country comparison to the world: 180

Natural gas—exports: 0 cu m (2013 est.)
country comparison to the world: 103

Natural gas—imports: 0 cu m (2013 est.)
country comparison to the world: 124

Natural gas—proved reserves: 0 cu m (1 January 2014 es)
country comparison to the world: 138

Carbon dioxide emissions from consumption of energy: 1.7 million Mt (2013 est.)
country comparison to the world: 156

COMMUNICATIONS

Telephones—fixed lines: *total subscriptions:* 74,182
subscriptions per 100 inhabitants: 8 (July 2016 est.)
country comparison to the world: 150

Telephones—mobile cellular: *total:* 927,793
subscriptions per 100 inhabitants: 101 (July 2016 est.)
country comparison to the world: 161

Telephone system: *general assessment:* modern local, interisland, and international (wire/radio integrated) public and special-purpose telephone, telegraph, and teleprinter facilities; regional radio communications center; subject to occasional devastating cyclones
domestic: telephone or radio telephone links to almost all inhabited islands; most towns and large villages have automatic telephone exchanges and direct dialing; combined fixed-line and mobile-cellular teledensity roughly 110 per 100 persons
international: country code—679; access to important cable links between US and Canada, as well as between NZ and Australia; satellite earth stations—2 Inmarsat (Pacific Ocean) (2016)

Broadcast media: Fiji TV, a publicly traded company, operates a free-to-air channel, as well as Sky Fiji and Sky Pacific multi-channel pay-TV services; state-owned commercial company, Fiji Broadcasting Corporation, Ltd, operates 6 radio stations—2 public broadcasters and 4 commercial broadcasters with multiple repeaters; 5 radio stations with repeaters operated by Communications Fiji, Ltd; transmissions of multiple international broadcasters are available (2009)

Internet country code: .fj
Internet users: total: 425,680
percent of population: 46.5% (July 2016 est.)
country comparison to the world: 139

TRANSPORTATION

National air transport system: *number of registered air carriers:* 2
inventory of registered aircraft operated by air carriers: 12
annual passenger traffic on registered air carriers: 1,336,976
annual freight traffic on registered air carriers: 83,686,504 mt-km (2015)
Civil aircraft registration country code prefix: DQ (2016)

Airports: 28 (2013)
country comparison to the world: 121

Airports—with paved runways: *total:* 4
over 3,047 m: 1
1,524 to 2,437 m: 1
914 to 1,523 m: 2 (2017)

Airports—with unpaved runways: *total:* 24
914 to 1,523 m: 5
under 914 m: 19 (2013)

Railways: *total:* 597 km
narrow gauge: 597 km 0.600-m gauge
note: belongs to the government-owned Fiji Sugar Corporation; used to haul sugarcane during the harvest season, which runs from May to December (2008)
country comparison to the world: 110

Roadways: *total:* 3,440 km
paved: 1,686 km
unpaved: 1,754 km (2011)
country comparison to the world: 162

Waterways: 203 km (122 km are navigable by motorized craft and 200-metric-ton barges) (2012)
country comparison to the world: 97

Merchant marine: *total:* 68
by type: bulk carrier 6, general cargo 25, oil tanker 2, other 35 (2017)
country comparison to the world: 101

Ports and terminals: *major seaport(s):* Lautoka, Levuka, Suva

MILITARY AND SECURITY

Military expenditures: 0.98% of GDP (2016)
1.07% of GDP (2015)
1.03% of GDP (2014)
1.39% of GDP (2013)
1.49% of GDP (2012)
country comparison to the world: 61

Military branches: Republic of Fiji Military Forces (RFMF): Land Forces, Naval Forces (2011)

Military service age and obligation: 18 years of age for voluntary military service; mandatory retirement at age 55 (2013)

TRANSNATIONAL ISSUES

Disputes—international: none

FINLAND

INTRODUCTION

Background: Finland was a province and then a grand duchy under Sweden from the 12th to the 19th centuries, and an autonomous grand duchy of Russia after 1809. It gained complete independence in 1917. During World War II, Finland successfully defended its independence through cooperation with Germany and resisted subsequent invasions by the Soviet Union—albeit with some loss of territory. In the subsequent half century, Finland transformed from a farm/forest economy to a diversified modern industrial economy; per capita income is among the highest in Western Europe. A member of the EU since 1995, Finland was the only Nordic state to join the euro single currency at its initiation in January 1999. In the 21st century, the key features of Finland's modern welfare state are high quality education, promotion of equality, and a national social welfare system—currently challenged by an aging population and the fluctuations of an export-driven economy.

GEOGRAPHY

Location: Northern Europe, bordering the Baltic Sea, Gulf of Bothnia, and Gulf of Finland, between Sweden and Russia

Geographic coordinates: 64 00 N, 26 00 E

Map references: Europe

Area: *total:* 338,145 sq km
land: 303,815 sq km
water: 34,330 sq km
country comparison to the world: 66

Area—comparative: slightly more than two times the size of Georgia; slightly smaller than Montana

Land boundaries: *total:* 2,563 km
border countries (3): Norway 709 km, Sweden 545 km, Russia 1,309 km

Coastline: 1,250 km

Maritime claims: *territorial sea:* 12 nm (in the Gulf of Finland—3 nm)
contiguous zone: 24 nm
exclusive fishing zone: 12 nm; extends to continental shelf boundary with Sweden, Estonia, and Russia
continental shelf: 200 m depth or to the depth of exploitation

Climate: cold temperate; potentially subarctic but comparatively mild because of moderating influence of the North Atlantic Current, Baltic Sea, and more than 60,000 lakes

Terrain: mostly low, flat to rolling plains interspersed with lakes and low hills

Elevation: *mean elevation:* 164 m

elevation extremes: *lowest point:* Baltic Sea 0 m
highest point: Halti (alternatively Haltia, Haltitunturi, Haltiatunturi) 1,328 m

Natural resources: timber, iron ore, copper, lead, zinc, chromite, nickel, gold, silver, limestone

Land use: *agricultural land:* 7.5%
arable land: 7.4%;
permanent crops: 0%;
permanent pasture: 0.1%
forest: 72.9%
other: 19.6% (2011 est.)

Irrigated land: 690 sq km (2012)

Population—distribution: the vast majority of people are found in the south; the northern interior areas remain sparsely populated

Natural hazards: severe winters in the north

Environment—current issues: air pollution from manufacturing and power plants contributing to acid rain; water pollution from industrial wastes, agricultural chemicals; habitat loss threatens wildlife populations

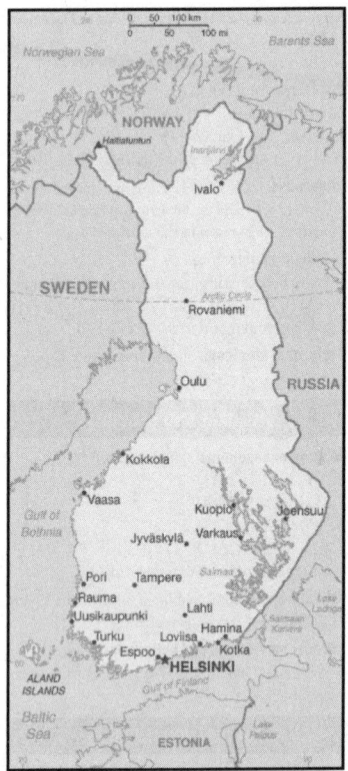

Environment—international agreements: *party to:* Air Pollution, Air Pollution-Nitrogen Oxides, Air Pollution-Persistent Organic Pollutants, Air Pollution-Sulfur 85, Air Pollution-Sulfur 94, Air Pollution-Volatile Organic Compounds, Antarctic-Environmental Protocol, Antarctic-Marine Living Resources, Antarctic Treaty, Biodiversity, Climate Change, Climate Change-Kyoto Protocol, Desertification, Endangered Species, Environmental Modification, Hazardous Wastes, Law of the Sea, Marine Dumping, Marine Life Conservation, Ozone Layer Protection, Ship Pollution, Tropical Timber 83, Tropical Timber 94, Wetlands, Whaling
signed, but not ratified: none of the selected agreements

Geography—note: long boundary with Russia; Helsinki is northernmost national capital on European continent; population concentrated on small southwestern coastal plain

PEOPLE AND SOCIETY

Population: 5,518,371 (July 2017 est.)
country comparison to the world: 117

Nationality: *noun:* Finn(s)
adjective: Finnish

Ethnic groups: Finn 93.4%, Swede 5.6%, Russian 0.5%, Estonian 0.3%, Romani 0.1%, Sami 0.1% (2006)

Languages: Finnish (official) 88.3%, Swedish (official) 5.3%, Russian 1.4%, other 5% (2016 est.)

Religions: Lutheran 72%, Orthodox 1.1%, other 1.6%, unspecified 25.3% (2016 est.)

Age structure: *0-14 years:* 16.43% (male 463,432/female 443,384)
15-24 years: 11.4% (male 321,609/female 307,458)
25-54 years: 37.78% (male 1,064,427/female 1,020,285)
55-64 years: 13.29% (male 360,821/female 372,794)
65 years and over: 21.1% (male 506,342/female 657,819) (2017 est.)

Dependency ratios: *total dependency ratio:* 57.9
youth dependency ratio: 25.9
elderly dependency ratio: 32
potential support ratio: 3.1 (2015 est.)

Median age: *total:* 42.5 years
male: 40.9 years
female: 44.3 years (2017 est.)
country comparison to the world: 25

Population growth rate: 0.36% (2017 est.)
country comparison to the world: 165

Birth rate: 10.7 births/1,000 population (2017 est.)
country comparison to the world: 185

Death rate: 10 deaths/1,000 population (2017 est.)
country comparison to the world: 40

Net migration rate: 2.9 migrant(s)/1,000 population (2017 est.)
country comparison to the world: 35

Population distribution: the vast majority of people are found in the south; the northern interior areas remain sparsely poplulated

Urbanization: *urban population:* 84.5% of total population (2017)
rate of urbanization: 0.46% annual rate of change (2015-20 est.)

Major urban areas—population: HELSINKI (capital) 1.18 million (2015)

Sex ratio: *at birth:* 1.05 male(s)/female
0-14 years: 1.05 male(s)/female
15-24 years: 1.04 male(s)/female
25-54 years: 1.04 male(s)/female
55-64 years: 0.97 male(s)/female
65 years and over: 0.76 male(s)/female
total population: 0.97 male(s)/female (2016 est.)

Mother's mean age at first birth: 28.8 years (2015 est.)

Maternal mortality ratio: 3 deaths/100,000 live births (2015 est.)
country comparison to the world: 181

Infant mortality rate: *total:* 2.5 deaths/1,000 live births
male: 2.7 deaths/1,000 live births
female: 2.4 deaths/1,000 live births (2017 est.)
country comparison to the world: 220

Life expectancy at birth: *total population:* 81 years
male: 78 years
female: 84.1 years (2017 est.)
country comparison to the world: 31

Total fertility rate: 1.75 children born/woman (2017 est.)
country comparison to the world: 162
Health expenditures: 9.7% of GDP (2014)
country comparison to the world: 29

Physicians density: 3.01 physicians/1,000 population (2013)

Hospital bed density: 4.53 beds/1,000 population (2014)

Drinking water source:
improved:
urban: 100% of population
rural: 100% of population
total: 100% of population
unimproved:
urban: 0% of population
rural: 0% of population
total: 0% of population (2015 est.)

Sanitation facility access:
improved:
urban: 99.4% of population
rural: 88% of population
total: 97.6% of population
unimproved:
urban: 0.6% of population
rural: 12% of population
total: 2.4% of population (2015 est.)

HIV/AIDS—adult prevalence rate: NA

HIV/AIDS—people living with HIV/AIDS: NA

HIV/AIDS—deaths: NA

Obesity—adult prevalence rate: 22.2% (2016)
country comparison to the world: 80

Education expenditures: 7.2% of GDP (2013)
country comparison to the world: 27

School life expectancy (primary to tertiary education): *total:* 19 years
male: 19 years
female: 20 years (2015)

Unemployment, youth ages 15-24: *total:* 22.5%
male: 25.4%
female: 19.7% (2015 est.)
country comparison to the world: 65

GOVERNMENT

Country name: *conventional long form:* Republic of Finland
conventional short form: Finland
local long form: Suomen tasavalta/Republiken Finland
local short form: Suomi/Finland
etymology: name may derive from the ancient Fenni peoples who are first described as living in northeastern Europe in the first centuries A.D.

Government type: parliamentary republic

Capital: *name:* Helsinki

geographic coordinates: 60 10 N, 24 56 E
time difference: UTC+2 (7 hours ahead of Washington, DC, during Standard Time)
daylight saving time: +1hr, begins last Sunday in March; ends last Sunday in October

Administrative divisions: 19 regions (maakunnat, singular—maakunta (Finnish); landskapen, singular—landskapet (Swedish)), Aland (Swedish), Ahvenanmaa (Finnish); Etela-Karjala (Finnish), Sodra Karelen (Swedish) [South Karelia]; Etela-Pohjanmaa (Finnish), Sodra Osterbotten (Swedish) [South Ostrobothnia]; Etela-Savo (Finnish), Sodra Savolax (Swedish) [South Savo]; Kanta-Hame (Finnish), Egentliga Tavastland (Swedish); Kainuu (Finnish), Kajanaland (Swedish); Keski-Pohjanmaa (Finnish), Mellersta Osterbotten (Swedish) [Central Ostrobothnia]; Keski-Suomi (Finnish), Mellersta Finland (Swedish) [Central Finland]; Kymenlaakso (Finnish), Kymmenedalen (Swedish); Lappi (Finnish), Lappland (Swedish); Paijat-Hame (Finnish), Paijanne-Tavastland (Swedish); Pirkanmaa (Finnish), Birkaland (Swedish) [Tampere]; Pohjanmaa (Finnish), Osterbotten (Swedish) [Ostrobothnia]; Pohjois-Karjala (Finnish), Norra Karelen (Swedish) [North Karelia]; Pohjois-Pohjanmaa (Finnish), Norra Osterbotten (Swedish) [North Ostrobothnia]; Pohjois-Savo (Finnish), Norra Savolax (Swedish) [North Savo]; Satakunta (Finnish and Swedish); Uusimaa (Finnish), Nyland (Swedish) [Newland]; Varsinais-Suomi (Finnish), Egentliga Finland (Swedish) [Southwest Finland]

Independence: 6 December 1917 (from Russia)

National holiday: Independence Day, 6 December (1917)

Constitution: history: previous 1906, 1919; latest drafted 17 June 1997, approved by Parliament 11 June 1999, entered into force 1 March 2000
amendments: proposed by Parliament; passage normally requires simple majority vote in two readings in the first parliamentary session and at least two-thirds majority vote in a single reading by the newly elected Parliament; proposals declared "urgent" by five-sixths of Parliament members can be passed by at least two-thirds majority vote in the first parliamentary session only; amended several times, last in 2012 (2016)

Legal system: civil law system based on the Swedish model

International law organization participation: accepts compulsory ICJ jurisdiction with reservations; accepts ICCt jurisdiction

Citizenship: *citizenship by birth:* no
citizenship by descent only: at least one parent must be a citizen of Finland
dual citizenship recognized: yes
residency requirement for naturalization: 6 years

Suffrage: 18 years of age; universal

Executive branch: *chief of state:* President Sauli NIINISTO (since 1 March 2012)

head of government: Prime Minister Juha SIPILA (since 28 May 2015)
cabinet: Council of State or Valtioneuvosto appointed by the president, responsible to Parliament
elections/appointments: president directly elected by absolute majority popular vote in 2 rounds if needed for a 6-year term (eligible for a second term); election last held on 28 January

2018 (next to be held in January 2024); prime minister appointed by Parliament in 2015
election results: Sauli NIINISTO reelected president; percent of vote Sauli NIINISTO (independent) 62.7%, Pekka HAAVISTO (Vihr) 12.4%, Laura HUHTASAARI (PS) 6.9%, Paavo VAYRYNEN (independent) 6.2%, Matti VANHANEN (Kesk) 4.1%, other 7.7%

Legislative branch: description: unicameral Parliament or Eduskunta (200 seats; 199 members directly elected in single- and multi-seat constituencies by proportional representation vote and 1 member in the province of Aland directly elected by simple majority vote; members serve 4-year terms)
elections: last held on 19 April 2015 (next to be held by April 2019)
election results: percent of vote by party/coalition—Kesk 21.1%, PS 17.6%, Kok 18.2%, SDP 16.5%, Vihr 8.5%, Vas 7.1%, SFP 4.9%, KD 3.5%, other 2.6%; seats by party/coalition—Kesk 49, PS 38, Kok 37, SDP 34, Vihr 15, Vas 12, SFP 9, KD 5, Aland Coalition 1

Judicial branch: *highest court(s):* Supreme Court or Korkein Oikeus (consists of the court president and 18 judges); Supreme Administrative Court (consists of 21 judges including the court president and organized into 3 chambers); note—Finland has a dual judicial system—courts with civil and criminal jurisdiction and administrative courts with jurisdiction for litigation between individuals and administrative organs of the state and communities
judge selection and term of office: Supreme Court and Supreme Administrative Court judges appointed by the president of the republic; judges serve until mandatory retirement at age 65
subordinate courts: 6 Courts of Appeal; 8 regional administrative courts; 27 district courts; special courts for issues relating to markets, labor, insurance, impeachment, land, tenancy, and water rights

Political parties and leaders: Aland Coalition (a coalition of several political parties on the Aland Islands)
Center Party or Kesk [Juha SIPILA]
Christian Democrats or KD [Sari ESSAYAH]
Finns Party or PS [Jussi HALLA-AHO]
Green League or Vihr [Ville NIINISTO]
Left Alliance or Vas [Li ANDERSSON]]
National Coalition Party or Kok [Petteri ORPO]
Social Democratic Party or SDP [Antti RINNE]
Swedish People's Party or SFP [Anna-Maja HENRIKSSON]

International organization participation: ADB (nonregional member), AfDB (nonregional member), Arctic Council, Australia Group, BIS, CBSS, CD, CE, CERN, EAPC, EBRD, ECB, EIB, EITI (implementing country), EMU, ESA, EU, FAO, FATF, G-9, IADB, IAEA, IBRD, ICAO, ICC (national committees), ICCt, ICRM, IDA, IEA, IFAD, IFC, IFRCS, IHO, ILO, IMF, IMO, IMSO, Interpol, IOC, IOM, IPU, ISO, ITSO, ITU, ITUC (NGOs), MIGA, MINUSMA, NC, NEA, NIB, NSG, OAS (observer), OECD, OPCW, OSCE,

Pacific Alliance (observer), Paris Club, PCA, PFP, Schengen Convention, UN, UNCTAD, UNESCO, UNHCR, UNIDO, UNIFIL, UNMIL, UNMOGIP, UNRWA, UNTSO, UPU, WCO, WFTU (NGOs), WHO, WIPO, WMO, WTO, ZC

Diplomatic representation in the US: *chief of mission:* Ambassador Kirsti KAUPPI (since 17 September 2015)
chancery: 3301 Massachusetts Avenue NW, Washington, DC 20008
telephone: [1] (202) 298-5800
FAX: [1] (202) 298-6030
consulate(s) general: Los Angeles, New York

Diplomatic representation from the US: *chief of mission:* Ambassador (vacant); Charge d'Affaires Donna Ann WELTON (since 20 January 2017)
embassy: Itainen Puistotie 14B, 00140 Helsinki
mailing address: APO AE 09723
telephone: [358] (9) 616250
FAX: [358] (9) 6162 5800

Flag description: white with a blue cross extending to the edges of the flag; the vertical part of the cross is shifted to the hoist side in the style of the Dannebrog (Danish flag); the blue represents the thousands of lakes scattered across the country, while the white is for the snow that covers the land in winter

National symbol(s): lion; national colors: blue, white

National anthem: name: "Maamme" (Our Land)
lyrics/music: Johan Ludvig RUNEBERG/Fredrik PACIUS
note: in use since 1848; although never officially adopted by law, the anthem has been popular since it was first sung by a student group in 1848; Estonia's anthem uses the same melody as that of Finland

ECONOMY

Economy—overview: Finland has a highly industrialized, largely free-market economy with per capita GDP almost as high as that of Austria and the Netherlands and slightly above that of Germany and Belgium. Trade is important, with exports accounting for over one-third of GDP in recent years. The government is open to, and actively takes steps to attract, foreign direct investment.

Finland is historically competitive in manufacturing—principally the wood, metals, engineering, telecommunications, and electronics industries. Finland excels in export of technology as well as promotion of startups in the information and communications technology, gaming, cleantech, and biotechnology sectors. Except for timber and several minerals, Finland depends on imports of raw materials, energy, and some components for manufactured goods. Because of the cold climate, agricultural development is limited to maintaining self-sufficiency in basic products. Forestry, an important export industry, provides a secondary occupation for the rural population.

Finland had been one of the best performing economies within the EU before 2009 and its banks and financial markets avoided the worst of global financial crisis. However, the world slowdown hit exports and domestic demand hard in that year, causing Finland's economy to contract from 2012 to 2014. The recession affected general government finances and the debt ratio. The economy returned to growth in 2016, posting a 1.9% GDP increase before growing 2.8% in 2017.

Finland's main challenges will be reducing high labor costs and boosting demand for its exports. In June 2016, the government enacted a Competitiveness Pact aimed at reducing labor costs, increasing hours worked, and introducing more flexibility into the wage bargaining system. The Government was also seeking to reform the health care system and social services. In the long term, Finland must address a rapidly aging population and decreasing productivity in traditional industries that threaten competitiveness, fiscal sustainability, and economic growth.

GDP (purchasing power parity): $242.4 billion (2017 est.)
$235.9 billion (2016 est.)
$231.5 billion (2015 est.)
note: data are in 2017 dollars
country comparison to the world: 63

GDP (official exchange rate): $251.5 billion (2016 est.)

GDP—real growth rate: 2.8% (2017 est.)
1.9% (2016 est.)
0% (2015 est.)
country comparison to the world: 124

GDP—per capita (PPP): $44,000 (2017 est.)
$43,000 (2016 est.)
$42,300 (2015 est.)
note: data are in 2017 dollars
country comparison to the world: 37

Gross national saving: 22.7% of GDP (2017 est.)
20.8% of GDP (2016 est.)
20.3% of GDP (2015 est.)
country comparison to the world: 67

GDP—composition, by end use:
household consumption: 54.8%
government consumption: 22.8%
investment in fixed capital: 22.1%
investment in inventories: 0.2%
exports of goods and services: 36.7%
imports of goods and services: -36.7% (2017 est.)

GDP—composition, by sector of origin:
agriculture: 2.6%
industry: 27.2%
services: 70.2% (2017 est.)

Agriculture—products: barley, wheat, sugar beets, potatoes; dairy cattle; fish

Industries: metals and metal products, electronics, machinery and scientific instruments, shipbuilding, pulp and paper, foodstuffs, chemicals, textiles, clothing

Industrial production growth rate: 2.2% (2017 est.)
country comparison to the world: 124

Labor force: 2.695 million (2017 est.)

country comparison to the world: 112

Labor force—by occupation: *agriculture:* 4.5%
industry: 24%
services: 71.5% (2014)

Unemployment rate: 8.7% (2017 est.)
8.8% (2016 est.)
country comparison to the world: 119

Population below poverty line: NA%

Household income or consumption by percentage share: *lowest 10%:* 4.2%
highest 10%: 21.5% (2015)

Distribution of family income—Gini index: 21.5 (2015)
26.8 (2008)
country comparison to the world: 150

Budget: *revenues:* $136.8 billion
expenditures: $140.7 billion
note: Central Government Budget (2017 est.)
Taxes and other revenues: 54.4% of GDP (2017 est.)
country comparison to the world: 10

Budget surplus (+) or deficit (-): -1.6% of GDP (2017 est.)
country comparison to the world: 72

Public debt: 63.8% of GDP (2017 est.)
63.6% of GDP (2016 est.)
note: data cover general government debt, and includes debt instruments issued (or owned) by government entities other than the treasury; the data include treasury debt held by foreign entities; the data include debt issued by subnational entities, as well as intra-governmental debt; intra-governmental debt consists of treasury borrowings from surpluses in the social funds, such as for retirement, medical care, and unemployment; debt instruments for the social funds are not sold at public auctions
country comparison to the world: 65

Fiscal year: calendar year

Inflation rate (consumer prices): 0.8% (2017 est.)
0.4% (2016 est.)
country comparison to the world: 30

Central bank discount rate: 0.25% (31 December 2016)
0.3% (31 December 2010)
note: this is the European Central Bank's rate on the marginal lending facility, which offers overnight credit to banks in the euro area
country comparison to the world: 140

Commercial bank prime lending rate: 1.6% (31 December 2017 est.)
1.79% (31 December 2016 est.)
country comparison to the world: 181

Stock of narrow money: $145.7 billion (31 December 2017 est.)
$124 billion (31 December 2016 est.)
note: see entry for the European Union for money supply for the entire euro area; the European Central Bank (ECB) controls monetary policy for the 18 members of the Economic and Monetary Union (EMU); individual members of the EMU do not control the quantity of money circulating within their own borders

country comparison to the world: 29

Stock of broad money: $176.4 billion (31 December 2017 est.)
$152.9 billion (31 December 2016 est.)
country comparison to the world: 45

Stock of domestic credit: $346.6 billion (31 December 2017 est.)
$351.6 billion (31 December 2016 est.)
country comparison to the world: 32

Market value of publicly traded shares: $133.7 billion (31 December 2016 est.)
$NA (31 December 2015 est.)
$154.4 billion (31 December 2014 est.)
country comparison to the world: 38

Current account balance: $922 million (2017 est.)
-$2.534 billion (2016 est.)
country comparison to the world: 40

Exports: $65.5 billion (2017 est.)
$58.32 billion (2016 est.)
country comparison to the world: 42

Exports—commodities: electrical and optical equipment, machinery, transport equipment, paper and pulp, chemicals, basic metals; timber

Exports—partners: Germany 13.1%, Sweden 10.6%, US 7.6%, Netherlands 6.7%, Russia 5.7%, China 5.2%, UK 4.8% (2016)

Imports: $62.82 billion (2017 est.)
$57.66 billion (2016 est.)
country comparison to the world: 45

Imports—commodities: foodstuffs, petroleum and petroleum products, chemicals, transport equipment, iron and steel, machinery, computers, electronic industry products, textile yarn and fabrics, grains

Imports—partners: Germany 16.9%, Sweden 16.1%, Russia 11.1%, Netherlands 8.6% (2016)

Reserves of foreign exchange and gold: $10.8 billion (31 December 2017 est.)
$10.48 billion (31 December 2016 est.)
country comparison to the world: 72

Debt—external: $544.7 billion (31 March 2016 est.)
$524.7 billion (31 March 2015 est.)
country comparison to the world: 21

Stock of direct foreign investment—at home: $110 billion (31 December 2017 est.)
$114.6 billion (31 December 2016 est.)
country comparison to the world: 45

Stock of direct foreign investment—abroad: $169.1 billion (31 December 2017 est.)
$153.7 billion (31 December 2016 est.)
country comparison to the world: 29

Exchange rates: euros (EUR) per US dollar—
0.906 (2017 est.)
0.9214 (2016 est.)
0.9214 (2015 est.)
0.885 (2014 est.)
0.7634 (2013 est.)

ENERGY

Electricity access: electrification—*total population:* 100% (2016)

Electricity—production: 65.17 billion kWh (2015 est.)
country comparison to the world: 42

Electricity—consumption: 79.07 billion kWh (2015 est.)
country comparison to the world: 37

Electricity—exports: 3.159 billion kWh (2016 est.)
country comparison to the world: 42

Electricity—imports: 22.11 billion kWh (2016 est.)
country comparison to the world: 9

Electricity—installed generating capacity: 15.88 million kW (2015 est.)
country comparison to the world: 51

Electricity—from fossil fuels: 44.5% of total installed capacity (2015 est.)
country comparison to the world: 162

Electricity—from nuclear fuels: 17.3% of total installed capacity (2015 est.)
country comparison to the world: 10

Electricity—from hydroelectric plants: 20.5% of total installed capacity (2015 est.)
country comparison to the world: 87

Electricity—from other renewable sources: 23.5% of total installed capacity (2015 est.)
country comparison to the world: 25

Crude oil—production: 0 bbl/day (2016 est.)
country comparison to the world: 136

Crude oil—exports: 0 bbl/day (2016 est.)
country comparison to the world: 121

Crude oil—imports: 220,400 bbl/day (2016 est.)
country comparison to the world: 28

Crude oil—proved reserves: 0 bbl (1 January 2017 es)
country comparison to the world: 135

Refined petroleum products—production: 303,600 bbl/day (2016 est.)
country comparison to the world: 41

Refined petroleum products—consumption: 200,700 bbl/day (2016 est.)
country comparison to the world: 55

Refined petroleum products—exports: 167,200 bbl/day (2016 est.)
country comparison to the world: 36

Refined petroleum products—imports: 147,600 bbl/day (2016 est.)
country comparison to the world: 47

Natural gas—production: 8 million cu m (2015 est.)
country comparison to the world: 97

Natural gas—consumption: 3.243 billion cu m (2015 est.)
country comparison to the world: 75

Natural gas—exports: 0 cu m (2016 est.)
country comparison to the world: 102

Natural gas—imports: 2.713 billion cu m (2015 est.)
country comparison to the world: 49

Natural gas—proved reserves: NA cu m (1 January 2016 es)

Carbon dioxide emissions from consumption of energy: 43 million Mt (2016 est.)
country comparison to the world: 66

COMMUNICATIONS

Telephones—fixed lines: *total subscriptions:* 457,300
subscriptions per 100 inhabitants: 8 (July 2016 est.)
country comparison to the world: 90

Telephones—mobile cellular: *total:* 7,366,100
subscriptions per 100 inhabitants: 134 (July 2016 est.)
country comparison to the world: 99

Telephone system: *general assessment:* modern system with excellent service
domestic: digital fiber-optic, fixed-line network and an extensive mobile-cellular network provide domestic needs
international: country code—358; submarine cables provide links to Estonia and Sweden; satellite earth stations—access to Intelsat transmission service via a Swedish satellite earth station, 1 Inmarsat (Atlantic and Indian Ocean regions); note—Finland shares the Inmarsat earth station with the other Nordic countries (Denmark, Iceland, Norway, and Sweden) (2015)

Broadcast media: a mix of 3 publicly operated TV stations and numerous privately owned TV stations; several free and special-interest pay-TV channels; cable and satellite multi-channel subscription services are available; all TV signals are broadcast digitally; Internet television, such as Netflix and others, is available; public broadcasting maintains a network of 13 national and 25 regional radio stations; a large number of private radio broadcasters and access to Internet radio (2017)

Internet country code: .fi; note—Aland Islands assigned .ax
Internet users: total: 4,822,132

percent of population: 87.7% (July 2016 est.)
country comparison to the world: 64

TRANSPORTATION

National air transport system: *number of registered air carriers:* 3
inventory of registered aircraft operated by air carriers: 73
annual passenger traffic on registered air carriers: 9,972,333
annual freight traffic on registered air carriers: 713.484 million mt-km (2015)
Civil aircraft registration country code prefix: OH (2016)

Airports: 148 (2013)
country comparison to the world: 39

Airports—with paved runways: *total:* 74
over 3,047 m: 3
2,438 to 3,047 m: 26
1,524 to 2,437 m: 10
914 to 1,523 m: 21
under 914 m: 14 (2017)

Airports—with unpaved runways: *total:* 74
914 to 1,523 m: 3
under 914 m: 71 (2013)

Pipelines: gas transmission pipes 1,286 km; distribution pipes 1,932 km (2016)

Railways: *total:* 5,923 km
broad gauge: 5,923 km 1.524-m gauge (3,262 km electrified) (2015)
country comparison to the world: 32

Roadways: *total:* 454,000 km
highways: 78,000 km (50,000 paved, including 700 km of expressways; 28,000 unpaved)
urban roads: 26,000 km
private and forest roads: 350,000 km (2012)
country comparison to the world: 16

Waterways: 8,000 km (includes Saimaa Canal system of 3,577 km; southern part leased from Russia; water transport used frequently in the summer and widely replaced with sledges on the ice in winter; there are 187,888 lakes in Finland that cover 31,500 km); Finland also maintains 8,200 km of coastal fairways (2013)
country comparison to the world: 17

Merchant marine: *total:* 267
by type: bulk carrier 7, container ship 1, general cargo 92, oil tanker 5, other 162 (2017)
country comparison to the world: 56

Ports and terminals: *major seaport(s):* Helsinki, Kotka, Naantali, Porvoo, Raahe, Rauma

MILITARY AND SECURITY

Military expenditures: 1.33% of GDP (2017 est.)
1.37% of GDP (2016)
1.29% of GDP (2015)
1.3% of GDP (2014)
1.41% of GDP (2013)
country comparison to the world: 62

Military branches: Finnish Defense Forces (FDF): Army (Puolustusvoimat), Navy (Merivoimat, includes Coastal Defense Forces), Air Force (Ilmavoimat) (2016)

Military service age and obligation: all Finnish men are called-up for military service the year they turn 18; at 18, women may volunteer for military service; service obligation 6-12 months; individuals enter the reserve upon completing their initial obligation; military obligation to age 60 (2016)

TRANSNATIONAL ISSUES

Disputes—international: various groups in Finland advocate restoration of Karelia and other areas ceded to the former Soviet Union, but the Finnish Government asserts no territorial demands

Refugees and internally displaced persons: *refugees (country of origin):* 6,781 (Iraq) (2016)
stateless persons: 2,671 (2016)

FRANCE

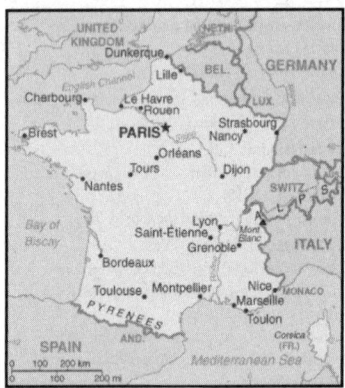

INTRODUCTION

Background: France today is one of the most modern countries in the world and is a leader among European nations. It plays an influential global role as a permanent member of the United Nations Security Council, NATO, the G-7, the G-20, the EU, and other multilateral organizations. France rejoined NATO's integrated military command structure in 2009, reversing DE GAULLE's 1966 decision to withdraw French forces from NATO. Since 1958, it has constructed a hybrid presidential-parliamentary governing system resistant to the instabilities experienced in earlier, more purely parliamentary administrations. In recent decades, its reconciliation and cooperation with Germany have proved central to the economic integration of Europe, including the introduction of a common currency, the euro, in January 1999. In the early 21st century, five French overseas entities—French Guiana, Guadeloupe, Martinique, Mayotte, and Reunion—became French regions and were made part of France proper.

GEOGRAPHY

Location: metropolitan France: Western Europe, bordering the Bay of Biscay and English Channel, between Belgium and Spain, southeast of the UK; bordering the Mediterranean Sea, between Italy and Spain
French Guiana: Northern South America, bordering the North Atlantic Ocean, between Brazil and Suriname
Guadeloupe: Caribbean, islands between the Caribbean Sea and the North Atlantic Ocean, southeast of Puerto Rico
Martinique: Caribbean, island between the Caribbean Sea and North Atlantic Ocean, north of Trinidad and Tobago
Mayotte: Southern Indian Ocean, island in the Mozambique Channel, about halfway between northern Madagascar and northern Mozambique
Reunion: Southern Africa, island in the Indian Ocean, east of Madagascar

Geographic coordinates: metropolitan France: 46 00 N, 2 00 E
French Guiana: 4 00 N, 53 00 W
Guadeloupe: 16 15 N, 61 35 W
Martinique: 14 40 N, 61 00 W
Mayotte: 12 50 S, 45 10 E
Reunion: 21 06 S, 55 36 E

Map references: metropolitan France: Europe
French Guiana: South America
Guadeloupe: Central America and the Caribbean
Martinique: Central America and the Caribbean
Mayotte: Africa
Reunion: World

Area: *total:* 643,801 sq km; 551,500 sq km (metropolitan France)
land: 640,427 sq km; 549,970 sq km (metropolitan France)
water: 3,374 sq km; 1,530 sq km (metropolitan France)
note: the first numbers include the overseas regions of French Guiana, Guadeloupe, Martinique, Mayotte, and Reunion
country comparison to the world: 44

Area—comparative: slightly more than four times the size of Georgia; slightly less than the size of Texas

Land boundaries: metropolitan France—total: 2,751 km
border countries (8): Andorra 55 km, Belgium 556 km, Germany 418 km, Italy 476 km, Luxembourg 69 km, Monaco 6 km, Spain 646 km, Switzerland 525 km
French Guiana—total: 1,205 km
border countries (2): Brazil 649 km, Suriname 556 km
Coastline: total: 4,853 km
metropolitan France: 3,427 km

Maritime claims: *territorial sea:* 12 nm
contiguous zone: 24 nm
exclusive economic zone: 200 nm (does not apply to the Mediterranean Sea)
continental shelf: 200-m depth or to the depth of exploitation

Climate: metropolitan France: generally cool winters and mild summers, but mild winters and hot summers along the Mediterranean; occasional strong, cold, dry, north-to-northwesterly wind known as mistral
French Guiana: tropical; hot, humid; little seasonal temperature variation
Guadeloupe and Martinique: subtropical tempered by trade winds; moderately high humidity; rainy season (June to October); vulnerable to devastating cyclones (hurricanes) every eight years on average
Mayotte: tropical; marine; hot, humid, rainy season during northeastern monsoon (November to May); dry season is cooler (May to November)

Reunion: tropical, but temperature moderates with elevation; cool and dry (May to November), hot and rainy (November to April)

Terrain: metropolitan France: mostly flat plains or gently rolling hills in north and west; remainder is mountainous, especially Pyrenees in south, Alps in east
French Guiana: low-lying coastal plains rising to hills and small mountains
Guadeloupe: Basse-Terre is volcanic in origin with interior mountains; Grande-Terre is low limestone formation; most of the seven other islands are volcanic in origin
Martinique: mountainous with indented coastline; dormant volcano
Mayotte: generally undulating, with deep ravines and ancient volcanic peaks
Reunion: mostly rugged and mountainous; fertile lowlands along coast

Elevation: *mean elevation:* 375 m

elevation extremes: *lowest point:* Rhone River delta -2 m
highest point: Mont Blanc 4,810 m
note: to assess the possible effects of climate change on the ice and snow cap of Mont Blanc, its surface and peak have been extensively measured in recent years; these new peak measurements have exceeded the traditional height of 4,807 m and have varied between 4,808 m and 4,811 m; the actual rock summit is 4,792 m and is 40 m away from the ice-covered summit

Natural resources: metropolitan France: coal, iron ore, bauxite, zinc, uranium, antimony, arsenic, potash, feldspar, fluorspar, gypsum, timber, arable land, fish

French Guiana: gold deposits, petroleum, kaolin, niobium, tantalum, clay

Land use: *agricultural land:* 52.7%
arable land: 33.4%;
permanent crops: 1.8%;
permanent pasture: 17.5%
forest: 29.2%
other: 18.1% (2011 est.)

Irrigated land: *total:* 26,420 sq km 26,950 sq km

metropolitan France: 26,000 sq km (2012)

Population—distribution: much of the population is concentrated in the north and southeast; although there are many urban agglomerations throughout the country, Paris is by far the largest city, with Lyon ranked a distant second

Natural hazards: metropolitan France: flooding; avalanches; midwinter windstorms; drought; forest fires in south near the Mediterranean

overseas departments: hurricanes (cyclones); flooding
volcanism: Montagne Pelee (1,394 m) on the island of Martinique in the Caribbean is the most active volcano of the Lesser Antilles arc, it last erupted in 1932; a catastrophic eruption in May

1902 destroyed the city of St. Pierre, killing an estimated 30,000 people; La Soufriere (1,467 m) on the island of Guadeloupe in the Caribbean last erupted from July 1976 to March 1977; these volcanoes are part of the volcanic island arc of the Lesser Antilles that extends from Saba in the north to Grenada in the south

Environment—current issues: some forest damage from acid rain; air pollution from industrial and vehicle emissions; water pollution from urban wastes, agricultural runoff

Environment—international agreements: *party to:* Air Pollution, Air Pollution-Nitrogen Oxides, Air Pollution-Persistent Organic Pollutants, Air Pollution-Sulfur 85, Air Pollution-Sulfur 94, Air Pollution-Volatile Organic Compounds, Antarctic-Environmental Protocol, Antarctic-Marine Living Resources, Antarctic Seals, Antarctic Treaty, Biodiversity, Climate Change, Climate Change-Kyoto Protocol, Desertification, Endangered Species, Hazardous Wastes, Law of the Sea, Marine Dumping, Marine Life Conservation, Ozone Layer Protection, Ship Pollution, Tropical Timber 83, Tropical Timber 94, Wetlands, Whaling *signed, but not ratified:* none of the selected agreements

Geography—note: largest West European nation; most major French rivers—the Meuse, Seine, Loire, Charente, Dordogne, and Garonne—flow northward or westward into the Atlantic Ocean, only the Rhone flows southward into the Mediterranean Sea

PEOPLE AND SOCIETY

Population: 67,106,161
note: the above figure is for metropolitan France and five overseas regions; the metropolitan France population is 62,814,233 (July 2017 est.)
country comparison to the world: 21

Nationality: *noun:* Frenchman(men), Frenchwoman(women)
adjective: French

Ethnic groups: Celtic and Latin with Teutonic, Slavic, North African, Indochinese, Basque minorities

overseas departments: black, white, mulatto, East Indian, Chinese, Amerindian

Languages: French (official) 100%, declining regional dialects and languages (Provencal, Breton, Alsatian, Corsican, Catalan, Basque, Flemish, Occitan, Picard)

overseas departments: French, Creole patois, Mahorian (a Swahili dialect)

Religions: Christian (overwhelmingly Roman Catholic) 63-66%, Muslim 7-9%, Buddhist 0.5-0.75%, Jewish 0.5-0.75%, other 0.5-1.0%, none 23-28%
note: France maintains a tradition of secularism and has not officially collected data on religious affiliation since the 1872 national census, which complicates assessments of France's religious composition; an 1872 law prohibiting state authorities from collecting data on individuals' ethnicity

or religious beliefs was reaffirmed by a 1978 law emphasizing the prohibition of the collection or exploitation of personal data revealing an individual's race, ethnicity, or political, philosophical, or religious opinions; a 1905 law codified France's separation of church and state (2015 est.)

Age structure: *0-14 years:* 18.53% (male 6,360,218/female 6,076,598)
15-24 years: 11.79% (male 4,045,901/female 3,864,395)
25-54 years: 37.78% (male 12,773,900/female 12,578,256)
55-64 years: 12.42% (male 4,020,507/female 4,315,407)
65 years and over: 19.48% (male 5,648,888/female 7,422,091) (2017 est.)

Dependency ratios: *total dependency ratio:* 59.2
youth dependency ratio: 29.1
elderly dependency ratio: 30.2
potential support ratio: 3.3 (2015 est.)

Median age: *total:* 41.4 years
male: 39.6 years
female: 43.1 years (2017 est.)
country comparison to the world: 39

Population growth rate: 0.39% (2017 est.)
country comparison to the world: 163

Birth rate: 12.2 births/1,000 population (2017 est.)
country comparison to the world: 163

Death rate: 9.3 deaths/1,000 population (2017 est.)
country comparison to the world: 60

Net migration rate: 1.1 migrant(s)/1,000 population (2017 est.)
country comparison to the world: 56

Population distribution: much of the population is concentrated in the north and southeast; although there are many urban agglomerations throughout the country, Paris is by far the largest city, with Lyon ranked a distant second

Urbanization: *urban population:* 80% of total population (2017)
rate of urbanization: 0.76% annual rate of change (2015-20 est.)

Major urban areas—population: PARIS (capital) 10.843 million; Lyon 1.609 million; Marseille-Aix-en-Provence 1.605 million; Lille 1.027 million; Nice-Cannes 967,000; Toulouse 938,000 (2015)

Sex ratio: *at birth:* 1.05 male(s)/female
0-14 years: 1.05 male(s)/female
15-24 years: 1.05 male(s)/female
25-54 years: 1.01 male(s)/female
55-64 years: 0.93 male(s)/female
65 years and over: 0.75 male(s)/female
total population: 0.96 male(s)/female (2016 est.)

Mother's mean age at first birth: 28.1 years (2010 est.)

Maternal mortality ratio: 8 deaths/100,000 live births (2015 est.)
country comparison to the world: 159

Infant mortality rate: *total:* 3.2 deaths/1,000 live births
male: 3.6 deaths/1,000 live births

female: 2.9 deaths/1,000 live births (2017 est.)
country comparison to the world: 213

Life expectancy at birth: *total population:* 81.9 years
male: 78.8 years
female: 85.2 years (2017 est.)
country comparison to the world: 17

Total fertility rate: 2.07 children born/woman (2017 est.)
country comparison to the world: 109

Contraceptive prevalence rate: 83% (2010/11)
Health expenditures: 11.5% of GDP (2014)
country comparison to the world: 8

Physicians density: 3.23 physicians/1,000 population (2015)

Hospital bed density: 6.4 beds/1,000 population (2011)

Drinking water source:
improved:
urban: 100% of population
rural: 100% of population
total: 100% of population
unimproved:
urban: 0% of population
rural: 0% of population
total: 0% of population (2015 est.)

Sanitation facility access:
improved:
urban: 98.6% of population
rural: 98.9% of population
total: 98.7% of population
unimproved:
urban: 1.4% of population
rural: 1.1% of population
total: 1.3% of population (2015 est.)

HIV/AIDS—adult prevalence rate: 0.4% (2016 est.)
country comparison to the world: 70

HIV/AIDS—people living with HIV/AIDS: 180,000 (2016 est.)
country comparison to the world: 30

HIV/AIDS—deaths: <1000 (2016 est.)

Obesity—adult prevalence rate: 21.6% (2016)
country comparison to the world: 87

Education expenditures: 5.5% of GDP (2013)
country comparison to the world: 43

School life expectancy (primary to tertiary education): *total:* 16 years
male: 16 years
female: 17 years (2014)

Unemployment, youth ages 15-24: *total:* 24.6%
male: 25%
female: 24% (2016 est.)
country comparison to the world: 39

GOVERNMENT

Country name: *conventional long form:* French Republic
conventional short form: France
local long form: Republique francaise
local short form: France

etymology: name derives from the Latin "Francia" meaning "Land of the Franks"; the Franks were a group of Germanic tribes located along the middle and lower Rhine River in the 3rd century A.D. who merged with Gallic-Roman populations in succeeding centuries and to whom they passed on their name

Government type: semi-presidential republic

Capital: *name:* Paris

geographic coordinates: 48 52 N, 2 20 E

time difference: UTC+1 (6 hours ahead of Washington, DC, during Standard Time)

daylight saving time: +1hr, begins last Sunday in March; ends last Sunday in October

note: applies to metropolitan France only, not to its overseas departments, collectivities, or territories

Administrative divisions: 18 regions (regions, singular—region); Auvergne-Rhone-Alpes, Bourgogne-Franche-Comte (Burgundy-Free County), Bretagne (Brittany), Centre-Val de Loire (Center-Loire Valley), Corse (Corsica), Grand Est (Grand East), Guadeloupe, Guyane (French Guiana), Hauts-de-France (Upper France), Ile-de-France, Martinique, Mayotte, Normandie (Normandy), Nouvelle-Aquitaine (New Aquitaine), Occitanie (Occitania), Pays de la Loire (Lands of the Loire), Provence-Alpes-Cote d'Azur, Reunion

note: France is divided into 13 metropolitan regions (including the "territorial collectivity" of Corse or Corsica) and 5 overseas regions (French Guiana, Guadeloupe, Martinique, Mayotte, and Reunion) and is subdivided into 96 metropolitan departments and 5 overseas departments (which are the same as the overseas regions)

Dependent areas: Clipperton Island, French Polynesia, French Southern and Antarctic Lands, New Caledonia, Saint Barthelemy, Saint Martin, Saint Pierre and Miquelon, Wallis and Futuna

note: the US Government does not recognize claims to Antarctica; New Caledonia has been considered a "sui generis" collectivity of France since 1998, a unique status falling between that of an independent country and a French overseas department

Independence: no official date of independence: 486 (Frankish tribes unified under Merovingian kingship); 10 August 843 (Western Francia established from the division of the Carolingian Empire); 14 July 1789 (French monarchy overthrown); 22 September 1792 (First French Republic founded); 4 October 1958 (Fifth French Republic established)

National holiday: Fete de la Federation, 14 July (1790); note—although often incorrectly referred to as Bastille Day, the celebration actually commemorates the holiday held on the first anniversary of the storming of the Bastille (on 14 July 1789) and the establishment of a constitutional monarchy; other names for the holiday are Fete Nationale (National Holiday) and quatorze juillet (14th of July)

Constitution: history: many previous; latest effective 4 October 1958

amendments: proposed by the president of the republic (upon recommendation of the prime minister and Parliament) or by Parliament; proposals submitted by Parliament members require passage by both houses followed by approval in a referendum; passage of proposals submitted by the government can bypass a referendum if submitted by the president to Parliament and passed by at least three-fifths majority vote by Parliament's National Assembly; amended many times, last in 2008 (2016)

Legal system: civil law; review of administrative but not legislative acts

International law organization participation: has not submitted an ICJ jurisdiction declaration; accepts ICCt jurisdiction

Citizenship: *citizenship by birth:* no

citizenship by descent only: at least one parent must be a citizen of France

dual citizenship recognized: yes

residency requirement for naturalization: 5 years

Suffrage: 18 years of age; universal

Executive branch: *chief of state:* President Emmanuel MACRON (since 14 May 2017)

head of government: Prime Minister Edouard PHILIPPE (since 15 May 2017)

cabinet: Council of Ministers appointed by the president at the suggestion of the prime minister

elections/appointments: president directly elected by absolute majority popular vote in 2 rounds if needed for a 5-year term (eligible for a second term); election last held on 23 April with a runoff on 7 May 2017 (next to be held in April 2022); prime minister appointed by the president

election results: Emmanuel MACRON elected president in second round; percent of vote in first round—Emmanuel MACRON (EM) 24.0%, Marine LE PEN (FN) 21.3%, Francois FILLON (LR) 20.0%, Jean-Luc MELENCHON (FI) 19.6%, Benoit HAMON (PS) 6.4%, other 8.7%; percent of vote in second round—MACRON 66.1%, LE PEN 33.9%

Legislative branch: description: bicameral Parliament or Parlement consists of the Senate or Senat (348 seats—328 for metropolitan France and overseas departments and regions of Guadeloupe, Martinique, French Guiana, Reunion, and Mayotte, 2 for New Caledonia, 2 for French Polynesia, 1 for Saint-Pierre and Miquelon, 1 for Saint-Barthelemy, 1 for Saint-Martin, 1 for Wallis and Futuna, and 12 for French nationals abroad; members indirectly elected by departmental electoral colleges using absolute majority vote in 2 rounds if needed for departments with 1-3 members and proportional representation vote in departments with 4 or more members; members serve 6-year terms with one-half of the membership renewed every 3 years) and the National Assembly or Assemblee Nationale (577 seats—556 for metropolitan France, 10 for overseas departments, and 11 for citizens abroad; members directly elected by absolute majority vote in 2 rounds if needed to serve 5-year terms)

elections: Senate—last held on 24 September 2017 (next to be held on 24 September 2020); National Assembly—last held on 11 and 18 June 2017 (next to be held in June 2022)

election results: Senate—percent of vote by party—NA; seats by party—LR 146, SOC 78, UC 49, REM 21, CRC 21, other 32

National Assembly—percent of vote by party first round—EM 28.2%, LR 15.8%. FN 13.2%, FI 11.0%, PS 7.4%, other 24.4%; percent of vote by party second round—EM 43.1%, LR 22.2%, FN 8.8%, MoDEM 6.1%, PS 5.7%. FI 4.9%, other 9.2%; seats by party—EM 308, LR 112, MoDEM 42, PS 29, UDI 18, FI 17, PCF 10, FN 8, other 33

Judicial branch: *highest court(s):* Court of Cassation or Cour de Cassation (consists of the court president, 6 divisional presiding judges, 120 trial judges, and 70 deputy judges organized into 6 divisions—3 civil, 1 commercial, 1 labor, and 1 criminal); Constitutional Council (consists of 9 members)

judge selection and term of office: Court of Cassation judges appointed by the president of the republic from nominations from the High Council of the Judiciary, presided over by the Court of Cassation and 15 appointed members; judges appointed for life; Constitutional Council members—3 appointed by the president of the republic and 3 each by the National Assembly and Senate presidents; members serve 9-year, non-renewable terms with one-third of the membership renewed every 3 years

subordinate courts: appellate courts or Cour d'Appel; regional courts or Tribunal de Grande Instance; first instance courts or Tribunal d'instance; administrative courts

Political parties and leaders: Democratic Movement or MoDEM [Francois BAYROU]

Europe Ecology—The Greens or EELV [David CORMAND]

French Communist Party or PCF [Pierre LAURENT]

La France Insoumise or FI [Jean-Luc MELENCHON]

Left Front Coalition or FDG [Jean-Luc MELENCHON]

Left Party or PG [linked with the movement La France Insoumise or FI [Jean-Luc MELENCHON]]

Left Radical Party or PRG [Sylvia PINEL] (formerly Radical Socialist Party or PRS and the Left Radical Movement or MRG)

Movement for France or MPF [Philippe DE VILLIERS]

National Front or FN [Marine LE PEN]

New Anticapitalist Party or NPA [collective leadership; main spokesperson Christine POUPIN; presidential candIdate Philippe POUTOU]

Rally for France or RPF [Igor KUREK]

Republican and Citizen Movement or MRC [Jean-Luc LAURENT]

Socialist Party or PS [Rachid TEMAL, interim leader]

Stand Up France (Debout La France) [Nicolas DUPONT-AIGNAN]

The Centrists [Herve MORIN] (formerly new Center of NC)

The Republic on the Move (La Republique en Marche) or REM [Christophe CASTANER]

The Republicans or LR (formerly Union for a Popular Movement or UMP) [Laurent WAUQUIEZ]

Union des Democrates et Independants or UDI [Jean-Christohe LAGARDE] and Democratic Movement or MoDem [Francois BAYROU] (previously Union for French Democracy or UDF); together known as UDI-Modem; Radical Party [Laurent HENART] is a member of UDI

United Republic or RS [Dominique DE VILLEPIN]

Worker's Struggle (Lutte Ouvriere) or LO; also known as Communist Union; [collective leadership; spokespersons Nathalie ARTHAUD and Arlette LAGUILLER]

Political pressure groups and leaders: French Confederation of Management—General Confederation of Executives) or CFE-CGC (Confederation francaise de l'encadrement—Confederation generale des cadres) [Francois HOMMERIL] (independent white-collar union with 140,000 members)

French Democratic Confederation of Labor or CFDT (Confederation Francaise Democratique du Travail) [Laurent BERGER] (left-leaning labor union with approximately 875,000 members)

French Confederation of Christian Workers or CFTC (Confederation francaise des travailleurs chretiens) [Philippe LOUIS] (independent labor union founded by Catholic workers that claims 142,000 members)

General Confederation of Labor or CGT (Confederation generale du travail) [Philippe MARTINEZ] (historically communist labor union with approximately 710,000 members)

General Confederation of Labor—Worker's Force) or FO (Confederation generale du travail—Force ouvriere) [Jean-Claude MAILLY] (independent labor union with an estimated 300,000 members)

Mouvement des entreprises de France or MEDEF [Pierre GATTAZ] (employers' union with claimed 750,000 companies as members)

French Guiana: conservationists; gold mining pressure groups; hunting pressure groups

Guadeloupe: Christian Movement for the Liberation of Guadeloupe or KLPG

General Federation of Guadeloupe Workers or CGT-G

General Union of Guadeloupe Workers or UGTG

Movement for an Independent Guadeloupe or MPGI

The Socialist Renewal Movement

Martinique: Caribbean Revolutionary Alliance or ARC

Central Union for Martinique Workers or CSTM Frantz Fanon Circle

League of Workers and Peasants

Proletarian Action Group or GAP

Reunion: NA

International organization participation: ADB (nonregional member), AfDB (nonregional member), Arctic Council (observer), Australia Group, BDEAC, BIS, BSEC (observer), CBSS (observer), CE, CERN, EAPC, EBRD, ECB, EIB, EITI (implementing country), EMU, ESA, EU, FAO, FATF, FZ, G-5, G-7, G-8, G-10, G-20, IADB, IAEA, IBRD, ICAO, ICC (national committees), ICCt, ICRM, IDA, IEA, IFAD, IFC, IFRCS, IGAD (partners), IHO, ILO, IMF, IMO, IMSO, InOC, Interpol, IOC, IOM, IPU, ISO, ITSO, ITU, ITUC (NGOs), MIGA, MINURSO, MINUSMA, MINUSTAH, MONUSCO, NATO, NEA, NSG, OAS (observer), OECD, OIF, OPCW, OSCE, Pacific Alliance (observer), Paris Club, PCA, PIF (partner), Schengen Convention, SELEC (observer), SPC, UN, UNCTAD, UNESCO, UNHCR, UNIDO, UNIFIL, Union Latina, UNMIL, UNOCI, UNRWA, UNSC (permanent), UNTSO, UNWTO, UPU, WCO, WFTU (NGOs), WHO, WIPO, WMO, WTO, ZC

Diplomatic representation in the US: chief of mission: Ambassador Gerard Roger ARAUD (since 18 September 2014)

chancery: 4101 Reservoir Road NW, Washington, DC 20007

telephone: [1] (202) 944-6000

FAX: [1] (202) 944-6166

consulate(s) general: Atlanta, Boston, Chicago, Houston, Los Angeles, Miami, New Orleans, New York, San Francisco, Washington DC

Diplomatic representation from the US: chief of mission: Ambassador Jamie D. McCOURT (since 18 December 2017); note—also accredited to Monaco

embassy: 2 Avenue Gabriel, 75382 Paris Cedex 08

mailing address: PSC 116, APO AE 09777

telephone: [33] (1) 43-12-22-22

FAX: [33] (1) 42 66 97 83

consulate(s) general: Marseille, Strasbourg

consulate(s): Bordeaux, Lyon, Rennes, Toulouse

Flag description: three equal vertical bands of blue (hoist side), white, and red; known as the "Le drapeau tricolore" (French Tricolor), the origin of the flag dates to 1790 and the French Revolution when the "ancient French color" of white was combined with the blue and red colors of the Parisian militia; the official flag for all French dependent areas

note: the design and/or colors are similar to a number of other flags, including those of Belgium, Chad, Cote d'Ivoire, Ireland, Italy, Luxembourg, and Netherlands

National symbol(s): Gallic rooster, fleur-de-lis, Marianne (female personification); national colors: blue, white, red

National anthem: name: "La Marseillaise" (The Song of Marseille)

lyrics/music: Claude-Joseph ROUGET de Lisle

note: adopted 1795, restored 1870; originally known as "Chant de Guerre pour l'Armee du Rhin" (War Song for the Army of the Rhine), the National Guard of Marseille made the song famous by singing it while marching into Paris in 1792 during the French Revolutionary Wars

ECONOMY

Economy—overview: The French economy is diversified across all sectors. The government has partially or fully privatized many large companies, including Air France, France Telecom, Renault, and Thales. However, the government maintains a strong presence in some sectors, particularly power, public transport, and defense industries. France is the most visited country in the world with 83 million foreign tourists in 2016, including 530,000 visitors for the 2016 Euro Cup. France's leaders remain committed to a capitalism in which they maintain social equity by means of laws, tax policies, and social spending that mitigate economic inequality.

France's real GDP grew by 1.6% in 2017, up from 1.2% the year before. The unemployment rate (including overseas territories) increased from 7.8% in 2008 to 10.2% in 2015, before falling to 9.5% in 2017. Youth unemployment in metropolitan France decreased from 24.6% in the fourth quarter of 2014 to 24% in the fourth quarter of 2016.

France's public finances have historically been strained by high spending and low growth. Despite measures to restore public finances, the budget deficit rose from 3.3% of GDP in 2008 to 7.5% of GDP in 2009. In 2017, the budget deficit improved to 2.9% of GDP, bringing it in compliance with the EU-mandated 3% deficit target. Meanwhile, France's public debt rose from 89.5% of GDP in 2012 to 96.9% in 2017.

Since entering office in May 2017, President Emmanuel MACRON launched a series of economic reforms to improve competitiveness and boost economic growth. President MACRON campaigned on reforming France's labor code and in late 2017 implemented a range of reforms to increase flexibility in the labor market by making it easier for firms to hire and fire and simplifying negotiations between employers and employees. In addition to labor reforms, President MACRON's proposed 2018 budget cuts public spending, taxes, and social security contributions to spur private investment and increase purchasing power.

GDP (purchasing power parity): $2.826 trillion (2017 est.)

$2.783 trillion (2016 est.)

$2.75 trillion (2015 est.)

note: data are in 2017 dollars

country comparison to the world: 11

GDP (official exchange rate): $2.575 trillion (2016 est.)

GDP—real growth rate: 1.6% (2017 est.)

1.2% (2016 est.)

1.1% (2015 est.)

country comparison to the world: 171

GDP—per capita (PPP): $43,600 (2017 est.)

$43,100 (2016 est.)

$42,700 (2015 est.)

note: data are in 2017 dollars

country comparison to the world: 39

Gross national saving: 22.1% of GDP (2017 est.)

22% of GDP (2016 est.)

22.3% of GDP (2015 est.)

country comparison to the world: 74

GDP—composition, by end use:

household consumption: 54.8%

government consumption: 23.5%

investment in fixed capital: 22%

investment in inventories: 1.3%
exports of goods and services: 30.3%
imports of goods and services: -32% (2017 est.)

GDP—composition, by sector of origin:
agriculture: 1.6%
industry: 19.4%
services: 78.9% (2017 est.)

Agriculture—products: wheat, cereals, sugar beets, potatoes, wine grapes; beef, dairy products; fish

Industries: machinery, chemicals, automobiles, metallurgy, aircraft, electronics; textiles, food processing; tourism

Industrial production growth rate: 1.1% (2017 est.)
country comparison to the world: 161

Labor force: 30.68 million (2017 est.)
country comparison to the world: 21

Labor force—by occupation: *agriculture:* 2.4%
industry: 18.3%
services: 79.3% (2015 est.)

Unemployment rate: 9.5% (2017 est.)
10% (2016 est.)
note: includes overseas territories
country comparison to the world: 133

Population below poverty line: 14% (2013 est.)

Household income or consumption by percentage share: *lowest 10%:* 3.6%
highest 10%: 25.4% (2013)

Distribution of family income—Gini index: 29.2 (2015)
30.5 (2012)
country comparison to the world: 130

Budget: *revenues:* $1.334 trillion
expenditures: $1.412 trillion (2017 est.)
Taxes and other revenues: 51.8% of GDP (2017 est.)
country comparison to the world: 13

Budget surplus (+) or deficit (-): -3.1% of GDP (2017 est.)
country comparison to the world: 117

Public debt: 96.1% of GDP (2017 est.)
96.4% of GDP (2016 est.)
note: data cover general government debt, and includes debt instruments issued (or owned) by government entities other than the treasury; the data include treasury debt held by foreign entities; the data include debt issued by subnational entities, as well as intra-governmental debt; intra-governmental debt consists of treasury borrowings from surpluses in the social funds, such as for retirement, medical care, and unemployment; debt instruments for the social funds are not sold at public auctions
country comparison to the world: 20

Fiscal year: calendar year

Inflation rate (consumer prices): 1.2% (2017 est.)
0.3% (2016 est.)
country comparison to the world: 50

Central bank discount rate: 0% (31 December 2016)
0.05% (31 December 2015)

note: this is the European Central Bank's rate on the marginal lending facility, which offers overnight credit to banks in the euro area
country comparison to the world: 158

Commercial bank prime lending rate: 1.4% (31 December 2017 est.)
1.6% (31 December 2016 est.)
country comparison to the world: 186

Stock of narrow money: $1.372 trillion (31 December 2017 est.)
$1.139 trillion (31 December 2016 est.)
note: see entry for the European Union for money supply for the entire euro area; the European Central Bank (ECB) controls monetary policy for the 18 members of the Economic and Monetary Union (EMU); individual members of the EMU do not control the quantity of money circulating within their own borders
country comparison to the world: 6

Stock of broad money: $2.338 trillion (31 December 2017 est.)
$1.982 trillion (31 December 2016 est.)
country comparison to the world: 7

Stock of domestic credit: $4.225 trillion (31 December 2017 est.)
$3.646 trillion (31 December 2016 est.)
country comparison to the world: 6

Market value of publicly traded shares: $1.591 trillion (31 March 2017 est.)
$2.088 trillion (31 December 2015 est.)
$2.086 trillion (31 December 2014 est.)
country comparison to the world: 9

Current account balance: -$28.92 billion (2017 est.)
-$24.66 billion (2016 est.)
country comparison to the world: 195

Exports: $541.3 billion (2017 est.)
$507 billion (2016 est.)
country comparison to the world: 7

Exports—commodities: machinery and transportation equipment, aircraft, plastics, chemicals, pharmaceutical products, iron and steel, beverages

Exports—partners: Germany 16%, Spain 7.6%, US 7.3%, Italy 7.2%, UK 7%, Belgium 6.8% (2016)

Imports: $576.3 billion (2017 est.)
$536.7 billion (2016 est.)
country comparison to the world: 7

Imports—commodities: machinery and equipment, vehicles, crude oil, aircraft, plastics, chemicals

Imports—partners: Germany 19.3%, Belgium 10.6%, Netherlands 7.9%, Italy 7.8%, Spain 7%, US 5.8%, China 5.1%, UK 4.2% (2016)

Reserves of foreign exchange and gold: $146.8 billion (31 December 2016 est.)
$138.2 billion (31 December 2015 est.)
country comparison to the world: 17

Debt—external: $5.36 trillion (31 March 2016 est.)
$5.25 trillion (31 March 2015 est.)
country comparison to the world: 4

Stock of direct foreign investment—at home: $842.5 billion (31 December 2017 est.)
$807.4 billion (31 December 2016 est.)
country comparison to the world: 13

Stock of direct foreign investment—abroad: $1.452 trillion (31 December 2017 est.)
$1.379 trillion (31 December 2016 est.)
country comparison to the world: 10

Exchange rates: euros (EUR) per US dollar—
0.906 (2017 est.)
0.9214 (2016 est.)
0.9214 (2015 est.)
0.885 (2014 est.)
0.7634 (2013 est.)

ENERGY

Electricity access: electrification—*total population:* 100% (2016)

Electricity—production: 536.1 billion kWh (2015 est.)
country comparison to the world: 10

Electricity—consumption: 436.1 billion kWh (2015 est.)
country comparison to the world: 11

Electricity—exports: 61.41 billion kWh (2016 est.)
country comparison to the world: 4

Electricity—imports: 20.79 billion kWh (2016 est.)
country comparison to the world: 11

Electricity—installed generating capacity: 129.3 million kW (2015 est.)
country comparison to the world: 10

Electricity—from fossil fuels: 16.1% of total installed capacity (2015 est.)
country comparison to the world: 196

Electricity—from nuclear fuels: 48.8% of total installed capacity (2015 est.)
country comparison to the world: 1

Electricity—from hydroelectric plants: 14% of total installed capacity (2015 est.)
country comparison to the world: 108

Electricity—from other renewable sources: 16.9% of total installed capacity (2015 est.)
country comparison to the world: 39

Crude oil—production: 16,420 bbl/day (2016 est.)
country comparison to the world: 74

Crude oil—exports: 0 bbl/day (2016 est.)
country comparison to the world: 127

Crude oil—imports: 1.096 million bbl/day (2016 est.)
country comparison to the world: 9

Crude oil—proved reserves: 72.35 million bbl (1 January 2017 es)
country comparison to the world: 77

Refined petroleum products—production: 1.27 million bbl/day (2016 est.)
country comparison to the world: 17

Refined petroleum products—consumption: 1.661 million bbl/day (2016 est.)
country comparison to the world: 15

Refined petroleum products—exports: 433,400 bbl/day (2016 est.)
country comparison to the world: 18

Refined petroleum products—imports: 854,200 bbl/day (2016 est.)
country comparison to the world: 9

Natural gas—production: 28 million cu m (2015 est.)
country comparison to the world: 90

Natural gas—consumption: 42.51 billion cu m (2015 est.)
country comparison to the world: 27

Natural gas—exports: 5.419 billion cu m (2015 est.)
country comparison to the world: 29

Natural gas—imports: 44.38 billion cu m (2015 est.)
country comparison to the world: 9

Natural gas—proved reserves: 8.608 billion cu m (1 January 2017 es)
country comparison to the world: 85

Carbon dioxide emissions from consumption of energy: 385.6 million Mt (2013 est.)
country comparison to the world: 17

COMMUNICATIONS

Telephones—fixed lines: *total subscriptions:* 39.006 million
subscriptions per 100 inhabitants: 58 (July 2016 est.)
country comparison to the world: 8

Telephones—mobile cellular: *total:* 67.571 million
subscriptions per 100 inhabitants: 101 (July 2016 est.)
country comparison to the world: 24

Telephone system: *general assessment:* highly developed
domestic: extensive cable and microwave radio relay; extensive use of fiber-optic cable; domestic satellite system
international: country code—33; numerous submarine cables provide links throughout Europe, Asia, Australia, the Middle East, and US; satellite earth stations—more than 3 (2 Intelsat (with total of 5 antennas—2 for Indian Ocean and 3 for Atlantic Ocean), NA Eutelsat, 1 Inmarsat—Atlantic Ocean region); HF radiotelephone communications with more than 20 countries

overseas departments: *country codes:* French Guiana—594; Guadeloupe—590; Martinique—596; Mayotte—262; Reunion—262 (2015)

Broadcast media: a mix of both publicly operated and privately owned TV stations; state-owned France television stations operate 4 networks, one of which is a network of regional stations, and has part-interest in several thematic cable/satellite channels and international channels; a large number of privately owned regional and local TV stations; multi-channel satellite and cable services provide a large number of channels; public broadcaster Radio France operates 7 national networks,

a series of regional networks, and operates services for overseas territories and foreign audiences; Radio France Internationale, under the Ministry of Foreign Affairs, is a leading international broadcaster; a large number of commercial FM stations, with many of them consolidating into commercial networks (2008)

Internet country code: metropolitan France—.fr; French Guiana—.gf; Guadeloupe—.gp; Martinique—.mq; Mayotte—.yt; Reunion—.re
Internet users: total: 57,226,585

percent of population: 85.6% (July 2016 est.)
country comparison to the world: 11

TRANSPORTATION

National air transport system: *number of registered air carriers:* 30
inventory of registered aircraft operated by air carriers: 485
annual passenger traffic on registered air carriers: 65,039,503
annual freight traffic on registered air carriers: 4,098.31 million mt-km (2015)
Civil aircraft registration country code prefix: F (2016)

Airports: 464 (2013)
country comparison to the world: 17

Airports—with paved runways: *total:* 294
over 3,047 m: 14
2,438 to 3,047 m: 25
1,524 to 2,437 m: 97
914 to 1,523 m: 83
under 914 m: 75 (2017)

Airports—with unpaved runways: *total:* 170
1,524 to 2,437 m: 1
914 to 1,523 m: 64
under 914 m: 105 (2013)

Heliports: 1 (2013)

Pipelines: gas 15,322 km; oil 2,939 km; refined products 5,084 km (2013)

Railways: *total:* 29,640 km
standard gauge: 29,473 km 1.435-m gauge (15,561 km electrified)
narrow gauge: 167 km 1.000-m gauge (63 km electrified) (2014)
country comparison to the world: 9

Roadways: *total:* 1,028,446 km (metropolitan France)
paved: 1,028,446 km (includes 11,416 km of expressways)
note: not included are 5,100 km of roadways in overseas departments (2010)
country comparison to the world: 8

Waterways: metropolitan France: 8,501 km (1,621 km navigable by craft up to 3,000 metric tons) (2010)

Merchant marine: *total:* 555
by type: container ship 24, general cargo 72, oil tanker 28, other 431 (2017)
country comparison to the world: 37

Ports and terminals: *major seaport(s):* Brest, Calais, Dunkerque, Le Havre, Marseille, Nantes,

river port(s): Paris, Rouen (Seine); Strasbourg (Rhine); Bordeaux (Garonne)
container port(s): Le Havre (2,215,262) (2011)
cruise/ferry port(s): Calais, Cherbourg, Le Havre
LNG terminal(s) (import): Fos Cavaou, Fos Tonkin, Montoir de Bretagne

MILITARY AND SECURITY

Military expenditures: 2.26% of GDP (2016)
2.27% of GDP (2015)
2.23% of GDP (2014)
2.22% of GDP (2013)
2.24% of GDP (2012)
country comparison to the world: 47

Military branches: Army (Armee de Terre; includes Marines, Foreign Legion, Army Light Aviation), Navy (Marine Nationale), Air Force (Armee de l'Air (AdlA); includes Air Defense) (2011)

Military service age and obligation: 18-25 years of age for male and female voluntary military service; no conscription; 1-year service obligation; women serve in noncombat posts (2013)

TERRORISM

Terrorist groups—foreign based: Basque Fatherland and Liberty (ETA): aim(s): establish an independent Basque homeland based on Marxist principles in what is now southwestern France and northern Spain
area(s) of operation: maintains a presence in the southwest, where the French and Spanish governments collaborate to arrest members and demand disarmament before engaging in negotiations; responsible for hundreds of deaths in France since its inception in 1959; continues to refrain from conducting attacks since its 20 October 2011 communique declaring a permanent cessation of violence, but had not formally disbanded or given up its weapons arsenal by early 2017; 79 members are currently in French prisons, with an unknown number present in the country; remains outlawed in France

Islamic State of Iraq and the Levant (ISIL): *aim(s):* destabilize France's economy and government
area(s) of operation: remains operational with known activities in at least Paris, Lyon, Nice, Tours, and Magnanville, where ISIL has either directed or inspired lethal attacks; three coordinated teams of suicide bombers and shooters conducted attacks on 13 November 2015 in Paris and its northern suburb Saint-Denis, killing at least 130 people and wounding approximately 360; as of early 2017, approximately 1,800 to 1,850 French citizens were fighting in Syria or Iraq alongside ISIL, planning to go to fight, or had returned from the fight; France is a top source country in Europe for ISIL recruits; recruits heavily in prisons

TRANSNATIONAL ISSUES

Disputes—international: Madagascar claims the French territories of Bassas da India, Europa Island, Glorioso Islands, and Juan de Nova Island; Comoros claims Mayotte; Mauritius claims

Tromelin Island; territorial dispute between Suriname and the French overseas department of French Guiana; France asserts a territorial claim in Antarctica (Adelie Land); France and Vanuatu claim Matthew and Hunter Islands, east of New Caledonia

Refugees and internally displaced persons: *refugees (country of origin):* 24,326 (Sri Lanka);

15,232 (Russia); 15,037 (Democratic Republic of the Congo); 13,154 (Serbia and Kosovo); 11,566 (Cambodia); 10,615 (Turkey); 8,991 (Syria); 8,008 (Vietnam); 7,685 (Afghanistan); 7,049 (Sudan); 6,841 (Laos); 6,823 (Guinea); 6,043 (Iraq); 5,183 (Mauritania) (2016)
stateless persons: 1,370 (2016)

Illicit drugs: metropolitan France: transshipment point for South American cocaine, Southwest Asian heroin, and European synthetics
French Guiana: small amount of marijuana grown for local consumption; minor transshipment point to Europe
Martinique: transshipment point for cocaine and marijuana bound for the US and Europe

FRENCH POLYNESIA

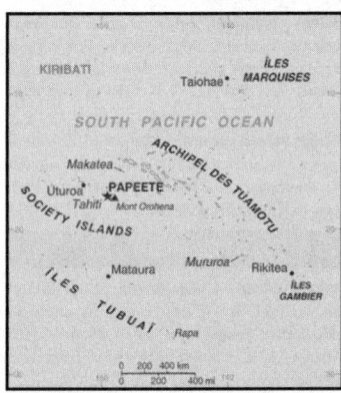

INTRODUCTION

Background: The French annexed various Polynesian island groups during the 19th century. In September 1995, France stirred up widespread protests by resuming nuclear testing on the Mururoa Atoll after a three-year moratorium. The tests were halted in January 1996. In recent years, French Polynesia's autonomy has been considerably expanded.

GEOGRAPHY

Location: Oceania, five archipelagoes (Archipel des Tuamotu, Iles Gambier, Iles Marquises, Iles Tubuai, Society Islands) in the South Pacific Ocean about halfway between South America and Australia

Geographic coordinates: 15 00 S, 140 00 W

Map references: Oceania

Area: *total:* 4,167 sq km (118 islands and atolls; 67 are inhabited)
land: 3,827 sq km
water: 340 sq km
country comparison to the world: 175

Area—comparative: slightly less than one-third the size of Connecticut

Land boundaries: 0 km

Coastline: 2,525 km

Maritime claims: *territorial sea:* 12 nm
exclusive economic zone: 200 nm

Climate: tropical, but moderate

Terrain: mixture of rugged high islands and low islands with reefs

Elevation: *mean elevation:* NA

elevation extremes: *lowest point:* Pacific Ocean 0 m
highest point: Mont Orohena 2,241 m

Natural resources: timber, fish, cobalt, hydropower

Land use: *agricultural land:* 12.5%
arable land: 0.7%;
permanent crops: 6.3%;
permanent pasture: 5.5%
forest: 43.7%
other: 43.8% (2011 est.)

Irrigated land: 10 sq km (2012)

Population—distribution: the majority of the population lives in the Society Islands, one of five archipelagos that includes the most populous island—Tahiti—with approximately 70% of the nation's population

Natural hazards: occasional cyclonic storms in January

Environment—current issues: sea level rise; extreme weather events (cyclones, storms, and tsunamis producing floods, landslides, erosion, and reef damage); droughts; fresh water scarcity

Geography—note: includes five archipelagoes: four volcanic (Iles Gambier, Iles Marquises, Iles Tubuai, Society Islands) and one coral (Archipel des Tuamotu); Makatea in the Tuamotu archipelago is one of the three great phosphate rock islands in the Pacific Ocean—the others are Banaba (Ocean Island) in Kiribati and Nauru

PEOPLE AND SOCIETY

Population: 287,881 (July 2017 est.)
country comparison to the world: 181

Nationality: *noun:* French Polynesian(s),
adjective: French Polynesian

Ethnic groups: Polynesian 78%, Chinese 12%, local French 6%, metropolitan French 4%

Languages: French (official) 70%, Polynesian (official) 28.2%, other 1.8% (2012 est.)

Religions: Protestant 54%, Roman Catholic 30%, other 10%, no religion 6%

Age structure: 0-14 years: 22.52% (male 33,340/female 31,481)

15-24 years: 15.73% (male 23,533/female 21,745)
25-54 years: 44.36% (male 65,464/female 62,254)
55-64 years: 9.42% (male 13,947/female 13,178)
65 years and over: 7.97% (male 11,090/female 11,849) (2017 est.)

Dependency ratios: *total dependency ratio:* 45.3
youth dependency ratio: 34.8
elderly dependency ratio: 10.5
potential support ratio: 9.5 (2015 est.)

Median age: *total:* 31.9 years
male: 31.7 years
female: 32.1 years (2017 est.)
country comparison to the world: 106

Population growth rate: 0.88% (2017 est.)
country comparison to the world: 123

Birth rate: 14.8 births/1,000 population (2017 est.)
country comparison to the world: 131

Death rate: 5.2 deaths/1,000 population (2017 est.)
country comparison to the world: 186

Net migration rate: -0.8 migrant(s)/1,000 population (2017 est.)
country comparison to the world: 131

Population distribution: the majority of the population lives in the Society Islands, one of five archipelagos that includes the most populous island—Tahiti—with approximately 70% of the nation's population

Urbanization: *urban population:* 55.7% of total population (2017)
rate of urbanization: 0.86% annual rate of change (2015-20 est.)

Major urban areas—population: PAPEETE (capital) 133,000 (2014)

Sex ratio: *at birth:* 1.05 male(s)/female
0-14 years: 1.06 male(s)/female
15-24 years: 1.08 male(s)/female
25-54 years: 1.05 male(s)/female
55-64 years: 1.06 male(s)/female
65 years and over: 0.94 male(s)/female
total population: 1.05 male(s)/female (2016 est.)

Infant mortality rate: *total:* 4.6 deaths/1,000 live births
male: 5.1 deaths/1,000 live births
female: 4.1 deaths/1,000 live births (2017 est.)
country comparison to the world: 178

Life expectancy at birth: *total population:* 77.4 years

male: 75.1 years
female: 79.8 years (2017 est.)
country comparison to the world: 71

Total fertility rate: 1.88 children born/woman (2017 est.)
country comparison to the world: 140

Physicians density: 3.17 physicians/1,000 population (2009)

Drinking water source:
improved:
urban: 100% of population
rural: 100% of population
total: 100% of population
unimproved:
urban: 0% of population
rural: 0% of population
total: 0% of population (2015 est.)

Sanitation facility access:
improved:
urban: 98.5% of population
rural: 98.5% of population
total: 98.5% of population
unimproved:
urban: 1.5% of population
rural: 1.5% of population
total: 1.5% of population (2015 est.)

HIV/AIDS—adult prevalence rate: NA

HIV/AIDS—people living with HIV/AIDS: NA

HIV/AIDS—deaths: NA

Unemployment, youth ages 15-24: *total:* 56.7%
male: 54.5%
female: 59.7% (2012 est.)

GOVERNMENT

Country name: *conventional long form:* Overseas Lands of French Polynesia
conventional short form: French Polynesia
local long form: Pays d'outre-mer de la Polynesie Francaise
local short form: Polynesie Francaise
former: French Colony of Oceania
etymology: the term "Polynesia" is an 18th-century construct composed of two Greek words, "poly" (many) and "nesoi" (islands), and refers to the more than 1,000 islands scattered over the central and southern Pacific Ocean

Dependency status: overseas lands of France; overseas territory of France from 1946-2003; overseas collectivity of France since 2003, though it is often referred to as an overseas country due to its degree of autonomy

Government type: parliamentary democracy (Assembly of French Polynesia); an overseas collectivity of France

Capital: *name:* Papeete (located on Tahiti)
geographic coordinates: 17 32 S, 149 34 W
time difference: UTC-10 (5 hours behind Washington, DC, during Standard Time)

Administrative divisions: 5 administrative subdivisions (subdivisions administratives, singular—subdivision administrative): Iles Australes (Austral Islands), Iles du Vent (Windward Islands), Iles

Marquises (Marquesas Islands), Iles Sous-le-Vent (Leeward Islands), Iles Tuamotu-Gambier; note—the Leeward Islands and the Windward Islands together make up the Society Islands (Iles de la Societe)

Independence: none (overseas lands of France)

National holiday: Fete de la Federation, 14 July (1790); note—the local holiday is Internal Autonomy Day, 29 June (1880)

Constitution: 4 October 1958 (French Constitution)

Legal system: the laws of France, where applicable, apply

Citizenship: see France

Suffrage: 18 years of age; universal

Executive branch: *chief of state:* President Emmanuel MACRON (since 14 May 2017), represented by High Commissioner of the Republic Rene BIDALL (since 30 May 2016)
head of government: President of French Polynesia Edouard FRITCH (since 12 September 2014)
cabinet: Council of Ministers approved by the Assembly from a list of its members submitted by the president
elections/appointments: French president directly elected by absolute majority popular vote in 2 rounds if needed for a 5-year term (eligible for a second term); high commissioner appointed by the French president on the advice of the French Ministry of Interior; French Polynesia president indirectly elected by Assembly of French Polynesia for a 5-year term (no term limits)

Legislative branch: description: unicameral Assembly of French Polynesia or Assemblee de la Polynesie Francaise (57 seats; elections held in 2 rounds; in the second round, 38 members directly elected in multi-seat constituencies by proportional representation vote; the party receiving the most votes gets an additional 19 seats; members serve 5-year terms)
elections: last held on 21 April 2013 and 5 May 2013 (next to be held in 2018)
election results: percent of vote by party—Popular Rally 45.1%, UPD 29.3%, A Tia Porinetia 25.6%; seats by party—Popular Rally 38, UPD 11, A Tia Porinetia 8
note: 2 seats were elected to the French Senate for a 6-year term; last election on 20 September 2014 (next to be held in September 2022); election results—percent of vote by party—NA; seats by party—Popular Rally 1, People's Servant Party 1; 3 seats were elected to the French National Assembly for a 5-year term; last election on 17 June 2012 (next to be held by June 2017); election results—percent of vote by party—NA; seats by party—Tapura Huiractura 2, Tavini Huiraatura 1

Judicial branch: *highest court(s):* Court of Appeal or Cour d'Appel (composition NA); note—appeals beyond the French Polynesia Court of Appeal are heard by the Court of Cassation (in Paris)
judge selection and term of office: judges assigned from France normally for 3 years

subordinate courts: Court of the First Instance or Tribunal de Premiere Instance; Court of Administrative Law or Tribunal Administratif

Political parties and leaders: A Tia Porinetia [Teva ROHFRITSCH]
Alliance for a New Democracy or ADN (includes The New Star [Philip SCHYLE], This Country is Yours [Nicole BOUTEAU])
New Fatherland Party (Ai'a Api) [Emile VERNAUDON]
Our Home alliance
People's Servant Party (Tavini Huiraatira) [Oscar TEMARU]
Popular Rally (Tahoeraa Huiraatira) [Gaston FLOSSE]
Tapura Huiraatira [Edouard FRITCH]
Tavini Huiraatira [James CHANCELOR]
Union for Democracy alliance or UPD [Oscar TEMARU]

International organization participation: ITUC (NGOs), PIF (associate member), SPC, UPU, WMO

Diplomatic representation in the US: none (overseas lands of France)

Diplomatic representation from the US: none (overseas lands of France)

Flag description: two red horizontal bands encase a wide white band in a 1:2:1 ratio; centered on the white band is a disk with a blue and white wave pattern depicting the sea on the lower half and a gold and white ray pattern depicting the sun on the upper half; a Polynesian canoe rides on the wave pattern; the canoe has a crew of five represented by five stars that symbolize the five island groups; red and white are traditional Polynesian colors
note: identical to the red-white-red flag of Tahiti, the largest and most populous of the islands in French Polynesia, but which has no emblem in the white band; the flag of France is used for official occasions

National symbol(s): outrigger canoe, Tahitian gardenia (Gardenia taitensis) flower; national colors: red, white

National anthem: name: "Ia Ora 'O Tahiti Nui" (Long Live Tahiti Nui)
lyrics/music: Maeva BOUGES, Irmine TEHEI, Angele TEROROTUA, Johanna NOUVEAU, Patrick AMARU, Louis MAMATUI, and Jean-Pierre CELESTIN (the compositional group created both the lyrics and music)
note: adopted 1993; serves as a local anthem; as a territory of France, "La Marseillaise" is official (see France)

Government—note: under certain acts of France, French Polynesia has acquired autonomy in all areas except those relating to police, monetary policy, tertiary education, immigration, and defense and foreign affairs; the duties of its president are fashioned after those of the French prime minister

ECONOMY

Economy—overview: Since 1962, when France stationed military personnel in the region, French

335

Polynesia has changed from a subsistence agricultural economy to one in which a high proportion of the work force is either employed by the military or supports the tourist industry. With the halt of French nuclear testing in 1996, the military contribution to the economy fell sharply.

After growing at an average yearly rate of 4.2% from 1997-2007, the economic and financial crisis in 2008 marked French Polynesia's entry into recession. However, since 2014, French Polynesia has shown signs of recovery. Business turnover reached 1.8% year-on-year in September 2016, tourism increased 1.8% in 2015, and GDP grew 2.0% in 2015.

French Polynesia's tourism-dominated service sector accounted for 85% of total value added for the economy in 2012. Tourism employs 17% of the workforce. Pearl farming is the second biggest industry, accounting for 54% of exports in 2015; however, the output has decreased to 12.5 tons – the lowest level since 2008. A small manufacturing sector predominantly processes commodities from French Polynesia's primary sector—8% of total economy in 2012—including agriculture and fishing.

France has agreed to finance infrastructure, marine businesses, and cultural and ecological sites at roughly $80 million per year between 2015 and 2020. Japan, the US, and China are French Polynesia's three largest trade partners.

GDP (purchasing power parity): $5.49 billion (2015 est.)
$5.383 billion (2014 est.)
$6.963 billion (2010 est.)
country comparison to the world: 173

GDP (official exchange rate): $4.795 billion (2012 est.)

GDP—real growth rate: 2% (2015 est.)
-2.7% (2014 est.)
-2.5% (2010 est.)
country comparison to the world: 157

GDP—per capita (PPP): $17,000 (2015 est.)
$20,100 (2014 est.)
$22,700 (2010)
country comparison to the world: 103

GDP—composition, by end use:
household consumption: 66.9%
government consumption: 33.6%
investment in fixed capital: 19.4%
investment in inventories: 0.1%
exports of goods and services: 17.5%
imports of goods and services: -37.5%

GDP—composition, by sector of origin:
agriculture: 2.5%
industry: 13%
services: 84.5% (2009)

Agriculture—products: coconuts, vanilla, vegetables, fruits, coffee; poultry, beef, dairy products; fish

Industries: tourism, pearls, agricultural processing, handicrafts, phosphates

Industrial production growth rate: NA%

Labor force: 126,300 (2016 est.)
country comparison to the world: 180

Labor force—by occupation: *agriculture:* 13%
industry: 19%
services: 68% (2013)

Unemployment rate: 21.8% (2012)
11.7% (2010)
country comparison to the world: 187

Population below poverty line: 19.7% (2009 est.)

Household income or consumption by percentage share: *lowest 10%:* NA%
highest 10%: NA%

Budget: *revenues:* $1.891 billion
expenditures: $1.833 billion (2012)
Taxes and other revenues: 39.4% of GDP (2012)
country comparison to the world: 37

Budget surplus (+) or deficit (-): 1.2% of GDP (2012)
country comparison to the world: 13

Fiscal year: calendar year

Inflation rate (consumer prices): 0% (2015 est.)
0.3% (2014 est.)
country comparison to the world: 10

Stock of broad money: $3.81 billion (2015 est.)
country comparison to the world: 138

Market value of publicly traded shares: $NA

Current account balance: $207.7 million (2014 est.)
$158.8 million (2013 est.)
country comparison to the world: 53

Exports: $1.245 billion (2014 est.)
$1.168 billion (2013 est.)
country comparison to the world: 152

Exports—commodities: cultured pearls, coconut products, mother-of-pearl, vanilla, shark meat

Exports—partners: Japan 22.2%, Hong Kong 21.7%, Kyrgyzstan 16.8%, France 13.3%, US 12.6% (2016)

Imports: $0 (2014 est.)
$2.271 billion (2013 est.)
country comparison to the world: 220

Imports—commodities: fuels, foodstuffs, machinery and equipment

Imports—partners: France 28.5%, South Korea 10.7%, US 9%, NZ 7.8%, China 7.2%, Singapore 5.9% (2016)

Debt—external: $NA

Stock of direct foreign investment—at home: $905 million (2015 est.)
$822.3 million (2014 est.)
country comparison to the world: 119

Stock of direct foreign investment—abroad: $349.3 million (2015)
$310.8 million (2014 est.)
country comparison to the world: 95

Exchange rates: Comptoirs Francais du Pacifique francs (XPF) per US dollar—
110.2 (2016 est.)
107.6 (2016 est.)
107.6 (2015 est.)
89.85 (2013 est.)
90.56 (2012 est.)

ENERGY

Electricity access: *population without electricity:* 116,981
electrification—total population: 59%
electrification—urban areas: 72%
electrification—rural areas: 45% (2012)

Electricity—production: 626 million kWh (2015 est.)
country comparison to the world: 161

Electricity—consumption: 582.2 million kWh (2015 est.)
country comparison to the world: 169

Electricity—exports: 0 kWh (2016 est.)
country comparison to the world: 138

Electricity—imports: 0 kWh (2016 est.)
country comparison to the world: 152

Electricity—installed generating capacity: 249,000 kW (2015 est.)
country comparison to the world: 160

Electricity—from fossil fuels: 71.1% of total installed capacity (2015 est.)
country comparison to the world: 102

Electricity—from nuclear fuels: 0% of total installed capacity (2015 est.)
country comparison to the world: 93

Electricity—from hydroelectric plants: 18.9% of total installed capacity (2015 est.)
country comparison to the world: 93

Electricity—from other renewable sources: 10.8% of total installed capacity (2015 est.)
country comparison to the world: 68

Crude oil—production: 0 bbl/day (2016 est.)
country comparison to the world: 137

Crude oil—exports: 0 bbl/day (2014 est.)
country comparison to the world: 126

Crude oil—imports: 0 bbl/day (2014 est.)
country comparison to the world: 129

Crude oil—proved reserves: 0 bbl (1 January 2017 es)
country comparison to the world: 136

Refined petroleum products—production: 0 bbl/day (2014 est.)
country comparison to the world: 146

Refined petroleum products—consumption: 7,000 bbl/day (2015 est.)
country comparison to the world: 165

Refined petroleum products—exports: 0 bbl/day (2014 est.)
country comparison to the world: 158

Refined petroleum products—imports: 6,636 bbl/day (2014 est.)
country comparison to the world: 154

Natural gas—production: 0 cu m (2013 est.)
country comparison to the world: 138

Natural gas—consumption: 0 cu m (2013 est.)
country comparison to the world: 183

Natural gas—exports: 0 cu m (2013 est.)
country comparison to the world: 106

Natural gas—imports: 0 cu m (2013 est.)
country comparison to the world: 127

Natural gas—proved reserves: 0 cu m (1 January 2014 es)
country comparison to the world: 142

Carbon dioxide emissions from consumption of energy: 1.1 million Mt (2013 est.)
country comparison to the world: 164

COMMUNICATIONS

Telephones—fixed lines: *total subscriptions:* 94,957
subscriptions per 100 inhabitants: 33 (July 2016 est.)
country comparison to the world: 159

Telephones—mobile cellular: *total:* 220,819
subscriptions per 100 inhabitants: 77 (July 2016 est.)
country comparison to the world: 180

Telephone system: *domestic:* combined fixed-line and mobile-cellular density is roughly 110 per 100 persons
international: country code—689; satellite earth station—1 Intelsat (Pacific Ocean) (2016)

Broadcast media: the publicly owned French Overseas Network (RFO), which operates in France's overseas departments and territories, broadcasts on 2 TV channels and 1 radio station; 1 government-owned TV station; a small number of privately owned radio stations (2008)

Internet country code: .pf
Internet users: total: 195,275

percent of population: 68.4% (July 2016 est.)
country comparison to the world: 163

TRANSPORTATION

National air transport system: *number of registered air carriers:* 2 (registered in France)
inventory of registered aircraft operated by air carriers: 21 (registered in France) (2015)
Civil aircraft registration country code prefix: F-OH (2016)

Airports: 54 (2013)
country comparison to the world: 87

Airports—with paved runways: *total:* 45
over 3,047 m: 2
1,524 to 2,437 m: 5
914 to 1,523 m: 33
under 914 m: 5 (2017)

Airports—with unpaved runways: *total:* 9
914 to 1,523 m: 4
under 914 m: 5 (2013)

Heliports: 1 (2013)

Roadways: *total:* 2,590 km
paved: 1,735 km
unpaved: 855 km (1999)
country comparison to the world: 171

Merchant marine: *total:* 17
by type: general cargo 8, other 9 (2017)
country comparison to the world: 138

Ports and terminals: *major seaport(s):* Papeete

MILITARY AND SECURITY

Military branches: no regular military forces (2011)

Military—note: defense is the responsibility of France

TRANSNATIONAL ISSUES

Disputes—international: none

FRENCH SOUTHERN AND ANTARCTIC LANDS

INTRODUCTION

Background: In February 2007, the Iles Eparses became an integral part of the French Southern and Antarctic Lands (TAAF). The Southern Lands are now divided into five administrative districts, two of which are archipelagos, Iles Crozet and Iles Kerguelen; the third is a district composed of two volcanic islands, Ile Saint-Paul and Ile Amsterdam; the fourth, Iles Eparses, consists of five scattered tropical islands around Madagascar. They contain no permanent inhabitants and are visited only by researchers studying the native fauna, scientists at the various scientific stations, fishermen, and military personnel. The fifth district is the Antarctic portion, which consists of "Adelie Land," a thin slice of the Antarctic continent discovered and claimed by the French in 1840.

Ile Amsterdam: Discovered but not named in 1522 by the Spanish, the island subsequently received the appellation of Nieuw Amsterdam from a Dutchman; it was claimed by France in 1843. A short-lived attempt at cattle farming began in 1871. A French meteorological station established on the island in 1949 is still in use.

Ile Saint Paul: Claimed by France since 1893, the island was a fishing industry center from 1843 to 1914. In 1928, a spiny lobster cannery was established, but when the company went bankrupt in 1931, seven workers were abandoned. Only two survived until 1934 when rescue finally arrived.

Iles Crozet: A large archipelago formed from the Crozet Plateau, Iles Crozet is divided into two main groups: L'Occidental (the West), which includes Ile aux Cochons, Ilots des Apotres, Ile des Pingouins, and the reefs Brisants de l'Heroine; and L'Oriental (the East), which includes Ile d'Est and Ile de la Possession (the largest island of the Crozets). Discovered and claimed by France in 1772, the islands were used for seal hunting and as a base for whaling. Originally administered as a dependency of Madagascar, they became part of the TAAF in 1955.

Iles Kerguelen: This island group, discovered in 1772, consists of one large island (Ile Kerguelen) and about 300 smaller islands. A permanent group of 50 to 100 scientists resides at the main base at Port-aux-Francais.

Adelie Land: The only non-insular district of the TAAF is the Antarctic claim known as "Adelie Land." The US Government does not recognize it as a French dependency.

Bassas da India: A French possession since 1897, this atoll is a volcanic rock surrounded by reefs and is awash at high tide.

Europa Island: This heavily wooded island has been a French possession since 1897; it is the site of a small military garrison that staffs a weather station.

Glorioso Islands: A French possession since 1892, the Glorioso Islands are composed of two lushly vegetated coral islands (Ile Glorieuse and Ile du Lys) and three rock islets. A military garrison operates a weather and radio station on Ile Glorieuse.

Juan de Nova Island: Named after a famous 15th-century Spanish navigator and explorer, the island has been a French possession since 1897. It has been exploited for its guano and phosphate. Presently a small military garrison oversees a meteorological station.

Tromelin Island: First explored by the French in 1776, the island came under the jurisdiction of Reunion in 1814. At present, it serves as a sea turtle sanctuary and is the site of an important meteorological station.

GEOGRAPHY

Location: southeast and east of Africa, islands in the southern Indian Ocean, some near Madagascar and others about equidistant between Africa,

Antarctica, and Australia; note—French Southern and Antarctic Lands include Ile Amsterdam, Ile Saint-Paul, Iles Crozet, Iles Kerguelen, Bassas da India, Europa Island, Glorioso Islands, Juan de Nova Island, and Tromelin Island in the southern Indian Ocean, along with the French-claimed sector of Antarctica, "Adelie Land"; the US does not recognize the French claim to "Adelie Land"

Geographic coordinates: Ile Amsterdam (Ile Amsterdam et Ile Saint-Paul): 37 50 S, 77 32 E
Ile Saint-Paul (Ile Amsterdam et Ile Saint-Paul): 38 72 S, 77 53 E
Iles Crozet: 46 25 S, 51 00 E
Iles Kerguelen: 49 15 S, 69 35 E
Bassas da India (Iles Eparses): 21 30 S, 39 50 E
Europa Island (Iles Eparses): 22 20 S, 40 22 E
Glorioso Islands (Iles Eparses): 11 30 S, 47 20 E
Juan de Nova Island (Iles Eparses): 17 03 S, 42 45 E
Tromelin Island (Iles Eparses): 15 52 S, 54 25 E

Map references: Antarctic Region, Africa

Area: Ile Amsterdam (Ile Amsterdam et Ile Saint-Paul): total—55 sq km; land—55 sq km; water—0 sq km
Ile Saint-Paul (Ile Amsterdam et Ile Saint-Paul): total—7 sq km; land—7 sq km; water—0 sq km
Iles Crozet: total—352 sq km; land—352 sq km; water—0 sq km
Iles Kerguelen: total—7,215 sq km; land—7,215 sq km; water—0 sq km
Bassas da India (Iles Eparses): total—80 sq km; land—0.2 sq km; water—79.8 sq km (lagoon)
Europa Island (Iles Eparses): total—28 sq km; land—28 sq km; water—0 sq km
Glorioso Islands (Iles Eparses): total—5 sq km; land—5 sq km; water—0 sq km
Juan de Nova Island (Iles Eparses): total—4.4 sq km; land—4.4 sq km; water—0 sq km
Tromelin Island (Iles Eparses): total—1 sq km; land—1 sq km; water—0 sq km
note: excludes "Adelie Land" claim of about 500,000 sq km in Antarctica that is not recognized by the US
country comparison to the world: 231

Area—comparative: Ile Amsterdam (Ile Amsterdam et Ile Saint-Paul): less than one-half the size of Washington, DC
Ile Saint-Paul (Ile Amsterdam et Ile Saint-Paul): more than 10 times the size of the National Mall in Washington, DC
Iles Crozet: about twice the size of Washington, DC
Iles Kerguelen: slightly larger than Delaware
Bassas da India (Iles Eparses): land area about one-third the size of the National Mall in Washington, DC
Europa Island (Iles Eparses): about one-sixth the size of Washington, DC
Glorioso Islands (Iles Eparses): about eight times the size of the National Mall in Washington, DC
Juan de Nova Island (Iles Eparses): about seven times the size of the National Mall in Washington, DC

Tromelin Island (Iles Eparses): about 1.7 times the size of the National Mall in Washington, DC

Land boundaries: 0 km

Coastline: Ile Amsterdam (Ile Amsterdam et Ile Saint-Paul): 28 km
Ile Saint-Paul (Ile Amsterdam et Ile Saint-Paul): Iles Kerguelen: 2,800 km
Bassas da India (Iles Eparses): 35.2 km
Europa Island (Iles Eparses): 22.2 km
Glorioso Islands (Iles Eparses): 35.2 km
Juan de Nova Island (Iles Eparses): 24.1 km
Tromelin Island (Iles Eparses): 3.7 km

Maritime claims: *territorial sea:* 12 nm
exclusive economic zone: 200 nm from Iles Kerguelen and Iles Eparses (does not include the rest of French Southern and Antarctic Lands); Juan de Nova Island and Tromelin Island claim a continental shelf of 200-m depth or to the depth of exploitation

Climate: Ile Amsterdam et Ile Saint-Paul: oceanic with persistent westerly winds and high humidity
Iles Crozet: windy, cold, wet, and cloudy
Iles Kerguelen: oceanic, cold, overcast, windy
Iles Eparses: tropical

Terrain: Ile Amsterdam (Ile Amsterdam et Ile Saint-Paul): a volcanic island with steep coastal cliffs; the center floor of the volcano is a large plateau
Ile Saint-Paul (Ile Amsterdam et Ile Saint-Paul): triangular in shape, the island is the top of a volcano, rocky with steep cliffs on the eastern side; has active thermal springs
Iles Crozet: a large archipelago formed from the Crozet Plateau is divided into two groups of islands
Iles Kerguelen: the interior of the large island of Ile Kerguelen is composed of high mountains, hills, valleys, and plains with peninsulas stretching off its coasts
Bassas da India (Iles Eparses): atoll, awash at high tide; shallow (15 m) lagoon
Europa Island, Glorioso Islands, Juan de Nova Island: low, flat, and sandy
Tromelin Island (Iles Eparses): low, flat, sandy; likely volcanic seamount

Elevation: *mean elevation:* NA

elevation extremes: *lowest point:* Indian Ocean 0 m
highest point: Mont de la Dives on Ile Amsterdam (Ile Amsterdam et Ile Saint-Paul) 867 m; unnamed location on Ile Saint-Paul (Ile Amsterdam et Ile Saint-Paul) 272 m; Pic Marion-Dufresne in Iles Crozet 1,090 m; Mont Ross in Iles Kerguelen 1,850 m; unnamed location on Bassas de India (Iles Eparses) 2.4 m; unnamed location on Europa Island (Iles Eparses) 24 m; unnamed location on Glorioso Islands (Iles Eparses) 12 m; unnamed location on Juan de Nova Island (Iles Eparses) 10 m; unnamed location on Tromelin Island (Iles Eparses) 7 m

Natural resources: fish, crayfish
note: Glorioso Islands and Tromelin Island (Iles Eparses) have guano, phosphates, and coconuts

Natural hazards: Ile Amsterdam and Ile Saint-Paul are inactive volcanoes; Iles Eparses subject

to periodic cyclones; Bassas da India is a maritime hazard since it is under water for a period of three hours prior to and following the high tide and surrounded by reefs
volcanism: Reunion Island—Piton de la Fournaise (2,632 m), which has erupted many times in recent years including 2010, 2015, and 2017, is one of the world's most active volcanoes; although rare, eruptions outside the volcano's caldera could threaten nearby cities

Environment—current issues: introduction of foreign species on Iles Crozet has caused severe damage to the original ecosystem; overfishing of Patagonian toothfish around Iles Crozet and Iles Kerguelen

Geography—note: islands' component is widely scattered across remote locations in the southern Indian Ocean
Bassas da India (Iles Eparses): atoll is a circular reef atop a long-extinct, submerged volcano
Europa Island and Juan de Nova Island (Iles Eparses): wildlife sanctuary for seabirds and sea turtles
Glorioso Island (Iles Eparses): islands and rocks are surrounded by an extensive reef system
Tromelin Island (Iles Eparses): climatologically important location for forecasting cyclones in the western Indian Ocean; wildlife sanctuary (seabirds, tortoises)

PEOPLE AND SOCIETY

Population: no indigenous inhabitants
Ile Amsterdam (Ile Amsterdam et Ile Saint-Paul): no permanent residents but has a meteorological station
Ile Saint-Paul (Ile Amsterdam et Ile Saint-Paul): uninhabited but is frequently visited by fishermen and has a scientific research cabin for short stays
Iles Crozet: uninhabited except for 18 to 30 people staffing the Alfred Faure research station on Ile del la Possession
Iles Kerguelen: 50 to 100 scientists are located at the main base at Port-aux-Francais on Ile Kerguelen
Bassas da India (Iles Eparses): uninhabitable
Europa Island, Glorioso Islands, Juan de Nova Island (Iles Eparses): a small French military garrison and a few meteorologists on each possession; visited by scientists
Tromelin Island (Iles Eparses): uninhabited, except for visits by scientists

GOVERNMENT

Country name: *conventional long form:* Territory of the French Southern and Antarctic Lands
conventional short form: French Southern and Antarctic Lands
local long form: Territoire des Terres Australes et Antarctiques Francaises
local short form: Terres Australes et Antarctiques Francaises
abbreviation: TAAF

etymology: self-descriptive name specifying the territories' affiliation and location in the Southern Hemisphere

Dependency status: overseas territory of France since 1955

note

Administrative divisions: none (overseas territory of France); there are no first-order administrative divisions as defined by the US Government, but there are 5 administrative districts named Iles Crozet, Iles Eparses, Iles Kerguelen, Ile Saint-Paul et Ile Amsterdam; the fifth district is the "Adelie Land" claim in Antarctica that is not recognized by the US

Legal system: the laws of France, where applicable, apply

Citizenship: see France

Executive branch: *chief of state:* President Emmanuel MACRON (since 14 May 2017), represented by Prefect Cecile POZZO DI BORGO (since 13 October 2014)

International organization participation: UPU

Diplomatic representation in the US: none (overseas territory of France)

Diplomatic representation from the US: none (overseas territory of France)

Flag description: the flag of France is used
National anthem: note: as a territory of France, "La Marseillaise" is official (see France)

ECONOMY

Economy—overview: Economic activity is limited to servicing meteorological and geophysical research stations, military bases, and French and other fishing fleets. The fish catches landed on Iles Kerguelen by foreign ships are exported to France and Reunion.

COMMUNICATIONS

Internet country code: .tf
Communications—note: has one or more meteorological stations on each possession

TRANSPORTATION

Airports: 4; note—one each on Europa Island, Glorioso Islands, Juan de Nova Island, and Tromelin Island in the Iles Eparses district (2013)

country comparison to the world: 191

Ports and terminals: none; offshore anchorage only

MILITARY AND SECURITY

Military—note: defense is the responsibility of France

TRANSNATIONAL ISSUES

Disputes—international: French claim to "Adelie Land" in Antarctica is not recognized by the US
Bassas da India, Europa Island, Glorioso Islands, Juan de Nova Island (Iles Eparses): claimed by Madagascar; the vegetated drying cays of Banc du Geyser, which were claimed by Madagascar in 1976, also fall within the EEZ claims of the Comoros and France (Glorioso Islands)
Tromelin Island (Iles Eparses): claimed by Mauritius

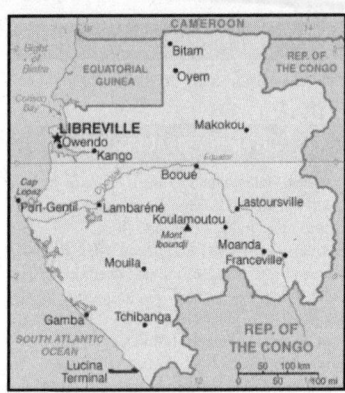

INTRODUCTION

Background: Following, independence from France in 1960, El Hadj Omar BONGO Ondimba—one of the longest-ruling heads of state in the world—dominated the country's political scene for four decades (1967-2009). President BONGO introduced a nominal multiparty system and a new constitution in the early 1990s. However, allegations of electoral fraud during local elections in December 2002 and the presidential election in 2005 exposed the weaknesses of formal political structures in Gabon. Following President BONGO's death in 2009, a new election brought his son, Ali BONGO Ondimba, to power. Despite constrained political conditions, Gabon's small population, abundant natural resources, and considerable foreign support have helped make it one of the more stable African countries.

President Ali BONGO Ondimba's controversial August 2016 reelection sparked unprecedented opposition protests that resulted in the burning of the parliament building. The election was contested by the opposition after fraudulent results were flagged by international election observers. Gabon's Constitutional Court reviewed the election results but ruled in favor of President BONGO, upholding his win and extending his mandate to 2023.

GEOGRAPHY

Location: Central Africa, bordering the Atlantic Ocean at the Equator, between Republic of the Congo and Equatorial Guinea

Geographic coordinates: 1 00 S, 11 45 E

Map references: Africa

Area: total: 267,667 sq km
land: 257,667 sq km
water: 10,000 sq km
country comparison to the world: 78

Area—comparative: slightly smaller than Colorado

Land boundaries: total: 3,261 km

border countries (3): Cameroon 349 km, Republic of the Congo 2,567 km, Equatorial Guinea 345 km

Coastline: 885 km

Maritime claims: territorial sea: 12 nm
contiguous zone: 24 nm
exclusive economic zone: 200 nm

Climate: tropical; always hot, humid

Terrain: narrow coastal plain; hilly interior; savanna in east and south

Elevation: mean elevation: 377 m

elevation extremes: lowest point: Atlantic Ocean 0 m
highest point: Mont Iboundji 1,575 m

Natural resources: petroleum, natural gas, diamond, niobium, manganese, uranium, gold, timber, iron ore, hydropower

Land use: agricultural land: 19%
arable land: 1.2%;
permanent crops: 0.6%;
permanent pasture: 17.2%
forest: 81%
other: 0% (2011 est.)
Irrigated land: 40 sq km (2012)

Population—distribution: the relatively small population is spread in pockets throughout the country; the largest urban center is the capital of Libreville, located along the Atlantic coast in the northwest

Natural hazards: none

Environment—current issues: deforestation; burgeoning population exacerbating disposal of solid waste; oil industry contributing to water pollution; wildlife poaching

Environment—international agreements: party to: Biodiversity, Climate Change, Climate Change-Kyoto Protocol, Desertification, Endangered Species, Hazardous Wastes, Law of the Sea, Marine Dumping, Ozone Layer Protection, Ship Pollution, Tropical Timber 83, Tropical Timber 94, Wetlands, Whaling
signed, but not ratified: none of the selected agreements

Geography—note: a small population and oil and mineral reserves have helped Gabon become one of Africa's wealthier countries; in general, these circumstances have allowed the country to maintain and conserve its pristine rain forest and rich biodiversity

PEOPLE AND SOCIETY

Population: 1,772,255
note: estimates for this country explicitly take into account the effects of excess mortality due to AIDS; this can result in lower life expectancy, higher infant mortality, higher death rates, lower population growth rates, and changes in the distribution of population by age and sex than would otherwise be expected (July 2017 est.)
country comparison to the world: 153

Nationality: noun: Gabonese (singular and plural)
adjective: Gabonese

Ethnic groups: Bantu tribes, including four major tribal groupings (Fang, Bapounou, Nzebi, Obamba); other Africans and Europeans, 154,000, including 10,700 French and 11,000 persons of dual nationality

Languages: French (official), Fang, Myene, Nzebi, Bapounou/Eschira, Bandjabi

Religions: Roman Catholic 42.3%, Protestant 12.3%, other Christian 27.4%, Muslim 9.8%, animist 0.6%, other 0.5%, none/no answer 7.1% (2012 est.)

Demographic profile: Gabon's oil revenues have given it one of the highest per capita income levels in sub-Saharan Africa, but the wealth is not evenly distributed and poverty is widespread. Unemployment is especially prevalent among the large youth population; more than 60% of the population is under the age of 25. With a fertility rate still averaging more than 4 children per woman, the youth population will continue to grow and further strain the mismatch between Gabon's supply of jobs and the skills of its labor force.

Gabon has been a magnet to migrants from neighboring countries since the 1960s because of the discovery of oil, as well as the country's political stability and timber, mineral, and natural gas resources. Nonetheless, income inequality and high unemployment have created slums in Libreville full of migrant workers from Senegal, Nigeria, Cameroon, Benin, Togo, and elsewhere in West Africa. In 2011, Gabon declared an end to refugee status for 9,500 remaining Congolese nationals to whom it had granted asylum during the Republic of the Congo's civil war between 1997 and 2003. About 5,400 of these refugees received permits to reside in Gabon.

Age structure: 0-14 years: 41.9% (male 373,307/female 369,237)
15-24 years: 20.46% (male 181,823/female 180,837)
25-54 years: 29.52% (male 262,511/female 260,673)
55-64 years: 4.36% (male 37,178/female 40,014)
65 years and over: 3.76% (male 28,664/female 38,011) (2017 est.)

Dependency ratios: total dependency ratio: 67.4
youth dependency ratio: 59.9
elderly dependency ratio: 7.6
potential support ratio: 13.2 (2015 est.)

Median age: total: 18.6 years
male: 18.4 years
female: 18.8 years (2017 est.)
country comparison to the world: 207

Population growth rate: 1.92% (2017 est.)
country comparison to the world: 51

Birth rate: 34.2 births/1,000 population (2017 est.)
country comparison to the world: 24

Death rate: 13 deaths/1,000 population (2017 est.)
country comparison to the world: 15

Net migration rate: 2 migrant(s)/1,000 population (2017 est.)
country comparison to the world: 161

Population distribution: the relatively small population is spread in pockets throughout the country; the largest urban center is the capital of Libreville, located along the Atlantic coast in the northwest

Urbanization: *urban population:* 87.6% of total population (2017)
rate of urbanization: 2.38% annual rate of change (2015-20 est.)

Major urban areas—population: LIBREVILLE (capital) 707,000 (2015)

Sex ratio: *at birth:* 1.03 male(s)/female
0-14 years: 1.01 male(s)/female
15-24 years: 1 male(s)/female
25-54 years: 1 male(s)/female
55-64 years: 0.93 male(s)/female
65 years and over: 0.75 male(s)/female
total population: 0.99 male(s)/female (2016 est.)

Mother's mean age at first birth: 20.3 years
note: median age at first birth among women 25-29 (2012 est.)

Maternal mortality ratio: 291 deaths/100,000 live births (2015 est.)
country comparison to the world: 42

Infant mortality rate: *total:* 44.1 deaths/1,000 live births
male: 50.8 deaths/1,000 live births
female: 37.3 deaths/1,000 live births (2017 est.)
country comparison to the world: 42

Life expectancy at birth: *total population:* 52.1 years
male: 51.7 years
female: 52.5 years (2017 est.)
country comparison to the world: 221

Total fertility rate: 4.39 children born/woman (2017 est.)
country comparison to the world: 23

Contraceptive prevalence rate: 31.1% (2012)
Health expenditures: 3.4% of GDP (2014)
country comparison to the world: 175

Hospital bed density: 6.3 beds/1,000 population (2010)

Drinking water source:
improved:
urban: 97.2% of population
rural: 66.7% of population
total: 93.2% of population
unimproved:
urban: 2.8% of population
rural: 33.3% of population
total: 6.8% of population (2015 est.)

Sanitation facility access:
improved:
urban: 43.4% of population
rural: 31.5% of population
total: 41.9% of population
unimproved:
urban: 56.6% of population
rural: 68.5% of population
total: 58.1% of population (2015 est.)

HIV/AIDS—adult prevalence rate: 3.6% (2016 est.)
country comparison to the world: 16

HIV/AIDS—people living with HIV/AIDS: 48,000 (2016 est.)
country comparison to the world: 57

HIV/AIDS—deaths: 1,500 (2016 est.)
country comparison to the world: 59

Major infectious diseases: *degree of risk:* very high
food or waterborne diseases: bacterial diarrhea, hepatitis A, and typhoid fever
vectorborne disease: malaria and dengue fever
water contact disease: schistosomiasis
animal contact disease: rabies (2016)

Obesity—adult prevalence rate: 15% (2016)
country comparison to the world: 127

Children under the age of 5 years underweight: 6.5% (2012)
country comparison to the world: 79

Education expenditures: 2.7% of GDP (2014)

Literacy: *definition:* age 15 and over can read and write
total population: 83.2%
male: 85.3%
female: 81% (2015 est.)

Unemployment, youth ages 15-24: *total:* 35.7%
male: 30.5%
female: 41.9% (2010 est.)

GOVERNMENT

Country name: *conventional long form:* Gabonese Republic
conventional short form: Gabon
local long form: Republique Gabonaise
local short form: Gabon
etymology: name originates from the Portuguese word "gabao" meaning "cloak," which is roughly the shape that the early explorers gave to the estuary of the Komo River by the capital of Libreville

Government type: presidential republic

Capital: *name:* Libreville

geographic coordinates: 0 23 N, 9 27 E
time difference: UTC+1 (6 hours ahead of Washington, DC, during Standard Time)

Administrative divisions: 9 provinces; Estuaire, Haut-Ogooue, Moyen-Ogooue, Ngounie, Nyanga, Ogooue-Ivindo, Ogooue-Lolo, Ogooue-Maritime, Woleu-Ntem

Independence: 17 August 1960 (from France)

National holiday: Independence Day, 17 August (1960)

Constitution: history: previous 1961; latest drafted May 1990, adopted 15 March 1991, promulgated 26 March 1991
amendments: proposed by the president of the republic, by the Council of Ministers, or by one-third of either house of Parliament; passage requires Constitutional Court evaluation, at least two-thirds majority vote of two-thirds of the Parliament membership convened in joint session, and approval in a referendum; constitutional

articles on Gabon's democratic form of government cannot be amended; amended several times, last in 2011 (2017)

Legal system: mixed legal system of French civil law and customary law

International law organization participation: has not submitted an ICJ jurisdiction declaration; accepts ICCt jurisdiction

Citizenship: *citizenship by birth:* no
citizenship by descent only: at least one parent must be a citizen of Gabon
dual citizenship recognized: no
residency requirement for naturalization: 10 years

Suffrage: 18 years of age; universal

Executive branch: *chief of state:* President Ali BONGO Ondimba (since 16 October 2009)

head of government: Prime Minister Emmanuel ISSOZE-NGONDET (since 29 September 2016)
cabinet: Council of Ministers appointed by the prime minister in consultation with the president
elections/appointments: president directly elected by simple majority popular vote for a 7-year term (no term limits); election last held on 27 August 2016 (next to be held in August 2023); prime minister appointed by the president
election results: Ali BONGO Ondimba reelected president; percent of vote—Ali BONGO Ondimba (PDG) 49.8%, Jean PING (UFC) 48.2%, other 2.0%

Legislative branch: description: bicameral Parliament or Parlement consists of the Senate or Senat (number of seats not fixed; members indirectly elected by municipal councils and departmental assemblies by absolute majority vote in 2 rounds; members serve 6-year terms) and the National Assembly or Assemblee Nationale (120 seats; members elected in single-seat constituencies by absolute majority vote in 2 rounds if needed; members serve 5-year terms)
elections: Senate—last held on 13 December 2014 (next to be held in January 2020); National Assembly—last held on 17 December 2011 (next originally scheduled on 27 December 2016, was rescheduled several times, latest to April 2018)
election results: Senate—percent of vote by party—NA; seats by party—PDG 81, CLR 7, PSD 2, ADERE-UPG 1, UPG 1, PGCI 1, independent 7; National Assembly—percent of vote by party—NA; seats by party—PDG 113, RPG 3, other 4

Judicial branch: *highest court(s):* Supreme Court (consists of 4 permanent specialized supreme courts—Supreme Court or Cour de Cassation, Administrative Supreme Court or Conseil d'Etat, Accounting Supreme Court or Cour des Comptes, Constitutional Court or Cour Constitutionnelle—and the non-permanent Court of State Security, initiated only for cases of high treason by the president and criminal activity by executive branch officials)
judge selection and term of office: appointment and tenure of Supreme, Administrative, Accounting, and State Security courts NA; Constitutional Court judges appointed—3 by the national

president, 3 by the president of the Senate, and 3 by the president of the National Assembly; judges serve 7-year, single renewable terms

subordinate courts: Courts of Appeal; county courts; military courts

Political parties and leaders: Circle of Liberal Reformers or CLR [General Jean-Boniface ASSELE]

Democratic and Republican Alliance or ADERE [DIDJOB Divungui di Ndinge]

Gabonese Democratic Party or PDG [Ali BONGO Ondimba]

Independent Center Party of Gabon or PGCI [Luccheri GAHILA]

Rally for Gabon or RPG

Social Democratic Party or PSD [Pierre Claver MAGANGA-MOUSSAVOU]

Union for the New Republic or UPRN [Louis Gaston MAYILA]

Union of Gabonese People or UPG [Richard MOULOMBA]

Union of Forces for Change or UFC [Jean PING]

Political pressure groups and leaders: Gabones Trade Union Confederation or GOSYGA [Martin ALLINI] (affiliated with the International Union Confederation)

National Convention of Trade Unions in the education sector or CONASYSED (banned by the governemnt in early 2017)

International organization participation: ACP, AfDB, AU, BDEAC, CEMAC, FAO, FZ, G-24, G-77, IAEA, IBRD, ICAO, ICCt, ICRM, IDA, IDB, IFAD, IFC, IFRCS, ILO, IMF, IMO, IMSO, Interpol, IOC, IOM, IPU, ISO, ITSO, ITU, ITUC (NGOs), MIGA, NAM, OIC, OIF, OPCW, UN, UNCTAD, UNESCO, UNIDO, UNWTO, UPU, WCO, WHO, WIPO, WMO, WTO

Diplomatic representation in the US: *chief of mission:* Ambassador Michael MOUSSA-NDONG (since September 9, 2011)

chancery: 2034 20th Street NW, Suite 200, Washington, DC 20009

telephone: [1] (202) 797-1000

FAX: [1] (301) 332-0668

Diplomatic representation from the US: *chief of mission:* Ambassador Cynthia AKUETTEH (since 13 August 2014); note—also accredited to Sao Tome and Principe

embassy: Boulevard du Bord de Mer, Libreville

mailing address: Centre Ville, B. P. 4000, Libreville; pouch: 2270 Libreville Place, Washington, DC 20521-2270

telephone: [241] 01-45-71-00

FAX: [241] 01-74-55-07

Flag description: three equal horizontal bands of green (top), yellow, and blue; green represents the country's forests and natural resources, gold represents the equator (which transects Gabon) as well as the sun, blue represents the sea

National symbol(s): black panther; national colors: green, yellow, blue

National anthem: name: "La Concorde" (The Concorde)

lyrics/music: Georges Aleka DAMAS

note: adopted 1960

ECONOMY

Economy—overview: Gabon enjoys a per capita income four times that of most sub-Saharan African nations, but because of high income inequality, a large proportion of the population remains poor. Gabon relied on timber and manganese exports until oil was discovered offshore in the early 1970s. From 2010 to 2016, oil accounted for approximately 80% of Gabon's exports, 45% of its GDP, and 60% of its state budget revenues.

Gabon faces fluctuating international prices for its oil, timber, and manganese exports. A rebound of oil prices from 2001 to 2013 helped growth, but declining production, as some fields passed their peak production, has hampered Gabon from fully realizing potential gains. GDP grew nearly 6% per year over the 2010-14 period, but slowed significantly from 2014 to just 1% in 2017 as oil prices declined. Low oil prices also weakened government revenue and negatively affected the trade and current account balances. In the wake of lower revenue, Gabon signed a 3-year agreement with the IMF in June 2017.

Despite an abundance of natural wealth, poor fiscal management and over-reliance on oil has stifled the economy. Power cuts and water shortages are frequent. Gabon is reliant on imports and the government heavily subsidizes commodities, including food, but will be hard pressed to tamp down public frustration with unemployment and corruption.

GDP (purchasing power parity): $36.75 billion (2017 est.)

$36.4 billion (2016 est.)

$35.66 billion (2015 est.)

note: data are in 2017 dollars

country comparison to the world: 124

GDP (official exchange rate): $14.47 billion (2016 est.)

GDP—real growth rate: 1% (2017 est.)

2.1% (2016 est.)

3.9% (2015 est.)

country comparison to the world: 188

GDP—per capita (PPP): $19,300 (2017 est.)

$19,400 (2016 est.)

$19,200 (2015 est.)

note: data are in 2017 dollars

country comparison to the world: 91

Gross national saving: 24.6% of GDP (2017 est.)

24% of GDP (2016 est.)

29.3% of GDP (2015 est.)

country comparison to the world: 54

GDP—composition, by end use:

household consumption: 39.9%

government consumption: 15.5%

investment in fixed capital: 28.3%

investment in inventories: 0.1%

exports of goods and services: 45.2%

imports of goods and services: -28.9% (2017 est.)

GDP—composition, by sector of origin:

agriculture: 4.5%

industry: 44%

services: 51.5% (2017 est.)

Agriculture—products: cocoa, coffee, sugar, palm oil, rubber; cattle; okoume (a tropical softwood); fish

Industries: petroleum extraction and refining; manganese, gold; chemicals, ship repair, food and beverages, textiles, lumbering and plywood, cement

Industrial production growth rate: 2% (2017 est.)

country comparison to the world: 130

Labor force: 557,800 (2017 est.)

country comparison to the world: 156

Labor force—by occupation: *agriculture:* 64%

industry: 12%

services: 24% (2005 est.)

Unemployment rate: 28% (2015 est.)

20.4% (2014 est.)

country comparison to the world: 199

Population below poverty line: 34.3% (2015 est.)

Household income or consumption by percentage share: *lowest 10%:* 2.5%

highest 10%: 32.7% (2005)

Budget: *revenues:* $3.122 billion

expenditures: $3.991 billion (2017 est.)

Taxes and other revenues: 21.6% of GDP (2017 est.)

country comparison to the world: 138

Budget surplus (+) or deficit (-): -6% of GDP (2017 est.)

country comparison to the world: 175

Public debt: 42.8% of GDP (2017 est.)

42.6% of GDP (2016 est.)

country comparison to the world: 127

Fiscal year: calendar year

Inflation rate (consumer prices): 2.5% (2017 est.)

2.1% (2016 est.)

country comparison to the world: 112

Central bank discount rate: 3% (31 December 2010)

4.25% (31 December 2009)

country comparison to the world: 109

Commercial bank prime lending rate: 15.5% (31 December 2017 est.)

15.5% (31 December 2016 est.)

country comparison to the world: 39

Stock of narrow money: $2.17 billion (31 December 2017 est.)

$2.053 billion (31 December 2016 est.)

country comparison to the world: 130

Stock of broad money: $3.372 billion (31 December 2017 est.)

$3.207 billion (31 December 2016 est.)

country comparison to the world: 142

Stock of domestic credit: $2.915 billion (31 December 2017 est.)

$3.097 billion (31 December 2016 est.)

country comparison to the world: 137

Market value of publicly traded shares: $NA

Current account balance: -$1.348 billion (2017 est.)

-$1.432 billion (2016 est.)

country comparison to the world: 141

Exports: $5.078 billion (2017 est.)
$4.364 billion (2016 est.)
country comparison to the world: 109

Exports—commodities: crude oil, timber, manganese, uranium

Exports—partners: US 45.7%, China 14.6%, South Korea 6.6%, Ireland 5.5%, Italy 5.1% (2016)

Imports: $3.224 billion (2017 est.)
$3.19 billion (2016 est.)
country comparison to the world: 142

Imports—commodities: machinery and equipment, foodstuffs, chemicals, construction materials

Imports—partners: France 24.7%, Belgium 14.7%, China 12.8%, Australia 6.7% (2016)

Reserves of foreign exchange and gold: $834.9 million (31 December 2017 est.)
$804.1 million (31 December 2016 est.)
country comparison to the world: 131

Debt—external: $5.599 billion (31 December 2017 est.)
$5.321 billion (31 December 2016 est.)
country comparison to the world: 132

Exchange rates: Cooperation Financiere en Afrique Centrale francs (XAF) per US dollar—
605.3 (2017 est.)
593.01 (2016 est.)
593.01 (2015 est.)
591.45 (2014 est.)
494.42 (2013 est.)

ENERGY

Electricity access: *population without electricity:* 200,000
electrification—*total population:* 89%
electrification—urban areas: 97%
electrification—rural areas: 38% (2013)

Electricity—production: 2.045 billion kWh (2015 est.)
country comparison to the world: 140

Electricity—consumption: 1.907 billion kWh (2015 est.)
country comparison to the world: 146

Electricity—exports: 0 kWh (2016 est.)
country comparison to the world: 140

Electricity—imports: 337 million kWh (2015 est.)
country comparison to the world: 87

Electricity—installed generating capacity: 670,000 kW (2015 est.)
country comparison to the world: 137

Electricity—from fossil fuels: 50.7% of total installed capacity (2015 est.)
country comparison to the world: 150

Electricity—from nuclear fuels: 0% of total installed capacity (2015 est.)
country comparison to the world: 95

Electricity—from hydroelectric plants: 49.3% of total installed capacity (2015 est.)
country comparison to the world: 40

Electricity—from other renewable sources: 0% of total installed capacity (2015 est.)
country comparison to the world: 182

Crude oil—production: 210,800 bbl/day (2016 est.)
country comparison to the world: 37

Crude oil—exports: 202,000 bbl/day (2014 est.)
country comparison to the world: 30

Crude oil—imports: 0 bbl/day (2014 est.)
country comparison to the world: 131

Crude oil—proved reserves: 2 billion bbl (1 January 2017 es)
country comparison to the world: 38

Refined petroleum products—production: 16,810 bbl/day (2014 est.)
country comparison to the world: 93

Refined petroleum products—consumption: 22,000 bbl/day (2015 est.)
country comparison to the world: 136

Refined petroleum products—exports: 5,118 bbl/day (2014 est.)
country comparison to the world: 95

Refined petroleum products—imports: 8,851 bbl/day (2014 est.)
country comparison to the world: 145

Natural gas—production: 378 million cu m (2015 est.)
country comparison to the world: 74

Natural gas—consumption: 957 million cu m (2015 est.)
country comparison to the world: 101

Natural gas—exports: 0 cu m (2013 est.)
country comparison to the world: 108

Natural gas—imports: 0 cu m (2013 est.)
country comparison to the world: 129

Natural gas—proved reserves: 28.32 billion cu m (1 January 2017 es)
country comparison to the world: 70

Carbon dioxide emissions from consumption of energy: 6 million Mt (2013 est.)
country comparison to the world: 122

COMMUNICATIONS

Telephones—fixed lines: *total subscriptions:* 18,946
subscriptions per 100 inhabitants: 1 (July 2016 est.)
country comparison to the world: 190

Telephones—mobile cellular: *total:* 2,582,542
subscriptions per 100 inhabitants: 149 (July 2016 est.)
country comparison to the world: 128

Telephone system: *general assessment:* adequate system of cable, microwave radio relay, tropospheric scatter, radiotelephone communication stations, and a domestic satellite system with 12 earth stations
domestic: a growing mobile cellular network with multiple providers is making telephone service more widely available with mobile cellular teledensity approaching 150 per 100 persons

international: country code—241; landing point for the SAT-3/WASC fiber-optic submarine cable that provides connectivity to Europe and Asia; satellite earth stations—3 Intelsat (Atlantic Ocean) (2016)

Broadcast media: state owns and operates 2 TV stations and 2 radio broadcast stations; a few private radio and TV stations; transmissions of at least 2 international broadcasters are accessible; satellite service subscriptions are available (2007)

Internet country code: .ga
Internet users: total: 835,408

percent of population: 48.1% (July 2016 est.)
country comparison to the world: 161

TRANSPORTATION

National air transport system: *number of registered air carriers:* 5
inventory of registered aircraft operated by air carriers: 7
annual passenger traffic on registered air carriers: 137,331
annual freight traffic on registered air carriers: 0 mt-km (2015)
Civil aircraft registration country code prefix: TR (2016)

Airports: 44 (2013)
country comparison to the world: 99

Airports—with paved runways: *total:* 14
over 3,047 m: 1
2,438 to 3,047 m: 2
1,524 to 2,437 m: 9
914 to 1,523 m: 1
under 914 m: 1 (2017)

Airports—with unpaved runways: *total:* 30
1,524 to 2,437 m: 7
914 to 1,523 m: 9
under 914 m: 14 (2013)

Pipelines: gas 807 km; oil 1,639 km; water 3 km (2013)

Railways: *total:* 649 km
standard gauge: 649 km 1.435-m gauge (2014)
country comparison to the world: 107

Roadways: *total:* 9,170 km
paved: 1,097 km
unpaved: 8,073 km (2007)
country comparison to the world: 140

Waterways: 1,600 km (310 km on Ogooue River) (2010)
country comparison to the world: 49

Merchant marine: *total:* 27
by type: general cargo 11, oil tanker 1, other 15 (2017)
country comparison to the world: 128

Ports and terminals: *major seaport(s):* Libreville, Owendo, Port-Gentil
oil terminal(s): Gamba, Lucina

MILITARY AND SECURITY

Military expenditures: 1.43% of GDP (2016)
1.19% of GDP (2015)
1.14% of GDP (2014)

1.6% of GDP (2013)

1.62% of GDP (2012)

country comparison to the world: 76

Military branches: Gabonese Defense Forces (Forces de Defense Gabonaise): Land Force (Force Terrestre), Gabonese Navy (Marine Gabonaise), Gabonese Air Forces (Forces Aerienne Gabonaises, FAG) (2012)

Military service age and obligation: 20 years of age for voluntary military service; no conscription (2012)

TRANSNATIONAL ISSUES

Disputes—international: UN urges Equatorial Guinea and Gabon to resolve the sovereignty dispute over Gabon-occupied Mbane Island and lesser islands and to establish a maritime boundary in hydrocarbon-rich Corisco Bay

Trafficking in persons: current situation: Gabon is primarily a destination and transit country for adults and children from West and Central African countries subjected to forced labor and sex trafficking; boys are forced to work as street vendors, mechanics, or in the fishing sector, while girls are subjected to domestic servitude or forced to work in markets or roadside restaurants; West African women are forced into domestic servitude or prostitution; men are reportedly forced to work on cattle farms; some foreign adults end up in forced labor in Gabon after initially seeking the help of human smugglers to help them migrate clandestinely; traffickers operate in loose, ethnic-based criminal networks, with female traffickers recruiting and facilitating the transport of victims from source countries; in some cases, families turn child victims over to traffickers, who promise paid jobs in Gabon

tier rating: Tier 2 Watch List—Gabon does not fully comply with the minimum standards for the elimination of trafficking; however, it is making significant efforts to do so; Gabon's existing laws do not prohibit all forms of trafficking, and the government failed to pass a legal amendment drafted in 2013 to criminalize the trafficking of adults; anti-trafficking law enforcement decreased in 2014, dropping from 50 investigations to 16, and the only defendant to face prosecution fled the country; government efforts to identify and refer victims to protective services declined from 50 child victims in 2013 to just 3 in 2014, none of whom was referred to a care facility; the government provided support to four centers offering services to orphans and vulnerable children—14 child victims identified by an NGO received government assistance; no adult victims have been identified since 2009 (2015)

GAMBIA, THE

INTRODUCTION

Background: The Gambia gained its independence from the UK in 1965. Geographically surrounded by Senegal, it formed a short-lived Confederation of Senegambia between 1982 and 1989. In 1991 the two nations signed a friendship and cooperation treaty, but tensions have flared up intermittently since then. Yahya JAMMEH led a military coup in 1994 that overthrew the president and banned political activity. A new constitution and presidential election in 1996, followed by parliamentary balloting in 1997, completed a nominal return to civilian rule. JAMMEH was elected president in all subsequent elections including most recently in late 2011. After 22 years of increasingly authoritarian rule, President JAMMEH was defeated in free and fair elections in December 2016. Due to The Gambia's poor human rights record under JAMMEH, international development partners had distanced themselves, and substantially reduced aid to the country. These channels may re-open under the administration of President

GEOGRAPHY

Location: Western Africa, bordering the North Atlantic Ocean and Senegal

Geographic coordinates: 13 28 N, 16 34 W

Map references: Africa

Area: *total:* 11,300 sq km

land: 10,120 sq km

water: 1,180 sq km

country comparison to the world: 166

Area—comparative: slightly less than twice the size of Delaware

Land boundaries: *total:* 749 km

border countries (1): Senegal 749 km

Coastline: 80 km

Maritime claims: *territorial sea:* 12 nm

contiguous zone: 18 nm

exclusive fishing zone: 200 nm

continental shelf: extent not specified

Climate: tropical; hot, rainy season (June to November); cooler, dry season (November to May)

Terrain: flood plain of the Gambia River flanked by some low hills

Elevation: *mean elevation:* 34 m

elevation extremes: *lowest point:* Atlantic Ocean 0 m

highest point: unnamed elevation 53 m

Natural resources: fish, clay, silica sand, titanium (rutile and ilmenite), tin, zircon

Land use: *agricultural land:* 56.1%

arable land: 41%;

permanent crops: 0.5%;

permanent pasture: 14.6%

forest: 43.9%

other: 0% (2011 est.)

Irrigated land: 50 sq km (2012)

Population—distribution: settlements are found scattered along the Gambia River; the largest communities, including the capital of Banjul, and the country's largest city, Serekunda, are found at the mouth of the Gambia River along the Atlantic coast

Natural hazards: droughts

Environment—current issues: deforestation; desertification; water-borne diseases prevalent

Environment—international agreements: *party to:* Biodiversity, Climate Change, Climate Change-Kyoto Protocol, Desertification, Endangered Species, Hazardous Wastes, Law of the Sea, Ozone Layer Protection, Ship Pollution, Wetlands, Whaling

signed, but not ratified: none of the selected agreements

Geography—note: almost an enclave of Senegal; smallest country on the African mainland

PEOPLE AND SOCIETY

Population: 2,051,363 (July 2017 est.)

country comparison to the world: 146

Nationality: *noun:* Gambian(s)

adjective: Gambian

Ethnic groups: Mandinka/Jahanka 34%, Fulani/Tukulur/Lorobo 22.4%, Wolof 12.6%, Jola/Karoninka 10.7%, Serahuleh 6.6%, Serer 3.2%, Manjago 2.1%, Bambara 1%, Creole/Aku Marabout 0.7%, other 0.9%, non-Gambian 5.2%, no answer 0.6% (2013 est.)

Languages: English (official), Mandinka, Wolof, Fula, other indigenous vernaculars

Religions: Muslim 95.7%, Christian 4.2%, none 0.1%, no response 0.1% (2013 est.)

Demographic profile: The Gambia's youthful age structure—almost 60% of the population is under the age of 25—is likely to persist because the country's total fertility rate remains strong at nearly 4 children per woman. The overall literacy rate is around 55%, and is significantly lower for women than for men. At least 70% of the populace are farmers who are reliant on rain-fed agriculture and cannot afford improved seeds and fertilizers. Crop failures caused by droughts between 2011 and

2013 have increased poverty, food shortages, and malnutrition.

The Gambia is a source country for migrants and a transit and destination country for migrants and refugees. Since the 1980s, economic deterioration, drought, and high unemployment, especially among youths, have driven both domestic migration (largely urban) and migration abroad (legal and illegal). Emigrants are largely skilled workers, including doctors and nurses, and provide a significant amount of remittances. The top receiving countries for Gambian emigrants are Spain, the US, Nigeria, Senegal, and the UK. While the Gambia and Spain do not share historic, cultural, or trade ties, rural Gambians have migrated to Spain in large numbers because of its proximity and the availability of jobs in its underground economy (this flow slowed following the onset of Spain's late 2007 economic crisis).

The Gambia's role as a host country to refugees is a result of wars in several of its neighboring West African countries. Since 2006, refugees from the Casamance conflict in Senegal have replaced their pattern of flight and return with permanent settlement in The Gambia, often moving in with relatives along the Senegal-Gambia border. The strain of providing for about 7,400 Casamance refugees has increased poverty among Gambian villagers.

Age structure: *0-14 years:* 37.44% (male 385,646/female 382,328)
15-24 years: 20.47% (male 207,611/female 212,366)
25-54 years: 34.4% (male 345,788/female 359,976)
55-64 years: 4.2% (male 41,295/female 44,865)
65 years and over: 3.48% (male 33,153/female 38,335) (2017 est.)

Dependency ratios: *total dependency ratio:* 92.3
youth dependency ratio: 87.8
elderly dependency ratio: 4.5
potential support ratio: 22.3 (2015 est.)

Median age: *total:* 21 years
male: 20.7 years
female: 21.3 years (2017 est.)
country comparison to the world: 186

Population growth rate: 2.05% (2017 est.)
country comparison to the world: 42

Birth rate: 29.4 births/1,000 population (2017 est.)
country comparison to the world: 41

Death rate: 7 deaths/1,000 population (2017 est.)
country comparison to the world: 133

Net migration rate: -1.9 migrant(s)/1,000 population (2017 est.)
country comparison to the world: 159

Population distribution: settlements are found scattered along the Gambia River; the largest communities, including the capital of Banjul, and the country's largest city, Serekunda, are found at the mouth of the Gambia River along the Atlantic coast

Urbanization: *urban population:* 60.8% of total population (2017)
rate of urbanization: 3.96% annual rate of change (2015-20 est.)

Major urban areas—population: BANJUL (capital) 504,000 (2015)

Sex ratio: *at birth:* 1.03 male(s)/female
0-14 years: 1.01 male(s)/female
15-24 years: 0.98 male(s)/female
25-54 years: 0.96 male(s)/female
55-64 years: 0.93 male(s)/female
65 years and over: 0.88 male(s)/female
total population: 0.98 male(s)/female (2016 est.)

Mother's mean age at first birth: 20.9 years
note: median age at first birth among women 25-29 (2013 est.)

Maternal mortality ratio: 706 deaths/100,000 live births (2015 est.)
country comparison to the world: 9

Infant mortality rate: *total:* 60.2 deaths/1,000 live births
male: 65.6 deaths/1,000 live births
female: 54.7 deaths/1,000 live births (2017 est.)
country comparison to the world: 17

Life expectancy at birth: *total population:* 65.1 years
male: 62.8 years
female: 67.5 years (2017 est.)
country comparison to the world: 180

Total fertility rate: 3.52 children born/woman (2017 est.)
country comparison to the world: 43

Contraceptive prevalence rate: 9% (2013)
Health expenditures: 7.3% of GDP (2014)
country comparison to the world: 73

Physicians density: 0.11 physicians/1,000 population (2008)

Hospital bed density: 1.1 beds/1,000 population (2011)

Drinking water source:
improved:
urban: 94.2% of population
rural: 84.4% of population
total: 90.2% of population
unimproved:
urban: 5.8% of population
rural: 15.6% of population
total: 9.8% of population (2015 est.)

Sanitation facility access:
improved:
urban: 61.5% of population
rural: 55% of population
total: 58.9% of population
unimproved:
urban: 38.5% of population
rural: 45% of population
total: 41.1% of population (2015 est.)

HIV/AIDS—adult prevalence rate: 1.7% (2016 est.)
country comparison to the world: 29

HIV/AIDS—people living with HIV/AIDS: 20,000 (2016 est.)
country comparison to the world: 77

HIV/AIDS—deaths: 1,100 (2016 est.)
country comparison to the world: 61

Major infectious diseases: *degree of risk:* very high

food or waterborne diseases: bacterial and protozoal diarrhea, hepatitis A, and typhoid fever
vectorborne diseases: malaria and dengue fever
water contact disease: schistosomiasis
respiratory disease: meningococcal meningitis
animal contact disease: rabies (2016)

Obesity—adult prevalence rate: 10.3% (2016)
country comparison to the world: 138

Children under the age of 5 years underweight: 16.4% (2013)
country comparison to the world: 38

Education expenditures: 2.8% of GDP (2013)
country comparison to the world: 109

Literacy: *definition:* age 15 and over can read and write
total population: 55.5%
male: 63.9%
female: 47.6% (2015 est.)

School life expectancy (primary to tertiary education): *total:* 9 years
male: 9 years
female: 9 years (2010)

Unemployment, youth ages 15-24: *total:* 44.3%
male: 38.1%
female: 49.5% (2012 est.)

GOVERNMENT

Country name: *conventional long form:* Republic of The Gambia
conventional short form: The Gambia
etymology: named for the Gambia River that flows through the heart of the country

Government type: presidential republic

Capital: *name:* Banjul
geographic coordinates: 13 27 N, 16 34 W
time difference: UTC 0 (5 hours ahead of Washington, DC, during Standard Time)

Administrative divisions: 5 regions, 1 city*, and 1 municipality**; Banjul*, Central River, Kanifing**, Lower River, North Bank, Upper River, West Coast

Independence: 18 February 1965 (from the UK)

National holiday: Independence Day, 18 February (1965)

Constitution: history: previous 1965 (independence act), 1970; latest adopted 8 April 1996, approved by referendum 8 August 1996, effective 16 January 1997
amendments: proposed by the National Assembly; passage requires at least three-fourths majority vote by the Assembly membership in each of several readings and approval by the president of the republic; a referendum is required for amendments affecting national sovereignty, fundamental rights and freedoms, government structures and authorities, taxation, and public funding; passage by referendum requires participation of at least 50% of eligible voters and approval by at least 75% of votes cast; amended 2001, 2004, 2010 (2017)

Legal system: mixed legal system of English common law, Islamic law, and customary law

345

International law organization participation: accepts compulsory ICJ jurisdiction with reservations; accepts ICCt jurisdiction

Citizenship: *citizenship by birth:* yes
citizenship by descent: yes
dual citizenship recognized: no
residency requirement for naturalization: 5 years

Suffrage: 18 years of age; universal

Executive branch: *chief of state:* President Adama BARROW (since 19 January 2017); Vice President Fatoumata JALLOW-TAMBAJANG (since 23 January 2017); note—the president is both chief of state and head of government

head of government: President Adama BARROW (since 19 January 2017); Vice President Fatoumata JALLOW-TAMBAJANG (since 23 January 2017)
cabinet: Cabinet appointed by the president
elections/appointments: president directly elected by simple majority popular vote for a 5-year term (no term limits); election last held on 24 November 2011 (next to be held on 1 December 2016); vice president appointed by the president
election results: Adama BARROW elected president; percent of vote—Adama BARROW (Coalition 2016) 43.3%, Yahya JAMMEH (APRC)39.6%, Mamma KANDEH (GDC) 17.1%

Legislative branch: description: unicameral National Assembly (58 seats; 53 members directly elected in single-seat constituencies by simple majority vote and 5 appointed by the president; members serve 5-year terms)
elections: last held on 6 April 2017 (next to be held in 2022)
election results: percent of vote by party—UDP 37.5%, GDC 17.4%, APRC 16%, PDOIS 9%, NRP 6.3%, PPP 2.5%, independent 9.6%; seats by party—UDP 31, APRC 5, GDC 5, NRP 5, PDOIS 4, PPP 2, independent 1

Judicial branch: *highest court(s):* Supreme Court of The Gambia (consists of the chief justice and 6 justices; court sessions held with 5 justices)
judge selection and term of office: justices appointed by the president after consultation with the Judicial Service Commission, a 6-member independent body of high-level judicial officials, a presidential appointee, and a National Assembly appointee; justices appointed for life or until mandatory retirement age
subordinate courts: Court of Appeal; High Court; Special Criminal Court; Khadis or Muslim courts; district tribunals; magistrates courts

Political parties and leaders: Alliance for Patriotic Reorientation and Construction or APRC [Fabakary JATTA]
Coalition 2016 [collective leadership] (electoral coalition including UDP, PDOIS, NRP, GMC, GDC, PPP, GPDP)
Gambia Democratic Congress or GDC [Mama KANDEH]
Gambia Moral Congress or GMC [Mai FATTY]
Gambia Party for Democracy and Progress or GPDP [Henry GOMEZ]

National Reconciliation Party or NRP [Samba JALLOW]
National Convention Party or NCP [Ebrima Janko SANYANG]
People's Democratic Organization for Independence and Socialism or PDOIS [Sidia JATTA]
People's Progressive Party or PPP [Yaya CEESAY]
United Democratic Party or UDP [Ousainou DARBOE]

Political pressure groups and leaders: The Association of Non-Governmental Organizations or TANGO
Female Lawyers Association of Gambia or FLAG
Gambia Committee on Traditional Practices or GAMCOTRAP
Gambia Press Union or GPU
West African Peace Building Network-Gambian Chapter or WANEB-GAMBIA
Youth Employment Network Gambia or YENGambia
other: special needs group advocates; teachers and principals

International organization participation: ACP, AfDB, AU, ECOWAS, FAO, G-77, IBRD, ICAO, ICCt, ICRM, IDA, IDB, IFAD, IFC, IFRCS, ILO, IMF, IMO, Interpol, IOC, IOM, IPU, ISO (correspondent), ITSO, ITU, ITUC (NGOs), MIGA, MINUSMA, NAM, OIC, OPCW, UN, UNAMID, UNCTAD, UNESCO, UNIDO, UNMIL, UNOCI, UNWTO, UPU, WCO, WFTU (NGOs), WHO, WIPO, WMO, WTO

Diplomatic representation in the US: *chief of mission:* Ambassador Dawda D. FADERA (since 24 January 2018)
chancery: 2233 Wisconsin Avenue NW, Georgetown Plaza, Suite 240, Washington, DC 20007
telephone: [1] (202) 785-1379, 1399, 1425
FAX: [1] (202) 342-0240

Diplomatic representation from the US: *chief of mission:* Ambassador C. Patricia ALSUP (since 11 January 2016)
embassy: Kairaba Avenue, Fajara, Banjul
mailing address: P.M.B. 19, Banjul
telephone: [220] 439-2856
FAX: [220] 439-2475

Flag description: three equal horizontal bands of red (top), blue with white edges, and green; red stands for the sun and the savannah, blue represents the Gambia River, and green symbolizes forests and agriculture; the white stripes denote unity and peace

National symbol(s): lion; national colors: red, blue, green, white

National anthem: name: "For The Gambia, Our Homeland"
lyrics/music: Virginia Julie HOWE/adapted by Jeremy Frederick HOWE
note: adopted 1965; the music is an adaptation of the traditional Mandinka song "Foday Kaba Dumbuya"

ECONOMY

Economy—overview: The government has invested in the agriculture sector because

three-quarters of the population depends on the sector for its livelihood and agriculture provides for about one-third of GDP, making The Gambia largely reliant on sufficient rainfall. The agricultural sector has untapped potential—less than half of arable land: is cultivated and agricultural productivity is low. Small-scale manufacturing activity features the processing of cashews, groundnuts, fish, and hides. The Gambia's reexport trade accounts for almost 80% of goods exports and China has been its largest trade partner for both exports and imports for several years.

The Gambia has sparse natural resource deposits. It relies heavily on remittances from workers overseas and tourist receipts. Remittance inflows to The Gambia amount to about one-fifth of the country's GDP. The Gambia's location on the ocean and proximity to Europe has made it one of the most frequented tourist destinations in West Africa, boosted by private sector investments in eco-tourism and facilities. Tourism normally brings in about 20% of GDP, but it suffered in 2014 from tourists' fears of Ebola virus in neighboring West African countries. Unemployment and underemployment remain high.

Economic progress depends on sustained bilateral and multilateral aid, on responsible government economic management, and on continued technical assistance from multilateral and bilateral donors. International donors and lenders were concerned about the quality of fiscal management under the administration of former President Yahya JAMMEH, who reportedly stole hundreds of millions of dollars of the country's funds during his 22 years in power, but anticipate significant improvements under the new administration of President Adama BARROW, who assumed power in early 2017. As of April 2017, the IMF, the World Bank, the European Union, and the African Development Bank were all negotiating with the new government of The Gambia to provide financial support in the coming months to ease the country's financial crisis.

The country faces a limited availability of foreign exchange, weak agricultural output, a border closure with Senegal, a slowdown in tourism, high inflation, a large fiscal deficit, and a high domestic debt burden that has crowded out private sector investment and driven interest rates to new highs. The government has committed to taking steps to reduce the deficit, including through expenditure caps, debt consolidation, and reform of state-owned enterprises.

GDP (purchasing power parity): $3.582 billion (2017 est.)
$3.478 billion (2016 est.)
$3.402 billion (2015 est.)
note: data are in 2017 dollars
country comparison to the world: 183

GDP (official exchange rate): $1.038 billion (2016 est.)

GDP—real growth rate: 3% (2017 est.)
2.2% (2016 est.)
4.3% (2015 est.)
country comparison to the world: 115

GDP—per capita (PPP): $1,700 (2017 est.)
$1,700 (2016 est.)
$1,700 (2015 est.)
note: data are in 2017 dollars
country comparison to the world: 216

Gross national saving: 10% of GDP (2017 est.)
9.8% of GDP (2016 est.)
4.7% of GDP (2015 est.)
country comparison to the world: 159

GDP—composition, by end use:
household consumption: 87.2%
government consumption: 10.5%
investment in fixed capital: 20.1%
investment in inventories: -8%
exports of goods and services: 21.9%
imports of goods and services: -31.7% (2017 est.)

GDP—composition, by sector of origin:
agriculture: 20.4%
industry: 14.2%
services: 65.4% (2017 est.)

Agriculture—products: rice, millet, sorghum, peanuts, corn, sesame, cassava (manioc, tapioca), palm kernels; cattle, sheep, goats

Industries: peanuts, fish, hides, tourism, beverages, agricultural machinery assembly, woodworking, metalworking, clothing

Industrial production growth rate: 3.9% (2017 est.)
country comparison to the world: 72

Labor force: 777,100 (2007 est.)
country comparison to the world: 151

Labor force—by occupation: *agriculture:* 75%
industry: 19%
services: 6% (1996)

Unemployment rate: NA%

Population below poverty line: 48.4% (2010 est.)

Household income or consumption by percentage share: *lowest 10%:* 2%
highest 10%: 36.9% (2003)

Distribution of family income—Gini index: 50.2 (1998)
country comparison to the world: 17

Budget: *revenues:* $187 million
expenditures: $369.9 million (2017 est.)
Taxes and other revenues: 18% of GDP (2017 est.)
country comparison to the world: 168

Budget surplus (+) or deficit (-): -17.6% of GDP (2017 est.)
country comparison to the world: 215

Public debt: 116.1% of GDP (2016 est.)
110.2% of GDP (2015 est.)
country comparison to the world: 10

Fiscal year: calendar year

Inflation rate (consumer prices): 8.3% (2017 est.)
7.2% (2016 est.)
country comparison to the world: 200

Central bank discount rate: 9% (31 December 2009)
11% (31 December 2008)
country comparison to the world: 34

Commercial bank prime lending rate: 30.6% (31 December 2017 est.)
30.4% (31 December 2016 est.)
country comparison to the world: 6

Stock of narrow money: $225.1 million (31 December 2017 est.)
$279.6 million (31 December 2016 est.)
country comparison to the world: 182

Stock of broad money: $435.6 million (31 December 2017 est.)
$529.9 million (31 December 2016 est.)
country comparison to the world: 187

Stock of domestic credit: $408.5 million (31 December 2017 est.)
$496.7 million (31 December 2016 est.)
country comparison to the world: 176

Market value of publicly traded shares: $NA

Current account balance: -$97 million (2017 est.)
-$86 million (2016 est.)
country comparison to the world: 79

Exports: $109.7 million (2017 est.)
$106.6 million (2016 est.)
country comparison to the world: 195

Exports—commodities: peanut products, fish, cotton lint, palm kernels

Exports—partners: Mali 36.3%, Guinea 24.5%, Senegal 12.3%, China 11.7%, Guinea-Bissau 5.8% (2016)

Imports: $316.1 million (2017 est.)
$326.7 million (2016 est.)
country comparison to the world: 196

Imports—commodities: foodstuffs, manufactures, fuel, machinery and transport equipment

Imports—partners: Cote dIvoire 13%, Brazil 12.3%, China 11%, Belgium 8.6%, India 5.7%, Spain 4.7%, Senegal 4.6% (2016)

Reserves of foreign exchange and gold: $22.8 million (31 December 2017 est.)
$87.64 million (31 December 2016 est.)
country comparison to the world: 174

Debt—external: g: $619.7 million (31 December 2017 est.)
$571.2 million (31 December 2016 est.)
country comparison to the world: 176

Exchange rates: dalasis (GMD) per US dollar—
49.74 (2017 est.)
43.8846 (2016 est.)
43.8846 (2015 est.)
41.89 (2014 est.)
41.733 (2013 est.)

ENERGY

Electricity access: *population without electricity:* 1,200,000
electrification—total population: 36%
electrification—urban areas: 60%
electrification—rural areas: 2% (2013)

Electricity—production: 240 million kWh (2015 est.)
country comparison to the world: 184

Electricity—consumption: 223.2 million kWh (2015 est.)
country comparison to the world: 186

Electricity—exports: 0 kWh (2016 est.)
country comparison to the world: 139

Electricity—imports: 0 kWh (2016 est.)
country comparison to the world: 153

Electricity—installed generating capacity: 114,000 kW (2015 est.)
country comparison to the world: 177

Electricity—from fossil fuels: 100% of total installed capacity (2015 est.)
country comparison to the world: 6

Electricity—from nuclear fuels: 0% of total installed capacity (2015 est.)
country comparison to the world: 94

Electricity—from hydroelectric plants: 0% of total installed capacity (2015 est.)
country comparison to the world: 176

Electricity—from other renewable sources: 0% of total installed capacity (2015 est.)
country comparison to the world: 181

Crude oil—production: 0 bbl/day (2016 est.)
country comparison to the world: 138

Crude oil—exports: 0 bbl/day (2014 est.)
country comparison to the world: 128

Crude oil—imports: 0 bbl/day (2014 est.)
country comparison to the world: 130

Crude oil—proved reserves: 0 bbl (1 January 2017 es)
country comparison to the world: 137

Refined petroleum products—production: 0 bbl/day (2014 est.)
country comparison to the world: 147

Refined petroleum products—consumption: 3,600 bbl/day (2015 est.)
country comparison to the world: 183

Refined petroleum products—exports: 41.62 bbl/day (2014 est.)
country comparison to the world: 125

Refined petroleum products—imports: 3,552 bbl/day (2014 est.)
country comparison to the world: 174

Natural gas—production: 0 cu m (2013 est.)
country comparison to the world: 139

Natural gas—consumption: 0 cu m (2013 est.)
country comparison to the world: 184

Natural gas—exports: 0 cu m (2013 est.)
country comparison to the world: 107

Natural gas—imports: 0 cu m (2013 est.)
country comparison to the world: 128

Natural gas—proved reserves: 0 cu m (1 January 2014 es)
country comparison to the world: 143

Carbon dioxide emissions from consumption of energy: 500,000 Mt (2013 est.)
country comparison to the world: 184

COMMUNICATIONS

Telephones—fixed lines: *total subscriptions:* 37,969
subscriptions per 100 inhabitants: 2 (July 2016 est.)
country comparison to the world: 158

Telephones—mobile cellular: *total:* 2,838,127

subscriptions per 100 inhabitants: 141 (July 2016 est.)

country comparison to the world: 146

Telephone system: *general assessment:* adequate microwave radio relay and open-wire network; state-owned Gambia Telecommunications partially privatized in 2007

domestic: combined fixed-line and mobile-cellular teledensity, aided by multiple mobile-cellular providers, is over 140 per 100 persons

international: country code—220; microwave radio relay links to Senegal and Guinea-Bissau; a landing station for the Africa Coast to Europe (ACE) undersea fiber-optic cable completed in 2011 and launched in 2012; satellite earth station—1 Intelsat (Atlantic Ocean) (2016)

Broadcast media: state-owned, single-channel TV service; state-owned radio station and 15 privately owned radio stations; 6 community radio stations; transmissions of multiple international broadcasters are available, some via shortwave radio; cable and satellite TV subscription services are obtainable in some parts of the country (2015)

Internet country code: .gm

Internet users: total: 371,785

percent of population: 18.5% (July 2016 est.)

country comparison to the world: 147

TRANSPORTATION

Civil aircraft registration country code prefix: C5 (2016)

Airports: 1 (2013)

country comparison to the world: 218

Airports—with paved runways: *total:* 1

over 3,047 m: 1 (2017)

Roadways: *total:* 3,740 km

paved: 711 km

unpaved: 3,029 km (2011)

country comparison to the world: 159

Waterways: 390 km (on River Gambia; small oceangoing vessels can reach 190 km) (2010)

country comparison to the world: 88

Merchant marine: *total:* 8

by type: other 8 (2017)

country comparison to the world: 32

Ports and terminals: *major seaport(s):* Banjul

MILITARY AND SECURITY

Military expenditures: 1.48% of GDP (2015)

1.72% of GDP (2014)

1.15% of GDP (2013)

1.22% of GDP (2012)

Military branches: Office of the Chief of Defense Staff: Gambian National Army (GNA), Gambian Navy (GN), Republican National Guard (RNG) (2010)

Military service age and obligation: 18 years of age for male and female voluntary military service; no conscription; service obligation 6 months (2012)

TRANSNATIONAL ISSUES

Disputes—international: attempts to stem refugees, cross-border raids, arms smuggling, and other illegal activities by separatists from southern Senegal's Casamance region, as well as from conflicts in other west African states

Refugees and internally displaced persons: *refugees (country of origin):* 7,530 (Senegal) (2017)

Trafficking in persons: current situation: The Gambia is a source and destination country for women and children subjected to forced labor and sex trafficking; Gambian women, girls, and, to a lesser extent, boys are exploited for prostitution and domestic servitude; women, girls, and boys from West African countries are trafficked to The Gambia for commercial sexual exploitation, particularly by European sex tourists; boys in some Koranic schools are forced into street vending or begging; some Gambian children have been identified as victims of forced labor in neighboring West African countries

tier rating: Tier 3—The Gambia does not fully comply with the minimum standards for the elimination of trafficking and is not making significant efforts to do so; the government demonstrated minimal anti-trafficking law enforcement efforts, investigating one trafficking case but not prosecuting or convicting any offenders in 2014; authorities did not investigate, prosecute, or convict any government employees complicit in trafficking, although corruption was a serious problem; the government identified and repatriated 19 Gambian girls subjected to domestic servitude in Lebanon but did not identify or provide protective services to any trafficking victims in The Gambia; a government program continued to provide resources and financial support to 12 Koranic schools on the condition that their students were not forced to beg (2015)

GAZA STRIP

INTRODUCTION

Background: Inhabited since at least the 15th century B.C., Gaza has been dominated by many different peoples and empires throughout its history; it was incorporated into the Ottoman Empire in

the early 16th century. Gaza fell to British forces during World War I, becoming a part of the British Mandate of Palestine. Following the 1948 Arab-Israeli War, Egypt administered the newly formed Gaza Strip; it was captured by Israel in the Six-Day War in 1967. Under a series of agreements known as the Oslo accords signed between 1994 and 1999, Israel transferred to the newly-created Palestinian Authority (PA) security and civilian responsibility for many Palestinian-populated areas of the Gaza Strip as well as the West Bank. Negotiations to determine the permanent status of the West Bank and Gaza Strip stalled in 2001, after which the area witnessed a violent intifada or uprising.

In early 2003, the "Quartet" of the US, EU, UN, and Russia presented a roadmap to a final peace settlement by 2005, calling for two states. Following PA President Yasir ARAFAT's death in late 2004 and the subsequent election of Mahmud ABBAS (head of the Fatah political faction) as the PA president in 2005, Israel and the Palestinians agreed to move the peace process forward. Israel by late 2005 unilaterally withdrew all of its settlers and soldiers and dismantled its military

facilities in the Gaza Strip, but it continues to control the Gaza Strip's land and maritime borders and airspace. In early 2006, the Islamic Resistance Movement (HAMAS) won a majority in the Palestinian Legislative Council election. Attempts to form a unity government between Fatah and HAMAS failed and violent clashes between their respective supporters ensued, culminating in HAMAS's violent seizure of all military and governmental institutions in the Gaza Strip in June 2007. Since HAMAS's takeover, Israel and Egypt have enforced tight restrictions on movement and access of goods and individuals into and out of the territory. Fatah and HAMAS have since reached a series of agreements aimed at restoring political unity between the Gaza Strip and the West Bank but have struggled to implement them. In April 2014, the two factions signed an agreement and two months later President ABBAS formed an interim government of independent technocrats, none of whom were affiliated with HAMAS. The factions have since met periodically for further negotiations, but they continue to disagree over how to implement the deal and HAMAS remains in de facto control of the Gaza Strip.

In July 2014, HAMAS and other Gaza-based militant groups engaged in a 51-day conflict with Israel —the third conflict since HAMAS's takeover in 2007 —culminating in late August with an open-ended truce that continues to hold despite the absence of a negotiated cease-fire and occasional violations by both sides. Reconstruction efforts since the end of the conflict have been hampered by Israeli restrictions on goods entering the Gaza Strip and inadequate donor aid. The UN in 2015 published a study assessing that the Gaza Strip could become uninhabitable by 2020 absent a substantial easing on border restrictions. In an attempt to reenergize peace talks between the Israelis and Palestinians, France in June 2016 hosted a ministerial meeting that included participants from 29 countries, although not Israel or the Palestinians, to lay the groundwork for an envisioned "multilateral peace conference" later in the year.

GEOGRAPHY

Location: Middle East, bordering the Mediterranean Sea, between Egypt and Israel

Geographic coordinates: 31 25 N, 34 20 E

Map references: Middle East

Area: *total:* 360 sq km
land: 360 sq km
water: 0 sq km
country comparison to the world: 207

Area—comparative: slightly more than twice the size of Washington, DC

Land boundaries: *total:* 72 km
border countries (2): Egypt 13 km, Israel 59 km

Coastline: 40 km

Maritime claims: see entry for Israel
note: effective 3 January 2009, the Gaza maritime area is closed to all maritime traffic and is under blockade imposed by Israeli Navy until further notice

Climate: temperate, mild winters, dry and warm to hot summers

Terrain: flat to rolling, sand- and dune-covered coastal plain

Elevation: *mean elevation:* NA

elevation extremes: *lowest point:* Mediterranean Sea 0 m
highest point: Abu 'Awdah (Joz Abu 'Awdah) 105 m

Natural resources: arable land, natural gas
Irrigated land: 240 sq km; note—includes the West Bank (2012)

Population—distribution: population concentrated in major cities, particularly Gaza City in the north

Natural hazards: droughts

Environment—current issues: desertification; salination of fresh water; sewage treatment; waterborne disease; soil degradation; depletion and contamination of underground water resources

Geography—note: strategic strip of land along Mideast-North African trade routes has experienced an incredibly turbulent history; the town of Gaza itself has been besieged countless times in its history; there are no Israeli settlements in the Gaza Strip; the Gaza Strip settlements were evacuated in 2005 (2017)

PEOPLE AND SOCIETY

Population: 1,795,183 (July 2017 est.)
country comparison to the world: 151

Nationality: *noun:* NA
adjective: NA

Ethnic groups: Palestinian Arab

Languages: Arabic, Hebrew (spoken by many Palestinians), English (widely understood)

Religions: Muslim 98.0—99.0% (predominantly Sunni), Christian <1.0%, other, unaffiliated, unspecified <1.0% (2012 est.)
note: dismantlement of Israeli settlements was completed in September 2005; Gaza has had no Jewish population since then

Age structure: *0-14 years:* 44.78% (male 412,644/female 391,275)
15-24 years: 21.25% (male 192,292/female 189,166)
25-54 years: 28.02% (male 246,518/female 256,543)
55-64 years: 3.4% (male 31,961/female 29,119)
65 years and over: 2.54% (male 23,729/female 21,936) (2017 est.)

Dependency ratios: *total dependency ratio:* 75.8
youth dependency ratio: 70.5
elderly dependency ratio: 5.2
potential support ratio: 19.1
note: data represent Gaza Strip and the West Bank (2015 est.)

Median age: *total:* 17.2 years
male: 16.8 years
female: 17.5 years (2017 est.)
country comparison to the world: 224

Population growth rate: 2.33% (2017 est.)
country comparison to the world: 31

Birth rate: 31.4 births/1,000 population (2017 est.)
country comparison to the world: 34

Death rate: 3.1 deaths/1,000 population (2017 est.)
country comparison to the world: 222

Net migration rate: -5.1 migrant(s)/1,000 population (2017 est.)
country comparison to the world: 191

Population distribution: population concentrated in major cities, particularly Gaza City in the north

Urbanization: *urban population:* 75.7% of total population (2017)
rate of urbanization: 2.75% annual rate of change (2015-20 est.)
note: data represent Gaza Strip and the West Bank

Sex ratio: *at birth:* 1.06 male(s)/female
0-14 years: 1.05 male(s)/female
15-24 years: 1.01 male(s)/female
25-54 years: 0.96 male(s)/female

55-64 years: 1.1 male(s)/female
65 years and over: 0.71 male(s)/female
total population: 1.02 male(s)/female (2016 est.)

Maternal mortality ratio: 45 deaths/100,000 live births
note: data represent Gaza Strip and the West Bank (2015 est.)
country comparison to the world: 98

Infant mortality rate: *total:* 16.6 deaths/1,000 live births
male: 17.6 deaths/1,000 live births
female: 15.4 deaths/1,000 live births (2017 est.)
country comparison to the world: 97

Life expectancy at birth: *total population:* 74.2 years
male: 72.5 years
female: 75.9 years (2017 est.)
country comparison to the world: 124

Total fertility rate: 4.13 children born/woman (2017 est.)
country comparison to the world: 31

Contraceptive prevalence rate: 57.2% (includes Gaza Strip and West Bank) (2014)

Physicians density: 2.1 physicians/1,000 population (2013)

Hospital bed density: 1.4 beds/1,000 population (2014)

Drinking water source:
improved:
urban: 50.7% of population
rural: 81.5% of population
total: 58.4% of population
unimproved:
urban: 49.3% of population
rural: 18.5% of population
total: 41.6% of population
note: includes Gaza Strip and the West Bank (2015 est.)

Sanitation facility access:
improved:
urban: 93% of population
rural: 90.2% of population
total: 92.3% of population
unimproved:
urban: 7% of population
rural: 9.8% of population
total: 7.7% of population
note: includes Gaza Strip and the West Bank (2015 est.)

HIV/AIDS—adult prevalence rate: NA

HIV/AIDS—people living with HIV/AIDS: NA

HIV/AIDS—deaths: NA

Children under the age of 5 years underweight: 1.4%
note: estimate is for Gaza and the West Bank (2014)

Education expenditures: 1.3% of GDP
note: includes West Bank (2015)

Literacy: *definition:* age 15 and over can read and write
total population: 96.9%
male: 98.6%

female: 95.2%
note: estimates are for Gaza and the West Bank (2016 est.)

School life expectancy (primary to tertiary education): *total:* 13 years
male: 12 years
female: 14 years
note: data represent Gaza and the West Bank (2015)

Unemployment, youth ages 15-24: *total:* 40.7%
male: 36.4%
female: 60.8%
note: includes the West Bank (2015 est.)
country comparison to the world: 14

GOVERNMENT

Country name: *conventional long form:* none
conventional short form: Gaza Strip
local long form: none
local short form: Qita' Ghazzah
etymology: named for the largest city in the region, Gaza, whose settlement can be traced back to at least the 15th century B.C. (as "Ghazzat")

ECONOMY

Economy—overview: Israeli security measures and Israeli-Palestinian violence continue to degrade economic conditions in the Gaza Strip, the smaller of the two areas comprising the Palestinian territories. Israeli-imposed border controls became more restrictive after HAMAS seized control of the territory in June 2007, resulting in high unemployment, elevated poverty rates, and a sharp contraction of the private sector, which had relied primarily on export markets.

Since April 2017, the Palestinian Authority has reduced payments for electricity supplied to Gaza and cut salaries for its employees there, exacerbating already poor economic conditions. Since 2014, Egypt's ongoing crackdown on the Gaza Strip's extensive tunnel-based smuggling network has exacerbated fuel, construction material, and consumer goods shortages in the territory. Donor support for reconstruction, following the 51-day conflict in 2014 between Israel and HAMAS and other Gaza-based militant groups, has fallen short of post-conflict needs; only 53% of pledged aid had been delivered as of December, 2017.

GDP (purchasing power parity): see entry for the West Bank

GDP (official exchange rate): $2.938 billion (2014 est.)
note: excludes the West Bank

GDP—real growth rate: -15.2% (2014 est.)
5.6% (2013)
7% (2012)
note: excludes the West Bank
country comparison to the world: 223

GDP—per capita (PPP): see entry for the the West Bank

GDP—composition, by end use:
household consumption: 91.3%
government consumption: 26.7%

investment in fixed capital: 23%
investment in inventories: 0%
exports of goods and services: 20%
imports of goods and services: -61%
note: data exclude the West Bank (2017 est.)

GDP—composition, by sector of origin:
agriculture: 3%
industry: 21.1%
services: 62.5%
note: data exclude the West Bank (2017 est.)

Agriculture—products: olives, fruit, vegetables, flowers; beef, dairy products

Industries: textiles, food processing, furniture

Industrial production growth rate: 4%
note: see entry for the West Bank (2017 est.)
country comparison to the world: 66

Labor force: 1.24 million
note: excludes the West Bank (2017 est.)
country comparison to the world: 140

Labor force—by occupation: *agriculture:* 5.2%
industry: 10%
services: 84.8%
note: data exclude the West Bank (2015 est.)

Unemployment rate: 26.7% (2017 est.)
26.9% (2016 est.)
note: data exclude the West Bank
country comparison to the world: 196

Population below poverty line: 30%
note: data exclude the West Bank (2011 est.)

Budget: see entry for the West Bank (2017 est.)

Fiscal year: calendar year

Inflation rate (consumer prices): 0.8% (2017 est.)
-0.2% (2016 est.)
note: 2.9% excludes the West Bank
country comparison to the world: 31

Commercial bank prime lending rate: see entry for the West Bank

Stock of narrow money: see entry for the West Bank

Stock of broad money: $2.901 billion (31 December 2017 est.)
$2.538 billion (31 December 2016 est.)
country comparison to the world: 144

Stock of domestic credit: $2.041 billion (31 December 2017 est.)
$1.712 billion (31 December 2016 est.)
country comparison to the world: 152

Current account balance: -$1.444 billion (2017 est.)
-$1.348 billion (2016 est.)
note: excludes the West Bank
country comparison to the world: 142

Exports: $1.955 billion (2017 est.)
$1.827 billion (2016 est.)
country comparison to the world: 142

Exports—commodities: strawberries, carnations, vegetables, fish (small and irregular shipments, as permitted to transit the Israeli-controlled Kerem Shalom crossing)

Imports: see entry for the West Bank

Imports—commodities: food, consumer goods, fuel

Reserves of foreign exchange and gold: $312.8 million (31 December 2016 est.)
$583 million (31 December 2015 est.)
country comparison to the world: 153

Debt—external: see entry for the West Bank

Exchange rates: see entry for the West Bank

ENERGY

Electricity access: *population without electricity:* 80,930
electrification—*total population:* 98%
electrification—urban areas: 99%
electrification—rural areas: 93%
note: data for Gaza Strip and West Bank combined (2012)

Electricity—production: 51,000 kWh (2011 est.)
country comparison to the world: 219

Electricity—consumption: 202,000 kWh (2009)
country comparison to the world: 216

Electricity—exports: 0 kWh (2011 est.)
country comparison to the world: 147

Electricity—imports: 193,000 kWh (2011 est.)
country comparison to the world: 115

Crude oil—proved reserves: 0 bbl (1 January 2010 es)
country comparison to the world: 138

COMMUNICATIONS

Telephones—fixed lines: 406,500 (includes the West Bank) (July 2016 est.)

Telephones—mobile cellular: *total:* 3,531,000 (includes the West Bank)
subscriptions per 100 inhabitants: 76 (includes the West Bank) (July 2016 est.)

Telephone system: *general assessment:* Israel has final say in allocating frequencies in the Gaza Strip and does not permit anything beyond a 2G network
domestic: Israeli company BEZEK and the Palestinian company PALTEL are responsible for fixed-line services; the Palestinian JAWWAL company provides cellular services; a slow 2G network allows calls and limited data transmission
international: country code—970 (2018)

Broadcast media: 1 TV station and about 10 radio stations; satellite TV accessible (2008)

Internet country code: .ps; *note*—same as the West Bank
Internet users: total: 2.673 million (includes the West Bank)

percent of population: 57.4% (includes the West Bank) (July 2016 est.)

TRANSPORTATION

Airports: 1 (2013)
country comparison to the world: 219

Airports—with paved runways: *total:* 1
over 3,047 m: 1 (2017)

Heliports: 1 (2013)

Roadways: note: see entry for the West Bank

Merchant marine: total: by type: (2017) country comparison to the world: 68

Ports and terminals: *major seaport(s):* Gaza

MILITARY AND SECURITY

Military branches: HAMAS does not have a conventional military in the Gaza Strip but maintains security forces in addition to its military wing, the 'Izz al-Din al-Qassam Brigades; the military wing reports to the Hamas Political Bureau leadership, which remains scattered throughout the region since relocating from its Damascus headquarters in early 2012 (2015)

TERRORISM

Terrorist groups—home based: *Army of Islam (AOI): aim(s):* stage attacks against Israel and Egypt from the Gaza Strip and, ultimately, establish an Islamic emirate in the region

area(s) of operation: headquartered in Gaza; heaviest presence and operational activity is in the Gaza Strip, from where operatives have a history of launching low-impact rockets into Israeli and Egyptian territory; kidnapped and subsequently released an American and New Zealander in Gaza working as Fox News journalists in 2006 and kidnapped and subsequently released a British journalist in 2007; rocket attacks have ebbed in recent years; most of the group's kidnappings are either for ransom or to negotiate with HAMAS to release AOI members from incarceration; membership was estimated in 2017 to number in the low hundreds; note—the Army of Islam (Jaish al-Islam, JAI) in Syria under Zahran ALLOUSH is unrelated to AOI

HAMAS: *aim(s):* bolster its staging capabilities in the Gaza Strip against Israel with the intent to lift Israel's blockade surrounding the Gaza Strip and, ultimately, destroy the state of Israel

area(s) of operation: headquartered in Gaza, where in 2006 HAMAS won the Palestinian legislative Council election in the Gaza Strip and took control of the ruling Palestinian Authority Government; Yahya al-SINWAR was elected in February 2017 in an internal election to head the Gaza Political Bureau; al-SINWAR leads with his deputy, Khalil al-HAYYA; HAMAS has an official political bureau in Qatar; launches rockets frequently into Israel from the Gaza Strip, which has resulted in numerous long-running lethal conflicts between HAMAS and Israeli forces; has dug numerous underground tunnels leading into Israel;

uses its primary media outlet, Al-Aqsa TV, to indoctrinate children in the Gaza Strip to become armed fighters and suicide bombers upon reaching adulthood

Mujahidin Shura Council in the Environs of Jerusalem (MSC): *aim(s):* bolster its staging capabilities in the Gaza Strip against Israel and, ultimately, destroy the state of Israel

area(s) of operation: headquartered in Gaza; although present in Egypt, Libya, Syria, and Israel, MSC was assessed in 2017 to be largely defunct; had previously conducted numerous rocket attacks on Israeli territory; majority of veteran members have defected to join other armed groups

Palestinian Islamic Jihad (PIJ): *aim(s):* enhance its staging capabilities in the Gaza Strip to launch attacks inside Israel to destroy it; create an Islamic state in all of historic Palestine, as defined by the British Mandate, which includes the Gaza Strip

area(s) of operation: stages rocket attacks against civilians and military personnel primarily in southern Israel; Akram AJURI is the supreme commander over the al-Quds Brigades, PIJ's armed wing; assessed in 2017 to have less than 5,000 members based in the Gaza Strip

Palestine Liberation Front (PLF): *aim(s):* bolster its staging capabilities in the Gaza Strip against Israel and, ultimately, destroy the state of Israel in order to establish a secular, Marxist Palestinian state with Jerusalem as its capital

area(s) of operation: based in Gaza; maintains a recruitment and limited paramilitary training presence in most of the refugee camps across the Gaza Strip; assessed in 2015 to have fewer than 500 members

Popular Front for the Liberation of Palestine (PFLP): *aim(s):* destroy the state of Israel and, ultimately, establish a secular, Marxist Palestinian state

area(s) of operation: headquartered in Gaza, recruiting and training fighters; stages limited attacks against Israel

PFLP-General Command (PFLP-GC): *aim(s):* bolster its staging capabilities to prepare fighters for deployment to Syria and to launch occasional attacks inside Israel; ultimately, seeks to establish a Palestinian state

area(s) of operation: headquartered in Gaza; as a longtime supporter of the Syrian Government, the group trains and deploys fighters to Syria to fight on behalf of President Bashar al-ASAD; provides training for pay to other armed groups, including HAMAS; stages occasional small-scale attacks inside Israel

Terrorist groups—foreign based: *Abdallah Azzam Brigades (AAB): aim(s):* bolster its staging capabilities in the Gaza Strip against Israel to continue its attempts to disrupt Israel's economy and its efforts to establish security

area(s) of operation: launches homemade rockets from the Gaza Strip into populated Israeli territory, primarily Nahariya and Ashkelon; operates as the Marwan Haddad Division

Al-Aqsa Martyrs Brigade (AAMB): *aim(s):* bolster its staging capabilities in the Gaza Strip against Israel and, ultimately, establish a Palestinian state comprising the West Bank, Gaza Strip, and Jerusalem

area(s) of operation: stages attacks in the Gaza Strip against Israeli soldiers and civilians inside Israel, including launching rockets and missiles into Israel; claimed in 2015 to have fired more than 500 rockets and missiles into Israel during Operation Pillar of Defense, the week-long Israeli Defense Force operation in Gaza; former leader Zaki al-SAKANI was released in late 2016 from HAMAS's custody in the Gaza Strip, where he had been held since 2008, only on the condition that he leave the Gaza Strip; since al-SAKANI's imprisonment, AAMB has operated under a decentralized power structure, with each cell reporting to a local leader

ISIL Sinai Province (formerly Ansar Bayt al-Maqdis): *aim(s):* bolster its staging capabilities in the Gaza Strip against Israel and, ultimately, establish a regional Islamic caliphate

area(s) of operation: stages attacks against Egyptian forces along the Gaza Strip-Egypt border and launches rockets into southern Israel from the border closest to Israel; moves fighters and supplies through underground tunnels that connect the Gaza Strip and Sinai Peninsula

TRANSNATIONAL ISSUES

Disputes—international: the status of the Gaza Strip is a final status issue to be resolved through negotiations; Israel removed settlers and military personnel from Gaza Strip in September 2005

Refugees and internally displaced persons: *refugees (country of origin):* 1,348,536 (Palestinian refugees) (2017)

IDPs: 193,000 (includes persons displaced within the Gaza Strip due to the intensification of the Israeli-Palestinian conflict since June 2014 and other Palestinian IDPs in the Gaza Strip and West Bank who fled as long ago as 1967, although confirmed cumulative data do not go back beyond 2006) (2016)

GEORGIA

INTRODUCTION

Background: The region of present day Georgia contained the ancient kingdoms of Colchis and Kartli-Iberia. The area came under Roman influence in the first centuries A.D., and Christianity became the state religion in the 330s. Domination by Persians, Arabs, and Turks was followed by a Georgian golden age (11th-13th centuries) that was cut short by the Mongol invasion of 1236. Subsequently, the Ottoman and Persian empires competed for influence in the region. Georgia was absorbed into the Russian Empire in the 19th century. Independent for three years (1918-1921) following the Russian revolution, it was forcibly incorporated into the USSR in 1921 and regained its independence when the Soviet Union dissolved in 1991.

Mounting public discontent over rampant corruption and ineffective government services, followed by an attempt by the incumbent Georgian Government to manipulate parliamentary elections in November 2003, touched off widespread protests that led to the resignation of Eduard SHEVARDNADZE, president since 1995. In the aftermath of that popular movement, which became known as the "Rose Revolution," new elections in early 2004 swept Mikheil SAAKASHVILI into power along with his United National Movement (UNM) party. Progress on market reforms and democratization has been made in the years since independence, but this progress has been complicated by Russian assistance and support to the separatist regions of Abkhazia and South Ossetia. Periodic flare-ups in tension and violence culminated in a five-day conflict in August 2008 between Russia and Georgia, including the invasion of large portions of undisputed Georgian territory. Russian troops pledged to pull back from most occupied Georgian territory, but in late August 2008 Russia unilaterally recognized the independence of Abkhazia and South Ossetia, and Russian military forces remain in those regions.

Billionaire philanthropist Bidzina IVANISH-VILI's unexpected entry into politics in October 2011 brought the divided opposition together under his Georgian Dream coalition, which won a majority of seats in the October 2012 parliamentary elections and removed UNM from power. Conceding defeat, SAAKASHVILI named IVANISHVILI as prime minister and allowed Georgian Dream to create a new government.

Giorgi MARGVELASHVILI was inaugurated as president on 17 November 2013, ending a tense year of power-sharing between SAAKASHVILI and IVANISHVILI. IVANISHVILI voluntarily resigned from office after the presidential succession, and Georgia's legislature on 20 November 2013 confirmed Irakli GARIBASHVILI as his replacement. GARIBASHVILI was replaced by Giorgi KVIRIKASHVILI in December 2015. KVIRIKASHVILI remained Prime Minister following Georgian Dream's success in the October 2016 parliamentary elections, where the party won a constitutional majority. These changes in leadership represent unique examples of a former Soviet state that emerged to conduct democratic and peaceful government transitions of power. Popular and government support for integration with the West is high in Georgia. Joining the EU and NATO are among the country's top foreign policy goals.

GEOGRAPHY

Location: Southwestern Asia, bordering the Black Sea, between Turkey and Russia, with a sliver of land north of the Caucasus extending into Europe; note—Georgia views itself as part of Europe; geopolitically, it can be classified as falling within Europe, the Middle East, or both

Geographic coordinates: 42 00 N, 43 30 E

Map references: Asia

Area: *total:* 69,700 sq km
land: 69,700 sq km
water: 0 sq km
note: approximately 12,560 sq km, or about 18% of Georgia's area, is Russian occupied; the seized area includes all of Abkhazia and the breakaway region of South Ossetia, which consists of the northern part of Shida Kartli, eastern slivers of the Imereti region and Racha-Lechkhumi and Kvemo Svaneti, and part of western Mtskheta-Mtianeti
country comparison to the world: 122

Area—comparative: slightly smaller than South Carolina; slightly larger than West Virginia

Land boundaries: *total:* 1,814 km
border countries (4): Armenia 219 km, Azerbaijan 428 km, Russia 894 km, Turkey 273 km

Coastline: 310 km

Maritime claims: *territorial sea:* 12 nm
exclusive economic zone: 200 nm

Climate: warm and pleasant; Mediterranean-like on Black Sea coast

Terrain: largely mountainous with Great Caucasus Mountains in the north and Lesser Caucasus Mountains in the south; Kolkhet'is Dablobi (Kolkhida Lowland) opens to the Black Sea in the west; Mtkvari River Basin in the east; fertile soils in river valley flood plains and foothills of Kolkhida Lowland

Elevation: *mean elevation:* 1,432 m

elevation extremes: *lowest point:* Black Sea 0 m
highest point: Mt'a Shkhara 5,193 m

Natural resources: timber, hydropower, manganese deposits, iron ore, copper, minor coal and oil deposits; coastal climate and soils allow for important tea and citrus growth

Land use: *agricultural land:* 35.5%
arable land: 5.8%;
permanent crops: 1.8%;
permanent pasture: 27.9%
forest: 39.4%
other: 25.1% (2011 est.)
Irrigated land: 4,330 sq km (2012)

Population—distribution: settlement coincides closely to the central valley, with emphasis on the capital city of Tbilisi in the east; smaller urban agglomerations dot the Black Sea coast, with Bat'umi being the largest

Natural hazards: earthquakes

Environment—current issues: air pollution, particularly in Rust'avi; heavy pollution of Mtkvari River and the Black Sea; inadequate supplies of potable water; soil pollution from toxic chemicals

Environment—international agreements: *party to:* Air Pollution, Biodiversity, Climate Change, Climate Change-Kyoto Protocol, Desertification, Endangered Species, Hazardous Wastes, Law of the Sea, Ozone Layer Protection, Ship Pollution, Wetlands
signed, but not ratified: none of the selected agreements

Geography—note: strategically located east of the Black Sea; Georgia controls much of the Caucasus Mountains and the routes through them; Krubera Cave in the western part of the country is the deepest-known cave in the world; at -2,197 m it is the only known cave on earth deeper than 2,000 m

PEOPLE AND SOCIETY

Population: 4,926,330 (July 2017 est.)
country comparison to the world: 124

Nationality: *noun:* Georgian(s)
adjective: Georgian

Ethnic groups: Georgian 86.8%, Azeri 6.3%, Armenian 4.5%, other 2.3% (includes Russian, Ossetian, Yazidi, Ukrainian, Kist, Greek) (2014 est.)

Languages: Georgian (official) 87.6%, Azeri 6.2%, Armenian 3.9%, Russian 1.2%, other 1% *note:* Abkhaz is the official language in Abkhazia (2014 est.)

Religions: Orthodox (official) 83.4%, Muslim 10.7%, Armenian Apostolic 2.9%, other 1.2% (includes Catholic, Jehovah's Witness, Yazidi, Protestant, Jewish), none 0.5%, unspecified/no answer 1.2% (2014 est.)

Age structure: *0-14 years:* 18.08% (male 466,426/ female 424,295)

15-24 years: 11.94% (male 310,970/female 277,434)

25-54 years: 40.96% (male 983,144/female 1,034,794)

55-64 years: 13.01% (male 286,539/female 354,247)

65 years and over: 16.01% (male 309,353/female 479,128) (2017 est.)

Dependency ratios: *total dependency ratio:* 50
youth dependency ratio: 28.1
elderly dependency ratio: 21.9
potential support ratio: 4.6 (2015 est.)

Median age: *total:* 38.1 years
male: 35.3 years
female: 40.9 years (2017 est.)
country comparison to the world: 61

Population growth rate: -0.02% (2017 est.)
country comparison to the world: 198

Birth rate: 12.3 births/1,000 population (2017 est.)
country comparison to the world: 162

Death rate: 10.9 deaths/1,000 population (2017 est.)
country comparison to the world: 30

Net migration rate: -1.6 migrant(s)/1,000 population (2017 est.)
country comparison to the world: 150

Population distribution: settlement coincides closely to the central valley, with emphasis on the capital city of Tbilisi in the east; smaller urban agglomerations dot the Black Sea coast, with Bat'umi being the largest

Urbanization: *urban population:* 54% of total population (2017)
rate of urbanization: -0.09% annual rate of change (2015-20 est.)
note: data include Abkhazia and South Ossetia

Major urban areas—population: TBILISI (capital) 1.147 million (2015)

Sex ratio: *at birth:* 1.08 male(s)/female
0-14 years: 1.11 male(s)/female
15-24 years: 1.11 male(s)/female
25-54 years: 0.95 male(s)/female
55-64 years: 0.81 male(s)/female
65 years and over: 0.64 male(s)/female
total population: 0.92 male(s)/female (2016 est.)

Mother's mean age at first birth: 24.5 years
note: data do not cover Abkhazia and South Ossetia (2014 est.)

Maternal mortality ratio: 36 deaths/100,000 live births (2015 est.)
country comparison to the world: 108

Infant mortality rate: *total:* 15.2 deaths/1,000 live births
male: 17.3 deaths/1,000 live births
female: 12.9 deaths/1,000 live births (2017 est.)
country comparison to the world: 100

Life expectancy at birth: *total population:* 76.4 years
male: 72.3 years
female: 80.7 years (2017 est.)
country comparison to the world: 86

Total fertility rate: 1.76 children born/woman (2017 est.)
country comparison to the world: 158

Contraceptive prevalence rate: 53.4%
note: percent of women aged 15-44 (2010)
Health expenditures: 7.4% of GDP (2014)
country comparison to the world: 69

Physicians density: 4.78 physicians/1,000 population (2014)

Hospital bed density: 2.6 beds/1,000 population (2012)

Drinking water source:
improved:
urban: 100% of population
rural: 100% of population
total: 100% of population
unimproved:
urban: 0% of population
rural: 0% of population
total: 0% of population (2015 est.)

Sanitation facility access:
improved:
urban: 95.2% of population
rural: 75.9% of population
total: 86.3% of population
unimproved:
urban: 4.8% of population
rural: 24.1% of population
total: 13.7% of population (2015 est.)

HIV/AIDS—adult prevalence rate: 0.5% (2016 est.)
country comparison to the world: 61

HIV/AIDS—people living with HIV/AIDS: 12,000 (2016 est.)
country comparison to the world: 89

HIV/AIDS—deaths: <500 (2016 est.)

Obesity—adult prevalence rate: 21.7% (2016)
country comparison to the world: 86

Children under the age of 5 years underweight: 1.1% (2009)
country comparison to the world: 131

Education expenditures: 2% of GDP (2012)
country comparison to the world: 167

Literacy: *definition:* age 15 and over can read and write
total population: 99.8%
male: 99.8%
female: 99.7% (2015 est.)

School life expectancy (primary to tertiary education): *total:* 15 years
male: 15 years
female: 16 years (2015)

Unemployment, youth ages 15-24: *total:* 35.6%
male: 28.6%
female: 30.8% (2015 est.)
country comparison to the world: 23

GOVERNMENT

Country name: *conventional long form:* none
conventional short form: Georgia
local long form: none
local short form: Sak'art'velo

former: Georgian Soviet Socialist Republic
etymology: the Western name may derive from the Persian designation "gurgan" meaning "Land of the Wolves"; the native name "Sak'art'velo" means "Land of the Kartvelians" and refers to the core central Georgian region of Kartli

Government type: semi-presidential republic

Capital: *name:* Tbilisi

geographic coordinates: 41 41 N, 44 50 E
time difference: UTC+4 (9 hours ahead of Washington, DC, during Standard Time)

Administrative divisions: 9 regions (mkharebi, singular—mkhare), 1 city (kalaki), and 2 autonomous republics (avtomnoy respubliki, singular—avtom respublika)
regions: Guria, Imereti, Kakheti, Kvemo Kartli, Mtskheta Mtianeti, Racha-Lechkhumi and Kvemo Svaneti, Samegrelo and Zemo Svaneti, Samtskhe-Javakheti, Shida Kartli; note—the breakaway region of South Ossetia consists of the northern part of Shida Kartli, eastern slivers of the Imereti region and Racha-Lechkhumi and Kvemo Svaneti, and part of western Mtskheta-Mtianeti
city: Tbilisi
autonomous republics: Abkhazia or Ap'khazet'is Avtonomiuri Respublika (Sokhumi), Ajaria or Acharis Avtonomiuri Respublika (Bat'umi)
note 1: the administrative centers of the two autonomous republics are shown in parentheses
note 2: the United States recognizes the breakaway regions of Abkhazia and South Ossetia to be part of Georgia

Independence: 9 April 1991 (from the Soviet Union); notable earlier date: A.D. 1008 (Georgia unified under King BAGRAT III)

National holiday: Independence Day, 26 May (1918); note—26 May 1918 was the date of independence from Soviet Russia, 9 April 1991 was the date of independence from the Soviet Union

Constitution: history: previous 1921, 1978 (based on 1977 Soviet Union constitution); latest approved 24 August 1995, effective 17 October 1995
amendments: proposed as a draft law supported by more than one-half of the Parliament membership or by petition of at least 200,000 voters; passage requires support by at least three-fourths of the Parliament membership in two successive sessions three months apart and the signature and promulgation by the president of Georgia; amended several times, last in 2017 (2018)

Legal system: civil law system

International law organization participation: accepts compulsory ICJ jurisdiction; accepts ICCt jurisdiction

Citizenship: *citizenship by birth:* no
citizenship by descent only: at least one parent must be a citizen of Georgia
dual citizenship recognized: no
residency requirement for naturalization: 10 years

Suffrage: 18 years of age; universal

353

Executive branch: *chief of state:* President Giorgi MARGVELASHVILI (since 17 November 2013)

head of government: Prime Minister Giorgi KVIRIKASHVILI (since 30 December 2015); First Deputy Prime Minister Dimitry KUMSISHVILI

cabinet: Cabinet of Ministers

elections/appointments: president directly elected by absolute majority popular vote in 2 rounds if needed for a 5-year term (eligible for a second term); election last held on 27 October 2013 (next to be held in October 2018); prime minister nominated by Parliament, appointed by the president

election results: Giorgi MARGVELASHVILI elected president in first round; percent of vote—Giorgi MARGVELASHVILI (independent), 62.1%, Davit BAKRADZE (UNM) 21.7%, Nino BURJANADZE 10.2%, other 6%

Legislative branch: description: unicameral Parliament or Sakartvelos Parlamenti (150 seats; 77 members directly elected in a single nationwide constituency by proportional representation vote and 73 directly elected in single-seat constituencies by simple majority vote; members serve 4-year terms)

elections: last held on 8 October and 30 October 2016 (next to be held in 2020)

election results: percent of vote by party—Georgian Dream 48.7%, UNM 27.1%, Alliance of Patriots 5%, other 19.2%; seats by party—Georgian Dream 115, UNM 27, Alliance of Patriots 6, IWSG 1, independent 1; note—European Georgia split from UNM in January 2017 taking 20 of 27 parliamentary members

Judicial branch: *highest court(s):* Supreme Court (organized into several specialized judicial chambers; number of judges determined by the president of Georgia); Constitutional Court (consists of 9 judges); note—the Abkhazian and Ajarian Autonomous republics each have a supreme court and a hierarchy of lower courts

judge selection and term of office: Supreme Court judges nominated by the president and appointed by the Parliament; judges serve not less than 10-year terms; Constitutional Court judges appointed by the president following candidate selection by the Justice Council of Georgia, a 12-member consultative body of high-level judges and presidential and parliamentary appointees; judges appointed for 10-year terms

subordinate courts: Courts of Appeal; regional (town) and district courts

Political parties and leaders: Alliance of Patriots [Irma INASHVILI]

European Georgia [Davit BAKRADZE] (split from UNM)

Georgian Dream-Democratic Georgia [Giorgi KVIRIKASHVILI]

Industry Will Save Georgia (Industrialists) or IWSG [Giorgi TOPADZE]

National Forum [Kakhaber SHARTAVA]

Free Democrats or FD [Shalva SHAVGULIDZE]

Republican Party [Khatuna SAMNIDZE]

State for the People Party [formerly Paata BUR-CHULADZE]

United Democratic Movement [Nino BURJANADZE]

United National Movement or UNM [Nika MELIA]

Political pressure groups and leaders: *other:* separatists in the Russian-occupied regions of Abkhazia and South Ossetia

International organization participation: ADB, BSEC, CD, CE, CPLP (associate), EAPC, EBRD, FAO, G-11, GCTU, GUAM, IAEA, IBRD, ICAO, ICC (national committees), ICCt, ICRM, IDA, IFAD, IFC, IFRCS, ILO, IMF, IMO, Interpol, IOC, IOM, IPU, ISO (correspondent), ITSO, ITU, ITUC (NGOs), MIGA, OAS (observer), OIF (observer), OPCW, OSCE, PFP, SELEC (observer), UN, UNCTAD, UNESCO, UNIDO, UNWTO, UPU, WCO, WHO, WIPO, WMO, WTO

Diplomatic representation in the US: *chief of mission:* Ambassador David BAKRADZE (since 18 January 2017)

chancery: 1824 R Street NW, Washington, DC 20009

telephone: [1] (202) 387-2390

FAX: [1] (202) 387-0864

consulate(s) general: New York

Diplomatic representation from the US: *chief of mission:* Ambassador Ian C. KELLY (since 17 September 2015)

embassy: 11 George Balanchine Street, T'bilisi 0131

mailing address: 7060 T'bilisi Place, Washington, DC 20521-7060

telephone: [995] (32) 227-70-00

FAX: [995] (32) 253-23-10

Flag description: white rectangle with a central red cross extending to all four sides of the flag; each of the four quadrants displays a small red bolnur-katskhuri cross; sometimes referred to as the Five-Cross Flag; although adopted as the official Georgian flag in 2004, the five-cross design appears to date back to the 14th century

National symbol(s): Saint George, lion; national colors: red, white

National anthem: name: "Tavisupleba" (Liberty)

lyrics/music: Davit MAGRADSE/Zakaria PALIASHVILI (adapted by Joseb KETSCHAKMADSE)

note: adopted 2004; after the Rose Revolution, a new anthem with music based on the operas "Abesalom da Eteri" and "Daisi" was adopted

ECONOMY

Economy—overview: Georgia's main economic activities include cultivation of agricultural products such as grapes, citrus fruits, and hazelnuts; mining of manganese, copper, and gold; and producing alcoholic and nonalcoholic beverages, metals, machinery, and chemicals in small-scale industries. The country imports nearly all of its needed supplies of natural gas and oil products. It has sizeable hydropower capacity that now provides most of its electricity needs.

Georgia has overcome the chronic energy shortages and gas supply interruptions of the past by renovating hydropower plants and by increasingly relying on natural gas imports from Azerbaijan instead of from Russia. Construction of the Baku-Tbilisi-Ceyhan oil pipeline, the South Caucasus gas pipeline, and the Baku-Tbilisi-Kars railroad are part of a strategy to capitalize on Georgia's strategic location between Europe and Asia and develop its role as a transit hub for gas, oil, and other goods.

Georgia's economy sustained GDP growth of more than 10% in 2006-07, based on strong inflows of foreign investment and robust government spending. However, GDP growth slowed following the August 2008 conflict with Russia, and sunk to negative 4% in 2009 as foreign direct investment and workers' remittances declined in the wake of the global financial crisis. The economy rebounded in the period 2010-17, but FDI inflows, the engine of Georgian economic growth prior to the 2008 conflict, have not recovered fully. Unemployment remains persistently high.

The country is pinning its hopes for faster growth on a continued effort to build up infrastructure, enhance support for entrepreneurship, simplify regulations, and improve professional education, in order to attract foreign investment and boost employment, with a focus on transportation projects, hydropower, agriculture, and tourism. Georgia has historically suffered from a chronic failure to collect tax revenues; however, since 2004 the government has simplified the tax code, increased tax enforcement, and cracked down on petty corruption, leading to higher revenues. The government has received high marks from the World Bank for improvements in business transparency. Since 2012, the Georgian Dream-led government has continued the previous administration's low-regulation, low-tax, free market policies, while modestly increasing social spending, strengthening anti-trust policy, and amending the labor code to comply with International Labor Standards. In mid-2014, Georgia concluded an association agreement with the EU, paving the way to free trade and visa-free travel. In 2017, Georgia signed Free Trade Agreement (FTA) with China as part of Tbilisi's efforts to diversify its economic ties. Georgia is seeking to develop its Black Sea ports to further facilitate East-West trade.

GDP (purchasing power parity): $39.32 billion (2017 est.)

$37.82 billion (2016 est.)

$36.81 billion (2015 est.)

note: data are in 2017 dollars

country comparison to the world: 121

GDP (official exchange rate): $15.23 billion (2016 est.)

GDP—real growth rate: 4% (2017 est.)

2.7% (2016 est.)

2.9% (2015 est.)

country comparison to the world: 65

GDP—per capita (PPP): $10,600 (2017 est.)

$10,200 (2016 est.)

$9,900 (2015 est.)

note: data are in 2017 dollars
country comparison to the world: 137

Gross national saving: 21.8% of GDP (2017 est.)
19.1% of GDP (2016 est.)
20.1% of GDP (2015 est.)
country comparison to the world: 77

GDP—composition, by end use:
household consumption: 63.4%
government consumption: 18.6%
investment in fixed capital: 29.7%
investment in inventories: 3.4%
exports of goods and services: 52.5%
imports of goods and services: -67.6% (2017 est.)

GDP—composition, by sector of origin:
agriculture: 9.6%
industry: 23.4%
services: 66.2% (2017 est.)

Agriculture—products: citrus, grapes, tea, hazelnuts, vegetables; livestock

Industries: steel, machine tools, electrical appliances, mining (manganese, copper, gold), chemicals, wood products, wine

Industrial production growth rate: 7% (2017 est.)
country comparison to the world: 27

Labor force: 1.998 million (2016 est.)
country comparison to the world: 125

Labor force—by occupation: *agriculture:* 55.6%
industry: 8.9%
services: 35.5% (2006 est.)

Unemployment rate: 11.5% (2017 est.)
11.8% (2016 est.)
country comparison to the world: 147

Population below poverty line: 9.2% (2010 est.)

Household income or consumption by percentage share: *lowest 10%:* 2%
highest 10%: 31.3% (2008)

Distribution of family income—Gini index: 40.1 (2014)
46 (2011)
country comparison to the world: 62

Budget: *revenues:* $4.26 billion
expenditures: $4.852 billion (2017 est.)
Taxes and other revenues: 28% of GDP (2017 est.)
country comparison to the world: 96

Budget surplus (+) or deficit (-): -3.9% of GDP (2017 est.)
country comparison to the world: 142

Public debt: 44.2% of GDP (2017 est.)
44.5% of GDP (2016 est.)
note: data cover general government debt, and includes debt instruments issued (or owned) by government entities other than the treasury; the data include treasury debt held by foreign entities; the data include debt issued by subnational entities; Georgia does not maintain intra-governmental debt or social funds
country comparison to the world: 119

Fiscal year: calendar year

Inflation rate (consumer prices): 6% (2017 est.)
2.1% (2016 est.)
country comparison to the world: 184

Central bank discount rate: 6.5% (7 Setpember 2016)
7% (23 September 2015)
note: this is the Refinancing Rate, the key monetary policy rate of the National Bank of Georgia
country comparison to the world: 57

Commercial bank prime lending rate: 11.5% (31 December 2017 est.)
12.62% (31 December 2016 est.)
country comparison to the world: 72

Stock of narrow money: $2.203 billion (31 December 2017 est.)
$2.389 billion (31 December 2016 est.)
country comparison to the world: 129

Stock of broad money: $2.419 billion (31 December 2017 est.)
$2.454 billion (31 December 2016 est.)
country comparison to the world: 148

Stock of domestic credit: $7.179 billion (31 December 2017 est.)
$7.753 billion (31 December 2016 est.)
country comparison to the world: 113

Market value of publicly traded shares: $1.155 billion (31 December 2015 est.)
$943.4 million (31 December 2012 est.)
$795.7 million (31 December 2011 est.)
country comparison to the world: 105

Current account balance: -$1.811 billion (2017 est.)
-$1.91 billion (2016 est.)
country comparison to the world: 154

Exports: $3.533 billion (2017 est.)
$2.831 billion (2016 est.)
country comparison to the world: 121

Exports—commodities: vehicles, ferro-alloys, fertilizers, nuts, scrap metal, gold, copper ores

Exports—partners: Russia 9.8%, Turkey 8.2%, China 8.1%, Bulgaria 7.3%, Azerbaijan 7.3%, Armenia 7.2%, Germany 4.1% (2016)

Imports: $7.846 billion (2017 est.)
$6.64 billion (2016 est.)
country comparison to the world: 108

Imports—commodities: fuels, vehicles, machinery and parts, grain and other foods, pharmaceuticals

Imports—partners: Canada 18.6%, Turkey 14%, Russia 7%, Ireland 6.5%, China 5.7%, Azerbaijan 5.1%, Germany 4.4%, Ukraine 4.3% (2016)

Reserves of foreign exchange and gold: $2.945 billion (31 December 2017 est.)
$2.756 billion (31 December 2016 est.)
country comparison to the world: 108

Debt—external: $14.15 billion (31 December 2017 est.)
$14.08 billion (31 December 2016 est.)
country comparison to the world: 105

Stock of direct foreign investment—at home: $16.2 billion (31 December 2017 est.)
$14.66 billion (31 December 2016 est.)
country comparison to the world: 87

Stock of direct foreign investment—abroad: $2.505 billion (31 December 2017 est.)
$2.185 billion (31 December 2016 est.)

country comparison to the world: 79

Exchange rates: laris (GEL) per US dollar—
2.535 (2017 est.)
2.3668 (2016 est.)
2.3668 (2015 est.)
2.2694 (2014 est.)
1.7657 (2013 est.)

ENERGY

Electricity access: electrification—*total population:* 100% (2016)

Electricity—production: 11.57 billion kWh (2016 est.)
country comparison to the world: 94

Electricity—consumption: 12.44 billion kWh (2016 est.)
country comparison to the world: 86

Electricity—exports: 560 million kWh (2016 est.)
country comparison to the world: 64

Electricity—imports: 478.9 million kWh (2016 est.)
country comparison to the world: 81

Electricity—installed generating capacity: 4.28 million kW (2015 est.)
country comparison to the world: 84

Electricity—from fossil fuels: 36.2% of total installed capacity (2015 est.)
country comparison to the world: 173

Electricity—from nuclear fuels: 0% of total installed capacity (2015 est.)
country comparison to the world: 96

Electricity—from hydroelectric plants: 63.8% of total installed capacity (2015 est.)
country comparison to the world: 24

Electricity—from other renewable sources: 0% of total installed capacity (2015 est.)
country comparison to the world: 183

Crude oil—production: 400 bbl/day (2016 est.)
country comparison to the world: 94

Crude oil—exports: 1,002 bbl/day (2014 est.)
country comparison to the world: 73

Crude oil—imports: 200 bbl/day (2014 est.)
country comparison to the world: 81

Crude oil—proved reserves: 35 million bbl (1 January 2017 es)
country comparison to the world: 83

Refined petroleum products—production: 0 bbl/day (2014 est.)
country comparison to the world: 148

Refined petroleum products—consumption: 23,000 bbl/day (2015 est.)
country comparison to the world: 135

Refined petroleum products—exports: 283.1 bbl/day (2014 est.)
country comparison to the world: 116

Refined petroleum products—imports: 23,910 bbl/day (2014 est.)
country comparison to the world: 111

Natural gas—production: 10 million cu m (2015 est.)
country comparison to the world: 95

Natural gas—consumption: 2.18 billion cu m (2015 est.)
country comparison to the world: 86

Natural gas—exports: 0 cu m (2013 est.)
country comparison to the world: 109

Natural gas—imports: 1.26 billion cu m (2015 est.)
country comparison to the world: 57

Natural gas—proved reserves: 8.495 billion cu m (1 January 2017 es)
country comparison to the world: 86

Carbon dioxide emissions from consumption of energy: 7 million Mt (2013 est.)
country comparison to the world: 118

COMMUNICATIONS

Telephones—fixed lines: *total subscriptions:* 831,346
subscriptions per 100 inhabitants: 17 (July 2016 est.)
country comparison to the world: 73

Telephones—mobile cellular: *total:* 5,532,701
subscriptions per 100 inhabitants: 112 (July 2016 est.)
country comparison to the world: 114

Telephone system: *general assessment:* fixed-line telecommunications network has limited coverage outside Tbilisi; multiple mobile-cellular providers provide services to an increasing subscribership throughout the country
domestic: cellular telephone networks cover the entire country; mobile-cellular teledensity roughly 110 per 100 persons; intercity facilities include a fiber-optic line between T'bilisi and K'ut'aisi
international: country code—995; the Georgia-Russia fiber-optic submarine cable provides connectivity to Russia; international service is available by microwave, landline, and satellite through the Moscow switch; international electronic mail and telex service are available (2015)

Broadcast media: Tbilisi-based Georgian Public Broadcaster (GPB) includes Channel 1, Channel 2, as well as the Batumi-based Adjara TV (also a part of GPB); all three are funded from the state budget; there are a number of independent commercial TV stations, including but not limited to Rustavi 2, Imedi, Maestro, Kavkasia, GDS, and TV1; the Georgian Orthodox Church also operates a satellite-based TV station called Unanimity; 26 regional TV broadcasters across Georgia are members of the Georgian Association of Regional Broadcasters (GARB) that seeks to strengthen the regional media's capacities and to distribute regional products; a nationwide digital switchover occurred in 2015; there are several dozen private radio stations; GPB operates 2 radio stations (2016)

Internet country code: .ge
Internet users: total: 2,464,107
percent of population: 50.0% (July 2016 est.)
country comparison to the world: 91

TRANSPORTATION

National air transport system: *number of registered air carriers:* 5
inventory of registered aircraft operated by air carriers: 13
annual passenger traffic on registered air carriers: 232,263
annual freight traffic on registered air carriers: 185,040 mt-km (2015)
Civil aircraft registration country code prefix: 4L (2016)

Airports: 22 (2013)
country comparison to the world: 135

Airports—with paved runways: *total:* 18
over 3,047 m: 1
2,438 to 3,047 m: 7
1,524 to 2,437 m: 3
914 to 1,523 m: 5
under 914 m: 2 (2017)

Airports—with unpaved runways: *total:* 4
1,524 to 2,437 m: 1
914 to 1,523 m: 2
under 914 m: 1 (2013)

Heliports: 2 (2013)

Pipelines: gas 1,596 km; oil 1,175 km (2013)

Railways: *total:* 1,363 km
broad gauge: 1,326 km 1.520-m gauge (1,251 km electrified)
narrow gauge: 37 km 0.912-m gauge (37 km electrified) (2014)
country comparison to the world: 82

Roadways: *total:* 19,109 km
paved: 19,109 km (includes 69 km of expressways) (2010)
country comparison to the world: 113

Merchant marine: *total:* 84
by type: bulk carrier 1, general cargo 24, oil tanker 2, other 57 (2017)
country comparison to the world: 90

Ports and terminals: *major seaport(s):* Black Sea—Bat'umi, P'ot'i

MILITARY AND SECURITY

Military expenditures: 2.23% of GDP (2016)
2.34% of GDP (2015)
2.26% of GDP (2014)
2.53% of GDP (2013)
3.1% of GDP (2012)
country comparison to the world: 27

Military branches: Georgian Armed Forces: Land Forces (include Air and Air Defense Forces); separatist Abkhazia Armed Forces: Ground Forces, Air Forces; separatist South Ossetia Armed Forces
note: Georgian naval forces have been incorporated into the Coast Guard, which is part of the Ministry of Internal Affairs rather than the Ministry of Defense (2015)

Military service age and obligation: 18 to 27 years of age for compulsory and voluntary active duty military service; conscript service obligation is 12 months (2017)

TRANSNATIONAL ISSUES

Disputes—international: Russia's military support and subsequent recognition of Abkhazia and South Ossetia independence in 2008 continue to sour relations with Georgia

Refugees and internally displaced persons: IDPs: 208,000 (displaced in the 1990s as a result of armed conflict in the breakaway republics of Abkhazia and South Ossetia; displaced in 2008 by fighting between Georgia and Russia over South Ossetia) (2016)
stateless persons: 250 (2016)

Illicit drugs: limited cultivation of cannabis and opium poppy, mostly for domestic consumption; used as transshipment point for opiates via Central Asia to Western Europe and Russia

GERMANY

INTRODUCTION

Background: As Europe's largest economy and second most populous nation (after Russia), Germany is a key member of the continent's economic, political, and defense organizations. European power struggles immersed Germany in two devastating World Wars in the first half of the 20th century and left the country occupied by the victorious Allied powers of the US, UK, France, and the Soviet Union in 1945. With the advent of the Cold War, two German states were formed in 1949: the western Federal Republic of Germany (FRG) and the eastern German Democratic Republic (GDR). The democratic FRG embedded itself in key western economic and security organizations, the EC, which became the EU, and NATO, while the communist GDR was on the front line of the Soviet-led Warsaw Pact. The decline of the USSR and the end of the Cold War allowed for German reunification in 1990. Since then, Germany has expended considerable funds to bring eastern productivity and wages up to western standards. In January 1999, Germany and 10 other EU countries introduced a common European exchange currency, the euro.

GEOGRAPHY

Location: Central Europe, bordering the Baltic Sea and the North Sea, between the Netherlands and Poland, south of Denmark

Geographic coordinates: 51 00 N, 9 00 E

Map references: Europe

Area: *total:* 357,022 sq km
land: 348,672 sq km
water: 8,350 sq km
country comparison to the world: 64

Area—comparative: three times the size of Pennsylvania; slightly smaller than Montana

Land boundaries: *total:* 3,714 km
border countries (9): Austria 801 km, Belgium 133 km, Czech Republic 704 km, Denmark 140 km, France 418 km, Luxembourg 128 km, Netherlands 575 km, Poland 467 km, Switzerland 348 km

Coastline: 2,389 km

Maritime claims: *territorial sea:* 12 nm
exclusive economic zone: 200 nm
continental shelf: 200-m depth or to the depth of exploitation

Climate: temperate and marine; cool, cloudy, wet winters and summers; occasional warm mountain (foehn) wind

Terrain: lowlands in north, uplands in center, Bavarian Alps in south

Elevation: *mean elevation:* 263 m
elevation extremes: lowest point: Neuendorf bei Wilster -3.5 m
highest point: Zugspitze 2,963 m

Natural resources: coal, lignite, natural gas, iron ore, copper, nickel, uranium, potash, salt, construction materials, timber, arable land

Land use: *agricultural land:* 48%
arable land: 34.1%;
permanent crops: 0.6%;
permanent pasture: 13.3%
forest: 31.8%
other: 20.2% (2011 est.)
Irrigated land: 6,500 sq km (2012)

Population—distribution: most populous country in Europe; a fairly even distribution throughout most of the country, with urban areas attracting larger and denser populations, particularly in the far western part of the industrial state of North Rhine-Westphalia

Natural hazards: flooding

Environment—current issues: emissions from coal-burning utilities and industries contribute to air pollution; acid rain, resulting from sulfur dioxide emissions, is damaging forests; pollution in the Baltic Sea from raw sewage and industrial effluents from rivers in eastern Germany; hazardous waste disposal; government established a mechanism for ending the use of nuclear power by 2022; government working to meet EU commitment to identify nature preservation areas in line with the EU's Flora, Fauna, and Habitat directive

Environment—international agreements: *party to:* Air Pollution, Air Pollution-Nitrogen Oxides, Air Pollution-Persistent Organic Pollutants, Air Pollution-Sulfur 85, Air Pollution-Sulfur 94, Air Pollution-Volatile Organic Compounds, Antarctic-Environmental Protocol, Antarctic-Marine Living Resources, Antarctic Seals, Antarctic Treaty, Biodiversity, Climate Change, Climate Change-Kyoto Protocol, Desertification, Endangered Species, Environmental Modification, Hazardous Wastes, Law of the Sea, Marine Dumping, Ozone Layer Protection, Ship Pollution, Tropical Timber 83, Tropical Timber 94, Wetlands, Whaling
signed, but not ratified: none of the selected agreements

Geography—note: strategic location on North European Plain and along the entrance to the Baltic Sea; most major rivers in Germany—the Rhine, Weser, Oder, Elbe—flow northward; the Danube, which originates in the Black Forest, flows eastward

PEOPLE AND SOCIETY

Population: 80,594,017 (July 2017 est.)
country comparison to the world: 19

Nationality: *noun:* German(s)
adjective: German

Ethnic groups: German 91.5%, Turkish 2.4%, other 6.1% (made up largely of Polish, Italian, Romanian, Syrian, and Greek)

Languages: German (official)
note: Danish, Frisian, Sorbian, and Romani are official minority languages; Low German, Danish, North Frisian, Sater Frisian, Lower Sorbian, Upper Sorbian, and Romani are recognized as regional languages under the European Charter for Regional or Minority Languages

Religions: Roman Catholic 29%, Protestant 27%, Muslim 4.4%, Orthodox Christian 1.9%, other 1.7%, none or members of unrecorded religious groups 36% (2015 est.)

Age structure: *0-14 years:* 12.82% (male 5,304,341/female 5,028,776)
15-24 years: 10.09% (male 4,145,486/female 3,986,302)
25-54 years: 40.45% (male 16,467,975/female 16,133,964)
55-64 years: 14.58% (male 5,834,179/female 5,913,322)
65 years and over: 22.06% (male 7,822,221/female 9,957,451) (2017 est.)

Dependency ratios: *total dependency ratio:* 52.1
youth dependency ratio: 19.9
elderly dependency ratio: 32.1
potential support ratio: 3.1 (2015 est.)

Median age: *total:* 47.1 years
male: 46 years
female: 48.2 years (2017 est.)
country comparison to the world: 3

Population growth rate: -0.16% (2017 est.)
country comparison to the world: 208

Birth rate: 8.6 births/1,000 population (2017 est.)
country comparison to the world: 213

Death rate: 11.7 deaths/1,000 population (2017 est.)
country comparison to the world: 24

Net migration rate: 1.5 migrant(s)/1,000 population (2017 est.)
country comparison to the world: 53

Population distribution: most populous country in Europe; a fairly even distribution throughout most of the country, with urban areas attracting larger and denser populations, particularly in the far western part of the industrial state of North Rhine-Westphalia

Urbanization: *urban population:* 75.7% of total population (2017)
rate of urbanization: 0.12% annual rate of change (2015-20 est.)

Major urban areas—population: BERLIN (capital) 3.563 million; Hamburg 1.831 million; Munich 1.438 million; Cologne 1.037 million (2015)

Sex ratio: *at birth:* 1.06 male(s)/female
0-14 years: 1.05 male(s)/female
15-24 years: 1.04 male(s)/female
25-54 years: 1.02 male(s)/female
55-64 years: 0.98 male(s)/female
65 years and over: 0.78 male(s)/female
total population: 0.97 male(s)/female (2016 est.)

Mother's mean age at first birth: 29.4 years (2015 est.)

Maternal mortality ratio: 6 deaths/100,000 live births (2015 est.)
country comparison to the world: 168

Infant mortality rate: *total:* 3.4 deaths/1,000 live births
male: 3.7 deaths/1,000 live births
female: 3.1 deaths/1,000 live births (2017 est.)
country comparison to the world: 205

Life expectancy at birth: *total population:* 80.8 years
male: 78.5 years
female: 83.3 years (2017 est.)
country comparison to the world: 34

Total fertility rate: 1.45 children born/woman (2017 est.)
country comparison to the world: 205
Health expenditures: 11.3% of GDP (2014)
country comparison to the world: 10

Physicians density: 4.13 physicians/1,000 population (2014)

Hospital bed density: 8.2 beds/1,000 population (2011)

Drinking water source:
improved:
urban: 100% of population

rural: 100% of population
total: 100% of population
unimproved:
urban: 0% of population
rural: 0% of population
total: 0% of population (2015 est.)

Sanitation facility access:
improved:
urban: 99.3% of population
rural: 99% of population
total: 99.2% of population
unimproved:
urban: 0.7% of population
rural: 1% of population
total: 0.8% of population (2015 est.)

HIV/AIDS—adult prevalence rate: NA

HIV/AIDS—people living with HIV/AIDS: NA (2016 est.)

HIV/AIDS—deaths: NA

Obesity—adult prevalence rate: 22.3% (2016)
country comparison to the world: 79

Education expenditures: 4.9% of GDP (2013)
country comparison to the world: 74

School life expectancy (primary to tertiary education): *total:* 17 years
male: 17 years
female: 17 years (2015)

Unemployment, youth ages 15-24: *total:* 7.2%
male: 7.9%
female: 6.5% (2015 est.)
country comparison to the world: 112

GOVERNMENT

Country name: *conventional long form:* Federal Republic of Germany
conventional short form: Germany
local long form: Bundesrepublik Deutschland
local short form: Deutschland
former: German Reich
etymology: the Gauls (Celts) of Western Europe may have referred to the newly arriving Germanic tribes who settled in neighboring areas east of the Rhine during the first centuries B.C. as "Germani", a term the Romans adopted as "Germania"; the native designation "Deutsch" comes from the Old High German "diutisc" meaning "of the people"

Government type: federal parliamentary republic

Capital: *name:* Berlin
geographic coordinates: 52 31 N, 13 24 E
time difference: UTC+1 (6 hours ahead of Washington, DC, during Standard Time)
daylight saving time: +1hr, begins last Sunday in March; ends last Sunday in October

Administrative divisions: 16 states (Laender, singular—Land); Baden-Wuerttemberg, Bayern (Bavaria), Berlin, Brandenburg, Bremen, Hamburg, Hessen (Hesse), Mecklenburg-Vorpommern (Mecklenburg-Western Pomerania), Niedersachsen (Lower Saxony), Nordrhein-Westfalen (North Rhine-Westphalia), Rheinland-Pfalz (Rhineland-Palatinate), Saarland, Sachsen (Saxony), Sachsen-Anhalt (Saxony-Anhalt), Schleswig-Holstein, Thueringen (Thuringia); note—Bayern,

Sachsen, and Thueringen refer to themselves as free states (Freistaaten, singular—Freistaat), while Hamburg prides itself on being a Free and Hanseatic City (Freie und Hansestadt)

Independence: 18 January 1871 (establishment of the German Empire); divided into four zones of occupation (UK, US, USSR, and France) in 1945 following World War II; Federal Republic of Germany (FRG or West Germany) proclaimed on 23 May 1949 and included the former UK, US, and French zones; German Democratic Republic (GDR or East Germany) proclaimed on 7 October 1949 and included the former USSR zone; West Germany and East Germany unified on 3 October 1990; all four powers formally relinquished rights on 15 March 1991; notable earlier dates: 10 August 843 (Eastern Francia established from the division of the Carolingian Empire); 2 February 962 (crowning of OTTO I, recognized as the first Holy Roman Emperor)

National holiday: German Unity Day, 3 October (1990)

Constitution: history: previous 1919 (Weimar Constitution); latest drafted 10 to 23 August 1948, approved 12 May 1949, promulgated 23 May 1949, entered into force 24 May 1949
amendments: proposed by Parliament; passage and enactment into law require two-thirds majority vote by both the Bundesrat (upper house) and the Bundestag (lower house) of Parliament; articles including those on basic human rights and freedoms cannot be amended; amended many times, last in 2012 (2016)

Legal system: civil law system

International law organization participation: accepts compulsory ICJ jurisdiction with reservations; accepts ICCt jurisdiction

Citizenship: *citizenship by birth:* no
citizenship by descent only: at least one parent must be a German citizen or a resident alien who has lived in Germany at least 8 years
dual citizenship recognized: yes, but requires prior permission from government
residency requirement for naturalization: 8 years

Suffrage: 18 years of age; universal; age 16 for some state and municipal elections

Executive branch: *chief of state:* President Frank-Walter STEINMEIER (since 19 March 2017; inaugurated 22 March 2017)
head of government: Chancellor Angela MERKEL (since 22 November 2005)
cabinet: Cabinet or Bundesminister (Federal Ministers) recommended by the chancellor, appointed by the president
elections/appointments: president indirectly elected by a Federal Convention consisting of all members of the Federal Parliament (Bundestag) and an equivalent number of delegates indirectly elected by the state parliaments; president serves a 5-year term (eligible for a second term); election last held on 12 February 2017 (next to be held in February 2022); following the most recent Federal Parliament election, the party or coalition with

the most representatives usually elects the chancellor and appointed by the president to serve a renewable 4-year term; Federal Parliament vote for chancellor last held on 17 December 2013 (next to be held in 2018)
election results: Frank-Walter STEINMEIER elected president; Federal Convention vote count—Frank-Walter STEINMEIER (SPD) 931, Christopher BUTTERWEGGE (The Left) 128, Albrecht GLASER (Alternative for Germany AfD) 42, Alexander HOLD (BVB/FW) 25, Engelbert SONNEBORN (Pirates) 10; Angela MERKEL (CDU) reelected chancellor; Federal Parliament vote—462 for, 150 against, 49 abstentions

Legislative branch: description: bicameral Parliament or Parlament consists of the Federal Council or Bundesrat (69 seats; members appointed by each of the 16 state governments) and the Federal Diet or Bundestag (709 seats—total seats can vary each electoral term; approximately one-half of members directly elected in multi-seat constituencies by proportional representation vote and approximately one-half directly elected in single-seat constituencies by simple majority vote; members serve 4-year terms)
elections: Bundestag—last held on 24 September 2017 (next to be held in 2021); most postwar German governments have been coalitions; note—there are no elections for the Bundesrat; composition is determined by the composition of the state-level governments; the composition of the Bundesrat has the potential to change any time one of the 16 states holds an election
election results: Bundestag—percent of vote by party—CDU/CSU 32.9%, SPD 20.5%, AfD 12.6%, FDP 10.8%, The Left 9.2%, Alliance '90/Greens 8.9%, other 5%; seats by party—CDU/CSU 246, SPD 153, FDP 80, The Left 69, Alliance '90/Greens 67

Judicial branch: *highest court(s):* Federal Court of Justice (court consists of 127 judges including the court president, vice-presidents, presiding judges, and other judges, and organized into 25 Senates subdivided into 12 civil panels, 5 criminal panels, and 8 special panels; Federal Constitutional Court or Bundesverfassungsgericht (consists of 2 Senates each subdivided into 3 chambers, each with a chairman and 8 members)
judge selection and term of office: Federal Court of Justice judges selected by the Judges Election Committee, which consists of the Secretaries of Justice from each of the 16 federated States and 16 members appointed by the Federal Parliament; judges appointed by the president of Germany; judges serve until mandatory retirement at age 65; Federal Constitutional Court judges—one-half elected by the House of Representatives and one-half by the Senate; judges appointed for 12-year terms with mandatory retirement at age 68
subordinate courts: Federal Administrative Court; Federal Finance Court; Federal Labor Court; Federal Social Court; each of the 16 German states or Land has its own constitutional court and a hierarchy of ordinary (civil, criminal, family) and specialized (administrative, finance, labor, social) courts

Political parties and leaders: Alliance '90/Greens [Annalena BAERBOCK and Robert HABECK] Alternative for Germany or AfD [Alexander GAULAND and Joerg MEUTHEN] Christian Democratic Union or CDU [Angela MERKEL] Christian Social Union or CSU [Horst SEEHOFER] Free Democratic Party or FDP [Christian LINDNER] The Left or Die Linke [Katja KIPPING and Bernd RIEXINGER] Social Democratic Party or SPD [Martin SCHULZ]

Political pressure groups and leaders: business associations and employers' organizations trade unions; religious, immigrant, expellee, and veterans groups

International organization participation: ADB (nonregional member), AfDB (nonregional member), Arctic Council (observer), Australia Group, BIS, BSEC (observer), CBSS, CD, CDB, CE, CERN, EAPC, EBRD, ECB, EIB, EITI (implementing country), EMU, ESA, EU, FAO, FATF, G-5, G-7, G-8, G-10, G-20, IADB, IAEA, IBRD, ICAO, ICC (national committees), ICCt, ICRM, IDA, IEA, IFAD, IFC, IFRCS, IGAD (partners), IHO, ILO, IMF, IMO, IMSO, Interpol, IOC, IOM, IPU, ISO, ITSO, ITU, ITUC (NGOs), MIGA, MINURSO, MINUSMA, NATO, NEA, NSG, OAS (observer), OECD, OPCW, OSCE, Pacific Alliance (observer), Paris Club, PCA, Schengen Convention, SELEC (observer), SICA (observer), UN, UNAMID, UNCTAD, UNESCO, UNHCR, UNIDO, UNIFIL, UNMISS, UNRWA, UNWTO, UPU, WCO, WHO, WIPO, WMO, WTO, ZC

Diplomatic representation in the US: *chief of mission:* Ambassador Hans Peter WITTIG (since 21 May 2014) *chancery:* 4645 Reservoir Road NW, Washington, DC 20007 *telephone:* [1] (202) 298-4000 *FAX:* [1] (202) 298-4249 *consulate(s) general:* Atlanta, Boston, Chicago, Houston, Los Angeles, Miami, New York, San Francisco

Diplomatic representation from the US: *chief of mission:* Ambassador (vacant); Charge d'Affaires Kent LOGSDON (since 20 January 2017) *embassy:* Pariser Platz 2 *mailing address:* Clayallee 170, 14191 Berlin *telephone:* [49] (30) 8305-0 *FAX:* [49] (30) 8305-1215 *consulate(s) general:* Dusseldorf, Frankfurt am Main, Hamburg, Leipzig, Munich

Flag description: three equal horizontal bands of black (top), red, and gold; these colors have played an important role in German history and can be traced back to the medieval banner of the Holy Roman Emperor—a black eagle with red claws and beak on a gold field

National symbol(s): eagle; national colors: black, red, yellow

National anthem: name: "Das Lied der Deutschen" (Song of the Germans) *lyrics/music:* August Heinrich HOFFMANN VON FALLERSLEBEN/Franz Joseph HAYDN *note:* adopted 1922; the anthem, also known as "Deutschlandlied" (Song of Germany), was originally adopted for its connection to the March 1848 liberal revolution; following appropriation by the Nazis of the first verse, specifically the phrase, "Deutschland, Deutschland ueber alles" (Germany, Germany above all) to promote nationalism, it was banned after 1945; in 1952, its third verse was adopted by West Germany as its national anthem; in 1990, it became the national anthem for the reunited Germany

ECONOMY

Economy—overview: The German economy—the fifth largest economy in the world in PPP terms and Europe's largest—is a leading exporter of machinery, vehicles, chemicals, and household equipment and benefits from a highly skilled labor force. Like its Western European neighbors, Germany faces significant demographic challenges to sustained long-term growth. Low fertility rates and a large increase in net immigration are increasing pressure on the country's social welfare system and necessitate structural reforms.

Reforms launched by the government of Chancellor Gerhard SCHROEDER (1998-2005), deemed necessary to address chronically high unemployment and low average growth, contributed to strong growth and falling unemployment. These advances, as well as a government subsidized, reduced working hour scheme, help explain the relatively modest increase in unemployment during the 2008-09 recession—the deepest since World War II. The German Government introduced a minimum wage in 2015 that increased to $9.79 (8.84 euros) in January 2017.

Stimulus and stabilization efforts initiated in 2008 and 2009 and tax cuts introduced in Chancellor Angela MERKEL's second term increased Germany's total budget deficit—including federal, state, and municipal—to 4.1% in 2010, but slower spending and higher tax revenues reduced the deficit to 0.8% in 2011 and in 2017 Germany reached a budget surplus of 0.7%. A constitutional amendment approved in 2009 limits the federal government to structural deficits of no more than 0.35% of GDP per annum as of 2016, though the target was already reached in 2012.

The German economy suffers from low levels of investment, and a government plan to invest 15 billion euros during 2016-18, largely in infrastructure, is intended to spur needed private investment. Following the March 2011 Fukushima nuclear disaster, Chancellor Angela MERKEL announced in May 2011 that eight of the country's 17 nuclear reactors would be shut down immediately and the remaining plants would close by 2022. Germany plans to replace nuclear power largely with renewable energy, which accounted for 29.5% of gross electricity consumption in 2016, up from 9% in 2000. Before the shutdown of the eight reactors, Germany relied on nuclear power for 23% of its electricity generating capacity and 46% of its base-load electricity production. Domestic consumption, bolstered by low energy prices and a weak euro, and exports are likely to drive German GDP growth again in 2018.

GDP (purchasing power parity): $4.15 trillion (2017 est.) $4.066 trillion (2016 est.) $3.992 trillion (2015 est.) *note:* data are in 2017 dollars *country comparison to the world:* 6

GDP (official exchange rate): $3.652 trillion (2016 est.)

GDP—real growth rate: 2.1% (2017 est.) 1.9% (2016 est.) 1.5% (2015 est.) *country comparison to the world:* 149

GDP—per capita (PPP): $50,200 (2017 est.) $49,300 (2016 est.) $48,900 (2015 est.) *note:* data are in 2017 dollars *country comparison to the world:* 27

Gross national saving: 27.6% of GDP (2017 est.) 27.5% of GDP (2016 est.) 27.7% of GDP (2015 est.) *country comparison to the world:* 39

GDP—composition, by end use: *household consumption:* 53.7% *government consumption:* 19.9% *investment in fixed capital:* 20.1% *investment in inventories:* -1% *exports of goods and services:* 47.3% *imports of goods and services:* -40% (2017 est.)

GDP—composition, by sector of origin: *agriculture:* 0.6% *industry:* 30.1% *services:* 69.3% (2017 est.)

Agriculture—products: potatoes, wheat, barley, sugar beets, fruit, cabbages; milk products; cattle, pigs, poultry

Industries: among the world's largest and most technologically advanced producers of iron, steel, coal, cement, chemicals, machinery, vehicles, machine tools, electronics, automobiles, food and beverages, shipbuilding, textiles

Industrial production growth rate: 1.4% (2017 est.) *country comparison to the world:* 156

Labor force: 45.9 million (2017 est.) *country comparison to the world:* 15

Labor force—by occupation: *agriculture:* 1.4% *industry:* 24.2% *services:* 74.3% (2016)

Unemployment rate: 3.8% (2017 est.) 4.2% (2016 est.) *country comparison to the world:* 44

Population below poverty line: 16.7% (2015 est.)

Household income or consumption by percentage share: *lowest 10%:* 3.6% *highest 10%:* 24% (2000)

Distribution of family income—Gini index: 27 (2006)

30 (1994)

country comparison to the world: 137

Budget: *revenues:* $1.598 trillion
expenditures: $1.573 trillion (2017 est.)
Taxes and other revenues: 43.8% of GDP (2017 est.)
country comparison to the world: 26

Budget surplus (+) or deficit (-): 0.7% of GDP (2017 est.)
country comparison to the world: 20

Public debt: 65.7% of GDP (2017 est.)
68.4% of GDP (2016 est.)
note: general government gross debt is defined in the Maastricht Treaty as consolidated general government gross debt at nominal value, outstanding at the end of the year in the following categories of government liabilities (as defined in ESA95): currency and deposits (AF.2), securities other than shares excluding financial derivatives (AF.3, excluding AF.34), and loans (AF.4); the general government sector comprises the sub-sectors of central government, state government, local government and social security funds; the series are presented as a percentage of GDP and in millions of euro; GDP used as a denominator is the gross domestic product at current market prices; data expressed in national currency are converted into euro using end-of-year exchange rates provided by the European Central Bank
country comparison to the world: 61

Fiscal year: calendar year

Inflation rate (consumer prices): 1.6% (2017 est.)
0.4% (2016 est.)
country comparison to the world: 69

Central bank discount rate: 0.25% (31 December 2016)
0.3% (31 December 2010)
note: this is the European Central Bank's rate on the marginal lending facility, which offers overnight credit to banks in the euro area
country comparison to the world: 135

Commercial bank prime lending rate: 1.8% (31 December 2017 est.)
1.6% (31 December 2016 est.)
country comparison to the world: 179

Stock of narrow money: $2.312 trillion (31 December 2017 est.)
$2.016 trillion (31 December 2016 est.)
note: see entry for the European Union for money supply for the entire euro area; the European Central Bank (ECB) controls monetary policy for the 18 members of the Economic and Monetary Union (EMU); individual members of the EMU do not control the quantity of money circulating within their own borders
country comparison to the world: 5

Stock of broad money: $3.282 trillion (31 December 2017 est.)
$2.908 trillion (31 December 2016 est.)
country comparison to the world: 5

Stock of domestic credit: $4.766 trillion (31 December 2017 est.)
$4.433 trillion (31 December 2016 est.)
country comparison to the world: 5

Market value of publicly traded shares: $1.716 trillion (31 December 2015 est.)
$1.739 trillion (31 December 2014 est.)
$1.936 trillion (31 December 2013 est.)
country comparison to the world: 7

Current account balance: $296 billion (2017 est.)
$290.4 billion (2016 est.)
country comparison to the world: 2

Exports: $1.401 trillion (2017 est.)
$1.322 trillion (2016 est.)
country comparison to the world: 4

Exports—commodities: motor vehicles, machinery, chemicals, computer and electronic products, electrical equipment, pharmaceuticals, metals, transport equipment, foodstuffs, textiles, rubber and plastic products

Exports—partners: US 8.9%, France 8.4%, UK 7.1%, Netherlands 6.5%, China 6.4%, Italy 5.1%, Austria 5%, Poland 4.5%, Switzerland 4.2% (2016)

Imports: $1.104 trillion (2017 est.)
$1.022 trillion (2016 est.)
country comparison to the world: 4

Imports—commodities: machinery, data processing equipment, vehicles, chemicals, oil and gas, metals, electric equipment, pharmaceuticals, foodstuffs, agricultural products

Imports—partners: Netherlands 13.3%, China 7.3%, France 7.3%, Belgium 6.1%, Italy 5.5%, Poland 5.2%, Czech Republic 4.7%, US 4.6%, Switzerland 4.4%, Austria 4.4%, UK 4.1% (2016)

Reserves of foreign exchange and gold: $185.3 billion (31 December 2016 est.)
$173.7 billion (31 December 2015 est.)
country comparison to the world: 15

Debt—external: $5.326 trillion (31 March 2016 est.)
$5.21 trillion (31 March 2015 est.)
country comparison to the world: 5

Stock of direct foreign investment—at home: $1.455 trillion (31 December 2017 est.)
$1.391 trillion (31 December 2016 est.)
country comparison to the world: 8

Stock of direct foreign investment—abroad: $2.074 trillion (31 December 2017 est.)
$1.981 trillion (31 December 2016 est.)
country comparison to the world: 4

Exchange rates: euros (EUR) per US dollar—
0.906 (2017 est.)
0.9214 (2016 est.)
0.9214 (2015 est.)
0.885 (2014 est.)
0.7634 (2013 est.)

ENERGY

Electricity access: electrification—total population: 100% (2016)

Electricity—production: 588.5 billion kWh (2015 est.)
country comparison to the world: 8

Electricity—consumption: 514.6 billion kWh (2015 est.)

country comparison to the world: 8

Electricity—exports: 78.86 billion kWh (2016 est.)
country comparison to the world: 2

Electricity—imports: 28.34 billion kWh (2016 est.)
country comparison to the world: 6

Electricity—installed generating capacity: 204.1 million kW (2015 est.)
country comparison to the world: 7

Electricity—from fossil fuels: 42.6% of total installed capacity (2015 est.)
country comparison to the world: 167

Electricity—from nuclear fuels: 5.3% of total installed capacity (2015 est.)
country comparison to the world: 23

Electricity—from hydroelectric plants: 2.2% of total installed capacity (2015 est.)
country comparison to the world: 136

Electricity—from other renewable sources: 49.9% of total installed capacity (2015 est.)
country comparison to the world: 3

Crude oil—production: 46,590 bbl/day (2016 est.)
country comparison to the world: 58

Crude oil—exports: 1,987 bbl/day (2016 est.)
country comparison to the world: 68

Crude oil—imports: 1.837 million bbl/day (2016 est.)
country comparison to the world: 6

Crude oil—proved reserves: 145.4 million bbl (1 January 2017 es)
country comparison to the world: 66

Refined petroleum products—production: 2.198 million bbl/day (2016 est.)
country comparison to the world: 10

Refined petroleum products—consumption: 2.41 million bbl/day (2016 est.)
country comparison to the world: 10

Refined petroleum products—exports: 474,300 bbl/day (2016 est.)
country comparison to the world: 17

Refined petroleum products—imports: 800,500 bbl/day (2016 est.)
country comparison to the world: 10

Natural gas—production: 8.73 billion cu m (2015 est.)
country comparison to the world: 44

Natural gas—consumption: 773.2 billion cu m (2015 est.)
country comparison to the world: 2

Natural gas—exports: 32.51 billion cu m (2015 est.)
country comparison to the world: 12

Natural gas—imports: 102.5 billion cu m (2015 est.)
country comparison to the world: 3

Natural gas—proved reserves: 41.99 billion cu m (1 January 2017 es)
country comparison to the world: 67

Carbon dioxide emissions from consumption of energy: 744 million Mt (2015 est.)

country comparison to the world: 7

COMMUNICATIONS

Telephones—fixed lines: *total subscriptions:* 44.31 million
subscriptions per 100 inhabitants: 55 (July 2016 est.)
country comparison to the world: 5
Telephones—mobile cellular: *total:* 94,432,800
subscriptions per 100 inhabitants: 117 (July 2016 est.)
country comparison to the world: 15
Telephone system: *general assessment:* one of the world's most technologically advanced telecommunications systems; as a result of intensive capital expenditures since reunification, the formerly backward system of the eastern part of the country, dating back to World War II, has been modernized and integrated with that of the western part
domestic: extensive system of automatic telephone exchanges connected by modern networks of fiber-optic cable, coaxial cable, microwave radio relay, and a domestic satellite system; cellular telephone service is widely available, expanding rapidly, and includes roaming service to many foreign countries
international: country code—49; Germany's international service is excellent worldwide, consisting of extensive land and undersea cable facilities as well as earth stations in the Inmarsat, Intelsat, Eutelsat, and Intersputnik satellite systems (2015)
Broadcast media: a mixture of publicly operated and privately owned TV and radio stations; national and regional public broadcasters compete with nearly 400 privately owned national and regional TV stations; more than 90% of households have cable or satellite TV; hundreds of radio stations including multiple national radio networks, regional radio networks, and a large number of local radio stations (2008)
Internet country code: .de
Internet users: total: 72,365,643
percent of population: 89.6% (July 2016 est.)
country comparison to the world: 8

TRANSPORTATION

National air transport system: *number of registered air carriers:* 20
inventory of registered aircraft operated by air carriers: 1,113
annual passenger traffic on registered air carriers: 115,540,886

annual freight traffic on registered air carriers: 6,985,007,915 mt-km (2015)
Civil aircraft registration country code prefix: D (2016)
Airports: 539 (2013)
country comparison to the world: 13
Airports—with paved runways: *total:* 318
over 3,047 m: 14
2,438 to 3,047 m: 49
1,524 to 2,437 m: 60
914 to 1,523 m: 70
under 914 m: 125 (2017)
Airports—with unpaved runways: *total:* 221
1,524 to 2,437 m: 1
914 to 1,523 m: 35
under 914 m: 185 (2013)
Heliports: 23 (2013)
Pipelines: condensate 37 km; gas 26,985 km; oil 2,826 km; refined products 4,479 km; water 8 km (2013)
Railways: *total:* 43,468.3 km
standard gauge: 43,209.3 km 1.435-m gauge (19,973 km electrified)
narrow gauge: 220 km 1.000-m gauge (79 km electrified); 15 km 0.900-m gauge; 24 km 0.750-m gauge (2014)
country comparison to the world: 6
Roadways: *total:* 645,000 km
paved: 645,000 km (includes 12,800 km of expressways)
note: includes local roads (2010)
country comparison to the world: 12
Waterways: 7,467 km (Rhine River carries most goods; Main-Danube Canal links North Sea and Black Sea) (2012)
country comparison to the world: 18
Merchant marine: *total:* 614
by type: bulk carrier 1, container ship 117, general cargo 87, oil tanker 34, other 375 (2017)
country comparison to the world: 35
Ports and terminals: *major seaport(s):* Baltic Sea—Rostock; North Sea—Wilhelmshaven
river port(s): Bremen (Weser); Bremerhaven (Geeste); Duisburg, Karlsruhe, Neuss-Dusseldorf (Rhine); Brunsbuttel, Hamburg (Elbe); Lubeck (Wakenitz)
oil terminal(s): Brunsbuttel Canal terminals
container port(s): Bremen/Bremerhaven (5,547,000), Hamburg (8,821,000) (2015)
LNG terminal(s) (import): Hamburg

MILITARY AND SECURITY

Military expenditures: 1.19% of GDP (2016 est.)
1.19% of GDP (2015)
1.19% of GDP (2014)
1.23% of GDP (2013)
1.31% of GDP (2012)
country comparison to the world: 74
Military branches: Federal Armed Forces (Bundeswehr): Army (Heer), Navy (Deutsche Marine, includes naval air arm), Air Force (Luftwaffe), Joint Support Service (Streitkraeftebasis, SKB), Central Medical Service (Zentraler Sanitaetsdienst, ZSanDstBw), Cyber and Information Space Command (Kommando Cyber- und Informationsraum, Kdo CIR) (2017)
Military service age and obligation: 17-23 years of age for male and female voluntary military service; conscription ended 1 July 2011; service obligation 8-23 months or 12 years; women have been eligible for voluntary service in all military branches and positions since 2001 (2013)

TERRORISM

Terrorist groups—foreign based: *Islamic State of Iraq and the Levant (ISIL): aim(s):* destabilize Germany's economy and government
area(s) of operation: police aggressively pursue and break up sleeper cells; as of early 2017, approximately 750 to 850 German citizens were fighting in Syria or Iraq alongside ISIL, planning to go to fight, or had returned from the fight; in December 2015, two operatives were arrested while assembling an IED intended for bombing the Israeli Embassy in Berlin

TRANSNATIONAL ISSUES

Disputes—international: none
Refugees and internally displaced persons: *refugees (country of origin):* 375,122 (Syria); 86,045 (Iraq); 46,292 (Afghanistan); 30,020 (Eritrea); 22,910 (Iran); 19,136 (Turkey); 9,189 (Serbia and Kosovo); 7,879 (Somalia); 5,255 (Russia); 5,169 (Pakistan) (2016); 10,305 (Ukraine) (2017)
note: estimate represents asylum applicants since Ukraine crisis began in 2014 until September 2017
stateless persons: 12,017 (2016)
Illicit drugs: source of precursor chemicals for South American cocaine processors; transshipment point for and consumer of Southwest Asian heroin, Latin American cocaine, and European-produced synthetic drugs; major financial center

GHANA

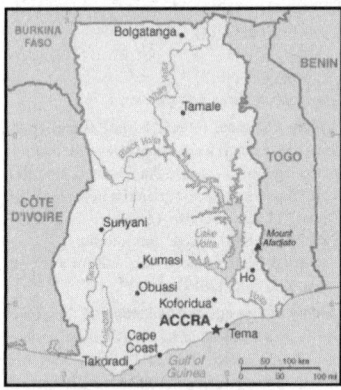

INTRODUCTION

Background: Formed from the merger of the British colony of the Gold Coast and the Togoland trust territory, Ghana in 1957 became the first sub-Saharan country in colonial Africa to gain its independence. Ghana endured a series of coups before Lt. Jerry RAWLINGS took power in 1981 and banned political parties. After approving a new constitution and restoring multiparty politics in 1992, RAWLINGS won presidential elections in 1992 and 1996 but was constitutionally prevented from running for a third term in 2000. John KUFUOR of the opposition New Patriotic Party (NPP) succeeded him and was reelected in 2004. John Atta MILLS of the National Democratic Congress won the 2008 presidential election and took over as head of state, but he died in July 2012 and was constitutionally succeeded by his vice president, John Dramani MAHAMA, who subsequently won the December 2012 presidential election. In 2016, however, Nana Addo Dankwa AKUFO-ADDO of the NPP defeated MAHAMA, marking the third time that the Ghana's presidency has changed parties since the return to democracy.

GEOGRAPHY

Location: Western Africa, bordering the Gulf of Guinea, between Cote d'Ivoire and Togo

Geographic coordinates: 8 00 N, 2 00 W

Map references: Africa

Area: *total:* 238,533 sq km
land: 227,533 sq km
water: 11,000 sq km
country comparison to the world: 83

Area—comparative: slightly smaller than Oregon

Land boundaries: *total:* 2,420 km
border countries (3): Burkina Faso 602 km, Cote d'Ivoire 720 km, Togo 1,098 km

Coastline: 539 km

Maritime claims: *territorial sea:* 12 nm

contiguous zone: 24 nm
exclusive economic zone: 200 nm
continental shelf: 200 nm

Climate: tropical; warm and comparatively dry along southeast coast; hot and humid in southwest; hot and dry in north

Terrain: mostly low plains with dissected plateau in south-central area

Elevation: *mean elevation:* 190 m

elevation extremes: *lowest point:* Atlantic Ocean 0 m
highest point: Mount Afadjato 885 m

Natural resources: gold, timber, industrial diamonds, bauxite, manganese, fish, rubber, hydropower, petroleum, silver, salt, limestone

Land use: *agricultural land:* 69.1%
arable land: 20.7%;
permanent crops: 11.9%;
permanent pasture: 36.5%
forest: 21.2%
other: 9.7% (2011 est.)
Irrigated land: 340 sq km (2012)

Population—distribution: population is concentrated in the southern half of the country, with the highest concentrations being on or near the Atlantic coast

Natural hazards: dry, dusty, northeastern harmattan winds from January to March; droughts

Environment—current issues: recurrent drought in north severely affects agricultural activities; deforestation; overgrazing; soil erosion; poaching and habitat destruction threatens wildlife populations; water pollution; inadequate supplies of potable water

Environment—international agreements: *party to:* Biodiversity, Climate Change, Climate Change-Kyoto Protocol, Desertification, Endangered Species, Environmental Modification, Hazardous Wastes, Law of the Sea, Ozone Layer Protection, Ship Pollution, Tropical Timber 83, Tropical Timber 94, Wetlands
signed, but not ratified: Marine Life Conservation

Geography—note: Lake Volta is the world's largest artificial lake (manmade reservoir) by surface area (8,482 sq km; 3,275 sq mi); the lake was created following the completion of the Akosombo Dam in 1965, which holds back the White Volta and Black Volta Rivers

PEOPLE AND SOCIETY

Population: 27,499,924
note: estimates for this country explicitly take into account the effects of excess mortality due to AIDS; this can result in lower life expectancy, higher infant mortality, higher death rates, lower population growth rates, and changes in the distribution of population by age and sex than would otherwise be expected (July 2017 est.)
country comparison to the world: 49

Nationality: *noun:* Ghanaian(s)
adjective: Ghanaian

Ethnic groups: Akan 47.5%, Mole-Dagbon 16.6%, Ewe 13.9%, Ga-Dangme 7.4%, Gurma 5.7%, Guan 3.7%, Grusi 2.5%, Mande 1.1%, other 1.4% (2010 est.)

Languages: Asante 16%, Ewe 14%, Fante 11.6%, Boron (Brong) 4.9%, Dagomba 4.4%, Dangme 4.2%, Dagarte (Dagaba) 3.9%, Kokomba 3.5%, Akyem 3.2%, Ga 3.1%, other 31.2%
note: English is the official language (2010 est.)

Religions: Christian 71.2% (Pentecostal/Charismatic 28.3%, Protestant 18.4%, Catholic 13.1%, other 11.4%), Muslim 17.6%, traditional 5.2%, other 0.8%, none 5.2% (2010 est.)

Demographic profile: Ghana has a young age structure, with approximately 57% of the population under the age of 25. Its total fertility rate fell significantly during the 1980s and 1990s but has stalled at around four children per woman for the last few years. Fertility remains higher in the northern region than the Greater Accra region. On average, desired fertility has remained stable for several years; urban dwellers want fewer children than rural residents. Increased life expectancy, due to better health care, nutrition, and hygiene, and reduced fertility have increased Ghana's share of elderly persons; Ghana's proportion of persons aged 60+ is among the highest in sub-Saharan Africa. Poverty has declined in Ghana, but it remains pervasive in the northern region, which is susceptible to droughts and floods and has less access to transportation infrastructure, markets, fertile farming land, and industrial centers. The northern region also has lower school enrollment, higher illiteracy, and fewer opportunities for women.

Ghana was a country of immigration in the early years after its 1957 independence, attracting labor migrants largely from Nigeria and other neighboring countries to mine minerals and harvest cocoa—immigrants composed about 12% of Ghana's population in 1960. In the late 1960s, worsening economic and social conditions discouraged immigration, and hundreds of thousands of immigrants, mostly Nigerians, were expelled.

During the 1970s, severe drought and an economic downturn transformed Ghana into a country of emigration; neighboring Cote d'Ivoire was the initial destination. Later, hundreds of thousands of Ghanaians migrated to Nigeria to work in its booming oil industry, but most were deported in 1983 and 1985 as oil prices plummeted. Many Ghanaians then turned to more distant destinations, including other parts of Africa, Europe, and North America, but the majority continued to migrate within West Africa. Since the 1990s, increased emigration of skilled Ghanaians, especially to the US and the UK, drained the country of its health care and education professionals. Internally, poverty and other developmental disparities continue to drive Ghanaians from the north to the south, particularly to its urban centers.

Age structure: *0-14 years:* 38.01% (male 5,253,430/female 5,198,892)
15-24 years: 18.63% (male 2,548,661/female 2,575,160)
25-54 years: 34.14% (male 4,554,972/female 4,834,765)
55-64 years: 4.97% (male 664,866/female 701,277)
65 years and over: 4.25% (male 538,790/female 629,111) (2017 est.)

Dependency ratios: *total dependency ratio:* 73
youth dependency ratio: 67.1
elderly dependency ratio: 5.9
potential support ratio: 17.1 (2015 est.)

Median age: *total:* 21.1 years
male: 20.6 years
female: 21.6 years (2017 est.)
country comparison to the world: 184

Population growth rate: 2.17% (2017 est.)
country comparison to the world: 36

Birth rate: 30.5 births/1,000 population (2017 est.)
country comparison to the world: 36

Death rate: 7 deaths/1,000 population (2017 est.)
country comparison to the world: 131

Net migration rate: -1.8 migrant(s)/1,000 population (2017 est.)
country comparison to the world: 155

Population distribution: population is concentrated in the southern half of the country, with the highest concentrations being on or near the Atlantic coast

Urbanization: *urban population:* 55.3% of total population (2017)
rate of urbanization: 3.07% annual rate of change (2015-20 est.)

Major urban areas—population: Kumasi 2.599 million; ACCRA (capital) 2.277 million (2015)

Sex ratio: *at birth:* 1.03 male(s)/female
0-14 years: 1.01 male(s)/female
15-24 years: 0.99 male(s)/female
25-54 years: 0.94 male(s)/female
55-64 years: 0.95 male(s)/female
65 years and over: 0.86 male(s)/female
total population: 0.97 male(s)/female (2016 est.)

Mother's mean age at first birth: 22.6 years
note: median age at first birth among women 25-29 (2014 est.)

Maternal mortality ratio: 319 deaths/100,000 live births (2015 est.)
country comparison to the world: 39

Infant mortality rate: *total:* 35.2 deaths/1,000 live births
male: 39.1 deaths/1,000 live births
female: 31.1 deaths/1,000 live births (2017 est.)
country comparison to the world: 53

Life expectancy at birth: *total population:* 67 years
male: 64.5 years
female: 69.6 years (2017 est.)
country comparison to the world: 172

Total fertility rate: 4 children born/woman (2017 est.)
country comparison to the world: 34

Contraceptive prevalence rate: 30.6% (2016)
Health expenditures: 3.6% of GDP (2014)
country comparison to the world: 170

Physicians density: 0.1 physicians/1,000 population (2010)

Hospital bed density: 0.9 beds/1,000 population (2011)

Drinking water source:
improved:
urban: 92.6% of population
rural: 84% of population
total: 88.7% of population
unimproved:
urban: 7.4% of population
rural: 16% of population
total: 11.3% of population (2015 est.)

Sanitation facility access:
improved:
urban: 20.2% of population
rural: 8.6% of population
total: 14.9% of population
unimproved:
urban: 79.8% of population
rural: 91.4% of population
total: 85.1% of population (2015 est.)

HIV/AIDS—adult prevalence rate: 1.6% (2016 est.)
country comparison to the world: 33

HIV/AIDS—people living with HIV/AIDS: 290,000 (2016 est.)
country comparison to the world: 20

HIV/AIDS—deaths: 15,000 (2016 est.)
country comparison to the world: 17

Major infectious diseases: *degree of risk:* very high
food or waterborne diseases: bacterial and protozoal diarrhea, hepatitis A, and typhoid fever
vectorborne diseases: malaria, dengue fever, and yellow fever
water contact disease: schistosomiasis
respiratory disease: meningococcal meningitis
animal contact disease: rabies (2016)

Obesity—adult prevalence rate: 10.9% (2016)
country comparison to the world: 136

Children under the age of 5 years underweight: 11% (2014)
country comparison to the world: 55

Education expenditures: 6.2% of GDP (2014)
country comparison to the world: 13

Literacy: *definition:* age 15 and over can read and write
total population: 76.6%
male: 82%
female: 71.4% (2015 est.)

School life expectancy (primary to tertiary education): *total:* 12 years
male: 12 years
female: 12 years (2015)

Unemployment, youth ages 15-24: *total:* 11.2%
male: 10.2%

female: 12% (2010 est.)

GOVERNMENT

Country name: *conventional long form:* Republic of Ghana
conventional short form: Ghana
former: Gold Coast
etymology: named for the medieval West African kingdom of the same name, but whose location was actually further north than the modern country

Government type: presidential republic

Capital: *name:* Accra
geographic coordinates: 5 33 N, 0 13 W
time difference: UTC 0 (5 hours ahead of Washington, DC, during Standard Time)

Administrative divisions: 10 regions; Ashanti, Brong-Ahafo, Central, Eastern, Greater Accra, Northern, Upper East, Upper West, Volta, Western

Independence: 6 March 1957 (from the UK)

National holiday: Independence Day, 6 March (1957)

Constitution: history: several previous; latest drafted 31 March 1992, approved and promulgated 28 April 1992, entered into force 7 January 1993
amendments: proposed by Parliament; consideration requires prior referral to the Council of State, a body of prominent citizens who advise the president of the republic; passage of amendments to "entrenched" constitutional articles (including those on national sovereignty, fundamental rights and freedoms, the structure and authorities of the branches of government, and amendment procedures) requires approval in a referendum by at least 40% participation of eligible voters and at least 75% of votes cast, followed by at least two-thirds majority vote in Parliament, and assent by the president; amendments to non-entrenched articles do not require referenda; amended 1996 (2017)

Legal system: mixed system of English common law and customary law

International law organization participation: has not submitted an ICJ jurisdiction declaration; accepts ICCt jurisdiction

Citizenship: *citizenship by birth:* no
citizenship by descent only: at least one parent or grandparent must be a citizen of Ghana
dual citizenship recognized: yes
residency requirement for naturalization: 5 years

Suffrage: 18 years of age; universal

Executive branch: *chief of state:* President Nana Addo Dankwa AKUFO-ADDO (since 7 January 2017); Vice President Mahamudu BAWUMIA (since 7 January 2017); the president is both chief of state and head of government

head of government: President Nana Addo Dankwa AKUFO-ADDO (since 7 January 2017); Vice President Mahamudu BAWUMIA (since 7 January 2017) *cabinet:* Council of Ministers; nominated by the president, approved by Parliament

elections/appointments: president and vice president directly elected on the same ballot by absolute majority popular vote in 2 rounds if needed for a 4-year term (eligible for a second term); election last held on 7 December 2016 (next to be held in December 2020)

election results: Nana Addo Dankwa AKUFO-ADDO elected president; percent of vote—Nana Addo Dankwa AKUFO-ADDO (NPP) 53.8%, John Dramani MAHAMA (NDC) 44.4%, other 1.8%

Legislative branch: description: unicameral Parliament (275 seats; members directly elected in single-seat constituencies by simple majority vote to serve 4-year terms)

elections: last held on 7 December 2016 (next to be held in December 2020)

election results: percent of vote by party—NA; seats by party—NPP 171, NDC 104

Judicial branch: *highest court(s):* Supreme Court (consists of a chief justice and 12 justices)

judge selection and term of office: chief justice appointed by the president in consultation with the Council of State (a small advisory body of prominent citizens) and with the approval of Parliament; other justices appointed by the president upon the advice of the Judicial Council (an 18-member independent body of judicial, military and police officials, and presidential nominees) and on the advice of the Council of State; justices can retire at age 60, with compulsory retirement at age 70

subordinate courts: Court of Appeal; High Court; Circuit Court; District Court; regional tribunals

Political parties and leaders: *note:* Ghana has more than 20 registered parties; included are 5 of the more popular parties as of May 2017

Convention People's Party or CPPm [Edmund DELLE]

National Democratic Congress or NDC [Kofi PORTUPHY]

New Patriotic Party or NPP Nana AKUFO-ADDO]

People's National Convention or PNC Edward MAHAMA]

Peoples Progressive Party or PPP [Dr. Papa Kwesi NDOUM]

Political pressure groups and leaders: public policy think tanks: Institute for Democratic Governance (IDEG); IMANI Center for Policy and Education; Ghana Center for Democratic Development; Institute for Economic Affairs

professional and trade groups: Ghana Bar Association; Ghana Trades Union Congress; American Chamber of Commerce; British Chamber of Commerce; and a host of religious organizations

other: wide range of international and domestic human rights and policy advocacy groups, environmental groups, business organizations, traditional leaders and youth groups

International organization participation: ACP, AfDB, AU, C, ECOWAS, EITI (compliant country), FAO, G-24, G-77, IAEA, IBRD, ICAO, ICC (national committees), ICCt, ICRM, IDA, IFAD, IFC, IFRCS, ILO, IMF, IMO, IMSO, Interpol, IOC, IOM, IPU, ISO, ITSO, ITU, ITUC (NGOs), MIGA, MINURSO, MINUSMA, MONUSCO, NAM, OAS (observer), OIF, OPCW, UN, UNAMID, UNCTAD, UNESCO, UNHCR, UNIDO, UNIFIL, UNISFA, UNMIL, UNMISS, UNOCI, UNWTO, UPU, WCO, WFTU (NGOs), WHO, WIPO, WMO, WTO

Diplomatic representation in the US: *chief of mission:* Ambassador Barfour ADJEI-BARWUAH (since 21 July 2017)

chancery: 3512 International Drive NW, Washington, DC 20008

telephone: [1] (202) 686-4520

FAX: [1] (202) 686-4527

consulate(s) general: New York

Diplomatic representation from the US: *chief of mission:* Ambassador Robert P. JACKSON (since 4 February 2016)

embassy: 24 Fourth Circular Rd., Cantonments, Accra

mailing address: P.O. Box 194, Accra

telephone: [233] 030-274-1000

FAX: [233] 030-274-1389

Flag description: three equal horizontal bands of red (top), yellow, and green, with a large black five-pointed star centered in the yellow band; red symbolizes the blood shed for independence, yellow represents the country's mineral wealth, while green stands for its forests and natural wealth; the black star is said to be the lodestar of African freedom

note: uses the popular Pan-African colors of Ethiopia; similar to the flag of Bolivia, which has a coat of arms centered in the yellow band

National symbol(s): black star, golden eagle; national colors: red, yellow, green, black

National anthem: name: "God Bless Our Homeland Ghana"

lyrics/music: unknown/Philip GBEHO

note: music adopted 1957, lyrics adopted 1966; the lyrics were changed twice, in 1960 when a republic was declared and after a 1966 coup

ECONOMY

Economy—overview: Ghana has a market-based economy with relatively few policy barriers to trade and investment in comparison with other countries in the region, and Ghana is well-endowed with natural resources. Ghana's economy was strengthened by a quarter century of relatively sound management, a competitive business environment, and sustained reductions in poverty levels, but in recent years has suffered the consequences of loose fiscal policy, high budget and current account deficits, and a depreciating currency.

Agriculture accounts for about 20% of GDP and employs more than half of the workforce, mainly small landholders. Gold and cocoa exports, and individual remittances, are major sources of foreign exchange. Expansion of Ghana's nascent oil industry has boosted economic growth, but the fall in oil prices since 2015 reduced by half Ghana's oil revenue. Production at Jubilee, Ghana's offshore oilfield, began in mid-December 2010. The country's first gas processing plant at Atubao is also producing natural gas from the Jubilee field, providing power to several of Ghana's thermal power plants.

As of 2017, key economic concerns facing the government include the lack of reliable electricity and the high debt burden. The AKUFO-ADDO administration has made some progress by committing to fiscal consolidation, but much work is still to be done in 2018. Ghana signed a $920 million extended credit facility with the IMF in April 2015 to help it address its growing economic crisis. The IMF fiscal targets require Ghana to reduce the deficit by cutting subsidies, decreasing the bloated public sector wage bill, strengthening revenue administration, and boosting tax revenues. Priorities for the new administration include rescheduling some of Ghana's $31 billion debt, stimulating economic growth, reducing inflation, and stabilizing the currency. Prospects for new oil and gas production and follow through on tighter fiscal management are likely to help Ghana's economy in 2018.

GDP (purchasing power parity): $130.2 billion (2017 est.)

$123 billion (2016 est.)

$118.8 billion (2015 est.)

note: data are in 2017 dollars

country comparison to the world: 81

GDP (official exchange rate): $45.46 billion (2016 est.)

GDP—real growth rate: 5.9% (2017 est.)

3.5% (2016 est.)

3.8% (2015 est.)

country comparison to the world: 27

GDP—per capita (PPP): $4,600 (2017 est.)

$4,500 (2016 est.)

$4,400 (2015 est.)

note: data are in 2017 dollars

country comparison to the world: 173

Gross national saving: 7.9% of GDP (2017 est.)

7.8% of GDP (2016 est.)

9% of GDP (2015 est.)

country comparison to the world: 166

GDP—composition, by end use:

household consumption: 82.1%

government consumption: 8.7%

investment in fixed capital: 13.9%

investment in inventories: 0.7%

exports of goods and services: 40.3%

imports of goods and services: -45.7% (2017 est.)

GDP—composition, by sector of origin:

agriculture: 18.3%

industry: 24.5%

services: 57.2% (2017 est.)

Agriculture—products: cocoa, rice, cassava (manioc, tapioca), peanuts, corn, shea nuts, bananas; timber

Industries: mining, lumbering, light manufacturing, aluminum smelting, food processing, cement, small commercial ship building, petroleum

Industrial production growth rate: 7.4% (2017 est.)

country comparison to the world: 23

Labor force: 12.49 million (2017 est.)
country comparison to the world: 47

Labor force—by occupation: *agriculture:* 44.7%
industry: 14.4%
services: 40.9% (2013 est.)

Unemployment rate: 11.9% (2015 est.)
5.2% (2013 est.)
country comparison to the world: 153

Population below poverty line: 24.2% (2013 est.)

Household income or consumption by percentage share: *lowest 10%:* 2%
highest 10%: 32.8% (2006)

Distribution of family income—Gini index: 42.3 (2012-13)
41.9 (2005-06)
country comparison to the world: 51

Budget: *revenues:* $9.236 billion
expenditures: $12.38 billion (2017 est.)
Taxes and other revenues: 20.3% of GDP (2017 est.)
country comparison to the world: 151

Budget surplus (+) or deficit (-): -6.9% of GDP (2017 est.)
country comparison to the world: 184

Public debt: 76.8% of GDP (2017 est.)
78.1% of GDP (2016 est.)
country comparison to the world: 45

Fiscal year: calendar year

Inflation rate (consumer prices): 11.8% (2017 est.)
17.5% (2016 est.)
country comparison to the world: 206

Central bank discount rate: 25.5% (31 December 2016)
26% (31 December 2015)
country comparison to the world: 2

Commercial bank prime lending rate: 30% (31 December 2017 est.)
31.3% (31 December 2016 est.)
country comparison to the world: 8

Stock of narrow money: $6.909 billion (31 December 2017 est.)
$6.472 billion (31 December 2016 est.)
country comparison to the world: 92

Stock of broad money: $14.93 billion (31 December 2017 est.)
$13.75 billion (31 December 2016 est.)
country comparison to the world: 99

Stock of domestic credit: $14.23 billion (31 December 2017 est.)
$13.67 billion (31 December 2016 est.)
country comparison to the world: 99

Market value of publicly traded shares: $12.55 billion (31 December 2016 est.)
$15.05 billion (31 December 2015 est.)
$3.465 billion (31 December 2012 est.)
country comparison to the world: 69

Current account balance: -$2.643 billion (2017 est.)
-$2.866 billion (2016 est.)
country comparison to the world: 163

Exports: $12.16 billion (2017 est.)
$11.06 billion (2016 est.)
country comparison to the world: 82

Exports—commodities: oil, gold, cocoa, timber, tuna, bauxite, aluminum, manganese ore, diamonds, horticultural products

Exports—partners: Switzerland 17.6%, India 14.7%, UAE 13.4%, China 8.9%, Vietnam 5.2%, Netherlands 4.2%, Burkina Faso 4% (2016)

Imports: $12.73 billion (2017 est.)
$12.75 billion (2016 est.)
country comparison to the world: 90

Imports—commodities: capital equipment, refined petroleum, foodstuffs

Imports—partners: China 17.3%, UK 9.7%, US 7.7%, Belgium 5.1%, India 4.6% (2016)

Reserves of foreign exchange and gold: $7.345 billion (31 December 2017 est.)
$6.162 billion (31 December 2016 est.)
country comparison to the world: 83

Debt—external: $23.1 billion (31 December 2017 est.)
$21.95 billion (31 December 2016 est.)
country comparison to the world: 90

Stock of direct foreign investment—at home: $19.85 billion (31 December 2013 est.)
$118 million (31 December 2012 est.)
country comparison to the world: 78

Stock of direct foreign investment—abroad: $16.62 billion (31 December 2013 est.)
$109 million (31 December 2012 est.)
country comparison to the world: 56

Exchange rates: cedis (GHC) per US dollar—
4.385 (2017 est.)
3.909 (2016 est.)
3.909 (2015 est.)
3.712 (2014 est.)
2.895 (2013 est.)

Energy

Electricity access: *population without electricity:* 7,300,000
electrification—*total population:* 72%
electrification—urban areas: 92%
electrification—rural areas: 50% (2013)

Electricity—production: 11.09 billion kWh (2015 est.)
country comparison to the world: 96

Electricity—consumption: 8.377 billion kWh (2015 est.)
country comparison to the world: 99

Electricity—exports: 552 million kWh (2015 est.)
country comparison to the world: 66

Electricity—imports: 223 million kWh (2015 est.)
country comparison to the world: 91

Electricity—installed generating capacity: 2.839 million kW (2015 est.)
country comparison to the world: 100

Electricity—from fossil fuels: 44.1% of total installed capacity (2015 est.)
country comparison to the world: 163

Electricity—from nuclear fuels: 0% of total installed capacity (2015 est.)

country comparison to the world: 97

Electricity—from hydroelectric plants: 55.7% of total installed capacity (2015 est.)
country comparison to the world: 32

Electricity—from other renewable sources: 1% of total installed capacity (2015 est.)
country comparison to the world: 138

Crude oil—production: 100,500 bbl/day (2016 est.)
country comparison to the world: 44

Crude oil—exports: 99,890 bbl/day (2015 est.)
country comparison to the world: 37

Crude oil—imports: 13,860 bbl/day (2014 est.)
country comparison to the world: 70

Crude oil—proved reserves: 660 million bbl (1 January 2017 es)
country comparison to the world: 44

Refined petroleum products—production: 2,815 bbl/day (2014 est.)
country comparison to the world: 103

Refined petroleum products—consumption: 79,000 bbl/day (2015 est.)
country comparison to the world: 90

Refined petroleum products—exports: 2,761 bbl/day (2014 est.)
country comparison to the world: 104

Refined petroleum products—imports: 80,350 bbl/day (2014 est.)
country comparison to the world: 65

Natural gas—production: 63.54 million cu m (2016 est.)
country comparison to the world: 84

Natural gas—consumption: 1.325 billion cu m (2015 est.)
country comparison to the world: 92

Natural gas—exports: 0 cu m (2015 est.)
country comparison to the world: 110

Natural gas—imports: 626 million cu m (2015 est.)
country comparison to the world: 66

Natural gas—proved reserves: 22.65 billion cu m (1 January 2017 es)
country comparison to the world: 75

Carbon dioxide emissions from consumption of energy: 11 million Mt (2013 est.)
country comparison to the world: 102

COMMUNICATIONS

Telephones—fixed lines: *total subscriptions:* 251,490
subscriptions per 100 inhabitants: 1 (July 2016 est.)
country comparison to the world: 120

Telephones—mobile cellular: *total:* 38,305,078
subscriptions per 100 inhabitants: 142 (July 2016 est.)
country comparison to the world: 42

Telephone system: *general assessment:* primarily microwave radio relay; wireless local loop has been installed; outdated and unreliable fixed-line infrastructure heavily concentrated in Accra

365

domestic: competition among multiple mobile-cellular providers has spurred growth with a sub-scribership of more than 140 per 100 persons and rising

international: country code—233; landing point for the SAT-3/WASC, Main One, and GLO-1 fiber-optic submarine cables that provide connectivity to South Africa, Europe, and Asia; satellite earth stations—4 Intelsat (Atlantic Ocean); microwave radio relay link to Panaftel system connects Ghana to its neighbors (2016)

Broadcast media: state-owned TV station, 2 state-owned radio networks; several privately owned TV stations and a large number of privately owned radio stations; transmissions of multiple international broadcasters are accessible; several cable and satellite TV subscription services are obtainable (2007)

Internet country code: .gh
Internet users: total: 9,328,018

percent of population: 34.7% (July 2016 est.)
country comparison to the world: 68

TRANSPORTATION

National air transport system: *number of registered air carriers:* 4

inventory of registered aircraft operated by air carriers: 8

annual passenger traffic on registered air carriers: 390,457

annual freight traffic on registered air carriers: 844,630 mt-km (2015)

Civil aircraft registration country code prefix: 9G (2016)

Airports: 10 (2013)
country comparison to the world: 156

Airports—with paved runways: *total:* 7
over 3,047 m: 1
2,438 to 3,047 m: 1
1,524 to 2,437 m: 3
914 to 1,523 m: 2 (2017)

Airports—with unpaved runways: *total:* 3
914 to 1,523 m: 3 (2013)

Pipelines: gas 394 km; oil 20 km; refined products 361 km (2013)

Railways: *total:* 947 km
narrow gauge: 947 km 1.067-m gauge (2014)
country comparison to the world: 92

Roadways: *total:* 109,515 km
paved: 13,787 km
unpaved: 95,728 km (2009)
country comparison to the world: 45

Waterways: 1,293 km (168 km for launches and lighters on Volta, Ankobra, and Tano Rivers; 1,125 km of arterial and feeder waterways on Lake Volta) (2011)
country comparison to the world: 56

Merchant marine: *total:* 44
by type: general cargo 6, oil tanker 2, other 36 (2017)
country comparison to the world: 63

Ports and terminals: *major seaport(s):* Takoradi, Tema

MILITARY AND SECURITY

Military expenditures: 0.38% of GDP (2016)
0.52% of GDP (2015)
0.68% of GDP (2014)
0.53% of GDP (2013)
0.8% of GDP (2012)
country comparison to the world: 125

Military branches: Ghana Army, Ghana Navy, Ghana Air Force (2012)

Military service age and obligation: 18-26 years of age for voluntary military service, with basic education certificate; no conscription; must be HIV/AIDS negative (2012)

TRANSNATIONAL ISSUES

Disputes—international: disputed maritime border between Ghana and Cote d'Ivoire

Refugees and internally displaced persons: *refugees (country of origin):* 6,656 (Cote d'Ivoire) (flight from 2010 post-election fighting) (2017)

Trafficking in persons: *current situation:* Ghana is a source, transit, and destination country for men, women, and children subjected to forced labor and sex trafficking; the trafficking of Ghanaians, particularly children, internally is more common than the trafficking of foreign nationals; Ghanaian children are subjected to forced labor in fishing, domestic service, street hawking, begging, portering, mining, quarrying, herding, and agriculture, with girls, and to a lesser extent boys, forced into prostitution; Ghanaian women, sometimes lured with legitimate job offers, and girls are sex trafficked in West Africa, the Middle East, and Europe; Ghanaian men fraudulently recruited for work in the Middle East are subjected to forced labor or prostitution, and a few Ghanaian adults have been identified as victims of false labor in the US; women and girls from Vietnam, China, and neighboring West African countries are sex trafficked in Ghana; the country is also a transit point for sex trafficking from West Africa to Europe

tier rating: Tier 2 Watch List—Ghana does not fully comply with the minimum standards for the elimination of trafficking; however, it is making significant efforts to do so; Ghana continued to investigate and prosecute trafficking offenses but was unable to ramp up its anti-trafficking efforts in 2014 because the government failed to provide law enforcement or protection agencies with operating budgets; victim protection efforts decreased in 2014, with significantly fewer victims identified; most child victims were referred to NGO-run facilities, but care for adults was lacking because the government did not provide any support to the country's Human Trafficking Fund for victim services or its two shelters; anti-trafficking prevention measures increased modestly, including reconvening of the Human Trafficking Management Board, public awareness campaigns on child labor and trafficking, and anti-trafficking TV and radio programs (2015)

Illicit drugs: illicit producer of cannabis for the international drug trade; major transit hub for Southwest and Southeast Asian heroin and, to a lesser extent, South American cocaine destined for Europe and the US; widespread crime and money-laundering problem, but the lack of a well-developed financial infrastructure limits the country's utility as a money-laundering center; significant domestic cocaine and cannabis use

GIBRALTAR

INTRODUCTION

Background: Strategically important, Gibraltar was reluctantly ceded to Great Britain by Spain in the 1713 Treaty of Utrecht; the British garrison was formally declared a colony in 1830. In a referendum held in 1967, Gibraltarians voted overwhelmingly to remain a British dependency. The subsequent granting of autonomy in 1969 by the UK led Spain to close the border and sever all communication links. Between 1997 and 2002, the UK and Spain held a series of talks on establishing temporary joint sovereignty over Gibraltar. In response to these talks, the Gibraltar Government called a referendum in late 2002 in which the majority of citizens voted overwhelmingly against any sharing of sovereignty with Spain. Since late 2004, Spain, the UK, and Gibraltar have held tripartite talks with the aim of cooperatively resolving problems that affect the local population, and work continues on cooperation agreements in areas such as taxation and financial services; communications and maritime security; policy, legal and customs services; environmental protection; and education and visa services. A new noncolonial constitution came into force in 2007, and the European Court of First Instance recognized Gibraltar's right to regulate its own tax regime in December 2008. The UK retains responsibility for defense, foreign relations, internal security, and financial stability.

Spain and the UK continue to spar over the territory. Throughout 2009, a dispute over Gibraltar's claim to territorial waters extending out three miles gave rise to periodic non-violent maritime confrontations between Spanish and UK naval

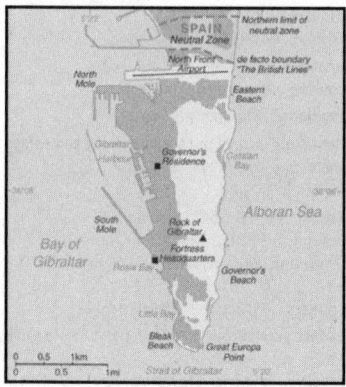

patrols and in 2013, the British reported a record number of entries by Spanish vessels into waters claimed by Gibraltar following a dispute over Gibraltar's creation of an artificial reef in those waters. Spain renewed its demands for an eventual return of Gibraltar to Spanish control after the UK's June 2016 vote to leave the EU, but London has dismissed any connection between the vote and its future commitment to Gibraltar. The European Commission has said that the UK will need to reach a separate bilateral agreement with Spain to allow Gibraltar to be covered by the UK's broader EU exit agreement.

GEOGRAPHY

Location: Southwestern Europe, bordering the Strait of Gibraltar, which links the Mediterranean Sea and the North Atlantic Ocean, on the southern coast of Spain

Geographic coordinates: 36 08 N, 5 21 W

Map references: Europe

Area: *total:* 6.5 sq km
land: 6.5 sq km
water: 0 sq km
country comparison to the world: 246

Area—comparative: more than 10 times the size of The National Mall in Washington, D.C.

Land boundaries: *total:* 1.2 km
border countries (1): Spain 1.2 km

Coastline: 12 km

Maritime claims: *territorial sea:* 3 nm

Climate: Mediterranean with mild winters and warm summers

Terrain: a narrow coastal lowland borders the Rock of Gibraltar

Elevation: *mean elevation:* NA

elevation extremes: *lowest point:* Mediterranean Sea 0 m
highest point: Rock of Gibraltar 426 m

Natural resources: none

Land use: *agricultural land:* 0%
arable land: 0%;
permanent crops: 0%;
permanent pasture: 0%

forest: 0%
other: 100% (2011 est.)
Irrigated land: NA

Natural hazards: occasional droughts; no streams or large bodies of water on the peninsula (all potable water comes from desalination)

Environment—current issues: limited natural freshwater resources: large concrete or natural rock water catchments collect rainwater (no longer used for drinking water) and adequate desalination plant

Geography—note: note 1: strategic location on Strait of Gibraltar that links the North Atlantic Ocean and Mediterranean Sea
note 2: one of only two British territories where traffic drives on the right, the other being the island of Diego Garcia in the British Indian Ocean Territory

PEOPLE AND SOCIETY

Population: 29,396 (July 2017 est.)
country comparison to the world: 218

Nationality: *noun:* Gibraltarian(s)
adjective: Gibraltar

Ethnic groups: Gibraltarian 79%, other British 13.2%, Spanish 2.1%, Moroccan 1.6%, other EU 2.4%, other 1.6% (2012 est.)

Languages: English (used in schools and for official purposes), Spanish, Italian, Portuguese

Religions: Roman Catholic 72.1%, Church of England 7.7%, other Christian 3.8%, Muslim 3.6%, Jewish 2.4%, Hindu 2%, other 1.1%, none 7.1%, unspecified 0.1% (2012 est.)

Age structure: *0-14 years:* 20.22% (male 3,045/female 2,899)
15-24 years: 14.34% (male 2,199/female 2,017)
25-54 years: 39.67% (male 5,958/female 5,703)
55-64 years: 9.68% (male 1,232/female 1,614)
65 years and over: 16.09% (male 2,329/female 2,400) (2017 est.)

Median age: *total:* 34.7 years
male: 33.8 years
female: 35.7 years (2017 est.)
country comparison to the world: 81

Population growth rate: 0.23% (2017 est.)
country comparison to the world: 181

Birth rate: 14 births/1,000 population (2017 est.)
country comparison to the world: 139

Death rate: 8.5 deaths/1,000 population (2017 est.)
country comparison to the world: 78

Net migration rate: -3.3 migrant(s)/1,000 population (2017 est.)
country comparison to the world: 179

Urbanization: *urban population:* 100% of total population (2017)
rate of urbanization: 0.01% annual rate of change (2015-20 est.)

Major urban areas—population: GIBRALTAR (capital) 29,000 (2014)

Sex ratio: *at birth:* 1.07 male(s)/female
0-14 years: 1.05 male(s)/female

15-24 years: 1.1 male(s)/female
25-54 years: 1.03 male(s)/female
55-64 years: 0.81 male(s)/female
65 years and over: 0.97 male(s)/female
total population: 1.01 male(s)/female (2016 est.)

Infant mortality rate: *total:* 5.9 deaths/1,000 live births
male: 6.6 deaths/1,000 live births
female: 5.2 deaths/1,000 live births (2017 est.)
country comparison to the world: 169

Life expectancy at birth: *total population:* 79.6 years
male: 76.7 years
female: 82.6 years (2017 est.)
country comparison to the world: 46

Total fertility rate: 1.9 children born/woman (2017 est.)
country comparison to the world: 136

HIV/AIDS—adult prevalence rate: NA

HIV/AIDS—people living with HIV/AIDS: NA

HIV/AIDS—deaths: NA

Education expenditures: NA

GOVERNMENT

Country name: *conventional long form:* none
conventional short form: Gibraltar
etymology: from the Spanish derivation of the Arabic "Jabal Tariq," which means "Mountain of Tariq" and which refers to the Rock of Gibraltar

Dependency status: overseas territory of the UK

Government type: parliamentary democracy (Parliament); self-governing overseas territory of the UK

Capital: *name:* Gibraltar

geographic coordinates: 36 08 N, 5 21 W
time difference: UTC+1 (6 hours ahead of Washington, DC, during Standard Time)
daylight saving time: +1hr, begins last Sunday in March; ends last Sunday in October

Administrative divisions: none (overseas territory of the UK)

Independence: none (overseas territory of the UK)

National holiday: National Day, 10 September (1967); note—day of the national referendum to decide whether to remain with the UK or join Spain

Constitution: history: previous 1969; latest passed by referendum 30 November 2006, entered into effect 14 December 2006, entered into force 2 January 2007
amendments: proposed by Parliament and require prior consent of the British monarch (through the Secretary of State); passage requires at least three-quarters majority vote in Parliament followed by simple majority vote in a referendum; note—only sections 1 through 15 in Chapter 1 (Protection of Fundamental Rights and Freedoms) can be amended by Parliament (2016)

Legal system: the laws of the UK, where applicable, apply

Citizenship: see United Kingdom

Suffrage: 18 years of age; universal; and British citizens with six months residence or more

Executive branch: *chief of state:* Queen ELIZABETH II (since 6 February 1952); represented by Governor Lt. Gen. Edward DAVIS (since 19 January 2016)

head of government: Chief Minister Fabian PICARDO (since 9 December 2011)

cabinet: Council of Ministers appointed from among the 17 elected members of Parliament by the governor in consultation with the chief minister

elections/appointments: the monarchy is hereditary; governor appointed by the monarch; following legislative elections, the leader of the majority party or majority coalition usually appointed chief minister by the governor

Legislative branch: description: unicameral Parliament (18 seats; 17 members directly elected in a single nationwide constituency by majority vote and 1 appointed by Parliament as speaker; members serve 4-year terms)

elections: last held on 26 November 2015 (next to be held not later than December 2019)

election results: percent of vote by party—GSLP-Liberal Alliance 68.4% (GSLP 47.8%, LPG 20.6%), GSD 31.6%; seats by party—GSLP-Liberal Alliance 10 (GSLP 7, LPG 3), GSD 7

Judicial branch: highest resident court(s): Court of Appeal (consists of at least 3 judges, including the court president); Supreme Court of Gibraltar (consists of the chief justice and 3 judges); note—appeals beyond the Court of Appeal are heard by the Judicial Committee of the Privy Council (in London)

judge selection and term of office: Court of Appeal and Supreme Court judges appointed by the governor upon the advice of the Judicial Service Commission, a 7-member body of judges and appointees of the governor; tenure of the Court of Appeal president based on terms of appointment; Supreme Court chief justice and judges normally appointed until retirement at age 67 but can be extended 3 years

subordinate courts: Court of First Instance; Magistrates' Court; specialized tribunals for issues relating to social security, taxes, and employment

Political parties and leaders: Gibraltar Liberal Party [Joseph GARCIA]

Gibraltar Social Democrats or GSD [Keith AZOPARDI]

Gibraltar Socialist Labor Party or GSLP [Fabian PICARDO]

GSLP-Liberal Alliance (includes GSLP and LPG)

Liberal Party of Gibraltar or LPG

Progressive Democratic Party [Nick CRUZ]

Political pressure groups and leaders: Chamber of Commerce

Gibraltar Representatives Organization

Women's Association

International organization participation: ICC (NGOs), Interpol (subbureau), UPU

Diplomatic representation in the US: none (overseas territory of the UK)

Diplomatic representation from the US: none (overseas territory of the UK)

Flag description: two horizontal bands of white (top, double width) and red with a three-towered red castle in the center of the white band; hanging from the castle gate is a gold key centered in the red band; the design is that of Gibraltar's coat of arms granted on 10 July 1502 by King Ferdinand and Queen Isabella of Spain; the castle symbolizes Gibraltar as a fortress, while the key represents Gibraltar's strategic importance—the key to the Mediterranean

National symbol(s): Barbary macaque; national colors: red, white, yellow

National anthem: name: "Gibraltar Anthem"

lyrics/music: Peter EMBERLEY

note: adopted 1994; serves as a local anthem; as a territory of the United Kingdom, "God Save the Queen" remains official (see United Kingdom)

ECONOMY

Economy—overview: Self-sufficient Gibraltar benefits from an extensive shipping trade, offshore banking, and its position as an international conference center. Tax rates are low to attract foreign investment. The British military presence has been sharply reduced and now contributes about 7% to the local economy, compared with 60% in 1984. In recent years, Gibraltar has seen major structural change from a public to a private sector economy, but changes in government spending still have a major impact on the level of employment.

The financial sector, tourism (over 11 million visitors in 2012), gaming revenues, shipping services fees, and duties on consumer goods also generate revenue. The financial sector, tourism, and the shipping sector contribute 30%, 30%, and 25%, respectively, of GDP. Telecommunications, e-commerce, and e-gaming account for the remaining 15%.

GDP (purchasing power parity): $2.044 billion (2014 est.)

$1.85 billion (2013 est.)

$2 billion (2012 est.)

note: data are in 2014 dollars

country comparison to the world: 197

GDP (official exchange rate): $2.044 billion (2013 est.)

GDP—per capita (PPP): $61,700 (2014 est.)

$43,000 (2008 est.)

$41,200 (2007 est.)

country comparison to the world: 16

GDP—composition, by sector of origin:

agriculture: 0%

industry: 0%

services: 100% (2008 est.)

Agriculture—products: none

Industries: tourism, banking and finance, ship repairing, tobacco

Industrial production growth rate: NA%

Labor force: 24,420 (2014 est.)

country comparison to the world: 210

Labor force—by occupation: *agriculture:* NEGL

industry: 1.8%

services: 98.2% (2014 est.)

Unemployment rate: 1% (2016 est.)

country comparison to the world: 5

Population below poverty line: NA%

Household income or consumption by percentage share: *lowest 10%:* NA%

highest 10%: NA%

Budget: *revenues:* $475.8 million

expenditures: $452.3 million (2008 est.)

Taxes and other revenues: 23.3% of GDP (2008 est.)

country comparison to the world: 127

Budget surplus (+) or deficit (-): 1.1% of GDP (2008 est.)

country comparison to the world: 14

Public debt: 7.5% of GDP (2008 est.)

8.4% of GDP (2006 est.)

country comparison to the world: 200

Fiscal year: 1 July—30 June

Inflation rate (consumer prices): 2.5% (2013 est.)

2.2% (2012 est.)

country comparison to the world: 113

Exports: $202.3 million (2014 est.)

$271 million (2004 est.)

country comparison to the world: 188

Exports—commodities: (principally reexports) petroleum 51%, manufactured goods (2010 est.)

Exports—partners: Spain 22.5%, Poland 16.7%, Netherlands 15.1%, UK 9.9%, Belgium 8.5%, Cote dIvoire 5%, Lebanon 4.2% (2016)

Imports: $2.967 billion (2004 est.)

country comparison to the world: 144

Imports—commodities: fuels, manufactured goods, foodstuffs

Imports—partners: US 22.3%, India 15.2%, Italy 11.2%, Spain 8.6%, Netherlands 7.2%, UK 6.1%, Greece 5.3%, France 4.3% (2016)

Debt—external: $NA

Exchange rates: Gibraltar pounds (GIP) per US dollar—

0.906 (2017 est.)

0.9214 (2016 est.)

0.9214 (2015 est.)

0.885 (2014 est.)

0.7634 (2013 est.)

ENERGY

Electricity—production: 194.6 million kWh (2015 est.)

country comparison to the world: 190

Electricity—consumption: 188.6 million kWh (2015 est.)

country comparison to the world: 191

Electricity—exports: 0 kWh (2016 est.)

country comparison to the world: 141

Electricity—imports: 0 kWh (2016 est.)

country comparison to the world: 154

Electricity—installed generating capacity: 43,000 kW (2015 est.)

country comparison to the world: 197

Electricity—from fossil fuels: 100% of total installed capacity (2015 est.)
country comparison to the world: 7

Electricity—from nuclear fuels: 0% of total installed capacity (2015 est.)
country comparison to the world: 98

Electricity—from hydroelectric plants: 0% of total installed capacity (2015 est.)
country comparison to the world: 177

Electricity—from other renewable sources: 0% of total installed capacity (2015 est.)
country comparison to the world: 184

Crude oil—production: 0 bbl/day (2016 est.)
country comparison to the world: 139

Crude oil—exports: 0 bbl/day (2014 est.)
country comparison to the world: 129

Crude oil—imports: 0 bbl/day (2014 est.)
country comparison to the world: 132

Crude oil—proved reserves: 0 bbl (1 January 2017 es)
country comparison to the world: 139

Refined petroleum products—production: 0 bbl/day (2014 est.)
country comparison to the world: 149

Refined petroleum products—consumption: 70,000 bbl/day (2015 est.)
country comparison to the world: 92

Refined petroleum products—exports: 0 bbl/day (2014 est.)
country comparison to the world: 159

Refined petroleum products—imports: 58,300 bbl/day (2014 est.)
country comparison to the world: 76

Natural gas—production: 0 cu m (2013 est.)
country comparison to the world: 140

Natural gas—consumption: 0 cu m (2013 est.)
country comparison to the world: 185

Natural gas—exports: 0 cu m (2013 est.)
country comparison to the world: 111

Natural gas—imports: 0 cu m (2013 est.)
country comparison to the world: 130

Natural gas—proved reserves: 0 cu m (1 January 2014 es)
country comparison to the world: 144

Carbon dioxide emissions from consumption of energy: 3.6 million Mt (2013 est.)
country comparison to the world: 139

COMMUNICATIONS

Telephones—fixed lines: *total subscriptions:* 17,027
subscriptions per 100 inhabitants: 58 (July 2016 est.)
country comparison to the world: 179

Telephones—mobile cellular: *total:* 45,714
subscriptions per 100 inhabitants: 156 (July 2016 est.)
country comparison to the world: 205

Telephone system: *general assessment:* adequate, automatic domestic system and adequate international facilities
domestic: automatic exchange facilities
international: country code—350; radiotelephone; microwave radio relay; satellite earth station—1 Intelsat (Atlantic Ocean) (2015)

Broadcast media: Gibraltar Broadcasting Corporation (GBC) provides TV and radio broadcasting services via 1 TV station and 4 radio stations; British Forces Broadcasting Service (BFBS) operates 1 radio station; broadcasts from Spanish radio and TV stations are accessible (2008)

Internet country code: .gi
Internet users: total: 27,699

percent of population: 94.4% (July 2016 est.)
country comparison to the world: 200

TRANSPORTATION

Civil aircraft registration country code prefix: VP-G (2016)

Airports: 1 (2013)
country comparison to the world: 220

Airports—with paved runways: total: 1
1,524 to 2,437 m: 1 (2017)

Roadways: total: 29 km
paved: 29 km (2007)
country comparison to the world: 221

Merchant marine: total: 291
by type: bulk carrier 8, container ship 31, general cargo 116, oil tanker 20, other 116 (2017)
country comparison to the world: 4

Ports and terminals: *major seaport(s):* Gibraltar

MILITARY AND SECURITY

Military branches: Royal Gibraltar Regiment (2013)

Military—note: defense is the responsibility of the UK; the Royal Gibraltar Regiment replaced the last British regular infantry forces in 1992

TRANSNATIONAL ISSUES

Disputes—international: in 2002, Gibraltar residents voted overwhelmingly by referendum to reject any "shared sovereignty" arrangement; the Government of Gibraltar insists on equal participation in talks between the UK and Spain; Spain disapproves of UK plans to grant Gibraltar even greater autonomy

GREECE

INTRODUCTION

Background: Greece achieved independence from the Ottoman Empire in 1830. During the second half of the 19th century and the first half of the 20th century, it gradually added neighboring islands and territories, most with Greek-speaking populations. In World War II, Greece was first invaded by Italy (1940) and subsequently occupied by Germany (1941-44); fighting endured in a protracted civil war between supporters of the king and other anti-communist and communist rebels. Following the latter's defeat in 1949, Greece joined NATO in 1952. In 1967, a group of military officers seized power, establishing a military dictatorship that suspended many political liberties and forced the king to flee the country. In 1974 following the collapse of the dictatorship, democratic elections and a referendum created a parliamentary republic and abolished the monarchy. In 1981, Greece joined the EC (now the EU); it became the 12th member of the European Economic and Monetary Union (EMU) in 2001. Greece has suffered a severe economic crisis since late 2009, due to nearly a decade of chronic overspending and structural rigidities. Since 2010, Greece has entered three bailout agreements with the European Commission, the European Central Bank (ECB), the IMF, and with the third, the European Stability Mechanism (ESM). The Greek Government agreed to its current, $96 billion bailout in August 2015, which will conclude August 2018.

GEOGRAPHY

Location: Southern Europe, bordering the Aegean Sea, Ionian Sea, and the Mediterranean Sea, between Albania and Turkey

Geographic coordinates: 39 00 N, 22 00 E

Map references: Europe

Area: *total:* 131,957 sq km

land: 130,647 sq km
water: 1,310 sq km
country comparison to the world: 98

Area—comparative: slightly smaller than Alabama

Land boundaries: *total:* 1,110 km
border countries (4): Albania 212 km, Bulgaria 472 km, Macedonia 234 km, Turkey 192 km

Coastline: 13,676 km

Maritime claims: *territorial sea:* 12 nm
continental shelf: 200-m depth or to the depth of exploitation

Climate: temperate; mild, wet winters; hot, dry summers

Terrain: mountainous with ranges extending into the sea as peninsulas or chains of islands

Elevation: *mean elevation:* 498 m

elevation extremes: *lowest point:* Mediterranean Sea 0 m
highest point: Mount Olympus 2,917 m

Natural resources: lignite, petroleum, iron ore, bauxite, lead, zinc, nickel, magnesite, marble, salt, hydropower potential

Land use: *agricultural land:* 63.4%
arable land: 19.7%;
permanent crops: 8.9%;
permanent pasture: 34.8%
forest: 30.5%
other: 6.1% (2011 est.)
Irrigated land: 15,550 sq km (2012)

Population—distribution: one-third of the population lives in and around metropolitan Athens; the remainder of the country has moderate population density mixed with sizeable urban clusters

Natural hazards: severe earthquakes
volcanism: Santorini (367 m) has been deemed a Decade Volcano by the International Association of Volcanology and Chemistry of the Earth's Interior, worthy of study due to its explosive history and close proximity to human populations; although there have been very few eruptions in recent centuries, Methana and Nisyros in the Aegean are classified as historically active

Environment—current issues: air pollution; water pollution

Environment—international agreements: *party to:* Air Pollution, Air Pollution-Nitrogen Oxides, Air Pollution-Sulfur 94, Antarctic-Environmental Protocol, Antarctic-Marine Living Resources, Antarctic Treaty, Biodiversity, Climate Change, Climate Change-Kyoto Protocol, Desertification, Endangered Species, Environmental Modification, Hazardous Wastes, Law of the Sea, Marine Dumping, Ozone Layer Protection, Ship Pollution, Tropical Timber 83, Tropical Timber 94, Wetlands
signed, but not ratified: Air Pollution-Persistent Organic Pollutants, Air Pollution-Volatile Organic Compounds

Geography—note: strategic location dominating the Aegean Sea and southern approach to Turkish Straits; a peninsular country, possessing an archipelago of about 2,000 islands

PEOPLE AND SOCIETY

Population: 10,768,477 (July 2017 est.)
country comparison to the world: 85

Nationality: *noun:* Greek(s)
adjective: Greek

Ethnic groups: population: Greek 93%, other (foreign citizens) 7% (2001 census)
note: data represent citizenship, since Greece does not collect data on ethnicity

Languages: Greek (official) 99%, other (includes English and French) 1%

Religions: Greek Orthodox (official) 98%, Muslim 1.3%, other 0.7%

Age structure: *0-14 years:* 13.83% (male 767,245/female 722,313)
15-24 years: 9.67% (male 532,179/female 509,487)
25-54 years: 42.45% (male 2,275,984/female 2,295,082)
55-64 years: 13.13% (male 692,420/female 721,641)
65 years and over: 20.91% (male 986,816/female 1,265,310) (2017 est.)

Dependency ratios: *total dependency ratio:* 52.7
youth dependency ratio: 22.2
elderly dependency ratio: 30.5
potential support ratio: 3.3 (2015 est.)

Median age: *total:* 44.5 years
male: 43.5 years
female: 45.6 years (2017 est.)
country comparison to the world: 7

Population growth rate: -0.06% (2017 est.)
country comparison to the world: 204

Birth rate: 8.4 births/1,000 population (2017 est.)
country comparison to the world: 218

Death rate: 11.3 deaths/1,000 population (2017 est.)
country comparison to the world: 27

Net migration rate: 2.3 migrant(s)/1,000 population (2017 est.)
country comparison to the world: 40

Population distribution: one-third of the population lives in and around metropolitan Athens; the remainder of the country has moderate population density mixed with sizeable urban clusters

Urbanization: *urban population:* 78.6% of total population (2017)
rate of urbanization: 0.31% annual rate of change (2015-20 est.)

Major urban areas—population: ATHENS (capital) 3.052 million (2015)

Sex ratio: *at birth:* 1.06 male(s)/female
0-14 years: 1.06 male(s)/female
15-24 years: 1.05 male(s)/female
25-54 years: 0.99 male(s)/female
55-64 years: 0.96 male(s)/female
65 years and over: 0.78 male(s)/female
total population: 0.95 male(s)/female (2016 est.)

Mother's mean age at first birth: 29.8 years (2014 est.)

Maternal mortality ratio: 3 deaths/100,000 live births (2015 est.)
country comparison to the world: 184

Infant mortality rate: *total:* 4.6 deaths/1,000 live births
male: 5 deaths/1,000 live births

female: 4.1 deaths/1,000 live births (2017 est.)
country comparison to the world: 179

Life expectancy at birth: *total population:* 80.7 years
male: 78 years
female: 83.4 years (2017 est.)
country comparison to the world: 36

Total fertility rate: 1.43 children born/woman (2017 est.)
country comparison to the world: 208
Health expenditures: 8.1% of GDP (2014)
country comparison to the world: 53

Physicians density: 6.26 physicians/1,000 population (2014)

Hospital bed density: 4.8 beds/1,000 population (2009)

Drinking water source:
improved:
urban: 100% of population
rural: 100% of population
total: 100% of population
unimproved:
urban: 0% of population
rural: 0% of population
total: 0% of population (2015 est.)

Sanitation facility access:
improved:
urban: 99.2% of population
rural: 98.1% of population
total: 99% of population
unimproved:
urban: 0.8% of population
rural: 1.9% of population
total: 1% of population (2015 est.)

HIV/AIDS—adult prevalence rate: NA

HIV/AIDS—people living with HIV/AIDS: NA (2016 est.)

HIV/AIDS—deaths: NA

Obesity—adult prevalence rate: 24.9% (2016)
country comparison to the world: 54

Literacy: *definition:* age 15 and over can read and write
total population: 97.7%
male: 98.5%
female: 96.9% (2015 est.)

School life expectancy (primary to tertiary education): *total:* 18 years
male: 18 years
female: 18 years (2014)

Unemployment, youth ages 15-24: *total:* 49.8%
male: 45.2%
female: 55% (2015 est.)
country comparison to the world: 3

GOVERNMENT

Country name: *conventional long form:* Hellenic Republic
conventional short form: Greece
local long form: Elliniki Dimokratia
local short form: Ellas or Ellada
former: Hellenic State, Kingdom of Greece

etymology: the English name derives from the Roman (Latin) designation "Graecia," meaning "Land of the Greeks"; the Greeks call their country "Hellas" or "Ellada"

Government type: parliamentary republic

Capital: *name:* Athens

geographic coordinates: 37 59 N, 23 44 E

time difference: UTC+2 (7 hours ahead of Washington, DC, during Standard Time)

daylight saving time: +1hr, begins last Sunday in March; ends last Sunday in October

Administrative divisions: 13 regions (perifereies, singular—perifereia) and 1 autonomous monastic state* (aftonomi monastiki politeia); Agion Oros* (Mount Athos), Anatoliki Makedonia kai Thraki (East Macedonia and Thrace), Attiki (Attica), Dytiki Ellada (West Greece), Dytiki Makedonia (West Macedonia), Ionia Nisia (Ionian Islands), Ipeiros (Epirus), Kentriki Makedonia (Central Macedonia), Kriti (Crete), Notio Aigaio (South Aegean), Peloponnisos (Peloponnese), Sterea Ellada (Central Greece), Thessalia (Thessaly), Voreio Aigaio (North Aegean)

Independence: 3 February 1830 (from the Ottoman Empire); note—25 March 1821, outbreak of the national revolt against the Ottomans; 3 February 1830, signing of the London Protocol recognizing Greek independence by Great Britain, France, and Russia

National holiday: Independence Day, 25 March (1821)

Constitution: history: many previous; latest entered into force 11 June 1975

amendments: proposed by at least 50 members of Parliament and agreed by three-fifths majority vote in two separate ballots at least 30 days apart; passage requires absolute majority vote by the next elected Parliament; entry into force finalized through a "special parliamentary resolution"; articles on human rights and freedoms and the form of government cannot be amended; amended 1986, 2001, 2008 (2016)

Legal system: civil legal system based on Roman law

International law organization participation: accepts compulsory ICJ jurisdiction with reservations; accepts ICCt jurisdiction

Citizenship: *citizenship by birth:* no

citizenship by descent only: at least one parent must be a citizen of Greece

dual citizenship recognized: yes

residency requirement for naturalization: 10 years

Suffrage: 17 years of age; universal and compulsory

Executive branch: *chief of state:* President Prokopios (Prokopis) PAVLOPOULOS (since 13 March 2015)

head of government: Prime Minister Alexios TSIPRAS (since 21 September 2015); note—Vassiliki THANOU-CHRISTOFILOU served as interim prime minister beginning on 27 August 2015 after the resignation of Alexios TSIPRAS

on 20 August 2015; she was Greece's first female prime minister

cabinet: Cabinet appointed by the president on the recommendation of the prime minister

elections/appointments: president elected by Hellenic Parliament for a 5-year term (eligible for a second term); election last held on 18 February 2015 (next to be held by February 2020); president appoints as prime minister the leader of the majority party or coalition in the Hellenic Parliament

election results: Prokopios PAVLOPOULOS (ND) elected president by Parliament—233 of 300 votes

Legislative branch: description: unicameral Hellenic Parliament or Vouli ton Ellinon (300 seats; 288 members directly elected in single- and multi-seat constituencies by proportional representation vote and 12 seats are filled from nationwide party lists; 50 seats allocated to the party with the highest total valid vote count and remaining seats are apportioned according to each party's or coalition's vote percentage; members serve up to 4 years)

elections: last held on 20 September 2015 (next to be held by 2019); note—snap elections were called because of upheaval in the governing SYRIZA party over a new bailout deal with international creditors

election results: percent of vote by party—SYRIZA 35.5%, ND 28.1%, Golden Dawn 7.0%, PASOK-DIMAR 6.3%, KKE 5.6%, To Potami (The River) 4.1%, ANEL 3.7%, EK 3.4%, other 6.3%; seats by party—SYRIZA 145, ND 75, Golden Dawn 18, PASOK-DIMAR 17, KKE 15, To Potami 11, ANEL 10, EK 9; note—only parties surpassing a 3% threshold are entitled to parliamentary seats; parties need 10 seats to become formal parliamentary groups but can retain that status if the party participated in the last election and received the minimum 3% threshold

Judicial branch: *highest court(s):* Supreme Civil and Criminal Court or Areios Pagos (consists of 56 judges including the court presidents); Council of State (supreme administrative court) consists of the president, vice president, 42 privy councillors, and 98 associate and reporting judges, organized into 5- and 7-member chambers; Hellenic Court of Audit (government audit and enforcement) consists of the president, 5 vice presidents, 20 councillors, and 90 associate and reporting judges

judge selection and term of office: Supreme Court judges appointed by presidential decree on the advice of the Supreme Judicial Council (SJC), which includes the president of the Supreme Court, other judges, and the prosecutor of the Supreme Court; judges appointed for life following a 2-year probationary period; Council of State president appointed by the Greek Cabinet to serve a 4-year term; other judge appointments and tenure NA; Court of Audit president appointed by decree of the president of the republic on the advice of the SJC to serve a 4-year term with an age limit of 67

subordinate courts: Courts of Appeal and Courts of First Instance(district courts)

Political parties and leaders: Anticapitalist Left Cooperation for the Overthrow or ANTARSYA [collective leadership]
Coalition of the Radical Left or SYRIZA [Alexios (Alexis) TSIPRAS]
Communist Party of Greece or KKE [Dimitrios KOUTSOUMBAS]
Democratic Left or DIMAR [Athanasios (Thanasis) THEOCHAROPOULOS]
Independent Greeks or ANEL [Panagiotis (Panos) KAMMENOS]
Movement of Democratic Socialists or KIDISO [Georgios PAPANDREOU]
New Democracy or ND [Kyriakos MITSOTAKIS]
Panhellenic Socialist Movement or PASOK [Foteini (Fofi) GENIMMATA]
People's Association-Golden Dawn [Nikolaos MICHALOLIAKOS]
Popular Unity or LAE [Panagiotis LAFAZANIS]
To Potami (The River) [Stavros THEODORAKIS]
Union of Centrists or EK [Vasilis LEVENTIS]

Political pressure groups and leaders: Supreme Administration of Civil Servants Unions or ADEDY [Spyros PAPASPYROS]
Federation of Greek Industries or SEV [Theodore FESSAS]
General Confederation of Greek Workers or GSEE [Ioannis PANAGOPOULOS]

International organization participation: Australia Group, BIS, BSEC, CD, CE, CERN, EAPC, EBRD, ECB, EIB, EMU, ESA, EU, FAO, FATF, IAEA, IBRD, ICAO, ICC (national committees), ICCt, ICRM, IDA, IEA, IFAD, IFC, IFRCS, IGAD (partners), IHO, ILO, IMF, IMO, IMSO, Interpol, IOC, IOM, IPU, ISO, ITSO, ITU, ITUC (NGOs), MIGA, NATO, NEA, NSG, OAS (observer), OECD, OIF, OPCW, OSCE, PCA, Schengen Convention, SELEC, UN, UNCTAD, UNESCO, UNHCR, UNIDO, UNIFIL, UNWTO, UPU, WCO, WFTU (NGOs), WHO, WIPO, WMO, WTO, ZC

Diplomatic representation in the US: *chief of mission:* Ambassador Theocharis LALAKOS (since 27 June 2016)

chancery: 2217 Massachusetts Avenue NW, Washington, DC 20008

telephone: [1] (202) 939-1300

FAX: [1] (202) 939-1324

consulate(s) general: Boston, Chicago, Los Angeles, New York, Tampa (FL), San Francisco

consulate(s): Atlanta, Houston

Diplomatic representation from the US: *chief of mission:* Ambassador Geoffrey R. PYATT (since 24 October 2016)

embassy: 91 Vasillisis Sophias Avenue, 10160 Athens

mailing address: PSC 108, APO AE 09842-0108

telephone: [30] (210) 721-2951

FAX: [30] (210) 645-6282

consulate(s) general: Thessaloniki

Flag description: nine equal horizontal stripes of blue alternating with white; a blue square bearing a white cross appears in the upper hoist-side corner; the cross symbolizes Greek Orthodoxy, the established religion of the country; there is no agreed upon meaning for the nine stripes or for the colors

note: Greek legislation states that the flag colors are cyan and white, but cyan can mean "blue" in Greek, so the exact shade of blue has never been set and has varied from a light to a dark blue over time; in general, the hue of blue normally encountered is a form of azure

National symbol(s): Greek cross (white cross on blue field, arms equal length); national colors: blue, white

National anthem: name: "Ymnos eis tin Eleftherian" (Hymn to Liberty)

lyrics/music: Dionysios SOLOMOS/Nikolaos MANTZAROS

note: adopted 1864; the anthem is based on a 158-stanza poem by the same name, which was inspired by the Greek Revolution of 1821 against the Ottomans (only the first two stanzas are used); Cyprus also uses "Hymn to Liberty" as its anthem

ECONOMY

Economy—overview: Greece has a capitalist economy with a public sector accounting for about 40% of GDP and with per capita GDP about two-thirds that of the leading euro-zone economies. Tourism provides 18% of GDP. Immigrants make up nearly one-fifth of the work force, mainly in agricultural and unskilled jobs. Greece is a major beneficiary of EU aid, equal to about 3.3% of annual GDP.

The Greek economy averaged growth of about 4% per year between 2003 and 2007, but the economy went into recession in 2009 as a result of the world financial crisis, tightening credit conditions, and Athens' failure to address a growing budget deficit. By 2013, the economy had contracted 26%, compared with the pre-crisis level of 2007. Greece met the EU's Growth and Stability Pact budget deficit criterion of no more than 3% of GDP in 2007-08, but violated it in 2009, when the deficit reached 15% of GDP. Deteriorating public finances, inaccurate and misreported statistics, and consistent underperformance on reforms prompted major credit rating agencies to downgrade Greece's international debt rating in late 2009 and led the country into a financial crisis. Under intense pressure from the EU and international market participants, the government accepted a bailout program that called on Athens to cut government spending, decrease tax evasion, overhaul the civil-service, health-care, and pension systems, and reform the labor and product markets. Austerity measures reduced the deficit to 1.3% in 2017. Successive Greek governments, however, failed to push through many of the most unpopular reforms in the face of widespread political opposition, including from the country's powerful labor unions and the general public.

In April 2010, a leading credit agency assigned Greek debt its lowest possible credit rating, and in May 2010, the IMF and euro-zone governments provided Greece emergency short- and medium-term loans worth $147 billion so that the country could make debt repayments to creditors. Greece, however, struggled to meet the targets set by the EU and the IMF, especially after Eurostat—the EU's statistical office—revised upward Greece's deficit and debt numbers for 2009 and 2010. European leaders and the IMF agreed in October 2011 to provide Athens a second bailout package of $169 billion. The second deal called for holders of Greek government bonds to write down a significant portion of their holdings to try to alleviate Greece's government debt burden. However, Greek banks, saddled with a significant portion of sovereign debt, were adversely affected by the write down and $60 billion of the second bailout package was set aside to ensure the banking system was adequately capitalized.

In 2014, the Greek economy began to turn the corner on the recession. Greece achieved three significant milestones: balancing the budget—not including debt repayments; issuing government debt in financial markets for the first time since 2010; and generating 0.7% GDP growth—the first economic expansion since 2007.

Despite the nascent recovery, widespread discontent with austerity measures helped propel the far-left Coalition of the Radical Left (SYRIZA) party into government in national legislative elections in January 2015. Between January and July 2015, frustrations between the SYRIZA-led government and Greece's EU and IMF creditors over the implementation of bailout measures and disbursement of funds led the Greek government to run up significant arrears to suppliers and Greek banks to rely on emergency lending, and also called into question Greece's future in the euro zone. To stave off a collapse of the banking system, Greece imposed capital controls in June 2015 shortly before rattling international financial markets by becoming the first developed nation to miss a loan payment to the IMF. Unable to reach an agreement with creditors, Prime Minister Alexios TSIPRAS held a nationwide referendum on 5 July on whether to accept the terms of Greece's bailout, campaigning for the ultimately successful "no" vote. The TSIPRAS government subsequently agreed, however, to a new $96 billion bailout in order to avert Greece's exit from the monetary bloc. On 20 August, Greece signed its third bailout which allowed it to cover significant debt payments to its EU and IMF creditors and ensure the banking sector retained access to emergency liquidity. The TSIPRAS government — which retook office on 20 September after calling new elections in late August—successfully secured disbursal of two delayed tranches of bailout funds. Despite the economic turmoil, Greek GDP did not contract as sharply as feared, with official estimates of a -0.2% contraction in 2015, boosted in part by a strong tourist season.

In 2017, Greece saw improvements in GDP and unemployment. Unfinished economic reforms, a massive non-performing loan problem, and ongoing uncertainty regarding the political direction of the country hold the economy back. Some estimates put Greece's black market at 20- to 25% of GDP, as more people have stopped reporting their income to avoid paying taxes that, in some cases, have risen to 70% of an individual's gross income. These issues will continue to be a drag on the economy in 2018 and further delay recovery from the financial crisis.

GDP (purchasing power parity): $299.5 billion (2017 est.)

$294.4 billion (2016 est.)

$294.3 billion (2015 est.)

note: data are in 2017 dollars

country comparison to the world: 59

GDP (official exchange rate): $204.3 billion (2016 est.)

GDP—real growth rate: 1.8% (2017 est.)

0% (2016 est.)

-0.2% (2015 est.)

country comparison to the world: 162

GDP—per capita (PPP): $27,800 (2017 est.)

$27,300 (2016 est.)

$27,100 (2015 est.)

note: data are in 2017 dollars

country comparison to the world: 72

Gross national saving: 10.5% of GDP (2017 est.)

9.9% of GDP (2016 est.)

9.9% of GDP (2015 est.)

country comparison to the world: 155

GDP—composition, by end use:

household consumption: 73.3%

government consumption: 19.5%

investment in fixed capital: 10.9%

investment in inventories: -1.7%

exports of goods and services: 31.5%

imports of goods and services: -33.6% (2017 est.)

GDP—composition, by sector of origin:

agriculture: 4%

industry: 16%

services: 80% (2017 est.)

Agriculture—products: wheat, corn, barley, sugar beets, olives, tomatoes, wine, tobacco, potatoes; beef, dairy products

Industries: tourism, food and tobacco processing, textiles, chemicals, metal products; mining, petroleum

Industrial production growth rate: 3% (2017 est.)

country comparison to the world: 101

Labor force: 4.769 million (2017 est.)

country comparison to the world: 85

Labor force—by occupation: *agriculture:* 12.6%

industry: 15%

services: 72.4% (30 October 2015 e)

Unemployment rate: 22.3% (2017 est.)

23.6% (2016 est.)

country comparison to the world: 188

Population below poverty line: 36% (2014 est.)

Household income or consumption by percentage share: *lowest 10%:* 1.7%

highest 10%: 26.7% (2015 est.)

Distribution of family income—Gini index: 36.7 (2012 est.)

35.7 (2011)

country comparison to the world: 83

Budget: *revenues:* $95.36 billion

expenditures: $98.08 billion (2017 est.)

Taxes and other revenues: 46.7% of GDP (2017 est.)
country comparison to the world: 20

Budget surplus (+) or deficit (-): -1.3% of GDP (2017 est.)
country comparison to the world: 64

Public debt: 180% of GDP (2017 est.)
179.4% of GDP (2016 est.)
country comparison to the world: 2

Fiscal year: calendar year

Inflation rate (consumer prices): 1.2% (2017 est.)
0% (2016 est.)
country comparison to the world: 54

Central bank discount rate: 0.05% (31 March 2016)
0.15% (11 June 2014)
note: this is the European Central Bank's rate on the marginal lending facility, which offers overnight credit to banks in the euro area
country comparison to the world: 145

Commercial bank prime lending rate: 5.5% (31 December 2017 est.)
5.62% (31 December 2016 est.)
country comparison to the world: 135

Stock of narrow money: $97.61 billion (31 December 2017 est.)
$86.53 billion (31 December 2016 est.)
note: see entry for the European Union for money supply for the entire euro area; the European Central Bank (ECB) controls monetary policy for the 18 members of the Economic and Monetary Union (EMU); individual members of the EMU do not control the quantity of money circulating within their own borders
country comparison to the world: 41

Stock of broad money: $156.9 billion (31 December 2017 est.)
$138.9 billion (31 December 2016 est.)
country comparison to the world: 50

Stock of domestic credit: $249.1 billion (31 December 2017 est.)
$231.4 billion (31 December 2016 est.)
country comparison to the world: 42

Market value of publicly traded shares: $42.08 billion (31 December 2015 est.)
$55.15 billion (31 December 2014 est.)
$82.59 billion (31 December 2013 est.)
country comparison to the world: 57

Current account balance: -$498 million (2017 est.)
-$1.238 billion (2016 est.)
country comparison to the world: 105

Exports: $29.23 billion (2017 est.)
$27.1 billion (2016 est.)
country comparison to the world: 63

Exports—commodities: food and beverages, manufactured goods, petroleum products, chemicals, textiles

Exports—partners: Italy 11.2%, Germany 7.7%, Cyprus 6.4%, Turkey 5.3%, Bulgaria 5.2%, US 4.3%, UK 4.2%, Lebanon 4.1% (2016)

Imports: $50.23 billion (2017 est.)

$45.45 billion (2016 est.)
country comparison to the world: 49

Imports—commodities: machinery, transport equipment, fuels, chemicals

Imports—partners: Germany 11.1%, Italy 8.8%, China 6.6%, Russia 6.4%, Netherlands 5.5%, Iraq 5.4%, France 4.4%, South Korea 4.1% (2016)

Reserves of foreign exchange and gold: $6.893 billion (31 December 2016 est.)
$6.026 billion (31 December 2015 est.)
country comparison to the world: 84

Debt—external: $506.6 billion (31 March 2016 est.)
$468.2 billion (31 March 2015 est.)
country comparison to the world: 22

Stock of direct foreign investment—at home: $34.18 billion (31 December 2017 est.)
$30.8 billion (31 December 2016 est.)
country comparison to the world: 68

Stock of direct foreign investment—abroad: $33.79 billion (31 December 2017 est.)
$32.91 billion (31 December 2016 est.)
country comparison to the world: 49

Exchange rates: euros (EUR) per US dollar—
0.906 (2017 est.)
0.9214 (2016 est.)
0.9214 (2015 est.)
0.885 (2014 est.)
0.7634 (2013 est.)

ENERGY

Electricity access: electrification—*total population:* 100% (2016)

Electricity—production: 48.34 billion kWh (2015 est.)
country comparison to the world: 54

Electricity—consumption: 53.05 billion kWh (2015 est.)
country comparison to the world: 48

Electricity—exports: 1.037 billion kWh (2016 est.)
country comparison to the world: 58

Electricity—imports: 9.833 billion kWh (2016 est.)
country comparison to the world: 26

Electricity—installed generating capacity: 18.94 million kW (2015 est.)
country comparison to the world: 46

Electricity—from fossil fuels: 56.8% of total installed capacity (2015 est.)
country comparison to the world: 137

Electricity—from nuclear fuels: 0% of total installed capacity (2015 est.)
country comparison to the world: 102

Electricity—from hydroelectric plants: 14.2% of total installed capacity (2015 est.)
country comparison to the world: 105

Electricity—from other renewable sources: 26.8% of total installed capacity (2015 est.)
country comparison to the world: 19

Crude oil—production: 3,172 bbl/day (2016 est.)
country comparison to the world: 85

Crude oil—exports: 3,082 bbl/day (2016 est.)
country comparison to the world: 65

Crude oil—imports: 477,400 bbl/day (2016 est.)
country comparison to the world: 20

Crude oil—proved reserves: 10 million bbl (1 January 2017 es)
country comparison to the world: 93

Refined petroleum products—production: 626,000 bbl/day (2016 est.)
country comparison to the world: 28

Refined petroleum products—consumption: 299,600 bbl/day (2016 est.)
country comparison to the world: 44

Refined petroleum products—exports: 351,700 bbl/day (2016 est.)
country comparison to the world: 23

Refined petroleum products—imports: 181,000 bbl/day (2016 est.)
country comparison to the world: 34

Natural gas—production: 4 million cu m (2015 est.)
country comparison to the world: 100

Natural gas—consumption: 4.354 billion cu m (2015 est.)
country comparison to the world: 71

Natural gas—exports: 0 cu m (2014 est.)
country comparison to the world: 115

Natural gas—imports: 3.162 billion cu m (2015 est.)
country comparison to the world: 43

Natural gas—proved reserves: 991.1 million cu m (1 January 2017 es)
country comparison to the world: 104

Carbon dioxide emissions from consumption of energy: 78 million Mt (2013 est.)
country comparison to the world: 46

COMMUNICATIONS

Telephones—fixed lines: *total subscriptions:* 5.126 million
subscriptions per 100 inhabitants: 48 (July 2016 est.)
country comparison to the world: 29

Telephones—mobile cellular: *total:* 12,538,927
subscriptions per 100 inhabitants: 116 (July 2016 est.)
country comparison to the world: 72

Telephone system: *general assessment:* adequate, modern networks reach all areas; good mobile telephone and international service
domestic: microwave radio relay trunk system; extensive open-wire connections; submarine cable to offshore islands
international: country code—30; landing point for the SEA-ME-WE-3 optical telecommunications submarine cable that provides links to Europe, Middle East, and Asia; a number of smaller submarine cables provide connectivity to various parts of Europe, the Middle East, and Cyprus; tropospheric scatter; satellite earth stations—4 (2 Intelsat—1 Atlantic Ocean and 1 Indian Ocean,

1 Eutelsat, and 1 Inmarsat—Indian Ocean region) (2015)

Broadcast media: Broadcast media dominated by the private sector; roughly 150 private TV channels, about ten of which broadcast nationwide; 1 government-owned terrestrial TV channel with national coverage; 3 privately owned satellite channels; multi-channel satellite and cable TV services available; upwards of 1,500 radio stations, all of them privately owned; government-owned broadcaster has 2 national radio stations (2014)

Internet country code: .gr
Internet users: total: 7,443,016
percent of population: 69.1% (July 2016 est.)
country comparison to the world: 56

TRANSPORTATION

National air transport system: *number of registered air carriers:* 9
inventory of registered aircraft operated by air carriers: 93
annual passenger traffic on registered air carriers: 12,583,541
annual freight traffic on registered air carriers: 27,452,961 mt-km (2015)
Civil aircraft registration country code prefix: SX (2016)

Airports: 77 (2013)
country comparison to the world: 69

Airports—with paved runways: total: 68
over 3,047 m: 6
2,438 to 3,047 m: 15
1,524 to 2,437 m: 19
914 to 1,523 m: 18
under 914 m: 10 (2017)

Airports—with unpaved runways: total: 9
914 to 1,523 m: 2
under 914 m: 7 (2013)

Heliports: 9 (2013)

Pipelines: gas 1,329 km; oil 94 km (2013)

Railways: total: 2,548 km
standard gauge: 1,565 km 1.435-m gauge (764 km electrified)
narrow gauge: 961 km 1.000-m gauge; 22 km 0.750-m gauge (2014)

country comparison to the world: 65

Roadways: total: 116,960 km
paved: 41,357 km (includes 1,091 km of expressways)
unpaved: 75,603 km (2010)
country comparison to the world: 41

Waterways: 6 km (the 6-km-long Corinth Canal crosses the Isthmus of Corinth; it shortens a sea voyage by 325 km) (2012)
country comparison to the world: 106

Merchant marine: total: 1,364
by type: bulk carrier 207, container ship 7, general cargo 127, oil tanker 423, other 600 (2017)
country comparison to the world: 21

Ports and terminals: *major seaport(s):* Aspropyrgos, Pachi, Piraeus, Thessaloniki
oil terminal(s): Agioi Theodoroi
container port(s): Piraeus (3,360,000) (2015)
LNG terminal(s) (import): Revithoussa

MILITARY AND SECURITY

Military expenditures: 2.56% of GDP (2016)
2.54% of GDP (2015)
2.34% of GDP (2014)
2.36% of GDP (2013)
2.41% of GDP (2012)
country comparison to the world: 48

Military branches: Hellenic Army (Ellinikos Stratos, ES), Hellenic Navy (Elliniko Polemiko Navtiko, EPN), Hellenic Air Force (Elliniki Polemiki Aeroporia, EPA) (2013)

Military service age and obligation: 19-45 years of age for compulsory military service; during wartime the law allows for recruitment beginning January of the year of inductee's 18th birthday, thus including 17 year olds; 18 years of age for volunteers; conscript service obligation is 1 year for the Army and 9 months for the Air Force and Navy; women are eligible for voluntary military service (2014)

TERRORISM

Terrorist groups—home based: *Revolutionary Struggle (RS): goals:* disrupt the influence of globalization and international capitalism on Greek

society, which RS blames for perceived unequal wealth distribution in Greece and, ultimately, overthrow the Greek Government
area(s) of operation: operates exclusively inside Greece, primarily in Athens; largely inactive in recent years, with the exception of shootouts with police officers trying to arrest members; RS claimed responsibility for a car bombing in central Athens on 10 April 2014 that resulted in no injuries but did cause substantial structural damage; has a history of conducting bombing and direct-fire attacks against Greek Government officials and buildings and officials' residences, multinational firms, domestic and foreign financial institutes, and embassies and diplomats; overall leader Panagiota ROUPA (a.k.a. Pola) was taken into Greek custody on 5 January 2017

TRANSNATIONAL ISSUES

Disputes—international: Greece and Turkey continue discussions to resolve their complex maritime, air, territorial, and boundary disputes in the Aegean Sea; Greece rejects the use of the name Macedonia or Republic of Macedonia; the mass migration of unemployed Albanians still remains a problem for developed countries, chiefly Greece and Italy

Refugees and internally displaced persons: *refugees (country of origin):* 14,420 (Syria); 11,440 (Afghanistan); 8,161 (Iraq) (2016)
stateless persons: 198 (2016)
note: 1,070,898 estimated refugee and migrant arrivals (January 2015—February 2018); as of December 2017, an estimated 49,927 migrants and refugees were stranded in Greece

Illicit drugs: a gateway to Europe for traffickers smuggling cannabis and heroin from the Middle East and Southwest Asia to the West and precursor chemicals to the East; some South American cocaine transits or is consumed in Greece; money laundering related to drug trafficking and organized crime

GREENLAND

INTRODUCTION

Background: Greenland, the world's largest island, is about 81% ice-capped. Vikings reached the island in the 10th century from Iceland; Danish colonization began in the 18th century, and Greenland became an integral part of the Danish Realm in 1953. It joined the European Community (now the EU) with Denmark in 1973 but withdrew in 1985 over a dispute centered on stringent fishing quotas. Greenland remains a member of the Overseas Countries and Territories Association of

the EU. Greenland was granted self-government in 1979 by the Danish parliament; the law went into effect the following year. Greenland voted in favor of increased self-rule in November 2008 and acquired greater responsibility for internal affairs when the Act on Greenland Self-Government was signed into law in June 2009. Denmark, however, continues to exercise control over several policy areas on behalf of Greenland, including foreign affairs, security, and financial policy in consultation with Greenland's Self-Rule Government.

GEOGRAPHY

Location: Northern North America, island between the Arctic Ocean and the North Atlantic Ocean, northeast of Canada

Geographic coordinates: 72 00 N, 40 00 W

Map references: Arctic Region

Area: *total:* 2,166,086 sq km
land: 2,166,086 sq km (410,449 sq km ice-free, 1,755,637 sq km ice-covered)
country comparison to the world: 13

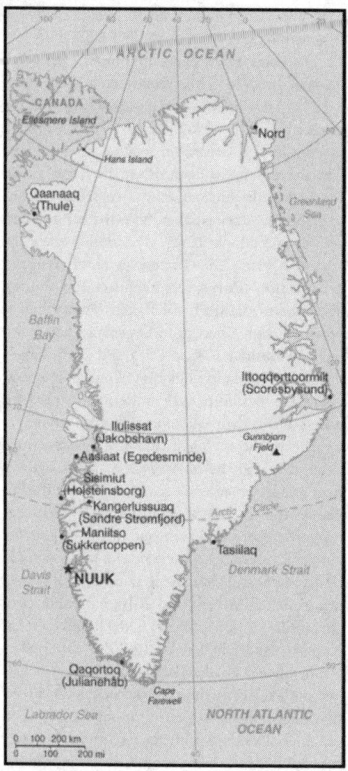

Area—comparative: slightly more than three times the size of Texas

Land boundaries: 0 km

Coastline: 44,087 km

Maritime claims: *territorial sea:* 3 nm
exclusive fishing zone: 200 nm or agreed boundaries or median line
continental shelf: 200 nm or agreed boundaries or median line

Climate: arctic to subarctic; cool summers, cold winters

Terrain: flat to gradually sloping icecap covers all but a narrow, mountainous, barren, rocky coast

Elevation: *mean elevation:* 1,792 m

elevation extremes: *lowest point:* Atlantic Ocean 0 m
highest point: Gunnbjorn Fjeld 3,694 m

Natural resources: coal, iron ore, lead, zinc, molybdenum, diamonds, gold, platinum, niobium, tantalite, uranium, fish, seals, whales, hydropower, possible oil and gas

Land use: *agricultural land:* 0.6%
arable land: 0%;
permanent crops: 0%;
permanent pasture: 0.6%
forest: 0%
other: 99.4% (2011 est.)
Irrigated land: NA

Population—distribution: settlement concentrated on the southwest shoreline, with limited settlements scattered along the remaining coast; interior is uninhabited

Natural hazards: continuous permafrost over northern two-thirds of the island

Environment—current issues: protection of the arctic environment; preservation of the Inuit traditional way of life, including whaling and seal hunting

Geography—note: dominates North Atlantic Ocean between North America and Europe; sparse population confined to small settlements along coast; close to one-quarter of the population lives in the capital, Nuuk; world's second largest ice sheet after that of Antarctica

PEOPLE AND SOCIETY

Population: 57,713 (July 2017 est.)
country comparison to the world: 206

Nationality: *noun:* Greenlander(s)
adjective: Greenlandic

Ethnic groups: Inuit 88%, Danish and other 12% (2010 est.)

Languages: Greenlandic (East Inuit) (official), Danish (official), English

Religions: Evangelical Lutheran, traditional Inuit spiritual beliefs

Age structure: *0-14 years:* 21.11% (male 6,195/female 5,986)
15-24 years: 15.48% (male 4,506/female 4,429)
25-54 years: 41.21% (male 12,473/female 11,309)
55-64 years: 12.96% (male 4,112/female 3,370)
65 years and over: 9.24% (male 2,862/female 2,471) (2017 est.)

Median age: *total:* 33.9 years
male: 35 years
female: 32.7 years (2017 est.)
country comparison to the world: 87

Population growth rate: -0.03% (2017 est.)
country comparison to the world: 200

Birth rate: 14.4 births/1,000 population (2017 est.)
country comparison to the world: 133

Death rate: 8.7 deaths/1,000 population (2017 est.)
country comparison to the world: 71

Net migration rate: -6 migrant(s)/1,000 population (2017 est.)
country comparison to the world: 197

Population distribution: settlement concentrated on the southwest shoreline, with limited settlements scattered along the remaining coast; interior is uninhabited

Urbanization: *urban population:* 87.2% of total population (2017)
rate of urbanization: 0.27% annual rate of change (2015-20 est.)

Major urban areas—population: NUUK (capital) 17,000 (2014)

Sex ratio: *at birth:* 1.05 male(s)/female
0-14 years: 1.03 male(s)/female
15-24 years: 1.02 male(s)/female
25-54 years: 1.1 male(s)/female
55-64 years: 1.26 male(s)/female
65 years and over: 1.15 male(s)/female
total population: 1.1 male(s)/female (2016 est.)

Infant mortality rate: *total:* 8.9 deaths/1,000 live births
male: 10.1 deaths/1,000 live births
female: 7.5 deaths/1,000 live births (2017 est.)
country comparison to the world: 148

Life expectancy at birth: *total population:* 72.6 years
male: 69.9 years
female: 75.5 years (2017 est.)
country comparison to the world: 146

Total fertility rate: 1.99 children born/woman (2017 est.)
country comparison to the world: 123

Physicians density: 1.73 physicians/1,000 population (2014)

Hospital bed density: 8.2 beds/1,000 population (2014)

Drinking water source:
improved:
urban: 100% of population
rural: 100% of population
total: 100% of population
unimproved:
urban: 0% of population
rural: 0% of population
total: 0% of population (2015 est.)

Sanitation facility access:
improved:
urban: 100% of population
rural: 100% of population
total: 100% of population
unimproved:
urban: 0% of population
rural: 0% of population
total: 0% of population (2015 est.)

HIV/AIDS—adult prevalence rate: NA

HIV/AIDS—people living with HIV/AIDS: NA

HIV/AIDS—deaths: NA

Literacy: *definition:* age 15 and over can read and write
total population: 100%
male: 100%
female: 100% (2015 est.)

GOVERNMENT

Country name: *conventional long form:* none
conventional short form: Greenland
local long form: none
local short form: Kalaallit Nunaat
note: named by Norwegian adventurer Erik THORVALDSSON (Erik the Red) in A.D. 985 in order to entice settlers to the island

Dependency status: part of the Kingdom of Denmark; self-governing overseas administrative division of Denmark since 1979

Government type: parliamentary democracy (Parliament of Greenland or Inatsisartut)

Capital: *name:* Nuuk (Godthaab)

geographic coordinates: 64 11 N, 51 45 W

time difference: UTC-3 (2 hours ahead of Washington, DC, during Standard Time)

daylight saving time: +1hr, begins last Sunday in March; ends last Sunday in October

note: Greenland has four time zones

Administrative divisions: 4 municipalities (kommuner, singular kommune); Kujalleq, Qaasuitsup, Qeqqata, Sermersooq

note: the North and East Greenland National Park (Avannaarsuani Tunumilu Nuna Allanngutsaaliugaq) and the Thule Air Base in Pituffik (in northwest Greenland) are two unincorporated areas; the national park's 972,000 sq km—about 46% of the island—makes it the largest national park in the world and also the most northerly

Independence: none (extensive self-rule as part of the Kingdom of Denmark; foreign affairs is the responsibility of Denmark, but Greenland actively participates in international agreements relating to Greenland)

National holiday: National Day, June 21; note—marks the summer solstice and the longest day of the year in the Northern Hemisphere

Constitution: previous 1953 (Greenland established as a constituency in the Danish constitution), 1979 (Greenland Home Rule Act); latest 21 June 2009 (Greenland Self-Government Act) (2016)

Legal system: the laws of Denmark apply where applicable and Greenlandic law applies to other areas

Citizenship: see Denmark

Suffrage: 18 years of age; universal

Executive branch: *chief of state:* Queen MARGRETHE II of Denmark (since 14 January 1972), represented by High Commissioner Mikaela ENGELL (since April 2011)

head of government: Premier Kim KIELSEN (since 30 September 2014)

cabinet: Self-rule Government (Naalakkersuisut) elected by the Parliament (Inatsisartut) on the basis of the strength of parties

elections/appointments: the monarchy is hereditary; high commissioner appointed by the monarch; premier indirectly elected by Parliament for a 4-year term

election results: Kim KIELSEN elected premier; Parliament vote—Kim KIELSEN (S) 34.3%, Sara OLSVIG (IA) 33.2%, Anda ULDUM (D) 11.8%, other 20.7%

Legislative branch: description: unicameral Parliament or Inatsisartut (31 seats; members directly elected in multi-seat constituencies by proportional representation vote to serve 4-year terms)

elections: last held on 28 November 2014 (next to be held by 2018)

election results: percent of vote by party—S 34.6%, IA 33.5%, D 11.9%, PN 11.7%, A 6.6%, other 1.7%; seats by party—S 11, IA 11, D 4, PN 3, A 2

note: 2 representatives were elected to the Danish Parliament on 18 June 2015 (next to be held by

June 2019); percent of vote by party—NA; seats by party—S 1, IA 1 (2013)

Judicial branch: *highest court(s):* High Court of Greenland (consists of the presiding professional judge and 2 lay assessors); note—appeals beyond the High Court of Greenland can be heard by the Supreme Court (in Copenhagen)

judge selection and term of office: judges appointed by the monarch upon the recommendation of the Judicial Appointments Council, a 6-member independent body of judges and lawyers; judges appointed for life with retirement at age 70

subordinate courts: Court of Greenland; 18 district or magistrates' courts

Political parties and leaders: Democrats Party or D (Demokraatit) [Randi VESTERGAARD EVALDSEN]

Forward Party or S (Siumut) [Kim KIELSEN]

Inuit Community or IA (Inuit Ataqatigiit) [Sara OLSVIG]

Inuit Party or PI (Partii Inuit) [Nikku OLSEN]

Partii Naleraq or PN [Hans ENOKSEN]

Solidarity Party or A (Atassut) [Siverth Karl HEILMANN]

Political pressure groups and leaders: conservationists; environmentalists; independence activists

International organization participation: Arctic Council, ICC, NC, NIB, UPU

Diplomatic representation in the US: none (self-governing overseas administrative division of Denmark); note—Greenland has an office in the Danish Embassy to the US; it also has offices in the Danish consulates of Chicago and New York

Diplomatic representation from the US: none (self-governing overseas administrative division of Denmark); note—the US Embassy in Copenhagen has an office devoted to Greenland

Flag description: two equal horizontal bands of white (top) and red with a large disk slightly to the hoist side of center—the top half of the disk is red, the bottom half is white; the design represents the sun reflecting off a field of ice; the colors are the same as those of the Danish flag and symbolize Greenland's links to the Kingdom of Denmark

National symbol(s): polar bear; national colors: red, white

National anthem: name: "Nunarput utoqqarsuanngoravit" ("Our Country, Who's Become So Old" also translated as "You Our Ancient Land")

lyrics/music: Henrik LUND/Jonathan PETERSEN

note: adopted 1916; the government also recognizes "Nuna asiilasooq" as a secondary anthem

ECONOMY

Economy—overview: Greenland's economy depends on exports of shrimp and fish, and on a substantial subsidy from the Danish Government. Fish account for over 90% of its exports, subjecting the economy to fluctuations in world demand. The subsidy from the Danish Government is budgeted

to be about $535 million in 2017, more than 50% of government revenues, and 25% of GDP.

The economy is expanding after a period of decline. In 2016 the economy grew 4.6% compared to 1.1% in 2015 and negative growth in the years 2013-14. For 2017 the economy is expected to continue to expand at a more subdued rate. The expansion has been driven by larger quotas for shrimp, the predominant Greenlandic export, and also by increased activity in the construction sector, especially in Nuuk, the capital, where the harbor is being enlarged and a prison is under construction. Private consumption and tourism also are contributing to GDP growth more than in previous years. Tourism in Greenland has grown annually around 20% in 2015 and 2016, largely a result of increasing numbers of cruise lines now operating in Greenland's western and southern waters during the peak summer tourism season.

The public sector, including publicly owned enterprises and the municipalities, plays a dominant role in Greenland's economy. During the last decade the Greenland Home Rule Government pursued conservative fiscal and monetary policies, but public pressure has increased for better schools, health care, and retirement systems. The budget was in deficit in 2014 and 2016, but public debt remains low at about 5% of GDP. The government plans a balanced budget for the 2017–20 period.

Significant challenges face the island, including low levels of qualified labor, geographic dispersion, lack of industry diversification, the long-term sustainability of the public budget, and a declining population due to emigration. Catches in fisheries have been declining in recent years. Hydrocarbon exploration has ceased with declining oil prices and currently only three mines are under development. The island has potential for natural resource exploitation with rare-earth, uranium, and iron ore mineral projects proposed.

GDP (purchasing power parity): $2.173 billion (2015 est.)

$2.137 billion (2014 est.)

$2.154 billion (2013 est.)

note: data are in 2015 US dollars

country comparison to the world: 195

GDP (official exchange rate): $2.221 billion (2011 est.)

GDP—real growth rate: 1.7% (2015 est.)

-0.8% (2014 est.)

-3% (2013 est.)

country comparison to the world: 166

GDP—per capita (PPP): $37,600 (2015 est.)

$37,000 (2014 est.)

$38,500 (2013 est.)

country comparison to the world: 51

GDP—composition, by end use:

household consumption: 24.8%

government consumption: 28%

investment in fixed capital: 14.3%

investment in inventories: -13.9%

exports of goods and services: 18.2%

imports of goods and services: 28.6% (2015 est.)

GDP—composition, by sector of origin:

agriculture: 15.9%

industry: 10.1%
services: 73.9% (2015 est.)

Agriculture—products: sheep, cow, reindeer, fish

Industries: fish processing (mainly shrimp and Greenland halibut); gold, zinc, anorthosite and ruby mining; handicrafts, hides and skins, small shipyards

Industrial production growth rate: NA%

Labor force: 26,840 (2015 est.)
country comparison to the world: 208

Labor force—by occupation: *agriculture:* 15.9%
industry: 10.1%
services: 73.9% (2015)

Unemployment rate: 9.1% (2015 est.)
10.3% (2014 est.)
country comparison to the world: 124

Population below poverty line: 16.2% (2015 est.)

Household income or consumption by percentage share: *lowest 10%:* NA%
highest 10%: NA%

Distribution of family income—Gini index: 33.9 (2015 est.)
34.3 (2014 est.)
country comparison to the world: 103

Budget: *revenues:* $1.578 billion
expenditures: $1.876 billion (2015 est.)
Taxes and other revenues: 71% of GDP (2015 est.)
country comparison to the world: 3

Budget surplus (+) or deficit (-): -13.5% of GDP (2015 est.)
country comparison to the world: 214

Public debt: 13% of GDP (2015 est.)
country comparison to the world: 195

Fiscal year: calendar year

Inflation rate (consumer prices): 0.3% (January 2017 est.)
1.2% (January 2016 est.)
country comparison to the world: 17

Central bank discount rate: NA%

Exports: $407.1 million (2015 est.)
$599.7 million (2014 est.)
country comparison to the world: 179

Exports—commodities: fish and fish products 91% (2015 est.)

Exports—partners: Denmark 81.2%, Portugal 8.3% (2016)

Imports: $783.5 million (2015 est.)
$866.1 million (2014 est.)
country comparison to the world: 182

Imports—commodities: machinery and transport equipment, manufactured goods, food, petroleum products

Imports—partners: Denmark 72.2%, Sweden 9.8% (2016)

Debt—external: $36.4 million (2010)
$58 million (2009)
country comparison to the world: 197

Exchange rates: Danish kroner (DKK) per US dollar—
6.586 (2016)

6.7309 (2016)
6.7309 (2015)
6.7236 (2014 est.)
5.6125 (2013 est.)

ENERGY

Electricity access: *electrification—total population:* 100% (2016)

Electricity—production: 625 million kWh (2015 est.)
country comparison to the world: 162

Electricity—consumption: 581.3 million kWh (2015 est.)
country comparison to the world: 170

Electricity—exports: 0 kWh (2016 est.)
country comparison to the world: 143

Electricity—imports: 0 kWh (2016 est.)
country comparison to the world: 156

Electricity—installed generating capacity: 187,000 kW (2015 est.)
country comparison to the world: 165

Electricity—from fossil fuels: 51.3% of total installed capacity (2015 est.)
country comparison to the world: 149

Electricity—from nuclear fuels: 0% of total installed capacity (2015 est.)
country comparison to the world: 100

Electricity—from hydroelectric plants: 48.7% of total installed capacity (2015 est.)
country comparison to the world: 41

Electricity—from other renewable sources: 0% of total installed capacity (2015 est.)
country comparison to the world: 185

Crude oil—production: 0 bbl/day (2016 est.)
country comparison to the world: 140

Crude oil—exports: 0 bbl/day (2014 est.)
country comparison to the world: 131

Crude oil—imports: 0 bbl/day (2014 est.)
country comparison to the world: 134

Crude oil—proved reserves: 0 bbl (1 January 2017 es)
country comparison to the world: 140

Refined petroleum products—production: 0 bbl/day (2014 est.)
country comparison to the world: 150

Refined petroleum products—consumption: 6,000 bbl/day (2015 est.)
country comparison to the world: 170

Refined petroleum products—exports: 0 bbl/day (2014 est.)
country comparison to the world: 161

Refined petroleum products—imports: 4,633 bbl/day (2014 est.)
country comparison to the world: 169

Natural gas—production: 0 cu m (2016 est.)
country comparison to the world: 142

Natural gas—consumption: 0 cu m (2013 est.)
country comparison to the world: 187

Natural gas—exports: 0 cu m (2016 est.)
country comparison to the world: 113

Natural gas—imports: 0 cu m (2013 est.)

country comparison to the world: 132

Natural gas—proved reserves: 0 cu m (1 January 2014 es)
country comparison to the world: 146

Carbon dioxide emissions from consumption of energy: 520,400 Mt (2015 est.)
country comparison to the world: 179

COMMUNICATIONS

Telephones—fixed lines: *total subscriptions:* 16,000
subscriptions per 100 inhabitants: 28 (July 2016 est.)
country comparison to the world: 191

Telephones—mobile cellular: *total:* 61,000
subscriptions per 100 inhabitants: 106 (July 2016 est.)
country comparison to the world: 200

Telephone system: *general assessment:* adequate domestic and international service provided by satellite, cables, and microwave radio relay; totally digital since 1995
domestic: microwave radio relay and satellite; the fundamental telecommunications infrastructure consists of a digital radio link from Nanortalik in south Greenland to Uummannaq in north Greenland; satellites cover north and east Greenland for domestic and foreign telecommunications; a marine cable connects south and west Greenland to the rest of the world, extending from Nuuk and Qaqortoq to Canada and Iceland
international: country code—299; satellite earth stations—15 (12 Intelsat, 1 Eutelsat, 2 Americom GE-2 (all Atlantic Ocean)) (2015)

Broadcast media: the Greenland Broadcasting Company provides public radio and TV services throughout the island with a broadcast station and a series of repeaters; a few private local TV and radio stations; Danish public radio rebroadcasts are available (2015)

Internet country code: .gl
Internet users: total: 39,544
percent of population: 68.5% (July 2016 est.)
country comparison to the world: 192

TRANSPORTATION

National air transport system: *number of registered air carriers:* 1 (registered in Denmark)
inventory of registered aircraft operated by air carriers: 8 (registered in Denmark) (2015)
Civil aircraft registration country code prefix: OY-H (2016)

Airports: 15 (2013)
country comparison to the world: 147

Airports—with paved runways: *total:* 10
2,438 to 3,047 m: 2
1,524 to 2,437 m: 1
914 to 1,523 m: 1
under 914 m: 6 (2017)

Airports—with unpaved runways: *total:* 5
1,524 to 2,437 m: 1
914 to 1,523 m: 2
under 914 m: 2 (2013)

Roadways: note: although there are short roads in towns, there are no roads between towns; inter-urban transport is either by sea or by air (2015)

Merchant marine: *total:* 8
by type: general cargo 1, other 7 (2017)
country comparison to the world: 151

Ports and terminals: *major seaport(s):* Sisimiut

MILITARY AND SECURITY

Military branches: no regular military forces or conscription; the Government of Denmark has responsibility for defense; as such the Danish military's Joint Arctic Command in Nuuk is responsible for territorial defense of Greenland (2016)

Military—note: defense is the responsibility of Denmark

TRANSNATIONAL ISSUES

Disputes—international: managed dispute between Canada and Denmark over Hans Island in the Kennedy Channel between Canada's Ellesmere Island and Greenland; Denmark (Greenland) and Norway have made submissions to the Commission on the Limits of the Continental Shelf (CLCS) and Russia is collecting additional data to augment its 2001 CLCS submission

GRENADA

INTRODUCTION

Background: Carib Indians inhabited Grenada when Christopher COLUMBUS discovered the island in 1498, but it remained uncolonized for more than a century. The French settled Grenada in the 17th century, established sugar estates, and imported large numbers of African slaves. Britain took the island in 1762 and vigorously expanded sugar production. In the 19th century, cacao eventually surpassed sugar as the main export crop; in the 20th century, nutmeg became the leading export. In 1967, Britain gave Grenada autonomy over its internal affairs. Full independence was attained in 1974 making Grenada one of the smallest independent countries in the Western Hemisphere. Grenada was seized by a Marxist military council on 19 October 1983. Six days later the island was invaded by US forces and those of six other Caribbean nations, which quickly captured the ringleaders and their hundreds of Cuban advisers. Free elections were reinstituted the following year and have continued since then.

GEOGRAPHY

Location: Caribbean, island between the Caribbean Sea and Atlantic Ocean, north of Trinidad and Tobago

Geographic coordinates: 12 07 N, 61 40 W

Map references: Central America and the Caribbean

Area: *total:* 344 sq km
land: 344 sq km
water: 0 sq km
country comparison to the world: 208

Area—comparative: twice the size of Washington, DC

Land boundaries: 0 km

Coastline: 121 km

Maritime claims: *territorial sea:* 12 nm
exclusive economic zone: 200 nm

Climate: tropical; tempered by northeast trade winds

Terrain: volcanic in origin with central mountains

Elevation: *mean elevation:* NA

elevation extremes: *lowest point:* Caribbean Sea 0 m
highest point: Mount Saint Catherine 840 m

Natural resources: timber, tropical fruit

Land use: *agricultural land:* 32.3%
arable land: 8.8%;
permanent crops: 20.6%;
permanent pasture: 2.9%
forest: 50%
other: 17.7% (2011 est.)
Irrigated land: 20 sq km (2012)

Population—distribution: approximately one-third of the population is found in the capital of St. George's; the island's population is concentrated along the coast

Natural hazards: lies on edge of hurricane belt; hurricane season lasts from June to November
volcanism: Mount Saint Catherine (840 m) lies on the island of Grenada; Kick 'em Jenny, an active submarine volcano (seamount) on the Caribbean Sea floor, lies about 8 km north of the island of Grenada; these two volcanoes are at the southern end of the volcanic island arc of the Lesser Antilles that extends up to the Netherlands dependency of Saba in the north

Environment—current issues: deforestation causing habitat destruction and species loss; coastal erosion and contamination; pollution and sedimentation; inadequate solid waste management

Environment—international agreements: *party to:* Biodiversity, Climate Change, Climate Change-Kyoto Protocol, Desertification, Endangered Species, Law of the Sea, Ozone Layer Protection, Whaling
signed, but not ratified: none of the selected agreements

Geography—note: the administration of the islands of the Grenadines group is divided between Saint Vincent and the Grenadines and Grenada

PEOPLE AND SOCIETY

Population: 111,724 (July 2017 est.)
country comparison to the world: 190

Nationality: *noun:* Grenadian(s)
adjective: Grenadian

Ethnic groups: African descent 82.4%, mixed 13.3%, East Indian 2.2%, other 1.3%, unspecified 0.9% (2011 est.)

Languages: English (official), French patois

Religions: Protestant 49.2% (includes Pentecostal 17.2%, Seventh Day Adventist 13.2%, Anglican 8.5%, Baptist 3.2%, Church of God 2.4%, Evangelical 1.9%, Methodist 1.6%, other 1.2%), Roman Catholic 36%, Jehovah's Witness 1.2%, Rastafarian 1.2%, other 5.5%, none 5.7%, unspecified 1.3% (2011 est.)

Age structure: *0-14 years:* 23.99% (male 13,914/female 12,893)
15-24 years: 15.03% (male 8,377/female 8,414)
25-54 years: 40.38% (male 23,099/female 22,013)
55-64 years: 10.52% (male 6,016/female 5,740)
65 years and over: 10.08% (male 5,210/female 6,048) (2017 est.)

Dependency ratios: *total dependency ratio:* 50.7
youth dependency ratio: 39.9
elderly dependency ratio: 10.8
potential support ratio: 9.3 (2015 est.)

Median age: *total:* 31.5 years
male: 31.5 years
female: 31.6 years (2017 est.)
country comparison to the world: 109

Population growth rate: 0.44% (2017 est.)
country comparison to the world: 159

Birth rate: 15.5 births/1,000 population (2017 est.)
country comparison to the world: 121

Death rate: 8.2 deaths/1,000 population (2017 est.)
country comparison to the world: 84

Net migration rate: -2.9 migrant(s)/1,000 population (2017 est.)
country comparison to the world: 173

Population distribution: approximately one-third of the population is found in the capital of St. George's; the island's population is concentrated along the coast

Urbanization: *urban population:* 35.7% of total population (2017)
rate of urbanization: 0.44% annual rate of change (2015-20 est.)

Major urban areas—population: SAINT GEORGE'S (capital) 38,000 (2014)

Sex ratio: *at birth:* 1.1 male(s)/female
0-14 years: 1.08 male(s)/female
15-24 years: 0.99 male(s)/female
25-54 years: 1.05 male(s)/female
55-64 years: 1.05 male(s)/female
65 years and over: 0.85 male(s)/female
total population: 1.03 male(s)/female (2016 est.)

Maternal mortality ratio: 27 deaths/100,000 live births (2015 est.)
country comparison to the world: 118

Infant mortality rate: *total:* 9.7 deaths/1,000 live births
male: 9.2 deaths/1,000 live births
female: 10.3 deaths/1,000 live births (2017 est.)
country comparison to the world: 141

Life expectancy at birth: *total population:* 74.5 years
male: 71.9 years
female: 77.4 years (2017 est.)
country comparison to the world: 123

Total fertility rate: 2.02 children born/woman (2017 est.)
country comparison to the world: 117
Health expenditures: 6.1% of GDP (2014)
country comparison to the world: 103

Hospital bed density: 3.5 beds/1,000 population (2012)

Drinking water source:
improved:
urban: 99% of population
rural: 95.3% of population
total: 96.6% of population
unimproved:
urban: 1% of population
rural: 4.7% of population
total: 3.4% of population (2015 est.)

Sanitation facility access:
improved:
urban: 97.5% of population
rural: 98.3% of population
total: 98% of population
unimproved:
urban: 2.5% of population

rural: 1.7% of population
total: 2% of population (2015 est.)

HIV/AIDS—adult prevalence rate: NA

HIV/AIDS—people living with HIV/AIDS: NA

HIV/AIDS—deaths: NA

Major infectious diseases: *note:* active local transmission of Zika virus by Aedes species mosquitoes has been identified in this country (as of August 2016); it poses an important risk (a large number of cases possible) among US citizens if bitten by an infective mosquito; other less common ways to get Zika are through sex, via blood transfusion, or during pregnancy, in which the pregnant woman passes Zika virus to her fetus (2016)

Obesity—adult prevalence rate: 21.3% (2016)
country comparison to the world: 90

School life expectancy (primary to tertiary education): *total:* 17 years
male: 17 years
female: 17 years (2015)

GOVERNMENT

Country name: *conventional long form:* none
conventional short form: Grenada
etymology: probably named for the Spanish city of Granada; in Spanish "granada" means "pomegranate"

Government type: parliamentary democracy (Parliament); a Commonwealth realm

Capital: *name:* Saint George's

geographic coordinates: 12 03 N, 61 45 W
time difference: UTC-4 (1 hour ahead of Washington, DC, during Standard Time)

Administrative divisions: 6 parishes and 1 dependency*; Carriacou and Petite Martinique*, Saint Andrew, Saint David, Saint George, Saint John, Saint Mark, Saint Patrick

Independence: 7 February 1974 (from the UK)

National holiday: Independence Day, 7 February (1974)

Constitution: previous 1967; latest presented 19 December 1973, effective 7 February 1974, suspended 1979 following a revolution, but restored in 1983; amended 1991 (Constitutional Judicature Act, 1991) (2017)

Legal system: common law based on English model

International law organization participation: has not submitted an ICJ jurisdiction declaration; accepts ICCt jurisdiction

Citizenship: *citizenship by birth:* yes
citizenship by descent: yes
dual citizenship recognized: yes
residency requirement for naturalization: 7 years for persons from a non-Caribbean state and 4 years for a person from a Caribbean state

Suffrage: 18 years of age; universal

Executive branch: *chief of state:* Queen ELIZABETH II (since 6 February 1952); represented by Governor General Cecile LA GRENADE (since 7 May 2013)

head of government: Prime Minister Keith MITCHELL (since 20 February 2013)
cabinet: Cabinet appointed by the governor general on the advice of the prime minister
elections/appointments: the monarchy is hereditary; governor general appointed by the monarch; following legislative elections, the leader of the majority party or majority coalition usually appointed prime minister by the governor general

Legislative branch: *description:* bicameral Parliament consists of the Senate (13 seats; members appointed by the governor general—10 on the advice of the prime minister and 3 on the advice of the opposition party leader; members serve 5-year terms) and the House of Representatives (15 seats; members directly elected in single-seat constituencies by simple majority vote to serve 5-year terms)
elections: last held on 19 February 2013 (next to be held in 2018)
election results: House of Representatives—percent of vote by party—NNP 58.8%, NDC 40.7%; other 0.5% seats by party—NNP 15

Judicial branch: *highest court(s):* the Eastern Caribbean Supreme Court (ECSC) is the superior court of the Organization of Eastern Caribbean States; the ECSC—headquartered on St. Lucia—consists of the Court of Appeal—headed by the chief justice and 4 judges—and the High Court with 18 judges; the Court of Appeal is itinerant, travelling to member states on a schedule to hear appeals from the High Court and subordinate courts; High Court judges reside at the member states with 2 in Grenada
judge selection and term of office: chief justice of Eastern Caribbean Supreme Court appointed by the Her Majesty, Queen ELIZABETH II; other justices and judges appointed by the Judicial and Legal Services Commission, and independent body of judicial officials; Court of Appeal justices appointed for life with mandatory retirement at age 65; High Court judges appointed for life with mandatory retirement at age 62
subordinate courts: magistrates' courts; Court of Magisterial Appeals

Political parties and leaders: Grenada United Labor Party or GULP [Wilfred HAYES]
National Democratic Congress or NDC [Nazim BURKE]
New National Party or NNP [Keith MITCHELL]

Political pressure groups and leaders: Committee for Human Rights in Grenada or CHRG
New Jewel Movement Support Group
The British Grenada Friendship Society
The New Jewel 19 Committee

International organization participation: ACP, AOSIS, C, Caricom, CDB, CELAC, FAO, G-77, IBRD, ICAO, ICCt (signatory), ICRM, IDA, IFAD, IFC, IFRCS, ILO, IMF, IMO, Interpol, IOC, ITU, ITUC, LAES, MIGA, NAM, OAS, OECS, OPANAL, OPCW, Petrocaribe, UN, UNCTAD, UNESCO, UNIDO, UPU, WHO, WIPO, WTO

Diplomatic representation in the US: *chief of mission:* Ambassador Ethelstan Angus FRIDAY (since 3 September 2013)

379

chancery: 1701 New Hampshire Avenue NW, Washington, DC 20009
telephone: [1] (202) 265-2561
FAX: [1] (202) 265-2468
consulate(s) general: Miami

Diplomatic representation from the US: *chief of mission:* the US does not have an embassy in Grenada; the US Ambassador to Barbados is accredited to Grenada
embassy: Lance-aux-Epines Stretch, Saint George's
mailing address: P. O. Box 54, Saint George's
telephone: [1] (473) 444-1173 through 1176
FAX: [1] (473) 444-4820

Flag description: a rectangle divided diagonally into yellow triangles (top and bottom) and green triangles (hoist side and outer side), with a red border around the flag; there are seven yellow, five-pointed stars with three centered in the top red border, three centered in the bottom red border, and one on a red disk superimposed at the center of the flag; there is also a symbolic nutmeg pod on the hoist-side triangle (Grenada is the world's second-largest producer of nutmeg, after Indonesia); the seven stars stand for the seven administrative divisions, with the central star denoting the capital, St. George; yellow represents the sun and the warmth of the people, green stands for vegetation and agriculture, and red symbolizes harmony, unity, and courage

National symbol(s): Grenada dove, Bougainvillea flower; national colors: red, yellow, green

National anthem: name: "Hail Grenada"
lyrics/music: Irva Merle BAPTISTE/Louis Arnold MASANTO
note: adopted 1974

ECONOMY

Economy—overview: Grenada relies on tourism as its main source of foreign exchange especially since the construction of an international airport in 1985. Strong performance in construction and manufacturing, together with the development of tourism and higher education—especially in medicine—contributed to growth in national output; however, economic growth remained stagnant in the 2010-14 period, after a sizable contraction in 2009, because of the global economic slowdown's effects on tourism and remittances. Gross national saving—and wealth—has been declining since 2010.

Hurricanes Ivan (2004) and Emily (2005) severely damaged the agricultural sector—particularly nutmeg and cocoa cultivation—which had been a key driver of economic growth. Grenada has rebounded from the devastating effects of the hurricanes but is now saddled with the debt burden from the rebuilding process. Public debt-to-GDP is about 110%, leaving the MITCHELL administration limited room to engage in public investments and social spending. MITCHELL in 2013 announced a structural adjustment program that includes a plan to increase tax revenue.

GDP (purchasing power parity): $1.59 billion (2017 est.)
$1.551 billion (2016 est.)
$1.495 billion (2015 est.)
note: data are in 2017 dollars
country comparison to the world: 199

GDP (official exchange rate): $1.111 billion (2016 est.)

GDP—real growth rate: 2.5% (2017 est.)
3.7% (2016 est.)
6.4% (2015 est.)
country comparison to the world: 134

GDP—per capita (PPP): $14,700 (2017 est.)
$14,500 (2016 est.)
$14,000 (2015 est.)
note: data are in 2017 dollars
country comparison to the world: 112

Gross national saving: 13.1% of GDP (2017 est.)
17% of GDP (2016 est.)
13.9% of GDP (2015 est.)
country comparison to the world: 137

GDP—composition, by end use:
household consumption: 84.4%
government consumption: 14.4%
investment in fixed capital: 15.9%
investment in inventories: -0.1%
exports of goods and services: 20.4%
imports of goods and services: -35.1% (2017 est.)

GDP—composition, by sector of origin:
agriculture: 9.1%
industry: 14.2%
services: 76.7% (2017 est.)

Agriculture—products: bananas, cocoa, nutmeg, mace, citrus, avocados, root crops, sugarcane, corn, vegetables

Industries: food and beverages, textiles, light assembly operations, tourism, construction

Industrial production growth rate: 0.6% (2017 est.)
country comparison to the world: 178

Labor force: 59,900 (2013 est.)
country comparison to the world: 188

Labor force—by occupation: *agriculture:* 11%
industry: 20%
services: 69% (2008 est.)

Unemployment rate: 33.5% (2013)
25% (2008)
country comparison to the world: 206

Population below poverty line: 38% (2008 est.)

Household income or consumption by percentage share: *lowest 10%:* NA%
highest 10%: NA%

Budget: *revenues:* $279.2 million
expenditures: $284.6 million (2017 est.)
Taxes and other revenues: 25.1% of GDP (2017 est.)
country comparison to the world: 113

Budget surplus (+) or deficit (-): -0.5% of GDP (2017 est.)
country comparison to the world: 49

Public debt: 84.4% of GDP (2016 est.)
91.7% of GDP (2015 est.)
country comparison to the world: 32

Fiscal year: calendar year

Inflation rate (consumer prices): 2.6% (2017 est.)
1.7% (2016 est.)
country comparison to the world: 120

Central bank discount rate: 6.5% (31 December 2009)
6.5% (31 December 2008)
country comparison to the world: 58

Commercial bank prime lending rate: 8.5% (31 December 2017 est.)
8.66% (31 December 2016 est.)
country comparison to the world: 99

Stock of narrow money: $223 million (31 December 2017 est.)
$214 million (31 December 2016 est.)
country comparison to the world: 183

Stock of broad money: $807.8 million (31 December 2017 est.)
$796.7 million (31 December 2016 est.)
country comparison to the world: 175

Stock of domestic credit: $574.2 million (31 December 2017 est.)
$566.3 million (31 December 2016 est.)
country comparison to the world: 173

Market value of publicly traded shares: $NA

Current account balance: -$79 million (2017 est.)
-$34 million (2016 est.)
country comparison to the world: 76

Exports: $43.4 million (2017 est.)
$44.2 million (2016 est.)
country comparison to the world: 206

Exports—commodities: nutmeg, bananas, cocoa, fruit and vegetables, clothing, mace

Exports—partners: US 28.4%, Japan 11%, Dominica 7.9%, St. Lucia 7.6%, Netherlands 5.2%, Barbados 4.9%, St. Kitts and Nevis 4.8% (2016)

Imports: $310.2 million (2017 est.)
$313.7 million (2016 est.)
country comparison to the world: 198

Imports—commodities: food, manufactured goods, machinery, chemicals, fuel

Imports—partners: US 32.7%, Trinidad and Tobago 23.5%, China 6%, Japan 4.6% (2016)

Reserves of foreign exchange and gold: $207.7 million (31 December 2016 est.)
$198 million (31 December 2015 est.)
country comparison to the world: 159

Debt—external: $679 million (2013 est.)
$538 million (2010 est.)
country comparison to the world: 174

Exchange rates: East Caribbean dollars (XCD) per US dollar—
2.7 (2017 est.)
2.7 (2016 est.)
2.7 (2015 est.)
2.7 (2014 est.)
2.7 (2013 est.)

ENERGY

Electricity access: *population without electricity:* 11,121
electrification—*total population:* 91%

electrification—urban areas: 100%
electrification—rural areas: 80% (2012)

Electricity—production: 200 million kWh (2015 est.)
country comparison to the world: 189

Electricity—consumption: 185 million kWh (2015 est.)
country comparison to the world: 192

Electricity—exports: 0 kWh (2016 est.)
country comparison to the world: 142

Electricity—imports: 0 kWh (2016 est.)
country comparison to the world: 155

Electricity—installed generating capacity: 50,000 kW (2015 est.)
country comparison to the world: 191

Electricity—from fossil fuels: 98% of total installed capacity (2015 est.)
country comparison to the world: 38

Electricity—from nuclear fuels: 0% of total installed capacity (2015 est.)
country comparison to the world: 99

Electricity—from hydroelectric plants: 0% of total installed capacity (2015 est.)
country comparison to the world: 178

Electricity—from other renewable sources: 2% of total installed capacity (2015 est.)
country comparison to the world: 122

Crude oil—production: 0 bbl/day (2016 est.)
country comparison to the world: 141

Crude oil—exports: 0 bbl/day (2014 est.)
country comparison to the world: 130

Crude oil—imports: 0 bbl/day (2014 est.)
country comparison to the world: 133

Crude oil—proved reserves: 0 bbl (1 January 2017 es)
country comparison to the world: 141

Refined petroleum products—production: 0 bbl/day (2014 est.)
country comparison to the world: 151

Refined petroleum products—consumption: 2,300 bbl/day (2015 est.)
country comparison to the world: 192

Refined petroleum products—exports: 0 bbl/day (2014 est.)

country comparison to the world: 160

Refined petroleum products—imports: 2,259 bbl/day (2014 est.)
country comparison to the world: 186

Natural gas—production: 0 cu m (2013 est.)
country comparison to the world: 141

Natural gas—consumption: 0 cu m (2013 est.)
country comparison to the world: 186

Natural gas—exports: 0 cu m (2013 est.)
country comparison to the world: 112

Natural gas—imports: 0 cu m (2013 est.)
country comparison to the world: 131

Natural gas—proved reserves: 0 cu m (1 January 2014 es)
country comparison to the world: 145

Carbon dioxide emissions from consumption of energy: 500,000 Mt (2013 est.)
country comparison to the world: 180

COMMUNICATIONS

Telephones—fixed lines: *total subscriptions:* 26,776
subscriptions per 100 inhabitants: 24 (July 2016 est.)
country comparison to the world: 174

Telephones—mobile cellular: *total:* 118,973
subscriptions per 100 inhabitants: 107 (July 2016 est.)
country comparison to the world: 186

Telephone system: *general assessment:* adequate, automatic, island-wide telephone system
domestic: interisland VHF and UHF radiotelephone links
international: country code—1-473; landing point for the East Caribbean Fiber System (ECFS) submarine cable with links to 13 other islands in the eastern Caribbean extending from the British Virgin Islands to Trinidad; SHF radiotelephone links to Trinidad and Tobago and Saint Vincent; VHF and UHF radio links to Trinidad (2015)

Broadcast media: the Grenada Broadcasting Network, jointly owned by the government and the Caribbean Communications Network of Trinidad and Tobago, operates a TV station and 2 radio stations; multi-channel cable TV subscription service

is available; a dozen private radio stations also broadcast (2007)

Internet country code: .gd
Internet users: total: 62,123
percent of population: 55.9% (July 2016 est.)
country comparison to the world: 183

TRANSPORTATION

National air transport system: *number of registered air carriers:* 0
inventory of registered aircraft operated by air carriers: 0
annual passenger traffic on registered air carriers: 0
annual freight traffic on registered air carriers: 0 mt-km (2015)
Civil aircraft registration country code prefix: J3 (2016)

Airports: 3 (2013)
country comparison to the world: 195

Airports—with paved runways: total: 3
2,438 to 3,047 m: 1
1,524 to 2,437 m: 1
under 914 m: 1 (2017)

Roadways: total: 1,127 km
paved: 687 km
unpaved: 440 km (2001)
country comparison to the world: 184

Merchant marine: *total:* 6
by type: general cargo 3, other 3 (2017)
country comparison to the world: 153

Ports and terminals: *major seaport(s):* Saint George's

MILITARY AND SECURITY

Military branches: no regular military forces; Royal Grenada Police Force (includes Coast Guard) (2010)

TRANSNATIONAL ISSUES

Disputes—international: none

Illicit drugs: small-scale cannabis cultivation; lesser transshipment point for marijuana and cocaine to US

GUAM

INTRODUCTION

Background: Spain ceded Guam to the US in 1898. Captured by the Japanese in 1941, it was retaken by the US three years later. The military installations on the island are some of the most strategically important US bases in the Pacific.

GEOGRAPHY

Location: Oceania, island in the North Pacific Ocean, about three-quarters of the way from Hawaii to the Philippines

Geographic coordinates: 13 28 N, 144 47 E

Map references: Oceania

Area: *total:* 544 sq km
land: 544 sq km
water: 0 sq km
country comparison to the world: 195

Area—comparative: three times the size of Washington, DC

Land boundaries: 0 km

Coastline: 125.5 km

Maritime claims: *territorial sea:* 12 nm

exclusive economic zone: 200 nm

Climate: tropical marine; generally warm and humid, moderated by northeast trade winds; dry season (January to June), rainy season (July to December); little seasonal temperature variation

Terrain: volcanic origin, surrounded by coral reefs; relatively flat coralline limestone plateau (source of most fresh water), with steep coastal cliffs and narrow coastal plains in north, low hills in center, mountains in south

Elevation: *mean elevation:* NA

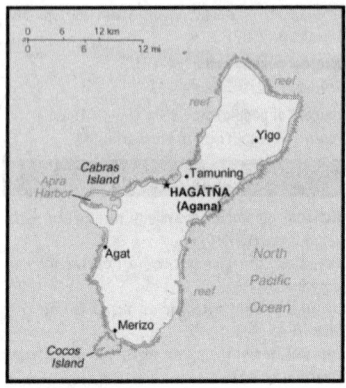

elevation extremes: *lowest point:* Pacific Ocean 0 m

highest point: Mount Lamlam 406 m

Natural resources: aquatic wildlife (supporting tourism), fishing (largely undeveloped)

Land use: *agricultural land:* 33.4%

arable land: 1.9%;

permanent crops: 16.7%;

permanent pasture: 14.8%

forest: 47.9%

other: 18.7% (2011 est.)

Irrigated land: 2 sq km (2012)

Population—distribution: no large cities exist on the island, though large villages (municipalities) attract much of the population; the largest of these is Dededo

Natural hazards: frequent squalls during rainy season; relatively rare but potentially destructive typhoons (June to December)

Environment—current issues: fresh water scarcity; reef damage; inadequate sewage treatment; extermination of native bird populations by the rapid proliferation of the brown tree snake, an exotic, invasive species

Geography—note: largest and southernmost island in the Mariana Islands archipelago and the largest island in Micronesia; strategic location in western North Pacific Ocean

PEOPLE AND SOCIETY

Population: 167,358 (July 2017 est.)

country comparison to the world: 186

Nationality: *noun:* Guamanian(s) (US citizens)

adjective: Guamanian

Ethnic groups: Chamorro 37.3%, Filipino 26.3%, white 7.1%, Chuukese 7%, Korean 2.2%, other Pacific Islander 2%, other Asian 2%, Chinese 1.6%, Palauan 1.6%, Japanese 1.5%, Pohnpeian 1.4%, mixed 9.4%, other 0.6% (2010 est.)

Languages: English 43.6%, Filipino 21.2%, Chamorro 17.8%, other Pacific island languages 10%, Asian languages 6.3%, other 1.1% (2010 est.)

Religions: Roman Catholic 85%, other 15% (1999 est.)

Age structure: *0-14 years:* 27.54% (male 23,896/female 22,190)

15-24 years: 16.63% (male 14,847/female 12,981)

25-54 years: 37.44% (male 32,295/female 30,356)

55-64 years: 9.8% (male 8,352/female 8,057)

65 years and over: 8.59% (male 6,706/female 7,678) (2017 est.)

Dependency ratios: *total dependency ratio:* 52.3

youth dependency ratio: 38.8

elderly dependency ratio: 13.6

potential support ratio: 7.4 (2015 est.)

Median age: *total:* 29 years

male: 28.3 years

female: 29.7 years (2017 est.)

country comparison to the world: 111

Population growth rate: 0.26% (2017 est.)

country comparison to the world: 177

Birth rate: 19.7 births/1,000 population (2017 est.)

country comparison to the world: 81

Death rate: 6 deaths/1,000 population (2017 est.)

country comparison to the world: 162

Net migration rate: -11.1 migrant(s)/1,000 population (2017 est.)

country comparison to the world: 212

Population distribution: no large cities exist on the island, though large villages (municipalities) attract much of the population; the largest of these is Dededo

Urbanization: *urban population:* 94.7% of total population (2017)

rate of urbanization: 1.27% annual rate of change (2015-20 est.)

Major urban areas—population: HAGATNA (capital) 143,000 (2014)

Sex ratio: *at birth:* 1.06 male(s)/female

0-14 years: 1.06 male(s)/female

15-24 years: 1.08 male(s)/female

25-54 years: 1.03 male(s)/female

55-64 years: 1.02 male(s)/female

65 years and over: 0.84 male(s)/female

total population: 1.03 male(s)/female (2016 est.)

Infant mortality rate: *total:* 12.6 deaths/1,000 live births

male: 12.3 deaths/1,000 live births

female: 12.8 deaths/1,000 live births (2017 est.)

country comparison to the world: 114

Life expectancy at birth: *total population:* 76 years

male: 73.6 years

female: 78.6 years (2017 est.)

country comparison to the world: 94

Total fertility rate: 2.96 children born/woman (2017 est.)

country comparison to the world: 57

Physicians density: 0.84 physicians/1,000 population (2007)

Drinking water source:

improved:

urban: 99.5% of population

rural: 99.5% of population

total: 99.5% of population

unimproved:

urban: 0.5% of population

rural: 0.5% of population

total: 0.5% of population (2015 est.)

Sanitation facility access:

improved:

urban: 89.8% of population

rural: 89.8% of population

total: 89.8% of population

unimproved:

urban: 10.2% of population

rural: 10.2% of population

total: 10.2% of population (2015 est.)

HIV/AIDS—adult prevalence rate: NA

HIV/AIDS—people living with HIV/AIDS: NA

HIV/AIDS—deaths: NA

Unemployment, youth ages 15-24: *total:* 29.4%

male: 29.7%

female: 28.9% (2011 est.)

country comparison to the world: 25

GOVERNMENT

Country name: *conventional long form:* Territory of Guam

conventional short form: Guam

local long form: Guahan

local short form: Guahan

etymology: the native Chamorro name for the island "Guahan" (meaning "we have" or "ours") was changed to Guam in the 1898 Treaty of Paris, whereby Spain relinquished Guam, Cuba, Puerto Rico, and the Philippines to the US

Dependency status: organized, unincorporated territory of the US with policy relations between Guam and the US under the jurisdiction of the Office of Insular Affairs, US Department of the Interior

Government type: presidential democracy; a self-governing unincorporated territory of the US

Capital: *name:* Hagatna (Agana)

geographic coordinates: 13 28 N, 144 44 E

time difference: UTC+10 (15 hours ahead of Washington, DC, during Standard Time)

Administrative divisions: none (territory of the US)

Independence: none (territory of the US)

National holiday: Discovery Day (or Magellan Day), first Monday in March (1521)

Constitution: effective 1 July 1950 (Guam Act of 1950 serves as a constitution); amended many times, last in 2015 (2016)

Legal system: common law modeled on US system; US federal laws apply

Citizenship: see United States

Suffrage: 18 years of age; universal; note—Guamanians are US citizens but do not vote in US presidential elections

Executive branch: *chief of state:* President Donald J. TRUMP (since 20 January 2017); Vice President Michael R. PENCE (since 20 January 2017)

head of government: Governor Eddie CALVO (since 3 January 2011); Lieutenant Governor Ray TENORIO (since 3 January 2011)

cabinet: Cabinet appointed by the governor with the consent of the Legislature

elections/appointments: president and vice president indirectly elected on the same ballot by an Electoral College of 'electors' chosen from each state to serve a 4-year term (eligible for a second term); under the US Constitution, residents of unincorporated territories, such as Guam, do not vote in elections for US president and vice president; however, they may vote in Democratic and Republican presidential primary elections; governor and lieutenant governor elected on the same ballot by absolute majority vote in 2 rounds if needed for a 4-year term (eligible for 2 consecutive terms); election last held on 8 November 2016 (next to be held in November 2020)

election results: Eddie CALVO reelected governor; percent of vote—Eddie CALVO (Republican Party) 63.9%, Carl GUTIERREZ (Democratic Party) 36.1%; Ray TENORIO (Republican Party) elected lieutenant governor

Legislative branch: description: unicameral Legislature of Guam or Liheslaturan Guahan (15 seats); members elected in a single countrywide constituency by simple majority vote to serve 2-year terms)

elections: last held on 8 November 2016 (next to be held in November 2018)

election results: percent of vote by party—NA; seats by party—Democratic Party 9, Republican Party 6

note: Guam directly elects 1 member by simple majority vote to serve a 2-year term as a delegate to the US House of Representatives; the delegate can vote when serving on a committee and when the House meets as the Committee of the Whole House, but not when legislation is submitted for a "full floor" House vote; election of delegate last held on 8 November 2016 (next to be held on 6 November 2018)

Judicial branch: *highest court(s):* Supreme Court of Guam (consists of 3 justices); note—appeals beyond the Supreme Court of Guam are referred to the US Supreme Court

judge selection and term of office: justices appointed by the governor and confirmed by the Guam legislature; justices appointed for life subject to retention election every 10 years

subordinate courts: Superior Court of Guam—includes several divisions; US Federal District Court for the District of Guam (a US territorial court; appeals beyond this court are heard before the US Court of Appeals for the Ninth Circuit)

Political parties and leaders: Democratic Party [Joaquin "Kim" PEREZ]
Republican Party [Victor CRUZ]

Political pressure groups and leaders: Guam Commission on Decolonization
Guam Federation of Teachers' Union
Guam Waterworks Authority Workers
We Are Guahan

International organization participation: AOSIS (observer), IOC, PIF (observer), SPC, UPU

Diplomatic representation in the US: none (territory of the US)

Diplomatic representation from the US: none (territory of the US)

Flag description: territorial flag is dark blue with a narrow red border on all four sides; centered is a red-bordered, pointed, vertical ellipse containing a beach scene, a proa or outrigger canoe with sail, and a palm tree with the word GUAM superimposed in bold red letters; the proa is sailing in Agana Bay with the promontory of Punta Dos Amantes, near the capital, in the background; the shape of the central emblem is that of a Chamorro sling stone, used as a weapon for defense or hunting; blue represents the sea and red the blood shed in the struggle against oppression

note: the US flag is the national flag

National symbol(s): coconut tree; national colors: deep blue, red

National anthem: name: "Fanohge Chamoru" (Stand Ye Guamanians)

lyrics/music: Ramon Manalisay SABLAN [English], Lagrimas UNTALAN [Chamoru]/Ramon Manalisay SABLAN

note: adopted 1919; the local anthem is also known as "Guam Hymn"; as a territory of the United States, "The Star-Spangled Banner," which generally follows the playing of "Stand Ye Guamanians," is official (see United States)

ECONOMY

Economy—overview: US national defense spending is the main driver of Guam's economy, followed by tourism and other services. Guam serves as a forward US base for the Western Pacific and is home to thousands of American military personnel. Total federal spending (defense and non-defense) amounted to $1.973 billion in 2014, or 40.4% of GDP. Of that total, federal grants amounted to $373.3 million in 2013, or 32.6% of Guam's total revenues for the fiscal year. Service exports, mainly spending by foreign tourists to Guam, amounted to $651 million in 2013, or 13.3% of GDP. In 2013, Guam's economy grew 0.6%. Despite slow growth, Guam's economy has been stable over the last decade. National defense spending cushions the island's economy against fluctuations in tourism.

GDP (purchasing power parity): $4.882 billion (2013 est.)
$4.756 billion (2012 est.)
$4.562 billion (2011 est.)
country comparison to the world: 178

GDP (official exchange rate): $4.6 billion (2010 est.)

GDP—real growth rate: 0.6% (2013 est.)
1.8% (2012)
-0.3% (2011)
country comparison to the world: 196

GDP—per capita (PPP): $30,500 (2013 est.)
$29,800 (2012 est.)
$28,600 (2011 est.)
country comparison to the world: 64

GDP—composition, by end use:
household consumption: 63.7%
government consumption: 64.9%

investment in fixed assets: 5.8%
investment in inventories: NA
exports of goods and services: 17%
imports of goods and services: -51.2% (2013)

GDP—composition, by sector of origin:
agriculture: NA%
industry: NA%
services: NA%

Agriculture—products: fruits, copra, vegetables; eggs, pork, poultry, beef

Industries: national defense, tourism, construction, transshipment services, concrete products, printing and publishing, food processing, textiles

Industrial production growth rate: NA%

Labor force: 70,490
note: includes only the civilian labor force (2013 est.)
country comparison to the world: 187

Labor force—by occupation: *agriculture:* 0.3%
industry: 21.6%
services: 78.1% (2013 est.)

Unemployment rate: 8.4% (2013 est.)
8.2% (2010 est.)
country comparison to the world: 115

Population below poverty line: 23% (2001 est.)

Household income or consumption by percentage share: *lowest 10%:* NA%
highest 10%: NA%

Budget: *revenues:* $1.147 billion
expenditures: $1.188 billion (2013 est.)
Taxes and other revenues: 24.9% of GDP (2013 est.)
country comparison to the world: 115

Budget surplus (+) or deficit (-): -0.9% of GDP (2013 est.)
country comparison to the world: 55

Public debt: 32.1% of GDP (2013)
35.8% of GDP (2012)
country comparison to the world: 157

Fiscal year: 1 October—30 September

Inflation rate (consumer prices): 1.8% (2014 est.)
4% (2011 est.)
country comparison to the world: 77

Exports: $828 million (2013 est.)
$795 million (2012)
country comparison to the world: 165

Exports—commodities: transshipments of refined petroleum products, construction materials, fish, foodstuffs and beverages

Exports—partners: Palau 20.3%, Japan 5.1% (2016)

Imports: $2.501 billion (2013 est.)
$2.438 billion (2012 est.)
country comparison to the world: 151

Imports—commodities: petroleum and petroleum products, food, manufactured goods

Imports—partners: Singapore 32.1%, Japan 30.6%, South Korea 8.4%, Hong Kong 8.1% (2016)

Debt—external: $NA

Exchange rates: the US dollar is used

ENERGY

Electricity access: *population without electricity:* 66,724
electrification—*total population:* 59%
electrification—urban areas: 60%
electrification—rural areas: 45% (2012)

Electricity—production: 1.623 billion kWh (2015 est.)
country comparison to the world: 144

Electricity—consumption: 1.509 billion kWh (2015 est.)
country comparison to the world: 148

Electricity—exports: 0 kWh (2016 est.)
country comparison to the world: 144

Electricity—imports: 0 kWh (2016 est.)
country comparison to the world: 157

Electricity—installed generating capacity: 552,000 kW (2015 est.)
country comparison to the world: 143

Electricity—from fossil fuels: 100% of total installed capacity (2015 est.)
country comparison to the world: 8

Electricity—from nuclear fuels: 0% of total installed capacity (2015 est.)
country comparison to the world: 101

Electricity—from hydroelectric plants: 0% of total installed capacity (2015 est.)
country comparison to the world: 179

Electricity—from other renewable sources: 0% of total installed capacity (2015 est.)
country comparison to the world: 186

Crude oil—production: 0 bbl/day (2016 est.)
country comparison to the world: 142

Crude oil—exports: 0 bbl/day (2014 est.)
country comparison to the world: 132

Crude oil—imports: 0 bbl/day (2014 est.)
country comparison to the world: 135

Crude oil—proved reserves: 0 bbl (1 January 2017 es)
country comparison to the world: 142

Refined petroleum products—production: 0 bbl/day (2014 est.)
country comparison to the world: 152

Refined petroleum products—consumption: 15,400 bbl/day (2015 est.)
country comparison to the world: 150

Refined petroleum products—exports: 0 bbl/day (2014 est.)
country comparison to the world: 162

Refined petroleum products—imports: 15,230 bbl/day (2014 est.)
country comparison to the world: 131

Natural gas—production: 0 cu m (2014 est.)
country comparison to the world: 143

Natural gas—consumption: 0 cu m (2014 est.)
country comparison to the world: 188

Natural gas—exports: 0 cu m (2014 est.)
country comparison to the world: 114

Natural gas—imports: 0 cu m (2014 est.)
country comparison to the world: 133

Natural gas—proved reserves: 0 cu m (1 January 2014 es)
country comparison to the world: 147

Carbon dioxide emissions from consumption of energy: 1.8 million Mt (2013 est.)
country comparison to the world: 152

COMMUNICATIONS

Telephones—fixed lines: *total subscriptions:* 68,000
subscriptions per 100 inhabitants: 42 (July 2016 est.)
country comparison to the world: 152

Telephones—mobile cellular: *total:* 181,000
subscriptions per 100 inhabitatnts: 113 (July 2016 est.)
country comparison to the world: 191

Telephone system: *general assessment:* modern system, integrated with US facilities for direct dialing, including free use of 800 numbers

domestic: three major companies provide both fixed-line and mobile services, as well as access to the Internet

international: country code—1-671; major landing point for submarine cables between Asia and the US (Guam is a transpacific communications hub for major carriers linking the US and Asia); satellite earth stations—2 Intelsat (Pacific Ocean) (2016)

Broadcast media: about a dozen TV channels, including digital channels; multi-channel cable TV services are available; roughly 20 radio stations (2009)

Internet country code: .gu
Internet users: total: 125,328

percent of population: 77.0% (July 2016 est.)
country comparison to the world: 168

TRANSPORTATION

Airports: 5 (2013)
country comparison to the world: 179

Airports—with paved runways: *total:* 4
over 3,047 m: 2
2,438 to 3,047 m: 1
914 to 1,523 m: 1 (2017)

Airports—with unpaved runways: *total:* 1
under 914 m: 1 (2013)

Roadways: *total:* 1,045 km (2008)
country comparison to the world: 186

Merchant marine: *total:* 3
by type: other 3 (2017)
country comparison to the world: 162

Ports and terminals: *major seaport(s):* Apra Harbor

MILITARY AND SECURITY

Military—note: defense is the responsibility of the US

TRANSNATIONAL ISSUES

Disputes—international: none

GUATEMALA

INTRODUCTION

Background: The Maya civilization flourished in Guatemala and surrounding regions during the first millennium A.D. After almost three centuries as a Spanish colony, Guatemala won its independence in 1821. During the second half of the 20th century, it experienced a variety of military and civilian governments, as well as a 36-year guerrilla war. In 1996, the government signed a peace agreement formally ending the internal conflict, which had left more than 200,000 people dead and had created, by some estimates, about 1 million refugees.

GEOGRAPHY

Location: Central America, bordering the North Pacific Ocean, between El Salvador and Mexico, and bordering the Gulf of Honduras (Caribbean Sea) between Honduras and Belize

Geographic coordinates: 15 30 N, 90 15 W

Map references: Central America and the Caribbean

Area: *total:* 108,889 sq km

land: 107,159 sq km
water: 1,730 sq km
country comparison to the world: 108

Area—comparative: slightly smaller than Pennsylvania

Land boundaries: *total:* 1,667 km
border countries (4): Belize 266 km, El Salvador 199 km, Honduras 244 km, Mexico 958 km

Coastline: 400 km

Maritime claims: *territorial sea:* 12 nm
exclusive economic zone: 200 nm

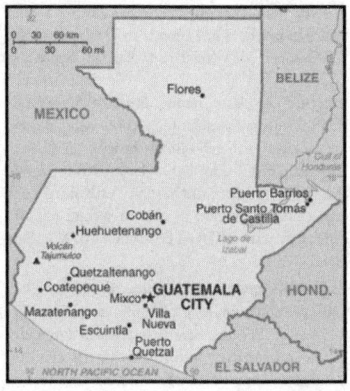

continental shelf: 200-m depth or to the depth of exploitation

Climate: tropical; hot, humid in lowlands; cooler in highlands

Terrain: two east-west trending mountain chains divide the country into three regions: the mountainous highlands, the Pacific coast south of mountains, and the vast northern Peten lowlands

Elevation: *mean elevation:* 759 m

elevation extremes: *lowest point:* Pacific Ocean 0 m

highest point: Volcan Tajumulco 4,220 m (highest point in Central America)

Natural resources: petroleum, nickel, rare woods, fish, chicle, hydropower

Land use: *agricultural land:* 41.2%
arable land: 14.2%;
permanent crops: 8.8%;
permanent pasture: 18.2%
forest: 33.6%
other: 25.2% (2011 est.)
Irrigated land: 3,375 sq km (2012)

Population—distribution: the vast majority of the populace resides in the southern half of the country, particularly in the mountainous regions; more than half of the population lives in rural areas

Natural hazards: numerous volcanoes in mountains, with occasional violent earthquakes; Caribbean coast extremely susceptible to hurricanes and other tropical storms

volcanism: significant volcanic activity in the Sierra Madre range; Santa Maria (3,772 m) has been deemed a Decade Volcano by the International Association of Volcanology and Chemistry of the Earth's Interior, worthy of study due to its explosive history and close proximity to human populations; Pacaya (2,552 m), which erupted in May 2010 causing an ashfall on Guatemala City and prompting evacuations, is one of the country's most active volcanoes with frequent eruptions since 1965; other historically active volcanoes include Acatenango, Almolonga, Atitlan, Fuego, and Tacana

Environment—current issues: deforestation in the Peten rainforest; soil erosion; water pollution

Environment—international agreements: *party to:* Antarctic Treaty, Biodiversity, Climate Change, Climate Change-Kyoto Protocol, Desertification, Endangered Species, Environmental Modification, Hazardous Wastes, Law of the Sea, Marine Dumping, Ozone Layer Protection, Ship Pollution, Wetlands, Whaling
signed, but not ratified: none of the selected agreements

Geography—note: there are no natural harbors on the west coast

PEOPLE AND SOCIETY

Population: 15,460,732 (July 2017 est.)
country comparison to the world: 70

Nationality: *noun:* Guatemalan(s)
adjective: Guatemalan

Ethnic groups: mestizo (mixed Amerindian-Spanish—in local Spanish called Ladino) and European 60.1%, Maya 39.3% (K'iche 11.3%, Q'eqchi 7.6%, Kaqchikel 7.4%, Mam 5.5%, other 7.5%), non-Maya, non-mestizo 0.15% (Xinca (indigenous, non-Maya), Garifuna (mixed West and Central African, Island Carib, and Arawak)), other 0.5% (2001 est.)

Languages: Spanish (official) 68.9%, Maya languages 30.9% (K'iche 8.7%, Q'eqchi 7%, Mam 4.6%, Kaqchikel 4.3%, other 6.3%), other 0.3% (includes Xinca and Garifuna)
note: the 2003 Law of National Languages officially recognized 23 indigenous languages, including 21 Maya languages, Xinka, and Garifuna (2001 est.)

Religions: Roman Catholic, Protestant, indigenous Mayan beliefs

Demographic profile: Guatemala is a predominantly poor country that struggles in several areas of health and development, including infant, child, and maternal mortality, malnutrition, literacy, and contraceptive awareness and use. The country's large indigenous population is disproportionately affected. Guatemala is the most populous country in Central America and has the highest fertility rate in Latin America. It also has the highest population growth rate in Latin America, which is likely to continue because of its large reproductive-age population and high birth rate. Almost half of Guatemala's population is under age 19, making it the youngest population in Latin America. Guatemala's total fertility rate has slowly declined during the last few decades due in part to limited government-funded health programs. However, the birth rate is still more close to three children per woman and is markedly higher among its rural and indigenous populations.

Guatemalans have a history of emigrating legally and illegally to Mexico, the United States, and Canada because of a lack of economic opportunity, political instability, and natural disasters. Emigration, primarily to the United States, escalated during the 1960 to 1996 civil war and accelerated after a peace agreement was signed. Thousands of Guatemalans who fled to Mexico returned after the war, but labor migration to southern Mexico continues.

Age structure: *0-14 years:* 34.5% (male 2,719,027/female 2,614,720)
15-24 years: 21.58% (male 1,677,634/female 1,658,941)
25-54 years: 34.12% (male 2,516,456/female 2,759,393)
55-64 years: 5.26% (male 384,967/female 428,198)
65 years and over: 4.54% (male 324,492/female 376,904) (2017 est.)

Dependency ratios: *total dependency ratio:* 68.7
youth dependency ratio: 61.1
elderly dependency ratio: 7.6
potential support ratio: 13.1 (2015 est.)

Median age: *total:* 22.1 years
male: 21.4 years
female: 22.8 years (2017 est.)
country comparison to the world: 180

Population growth rate: 1.75% (2017 est.)
country comparison to the world: 59

Birth rate: 24.1 births/1,000 population (2017 est.)
country comparison to the world: 52

Death rate: 4.7 deaths/1,000 population (2017 est.)
country comparison to the world: 200

Net migration rate: -1.9 migrant(s)/1,000 population (2017 est.)
country comparison to the world: 157

Population distribution: the vast majority of the populace resides in the southern half of the country, particularly in the mountainous regions; more than half of the population lives in rural areas

Urbanization: *urban population:* 52.5% of total population (2017)
rate of urbanization: 3.23% annual rate of change (2015-20 est.)

Major urban areas—population: GUATEMALA CITY (capital) 2.918 million (2015)

Sex ratio: *at birth:* 1.05 male(s)/female
0-14 years: 1.04 male(s)/female
15-24 years: 1.01 male(s)/female
25-54 years: 0.91 male(s)/female
55-64 years: 0.91 male(s)/female
65 years and over: 0.87 male(s)/female
total population: 0.97 male(s)/female (2016 est.)

Mother's mean age at first birth: 21.2 years
note: median age at first birth among women 25-29 (2014/15 est.)

Maternal mortality ratio: 88 deaths/100,000 live births (2015 est.)
country comparison to the world: 78

Infant mortality rate: *total:* 21.3 deaths/1,000 live births
male: 23.2 deaths/1,000 live births
female: 19.3 deaths/1,000 live births (2017 est.)
country comparison to the world: 78

Life expectancy at birth: *total population:* 72.6 years
male: 70.6 years
female: 74.7 years (2017 est.)
country comparison to the world: 147

385

Total fertility rate: 2.77 children born/woman (2017 est.)
country comparison to the world: 63

Contraceptive prevalence rate: 60.6% (2014/15)
Health expenditures: 6.2% of GDP (2014)
country comparison to the world: 101

Physicians density: 0.9 physicians/1,000 population (2009)

Hospital bed density: 0.6 beds/1,000 population (2011)

Drinking water source:
improved:
urban: 98.4% of population
rural: 86.8% of population
total: 92.8% of population
unimproved:
urban: 1.6% of population
rural: 13.2% of population
total: 7.2% of population (2015 est.)

Sanitation facility access:
improved:
urban: 77.5% of population
rural: 49.3% of population
total: 63.9% of population
unimproved:
urban: 22.5% of population
rural: 50.7% of population
total: 36.1% of population (2015 est.)

HIV/AIDS—adult prevalence rate: 0.5% (2016 est.)
country comparison to the world: 64

HIV/AIDS—people living with HIV/AIDS: 46,000
country comparison to the world: 59

HIV/AIDS—deaths: 1,600 (2016 est.)
country comparison to the world: 57

Major infectious diseases: *degree of risk:* high
food or waterborne diseases: bacterial diarrhea, hepatitis A, and typhoid fever
vectorborne disease: dengue fever and malaria
note: active local transmission of Zika virus by Aedes species mosquitoes has been identified in this country (as of August 2016); it poses an important risk (a large number of cases possible) among US citizens if bitten by an infective mosquito; other less common ways to get Zika are through sex, via blood transfusion, or during pregnancy, in which the pregnant woman passes Zika virus to her fetus (2016)

Obesity—adult prevalence rate: 21.2% (2016)
country comparison to the world: 93

Children under the age of 5 years underweight: 12.6% (2015)
country comparison to the world: 57

Education expenditures: 3% of GDP (2015)
country comparison to the world: 139

Literacy: *definition:* age 15 and over can read and write
total population: 81.5%
male: 87.4%
female: 76.3% (2015 est.)

School life expectancy (primary to tertiary education): *total:* 11 years
male: 11 years

female: 10 years (2013)

Unemployment, youth ages 15-24: *total:* 4.8%
male: 3.6%
female: 7.5% (2015 est.)
country comparison to the world: 117

GOVERNMENT

Country name: *conventional long form:* Republic of Guatemala
conventional short form: Guatemala
local long form: Republica de Guatemala
local short form: Guatemala
etymology: name derives from the Maya word meaning "Land of Trees"

Government type: presidential republic

Capital: *name:* Guatemala City

geographic coordinates: 14 37 N, 90 31 W
time difference: UTC-6 (1 hour behind Washington, DC, during Standard Time)

Administrative divisions: 22 departments (departamentos, singular—departamento); Alta Verapaz, Baja Verapaz, Chimaltenango, Chiquimula, El Progreso, Escuintla, Guatemala, Huehuetenango, Izabal, Jalapa, Jutiapa, Peten, Quetzaltenango, Quiche, Retalhuleu, Sacatepequez, San Marcos, Santa Rosa, Solola, Suchitepequez, Totonicapan, Zacapa

Independence: 15 September 1821 (from Spain)

National holiday: Independence Day, 15 September (1821)

Constitution: several previous; latest adopted 31 May 1985, effective 14 January 1986; suspended, reinstated, and amended in 1994 (2016)

Legal system: civil law system; judicial review of legislative acts

International law organization participation: has not submitted an ICJ jurisdiction declaration; accepts ICCt jurisdiction

Citizenship: *citizenship by birth:* yes
citizenship by descent: yes
dual citizenship recognized: yes
residency requirement for naturalization: 5 years with no absences of six consecutive months or longer or absences totaling more than a year

Suffrage: 18 years of age; universal; note—active duty members of the armed forces and police by law cannot vote and are restricted to their barracks on election day

Executive branch: *chief of state:* President Jimmy Ernesto MORALES Cabrera (since 14 January 2016); Vice President Jafeth CABRERA Franco (since 14 January 2016); note—the president is both chief of state and head of government

head of government: President Jimmy Ernesto MORALES Cabrera (since 14 January 2016); Vice President Jafeth CABRERA Franco (since 14 January 2016)

cabinet: Council of Ministers appointed by the president
elections/appointments: president and vice president directly elected on the same ballot by absolute majority popular vote in 2 rounds if needed for

a 4-year term (not eligible for consecutive terms); election last held in 2 rounds on 6 September and 25 October 2015 (next to be held in September 2019)
election results: Jimmy Ernesto MORALES Cabrera elected president in second round; percent of vote in first round—Jimmy Ernesto MORALES Cabrera (FNC) 23.9%, Sandra TORRES (UNE) 19.8%, Manuel BALDIZON (LIDER) 19.6%, other 36.7%; percent of vote in second round—Jimmy Ernesto MORALES Cabrera 67.4%, Sandra TORRES 32.6%

Legislative branch: description: unicameral Congress of the Republic or Congreso de la Republica (158 seats; 127 members directly elected in multiseat constituencies within each of the country's 22 departments by simple majority vote and 31 directly elected in a single nationwide constituency by proportional representation vote; members serve 4-year terms)
elections: last held on 6 September 2015 (next to be held in September 2019)
election results: percent of vote by party—LIDER 19.1%, UNE 14.8%, TODOS 9.7%, PP 9.4%, FCN 8.8%, EG 6.2%, CREO-PU 5.7%, UCN 5.4%, Winaq-URNG-MAIZ 4.3%, Convergence 3.8%, VIVA 3.7%, PAN 3.4%, FUERZA 2.1%, other 3.5%; seats by party—LIDER 44, UNE 36, TODOS 18, PP 17, FCN 11, EG 7, UCN 6, CREO-PU 5, Winaq-URNG-MAIZ 3, Convergence 3, VIVA 3, PAN 3, FUERZA 2; note—seats by party as of 6 January 2016—FCN 37, UNE 32, MR 20, TODOS 17, AC 12, EG 7, UCN 6, CREO 5, LIDER 5, VIVA 4, Convergence 3, PAN 3, PP 2, FUERZA 1, PU 1, URNG 1, Winaq 1, independent 1

Judicial branch: *highest court(s):* Supreme Court of Justice or Corte Suprema de Justicia (consists of 13 magistrates including the court president and organized into 3 chambers); note—the court president also supervises trial judges countrywide; Constitutional Court or Corte de Constitucionalidad (consists of 5 judges and 5 alternates)
judge selection and term of office: Supreme Court magistrates elected by the Congress of the Republic from candidates proposed by the Postulation Committee, an independent body of deans of the country's university law schools, representatives of the country's law associations, and representatives of the Courts of Appeal; magistrates elected for concurrent, renewable 5-year terms; Constitutional Court judges—1 elected by the Congress of the Republic, 1 by the Supreme Court, 1 by the president of the republic, 1 by the (public) University of San Carlos, and 1 by the lawyers bar association; judges elected for concurrent, renewable 5-year terms; the presidency of the court rotates among the magistrates for a single 1-year term
subordinate courts: numerous first instance and appellate courts

Political parties and leaders: Citizen Alliance or AC
Commitment, Renewal, and Order or CREO [Richard LEE Abularach]
Convergence [Pablo MONSANTO]

Encounter for Guatemala or EG [Nineth MONTENEGRO Cottom]

Everyone Together for Guatemala or TODOS [Felipe ALEJOS]

FUERZA [Maurico REDFORD]

Grand National Alliance or GANA [Carlos Alberto MARTINEZ Castellanos]

Guatemalan National Revolutionary Unity or Winaq-URNG [Angel SANCHEZ Viesca]

Heart New Nation or CNN [Mario Roberto CHU Catalan]

My Country or Mi Pais [Alfredo RABBE]

National Advancement Party or PAN [Juan GUTIERREZ Strauss]

National Unity for Hope or UNE [Sandra TORRES]

National Convergence Front or FCN [Edgar Justino OVALLE Maldonado]

National Welfare or BIEN [Fidel REYES Lee]

Nationalist Change Union or UCN [Mario ESTRADA]

Patriot Party or PP [Ingrid Roxana BALDETTI Elias]

Political Movement Winaq or WINAQ [Amilcar de Jesus POP Ac]

Productivity and Labor Party or PPT [Edgar Alfredo RODRIGUEZ]

Progressive Liberating Party or PLP [Ana BERNAT]

Reform Movement or MR [Jose Raul VIGIL Arias]

Renewed Democratic Liberty or LIDER [Manuel BALDIZON]

Unionista Party or PU [Alvaro ARZU Escobar]

UNITED [Mario Rolando TORRES Marroquin]

Victoria (Victory) [Manuel de Jesus RIVERA]

Vision with Values or VIVA [Cromwell CUESTAS Paz]

Political pressure groups and leaders: Alliance Against Impunity or AI (includes Center for Legal Action on Human Rights or CALDH, Family and Friends of the Disappeared of Guatemala or FAMDEGUA)

Civic and Political Convergence of Women

Committee for Campesino Unity or CUC

Coordinating Committee of Agricultural, Commercial, Industrial, and Financial Associations or CACIF

Foundation for the Development of Guatemala or FUNDESA

Guatemala Visible

Mutual Support Group or GAM

Movimiento PRO-Justicia

National Union of Agriculture Workers or UNAGRO

International organization participation: BCIE, CACM, CD, CELAC, EITI (compliant country), FAO, G-24, G-77, IADB, IAEA, IBRD, ICAO, ICC (national committees), ICCt (signatory), ICRM, IDA, IFAD, IFC, IFRCS, IHO, ILO, IMF, IMO, Interpol, IOC, IOM, IPU, ISO (correspondent), ITSO, ITU, ITUC (NGOs), LAES, LAIA (observer), MIGA, MINUSTAH, MONUSCO, NAM, OAS, OPANAL, OPCW, Pacific Alliance (observer), PCA, Petrocaribe, SICA, UN, UNCTAD, UNESCO, UNIDO, UNIFIL, Union Latina, UNISFA, UNITAR, UNMISS, UNOCI, UNWTO, UPU, WCO, WFTU (NGOs), WHO, WIPO, WMO, WTO

Diplomatic representation in the US: *chief of mission:* Ambassador Manuel Alfredo ESPINA Pinto (since 8 September 2017)

chancery: 2220 R Street NW, Washington, DC 20008

telephone: [1] (202) 745-4952

FAX: [1] (202) 745-1908

consulate(s): Del Rio (TX), San Bernardino (CA), Silver Spring (MD), Tucson (AZ)

consulate(s) general: Atlanta, Chicago, Denver, Houston, Lake Worth (FL), Los Angeles, McAllen (TX), Miami, New York, Phoenix, Providence (RI), San Francisco, Silver Spring (MD), Tucson (AZ)

Diplomatic representation from the US: *chief of mission:* Ambassador Luis ARREAGA (since 4 October 2017)

embassy: 7-01 Avenida Reforma, Zone 10, Guatemala City

mailing address: DPO AA 34024

telephone: [502] 2326-4000

FAX: [502] 2326-4654

Flag description: three equal vertical bands of light blue (hoist side), white, and light blue, with the coat of arms centered in the white band; the coat of arms includes a green and red quetzal (the national bird) representing liberty and a scroll bearing the inscription LIBERTAD 15 DE SEPTIEMBRE DE 1821 (the original date of independence from Spain) all superimposed on a pair of crossed rifles signifying Guatemala's willingness to defend itself and a pair of crossed swords representing honor and framed by a laurel wreath symbolizing victory; the blue bands represent the Pacific Ocean and Caribbean Sea; the white band denotes peace and purity

note: one of only two national flags featuring a firearm, the other is Mozambique

National symbol(s): quetzal (bird); national colors: blue, white

National anthem: name: "Himno Nacional de Guatemala" (National Anthem of Guatemala)

lyrics/music: Jose Joaquin PALMA/Rafael Alvarez OVALLE

note: adopted 1897, modified lyrics adopted 1934; Cuban poet Jose Joaquin PALMA anonymously submitted lyrics to a public contest calling for a national anthem; his authorship was not discovered until 1911

ECONOMY

Economy—overview: Guatemala is the most populous country in Central America with a GDP per capita roughly half the average for Latin America and the Caribbean. The agricultural sector accounts for 13.5% of GDP and 31% of the labor force; key agricultural exports include sugar, coffee, bananas, and vegetables. Guatemala is the top remittance recipient in Central America as a result of Guatemala's large expatriate community in the US. These inflows are a primary source of foreign income, equivalent to over one-half of the country's exports and one-tenth of its GDP.

The 1996 peace accords, which ended 36 years of civil war, removed a major obstacle to foreign investment, and Guatemala has since pursued important reforms and macroeconomic stabilization. The Dominican Republic-Central America Free Trade Agreement (CAFTA-DR) entered into force in July 2006, spurring increased investment and diversification of exports, with the largest increases in ethanol and non-traditional agricultural exports. While CAFTA-DR has helped improve the investment climate, concerns over security, the lack of skilled workers, and poor infrastructure continue to hamper foreign direct investment.

The distribution of income remains highly unequal with the richest 20% of the population accounting for more than 51% of Guatemala's overall consumption. More than half of the population is below the national poverty line, and 23% of the population lives in extreme poverty. Poverty among indigenous groups, which make up more than 40% of the population, averages 79%, with 40% of the indigenous population living in extreme poverty. Nearly one-half of Guatemala's children under age five are chronically malnourished, one of the highest malnutrition rates in the world.

Guatemala is facing growing fiscal pressures, exacerbated by multiple corruption scandals that led to the resignation of the president, vice president, and numerous high-level economic officials in 2015.

GDP (purchasing power parity): $138.3 billion (2017 est.)

$134 billion (2016 est.)

$130 billion (2015 est.)

note: data are in 2017 dollars

country comparison to the world: 78

GDP (official exchange rate): $70.81 billion (2016 est.)

GDP—real growth rate: 3.2% (2017 est.)

3.1% (2016 est.)

4.1% (2015 est.)

country comparison to the world: 107

GDP—per capita (PPP): $8,200 (2017 est.)

$8,100 (2016 est.)

$8,000 (2015 est.)

note: data are in 2017 dollars

country comparison to the world: 152

Gross national saving: 13.5% of GDP (2017 est.)

13.9% of GDP (2016 est.)

13.3% of GDP (2015 est.)

country comparison to the world: 134

GDP—composition, by end use:

household consumption: 85.4%

government consumption: 9.8%

investment in fixed capital: 12.5%

investment in inventories: 0.5%

exports of goods and services: 19.3%

imports of goods and services: -27.5% (2017 est.)

GDP—composition, by sector of origin:

agriculture: 13.2%

industry: 23.6%
services: 63.2% (2017 est.)

Agriculture—products: sugarcane, corn, bananas, coffee, beans, cardamom; cattle, sheep, pigs, chickens

Industries: sugar, textiles and clothing, furniture, chemicals, petroleum, metals, rubber, tourism

Industrial production growth rate: 3.1% (2017 est.)
country comparison to the world: 92

Labor force: 6.664 million (2017 est.)
country comparison to the world: 70

Labor force—by occupation: *agriculture:* 30.5%
industry: 13.7%
services: 55.8% (2016 est.)

Unemployment rate: 2.4% (2016 est.)
2.7% (2015 est.)
country comparison to the world: 21

Population below poverty line: 59.3% (2014 est.)

Household income or consumption by percentage share: *lowest 10%:* 1.6%
highest 10%: 38.4% (2014)

Distribution of family income—Gini index: 53 (2014 est.)
56 (2011)
country comparison to the world: 11

Budget: *revenues:* $8.335 billion
expenditures: $9.6 billion (2017 est.)
Taxes and other revenues: 11.8% of GDP (2017 est.)
country comparison to the world: 207

Budget surplus (+) or deficit (-): -1.8% of GDP (2017 est.)
country comparison to the world: 77

Public debt: 30.1% of GDP (2017 est.)
29.2% of GDP (2016 est.)
country comparison to the world: 161

Fiscal year: calendar year

Inflation rate (consumer prices): 4.4% (2017 est.)
4.4% (2016 est.)
country comparison to the world: 166

Central bank discount rate: 7.53% (31 December 2015 est.)
6.5% (31 December 2010)
country comparison to the world: 42

Commercial bank prime lending rate: 13.5% (31 December 2017 est.)
13.1% (31 December 2016 est.)
country comparison to the world: 58

Stock of narrow money: $12.13 billion (31 December 2017 est.)
$10.81 billion (31 December 2016 est.)
country comparison to the world: 81

Stock of broad money: $28.42 billion (31 December 2017 est.)
$25.35 billion (31 December 2016 est.)
country comparison to the world: 80

Stock of domestic credit: $35.27 billion (31 December 2017 est.)
$30.44 billion (31 December 2016 est.)
country comparison to the world: 76

Market value of publicly traded shares: $NA

Current account balance: $364 million (2017 est.)
$644 million (2016 est.)
country comparison to the world: 48

Exports: $10.53 billion (2017 est.)
$10.58 billion (2016 est.)
country comparison to the world: 88

Exports—commodities: sugar, coffee, petroleum, apparel, bananas, fruits and vegetables, cardamom, manufacturing products, precious stones and metals, electricity

Exports—partners: US 34%, El Salvador 11.5%, Honduras 7.1%, Nicaragua 6%, Costa Rica 4.5%, Mexico 4.3% (2016)

Imports: $17.48 billion (2017 est.)
$17.64 billion (2016 est.)
country comparison to the world: 80

Imports—commodities: fuels, machinery and transport equipment, construction materials, grain, fertilizers, electricity, mineral products, chemical products, plastic materials and products

Imports—partners: US 38.1%, Mexico 11%, China 9.9%, El Salvador 5%, Panama 4.2% (2016)

Reserves of foreign exchange and gold: $10.05 billion (31 December 2017 est.)
$9.156 billion (31 December 2016 est.)
country comparison to the world: 74

Debt—external: $23.54 billion (31 December 2017 est.)
$21.45 billion (31 December 2016 est.)
country comparison to the world: 89

Stock of direct foreign investment—at home: $13.19 billion (2015 est.)
$11.98 billion (2014 est.)
country comparison to the world: 92

Exchange rates: quetzales (GTQ) per US dollar—
7.323 (2017 est.)
7.5999 (2016 est.)
7.5999 (2015 est.)
7.6548 (2014 est.)
7.7322 (2013 est.)

ENERGY

Electricity access: *population without electricity:* 1,600,000
electrification—*total population:* 78%
electrification—urban areas: 85%
electrification—rural areas: 72% (2013)

Electricity—production: 10.88 billion kWh (2016 est.)
country comparison to the world: 97

Electricity—consumption: 9.833 billion kWh (2016 est.)
country comparison to the world: 95

Electricity—exports: 1.335 billion kWh (2016 est.)
country comparison to the world: 52

Electricity—imports: 746.9 million kWh (2016 est.)
country comparison to the world: 73

Electricity—installed generating capacity: 4.139 million kW (2016 est.)
country comparison to the world: 86

Electricity—from fossil fuels: 42.9% of total installed capacity (2015 est.)
country comparison to the world: 166

Electricity—from nuclear fuels: 0% of total installed capacity (2015 est.)
country comparison to the world: 103

Electricity—from hydroelectric plants: 28.3% of total installed capacity (2015 est.)
country comparison to the world: 75

Electricity—from other renewable sources: 34.4% of total installed capacity (2015 est.)
country comparison to the world: 8

Crude oil—production: 8,977 bbl/day (2016 est.)
country comparison to the world: 80

Crude oil—exports: 7,407 bbl/day (2016 est.)
country comparison to the world: 60

Crude oil—imports: 17,220 bbl/day (2014 est.)
country comparison to the world: 66

Crude oil—proved reserves: 83.07 million bbl (1 January 2017 es)
country comparison to the world: 75

Refined petroleum products—production: 1,069 bbl/day (2016 est.)
country comparison to the world: 105

Refined petroleum products—consumption: 91,900 bbl/day (2016 est.)
country comparison to the world: 84

Refined petroleum products—exports: 11,780 bbl/day (2016 est.)
country comparison to the world: 81

Refined petroleum products—imports: 104,200 bbl/day (2016 est.)
country comparison to the world: 56

Natural gas—production: 0 cu m (2013 est.)
country comparison to the world: 144

Natural gas—consumption: 0 cu m (2013 est.)
country comparison to the world: 189

Natural gas—exports: 0 cu m (2013 est.)
country comparison to the world: 116

Natural gas—imports: 0 cu m (2013 est.)
country comparison to the world: 134

Natural gas—proved reserves: 2.96 billion cu m (1 January 2006 es)
country comparison to the world: 98

Carbon dioxide emissions from consumption of energy: 13.6 million Mt (2013 est.)
country comparison to the world: 95

COMMUNICATIONS

Telephones—fixed lines: *total subscriptions:* 1.675 million
subscriptions per 100 inhabitants: 11 (July 2016 est.)
country comparison to the world: 65

Telephones—mobile cellular: *total:* 19,208,673
subscriptions per 100 inhabitants: 126 (July 2016 est.)
country comparison to the world: 63

Telephone system: *general assessment:* fairly modern network centered in the city of Guatemala *domestic:* state-owned telecommunications company privatized in the late 1990s opened the way for competition; fixed-line teledensity roughly 10 per 100 persons; fixed-line investments are being concentrated on improving rural connectivity; mobile-cellular teledensity about 125 per 100 persons

international: country code—502; landing point for both the Americas Region Caribbean Ring System (ARCOS-1) and the SAM-1 fiber-optic submarine cable system that, together, provide connectivity to South and Central America, parts of the Caribbean, and the US; connected to Central American Microwave System; satellite earth station—1 Intelsat (Atlantic Ocean) (2017)

Broadcast media: 4 privately owned national terrestrial TV channels dominate TV broadcasting; multi-channel satellite and cable services are available; 1 government-owned radio station and hundreds of privately owned radio stations (2007)

Internet country code: .gt

Internet users: total: 5,241,952

percent of population: 34.5% (July 2016 est.)
country comparison to the world: 90

TRANSPORTATION

National air transport system: *number of registered air carriers:* 3

inventory of registered aircraft operated by air carriers: 8

annual passenger traffic on registered air carriers: 93,129

annual freight traffic on registered air carriers: 455,520 mt-km (2015)

Civil aircraft registration country code prefix: TG (2016)

Airports: 291 (2013)
country comparison to the world: 23

Airports—with paved runways: *total:* 16
2,438 to 3,047 m: 2
1,524 to 2,437 m: 4
914 to 1,523 m: 6

under 914 m: 4 (2017)

Airports—with unpaved runways: *total:* 275
2,438 to 3,047 m: 1
1,524 to 2,437 m: 2
914 to 1,523 m: 77
under 914 m: 195 (2013)

Heliports: 1 (2013)

Pipelines: oil 480 km (2013)

Railways: *total:* 800 km
narrow gauge: 800 km 0.914-m gauge (2014)
country comparison to the world: 96

Roadways: *total:* 17,621 km
paved: 7,489 km
unpaved: 10,132 km (includes 4,960 km of rural roads) (2016)
country comparison to the world: 118

Waterways: 990 km (260 km navigable year round; additional 730 km navigable during high-water season) (2012)
country comparison to the world: 65

Merchant marine: *total:* 9
by type: oil tanker 1, other 8 (2017)
country comparison to the world: 148

Ports and terminals: *major seaport(s):* Puerto Quetzal, Santo Tomas de Castilla

MILITARY AND SECURITY

Military expenditures: 0.39% of GDP (2016)
0.43% of GDP (2015)
0.45% of GDP (2014)
0.46% of GDP (2013)
0.45% of GDP (2012)
country comparison to the world: 129

Military branches: National Army of Guatemala (Ejercito Nacional de Guatemala, ENG, includes Guatemalan Navy (Fuerza de Mar, including Marines) and Guatemalan Air Force (Fuerza Aerea Guatemalteca, FAG)) (2013)

Military service age and obligation: all male citizens between the ages of 18 and 50 are eligible for

military service; in practice, most of the force is volunteer, however, a selective draft system is employed, resulting in a small portion of 17-21 year-olds conscripted; conscript service obligation varies from 1 to 2 years; women can serve as officers (2013)

TRANSNATIONAL ISSUES

Disputes—international: annual ministerial meetings under the Organization of American States-initiated Agreement on the Framework for Negotiations and Confidence Building Measures continue to address Guatemalan land and maritime claims in Belize and the Caribbean Sea; Guatemala persists in its territorial claim to half of Belize, but agrees to Line of Adjacency to keep Guatemalan squatters out of Belize's forested interior; both countries agreed in April 2012 to hold simultaneous referenda, scheduled for 6 October 2013, to decide whether to refer the dispute to the ICJ for binding resolution, but this vote was suspended indefinitely; Mexico must deal with thousands of impoverished Guatemalans and other Central Americans who cross the porous border looking for work in Mexico and the US

Refugees and internally displaced persons: IDPs: 257,000 (more than three decades of internal conflict that ended in 1996 displaced mainly the indigenous Maya population and rural peasants; ongoing drug cartel and gang violence) (2016)

Illicit drugs: major transit country for cocaine and heroin; it is estimated that 1,000 mt of cocaine are smuggled through the country each year, primarily destined for the US market; in 2016, the Guatemalan government estimated that an average of 4,500 hectares of opium poppy were being cultivated; marijuana cultivation for mostly domestic consumption; proximity to Mexico makes Guatemala a major staging area for drugs (particularly for cocaine); money laundering is a serious problem; corruption is a major problem

GUERNSEY

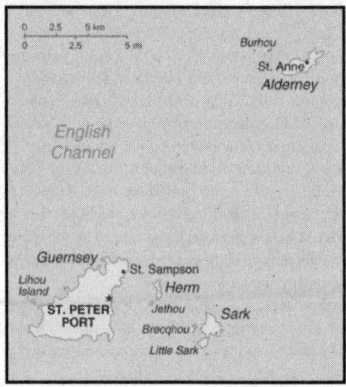

INTRODUCTION

Background: Guernsey and the other Channel Islands represent the last remnants of the medieval Dukedom of Normandy, which held sway in both France and England. The islands were the only British soil occupied by German troops in World War II. The Bailiwick of Guernsey is a British crown dependency but is not part of the UK or of the EU. However, the UK Government is constitutionally responsible for its defense and international representation. The Bailiwick of Guernsey consists of the main island of Guernsey and a number of smaller islands including Alderney, Sark, Herm, Jethou, Brecqhou, and Lihou.

GEOGRAPHY

Location: Western Europe, islands in the English Channel, northwest of France

Geographic coordinates: 49 28 N, 2 35 W

Map references: Europe

Area: *total:* 78 sq km
land: 78 sq km
water: 0 sq km
note: includes Alderney, Guernsey, Herm, Sark, and some other smaller islands
country comparison to the world: 228

Area—comparative: about one-half the size of Washington, DC

Land boundaries: 0 km

Coastline: 50 km

Maritime claims: *territorial sea:* 3 nm
exclusive fishing zone: 12 nm

Climate: temperate with mild winters and cool summers; about 50% of days are overcast

Terrain: mostly flat with low hills in southwest

Elevation: *mean elevation:* NA

elevation extremes: *lowest point:* English Channel 0 m
highest point: Le Moulin on Sark 114 m

Natural resources: cropland
Irrigated land: NA

Natural hazards: very large tidal variation and fast currents can make local waters dangerous

Environment—current issues: coastal erosion, coastal flooding; declining biodiversity due to land abandonment and succession to scrub or woodland

Geography—note: large, deepwater harbor at Saint Peter Port

PEOPLE AND SOCIETY

Population: 66,502 (July 2017 est.)
country comparison to the world: 204

Nationality: *noun:* Channel Islander(s)
adjective: Channel Islander

Ethnic groups: British and Norman-French descent with small percentages from other European countries

Languages: English, French, Norman-French dialect spoken in country districts

Religions: Protestant (Anglican, Presbyterian, Baptist, Congregational, Methodist), Roman Catholic

Age structure: *0-14 years:* 14.51% (male 4,984/female 4,665)
15-24 years: 11.13% (male 3,780/female 3,620)
25-54 years: 41.67% (male 13,995/female 13,719)
55-64 years: 13.11% (male 4,332/female 4,387)
65 years and over: 19.58% (male 5,929/female 7,091) (2017 est.)

Dependency ratios: *total dependency ratio:* 47.1
youth dependency ratio: 21.6
elderly dependency ratio: 25.4
potential support ratio: 3.9
note: data represent the Guernsey and Jersey (2015 est.)

Median age: *total:* 43.8 years
male: 42.5 years
female: 45.1 years (2017 est.)
country comparison to the world: 15

Population growth rate: 0.3% (2017 est.)
country comparison to the world: 172

Birth rate: 9.8 births/1,000 population (2017 est.)
country comparison to the world: 196

Death rate: 9 deaths/1,000 population (2017 est.)
country comparison to the world: 65

Net migration rate: 2.2 migrant(s)/1,000 population (2017 est.)
country comparison to the world: 45

Urbanization: *urban population:* 31.7% of total population (2017)

rate of urbanization: 0.86% annual rate of change (2015-20 est.)
note: data are for Guernsey and Jersey

Sex ratio: *at birth:* 1.05 male(s)/female
0-14 years: 1.07 male(s)/female
15-24 years: 1.04 male(s)/female
25-54 years: 1.02 male(s)/female
55-64 years: 0.99 male(s)/female
65 years and over: 0.83 male(s)/female
total population: 0.99 male(s)/female (2016 est.)

Infant mortality rate: *total:* 3.4 deaths/1,000 live births
male: 3.7 deaths/1,000 live births
female: 3.1 deaths/1,000 live births (2017 est.)
country comparison to the world: 206

Life expectancy at birth: *total population:* 82.6 years
male: 79.9 years
female: 85.4 years (2017 est.)
country comparison to the world: 9

Total fertility rate: 1.56 children born/woman (2017 est.)
country comparison to the world: 188

HIV/AIDS—adult prevalence rate: NA

HIV/AIDS—people living with HIV/AIDS: NA

HIV/AIDS—deaths: NA

GOVERNMENT

Country name: *conventional long form:* Bailiwick of Guernsey
conventional short form: Guernsey
etymology: the name is of Old Norse origin, but the meaning of the root "Guern(s)" is uncertain; the "-ey" ending means "island"

Dependency status: British crown dependency

Government type: parliamentary democracy (States of Deliberation); a Crown dependency of the UK

Capital: *name:* Saint Peter Port
geographic coordinates: 49 27 N, 2 32 W
time difference: UTC 0 (5 hours ahead of Washington, DC, during Standard Time)
daylight saving time: +1hr, begins last Sunday in March; ends last Sunday in October

Administrative divisions: none (British crown dependency); there are no first-order administrative divisions as defined by the US Government, but there are 10 parishes: Castel, Forest, Saint Andrew, Saint Martin, Saint Peter Port, Saint Pierre du Bois, Saint Sampson, Saint Saviour, Torteval, Vale
note: two additional parishes for Guernsey are sometimes listed—the parish of Saint Anne on the island of Alderney and the parish of Saint Peter on the island of Sark—but they are generally not included in the enumeration of parishes

Independence: none (British crown dependency)

National holiday: Liberation Day, 9 May (1945)

Constitution: *history:* unwritten; includes royal charters, statutes, and common law and practice

amendments: new laws or changes to existing laws are initiated by the States of Deliberation; passage requires majority vote (2016)

Legal system: customary legal system based on Norman customary law, and includes elements of the French civil code and English common law

Citizenship: see United Kingdom

Suffrage: 16 years of age; universal

Executive branch: *chief of state:* Queen ELIZABETH II (since 6 February 1952); represented by Lieutenant Governor Vice Admiral Ian CORDER (since 14 March 2016)

head of government: Chief Minister Gavin ST PIER (since 6 May 2016); Bailiff Sir Richard COLLAS (since 23 March 2012); note—the chief minister is the president of the Policy and Resources Committee and is the de facto head of government; the Policy and Resources Committee, elected by the States of Deliberation, functions as the executive; the 5 members all have equal voting rights
cabinet: none
elections/appointments: the monarchy is hereditary; lieutenant governor and bailiff appointed by the monarch; chief minister, who is the president of the Policy and Resources Committee indirectly elected by the States of Deliberation for a 4-year term; last held on 6 May 2016 (next to be held in 2020)
election results: Gavin ST PIER (independent) elected president of the Policy and Resources Committee and chief minister

Legislative branch: *description:* unicameral States of Deliberation (40 seats; 38 People's Deputies and 2 representatives of the States of Alderney; members directly elected by majority vote to serve 4-year terms); note—non-voting members include the bailiff (presiding officer), attorney-general, and solicitor-general
elections: last held on 27 April 2016 (next to be held in 2020)
election results: percent of vote—NA; seats—independent 38

Judicial branch: *highest resident court(s):* Guernsey Court of Appeal (consists of the Bailiff of Guernsey, who is the ex-officio president of the Guernsey Court of Appeal, and at least 12 judges); Royal Court (organized into 3 divisions—Full Court sits with 1 judge and 7 to 12 jurats acting as judges of fact, Ordinary Court sits with 1 judge and normally 3 jurats, and Matrimonial Causes Division sits with 1 judge and 4 jurats); note—appeals beyond Guernsey courts are heard by the Judicial Committee of the Privy Council (in London)
judge selection and term of office: Royal Court Bailiff, Deputy Bailiff, and Court of Appeal justices appointed by the British Crown and hold office at Her Majesty's pleasure; jurats elected by the States of Election, a body chaired by the Bailiff and a number of jurats
subordinate courts: Court of Alderney; Court of the Seneschal of Sark; Magistrate's Court (includes Juvenile Court); Contracts Court; Ecclesiastical Court; Court of Chief Pleas

Political parties and leaders: none; all independents

Political pressure groups and leaders: Stop Traffic Endangering Pedestrian Safety or STEPS

International organization participation: UPU

Diplomatic representation in the US: none (British crown dependency)

Diplomatic representation from the US: none (British crown dependency)

Flag description: white with the red cross of Saint George (patron saint of England) extending to the edges of the flag and a yellow equal-armed cross of William the Conqueror superimposed on the Saint George cross; the red cross represents the old ties with England and the fact that Guernsey is a British Crown dependency; the gold cross is a replica of the one used by Duke William of Normandy at the Battle of Hastings

National symbol(s): Guernsey cow, donkey; national colors: red, white, yellow

National anthem: name: "Sarnia Cherie" (Guernsey Dear)
lyrics/music: George DEIGHTON/Domencio SANTANGELO
note: adopted 1911; serves as a local anthem; as a British crown dependency, "God Save the Queen" remains official (see United Kingdom)

Economy—overview: Financial services account for about 40% of employment and about 55% of total income in this tiny, prosperous Channel Island economy. Tourism, manufacturing, and horticulture, mainly tomatoes and cut flowers, have been declining. Financial services, construction, retail, and the public sector have been growing. Light tax and death duties make Guernsey a popular tax haven. In October 2014, Guernsey signed an OECD agreement to automatically exchange some financial account information to limit tax avoidance and evasion.

GDP (purchasing power parity): $3.465 billion (2015 est.)
$3.451 billion (2014 est.)
$3.42 billion (2013 est.)
note: data are in 2015 dollars
country comparison to the world: 184

GDP (official exchange rate): $2.742 billion (2005 est.)

GDP—real growth rate: 0.4% (2015 est.)
1.2% (2014 est.)
4.2% (2012 est.)
country comparison to the world: 197

GDP—per capita (PPP): $52,500 (2014 est.)
$52,500 (2014 est.)
country comparison to the world: 23

GDP—composition, by sector of origin:
agriculture: 3%
industry: 10%
services: 87% (2000)

Agriculture—products: tomatoes, greenhouse flowers, sweet peppers, eggplant, fruit; Guernsey cattle

Industries: tourism, banking

Industrial production growth rate: NA%

Labor force: 31,470 (March 2006)
country comparison to the world: 204

Unemployment rate: 1.2% (2016 est.)
country comparison to the world: 9

Population below poverty line: NA%

Household income or consumption by percentage share: *lowest 10%:* NA%
highest 10%: NA%

Budget: *revenues:* $563.6 million
expenditures: $530.9 million (2005)
Taxes and other revenues: 20.6% of GDP (2005)
country comparison to the world: 149

Budget surplus (+) or deficit (-): 1.2% of GDP (2005)
country comparison to the world: 12

Fiscal year: calendar year

Inflation rate (consumer prices): 3.4% (June 2006 est.)
country comparison to the world: 140

Exports: $NA

Exports—commodities: tomatoes, flowers and ferns, sweet peppers, eggplant, other vegetables

Imports: $NA

Imports—commodities: coal, gasoline, oil, machinery, and equipment

Debt—external: $NA

Exchange rates: Guernsey pound per US dollar
0.7836 (2017)
0.738 (2016)
0.738 (2015)
0.6542 (2014)
0.607 (2013)

Electricity access: electrification—*total population:* 100% (2016)

Telephones—fixed lines: *total subscriptions:* 36,547
subscriptions per 100 inhabitants: 60 (July 2016 est.)
country comparison to the world: 165

Telephones—mobile cellular: *total:* 71,249
subscriptions per 100 inhabitants: 113 (July 2016 est.)
country comparison to the world: 203
Telephone system: domestic: fixed-line and mobile-cellular services widely available
international: country code—44; 1 submarine cable (2015)

Broadcast media: multiple UK terrestrial TV broadcasts are received via a transmitter in Jersey with relays in Jersey, Guernsey, and Alderney; satellite packages are available; BBC Radio Guernsey and 1 other radio station operating (2009)

Internet country code: .gg
Internet users: total: 55,050

percent of population: 83.3% (July 2016 est.)
country comparison to the world: 185

National air transport system: *number of registered air carriers:* 2 (registered in UK)
inventory of registered aircraft operated by air carriers: 11 (registered in UK) (2015)

Airports: 2 (2013)
country comparison to the world: 200

Airports—with paved runways: *total:* 2
1,524 to 2,437 m: 1
under 914 m: 1 (2017)

Ports and terminals: *major seaport(s):* Braye Bay, Saint Peter Port

Military—note: defense is the responsibility of the UK

Disputes—international: none

GUINEA

Background: Guinea is at a turning point after decades of authoritarian rule since gaining its independence from France in 1958. Sekou TOURE ruled the country as president from independence to his death in 1984. Lansana CONTE came to power in 1984 when the military seized the government after TOURE's death. Gen. CONTE organized and won presidential elections in 1993, 1998, and 2003, though all the polls were rigged. Upon CONTE's death in December 2008, Capt. Moussa Dadis CAMARA led a military coup, seizing power and suspending the constitution. His unwillingness to yield to domestic and international pressure to step down led to heightened political tensions that peaked in September 2009 when presidential guards opened fire on an opposition rally killing more than 150 people. In early December 2009, CAMARA was wounded in an assassination attempt and exiled to Burkina Faso. A transitional government led by Gen. Sekouba KONATE paved the way for Guinea's transition to a fledgling democracy. The country held its first free and competitive democratic presidential and legislative elections in 2010 and 2013 respectively, and in October 2015 held a second consecutive presidential election. Alpha CONDE was reelected to a second five-year term as president in 2015, and the National Assembly was seated in January 2014. CONDE's first cabinet is the first all-civilian government in Guinea. The country held a successful political dialogue in August and September 2016 that brought together the government and opposition to address long-standing tensions.

GEOGRAPHY

Location: Western Africa, bordering the North Atlantic Ocean, between Guinea-Bissau and Sierra Leone

Geographic coordinates: 11 00 N, 10 00 W

Map references: Africa

Area: *total:* 245,857 sq km
land: 245,717 sq km
water: 140 sq km
country comparison to the world: 80

Area—comparative: slightly smaller than Oregon

Land boundaries: *total:* 4,046 km
border countries (6): Cote d'Ivoire 816 km, Guinea-Bissau 421 km, Liberia 590 km, Mali 1,062 km, Senegal 363 km, Sierra Leone 794 km

Coastline: 320 km

Maritime claims: *territorial sea:* 12 nm
exclusive economic zone: 200 nm

Climate: generally hot and humid; monsoonal-type rainy season (June to November) with southwesterly winds; dry season (December to May) with northeasterly harmattan winds

Terrain: generally flat coastal plain, hilly to mountainous interior

Elevation: *mean elevation:* 472 m

elevation extremes: *lowest point:* Atlantic Ocean 0 m
highest point: Mont Nimba 1,752 m

Natural resources: bauxite, iron ore, diamonds, gold, uranium, hydropower, fish, salt

Land use: *agricultural land:* 58.1%

arable land: 11.8%;
permanent crops: 2.8%;
permanent pasture: 43.5%
forest: 26.5%
other: 15.4% (2011 est.)
Irrigated land: 950 sq km (2012)

Population—distribution: areas of highest density are in the west and south; interior is sparsely populated

Natural hazards: hot, dry, dusty harmattan haze may reduce visibility during dry season

Environment—current issues: deforestation; inadequate potable water; desertification; soil contamination and erosion; overfishing, overpopulation in forest region; poor mining practices have led to environmental damage

Environment—international agreements: *party to:* Biodiversity, Climate Change, Climate Change-Kyoto Protocol, Desertification, Endangered Species, Hazardous Wastes, Law of the Sea, Ozone Layer Protection, Ship Pollution, Wetlands, Whaling
signed, but not ratified: none of the selected agreements

Geography—note: the Niger and its important tributary the Milo River have their sources in the Guinean highlands

PEOPLE AND SOCIETY

Population: 12,413,867 (July 2017 est.)
country comparison to the world: 74

Nationality: *noun:* Guinean(s)
adjective: Guinean

Ethnic groups: Fulani (Peul) 32.1%, Malinke 29.8%, Susu 19.8%, Guerze 6.2%, Kissi 4.7%, Toma 2.8%, other/no answer 4.6% (2012 est.)

Languages: French (official)
note: each ethnic group has its own language

Religions: Muslim 86.2%, Christian 9.7%, animist/other/none 4.1% (2012 est.)

Demographic profile: Guinea's strong population growth is a result of declining mortality rates and sustained elevated fertility. The population growth rate was somewhat tempered in the 2000s because of a period of net outmigration. Although life expectancy and mortality rates have improved over the last two decades, the nearly universal practice of female genital cutting continues to contribute to high infant and maternal mortality rates. Guinea's total fertility remains high at about 5 children per woman because of the ongoing preference for larger families, low contraceptive usage and availability, a lack of educational attainment and empowerment among women, and poverty. A lack of literacy and vocational training programs limit job prospects for youths, but even those with university degrees often have no option but to work in the informal sector. About 60% of the country's large youth population is unemployed.

Tensions and refugees have spilled over Guinea's borders with Sierra Leone, Liberia, and Cote d'Ivoire. During the 1990s Guinea harbored as many as half a million refugees from Sierra Leone

and Liberia, more refugees than any other African country for much of that decade. About half sought refuge in the volatile "Parrot's Beak" region of southwest Guinea, a wedge of land jutting into Sierra Leone near the Liberian border. Many were relocated within Guinea in the early 2000s because the area suffered repeated cross-border attacks from various government and rebel forces, as well as anti-refugee violence.

Age structure: *0-14 years:* 41.52% (male 2,603,506/female 2,550,714)
15-24 years: 19.73% (male 1,236,092/female 1,212,936)
25-54 years: 30.59% (male 1,905,249/female 1,892,638)
55-64 years: 4.48% (male 266,848/female 289,697)
65 years and over: 3.67% (male 201,598/female 254,589) (2017 est.)

Dependency ratios: *total dependency ratio:* 84.2
youth dependency ratio: 78.6
elderly dependency ratio: 5.6
potential support ratio: 17.8 (2015 est.)

Median age: *total:* 18.9 years
male: 18.7 years
female: 19.1 years (2017 est.)
country comparison to the world: 204

Population growth rate: 2.61% (2017 est.)
country comparison to the world: 15

Birth rate: 35.1 births/1,000 population (2017 est.)
country comparison to the world: 20

Death rate: 9 deaths/1,000 population (2017 est.)
country comparison to the world: 66

Net migration rate: 0 migrant(s)/1,000 population (2017 est.)
country comparison to the world: 83

Population distribution: areas of highest density are in the west and south; interior is sparsely populated

Urbanization: *urban population:* 38.2% of total population (2017)
rate of urbanization: 3.73% annual rate of change (2015-20 est.)

Major urban areas—population: CONAKRY (capital) 1.936 million (2015)

Sex ratio: *at birth:* 1.03 male(s)/female
0-14 years: 1.02 male(s)/female
15-24 years: 1.02 male(s)/female
25-54 years: 1.01 male(s)/female
55-64 years: 0.92 male(s)/female
65 years and over: 0.79 male(s)/female
total population: 1 male(s)/female (2016 est.)

Mother's mean age at first birth: 18.9 years
note: median age at first birth among women 25-29 (2012 est.)

Maternal mortality ratio: 679 deaths/100,000 live births (2015 est.)
country comparison to the world: 11

Infant mortality rate: *total:* 50 deaths/1,000 live births
male: 52.6 deaths/1,000 live births
female: 47.3 deaths/1,000 live births (2017 est.)
country comparison to the world: 29

Life expectancy at birth: *total population:* 61 years
male: 59.5 years
female: 62.6 years (2017 est.)
country comparison to the world: 201

Total fertility rate: 4.77 children born/woman (2017 est.)
country comparison to the world: 19

Contraceptive prevalence rate: 5.6% (2012)
Health expenditures: 5.6% of GDP (2014)
country comparison to the world: 118

Hospital bed density: 0.3 beds/1,000 population (2011)

Drinking water source:
improved:
urban: 92.7% of population
rural: 67.4% of population
total: 76.8% of population
unimproved:
urban: 7.3% of population
rural: 32.6% of population
total: 23.2% of population (2015 est.)

Sanitation facility access:
improved:
urban: 34.1% of population
rural: 11.8% of population
total: 20.1% of population
unimproved:
urban: 65.9% of population
rural: 88.2% of population
total: 79.9% of population (2015 est.)

HIV/AIDS—adult prevalence rate: 1.5% (2016 est.)
country comparison to the world: 34

HIV/AIDS—people living with HIV/AIDS: 120,000 (2016 est.)
country comparison to the world: 36

HIV/AIDS—deaths: 5,800 (2016 est.)
country comparison to the world: 28

Major infectious diseases: *degree of risk:* very high
food or waterborne diseases: bacterial and protozoal diarrhea, hepatitis A, and typhoid fever
vectorborne diseases: malaria, dengue fever, and yellow fever
water contact disease: schistosomiasis
aerosolized dust or soil contact disease: Lassa fever
animal contact disease: rabies (2016)

Obesity—adult prevalence rate: 7.7% (2016)
country comparison to the world: 158

Children under the age of 5 years underweight: 18.7% (2012)
country comparison to the world: 33

Education expenditures: 3.2% of GDP (2014)
country comparison to the world: 156

Literacy: *definition:* age 15 and over can read and write
total population: 30.4%
male: 38.1%
female: 22.8% (2015 est.)

School life expectancy (primary to tertiary education): *total:* 9 years
male: 10 years
female: 8 years (2014)

Unemployment, youth ages 15-24: *total:* 1%
male: 1.5%
female: 0.6% (2012 est.)

GOVERNMENT

Country name: *conventional long form:* Republic of Guinea
conventional short form: Guinea
local long form: Republique de Guinee
local short form: Guinee
former: French Guinea
etymology: the country is named after the Guinea region of West Africa that lies along the Gulf of Guinea and stretches north to the Sahel

Government type: presidential republic

Capital: *name:* Conakry
geographic coordinates: 9 30 N, 13 42 W
time difference: UTC 0 (5 hours ahead of Washington, DC, during Standard Time)

Administrative divisions: 7 regions administrative and 1 gouvenorat*; Boke, Conakry*, Faranah, Kankan, Kindia, Labe, Mamou, N'Zerekore

Independence: 2 October 1958 (from France)

National holiday: Independence Day, 2 October (1958)

Constitution: history: previous 1958, 1990; latest promulgated 19 April 2010, approved 7 May 2010
amendments: proposed by the National Assembly or by the president of the republic; consideration of proposals requires approval by simple majority vote by the Assembly; passage requires approval in referendum; the president can opt to submit amendments directly to the Assembly, in which case approval requires at least two-thirds majority vote (2017)

Legal system: civil law system based on the French model

International law organization participation: accepts compulsory ICJ jurisdiction with reservations; accepts ICCt jurisdiction

Citizenship: *citizenship by birth:* no
citizenship by descent only: at least one parent must be a citizen of Guinea
dual citizenship recognized: no
residency requirement for naturalization: na

Suffrage: 18 years of age; universal

Executive branch: *chief of state:* President Alpha CONDE (since 21 December 2010)
head of government: Prime Minister Mamady YOULA (since 26 December 2015)
cabinet: Council of Ministers appointed by the president
elections/appointments: president directly elected by absolute majority popular vote in 2 rounds if needed for a 5-year term (eligible for a second term); election last held on 11 October 2015 (next scheduled for 2020); prime minister appointed by the president
election results: Alpha CONDE reelected president; percent of vote—Alpha CONDE (RPG) 57.8%, Cellou Dalein DIALLO (UFDG) 31.4%, other 10.8%

Legislative branch: description: unicameral People's National Assembly or Assemblee Nationale Populaire (114 seats; 76 members directly elected in a single nationwide constituency by proportional representation vote and 38 directly elected in single-seat constituencies by simple majority vote; members serve 5-year terms)
elections: last held on 28 September 2013 (next to be held in 2018)
election results: percent of vote by party—NA; seats by party—RPG 53, UFDG 37, UFR 10, PEDN 2, UPG 2, other parties 10

Judicial branch: *highest court(s):* Supreme Court or Cour Supreme (organized into Administrative Chamber and Civil, Penal, and Social Chamber; court consists of the first president, 2 chamber presidents, at least 4 councillors, the solicitor general, and NA deputies); Constitutional Court (consists of 9 members)
judge selection and term of office: Supreme Court first president appointed by the national president after consultation with the National Assembly; other members appointed by presidential decree; members serve until age 65; Constitutional Court member appointments—2 by the National Assembly and the president of the republic, 3 experienced judges designated by their peers, 1 experienced lawyer, 1 university professor with expertise in public law designated by peers, and 2 experienced representatives of the Independent National Institution of Human Rights; members serve single 9-year terms
subordinate courts: includes Court of Appeal or Cour d'Appel; courts of first instance or Tribunal de Premiere Instance; High Court of Justice or Cour d'Assises; labor court; military tribunal; justices of the peace; specialized courts

Political parties and leaders: Bloc Liberal or BL [Faya MILLIMONO]
National Party for Hope and Development or PEDN [Lansana KOUYATE]
Rally for the Guinean People or RPG [Alpha CONDE]
Union for the Progress of Guinea or UPG
Union of Democratic Forces of Guinea or UFDG [Cellou Dalein DIALLO]
Union of Republican Forces or UFR [Sidya TOURE]

Political pressure groups and leaders: National Confederation of Guinean Workers-Labor Union of Guinean Workers or CNTG-USTG Alliance
Syndicate of Guinean Teachers and Researchers or SLECG

International organization participation: ACP, AfDB, AU, ECOWAS, EITI (compliant country), FAO, G-77, IBRD, ICAO, ICCt, ICRM, IDA, IDB, IFAD, IFC, IFRCS, ILO, IMF, IMO, Interpol, IOC, IOM, IPU, ISO (correspondent), ITSO, ITU, ITUC (NGOs), MIGA, MINURSO, MINUSMA, MONUSCO, NAM, OIC, OIF, OPCW, UN, UNCTAD, UNESCO, UNHCR, UNIDO, UNISFA, UNMISS, UNOCI,

UNWTO, UPU, WCO, WFTU (NGOs), WHO, WIPO, WMO, WTO

Diplomatic representation in the US: *chief of mission:* Ambassador Kerfalla YANSANE (since 24 January 2018)
chancery: 2112 Leroy Place NW, Washington, DC 20008
telephone: [1] (202) 986-4300
FAX: [1] (202) 986-3800

Diplomatic representation from the US: *chief of mission:* Ambassador Dennis B. HANKINS (since December 2015)
embassy: Koloma, Conakry, across from the Radio Television de Guinee
mailing address: P.O. Box 603, Transversale No. 2, Centre Administratif de Koloma, Commune de Ratoma, Conakry
telephone: [224] 655-10-40-00
FAX: [224] 655-10-42-97

Flag description: three equal vertical bands of red (hoist side), yellow, and green; red represents the people's sacrifice for liberation and work; yellow stands for the sun, for the riches of the earth, and for justice; green symbolizes the country's vegetation and unity
note: uses the popular Pan-African colors of Ethiopia; the colors from left to right are the reverse of those on the flags of neighboring Mali and Senegal

National symbol(s): elephant; national colors: red, yellow, green

National anthem: *name:* "Liberte" (Liberty)
lyrics/music: unknown/Fodeba KEITA
note: adopted 1958

ECONOMY

Economy—overview: Guinea is a poor country of approximately 12.9 million people in 2016 that possesses the world's largest reserves of bauxite and largest untapped high-grade iron ore reserves, as well as gold and diamonds. In addition, Guinea has fertile soil, ample rainfall, and is the source of several West African rivers, including the Senegal, Niger, and Gambia. Guinea's hydro potential is enormous and the country could be a major exporter of electricity. The country also has tremendous agriculture potential. Gold, bauxite, and diamonds are Guinea's main exports. International investors have shown interest in Guinea's unexplored mineral reserves, which have the potential to propel Guinea's future growth.

Following the death of long-term President Lansana CONTE in 2008 and the coup that followed, international donors, including the G-8, the IMF, and the World Bank, significantly curtailed their development programs in Guinea. However, the IMF approved a 3-year Extended Credit Facility arrangement in 2012, following the December 2010 presidential elections. In September 2012, Guinea achieved Heavily Indebted Poor Countries completion point status. Future access to international assistance and investment will depend on the government's ability to be transparent, combat corruption, reform its banking system, improve its business environment, and build infrastructure. In April 2013, the government amended its mining code to reduce taxes and royalties. In 2014, Guinea also complied with requirements of the Extractive Industries Transparency Initiative by publishing its mining contracts and was found to be compliant. Guinea completed its program with the IMF in October 2016 even though some targeted reforms have been delayed. Currently Guinea is negotiating a new IMF program which will be based on Guinea's new five-year economic plan, focusing on the development of higher value-added products, including from the agro-business sector and development of the rural economy.

The biggest threats to Guinea's economy are political instability, a reintroduction of the Ebola virus epidemic, and low international commodity prices. Economic recovery will be a long process while the government adjusts to lower inflows of international donor aid following the surge of Ebola-related emergency support. Ebola stalled promising economic growth in the 2014-15 period and impeded several projects, such as offshore oil exploration and the Simandou iron ore project. The economy, however, grew by 6.6% in 2016 and 6.7% in 2017, mainly due to growth from bauxite mining and thermal energy generation as well as the resiliency of the agricultural sector. The 240-megawatt Kaleta Dam, inaugurated in September 2015, has expanded access to electricity for residents of Conakry. An enduring legacy of corruption, inefficiency, and lack of government transparency, combined with fears of Ebola virus, continue to undermine Guinea's economic viability.

Guinea's iron ore industry took a hit in 2016 when investors in the Simandou iron ore project announced plans to divest from the project. In 2017, agriculture output and public investment boosted economic growth, while the mining sector continued to play a prominent role in economic performance.

Successive governments have failed to address the country's crumbling infrastructure. Guinea suffers from chronic electricity shortages; poor roads, rail lines and bridges; and a lack of access to clean water—all of which continue to plague economic development. The present government, led by President Alpha CONDE, is working to create an environment to attract foreign investment and hopes to have greater participation from western countries and firms in Guinea's economic development.

GDP (purchasing power parity): $26.45 billion (2017 est.)
$24.8 billion (2016 est.)
$23.26 billion (2015 est.)
note: data are in 2017 dollars
country comparison to the world: 140

GDP (official exchange rate): $9.183 billion (2016 est.)

GDP—real growth rate: 6.7% (2017 est.)
6.6% (2016 est.)
3.5% (2015 est.)
country comparison to the world: 14

GDP—per capita (PPP): $2,000 (2017 est.)
$2,000 (2016 est.)
$1,900 (2015 est.)
note: data are in 2017 dollars
country comparison to the world: 208

Gross national saving: -1.8% of GDP (2017 est.)
-6.7% of GDP (2016 est.)
-8.1% of GDP (2015 est.)
country comparison to the world: 178

GDP—composition, by end use:
household consumption: 106.1%
government consumption: 7.6%
investment in fixed capital: 13.6%
investment in inventories: 0%
exports of goods and services: 33.3%
imports of goods and services: -60.6% (2017 est.)

GDP—composition, by sector of origin:
agriculture: 19.5%
industry: 38.4%
services: 42.1% (2017 est.)

Agriculture—products: rice, coffee, pineapples, mangoes, palm kernels, cocoa, cassava (manioc, tapioca), bananas, potatoes, sweet potatoes; cattle, sheep, goats; timber

Industries: bauxite, gold, diamonds, iron ore; light manufacturing, agricultural processing

Industrial production growth rate: 8% (2017 est.)
country comparison to the world: 19

Labor force: 5.558 million (2017 est.)
country comparison to the world: 75

Labor force—by occupation: *agriculture:* 76%
industry and services: 24% (2006 est.)

Unemployment rate: 2.8% (2017 est.)
2.4% (2016 est.)
country comparison to the world: 29

Population below poverty line: 47% (2006 est.)

Household income or consumption by percentage share: *lowest 10%:* 2.7%
highest 10%: 30.3% (2007)

Distribution of family income—Gini index: 39.4 (2007)
40.3 (1994)
country comparison to the world: 67

Budget: *revenues:* $1.559 billion
expenditures: $1.868 billion (2017 est.)
Taxes and other revenues: 17% of GDP (2017 est.)
country comparison to the world: 177

Budget surplus (+) or deficit (-): -3.4% of GDP (2017 est.)
country comparison to the world: 131

Public debt: 56% of GDP (2016 est.)
54.7% of GDP (2015 est.)
country comparison to the world: 85

Fiscal year: calendar year

Inflation rate (consumer prices): 8.5% (2017 est.)
8.2% (2016 est.)
country comparison to the world: 201

Central bank discount rate: 22.25% (31 December 2005)
country comparison to the world: 4

Commercial bank prime lending rate: 21.5% (31 December 2017 est.)
21.7% (31 December 2016 est.)
country comparison to the world: 13

Stock of narrow money: $1.771 billion (31 December 2017 est.)
$1.61 billion (31 December 2016 est.)
country comparison to the world: 139

Stock of broad money: $2.315 billion (31 December 2017 est.)
$2.12 billion (31 December 2016 est.)
country comparison to the world: 152

Stock of domestic credit: $1.808 billion (31 December 2017 est.)
$1.931 billion (31 December 2016 est.)
country comparison to the world: 148

Market value of publicly traded shares: $NA

Current account balance: -$2.297 billion (2017 est.)
-$2.706 billion (2016 est.)
country comparison to the world: 161

Exports: $2.115 billion (2017 est.)
$1.954 billion (2016 est.)
country comparison to the world: 139

Exports—commodities: bauxite, gold, diamonds, coffee, fish, agricultural products

Exports—partners: China 24.6%, Ghana 17.9%, Switzerland 10.1%, UAE 7.7%, France 5.2%, Spain 4.3%, India 4.1% (2016)

Imports: $2.475 billion (2017 est.)
$2.109 billion (2016 est.)
country comparison to the world: 152

Imports—commodities: petroleum products, metals, machinery, transport equipment, textiles, grain and other foodstuffs

Imports—partners: Netherlands 14.6%, China 13.5%, India 12.4%, Belgium 8.6%, France 6.9%, UAE 5.4%, Singapore 4.9% (2016)

Reserves of foreign exchange and gold: $416.1 million (31 December 2017 est.)
$383.4 million (31 December 2016 est.)
country comparison to the world: 145

Debt—external: $1.53 billion (31 December 2017 est.)
$1.462 billion (31 December 2016 est.)
country comparison to the world: 159

Stock of direct foreign investment—abroad: $69.91 million (31 December 2017 est.)
$69.19 million (31 December 2016 est.)
country comparison to the world: 105

Exchange rates: Guinean francs (GNF) per US dollar—
9,230 (2017 est.)
9,085 (2016 est.)
9,085 (2015 est.)
7,485.5 (2014 est.)
7,014.1 (2013 est.)

ENERGY

Electricity access: *population without electricity:* 8,700,000
electrification—*total population:* 26%

electrification—urban areas: 53%
electrification—rural areas: 11% (2013)

Electricity—production: 1 billion kWh (2015 est.)
country comparison to the world: 151

Electricity—consumption: 930 million kWh (2015 est.)
country comparison to the world: 157

Electricity—exports: 0 kWh (2016 est.)
country comparison to the world: 145

Electricity—imports: 0 kWh (2016 est.)
country comparison to the world: 158

Electricity—installed generating capacity: 740,000 kW (2015 est.)
country comparison to the world: 135

Electricity—from fossil fuels: 50% of total installed capacity (2015 est.)
country comparison to the world: 152

Electricity—from nuclear fuels: 0% of total installed capacity (2015 est.)
country comparison to the world: 104

Electricity—from hydroelectric plants: 49.7% of total installed capacity (2015 est.)
country comparison to the world: 39

Electricity—from other renewable sources: 0.3% of total installed capacity (2015 est.)
country comparison to the world: 155

Crude oil—production: 0 bbl/day (2016 est.)
country comparison to the world: 143

Crude oil—exports: 0 bbl/day (2014 est.)
country comparison to the world: 133

Crude oil—imports: 0 bbl/day (2014 est.)
country comparison to the world: 136

Crude oil—proved reserves: 0 bbl (1 January 2017 es)
country comparison to the world: 143

Refined petroleum products—production: 0 bbl/day (2014 est.)
country comparison to the world: 153

Refined petroleum products—consumption: 16,000 bbl/day (2015 est.)
country comparison to the world: 148

Refined petroleum products—exports: 0 bbl/day (2014 est.)
country comparison to the world: 163

Refined petroleum products—imports: 16,130 bbl/day (2014 est.)
country comparison to the world: 125

Natural gas—production: 0 cu m (2013 est.)
country comparison to the world: 145

Natural gas—consumption: 0 cu m (2013 est.)
country comparison to the world: 190

Natural gas—exports: 0 cu m (2013 est.)
country comparison to the world: 117

Natural gas—imports: 0 cu m (2013 est.)
country comparison to the world: 135

Natural gas—proved reserves: 0 cu m (1 January 2014 es)
country comparison to the world: 148

Carbon dioxide emissions from consumption of energy: 1.4 million Mt (2013 est.)
country comparison to the world: 158

COMMUNICATIONS

Telephones—fixed lines: *total subscriptions:* 0 *subscriptions per 100 inhabitants:* less than 1 (July 2016 est.)
country comparison to the world: 219

Telephones—mobile cellular: *total:* 10.8 million *subscriptions per 100 inhabitants:* 89 (July 2016 est.)
country comparison to the world: 93

Telephone system: *general assessment:* huge improvement over the last 10 years; the capital and the regional administrative centers have 3G access
domestic: there is national coverage and Conakry is reasonably well-served; coverage elsewhere remains inadequate but is improving; fixed-line teledensity less than 1 per 100 persons; mobile-cellular subscribership is expanding rapidly and now approaches 90 per 100 persons
international: country code—224; satellite earth station—1 Intelsat (Atlantic Ocean) (2017)

Broadcast media: government maintains marginal control over broadcast media; single state-run TV station; state-run radio broadcast station also operates several stations in rural areas; a steadily increasing number of privately owned radio stations, nearly all in Conakry, and about a dozen community radio stations; foreign TV programming available via satellite and cable subscription services (2011)

Internet country code: .gn
Internet users: total: 1,185,148

percent of population: 9.8% (July 2016 est.)
country comparison to the world: 156

TRANSPORTATION

Civil aircraft registration country code prefix: 3X (2016)

Airports: 16 (2013)
country comparison to the world: 144

Airports—with paved runways: *total:* 4
over 3,047 m: 1
1,524 to 2,437 m: 3 (2017)

Airports—with unpaved runways: *total:* 12
1,524 to 2,437 m: 7
914 to 1,523 m: 3
under 914 m: 2 (2013)

Railways: *total:* 1,086 km
standard gauge: 279 km 1.435-m gauge
narrow gauge: 807 km 1.000-m gauge (2017)
country comparison to the world: 105

Roadways: *total:* 44,348 km
paved: 4,342 km
unpaved: 40,006 km (2003)
country comparison to the world: 81

Waterways: 1,300 km (navigable by shallow-draft native craft in the northern part of the Niger River system) (2011)
country comparison to the world: 53

Merchant marine: *total:* 1
by type: other 1 (2017)

country comparison to the world: 165

Ports and terminals: *major seaport(s):* Conakry, Kamsar

MILITARY AND SECURITY

Military expenditures: 2.49% of GDP (2016)
3.31% of GDP (2015)
2.97% of GDP (2014)
3.16% of GDP (2013)
2.98% of GDP (2012)

Military branches: National Armed Forces: Army, Guinean Navy (Armee de Mer or Marine Guineenne, includes Marines), Guinean Air Force (Force Aerienne de Guinee) (2009)

Military service age and obligation: no compulsory military service (2017)

TRANSNATIONAL ISSUES

Disputes—international: Sierra Leone considers Guinea's definition of the flood plain limits to define the left bank boundary of the Makona and Moa Rivers excessive and protests Guinea's continued occupation of these lands, including the hamlet of Yenga, occupied since 1998

Trafficking in persons: current situation: Guinea is a source, transit, and, to a lesser extent, a destination country for men, women, and children subjected to forced labor and sex trafficking; the majority of trafficking victims are Guinean children, and trafficking is more prevalent among Guineans than foreign national migrants; Guinean girls are subjected to domestic servitude and commercial sexual exploitation, while boys are forced to beg or to work as street vendors, shoe shiners, or miners; Guinea is a source country and transit point for West African children forced to work as miners in the region; Guinean women and girls are subjected to domestic servitude and sex trafficking in West Africa, the Middle East, the US, and increasingly Europe, while Thai, Chinese, and Vietnamese women are forced into prostitution and some West Africans are forced into domestic servitude in Guinea

tier rating: Tier 2 Watch List—Guinea does not fully comply with the minimum standards for the elimination of trafficking; however, it is making significant efforts to do so; in 2014, Guinea was granted a waiver from an otherwise required downgrade to Tier 3 because its government has a written plan that, if implemented would constitute making significant efforts to bring itself into compliance with the minimum standards for the elimination of trafficking; no new investigations were conducted in 2014, and the one ongoing case led to the prosecution of four offenders for forced child labor, three of whom were convicted but given inadequate sentences for the crime; the government did not identify or provide protective services to victims and did not support NGOs that assisted victims but continued to refer child victims to NGOs on an ad hoc basis; Guinean law does not prohibit all forms of trafficking, excluding, for example, debt bondage; the 2014 Ebolavirus outbreak negatively affected Guinea's ability to address human trafficking (2015)

GUINEA-BISSAU

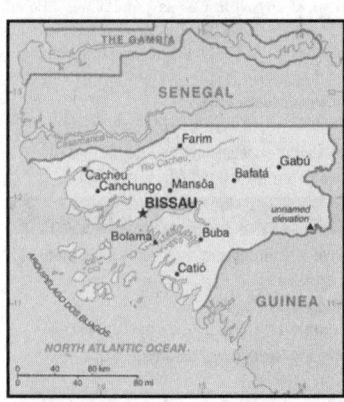

INTRODUCTION

Background: Since independence from Portugal in 1974, Guinea-Bissau has experienced considerable political and military upheaval. In 1980, a military coup established authoritarian General Joao Bernardo 'Nino' VIEIRA as president. Despite eventually setting a path to a market economy and multiparty system, VIEIRA's regime was characterized by the suppression of political opposition and the purging of political rivals. Several coup attempts through the 1980s and early 1990s failed to unseat him. In 1994 VIEIRA was elected president in the country's first free, multiparty election. A military mutiny and resulting civil war in 1998 eventually led to VIEIRA's ouster in May 1999. In February 2000, a transitional government turned over power to opposition leader Kumba YALA after he was elected president in transparent polling. In September 2003, after only three years in office, YALA was overthrown in a bloodless military coup, and businessman Henrique ROSA was sworn in as interim president. In 2005, former President VIEIRA was reelected, pledging to pursue economic development and national reconciliation; he was assassinated in March 2009. Malam Bacai SANHA was elected in an emergency election held in June 2009, but he passed away in January 2012 from a long-term illness. A military coup in April 2012 prevented Guinea-Bissau's second-round presidential election—to determine SANHA's successor—from taking place. Following mediation by the Economic Community of Western African States, a civilian transitional government assumed power in 2012 and remained until Jose Mario VAZ won a free and fair election in 2014. A long-running dispute between factions in the ruling PAIGC party has brought the government to a political impasse; there have been five prime ministers since August 2015.

GEOGRAPHY

Location: Western Africa, bordering the North Atlantic Ocean, between Guinea and Senegal

Geographic coordinates: 12 00 N, 15 00 W

Map references: Africa

Area: *total:* 36,125 sq km
land: 28,120 sq km
water: 8,005 sq km
country comparison to the world: 138

Area—comparative: slightly less than three times the size of Connecticut

Land boundaries: *total:* 762 km

border countries (2): Guinea 421 km, Senegal 341 km

Coastline: 350 km

Maritime claims: *territorial sea:* 12 nm
exclusive economic zone: 200 nm

Climate: tropical; generally hot and humid; monsoonal-type rainy season (June to November) with southwesterly winds; dry season (December to May) with northeasterly harmattan winds

Terrain: mostly low-lying coastal plain with a deeply indented estuarine coastline rising to savanna in east; numerous off-shore islands including the Arquipelago Dos Bijagos consisting of 18 main islands and many small islets

Elevation: *mean elevation:* 70 m

elevation extremes: *lowest point:* Atlantic Ocean 0 m
highest point: unnamed elevation in the eastern part of the country 300 m

Natural resources: fish, timber, phosphates, bauxite, clay, granite, limestone, unexploited deposits of petroleum

Land use: *agricultural land:* 44.8%
arable land: 8.2%;
permanent crops: 6.9%;
permanent pasture: 29.7%
forest: 55.2%
other: 0% (2011 est.)
Irrigated land: 250 sq km (2012)

Population—distribution: approximately one-fifth of the population lives in the capital city of Bissau along the Atlantic coast; the remainder is distributed among the eight other, mainly rural, regions

Natural hazards: hot, dry, dusty harmattan haze may reduce visibility during dry season; brush fires

Environment—current issues: deforestation; soil erosion; overgrazing; overfishing

Environment—international agreements: *party to:* Biodiversity, Climate Change, Climate Change-Kyoto Protocol, Desertification, Endangered Species, Hazardous Wastes, Law of the Sea, Ozone Layer Protection, Wetlands

signed, but not ratified: none of the selected agreements

Geography—note: this small country is swampy along its western coast and low-lying inland

PEOPLE AND SOCIETY

Population: 1,792,338 (July 2017 est.)
country comparison to the world: 152

Nationality: *noun:* Bissau-Guinean(s)
adjective: Bissau-Guinean

Ethnic groups: Fulani 28.5%, Balanta 22.5%, Mandinga 14.7%, Papel 9.1%, Manjaco 8.3%, Beafada 3.5%, Mancanha 3.1%, Bijago 2.1%, Felupe 1.7%, Mansoanca 1.4%, Balanta Mane 1%, other 1.8%, none 2.2% (2008 est.)

Languages: Crioulo (lingua franca), Portuguese (official; largely used as a second or third language), Pular (a Fula language), Mandingo

Religions: Muslim 45.1%, Christian 22.1%, animist 14.9%, none 2%, unspecified 15.9% (2008 est.)

Demographic profile: Guinea-Bissau's young and growing population is sustained by high fertility; approximately 60% of the population is under the age of 25. Its large reproductive-age population and total fertility rate of more than 4 children per woman offsets the country's high infant and maternal mortality rates. The latter is among the world's highest because of the prevalence of early childbearing, a lack of birth spacing, the high percentage of births outside of health care facilities, and a shortage of medicines and supplies.

Guinea-Bissau's history of political instability, a civil war, and several coups (the latest in 2012) have resulted in a fragile state with a weak economy, high unemployment, rampant corruption, widespread poverty, and thriving drug and child trafficking. With the country lacking educational infrastructure, school funding and materials, and qualified teachers, and with the cultural emphasis placed on religious education, parents frequently send boys to study in residential Koranic schools (daaras) in Senegal and The Gambia. They often are extremely deprived and are forced into street begging or agricultural work by marabouts (Muslim religious teachers), who enrich themselves at the expense of the children. Boys who leave their marabouts often end up on the streets of Dakar or other large Senegalese towns and are vulnerable to even worse abuse.

Some young men lacking in education and job prospects become involved in the flourishing international drug trade. Local drug use and associated violent crime are growing.

Age structure: *0-14 years:* 39.03% (male 349,256/female 350,327)
15-24 years: 20.18% (male 179,389/female 182,242)
25-54 years: 32.77% (male 292,736/female 294,526)
55-64 years: 4.57% (male 32,156/female 49,761)
65 years and over: 3.46% (male 22,574/female 39,371) (2017 est.)

Dependency ratios: *total dependency ratio:* 80.4
youth dependency ratio: 75.2
elderly dependency ratio: 5.2
potential support ratio: 19.3 (2015 est.)

Median age: *total:* 20.1 years
male: 19.7 years
female: 20.6 years (2017 est.)
country comparison to the world: 190

Population growth rate: 1.86% (2017 est.)
country comparison to the world: 53

Birth rate: 32.5 births/1,000 population (2017 est.)
country comparison to the world: 30

Death rate: 13.9 deaths/1,000 population (2017 est.)
country comparison to the world: 6

Net migration rate: 0 migrant(s)/1,000 population (2017 est.)
country comparison to the world: 84

Population distribution: approximately one-fifth of the population lives in the capital city of Bissau along the Atlantic coast; the remainder is distributed among the eight other, mainly rural, regions

Urbanization: *urban population:* 50.8% of total population (2017)
rate of urbanization: 3.69% annual rate of change (2015-20 est.)

Major urban areas—population: BISSAU (capital) 492,000 (2015)

Sex ratio: *at birth:* 1.03 male(s)/female
0-14 years: 1 male(s)/female
15-24 years: 0.98 male(s)/female
25-54 years: 0.99 male(s)/female
55-64 years: 0.62 male(s)/female
65 years and over: 0.6 male(s)/female
total population: 0.96 male(s)/female (2016 est.)

Maternal mortality ratio: 549 deaths/100,000 live births (2015 est.)
country comparison to the world: 18

Infant mortality rate: *total:* 85.7 deaths/1,000 live births
male: 95.1 deaths/1,000 live births
female: 76 deaths/1,000 live births (2017 est.)
country comparison to the world: 4

Life expectancy at birth: *total population:* 51 years
male: 48.9 years
female: 53.1 years (2017 est.)
country comparison to the world: 223

Total fertility rate: 4.09 children born/woman (2017 est.)
country comparison to the world: 32

Contraceptive prevalence rate: 16% (2014)
Health expenditures: 5.6% of GDP (2014)
country comparison to the world: 123

Physicians density: 0.08 physicians/1,000 population (2009)

Hospital bed density: 1 beds/1,000 population (2009)

Drinking water source:
improved:
urban: 98.8% of population
rural: 60.3% of population
total: 79.3% of population
unimproved:
urban: 1.2% of population
rural: 39.7% of population
total: 20.7% of population (2015 est.)

Sanitation facility access:
improved:
urban: 33.5% of population
rural: 8.5% of population
total: 20.8% of population
unimproved:
urban: 66.5% of population
rural: 91.5% of population
total: 79.2% of population (2015 est.)

HIV/AIDS—adult prevalence rate: 3.1% (2016 est.)
country comparison to the world: 20

HIV/AIDS—people living with HIV/AIDS: 36,000 (2016 est.)
country comparison to the world: 62

HIV/AIDS—deaths: 2,000 (2016 est.)
country comparison to the world: 52

Major infectious diseases: *degree of risk:* very high
food or waterborne diseases: bacterial and protozoal diarrhea, hepatitis A, and typhoid fever
vectorborne diseases: malaria, dengue fever, and yellow fever
water contact disease: schistosomiasis
animal contact disease: rabies (2016)

Obesity—adult prevalence rate: 9.5% (2016)
country comparison to the world: 144

Children under the age of 5 years underweight: 17% (2014)
country comparison to the world: 35

Education expenditures: 2.2% of GDP (2013)

Literacy: *definition:* age 15 and over can read and write
total population: 59.9%
male: 71.8%
female: 48.3% (2015 est.)

GOVERNMENT

Country name: *conventional long form:* Republic of Guinea-Bissau
conventional short form: Guinea-Bissau
local long form: Republica da Guine-Bissau
local short form: Guine-Bissau
former: Portuguese Guinea
etymology: the country is named after the Guinea region of West Africa that lies along the Gulf of Guinea and stretches north to the Sahel; "Bissau," the name of the capital city, distinguishes the country from neighboring Guinea

Government type: semi-presidential republic

Capital: *name:* Bissau

geographic coordinates: 11 51 N, 15 35 W

time difference: UTC 0 (5 hours ahead of Washington, DC, during Standard Time)

Administrative divisions: 9 regions (regioes, singular—regiao); Bafata, Biombo, Bissau, Bolama/Bijagos, Cacheu, Gabu, Oio, Quinara, Tombali

Independence: 24 September 1973 (declared); 10 September 1974 (from Portugal)

National holiday: Independence Day, 24 September (1973)

Constitution: history: promulgated 16 May 1984; note—constitution suspended following military coup in April 2012 and restored in 2014

amendments: proposed by the National People's Assembly if supported by at least one-third of its members, by the Council of State (a presidential consultant body), or by the government; passage requires approval by at least two-thirds majority vote of the Assembly; constitutional articles on the republican and secular form of government and national sovereignty cannot be amended; amended 1991, 1993, 1996 (2017)

Legal system: mixed legal system of civil law, which incorporated Portuguese law at independence and influenced by early French civil code and customary law

International law organization participation: accepts compulsory ICJ jurisdiction; non-party state to the ICCt

Citizenship: *citizenship by birth:* yes
citizenship by descent: yes
dual citizenship recognized: no
residency requirement for naturalization: 5 years

Suffrage: 18 years of age; universal

Executive branch: *chief of state:* President Jose Mario VAZ (since 17 June 2014)

head of government: Prime Minister Artur SILVA (since 31 January 2018); note—President Umaro SISSOCO Embalo (since 18 November 2016) resigned on 13 January 2018

cabinet: Cabinet nominated by the prime minister, appointed by the president

elections/appointments: president directly elected by absolute majority popular vote in 2 rounds if needed for a 5-year term (no term limits); election last held on 13 April 2014 with a runoff on 18 May 2014 (next to be held in 2019); prime minister appointed by the president after consultation with party leaders in the National People's Assembly

election results: Jose Mario VAZ elected president in second round; percent of vote in first round—Jose Mario VAZ (PAIGC) 41%, Nuno Gomez NABIAM (independent) 25.1%, other 33.9%; percent of vote in second round—Jose Mario VAZ 61.9%, Nuno Gomez NABIAM 38.1%

Legislative branch: description: unicameral National People's Assembly or Assembleia Nacional Popular (102 seats; members directly elected in 2 single- and 27 multi-seat constituencies by closed party-list proportional representation vote to serve 4-year terms)

elections: last held on 13 April 2014 (next to be held in 2018)

election results: percent of vote by party—PAIGC 48.0%, PRS 30.8%, other 21.2%; seats by party—PAIGC 57, PRS 41, other 4

Judicial branch: *highest court(s):* Supreme Court or Suprema da Tribunal Justica (consists of 9 judges and organized into Civil, Criminal, and Social and Administrative Disputes Chambers); note—the Supreme Court has both appellate and constitutional jurisdiction

judge selection and term of office: judges nominated by the Higher Council of the Magistrate, a major government organ responsible for judge appointments, dismissals, and judiciary discipline; judges appointed by the president for life

subordinate courts: Appeal Court; regional (first instance) courts; military court

Political parties and leaders: African Party for the Independence of Guinea-Bissau and Cabo Verde or PAIGC [Domingos SIMOES PEREIRA]
Democratic Convergence Party or PCD [Vicente FERNANDES]
New Democracy Party or PND [Mamadu Iaia DJALO]
Party for Social Renewal or PRS [Alberto NAMBEIA]
Republican Party for Independence and Development or PRID [Aristides GOMES]
Union for Change or UM [Agnelo REGALA]

Political pressure groups and leaders: Chamber of Commerce of Agriculture, Industry, and Services [Braima CAMARA]

International organization participation: ACP, AfDB, AOSIS, AU, CPLP, ECOWAS, FAO, FZ, G-77, IBRD, ICAO, ICRM, IDA, IDB, IFAD, IFC, IFRCS, ILO, IMF, IMO, Interpol, IOC, IOM, IPU, ITSO, ITU, ITUC (NGOs), MIGA, MINUSMA, NAM, OIC, OIF, OPCW, UN, UNCTAD, UNESCO, UNIDO, UNWTO, UPU, WADB (regional), WAEMU, WCO, WFTU (NGOs), WHO, WIPO, WMO, WTO

Diplomatic representation in the US: *chief of mission:* none; note—Guinea-Bissau does not have official representation in Washington, DC

Diplomatic representation from the US: the US Embassy suspended operations on 14 June 1998 in the midst of violent conflict between forces loyal to then President VIEIRA and a military-led junta; the US Ambassador to Senegal is accredited to Guinea-Bissau

Flag description: two equal horizontal bands of yellow (top) and green with a vertical red band on the hoist side; there is a black five-pointed star centered in the red band; yellow symbolizes the sun; green denotes hope; red represents blood shed during the struggle for independence; the black star stands for African unity
note: uses the popular Pan-African colors of Ethiopia; the flag design was heavily influenced by the Ghanaian flag

National symbol(s): black star; national colors: red, yellow, green, black

National anthem: name: "Esta e a Nossa Patria Bem Amada" (This Is Our Beloved Country)
lyrics/music: Amilcar Lopes CABRAL/XIAO He
note: adopted 1974; a delegation from then Portuguese Guinea visited China in 1963 and heard music by XIAO He; Amilcar Lopes CABRAL, the leader of Guinea-Bissau's independence movement, asked the composer to create a piece that would inspire his people to struggle for independence

ECONOMY

Economy—overview: Guinea-Bissau is highly dependent on subsistence agriculture, cashew nut exports, and foreign assistance. Two out of three Bissau-Guineans remain below the absolute poverty line. The legal economy is based on cashews and fishing. Illegal logging and trafficking in narcotics also play significant roles. The combination of limited economic prospects, weak institutions, and favorable geography have made this West African country a way station for drugs bound for Europe.

Guinea-Bissau has substantial potential for development of mineral resources, including phosphates, bauxite, and mineral sands. Offshore oil and gas exploration has begun. The country's climate and soil make it feasible to grow a wide range of cash crops, fruit, vegetables, and tubers; however, cashews generate more than 80% of export receipts and are the main source of income for many rural communities.

With renewed donor support following elections in April-May 2014 and a successful regional bond issuance, the Government of Guinea-Bissau began to make progress paying salaries, settling domestic arrears, and gaining more control over revenues and expenditures, but it was deposed by the president in August 2015. A political stalemate since then has resulted in weak governance and reduced donor support.

The country is participating in a three-year, IMF extended credit facility program that was suspended because of a planned bank bailout. The program was renewed in 2017, but the major donors of direct budget support (the EU, World Bank, and African Development Bank) have halted their programs indefinitely. Diversification of the economy remains a key policy goal, but Guinea-Bissau's poor infrastructure and business climate will constrain this effort.

GDP (purchasing power parity): $3.071 billion (2017 est.)
$2.925 billion (2016 est.)
$2.783 billion (2015 est.)
note: data are in 2017 dollars
country comparison to the world: 189

GDP (official exchange rate): $1.295 billion (2016 est.)

GDP—real growth rate: 5% (2017 est.)
5.1% (2016 est.)
5.1% (2015 est.)
country comparison to the world: 41

GDP—per capita (PPP): $1,800 (2017 est.)
$1,800 (2016 est.)
$1,700 (2015 est.)
note: data are in 2017 dollars
country comparison to the world: 213

Gross national saving: 11.2% of GDP (2017 est.)
14% of GDP (2016 est.)
11.9% of GDP (2015 est.)
country comparison to the world: 150

GDP—composition, by end use:
household consumption: 86.7%
government consumption: 10.8%
investment in fixed capital: 11.1%
investment in inventories: 0.1%
exports of goods and services: 28.9%
imports of goods and services: -37.7% (2017 est.)

GDP—composition, by sector of origin:
agriculture: 44.1%
industry: 12.9%
services: 43% (2017 est.)

Agriculture—products: rice, corn, beans, cassava (manioc, tapioca), cashew nuts, peanuts, palm kernels, cotton; timber; fish

Industries: agricultural products processing, beer, soft drinks

Industrial production growth rate: 1.9% (2017 est.)
country comparison to the world: 142

Labor force: 731,300 (2013 est.)
country comparison to the world: 152

Labor force—by occupation: *agriculture:* 82%
industry and services: 18% (2000 est.)

Unemployment rate: NA%

Population below poverty line: 67% (2015 est.)

Household income or consumption by percentage share: *lowest 10%:* 2.9%
highest 10%: 28% (2002)

Budget: *revenues:* $226 million
expenditures: $267 million (2017 est.)
Taxes and other revenues: 17.5% of GDP (2017 est.)
country comparison to the world: 173

Budget surplus (+) or deficit (-): -3.2% of GDP (2017 est.)
country comparison to the world: 119

Public debt: 46.3% of GDP (2016 est.)
46.8% of GDP (2015 est.)
country comparison to the world: 112

Fiscal year: calendar year

Inflation rate (consumer prices): 2.8% (2017 est.)
1.5% (2016 est.)
country comparison to the world: 125

Central bank discount rate: 4.25% (31 December 2009)
4.75% (31 December 2008)
country comparison to the world: 92

Commercial bank prime lending rate: 15% (31 December 2017 est.)
5.3% (31 December 2016 est.)
country comparison to the world: 43

Stock of narrow money: $653.4 million (31 December 2017 est.)
$525.2 million (31 December 2016 est.)

country comparison to the world: 164

Stock of broad money: $685.5 million (31 December 2017 est.)
$560 million (31 December 2016 est.)
country comparison to the world: 180

Stock of domestic credit: $275.3 million (31 December 2017 est.)
$241 million (31 December 2016 est.)
country comparison to the world: 181

Market value of publicly traded shares: $NA

Current account balance: $1 million (2017 est.)
$11 million (2016 est.)
country comparison to the world: 60

Exports: $281.2 million (2017 est.)
$278.6 million (2016 est.)
country comparison to the world: 183

Exports—commodities: fish, shrimp; cashews, peanuts, palm kernels, raw and sawn lumber

Exports—partners: India 64.6%, Vietnam 9.4%, Belarus 9.4%, Nigeria 4.7% (2016)

Imports: $241.2 million (2017 est.)
$221.8 million (2016 est.)
country comparison to the world: 202

Imports—commodities: foodstuffs, machinery and transport equipment, petroleum products

Imports—partners: Portugal 44.2%, Senegal 19.2%, China 7.2%, Pakistan 6.7%, Netherlands 4.4% (2016)

Debt—external: $1.095 billion (31 December 2010 est.)
$941.5 million (31 December 2000 est.)
country comparison to the world: 166

Exchange rates: Communaute Financiere Africaine francs (XOF) per US dollar—
605.3 (2017 est.)
593.01 (2016 est.)
593.01 (2015 est.)
591.45 (2014 est.)
494.42 (2013 est.)

ENERGY

Electricity access: *population without electricity:* 1,300,000
electrification—*total population:* 21%
electrification—urban areas: 37%
electrification—rural areas: 6% (2013)

Electricity—production: 34 million kWh (2015 est.)
country comparison to the world: 209

Electricity—consumption: 31.62 million kWh (2015 est.)
country comparison to the world: 208

Electricity—exports: 0 kWh (2016 est.)
country comparison to the world: 185

Electricity—imports: 0 kWh (2016 est.)
country comparison to the world: 189

Electricity—installed generating capacity: 28,000 kW (2015 est.)
country comparison to the world: 202

Electricity—from fossil fuels: 100% of total installed capacity (2015 est.)

country comparison to the world: 17

Electricity—from nuclear fuels: 0% of total installed capacity (2015 est.)
country comparison to the world: 168

Electricity—from hydroelectric plants: 0% of total installed capacity (2015 est.)
country comparison to the world: 196

Electricity—from other renewable sources: 0% of total installed capacity (2015 est.)
country comparison to the world: 202

Crude oil—production: 0 bbl/day (2016 est.)
country comparison to the world: 144

Crude oil—exports: 0 bbl/day (2014 est.)
country comparison to the world: 178

Crude oil—imports: 0 bbl/day (2014 est.)
country comparison to the world: 178

Crude oil—proved reserves: 0 bbl (1 January 2017 es)
country comparison to the world: 144

Refined petroleum products—production: 0 bbl/day (2014 est.)
country comparison to the world: 154

Refined petroleum products—consumption: 2,500 bbl/day (2015 est.)
country comparison to the world: 190

Refined petroleum products—exports: 0 bbl/day (2014 est.)
country comparison to the world: 190

Refined petroleum products—imports: 2,423 bbl/day (2014 est.)
country comparison to the world: 183

Natural gas—production: 0 cu m (2013 est.)
country comparison to the world: 186

Natural gas—consumption: 0 cu m (2013 est.)
country comparison to the world: 124

Natural gas—exports: 0 cu m (2013 est.)
country comparison to the world: 169

Natural gas—imports: 0 cu m (2013 est.)
country comparison to the world: 177

Natural gas—proved reserves: 0 cu m (1 January 2014 es)
country comparison to the world: 187

Carbon dioxide emissions from consumption of energy: 500,000 Mt (2013 est.)
country comparison to the world: 182

COMMUNICATIONS

Telephones—fixed lines: *total subscriptions:* 0
subscriptions per 100 inhabitants: less than 1 (July 2016 est.)
country comparison to the world: 208

Telephones—mobile cellular: *total:* 1,285,835
subscriptions per 100 inhabitants: 73 (July 2016 est.)
country comparison to the world: 156

Telephone system: *general assessment:* small system including a combination of microwave radio relay, open-wire lines, radiotelephone, and mobile cellular communications

399

domestic: fixed-line teledensity less than 1 per 100 persons; mobile cellular teledensity is roughly 70 per 100 persons

international: country code—245 (2015)

Broadcast media: 1 state-owned TV station and a second station, Radio e Televisao de Portugal (RTP) Africa, is operated by Portuguese public broadcaster (RTP); 1 state-owned radio station, several private radio stations, and some community radio stations; multiple international broadcasters are available (2007)

Internet country code: .gw

Internet users: total: 66,169

percent of population: 3.8% (July 2016 est.)
country comparison to the world: 181

TRANSPORTATION

Civil aircraft registration country code prefix: J5 (2016)

Airports: 8 (2013)
country comparison to the world: 160

Airports—with paved runways: *total:* 2
over 3,047 m: 1
1,524 to 2,437 m: 1 (2017)

Airports—with unpaved runways: *total:* 6
1,524 to 2,437 m: 1
914 to 1,523 m: 2
under 914 m: 3 (2013)

Roadways: *total:* 3,455 km
paved: 965 km
unpaved: 2,490 km (2002)
country comparison to the world: 161

Waterways: (rivers are partially navigable; many inlets and creeks provide shallow-water access to much of interior) (2012)

Merchant marine: *total:* 9
by type: general cargo 5, other 4 (2017)
country comparison to the world: 145

Ports and terminals: *major seaport(s):* Bissau, Buba, Cacheu, Farim

MILITARY AND SECURITY

Military expenditures: 1.76% of GDP (2015)
1.94% of GDP (2014)
2.11% of GDP (2013)
2.46% of GDP (2012)
1.58% of GDP (2011)
country comparison to the world: 45

Military branches: People's Revolutionary Armed Force (FARP): Army, Navy, National Air Force (Forca Aerea Nacional); Presidential Guard (2012)

Military service age and obligation: 18-25 years of age for selective compulsory military service (Air Force service is voluntary); 16 years of age or younger, with parental consent, for voluntary service (2013)

TRANSNATIONAL ISSUES

Disputes—international: a longstanding low-grade conflict continues in parts of

Refugees and internally displaced persons: *refugees (country of origin):* 8,572 (Senegal) (2017)

Trafficking in persons: current situation: Guinea-Bissau is a source country for children subjected to forced labor and sex trafficking; the extent to which adults are trafficked for forced labor or forced prostitution is unclear; boys are forced into street vending in Guinea-Bissau and manual labor, agriculture, and mining in Senegal, while girls may be forced into street vending, domestic service, and, to a lesser extent, prostitution in Guinea and Senegal; some Bissau-Guinean boys at Koranic schools are forced into begging by religious teachers

tier rating: Tier 3—Guinea-Bissau does not fully comply with the minimum standards for the elimination of trafficking and is not making significant efforts to do so; despite enacting an anti-trafficking law and adopting a national action plan in 2011, the country failed to demonstrate any notable anti-trafficking efforts for the third consecutive year; existing laws prohibiting all forms of trafficking were not used to prosecute any trafficking offenders in 2014, and only one case of potential child labor trafficking was under investigation; authorities continued to rely entirely on NGOs and international organizations to provide victims with protective services; no trafficking prevention activities were conducted (2015)

Illicit drugs: increasingly important transit country for South American cocaine en route to Europe; enabling environment for trafficker operations due to pervasive corruption; archipelago-like geography near the capital facilitates drug smuggling

---

GUYANA

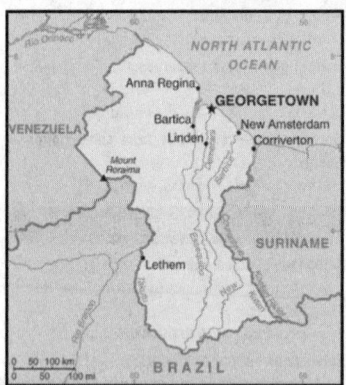

INTRODUCTION

Background: Originally a Dutch colony in the 17th century, by 1815 Guyana had become a British possession. The abolition of slavery led to settlement of urban areas by former slaves and the importation of indentured servants from India to work the sugar plantations. The resulting ethno-cultural divide has persisted and has led to turbulent politics. Guyana achieved independence from the UK in 1966, and since then it has been ruled mostly by socialist-oriented governments. In 1992, Cheddi JAGAN was elected president in what is considered the country's first free and fair election since independence. After his death five years later, his wife, Janet JAGAN, became president but resigned in 1999 due to poor health. Her successor, Bharrat JAGDEO, was elected in 2001 and again in 2006. Early elections held in May 2015 resulted in the first change in governing party and the replacement of President Donald RAMOTAR by current President David GRANGER

GEOGRAPHY

Location: Northern South America, bordering the North Atlantic Ocean, between Suriname and Venezuela

Geographic coordinates: 5 00 N, 59 00 W

Map references: South America

Area: *total:* 214,969 sq km
land: 196,849 sq km

water: 18,120 sq km
country comparison to the world: 86

Area—comparative: slightly smaller than Idaho

Land boundaries: *total:* 2,933 km
border countries (3): Brazil 1,308 km, Suriname 836 km, Venezuela 789 km

Coastline: 459 km

Maritime claims: *territorial sea:* 12 nm
exclusive economic zone: 200 nm
continental shelf: 200 nm or to the outer edge of the continental margin

Climate: tropical; hot, humid, moderated by northeast trade winds; two rainy seasons (May to August, November to January)

Terrain: mostly rolling highlands; low coastal plain; savanna in south

Elevation: *mean elevation:* 207 m

elevation extremes: *lowest point:* Atlantic Ocean 0 m

highest point: Laberintos del Norte on Mount Roraima 2,775 m

Natural resources: bauxite, gold, diamonds, hardwood timber, shrimp, fish

Land use: *agricultural land:* 8.4%
arable land: 2.1%;
permanent crops: 0.1%;
permanent pasture: 6.2%
forest: 77.4%
other: 14.2% (2011 est.)
Irrigated land: 1,430 sq km (2012)

Population—distribution: population is heavily concentrated in the northeast in and around Georgetown, with notable concentrations along the Berbice River to the east; the remainder of the country is sparsely populated

Natural hazards: flash flood threat during rainy seasons

Environment—current issues: water pollution from sewage and agricultural and industrial chemicals; deforestation

Environment—international agreements: *party to:* Biodiversity, Climate Change, Climate Change-Kyoto Protocol, Desertification, Endangered Species, Hazardous Wastes, Law of the Sea, Ozone Layer Protection, Ship Pollution, Tropical Timber 83, Tropical Timber 94
signed, but not ratified: none of the selected agreements

Geography—note: the third-smallest country in South America after Suriname and Uruguay; substantial portions of its western and eastern territories are claimed by Venezuela and Suriname respectively; contains some of the largest unspoiled rainforests on the continent

PEOPLE AND SOCIETY

Population: 737,718
note: estimates for this country explicitly take into account the effects of excess mortality due to AIDS; this can result in lower life expectancy, higher infant mortality, higher death rates, lower population growth rates, and changes in the distribution of population by age and sex than would otherwise be expected (July 2017 est.)
country comparison to the world: 166

Nationality: *noun:* Guyanese (singular and plural)
adjective: Guyanese

Ethnic groups: East Indian 39.8%, black (African) 29.3%, mixed 19.9%, Amerindian 10.5%, other 0.5% (includes Portuguese, Chinese, white) (2012 est.)

Languages: English (official), Guyanese Creole, Amerindian languages (including Caribbean and Arawak languages), Indian languages (including Caribbean Hindustani, a dialect of Hindi), Chinese (2014 est.)

Religions: Protestant 34.8% (Pentecostal 22.8%, Seventh Day Adventist 5.4%, Anglican 5.2%, Methodist 1.4%), Hindu 24.8%, Roman Catholic 7.1%, Muslim 6.8%, Jehovah's Witness 1.3%, Rastafarian 0.5%, other Christian 20.8%, other 0.9%, none 3.1% (2012 est.)

Demographic profile: Guyana is the only English-speaking country in South America and shares cultural and historical bonds with the Anglophone Caribbean. Guyana's two largest ethnic groups

are the Afro-Guyanese (descendants of African slaves) and the Indo-Guyanese (descendants of Indian indentured laborers), which together comprise about three quarters of Guyana's population. Tensions periodically have boiled over between the two groups, which back ethnically based political parties and vote along ethnic lines. Poverty reduction has stagnated since the late 1990s. About one-third of the Guyanese population lives below the poverty line; indigenous people are disproportionately affected. Although Guyana's literacy rate is reported to be among the highest in the Western Hemisphere, the level of functional literacy is considerably lower, which has been attributed to poor education quality, teacher training, and infrastructure.

Guyana's emigration rate is among the highest in the world—more than 55% of its citizens reside abroad—and it is one of the largest recipients of remittances relative to GDP among Latin American and Caribbean counties. Although remittances are a vital source of income for most citizens, the pervasive emigration of skilled workers deprives Guyana of professionals in healthcare and other key sectors. More than 80% of Guyanese nationals with tertiary level educations have emigrated. Brain drain and the concentration of limited medical resources in Georgetown hamper Guyana's ability to meet the health needs of its predominantly rural population. Guyana has one of the highest HIV prevalence rates in the region and continues to rely on international support for its HIV treatment and prevention programs.

Age structure: *0-14 years:* 26.22% (male 98,506/female 94,949)
15-24 years: 21.56% (male 81,487/female 77,567)
25-54 years: 38.1% (male 146,915/female 134,145)
55-64 years: 8.03% (male 26,924/female 32,345)
65 years and over: 6.08% (male 18,421/female 26,459) (2017 est.)

Dependency ratios: *total dependency ratio:* 53.5
youth dependency ratio: 45.8
elderly dependency ratio: 7.7
potential support ratio: 13.3 (2015 est.)

Median age: *total:* 26.2 years
male: 25.9 years
female: 26.6 years (2017 est.)
country comparison to the world: 150

Population growth rate: 0.32% (2017 est.)
country comparison to the world: 167

Birth rate: 15.4 births/1,000 population (2017 est.)
country comparison to the world: 123

Death rate: 7.4 deaths/1,000 population (2017 est.)
country comparison to the world: 112

Net migration rate: -4.8 migrant(s)/1,000 population (2017 est.)
country comparison to the world: 189

Population distribution: population is heavily concentrated in the northeast in and around Georgetown, with noteable concentrations along the Berbice River to the east; the remainder of the country is sparsely populated

Urbanization: *urban population:* 28.8% of total population (2017)
rate of urbanization: 0.91% annual rate of change (2015-20 est.)

Major urban areas—population: GEORGETOWN (capital) 124,000 (2014)

Sex ratio: *at birth:* 1.05 male(s)/female
0-14 years: 1.04 male(s)/female
15-24 years: 1.05 male(s)/female
25-54 years: 1.09 male(s)/female
55-64 years: 0.82 male(s)/female
65 years and over: 0.71 male(s)/female
total population: 1.02 male(s)/female (2016 est.)

Mother's mean age at first birth: 20.8 years
note: median age at first birth among women 25-29 (2009 est.)

Maternal mortality ratio: 229 deaths/100,000 live births (2015 est.)
country comparison to the world: 47

Infant mortality rate: *total:* 30.4 deaths/1,000 live births
male: 34.2 deaths/1,000 live births
female: 26.5 deaths/1,000 live births (2017 est.)
country comparison to the world: 63

Life expectancy at birth: *total population:* 68.6 years
male: 65.6 years
female: 71.8 years (2017 est.)
country comparison to the world: 165

Total fertility rate: 2 children born/woman (2017 est.)
country comparison to the world: 121

Contraceptive prevalence rate: 33.9% (2014)
Health expenditures: 5.2% of GDP (2014)
country comparison to the world: 134

Physicians density: 0.21 physicians/1,000 population (2010)

Hospital bed density: 2 beds/1,000 population (2009)

Drinking water source:
improved:
urban: 98.2% of population
rural: 98.3% of population
total: 98.3% of population
unimproved:
urban: 1.8% of population
rural: 1.7% of population
total: 1.7% of population (2015 est.)

Sanitation facility access:
improved:
urban: 87.9% of population
rural: 82% of population
total: 83.7% of population
unimproved:
urban: 12.1% of population
rural: 18% of population
total: 16.3% of population (2015 est.)

HIV/AIDS—adult prevalence rate: 1.6% (2016 est.)
country comparison to the world: 32

HIV/AIDS—people living with HIV/AIDS: 8,500 (2016 est.)
country comparison to the world: 99

HIV/AIDS—deaths: <200 (2016 est.)

Major infectious diseases: *degree of risk:* very high

food or waterborne diseases: bacterial and protozoal diarrhea, hepatitis A, and typhoid fever

vectorborne diseases: dengue fever and malaria

note: active local transmission of Zika virus by Aedes species mosquitoes has been identified in this country (as of August 2016); it poses an important risk (a large number of cases possible) among US citizens if bitten by an infective mosquito; other less common ways to get Zika are through sex, via blood transfusion, or during pregnancy, in which the pregnant woman passes Zika virus to her fetus (2016)

Obesity—adult prevalence rate: 20.2% (2016)
country comparison to the world: 101

Children under the age of 5 years underweight: 8.5% (2014)
country comparison to the world: 67

Education expenditures: 3.2% of GDP (2012)
country comparison to the world: 136

Literacy: *definition:* age 15 and over has ever attended school
total population: 88.5%
male: 87.2%
female: 89.8% (2015 est.)

School life expectancy (primary to tertiary education): *total:* 10 years
male: 10 years
female: 10 years (2012)

GOVERNMENT

Country name: *conventional long form:* Cooperative Republic of Guyana
conventional short form: Guyana
former: British Guiana
etymology: the name is derived from Guiana, the original name for the region that included British Guiana, Dutch Guiana, and French Guiana; ultimately the word is derived from an indigenous Amerindian language and means "Land of Many Waters" (referring to the area's multitude of rivers and streams)

Government type: parliamentary republic

Capital: *name:* Georgetown

geographic coordinates: 6 48 N, 58 09 W
time difference: UTC-4 (1 hour ahead of Washington, DC, during Standard Time)

Administrative divisions: 10 regions; Barima-Waini, Cuyuni-Mazaruni, Demerara-Mahaica, East Berbice-Corentyne, Essequibo Islands-West Demerara, Mahaica-Berbice, Pomeroon-Supenaam, Potaro-Siparuni, Upper Demerara-Berbice, Upper Takutu-Upper Essequibo

Independence: 26 May 1966 (from the UK)

National holiday: Republic Day, 23 February (1970)

Constitution: several previous; latest promulgated 6 October 1980; amended many times, last in 2009 (2017)

Legal system: common law system, based on the English model, with some Roman-Dutch civil law influence

International law organization participation: has not submitted an ICJ jurisdiction declaration; accepts ICCt jurisdiction

Citizenship: *citizenship by birth:* yes
citizenship by descent: yes
dual citizenship recognized: no
residency requirement for naturalization: na

Suffrage: 18 years of age; universal

Executive branch: *chief of state:* President David GRANGER (since 16 May 2015); note—the president is both chief of state and head of government

head of government: President David GRANGER (since 16 May 2015)
cabinet: Cabinet of Ministers appointed by the president, responsible to the National Assembly
elections/appointments: the predesignated candidate of the winning party in the last National Assembly election becomes president for a 5-year term (no term limits); election last held on 11 May 2015 (next to be held no later than 2020); prime minister appointed by the president
election results: David GRANGER (APNU-AFC) designated president by the majority party in the National Assembly

Legislative branch: description: unicameral National Assembly (65 seats; members directly elected in multi-seat constituencies and a single nationwide constituency by proportional representation vote; members serve 5-year terms)
elections: last held on 11 May 2015 (next to be held by May 2020)
election results: percent of vote by party—APNU-AFC 50.3%, PPP/C 49.2%, other 0.5%; seats by party—APNU-AFC 33, PPP/C 32

Judicial branch: *highest court(s):* Supreme Court of Judicature (consists of the Court of Appeal with a chief justice and 3 justices, and the High Court with a chief justice and 10 justices organized into 3- or 5-judge panels); note—in 2009, Guyana ceased final appeals in civil and criminal cases to the Judicial Committee of the Privy Council (in London), replacing it with the Caribbean Court of Justice, the judicial organ of the Caribbean Community
judge selection and term of office: Court of Appeal and High Court chief justices appointed by the president; other judges of both courts appointed by the Judicial Service Commission, a body appointed by the president; judges appointed for life with retirement at age 65
subordinate courts: Land Court; magistrates' courts

Political parties and leaders: A Partnership for National Unity or APNU [David A. GRANGER]
Alliance for Change or AFC [Raphael TROTMAN]
Justice for All Party [C.N. SHARMA]
National Independent Party or NIP [Saphier Husain SUBEDAR]
People's Progressive Party/Civic or PPP/C [Donald RAMOTAR]

The United Force or TUF [Manzoor NADIR]
United Republican Party or URP [Vishnu BANDHU]

Political pressure groups and leaders: Amerindian People's Association
Guyana Bar Association
Guyana Citizens Initiative
Guyana Human Rights Association
Guyana Public Service Union or GPSU
Guyana Trans United
Private Sector Commission
Society Against Sexual Orientation Discrimination or SASOD
Trades Union Congress

International organization participation: ACP, AOSIS, C, Caricom, CD, CDB, CELAC, FAO, G-77, IADB, IBRD, ICAO, ICCt, ICRM, IDA, IFAD, IFC, IFRCS, ILO, IMF, IMO, Interpol, IOC, IOM, ISO (correspondent), ITU, LAES, MIGA, NAM, OAS, OIC, OPANAL, OPCW, PCA, Petrocaribe, UN, UNASUR, UNCTAD, UNESCO, UNIDO, UPU, WCO, WFTU (NGOs), WHO, WIPO, WMO, WTO

Diplomatic representation in the US: *chief of mission:* Ambassador Riyad David INSANALLY (since 16 Sept 2016)
chancery: 2490 Tracy Place NW, Washington, DC 20008
telephone: [1] (202) 265-6900
FAX: [1] (202) 232-1297
consulate(s) general: New York

Diplomatic representation from the US: *chief of mission:* Ambassador Perry L. HOLLOWAY (since 2 October 2015)
embassy: US Embassy, 100 Young and Duke Streets, Kingston, Georgetown
mailing address: P. O. Box 10507, Georgetown; US Embassy, 3170 Georgetown Place, Washington DC 20521-3170
telephone: [592] 225-4900 through 4909
FAX: [592] 225-8497

Flag description: green with a red isosceles triangle (based on the hoist side) superimposed on a long, yellow arrowhead; there is a narrow, black border between the red and yellow, and a narrow, white border between the yellow and the green; green represents forest and foliage; yellow stands for mineral resources and a bright future; white symbolizes Guyana's rivers; red signifies zeal and the sacrifice of the people; black indicates perseverance

National symbol(s): Canje pheasant (hoatzin), jaguar, Victoria Regia water lily; national colors: red, yellow, green, black, white

National anthem: name: "Dear Land of Guyana, of Rivers and Plains"
lyrics/music: Archibald Leonard LUKERL/Robert Cyril Gladstone POTTER
note: adopted 1966

ECONOMY

Economy—overview: The Guyanese economy exhibited moderate economic growth in recent years and is based largely on agriculture and extractive industries. The economy is heavily dependent upon the export of six commodities—sugar, gold, bauxite, shrimp, timber, and rice—which represent nearly 60% of the country's GDP and are highly susceptible to adverse weather conditions and fluctuations in commodity prices. Much of Guyana's growth in recent years has come from a surge in gold production in response to global prices, although downward trends in gold prices may threaten future growth. In 2014, production of sugar dropped to a 24-year low.

Guyana's entrance into the Caricom Single Market and Economy in January 2006 broadened the country's export market, primarily in the raw materials sector. Guyana has experienced positive growth almost every year over the past decade. Inflation has been kept under control. Recent years have seen the government's stock of debt reduced significantly—with external debt now less than half of what it was in the early 1990s. Despite recent improvements, the government is still juggling a sizable external debt against the urgent need for expanded public investment. In March 2007, the Inter-American Development Bank, Guyana's principal donor, canceled Guyana's nearly $470 million debt, equivalent to 21% of GDP, which along with other Highly Indebted Poor Country debt forgiveness, brought the debt-to-GDP ratio down from 183% in 2006 to 52% in 2017. Guyana had become heavily indebted as a result of the inward-looking, state-led development model pursued in the 1970s and 1980s. Chronic problems include a shortage of skilled labor and a deficient infrastructure.

GDP (purchasing power parity): $6.367 billion (2017 est.)
$6.15 billion (2016 est.)
$5.953 billion (2015 est.)
note: data are in 2017 dollars
country comparison to the world: 171

GDP (official exchange rate): $3.591 billion (2016 est.)

GDP—real growth rate: 3.5% (2017 est.)
3.3% (2016 est.)
3.1% (2015 est.)
country comparison to the world: 91

GDP—per capita (PPP): $8,300 (2017 est.)
$8,000 (2016 est.)
$7,800 (2015 est.)
note: data are in 2017 dollars
country comparison to the world: 150

Gross national saving: 14.8% of GDP (2017 est.)
15.3% of GDP (2016 est.)
8.2% of GDP (2015 est.)
country comparison to the world: 127

GDP—composition, by end use:
household consumption: 73.3%
government consumption: 19.1%
investment in fixed capital: 23.1%
investment in inventories: 3.2%
exports of goods and services: 51.4%
imports of goods and services: -70.1% (2017 est.)

GDP—composition, by sector of origin:
agriculture: 17.5%
industry: 37.8%

services: 44.7% (2017 est.)

Agriculture—products: sugarcane, rice, edible oils; beef, pork, poultry; shrimp, fish

Industries: bauxite, sugar, rice milling, timber, textiles, gold mining

Industrial production growth rate: 9% (2017 est.)
country comparison to the world: 11

Labor force: 313,800 (2013 est.)
country comparison to the world: 163

Labor force—by occupation: *agriculture:* NA%
industry: NA%
services: NA%

Unemployment rate: 11.1% (2013)
11.3% (2012)
country comparison to the world: 143

Population below poverty line: 35% (2006 est.)

Household income or consumption by percentage share: *lowest 10%:* 1.3%
highest 10%: 33.8% (1999)

Distribution of family income—Gini index: 44.6 (2007)
43.2 (1999)
country comparison to the world: 42

Budget: *revenues:* $939.1 million
expenditures: $1.152 billion (2017 est.)
Taxes and other revenues: 26.2% of GDP (2017 est.)
country comparison to the world: 108

Budget surplus (+) or deficit (-): -5.9% of GDP (2017 est.)
country comparison to the world: 174

Public debt: 52.3% of GDP (2017 est.)
46.8% of GDP (2016 est.)
country comparison to the world: 95

Fiscal year: calendar year

Inflation rate (consumer prices): 2.3% (2017 est.)
0.8% (2016 est.)
country comparison to the world: 108

Central bank discount rate: 5.5% (31 December 2011)
4.25% (31 December 2010)
country comparison to the world: 74

Commercial bank prime lending rate: 13.3% (31 December 2017 est.)
13% (31 December 2016 est.)
country comparison to the world: 59

Stock of narrow money: $772.3 million (31 December 2017 est.)
$701.4 million (31 December 2016 est.)
country comparison to the world: 160

Stock of broad money: $1.735 billion (31 December 2017 est.)
$1.7 billion (31 December 2016 est.)
country comparison to the world: 163

Stock of domestic credit: $1.986 billion (31 December 2017 est.)
$1.875 billion (31 December 2016 est.)
country comparison to the world: 149

Market value of publicly traded shares: $610.9 million (31 December 2012 est.)
$440.4 million (31 December 2011 est.)

$339.8 million (31 December 2010 est.)
country comparison to the world: 111

Current account balance: -$70 million (2017 est.)
$14 million (2016 est.)
country comparison to the world: 75

Exports: $1.474 billion (2017 est.)
$1.38 billion (2016 est.)
country comparison to the world: 150

Exports—commodities: sugar, gold, bauxite, alumina, rice, shrimp, molasses, rum, timber

Exports—partners: Canada 30.6%, US 20.7%, Trinidad and Tobago 11.4% (2016)

Imports: $1.776 billion (2017 est.)
$1.555 billion (2016 est.)
country comparison to the world: 164

Imports—commodities: manufactures, machinery, petroleum, food

Imports—partners: Trinidad and Tobago 29%, US 27.5%, China 7.3%, Suriname 5.5% (2016)

Reserves of foreign exchange and gold: $607.7 million (31 December 2017 est.)
$581 million (31 December 2016 est.)
country comparison to the world: 136

Debt—external: $1.726 billion (31 December 2017 est.)

$1.542 billion (31 December 2016 est.)
country comparison to the world: 153

Exchange rates: Guyanese dollars (GYD) per US dollar—
207 (2017 est.)
206.5 (2016 est.)
206.5 (2015 est.)
206.5 (2014 est.)
206.45 (2013 est.)

ENERGY

Electricity access: *population without electricity:* 154,540
electrification—total population: 79%
electrification—urban areas: 91%
electrification—rural areas: 75% (2012)

Electricity—production: 1 billion kWh (2015 est.)
country comparison to the world: 150

Electricity—consumption: 800 million kWh (2015 est.)
country comparison to the world: 162

Electricity—exports: 0 kWh (2016 est.)
country comparison to the world: 146

Electricity—imports: 0 kWh (2016 est.)
country comparison to the world: 159

Electricity—installed generating capacity: 438,000 kW (2015 est.)
country comparison to the world: 149

Electricity—from fossil fuels: 86.8% of total installed capacity (2015 est.)
country comparison to the world: 71

Electricity—from nuclear fuels: 0% of total installed capacity (2015 est.)
country comparison to the world: 105

Electricity—from hydroelectric plants: 0.2% of total installed capacity (2015 est.)

country comparison to the world: 153

Electricity—from other renewable sources: 13% of total installed capacity (2015 est.)
country comparison to the world: 55

Crude oil—production: 0 bbl/day (2016 est.)
country comparison to the world: 145

Crude oil—exports: 0 bbl/day (2014 est.)
country comparison to the world: 134

Crude oil—imports: 0 bbl/day (2014 est.)
country comparison to the world: 137

Crude oil—proved reserves: 2.5 billion bbl (1 January 2017 es)
country comparison to the world: 35

Refined petroleum products—production: 0 bbl/day (2014 est.)
country comparison to the world: 155

Refined petroleum products—consumption: 13,000 bbl/day (2015 est.)
country comparison to the world: 154

Refined petroleum products—exports: 0 bbl/day (2014 est.)
country comparison to the world: 164

Refined petroleum products—imports: 13,250 bbl/day (2014 est.)
country comparison to the world: 134

Natural gas—production: 0 cu m (2013 est.)
country comparison to the world: 146

Natural gas—consumption: 0 cu m (2013 est.)
country comparison to the world: 191

Natural gas—exports: 0 cu m (2013 est.)
country comparison to the world: 118

Natural gas—imports: 0 cu m (2013 est.)
country comparison to the world: 136

Natural gas—proved reserves: 0 cu m (1 January 2014 es)
country comparison to the world: 149

Carbon dioxide emissions from consumption of energy: 1.7 million Mt (2013 est.)
country comparison to the world: 155

COMMUNICATIONS

Telephones—fixed lines: *total subscriptions:* 153,000
subscriptions per 100 inhabitants: 21 (July 2016 est.)
country comparison to the world: 134

Telephones—mobile cellular: *total:* 539,000
subscriptions per 100 inhabitants: 73 (July 2016 est.)
country comparison to the world: 167

Telephone system: *general assessment:* reliable international long distance service; 100% digital network; national transmission supported by fiber optic cable and rural network by microwaves; more than 150,000 lines; many areas still lack fixed-line telephone services
domestic: fixed-line teledensity is about 20 per 100 persons; mobile-cellular teledensity about 75 per 100 persons

international: country code—592; SIP trunking to most providers; international calls via diverse fiber optic cables; satellite earth station—1 Intelsat (Atlantic Ocean) (2017)

Broadcast media: government-dominated broadcast media; the National Communications Network (NCN) TV is state-owned; a few private TV stations relay satellite services; the state owns and operates 2 radio stations broadcasting on multiple frequencies capable of reaching the entire country; government limits on licensing of new private radio stations has constrained competition in broadcast media (2017)

Internet country code: .gy
Internet users: total: 262,425

percent of population: 35.7% (July 2016 est.)
country comparison to the world: 149

TRANSPORTATION

National air transport system: *number of registered air carriers:* 2
inventory of registered aircraft operated by air carriers: 12
annual passenger traffic on registered air carriers: 43,835
annual freight traffic on registered air carriers: 0 mt-km (2015)
Civil aircraft registration country code prefix: 8R (2016)

Airports: 117 (2013)
country comparison to the world: 50

Airports—with paved runways: *total:* 11
1,524 to 2,437 m: 2
914 to 1,523 m: 1
under 914 m: 8 (2017)

Airports—with unpaved runways: *total:* 106
1,524 to 2,437 m: 1
914 to 1,523 m: 16
under 914 m: 89 (2013)

Roadways: *total:* 7,970 km
paved: 590 km
unpaved: 7,380 km (2001)
country comparison to the world: 141

Waterways: 330 km (the Berbice, Demerara, and Essequibo Rivers are navigable by oceangoing vessels for 150 km, 100 km, and 80 km respectively) (2012)
country comparison to the world: 91

Merchant marine: *total:* 55
by type: general cargo 26, oil tanker 6, other 23 (2017)
country comparison to the world: 109

Ports and terminals: *major seaport(s):* Georgetown

MILITARY AND SECURITY

Military expenditures: 1.42% of GDP (2016)
1.46% of GDP (2015)
1.28% of GDP (2014)
1.18% of GDP (2013)

1.18% of GDP (2012)
country comparison to the world: 93

Military branches: Guyana Defense Force: Army (includes Air Corps, Coast Guard) (2012)

Military service age and obligation: 18 years of age or older for voluntary military service; no conscription (2014)

TRANSNATIONAL ISSUES

Disputes—international: all of the area west of the Essequibo River is claimed by Venezuela preventing any discussion of a maritime boundary; Guyana has expressed its intention to join Barbados in asserting claims before UN Convention on the Law of the Sea (UNCLOS) that Trinidad and Tobago's maritime boundary with Venezuela extends into their waters; Suriname claims a triangle of land between the New and Kutari/Koetari Rivers in a historic dispute over the headwaters of the Courantyne

Trafficking in persons: current situation: Guyana is a source and destination country for men, women, and children subjected to sex trafficking and forced labor—children are particularly vulnerable; women and girls from Guyana, Venezuela, Suriname, Brazil, and the Dominican Republic are forced into prostitution in Guyana's interior mining communities and urban areas; forced labor is reported in mining, agriculture, forestry, domestic service, and shops; Guyanese nationals are also trafficked to Suriname, Jamaica, and other Caribbean countries for sexual exploitation and forced labor

tier rating: Tier 2 Watch List—Guyana does not fully comply with the minimum standards for the elimination of trafficking; however, it is making significant efforts to do so; in 2014, Guyana was granted a waiver from an otherwise required downgrade to Tier 3 because its government has a written plan that, if implemented would constitute making significant efforts to bring itself into compliance with the minimum standards for the elimination of trafficking; the government released its anti-trafficking action plan in June 2014 but made uneven efforts to implement it; law enforcement was weak, investigating seven trafficking cases, prosecuting four alleged traffickers, and convicting one trafficker—a police officer—who was released on bail pending appeal; in 2014, as in previous years, Guyanese courts dismissed the majority of ongoing trafficking prosecutions; the government referred some victims to care services, which were provided by NGOs with little or no government support (2015)

Illicit drugs: transshipment point for narcotics from South America—primarily Venezuela—to Europe and the US; producer of cannabis; rising money laundering related to drug trafficking and human smuggling

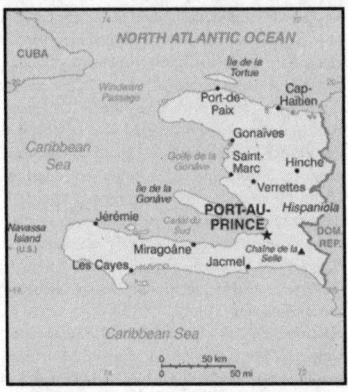

INTRODUCTION

Background: The native Taino—who inhabited the island of Hispaniola when it was discovered by Christopher COLUMBUS in 1492—were virtually annihilated by Spanish settlers within 25 years. In the early 17th century, the French established a presence on Hispaniola. In 1697, Spain ceded to the French the western third of the island, which later became Haiti. The French colony, based on forestry and sugar-related industries, became one of the wealthiest in the Caribbean but only through the heavy importation of African slaves and considerable environmental degradation. In the late 18th century, Haiti's nearly half million slaves revolted under Toussaint L'OUVERTURE. After a prolonged struggle, Haiti became the first postcolonial black-led nation in the world, declaring its independence in 1804. Currently the poorest country in the Western Hemisphere, Haiti has experienced political instability for most of its history. A massive magnitude 7.0 earthquake struck Haiti in January 2010 with an epicenter about 25 km (15 mi) west of the capital, Port-au-Prince. Estimates are that over 300,000 people were killed and some 1.5 million left homeless. The earthquake was assessed as the worst in this region over the last 200 years. President Michel MARTELLY resigned in February 2016 and was replaced by Interim President Jocelerme PRIVERT. President Jovenel MOISE won the November 2016 elections and assumed office in February 2017.

GEOGRAPHY

Location: Caribbean, western one-third of the island of Hispaniola, between the Caribbean Sea and the North Atlantic Ocean, west of the Dominican Republic

Geographic coordinates: 19 00 N, 72 25 W

Map references: Central America and the Caribbean

Area: total: 27,750 sq km
land: 27,560 sq km
water: 190 sq km

country comparison to the world: 148

Area—comparative: slightly smaller than Maryland

Land boundaries: total: 376 km
border countries (1): Dominican Republic 376 km

Coastline: 1,771 km

Maritime claims: territorial sea: 12 nm
contiguous zone: 24 nm
exclusive economic zone: 200 nm
continental shelf: to depth of exploitation

Climate: tropical; semiarid where mountains in east cut off trade winds

Terrain: mostly rough and mountainous

Elevation: mean elevation: 470 m

elevation extremes: lowest point: Caribbean Sea 0 m
highest point: Chaine de la Selle 2,680 m

Natural resources: bauxite, copper, calcium carbonate, gold, marble, hydropower, arable land

Land use: agricultural land: 66.4%
arable land: 38.5%;
permanent crops: 10.2%;
permanent pasture: 17.7%
forest: 3.6%
other: 30% (2011 est.)
Irrigated land: 970 sq km (2012)

Population—distribution: fairly even distribution; largest concentrations located near coastal areas

Natural hazards: lies in the middle of the hurricane belt and subject to severe storms from June to October; occasional flooding and earthquakes; periodic droughts

Environment—current issues: extensive deforestation (much of the remaining forested land is being cleared for agriculture and used as fuel); soil erosion; inadequate supplies of potable water

Environment—international agreements: party to: Biodiversity, Climate Change, Climate Change-Kyoto Protocol, Desertification, Law of the Sea, Marine Dumping, Marine Life Conservation, Ozone Layer Protection
signed, but not ratified: Hazardous Wastes

Geography—note: shares island of Hispaniola with Dominican Republic (western one-third is Haiti, eastern two-thirds is the Dominican Republic); it is the most mountainous nation in the Caribbean

PEOPLE AND SOCIETY

Population: 10,646,714
note: estimates for this country explicitly take into account the effects of excess mortality due to AIDS; this can result in lower life expectancy, higher infant mortality, higher death rates, lower population growth rates, and changes in the distribution of population by age and sex than would otherwise be expected (July 2017 est.)
country comparison to the world: 88

Nationality: noun: Haitian(s)
adjective: Haitian

Ethnic groups: black 95%, mulatto and white 5%

Languages: French (official), Creole (official)

Religions: Roman Catholic (official) 54.7%, Protestant 28.5% (Baptist 15.4%, Pentecostal 7.9%, Adventist 3%, Methodist 1.5%, other 0.7%), voodoo (official) 2.1%, other 4.6%, none 10.2% (2003 est.)
note: many Haitians practice elements of voodoo in addition to another religion, most often Roman Catholicism; voodoo was recognized as an official religion in 2003

Age structure: 0-14 years: 32.81% (male 1,740,291/female 1,752,663)
15-24 years: 21.25% (male 1,132,386/female 1,129,844)
25-54 years: 36.78% (male 1,943,683/female 1,972,347)
55-64 years: 5.01% (male 254,352/female 279,431)
65 years and over: 4.15% (male 194,535/female 247,182) (2017 est.)

Dependency ratios: total dependency ratio: 62.3
youth dependency ratio: 54.8
elderly dependency ratio: 7.5
potential support ratio: 13.3 (2015 est.)

Median age: total: 23 years
male: 22.7 years
female: 23.2 years (2017 est.)
country comparison to the world: 173

Population growth rate: 1.34% (2017 est.)
country comparison to the world: 83

Birth rate: 23 births/1,000 population (2017 est.)
country comparison to the world: 66

Death rate: 7.6 deaths/1,000 population (2017 est.)
country comparison to the world: 106

Net migration rate: -2 migrant(s)/1,000 population (2017 est.)
country comparison to the world: 163

Population distribution: fairly even distribution; largest concentrations located near coastal areas

Urbanization: urban population: 60.9% of total population (2017)
rate of urbanization: 2.93% annual rate of change (2015-20 est.)

Major urban areas—population: PORT-AU-PRINCE (capital) 2.44 million (2015)

Sex ratio: at birth: 1.01 male(s)/female
0-14 years: 0.99 male(s)/female
15-24 years: 1 male(s)/female
25-54 years: 0.99 male(s)/female
55-64 years: 0.91 male(s)/female
65 years and over: 0.81 male(s)/female
total population: 0.98 male(s)/female (2016 est.)

Mother's mean age at first birth: 22.7 years
note: median age at first birth among women 25-29 (2012 est.)

Maternal mortality ratio: 359 deaths/100,000 live births (2015 est.)
country comparison to the world: 33

Infant mortality rate: *total:* 46.8 deaths/1,000 live births
male: 53.1 deaths/1,000 live births
female: 40.5 deaths/1,000 live births (2017 est.)
country comparison to the world: 36

Life expectancy at birth: *total population:* 64.2 years
male: 61.6 years
female: 66.8 years (2017 est.)
country comparison to the world: 188

Total fertility rate: 2.72 children born/woman (2017 est.)
country comparison to the world: 64

Contraceptive prevalence rate: 34.5% (2012)

Health expenditures: 7.6% of GDP (2014)
country comparison to the world: 62

Hospital bed density: 1.3 beds/1,000 population (2007)

Drinking water source:
improved:
urban: 64.9% of population
rural: 47.6% of population
total: 57.7% of population
unimproved:
urban: 35.1% of population
rural: 52.4% of population
total: 42.3% of population (2015 est.)

Sanitation facility access:
improved:
urban: 33.6% of population
rural: 19.2% of population
total: 27.6% of population
unimproved:
urban: 66.4% of population
rural: 80.8% of population
total: 72.4% of population (2015 est.)

HIV/AIDS—adult prevalence rate: 2.1% (2016 est.)
country comparison to the world: 24

HIV/AIDS—people living with HIV/AIDS: 150,000 (2016 est.)
country comparison to the world: 31

HIV/AIDS—deaths: 4,600 (2016 est.)
country comparison to the world: 31

Major infectious diseases: *degree of risk:* very high
food or waterborne diseases: bacterial and protozoal diarrhea, hepatitis A and E, and typhoid fever
vectorborne diseases: dengue fever and malaria
note: active local transmission of Zika virus by Aedes species mosquitoes has been identified in this country (as of August 2016); it poses an important risk (a large number of cases possible) among US citizens if bitten by an infective mosquito; other less common ways to get Zika are through sex, via blood transfusion, or during pregnancy, in which the pregnant woman passes Zika virus to her fetus (2016)

Obesity—adult prevalence rate: 22.7% (2016)
country comparison to the world: 73

Children under the age of 5 years underweight: 11.6% (2012)
country comparison to the world: 64

Education expenditures: NA

Literacy: *definition:* age 15 and over can read and write
total population: 60.7%
male: 64.3%
female: 57.3% (2015 est.)

GOVERNMENT

Country name: *conventional long form:* Republic of Haiti
conventional short form: Haiti
local long form: Republique d'Haiti/Repiblik d Ayiti
local short form: Haiti/Ayiti
etymology: the native Taino name means "Land of High Mountains" and was originally applied to the entire island of Hispaniola

Government type: semi-presidential republic

Capital: *name:* Port-au-Prince
geographic coordinates: 18 32 N, 72 20 W
time difference: UTC-5 (same time as Washington, DC, during Standard Time)
daylight saving time: +1hr, begins second Sunday in March; ends first Sunday in November

Administrative divisions: 10 departments (departements, singular—departement); Artibonite, Centre, Grand'Anse, Nippes, Nord, Nord-Est, Nord-Ouest, Ouest, Sud, Sud-Est

Independence: 1 January 1804 (from France)

National holiday: Independence Day, 1 January (1804)

Constitution: many previous (23 total); latest adopted 10 March 1987; amended 2012 (2016)

Legal system: civil law system strongly influenced by Napoleonic Code

International law organization participation: accepts compulsory ICJ jurisdiction; non-party state to the ICCt

Citizenship: *citizenship by birth:* no
citizenship by descent only: at least one parent must be a native-born citizen of Haiti
dual citizenship recognized: no
residency requirement for naturalization: 5 years

Suffrage: 18 years of age; universal

Executive branch: *chief of state:* President Jovenel MOISE (since 7 February 2017)
head of government: Prime Minister Dr. Jack Guy LAFONTANT (since 21 March 2017)
cabinet: Cabinet chosen by the prime minister in consultation with the president; parliament must ratify the Cabinet and Prime Minister's governing policy
elections/appointments: president directly elected by absolute majority popular vote in 2 rounds if needed for a 5-year term (eligible for a single non-consecutive term); last election originally scheduled for 9 October 2016 but postponed to 20 November 2016 due to Hurricane Matthew
election results: Jovenel MOISE elected president in first round; percent of vote—Jovenel MOISE (PHTK) 55.6%, Jude CELESTIN (LAPEH)

19.6%, Jean-Charles MOISE (PPD) 11%, Maryse NARCISSE (FL) 9%; other 4.8%

Legislative branch: *description:* bicameral legislature or le Corps Legislatif ou parlement consists of le Senat or Senate (30 seats; members directly elected in multi-seat constituencies by absolute majority vote in 2 rounds if needed; members serve 6-year terms with one-third of the membership renewed every 2 years) and la Chambre de deputes or Chamber of Deputies (118 seats; members directly elected in single-seat constituencies by absolute majority vote in 2 rounds if needed; members serve 4-year terms); note—when the 2 chambers meet collectively it is known as L'Assemblee Nationale or the National Assembly and is convened for specific purposes spelled out in the constitution
elections: Senate—last held on 9 August 2015 with run-off election on 25 October 2015 (next possible election in 2017); Chamber of Deputies—last held on 9 August 2015 with run-off election on 25 October 2015 (next regular election may be held in 2017)
election results: Senate—percent of vote by party—NA; seats by party—NA; Chamber of Deputies—percent of vote by party—NA; seats by party—NA

Judicial branch: *highest court(s):* Supreme Court or Cour de Cassation (consists of a chief judge and other judges); note—Haiti is a member of the Caribbean Court of Justice
judge selection and term of office: judges appointed by the president from candidate lists submitted by the Senate of the National Assembly; note—Article 174 of the Haiti Constitution states that judges of the Supreme Court are appointed for 10 years, whereas Article 177 states that judges of the Supreme Court are appointed for life
subordinate courts: Courts of Appeal; Courts of First Instance; magistrates' courts; special courts

Political parties and leaders: Alternative League for Haitian Progress and Empowerment or LAPEH [Jude CELESTIN]
Christian Movement for a New Haiti or MCNH [Luc MESADIEU]
Christian National Movement for the Reconstruction of Haiti or UNCRH [Chavannes JEUNE]
Convention for Democratic Unity or KID [Evans PAUL]
Cooperative Action to Rebuild Haiti or KONBA [Jean William JEANTY]
December 16 Platform or Platfom 16 Desanm [Dr. Gerard BLOT]
Democratic Alliance Party or ALYANS [Evans PAUL] (coalition includes KID and PPRH)
Democratic Centers' National Council or CONACED [Osner FEVRY]
Dessalinian Patriotic and Popular Movement or MOPOD [Jean Andre VICTOR]
Effort and Solidarity to Create an Alternative for the People or ESKAMP [Joseph JASME]
Fanmi Lavalas or FL [Jean-Bertrand ARISTIDE]
For Us All or PONT [Jean-Marie CHERESTAL]
Fusion of Haitian Social Democrats or FHSD [Edmonde Supplice BEAUZILE]

Grouping of Citizens for Hope or RESPE [Charles-Henri BAKER]

Haitians for Haiti [Yvon NEPTUNE]

Haitian Tet Kale Party or PHTK [Ann Valerie Timothee MILFORT]

Haiti in Action or AAA [Youri LATORTUE]

Independent Movement for National Reconstruction or MIRN [Luc FLEURINORD]

Konbit Pou refe Ayiti or KONBIT

Lavni Organization or LAVNI [Yves CRISTALIN]

Liberal Party of Haiti or PLH [Jean Andre VICTOR]

Love Haiti or Renmen Ayiti [Jean-Henry CEANT and Camille LEBLANC]

Mobilization for National Development or MDN [Hubert de RONCERAY]

New Christian Movement for a New Haiti or MOCHRENA [Luc MESADIEU]

Organization for the Advancement of Haiti and Haitians or OLAHH

Party for the Integral Advancement of the Haitian People or PAIPH

Patriotic Unity or IP [Marie Denise CLAUDE]

Peasant's Response or Repons Peyizan [Michel MARTELLY]

Platform Alternative for Progress and Democracy or ALTENATIV [Victor BENOIT and Evans PAUL]

Platform of Haitian Patriots or PLAPH [Dejean BELISAIRE and Himmler REBU]

Platform Pitit Desaline or PPD [Jean-Charles MOISE]

Pont

Popular Party for the Renewal of Haiti or PPRH [Claude ROMAIN]

PPG18

Rally of Progressive National Democrats or RDNP [Mirlande MANIGAT]

Renmen Ayiti or RA [Jean-Henry CEANT]

Reseau National Bouclier or BOUCLIER

Respect or RESPE

Strength in Unity or Ansanm Nou Fo [Leslie VOLTAIRE]

Struggling People's Organization or OPL [Jacques-Edouard ALEXIS]

Truth (Verite)

Union [Chavannes JEUNE]

Unity or Inite [Levaillant LOUIS-JEUNE] (coalition that includes Front for Hope or L'ESPWA)

Vigilance or Veye Yo [Lavarice GAUDIN]

Political pressure groups and leaders: Haitian Self-Employed Workers Union or CATH [Fignole ST-CYR]

Confederation of Haitian Workers or CTH

Private Sector Economic Forum or PSEF [Reginald BOULOS]

Federation of Workers Trade Unions or FOS

General Organization of Independent Haitian Workers or OGITH [Patrick NUMAS]

Grand-Anse Resistance Committee or KOREGA

Haitian Association of Industries or ADIH [Georges SASSINE]

National Popular Assembly or APN

Papaye Peasants Movement or MPP [Chavannes JEAN-BAPTISTE]

Popular Organizations Gathering Power or PROP

Protestant Federation of Haiti

Roman Catholic Church

International organization participation: ACP, AOSIS, Caricom, CD, CDB, CELAC, FAO, G-77, IADB, IAEA, IBRD, ICAO, ICC (NGOs), ICRM, IDA, IFAD, IFC, IFRCS, ILO, IMF, IMO, Interpol, IOC, IOM, IPU, ITSO, ITU, ITUC (NGOs), LAES, MIGA, NAM, OAS, OIF, OPANAL, OPCW, PCA, Petrocaribe, UN, UNCTAD, UNESCO, UNIDO, Union Latina, UNWTO, UPU, WCO, WFTU (NGOs), WHO, WIPO, WMO, WTO

Diplomatic representation in the US: *chief of mission:* Ambassador Paul Getty ALTIDOR (since 2 May 2012)

chancery: 2311 Massachusetts Avenue NW, Washington, DC 20008

telephone: [1] (202) 332-4090

FAX: [1] (202) 745-7215

consulate(s) general: Atlanta, Boston, Chicago, Miami, Orlando (FL), New York, San Juan (Puerto Rico)

Diplomatic representation from the US: *chief of mission:* Ambassador (vacant); Charge d'Affaires Robin DIALLO (since August 2017)

embassy: Tabarre 41, Route de Tabarre, Port-au-Prince

mailing address: (in Haiti) P.O. Box 1634, Port-au-Prince, Haiti; (from abroad) 3400 Port-au-Prince, State Department, Washington, DC 20521-3400

telephone: [509] 2229-8000

FAX: [509] 229-8028

Flag description: two equal horizontal bands of blue (top) and red with a centered white rectangle bearing the coat of arms, which contains a palm tree flanked by flags and two cannons above a scroll bearing the motto L'UNION FAIT LA FORCE (Union Makes Strength); the colors are taken from the French Tricolor and represent the union of blacks and mulattoes

National symbol(s): Hispaniolan trogon (bird), hibiscus flower; national colors: blue, red

National anthem: name: "La Dessalinienne" (The Dessalines Song)

lyrics/music: Justin LHERISSON/Nicolas GEFFRARD

note: adopted 1904; named for Jean-Jacques DESSALINES, a leader in the Haitian Revolution and first ruler of an independent Haiti

ECONOMY

Economy—overview: Haiti is a free market economy with low labor costs and tariff-free access to the US for many of its exports. Two-fifths of all Haitians depend on the agricultural sector, mainly small-scale subsistence farming, which remains vulnerable to damage from frequent natural disasters. Poverty, corruption, vulnerability to natural disasters, and low levels of education for much of the population represent some of the most serious impediments to Haiti's economic growth. Remittances are the primary source of foreign exchange, equivalent to more than a quarter of GDP, and nearly double the combined value of Haitian exports and foreign direct investment.

Currently the poorest country in the Western Hemisphere, with close to 60% of the population living under the national poverty line, Haiti's GDP growth rose to 5.5% in 2011 as the Haitian economy began recovering from the devastating January 2010 earthquake that destroyed much of its capital city, Port-au-Prince, and neighboring areas. However, growth slowed to below 2% in 2015 and 2016 as political uncertainty, drought conditions, decreasing foreign aid, and the depreciation of the national currency took a toll on investment and economic growth. Hurricane Matthew, the fiercest Caribbean storm in nearly a decade, made landfall in Haiti on 4 October 2016, with 140 mile-per-hour winds, creating a new humanitarian emergency. An estimated 2.1 million people were affected by the category 4 storm, which caused extensive damage to crops, houses, livestock, and infrastructure across Haiti's southern peninsula.

US economic engagement under the Caribbean Basin Trade Partnership Act (CBTPA) and the 2008 Haitian Hemispheric Opportunity through Partnership Encouragement Act (HOPE II) have contributed to an increase in apparel exports and investment by providing duty-free access to the US. The Haiti Economic Lift Program (HELP) Act of 2010 extended the CBTPA and HOPE II until 2020, while the Trade Preferences Extension Act of 2015 extended trade benefits provided to Haiti in the HOPE and HELP Acts through September 2025. Apparel sector exports in 2016 reached approximately $850 million and account for over 90% of Haitian exports and more than 10% of the GDP.

Investment in Haiti is hampered by the difficulty of doing business and weak infrastructure, including access to electricity. Haiti's outstanding external debt was cancelled by donor countries following the 2010 earthquake, but has since risen to $2.6 billion as of December 2017, the majority of which is owed to Venezuela under the PetroCaribe program. Although the government has increased its revenue collection, it continues to rely on formal international economic assistance for fiscal sustainability, with over 20% of its annual budget coming from foreign aid or direct budget support.

GDP (purchasing power parity): $19.88 billion (2017 est.)

$19.69 billion (2016 est.)

$19.41 billion (2015 est.)

note: data are in 2017 dollars

country comparison to the world: 149

GDP (official exchange rate): $8.36 billion (2016 est.)

GDP—real growth rate: 1% (2017 est.)

1.4% (2016 est.)

1.2% (2015 est.)

country comparison to the world: 186

GDP—per capita (PPP): $1,800 (2017 est.)

$1,800 (2016 est.)

$1,800 (2015 est.)

note: data are in 2017 dollars

country comparison to the world: 214

Gross national saving: 28.2% of GDP (2017 est.)
29.3% of GDP (2016 est.)
29.3% of GDP (2015 est.)
country comparison to the world: 33

GDP—composition, by end use:
household consumption: 99.1%
government consumption: 10%
investment in fixed capital: 32.6%
investment in inventories: -1.4%
exports of goods and services: 20%
imports of goods and services: -60.3%
note: figure for household consumption also
includes government consumption (2017 est.)

GDP—composition, by sector of origin:
agriculture: 21.9%
industry: 20.8%
services: 57.3% (2017 est.)

Agriculture—products: coffee, mangoes, cocoa,
sugarcane, rice, corn, sorghum; wood, vetiver

Industries: textiles, sugar refining, flour milling,
cement, light assembly using imported parts

Industrial production growth rate: 4% (2017 est.)
country comparison to the world: 67

Labor force: 4.594 million
note: shortage of skilled labor, unskilled labor
abundant (2014 est.)
country comparison to the world: 89

Labor force—by occupation: *agriculture:* 38.1%
industry: 11.5%
services: 50.4% (2010)

Unemployment rate: 40.6% (2010 est.)
note: widespread unemployment and underemployment; more than two-thirds of the labor force
do not have formal jobs
country comparison to the world: 212

Population below poverty line: 58.5% (2012 est.)

**Household income or consumption by percentage
share:** *lowest 10%:* 0.7%
highest 10%: 47.7% (2001)

Distribution of family income—Gini index: 60.8
(2012)
59.2 (2001)
country comparison to the world: 5

Budget: *revenues:* $1.58 billion
expenditures: $2.251 billion (2017 est.)
Taxes and other revenues: 18.9% of GDP (2017
est.)
country comparison to the world: 162

Budget surplus (+) or deficit (-): -8% of GDP
(2017 est.)
country comparison to the world: 197

Public debt: 33.5% of GDP (2016 est.)
30.2% of GDP (2015 est.)
country comparison to the world: 149

Fiscal year: 1 October–30 September

Inflation rate (consumer prices): 14.7% (2017
est.)
13.4% (2016 est.)
country comparison to the world: 212

Commercial bank prime lending rate: 14% (31
December 2017 est.)

13.23% (31 December 2016 est.)
country comparison to the world: 50

Stock of narrow money: $1.258 billion (31 Decem-
ber 2017 est.)
$1.049 billion (31 December 2016 est.)
country comparison to the world: 150

Stock of broad money: $2.155 billion (31 Decem-
ber 2017 est.)
$1.742 billion (31 December 2016 est.)
country comparison to the world: 155

Stock of domestic credit: $3.178 billion (31
December 2017 est.)
$2.253 billion (31 December 2016 est.)
country comparison to the world: 144

Market value of publicly traded shares: $NA

Current account balance: -$91 million (2017 est.)
-$72 million (2016 est.)
country comparison to the world: 78

Exports: $960.1 million (2017 est.)
$995 million (2016 est.)
country comparison to the world: 161

Exports—commodities: apparel, manufactures,
oils, cocoa, mangoes, coffee

Exports—partners: US 80.8%, Dominican Republic 5.1% (2016)

Imports: $3.621 billion (2017 est.)
$3.183 billion (2016 est.)
country comparison to the world: 136

Imports—commodities: food, manufactured
goods, machinery and transport equipment, fuels,
raw materials

Imports—partners: US 19.3%, China 18.9%,
Netherlands Antilles 18.1%, Indonesia 6.5%,
Colombia 4.8% (2016)

Reserves of foreign exchange and gold: $2.044
billion (31 December 2017 est.)
$2.11 billion (31 December 2016 est.)
country comparison to the world: 119

Debt—external: $2.607 billion (31 December
2017 est.)
$2.17 billion (31 December 2016 est.)
country comparison to the world: 148

Stock of direct foreign investment—at home:
$1.46 billion (31 December 2017 est.)
$1.37 billion (31 December 2016 est.)
country comparison to the world: 117

Exchange rates: gourdes (HTG) per US dollar—
65.21 (2017 est.)
63.34 (2016 est.)
63.34 (2015 est.)
50.71 (2014 est.)
45.22 (2013 est.)

ENERGY

Electricity access: *population without electricity:* 7,400,000
electrification—*total population:* 38%
electrification—urban areas: 72%
electrification—rural areas: 15% (2013)

Electricity—production: 979.7 million kWh (2015
est.)
country comparison to the world: 152

Electricity—consumption: 371.7 million kWh
(2015 est.)
country comparison to the world: 177

Electricity—exports: 0 kWh (2016 est.)
country comparison to the world: 148

Electricity—imports: 0 kWh (2016 est.)
country comparison to the world: 160

Electricity—installed generating capacity:
313,000 kW (2016 est.)
country comparison to the world: 156

Electricity—from fossil fuels: 80.9% of total
installed capacity (2015 est.)
country comparison to the world: 84

Electricity—from nuclear fuels: 0% of total
installed capacity (2015 est.)
country comparison to the world: 106

Electricity—from hydroelectric plants: 18.8% of
total installed capacity (2015 est.)
country comparison to the world: 94

Electricity—from other renewable sources: 0.3%
of total installed capacity (2015 est.)
country comparison to the world: 158

Crude oil—production: 0 bbl/day (2016 est.)
country comparison to the world: 146

Crude oil—exports: 0 bbl/day (2014 est.)
country comparison to the world: 135

Crude oil—imports: 0 bbl/day (2014 est.)
country comparison to the world: 138

Crude oil—proved reserves: 0 bbl (1 January 2017
es)
country comparison to the world: 145

Refined petroleum products—production: 0 bbl/
day (2014 est.)
country comparison to the world: 156

Refined petroleum products—consumption:
19,000 bbl/day (2015 est.)
country comparison to the world: 140

Refined petroleum products—exports: 0 bbl/day
(2014 est.)
country comparison to the world: 165

Refined petroleum products—imports: 19,020 bbl/
day (2014 est.)
country comparison to the world: 120

Natural gas—production: 0 cu m (2013 est.)
country comparison to the world: 147

Natural gas—consumption: 0 cu m (2013 est.)
country comparison to the world: 192

Natural gas—exports: 0 cu m (2013 est.)
country comparison to the world: 119

Natural gas—imports: 0 cu m (2013 est.)
country comparison to the world: 137

Natural gas—proved reserves: 0 cu m (1 January
2014 es)
country comparison to the world: 150

**Carbon dioxide emissions from consumption of
energy:** 2.1 million Mt (2013 est.)
country comparison to the world: 148

COMMUNICATIONS

Telephones—fixed lines: *total subscriptions:*
5,692

subscriptions per 100 inhabitants: less than 1 (July 2016 est.)
country comparison to the world: 167

Telephones—mobile cellular: total: 6,504,010
subscriptions per 100 inhabitants: 62 (July 2016 est.)
country comparison to the world: 107

Telephone system: general assessment: telecommunications infrastructure is among the least-developed in Latin America and the Caribbean; domestic cell service is functional
domestic: mobile-cellular telephone services have expanded greatly in the last five years due to low-cost GSM phones and pay-as-you-go plans; mobile-cellular teledensity is over 60 per 100 persons
international: country code—509; satellite earth station—1 Intelsat (Atlantic Ocean) (2016)

Broadcast media: 130 television stations throughout the country, including 1 government-owned; cable TV subscription service available; 495 radio stations (of them, only 135 are licensed), including 1 government-owned; more than 250 private and community radio stations; over 50 FM stations in Port-au-Prince alone (2015)

Internet country code: .ht
Internet users: total: 1,282,686

percent of population: 12.2% (July 2016 est.)
country comparison to the world: 119

TRANSPORTATION

National air transport system: number of registered air carriers: 1
inventory of registered aircraft operated by air carriers: 1 (2015)
Civil aircraft registration country code prefix: HH (2016)

Airports: 14 (2013)
country comparison to the world: 148

Airports—with paved runways: total: 4
2,438 to 3,047 m: 2
914 to 1,523 m: 2 (2017)

Airports—with unpaved runways: total: 10
914 to 1,523 m: 2
under 914 m: 8 (2013)

Roadways: total: 4,266 km
paved: 768 km
unpaved: 3,498 km (2009)
country comparison to the world: 155

Merchant marine: total: 4
by type: general cargo 3, other 1 (2017)
country comparison to the world: 160

Ports and terminals: major seaport(s): Cap-Haitien, Gonaives, Jacmel, Port-au-Prince

MILITARY AND SECURITY

Military branches: no regular military forces—small Coast Guard; a Ministry of National Defense established May 2012; the regular Haitian Armed Forces (FAdH)—Army, Navy, and Air Force—have been demobilized but still exist on paper until or unless they are constitutionally abolished (2011)

TRANSNATIONAL ISSUES

Disputes—international: since 2004, peacekeepers from the UN Stabilization Mission in Haiti have assisted in maintaining civil order in Haiti; the mission currently includes 6,685 military, 2,607 police, and 443 civilian personnel; despite efforts to control illegal migration, Haitians cross into the Dominican Republic and sail to neighboring countries; Haiti claims US-administered Navassa Island
Refugees and internally displaced persons: IDPs: 37,667 (includes only IDPs from the 2010 earthquake living in camps or camp-like situations; information is lacking about IDPs living outside of camps or who have left camps) (2017)
stateless persons: 2,302 (2016)
note: stateless persons are individuals without a nationality who were born in the Dominican Republic prior to January 2010

Trafficking in persons: current situation: Haiti is a source, transit, and destination country for men,

women, and children subjected to forced labor and sex trafficking; most of Haiti's trafficking cases involve children in domestic servitude vulnerable to physical and sexual abuse; dismissed and runaway child domestic servants often end up in prostitution, begging, or street crime; other exploited populations included low-income Haitians, child laborers, and women and children living in IDP camps dating to the 2010 earthquake; Haitian adults are vulnerable to fraudulent labor recruitment abroad and, along with children, may be subjected to forced labor in the Dominican Republic, elsewhere in the Caribbean, South America, and the US; Dominicans are exploited in sex trafficking and forced labor in Haiti

tier rating: Tier 2 Watch List – Haiti does not fully comply with the minimum standards for the elimination of trafficking; however, it is making significant efforts to do so; in 2014, Haiti was granted a waiver from an otherwise required downgrade to Tier 3 because its government has a written plan that, if implemented would constitute making significant efforts to bring itself into compliance with the minimum standards for the elimination of trafficking; in 2014, Haiti developed a national anti-trafficking action plan and enacted a law prohibiting all forms of human trafficking, although judicial corruption hampered its implementation; progress was made in investigating and prosecuting suspected traffickers, but no convictions were made; the government sustained limited efforts to identify and refer victims to protective services, which were provided mostly by NGOs without government support; campaigns to raise awareness about child labor and child trafficking continued (2015)

Illicit drugs: Caribbean transshipment point for cocaine en route to the US and Europe; substantial bulk cash smuggling activity; Colombian narcotics traffickers favor Haiti for illicit financial transactions; pervasive corruption; significant consumer of cannabis

HEARD ISLAND AND MCDONALD ISLANDS

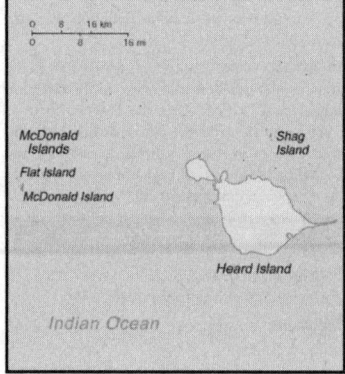

INTRODUCTION

Background: The UK transferred these uninhabited, barren, sub-Antarctic islands to Australia in 1947. Populated by large numbers of seal and bird species, the islands have been designated a nature preserve.

GEOGRAPHY

Location: islands in the Indian Ocean, about two-thirds of the way from Madagascar to Antarctica
Geographic coordinates: 53 06 S, 72 31 E
Map references: Antarctic Region
Area: total: 412 sq km

land: 412 sq km
water: 0 sq km
country comparison to the world: 203

Area—comparative: slightly more than two times the size of Washington, DC

Land boundaries: 0 km

Coastline: 101.9 km

Maritime claims: territorial sea: 12 nm
exclusive fishing zone: 200 nm

Climate: antarctic

Terrain: Heard Island—80% ice-covered, bleak and mountainous, dominated by a large massif (Big Ben) and an active volcano (Mawson Peak); McDonald Islands—small and rocky

Elevation: *mean elevation:* NA

elevation extremes: *lowest point:* Indian Ocean 0 m

highest point: Mawson Peak on Big Ben volcano 2,745 m

Natural resources: fish

Land use: *agricultural land:* 0%
arable land: 0%;
permanent crops: 0%;
permanent pasture: 0%;
forest: 0%
other: 100% (2011 est.)

Natural hazards: Mawson Peak, an active volcano, is on Heard Island

Environment—current issues: none; uninhabited and mostly ice covered

Geography—note: Mawson Peak on Heard Island is the highest Australian mountain (at 2,745 meters, it is taller than Mt. Kosciuszko in Australia proper), and one of only two active volcanoes located in Australian territory, the other being McDonald Island; in 1992, McDonald Island broke its dormancy and began erupting; it has erupted several times since, most recently in 2005

PEOPLE AND SOCIETY

Population: uninhabited

GOVERNMENT

Country name: *conventional long form:* Territory of Heard Island and McDonald Islands
conventional short form: Heard Island and McDonald Islands
abbreviation: HIMI
etymology: named after American Captain John HEARD, who sighted the island on 25 November 1853, and American Captain William McDONALD, who discovered the islands on 4 January 1854

Dependency status: territory of Australia; administered from Canberra by the Department of Sustainability, Environment, Water, Population and Communities (Australian Antarctic Division)

Legal system: the laws of Australia, where applicable, apply

Diplomatic representation in the US: none (territory of Australia)

Diplomatic representation from the US: none (territory of Australia)

Flag description: the flag of Australia is used

ECONOMY

Economy—overview: The islands have no indigenous economic activity, but the Australian Government allows limited fishing in the surrounding waters. Visits to Heard Island typically focus on terrestrial and marine research and infrequent private expeditions.

COMMUNICATIONS

Internet country code: .hm

TRANSPORTATION

Ports and terminals: none; offshore anchorage only

MILITARY AND SECURITY

Military—note: defense is the responsibility of Australia; Australia conducts fisheries patrols

TRANSNATIONAL ISSUES

Disputes—international: none

HOLY SEE (VATICAN CITY)

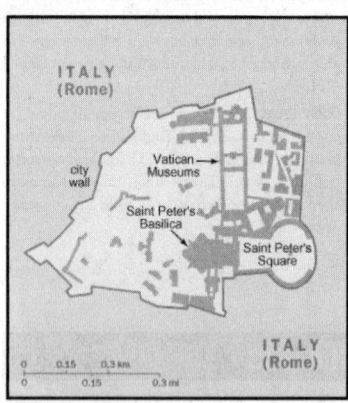

ITALY (Rome)

city wall

Vatican Museums

Saint Peter's Basilica

Saint Peter's Square

ITALY (Rome)

0   0.15   0.3 km
0   0.15   0.3 mi

INTRODUCTION

Background: Popes in their secular role ruled portions of the Italian peninsula for more than a thousand years until the mid-19th century, when many of the Papal States were seized by the newly united Kingdom of Italy. In 1870, the pope's holdings were further circumscribed when Rome itself was annexed. Disputes between a series of "prisoner" popes and Italy were resolved in 1929 by three Lateran Treaties, which established the independent state of Vatican City and granted Roman Catholicism special status in Italy. In 1984, a concordat between the Holy See and Italy modified certain of the earlier treaty provisions, including the primacy

of Roman Catholicism as the Italian state religion. Present concerns of the Holy See include religious freedom, threats against minority Christian communities in Africa and the Middle East, the plight of refugees and migrants, sexual misconduct by clergy, international development, interreligious dialogue and reconciliation, and the application of church doctrine in an era of rapid change and globalization. About 1.2 billion people worldwide profess Catholicism—the world's largest Christian faith.

GEOGRAPHY

Location: Southern Europe, an enclave of Rome (Italy)

Geographic coordinates: 41 54 N, 12 27 E

Map references: Europe

Area: *total:* 0.44 sq km
land: 0.44 sq km
water: 0 sq km
country comparison to the world: 254

Area—comparative: about 0.7 times the size of the National Mall in Washington, DC

Land boundaries: *total:* 3.4 km
border countries (1): Italy 3.4 km

Coastline: 0 km (landlocked)

Maritime claims: none (landlocked)

Climate: temperate; mild, rainy winters (September to May) with hot, dry summers (May to September)

Terrain: urban; low hill

Elevation: *mean elevation:* NA

elevation extremes: *lowest point:* Saint Peter's Square 19 m

highest point: Vatican Gardens (Vatican Hill) 78 m

Natural resources: none

Land use: *agricultural land:* 0%
arable land: 0%;
permanent crops: 0%;
permanent pasture: 0%;
forest: 0%
other: 100% (urban area) (2011 est.)

Natural hazards: occasional earthquakes

Environment—current issues: some air pollution from the surrounding city of Rome

Environment—international agreements: *party to:* Ozone Layer Protection
signed, but not ratified: Air Pollution, Environmental Modification

Geography—note: landlocked; enclave in Rome, Italy; world's smallest state; beyond the territorial boundary of Vatican City, the Lateran Treaty of 1929 grants the Holy See extraterritorial authority over 23 sites in Rome and five outside of Rome, including the Pontifical Palace at Castel Gandolfo (the Pope's summer residence)

PEOPLE AND SOCIETY

Population: 1,000 (2017 est.)
country comparison to the world: 235

Nationality: *noun:* none
adjective: none

Ethnic groups: Italian, Swiss, Argentinian, and other nationalities from around the world (2017)

Languages: Italian, Latin, French, various other languages

Religions: Roman Catholic

Population growth rate: 0% (2014 est.)
country comparison to the world: 193

Urbanization: *urban population:* 100% of total population (2017)
rate of urbanization: 0.1% annual rate of change (2015-20 est.)

Major urban areas—population: VATICAN CITY (capital) 1,000 (2014)

HIV/AIDS—adult prevalence rate: NA

HIV/AIDS—people living with HIV/AIDS: NA

HIV/AIDS—deaths: NA

Education expenditures: NA

GOVERNMENT

Country name: *conventional long form:* The Holy See (Vatican City State)
conventional short form: Holy See (Vatican City)
local long form: La Santa Sede (Stato della Citta del Vaticano)
local short form: Santa Sede (Citta del Vaticano)
etymology: "holy" comes from the Greek word "hera" meaning "sacred"; "see" comes from the Latin word "sedes" meaning "seat," and refers to the episcopal chair; the term "Vatican" derives from the hill Mons Vaticanus on which the Vatican is located and which comes from the Latin "vaticinari" (to prophecy), referring to the fortune tellers and soothsayers who frequented the area in Roman times

Government type: ecclesiastical elective monarchy; self-described as an "absolute monarchy"

Capital: *name:* Vatican City

geographic coordinates: 41 54 N, 12 27 E
time difference: UTC+1 (6 hours ahead of Washington, DC, during Standard Time)
daylight saving time: +1hr, begins last Sunday in March; ends last Sunday in October

Administrative divisions: none

Independence: 11 February 1929; note—the three treaties signed with Italy on 11 February 1929 acknowledged, among other things, the full sovereignty of the Holy See and established its territorial extent; however, the origin of the Papal States, which over centuries varied considerably in extent, may be traced back to A.D. 754

National holiday: Election Day of Pope FRANCIS, 13 March (2013)

Constitution: history: previous 1929, 1963; latest adopted 26 November 2000, effective 22 February 2001 (Fundamental Law of Vatican City State); note—in October 2013, Pope Francis instituted a 9-member Council of Cardinal Advisors to reform the administrative apparatus of the Holy See (Roman Curia) to include writing a new constitution

amendments: note—although the Fundamental Law of Vatican City State makes no mention of amendments, Article Four (drafting laws), states that this legislative responsibility resides with the Pontifical Commission for Vatican City State; draft legislation is submitted through the Secretariat of State and considered by the pope (2016)

Legal system: religious legal system based on canon (religious) law

International law organization participation: has not submitted an ICJ jurisdiction declaration; non-party state to the ICCt

Citizenship: *citizenship by birth:* no
citizenship by descent: no
dual citizenship recognized: no
residency requirement for naturalization: not applicable
note: in the Holy See, citizenship is acquired by law, ex iure, or by adminstrative decision; in the first instance, citizenship is a function of holding office within the Holy See as in the case of cardinals resident in Vatican City or diplomats of the Holy See; in the second instance, citizenship may be requested in a limited set of circumstances for those who reside within Vatican City under papal authorization, as a function of their office or service, or as the spouses and children of current citizens; citizenship is lost once an individual no longer permanently resides in Vatican City, normally reverting to the citizenship previously held

Suffrage: election of the pope is limited to cardinals less than 80 years old

Executive branch: *chief of state:* Pope FRANCIS (since 13 March 2013)

head of government: Secretary of State Cardinal Pietro PAROLIN (since 15 October 2013); note—Head of Government of Vatican City is President Cardinal Giuseppe BERTELLO (since 1 October 2011)
cabinet: Pontifical Commission for the State of Vatican City appointed by the pope
elections/appointments: pope elected by the College of Cardinals, usually for life or until voluntary resignation; election last held on 13 March 2013 (next to be held after the death or resignation of the current pope); Secretary of State appointed by the pope
election results: Jorge Mario BERGOGLIO, former Archbishop of Buenos Aires, elected Pope FRANCIS

Legislative branch: *description:* unicameral Pontifical Commission for Vatican City State or Pontificia Commissione per lo Stato della Citta del Vaticano (7 seats; members appointed by the pope to serve 5-year terms)
elections: last held on 1 June 2013

Judicial branch: *highest court(s):* Supreme Court or Supreme Tribunal of the Apostolic Signatura (consists of the cardinal prefect, who serves as ex-officio president of the court, and 2 other cardinals of the Prefect Signatura); note—judicial duties were established by the Motu Proprio, papal directive, of Pope PIUS XII on 1 May 1946; most

Vatican City criminal matters are handled by the Republic of Italy courts
judge selection and term of office: cardinal prefect appointed by the pope; the other 2 cardinals of the court appointed by the cardinal prefect on a yearly basis
subordinate courts: Appellate Court of Vatican City; Tribunal of Vatican City

Political parties and leaders: none

Political pressure groups and leaders: none (exclusive of influence exercised by church officers)

International organization participation: CE (observer), IAEA, Interpol, IOM, ITSO, ITU, ITUC (NGOs), OAS (observer), OPCW, OSCE, Schengen Convention (de facto member), SICA (observer), UN (observer), UNCTAD, UNHCR, Union Latina (observer), UNWTO (observer), UPU, WIPO, WTO (observer)

Diplomatic representation in the US: *chief of mission:* Apostolic Nuncio Archbishop Christophe PIERRE (since 27 June 2016)
chancery: 3339 Massachusetts Avenue NW, Washington, DC 20008
telephone: [1] (202) 333-7121
FAX: [1] (202) 337-4036

Diplomatic representation from the US: *chief of mission:* Ambassador Callista GINGRICH (since 22 December 2017)
embassy: American Embassy to the Holy See, Via Sallustiana, 49, 00187 Rome, Italy
mailing address: Unit 5660, Box 66, DPO AE 09624-0066
telephone: [39] (06) 4674-1
FAX: [39] (06) 4674-3412

Flag description: two vertical bands of yellow (hoist side) and white with the arms of the Holy See, consisting of the crossed keys of Saint Peter surmounted by the three-tiered papal tiara, centered in the white band; the yellow color represents the pope's spiritual power, the white his worldly power

National symbol(s): crossed keys beneath a papal tiara; national colors: yellow, white

National anthem: name: "Inno e Marcia Pontificale" (Hymn and Pontifical March); often called The Pontifical Hymn
lyrics/music: Raffaello LAVAGNA/Charles-Francois GOUNOD
note: adopted 1950

ECONOMY

Economy—overview: The Holy See is supported financially by a variety of sources, including investments, real estate income, and donations from Catholic individuals, dioceses, and institutions; these help fund the Roman Curia (Vatican bureaucracy), diplomatic missions, and media outlets. Moreover, an annual collection taken up in dioceses and from direct donations go to a non-budgetary fund, known as Peter's Pence, which is used directly by the pope for charity, disaster relief, and aid to churches in developing nations.

The separate Vatican City State budget includes the Vatican museums and post office and is supported financially by the sale of stamps, coins, medals, and tourist mementos as well as fees for admission to museums and publication sales. Revenues increased between 2010 and 2011 because of expanded operating hours and a growing number of visitors. However, the Holy See did not escape the financial difficulties experienced by other European countries; in 2012, it started a spending review to determine where to cut costs to reverse its 2011 budget deficit of $20 million. The Holy See generated a modest surplus in 2012 before recording a $32 million deficit in 2013, driven primarily by the decreasing value of gold. The incomes and living standards of lay workers are comparable to those of counterparts who work in the city of Rome so most public expenditures go to wages and other personnel costs;. In February 2014, Pope FRANCIS created the Secretariat of the Economy to oversee financial and administrative operations of the Holy See, part of a broader campaign to reform the Holy See's finances.

GDP (purchasing power parity): $NA

Industries: printing; production of coins, medals, postage stamps; mosaics, staff uniforms; worldwide banking and financial activities

Labor force: 4,822 (2016)
country comparison to the world: 222
Labor force—by occupation: note: essentially services with a small amount of industry; nearly all dignitaries, priests, nuns, guards, and the approximately 3,000 lay workers live outside the Vatican

Population below poverty line: NA%

Budget: *revenues:* $315 million
expenditures: $348 million (2013)
Taxes and other revenues: NA%

Budget surplus (+) or deficit (-): NA%

Fiscal year: calendar year

Exchange rates: euros (EUR) per US dollar—
0.906 (2017 est.)
0.9214 (2016 est.)
0.9214 (2015 est.)
0.885 (2014 est.)
0.7634 (2013 est.)

COMMUNICATIONS

Telephone system: *general assessment:* automatic digital exchange
domestic: connected via fiber-optic cable to Telecom Italia network
international: country code—39; uses Italian system (2015)

Broadcast media: the Vatican Television Center (CTV) transmits live broadcasts of the Pope's Sunday and Wednesday audiences, as well as the Pope's public celebrations; CTV also produces documentaries; Vatican Radio is the Holy See's official broadcasting service broadcasting via shortwave, AM and FM frequencies, and via satellite and Internet connections (2017)

Internet country code: .va

MILITARY AND SECURITY

Military branches: Pontifical Swiss Guard Corps (Corpo della Guardia Svizzera Pontificia) (2013)

Military service age and obligation: Pontifical Swiss Guard Corps (Corpo della Guardia Svizzera Pontificia): 19-30 years of age for voluntary military service; no conscription; must be Roman Catholic, a Swiss citizen, with a secondary education (2013)

Military—note: defense is the responsibility of Italy; ceremonial and limited security duties performed by Pontifical Swiss Guard

TRANSNATIONAL ISSUES

Disputes—international: none

HONDURAS

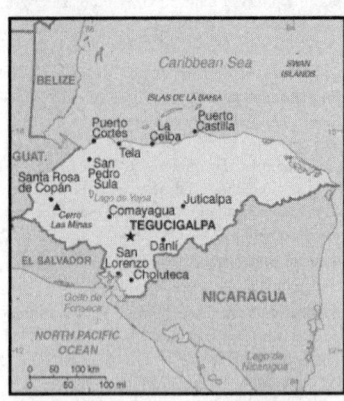

INTRODUCTION

Background: Once part of Spain's vast empire in the New World, Honduras became an independent nation in 1821. After two and a half decades of mostly military rule, a freely elected civilian government came to power in 1982. During the 1980s, Honduras proved a haven for anti-Sandinista contras fighting the Marxist Nicaraguan Government and an ally to Salvadoran Government forces fighting leftist guerrillas. The country was devastated by Hurricane Mitch in 1998, which killed about 5,600 people and caused approximately $2 billion in damage. Since then, the economy has slowly rebounded.

GEOGRAPHY

Location: Central America, bordering the Caribbean Sea, between Guatemala and Nicaragua and bordering the Gulf of Fonseca (North Pacific Ocean), between El Salvador and Nicaragua

Geographic coordinates: 15 00 N, 86 30 W

Map references: Central America and the Caribbean

Area: *total:* 112,090 sq km
land: 111,890 sq km
water: 200 sq km
country comparison to the world: 104

Area—comparative: slightly larger than Tennessee

Land boundaries: *total:* 1,575 km
border countries (3): Guatemala 244 km, El Salvador 391 km, Nicaragua 940 km

Coastline: 823 km (Caribbean Sea 669 km, Gulf of Fonseca 163 km)

Maritime claims: *territorial sea:* 12 nm
contiguous zone: 24 nm
exclusive economic zone: 200 nm
continental shelf: natural extension of territory or to 200 nm

Climate: subtropical in lowlands, temperate in mountains

Terrain: mostly mountains in interior, narrow coastal plains

Elevation: *mean elevation:* 684 m

elevation extremes: *lowest point:* Caribbean Sea 0 m
highest point: Cerro Las Minas 2,870 m

Natural resources: timber, gold, silver, copper, lead, zinc, iron ore, antimony, coal, fish, hydropower

Land use: *agricultural land:* 28.8%
arable land: 9.1%;
permanent crops: 4%;
permanent pasture: 15.7%
forest: 45.3%
other: 25.9% (2011 est.)
Irrigated land: 900 sq km (2012)

Population—distribution: most residents live in the mountainous western half of the country; unlike other Central American nations, Honduras is the only one with an urban population that is distributed between two large centers—the capital of Tegucigalpa and the city of San Pedro Sula; the Rio Ulua valley in the north is the only densely populated lowland area

Natural hazards: frequent, but generally mild, earthquakes; extremely susceptible to damaging hurricanes and floods along the Caribbean coast

Environment—current issues: urban population expanding; deforestation results from logging and the clearing of land for agricultural purposes; further land degradation and soil erosion hastened by uncontrolled development and improper land use practices such as farming of marginal lands; mining activities polluting Lago de Yojoa (the country's largest source of fresh water), as well as several rivers and streams, with heavy metals

Environment—international agreements: *party to:* Biodiversity, Climate Change, Climate Change-Kyoto Protocol, Desertification, Endangered Species, Hazardous Wastes, Law of the Sea, Marine Dumping, Ozone Layer Protection, Ship Pollution, Tropical Timber 83, Tropical Timber 94, Wetlands *signed, but not ratified:* none of the selected agreements

Geography—note: has only a short Pacific coast but a long Caribbean shoreline, including the virtually uninhabited eastern Mosquito Coast

PEOPLE AND SOCIETY

Population: 9,038,741
note: estimates for this country explicitly take into account the effects of excess mortality due to AIDS; this can result in lower life expectancy, higher infant mortality, higher death rates, lower population growth rates, and changes in the distribution of population by age and sex than would otherwise be expected (July 2017 est.)
country comparison to the world: 94

Nationality: *noun:* Honduran(s)
adjective: Honduran

Ethnic groups: mestizo (mixed Amerindian and European) 90%, Amerindian 7%, black 2%, white 1%

Languages: Spanish (official), Amerindian dialects

Religions: Roman Catholic 46%, Protestant 41%, atheist 1%, other 2%, none 9% (2014 est.)

Demographic profile: Honduras is one of the poorest countries in Latin America and has the one of the world's highest murder rates. More than half of the population lives in poverty and per capita income is one of the lowest in the region. Poverty rates are higher among rural and indigenous people and in the south, west, and along the eastern border than in the north and central areas where most of Honduras' industries and infrastructure are concentrated. The increased productivity needed to break Honduras' persistent high poverty rate depends, in part, on further improvements in educational attainment. Although primary-school enrollment is near 100%, educational quality is poor, the drop-out rate and grade repetition remain high, and teacher and school accountability is low.

Honduras' population growth rate has slowed since the 1990s, but it remains high at nearly 2% annually because the birth rate averages approximately three children per woman and more among rural, indigenous, and poor women. Consequently, Honduras' young adult population—ages 15 to 29—is projected to continue growing rapidly for the next three decades and then stabilize or slowly shrink. Population growth and limited job prospects outside of agriculture will continue to drive emigration. Remittances represent about a fifth of GDP.

Age structure: *0-14 years:* 32.95% (male 1,521,300/female 1,456,727)
15-24 years: 21% (male 968,013/female 930,060)

25-54 years: 36.63% (male 1,675,574/female 1,635,241)
55-64 years: 5.13% (male 218,342/female 245,447)
65 years and over: 4.29% (male 167,957/female 220,080) (2017 est.)

Dependency ratios: *total dependency ratio:* 59.8
youth dependency ratio: 52.7
elderly dependency ratio: 7.1
potential support ratio: 14.2 (2015 est.)

Median age: *total:* 23 years
male: 22.6 years
female: 23.3 years (2017 est.)
country comparison to the world: 174

Population growth rate: 1.6% (2017 est.)
country comparison to the world: 67

Birth rate: 22.4 births/1,000 population (2017 est.)
country comparison to the world: 68

Death rate: 5.3 deaths/1,000 population (2017 est.)
country comparison to the world: 184

Net migration rate: -1.1 migrant(s)/1,000 population (2017 est.)
country comparison to the world: 141

Population distribution: most residents live in the mountainous western half of the country; unlike other Central American nations, Honduras is the only one with an urban population that is distributed between two large centers—the capital of Tegucigalpa and the city of San Pedro Sula; the Rio Ulua valley in the north is the only densely populated lowland area

Urbanization: *urban population:* 55.9% of total population (2017)
rate of urbanization: 2.85% annual rate of change (2015-20 est.)

Major urban areas—population: TEGUCIGALPA (capital) 1.123 million; San Pedro Sula 852,000 (2015)

Sex ratio: *at birth:* 1.05 male(s)/female
0-14 years: 1.04 male(s)/female
15-24 years: 1.04 male(s)/female
25-54 years: 1.02 male(s)/female
55-64 years: 0.88 male(s)/female
65 years and over: 0.77 male(s)/female
total population: 1.01 male(s)/female (2016 est.)

Mother's mean age at first birth: 20.4 years
note: median age a first birth among women 25-29 (2011/12 est.)

Maternal mortality ratio: 129 deaths/100,000 live births (2015 est.)
country comparison to the world: 65

Infant mortality rate: *total:* 17.2 deaths/1,000 live births
male: 19.4 deaths/1,000 live births
female: 14.8 deaths/1,000 live births (2017 est.)
country comparison to the world: 95

Life expectancy at birth: *total population:* 71.2 years
male: 69.5 years
female: 72.9 years (2017 est.)
country comparison to the world: 151

Total fertility rate: 2.67 children born/woman (2017 est.)
country comparison to the world: 70

Contraceptive prevalence rate: 73.2% (2011/12)

Health expenditures: 8.7% of GDP (2014)
country comparison to the world: 45

Hospital bed density: 0.7 beds/1,000 population (2012)

Drinking water source:
improved:
urban: 97.4% of population
rural: 83.8% of population
total: 91.2% of population
unimproved:
urban: 2.6% of population
rural: 16.2% of population
total: 8.8% of population (2015 est.)

Sanitation facility access:
improved:
urban: 86.7% of population
rural: 77.7% of population
total: 82.6% of population
unimproved:
urban: 13.3% of population
rural: 22.3% of population
total: 17.4% of population (2015 est.)

HIV/AIDS—adult prevalence rate: 0.4% (2016 est.)
country comparison to the world: 69

HIV/AIDS—people living with HIV/AIDS: 21,000 (2016 est.)
country comparison to the world: 75

HIV/AIDS—deaths: <1000 (2016 est.)

Major infectious diseases: *degree of risk:* high *food or waterborne diseases:* bacterial diarrhea, hepatitis A, and typhoid fever
vectorborne diseases: dengue fever and malaria
note: active local transmission of Zika virus by Aedes species mosquitoes has been identified in this country (as of August 2016); it poses an important risk (a large number of cases possible) among US citizens if bitten by an infective mosquito; other less common ways to get Zika are through sex, via blood transfusion, or during pregnancy, in which the pregnant woman passes Zika virus to her fetus (2016)

Obesity—adult prevalence rate: 21.4% (2016)
country comparison to the world: 89

Children under the age of 5 years underweight: 7.1% (2012)
country comparison to the world: 76

Education expenditures: 5.9% of GDP (2013)

Literacy: *definition:* age 15 and over can read and write
total population: 89%
male: 89%
female: 88.9% (2015 est.)

School life expectancy (primary to tertiary education): *total:* 11 years
male: 11 years
female: 12 years (2014)

Unemployment, youth ages 15-24: *total:* 14.2%
male: 7.6%

female: 25.6% (2015 est.)
country comparison to the world: 113

GOVERNMENT

Country name: *conventional long form:* Republic of Honduras
conventional short form: Honduras
local long form: Republica de Honduras
local short form: Honduras
etymology: the name means "depths" in Spanish and refers to the deep anchorage in the northern Bay of Trujillo

Government type: presidential republic

Capital: *name:* Tegucigalpa

geographic coordinates: 14 06 N, 87 13 W
time difference: UTC-6 (1 hour behind Washington, DC during Standard Time)

Administrative divisions: 18 departments (departamentos, singular—departamento); Atlantida, Choluteca, Colon, Comayagua, Copan, Cortes, El Paraiso, Francisco Morazan, Gracias a Dios, Intibuca, Islas de la Bahia, La Paz, Lempira, Ocotepeque, Olancho, Santa Barbara, Valle, Yoro

Independence: 15 September 1821 (from Spain)

National holiday: Independence Day, 15 September (1821)

Constitution: several previous; latest approved 11 January 1982, effective 20 January 1982; amended many times, last in 2012; note—in 2015, the Honduran Supreme Court struck down several constitutional articles on presidential term limits (2016)

Legal system: civil law system

International law organization participation: accepts compulsory ICJ jurisdiction with reservations; accepts ICCt jurisdiction

Citizenship: *citizenship by birth:* yes
citizenship by descent: yes
dual citizenship recognized: yes
residency requirement for naturalization: 1 to 3 years

Suffrage: 18 years of age; universal and compulsory

Executive branch: *chief of state:* President Juan Orlando HERNANDEZ Alvarado (since 27 January 2014); Vice Presidents Ricardo ALVAREZ, Rossana GUEVARA, and Lorena HERRERA (since 27 January 2014); note—the president is both chief of state and head of government

head of government: President Juan Orlando HERNANDEZ Alvarado (since 27 January 2014); Vice Presidents Ricardo ALVAREZ, Rossana GUEVARA, and Lorena HERRERA (since 27 January 2014)

cabinet: Cabinet appointed by president
elections/appointments: president directly elected by simple majority popular vote for a single 4-year term; election last held on 26 November 2017 (next to be held in November 2021); note—in 2015, the Constitutional Chamber of the Honduran Supreme Court struck down the constitutional provisions on presidential term limits
election results: Juan Orlando HERNANDEZ Alvarado reelected president; percent of vote Juan

Orlando HERNANDEZ Alvarado (PNH) 43%, Salvador NASRALLA (Alliance Against the Dictatorship) 41.4%, Luis Orlando ZELAYA Medrano (PL) 14.7%, other .9%

Legislative branch: *description:* unicameral National Congress or Congreso Nacional (128 seats; members directly elected in multi-seat constituencies by proportional representation vote; members serve 4-year terms)
elections: last held on 24 November 2013 (next to be held on 26 November 2017)
election results: percent of vote by party—PNH 33.6%, LIBRE 27.5%, PL 17.0%, PAC 15.2%, PINU 1.9%, UD 1.7%, DC 1.6%, other 1.5%; seats by party—PNH 48, LIBRE 37, PL 27, PAC 13, PINU 1, UD 1, DC 1; note—seats by party as of 6 January 2016—PNH 49, PL 27, LIBRE 31, PAC 13, VAMOS 4, PINU 1, UD 1, independents 2

Judicial branch: *highest court(s):* Supreme Court of Justice or Corte Suprema de Justicia (15 principal judges—including the court president—and 7 alternates; court organized into civil, criminal, constitutional, and labor chambers); note—the court has both judicial and constitutional jurisdiction
judge selection and term of office: court president elected by his peers; judges elected by the National Congress from candidates proposed by the Nominating Board, a diverse 7-member group of judicial officials, and other government and non-government officials selected by each of their organizations; judges elected by Congress for renewable, 7-year terms
subordinate courts: courts of appeal; courts of first instance; peace courts

Political parties and leaders: Alliance against the Dictatorship [Salvador NASRALLA] (electoral coalition)
Anti-Corruption Party or PAC [Marlene ALVARENGA]
Christian Democratic Party or DC [Felicito AVILA Ordonez]
Democratic Unification Party or UD [Cesar HAM]
Freedom and Refoundation Party or LIBRE [Jose Manuel ZELAYA Rosales]
Go Solidarity Movement or VAMOS [Augusto CRUZ Asensio]
Liberal Party or PL [Luis Orlando ZELAYA Medrano]
National Party of Honduras or PNH [Gladis Aurora LOPEZ]
Innovation and Unity Party or PINU [Guillermo VALLE]

Political pressure groups and leaders: Beverage and Related Industries Syndicate or STIBYS
Committee for the Defense of Human Rights in Honduras or CODEH
Committee of the Relatives of the Disappeared in Honduras or COFADEH
Confederation of Honduran Workers or CTH
Coordinating Committee of Popular Organizations or CCOP
General Workers Confederation or CGT

Honduras Council of Private Enterprise or COHEP
National Association of Honduran Campesinos or ANACH
National Union of Campesinos or UNC
Popular Bloc or BP
United Confederation of Honduran Workers or CUTH
United Farm Workers' Movement of the Aguan OR MUCA

International organization participation: BCIE, CACM, CD, CELAC, EITI (candidate country), FAO, G-11, G-77, IADB, IAEA, IBRD, ICAO, ICCt, ICRM, IDA, IFAD, IFC, IFRCS, ILO, IMF, IMO, Interpol, IOC (suspended), IOM, IPU, ISO (subscriber), ITSO, ITU, ITUC (NGOs), LAES, LAIA (observer), MIGA, MINURSO, MINUSTAH, NAM, OAS, OPANAL, OPCW, Pacific Alliance (observer), PCA, Petrocaribe, SICA, UN, UNCTAD, UNESCO, UNIDO, Union Latina, UNWTO, UPU, WCO (suspended), WFTU (NGOs), WHO, WIPO, WMO, WTO

Diplomatic representation in the US: *chief of mission:* Ambassador Marlon Ramsses TABORA Munoz (since 24 April 2017)
chancery: Suite 4-M, 3007 Tilden Street NW, Washington, DC 20008
telephone: [1] (202) 966-2604
FAX: [1] (202) 966-9751
consulate(s): Dallas, McAllen (TX)
consulate(s) general: Atlanta, Chicago, Houston, Los Angeles, Miami, New Orleans, New York, San Francisco

Diplomatic representation from the US: *chief of mission:* Ambassador (vacant); Charge d'Affaires Heide B. FULTON (since June 2017)
embassy: Avenida La Paz, Apartado Postal No. 3453, Tegucigalpa
mailing address: American Embassy, APO AA 34022, Tegucigalpa
telephone: [504] 2236-9320, 2238-5114
FAX: [504] 2236-9037

Flag description: three equal horizontal bands of cerulean blue (top), white, and cerulean blue, with five cerulean, five-pointed stars arranged in an X pattern centered in the white band; the stars represent the members of the former Federal Republic of Central America: Costa Rica, El Salvador, Guatemala, Honduras, and Nicaragua; the blue bands symbolize the Pacific Ocean and the Caribbean Sea; the white band represents the land between the two bodies of water and the peace and prosperity of its people
note: similar to the flag of El Salvador, which features a round emblem encircled by the words REPUBLICA DE EL SALVADOR EN LA AMERICA CENTRAL centered in the white band; also similar to the flag of Nicaragua, which features a triangle encircled by the words REPUBLICA DE NICARAGUA on top and AMERICA CENTRAL on the bottom, centered in the white band

National symbol(s): scarlet macaw, white-tailed deer; national colors: blue, white

National anthem: name: "Himno Nacional de Honduras" (National Anthem of Honduras)
lyrics/music: Augusto Constancio COELLO/Carlos HARTLING
note: adopted 1915; the anthem's seven verses chronicle Honduran history; on official occasions, only the chorus and last verse are sung

ECONOMY

Economy—overview: Honduras, the second poorest country in Central America, suffers from extraordinarily unequal distribution of income, as well as high underemployment. While historically dependent on the export of bananas and coffee, Honduras has diversified its export base to include apparel and automobile wire harnessing.

Honduras's economy depends heavily on US trade and remittances. The US-Central America-Dominican Republic Free Trade Agreement came into force in 2006 and has helped foster foreign direct investment, but physical and political insecurity, as well as crime and perceptions of corruption, may deter potential investors; about 15% of foreign direct investment is from US firms.

The economy registered modest economic growth of 3.1%-4.0% from 2010 to 2017, insufficient to improve living standards for the nearly 65% of the population in poverty. In 2017, Honduras faced rising public debt, but its economy has performed better than expected due to low oil prices and improved investor confidence. Haiti signed a three-year standby arrangement with the IMF in December 2014, aimed at easing Honduras's poor fiscal position.

GDP (purchasing power parity): $45.68 billion (2017 est.)
$43.92 billion (2016 est.)
$42.39 billion (2015 est.)
note: data are in 2017 dollars
country comparison to the world: 112

GDP (official exchange rate): $22.68 billion (2016 est.)

GDP—real growth rate: 4% (2017 est.)
3.6% (2016 est.)
3.6% (2015 est.)
country comparison to the world: 64

GDP—per capita (PPP): $5,500 (2017 est.)
$5,400 (2016 est.)
$5,200 (2015 est.)
note: data are in 2017 dollars
country comparison to the world: 170

Gross national saving: 21.5% of GDP (2017 est.)
19.5% of GDP (2016 est.)
19.3% of GDP (2015 est.)
country comparison to the world: 79

GDP—composition, by end use:
household consumption: 78%
government consumption: 14.9%
investment in fixed capital: 22.3%
investment in inventories: 1.2%
exports of goods and services: 42.5%
imports of goods and services: -58.9% (2017 est.)

GDP—composition, by sector of origin:
agriculture: 13.8%

industry: 28.4%
services: 57.8% (2017 est.)

Agriculture—products: bananas, coffee, citrus, corn, African palm; beef; timber; shrimp, tilapia, lobster, sugar, oriental vegetables

Industries: sugar processing, coffee, woven and knit apparel, wood products, cigars

Industrial production growth rate: 4.8% (2017 est.)
country comparison to the world: 51

Labor force: 3.735 million (2017 est.)
country comparison to the world: 97

Labor force—by occupation: *agriculture:* 39.2%
industry: 20.9%
services: 39.8% (2005 est.)

Unemployment rate: 5.9% (2017 est.)
6.3% (2016 est.)
note: about one-third of the people are underemployed
country comparison to the world: 82

Population below poverty line: 29.6% (2014)

Household income or consumption by percentage share: *lowest 10%:* 1.2%
highest 10%: 38.4% (2014)

Distribution of family income—Gini index: 47.1 (2014)
45.7 (2009)
country comparison to the world: 27

Budget: *revenues:* $4.376 billion
expenditures: $5.086 billion (2017 est.)
Taxes and other revenues: 19.3% of GDP (2017 est.)
country comparison to the world: 159

Budget surplus (+) or deficit (-): -3.1% of GDP (2017 est.)
country comparison to the world: 116

Public debt: 51.9% of GDP (2017 est.)
47.7% of GDP (2016 est.)
country comparison to the world: 96

Fiscal year: calendar year

Inflation rate (consumer prices): 4% (2017 est.)
2.7% (2016 est.)
country comparison to the world: 154

Central bank discount rate: 6.25% (31 December 2010)
country comparison to the world: 68

Commercial bank prime lending rate: 19.7% (31 December 2017 est.)
19.33% (31 December 2016 est.)
country comparison to the world: 18

Stock of narrow money: $2.729 billion (31 December 2017 est.)
$2.455 billion (31 December 2016 est.)
country comparison to the world: 123

Stock of broad money: $9.334 billion (31 December 2017 est.)
$8.602 billion (31 December 2016 est.)
country comparison to the world: 107

Stock of domestic credit: $13.72 billion (31 December 2017 est.)
$12.65 billion (31 December 2016 est.)
country comparison to the world: 101

Market value of publicly traded shares: $NA

Current account balance: -$917 million (2017 est.)
-$811 million (2016 est.)
country comparison to the world: 129

Exports: $8.173 billion (2017 est.)
$7.841 billion (2016 est.)
country comparison to the world: 96

Exports—commodities: coffee, apparel, coffee, shrimp, automobile wire harnesses, cigars, bananas, gold, palm oil, fruit, lobster, lumber

Exports—partners: US 36.7%, Germany 10.7%, El Salvador 8.6%, Guatemala 6.5%, Netherlands 5.4%, Nicaragua 5.3% (2016)

Imports: $10.87 billion (2017 est.)
$10.56 billion (2016 est.)
country comparison to the world: 94

Imports—commodities: communications equipment, machinery and transport, industrial raw materials, chemical products, fuels, foodstuffs

Imports—partners: US 32.8%, China 14.1%, Guatemala 8.9%, Mexico 7.3%, El Salvador 5.7% (2016)

Reserves of foreign exchange and gold: $4.46 billion (31 December 2017 est.)
$3.814 billion (31 December 2016 est.)
country comparison to the world: 96

Debt—external: $9.025 billion (31 December 2017 est.)
$7.852 billion (31 December 2016 est.)
country comparison to the world: 118

Exchange rates: lempiras (HNL) per US dollar—
23.74 (2017 est.)
22.995 (2016 est.)
22.995 (2015 est.)
22.098 (2014 est.)
21.137 (2013 est.)

ENERGY

Electricity access: *population without electricity:* 900,000
electrification—*total population:* 82%
electrification—urban areas: 97%
electrification—rural areas: 66% (2013)

Electricity—production: 8.367 billion kWh (2015 est.)
country comparison to the world: 108

Electricity—consumption: 7.215 billion kWh (2015 est.)
country comparison to the world: 108

Electricity—exports: 536 million kWh (2015 est.)
country comparison to the world: 67

Electricity—imports: 679 million kWh (2015 est.)
country comparison to the world: 76

Electricity—installed generating capacity: 2.499 million kW (2015 est.)
country comparison to the world: 105

Electricity—from fossil fuels: 45.6% of total installed capacity (2015 est.)
country comparison to the world: 157

Electricity—from nuclear fuels: 0% of total installed capacity (2015 est.)

country comparison to the world: 108

Electricity—from hydroelectric plants: 25.2% of total installed capacity (2015 est.)
country comparison to the world: 79

Electricity—from other renewable sources: 32% of total installed capacity (2015 est.)
country comparison to the world: 12

Crude oil—production: 0 bbl/day (2016 est.)
country comparison to the world: 147

Crude oil—exports: 0 bbl/day (2014 est.)
country comparison to the world: 137

Crude oil—imports: 0 bbl/day (2014 est.)
country comparison to the world: 140

Crude oil—proved reserves: 0 bbl (1 January 2017 es)
country comparison to the world: 146

Refined petroleum products—production: 0 bbl/day (2014 est.)
country comparison to the world: 157

Refined petroleum products—consumption: 52,000 bbl/day (2015 est.)
country comparison to the world: 105

Refined petroleum products—exports: 13,160 bbl/day (2014 est.)
country comparison to the world: 77

Refined petroleum products—imports: 64,820 bbl/day (2014 est.)
country comparison to the world: 71

Natural gas—production: 0 cu m (2013 est.)
country comparison to the world: 149

Natural gas—consumption: 0 cu m (2013 est.)
country comparison to the world: 193

Natural gas—exports: 0 cu m (2013 est.)
country comparison to the world: 121

Natural gas—imports: 0 cu m (2013 est.)
country comparison to the world: 138

Natural gas—proved reserves: 0 cu m (1 January 2014 es)
country comparison to the world: 152

Carbon dioxide emissions from consumption of energy: 10 million Mt (2013 est.)
country comparison to the world: 103

COMMUNICATIONS

Telephones—fixed lines: *total subscriptions:* 442,929
subscriptions per 100 inhabitants: 5 (July 2016 est.)
country comparison to the world: 95

Telephones—mobile cellular: *total:* 7,832,802
subscriptions per 100 inhabitants: 88 (July 2016 est.)
country comparison to the world: 97

Telephone system: *general assessment:* fixed-line connections are increasing but still limited; competition among multiple providers of mobile-cellular services is contributing to a sharp increase in subscribership
domestic: beginning in 2003, private sub-operators allowed to provide fixed lines in order to expand telephone coverage contributing to a small increase in fixed-line teledensity; mobile-cellular subscribership is roughly 90 per 100 persons
international: country code—504; landing point for both the Americas Region Caribbean Ring System (ARCOS-1) and the MAYA-1 fiber-optic submarine cable system that together provide connectivity to South and Central America, parts of the Caribbean, and the US; satellite earth stations—2 Intelsat (Atlantic Ocean); connected to Central American Microwave System (2016)

Broadcast media: multiple privately owned terrestrial TV networks, supplemented by multiple cable TV networks; Radio Honduras is the lone government-owned radio network; roughly 300 privately owned radio stations (2007)

Internet country code: .hn
Internet users: total: 2,667,978

percent of population: 30.0% (July 2016 est.)
country comparison to the world: 103

TRANSPORTATION

National air transport system: *number of registered air carriers:* 5
inventory of registered aircraft operated by air carriers: 10
annual passenger traffic on registered air carriers: 251,149
annual freight traffic on registered air carriers: 502,372 mt-km (2015)
Civil aircraft registration country code prefix: HR (2016)

Airports: 103 (2013)
country comparison to the world: 54

Airports—with paved runways: *total:* 13
2,438 to 3,047 m: 3
1,524 to 2,437 m: 3
914 to 1,523 m: 4
under 914 m: 3 (2017)

Airports—with unpaved runways: *total:* 90
1,524 to 2,437 m: 1
914 to 1,523 m: 16
under 914 m: 73 (2013)

Railways: *total:* 699 km
narrow gauge: 164 km 1.067-m gauge; 115 km 1.057-m gauge; 420 km 0.914-m gauge (2014)
country comparison to the world: 101

Roadways: *total:* 14,742 km
paved: 3,367 km

unpaved: 11,375 km (1,543 km summer only)
note: an additional 8,951 km of non-official roads used by the coffee industry (2012)
country comparison to the world: 125

Waterways: 465 km (most navigable only by small craft) (2012)
country comparison to the world: 84

Merchant marine: *total:* 552
by type: container ship 1, general cargo 250, oil tanker 90, other 211 (2017)
country comparison to the world: 38

Ports and terminals: *major seaport(s):* La Ceiba, Puerto Cortes, San Lorenzo, Tela

MILITARY AND SECURITY

Military expenditures: 1.59% of GDP (2016)
1.52% of GDP (2015)
1.62% of GDP (2014)
1.55% of GDP (2013)
1.15% of GDP (2012)
country comparison to the world: 96

Military branches: Honduran Armed Forces (Fuerzas Armadas de Honduras, FFAA): Army, Navy (includes Naval Infantry), Honduran Air Force (Fuerza Aerea Hondurena, FAH) (2012)

Military service age and obligation: 18 years of age for voluntary 2- to 3-year military service; no conscription (2012)

TRANSNATIONAL ISSUES

Disputes—international: International Court of Justice (ICJ) ruled on the delimitation of "bolsones" (disputed areas) along the El Salvador-Honduras border in 1992 with final settlement by the parties in 2006 after an Organization of American States survey and a further ICJ ruling in 2003; the 1992 ICJ ruling advised a tripartite resolution to a maritime boundary in the Gulf of Fonseca with consideration of Honduran access to the Pacific; El Salvador continues to claim tiny Conejo Island, not mentioned in the ICJ ruling, off Honduras in the Gulf of Fonseca; Honduras claims the Belizean-administered Sapodilla Cays off the coast of Belize in its constitution, but agreed to a joint ecological park around the cays should Guatemala consent to a maritime corridor in the Caribbean under the OAS-sponsored 2002 Belize-Guatemala Differendum
Refugees and internally displaced persons: IDPs: 190,000 (violence, extortion, threats, forced recruitment by urban gangs) (2016)

Illicit drugs: transshipment point for drugs and narcotics; illicit producer of cannabis, cultivated on small plots and used principally for local consumption; corruption is a major problem; some money-laundering activity

HONG KONG

INTRODUCTION

Background: Occupied by the UK in 1841, Hong Kong was formally ceded by China the following year; various adjacent lands were added later in the 19th century. Pursuant to an agreement signed by China and the UK on 19 December 1984, Hong Kong became the Hong Kong Special Administrative Region of the People's Republic of China on 1 July 1997. In this agreement, China promised that, under its "one country, two systems" formula, China's socialist economic system would not be imposed on Hong Kong and that Hong Kong would enjoy a "high degree of autonomy" in all matters except foreign and defense affairs for the subsequent 50 years.

GEOGRAPHY

Location: Eastern Asia, bordering the South China Sea and China

Geographic coordinates: 22 15 N, 114 10 E

Map references: Southeast Asia

Area: *total:* 1,108 sq km
land: 1,073 sq km
water: 35 sq km
country comparison to the world: 184

Area—comparative: six times the size of Washington, DC

Land boundaries: *total:* 33 km
regional border(s) (1): China 33 km

Coastline: 733 km

Maritime claims: *territorial sea:* 12 nm

Climate: subtropical monsoon; cool and humid in winter, hot and rainy from spring through summer, warm and sunny in fall

Terrain: hilly to mountainous with steep slopes; lowlands in north

Elevation: *mean elevation:* NA

elevation extremes: *lowest point:* South China Sea 0 m
highest point: Tai Mo Shan 958 m

Natural resources: outstanding deepwater harbor, feldspar

Land use: *agricultural land:* 5%
arable land: 3.2%;
permanent crops: 0.9%;
permanent pasture: 0.9%
forest: 0%
other: 95% (2011 est.)
Irrigated land: 10 sq km (2012)

Population—distribution: population fairly evenly distributed

Natural hazards: occasional typhoons

Environment—current issues: air and water pollution from rapid urbanization

Environment—international agreements: *party to:* Marine Dumping (associate member), Ship Pollution (associate member)

Geography—note: consists of a mainland area (the New Territories) and more than 200 islands

PEOPLE AND SOCIETY

Population: 7,191,503 (July 2017 est.)
country comparison to the world: 100

Nationality: *noun:* Chinese/Hong Konger
adjective: Chinese/Hong Kong

Ethnic groups: Chinese 92%, Filipino 2.5%, Indonesian 2.1%, other 3.4% (2016 est.)

Languages: Cantonese (official) 88.9%, English (official) 4.3%, Mandarin (official) 1.9%, other Chinese dialects 3.1%, other 1.9% (2016 est.)

Religions: eclectic mixture of local religions 90%, Christian 10%

Age structure: *0-14 years:* 12.19% (male 462,748/female 414,023)
15-24 years: 10.43% (male 392,167/female 357,821)
25-54 years: 44.68% (male 1,370,206/female 1,842,825)
55-64 years: 16.17% (male 559,421/female 603,771)
65 years and over: 16.53% (male 559,512/female 629,009) (2017 est.)

Dependency ratios: *total dependency ratio:* 35.9
youth dependency ratio: 15.2
elderly dependency ratio: 20.7
potential support ratio: 4.8 (2015 est.)

Median age: *total:* 44.4 years
male: 43.5 years
female: 45 years (2017 est.)
country comparison to the world: 10

Population growth rate: 0.32% (2017 est.)
country comparison to the world: 166

Birth rate: 8.9 births/1,000 population (2017 est.)
country comparison to the world: 208

Death rate: 7.4 deaths/1,000 population (2017 est.)
country comparison to the world: 117

Net migration rate: 1.7 migrant(s)/1,000 population (2017 est.)
country comparison to the world: 51

Population distribution: population fairly evenly distributed

Urbanization: *urban population:* 100% of total population (2017)
rate of urbanization: 0.64% annual rate of change (2015-20 est.)

Major urban areas—population: Hong Kong 7.26 million (2014)

Sex ratio: *at birth:* 1.12 male(s)/female
0-14 years: 1.12 male(s)/female
15-24 years: 1.08 male(s)/female
25-54 years: 0.74 male(s)/female
55-64 years: 0.94 male(s)/female
65 years and over: 0.89 male(s)/female
total population: 0.87 male(s)/female (2016 est.)

Mother's mean age at first birth: 29.8 years (2008 est.)

Infant mortality rate: *total:* 2.7 deaths/1,000 live births
male: 3 deaths/1,000 live births
female: 2.5 deaths/1,000 live births (2017 est.)
country comparison to the world: 216

Life expectancy at birth: *total population:* 83 years
male: 80.4 years
female: 85.9 years (2017 est.)
country comparison to the world: 7

Total fertility rate: 1.19 children born/woman (2017 est.)
country comparison to the world: 221

Contraceptive prevalence rate: 74.8% (2012)

Physicians density: 1.78 physicians/1,000 population WHO, Western Pacific Region, Health Information and Intelligence Platform, accessed 3/7/17 (2010)

HIV/AIDS—people living with HIV/AIDS: NA

HIV/AIDS—deaths: NA

Education expenditures: 3.3% of GDP (2015)
country comparison to the world: 124

School life expectancy (primary to tertiary education): *total:* 16 years
male: 16 years
female: 16 years (2014)

Unemployment, youth ages 15-24: *total:* 9.9%
male: 10.9%
female: 8.5% (2016 est.)
country comparison to the world: 106

GOVERNMENT

Country name: *conventional long form:* Hong Kong Special Administrative Region
conventional short form: Hong Kong
local long form: Heung Kong Takpit Hangching Ku (Eitel/Dyer-Ball); Xianggang Tebie Xingzhengqu (Hanyu Pinyin)

local short form: Heung Kong (Eitel/Dyer-Ball); Xianggang (Hanyu Pinyin)

abbreviation: HK

etymology: probably an imprecise phonetic rendering of the Cantonese name meaning "fragrant harbor"

Dependency status: special administrative region of the People's Republic of China

Government type: presidential limited democracy; a special administrative region of the People's Republic of China

Administrative divisions: none (special administrative region of the People's Republic of China)

Independence: none (special administrative region of China)

National holiday: National Day (Anniversary of the Founding of the People's Republic of China), 1 October (1949); note—1 July (1997) is celebrated as Hong Kong Special Administrative Region Establishment Day

Constitution: several previous (governance documents while under British authority); latest drafted April 1988 to February 1989, approved March 1990, effective 1 July 1997 (Basic Law of the Hong Kong Special Administrative Region of the People's Republic of China serves as the constitution); note—since 1990, the PRC National People's Congress has interpreted specific articles of the Basic Law (2016)

Legal system: mixed legal system of common law based on the English model and Chinese customary law (in matters of family and land tenure)

Citizenship: see China

Suffrage: 18 years of age in direct elections for half of the Legislative Council seats and all of the seats in 18 district councils; universal for permanent residents living in the territory of Hong Kong for the past 7 years; note—in indirect elections, suffrage is limited to about 220,000 members of functional constituencies for the other half of the legislature and a 1,200-member election committee for the chief executive drawn from broad sectoral groupings, central government bodies, municipal organizations, and elected Hong Kong officials

Executive branch: *chief of state:* President of China XI Jinping (since 14 March 2013)

head of government: Chief Executive Carrie LAM (since 1 July 2017)

cabinet: Executive Council or ExCo appointed by the chief executive

elections/appointments: president indirectly elected by National People's Congress for a 5-year term (eligible for a second term); election last held on 5-17 March 2013 (next to be held in March 2018); chief executive indirectly elected by the Election Committee and appointed by the PRC Government for a 5-year term (eligible for a second term); election last held on 26 March 2017 (next to be held in 2022)

election results: Carrie LAM elected chief executive; Election Committee vote—Carrie LAM 777, John TSANG 365, WOO Kwok-hing 21, invalid 23

note: the Legislative Council voted in June 2010 to expand the Election Committee to 1,200 members

Legislative branch: *description:* unicameral Legislative Council or LegCo (70 seats; 35 members directly elected in multi-seat constituencies by party-list proportional representation vote; 30 members indirectly elected by the approximately 220,000 members of various functional constituencies based on a variety of methods; five at large "super-seat" members directly elected by all of Hong Kong's eligible voters who do not participate in a functional constituency; members serve 4-year terms)

elections: last held on 4 September 2016; (next to be held in September 2020); note—by-election to be held on 11 March 2018 to fill 4 seats left vacant after 4 legislators were removed from office

election results: percent of vote by block—pro-democracy 36.0%; pro-Beijing 40.2%, localist 19.0%; other 4.8%; seats by block/party—pro-Beijing 40 (DAB 12, BPA 7, FTU 5, Liberal Party 4, NPP 3, other 9); pro-democracy 23 (Democratic Party 7, Civic Party 6, PP-LSD 2, Professional Commons 2, Labor 1, NWSC 1, PTU 1, other democrats 3), localists 6 (ALLin HK 2, CP-PPI-HKRO 1, Demosisto 1, Democracy Groundwork 1, other localist 1), non-aligned independent 1; note—2 localists were barred from taking office in November 2016 and 4 pro-democracy legislators were removed in July 2017

Judicial branch: *highest court(s):* Court of Final Appeal (consists of the chief justice, 3 permanent judges, and 20 non-permanent judges); note—a sitting bench consists of the chief justice and 3 permanent judges and 1 non-permanent judge

judge selection and term of office: all judges appointed by the Hong Kong Chief Executive upon the recommendation of the Judicial Officers Recommendation Commission, an independent body consisting of the Secretary for Justice, other judges, and judicial and legal professionals; permanent judges appointed until normal retirement at age 65, but can be extended; non-permanent judges appointed for renewable 3-year terms without age limit

subordinate courts: High Court (consists of the Court of Appeal and Court of First Instance); District Courts (includes Family and Land Courts); magistrates' courts; specialized tribunals

Political parties and leaders: parties: ALLinHK (alliance of 6 localist groups)

Business and Professional Alliance or BPA [Andrew LEUNG Kwan-yuen]

Civic Party [Alan LEONG Kah-kit]

Civic Passion or CP [CHENG Chung-tai] (part of Civic Passion-Proletariat Political Institute-Hong Kong Resurgence Order alliance or CP-PPI-HKRO that dissolved after the 2016 election)

Democracy Groundwork [LAU Siu-lai]

Democratic Alliance for the Betterment and Progress of Hong Kong or DAB [Starry LEE Wai-king]

Democratic Party [WU Chi-wai]

Demosisto [Nathan LAW]

Federation of Trade Unions or FTU [Stanley NG Chau-pei]

Labor Party [Acting Chairman CHIU Shi-shun]

League of Social Democrats or LSD [Avery NG Man-yuen]

Liberal Party [Felix CHUNG Kwok-pan]

Neighborhood and Workers Service Center or NWSC [LEUNG Yui-chung]

New People's Party or NPP [Regina IP Lau Su-yee]

People Power or PP [Erica YUEN Mi-ming]

Youngspiration [Sixtus "Baggio" LEUNG Chung-hang]

others: Professional Commons (think tank) [Charles Peter MOK]

Professional Teachers Union or PTU

note: political blocks include: pro-democracy—Civic Party, Democratic Party, Labor Party, LSD, NWSC, PP, Professional Commons, PTU; pro-Beijing—DAB, FTU, Liberal Party, NPP, BPA; localist—ALLinHK, CP, Democracy Groundwork, Demosisto; there is no political party ordinance, so there are no registered political parties; politically active groups register as societies or companies

Political pressure groups and leaders: Chinese General Chamber of Commerce (pro-China) Chinese Manufacturers' Association of Hong Kong

Civic Act-up (pro-democracy)

Federation of Hong Kong Industries

Hong Kong Alliance in Support of the Patriotic Democratic Movement in China [Albert HO] (pro-China)

Hong Kong and Kowloon Trade Union Council or HKTUC (pro-democracy)

Hong Kong General Chamber of Commerce or HKGCC

Hong Kong Professional Teachers' Union or HKPTU [FUNG Wai-wah]

International organization participation: ADB, APEC, BIS, FATF, ICC (national committees), IHO, IMF, IMO (associate), Interpol (subbureau), IOC, ISO (correspondent), ITUC (NGOs), UNWTO (associate), UPU, WCO, WMO, WTO

Diplomatic representation in the US: none (Special Administrative Region of China); Hong Kong Economic and Trade Office (HKETO) carries out normal liaison activities and communication with the US Government and other US entities

commissioner: Clement C.M. LEUNG

office: 1520 18th Street NW, Washington, DC 20036

telephone: [1] 202 331-8947

FAX: [1] 202 331-8958

HKETO offices: New York, San Francisco

Diplomatic representation from the US: *chief of mission:* Consul General Kurt W. TONG (since 27 August 2016); note—also accredited to Macau

consulate(s) general: 26 Garden Road, Hong Kong

mailing address: Unit 8000, Box 1, DPO AP 96521-0006

telephone: [852] 2523-9011

FAX: [852] 2845-1598

Flag description: red with a stylized, white, five-petal Bauhinia flower in the center; each petal contains a small, red, five-pointed star in its middle; the red color is the same as that on the Chinese flag and represents the motherland; the fragrant Bauhinia—developed in Hong Kong the late 19th century—has come to symbolize the region; the five stars echo those on the flag of China

National symbol(s): orchid tree flower; national colors: red, white

National anthem: *note:* as a Special Administrative Region of China, "Yiyongjun Jinxingqu" is the official anthem (see China)

ECONOMY

Economy—overview: Hong Kong has a free market economy, highly dependent on international trade and finance—the value of goods and services trade, including the sizable share of reexports, is about four times GDP. Hong Kong has no tariffs on imported goods, and it levies excise duties on only four commodities, whether imported or produced locally: hard alcohol, tobacco, hydrocarbon oil, and methyl alcohol. There are no quotas or dumping laws. Hong Kong continues to link its currency closely to the US dollar, maintaining an arrangement established in 1983.

Hong Kong's open economy left it exposed to the global economic slowdown that began in 2008. Although increasing integration with China through trade, tourism, and financial links aided a more rapid initial recovery than many observers anticipated, its continued reliance on foreign trade and investment leaves it vulnerable to renewed global financial market volatility or a slowdown in the global economy.

The Hong Kong Government is promoting the Special Administrative Region (SAR) as the site for Chinese renminbi (RMB) internationalization. Hong Kong residents are allowed to establish RMB-denominated savings accounts; RMB-denominated corporate and Chinese government bonds have been issued in Hong Kong; and RMB trade settlement is allowed. The territory far exceeded the RMB conversion quota set by Beijing for trade settlements in 2010 due to the growth of earnings from exports to the mainland. RMB deposits grew to roughly 9.4% of total system deposits in Hong Kong by the end of 2015. The government is pursuing efforts to introduce additional use of RMB in Hong Kong financial markets and is seeking to expand the RMB quota.

The mainland has long been Hong Kong's largest trading partner, accounting for about half of Hong Kong's total trade by value. Hong Kong's natural resources are limited, and food and raw materials must be imported. As a result of China's easing of travel restrictions, the number of mainland tourists to the territory has surged from 4.5 million in 2001 to 47.3 million in 2014, outnumbering visitors from all other countries combined. Mainland visitors to Hong Kong declined 3% in 2015 to approximately 45.7 million, reflecting an overall drop of 2.5% in total visitors to Hong Kong. Hong Kong has also established itself as the premier stock market for Chinese firms seeking to list abroad. In 2015, mainland Chinese companies constituted about 51% of the firms listed on the Hong Kong Stock Exchange and accounted for about 62.1% of the exchange's market capitalization. During the past decade, as Hong Kong's manufacturing industry moved to the mainland, its service industry has grown rapidly. In 2014, Hong Kong and China signed a new agreement on achieving basic liberalization of trade in services in Guangdong Province under the Closer Economic Partnership Agreement, adopted in 2003 to forge closer ties between Hong Kong and the mainland. The new measures, which took effect in March 2015, cover a negative list and a most-favored treatment provision, and will improve access to the mainland's service sector for Hong Kong-based companies.

Credit expansion and a tight housing supply have caused Hong Kong property prices to rise rapidly; consumer prices increased 2.6% in 2016, but slowed to 2.0% in 2017. Lower- and middle-income segments of the population are increasingly unable to afford adequate housing.

Hong Kong's economic integration with the mainland continues to be most evident in the banking and finance sector. Initiatives like the Hong Kong-Shanghai Stock Connect, the Mutual Recognition of Funds, and The Hong Kong Shanghai Gold Connect are all important steps towards opening up the Mainland's capital markets and has reinforced Hong Kong's leading role as China's offshore RMB market. Additional connect schemes from bonds to commodities and other investment products are also under exploration by Hong Kong authorities. In 2017, Chief Executive Lam announced plans to increase government spending on research and development, education, and technological innovation with the aim of spurring continued economic growth through greater sector diversification.

GDP (purchasing power parity): $453 billion (2017 est.)
$437.5 billion (2016 est.)
$428.8 billion (2015 est.)
note: data are in 2017 dollars
country comparison to the world: 44

GDP (official exchange rate): $334.1 billion (2016 est.)

GDP—real growth rate: 3.5% (2017 est.)
2% (2016 est.)
2.4% (2015 est.)
country comparison to the world: 90

GDP—per capita (PPP): $61,000 (2017 est.)
$59,400 (2016 est.)
$58,700 (2015 est.)
note: data are in 2017 dollars
country comparison to the world: 18

Gross national saving: 24.9% of GDP (2017 est.)
26.4% of GDP (2016 est.)
24.9% of GDP (2015 est.)
country comparison to the world: 52

GDP—composition, by end use:
household consumption: 66.6%
government consumption: 10%

investment in fixed capital: 22.3%
investment in inventories: 0.7%
exports of goods and services: 191.9%
imports of goods and services: -191.3% (2017 est.)

GDP—composition, by sector of origin:
agriculture: 0.1%
industry: 7.2%
services: 92.7% (2017 est.)

Agriculture—products: fresh vegetables and fruit; poultry, pork; fish

Industries: textiles, clothing, tourism, banking, shipping, electronics, plastics, toys, watches, clocks

Industrial production growth rate: 3% (2017 est.)
country comparison to the world: 102

Labor force: 3.965 million (2017 est.)
country comparison to the world: 95

Labor force—by occupation: *manufacturing:* 3.8%
construction: 2.8%
wholesale and retail trade, restaurants, and hotels: 53.3%
financing, insurance, and real estate: 12.5%
transport and communications: 10.1%
community and social services: 17.1%
note: above data exclude public sector (2013 est.)

Unemployment rate: 2.6% (2017 est.)
2.7% (2016 est.)
country comparison to the world: 25

Population below poverty line: 19.6% (2012 est.)

Household income or consumption by percentage share: *lowest 10%:* NA%
highest 10%: NA%

Distribution of family income—Gini index: 53.7 (2011)
53.3 (2007)
country comparison to the world: 9

Budget: *revenues:* $66.19 billion
expenditures: $62.86 billion (2017 est.)
Taxes and other revenues: 19.8% of GDP (2017 est.)
country comparison to the world: 155

Budget surplus (+) or deficit (-): 1% of GDP (2017 est.)
country comparison to the world: 15

Public debt: 43.6% of GDP (2017 est.)
44.8% of GDP (2016 est.)
country comparison to the world: 121

Fiscal year: 1 April—31 March

Inflation rate (consumer prices): 2% (2017 est.)
2.6% (2016 est.)
country comparison to the world: 92

Central bank discount rate: 0.5% (31 December 2013)
0.5% (31 December 2012)
country comparison to the world: 132

Commercial bank prime lending rate: 5.1% (31 December 2017 est.)
5% (31 December 2016 est.)
country comparison to the world: 144

419

Stock of narrow money: $310.3 billion (31 December 2017 est.)

$285.5 billion (31 December 2016 est.)

country comparison to the world: 17

Stock of broad money: $1.736 trillion (31 December 2017 est.)

$1.613 trillion (31 December 2016 est.)

country comparison to the world: 10

Stock of domestic credit: $719.2 billion (31 December 2017 est.)

$676.5 billion (31 December 2016 est.)

country comparison to the world: 21

Market value of publicly traded shares: $3.185 trillion (31 December 2015 est.)

$3.233 trillion (31 December 2014 est.)

$3.101 trillion (31 December 2013 est.)

country comparison to the world: 5

Current account balance: $10.06 billion (2017 est.)

$14.88 billion (2016 est.)

country comparison to the world: 21

Exports: $540 billion (2017 est.)

$502.5 billion (2016 est.)

country comparison to the world: 8

Exports—commodities: electrical machinery and appliances, textiles, apparel, footwear, watches and clocks, toys, plastics, precious stones, printed material

Exports—partners: China 54.2%, US 9% (2016)

Imports: $561.4 billion (2017 est.)

$520.1 billion (2016 est.)

country comparison to the world: 8

Imports—commodities: raw materials and semi-manufactures, consumer goods, capital goods, foodstuffs, fuel (most is reexported)

Imports—partners: China 47.8%, Singapore 6.5%, Japan 6.2%, US 5.2%, South Korea 4.9% (2016)

Reserves of foreign exchange and gold: $398.3 billion (31 December 2017 est.)

$386.3 billion (31 December 2016 est.)

country comparison to the world: 9

Debt—external: $494.5 billion (31 December 2017 est.)

$505.9 billion (31 December 2016 est.)

country comparison to the world: 23

Stock of direct foreign investment—at home:

$1.901 trillion (31 December 2017 est.)

$1.786 trillion (31 December 2016 est.)

country comparison to the world: 5

Stock of direct foreign investment—abroad:

$1.806 trillion (31 December 2017 est.)

$1.723 trillion (31 December 2016 est.)

country comparison to the world: 5

Exchange rates: Hong Kong dollars (HKD) per US dollar—

7.802 (2017 est.)

7.762 (2016 est.)

7.762 (2015 est.)

7.752 (2014 est.)

7.754 (2013 est.)

ENERGY

Electricity access: electrification—*total population:* 100% (2016)

Electricity—production: 35.75 billion kWh (2015 est.)

country comparison to the world: 61

Electricity—consumption: 41.74 billion kWh (2015 est.)

country comparison to the world: 55

Electricity—exports: 1.205 billion kWh (2016 est.)

country comparison to the world: 55

Electricity—imports: 11.62 billion kWh (2016 est.)

country comparison to the world: 23

Electricity—installed generating capacity: 12.63 million kW (2015 est.)

country comparison to the world: 55

Electricity—from fossil fuels: 100% of total installed capacity (2015 est.)

country comparison to the world: 9

Electricity—from nuclear fuels: 0% of total installed capacity (2015 est.)

country comparison to the world: 107

Electricity—from hydroelectric plants: 0% of total installed capacity (2015 est.)

country comparison to the world: 180

Electricity—from other renewable sources: 0% of total installed capacity (2015 est.)

country comparison to the world: 187

Crude oil—production: 0 bbl/day (2016 est.)

country comparison to the world: 148

Crude oil—exports: 0 bbl/day (2014 est.)

country comparison to the world: 136

Crude oil—imports: 0 bbl/day (2014 est.)

country comparison to the world: 139

Crude oil—proved reserves: 0 bbl (1 January 2017 es)

country comparison to the world: 147

Refined petroleum products—production: 0 bbl/day (2014 est.)

country comparison to the world: 158

Refined petroleum products—consumption: 388,500 bbl/day (2015 est.)

country comparison to the world: 39

Refined petroleum products—exports: 9,625 bbl/day (2014 est.)

country comparison to the world: 84

Refined petroleum products—imports: 332,000 bbl/day (2014 est.)

country comparison to the world: 25

Natural gas—production: 0 cu m (2013 est.)

country comparison to the world: 148

Natural gas—consumption: 4.49 billion cu m (2015 est.)

country comparison to the world: 69

Natural gas—exports: 0 cu m (2013 est.)

country comparison to the world: 120

Natural gas—imports: 3.243 billion cu m (2015 est.)

country comparison to the world: 42

Natural gas—proved reserves: 0 cu m (1 January 2014 es)

country comparison to the world: 151

Carbon dioxide emissions from consumption of energy: 90 million Mt (2013 est.)

country comparison to the world: 43

COMMUNICATIONS

Telephones—fixed lines: *total subscriptions:* 4,323,291

subscriptions per 100 inhabitants: 60 (July 2016 est.)

country comparison to the world: 36

Telephones—mobile cellular: *total:* 16.736 million

subscriptions per 100 inhabitants: 234 (July 2016 est.)

country comparison to the world: 60

Telephone system: *general assessment:* modern facilities provide excellent domestic and international services

domestic: microwave radio relay links and extensive fiber-optic network

international: country code—852; multiple international submarine cables provide connections to Asia, US, Australia, the Middle East, and Western Europe; satellite earth stations—3 Intelsat (1 Pacific Ocean and 2 Indian Ocean); coaxial cable to Guangzhou, China (2015)

Broadcast media: 2 commercial terrestrial TV networks each with multiple stations; multi-channel satellite and cable TV systems available; 3 radio networks, one of which is government funded, operate about 15 radio stations (2012)

Internet country code: .hk

Internet users: total: 6.066 million

percent of population: 85% (July 2016 est.)

country comparison to the world: 61

TRANSPORTATION

National air transport system: *number of registered air carriers:* 7 (registered in China)

inventory of registered aircraft operated by air carriers: 253 (registered in China)

annual passenger traffic on registered air carriers: 41,867,157

annual freight traffic on registered air carriers: 11.294 billion mt-km (2015)

Civil aircraft registration country code prefix: B-H (2016)

Airports: 2 (2013)

country comparison to the world: 201

Airports—with paved runways: *total:* 2

over 3,047 m: 1

1,524 to 2,437 m: 1 (2017)

Heliports: 9 (2013)

Roadways: *total:* 2,100 km

paved: 2,100 km (2015)

country comparison to the world: 174

Merchant marine: total: 2,576

by type: bulk carrier 1,142, container ship 471, general cargo 226, oil tanker 346, other 391 (2017)
country comparison to the world: 9

Ports and terminals: *major seaport(s):* Hong Kong

MILITARY AND SECURITY

Military branches: no regular indigenous military forces; Hong Kong garrison of China's People's Liberation Army (PLA) includes elements of the

PLA Army, PLA Navy, and PLA Air Force; these forces are under the direct leadership of the Central Military Commission in Beijing and under administrative control of the adjacent Southern Command (2016)

Military—note: defense is the responsibility of China

TRANSNATIONAL ISSUES

Disputes—international: Hong Kong plans to reduce its 2,800-hectare Frontier Closed Area

(FCA) to 400 hectares by 2015; the FCA was established in 1951 as a buffer zone between Hong Kong and mainland China to prevent illegal migration from and the smuggling of goods

Illicit drugs: despite strenuous law enforcement efforts, faces difficult challenges in controlling transit of heroin and methamphetamine to regional and world markets; modern banking system provides conduit for money laundering; rising indigenous use of synthetic drugs, especially among young people

HUNGARY

INTRODUCTION

Background: Hungary became a Christian kingdom in A.D. 1000 and for many centuries served as a bulwark against Ottoman Turkish expansion in Europe. The kingdom eventually became part of the polyglot Austro-Hungarian Empire, which collapsed during World War I. The country fell under communist rule following World War II. In 1956, a revolt and an announced withdrawal from the Warsaw Pact were met with a massive military intervention by Moscow. Under the leadership of Janos KADAR in 1968, Hungary began liberalizing its economy, introducing so-called "Goulash Communism." Hungary held its first multiparty elections in 1990 and initiated a free market economy. It joined NATO in 1999 and the EU five years later.

GEOGRAPHY

Location: Central Europe, northwest of Romania

Geographic coordinates: 47 00 N, 20 00 E

Map references: Europe

Area: total: 93,028 sq km
land: 89,608 sq km
water: 3,420 sq km
country comparison to the world: 111

Area—comparative: slightly smaller than Virginia; about the same size as Indiana

Land boundaries: total: 2,106 km
border countries (7): Austria 321 km, Croatia 348 km, Romania 424 km, Serbia 164 km, Slovakia 627 km, Slovenia 94 km, Ukraine 128 km

Coastline: 0 km (landlocked)

Maritime claims: none (landlocked)

Climate: temperate; cold, cloudy, humid winters; warm summers

Terrain: mostly flat to rolling plains; hills and low mountains on the Slovakian border

Elevation: *mean elevation:* 143 m

elevation extremes: *lowest point:* Tisza River 78 m
highest point: Kekes 1,014 m

Natural resources: bauxite, coal, natural gas, fertile soils, arable land

Land use: *agricultural land:* 58.9%
arable land: 48.5%;
permanent crops: 2%;
permanent pasture: 8.4%
forest: 22.5%
other: 18.6% (2011 est.)
Irrigated land: 1,721 sq km (2012)

Population—distribution: a fairly even distribution throughout most of the country, with urban areas attracting larger and denser populations

Environment—current issues: the upgrading of Hungary's standards in waste management, energy efficiency, and air, soil, and water pollution to meet EU requirements will require large investments

Environment—international agreements: *party to:* Air Pollution, Air Pollution-Nitrogen Oxides, Air Pollution-Persistent Organic Pollutants, Air Pollution-Sulfur 85, Air Pollution-Sulfur 94, Air Pollution-Volatile Organic Compounds, Antarctic Treaty, Biodiversity, Climate Change, Climate Change-Kyoto Protocol, Desertification, Endangered Species, Environmental Modification, Hazardous Wastes, Law of the Sea, Marine Dumping, Ozone Layer Protection, Ship Pollution, Wetlands, Whaling
signed, but not ratified: none of the selected agreements

Geography—note: landlocked; strategic location astride main land routes between Western Europe and Balkan Peninsula as well as between Ukraine and Mediterranean basin; the north-south flowing Duna (Danube) and Tisza Rivers divide the country into three large regions

PEOPLE AND SOCIETY

Population: 9,850,845 (July 2017 est.)

country comparison to the world: 92

Nationality: *noun:* Hungarian(s)
adjective: Hungarian

Ethnic groups: Hungarian 85.6%, Romani 3.2%, German 1.9%, other 2.6%, unspecified 14.1% (2011 est.)

note: percentages add up to more than 100% because respondents were able to identify more than one ethnic group; Romani populations are usually underestimated in official statistics and may represent 5–10% of Hungary's population

Languages: Hungarian (official) 99.6%, English 16%, German 11.2%, Russian 1.6%, Romanian 1.3%, French 1.2%, other 4.2%

note: shares sum to more than 100% because some respondents gave more than one answer on the census; Hungarian is the mother tongue of 98.9% of Hungarian speakers (2011 est.)

Religions: Roman Catholic 37.2%, Calvinist 11.6%, Lutheran 2.2%, Greek Catholic 1.8%, other 1.9%, none 18.2%, unspecified 27.2% (2011 est.)

Age structure: *0-14 years:* 14.71% (male 746,043/female 702,792)
15-24 years: 10.96% (male 557,655/female 522,324)
25-54 years: 41.88% (male 2,075,101/female 2,050,478)
55-64 years: 13.4% (male 608,734/female 711,602)
65 years and over: 19.05% (male 708,214/female 1,167,902) (2017 est.)

Dependency ratios: *total dependency ratio:* 46.9
youth dependency ratio: 21.2
elderly dependency ratio: 25.7
potential support ratio: 3.9 (2015 est.)

Median age: *total:* 42.3 years
male: 40.4 years
female: 44.3 years (2017 est.)
country comparison to the world: 31

Population growth rate: -0.25% (2017 est.)
country comparison to the world: 214

Birth rate: 9 births/1,000 population (2017 est.)
country comparison to the world: 205

Death rate: 12.8 deaths/1,000 population (2017 est.)

country comparison to the world: 16

Net migration rate: 1.3 migrant(s)/1,000 population (2017 est.)
country comparison to the world: 54

Population distribution: a fairly even distribution throughout most of the country, with urban areas attracting larger and denser populations

Urbanization: *urban population:* 72.1% of total population (2017)
rate of urbanization: 0.36% annual rate of change (2015-20 est.)

Major urban areas—population: BUDAPEST (capital) 1.714 million (2015)

Sex ratio: *at birth:* 1.06 male(s)/female
0-14 years: 1.06 male(s)/female
15-24 years: 1.07 male(s)/female
25-54 years: 1.01 male(s)/female
55-64 years: 0.85 male(s)/female
65 years and over: 0.6 male(s)/female
total population: 0.91 male(s)/female (2016 est.)

Mother's mean age at first birth: 28.3 years (2014 est.)

Maternal mortality ratio: 17 deaths/100,000 live births (2015 est.)
country comparison to the world: 131

Infant mortality rate: *total:* 4.9 deaths/1,000 live births
male: 5.2 deaths/1,000 live births
female: 4.6 deaths/1,000 live births (2017 est.)
country comparison to the world: 177

Life expectancy at birth: *total population:* 76.1 years
male: 72.4 years
female: 80 years (2017 est.)
country comparison to the world: 91

Total fertility rate: 1.45 children born/woman (2017 est.)
country comparison to the world: 204

Health expenditures: 7.4% of GDP (2014)
country comparison to the world: 70

Physicians density: 3.32 physicians/1,000 population (2014)

Hospital bed density: 7.2 beds/1,000 population (2011)

Drinking water source:
improved:
urban: 100% of population
rural: 100% of population
total: 100% of population
unimproved:
urban: 0% of population
rural: 0% of population
total: 0% of population (2015 est.)

Sanitation facility access:
improved:
urban: 97.8% of population
rural: 98.6% of population
total: 98% of population
unimproved:
urban: 2.2% of population
rural: 1.4% of population
total: 2% of population (2015 est.)

HIV/AIDS—adult prevalence rate: NA

HIV/AIDS—people living with HIV/AIDS: NA

HIV/AIDS—deaths: NA

Major infectious diseases: *degree of risk:* intermediate
vectorborne diseases: tickborne encephalitis (2016)

Obesity—adult prevalence rate: 26.4% (2016)
country comparison to the world: 42

Education expenditures: 4.2% of GDP (2013)
country comparison to the world: 81

Literacy: *definition:* age 15 and over can read and write
total population: 99.1%
male: 99.1%
female: 99% (2015 est.)

School life expectancy (primary to tertiary education): *total:* 15 years
male: 15 years
female: 16 years (2015)

Unemployment, youth ages 15-24: *total:* 17.3%
male: 18.3%
female: 16% (2015 est.)
country comparison to the world: 31

GOVERNMENT

Country name: *conventional long form:* none
conventional short form: Hungary
local long form: none
local short form: Magyarorszag
etymology: the Byzantine Greeks refered to the tribes that arrived on the steppes of Eastern Europe in the 9th century as the "Oungroi," a name that was later Latinized to "Ungri" and which became "Hungari"; the name originally meant an "[alliance of] ten tribes"; the Hungarian name "Magyarorszag" means "Country of the Magyars"; the term may derive from the most prominent of the Hungarian tribes, the Megyer

Government type: parliamentary republic

Capital: *name:* Budapest

geographic coordinates: 47 30 N, 19 05 E
time difference: UTC+1 (6 hours ahead of Washington, DC, during Standard Time)
daylight saving time: +1hr, begins last Sunday in March; ends last Sunday in October

Administrative divisions: 19 counties (megyek, singular—megye), 23 cities with county rights (megyei jogu varosok, singular—megyei jogu varos), and 1 capital city (fovaros)
counties: Bacs-Kiskun, Baranya, Bekes, Borsod-Abauj-Zemplen, Csongrad, Fejer, Gyor-Moson-Sopron, Hajdu-Bihar, Heves, Jasz-Nagykun-Szolnok, Komarom-Esztergom, Nograd, Pest, Somogy, Szabolcs-Szatmar-Bereg, Tolna, Vas, Veszprem, Zala
cities with county rights: Bekescsaba, Debrecen, Dunaujvaros, Eger, Erd, Gyor, Hodmezovasarhely, Kaposvar, Kecskemet, Miskolc, Nagykanizsa, Nyiregyhaza, Pecs, Salgotarjan, Sopron, Szeged, Szekesfehervar, Szekszard, Szolnok, Szombathely, Tatabanya, Veszprem, Zalaegerszeg
capital city: Budapest

Independence: 16 November 1918 (republic proclaimed); notable earlier dates: 25 December 1000 (crowning of King STEPHEN I, traditional founding date); 30 March 1867 (Austro-Hungarian dual monarchy established)

National holiday: Saint Stephen's Day, 20 August (1083); note—commemorates his cannonization and the transfer of his remains to Buda (now Budapest) in 1083

Constitution: history: previous 1949 (heavily amended in 1989 following the collapse of communism); latest approved 18 April 2011, signed 25 April 2011, effective 1 January 2012
amendments: proposed by the president of the republic, by the government, by parliamentary committee, or by Parliament members; passage requires two-thirds majority vote of Parliament members and approval by the president; amended several times, last in 2016 (2017)

Legal system: civil legal system influenced by the German model

International law organization participation: accepts compulsory ICJ jurisdiction with reservations; accepts ICCt jurisdiction

Citizenship: *citizenship by birth:* no
citizenship by descent only: at least one parent must be a citizen of Hungary
dual citizenship recognized: yes
residency requirement for naturalization: 8 years

Suffrage: 18 years of age, 16 if married and marriage registered in Hungary; universal

Executive branch: *chief of state:* Janos ADER (since 10 May 2012)

head of government: Prime Minister Viktor ORBAN (since 29 May 2010)
cabinet: Cabinet of Ministers proposed by the prime minister and appointed by the president
elections/appointments: president indirectly elected by the National Assembly with two-thirds majority vote in first round or simple majority vote in second round for a 5-year term (eligible for a second term); election last held on 13 March 2017 (next to be held by spring 2022); prime minister elected by the National Assembly on the recommendation of the president
election results: Janos ADER (Fidesz) reelected president; National Assembly vote—131 to 39; Viktor ORBAN (Fidesz) reelected prime minister; National Assembly vote—130 to 57

Legislative branch: *description:* unicameral National Assembly or Orszaggyules (199 seats; 106 members directly elected in single-member constituencies by simple majority vote and 93 members directly elected in a single nationwide constituency by party list proportional representation vote; members serve 4-year terms)
elections: last held on 6 April 2014 (next to be held on 8 April 2018)
election results: percent of vote by party—Fidesz-KDNP 66.8%, Unity 19.1%, Jobbik 11.6%, LMP 2.5%; seats by party—Fidesz-KDNP 133, Unity 38, Jobbik 23, LMP 5

Judicial branch: *highest court(s):* Curia or Supreme Judicial Court (consists of the president, vice president, department heads, and approximately 91 judges and is organized into civil, criminal, and administrative-labor departments; Constitutional Court (consists of 15 judges including the court president and vice president)

judge selection and term of office: Curia president elected by the National Assembly on the recommendation of the president of the republic; other Curia judges appointed by the president upon the recommendation of the National Judicial Council, a separate 15-member administrative body; judge tenure based on interim evaluations until normal retirement age; Constitutional Court judges, including the president of the court elected by the National Assembly; court vice president elected by the court itself; members serve 12-year terms with mandatory retirement at age 70

subordinate courts: 5 regional courts of appeal; 19 regional or county courts (including Budapest Metropolitan Court); 20 administrative-labor courts; 111 district or local courts

Political parties and leaders: Christian Democratic People's Party or KDNP [Zsolt SEMJEN] Democratic Coalition or DK [Ferenc GYURCSANY]
Dialogue for Hungary or PM [Gergely KARACSONY, Timea SZABO]
Fidesz-Hungarian Civic Alliance or Fidesz [Viktor ORBAN]
Hungarian Liberal Party or MLP [Gabor FODOR]
Hungarian Socialist Party or MSZP [Gyula MOLNAR]
Movement for a Better Hungary or Jobbik [Gabor VONA]
Politics Can Be Different or LMP [Akos HADHAZI, Bernadett SZEL]
Together 2014 or Egyutt or E14 [Peter JUHASZ]
Momentum (Momentum Mozgalom) [Andras FEKETE-GYOR]
Unity (electoral coalition of MSZP, E14, DK, PM, MLP)

Political pressure groups and leaders: Civil Osszefogas Forum ("Civil Unity Forum," nominally independent organization that serves as the steering committee for the pro-government mass organization Bekemenet (Peace March), supporting ORBAN government's policies; increasingly inactive in Orban's second consecutive term from 2014)
Hungarian Civil Liberties Union (Tarsasag a Szabadsagjogokert) or TASZ (freedom of expression, information privacy)
Hungarian Helsinki Committee (asylum seekers' rights, human rights in law enforcement and the judicial system)
MigSzol (Migrant Solidarity Group of Hungary) (independent advocacy group on migration crisis)
MostMi ("Now Us") [Bori TAKACS](Facebook group that was a major participant at anti-government demonstrations in late 2014-early 2015; pro-Europe, anti-establishment movement that blames Fidesz for the state of the country but also blames all established political parties for perceived

political and economic failures since the fall of communism)
Okotars (empowerment of civil society in Hungary)
other: Energy Club (Energia Klub)
Greenpeace Hungary (Greenpeace Magyarorszag)

International organization participation: Australia Group, BIS, CD, CE, CEI, CERN, EAPC, EBRD, ECB, EIB, ESA (cooperating state), EU, FAO, G-9, IAEA, IBRD, ICAO, ICC (national committees), ICCt, ICRM, IDA, IEA, IFAD, IFC, IFRCS, ILO, IMF, IMO, IMSO, Interpol, IOC, IOM, IPU, ISO, ITSO, ITU, ITUC (NGOs), MIGA, MINURSO, NATO, NEA, NSG, OAS (observer), OECD, OIF (observer), OPCW, OSCE, PCA, Schengen Convention, SELEC, UN, UNCTAD, UNESCO, UNFICYP, UNHCR, UNIDO, UNIFIL, UNWTO, UPU, WCO, WFTU (NGOs), WHO, WIPO, WMO, WTO, ZC

Diplomatic representation in the US: *chief of mission:* Ambassador Laszlo SZABO (since 8 September 2017)
chancery: 3910 Shoemaker Street NW, Washington, DC 20008
telephone: [1] (202) 362-6730
FAX: [1] (202) 966-8135
consulate(s) general: Los Angeles, New York
consulate(s): Boston

Diplomatic representation from the US: *chief of mission:* Ambassador (vacant); Charge d'Affaires David KOSTELANCIK (since 20 January 2017)
embassy: Szabadsag ter 12, H-1054 Budapest
mailing address: pouch: American Embassy Budapest, 5270 Budapest Place, US Department of State, Washington, DC 20521-5270
telephone: [36] (1) 475-4400
FAX: [36] (1) 475-4248

Flag description: three equal horizontal bands of red (top), white, and green; the flag dates to the national movement of the 18th and 19th centuries, and fuses the medieval colors of the Hungarian coat of arms with the revolutionary tricolor form of the French flag; folklore attributes virtues to the colors: red for strength, white for faithfulness, and green for hope; alternatively, the red is seen as being for the blood spilled in defense of the land, white for freedom, and green for the pasturelands that make up so much of the country

National symbol(s): Holy Crown of Hungary (Crown of Saint Stephen); national colors: red, white, green

National anthem: name: "Himnusz" (Hymn)
lyrics/music: Ferenc KOLCSEY/Ferenc ERKEL
note: adopted 1844

ECONOMY

Economy—overview: Hungary has transitioned from a centrally planned to a market-driven economy with a per capita income approximately two-thirds of the EU-28 average; however, in recent years the government has become more involved in managing the economy. Budapest has implemented unorthodox economic policies to boost

household consumption and has relied on EU-funded development projects to generate growth.

The economy is largely driven by exports, making it vulnerable to external market shocks. Following the fall of communism in 1990, Hungary experienced a drop-off in exports and financial assistance from the former Soviet Union. Hungary embarked on a series of economic reforms, including privatization of state-owned enterprises and reduction of social spending programs, to shift from a centrally planned to a market-driven economy, and to reorient its economy towards trade with the West. These efforts helped to spur growth, attract investment, and reduce Hungary's debt burden and fiscal deficits. However, living conditions for the average Hungarian initially deteriorated as inflation increased and unemployment reached double digits. Conditions slowly improved over the 1990s as the reforms came to fruition and export growth accelerated. Economic policies instituted during that decade helped position Hungary to join the European Union in 2004; Hungary has yet to join the euro-zone, however. Hungary suffered a historic economic contraction as a result of the global economic slowdown in 2008-09 as export demand and domestic consumption dropped, prompting it to take an IMF-EU financial assistance package.

Since 2010, the government has backpedaled on reforms and taken a more nationalist and populist approach towards economic management. The government has favored national industries, and specifically government-linked businesses, through legislation, regulation, and public procurements. In 2010 and 2012, the government increased taxes on foreign-dominated sectors, such as banking and retail, because the move helped to raise revenues and decrease the budget deficit, thereby allowing Hungary to maintain access to EU development funds. The policy deterred private investment, however. In 2011 and 2014, Hungary nationalized private pension funds. The move squeezed financial service providers out of the system, but it also helped Hungary curb its public debt and lower its budget deficit to below 3% of GDP, as subsequent pension contributions have been channeled into the state-managed pension fund. Hungary's public debt (at 73.9% of GDP) is still high compared to EU peers in Central Europe. Despite these reversals, real GDP growth has remained robust in the past several years because EU funding increased, EU demand for Hungarian exports rose, and domestic household consumption rebounded. To further boost household consumption ahead of an anticipated 2018 election, the government has announced plans to increase the minimum wage and public sector salaries, decrease taxes on foodstuffs and services, cut the personal income tax from 16% to 15%, and introduce a uniform 9% business tax for small and medium-sized enterprises and large companies. Real GDP growth slowed in 2016 due to a cyclical decrease in EU funding, but increased to 3.8% in 2017, in part as Budapest front-loaded drawdowns of EU funds ahead of the planned 2018 election.

Systemic economic challenges include pervasive corruption, long-term and youth unemployment, skilled labor shortages, widespread poverty in rural areas, vulnerabilities to changes in demand for exports, and a heavy reliance on Russian energy imports.

GDP (purchasing power parity): $283.6 billion (2017 est.)
$274.8 billion (2016 est.)
$269.5 billion (2015 est.)
note: data are in 2017 dollars
country comparison to the world: 61

GDP (official exchange rate): $132 billion (2016 est.)

GDP—real growth rate: 3.2% (2017 est.)
2% (2016 est.)
3.1% (2015 est.)
country comparison to the world: 106

GDP—per capita (PPP): $28,900 (2017 est.)
$28,000 (2016 est.)
$27,300 (2015 est.)
note: data are in 2017 dollars
country comparison to the world: 69

Gross national saving: 24.4% of GDP (2017 est.)
24.5% of GDP (2016 est.)
25.1% of GDP (2015 est.)
country comparison to the world: 57

GDP—composition, by end use:
household consumption: 52.3%
government consumption: 19.9%
investment in fixed capital: 19%
investment in inventories: -1.2%
exports of goods and services: 94.1%
imports of goods and services: -84.1% (2017 est.)

GDP—composition, by sector of origin:
agriculture: 4.4%
industry: 30.9%
services: 64.7% (2017 est.)

Agriculture—products: wheat, corn, sunflower seed, potatoes, sugar beets; pigs, cattle, poultry, dairy products

Industries: mining, metallurgy, construction materials, processed foods, textiles, chemicals (especially pharmaceuticals), motor vehicles

Industrial production growth rate: 5.5% (2017 est.)
country comparison to the world: 37

Labor force: 4.599 million (2017 est.)
country comparison to the world: 88

Labor force—by occupation: agriculture: 4.9%
industry: 30.3%
services: 64.5% (2015 est.)

Unemployment rate: 4.4% (2017 est.)
5.1% (2016 est.)
country comparison to the world: 59

Population below poverty line: 14.9% (2015 est.)

Household income or consumption by percentage share: lowest 10%: 3.3%
highest 10%: 22.4% (2015)

Distribution of family income—Gini index: 28.2 (2015 est.)
28.6 (2014)
country comparison to the world: 133

Budget: revenues: $63.63 billion
expenditures: $66.96 billion (2017 est.)

Taxes and other revenues: 48.2% of GDP (2017 est.)
country comparison to the world: 19

Budget surplus (+) or deficit (-): -2.5% of GDP
note: Hungary has been under the EU Excessive Deficit Procedure since it joined the EU in 2004; in March 2012 the EU elevated its Excessive Deficit Procedure against Hungary and proposed freezing 30% of the country's Cohesion Funds because 2011 deficit reductions were not achieved in a sustainable manner; in June 2012, the EU lifted the freeze, recognizing that steps had been taken to reduce the deficit; the Hungarian deficit increased above 3% both in 2013 and in 2014 due to sluggish growth and the government's fiscal tightening (2017 est.)
country comparison to the world: 100

Public debt: 73.9% of GDP (2017 est.)
74.1% of GDP (2016 est.)
note: general government gross debt is defined in the Maastricht Treaty as consolidated general government gross debt at nominal value, outstanding at the end of the year in the following categories of government liabilities: currency and deposits, securities other than shares excluding financial derivatives, and government, state government, local government, and social security funds.
country comparison to the world: 47

Fiscal year: calendar year

Inflation rate (consumer prices): 2.5% (2017 est.)
0.4% (2016 est.)
country comparison to the world: 114

Central bank discount rate: 0.9% (31 December 2016)
1.35% (31 December 2015)
country comparison to the world: 129

Commercial bank prime lending rate: 1.6% (31 December 2017 est.)
2.09% (31 December 2016 est.)
country comparison to the world: 182

Stock of narrow money: $68.36 billion (31 December 2017 est.)
$55.64 billion (31 December 2016 est.)
country comparison to the world: 47

Stock of broad money: $80.77 billion (31 December 2017 est.)
$69.25 billion (31 December 2016 est.)
country comparison to the world: 59

Stock of domestic credit: $77.36 billion (31 December 2017 est.)
$70.11 billion (31 December 2016 est.)
country comparison to the world: 60

Market value of publicly traded shares: $21.59 billion (31 December 2016 est.)
$17.69 billion (31 December 2015 est.)
$14.51 billion (31 December 2014 est.)
country comparison to the world: 64

Current account balance: $6.339 billion (2017 est.)
$6.797 billion (2016 est.)
country comparison to the world: 26

Exports: $98.72 billion (2017 est.)
$91.6 billion (2016 est.)

country comparison to the world: 37

Exports—commodities: machinery and equipment 53.4%, other manufactures 31.2%, food products 8.4%, raw materials 3.4%, fuels and electricity 3.9% (2012 est.)

Exports—partners: Germany 28.2%, Romania 5.2%, Slovakia 5%, Austria 4.9%, France 4.8%, Italy 4.8%, Czech Republic 4.2%, Poland 4.2% (2016)

Imports: $93.28 billion (2017 est.)
$85.78 billion (2016 est.)
country comparison to the world: 36

Imports—commodities: machinery and equipment 45.4%, other manufactures 34.3%, fuels and electricity 12.6%, food products 5.3%, raw materials 2.5% (2012)

Imports—partners: Germany 26.3%, Austria 6.4%, China 6.3%, Poland 5.5%, Slovakia 5.3%, Netherlands 4.9%, Czech Republic 4.9%, France 4.8%, Italy 4.8% (2016)

Reserves of foreign exchange and gold: $27.02 billion (31 December 2017 est.)
$25.82 billion (31 December 2016 est.)
country comparison to the world: 53

Debt—external: $131.8 billion (31 December 2017 est.)
$131.3 billion (31 December 2016 est.)
country comparison to the world: 45

Stock of direct foreign investment—at home: $302.9 billion (31 December 2017 est.)
$298.2 billion (31 December 2016 est.)
country comparison to the world: 22

Stock of direct foreign investment—abroad: $225.3 billion (31 December 2017 est.)
$222.6 billion (31 December 2016 est.)
country comparison to the world: 25

Exchange rates: forints (HUF) per US dollar—
279.5 (2017 est.)
281.52 (2016 est.)
281.52 (2015 est.)
279.33 (2014 est.)
232.6 (2013 est.)

ENERGY

Electricity access: electrification—total population: 100% (2016)

Electricity—production: 28.67 billion kWh (2015 est.)
country comparison to the world: 66

Electricity—consumption: 38.66 billion kWh (2015 est.)
country comparison to the world: 58

Electricity—exports: 5.24 billion kWh (2016 est.)
country comparison to the world: 35

Electricity—imports: 17.95 billion kWh (2016 est.)
country comparison to the world: 13

Electricity—installed generating capacity: 8.468 million kW (2015 est.)
country comparison to the world: 68

Electricity—from fossil fuels: 64.5% of total installed capacity (2015 est.)

country comparison to the world: 115

Electricity—from nuclear fuels: 22.3% of total installed capacity (2015 est.)
country comparison to the world: 7

Electricity—from hydroelectric plants: 0.7% of total installed capacity (2015 est.)
country comparison to the world: 148

Electricity—from other renewable sources: 14.1% of total installed capacity (2015 est.)
country comparison to the world: 52

Crude oil—production: 13,830 bbl/day (2016 est.)
country comparison to the world: 77

Crude oil—exports: 1,042 bbl/day (2016 est.)
country comparison to the world: 72

Crude oil—imports: 120,400 bbl/day (2016 est.)
country comparison to the world: 40

Crude oil—proved reserves: 25.1 million bbl (1 January 2017 es)
country comparison to the world: 85

Refined petroleum products—production: 156,100 bbl/day (2016 est.)
country comparison to the world: 58

Refined petroleum products—consumption: 157,200 bbl/day (2016 est.)
country comparison to the world: 67

Refined petroleum products—exports: 50,510 bbl/day (2016 est.)
country comparison to the world: 53

Refined petroleum products—imports: 67,860 bbl/day (2016 est.)
country comparison to the world: 70

Natural gas—production: 1.772 billion cu m (2015 est.)
country comparison to the world: 60

Natural gas—consumption: 17.14 billion cu m (2015 est.)
country comparison to the world: 47

Natural gas—exports: 545 million cu m (2015 est.)
country comparison to the world: 42

Natural gas—imports: 6.79 billion cu m (2015 est.)
country comparison to the world: 31

Natural gas—proved reserves: 7.702 billion cu m (1 January 2017 es)
country comparison to the world: 87

Carbon dioxide emissions from consumption of energy: 44.2 million Mt (2015 est.)
country comparison to the world: 64

COMMUNICATIONS

Telephones—fixed lines: *total subscriptions:* 3,119,735
subscriptions per 100 inhabitants: 32 (July 2016 est.)
country comparison to the world: 49

Telephones—mobile cellular: *total:* 11,779,908
subscriptions per 100 inhabitants: 119 (July 2016 est.)
country comparison to the world: 78

Telephone system: *general assessment:* modern telephone system is digital and highly automated; trunk services are carried by fiber-optic cable and digital microwave radio relay
domestic: competition among mobile-cellular service providers has led to a sharp increase in the use of mobile-cellular phones since 2000 and a decrease in the number of fixed-line connections
international: country code—36; Hungary has fiber-optic cable connections with all neighboring countries; the international switch is in Budapest; satellite earth stations—2 Intelsat (Atlantic Ocean and Indian Ocean regions), 1 Inmarsat, 1 very small aperture terminal (VSAT) system of ground terminals (2015)

Broadcast media: mixed system of state-supported public service broadcast media and private broadcasters; the 5 publicly owned TV channels and the 2 main privately owned TV stations are the major national broadcasters; a large number of special interest channels; highly developed market for satellite and cable TV services with about two-thirds of viewers utilizing their services; 4 state-supported public-service radio networks; a large number of local stations including commercial, public service, nonprofit, and community radio stations; digital transition completed at the end of 2013; government-linked businesses have greatly consolidated ownership in broadcast and print media (2016)

Internet country code: .hu
Internet users: total: 7,826,695

percent of population: 79.3% (July 2016 est.)
country comparison to the world: 50

TRANSPORTATION

National air transport system: *number of registered air carriers:* 5
inventory of registered aircraft operated by air carriers: 75
annual passenger traffic on registered air carriers: 20,042,185
annual freight traffic on registered air carriers: 0 mt-km (2015)
Civil aircraft registration country code prefix: HA (2016)

Airports: 41 (2013)
country comparison to the world: 104

Airports—with paved runways: *total:* 20
over 3,047 m: 2
2,438 to 3,047 m: 6
1,524 to 2,437 m: 6
914 to 1,523 m: 5
under 914 m: 1 (2017)

Airports—with unpaved runways: *total:* 21
1,524 to 2,437 m: 2
914 to 1,523 m: 8
under 914 m: 11 (2013)

Heliports: 3 (2013)

Pipelines: gas (high-pressure transmission system) 5,873 km; gas (low-pressure distribution network) 83,619 km (2015); oil 850 km; refined products 1,200 km (2016)

Railways: *total:* 8,049 km
broad gauge: 36 km 1.524-m gauge
standard gauge: 7,794 km 1.435-m gauge (2,889 km electrified)
narrow gauge: 219 km 0.760-m gauge (2014)
country comparison to the world: 28

Roadways: *total:* 203,601 km
paved: 77,087 km (includes 1,582 km of expressways)
unpaved: 126,514 km (2014)
country comparison to the world: 26

Waterways: 1,622 km (most on Danube River) (2011)
country comparison to the world: 47

Ports and terminals: river port(s): Baja, Csepel (Budapest), Dunaujvaros, Gyor-Gonyu, Mohacs (Danube)

MILITARY AND SECURITY

Military expenditures: 1.01% of GDP (2016)
0.93% of GDP (2015)
0.87% of GDP (2014)
0.95% of GDP (2013)
1.04% of GDP (2012)
country comparison to the world: 113

Military branches: Hungarian Defense Forces: Land Forces, Hungarian Air Force (Magyar Legiero, ML) (2011)

Military service age and obligation: 18-25 years of age for voluntary military service; no conscription; 6-month service obligation (2012)

TRANSNATIONAL ISSUES

Disputes—international: bilateral government, legal, technical and economic working group negotiations continue in 2006 with Slovakia over Hungary's failure to complete its portion of the Gabcikovo-Nagymaros hydroelectric dam project along the Danube; as a member state that forms part of the EU's external border, Hungary has implemented the strict Schengen border rules

Refugees and internally displaced persons: *refugees (countries of origin):* 5,950 applicants for forms of legal stay other than asylum (Ukraine) (2015)
stateless persons: 135 (2016)
note: 432,428 estimated refugee and migrant arrivals (January 2015—February 2018); Hungary is predominantly a transit country and hosts fewer than 600 migrants and asylum seekers as of November 2017

Illicit drugs: transshipment point for Southwest Asian heroin and cannabis and for South American cocaine destined for Western Europe; limited producer of precursor chemicals, particularly for amphetamine and methamphetamine; efforts to counter money laundering, related to organized crime and drug trafficking are improving but remain vulnerable; significant consumer of ecstasy

INTRODUCTION

Background: Settled by Norwegian and Celtic (Scottish and Irish) immigrants during the late 9th and 10th centuries A.D., Iceland boasts the world's oldest functioning legislative assembly, the Althingi, established in 930. Independent for over 300 years, Iceland was subsequently ruled by Norway and Denmark. Fallout from the Askja volcano of 1875 devastated the Icelandic economy and caused widespread famine. Over the next quarter century, 20% of the island's population emigrated, mostly to Canada and the US. Denmark granted limited home rule in 1874 and complete independence in 1944. The second half of the 20th century saw substantial economic growth driven primarily by the fishing industry. The economy diversified greatly after the country joined the European Economic Area in 1994, but Iceland was especially hard hit by the global financial crisis in the years following 2008. The economy is now on an upward trajectory, fueled primarily by a tourism and construction boom. Literacy, longevity, and social cohesion are first rate by world standards.

GEOGRAPHY

Location: Northern Europe, island between the Greenland Sea and the North Atlantic Ocean, northwest of the United Kingdom

Geographic coordinates: 65 00 N, 18 00 W

Map references: Arctic Region

Area: *total:* 103,000 sq km
land: 100,250 sq km
water: 2,750 sq km
country comparison to the world: 109

Area—comparative: slightly smaller than Pennsylvania; about the same size as Kentucky

Land boundaries: 0 km

Coastline: 4,970 km

Maritime claims: *territorial sea:* 12 nm
exclusive economic zone: 200 nm
continental shelf: 200 nm or to the edge of the continental margin

Climate: temperate; moderated by North Atlantic Current; mild, windy winters; damp, cool summers

Terrain: mostly plateau interspersed with mountain peaks, icefields; coast deeply indented by bays and fiords

Elevation: *mean elevation:* 557 m

elevation extremes: *lowest point:* Atlantic Ocean 0 m
highest point: Hvannadalshnukur 2,110 m (at Vatnajokull Glacier)

Natural resources: fish, hydropower, geothermal power, diatomite

Land use: *agricultural land:* 18.7%
arable land: 1.2%;
permanent crops: 0%;
permanent pasture: 17.5%
forest: 0.3%
other: 81% (2011 est.)
Irrigated land: NA

Population—distribution: Iceland is almost entirely urban with half of the population located in and around the capital of Reykjavik; smaller clusters are primarily found along the coast in the north and west

Natural hazards: earthquakes and volcanic activity
volcanism: Iceland, situated on top of a hotspot, experiences severe volcanic activity; Eyjafjallajokull (1,666 m) erupted in 2010, sending ash high into the atmosphere and seriously disrupting European air traffic; scientists continue to monitor nearby Katla (1,512 m), which has a high probability of eruption in the very near future, potentially disrupting air traffic; Grimsvoetn and Hekla are Iceland's most active volcanoes; other historically active volcanoes include Askja, Bardarbunga, Brennisteinsfjoll, Esjufjoll, Hengill, Krafla, Krisuvik, Kverkfjoll, Oraefajokull, Reykjanes, Torfajokull, and Vestmannaeyjar

Environment—current issues: water pollution from fertilizer runoff; inadequate wastewater treatment

Environment—international agreements: *party to:* Air Pollution, Air Pollution-Persistent Organic Pollutants, Biodiversity, Climate Change, Climate Change-Kyoto Protocol, Desertification, Endangered Species, Hazardous Wastes, Kyoto Protocol, Law of the Sea, Marine Dumping, Ozone Layer Protection, Ship Pollution, Transboundary Air Pollution, Wetlands, Whaling
signed, but not ratified: Environmental Modification, Marine Life Conservation

Geography—note: strategic location between Greenland and Europe; westernmost European country; Reykjavik is the northernmost national capital in the world; more land covered by glaciers than in all of continental Europe

PEOPLE AND SOCIETY

Population: 339,747 (July 2017 est.)
country comparison to the world: 178

Nationality: *noun:* Icelander(s)
adjective: Icelandic

Ethnic groups: homogeneous mixture of descendants of Norse and Celts 94%, population of foreign origin 6%

Languages: Icelandic, English, Nordic languages, German widely spoken

Religions: Evangelical Lutheran Church of Iceland (official) 69.9%, Roman Catholic 3.8%, Reykjavik Free Church 2.9%, Hafnarfjorour Free Church 2%, Asatru Association 1.1%, The Independent Congregation 1%, other religions 4% (includes Zuist and Pentecostal), none 6.1%, other or unspecified 9.2% (2017 est.)

Age structure: *0-14 years:* 20.4% (male 35,418/female 33,887)
15-24 years: 13.5% (male 23,190/female 22,659)
25-54 years: 39.88% (male 68,579/female 66,899)
55-64 years: 11.81% (male 20,119/female 20,007)
65 years and over: 14.42% (male 22,936/female 26,053) (2017 est.)

Dependency ratios: *total dependency ratio:* 51.6
youth dependency ratio: 30.8
elderly dependency ratio: 20.8
potential support ratio: 4.8 (2015 est.)

Median age: *total:* 36.5 years
male: 35.9 years
female: 37.1 years (2017 est.)
country comparison to the world: 70

Population growth rate: 1.13% (2017 est.)
country comparison to the world: 101

Birth rate: 13.7 births/1,000 population (2017 est.)
country comparison to the world: 141

Death rate: 6.4 deaths/1,000 population (2017 est.)
country comparison to the world: 148

Net migration rate: 4 migrant(s)/1,000 population (2017 est.)
country comparison to the world: 28

Population distribution: Iceland is almost entirely urban with half of the population located in and around the capital of Reykjavik; smaller clusters are primarily found along the coast in the north and west

Urbanization: *urban population:* 94.3% of total population (2017)
rate of urbanization: 1.1% annual rate of change (2015-20 est.)

Major urban areas—population: REYKJAVIK (capital) 184,000 (2014)

Sex ratio: *at birth:* 1.05 male(s)/female
0-14 years: 1.05 male(s)/female
15-24 years: 1.03 male(s)/female
25-54 years: 1.02 male(s)/female
55-64 years: 1.01 male(s)/female
65 years and over: 0.88 male(s)/female
total population: 1.01 male(s)/female (2016 est.)

Mother's mean age at first birth: 27.4 years (2015 est.)

Maternal mortality ratio: 3 deaths/100,000 live births (2015 est.)
country comparison to the world: 183

Infant mortality rate: total: 2.1 deaths/1,000 live births
male: 2.2 deaths/1,000 live births
female: 1.9 deaths/1,000 live births (2017 est.)
country comparison to the world: 223

Life expectancy at birth: *total population:* 83.1 years
male: 80.9 years
female: 85.4 years (2017 est.)
country comparison to the world: 6

Total fertility rate: 2 children born/woman (2017 est.)
country comparison to the world: 120

Health expenditures: 8.9% of GDP (2014)
country comparison to the world: 43

Physicians density: 3.79 physicians/1,000 population (2015)

Hospital bed density: 3.18 beds/1,000 population (2014)

Drinking water source:
improved:
urban: 100% of population
rural: 100% of population
total: 100% of population
unimproved:
urban: 0% of population
rural: 0% of population
total: 0% of population (2015 est.)

Sanitation facility access:
improved:
urban: 98.7% of population
rural: 100% of population
total: 98.8% of population
unimproved:
urban: 1.3% of population
rural: 0% of population
total: 1.2% of population (2015 est.)

HIV/AIDS—adult prevalence rate: NA

HIV/AIDS—people living with HIV/AIDS: NA

HIV/AIDS—deaths: NA

Obesity—adult prevalence rate: 21.9% (2016)
country comparison to the world: 83

Education expenditures: 7.8% of GDP (2013)
country comparison to the world: 14

School life expectancy (primary to tertiary education): *total:* 20 years
male: 18 years
female: 21 years (2013)

Unemployment, youth ages 15-24: *total:* 6.5%
male: 6.7%
female: 6.4% (2016 est.)
country comparison to the world: 85

GOVERNMENT

Country name: *conventional long form:* Republic of Iceland
conventional short form: Iceland
local long form: Lydveldid Island
local short form: Island

etymology: Floki VILGERDARSON, an early explorer of the island (9th century), applied the name "Land of Ice" after spotting a fjord full of drift ice to the north and spending a bitter winter on the island; he eventually settled on the island, however, after he saw how it greened up in the summer and that it was, in fact, habitable

Government type: parliamentary republic

Capital: name: Reykjavik

geographic coordinates: 64 09 N, 21 57 W
time difference: UTC 0 (5 hours ahead of Washington, DC, during Standard Time)

Administrative divisions: 8 regions; Austurland, Hofudhborgarsvaedhi, Nordhurland Eystra, Nordhurland Vestra, Sudhurland, Sudhurnes, Vestfirdhir, Vesturland

Independence: 1 December 1918 (became a sovereign state under the Danish Crown); 17 June 1944 (from Denmark; birthday of Jon SIGURDSSON, leader of Iceland's 19th Century independence movement)

National holiday: Independence Day, 17 June (1944)

Constitution: history: several previous; latest ratified 16 June 1944, effective 17 June 1944 (at independence)
amendments: proposed by the Althingi; passage requires approval by the Althingi and by the next elected Althingi, and confirmation by the president of the republic; proposed amendments to Article 62 of the constitution—that the Evangelical Lutheran Church shall be the state church of Iceland—also require passage by referendum; amended many times, last in 2013 (2016)

Legal system: civil law system influenced by the Danish model

International law organization participation: has not submitted an ICJ jurisdiction declaration; accepts ICCt jurisdiction

Citizenship: *citizenship by birth:* no
citizenship by descent only: at least one parent must be a citizen of Iceland
dual citizenship recognized: yes
residency requirement for naturalization: 3 to 7 years

Suffrage: 18 years of age; universal

Executive branch: *chief of state:* President Gudni Thorlacius JOHANNESSON (since 1 August 2016)

head of government: Prime Minister Katrin JAKOBSDOTTIR (since 30 November 2017)
cabinet: Cabinet appointed by the prime minister
elections/appointments: president directly elected by simple majority popular vote for a 4-year term (no term limits); election last held on 25 June 2016 (next to be held in June 2020); following legislative elections, the leader of the majority party or majority coalition becomes prime minister
election results: Gudni Thorlacius JOHANNESSON elected president; percent of vote—Gudni Thorlacius JOHANNESSON (IP) 39.1%, Halla TOMASDOTTIR (independent) 27.9%, Andri Snaer MAGNASON (independent) 14.3%,

David ODDSSON (IP) 13.7%, Sturla JONSSON (Sturla Jonsson) 3.5%, invalid 1.5%

Legislative branch: *description:* unicameral Althingi or Parliament (63 seats; members directly elected in multi-seat constituencies by proportional representation vote to serve 4-year terms)
elections: last held on 28 October 2016 (next to be held on 28 October 2017)
election results: percent of vote by party—IP 25.2%, LGM 16.9%, SDA 12.1%, CP 10.9%, PP 10.7%, Pirate Party 9.2%, People's Party 6.9%, Reform Party 6.7%. other 1.5%; seats by party—IP 16, LGM 11, SDA 7, CP 7, PP 8, Pirate Party 6, Reform Party 4, People's Party 4

Judicial branch: *highest court(s):* Supreme Court or Haestirettur (consists of 9 judges)
judge selection and term of office: judges proposed by Ministry of Interior selection committee and appointed by the president; judges appointed for an indefinite period
subordinate courts: 8 district courts; Labor Court

Political parties and leaders: Bright Future (Bjort framtid) or BF [Biort OLAFSDOTTIR]
Centrist Party (Midflokkurinn) or CP [Sigmundur David GUNNLAUGSSON]
Independence Party (Sjalfstaedisflokkurinn) or IP [Bjarni BENEDIKTSSON]
Left-Green Movement (Vinstrihreyfingin-graent frambod) or LGM [Katrin JAKOBSDOTTIR]
People's Party (Flokkur Folksins) [Inga SAELAND]
Pirate Party (Piratar) [Birgitta JONSDOTTIR]
Progressive Party (Framsoknarflokkurinn) or PP [Sigurdur Ingi JOHANNSSON]
Reform (Vidreisn) [Thorgerdur Katrin GUNNARSDOTTIR]
Social Democratic Alliance (Samfylkingin) or SDA [Logi Mar EINARSSON]

International organization participation: Arctic Council, Australia Group, BIS, CBSS, CD, CE, EAPC, EBRD, EFTA, FAO, FATF, IAEA, IBRD, ICAO, ICC (national committees), ICCt, ICRM, IDA, IFAD, IFC, IFRCS, IHO, ILO, IMF, IMO, IMSO, Interpol, IOC, IOM, IPU, ISO, ITSO, ITU, ITUC (NGOs), MIGA, NATO, NC, NEA, NIB, NSG, OAS (observer), OECD, OPCW, OSCE, PCA, Schengen Convention, UN, UNCTAD, UNESCO, UPU, WCO, WHO, WIPO, WMO, WTO

Diplomatic representation in the US: *chief of mission:* Ambassador Geir Hilmar HAARDE (since 23 February 2015)
chancery: House of Sweden, 2900 K Street NW
telephone: [1] (202) 265-6653
FAX: [1] (202) 265-6656
consulate(s) general: New York

Diplomatic representation from the US: *chief of mission:* Ambassador (vacant); Charge d'Affaires Jill ESPOSITO (since 20 January 2017)
embassy: Laufasvegur 21, 101 Reykjavik
mailing address: US Department of State, 5640 Reykjavik Place, Washington, D.C. 20521-5640
telephone: [354] 595-22-00
FAX: [354] 562-9118

427

Flag description: blue with a red cross outlined in white extending to the edges of the flag; the vertical part of the cross is shifted to the hoist side in the style of the Dannebrog (Danish flag); the colors represent three of the elements that make up the island: red is for the island's volcanic fires, white recalls the snow and ice fields of the island, and blue is for the surrounding ocean

National symbol(s): gyrfalcon; national colors: blue, white, red

National anthem: name: "Lofsongur" (Song of Praise)
lyrics/music: Matthias JOCHUMSSON/Sveinbjorn SVEINBJORNSSON
note: adopted 1944; also known as "O, Gud vors lands" (O, God of Our Land), the anthem was originally written and performed in 1874

ECONOMY

Economy—overview: Iceland's economy combines a capitalist structure and free-market principles with an extensive welfare system. Except for a brief period during the 2008 crisis, Iceland has achieved high growth, low unemployment, and a remarkably even distribution of income. The economy depends heavily on the fishing industry, which provides 40% of merchandise export earnings, more than 12% of GDP, and employs nearly 5% of the work force. It remains sensitive to declining fish stocks, as well as to fluctuations in world prices for its main exports: fish and fish products, aluminum, and ferrosilicon. Since 2010, tourism has become the main pillar of Icelandic economic growth, with the number of tourists reaching 4.5 times the Icelandic population in 2016.

Iceland's economy has been diversifying into manufacturing and service industries in the last decade, particularly within the fields of tourism, software production, and biotechnology. In fall 2013, the Icelandic Government approved a joint application by Icelandic, Chinese, and Norwegian energy firms to conduct oil exploration off Iceland's northeast coast, although no exploration has yet taken place. Abundant geothermal and hydropower sources have attracted substantial foreign investment in the aluminum sector, boosted economic growth, and sparked some interest from high-tech firms looking to establish data centers using cheap green energy, although the financial crisis has put several investment projects on hold.

Following the privatization of the banking sector in the early 2000s, domestic banks expanded aggressively in foreign markets, and consumers and businesses borrowed heavily in foreign currencies. Worsening global financial conditions throughout 2008 resulted in a sharp depreciation of the krona vis-a-vis other major currencies. The foreign exposure of Icelandic banks, whose loans and other assets totaled more than 10 times the country's GDP, became unsustainable. Iceland's three largest banks collapsed in late 2008. The country secured over $10 billion in loans from the IMF and other countries to stabilize its currency and financial sector, and to back government guarantees for foreign deposits in Icelandic banks. GDP fell 6.8% in 2009, and unemployment peaked at 9.4% in

February 2009. Three new banks were established to take over the domestic assets of the collapsed banks. Two of them have majority ownership by the state, which intends to re-privatize them.

Since the collapse of Iceland's financial sector, government economic priorities have included stabilizing the krona, implementing capital controls, reducing Iceland's high budget deficit, containing inflation, addressing high household debt, restructuring the financial sector, and diversifying the economy. Capital controls were lifted in March 2017, but some financial protections (e.g., reserve requirements for specified investments connected to new inflows of foreign currency) remain in place. Iceland's financial woes prompted an initial increase in public support to join the EU and the euro zone, with accession negotiations beginning in July 2010, but negotiations were suspended under the center-right government that took power in 2013. The current ruling coalition does not intend to restart accession talks, but has signaled that it would allow a vote on the question of EU membership, if a bill came before parliament near the end of the current parliamentary term. Most macroeconomic indicators and employment have rebounded to pre-crisis levels, driven primarily by the unprecedented growth in tourism—averaging over 20% annually—following the well-publicized volcanic eruption in 2010.

GDP (purchasing power parity): $17.73 billion (2017 est.)
$16.8 billion (2016 est.)
$15.67 billion (2015 est.)
note: data are in 2017 dollars
country comparison to the world: 153

GDP (official exchange rate): $24.85 billion (2016 est.)

GDP—real growth rate: 5.5% (2017 est.)
7.2% (2016 est.)
4.1% (2015 est.)
country comparison to the world: 29

GDP—per capita (PPP): $52,100 (2017 est.)
$50,000 (2016 est.)
$47,100 (2015 est.)
note: data are in 2017 dollars
country comparison to the world: 24

Gross national saving: 28.1% of GDP (2017 est.)
29.3% of GDP (2016 est.)
24.5% of GDP (2015 est.)
country comparison to the world: 34

GDP—composition, by end use:
household consumption: 49%
government consumption: 22.2%
investment in fixed capital: 21.9%
investment in inventories: 0.1%
exports of goods and services: 49.6%
imports of goods and services: -42.6% (2017 est.)

GDP—composition, by sector of origin:
agriculture: 5.8%
industry: 19.8%
services: 74.4% (2017 est.)

Agriculture—products: potatoes, carrots, green vegetables, tomatoes, cucumbers; mutton, chicken, pork, beef, dairy products; fish

Industries: tourism, fish processing; aluminum smelting;; geothermal power, hydropower; medical/pharmaceutical products

Industrial production growth rate: 2.4% (2017 est.)
country comparison to the world: 118

Labor force: 198,700 (2017 est.)
country comparison to the world: 172

Labor force—by occupation: *agriculture:* 4.8%
industry: 22.2%
services: 73% (2008)

Unemployment rate: 2.8% (2017 est.)
3% (2016 est.)
country comparison to the world: 31

Population below poverty line: NA%
note: 332,100 families (2011 est.)

Household income or consumption by percentage share: *lowest 10%:* NA%
highest 10%: NA%

Distribution of family income—Gini index: 28 (2006)
25 (2005)
country comparison to the world: 135

Budget: *revenues:* $9.962 billion
expenditures: $9.735 billion (2017 est.)
Taxes and other revenues: 40.1% of GDP (2017 est.)
country comparison to the world: 34

Budget surplus (+) or deficit (-): 0.9% of GDP (2017 est.)
country comparison to the world: 17

Public debt: 47.4% of GDP (2017 est.)
54.5% of GDP (2016 est.)
country comparison to the world: 106

Fiscal year: calendar year

Inflation rate (consumer prices): 1.8% (2017 est.)
1.7% (2016 est.)
country comparison to the world: 82

Central bank discount rate: 5.4% (31 January 2012)
5.75% (31 December 2010)
country comparison to the world: 77

Commercial bank prime lending rate: 7.6% (31 December 2017 est.)
8.24% (31 December 2016 est.)
country comparison to the world: 113

Stock of narrow money: $4.653 billion (31 December 2017 est.)
$4.251 billion (31 December 2016 est.)
country comparison to the world: 108

Stock of broad money: $8.506 billion (31 December 2016 est.)
$8.693 billion (31 December 2016 est.)
country comparison to the world: 111

Stock of domestic credit: $19.78 billion (31 December 2017 est.)
$21.18 billion (31 December 2016 est.)
country comparison to the world: 86

Market value of publicly traded shares: $2.825 billion (31 December 2012 est.)
$2.021 billion (31 December 2011 est.)
$1.996 billion (31 December 2010 est.)
country comparison to the world: 96

Current account balance: $1.54 billion (2017 est.)
$1.589 billion (2016 est.)
country comparison to the world: 34

Exports: $4.6 billion (2017 est.)
$4.483 billion (2016 est.)
country comparison to the world: 113

Exports—commodities: fish and fish products (42%), aluminum (38%), agricultural products, medicinal and medical products, ferro-silicon (2015)

Exports—partners: Netherlands 25.4%, UK 11.3%, Spain 10.5%, US 7.8%, Germany 7%, France 6.7%, Norway 4.2% (2016)

Imports: $5.674 billion (2017 est.)
$5.315 billion (2016 est.)
country comparison to the world: 117

Imports—commodities: machinery and equipment, petroleum products, foodstuffs, textiles

Imports—partners: Germany 10.1%, US 10%, Norway 9.1%, Netherlands 7.5%, China 7.4%, Denmark 6.1%, UK 5.8% (2016)

Reserves of foreign exchange and gold: $6.14 billion (31 December 2017 est.)
$7.226 billion (31 December 2016 est.)
country comparison to the world: 89

Debt—external: $27.14 billion (31 December 2017 est.)
$25.02 billion (31 December 2016 est.)
country comparison to the world: 86

Stock of direct foreign investment—at home:
$12.89 billion (31 December 2017 est.)
$13.89 billion (31 December 2016 est.)
country comparison to the world: 94

Stock of direct foreign investment—abroad:
$15.54 billion (31 December 2017 est.)
$17.64 billion (31 December 2016 est.)
country comparison to the world: 59

Exchange rates: Icelandic kronur (ISK) per US dollar—
111.7 (2017 est.)
120.81 (2016 est.)
120.81 (2015 est.)
131.92 (2014 est.)
116.77 (2013 est.)

ENERGY

Electricity access: electrification—*total population:* 100% (2016)

Electricity—production: 18.56 billion kWh (2015 est.)
country comparison to the world: 78

Electricity—consumption: 17.98 billion kWh (2015 est.)
country comparison to the world: 73

Electricity—exports: 0 kWh (2016 est.)
country comparison to the world: 149

Electricity—imports: 0 kWh (2016 est.)
country comparison to the world: 161

Electricity—installed generating capacity: 2.772 million kW (2015 est.)
country comparison to the world: 101

Electricity—from fossil fuels: 4.2% of total installed capacity (2015 est.)
country comparison to the world: 206

Electricity—from nuclear fuels: 0% of total installed capacity (2015 est.)
country comparison to the world: 110

Electricity—from hydroelectric plants: 71.7% of total installed capacity (2015 est.)
country comparison to the world: 18

Electricity—from other renewable sources: 24.1% of total installed capacity (2015 est.)
country comparison to the world: 24

Crude oil—production: 0 bbl/day (2016 est.)
country comparison to the world: 149

Crude oil—exports: 0 bbl/day (2016 est.)
country comparison to the world: 139

Crude oil—imports: 0 bbl/day (2016 est.)
country comparison to the world: 141

Crude oil—proved reserves: 0 bbl (1 January 2017 es)
country comparison to the world: 148

Refined petroleum products—production: 0 bbl/day (2016 est.)
country comparison to the world: 159

Refined petroleum products—consumption: 19,800 bbl/day (2016 est.)
country comparison to the world: 139

Refined petroleum products—exports: 2,845 bbl/day (2016 est.)
country comparison to the world: 103

Refined petroleum products—imports: 19,530 bbl/day (2016 est.)
country comparison to the world: 119

Natural gas—production: 0 cu m (2014 est.)
country comparison to the world: 150

Natural gas—consumption: 0 cu m (2014 est.)
country comparison to the world: 194

Natural gas—exports: 0 cu m (2014 est.)
country comparison to the world: 122

Natural gas—imports: 0 cu m (2014 est.)
country comparison to the world: 139

Natural gas—proved reserves: 0 cu m (1 January 2014 es)
country comparison to the world: 153

Carbon dioxide emissions from consumption of energy: 3.3 million Mt (2013 est.)
country comparison to the world: 141

COMMUNICATIONS

Telephones—fixed lines: *total subscriptions:* 164,566
subscriptions per 100 inhabitants: 49 (July 2016 est.)
country comparison to the world: 131

Telephones—mobile cellular: *total:* 401,613
subscriptions per 100 inhabitants: 120 (July 2016 est.)
country comparison to the world: 175

Telephone system: *general assessment:* telecommunications infrastructure is modern and fully digitized, with satellite-earth stations, fiber-optic cables, and an extensive broadband network
domestic: liberalization of the telecommunications sector beginning in the late 1990s has led to increased competition especially in the mobile services segment of the market
international: country code—354; the CANTAT-3 and FARICE-1 submarine cable systems provide connectivity to Canada, the Faroe Islands, UK, Denmark, and Germany; a planned new section of the Hibernia-Atlantic submarine cable will provide additional connectivity to Canada, US, and Ireland; satellite earth stations—2 Intelsat (Atlantic Ocean), 1 Inmarsat (Atlantic and Indian Ocean regions); note—Iceland shares the Inmarsat earth station with the other Nordic countries (Denmark, Finland, Norway, and Sweden) (2015)

Broadcast media: state-owned public TV broadcaster operates 1 TV channel nationally; several privately owned TV stations broadcast nationally and roughly another half-dozen operate locally; about one-half the households utilize multi-channel cable or satellite TV services; state-owned public radio broadcaster operates 2 national networks and 4 regional stations; 2 privately owned radio stations operate nationally and another 15 provide more limited coverage (2007)

Internet country code: .is
Internet users: total: 329,967

percent of population: 98.2% (July 2016 est.)
country comparison to the world: 141

TRANSPORTATION

National air transport system: *number of registered air carriers:* 5
inventory of registered aircraft operated by air carriers: 43
annual passenger traffic on registered air carriers: 3,413,950
annual freight traffic on registered air carriers: 102,356,809 mt-km (2015)
Civil aircraft registration country code prefix: TF (2016)

Airports: 96 (2013)
country comparison to the world: 60

Airports—with paved runways: *total:* 7
over 3,047 m: 1
1,524 to 2,437 m: 3
914 to 1,523 m: 3 (2017)

Airports—with unpaved runways: *total:* 89
1,524 to 2,437 m: 3
914 to 1,523 m: 26
under 914 m: 60 (2013)

Roadways: *total:* 12,890 km
paved/oiled gravel: 4,782 km (excludes urban roads)
unpaved: 8,108 km (2012)
country comparison to the world: 127

Merchant marine: *total:* 33
by type: general cargo 6, oil tanker 1, other 26 (2017)
country comparison to the world: 122

Ports and terminals: *major seaport(s):* Grundartangi, Hafnarfjordur, Reykjavik

MILITARY AND SECURITY

Military expenditures: 0.1% of GDP (2016)
0.13% of GDP (2012)
0.14% of GDP (2011)
0.13% of GDP (2010)
country comparison to the world: 131

Military branches: no regular military forces; Icelandic National Police; Icelandic Coast Guard (2016)

Military—note: Iceland is the only NATO member that has no standing military force; all US military forces in Iceland were withdrawn as of October 2006; defense of Iceland remains a NATO commitment and NATO maintains an air policing presence in Icelandic airspace; Iceland participates in international peacekeeping missions with the civilian-manned Icelandic Crisis Response Unit (ICRU)

TRANSNATIONAL ISSUES

Disputes—international: Iceland, the UK, and Ireland dispute Denmark's claim that the Faroe Islands' continental shelf extends beyond 200 nm; the European Free Trade Association Surveillance Authority filed a suit against Iceland, claiming the country violated the Agreement on the European Economic Area in failing to pay minimum compensation to Icesave depositors

Refugees and internally displaced persons: *stateless persons:* 131 (2016)

INDIA

INTRODUCTION

Background: The Indus Valley civilization, one of the world's oldest, flourished during the 3rd and 2nd millennia B.C. and extended into northwestern India. Aryan tribes from the northwest infiltrated the Indian subcontinent about 1500 B.C.; their merger with the earlier Dravidian inhabitants created the classical Indian culture. The Maurya Empire of the 4th and 3rd centuries B.C.—which reached its zenith under ASHOKA—united much of South Asia. The Golden Age ushered in by the Gupta dynasty (4th to 6th centuries A.D.) saw a flowering of Indian science, art, and culture. Islam spread across the subcontinent over a period of 700 years. In the 10th and 11th centuries, Turks and Afghans invaded India and established the Delhi Sultanate. In the early 16th century, the Emperor BABUR established the Mughal Dynasty, which ruled India for more than three centuries. European explorers began establishing footholds in India during the 16th century.

By the 19th century, Great Britain had become the dominant political power on the subcontinent. The British Indian Army played a vital role in both World Wars. Years of nonviolent resistance to British rule, led by Mohandas GANDHI and Jawaharlal NEHRU, eventually resulted in Indian independence, which was granted in 1947. Large-scale communal violence took place before and after the subcontinent partition into two separate states—India and Pakistan. The neighboring nations have fought three wars since independence, the last of which was in 1971 and resulted in East Pakistan becoming the separate nation of Bangladesh. India's nuclear weapons tests in 1998 emboldened Pakistan to conduct its own tests that same year. In November 2008, terrorists originating from Pakistan conducted a series of coordinated attacks in Mumbai, India's financial capital. Despite pressing problems such as significant overpopulation, environmental degradation, extensive poverty, and widespread corruption, economic growth following the launch of economic reforms in 1991 and a massive youthful population are driving India's emergence as a regional and global power.

GEOGRAPHY

Location: Southern Asia, bordering the Arabian Sea and the Bay of Bengal, between Burma and Pakistan

Geographic coordinates: 20 00 N, 77 00 E

Map references: Asia

Area: *total:* 3,287,263 sq km
land: 2,973,193 sq km
water: 314,070 sq km
country comparison to the world: 8

Area—comparative: slightly more than one-third the size of the US

Land boundaries: *total:* 13,888 km
border countries (6): Bangladesh 4,142 km, Bhutan 659 km, Burma 1,468 km, China 2,659 km, Nepal 1,770 km, Pakistan 3,190 km

Coastline: 7,000 km

Maritime claims: *territorial sea:* 12 nm
contiguous zone: 24 nm
exclusive economic zone: 200 nm
continental shelf: 200 nm or to the edge of the continental margin

Climate: varies from tropical monsoon in south to temperate in north

Terrain: upland plain (Deccan Plateau) in south, flat to rolling plain along the Ganges, deserts in west, Himalayas in north

Elevation: *mean elevation:* 160 m

elevation extremes: *lowest point:* Indian Ocean 0 m
highest point: Kanchenjunga 8,586 m

Natural resources: coal (fourth-largest reserves in the world), iron ore, manganese, mica, bauxite, rare earth elements, titanium ore, chromite, natural gas, diamonds, petroleum, limestone, arable land

Land use: *agricultural land:* 60.5%
arable land: 52.8%;
permanent crops: 4.2%;
permanent pasture: 3.5%
forest: 23.1%
other: 16.4% (2011 est.)
Irrigated land: 667,000 sq km (2012)

Population—distribution: with the notable exception of the deserts in the northwest, including the Thar Desert, and the mountain fringe in the north, a very high population density exists throughout most of the country; the core of the population is in the north along the banks of the Ganges, with other river valleys and southern coastal areas also having large population concentrations

Natural hazards: droughts; flash floods, as well as widespread and destructive flooding from monsoonal rains; severe thunderstorms; earthquakes
volcanism: Barren Island (354 m) in the Andaman Sea has been active in recent years

Environment—current issues: deforestation; soil erosion; overgrazing; desertification; air pollution from industrial effluents and vehicle emissions; water pollution from raw sewage and runoff of agricultural pesticides; tap water is not potable throughout the country; huge and growing population is overstraining natural resources

Environment—international agreements: *party to:* Antarctic-Environmental Protocol, Antarctic-Marine Living Resources, Antarctic Treaty, Biodiversity, Climate Change, Climate Change-Kyoto Protocol, Desertification, Endangered Species, Environmental Modification, Hazardous Wastes, Law of the Sea, Ozone Layer Protection, Ship Pollution, Tropical Timber 83, Tropical Timber 94, Wetlands, Whaling *signed, but not ratified:* none of the selected agreements

Geography—note: dominates South Asian subcontinent; near important Indian Ocean trade routes; Kanchenjunga, third tallest mountain in the world, lies on the border with Nepal

PEOPLE AND SOCIETY

Population: 1,281,935,911 (July 2017 est.)
country comparison to the world: 2

Nationality: *noun:* Indian(s)
adjective: Indian

Ethnic groups: Indo-Aryan 72%, Dravidian 25%, Mongoloid and other 3% (2000)

Languages: Hindi 41%, Bengali 8.1%, Telugu 7.2%, Marathi 7%, Tamil 5.9%, Urdu 5%, Gujarati 4.5%, Kannada 3.7%, Malayalam 3.2%, Oriya 3.2%, Punjabi 2.8%, Assamese 1.3%, Maithili 1.2%, other 5.9%

note: English enjoys the status of subsidiary official language but is the most important language for national, political, and commercial communication; Hindi is the most widely spoken language and primary tongue of 41% of the people; there are 14 other official languages: Bengali, Telugu, Marathi, Tamil, Urdu, Gujarati, Malayalam, Kannada, Oriya, Punjabi, Assamese, Kashmiri, Sindhi, and Sanskrit; Hindustani is a popular variant of Hindi/Urdu spoken widely throughout northern India but is not an official language (2001 est.)

Religions: Hindu 79.8%, Muslim 14.2%, Christian 2.3%, Sikh 1.7%, other and unspecified 2% (2011 est.)

Age structure: *0-14 years:* 27.34% (male 186,087,665/female 164,398,204)
15-24 years: 17.9% (male 121,879,786/female 107,583,437)
25-54 years: 41.08% (male 271,744,709/female 254,834,569)
55-64 years: 7.45% (male 47,846,122/female 47,632,532)
65 years and over: 6.24% (male 37,837,801/female 42,091,086) (2017 est.)

Dependency ratios: *total dependency ratio:* 52.2
youth dependency ratio: 43.6
elderly dependency ratio: 8.6
potential support ratio: 11.7 (2015 est.)

Median age: *total:* 27.9 years
male: 27.2 years
female: 28.6 years (2017 est.)
country comparison to the world: 140

Population growth rate: 1.17% (2017 est.)
country comparison to the world: 96

Birth rate: 19 births/1,000 population (2017 est.)
country comparison to the world: 87

Death rate: 7.3 deaths/1,000 population (2017 est.)
country comparison to the world: 118

Net migration rate: 0 migrant(s)/1,000 population (2017 est.)
country comparison to the world: 85

Population distribution: with the notable exception of the deserts in the northwest, including the Thar Desert, and the mountain fringe in the north, a very high population density exists throughout most of the country; the core of the population is in the north along the banks of the Ganges, with other river valleys and southern coastal areas also having large population concentrations

Urbanization: *urban population:* 33.5% of total population (2017)
rate of urbanization: 2.28% annual rate of change (2015-20 est.)

Major urban areas—population: NEW DELHI (capital) 25.703 million; Mumbai 21.043 million; Kolkata 11.766 million; Bangalore 10.087 million; Chennai 9.62 million; Hyderabad 8.944 million (2015)

Sex ratio: *at birth:* 1.12 male(s)/female
0-14 years: 1.13 male(s)/female
15-24 years: 1.13 male(s)/female
25-54 years: 1.06 male(s)/female
55-64 years: 1.01 male(s)/female
65 years and over: 0.9 male(s)/female
total population: 1.08 male(s)/female (2016 est.)

Maternal mortality ratio: 174 deaths/100,000 live births (2015 est.)
country comparison to the world: 56

Infant mortality rate: *total:* 39.1 deaths/1,000 live births
male: 38 deaths/1,000 live births
female: 40.4 deaths/1,000 live births (2017 est.)
country comparison to the world: 47

Life expectancy at birth: *total population:* 68.8 years
male: 67.6 years
female: 70.1 years (2017 est.)
country comparison to the world: 164

Total fertility rate: 2.43 children born/woman (2017 est.)
country comparison to the world: 81

Contraceptive prevalence rate: 53.5% (2015/16)

Health expenditures: 4.7% of GDP (2014)
country comparison to the world: 149

Physicians density: 0.73 physicians/1,000 population (2014)

Hospital bed density: 0.7 beds/1,000 population (2011)

Drinking water source:
improved:
urban: 97.1% of population
rural: 92.6% of population
total: 94.1% of population
unimproved:
urban: 2.9% of population
rural: 7.4% of population
total: 5.9% of population (2015 est.)

Sanitation facility access:
improved:
urban: 62.6% of population
rural: 28.5% of population
total: 39.6% of population
unimproved:
urban: 37.4% of population

rural: 71.5% of population
total: 60.4% of population (2015 est.)

HIV/AIDS—adult prevalence rate: 0.3% (2016 est.)
country comparison to the world: 80

HIV/AIDS—people living with HIV/AIDS: 2.1 million (2016 est.)
country comparison to the world: 3

HIV/AIDS—deaths: 62,000 (2016 est.)
country comparison to the world: 3

Major infectious diseases: *degree of risk:* very high
food or waterborne diseases: bacterial diarrhea, hepatitis A and E, and typhoid fever
vectorborne diseases: dengue fever, Japanese encephalitis, and malaria
water contact disease: leptospirosis
animal contact disease: rabies (2016)

Obesity—adult prevalence rate: 3.9% (2016)
country comparison to the world: 189

Children under the age of 5 years underweight: 35.7% (2015)
country comparison to the world: 2

Education expenditures: 3.8% of GDP (2013)
country comparison to the world: 134

Literacy: *definition:* age 15 and over can read and write
total population: 71.2%
male: 81.3%
female: 60.6% (2015 est.)

School life expectancy (primary to tertiary education): *total:* 12 years
male: 12 years
female: 12 years (2014)

Unemployment, youth ages 15-24: *total:* 10.7%
male: 10.4%
female: 11.6% (2012 est.)
country comparison to the world: 97

GOVERNMENT

Country name: *conventional long form:* Republic of India
conventional short form: India
local long form: Republic of India/Bharatiya Ganarajya
local short form: India/Bharat
etymology: the English name derives from the Indus River; the Indian name "Bharat" may derive from the "Bharatas" tribe mentioned in the Vedas of the second millennium B.C.; the name is also associated with Emperor Bharata, the legendary conqueror of all of India

Government type: federal parliamentary republic

Capital: *name:* New Delhi

geographic coordinates: 28 36 N, 77 12 E
time difference: UTC+5.5 (10.5 hours ahead of Washington, DC, during Standard Time)

Administrative divisions: 29 states and 7 union territories*; Andaman and Nicobar Islands*, Andhra Pradesh, Arunachal Pradesh, Assam, Bihar, Chandigarh*, Chhattisgarh, Dadra and Nagar Haveli*, Daman and Diu*, Delhi*, Goa,

Gujarat, Haryana, Himachal Pradesh, Jammu and Kashmir, Jharkhand, Karnataka, Kerala, Lakshadweep*, Madhya Pradesh, Maharashtra, Manipur, Meghalaya, Mizoram, Nagaland, Odisha, Puducherry*, Punjab, Rajasthan, Sikkim, Tamil Nadu, Telangana, Tripura, Uttar Pradesh, Uttarakhand, West Bengal

note: although its status is that of a union territory, the official name of Delhi is National Capital Territory of Delhi

Independence: 15 August 1947 (from the UK)

National holiday: Republic Day, 26 January (1950)

Constitution: history: previous 1935 (preindependence); latest draft completed 4 November 1949, adopted 26 November 1949, effective 26 January 1950

amendments: proposed by either the Council of States or the House of the People; passage requires majority participation of the total membership in each house and at least two-thirds majority of voting members of each house, followed by assent of the president of India; proposed amendments to the constitutional amendment procedures also must be ratified by at least one-half of the India state legislatures before presidential assent; amended many times, last in 2016 (2017)

Legal system: common law system based on the English model; separate personal law codes apply to Muslims, Christians, and Hindus; judicial review of legislative acts

International law organization participation: accepts compulsory ICJ jurisdiction with reservations; non-party state to the ICCt

Citizenship: *citizenship by birth:* no
citizenship by descent only: at least one parent must be a citizen of India
dual citizenship recognized: no
residency requirement for naturalization: 5 years

Suffrage: 18 years of age; universal

Executive branch: *chief of state:* President Ram Nath KOVIND (since 25 July 2017); Vice President M. Venkaiah NAIDU (since 11 August 2017)

head of government: Prime Minister Narendra MODI (since 26 May 2014)

cabinet: Union Council of Ministers recommended by the prime minister, appointed by the president

elections/appointments: president indirectly elected by an electoral college consisting of elected members of both houses of Parliament and state legislatures for a 5-year term (no term limits); election last held on 17 July 2017 (next to be held in July 2022); vice president indirectly elected by an electoral college consisting of elected members of both houses of Parliament and state legislatures for a 5-year term (no term limits); election last held on 5 August 2017 (next to be held in August 2022); following legislative elections, the prime minister is elected by parliamentary members of the majority party

election results: Ram Nath KOVIND elected president; percent of electoral college vote—Ram Nath KOVIND (BJP) 65.7% Meira KUMAR

(INC) 34.3%; Mohammad Hamid ANSARI reelected vice president (2012 election); electoral college vote—Mohammad Hamid ANSARI 490, Jaswant SINGH 238

Legislative branch: *description:* bicameral Parliament or Sansad consists of the Council of States or Rajya Sabha (245 seats; 233 members indirectly elected by state and territorial assemblies by proportional representation vote, and 12 members appointed by the president; members serve 6-year terms) and the House of the People or Lok Sabha (545 seats; 543 members directly elected in single-seat constituencies by simple majority vote and 2 appointed by the president; members serve 5-year terms)

elections: House of the People—last held April-May 2014 in 9 phases; (next must be held by May 2019)

election results: House of the People—percent of vote by party—BJP 31.0%, INC 19.3%, AITC 3.8%, SP 3.4%, AIADMK 3.3%, CPI(M) 3.3%, TDP 2.6%, YSRC 2.5%, AAP 2.1%, SAD 1.8%, BJD 1.7%, SS 1.7%, NCP 1.6%, RJD 1.3%, TRS 1.3%, LJP 0.4%, other 15.9%, independent 3.0%; seats by party—BJP 282, INC 44, AIADMK 37, AITC 34, BJD 20, SS 18, TDP 16, TRS 11, CPI(M) 9, YSRC 9, LJP 6, NCP 6, SP 5, AAP 4, RJD 4, SAD 4, other 33, independent 3

Judicial branch: *highest court(s):* Supreme Court (the chief justice and 25 associate justices)

judge selection and term of office: justices appointed by the president to serve until age 65

subordinate courts: High Courts; District Courts; Labour Court

note: in mid-2011, India's Cabinet approved the "National Mission for Justice Delivery and Legal Reform" to eliminate judicial corruption and reduce the backlog of cases

Political parties and leaders: Aam Aadmi Party or AAP [Arvind KEJRIWAL]
All India Anna Dravida Munnetra Kazhagam or AIADMK [Edappadi PALANISWAMY, Occhaathevar PANNEERSELVAM]
All India Trinamool Congress or AITC [Mamata BANERJEE]
Bahujan Samaj Party or BSP [MAYAWATI]
Bharatiya Janata Party or BJP [Amit SHAH]
Biju Janata Dal or BJD [Naveen PATNAIK]
Communist Party of India-Marxist or CPI(M) [Prakash KARAT]
Indian National Congress or INC [Rahul GANDHI]
Lok Janshakti Party (LJP) [Ram Vilas PASWAN]
Nationalist Congress Party or NCP [Sharad PAWAR]
Rashtriya Janata Dal or RJD [Lalu Prasad YADAV]
Samajwadi Party or SP [Akhilesh YADAV]
Shiromani Akali Dal or SAD [Parkash Singh BADAL]
Shiv Sena or SS [Uddhav THACKERAY]
Telegana Rashtra Samithi or TRS [K. Chandrashekar RAO]
Telugu Desam Party or TDP [Chandrababu NAIDU]
YSR Congress or YSRC [Jagan Mohan REDDY]

note: India has dozens of national and regional political parties

Political pressure groups and leaders: All Parties Hurriyat Conference in the Kashmir Valley (separatist group)
Bajrang Dal (militant religious organization)
Jamiat Ulema-e Hind [Mahmood MADANI] (religious organization)
Rashtriya Swayamsevak Sangh or RSS [Mohan BHAGWAT] (nationalist organization)
Vishwa Hindu Parishad [Pravin TOGADIA] (militant religious organization)
other: hundreds of social reform, anti-corruption, and environmental groups at state and local level; numerous religious or militant/chauvinistic organizations; various separatist groups seeking greater communal and/or regional autonomy

International organization participation: ADB, AfDB (nonregional member), Arctic Council (observer), ARF, ASEAN (dialogue partner), BIMSTEC, BIS, BRICS, C, CD, CERN (observer), CICA, CP, EAS, FAO, FATF, G-15, G-20, G-24, G-5, G-77, IAEA, IBRD, ICAO, ICC (national committees), ICRM, IDA, IFAD, IFC, IFRCS, IHO, ILO, IMF, IMO, IMSO, Interpol, IOC, IOM, IPU, ISO, ITSO, ITU, ITUC (NGOs), LAS (observer), MIGA, MINURSO, MONUSCO, NAM, OAS (observer), OECD, OPCW, Pacific Alliance (observer), PCA, PIF (partner), SAARC, SACEP, SCO (observer), UN, UNCTAD, UNDOF, UNESCO, UNHCR, UNIDO, UNIFIL, UNISFA, UNITAR, UNMISS, UNOCI, UNWTO, UPU, WCO, WFTU (NGOs), WHO, WIPO, WMO, WTO

Diplomatic representation in the US: *chief of mission:* Ambassador Navtej Singh SARNA (since 18 January 2017)

chancery: 2107 Massachusetts Avenue NW, Washington, DC 20008; note—Consular Wing located at 2536 Massachusetts Avenue NW, Washington, DC 20008; telephone: [1](202) 939-7000

telephone: [1] (202) 939-7000

FAX: [1] (202) 265-4351

consulate(s) general: Atlanta, Chicago, Houston, New York, San Francisco

Diplomatic representation from the US: *chief of mission:* Ambassador Kenneth I. JUSTER (since 23 November 2017)

embassy: Shantipath, Chanakyapuri, New Delhi 110021

mailing address: use embassy street address

telephone: [91] (11) 2419-8000

FAX: [91] (11) 2419-0017

consulate(s) general: Chennai (Madras), Hyderabad, Kolkata (Calcutta), Mumbai (Bombay)

Flag description: three equal horizontal bands of saffron (subdued orange) (top), white, and green, with a blue chakra (24-spoked wheel) centered in the white band; saffron represents courage, sacrifice, and the spirit of renunciation; white signifies purity and truth; green stands for faith and fertility; the blue chakra symbolizes the wheel of life in movement and death in stagnation note: similar to the flag of Niger, which has a small orange disk centered in the white band

National symbol(s): the Lion Capital of Ashoka, which depicts four Asiatic lions standing back to back mounted on a circular abacus, is the official emblem; Bengal tiger; lotus flower; national colors: saffron, white, green

National anthem: name: "Jana-Gana-Mana" (Thou Art the Ruler of the Minds of All People) *lyrics/music:* Rabindranath TAGORE *note:* adopted 1950; Rabindranath TAGORE, a Nobel laureate, also wrote Bangladesh's national anthem

ECONOMY

Economy—overview: India's diverse economy encompasses traditional village farming, modern agriculture, handicrafts, a wide range of modern industries, and a multitude of services. Slightly less than half of the workforce is in agriculture, but services are the major source of economic growth, accounting for nearly two-thirds of India's output but employing less than one-third of its labor force. India has capitalized on its large educated English-speaking population to become a major exporter of information technology services, business outsourcing services, and software workers. Nevertheless, per capita income remains below the world average.

India is developing into an open-market economy, yet traces of its past autarkic policies remain. Economic liberalization measures, including industrial deregulation, privatization of state-owned enterprises, and reduced controls on foreign trade and investment, began in the early 1990s and served to accelerate the country's growth, which averaged nearly 7% per year from 1997 to 2017. India's economic growth slowed in 2011 because of a decline in investment caused by high interest rates, rising inflation, and investor pessimism about the government's commitment to further economic reforms and about slow world growth. Rising macroeconomic imbalances in India and improving economic conditions in Western countries led investors to shift capital away from India, prompting a sharp depreciation of the rupee through 2016.

Growth rebounded in 2014 through 2016, exceeding 7% each year, but slowed in 2017. Investors' perceptions of India improved in early 2014, due to a reduction of the current account deficit and expectations of post-election economic reform, resulting in a surge of inbound capital flows and stabilization of the rupee. Since the election, the government has passed an important goods and services tax bill and raised foreign direct investment caps in some sectors, but most economic reforms have focused on administrative and governance changes largely because the ruling party remains a minority in India's upper house of Parliament, which must approve most bills. Despite a high growth rate compared to the rest of the world, India's government-owned banks faced mounting bad debt in 2015 and 2016, resulting in low credit growth and restrained economic growth.

The outlook for India's long-term growth is moderately positive due to a young population and corresponding low dependency ratio, healthy savings and investment rates, and increasing integration into the global economy. However, long-term challenges remain significant, including: India's discrimination against women and girls, an inefficient power generation and distribution system, ineffective enforcement of intellectual property rights, decades-long civil litigation dockets, inadequate transport and agricultural infrastructure, limited non-agricultural employment opportunities, high spending and poorly targeted subsidies, inadequate availability of quality basic and higher education, and accommodating rural-to-urban migration.

GDP (purchasing power parity): $9.447 trillion (2017 est.)
$8.852 trillion (2016 est.)
$8.265 trillion (2015 est.)
note: data are in 2017 dollars
country comparison to the world: 4

GDP (official exchange rate): $2.439 trillion (2016 est.)

GDP—real growth rate: 6.7% (2017 est.)
7.1% (2016 est.)
8% (2015 est.)
country comparison to the world: 15

GDP—per capita (PPP): $7,200 (2017 est.)
$6,800 (2016 est.)
$6,400 (2015 est.)
note: data are in 2017 dollars
country comparison to the world: 157

Gross national saving: 28.6% of GDP (2017 est.)
29.7% of GDP (2016 est.)
31.8% of GDP (2015 est.)
country comparison to the world: 32

GDP—composition, by end use:
household consumption: 58.7%
government consumption: 11.6%
investment in fixed capital: 27.5%
investment in inventories: 4%
exports of goods and services: 18.4%
imports of goods and services: -20.2% (2017 est.)

GDP—composition, by sector of origin:
agriculture: 16.8%
industry: 28.9%
services: 46.6% (2017 est.)

Agriculture—products: rice, wheat, oilseed, cotton, jute, tea, sugarcane, lentils, onions, potatoes; dairy products, sheep, goats, poultry; fish

Industries: textiles, chemicals, food processing, steel, transportation equipment, cement, mining, petroleum, machinery, software, pharmaceuticals

Industrial production growth rate: 7.5% (2017 est.)
country comparison to the world: 21

Labor force: 521.9 million (2017 est.)
country comparison to the world: 2

Labor force—by occupation: *agriculture:* 47%
industry: 22%
services: 31% (FY 2014 est.)

Unemployment rate: 8.8% (2017 est.)
8% (2016 est.)

country comparison to the world: 120

Population below poverty line: 21.9% (2011 est.)

Household income or consumption by percentage share: *lowest 10%:* 3.6%
highest 10%: 29.8% (2011)

Distribution of family income—Gini index: 35.2 (2011)
37.8 (1997)
country comparison to the world: 93

Budget: *revenues:* $248.7 billion
expenditures: $330.3 billion (2017 est.)
Taxes and other revenues: 10.2% of GDP (2017 est.)
country comparison to the world: 213

Budget surplus (+) or deficit (-): -3.3% of GDP (2017 est.)
country comparison to the world: 125

Public debt: 50.1% of GDP (2017 est.)
50.3% of GDP (2016 est.)
note: data cover central government debt, and exclude debt instruments issued (or owned) by government entities other than the treasury; the data include treasury debt held by foreign entities; the data exclude debt issued by subnational entities, as well as intra-governmental debt; intra-governmental debt consists of treasury borrowings from surpluses in the social funds, such as for retirement, medical care, and unemployment; debt instruments for the social funds are not sold at public auctions
country comparison to the world: 102

Fiscal year: 1 April—31 March

Inflation rate (consumer prices): 3.8% (2017 est.)
4.5% (2016 est.)
country comparison to the world: 153

Central bank discount rate: 6.25% (31 December 2016)
7.75% (31 December 2014)
note: this is the Indian central bank's policy rate—the repurchase rate
country comparison to the world: 69

Commercial bank prime lending rate: 9.6% (31 December 2017 est.)
9.67% (31 December 2016 est.)
country comparison to the world: 88

Stock of narrow money: $429.3 billion (31 December 2017 est.)
$294.4 billion (31 December 2016 est.)
country comparison to the world: 14

Stock of broad money: $2.063 trillion (31 December 2017 est.)
$1.773 trillion (31 December 2016 est.)
country comparison to the world: 9

Stock of domestic credit: $1.795 trillion (31 December 2017 est.)
$1.622 trillion (31 December 2016 est.)
country comparison to the world: 14

Market value of publicly traded shares: $1.516 trillion (31 December 2015 est.)
$1.558 trillion (31 December 2014 est.)
$1.139 trillion (31 December 2013 est.)
country comparison to the world: 11

Current account balance: -$33.68 billion (2017 est.)

-$15.23 billion (2016 est.)

country comparison to the world: 197

Exports: $299.3 billion (2017 est.)

$268.6 billion (2016 est.)

country comparison to the world: 21

Exports—commodities: petroleum products, precious stones, vehicles, machinery, iron and steel, chemicals, pharmaceutical products, cereals, apparel

Exports—partners: US 16%, UAE 11.7%, Hong Kong 5.1% (2016)

Imports: $426.8 billion (2017 est.)

$376.1 billion (2016 est.)

country comparison to the world: 12

Imports—commodities: crude oil, precious stones, machinery, chemicals, fertilizer, plastics, iron and steel

Imports—partners: China 17%, US 5.8%, UAE 5.4%, Saudi Arabia 5.2%, Switzerland 4.2% (2016)

Reserves of foreign exchange and gold: $407.2 billion (31 December 2017 est.)

$359.7 billion (31 December 2016 est.)

country comparison to the world: 8

Debt—external: $483.4 billion (31 December 2017 est.)

$456.4 billion (31 December 2016 est.)

country comparison to the world: 25

Stock of direct foreign investment—at home: $367.5 billion (31 December 2017 est.)

$318.5 billion (31 December 2016 est.)

country comparison to the world: 21

Stock of direct foreign investment—abroad: $156.1 billion (31 December 2017 est.)

$144.1 billion (31 December 2016 est.)

country comparison to the world: 31

Exchange rates: Indian rupees (INR) per US dollar—

65.17 (2017 est.)

67.195 (2016 est.)

67.195 (2015 est.)

64.152 (2014 est.)

61.03 (2013 est.)

ENERGY

Electricity access: *population without electricity:* 237,400,000

electrification—total population: 79%

electrification—urban areas: 98%

electrification—rural areas: 70% (2013)

Electricity—production: 1.289 trillion kWh (2015 est.)

country comparison to the world: 4

Electricity—consumption: 1.048 trillion kWh (2015 est.)

country comparison to the world: 4

Electricity—exports: 5.15 billion kWh (2015 est.)

country comparison to the world: 37

Electricity—imports: 5.244 billion kWh (2015 est.)

country comparison to the world: 38

Electricity—installed generating capacity: 308.8 million kW (30 November 2016)

country comparison to the world: 5

Electricity—from fossil fuels: 71.5% of total installed capacity (2015 est.)

country comparison to the world: 101

Electricity—from nuclear fuels: 1.6% of total installed capacity (2015 est.)

country comparison to the world: 29

Electricity—from hydroelectric plants: 14.4% of total installed capacity (2015 est.)

country comparison to the world: 104

Electricity—from other renewable sources: 14.6% of total installed capacity (2015 est.)

country comparison to the world: 49

Crude oil—production: 734,500 bbl/day (2016 est.)

country comparison to the world: 25

Crude oil—exports: 0 bbl/day (2014 est.)

country comparison to the world: 140

Crude oil—imports: 3.789 million bbl/day (2014 est.)

country comparison to the world: 3

Crude oil—proved reserves: 4.621 billion bbl (1 January 2017 es)

country comparison to the world: 25

Refined petroleum products—production: 4.793 million bbl/day (2014 est.)

country comparison to the world: 5

Refined petroleum products—consumption: 4.142 million bbl/day (2015 est.)

country comparison to the world: 4

Refined petroleum products—exports: 1.371 million bbl/day (2014 est.)

country comparison to the world: 7

Refined petroleum products—imports: 481,900 bbl/day (2014 est.)

country comparison to the world: 18

Natural gas—production: 31.24 billion cu m (2015 est.)

country comparison to the world: 25

Natural gas—consumption: 102.3 billion cu m (2015 est.)

country comparison to the world: 14

Natural gas—exports: 270 million cu m (2015 est.)

country comparison to the world: 46

Natural gas—imports: 18.67 billion cu m (2015 est.)

country comparison to the world: 19

Natural gas—proved reserves: 1.227 trillion cu m (1 January 2017 es)

country comparison to the world: 24

Carbon dioxide emissions from consumption of energy: 1.887 billion Mt (2013 est.)

country comparison to the world: 4

COMMUNICATIONS

Telephones—fixed lines: *total subscriptions:* 24.404 million

subscriptions per 100 inhabitants: 2 (July 2016 est.)

country comparison to the world: 13

Telephones—mobile cellular: *total:* 1,127.809 million

subscriptions per 100 inhabitants: 89 (July 2016 est.)

country comparison to the world: 2

Telephone system: *general assessment:* supported by recent deregulation and liberalization of telecommunications laws and policies, India has emerged as one of the fastest-growing telecom markets in the world; total telephone subscribership base exceeded 1 billion in 2015, an overall teledensity of roughly 80%, and subscribership is currently growing at roughly 5 million per month; urban teledensity now exceeds 100%, and rural teledensity has reached 50%

domestic: mobile cellular service introduced in 1994 and organized nationwide into four metropolitan areas and 19 telecom circles, each with multiple private service providers and one or more state-owned service providers; in recent years significant trunk capacity added in the form of fiber-optic cable and one of the world's largest domestic satellite systems, the Indian National Satellite system (INSAT), with 6 satellites supporting 33,000 very small aperture terminals (VSAT)

international: country code—91; a number of major international submarine cable systems, including SEA-ME-WE-3 with landing sites at Cochin and Mumbai (Bombay), SEA-ME-WE-4 with a landing site at Chennai, Fiber-Optic Link Around the Globe (FLAG) with a landing site at Mumbai (Bombay), South Africa—Far East (SAFE) with a landing site at Cochin, the i2i cable network linking to Singapore with landing sites at Mumbai (Bombay) and Chennai (Madras), and Tata Indicom linking Singapore and Chennai (Madras), provide a significant increase in the bandwidth available for both voice and data traffic; satellite earth stations—8 Intelsat (Indian Ocean) and 1 Inmarsat (Indian Ocean region); 9 gateway exchanges operating from Mumbai (Bombay), New Delhi, Kolkata (Calcutta), Chennai (Madras), Jalandhar, Kanpur, Gandhinagar, Hyderabad, and Ernakulam (2015)

Broadcast media: Doordarshan, India's public TV network, operates about 20 national, regional, and local services; a large and increasing number of privately owned TV stations are distributed by cable and satellite service providers; in 2015, more than 230 million homes had access to cable and satellite TV offering more than 700 TV channels; government controls AM radio with All India Radio operating domestic and external networks; news broadcasts via radio are limited to the All India Radio Network; since 2000, privately owned FM stations have been permitted and their numbers have increased rapidly (2015)

Internet country code: .in

Internet users: total: 374,328,160

percent of population: 29.5% (July 2016 est.)

country comparison to the world: 4

TRANSPORTATION

National air transport system: *number of registered air carriers:* 20
inventory of registered aircraft operated by air carriers: 485
annual passenger traffic on registered air carriers: 98,927,860
annual freight traffic on registered air carriers: 1,833,847,614 mt-km (2015)
Civil aircraft registration country code prefix: VT (2016)

Airports: 346 (2013)
country comparison to the world: 21

Airports—with paved runways: *total:* 253
over 3,047 m: 22
2,438 to 3,047 m: 59
1,524 to 2,437 m: 76
914 to 1,523 m: 82
under 914 m: 14 (2017)

Airports—with unpaved runways: *total:* 93
over 3,047 m: 1
2,438 to 3,047 m: 3
1,524 to 2,437 m: 6
914 to 1,523 m: 38
under 914 m: 45 (2013)

Heliports: 45 (2013)

Pipelines: condensate/gas 9 km; gas 13,581 km; liquid petroleum gas 2,054 km; oil 8,943 km; oil/gas/water 20 km; refined products 11,069 km (2013)

Railways: *total:* 68,525 km
broad gauge: 58,404 km 1.676-m gauge (23,654 electrified)
narrow gauge: 9,499 km 1.000-m gauge; 622 km 0.762-m gauge (2014)
country comparison to the world: 5

Roadways: *total:* 4,699,024 km
note: includes 96,214 km of national highways and expressways, 147,800 km of state highways, and 4,455,010 km of other roads (2015)
country comparison to the world: 2

Waterways: 14,500 km (5,200 km on major rivers and 485 km on canals suitable for mechanized vessels) (2012)
country comparison to the world: 9

Merchant marine: *total:* 1,674
by type: bulk carrier 74, container ship 20, general cargo 571, oil tanker 126, other 883 (2017)
country comparison to the world: 15

Ports and terminals: *major seaport(s):* Chennai, Jawaharal Nehru Port, Kandla, Kolkata (Calcutta), Mumbai (Bombay), Sikka, Vishakhapatnam
container port(s) (TEUs): Chennai (1,571,000), Jawaharal Nehru Port (4,492,000) (2015)
LNG terminal(s) (import): Dabhol, Dahej, Hazira

MILITARY AND SECURITY

Military expenditures: 2.47% of GDP (2016)
2.41% of GDP (2015)
2.5% of GDP (2014)
2.47% of GDP (2013)

2.54% of GDP (2012)
country comparison to the world: 31

Military branches: Army, Navy (includes naval air arm), Air Force, Coast Guard (2011)

Military service age and obligation: 16-18 years of age for voluntary military service (Army 17 1/2, Air Force 17, Navy 16 1/2); no conscription; women may join as officers, currently serve in combat roles as pilots, and will soon be allowed in all combat roles (2016)

TERRORISM

Terrorist groups—home based: *Indian Mujahedeen (IM): aim(s):* establish Islamic rule in India and, ultimately, convert all non-Muslims to Islam; stated goal is to carry out terrorist actions against Indians for perceived atrocities against Indian Muslims
area(s) of operation: based in the western state of Maharashtra, India's third-largest state and its second most populous state; in recent years, IM's small and loosely connected networks have diminished throughout the country; known for carrying out numerous coordinated bombings in crowded areas against economic and civilian targets in order to maximize casualties, resulting in hundreds of deaths and thousands of injuries; on 13 July 2011, three coordinated bombings in Mumbai, India, resulted in 26 civilian deaths and at least 130 more injured; on 13 February 2010, operatives bombed a German bakery in Pune, Maharashtra State, killing 17 civilians; outlawed in India

Terrorist groups—foreign based: *al-Qa'ida (AQ): aim(s):* overthrow the Indian Government and, ultimately, establish a pan-Islamic caliphate under a strict Salafi Muslim interpretation of Sharia
area(s) of operation: maintains an operational presence as al-Qa'ida in the Indian Subcontinent under Pakistani Asim UMAR

al-Qa'ida in the Indian Subcontinent (AQIS): *aim(s):* establish an Islamic caliphate in the Indian subcontinent
area(s) of operation: targets primarily military and security personnel, especially in the states of Assam, Gujarat, and Kashmir; present in large cities, including Delhi; overall leader Asim UMAR issued a public statement in 2016 encouraging Muslims in India to kill Indian officials; actively recruits Indian youth

Harakat ul-Jihad-i-Islami (HUJI): *aim(s):* enhance its networks and operational capabilities in India
area(s) of operation: maintains a limited operational presence, especially in the south, where operatives continue to conduct targeted killings of important Hindu personalities, including in Bangalore and Hubli; on 7 September 2011, operatives bombed the New Delhi High Court in New Delhi, killing at least 11 people and injuring 76; the group sent an email to the press stating that the bombing was intended to force India to repeal a death sentence of a HUJI member

Harakat ul-Jihad-i-Islami/Bangladesh (HUJI-B): *aim(s):* enhance its networks in India and, ultimately, install an Islamic state in Bangladesh

area(s) of operation: maintains a low-profile presence

Harakat ul-Mujahidin (HUM): *aim(s):* enhance its networks and paramilitary training in India and, ultimately, annex Kashmir into Pakistan and establish an Islamic state in Kashmir
area(s) of operation: conducted numerous attacks against Indian troops and civilians in Kashmir, especially between 2005 and 2013; attacks have ebbed in recent years

Islamic State of Iraq and the Levant (ISIL): *aim(s):* bolster its networks in India and, ultimately, unite Kashmir with Pakistan
area(s) of operation: maintains a limited recruitment presence in major cities

Jaish-e-Mohammed (JEM): *aim(s):* unite the Indian-administered state of Jammu and Kashmir with Pakistan
area(s) of operation: operationally active throughout India, primarily in the state of Jammu and Kashmir; responsible for participating in multiple lethal suicide attacks in India, including the attacks against Indian military personnel on 18 September 2016 in Uri that killed 18 soldiers and on 2 January 2016 at the Pathankot airbase that killed seven soldiers; the September attack marked the deadliest attack on Indian security forces in Kashmir since the mid-1990s; outlawed in India

Lashkar-e Tayyiba (LeT): *aim(s):* annex India's state of Jammu and Kashmir to Pakistan's control and, ultimately, install Islamic rule over parts of India and Pakistan
area(s) of operation: operational throughout India, especially in the north in the state of Jammu and Kashmir since at least 1993; conducts lethal attacks against Indian troops and civilians; continues to be one of the largest and most proficient of the anti-India-focused armed groups; LeT bombing and shooting attacks have killed hundreds and wounded thousands of Indian civilians in recent years; Chairman Hafiz Mohammad SAEED is wanted for arrest in India for his alleged role in masterminding the 26 November 2008 Mumbai attacks that killed 166 people and injured over 300; LeT changed its name to Kashmir Tehrik Azadi in early 2017

Liberation Tigers of Tamil Eelam (LTTE): *aim(s):* enhance its networks in India and, ultimately, revive the movement to establish a Tamil homeland
area(s) of operation: maintains safehavens, transit routes, human trafficking, and an operational presence in an effort to revive the movement and conduct attacks; authorities continue in 2017 to pursue leaders, operatives, and supporters for arrest; in 2014, authorities arrested operatives for plotting imminent attacks in India's southern cities of Chennai and Bangalore

TRANSNATIONAL ISSUES

Disputes—international: since China and India launched a security and foreign policy dialogue in 2005, consolidated discussions related to the dispute over most of their rugged, militarized boundary, regional nuclear proliferation, Indian claims that China transferred missiles to Pakistan, and other matters continue

Kashmir remains the site of the world's largest and most militarized territorial dispute with portions under the de facto administration of China (Aksai Chin), India (Jammu and Kashmir), and Pakistan (Azad Kashmir and Northern Areas)

India and Pakistan resumed bilateral dialogue in February 2011 after a two-year hiatus, have maintained the 2003 cease-fire in Kashmir, and continue to have disputes over water sharing of the Indus River and its tributaries

UN Military Observer Group in India and Pakistan has maintained a small group of peacekeepers since 1949; India does not recognize Pakistan's ceding historic Kashmir lands to China in 1964; to defuse tensions and prepare for discussions on a

maritime boundary, India and Pakistan seek technical resolution of the disputed boundary in Sir Creek estuary at the mouth of the Rann of Kutch in the Arabian Sea; Pakistani maps continue to show its Junagadh claim in Indian Gujarat State; Prime Minister Singh's September 2011 visit to Bangladesh resulted in the signing of a Protocol to the 1974 Land Boundary Agreement between India and Bangladesh, which had called for the settlement of longstanding boundary disputes over undemarcated areas and the exchange of territorial enclaves, but which had never been implemented; Bangladesh referred its maritime boundary claims with Burma and India to the International Tribunal on the Law of the Sea; Joint Border Committee with Nepal continues to examine contested boundary sections, including the 400 sq km dispute over the source of the Kalapani River; India

maintains a strict border regime to keep out Maoist insurgents and control illegal cross-border activities from Nepal

Refugees and internally displaced persons: refugees (country of origin): 110,098 (Tibet/China); 63,162 (Sri Lanka); 15,561 (Burma); 7,693 (Afghanistan) (2015)
IDPs: 796,000 (armed conflict and intercommunal violence) (2016)

Illicit drugs: world's largest producer of licit opium for the pharmaceutical trade, but an undetermined quantity of opium is diverted to illicit international drug markets; transit point for illicit narcotics produced in neighboring countries and throughout Southwest Asia; illicit producer of methaqualone; vulnerable to narcotics money laundering through the hawala system; licit ketamine and precursor production

INDIAN OCEAN

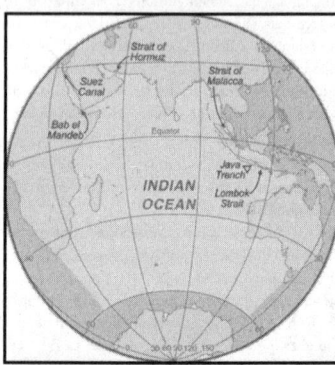

INTRODUCTION

Background: The Indian Ocean is the third largest of the world's five oceans (after the Pacific Ocean and Atlantic Ocean, but larger than the Southern Ocean and Arctic Ocean). Four critically important access waterways are the Suez Canal (Egypt), Bab el Mandeb (Djibouti-Yemen), Strait of Hormuz (Iran-Oman), and Strait of Malacca (Indonesia-Malaysia). The decision by the International Hydrographic Organization in the spring of 2000 to delimit a fifth ocean, the Southern Ocean, removed the portion of the Indian Ocean south of 60 degrees south latitude.

GEOGRAPHY

Location: body of water between Africa, the Southern Ocean, Asia, and Australia

Geographic coordinates: 20 00 S, 80 00 E

Map references: Political Map of the World

Area: total: 68.556 million sq km
note: includes Andaman Sea, Arabian Sea, Bay of Bengal, Flores Sea, Great Australian Bight, Gulf of Aden, Gulf of Oman, Java Sea, Mozambique

Channel, Persian Gulf, Red Sea, Savu Sea, Strait of Malacca, Timor Sea, and other tributary water bodies

Area—comparative: almost 7 times the size of the US

Coastline: 66,526 km

Climate: northeast monsoon (December to April), southwest monsoon (June to October); tropical cyclones occur during May/June and October/November in the northern Indian Ocean and January/February in the southern Indian Ocean

Terrain: surface dominated by a major gyre (broad, circular system of currents) in the southern Indian Ocean and a unique reversal of surface currents in the northern Indian Ocean; ocean floor is dominated by the Mid-Indian Ocean Ridge and subdivided by the Southeast Indian Ocean Ridge, Southwest Indian Ocean Ridge, and Ninetyeast Ridge
major surface currents: the counterclockwise Indian Ocean Gyre comprised of the warm Agulhas and East Madagascar Currents in the west, the South Indian Current in the south, the cold West Australian Current in the east, and the South Equatorial Current in the north; a distinctive annual reversal of surface currents occurs in the northern Indian Ocean; low atmospheric pressure over southwest Asia from hot, rising, summer air results in the southwest monsoon and southwest-to-northeast winds and clockwise currents, while high pressure over northern Asia from cold, falling, winter air results in the northeast monsoon and northeast-to-southwest winds and counterclockwise currents

Elevation: mean depth: -3,741 m

elevation extremes: lowest point: Java Trench -7,258 m
highest point: sea level 0 m

Natural resources: oil and gas fields, fish, shrimp, sand and gravel aggregates, placer deposits, polymetallic nodules

Natural hazards: occasional icebergs pose navigational hazard in southern reaches

Environment—current issues: endangered marine species include the dugong, seals, turtles, and whales; oil pollution in the Arabian Sea, Persian Gulf, and Red Sea

Geography—note: major chokepoints include Bab el Mandeb, Strait of Hormuz, Strait of Malacca, southern access to the Suez Canal, and the Lombok Strait

GOVERNMENT

Country name: etymology: named for the country of India, which makes up much of its northern border

ECONOMY

Economy—overview: The Indian Ocean provides major sea routes connecting the Middle East, Africa, and East Asia with Europe and the Americas. It carries a particularly heavy traffic of petroleum and petroleum products from the oilfields of the Persian Gulf and Indonesia. Its fish are of great and growing importance to the bordering countries for domestic consumption and export. Fishing fleets from Russia, Japan, South Korea, and Taiwan also exploit the Indian Ocean, mainly for shrimp and tuna. Large reserves of hydrocarbons are being tapped in the offshore areas of Saudi Arabia, Iran, India, and western Australia. An estimated 40% of the world's offshore oil production comes from the Indian Ocean. Beach sands rich in heavy minerals and offshore placer deposits are actively exploited by bordering countries, particularly India, South Africa, Indonesia, Sri Lanka, and Thailand.

TRANSPORTATION

Ports and terminals: major seaport(s): Chennai (Madras, India); Colombo (Sri Lanka); Durban (South Africa); Jakarta (Indonesia); Kolkata

(Calcutta, India); Melbourne (Australia); Mumbai (Bombay, India); Richards Bay (South Africa)

MILITARY AND SECURITY

Maritime threats: although the number of reported incidents of piracy continued to drop in 2016, the International Maritime Bureau continues to report the territorial waters of littoral states and offshore waters as high risk for piracy and armed robbery against ships, particularly in the Gulf of Aden, along the east coast of Africa, the Bay of Bengal, and the Strait of Malacca; the presence of several naval task forces in the Gulf of Aden and additional anti-piracy measures on the part of ship operators, including the use of on-board armed security teams, have reduced incidents of piracy; in response, Somali-based pirates, using hijacked fishing trawlers as "mother ships" to extend their range, shifted operations as far south as the Mozambique Channel, eastward to the vicinity of the Maldives, and northeastward to the Strait of Hormuz; Operation Ocean Shield, the NATO naval task force established in 2009 to combat Somali piracy, concluded its operations in December 2016 as a result of the drop in reported incidents over the last few years; the EU naval mission continues its operatons in the Gulf of Aden and Indian Ocean; the first half of 2017 has seen an increase in attacks with two incidents in the Gulf of Aden, one in the Red Sea, and four off the coast of Somalia

TRANSNATIONAL ISSUES

Disputes—international: some maritime disputes (see littoral states)

INDONESIA

Geographic coordinates: 5 00 S, 120 00 E

Map references: Southeast Asia

Area: *total:* 1,904,569 sq km
land: 1,811,569 sq km
water: 93,000 sq km
country comparison to the world: 16

Area—comparative: slightly less than three times the size of Texas

Land boundaries: *total:* 2,958 km
border countries (3): Malaysia 1,881 km, Papua New Guinea 824 km, Timor-Leste 253 km

Coastline: 54,716 km

Maritime claims: measured from claimed archipelagic straight baselines
territorial sea: 12 nm
exclusive economic zone: 200 nm

Climate: tropical; hot, humid; more moderate in highlands

Terrain: mostly coastal lowlands; larger islands have interior mountains

Elevation: *mean elevation:* 367 m

elevation extremes: *lowest point:* Indian Ocean 0 m
highest point: Puncak Jaya 4,884 m

Natural resources: petroleum, tin, natural gas, nickel, timber, bauxite, copper, fertile soils, coal, gold, silver

Land use: *agricultural land:* 31.2%
arable land: 13%;
permanent crops: 12.1%;
permanent pasture: 6.1%;
forest: 51.7%
other: 17.1% (2011 est.)
Irrigated land: 67,220 sq km (2012)

Population—distribution: major concentration on the island of Java, which is considered one of the most densely populated places on earth; of the outer islands (those surrounding Java and Bali), Sumatra contains some of the most significant clusters, particularly in the south near the Selat Sunda, and along the northeastern coast near Medan; the cities of Makasar (Sulawesi), Banjarmasin (Kalimantan) are also heavily populated

Natural hazards: occasional floods; severe droughts; tsunamis; earthquakes; volcanoes; forest fires

volcanism: Indonesia contains the most volcanoes of any country in the world—some 76 are historically active; significant volcanic activity occurs on Java, Sumatra, the Sunda Islands, Halmahera Island, Sulawesi Island, Sangihe Island, and in the Banda Sea; Merapi (2,968 m), Indonesia's most active volcano and in eruption since 2010, has been deemed a Decade Volcano by the International Association of Volcanology and Chemistry of the Earth's Interior, worthy of study due to its explosive history and close proximity to human populations; other notable historically active volcanoes include Agung, Awu, Karangetang, Krakatau (Krakatoa), Makian, Raung, and Tambora

Environment—current issues: deforestation; water pollution from industrial wastes, sewage; air pollution in urban areas; smoke and haze from forest fires

Environment—international agreements: *party to:* Biodiversity, Climate Change, Climate Change-Kyoto Protocol, Desertification, Endangered Species, Hazardous Wastes, Law of the Sea, Ozone Layer Protection, Ship Pollution, Tropical Timber 83, Tropical Timber 94, Wetlands
signed, but not ratified: Marine Life Conservation

Geography—note: according to Indonesia's National Coordinating Agency for Survey and Mapping, the total number of islands in the archipelago is 13,466, of which 922 are permanently inhabited (Indonesia is the world's largest country comprised solely of islands); the country straddles the equator and occupies a strategic location astride or along major sea lanes from the Indian Ocean to the Pacific Ocean; despite having the fourth largest population in the world, Indonesia is the most heavily forested region on earth after the Amazon

PEOPLE AND SOCIETY

Population: 260,580,739 (July 2017 est.)
country comparison to the world: 4

Nationality: *noun:* Indonesian(s)
adjective: Indonesian

Ethnic groups: Javanese 40.1%, Sundanese 15.5%, Malay 3.7%, Batak 3.6%, Madurese 3%, Betawi 2.9%, Minangkabau 2.7%, Buginese 2.7%,

INTRODUCTION

Background: The Dutch began to colonize Indonesia in the early 17th century; Japan occupied the islands from 1942 to 1945. Indonesia declared its independence shortly before Japan's surrender, but it required four years of sometimes brutal fighting, intermittent negotiations, and UN mediation before the Netherlands agreed to transfer sovereignty in 1949. A period of sometimes unruly parliamentary democracy ended in 1957 when President SOEKARNO declared martial law and instituted "Guided Democracy." After an abortive coup in 1965 by alleged communist sympathizers, SOEKARNO was gradually eased from power. From 1967 until 1998, President SUHARTO ruled Indonesia with his "New Order" government. After street protests toppled SUHARTO in 1998, free and fair legislative elections took place in 1999. Indonesia is now the world's third most populous democracy, the world's largest archipelagic state, and the world's largest Muslim-majority nation. Current issues include: alleviating poverty, improving education, preventing terrorism, consolidating democracy after four decades of authoritarianism, implementing economic and financial reforms, stemming corruption, reforming the criminal justice system, addressing climate change, and controlling infectious diseases, particularly those of global and regional importance. In 2005, Indonesia reached a historic peace agreement with armed separatists in Aceh, which led to democratic elections in Aceh in December 2006. Indonesia continues to face low intensity armed resistance in Papua by the separatist Free Papua Movement.

GEOGRAPHY

Location: Southeastern Asia, archipelago between the Indian Ocean and the Pacific Ocean

Bantenese 2%, Banjarese 1.7%, Balinese 1.7%, Acehnese 1.4%, Dayak 1.4%, Sasak 1.3%, Chinese 1.2%, other 15% (2010 est.)

Languages: Bahasa Indonesia (official, modified form of Malay), English, Dutch, local dialects (of which the most widely spoken is Javanese)
note: more than 700 languages are used in Indonesia

Religions: Muslim 87.2%, Protestant 7%, Roman Catholic 2.9%, Hindu 1.7%, other 0.9% (includes Buddhist and Confucian), unspecified 0.4% (2010 est.)

Age structure: 0-14 years: 25.02% (male 33,205,805/female 31,994,844)
15-24 years: 16.99% (male 22,537,842/female 21,738,210)
25-54 years: 42.4% (male 56,493,414/female 53,980,979)
55-64 years: 8.58% (male 10,192,430/female 12,177,931)
65 years and over: 7.01% (male 7,954,795/female 10,304,489) (2017 est.)

Dependency ratios: total dependency ratio: 49.2
youth dependency ratio: 41.6
elderly dependency ratio: 7.6
potential support ratio: 13.2 (2015 est.)

Median age: total: 30.2 years
male: 29.6 years
female: 30.8 years (2017 est.)
country comparison to the world: 117

Population growth rate: 0.86% (2017 est.)
country comparison to the world: 125

Birth rate: 16.2 births/1,000 population (2017 est.)
country comparison to the world: 113

Death rate: 6.5 deaths/1,000 population (2017 est.)
country comparison to the world: 145

Net migration rate: -1.1 migrant(s)/1,000 population (2017 est.)
country comparison to the world: 139

Population distribution: major concentration on the island of Java, which is considered one of the most densely populated places on earth; of the outer islands (those surrounding Java and Bali), Sumatra contains some of the most significant clusters, particularly in the south near the Selat Sunda, and along the northeastern coast near Medan; the cities of Makasar (Sulawesi), Banjarmasin (Kalimantan) are also heavily populated

Urbanization: urban population: 55.2% of total population (2017)
rate of urbanization: 2.3% annual rate of change (2015-20 est.)

Major urban areas—population: JAKARTA (capital) 10.323 million; Surabaya 2.853 million; Bandung 2.544 million; Medan 2.204 million; Semarang 1.63 million; Makassar 1.489 million (2015)

Sex ratio: at birth: 1.05 male(s)/female
0-14 years: 1.04 male(s)/female
15-24 years: 1.04 male(s)/female
25-54 years: 1.04 male(s)/female
55-64 years: 0.84 male(s)/female

65 years and over: 0.77 male(s)/female
total population: 1 male(s)/female (2016 est.)

Mother's mean age at first birth: 22.8 years
note: median age at first birth among women 25-29 (2012 est.)

Maternal mortality ratio: 126 deaths/100,000 live births (2015 est.)
country comparison to the world: 67

Infant mortality rate: total: 22.7 deaths/1,000 live births
male: 26.6 deaths/1,000 live births
female: 18.6 deaths/1,000 live births (2017 est.)
country comparison to the world: 71

Life expectancy at birth: total population: 73 years
male: 70.4 years
female: 75.7 years (2017 est.)
country comparison to the world: 143

Total fertility rate: 2.11 children born/woman (2017 est.)
country comparison to the world: 105

Contraceptive prevalence rate: 61.1% (2015)

Health expenditures: 2.8% of GDP (2014)
country comparison to the world: 184

Physicians density: 0.2 physicians/1,000 population (2012)

Hospital bed density: 0.9 beds/1,000 population (2012)

Drinking water source:
improved:
urban: 94.2% of population
rural: 79.5% of population
total: 87.4% of population
unimproved:
urban: 5.8% of population
rural: 20.5% of population
total: 12.6% of population (2015 est.)

Sanitation facility access:
improved:
urban: 72.3% of population
rural: 47.5% of population
total: 60.8% of population
unimproved:
urban: 27.7% of population
rural: 52.5% of population
total: 39.2% of population (2015 est.)

HIV/AIDS—adult prevalence rate: 0.4% (2016 est.)
country comparison to the world: 68

HIV/AIDS—people living with HIV/AIDS: 620,000 (2016 est.)
country comparison to the world: 13

HIV/AIDS—deaths: 38,000 (2016 est.)
country comparison to the world: 5

Major infectious diseases: degree of risk: very high
food or waterborne diseases: bacterial diarrhea, hepatitis A, and typhoid fever
vectorborne diseases: dengue fever and malaria (2016)

Obesity—adult prevalence rate: 6.9% (2016)
country comparison to the world: 162

Children under the age of 5 years underweight: 19.9% (2013)
country comparison to the world: 31

Education expenditures: 3.3% of GDP (2014)
country comparison to the world: 143

Literacy: definition: age 15 and over can read and write
total population: 95.4%
male: 97.2%
female: 93.6% (2016 est.)

School life expectancy (primary to tertiary education): total: 13 years
male: 13 years
female: 13 years (2014)

Unemployment, youth ages 15-24: total: 22.6%
male: 22.3%
female: 23.1% (2015 est.)
country comparison to the world: 49

GOVERNMENT

Country name: conventional long form: Republic of Indonesia
conventional short form: Indonesia
local long form: Republik Indonesia
local short form: Indonesia
former: Netherlands East Indies, Dutch East Indies
etymology: the name is an 18th-century construct of two Greek words, "Indos" (India) and "nesoi" (islands), meaning "Indian islands"

Government type: presidential republic

Capital: name: Jakarta
geographic coordinates: 6 10 S, 106 49 E
time difference: UTC+7 (12 hours ahead of Washington, DC, during Standard Time)
note: Indonesia has three time zones

Administrative divisions: 31 provinces (provinsi-provinsi, singular—provinsi), 1 autonomous province*, 1 special region** (daerah-daerah istimewa, singular—daerah istimewa), and 1 national capital district*** (daerah khusus ibukota); Aceh*, Bali, Banten, Bengkulu, Gorontalo, Jakarta Raya***, Jambi, Jawa Barat (West Java), Jawa Tengah (Central Java), Jawa Timur (East Java), Kalimantan Barat (West Kalimantan), Kalimantan Selatan (South Kalimantan), Kalimantan Tengah (Central Kalimantan), Kalimantan Timur (East Kalimantan), Kalimantan Utara (North Kalimantan), Kepulauan Bangka Belitung (Bangka Belitung Islands), Kepulauan Riau (Riau Islands), Lampung, Maluku, Maluku Utara (North Maluku), Nusa Tenggara Barat (West Nusa Tenggara), Nusa Tenggara Timur (East Nusa Tenggara), Papua, Papua Barat (West Papua), Riau, Sulawesi Barat (West Sulawesi), Sulawesi Selatan (South Sulawesi), Sulawesi Tengah (Central Sulawesi), Sulawesi Tenggara (Southeast Sulawesi), Sulawesi Utara (North Sulawesi), Sumatera Barat (West Sumatra), Sumatera Selatan (South Sumatra), Sumatera Utara (North Sumatra), Yogyakarta**
note: following the implementation of decentralization beginning on 1 January 2001, regencies and municipalities have become the key

administrative units responsible for providing most government services

Independence: 17 August 1945 (declared independence from the Netherlands)

National holiday: Independence Day, 17 August (1945)

Constitution: drafted July to August 1945, effective 17 August 1945, abrogated by 1949 and 1950 constitutions, 1945 constitution restored 5 July 1959; amended several times, last in 2002; note—an amendment on "national character building and national consciousness awareness" was pending parliamentary review in early 2016 (2016)

Legal system: civil law system based on the Roman-Dutch model and influenced by customary law

International law organization participation: has not submitted an ICJ jurisdiction declaration; non-party state to the ICCt

Citizenship: *citizenship by birth:* no
citizenship by descent only: at least one parent must be a citizen of Indonesia
dual citizenship recognized: no
residency requirement for naturalization: 5 continuous years

Suffrage: 17 years of age; universal and married persons regardless of age

Executive branch: *chief of state:* President Joko WIDODO (since 20 October 2014); Vice President Jusuf KALLA (since 20 October 2014); note—the president is both chief of state and head of government

head of government: President Joko WIDODO (since 20 October 2014); Vice President Jusuf KALLA (since 20 October 2014)
cabinet: Cabinet appointed by the president
elections/appointments: president and vice president directly elected by absolute majority popular vote for a 5-year term (eligible for a second term); election last held on 9 July 2014 (next to be held in 2019)
election results: Joko WIDODO elected president; percent of vote—Joko WIDODO (PDI-P) 53.2%, PRABOWO Subianto (GERINDRA) 46.8%

Legislative branch: *description:* bicameral People's Consultative Assembly or Majelis Permusyawaratan Rakyat consists of the Regional Representative Council or Dewan Perwakilan Daerah (132 seats; non-partisan members directly elected in multi-seat constituencies—4 each from the country's 33 electoral districts—by proportional representation vote to serve 5-year terms) and the House of Representatives or Dewan Perwakilan Rakyat (560 seats; members directly elected in multi-seat constituencies by single non-transferable vote to serve 5-year terms); note—the Regional Council has no legislative authority
elections: last held on 9 April 2014 (next to be held in 2019)
election results: Regional Representative Council—all seats elected on a non-partisan basis; House of Representatives—percent of vote by party—PDI-P 19.0%, Golkar 14.8%, Gerindra 11.8%, PD 10.2%, PKB 9.0%, PAN 2.6%, PKS

6.8%, NasDem 6.7%, PPP 6.5%, Hanura 5.3%, other 7.9%; seats by party—PDI-P 109, Golkar 91, Gerindra 73, PD 61, PAN 48, PKB 47, PKS 40, PPP 39, NasDem 36, Hanura 16

Judicial branch: *highest court(s):* Supreme Court or Mahkamah Agung (51 judges divided into 8 chambers); Constitutional Court or Mahkamah Konstitusi (consists of 9 judges)
judge selection and term of office: Supreme Court judges nominated by Judicial Commission, appointed by president with concurrence of parliament; judges serve until retirement at age 65; Constitutional Court judges—3 nominated by president, 3 by Supreme Court, and 3 by parliament; judges appointed by the president; judges serve until mandatory retirement at age 70
subordinate courts: High Courts of Appeal, district courts, religious courts

Political parties and leaders: Democrat Party or PD [Susilo Bambang YUDHOYONO]
Functional Groups Party or GOLKAR [Setya NOVANTO]
Great Indonesia Movement Party or GERINDRA [PRABOWO Subianto Djojohadikusumo]
Indonesia Democratic Party-Struggle or PDI-P [MEGAWATI Sukarnoputri]
National Awakening Party or PKB [Muhaiman ISKANDAR]
National Democratic Party or Nasdem [Surya PALOH]
National Mandate Party or PAN [Zulkifli HASAN]
People's Conscience Party or HANURA [WIRANTO]
Prosperous Justice Party or PKS [Muhammad Sohibul IMAN]
United Development Party or PPP [Muhammad ROMAHURMUZIY]

Political pressure groups and leaders: Commission for the "Disappeared" and Victims of Violence or KontraS
Indonesia Corruption Watch or ICW
Indonesian Forum for the Environment or WALHI

International organization participation: ADB, APEC, ARF, ASEAN, BIS, CD, CICA (observer), CP, D-8, EAS, EITI (compliant country), FAO, G-11, G-15, G-20, G-77, IAEA, IBRD, ICAO, ICC (national committees), ICRM, IDA, IDB, IFAD, IFC, IFRCS, IHO, ILO, IMF, IMO, IMSO, Interpol, IOC, IOM (observer), IORA, IPU, ISO, ITSO, ITU, ITUC (NGOs), MIGA, MINURSO, MINUSTAH, MONUSCO, MSG (associate member), NAM, OECD (enhanced engagement), OIC, OPCW, PIF (partner), UN, UNA-MID, UNCTAD, UNESCO, UNIDO, UNIFIL, UNISFA, UNMIL, UNWTO, UPU, WCO, WFTU (NGOs), WHO, WIPO, WMO, WTO

Diplomatic representation in the US: *chief of mission:* Ambassador Budi BOWOLEKSONO (since 21 May 2014)
chancery: 2020 Massachusetts Avenue NW, Washington, DC 20036
telephone: [1] (202) 775-5200
FAX: [1] (202) 775-5365

consulate(s) general: Chicago, Houston, Los Angeles, New York, San Francisco

Diplomatic representation from the US: *chief of mission:* Ambassador Joseph R. DONOVAN, Jr. (since 12 January 2017)
embassy: Jalan Medan Merdeka Selatan 3-5, Jakarta 10110
mailing address: Unit 8129, Box 1, FPO AP 96520
telephone: [62] (21) 3435-9000
FAX: [62] (21) 386-2259
consulate general: Surabaya
consulate: Medan

Flag description: two equal horizontal bands of red (top) and white; the colors derive from the banner of the Majapahit Empire of the 13th-15th centuries; red symbolizes courage, white represents purity
note: similar to the flag of Monaco, which is shorter; also similar to the flag of Poland, which is white (top) and red

National symbol(s): garuda (mythical bird); national colors: red, white

National anthem: *name:* "Indonesia Raya" (Great Indonesia)
lyrics/music: Wage Rudolf SOEPRATMAN
note: adopted 1945

ECONOMY

Economy—overview: Indonesia, the largest economy in Southeast Asia, has seen a slowdown in growth since 2012, mostly due to the end of the commodities export boom. During the global financial crisis, Indonesia outperformed its regional neighbors and joined China and India as the only G20 members posting growth. Indonesia's annual budget deficit is capped at 3% of GDP, and the Government of Indonesia lowered its debt-to-GDP ratio from a peak of 100% shortly after the Asian financial crisis in 1999 to 33% today. While Fitch and Moody's Investors upgraded Indonesia's credit rating to investment grade in December 2011, Standard & Poor's has yet to raise Indonesia's rating to this status amid several constraints to foreign direct investment in the country, such as a high level of protectionism.

Indonesia still struggles with poverty and unemployment, inadequate infrastructure, corruption, a complex regulatory environment, and unequal resource distribution among its regions. President Joko WIDODO—elected in July 2014—seeks to develop Indonesia's maritime resources and pursue other infrastructure development, including significantly increasing its electrical power generation capacity. Fuel subsidies were significantly reduced in early 2015, a move which has helped the government redirect its spending to development priorities. Indonesia, with the nine other ASEAN members, will continue to move towards participation in the ASEAN Economic Community, though full implementation of economic integration has not yet materialized.

GDP (purchasing power parity): $3.243 trillion (2017 est.)

$3.084 trillion (2016 est.)
$2.937 trillion (2015 est.)
note: data are in 2017 dollars
country comparison to the world: 8

GDP (official exchange rate): $1.011 trillion (2016 est.)

GDP—real growth rate: 5.2% (2017 est.)
5% (2016 est.)
4.9% (2015 est.)
country comparison to the world: 37

GDP—per capita (PPP): $12,400 (2017 est.)
$11,900 (2016 est.)
$11,500 (2015 est.)
note: data are in 2017 dollars
country comparison to the world: 125

Gross national saving: 32.6% of GDP (2017 est.)
32.5% of GDP (2016 est.)
32.1% of GDP (2015 est.)
country comparison to the world: 20

GDP—composition, by end use:
household consumption: 57.5%
government consumption: 8.9%
investment in fixed capital: 32.1%
investment in inventories: 0.7%
exports of goods and services: 19.2%
imports of goods and services: -18.4% (2017 est.)

GDP—composition, by sector of origin:
agriculture: 13.9%
industry: 40.3%
services: 45.9% (2017 est.)

Agriculture—products: rubber and similar products, palm oil, poultry, beef, forest products, shrimp, cocoa, coffee, medicinal herbs, essential oil, fish and its similar products, and spices

Industries: petroleum and natural gas, textiles, automotive, electrical appliances, apparel, footwear, mining, cement, medical instruments and appliances, handicrafts, chemical fertilizers, plywood, rubber, processed food, jewelry, and tourism

Industrial production growth rate: 3.8% (2017 est.)
country comparison to the world: 76

Labor force: 126.1 million (2017 est.)
country comparison to the world: 5

Labor force—by occupation: *agriculture:* 32%
industry: 21%
services: 47% (2016 est.)

Unemployment rate: 5.4% (2017 est.)
5.6% (2016 est.)
country comparison to the world: 72

Population below poverty line: 10.9% (2016 est.)

Household income or consumption by percentage share: *lowest 10%:* 3.4%
highest 10%: 28.2% (2010)

Distribution of family income—Gini index: 36.8 (2009)
39.4 (2005)
country comparison to the world: 81

Budget: *revenues:* $130.6 billion
expenditures: $154.8 billion (2017 est.)
Taxes and other revenues: 12.9% of GDP (2017 est.)
country comparison to the world: 202

Budget surplus (+) or deficit (-): -2.4% of GDP (2017 est.)
country comparison to the world: 97

Public debt: 33.1% of GDP (2017 est.)
31.5% of GDP (2016 est.)
country comparison to the world: 151

Fiscal year: calendar year

Inflation rate (consumer prices): 4% (2017 est.)
3.5% (2016 est.)
country comparison to the world: 157

Central bank discount rate: 6.37% (31 December 2010)
6.46% (31 December 2009)
note: this figure represents the 3-month SBI rate; the Bank of Indonesia has not employed the one-month SBI since September 2010
country comparison to the world: 65

Commercial bank prime lending rate: 11.3% (31 December 2017 est.)
11.89% (31 December 2016 est.)
note: these figures represent the average annualized rate on working capital loans
country comparison to the world: 73

Stock of narrow money: $107.6 billion (31 December 2017 est.)
$92.11 billion (31 December 2016 est.)
country comparison to the world: 36

Stock of broad money: $407.6 billion (31 December 2017 est.)
$372.5 billion (31 December 2016 est.)
country comparison to the world: 27

Stock of domestic credit: $436.7 billion (31 December 2017 est.)
$397.7 billion (31 December 2016 est.)
country comparison to the world: 28

Market value of publicly traded shares: $428.2 billion (31 December 2016 est.)
$353.3 billion (31 December 2015 est.)
$422.1 billion (31 December 2014 est.)
country comparison to the world: 23

Current account balance: -$17.03 billion (2017 est.)
-$16.77 billion (2016 est.)
country comparison to the world: 189

Exports: $157.8 billion (2017 est.)
$144.4 billion (2016 est.)
country comparison to the world: 31

Exports—commodities: mineral fuels, animal or vegetable fats (includes palm oil), electrical machinery, rubber, machinery and mechanical appliance parts

Exports—partners: China 11.6%, US 11.2%, Japan 11.1%, Singapore 7.8%, India 7%, Malaysia 4.9%, South Korea 4.8% (2016)

Imports: $142.3 billion (2017 est.)
$129 billion (2016 est.)
country comparison to the world: 32

Imports—commodities: mineral fuels, boilers, machinery, and mechanical parts, electric machinery, iron and steel, foodstuffs

Imports—partners: China 22.9%, Singapore 10.8%, Japan 9.6%, Thailand 6.4%, US 5.4%, Malaysia 5.4%, South Korea 5% (2016)

Reserves of foreign exchange and gold: $122.5 billion (31 December 2017 est.)
$116.4 billion (31 December 2016 est.)
country comparison to the world: 21

Debt—external: $322.6 billion (31 December 2017 est.)
$316.5 billion (31 December 2016 est.)
country comparison to the world: 33

Stock of direct foreign investment—at home: $247.7 billion (31 December 2017 est.)
$229.1 billion (31 December 2016 est.)
country comparison to the world: 25

Stock of direct foreign investment—abroad: $19.96 billion (31 December 2017 est.)
$18.42 billion (31 December 2016 est.)
country comparison to the world: 53

Exchange rates: Indonesian rupiah (IDR) per US dollar—
13,360.1 (2017 est.)
13,308.3 (2016 est.)
13,308.3 (2015 est.)
13,389.4 (2014 est.)
11,865.2 (2013 est.)

ENERGY

Electricity access: *population without electricity:* 48,700,000
electrification—*total population:* 81%
electrification—urban areas: 94%
electrification—rural areas: 66% (2013)

Electricity—production: 221.3 billion kWh (2015 est.)
country comparison to the world: 22

Electricity—consumption: 199.3 billion kWh (2015 est.)
country comparison to the world: 22

Electricity—exports: 0 kWh (2016 est.)
country comparison to the world: 150

Electricity—imports: 13 million kWh (2015 est.)
country comparison to the world: 112

Electricity—installed generating capacity: 57.35 million kW (2015 est.)
country comparison to the world: 20

Electricity—from fossil fuels: 85.1% of total installed capacity (2015 est.)
country comparison to the world: 76

Electricity—from nuclear fuels: 0% of total installed capacity (2015 est.)
country comparison to the world: 111

Electricity—from hydroelectric plants: 9.4% of total installed capacity (2015 est.)
country comparison to the world: 120

Electricity—from other renewable sources: 5.9% of total installed capacity (2015 est.)
country comparison to the world: 90

Crude oil—production: 831,100 bbl/day (2016 est.)
country comparison to the world: 24

Crude oil—exports: 289,300 bbl/day (2014 est.)

country comparison to the world: 26

Crude oil—imports: 507,900 bbl/day (2014 est.)
country comparison to the world: 17

Crude oil—proved reserves: 3.23 billion bbl (1 January 2017 es)
country comparison to the world: 30

Refined petroleum products—production: 990,700 bbl/day (2014 est.)
country comparison to the world: 21

Refined petroleum products—consumption: 1.708 million bbl/day (2015 est.)
country comparison to the world: 14

Refined petroleum products—exports: 98,780 bbl/day (2014 est.)
country comparison to the world: 42

Refined petroleum products—imports: 668,500 bbl/day (2014 est.)
country comparison to the world: 12

Natural gas—production: 72.8 billion cu m (2015 est.)
country comparison to the world: 12

Natural gas—consumption: 53.15 billion cu m (2015 est.)
country comparison to the world: 21

Natural gas—exports: 30.29 billion cu m (2015 est.)
country comparison to the world: 13

Natural gas—imports: 1.8 billion cu m (2014 est.)
country comparison to the world: 52

Natural gas—proved reserves: 2.775 trillion cu m (1 January 2017 es)
country comparison to the world: 14

Carbon dioxide emissions from consumption of energy: 442 million Mt (2013 est.)
country comparison to the world: 16

COMMUNICATIONS

Telephones—fixed lines: *total subscriptions:* 10,372,912
subscriptions per 100 inhabitants: 4 (July 2016 est.)
country comparison to the world: 11

Telephones—mobile cellular: *total:* 385,573,398
subscriptions per 100 inhabitants: 149 (July 2016 est.)
country comparison to the world: 4

Telephone system: *general assessment:* domestic service includes an interisland microwave system, an HF radio police net, and a domestic satellite communications system; international service good
domestic: coverage provided by existing network has been expanded by use of over 200,000 telephone kiosks many located in remote areas; mobile-cellular subscribership growing rapidly
international: country code—62; landing point for both the SEA-ME-WE-3 and SEA-ME-WE-4 submarine cable networks that provide links throughout Asia, the Middle East, and Europe; satellite earth stations—2 Intelsat (1 Indian Ocean and 1 Pacific Ocean) (2015)

Broadcast media: mixture of about a dozen national TV networks—2 public broadcasters, the remainder private broadcasters—each with multiple transmitters; more than 100 local TV stations; widespread use of satellite and cable TV systems; public radio broadcaster operates 6 national networks, as well as regional and local stations; overall, more than 700 radio stations with more than 650 privately operated (2008)

Internet country code: .id
Internet users: total: 65,525,226

percent of population: 25.4% (July 2016 est.)
country comparison to the world: 14

TRANSPORTATION

National air transport system: *number of registered air carriers:* 29
inventory of registered aircraft operated by air carriers: 550
annual passenger traffic on registered air carriers: 88,685,767
annual freight traffic on registered air carriers: 747,473,207 mt-km (2015)
Civil aircraft registration country code prefix: PK (2016)

Airports: 673 (2013)
country comparison to the world: 10

Airports—with paved runways: *total:* 186
over 3,047 m: 5
2,438 to 3,047 m: 21
1,524 to 2,437 m: 51
914 to 1,523 m: 72
under 914 m: 37 (2017)

Airports—with unpaved runways: *total:* 487
1,524 to 2,437 m: 4
914 to 1,523 m: 23
under 914 m: 460 (2013)

Heliports: 76 (2013)

Pipelines: condensate 1,064 km; condensate/gas 150 km; gas 11,702 km; liquid petroleum gas 119 km; oil 7,767 km; oil/gas/water 77 km; refined products 728 km; unknown 53 km; water 44 km (2013)

Railways: *total:* 8,159 km
narrow gauge: 8,159 km 1.067-m gauge (565 km electrified)
note: 4,816 km operational (2014)
country comparison to the world: 27

Roadways: *total:* 496,607 km
paved: 283,102 km
unpaved: 213,505 km (2011)
country comparison to the world: 14

Waterways: 21,579 km (2011)
country comparison to the world: 7

Merchant marine: *total:* 8,782
by type: bulk carrier 81, container ship 194, general cargo 2,142, oil tanker 544, other 5,821 (2017)
country comparison to the world: 1

Ports and terminals: *major seaport(s):* Banjarmasin, Belawan, Kotabaru, Krueg Geukueh, Palembang, Panjang, Sungai Pakning, Tanjung Perak, Tanjung Priok

container port(s) (TEUs): Belawan (1,197,000), Tanjung Priok (5,154,000) (2015)
LNG terminal(s) (export): Bontang, Tangguh
LNG terminal(s) (import): Arun, Lampung, West Java

MILITARY AND SECURITY

Military expenditures: 0.88% of GDP (2016)
0.89% of GDP (2015)
0.78% of GDP (2014)
0.92% of GDP (2013)
0.71% of GDP (2012)
country comparison to the world: 116

Military branches: Indonesian Armed Forces (Tentara Nasional Indonesia, TNI): Army (TNI-Angkatan Darat (TNI-AD)), Navy (TNI-Angkatan Laut (TNI-AL)), includes marines (Korps Marinir, KorMar), naval air arm), Air Force (TNI-Angkatan Udara (TNI-AU)), National Air Defense Command (Kommando Pertahanan Udara Nasional (Kohanudnas)) (2013)

Military service age and obligation: 18-45 years of age for voluntary military service, with selective conscription authorized; 2-year service obligation, with reserve obligation to age 45 (officers); Indonesian citizens only (2012)

Maritime threats: the International Maritime Bureau continues to report the territorial and offshore waters in the Strait of Malacca and South China Sea as high risk for piracy and armed robbery against ships; attacks declined dramatically from 108 incidents in 2015 to 49 in 2016, although Indonesian waters remained the most dangerous in the world; in 2016, 45 commercial vessels were boarded and one hijacked; during 2016 37 crew members were taken hostage; hijacked vessels are often disguised and cargo diverted to ports in East Asia; crews have been murdered or cast adrift; Indonesia remains the most dangerous area during the first half of 2017 with more than 20% of all incidents reported world-wide

TERRORISM

Terrorist groups—home based: *Jemaah Anshorut Tauhid (JAT): aim(s):* establish an Islamic caliphate in Indonesia
area(s) of operation: headquartered in Indonesia; a group member in Jamaah Ansharut Daulah, an Indonesian-based coalition of armed groups aligned with ISIL; has conducted multiple small-scale bombing and shooting attacks over the years on Indonesian Government personnel, police, military, and civilians, resulting in the deaths of several Indonesian police and civilians

Jemaah Islamiya (JI): *aim(s):* overthrow the Indonesian Government and, ultimately, establish a pan-Islamic state across Southeast Asia
area(s) of operation: headquartered in Indonesia; on 5 August 2003, a suicide bomber detonated a VBIED outside the J.W. Marriott Hotel in Megakuningan, Jakarta, Indonesia, killing 12 people and injuring 150; on 12 October 2002, a suicide bomber detonated explosives in a busy nightclub frequented by foreigners on the resort island of

Bali, followed by operatives detonating a vehicle-borne improvised explosive device when patrons fled the burning scene, killing at least 202 people; as of early 2017, the attack remains the deadliest in Indonesia; JI attacks have ebbed in recent years; incarcerated recruiters radicalize and recruit fellow prisoners

Terrorist groups—foreign based: *Islamic State of Iraq and the Levant (ISIL): aim(s):* replace the Indonesian Government with an Islamic state and implement ISIL's strict interpretation of Sharia *area(s) of operation:* claimed responsibility for coordinated attacks against a police traffic post and numerous civilian targets on 14 January 2016 in Central Jakarta, where operatives used gunfire, suicide bombers, and explosives that killed five people and wounded over 24; marked the first attack in Southeast Asia claimed by ISIL; recruits heavily in prisons; ISIL's leader in Indonesia, Aman ABDURRAHMAN, was in an Indonesian prison as of early 2017; incarcerated members radicalize and recruit fellow prisoners; the majority of Southeast Asians fighting alongside ISIL are from Indonesia

TRANSNATIONAL ISSUES

Disputes—international: Indonesia has a stated foreign policy objective of establishing stable fixed land and maritime boundaries with all of its neighbors; three stretches of land borders with Timor-Leste have yet to be delimited, two of which are in the Oecussi exclave area, and no maritime or Exclusive Economic Zone (EEZ) boundaries have been established between the countries; all borders between Indonesia and Australia have been agreed upon bilaterally, but a 1997 treaty that would settle the last of their maritime and EEZ boundary has yet to be ratified by Indonesia's legislature; Indonesian groups challenge Australia's claim to Ashmore Reef; Australia has closed parts of the Ashmore and Cartier Reserve to Indonesian traditional fishing and placed restrictions on certain catches; land and maritime negotiations with Malaysia are ongoing, and disputed areas include the controversial Tanjung Datu and Camar Wulan border area in Borneo and the maritime boundary in the Ambalat oil block in the Celebes Sea; Indonesia and Singapore continue to work on finalizing their 1973 maritime boundary agreement by defining unresolved areas north of Indonesia's Batam Island; Indonesian secessionists, squatters, and illegal migrants create repatriation problems for Papua New Guinea; maritime delimitation talks continue with Palau; EEZ negotiations with Vietnam are ongoing, and the two countries in Fall 2011 agreed to work together to reduce illegal fishing along their maritime boundary

Refugees and internally displaced persons: IDPs: 7,100 (inter-communal, inter-faith, and separatist violence between 1998 and 2004 in Aceh and Papua; religious attacks and land conflicts in 2012 and 2013; most IDPs in Aceh, Maluku, East Nusa Tengarra) (2016) (2011)

Illicit drugs: illicit producer of cannabis largely for domestic use; producer of methamphetamine and ecstasy; President WIDODO's war on drugs has led to an increase in death sentences and executions, particularly of foreign drug traffickers

IRAN

INTRODUCTION

Background: Known as Persia until 1935, Iran became an Islamic republic in 1979 after the ruling monarchy was overthrown and Shah Mohammad Reza PAHLAVI was forced into exile. Conservative clerical forces led by Ayatollah Ruhollah KHOMEINI established a theocratic system of government with ultimate political authority vested in a learned religious scholar referred to commonly as the Supreme Leader who, according to the constitution, is accountable only to the Assembly of Experts (AOE)—a popularly elected 86-member body of clerics. US-Iranian relations became strained when a group of Iranian students seized the US Embassy in Tehran in November 1979 and held embassy personnel hostages until mid-January 1981. The US cut off diplomatic relations with Iran in April 1980. During the period 1980-88, Iran fought a bloody, indecisive war with Iraq that eventually expanded into the Persian Gulf and led to clashes between US Navy and Iranian military forces. Iran has been designated a state sponsor of terrorism for its activities in Lebanon and elsewhere in the world and remains subject to US, UN, and EU economic sanctions and export controls because of its continued involvement in terrorism and concerns over possible military dimensions of its nuclear program. Following the election of reformer Hojjat ol-Eslam Mohammad KHATAMI as president in 1997 and a reformist Majles (legislature) in 2000, a campaign to foster political reform in response to popular dissatisfaction was initiated. The movement floundered as conservative politicians, supported by the Supreme Leader, unelected institutions of authority like the Council of Guardians, and the security services reversed and blocked reform measures while increasing security repression.

Starting with nationwide municipal elections in 2003 and continuing through Majles elections in 2004, conservatives reestablished control over Iran's elected government institutions, which culminated with the August 2005 inauguration of hardliner Mahmud AHMADI-NEJAD as president. His controversial reelection in June 2009 sparked nationwide protests over allegations of electoral fraud, but the protests were quickly suppressed. Deteriorating economic conditions due primarily to government mismanagement and international sanctions prompted at least two major economically based protests in July and October 2012, but Iran's internal security situation remained stable. President AHMADI-NEJAD's independent streak angered regime establishment figures, including the Supreme Leader, leading to conservative opposition to his agenda for the last year of his presidency, and an alienation of his political supporters. In June 2013 Iranians elected a moderate conservative cleric Dr. Hasan Fereidun RUHANI to the presidency. He is a longtime senior member in the regime, but has made promises of reforming society and Iran's foreign policy. The UN Security Council has passed a number of resolutions calling for Iran to suspend its uranium enrichment and reprocessing activities and comply with its IAEA obligations and responsibilities, and in July 2015 Iran and the five permanent members, plus Germany (P5+1) signed the Joint Comprehensive Plan of Action (JCPOA) under which Iran agreed to restrictions on its nuclear program in exchange for sanctions relief. Iran held elections in 2016 for the AOE and Majles, resulting in a conservative-controlled AOE and a Majles that many Iranians perceive as more supportive of the RUHANI administration than the previous, conservative-dominated body. Iran will hold presidential elections in May 2017. RUHANI is currently favored to win a second term.

GEOGRAPHY

Location: Middle East, bordering the Gulf of Oman, the Persian Gulf, and the Caspian Sea, between Iraq and Pakistan

Geographic coordinates: 32 00 N, 53 00 E

Map references: Middle East

Area: *total:* 1,648,195 sq km
land: 1,531,595 sq km
water: 116,600 sq km
country comparison to the world: 19

Area—comparative: almost 2.5 times the size of Texas; slightly smaller than Alaska

Land boundaries: *total:* 5,894 km
border countries (7): Afghanistan 921 km, Armenia 44 km, Azerbaijan 689 km, Iraq 1,599 km, Pakistan 959 km, Turkey 534 km, Turkmenistan 1,148 km

Coastline: 2,440 km; note—Iran also borders the Caspian Sea (740 km)

Maritime claims: *territorial sea:* 12 nm
contiguous zone: 24 nm
exclusive economic zone: bilateral agreements or median lines in the Persian Gulf
continental shelf: natural prolongation

Climate: mostly arid or semiarid, subtropical along Caspian coast

Terrain: rugged, mountainous rim; high, central basin with deserts, mountains; small, discontinuous plains along both coasts

Elevation: *mean elevation:* 1,305 m
elevation extremes: lowest point: Caspian Sea -28 m
highest point: Kuh-e Damavand 5,625 m

Natural resources: petroleum, natural gas, coal, chromium, copper, iron ore, lead, manganese, zinc, sulfur

Land use: *agricultural land:* 30.1%
arable land: 10.8%;
permanent crops: 1.2%;
permanent pasture: 18.1%
forest: 6.8%
other: 63.1% (2011 est.)
Irrigated land: 95,530 sq km (2012)

Population—distribution: population is concentrated in the north, northwest, and west, reflecting the position of the Zagros and Elburz Mountains; the vast dry areas in the center and eastern parts of the country, around the deserts of the Dasht-e Kavir and Dasht-e Lut, have a much lower population density

Natural hazards: periodic droughts, floods; dust storms, sandstorms; earthquakes

Environment—current issues: air pollution, especially in urban areas, from vehicle emissions, refinery operations, and industrial effluents; deforestation; overgrazing; desertification; oil pollution in the Persian Gulf; wetland losses from drought; soil degradation (salination); inadequate supplies of potable water; water pollution from raw sewage and industrial waste; urbanization

Environment—international agreements: *party to:* Biodiversity, Climate Change, Climate Change-Kyoto Protocol, Desertification, Endangered Species, Hazardous Wastes, Marine Dumping, Ozone Layer Protection, Ship Pollution, Wetlands
signed, but not ratified: Environmental Modification, Law of the Sea, Marine Life Conservation

Geography—note: strategic location on the Persian Gulf and Strait of Hormuz, which are vital maritime pathways for crude oil transport

PEOPLE AND SOCIETY

Population: 82,021,564 (July 2017 est.)
country comparison to the world: 17

Nationality: *noun:* Iranian(s)
adjective: Iranian

Ethnic groups: Persian, Azeri, Kurd, Lur, Baloch, Arab, Turkmen and Turkic tribes

Languages: Persian (official), Azeri Turkic and Turkic dialects, Kurdish, Gilaki and Mazandarani, Luri, Balochi, Arabic, other

Religions: Muslim (official) 99.4% (Shia 90-95%, Sunni 5-10%), other (includes Zoroastrian, Jewish, and Christian) 0.3%, unspecified 0.4% (2011 est.)

Age structure: *0-14 years:* 24.19% (male 10,154,424/female 9,690,512)
15-24 years: 14.69% (male 6,174,435/female 5,878,475)
25-54 years: 48.57% (male 20,316,773/female 19,522,673)
55-64 years: 7.22% (male 2,920,111/female 2,999,525)
65 years and over: 5.32% (male 2,026,594/female 2,338,042) (2017 est.)

Dependency ratios: *total dependency ratio:* 40.2
youth dependency ratio: 33.1
elderly dependency ratio: 7.1
potential support ratio: 14.2 (2015 est.)

Median age: *total:* 30.3 years
male: 30 years
female: 30.5 years (2017 est.)
country comparison to the world: 122

Population growth rate: 1.24% (2017 est.)
country comparison to the world: 90

Birth rate: 17.9 births/1,000 population (2017 est.)
country comparison to the world: 101

Death rate: 5.3 deaths/1,000 population (2017 est.)
country comparison to the world: 183

Net migration rate: -0.2 migrant(s)/1,000 population (2017 est.)
country comparison to the world: 111

Population distribution: population is concentrated in the north, northwest, and west, reflecting the position of the Zagros and Elburz Mountains; the vast dry areas in the center and eastern parts of the country, around the deserts of the Dasht-e Kavir and Dasht-e Lut, have a much lower population density

Urbanization: *urban population:* 74.4% of total population (2017)
rate of urbanization: 1.78% annual rate of change (2015-20 est.)

Major urban areas—population: TEHRAN (capital) 8.432 million; Mashhad 3.014 million; Esfahan 1.88 million; Karaj 1.807 million; Shiraz 1.661 million; Tabriz 1.572 million (2015)

Sex ratio: *at birth:* 1.05 male(s)/female
0-14 years: 1.05 male(s)/female
15-24 years: 1.05 male(s)/female
25-54 years: 1.04 male(s)/female
55-64 years: 0.97 male(s)/female
65 years and over: 0.86 male(s)/female
total population: 1.03 male(s)/female (2016 est.)

Maternal mortality ratio: 25 deaths/100,000 live births (2015 est.)

country comparison to the world: 123

Infant mortality rate: *total:* 15.9 deaths/1,000 live births
male: 17 deaths/1,000 live births
female: 14.8 deaths/1,000 live births (2017 est.)
country comparison to the world: 99

Life expectancy at birth: *total population:* 74 years
male: 72.7 years
female: 75.5 years (2017 est.)
country comparison to the world: 129

Total fertility rate: 1.97 children born/woman (2017 est.)
country comparison to the world: 124

Contraceptive prevalence rate: 77.4% (2010/11)

Health expenditures: 6.9% of GDP (2014)
country comparison to the world: 84

Physicians density: 1.49 physicians/1,000 population (2014)

Hospital bed density: 0.1 beds/1,000 population (2012)

Drinking water source:
improved:
urban: 97.7% of population
rural: 92.1% of population
total: 96.2% of population
unimproved:
urban: 2.3% of population
rural: 7.9% of population
total: 3.8% of population (2015 est.)

Sanitation facility access:
improved:
urban: 92.8% of population
rural: 82.3% of population
total: 90% of population
unimproved:
urban: 7.2% of population
rural: 17.7% of population
total: 10% of population (2015 est.)

HIV/AIDS—adult prevalence rate: 0.1% (2016 est.)
country comparison to the world: 103

HIV/AIDS—people living with HIV/AIDS: 66,000 (2016 est.)
country comparison to the world: 52

HIV/AIDS—deaths: 4,000 (2016 est.)
country comparison to the world: 34

Major infectious diseases: *degree of risk:* intermediate
food or waterborne diseases: bacterial diarrhea
vectorborne diseases: Crimean-Congo hemorrhagic fever (2016)

Obesity—adult prevalence rate: 25.8% (2016)
country comparison to the world: 47

Children under the age of 5 years underweight: 4.1% (2011)
country comparison to the world: 93

Education expenditures: 2.9% of GDP (2015)
country comparison to the world: 119

Literacy: *definition:* age 15 and over can read and write
total population: 86.8%

male: 91.2%
female: 82.5% (2015 est.)

School life expectancy (primary to tertiary education): *total:* 15 years
male: 15 years
female: 15 years (2015)

Unemployment, youth ages 15-24: *total:* 26.1%
male: 22.3%
female: 42.8% (2015 est.)
country comparison to the world: 44

GOVERNMENT

Country name: *conventional long form:* Islamic Republic of Iran
conventional short form: Iran
local long form: Jomhuri-ye Eslami-ye Iran
local short form: Iran
former: Persia
etymology: name derives from the Avestan term "aryanam" meaning "Land of the noble [ones]"

Government type: theocratic republic

Capital: name: Tehran

geographic coordinates: 35 42 N, 51 25 E
time difference: UTC+3.5 (8.5 hours ahead of Washington, DC, during Standard Time)
daylight saving time: +1hr, begins fourth Wednesday in March; ends fourth Friday in September

Administrative divisions: 31 provinces (ostanha, singular—ostan); Alborz, Ardabil, Azarbayjan-e Gharbi (West Azerbaijan), Azarbayjan-e Sharqi (East Azerbaijan), Bushehr, Chahar Mahal va Bakhtiari, Esfahan, Fars, Gilan, Golestan, Hamadan, Hormozgan, Ilam, Kerman, Kermanshah, Khorasan-e Jonubi (South Khorasan), Khorasan-e Razavi (Razavi Khorasan), Khorasan-e Shomali (North Khorasan), Khuzestan, Kohgiluyeh va Bowyer Ahmad, Kordestan, Lorestan, Markazi, Mazandaran, Qazvin, Qom, Semnan, Sistan va Baluchestan, Tehran, Yazd, Zanjan

Independence: 1 April 1979 (Islamic Republic of Iran proclaimed); notable earlier dates: ca. 550 B.C. (Achaemenid (Persian) Empire established); A.D. 1501 (Iran reunified under the Safavid Dynasty); 1794 (beginning of Qajar Dynasty); 12 December 1925 (modern Iran established under the PAHLAVI Dynasty)

National holiday: Republic Day, 1 April (1979)

Constitution: history: previous 1906; latest adopted 24 October 1979, effective 3 December 1979
amendments: proposed by the supreme leader—after consultation with the Exigency Council—and submitted as an edict to the "Council for Revision of the Constitution," a body consisting of various executive, legislative, judicial, and academic leaders and members; passage requires absolute majority vote in a referendum and approval of the supreme leader; articles including Iran's political system, its religious basis, and its form of government cannot be amended; amended 1989 (2016)

Legal system: religious legal system based on secular and Islamic law

International law organization participation: has not submitted an ICJ jurisdiction declaration; non-party state to the ICCt

Citizenship: *citizenship by birth:* no
citizenship by descent only: the father must be a citizen of Iran
dual citizenship recognized: no
residency requirement for naturalization: 5 years

Suffrage: 18 years of age; universal

Executive branch: *chief of state:* Supreme Leader Ali Hoseini-KHAMENEI (since 4 June 1989)

head of government: President Hasan Fereidun RUHANI (since 3 August 2013); First Vice President Eshaq JAHANGIRI (since 5 August 2013)
cabinet: Council of Ministers selected by the president with legislative approval; the supreme leader has some control over appointments to several ministries
elections/appointments: supreme leader appointed for life by Assembly of Experts; president directly elected by absolute majority popular vote in 2 rounds if needed for a 4-year term (eligible for a second term and an additional nonconsecutive term); election last held on 19 May 2017 (next to be held in 2021)
election results: Hasan Fereidun RUHANI reelected president; percent of vote—Hasan Fereidun RUHANI (Moderation and Development Party) 50.7%, Mohammad Bagher GHALIBAF (PJP) 16.6%, Mohsen REZAI (Resistance Front of Islamic Iran) 10.6%, Saeed JALILI (Front of Islamic Revolutionary Stability 11.4% other 10.7%
note: 3 oversight bodies are also considered part of the executive branch of government

Legislative branch: *description:* unicameral Islamic Consultative Assembly or Majles-e Shuraye Eslami or Majles (290 seats; 285 members directly elected in single- and multi-seat constituencies by 2-round vote, and 1 seat each for Zoroastrians, Jews, Assyrian and Chaldean Christians, Armenians in the north of the country and Armenians in the South; members serve 4-year terms); note—all candidates to the Majles must be approved by the Guardians Council, a 12-member group of which 6 are appointed by the supreme leader and 6 are jurists nominated by the judiciary and elected by the Majles
elections: first round held on 26 February 2016 and second round for 68 remaining seats held on 29 April 2016; (next full Majles election to be held in 2020)
election results: percent of vote by coalition—List of Hope 37.2%, Principlists Grand Coalition 25.9%, People's Voice Coalition 4.5%, joint Hope/People's Voice 4.1%, joint People's Voice/Principlist 0.3%, religious minorities 1.7%, independent 26.4%; seats by coalition—List of Hope 108, Principlists Grand Coalition 75, People's Voice Coalition 13, joint Hope/People's Voice 12, joint People's Voice/Principlist 1, religious minorities 5, independent 76

Judicial branch: *highest court(s):* Supreme Court (consists of the president and NA judges)

judge selection and term of office: Supreme Court president appointed by the head of the High Judicial Council (HJC), a 5-member body to include the Supreme Court chief justice, the prosecutor general, and 3 clergy, in consultation with judges of the Supreme Court; president appointed for a 5-year term; other judges appointed by the HJC; judge tenure NA
subordinate courts: Penal Courts I and II; Islamic Revolutionary Courts; Courts of Peace; Special Clerical Court (functions outside the judicial system and handles cases involving clerics); military courts

Political parties and leaders: Followers of Walayat [Ali LARIJANI]

Front of Islamic Revolutionary Stability [Morteza AGHA-TEHRANI, general secretary]

Pervasive Coalition of Reformists: The Second Step [Ali SOUFI, chairman] (includes Council for Coordinating the Reforms Front, National Trust Party, Union of Islamic Iran People Party, Moderation and Development Party)

Principlists Grand Coalition [Alireza ZAKANI] (includes Combatant Clergy Association and Islamic Coalition Party, Society of Devotees and Pathseekers of the Islamic Revolution, Front of Islamic Revolution Stability)

Progress and Justice Population of Islamic Iran or PJP [Hossein GHORBANZADEH, General Secretary]

Resistance Front of Islamic Iran [Yadollah HABIBI, general secretary]

Political pressure groups and leaders: political groups that support the Islamic Republic: Ansar-e Hizballah

Democracy Party (Hezb-e Mardom Salari)

Executives of Construction Party (Kargozaran)

Followers of the Guardianship of the Jurisprudent (Rahrovan)

Followers of the Line of the Imam and the Leader (Peyrovan)

Islamic Iran Freedom Party (Hezb-e Azadegi)

Islamic Coalition Party (Motalefeh)

Islamic Labor Party (Hezb-e Kar)

Militant Clerics Society or MCS (Ruhaniyun)

Moderation and Development Party (Hezb-e Etedal va Tose-eh)

Nation of Iran Unity Party (Hezb-e Etehad)

National Trust Party (Hezb-e Etemad-e Meli)

Qom Theological Lecturers Association

Reform Front Coordination Council (Shora-ye Hamahangi Eslahat)

Society of Devotees (Isargaran)

Society of Modern Thinking Muslim Women of Iran (Jamiat-e Zanan-e Noandish)

Steadfastness Front (Paydari)

Tehran Militant Clergy Association or MCA (Ruhaniyat)

Voice of Iranians (Neda)

Wayfarers of the Islamic Revolution (Rahpuyan);

armed political groups repressed by the government: Democratic Party of Iranian Kurdistan or KDPI

Harekat-e Ansar-e Iran (splinter faction of Jundallah)

Jaysh l-Adl (formerly known as Jundallah)
Komala
Mojahedin-e Khalq Organization or MEK (MKO)
People's Fedayeen
People's Free Life Party of Kurdistan or PJAK

International organization participation: CICA, CP, D-8, ECO, FAO, G-15, G-24, G-77, IAEA, IBRD, ICAO, ICC (national committees), ICRM, IDA, IDB, IFAD, IFC, IFRCS, IHO, ILO, IMF, IMO, IMSO, Interpol, IOC, IOM, IPU, ISO, ITSO, ITU, MIGA, NAM, OIC, OPCW, OPEC, PCA, SAARC (observer), SCO (observer), UN, UNAMID, UNCTAD, UNESCO, UNHCR, UNIDO, UNITAR, UNWTO, UPU, WCO, WFTU (NGOs), WHO, WIPO, WMO, WTO (observer)

Diplomatic representation in the US: none; note—Iran has an Interests Section in the Pakistani Embassy; address: Iranian Interests Section, Pakistani Embassy, 2209 Wisconsin Avenue NW, Washington, DC 20007; telephone: [1] (202) 965-4990; FAX [1] (202) 965-1073

Diplomatic representation from the US: none; note—the US Interests Section is located in the Embassy of Switzerland, No. 39 Shahid Mousavi (Golestan 5th), Pasdaran Ave., Tehran, Iran; telephone [98] 21 2254 2178/2256 5273; FAX [98] 21 2258 0432

Flag description: three equal horizontal bands of green (top), white, and red; the national emblem (a stylized representation of the word Allah in the shape of a tulip, a symbol of martyrdom) in red is centered in the white band; ALLAH AKBAR (God is Great) in white Arabic script is repeated 11 times along the bottom edge of the green band and 11 times along the top edge of the red band; green is the color of Islam and also represents growth, white symbolizes honesty and peace, red stands for bravery and martyrdom

National symbol(s): lion; national colors: green, white, red

National anthem: name: "Soroud-e Melli-ye Jomhouri-ye Eslami-ye Iran" (National Anthem of the Islamic Republic of Iran)
lyrics/music: multiple authors/Hassan RIAHI
note: adopted 1990

ECONOMY

Economy—overview: Iran's economy is marked by statist policies, inefficiencies, and reliance on oil and gas exports, but Iran also possesses significant agricultural, industrial, and service sectors. The Iranian government directly owns and operates hundreds of state-owned enterprises and indirectly controls many companies affiliated with the country's security forces. Distortions—including corruption, price controls, subsidies, and a banking system holding billions of dollars of non-performing loans—weigh down the economy, undermining the potential for private-sector-led growth.

Private sector activity includes small-scale workshops, farming, some manufacturing, and services, in addition to medium-scale construction, cement production, mining, and metalworking.

Significant informal market activity flourishes and corruption is widespread.

The lifting of most nuclear-related sanctions under the Joint Comprehensive Plan of Action (JCPOA) in January 2016 sparked a restoration of Iran's oil production and revenue that drove rapid GDP growth, but economic growth declined in 2017 as oil production plateaued. The economy continues to suffer from low levels of investment and declines in productivity since before the JCPOA, and from high levels of unemployment, especially among women and college-educated Iranian youth.

In May 2017, the re-election of President Hasan RUHANI generated widespread public expectations that the economic benefits of the JCPOA would expand and reach all levels of society. RUHANI will need to implement structural reforms that strengthen the banking sector and improve Iran's business climate to attract foreign investment and encourage the growth of the private sector. Sanctions that are not related to Iran's nuclear program remain in effect, and these—plus fears over the possible re-imposition of nuclear-related sanctions—will continue to deter foreign investors from engaging with Iran.

GDP (purchasing power parity): $1.631 trillion (2017 est.)
$1.576 trillion (2016 est.)
$1.401 trillion (2015 est.)
note: data are in 2017 dollars
country comparison to the world: 19

GDP (official exchange rate): $427.7 billion (2016 est.)

GDP—real growth rate: 3.5% (2017 est.)
12.5% (2016 est.)
-1.6% (2015 est.)
country comparison to the world: 89

GDP—per capita (PPP): $20,000 (2017 est.)
$19,600 (2016 est.)
$17,600 (2015 est.)
note: data are in 2017 dollars
country comparison to the world: 88

Gross national saving: 41.5% of GDP (2017 est.)
37.6% of GDP (2016 est.)
37.3% of GDP (2015 est.)
country comparison to the world: 7

GDP—composition, by end use:
household consumption: 50.2%
government consumption: 13.3%
investment in fixed capital: 21.3%
investment in inventories: 14.1%
exports of goods and services: 22.5%
imports of goods and services: -21.3% (2017 est.)

GDP—composition, by sector of origin:
agriculture: 9.8%
industry: 35.9%
services: 54.3% (2017 est.)

Agriculture—products: wheat, rice, other grains, sugar beets, sugarcane, fruits, nuts, cotton; dairy products, wool; caviar

Industries: petroleum, petrochemicals, gas, fertilizer, caustic soda, textiles, cement and other construction materials, food processing (particularly sugar refining and vegetable oil production), ferrous and nonferrous metal fabrication, armaments

Industrial production growth rate: 7.1% (2017 est.)
country comparison to the world: 24

Labor force: 30.5 million
note: shortage of skilled labor (2017 est.)
country comparison to the world: 22

Labor force—by occupation: *agriculture:* 16.3%
industry: 35.1%
services: 48.6% (2013 est.)

Unemployment rate: 12.4% (2017 est.)
12.5% (2016 est.)
note: data are Iranian government numbers
country comparison to the world: 160

Population below poverty line: 18.7% (2007 est.)

Household income or consumption by percentage share: *lowest 10%:* 2.6%
highest 10%: 29.6% (2005)

Distribution of family income—Gini index: 44.5 (2006)
country comparison to the world: 44

Budget: *revenues:* $77.22 billion
expenditures: $86.26 billion (2017 est.)
Taxes and other revenues: 18.1% of GDP (2017 est.)
country comparison to the world: 167

Budget surplus (+) or deficit (-): -2.1% of GDP (2017 est.)
country comparison to the world: 91

Public debt: 14.2% of GDP (2017 est.)
13.4% of GDP (2016 est.)
note: includes publicly guaranteed debt
country comparison to the world: 194

Fiscal year: 21 March—20 March

Inflation rate (consumer prices): 10.5% (2017 est.)
9% (2016 est.)
note: official Iranian estimate
country comparison to the world: 204

Central bank discount rate: NA%

Commercial bank prime lending rate: 13% (31 December 2017 est.)
18% (31 December 2016 est.)
country comparison to the world: 60

Stock of narrow money: $51.61 billion (31 December 2017 est.)
$47.59 billion (31 December 2016 est.)
country comparison to the world: 55

Stock of broad money: $436.3 billion (31 December 2017 est.)
$366 billion (31 December 2016 est.)
country comparison to the world: 26

Stock of domestic credit: $366.1 billion (31 December 2017 est.)
$315.4 billion (31 December 2016 est.)
country comparison to the world: 35

Market value of publicly traded shares: $89.43 billion (31 December 2015 est.)
$116.6 billion (31 December 2014 est.)
$345.8 billion (31 December 2013 est.)
country comparison to the world: 41

Current account balance: $21.6 billion (2017 est.)

$16.39 billion (2016 est.)
country comparison to the world: 16

Exports: $91.99 billion (2017 est.)
$83.98 billion (2016 est.)
country comparison to the world: 38

Exports—commodities: petroleum 60%, chemical and petrochemical products, fruits and nuts, carpets, cement, ore

Exports—partners: China 30.1%, India 16.7%, South Korea 9.7%, Turkey 9.5%, Japan 6.8% (2016)

Imports: $70.53 billion (2017 est.)
$63.14 billion (2016 est.)
country comparison to the world: 43

Imports—commodities: industrial supplies, capital goods, foodstuffs and other consumer goods, technical services

Imports—partners: UAE 27.4%, China 13.2%, Turkey 7.8%, South Korea 4.3%, Germany 4% (2016)

Reserves of foreign exchange and gold: $132.6 billion (31 December 2017 est.)
$133.7 billion (31 December 2016 est.)
country comparison to the world: 20

Debt—external: $10.56 billion (31 December 2017 est.)
$8.196 billion (31 December 2016 est.)
country comparison to the world: 112

Stock of direct foreign investment—at home: $50.33 billion (31 December 2017 est.)
$46.02 billion (31 December 2016 est.)
country comparison to the world: 58

Stock of direct foreign investment—abroad: $5.226 billion (31 December 2017 est.)
$4.656 billion (31 December 2016 est.)
country comparison to the world: 71

Exchange rates: Iranian rials (IRR) per US dollar—
32,769.7 (2017 est.)
30,914.9 (2016 est.)
30,914.9 (2015 est.)
29,011.5 (2014 est.)
25,912 (2013 est.)

ENERGY

Electricity access: *population without electricity:* 1,100,000

electrification—total population: 98.6%
electrification—urban areas: 100%
electrification—rural areas: 95% (2013)

Electricity—production: 265.1 billion kWh (2015 est.)
country comparison to the world: 17

Electricity—consumption: 220.9 billion kWh (2015 est.)
country comparison to the world: 19

Electricity—exports: 6.822 billion kWh (2015 est.)
country comparison to the world: 29

Electricity—imports: 4.148 billion kWh (2015 est.)
country comparison to the world: 46

Electricity—installed generating capacity: 72.94 million kW (2015 est.)
country comparison to the world: 16

Electricity—from fossil fuels: 83.2% of total installed capacity (2015 est.)
country comparison to the world: 80

Electricity—from nuclear fuels: 1.3% of total installed capacity (2015 est.)
country comparison to the world: 31

Electricity—from hydroelectric plants: 13.9% of total installed capacity (2015 est.)
country comparison to the world: 109

Electricity—from other renewable sources: 0.2% of total installed capacity (2015 est.)
country comparison to the world: 161

Crude oil—production: 4.068 million bbl/day (2016 est.)
country comparison to the world: 5

Crude oil—exports: 1.342 million bbl/day (2014 est.)
country comparison to the world: 12

Crude oil—imports: 33,710 bbl/day (2014 est.)
country comparison to the world: 59

Crude oil—proved reserves: 158.4 billion bbl (1 January 2017 es)
country comparison to the world: 4

Refined petroleum products—production: 1.801 million bbl/day (2014 est.)
country comparison to the world: 12

Refined petroleum products—consumption: 1.922 million bbl/day (2015 est.)
country comparison to the world: 13

Refined petroleum products—exports: 272,600 bbl/day (2014 est.)
country comparison to the world: 28

Refined petroleum products—imports: 47,750 bbl/day (2014 est.)
country comparison to the world: 85

Natural gas—production: 184.8 billion cu m (2015 est.)
country comparison to the world: 3

Natural gas—consumption: 186 billion cu m (2015 est.)
country comparison to the world: 9

Natural gas—exports: 8.38 billion cu m (2015 est.)
country comparison to the world: 25

Natural gas—imports: 9.55 billion cu m (2015 est.)
country comparison to the world: 29

Natural gas—proved reserves: 33.5 trillion cu m (1 January 2017 es)
country comparison to the world: 2

Carbon dioxide emissions from consumption of energy: 650.4 million Mt (2014 est.)
country comparison to the world: 8

COMMUNICATIONS

Telephones—fixed lines: *total subscriptions:* 30,818,011

subscriptions per 100 inhabitants: 37 (July 2016 est.)
country comparison to the world: 10

Telephones—mobile cellular: *total:* 74.219 million
subscriptions per 100 inhabitants: 91 (July 2016 est.)
country comparison to the world: 22

Telephone system: *general assessment:* currently being modernized and expanded with the goal of not only improving the efficiency and increasing the volume of the urban service but also bringing telephone service to several thousand villages not presently connected
domestic: heavy investment by Iran's state-owned telecom company has greatly improved and expanded both the fixed-line and mobile cellular networks; a huge percentage of the cell phones in the market have been smuggled into the country
international: country code—98; submarine fiber-optic cable to UAE with access to Fiber-Optic Link Around the Globe (FLAG); Trans-Asia-Europe (TAE) fiber-optic line runs from Azerbaijan through the northern portion of Iran to Turkmenistan with expansion to Georgia and Azerbaijan; HF radio and microwave radio relay to Turkey, Azerbaijan, Pakistan, Afghanistan, Turkmenistan, Syria, Kuwait, Tajikistan, and Uzbekistan; satellite earth stations—13 (9 Intelsat and 4 Inmarsat) (2015)

Broadcast media: state-run broadcast media with no private, independent broadcasters; Islamic Republic of Iran Broadcasting (IRIB), the state-run TV broadcaster, operates 5 nationwide channels, a news channel, about 30 provincial channels, and several international channels; about 20 foreign Persian-language TV stations broadcasting on satellite TV are capable of being seen in Iran; satellite dishes are illegal and, while their use had been tolerated, authorities began confiscating satellite dishes following the unrest stemming from the 2009 presidential election; IRIB operates 8 nationwide radio networks, a number of provincial stations, and an external service; most major international broadcasters transmit to Iran (2009)

Internet country code: .ir
Internet users: total: 36.07 million

percent of population: 44.1% (July 2016 est.)
country comparison to the world: 26

TRANSPORTATION

National air transport system: *number of registered air carriers:* 15
inventory of registered aircraft operated by air carriers: 228
annual passenger traffic on registered air carriers: 15,003,958
annual freight traffic on registered air carriers: 107,184,869 mt-km (2015)
Civil aircraft registration country code prefix: EP (2016)

Airports: 319 (2013)
country comparison to the world: 22

Airports—with paved runways: *total:* 140

over 3,047 m: 42
2,438 to 3,047 m: 29
1,524 to 2,437 m: 26
914 to 1,523 m: 36
under 914 m: 7 (2017)

Airports—with unpaved runways: *total:* 179
over 3,047 m: 1
2,438 to 3,047 m: 2
1,524 to 2,437 m: 9
914 to 1,523 m: 135
under 914 m: 32 (2013)

Heliports: 26 (2013)

Pipelines: condensate 7 km; condensate/gas 973 km; gas 20,794 km; liquid petroleum gas 570 km; oil 8,625 km; refined products 7,937 km (2013)

Railways: *total:* 8,483.5 km
broad gauge: 94 km 1.676-m gauge
standard gauge: 8,389.5 km 1.435-m gauge (189.5 km electrified) (2014)
country comparison to the world: 25

Roadways: *total:* 198,866 km
paved: 160,366 km (includes 1,948 km of expressways)
unpaved: 38,500 km (2010)
country comparison to the world: 27

Waterways: 850 km (on Karun River; some navigation on Lake Urmia) (2012)
country comparison to the world: 69

Merchant marine: *total:* 739
by type: bulk carrier 32, container ship 28, general cargo 340, oil tanker 26, other 313 (2017)
country comparison to the world: 30

Ports and terminals: *major seaport(s):* Bandar-e Asaluyeh, Bandar Abbas, Bandar Emam
container port(s) (TEUs): Bandar Abbas (2,752,460)

MILITARY AND SECURITY

Military expenditures: 2.69% of GDP (2015)
2.33% of GDP (2014)
2.35% of GDP (2013)
2.81% of GDP (2012)
2.41% of GDP (2011)

Military branches: *Islamic Republic of Iran Regular Forces (Artesh):* Ground Forces, Navy, Air Force (IRIAF), Khatemolanbia Air Defense Headquarters; Islamic Revolutionary Guard Corps

(Sepah-e Pasdaran-e Enqelab-e Eslami, IRGC): Ground Resistance Forces, Navy, Aerospace Force, Qods Force (special operations); Law Enforcement Forces (2015)

Military service age and obligation: 18 years of age for compulsory military service; 16 years of age for volunteers; 17 years of age for Law Enforcement Forces; 15 years of age for Basij Forces (Popular Mobilization Army); conscript military service obligation is 18 months; women exempt from military service (2012)

TERRORISM

Terrorist groups—foreign based: *Jundallah:* *aim(s):* secure recognition of Balochi cultural, economic, and political rights and greater autonomy from the Iranian Government
area(s) of operation: based in Sistan va Baluchestan Province in the southeast; targets Shia Muslims, primarily Iranian soldiers and security personnel

Kurdistan Workers Party (PKK) (Kongra-Gel): *aim(s):* establish Kurdistan, which comprises territory in northwestern Iran
area(s) of operation: has maintained an operational presence under the name Party of Free Life of Kurdistan (PJAK) since circa 2004; targets Iranian Government personnel, primarily in the northwest in the Kurdish-populated region; PJAK's attack tempo has ebbed since 2011

TRANSNATIONAL ISSUES

Disputes—international: Iran protests Afghanistan's limiting flow of dammed Helmand River tributaries during drought; Iraq's lack of a maritime boundary with Iran prompts jurisdiction disputes beyond the mouth of the Shatt al Arab in the Persian Gulf; Iran and UAE dispute Tunb Islands and Abu Musa Island, which are occupied by Iran; Azerbaijan, Kazakhstan, and Russia ratified Caspian seabed delimitation treaties based on equidistance, while Iran continues to insist on a one-fifth slice of the sea; Afghan and Iranian commissioners have discussed boundary monument densification and resurvey

Refugees and internally displaced persons: refugees (country of origin): 2.5-3.0 (1

million registered, 1.5-2.0 million undocumented) (Afghanistan); 28,268 (Iraq) (2016)

Trafficking in persons: current situation: Iran is a source, transit, and destination country for men, women, and children subjected to sex trafficking and forced labor; organized groups sex traffic Iranian women and children in Iran and to the UAE and Europe; the transport of girls from and through Iran en route to the Gulf for sexual exploitation or forced marriages is on the rise; Iranian children are also forced to work as beggars, street vendors, and in domestic workshops; Afghan boys forced to work in construction or agriculture are vulnerable to sexual abuse by their employers; Pakistani and Afghan migrants being smuggled to Europe often are subjected to forced labor, including debt bondage

tier rating: Tier 3—Iran does not comply with the minimum standards for the elimination of trafficking, and is not making significant efforts to do so; the government does not share information on its anti-trafficking efforts, but publically available information from NGOs, the media, and international organizations indicates that Iran is not taking adequate measures to address its trafficking problems, particularly protecting victims; Iranian law does not prohibit all forms of human trafficking; female victims find it extremely difficult to get justice because Iranian courts accord women's testimony half the weight of men's, and female victims of sexual abuse, including trafficking, are likely to be prosecuted for adultery; the government did not identify or provide protection services to any victims and continued to punish victims for unlawful acts committed as a direct result of being trafficked; the government made some effort to cooperate with neighboring governments and an international organization to combat human trafficking and other crimes (2015)

Illicit drugs: despite substantial interdiction efforts and considerable control measures along the border with Afghanistan, Iran remains one of the primary transshipment routes for Southwest Asian heroin to Europe; suffers one of the highest opiate addiction rates in the world, and has an increasing problem with synthetic drugs; regularly enforces the death penalty for drug offences; lacks anti-money laundering laws; has reached out to neighboring countries to share counter-drug intelligence

IRAQ

INTRODUCTION

Background: Formerly part of the Ottoman Empire, Iraq was occupied by the United Kingdom during the course of World War I; in 1920, it was declared a League of Nations mandate under UK administration. In stages over the next dozen years, Iraq attained its independence as a kingdom in 1932. A "republic" was proclaimed in 1958, but in actuality a series of strongmen ruled the country

until 2003. The last was SADDAM Husayn from 1979 to 2003. Territorial disputes with Iran led to an inconclusive and costly eight-year war (1980-88). In August 1990, Iraq seized Kuwait but was expelled by US-led UN coalition forces during the Gulf War of January-February 1991. Following Kuwait's liberation, the UN Security Council (UNSC) required Iraq to scrap all weapons of mass destruction and long-range missiles and to allow UN verification inspections. Continued

Iraqi noncompliance with UNSC resolutions over a period of 12 years led to the US-led invasion of Iraq in March 2003 and the ouster of the SADDAM Husayn regime. US forces remained in Iraq under a UNSC mandate through 2009 and under a bilateral security agreement thereafter, helping to provide security and to train and mentor Iraqi security forces.

In October 2005, Iraqis approved a constitution in a national referendum and, pursuant to

447

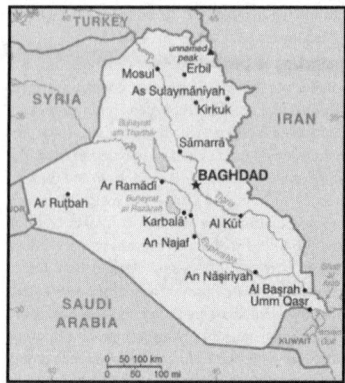

this document, elected a 275-member Council of Representatives (COR) in December 2005. The COR approved most cabinet ministers in May 2006, marking the transition to Iraq's first constitutional government in nearly a half century. Nearly nine years after the start of the Second Gulf War in Iraq, US military operations there ended in mid-December 2011. In January 2009 and April 2013, Iraq held elections for provincial councils in all governorates except for the three comprising the Kurdistan Regional Government and Kirkuk Governorate. Iraq held a national legislative election in March 2010—choosing 325 legislators in an expanded COR—and, after nine months of deadlock, the COR approved the new government in December 2010. In April 2014, Iraq held a national legislative election and expanded the COR to 328 legislators. Prime Minister Nuri al-MALIKI dropped his bid for a third term in office, enabling new Prime Minister Haydar al-ABADI, a Shia Muslim from Baghdad, to win legislative approval of his new cabinet in September 2014. Since 2014, Iraq has been engaged in a military campaign against ISIS to recapture territory lost in the western and northern portion of the country.

GEOGRAPHY

Location: Middle East, bordering the Persian Gulf, between Iran and Kuwait

Geographic coordinates: 33 00 N, 44 00 E

Map references: Middle East

Area: *total:* 438,317 sq km
land: 437,367 sq km
water: 950 sq km
country comparison to the world: 60

Area—comparative: slightly more than three times the size of New York state

Land boundaries: *total:* 3,809 km
border countries (6): Iran 1,599 km, Jordan 179 km, Kuwait 254 km, Saudi Arabia 811 km, Syria 599 km, Turkey 367 km

Coastline: 58 km

Maritime claims: *territorial sea:* 12 nm
continental shelf: not specified

Climate: mostly desert; mild to cool winters with dry, hot, cloudless summers; northern mountainous

regions along Iranian and Turkish borders experience cold winters with occasionally heavy snows that melt in early spring, sometimes causing extensive flooding in central and southern Iraq

Terrain: mostly broad plains; reedy marshes along Iranian border in south with large flooded areas; mountains along borders with Iran and Turkey

Elevation: *mean elevation:* 312 m

elevation extremes: *lowest point:* Persian Gulf 0 m
highest point: Cheekha Dar (Kurdish for "Black Tent") 3,611 m

Natural resources: petroleum, natural gas, phosphates, sulfur

Land use: *agricultural land:* 18.1%
arable land: 8.4%;
permanent crops: 0.5%;
permanent pasture: 9.2%
forest: 1.9%
other: 80% (2011 est.)
Irrigated land: 35,250 sq km (2012)

Population—distribution: population is concentrated in the north, center, and eastern parts of the country, with many of the larger urban agglomerations found along extensive parts of the Tigris and Euphrates Rivers; much of the western and southern areas are either lightly populated or uninhabited

Natural hazards: dust storms; sandstorms; floods

Environment—current issues: government water control projects drained most of the inhabited marsh areas east of An Nasiriyah by drying up or diverting the feeder streams and rivers; a once sizable population of Marsh Arabs, who inhabited these areas for thousands of years, has been displaced; furthermore, the destruction of the natural habitat poses serious threats to the area's wildlife populations; inadequate supplies of potable water; development of the Tigris and Euphrates rivers system contingent upon agreements with upstream riparian Turkey; air and water pollution; soil degradation (salination) and erosion; desertification

Environment—international agreements: *party to:* Biodiversity, Law of the Sea, Ozone Layer Protection
signed, but not ratified: Environmental Modification

Geography—note: strategic location on Shatt al Arab waterway and at the head of the Persian Gulf

PEOPLE AND SOCIETY

Population: 39,192,111 (July 2017 est.)
country comparison to the world: 35

Nationality: *noun:* Iraqi(s)
adjective: Iraqi

Ethnic groups: Arab 75-80%, Kurdish 15-20%, other 5% (includes Turkmen, Yezidi, Shabak, Kaka'i, bedouin, Romani, Assyrian, Circassian, Sabaean-Mandaean, Persian)
note: data is a 1987 government estimate; no more recent reliable numbers are available

Languages: Arabic (official), Kurdish (official), Turkmen (a Turkish dialect), Syriac (Neo-Aramaic), and Armenian are official in areas where native speakers of these languages constitute a majority of the population)

Religions: Muslim (official) 95-98% (Shia 64-69%, Sunni 29-34%), Christian 1% (includes Catholic, Orthodox, Protestant, Assyrian Church of the East), other 1-4%
note: while there has been voluntary relocation of many Christian families to northern Iraq, recent reporting indicates that the overall Christian population may have dropped by as much as 50% since the fall of the SADDAM Husayn regime in 2003, with many fleeing to Syria, Jordan, and Lebanon (2015 est.)

Age structure: *0-14 years:* 39.46% (male 7,895,522/female 7,569,205)
15-24 years: 19.25% (male 3,841,375/female 3,702,187)
25-54 years: 33.84% (male 6,704,201/female 6,558,108)
55-64 years: 3.99% (male 752,598/female 812,683)
65 years and over: 3.46% (male 601,937/female 754,295) (2017 est.)

Dependency ratios: *total dependency ratio:* 77.7
youth dependency ratio: 72.3
elderly dependency ratio: 5.5
potential support ratio: 18.3 (2015 est.)

Median age: *total:* 20 years
male: 19.8 years
female: 20.3 years (2017 est.)
country comparison to the world: 191

Population growth rate: 2.55% (2017 est.)
country comparison to the world: 17

Birth rate: 30.4 births/1,000 population (2017 est.)
country comparison to the world: 37

Death rate: 3.8 deaths/1,000 population (2017 est.)
country comparison to the world: 212

Net migration rate: -1.2 migrant(s)/1,000 population (2017 est.)
country comparison to the world: 142

Population distribution: population is concentrated in the north, center, and eastern parts of the country, with many of the larger urban agglomerations found along extensive parts of the Tigris and Euphrates Rivers; much of the western and southern areas are either lightly populated or uninhabited

Urbanization: *urban population:* 69.7% of total population (2017)
rate of urbanization: 2.97% annual rate of change (2015-20 est.)

Major urban areas—population: BAGHDAD (capital) 6.643 million; Mosul 1.694 million; Erbil 1.166 million; Basra 1.019 million; As Sulaymaniyah 1.004 million; Najaf 889,000 (2015)

Sex ratio: *at birth:* 1.05 male(s)/female
0-14 years: 1.04 male(s)/female
15-24 years: 1.04 male(s)/female
25-54 years: 1.02 male(s)/female

55-64 years: 0.91 male(s)/female
65 years and over: 0.8 male(s)/female
total population: 1.02 male(s)/female (2016 est.)

Maternal mortality ratio: 50 deaths/100,000 live births (2015 est.)
country comparison to the world: 96

Infant mortality rate: *total:* 37.5 deaths/1,000 live births
male: 40.6 deaths/1,000 live births
female: 34.2 deaths/1,000 live births (2017 est.)
country comparison to the world: 48

Life expectancy at birth: *total population:* 74.9 years
male: 72.6 years
female: 77.2 years (2017 est.)
country comparison to the world: 117

Total fertility rate: 4 children born/woman (2017 est.)
country comparison to the world: 35

Contraceptive prevalence rate: 52.5% (2011)

Health expenditures: 5.5% of GDP (2014)
country comparison to the world: 124

Physicians density: 0.85 physicians/1,000 population (2014)

Hospital bed density: 1.3 beds/1,000 population (2012)

Drinking water source:
improved:
urban: 93.8% of population
rural: 70.1% of population
total: 86.6% of population
unimproved:
urban: 6.1% of population
rural: 31.5% of population
total: 14.6% of population (2015 est.)

Sanitation facility access:
improved:
urban: 86.4% of population
rural: 83.8% of population
total: 85.6% of population
unimproved:
urban: 13.6% of population
rural: 16.2% of population
total: 14.4% of population (2015 est.)

HIV/AIDS—adult prevalence rate: NA

HIV/AIDS—people living with HIV/AIDS: NA

HIV/AIDS—deaths: NA

Major infectious diseases: *degree of risk:* intermediate
food or waterborne diseases: bacterial diarrhea, hepatitis A, and typhoid fever (2016)

Obesity—adult prevalence rate: 30.4% (2016)
country comparison to the world: 23

Children under the age of 5 years underweight: 8.5% (2011)
country comparison to the world: 74

Education expenditures: NA

Literacy: *definition:* age 15 and over can read and write
total population: 79.7%
male: 85.7%
female: 73.7% (2015 est.)

GOVERNMENT

Country name: *conventional long form:* Republic of Iraq
conventional short form: Iraq
local long form: Jumhuriyat al-Iraq/Komar-i Eraq
local short form: Al Iraq/Eraq
etymology: the name probably derives from "Uruk" (Biblical "Erech"), the ancient Sumerian and Babylonian city on the Euphrates River

Government type: federal parliamentary republic

Capital: name: Baghdad

geographic coordinates: 33 20 N, 44 24 E
time difference: UTC+3 (8 hours ahead of Washington, DC, during Standard Time)

Administrative divisions: 18 governorates (muhafazat, singular—muhafazah (Arabic); parezgakan, singular—parezga (Kurdish)) and 1 region*; Al Anbar; Al Basrah; Al Muthanna; Al Qadisiyah (Ad Diwaniyah); An Najaf; Arbil (Erbil) (Arabic), Hewler (Kurdish); As Sulaymaniyah (Arabic), Slemani (Kurdish); Babil; Baghdad; Dahuk (Arabic), Dihok (Kurdish); Dhi Qar; Diyala; Karbala'; Kirkuk; Kurdistan Regional Government*; Maysan; Ninawa; Salah ad Din; Wasit

Independence: 3 October 1932 (from League of Nations mandate under British administration); note—on 28 June 2004 the Coalition Provisional Authority transferred sovereignty to the Iraqi Interim Government

National holiday: Independence Day, 3 October (1932); Republic Day, 14 July (1958)

Constitution: history: several previous; latest adopted by referendum 15 October 2005
amendments: proposed by the president of the republic and the Council of Minsters collectively, or by one-fifth of the Council of Representatives members; passage requires at least a two-thirds majority vote by the Council of Representatives, approval by referendum, and ratification by the president; passage of amendments to articles on citizen rights and liberties requires a two-thirds majority vote of Council of Representatives members after two successive electoral terms, approval in a referendum, and ratification by the president (2016)

Legal system: mixed legal system of civil and Islamic law

International law organization participation: has not submitted an ICJ jurisdiction declaration; non-party state to the ICCt

Citizenship: *citizenship by birth:* no
citizenship by descent only: at least one parent must be a citizen of Iraq
dual citizenship recognized: yes
residency requirement for naturalization: 10 years

Suffrage: 18 years of age; universal

Executive branch: *chief of state:* President Fuad MASUM (since 24 July 2014); Vice Presidents Ayad ALLAWI (since 9 September 2014), Nuri al-MALIKI (since 8 September 2014), Usama al-NUJAYFI (since 9 September 2014)

head of government: Prime Minister Haydar al-ABADI (since 8 September 2014)
cabinet: Council of Ministers proposed by the prime minister, approved by Council of Representatives
elections/appointments: president indirectly elected by Council of Representatives (COR) to serve a 4-year term (eligible for a second term); election last held on 30 April 2014 (next to be held in April 2018); prime minister nominated by the majority COR bloc and submission of COR minister nominees for majority COR approval; disapproval requires designation of a new prime minister candidate
election results: Fuad MASUM elected president; Council of Representatives vote—Fuad MASUM (PUK) 211, Barham SALIH (PUK) 17

Legislative branch: *description:* unicameral Council of Representatives or Majlis an-Nuwwab al-Iraqiyy (328 seats; 320 members directly elected in multi-seat constituencies by proportional representation vote and 8 seats reserved for minorities; members serve 4-year terms); note—Iraq's constitution calls for the establishment of an upper house, the Federation Council, but it has not been instituted
elections: last held on 30 April 2014 (next to be held in May 2018)
election results: percent of vote by party/coalition—NA; seats by party/coalition—State of Law Coalition 95, Ahrar Bloc/Sadrist Trend 34, ISCI/Muwatin 31, United for Reform Coalition/Muttahidun 28, KDP 25, PUK 21, Nationalism Coalition/Wataniyah 21, other Sunni coalitions/parties 19, Al-Arabiyah Coalition 10, Goran 9, other Shia parties/coalitions 8, Fadilah 6, National Reform Trend 6, Diyala is Our Identity 5, Iraq Coalition 5, KIU 4, other 5

Judicial branch: *highest court(s):* Federal Supreme Court or FSC (consists of 9 judges); note—court jurisdiction limited to constitutional issues and disputes between regions or governorates and the central government; Court of Cassation (consists of a court president, 5 vice-presidents, and at least 24 judges)
judge selection and term of office: Federal Supreme Court and Court of Cassation judges selected by the president of the republic from nominees selected by the Supreme Judicial Council (SJC), a 25-member committee of judicial officials that manage the judiciary and prosecutors; FSC members appointed for life; Court of Cassation judges appointed by the SJC and confirmed by the Council of Representatives to serve until retirement nominally at age 63
subordinate courts: Courts of Appeal (governorate level); civil courts including first instance, personal status, labor, and customs; criminal courts including felony, misdemeanor, investigative, major crimes, juvenile, and traffic; religious courts

Political parties and leaders: Al-Arabiyah Coalition [Salih al-MUTLAQI]
Badr Organization [Hadi al-AMIRI]
Da`wa Party [Haider al-ABADI]
Da`wa Tanzim [Khalid al-ASADI]

Diyala is Our Identity [Salim al-JABOURI]

Fadilah Party [Muhammad al-YAQUBI]

Goran Party [Omar SAYYID ALI]

Iraq Coalition [Fadhil al-DABBITS] (electoral coalition)

Islamic Supreme Council of Iraq or ISCI/Muwatin Coalition [Ammar al-HAKIM]

Kurdistan Democratic Party or KDP [Masud BARZANI]

Kurdistan Islamic Union or KIU [Salahaddin Muhammad Bahaaeddin SADIQ]

Nationalism Coalition/Wataniyah [Ayad ALLAWI]

National Reform Trend [Ibrahim al-JAFARI]

Patriotic Union of Kurdistan or PUK [KOSRAT Rasul Ali, acting]

Sadrist Trend or Ahrar Bloc [Muqtada al-SADR]

State of Law Coalition [Nuri al MALIKI]

United for Reform Coalition/Muttahidun Lil Islah [Usama al-NUJAYFI]

note: numerous smaller local, tribal, and minority parties

Political pressure groups and leaders: Sunni militias; Shia militias, some associated with political parties

International organization participation: ABEDA, AFESD, AMF, CAEU, CICA, EITI (compliant country), FAO, G-77, IAEA, IBRD, ICAO, ICRM, IDA, IDB, IFAD, IFC, IFRCS, ILO, IMF, IMO, IMSO, Interpol, IOC, IPU, ISO, ITSO, ITU, LAS, MIGA, NAM, OAPEC, OIC, OPCW, OPEC, PCA, UN, UNCTAD, UNESCO, UNIDO, UNWTO, UPU, WCO, WFTU (NGOs), WHO, WIPO, WMO, WTO (observer)

Diplomatic representation in the US: *chief of mission:* Ambassador Farid YASIN (since 18 January 2017)

chancery: 3421 Massachusetts Avenue, NW, Washington, DC 20007

telephone: [1] (202) 742-1600

FAX: [1] (202) 333-1129

consulate(s) general: Detroit, Los Angeles

Diplomatic representation from the US: *chief of mission:* Ambassador Douglas A. SILLIMAN (since 1 September 2016)

embassy: Al-Kindi Street, International Zone, Baghdad

mailing address: APO AE 09316

telephone: 0760-030-3000

FAX: NA

Flag description: three equal horizontal bands of red (top), white, and black; the Takbir (Arabic expression meaning "God is great") in green Arabic script is centered in the white band; the band colors derive from the Arab Liberation flag and represent oppression (black), overcome through bloody struggle (red), to be replaced by a bright future (white); the Council of Representatives approved this flag in 2008 as a compromise temporary replacement for the Ba'thist SADDAM-era flag

note: similar to the flag of Syria, which has two stars but no script; Yemen, which has a plain white band; and that of Egypt, which has a golden Eagle of Saladin centered in the white band

National symbol(s): golden eagle; national colors: red, white, black

National anthem: *name:* "Mawtini" (My Homeland)

lyrics/music: Ibrahim TOUQAN/Mohammad FLAYFEL

note: adopted 2004; following the ouster of SADDAM Husayn, Iraq adopted "Mawtini," a popular folk song throughout the Arab world; also serves as an unofficial anthem of the Palestinian people

ECONOMY

Economy—overview: Iraq's GDP growth slowed to 1.1% in 2017, a marked decline compared to the previous two years as domestic consumption and investment fell because of civil violence and a sluggish oil market. The Iraqi Government received its third tranche of funding from its 2016 Stand-By Arrangement (SBA) with the IMF in August 2017, which is intended to stabilize its finances by encouraging improved fiscal management, needed economic reform, and expenditure reduction. Additionally, in late 2017 Iraq received more than $1.4 billion in financing from international lenders, part of which was generated by issuing a $1 billion bond for reconstruction and rehabilitation in areas liberated from ISIL. Investment and key sector diversification are crucial components to Iraq's long-term economic development and require a strengthened business climate with enhanced legal and regulatory oversight to bolster private-sector engagement. Sustained improvements in the overall standard of living depend heavily on global oil prices, the central government passage of major policy reforms, a stable security environment post-ISIS, and the resolution of civil discord with the Kurdish Regional Government (KRG).

Iraq's largely state-run economy is dominated by the oil sector, which provides roughly 90% of government revenue and 80% of foreign exchange earnings, and is a major determinant of the economy's fortunes. Iraq's contracts with major oil companies have the potential to further expand oil exports and revenues, but Iraq will need to make significant upgrades to its oil processing, pipeline, and export infrastructure to enable these deals to reach their economic potential.

In 2017, Iraqi oil exports from northern fields were disrupted following a KRG referendum that resulted in the Iraqi Government reasserting federal control over disputed oil fields and energy infrastructure in Kirkuk. The Iraqi government and the KRG dispute the role of federal and regional authorities in the development and export of natural resources. In 2007, the KRG passed an oil law to develop IKR oil and gas reserves independent of the federal government. The KRG has signed about 50 contracts with foreign energy companies to develop its reserves, some of which lie in territories taken by Baghdad in October 2017. The KRG is able to unilaterally export oil from the fields it retains control of through its own pipeline to Turkey, which Baghdad claims is illegal. In the absence of a national hydrocarbons law, the two

sides have entered into five provisional oil- and revenue-sharing deals since 2009, all of which collapsed.

Iraq is making slow progress enacting laws and developing the institutions needed to implement economic policy, and political reforms are still needed to assuage investors' concerns regarding the uncertain business climate. The Government of Iraq is eager to attract additional foreign direct investment, but it faces a number of obstacles, including a tenuous political system and concerns about security and societal stability. Rampant corruption, outdated infrastructure, insufficient essential services, skilled labor shortages, and antiquated commercial laws stifle investment and continue to constrain growth of private, nonoil sectors. Under the Iraqi constitution, some competencies relevant to the overall investment climate are either shared by the federal government and the regions or are devolved entirely to local governments. Investment in the IKR operates within the framework of the Kurdistan Region Investment Law (Law 4 of 2006) and the Kurdistan Board of Investment, which is designed to provide incentives to help economic development in areas under the authority of the KRG.

Inflation has remained under control since 2006. However, Iraqi leaders remain hard-pressed to translate macroeconomic gains into an improved standard of living for the Iraqi populace. Unemployment remains a problem throughout the country despite a bloated public sector. Encouraging private enterprise through deregulation would make it easier for Iraqi citizens and foreign investors to start new businesses. Rooting out corruption and implementing reforms—such as restructuring banks and developing the private sector—would be important steps in this direction.

GDP (purchasing power parity): $660.7 billion (2017 est.)

$663.7 billion (2016 est.)

$598 billion (2015 est.)

note: data are in 2017 dollars

country comparison to the world: 35

GDP (official exchange rate): $192.7 billion (2016 est.)

GDP—real growth rate: -0.4% (2017 est.)

11% (2016 est.)

4.8% (2015 est.)

country comparison to the world: 204

GDP—per capita (PPP): $17,000 (2017 est.)

$17,500 (2016 est.)

$16,200 (2015 est.)

note: data are in 2017 dollars

country comparison to the world: 102

Gross national saving: 13.4% of GDP (2017 est.)

11.9% of GDP (2016 est.)

18% of GDP (2015 est.)

country comparison to the world: 135

GDP—composition, by end use:

household consumption: 50.4%

government consumption: 18.8%

investment in fixed capital: 23.5%

investment in inventories: -4.5%

exports of goods and services: 39.7%

imports of goods and services: -27.9% (2013 est.)

GDP—composition, by sector of origin:
agriculture: 4.8%
industry: 40.6%
services: 54.6% (2017 est.)

Agriculture—products: wheat, barley, rice, vegetables, dates, cotton; cattle, sheep, poultry

Industries: petroleum, chemicals, textiles, leather, construction materials, food processing, fertilizer, metal fabrication/processing

Industrial production growth rate: 0.8% (2017 est.)
country comparison to the world: 174

Labor force: 8.9 million (2010 est.)
country comparison to the world: 57

Labor force—by occupation: *agriculture:* 21.6%
industry: 18.7%
services: 59.8% (2008 est.)

Unemployment rate: 16% (2012 est.)
15% (2010 est.)
country comparison to the world: 173

Population below poverty line: 23% (2014 est.)

Household income or consumption by percentage share: *lowest* 10%: 3.6%
highest 10%: 25.7% (2007 est.)

Budget: *revenues:* $63.97 billion
expenditures: $76.35 billion (2017 est.)
Taxes and other revenues: 33.2% of GDP (2017 est.)
country comparison to the world: 66

Budget surplus (+) or deficit (-): -6.4% of GDP (2017 est.)
country comparison to the world: 181

Public debt: 63.7% of GDP (2016 est.)
55% of GDP (2015 est.)
country comparison to the world: 66

Fiscal year: calendar year

Inflation rate (consumer prices): 2% (2017 est.)
0.4% (2016 est.)
country comparison to the world: 91

Central bank discount rate: 6% (2016)
6% (2015)
country comparison to the world: 70

Commercial bank prime lending rate: 4% (31 December 2017 est.)
4% (31 December 2016 est.)
country comparison to the world: 160

Stock of narrow money: $62.01 billion (31 December 2017 est.)
$59.84 billion (31 December 2016 est.)
country comparison to the world: 50

Stock of broad money: $77.06 billion (31 December 2017 est.)
$74.52 billion (31 December 2016 est.)
country comparison to the world: 62

Stock of domestic credit: $3.504 billion (31 December 2017 est.)
$3.191 billion (31 December 2016 est.)
country comparison to the world: 136

Market value of publicly traded shares: $4 billion (9 December 2011)
$2.6 billion (31 July 2010)

$2 billion (31 July 2009 est.)
country comparison to the world: 93

Current account balance: -$12.22 billion (2017 est.)
-$14.9 billion (2016 est.)
country comparison to the world: 188

Exports: $56.74 billion (2017 est.)
$28.36 billion (2016 est.)
country comparison to the world: 48

Exports—commodities: crude oil 99%, crude materials excluding fuels, food, live animals

Exports—partners: China 25.4%, India 17.3%, US 14.3%, South Korea 12%, Italy 6.5%, Greece 6.1% (2016)

Imports: $36.47 billion (2017 est.)
$19.57 billion (2016 est.)
country comparison to the world: 59

Imports—commodities: food, medicine, manufactures

Imports—partners: China 23.5%, Turkey 23%, Iran 20%, South Korea 5%, US 4% (2016)

Reserves of foreign exchange and gold: $47.02 billion (31 December 2017 est.)
$45.36 billion (31 December 2016 est.)
country comparison to the world: 41

Debt—external: $73.43 billion (31 December 2017 est.)
$64.16 billion (31 December 2016 est.)
country comparison to the world: 60

Stock of direct foreign investment—at home: $26.63 billion (2015 est.)
$23.16 billion (2014 est.)
country comparison to the world: 71

Stock of direct foreign investment—abroad: $2.109 billion (2015 est.)
$1.956 billion (2014 est.)
country comparison to the world: 82

Exchange rates: Iraqi dinars (IQD) per US dollar—
1,184 (2017 est.)
1,182 (2016 est.)
1,182 (2015 est.)
1,167.63 (2014 est.)
1,213.72 (2013 est.)

ENERGY

Electricity access: *population without electricity:* 600,000
electrification—*total population:* 98%
electrification—urban areas: 99.6%
electrification—rural areas: 95.4% (2013)

Electricity—production: 84 billion kWh (2016 est.)
country comparison to the world: 38

Electricity—consumption: 66 billion kWh (2016 est.)
country comparison to the world: 41

Electricity—exports: 0 kWh (2016 est.)
country comparison to the world: 151

Electricity—imports: 12 billion kWh (2016 est.)
country comparison to the world: 22

Electricity—installed generating capacity: 28 million kW (2017 est.)
country comparison to the world: 35

Electricity—from fossil fuels: 87.3% of total installed capacity (2017 est.)
country comparison to the world: 67

Electricity—from nuclear fuels: 0% of total installed capacity (2017 est.)
country comparison to the world: 115

Electricity—from hydroelectric plants: 6.2% of total installed capacity (2017 est.)
country comparison to the world: 127

Electricity—from other renewable sources: 0% of total installed capacity (2017 est.)
country comparison to the world: 189

Crude oil—production: 4.452 million bbl/day (2016 est.)
country comparison to the world: 4

Crude oil—exports: 2.792 million bbl/day (2014 est.)
country comparison to the world: 3

Crude oil—imports: 0 bbl/day (2014 est.)
country comparison to the world: 142

Crude oil—proved reserves: 142.5 billion bbl (1 January 2017 es)
country comparison to the world: 5

Refined petroleum products—production: 484,800 bbl/day (2014 est.)
country comparison to the world: 32

Refined petroleum products—consumption: 850,000 bbl/day (2015 est.)
country comparison to the world: 26

Refined petroleum products—exports: 7,080 bbl/day (2014 est.)
country comparison to the world: 89

Refined petroleum products—imports: 295,300 bbl/day (2014 est.)
country comparison to the world: 26

Natural gas—production: 1.002 billion cu m (2015 est.)
country comparison to the world: 68

Natural gas—consumption: 1.27 billion cu m (2015 est.)
country comparison to the world: 93

Natural gas—exports: 0 cu m (2013 est.)
country comparison to the world: 124

Natural gas—imports: 0 cu m (2013 est.)
country comparison to the world: 141

Natural gas—proved reserves: 3.158 trillion cu m (1 January 2017 es)
country comparison to the world: 12

Carbon dioxide emissions from consumption of energy: 137 million Mt (2013 est.)
country comparison to the world: 35

COMMUNICATIONS

Telephones—fixed lines: *total subscriptions:* 2.031 million
subscriptions per 100 inhabitants: 5 (July 2016 est.)
country comparison to the world: 59

Telephones—mobile cellular: total: 30,203,100 *subscriptions per 100 inhabitants:* 79 (July 2016 est.)
country comparison to the world: 36

Telephone system: *general assessment:* the 2003 liberation of Iraq severely disrupted telecommunications throughout Iraq; widespread government efforts to rebuild domestic and international communications have slowed due to the conflict with ISIS/ISIL

domestic: the mobile cellular market continues to expand (cell phones were banned prior to 2003 under the SADDAM regime); 3G services offered by three major mobile operators in 2015; conflict has destroyed infrastructure in areas

international: country code—964; satellite earth stations—4 (2 Intelsat—1 Atlantic Ocean and 1 Indian Ocean, 1 Intersputnik—Atlantic Ocean region, and 1 Arabsat (inoperative)); local microwave radio relay connects border regions to Jordan, Kuwait, Syria, and Turkey; international terrestrial fiber-optic connections have been established with Saudi Arabia, Turkey, Kuwait, Jordan, and Iran; links to the Fiber-Optic Link Around the Globe (FLAG) and the Gulf Bridge International (GBI) submarine fiber-optic cables have been established (2017)

Broadcast media: the number of private radio and TV stations has increased rapidly since 2003; government-owned TV and radio stations are operated by the publicly funded Iraqi Media Network; private broadcast media are mostly linked to political, ethnic, or religious groups; satellite TV is available to an estimated 70% of viewers and many of the broadcasters are based abroad; transmissions of multiple international radio broadcasters are accessible (2015)

Internet country code: .iq
Internet users: total: 8,098,401

percent of population: 21.2% (July 2016 est.)
country comparison to the world: 87

TRANSPORTATION

National air transport system: *number of registered air carriers:* 4
inventory of registered aircraft operated by air carriers: 39
annual passenger traffic on registered air carriers: 484,803
annual freight traffic on registered air carriers: 10,758,230 mt-km (2015)
Civil aircraft registration country code prefix: YI (2016)

Airports: 102 (2013)
country comparison to the world: 55

Airports—with paved runways: *total:* 72
over 3,047 m: 20
2,438 to 3,047 m: 34
1,524 to 2,437 m: 4
914 to 1,523 m: 7
under 914 m: 7 (2017)

Airports—with unpaved runways: *total:* 30
over 3,047 m: 3
2,438 to 3,047 m: 5

1,524 to 2,437 m: 3
914 to 1,523 m: 13
under 914 m: 6 (2013)

Heliports: 16 (2013)

Pipelines: gas 2,455 km; liquid petroleum gas 913 km; oil 5,432 km; refined products 1,637 km (2013)

Railways: *total:* 2,272 km
standard gauge: 2,272 km 1.435-m gauge (2014)
country comparison to the world: 67

Roadways: *total:* 59,623 km
paved: 59,623 km (includes Kurdistan Region) (2012)
country comparison to the world: 71

Waterways: 5,279 km (the Euphrates River (2,815 km), Tigris River (1,899 km), and Third River (565 km) are the principal waterways) (2012)
country comparison to the world: 22

Merchant marine: *total:* 77
by type: general cargo 1, oil tanker 6, other 70 (2017)
country comparison to the world: 98

Ports and terminals: river port(s): Al Basrah (Shatt al-'Arab); Khawr az Zubayr, Umm Qasr (Khawr az Zubayr waterway)

MILITARY AND SECURITY

Military expenditures: 3.63% of GDP (2016)
5.35% of GDP (2015)
2.95% of GDP (2014)
3.32% of GDP (2013)
1.9% of GDP (2012)
country comparison to the world: 2

Military branches: *Ministry of Defense:* Iraqi Army (includes Army Aviation Directorate), Iraqi Navy, Iraqi Air Force; National-Level Security Forces: Iraqi Counterterrorism Service, Iraqi Federal Police (includes Emergency Response Division), Iraqi Border Guard Force, Popular Mobilization Committee Forces (2017)

Military service age and obligation: 18-40 years of age for voluntary military service; no conscription (2013)

TERRORISM

Terrorist groups—home based: *Ansar al-Islam (AAI):* aim(s): expel western interests from Iraq and establish an independent Iraqi state based on its interpretation of Sharia

area(s) of operation: headquartered in northern Iraq with its heaviest presence in Kirkuk, Tikrit, and Mosul; active in the western and central regions of the country; primarily targets Iraqi government, security, and police personnel for attacks and Iraqi citizens and politicians for kidnappings, executions, and assassinations; operates a paramilitary training camp in Ninawa Province, in the northwest along the border with western Syria; on 1 February 2004, two suicide bombers carried out simultaneous attacks at the headquarters of the Kurdistan Democratic Party (KDP) and Patriotic Union of Kurdistan (PUK) regional offices in Erbil, where party leaders greeted hundreds

of people gathered to attend the KDP and PUK reception to celebrate the beginning of Eid; at least 101 people were killed and over 130 others were injured, including scores of senior KDP and PUK officials; in another high-profile attack, on 21 December 2004, a suicide bomber killed 14 US soldiers, four contractors, and injured 70 more soldiers and civilians when he detonated his vest in Forward Operating Base Marez's mess hall in Mosul; majority of members are Iraqi Kurds or Iraqi Arabs who are Sunni Muslim

Jaysh Rijal al-Tariq al Naqshabandi (JRTN): *aim(s):* end external influence in Iraq and, ultimately, overthrow the government of Iraq to install a secular Ba'athist state within the internationally recognized borders of Iraq

area(s) of operation: continues to attack Kurds who belong to any of the separatist Kurdish groups, Iraqi Government military and security forces and facilities, and foreign military personnel; joined ISIL paramilitary forces in opposition to the Iraqi Government and played a major role in ISIL capturing Mosul from Iraqi security forces in 2014; JRTN and ISIL's relationship collapsed soon after ISIL took control of Mosul, denying JRTN a share in the take over; assessed in 2016 to have fewer than 5,000 members; majority of fighters are Iraqi Sunni Muslims following Naqshabandi Sufi Islam ideals

Kata'ib Hizballah (KH): *aim(s):* counter US influence and, ultimately, overthrow the Iraqi Government to install a government based on Shia Muslim laws and precepts

area(s) of operation: headquartered in the Shia Muslim areas of Baghdad, with fighters increasingly active in Ninawa, Al Anbar, and Babil governorates in response to ISIL's territorial gains; targets mostly ISIL members, Sunni Muslims, and US personnel and interests; when fighting alongside the Iraqi army during the month-long offensive in May-June 2016 to retake the Shia Muslim-dominated city of Fallujah from ISIL, KH was among the Shia Muslim militias accused of beating and executing dozens of Sunni civilians in the recaptured city; until US military forces left the country in December 2011, KH earned a reputation for conducting numerous lethal IED and improvised rocket-assisted mortar (IRAM) attacks against US and coalition forces; an IRAM attack that killed a US civilian on 19 February 2008 at a US military base southeast of Baghdad was the group's first-known attack against anyone; the Iraqi Hizballah group that the late Secretary General Bassem al-MOUSAWI led is frequently confused with KH—the two groups are not affiliated; al-MOUSAWI was killed in early February 2017 in Basra Governorate

Kurdistan Workers Party (PKK) (Kongra-Gel): *aim(s):* establish Kurdistan, comprising territory in northern Iraq, eastern and southeastern Turkey, northern Syria, and northwestern Iran

area(s) of operation: headquartered in northern Iraq in the Qandil Mountains, where it has strongholds in As Sulaymaniyah and Arbil governorates and on the Iraq-Iran border; stages attacks inside

Turkey from Iraq, which has drawn Turkish forces on occasion into Iraq to combat Kurdistan Workers Party fighters; enjoys escalating influence in Iraq in recent years as leaders deepen ties to Iraqi political leaders and religious parties throughout the country, especially in the areas of Sinjar and Rabi'ah in Nineveh Governorate, northwestern Kirkuk, and Tuz Khurmatu District in Salah ad Din Governorate; engages heavily in recruiting Iraqi Kurdish youths

Terrorist groups—foreign based: *Islamic State of Iraq and the Levant (ISIL): aim(s):* replace the Iraqi Government with an Islamic state and implement ISIL's strict interpretation of Sharia; declared its intention to wipe out the Yazidi community, whose faith is one of the country's oldest

area(s) of operation: operationally active throughout most of Iraq, particularly along the Iraq-Syria border; the country's second largest city, Mosul, was ISIL's most significant stronghold until recently; increasingly losing control over all of Mosul, but remained in control of western Mosul in early 2017, with fewer than 2,000 fighters in the city; assessed to have displaced at least 160,000 of the remaining civilians living in the city; 5,000-6,000 fighters had been stationed in Mosul as of late 2016; overall leader Abu Bakr al-BAGHDADI is reportedly based in the north, along with some of the other top leaders; targets religious and ethnic minorities and all groups or governments that oppose ISIL's hardline Sunni

jihadist ideology, including perceived Sunni rivals; has killed thousands who refused to convert to Islam; has exploited natural resources, especially oil and wheat, and levied taxes and fees on companies and individuals in areas under its influence; fighters have ransacked and demolished numerous ancient sites that pre-date Islam, denouncing them as idolatrous; an estimated 3 million Iraqis have fled their homes because of ISIL and remained displaced inside Iraq as of early 2017; responsible for the deadliest single attack in Iraq since 2007 when operatives conducting coordinated bombings using IEDs and vehicle-borne improvised explosive devices on 3 July 2016 in Karrada District in Baghdad, while the district was teeming with late-night shoppers during Ramadan; at least 320 people were killed, mostly Shia Muslims, and over 225 injured; mass grave sites have been found throughout regions under ISIL's control, some containing hundreds of bodies and others containing thousands; has used mustard and chlorine gas against civilian and military targets in Iraq; senior leaders Attallah Salman 'Abd Kafi al-JABURI and Marwan Ibrahim Hussayn Tah al-AZAWI are connected with the group's chemical weapons development; recruits heavily in prisons

TRANSNATIONAL ISSUES

Disputes—international: Iraq's lack of a maritime boundary with Iran prompts jurisdiction disputes beyond the mouth of the Shatt al Arab in the

Persian Gulf; Turkey has expressed concern over the autonomous status of Kurds in Iraq

Refugees and internally displaced persons: refugees (country of origin): 15,692 (Turkey); 7,703 (West Bank and Gaza Strip); 7,545 (Iran) (2016); 246,974 (Syria) (2017)

IDPs: 3,570,116 (includes displacement between 2006 and 2008 due to ethno-sectarian violence and displacement in central and northern Iraq since January 2014) (2017)

stateless persons: 48,200 (2016); note—in the 1970s and 1980s under SADDAM Husayn's regime, thousands of Iraq's Faili Kurds, followers of Shia Islam, were stripped of their Iraqi citizenship, had their property seized by the government, and many were deported; some Faili Kurds had their citizenship reinstated under the 2006 Iraqi Nationality Law, but others lack the documentation to prove their Iraqi origins; some Palestinian refugees persecuted by the SADDAM regime remain stateless

note: estimate revised to reflect the reduction of statelessness in line with Law 26 of 2006, which allows stateless persons to apply for nationality in certain circumstances; more accurate studies of statelessness in Iraq are pending (2015)

IRELAND

INTRODUCTION

Background: Celtic tribes arrived on the island between 600 and 150 B.C. Invasions by Norsemen that began in the late 8th century were finally ended when King Brian BORU defeated the Danes in 1014. Norman invasions began in the 12th century and set off more than seven centuries of Anglo-Irish struggle marked by fierce rebellions and harsh repressions. The Irish famine of the mid-19th century saw the population of the

island drop by one third through starvation and emigration. For more than a century after that the population of the island continued to fall only to begin growing again in the 1960s. Over the last 50 years, Ireland's high birthrate has made it demographically one of the youngest populations in the EU. The modern Irish state traces its origins to the failed 1916 Easter Monday Uprising that touched off several years of guerrilla warfare resulting in independence from the UK in 1921 for 26 southern counties; six northern (Ulster) counties remained part of the UK. Deep sectarian divides between the Catholic and Protestant populations and systemic discrimination in Northern Ireland erupted into years of violence known as the "Troubles" that began in the 1960s. The Government of Ireland was part of a process along with the UK and US Governments that helped broker the Good Friday Agreement in Northern Ireland in 1998. This initiated a new phase of cooperation between the Irish and British Governments. Ireland was neutral in World War II and continues its policy of military neutrality. Ireland joined the European Community in 1973 and the euro-zone currency union in 1999. The economic boom years of the Celtic Tiger (1995-2007) saw rapid economic growth, which came to an abrupt end in 2008 with the meltdown of the Irish banking system. Today the economy is recovering, fueled

by large and growing foreign direct investment, especially from US multi-nationals.

GEOGRAPHY

Location: Western Europe, occupying five-sixths of the island of Ireland in the North Atlantic Ocean, west of Great Britain

Geographic coordinates: 53 00 N, 8 00 W

Map references: Europe

Area: *total:* 70,273 sq km
land: 68,883 sq km
water: 1,390 sq km
country comparison to the world: 121

Area—comparative: slightly larger than West Virginia

Land boundaries: *total:* 443 km
border countries (1): UK 443 km

Coastline: 1,448 km

Maritime claims: *territorial sea:* 12 nm
exclusive fishing zone: 200 nm

Climate: temperate maritime; modified by North Atlantic Current; mild winters, cool summers; consistently humid; overcast about half the time

Terrain: mostly flat to rolling interior plain surrounded by rugged hills and low mountains; sea cliffs on west coast

453

Elevation: *mean elevation:* 118 m

elevation extremes: *lowest point:* Atlantic Ocean 0 m

highest point: Carrauntoohil 1,041 m

Natural resources: natural gas, peat, copper, lead, zinc, silver, barite, gypsum, limestone, dolomite

Land use: *agricultural land:* 66.1%
arable land: 15.4%;
permanent crops: 0%;
permanent pasture: 50.7%
forest: 10.9%
other: 23% (2011 est.)
Irrigated land: 0 sq km (2012)

Population—distribution: population distribution is weighted to the eastern side of the island, with the largest concentration being in and around Dublin; populations in the west are small due to mountainous land, poorer soil, lack of good transport routes, and fewer job opportunities

Natural hazards: rare extreme weather events

Environment—current issues: water pollution, especially of lakes, from agricultural runoff

Environment—international agreements: *party to:* Air Pollution, Air Pollution-Nitrogen Oxides, Air Pollution-Sulfur 94, Biodiversity, Climate Change, Climate Change-Kyoto Protocol, Desertification, Endangered Species, Environmental Modification, Hazardous Wastes, Law of the Sea, Marine Dumping, Ozone Layer Protection, Ship Pollution, Tropical Timber 83, Tropical Timber 94, Wetlands, Whaling

signed, but not ratified: Air Pollution-Persistent Organic Pollutants, Marine Life Conservation

Geography—note: strategic location on major air and sea routes between North America and northern Europe; over 40% of the population resides within 100 km of Dublin

PEOPLE AND SOCIETY

Population: 5,011,102 (July 2017 est.)
country comparison to the world: 121

Nationality: *noun:* Irishman(men), Irishwoman(women), Irish (collective plural)
adjective: Irish

Ethnic groups: Irish 82.2%, Irish travelers 0.7%, other white 9.5%, Asian 2.1%, black 1.4%, other 1.5%, unspecified 2.6% (2016 est.)

Languages: English (official, the language generally used), Irish (Gaelic or Gaeilge) (official, spoken by approximately 39.8% of the population as of 2016; mainly spoken in areas along Ireland's western coast known as gaeltachtai, which are officially recognized regions where Irish is the predominant language)

Religions: Roman Catholic 78.3%, Church of Ireland 2.7%, other Christian 1.6%, Orthodox 1.3%, Muslim 1.3%, other 2.4%, none 9.8%, unspecified 2.6% (2016 est.)

Age structure: *0-14 years:* 21.46% (male 549,864/female 525,608)
15-24 years: 11.84% (male 301,114/female 292,055)

25-54 years: 43.2% (male 1,087,587/female 1,077,383)
55-64 years: 10.42% (male 261,650/female 260,737)
65 years and over: 13.07% (male 303,078/female 352,026) (2017 est.)

Dependency ratios: *total dependency ratio:* 53.8
youth dependency ratio: 33.4
elderly dependency ratio: 20.3
potential support ratio: 4.9 (2015 est.)

Median age: *total:* 36.8 years
male: 36.4 years
female: 37.1 years (2017 est.)
country comparison to the world: 68

Population growth rate: 1.15% (2017 est.)
country comparison to the world: 99

Birth rate: 14.1 births/1,000 population (2017 est.)
country comparison to the world: 137

Death rate: 6.6 deaths/1,000 population (2017 est.)
country comparison to the world: 142

Net migration rate: 4 migrant(s)/1,000 population (2017 est.)
country comparison to the world: 27

Population distribution: population distribution is weighted to the eastern side of the island, with the largest concentration being in and around Dublin; populations in the west are small due to mountainous land, poorer soil, lack of good transport routes, and fewer job opportunities

Urbanization: *urban population:* 63.8% of total population (2017)
rate of urbanization: 1.45% annual rate of change (2015-20 est.)

Major urban areas—population: DUBLIN (capital) 1.169 million (2015)

Sex ratio: *at birth:* 1.06 male(s)/female
0-14 years: 1.05 male(s)/female
15-24 years: 1.03 male(s)/female
25-54 years: 1.01 male(s)/female
55-64 years: 1 male(s)/female
65 years and over: 0.86 male(s)/female
total population: 1 male(s)/female (2016 est.)

Mother's mean age at first birth: 30.7 years (2015 est.)

Maternal mortality ratio: 8 deaths/100,000 live births (2015 est.)
country comparison to the world: 156

Infant mortality rate: *total:* 3.6 deaths/1,000 live births
male: 4 deaths/1,000 live births
female: 3.3 deaths/1,000 live births (2017 est.)
country comparison to the world: 198

Life expectancy at birth: *total population:* 80.9 years
male: 78.6 years
female: 83.4 years (2017 est.)
country comparison to the world: 33

Total fertility rate: 1.97 children born/woman (2017 est.)
country comparison to the world: 125

Health expenditures: 7.8% of GDP (2014)

country comparison to the world: 57

Physicians density: 2.79 physicians/1,000 population (2015)

Hospital bed density: 2.9 beds/1,000 population (2011)

Drinking water source:
improved:
urban: 97.9% of population
rural: 97.8% of population
total: 97.9% of population
unimproved:
urban: 2.1% of population
rural: 2.2% of population
total: 2.1% of population (2015 est.)

Sanitation facility access:
improved:
urban: 89.1% of population
rural: 92.9% of population
total: 90.5% of population
unimproved:
urban: 10.9% of population
rural: 7.1% of population
total: 9.5% of population (2015 est.)

HIV/AIDS—adult prevalence rate: 0.2% (2016 est.)
country comparison to the world: 89

HIV/AIDS—people living with HIV/AIDS: 6,200 (2016 est.)
country comparison to the world: 105

HIV/AIDS—deaths: NA

Obesity—adult prevalence rate: 25.3% (2016)
country comparison to the world: 51

Education expenditures: 5.3% of GDP (2013)
country comparison to the world: 31

School life expectancy (primary to tertiary education): *total:* 19 years
male: 19 years
female: 19 years (2014)

Unemployment, youth ages 15-24: *total:* 20.9%
male: 23.6%
female: 17.6% (2015 est.)
country comparison to the world: 38

GOVERNMENT

Country name: *conventional long form:* none
conventional short form: Ireland
local long form: none
local short form: Eire
etymology: the modern Irish name "Eire" evolved from the Gaelic "Eriu," the name of the matron goddess of Ireland (goddess of the land); the names "Ireland" in English and "Eire" in Irish are direct translations of each other

Government type: parliamentary republic

Capital: *name:* Dublin

geographic coordinates: 53 19 N, 6 14 W
time difference: UTC 0 (5 hours ahead of Washington, DC, during Standard Time)
daylight saving time: +1hr, begins last Sunday in March; ends last Sunday in October

Administrative divisions: 28 counties and 3 cities*; Carlow, Cavan, Clare, Cork, Cork*, Donegal,

Dublin*, Dun Laoghaire-Rathdown, Fingal, Galway, Galway*, Kerry, Kildare, Kilkenny, Laois, Leitrim, Limerick, Longford, Louth, Mayo, Meath, Monaghan, Offaly, Roscommon, Sligo, South Dublin, Tipperary, Waterford, Westmeath, Wexford, Wicklow

Independence: 6 December 1921 (from the UK by treaty)

National holiday: Saint Patrick's Day, 17 March; note—marks the traditional death date of Saint Patrick, patron saint of Ireland, during the latter half of the fifth century A.D. (most commonly cited years are c. 461 and c. 493); although Saint Patrick's feast day was celebrated in Ireland as early as the ninth century, it only became an official public holiday in Ireland in 1903

Constitution: history: previous 1922; latest drafted 14 June 1937, adopted by plebiscite 1 July 1937, effective 29 December 1937
amendments: proposed as bills by Parliament; passage requires majority vote by both the Senate and House of Representatives, majority vote in a referendum, and presidential signature; amended many times, last in 2015 (2016)

Legal system: common law system based on the English model but substantially modified by customary law; judicial review of legislative acts by Supreme Court

International law organization participation: accepts compulsory ICJ jurisdiction with reservations; accepts ICCt jurisdiction

Citizenship: *citizenship by birth:* yes
citizenship by descent: yes
dual citizenship recognized: yes
residency requirement for naturalization: 4 of the previous 8 years

Suffrage: 18 years of age; universal

Executive branch: *chief of state:* President Michael D. HIGGINS (since 11 November 2011)

head of government: Taoiseach (Prime Minister) Leo VARADKAR (since 14 June 2017)
cabinet: Cabinet nominated by the prime minister, appointed by the president, approved by the Dali Eireann (lower house of Parliament)
elections/appointments: president directly elected by majority popular vote for a 7-year term (eligible for a second term); election last held on 29 October 2011 (next to be held no later than 10 November 2018); taoiseach (prime minister) nominated by the House of Representatives (Dail Eireann), appointed by the president
election results: Michael D. HIGGINS elected president; percent of vote—Michael D. HIGGINS (Labor Party) 39.6%, Sean GALLAGHER (independent) 28.5%, Martin MCGUINNESS (Sinn Fein) 13.7%, Gay MITCHELL (Fine Gael) 6.4%, David NORRIS (independent) 6.2%, other 5.6%

Legislative branch: *description:* bicameral Parliament or Oireachtas consists of the Senate or Seanad Eireann (60 seats; 43 members indirectly elected from 5 vocational panels of nominees by an electoral college consisting of members from the House of Representatives, outgoing Senate members, and city and county council members,

11 appointed by the prime minister, and 6 elected by 2 university constituencies—3 each from the University of Dublin (Trinity College) and the National University of Ireland); and the House of Representatives or Dail Eireann (158 seats; members directly elected in multi-seat constituencies by proportional representation vote; all Parliament members serve 5-year terms)
elections: Senate—last held in April and May 2016 (next to be held no later than 2021); House of Representatives—last held on 26 February 2016 (next to be held no later than 2021)
election results: Senate—percent of vote by party—NA; seats by party—Fine Gael 19, Fianna Fail 14, Sinn Fein 7, Labor Party 5, Green Party 1, independent 14
House of Representatives—percent of vote by party—Fine Gael 25.5%, Fianna Fail 24.4%, Sinn Fein 13.8%, Labor Party 6.6%, AAA-PBD 4.0%, Social Democrats 3.0%, Green Party 2.7%, Renua Ireland 2.2% independent 17.8%; seats by party—Fine Gael 50, Fianna Fail 44, Sinn Fein 23, Labor Party 7, AAA-PBP 6, Social Democrats 3, Green Party 2, independent 23

Judicial branch: *highest court(s):* Supreme Court of Ireland (consists of the chief justice, 9 judges, 2 ex-officio members—the presidents of the High Court and Court of Appeal—and organized in 3-, 5-, or 7-judge panels, depending on the importance or complexity of an issue of law)
judge selection and term of office: judges nominated by the prime minister and Cabinet and appointed by the president; chief justice serves in the position for 7 years; judges can serve until age 70
subordinate courts: High Court, Court of Appeal; circuit and district courts; criminal courts

Political parties and leaders: Solidarity-People Before Profit or AAAS-PBP [collective leadership]
Fianna Fail [Micheal MARTIN]
Fine Gael [Leo VARADKAR]
Green Party [Eamon RYAN]
Labor (Labour) Party [Brendan HOWLIN]
Renua Ireland [John LEAHY]
Sinn Fein [Mary Lou MCDONALD]
Social Democrats [Catherine MURPHY, Roisin SHORTALL]
Socialist Party [collective leadership]
The Workers' Party [Michael DONNELLY]

Political pressure groups and leaders: Continuity IRA (terrorist group)
Families Acting for Innocent Relatives or FAIR [Brian MCCONNELL] (seek compensation for victims of violence)
Iona Institute [David QUINN] (a conservative Catholic think tank)
Irish Anti-War Movement [Richard BOYD BARRETT] (campaigns against wars around the world)
Keep Ireland Open (environmental group)
Oglaigh na hEireann (terrorist group)
Midland Railway Action Group or MRAG [Willie ALLEN] (transportation promoters)
New Irish Republican Army (terrorist group combining elements of the former Real IRA and Republican Action Against Drugs)

Peace and Neutrality Alliance or PANA [Roger COLE] (campaigns to protect Irish neutrality)
Rail Users Ireland (formerly the Platform 11—transportation promoters)
32 Country Sovereignty Movement or 32CSM (supports unifying Northern Ireland with the rest of the island under Irish government sovereignty)

International organization participation: ADB (nonregional member), Australia Group, BIS, CD, CE, EAPC, EBRD, ECB, EIB, EMU, ESA, EU, FAO, FATF, IAEA, IBRD, ICAO, ICC (national committees), ICCt, ICRM, IDA, IEA, IFAD, IFC, IFRCS, IGAD (partners), IHO, ILO, IMF, IMO, Interpol, IOC, IOM, IPU, ISO, ITSO, ITU, ITUC (NGOs), MIGA, MINURSO, MONUSCO, NEA, NSG, OAS (observer), OECD, OPCW, OSCE, Paris Club, PCA, PFP, UN, UNCTAD, UNDOF, UNESCO, UNHCR, UNIDO, UNIFIL, UNOCI, UNRWA, UNTSO, UPU, WCO, WHO, WIPO, WMO, WTO, ZC

Diplomatic representation in the US: *chief of mission:* Ambassador Daniel Gerard MULHALL (since 8 September 2017)
chancery: 2234 Massachusetts Avenue NW, Washington, DC 20008
telephone: [1] (202) 462-3939
FAX: [1] (202) 232-5993
consulate(s) general: Atlanta, Austin (TX), Boston, Chicago, New York, San Francisco

Diplomatic representation from the US: *chief of mission:* Ambassador (vacant) Charge d'Affaires L. Reece SMYTH (since 20 January 2017)
embassy: 42 Elgin Road, Ballsbridge, Dublin 4
mailing address: use embassy street address
telephone: [353] (1) 668-7777
FAX: [353] (1) 668-9946

Flag description: three equal vertical bands of green (hoist side), white, and orange; officially the flag colors have no meaning, but a common interpretation is that the green represents the Irish nationalist (Gaelic) tradition of Ireland; orange represents the Orange tradition (minority supporters of William of Orange); white symbolizes peace (or a lasting truce) between the green and the orange
note: similar to the flag of Cote d'Ivoire, which is shorter and has the colors reversed—orange (hoist side), white, and green; also similar to the flag of Italy, which is shorter and has colors of green (hoist side), white, and red

National symbol(s): harp, shamrock (trefoil); national colors: blue, green

National anthem: name: "Amhran na bhFiann" (The Soldier's Song)
lyrics/music: Peadar KEARNEY [English], Liam O RINN [Irish]/Patrick HEENEY and Peadar KEARNEY
note: adopted 1926; instead of "Amhran na bhFiann," the song "Ireland's Call" is often used at athletic events where citizens of Ireland and Northern Ireland compete as a unified team

ECONOMY

Economy—overview: Ireland is a small, modern, trade-dependent economy. Ireland was among the initial group of 12 EU nations that began circulating the euro on 1 January 2002. GDP growth averaged 6% in 1995-2007, but economic activity dropped sharply during the world financial crisis and the subsequent collapse of its domestic property market and construction industry. Faced with sharply reduced revenues and a burgeoning budget deficit from efforts to stabilize its fragile banking sector, the Irish Government introduced the first in a series of draconian budgets in 2009. These measures were not sufficient to stabilize Ireland's public finances. In 2010, the budget deficit reached 32.4% of GDP—the world's largest deficit, as a percentage of GDP. In late 2010, the former COWEN government agreed to a $92 billion loan package from the EU and IMF to help Dublin recapitalize Ireland's banking sector and avoid defaulting on its sovereign debt. In March 2011, the KENNY government intensified austerity measures to meet the deficit targets under Ireland's EU-IMF bailout program.

In late 2013, Ireland formally exited its EU-IMF bailout program, benefiting from its strict adherence to deficit-reduction targets and success in refinancing a large amount of banking-related debt. In 2014, the economy rapidly picked up and GDP grew by 25% in 2015. In late 2014, the government introduced a fiscally neutral budget, marking the end of the austerity program. Continued growth of tax receipts has allowed the government to lower some taxes and increase public spending while keeping to its deficit-reduction targets. In 2015, GDP growth exceeded 26%. This increase reflected one-off statistical revisions, multinational corporate restructurings, and the aircraft leasing sector, rather than gains in the on the ground economy. Growth moderated to around 4.1% in 2017, but the recovering economy assisted lowering the deficit to 0.6% of GDP.

In the wake of the collapse of the construction sector and the downturn in consumer spending and business investment, the export sector, dominated by foreign multinationals, has become an even more important component of Ireland's economy. Ireland's low corporation tax of 12.5% and a talented pool of high-tech laborers have been key factors in encouraging business investment. Loose tax residency requirements made Ireland a common destination for international firms seeking to avoid taxation. In 2014, amid growing international pressure, the government announced it would phase in more stringent tax laws, effectively closing a commonly used loophole.

GDP (purchasing power parity): $344.8 billion (2017 est.)
$331.2 billion (2016 est.)
$315.1 billion (2015 est.)
note: data are in 2017 dollars
country comparison to the world: 52

GDP (official exchange rate): $325.6 billion (2016 est.)

GDP—real growth rate: 4.1% (2017 est.)
5.1% (2016 est.)
25.5% (2015 est.)
country comparison to the world: 61

GDP—per capita (PPP): $72,600 (2017 est.)

$70,500 (2016 est.)
$67,700 (2015 est.)
note: data are in 2017 dollars
country comparison to the world: 11

Gross national saving: 37.1% of GDP (2017 est.)
35.7% of GDP (2016 est.)
32.1% of GDP (2015 est.)
country comparison to the world: 12

GDP—composition, by end use:
household consumption: 34.6%
government consumption: 10.3%
investment in fixed capital: 33.1%
investment in inventories: 0.8%
exports of goods and services: 120.7%
imports of goods and services: -99.5% (2017 est.)

GDP—composition, by sector of origin:
agriculture: 1%
industry: 38.2%
services: 60.7% (2017 est.)

Agriculture—products: barley, potatoes, wheat; beef, dairy products

Industries: pharmaceuticals, chemicals, computer hardware and software, food products, beverages and brewing; medical devices

Industrial production growth rate: 1.5% (2017 est.)
country comparison to the world: 153

Labor force: 2.226 million (2017 est.)
country comparison to the world: 122

Labor force—by occupation: *agriculture:* 5%
industry: 11%
services: 84% (2015 est.)

Unemployment rate: 6.4% (2017 est.)
7.9% (2016 est.)
country comparison to the world: 87

Population below poverty line: 8.2% (2013 est.)

Household income or consumption by percentage share: *lowest 10%:* 2.9%
highest 10%: 27.2% (2000)

Distribution of family income—Gini index: 31.3 (2013 est.)
35.9 (1987 est.)
country comparison to the world: 119

Budget: *revenues:* $85.41 billion
expenditures: $87.22 billion (2017 est.)
Taxes and other revenues: 26.2% of GDP (2017 est.)
country comparison to the world: 107

Budget surplus (+) or deficit (-): -0.6% of GDP (2017 est.)
country comparison to the world: 50

Public debt: 69.5% of GDP (2017 est.)
72.9% of GDP (2016 est.)
note: data cover general government debt, and includes debt instruments issued (or owned) by government entities other than the treasury; the data include treasury debt held by foreign entities; the data include debt issued by subnational entities, as well as intra-governmental debt; intra-governmental debt consists of treasury borrowings from surpluses in the social funds, such as for retirement, medical care, and unemployment; debt instruments for the social funds are not sold at public auctions

country comparison to the world: 51

Fiscal year: calendar year

Inflation rate (consumer prices): 0.4% (2017 est.)
-0.2% (2016 est.)
country comparison to the world: 18

Central bank discount rate: 0.05% (31 December 2015)
0.15% (31 August 2014)
note: this is the European Central Bank's rate on the marginal lending facility, which offers overnight credit to banks in the euro area
country comparison to the world: 146

Commercial bank prime lending rate: 3.8% (31 December 2017 est.)
3.48% (31 December 2016 est.)
country comparison to the world: 162

Stock of narrow money: $180 billion (31 December 2017 est.)
$156.2 billion (31 December 2016 est.)
note: see entry for the European Union for money supply for the entire euro area; the European Central Bank (ECB) controls monetary policy for the 18 members of the Economic and Monetary Union (EMU); individual members of the EMU do not control the quantity of money circulating within their own borders
country comparison to the world: 27

Stock of broad money: $233.9 billion (31 December 2017 est.)
$204.9 billion (31 December 2016 est.)
country comparison to the world: 36

Stock of domestic credit: $305.3 billion (31 December 2017 est.)
$287.1 billion (31 December 2016 est.)
country comparison to the world: 37

Market value of publicly traded shares: $128 billion (31 December 2015 est.)
$143.5 billion (31 December 2014 est.)
$170.1 billion (31 December 2013 est.)
country comparison to the world: 39

Current account balance: $10.94 billion (2017 est.)
$10.17 billion (2016 est.)
country comparison to the world: 20

Exports: $225.1 billion (2017 est.)
$206 billion (2016 est.)
country comparison to the world: 24

Exports—commodities: machinery and equipment, computers, chemicals, medical devices, pharmaceuticals; foodstuffs, animal products

Exports—partners: US 26%, UK 12.7%, Belgium 12.6%, Germany 6.7%, Switzerland 5.4%, Netherlands 5.1%, France 4.2% (2016)

Imports: $96.03 billion (2017 est.)
$92.09 billion (2016 est.)
country comparison to the world: 34

Imports—commodities: data processing equipment, other machinery and equipment, chemicals, petroleum and petroleum products, textiles, clothing

Imports—partners: UK 28.8%, US 15.9%, France 12.6%, Germany 10.1%, Netherlands 4.7% (2016)

Reserves of foreign exchange and gold: $3.591 billion (31 December 2016 est.)
$2.203 billion (31 December 2015 est.)
country comparison to the world: 101

Debt—external: $2.47 trillion (31 March 2016 est.)
$2.35 trillion (31 March 2015 est.)
country comparison to the world: 9

Stock of direct foreign investment—at home: $1.477 trillion (31 December 2017 est.)
$1.411 trillion (31 December 2016 est.)
country comparison to the world: 7

Stock of direct foreign investment—abroad: $1.49 trillion (31 December 2017 est.)
$1.404 trillion (31 December 2016 est.)
country comparison to the world: 9

Exchange rates: euros (EUR) per US dollar—
0.906 (2017 est.)
0.9214 (2016 est.)
0.9214 (2015 est.)
0.885 (2014 est.)
0.7634 (2013 est.)

ENERGY

Electricity access: *electrification—total population:* 100% (2016)

Electricity—production: 25.2 billion kWh (2015 est.)
country comparison to the world: 70

Electricity—consumption: 23.79 billion kWh (2015 est.)
country comparison to the world: 69

Electricity—exports: 1.583 billion kWh (2016 est.)
country comparison to the world: 48

Electricity—imports: 871 million kWh (2016 est.)
country comparison to the world: 70

Electricity—installed generating capacity: 9.557 million kW (2015 est.)
country comparison to the world: 63

Electricity—from fossil fuels: 68.1% of total installed capacity (2015 est.)
country comparison to the world: 106

Electricity—from nuclear fuels: 0% of total installed capacity (2015 est.)
country comparison to the world: 83

Electricity—from hydroelectric plants: 2.5% of total installed capacity (2015 est.)
country comparison to the world: 135

Electricity—from other renewable sources: 29.7% of total installed capacity (2015 est.)
country comparison to the world: 15

Crude oil—production: 0 bbl/day (2016 est.)
country comparison to the world: 150

Crude oil—exports: 0 bbl/day (2016 est.)
country comparison to the world: 117

Crude oil—imports: 65,390 bbl/day (2016 est.)
country comparison to the world: 49

Crude oil—proved reserves: 0 bbl (1 January 2017 es)
country comparison to the world: 149

Refined petroleum products—production: 64,310 bbl/day (2016 est.)
country comparison to the world: 77

Refined petroleum products—consumption: 151,700 bbl/day (2016 est.)
country comparison to the world: 69

Refined petroleum products—exports: 31,540 bbl/day (2016 est.)
country comparison to the world: 61

Refined petroleum products—imports: 119,600 bbl/day (2016 est.)
country comparison to the world: 54

Natural gas—production: 132 million cu m (2015 est.)
country comparison to the world: 80

Natural gas—consumption: 5.06 billion cu m (2015 est.)
country comparison to the world: 64

Natural gas—exports: 0 cu m (2014 est.)
country comparison to the world: 97

Natural gas—imports: 4.234 billion cu m (2015 est.)
country comparison to the world: 36

Natural gas—proved reserves: 9.911 billion cu m (1 January 2017 es)
country comparison to the world: 84

Carbon dioxide emissions from consumption of energy: 34 million Mt (2013 est.)
country comparison to the world: 74

COMMUNICATIONS

Telephones—fixed lines: *total subscriptions:* 1,897,134
subscriptions per 100 inhabitants: 38 (July 2016 est.)
country comparison to the world: 57

Telephones—mobile cellular: *total:* 4,950,118
subscriptions per 100 inhabitants: 100 (July 2016 est.)
country comparison to the world: 119

Telephone system: *general assessment:* modern digital system using cable and microwave radio relay
domestic: system privatized but dominated by former state monopoly operator; increasing levels of broadband access particularly in urban areas
international: country code—353; landing point for the Hibernia-Atlantic submarine cable with links to the US, Canada, and UK; satellite earth stations—81 (2014)

Broadcast media: publicly owned broadcaster Radio Telefis Eireann (RTE) operates 2 TV stations; commercial TV stations are available; about 75% of households utilize multi-channel satellite and TV services that provide access to a wide range of stations; RTE operates 4 national radio stations and has launched digital audio broadcasts on several stations; a number of commercial broadcast stations operate at the national, regional, and local levels (2014)

Internet country code: .ie
Internet users: total: 4,069,432

percent of population: 82.2% (July 2016 est.)
country comparison to the world: 79

TRANSPORTATION

National air transport system: *number of registered air carriers:* 6
inventory of registered aircraft operated by air carriers: 431
annual passenger traffic on registered air carriers: 113,144,501
annual freight traffic on registered air carriers: 138.58 million mt-km (2015)
Civil aircraft registration country code prefix: EI (2016)

Airports: 40 (2013)
country comparison to the world: 105

Airports—with paved runways: *total:* 16
over 3,047 m: 1
2,438 to 3,047 m: 1
1,524 to 2,437 m: 4
914 to 1,523 m: 5
under 914 m: 5 (2017)

Airports—with unpaved runways: *total:* 24
2,438 to 3,047 m: 1
914 to 1,523 m: 2
under 914 m: 21 (2013)

Pipelines: gas 2,147 km (2013)

Railways: *total:* 3,237 km
broad gauge: 1,872 km 1.600-m gauge (49 km electrified)
narrow gauge: 1,365 km 0.914-m gauge (operated by the Irish Peat Board to transport peat to power stations and briquetting plants) (2014)
country comparison to the world: 55

Roadways: *total:* 96,036 km
paved: 96,036 km (includes 1,224 km of expressways) (2014)
country comparison to the world: 51

Waterways: 956 km (pleasure craft only) (2010)
country comparison to the world: 67

Merchant marine: *total:* 83
by type: bulk carrier 9, general cargo 28, oil tanker 1, other 45 (2017)
country comparison to the world: 91

Ports and terminals: *major seaport(s):* Dublin, Shannon Foynes
river port(s): Cork (Lee), Waterford (Suir)
container port(s) (TEUs): Dublin (1,931,001)

MILITARY AND SECURITY

Military expenditures: 0.34% of GDP (2016)
0.35% of GDP (2015)
0.47% of GDP (2014)
0.5% of GDP (2013)
0.51% of GDP (2012)
country comparison to the world: 126

Military branches: Irish Defence Forces (Oglaigh na h-Eireannn), Permanent Defence Forces (PDF): Army, Naval Service, Air Corps; Reserve Defence Forces (RDF): Army, Naval Service Reserves (2014)

Military service age and obligation: 18-25 years of age for male and female voluntary military service recruits to the Permanent Defence Forces (PDF; 18-27 years of age for the Naval Service); 18-28 for cadetship (officer) applicants; 18-35 years of age for the Reserve Defence Forces (RDF); maximum obligation 12 years (PDF officers), 5 years (PDF enlisted), 3 years RDF (4 years for Naval Service Reserves); EU citizenship, refugee status, or 5-year residence in Ireland required (2014)

TERRORISM

Terrorist groups—foreign based: *Continuity Irish Republican Army (CIRA): aim(s):* to bring about a united Ireland
area(s) of operation: maintains a limited operational presence; in December 2016, authorities found a large CIRA weapons cache in Monaghan

County, which borders Northern Ireland; on 5 February 2016, gunmen opened fire in Dublin at a boxing weigh-in taking place in the Regency Hotel, killing one man and injuring two others; CIRA claimed responsibility accusing the deceased of being involved in the 2009 murder of fellow Republican and Real IRA senior member Alan RYAN

Real Irish Republican Army (RIRA): *aim(s):* to bring about a united Ireland
area(s) of operation: maintains a limited operational presence, centered primarily on generating revenue from smuggling and other illegal activities

TRANSNATIONAL ISSUES

Disputes—international: Ireland, Iceland, and the UK dispute Denmark's claim that the Faroe Islands' continental shelf extends beyond 200 nm

Refugees and internally displaced persons: *stateless persons:* 99 (2016)

Illicit drugs: transshipment point for and consumer of hashish from North Africa to the UK and Netherlands and of European-produced synthetic drugs; increasing consumption of South American cocaine; minor transshipment point for heroin and cocaine destined for Western Europe; despite recent legislation, narcotics-related money laundering—using bureaux de change, trusts, and shell companies involving the offshore financial community—remains a concern

ISLE OF MAN

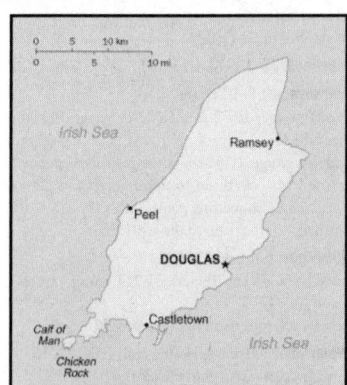

INTRODUCTION

Background: Part of the Norwegian Kingdom of the Hebrides until the 13th century when it was ceded to Scotland, the isle came under the British Crown in 1765. Current concerns include reviving the almost extinct Manx Gaelic language. Isle of Man is a British Crown dependency but is not part of the UK or of the EU. However, the UK Government remains constitutionally responsible for its defense and international representation.

GEOGRAPHY

Location: Western Europe, island in the Irish Sea, between Great Britain and Ireland

Geographic coordinates: 54 15 N, 4 30 W

Map references: Europe

Area: *total:* 572 sq km
land: 572 sq km
water: 0 sq km
country comparison to the world: 194

Area—comparative: slightly more than three times the size of Washington, DC

Land boundaries: 0 km

Coastline: 160 km

Maritime claims: *territorial sea:* 12 nm
exclusive fishing zone: 12 nm

Climate: temperate; cool summers and mild winters; overcast about a third of the time

Terrain: hills in north and south bisected by central valley

Elevation: *mean elevation:* NA

elevation extremes: *lowest point:* Irish Sea 0 m
highest point: Snaefell 621 m

Natural resources: none

Land use: *agricultural land:* 74.7%
arable land: 43.8%;
permanent crops: 0%;
permanent pasture: 30.9%
forest: 6.1%
other: 19.2% (2011 est.)
Irrigated land: 0 sq km (2012)

Population—distribution: most people concentrated in cities and large towns of which Douglas, in the southeast, is the largest

Natural hazards: occasional high winds and rough seas

Environment—current issues: waste disposal (both household and industrial); transboundary air pollution

Geography—note: one small islet, the Calf of Man, lies to the southwest and is a bird sanctuary

PEOPLE AND SOCIETY

Population: 88,815 (July 2017 est.)
country comparison to the world: 199

Nationality: *noun:* Manxman(men), Manxwoman (women)

adjective: Manx

Ethnic groups: white 96.5%, Asian/Asian British 1.9%, other 1.5% (2011 est.)

Languages: English, Manx Gaelic (about 2% of the population has some knowledge)

Religions: Protestant (Anglican, Methodist, Baptist, Presbyterian, Society of Friends), Roman Catholic

Age structure: *0-14 years:* 16.28% (male 7,547/ female 6,916)
15-24 years: 11.43% (male 5,355/female 4,800)
25-54 years: 38.79% (male 17,215/female 17,234)
55-64 years: 13.13% (male 5,891/female 5,772)
65 years and over: 20.36% (male 8,469/female 9,616) (2017 est.)

Median age: *total:* 44.2 years
male: 43.3 years
female: 44.9 years (2017 est.)
country comparison to the world: 11

Population growth rate: 0.68% (2017 est.)
country comparison to the world: 146

Birth rate: 11 births/1,000 population (2017 est.)
country comparison to the world: 180

Death rate: 10.2 deaths/1,000 population (2017 est.)
country comparison to the world: 37

Net migration rate: 6 migrant(s)/1,000 population (2017 est.)
country comparison to the world: 16

Population distribution: most people concentrated in cities and large towns of which Douglas, in the southeast, is the largest

Urbanization: *urban population:* 52.4% of total population (2017)
rate of urbanization: 0.81% annual rate of change (2015-20 est.)

Major urban areas—population: DOUGLAS (capital) 29,000 (2014)

Sex ratio: *at birth:* 1.08 male(s)/female
0-14 years: 1.1 male(s)/female
15-24 years: 1.1 male(s)/female
25-54 years: 1 male(s)/female
55-64 years: 1.02 male(s)/female
65 years and over: 0.87 male(s)/female
total population: 1 male(s)/female (2016 est.)

Infant mortality rate: *total:* 4 deaths/1,000 live births
male: 4 deaths/1,000 live births
female: 4.1 deaths/1,000 live births (2017 est.)
country comparison to the world: 193

Life expectancy at birth: *total population:* 81.3 years
male: 79.6 years
female: 83.2 years (2017 est.)
country comparison to the world: 29

Total fertility rate: 1.92 children born/woman (2017 est.)
country comparison to the world: 132

HIV/AIDS—adult prevalence rate: NA

HIV/AIDS—people living with HIV/AIDS: NA

HIV/AIDS—deaths: NA

Unemployment, youth ages 15-24: *total:* 10.1%
male: 11.8%
female: 8.2% (2011 est.)
country comparison to the world: 118

GOVERNMENT

Country name: *conventional long form:* none
conventional short form: Isle of Man
abbreviation: I.O.M.
etymology: the name "man" may be derived from the Celtic word for "mountain"

Dependency status: British Crown dependency

Government type: parliamentary democracy (Tynwald); a Crown dependency of the UK

Capital: *name:* Douglas

geographic coordinates: 54 09 N, 4 29 W
time difference: UTC 0 (5 hours ahead of Washington, DC, during Standard Time)
daylight saving time: +1hr, begins last Sunday in March; ends last Sunday in October

Administrative divisions: none; there are no first-order administrative divisions as defined by the US Government, but there are 24 local authorities each with its own elections

Independence: none (British crown dependency)

National holiday: Tynwald Day, 5 July (1417); date Tynwald Day was first recorded

Constitution: *history:* development of the Isle of Man constitution dates to at least the 14th century
amendments: proposed as a bill in the House of Keys, by the "Government," by a "Member of the House," or through petition to the House or Legislative Council; passage normally requires three separate readings and approval of at least 13 House members; following both House and Council agreement, assent is required by the lieutenant governor on behalf of the Crown; the constitution has been expanded and amended many times, last in 2015 (2016)

Legal system: the laws of the UK, where applicable, apply and include Manx statutes

Citizenship: see United Kingdom

Suffrage: 16 years of age; universal

Executive branch: *chief of state:* Lord of Mann Queen ELIZABETH II (since 6 February 1952); represented by Lieutenant Governor Sir Richard GOZNEY (since 27 May 2016)

head of government: Chief Minister Howard QUAYLE (since 4 October 2016)
cabinet: Council of Ministers appointed by the lieutenant governor
elections/appointments: the monarchy is hereditary; lieutenant governor appointed by the monarch; chief minister indirectly elected by the Tynwald for a 5-year term (eligible for second term); election last held on 4 October 2016 (next to be held in 2021)
election results: Howard QUAYLE (independent) elected chief minister; Tynwald vote—21 of 33

Legislative branch: *description:* bicameral Tynwald or the High Court of Tynwald consists of the Legislative Council (11 seats; includes the President of Tynwald, 2 ex-officio members—the Lord Bishop of Sodor and Man and the attorney general (non-voting)—and 8 members indirectly elected by the House of Keys with renewal of 4 members every 2 years; elected members serve 4-year terms) and the House of Keys (24 seats; 2 members directly elected by simple majority vote from 12 constituencies to serve 5-year terms)
elections: House of Keys—last held on 22 September 2016 (next to be held in September 2021)
election results: House of Keys—percent of vote by party—Liberal Vannin 6.4%, independent 92.3%; seats by party—Liberal Vannin 3, other 1.3% independent 21

Judicial branch: *highest resident court(s):* Isle of Man High Court of Justice (consists of 3 permanent judges or "deemsters" and 1 judge of appeal; organized into the Staff of Government Division or Court of Appeal and the Civil Division); the Court of General Gaol Delivery is not formally part of the High Court but is administered as though part of the High Court and deals with serious criminal cases; note—appeals beyond the Court of Appeal are referred to the Judicial Committee of the Privy Council (in London)
judge selection and term of office: deemsters appointed by the Lord Chancellor of England on the nomination of the lieutenant governor; deemsters can serve until age 70
subordinate courts: High Court; Court of Summary Gaol Delivery; Summary Courts; Magistrate's Court; specialized courts

Political parties and leaders: Liberal Vannin Party [Kate BEECROFT]
Manx Labor Party
Mec Vannin [Bernard MOFFATT]; (sometimes referred to as the Manx Nationalist Party)
note: most members sit as independents

Political pressure groups and leaders: Alliance for Progressive Government or APG (a government watchdog)

International organization participation: UPU

Diplomatic representation in the US: none (British Crown dependency)

Diplomatic representation from the US: none (British Crown dependency)

Flag description: red with the Three Legs of Man emblem (triskelion), in the center; the three legs are joined at the thigh and bent at the knee; in order to have the toes pointing clockwise on both sides of the flag, a two-sided emblem is used; the flag is based on the coat-of-arms of the last recognized Norse King of Mann, Magnus III (r. 1252-65); the triskelion has its roots in an early Celtic sun symbol

National symbol(s): triskelion (a motif of three legs); national colors: red, white

National anthem: *name:* "Arrane Ashoonagh dy Vannin" (O Land of Our Birth)
lyrics/music: William Henry GILL [English], John J. KNEEN [Manx]/traditional
note: adopted 2003, in use since 1907; serves as a local anthem; as a British Crown dependency, "God Save the Queen" is official (see United Kingdom) and is played when the sovereign, members of the royal family, or the lieutenant governor are present

ECONOMY

Economy—overview: Financial services, manufacturing, and tourism are key sectors of the economy. The government offers low taxes and other incentives to high-technology companies and financial institutions to locate on the island; this has paid off in expanding employment opportunities in high-income industries. As a result, agriculture and fishing, once the mainstays of the economy, have declined in their contributions to GDP. The Isle of Man also attracts online gambling sites and the film industry. Online gambling sites provided about 10% of the islands income in 2014. The Isle of Man currently enjoys free access to EU markets and trade is mostly with the UK. The Isle of Man's trade relationship with the EU derives from the United Kingdom's EU membership and will need to be renegotiated in light of the United Kingdom's decision to withdraw from the bloc.

GDP (purchasing power parity): $7.428 billion (2014 est.)
$6.298 billion (2013 est.)
$5.85 billion (2012 est.)
note: data are in 2014 US dollars
country comparison to the world: 168

GDP (official exchange rate): $6.615 billion (2007 est.)

GDP—real growth rate: 2.2% (2012)
3.4% (2011)
2.1% (2010)
country comparison to the world: 147

GDP—per capita (PPP): $84,600 (2014 est.)
$73,100 (2013 est.)
$68,500 (2012 est.)
country comparison to the world: 9

GDP—composition, by sector of origin:
agriculture: 1%
industry: 13%
services: 86% (FY12/13 est.)

Agriculture—products: cereals, vegetables; cattle, sheep, pigs, poultry

Industries: financial services, light manufacturing, tourism

Labor force: 41,790 (2006)
country comparison to the world: 195

Labor force—by occupation: agriculture, forestry, and fishing: 2%
manufacturing: 5%
construction: 8%
gas, electricity, and water: 1%
transport and communication: 9%
wholesale and retail distribution: 11%
professional and scientific services: 20%
public administration: 7%
banking and finance: 23%
tourism: 1%
entertainment and catering: 5%
miscellaneous services: 8% (2006)

Unemployment rate: 2.7% (2013 est.)
2% (April 2011 est.)
country comparison to the world: 26

Population below poverty line: NA%

Household income or consumption by percentage share: *lowest 10%:* NA%
highest 10%: NA%

Budget: *revenues:* $965 million
expenditures: $943 million (FY05/06 est.)
Taxes and other revenues: 14.6% of GDP
(FY05/06 est.)

country comparison to the world: 196

Budget surplus (+) or deficit (-): 0.3% of GDP (FY05/06 est.)
country comparison to the world: 28

Fiscal year: 1 April–31 March

Inflation rate (consumer prices): 5% (2010 est.)
3.1% (2006)
country comparison to the world: 172

Market value of publicly traded shares: $NA

Exports: $NA

Exports—commodities: tweeds, herring, processed shellfish, beef, lamb

Imports: $NA

Imports—commodities: timber, fertilizers, fish

Debt—external: $NA

Exchange rates: Manx pounds (IMP) per US dollar—
0.7836 (2017)
0.738 (2016)
0.738 (2015)
0.6542 (2014)
0.6472 (2013 est.)

ENERGY

Electricity access: *electrification—total population:* 100% (2016)

COMMUNICATIONS

Telephone system: *domestic:* landline, telefax, mobile cellular telephone system
international: country code—44; fiber-optic cable, microwave radio relay, satellite earth station, submarine cable

Broadcast media: national public radio broadcasts over 3 FM stations and 1 AM station; 2 commercial broadcasters operating with 1 having multiple FM stations; receives radio and TV services via relays from British TV and radio broadcasters (2008)

Internet country code: .im

TRANSPORTATION

Civil aircraft registration country code prefix: M (2016)

Airports: 1 (2013)
country comparison to the world: 221

Airports—with paved runways: *total:* 1
1,524 to 2,437 m: 1 (2017)

Railways: *total:* 63 km
narrow gauge: 6 km 1.076-m gauge (6 km electrified); 57 km 0.914-m gauge (29 km electrified)
note: primarily summer tourist attractions (2008)
country comparison to the world: 130

Roadways: *total:* 500 km (2008)
country comparison to the world: 197

Ports and terminals: *major seaport(s):* Douglas, Ramsey

MILITARY AND SECURITY

Military—note: defense is the responsibility of the UK

TRANSNATIONAL ISSUES

Disputes—international: none

ISRAEL

INTRODUCTION

Background: Following World War II, Britain withdrew from its mandate of Palestine, and the UN proposed partitioning the area into Arab and Jewish states, an arrangement rejected by the Arabs. Nonetheless, an Israeli state was declared in 1948, and Israel subsequently defeated the Arab armies in a series of wars that did not end deep tensions between the two sides. (The territories Israel has occupied since the 1967 war are not included in the Israel country profile, unless otherwise noted.) On 25 April 1982, Israel withdrew from the Sinai Peninsula pursuant to the 1979 Israel-Egypt Peace Treaty. In keeping with the framework established at the Madrid Conference in October 1991, Israel conducted bilateral negotiations with Palestinian representatives and Syria to achieve a permanent settlement with each. Israel and Palestinian officials on 13 September 1993 signed a Declaration of Principles (also known as the "Oslo Accords"), enshrining the idea of a two-state solution to their conflict and guiding an interim period of Palestinian self-rule. The parties achieved six

additional significant interim agreements between 1994 and 1999 aimed at creating the conditions for a two-state solution, but most were never fully realized. Outstanding territorial and other disputes with Jordan were resolved in the 26 October 1994 Israel-Jordan Peace Treaty.

Progress toward a final status agreement with the Palestinians was undermined by Israeli-Palestinian violence between 2001 and February 2005. Israel in 2005 unilaterally disengaged from the Gaza Strip, evacuating settlers and its military while retaining control over most points of entry into the Gaza Strip. The election of HAMAS to head the Palestinian Legislative Council in 2006 temporarily froze relations between Israel and the Palestinian Authority (PA). Israel engaged in a 34-day conflict with Hizballah in Lebanon from July-August 2006 and a 23-day conflict with HAMAS in the Gaza Strip from December 2008-January 2009. In November 2012, Israel engaged in a seven-day conflict with HAMAS in the Gaza Strip. Direct talks with the Palestinians most recently launched in July 2013 but were suspended in April 2014. The talks represented

the fourth concerted effort to resolve final status issues between the sides since they were first discussed at Camp David in 2000. Three months later HAMAS and other militant groups launched rockets into Israel, which led to a 51-day conflict between Israel and militants in Gaza.

GEOGRAPHY

Location: Middle East, bordering the Mediterranean Sea, between Egypt and Lebanon

Geographic coordinates: 31 30 N, 34 45 E

Map references: Middle East

Area: *total:* 20,770 sq km
land: 20,330 sq km
water: 440 sq km
country comparison to the world: 154

Area—comparative: slightly larger than New Jersey

Land boundaries: *total:* 1,068 km
border countries (6): Egypt 208 km, Gaza Strip 59 km, Jordan 307 km, Lebanon 81 km, Syria 83 km, West Bank 330 km

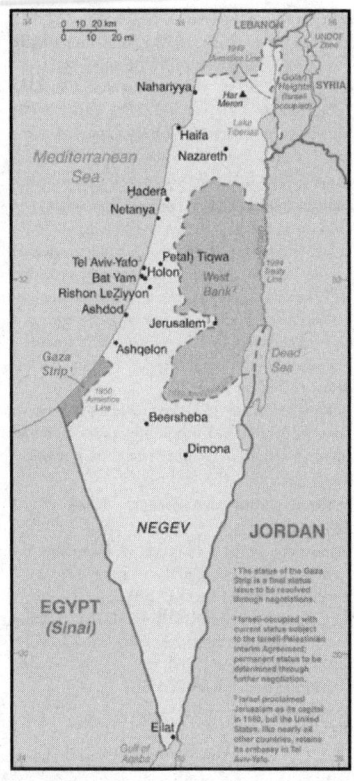

Coastline: 273 km

Maritime claims: *territorial sea:* 12 nm
continental shelf: to depth of exploitation

Climate: temperate; hot and dry in southern and eastern desert areas

Terrain: Negev desert in the south; low coastal plain; central mountains; Jordan Rift Valley

Elevation: *mean elevation:* 508 m

elevation extremes: *lowest point:* Dead Sea -431 m
highest point: Har Meron 1,208 m

Natural resources: timber, potash, copper ore, natural gas, phosphate rock, magnesium bromide, clays, sand

Land use: *agricultural land:* 23.8%
arable land: 13.7%;
permanent crops: 3.8%;
permanent pasture: 6.3%
forest: 7.1%
other: 69.1% (2011 est.)
Irrigated land: 2,250 sq km (2012)

Population—distribution: population concentrated in and around Tel-Aviv, as well as around the Sea of Galilee; the south remains sparsely populated with the exception of the shore of the Gulf of Aqaba

Natural hazards: sandstorms may occur during spring and summer; droughts; periodic earthquakes

Environment—current issues: limited arable land: and restricted natural freshwater resources; desertification; air pollution from industrial and vehicle emissions; groundwater pollution from industrial and domestic waste, chemical fertilizers, and pesticides

Environment—international agreements: *party to:* Biodiversity, Climate Change, Climate Change-Kyoto Protocol, Desertification, Endangered Species, Hazardous Wastes, Ozone Layer Protection, Ship Pollution, Wetlands, Whaling
signed, but not ratified: Marine Life Conservation

Geography—note: Lake Tiberias (Sea of Galilee) is an important freshwater source; the Dead Sea is the second saltiest body of water in the world (after Lake Assal in Djibouti); in 2017, there were 422 settlements in the Israeli-occupied territories—42 settlements in the Golan Heights, 380 sites in the occupied Palestinian territories to include 213 settlements and 132 outposts in the West Bank, and 35 settlements in East Jerusalem; there are no Israeli settlements in the Gaza Strip, as all were evacuated in 2005 (2017)

PEOPLE AND SOCIETY

Population: 8,299,706 (July 2017 est.) (includes populations of the Golan Heights of Golan Sub-District and also East Jerusalem, which was annexed by Israel after 1967)
note: approximately 22,000 Israeli settlers live in the Golan Heights (2016); approximately 201,000 Israeli settlers live in East Jerusalem (2014)
country comparison to the world: 97

Nationality: *noun:* Israeli(s)
adjective: Israeli

Ethnic groups: Jewish 74.7% (of which Israel-born 76.3%, Europe/America/Oceania-born 16.2%, Africa-born 4.8%, Asia-born 2.7%), non-Jewish 25.2% (mostly Arab) (2016 est.)

Languages: Hebrew (official), Arabic (used officially for Arab minority), English (most commonly used foreign language)

Religions: Jewish 74.7%, Muslim 17.7%, Christian 2%, Druze 1.6%, other 4% (2016 est.)

Age structure: *0-14 years:* 27.51% (male 1,168,351/female 1,114,902)
15-24 years: 15.53% (male 658,572/female 630,675)
25-54 years: 37.17% (male 1,577,187/female 1,507,793)
55-64 years: 8.46% (male 344,922/female 357,301)
65 years and over: 11.33% (male 421,660/female 518,343) (2017 est.)

Dependency ratios: *total dependency ratio:* 64.2
youth dependency ratio: 45.7
elderly dependency ratio: 18.4
potential support ratio: 5.4 (2015 est.)

Median age: *total:* 29.9 years
male: 29.3 years
female: 30.6 years (2017 est.)
country comparison to the world: 118

Population growth rate: 1.51% (2017 est.)

country comparison to the world: 76

Birth rate: 18.1 births/1,000 population (2017 est.)
country comparison to the world: 96

Death rate: 5.2 deaths/1,000 population (2017 est.)
country comparison to the world: 187

Net migration rate: 2.2 migrant(s)/1,000 population (2017 est.)
country comparison to the world: 43

Population distribution: population concentrated in and around Tel-Aviv, as well as around the Sea of Galilee; the south remains sparsely populated with the exception of the shore of the Gulf of Aqaba

Urbanization: *urban population:* 92.3% of total population (2017)
rate of urbanization: 1.5% annual rate of change (2015-20 est.)

Major urban areas—population: Tel Aviv-Yafo 3.608 million; Haifa 1.097 million; JERUSALEM (proclaimed capital) 839,000 (2015)

Sex ratio: *at birth:* 1.05 male(s)/female
0-14 years: 1.05 male(s)/female
15-24 years: 1.05 male(s)/female
25-54 years: 1.05 male(s)/female
55-64 years: 0.96 male(s)/female
65 years and over: 0.81 male(s)/female
total population: 1.01 male(s)/female (2016 est.)

Mother's mean age at first birth: 27.6 years (2015 est.)

Maternal mortality ratio: 5 deaths/100,000 live births (2015 est.)
country comparison to the world: 170

Infant mortality rate: *total:* 3.4 deaths/1,000 live births
male: 3.4 deaths/1,000 live births
female: 3.5 deaths/1,000 live births (2017 est.)
country comparison to the world: 204

Life expectancy at birth: *total population:* 82.5 years
male: 80.7 years
female: 84.5 years (2017 est.)
country comparison to the world: 12

Total fertility rate: 2.64 children born/woman (2017 est.)
country comparison to the world: 71

Health expenditures: 7.8% of GDP (2014)
country comparison to the world: 59

Physicians density: 3.62 physicians/1,000 population (2014)

Hospital bed density: 3.3 beds/1,000 population (2012)

Drinking water source:
improved:
urban: 100% of population
rural: 100% of population
total: 100% of population
unimproved:
urban: 0% of population
rural: 0% of population
total: 0% of population (2015 est.)

Sanitation facility access:

improved:

urban: 100% of population

rural: 100% of population

total: 100% of population

unimproved:

urban: 0% of population

rural: 0% of population

total: 0% of population (2015 est.)

HIV/AIDS—adult prevalence rate: NA

HIV/AIDS—people living with HIV/AIDS: NA

HIV/AIDS—deaths: NA

Obesity—adult prevalence rate: 26.1% (2016)

country comparison to the world: 45

Education expenditures: 5.9% of GDP (2013)

country comparison to the world: 57

Literacy: *definition:* age 15 and over can read and write

total population: 97.8%

male: 98.7%

female: 96.8% (2011 est.)

School life expectancy (primary to tertiary education): *total:* 16 years

male: 16 years

female: 16 years (2014)

Unemployment, youth ages 15-24: *total:* 8.6%

male: 8.2%

female: 9.1% (2016 est.)

country comparison to the world: 90

GOVERNMENT

Country name: *conventional long form:* State of Israel

conventional short form: Israel

local long form: Medinat Yisra'el

local short form: Yisra'el

etymology: named after the ancient Kingdom of Israel; according to Biblical tradition, the Jewish patriarch Jacob received the name "Israel" ("He who struggles with God") after he wrestled an entire night with an angel of the Lord; Jacob's 12 sons became the ancestors of the Israelites, also known as the Twelve Tribes of Israel, who formed the Kingdom of Israel

Government type: parliamentary democracy

Capital: name: Jerusalem; note—the US recognized Jerusalem as Israel's capital in December 2017 without taking a position on the specific boundaries of Israeli sovereignty

geographic coordinates: 31 46 N, 35 14 E

time difference: UTC+2 (7 hours ahead of Washington, DC, during Standard Time)

daylight saving time: +1hr, Friday before the last Sunday in March; ends the last Sunday in October

Administrative divisions: 6 districts (mehozot, singular—mehoz); Central, Haifa, Jerusalem, Northern, Southern, Tel Aviv

Independence: 14 May 1948 (from League of Nations mandate under British administration)

National holiday: Independence Day, 14 May (1948); note—Israel declared independence on 14 May 1948, but the Jewish calendar is lunar and the holiday may occur in April or May

Constitution: history: no formal constitution; some functions of a constitution are filled by the Declaration of Establishment (1948), the Basic Laws, and the Law of Return (as amended)

amendments: proposed by Government of Israel ministers or by the Knesset; passage requires a majority vote of Knesset members and subject to Supreme Court judicial review; 11 of the 13 Basic Laws have been amended at least once, latest in 2018 (2018)

Legal system: mixed legal system of English common law, British Mandate regulations, and Jewish, Christian, and Muslim religious laws

International law organization participation: has not submitted an ICJ jurisdiction declaration; withdrew acceptance of International Criminal Court jurisdiction in 2002

Citizenship: *citizenship by birth:* no

citizenship by descent only: at least one parent must be a citizen of Israel

dual citizenship recognized: yes, but naturalized citizens are not allowed to maintain dual citizenship

residency requirement for naturalization: 3 out of the 5 years preceding the application for naturalization

note: Israeli law (Law of Return, 5 July 1950) provides for the granting of citizenship to any Jew—defined as a person being born to a Jewish mother or having converted to Judaism while renouncing any other religion—who immigrates to and expresses a desire to settle in Israel on the basis of the Right of aliyah; the 1970 amendment of this act extended the right to family members including the spouse of a Jew, any child or grandchild, and the spouses of children and grandchildren

Suffrage: 18 years of age; universal; 17 years of age for municipal elections

Executive branch: *chief of state:* President Reuven RIVLIN (since 27 July 2014)

head of government: Prime Minister Binyamin NETANYAHU (since 31 March 2009)

cabinet: Cabinet selected by prime minister and approved by the Knesset

elections/appointments: president indirectly elected by the Knesset for a 7-year term (limited to 1 term); election last held on 10 June 2014 (next to be held in 2021 but can be called earlier); following legislative elections, the president, in consultation with party leaders, tasks a Knesset member (usually the member of the largest party) with forming a government

election results: Reuven RIVLIN elected president in second round; Knesset vote—Reuven RIVLIN (Likud) 63, Meir SHEETRIT (The Movement) 53, other/invalid 4

Legislative branch: *description:* unicameral Knesset (120 seats; members directly elected in a single nationwide constituency by proportional representation vote; members serve 4-year terms)

elections: last held on 17 March 2015 (next to be held by 5 November 2019 but can be called earlier)

election results: percent of vote by party—Likud 23.4%, Zionist Camp 18.7%, Joint List 10.5%, Yesh Atid 8.8%, Kulanu 7.5%, The Jewish Home 6.7%, Shas, 5.7%, Yisrael Beitenu 5.1%, UTJ 5.0%, Meretz 3.9%, Yachad 3.0%, other 1.7%; seats by party—Likud 30, Zionist Camp 24, Joint List 13, Yesh Atid 11, Kulanu 10, The Jewish Home 8, Shas 7, Yisrael Beitenu 6, UTJ 6, Meretz 5

Judicial branch: *highest court(s):* Supreme Court (consists of the chief justice and 14 judges)

judge selection and term of office: judges selected by the Judicial Selection Committee consisting of 3 Supreme Court judges, 2 Cabinet members including the Minister of Justice as chairman, 2 Knesset members, and 2 representatives from the Israel Bar Association; judges can serve up to mandatory retirement at age 70

subordinate courts: Court for Administrative Matters; district and magistrate courts; national and regional labor courts; special and religious courts

Political parties and leaders: Balad [Jamal ZAHALKA]

Democratic Front for Peace and Equality or HADASH [Ayman ODEH]

Israeli Labor Party [Avi GABBAY]

Joint List [Ayman ODEH] (coalition includes Balad, HADASH, United Arab List, and Ta'al))

Kulanu [Moshe KAHLON]

Likud [Binyamin NETANYAHU]

Meretz [Zehava GALON]

SHAS [Arye DERI]

Ta'al (Arab Movement for Renewal) [Ahmad TIBI]

Tekumah/National Union (Ichud Leumi) [Uri ARIEL]

The Jewish Home (Habayit Hayehudi) [Naftali BENNETT]

The Movement (Hatnuah) [Tzipora "Tzipi" LIVNI]

United Arab List [Masud GANAIM]

United Torah Judaism or UTJ [Yaakov LITZMAN] (an alliance of three parties)

Yachad [Eli YISHAI]

Yesh Atid [Yair LAPID]

Yisrael Beiteinu [Avigdor LIEBERMAN]

Political pressure groups and leaders: Breaking the Silence or BtS [Yehuda SHAUL] collects testimonies from soldiers who served in the West Bank and Gaza Strip

B'Tselem [Hagai EL-AD] (monitors human rights abuses)

Peace Now [Yariv OPPENHEIMER] (supports territorial concessions in the West Bank and Gaza Strip)

YESHA Council [Avi ROEHD] (promotes settler interests and opposes territorial compromise)

International organization participation: BIS, BSEC (observer), CE (observer), CERN, CICA, EBRD, FAO, IADB, IAEA, IBRD, ICAO, ICC (national committees), ICRM, IDA, IFAD, IFC, IFRCS, ILO, IMF, IMO, IMSO, Interpol, IOC, IOM, IPU, ISO, ITSO, ITU, ITUC (NGOs), MIGA, OAS (observer), OECD, OPCW (signatory), OSCE (partner), Pacific Alliance (observer), Paris Club, PCA, SELEC (observer), UN, UNCTAD, UNESCO, UNHCR, UNIDO, UNWTO, UPU, WCO, WHO, WIPO, WMO, WTO

Diplomatic representation in the US: *chief of mission:* Ambassador Ron DERMER (since 3 December 2013)
chancery: 3514 International Drive NW, Washington, DC 20008
telephone: [1] (202) 364-5500
FAX: [1] (202) 364-5607
consulate(s) general: Atlanta, Boston, Chicago, Houston, Los Angeles, Miami, New York, Philadelphia, San Francisco

Diplomatic representation from the US: *chief of mission:* Ambassador David FRIEDMAN (since 23 May 2017)
embassy: 71 HaYarkon Street, Tel Aviv 6343229
telephone: [972] (3) 519-7475
FAX: [972] (3) 516-4390
consular agent: Haifa

Flag description: white with a blue hexagram (six-pointed linear star) known as the Magen David (Star of David or Shield of David) centered between two equal horizontal blue bands near the top and bottom edges of the flag; the basic design resembles a traditional Jewish prayer shawl (tallit), which is white with blue stripes; the hexagram as a Jewish symbol dates back to medieval times
note: the Israeli flag proclamation states that the flag colors are sky blue and white, but the exact shade of blue has never been set and can vary from a light to a dark blue

National symbol(s): Star of David (Magen David), menorah (seven-branched lampstand); national colors: blue, white

National anthem: name: "Hatikvah" (The Hope)
lyrics/music: Naftali Herz IMBER/traditional, arranged by Samuel COHEN
note: adopted 2004, unofficial since 1948; used as the anthem of the Zionist movement since 1897; the 1888 arrangement by Samuel COHEN is thought to be based on the Romanian folk song "Carul cu boi" (The Ox Driven Cart)

ECONOMY

Economy—overview: Israel has a technologically advanced free market economy. Cut diamonds, high-technology equipment, and pharmaceuticals are among its leading exports. Its major imports include crude oil, grains, raw materials, and military equipment. Israel usually posts sizable trade deficits, which are offset by tourism and other service exports, as well as significant foreign investment inflows.

Between 2004 and 2013, growth averaged nearly 5% per year, led by exports. The global financial crisis of 2008-09 spurred a brief recession in Israel, but the country entered the crisis with solid fundamentals, following years of prudent fiscal policy and a resilient banking sector. Israel's economy also weathered the 2011 Arab Spring because strong trade ties outside the Middle East insulated the economy from spillover effects.

Slowing domestic and international demand and decreased investment resulting from Israel's uncertain security situation reduced GDP growth to an average of roughly 2.8% per year during the period 2014-17. Natural gas fields discovered off Israel's coast since 2009 have brightened Israel's energy security outlook. The Tamar and Leviathan fields were some of the world's largest offshore natural gas finds in the last decade. Political and regulatory issues have delayed the development of the massive Leviathan field, but production from Tamar provided a 0.8% boost to Israel's GDP in 2013 and a 0.3% boost in 2014. One of the most carbon intense OECD countries, Israel generates about 57% of its power from coal and only 2.6% from renewable sources.

Income inequality and high housing and commodity prices continue to be a concern for many Israelis. Israel's income inequality and poverty rates are among the highest of OECD countries, and there is a broad perception among the public that a small number of "tycoons" have a cartel-like grip over the major parts of the economy. Government officials have called for reforms to boost the housing supply and to increase competition in the banking sector to address these public grievances. Despite calls for reforms, the restricted housing supply continues to impact the well-being of younger Israelis seeking to purchase homes. Tariffs and non-tariff barriers, coupled with guaranteed prices and customs tariffs for farmers kept food prices high in 2016. Private consumption is expected to drive growth through 2018 with consumers benefitting from low inflation and a strong currency.

In the long term, Israel faces structural issues, including low labor participation rates for its fastest growing social segments—the ultraorthodox and Arab-Israeli communities. Also, Israel's progressive, globally competitive, knowledge-based technology sector employs only about 8% of the workforce, with the rest mostly employed in manufacturing and services—sectors which face downward wage pressures from global competition. Expenditures on educational institutions remain low compared to most other OECD countries with similar GDP per capita.

GDP (purchasing power parity): $315.6 billion (2017 est.)
$306.1 billion (2016 est.)
$294.5 billion (2015 est.)
note: data are in 2017 dollars
country comparison to the world: 55

GDP (official exchange rate): $348 billion (2016 est.)

GDP—real growth rate: 3.1% (2017 est.)
4% (2016 est.)
2.6% (2015 est.)
country comparison to the world: 111

GDP—per capita (PPP): $36,200 (2017 est.)
$35,800 (2016 est.)
$35,200 (2015 est.)
note: data are in 2017 dollars
country comparison to the world: 53

Gross national saving: 24.2% of GDP (2017 est.)

24.1% of GDP (2016 est.)
24.6% of GDP (2015 est.)
country comparison to the world: 58

GDP—composition, by end use:
household consumption: 55.4%
government consumption: 22%
investment in fixed capital: 20.5%
investment in inventories: 0.2%
exports of goods and services: 29.8%
imports of goods and services: -27.9% (2017 est.)

GDP—composition, by sector of origin:
agriculture: 2.3%
industry: 26.6%
services: 69.5% (2017 est.)

Agriculture—products: citrus, vegetables, cotton; beef, poultry, dairy products

Industries: high-technology products (including aviation, communications, computer-aided design and manufactures, medical electronics, fiber optics), wood and paper products, potash and phosphates, food, beverages, and tobacco, caustic soda, cement, pharmaceuticals, construction, metal products, chemical products, plastics, cut diamonds, textiles, footwear

Industrial production growth rate: 4% (2017 est.)
country comparison to the world: 68

Labor force: 4.021 million (2017 est.)
country comparison to the world: 93

Labor force—by occupation: *agriculture:* 1.1%
industry: 17.3%
services: 81.6% (2015)

Unemployment rate: 4.3% (2017 est.)
4.8% (2016 est.)
country comparison to the world: 56

Population below poverty line: 22%
note: Israel's poverty line is $7.30 per person per day (2014 est.)

Household income or consumption by percentage share: *lowest 10%:* 1.7%
highest 10%: 31.3% (2010)

Distribution of family income—Gini index: 42.8 (2013)
39.2 (2008)
country comparison to the world: 47

Budget: *revenues:* $92.82 billion
expenditures: $102.1 billion (2017 est.)
Taxes and other revenues: 26.7% of GDP (2017 est.)
country comparison to the world: 106

Budget surplus (+) or deficit (-): -2.7% of GDP (2017 est.)
country comparison to the world: 104

Public debt: 59.5% of GDP (2017 est.)
60.7% of GDP (2016 est.)
country comparison to the world: 75

Fiscal year: calendar year

Inflation rate (consumer prices): 0.2% (2017 est.)
-0.5% (2016 est.)
country comparison to the world: 15

Central bank discount rate: 0.1% (15 December 2015)
0.25% (31 December 2014)

country comparison to the world: 144

Commercial bank prime lending rate: 3.3% (31 December 2017 est.)
3.42% (31 December 2016 est.)
country comparison to the world: 166

Stock of narrow money: $98.28 billion (31 December 2017 est.)
$79.58 billion (31 December 2016 est.)
country comparison to the world: 40

Stock of broad money: $223.1 billion (31 December 2017 est.)
$189 billion (31 December 2016 est.)
country comparison to the world: 37

Stock of domestic credit: $280.8 billion (31 December 2017 est.)
$257.5 billion (31 December 2016 est.)
country comparison to the world: 40

Market value of publicly traded shares: $243.9 billion (31 December 2015 est.)
$200.5 billion (31 December 2014 est.)
$203.3 billion (31 December 2013 est.)
country comparison to the world: 31

Current account balance: $14.28 billion (2017 est.)
$11.57 billion (2016 est.)
country comparison to the world: 19

Exports: $60.6 billion (2017 est.)
$56.17 billion (2016 est.)
country comparison to the world: 46

Exports—commodities: machinery and equipment, software, cut diamonds, agricultural products, chemicals, textiles and apparel

Exports—partners: US 29.3%, Hong Kong 7.4%, UK 6.5%, China 5.5%, Belgium 4.2% (2016)

Imports: $66.76 billion (2017 est.)
$63.54 billion (2016 est.)
country comparison to the world: 44

Imports—commodities: raw materials, military equipment, investment goods, rough diamonds, fuels, grain, consumer goods

Imports—partners: US 12.2%, China 8.9%, Switzerland 6.4%, Germany 6.1%, Belgium 5.9%, UK 5.5%, Netherlands 4.1%, Italy 4% (2016)

Reserves of foreign exchange and gold: $113 billion (31 December 2017 est.)
$95.45 billion (31 December 2016 est.)
country comparison to the world: 24

Debt—external: $93.02 billion (31 December 2017 est.)
$87.96 billion (31 December 2016 est.)
country comparison to the world: 51

Stock of direct foreign investment—at home: $119.4 billion (31 December 2017 est.)
$107.3 billion (31 December 2016 est.)
country comparison to the world: 43

Stock of direct foreign investment—abroad: $106.9 billion (31 December 2017 est.)
$98.11 billion (31 December 2016 est.)
country comparison to the world: 35

Exchange rates: new Israeli shekels (ILS) per US dollar—
3.606 (2017 est.)

3.8406 (2016 est.)
3.8406 (2015 est.)
3.8869 (2014 est.)
3.5779 (2013 est.)

ENERGY

Electricity access: *electrification—total population:* 100% (2016)

Electricity—production: 60.44 billion kWh (2015 est.)
country comparison to the world: 48

Electricity—consumption: 52.78 billion kWh (2015 est.)
country comparison to the world: 49

Electricity—exports: 5.2 billion kWh (2016 est.)
country comparison to the world: 36

Electricity—imports: 0 kWh (2016 est.)
country comparison to the world: 162

Electricity—installed generating capacity: 17.22 million kW (2015 est.)
country comparison to the world: 47

Electricity—from fossil fuels: 95.5% of total installed capacity (2015 est.)
country comparison to the world: 53

Electricity—from nuclear fuels: 0% of total installed capacity (2015 est.)
country comparison to the world: 112

Electricity—from hydroelectric plants: 0% of total installed capacity (2015 est.)
country comparison to the world: 181

Electricity—from other renewable sources: 4.9% of total installed capacity (2015 est.)
country comparison to the world: 99

Crude oil—production: 390 bbl/day (2016 est.)
country comparison to the world: 95

Crude oil—exports: 0 bbl/day (2016 est.)
country comparison to the world: 141

Crude oil—imports: 215,600 bbl/day (2016 est.)
country comparison to the world: 30

Crude oil—proved reserves: 12.73 million bbl (1 January 2017 es)
country comparison to the world: 90

Refined petroleum products—production: 278,300 bbl/day (2016 est.)
country comparison to the world: 44

Refined petroleum products—consumption: 199,900 bbl/day (2016 est.)
country comparison to the world: 56

Refined petroleum products—exports: 115,700 bbl/day (2016 est.)
country comparison to the world: 41

Refined petroleum products—imports: 98,020 bbl/day (2016 est.)
country comparison to the world: 58

Natural gas—production: 8.5 billion cu m (2015 est.)
country comparison to the world: 45

Natural gas—consumption: 13.61 billion cu m (2015 est.)
country comparison to the world: 49

Natural gas—exports: 2.605 billion cu m (2011 est.)
country comparison to the world: 36

Natural gas—imports: 160 million cu m (2015 est.)
country comparison to the world: 73

Natural gas—proved reserves: 176 billion cu m (1 January 2017 es)
country comparison to the world: 47

Carbon dioxide emissions from consumption of energy: 62.5 million Mt (2014 est.)
country comparison to the world: 54

COMMUNICATIONS

Telephones—fixed lines: *total subscriptions:* 3,340,223
subscriptions per 100 inhabitants: 41 (July 2016 est.)
country comparison to the world: 50

Telephones—mobile cellular: *total:* 10.57 million
subscriptions per 100 inhabitants: 129 (July 2016 est.)
country comparison to the world: 88

Telephone system: *general assessment:* most highly developed system in the Middle East
domestic: good system of coaxial cable and microwave radio relay; all systems are digital; competition among both fixed-line and mobile cellular providers results in good coverage countrywide; Israeli cellular providers upgraded to 4G in 2014
international: country code—972; submarine cables provide links to Europe, Cyprus, and parts of the Middle East; satellite earth stations—3 Intelsat (2 Atlantic Ocean and 1 Indian Ocean) (2018)

Broadcast media: state broadcasting network, operated by the Israel Broadcasting Authority (IBA), broadcasts on 2 channels, one in Hebrew and the other in Arabic; 5 commercial channels including a channel broadcasting in Russian, a channel broadcasting Knesset proceedings, and a music channel supervised by a public body; multichannel satellite and cable TV packages provide access to foreign channels; IBA broadcasts on 8 radio networks with multiple repeaters and Israel Defense Forces Radio broadcasts over multiple stations; about 15 privately owned radio stations; overall more than 100 stations and repeater stations (2008)

Internet country code: .il
Internet users: total: 6,521,539

percent of population: 79.8% (July 2016 est.)
country comparison to the world: 58

TRANSPORTATION

National air transport system: *number of registered air carriers:* 6
inventory of registered aircraft operated by air carriers: 60
annual passenger traffic on registered air carriers: 6,064,478
annual freight traffic on registered air carriers: 758,633,996 mt-km (2015)

Civil aircraft registration country code prefix: 4X (2016)

Airports: 47 (2013)
country comparison to the world: 94

Airports—with paved runways: total: 29
over 3,047 m: 2
2,438 to 3,047 m: 5
1,524 to 2,437 m: 6
914 to 1,523 m: 11
under 914 m: 5 (2017)

Airports—with unpaved runways: total: 18
1,524 to 2,437 m: 1
914 to 1,523 m: 3
under 914 m: 14 (2013)

Heliports: 3 (2013)

Pipelines: gas 763 km; oil 442 km; refined products 261 km (2013)

Railways: total: 1,250 km
standard gauge: 1,250 km 1.435-m gauge (2014)
country comparison to the world: 83

Roadways: total: 18,566 km
paved: 18,566 km (includes 449 km of expressways) (2011)
country comparison to the world: 115

Merchant marine: total: 42
by type: container ship 5, general cargo 4, oil tanker 3, other 30 (2017)
country comparison to the world: 116

Ports and terminals: major seaport(s): Ashdod, Elat (Eilat), Hadera, Haifa
container port(s) (TEUs): Ashdod (1,176,000), Haifa (1,238,000)

MILITARY AND SECURITY

Military expenditures: 5.64% of GDP (2016)
5.6% of GDP (2015)
5.86% of GDP (2014)
5.75% of GDP (2013)
5.72% of GDP (2012)
country comparison to the world: 5

Military branches: Israel Defense Forces (IDF), Israel Naval Force (IN), Israel Air Force (IAF) (2010)

Military service age and obligation: 18 years of age for compulsory (Jews, Druze) military service; 17 years of age for voluntary (Christians, Muslims, Circassians) military service; both sexes are obligated to military service; conscript service obligation—32 months for enlisted men and 24 months for enlisted women (varies based on military occupation), 48 months for officers; pilots commit to 9-year service; reserve obligation to age 41-51 (men), age 24 (women) (2015)

TERRORISM

Terrorist groups—home based: *Kahane Chai (Kach):* aim(s): expel Arabs from Israel's biblical lands and, ultimately, restore the biblical state of Israel
area(s) of operation: Israel and West Bank settlements, where operatives have conducted bombings and shootings against Israeli Arabs and Palestinians; considered to be operationally inactive in recent years

Terrorist groups—foreign based: *Abdallah Azzam Brigades (AAB):* aim(s): disrupt Israel's efforts to establish security
area(s) of operation: responsible over the years for numerous lethal rocket attacks fired into Israeli territory from Lebanon into densely populated areas, especially Nahariyya and Ashqelon

Al-Aqsa Martyrs Brigade (AAMB): aim(s): drive the Israeli military and West Bank settlers from the West Bank and impel Israelis to leave Jerusalem and, ultimately, establish a Palestinian state comprising the West Bank, Gaza Strip, and Jerusalem
area(s) of operation: launches rockets and missiles into southern Israel from the Gaza Strip; conducts suicide bombings in Tel Aviv and Jerusalem; on 27 January 2002, operative Wafa IDRIS became the first known Palestinian female suicide bomber and the first known female suicide bomber to conduct an attack inside Israel, when she detonated her vest in Jerusalem, killing an 81-year-old woman and wounding at least 100 other people

Army of Islam (AOI): aim(s): disrupt Israel's efforts to provide security and, ultimately, destroy the state of Israel to establish a regional Islamic caliphate

area(s) of operation: has a history of launching rocket attacks into Israeli territory mostly from the Gaza Strip; attacks have ebbed in recent years

Hizballah: aim(s): destroy the state of Israel
area(s) of operation: has been operational across Israel at various times since Hizballah's inception in 1982, especially in the north, and launching numerous rockets and other airborne projectiles and devices into Israeli towns in many regions; on 12 July 2006, a 34-day military conflict between Hizballah and Israel was precipitated when Hizballah fired rockets on several Israeli towns, while operatives crossed into northern Israel from southern Lebanon to attack an Israeli army convoy, killing eight and abducting two soldiers; intense fighting took place in Lebanon, northern Israel, and the Golan Heights until a UN-brokered ceasefire went into effect on 14 August 2006; responsible for hundreds of Israeli deaths over the years

ISIL Sinai Province (formerly Ansar Bayt al-Maqdis): aim(s): destroy the state of Israel and, ultimately, establish a regional Islamic caliphate

area(s) of operation: launches rockets into southern Israel from the Sinai Peninsula, primarily in the Eshkol region and approaching the southern city of Elat; outlawed in Israel

HAMAS: aim(s): lift Israel's blockade surrounding the Gaza Strip and, ultimately, destroy the state of Israel
area(s) of operation: operatives have launched tens of thousands of projectiles directed at Israeli urban areas over the years, resulting in numerous long-running lethal conflicts between HAMAS and Israeli forces; primarily stages projectile attacks from the Gaza Strip into Israel; regularly digs underground tunnels leading to Israeli territory for the purpose of smuggling fighters or supplies in and out of the country; on 25 June 2006, operatives kidnapped Israeli soldier Corporal Gilad SCHALIT near the Kerem Shalom crossing in southern Israel and held him until 18 October 2011, when he was released as part of a prisoner exchange; two soldiers were killed and two others injured during the kidnapping

Mujahidin Shura Council in the Environs of Jerusalem (MSC): aim(s): destroy the state of Israel
area(s) of operation: primarily operational in the south, with a limited presence by 2017; the majority of veteran members have defected to join other groups; had previously participated in numerous rocket attacks into southern Israel's populated areas, such as Sderot, from the Gaza Strip and Egypt; most of the launchings were in coordination alongside the Army of Islam (AOI), another US-designated foreign terrorist organization

Palestinian Islamic Jihad (PIJ): aim(s): committed to the destruction of Israel and creation of an Islamic state in all of historic Palestine as defined by the British Mandate, including contemporary Israel, the Gaza Strip, and the West Bank
area(s) of operation: launches attacks from the Gaza Strip into Israel; responsible for thousands of rocket attacks and numerous suicide bombings against Israeli civilians and military personnel over the years, primarily in southern Israel; PIJ's first female suicide bomber killed 22 people and wounded 60 others on 2 October 2003, when she detonated a powerful explosive at the Maxim Restaurant in Haifa

Palestine Liberation Front (PLF): aim(s): destroy Israel and, ultimately, establish a Palestinian state
area(s) of operation: maintains a limited operational presence; until recent years, operatives conducted occasional shooting and IED attacks against Israeli military and security targets inside Israel, including bombing Israeli planes

PFLP-General Command (PFLP-GC): aim(s): destroy the state of Israel
area(s) of operation: primarily northern Israel; attacks have ebbed in recent years

Popular Front for the Liberation of Palestine (PFLP): aim(s): destroy the state of Israel and, ultimately, establish a secular, Marxist Palestinian state
area(s) of operation: mostly active near Jerusalem; on 18 November 2014, four members with guns, axes, and knives stormed the Kehilat Bnei Torah Synagogue in West Jerusalem, during prayer services, killing four rabbis and a congregant and wounding at least eight; responsible for several attacks on citizens over the years

TRANSNATIONAL ISSUES

Disputes—international: West Bank and Gaza Strip are Israeli-occupied with current status subject to the Israeli-Palestinian Interim Agreement—permanent status to be determined through further negotiation; Israel continues construction of a "seam line" separation barrier along parts of the Green Line and within the

West Bank; Israel withdrew its settlers and military from the Gaza Strip and from four settlements in the West Bank in August 2005; Golan Heights is Israeli-occupied (Lebanon claims the Shab'a Farms area of Golan Heights); since 1948, about 350 peacekeepers from the UN Truce Supervision Organization headquartered in Jerusalem monitor ceasefires, supervise armistice agreements, prevent isolated incidents from escalating, and assist other UN personnel in the region

Refugees and internally displaced persons: refugees (country of origin): 27,812 (Eritrea) (2016)

stateless persons: 42 (2016)

Illicit drugs: increasingly concerned about ecstasy, cocaine, and heroin abuse; drugs arrive in country from Lebanon and, increasingly, from Jordan; money-laundering center

ITALY

INTRODUCTION

Background: Italy became a nation-state in 1861 when the regional states of the peninsula, along with Sardinia and Sicily, were united under King Victor EMMANUEL II. An era of parliamentary government came to a close in the early 1920s when Benito MUSSOLINI established a Fascist dictatorship. His alliance with Nazi Germany led to Italy's defeat in World War II. A democratic republic replaced the monarchy in 1946 and economic revival followed. Italy is a charter member of NATO and the European Economic Community (EEC) and its subsequent successors the EC and the EU. It has been at the forefront of European economic and political unification, joining the Economic and Monetary Union in 1999. Persistent problems include sluggish economic growth, high youth and female unemployment, organized crime, corruption, and economic disparities between southern Italy and the more prosperous north.

GEOGRAPHY

Location: Southern Europe, a peninsula extending into the central Mediterranean Sea, northeast of Tunisia

Geographic coordinates: 42 50 N, 12 50 E

Map references: Europe

Area: *total:* 301,340 sq km
land: 294,140 sq km
water: 7,200 sq km
note: includes Sardinia and Sicily
country comparison to the world: 73

Area—comparative: almost twice the size of Georgia; slightly larger than Arizona

Land boundaries: *total:* 1,836.4 km
border countries (6): Austria 404 km, France 476 km, Holy See (Vatican City) 3.4 km, San Marino 37 km, Slovenia 218 km, Switzerland 698 km

Coastline: 7,600 km

Maritime claims: *territorial sea:* 12 nm
continental shelf: 200-m depth or to the depth of exploitation

Climate: predominantly Mediterranean; alpine in far north; hot, dry in south

Terrain: mostly rugged and mountainous; some plains, coastal lowlands

Elevation: *mean elevation:* 538 m

elevation extremes: *lowest point:* Mediterranean Sea 0 m
highest point: Mont Blanc (Monte Bianco) de Courmayeur 4,748 m (a secondary peak of Mont Blanc)

Natural resources: coal, mercury, zinc, potash, marble, barite, asbestos, pumice, fluorspar, feldspar, pyrite (sulfur), natural gas and crude oil reserves, fish, arable land

Land use: *agricultural land:* 47.1%
arable land: 22.8%;
permanent crops: 8.6%;
permanent pasture: 15.7%
forest: 31.4%
other: 21.5% (2011 est.)
Irrigated land: 39,500 sq km (2012)

Population—distribution: despite a distinctive pattern with an industrial north and an agrarian south, a fairly even population distribution exists throughout most of the country, with coastal areas, the Po River Valley, and urban centers (particularly Milan, Rome, and Naples), attracting larger and denser populations

Natural hazards: regional risks include landslides, mudflows, avalanches, earthquakes, volcanic eruptions, flooding; land subsidence in Venice
volcanism: significant volcanic activity; Etna (3,330 m), which is in eruption as of 2010, is Europe's most active volcano; flank eruptions pose a threat to nearby Sicilian villages; Etna, along with the famous Vesuvius, which remains a threat to the millions of nearby residents in the Bay of Naples area, have both been deemed Decade Volcanoes by the International Association of Volcanology and Chemistry of the Earth's Interior, worthy of study due to their explosive history and close

proximity to human populations; Stromboli, on its namesake island, has also been continuously active with moderate volcanic activity; other historically active volcanoes include Campi Flegrei, Ischia, Larderello, Pantelleria, Vulcano, and Vulsini

Environment—current issues: air pollution from industrial emissions such as sulfur dioxide; coastal and inland rivers polluted from industrial and agricultural effluents; acid rain damaging lakes; inadequate industrial waste treatment and disposal facilities

Environment—international agreements: *party to:* Air Pollution, Air Pollution-Nitrogen Oxides, Air Pollution-Persistent Organic Pollutants, Air Pollution-Sulfur 85, Air Pollution-Sulfur 94, Air Pollution-Volatile Organic Compounds, Antarctic-Environmental Protocol, Antarctic-Marine Living Resources, Antarctic Seals, Antarctic Treaty, Biodiversity, Climate Change, Climate Change-Kyoto Protocol, Desertification, Endangered Species, Environmental Modification, Hazardous Wastes, Law of the Sea, Marine Dumping, Ozone Layer Protection, Ship Pollution, Tropical Timber 83, Tropical Timber 94, Wetlands, Whaling
signed, but not ratified: none of the selected agreements

Geography—note: strategic location dominating central Mediterranean as well as southern sea and air approaches to Western Europe

PEOPLE AND SOCIETY

Population: 62,137,802 (July 2017 est.)
country comparison to the world: 23

Nationality: *noun:* Italian(s)
adjective: Italian

Ethnic groups: Italian (includes small clusters of German-, French-, and Slovene-Italians in the north and Albanian-Italians and Greek-Italians in the south)

Languages: Italian (official), German (parts of Trentino-Alto Adige region are predominantly German speaking), French (small French-speaking minority in Valle d'Aosta region), Slovene (Slovene-speaking minority in the Trieste-Gorizia area)

Religions: Christian 80% (overwhelmingly Roman Catholic with very small groups of Jehovah's Witnesses and Protestants), Muslim (about 800,000 to 1 million), atheist and agnostic 20%

Age structure: *0-14 years:* 13.65% (male 4,334,457/female 4,146,726)

15-24 years: 9.66% (male 3,008,228/female 2,996,854)

25-54 years: 42.16% (male 12,933,634/female 13,265,541)

55-64 years: 12.99% (male 3,914,061/female 4,159,859)

65 years and over: 21.53% (male 5,758,197/female 7,620,245) (2017 est.)

Dependency ratios: *total dependency ratio:* 56.5
youth dependency ratio: 21.5
elderly dependency ratio: 35
potential support ratio: 2.9 (2015 est.)

Median age: *total:* 45.5 years
male: 44.4 years
female: 46.5 years (2017 est.)
country comparison to the world: 6

Population growth rate: 0.19% (2017 est.)
country comparison to the world: 183

Birth rate: 8.6 births/1,000 population (2017 est.)
country comparison to the world: 215

Death rate: 10.4 deaths/1,000 population (2017 est.)
country comparison to the world: 32

Net migration rate: 3.7 migrant(s)/1,000 population (2017 est.)
country comparison to the world: 31

Population distribution: despite a distinctive pattern with an industrial north and an agrarian south, a fairly even population distribution exists throughout most of the country, with coastal areas, the Po River Valley, and urban centers (particularly Milan, Rome, and Naples), attracting larger and denser populations

Urbanization: *urban population:* 69.3% of total population (2017)
rate of urbanization: 0.32% annual rate of change (2015-20 est.)

Major urban areas—population: ROME (capital) 3.718 million; Milan 3.099 million; Naples 2.202 million; Turin 1.765 million; Palermo 853,000; Bergamo 840,000 (2015)

Sex ratio: *at birth:* 1.06 male(s)/female
0-14 years: 1.04 male(s)/female
15-24 years: 1 male(s)/female
25-54 years: 0.98 male(s)/female
55-64 years: 0.94 male(s)/female
65 years and over: 0.75 male(s)/female
total population: 0.93 male(s)/female (2016 est.)

Mother's mean age at first birth: 30.7 years (2014 est.)

Maternal mortality ratio: 4 deaths/100,000 live births (2015 est.)
country comparison to the world: 178

Infant mortality rate: *total:* 3.3 deaths/1,000 live births
male: 3.5 deaths/1,000 live births
female: 3 deaths/1,000 live births (2017 est.)
country comparison to the world: 210

Life expectancy at birth: *total population:* 82.3 years
male: 79.6 years
female: 85.1 years (2017 est.)
country comparison to the world: 15

Total fertility rate: 1.44 children born/woman (2017 est.)
country comparison to the world: 206

Health expenditures: 9.2% of GDP (2014)
country comparison to the world: 36

Physicians density: 3.95 physicians/1,000 population (2014)

Hospital bed density: 3.4 beds/1,000 population (2011)

Drinking water source:
improved:
urban: 100% of population
rural: 100% of population
total: 100% of population
unimproved:
urban: 0% of population
rural: 0% of population
total: 0% of population (2015 est.)

Sanitation facility access:
improved:
urban: 99.5% of population
rural: 99.6% of population
total: 99.5% of population
unimproved:: urban: 0.5% of population
rural: 0.4% of population
total: 0.5% of population (2015 est.)

HIV/AIDS—adult prevalence rate: 0.3% (2016 est.)
country comparison to the world: 85

HIV/AIDS—people living with HIV/AIDS: 130,000 (2016 est.)
country comparison to the world: 34

HIV/AIDS—deaths: Obesity—adult prevalence rate: 19.9% (2016)
country comparison to the world: 107

Education expenditures: 4.2% of GDP (2013)
country comparison to the world: 93

Literacy: *definition:* age 15 and over can read and write
total population: 99.2%
male: 99.4%
female: 99% (2015 est.)

School life expectancy (primary to tertiary education): *total:* 16 years
male: 16 years
female: 17 years (2014)

Unemployment, youth ages 15-24: *total:* 40.3%
male: 38.8%
female: 42.6% (2015 est.)
country comparison to the world: 17

GOVERNMENT

Country name: *conventional long form:* Italian Republic
conventional short form: Italy
local long form: Repubblica Italiana
local short form: Italia
former: Kingdom of Italy
etymology: derivation is unclear, but the Latin "Italia" may come from the Oscan "Viteliu" meaning "[Land] of Young Cattle" (the bull was a symbol of southern Italic tribes)

Government type: parliamentary republic

Capital: name: Rome

geographic coordinates: 41 54 N, 12 29 E
time difference: UTC+1 (6 hours ahead of Washington, DC, during Standard Time)
daylight saving time: +1hr, begins last Sunday in March; ends last Sunday in October

Administrative divisions: 15 regions (regioni, singular—regione) and 5 autonomous regions (regioni autonome, singular—regione autonoma)
regions: Abruzzo, Basilicata, Calabria, Campania, Emilia-Romagna, Lazio (Latium), Liguria, Lombardia, Marche, Molise, Piemonte (Piedmont), Puglia (Apulia), Toscana (Tuscany), Umbria, Veneto
autonomous regions: Friuli-Venezia Giulia; Sardegna (Sardinia); Sicilia (Sicily); Trentino-Alto Adige (Trentino-South Tyrol) or Trentino-Suedtirol (German); Valle d'Aosta (Aosta Valley) or Vallee d'Aoste (French)

Independence: 17 March 1861 (Kingdom of Italy proclaimed; Italy was not finally unified until 1871)

National holiday: Republic Day, 2 June (1946)

Constitution: history: previous 1848 (originally for the Kingdom of Sardinia and adopted by the Kingdom of Italy in 1861); latest enacted 22 December 1947, adopted 27 December 1947, entered into force 1 January 1948
amendments: proposed by both houses of Parliament; passage requires two successive debates and approval by absolute majority of each house on the second vote; a referendum is only required when requested by one-fifth of the members of either house, by voter petition, or by five Regional Councils (elected legislative assemblies of the 15 first-level administrative regions and 5 autonomous regions of Italy); referendum not required if an amendment has been approved by a two-thirds majority in each house in the second vote; amended many times, last in 2012; note—a referendum held on 4 December 2016 on constitutional amendments was defeated (2017)

Legal system: civil law system; judicial review of legislation under certain conditions in Constitutional Court

International law organization participation: accepts compulsory ICJ jurisdiction with reservations; accepts ICCt jurisdiction

Citizenship: *citizenship by birth:* no
citizenship by descent only: at least one parent must be a citizen of Italy
dual citizenship recognized: yes
residency requirement for naturalization: 4 years for EU nationals, 5 years for refugees and specified exceptions, 10 years for all others

Suffrage: 18 years of age; universal except in senatorial elections, where minimum age is 25

Executive branch: *chief of state:* President Sergio MATTARELLA (since 3 February 2015)

head of government: Prime Minister Paolo GENTILONI (since 12 December 2016); the prime minister's official title is President of the Council of Ministers
cabinet: Council of Ministers proposed by the prime minister, known officially as the President of the Council of Ministers and locally as the Premier; nominated by the president

elections/appointments: president indirectly elected by an electoral college consisting of both houses of Parliament and 58 regional representatives for a 7-year term (no term limits); election last held on 31 January 2015 (next to be held in 2022); prime minister appointed by the president, confirmed by parliament

election results: Sergio MATTARELLA (PD) elected president; electoral college vote count in fourth round—665 out of 1,009 (505-vote threshold)

Legislative branch: *description:* bicameral Parliament or Parlamento consists of the Senate or Senato della Repubblica (322 seats; 315 members directly elected in single- and multi-seat constituencies by proportional representation vote to serve 5-year terms and 7 ex-officio members appointed by the president of the Republic to serve for life) and the Chamber of Deputies or Camera dei Deputati (630 seats; 629 members directly elected in single- and multi-seat constituencies by proportional representation vote and 1 member from Valle d'Aosta elected by simple majority vote; members serve 5-year terms)

elections: Senate—last held on 24-25 February 2013 (next to be held by 20 May 2018); Chamber of Deputies—last held on 24-25 February 2013 (next to be held by 4 March 2018); President MATTARELLA dissolved parliament on 28 December 2017, triggering an early election

election results: Senate—percent of vote by party—NA; seats by party—center-left coalition 123 (PD 111, SEL 7, SVP 2, other 3), center-right coalition 117 (PdL 98, LN 18, other 1), M5S 54, centrist coalition 19, other 2

Chamber of Deputies—percent of vote by party—NA; seats by party—center-left coalition 345 (PD 297, SEL 37, CD 6 SVP 5), center-right coalition 125 (PdL 98, LN 18, FdI-AN 9), M5S 109, centrist coalition 47, other 3

Judicial branch: *highest court(s):* Supreme Court of Cassation or Corte Suprema di Cassazione consists of the first president (chief justice), deputy president, 54 justices presiding over 6 civil and 7 criminal divisions, and 288 judges; an additional 30 judges of lower courts serve as supporting judges; cases normally heard by 5-judge panels; more complex cases heard by 9-judge panels; Constitutional Court or Corte Costituzionale (consists of the court president and 14 judges)

judge selection and term of office: Supreme Court judges appointed by the High Council of the Judiciary, headed by the president of the republic; judges may serve for life; Constitutional Court judges—5 appointed by the president, 5 elected by parliament, 5 elected by select higher courts; judges serve up to 9 years

subordinate courts: various lower civil and criminal courts (primary and secondary tribunals, courts, and courts of appeal)

Political parties and leaders: Ruling left-center-right coalition: Civic Choice or SC [Enrico ZANETTI]
Democratic Centre or CD [Bruno TABACCI]
Democratic Party or PD [Matteo RENZI]
Popular Alliance or AP [Angelino ALFANO] (formerly New Center-Right or NCD)
Union of the Center or UdC [Pier Fernando CASSINI]

Center-right opposition: Brothers of Italy-National Alliance or FdI-AN [Giorgia MELONI, Ignazio LA RUSSA, and Guido CROSETTO]
Forza Italia or FI [Silvio BERLUSCONI] (formerly People of Freedom or PdL)
Northern League or LN [Matteo SALVINI]
Other parties and parliamentary groups: Five Star Movement or M5S [Luigi DI MAIO]
Liberal Popular Alliance or ALA [Denis VERDINI]
Democratic and Progressive Movement or MDP [Roberto SPERANZA]
Sinistra Italiani or SI [Nicola FRATOIANNI] (formerly Sinistra Ecologia Liberta or SEL)
South Tyrolean People's Party or SVP [Philipp ACHAMMER]

Political pressure groups and leaders: manufacturers and merchants associations: Confcommercio Confindustria
organized farm groups: Confcoltivatori Confagricoltura
major trade union confederations: Confederazione Generale Italiana del Lavoro or CGIL [Susanna CAMUSSO] (left wing)
Confederazione Italiana dei Sindacati Lavoratori or CISL [Raffaele BONANNI] (Roman Catholic centrist)
Unione Italiana del Lavoro or UIL [Luigi ANGELETTI] (lay centrist)
other: Roman Catholic Church

International organization participation: ADB (nonregional member), AfDB (nonregional member), Arctic Council (observer), Australia Group, BIS, BSEC (observer), CBSS (observer), CD, CDB, CE, CEI, CERN, EAPC, EBRD, ECB, EIB, EITI (implementing country), EMU, ESA, EU, FAO, FATF, G-7, G-8, G-10, G-20, IADB, IAEA, IBRD, ICAO, ICC (national committees), ICCt, ICRM, IDA, IEA, IFAD, IFC, IFRCS, IGAD (partners), IHO, ILO, IMF, IMO, IMSO, Interpol, IOC, IOM, IPU, ISO, ITSO, ITU, ITUC (NGOs), LAIA (observer), MIGA, MINURSO, MINUSMA, NATO, NEA, NSG, OAS (observer), OECD, OPCW, OSCE, Pacific Alliance (observer), Paris Club, PCA, PIF (partner), Schengen Convention, SELEC (observer), SICA (observer), UN, UN Security Council (temporary), UNCTAD, UNESCO, UNHCR, UNIDO, UNIFIL, Union Latina, UNMOGIP, UNRWA, UNTSO, UNWTO, UPU, WCO, WHO, WIPO, WMO, WTO, ZC

Diplomatic representation in the US: *chief of mission:* Ambassador Armando VARRICCHIO (since 2 March 2016)
chancery: 3000 Whitehaven Street NW, Washington, DC 20008
telephone: [1] (202) 612-4400
FAX: [1] (202) 518-2151
consulate(s) general: Boston, Chicago, Detroit, Houston, Miami, New York, Los Angeles, Philadelphia, San Francisco
consulate(s): Charlotte (NC), Cleveland (OH), Detroit (MI), Hattiesburg (MS), Honolulu (HI), New Orleans, Newark (NJ), Norfolk (VA), Pittsburgh (PA), Portland (OR), Seattle

Diplomatic representation from the US: *chief of mission:* Ambassador Lewis EISENBERG (since 4 October 2017); note—also accredited to San Marino

embassy: Via Vittorio Veneto 121, 00187-Rome
mailing address: PSC 59, Box 100, APO AE 09624
telephone: (+39)06.46741
FAX: [39] (06) 4674-2244
consulate(s) general: Florence, Milan, Naples

Flag description: three equal vertical bands of green (hoist side), white, and red; design inspired by the French flag brought to Italy by Napoleon in 1797; colors are those of Milan (red and white) combined with the green uniform color of the Milanese civic guard
note: similar to the flag of Mexico, which is longer, uses darker shades of red and green, and has its coat of arms centered on the white band; Ireland, which is longer and is green (hoist side), white, and orange; also similar to the flag of the Cote d'Ivoire, which has the colors reversed—orange (hoist side), white, and green

National symbol(s): white, five-pointed star (Stella d'Italia); national colors: red, white, green

National anthem: name: "Il Canto degli Italiani" (The Song of the Italians)
lyrics/music: Goffredo MAMELI/Michele NOVARO
note: adopted 1946; the anthem, originally written in 1847, is also known as "L'Inno di Mameli" (Mameli's Hymn), and "Fratelli D'Italia" (Brothers of Italy)

ECONOMY

Economy—overview: Italy's economy compromises a developed industrial north, dominated by private companies, and a less-developed, highly subsidized, agricultural south, with a legacy of unemployment and underdevelopment. The Italian economy is driven in large part by the manufacture of high-quality consumer goods produced by small and medium-sized enterprises, many of them family-owned. Italy also has a sizable underground economy, which by some estimates accounts for as much as 17% of GDP. These activities are most common within the agriculture, construction, and service sectors.

Italy is the third-largest economy in the euro zone, but its exceptionally high public debt and structural impediments to growth have rendered it vulnerable to scrutiny by financial markets. Public debt has increased steadily since 2007, reaching 131% of GDP in 2017. Investor concerns about Italy and the broader euro-zone crisis eased in 2013, bringing down Italy's borrowing costs on sovereign government debt from euro-era records. The government still faces pressure from investors and European partners to sustain its efforts to address Italy's longstanding structural economic problems, including labor market inefficiencies, a sluggish judicial system, and a weak banking sector. Italy's economy returned to modest growth in late 2014 for the first time since 2011. In 2015-16, Italy's economy grew at about 1% each year, and in 2017 growth accelerated to 1.5% of GDP. In 2017, overall unemployment was 11.4%, but youth unemployment remained high at 37.1%.

GDP (purchasing power parity): $2.307 trillion (2017 est.)

$2.273 trillion (2016 est.)
$2.253 trillion (2015 est.)
note: data are in 2017 dollars
country comparison to the world: 13

GDP (official exchange rate): $1.921 trillion (2016 est.)

GDP—real growth rate: 1.5% (2017 est.)
0.9% (2016 est.)
0.8% (2015 est.)
country comparison to the world: 175

GDP—per capita (PPP): $38,000 (2017 est.)
$37,500 (2016 est.)
$37,100 (2015 est.)
note: data are in 2017 dollars
country comparison to the world: 49

Gross national saving: 19.6% of GDP (2017 est.)
19.6% of GDP (2016 est.)
18.8% of GDP (2015 est.)
country comparison to the world: 94

GDP—composition, by end use:
household consumption: 60.2%
government consumption: 18.7%
investment in fixed capital: 17.2%
investment in inventories: 0.1%
exports of goods and services: 31.8%
imports of goods and services: -28% (2017 est.)

GDP—composition, by sector of origin:
agriculture: 2.1%
industry: 24%
services: 73.9% (2017 est.)

Agriculture—products: fruits, vegetables, grapes, potatoes, sugar beets, soybeans, grain, olives; beef, dairy products; fish

Industries: tourism, machinery, iron and steel, chemicals, food processing, textiles, motor vehicles, clothing, footwear, ceramics

Industrial production growth rate: 0.8% (2017 est.)
country comparison to the world: 172

Labor force: 25.94 million (2017 est.)
country comparison to the world: 25

Labor force—by occupation: *agriculture:* 3.9%
industry: 28.3%
services: 67.8% (2011)

Unemployment rate: 11.4% (2017 est.)
11.7% (2016 est.)
country comparison to the world: 146

Population below poverty line: 29.9% (2012 est.)

Household income or consumption by percentage share: *lowest 10%:* 2.3%
highest 10%: 26.8% (2000)

Distribution of family income—Gini index: 31.9 (2012 est.)
27.3 (1995)
country comparison to the world: 116

Budget: *revenues:* $884.4 billion
expenditures: $927.7 billion (2017 est.)
Taxes and other revenues: 46% of GDP (2017 est.)
country comparison to the world: 21

Budget surplus (+) or deficit (-): -2.3% of GDP (2017 est.)
country comparison to the world: 94

Public debt: 131.2% of GDP (2017 est.)
132.5% of GDP (2016 est.)
note: Italy reports its data on public debt according to guidelines set out in the Maastricht Treaty; general government gross debt is defined in the Maastricht Treaty as consolidated general government gross debt at nominal value, outstanding at the end of the year, in the following categories of government liabilities (as defined in ESA95): currency and deposits (AF.2), securities other than shares excluding financial derivatives (AF.3, excluding AF.34), and loans (AF.4); the general government sector comprises the central government, state government, local government and social security funds
country comparison to the world: 5

Fiscal year: calendar year

Inflation rate (consumer prices): 1.4% (2017 est.)
-0.1% (2016 est.)
country comparison to the world: 57

Central bank discount rate: 0.25% (31 December 2013)
0.75% (31 December 2012)
note: this is the European Central Bank's rate on the marginal lending facility, which offers overnight credit to banks in the euro area
country comparison to the world: 137

Commercial bank prime lending rate: 3.3% (31 December 2017 est.)
3.5% (31 December 2016 est.)
country comparison to the world: 167

Stock of narrow money: $1.238 trillion (31 December 2017 est.)
$1.101 trillion (31 December 2016 est.)
note: see entry for the European Union for money supply for the entire euro area; the European Central Bank (ECB) controls monetary policy for the 18 members of the Economic and Monetary Union (EMU); individual members of the EMU do not control the quantity of money circulating within their own borders
country comparison to the world: 7

Stock of broad money: $1.694 trillion (31 December 2017 est.)
$1.519 trillion (31 December 2016 est.)
country comparison to the world: 11

Stock of domestic credit: $3.264 trillion (31 December 2017 est.)
$3.024 trillion (31 December 2016 est.)
country comparison to the world: 7

Market value of publicly traded shares: $587.3 billion (31 December 2014 est.)
$615.5 billion (31 December 2013 est.)
$480.5 billion (31 December 2012 est.)
country comparison to the world: 20

Current account balance: $52.83 billion (2017 est.)
$47.31 billion (2016 est.)
country comparison to the world: 10

Exports: $499.1 billion (2017 est.)
$454.1 billion (2016 est.)
country comparison to the world: 10

Exports—commodities: engineering products, textiles and clothing, production machinery, motor vehicles, transport equipment, chemicals; foodstuffs, beverages, and tobacco; minerals, nonferrous metals

Exports—partners: Germany 12.6%, France 10.5%, US 8.9%, UK 5.4%, Spain 5%, Switzerland 4.6% (2016)

Imports: $426.7 billion (2017 est.)
$387.1 billion (2016 est.)
country comparison to the world: 13

Imports—commodities: engineering products, chemicals, transport equipment, energy products, minerals and nonferrous metals, textiles and clothing; food, beverages, tobacco

Imports—partners: Germany 16.3%, France 8.9%, China 7.5%, Netherlands 5.5%, Spain 5.3%, Belgium 4.9% (2016)

Reserves of foreign exchange and gold: $136 billion (31 December 2016 est.)
$130.6 billion (31 December 2015 est.)
country comparison to the world: 18

Debt—external: $2.444 trillion (31 March 2016 est.)
$2.3 trillion (31 March 2015 est.)
country comparison to the world: 10

Stock of direct foreign investment—at home: $495.2 billion (31 December 2017 est.)
$471.7 billion (31 December 2016 est.)
country comparison to the world: 18

Stock of direct foreign investment—abroad: $607.8 billion (31 December 2017 est.)
$584.1 billion (31 December 2016 est.)
country comparison to the world: 16

Exchange rates: euros (EUR) per US dollar—
0.906 (2017 est.)
0.9214 (2016 est.)
0.9214 (2015 est.)
0.885 (2014 est.)
0.7634 (2013 est.)

ENERGY

Electricity access: *electrification—total population:* 100% (2016)

Electricity—production: 269.3 billion kWh (2015 est.)
country comparison to the world: 15

Electricity—consumption: 296 billion kWh (2015 est.)
country comparison to the world: 13

Electricity—exports: 6.155 billion kWh (2016 est.)
country comparison to the world: 31

Electricity—imports: 43.18 billion kWh (2016 est.)
country comparison to the world: 3

Electricity—installed generating capacity: 117 million kW (2015 est.)
country comparison to the world: 11

Electricity—from fossil fuels: 52.8% of total installed capacity (2015 est.)
country comparison to the world: 146

Electricity—from nuclear fuels: 0% of total installed capacity (2015 est.)
country comparison to the world: 113

Electricity—from hydroelectric plants: 12.5% of total installed capacity (2015 est.)
country comparison to the world: 114

Electricity—from other renewable sources: 28.6% of total installed capacity (2015 est.)
country comparison to the world: 18

Crude oil—production: 70,670 bbl/day (2016 est.)
country comparison to the world: 49

Crude oil—exports: 11,610 bbl/day (2016 est.)
country comparison to the world: 58

Crude oil—imports: 1.231 million bbl/day (2016 est.)
country comparison to the world: 8

Crude oil—proved reserves: 556.7 million bbl (1 January 2017 es)
country comparison to the world: 48

Refined petroleum products—production: 1.567 million bbl/day (2016 est.)
country comparison to the world: 13

Refined petroleum products—consumption: 1.253 million bbl/day (2016 est.)
country comparison to the world: 20

Refined petroleum products—exports: 572,000 bbl/day (2016 est.)
country comparison to the world: 14

Refined petroleum products—imports: 449,600 bbl/day (2016 est.)
country comparison to the world: 19

Natural gas—production: 5.785 billion cu m (2016 est.)
country comparison to the world: 49

Natural gas—consumption: 70.91 billion cu m (2016 est.)
country comparison to the world: 18

Natural gas—exports: 21.2 million cu m (2016 est.)
country comparison to the world: 53

Natural gas—imports: 65.28 billion cu m (2016 est.)
country comparison to the world: 6

Natural gas—proved reserves: 49.13 billion cu m (1 January 2017 es)
country comparison to the world: 65

Carbon dioxide emissions from consumption of energy: 362 million Mt (2013 est.)
country comparison to the world: 19

COMMUNICATIONS

Telephones—fixed lines: *total subscriptions:* 20,267,172
subscriptions per 100 inhabitants: 33 (July 2016 est.)
country comparison to the world: 15

Telephones—mobile cellular: *total:* 85,955,905
subscriptions per 100 inhabitants: 139 (July 2016 est.)
country comparison to the world: 18

Telephone system: *general assessment:* modern, well-developed, fast; fully automated telephone, telex, and data services
domestic: high-capacity cable and microwave radio relay trunks
international: country code—39; a series of submarine cables provide links to Asia, Middle East, Europe, North Africa, and US; satellite earth stations—3 Intelsat (with a total of 5 antennas—3 for Atlantic Ocean and 2 for Indian Ocean), 1 Inmarsat (Atlantic Ocean region), and NA Eutelsat (2015)

Broadcast media: two Italian media giants dominate—the publicly owned Radiotelevisione Italiana (RAI) with 3 national terrestrial stations and privately owned Mediaset with 3 national terrestrial stations; a large number of private stations and Sky Italia—a satellite TV network; RAI operates 3 AM/FM nationwide radio stations; about 1,300 commercial radio stations (2007)

Internet country code: .it
Internet users: total: 38,025,661

percent of population: 61.3% (July 2016 est.)
country comparison to the world: 18

TRANSPORTATION

National air transport system: *number of registered air carriers:* 9
inventory of registered aircraft operated by air carriers: 382
annual passenger traffic on registered air carriers: 26,036,010
annual freight traffic on registered air carriers: 945,433,732 mt-km (2015)
Civil aircraft registration country code prefix: I (2016)

Airports: 129 (2013)
country comparison to the world: 45

Airports—with paved runways: *total:* 98
over 3,047 m: 9
2,438 to 3,047 m: 31
1,524 to 2,437 m: 18
914 to 1,523 m: 29
under 914 m: 11 (2017)

Airports—with unpaved runways: *total:* 31
1,524 to 2,437 m: 1
914 to 1,523 m: 10
under 914 m: 20 (2013)

Heliports: 5 (2013)

Pipelines: gas 20,223 km; oil 1,393 km; refined products 1,574 km (2013)

Railways: *total:* 20,181.7 km
standard gauge: 18,770.1 km 1.435-m gauge (12,893.6 km electrified)
narrow gauge: 122.3 km 1.000-m gauge (122.3 km electrified); 1,289.3 km 0.950-m gauge (151.3 km electrified) (2014)
country comparison to the world: 14

Roadways: *total:* 487,700 km
paved: 487,700 km (includes 6,700 km of expressways) (2007)
country comparison to the world: 15

Waterways: 2,400 km (used for commercial traffic; of limited overall value compared to road and rail) (2012)
country comparison to the world: 36

Merchant marine: *total:* 1,430
by type: bulk carrier 65, container ship 10, general cargo 145, oil tanker 135, other 1,075 (2017)
country comparison to the world: 20

Ports and terminals: *major seaport(s):* Augusta, Cagliari, Genoa, Livorno, Taranto, Trieste, Venice
oil terminal(s): Melilli (Santa Panagia) oil terminal, Sarroch oil terminal
container port(s) (TEUs): Genoa (2,243,000), Gioia Tauro (3,512,000), La Spezia (1,300,000) (2015)
LNG terminal(s) (import): La Spezia, Panigaglia, Porto Levante

MILITARY AND SECURITY

Military expenditures: 1.51% of GDP (2016)
1.39% of GDP (2015)
1.47% of GDP (2014)
1.59% of GDP (2013)
1.63% of GDP (2012)
country comparison to the world: 52

Military branches: Italian Armed Forces: Army (Esercito Italiano, EI), Navy (Marina Militare Italiana, MMI), Italian Air Force (Aeronautica Militare Italiana, AMI), Carabinieri Corps (Arma dei Carabinieri, CC), Financial Guard (Guardia di Finanza) (2015)

Military service age and obligation: 18-25 years of age for voluntary military service; women may serve in any military branch; Italian citizenship required; 1-year service obligation (2013)

TERRORISM

Terrorist groups—foreign based: *Islamic State of Iraq and the Levant (ISIL): aim(s):* enhance its networks in Italy and, ultimately, establish a global Islamic caliphate
area(s) of operation: maintains an operational presence, primarily in large cities; authorities have foiled an increasing number of plots in recent years; has a growing recruitment network targeting Muslim youths; the number of Italians fighting alongside ISIS remains low compared to other Western European nations; authorities continue to pursue and prosecute Italian recruits who have either fought in Syria or elsewhere alongside ISIL or attempt to leave Italy to fight

TRANSNATIONAL ISSUES

Disputes—international: Italy's long coastline and developed economy entices tens of thousands of illegal immigrants from southeastern Europe and northern Africa
Refugees and internally displaced persons: refugees (country of origin): 16,033 (Afghanistan); 14,336 (Somalia); 14,247 (Nigeria); 13,412 (Pakistan); 11,327 (Mali); 10,049 (Eritrea); 7,723 (Gambia); 5,805 (Cote d'Ivoire) (2016); 10,410 (Ukraine) (2017); note: estimate represents asylum applicants since Ukraine crisis began in 2014 until September 2017
stateless persons: 701 (2016)
note: 459,370 estimated refugee and migrant arrivals by sea (January 2015—February 2018)

Illicit drugs: important gateway for and consumer of Latin American cocaine and Southwest Asian heroin entering the European market; money laundering by organized crime and from smuggling

INTRODUCTION

Background: The island—discovered by Christopher COLUMBUS in 1494—was settled by the Spanish early in the 16th century. The native Taino, who had inhabited Jamaica for centuries, were gradually exterminated and replaced by African slaves. England seized the island in 1655 and established a plantation economy based on sugar, cocoa, and coffee. The abolition of slavery in 1834 freed a quarter million slaves, many of whom became small farmers. Jamaica gradually increased its independence from Britain. In 1958 it joined other British Caribbean colonies in forming the Federation of the West Indies. Jamaica gained full independence when it withdrew from the Federation in 1962. Deteriorating economic conditions during the 1970s led to recurrent violence as rival gangs affiliated with the major political parties evolved into powerful organized crime networks involved in international drug smuggling and money laundering. Violent crime, drug trafficking, and poverty pose significant challenges to the government today. Nonetheless, many rural and resort areas remain relatively safe and contribute substantially to the economy.

GEOGRAPHY

Location: Caribbean, island in the Caribbean Sea, south of Cuba

Geographic coordinates: 18 15 N, 77 30 W

Map references: Central America and the Caribbean

Area: *total:* 10,991 sq km
land: 10,831 sq km
water: 160 sq km
country comparison to the world: 167

Area—comparative: about half the size of New Jersey; slightly smaller than Connecticut

Land boundaries: 0 km

Coastline: 1,022 km

Maritime claims: measured from claimed archipelagic straight baselines
territorial sea: 12 nm
contiguous zone: 24 nm
exclusive economic zone: 200 nm
continental shelf: 200 nm or to edge of the continental margin

Climate: tropical; hot, humid; temperate interior

Terrain: mostly mountains, with narrow, discontinuous coastal plain

Elevation: *mean elevation:* 18 m

elevation extremes: *lowest point:* Caribbean Sea 0 m
highest point: Blue Mountain Peak 2,256 m

Natural resources: bauxite, gypsum, limestone

Land use: *agricultural land:* 41.4%
arable land: 11.1%;
permanent crops: 9.2%;
permanent pasture: 21.1%
forest: 31.1%
other: 27.5% (2011 est.)
Irrigated land: 250 sq km (2012)

Population—distribution: population density is high throughout, but increases in and around Kingston, Montego Bay, and Port Esquivel

Natural hazards: hurricanes (especially July to November)

Environment—current issues: heavy rates of deforestation; coastal waters polluted by industrial waste, sewage, and oil spills; damage to coral reefs; air pollution in Kingston from vehicle emissions

Environment—international agreements: *party to:* Biodiversity, Climate Change, Climate Change-Kyoto Protocol, Desertification, Endangered Species, Hazardous Wastes, Law of the Sea, Marine Dumping, Marine Life Conservation, Ozone Layer Protection, Ship Pollution, Wetlands
signed, but not ratified: none of the selected agreements

Geography—note: third largest island in the Caribbean (after Cuba and Hispaniola); strategic location between Cayman Trench and Jamaica Channel, the main sea lanes for the Panama Canal

PEOPLE AND SOCIETY

Population: 2,990,561 (July 2017 est.)
country comparison to the world: 138

Nationality: *noun:* Jamaican(s)
adjective: Jamaican

Ethnic groups: black 92.1%, mixed 6.1%, East Indian 0.8%, other 0.4%, unspecified 0.7% (2011 est.)

Languages: English, English patois

Religions: Protestant 64.8% (includes Seventh Day Adventist 12.0%, Pentecostal 11.0%, Other Church of God 9.2%, New Testament Church of God 7.2%, Baptist 6.7%, Church of God in Jamaica 4.8%, Church of God of Prophecy 4.5%, Anglican 2.8%, United Church 2.1%, Methodist 1.6%, Revived 1.4%, Brethren 0.9%, and Moravian 0.7%), Roman Catholic 2.2%, Jehovah's Witness 1.9%, Rastafarian 1.1%, other 6.5%, none 21.3%, unspecified 2.3% (2011 est.)

Age structure: *0-14 years:* 27.17% (male 413,325/female 399,190)
15-24 years: 20.79% (male 312,400/female 309,477)
25-54 years: 38.17% (male 564,414/female 577,059)
55-64 years: 5.85% (male 84,271/female 90,612)

65 years and over: 8.02% (male 107,310/female 132,503) (2017 est.)

Dependency ratios: *total dependency ratio:* 48.7
youth dependency ratio: 34.9
elderly dependency ratio: 13.8
potential support ratio: 7.2 (2015 est.)

Median age: *total:* 26 years
male: 25.5 years
female: 26.5 years (2017 est.)
country comparison to the world: 151

Population growth rate: 0.68% (2017 est.)
country comparison to the world: 145

Birth rate: 17.9 births/1,000 population (2017 est.)
country comparison to the world: 99

Death rate: 6.8 deaths/1,000 population (2017 est.)
country comparison to the world: 135

Net migration rate: -4.3 migrant(s)/1,000 population (2017 est.)
country comparison to the world: 184

Population distribution: population density is high throughout, but increases in and around Kingston, Montego Bay, and Port Esquivel

Urbanization: *urban population:* 55.3% of total population (2017)
rate of urbanization: 0.93% annual rate of change (2015-20 est.)

Major urban areas—population: KINGSTON (capital) 588,000 (2015)

Sex ratio: *at birth:* 1.05 male(s)/female
0-14 years: 1.04 male(s)/female
15-24 years: 1.01 male(s)/female
25-54 years: 0.98 male(s)/female
55-64 years: 0.93 male(s)/female
65 years and over: 0.81 male(s)/female
total population: 0.98 male(s)/female (2016 est.)

Mother's mean age at first birth: 21.2 years
note: median age at first birth among women 25-29 (2008 est.)

Maternal mortality ratio: 89 deaths/100,000 live births (2015 est.)
country comparison to the world: 77

Infant mortality rate: *total:* 12.8 deaths/1,000 live births
male: 13.4 deaths/1,000 live births
female: 12.3 deaths/1,000 live births (2017 est.)
country comparison to the world: 111

Life expectancy at birth: *total population:* 73.7 years
male: 72.1 years
female: 75.4 years (2017 est.)
country comparison to the world: 130

Total fertility rate: 1.96 children born/woman (2017 est.)
country comparison to the world: 126

Contraceptive prevalence rate: 72.5% (2008/09)

Health expenditures: 5.4% of GDP (2014)
country comparison to the world: 130

Physicians density: 0.41 physicians/1,000 population (2008)

Hospital bed density: 1.7 beds/1,000 population (2012)

Drinking water source:
improved:
urban: 97.5% of population
rural: 89.4% of population
total: 93.8% of population
unimproved:
urban: 2.5% of population
rural: 10.6% of population
total: 6.2% of population (2015 est.)

Sanitation facility access:
improved:
urban: 79.9% of population
rural: 84.1% of population
total: 81.8% of population
unimproved:
urban: 20.1% of population
rural: 15.9% of population
total: 18.2% of population (2015 est.)

HIV/AIDS—adult prevalence rate: 1.7% (2016 est.)
country comparison to the world: 30

HIV/AIDS—people living with HIV/AIDS: 30,000 (2016 est.)
country comparison to the world: 67

HIV/AIDS—deaths: 1,300 (2016 est.)
country comparison to the world: 60

Major infectious diseases: note: active local transmission of Zika virus by Aedes species mosquitoes has been identified in this country (as of August 2016); it poses an important risk (a large number of cases possible) among US citizens if bitten by an infective mosquito; other less common ways to get Zika are through sex, via blood transfusion, or during pregnancy, in which the pregnant woman passes Zika virus to her fetus (2016)

Obesity—adult prevalence rate: 24.7% (2016)
country comparison to the world: 55

Children under the age of 5 years underweight: 2.5% (2012)
country comparison to the world: 112

Education expenditures: 5.4% of GDP (2015)
country comparison to the world: 40

Literacy: definition: age 15 and over has ever attended school
total population: 88.7%
male: 84%
female: 93.1% (2015 est.)

Unemployment, youth ages 15-24: total: 37.8%
male: 32.4%
female: 43.8% (2013 est.)
country comparison to the world: 20

GOVERNMENT

Country name: conventional long form: none
conventional short form: Jamaica
etymology: from the native Taino word "haymaca" meaning "Land of Wood and Water" or possibly "Land of Springs"

Government type: parliamentary democracy (Parliament) under a constitutional monarchy; a Commonwealth realm

Capital: name: Kingston
geographic coordinates: 18 00 N, 76 48 W
time difference: UTC-5 (same time as Washington, DC, during Standard Time)

Administrative divisions: 14 parishes; Clarendon, Hanover, Kingston, Manchester, Portland, Saint Andrew, Saint Ann, Saint Catherine, Saint Elizabeth, Saint James, Saint Mary, Saint Thomas, Trelawny, Westmoreland
note: for local government purposes, Kingston and Saint Andrew were amalgamated in 1923 into the present single corporate body known as the Kingston and Saint Andrew Corporation

Independence: 6 August 1962 (from the UK)

National holiday: Independence Day, 6 August (1962)

Constitution: several previous (preindependence); latest drafted 1961-62, submitted to British Parliament 24 July 1962, entered into force 6 August 1962 (at independence); amended many times, last in 2015 (2016)

Legal system: common law system based on the English model

International law organization participation: has not submitted an ICJ jurisdiction declaration; non-party state to the ICCt

Citizenship: citizenship by birth: yes
citizenship by descent: yes
dual citizenship recognized: yes
residency requirement for naturalization: 4 out of the previous 5 years

Suffrage: 18 years of age; universal

Executive branch: chief of state: Queen ELIZABETH II (since 6 February 1952); represented by Governor General Dr. Patrick L. ALLEN (since 26 February 2009)

head of government: Prime Minister Andrew HOLNESS (since 3 March 2016)
cabinet: Cabinet appointed by the governor general on the advice of the prime minister
elections/appointments: the monarchy is hereditary; governor general appointed by the monarch on the recommendation of the prime minister; following legislative elections, the leader of the majority party or majority coalition in the House of Representatives is appointed prime minister by the governor general

Legislative branch: description: bicameral Parliament consists of the Senate (21 seats; members appointed by the governor general on the recommendation of the prime minister and the minority party leader, 13 seats allocated to the ruling party, and 8 seats allocated to the minority party; members serve 5-year terms) and the House of Representatives (63 seats; members directly elected in single-seat constituencies by simple majority vote to serve 5-year terms)
elections: last held on 25 February 2016 (next to be held no later than February 2021)

election results: percent of vote by party—JLP 50.1%, PNP 49.7%, other 0.2%; seats by party—JLP 32, PNP 31

Judicial branch: highest resident court(s): Court of Appeal (consists of president of the court and a minimum of 4 judges; Supreme Court (40 judges organized in specialized divisions); note—appeals beyond Jamaica's highest courts are referred to the Judicial Committee of the Privy Council (in London) rather than to the Caribbean Court of Justice (the appellate court implemented for member states of the Caribbean Community)
judge selection and term of office: chief justice of the Supreme Court and president of the Court of Appeal appointed by the governor-general on the advice of the prime minister; other judges of both courts appointed by the governor-general on the advice of the Judicial Service Commission; judges of both courts serve till age 70
subordinate courts: resident magistrate courts, district courts, and petty sessions courts

Political parties and leaders: Jamaica Labor Party or JLP [Andrew HOLNESS]
People's National Party or PNP [Dr. Peter David PHILLIPS]
National Democratic Movement or NDM [Peter TOWNSEND]
Political pressure groups and leaders: New Beginnings Movement or NBM
Rastafarians

International organization participation: ACP, AOSIS, C, Caricom, CDB, CELAC, FAO, G-15, G-77, IADB, IAEA, IBRD, ICAO, ICC (NGOs), ICRM, IDA, IFAD, IFC, IFRCS, IHO, ILO, IMF, IMO, Interpol, IOC, IOM, ISO, ITSO, ITU, LAES, MIGA, NAM, OAS, OPANAL, OPCW, Petrocaribe, UN, UNCTAD, UNESCO, UNIDO, UNITAR, UNWTO, UPU, WCO, WFTU (NGOs), WHO, WIPO, WMO, WTO

Diplomatic representation in the US: chief of mission: Ambassador Audrey Patrice MARKS (since 18 January 2017)
chancery: 1520 New Hampshire Avenue NW, Washington, DC 20036
telephone: [1] (202) 452-0660
FAX: [1] (202) 452-0036
consulate(s) general: Miami, New York
consulate(s): Atlanta, Boston, Chicago, Concord (MA), Houston, Los Angeles, Philadelphia (PA), Richmond (VA), San Francisco, Seattle

Diplomatic representation from the US: chief of mission: Ambassador (vacant); Charge d'Affaires Eric KHANT (since 30 June 2017)
embassy: 142 Old Hope Road, Kingston 6
mailing address: P.O. Box 541, Kingston 5
telephone: [1] (876) 702-6000
FAX: [1] (876) 702-6348

Flag description: diagonal yellow cross divides the flag into four triangles—green (top and bottom) and black (hoist side and fly side); green represents hope, vegetation, and agriculture, black reflects hardships overcome and to be faced, and yellow recalls golden sunshine and the island's natural resources

National symbol(s): green-and-black streamertail (bird), Guaiacum officinale (Guaiacwood); national colors: green, yellow, black

National anthem: name: "Jamaica, Land We Love" *lyrics/music:* Hugh Braham SHERLOCK/Robert Charles LIGHTBOURNE *note:* adopted 1962

ECONOMY

Economy—overview: The Jamaican economy is heavily dependent on services, which accounts for more than 70% of GDP. The country continues to derive most of its foreign exchange from tourism, remittances, and bauxite/alumina. Earnings from remittances and tourism each account for about 15% of GDP, while bauxite/alumina exports have declined to less than 5% of GDP.

Jamaica's economy has grown on average less than 1% a year for the last three decades and many impediments remain to growth: a bloated public sector which crowds out spending on important projects; high crime and corruption; red-tape; and a high debt-to-GDP ratio. Jamaica, however, has made steady progress in reducing its debt-to-GDP ratio from a high of almost 150% in 2012 to about 115% in 2017, in close collaboration with the International Monetary Fund. The existing Stand By Agreement requires Jamaica to produce an annual primary surplus of 7%, in an attempt to reduce its debt burden below 60% by 2025.

Economic growth reached 1.6% in 2016. The HOLNESS administration faces the difficult prospect of maintaining fiscal discipline to make debt payments while simultaneously attacking a serious crime problem. High unemployment exacerbates the crime problem, including gang violence fueled by the drug trade.

GDP (purchasing power parity): $26.2 billion (2017 est.)
$25.77 billion (2016 est.)
$25.44 billion (2015 est.)
note: data are in 2017 dollars
country comparison to the world: 141

GDP (official exchange rate): $14.29 billion (2016 est.)

GDP—real growth rate: 1.7% (2017 est.)
1.3% (2016 est.)
0.9% (2015 est.)
country comparison to the world: 168

GDP—per capita (PPP): $9,200 (2017 est.)
$9,100 (2016 est.)
$9,000 (2015 est.)
note: data are in 2017 dollars
country comparison to the world: 143

Gross national saving: 16.5% of GDP (2017 est.)
17% of GDP (2016 est.)
18.1% of GDP (2015 est.)
country comparison to the world: 113

GDP—composition, by end use:
household consumption: 81.9%
government consumption: 13.5%
investment in fixed capital: 21.1%
investment in inventories: 0.1%
exports of goods and services: 29.4%

imports of goods and services: -46% (2017 est.)

GDP—composition, by sector of origin:
agriculture: 7.5%
industry: 21.3%
services: 71.2% (2017 est.)

Agriculture—products: sugarcane, bananas, coffee, citrus, yams, ackees, vegetables; poultry, goats, milk; shellfish

Industries: tourism, bauxite/alumina, agricultural-processing, light manufactures, rum, cement, metal, paper, chemical products, telecommunications

Industrial production growth rate: 1.7% (2017 est.)
country comparison to the world: 145

Labor force: 1.325 million (2017 est.)
country comparison to the world: 136

Labor force—by occupation: *agriculture:* 17%
industry: 19%
services: 64% (2006)

Unemployment rate: 12.2% (2017 est.)
12.8% (2016 est.)
country comparison to the world: 157

Population below poverty line: 16.5% (2009 est.)

Household income or consumption by percentage share: *lowest 10%:* 2.1%
highest 10%: 35.8% (2004)

Distribution of family income—Gini index: 45.5 (2004)
37.9 (2000)
country comparison to the world: 38

Budget: *revenues:* $4.207 billion
expenditures: $4.15 billion (2017 est.)
Taxes and other revenues: 29.4% of GDP (2017 est.)
country comparison to the world: 85

Budget surplus (+) or deficit (-): 0.4% of GDP (2017 est.)
country comparison to the world: 25

Public debt: 117.8% of GDP (2017 est.)
127.1% of GDP (2016 est.)
country comparison to the world: 9

Fiscal year: 1 April—31 March

Inflation rate (consumer prices): 3.4% (2017 est.)
2.3% (2016 est.)
country comparison to the world: 138

Central bank discount rate: 2% (31 December 2010)
country comparison to the world: 115

Commercial bank prime lending rate: 16.6% (31 December 2017 est.)
16.5% (31 December 2016 est.)
country comparison to the world: 29

Stock of narrow money: $3.634 billion (31 December 2017 est.)
$3.409 billion (31 December 2016 est.)
country comparison to the world: 113

Stock of broad money: $8.888 billion (31 December 2017 est.)
$8.429 billion (31 December 2016 est.)
country comparison to the world: 110

Stock of domestic credit: $7.902 billion (31 December 2017 est.)

$7.343 billion (31 December 2016 est.)
country comparison to the world: 114

Market value of publicly traded shares: $6.39 billion (31 December 2012 est.)
$7.223 billion (31 December 2011 est.)
$6.626 billion (31 December 2010 est.)
country comparison to the world: 82

Current account balance: -$390 million (2017 est.)
-$309 million (2016 est.)
country comparison to the world: 98

Exports: $1.123 billion (2017 est.)
$1.195 billion (2016 est.)
country comparison to the world: 156

Exports—commodities: alumina, bauxite, sugar, rum, coffee, yams, beverages, chemicals, apparel, mineral fuels

Exports—partners: US 40.8%, Canada 11.9%, Netherlands 10.2%, Russia 5.8%, UK 4.1% (2016)

Imports: $4.197 billion (2017 est.)
$4.169 billion (2016 est.)
country comparison to the world: 130

Imports—commodities: food and other consumer goods, industrial supplies, fuel, parts and accessories of capital goods, machinery and transport equipment, construction materials

Imports—partners: US 39%, Trinidad and Tobago 7.2%, China 6.4%, Japan 6.2%, Mexico 4.1% (2016)

Reserves of foreign exchange and gold: $3.1 billion (31 December 2017 est.)
$3.291 billion (31 December 2016 est.)
country comparison to the world: 105

Debt—external: $14.9 billion (31 December 2017 est.)
$15.17 billion (31 December 2016 est.)
country comparison to the world: 102

Exchange rates: Jamaican dollars (JMD) per US dollar—
128.5 (2017 est.)
125.126 (2016 est.)
125.126 (2015 est.)
116.898 (2014 est.)
110.935 (2013 est.)

ENERGY

Electricity access: *population without electricity:* 200,000

electrification—total population: 93%
electrification—urban areas: 98%
electrification—rural areas: 87% (2013)

Electricity—production: 3.894 billion kWh (2015 est.)
country comparison to the world: 126

Electricity—consumption: 2.757 billion kWh (2015 est.)
country comparison to the world: 138

Electricity—exports: 0 kWh (2016 est.)
country comparison to the world: 153

Electricity—imports: 0 kWh (2016 est.)
country comparison to the world: 164

473

Electricity—installed generating capacity: 988,000 kW (2015 est.)
country comparison to the world: 128

Electricity—from fossil fuels: 88.5% of total installed capacity (2015 est.)
country comparison to the world: 65

Electricity—from nuclear fuels: 0% of total installed capacity (2015 est.)
country comparison to the world: 116

Electricity—from hydroelectric plants: 3% of total installed capacity (2015 est.)
country comparison to the world: 133

Electricity—from other renewable sources: 13% of total installed capacity (2015 est.)
country comparison to the world: 56

Crude oil—production: 0 bbl/day (2016 est.)
country comparison to the world: 151

Crude oil—exports: 0 bbl/day (2014 est.)
country comparison to the world: 143

Crude oil—imports: 19,160 bbl/day (2014 est.)
country comparison to the world: 63

Crude oil—proved reserves: 0 bbl (1 January 2017 es)
country comparison to the world: 150

Refined petroleum products—production: 19,760 bbl/day (2014 est.)
country comparison to the world: 91

Refined petroleum products—consumption: 54,000 bbl/day (2015 est.)
country comparison to the world: 102

Refined petroleum products—exports: 845.3 bbl/day (2014 est.)
country comparison to the world: 110

Refined petroleum products—imports: 34,170 bbl/day (2014 est.)
country comparison to the world: 98

Natural gas—production: 0 cu m (2013 est.)
country comparison to the world: 151

Natural gas—consumption: 0 cu m (2013 est.)
country comparison to the world: 195

Natural gas—exports: 0 cu m (2013 est.)
country comparison to the world: 126

Natural gas—imports: 0 cu m (2013 est.)
country comparison to the world: 142

Natural gas—proved reserves: 0 cu m (1 January 2014 es)
country comparison to the world: 154

Carbon dioxide emissions from consumption of energy: 13 million Mt (2013 est.)
country comparison to the world: 97

COMMUNICATIONS

Telephones—fixed lines: *total subscriptions:* 310,213
subscriptions per 100 inhabitants: 10 (July 2016 est.)
country comparison to the world: 122

Telephones—mobile cellular: *total:* 3,267,344
subscriptions per 100 inhabitants: 110 (July 2016 est.)
country comparison to the world: 140

Telephone system: *general assessment:* fully automatic domestic telephone network
domestic: the 1999 agreement to open the market for telecommunications services resulted in rapid growth in mobile-cellular telephone usage while the number of fixed lines in use has declined; combined fixed-line and mobile cellular teledensity exceeds 120 per 100 persons
international: country code—1-876; the Fibralink submarine cable network provides enhanced delivery of business and broadband traffic and is linked to the Americas Region Caribbean Ring System (ARCOS-1) submarine cable in the Dominican Republic; the link to ARCOS-1 provides seamless connectivity to US, parts of the Caribbean, Central America, and South America; the ALBA-1 fiber-optic submarine cable links Jamaica, Cuba, and Venezuela; satellite earth stations—2 Intelsat (Atlantic Ocean) (2016)

Broadcast media: 3 free-to-air TV stations, subscription cable services, and roughly 30 radio stations (2013)

Internet country code: .jm
Internet users: total: 1,336,653
percent of population: 45.0% (July 2016 est.)
country comparison to the world: 109

TRANSPORTATION

National air transport system: *number of registered air carriers:* 2
inventory of registered aircraft operated by air carriers: 5
annual passenger traffic on registered air carriers: 92,836
annual freight traffic on registered air carriers: 0 mt-km (2015)
Civil aircraft registration country code prefix: 6Y (2016)

Airports: 28 (2013)
country comparison to the world: 123

Airports—with paved runways: *total:* 11
2,438 to 3,047 m: 2
914 to 1,523 m: 4
under 914 m: 5 (2017)

Airports—with unpaved runways: *total:* 17
914 to 1,523 m: 1
under 914 m: 16 (2013)

Roadways: *total:* 22,121 km (includes 44 km of expressways)
paved: 16,148 km
unpaved: 5,973 km (2011)
country comparison to the world: 104

Merchant marine: *total:* 41
by type: bulk carrier 3, container ship 8, general cargo 11, other 19 (2017)

country comparison to the world: 117

Ports and terminals: *major seaport(s):* Discovery Bay (Port Rhoades), Kingston, Montego Bay, Port Antonio, Port Esquivel, Port Kaiser, Rocky Point
container port(s) (TEUs): Kingston (1,724,928)

MILITARY AND SECURITY

Military expenditures: 0.82% of GDP (2016)
0.83% of GDP (2015)
0.87% of GDP (2014)
0.9% of GDP (2013)
0.93% of GDP (2012)
country comparison to the world: 111

Military branches: Jamaica Defense Force: Ground Forces, Coast Guard, Air Wing (2010)

Military service age and obligation: 17 1/2 is the legal minimum age for voluntary military service; no conscription (2012)

TRANSNATIONAL ISSUES

Disputes—international: none

Trafficking in persons: current situation: Jamaica is a source and destination country for children and adults subjected to sex trafficking and forced labor; sex trafficking of children and adults occurs on the street, in night clubs, bars, massage parlors, and private homes; child sex tourism is a problem in resort areas; Jamaicans have been subjected to sexual exploitation or forced labor in the Caribbean, Canada, the US, and the UK, while foreigners have endured conditions of forced labor in Jamaica or aboard foreign-flagged fishing vessels operating in Jamaican waters; a high number of Jamaican children are reported missing
tier rating: Tier 2 Watch List—Jamaica does not fully comply with the minimum standards for the elimination of trafficking; however, it is making significant efforts to do so; in 2014, the government made significant efforts to raise public awareness of human trafficking, and named a national trafficking-in-persons rapporteur—the first in the region; authorities initiated more new trafficking investigations than in 2013 and concluded a trafficking case in the Supreme Court, but chronic delays impeded prosecutions and no offenders were convicted for the sixth consecutive year; more adult trafficking victims were identified than in previous years, but only one child victim was identified, which was exceptionally low relative to the number of vulnerable children (2015)

Illicit drugs: transshipment point for cocaine from South America to North America and Europe; illicit cultivation and consumption of cannabis; government has an active manual cannabis eradication program; corruption is a major concern; substantial money-laundering activity; Colombian narcotics traffickers favor Jamaica for illicit financial transactions

JAN MAYEN

INTRODUCTION

Background: This desolate, arctic, mountainous island was named after a Dutch whaling captain who indisputably discovered it in 1614 (earlier claims are inconclusive). Visited only occasionally by seal hunters and trappers over the following centuries, the island came under Norwegian sovereignty in 1929. The long dormant Beerenberg volcano, the northernmost active volcano on earth, resumed activity in 1970 and the most recent eruption occurred in 1985.

GEOGRAPHY

Location: Northern Europe, island between the Greenland Sea and the Norwegian Sea, northeast of Iceland

Geographic coordinates: 71 00 N, 8 00 W

Map references: Arctic Region

Area: *total:* 377 sq km
land: 377 sq km
water: 0 sq km
country comparison to the world: 206

Area—comparative: slightly more than twice the size of Washington, DC

Land boundaries: 0 km

Coastline: 124.1 km

Maritime claims: *territorial sea:* 12 nm

contiguous zone: 24 nm
exclusive economic zone: 200 nm
continental shelf: 200-m depth or to the depth of exploitation

Climate: arctic maritime with frequent storms and persistent fog

Terrain: volcanic island, partly covered by glaciers

Elevation: *mean elevation:* NA

elevation extremes: *lowest point:* Norwegian Sea 0 m
highest point: Haakon VII Toppen on Beerenberg 2,277 m
note: Beerenberg volcano has numerous peaks; the highest point on the volcano rim is named Haakon VII Toppen, after Norway's first king following the reestablishment of Norwegian independence in 1905

Natural resources: none

Land use: *agricultural land:* 0%
arable land: 0%;
permanent crops: 0%;
permanent pasture: 0%
forest: 0%
other: 100% (2011 est.)
Irrigated land: 0 sq km (2012)

Natural hazards: dominated by the volcano Beerenberg
volcanism: Beerenberg (2,227 m) is Norway's only active volcano; volcanic activity resumed in 1970; the most recent eruption occurred in 1985

Environment—current issues: pollutants transported from southerly latitudes by winds, ocean currents, and rivers accumulate in the food chains of native animals
Geography—note: barren volcanic spoon-shaped island with some moss and grass flora; island consists of two parts: a larger northeast Nord-Jan (the spoon "bowl") and the smaller Sor-Jan (the "handle"), linked by a 2.5 km-wide isthmus (the "stem") with two large lakes, Sorlaguna (South Lagoon) and Nordlaguna (North Lagoon)

PEOPLE AND SOCIETY

Population: no indigenous inhabitants
note: personnel operate the Long Range Navigation (Loran-C) base and the weather and coastal services radio station

GOVERNMENT

Country name: *conventional long form:* none
conventional short form: Jan Mayen
etymology: named after Dutch Captain Jan Jacobszoon MAY, one of the first explorers to reach the island in 1614

Dependency status: territory of Norway; since August 1994, administered from Oslo through the county governor (fylkesmann) of Nordland; however, authority has been delegated to a station commander of the Norwegian Defense Communication Service; in 2010 Norway designated the majority of Jan Mayen as a nature reserve

Legal system: the laws of Norway, where applicable, apply

Flag description: the flag of Norway is used

ECONOMY

Economy—overview: Jan Mayen is a volcanic island with no exploitable natural resources, although surrounding waters contain substantial fish stocks and potential untapped petroleum resources. Economic activity is limited to providing services for employees of Norway's radio and meteorological stations on the island.

COMMUNICATIONS

Broadcast media: a coastal radio station has been remotely operated since 1994 (2008)

TRANSPORTATION

Airports: 1 (2013)
country comparison to the world: 222

Airports—with unpaved runways: *total:* 1
1,524 to 2,437 m: 1 (2013)

Ports and terminals: none; offshore anchorage only

MILITARY AND SECURITY

Military—note: defense is the responsibility of Norway

TRANSNATIONAL ISSUES

Disputes—international: none

JERSEY

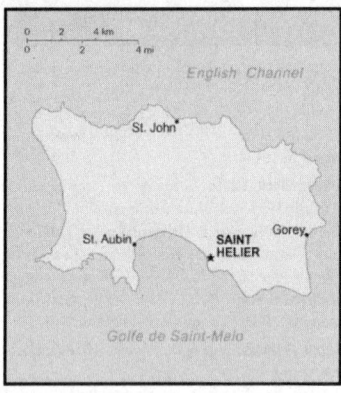

INTRODUCTION

Background: Jersey and the other Channel Islands represent the last remnants of the medieval Dukedom of Normandy that held sway in both France and England. These islands were the only British soil occupied by German troops in World War II. The Bailiwick of Jersey is a British Crown dependency but is not part of the UK or of the EU. However, the UK Government is constitutionally responsible for its defense and international representation.

GEOGRAPHY

Location: Western Europe, island in the English Channel, northwest of France

Geographic coordinates: 49 15 N, 2 10 W

Map references: Europe

Area: *total:* 116 sq km
land: 116 sq km
water: 0 sq km
country comparison to the world: 225

Area—comparative: about two-thirds the size of Washington, DC

Land boundaries: 0 km

Coastline: 70 km

Maritime claims: *territorial sea:* 12 nm
exclusive fishing zone: 12 nm

Climate: temperate; mild winters and cool summers

Terrain: gently rolling plain with low, rugged hills along north coast

Elevation: *mean elevation:* NA

elevation extremes: *lowest point:* English Channel 0 m
highest point: Les Platons 136 m

Natural resources: arable land

Land use: *agricultural land:* 66%
arable land: 66%;
permanent crops: 0%;

permanent pasture: 0%
forest: 0%
other: 34% (2011 est.)
Irrigated land: NA

Population—distribution: fairly even distribution; no notable trends

Natural hazards: very large tidal variation can be hazardous to navigation

Environment—current issues: habitat and species depletion due to human encroachment; water pollution; improper solid waste disposal
Geography—note: largest and southernmost of Channel Islands; about 30% of population concentrated in Saint Helier

PEOPLE AND SOCIETY

Population: 98,840 (July 2017 est.)
country comparison to the world: 196

Nationality: *noun:* Channel Islander(s)
adjective: Channel Islander

Ethnic groups: Jersey 46.4%, British 32.7%, Portuguese/Madeiran 8.2%, Polish 3.3%, Irish, French, and other white 7.1%, other 2.4% (2011 est.)

Languages: English 94.5% (official), Portuguese 4.6%, other 0.9% (2001 census)

Religions: Protestant (Anglican, Baptist, Congregational New Church, Methodist, Presbyterian), Roman Catholic

Age structure: *0-14 years:* 16.23% (male 8,300/female 7,740)
15-24 years: 13.91% (male 7,094/female 6,658)
25-54 years: 40.99% (male 20,318/female 20,200)
55-64 years: 12.53% (male 6,042/female 6,339)
65 years and over: 16.34% (male 6,879/female 9,270) (2017 est.)

Dependency ratios: *total dependency ratio:* 47.1
youth dependency ratio: 21.6
elderly dependency ratio: 25.4
potential support ratio: 3.9
note: data represent the Guernsey and Jersey (2015 est.)

Median age: *total:* 38 years
male: 36 years
female: 40.7 years (2017 est.)
country comparison to the world: 59

Population growth rate: 0.78% (2017 est.)
country comparison to the world: 133

Birth rate: 12.4 births/1,000 population (2017 est.)
country comparison to the world: 160

Death rate: 7.8 deaths/1,000 population (2017 est.)
country comparison to the world: 98

Net migration rate: 3.2 migrant(s)/1,000 population (2017 est.)
country comparison to the world: 33

Population distribution: fairly even distribution; no notable trends

Urbanization: *urban population:* 31.7% of total population (2017)
rate of urbanization: 0.86% annual rate of change (2015-20 est.)
note: data are for Guernsey and Jersey

Sex ratio: *at birth:* 1.06 male(s)/female
0-14 years: 1.07 male(s)/female
15-24 years: 1.06 male(s)/female
25-54 years: 1 male(s)/female
55-64 years: 0.96 male(s)/female
65 years and over: 0.74 male(s)/female
total population: 0.97 male(s)/female (2016 est.)

Infant mortality rate: *total:* 3.8 deaths/1,000 live births
male: 4 deaths/1,000 live births
female: 3.5 deaths/1,000 live births (2017 est.)
country comparison to the world: 195

Life expectancy at birth: *total population:* 81.9 years
male: 79.5 years
female: 84.6 years (2017 est.)
country comparison to the world: 20

Total fertility rate: 1.66 children born/woman (2017 est.)
country comparison to the world: 176

HIV/AIDS—adult prevalence rate: NA

HIV/AIDS—people living with HIV/AIDS: NA

HIV/AIDS—deaths: NA

GOVERNMENT

Country name: *conventional long form:* Bailiwick of Jersey
conventional short form: Jersey
etymology: the name is of Old Norse origin, but the meaning of the root "Jer(s)" is uncertain; the "-ey" ending means "island"

Dependency status: British crown dependency

Government type: parliamentary democracy (Assembly of the States of Jersey); a Crown dependency of the UK

Capital: *name:* Saint Helier
geographic coordinates: 49 11 N, 2 06 W
time difference: UTC 0 (5 hours ahead of Washington, DC, during Standard Time)
daylight saving time: +1hr, begins last Sunday in March; ends last Sunday in October

Administrative divisions: none (British crown dependency); there are no first-order administrative divisions as defined by the US Government, but there are 12 parishes; Grouville, Saint Brelade, Saint Clement, Saint Helier, Saint John, Saint Lawrence, Saint Martin, Saint Mary, Saint Ouen, Saint Peter, Saint Saviour, and Trinity

Independence: none (British crown dependency)

National holiday: Liberation Day, 9 May (1945)

Constitution: history: unwritten; partly statutes, partly common law and practice *amendments:* proposed by a government minister to the Assembly of the States of Jersey, by an Assembly member, or by an elected parish head; passage requires several Assembly readings, a majority vote by the Assembly, review by the UK Ministry of Justice, and approval by the British monarch (Royal Assent) (2016)

Legal system: the laws of the UK, where applicable, apply; local statutes

Citizenship: see United Kingdom

Suffrage: 16 years of age; universal

Executive branch: *chief of state:* Queen ELIZABETH II (since 6 February 1952); represented by Lieutenant Governor Sir Stephen DALTON (since 13 March 2017) 2017

head of government: Chief Minister Ian GORST (since 18 November 2011); Bailiff William BAILHACHE (since 29 January 2015)
cabinet: Council of Ministers appointed individually by the states
elections/appointments: the monarchy is hereditary; Council of Ministers, including the chief minister, indirectly elected by the Assembly of States; lieutenant governor and bailiff appointed by the monarch

Legislative branch: *description:* unicameral Assembly of the States of Jersey (49 elected members; 8 senators to serve 4-year terms, and 29 deputies and 12 connetables, or heads of parishes, to serve 4-year terms; 5 non-voting members appointed by the monarch include the bailiff, lieutenant governor, dean of Jersey, attorney general, and the solicitor general)
elections: last held on 15 October 2014 (next to be held in May 2018)
election results: percent of vote—NA; seats—independents 49

Judicial branch: *highest court(s):* Jersey Court of Appeal (consists of the bailiff, deputy bailiff, and 12 judges); Royal Court (consists of the bailiff, deputy bailiff, 6 commissioners and lay people referred to as jurats, and is organized into Heritage, Family, Probate, and Samedi Divisions); appeals beyond the Court of Appeal are heard by the Judicial Committe of the Privy Council in London
judge selection and term of office: Jersey Court of Appeal bailiffs and judges appointed by the Crown upon the advice of the Secretary of State for Justice; bailiffs and judges appointed for extent of good behavior; Royal Court bailiffs appointed by the Crown upon the advice of the Secretary of State for Justice; commissioners appointed by the bailiff; jurats appointed by the Electoral College; bailiffs and commissioners appointed for extent of good behavior; jurats appointed until retirement at age 72
subordinate courts: Magistrate's Court; Youth Court; Petty Debts Court; Parish Hall Enquires (a process of preliminary investigation into youth and minor adult offenses to determine need for presentation before a court)

Political parties and leaders: one registered party: Reform Jersey [Sam MEZEC]

note: most senators and deputies sit as independents

Political pressure groups and leaders: Institute of Directors, Jersey branch (provides business support)
Jersey Hospitality Association or JHa [Fiona KERLEY] (trade association)
Jersey Rights Association [David ROTHERHAM] (human rights)
La Societe Jersiaise (education and conservation group)
Progress Jersey [Daren O'TOOLE, Gino RISOLI] (human rights)
Royal Jersey Agriculture and Horticultural Society or RJA&HS (development and management of the Jersey breed of cattle)
Save Jersey's Heritage (protects heritage through building preservation)

Diplomatic representation in the US: none (British Crown dependency)

Diplomatic representation from the US: none (British Crown dependency)

Flag description: white with a diagonal red cross extending to the corners of the flag; in the upper quadrant, surmounted by a yellow crown, a red shield with three lions in yellow; according to tradition, the ships of Jersey—in an attempt to differentiate themselves from English ships flying the horizontal cross of St. George—rotated the cross to the "X" (saltire) configuration; because this arrangement still resembled the Irish cross of St. Patrick, the yellow Plantagenet crown and Jersey coat of arms were added

National symbol(s): Jersey cow; national colors: red, white

National anthem: *name:* "Isle de Siez Nous" (Island Home)
lyrics/music: Gerard LE FEUVRE
note: adopted 2008; serves as a local anthem; as a British Crown dependency, "God Save the Queen" is official (see United Kingdom)

ECONOMY

Economy—overview: Jersey's economy is based on international financial services, agriculture, and tourism. In 2010, the financial services sector accounted for about 50% of the island's output. Potatoes, cauliflower, tomatoes, and especially flowers are important export crops, shipped mostly to the UK. The Jersey breed of dairy cattle is known worldwide and represents an important export income earner. Tourism accounts for one-quarter of GDP. Living standards come close to those of the UK. In recent years, the government has encouraged light industry to locate in Jersey with the result that an electronics industry has developed, displacing more traditional industries. All raw material and energy requirements are imported as well as a large share of Jersey's food needs. Light taxes and death duties make the island a popular tax haven. In October 2014, Jersey signed an OECD agreement to automatically exchange some financial account information to limit tax avoidance and evasion.

GDP (purchasing power parity): $5.08 billion (2015 est.)
$4.98 billion (2014)
note: data are in 2015 US dollars
country comparison to the world: 175

GDP (official exchange rate): $4.524 billion (FY12/13 est.)

GDP—real growth rate: 2% (2015 est.)
country comparison to the world: 155

GDP—per capita (PPP): $49,500 (2015 est.)
country comparison to the world: 32

GDP—composition, by sector of origin:
agriculture: 2%
industry: 2%
services: 96% (2010)

Agriculture—products: potatoes, cauliflower, tomatoes; beef, dairy products

Industries: tourism, banking and finance, dairy, electronics

Industrial production growth rate: NA%

Labor force: 53,380 (June 2012)
country comparison to the world: 190

Unemployment rate: 4% (2015 est.)
1.7% (2012 est.)
country comparison to the world: 47

Population below poverty line: NA%

Household income or consumption by percentage share: *lowest 10%:* NA%
highest 10%: NA%

Budget: *revenues:* $829 million
expenditures: $851 million (2005)
Taxes and other revenues: 18.3% of GDP (2005)
country comparison to the world: 164

Budget surplus (+) or deficit (-): -0.5% of GDP (2005)
country comparison to the world: 48

Fiscal year: 1 April—31 March

Inflation rate (consumer prices): 3.7% (2006)
country comparison to the world: 147

Market value of publicly traded shares: $NA

Exports: $NA

Exports—commodities: light industrial and electrical goods, dairy cattle, foodstuffs, textiles, flowers

Imports: $NA

Imports—commodities: machinery and transport equipment, manufactured goods, foodstuffs, mineral fuels, chemicals

Debt—external: $NA

Exchange rates: Jersey pounds (JEP) per US dollar
0.7836 (2017)
0.738 (2016)
0.738 (2015)
0.6542 (2012)
0.6391 (2011 est.)

ENERGY

Electricity access: electrification—*total population:* 100% (2016)

Electricity—consumption: 630.1 million kWh (2004 est.)
country comparison to the world: 166

Communications

Telephones—fixed lines: *total subscriptions:* 55,938
subscriptions per 100 inhabitants: 58 (July 2016 est.)
country comparison to the world: 148

Telephones—mobile cellular: *total:* 122,668
subscriptions per 100 inhabitants: 119 (July 2016 est.)
country comparison to the world: 194

Telephone system: *general assessment:* modern system with broadband access
domestic: fixed-line and mobile-cellular services widely available

international: country code—44; submarine cable connectivity to Guernsey, the UK, and France (2015)

Broadcast media: multiple UK terrestrial TV broadcasts are received via a transmitter in Jersey; satellite packages available; BBC Radio Jersey and 1 other radio station operating (2009)

Internet country code: .je
Internet users: total: 58,000

percent of population: 59.6% (July 2016 est.)
country comparison to the world: 197

TRANSPORTATION

National air transport system: *number of registered air carriers:* 2 (registered in UK)
inventory of registered aircraft operated by air carriers: 11 (registered in UK) (2015)

Airports: 1 (2013)
country comparison to the world: 223

Airports—with paved runways: *total:* 1
1,524 to 2,437 m: 1 (2017)

Roadways: *total:* 576 km (2010)
country comparison to the world: 193

Ports and terminals: *major seaport(s):* Gorey, Saint Aubin, Saint Helier

MILITARY AND SECURITY

Military—note: defense is the responsibility of the UK

TRANSNATIONAL ISSUES

Disputes—international: none

JORDAN

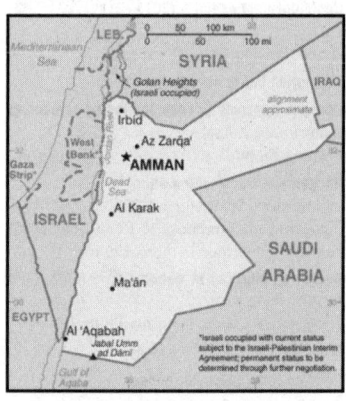

INTRODUCTION

Background: Following World War I and the dissolution of the Ottoman Empire, the League of Nations awarded Britain the mandate to govern much of the Middle East. Britain demarcated a semi-autonomous region of Transjordan from Palestine in the early 1920s. The area gained its independence in 1946 and thereafter became The Hashemite Kingdom of Jordan. The country's long-time ruler, King HUSSEIN (1953-99), successfully navigated competing pressures from the major powers (US, USSR, and UK), various Arab states, Israel, and a large internal Palestinian population. Jordan lost the West Bank to Israel in the 1967 Six-Day War. King HUSSEIN in 1988 permanently relinquished Jordanian claims to the West Bank; in 1994 he signed a peace treaty with Israel. King ABDALLAH II, King HUSSEIN's eldest son, assumed the throne following his father's death in 1999. He has implemented modest political and economic reforms, including the passage of a new electoral law in early 2016 ahead

of legislative elections held in September. The Islamic Action Front, which is the political arm of the Jordanian Muslim Brotherhood, returned to parliament with 15 seats after boycotting the previous two elections in 2010 and 2013.

GEOGRAPHY

Location: Middle East, northwest of Saudi Arabia, between Israel (to the west) and Iraq

Geographic coordinates: 31 00 N, 36 00 E

Map references: Middle East

Area: *total:* 89,342 sq km
land: 88,802 sq km
water: 540 sq km
country comparison to the world: 113

Area—comparative: about three-quarters the size of Pennsylvania; slightly smaller than Indiana

Land boundaries: *total:* 1,744 km
border countries (5): Iraq 179 km, Israel 307 km, Saudi Arabia 731 km, Syria 379 km, West Bank 148 km

Coastline: 26 km

Maritime claims: *territorial sea:* 3 nm

Climate: mostly arid desert; rainy season in west (November to April)

Terrain: mostly desert plateau in east, highland area in west; Great Rift Valley separates eastern and western banks of the Jordan River

Elevation: *mean elevation:* 812 m

elevation extremes: *lowest point:* Dead Sea -431 m
highest point: Jabal Umm ad Dami 1,854 m

Natural resources: phosphates, potash, shale oil

Land use: *agricultural land:* 11.4%
arable land: 2%;
permanent crops: 1%;
permanent pasture: 8.4%
forest: 1.1%

other: 87.5% (2011 est.)
Irrigated land: 964 sq km (2012)

Population—distribution: population heavily concentrated in the west, and particularly the northwest, in and around the capital of Amman; a sizeable, but smaller population is located in the southwest along the shore of the Gulf of Aqaba

Natural hazards: droughts; periodic earthquakes; flash floods

Environment—current issues: limited natural freshwater resources; deforestation; overgrazing; soil erosion; desertification

Environment—international agreements: *party to:* Biodiversity, Climate Change, Climate Change-Kyoto Protocol, Desertification, Endangered Species, Hazardous Wastes, Law of the Sea, Marine Dumping, Ozone Layer Protection, Wetlands
signed, but not ratified: none of the selected agreements
Geography—note: strategic location at the head of the Gulf of Aqaba and as the Arab country that shares the longest border with Israel and the occupied West Bank

PEOPLE AND SOCIETY

Population: 10,248,069
note: increased estimate reflects revised assumptions about the net migration rate due to the increased flow of Syrian refugees (July 2017 est.)
country comparison to the world: 89

Nationality: *noun:* Jordanian(s)
adjective: Jordanian

Ethnic groups: Arab 98%, Circassian 1%, Armenian 1%

Languages: Arabic (official), English (widely understood among upper and middle classes)

Religions: Muslim 97.2% (official; predominantly Sunni), Christian 2.2% (majority Greek Orthodox, but some Greek and Roman Catholics, Syrian

Orthodox, Coptic Orthodox, Armenian Orthodox, and Protestant denominations), Buddhist 0.4%, Hindu 0.1%, Jewish <0.1, folk religionist <0.1, unaffiliated <0.1, other <0.1 (2010 est.)

Age structure: 0-14 years: 34.68% (male 1,827,554/female 1,726,691)
15-24 years: 20.07% (male 1,103,042/female 953,704)
25-54 years: 37.36% (male 2,073,211/female 1,755,290)
55-64 years: 4.44% (male 236,435/female 218,469)
65 years and over: 3.45% (male 174,470/female 179,203) (2017 est.)

Dependency ratios: total dependency ratio: 66.1
youth dependency ratio: 59.8
elderly dependency ratio: 6.2
potential support ratio: 16 (2015 est.)

Median age: total: 22.5 years
male: 22.9 years
female: 22 years (2017 est.)
country comparison to the world: 177

Population growth rate: 2.05% (2017 est.)
country comparison to the world: 43

Birth rate: 23.9 births/1,000 population (2017 est.)
country comparison to the world: 58

Death rate: 3.4 deaths/1,000 population (2017 est.)
country comparison to the world: 218

Net migration rate: 0 migrant(s)/1,000 population (2017 est.)
country comparison to the world: 87

Population distribution: population heavily concentrated in the west, and particularly the northwest, in and around the capital of Amman; a sizeable, but smaller population is located in the southwest along the shore of the Gulf of Aqaba

Urbanization: urban population: 84.1% of total population (2017)
rate of urbanization: 1.26% annual rate of change (2015-20 est.)

Major urban areas—population: AMMAN (capital) 1.155 million (2015)

Sex ratio: at birth: 1.06 male(s)/female
0-14 years: 1.05 male(s)/female
15-24 years: 1.05 male(s)/female
25-54 years: 1 male(s)/female
55-64 years: 0.95 male(s)/female
65 years and over: 0.89 male(s)/female
total population: 1.02 male(s)/female (2016 est.)

Mother's mean age at first birth: 24.7 years
note: median age at first birth among women 25-29 (2012 est.)

Maternal mortality ratio: 58 deaths/100,000 live births (2015 est.)
country comparison to the world: 90

Infant mortality rate: total: 14.2 deaths/1,000 live births
male: 15 deaths/1,000 live births
female: 13.3 deaths/1,000 live births (2017 est.)
country comparison to the world: 104

Life expectancy at birth: total population: 74.8 years

male: 73.4 years
female: 76.3 years (2017 est.)
country comparison to the world: 119

Total fertility rate: 3.19 children born/woman (2017 est.)
country comparison to the world: 49

Contraceptive prevalence rate: 61.2% (2012)

Health expenditures: 7.5% of GDP (2014)
country comparison to the world: 66

Physicians density: 2.65 physicians/1,000 population (2014)

Hospital bed density: 1.8 beds/1,000 population (2012)

Drinking water source:
improved:
urban: 97.8% of population
rural: 92.3% of population
total: 96.9% of population
unimproved:
urban: 2.2% of population
rural: 7.7% of population
total: 3.1% of population (2015 est.)

Sanitation facility access:
improved:
urban: 98.6% of population
rural: 98.9% of population
total: 98.6% of population
unimproved:
urban: 1.4% of population
rural: 1.1% of population
total: 1.4% of population (2015 est.)

HIV/AIDS—adult prevalence rate: <.1% (2016 est.)

HIV/AIDS—people living with HIV/AIDS: <500 (2016 est.)

HIV/AIDS—deaths: <100 (2016 est.)

Obesity—adult prevalence rate: 35.5% (2016)
country comparison to the world: 13

Children under the age of 5 years underweight: 3% (2012)
country comparison to the world: 114

Education expenditures: NA

Literacy: definition: age 15 and over can read and write
total population: 95.4%
male: 97.7%
female: 92.9% (2015 est.)

School life expectancy (primary to tertiary education): total: 13 years
male: 12 years
female: 13 years (2012)

Unemployment, youth ages 15-24: total: 29.3%
male: 25.2%
female: 48.8% (2012 est.)
country comparison to the world: 27

GOVERNMENT

Country name: conventional long form: Hashemite Kingdom of Jordan
conventional short form: Jordan
local long form: Al Mamlakah al Urduniyah al Hashimiyah

local short form: Al Urdun
former: Transjordan
etymology: named for the Jordan River, which makes up part of Jordan's northwest border

Government type: parliamentary constitutional monarchy

Capital: name: Amman
geographic coordinates: 31 57 N, 35 56 E
time difference: UTC+2 (7 hours ahead of Washington, DC, during Standard Time)
daylight saving time: +1hr, begins last Friday in March; ends last Friday in October

Administrative divisions: 12 governorates (muhafazat, singular—muhafazah); 'Ajlun, Al 'Aqabah, Al Balqa', Al Karak, Al Mafraq, Al Asimah (Amman), At Tafilah, Az Zarqa', Irbid, Jarash, Ma'an, Madaba

Independence: 25 May 1946 (from League of Nations mandate under British administration)

National holiday: Independence Day, 25 May (1946)

Constitution: history: previous 1928 (preindependence); latest initially adopted 28 November 1947, revised and ratified 1 January 1952
amendments: proposed by 10 or more members of the Senate or by the House of Representatives followed by referral to the relevant House committee for its review and opinion; if accepted, the proposal is referred to the government for restatement as a draft; passage requires two-thirds majority vote of both the Senate and the House and ratification by the king; amended several times, last in 2016 (2016)

Legal system: mixed system developed from codes instituted by the Ottoman Empire (based on French law), British common law, and Islamic law

International law organization participation: has not submitted an ICJ jurisdiction declaration; accepts ICCt jurisdiction

Citizenship: citizenship by birth: no
citizenship by descent only: the father must be a citizen of Jordan
dual citizenship recognized: yes
residency requirement for naturalization: 15 years

Suffrage: 18 years of age; universal

Executive branch: chief of state: King ABDALLAH II (since 7 February 1999); Crown Prince HUSSEIN (born 28 June 1994), eldest son of King ABDALLAH II

head of government: Prime Minister Hani MULKI (since 1 June 2016)
cabinet: Cabinet appointed by the prime minister in consultation with the monarch
elections/appointments: the monarchy is hereditary; prime minister appointed by the monarch

Legislative branch: description: bicameral National Assembly or Majlis al-'Umma consists of the Senate, or the House of Notables or Majlis al-Ayan (65 seats; members appointed by the monarch to serve 4-year terms) and the Chamber of Deputies or House of Representatives or Majlis al-Nuwaab (130 seats; 115 members directly

479

elected in single- and multi-seat constituencies by open-list proportional representation vote and 15 seats for women; 12 of the 115 seats reserved for Christian, Chechen, and Circassian candidates; members serve 4-year terms)

elections: Chamber of Deputies—last held on 20 September 2016 (next to be held in 2020)

election results: Chamber of Deputies—percent of vote by party—NA; seats by party—NA

Judicial branch: *highest court(s):* Court of Cassation or Supreme Court (consists of 15 judges including the chief justice; 7-judge panels for important cases and 5 judge panels for most appeals cases); Constitutional Court (consists of 9 members including the court chairman)

judge selection and term of office: Supreme Court chief justice appointed by the king; other judges nominated by the Judicial Council, an 11-member judicial policy-making body consisting of high-level judicial officials and judges, and approved by the king; judge tenure NA; Constitutional Court members appointed by the king for 6-year non-renewable terms with one-third of the membership renewed every 2 years

subordinate courts: Courts of Appeal; Major Felonies Court; Courts of First Instance; Magistrate Courts; religious courts; state security courts

Political parties and leaders: Al-Hayah Jordanian Party [Zahier AMR]
Arab Ba'ath Socialist Party [Akram al-HIMSI]
Ba'ath Arab Progressive Party [Fuad DABBOUR]
Democratic People's Party [Ablah ABU ULBAH]
Democratic Popular Unity Party [Sa'id DIAB]
Du'a Party [Muhammed ABU BAKR]
Islamic Action Front or IAF [Hamzah MANSOUR]
Islamic Centrist Party [Muhammad al-HAJ]
Jordanian Communist Party [Munir HAMARNAH]
Jordanian National Party [Muna ABU BAKR]
Jordanian United Front [Amjad al-MAJALI]
Muslim Center Party [Haitham ALAMAERAH]
National Congress Party [Raheeh GHARAYBEH]
National Constitution Party [Ahmad al-SHUNAQ]
National Current Party [Abd al-Hadi al-MAJALI]
National Movement for Direct Democracy [Muhammad al-QAQ]
Risalah Party [Hazem QASHOU]
The Direct Democratic Nationalists Movement Party [Nash'at KHALIFAH]

Political pressure groups and leaders: 15 April Movement [Mohammad SUNEID]
24 March Movement [Mu'az al-KHAWALIDAH, Abdel Rahman HASANEIN]
1952 Constitution Movement
Anti-Normalization Committee [Saleh al-ARMOUTI]
Economic and Social Association of Retired Servicemen and Veterans or ESARSV [Abdulsalam al-HASSANAT]
Group of 36
Higher Coordination Committee of Opposition Parties [Said DIAB]

Higher National Committee for Military Retirees or HNCMR [Ali al-HABASHNEH]
Hirak
Jordan Bar Association [Samir KHIRFAN]
Jordanian Campaign for Change or Jayin
Jordanian Muslim Brotherhood [Dr. Hamam SAID]
Jordanian Press Association [Sayf al-SHARIF]
National Front for Reform or NFR [Ahmad OBEIDAT]
Popular Gathering for Reform
Professional Associations Council [Abd al-Hadi al-FALAHAT]
Sons of Jordan

International organization participation: ABEDA, AFESD, AMF, CAEU, CD, CICA, EBRD, FAO, G-11, G-77, IAEA, IBRD, ICAO, ICC (national committees), ICCt, ICRM, IDA, IDB, IFAD, IFC, IFRCS, ILO, IMF, IMO, IMSO, Interpol, IOC, IOM, IPU, ISO, ITSO, ITU, ITUC (NGOs), LAS, MIGA, MINUSTAH, MINUSMA, MONUSCO, NAM, OIC, OPCW, OSCE (partner), PCA, UN, UN Security Council (temporary), UNAMID, UNCTAD, UNESCO, UNHCR, UNIDO, UNMIL, UNMISS, UNOCI, UNRWA, UNWTO, UPU, WCO, WFTU (NGOs), WHO, WIPO, WMO, WTO

Diplomatic representation in the US: *chief of mission:* Ambassador Dina Khalil Tawiq KAWAR (since 27 June 2016)
chancery: 3504 International Drive NW, Washington, DC 20008
telephone: [1] (202) 966-2664
FAX: [1] (202) 966-3110

Diplomatic representation from the US: *chief of mission:* Ambassador (vacant); Charge d'Affaires Henry T. WOOSTER (since 24 March 2017)
embassy: Abdoun, Al-Umawyeen St., Amman
mailing address: P. O. Box 354, Amman 11118 Jordan; Unit 70200, Box 5, DPO AE 09892-0200
telephone: [962] (6) 590-6000
FAX: [962] (6) 592-0163

Flag description: three equal horizontal bands of black (top), representing the Abbassid Caliphate, white, representing the Ummayyad Caliphate, and green, representing the Fatimid Caliphate; a red isosceles triangle on the hoist side, representing the Great Arab Revolt of 1916, and bearing a small white seven-pointed star symbolizing the seven verses of the opening Sura (Al-Fatiha) of the Holy Koran; the seven points on the star represent faith in One God, humanity, national spirit, humility, social justice, virtue, and aspirations; design is based on the Arab Revolt flag of World War I

National symbol(s): eagle; national colors: black, white, green, red

National anthem: name: "As-salam al-malaki al-urdoni" (Long Live the King of Jordan)
lyrics/music: Abdul-Mone'm al-RIFAI'/Abdul-Qader al-TANEER
note: adopted 1946; the shortened version of the anthem is used most commonly, while the full version is reserved for special occasions

Economy—overview: Jordan's economy is among the smallest in the Middle East, with insufficient supplies of water, oil, and other natural resources, underlying the government's heavy reliance on foreign assistance. Other economic challenges for the government include chronic high rates of poverty, unemployment and underemployment, budget and current account deficits, and government debt.

King ABDALLAH, during the first decade of the 2000s, implemented significant economic reforms, such as expanding foreign trade and privatizing state-owned companies that attracted foreign investment and contributed to average annual economic growth of 8% for 2004 through 2008. The global economic slowdown and regional turmoil contributed to slower growth from 2010 to 2017—with growth averaging 2.6% per year—and hurt export-oriented sectors, construction, and tourism. Since the onset of the civil war in Syria and resulting refugee crisis, one of Jordan's most pressing socioeconomic challenges has been managing the influx of 650,000 UN-registered refugees, more than 80% of whom live in Jordan's urban areas. Jordan's own official census estimated the refugee number at 1.3 million as of early 2016.

Jordan is nearly completely dependent on imported energy—mostly natural gas—and energy consistently makes up 25-30 percent of Jordan's imports. To diversify its energy mix, Jordan has secured several contracts for liquefied natural gas and is currently exploring nuclear power generation, exploitation of abundant oil shale reserves and renewable technologies, as well as the import of Israeli offshore gas. In August 2016, Jordan and the IMF agreed to a $723 million Extended Fund Facility that aims to build on the three-year, $2.1 billion IMF program that ended in August 2015 with the goal of helping Jordan correct budgetary and balance of payments imbalances.

GDP (purchasing power parity): $89.05 billion (2017 est.)
$87.04 billion (2016 est.)
$85.33 billion (2015 est.)
note: data are in 2017 dollars
country comparison to the world: 89

GDP (official exchange rate): $40.49 billion (2016 est.)

GDP—real growth rate: 2.3% (2017 est.)
2% (2016 est.)
2.4% (2015 est.)
country comparison to the world: 142

GDP—per capita (PPP): $12,500 (2017 est.)
$12,500 (2016 est.)
$12,500 (2015 est.)
note: data are in 2017 dollars
country comparison to the world: 123

Gross national saving: 11.8% of GDP (2017 est.)
9.5% of GDP (2016 est.)
10.2% of GDP (2015 est.)
country comparison to the world: 147

GDP—composition, by end use:
household consumption: 79.1%

government consumption: 19.3%
investment in fixed capital: 22.4%
investment in inventories: 1.9%
exports of goods and services: 32.7%
imports of goods and services: -55.4% (2017 est.)

GDP—composition, by sector of origin:
agriculture: 4.3%
industry: 28.9%
services: 66.8% (2017 est.)

Agriculture—products: citrus, tomatoes, cucumbers, olives, strawberries, stone fruits; sheep, poultry, dairy

Industries: tourism, information technology, clothing, fertilizer, potash, phosphate mining, pharmaceuticals, petroleum refining, cement, inorganic chemicals, light manufacturing

Industrial production growth rate: 2.2% (2017 est.)
country comparison to the world: 123

Labor force: 2.295 million (2017 est.)
country comparison to the world: 118

Labor force—by occupation: *agriculture:* 2%
industry: 20%
services: 78% (2013 est.)

Unemployment rate: 16.5% (2017 est.)
15.3% (2016 est.)
note: official rate; unofficial rate is approximately 30%
country comparison to the world: 176

Population below poverty line: 14.2% (2002 est.)

Household income or consumption by percentage share: *lowest 10%:* 3.4%
highest 10%: 28.7% (2010 est.)

Distribution of family income—Gini index: 39.7 (2007)
36.4 (1997)
country comparison to the world: 64

Budget: *revenues:* $9.157 billion
expenditures: $11.81 billion (2017 est.)
Taxes and other revenues: 22.6% of GDP (2017 est.)
country comparison to the world: 133

Budget surplus (+) or deficit (-): -6.5% of GDP (2017 est.)
country comparison to the world: 182

Public debt: 86% of GDP (2017 est.)
87.7% of GDP (2016 est.)
note: data cover central government debt, and include debt instruments issued (or owned) by government entities other than the treasury; the data include treasury debt held by foreign entities; the data exclude debt issued by subnational entities, as well as intra-governmental debt; intra-governmental debt consists of treasury borrowings from surpluses in the social funds, such as for retirement, medical care, and unemployment; debt instruments for the social funds are not sold at public auctions
country comparison to the world: 31

Fiscal year: calendar year

Inflation rate (consumer prices): 3.3% (2017 est.)
-0.8% (2016 est.)
country comparison to the world: 137

Central bank discount rate: 3.75% (31 December 2015)
0.3% (31 December 2010)
country comparison to the world: 99

Commercial bank prime lending rate: 8.5% (31 December 2017 est.)
7.83% (31 December 2016 est.)
country comparison to the world: 100

Stock of narrow money: $14.98 billion (31 December 2017 est.)
$14.63 billion (31 December 2016 est.)
country comparison to the world: 72

Stock of broad money: $47.29 billion (31 December 2017 est.)
$46.3 billion (31 December 2016 est.)
country comparison to the world: 70

Stock of domestic credit: $44.59 billion (31 December 2017 est.)
$41.87 billion (31 December 2016 est.)
country comparison to the world: 69

Market value of publicly traded shares: $24.25 billion (31 December 2016 est.)
$25.45 billion (31 December 2015 est.)
$25.55 billion (31 December 2014 est.)
country comparison to the world: 63

Current account balance: -$3.412 billion (2017 est.)
-$3.613 billion (2016 est.)
country comparison to the world: 170

Exports: $7.734 billion (2017 est.)
$7.509 billion (2016 est.)
country comparison to the world: 98

Exports—commodities: textiles, fertilizers, potash, phosphates, vegetables, pharmaceuticals

Exports—partners: US 25.2%, Saudi Arabia 14.2%, India 8.4%, Iraq 6.8%, UAE 5.6%, Kuwait 5.1% (2016)

Imports: $17.61 billion (2017 est.)
$17.03 billion (2016 est.)
country comparison to the world: 79

Imports—commodities: crude oil, refined petroleum products, machinery, transport equipment, iron, cereals

Imports—partners: China 14%, Saudi Arabia 11.8%, US 7.4%, Germany 4.8%, Italy 4.7%, UAE 4.4% (2016)

Reserves of foreign exchange and gold: $15.98 billion (31 December 2017 est.)
$15.54 billion (31 December 2016 est.)
country comparison to the world: 67

Debt—external: $27.72 billion (31 December 2017 est.)
$26.38 billion (31 December 2016 est.)
country comparison to the world: 84

Stock of direct foreign investment—at home: $33.96 billion (31 December 2017 est.)
$32.15 billion (31 December 2016 est.)
country comparison to the world: 69

Stock of direct foreign investment—abroad: $646.5 million (31 December 2017 est.)
$612.5 million (31 December 2016 est.)
country comparison to the world: 90

Exchange rates: Jordanian dinars (JOD) per US dollar—
0.71 (2017 est.)
0.71 (2016 est.)
0.71 (2015 est.)
0.71 (2014 est.)
0.71 (2013 est.)

ENERGY

Electricity access: *population without electricity:* 40,926
electrification—*total population:* 99.5%
electrification—urban areas: 99%
electrification—rural areas: 99.4% (2012)

Electricity—production: 17.76 billion kWh (2015 est.)
country comparison to the world: 80

Electricity—consumption: 16.13 billion kWh (2015 est.)
country comparison to the world: 74

Electricity—exports: 50 million kWh (2015 est.)
country comparison to the world: 87

Electricity—imports: 604 million kWh (2015 est.)
country comparison to the world: 78

Electricity—installed generating capacity: 4.382 million kW (2015 est.)
country comparison to the world: 83

Electricity—from fossil fuels: 96.3% of total installed capacity (2015 est.)
country comparison to the world: 47

Electricity—from nuclear fuels: 0% of total installed capacity (2015 est.)
country comparison to the world: 117

Electricity—from hydroelectric plants: 0.3% of total installed capacity (2015 est.)
country comparison to the world: 152

Electricity—from other renewable sources: 9.5% of total installed capacity (2015 est.)
country comparison to the world: 72

Crude oil—production: 22 bbl/day (2016 est.)
country comparison to the world: 100

Crude oil—exports: 0 bbl/day (2014 est.)
country comparison to the world: 144

Crude oil—imports: 63,220 bbl/day (2014 est.)
country comparison to the world: 50

Crude oil—proved reserves: 1 million bbl (1 January 2017 es)
country comparison to the world: 99

Refined petroleum products—production: 65,150 bbl/day (2014 est.)
country comparison to the world: 76

Refined petroleum products—consumption: 160,000 bbl/day (2015 est.)
country comparison to the world: 64

Refined petroleum products—exports: 0 bbl/day (2014 est.)
country comparison to the world: 166

Refined petroleum products—imports: 93,860 bbl/day (2014 est.)
country comparison to the world: 60

Natural gas—production: 151 million cu m (2015 est.)
country comparison to the world: 79

Natural gas—consumption: 3.509 billion cu m (2015 est.)
country comparison to the world: 73

Natural gas—exports: 0 cu m (2013 est.)
country comparison to the world: 127

Natural gas—imports: 2.746 billion cu m (2015 est.)
country comparison to the world: 47

Natural gas—proved reserves: 6.031 billion cu m (1 January 2017 es)
country comparison to the world: 92

Carbon dioxide emissions from consumption of energy: 19 million Mt (2013 est.)
country comparison to the world: 83

COMMUNICATIONS

Telephones—fixed lines: *total subscriptions:* 355,821
subscriptions per 100 inhabitants: 4 (July 2016 est.)
country comparison to the world: 107

Telephones—mobile cellular: *total:* 15.352 million
subscriptions per 100 inhabitants: 188 (July 2016 est.)
country comparison to the world: 81

Telephone system: *general assessment:* service has improved recently with increased use of digital switching equipment; microwave radio relay transmission and coaxial and fiber-optic cable are employed on trunk lines; growing mobile-cellular usage in both urban and rural areas is reducing use of fixed-line services
domestic: 1995 telecommunications law opened all non-fixed-line services to private competition; in 2005, monopoly over fixed-line services terminated and the entire telecommunications sector was opened to competition; currently multiple mobile-cellular providers with subscribership up to 185 per 100 persons

international: country code—962; landing point for the Fiber-Optic Link Around the Globe (FLAG) FEA and FLAG Falcon submarine cable networks; satellite earth stations—33 (3 Intelsat, 1 Arabsat, and 29 land and maritime Inmarsat terminals); fiber-optic cable to Saudi Arabia and microwave radio relay link with Egypt and Syria; participant in Medarabtel (2016)

Broadcast media: radio and TV dominated by the government-owned Jordan Radio and Television Corporation (JRTV) that operates a main network, a sports network, a film network, and a satellite channel; first independent TV broadcaster aired in 2007; international satellite TV and Israeli and Syrian TV broadcasts are available; roughly 30 radio stations with JRTV operating the main government-owned station; transmissions of multiple international radio broadcasters are available (2007)

Internet country code: .jo
Internet users: total: 5,099,674
percent of population: 62.3% (July 2016 est.)
country comparison to the world: 82

TRANSPORTATION

National air transport system: *number of registered air carriers:* 7
inventory of registered aircraft operated by air carriers: 40
annual passenger traffic on registered air carriers: 3,065,145
annual freight traffic on registered air carriers: 169.105 million mt-km (2015)
Civil aircraft registration country code prefix: JY (2016)

Airports: 18 (2013)
country comparison to the world: 140

Airports—with paved runways: *total:* 16
over 3,047 m: 8
2,438 to 3,047 m: 5
1,524 to 2,437 m: 2
914 to 1,523 m: 1 (2017)

Airports—with unpaved runways: *total:* 2
under 914 m: 2 (2013)

Heliports: 1 (2012)

Pipelines: gas 473 km; oil 49 km (2013)

Railways: *total:* 509 km
narrow gauge: 509 km 1.050-m gauge (2014)
country comparison to the world: 114

Roadways: *total:* 7,203 km
paved: 7,203 km (2011)
country comparison to the world: 144

Merchant marine: *total:* 31
by type: general cargo 9, oil tanker 1, other 21 (2017)
country comparison to the world: 123

Ports and terminals: *major seaport(s):* Al 'Aqabah

MILITARY AND SECURITY

Military expenditures: 4.58% of GDP (2016)
4.31% of GDP (2015)
4.32% of GDP (2014)
4.3% of GDP (2013)
4.76% of GDP (2012)
country comparison to the world: 7

Military branches: Jordanian Armed Forces (JAF): Royal Jordanian Land Force (RJLF), Royal Jordanian Navy, Royal Jordanian Air Force (Al-Quwwat al-Jawwiya al-Malakiya al-Urduniya, RJAF), Special Operations Command (Socom); Public Security Directorate (normally falls under Ministry of Interior, but comes under JAF in wartime or crisis) (2013)

Military service age and obligation: 17 years of age for voluntary male military service; initial service term 2 years, with option to reenlist for 18 years; conscription at age 18 suspended in 1999; women are not conscripted, but can volunteer to serve in noncombat military positions in the Royal Jordanian Arab Army Women's Corps and RJAF (2013)

TRANSNATIONAL ISSUES

Disputes—international: 2004 Agreement settles border dispute with Syria pending demarcation

Refugees and internally displaced persons: refugees (country of origin): 2,175,491 (Palestinian refugees) (2017); 657,628 (Syria); 66,262 (Iraq) (2018)

KAZAKHSTAN

INTRODUCTION

Background: Ethnic Kazakhs, a mix of Turkic and Mongol nomadic tribes who migrated to the region by the 13th century, were rarely united as a single nation. The area was conquered by Russia in the 18th century, and Kazakhstan became a Soviet Republic in 1936. Soviet policies reduced the number of ethnic Kazakhs in the 1930s and enabled non-ethnic Kazakhs to outnumber natives. During the 1950s and 1960s agricultural "Virgin Lands" program, Soviet citizens were encouraged to help cultivate Kazakhstan's northern pastures. This influx of immigrants (mostly Russians, but also some other deported nationalities) further skewed the ethnic mixture. Non-Muslim ethnic minorities departed Kazakhstan in large numbers from the mid-1990s through the mid-2000s and a national program has repatriated about a million ethnic Kazakhs back to Kazakhstan. These trends have allowed Kazakhs to become the titular majority again. This dramatic demographic shift has also undermined the previous religious diversity and made the country more than 70% Muslim.

Kazakhstan's economy is larger than those of all the other Central Asian states largely due to the country's vast natural resources. Current issues include: developing a cohesive national identity, expanding the development of the country's vast energy resources and exporting them to world markets, diversifying the economy, enhancing Kazakhstan's economic competitiveness, and strengthening relations with neighboring states and foreign powers. Astana successfully hosted an internationally recognized exposition in 2017. The three-month Expo 2017, themed Future Energy, was the first such exhibition by a former Soviet country.

GEOGRAPHY

Location: Central Asia, northwest of China; a small portion west of the Ural (Zhayyq) River in easternmost Europe

Geographic coordinates: 48 00 N, 68 00 E

Map references: Asia

Area: *total:* 2,724,900 sq km
land: 2,699,700 sq km
water: 25,200 sq km
country comparison to the world: 10

Area—comparative: slightly less than four times the size of Texas

Land boundaries: *total:* 13,364 km

border countries (5): China 1,765 km, Kyrgyzstan 1,212 km, Russia 7,644 km, Turkmenistan 413 km, Uzbekistan 2,330 km

Coastline: 0 km (landlocked); note—Kazakhstan borders the Aral Sea, now split into two bodies of water (1,070 km), and the Caspian Sea (1,894 km)

Maritime claims: none (landlocked)

Climate: continental, cold winters and hot summers, arid and semiarid

Terrain: vast flat steppe extending from the Volga in the west to the Altai Mountains in the east and from the plains of western Siberia in the north to oases and deserts of Central Asia in the south

Elevation: *mean elevation:* 387 m

elevation extremes: *lowest point:* Vpadina Kaundy -132 m
highest point: Khan Tangiri Shyngy (Pik Khan-Tengri) 6,995 m

Natural resources: major deposits of petroleum, natural gas, coal, iron ore, manganese, chrome ore, nickel, cobalt, copper, molybdenum, lead, zinc, bauxite, gold, uranium

Land use: *agricultural land:* 77.4%
arable land: 8.9%;
permanent crops: 0%;
permanent pasture: 68.5%
forest: 1.2%
other: 21.4% (2011 est.)
Irrigated land: 20,660 sq km (2012)

Population—distribution: most of the country displays a low population density, particularly the interior; population clusters appear in urban agglomerations in the far northern and southern portions of the country

Natural hazards: earthquakes in the south; mudslides around Almaty

Environment—current issues: radioactive or toxic chemical sites associated with former defense industries and test ranges scattered throughout the country pose health risks for humans and animals; industrial pollution is severe in some cities; because the two main rivers that flowed into the Aral Sea have been diverted for irrigation, it is drying up and leaving behind a harmful layer of chemical pesticides and natural salts; these substances are then picked up by the wind and blown into noxious dust storms; pollution in the Caspian Sea; soil pollution from overuse of agricultural chemicals and salination from poor infrastructure and wasteful irrigation practices

Environment—international agreements: *party to:* Air Pollution, Biodiversity, Climate Change, Desertification, Endangered Species, Environmental Modification, Hazardous Wastes, Ozone Layer Protection, Ship Pollution, Wetlands
signed, but not ratified: Climate Change-Kyoto Protocol

Geography—note: world's largest landlocked country and one of only two landlocked countries in the world that extends into two continents (the

other is Azerbaijan); Russia leases approximately 6,000 sq km of territory enclosing the Baykonur Cosmodrome; in January 2004, Kazakhstan and Russia extended the lease to 2050

PEOPLE AND SOCIETY

Population: 18,556,698 (July 2017 est.)
country comparison to the world: 62

Nationality: *noun:* Kazakhstani(s)
adjective: Kazakhstani

Ethnic groups: Kazakh (Qazaq) 63.1%, Russian 23.7%, Uzbek 2.9%, Ukrainian 2.1%, Uighur 1.4%, Tatar 1.3%, German 1.1%, other 4.4% (2009 est.)

Languages: Kazakh (official, Qazaq) 74% (understand spoken language), Russian (official, used in everyday business, designated the "language of interethnic communication") 94.4% (understand spoken language) (2009 est.)

Religions: Muslim 70.2%, Christian 26.2% (mainly Russian Orthodox), other 0.2%, atheist 2.8%, unspecified 0.5% (2009 est.)

Age structure: *0-14 years:* 25.91% (male 2,374,427/female 2,434,212)
15-24 years: 14.05% (male 1,329,376/female 1,277,615)
25-54 years: 42.42% (male 3,847,282/female 4,024,052)
55-64 years: 9.97% (male 810,019/female 1,040,917)
65 years and over: 7.65% (male 494,064/female 924,734) (2017 est.)

Dependency ratios: *total dependency ratio:* 50.4
youth dependency ratio: 40.3
elderly dependency ratio: 10.2
potential support ratio: 9.8 (2015 est.)

Median age: *total:* 30.6 years
male: 29.3 years
female: 31.9 years (2017 est.)
country comparison to the world: 113

Population growth rate: 1.04% (2017 est.)
country comparison to the world: 109

Birth rate: 18.1 births/1,000 population (2017 est.)
country comparison to the world: 98

Death rate: 8.1 deaths/1,000 population (2017 est.)
country comparison to the world: 88

Net migration rate: 0.4 migrant(s)/1,000 population (2017 est.)
country comparison to the world: 63

Population distribution: most of the country displays a low population density, particularly the interior; population clusters appear in urban agglomerations in the far northern and southern portions of the country

Urbanization: *urban population:* 53.2% of total population (2017)
rate of urbanization: 0.94% annual rate of change (2015-20 est.)

Major urban areas—population: Almaty 1.523 million; ASTANA (capital) 759,000 (2015)

Sex ratio: *at birth:* 0.94 male(s)/female
0-14 years: 0.98 male(s)/female
15-24 years: 1.04 male(s)/female
25-54 years: 0.95 male(s)/female
55-64 years: 0.78 male(s)/female
65 years and over: 0.53 male(s)/female
total population: 0.92 male(s)/female (2016 est.)

Mother's mean age at first birth: 25 years (2014 est.)

Maternal mortality ratio: 12 deaths/100,000 live births (2015 est.)
country comparison to the world: 142

Infant mortality rate: *total:* 19.6 deaths/1,000 live births
male: 22.3 deaths/1,000 live births
female: 17.2 deaths/1,000 live births (2017 est.)
country comparison to the world: 82

Life expectancy at birth: *total population:* 71.1 years
male: 65.9 years
female: 76 years (2017 est.)
country comparison to the world: 152

Total fertility rate: 2.25 children born/woman (2017 est.)
country comparison to the world: 94

Contraceptive prevalence rate: 55.7% (2015)

Health expenditures: 4.4% of GDP (2014)
country comparison to the world: 158

Physicians density: 3.27 physicians/1,000 population (2014)

Hospital bed density: 7.2 beds/1,000 population (2012)

Drinking water source:
improved:
urban: 99.4% of population
rural: 85.6% of population
total: 92.9% of population
unimproved:
urban: 0.6% of population
rural: 14.4% of population
total: 7.1% of population (2015 est.)

Sanitation facility access:
improved:
urban: 97% of population
rural: 98.1% of population
total: 97.5% of population
unimproved:
urban: 3% of population
rural: 1.9% of population
total: 2.5% of population (2015 est.)

HIV/AIDS—adult prevalence rate: 0.2% (2016 est.)
country comparison to the world: 90

HIV/AIDS—people living with HIV/AIDS: 26,000 (2016 est.)
country comparison to the world: 68

HIV/AIDS—deaths: <1000 (2016 est.)

Obesity—adult prevalence rate: 21% (2016)
country comparison to the world: 94

Children under the age of 5 years underweight: 2% (2015)
country comparison to the world: 100

Education expenditures: 3.1% of GDP (2009)
country comparison to the world: 138

Literacy: *definition:* age 15 and over can read and write
total population: 99.8%
male: 99.8%
female: 99.8% (2015 est.)

School life expectancy (primary to tertiary education): *total:* 15 years
male: 15 years
female: 15 years (2016)

Unemployment, youth ages 15-24: *total:* 3.9%
male: 3.6%
female: 4.3% (2013 est.)
country comparison to the world: 128

GOVERNMENT

Country name: *conventional long form:* Republic of Kazakhstan
conventional short form: Kazakhstan
local long form: Qazaqstan Respublikasy
local short form: Qazaqstan
former: Kazakh Soviet Socialist Republic
etymology: the name "Kazakh" derives from the Turkic word "kaz" meaning "to wander," recalling the Kazakh's nomadic lifestyle; the Persian suffix "-stan" means "place of" or "country," so the word Kazakhstan literally means "Land of the Wanderers"

Government type: presidential republic

Capital: *name:* Astana
geographic coordinates: 51 10 N, 71 25 E
time difference: UTC+6 (11 hours ahead of Washington, DC, during Standard Time)
note: Kazakhstan has two time zones

Administrative divisions: 14 provinces (oblyslar, singular—oblys) and 2 cities* (qalalar, singular—qala); Almaty (Taldyqorghan), Almaty*, Aqmola (Kokshetau), Aqtobe, Astana*, Atyrau, Batys Qazaqstan [West Kazakhstan] (Oral), Mangghystau (Aqtau), Ongtustik Qazaqstan [South Kazakhstan] (Shymkent), Pavlodar, Qaraghandy, Qostanay, Qyzylorda, Shyghys Qazaqstan [East Kazakhstan] (Oskemen), Soltustik Qazaqstan [North Kazakhstan] (Petropavl), Zhambyl (Taraz)
note: administrative divisions have the same names as their administrative centers (exceptions have the administrative center name following in parentheses); in 1995, the Governments of Kazakhstan and Russia entered into an agreement whereby Russia would lease for a period of 20 years an area of 6,000 sq km enclosing the Baykonur space launch facilities and the city of Bayqongyr (Baykonur, formerly Leninsk); in 2004, a new agreement extended the lease to 2050

Independence: 16 December 1991 (from the Soviet Union)

National holiday: Independence Day, 16 December (1991)

Constitution: history: previous 1937, 1978 (preindependence), 1993; latest approved by referendum 30 August 1995, effective 5 September 1995
amendments: proposed by the president of the republic on the recommendation of Parliament or the government; the president has the option of submitting draft amendments to Parliament or directly to a referendum; passage of amendments to Parliament requires three-fourths majority vote of both houses and the signature of the president; passage by referendum requires absolute majority vote by more than one-half of the voters in at least two-thirds of the oblasts, major cities, and the capital, followed by the signature of the president; amended several times, last in 2017 (2017)

Legal system: civil law system influenced by Roman-Germanic law and by the theory and practice of the Russian Federation

International law organization participation: has not submitted an ICJ jurisdiction declaration; non-party state to the ICCt

Citizenship: *citizenship by birth:* no
citizenship by descent only: at least one parent must be a citizen of Kazakhstan
dual citizenship recognized: no
residency requirement for naturalization: 5 years

Suffrage: 18 years of age; universal

Executive branch: *chief of state:* President Nursultan Abishuly NAZARBAYEV (chairman of the Supreme Soviet from 22 February 1990, elected president 1 December 1991)

head of government: Prime Minister Bakytzhan SAGINTAYEV (since 9 September 2016); First Deputy Prime Minister Askar MAMIN (since 13 September 2016)
cabinet: Council of Ministers appointed by the president
elections/appointments: president directly elected by simple majority popular vote for a 5-year term (eligible for a second consecutive term); election last held on 26 April 2015 (next scheduled for 2020); prime minister and deputy prime minister appointed by the president, approved by the Mazhilis; note—constitutional amendments in May 2007 shortened the presidential term from 7 to 5 years and established a 2-consecutive-term limit; NAZARBAYEV has official status as the "First President of Kazakhstan" and is allowed unlimited terms
election results: Nursultan Abishuly NAZARBAYEV reelected president; percent of vote—Nursultan Abishuly NAZARBAYEV (Nur Otan) 97.8%, other 2.2%

Legislative branch: *description:* bicameral Parliament consists of the Senate (47 seats; 32 members indirectly elected by majority 2-round vote by the oblast-level assemblies and 15 members appointed by the president; members serve 6-year terms, with one-half of the membership renewed every 3 years) and the Mazhilis (107 seats; 98 members directly elected in a single national constituency by proportional representation vote to serve 5-year terms and 9 indirectly elected by the Assembly of

People of Kazakhstan, a 350-member, presidentially appointed advisory body designed to represent the country's ethnic minorities)

elections: Senate—last held on 28 June 2017 (next to be held in 2020); Mazhilis—last held on 20 March 2016 (next to be held by 2021)

election results: Senate—percent of vote by party—NA; seats by party—Nur Otan 16; Mazhilis—percent of vote by party—Nur Otan 82.2%, Ak Zhol 7.2%, Communist People's Party 7.1%, other 3.5%; seats by party—Nur Otan 84, Ak Zhol 7, Communist People's Party 7

Judicial branch: *highest court(s):* Supreme Court of the Republic (consists of 44 members); Constitutional Council (consists of 7 members)

judge selection and term of office: Supreme Court judges proposed by the president of the republic on recommendation of the Supreme Judicial Council and confirmed by the Senate; judges normally serve until age 65 but can be extended to age 70; Constitutional Council—the president of the republic, the Senate chairperson, and the Majilis chairperson each appoints 1 member for a 3-year term and each appoints 1 member for a 6-year term; chairperson of the Constitutional Council appointed by the president of the republic for a 6-year term

subordinate courts: regional and local courts

Political parties and leaders: Ak Zhol (Bright Path) Party or Democratic Party of Kazakhstan Ak Zhol [Azat PERUASHEV]
Auyl National Patriotic Party [Ali BEKTAYEV] (a merger of the Patriots' Party and the Auyl Social Democratic Party)
Birlik (Unity) [Serik SULTANGALI] (a merger of Adilet (Justice; formerly Democratic Party of Kazakhstan) and Rukhaniyat (Spirituality))
Communist People's Party of Kazakhstan [Vladislav KOSAREV]
National Social Democratic Party or NSDP [Zharmakhan TUYAKBAY]
Nur Otan (Radiant Fatherland) Democratic People's Party [Nursultan NAZARBAYEV] (the Agrarian, Asar, and Civic parties merged with Otan)

Political pressure groups and leaders: Adil-Soz [Tamara KALEYEVA]
Chairman of Bureau's Council [Roza AKYLBEKOVA]
Foundation for Support of Civil Initiatives [Nurul RAKHIMBEK]
International Legal Initiative [Aina SHORMANBAYEVA]
Kazakhstan International Bureau on Human Rights and Rule of Law or KIBHR [Rosa AKYLBEKOVA]
Legal Media Centre (sometimes known as the North Kazakhstan Legal Media Centre) [Diana OKREMOVA]
Public Foundation for Parliamentary Development [Zauresh BATTALOVA]
Republican Network of International Monitors or RNIM [Daniyar LIVAZOV]
Transparency International [Natalya KOVALEVA]

International organization participation: ADB, CICA, CIS, CSTO, EAEU, EAPC, EBRD, ECO, EITI (compliant country), FAO, GCTU, IAEA, IBRD, ICAO, ICC (NGOs), ICRM, IDA, IDB, IFAD, IFC, IFRCS, ILO, IMF, IMO, Interpol, IOC, IOM, IPU, ISO, ITSO, ITU, MIGA, MINURSO, NAM (observer), NSG, OAS (observer), OIC, OPCW, OSCE, PFP, SCO, UN, UN Security Council (temporary), UNCTAD, UNESCO, UNIDO, UNWTO, UPU, WCO, WFTU (NGOs), WHO, WIPO, WMO, WTO (observer), ZC

Diplomatic representation in the US: *chief of mission:* Ambassador Erzhar KAZYKHANOV (since 24 April 2017)
chancery: 1401 16th Street NW, Washington, DC 20036
telephone: [1] (202) 232-5488
FAX: [1] (202) 232-5845
consulate(s) general: New York

Diplomatic representation from the US: *chief of mission:* Ambassador George KROL (since 18 March 2015)
embassy: Rakhymzhan Koshkarbayev Ave. No 3, Astana 010010
mailing address: use embassy street address
telephone: [7] (7172) 70-21-00
FAX: [7] (7172) 54-09-14
Consulate(s) General: Almaty

Flag description: a gold sun with 32 rays above a soaring golden steppe eagle, both centered on a sky blue background; the hoist side displays a national ornamental pattern "koshkar-muiz" (the horns of the ram) in gold; the blue color is of religious significance to the Turkic peoples of the country, and so symbolizes cultural and ethnic unity; it also represents the endless sky as well as water; the sun, a source of life and energy, exemplifies wealth and plenitude; the sun's rays are shaped like grain, which is the basis of abundance and prosperity; the eagle has appeared on the flags of Kazakh tribes for centuries and represents freedom, power, and the flight to the future

National symbol(s): golden eagle; national colors: blue, yellow

National anthem: name: "Menin Qazaqstanim" (My Kazakhstan)
lyrics/music: Zhumeken NAZHIMEDENOV and Nursultan NAZARBAYEV/Shamshi KALDAYAKOV
note: adopted 2006; President Nursultan NAZARBAYEV played a role in revising the lyrics

ECONOMY

Economy—overview: Kazakhstan, geographically the largest of the former Soviet republics, excluding Russia, possesses substantial fossil fuel reserves and other minerals and metals, such as uranium, copper, and zinc. It also has a large agricultural sector featuring livestock and grain. The government realizes that its economy suffers from an over-reliance on oil and extractive industries and has made initial attempts to diversify its economy by targeting sectors like transport, pharmaceuticals,

telecommunications, petrochemicals and food processing for greater development and investment.

Kazakhstan's vast hydrocarbon and mineral reserves form the backbone of its economy. Chevron-led Tengizchevroil announced a $36.8 billion expansion of Kazakhstan's premiere Tengiz oil field in July 2016. Meanwhile, the super-giant Kashagan field finally launched production in October 2016 after years of delay and an estimated $55 billion in development costs.

Kazakhstan is landlocked and depends on Russia to export its oil to Europe. It also exports oil directly to China. In 2010, Kazakhstan joined Russia and Belarus to establish a Customs Union in an effort to boost foreign investment and improve trade. The Customs Union evolved into a Single Economic Space in 2012 and the Eurasian Economic Union (EAEU) in January 2015. In part due to weak commodity prices, Kazakhstan's exports to EAEU countries declined 23.5% in 2016. Imports from EAEU countries to Kazakhstan declined 13.7%.

The economic downturn of its EAEU partner, Russia, and the decline in global commodity prices from 2014 to 2015 contributed to an economic slowdown in Kazakhstan, which continues to experience its slowest economic growth since the financial crises of 2008-09. In 2014, Kazakhstan devalued its currency, the tenge, and announced a stimulus package to cope with its economic challenges. In the face of further decline in the ruble, oil prices, and the regional economy, Kazakhstan announced in 2015 it would replace its currency band with a floating exchange rate, leading to a sharp fall in the value of the tenge. Since reaching a low of 391 to the dollar in January 2016, the tenge has modestly appreciated, helped by somewhat higher oil prices.

Despite some positive institutional and legislative changes in the last several years, investors remain concerned about corruption, bureaucracy, and arbitrary law enforcement, especially at the regional and municipal levels. An additional concern is the condition of the country's banking sector, which suffers from low liquidity, poor asset quality, and a lack of transparency. Investors also question the potentially negative effects on the economy of a contested presidential succession as Kazakhstan's first president, Nursultan NAZARBAYEV, who turned 77 in 2017, has not announced whether he will seek reelection in 2019.

GDP (purchasing power parity): $474.3 billion (2017 est.)
$459 billion (2016 est.)
$454.1 billion (2015 est.)
note: data are in 2017 dollars
country comparison to the world: 42

GDP (official exchange rate): $156.2 billion (2016 est.)

GDP—real growth rate: 3.3% (2017 est.)
1.1% (2016 est.)
1.2% (2015 est.)
country comparison to the world: 103

GDP—per capita (PPP): $26,100 (2017 est.)

485

$25,600 (2016 est.)
$25,700 (2015 est.)
note: data are in 2017 dollars
country comparison to the world: 77

Gross national saving: 22.8% of GDP (2017 est.)
22.3% of GDP (2016 est.)
26.6% of GDP (2015 est.)
country comparison to the world: 66

GDP—composition, by end use:
household consumption: 57.5%
government consumption: 12.6%
investment in fixed capital: 23.9%
investment in inventories: 0.7%
exports of goods and services: 35.2%
imports of goods and services: -30% (2017 est.)

GDP—composition, by sector of origin:
agriculture: 4.8%
industry: 34.4%
services: 60.8% (2017 est.)

Agriculture—products: grain (mostly spring wheat and barley), potatoes, vegetables, melons; livestock

Industries: oil, coal, iron ore, manganese, chromite, lead, zinc, copper, titanium, bauxite, gold, silver, phosphates, sulfur, uranium, iron and steel; tractors and other agricultural machinery, electric motors, construction materials

Industrial production growth rate: 4.9% (2017 est.)
country comparison to the world: 49

Labor force: 9.147 million (2017 est.)
country comparison to the world: 54

Labor force—by occupation: *agriculture:* 18.1%
industry: 20.4%
services: 61.6% (2017 est.)

Unemployment rate: 5% (2017 est.)
5% (2016 est.)
country comparison to the world: 68

Population below poverty line: 2.7% (2015 est.)

Household income or consumption by percentage share: *lowest 10%:* 4.3%
highest 10%: 22% (2013 est.)

Distribution of family income—Gini index: 26.3 (2013)
31.5 (2003)
country comparison to the world: 141

Budget: *revenues:* $34.13 billion
expenditures: $37.89 billion (2017 est.)
Taxes and other revenues: 21.9% of GDP (2017 est.)
country comparison to the world: 137

Budget surplus (+) or deficit (-): -2.4% of GDP (2017 est.)
country comparison to the world: 96

Public debt: 27.5% of GDP (2017 est.)
26.2% of GDP (2016 est.)
country comparison to the world: 170

Fiscal year: calendar year

Inflation rate (consumer prices): 7.3% (2017 est.)
14.6% (2016 est.)
country comparison to the world: 194

Central bank discount rate: 11% (10 April 2017)
12% (9 January 2017)

country comparison to the world: 19

Commercial bank prime lending rate: 14.1% (31 December 2017 est.)
15.33% (31 December 2016 est.)
country comparison to the world: 49

Stock of narrow money: $15.58 billion (31 December 2017 est.)
$13.81 billion (31 December 2016 est.)
country comparison to the world: 71

Stock of broad money: $42.11 billion (31 December 2017 est.)
$37.78 billion (31 December 2016 est.)
country comparison to the world: 73

Stock of domestic credit: $55.99 billion (31 December 2017 est.)
$55.53 billion (31 December 2016 est.)
country comparison to the world: 63

Market value of publicly traded shares: $744 million (31 December 2016 est.)
$4.737 billion (31 December 2015 est.)
$26.23 billion (31 December 2013 est.)
country comparison to the world: 109

Current account balance: -$8.291 billion (2017 est.)
-$8.518 billion (2016 est.)
country comparison to the world: 182

Exports: $44.11 billion (2017 est.)
$37.3 billion (2016 est.)
country comparison to the world: 52

Exports—commodities: oil and oil products, natural gas, ferrous metals, chemicals, machinery, grain, wool, meat, coal

Exports—partners: Italy 20.3%, China 11.5%, Russia 9.5%, Netherlands 8.9%, Switzerland 7.3%, France 4.9% (2016)

Imports: $31.09 billion (2017 est.)
$27.87 billion (2016 est.)
country comparison to the world: 61

Imports—commodities: machinery and equipment, metal products, foodstuffs

Imports—partners: Russia 36.2%, China 14.5%, Germany 5.7%, US 5.1% (2016)

Reserves of foreign exchange and gold: $31.44 billion (31 December 2017 est.)
$29.53 billion (31 December 2016 est.)
country comparison to the world: 50

Debt—external: $159.2 billion (31 December 2017 est.)
$163.8 billion (31 December 2016 est.)
country comparison to the world: 41

Stock of direct foreign investment—at home: $156.2 billion (31 December 2017 est.)
$143.2 billion (31 December 2016 est.)
country comparison to the world: 35

Stock of direct foreign investment—abroad: $34.74 billion (31 December 2017 est.)
$32.74 billion (31 December 2016 est.)
country comparison to the world: 48

Exchange rates: tenge (KZT) per US dollar—326.3 (2017 est.)
342.13 (2016 est.)
342.13 (2015 est.)

221.73 (2014 est.)
179.19 (2013 est.)

ENERGY

Electricity access: electrification—*total population:* 100% (2016)

Electricity—production: 100.4 billion kWh (2015 est.)
country comparison to the world: 36

Electricity—consumption: 95.26 billion kWh (2015 est.)
country comparison to the world: 34

Electricity—exports: 1.614 billion kWh (2015 est.)
country comparison to the world: 47

Electricity—imports: 1.618 billion kWh (2015 est.)
country comparison to the world: 58

Electricity—installed generating capacity: 22.06 million kW (2016 est.)
country comparison to the world: 39

Electricity—from fossil fuels: 86.1% of total installed capacity (2015 est.)
country comparison to the world: 74

Electricity—from nuclear fuels: 0% of total installed capacity (2015 est.)
country comparison to the world: 124

Electricity—from hydroelectric plants: 13.3% of total installed capacity (2015 est.)
country comparison to the world: 111

Electricity—from other renewable sources: 0.8% of total installed capacity (2015 est.)
country comparison to the world: 146

Crude oil—production: 1.595 million bbl/day (2016 est.)
country comparison to the world: 16

Crude oil—exports: 1.292 million bbl/day (2016 est.)
country comparison to the world: 13

Crude oil—imports: 145,800 bbl/day (2014 est.)
country comparison to the world: 36

Crude oil—proved reserves: 30 billion bbl (1 January 2017 es)
country comparison to the world: 12

Refined petroleum products—production: 228,600 bbl/day (2016 est.)
country comparison to the world: 47

Refined petroleum products—consumption: 186,300 bbl/day (2016 est.)
country comparison to the world: 57

Refined petroleum products—exports: 846 bbl/day (2015 est.)
country comparison to the world: 109

Refined petroleum products—imports: 44,490 bbl/day (2015 est.)
country comparison to the world: 89

Natural gas—production: 21.38 billion cu m (2016 est.)
country comparison to the world: 30

Natural gas—consumption: 13.1 billion cu m (2016 est.)

country comparison to the world: 50

Natural gas—exports: 13.7 billion cu m (2016 est.)
country comparison to the world: 20

Natural gas—imports: 4.7 billion cu m (2015 est.)
country comparison to the world: 34

Natural gas—proved reserves: 2.407 trillion cu m (1 January 2017 es)
country comparison to the world: 15

Carbon dioxide emissions from consumption of energy: 257.8 million Mt (2014 est.)
country comparison to the world: 25

COMMUNICATIONS

Telephones—fixed lines: *total subscriptions:* 3,931,100
subscriptions per 100 inhabitants: 21 (July 2016 est.)
country comparison to the world: 39

Telephones—mobile cellular: *total:* 25.395 million
subscriptions per 100 inhabitants: 138 (July 2016 est.)
country comparison to the world: 45

Telephone system: *general assessment:* inherited an outdated telecommunications network from the Soviet era requiring modernization
domestic: intercity by landline and microwave radio relay; number of fixed-line connections is inadequate; mobile-cellular usage increased rapidly and the subscriber base approaches 140 per 100 persons
international: country code—7; international traffic with other former Soviet republics and China carried by landline and microwave radio relay and with other countries by satellite and by the Trans-Asia-Europe (TAE) fiber-optic cable; satellite earth stations—2 Intelsat (2017)

Broadcast media: state owns nearly all radio and TV transmission facilities and operates national TV and radio networks; there are 3 TV channels: Kazakhstan, KAZsport, Balapan; and 4 radio stations: Kazakh Radiosy, Shalkar, Astana, and Classic; some former state-owned media outlets have been privatized; households with satellite dishes have access to foreign media; a small number of commercial radio stations operate along with state-run radio stations; recent legislation requires all media outlets to register with the government

and all TV providers to broadcast in digital format by 2018; broadcasts reach 98.63% of the population as well as neighboring countries (2017)

Internet country code: .kz
Internet users: total: 14,100,751

percent of population: 76.8% (July 2016 est.)
country comparison to the world: 45

TRANSPORTATION

National air transport system: *number of registered air carriers:* 10
inventory of registered aircraft operated by air carriers: 71
annual passenger traffic on registered air carriers: 5,081,631
annual freight traffic on registered air carriers: 37,669,008 mt-km (2015)
Civil aircraft registration country code prefix: UP (2016)

Airports: 96 (2013)
country comparison to the world: 59

Airports—with paved runways: *total:* 63
over 3,047 m: 10
2,438 to 3,047 m: 25
1,524 to 2,437 m: 15
914 to 1,523 m: 5
under 914 m: 8 (2017)

Airports—with unpaved runways: *total:* 33
over 3,047 m: 5
2,438 to 3,047 m: 7
1,524 to 2,437 m: 3
914 to 1,523 m: 5
under 914 m: 13 (2013)

Heliports: 3 (2013)

Pipelines: condensate 658 km; gas 12,432 km; oil 11,313 km; refined products 1,095 km; water 1,465 km (2013)

Railways: *total:* 14,184 km
broad gauge: 14,184 km 1.520-m gauge (4,056 km electrified) (2014)
country comparison to the world: 19

Roadways: *total:* 97,418 km
paved: 87,140 km
unpaved: 10,278 km (2012)
country comparison to the world: 48

Waterways: 4,000 km (on the Ertis (Irtysh) River (80%) and Syr Darya (Syrdariya) River) (2010)
country comparison to the world: 25

Merchant marine: *total:* 119
by type: general cargo 4, oil tanker 10, other 105 (2017)
country comparison to the world: 77

Ports and terminals: *major seaport(s):* Caspian Sea—Aqtau (Shevchenko), Atyrau (Gur'yev)
river port(s): Oskemen (Ust-Kamenogorsk), Pavlodar, Semey (Semipalatinsk) (Irtysh River)

MILITARY AND SECURITY

Military expenditures: 0.82% of GDP (2016)
3.45% of GDP (2015)
1.04% of GDP (2014)
1.08% of GDP (2013)
1.05% of GDP (2012)
country comparison to the world: 81

Military branches: Kazakhstan Armed Forces: Land Forces, Navy, Air Defense Forces (2017)

Military service age and obligation: 18 is the legal minimum age for compulsory military service; conscript service obligation is 2 years, but Kazakhstan is transitioning to a largely contract force; military cadets in intermediate (ages 15-17) and higher (ages 17-21) education institutes are classified as military service personnel (2017)

TRANSNATIONAL ISSUES

Disputes—international: Kyrgyzstan has yet to ratify the 2001 boundary delimitation with Kazakhstan; field demarcation of the boundaries commenced with Uzbekistan in 2004 and with Turkmenistan in 2005; ongoing demarcation with Russia began in 2007; demarcation with China was completed in 2002; creation of a seabed boundary with Turkmenistan in the Caspian Sea remains under discussion; Azerbaijan, Kazakhstan, and Russia ratified Caspian seabed delimitation treaties based on equidistance, while Iran continues to insist on a one-fifth slice of the sea

Refugees and internally displaced persons: *stateless persons:* 8,451 (2016)

Illicit drugs: significant illicit cultivation of cannabis for CIS markets, as well as limited cultivation of opium poppy and ephedra (for the drug ephedrine); limited government eradication of illicit crops; transit point for Southwest Asian narcotics bound for Russia and the rest of Europe; significant consumer of opiates

KENYA

INTRODUCTION

Background: Founding president and liberation struggle icon Jomo KENYATTA led Kenya from independence in 1963 until his death in 1978, when Vice President Daniel MOI took power in a constitutional succession. The country was a de facto one-party state from 1969 until 1982, after which time the ruling Kenya African National

Union (KANU) changed the constitution to make itself the sole legal party in Kenya. MOI acceded to internal and external pressure for political liberalization in late 1991. The ethnically fractured opposition failed to dislodge KANU from power in elections in 1992 and 1997, which were marred by violence and fraud, but were viewed as having generally reflected the will of the Kenyan

people. President MOI stepped down in December 2002 following fair and peaceful elections. Mwai KIBAKI, running as the candidate of the multiethnic, united opposition group, the National Rainbow Coalition (NARC), defeated KANU candidate Uhuru KENYATTA, the son of founding president Jomo KENYATTA, and assumed the

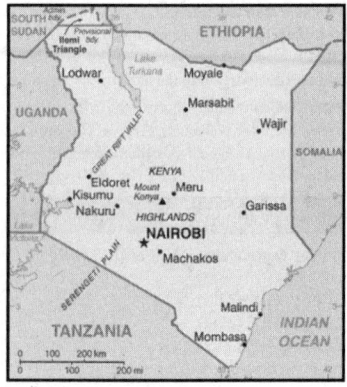

presidency following a campaign centered on an anticorruption platform.

KIBAKI's reelection in December 2007 brought charges of vote rigging from Orange Democratic Movement (ODM) candidate Raila ODINGA and unleashed two months of violence in which approximately 1,100 people died. African Union-sponsored mediation led by former UN Secretary General Kofi ANNAN in late February 2008 resulted in a power-sharing accord bringing ODINGA into the government in the restored position of prime minister. The power sharing accord included a broad reform agenda, the centerpiece of which was constitutional reform. In August 2010, Kenyans overwhelmingly adopted a new constitution in a national referendum. The new constitution introduced additional checks and balances to executive power and significant devolution of power and resources to 47 newly created counties. It also eliminated the position of prime minister following the first presidential election under the new constitution, which occurred in March 2013. Uhuru KENYATTA won the election and was sworn into office in April 2013; he began a second term in November 2017.

GEOGRAPHY

Location: Eastern Africa, bordering the Indian Ocean, between Somalia and Tanzania

Geographic coordinates: 1 00 N, 38 00 E

Map references: Africa

Area: *total:* 580,367 sq km
land: 569,140 sq km
water: 11,227 sq km
country comparison to the world: 50

Area—comparative: five times the size of Ohio; slightly more than twice the size of Nevada

Land boundaries: *total:* 3,457 km
border countries (5): Ethiopia 867 km, Somalia 684 km, South Sudan 317 km, Tanzania 775 km, Uganda 814 km

Coastline: 536 km

Maritime claims: *territorial sea:* 12 nm
exclusive economic zone: 200 nm
continental shelf: 200-m depth or to the depth of exploitation

Climate: varies from tropical along coast to arid in interior

Terrain: low plains rise to central highlands bisected by Great Rift Valley; fertile plateau in west

Elevation: *mean elevation:* 762 m

elevation extremes: *lowest point:* Indian Ocean 0 m
highest point: Mount Kenya 5,199 m

Natural resources: limestone, soda ash, salt, gemstones, fluorspar, zinc, diatomite, gypsum, wildlife, hydropower

Land use: *agricultural land:* 48.1%
arable land: 9.8%;
permanent crops: 0.9%;
permanent pasture: 37.4%
forest: 6.1%
other: 45.8% (2011 est.)
Irrigated land: 1,030 sq km (2012)

Population—distribution: population heavily concentrated in the west along the shore of Lake Victoria; other areas of high density include the capital of Nairobi, and in the southeast along the Indian Ocean coast

Natural hazards: recurring drought; flooding during rainy seasons
volcanism: limited volcanic activity; the Barrier (1,032 m) last erupted in 1921; South Island is the only other historically active volcano

Environment—current issues: water pollution from urban and industrial wastes; degradation of water quality from increased use of pesticides and fertilizers; water hyacinth infestation in Lake Victoria; deforestation; soil erosion; desertification; poaching

Environment—international agreements: *party to:* Biodiversity, Climate Change, Climate Change-Kyoto Protocol, Desertification, Endangered Species, Hazardous Wastes, Law of the Sea, Marine Dumping, Marine Life Conservation, Ozone Layer Protection, Ship Pollution, Wetlands, Whaling
signed, but not ratified: none of the selected agreements

Geography—note: the Kenyan Highlands comprise one of the most successful agricultural production regions in Africa; glaciers are found on Mount Kenya, Africa's second highest peak; unique physiography supports abundant and varied wildlife of scientific and economic value

PEOPLE AND SOCIETY

Population: 47,615,739
note: estimates for this country explicitly take into account the effects of excess mortality due to AIDS; this can result in lower life expectancy, higher infant mortality, higher death rates, lower population growth rates, and changes in the distribution of population by age and sex than would otherwise be expected (July 2017 est.)
country comparison to the world: 30

Nationality: *noun:* Kenyan(s)
adjective: Kenyan

Ethnic groups: Kikuyu 22%, Luhya 14%, Luo 13%, Kalenjin 12%, Kamba 11%, Kisii 6%, Meru 6%, other African 15%, non-African (Asian, European, and Arab) 1%

Languages: English (official), Kiswahili (official), numerous indigenous languages

Religions: Christian 83% (Protestant 47.7%, Catholic 23.4%, other Christian 11.9%), Muslim 11.2%, Traditionalists 1.7%, other 1.6%, none 2.4%, unspecified 0.2% (2009 est.)

Demographic profile: Kenya has experienced dramatic population growth since the mid-20th century as a result of its high birth rate and its declining mortality rate. More than 40% of Kenyans are under the age of 15 because of sustained high fertility, early marriage and childbearing, and an unmet need for family planning. Kenya's persistent rapid population growth strains the labor market, social services, arable land, and natural resources. Although Kenya in 1967 was the first sub-Saharan country to launch a nationwide family planning program, progress in reducing the birth rate has largely stalled since the late 1990s, when the government decreased its support for family planning to focus on the HIV epidemic. Government commitment and international technical support spurred Kenyan contraceptive use, decreasing the fertility rate (children per woman) from about 8 in the late 1970s to less than 5 children twenty years later, but it has plateaued at just over 3 children today.

Kenya is a source of emigrants and a host country for refugees. In the 1960s and 1970s, Kenyans pursued higher education in the UK because of colonial ties, but as British immigration rules tightened, the US, the then Soviet Union, and Canada became attractive study destinations. Kenya's stagnant economy and political problems during the 1980s and 1990s led to an outpouring of Kenyan students and professionals seeking permanent opportunities in the West and southern Africa. Nevertheless, Kenya's relative stability since its independence in 1963 has attracted hundreds of thousands of refugees escaping violent conflicts in neighboring countries; Kenya shelters more than 300,000 Somali refugees as of April 2017.

Age structure: *0-14 years:* 40.02% (male 9,557,274/female 9,497,870)
15-24 years: 19.15% (male 4,552,448/female 4,567,894)
25-54 years: 33.91% (male 8,170,264/female 7,976,751)
55-64 years: 3.92% (male 856,092/female 1,009,075)
65 years and over: 3% (male 614,751/female 813,320) (2017 est.)

Dependency ratios: *total dependency ratio:* 78.3
youth dependency ratio: 73.7
elderly dependency ratio: 4.6
potential support ratio: 21.7 (2015 est.)

Median age: *total:* 19.7 years
male: 19.6 years
female: 19.9 years (2017 est.)
country comparison to the world: 199

Population growth rate: 1.69% (2017 est.)
country comparison to the world: 63

Birth rate: 23.9 births/1,000 population (2017 est.)
country comparison to the world: 59

Death rate: 6.7 deaths/1,000 population (2017 est.)
country comparison to the world: 140

Net migration rate: -0.2 migrant(s)/1,000 population (2017 est.)
country comparison to the world: 107

Population distribution: population heavily concentrated in the west along the shore of Lake Victoria; other areas of high density include the capital of Nairobi, and in the southeast along the Indian Ocean coast

Urbanization: *urban population:* 26.5% of total population (2017)
rate of urbanization: 4.15% annual rate of change (2015-20 est.)

Major urban areas—population: NAIROBI (capital) 3.915 million; Mombassa 1.104 million (2015)

Sex ratio: *at birth:* 1.02 male(s)/female
0-14 years: 1.01 male(s)/female
15-24 years: 1 male(s)/female
25-54 years: 1.02 male(s)/female
55-64 years: 0.84 male(s)/female
65 years and over: 0.77 male(s)/female
total population: 1 male(s)/female (2016 est.)

Mother's mean age at first birth: 20.3 years
note: median age at first birth among women 25-29 (2014 est.)

Maternal mortality ratio: 510 deaths/100,000 live births (2015 est.)
country comparison to the world: 19

Infant mortality rate: *total:* 37.1 deaths/1,000 live births
male: 41.5 deaths/1,000 live births
female: 32.7 deaths/1,000 live births (2017 est.)
country comparison to the world: 49

Life expectancy at birth: *total population:* 64.3 years
male: 62.8 years
female: 65.8 years (2017 est.)
country comparison to the world: 186

Total fertility rate: 2.98 children born/woman (2017 est.)
country comparison to the world: 56

Contraceptive prevalence rate: 66.3% (2015)

Health expenditures: 5.7% of GDP (2014)
country comparison to the world: 114

Physicians density: 0.2 physicians/1,000 population (2013)

Hospital bed density: 1.4 beds/1,000 population (2010)

Drinking water source:
improved:
urban: 81.6% of population
rural: 56.8% of population
total: 63.2% of population
unimproved:
urban: 18.4% of population
rural: 43.2% of population

total: 36.8% of population (2015 est.)

Sanitation facility access:
improved:
urban: 31.2% of population
rural: 29.7% of population
total: 30.1% of population
unimproved:
urban: 68.8% of population
rural: 70.3% of population
total: 69.9% of population (2015 est.)

HIV/AIDS—adult prevalence rate: 5.4% (2016 est.)
country comparison to the world: 12

HIV/AIDS—people living with HIV/AIDS: 1.6 million (2016 est.)
country comparison to the world: 5

HIV/AIDS—deaths: 36,000 (2016 est.)
country comparison to the world: 6

Major infectious diseases: *degree of risk:* very high
food or waterborne diseases: bacterial and protozoal diarrhea, hepatitis A, and typhoid fever
vectorborne disease: malaria, dengue fever, and Rift Valley fever

water contact disease: schistosomiasis
animal contact disease: rabies (2016)

Obesity—adult prevalence rate: 7.1% (2016)
country comparison to the world: 161

Children under the age of 5 years underweight: 11% (2014)
country comparison to the world: 42

Education expenditures: 5.3% of GDP (2015)
country comparison to the world: 28

Literacy: *definition:* age 15 and over can read and write
total population: 78%
male: 81.1%
female: 74.9% (2015 est.)

School life expectancy (primary to tertiary education): *total:* 11 years
male: 11 years
female: 11 years (2009)

GOVERNMENT

Country name: *conventional long form:* Republic of Kenya
conventional short form: Kenya
local long form: Republic of Kenya/Jamhuri ya Kenya
local short form: Kenya
former: British East Africa
etymology: named for Mount Kenya; the meaning of the name is unclear but may derive from the Kikuyu, Embu, and Kamba words "kirinyaga," "kirenyaa," and "kiinyaa"—all of which mean "God's resting place"

Government type: presidential republic

Capital: *name:* Nairobi

geographic coordinates: 1 17 S, 36 49 E
time difference: UTC+3 (8 hours ahead of Washington, DC, during Standard Time)

Administrative divisions: 47 counties; Baringo, Bomet, Bungoma, Busia, Elgeyo/Marakwet, Embu, Garissa, Homa Bay, Isiolo, Kajiado, Kakamega, Kericho, Kiambu, Kilifi, Kirinyaga, Kisii, Kisumu, Kitui, Kwale, Laikipia, Lamu, Machakos, Makueni, Mandera, Marsabit, Meru, Migori, Mombasa, Murang'a, Nairobi City, Nakuru, Nandi, Narok, Nyamira, Nyandarua, Nyeri, Samburu, Siaya, Taita/Taveta, Tana River, Tharaka-Nithi, Trans Nzoia, Turkana, Uasin Gishu, Vihiga, Wajir, West Pokot

Independence: 12 December 1963 (from the UK)

National holiday: Jamhuri Day (Independence Day), 12 December (1963); note—Madaraka Day, 1 June (1963) marks the day Kenya attained internal self-rule

Constitution: *history:* previous 1963, 1969; latest drafted 6 May 2010, passed by referendum 4 August 2010, promulgated 27 August 2010
amendments: proposed by either house of Parliament or by petition of at least one million eligible voters; passage of amendments by Parliament requires approval by at least two-thirds majority vote of both houses in each of two readings, approval in a referendum by majority of votes cast by at least 20% participation of eligible voters in at least one-half of Kenya's counties, and approval by the president; passage of amendments introduced by petition requires approval by a majority of county assemblies, approval by majority vote of both houses, and approval by the president (2017)

Legal system: mixed legal system of English common law, Islamic law, and customary law; judicial review in a new Supreme Court established pursuant to the new constitution

International law organization participation: accepts compulsory ICJ jurisdiction with reservations; accepts ICCt jurisdiction

Citizenship: *citizenship by birth:* no
citizenship by descent only: at least one parent must be a citizen of Kenya
dual citizenship recognized: yes
residency requirement for naturalization: 4 out of the previous 7 years

Suffrage: 18 years of age; universal

Executive branch: *chief of state:* President Uhuru KENYATTA (since 9 April 2013); Deputy President William RUTO (since 9 April 2013); note—the president is both chief of state and head of government

head of government: President Uhuru KENYATTA (since 9 April 2013); Deputy President William RUTO (since 9 April 2013); note—position of the prime minister abolished after the March 2013 elections
cabinet: Cabinet appointed by the president, subject to confirmation by the National Assembly
elections/appointments: president and deputy president directly elected on the same ballot by qualified majority popular vote for a 5-year term (eligible for a second term); in addition to receiving an absolute majority popular vote, the presidential candidate must also win at least 25% of the votes cast in at least 24 of the 47 counties to avoid

a runoff; election last held on 26 October 2017 (next to be held in 2022)

election results: Uhuru KENYATTA reelected president in vote held 26 October 2017; percent of vote—Uhuru KENYATTA (Jubilee Party) 98.3%, Raila ODINGA (ODM) 1%, other 0.7%; note—Kenya held a previous presidential electin on 8 August 2017, but Kenya's Supreme Court on 1 September 2017 nullified the results, citing irregularities; the political opposition boycotted the October vote

Legislative branch: *description:* bicameral parliament consists of the Senate (67 seats; 47 members directly elected in single-seat constituencies by simple majority vote and 20 directly elected by proportional representation vote—16 women, 2 representing youth, and 2 representing the disabled; members serve 5-year terms) and the National Assembly (349 seats; 290 members directly elected in single-seat constituencies by simple majority vote, 47 women in single-seat constituencies elected by simple majority vote, and 12 members nominated by the National Assembly—6 representing youth and 6 representing the disabled; members serve 5-year terms)

elections: last held on 8 August 2017 (next to be held in August 2021)

election results: Senate—percent of vote by party/coalition—NA; seats by party/coalition—Jubilee Party 24; National Super Alliance 28, other 14, independent 1

National Assembly—percent of vote by party/coalition—NA; seats by party/coalition—Jubilee Party 140, National Super Alliance 62, other 118

Judicial branch: *highest court(s):* Supreme Court (consists of chief and deputy chief justices and 5 judges)

judge selection and term of office: chief and deputy chief justices nominated by Judicial Service Commission (JSC) and appointed by president with approval of the National Assembly; other judges nominated by the JSC and appointed by president; chief justice serves a nonrenewable 10-year term or till age 70 whichever comes first; other judges serve till age 70

subordinate courts: High Court; Court of Appeal; military courts; magistrates' courts; religious courts

Political parties and leaders: Alliance Party of Kenya or APK [Kiraitu MURUNGI]
Amani National Congress [Musalia MUDAVADI]
Federal Party of Kenya or FPK [Cyrus JIRONGA]
Forum for the Restoration of Democracy-Kenya or FORD-K [Moses WETANGULA]
Forum for the Restoration of Democracy-People or FORD-P [Henry OBWOCHA]
Jubilee Party [Uhuru KENYATTA]
Kenya African National Union or KANU [Gideon MOI]
National Rainbow Coalition or NARC [Charity NGILU]
National Super Alliance (includes ODM, ANC, WDM-K, FORD-K) [Raila ODINGA]
Orange Democratic Movement Party of Kenya or ODM [Raila ODINGA]

Wiper Democratic Movement-K or WDM-K (formerly Orange Democratic Movement-Kenya or ODM-K) [Kalonzo MUSYOKA]

Political pressure groups and leaders: African Center for Open Governance or AfriCOG [Gladwell OTIENO]
Anglican Church of Kenya [Archbishop Jackson Nasoore Ole SAPIT]
Council of Imams and Preachers of Kenya or CIPK [Sheikh Mohammed KHALIFA]
Federation of Women Lawyers in Kenya
Kenya Association of Manufacturers
Kenya Human Rights Commission or KHRC [George KEGORO]
Kenya Private Sector Alliance
Kenyans for Peace with Truth and Justice (umbrella group of more than 30 NGOs)
Muslim Human Rights Forum [Ali-Amin KIMATHI]
National Muslim Leaders Forum or NAMLEF [Abdullahi ABDI]
Protestant National Council of Churches of Kenya or NCCK [Canon Peter Karanja MWANGI]
Roman Catholic Church [Cardinal John NJUE]
Supreme Council of Kenya Muslims or SUPKEM [Adan WACHU]
other: labor unions, other Christian churches

International organization participation: ACP, AfDB, AU, C, CD, COMESA, EAC, EADB, FAO, G-15, G-77, IAEA, IBRD, ICAO, ICCt, ICRM, IDA, IFAD, IFC, IFRCS, IGAD, ILO, IMF, IMO, IMSO, Interpol, IOC, IOM, IPU, ISO, ITSO, ITU, ITUC (NGOs), MIGA, MINUSMA, MONUSCO, NAM, OPCW, PCA, UN, UNAMID, UNCTAD, UNESCO, UNHCR, UNIDO, UNIFIL, UNMIL, UNMISS, UNWTO, UPU, WCO, WHO, WMO, WTO

Diplomatic representation in the US: *chief of mission:* Ambassador Robinson Njeru GITHAE (since 18 November 2014)
chancery: 2249 R Street NW, Washington, DC 20008
telephone: [1] (202) 387-6101
FAX: [1] (202) 462-3829
consulate(s) general: Los Angeles
consulate(s): New York

Diplomatic representation from the US: *chief of mission:* Ambassador Robert F. GODEC (since 16 January 2013)
embassy: United Nations Avenue, Nairobi; P.O. Box 606 Village Market, Nairobi 00621
mailing address: American Embassy Nairobi, U.S. Department of State, Washington, DC 20521-8900
telephone: [254] (20) 363-6000
FAX: [254] (20) 363-6157

Flag description: three equal horizontal bands of black (top), red, and green; the red band is edged in white; a large Maasai warrior's shield covering crossed spears is superimposed at the center; black symbolizes the majority population, red the blood shed in the struggle for freedom, green stands for natural wealth, and white for peace; the shield and crossed spears symbolize the defense of freedom

National symbol(s): lion; national colors: black, red, green, white

National anthem: name: "Ee Mungu Nguvu Yetu" (Oh God of All Creation)
lyrics/music: Graham HYSLOP, Thomas KALUME, Peter KIBUKOSYA, Washington OMONDI, and George W. SENOGA-ZAKE/traditional, adapted by Graham HYSLOP, Thomas KALUME, Peter KIBUKOSYA, Washington OMONDI, and George W. SENOGA-ZAKE
note: adopted 1963; based on a traditional Kenyan folk song

ECONOMY

Economy—overview: Kenya is the economic, financial, and transport hub of East Africa. Kenya's real GDP growth has averaged over 5% for the last eight years. Since 2014, Kenya has been ranked as a lower middle income country because its per capita GDP crossed a World Bank threshold. While Kenya has a growing entrepreneurial middle class and steady growth, its economic and development trajectory could be impaired by weak governance and corruption. Although reliable numbers are hard to find, unemployment and under-employment are extremely high, and could be near 40% of the population.

Agriculture remains the backbone of the Kenyan economy, contributing one-third of GDP. About 75% of Kenya's population of roughly 44.2 million work at least part-time in the agricultural sector, including livestock and pastoral activities. Over 75% of agricultural output is from small-scale, rain-fed farming or livestock production.

Inadequate infrastructure continues to hamper Kenya's efforts to improve its annual growth to the 8%-10% range so that it can meaningfully address poverty and unemployment. The KENYATTA administration has been successful in courting external investment for infrastructure development. International financial institutions and donors remain important to Kenya's economic growth and development, but Kenya has also successfully raised capital in the global bond market. Kenya issued its first sovereign bond offering in mid-2014. Nairobi has contracted with a Chinese company to construct a new standard gauge railway connecting Mombasa and Nairobi, with completion expected in June 2017. In 2013, the country adopted a devolved system of government with the creation of 47 counties, and is in the process of devolving state revenues and responsibilities to the counties. Inflationary pressures and sharp currency depreciation peaked in early 2012 but have since abated following low global food and fuel prices and monetary interventions by the Central Bank. Drought-like conditions in parts of the country have pushed 2017 inflation above 8%. Chronic budget deficits, including a shortage of funds in mid-2015, hampered the government's ability to implement proposed development programs, but the economy is back in balance with many indicators, including foreign exchange reserves, interest rates, and FDI moving in the right direction. Underlying weaknesses were exposed in the banking sector in 2016 when the government was forced to take over three small and undercapitalized banks. In 2016, the government enacted legislation that limits interest rates banks can charge on loans and set a rate that banks must pay their depositors. This measure led to a sharp shrinkage of credit in the economy.

Tourism holds a significant place in Kenya's economy. A spate of terrorist attacks by the Somalia-based group al-

GDP (purchasing power parity): $163.4 billion (2017 est.)
$155.6 billion (2016 est.)
$147 billion (2015 est.)
note: data are in 2017 dollars
country comparison to the world: 75

GDP (official exchange rate): $78.4 billion (2016 est.)

GDP—real growth rate: 5% (2017 est.)
5.8% (2016 est.)
5.7% (2015 est.)
country comparison to the world: 43

GDP—per capita (PPP): $3,500 (2017 est.)
$3,400 (2016 est.)
$3,300 (2015 est.)
note: data are in 2017 dollars
country comparison to the world: 187

Gross national saving: 15.4% of GDP (2017 est.)
15.5% of GDP (2016 est.)
10.9% of GDP (2015 est.)
country comparison to the world: 125

GDP—composition, by end use:
household consumption: 77%
government consumption: 13.7%
investment in fixed capital: 17.1%
investment in inventories: -0.1%
exports of goods and services: 13.9%
imports of goods and services: -21.7% (2017 est.)

GDP—composition, by sector of origin:
agriculture: 35%
industry: 17.6%
services: 47.7% (2017 est.)

Agriculture—products: tea, coffee, corn, wheat, sugarcane, fruit, vegetables; dairy products, beef, fish, pork, poultry, eggs

Industries: small-scale consumer goods (plastic, furniture, batteries, textiles, clothing, soap, cigarettes, flour), agricultural products, horticulture, oil refining; aluminum, steel, lead; cement, commercial ship repair, tourism, information technology

Industrial production growth rate: 7% (2017 est.)
country comparison to the world: 25

Labor force: 19.82 million (2017 est.)
country comparison to the world: 32

Labor force—by occupation: *agriculture:* 61.1%
industry: 6.7%
services: 32.2% (2005 est.)

Unemployment rate: 40% (2013 est.)
40% (2001 est.)
country comparison to the world: 211

Population below poverty line: 43.4% (2012 est.)

Household income or consumption by percentage share: *lowest 10%:* 1.8%
highest 10%: 37.8% (2005)

Distribution of family income—Gini index: 42.5 (2008 est.)
44.9 (1997)
country comparison to the world: 49

Budget: *revenues:* $15.37 billion
expenditures: $20.18 billion (2017 est.)
Taxes and other revenues: 19.6% of GDP (2017 est.)
country comparison to the world: 156

Budget surplus (+) or deficit (-): -6.1% of GDP (2017 est.)
country comparison to the world: 177

Public debt: 52.6% of GDP (2017 est.)
53.5% of GDP (2016 est.)
country comparison to the world: 92

Fiscal year: 1 July—30 June

Inflation rate (consumer prices): 8% (2017 est.)
6.3% (2016 est.)
country comparison to the world: 198

Central bank discount rate: 11.5% (20 January 2016)
7% (31 December 2010)
country comparison to the world: 16

Commercial bank prime lending rate: 14.3% (31 December 2017 est.)
16.58% (31 December 2016 est.)
country comparison to the world: 48

Stock of narrow money: $13.03 billion (31 December 2017 est.)
$12.77 billion (31 December 2016 est.)
country comparison to the world: 78

Stock of broad money: $29.29 billion (31 December 2017 est.)
$22.86 billion (31 December 2016 est.)
country comparison to the world: 78

Stock of domestic credit: $36.59 billion (31 December 2017 est.)
$29.88 billion (31 December 2016 est.)
country comparison to the world: 78

Market value of publicly traded shares: $26.16 billion (31 December 2014 est.)
$22.09 billion (31 December 2013 est.)
$14.79 billion (31 December 2012 est.)
country comparison to the world: 61

Current account balance: -$4.75 billion (2017 est.)
-$3.653 billion (2016 est.)
country comparison to the world: 174

Exports: $6.397 billion (2017 est.)
$5.747 billion (2016 est.)
country comparison to the world: 102

Exports—commodities: tea, horticultural products, coffee, petroleum products, fish, cement, apparel

Exports—partners: Uganda 10.1%, Tanzania 8.6%, US 7.7%, Netherlands 7.4%, UK 7.3%, UAE 4.6%, Pakistan 4.5% (2016)

Imports: $14.52 billion (2017 est.)
$13.64 billion (2016 est.)

country comparison to the world: 87

Imports—commodities: machinery and transportation equipment, oil, petroleum products, motor vehicles, iron and steel, resins and plastics

Imports—partners: China 24.1%, India 11.2%, UAE 7.7%, Japan 5.4% (2016)

Reserves of foreign exchange and gold: $7.592 billion (31 December 2017 est.)
$7.601 billion (31 December 2016 est.)
country comparison to the world: 79

Debt—external: $24.99 billion (31 December 2017 est.)
$22.6 billion (31 December 2016 est.)
country comparison to the world: 88

Stock of direct foreign investment—at home: $6.196 billion (31 December 2017 est.)
$5.317 billion (31 December 2016 est.)
country comparison to the world: 101

Stock of direct foreign investment—abroad: $NA (31 December 2017 est.)
$NA (31 December 2016 est.)

Exchange rates: Kenyan shillings (KES) per US dollar—
104 (2017 est.)
101.504 (2016 est.)
101.504 (2015 est.)
98.179 (2014 est.)
87.921 (2013 est.)

ENERGY

Electricity access: *population without electricity:* 35,400,000
electrification—*total population:* 20%
electrification—urban areas: 60%
electrification—rural areas: 7% (2013)

Electricity—production: 9.548 billion kWh (2015 est.)
country comparison to the world: 104

Electricity—consumption: 7.666 billion kWh (2015 est.)
country comparison to the world: 105

Electricity—exports: 45 million kWh (2015 est.)
country comparison to the world: 89

Electricity—imports: 67 million kWh (2015 est.)
country comparison to the world: 102

Electricity—installed generating capacity: 2.301 million kW (2015 est.)
country comparison to the world: 109

Electricity—from fossil fuels: 31.9% of total installed capacity (2015 est.)
country comparison to the world: 183

Electricity—from nuclear fuels: 0% of total installed capacity (2015 est.)
country comparison to the world: 118

Electricity—from hydroelectric plants: 35.6% of total installed capacity (2015 est.)
country comparison to the world: 58

Electricity—from other renewable sources: 53.6% of total installed capacity (2015 est.)
country comparison to the world: 1

Crude oil—production: 0 bbl/day (2016 est.)

country comparison to the world: 152

Crude oil—exports: 0 bbl/day (2014 est.)
country comparison to the world: 145

Crude oil—imports: 11,870 bbl/day (2014 est.)
country comparison to the world: 71

Crude oil—proved reserves: 0 bbl (1 January 2017 es)
country comparison to the world: 151

Refined petroleum products—production: 14,320 bbl/day (2014 est.)
country comparison to the world: 97

Refined petroleum products—consumption: 93,000 bbl/day (2015 est.)
country comparison to the world: 83

Refined petroleum products—exports: 345.2 bbl/day (2014 est.)
country comparison to the world: 114

Refined petroleum products—imports: 76,090 bbl/day (2014 est.)
country comparison to the world: 66

Natural gas—production: 0 cu m (2013 est.)
country comparison to the world: 152

Natural gas—consumption: 0 cu m (2013 est.)
country comparison to the world: 196

Natural gas—exports: 0 cu m (2013 est.)
country comparison to the world: 128

Natural gas—imports: 0 cu m (2013 est.)
country comparison to the world: 143

Natural gas—proved reserves: 0 cu m (1 January 2014 es)
country comparison to the world: 155

Carbon dioxide emissions from consumption of energy: 13 million Mt (2013 est.)
country comparison to the world: 96

COMMUNICATIONS

Telephones—fixed lines: *total subscriptions:* 72,801
subscriptions per 100 inhabitants: less than 1 (July 2016 est.)
country comparison to the world: 129

Telephones—mobile cellular: *total:* 38,982,188
subscriptions per 100 inhabitants: 83 (July 2016 est.)
country comparison to the world: 35

Telephone system: *general assessment:* the mobile-cellular system is generally good, especially is urban areas; fixed-line telephone system is small and inefficient; trunks are primarily microwave radio relay; business data commonly transferred by a very small aperture terminal (VSAT) system
domestic: sole fixed-line provider, Telkom Kenya, privatized in 2013 and is now 60% owned by Helios Investment Partners, a London-based equity fund, and 40% owned by the Kenyan Government; multiple providers in the mobile-cellular segment of the market fostering a boom in mobile-cellular telephone usage with teledensity reaching 83 per 100 persons in 2016
international: country code—254; landing point for the EASSy, TEAMS and SEACOM fiber-optic submarine cable systems; satellite earth stations—4 Intelsat (2016)

Broadcast media: about a half-dozen large-scale privately owned media companies with TV and radio stations, as well as a state-owned TV broadcaster, provide service nationwide; satellite and cable TV subscription services available; state-owned radio broadcaster operates 2 national radio channels and provides regional and local radio services in multiple languages; many private radio stations broadcast on a national level along with over 100 private and non-profit provincial stations broadcasting in local languages; transmissions of several international broadcasters available (2014)

Internet country code: .ke
Internet users: total: 12,165,597

percent of population: 26.0% (July 2016 est.)
country comparison to the world: 33

TRANSPORTATION

National air transport system: *number of registered air carriers:* 16
inventory of registered aircraft operated by air carriers: 106
annual passenger traffic on registered air carriers: 4,874,590
annual freight traffic on registered air carriers: 286,414,683 mt-km (2015)
Civil aircraft registration country code prefix: 5Y (2016)

Airports: 197 (2013)
country comparison to the world: 28

Airports—with paved runways: *total:* 16
over 3,047 m: 5
2,438 to 3,047 m: 2
1,524 to 2,437 m: 2
914 to 1,523 m: 6
under 914 m: 1 (2017)

Airports—with unpaved runways: *total:* 181
1,524 to 2,437 m: 14
914 to 1,523 m: 107
under 914 m: 60 (2013)

Pipelines: oil 4 km; refined products 928 km (2013)

Railways: *total:* 3,806 km
narrow gauge: 3,334 km 1.000-m gauge
standard gauge: 472 km 1.435-m gauge (2014)
country comparison to the world: 54

Roadways: *total:* 161,452 km
paved: 14,420 km (8,500 km highways, 1,872 urban roads, and 4,048 rural roads)
unpaved: 147,032 km (2017)
country comparison to the world: 32

Waterways: none specifically; the only significant inland waterway is the part of Lake Victoria within the boundaries of Kenya; Kisumu is the main port and has ferry connections to Uganda and Tanzania (2011)

Merchant marine: *total:* 20
by type: oil tanker 2, other 18 (2017)
country comparison to the world: 134

Ports and terminals: *major seaport(s):* Kisumu, Mombasa

LNG terminal(s) (import): Mombasa

MILITARY AND SECURITY

Military expenditures: 1.4% of GDP (2017)
1.32% of GDP (2016)
1.32% of GDP (2015)
1.33% of GDP (2014)
1.56% of GDP (2013)
country comparison to the world: 41

Military branches: Kenya Defence Forces: Kenya Army, Kenya Navy, Kenya Air Force (2012)

Military service age and obligation: 18-26 years of age for male and female voluntary service (under 18 with parental consent), with a 9-year obligation (7 years for Kenyan Navy); applicants must be Kenyan citizens and provide a national identity card (obtained at age 18) and a school-leaving certificate; women serve under the same terms and conditions as men; mandatory retirement at age 55 (2012)

TERRORISM

Terrorist groups—foreign based: *al-Qa'ida (AQ):*
aim(s): drive US Government personnel, US business people, and other US influences out of Kenya and, ultimately, establish a pan-Islamic caliphate under a strict Salafi Muslim interpretation
area(s) of operation: maintains a limited presence; on 7 August 1998, operatives detonated truck bombs that exploded and killed and injured scores of workers and severely damaged the US Embassy in Nairobi, killing approximately 213 people and injuring a few thousand others; almost all of the dead and injured were Kenyans

al-Shabaab: *aim(s):* avenge Kenya's 2011 decision to send troops to Somalia to combat al-Shabaab; establish Islamic rule in Kenya and Somalia's border regions
area(s) of operation: maintains an operational and recruitment presence, mostly in the northeast; on 2 April 2015, gunmen stormed Garissa University and shot and killed 148 people and injured approximately 80; gunmen took over 700 students hostage and killed those who identified as Christian, making it one of Kenya's deadliest attacks; on 21 September 2013, at the upscale Westgate Mall in Nairobi, gunmen injured 200 people and killed six soldiers and police officers and approximately 65 civilians, including foreign nationals from 13 countries; leadership claimed the attack on the mall was in retaliation for Kenya's support for the African Union Mission for Somalia, a regional peacekeeping force operated by the African Union with the approval of the UN

TRANSNATIONAL ISSUES

Disputes—international: Kenya served as an important mediator in brokering Sudan's north-south separation in February 2005; Kenya provides shelter to an estimated 580,000 refugees, including Ugandans who flee across the border periodically to seek protection from Lord's Resistance Army rebels; Kenya works hard to prevent the clan and militia fighting in Somalia from spreading across the border, which has long been open to nomadic pastoralists; the boundary that separates Kenya's and Sudan's sovereignty is unclear in the "Ilemi Triangle," which Kenya has administered since colonial times

Refugees and internally displaced persons: refugees (country of origin): 284,346 (Somalia) (refugees and asylum seekers); 112,425 (South Sudan) (refugees and asylum seekers); 35,710 (Democratic Republic of the Congo) (refugees and asylum seekers); 27,880 (Ethiopia) (refugees and asylum seekers); 12,828 (Burundi) (refugees and asylum seekers); 10,008 (Sudan) (refugees and asylum seekers) (2017)

IDPs: 138,000 (represents people displaced since the 1990s by ethnic and political violence and land disputes and who sought refuge mostly in camps; persons who took refuge in host communities or were evicted in urban areas are not included in the data; data is not available on pastoralists displaced by cattle rustling, violence, natural disasters, and development projects; the largest displacement resulted from 2007-08 post-election violence (2016)

stateless persons: 20,000 (2016); note—the stateless population consists of Nubians, Kenyan Somalis, and coastal Arabs; the Nubians are descendants of Sudanese soldiers recruited by the British to fight for them in East Africa more than a century

ago; Nubians did not receive Kenyan citizenship when the country became independent in 1963; only recently have Nubians become a formally recognized tribe and had less trouble obtaining national IDs; Galjeel and other Somalis who have lived in Kenya for decades are included with more recent Somali refugees and denied ID cards

Illicit drugs: widespread harvesting of small plots of marijuana; transit country for South Asian heroin destined for Europe and North America; Indian methaqualone also transits on way to South Africa; significant potential for money-laundering activity given the country's status as a regional financial center; massive corruption, and relatively high levels of narcotics-associated activities

KIRIBATI

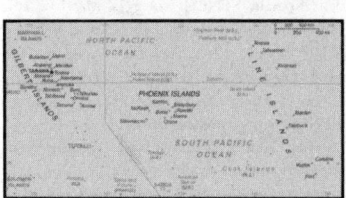

INTRODUCTION

Background: The Gilbert Islands became a British protectorate in 1892 and a colony in 1915; they were captured by the Japanese in the Pacific War in 1941. The islands of Makin and Tarawa were the sites of major US amphibious victories over entrenched Japanese garrisons in 1943. The Gilbert Islands were granted self-rule by the UK in 1971 and complete independence in 1979 under the new name of Kiribati. The US relinquished all claims to the sparsely inhabited Phoenix and Line Island groups in a 1979 treaty of friendship with Kiribati.

GEOGRAPHY

Location: Oceania, group of 33 coral atolls in the Pacific Ocean, straddling the Equator; the capital Tarawa is about halfway between Hawaii and Australia

Geographic coordinates: 1 25 N, 173 00 E

Map references: Oceania

Area: *total:* 811 sq km
land: 811 sq km
water: 0 sq km
note: includes three island groups—Gilbert Islands, Line Islands, and Phoenix Islands—dispersed over about 3.5 million sq km (1.35 million sq mi)
country comparison to the world: 187

Area—comparative: four times the size of Washington, DC

Land boundaries: 0 km

Coastline: 1,143 km

Maritime claims: *territorial sea:* 12 nm
exclusive economic zone: 200 nm

Climate: tropical; marine, hot and humid, moderated by trade winds

Terrain: mostly low-lying coral atolls surrounded by extensive reefs

Elevation: *mean elevation:* 2 m

elevation extremes: *lowest point:* Pacific Ocean 0 m
highest point: unnamed elevation on Banaba 81 m

Natural resources: phosphate (production discontinued in 1979), coconuts (copra), fish

Land use: *agricultural land:* 42%
arable land: 2.5%;
permanent crops: 39.5%;
permanent pasture: 0%
forest: 15%
other: 43% (2011 est.)
Irrigated land: 0 sq km (2012)

Population—distribution: consists of three achipelagos spread out over an area roughly the size of India; the eastern Line Islands and central Phoenix Islands are sparsely populated, but the western Gilbert Islands are some of the most densely settled places on earth, with the main island of South Tarawa boasting a population density similar to Tokyo or Hong Kong

Natural hazards: typhoons can occur any time, but usually November to March; occasional tornadoes; low level of some of the islands make them sensitive to changes in sea level

Environment—current issues: heavy pollution in lagoon of south Tarawa atoll due to heavy migration mixed with traditional practices such as lagoon latrines and open-pit dumping; ground water at risk

Environment—international agreements: *party to:* Biodiversity, Climate Change, Climate Change-Kyoto Protocol, Desertification, Hazardous Wastes, Law of the Sea, Marine Dumping, Ozone Layer Protection, Whaling

signed, but not ratified: none of the selected agreements

Geography—note: 21 of the 33 islands are inhabited; Banaba (Ocean Island) in Kiribati is one of the three great phosphate rock islands in the Pacific Ocean—the others are Makatea in French Polynesia, and Nauru; Kiribati is the only country in the world to fall into all four hemispheres (northern, southern, eastern, and western)

PEOPLE AND SOCIETY

Population: 108,145 (July 2017 est.)
country comparison to the world: 191

Nationality: *noun:* I-Kiribati (singular and plural)
adjective: I-Kiribati

Ethnic groups: I-Kiribati 96.2%, I-Kiribati/mixed 1.8%, Tuvaluan 0.2%, other 1.8% (2015 est.)

Languages: I-Kiribati, English (official)

Religions: Roman Catholic 57.3%, Kiribati Uniting Church 31.3%, Mormon 5.3%, Baha'i 2.1%, Seventh Day Adventist 1.9%, other 2.1% (2015 est.)

Age structure: *0-14 years:* 29.68% (male 16,360/ female 15,734)
15-24 years: 21.07% (male 11,282/female 11,503)
25-54 years: 38.98% (male 20,300/female 21,860)
55-64 years: 6.04% (male 2,942/female 3,590)
65 years and over: 4.23% (male 1,802/female 2,772) (2017 est.)

Dependency ratios: *total dependency ratio:* 63
youth dependency ratio: 57
elderly dependency ratio: 6
potential support ratio: 16.6 (2015 est.)

Median age: *total:* 24.6 years
male: 23.8 years
female: 25.5 years (2017 est.)
country comparison to the world: 158

Population growth rate: 1.13% (2017 est.)
country comparison to the world: 100

Birth rate: 21.2 births/1,000 population (2017 est.)
country comparison to the world: 76

Death rate: 7 deaths/1,000 population (2017 est.)
country comparison to the world: 130

Net migration rate: -2.9 migrant(s)/1,000 population (2017 est.)
country comparison to the world: 172

Population distribution: consists of three achipelagos spread out over an area roughly the size of India; the eastern Line Islands and central Phoenix Islands are sparsely populated, but the western Gilbert Islands are some of the most densely settled places on earth, with the main island of South Tarawa boasting a population density similar to Tokyo or Hong Kong

Urbanization: *urban population:* 44.6% of total population (2017)
rate of urbanization: 1.9% annual rate of change (2015-20 est.)

Major urban areas—population: TARAWA (capital) 46,000 (2014)

Sex ratio: *at birth:* 1.05 male(s)/female
0-14 years: 1.04 male(s)/female
15-24 years: 0.99 male(s)/female
25-54 years: 0.93 male(s)/female
55-64 years: 0.82 male(s)/female
65 years and over: 0.65 male(s)/female
total population: 0.95 male(s)/female (2016 est.)

Mother's mean age at first birth: 23.1 years
note: median age at first birth among women 25-29 (2009 est.)

Maternal mortality ratio: 90 deaths/100,000 live births (2015 est.)
country comparison to the world: 76

Infant mortality rate: *total:* 32.1 deaths/1,000 live births
male: 33.3 deaths/1,000 live births
female: 30.9 deaths/1,000 live births (2017 est.)
country comparison to the world: 58

Life expectancy at birth: *total population:* 66.5 years
male: 64 years
female: 69.1 years (2017 est.)
country comparison to the world: 174

Total fertility rate: 2.39 children born/woman (2017 est.)
country comparison to the world: 85

Contraceptive prevalence rate: 22.3% (2009)

Health expenditures: 10.2% of GDP (2014)
country comparison to the world: 24

Physicians density: 0.2 physicians/1,000 population (2013)

Hospital bed density: 1.3 beds/1,000 population (2011)

Drinking water source:
improved:
urban: 87.3% of population
rural: 50.6% of population
total: 66.9% of population
unimproved:
urban: 12.7% of population
rural: 49.4% of population
total: 33.1% of population (2015 est.)

Sanitation facility access:

improved:
urban: 51.2% of population
rural: 30.6% of population
total: 39.7% of population
unimproved:
urban: 48.8% of population
rural: 69.4% of population
total: 60.3% of population (2015 est.)

HIV/AIDS—adult prevalence rate: NA

HIV/AIDS—people living with HIV/AIDS: NA

HIV/AIDS—deaths: NA

Obesity—adult prevalence rate: 46% (2016)
country comparison to the world: 9

Children under the age of 5 years underweight: 14.9% (2009)
country comparison to the world: 48

School life expectancy (primary to tertiary education): *total:* 12 years
male: 11 years
female: 12 years (2008)

Unemployment, youth ages 15-24: *total:* 54%
male: 47.6%
female: 61.8% (2010 est.)

GOVERNMENT

Country name: *conventional long form:* Republic of Kiribati
conventional short form: Kiribati
local long form: Republic of Kiribati
local short form: Kiribati
note: pronounced keer-ree-bahss
former: Gilbert Islands
etymology: the name is the local pronunciation of "Gilberts," the former designation of the islands; originally named after explorer Thomas GILBERT, who mapped many of the islands in 1788

Government type: presidential republic

Capital: *name:* Tarawa
geographic coordinates: 1 21 N, 173 02 E
time difference: UTC+12 (17 hours ahead of Washington, DC, during Standard Time)
note: on 1 January 1995, Kiribati proclaimed that all of its territory was in the same time zone as its Gilbert Islands group (UTC +12) even though the Phoenix Islands and the Line Islands under its jurisdiction are on the other side of the International Date Line

Administrative divisions: 3 geographical units: Gilbert Islands, Line Islands, Phoenix Islands; note—there are no first-order administrative divisions, but there are 6 districts (Banaba, Central Gilberts, Line Islands, Northern Gilberts, Southern Gilberts, Tarawa) and 21 island councils—one for each of the inhabited islands (Abaiang, Abemama, Aranuka, Arorae, Banaba, Beru, Butaritari, Kanton, Kiritimati, Kuria, Maiana, Makin, Marakei, Nikunau, Nonouti, Onotoa, Tabiteuea, Tabuaeran, Tamana, Tarawa, Teraina)

Independence: 12 July 1979 (from the UK)

National holiday: Independence Day, 12 July (1979)

Constitution: The Gilbert and Ellice Islands Order in Council 1915, The Gilbert Islands Order in Council 1975 (preindependence); latest promulgated 12 July 1979 (at independence); amended 1995, 2013 (2016)

Legal system: English common law supplemented by customary law

International law organization participation: has not submitted an ICJ jurisdiction declaration; non-party state to the ICCt

Citizenship: *citizenship by birth:* no
citizenship by descent only: at least one parent must be a native-born citizen of Kiribati
dual citizenship recognized: no
residency requirement for naturalization: 7 years

Suffrage: 18 years of age; universal

Executive branch: *chief of state:* President Taneti MAAMAU (since 11 March 2016); Vice President Kourabi NENEM (since 17 March 2016); note—the president is both chief of state and head of government

head of government: President Taneti MAAMAU (since 11 March 2016); Vice President Kourabi NENEM (since 17 March 2016)
cabinet: Cabinet appointed by the president from among House of Assembly members
elections/appointments: president directly elected by simple majority popular vote following nomination of candidates from among House of Assembly members; term is 4 years (eligible for 2 additional terms); election last held on 9 March 2016 (next to be held in 2020); vice president appointed by the president
election results: Taneti MAAMAU elected president; percent of vote—Taneti MAAMAU 60%, Rimeta BENIAMINA (BTK) 38.6%, Taneti IOANE (BTK) 1.4%

Legislative branch: *description:* unicameral House of Assembly or Maneaba Ni Maungatabu (46 seats; 44 members directly elected in single- and multiseat constituencies by absolute majority vote in two-rounds if needed; 1 member appointed by the Rabi Council of Leaders—representing Banaba Island, and 1 ex officio member—the attorney general; members serve 4-year terms)
elections: legislative elections were held in two rounds—the first on 21 October 2011 and the second on 28 October 2011 (next to be held in 2015)
election results: percent of vote by party—NA; seats by party—BTK 26, KTK and MKP 19, , other 2 (includes attorney general)

Judicial branch: *highest court(s):* High Court (consists of a chief justice and other judges as prescribed by the president); note—the High Court has jurisdiction on constitutional issues
judge selection and term of office: chief justice appointed by the president on the advice of the cabinet in consultation with the Public Service Commission (PSC); other judges appointed by the president on the advice of the chief justice along with the PSC
subordinate courts: Court of Appeal; magistrates' courts

Political parties and leaders: Boutokaan Te Koaua Party or BTK [Anote TONG]

Kamaeuraoan Te I-Kiribati Party or KTK [Tetaua TAITAI]

Maurin Kiribati Pati or MKP [Rimeta BENIAMINA]

note: there is no tradition of formally organized political parties in Kiribati; they more closely resemble factions or interest groups because they have no party headquarters, formal platforms, or party structures

International organization participation: ABEDA, ACP, ADB, AOSIS, C, FAO, IBRD, ICAO, ICRM, IDA, IFAD, IFC, IFRCS, ILO, IMF, IMO, IOC, ITU, ITUC (NGOs), OPCW, PIF, Sparteca, SPC, UN, UNCTAD, UNESCO, UPU, WHO, WIPO, WMO

Diplomatic representation in the US: none; the Kiribati Permanent Mission to the UN serves as the Embassy; it is headed by Teburoro TITO (since 24 January 2018); address: 800 Second Avenue, Suite 400A, New York, NY 10017; telephone: [1] (212)867-3310; FAX: [1](212)867-3320

note: honorary consulate in Honolulu

Diplomatic representation from the US: the US does not have an embassy in Kiribati; the US Ambassador to Fiji is accredited to Kiribati

Flag description: the upper half is red with a yellow frigatebird flying over a yellow rising sun, and the lower half is blue with three horizontal wavy white stripes to represent the Pacific ocean; the white stripes represent the three island groups—the Gilbert, Line, and Phoenix Islands; the 17 rays of the sun represent the 16 Gilbert Islands and Banaba (formerly Ocean Island); the frigatebird symbolizes authority and freedom

National symbol(s): frigatebird; national colors: red, white, blue, yellow

National anthem: name: "Teirake kaini Kiribati" (Stand Up, Kiribati)

lyrics/music: Urium Tamuera IOTEBA

note: adopted 1979

ECONOMY

Economy—overview: A remote country of 33 scattered coral atolls, Kiribati has few natural resources and is one of the least developed Pacific Island countries. Commercially viable phosphate deposits were exhausted by the time of independence from the United Kingdom in 1979. Earnings from fishing licenses and seafarer remittances are important sources of income, however, remittances and the number of seafarers employed declined in the global crisis, but has since improved. Fishing license revenues remain a main source of income for the Kiribati government.

Economic development is constrained by a shortage of skilled workers, weak infrastructure, and remoteness from international markets. The public sector dominates economic activity, with ongoing capital projects in infrastructure including road rehabilitation, water and sanitation projects, and renovations to the international airport,

spurring some growth. Public debt increased from 23% of GDP at the end of 2015 to 25.8% in 2016.

Kiribati is dependent on foreign aid, which was estimated to have contributed over 43% in 2013 to the government's finances. The country's sovereign fund, the Revenue Equalization Reserve Fund (RERF), which is held offshore, had an estimated balance of $855.5 million in late July 2016. The RERF seeks to avoid exchange rate risk by holding investments in more than 20 currencies, including the Australian dollar, US dollar, the Japanese yen, and the Euro. Drawdowns from the RERF helped finance the government's annual budget.

GDP (purchasing power parity): $224 million (2017 est.)

$218 million (2016 est.)

$209.2 million (2015 est.)

note: data are in 2017 dollars

country comparison to the world: 220

GDP (official exchange rate): $186 million (2016 est.)

GDP—real growth rate: 2.8% (2017 est.)

4.2% (2016 est.)

7.5% (2015 est.)

country comparison to the world: 122

GDP—per capita (PPP): $1,900 (2017 est.)

$1,900 (2016 est.)

$1,900 (2015 est.)

note: data are in 2017 dollars

country comparison to the world: 210

GDP—composition, by sector of origin:

agriculture: 26.3%

industry: 9.2%

services: 64.5% (2012 est.)

Agriculture—products: copra, breadfruit, fish

Industries: fishing, handicrafts

Industrial production growth rate: 1.1% (2012 est.)

country comparison to the world: 162

Labor force: 39,000

note: economically active, not including subsistence farmers (2010 est.)

country comparison to the world: 199

Labor force—by occupation: *agriculture:* 15%

industry: 10%

services: 75% (2010)

Unemployment rate: 30.6% (2010 est.)

6.1% (2005)

country comparison to the world: 205

Population below poverty line: NA%

Household income or consumption by percentage share: *lowest 10%:* NA%

highest 10%: NA%

Budget: *revenues:* $197.9 million

expenditures: $179.9 million (2013 est.)

Taxes and other revenues: 106.4% of GDP (2013 est.)

country comparison to the world: 2

Budget surplus (+) or deficit (-): 9.7% of GDP (2013 est.)

country comparison to the world: 2

Public debt: 26.8% of GDP (2016 est.)

23.1% of GDP (2015 est.)

country comparison to the world: 172

Fiscal year: NA

Inflation rate (consumer prices): 2.2% (2017 est.)

1.9% (2016 est.)

country comparison to the world: 102

Market value of publicly traded shares: $NA

Current account balance: -$9 million (2017 est.)

$27 million (2016 est.)

country comparison to the world: 64

Exports: $84.75 million (2013 est.)

$62.31 million (2012 est.)

country comparison to the world: 198

Exports—commodities: fish, coconut products

Exports—partners: Morocco 19.8%, Fiji 17.3%, Philippines 10.2%, US 10.1%, Vietnam 7.9%, Australia 4.2% (2016)

Imports: $182.2 million (2013 est.)

$172.5 million (2012 est.)

country comparison to the world: 205

Imports—commodities: food, machinery and equipment, miscellaneous manufactured goods, fuel

Imports—partners: Australia 22.9%, NZ 20.9%, Fiji 14.1%, Singapore 10.5%, Japan 8.1%, China 6.9% (2016)

Reserves of foreign exchange and gold: $7.479 million (31 December 2015 est.)

$8.37 million (31 December 2010 est.)

country comparison to the world: 175

Debt—external: $13.6 million (2013 est.)

$14.1 million (2012 est.)

country comparison to the world: 200

Stock of direct foreign investment—at home: $NA

Exchange rates: Australian dollars (AUD) per US dollar—

1.311 (2017 est.)

1.3383 (2016 est.)

1.3383 (2015 est.)

1.3291 (2014 est.)

1.1094 (2013 est.)

note: the Australian dollar circulates as legal tender

ENERGY

Electricity access: *population without electricity:* 43,839

electrification—total population: 59%

electrification—urban areas: 77%

electrification—rural areas: 45% (2012)

Electricity—production: 24 million kWh (2015 est.)

country comparison to the world: 212

Electricity—consumption: 22.32 million kWh (2015 est.)

country comparison to the world: 212

Electricity—exports: 0 kWh (2016 est.)

country comparison to the world: 155

Electricity—imports: 0 kWh (2016 est.)

country comparison to the world: 166

Electricity—installed generating capacity: 8,000 kW (2015 est.)
country comparison to the world: 210

Electricity—from fossil fuels: 62.5% of total installed capacity (2015 est.)
country comparison to the world: 121

Electricity—from nuclear fuels: 0% of total installed capacity (2015 est.)
country comparison to the world: 121

Electricity—from hydroelectric plants: 0% of total installed capacity (2015 est.)
country comparison to the world: 182

Electricity—from other renewable sources: 37.5% of total installed capacity (2015 est.)
country comparison to the world: 6

Crude oil—production: 0 bbl/day (2016 est.)
country comparison to the world: 153

Crude oil—exports: 0 bbl/day (2014 est.)
country comparison to the world: 147

Crude oil—imports: 0 bbl/day (2014 est.)
country comparison to the world: 143

Crude oil—proved reserves: 0 bbl (1 January 2017 es)
country comparison to the world: 152

Refined petroleum products—production: 0 bbl/day (2014 est.)
country comparison to the world: 160

Refined petroleum products—consumption: 400 bbl/day (2015 est.)
country comparison to the world: 212

Refined petroleum products—exports: 0 bbl/day (2014 est.)
country comparison to the world: 168

Refined petroleum products—imports: 509.6 bbl/day (2014 est.)
country comparison to the world: 206

Natural gas—production: 0 cu m (2013 est.)
country comparison to the world: 154

Natural gas—consumption: 0 cu m (2013 est.)
country comparison to the world: 198

Natural gas—exports: 0 cu m (2013 est.)
country comparison to the world: 131

Natural gas—imports: 0 cu m (2013 est.)
country comparison to the world: 145

Natural gas—proved reserves: 0 cu m (1 January 2014 es)
country comparison to the world: 157

Carbon dioxide emissions from consumption of energy: 58,450 Mt (2012 est.)
country comparison to the world: 210

COMMUNICATIONS

Telephones—fixed lines: *total subscriptions:* 1,000
subscriptions per 100 inhabitants: 1 (July 2016 est.)
country comparison to the world: 200

Telephones—mobile cellular: *total:* 55,000
subscriptions per 100 inhabitants: 51 (July 2016 est.)
country comparison to the world: 211

Telephone system: *general assessment:* generally good quality national and international service
domestic: wireline service available on Tarawa and Kiritimati (Christmas Island); connections to outer islands by HF/VHF radiotelephone; recently formed Amalgamated Telecom Holdings Kiribati Limited is implementing the first phase of improvements with 3G and 4G upgrades on some islands
international: country code—686; satellite earth station—1 Intelsat (Pacific Ocean) (2016)

Broadcast media: multi-channel TV packages provide access to Australian and US stations; 1 government-operated radio station broadcasts on AM, FM, and shortwave (2017)

Internet country code: .ki
Internet users: total: 14,649

percent of population: 13.7% (July 2016 est.)
country comparison to the world: 204

TRANSPORTATION

Civil aircraft registration country code prefix: T3 (2016)

Airports: 19 (2013)
country comparison to the world: 138

Airports—with paved runways: *total:* 4
1,524 to 2,437 m: 4 (2017)

Airports—with unpaved runways: *total:* 15
914 to 1,523 m: 10
under 914 m: 5 (2013)

Roadways: *total:* 670 km (2017)
country comparison to the world: 192

Waterways: 5 km (small network of canals in Line Islands) (2012)
country comparison to the world: 107

Merchant marine: *total:* 133
by type: bulk carrier 5, general cargo 51, oil tanker 22, other 55 (2017)
country comparison to the world: 76

Ports and terminals: *major seaport(s):* Betio (Tarawa Atoll), Canton Island, English Harbor

MILITARY AND SECURITY

Military branches: no regular military forces (establishment prevented by the constitution); Police Force (2011)

Military—note: Kiribati does not have military forces; defense assistance is provided by Australia and NZ

TRANSNATIONAL ISSUES

Disputes—international: none

KOREA, NORTH

INTRODUCTION

Background: An independent kingdom for much of its long history, Korea was occupied by Japan beginning in 1905 following the Russo-Japanese War. Five years later, Japan formally annexed the entire peninsula. Following World War II, Korea was split with the northern half coming under Soviet-sponsored communist control. After failing in the Korean War (1950-53) to conquer the US-backed Republic of Korea (ROK) in the southern portion by force, North Korea (DPRK), under its founder President KIM Il Sung, adopted a policy of ostensible diplomatic and economic "self-reliance" as a check against outside influence. The DPRK demonized the US as the ultimate threat to its social system through state-funded propaganda, and molded political, economic, and military policies around the core ideological objective of eventual unification of Korea under Pyongyang's control. KIM Il Sung's son, KIM Jong Il, was officially designated as his father's successor in 1980, assuming a growing political and managerial role until the elder KIM's death in 1994. KIM Jong Un was publicly unveiled as his father's successor in 2010.

Following KIM Jong Il's death in 2011, KIM Jong Un quickly assumed power and has now taken on most of his father's former titles and duties. After decades of economic mismanagement and resource misallocation, the DPRK since the mid-1990s has faced chronic food shortages. In recent years, the North's domestic agricultural production has increased, but still falls far short of producing sufficient food to provide for its entire population. The DPRK began to ease restrictions to allow semi-private markets, starting in 2002, but has made few other efforts to meet its goal of improving the overall standard of living. North Korea's history of regional military provocations; proliferation of military-related items; long-range missile development; WMD programs including tests of nuclear devices in 2006, 2009, 2013, 2016, and 2017; and massive conventional armed forces are of major concern to the international community and have limited the DPRK's international engagement, particularly economically. The regime abides by a policy calling for the simultaneous development of its nuclear weapons program and its economy.

GEOGRAPHY

Location: Eastern Asia, northern half of the Korean Peninsula bordering the Korea Bay and the Sea of Japan, between China and South Korea

Geographic coordinates: 40 00 N, 127 00 E

Map references: Asia

Area: *total:* 120,538 sq km
land: 120,408 sq km
water: 130 sq km
country comparison to the world: 100

Area—comparative: slightly larger than Virginia; slightly smaller than Mississippi

Land boundaries: *total:* 1,607 km
border countries (3): China 1,352 km, South Korea 237 km, Russia 18 km

Coastline: 2,495 km

Maritime claims: *territorial sea:* 12 nm
exclusive economic zone: 200 nm
note: military boundary line 50 nm in the Sea of Japan and the exclusive economic zone limit in the Yellow Sea where all foreign vessels and aircraft without permission are banned

Climate: temperate, with rainfall concentrated in summer; long, bitter winters

Terrain: mostly hills and mountains separated by deep, narrow valleys; wide coastal plains in west, discontinuous in east

Elevation: *mean elevation:* 600 m

elevation extremes: *lowest point:* Sea of Japan 0 m
highest point: Paektu-san 2,744 m

Natural resources: coal, iron ore, limestone, magnesite, graphite, copper, zinc, lead, precious metals, hydropower

Land use: *agricultural land:* 21.8%
arable land: 19.5%;
permanent crops: 1.9%;
permanent pasture: 0.4%
forest: 46%
other: 32.2% (2011 est.)
Irrigated land: 14,600 sq km (2012)

Population—distribution: population concentrated in the plains and lowlands; least populated regions are the mountainous provinces adjacent to the Chinese border; largest concentrations are in the western provinces, particularly the municipal district of Pyongyang, and around Hungnam and Wonsan in the east

Natural hazards: late spring droughts often followed by severe flooding; occasional typhoons during the early fall
volcanism: Changbaishan (2,744 m) (also known as Baitoushan, Baegdu or P'aektu-san), on the Chinese border, is considered historically active

Environment—current issues: water pollution; inadequate supplies of potable water; waterborne disease; deforestation; soil erosion and degradation

Environment—international agreements: *party to:* Antarctic Treaty, Biodiversity, Climate Change, Climate Change-Kyoto Protocol, Desertification, Environmental Modification, Hazardous Wastes, Ozone Layer Protection, Ship Pollution
signed, but not ratified: Law of the Sea

Geography—note: strategic location bordering China, South Korea, and Russia; mountainous interior is isolated and sparsely populated

PEOPLE AND SOCIETY

Population: 25,248,140 (July 2017 est.)
country comparison to the world: 51

Nationality: *noun:* Korean(s)
adjective: Korean

Ethnic groups: racially homogeneous; there is a small Chinese community and a few ethnic Japanese

Languages: Korean

Religions: traditionally Buddhist and Confucianist, some Christian and syncretic Chondogyo (Religion of the Heavenly Way)
note: autonomous religious activities now almost nonexistent; government-sponsored religious groups exist to provide illusion of religious freedom

Age structure: *0-14 years:* 20.78% (male 2,670,884/female 2,576,846)
15-24 years: 15.59% (male 1,982,045/female 1,955,220)
25-54 years: 44.28% (male 5,608,520/female 5,572,000)
55-64 years: 9.77% (male 1,166,680/female 1,301,201)
65 years and over: 9.56% (male 826,735/female 1,588,009) (2017 est.)

Dependency ratios: *total dependency ratio:* 44.5
youth dependency ratio: 30.5
elderly dependency ratio: 14
potential support ratio: 7.1 (2015 est.)

Median age: *total:* 34 years
male: 32.5 years
female: 35.6 years (2017 est.)
country comparison to the world: 86

Population growth rate: 0.53% (2017 est.)
country comparison to the world: 151

Birth rate: 14.6 births/1,000 population (2017 est.)
country comparison to the world: 132

Death rate: 9.3 deaths/1,000 population (2017 est.)
country comparison to the world: 61

Net migration rate: 0 migrant(s)/1,000 population (2017 est.)
country comparison to the world: 88

Population distribution: population concentrated in the plains and lowlands; least populated regions are the mountainous provinces adjacent to the Chinese border; largest concentrations are in the western provinces, particularly the municipal district of Pyongyang, and around Hungnam and Wonsan in the east

Urbanization: *urban population:* 61.2% of total population (2017)
rate of urbanization: 0.8% annual rate of change (2015-20 est.)

Major urban areas—population: PYONGYANG (capital) 2.863 million (2015)

Sex ratio: *at birth:* 1.05 male(s)/female
0-14 years: 1.03 male(s)/female
15-24 years: 1.02 male(s)/female
25-54 years: 1.01 male(s)/female
55-64 years: 0.9 male(s)/female
65 years and over: 0.53 male(s)/female
total population: 0.94 male(s)/female (2016 est.)

Maternal mortality ratio: 82 deaths/100,000 live births (2015 est.)
country comparison to the world: 79

Infant mortality rate: *total:* 22.1 deaths/1,000 live births
male: 24.6 deaths/1,000 live births
female: 19.5 deaths/1,000 live births (2017 est.)
country comparison to the world: 73

Life expectancy at birth: *total population:* 70.7 years
male: 66.9 years
female: 74.8 years (2017 est.)
country comparison to the world: 157

Total fertility rate: 1.95 children born/woman (2017 est.)
country comparison to the world: 127

Contraceptive prevalence rate: 78.2%
note: percent of women aged 20-49 (2014)

Physicians density: 2.78 physicians/1,000 population (2011)

Hospital bed density: 13.2 beds/1,000 population (2012)

Drinking water source:
improved:
urban: 99.9% of population
rural: 99.4% of population
total: 99.7% of population
unimproved:
urban: 0.1% of population
rural: 0.6% of population
total: 0.3% of population (2015 est.)

Sanitation facility access:
improved:
urban: 87.9% of population
rural: 72.5% of population
total: 81.9% of population
unimproved:
urban: 12.1% of population
rural: 27.5% of population
total: 18.1% of population (2015 est.)

HIV/AIDS—adult prevalence rate: NA

HIV/AIDS—deaths: NA

Obesity—adult prevalence rate: 6.8% (2016)

country comparison to the world: 163

Children under the age of 5 years underweight: 15.2% (2012)

country comparison to the world: 46

Education expenditures: NA

Literacy: *definition:* age 15 and over can read and write

total population: 100%

male: 100%

female: 100% (2015 est.)

School life expectancy (primary to tertiary education): *total:* 11 years

male: 11 years

female: 11 years (2015)

GOVERNMENT

Country name: *conventional long form:* Democratic People's Republic of Korea

conventional short form: North Korea

local long form: Choson-minjujuui-inmin-konghwaguk

local short form: Choson

abbreviation: DPRK

etymology: derived from the Chinese name for Goryeo, which was the Korean dynasty that united the peninsula in the 10th century A.D.; the North Korean name "Choson" means "[Land of the] Morning Calm"

Government type: single-party state; official state ideology of "Juche" or "national self-reliance

Capital: *name:* Pyongyang

geographic coordinates: 39 01 N, 125 45 E

time difference: UTC+8.5 (13.5 hours ahead of Washington, DC, during Standard Time)

note: on 15 August 2015, North Korea reverted to UTC+8.5, a time zone that had been observed during pre-colonial times

Administrative divisions: 9 provinces (do, singular and plural) and 3 cities (si, singular and plural)

provinces: Chagang, Hambuk (North Hamgyong), Hamnam (South Hamgyong), Hwangbuk (North Hwanghae), Hwangnam (South Hwanghae), Kangwon, P'yongbuk (North Pyongan), P'yongnam (South Pyongan), Ranggang

cities: Namp'o, P'yongyang, Rason

note: Namp'o is sometimes designated as a metropolitan city, P'yongyang as a directly controlled city, and Rason as a city

Independence: 15 August 1945 (from Japan)

National holiday: Founding of the Democratic People's Republic of Korea (DPRK), 9 September (1948)

Constitution: previous 1948, 1972; latest adopted 1998; revised 2009, 2012, 2013 (2016)

Legal system: civil law system based on the Prussian model; system influenced by Japanese traditions and Communist legal theory

International law organization participation: has not submitted an ICJ jurisdiction declaration; non-party state to the ICCt

Citizenship: *citizenship by birth:* no

citizenship by descent only: at least one parent must be a citizen of North Korea

dual citizenship recognized: no

residency requirement for naturalization: unknown

Suffrage: 17 years of age; universal and compulsory

Executive branch: *chief of state:* Supreme People's Assembly President KIM Yong Nam (since 5 September 1998); note—functions as the technical head of state and performs related duties, such as receiving ambassadors' credentials

head of government: State Affairs Commission Chairman KIM Jong Un (since 17 December 2011); note—functions as the commander-in-chief and chief executive

cabinet: Cabinet or Naegak members appointed by the Supreme People's Assembly except the Minister of People's Armed Forces

elections/appointments: chief of state and premier indirectly elected by the Supreme People's Assembly; election last held on 9 March 2014 (next election NA)

election results: KIM Jong Un reelected unopposed

note: the Korean Workers' Party continues to list deceased leaders KIM Il Sung and KIM Jong Il as Eternal President and Eternal General Secretary respectively

Legislative branch: *description:* unicameral Supreme People's Assembly or Ch'oego Inmin Hoeui (687 seats); members directly elected by absolute majority vote to serve 5-year terms); note—the Korean Workers' Party selects all candidates

elections: last held on 9 March 2014 (next to be held in March 2019)

election results: percent of vote by party—NA; seats by party—KWP 607, KSDF 50, Chondoist Chongu Party 22, Chongryon 5, religious associations 3; ruling party approves a list of candidates who are elected without opposition; KWP, KSDP, Chondoist Chongu Party, and Chongryon are part of the DFRF; a token number of seats are reserved for minor parties

Judicial branch: *highest court(s):* Supreme Court or Central Court (consists of one judge and 2 "People's Assessors" or for some cases, 3 judges)

judge selection and term of office: judges elected by the Supreme People's Assembly for 5-year terms

subordinate courts: lower provincial courts as determined by the Supreme People's Assembly

Political parties and leaders: major parties: Democratic Front for the Reunification of the Fatherland or DFRF

Korean Workers' Party or KWP [KIM Jong Un]

General Association of Korean Residents in Japan or Chongryon

minor parties: Chondoist Chongu Party (under KWP control)

Social Democratic Party or KSDP [KIM Yong Dae] (under KWP control)

Political pressure groups and leaders: none

International organization participation: ARF, FAO, G-77, ICAO, ICRM, IFAD, IFRCS, IHO, IMO, IMSO, IOC, IPU, ISO, ITSO, ITU, NAM, UN, UNCTAD, UNESCO, UNIDO, UNWTO, UPU, WFTU (NGOs), WHO, WIPO, WMO

Diplomatic representation in the US: none; North Korea has a Permanent Mission to the UN in New York

Diplomatic representation from the US: none; note—Swedish Embassy in Pyongyang represents the US as consular protecting power

Flag description: three horizontal bands of blue (top), red (triple width), and blue; the red band is edged in white; on the hoist side of the red band is a white disk with a red five-pointed star; the broad red band symbolizes revolutionary traditions; the narrow white bands stand for purity, strength, and dignity; the blue bands signify sovereignty, peace, and friendship; the red star represents socialism

National symbol(s): red star, chollima (winged horse); national colors: red, white, blue

National anthem: name: "Aegukka" (Patriotic Song)

lyrics/music: PAK Se Yong/KIM Won Gyun

note: adopted 1947; both North Korea's and South Korea's anthems share the same name and have a vaguely similar melody but have different lyrics; the North Korean anthem is also known as "Ach'imun pinnara" (Let Morning Shine)

ECONOMY

Economy—overview: North Korea, one of the world's most centrally directed and least open economies, faces chronic economic problems. Industrial capital stock is nearly beyond repair as a result of years of underinvestment, shortages of spare parts, and poor maintenance. Large-scale military spending and development of its ballistic missile and nuclear program severely draws off resources needed for investment and civilian consumption. Industrial and power outputs have stagnated for years at a fraction of pre-1990 levels. Frequent weather-related crop failures aggravated chronic food shortages caused by on-going systemic problems, including a lack of arable land, collective farming practices, poor soil quality, insufficient fertilization, and persistent shortages of tractors and fuel.

The mid 1990s through mid 2000s were marked by severe famine and widespread starvation. Significant food aid was provided by the international community through 2009. Since that time, food assistance has declined significantly. In the last few years, domestic corn and rice production has improved, although domestic production does not fully satisfy demand. A large portion of the population continues to suffer from prolonged malnutrition and poor living conditions. Since 2002, the government has allowed semi-private markets to begin selling a wider range of goods, allowing North Koreans to partially make up for diminished public distribution system rations. It also implemented changes in the management process of communal farms in an effort to boost agricultural output.

In December 2009, North Korea carried out a redenomination of its currency, capping the amount of North Korean won that could be exchanged for the new notes, and limiting the exchange to a one-week window. A concurrent crackdown on markets and foreign currency use yielded severe shortages and inflation, forcing Pyongyang to ease the restrictions by February 2010. In response to the sinking of the South Korean warship Cheonan and the shelling of Yeonpyeong Island in 2010, South Korea's government cut off most aid, trade, and bilateral cooperation activities. In February 2016, South Korea ceased its remaining bilateral economic activity by closing the Kaesong Industrial Complex in response to North Korea's fourth nuclear test a month earlier. This nuclear test and another in September 2016 resulted in two United Nations Security Council Resolutions that targeted North Korea's foreign currency earnings, particularly coal and other mineral exports. Over the last decade, China has been North Korea's primary trading partner.

The North Korean Government continues to stress its goal of improving the overall standard of living, but has taken few steps to make that goal a reality for its populace. In 2016, the regime used two mass mobilizations—one totaling 70 days and another 200 days—to spur the population to increase production and complete construction projects quickly. The regime released a five-year economic development strategy in May 2016 that outlined plans for promoting growth across sectors. Firm political control remains the government's overriding concern, which likely will inhibit formal changes to North Korea's current economic system.

GDP (purchasing power parity): $40 billion (2015 est.)
$40 billion (2014 est.)
$40 billion (2013 est.)
note: data are in 2015 US dollars;
North Korea does not publish reliable National Income Accounts data; the data shown are derived from purchasing power parity (PPP) GDP estimates for North Korea that were made by Angus MADDISON in a study conducted for the OECD; his figure for 1999 was extrapolated to 2015 using estimated real growth rates for North Korea's GDP and an inflation factor based on the US GDP deflator; the results were rounded to the nearest $10 billion.
country comparison to the world: 118

GDP (official exchange rate): $28 billion (2013 est.)

GDP—real growth rate: -1.1% (2015 est.)
1% (2014 est.)
1.1% (2013 est.)
country comparison to the world: 207

GDP—per capita (PPP): $1,700 (2015 est.)
$1,800 (2014 est.)
$1,800 (2013 est.)
note: data are in 2015 US dollars
country comparison to the world: 215

Gross national saving: NA%

GDP—composition, by end use:

household consumption: NA%
government consumption: NA%
investment in fixed capital: NA%
investment in inventories: NA%
exports of goods and services: 5.9%
imports of goods and services: -11.1% (2014 est.)

GDP—composition, by sector of origin:
agriculture: 25.4%
industry: 41%
services: 33.5% (2017 est.)

Agriculture—products: rice, corn, potatoes, wheat, soybeans, pulses, beef, pork, eggs

Industries: military products; machine building, electric power, chemicals; mining (coal, iron ore, limestone, magnesite, graphite, copper, zinc, lead, and precious metals), metallurgy; textiles, food processing; tourism

Industrial production growth rate: 1% (2017 est.)
country comparison to the world: 163

Labor force: 14 million
note: estimates vary widely (2014 est.)
country comparison to the world: 42

Labor force—by occupation: *agriculture:* 37%
industry and services: 63% (2008 est.)

Unemployment rate: 25.6% (2013 est.)
25.5% (2012 est.)
country comparison to the world: 193

Population below poverty line: NA%

Household income or consumption by percentage share: *lowest 10%:* NA%
highest 10%: NA%

Budget: *revenues:* $3.2 billion
expenditures: $3.3 billion (2007 est.)
Taxes and other revenues: 11.4% of GDP
note: excludes earnings from state-operated enterprises (2007 est.)
country comparison to the world: 209

Budget surplus (+) or deficit (-): -0.4% of GDP (2007 est.)
country comparison to the world: 44

Fiscal year: calendar year

Inflation rate (consumer prices): NA%

Exports: $2.985 billion (2016 est.)
$2.908 billion (2015 est.)
country comparison to the world: 126

Exports—commodities: minerals, metallurgical products, manufactures (including armaments), textiles, agricultural and fishery products

Exports—partners: China 85.6% (2016)

Imports: $3.752 billion (2016 est.)
$3.711 billion (2015 est.)
country comparison to the world: 135

Imports—commodities: petroleum, coking coal, machinery and equipment, textiles, grain

Imports—partners: China 90.3% (2016)

Debt—external: $5 billion (2013 est.)
country comparison to the world: 136

Exchange rates: North Korean won (KPW) per US dollar (average market rate)
135 (2017 est.)
130 (2016 est.)
130 (2015 est.)
98.5 (2013 est.)
155.5 (2012 est.)

ENERGY

Electricity access: *population without electricity:* 18,400,000
electrification—*total population:* 30%
electrification—urban areas: 41%
electrification—rural areas: 13% (2013)

Electricity—production: 13.41 billion kWh (2015 est.)
country comparison to the world: 88

Electricity—consumption: 11.24 billion kWh (2015 est.)
country comparison to the world: 90

Electricity—exports: 0 kWh (2016 est.)
country comparison to the world: 154

Electricity—imports: 0 kWh (2016 est.)
country comparison to the world: 165

Electricity—installed generating capacity: 10 million kW (2015 est.)
country comparison to the world: 61

Electricity—from fossil fuels: 45% of total installed capacity (2015 est.)
country comparison to the world: 160

Electricity—from nuclear fuels: 0% of total installed capacity (2015 est.)
country comparison to the world: 120

Electricity—from hydroelectric plants: 55% of total installed capacity (2015 est.)
country comparison to the world: 34

Electricity—from other renewable sources: 0% of total installed capacity (2015 est.)
country comparison to the world: 191

Crude oil—production: 0 bbl/day (2016 est.)
country comparison to the world: 154

Crude oil—exports: 0 bbl/day (2014 est.)
country comparison to the world: 146

Crude oil—imports: 10,640 bbl/day (2014 est.)
country comparison to the world: 73

Crude oil—proved reserves: 0 bbl (1 January 2017 es)
country comparison to the world: 153

Refined petroleum products—production: 11,270 bbl/day (2014 est.)
country comparison to the world: 100

Refined petroleum products—consumption: 18,000 bbl/day (2015 est.)
country comparison to the world: 144

Refined petroleum products—exports: 0 bbl/day (2014 est.)
country comparison to the world: 167

Refined petroleum products—imports: 5,976 bbl/day (2014 est.)
country comparison to the world: 160

Natural gas—production: 0 cu m (2014 est.)
country comparison to the world: 153

Natural gas—consumption: 0 cu m (2014 est.)
country comparison to the world: 197

Natural gas—exports: 0 cu m (2014 est.)

country comparison to the world: 130

Natural gas—imports: 0 cu m (2014 est.)
country comparison to the world: 144

Natural gas—proved reserves: 0 cu m (1 January 2014 es)
country comparison to the world: 156

Carbon dioxide emissions from consumption of energy: 50 million Mt (2013 est.)
country comparison to the world: 59

COMMUNICATIONS

Telephones—fixed lines: *total subscriptions:* 1.18 million
subscriptions per 100 inhabitants: 5 (July 2016 est.)
country comparison to the world: 70

Telephones—mobile cellular: *total:* 3.24 million
subscriptions per 100 inhabitants: 13 (July 2016 est.)
country comparison to the world: 142

Telephone system: *general assessment:* adequate system; nationwide fiber-optic network; mobile-cellular service expanded beyond Pyongyang
domestic: fiber-optic links installed down to the county level; telephone directories unavailable; mobile service launched in late 2008 for the Pyongyang area and considerable progress in expanding to other parts of the country since
international: country code—850; satellite earth stations—2 (1 Intelsat—Indian Ocean, 1 Russian—Indian Ocean region); other international connections through Moscow and Beijing (2015)

Broadcast media: no independent media; radios and TVs are pre-tuned to government stations; 4 government-owned TV stations; the Korean Workers' Party owns and operates the Korean Central Broadcasting Station, and the state-run Voice of Korea operates an external broadcast service; the government prohibits listening to and jams foreign broadcasts (2015)

Internet country code: .kp

TRANSPORTATION

National air transport system: *number of registered air carriers:* 1
inventory of registered aircraft operated by air carriers: 17
annual passenger traffic on registered air carriers: 223,418
annual freight traffic on registered air carriers: 1,574,719 mt-km (2015)
Civil aircraft registration country code prefix: P (2016)

Airports: 82 (2013)
country comparison to the world: 67

Airports—with paved runways: *total:* 39
over 3,047 m: 3
2,438 to 3,047 m: 22
1,524 to 2,437 m: 8
914 to 1,523 m: 2
under 914 m: 4 (2017)

Airports—with unpaved runways: *total:* 43
2,438 to 3,047 m: 3
1,524 to 2,437 m: 17
914 to 1,523 m: 15
under 914 m: 8 (2013)

Heliports: 23 (2013)

Pipelines: oil 6 km (2013)

Railways: *total:* 7,435 km
standard gauge: 7,435 km 1.435-m gauge (5,400 km electrified)
note: figures are approximate; some narrow-gauge railway also exists (2014)
country comparison to the world: 29

Roadways: *total:* 25,554 km
paved: 724 km
unpaved: 24,830 km (2006)
country comparison to the world: 100

Waterways: 2,250 km (most navigable only by small craft) (2011)
country comparison to the world: 38

Merchant marine: *total:* 248
by type: bulk carrier 6, container ship 3, general cargo 184, oil tanker 25, other 30 (2017)
country comparison to the world: 60

Ports and terminals: *major seaport(s):* Ch'ongjin, Haeju, Hungnam, Namp'o, Songnim, Sonbong (formerly Unggi), Wonsan

MILITARY AND SECURITY

Military branches: North Korean People's Army: Ground Forces, Navy, Air Force; civil security forces (2005)

Military service age and obligation: 17 years of age for compulsory male and female military service; service obligation 10 years for men, to age 23 for women (2017)

TRANSNATIONAL ISSUES

Disputes—international: risking arrest, imprisonment, and deportation, tens of thousands of North Koreans cross into China to escape famine, economic privation, and political oppression; North Korea and China dispute the sovereignty of certain islands in Yalu and Tumen Rivers; Military Demarcation Line within the 4-km-wide Demilitarized Zone has separated North from South Korea since 1953; periodic incidents in the Yellow Sea with South Korea which claims the Northern Limiting Line as a maritime boundary; North Korea supports South Korea in rejecting Japan's claim to Liancourt Rocks (Tok-do/Take-shima)

Refugees and internally displaced persons: IDPs: undetermined (periodic flooding and famine during mid-1990s) (2017)

Trafficking in persons: current situation: North Korea is a source country for men, women, and children who are subjected to forced labor and sex trafficking; many North Korean workers recruited to work abroad under bilateral contracts with foreign governments, most often Russia and China, are subjected to forced labor and do not have a choice in the work the government assigns them, are not free to change jobs, and face government reprisals if they try to escape or complain to outsiders; tens of thousands of North Koreans, including children, held in prison camps are subjected to forced labor, including logging, mining, and farming; many North Korean women and girls, lured by promises of food, jobs, and freedom, have migrated to China illegally to escape poor social and economic conditions only to be forced into prostitution, domestic service, or agricultural work through forced marriages

tier rating: Tier 3—North Korea does not fully comply with minimum standards for the elimination of trafficking and is not making significant efforts to do so; the government continued to participate in human trafficking through its use of domestic forced labor camps and the provision of forced labor to foreign governments through bilateral contracts; officials did not demonstrate any efforts to address human trafficking through prosecution, protection, or prevention measures; no known investigations, prosecutions, or convictions of trafficking offenders or officials complicit in trafficking-related offenses were conducted; the government also made no efforts to identify or protect trafficking victims and did not permit NGOs to assist victims (2015)

Illicit drugs: at present there is insufficient information to determine the current level of involvement of government officials in the production or trafficking of illicit drugs, but for years, from the 1970s into the 2000s, citizens of the Democratic People's Republic of (North) Korea (DPRK), many of them diplomatic employees of the government, were apprehended abroad while trafficking in narcotics; police investigations in Taiwan and Japan in recent years have linked North Korea to large illicit shipments of heroin and methamphetamine

KOREA, SOUTH

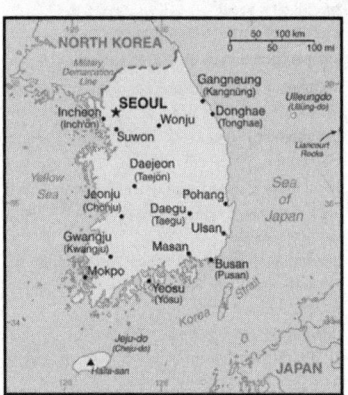

INTRODUCTION

Background: An independent kingdom for much of its long history, Korea was occupied by Japan beginning in 1905 following the Russo-Japanese War. In 1910, Tokyo formally annexed the entire Peninsula. Korea regained its independence following Japan's surrender to the US in 1945. After World War II, a democratic-based government (Republic of Korea, ROK) was set up in the southern half of the Korean Peninsula while a communist-style government was installed in the north (Democratic People's Republic of Korea, DPRK). During the Korean War (1950-53), US troops and UN forces fought alongside ROK soldiers to defend South Korea from a DPRK invasion supported by China and the Soviet Union. A 1953 armistice split the Peninsula along a demilitarized zone at about the 38th parallel. PARK Chung-hee took over leadership of the country in a 1961 coup. During his regime, from 1961 to 1979, South Korea achieved rapid economic growth, with per capita income rising to roughly 17 times the level of North Korea.

South Korea held its first free presidential election under a revised democratic constitution in 1987, with former ROK Army general ROH Tae-woo winning a close race. In 1993, KIM Young-sam (1993-98) became the first civilian president of South Korea's new democratic era. President KIM Dae-jung (1998-2003) won the Nobel Peace Prize in 2000 for his contributions to South Korean democracy and his "Sunshine" policy of engagement with North Korea. President PARK Geun-hye, daughter of former ROK President PARK Chung-hee, took office in February 2013 as South Korea's first female leader. In December 2016, the National Assembly passed an impeachment motion against President PARK over her alleged involvement in a corruption and influence-peddling scandal, immediately suspending her presidential authorities. The impeachment was upheld in March 2017, triggering an early presidential election in May 2017 won by MOON Jae-in. South Korea will host the Winter Olympic Games in February 2018. Discord with North Korea has permeated inter-Korean relations for much of the past decade, highlighted by the North's attacks on a South Korean ship and island in 2010, the exchange of artillery fire across the DMZ in 2015, and multiple nuclear and missile tests in 2016 and 2017.

GEOGRAPHY

Location: Eastern Asia, southern half of the Korean Peninsula bordering the Sea of Japan and the Yellow Sea

Geographic coordinates: 37 00 N, 127 30 E

Map references: Asia

Area: *total:* 99,720 sq km
land: 96,920 sq km
water: 2,800 sq km
country comparison to the world: 110

Area—comparative: slightly smaller than Pennsylvania; slightly larger than Indiana

Land boundaries: *total:* 237 km
border countries (1): North Korea 237 km

Coastline: 2,413 km

Maritime claims: *territorial sea:* 12 nm; between 3 nm and 12 nm in the Korea Strait
contiguous zone: 24 nm
exclusive economic zone: 200 nm
continental shelf: not specified

Climate: temperate, with rainfall heavier in summer than winter; cold winters

Terrain: mostly hills and mountains; wide coastal plains in west and south

Elevation: *mean elevation:* 282 m

elevation extremes: *lowest point:* Sea of Japan 0 m
highest point: Halla-san 1,950 m

Natural resources: coal, tungsten, graphite, molybdenum, lead, hydropower potential

Land use: *agricultural land:* 18.1%
arable land: 15.3%;
permanent crops: 2.2%;
permanent pasture: 0.6%
forest: 63.9%
other: 18% (2011 est.)
Irrigated land: 7,780 sq km (2012)

Population—distribution: with approximately 70% of the country considered mountainous, the country's population is primarily concentrated in the lowland areas, where density is quite high; Gyeonggi Province in the northwest, which surrounds the capital of Seoul and contains the port of Incheon, is the most densely populated province; Gangwon in the northeast is the least populated

Natural hazards: occasional typhoons bring high winds and floods; low-level seismic activity common in southwest
volcanism: Halla (1,950 m) is considered historically active although it has not erupted in many centuries

Environment—current issues: air pollution in large cities; acid rain; water pollution from the discharge of sewage and industrial effluents; drift net fishing

Environment—international agreements: *party to:* Antarctic-Environmental Protocol, Antarctic-Marine Living Resources, Antarctic Treaty, Biodiversity, Climate Change, Climate Change-Kyoto Protocol, Desertification, Endangered Species, Environmental Modification, Hazardous Wastes, Law of the Sea, Marine Dumping, Ozone Layer Protection, Ship Pollution, Tropical Timber 83, Tropical Timber 94, Wetlands, Whaling
signed, but not ratified: none of the selected agreements

Geography—note: strategic location on Korea Strait; about 3,000 mostly small and uninhabited islands lie off the western and southern coasts

PEOPLE AND SOCIETY

Population: 51,181,299 (July 2017 est.)
country comparison to the world: 27

Nationality: *noun:* Korean(s)
adjective: Korean

Ethnic groups: homogeneous

Languages: Korean, English (widely taught in junior high and high school)

Religions: Protestant 19.7%, Buddhist 15.5%, Catholic 7.9%, none 56.9%
note: many people practice Confucianism, regardless of their religion or not having a religious affiliation (2015 est.)

Age structure: *0-14 years:* 13.21% (male 3,484,398/female 3,276,984)
15-24 years: 12.66% (male 3,415,998/female 3,065,144)
25-54 years: 45.52% (male 11,992,462/female 11,303,726)
55-64 years: 14.49% (male 3,660,888/female 3,756,947)
65 years and over: 14.12% (male 3,080,601/female 4,144,151) (2017 est.)

Dependency ratios: *total dependency ratio:* 36.7
youth dependency ratio: 19
elderly dependency ratio: 17.7
potential support ratio: 5.6 (2015 est.)

Median age: *total:* 41.8 years
male: 40.2 years
female: 43.4 years (2017 est.)
country comparison to the world: 40

Population growth rate: 0.48% (2017 est.)
country comparison to the world: 155

Birth rate: 8.3 births/1,000 population (2017 est.)
country comparison to the world: 220

Death rate: 6 deaths/1,000 population (2017 est.)
country comparison to the world: 167

Net migration rate: 2.5 migrant(s)/1,000 population (2017 est.)
country comparison to the world: 36

Population distribution: with approximately 70% of the country considered mountainous, the country's population is primarily concentrated in the lowland areas, where density is quite high; Gyeonggi Province in the northwest, which surrounds the capital of Seoul and contains the port of Incheon, is the most densely populated province; Gangwon in the northeast is the least populated

Urbanization: *urban population:* 82.7% of total population (2017)
rate of urbanization: 0.55% annual rate of change (2015-20 est.)

Major urban areas—population: SEOUL (capital) 9.774 million; Busan (Pusan) 3.216 million; Incheon (Inch'on) 2.685 million; Daegu (Taegu) 2.244 million; Daejon (Taejon) 1.564 million; Gwangju (Kwangju) 1.536 million (2015)

Sex ratio: *at birth:* 1.07 male(s)/female
0-14 years: 1.07 male(s)/female
15-24 years: 1.12 male(s)/female
25-54 years: 1.06 male(s)/female
55-64 years: 0.98 male(s)/female
65 years and over: 0.71 male(s)/female
total population: 1 male(s)/female (2016 est.)

Mother's mean age at first birth: 31 years (2014 est.)

Maternal mortality ratio: 11 deaths/100,000 live births (2015 est.)
country comparison to the world: 145

Infant mortality rate: *total:* 3 deaths/1,000 live births
male: 3.2 deaths/1,000 live births
female: 2.8 deaths/1,000 live births (2017 est.)
country comparison to the world: 215

Life expectancy at birth: *total population:* 82.5 years
male: 79.3 years
female: 85.8 years (2017 est.)
country comparison to the world: 11

Total fertility rate: 1.26 children born/woman (2017 est.)
country comparison to the world: 219

Contraceptive prevalence rate: 80%
note: percent of women aged 15-44 (2009)

Health expenditures: 7.4% of GDP (2014)
country comparison to the world: 72

Physicians density: 2.23 physicians/1,000 population (2014)

Hospital bed density: 10.3 beds/1,000 population (2009)

Drinking water source:
improved:
urban: 99.7% of population
rural: 87.9% of population
total: 97.8% of population

unimproved:
urban: 0.3% of population
rural: 12.1% of population
total: 2.2% of population (2012 est.)

Sanitation facility access:
improved:
urban: 100% of population
rural: 100% of population
total: 100% of population
unimproved:
urban: 0% of population
rural: 0% of population
total: 0% of population (2015 est.)

HIV/AIDS—adult prevalence rate: NA

HIV/AIDS—people living with HIV/AIDS: NA

HIV/AIDS—deaths: NA

Obesity—adult prevalence rate: 4.7% (2016)
country comparison to the world: 184

Children under the age of 5 years underweight: 0.7% (2010)
country comparison to the world: 135

Education expenditures: 4.6% of GDP (2012)
country comparison to the world: 75

School life expectancy (primary to tertiary education): *total:* 17 years
male: 17 years
female: 16 years (2013)

Unemployment, youth ages 15-24: *total:* 10.7%
male: 11%
female: 10.5% (2016 est.)
country comparison to the world: 107

GOVERNMENT

Country name: *conventional long form:* Republic of Korea
conventional short form: South Korea
local long form: Taehan-min'guk
local short form: Han'guk
abbreviation: ROK
etymology: derived from the Chinese name for Goryeo, which was the Korean dynasty that united the peninsula in the 10th century A.D.; the South Korean name "Han'guk" means "Land of the Han," where "han" may have its origins in the native root for "great [leader]" (similar to the title "khan")

Government type: presidential republic

Capital: *name:* Seoul; note—Sejong, located some 120 km (75 mi) south of Seoul, is being developed as a new capital

geographic coordinates: 37 33 N, 126 59 E
time difference: UTC+9 (14 hours ahead of Washington, DC, during Standard Time)

Administrative divisions: 9 provinces (do, singular and plural), 6 metropolitan cities (gwangyeoksi, singular and plural), 1 special city (teugbyeolsi), and 1 special self-governing city (teukbyeoljachisi)
provinces: Chungbuk (North Chungcheong), Chungnam (South Chungcheong), Gangwon, Gyeongbuk (North Gyeongsang), Gyeonggi, Gyeongnam (South Gyeongsang), Jeju, Jeonbuk (North Jeolla), Jeonnam (South Jeolla)

metropolitan cities: Busan (Pusan), Daegu (Taegu), Daejeon (Taejon), Gwangju (Kwangju), Incheon (Inch'on), Ulsan
special city: Seoul
special self-governing city: Sejong

Independence: 15 August 1945 (from Japan)

National holiday: Liberation Day, 15 August (1945)

Constitution: effective 17 July 1948; amended many times, last in 1987 (2017)

Legal system: mixed legal system combining European civil law, Anglo-American law, and Chinese classical thought

International law organization participation: has not submitted an ICJ jurisdiction declaration; accepts ICCt jurisdiction

Citizenship: *citizenship by birth:* no
citizenship by descent only: at least one parent must be a citizen of South Korea
dual citizenship recognized: no
residency requirement for naturalization: 5 years

Suffrage: 19 years of age; universal

Executive branch: *chief of state:* President MOON Jae-in (since 10 May 2017); note—President PARK Geun-hye (since 25 February 2013) was impeached by the National Assembly on 9 December 2016; PARK's impeachment was upheld by the Constitutional Court and she was removed from office on 9 March 2017

head of government: Prime Minister LEE Nak-yon (since 1 June 2017); Deputy Prime Ministers KIM Dong-yeon (since 9 June 2017), KIM Sang-kon (since 4 July 2017)
cabinet: State Council appointed by the president on the prime minister's recommendation
elections/appointments: president directly elected by simple majority popular vote for a single 5-year term; election last held on 9 May 2017 (next to be held in 2022); prime minister appointed by president with consent of National Assembly
election results: MOON Jae-in elected president; percent of vote—MOON Jae-in (DP) 41.1%, HONG Joon-pyo (LKP) 25.5%, AHN Cheol-soo (PP) 21.4%, other 12.0%

Legislative branch: *description:* unicameral National Assembly or Kuk Hoe (300 seats; 246 members directly elected in single-seat constituencies by simple majority vote and 54 directly elected in a single national constituency by proportional representation vote; members serve 4-year terms)
elections: last held on 13 April 2016 (next to be held in 2020)
election results: percent of vote by party—NFP 33.5%, PP 26.7%, MPK 25.5%, JP 7.2%, other 7.1%; seats by party—MPK 123, NFP 122, PP 38, JP 6, independent 11
note: as of February 2018, seats by party—DP 108, LKP 100, PP 14, BP 9, JP 2, MP 1, Patriotic Party 1, independent 3, vacant

Judicial branch: *highest court(s):* Supreme Court of South Korea (consists of a chief justice and 13 justices); Constitutional Court (consists of a court head and 8 justices)

judge selection and term of office: Supreme Court chief justice appointed by the president with the consent of the National Assembly; other justices appointed by the president upon the recommendation of the chief justice and consent of the National Assembly; position of the chief justice is a 6-year non-renewable term; other justices serve 6-year renewable terms; Constitutional Court justices appointed—3 by the president, 3 by the National Assembly, and 3 by the Supreme Court chief justice; court head serves until retirement at age 70, while other justices serve 6-year renewable terms with mandatory retirement at age 65

subordinate courts: High Courts; District Courts; Branch Courts (organized under the District Courts); specialized courts for family and administrative issues

Political parties and leaders: Bareun Party or BP [YOO Seong-min] (split from the NFP)

Democratic Party or DP [CHOO Mi-ae] (renamed from Minjoo Party of Korea or MPK in October 2016; formerly New Politics Alliance for Democracy or NPAD, which was a merger of the Democratic Party or DP (formerly DUP) [KIM Han-gil] and the New Political Vision Party or NPVP [AHN Cheol-soo] in March 2014)

Justice Party or JP [SIM Sang-jeong]

Liberty Korea Party or LKP [HONG Joon-pyo] (formerly the New Frontier Party (NFP) or Saenuri and before that the Grand National Party [HONG Joon-Pyo])

Minjung Party or MP (formed from the merger of the New People's Party (formerly the New People's Political Party or NPP) and the People's United Party or PUP)

Patriotic Party

People's Party or PP [AHN Cheol-soo]

Saenuri Party [CHUNG Kwang-Taek) (split from Liberty Korea Party in April 2017)

Political pressure groups and leaders: Christian Council of Korea

Citizen's Coalition for Economic Justice

Federation of Korean Trade Unions

Korea Women's Association United

Korea Women's Hotline

Korean Confederation of Trade Unions

Korean Veterans' Association

Lawyers for a Democratic Society

National Council of Churches in Korea

People's Solidarity for Participatory Democracy

International organization participation: ADB, AfDB (nonregional member), APEC, Arctic Council (observer), ARF, ASEAN (dialogue partner), Australia Group, BIS, CD, CICA, CP, EAS, EBRD, FAO, FATF, G-20, IADB, IAEA, IBRD, ICAO, ICC (national committees), ICCt, ICRM, IDA, IEA, IFAD, IFC, IFRCS, IHO, ILO, IMF, IMO, IMSO, Interpol, IOC, IOM, IPU, ISO, ITSO, ITU, ITUC (NGOs), LAIA (observer), MIGA, MINURSO, MINUSTAH, NEA, NSG, OAS (observer), OECD, OPCW, OSCE (partner), Pacific Alliance (observer), Paris Club (associate), PCA, PIF (partner), SAARC (observer),

SICA (observer), UN, UNAMID, UNCTAD, UNESCO, UNHCR, UNIDO, UNIFIL, UNMIL, UNMISS, UNMOGIP, UNOCI, UNWTO, UPU, WCO, WHO, WIPO, WMO, WTO, ZC

Diplomatic representation in the US: *chief of mission:* Ambassador CHO Yoon-je (since 29 November 2017)

chancery: 2450 Massachusetts Avenue NW, Washington, DC 20008

telephone: [1] (202) 939-5600

FAX: [1] (202) 797-0595

consulate(s) general: Agana (Guam), Anchorage (AK), Atlanta, Boston, Chicago, Honolulu, Houston, Los Angeles, New York, San Francisco, Seattle

Diplomatic representation from the US: *chief of mission:* Ambassador (vacant); Charge d'Affaires Marc KNAPPER (since 20 January 2017)

embassy: 188 Sejong-daero, Jongno-gu, Seoul 110-710

mailing address: US Embassy Seoul, Unit

telephone: [82] (2) 397-4114

FAX: [82] (2) 725-0152

Flag description: white with a red (top) and blue yin-yang symbol in the center; there is a different black trigram from the ancient I Ching (Book of Changes) in each corner of the white field; the South Korean national flag is called Taegukki; white is a traditional Korean color and represents peace and purity; the blue section represents the negative cosmic forces of the yin, while the red symbolizes the opposite positive forces of the yang; each trigram (kwae) denotes one of the four universal elements, which together express the principle of movement and harmony

National symbol(s): taegeuk (yin yang symbol), Hibiscus syriacus (Rose of Sharon); national colors: red, white, blue, black

National anthem: name: "Aegukga" (Patriotic Song)

lyrics/music: YUN Ch'i-Ho or AN Ch'ang-Ho/AHN Eaktay

note: adopted 1948, well-known by 1910; both North Korea's and South Korea's anthems share the same name and have a vaguely similar melody but have different lyrics

ECONOMY

Economy—overview: After emerging from the 1950-53 war with North Korea, South Korea emerged as one of the 20th century's most remarkable economic success stories, becoming a developed, globally connected, high-technology society within decades. In the 1960s, GDP per capita was comparable with levels in the poorest countries in the world. In 2004, South Korea joined the trillion-dollar club of world economies.

Beginning in the 1960s under President PARK Chung-hee, the government promoted the import of raw materials and technology, encouraged saving and investment over consumption, kept wages low, and directed resources to export-oriented industries that remain important to the economy to this day. Growth surged under these policies,

and frequently reached double-digits in the 1960s and 1970s. Growth gradually moderated in the 1990s as the economy matured, but remained strong enough to propel South Korea into the ranks of the advanced economies of the OECD by 1997. These policies also led to the emergence of family-owned chaebol conglomerates such as Daewoo, Hyundai, and Samsung, which retained their dominant positions even as the government loosened its grip on the economy amid the political changes of the 1980s and 1990s.

The Asian financial crisis of 1997-98 hit South Korea's companies hard because of their excessive reliance on short-term borrowing, and GDP ultimately plunged by 7% in 1998. South Korea tackled difficult economic reforms following the crisis, including restructuring some chaebols, increasing labor market flexibility, and opening up to more foreign investment and imports. These steps lead to a relatively rapid economic recovery. South Korea also began expanding its network of free trade agreements to help bolster exports, and has since implemented 16 free trade agreements covering 58 countries—including the United State and China—that collectively cover more than three-quarters of global GDP.

In 2017, the election of President MOON Jae-in brought a surge in consumer confidence, in part, because of his successful efforts to increase wages and government spending. These factors combined with an uptick in export growth to drive real GDP growth to more than 3%, despite disruptions in South Korea's trade with China over the deployment of a US missile defense system in South Korea.

In 2018 and beyond, South Korea will contend with gradually slowing economic growth—in the 2-3% range—not uncommon for advanced economies. This could be partially offset by efforts to address challenges arising from its rapidly aging population, inflexible labor market, continued dominance of the chaebols, and heavy reliance on exports rather than domestic consumption. Socioeconomic problems also persist, and include rising inequality, poverty among the elderly, high youth unemployment, long working hours, low worker productivity, and corruption.

GDP (purchasing power parity): $2.027 trillion (2017 est.)

$1.967 trillion (2016 est.)

$1.913 trillion (2015 est.)

note: data are in 2017 dollars

country comparison to the world: 15

GDP (official exchange rate): $1.53 trillion (2016 est.)

GDP—real growth rate: 3% (2017 est.)

2.8% (2016 est.)

2.8% (2015 est.)

country comparison to the world: 114

GDP—per capita (PPP): $39,400 (2017 est.)

$38,400 (2016 est.)

$37,500 (2015 est.)

note: data are in 2017 dollars

country comparison to the world: 45

Gross national saving: 37.2% of GDP (2017 est.)

36.2% of GDP (2016 est.)
36.6% of GDP (2015 est.)
country comparison to the world: 11

GDP—composition, by end use:
household consumption: 47.8%
government consumption: 15.2%
investment in fixed capital: 29.4%
investment in inventories: 0.3%
exports of goods and services: 43.9%
imports of goods and services: -36.7% (2017 est.)

GDP—composition, by sector of origin:
agriculture: 2.2%
industry: 38.8%
services: 59.1% (2017 est.)

Agriculture—products: rice, root crops, barley, vegetables, fruit, cattle, pigs, chickens, milk, eggs, fish

Industries: electronics, telecommunications, automobile production, chemicals, shipbuilding, steel

Industrial production growth rate: 3.5% (2017 est.)
country comparison to the world: 87

Labor force: 27.47 million (2017 est.)
country comparison to the world: 24

Labor force—by occupation: *agriculture:* 4.9%
industry: 24.1%
services: 71% (2016 est.)

Unemployment rate: 3.8% (2017 est.)
3.7% (2016 est.)
country comparison to the world: 45

Population below poverty line: 12.5% (2015 est.)

Household income or consumption by percentage share: *lowest 10%:* 6.8%
highest 10%: 48.5% (2015 est.)

Distribution of family income—Gini index: 34.1 (2015 est.)
34.1 (2014 est.)
country comparison to the world: 99

Budget: *revenues:* $351.6 billion
expenditures: $338 billion (2017 est.)
Taxes and other revenues: 23% of GDP (2017 est.)
country comparison to the world: 130

Budget surplus (+) or deficit (-): 0.9% of GDP (2017 est.)
country comparison to the world: 19

Public debt: 43.3% of GDP (2017 est.)
45.6% of GDP (2016 est.)
country comparison to the world: 123

Fiscal year: calendar year

Inflation rate (consumer prices): 1.9% (2017 est.)
1% (2016 est.)
country comparison to the world: 84

Central bank discount rate: 1.25% (31 December 2016 est.)
1.5% (31 December 2015 est.)
country comparison to the world: 125

Commercial bank prime lending rate: 3.4% (31 December 2017 est.)
3.37% (31 December 2016 est.)
country comparison to the world: 165

Stock of narrow money: $742.5 billion (31 December 2017 est.)
$658.7 billion (31 December 2016 est.)
country comparison to the world: 9

Stock of broad money: $2.167 trillion (31 December 2017 est.)
$1.993 trillion (31 December 2016 est.)
country comparison to the world: 8

Stock of domestic credit: $2.683 trillion (31 December 2017 est.)
$2.515 trillion (31 December 2016 est.)
country comparison to the world: 10

Market value of publicly traded shares: $1.305 trillion (31 December 2016 est.)
$1.28 trillion (31 December 2015 est.)
$1.269 trillion (31 December 2014 est.)
country comparison to the world: 12

Current account balance: $85.14 billion (2017 est.)
$98.68 billion (2016 est.)
country comparison to the world: 5

Exports: $552.3 billion (2017 est.)
$511.8 billion (2016 est.)
country comparison to the world: 6

Exports—commodities: semiconductors, petrochemicals, automobile/auto parts, ships, wireless communication equipment, flat displays, steel, electronics, plastics, computers

Exports—partners: China 25.1%, US 13.5%, Vietnam 6.6%, Hong Kong 6.6%, Japan 4.9% (2016)

Imports: $448.4 billion (2017 est.)
$391.3 billion (2016 est.)
country comparison to the world: 9

Imports—commodities: crude oil/petroleum products, semiconductors, natural gas, coal, steel, computers, wireless communication equipment, automobiles, fine chemicals, textiles

Imports—partners: China 21.4%, Japan 11.7%, US 10.7%, Germany 4.7% (2016)

Reserves of foreign exchange and gold: $374.8 billion (31 December 2017 est.)
$371.1 billion (31 December 2016 est.)
country comparison to the world: 11

Debt—external: $376.9 billion (31 December 2017 est.)
$358.2 billion (31 December 2016 est.)
country comparison to the world: 31

Stock of direct foreign investment—at home: $193.6 billion (31 December 2017 est.)
$185 billion (31 December 2016 est.)
country comparison to the world: 31

Stock of direct foreign investment—abroad: $342.4 billion (31 December 2017 est.)
$310.3 billion (31 December 2016 est.)
country comparison to the world: 21

Exchange rates: South Korean won (KRW) per US dollar-
1,136.7 (2017 est.)
1,160.77 (2016 est.)
1,160.77 (2015 est.)
1,130.95 (2014 est.)
1,052.96 (2013 est.)

ENERGY

Electricity access: *electrification—total population:* 100% (2016)

Electricity—production: 528.1 billion kWh (2016 est.)
country comparison to the world: 11

Electricity—consumption: 497 billion kWh (2016 est.)
country comparison to the world: 10

Electricity—exports: 0 kWh (2016 est.)
country comparison to the world: 156

Electricity—imports: 0 kWh (2016 est.)
country comparison to the world: 167

Electricity—installed generating capacity: 103 million kW (2015 est.)
country comparison to the world: 13

Electricity—from fossil fuels: 67.1% of total installed capacity (2015 est.)
country comparison to the world: 110

Electricity—from nuclear fuels: 21.1% of total installed capacity (2015 est.)
country comparison to the world: 8

Electricity—from hydroelectric plants: 1.7% of total installed capacity (2015 est.)
country comparison to the world: 139

Electricity—from other renewable sources: 7.2% of total installed capacity (2015 est.)
country comparison to the world: 81

Crude oil—production: 0 bbl/day (2016 est.)
country comparison to the world: 155

Crude oil—exports: 0 bbl/day (2016 est.)
country comparison to the world: 148

Crude oil—imports: 2.942 million bbl/day (2016 est.)
country comparison to the world: 5

Crude oil—proved reserves: NA bbl (1 January 2017 es)

Refined petroleum products—production: 3.114 million bbl/day (2016 est.)
country comparison to the world: 7

Refined petroleum products—consumption: 2.63 million bbl/day (2016 est.)
country comparison to the world: 9

Refined petroleum products—exports: 1.343 million bbl/day (2016 est.)
country comparison to the world: 8

Refined petroleum products—imports: 935,500 bbl/day (2016 est.)
country comparison to the world: 8

Natural gas—production: 188 million cu m (2015 est.)
country comparison to the world: 78

Natural gas—consumption: 69.63 billion cu m (2015 est.)
country comparison to the world: 19

Natural gas—exports: 0 cu m (2014 est.)
country comparison to the world: 132

Natural gas—imports: 43.43 billion cu m (2015 est.)
country comparison to the world: 10

Natural gas—proved reserves: 7.079 billion cu m (1 January 2017 es)
country comparison to the world: 88

Carbon dioxide emissions from consumption of energy: 599.3 million Mt (2014 est.)
country comparison to the world: 9

COMMUNICATIONS

Telephones—fixed lines: *total subscriptions:* 28,035,600
subscriptions per 100 inhabitants: 55 (July 2016 est.)
country comparison to the world: 12

Telephones—mobile cellular: *total:* 58.935 million
subscriptions per 100 inhabitants: 120 (July 2016 est.)
country comparison to the world: 27

Telephone system: *general assessment:* excellent domestic and international services featuring rapid incorporation of new technologies
domestic: fixed-line and mobile-cellular services widely available with the latter subscribership up to about 120 per 100 persons; rapid assimilation of a full range of telecommunications technologies leading to a boom in e-commerce
international: country code—82; numerous submarine cables provide links throughout Asia, Australia, the Middle East, Europe, and US; satellite earth stations—66 (2016)

Broadcast media: multiple national TV networks with 2 of the 3 largest networks publicly operated; the largest privately owned network, Seoul Broadcasting Service (SBS), has ties with other commercial TV networks; cable and satellite TV subscription services available; publicly operated radio broadcast networks and many privately owned radio broadcasting networks, each with multiple affiliates, and independent local stations (2017)

Internet country code: .kr
Internet users: total: 44.153 million

percent of population: 89.9% (July 2016 est.)
country comparison to the world: 13

TRANSPORTATION

National air transport system: *number of registered air carriers:* 12

inventory of registered aircraft operated by air carriers: 348
annual passenger traffic on registered air carriers: 65,482,307
annual freight traffic on registered air carriers: 11.297 billion mt-km (2015)
Civil aircraft registration country code prefix: HL (2016)

Airports: 111 (2013)
country comparison to the world: 53

Airports—with paved runways: *total:* 71
over 3,047 m: 4
2,438 to 3,047 m: 19
1,524 to 2,437 m: 12
914 to 1,523 m: 13
under 914 m: 23 (2017)

Airports—with unpaved runways: *total:* 40
914 to 1,523 m: 2
under 914 m: 38 (2013)

Heliports: 466 (2013)

Pipelines: gas 2,216 km; oil 16 km; refined products 889 km (2013)

Railways: *total:* 3,874 km
standard gauge: 3,874 km 1.435-m gauge (2,727 km electrified) (2015)
country comparison to the world: 52

Roadways: *total:* 99,025 km
paved: 91,195 km (includes 4,193 km of expressways)
unpaved: 7,830 km (2015)
country comparison to the world: 46

Waterways: 1,600 km (most navigable only by small craft) (2011)
country comparison to the world: 50

Merchant marine: *total:* 1,907
by type: bulk carrier 100, container ship 89, general cargo 394, oil tanker 201, other 1,123 (2017)
country comparison to the world: 12

Ports and terminals: *major seaport(s):* Busan, Incheon, Gunsan, Kwangyang, Mokpo, Pohang, Ulsan, Yeosu
container port(s) (TEUs): Busan (19,469,000), Kwangyang (2,327,000), Incheon (2,368,000) (2015)
LNG terminal(s) (import): Incheon, Kwangyang, Pyeongtaek, Samcheok, Tongyeong, Yeosu

MILITARY AND SECURITY

Military expenditures: 2.3% of GDP (2016)
2.3% of GDP (2015)
2.64% of GDP (2014)
2.63% of GDP (2013)
2.61% of GDP (2012)
country comparison to the world: 25

Military branches: Republic of Korea Army, Navy (includes Marine Corps), Air Force (2011)

Military service age and obligation: 18-35 years of age for compulsory military service, with middle school education required; minimum conscript service obligation—21 months (Army, Marines), 23 months (Navy), 24 months (Air Force); 18-26 years of age for voluntary military service; women, in service since 1950, admitted to 7 service branches, including infantry, but excluded from artillery, armor, anti-air, and chaplaincy corps; HIV-positive individuals are exempt from military service (2017)

TRANSNATIONAL ISSUES

Disputes—international: Military Demarcation Line within the 4-km-wide Demilitarized Zone has separated North from South Korea since 1953; periodic incidents with North Korea in the Yellow Sea over the Northern Limit Line, which South Korea claims as a maritime boundary; South Korea and Japan claim Liancourt Rocks (Tok-do/Takeshima), occupied by South Korea since 1954

Refugees and internally displaced persons: *stateless persons:* 197 (2016)

KOSOVO

INTRODUCTION

Background: The central Balkans were part of the Roman and Byzantine Empires before ethnic Serbs migrated to the territories of modern Kosovo in the 7th century. During the medieval period, Kosovo became the center of a Serbian Empire and saw the construction of many important Serb religious sites, including many architecturally significant Serbian Orthodox monasteries. The defeat of Serbian forces at the Battle of Kosovo in 1389 led to five centuries of Ottoman rule during which large numbers of Turks and Albanians moved to Kosovo. By the end of the 19th century, Albanians replaced Serbs as the dominant ethnic group in Kosovo. Serbia reacquired control over the region from the Ottoman Empire during the First Balkan War of 1912. After World War II,

Kosovo's present-day boundaries were established when Kosovo became an autonomous province of Serbia in the Socialist Federal Republic of Yugoslavia (S.F.R.Y.). Despite legislative concessions, Albanian nationalism increased in the 1980s, which led to riots and calls for Kosovo's independence. The Serbs—many of whom viewed Kosovo as their cultural heartland—instituted a new constitution in 1989 revoking Kosovo's autonomous status. Kosovo's Albanian leaders responded in 1991 by organizing a referendum declaring Kosovo independent. Serbia undertook repressive measures against the Kosovar Albanians in the 1990s, provoking a Kosovar Albanian insurgency.

Beginning in 1998, Serbia conducted a brutal counterinsurgency campaign that resulted in massacres and massive expulsions of ethnic Albanians (some 800,000 ethnic Albanians were forced from their homes in Kosovo). After international attempts to mediate the conflict failed, a three-month NATO military operation against Serbia beginning in March 1999 forced the Serbs to agree to withdraw their military and police forces from Kosovo. UN Security Council Resolution 1244 (1999) placed Kosovo under a transitional administration, the UN Interim Administration Mission in Kosovo (UNMIK), pending a determination of Kosovo's future status. A UN-led process began in late 2005 to determine Kosovo's final status. The 2006-07 negotiations ended without agreement between Belgrade and Pristina, though the UN issued a comprehensive report on Kosovo's final status that endorsed independence. On 17 February 2008, the Kosovo Assembly declared Kosovo independent. Since then, over 110 countries have recognized Kosovo, and it has joined numerous international organizations. In October 2008, Serbia sought an advisory opinion from the International Court of Justice (ICJ) on the legality under international law of Kosovo's declaration of independence. The ICJ released the advisory opinion in July 2010 affirming that Kosovo's declaration of independence did not violate general principles of international law, UN Security Council Resolution 1244, or the Constitutive Framework. The opinion was closely tailored to Kosovo's unique history and circumstances.

Demonstrating Kosovo's development into a sovereign, multi-ethnic, democratic country the international community ended the period of Supervised Independence in 2012. Elections were held throughout Kosovo in 2013 and 2014, at the municipal and national level respectively. Serbia continues to reject Kosovo's independence, but the two countries reached an agreement to normalize their relations in April 2013 through EU-facilitated talks and are currently engaged in the implementation process. Kosovo seeks full integration into the international community, and has pursued bilateral recognitions and eventual membership in international organizations, such as the UN, EU, and NATO.

GEOGRAPHY

Location: Southeast Europe, between Serbia and Macedonia

Geographic coordinates: 42 35 N, 21 00 E

Map references: Europe

Area: *total:* 10,887 sq km
land: 10,887 sq km
water: 0 sq km
country comparison to the world: 168

Area—comparative: slightly larger than Delaware

Land boundaries: *total:* 714 km
border countries (4): Albania 112 km, Macedonia 160 km, Montenegro 76 km, Serbia 366 km

Coastline: 0 km (landlocked)

Maritime claims: none (landlocked)

Climate: influenced by continental air masses resulting in relatively cold winters with heavy snowfall and hot, dry summers and autumns;

Mediterranean and alpine influences create regional variation; maximum rainfall between October and December

Terrain: flat fluvial basin at an elevation of 400-700 m above sea level surrounded by several high mountain ranges with elevations of 2,000 to 2,500 m

Elevation: *mean elevation:* 450 m

elevation extremes: *lowest point:* Drini i Bardhe/Beli Drim 297 m (located on the border with Albania)
highest point: Gjeravica/Deravica 2,656 m

Natural resources: nickel, lead, zinc, magnesium, lignite, kaolin, chrome, bauxite

Land use: *agricultural land:* 52.8%
arable land: 27.4%;
permanent crops: 1.9%;
permanent pasture: 23.5%
forest: 41.7%
other: 5.5% (2001 est.)
Irrigated land: NA

Population—distribution: population clusters exist throughout the country, the largest being in the east in and around the capital of Pristina

Geography—note: the 41-km long Nerodimka River divides into two branches each of which flows into a different sea: the northern branch flows into the Sitnica River, which via the Ibar, Morava, and Danube Rivers ultimately flows into the Black Sea; the southern branch flows via the Lepenac and Vardar Rivers into the Aegean Sea

PEOPLE AND SOCIETY

Population: 1,895,250 (July 2017 est.)
country comparison to the world: 150

Nationality: *noun:* Kosovar (Albanian), Kosovac (Serbian)
adjective: Kosovar (Albanian), Kosovski (Serbian)
note: Kosovan, a neutral term, is sometimes also used as a noun or adjective

Ethnic groups: Albanians 92.9%, Bosniaks 1.6%, Serbs 1.5%, Turk 1.1%, Ashkali 0.9%, Egyptian 0.7%, Gorani 0.6%, Romani 0.5%, other/unspecified 0.2%
note: these estimates may under-represent Serb, Romani, and some other ethnic minorities because they are based on the 2011 Kosovo national census, which excluded northern Kosovo (a largely Serb-inhabited region) and was partially boycotted by Serb and Romani communities in southern Kosovo (2011 est.)

Languages: Albanian (official) 94.5%, Bosnian 1.7%, Serbian (official) 1.6%, Turkish 1.1%, other 0.9% (includes Romani), unspecified 0.1%
note: in municipalities where a community's mother tongue is not one of Kosovo's official languages, the language of that community may be given official status according to the 2006 Law on the Use of Languages (2011 est.)

Religions: Muslim 95.6%, Roman Catholic 2.2%, Orthodox 1.5%, other 0.07%, none 0.07%, unspecified 0.6% (2011 est.)

Age structure: *0-14 years:* 25.01% (male 246,281/female 227,718)
15-24 years: 17.22% (male 170,515/female 155,840)
25-54 years: 42.57% (male 425,815/female 381,037)
55-64 years: 7.92% (male 75,964/female 74,170)
65 years and over: 7.28% (male 57,965/female 79,945) (2017 est.)

Median age: *total:* 29.1 years
male: 28.8 years
female: 29.5 years (2017 est.)
country comparison to the world: 126

Population distribution: population clusters exist throughout the country, the largest being in the east in and around the capital of Pristina

Major urban areas—population: PRISTINA (capital) 207,062 (2014)

Sex ratio: *at birth:* 1.08 male(s)/female
0-14 years: 1.08 male(s)/female
15-24 years: 1.1 male(s)/female
25-54 years: 1.12 male(s)/female
55-64 years: 1.01 male(s)/female
65 years and over: 0.72 male(s)/female
total population: 1.06 male(s)/female (2016 est.)

Unemployment, youth ages 15-24: *total:* 57.7%
male: 54.2%
female: 67.2% (2015 est.)
country comparison to the world: 2

GOVERNMENT

Country name: *conventional long form:* Republic of Kosovo
conventional short form: Kosovo
local long form: Republika e Kosoves (Republika Kosovo)
local short form: Kosova (Kosovo)
etymology: name derives from the Serbian "kos" meaning "blackbird," an ellipsis (linguistic omission) for "kosove polje" or "field of the blackbirds"

Government type: parliamentary republic

Capital: *name:* Pristina (Prishtine, Prishtina)
geographic coordinates: 42 40 N, 21 10 E
time difference: UTC+1 (6 hours ahead of Washington, DC, during Standard Time)
daylight saving time: +1hr, begins last Sunday in March; ends last Sunday in October

Administrative divisions: 38 municipalities (komunat, singular—komuna (Albanian); opstine, singular—opstina (Serbian)); Decan (Decani), Dragash (Dragas), Ferizaj (Urosevac), Fushe Kosove (Kosovo Polje), Gjakove (Dakovica), Gjilan (Gnjilane), Gllogovc (Glogovac), Gracanice (Gracanica), Hani i Elezit (Deneral Jankovic), Istog (Istok), Junik, Kacanik, Kamenice (Kamenica), Kline (Klina), Kllokot (Klokot), Leposaviq (Leposavic), Lipjan (Lipljan), Malisheve (Malisevo), Mamushe (Mamusa), Mitrovice e Jug (Juzna Mitrovica) [South Mitrovica], Mitrovice e Veriut (Severna Mitrovica) [North Mitrovica], Novoberde (Novo Brdo), Obiliq (Obilic), Partesh (Partes), Peje (Pec), Podujeve (Podujevo), Prishtine (Pristina), Prizren, Rahovec (Orahovac),

Ranillug (Ranilug), Shterpce (Strpce), Shtime (Stimlje), Skenderaj (Srbica), Suhareke (Suva Reka), Viti (Vitina), Vushtrri (Vucitrn), Zubin Potok, Zvecan

Independence: 17 February 2008 (from Serbia)

National holiday: Independence Day, 17 February (2008)

Constitution: history: previous 1974, 1990; latest (postindependence) draft finalized 2 April 2008, signed 7 April 2008, ratified 9 April 2008, entered into force 15 June 2008; note—amendment 24, passed by the Assembly in August 2015, established the Kosovo Relocated Specialist Institution, a court established to try war crimes allegedly committed by the Kosovo Liberation Army in the late 1990s

amendments: proposed by the government, by the president of the republic, or by one-fourth of Assembly deputies; passage requires two-thirds majority vote of the Assembly, including two-thirds majority vote of deputies representing non-majority communities, followed by a favorable Constitutional Court assessment; amended several times, last in 2016 (2016)

Legal system: civil law system; note—the European Union Rule of Law Mission (EULEX) retains limited executive powers related to the investigation of such issues as war crimes

International law organization participation: has not submitted an ICJ jurisdiction declaration; non-party state to the ICCt

Citizenship: *citizenship by birth:* no
citizenship by descent only: at least one parent must be a citizen of Kosovo
dual citizenship recognized: yes
residency requirement for naturalization: 5 years

Suffrage: 18 years of age; universal

Executive branch: *chief of state:* President Hashim THACI (since 7 April 2016)

head of government: Prime Minister Ramush HARADINAJ (since 9 September 2017); note—Prime Minister Isa MUSTAFA lost no-confidence vote on 10 May 2017
cabinet: Cabinet elected by the Assembly
elections/appointments: president indirectly elected by at least two-thirds majority vote of the Assembly for a 5-year term; if a candidate does not attain a two-thirds threshold in the first two ballots, the candidate winning a simple majority vote in the third ballot is elected (eligible for a second term); election last held on 26 February 2016 (next to be held in 2021); prime minister indirectly elected by the Assembly
election results: Hashim THACI elected president in the third ballot; Assembly vote—Hashim THACI (PDK) 71, Rafet RAMA (PDK) 0, invalid 10; Isa MUSTAFA (LDK) selected prime minister by the president in consultation with the LDK/PDK/PD/LB/PSHDK/PK coalition

Legislative branch: *description:* unicameral Assembly or Kuvendi i Kosoves/Skupstina Kosova (120 seats; 100 members directly elected by proportional representation vote with 20 seats reserved for ethnic minorities—10 for Serbs and 10 for other ethnic minorities; members serve 4-year terms)

elections: last held on 11 June 2017 (next to be held in 2021); note—early elections were held after a no-confidence vote on 10 May 2017 led to the dismissal of Prime Minister Isa MUSTAFA

election results: percent of vote by party/coalition—PAN Coalition 33.7%, VV 27.5%, LAA Coalition 25.5%, Serb List 6.1%, KDTP 1.1%, VAKAT 1.1%, other 5%; seats by party/coalition—PAN Coalition 39, VV 32, LAA Coalition 29, Serb List 9, KDTP 2, VAKAT 2, other 7

Judicial branch: *highest court(s):* Supreme Court (consists of the court president and NA judges); Constitutional Court (consists of the court president, vice president, and 7 judges)

judge selection and term of office: Supreme Court judges nominated by the Kosovo Judicial Council, a 13-member independent body staffed by judges and lay members, and also responsible for overall administration of Kosovo's judicial system; judges appointed by the president of the Republic of Kosovo; judges appointed until mandatory retirement age; Constitutional Court judges nominated by the Kosovo Assembly and appointed by the president of the republic to serve single, 9-year terms

subordinate courts: subordinate courts: Court of Appeals (organized into 4 departments: General, Serious Crime, Commercial Matters, and Administrative Matters; Basic Court (located in 7 municipalities, each with several branches)

note: in August 2015, the Kosovo Assembly approved a constitutional amendment that establishes the Kosovo Relocated Specialist Judicial Institution; the court, located at the Hague in the Netherlands, began operating in late 2016 and tries crimes by members of the Kosovo Liberation Army during the late 1990s

Political parties and leaders: Albanian Christian Democratic Party of Kosovo or PSHDK [Uke BERISHA]
Alliance for the Future of Kosovo or AAK [Ramush HARADINAJ]
Conservative Party of Kosovo or PK [Munir BASHA]
Democratic League of Kosovo or LDK [Isa MUSTAFA]
Democratic Party of Kosovo or PDK [Kadri VESELI]
Independent Liberal Party or SLS [Slobodan PETROVIC]
Initiative for Kosovo or NISMA [Fatmir LIMAJ]
Justice Party of Kosovo or PD [Ferid AGANI]
LAA Coalition [Isa MUSTAFA] (includes LDK, AKR, The Alternative]
Movement for Self-Determination (Vetevendosje) or VV [Visar YMERI]
Movement for Unification or LB [Valon MURATI]
New Kosovo Alliance or AKR [Behgjet PACOLLI]
New Kosovo Coalition
PAN Coalition [Kadri VESELI] (includes PDK, AAK, NISMA)
Self-Determination (Vetevendosje) (Visar YMERI)
Serb List [Slavko SIMIC]

The Alternative [Mimoza KUSATI-LILA]
Turkish Democratic Party of Kosovo or KDTP [Mahir YAGCILAR]
Vakat Coalition or VAKAT [Rasim DEMIRI]

Political pressure groups and leaders: CiviKos Platform [Valdete IDRIZI]
Council for the Defense of Human Rights and Freedom or CDHRF [Behxhet SHALA]
Group for Political and Legal Studies or GLPS [Fisnik KORENICA]
KLA War Veterans Organization [Muharrem XHEMAJLI]
Kosova Women's Network or KWN [Igballe ROGOVA]
Kosovar Civil Society Foundation or KCFS [Venera HAJRULLAHU]
Kosovo Democratic Institute or KDI [Ismet KRYEZIU]
Organization for Democracy, Anti-Corruption and Dignity Rise! or COHU [Arton DEMHASAJ]
Serb National Council (SNV)
Speak Up or FOL [Petrit ZOGAJ] (think tank)

International organization participation: IBRD, IDA, IFC, IMF, ITUC (NGOs), MIGA, OIF (observer)

Diplomatic representation in the US: *chief of mission:* Ambassador Vlora CITAKU (since 17 September 2015)
chancery: 2175 K Street, NW, Suite 300, Washington, DC 20037
telephone: 202-450-2130
FAX: 202-735-0609
consulate(s) general: New York
consulate(s): Des Moines (IA)

Diplomatic representation from the US: *chief of mission:* Ambassador Gregory T. DELAWIE (since 21 August 2015)
embassy: Arberia/Dragodan, Nazim Hikmet 30, Pristina, Kosovo
mailing address: use embassy street address
telephone: [381] 38 59 59 3000
FAX: [381] 38 549 890

Flag description: centered on a dark blue field is a gold-colored silhouette of Kosovo surmounted by six white, five-pointed stars arrayed in a slight arc; each star represents one of the major ethnic groups of Kosovo: Albanians, Serbs, Turks, Gorani, Roma, and Bosniaks
note: one of only two national flags that uses a map as a design element; the flag of Cyprus is the other

National symbol(s): six, five-pointed, white stars; national colors: blue, gold, white

National anthem: name: "Europe"
lyrics/music: no lyrics/Mendi MENGJIQI
note: adopted 2008; Kosovo chose to exclude lyrics in its anthem so as not to offend the country's minority ethnic groups

ECONOMY

Economy—overview: Kosovo's economy has shown progress in transitioning to a market-based system and maintaining macroeconomic stability, but it is still highly dependent on the international community and the diaspora for financial and technical assistance. Remittances from the diaspora—located mainly in Germany, Switzerland, and the Nordic countries—are estimated to account for about 17% of GDP and international donor assistance accounts for approximately 10% of GDP. With international assistance, Kosovo has been able to privatize a majority of its state-owned enterprises.

Kosovo's citizens are the second poorest in Europe, after Moldova, with a per capita GDP (PPP) of $10,400 in 2017. An unemployment rate of 33%, and a youth unemployment rate near 60%, in a country where the average age is 26, encourages emigration and fuels a significant informal, unreported economy. Emigration remains challenging, however, because Kosovo lacks visa-free travel to the EU. Most of Kosovo's population lives in rural towns outside of the capital, Pristina. Inefficient, near-subsistence farming is common—the result of small plots, limited mechanization, and a lack of technical expertise. Kosovo enjoys lower labor costs than the rest of the region. However, high levels of corruption, little contract enforcement, and unreliable electricity supply have discouraged potential investors. The official currency of Kosovo is the euro, but the Serbian dinar is also used illegally in Serb majority communities. Kosovo's tie to the euro has helped keep core inflation low.

Minerals and metals production—including lignite, lead, zinc, nickel, chrome, aluminum, magnesium, and a wide variety of construction materials—once the backbone of industry, has declined because of aging equipment and insufficient investment, problems exacerbated by competing and unresolved ownership claims of Kosovo's largest mines. A limited and unreliable electricity supply is a major impediment to economic development, but Kosovo has received technical assistance to help improve the sector's performance and has worked to improve infrastructure connections with its neighbors. In 2012, Kosovo privatized its electricity supply and distribution network. The US Government is cooperating with the Ministry of Economic Development (MED) and the World Bank to conclude a commercial tender for the construction of Kosovo C, a new lignite-fired power plant that would leverage Kosovo's large lignite reserves. MED also has plans for the rehabilitation of an older coal power plant, Kosovo B, and the development of a coal mine that could supply both plants.

In June 2009, Kosovo joined the World Bank and International Monetary Fund, and began servicing its share of the former Yugoslavia's debt. In order to help integrate Kosovo into regional economic structures, UNMIK signed (on behalf of Kosovo) its accession to the Central Europe Free Trade Area (CEFTA) in 2006. Kosovo joined the European Bank for Reconstruction and Development in 2012 and the Council of Europe Development Bank in 2013. In 2016, Kosovo implemented the Stabilization and Association Agreement (SAA) negotiations with the EU, focused on trade liberalization. Under the SAA, Kosovo—which gets approximately 58% of government revenue

from tariffs on imports—is required to phase out tariffs on EU goods over the next seven years. In 2014, nearly 60% of customs duty-eligible imports into Kosovo were EU goods. In 2015, Kosovo negotiated a $185 million Stand-by Arrangement (SBA) with the IMF following the conclusion of its previous SBA in 2014. The IMF requested an extension of the current SBA to August 2017 to facilitate policy continuity and allow sufficient time for ongoing structural reforms to progress. In August 2015, as part of its EU-facilitated normalization process with Serbia, Kosovo signed agreements on telecommunications and energy distribution, but disagreements over who owns economic assets, such as the Trepca mining conglomerate, within Kosovo continue.

Kosovo experienced its first federal budget deficit in 2012, when government expenditures climbed sharply. In May 2014, the government introduced a 25% salary increase for public sector employees and an equal increase in certain social benefits. Central revenues could not sustain these increases, and the government was forced to reduce its planned capital investments. The government, led by Prime Minister MUSTAFA—a trained economist—recently made several changes to its fiscal policy, expanding the list of duty-free imports, decreasing the Value Added Tax (VAT) for basic food items and public utilities, and increasing the VAT for all other goods.

While Kosovo's economy continued to make progress, it needs further reform and investment to enable the level of growth required to reduce unemployment and raise living standards in a meaningful way.

GDP (purchasing power parity): $19.38 billion (2017 est.)
$18.73 billion (2016 est.)
$18.11 billion (2015 est.)
note: data are in 2017 dollars
country comparison to the world: 151

GDP (official exchange rate): $6.684 billion (2016 est.)

GDP—real growth rate: 3.5% (2017 est.)
3.4% (2016 est.)
4.1% (2015 est.)
country comparison to the world: 99

GDP—per capita (PPP): $10,400 (2017 est.)
$10,200 (2016 est.)
$9,900 (2015 est.)
note: data are in 2016 US dollars
country comparison to the world: 138

Gross national saving: 12.5% of GDP (2017 est.)
12.7% of GDP (2016 est.)
12.5% of GDP (2015 est.)
country comparison to the world: 143

GDP—composition, by end use:
household consumption: 90.5%
government consumption: 16%
investment in fixed capital: 28.2%
investment in inventories: 3%
exports of goods and services: 5.8%
imports of goods and services: -43.5% (2012 est.)

GDP—composition, by sector of origin:

agriculture: 12.9%
industry: 22.6%
services: 64.5% (2009 est.)

Agriculture—products: wheat, corn, berries, potatoes, peppers, fruit; dairy, livestock; fish

Industries: mineral mining, construction materials, base metals, leather, machinery, appliances, foodstuffs and beverages, textiles

Labor force: 483,200
note: includes those estimated to be employed in the grey economy (2013 est.)
country comparison to the world: 157

Labor force—by occupation: *agriculture:* 5.9%
industry: 16.8%
services: 77.3% (2013)

Unemployment rate: 34.8% (2016 est.)
34.6% (2015 est.)
note: Kosovo has a large informal sector that may not be reflected in these data
country comparison to the world: 207

Population below poverty line: 30% (2013 est.)

Distribution of family income—Gini index: 30 (FY05/06)
country comparison to the world: 127

Budget: *revenues:* $1.396 billion
expenditures: $1.61 billion (2014 est.)
Taxes and other revenues: 20.9% of GDP (2014 est.)
country comparison to the world: 145

Budget surplus (+) or deficit (-): -3.2% of GDP (2014 est.)
country comparison to the world: 120

Public debt: 20.6% of GDP (2016 est.)
18.9% of GDP (2015 est.)
country comparison to the world: 185

Inflation rate (consumer prices): 1.4% (2017 est.)
0.3% (2016 est.)
country comparison to the world: 58

Commercial bank prime lending rate: 12.8% (30 June 2013 est.)
13.7% (31 December 2012 est.)
country comparison to the world: 63

Stock of broad money: $2.511 billion (2014 est.)
$2.773 billion (2012 est.)
country comparison to the world: 147

Stock of domestic credit: $2.02 billion (2014 est.)
$2.505 billion (2013 est.)
country comparison to the world: 145

Current account balance: -$738 million (2017 est.)
-$651 million (2016 est.)
country comparison to the world: 117

Exports: $349 million (2014 est.)
$408 million (2013 est.)
country comparison to the world: 181

Exports—commodities: mining and processed metal products, scrap metals, leather products, machinery, appliances, prepared foodstuffs, beverages and tobacco, vegetable products, textiles and apparel

Exports—partners: Albania 24.2%, Macedonia, The Former Yugo Rep of 17.3%, Germany 8.8%,

Switzerland 7.7%, Bulgaria 7.5%, Netherlands 6.9%, Turkey 4.6%, Austria 4.4% (2016)

Imports: $2.687 billion (2014 est.)
$3.398 billion (2013 est.)
country comparison to the world: 148

Imports—commodities: foodstuffs, livestock, wood, petroleum, chemicals, machinery, minerals, textiles, stone, ceramic and glass products, electrical equipment

Imports—partners: Macedonia, The Former Yugo Rep of 34.1%, Turkey 12%, Germany 9.4%, Albania 7.4%, Slovenia 6.9%, Italy 4.6% (2016)

Reserves of foreign exchange and gold: $NA

Debt—external: $1.4 billion (2016 est.)
$1.3 billion (2015 est.)
country comparison to the world: 160

Stock of direct foreign investment—at home: $21.2 billion (31 December 2017 est.)
$39.02 billion (31 December 2016 est.)
country comparison to the world: 77

Exchange rates: euros (EUR) per US dollar—
0.906 (2017 est.)
0.9214 (2016 est.)
0.9214 (2015 est.)
0.885 (2014 est.)
0.7634 (2013 est.)

ENERGY

Electricity access: *electrification—total population:* 100% (2016)

Electricity—production: 5.759 billion kWh (2015 est.)
country comparison to the world: 116

Electricity—consumption: 4.89 billion kWh (2015 est.)
country comparison to the world: 122

Electricity—exports: 553 million kWh (2015 est.)
country comparison to the world: 65

Electricity—imports: 684 million kWh (2015 est.)
country comparison to the world: 75

Electricity—installed generating capacity: 1.565 million kW (2015 est.)
country comparison to the world: 120

Electricity—from fossil fuels: 97.1% of total installed capacity (2015 est.)
country comparison to the world: 43

Electricity—from nuclear fuels: 0% of total installed capacity (2015 est.)
country comparison to the world: 123

Electricity—from hydroelectric plants: 2.9% of total installed capacity (2015 est.)
country comparison to the world: 134

Electricity—from other renewable sources: 0% of total installed capacity (2015 est.)
country comparison to the world: 193

Crude oil—production: 0 bbl/day (2016 est.)
country comparison to the world: 156

Crude oil—exports: 0 bbl/day (2014 est.)
country comparison to the world: 149

Crude oil—imports: 0 bbl/day (2014 est.)
country comparison to the world: 145

Crude oil—proved reserves: NA bbl (1 January 2017 es)

Refined petroleum products—production: 0 bbl/day (2014 est.)
country comparison to the world: 161

Refined petroleum products—consumption: 12,000 bbl/day (2015 est.)
country comparison to the world: 157

Refined petroleum products—exports: 38.36 bbl/day (2014 est.)
country comparison to the world: 126

Refined petroleum products—imports: 11,430 bbl/day (2014 est.)
country comparison to the world: 139

Natural gas—production: 0 cu m (2016)
country comparison to the world: 155

Natural gas—consumption: 0 cu m (2016)
country comparison to the world: 199

Natural gas—proved reserves: NA cu m

Carbon dioxide emissions from consumption of energy: 7.576 million Mt (2012 est.)
country comparison to the world: 114

COMMUNICATIONS

Telephones—fixed lines: *total:* 831,470
subscriptions per 100 inhabitants: 45 (July 2016 est.)
country comparison to the world: 143

Telephones—mobile cellular: *total:* 562,000
subscriptions per 100 inhabitants: 31 (July 2016 est.)
country comparison to the world: 168

TRANSPORTATION

Civil aircraft registration country code prefix: Z6 (2016)

Airports: 6 (2013)
country comparison to the world: 172

Airports—with paved runways: *total:* 3
2,438 to 3,047 m: 1
1,524 to 2,437 m: 1
under 914 m: 1 (2017)

Airports—with unpaved runways: *total:* 3
under 914 m: 3 (2013)

Heliports: 2 (2013)

Railways: *total:* 333 km
standard gauge: 333 km 1.435-m gauge (2015)
country comparison to the world: 121

Roadways: *total:* 2,012 km
paved: 1,921 km (includes 78 km of expressways)
unpaved: 91 km (2015)
country comparison to the world: 176

MILITARY AND SECURITY

Military expenditures: 0.79% of GDP (2016)
0.78% of GDP (2015)
0.73% of GDP (2014)
0.69% of GDP (2013)
0.67% of GDP (2012)

Military branches: Kosovo does not have a military force; the Kosovo Security Force was established in 2009 and maintains a non-military mandate in four core competencies: search-and-rescue, firefighting, demining, and hazardous material response (2015)

TRANSNATIONAL ISSUES

Disputes—international: Serbia with several other states protest the US and other states' recognition of Kosovo's declaration of its status as a sovereign and independent state in February 2008; ethnic Serbian municipalities along Kosovo's northern border challenge final status of Kosovo-Serbia boundary; several thousand NATO-led Kosovo Force peacekeepers under UN Interim Administration Mission in Kosovo authority continue to keep the peace within Kosovo between the ethnic Albanian majority and the Serb minority in Kosovo; Kosovo and Macedonia completed demarcation of their boundary in September 2008

Refugees and internally displaced persons: IDPs: 17,000 (primarily ethnic Serbs displaced during the 1998-1999 war fearing reprisals from the majority ethnic-Albanian population; a smaller number of ethnic Serbs, Roma, Ashkali, and Egyptians fled their homes in 2004 as a result of violence) (2015)

KUWAIT

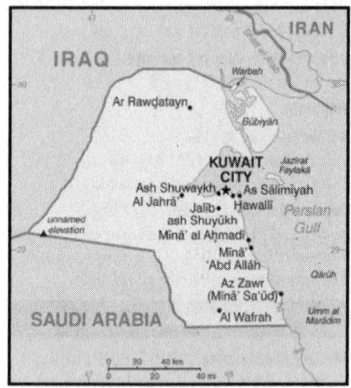

INTRODUCTION

Background: Kuwait has been ruled by the AL-SABAH dynasty since the 18th century. The threat of Ottoman invasion in 1899 prompted Amir Mubarak AL-SABAH to seek protection from Britain, ceding foreign and defense responsibility to Britain until 1961, when the country attained its independence. Kuwait was attacked and overrun by Iraq on 2 August 1990. Following several weeks of aerial bombardment, a US-led UN coalition began a ground assault on 23 February 1991 that liberated Kuwait in four days. Kuwait spent more than $5 billion to repair oil infrastructure damaged during 1990-91. The AL-SABAH family returned to power in 1991 and established one of the most independent legislatures in the Arab World. The country witnessed the historic election in 2009 of four women to its National Assembly. Amid the 2010-11 uprisings and protests across the Arab world, stateless Arabs, known as bidoon, staged small protests in early 2011 demanding citizenship, jobs, and other benefits available to Kuwaiti nationals. Youth activist groups' repeated rallies in 2011 for the dismissal of a prime minister seen as being corrupt, ultimately led to his resignation in late 2011. Demonstrations renewed in late 2012 in response to an Amiri decree amending the electoral law. The opposition, led by a coalition of Sunni Islamists, tribalists, some liberals, and myriad youth groups, largely boycotted legislative elections in 2012 and 2013, which ushered in a legislature more amenable to the government's agenda. However, the opposition, expressing strong opposition to the government's fiscal reforms, participated in the November 2016 National Assembly election and won almost half of the positions. Since coming to power in 2006, the Amir has dissolved the National Assembly on seven occasions (the Constitutional Court annulled the Assembly in June 2012 and again in June 2013) and shuffled the cabinet over a dozen times, usually citing political

stagnation and gridlock between the legislature and the government.

GEOGRAPHY

Location: Middle East, bordering the Persian Gulf, between Iraq and Saudi Arabia

Geographic coordinates: 29 30 N, 45 45 E

Map references: Middle East

Area: *total:* 17,818 sq km
land: 17,818 sq km
water: 0 sq km
country comparison to the world: 158

Area—comparative: slightly smaller than New Jersey

Land boundaries: *total:* 475 km
border countries (2): Iraq 254 km, Saudi Arabia 221 km

Coastline: 499 km

Maritime claims: *territorial sea:* 12 nm

Climate: dry desert; intensely hot summers; short, cool winters

Terrain: flat to slightly undulating desert plain

Elevation: *mean elevation:* 108 m

elevation extremes: *lowest point:* Persian Gulf 0 m
highest point: 3.6 km W. of Al-Salmi Border Post 300 m

Natural resources: petroleum, fish, shrimp, natural gas

Land use: *agricultural land:* 8.5%
arable land: 0.6%;
permanent crops: 0.3%;
permanent pasture: 7.6%
forest: 0.4%
other: 91.1% (2011 est.)
Irrigated land: 105 sq km (2012)

Population—distribution: densest settlement is along the Persian Gulf, particularly in Kuwait City and on Bubiyan Island; significant population threads extend south and west along highways that radiate from the capital, particularly in the southern half of the country

Natural hazards: sudden cloudbursts are common from October to April and bring heavy rain, which can damage roads and houses; sandstorms and dust storms occur throughout the year but are most common between March and August

Environment—current issues: limited natural freshwater resources; some of world's largest and most sophisticated desalination facilities provide much of the water; air and water pollution; desertification

Environment—international agreements: *party to:* Biodiversity, Climate Change, Climate Change-Kyoto Protocol, Desertification, Endangered Species, Environmental Modification, Hazardous Wastes, Law of the Sea, Ozone Layer Protection

signed, but not ratified: Marine Dumping

Geography—note: strategic location at head of Persian Gulf

PEOPLE AND SOCIETY

Population: 2,875,422 (July 2017 est.)
note: Kuwait's Public Authority for Civil Information estimates the country's total population to be 4,437,590 for 2017, with immigrants accounting more than 69.5%
country comparison to the world: 139

Nationality: *noun:* Kuwaiti(s)
adjective: Kuwaiti

Ethnic groups: Kuwaiti 31.3%, other Arab 27.9%, Asian 37.8%, African 1.9%, other 1.1% (includes European, North American, South American, and Australian) (2013 est.)

Languages: Arabic (official), English widely spoken

Religions: Muslim (official) 76.7%, Christian 17.3%, other and unspecified 5.9%
note: represents the total population; about 69% of the population consists of immigrants (2013 est.)

Age structure: *0-14 years:* 25.02% (male 374,259/female 345,104)
15-24 years: 15.1% (male 238,451/female 195,700)
25-54 years: 52.27% (male 948,902/female 554,050)
55-64 years: 5.07% (male 82,366/female 63,505)
65 years and over: 2.54% (male 33,561/female 39,524) (2017 est.)

Dependency ratios: *total dependency ratio:* 29.8
youth dependency ratio: 27.1
elderly dependency ratio: 2.7
potential support ratio: 37.3 (2015 est.)

Median age: *total:* 29.3 years
male: 30.4 years
female: 27.4 years (2017 est.)
country comparison to the world: 123

Population growth rate: 1.46% (2017 est.)
country comparison to the world: 78

Birth rate: 19.2 births/1,000 population (2017 est.)
country comparison to the world: 84

Death rate: 2.2 deaths/1,000 population (2017 est.)
country comparison to the world: 224

Net migration rate: -2.4 migrant(s)/1,000 population (2017 est.)
country comparison to the world: 168

Population distribution: densest settlement is along the Persian Gulf, particularly in Kuwait City and on Bubiyan Island; significant population threads extend south and west along highways that radiate from the capital, particularly in the southern half of the country

Urbanization: *urban population:* 98.4% of total population (2017)

rate of urbanization: 2.29% annual rate of change (2015-20 est.)

Major urban areas—population: KUWAIT (capital) 2.779 million (2015)

Sex ratio: at birth: 1.05 male(s)/female
0-14 years: 1.08 male(s)/female
15-24 years: 1.22 male(s)/female
25-54 years: 1.72 male(s)/female
55-64 years: 1.31 male(s)/female
65 years and over: 0.89 male(s)/female
total population: 1.41 male(s)/female (2016 est.)

Maternal mortality ratio: 4 deaths/100,000 live births (2015 est.)
country comparison to the world: 179

Infant mortality rate: total: 7 deaths/1,000 live births
male: 6.8 deaths/1,000 live births
female: 7.2 deaths/1,000 live births (2017 est.)
country comparison to the world: 162

Life expectancy at birth: total population: 78.2 years
male: 76.8 years
female: 79.6 years (2017 est.)
country comparison to the world: 64

Total fertility rate: 2.4 children born/woman (2017 est.)
country comparison to the world: 84

Health expenditures: 3% of GDP (2014)
country comparison to the world: 182

Physicians density: 1.95 physicians/1,000 population (2014)

Hospital bed density: 2.2 beds/1,000 population (2012)

Drinking water source:
improved:
urban: 99% of population
rural: 99% of population
total: 99% of population
unimproved:
urban: 1% of population
rural: 1% of population
total: 1% of population (2015 est.)

Sanitation facility access:
improved:
urban: 100% of population
rural: 100% of population
total: 100% of population
unimproved:
urban: 0% of population
rural: 0% of population
total: 0% of population (2015 est.)

HIV/AIDS—adult prevalence rate: <.1% (2016 est.)

HIV/AIDS—people living with HIV/AIDS: <500 (2016 est.)

HIV/AIDS—deaths: <100 (2016 est.)

Obesity—adult prevalence rate: 37.9% (2016)
country comparison to the world: 11

Children under the age of 5 years underweight: 3% (2014)
country comparison to the world: 120

Literacy: definition: age 15 and over can read and write
total population: 95.7%
male: 96.4%
female: 94.5% (2016 est.)

School life expectancy (primary to tertiary education): total: 13 years
male: 13 years
female: 14 years (2013)

Unemployment, youth ages 15-24: total: 14.6%
male: N/A
female: N/A (2011 est.)
country comparison to the world: 94

GOVERNMENT

Country name: conventional long form: State of Kuwait
conventional short form: Kuwait
local long form: Dawlat al Kuwayt
local short form: Al Kuwayt
etymology: the name derives from the capital city, which is from Arabic "al-Kuwayt" a diminutive of "kut" meaning "fortress encircled by water"

Government type: constitutional monarchy

Capital: name: Kuwait City
geographic coordinates: 29 22 N, 47 58 E
time difference: UTC+3 (8 hours ahead of Washington, DC, during Standard Time)

Administrative divisions: 6 governorates (muhafazat, singular—muhafazah); Al Ahmadi, Al 'Asimah, Al Farwaniyah, Al Jahra', Hawalli, Mubarak al Kabir

Independence: 19 June 1961 (from the UK)

National holiday: National Day, 25 February (1950)

Constitution: history: approved and promulgated 11 November 1962
amendments: proposed by the amir or supported by at least one-third of the National Assembly; passage requires two-thirds consent by the Assembly membership and promulgation by the amir; constitutional articles on the initiation, approval, and promulgation of general legislation cannot be amended (2016)

Legal system: mixed legal system consisting of English common law, French civil law, and Islamic religious law

International law organization participation: has not submitted an ICJ jurisdiction declaration; non-party state to the ICCt

Citizenship: citizenship by birth: no
citizenship by descent only: at least one parent must be a citizen of Kuwait
dual citizenship recognized: no
residency requirement for naturalization: not specified

Suffrage: 21 years of age and at least 20-year citizenship; universal; note—in early 2017, legislation was introduced to lower the voting age to 18 and instate suffrage for the armed forces and police

Executive branch: chief of state: Amir SABAH al-Ahmad al-Jabir al-Sabah (since 29 January 2006); Crown Prince NAWAF al-Ahmad al-Sabah (born 25 June 1937)

head of government: Prime Minister JABIR AL-MUBARAK al-Hamad al-Sabah (since 30 November 2011); First Deputy Prime Minister NASIR al-Sabah al-Ahmad al-Sabah (since 12 December 2017); Deputy Prime Ministers SABAH al-KHALD al-Sabah (since 4 August 2013), KHALD al-Jarrah al-Sabah (since December 2016), Anas al-SALEH (since 2015)
cabinet: Council of Ministers appointed by the prime minister, approved by the amir
elections/appointments: amir chosen from within the ruling family, confirmed by the National Assembly; prime minister and deputy prime ministers appointed by the amir

Legislative branch: description: unicameral National Assembly or Majlis al-Umma (65 seats; 50 members directly elected in multi-seat constituencies by simple majority vote and 15 ex-officio members—cabinet ministers—appointed by the prime minister; members serve 4-year terms)
elections: last held on 26 November 2016 (next to be held in 2020)
election results: preliminary results—opposition groups including those linked to the Muslim Brotherhood and Salafists 24 seats, other 26

Judicial branch: highest court(s): Constitutional Court (consists of 5 judges); Supreme Court or Court of Cassation (organized into several circuits, each with 5 judges)
judge selection and term of office: all Kuwaiti judges appointed by the Amir upon recommendation of the Supreme Judicial Council, a consultative body comprised of Kuwaiti judges and Ministry of Justice officials
subordinate courts: High Court of Appeal; Court of First Instance; Summary Court

Political parties and leaders: none; while the formation of political parties is not permitted, they are not forbidden by law

Political pressure groups and leaders: Islamists; merchants; political groups; secular liberals and pro-governmental deputies; Shia activists; tribal groups

International organization participation: ABEDA, AfDB (nonregional member), AFESD, AMF, BDEAC, CAEU, CD, FAO, G-77, GCC, IAEA, IBRD, ICAO, ICC (national committees), ICRM, IDA, IDB, IFAD, IFC, IFRCS, IHO, ILO, IMF, IMO, IMSO, Interpol, IOC, IPU, ISO, ITSO, ITU, ITUC (NGOs), LAS, MIGA, NAM, OAPEC, OIC, OPCW, OPEC, Paris Club (associate), PCA, UN, UNCTAD, UNESCO, UNIDO, UNRWA, UNWTO, UPU, WCO, WFTU (NGOs), WHO, WIPO, WMO, WTO

Diplomatic representation in the US: chief of mission: Ambassador SALIM al-Abdallah al-Jabir al-Sabah (since 10 October 2001)
chancery: 2940 Tilden Street NW, Washington, DC 20008
telephone: [1] (202) 966-0702
FAX: [1] (202) 966-8468
consulate(s) general: Los Angeles

Diplomatic representation from the US: *chief of mission:* Ambassador Lawrence R. SILVERMAN (since 5 October 2016)
embassy: Bayan 36302, Block 13, Al-Masjed Al-Aqsa Street (near the Bayan palace), Kuwait City
mailing address: P. O. Box 77 Safat 13001 Kuwait; or PSC 1280 APO AE 09880-9000
telephone: [965] 2259-1001
FAX: [965] 2538-6562

Flag description: three equal horizontal bands of green (top), white, and red with a black trapezoid based on the hoist side; colors and design are based on the Arab Revolt flag of World War I; green represents fertile fields, white stands for purity, red denotes blood on Kuwaiti swords, black signifies the defeat of the enemy

National symbol(s): golden falcon; national colors: green, white, red, black

National anthem: *name:* "Al-Nasheed Al-Watani" (National Anthem)
lyrics/music: Ahmad MUSHARI al-Adwani/Ibrahim Nasir al-SOULA
note: adopted 1978; the anthem is only used on formal occasions

ECONOMY

Economy—overview: Kuwait has a geographically small, but wealthy, relatively open economy with crude oil reserves of about 102 billion barrels—more than 6% of world reserves. Kuwaiti officials plan to increase production to 4 million barrels of oil equivalent per day by 2020. Petroleum accounts for over half of GDP, 92% of export revenues, and 90% of government income.

In 2015, Kuwait, for the first time in 15 years, realized a budget deficit after decades of high oil prices; in 2016, the deficit grew to 16.5% of GDP. Kuwaiti authorities announced cuts to fuel subsidies in August 2016, provoking outrage among the public and National Assembly, and the Amir dissolved the government for the seventh time in ten years. In 2017 the deficit was reduced to 7.2% of GDP, and the government raised $8 billion by issuing international bonds. Despite Kuwait's dependence on oil, the government has cushioned itself against the impact of lower oil prices, by saving annually at least 10% of government revenue in the Fund for Future Generations.

Kuwait has failed to diversify its economy or bolster the private sector, because of a poor business climate, a large public sector that employs about 74% of citizens, and an acrimonious relationship between the National Assembly and the executive branch that has stymied most economic reforms. The Kuwaiti Government has made little progress on its long-term economic development plan first passed in 2010. While the government planned to spend up to $104 billion over four years to diversify the economy, attract more investment, and boost private sector participation in the economy, many of the projects did not materialize because of an uncertain political situation or delays in awarding contracts. To increase non-oil revenues, the Kuwaiti Government in August 2017 approved draft bills supporting a Gulf Cooperation Council-wide value added tax scheduled to take effect in 2018.

GDP (purchasing power parity): $302.5 billion (2017 est.)
$308.9 billion (2016 est.)
$301.5 billion (2015 est.)
note: data are in 2017 dollars
country comparison to the world: 57

GDP (official exchange rate): $118.3 billion (2016 est.)

GDP—real growth rate: -2.1% (2017 est.)
2.5% (2016 est.)
2.1% (2015 est.)
country comparison to the world: 212

GDP—per capita (PPP): $69,700 (2017 est.)
$73,100 (2016 est.)
$73,400 (2015 est.)
note: data are in 2017 dollars
country comparison to the world: 13

Gross national saving: 24.1% of GDP (2017 est.)
25.1% of GDP (2016 est.)
30.8% of GDP (2015 est.)
country comparison to the world: 59

GDP—composition, by end use:
household consumption: 43%
government consumption: 24.5%
investment in fixed capital: 28%
investment in inventories: 0%
exports of goods and services: 50.2%
imports of goods and services: -45.7% (2017 est.)

GDP—composition, by sector of origin:
agriculture: 0.4%
industry: 58.7%
services: 40.9% (2017 est.)

Agriculture—products: fish

Industries: petroleum, petrochemicals, cement, shipbuilding and repair, water desalination, food processing, construction materials

Industrial production growth rate: -1.5% (2017 est.)
country comparison to the world: 192

Labor force: 2.695 million
note: non-Kuwaitis represent about 60% of the labor force (2017 est.)
country comparison to the world: 113

Labor force—by occupation: *agriculture:* NA%
industry: NA%
services: NA%

Unemployment rate: 2.1% (2017 est.)
2.1% (2016 est.)
country comparison to the world: 16

Population below poverty line: NA%

Household income or consumption by percentage share: *lowest 10%:* NA%
highest 10%: NA%

Budget: *revenues:* $52.87 billion
expenditures: $61.39 billion (2017 est.)
Taxes and other revenues: 44.7% of GDP (2017 est.)
country comparison to the world: 24

Budget surplus (+) or deficit (-): -7.2% of GDP (2017 est.)
country comparison to the world: 192

Public debt: 26.2% of GDP (2017 est.)
17.3% of GDP (2016 est.)
country comparison to the world: 174

Fiscal year: 1 April—31 March

Inflation rate (consumer prices): 2.5% (2017 est.)
3.5% (2016 est.)
country comparison to the world: 115

Central bank discount rate: 2.5% (31 December 2016)
1.25% (31 December 2010)
country comparison to the world: 111

Commercial bank prime lending rate: 5.2% (31 December 2017 est.)
4.5% (31 December 2016 est.)
country comparison to the world: 143

Stock of narrow money: $33.35 billion (31 December 2017 est.)
$31.87 billion (31 December 2016 est.)
country comparison to the world: 61

Stock of broad money: $121.5 billion (31 December 2017 est.)
$116.9 billion (31 December 2016 est.)
country comparison to the world: 55

Stock of domestic credit: $102.2 billion (31 December 2017 est.)
$98.92 billion (31 December 2016 est.)
country comparison to the world: 56

Market value of publicly traded shares: $81.78 billion (31 December 2016 est.)
$83.13 billion (31 December 2015 est.)
$99.77 billion (31 December 2014 est.)
country comparison to the world: 44

Current account balance: -$714 million (2017 est.)
-$4.997 billion (2016 est.)
country comparison to the world: 115

Exports: $54.09 billion (2017 est.)
$46.26 billion (2016 est.)
country comparison to the world: 50

Exports—commodities: oil and refined products, fertilizers

Exports—partners: South Korea 16.8%, China 14.4%, Japan 9.6%, India 9.2%, US 7.5%, Singapore 5.6% (2016)

Imports: $29.36 billion (2017 est.)
$30.82 billion (2016 est.)
country comparison to the world: 64

Imports—commodities: food, construction materials, vehicles and parts, clothing

Imports—partners: China 14.1%, US 11.9%, UAE 8.3%, Japan 6.5%, Germany 6.2%, India 5.4%, Italy 5%, Saudi Arabia 4.4%, South Korea 4.4% (2016)

Reserves of foreign exchange and gold: $33.13 billion (31 December 2017 est.)
$31.13 billion (31 December 2016 est.)
country comparison to the world: 49

Debt—external: $48.91 billion (31 December 2017 est.)
$38.34 billion (31 December 2016 est.)
country comparison to the world: 64

Stock of direct foreign investment—at home:
$13.07 billion (31 December 2017 est.)
$12.62 billion (31 December 2016 est.)
country comparison to the world: 93

Stock of direct foreign investment—abroad:
$79.62 billion (31 December 2017 est.)
$74.13 billion (31 December 2016 est.)
country comparison to the world: 38

Exchange rates: Kuwaiti dinars (KD) per US dollar—
0.3041 (2017 est.)
0.3022 (2016 est.)
0.3022 (2015 est.)
0.3009 (2014 est.)
0.2845 (2013 est.)

ENERGY

Electricity access: *population without electricity:* 56,655
electrification—*total population:* 98%
electrification—urban areas: 98%
electrification—rural areas: 93% (2012)

Electricity—production: 63.84 billion kWh (2015 est.)
country comparison to the world: 46

Electricity—consumption: 54.11 billion kWh (2015 est.)
country comparison to the world: 46

Electricity—exports: 0 kWh (2016 est.)
country comparison to the world: 157

Electricity—imports: 0 kWh (2016 est.)
country comparison to the world: 168

Electricity—installed generating capacity: 16 million kW (2016 est.)
country comparison to the world: 50

Electricity—from fossil fuels: 100% of total installed capacity (2016 est.)
country comparison to the world: 10

Electricity—from nuclear fuels: 0% of total installed capacity (2016 est.)
country comparison to the world: 122

Electricity—from hydroelectric plants: 0% of total installed capacity (2016 est.)
country comparison to the world: 183

Electricity—from other renewable sources: 0% of total installed capacity (2016 est.)
country comparison to the world: 192

Crude oil—production: 2.924 million bbl/day (2016 est.)
country comparison to the world: 9

Crude oil—exports: 1.656 million bbl/day (2014 est.)
country comparison to the world: 9

Crude oil—imports: 0 bbl/day (2014 est.)
country comparison to the world: 144

Crude oil—proved reserves: 101.5 billion bbl (1 January 2017 es)
country comparison to the world: 6

Refined petroleum products—production: 920,000 bbl/day (2016 est.)
country comparison to the world: 23

Refined petroleum products—consumption: 500,000 bbl/day (2016 est.)
country comparison to the world: 35

Refined petroleum products—exports: 400,000 bbl/day (2013 est.)
country comparison to the world: 20

Refined petroleum products—imports: 11,900 bbl/day (2016 est.)
country comparison to the world: 137

Natural gas—production: 16.91 billion cu m (2015 est.)
country comparison to the world: 35

Natural gas—consumption: 33.18 billion cu m (2015 est.)
country comparison to the world: 36

Natural gas—exports: 0 cu m (2013 est.)
country comparison to the world: 133

Natural gas—imports: 4 billion cu m (2015 est.)
country comparison to the world: 37

Natural gas—proved reserves: 1.798 trillion cu m (1 January 2017 es)
country comparison to the world: 21

Carbon dioxide emissions from consumption of energy: 107 million Mt (2013 est.)
country comparison to the world: 38

COMMUNICATIONS

Telephones—fixed lines: *total subscriptions:* 403,234
subscriptions per 100 inhabitants: 14 (July 2016 est.)
country comparison to the world: 97

Telephones—mobile cellular: *total:* 5,392,806
subscriptions per 100 inhabitants: 190 (July 2016 est.)
country comparison to the world: 100

Telephone system: *general assessment:* the quality of service is excellent
domestic: new telephone exchanges provide a large capacity for new subscribers; trunk traffic is carried by microwave radio relay, coaxial cable, and open-wire and fiber-optic cable; a 4G LTE mobile-cellular telephone system operates throughout Kuwait, and the country is well-supplied with pay telephones
international: country code—965; linked to international submarine cable Fiber-Optic Link Around the Globe (FLAG); linked to Bahrain, Qatar, UAE via the Fiber-Optic Gulf (FOG) cable; coaxial cable and microwave radio relay to Saudi Arabia; satellite earth stations—6 (3 Intelsat—1 Atlantic Ocean and 2 Indian Ocean, 1 Inmarsat—Atlantic Ocean, and 2 Arabsat) (2017)

Broadcast media: state-owned TV broadcaster operates 4 networks and a satellite channel; several private TV broadcasters have emerged since 2003; satellite TV available with pan-Arab TV stations are especially popular; state-owned Radio Kuwait broadcasts on a number of channels in Arabic and English; first private radio station emerged in 2005; transmissions of at least 2 international radio broadcasters are available (2007)

Internet country code: .kw

Internet users: total: 2,219,972

percent of population: 78.4% (July 2016 est.)
country comparison to the world: 93

TRANSPORTATION

National air transport system: *number of registered air carriers:* 3
inventory of registered aircraft operated by air carriers: 31
annual passenger traffic on registered air carriers: 3,655,366
annual freight traffic on registered air carriers: 275,777,666 mt-km (2015)
Civil aircraft registration country code prefix: 9K (2016)

Airports: 7 (2013)
country comparison to the world: 168

Airports—with paved runways: *total:* 4
over 3,047 m: 1
2,438 to 3,047 m: 2
914 to 1,523 m: 1 (2017)

Airports—with unpaved runways: *total:* 3
1,524 to 2,437 m: 1
under 914 m: 2 (2013)

Heliports: 4 (2013)

Pipelines: gas 261 km; oil 540 km; refined products 57 km (2013)

Roadways: *total:* 6,608 km (2010)
country comparison to the world: 148

Merchant marine: *total:* 161
by type: container ship 1, general cargo 18, oil tanker 27, other 115 (2017)
country comparison to the world: 70

Ports and terminals: *major seaport(s):* Ash Shu'aybah, Ash Shuwaykh, Az Zawr (Mina' Sa'ud), Mina' 'Abd Allah, Mina' al Ahmadi

MILITARY AND SECURITY

Military expenditures: 4.83% of GDP (2015)
3.65% of GDP (2014)
3.27% of GDP (2013)
3.41% of GDP (2012)
3.5% of GDP (2011)
country comparison to the world: 132

Military branches: Kuwaiti Land Forces (KLF), Kuwaiti Navy, Kuwaiti Air Force (Al-Quwwat al-Jawwiya al-Kuwaitiya; includes Kuwaiti Air Defense Force, KADF), Kuwaiti National Guard (KNG) (2013)

Military service age and obligation: 17-21 years of age for voluntary military service; conscription suspended (2012)

TERRORISM

Terrorist groups—foreign based: *Islamic State of Iraq and the Levant (ISIL):* aim(s): replace the Kuwaiti Government with an Islamic state and implement ISIL's strict interpretation of Sharia
area(s) of operation: maintains an operational and recruitment presence, primarily in large cities; a suicide bomber killed 27 Shia Muslim worshippers and injured 227 inside the Iman al-Sadeq

Mosque on 25 June 2015 in Kuwait City; the attack remains the most violent to occur in modern Kuwait; operatives continue to smuggle weapons, ammunition, and explosives into Iraq along the Kuwait-Iraq border

TRANSNATIONAL ISSUES

Disputes—international: Kuwait and Saudi Arabia continue negotiating a joint maritime boundary with Iran; no maritime boundary exists with Iraq in the Persian Gulf

Refugees and internally displaced persons: *stateless persons:* 93,000 (2016); note—Kuwait's 1959 Nationality Law defined citizens as persons who settled in the country before 1920 and who had maintained normal residence since then; one-third of the population, descendants of Bedouin tribes, missed the window of opportunity to register for nationality rights after Kuwait became independent in 1961 and were classified as bidun (meaning without); since the 1980s Kuwait's

bidun have progressively lost their rights, including opportunities for employment and education, amid official claims that they are nationals of other countries who have destroyed their identification documents in hopes of gaining Kuwaiti citizenship; Kuwaiti authorities have delayed processing citizenship applications and labeled biduns as "illegal residents," denying them access to civil documentation, such as birth and marriage certificates

Trafficking in persons: current situation: Kuwait is a destination country for men and women subjected to forced labor and, to a lesser degree, forced prostitution; men and women migrate from South and Southeast Asia, Egypt, the Middle East, and increasingly Africa to work in Kuwait, most of them in the domestic service, construction, and sanitation sectors; although most of these migrants enter Kuwait voluntarily, upon arrival some are subjected to conditions of forced labor by their sponsors and labor agents, including debt bondage; Kuwait's sponsorship law restricts workers' movements and penalizes them for running away

from abusive workplaces, making domestic workers particularly vulnerable to forced labor in private homes

tier rating: Tier 3—Kuwait does not fully comply with the minimum standards for the elimination of trafficking and is not making sufficient efforts to do so; although investigations into visa fraud rings lead to the referral of hundreds of people for prosecution, including complicit officials, the government has not prosecuted or convicted any suspected traffickers; authorities made no effort to enforce the prohibition against withholding workers' passports, as mandated under Kuwaiti law; punishment of forced labor cases was limited to shutting down labor recruitment firms, assessing fines, and ordering the return of withheld passports and the paying of back-wages; the government made progress in victims' protection by opening a high-capacity shelter for runaway domestic workers but still lacks formal procedures to identify and refer victims to care services (2015)

KYRGYZSTAN

INTRODUCTION

Background: A Central Asian country of incredible natural beauty and proud nomadic traditions, most of the territory of present-day Kyrgyzstan was formally annexed to the Russian Empire in 1876. The Kyrgyz staged a major revolt against the Tsarist Empire in 1916 in which almost one-sixth of the Kyrgyz population was killed. Kyrgyzstan became a Soviet republic in 1936 and achieved independence in 1991 when the USSR dissolved. Nationwide demonstrations in 2005 and 2010 resulted in the ouster of Kyrgyzstan's first two presidents, Askar AKAEV and Kurmanbek BAKIEV. In 2017, Almazbek ATAMBAEV became the first Kyrgyzstani president to step down after serving a full term as required in the country's constitution. Former Prime Minister and ruling Social-Democratic Party of Kyrgyzstan member Sooronbay JEENBEKOV replaced him after winning an October 2017 presidential election that was the most competitive in Kyrgyzstan's history, although it was marred by allegations of illicit government interference to benefit JEENBEKOV. The president holds substantial powers as head of state even though the prime minister oversees Kyrgyzstan's government and selects most cabinet members. The president represents the country internationally and can sign or veto laws, call for new elections, and nominate

supreme court judges, cabinet members for posts related to security or defense, and numerous other high-level positions. Continuing concerns for Kyrgyzstan include the trajectory of democratization, endemic corruption, poor interethnic relations, border security vulnerabilities, and potential terrorist threats.

GEOGRAPHY

Location: Central Asia, west of China, south of Kazakhstan

Geographic coordinates: 41 00 N, 75 00 E

Map references: Asia

Area: *total:* 199,951 sq km
land: 191,801 sq km
water: 8,150 sq km
country comparison to the world: 88

Area—comparative: slightly smaller than South Dakota

Land boundaries: *total:* 4,573 km
border countries (4): China 1,063 km, Kazakhstan 1,212 km, Tajikistan 984 km, Uzbekistan 1,314 km

Coastline: 0 km (landlocked)

Maritime claims: none (landlocked)

Climate: dry continental to polar in high Tien Shan Mountains; subtropical in southwest (Fergana Valley); temperate in northern foothill zone

Terrain: peaks of the Tien Shan mountain range and associated valleys and basins encompass the entire country

Elevation: *mean elevation:* 2,988 m

elevation extremes: *lowest point:* Kara-Daryya (Karadar'ya) 132 m
highest point: Jengish Chokusu (Pik Pobedy) 7,439 m

Natural resources: abundant hydropower; gold, rare earth metals; locally exploitable coal, oil, and natural gas; other deposits of nepheline, mercury, bismuth, lead, and zinc

Land use: *agricultural land:* 55.4%
arable land: 6.7%;
permanent crops: 0.4%;
permanent pasture: 48.3%
forest: 5.1%
other: 39.5% (2011 est.)
Irrigated land: 10,233 sq km (2012)

Population—distribution: the vast majority of Kyrgyzstanis live in rural areas; densest population settlement is to the north in and around the capital, Bishkek, followed by Osh in the west; the least densely populated area is the east, southeast in the Tien Shan mountains

Natural hazards: major flooding during snow melt; prone to earthquakes

Environment—current issues: water pollution; many people get their water directly from contaminated streams and wells; as a result, water-borne diseases are prevalent; increasing soil salinity from faulty irrigation practices

Environment—international agreements: *party to:* Air Pollution, Biodiversity, Climate Change, Climate Change-Kyoto Protocol, Desertification, Hazardous Wastes, Ozone Layer Protection, Wetlands
signed, but not ratified: none of the selected agreements

Geography—note: landlocked; entirely mountainous, dominated by the Tien Shan range; 94% of the country is 1,000 m above sea level with an average elevation of 2,750 m; many tall peaks, glaciers, and high-altitude lakes

PEOPLE AND SOCIETY

Population: 5,789,122 (July 2017 est.)
country comparison to the world: 114

Nationality: *noun:* Kyrgyzstani(s)
adjective: Kyrgyzstani

Ethnic groups: Kyrgyz 73.2%, Uzbek 14.6%, Russian 5.8%, Dungan 1.1%, other 5.3% (includes Uyghur, Tajik, Turk, Kazakh, Tatar, Ukrainian, Korean, German) (2017 est.)

Languages: Kyrgyz (official) 71.4%, Uzbek 14.4%, Russian (official) 9%, other 5.2% (2009 est.)

Religions: Muslim 75%, Russian Orthodox 20%, other 5%

Age structure: 0-14 *years:* 30.3% (male 899,545/female 854,745)
15-24 years: 16.79% (male 493,924/female 478,217)
25-54 years: 39.84% (male 1,130,422/female 1,175,729)
55-64 years: 7.8% (male 196,856/female 254,694)
65 years and over: 5.27% (male 116,584/female 188,406) (2017 est.)

Dependency ratios: *total dependency ratio:* 54.7
youth dependency ratio: 48.1
elderly dependency ratio: 6.6
potential support ratio: 15.1 (2015 est.)

Median age: *total:* 26.5 years
male: 25.4 years
female: 27.6 years (2017 est.)
country comparison to the world: 148

Population growth rate: 1.05% (2017 est.)
country comparison to the world: 107

Birth rate: 22.1 births/1,000 population (2017 est.)
country comparison to the world: 72

Death rate: 6.5 deaths/1,000 population (2017 est.)
country comparison to the world: 143

Net migration rate: -5.1 migrant(s)/1,000 population (2017 est.)
country comparison to the world: 192

Population distribution: the vast majority of Kyrgyzstanis live in rural areas; densest population settlement is to the north in and around the capital, Bishkek, followed by Osh in the west; the least densely populated area is the east, southeast in the Tien Shan mountains

Urbanization: *urban population:* 36% of total population (2017)
rate of urbanization: 2.04% annual rate of change (2015-20 est.)

Major urban areas—population: BISHKEK (capital) 865,000 (2015)

Sex ratio: *at birth:* 1.07 male(s)/female
0-14 years: 1.05 male(s)/female
15-24 years: 1.03 male(s)/female
25-54 years: 0.96 male(s)/female
55-64 years: 0.77 male(s)/female
65 years and over: 0.62 male(s)/female
total population: 0.96 male(s)/female (2016 est.)

Mother's mean age at first birth: 23.2 years (2014 est.)

Maternal mortality ratio: 76 deaths/100,000 live births (2015 est.)
country comparison to the world: 82

Infant mortality rate: *total:* 25.9 deaths/1,000 live births
male: 30 deaths/1,000 live births
female: 21.5 deaths/1,000 live births (2017 est.)
country comparison to the world: 68

Life expectancy at birth: *total population:* 70.9 years
male: 66.8 years
female: 75.4 years (2017 est.)
country comparison to the world: 156

Total fertility rate: 2.61 children born/woman (2017 est.)
country comparison to the world: 76

Contraceptive prevalence rate: 42% (2014)

Health expenditures: 6.5% of GDP (2014)
country comparison to the world: 91

Physicians density: 1.85 physicians/1,000 population (2014)

Hospital bed density: 4.8 beds/1,000 population (2012)

Drinking water source:
improved:
urban: 96.7% of population
rural: 86.2% of population
total: 90% of population
unimproved:
urban: 3.3% of population
rural: 13.8% of population
total: 10% of population (2015 est.)

Sanitation facility access:
improved:
urban: 89.1% of population
rural: 95.6% of population
total: 93.3% of population
unimproved:
urban: 10.9% of population
rural: 4.4% of population
total: 6.7% of population (2015 est.)

HIV/AIDS—adult prevalence rate: 0.2% (2016 est.)
country comparison to the world: 91

HIV/AIDS—people living with HIV/AIDS: 8,500 (2016 est.)
country comparison to the world: 100

HIV/AIDS—deaths: <500 (2016 est.)

Obesity—adult prevalence rate: 16.6% (2016)
country comparison to the world: 121

Children under the age of 5 years underweight: 2.8% (2014)
country comparison to the world: 101

Education expenditures: 5.5% of GDP (2014)
country comparison to the world: 25

Literacy: *definition:* age 15 and over can read and write
total population: 99.5%
male: 99.6%
female: 99.4% (2015 est.)

School life expectancy (primary to tertiary education): *total:* 13 years

male: 13 years
female: 13 years (2014)

Unemployment, youth ages 15-24: *total:* 15%
male: 12.5%
female: 19.1% (2015 est.)
country comparison to the world: 80

GOVERNMENT

Country name: *conventional long form:* Kyrgyz Republic
conventional short form: Kyrgyzstan
local long form: Kyrgyz Respublikasy
local short form: Kyrgyzstan
former: Kirghiz Soviet Socialist Republic
etymology: a combination of the Turkic words "kyrg" (forty) and "-yz" (tribes) with the Persian suffix "-stan" (country) creating the meaning "Land of the Forty Tribes"; the name refers to the forty clans united by the legendary Kyrgyz hero, MANAS

Government type: parliamentary republic

Capital: *name:* Bishkek
geographic coordinates: 42 52 N, 74 36 E
time difference: UTC+6 (11 hours ahead of Washington, DC, during Standard Time)

Administrative divisions: 7 provinces (oblustar, singular—oblus) and 2 cities* (shaarlar, singular—shaar); Batken Oblusu, Bishkek Shaary*, Chuy Oblusu (Bishkek), Jalal-Abad Oblusu, Naryn Oblusu, Osh Oblusu, Osh Shaary*, Talas Oblusu, Ysyk-Kol Oblusu (Karakol)
note: administrative divisions have the same names as their administrative centers (exceptions have the administrative center name following in parentheses)

Independence: 31 August 1991 (from the Soviet Union)

National holiday: Independence Day, 31 August (1991)

Constitution: history: previous 1993; latest adopted by referendum 27 June 2010, effective 2 July 2010; note—constitutional amendments that transferred some presidential powers to the prime minister passed in a referendum in December 2016 and became effective December 2017
amendments: proposed as a draft law by the majority of the Supreme Council membership or by petition of 300,000 voters; passage requires at least two-thirds majority vote of the Council membership in each of at least three readings of the draft two months apart; the draft may be submitted to a referendum if approved by two-thirds of the Council membership; adoption requires the signature of the president; amended 2017 (2017)

Legal system: civil law system, which includes features of French civil law and Russian Federation laws

International law organization participation: has not submitted an ICJ jurisdiction declaration; non-party state to the ICCt

Citizenship: *citizenship by birth:* no
citizenship by descent only: at least one parent must be a citizen of Kyrgyzstan

dual citizenship recognized: yes, but only if a mutual treaty on dual citizenship is in force
residency requirement for naturalization: 5 years

Suffrage: 18 years of age; universal

Executive branch: *chief of state:* President Sooronbay JEENBEKOV (since 24 November 2017)

head of government: Prime Minister Sapar ISAKOV (since 26 August 2017)
cabinet: Cabinet of Ministers proposed by the prime minister, appointed by the president; defense and security committee chairs appointed by the president
elections/appointments: president directly elected by absolute majority popular vote in 2 rounds if needed for a single 6-year term; election last held on 15 October 2017 (next to be held in October 2023); prime minister nominated by the majority party or majority coalition in the Supreme Council, appointed by the president
election results: Sooronbay JEENBEKOV elected president in first round; percent of vote—Sooronbay JEENBEKOV (SDPK) 54.2%, Omurbek BABANOV (Respublika) 33.5%, Adakhan MADUMAROV (Butun Kyrgyzstan) 6.6%, Temir SARIYEV (Akshumar) 2.5%, other 3.2%; note—Sapar ISAKOV elected prime minister; Supreme Council vote—97 to 5

Legislative branch: *description:* unicameral Supreme Council or Jogorku Kenesh (120 seats); members directly elected in a single nationwide constituency by proportional representation vote to serve 5-year terms)
elections: last held on 4 October 2015 (next to be held in 2020)
election results: percent of vote by party—SDPK 27.4%, Respublika-Ata-Jurt 20.1%, Kyrgyzstan Party 12.9%, Onuguu-Progress 9.3%, Bir Bol 8.5%, Ata-Meken 7.7%, other 14.1%; seats by party—SDPK 38, Respublika-Ata-Jurt 28, Kyrgyzstan Party 18, Onuguu-Progress 13, Bir Bol 12, Ata-Meken 11

Judicial branch: *highest court(s):* Supreme Court (consists of 25 judges); Constitutional Chamber of the Supreme Court (consists of the chairperson, deputy chairperson, and 9 judges)
judge selection and term of office: Supreme Court and Constitutional Court judges appointed by the Supreme Council on the recommendation of the president; Supreme Court judges serve for 10 years, Constitutional Court judges serve for 15 years; mandatory retirement at age 70 for judges of both courts
subordinate courts: Higher Court of Arbitration; oblast (provincial) and city courts

Political parties and leaders: Ata-Jurt (Homeland) [Kamchybek TASHIEV]
Ata-Meken (Fatherland) [Almambet SHYKMAMATOV]
Bir Bol (Stay United) [Altynbek SULAIMANOV]
Butun Kyrgyzstan (United Kyrgyzstan) [Adakhan MADUMAROV]
Kyrgyzstan Party [Almazbek BAATYRBEKOV]
Onuguu-Progress [Bakyt TOROBAEV]
Respublika (Republic) [Ruslan KAZAKBAEV]

Respublika-Ata-Jurt (Republic-Homeland) [Ruslan KAZAKBAEV] (parliamentary faction)
Social-Democratic Party of Kyrgyzstan or SDPK [Isa OMURKULOV]

Political pressure groups and leaders: Adilet (Justice) Legal Clinic [Cholpon JAKUPOVA]
Bir Duino [Tolekan ISMAILOVA] (formerly Citizens Against Corruption)
Coalition for Democracy and Civil Society [Dinara OSHURAKHUNOVA]
Kylym Shamy (Torch of the Century) [Aziza ABDIRASULOVA] (human rights)
Precedent Partnership Group [Nurbek TOKTAKUNOV]
Societal Analysis Public Association [Rita KARASARTOVA]

International organization participation: ADB, CICA, CIS, CSTO, EAEC, EAEU, EAPC, EBRD, ECO, EITI (compliant country), FAO, GCTU, IAEA, IBRD, ICAO, ICC (NGOs), ICRM, IDA, IDB, IFAD, IFC, IFRCS, ILO, IMF, Interpol, IOC, IOM, IPU, ISO (correspondent), ITSO, ITU, MIGA, NAM (observer), OIC, OPCW, OSCE, PCA, PFP, SCO, UN, UNAMID, UNCTAD, UNESCO, UNIDO, UNISFA, UNMIL, UNMISS, UNWTO, UPU, WCO, WFTU (NGOs), WHO, WIPO, WMO, WTO

Diplomatic representation in the US: *chief of mission:* Ambassador Kadyr TOKTOGULOV (since 23 February 2015)
chancery: 2360 Massachusetts Ave. NW, Washington, DC 20008
telephone: [1] (202) 449-9822
FAX: [1] (202) 449-8275
consulate(s): New York

Diplomatic representation from the US: *chief of mission:* Ambassador (vacant); Charge d'Affaires Alan MELTZER (since 4 August 2017)
embassy: 171 Prospect Mira, Bishkek 720016
mailing address: use embassy street address
telephone: [996] (312) 597-000
FAX: [996] (312) 597-744

Flag description: red field with a yellow sun in the center having 40 rays representing the 40 Kyrgyz tribes; on the obverse side the rays run counterclockwise, on the reverse, clockwise; in the center of the sun is a red ring crossed by two sets of three lines, a stylized representation of a "tunduk"—the crown of a traditional Kyrgyz yurt; red symbolizes bravery and valor, the sun evinces peace and wealth

National symbol(s): gyrfalcon; national colors: red, yellow

National anthem: name: "Kyrgyz Respublikasynyn Mamlekettik Gimni" (National Anthem of the Kyrgyz Republic)
lyrics/music: Djamil SADYKOV and Eshmambet KULUEV/Nasyr DAVLESOV and Kalyi MOLDOBASANOV
note: adopted 1992

ECONOMY

Economy—overview: Kyrgyzstan is a landlocked, mountainous, lower middle income country with an economy dominated by minerals extraction, agriculture, and reliance on remittances from citizens working abroad. Cotton, wool, and meat are the main agricultural products, although only cotton is exported in any quantity. Other exports include gold, mercury, uranium, natural gas, and—in some years—electricity. The country has sought to attract foreign investment to expand its export base, including construction of hydroelectric dams, but a difficult investment climate and an ongoing legal battle over a Canadian firm over the joint ownership structure of the nation's largest gold mine deter potential investors. Remittances from Kyrgyz migrant workers, predominantly in Russia and Kazakhstan, are equivalent to over one-quarter of Kyrgyzstan's GDP.

Following independence, Kyrgyzstan rapidly implemented market reforms, such as improving the regulatory system and instituting land reform. In 1998, Kyrgyzstan was the first Commonwealth of Independent States country to be accepted into the World Trade Organization. The government has privatized much of its ownership shares in public enterprises. Despite these reforms, the country suffered a severe drop in production in the early 1990s and has again faced slow growth in recent years as the global financial crisis, declining oil prices, and regional economic headwinds have damaged economies across Central Asia. The Kyrgyz government remains dependent on foreign donor support to finance its annual budget deficit of approximately 3 to 5% of GDP.

Kyrgyz leaders hope the country's August 2015 accession to the Eurasian Economic Union (EAEU) will bolster trade and investment, but slowing economies in Russia and China and low commodity prices continue to hamper economic growth. While joining the EAEU has increased Kyrgyz labor mobility within member states, large-scale trade and investment pledged by Kyrgyz leaders has been slow in developing since accession. Kyrgyz entrepreneurs and politicians alike often contend that non-tariff measures imposed by other EAEU member states, particularly Kazakhstan, are negatively impacting sectors of the Kyrgyz economy that enjoy a comparative advantage, such as meat and dairy production. Since acceding to the EAEU, the Kyrgyz Republic has continued harmonizing its laws and regulations to conform to EAEU standards, though many local entrepreneurs have criticized this process as disjointed and incomplete. The keys to future growth include progress in fighting corruption, improving administrative transparency, restructuring and diversifying domestic industries, and attracting foreign aid and investment.

GDP (purchasing power parity): $22.64 billion (2017 est.)
$21.87 billion (2016 est.)
$21.08 billion (2015 est.)
note: data are in 2017 dollars
country comparison to the world: 144

GDP (official exchange rate): $7.061 billion (2016 est.)

GDP—real growth rate: 3.5% (2017 est.)

3.8% (2016 est.)
3.5% (2015 est.)
country comparison to the world: 98

GDP—per capita (PPP): $3,700 (2017 est.)
$3,600 (2016 est.)
$3,500 (2015 est.)
note: data are in 2017 dollars
country comparison to the world: 185

Gross national saving: 22.3% of GDP (2017 est.)
23.8% of GDP (2016 est.)
18.3% of GDP (2015 est.)
country comparison to the world: 73

GDP—composition, by end use:
household consumption: 85.8%
government consumption: 18%
investment in fixed capital: 32.7%
investment in inventories: 2.9%
exports of goods and services: 37.2%
imports of goods and services: -76.5% (2017 est.)

GDP—composition, by sector of origin:
agriculture: 14.3%
industry: 32.5%
services: 53.2% (2017 est.)

Agriculture—products: cotton, potatoes, vegetables, grapes, fruits and berries; sheep, goats, cattle, wool

Industries: small machinery, textiles, food processing, cement, shoes, lumber, refrigerators, furniture, electric motors, gold, rare earth metals

Industrial production growth rate: 17.3% (2017 est.)
country comparison to the world: 2

Labor force: 2.841 million (2017 est.)
country comparison to the world: 107

Labor force—by occupation: *agriculture:* 48%
industry: 12.5%
services: 39.5% (2005 est.)

Unemployment rate: 7.4% (2017 est.)
7.5% (2016 est.)
country comparison to the world: 104

Population below poverty line: 32.1% (2015 est.)

Household income or consumption by percentage share: *lowest 10%:* 4.4%
highest 10%: 22.9% (2014 est.)

Distribution of family income—Gini index: 33.4 (2007)
29 (2001)
country comparison to the world: 107

Budget: *revenues:* $2.05 billion
expenditures: $2.304 billion (2017 est.)
Taxes and other revenues: 29% of GDP (2017 est.)
country comparison to the world: 89

Budget surplus (+) or deficit (-): -3.6% of GDP (2017 est.)
country comparison to the world: 135

Public debt: 58.4% of GDP (2017 est.)
58.5% of GDP (2016 est.)
country comparison to the world: 79

Fiscal year: calendar year

Inflation rate (consumer prices): 3.8% (2017 est.)
0.4% (2016 est.)

country comparison to the world: 148

Central bank discount rate: 5% (31 December 2016)
8% (31 December 2015)
country comparison to the world: 79

Commercial bank prime lending rate: 20.1% (31 December 2017 est.)
22.23% (31 December 2016 est.)
country comparison to the world: 15

Stock of narrow money: $1.82 billion (31 December 2017 est.)
$1.411 billion (31 December 2016 est.)
country comparison to the world: 137

Stock of broad money: $2.176 billion (31 December 2017 est.)
$1.667 billion (31 December 2016 est.)
country comparison to the world: 154

Stock of domestic credit: $1.944 billion (31 December 2017 est.)
$1.444 billion (31 December 2016 est.)
country comparison to the world: 159

Market value of publicly traded shares: $165 million (31 December 2012 est.)
$165 million (31 December 2011 est.)
$79 million (31 December 2010 est.)
country comparison to the world: 120

Current account balance: -$817 million (2017 est.)
-$633 million (2016 est.)
country comparison to the world: 123

Exports: $1.768 billion (2017 est.)
$1.544 billion (2016 est.)
country comparison to the world: 145

Exports—commodities: gold, cotton, wool, garments, meat; mercury, uranium, electricity; machinery; shoes

Exports—partners: Switzerland 44.9%, Kazakhstan 10.5%, Russia 10.1%, Uzbekistan 8.7%, Turkey 6.2%, China 5.5% (2016)

Imports: $4.326 billion (2017 est.)
$3.644 billion (2016 est.)
country comparison to the world: 129

Imports—commodities: oil and gas, machinery and equipment, chemicals, foodstuffs

Imports—partners: China 37.8%, Russia 20.7%, Kazakhstan 16.4%, Turkey 4.9% (2016)

Reserves of foreign exchange and gold: $2.411 billion (31 December 2017 est.)
$1.97 billion (31 December 2016 est.)
country comparison to the world: 113

Debt—external: $8.679 billion (31 December 2017 est.)
$8.182 billion (31 December 2016 est.)
country comparison to the world: 119

Stock of direct foreign investment—at home: $5.86 billion (31 December 2017 est.)
$5.21 billion (31 December 2016 est.)
country comparison to the world: 103

Stock of direct foreign investment—abroad: $675.5 million (31 December 2017 est.)
$655.5 million (31 December 2016 est.)
country comparison to the world: 88

Exchange rates: soms (KGS) per US dollar—
68.35 (2017 est.)
69.914 (2016 est.)
69.914 (2015 est.)
64.462 (2014 est.)
53.654 (2013 est.)

ENERGY

Electricity access: *electrification—total population:* 100% (2016)

Electricity—production: 12.8 billion kWh (2015 est.)
country comparison to the world: 90

Electricity—consumption: 10.68 billion kWh (2015 est.)
country comparison to the world: 91

Electricity—exports: 184 million kWh (2015 est.)
country comparison to the world: 76

Electricity—imports: 729 million kWh (2015 est.)
country comparison to the world: 74

Electricity—installed generating capacity: 3.89 million kW (2015 est.)
country comparison to the world: 91

Electricity—from fossil fuels: 20.6% of total installed capacity (2015 est.)
country comparison to the world: 195

Electricity—from nuclear fuels: 0% of total installed capacity (2015 est.)
country comparison to the world: 119

Electricity—from hydroelectric plants: 79.4% of total installed capacity (2015 est.)
country comparison to the world: 15

Electricity—from other renewable sources: 0% of total installed capacity (2015 est.)
country comparison to the world: 190

Crude oil—production: 1,000 bbl/day (2016 est.)
country comparison to the world: 91

Crude oil—exports: 19.65 bbl/day (2014 est.)
country comparison to the world: 83

Crude oil—imports: 100 bbl/day (2014 est.)
country comparison to the world: 83

Crude oil—proved reserves: 40 million bbl (1 January 2017 es)
country comparison to the world: 82

Refined petroleum products—production: 1,776 bbl/day (2014 est.)
country comparison to the world: 104

Refined petroleum products—consumption: 33,000 bbl/day (2015 est.)
country comparison to the world: 118

Refined petroleum products—exports: 2,698 bbl/day (2014 est.)
country comparison to the world: 105

Refined petroleum products—imports: 31,960 bbl/day (2014 est.)
country comparison to the world: 99

Natural gas—production: 30 million cu m (2015 est.)
country comparison to the world: 89

Natural gas—consumption: 773 million cu m (2015 est.)

517

country comparison to the world: 105

Natural gas—exports: 0 cu m (2013 est.)
country comparison to the world: 129

Natural gas—imports: 160 million cu m (2015 est.)
country comparison to the world: 74

Natural gas—proved reserves: 5.663 billion cu m (1 January 2017 es)
country comparison to the world: 95

Carbon dioxide emissions from consumption of energy: 9.4 million Mt (2013 est.)
country comparison to the world: 106

COMMUNICATIONS

Telephones—fixed lines: *total subscriptions:* 382,149
subscriptions per 100 inhabitants: 7 (July 2016 est.)
country comparison to the world: 100

Telephones—mobile cellular: *total:* 7,613,528
subscriptions per 100 inhabitants: 133 (July 2016 est.)
country comparison to the world: 101

Telephone system: *general assessment:* telecommunications infrastructure is being upgraded; loans from the European Bank for Reconstruction and Development (EBRD) are being used to install a digital network, digital radio-relay stations, and fiber-optic links
domestic: fixed-line penetration remains low and concentrated in urban areas; multiple mobile-cellular service providers with growing coverage; mobile-cellular subscribership up to over 130 per 100 persons
international: country code—996; connections with other CIS countries by landline or microwave radio relay and with other countries by leased connections with Moscow international gateway switch and by satellite; satellite earth stations—2 (1 Intersputnik, 1 Intelsat); connected internationally by the Trans-Asia-Europe (TAE) fiber-optic line (2016)

Broadcast media: state-run TV broadcaster operates 2 nationwide networks and 6 regional stations; roughly 20 private TV stations operating with most rebroadcasting other channels; state-run radio broadcaster operates 2 networks; about 20 private radio stations (2007)

Internet country code: .kg
Internet users: total: 1,976,006

percent of population: 34.5% (July 2016 est.)
country comparison to the world: 113

TRANSPORTATION

National air transport system: *number of registered air carriers:* 3
inventory of registered aircraft operated by air carriers: 10
annual passenger traffic on registered air carriers: 625,294
annual freight traffic on registered air carriers: 69,290 mt-km (2015)
Civil aircraft registration country code prefix: EX (2016)

Airports: 28 (2013)
country comparison to the world: 122

Airports—with paved runways: *total:* 18
over 3,047 m: 1
2,438 to 3,047 m: 3
1,524 to 2,437 m: 11
under 914 m: 3 (2017)

Airports—with unpaved runways: *total:* 10
1,524 to 2,437 m: 1
914 to 1,523 m: 1
under 914 m: 8 (2013)

Pipelines: gas 480 km; oil 16 km (2013)

Railways: *total:* 470 km
broad gauge: 470 km 1.520-m gauge (2014)
country comparison to the world: 116

Roadways: *total:* 34,000 km (2007)
country comparison to the world: 94

Waterways: 600 km (2010)
country comparison to the world: 78

Ports and terminals: lake port(s): Balykchy (Ysyk-Kol or Rybach'ye)(Lake Ysyk-Kol)

MILITARY AND SECURITY

Military expenditures: 3.15% of GDP (2016)
3.45% of GDP (2015)
3.38% of GDP (2014)
3.2% of GDP (2013)
3.21% of GDP (2012)

Military branches: State Committee on Defense Affairs (GKDO): Ground Forces, Air Force (includes Air Defense Forces) (2015)

Military service age and obligation: 18-27 years of age for compulsory or voluntary male military service in the Armed Forces or Interior Ministry; 1-year service obligation, with optional fee-based 3-year service in the call-up mobilization reserve; women may volunteer at age 19; 16-17 years of age for military cadets, who cannot take part in military operations (2013)

TRANSNATIONAL ISSUES

Disputes—international: Kyrgyzstan has yet to ratify the 2001 boundary delimitation with Kazakhstan; disputes in Isfara Valley delay completion of delimitation with Tajikistan; delimitation of 130 km of border with Uzbekistan is hampered by serious disputes over enclaves and other areas

Refugees and internally displaced persons: *stateless persons:* 2,334 (2016); note—most stateless people were born in Kyrgyzstan, have lived there many years, or married Kyrgyz citizens; in 2009, Kyrgyzstan adopted a national action plan to speed up the exchange of old Soviet passports for Kyrgyz ones; between 2014 and 2016, Kyrgyzstan has resolved nearly 9,000 stateless cases; stateless people are unable to register marriages and births, to travel within the country or abroad, to own property, or to receive social benefits

Illicit drugs: limited illicit cultivation of cannabis and opium poppy for CIS markets; limited government eradication of illicit crops; transit point for Southwest Asian narcotics bound for Russia and the rest of Europe; major consumer of opiates

INTRODUCTION

Background: Modern-day Laos has its roots in the ancient Lao kingdom of Lan Xang, established in the 14th century under King FA NGUM. For 300 years Lan Xang had influence reaching into present-day Cambodia and Thailand, as well as over all of what is now Laos. After centuries of gradual decline, Laos came under the domination of Siam (Thailand) from the late 18th century until the late 19th century, when it became part of French Indochina. The Franco-Siamese Treaty of 1907 defined the current Lao border with Thailand. In 1975, the communist Pathet Lao took control of the government, ending a six-century-old monarchy and instituting a strict socialist regime closely aligned to Vietnam. A gradual, limited return to private enterprise and the liberalization of foreign investment laws began in 1988. Laos became a member of ASEAN in 1997 and the WTO in 2013.

GEOGRAPHY

Location: Southeastern Asia, northeast of Thailand, west of Vietnam

Geographic coordinates: 18 00 N, 105 00 E

Map references: Southeast Asia

Area: *total:* 236,800 sq km
land: 230,800 sq km
water: 6,000 sq km
country comparison to the world: 85

Area—comparative: about twice the size of Pennsylvania; slightly larger than Utah

Land boundaries: *total:* 5,274 km
border countries (5): Burma 238 km, Cambodia 555 km, China 475 km, Thailand 1,845 km, Vietnam 2,161 km

Coastline: 0 km (landlocked)

Maritime claims: none (landlocked)

Climate: tropical monsoon; rainy season (May to November); dry season (December to April)

Terrain: mostly rugged mountains; some plains and plateaus

Elevation: *mean elevation:* 710 m

elevation extremes: *lowest point:* Mekong River 70 m
highest point: Phu Bia 2,817 m

Natural resources: timber, hydropower, gypsum, tin, gold, gemstones

Land use: *agricultural land:* 10.6%
arable land: 6.2%;
permanent crops: 0.7%;
permanent pasture: 3.7%
forest: 67.9%
other: 21.5% (2011 est.)
Irrigated land: 3,100 sq km (2012)

Population—distribution: most densely populated area is in and around the capital city of Vientiane; large communities are primarily found along the Mekong River along the southwestern border; overall density is considered one of the lowest in Southeast Asia

Natural hazards: floods, droughts

Environment—current issues: unexploded ordnance; deforestation; soil erosion; most of the population does not have access to potable water

Environment—international agreements: *party to:* Biodiversity, Climate Change, Climate Change-Kyoto Protocol, Desertification, Endangered Species, Environmental Modification, Law of the Sea, Ozone Layer Protection
signed, but not ratified: none of the selected agreements

Geography—note: landlocked; most of the country is mountainous and thickly forested; the Mekong River forms a large part of the western boundary with Thailand

PEOPLE AND SOCIETY

Population: 7,126,706 (July 2017 est.)
country comparison to the world: 101

Nationality: *noun:* Lao(s) or Laotian(s)
adjective: Lao or Laotian

Ethnic groups: Lao 53.2%, Khmou 11%, Hmong 9.2%, Phouthay 3.4%, Tai 3.1%, Makong 2.5%, Katong 2.2%, Lue 2%, Akha 1.8%, other 11.6%
note: the Laos Government officially recognizes 49 ethnic groups, but the total number of ethnic groups is estimated to be well over 200 (2015 est.)

Languages: Lao (official), French, English, various ethnic languages

Religions: Buddhist 64.7%, Christian 1.7%, none 31.4%, other/not stated 2.1% (2015 est.)

Age structure: *0-14 years:* 32.76% (male 1,180,227/female 1,154,550)
15-24 years: 21.17% (male 749,312/female 759,677)
25-54 years: 36.7% (male 1,290,768/female 1,324,390)

55-64 years: 5.48% (male 190,627/female 199,673)
65 years and over: 3.89% (male 125,682/female 151,800) (2017 est.)

Dependency ratios: *total dependency ratio:* 60.2
youth dependency ratio: 54
elderly dependency ratio: 6.2
potential support ratio: 16.1 (2015 est.)

Median age: *total:* 23 years
male: 22.7 years
female: 23.3 years (2017 est.)
country comparison to the world: 172

Population growth rate: 1.51% (2017 est.)
country comparison to the world: 77

Birth rate: 23.6 births/1,000 population (2017 est.)
country comparison to the world: 63

Death rate: 7.4 deaths/1,000 population (2017 est.)
country comparison to the world: 115

Net migration rate: -1.1 migrant(s)/1,000 population (2017 est.)
country comparison to the world: 138

Population distribution: most densely populated area is in and around the capital city of Vientiane; large communities are primarily found along the Mekong River along the southwestern border; overall density is considered one of the lowest in Southeast Asia

Urbanization: *urban population:* 40.7% of total population (2017)
rate of urbanization: 4.13% annual rate of change (2015-20 est.)

Major urban areas—population: VIENTIANE (capital) 997,000 (2015)

Sex ratio: *at birth:* 1.04 male(s)/female
0-14 years: 1.02 male(s)/female
15-24 years: 0.99 male(s)/female
25-54 years: 0.97 male(s)/female
55-64 years: 0.96 male(s)/female
65 years and over: 0.83 male(s)/female
total population: 0.99 male(s)/female (2016 est.)

Maternal mortality ratio: 197 deaths/100,000 live births (2015 est.)
country comparison to the world: 52

Infant mortality rate: *total:* 49.9 deaths/1,000 live births
male: 55.2 deaths/1,000 live births
female: 44.4 deaths/1,000 live births (2017 est.)
country comparison to the world: 30

Life expectancy at birth: *total population:* 64.6 years
male: 62.6 years
female: 66.7 years (2017 est.)
country comparison to the world: 184

Total fertility rate: 2.7 children born/woman (2017 est.)
country comparison to the world: 67

Contraceptive prevalence rate: 49.8% (2011/12)

Health expenditures: 1.9% of GDP (2014)

country comparison to the world: 191

Physicians density: 0.18 physicians/1,000 population (2012)

Hospital bed density: 1.5 beds/1,000 population (2012)

Drinking water source:
improved:
urban: 85.6% of population
rural: 69.4% of population
total: 75.7% of population
unimproved:
urban: 14.4% of population
rural: 30.6% of population
total: 24.3% of population (2015 est.)

Sanitation facility access:
improved:
urban: 94.5% of population
rural: 56% of population
total: 70.9% of population
unimproved:
urban: 5.5% of population
rural: 44% of population
total: 29.1% of population (2015 est.)

HIV/AIDS—adult prevalence rate: 0.3% (2016 est.)
country comparison to the world: 86

HIV/AIDS—people living with HIV/AIDS: 11,000 (2016 est.)
country comparison to the world: 94

HIV/AIDS—deaths: <500 (2016 est.)

Major infectious diseases: *degree of risk:* very high
food or waterborne diseases: bacterial and protozoal diarrhea, hepatitis A, and typhoid fever
vectorborne diseases: dengue fever and malaria (2016)

Obesity—adult prevalence rate: 5.3% (2016)
country comparison to the world: 180

Children under the age of 5 years underweight: 26.5% (2011)
country comparison to the world: 22

Education expenditures: 3.3% of GDP (2014)
country comparison to the world: 147

Literacy: *definition:* age 15 and over can read and write
total population: 79.9%
male: 87.1%
female: 72.8% (2015 est.)

School life expectancy (primary to tertiary education): *total:* 11 years
male: 11 years
female: 11 years (2015)

GOVERNMENT

Country name: *conventional long form:* Lao People's Democratic Republic
conventional short form: Laos
local long form: Sathalanalat Paxathipatai Paxaxon Lao
local short form: Mueang Lao (unofficial)
etymology: name means "Land of the Lao [people]"

Government type: communist state

Capital: *name:* Vientiane (Viangchan)

geographic coordinates: 17 58 N, 102 36 E
time difference: UTC+7 (12 hours ahead of Washington, DC, during Standard Time)

Administrative divisions: 17 provinces (khoueng, singular and plural) and 1 capital city* (nakhon luang, singular and plural); Attapu, Bokeo, Bolikhamxai, Champasak, Houaphan, Khammouan, Louangnamtha, Louangphabang, Oudomxai, Phongsali, Salavan, Savannakhet, Viangchan (Vientiane)*, Viangchan, Xaignabouli, Xaisomboun, Xekong, Xiangkhouang

Independence: 19 July 1949 (from France)

National holiday: Republic Day (National Day), 2 December (1975)

Constitution: previous 1947 (preindependence); latest promulgated 13-15 August 1991; amended 2003, 2015 (2016)

Legal system: civil law system similar in form to the French system

International law organization participation: has not submitted an ICJ jurisdiction declaration; non-party state to the ICCt

Citizenship: *citizenship by birth:* no
citizenship by descent only: at least one parent must be a citizen of Laos
dual citizenship recognized: no
residency requirement for naturalization: 10 years

Suffrage: 18 years of age; universal

Executive branch: *chief of state:* President BOUNNYANG Vorachit (since 20 April 2016); Vice President PHANKHAM Viphavan (since 20 April 2016)

head of government: Prime Minister THONGLOUN Sisoulit (since 20 April 2016); Deputy Prime Ministers BOUNTHONG Chitmani, SONXAI Siphandon, SOMDI Douangdi (since 20 April 2016)
cabinet: Council of Ministers appointed by the president, approved by the National Assembly
elections/appointments: president and vice president indirectly elected by the National Assembly for a 5-year term (no term limits); election last held on 20 April 2016 (next to be held in 2021); prime minister nominated by the president, elected by the National Assembly for 5-year term
election results: BOUNNYANG Vorachit (LPRP) elected president; PHANKHAM Viphavan (LPRP) elected vice president; percent of National Assembly vote—NA; THONGLOUN Sisoulit (LPRP) elected prime minister; percent of National Assembly vote—NA

Legislative branch: *description:* unicameral National Assembly or Sapha Heng Xat (149 seats; members directly elected in multi-seat constituencies by simple majority vote from candidate lists provided by the Lao People's Revolutionary Party; members serve 5-year terms)
elections: last held on 20 March 2016 (next to be held in 2021)

election results: percent of vote by party—NA; seats by party—LPRP 144, independent 5

Judicial branch: *highest court(s):* People's Supreme Court (consists of the court president and organized into criminal, civil, administrative, commercial, family, and juvenile chambers, each with a vice president and several judges)
judge selection and term of office: president of People's Supreme Court appointed by National Assembly on recommendation of the president of the republic for a 5-year term; vice presidents of People's Supreme Court appointed by the president of the republic on recommendation of the National Assembly; appointment of chamber judges NA; tenure of court vice presidents and chamber judges NA
subordinate courts: appellate courts; provincial, municipal, district, and military courts

Political parties and leaders: Lao People's Revolutionary Party or LPRP [BOUNNYANG Vorachit]
note: other parties proscribed

Political pressure groups and leaders: International Labor Organization

International organization participation: ADB, ARF, ASEAN, CP, EAS, FAO, G-77, IAEA, IBRD, ICAO, ICRM, IDA, IFAD, IFC, IFRCS, ILO, IMF, Interpol, IOC, IPU, ISO (subscriber), ITU, MIGA, NAM, OIF, OPCW, PCA, UN, UNCTAD, UNESCO, UNIDO, UNWTO, UPU, WCO, WFTU (NGOs), WHO, WIPO, WMO, WTO

Diplomatic representation in the US: *chief of mission:* Ambassador MAI Xaignavong (since 3 August 2015)
chancery: 2222 S Street NW, Washington, DC 20008
telephone: [1] (202) 332-6416
FAX: [1] (202) 332-4923
consulate(s): New York

Diplomatic representation from the US: *chief of mission:* Ambassador Rena BITTER (since 2 November 2016)
embassy: Thadeua Road, Kilometer 9, Ban Somvang Tai, Hatsayfong District, Vientiane
mailing address: American Embassy Vientiane, Unit 46222, APO AP 96546-6222
telephone: [856] 21-48-7000
FAX: [856] 21-48-7190

Flag description: three horizontal bands of red (top), blue (double width), and red with a large white disk centered in the blue band; the red bands recall the blood shed for liberation; the blue band represents the Mekong River and prosperity; the white disk symbolizes the full moon against the Mekong River, but also signifies the unity of the people under the Lao People's Revolutionary Party, as well as the country's bright future

National symbol(s): elephant; national colors: red, white, blue

National anthem: *name:* "Pheng Xat Lao" (Hymn of the Lao People)
lyrics/music: SISANA Sisane/THONGDY Sounthonevichit

note: music adopted 1945, lyrics adopted 1975; the anthem's lyrics were changed following the 1975 Communist revolution that overthrew the monarchy

ECONOMY

Economy—overview: The government of Laos, one of the few remaining one-party communist states, began decentralizing control and encouraging private enterprise in 1986. Economic growth averaged more than 6% per year in the period 1988-2008, and Laos' growth has more recently been amongst the fastest in Asia, averaging more than 7% per year for most of the last decade.

Nevertheless, Laos remains a country with an underdeveloped infrastructure, particularly in rural areas. It has a basic, but improving, road system, and limited external and internal land-line telecommunications. Electricity is available to 83% of the population. Agriculture, dominated by rice cultivation in lowland areas, accounts for about 20% of GDP and 73% of total employment. Recently, the country has faced a persistent current account deficit, falling foreign currency reserves, and growing public debt.

Laos' economy is heavily dependent on capital-intensive natural resource exports. The economy has benefited from high-profile foreign direct investment in hydropower dams along the Mekong River, copper and gold mining, logging, and construction, although some projects in these industries have drawn criticism for their environmental impacts.

Laos gained Normal Trade Relations status with the US in 2004 and applied for Generalized System of Preferences trade benefits in 2013 after being admitted to the World Trade Organization earlier in the year. Laos held the chairmanship of ASEAN in 2016. Laos is in the process of implementing a value-added tax system. The government appears committed to raising the country's profile among foreign investors and has developed special economic zones replete with generous tax incentives, but a limited labor pool, a small domestic market, and corruption remain impediments to investment. Laos also has ongoing problems with the business environment, including onerous registration requirements, a gap between legislation and implementation, and unclear or conflicting regulations.

GDP (purchasing power parity): $49.21 billion (2017 est.)
$46.03 billion (2016 est.)
$43.01 billion (2015 est.)
note: data are in 2017 dollars
country comparison to the world: 111

GDP (official exchange rate): $17.15 billion (2016 est.)

GDP—real growth rate: 6.9% (2017 est.)
7% (2016 est.)
7.3% (2015 est.)
country comparison to the world: 11

GDP—per capita (PPP): $7,400 (2017 est.)
$7,000 (2016 est.)
$6,600 (2015 est.)

note: data are in 2017 dollars
country comparison to the world: 156

Gross national saving: 18% of GDP (2017 est.)
14.8% of GDP (2016 est.)
14.5% of GDP (2015 est.)
country comparison to the world: 101

GDP—composition, by end use:
household consumption: 62.6%
government consumption: 13.4%
investment in fixed capital: 36%
investment in inventories: 3.1%
exports of goods and services: 35.7%
imports of goods and services: -50.8% (2017 est.)

GDP—composition, by sector of origin:
agriculture: 20.9%
industry: 33.2%
services: 39.1% (2017 est.)

Agriculture—products: sweet potatoes, vegetables, corn, coffee, sugarcane, tobacco, cotton, tea, peanuts, rice; cassava (manioc, tapioca), water buffalo, pigs, cattle, poultry

Industries: mining (copper, tin, gold, gypsum); timber, electric power, agricultural processing, rubber, construction, garments, cement, tourism

Industrial production growth rate: 8% (2017 est.)
country comparison to the world: 20

Labor force: 3.582 million (2017 est.)
country comparison to the world: 101

Labor force—by occupation: *agriculture:* 73.1%
industry: 6.1%
services: 20.6% (2012 est.)

Unemployment rate: 1.5% (2016 est.)
1.5% (2016 est.)
country comparison to the world: 10

Population below poverty line: 22% (2013 est.)

Household income or consumption by percentage share: *lowest 10%:* 3.3%
highest 10%: 30.3% (2008)

Distribution of family income—Gini index: 36.7 (2008)
34.6 (2002)
country comparison to the world: 84

Budget: *revenues:* $3.144 billion
expenditures: $4.098 billion (2017 est.)
Taxes and other revenues: 18.3% of GDP (2017 est.)
country comparison to the world: 165

Budget surplus (+) or deficit (-): -5.6% of GDP (2017 est.)
country comparison to the world: 171

Public debt: 67.3% of GDP (2016 est.)
65.6% of GDP (2015 est.)
country comparison to the world: 54

Fiscal year: 1 October–30 September

Inflation rate (consumer prices): 2.3% (2017 est.)
2% (2016 est.)
country comparison to the world: 109

Central bank discount rate: 4.3% (31 December 2010)
4% (31 December 2009)
country comparison to the world: 84

Commercial bank prime lending rate: 18.5% (31 December 2017 est.)
18% (31 December 2016 est.)
country comparison to the world: 23

Stock of narrow money: $1.303 billion (31 December 2017 est.)
$1.243 billion (31 December 2016 est.)
country comparison to the world: 149

Stock of broad money: $9.193 billion (31 December 2017 est.)
$8.197 billion (31 December 2016 est.)
country comparison to the world: 109

Stock of domestic credit: $9.52 billion (31 December 2017 est.)
$8.381 billion (31 December 2016 est.)
country comparison to the world: 112

Market value of publicly traded shares: $1.012 billion (2012 est.)
$576.8 million (2011 est.)
country comparison to the world: 106

Current account balance: -$1.653 billion (2017 est.)
-$1.678 billion (2016 est.)
country comparison to the world: 151

Exports: $2.881 billion (2017 est.)
$2.705 billion (2016 est.)
country comparison to the world: 129

Exports—commodities: wood products, coffee, electricity, tin, copper, gold, cassava

Exports—partners: Thailand 40.1%, China 28.5%, Vietnam 13.7% (2016)

Imports: $5.852 billion (2017 est.)
$5.547 billion (2016 est.)
country comparison to the world: 116

Imports—commodities: machinery and equipment, vehicles, fuel, consumer goods

Imports—partners: Thailand 64.6%, China 16.5%, Vietnam 9.4% (2016)

Reserves of foreign exchange and gold: $989.8 million (31 December 2017 est.)
$940.1 million (31 December 2016 est.)
country comparison to the world: 125

Debt—external: $13.64 billion (31 December 2017 est.)
$12.9 billion (31 December 2016 est.)
country comparison to the world: 106

Stock of direct foreign investment—at home: $15.14 billion (31 December 2012 est.)
$12.44 billion (31 December 2011 est.)
country comparison to the world: 90

Exchange rates: kips (LAK) per US dollar—
8,231.1 (2017 est.)
8,129.1 (2016 est.)
8,129.1 (2015 est.)
8,147.9 (2014 est.)
8,049 (2013 est.)

ENERGY

Electricity access: *population without electricity:* 900,000
electrification—*total population:* 87%
electrification—*urban areas:* 97%

521

electrification—rural areas: 82% (2013)

Electricity—production: 11.46 billion kWh (2015 est.)
country comparison to the world: 95

Electricity—consumption: 4.239 billion kWh (2015 est.)
country comparison to the world: 126

Electricity—exports: 8.469 billion kWh (2015 est.)
country comparison to the world: 26

Electricity—imports: 2.05 billion kWh (2015 est.)
country comparison to the world: 55

Electricity—installed generating capacity: 4.541 million kW (2015 est.)
country comparison to the world: 81

Electricity—from fossil fuels: 1.1% of total installed capacity (2015 est.)
country comparison to the world: 210

Electricity—from nuclear fuels: 0% of total installed capacity (2015 est.)
country comparison to the world: 125

Electricity—from hydroelectric plants: 98.2% of total installed capacity (2015 est.)
country comparison to the world: 5

Electricity—from other renewable sources: 0.7% of total installed capacity (2015 est.)
country comparison to the world: 147

Crude oil—production: 0 bbl/day (2016 est.)
country comparison to the world: 157

Crude oil—exports: 0 bbl/day (2014 est.)
country comparison to the world: 150

Crude oil—imports: 0 bbl/day (2014 est.)
country comparison to the world: 146

Crude oil—proved reserves: 0 bbl (1 January 2017 es)
country comparison to the world: 154

Refined petroleum products—production: 0 bbl/day (2014 est.)
country comparison to the world: 162

Refined petroleum products—consumption: 3,500 bbl/day (2015 est.)
country comparison to the world: 184

Refined petroleum products—exports: 0 bbl/day (2014 est.)
country comparison to the world: 169

Refined petroleum products—imports: 3,480 bbl/day (2014 est.)
country comparison to the world: 175

Natural gas—production: 0 cu m (2013 est.)
country comparison to the world: 156

Natural gas—consumption: 0 cu m (2013 est.)
country comparison to the world: 200

Natural gas—exports: 0 cu m (2013 est.)
country comparison to the world: 134

Natural gas—imports: 0 cu m (2013 est.)
country comparison to the world: 146

Natural gas—proved reserves: 0 cu m (1 January 2014 es)
country comparison to the world: 158

Carbon dioxide emissions from consumption of energy: 500,000 Mt (2013 est.)

country comparison to the world: 185

COMMUNICATIONS

Telephones—fixed lines: *total subscriptions:* 1,266,605
subscriptions per 100 inhabitants: 18 (July 2016 est.)
country comparison to the world: 81

Telephones—mobile cellular: *total:* 3.727 million
subscriptions per 100 inhabitants: 54 (July 2016 est.)
country comparison to the world: 122

Telephone system: *general assessment:* service to public is generally improving; the government relies on a radiotelephone network to communicate with remote areas
domestic: mobile cellular network coverage including 3G is relatively widespread, although usage has slowed as the regulator imposed a strict policy on pricing and competition is effectively discouraged; network performance has suffered because of insufficient maintenance and upgrades
international: country code—856; satellite earth station—1 Intersputnik (Indian Ocean region) and a second to be developed by China (2017)

Broadcast media: 6 TV stations operating out of Vientiane—3 government-operated and the others commercial; 17 provincial stations operating with nearly all programming relayed via satellite from the government-operated stations in Vientiane; Chinese and Vietnamese programming relayed via satellite from Lao National TV; broadcasts available from stations in Thailand and Vietnam in border areas; multi-channel satellite and cable TV systems provide access to a wide range of foreign stations; state-controlled radio with state-operated Lao National Radio (LNR) broadcasting on 5 frequencies—1 AM, 1 SW, and 3 FM; LNR's AM and FM programs are relayed via satellite constituting a large part of the programming schedules of the provincial radio stations; Thai radio broadcasts available in border areas and transmissions of multiple international broadcasters are also accessible (2012)

Internet country code: .la
Internet users: total: 1.258 million

percent of population: 18.2% (July 2016 est.)
country comparison to the world: 142

TRANSPORTATION

National air transport system: *number of registered air carriers:* 1
inventory of registered aircraft operated by air carriers: 11
annual passenger traffic on registered air carriers: 1,181,187
annual freight traffic on registered air carriers: 1,356,074 mt-km (2015)
Civil aircraft registration country code prefix: RDPL (2016)

Airports: 41 (2013)
country comparison to the world: 103

Airports—with paved runways: *total:* 8

2,438 to 3,047 m: 3
1,524 to 2,437 m: 4
914 to 1,523 m: 1 (2017)

Airports—with unpaved runways: *total:* 33
1,524 to 2,437 m: 2
914 to 1,523 m: 9
under 914 m: 22 (2013)

Pipelines: refined products 540 km (2013)

Roadways: *total:* 39,586 km
paved: 5,415 km
unpaved: 34,171 km (2009)
country comparison to the world: 89

Waterways: 4,600 km (primarily on the Mekong River and its tributaries; 2,900 additional km are intermittently navigable by craft drawing less than 0.5 m) (2012)
country comparison to the world: 23

Merchant marine: *total:* 1
by type: general cargo 1 (2017)
country comparison to the world: 167

MILITARY AND SECURITY

Military expenditures: 0.2% of GDP (2013)
0.22% of GDP (2012)
0.23% of GDP (2011)

Military branches: Lao People's Armed Forces (LPAF): Lao People's Army (LPA, includes Riverine Force), Air Force (2011)

Military service age and obligation: 18 years of age for compulsory or voluntary military service; conscript service obligation—minimum 18-months (2012)

Military—note: serving one of the world's least developed countries, the Lao People's Armed Forces (LPAF) is small, poorly funded, and ineffectively resourced; its mission focus is border and internal security, primarily in countering ethnic Hmong insurgent groups; together with the Lao People's Revolutionary Party and the government, the Lao People's Army (LPA) is the third pillar of state machinery, and as such is expected to suppress political and civil unrest and similar national emergencies; there is no perceived external threat to the state and the LPA maintains strong ties with the neighboring Vietnamese military (2012)

TRANSNATIONAL ISSUES

Disputes—international: southeast Asian states have enhanced border surveillance to check the spread of avian flu; talks continue on completion of demarcation with Thailand but disputes remain over islands in the Mekong River; Cambodia and Laos have a longstanding border demarcation dispute; concern among Mekong River Commission members that China's construction of eight dams on the Upper Mekong River and construction of more dams on its tributaries will affect water levels, sediment flows, and fisheries; Cambodia and Vietnam are concerned about Laos' extensive plans for upstream dam construction for the same reasons

Trafficking in persons: current situation: Laos is a source and, to a lesser extent, transit and destination country for men, women, and children subjected to forced labor and sex trafficking; Lao economic migrants may encounter conditions of forced labor or sexual exploitation in destination countries, most often Thailand; Lao women and girls are exploited in Thailand's commercial sex trade, domestic service, factories, and agriculture; a small, possibly growing, number of Lao women and girls are sold as brides in China and South Korea and subsequently sex trafficked; Lao men and boys are victims of forced labor in the Thai fishing, construction, and agriculture industries; some Lao children, as well as Vietnamese and Chinese women and girls, are subjected to sex trafficking in Laos; other Vietnamese and Chinese, and possibly Burmese, adults and girls transit Laos for sexual and labor exploitation in neighboring countries, particularly Thailand

tier rating: Tier 2 Watch List—Laos does not fully comply with the minimum standards for the elimination of trafficking; however, it is making significant efforts to do so; authorities sustained moderate efforts to investigate, prosecute, and convict trafficking offenders; the government failed to make progress in proactively identifying victims exploited within the country or among those deported from abroad; the government continues to rely almost entirely on local and international organizations to provide and fund services to trafficking victims; although Lao men and boys are trafficked, most protective services are only available to women and girls, and long-term support is lacking; modest prevention efforts include the promotion of anti-trafficking awareness on state-controlled media (2015)

Illicit drugs: estimated opium poppy cultivation in 2015 was estimated to be 5,700 hectares, compared with 6,200 hectares in 2014; estimated potential production of between 84 and 176 mt of raw opium; unsubstantiated reports of domestic methamphetamine production; growing domestic methamphetamine problem

LATVIA

Area: *total:* 64,589 sq km
land: 62,249 sq km
water: 2,340 sq km
country comparison to the world: 125

Area—comparative: slightly larger than West Virginia

Land boundaries: *total:* 1,370 km
border countries (4): Belarus 161 km, Estonia 333 km, Lithuania 544 km, Russia 332 km

Coastline: 498 km

Maritime claims: *territorial sea:* 12 nm
exclusive economic zone: limits as agreed to by Estonia, Finland, Latvia, Sweden, and Russia
continental shelf: 200 m depth or to the depth of exploitation

Climate: maritime; wet, moderate winters

Terrain: low plain

Elevation: *mean elevation:* 87 m

elevation extremes: *lowest point:* Baltic Sea 0 m
highest point: Gaizina Kalns 312 m

Natural resources: peat, limestone, dolomite, amber, hydropower, timber, arable land

Land use: *agricultural land:* 29.2%
arable land: 18.6%;
permanent crops: 0.1%;
permanent pasture: 10.5%
forest: 54.1%
other: 16.7% (2011 est.)
Irrigated land: 12 sq km
note: land in Latvia is often too wet and in need of drainage not irrigation; approximately 16,000 sq km or 85% of agricultural land has been improved by drainage (2012)

Population—distribution: largest concentration of people is found in and around the port and capital city of Riga; small agglomerations are scattered throughout the country

Natural hazards: large percentage of agricultural fields can become waterlogged and require drainage

Environment—current issues: Latvia's environment has benefited from a shift to service industries after the country regained independence; improvements have occurred in drinking water quality, sewage treatment, household and hazardous waste management, as well as reduction of air pollution

Environment—international agreements: *party to:* Air Pollution, Air Pollution-Persistent Organic Pollutants, Biodiversity, Climate Change, Climate Change-Kyoto Protocol, Desertification, Endangered Species, Hazardous Wastes, Law of the Sea, Ozone Layer Protection, Ship Pollution, Wetlands
signed, but not ratified: none of the selected agreements

Geography—note: most of the country is composed of fertile low-lying plains with some hills in the east

INTRODUCTION

Background: Several eastern Baltic tribes merged in medieval times to form the ethnic core of the Latvian people (ca. 8th-12th centuries A.D.). The region subsequently came under the control of Germans, Poles, Swedes, and finally, Russians. A Latvian republic emerged following World War I, but it was annexed by the USSR in 1940—an action never recognized by the US and many other countries. Latvia reestablished its independence in 1991 following the breakup of the Soviet Union. Although the last Russian troops left in 1994, the status of the Russian minority (some 26% of the population) remains of concern to Moscow. Latvia acceded to both NATO and the EU in the spring of 2004; it joined the euro zone in 2014 and the OECD in 2016. A dual citizenship law was adopted in 2013, easing naturalization for non-citizen children.

GEOGRAPHY

Location: Eastern Europe, bordering the Baltic Sea, between Estonia and Lithuania

Geographic coordinates: 57 00 N, 25 00 E

Map references: Europe

PEOPLE AND SOCIETY

Population: 1,944,643 (July 2017 est.)
country comparison to the world: 149

Nationality: *noun:* Latvian(s)
adjective: Latvian

Ethnic groups: Latvian 61.8%, Russian 25.6%, Belarusian 3.4%, Ukrainian 2.3%, Polish 2.1%, Lithuanian 1.2%, other 3.6% (2016 est.)

Languages: Latvian (official) 56.3%, Russian 33.8%, other 0.6% (includes Polish, Ukrainian, and Belarusian), unspecified 9.4%
note: data represent language usually spoken at home (2011 est.)

Religions: Lutheran 19.6%, Orthodox 15.3%, other Christian 1%, other 0.4%, unspecified 63.7% (2006)

Age structure: *0-14 years:* 15.15% (male 151,195/female 143,388)
15-24 years: 9.45% (male 94,779/female 88,952)
25-54 years: 41.75% (male 403,699/female 408,277)
55-64 years: 14.1% (male 121,993/female 152,260)
65 years and over: 19.55% (male 124,570/female 255,530) (2017 est.)

Dependency ratios: *total dependency ratio:* 52.5

youth dependency ratio: 23.1
elderly dependency ratio: 29.4
potential support ratio: 3.4 (2015 est.)

Median age: *total:* 43.6 years
male: 39.7 years
female: 46.9 years (2017 est.)
country comparison to the world: 17

Population growth rate: -1.08% (2017 est.)
country comparison to the world: 229

Birth rate: 9.7 births/1,000 population (2017 est.)
country comparison to the world: 198

Death rate: 14.5 deaths/1,000 population (2017 est.)
country comparison to the world: 4

Net migration rate: -6.1 migrant(s)/1,000 population (2017 est.)
country comparison to the world: 199

Population distribution: largest concentration of people is found in and around the port and capital city of Riga; small agglomerations are scattered throughout the country

Urbanization: *urban population:* 67.4% of total population (2017)
rate of urbanization: -0.56% annual rate of change (2015-20 est.)

Major urban areas—population: RIGA (capital) 621,000 (2015)

Sex ratio: *at birth:* 1.05 male(s)/female
0-14 years: 1.05 male(s)/female
15-24 years: 1.07 male(s)/female
25-54 years: 0.98 male(s)/female
55-64 years: 0.79 male(s)/female
65 years and over: 0.48 male(s)/female
total population: 0.85 male(s)/female (2016 est.)

Mother's mean age at first birth: 27.2 years (2014 est.)

Maternal mortality ratio: 18 deaths/100,000 live births (2015 est.)
country comparison to the world: 130

Infant mortality rate: *total:* 5.2 deaths/1,000 live births
male: 5.6 deaths/1,000 live births
female: 4.8 deaths/1,000 live births (2017 est.)
country comparison to the world: 175

Life expectancy at birth: *total population:* 74.7 years
male: 70.1 years
female: 79.5 years (2017 est.)
country comparison to the world: 121

Total fertility rate: 1.51 children born/woman (2017 est.)
country comparison to the world: 196

Health expenditures: 5.9% of GDP (2014)
country comparison to the world: 106

Physicians density: 3.22 physicians/1,000 population (2014)

Hospital bed density: 5.9 beds/1,000 population (2011)

Drinking water source:
improved:
urban: 99.8% of population
rural: 98.3% of population

total: 99.3% of population
unimproved:
urban: 0.2% of population
rural: 1.7% of population
total: 0.7% of population (2015 est.)

Sanitation facility access:
improved:
urban: 90.8% of population
rural: 81.5% of population
total: 87.8% of population
unimproved:
urban: 9.2% of population
rural: 18.5% of population
total: 12.2% of population (2015 est.)

HIV/AIDS—adult prevalence rate: 0.7% (2016 est.)
country comparison to the world: 52

HIV/AIDS—people living with HIV/AIDS: 6,600 (2016 est.)
country comparison to the world: 104

HIV/AIDS—deaths: <500 (2016 est.)

Major infectious diseases: *degree of risk:* intermediate
vectorborne diseases: tickborne encephalitis (2016)

Obesity—adult prevalence rate: 23.6% (2016)
country comparison to the world: 65

Education expenditures: 4.9% of GDP (2013)
country comparison to the world: 77

Literacy: *definition:* age 15 and over can read and write
total population: 99.9%
male: 99.9%
female: 99.9% (2015 est.)

School life expectancy (primary to tertiary education): *total:* 16 years
male: 16 years
female: 17 years (2014)

Unemployment, youth ages 15-24: *total:* 16.3%
male: 18%
female: 14.1% (2015 est.)
country comparison to the world: 28

GOVERNMENT

Country name: *conventional long form:* Republic of Latvia
conventional short form: Latvia
local long form: Latvijas Republika
local short form: Latvija
former: Latvian Soviet Socialist Republic
etymology: the name "Latvia" originates from the ancient Latgalians, one of four eastern Baltic tribes that formed the ethnic core of the Latvian people (ca. 8th-12th centuries A.D.)

Government type: parliamentary republic

Capital: *name:* Riga
geographic coordinates: 56 57 N, 24 06 E
time difference: UTC+2 (7 hours ahead of Washington, DC, during Standard Time)
daylight saving time: +1hr, begins last Sunday in March; ends last Sunday in October

Administrative divisions: 110 municipalities (novadi, singular—novads) and 9 cities
municipalities: Adazu Novads, Aglonas Novads, Aizkraukles Novads, Aizputes Novads, Aknistes Novads, Alojas Novads, Alsungas Novads, Aluksnes Novads, Amatas Novads, Apes Novads, Auces Novads, Babites Novads, Baldones Novads, Baltinavas Novads, Balvu Novads, Bauskas Novads, Beverinas Novads, Brocenu Novads, Burtnieku Novads, Carnikavas Novads, Cesu Novads, Cesvaines Novads, Ciblas Novads, Dagdas Novads, Daugavpils Novads, Dobeles Novads, Dundagas Novads, Durbes Novads, Engures Novads, Erglu Novads, Garkalnes Novads, Grobinas Novads, Gulbenes Novads, Iecavas Novads, Ikskiles Novads, Ilukstes Novads, Incukalna Novads, Jaunjelgavas Novads, Jaunpiebalgas Novads, Jaunpils Novads, Jekabpils Novads, Jelgavas Novads, Kandavas Novads, Karsavas Novads, Keguma Novads, Kekavas Novads, Kocenu Novads, Kokneses Novads, Kraslavas Novads, Krimuldas Novads, Krustpils Novads, Kuldigas Novads, Lielvardes Novads, Ligatnes Novads, Limbazu Novads, Livanu Novads, Lubanas Novads, Ludzas Novads, Madonas Novads, Malpils Novads, Marupes Novads, Mazsalacas Novads, Mersraga Novads, Nauksenu Novads, Neretas Novads, Nicas Novads, Ogres Novads, Olaines Novads, Ozolnieku Novads, Pargaujas Novads, Pavilostas Novads, Plavinu Novads, Preilu Novads, Priekules Novads, Priekulu Novads, Raunas Novads, Rezeknes Novads, Riebinu Novads, Rojas Novads, Ropazu Novads, Rucavas Novads, Rugaju Novads, Rujienas Novads, Rundales Novads, Salacgrivas Novads, Salas Novads, Salaspils Novads, Saldus Novads, Saulkrastu Novads, Sejas Novads, Siguldas Novads, Skriveru Novads, Skrundas Novads, Smiltenes Novads, Stopinu Novads, Strencu Novads, Talsu Novads, Tervetes Novads, Tukuma Novads, Vainodes Novads, Valkas Novads, Varaklanu Novads, Varkavas Novads, Vecpiebalgas Novads, Vecumnieku Novads, Ventspils Novads, Viesites Novads, Vilakas Novads, Vilanu Novads, Zilupes Novads
cities: Daugavpils, Jekabpils, Jelgava, Jurmala, Liepaja, Rezekne, Riga, Valmiera, Ventspils

Independence: 4 May 1990 (declared independence from the Soviet Union); 6 September 1991 (recognized by the Soviet Union)

National holiday: Independence Day (Republic of Latvia Proclamation Day), 18 November (1918); note—18 November 1918 was the date Latvia established its statehood and its concomitant independence from Soviet Russia; 4 May 1990 was the date it declared the restoration of Latvian statehood and its concomitant independence from the Soviet Union

Constitution: history: several previous (pre-1991 independence); note—following the restoration of independence in 1991, parts of the 1922 constitution were reintroduced 4 May 1990 and fully reintroduced 6 July 1993
amendments: proposed by two-thirds of Parliament members or by petition of one-tenth of qualified voters submitted through the president;

passage requires at least two-thirds majority vote of Parliament in each of three readings; amendment of constitutional articles including national sovereignty, language, the parliamentary electoral system, and constitutional amendment procedures requires passage in a referendum by majority vote of at least one-half of the electorate; amended several times, last in 2014 (2016)

Legal system: civil law system with traces of socialist legal traditions and practices

International law organization participation: has not submitted an ICJ jurisdiction declaration; accepts ICCt jurisdiction

Citizenship: *citizenship by birth:* no
citizenship by descent only: at least one parent must be a citizen of Latvia
dual citizenship recognized: no
residency requirement for naturalization: 5 years

Suffrage: 18 years of age; universal

Executive branch: *chief of state:* President Raimonds VEJONIS (since 8 July 2015)

head of government: Prime Minister Maris KUCINSKIS (since 11 February 2016); Deputy Prime Minister Arvils ASERADENS (since 11 February 2016)
cabinet: Cabinet of Ministers nominated by the prime minister, appointed by Parliament
elections/appointments: president indirectly elected by Parliament for a 4-year term (eligible for a second term); election last held on 3 June 2015 (next to be held in 2019); prime minister appointed by the president, confirmed by Parliament
election results: Raimonds VEJONIS elected president; Parliament vote—Raimonds VEJONIS 55 of 100

Legislative branch: *description:* unicameral Parliament or Saeima (100 seats; members directly elected in multi-seat constituencies by proportional representation vote; members serve 4-year terms)
elections: last held on 4 October 2014 (next to be held in October 2018)
election results: percent of vote by party—SC 23%, Unity 21.9%, ZZS 19.5%, NA 16.6%, NSL 6.9%, LRA 6.7%, other 5.4%; seats by party—SC 24, Unity 23, ZZS 21, NA 17, LRA 8, NSL 7

Judicial branch: *highest court(s):* Supreme Court (consists of the Senate with 27 judges and Supreme Court of Chambers with 22 judges); Constitutional Court (consists of 7 judges)
judge selection and term of office: Supreme Court judges nominated by chief justice and confirmed by the Saeima; judges serve until age 70, but term can be extended 2 years; Constitutional Court judges—3 nominated by Saeima members, 2 by Cabinet ministers, and 2 by plenum of Supreme Court; all judges confirmed by Saeima majority vote; Constitutional Court president and vice president serve in their positions for 3 years; all judges serve 10-year terms; mandatory retirement at age 70
subordinate courts: district (city) and regional courts

Political parties and leaders: Alliance of Regions or LRA [Martins BONDARS]

For Latvia from the Heart or NSL [Inguna SUDRABA]
Social Democratic Party "Harmony" or SC [Nils USAKOVS]
National Alliance "All For Latvia!"-"For Fatherland and Freedom/LNNK" or NA [Gaidis BERZINS, Raivis DZINTARS]
Union of Greens and Farmers or ZZS [Augusts BRIGMANIS]
Unity [Andris PIEBALGS]

Political pressure groups and leaders: Latvian Employers' Confederation or LDDK [Vitalijs GAVRILOVS]
Farmers' Parliament or ZSA [Juris LAZDINS]
Free Trade Union Confederation of Latvia or LBAS [Egils BALDZENS]

International organization participation: Australia Group, BA, BIS, CBSS, CD, CE, EAPC, EBRD, ECB, EIB, EMU, ESA (cooperating state), EU, FAO, IAEA, IBRD, ICAO, ICC (NGOs), ICCt, ICRM, IDA, IFC, IFRCS, IHO, ILO, IMF, IMO, IMSO, Interpol, IOC, IOM, IPU, ISO (correspondent), ITU, ITUC (NGOs), MIGA, NATO, NIB, NSG, OAS (observer), OIF (observer), OPCW, OSCE, PCA, Schengen Convention, UN, UNCTAD, UNESCO, UNHCR, UNWTO, UPU, WCO, WHO, WIPO, WMO, WTO

Diplomatic representation in the US: *chief of mission:* Ambassador Andris TEIKMANIS (since 16 September 2016)
chancery: 2306 Massachusetts Ave. NW, Washington, DC 20008
telephone: [1] (202) 328-2840
FAX: [1] (202) 328-2860

Diplomatic representation from the US: *chief of mission:* Ambassador Nancy Bikoff PETTIT (since 8 September 2015)
embassy: 1 Samnera Velsa St, Riga LV-1510
mailing address: Embassy of the United States of America, 1 Samnera Velsa St, Riga, LV-1510, Latvia
telephone: [371] 6710-7000
FAX: [371] 6710-7050

Flag description: three horizontal bands of maroon (top), white (half-width), and maroon; the flag is one of the older banners in the world; a medieval chronicle mentions a red standard with a white stripe being used by Latvian tribes in about 1280

National symbol(s): white wagtail (bird); national colors: maroon, white

National anthem: name: "Dievs, sveti Latviju!" (God Bless Latvia)
lyrics/music: Karlis BAUMANIS
note: adopted 1920, restored 1990; first performed in 1873 while Latvia was a part of Russia; banned during the Soviet occupation from 1940 to 1990

ECONOMY

Economy—overview: Latvia is a small, open economy with exports contributing more than half of GDP. Due to its geographical location, transit services are highly-developed, along with timber and wood-processing, agriculture and food products, and manufacturing of machinery and electronics

industries. Corruption continues to be an impediment to attracting foreign direct investment and Latvia's low birth rate and decreasing population are major challenges to its long-term economic vitality.

Latvia's economy experienced GDP growth of more than 10% per year during 2006-07, but entered a severe recession in 2008 as a result of an unsustainable current account deficit and large debt exposure amid the slowing world economy. Triggered by the collapse of the second largest bank, GDP plunged by more than 14% in 2009 and, despite strong growth since 2011, the economy took until 2017 return to pre-crisis levels in real terms. Strong investment and consumption, the latter stoked by rising wages, helped the economy grow by more than 4% in 2017, while inflation rose to 3%. Continued gains in competitiveness and investment will be key to maintaining economic growth, especially in light of unfavorable demographic trends, including the emigration of skilled workers, and one of the highest levels of income inequality in the EU.

In the wake of the 2008-09 crisis, the IMF, EU, and other international donors provided substantial financial assistance to Latvia as part of an agreement to defend the currency's peg to the euro in exchange for the government's commitment to stringent austerity measures. The IMF/EU program successfully concluded in December 2011, although, the austerity measures imposed large social costs. The majority of companies, banks, and real estate have been privatized, although the state still holds sizable stakes in a few large enterprises, including 80% ownership of the Latvian national airline. Latvia officially joined the World Trade Organization in February 1999 and the EU in May 2004. Latvia also joined the euro zone in 2014 and the OECD in 2016.

GDP (purchasing power parity): $53.47 billion (2017 est.)
$51.49 billion (2016 est.)
$50.5 billion (2015 est.)
note: data are in 2017 dollars
country comparison to the world: 109

GDP (official exchange rate): $30.18 billion (2016 est.)

GDP—real growth rate: 3.8% (2017 est.)
2% (2016 est.)
2.7% (2015 est.)
country comparison to the world: 81

GDP—per capita (PPP): $27,300 (2017 est.)
$26,100 (2016 est.)
$25,400 (2015 est.)
note: data are in 2017 dollars
country comparison to the world: 73

Gross national saving: 20.9% of GDP (2017 est.)
21.4% of GDP (2016 est.)
21.3% of GDP (2015 est.)
country comparison to the world: 83

GDP—composition, by end use:
household consumption: 63.1%
government consumption: 17.8%
investment in fixed capital: 19.7%
investment in inventories: 0%

exports of goods and services: 60.3%
imports of goods and services: -61% (2017 est.)

GDP—composition, by sector of origin:
agriculture: 3.2%
industry: 21.6%
services: 75.2% (2017 est.)

Agriculture—products: grain, rapeseed, potatoes, vegetables; pork, poultry, milk, eggs; fish

Industries: processed foods, processed wood products, textiles, processed metals, pharmaceuticals, railroad cars, synthetic fibers, electronics

Industrial production growth rate: 2.4% (2017 est.)
country comparison to the world: 119

Labor force: 990,000 (2017 est.)
country comparison to the world: 144

Labor force—by occupation: *agriculture:* 7.7%
industry: 24.1%
services: 68.1% (2016 est.)

Unemployment rate: 9% (2017 est.)
9.6% (2016 est.)
country comparison to the world: 123

Population below poverty line: 25.5% (2015)

Household income or consumption by percentage share: *lowest 10%:* 2.2%
highest 10%: 26.3% (2015)

Distribution of family income—Gini index: 34.5 (2015)
35.4 (2014)
country comparison to the world: 97

Budget: *revenues:* $10.13 billion
expenditures: $10.43 billion (2017 est.)
Taxes and other revenues: 33.6% of GDP (2017 est.)
country comparison to the world: 63

Budget surplus (+) or deficit (-): -1% of GDP (2017 est.)
country comparison to the world: 59

Public debt: 38.9% of GDP (2017 est.)
40.1% of GDP (2016 est.)
note: data cover general government debt, and includes debt instruments issued (or owned) by government entities, including sub-sectors of central government, state government, local government, and social security funds
country comparison to the world: 139

Fiscal year: calendar year

Inflation rate (consumer prices): 3% (2017 est.)
0.1% (2016 est.)
country comparison to the world: 129

Central bank discount rate: 0% (31 December 2016 est.)
0.05% (31 December 2015 est.)
country comparison to the world: 156

Commercial bank prime lending rate: 4.6% (31 December 2017 est.)
4.5% (31 December 2016 est.)
country comparison to the world: 149

Stock of narrow money: $12.77 billion (31 December 2017 est.)
$10.71 billion (31 December 2016 est.)
country comparison to the world: 79

Stock of broad money: $15.25 billion (31 December 2017 est.)
$12.97 billion (31 December 2016 est.)
country comparison to the world: 98

Stock of domestic credit: $17.12 billion (31 December 2017 est.)
$15.11 billion (31 December 2016 est.)
country comparison to the world: 94

Market value of publicly traded shares: $6.76 billion (31 December 2016 est.)
$6.799 billion (31 December 2015 est.)
$7.127 billion (31 December 2014 est.)
country comparison to the world: 79

Current account balance: -$100 million (2017 est.)
$409 million (2016 est.)
country comparison to the world: 80

Exports: $12.34 billion (2017 est.)
$11.35 billion (2016 est.)
country comparison to the world: 81

Exports—commodities: foodstuffs, wood and wood products, metals, machinery and equipment, textiles

Exports—partners: Lithuania 17.3%, Estonia 11.5%, Russia 11.4%, Germany 6.8%, Sweden 5.7%, UK 5.3%, Poland 5%, Denmark 4.4% (2016)

Imports: $15.13 billion (2017 est.)
$13.28 billion (2016 est.)
country comparison to the world: 86

Imports—commodities: machinery and equipment, consumer goods, chemicals, fuels, vehicles

Imports—partners: Lithuania 16.9%, Germany 12.3%, Poland 10.4%, Estonia 7.9%, Russia 7.4%, Finland 4.3%, Netherlands 4.3% (2016)

Reserves of foreign exchange and gold: $3.595 billion (31 December 2017 est.)
$3.514 billion (31 December 2016 est.)
country comparison to the world: 100

Debt—external: $40.02 billion (31 March 2016 est.)
$38.19 billion (31 March 2015 est.)
country comparison to the world: 71

Stock of direct foreign investment—at home:
$16.22 billion (31 December 2017 est.)
$15.36 billion (31 December 2016 est.)
country comparison to the world: 86

Stock of direct foreign investment—abroad:
$2.755 billion (31 December 2017 est.)
$2.485 billion (31 December 2016 est.)
country comparison to the world: 78

Exchange rates: lati (LVL) per US dollar—
0.906 (2017 est.)
0.9037 (2016 est.)
0.9037 (2015 est.)
0.9012 (2014 est.)
0.7525 (2013 est.)

ENERGY

Electricity access: electrification—*total population:* 100% (2016)

Electricity—production: 5.342 billion kWh (2015 est.)
country comparison to the world: 119

Electricity—consumption: 6.712 billion kWh (2015 est.)
country comparison to the world: 111

Electricity—exports: 3.795 billion kWh (2016 est.)
country comparison to the world: 38

Electricity—imports: 4.828 billion kWh (2016 est.)
country comparison to the world: 41

Electricity—installed generating capacity: 2.935 million kW (2015 est.)
country comparison to the world: 98

Electricity—from fossil fuels: 39.1% of total installed capacity (2015 est.)
country comparison to the world: 169

Electricity—from nuclear fuels: 0% of total installed capacity (2015 est.)
country comparison to the world: 127

Electricity—from hydroelectric plants: 54.1% of total installed capacity (2015 est.)
country comparison to the world: 35

Electricity—from other renewable sources: 6.7% of total installed capacity (2015 est.)
country comparison to the world: 85

Crude oil—production: 0 bbl/day (2016 est.)
country comparison to the world: 158

Crude oil—exports: 0 bbl/day (2016 est.)
country comparison to the world: 152

Crude oil—imports: 0 bbl/day (2016 est.)
country comparison to the world: 148

Crude oil—proved reserves: 0 bbl (1 January 2017 es)
country comparison to the world: 155

Refined petroleum products—production: 0 bbl/day (2016 est.)
country comparison to the world: 163

Refined petroleum products—consumption: 37,680 bbl/day (2016 est.)
country comparison to the world: 117

Refined petroleum products—exports: 22,640 bbl/day (2016 est.)
country comparison to the world: 69

Refined petroleum products—imports: 54,060 bbl/day (2016 est.)
country comparison to the world: 79

Natural gas—production: 0 cu m (2014 est.)
country comparison to the world: 158

Natural gas—consumption: 2.2 billion cu m (2015 est.)
country comparison to the world: 85

Natural gas—exports: 0 cu m (2014 est.)
country comparison to the world: 136

Natural gas—imports: 1.306 billion cu m (2015 est.)
country comparison to the world: 56

Natural gas—proved reserves: 0 cu m (2014 est.)
country comparison to the world: 160

Carbon dioxide emissions from consumption of energy: 7.6 million Mt (2013 est.)
country comparison to the world: 113

COMMUNICATIONS

Telephones—fixed lines: *total subscriptions:* 367,195
subscriptions per 100 inhabitants: 19 (July 2016 est.)
country comparison to the world: 106
Telephones—mobile cellular: *total:* 2,650,273
subscriptions per 100 inhabitants: 135 (July 2016 est.)
country comparison to the world: 145
Telephone system: *general assessment:* recent efforts focused on bringing competition to the telecommunications sector; the number of fixed lines is decreasing as mobile-cellular telephone service expands
domestic: number of telecommunications operators has grown rapidly since the fixed-line market opened to competition in 2003; combined fixed-line and mobile-cellular subscribership roughly 150 per 100 persons
international: country code—371; the Latvian network is now connected via fiber-optic cable to Estonia, Finland, and Sweden (2016)

Broadcast media: several national and regional commercial TV stations are foreign-owned, 2 national TV stations are publicly owned; system supplemented by privately owned regional and local TV stations; cable and satellite multi-channel TV services with domestic and foreign broadcasts available; publicly owned broadcaster operates 4 radio networks with dozens of stations throughout the country; dozens of private broadcasters also operate radio stations (2007)

Internet country code: .lv
Internet users: total: 1,570,374
percent of population: 79.9% (July 2016 est.)
country comparison to the world: 110

TRANSPORTATION

National air transport system: *number of registered air carriers:* 3
inventory of registered aircraft operated by air carriers: 47

annual passenger traffic on registered air carriers: 2,527,368
annual freight traffic on registered air carriers: 2,277,996 mt-km (2015)
Civil aircraft registration country code prefix: YL (2016)

Airports: 42 (2013)
country comparison to the world: 101
Airports—with paved runways: *total:* 18
over 3,047 m: 1
2,438 to 3,047 m: 3
1,524 to 2,437 m: 4
914 to 1,523 m: 3
under 914 m: 7 (2017)
Airports—with unpaved runways: *total:* 24
under 914 m: 24 (2013)

Heliports: 1 (2013)

Pipelines: gas 928 km; refined products 415 km (2013)

Railways: *total:* 2,239 km
broad gauge: 2,206 km 1.520-m gauge
narrow gauge: 33 km 0.750-m gauge (2008)
country comparison to the world: 68

Roadways: *total:* 72,440 km
paved: 14,707 km
unpaved: 57,733 km (2013)
country comparison to the world: 65

Waterways: 300 km (navigable year-round) (2010)
country comparison to the world: 92

Merchant marine: *total:* 65
by type: general cargo 15, oil tanker 8, other 42 (2017)
country comparison to the world: 103

Ports and terminals: *major seaport(s):* Riga, Ventspils

MILITARY AND SECURITY

Military expenditures: 1.47% of GDP (2016)
1.05% of GDP (2015)
0.94% of GDP (2014)
0.94% of GDP (2013)
0.91% of GDP (2012)
country comparison to the world: 105

Military branches: National Armed Forces (Nacionalie Brunotie Speki): Land Forces (Latvijas Sauszemes Speki), Navy (Latvijas Juras Speki, includes Coast Guard (Latvijas Kara Flote)),

Latvian Air Force (Latvijas Gaisa Speki), Latvian Home Guard (Latvijas Zemessardze) (2017)

Military service age and obligation: 18 years of age for voluntary male and female military service; no conscription; under current law, every citizen is entitled to serve in the armed forces for life (2016)

TRANSNATIONAL ISSUES

Disputes—international: Russia demands better Latvian treatment of ethnic Russians in Latvia; boundary demarcated with Latvia and Lithuania; the Latvian parliament has not ratified its 1998 maritime boundary treaty with Lithuania, primarily due to concerns over oil exploration rights; as a member state that forms part of the EU's external border, Latvia has implemented the strict Schengen border rules with Russia
Refugees and internally displaced persons: stateless persons: 242,736 (2016); note—individuals who were Latvian citizens prior to the 1940 Soviet occupation and their descendants were recognized as Latvian citizens when the country's independence was restored in 1991; citizens of the former Soviet Union residing in Latvia who have neither Latvian nor other citizenship are considered non-citizens (officially there is no statelessness in Latvia) and are entitled to non-citizen passports; children born after Latvian independence to stateless parents are entitled to Latvian citizenship upon their parents' request; non-citizens cannot vote or hold certain government jobs and are exempt from military service but can travel visa-free in the EU under the Schengen accord like Latvian citizens; non-citizens can obtain naturalization if they have been permanent residents of Latvia for at least five years, pass tests in Latvian language and history, and know the words of the Latvian national anthem

Illicit drugs: transshipment and destination point for cocaine, synthetic drugs, opiates, and cannabis from Southwest Asia, Western Europe, Latin America, and neighboring Baltic countries; despite improved legislation, vulnerable to money laundering due to nascent enforcement capabilities and comparatively weak regulation of offshore companies and the gaming industry; CIS organized crime (including counterfeiting, corruption, extortion, stolen cars, and prostitution) accounts for most laundered proceeds

LEBANON

INTRODUCTION

Background: Following World War I, France acquired a mandate over the northern portion of the former Ottoman Empire province of Syria. The French demarcated the region of Lebanon in 1920 and granted this area independence in 1943. Since independence the country has been marked by periods of political turmoil interspersed with

prosperity built on its position as a regional center for finance and trade. The country's 1975-90 civil war that resulted in an estimated 120,000 fatalities, was followed by years of social and political instability. Sectarianism is a key element of Lebanese political life. Neighboring Syria has historically influenced Lebanon's foreign policy and internal policies, and its military occupied Lebanon from 1976 until 2005. The Lebanon-based Hizballah

militia and Israel continued attacks and counterattacks against each other after Syria's withdrawal, and fought a brief war in 2006. Lebanon's borders with Syria and Israel remain unresolved.

GEOGRAPHY

Location: Middle East, bordering the Mediterranean Sea, between Israel and Syria

Geographic coordinates: 33 50 N, 35 50 E

Map references: Middle East

Area: *total:* 10,400 sq km
land: 10,230 sq km
water: 170 sq km
country comparison to the world: 169

Area—comparative: about one-third the size of Maryland

Land boundaries: *total:* 484 km
border countries (2): Israel 81 km, Syria 403 km

Coastline: 225 km

Maritime claims: *territorial sea:* 12 nm

Climate: Mediterranean; mild to cool, wet winters with hot, dry summers; the Lebanon Mountains experience heavy winter snows

Terrain: narrow coastal plain; El Beqaa (Bekaa Valley) separates Lebanon and Anti-Lebanon Mountains

Elevation: *mean elevation:* 1,250 m

elevation extremes: *lowest point:* Mediterranean Sea 0 m
highest point: Qornet es Saouda 3,088 m

Natural resources: limestone, iron ore, salt, water-surplus state in a water-deficit region, arable land

Land use: *agricultural land:* 63.3%
arable land: 11.9%;
permanent crops: 12.3%;
permanent pasture: 39.1%
forest: 13.4%
other: 23.3% (2011 est.)
Irrigated land: 1,040 sq km (2012)

Population—distribution: the majority of the people live on or near the Mediterranean coast, and of these most live in and around the capital, Beirut; favorable growing conditions in the Bekaa Valley, on the southeastern side of the Lebanon Mountains, have attracted farmers and thus the area exhibits a smaller population density

Natural hazards: earthquakes; dust storms, sandstorms

Environment—current issues: deforestation; soil erosion; desertification; air pollution in Beirut from vehicular traffic and the burning of industrial wastes; pollution of coastal waters from raw sewage and oil spills

Environment—international agreements: *party to:* Biodiversity, Climate Change, Climate Change-Kyoto Protocol, Desertification, Hazardous Wastes, Law of the Sea, Ozone Layer Protection, Ship Pollution, Wetlands
signed, but not ratified: Environmental Modification, Marine Life Conservation

Geography—note: smallest country in continental Asia; Nahr el Litani is the only major river in Near East not crossing an international boundary; rugged terrain historically helped isolate, protect, and develop numerous factional groups based on religion, clan, and ethnicity

PEOPLE AND SOCIETY

Population: 6,229,794 (July 2017 est.)
country comparison to the world: 107

Nationality: *noun:* Lebanese (singular and plural)
adjective: Lebanese

Ethnic groups: Arab 95%, Armenian 4%, other 1%
note: many Christian Lebanese do not identify themselves as Arab but rather as descendants of the ancient Canaanites and prefer to be called Phoenicians

Languages: Arabic (official), French, English, Armenian

Religions: Muslim 54% (27% Sunni, 27% Shia), Christian 40.5% (includes 21% Maronite Catholic, 8% Greek Orthodox, 5% Greek Catholic, 6.5% other Christian), Druze 5.6%, very small numbers of Jews, Baha'is, Buddhists, Hindus, and Mormons
note: 18 religious sects recognized (2012 est.)

Age structure: *0-14 years:* 24.09% (male 768,282/female 732,773)
15-24 years: 16.42% (male 523,380/female 499,582)
25-54 years: 44.79% (male 1,412,114/female 1,378,464)
55-64 years: 7.91% (male 232,198/female 260,685)
65 years and over: 6.78% (male 183,995/female 238,321) (2017 est.)

Dependency ratios: *total dependency ratio:* 47.3
youth dependency ratio: 35.3
elderly dependency ratio: 12
potential support ratio: 8.3 (2015 est.)

Median age: *total:* 30.5 years
male: 29.9 years
female: 31.1 years (2017 est.)
country comparison to the world: 115

Population growth rate: -1.1% (2017 est.)
country comparison to the world: 231

Birth rate: 14.3 births/1,000 population (2017 est.)
country comparison to the world: 135

Death rate: 5 deaths/1,000 population (2017 est.)
country comparison to the world: 193

Net migration rate: -20.3 migrant(s)/1,000 population (2017 est.)
country comparison to the world: 219

Population distribution: the majority of the people live on or near the Mediterranean coast, and of these most live in and around the capital, Beirut; favorable growing conditions in the Bekaa Valley, on the southeastern side of the Lebanon Mountains, have attracted farmers and thus the area exhibits a smaller population density

Urbanization: *urban population:* 88% of total population (2017)
rate of urbanization: -0.57% annual rate of change (2015-20 est.)

Major urban areas—population: BEIRUT (capital) 2.226 million (2015)

Sex ratio: *at birth:* 1.05 male(s)/female
0-14 years: 1.05 male(s)/female
15-24 years: 1.05 male(s)/female
25-54 years: 1.02 male(s)/female
55-64 years: 0.88 male(s)/female
65 years and over: 0.79 male(s)/female
total population: 1 male(s)/female (2016 est.)

Maternal mortality ratio: 15 deaths/100,000 live births (2015 est.)
country comparison to the world: 137

Infant mortality rate: *total:* 7.4 deaths/1,000 live births
male: 7.8 deaths/1,000 live births
female: 7 deaths/1,000 live births (2017 est.)
country comparison to the world: 161

Life expectancy at birth: *total population:* 77.8 years
male: 76.5 years
female: 79.1 years (2017 est.)
country comparison to the world: 68
Total fertility rate: 1.72 children born/woman (2017 est.)
country comparison to the world: 169

Contraceptive prevalence rate: 54.5% (2009)

Health expenditures: 6.4% of GDP (2014)
country comparison to the world: 95

Physicians density: 2.38 physicians/1,000 population (2014)

Hospital bed density: 3.5 beds/1,000 population (2012)

Drinking water source:
improved:
urban: 99% of population
rural: 99% of population
total: 99% of population
unimproved:
urban: 1% of population
rural: 1% of population
total: 1% of population (2015 est.)

Sanitation facility access:
improved:
urban: 80.7% of population
rural: 80.7% of population
total: 80.7% of population
unimproved:
urban: 19.3% of population
rural: 19.3% of population
total: 19.3% of population (2015 est.)

HIV/AIDS—adult prevalence rate: <.1% (2016 est.)

HIV/AIDS—people living with HIV/AIDS: 2,200 (2016 est.)
country comparison to the world: 117

HIV/AIDS—deaths: <100 (2016 est.)

Obesity—adult prevalence rate: 32% (2016)
country comparison to the world: 19

Education expenditures: 2.6% of GDP (2013)
country comparison to the world: 162

Literacy: *definition:* age 15 and over can read and write
total population: 93.9%
male: 96%
female: 91.8% (2015 est.)

School life expectancy (primary to tertiary education): *total:* 11 years
male: 12 years
female: 11 years (2014)

Unemployment, youth ages 15-24: *total:* 22.1%
male: 22.3%
female: 21.6% (2007 est.)
country comparison to the world: 71

GOVERNMENT

Country name: *conventional long form:* Lebanese Republic
conventional short form: Lebanon
local long form: Al Jumhuriyah al Lubnaniyah
local short form: Lubnan
former: Greater Lebanon
etymology: derives from the Semitic root "lbn" meaning "white" and refers to snow-capped Mount Lebanon

Government type: parliamentary republic

Capital: *name:* Beirut
geographic coordinates: 33 52 N, 35 30 E
time difference: UTC+2 (7 hours ahead of Washington, DC, during Standard Time)
daylight saving time: +1hr, begins last Sunday in March; ends last Sunday in October

Administrative divisions: 8 governorates (mohafazat, singular—mohafazah); Aakkar, Baalbek-Hermel, Beqaa (Bekaa), Beyrouth (Beirut), Liban-Nord (North Lebanon), Liban-Sud (South Lebanon), Mont-Liban (Mount Lebanon), Nabatiye

Independence: 22 November 1943 (from League of Nations mandate under French administration)

National holiday: Independence Day, 22 November (1943)

Constitution: history: drafted 15 May 1926, adopted 23 May 1926
amendments: proposed by the president of the republic and introduced as a government bill to the Chamber of Deputies or proposed by at least 10 members of the Chamber of Deputies and agreed upon by two-thirds of its members; following government review and approval, the proposal is prepared as a draft amendment and submitted to the Chamber of Deputies for discussion and vote; passage requires at least two-thirds majority vote of a required two-thirds quorum of the chamber

membership and promulgation by the president; amended several times, last in 2004 (2016)

Legal system: mixed legal system of civil law based on the French civil code, Ottoman legal tradition, and religious laws covering personal status, marriage, divorce, and other family relations of the Jewish, Islamic, and Christian communities

International law organization participation: has not submitted an ICJ jurisdiction declaration; non-party state to the ICCt

Citizenship: *citizenship by birth:* no
citizenship by descent only: the father must be a citizen of Lebanon
dual citizenship recognized: yes
residency requirement for naturalization: unknown

Suffrage: 21 years of age; compulsory for all males; authorized for women at age 21 with elementary education; excludes military personnel

Executive branch: *chief of state:* President Michel AWN (since 31 October 2016)

head of government: Prime Minister Saad al-HARIRI (since 18 December 2016); Deputy Prime Minister Ghassan HASBANI (since 18 December 2016)
cabinet: Cabinet chosen by the prime minister in consultation with the president and National Assembly
elections/appointments: president indirectly elected by the National Assembly with two-thirds majority vote in the first round and if needed absolute majority vote in a second round for a 6-year term (eligible for non-consecutive terms); last held on 31 October 2016 (next to be held in 2022); prime minister and deputy prime minister appointed by the president in consultation with the National Assembly
election results: Michel AWN elected president in second round; National Assembly vote—Michel AWN (FPM) 83; note—in the initial election held on 23 April 2014, no candidate received the required two-thirds vote, and subsequent attempts failed because the Assembly lacked the necessary quorum to hold a vote; the president was finally elected in its 46th attempt on 31 October 2016

Legislative branch: *description:* unicameral National Assembly or Majlis al-Nuwab in Arabic or Assemblee Nationale in French (128 seats; members directly elected in multi-seat constituencies by majority vote; members serve 4-year terms); note—seats are apportioned among the Christian and Muslim denominations
note: Lebanon's Constitution states the National Assembly cannot conduct regular business until it elects a president when the position is vacant
elections: last held on 7 June 2009 (next originally scheduled in 2014, but postponed till 2018)
election results: percent of vote by coalition—March 8 Coalition 54.7%, March 14 Coalition 45.3%; seats by coalition—March 14 Coalition 71; March 8 Coalition 57; seats by coalition following 16 July 2012 byelection held to fill one seat—March 14 Coalition 72, March 8 Coalition 56

Judicial branch: *highest court(s):* Court of Cassation or Supreme Court (organized into 8 chambers, each with a presiding judge and 2 associate judges); Constitutional Council (consists of 10 members)
judge selection and term of office: Court of Cassation judges appointed by Supreme Judicial Council, a 10-member body headed by the chief justice, and includes other judicial officials; judge tenure NA; Constitutional Council members appointed—5 by the Council of Ministers and 5 by parliament; members serve 5-year terms
subordinate courts: Courts of Appeal; Courts of First Instance; specialized tribunals, religious courts; military courts

Political parties and leaders: March 14 Coalition:
Future Movement Bloc [Sa'ad al-HARIRI]
Kata'ib Party [Sami GEMAYEL]
Lebanese Forces or LF [Samir JA'JA]
Marada Movement [Sulayman FRANJIEH]
Social Democrat Hunshaqian Party [Sebouh KELPAKIAN]
Hizballah-led bloc (formerly March 8 Coalition):
Amal Movement [Nabih BERRI]
Ba'th Arab Socialist Party of Lebanon [Fayez SHUKR]
Free Patriotic Movement or FPM [Gibran BASSIL]
Hizballah [Hassan NASRALLAH]
Islamic Actions Front [Sheikh Zuhair al-JU'AYD]
Marada Movement [Sulayman FRANJIEH]
Syrian Social Nationalist Party [Ali QANSO]
Tashnag or Armenian Revolutionary Federation [Hagop PAKRADOUNIAN]

Independent: Progressive Socialist Party or PSP [Walid JUNBLATT]

Political pressure groups and leaders: Grand Mufti of Lebanon [Sheikh Abdul Latif DERIAN]
Maronite Church [Patriarch Moran Mor Bechora Boutros al-RAHI]
note: most sects retain militias and a number of Sunni militant groups operate in Palestinian refugee camps

International organization participation: ABEDA, AFESD, AMF, CAEU, FAO, G-24, G-77, IAEA, IBRD, ICAO, ICC (national committees), ICRM, IDA, IDB, IFAD, IFC, IFRCS, ILO, IMF, IMO, IMSO, Interpol, IOC, IPU, ISO, ITSO, ITU, LAS, MIGA, NAM, OAS (observer), OIC, OIF, OPCW, PCA, UN, UNCTAD, UNESCO, UNHCR, UNIDO, UNRWA, UNWTO, UPU, WCO, WFTU (NGOs), WHO, WIPO, WMO, WTO (observer)

Diplomatic representation in the US: *chief of mission:* Ambassador Gabriel Naoum ISSA (since 28 January 2016)
chancery: 2560 28th Street NW, Washington, DC 20008
telephone: [1] (202) 939-6300
FAX: [1] (202) 939-6324
consulate(s) general: Detroit, New York, Los Angeles

Diplomatic representation from the US: *chief of mission:* Ambassador Elizabeth H. RICHARD (since 17 May 2016)

embassy: Awkar, Lebanon (Awkar facing the Municipality)
mailing address: P. O. Box 70-840, Antelias, Lebanon; from US: US Embassy Beirut, 6070 Beirut Place, Washington, DC 20521-6070
telephone: [961] (4) 542600, 543600
FAX: [961] (4) 544136

Flag description: three horizontal bands consisting of red (top), white (middle, double width), and red (bottom) with a green cedar tree centered in the white band; the red bands symbolize blood shed for liberation, the white band denotes peace, the snow of the mountains, and purity; the green cedar tree is the symbol of Lebanon and represents eternity, steadiness, happiness, and prosperity

National symbol(s): cedar tree; national colors: red, white, green

National anthem: *name:* "Kulluna lil-watan" (All Of Us, For Our Country!)
lyrics/music: Rachid NAKHLE/Wadih SABRA
note: adopted 1927; chosen following a nation-wide competition

ECONOMY

Economy—overview: Lebanon has a free-market economy and a strong laissez-faire commercial tradition. The government does not restrict foreign investment; however, the investment climate suffers from red tape, corruption, arbitrary licensing decisions, complex customs procedures, high taxes, tariffs, and fees, archaic legislation, and weak intellectual property rights. The Lebanese economy is service-oriented; main growth sectors include banking and tourism.

The 1975-90 civil war seriously damaged Lebanon's economic infrastructure, cut national output by half, and derailed Lebanon's position as a Middle Eastern entrepot and banking hub. Following the civil war, Lebanon rebuilt much of its war-torn physical and financial infrastructure by borrowing heavily, mostly from domestic banks, which saddled the government with a huge debt burden. Pledges of economic and financial reforms made at separate international donor conferences during the 2000s have mostly gone unfulfilled, including those made during the Paris III Donor Conference in 2007, following the July 2006 war.

Spillover from the Syrian conflict, including the influx of more than 1.1 million registered Syrian refugees, has increased internal tension and slowed economic growth to the 1-2% range in 2011-17, after four years of averaging 8% growth. Syrian refugees have increased the labor supply, but are blamed for pushing more Lebanese into unemployment. Chronic fiscal deficits have increased Lebanon's debt-to-GDP ratio, the third highest in the world; most of the debt is held internally by Lebanese banks. Weak economic growth limits tax revenues, while the largest government expenditures remain debt servicing, salaries for government workers, and transfers to the electricity sector. These limitations constrain other government spending, limiting its ability to invest in necessary infrastructure improvements, such as water, electricity, and transportation. The

Lebanese government in 2017 passed initiatives to encourage foreign investment to improve the country's infrastructure and exploit offshore energy resources.

GDP (purchasing power parity): $87.89 billion (2017 est.)
$86.59 billion (2016 est.)
$85.73 billion (2015 est.)
note: data are in 2017 dollars
country comparison to the world: 91

GDP (official exchange rate): $52.7 billion (2016 est.)

GDP—real growth rate: 1.5% (2017 est.)
1% (2016 est.)
0.8% (2015 est.)
country comparison to the world: 173

GDP—per capita (PPP): $19,500 (2017 est.)
$19,400 (2016 est.)
$19,400 (2015 est.)
note: data are in 2017 dollars
country comparison to the world: 90

Gross national saving: 3.3% of GDP (2017 est.)
4.7% of GDP (2016 est.)
2.5% of GDP (2015 est.)
country comparison to the world: 171

GDP—composition, by end use:
household consumption: 83.6%
government consumption: 12.8%
investment in fixed capital: 19.4%
investment in inventories: 0.5%
exports of goods and services: 26.4%
imports of goods and services: -42.7% (2017 est.)

GDP—composition, by sector of origin:
agriculture: 5.7%
industry: 21%
services: 73.3% (2017 est.)

Agriculture—products: citrus, grapes, tomatoes, apples, vegetables, potatoes, olives, tobacco; sheep, goats

Industries: banking, tourism, real estate and construction, food processing, wine, jewelry, cement, textiles, mineral and chemical products, wood and furniture products, oil refining, metal fabricating

Industrial production growth rate: 2.1% (2017 est.)
country comparison to the world: 127

Labor force: 2.166 million
note: excludes as many as 1 million foreign workers and refugees (2016 est.)
country comparison to the world: 123

Labor force—by occupation: *agriculture:* NA%
industry: NA%
services: NA%

Unemployment rate: NA%

Population below poverty line: 28.6% (2004 est.)

Household income or consumption by percentage share: *lowest 10%:* NA%
highest 10%: NA%

Budget: *revenues:* $10.9 billion
expenditures: $15.99 billion (2017 est.)
Taxes and other revenues: 20.7% of GDP (2017 est.)
country comparison to the world: 146

Budget surplus (+) or deficit (-): -9.7% of GDP (2017 est.)
country comparison to the world: 205

Public debt: 142.2% of GDP (2017 est.)
146.6% of GDP (2016 est.)
note: data cover central government debt, and exclude debt instruments issued (or owned) by government entities other than the treasury; the data include treasury debt held by foreign entities; the data include debt issued by subnational entities, as well as intra-governmental debt; intra-governmental debt consists of treasury borrowings from surpluses in the social funds, such as for retirement, medical care, and unemployment
country comparison to the world: 3

Fiscal year: calendar year

Inflation rate (consumer prices): 3.1% (2017 est.)
-0.8% (2016 est.)
country comparison to the world: 130

Central bank discount rate: 3.5% (31 December 2010)
10% (31 December 2009)
country comparison to the world: 102

Commercial bank prime lending rate: 8.6% (31 December 2017 est.)
8.35% (31 December 2016 est.)
country comparison to the world: 97

Stock of narrow money: $7.366 billion (31 December 2017 est.)
$6.739 billion (31 December 2016 est.)
country comparison to the world: 89

Stock of broad money: $56.65 billion (31 December 2017 est.)
$54.68 billion (31 December 2016 est.)
country comparison to the world: 65

Stock of domestic credit: $112.2 billion (31 December 2017 est.)
$104 billion (31 December 2016 est.)
country comparison to the world: 55

Market value of publicly traded shares: $11.22 billion (30 December 2014 est.)
$10.54 billion (30 December 2013 est.)
$10.42 billion (28 December 2012 est.)
country comparison to the world: 73

Current account balance: -$9.488 billion (2017 est.)
-$9.382 billion (2016 est.)
country comparison to the world: 183

Exports: $4.051 billion (2017 est.)
$3.689 billion (2016 est.)
country comparison to the world: 116

Exports—commodities: jewelry, base metals, chemicals, consumer goods, fruit and vegetables, tobacco, construction minerals, electric power machinery and switchgear, textile fibers, paper

Exports—partners: South Africa 21.1%, Saudi Arabia 9%, UAE 8%, Syria 6.7%, Iraq 5.4% (2016)

Imports: $18.05 billion (2017 est.)
$17.33 billion (2016 est.)
country comparison to the world: 77

Imports—commodities: petroleum products, cars, medicinal products, clothing, meat and live animals, consumer goods, paper, textile fabrics, tobacco, electrical machinery and equipment, chemicals

Imports—partners: China 11.2%, Italy 7.5%, US 6.3%, Germany 6.2%, Greece 5.7%, Egypt 4.1% (2016)

Reserves of foreign exchange and gold: $53.1 billion (31 December 2017 est.)
$54.04 billion (31 December 2016 est.)
country comparison to the world: 38

Debt—external: $39.46 billion (31 December 2017 est.)
$36.6 billion (31 December 2016 est.)
country comparison to the world: 73

Stock of direct foreign investment—at home: $NA

Stock of direct foreign investment—abroad: $NA

Exchange rates: Lebanese pounds (LBP) per US dollar—
1,507.5 (2017 est.)
1,507.5 (2016 est.)
1,507.5 (2015 est.)
1,507.5 (2014 est.)
1,507.5 (2013 est.)

ENERGY

Electricity access: electrification—*total population:* 100% (2016)

Electricity—production: 17.32 billion kWh (2015 est.)
country comparison to the world: 81

Electricity—consumption: 15.66 billion kWh (2015 est.)
country comparison to the world: 77

Electricity—exports: 0 kWh (2016 est.)
country comparison to the world: 158

Electricity—imports: 268 million kWh (2015 est.)
country comparison to the world: 89

Electricity—installed generating capacity: 2.337 million kW (2015 est.)
country comparison to the world: 108

Electricity—from fossil fuels: 87.2% of total installed capacity (2015 est.)
country comparison to the world: 68

Electricity—from nuclear fuels: 0% of total installed capacity (2015 est.)
country comparison to the world: 126

Electricity—from hydroelectric plants: 12.2% of total installed capacity (2015 est.)
country comparison to the world: 115

Electricity—from other renewable sources: 0.9% of total installed capacity (2015 est.)
country comparison to the world: 142

Crude oil—production: 0 bbl/day (2016 est.)
country comparison to the world: 159

Crude oil—exports: 0 bbl/day (2014 est.)
country comparison to the world: 151

Crude oil—imports: 0 bbl/day (2014 est.)
country comparison to the world: 147

Crude oil—proved reserves: 0 bbl (1 January 2017 es)
country comparison to the world: 156

Refined petroleum products—production: 0 bbl/day (2014 est.)
country comparison to the world: 164

Refined petroleum products—consumption: 143,000 bbl/day (2015 est.)
country comparison to the world: 71

Refined petroleum products—exports: 0 bbl/day (2014 est.)
country comparison to the world: 170

Refined petroleum products—imports: 148,800 bbl/day (2014 est.)
country comparison to the world: 46

Natural gas—production: 0 cu m (2013 est.)
country comparison to the world: 157

Natural gas—consumption: 150.1 million cu m (2010 est.)
country comparison to the world: 112

Natural gas—exports: 0 cu m (2013 est.)
country comparison to the world: 135

Natural gas—imports: 150.1 million cu m (2010 est.)
country comparison to the world: 75

Natural gas—proved reserves: 0 cu m (1 January 2014 es)
country comparison to the world: 159

Carbon dioxide emissions from consumption of energy: 16 million Mt (2013 est.)
country comparison to the world: 89

COMMUNICATIONS

Telephones—fixed lines: *total subscriptions:* 1.068 million
subscriptions per 100 inhabitants: 17 (July 2016 est.)
country comparison to the world: 77

Telephones—mobile cellular: *total:* 4,890,534
subscriptions per 100 inhabitants: 78 (July 2016 est.)
country comparison to the world: 125

Telephone system: *general assessment:* repair of the telecommunications system, severely damaged during the civil war, now complete
domestic: two mobile-cellular networks provide good service; combined fixed-line and mobile-cellular subscribership about 95 per 100 persons
international: country code—961; submarine cable links to Cyprus, Egypt, and Syria; satellite earth stations—2 Intelsat (1 Indian Ocean and 1 Atlantic Ocean); coaxial cable to Syria (2016)

Broadcast media: 7 TV stations, 1 of which is state owned; more than 30 radio stations, 1 of which is state owned; satellite and cable TV services available; transmissions of at least 2 international broadcasters are accessible through partner stations (2007)

Internet country code: .lb
Internet users: total: 4,747,542

percent of population: 76.1% (July 2016 est.)
country comparison to the world: 76

TRANSPORTATION

National air transport system: *number of registered air carriers:* 2
inventory of registered aircraft operated by air carriers: 21
annual passenger traffic on registered air carriers: 2,583,274

annual freight traffic on registered air carriers: 53,902,026 mt-km (2015)
Civil aircraft registration country code prefix: OD (2016)

Airports: 8 (2013)
country comparison to the world: 161

Airports—with paved runways: total: 5
over 3,047 m: 1
2,438 to 3,047 m: 2
1,524 to 2,437 m: 1
under 914 m: 1 (2017)

Airports—with unpaved runways: total: 3
914 to 1,523 m: 2
under 914 m: 1 (2013)

Heliports: 1 (2013)

Pipelines: gas 88 km (2013)

Railways: *total:* 401 km
standard gauge: 319 km 1.435-m gauge
narrow gauge: 82 km 1.050-m gauge
note: rail system is still unusable due to damage sustained from fighting in the 1980s and in 2006 (2017)
country comparison to the world: 120

Roadways: *total:* 6,970 km (includes 170 km of expressways) (2005)
country comparison to the world: 146

Merchant marine: *total:* 54
by type: bulk carrier 1, container ship 1, general cargo 39, oil tanker 1, other 12 (2017)
country comparison to the world: 111

Ports and terminals: *major seaport(s):* Beirut, Tripoli
container port(s) (TEUs): Beirut (1,034,249)

MILITARY AND SECURITY

Military expenditures: 4.76% of GDP (2015)
4.96% of GDP (2014)
4.36% of GDP (2013)
4.07% of GDP (2012)
4.06% of GDP (2011)
country comparison to the world: 11

Military branches: Lebanese Armed Forces (LAF): Lebanese Army ((Al Jaysh al Lubnani) includes Lebanese Navy (Al Quwwat al Bahiriyya al Lubnaniya), Lebanese Air Force (Al Quwwat al Jawwiya al Lubnaniya)) (2013)

Military service age and obligation: 17-30 years of age for voluntary military service; 18-24 years of age for officer candidates; no conscription (2013)

TERRORISM

Terrorist groups—home based: *Abdallah Azzam Brigades (AAB):* aim(s): enhance its networks in Lebanon to combat Shia Muslim influence in the country, including Hizballah; seeks to disrupt Israel's economy and its efforts to establish security and attack Western interests in the Middle East
area(s) of operation: headquartered in the Ayn al-Hilwah Palestinian refugee camp near Sidon in the south; responsible for several blasts and suicide attacks in Beirut's Shia Muslim-populated suburbs, such as Dahiyeh, that frequently kill or

injure dozens of innocent civilians; responsible for numerous rocket attacks fired from Lebanon into populated Israeli territory; assessed in 2017 to have dozens of members

Asbat al-Ansar (AAA): *aim(s):* overthrow the Lebanese Government, rid Lebanon of Western influences, and destroy the state of Israel to seize Jerusalem and, ultimately, establish an Islamic state in the Levant region

area(s) of operation: headquartered in the Ayn al-Hilwah Palestinian refugee camp near Sidon in the south; this group is essentially defunct; active primarily as recruiters in Lebanon's Palestinian refugee camps; until the mid-2000s, operatives conducted small-scale bombing and shooting attacks in Lebanon against Christian, secular, and Shia Muslim figures and institutions, elements of foreign influence inside the country, and Lebanese Government officials (including the assassination of judges); assessed in 2017 to have a few dozen members

Hizballah: *aim(s):* destroy the state of Israel, counter the West, provide paramilitary support to Syrian President Bashar al-ASAD's regime, and accrue military resources, and defend its position of strength in Lebanon

area(s) of operation: headquartered in Beirut, with considerable support from Iran; Iran's Islamic Revolutionary Guard Corps has had a presence in Lebanon since the early 1980s and coordinates closely with Hizballah on military operations and training; remains the most capable terrorist group in the country, enjoying popular support among many Lebanese Shia and allied Christians; engages in terrorist activity against Israel, including an incident on 28 January 2015, when operatives attacked an Israeli military convoy near Lebanon's Shebaa Farms area, killing two Israeli soldiers and wounding several others; the attack was the most severe eruption of violence between Israel and Hizballah since their lethal 34-day conflict in 2006; continues to operate as an armed militia beyond the control of the state and as a powerful political actor in Lebanon; receives funds from Lebanese donors and the Lebanese diaspora

Terrorist groups—foreign based: *Al-Aqsa Martyrs Brigade (AAMB):* aim(s): bolster its recruitment presence in Lebanon and, ultimately, establish a Palestinian state comprising the West Bank, Gaza Strip, and Jerusalem

area(s) of operation: recruits youths in Palestinian refugee camps

al-Nusrah Front: *aim(s):* bolster networks in Lebanon and, ultimately, establish a regional Islamic caliphate

area(s) of operation: targets Lebanese Armed Forces, especially in the east in the Beqaa Valley

and along the Lebanon-Syria border; has claimed responsibility for multiple attacks against Shia Muslims, including suicide bombings aimed at Hizballah members; fighters transit Lebanon to fight in Syria

Islamic State of Iraq and the Levant (ISIL): *aim(s):* replace the Lebanese Government with an Islamic state and implement ISIL's strict interpretation of Sharia

area(s) of operation: operational primarily in the east along the border with Syria; targets Lebanese army personnel and Shia Muslims, including Hizballah members and facilities; the Lebanese army has intensified offenses against ISIL since it claimed responsibility for double suicide bombings in Beirut on 12 November 2015, killing 43 civilians and wounding over 200 in the worst attack in years to hit the city

Palestine Liberation Front (PLF): *aim(s):* enhance its networks in Lebanon and, ultimately, destroy the state of Israel to establish a secular, Marxist Palestinian state with Jerusalem as its capital

area(s) of operation: maintains a recruitment and limited training presence in many refugee camps

Popular Front for the Liberation of Palestine (PFLP): *aim(s):* enhance its recruitment network in Lebanon and, ultimately, establish a secular, Marxist Palestinian nation

area(s) of operation: recruits youth residing in the country's Palestinian refugee camps

PFLP-General Command (PFLP-GC): *aim(s):* enhance recruitment and operational networks in Lebanon

area(s) of operation: recruits young men living in Palestinian refugee camps, including camps in the Beqaa Valley; operates paramilitary bases; receives funds and training from Hizballah and Iranian elements working with Hizballah

TRANSNATIONAL ISSUES

Disputes—international: lacking a treaty or other documentation describing the boundary, portions of the Lebanon-Syria boundary are unclear with several sections in dispute; since 2000, Lebanon has claimed Shab'a Farms area in the Israeli-occupied Golan Heights; the roughly 2,000-strong UN Interim Force in Lebanon has been in place since 1978

Refugees and internally displaced persons: refugees (country of origin): 6,454 (Iraq) (2016); 997,552 (Syria); 463,664 (Palestinian refugees) (2017)

IDPs: 12,000 (2007 Lebanese security forces' destruction of Palestinian refugee camp) (2016)

stateless persons: undetermined (2016); note—tens of thousands of persons are stateless in Lebanon, including many Palestinian refugees and their descendants, Syrian Kurds denaturalized in Syria in 1962, children born to Lebanese women married to foreign or stateless men; most babies born to Syrian refugees, and Lebanese children whose births are unregistered

Trafficking in persons: current situation: Lebanon is a source and destination country for women and children subjected to forced labor and sex trafficking and a transit point for Eastern European women and children subjected to sex trafficking in other Middle Eastern countries; women and girls from South and Southeast Asia and an increasing number from East and West Africa are recruited by agencies to work in domestic service but are subject to conditions of forced labor; under Lebanon's artiste visa program, women from Eastern Europe, North Africa, and the Dominican Republic enter Lebanon to work in the adult entertainment industry but are often forced into the sex trade; Lebanese children are reportedly forced into street begging and commercial sexual exploitation, with small numbers of Lebanese girls sex trafficked in other Arab countries; Syrian refugees are vulnerable to forced labor and prostitution

tier rating: Tier 2 Watch List—Lebanon does not fully comply with the minimum standards for the elimination of trafficking; however, it is making significant efforts to do so; in 2014, Lebanon was granted a waiver from an otherwise required downgrade to Tier 3 because its government has a written plan that, if implemented would constitute making significant efforts to bring itself into compliance with the minimum standards for the elimination of trafficking; law enforcement efforts in 2014 were uneven; the number of convicted traffickers increased, but judges lack of familiarity with anti-trafficking law meant that many offenders were not brought to justice; the government relied heavily on an NGO to identify and provide service to trafficking victims; and its lack of thoroughly implemented victim identification procedures resulted in victims continuing to be arrested, detained, and deported for crimes committed as a direct result of being trafficked (2015)

Illicit drugs: Lebanon is a transit country for hashish, cocaine, heroin, and fenethylene; fenethylene, cannabis, hashish, and some opium are produced in the Bekaa Valley; small amounts of Latin American cocaine and Southwest Asian heroin transit country on way to European markets and for Middle Eastern consumption; money laundering of drug proceeds fuels concern that extremists are benefiting from drug trafficking

LESOTHO

INTRODUCTION

Background: Basutoland was renamed the Kingdom of Lesotho upon independence from the UK in 1966. The Basutho National Party ruled the country during its first two decades. King MOSHOESHOE was exiled in 1990, but returned to Lesotho in 1992 and was reinstated in 1995 and subsequently succeeded by his son, King LETSIE III, in 1996. Constitutional government was restored in 1993 after seven years of military rule. In 1998, violent protests and a military mutiny following a contentious election prompted a brief but bloody intervention by South African and Batswana military forces under the aegis of the Southern African Development Community. Subsequent constitutional reforms restored relative political stability. Peaceful parliamentary elections were held in 2002, but the National Assembly elections in 2007 were hotly contested and aggrieved parties disputed how the electoral law was applied to award proportional seats in the Assembly. In 2012, competitive elections involving 18 parties saw Prime Minister Motsoahae Thomas THABANE form a coalition government—the first in the country's history—that ousted the 14-year incumbent, Pakalitha MOSISILI, who peacefully transferred power the following month. MOSISILI returned to power in snap elections in February 2015 after the collapse of THABANE's coalition government and an alleged attempted military coup.

GEOGRAPHY

Location: Southern Africa, an enclave of South Africa

Geographic coordinates: 29 30 S, 28 30 E

Map references: Africa

Area: *total:* 30,355 sq km
land: 30,355 sq km
water: 0 sq km
country comparison to the world: 142

Area—comparative: slightly smaller than Maryland

Land boundaries: *total:* 1,106 km
border countries (1): South Africa 1,106 km

Coastline: 0 km (landlocked)

Maritime claims: none (landlocked)

Climate: temperate; cool to cold, dry winters; hot, wet summers

Terrain: mostly highland with plateaus, hills, and mountains

Elevation: *mean elevation:* 2,161 m

elevation extremes: *lowest point:* junction of the Orange and Makhaleng Rivers 1,400 m
highest point: Thabana Ntlenyana 3,482 m

Natural resources: water, agricultural and grazing land, diamonds, sand, clay, building stone

Land use: *agricultural land:* 76.1%
arable land: 10.1%;
permanent crops: 0.1%;
permanent pasture: 65.9%
forest: 1.5%
other: 22.4% (2011 est.)
Irrigated land: 30 sq km (2012)

Population—distribution: relatively higher population density in the western half of the nation, with the capital of Maseru, and the smaller cities of Mafeteng, Teyateyaneng, and Leribe attracting the most people

Natural hazards: periodic droughts

Environment—current issues: population pressure forcing settlement in marginal areas results in overgrazing, severe soil erosion, and soil exhaustion; desertification; Highlands Water Project controls, stores, and redirects water to South Africa

Environment—international agreements: *party to:* Biodiversity, Climate Change, Climate Change-Kyoto Protocol, Desertification, Endangered Species, Hazardous Wastes, Law of the Sea, Marine Life Conservation, Ozone Layer Protection, Wetlands
signed, but not ratified: none of the selected agreements

Geography—note: landlocked, completely surrounded by South Africa; mountainous, more than 80% of the country is 1,800 m above sea level

PEOPLE AND SOCIETY

Population: 1,958,042
note: estimates for this country explicitly take into account the effects of excess mortality due to AIDS; this can result in lower life expectancy, higher infant mortality, higher death rates, lower population growth rates, and changes in the distribution of population by age and sex than would otherwise be expected (July 2017 est.)
country comparison to the world: 148

Nationality: *noun:* Mosotho (singular), Basotho (plural)

adjective: Basotho

Ethnic groups: Sotho 99.7%, Europeans, Asians, and other 0.3%

Languages: Sesotho (official) (southern Sotho), English (official), Zulu, Xhosa

Religions: Christian 80%, indigenous beliefs 20%

Demographic profile: Lesotho faces great socioeconomic challenges. More than half of its population lives below the property line, and the country's HIV/AIDS prevalence rate is the second highest in the world. In addition, Lesotho is a small, mountainous, landlocked country with little arable land, leaving its population vulnerable to food shortages and reliant on remittances. Lesotho's persistently high infant, child, and maternal mortality rates have been increasing during the last decade, according to the last two Demographic and Health Surveys. Despite these significant shortcomings, Lesotho has made good progress in education; it is on-track to achieve universal primary education and has one of the highest adult literacy rates in Africa.

Lesotho's migration history is linked to its unique geography; it is surrounded by South Africa with which it shares linguistic and cultural traits. Lesotho at one time had more of its workforce employed outside its borders than any other country. Today remittances equal about 17% of its GDP. With few job options at home, a high rate of poverty, and higher wages available across the border, labor migration to South Africa replaced agriculture as the prevailing Basotho source of income decades ago. The majority of Basotho migrants are single men contracted to work as gold miners in South Africa. However, migration trends changed in the 1990s, and fewer men found mining jobs in South Africa because of declining gold prices, stricter immigration policies, and a preference for South African workers.

Although men still dominate cross-border labor migration, more women are working in South Africa, mostly as domestics, because they are widows or their husbands are unemployed. Internal rural-urban flows have also become more frequent, with more women migrating within the country to take up jobs in the garment industry or moving to care for loved ones with HIV/AIDS. Lesotho's small population of immigrants is increasingly composed of Taiwanese and Chinese migrants who are involved in the textile industry and small retail businesses.

Age structure: *0-14 years:* 32.12% (male 316,106/female 312,869)
15-24 years: 19.43% (male 181,481/female 199,190)
25-54 years: 37.94% (male 362,798/female 380,001)
55-64 years: 5.01% (male 52,293/female 45,828)
65 years and over: 5.5% (male 55,163/female 52,464) (2017 est.)

Dependency ratios: *total dependency ratio:* 66.9
youth dependency ratio: 59.5
elderly dependency ratio: 7.4
potential support ratio: 13.5 (2015 est.)

Median age: *total:* 24.2 years
male: 24.2 years
female: 24.2 years (2017 est.)
country comparison to the world: 161

Population growth rate: 0.28% (2017 est.)
country comparison to the world: 173

Birth rate: 24.6 births/1,000 population (2017 est.)
country comparison to the world: 50

Death rate: 15 deaths/1,000 population (2017 est.)
country comparison to the world: 1

Net migration rate: -6.8 migrant(s)/1,000 population (2017 est.)
country comparison to the world: 203

Population distribution: relatively higher population density in the western half of the nation, with the capital of Maseru, and the smaller cities of Mafeteng, Teyateyaneng, and Leribe attracting the most people

Urbanization: *urban population:* 28.4% of total population (2017)
rate of urbanization: 2.85% annual rate of change (2015-20 est.)

Major urban areas—population: MASERU (capital) 267,000 (2014)

Sex ratio: *at birth:* 1.03 male(s)/female
0-14 years: 1.01 male(s)/female
15-24 years: 0.91 male(s)/female
25-54 years: 0.96 male(s)/female
55-64 years: 1.14 male(s)/female
65 years and over: 1.03 male(s)/female
total population: 0.98 male(s)/female (2016 est.)

Mother's mean age at first birth: 21 years
note: median age at first birth among women 25-29 (2014 est.)

Maternal mortality ratio: 487 deaths/100,000 live births (2015 est.)
country comparison to the world: 22

Infant mortality rate: *total:* 46.1 deaths/1,000 live births
male: 49.7 deaths/1,000 live births
female: 42.4 deaths/1,000 live births (2017 est.)
country comparison to the world: 37

Life expectancy at birth: *total population:* 53 years
male: 53 years
female: 53.1 years (2017 est.)
country comparison to the world: 216

Total fertility rate: 2.63 children born/woman (2017 est.)
country comparison to the world: 74

Contraceptive prevalence rate: 60.2% (2014)

Health expenditures: 10.6% of GDP (2014)
country comparison to the world: 19

Hospital bed density: 1.3 beds/1,000 population (2006)

Drinking water source:
improved:
urban: 94.6% of population

rural: 77% of population
total: 81.8% of population
unimproved:
urban: 5.4% of population
rural: 23% of population
total: 18.2% of population (2015 est.)

Sanitation facility access:
improved:
urban: 37.3% of population
rural: 27.6% of population
total: 30.3% of population
unimproved:
urban: 62.7% of population
rural: 72.4% of population
total: 69.7% of population (2015 est.)

HIV/AIDS—adult prevalence rate: 25% (2016 est.)
country comparison to the world: 2

HIV/AIDS—people living with HIV/AIDS: 330,000 (2016 est.)
country comparison to the world: 19

HIV/AIDS—deaths: 9,900 (2016 est.)
country comparison to the world: 21

Obesity—adult prevalence rate: 16.6% (2016)
country comparison to the world: 122

Children under the age of 5 years underweight: 10.3% (2014)
country comparison to the world: 54

Education expenditures: 13% of GDP (2008)
country comparison to the world: 1

Literacy: *definition:* age 15 and over can read and write
total population: 79.4%
male: 70.1%
female: 88.3% (2015 est.)

School life expectancy (primary to tertiary education): *total:* 11 years
male: 10 years
female: 11 years (2014)

Unemployment, youth ages 15-24: *total:* 34.4%
male: NA
female: NA (2013 est.)
country comparison to the world: 18

GOVERNMENT

Country name: *conventional long form:* Kingdom of Lesotho
conventional short form: Lesotho
local long form: Kingdom of Lesotho
local short form: Lesotho
former: Basutoland
etymology: the name translates as "Land of the Sesotho Speakers"

Government type: parliamentary constitutional monarchy

Capital: *name:* Maseru

geographic coordinates: 29 19 S, 27 29 E
time difference: UTC+2 (7 hours ahead of Washington, DC, during Standard Time)

Administrative divisions: 10 districts; Berea, Butha-Buthe, Leribe, Mafeteng, Maseru, Mohale's Hoek, Mokhotlong, Qacha's Nek, Quthing, Thaba-Tseka

Independence: 4 October 1966 (from the UK)

National holiday: Independence Day, 4 October (1966)

Constitution: history: previous 1959, 1967; latest adopted 2 April 1993 (effectively restoring the 1967 version)
amendments: proposed by Parliament; passage of amendments affecting constitutional provisions including fundamental rights and freedoms, sovereignty of the kingdom, the office of the king, and powers of Parliament requires a majority vote by the National Assembly, approval by the Senate, approval in a referendum by a majority of qualified voters, and assent by the king; passage of amendments other than those specified provisions requires at least a two-thirds majority vote in both Parliament houses; amended several times, last in 2011 (2017)

Legal system: mixed legal system of English common law and Roman-Dutch law; judicial review of legislative acts in High Court and Court of Appeal

International law organization participation: accepts compulsory ICJ jurisdiction with reservations; accepts ICCt jurisdiction

Citizenship: *citizenship by birth:* yes
citizenship by descent: yes
dual citizenship recognized: no
residency requirement for naturalization: 5 years

Suffrage: 18 years of age; universal

Executive branch: *chief of state:* King LETSIE III (since 7 February 1996); note—King LETSIE III formerly occupied the throne from November 1990 to February 1995 while his father was in exile

head of government: Prime Minister Thomas Motsoahae THABANE (since 16 June 2017)
cabinet: consists of the Prime Minister, appointed by the King on the advice of the Council of State, and 25 other Ministers
elections/appointments: the monarchy is hereditary, but under the terms of the constitution that came into effect after the March 1993 election, the monarch is a "living symbol of national unity" with no executive or legislative powers; under traditional law, the college of chiefs has the power to depose the monarch, to determine next in line of succession, or to serve as regent in the event that a successor is not of mature age; following legislative elections, the leader of the majority party or majority coalition in the Assembly automatically becomes prime minister

Legislative branch: *description:* bicameral Parliament consists of the Senate (33 seats; 22 principal chiefs and 11 other senators nominated by the king with the advice of the Council of State, a 13-member body of key government and nongovernment officials; members serve 5-year terms) and the National Assembly (120 seats; 80 members directly elected in single-seat constituencies by simple majority vote and 40 elected through proportional representation; members serve 5-year terms)
elections: last held on 3 June 2017 (next to be held in 2022)

election results: National Assembly—percent of votes by party—ABC 40.5%, DC 25.8%, LCD 9.0%, AD 7.3%, MEC 5.1%, BNP 4.1, PFD 2.3%, other 5.9%; seats by party—ABC 48, DC 30, LCD 11, AD 9, MEC 6, BNP 5, PFD 3, other 5, vacant 3

Judicial branch: *highest court(s):* Court of Appeal (consists of the court president, such number of justices of appeal as set by Parliament, and the Chief Justice and the puisne judges of the High Court ex officio); High Court (consists of the chief justice and such number of puisne judges as set by Parliament); note—both the Court of Appeal and the High Court have jurisdiction in constitutional issues

judge selection and term of office: Court of Appeal president and High Court chief justice appointed by the monarch on the advice of the prime minister; puisne judges appointed by the monarch on advice of the Judicial Service Commission, an independent body of judicial officers and officials designated by the monarch; judges of both courts can serve until age 75

subordinate courts: Magistrate Courts; customary or traditional courts; military courts

Political parties and leaders: All Basotho Convention or ABC [Thomas Motsoahae THABANE] Alliance of Democrats or AD [Monyane MOLELEKI]
Basotho Congress Party or BCP [Thulo MAHLAKENG]
Basotho National Party or BNP [Thesele MASERIBANE]
Democratic Congress or DC [Pakalitha MOSISILI]
Lesotho Congress for Democracy or LCD [Mothetjoa METSING]
Lesotho Peoples Congress or LPC [Mabusetsa MAKHARILELE]
Maremaltou Freedom Party or MFP [Tlhoriso LEKATSA]
Movement of Economic Change or MEC [Selibe MOCHOBOROANE]
National Independent Party or NIP [Kimetso MATHABA]
Popular Front for Democracy of PFD [Lekhetho RAKUOANE]
Reformed Congress of Lesotho or RCL [Keketso RANTSO]
Truth Reconciliation Unity or TRU [Tlali KHASU]
Political pressure groups and leaders: Media Institute of Southern Africa or MISA, Lesotho chapter [Tsebo MATASA] (media freedom advocates)

International organization participation: ACP, AfDB, AU, C, CD, FAO, G-77, IAEA, IBRD, ICAO, ICCt, ICRM, IDA, IFAD, IFC, IFRCS, ILO, IMF, Interpol, IOC, IOM, IPU, ISO (correspondent), ITU, MIGA, NAM, OPCW, SACU, SADC, UN, UNAMID, UNCTAD, UNESCO, UNHCR, UNIDO, UNWTO, UPU, WCO, WFTU (NGOs), WHO, WIPO, WMO, WTO

Diplomatic representation in the US: *chief of mission:* Ambassador Eliachim Molapi SEBATANE (since 18 January 2012)
chancery: 2511 Massachusetts Avenue NW, Washington, DC 20008

telephone: [1] (202) 797-5533
FAX: [1] (202) 234-6815

Diplomatic representation from the US: *chief of mission:* Ambassador Matthew T. HARRINGTON (October 2014)
embassy: 254 Kingsway Road, Maseru West (Consular Section)
mailing address: P.O. Box 333, Maseru 100, Lesotho
telephone: [266] 22 312 666
FAX: [266] 22 310 116

Flag description: three horizontal stripes of blue (top), white, and green in the proportions of 3:4:3; the colors represent rain, peace, and prosperity respectively; centered in the white stripe is a black Basotho hat representing the indigenous people; the flag was unfurled in October 2006 to celebrate 40 years of independence

National symbol(s): mokorotio (Basotho hat); national colors: blue, white, green, black

National anthem: *name:* "Lesotho fatse la bo ntat'a rona" (Lesotho, Land of Our Fathers)
lyrics/music: Francois COILLARD/Ferdinand-Samuel LAUR
note: adopted 1967; music derives from an 1823 Swiss songbook

ECONOMY

Economy—overview: Small, mountainous, and completely landlocked by South Africa, Lesotho depends on a narrow economic base of textile manufacturing, agriculture, remittances, and regional customs revenue. About three-fourths of the people live in rural areas and engage in animal herding and subsistence agriculture, although Lesotho produces less than 20% of the nation's demand for food. Agriculture is vulnerable to weather and climate variability.

Lesotho relies on South Africa for much of its economic activity; Lesotho imports 85% of the goods it consumes from South Africa, including most agricultural inputs. Households depend heavily on remittances from family members working in South Africa in mines, on farms, and as domestic workers, though mining employment has declined substantially since the 1990s. Lesotho is a member of the Southern Africa Customs Union (SACU), and revenues from SACU accounted for roughly 26% of total GDP in 2016; however, SACU revenues are volatile and expected to decline over the next 5 years. Lesotho also gains royalties from the South African Government for water transferred to South Africa from a dam and reservoir system in Lesotho. However, the government continues to strengthen its tax system to reduce dependency on customs duties and other transfers.

The government maintains a large presence in the economy—government consumption accounted for about 26% of GDP in 2017. The government remains Lesotho's largest employer; in 2016, the government wage bill rose to 23% of GDP—the largest in sub-Saharan Africa. Lesotho's largest private employer is the textile and garment industry—approximately 36,000 Basotho, mainly women, work in factories producing garments for

export to South Africa and the US. Diamond mining in Lesotho has grown in recent years and accounted for nearly 35% of total exports in 2015. Lesotho managed steady GDP growth at an average of 4.5% from 2010 to 2014, dropping to about 2.5% in 2015-16, but poverty remains widespread around 57% of the total population.

GDP (purchasing power parity): $7.448 billion (2017 est.)
$7.118 billion (2016 est.)
$6.954 billion (2015 est.)
note: data are in 2017 dollars
country comparison to the world: 167

GDP (official exchange rate): $2.721 billion (2016 est.)

GDP—real growth rate: 4.6% (2017 est.)
2.4% (2016 est.)
2.5% (2015 est.)
country comparison to the world: 50

GDP—per capita (PPP): $3,900 (2017 est.)
$3,700 (2016 est.)
$3,600 (2015 est.)
note: data are in 2017 dollars
country comparison to the world: 180

Gross national saving: 20.3% of GDP (2017 est.)
21% of GDP (2016 est.)
23.8% of GDP (2015 est.)
country comparison to the world: 87

GDP—composition, by end use:
household consumption: 69.2%
government consumption: 26.4%
investment in fixed capital: 31.4%
investment in inventories: -13.4%
exports of goods and services: 40.8%
imports of goods and services: -54.4% (2017 est.)

GDP—composition, by sector of origin:
agriculture: 5.3%
industry: 34.6%
services: 60.1% (2017 est.)

Agriculture—products: corn, wheat, pulses, sorghum, barley; livestock

Industries: food, beverages, textiles, apparel assembly, handicrafts, construction, tourism

Industrial production growth rate: 8.2% (2017 est.)
country comparison to the world: 17

Labor force: 930,800 (2017 est.)
country comparison to the world: 149

Labor force—by occupation: *agriculture:* 86%
industry and services: 14%
note: most of the resident population is engaged in subsistence agriculture; roughly 35% of the active male wage earners work in South Africa (2002 est.)

Unemployment rate: 28.1% (2014 est.)
25% (2008 est.)
country comparison to the world: 202

Population below poverty line: 57% (2016 est.)

Household income or consumption by percentage share: *lowest 10%:* 1%
highest 10%: 39.4% (2003)

Distribution of family income—Gini index: 63.2 (1995)

56 (1986-87)
country comparison to the world: 1

Budget: *revenues:* $1.057 billion
expenditures: $1.16 billion (2017 est.)
Taxes and other revenues: 38.8% of GDP (2017 est.)
country comparison to the world: 40

Budget surplus (+) or deficit (-): -3.8% of GDP (2017 est.)
country comparison to the world: 139

Public debt: 47.8% of GDP (2016 est.)
49.5% of GDP (2015 est.)
country comparison to the world: 105

Fiscal year: 1 April—31 March

Inflation rate (consumer prices): 6.6% (2017 est.)
6.4% (2016 est.)
country comparison to the world: 190

Central bank discount rate: 6.75% (2 February 2016)
6.25% (31 December 2015)
country comparison to the world: 53

Commercial bank prime lending rate: 12% (31 December 2017 est.)
11.58% (31 December 2016 est.)
country comparison to the world: 67

Stock of narrow money: $301.5 million (31 December 2017 est.)
$356.3 million (31 December 2016 est.)
country comparison to the world: 179

Stock of broad money: $703.2 million (31 December 2017 est.)
$725.2 million (31 December 2016 est.)
country comparison to the world: 178

Stock of domestic credit: $225.4 million (31 December 2017 est.)
$230.9 million (31 December 2016 est.)
country comparison to the world: 182

Current account balance: -$232 million (2017 est.)
-$174 million (2016 est.)
country comparison to the world: 91

Exports: $1.031 billion (2017 est.)
$894 million (2016 est.)
country comparison to the world: 157

Exports—commodities: manufactures (clothing, footwear), wool and mohair, food and live animals, electricity, water, diamonds

Exports—partners: South Africa 56.5%, US 35.4% (2016)

Imports: $1.718 billion (2017 est.)
$1.613 billion (2016 est.)
country comparison to the world: 165

Imports—commodities: food; building materials, vehicles, machinery, medicines, petroleum products

Imports—partners: South Africa 84.5% (2016)

Reserves of foreign exchange and gold: $983 million (31 December 2017 est.)
$925.2 million (31 December 2016 est.)
country comparison to the world: 126

Debt—external: $952.5 million (31 December 2017 est.)

$921.3 million (31 December 2016 est.)
country comparison to the world: 168

Stock of direct foreign investment—at home: $532.5 million (31 December 2017 est.)
$456.5 million (31 December 2016 est.)
country comparison to the world: 123

Exchange rates: maloti (LSL) per US dollar—
14.48 (2017 est.)
14.71 (2016 est.)
14.71 (2015 est.)
12.76 (2014 est.)
10.85 (2013 est.)

ENERGY

Electricity access: *population without electricity:* 1,700,000
electrification—*total population:* 17%
electrification—urban areas: 43%
electrification—rural areas: 8% (2013)

Electricity—production: 600 million kWh (2015 est.)
country comparison to the world: 166

Electricity—consumption: 763 million kWh (2015 est.)
country comparison to the world: 163

Electricity—exports: 0 kWh (2016 est.)
country comparison to the world: 161

Electricity—imports: 205 million kWh (2015 est.)
country comparison to the world: 92

Electricity—installed generating capacity: 80,000 kW (2015 est.)
country comparison to the world: 184

Electricity—from fossil fuels: 0% of total installed capacity (2015 est.)
country comparison to the world: 215

Electricity—from nuclear fuels: 0% of total installed capacity (2015 est.)
country comparison to the world: 130

Electricity—from hydroelectric plants: 100% of total installed capacity (2015 est.)
country comparison to the world: 1

Electricity—from other renewable sources: 0% of total installed capacity (2015 est.)
country comparison to the world: 195

Crude oil—production: 0 bbl/day (2016 est.)
country comparison to the world: 160

Crude oil—exports: 0 bbl/day (2014 est.)
country comparison to the world: 154

Crude oil—imports: 0 bbl/day (2014 est.)
country comparison to the world: 150

Crude oil—proved reserves: 0 bbl (1 January 2017 es)
country comparison to the world: 157

Refined petroleum products—production: 0 bbl/day (2014 est.)
country comparison to the world: 165

Refined petroleum products—consumption: 5,000 bbl/day (2015 est.)
country comparison to the world: 178

Refined petroleum products—exports: 0 bbl/day (2014 est.)

country comparison to the world: 172

Refined petroleum products—imports: 5,121 bbl/day (2014 est.)
country comparison to the world: 166

Natural gas—production: 0 cu m (2013 est.)
country comparison to the world: 161

Natural gas—consumption: 0 cu m (2013 est.)
country comparison to the world: 202

Natural gas—exports: 0 cu m (2013 est.)
country comparison to the world: 139

Natural gas—imports: 0 cu m (2013 est.)
country comparison to the world: 148

Natural gas—proved reserves: 0 cu m (1 January 2014 es)
country comparison to the world: 163

Carbon dioxide emissions from consumption of energy: 300,000 Mt (2013 est.)
country comparison to the world: 193

COMMUNICATIONS

Telephones—fixed lines: *total subscriptions:* 41,158
subscriptions per 100 inhabitants: 2 (July 2016 est.)
country comparison to the world: 161

Telephones—mobile cellular: *total:* 2,282,917
subscriptions per 100 inhabitants: 117 (July 2016 est.)
country comparison to the world: 151

Telephone system: *general assessment:* rudimentary system consisting of a modest number of landlines, a small microwave radio relay system, and a small radiotelephone communication system; mobile-cellular telephone system is expanding
domestic: Econet Telecom Lesotho provides telecom services; fixed-line density is low; mobile-cellular service dominates the market with a subscribership now over 115 per 100 persons
international: country code—266; satellite earth station—1 Intelsat (Atlantic Ocean) (2016)

Broadcast media: 1 state-owned TV station and 2 state-owned radio stations; government controls most private broadcast media; satellite TV subscription service available; transmissions of multiple international broadcasters obtainable (2008)

Internet country code: .ls
Internet users: total: 534,360

percent of population: 27.4% (July 2016 est.)
country comparison to the world: 169

TRANSPORTATION

Civil aircraft registration country code prefix: 7P (2016)

Airports: 24 (2013)
country comparison to the world: 132

Airports—with paved runways: *total:* 3
over 3,047 m: 1
914 to 1,523 m: 1
under 914 m: 1 (2017)

Airports—with unpaved runways: *total:* 21
914 to 1,523 m: 5
under 914 m: 16 (2013)

Roadways: *total:* 5,940 km
paved: 1,069 km
unpaved: 4,871 km (2011)
country comparison to the world: 150

MILITARY AND SECURITY

Military expenditures: 1.85% of GDP (2016)
1.89% of GDP (2015)
1.89% of GDP (2014)
1.89% of GDP (2013)
1.99% of GDP (2012)
country comparison to the world: 43

Military branches: Lesotho Defense Force (LDF): Army (includes Air Wing) (2012)

Military service age and obligation: 18-24 years of age for voluntary military service; no conscription; women serve as commissioned officers (2012)

Military—note: Lesotho's declared policy for its military is the maintenance of the country's sovereignty and the preservation of internal security; in practice, external security is guaranteed by South Africa

TRANSNATIONAL ISSUES

Disputes—international: South Africa has placed military units to assist police operations along the border of Lesotho, Zimbabwe, and Mozambique to control smuggling, poaching, and illegal migration

Trafficking in persons: current situation: Lesotho is a source, transit, and destination country for women and children subjected to forced labor and sex trafficking and for men subjected to forced labor; in Lesotho and South Africa, Basotho women and children are subjected to domestic servitude, and Basotho children increasingly endure commercial sexual exploitation; some Basotho men who voluntarily migrate to South Africa for work become victims of forced labor in agriculture and mining or are coerced into committing crimes; foreign nationals continue to traffic fellow citizens in Lesotho

tier rating: Tier 2 Watch List—Lesotho does not fully comply with the minimum standards for the elimination of trafficking; however, it is making significant efforts to do so; in 2014, Lesotho was granted a waiver from an otherwise required downgrade to Tier 3 because its government has a written plan that, if implemented would constitute making significant efforts to bring itself into compliance with the minimum standards for the elimination of trafficking; the government failed to initiate any prosecutions against alleged traffickers and has not convicted any offenders under the 2011 anti-trafficking act, which remains unimplemented for a fifth year; authorities did not develop formal victim identification and referral procedures, did not establish victim care centers, as required under the 2011 anti-trafficking act, and did not support NGOs offering victims protective services (2015)

LIBERIA

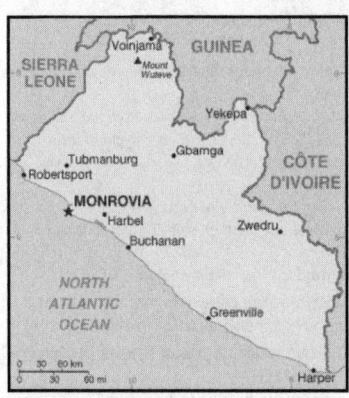

INTRODUCTION

Background: Settlement of freed slaves from the US in what is today Liberia began in 1822; by 1847, the Americo-Liberians were able to establish a republic. William TUBMAN, president from 1944-71, did much to promote foreign investment and to bridge the economic, social, and political gaps between the descendants of the original settlers and the inhabitants of the interior. In 1980, a military coup led by Samuel DOE ushered in a decade of authoritarian rule. In December 1989, Charles TAYLOR launched a rebellion against DOE's regime that led to a prolonged civil war in which DOE was killed. A period of relative peace in 1997 allowed for an election that brought TAYLOR to power, but major fighting resumed in 2000. An August 2003 peace agreement ended the war and prompted the resignation of former president Charles TAYLOR, who was convicted by the UN-backed Special Court for Sierra Leone in The Hague for his involvement in Sierra Leone's civil war. After two years of rule by a transitional government, democratic elections in late 2005 brought President Ellen JOHNSON SIRLEAF to power. She subsequently won reelection in 2011 but was challenged to rebuild Liberia's economy, particularly following the 2014-15 Ebola epidemic, and to reconcile a nation still recovering from 14 years of fighting. In July 2016, the UN handed over peacekeeping responsibility to Liberia and reduced the UN troop presence, which now serves a support role. Constitutional term limits barred President JOHNSON SIRLEAF from running for re-election. The November 2017 presidential run-off election was halted pending a ruling on fraud allegations.

GEOGRAPHY

Location: Western Africa, bordering the North Atlantic Ocean, between Cote d'Ivoire and Sierra Leone

Geographic coordinates: 6 30 N, 9 30 W

Map references: Africa

Area: *total:* 111,369 sq km
land: 96,320 sq km
water: 15,049 sq km
country comparison to the world: 105

Area—comparative: slightly larger than Tennessee

Land boundaries: *total:* 1,667 km
border countries (3): Guinea 590 km, Cote d'Ivoire 778 km, Sierra Leone 299 km

Coastline: 579 km

Maritime claims: *territorial sea:* 200 nm

Climate: tropical; hot, humid; dry winters with hot days and cool to cold nights; wet, cloudy summers with frequent heavy showers

Terrain: mostly flat to rolling coastal plains rising to rolling plateau and low mountains in northeast

Elevation: *mean elevation:* 243 m

elevation extremes: *lowest point:* Atlantic Ocean 0 m
highest point: Mount Wuteve 1,447 m

Natural resources: iron ore, timber, diamonds, gold, hydropower

Land use: *agricultural land:* 28.1%
arable land: 5.2%;
permanent crops: 2.1%;
permanent pasture: 20.8%;
forest: 44.6%
other: 27.3% (2011 est.)
Irrigated land: 30 sq km (2012)

Population—distribution: more than half of the population lives in urban areas, with approximately one-third living within an 80-km radius of Monrovia

Natural hazards: dust-laden harmattan winds blow from the Sahara (December to March)

Environment—current issues: tropical rain forest deforestation; soil erosion; loss of biodiversity; pollution of coastal waters from oil residue and raw sewage

Environment—international agreements: *party to:* Biodiversity, Climate Change, Climate Change-Kyoto Protocol, Desertification, Endangered Species, Hazardous Wastes, Law of the Sea, Ozone Layer Protection, Ship Pollution, Tropical Timber 83, Tropical Timber 94, Wetlands
signed, but not ratified: Environmental Modification, Marine Life Conservation

Geography—note: facing the Atlantic Ocean, the coastline is characterized by lagoons, mangrove

537

swamps, and river-deposited sandbars; the inland grassy plateau supports limited agriculture

PEOPLE AND SOCIETY

Population: 4,689,021 (July 2017 est.)
country comparison to the world: 125

Nationality: *noun:* Liberian(s)
adjective: Liberian

Ethnic groups: Kpelle 20.3%, Bassa 13.4%, Grebo 10%, Gio 8%, Mano 7.9%, Kru 6%, Lorma 5.1%, Kissi 4.8%, Gola 4.4%, other 20.1% (2008 Census)

Languages: English 20% (official), some 20 ethnic group languages few of which can be written or used in correspondence

Religions: Christian 85.6%, Muslim 12.2%, Traditional 0.6%, other 0.2%, none 1.4% (2008 Census)

Demographic profile: Liberia's high fertility rate of nearly 5 children per woman and large youth cohort—more than 60% of the population is under the age of 25—will sustain a high dependency ratio for many years to come. Significant progress has been made in preventing child deaths, despite a lack of health care workers and infrastructure. Infant and child mortality have dropped nearly 70% since 1990; the annual reduction rate of about 5.4% is the highest in Africa.

Nevertheless, Liberia's high maternal mortality rate remains among the world's worst; it reflects a high unmet need for family planning services, frequency of early childbearing, lack of quality obstetric care, high adolescent fertility, and a low proportion of births attended by a medical professional. Female mortality is also increased by the prevalence of female genital cutting (FGC), which is practiced by 10 of Liberia's 16 tribes and affects more than two-thirds of women and girls. FGC is an initiation ritual performed in rural bush schools, which teach traditional beliefs on marriage and motherhood and are an obstacle to formal classroom education for Liberian girls.

Liberia has been both a source and a destination for refugees. During Liberia's 14-year civil war (1989-2003), more than 250,000 people became refugees and another half million were internally displaced. Between 2004 and the cessation of refugee status for Liberians in June 2012, the UNHCR helped more than 155,000 Liberians to voluntarily repatriate, while others returned home on their own. Some Liberian refugees spent more than two decades living in other West African countries. Liberia hosted more than 125,000 Ivoirian refugees escaping post-election violence in 2010-11; as of mid-2017, about 12,000 Ivoirian refugees were still living in Liberia as of October 2017 because of instability.

Age structure: *0-14 years:* 43.82% (male 1,038,452/female 1,016,491)
15-24 years: 19.56% (male 457,806/female 459,289)
25-54 years: 30.33% (male 699,879/female 722,244)
55-64 years: 3.43% (male 82,616/female 78,003)

65 years and over: 2.86% (male 65,979/female 68,262) (2017 est.)

Dependency ratios: *total dependency ratio:* 83.2
youth dependency ratio: 77.6
elderly dependency ratio: 5.5
potential support ratio: 18.1 (2015 est.)

Median age: *total:* 17.8 years
male: 17.5 years
female: 18 years (2017 est.)
country comparison to the world: 211

Population growth rate: 2.5% (2017 est.)
country comparison to the world: 19

Birth rate: 38.3 births/1,000 population (2017 est.)
country comparison to the world: 10

Death rate: 7.6 deaths/1,000 population (2017 est.)
country comparison to the world: 105

Net migration rate: -5.7 migrant(s)/1,000 population (2017 est.)
country comparison to the world: 194

Population distribution: more than half of the population lives in urban areas, with approximately one-third living within an 80-km radius of Monrovia

Urbanization: *urban population:* 50.5% of total population (2017)
rate of urbanization: 3.24% annual rate of change (2015-20 est.)

Major urban areas—population: MONROVIA (capital) 1.264 million (2015)

Sex ratio: *at birth:* 1.03 male(s)/female
0-14 years: 1.02 male(s)/female
15-24 years: 0.97 male(s)/female
25-54 years: 0.99 male(s)/female
55-64 years: 0.93 male(s)/female
65 years and over: 0.97 male(s)/female
total population: 0.99 male(s)/female (2016 est.)

Mother's mean age at first birth: 19.2 years
note: median age at first birth among women 25-29 (2013 est.)

Maternal mortality ratio: 725 deaths/100,000 live births (2015 est.)
country comparison to the world: 7

Infant mortality rate: *total:* 52.2 deaths/1,000 live births
male: 56.7 deaths/1,000 live births
female: 47.6 deaths/1,000 live births (2017 est.)
country comparison to the world: 24

Life expectancy at birth: *total population:* 63.3 years
male: 61.2 years
female: 65.5 years (2017 est.)
country comparison to the world: 195

Total fertility rate: 5.06 children born/woman (2017 est.)
country comparison to the world: 14

Contraceptive prevalence rate: 20.2% (2013)

Health expenditures: 10% of GDP (2014)
country comparison to the world: 25

Physicians density: 0.01 physicians/1,000 population (2008)

Hospital bed density: 0.8 beds/1,000 population (2010)

Drinking water source:
improved:
urban: 88.6% of population
rural: 62.6% of population
total: 75.6% of population
unimproved:
urban: 11.4% of population
rural: 37.4% of population
total: 24.4% of population (2015 est.)

Sanitation facility access:
improved:
urban: 28% of population
rural: 5.9% of population
total: 16.9% of population
unimproved:
urban: 72% of population
rural: 94.1% of population
total: 83.1% of population (2015 est.)

HIV/AIDS—adult prevalence rate: 1.6% (2016 est.)
country comparison to the world: 31

HIV/AIDS—people living with HIV/AIDS: 43,000 (2016 est.)
country comparison to the world: 60

HIV/AIDS—deaths: 2,800 (2016 est.)
country comparison to the world: 45

Major infectious diseases: *degree of risk:* very high
food or waterborne diseases: bacterial and protozoal diarrhea, hepatitis A, and typhoid fever
vectorborne diseases: malaria, dengue fever, and yellow fever
water contact disease: schistosomiasis
aerosolized dust or soil contact disease: Lassa fever
animal contact disease: rabies (2016)

Obesity—adult prevalence rate: 9.9% (2016)
country comparison to the world: 141

Children under the age of 5 years underweight: 15.3% (2013)
country comparison to the world: 28

Education expenditures: 2.8% of GDP (2012)
country comparison to the world: 144

Literacy: *definition:* age 15 and over can read and write
total population: 47.6%
male: 62.4%
female: 32.8% (2015 est.)

Unemployment, youth ages 15-24: *total:* 6%
male: 4.3%
female: 7.6% (2010 est.)
country comparison to the world: 126

GOVERNMENT

Country name: *conventional long form:* Republic of Liberia
conventional short form: Liberia
etymology: name derives from the Latin word "liber" meaning "free"; so named because the nation was created as a homeland for liberated African-American slaves

Government type: presidential republic

Capital: *name:* Monrovia

geographic coordinates: 6 18 N, 10 48 W

time difference: UTC 0 (5 hours ahead of Washington, DC, during Standard Time)

Administrative divisions: 15 counties; Bomi, Bong, Gbarpolu, Grand Bassa, Grand Cape Mount, Grand Gedeh, Grand Kru, Lofa, Margibi, Maryland, Montserrado, Nimba, River Cess, River Gee, Sinoe

Independence: 26 July 1847

National holiday: Independence Day, 26 July (1847)

Constitution: history: previous 1847 (at independence); latest drafted 19 October 1983, revised version adopted by referendum 3 July 1984, effective 6 January 1986

amendments: proposed by agreement of at least two-thirds of both National Assembly houses or by petition of at least 10,000 citizens; passage requires at least two-thirds majority approval of both houses and approval in a referendum by at least two-thirds majority of registered voters; amended 2011; note—a series of amendment proposals approved by the Constitution Review Conference in early 2015 are pending a referendum ahead of October 2017 elections (2017)

Legal system: mixed legal system of common law (based on Anglo-American law) and customary law

International law organization participation: accepts compulsory ICJ jurisdiction with reservations; accepts ICCt jurisdiction

Citizenship: *citizenship by birth:* no

citizenship by descent only: at least one parent must be a citizen of Liberia

dual citizenship recognized: no

residency requirement for naturalization: 2 years

Suffrage: 18 years of age; universal

Executive branch: *chief of state:* President George WEAH (since 22 January 2018); Vice President Jewel TAYLOR (since 22 January 2018); note—the president is both chief of state and head of government

head of government: President George WEAH (since 22 January 2018); Vice President Jewel Taylor (since 22 January 2018)

cabinet: Cabinet appointed by the president, confirmed by the Senate

elections/appointments: president directly elected by absolute majority popular vote in 2 rounds if needed for a 6-year term (eligible for a second term); election last held on 10 October 2017 (run-off scheduled for 26 December 2017); the runoff originally scheduled for 7 November 2017 was been halted pending a ruling on fraud allegations

election results: George WEAH elected president in second round; percent of vote in first round—George WEAH (Coalition for Democratic Change) 38.4%, Joseph BOAKAI (UP) 28.8%, Charles BRUMSKINE (LP) 9.6%, Prince JOHNSON (MDR) 8.2%, Alexander B. CUMMINGS (ANC) 7.2%, other 7.8%; percentage of vote in second round—George WEAH 61.5%, Joseph BOAKAI 38.5%

Legislative branch: *description:* bicameral National Assembly consists of the Senate (30 seats; members directly elected in 15 2-seat districts by simple majority vote to serve 9-year staggered terms; each district elects 1 senator and elects the second senator 3 years later, followed by a 6-year hiatus, after which the first Senate seat is up for election) and the House of Representatives (73 seats; members directly elected in single-seat districts by simple majority vote to serve 6-year terms; eligible for a second term)

elections: Senate—last held on 20 December 2014 (originally scheduled for 14 October 2014 but postponed due to Ebola-virus epidemic; next to be held in October 2020); House of Representatives—last held on 10 October 2017 (next to be held in October 2023)

election results: Senate—percent of vote by party—CDC 29.8%, UP 10.3%, LP 11.5%, NPP 6.1%, PUP 4.9%, ANC 4.2%, NDC 1.3%, other 7.6%, independent 24.3%; seats by party—UP 4, CDC 2, LP 2, ANC 1, NDC 1, NPP 1, PUP 1, independent 3

House of Representatives—percent of vote by party/coalition—Coalition for Democratic Change 15.6%, UP 14%, LP 8.7%, ANC 6.1%, PUP 5.9%, ALP 5.1%, MDR 3.4%, other 41.2%; seats by party/coalition—Coalition for Democratic Change 21, UP 19, PUP 5, LP 3, ALP 3, MDR 2, independent 12, other 6, vacant 2

Judicial branch: *highest court(s):* Supreme Court (consists of a chief justice and 4 associate justices); note—the Supreme Court has jurisdiction for all constitutional cases

judge selection and term of office: chief justice and associate justices appointed by the president of Liberia with consent of the Senate; judges can serve until age 70

subordinate courts: judicial circuit courts; special courts including criminal, civil, labor, traffic; magistrate and traditional or customary courts

Political parties and leaders: Alliance for Peace and Democracy or APD [Marcus S. G. DAHN]
All Liberian Party or ALL [Benoi UREY]
Alternative National Congress or ANC [Orishil GOULD]
Coalition for Democratic Change [George WEAH] (includes CDC, NPP, LPDP)
Congress for Democratic Change or CDC [George WEAH]
Liberia Destiny Party or LDP [Nathaniel BARNES]
Liberia National Union or LINU [Nathaniel BLAMA]
Liberia Transformation Party or LTP [Julius SUKU]
Liberia People Democratic Party or LPDP [Alex J. TYLER]
Liberian People's Party or LPP
Liberty Party or LP [J. Fonati KOFFA]

Movement for Democracy and Reconstruction or MDR [Prince Y. JOHNSON]
Movement for Economic Empowerment [J. Mill JONES, Dr.]
Movement for Progressive Change or MPC [Simeon FREEMAN]
National Democratic Coalition or NDC [Dew MAYSON]
National Democratic Party of Liberia or NDPL [D. Nyandeh SIEH]
National Patriotic Party or NPP [Jewel HOWARD TAYLOR]
National Reformist Party or NRP [Maximillian T. W. DIABE]
National Union for Democratic Progress or NUDP [Victor BARNEY]
People's Unification Party or PUP [Isobe GBORKORKOLLIE]
Unity Party or UP [Varney SHERMAN]
United People's Party [MacDonald WENTO]
Victory for Change Party [Marcus R. JONES]

Political pressure groups and leaders: Liberian Federation of Labor Unions or LFLU [Aloysius KIE]
MCSS Teachers Association
National Health Workers Association of Liberia
National Teachers Association of Liberia or NTAL [Mary MULBAH]
other: demobilized former military officers

International organization participation: ACP, AfDB, AU, ECOWAS, EITI (compliant country), FAO, G-77, IAEA, IBRD, ICAO, ICC (NGOs), ICCt, ICRM, IDA, IFAD, IFC, IFRCS, ILO, IMF, IMO, IMSO, Interpol, IOC, IOM, ISO (correspondent), ITU, ITUC (NGOs), MIGA, MINUSMA, NAM, OPCW, UN, UNCTAD, UNESCO, UNIDO, UNWTO, UPU, WCO, WFTU (NGOs), WHO, WIPO, WMO, WTO (observer)

Diplomatic representation in the US: *chief of mission:* Ambassador Lois Cheche BRUTUS (since 29 November 2017)

chancery: 5201 16th Street NW, Washington, DC 20011

telephone: [1] (202) 723-0437

FAX: [1] (202) 723-0436

consulate(s) general: New York

Diplomatic representation from the US: *chief of mission:* Ambassador Christine A. ELDER (since 23 June 2016)

embassy: U.S. Embassy, 502 Benson Street, Monrovia

mailing address: P.O. Box 98, Monrovia

telephone: [231] 77-677-7000

FAX: [231] 77-677-7370

Flag description: 11 equal horizontal stripes of red (top and bottom) alternating with white; a white five-pointed star appears on a blue square in the upper hoist-side corner; the stripes symbolize the signatories of the Liberian Declaration of Independence; the blue square represents the African mainland, and the star represents the freedom granted to the ex-slaves; according to the constitution, the blue color signifies liberty, justice, and fidelity, the white color purity, cleanliness, and

539

guilelessness, and the red color steadfastness, valor, and fervor

note: the design is based on the US flag

National symbol(s): white star; national colors: red, white, blue

National anthem: name: "All Hail, Liberia Hail!" *lyrics/music:* Daniel Bashiel WARNER/Olmstead LUCA

note: lyrics adopted 1847, music adopted 1860; the anthem's author later became the third president of Liberia

ECONOMY

Economy—overview: Liberia is a low-income country that relies heavily on foreign assistance and remittances from the diaspora. It is richly endowed with water, mineral resources, forests, and a climate favorable to agriculture. Its principal exports are iron ore, rubber, diamonds, and gold. Palm oil and cocoa are emerging as new export products. The government has attempted to revive raw timber extraction and is encouraging oil exploration.

In the 1990s and early 2000s, civil war and government mismanagement destroyed much of Liberia's economy, especially infrastructure in and around the capital. Much of the conflict was fueled by control over Liberia's natural resources. With the conclusion of fighting and the installation of a democratically elected government in 2006, businesses that had fled the country began to return. The country achieved high growth during the period 2010-13 due to favorable world prices for its commodities. However, during the 2014-2015 Ebola crisis, the economy declined and many foreign-owned businesses departed with their capital and expertise. The epidemic forced the government to divert scarce resources to combat the spread of the virus, reducing funds available for needed public investment. The cost of addressing the Ebola epidemic coincided with decreased economic activity reducing government revenue, although higher donor support significantly offset this loss. During the same period, global commodities prices for key exports fell and have yet to recover to pre-Ebola levels.

In 2017, gold was a key driver of growth, as a new mining project began its first full year of production; iron ore exports are also increased as Arcelor Mittal opened new mines at Mount Gangra. The completion of the rehabilitation of the Mount Coffee Hydroelectric Dam increased electricity production to support ongoing and future economic activity, although electricity tariffs remain high relative to other countries in the region and transmission infrastructure is limited. Presidential and legislative elections in October 2017 generated election-related spending pressures.

Revitalizing the economy in the future will depend on economic diversification, increasing investment and trade, higher global commodity prices, sustained foreign aid and remittances, development of infrastructure and institutions,

combating corruption, and maintaining political stability and security.

GDP (purchasing power parity): $3.906 billion (2017 est.)
$3.808 billion (2016 est.)
$3.871 billion (2015 est.)
note: data are in 2017 dollars
country comparison to the world: 179

GDP (official exchange rate): $2.14 billion (2016 est.)

GDP—real growth rate: 2.6% (2017 est.)
-1.6% (2016 est.)
0% (2015 est.)
country comparison to the world: 128

GDP—per capita (PPP): $900 (2017 est.)
$900 (2016 est.)
$900 (2015 est.)
note: data are in 2017 dollars
country comparison to the world: 226

Gross national saving: NA% (2017 est.)
-21.9% of GDP (2016 est.)
-2.3% of GDP (2017 est.)

GDP—composition, by end use:
household consumption: 128.8%
government consumption: 16.7%
investment in fixed capital: 19.5%
investment in inventories: 6.7%
exports of goods and services: 17.5%
imports of goods and services: -89.2% (2016 est.)

GDP—composition, by sector of origin:
agriculture: 36.1%
industry: 10.5%
services: 53.4% (2017 est.)

Agriculture—products: rubber, coffee, cocoa, rice, cassava (manioc, tapioca), palm oil, sugarcane, bananas; sheep, goats; timber

Industries: mining (iron ore and gold), rubber processing, palm oil processing, diamonds

Industrial production growth rate: 3.2% (2017 est.)
country comparison to the world: 91

Labor force: 1.677 million (2017 est.)
country comparison to the world: 128

Labor force—by occupation: *agriculture:* 70%
industry: 8%
services: 22% (2000 est.)

Unemployment rate: 2.8% (2014 est.)
country comparison to the world: 30

Population below poverty line: 54.1% (2014 est.)

Household income or consumption by percentage share: *lowest 10%:* 2.4%
highest 10%: 30.1% (2007)

Distribution of family income—Gini index: 32 (2014)
38.2 (2007)
country comparison to the world: 115

Budget: *revenues:* $626.1 million
expenditures: $727.6 million (2017 est.)
Taxes and other revenues: 29.3% of GDP (2017 est.)
country comparison to the world: 87

Budget surplus (+) or deficit (-): -4.7% of GDP (2017 est.)

country comparison to the world: 155

Public debt: 46.5% of GDP (2017 est.)
42.3% of GDP (2016 est.)
country comparison to the world: 111

Fiscal year: calendar year

Inflation rate (consumer prices): 12.8% (2017 est.)
8.8% (2016 est.)
country comparison to the world: 209

Central bank discount rate: 3.2% (2016)
country comparison to the world: 105

Commercial bank prime lending rate: 15.2% (31 December 2017 est.)
13.59% (31 December 2016 est.)
country comparison to the world: 41

Stock of narrow money: $425.9 million (31 December 2017 est.)
$436.4 million (31 December 2016 est.)
country comparison to the world: 171

Stock of broad money: $557 million (31 December 2017 est.)
$639 million (31 December 2016 est.)
country comparison to the world: 183

Stock of domestic credit: $706.1 million (31 December 2017 est.)
$789.4 million (31 December 2016 est.)
country comparison to the world: 170

Market value of publicly traded shares: $NA

Current account balance: -$571 million (2017 est.)
-$520 million (2016 est.)
country comparison to the world: 108

Exports: $202.1 million (2017 est.)
$169.8 million (2016 est.)
country comparison to the world: 189

Exports—commodities: rubber, timber, iron, diamonds, cocoa, coffee

Exports—partners: Poland 18.5%, Switzerland 9.7%, UAE 9.4%, Netherlands 8.9%, Germany 6.1%, US 5.9%, South Africa 5%, China 4.4%, Ghana 4.2% (2016)

Imports: $1.247 billion (2017 est.)
$1.21 billion (2016 est.)
country comparison to the world: 173

Imports—commodities: fuels, chemicals, machinery, transportation equipment, manufactured goods; foodstuffs

Imports—partners: South Korea 38.3%, Singapore 18%, China 15.9%, Japan 10.9% (2016)

Debt—external: $1.049 billion (31 December 2017 est.)
$938.9 million (31 December 2016 est.)
country comparison to the world: 167

Stock of direct foreign investment—at home: $17.01 billion (31 December 2015 est.)
$16.56 billion (31 December 2014 est.)
country comparison to the world: 83

Stock of direct foreign investment—abroad: $201 million (31 December 2013 est.)
$201 million (31 December 2012 est.)
country comparison to the world: 101

Exchange rates: Liberian dollars (LRD) per US dollar—
109.4 (2017 est.)
93.4 (2016 est.)
93.4 (31 December 2015 est.)
85.3 (2014 est.)
83.893 (2013 est.)

ENERGY

Electricity access: *population without electricity:* 3,900,000
electrification—*total population:* 10%
electrification—urban areas: 17%
electrification—rural areas: 3% (2013)

Electricity—production: 70.07 million kWh
note: according to a 2014 household survey, only 4.5% of Liberians use Liberia Electricity Corporation (LEC)power. 4.9% use a community generator, 4.4% have their own generator, 3.9% use vehicle batteries, and 0.8% use other sources of electricity. 81.3% have no access to electricity. LEC accounts for roughly 70 million kWh of ouput. (2016 est.)
country comparison to the world: 202

Electricity—consumption: 39 million kWh (2016 est.)
country comparison to the world: 207

Electricity—exports: 0 kWh (2016 est.)
country comparison to the world: 159

Electricity—imports: 0 kWh (2016 est.)
country comparison to the world: 169

Electricity—installed generating capacity: 125,000 kW (2015 est.)
country comparison to the world: 176

Electricity—from fossil fuels: 63.3% of total installed capacity (2016 est.)
country comparison to the world: 119

Electricity—from nuclear fuels: 0% of total installed capacity (2016 est.)
country comparison to the world: 129

Electricity—from hydroelectric plants: 36.7% of total installed capacity (2016 est.)
country comparison to the world: 57

Electricity—from other renewable sources: 0% of total installed capacity (2016 est.)
country comparison to the world: 194

Crude oil—production: 0 bbl/day (2016 est.)
country comparison to the world: 161

Crude oil—exports: 0 bbl/day (2014 est.)
country comparison to the world: 153

Crude oil—imports: 0 bbl/day (2014 est.)
country comparison to the world: 149

Crude oil—proved reserves: 0 bbl (1 January 2017 es)
country comparison to the world: 158

Refined petroleum products—production: 0 bbl/day (2014 est.)
country comparison to the world: 166

Refined petroleum products—consumption: 6,600 bbl/day (2015 est.)
country comparison to the world: 167

Refined petroleum products—exports: 0 bbl/day (2014 est.)
country comparison to the world: 171

Refined petroleum products—imports: 6,611 bbl/day (2014 est.)
country comparison to the world: 155

Natural gas—production: 0 cu m (2013 est.)
country comparison to the world: 160

Natural gas—consumption: 0 cu m (2013 est.)
country comparison to the world: 201

Natural gas—exports: 0 cu m (2013 est.)
country comparison to the world: 138

Natural gas—imports: 0 cu m (2013 est.)
country comparison to the world: 147

Natural gas—proved reserves: 0 cu m (1 January 2014 es)
country comparison to the world: 162

Carbon dioxide emissions from consumption of energy: 600,000 Mt (2013 est.)
country comparison to the world: 174

COMMUNICATIONS

Telephones—fixed lines: *total subscriptions:* 8,000
subscriptions per 100 inhabitants: less than 1 (July 2016 est.)
country comparison to the world: 198

Telephones—mobile cellular: *total:* 3,834,600
subscriptions per 100 inhabitants: 89 (July 2016 est.)
country comparison to the world: 136

Telephone system: *general assessment:* the limited services available are found almost exclusively in the capital, Monrovia; fixed-line service stagnant and extremely limited; telephone coverage extended to a number of other towns and rural areas by four mobile-cellular network operators
domestic: mobile-cellular subscription base growing and teledensity approached 90 per 100 persons in 2016
international: country code—231; satellite earth station—1 Intelsat (Atlantic Ocean) (2015)

Broadcast media: 8 private and 1 government-owned TV station; satellite TV service available; 1 state-owned radio station; 19 independent radio stations broadcasting in Monrovia, with another 77 local stations operating in other areas; transmissions of 4 international broadcasters are available (2017)

Internet country code: .lr
Internet users: total: 314,717

percent of population: 7.3% (July 2016 est.)
country comparison to the world: 158

TRANSPORTATION

Civil aircraft registration country code prefix: A8 (2016)

Airports: 29 (2013)
country comparison to the world: 117

Airports—with paved runways: *total:* 2
over 3,047 m: 1
1,524 to 2,437 m: 1 (2017)

Airports—with unpaved runways: *total:* 27
1,524 to 2,437 m: 5
914 to 1,523 m: 8
under 914 m: 14 (2013)

Pipelines: oil 4 km (2013)

Railways: *total:* 429 km
standard gauge: 345 km 1.435-m gauge
narrow gauge: 84 km 1.067-m gauge
note: most sections of the railways inoperable due to damage sustained during the civil wars from 1980 to 2003, but many are being rebuilt (2008)
country comparison to the world: 119

Roadways: *total:* 10,600 km
paved: 657 km
unpaved: 9,943 km (2000)
country comparison to the world: 134

Merchant marine: *total:* 3,296
by type: bulk carrier 984, container ship 892, general cargo 120, oil tanker 750, other 550 (2017)
country comparison to the world: 7

Ports and terminals: *major seaport(s):* Buchanan, Monrovia

MILITARY AND SECURITY

Military expenditures: 0.62% of GDP (2016)
0.66% of GDP (2015)
0.71% of GDP (2014)
0.78% of GDP (2013)
0.87% of GDP (2012)
country comparison to the world: 114

Military branches: Armed Forces of Liberia (AFL): Army, Navy, Air Force (2014)

Military service age and obligation: 18 years of age for voluntary military service; no conscription (2012)

TRANSNATIONAL ISSUES

Disputes—international: as the UN Mission in Liberia (UNMIL) continues to drawdown prior to the 1 March 2018 closure date, the peacekeeping force is being reduced to 434 soldiers and two police units; some Liberian refugees still remain in Guinea, Cote d'Ivoire, Sierra Leone, and Ghana; Liberia shelters almost 15,000 Ivoirian refugees, as of May 2017; in 2017, Liberia's 3 refugee camps will be converted into "settlements" and remaining Ivoirian refugees will be integrated into local communities

Refugees and internally displaced persons: refugees (country of origin): 11,063 (Cote d'Ivoire) (2017)
IDPs: up to 23,000 (civil war from 1990-2004; post-election violence in March and April 2011; many dwell in slums in Monrovia) (2014)

Illicit drugs: transshipment point for Southeast and Southwest Asian heroin and South American cocaine for the European and US markets; corruption, criminal activity, arms-dealing, and diamond trade provide significant potential for money laundering, but the lack of well-developed financial system limits the country's utility as a major money-laundering center

LIBYA

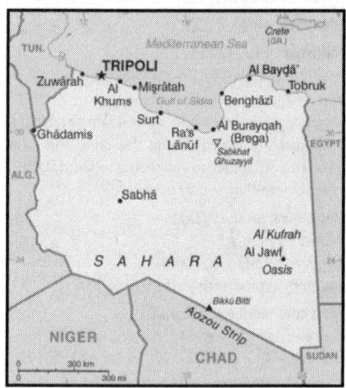

INTRODUCTION

Background: The Italians supplanted the Ottoman Turks in the area around Tripoli in 1911 and did not relinquish their hold until 1943 when they were defeated in World War II. Libya then passed to UN administration and achieved independence in 1951. Following a 1969 military coup, Col. Muammar al-QADHAFI assumed leadership and began to espouse his political system at home, which was a combination of socialism and Islam. During the 1970s, QADHAFI used oil revenues to promote his ideology outside Libya, supporting subversive and terrorist activities that included the downing of two airliners—one over Scotland, another in Northern Africa—and a discotheque bombing in Berlin. UN sanctions in 1992 isolated QADHAFI politically and economically following the attacks; sanctions were lifted in 2003 following Libyan acceptance of responsibility for the bombings and agreement to claimant compensation. QADHAFI also agreed to end Libya's program to develop weapons of mass destruction, and he made significant strides in normalizing relations with Western nations.

Unrest that began in several Middle Eastern and North African countries in late 2010 erupted in Libyan cities in early 2011. QADHAFI's brutal crackdown on protesters spawned a civil war that triggered UN authorization of air and naval intervention by the international community. After months of seesaw fighting between government and opposition forces, the QADHAFI regime was toppled in mid-2011 and replaced by a transitional government known as the National Transitional Council (NTC). In 2012, the NTC handed power to an elected parliament, the General National Congress (GNC). Voters chose a new parliament to replace the GNC in June 2014—the House of Representatives (HoR), which relocated to the eastern city of Tobruk after fighting broke out in Tripoli.

In October 2015, the UN brokered an agreement among a broad array of Libyan political parties and social groups—known as the Libyan Political Agreement (LPA). Members of the Libyan Political Dialogue, including representatives of the HoR and ex-GNC, signed the LPA in December 2015. The LPA called for the formation of an interim Government of National Accord or GNA, with a nine-member Presidency Council, the HoR, and an advisory High Council of State that most ex-GNC members joined. The LPA's roadmap for a two-year transition to a new constitution and elected government was subsequently endorsed by UN Security Council Resolution 2259, which also called upon member states to cease official contact with parallel institutions. In January 2016, the HoR voted to approve the LPA, including the Presidency Council, while voting against a controversial provision on security leadership positions. In March 2016, the GNA Presidency Council seated itself in Tripoli. In 2016, the GNA twice announced a slate of ministers who operate de facto, but the HoR did not endorse the ministerial list. HoR and ex-GNC-affiliated hardliners continued to oppose the GNA and hamper the LPA's implementation. In September 2017, UN Special Representative Ghassan SALAME announced a new roadmap for political reconciliation. SALAME's plan called for amendments to the LPA, a national conference of Libyan leaders, and a constitutional referendum and general elections within a year

GEOGRAPHY

Location: Northern Africa, bordering the Mediterranean Sea, between Egypt, Tunisia, and Algeria

Geographic coordinates: 25 00 N, 17 00 E

Map references: Africa

Area: *total:* 1,759,540 sq km
land: 1,759,540 sq km
water: 0 sq km
country comparison to the world: 18

Area—comparative: about 2.5 times the size of Texas; slightly larger than Alaska

Land boundaries: *total:* 4,339 km
border countries (6): Algeria 989 km, Chad 1,050 km, Egypt 1,115 km, Niger 342 km, Sudan 382 km, Tunisia 461 km

Coastline: 1,770 km

Maritime claims: *territorial sea:* 12 nm
note: Gulf of Sidra closing line—32 degrees, 30 minutes north
exclusive fishing zone: 62 nm

Climate: Mediterranean along coast; dry, extreme desert interior

Terrain: mostly barren, flat to undulating plains, plateaus, depressions

Elevation: *mean elevation:* 423 m

elevation extremes: lowest point: Sabkhat Ghuzayyil -47 m
highest point: Bikku Bitti 2,267 m

Natural resources: petroleum, natural gas, gypsum

Land use: *agricultural land:* 8.8%
arable land: 1%;
permanent crops: 0.2%;
permanent pasture: 7.6%
forest: 0.1%
other: 91.1% (2011 est.)
Irrigated land: 4,700 sq km (2012)

Population—distribution: well over 90% of the population lives along the Mediterranean coast in and between Tripoli to the west and Al Bayda to the east; the interior remains vastly underpopulated due to the Sahara and lack of surface water

Natural hazards: hot, dry, dust-laden ghibli is a southern wind lasting one to four days in spring and fall; dust storms, sandstorms

Environment—current issues: desertification; limited natural freshwater resources; the Great Manmade River Project, the largest water development scheme in the world, brings water from large aquifers under the Sahara to coastal cities

Environment—international agreements: *party to:* Biodiversity, Climate Change, Climate Change-Kyoto Protocol, Desertification, Endangered Species, Hazardous Wastes, Marine Dumping, Ozone Layer Protection, Ship Pollution, Wetlands
signed, but not ratified: Law of the Sea

Geography—note: more than 90% of the country is desert or semidesert

PEOPLE AND SOCIETY

Population: 6,653,210 (July 2017 est.)
note: immigrants make up just over 12% of the total population, according to UN data (2017)
country comparison to the world: 106

Nationality: *noun:* Libyan(s)
adjective: Libyan

Ethnic groups: Berber and Arab 97%, other 3% (includes Greeks, Maltese, Italians, Egyptians, Pakistanis, Turks, Indians, and Tunisians)

Languages: Arabic (official), Italian, English (all widely understood in the major cities); Berber (Nafusi, Ghadamis, Suknah, Awjilah, Tamasheq)

Religions: Muslim (official; virtually all Sunni) 96.6%, Christian 2.7%, Buddhist 0.3%, Hindu <0.1, Jewish <0.1, folk religion <0.1, unaffiliated 0.2%, other <0.1
note: non-Sunni Muslims include native Ibadhi Muslims (<1% of the population) and foreign Muslims (2010 est.)

Demographic profile: Despite continuing unrest, Libya remains a destination country for economic migrants. It is also a hub for transit migration to Europe because of its proximity to southern Europe and its lax border controls. Labor migrants have been drawn to Libya since the development of its oil sector in the 1960s. Until the latter part of the 1990s, most migrants to Libya were Arab (primarily Egyptians and Sudanese). However, international isolation stemming from Libya's involvement in international terrorism and a perceived lack of support from Arab countries led QADHAFI in 1998 to adopt a decade-long pan-African policy that enabled large numbers of sub-Saharan migrants to enter Libya without visas to work in the construction and agricultural industries. Although sub-Saharan Africans provided a cheap labor source, they were poorly treated and were subjected to periodic mass expulsions.

By the mid-2000s, domestic animosity toward African migrants and a desire to reintegrate into the international community motivated QADHAFI to impose entry visas on Arab and African immigrants and to agree to joint maritime patrols and migrant repatriations with Italy, the main recipient of illegal migrants departing Libya. As his regime neared collapse in 2011, QADHAFI reversed his policy of cooperating with Italy to curb illegal migration and sent boats loaded with migrants and asylum seekers to strain European resources. Libya's 2011 revolution decreased immigration drastically and prompted nearly 800,000 migrants to flee to third countries, mainly Tunisia and Egypt, or to their countries of origin. The inflow of migrants declined in 2012 but returned to normal levels by 2013, despite continued hostility toward sub-Saharan Africans and a less-inviting job market.

While Libya is not an appealing destination for migrants, since 2014, transiting migrants—primarily from East and West Africa—continue to exploit its political instability and weak border controls and use it as a primary departure area to migrate across the central Mediterranean to Europe in growing numbers. In addition, more than 200,000 people were displaced internally as of August 2017 by fighting between armed groups in eastern and western Libya and, to a lesser extent, by intertribal clashes in the country's south.

Age structure: *0-14 years:* 25.84% (male 879,311/female 839,824)
15-24 years: 17.09% (male 584,117/female 552,680)
25-54 years: 47.28% (male 1,651,362/female 1,494,106)
55-64 years: 5.48% (male 185,679/female 179,224)
65 years and over: 4.31% (male 141,867/female 145,040) (2017 est.)

Dependency ratios: *total dependency ratio:* 49.1
youth dependency ratio: 42.6
elderly dependency ratio: 6.4
potential support ratio: 15.5 (2015 est.)

Median age: *total:* 28.9 years
male: 29.1 years
female: 28.7 years (2017 est.)
country comparison to the world: 129

Population growth rate: 1.58% (2017 est.)
country comparison to the world: 68

Birth rate: 17.5 births/1,000 population (2017 est.)

country comparison to the world: 106

Death rate: 3.6 deaths/1,000 population (2017 est.)
country comparison to the world: 215

Net migration rate: 1.9 migrant(s)/1,000 population (2017 est.)
country comparison to the world: 48

Population distribution: well over 90% of the population lives along the Mediterranean coast in and between Tripoli to the west and Al Bayda to the east; the interior remains vastly underpopulated due to the Sahara and lack of surface water

Urbanization: *urban population:* 79% of total population (2017)
rate of urbanization: 1.64% annual rate of change (2015-20 est.)

Major urban areas—population: TRIPOLI (capital) 1.126 million (2015)

Sex ratio: *at birth:* 1.05 male(s)/female
0-14 years: 1.05 male(s)/female
15-24 years: 1.06 male(s)/female
25-54 years: 1.1 male(s)/female
55-64 years: 1.04 male(s)/female
65 years and over: 1.01 male(s)/female
total population: 1.07 male(s)/female (2016 est.)

Maternal mortality ratio: 9 deaths/100,000 live births (2015 est.)
country comparison to the world: 152

Infant mortality rate: *total:* 10.8 deaths/1,000 live births
male: 11.7 deaths/1,000 live births
female: 9.9 deaths/1,000 live births (2017 est.)
country comparison to the world: 130

Life expectancy at birth: *total population:* 76.7 years
male: 74.9 years
female: 78.5 years (2017 est.)
country comparison to the world: 85

Total fertility rate: 2.04 children born/woman (2017 est.)
country comparison to the world: 114

Contraceptive prevalence rate: 41.9% (2007)

Health expenditures: 5% of GDP (2014)
country comparison to the world: 143

Physicians density: 2.09 physicians/1,000 population (2014)

Hospital bed density: 3.7 beds/1,000 population (2012)

Drinking water source:
improved:
urban: 54.2% of population
rural: 54.9% of population
total: 54.4% of population
unimproved:
urban: 45.8% of population
rural: 45.1% of population
total: 45.6% of population (2001 est.)

Sanitation facility access:
improved:
urban: 96.8% of population
rural: 95.7% of population
total: 96.6% of population

unimproved:
urban: 3.2% of population
rural: 4.3% of population
total: 3.4% of population (2015 est.)

HIV/AIDS—people living with HIV/AIDS: NA

HIV/AIDS—deaths: NA

Obesity—adult prevalence rate: 32.5% (2016)
country comparison to the world: 16

Children under the age of 5 years underweight: 5.6% (2007)
country comparison to the world: 86

Education expenditures: NA

Literacy: *definition:* age 15 and over can read and write
total population: 91%
male: 96.7%
female: 85.6% (2015 est.)

Unemployment, youth ages 15-24: *total:* 48.7%
male: 40.8%
female: 67.8% (2012 est.)

GOVERNMENT

Country name: *conventional long form:* none
conventional short form: Libya
local long form: none
local short form: Libiya
etymology: name derives from the Libu, an ancient Libyan tribe first mentioned in texts from the 13th century B.C.

Government type: in transition

Capital: *name:* Tripoli (Tarabulus)
geographic coordinates: 32 53 N, 13 10 E
time difference: UTC+2 (7 hours ahead of Washington, DC, during Standard Time)

Administrative divisions: 22 districts (shabiyat, singular—shabiyat); Al Butnan, Al Jabal al Akhdar, Al Jabal al Gharbi, Al Jafarah, Al Jufrah, Al Kufrah, Al Marj, Al Marqab, Al Wahat, An Nuqat al Khams, Az Zawiyah, Banghazi, Darnah, Ghat, Misratah, Murzuq, Nalut, Sabha, Surt, Tarabulus, Wadi al Hayat, Wadi ash Shati

Independence: 24 December 1951 (from UN trusteeship)

National holiday: Liberation Day, 23 October (2011)

Constitution: history: previous 1951, 1977; drafting of a new constitution by the Constitution Drafting Assembly continued into 2017 (2017)

Legal system: Libya's post-revolution legal system is in flux and driven by state and non-state entities

International law organization participation: has not submitted an ICJ jurisdiction declaration; non-party state to the ICCt

Citizenship: *citizenship by birth:* no
citizenship by descent only: at least one parent or grandparent must be a citizen of Libya
dual citizenship recognized: no
residency requirement for naturalization: varies from 3 to 5 years

Suffrage: 18 years of age, universal

543

Executive branch: *chief of state:* Chairman, Presidential Council, Fayiz al-SARAJ (since December 2015)

head of government: Prime Minister Fayiz al-SARAJ (since December 2015)

cabinet: new cabinet awaiting approval by the House of Representatives

elections/appointments: NA

election results: NA

Legislative branch: *description:* unicameral House of Representative or Majlis Al Nuwab (200 seats including 32 reserved for women; members elected by direct popular vote; member term NA)

elections: election last held in June 2014; note—the Libyan Supreme Court in November 2014 declared the Council election unconstitutional, but the Council rejected the ruling

election results: percent of vote by party—NA; seats by party—independent 200; note—not all 200 seats were filled in the June election because of boycotts and lack of security at some polling stations; some elected members of the House also boycotted the election

Judicial branch: *highest court(s):* NA; note—government is in transition

Political parties and leaders: NA

Political pressure groups and leaders: NA

International organization participation: ABEDA, AfDB, AFESD, AMF, AMU, AU, BDEAC, CAEU, COMESA, FAO, G-77, IAEA, IBRD, ICAO, ICC (NGOs), ICRM, IDA, IDB, IFAD, IFC, IFRCS, ILO, IMF, IMO, IMSO, Interpol, IOC, IOM, IPU, ISO, ITSO, ITU, LAS, MIGA, NAM, OAPEC, OIC, OPCW, OPEC, PCA, UN, UNCTAD, UNESCO, UNIDO, UNWTO, UPU, WCO, WFTU (NGOs), WHO, WIPO, WMO, WTO (observer)

Diplomatic representation in the US: *chief of mission:* Ambassador Wafa M.T. BUGHAIGHIS (since 29 November 2017)

chancery: 2600 Virginia Avenue NW, Suite 400, Washington, DC 20037

telephone: [1] (202) 944-9601

FAX: [1] (202) 944-9606

Diplomatic representation from the US: *chief of mission:* Ambassador Peter William BODDE (since 21 December 2015)

note: the embassy closed in July 2014 due to major fighting near the embassy related to the Libyan civil war; embassy staff and operations temporarily moved to Tunis, Tunisia

embassy: Sidi Slim Area/Walie Al-Ahed Road, Tripoli

mailing address: US Embassy, 8850 Tripoli Place, Washington, DC 20521-8850

telephone: [218] (0) 91-220-3239

Flag description: three horizontal bands of red (top), black (double width), and green with a white crescent and star centered on the black stripe; the National Transitional Council reintroduced this flag design of the former Kingdom of Libya (1951-1969) on 27 February 2011; it replaced the former all-green banner promulgated by the QADHAFI regime in 1977; the colors represent the three

major regions of the country: red stands for Fezzan, black symbolizes Cyrenaica, and green denotes Tripolitania; the crescent and star represent Islam, the main religion of the country

National symbol(s): star and crescent, hawk; national colors: red, black, green

National anthem: name: "Libya, Libya, Libya"

lyrics/music: Al Bashir AL AREBI/Mohamad Abdel WAHAB

note: also known as "Ya Beladi" or "Oh, My Country!"; adopted 1951; readopted 2011 with some modification to the lyrics; during the QADHAFI years between 1969 and 2011, the anthem was "Allahu Akbar," (God is Great) a marching song of the Egyptian Army in the 1956 Suez War

ECONOMY

Economy—overview: Libya's economy, almost entirely dependent on oil and gas exports, struggled during the period 2014-16 as the country plunged into civil war and world oil prices dropped to seven-year lows. In early 2015, armed conflict between rival forces for control of the country's largest oil terminals caused a decline in Libyan crude oil production, which never recovered to more than one-third of the average pre-Revolution highs of 1.6 million barrels per day. The Central Bank of Libya continued to pay government salaries to a majority of the Libyan workforce and to fund subsidies for fuel and food, resulting in an estimated budget deficit of about 17% of GDP in 2017. The economy recovered handsomely in 2017 as conflict subsided.

Libya's economic transition away from QADHAFI's notionally socialist model has completely stalled as political chaos persists and security continues to deteriorate. Libya's leaders have hindered economic development by failing to use its financial resources to invest in national infrastructure. The country suffers from widespread power outages in its largest cities, caused by shortages of fuel for power generation. Living conditions, including access to clean drinking water, medical services, and safe housing, have all declined as the civil war has forced more people to become internally displaced, further straining local resources.

Extremists affiliated with the Islamic State of Iraq and the Levant (ISIL) attacked Libyan oilfields in the first half of 2015; ISIL has a presence in many cities across Libya including near oil infrastructure, threatening future government revenues from oil and gas.

GDP (purchasing power parity): $63.14 billion (2017 est.)

$40.72 billion (2016 est.)

$41.96 billion (2015 est.)

note: data are in 2017 dollars

country comparison to the world: 107

GDP (official exchange rate): $33.31 billion (2016 est.)

GDP—real growth rate: 55.1% (2017 est.)

-3% (2016 est.)

-10.3% (2015 est.)

country comparison to the world: 1

GDP—per capita (PPP): $9,800 (2017 est.)

$6,400 (2016 est.)

$6,600 (2015 est.)

note: data are in 2017 dollars

country comparison to the world: 142

Gross national saving: 1.9% of GDP (2017 est.)

-11% of GDP (2016 est.)

-8% of GDP (2015 est.)

country comparison to the world: 175

GDP—composition, by end use:

household consumption: 76.1%

government consumption: 19.4%

investment in fixed capital: 2.8%

investment in inventories: 1.4%

exports of goods and services: 39.7%

imports of goods and services: -39.5% (2017 est.)

GDP—composition, by sector of origin:

agriculture: 1.3%

industry: 63.8%

services: 34.9% (2017 est.)

Agriculture—products: wheat, barley, olives, dates, citrus, vegetables, peanuts, soybeans; cattle

Industries: petroleum, petrochemicals, aluminum, iron and steel, food processing, textiles, handicrafts, cement

Industrial production growth rate: 76.5% (2017 est.)

country comparison to the world: 1

Labor force: 1.114 million (2017 est.)

country comparison to the world: 143

Labor force—by occupation: *agriculture:* 17%

industry: 23%

services: 59% (2004 est.)

Unemployment rate: 30% (2004 est.)

country comparison to the world: 204

Population below poverty line: NA%

note: about one-third of Libyans live at or below the national poverty line

Household income or consumption by percentage share: *lowest 10%:* NA%

highest 10%: NA%

Budget: *revenues:* $16.33 billion

expenditures: $22.32 billion (2017 est.)

Taxes and other revenues: 49% of GDP (2017 est.)

country comparison to the world: 16

Budget surplus (+) or deficit (-): -18% of GDP (2017 est.)

country comparison to the world: 216

Public debt: 5.1% of GDP (2017 est.)

7.4% of GDP (2016 est.)

country comparison to the world: 203

Fiscal year: calendar year

Inflation rate (consumer prices): 32.8% (2017 est.)

27.1% (2016 est.)

country comparison to the world: 224

Central bank discount rate: 9.52% (31 December 2010)

3% (31 December 2009)

country comparison to the world: 26

Commercial bank prime lending rate: 7.3% (31 December 2017 est.)

6% (31 December 2016 est.)

country comparison to the world: 116

Stock of narrow money: $76.35 billion (31 December 2017 est.)

$62.57 billion (31 December 2016 est.)

country comparison to the world: 46

Stock of broad money: $77.89 billion (31 December 2017 est.)
$63.76 billion (31 December 2016 est.)
country comparison to the world: 60

Stock of domestic credit: $16.82 billion (31 December 2017 est.)
$14.14 billion (31 December 2016 est.)
country comparison to the world: 96

Market value of publicly traded shares: $NA

Current account balance: $591 million (2017 est.)
-$4.575 billion (2016 est.)
country comparison to the world: 45

Exports: $19.72 billion (2017 est.)
$11.99 billion (2016 est.)
country comparison to the world: 70

Exports—commodities: crude oil, refined petroleum products, natural gas, chemicals

Exports—partners: Italy 24.2%, Egypt 21.1%, Spain 9.5%, France 7.8%, Croatia 5%, Netherlands 5%, China 4.3% (2016)

Imports: $12.66 billion (2017 est.)
$11.01 billion (2016 est.)
country comparison to the world: 91

Imports—commodities: machinery, semi-finished goods, food, transport equipment, consumer products

Imports—partners: China 14.4%, South Korea 13.3%, Turkey 10.4%, Italy 5.9% (2016)

Reserves of foreign exchange and gold: $69.35 billion (31 December 2017 est.)
$66.05 billion (31 December 2016 est.)
country comparison to the world: 31

Debt—external: $2.927 billion (31 December 2017 est.)
$3.116 billion (31 December 2016 est.)
country comparison to the world: 144

Stock of direct foreign investment—at home: $19.07 billion (31 December 2017 est.)
$18.96 billion (31 December 2016 est.)
country comparison to the world: 80

Stock of direct foreign investment—abroad: $22.77 billion (31 December 2017 est.)
$22.19 billion (31 December 2016 est.)
country comparison to the world: 52

Exchange rates: Libyan dinars (LYD) per US dollar—
1.413 (2017 est.)
1.3904 (2016 est.)
1.3904 (2015 est.)
1.379 (2014 est.)
1.2724 (2013 est.)

ENERGY

Electricity access: *population without electricity:* 13,083
electrification—*total population:* 99.8%
electrification—urban areas: 100%
electrification—rural areas: 99.1% (2013)

Electricity—production: 35.45 billion kWh

note: persistent electricity shortages have contributed to the ongoing instability throughout the country (2015 est.)
country comparison to the world: 62

Electricity—consumption: 8.131 billion kWh (2015 est.)
country comparison to the world: 104

Electricity—exports: 0 kWh (2015 est.)
country comparison to the world: 162

Electricity—imports: 88 million kWh (2015 est.)
country comparison to the world: 100

Electricity—installed generating capacity: 9.46 million kW (2015 est.)
country comparison to the world: 64

Electricity—from fossil fuels: 99.9% of total installed capacity (2015 est.)
country comparison to the world: 23

Electricity—from nuclear fuels: 0% of total installed capacity (2015 est.)
country comparison to the world: 132

Electricity—from hydroelectric plants: 0% of total installed capacity (2015 est.)
country comparison to the world: 184

Electricity—from other renewable sources: 0.1% of total installed capacity (2015 est.)
country comparison to the world: 168

Crude oil—production: 384,700 bbl/day (2016 est.)
country comparison to the world: 30

Crude oil—exports: 383,500 bbl/day
note: Libyan crude oil export values are highly volatile because of continuing protests and other disruptions across the country (2014 est.)
country comparison to the world: 24

Crude oil—imports: 0 bbl/day (2014 est.)
country comparison to the world: 152

Crude oil—proved reserves: 48.36 billion bbl (1 January 2017 es)
country comparison to the world: 9

Refined petroleum products—production: 102,100 bbl/day (2014 est.)
country comparison to the world: 69

Refined petroleum products—consumption: 262,000 bbl/day (2015 est.)
country comparison to the world: 49

Refined petroleum products—exports: 16,450 bbl/day (2014 est.)
country comparison to the world: 74

Refined petroleum products—imports: 169,400 bbl/day (2014 est.)
country comparison to the world: 38

Natural gas—production: 11.6 billion cu m (2015 est.)
country comparison to the world: 40

Natural gas—consumption: 7.55 billion cu m (2015 est.)
country comparison to the world: 61

Natural gas—exports: 7.11 billion cu m (2015 est.)
country comparison to the world: 28

Natural gas—imports: 0 cu m (2013 est.)

country comparison to the world: 149

Natural gas—proved reserves: 1.505 trillion cu m (1 January 2017 es)
country comparison to the world: 22

Carbon dioxide emissions from consumption of energy: 57 million Mt (2013 est.)
country comparison to the world: 56

COMMUNICATIONS

Telephones—fixed lines: *total subscriptions:* 1,374,408
subscriptions per 100 inhabitants: 21 (July 2016 est.)
country comparison to the world: 89

Telephones—mobile cellular: *total:* 7,660,068
subscriptions per 100 inhabitants: 117 (July 2016 est.)
country comparison to the world: 85

Telephone system: *general assessment:* Libya's civil war has disrupted its telecommunications sector, but much of its infrastructure remains superior to that in most other African countries
domestic: combined fixed-line and mobile-cellular service generally adequate, but pressure to rebuild damaged infrastructure growing
international: country code—218; satellite earth stations—4 Intelsat, NA Arabsat, and NA Intersputnik; submarine cable to France and Italy; microwave radio relay to Tunisia and Egypt; tropospheric scatter to Greece; participant in Medarabtel (2015)

Broadcast media: state-funded and private TV stations; some provinces operate local TV stations; pan-Arab satellite TV stations are available; state-funded radio (2012)

Internet country code: .ly
Internet users: total: 1,326,194

percent of population: 20.3% (July 2016 est.)
country comparison to the world: 114

TRANSPORTATION

National air transport system: *number of registered air carriers:* 8
inventory of registered aircraft operated by air carriers: 23
annual passenger traffic on registered air carriers: 2,566,465
annual freight traffic on registered air carriers: 3,833,542 mt-km (2015)
Civil aircraft registration country code prefix: 5A (2016)

Airports: 146 (2013)
country comparison to the world: 41

Airports—with paved runways: *total:* 68
over 3,047 m: 23
2,438 to 3,047 m: 7
1,524 to 2,437 m: 30
914 to 1,523 m: 7
under 914 m: 1 (2017)

Airports—with unpaved runways: *total:* 78
over 3,047 m: 2
2,438 to 3,047 m: 5
1,524 to 2,437 m: 14

914 to 1,523 m: 37
under 914 m: 20 (2013)

Heliports: 2 (2013)

Pipelines: condensate 882 km; gas 3,743 km; oil 7,005 km (2013)

Roadways: total: 100,024 km
paved: 57,214 km
unpaved: 42,810 km (2003)
country comparison to the world: 47

Merchant marine: total: 98
by type: general cargo 2, oil tanker 16, other 80 (2017)
country comparison to the world: 85

Ports and terminals: major seaport(s): Marsa al Burayqah (Marsa el Brega), Tripoli
oil terminal(s): Az Zawiyah, Ra's Lanuf
LNG terminal(s) (export): Marsa el Brega

MILITARY AND SECURITY

Military branches: note—in transition; government has affiliated Army, Air Force, Navy, and Coast Guard forces (2016)

Military service age and obligation: 18 years of age for mandatory or voluntary service (2012)

TERRORISM

Terrorist groups—home based: Ansar al-Shari'a in Benghazi: aim(s): install Sharia in Libya
area(s) of operation: engages in frequent assassinations of security officials and political figures in the east, mostly in Benghazi; operates as a member of the Benghazi Revolutionaries Shura Council, a coalition of jihadist groups combating the Libyan Ground Forces; on 11 September 2012, members participated in launching mortar attacks and ransackings at the US Special Mission and Annex in Benghazi that killed four people, including US Ambassador Christopher STEVENS; majority of members are Libyans and some are former Libyan Islamic Fighting Group members

Ansar al-Shari'a in Darnah: aim(s): install Sharia in Libya
area(s) of operation: engages in frequent assassinations of security officials and political figures in the east, mostly in Darnah; operates as a member group of the Darnah Mujahidin Shura Council, a coalition of jihadist groups combating the Libyan Ground Forces; on 11 September 2012, members participated in launching mortar attacks and ransackings at the US Special Mission and Annex in Benghazi that killed four people, including US Ambassador Christopher STEVENS; majority of members are Libyans and some are former Libyan Islamic Fighting Group members

Islamic State of Iraq and the Levant's Branch in Libya (ISIL-Libya): aim(s): prevent a unitary Libyan state from reconstituting, secure control over the country's critical resources and, ultimately, establish an Islamic caliphate in Libya
area(s) of operation: based in Libya since circa 2015, with its original headquarters in Sirte; organized in the following Libya-based wilayats (provinces): Wilayat Tarabulus (west), Wilayat Barqa (northeast), and Wilayat Fezzan (southeast); ISIL-Libya no longer controls territory in Libya, but does maintain a low-profile presence throughout much of the country; was previously known before 2017 to have operated paramilitary training camps, collected taxes, directed religious education, broadcasted its messages on radio, and enforced its strict interpretation of Sharia; prior to Libyan military and security forces and their foreign allies confronting ISIL-Libya, the group was assessed in 2016 to have had a growing presence with 1,000 of the 4,000-6,000 fighters based in Surt, a key oil exporting center, dedicated to taking control of oil fields to generate revenue; Libyan Government officials and Western allies collaborated to keep chemical weapons left over from the al-QADHAFI regime out of the group's reach; has engaged heavily in recruiting Libyan youth, including some from Colonel Muammar al-QADHAFI's tribe, and among his former army officers; current personnel strength is unknown

Terrorist groups—foreign based: al-Mulathamun Battalion: aim(s): replace regional governments, including Libya's transitional government, with an Islamic state
area(s) of operation: maintains an operational presence; engages heavily in kidnappings for ransom

al-Qa'ida (AQ): aim(s): bolster networks in Libya and, ultimately, establish a pan-Islamic caliphate under a strict Salafi Muslim interpretation of Sharia
area(s) of operation: maintains a growing presence operating training camps and safehavens; stages attacks in Libya against Egypt and Tunisia

al-Qaida in the Islamic Maghreb (AQIM): aim(s): replace Libya's transitional government with Sharia and, ultimately, establish a regional Islamic caliphate across all of North and West Africa
area(s) of operation: maintains an operational presence, primarily in the western and southern regions; centered mostly on kidnappings for ransom

Islamic State of Iraq and the Levant (ISIL): aim(s): bolster its affiliate ISIL-Libya and enhance operational planning and logistics networks for staging attacks inside Tunisia
area(s) of operation: stages attacks in Libya against Tunisia along the Libya-Tunisia border; collaborates with its affiliate ISIL-Libya

Mujahidin Shura Council in the Environs of Jerusalem (MSC): aim(s): enhance its networks in Libya and, ultimately, destroy the state of Israel
area(s) of operation: maintains limited networks for operational planning, logistics, transferring funds, and smuggling fighters and arms to be used against Israel; by 2017, the majority of veteran members had defected to join other groups

TRANSNATIONAL ISSUES

Disputes—international: dormant disputes include Libyan claims of about 32,000 sq km still reflected on its maps of southeastern Algeria and the FLN's assertions of a claim to Chirac Pastures in southeastern Morocco; various Chadian rebels from the Aozou region reside in southern Libya

Refugees and internally displaced persons: refugees (country of origin): 5,298 (West Bank and Gaza Strip) (2018)
IDPs: 180,937 (conflict between pro-QADHAFI and anti-QADHAFI forces in 2011; post-QADHAFI tribal clashes 2014) (2017)

Trafficking in persons: current situation: Libya is a destination and transit country for men and women from sub-Saharan Africa and Asia subjected to forced labor and forced prostitution; migrants who seek employment in Libya as laborers and domestic workers or who transit Libya en route to Europe are vulnerable to forced labor; private employers also exploit migrants from detention centers as forced laborers on farms and construction sites, returning them to detention when they are no longer needed; some sub-Saharan women are reportedly forced to work in Libyan brothels, particularly in the country's south; since 2013, militia groups and other informal armed groups, including some affiliated with the government, are reported to conscript Libyan children under the age of 18; large-scale violence driven by militias, civil unrest, and increased lawlessness increased in 2014, making it more difficult to obtain information on human trafficking

tier rating: Tier 3—the Libyan Government does not fully comply with the minimum standards for the elimination of trafficking and is not making significant efforts to do so; in 2014, the government's capacity to address human trafficking was hampered by the ongoing power struggle and violence; the judicial system was not functioning, preventing any efforts to investigate, prosecute, or convict traffickers, complicit detention camp guards or government officials, or militias or armed groups that used child soldiers; the government failed to identify or provide protection to trafficking victims, including child conscripts, and continued to punish victims for unlawful acts committed as a direct result of being trafficked; no public anti-trafficking awareness campaigns were conducted (2015)

LIECHTENSTEIN

INTRODUCTION

Background: The Principality of Liechtenstein was established within the Holy Roman Empire in 1719. Occupied by both French and Russian troops during the Napoleonic Wars, it became a sovereign state in 1806 and joined the German Confederation in 1815. Liechtenstein became fully independent in 1866 when the Confederation dissolved. Until the end of World War I, it was closely tied to Austria, but the economic devastation caused by that conflict forced Liechtenstein to enter into a customs and monetary union with Switzerland. Since World War II (in which Liechtenstein remained neutral), the country's low taxes have spurred outstanding economic growth. In 2000, shortcomings in banking regulatory oversight resulted in concerns about the use of financial institutions for money laundering. However, Liechtenstein implemented anti-money laundering legislation and a Mutual Legal Assistance Treaty with the US that went into effect in 2003.

GEOGRAPHY

Location: Central Europe, between Austria and Switzerland

Geographic coordinates: 47 16 N, 9 32 E

Map references: Europe

Area: *total:* 160 sq km
land: 160 sq km
water: 0 sq km
country comparison to the world: 219

Area—comparative: about 0.9 times the size of Washington, DC

Land boundaries: *total:* 75 km
border countries (2): Austria 34 km, Switzerland 41 km

Coastline: 0 km (doubly landlocked)

Maritime claims: none (landlocked)

Climate: continental; cold, cloudy winters with frequent snow or rain; cool to moderately warm, cloudy, humid summers

Terrain: mostly mountainous (Alps) with Rhine Valley in western third

Elevation: *mean elevation:* NA

elevation extremes: *lowest point:* Ruggeller Riet 430 m
highest point: Vorder-Grauspitz 2,599 m

Natural resources: hydroelectric potential, arable land

Land use: *agricultural land:* 37.6%
arable land: 18.8%;
permanent crops: 0%;
permanent pasture: 18.8%
forest: 43.1%
other: 19.3% (2011 est.)
Irrigated land: 0 sq km (2012)

Population—distribution: most of the population is found in the western half of the country along the Rhine River

Natural hazards: avalanches, landslides

Environment—current issues: some air pollution generated locally, some transfered from surrounding countries

Environment—international agreements: *party to:* Air Pollution, Air Pollution-Nitrogen Oxides, Air Pollution-Persistent Organic Pollutants, Air Pollution-Sulfur 85, Air Pollution-Sulfur 94, Air Pollution-Volatile Organic Compounds, Biodiversity, Climate Change, Climate Change-Kyoto Protocol, Desertification, Endangered Species, Hazardous Wastes, Ozone Layer Protection, Wetlands
signed, but not ratified: Law of the Sea

Geography—note: along with Uzbekistan, one of only two doubly landlocked countries in the world; variety of microclimatic variations based on elevation

PEOPLE AND SOCIETY

Population: 38,244 (July 2017 est.)
country comparison to the world: 213

Nationality: *noun:* Liechtensteiner(s)
adjective: Liechtenstein

Ethnic groups: Liechtensteiner 66%, other 34% (2013 est.)

Languages: German 94.5% (official) (Alemannic is the main dialect), Italian 1.1%, other 4.3% (2010 est.)

Religions: Roman Catholic (official) 75.9%, Protestant Reformed 6.5%, Muslim 5.4%, Lutheran 1.3%, other 2.9%, none 5.4%, unspecified 2.6% (2010 est.)

Age structure: *0-14 years:* 15.26% (male 3,148/female 2,689)
15-24 years: 11.65% (male 2,239/female 2,217)
25-54 years: 41.64% (male 7,956/female 7,969)
55-64 years: 14.03% (male 2,607/female 2,760)

65 years and over: 17.41% (male 3,058/female 3,601) (2017 est.)

Median age: *total:* 43.2 years
male: 41.7 years
female: 44.5 years (2017 est.)
country comparison to the world: 19

Population growth rate: 0.8% (2017 est.)
country comparison to the world: 131

Birth rate: 10.4 births/1,000 population (2017 est.)
country comparison to the world: 188

Death rate: 7.4 deaths/1,000 population (2017 est.)
country comparison to the world: 116

Net migration rate: 5 migrant(s)/1,000 population (2017 est.)
country comparison to the world: 24

Population distribution: most of the population is found in the western half of the country along the Rhine River

Urbanization: *urban population:* 14.3% of total population (2017)
rate of urbanization: 0.79% annual rate of change (2015-20 est.)

Major urban areas—population: VADUZ (capital) 5,000 (2014)

Sex ratio: *at birth:* 1.26 male(s)/female
0-14 years: 1.17 male(s)/female
15-24 years: 0.99 male(s)/female
25-54 years: 1 male(s)/female
55-64 years: 0.95 male(s)/female
65 years and over: 0.84 male(s)/female
total population: 0.99 male(s)/female (2016 est.)

Infant mortality rate: *total:* 4.2 deaths/1,000 live births
male: 4.5 deaths/1,000 live births
female: 3.9 deaths/1,000 live births (2017 est.)
country comparison to the world: 190

Life expectancy at birth: *total population:* 81.9 years
male: 79.7 years
female: 84.7 years (2017 est.)
country comparison to the world: 19

Total fertility rate: 1.69 children born/woman (2017 est.)
country comparison to the world: 174

HIV/AIDS—adult prevalence rate: NA

HIV/AIDS—people living with HIV/AIDS: NA

HIV/AIDS—deaths: NA

Education expenditures: 2.6% of GDP (2011)
country comparison to the world: 166

School life expectancy (primary to tertiary education): *total:* 15 years
male: 16 years
female: 13 years (2015)

GOVERNMENT

Country name: *conventional long form:* Principality of Liechtenstein
conventional short form: Liechtenstein
local long form: Fürstentum Liechtenstein

547

local short form: Liechtenstein

etymology: named after the Liechtenstein dynasty that purchased and united the counties of Schellenburg and Vaduz and that was allowed by the Holy Roman Emperor in 1719 to rename the new property after their family; the name in German means "light (bright) stone"

Government type: constitutional monarchy

Capital: *name:* Vaduz

geographic coordinates: 47 08 N, 9 31 E

time difference: UTC+1 (6 hours ahead of Washington, DC, during Standard Time)

daylight saving time: +1hr, begins last Sunday in March; ends last Sunday in October

Administrative divisions: 11 communes (Gemeinden, singular—Gemeinde); Balzers, Eschen, Gamprin, Mauren, Planken, Ruggell, Schaan, Schellenberg, Triesen, Triesenberg, Vaduz

Independence: 23 January 1719 (Principality of Liechtenstein established); 12 July 1806 (independence from the Holy Roman Empire); 24 August 1866 (independence from the German Confederation)

National holiday: National Day, 15 August (1940); note—a National Day was originally established in 1940 to combine celebrations for the Feast of the Assumption (15 August) with those honoring the birthday of former Prince Franz Josef II (1906-1989) whose birth fell on 16 August; after the prince's death, National Day became the official national holiday by law in 1990

Constitution: history: previous 1862; latest adopted 5 October 1921

amendments: proposed by Parliament, by the reigning prince (in the form of "Government" proposals), by petition of at least 1,500 qualified voters, or by at least four communes; passage requires unanimous approval of Parliament members in one sitting or three-quarters majority vote in two successive sittings; referendum required only if petitioned by at least 1,500 voters or by at least four communes; passage by referendum requires absolute majority of votes cast; amended several times, last in 2011 (2016)

Legal system: civil law system influenced by Swiss, Austrian, and German law

International law organization participation: accepts compulsory ICJ jurisdiction with reservations; accepts ICCt jurisdiction

Citizenship: *citizenship by birth:* no

citizenship by descent only: the father must be a citizen of Liechtenstein; in the case of a child born out of wedlock, the mother must be a citizen

dual citizenship recognized: no

residency requirement for naturalization: 5 years

Suffrage: 18 years of age; universal

Executive branch: *chief of state:* Prince HANS-ADAM II (since 13 November 1989, assumed executive powers on 26 August 1984); Heir Apparent Prince ALOIS, son of the monarch (born 11 June 1968); note—on 15 August 2004, HANS-ADAM II transferred the official duties of the ruling prince to ALOIS, but HANS-ADAM II retains status of chief of state

head of government: Prime Minister Adrian HASLER (since 27 March 2013)

cabinet: Cabinet elected by the Parliament, confirmed by the monarch

elections/appointments: the monarchy is hereditary; following legislative elections, the leader of the majority party in the Parliament usually appointed the head of government by the monarch, and the leader of the largest minority party in the Landtag usually appointed the deputy head of government by the monarch if there is a coalition government

Legislative branch: *description:* unicameral Parliament or Landtag (25 seats; members directly elected in 2 multi-seat constituencies by proportional representation vote to serve 4-year terms)

elections: last held on 5 February 2017 (next to be held in February 2021)

election results: percent of vote by party—FBP 35.2%, VU 33.7%, DU 18.4% FL 12.6%; seats by party—FBP 9, VU 8, DU 5, FL 3

Judicial branch: *highest court(s):* Supreme Court or Oberster Gerichtshof (consists of 5 judges); Constitutional Court or Verfassungsgericht (consists of 5 judges and 5 alternates)

judge selection and term of office: judges of both courts elected by the Landtag and appointed by the monarch; Supreme Court judges serve 4-year renewable terms; Constitutional Court judges appointed for renewable 5-year terms

subordinate courts: Court of Appeal or Obergericht (second instance), Court of Justice (first instance), Administrative Court, county courts

Political parties and leaders: Fatherland Union (Vaterlaendische Union) or VU [Guenther FRITZ]

Progressive Citizens' Party (Fortschrittliche Buergerpartei) or FBP [Thomas BANZER]

The Free List (Die Freie Liste) or FL [Pepo FRICK]

The Independents (Die Unabhaengigen) or DU [Harry QUADERER]

International organization participation: CD, CE, EBRD, EFTA, IAEA, ICCt, ICRM, IFRCS, Interpol, IOC, IPU, ITSO, ITU, ITUC (NGOs), OAS (observer), OPCW, OSCE, PCA, Schengen Convention, UN, UNCTAD, UPU, WIPO, WTO

Diplomatic representation in the US: *chief of mission:* Ambassador Kurt JAEGER (since 16 September 2016)

chancery: 2900 K Street, NW, Suite 602B, Washington, DC 20007

telephone: [1] (202) 331-0590

FAX: [1] (202) 331-3221

Diplomatic representation from the US: the US does not have an embassy in Liechtenstein; the US Ambassador to Switzerland is accredited to Liechtenstein

Flag description: two equal horizontal bands of blue (top) and red with a gold crown on the hoist side of the blue band; the colors may derive from the blue and red livery design used in the principality's household in the 18th century; the prince's crown was introduced in 1937 to distinguish the flag from that of Haiti

National symbol(s): princely hat (crown); national colors: blue, red

National anthem: name: "Oben am jungen Rhein" (High Above the Young Rhine)

lyrics/music: Jakob Joseph JAUCH/Josef FROMMELT

note: adopted 1850, revised 1963; uses the tune of "God Save the Queen"

ECONOMY

Economy—overview: Despite its small size and lack of natural resources, Liechtenstein has developed into a prosperous, highly industrialized, free-enterprise economy with a vital financial service sector and the third highest per capita income in the world, after Qatar and Luxembourg. The Liechtenstein economy is widely diversified with a large number of small businesses. Low business taxes—a flat tax of 12.5% on the income is applied—and easy incorporation rules have induced many holding companies to establish nominal offices in Liechtenstein, providing 30% of state revenues.

The country participates in a customs union with Switzerland and uses the Swiss franc as its national currency. It imports more than 90% of its energy requirements. Liechtenstein has been a member of the European Economic Area (an organization serving as a bridge between the European Free Trade Association and the EU) since May 1995. The government is working to harmonize its economic policies with those of an integrated Europe.

Since 2008, Liechtenstein has faced renewed international pressure—particularly from Germany and the US—to improve transparency in its banking and tax systems. In December 2008, Liechtenstein signed a Tax Information Exchange Agreement with the US. Upon Liechtenstein's conclusion of 12 bilateral information-sharing agreements, the OECD in October 2009 removed the principality from its "grey list" of countries that had yet to implement the organization's Model Tax Convention. By the end of 2010, Liechtenstein had signed 25 Tax Information Exchange Agreements or Double Tax Agreements. In 2011, Liechtenstein joined the Schengen area, which allows passport-free travel across 26 European countries.

GDP (purchasing power parity): $4.978 billion (2014 est.)

$3.2 billion (2009 est.)

$3.216 billion (2008 est.)

country comparison to the world: 176

GDP (official exchange rate): $6.672 billion (2010 est.)

GDP—real growth rate: 1.8% (2012 est.)

-0.5% (2011 est.)

3.1% (2007 est.)

country comparison to the world: 163

GDP—per capita (PPP): $139,100 (2009 est.)

$90,100 (2008 est.)

$91,300 (2007 est.)

country comparison to the world: 1

GDP—composition, by sector of origin:
agriculture: 7%
industry: 41%
services: 52% (2014)

Agriculture—products: wheat, barley, corn, potatoes; livestock, dairy products

Industries: electronics, metal manufacturing, dental products, ceramics, pharmaceuticals, food products, precision instruments, tourism, optical instruments

Industrial production growth rate: NA%

Labor force: 38,520 (2012)
note: 51% of the labor force in Liechtenstein commute daily from Austria, Switzerland, and Germany (2015 est.)
country comparison to the world: 200

Labor force—by occupation: *agriculture:* 0.8%
industry: 36.9%
services: 62.3% (2015)

Unemployment rate: 2.4% (2015)
2.4% (2014)
country comparison to the world: 20

Population below poverty line: NA%

Household income or consumption by percentage share: *lowest 10%:* NA%
highest 10%: NA%

Budget: *revenues:* $995.3 million
expenditures: $890.4 million (2012 est.)
Taxes and other revenues: 14.9% of GDP (2012 est.)
country comparison to the world: 190

Budget surplus (+) or deficit (-): 1.6% of GDP (2012 est.)
country comparison to the world: 10

Fiscal year: calendar year

Inflation rate (consumer prices): -0.4% (2016 est.)
-0.2% (2013)
country comparison to the world: 4

Market value of publicly traded shares: $NA

Exports: $3.217 billion (2015 est.)
$3.774 billion (2014 est.)
note: trade data exclude trade with Switzerland
country comparison to the world: 122

Exports—commodities: small specialty machinery, connectors for audio and video, parts for motor vehicles, dental products, hardware, prepared foodstuffs, electronic equipment, optical products

Imports: $0 (2015 est.)
$2.23 billion (2014 est.)
note: trade data exclude trade with Switzerland
country comparison to the world: 222

Imports—commodities: agricultural products, raw materials, energy products, machinery, metal goods, textiles, foodstuffs, motor vehicles

Debt—external: $0 (2015 est.)
note: public external debt only; private external debt unavailable
country comparison to the world: 206

Exchange rates: Swiss francs (CHF) per US dollar—
0.9875 (2017)
0.9852 (2016)
0.9852 (2015)
0.9627 (2014 est.)
0.9152 (2013 est.)

ENERGY

Electricity access: electrification—*total population:* 100% (2016)

Electricity—production: 68.43 million kWh (2015)
country comparison to the world: 203

Electricity—consumption: 393.6 million kWh (2015)
country comparison to the world: 175

Electricity—exports: 0 kWh (2015 est.) (2015 est.)
country comparison to the world: 160

Electricity—imports: 325.2 million kWh (2015)
country comparison to the world: 88

COMMUNICATIONS

Telephones—fixed lines: *total subscriptions:* 16,600
subscriptions per 100 inhabitants: 44 (July 2016 est.)
country comparison to the world: 187

Telephones—mobile cellular: *total:* 43,914
subscriptions per 100 inhabitants: 116 (July 2016 est.)
country comparison to the world: 204

Telephone system: *general assessment:* automatic telephone system

domestic: fixed-line and mobile-cellular services widely available; combined telephone service subscribership exceeds 155 per 100 persons
international: country code—423; linked to Swiss networks by cable and microwave radio relay (2016)

Broadcast media: relies on foreign terrestrial and satellite broadcasters for most broadcast media services; first Liechtenstein-based TV station established August 2008; Radio Liechtenstein operates multiple radio stations; a Swiss-based broadcaster operates several radio stations in Liechtenstein (2008)

Internet country code: .li
Internet users: total: 37,214

percent of population: 98.1% (July 2016 est.)
country comparison to the world: 193

TRANSPORTATION

Civil aircraft registration country code prefix: HB (2016)

Pipelines: gas 20 km (2013)

Railways: total: 9 km
standard gauge: 9 km 1.435-m gauge (electrified)
note: belongs to the Austrian Railway System connecting Austria and Switzerland (2008)
country comparison to the world: 136

Roadways: total: 380 km
paved: 380 km (2012)
country comparison to the world: 203

Waterways: 28 km (2010)
country comparison to the world: 105

MILITARY AND SECURITY

Military branches: no regular military forces; National Police maintain close relations with neighboring forces (2016)

Military—note: Liechtenstein has no military forces, but the modern National Police maintain close relations with neighboring forces (2013)

TRANSNATIONAL ISSUES

Disputes—international: none

Illicit drugs: has strengthened money laundering controls, but money laundering remains a concern due to Liechtenstein's sophisticated offshore financial services sector

LITHUANIA

INTRODUCTION

Background: Lithuanian lands were united under MINDAUGAS in 1236; over the next century, through alliances and conquest, Lithuania extended its territory to include most of present-day Belarus and Ukraine. By the end of the 14th century Lithuania was the largest state in Europe. An alliance with Poland in 1386 led the two countries into a union through the person of a common ruler. In 1569, Lithuania and Poland formally united into a single dual state, the Polish-Lithuanian Commonwealth. This entity survived until 1795 when its remnants were partitioned by surrounding countries. Lithuania regained its independence following World War I but was annexed by the USSR in 1940—an action never recognized by the US and many other countries. On 11 March 1990, Lithuania became the first of the Soviet republics to declare its independence, but Moscow did not recognize this proclamation until September of 1991 (following the abortive coup in Moscow). The last Russian troops withdrew in 1993. Lithuania subsequently restructured

549

its economy for integration into Western European institutions; it joined both NATO and the EU in the spring of 2004. In 2015, Lithuania joined the euro zone.

GEOGRAPHY

Location: Eastern Europe, bordering the Baltic Sea, between Latvia and Russia, west of Belarus

Geographic coordinates: 56 00 N, 24 00 E

Map references: Europe

Area: *total:* 65,300 sq km
land: 62,680 sq km
water: 2,620 sq km
country comparison to the world: 124

Area—comparative: slightly larger than West Virginia

Land boundaries: *total:* 1,549 km
border countries (4): Belarus 640 km, Latvia 544 km, Poland 104 km, Russia (Kaliningrad) 261 km

Coastline: 90 km

Maritime claims: *territorial sea:* 12 nm

Climate: transitional, between maritime and continental; wet, moderate winters and summers

Terrain: lowland, many scattered small lakes, fertile soil

Elevation: *mean elevation:* 110 m

elevation extremes: *lowest point:* Baltic Sea 0 m
highest point: Aukstojas 294 m

Natural resources: peat, arable land, amber

Land use: *agricultural land:* 44.8%
arable land: 34.9%;
permanent crops: 0.5%;
permanent pasture: 9.4%
forest: 34.6%
other: 20.6% (2011 est.)
Irrigated land: 44 sq km (2012)

Population—distribution: fairly even population distribution throughout the country, but somewhat greater concentrations in the southern cities of Vilnius and Kaunas, and the western port of Klaipeda

Natural hazards: occasional floods, droughts

Environment—current issues: contamination of soil and groundwater with petroleum products and chemicals at military bases

Environment—international agreements: *party to:* Air Pollution, Air Pollution-Nitrogen Oxides, Air Pollution-Persistent Organic Pollutants, Air Pollution-Sulphur 85, Air Pollution-Sulphur 94, Air Pollution-Volatile Organic Compounds, Biodiversity, Climate Change, Climate Change-Kyoto Protocol, Desertification, Endangered Species, Environmental Modification, Hazardous Wastes, Law of the Sea, Ozone Layer Protection, Ship Pollution, Wetlands
signed, but not ratified: none of the selected agreements

Geography—note: fertile central plains are separated by hilly uplands that are ancient glacial deposits

PEOPLE AND SOCIETY

Population: 2,823,859 (July 2017 est.)
country comparison to the world: 140

Nationality: *noun:* Lithuanian(s)
adjective: Lithuanian

Ethnic groups: Lithuanian 84.1%, Polish 6.6%, Russian 5.8%, Belarusian 1.2%, other 1.1%, unspecified 1.2% (2011 est.)

Languages: Lithuanian (official) 82%, Russian 8%, Polish 5.6%, other 0.9%, unspecified 3.5% (2011 est.)

Religions: Roman Catholic 77.2%, Russian Orthodox 4.1%, Old Believer 0.8%, Evangelical Lutheran 0.6%, Evangelical Reformist 0.2%, other (including Sunni Muslim, Jewish, Greek Catholic, and Karaite) 0.8%, none 6.1%, unspecified 10.1% (2011 est.)

Age structure: *0-14 years:* 15.01% (male 217,438/female 206,533)
15-24 years: 11.09% (male 161,965/female 151,197)
25-54 years: 40.05% (male 557,504/female 573,364)
55-64 years: 14.17% (male 177,157/female 223,110)
65 years and over: 19.67% (male 187,859/female 367,732) (2017 est.)

Dependency ratios: *total dependency ratio:* 49.9
youth dependency ratio: 21.9
elderly dependency ratio: 28
potential support ratio: 3.6 (2015 est.)

Median age: *total:* 43.7 years
male: 39.7 years
female: 47.1 years (2017 est.)
country comparison to the world: 16

Population growth rate: -1.08% (2017 est.)
country comparison to the world: 228

Birth rate: 9.9 births/1,000 population (2017 est.)
country comparison to the world: 195

Death rate: 14.6 deaths/1,000 population (2017 est.)
country comparison to the world: 2

Net migration rate: -6.1 migrant(s)/1,000 population (2017 est.)
country comparison to the world: 198

Population distribution: fairly even population distribution throughout the country, but somewhat greater concentrations in the southern cities of Vilnius and Kaunas, and the western port of Klaipeda

Urbanization: *urban population:* 66.5% of total population (2017)
rate of urbanization: -0.34% annual rate of change (2015-20 est.)

Major urban areas—population: VILNIUS (capital) 517,000 (2015)

Sex ratio: *at birth:* 1.06 male(s)/female
0-14 years: 1.05 male(s)/female
15-24 years: 1.07 male(s)/female
25-54 years: 0.97 male(s)/female
55-64 years: 0.79 male(s)/female
65 years and over: 0.51 male(s)/female
total population: 0.86 male(s)/female (2016 est.)

Mother's mean age at first birth: 27 years (2014 est.)

Maternal mortality ratio: 10 deaths/100,000 live births (2015 est.)
country comparison to the world: 147

Infant mortality rate: *total:* 3.8 deaths/1,000 live births
male: 4.3 deaths/1,000 live births
female: 3.3 deaths/1,000 live births (2017 est.)
country comparison to the world: 197

Life expectancy at birth: *total population:* 75 years
male: 69.7 years
female: 80.7 years (2017 est.)
country comparison to the world: 112

Total fertility rate: 1.59 children born/woman (2017 est.)
country comparison to the world: 185

Health expenditures: 6.6% of GDP (2014)
country comparison to the world: 89

Physicians density: 4.33 physicians/1,000 population (2014)

Hospital bed density: 7 beds/1,000 population (2011)

Drinking water source:
improved:
urban: 99.7% of population
rural: 90.4% of population
total: 96.6% of population
unimproved:
urban: 0.3% of population
rural: 9.6% of population
total: 3.4% of population (2015 est.)

Sanitation facility access:
improved:
urban: 97.2% of population
rural: 82.8% of population
total: 92.4% of population
unimproved:
urban: 2.8% of population
rural: 17.2% of population
total: 7.6% of population (2015 est.)

HIV/AIDS—adult prevalence rate: 0.2% (2016 est.)
country comparison to the world: 92

HIV/AIDS—people living with HIV/AIDS: 2,900 (2016 est.)
country comparison to the world: 113

HIV/AIDS—deaths: <200

Major infectious diseases: *degree of risk:* intermediate
vectorborne diseases: tickborne encephalitis (2016)

Obesity—adult prevalence rate: 26.3% (2016)
country comparison to the world: 43

Education expenditures: 4.6% of GDP (2013)
country comparison to the world: 61

Literacy: *definition:* age 15 and over can read and write
total population: 99.8%
male: 99.8%
female: 99.8% (2015 est.)

School life expectancy (primary to tertiary education): *total:* 17 years
male: 16 years
female: 17 years (2014)

Unemployment, youth ages 15-24: *total:* 16.3%
male: 16%
female: 16.6% (2015 est.)
country comparison to the world: 35

GOVERNMENT

Country name: *conventional long form:* Republic of Lithuania
conventional short form: Lithuania
local long form: Lietuvos Respublika
local short form: Lietuva
former: Lithuanian Soviet Socialist Republic
etymology: meaning of the name "Lietuva" remains unclear; it may derive from the Lietava, a stream in east central Lithuania

Government type: semi-presidential republic

Capital: *name:* Vilnius
geographic coordinates: 54 41 N, 25 19 E
time difference: UTC+2 (7 hours ahead of Washington, DC, during Standard Time)
daylight saving time: +1hr, begins last Sunday in March; ends last Sunday in October

Administrative divisions: 60 municipalities (savivaldybe, singular—savivaldybe); Akmene, Alytaus Miestas, Alytus, Anksciai, Birstono, Birzai, Druskininkai, Elektrenai, Ignalina, Jonava, Joniskis, Jurbarkas, Kaisiadorys, Kalvarijos, Kauno Miestas, Kaunas, Kazlu Rudos, Kedainiai, Kelme, Klaipedos Miestas, Klaipeda, Kretinga, Kupiskis, Lazdijai, Marijampole, Mazeikiai, Moletai, Neringa, Pagegiai, Pakruojis, Palangos Miestas, Panevezio Miestas, Panevezys, Pasvalys, Plunge, Prienai, Radviliskis, Raseiniai, Rietavo, Rokiskis, Sakiai, Salcininkai, Siauliu Miestas, Siauliai, Silale, Silute, Sirvintos, Skuodas, Svencionys, Taurage, Telsiai, Trakai, Ukmerge, Utena, Varena, Vilkaviskis, Vilniaus Miestas, Vilnius, Visaginas, Zarasai

Independence: 11 March 1990 (declared independence from the Soviet Union); 6 September 1991 (recognized by the Soviet Union); notable earlier dates: 6 July 1253 (coronation of MINDAUGAS, traditional founding date); 1 July 1569 (Polish-Lithuanian Commonwealth created); 16 February 1918 (independence from Soviet Russia)

National holiday: Independence Day (or National Day), 16 February (1918); note—16 February 1918 was the date Lithuania established its statehood and its concomitant independence from Soviet Russia and Germany; 11 March 1990 was the date it declared the restoration of Lithuanian statehood and its concomitant independence from the Soviet Union

Constitution: history: several previous; latest adopted by referendum 25 October 1992, entered into force 2 November 1992
amendments: proposed by at least one-fourth of all Parliament members or by petition of at least 300,000 voters; passage requires two-thirds majority vote of Parliament in each of two readings three months apart and a presidential signature; amendments to constitutional articles on national sovereignty and constitutional amendment procedure also require three-fourths voter approval in a referendum; amended 1996, 2003, 2006 (2016)

Legal system: civil law system; legislative acts can be appealed to the Constitutional Court

International law organization participation: accepts compulsory ICJ jurisdiction with reservations; accepts ICCt jurisdiction

Citizenship: *citizenship by birth:* no
citizenship by descent only: at least one parent must be a citizen of Lithuania
dual citizenship recognized: no
residency requirement for naturalization: 10 years

Suffrage: 18 years of age; universal

Executive branch: *chief of state:* President Dalia GRYBAUSKAITE (since 12 July 2009)

head of government: Prime Minister Saulius SKVERNELIS (since 13 December 2016)
cabinet: Council of Ministers nominated by the prime minister, appointed by the president, and approved by Parliament
elections/appointments: president directly elected by absolute majority popular vote in 2 rounds if needed for a 5-year term (eligible for a second term); election last held on 11 and 25 May 2014 (next to be held in May 2019); prime minister appointed by the president, approved by Parliament
election results: Dalia GRYBAUSKAITE reelected president in second reound; percent of vote—Dalia GRYBAUSKAITE (independent) 57.9%, Zigmantas BALCYTIS (LSDP) 40.1%, invalid 2%; Saulius SKVERNELIS (LVZS) approved as prime minister by Parliament vote—90 to 4

Legislative branch: *description:* unicameral Parliament or Seimas (141 seats; 71 members directly elected in single-seat constituencies by absolute majority vote and 70 directly elected in a single nationwide constituency by proportional representation vote; members serve 4-year terms)
elections: last held on 9 and 23 October 2016 (next to be held in October 2020)
election results: percent of vote by party—LVLS 22.5%, TS-LKD 22.6%, LSDP 15%, LS 9.5%, LCP-LPP 6.3%, LLRA 5.7%, TT 5.6%, DP 4.9%, LZP 2%, Lithuanian List 1.8%, other 4.1%; seats by party—LVLS 54, TS-LKD 31, LSDP 17, LS 14, LLRA 8, TT 8, DP 2, LCP-LPP 1, LZP 1, Lithuanian List 1, independent 4

Judicial branch: *highest court(s):* Supreme Court (consists of 37 judges); Constitutional Court (consists of 9 judges)
judge selection and term of office: Supreme Court judges nominated by the president and appointed by the Seimas; judges serve 5-year renewable terms; Constitutional Court judges appointed by the Seimas from nominations—three each by the president of the republic, by the Seimas chairperson, and by the Supreme Court president; judges serve 9-year, nonrenewable terms; one-third of membership reconstituted every 3 years
subordinate courts: Court of Appeals; district and local courts

Political parties and leaders: Anti-Corruption Coalition or LCP-LPP [Naglis PUTEIKIS and Kristupas KRIVICKAS]
Electoral Action of Lithuanian Poles or LLRA [Valdemar TOMASEVSKI]
Homeland Union-Lithuanian Christian Democrats or TS-LKD [Gabrielius LANDSBERGIS]
Labor Party or DP [Valentinas MAZURONIS]
Liberal Movement or LS or LRLS (vacant)
Lithuanian Center Party or LCP [Naglis PUTEIKIS]
Lithuanian Green Party or LZP [Linas BALSYS]
Lithuanian List [Darius KUOLYS]
Lithuanian Pensioners Party or LPP [Kristupas KRIVICKAS]
Lithuanian Social Democratic Party or LSDP [Algirdas BUTKEVICIUS]
Order and Justice Party or TT [Remigijus ZEMAITAITIS]
Peasant and Greens Union or LVZS [Ramunas KARBAUSKIS] (formerly LVLS)
Way of Courage or DK [Jonas VARKALA]

International organization participation: Australia Group, BA, BIS, CBSS, CD, CE, EAPC, EBRD, ECB, EIB, EU, FAO, IAEA, IBRD, ICAO, ICC (national committees), ICCt, ICRM, IDA, IFC, IFRCS, ILO, IMF, IMO, Interpol, IOC, IOM, IPU, ISO, ITU, ITUC (NGOs), MIGA, NATO, NIB, NSG, OAS (observer), OIF (observer), OPCW, OSCE, PCA, Schengen Convention, UN, UN Security Council (non-permanent), UNCTAD, UNESCO, UNIDO, UNWTO, UPU, WCO, WHO, WIPO, WMO, WTO

Diplomatic representation in the US: *chief of mission:* Ambassador Rolandas KRISCIUNAS (since 17 September 2015)
chancery: 2622 16th Street NW, Washington, DC 20009
telephone: [1] (202) 234-5860
FAX: [1] (202) 328-0466

consulate(s) general: Chicago, Los Angeles, New York

Diplomatic representation from the US: *chief of mission:* Ambassador Anne HALL (since 7 October 2016)
embassy: Akmenu gatve 6, Vilnius, LT-03106
mailing address: American Embassy, Akmenu Gatve 6, Vilnius LT-03106
telephone: [370] (5) 266-5500
FAX: [370] (5) 266-5510

Flag description: three equal horizontal bands of yellow (top), green, and red; yellow symbolizes golden fields, as well as the sun, light, and goodness; green represents the forests of the countryside, in addition to nature, freedom, and hope; red stands for courage and the blood spilled in defense of the homeland

National symbol(s): mounted knight known as Vytis (the Chaser), white stork; national colors: yellow, green, red

National anthem: name: "Tautiska giesme" (The National Song)
lyrics/music: Vincas KUDIRKA
note: adopted 1918, restored 1990; written in 1898 while Lithuania was a part of Russia; banned during the Soviet occupation from 1940 to 1990

ECONOMY

Economy—overview: After the country declared independence from the Soviet Union in 1990, Lithuania faced an initial dislocation that is typical during transitions from a planned economy to a free-market economy. Macroeconomic stabilization policies, including privatization of most state-owned enterprises, and a strong commitment to a currency board arrangement led to an open and rapidly growing economy and rising consumer demand. Foreign investment and EU funding aided in the transition. Lithuania joined the WTO in May 2001, the EU in May 2004, and the euro zone in January 2015, and is now working to complete the OECD accession roadmap it received in July 2015. In 2017, joined the OECD Working Group on Bribery, an important step in the OECD accession process.

The Lithuanian economy was severely hit by the 2008-09 global financial crisis, but it has rebounded and become one of the fastest growing in the EU. Increases in exports, investment, and wage growth that supported consumption helped the economy grow by 3.6% in 2017. In 2015, Russia was Lithuania's largest trading partner, followed by Poland, Germany, and Latvia; goods and services trade between the US and Lithuania totaled $2.2 billion. Lithuania opened a self-financed liquefied natural gas terminal in January 2015, providing the first non-Russian supply of natural gas to the Baltic States and reducing Lithuania's dependence on Russian gas from 100% to approximately 30% in 2016.

Lithuania's ongoing recovery hinges on improving the business environment, especially by liberalizing labor laws, and improving competitiveness and export growth, the latter hampered by economic slowdowns in the EU and Russia. In addition, a steady outflow of young and highly educated people is causing a shortage of skilled labor, which, combined with a rapidly aging population, could stress public finances and constrain long-term growth.

GDP (purchasing power parity): $90.63 billion (2017 est.)
$87.55 billion (2016 est.)
$85.58 billion (2015 est.)
note: data are in 2017 dollars
country comparison to the world: 88

GDP (official exchange rate): $46.67 billion (2016 est.)

GDP—real growth rate: 3.5% (2017 est.)
2.3% (2016 est.)
1.8% (2015 est.)
country comparison to the world: 97

GDP—per capita (PPP): $31,900 (2017 est.)
$30,500 (2016 est.)
$29,500 (2015 est.)
note: data are in 2017 dollars
country comparison to the world: 60

Gross national saving: 16% of GDP (2017 est.)
15.5% of GDP (2016 est.)
17.6% of GDP (2015 est.)
country comparison to the world: 121

GDP—composition, by end use:
household consumption: 66.3%
government consumption: 17.7%
investment in fixed capital: 18.8%
investment in inventories: -0.5%
exports of goods and services: 75.9%
imports of goods and services: -78.2% (2017 est.)

GDP—composition, by sector of origin:
agriculture: 3.3%
industry: 28.5%
services: 68.3% (2017 est.)

Agriculture—products: grain, potatoes, sugar beets, flax, vegetables; beef, milk, eggs, pork, cheese; fish

Industries: metal-cutting machine tools, electric motors, televisions, refrigerators and freezers, petroleum refining, shipbuilding (small ships), furniture, textiles, food processing, fertilizer, agricultural machinery, optical equipment, lasers, electronic components, computers, amber jewelry, information technology, video game development, app/software development, biotechnology

Industrial production growth rate: 2.8% (2017 est.)
country comparison to the world: 106

Labor force: 1.467 million (2017 est.)
country comparison to the world: 133

Labor force—by occupation: *agriculture:* 9.1%
industry: 25.2%
services: 65.8% (2015 est.)

Unemployment rate: 7% (2017 est.)
7.9% (2016 est.)
country comparison to the world: 102

Population below poverty line: 22.2% (2015 est.)

Household income or consumption by percentage share: *lowest 10%:* 2.2%
highest 10%: 28.8% (2015)

Distribution of family income—Gini index: 37.9 (2015)
35 (2014)
country comparison to the world: 75

Budget: *revenues:* $16.18 billion
expenditures: $16.63 billion (2017 est.)
Taxes and other revenues: 34.7% of GDP (2017 est.)
country comparison to the world: 57

Budget surplus (+) or deficit (-): -1% of GDP (2017 est.)
country comparison to the world: 58

Public debt: 38.9% of GDP (2017 est.)
40.2% of GDP (2016 est.)
note: official data; data cover general government debt, and includes debt instruments issued (or owned) by government entities other than the treasury; the data include treasury debt held by foreign entities, debt issued by subnational entities, as well as intra-governmental debt; intra-governmental debt consists of treasury borrowings from surpluses in the social funds, such as for retirement, medical care, and unemployment; debt instruments for the social funds are sold at public auctions
country comparison to the world: 138

Fiscal year: calendar year

Inflation rate (consumer prices): 3.5% (2017 est.)
0.7% (2016 est.)
country comparison to the world: 142

Central bank discount rate: 0% (31 December 2016 est.)
0.05% (31 December 2015 est.)
country comparison to the world: 155

Commercial bank prime lending rate: 2.9% (31 December 2017 est.)
2.83% (31 December 2016 est.)
country comparison to the world: 172

Stock of narrow money: $24.73 billion (31 December 2017 est.)
$20.93 billion (31 December 2016 est.)
country comparison to the world: 66

Stock of broad money: $28.27 billion (31 December 2017 est.)
$24.87 billion (31 December 2016 est.)
country comparison to the world: 81

Stock of domestic credit: $34.78 billion (31 December 2017 est.)
$28.55 billion (31 December 2016 est.)
country comparison to the world: 80

Market value of publicly traded shares: $6.76 billion (31 December 2016 est.)
$6.799 billion (31 December 2015 est.)
$7.127 billion (31 December 2014 est.)
country comparison to the world: 81

Current account balance: -$747 million (2017 est.)
-$379 million (2016 est.)
country comparison to the world: 118

Exports: $26.38 billion (2017 est.)
$24.23 billion (2016 est.)
country comparison to the world: 66

Exports—commodities: refined fuel, machinery and equipment, chemicals, textiles, foodstuffs, plastics

Exports—partners: Russia 13.5%, Latvia 9.9%, Poland 9.1%, Germany 7.7%, Estonia 5.3%, US 5.2%, Sweden 4.8%, UK 4.3% (2016)

Imports: $30.39 billion (2017 est.)
$26.35 billion (2016 est.)

country comparison to the world: 63

Imports—commodities: oil, natural gas, machinery and equipment, transport equipment, chemicals, textiles and clothing, metals

Imports—partners: Russia 14.4%, Germany 12.1%, Poland 10.8%, Latvia 8%, Italy 5.4%, Netherlands 4.8%, Sweden 4.4% (2016)

Reserves of foreign exchange and gold: $2.602 billion (31 December 2016 est.) $1.697 billion (31 December 2015 est.) *country comparison to the world:* 110

Debt—external: $34.48 billion (31 March 2016 est.) $31.6 billion (31 March 2015 est.) *country comparison to the world:* 78

Stock of direct foreign investment—at home: $16.57 billion (31 December 2017 est.) $15.87 billion (31 December 2016 est.) *country comparison to the world:* 84

Stock of direct foreign investment—abroad: $4.82 billion (31 December 2017 est.) $4.48 billion (31 December 2016 est.) *country comparison to the world:* 72

Exchange rates: litai (LTL) per US dollar— 0.884 (2017 est.) 0.9037 (2016 est.) 0.9037 (2015 est.) 0.9012 (2014 est.) 0.7525 (2013 est.)

ENERGY

Electricity access: electrification—*total population:* 100% (2016)

Electricity—production: 3.433 billion kWh (2015 est.) *country comparison to the world:* 129

Electricity—consumption: 9.848 billion kWh (2015 est.) *country comparison to the world:* 94

Electricity—exports: 730 million kWh (2015 est.) *country comparison to the world:* 61

Electricity—imports: 7.938 billion kWh (2015 est.) *country comparison to the world:* 31

Electricity—installed generating capacity: 3.641 million kW (2015 est.) *country comparison to the world:* 94

Electricity—from fossil fuels: 59.9% of total installed capacity (2015 est.) *country comparison to the world:* 129

Electricity—from nuclear fuels: 0% of total installed capacity (2015 est.) *country comparison to the world:* 128

Electricity—from hydroelectric plants: 3.2% of total installed capacity (2015 est.) *country comparison to the world:* 132

Electricity—from other renewable sources: 18.3% of total installed capacity (2015 est.) *country comparison to the world:* 35

Crude oil—production: 2,000 bbl/day (2016 est.) *country comparison to the world:* 90

Crude oil—exports: 1,238 bbl/day (2014 est.) *country comparison to the world:* 70

Crude oil—imports: 160,800 bbl/day (2014 est.) *country comparison to the world:* 34

Crude oil—proved reserves: 12 million bbl (1 January 2017 es) *country comparison to the world:* 91

Refined petroleum products—production: 174,800 bbl/day (2014 est.) *country comparison to the world:* 55

Refined petroleum products—consumption: 53,000 bbl/day (2015 est.) *country comparison to the world:* 103

Refined petroleum products—exports: 145,600 bbl/day (2014 est.) *country comparison to the world:* 37

Refined petroleum products—imports: 27,520 bbl/day (2014 est.) *country comparison to the world:* 103

Natural gas—production: 0 cu m (2014 est.) *country comparison to the world:* 159

Natural gas—consumption: 2.93 billion cu m (2015 est.) *country comparison to the world:* 78

Natural gas—exports: 0 cu m (2014 est.) *country comparison to the world:* 137

Natural gas—imports: 2.2 billion cu m (2015 est.) *country comparison to the world:* 50

Natural gas—proved reserves: 0 cu m (2016 est.) *country comparison to the world:* 161

Carbon dioxide emissions from consumption of energy: 11.2 million Mt (2015 est.) *country comparison to the world:* 99

COMMUNICATIONS

Telephones—fixed lines: *total subscriptions:* 530,871 *subscriptions per 100 inhabitants:* 19 (July 2016 est.) *country comparison to the world:* 93

Telephones—mobile cellular: *total:* 4,204,692 *subscriptions per 100 inhabitants:* 147 (July 2016 est.) *country comparison to the world:* 124

Telephone system: *general assessment:* adequate; being modernized to provide improved international capability and better residential access *domestic:* rapid expansion of mobile-cellular services has resulted in a steady decline in the number of fixed-line connections; mobile-cellular teledensity stands at about 145 per 100 persons *international:* country code—370; major international connections to Denmark, Sweden, and Norway by submarine cable for further transmission by satellite; landline connections to Latvia and Poland (2016)

Broadcast media: public broadcaster operates 3 channels with the third channel—a satellite channel—introduced in 2007; various privately owned commercial TV broadcasters operate national and multiple regional channels; many privately owned local TV stations; multi-channel cable and satellite TV services available; publicly owned broadcaster operates 3 radio networks; many privately owned commercial broadcasters, with repeater stations in various regions throughout the country (2007)

Internet country code: .lt *Internet users:* total: 2,122,884

percent of population: 74.4% (July 2016 est.) *country comparison to the world:* 97

TRANSPORTATION

National air transport system: *number of registered air carriers:* 2 *inventory of registered aircraft operated by air carriers:* 52 *annual passenger traffic on registered air carriers:* 1,363,950 *annual freight traffic on registered air carriers:* 565,642 mt-km (2015) *Civil aircraft registration country code prefix:* LY (2016)

Airports: 61 (2013) *country comparison to the world:* 79

Airports—with paved runways: *total:* 22 *over 3,047 m:* 3 *2,438 to 3,047 m:* 1 *1,524 to 2,437 m:* 7 *914 to 1,523 m:* 2 *under 914 m:* 9 (2017)

Airports—with unpaved runways: *total:* 39 *over 3,047 m:* 1 *914 to 1,523 m:* 2 *under 914 m:* 36 (2013)

Pipelines: gas 1,921 km; refined products 121 km (2013)

Railways: *total:* 1,768 km *broad gauge:* 1,746 km 1.520-m gauge (122 km electrified) *standard gauge:* 22 km 1.435-m gauge (2014) *country comparison to the world:* 77

Roadways: *total:* 84,166 km *paved:* 72,297 km (includes 312 km of expressways) *unpaved:* 11,869 km (2012) *country comparison to the world:* 58

Waterways: 441 km (navigable year-round) (2007) *country comparison to the world:* 86

Merchant marine: *total:* 60 *by type:* container ship 2, general cargo 27, oil tanker 2, other 29 (2017) *country comparison to the world:* 105

Ports and terminals: *major seaport(s):* Klaipeda *oil terminal(s):* Butinge oil terminal *LNG terminal(s) (import):* Klaipeda

MILITARY AND SECURITY

Military expenditures: 1.49% of GDP (2016) 1.14% of GDP **(2015)** **0.88% of GDP (2014)** **0.76% of GDP (2013)** **0.77% of GDP (2012)** *country comparison to the world:* 103

Military branches: Lithuanian Armed Forces (Lietuvos Ginkluotosios Pajegos): Land Forces (Sausumos Pajegos), Naval Forces (Karines Juru Pajegos), Air Forces (Karines Oro Pajegos), Special Forces (Specialiuju Operaciju Pajegos); Volunteer Forces (Savanoriu Pajegos) (2016)

Military service age and obligation: 18 years of age for military service; 9-month service obligation; in 2015, Lithuania reinstated conscription after having converted to a professional military in the fall of 2008 (2016)

TRANSNATIONAL ISSUES

Disputes—international: Lithuania and Russia committed to demarcating their boundary in 2006

in accordance with the land and maritime treaty ratified by Russia in May 2003 and by Lithuania in 1999; Lithuania operates a simplified transit regime for Russian nationals traveling from the Kaliningrad coastal exclave into Russia, while still conforming, as a EU member state having an external border with a non-EU member, to strict Schengen border rules; boundary demarcated with Latvia and Lithuania; as of January 2007, ground demarcation of the boundary with Belarus was complete and mapped with final ratification documents in preparation

Refugees and internally displaced persons: stateless persons: 3,466 (2016)

Illicit drugs: transshipment and destination point for cannabis, cocaine, ecstasy, and opiates from Southwest Asia, Latin America, Western Europe, and neighboring Baltic countries; growing production of high-quality amphetamines, but limited production of cannabis, methamphetamines; susceptible to money laundering despite changes to banking legislation

LUXEMBOURG

INTRODUCTION

Background: Founded in 963, Luxembourg became a grand duchy in 1815 and an independent state under the Netherlands. It lost more than half of its territory to Belgium in 1839 but gained a larger measure of autonomy. In 1867, Luxembourg attained full independence under the condition that it promise perpetual neutrality. Overrun by Germany in both world wars, it ended its neutrality in 1948 when it entered into the Benelux Customs Union and when it joined NATO the following year. In 1957, Luxembourg became one of the six founding countries of the EEC (later the EU), and in 1999 it joined the euro currency zone.

GEOGRAPHY

Location: Western Europe, between France and Germany

Geographic coordinates: 49 45 N, 6 10 E

Map references: Europe

Area: *total:* 2,586 sq km
land: 2,586 sq km
water: 0 sq km
country comparison to the world: 179

Area—comparative: slightly smaller than Rhode Island; about half the size of Delaware

Land boundaries: *total:* 327 km
border countries (3): Belgium 130 km, France 69 km, Germany 128 km

Coastline: 0 km (landlocked)

Maritime claims: none (landlocked)

Climate: modified continental with mild winters, cool summers

Terrain: mostly gently rolling uplands with broad, shallow valleys; uplands to slightly mountainous in the north; steep slope down to Moselle flood plain in the southeast

Elevation: *mean elevation:* 325 m

elevation extremes: *lowest point:* Moselle River 133 m
highest point: Buurgplaatz 559 m

Natural resources: iron ore (no longer exploited), arable land

Land use: *agricultural land:* 50.7%
arable land: 24%;
permanent crops: 0.6%;
permanent pasture: 26.1%
forest: 33.5%
other: 15.8% (2011 est.)
Irrigated land: 0 sq km (2012)

Population—distribution: most people live in the south, on or near the border with France

Natural hazards: occasional flooding

Environment—current issues: air and water pollution in urban areas, soil pollution of farmland

Environment—international agreements: *party to:* Air Pollution, Air Pollution-Nitrogen Oxides, Air Pollution-Persistent Organic Pollutants, Air Pollution-Sulfur 85, Air Pollution-Sulfur 94, Air Pollution-Volatile Organic Compounds, Biodiversity, Climate Change, Climate Change-Kyoto Protocol, Desertification, Endangered Species, Hazardous Wastes, Law of the Sea, Marine Dumping, Ozone Layer Protection, Ship Pollution, Tropical Timber 83, Tropical Timber 94, Wetlands

signed, but not ratified: Environmental Modification

Geography—note: landlocked; the only grand duchy in the world

PEOPLE AND SOCIETY

Population: 594,130 (July 2017 est.)
country comparison to the world: 171

Nationality: *noun:* Luxembourger(s)
adjective: Luxembourg

Ethnic groups: Luxembourger 53.3%, Portuguese 16.2%, French 7.2%, Italian 3.5%, Belgian 3.4%, German 2.2%, British 1.1%, other 13.2%
note: data represent population by nationality (2016 est.)

Languages: Luxembourgish (official administrative and judicial language and national language (spoken vernacular)) 55.8%, Portuguese 15.7%, French (official administrative, judicial, and legislative language) 12.1%, German (official administrative and judicial language) 3.1%, Italian 2.9%, English 2.1%, other 8.4% (2011 est.)

Religions: Christian (predominantly Roman Catholic) 70.4%, Muslim 2.3%, other (includes Buddhist, folk religions, Hindu, Jewish) 0.5%, none 26.8% (2010 est.)

Age structure: *0-14 years:* 16.77% (male 51,333/female 48,296)
15-24 years: 12.18% (male 37,047/female 35,310)
25-54 years: 44.27% (male 134,986/female 128,028)
55-64 years: 11.77% (male 35,450/female 34,457)
65 years and over: 15.02% (male 39,786/female 49,437) (2017 est.)

Dependency ratios: *total dependency ratio:* 43.6
youth dependency ratio: 23.5
elderly dependency ratio: 20.1
potential support ratio: 5 (2015 est.)

Median age: *total:* 39.3 years
male: 38.7 years
female: 39.9 years (2017 est.)
country comparison to the world: 54

Population growth rate: 1.98% (2017 est.)
country comparison to the world: 47

Birth rate: 11.5 births/1,000 population (2017 est.)
country comparison to the world: 170

Death rate: 7.3 deaths/1,000 population (2017 est.)
country comparison to the world: 123

Net migration rate: 15.5 migrant(s)/1,000 population (2017 est.)
country comparison to the world: 2

Population distribution: most people live in the south, on or near the border with France

Urbanization: *urban population:* 90.7% of total population (2017)
rate of urbanization: 1.46% annual rate of change (2015-20 est.)

Major urban areas—population: LUXEMBOURG (capital) 107,000 (2014)

Sex ratio: *at birth:* 1.06 male(s)/female
0-14 years: 1.06 male(s)/female
15-24 years: 1.05 male(s)/female
25-54 years: 1.05 male(s)/female
55-64 years: 1.03 male(s)/female
65 years and over: 0.79 male(s)/female
total population: 1.01 male(s)/female (2016 est.)

Mother's mean age at first birth: 30.1 years (2015 est.)

Maternal mortality ratio: 10 deaths/100,000 live births (2015 est.)
country comparison to the world: 150

Infant mortality rate: *total:* 3.4 deaths/1,000 live births
male: 3.8 deaths/1,000 live births
female: 3 deaths/1,000 live births (2017 est.)
country comparison to the world: 209

Life expectancy at birth: *total population:* 82.3 years
male: 79.9 years
female: 84.9 years (2017 est.)
country comparison to the world: 13

Total fertility rate: 1.62 children born/woman (2017 est.)
country comparison to the world: 178

Health expenditures: 6.6% of GDP (2014)
country comparison to the world: 90

Physicians density: 2.92 physicians/1,000 population (2015)

Hospital bed density: 5.4 beds/1,000 population (2010)

Drinking water source:
improved:
urban: 100% of population
rural: 100% of population
total: 100% of population
unimproved:
urban: 0% of population
rural: 0% of population
total: 0% of population (2015 est.)

Sanitation facility access:
improved:
urban: 97.5% of population
rural: 98.5% of population

total: 97.6% of population
unimproved:
urban: 2.5% of population
rural: 1.5% of population
total: 2.4% of population (2015 est.)

HIV/AIDS—adult prevalence rate: NA

HIV/AIDS—people living with HIV/AIDS: NA

HIV/AIDS—deaths: <100 (2016 est.)

Obesity—adult prevalence rate: 22.6% (2016)
country comparison to the world: 74

Education expenditures: 4.1% of GDP (2012)
country comparison to the world: 118

School life expectancy (primary to tertiary education): *total:* 14 years
male: 14 years
female: 14 years (2012)

Unemployment, youth ages 15-24: *total:* 17.4%
male: 18.9%
female: 15.7% (2015 est.)
country comparison to the world: 59

GOVERNMENT

Country name: *conventional long form:* Grand Duchy of Luxembourg
conventional short form: Luxembourg
local long form: Grand Duche de Luxembourg
local short form: Luxembourg
etymology: from the Celtic "lucilem" (little) and the German "burg" (castle or fortress) to produce the meaning of the "little castle"

Government type: constitutional monarchy

Capital: *name:* Luxembourg

geographic coordinates: 49 36 N, 6 07 E
time difference: UTC+1 (6 hours ahead of Washington, DC, during Standard Time)
daylight saving time: +1hr, begins last Sunday in March; ends last Sunday in October

Administrative divisions: 12 cantons (cantons, singular—canton); Capellen, Clervaux, Diekirch, Echternach, Esch-sur-Alzette, Grevenmacher, Luxembourg, Mersch, Redange, Remich, Vianden, Wiltz

Independence: 1839 (from the Netherlands)

National holiday: National Day (Birthday of Grand Duke HENRI), 23 June; note—this date of birth is not the true date of birth for any of the Royals, but the national festivities were shifted in 1962 to allow observance during a more favorable time of year

Constitution: history: previous 1842 (heavily amended 1848, 1856); latest effective 17 October 1868
amendments: proposed by the Chamber of Deputies or by the monarch to the Chamber; passage requires at least two-thirds majority vote by the Chamber in two successive readings three months apart; a referendum can be substituted for the second reading if approved by more than one-quarter of the Chamber members or by 25,000 valid voters; adoption by referendum requires a majority of all valid voters; amended many times, last in 2009 (2016)

Legal system: civil law system

International law organization participation: accepts compulsory ICJ jurisdiction; accepts ICCt jurisdiction

Citizenship: *citizenship by birth:* limited to situations where the parents are either unknown, stateless, or when the nationality law of the parents' state of origin does not permit acquisition of citizenship by descent when the birth occurs outside of national territory
citizenship by descent: at least one parent must be a citizen of Luxembourg
dual citizenship recognized: yes
residency requirement for naturalization: 7 years

Suffrage: 18 years of age; universal and compulsory

Executive branch: *chief of state:* Grand Duke HENRI (since 7 October 2000); Heir Apparent Prince GUILLAUME, son of the monarch, born 11 November 1981

head of government: Prime Minister Xavier BETTEL (since 4 December 2013); Deputy Prime Minister Etienne SCHNEIDER (since 4 December 2013)
cabinet: Council of Ministers recommended by the prime minister, appointed by the monarch
elections/appointments: the monarchy is hereditary; following elections to the Chamber of Deputies, the leader of the majority party or majority coalition usually appointed prime minister by the monarch; deputy prime minister appointed by the monarch; prime minister and deputy prime minister are responsible to the Chamber of Deputies

Legislative branch: *description:* unicameral Chamber of Deputies or Chambre des Deputes (60 seats; members directly elected in multi-seat constituencies by proportional representation vote; members serve 5-year terms); note—a 21-member Council of State appointed by the Grand Duke on the advice of the prime minister serves as an advisory body to the Chamber of Deputies
elections: last held on 20 October 2013 (next to be held by October 2018)
election results: percent of vote by party—CSV 33.7%, LSAP 20.3%, DP 18.3%, Green Party 10.1%, ADR 6.6%, The Left 4.9%, other 6.1%; seats by party—CSV 23, LSAP 13, DP 13, Green Party 6, ADR 3, The Left 2

Judicial branch: *highest court(s):* Supreme Court of Justice includes Court of Appeal and Court of Cassation (consists of 27 judges on 9 benches); Constitutional Court (consists of 9 members)
judge selection and term of office: judges of both courts appointed by the monarch for life
subordinate courts: Court of Accounts; district and local tribunals and courts

Political parties and leaders: Alternative Democratic Reform Party or ADR [Jean SCHOOS]
Christian Social People's Party or CSV [Marc SPAUTZ]
Democratic Party or DP [Corinne CAHEN]
Green Party [Francoise FOLMER and Christian KMIOTEK]

Luxembourg Socialist Workers' Party or LSAP [Claude HAAGEN]

The Left (dei Lenk/la Gauche) [collective leadership, Central Committee]

other minor parties

Political pressure groups and leaders: Business Federation Luxembourg or FEDIL [Nicolas BUCK] Centrale Paysanne [Marc FISCH] (federation of agricultural producers) Chamber of Artisans (Chambre des Metiers) [Tom OBERWEIS] Chamber of Commerce (Chambre de Commerce) [Carlo THELEN] Chambre des Salaries or CSL [Jean-Claude REDING] General Association of Officials (Confederation Generale de la Fonction Publique or CGFP) [Romain WOLFF] (trade union representing civil service) Greenpeace [Raymond AENDEKERK] Luxembourg Confederation of Christian Trade Unions or LCGB [Patrick DURY] (center-right trade union) Luxembourg Association of Bankers and Insurance Employees or ALEBA [Roberto SCOLATI] Luxembourg Bankers Association or ABBL [Yves MAAS] Mouvement Ecologique [Blanche WEBER] (environmental protection) Confederation of Independent Trade Unions or OGB-L [Andre ROELTGEN] (center-left trade union)

International organization participation: ADB (nonregional member), Australia Group, Benelux, BIS, CD, CE, EAPC, EBRD, ECB, EIB, EMU, ESA, EU, FAO, FATF, IAEA, IBRD, ICAO, ICC (national committees), ICCt, ICRM, IDA, IEA, IFAD, IFC, IFRCS, ILO, IMF, IMO, Interpol, IOC, IOM, IPU, ISO, ITSO, ITU, ITUC (NGOs), MIGA, NATO, NEA, NSG, OAS (observer), OECD, OIF, OPCW, OSCE, PCA, Schengen Convention, UN, UNCTAD, UNESCO, UNHCR, UNIDO, UNRWA, UPU, WCO, WHO, WIPO, WMO, WTO, ZC

Diplomatic representation in the US: *chief of mission:* Ambassador Sylvie LUCAS (since 16 September 2016) *chancery:* 2200 Massachusetts Avenue NW, Washington, DC 20008 *telephone:* [1] (202) 265-4171 *FAX:* [1] (202) 328-8270 *consulate(s) general:* New York, San Francisco

Diplomatic representation from the US: US chief of mission: Ambassador (vacant); Charge d'Affaires Kerri HANNAN (since late June 2017) *embassy:* 22 Boulevard Emmanuel Servais, L-2535 Luxembourg City *mailing address:* Unit 3560, APO-AE 09126-3560 (official mail) *telephone:* [352] 46-01-23 00 *FAX:* [352] 46-14-01

Flag description: three equal horizontal bands of red (top), white, and light blue; similar to the flag of the Netherlands, which uses a darker blue and is shorter; the coloring is derived from the Grand

Duke's coat of arms (a red lion on a white and blue striped field)

National symbol(s): red, rampant lion; national colors: red, white, light blue

National anthem: name: "Ons Heemecht" (Our Motherland); "De Wilhelmus" (The William) *lyrics/music:* Michel LENTZ/Jean-Antoine ZINNEN; Nikolaus WELTER/unknown *note:* "Ons Heemecht," adopted 1864, is the national anthem, while "De Wilhelmus," adopted 1919, serves as a royal anthem for use when members of the grand ducal family enter or exit a ceremony in Luxembourg

ECONOMY

Economy—overview: This small, stable, high-income economy has historically featured solid growth, low inflation, and low unemployment. Luxembourg, the only Grand Duchy in the world, is a landlocked country in northwestern Europe surrounded by Belgium, France, and Germany. Despite its small landmass and small population, Luxembourg is the second-wealthiest country in the world when measured on a gross domestic product (PPP) per capita basis. Luxembourg has one of the highest current account surpluses as a share of GDP in the euro zone, and it maintains a healthy budgetary position, with a 2017 surplus of 0.5% of GDP, and the lowest public debt level in the region.

Since 2002, Luxembourg's government has proactively implemented policies and programs to support economic diversification and to attract foreign direct investment. The government focused on key innovative industries that showed promise for supporting economic growth: logistics, information and communications technology (ICT); health technologies, including biotechnology and biomedical research; clean energy technologies, and more recently, space technology and financial services technologies. The economy has evolved and flourished, posting strong GDP growth of 3.4% in 2017, far outpacing the European average of 1.8%.

Luxembourg remains a financial powerhouse—the financial sector accounts for more than 35% of GDP—because of the exponential growth of the investment fund sector through the launch and development of cross-border funds (UCITS) in the 1990s. Luxembourg is the world's second-largest investment fund asset domicile, after the US, with $4 trillion of assets in custody in financial institutions.

Luxembourg has lost some of its advantage as a favorable tax location because of OECD and EU pressure, as well as the "LuxLeaks" scandal, which revealed advantageous tax treatments offered to foreign corporations. In 2015, the government's compliance with EU requirements to implement automatic exchange of tax information on savings accounts—thus ending banking secrecy—has constricted banking activity. Likewise, changes to the way EU members collect taxes from e-commerce has cut Luxembourg's sales tax revenues, requiring the government to raise additional levies and

to reduce some direct social benefits as part of the tax reform package of 2017. The tax reform package also included reductions in the corporate tax rate and increases in deductions for families, both intended to increase purchasing power and increase competitiveness.

GDP (purchasing power parity): $64.39 billion (2017 est.) $61.99 billion (2016 est.) $59.5 billion (2015 est.) *note:* data are in 2017 dollars *country comparison to the world:* 105

GDP (official exchange rate): $63.52 billion (2016 est.)

GDP—real growth rate: 3.9% (2017 est.) 4.2% (2016 est.) 4% (2015 est.) *country comparison to the world:* 74

GDP—per capita (PPP): $109,100 (2017 est.) $107,600 (2016 est.) $105,700 (2015 est.) *note:* data are in 2017 dollars *country comparison to the world:* 5

Gross national saving: 23.2% of GDP (2017 est.) 22.8% of GDP (2016 est.) 24% of GDP (2015 est.) *country comparison to the world:* 62

GDP—composition, by end use: *household consumption:* 28.2% *government consumption:* 15.9% *investment in fixed capital:* 16.8% *investment in inventories:* 0.9% *exports of goods and services:* 230.8% *imports of goods and services:* -192.8% (2017 est.)

GDP—composition, by sector of origin: *agriculture:* 0.2% *industry:* 11.9% *services:* 87.9% (2017 est.)

Agriculture—products: grapes, barley, oats, potatoes, wheat, fruits; dairy and livestock products

Industries: banking and financial services, construction, real estate services, iron, metals, and steel, information technology, telecommunications, cargo transportation and logistics, chemicals, engineering, tires, glass, aluminum, tourism, biotechnology

Industrial production growth rate: 0.1% (2017 est.) *country comparison to the world:* 185

Labor force: 282,800 *note:* data exclude foreign workers; in addition to the figure for domestic labor force, about 150,000 workers commute daily from France, Belgium, and Germany (2017 est.) *country comparison to the world:* 166

Labor force—by occupation: *agriculture:* 1.1% *industry:* 20% *services:* 78.9% (2013 est.)

Unemployment rate: 5.9% (2017 est.) 6.4% (2016 est.) *country comparison to the world:* 81

Population below poverty line: NA%

Household income or consumption by percentage share: *lowest 10%:* 3.5%
highest 10%: 23.8% (2000)

Distribution of family income—Gini index: 30.4 (2013 est.)
26 (2005 est.)
country comparison to the world: 124

Budget: *revenues:* $27.6 billion
expenditures: $27.38 billion (2017 est.)
Taxes and other revenues: 43.5% of GDP (2017 est.)
country comparison to the world: 27

Budget surplus (+) or deficit (-): 0.4% of GDP (2017 est.)
country comparison to the world: 26

Public debt: 19.3% of GDP (2017 est.)
20% of GDP (2016 est.)
note: data cover general government debt, and includes debt instruments issued (or owned) by government entities other than the treasury; the data include treasury debt held by foreign entities; the data include debt issued by subnational entities, as well as intra-governmental debt; intra-governmental debt consists of treasury borrowings from surpluses in the social funds, such as for retirement, medical care, and unemployment; debt instruments for the social funds are not sold at public auctions
country comparison to the world: 188

Fiscal year: calendar year

Inflation rate (consumer prices): 1.2% (2017 est.)
0% (2016 est.)
country comparison to the world: 52

Central bank discount rate: 0.25% (31 December 2016)
0.3% (31 December 2010)
note: this is the European Central Bank's rate on the marginal lending facility, which offers overnight credit to banks in the euro area
country comparison to the world: 139

Stock of narrow money: $281 billion (31 December 2017 est.)
$229.2 billion (31 December 2016 est.)
note: see entry for the EU for money supply for the entire euro area; the European Central Bank (ECB) controls monetary policy for the 18 members of the Economic and Monetary Union (EMU); individual members of the EMU do not control the quantity of money circulating within their own borders
country comparison to the world: 18

Stock of broad money: $312.7 billion (31 December 2017 est.)
$271.4 billion (31 December 2016 est.)
country comparison to the world: 34

Stock of domestic credit: $127.7 billion (31 December 2017 est.)
$109.9 billion (31 December 2016 est.)
country comparison to the world: 53

Market value of publicly traded shares: $47.13 billion (31 December 2015 est.)
$63.17 billion (31 December 2014 est.)
$78.64 billion (31 December 2013 est.)

country comparison to the world: 53

Current account balance: $2.967 billion (2017 est.)
$2.823 billion (2016 est.)
country comparison to the world: 30

Exports: $18.4 billion (2017 est.)
$16.37 billion (2016 est.)
country comparison to the world: 72

Exports—commodities: machinery and equipment, steel products, chemicals, rubber products, glass

Exports—partners: Germany 23.1%, Belgium 16.6%, France 15.4%, Netherlands 5.1% (2016)

Imports: $22.4 billion (2017 est.)
$19.97 billion (2016 est.)
country comparison to the world: 70

Imports—commodities: commercial aircraft, minerals, chemicals, metals, foodstuffs, luxury consumer goods

Imports—partners: Belgium 29.4%, Germany 24.3%, France 10.3%, US 7%, China 5.8%, Netherlands 4.3%, Mexico 4.3% (2016)

Reserves of foreign exchange and gold: $1 billion (31 December 2017 est.)
$974 million (31 December 2016 est.)
country comparison to the world: 124

Debt—external: $3.781 trillion (31 March 2016 est.)
$3.806 trillion (31 March 2015 est.)
country comparison to the world: 7

Stock of direct foreign investment—at home: $11.21 billion (31 December 2008 est.)
country comparison to the world: 95

Stock of direct foreign investment—abroad: $NA

Exchange rates: euros (EUR) per US dollar—
0.906 (2017 est.)
0.9214 (2016 est.)
0.9214 (2015 est.)
0.885 (2014 est.)
0.7634 (2013 est.)

ENERGY

Electricity access: *electrification—total population:* 100% (2016)

Electricity—production: 735 million kWh (2015 est.)
country comparison to the world: 158

Electricity—consumption: 6.178 billion kWh (2015 est.)
country comparison to the world: 114

Electricity—exports: 1.42 billion kWh (2016 est.)
country comparison to the world: 51

Electricity—imports: 7.718 billion kWh (2016 est.)
country comparison to the world: 32

Electricity—installed generating capacity: 2.023 million kW (2015 est.)
country comparison to the world: 113

Electricity—from fossil fuels: 23.7% of total installed capacity (2015 est.)
country comparison to the world: 192

Electricity—from nuclear fuels: 0% of total installed capacity (2015 est.)
country comparison to the world: 131

Electricity—from hydroelectric plants: 1.7% of total installed capacity (2015 est.)
country comparison to the world: 140

Electricity—from other renewable sources: 12.7% of total installed capacity (2015 est.)
country comparison to the world: 60

Crude oil—production: 0 bbl/day (2016 est.)
country comparison to the world: 162

Crude oil—exports: 0 bbl/day (2016 est.)
country comparison to the world: 155

Crude oil—imports: 0 bbl/day (2016 est.)
country comparison to the world: 151

Crude oil—proved reserves: 0 bbl (1 January 2017 es)
country comparison to the world: 159

Refined petroleum products—production: 0 bbl/day (2016 est.)
country comparison to the world: 167

Refined petroleum products—consumption: 56,120 bbl/day (2016 est.)
country comparison to the world: 99

Refined petroleum products—exports: 0 bbl/day (2016 est.)
country comparison to the world: 173

Refined petroleum products—imports: 55,900 bbl/day (2016 est.)
country comparison to the world: 77

Natural gas—production: 6 million cu m (2015 est.)
country comparison to the world: 98

Natural gas—consumption: 1.108 billion cu m (2015 est.)
country comparison to the world: 96

Natural gas—exports: 0 cu m (2014 est.)
country comparison to the world: 140

Natural gas—imports: 875 million cu m (2015 est.)
country comparison to the world: 61

Natural gas—proved reserves: 0 cu m (1 January 2014 es)
country comparison to the world: 164

Carbon dioxide emissions from consumption of energy: 11 million Mt (2013 est.)
country comparison to the world: 100

COMMUNICATIONS

Telephones—fixed lines: *total subscriptions:* 280,000
subscriptions per 100 inhabitants: 48 (July 2016 est.)
country comparison to the world: 119

Telephones—mobile cellular: *total:* 813,000
subscriptions per 100 inhabitants: 140 (July 2016 est.)
country comparison to the world: 162

Telephone system: *general assessment:* highly developed, completely automated and efficient system, mainly buried cables

557

domestic: fixed-line teledensity about 50 per 100 persons; nationwide mobile-cellular telephone system with market for mobile-cellular phones virtually saturated

international: country code—352 (2016)

Broadcast media: Luxembourg has a long tradition of operating radio and TV services for pan-European audiences and is home to Europe's largest privately owned broadcast media group, the RTL Group, which operates 46 TV stations and 29 radio stations in Europe; also home to Europe's largest satellite operator, Societe Europeenne des Satellites (SES); domestically, the RTL Group operates TV and radio networks; other domestic private radio and TV operators and French and German stations available; satellite and cable TV services available (2016)

Internet country code: .lu

Internet users: total: 567,698

percent of population: 97.5% (July 2016 est.)
country comparison to the world: 130

TRANSPORTATION

National air transport system: *number of registered air carriers:* 3
inventory of registered aircraft operated by air carriers: 119

annual passenger traffic on registered air carriers: 1,830,972
annual freight traffic on registered air carriers: 6,309,473,324 mt-km (2015)
Civil aircraft registration country code prefix: LX (2016)

Airports: 2 (2013)
country comparison to the world: 202

Airports—with paved runways: *total:* 1
over 3,047 m: 1 (2017)

Airports—with unpaved runways: *total:* 1
under 914 m: 1 (2013)

Heliports: 1 (2013)

Pipelines: gas 142 km; refined products 27 km (2013)

Railways: *total:* 275 km
standard gauge: 275 km 1.435-m gauge (275 km electrified) (2014)
country comparison to the world: 125

Roadways: *total:* 2,899 km
paved: 2,899 km (includes 152 km of expressways) (2011)
country comparison to the world: 167

Waterways: 37 km (on Moselle River) (2010)
country comparison to the world: 104

Merchant marine: *total:* 152

by type: bulk carrier 3, container ship 21, general cargo 2, other 126 (2017)
country comparison to the world: 72

Ports and terminals: river port(s): Mertert (Moselle)

MILITARY AND SECURITY

Military expenditures: 0.49% of GDP (2016)
0.48% of GDP (2015)
0.42% of GDP (2014)
0.42% of GDP (2013)
0.42% of GDP (2012)
country comparison to the world: 123

Military branches: Luxembourg Army (Armee Luxembourgeoise) (2015)

Military service age and obligation: 18-24 years of age for male and female voluntary military service; no conscription; Luxembourg citizen or EU citizen with 3-year residence in Luxembourg (2017)

TRANSNATIONAL ISSUES

Disputes—international: none
Refugees and internally displaced persons: stateless persons: 83 (2016)

INTRODUCTION

Background: Colonized by the Portuguese in the 16th century, Macau was the first European settlement in the Far East. Pursuant to an agreement signed by China and Portugal on 13 April 1987, Macau became the Macau Special Administrative Region of the People's Republic of China on 20 December 1999. In this agreement, China promised that, under its "one country, two systems" formula, China's political and economic system would not be imposed on Macau, and that Macau would enjoy a "high degree of autonomy" in all matters except foreign affairs and defense for the subsequent 50 years.

GEOGRAPHY

Location: Eastern Asia, bordering the South China Sea and China

Geographic coordinates: 22 10 N, 113 33 E

Map references: Southeast Asia

Area: *total:* 28.2 sq km
land: 28.2 sq km
water: 0 sq km
country comparison to the world: 238

Area—comparative: less than one-sixth the size of Washington, DC

Land boundaries: *total:* 3 km
regional border(s) (1): China 3 km

Coastline: 41 km

Maritime claims: not specified

Climate: subtropical; marine with cool winters, warm summers

Terrain: generally flat

Elevation: *mean elevation:* NA

elevation extremes: *lowest point:* South China Sea 0 m
highest point: Alto Coloane 172 m

Natural resources: NEGL

Land use: *agricultural land:* 0%
arable land: 0%;
permanent crops: 0%;

permanent pasture: 0%
forest: 0%
other: 100% (urban area) (2011 est.)
Irrigated land: 0 sq km (2012)

Population—distribution: population fairly equally distributed

Natural hazards: typhoons

Environment—current issues: air pollution; coastal waters pollution; insufficient policies in reducing and recycling solid wastes; increasing population density worsening noise pollution

Environment—international agreements: *party to:* Marine Dumping (associate member), Ship Pollution (associate member)

Geography—note: essentially urban; an area of land reclaimed from the sea measuring 5.2 sq km and known as Cotai now connects the islands of Coloane and Taipa; the island area is connected to the mainland peninsula by three bridges

PEOPLE AND SOCIETY

Population: 601,969 (July 2017 est.)
note: Macau's statistical agency estimated the total population to be approximately 648,55 as of September 2017
country comparison to the world: 170

Nationality: *noun:* Chinese
adjective: Chinese

Ethnic groups: Chinese 88.7%, Portuguese 1.1%, mixed 1.1%, other 9.2% (includes Macanese—mixed Portuguese and Asian ancestry) (2016 est.)

Languages: Cantonese 80.1%, Mandarin 5.5%, other Chinese dialects 5.3%, Tagalog 3%, English 2.8%, Portuguese 0.6%, other 2.8%
note: Chinese and Portuguese are official languages (2016 est.)

Religions: Buddhist 50%, Roman Catholic 15%, none or other 35% (1997 est.)

Age structure: *0-14 years:* 14.1% (male 44,133/female 40,764)
15-24 years: 11.73% (male 37,194/female 33,418)
25-54 years: 50.1% (male 134,244/female 167,318)
55-64 years: 13.5% (male 40,837/female 40,423)
65 years and over: 10.57% (male 29,764/female 33,874) (2017 est.)

Dependency ratios: *total dependency ratio:* 26.6
youth dependency ratio: 15.7
elderly dependency ratio: 10.9
potential support ratio: 9.2 (2015 est.)

Median age: *total:* 39.3 years
male: 39.5 years
female: 39.1 years (2017 est.)
country comparison to the world: 57

Population growth rate: 0.74% (2017 est.)
country comparison to the world: 138

Birth rate: 8.6 births/1,000 population (2017 est.)
country comparison to the world: 216

Death rate: 4.5 deaths/1,000 population (2017 est.)
country comparison to the world: 205

Net migration rate: 3.3 migrant(s)/1,000 population (2017 est.)
country comparison to the world: 32

Population distribution: population fairly equally distributed

Urbanization: *urban population:* 100% of total population (2017)
rate of urbanization: 1.39% annual rate of change (2015-20 est.)

Sex ratio: *at birth:* 1.05 male(s)/female
0-14 years: 1.09 male(s)/female
15-24 years: 1.11 male(s)/female
25-54 years: 0.8 male(s)/female
55-64 years: 1.01 male(s)/female
65 years and over: 0.88 male(s)/female
total population: 0.91 male(s)/female (2016 est.)

Infant mortality rate: *total:* 3.1 deaths/1,000 live births
male: 3.3 deaths/1,000 live births
female: 2.9 deaths/1,000 live births (2017 est.)
country comparison to the world: 214

Life expectancy at birth: *total population:* 84.6 years
male: 81.6 years
female: 87.7 years (2017 est.)
country comparison to the world: 4

Total fertility rate: 0.95 children born/woman (2017 est.)
country comparison to the world: 223

Physicians density: 3.11 physicians/1,000 population (2010)

HIV/AIDS—adult prevalence rate: NA

HIV/AIDS—people living with HIV/AIDS: NA

HIV/AIDS—deaths: NA

Education expenditures: 2% of GDP (2014)
country comparison to the world: 148

Literacy: *definition:* age 15 and over can read and write
total population: 96.5%
male: 98.2%
female: 95% (2016 est.)

School life expectancy (primary to tertiary education): *total:* 15 years
male: 14 years
female: 15 years (2015)

Unemployment, youth ages 15-24: *total:* 4.5%
male: 5.7%
female: 3.8% (2015 est.)
country comparison to the world: 123

GOVERNMENT

Country name: *conventional long form:* Macau Special Administrative Region
conventional short form: Macau

official long form: Aomen Tebie Xingzhengqu (Chinese); Regiao Administrativa Especial de Macau (Portuguese)

official short form: Aomen (Chinese); Macau (Portuguese)

etymology: name is thought to derive from the A-Ma Temple—built in 1488 and dedicated to Mazu, the goddess of seafarers and fishermen—which is referred to locally as "Maa Gok"—and in Portuguese became "Macau"; the Chinese name Aomen means "inlet gates"

Dependency status: special administrative region of the People's Republic of China

Government type: presidential limited democracy; a special administrative region of the People's Republic of China

Administrative divisions: none (special administrative region of the People's Republic of China)

Independence: none (special administrative region of China)

National holiday: National Day (anniversary of the Founding of the People's Republic of China), 1 October (1949); note—20 December (1999) is celebrated as Macau Special Administrative Region Establishment Day

Constitution: previous 1976 (Organic Statute of Macau, under Portuguese authority); latest adopted 31 March 1993, effective 20 December 1999 (Basic Law of the Macau Special Administrative Region of the People's Republic of China serves as Macau's constitution); amended 2005, 2012 (2016)

Legal system: civil law system based on the Portuguese model

Citizenship: see China

Suffrage: 18 years of age in direct elections for some legislative positions, universal for permanent residents living in Macau for the past 7 years; note—indirect elections are limited to organizations registered as "corporate voters" and an election committee for the chief executive drawn from broad regional groupings, municipal organizations, central government bodies, and elected Macau officials

Executive branch: *chief of state:* President of China XI Jinping (since 14 March 2013)

head of government: Chief Executive Fernando CHUI Sai On (since 20 December 2009)

cabinet: Executive Council appointed by the chief executive

elections/appointments: president indirectly elected by National People's Congress for a 5-year term (eligible for a second term); election last held on 5-17 March 2013 (next to be held in March 2018);chief executive chosen by a 400-member Election Committee for a 5-year term (eligible for a second term); election last held on 29 August 2014 (next to be held in 2019); note—the Legislative Assembly in August 2012 voted to expand the Election Committee to 400 from 300 seats for the 2014 election

election results: Fernando CHUI Sai On reelected chief executive; Election Committee vote count—380 of 396

Legislative branch: *description:* unicameral Legislative Council or Regiao Administrativa Especial de Macau (33 seats; 14 members directly elected by proportional representation vote, 12 indirectly elected by an electoral college of professional and commercial interest groups, and 7 appointed by the chief executive; members serve 4-year terms)

elections: last held on 17 September 2017 (next to be held in 2021)

election results: percent of vote—UMG 10%, UPD 9.7%, ACUM 8.6%, NE 8.3%, UPP 7.2, ANMD 6.6%, NUDM 6.1%, ACDM 5.9%, APMD 5.8%, Civic Watch 5.6%, ABL 5.5%, ANPM 5.3%, other 15.4%; seats by political group—UMG 2, UPD 2, ABL 1, ACDM 1, ACUM 1, ANMD 1, ANPM 1, APMD 1, Civic Watch 1, NE 1, NUDM 1, UPP 1; 12 seats filled by professional and business groups; 7 members appointed by the chief executive

Judicial branch: *highest court(s):* Court of Final Appeal of Macau Special Administrative Region (consists of the court president and 2 associate justices)

judge selection and term of office: justices appointed by the Macau chief executive upon the recommendation of an independent commission of judges, lawyers, and "eminent" persons; judge tenure NA

subordinate courts: Court of Second Instance; Court of First instance; Lower Court; Administrative Court

Political parties and leaders: Alliance for Change or APM [Melinda CHAN Mei-yi]

Alliance for a Happy Home or ABL [WONG Kit-cheng] (an electoral list of UPP)

Civic Watch or Civico [Agnes LAM Iok-fong]

Macau-Guangdong Union or UMG [MAK Soi-kun]

Macau Citizens' Development Association or ACDM [Becky SONG Pek-kei] (an electoral list of ACUM)

New Democratic Macau Association or ANMD [AU Kam-san]

New Hope or NE [Jose Maria Pereira COUTINHO]

New Macau Association or AMN [Sulu SOU Ka-hou]

New Union for Macau's Development or NUDM [Angela LEONG On-kei]

Prosperous Democratic Macau Association or APMD (an electoral list of the AMN)

Union for Development or UPD [Ella LEI Cheng-I]

Union for Promoting Progress or UPP [HO Ion-sang]

United Citizens Association of Macau or ACUM [CHAN Meng-kam]

note: there is no political party ordinance, so there are no registered political parties; politically active groups register as societies or companies

Political pressure groups and leaders: Bar-Bending Workers' Association [WONG Wai-Man]

Democratic Action [LEE Kin-yun]

Macau New Chinese Youth Association (Associacao de Nova Juventude Chinesa de Macau) or ANJCM [LEONG Sin-man]

Macau Workers' Union [HO Heng-kuok]

New Macau Association [Antonio NG Kuok-cheong]

Workers' Self-Help Union [CHEONG Weng-fat]

International organization participation: ICC (national committees), IHO, IMF, IMO (associate), Interpol (subbureau), ISO (correspondent), UNESCO (associate), UNWTO (associate), UPU, WCO, WMO, WTO

Diplomatic representation in the US: none (Special Administrative Region of China)

Diplomatic representation from the US: the US has no offices in Macau; US Consulate General in Hong Kong is accredited to Macau

Flag description: green with a lotus flower above a stylized bridge and water in white, beneath an arc of five gold, five-pointed stars: one large in the center of the arc and two smaller on either side; the lotus is the floral emblem of Macau, the three petals represent the peninsula and two islands that make up Macau; the five stars echo those on the flag of China

National symbol(s): lotus blossom; national colors: green, white, yellow

National anthem: *note:* as a Special Administrative Region of China, "Yiyongjun Jinxingqu" is the official anthem (see China)

ECONOMY

Economy—overview: Since opening up its locally-controlled casino industry to foreign competition in 2001, Macau has attracted tens of billions of dollars in foreign investment, transforming the territory into one of the world's largest gaming centers. Macau's gaming and tourism businesses were fueled by China's decision to relax travel restrictions on Chinese citizens wishing to visit Macau. In 2016, Macau's gaming-related taxes accounted for more than 76% of total government revenue.

Macau's economy slowed dramatically in 2009 as a result of the global economic slowdown, but strong growth resumed in the 2010-13 period, largely on the back of tourism from mainland China and the gaming sectors. In 2015, this city of 646,800 hosted nearly 30.7 million visitors. Almost 67% came from mainland China. Macau's traditional manufacturing industry has slowed greatly since the termination of the Multi-Fiber Agreement in 2005. Services export—primarily gaming—increasingly has driven Macau's economic performance. Mainland China's anti-corruption campaign brought Macau's gambling boom to a halt in 2014, with spending in casinos contracting 34.3% in 2015. As a result, Macau's inflation-adjusted GDP contracted 21.5% in 2015 and another 2.1% in 2016—down from double-digit expansion rates in the period 2010-13—but the economy recovered handsomely in 2017.

Macau continues to face the challenges of managing its growing casino industry, risks from money-laundering activities, and the need to diversify the economy away from heavy dependence on gaming revenues. Macau's currency, the pataca, is closely tied to the Hong Kong dollar, which is also freely accepted in the territory.

GDP (purchasing power parity): $73.58 billion (2017 est.)
$64.86 billion (2016 est.)
$66.28 billion (2015 est.)
note: data are in 2017 dollars
country comparison to the world: 97

GDP (official exchange rate): $51.16 billion (2016 est.)

GDP—real growth rate: 13.4% (2017 est.)
-2.1% (2016 est.)
-21.5% (2015 est.)
country comparison to the world: 2

GDP—per capita (PPP): $114,400 (2017 est.)
$100,600 (2016 est.)
$102,400 (2015 est.)
country comparison to the world: 4

GDP—composition, by end use:
household consumption: 24.5%
government consumption: 9.4%
investment in fixed capital: 17.7%
investment in inventories: 0%
exports of goods and services: 79.3%
imports of goods and services: -30.8% (2017 est.)

GDP—composition, by sector of origin:
agriculture: 0%
industry: 11.3%
services: 88.7% (2017 est.)

Agriculture—products: only 2% of land area is cultivated, mainly by vegetable growers; fishing, mostly for crustaceans, is important; some of the catch is exported to Hong Kong

Industries: tourism, gambling, clothing, textiles, electronics, footwear, toys

Industrial production growth rate: 2% (2017 est.)
country comparison to the world: 137

Labor force: 400,000 (2017 est.)
country comparison to the world: 160

Labor force—by occupation: manufacturing: 2.5%
construction: 9.8%
transport and communications: 4.4%
wholesale and retail trade: 12.4%
restaurants and hotels: 15%
gambling: 25.9%
public sector: 7.1%
financial services: 2.6%
other services: 20.3% (2013)

Unemployment rate: 2% (2017 est.)
1.9% (2016 est.)
country comparison to the world: 13

Population below poverty line: NA%

Household income or consumption by percentage share: lowest 10%: NA%
highest 10%: NA%

Distribution of family income—Gini index: 35 (2013)
38 (2008)
country comparison to the world: 94

Budget: revenues: $14.24 billion
expenditures: $10.55 billion (2017 est.)
Taxes and other revenues: 27.8% of GDP (2017 est.)
country comparison to the world: 97

Budget surplus (+) or deficit (-): 7.2% of GDP (2017 est.)
country comparison to the world: 4

Public debt: 0% of GDP (2016 est.)
0% of GDP (2015 est.)
country comparison to the world: 206

Fiscal year: calendar year

Inflation rate (consumer prices): 1.5% (2017 est.)
2.4% (2016 est.)
country comparison to the world: 63

Commercial bank prime lending rate: 5.5% (31 December 2017 est.)
5.25% (31 December 2016 est.)
country comparison to the world: 134

Stock of narrow money: $8.993 billion (31 December 2017 est.)
$7.783 billion (31 December 2016 est.)
country comparison to the world: 87

Stock of broad money: $77.31 billion (31 December 2017 est.)
$66.57 billion (31 December 2016 est.)
country comparison to the world: 61

Stock of domestic credit: $20.18 billion (31 December 2017 est.)
$17.16 billion (31 December 2016 est.)
country comparison to the world: 93

Market value of publicly traded shares: $85.5 billion (2 March 2012 est.)
$46.1 billion (31 February 2011 est.)
$2.3 billion (31 December 2008 est.)
country comparison to the world: 43

Current account balance: $16.86 billion (2017 est.)
$12.31 billion (2016 est.)
country comparison to the world: 18

Exports: $1.137 billion (2013 est.)
$1.959 billion (2015 est.)
note: includes reexports
country comparison to the world: 155

Exports—commodities: clothing, textiles, footwear, toys, electronics, machinery and parts

Exports—partners: Hong Kong 64.1%, China 20.2% (2016)

Imports: $0 (2014 est.)
$13.52 billion (2015 est.)
country comparison to the world: 221

Imports—commodities: raw materials and semi-manufactured goods, consumer goods (foodstuffs, beverages, tobacco, garments and footwear, motor vehicles), capital goods, mineral fuels and oils

Imports—partners: China 36.7%, Hong Kong 8.6%, Italy 7.9%, Switzerland 7.6%, France 7.4%, Japan 6.3%, US 5.8% (2016)

Reserves of foreign exchange and gold: $19.49 billion (31 December 2016 est.)
$18.89 billion (31 December 2015 est.)

note: the Fiscal Reserves Act that came into force on 1 January 2012 requires the fiscal reserves to be separated from the foreign exchange reserves and to be managed separately; the transfer of assets took place in February 2012
country comparison to the world: 62

Debt—external: $0 (31 December 2013)
$0 (31 December 2012)
country comparison to the world: 205

Stock of direct foreign investment—at home: $18.91 billion (31 December 2011 est.)
$14.91 billion (31 December 2011 est.)
country comparison to the world: 81

Stock of direct foreign investment—abroad: $1.166 billion (2012 est.)
$667.8 million (2011 est.)
country comparison to the world: 84

Exchange rates: patacas (MOP) per US dollar—
8 (2017 est.)
7.9951 (2016 est.)
7.9951 (2015 est.)
7.985 (2014 est.)
7.9871 (2013 est.)

ENERGY

Electricity access: population without electricity: 59,742
electrification—total population: 91%
electrification—urban areas: 91%
electrification—rural areas: 72% (2012)

Electricity—production: 904 million kWh (2015 est.)
country comparison to the world: 156

Electricity—consumption: 4.834 billion kWh (2015 est.)
country comparison to the world: 123

Electricity—exports: 0 kWh (2016 est.)
country comparison to the world: 164

Electricity—imports: 4.306 billion kWh (2016 est.)
country comparison to the world: 44

Electricity—installed generating capacity: 472,000 kW (2015 est.)
country comparison to the world: 148

Electricity—from fossil fuels: 100% of total installed capacity (2015 est.)
country comparison to the world: 11

Electricity—from nuclear fuels: 0% of total installed capacity (2015 est.)
country comparison to the world: 134

Electricity—from hydroelectric plants: 0% of total installed capacity (2015 est.)
country comparison to the world: 185

Electricity—from other renewable sources: 0% of total installed capacity (2015 est.)
country comparison to the world: 196

Crude oil—production: 0 bbl/day (2016 est.)
country comparison to the world: 163

Crude oil—exports: 0 bbl/day (2014 est.)
country comparison to the world: 157

Crude oil—imports: 0 bbl/day (2014 est.)
country comparison to the world: 154

Crude oil—proved reserves: 0 bbl (1 January 2017 es)
country comparison to the world: 160

Refined petroleum products—production: 0 bbl/day (2014 est.)
country comparison to the world: 168

Refined petroleum products—consumption: 12,700 bbl/day (2015 est.)
country comparison to the world: 156

Refined petroleum products—exports: 0 bbl/day (2014 est.)
country comparison to the world: 175

Refined petroleum products—imports: 10,760 bbl/day (2014 est.)
country comparison to the world: 141

Natural gas—production: 0 cu m (2013 est.)
country comparison to the world: 163

Natural gas—consumption: 355,000 cu m (2013 est.)
country comparison to the world: 115

Natural gas—exports: 0 cu m (2013 est.)
country comparison to the world: 142

Natural gas—imports: 371,000 cu m (2013 est.)
country comparison to the world: 78

Natural gas—proved reserves: 0 cu m (1 January 2014 es)
country comparison to the world: 165

Carbon dioxide emissions from consumption of energy: 1.8 million Mt (2013 est.)
country comparison to the world: 153

COMMUNICATIONS

Telephones—fixed lines: *total:* 142,000

subscriptions per 100 inhabitants: 24 (July 2016 est.)
country comparison to the world: 133

Telephones—mobile cellular: *total:* 1.896 million
subscriptions per 100 inhabitants: 320 (July 2016 est.)
country comparison to the world: 154

Telephone system: *general assessment:* fairly modern communication facilities maintained for domestic and international services
domestic: termination of monopoly over mobile-cellular telephone services in 2001 spurred sharp increase in subscriptions with mobile-cellular teledensity exceeding 300 per 100 persons; fixed-line subscribership appears to have peaked and is now in decline
international: country code—853; landing point for the SEA-ME-WE-3 submarine cable network that provides links to Asia, the Middle East, and Europe; HF radiotelephone communication facility; satellite earth station—1 Intelsat (Indian Ocean) (2016)

Broadcast media: local government dominates broadcast media; 2 television stations operated by the government with one broadcasting in Portuguese and the other in Cantonese and Mandarin; 1 cable TV and 4 satellite TV services available; 3 radio stations broadcasting, of which 2 are government-operated (2015)

Internet country code: .mo
Internet users: total: 460,000
percent of population: 77.6% (July 2016 est.)
country comparison to the world: 150

TRANSPORTATION

National air transport system: *number of registered air carriers:* 1 (registered in China)
inventory of registered aircraft operated by air carriers: 17 (registered in China)
annual passenger traffic on registered air carriers: 2,276,436
annual freight traffic on registered air carriers: 25.435 million mt-km (2015)
Civil aircraft registration country code prefix: B-M (2016)

Airports: 1 (2013)
country comparison to the world: 224

Airports—with paved runways: *total:* 1
over 3,047 m: 1 (2017)

Heliports: 2 (2013)

Roadways: *total:* 424 km
paved: 424 km (2014)
country comparison to the world: 200

Ports and terminals: *major seaport(s):* Macau

MILITARY AND SECURITY

Military branches: no regular indigenous military forces

Military—note: defense is the responsibility of China

TRANSNATIONAL ISSUES

Disputes—international: none

Illicit drugs: transshipment point for drugs going into mainland China; consumer of opiates and amphetamines

MACEDONIA

INTRODUCTION

Background: Macedonia gained its independence peacefully from Yugoslavia in 1991. Greek objection to Macedonia's name, insisting it implies territorial pretensions to the northern Greek province of the same name, and democratic backsliding have stalled the country's movement toward Euro-Atlantic integration. Immediately after Macedonia declared independence, Greece sought to block Macedonian efforts to gain UN membership if the name "Macedonia" was used. Macedonia was eventually admitted to the UN in 1993 as "The Former Yugoslav Republic of Macedonia," and at the same time it agreed to UN-sponsored negotiations on the name dispute. In 1995, Greece lifted a 20-month trade embargo and the two countries agreed to normalize relations, but the issue of the name remained unresolved and negotiations for a solution are ongoing. Since 2004, the US and over 130 other nations have recognized Macedonia by its constitutional name, Republic of Macedonia. Ethnic Albanian grievances over perceived political and economic inequities escalated into an insurgency in 2001 that eventually led to the internationally brokered Ohrid Framework Agreement (OFA), which ended the fighting and established guidelines for constitutional amendments and the creation of new laws that enhanced the rights of minorities. Relations between ethnic Macedonians and ethnic Albanians remain fragile, however.

A nearly three-year political crisis that engulfed Macedonia finally ended in June 2017 following a six-month-long government formation period after a closely contested early legislative election in December 2016. The crisis began after the 2014 legislative and presidential election, and escalated in 2015 when the opposition party began releasing wiretap content that it alleged showed widespread government corruption. Although Macedonia became an EU candidate in 2005, the country still faces challenges, including overcoming the political crisis, fully implementing the OFA, resolving the outstanding name dispute with Greece, improving relations with Bulgaria, halting democratic backsliding, and stimulating economic growth and development. At the 2008 NATO Summit in Bucharest, Romania, the Allies agreed that Macedonia would be invited to join the Alliance as soon as a mutually acceptable resolution to the name dispute was reached with Greece.

GEOGRAPHY

Location: Southeastern Europe, north of Greece

Geographic coordinates: 41 50 N, 22 00 E

Map references: Europe

Area: *total:* 25,713 sq km
land: 25,433 sq km
water: 280 sq km
country comparison to the world: 150

Area—comparative: slightly larger than Vermont

Land boundaries: *total:* 838 km
border countries (5): Albania 181 km, Bulgaria 162 km, Greece 234 km, Kosovo 160 km, Serbia 101 km

Coastline: 0 km (landlocked)

Maritime claims: none (landlocked)

Climate: warm, dry summers and autumns; relatively cold winters with heavy snowfall

Terrain: mountainous with deep basins and valleys; three large lakes, each divided by a frontier line; country bisected by the Vardar River

Elevation: *mean elevation:* 741 m

elevation extremes: *lowest point:* Vardar River 50 m
highest point: Golem Korab (Maja e Korabit) 2,764 m

Natural resources: low-grade iron ore, copper, lead, zinc, chromite, manganese, nickel, tungsten, gold, silver, asbestos, gypsum, timber, arable land

Land use: *agricultural land:* 44.3%
arable land: 16.4%;
permanent crops: 1.4%;
permanent pasture: 26.5%
forest: 39.8%
other: 15.9% (2011 est.)
Irrigated land: 1,280 sq km (2012)

Population—distribution: a fairly even distribution throughout most of the country, with urban areas attracting larger and denser populations

Natural hazards: high seismic risks

Environment—current issues: air pollution from metallurgical plants

Environment—international agreements: *party to:* Air Pollution, Biodiversity, Climate Change, Climate Change-Kyoto Protocol, Desertification, Endangered Species, Hazardous Wastes, Law of the Sea, Ozone Layer Protection, Wetlands
signed, but not ratified: none of the selected agreements

Geography—note: landlocked; major transportation corridor from Western and Central Europe to Aegean Sea and Southern Europe to Western Europe

PEOPLE AND SOCIETY

Population: 2,103,721 (July 2017 est.)
country comparison to the world: 145

Nationality: *noun:* Macedonian(s)
adjective: Macedonian

Ethnic groups: Macedonian 64.2%, Albanian 25.2%, Turkish 3.9%, Romani 2.7%, Serb 1.8%, other 2.2% (2002 est.)
note: Romani populations are usually underestimated in official statistics and may represent 6.5–13% of Macedonia's population

Languages: Macedonian (official) 66.5%, Albanian 25.1%, Turkish 3.5%, Romani 1.9%, Serbian 1.2%, other 1.8% (2002 est.)
note: minority languages are co-official with Macedonian in municipalities where they are spoken by at least 20% of the population; Albanian is co-official in Tetovo, Brvenica, Vrapciste, and other municipalities; Turkish is co-official in Centar Zupa and Plasnica; Romani is co-official in Suto Orizari; Aromanian is co-official in Drusevo; Serbian is co-official in Cucer Sandevo

Religions: Macedonian Orthodox 64.8%, Muslim 33.3%, other Christian 0.4%, other and unspecified 1.5% (2002 est.)

Age structure: *0-14 years:* 17.17% (male 187,063/ female 174,196)
15-24 years: 13.41% (male 145,716/female 136,444)
25-54 years: 43.6% (male 465,862/female 451,321)
55-64 years: 12.41% (male 128,024/female 132,955)
65 years and over: 13.41% (male 121,019/female 161,121) (2017 est.)

Dependency ratios: *total dependency ratio:* 41.6
youth dependency ratio: 23.8
elderly dependency ratio: 17.7
potential support ratio: 5.6 (2015 est.)

Median age: *total:* 37.9 years
male: 36.8 years
female: 39 years (2017 est.)
country comparison to the world: 65

Population growth rate: 0.17% (2017 est.)
country comparison to the world: 187

Birth rate: 11.4 births/1,000 population (2017 est.)
country comparison to the world: 172

Death rate: 9.2 deaths/1,000 population (2017 est.)
country comparison to the world: 63

Net migration rate: -0.5 migrant(s)/1,000 population (2017 est.)
country comparison to the world: 122

Population distribution: a fairly even distribution throughout most of the country, with urban areas attracting larger and denser populations

Urbanization: *urban population:* 57.3% of total population (2017)
rate of urbanization: 0.24% annual rate of change (2015-20 est.)

Major urban areas—population: SKOPJE (capital) 503,000 (2015)

Sex ratio: *at birth:* 1.08 male(s)/female
0-14 years: 1.07 male(s)/female
15-24 years: 1.07 male(s)/female
25-54 years: 1.03 male(s)/female
55-64 years: 0.96 male(s)/female
65 years and over: 0.75 male(s)/female

total population: 0.99 male(s)/female (2016 est.)

Mother's mean age at first birth: 26.8 years (2014 est.)

Maternal mortality ratio: 8 deaths/100,000 live births (2015 est.)
country comparison to the world: 157

Infant mortality rate: *total:* 7.4 deaths/1,000 live births
male: 7.6 deaths/1,000 live births
female: 7.1 deaths/1,000 live births (2017 est.)
country comparison to the world: 160

Life expectancy at birth: *total population:* 76.4 years
male: 73.8 years
female: 79.2 years (2017 est.)
country comparison to the world: 88

Total fertility rate: 1.6 children born/woman (2017 est.)
country comparison to the world: 180

Contraceptive prevalence rate: 40.2% (2011)

Health expenditures: 6.5% of GDP (2014)
country comparison to the world: 93

Physicians density: 2.8 physicians/1,000 population (2013)

Hospital bed density: 4.5 beds/1,000 population (2011)

Drinking water source:
improved:
urban: 99.8% of population
rural: 98.9% of population
total: 99.4% of population
unimproved:
urban: 0.2% of population
rural: 1.1% of population
total: 0.6% of population (2015 est.)

Sanitation facility access:
improved:
urban: 97.2% of population
rural: 82.6% of population
total: 90.9% of population
unimproved:
urban: 2.8% of population
rural: 17.4% of population
total: 9.1% of population (2015 est.)

HIV/AIDS—adult prevalence rate: <.1% (2016 est.)

HIV/AIDS—people living with HIV/AIDS: <500 (2016 est.)

HIV/AIDS—deaths: <100 (2016 est.)

Obesity—adult prevalence rate: 22.4% (2016)
country comparison to the world: 77

Children under the age of 5 years underweight: 1.3% (2011)
country comparison to the world: 128

Literacy: *definition:* age 15 and over can read and write
total population: 97.8%
male: 98.8%
female: 96.8% (2015 est.)

School life expectancy (primary to tertiary education): *total:* 13 years
male: 13 years

female: 13 years (2014)

Unemployment, youth ages 15-24: *total:* 47.3%
male: 49.7%
female: 43.3% (2014 est.)
country comparison to the world: 4

GOVERNMENT

Country name: *conventional long form:* Republic of Macedonia
conventional short form: Macedonia
local long form: Republika Makedonija
local short form: Makedonija
note: the provisional designation used by the UN, EU, and NATO is the "former Yugoslav Republic of Macedonia" (FYROM)
former: People's Republic of Macedonia, Socialist Republic of Macedonia
etymology: the country name derives from the ancient kingdom of Macedon (7th to 2nd centuries B.C.)

Government type: parliamentary republic

Capital: *name:* Skopje
geographic coordinates: 42 00 N, 21 26 E
time difference: UTC+1 (6 hours ahead of Washington, DC, during Standard Time)
daylight saving time: +1hr, begins last Sunday in March; ends last Sunday in October

Administrative divisions: 70 municipalities (opstini, singular—opstina) and 1 city* (grad); Aracinovo, Berovo, Bitola, Bogdanci, Bogovinje, Bosilovo, Brvenica, Caska, Centar Zupa, Cesinovo-Oblesevo, Cucer Sandevo, Debar, Debarca, Delcevo, Demir Hisar, Demir Kapija, Dojran, Dolneni, Gevgelija, Gostivar, Gradsko, Ilinden, Jegunovce, Karbinci, Kavadarci, Kicevo, Kocani, Konce, Kratovo, Kriva Palanka, Krivogastani, Krusevo, Kumanovo, Lipkovo, Lozovo, Makedonska Kamenica, Makedonski Brod, Mavrovo i Rostusa, Mogila, Negotino, Novaci, Novo Selo, Ohrid, Pehcevo, Petrovec, Plasnica, Prilep, Probistip, Radovis, Rankovce, Resen, Rosoman, Skopje*, Sopiste, Staro Nagoricane, Stip, Struga, Strumica, Studenicani, Sveti Nikole, Tearce, Tetovo, Valandovo, Vasilevo, Veles, Vevcani, Vinica, Vrapciste, Zelenikovo, Zelino, Zrnovci

Independence: 8 September 1991 (referendum by registered voters endorsed independence from Yugoslavia)

National holiday: Independence Day, 8 September (1991); also known as National Day

Constitution: history: several previous; latest adopted 17 November 1991, effective 20 November 1991
amendments: proposed by the president of the republic, by the government, by at least 30 members of the Assembly, or by petition of at least 150,000 citizens; draft amendments require approval by majority vote of Assembly members, followed by public debate; final passage requires two-thirds majority vote of the Assembly; amended several times, last in 2015 (2016)

Legal system: civil law system; judicial review of legislative acts

International law organization participation: has not submitted an ICJ jurisdiction declaration; accepts ICCt jurisdiction

Citizenship: *citizenship by birth:* no
citizenship by descent only: at least one parent must be a citizen of Macedonia
dual citizenship recognized: no
residency requirement for naturalization: 8 years

Suffrage: 18 years of age; universal

Executive branch: *chief of state:* President Gjorge IVANOV (since 12 May 2009)

head of government: Prime Minister Zoran ZAEV (since 31 May 2017)
cabinet: Council of Ministers elected by the Assembly by simple majority vote; note—the 2014 cabinet formed by the government coalition parties VMRO-DPMNE, DUI, and several small parties; as a result of an agreement reached in July 2015 between the largest parties to resolve a 16-month opposition boycott of the Assembly, several minister and deputy minister positions were also given to the opposition SDSM from November 2015 through May 2016 in preparation for parliamentary elections originally scheduled for 24 April 2016, and pushed back to 5 June 2016, and again from September to December 2016
elections/appointments: president directly elected by absolute majority popular vote in 2 rounds if needed for a 5-year term (eligible for a second term); election last held on 13 and 27 April 2014 (next to be held in 2019); following legislative elections, the leader of the majority party or majority coalition is usually elected prime minister by the Assembly
election results: Gjorge IVANOV reelected president in second round; percent of vote—Gjorge IVANOV (independent) 55.3%, Stevo PENDAROVSKI (SDSM) 41.1%, other 3.6%

Legislative branch: *description:* unicameral Assembly or Sobranie (123 seats; 120 members directly elected in multi-seat constituencies by proportional representation vote and 3 directly elected in diaspora constituencies worldwide by simple majority vote, provided candidates meet a specified minimum vote count; members serve 4-year terms)
elections: last held on 11 December 2016, with a second round held in one polling station on 25 December 2016 (next to be held in 2020)
election results: percent of vote by party—VMRO-DPMNE 38.1%, SDSM coalition 36.7%, BDI 7.3%, Besa Movement 4.9%, Alliance for Albanians 3.1%, PDSh 2.7%, other 7.2%; seats by party—VMRO-DPMNE 51, SDSM coalition 49, BDI 10, Besa Movement 5, Alliance for Albanians 3, PDSh 2

Judicial branch: *highest court(s):* Supreme Court (consists of 22 judges); Constitutional Court (consists of 9 judges)
judge selection and term of office: Supreme Court judges nominated by the Judicial Council, a 7-member body of legal professionals, and appointed by the Assembly; judge tenure NA; Constitutional Court judges appointed by the Assembly for nonrenewable, 9-year terms
subordinate courts: Courts of Appeal; Basic Courts

Political parties and leaders: Alliance for Albanians [Ziadin SELA]
Besa Movement [Bilal KASAMI]
Democratic Party of Albanians or PDSh [Menduh THACI]
Democratic Union for Integration or BDI [Ali AHMETI]
Internal Macedonian Revolutionary Organization—Democratic Party for Macedonian National Unity or VMRO-DPMNE [Hristijan MICKOSKI]
Social Democratic Union of Macedonia or SDSM [Zoran ZAEV]
note: during the 2016 parliamentary elections VMRO-DPMNE and SDSM each led coalitions

Political pressure groups and leaders: Confederation of Free Trade Unions or KSS [Blagoja RALPOVSKI]
Federation of Trade Unions of Macedonia or SSM [Zivko MITREVSKI]
Trade Union of Education, Science and Culture or SONK [Jakim NEDELKOV]
Student Plenum
Eco Guerilla [Arianit XHAFERI]

International organization participation: BIS, CD, CE, CEI, EAPC, EBRD, EU (candidate country), FAO, IAEA, IBRD, ICAO, ICC (NGOs), ICCt, ICRM, IDA, IFAD, IFC, IFRCS, ILO, IMF, IMO, Interpol, IOC, IOM, IPU, ISO, ITU, ITUC (NGOs), MIGA, OAS (observer), OIF, OPCW, OSCE, PCA, PFP, SELEC, UN, UNCTAD, UNESCO, UNHCR, UNIDO, UNIFIL, UNWTO, UPU, WCO, WHO, WIPO, WMO, WTO

Diplomatic representation in the US: *chief of mission:* Ambassador Vasko NAUMOVSKI (since 18 November 2014)
chancery: 2129 Wyoming Avenue NW, Washington, DC 20008
telephone: [1] (202) 667-0501
FAX: [1] (202) 667-2131
consulate(s) general: Chicago, Detroit, New York

Diplomatic representation from the US: *chief of mission:* Ambassador Jess L. BAILY (since 12 February 2015)
embassy: Str. Samolilova, Nr. 21, 1000 Skopje
mailing address: American Embassy Skopje, US Department of State, 7120 Skopje Place, Washington, DC 20521-7120 (pouch)
telephone: [389] (2) 310-2000
FAX: [389] (2) 310-2499

Flag description: a yellow sun (the Sun of Liberty) with eight broadening rays extending to the edges of the red field; the red and yellow colors have long been associated with Macedonia

National symbol(s): eight-rayed sun; national colors: red, yellow

National anthem: *name:* "Denes nad Makedonija" (Today Over Macedonia)
lyrics/music: Vlado MALESKI/Todor SKALOVSKI

note: written in 1943 and adopted in 1991, the song previously served as the anthem of the Socialist Republic of Macedonia while part of Yugoslavia

ECONOMY

Economy—overview: Since its independence in 1991, Macedonia has made progress in liberalizing its economy and improving its business environment. Its low tax rates and free economic zones have helped to attract foreign investment, which is still low relative to the rest of Europe. Corruption and weak rule of law remain significant problems. Some businesses complain of opaque regulations and unequal enforcement of the law.

Macedonia's economy is closely linked to Europe as a customer for exports and source of investment, and has suffered as a result of prolonged weakness in the euro zone. Unemployment has remained consistently high at about 23%, but may be overstated based on the existence of an extensive gray market, estimated to be between 20% and 45% of GDP, which is not captured by official statistics.

Macedonia is working to build a country-wide natural gas pipeline and distribution network. Currently, Macedonia receives its small natural gas supplies from Russia via Bulgaria. In 2016, Macedonia signed a memorandum of understanding with Greece to build an interconnector that could connect to the Trans Adriatic Pipeline that will traverse the region once complete, or to an LNG import terminal in Greece.

Macedonia maintained macroeconomic stability through the global financial crisis by conducting prudent monetary policy, which keeps the domestic currency pegged to the euro, and inflation at a low level. However, in the last two years, the internal political crisis has hampered economic performance, with GDP growth slowing in 2016 and 2017, and both domestic private and public investments declining. Fiscal policies were lax, with unproductive public expenditures, including subsidies and pension increases, and rising guarantees for the debt of state owned enterprises, and fiscal targets were consistently missed. In 2017, public debt stabilized at about 47% of GDP, still relatively low compared to its Western Balkan neighbors and the rest of Europe.

GDP (purchasing power parity): $31.55 billion (2017 est.)
$30.78 billion (2016 est.)
$30.06 billion (2015 est.)
note: data are in 2017 dollars; Macedonia has a large informal sector that may not be reflected in these data
country comparison to the world: 130

GDP (official exchange rate): $11.42 billion (2016 est.)

GDP—real growth rate: 2.5% (2017 est.)
2.4% (2016 est.)
3.8% (2015 est.)
country comparison to the world: 135

GDP—per capita (PPP): $15,200 (2017 est.)
$14,900 (2016 est.)
$14,500 (2015 est.)

note: data are in 2017 dollars
country comparison to the world: 109

Gross national saving: 26.1% of GDP (2017 est.)
30.5% of GDP (2016 est.)
29% of GDP (2015 est.)
country comparison to the world: 45

GDP—composition, by end use:
household consumption: 65.6%
government consumption: 15.6%
investment in fixed capital: 13.6%
investment in inventories: 20.2%
exports of goods and services: 54%
imports of goods and services: -69% (2017 est.)

GDP—composition, by sector of origin:
agriculture: 10%
industry: 30%
services: 60% (2017 est.)

Agriculture—products: grapes, tobacco, vegetables, fruits; milk, eggs

Industries: food processing, beverages, textiles, chemicals, iron, steel, cement, energy, pharmaceuticals, automotive parts

Industrial production growth rate: 3% (2017 est.)
country comparison to the world: 103

Labor force: 950,800 (2017 est.)
country comparison to the world: 147

Labor force—by occupation: *agriculture:* 16.6%
industry: 29.6%
services: 53.8% (2016 est.)

Unemployment rate: 23.4% (2017 est.)
23.6% (2016 est.)
country comparison to the world: 192

Population below poverty line: 21.5% (2015 est.)

Household income or consumption by percentage share: *lowest 10%:* 2.2%
highest 10%: 34.5% (2009 est.)

Distribution of family income—Gini index: 33.7 (2015)
35.2 (2014)
country comparison to the world: 105

Budget: *revenues:* $3.314 billion
expenditures: $3.655 billion (2017 est.)
Taxes and other revenues: 29% of GDP (2017 est.)
country comparison to the world: 88

Budget surplus (+) or deficit (-): -3% of GDP (2017 est.)
country comparison to the world: 114

Public debt: 47.3% of GDP (2017 est.)
47.8% of GDP (2016 est.)
note: official data from Ministry of Finance; data cover central government debt; this data excludes debt instruments issued (or owned) by government entities other than the treasury; includes treasury debt held by foreign entitites; excludes debt issued by sub-national entities; there are no debt instruments sold for social funds
country comparison to the world: 107

Fiscal year: calendar year

Inflation rate (consumer prices): 0.3% (2017 est.)
-0.2% (2016 est.)
country comparison to the world: 16

Central bank discount rate: 3.25% (31 March 2017)
3.75% (31 December 2016)
note: series discontinued in January 2010; the discount rate has been replaced by a referent rate for calculating the penalty rate
country comparison to the world: 104

Commercial bank prime lending rate: 6.2% (31 December 2017 est.)
6.61% (31 December 2016 est.)
country comparison to the world: 124

Stock of narrow money: $2.155 billion (31 December 2017 est.)
$1.909 billion (31 December 2016 est.)
country comparison to the world: 132

Stock of broad money: $5.036 billion (31 December 2017 est.)
$4.574 billion (31 December 2016 est.)
country comparison to the world: 128

Stock of domestic credit: $5.2 billion (31 December 2017 est.)
$5.01 billion (31 December 2016 est.)
country comparison to the world: 127

Market value of publicly traded shares: $2.078 billion (31 December 2016)
$1.853 billion (31 December 2015)
$2.269 billion (31 December 2014)
country comparison to the world: 99

Current account balance: -$261 million (2017 est.)
-$336 million (2016 est.)
country comparison to the world: 93

Exports: $4.276 billion (2017 est.)
$3.75 billion (2016 est.)
country comparison to the world: 114

Exports—commodities: foodstuffs, beverages, tobacco; textiles, miscellaneous manufactures, iron, steel; automotive parts

Exports—partners: Germany 40.9%, Kosovo 13.5%, Serbia 7.7%, Bulgaria 4.5% (2016)

Imports: $6.446 billion (2017 est.)
$5.805 billion (2016 est.)
country comparison to the world: 112

Imports—commodities: machinery and equipment, automobiles, chemicals, fuels, food products

Imports—partners: Germany 12.2%, UK 10.7%, Serbia 7.9%, Greece 7.3%, China 6.2%, Italy 5.6%, Turkey 5.1%, Bulgaria 4.6% (2016)

Reserves of foreign exchange and gold: $2.794 billion (31 December 2017 est.)
$2.755 billion (31 December 2016 est.)
country comparison to the world: 109

Debt—external: $8.07 billion (31 December 2017 est.)
$7.685 billion (31 December 2016 est.)
country comparison to the world: 123

Stock of direct foreign investment—at home: $7.15 billion (31 December 2017 est.)
$6.8 billion (31 December 2016 est.)
country comparison to the world: 98

Stock of direct foreign investment—abroad: $899.1 million (31 December 2017 est.)

$849.1 million (31 December 2016 est.)
country comparison to the world: 86

Exchange rates: Macedonian denars (MKD) per US dollar—
55.8 (2017 est.)
55.733 (2016 est.)
55.733 (2015 est.)
55.537 (2014 est.)
46.437 (31 December 2013 est.)

ENERGY

Electricity access: electrification—*total population:* 100% (2016)

Electricity—production: 5.303 billion kWh (2016 est.)
country comparison to the world: 120

Electricity—consumption: 6.455 billion kWh (2016 est.)
country comparison to the world: 112

Electricity—exports: 58.5 million kWh (2016 est.)
country comparison to the world: 83

Electricity—imports: 2.191 billion kWh (2016 est.)
country comparison to the world: 54

Electricity—installed generating capacity: 2.057 million kW (2016 est.)
country comparison to the world: 112

Electricity—from fossil fuels: 64.3% of total installed capacity (2016 est.)
country comparison to the world: 116

Electricity—from nuclear fuels: 0% of total installed capacity (2016 est.)
country comparison to the world: 140

Electricity—from hydroelectric plants: 32.8% of total installed capacity (2016 est.)
country comparison to the world: 65

Electricity—from other renewable sources: 2.9% of total installed capacity (2016 est.)
country comparison to the world: 113

Crude oil—production: 0 bbl/day (2016 est.)
country comparison to the world: 164

Crude oil—exports: 142.3 bbl/day (2014 est.)
country comparison to the world: 80

Crude oil—imports: 0 bbl/day (2014 est.)
country comparison to the world: 159

Crude oil—proved reserves: 0 bbl (1 January 2017 es)
country comparison to the world: 161

Refined petroleum products—production: 0 bbl/day (2016 est.)
country comparison to the world: 169

Refined petroleum products—consumption: 20,700 bbl/day (2016 est.)
country comparison to the world: 138

Refined petroleum products—exports: 3,900 bbl/day (2016 est.)
country comparison to the world: 100

Refined petroleum products—imports: 23,400 bbl/day (2016 est.)
country comparison to the world: 112

Natural gas—production: 0 cu m (2016)
country comparison to the world: 168

Natural gas—consumption: 471 million cu m (2015 est.)
country comparison to the world: 108

Natural gas—exports: 0 cu m (2016)
country comparison to the world: 148

Natural gas—imports: 60 million cu m (2015 est.)
country comparison to the world: 76

Natural gas—proved reserves: 0 cu m (31 December 2016)
country comparison to the world: 171

Carbon dioxide emissions from consumption of energy: 7.9 million Mt (2013 est.)
country comparison to the world: 111

COMMUNICATIONS

Telephones—fixed lines: *total subscriptions:* 368,070
subscriptions per 100 inhabitants: 18 (July 2016 est.)
country comparison to the world: 105

Telephones—mobile cellular: *total:* 2.223 million
subscriptions per 100 inhabitants: 106 (July 2016 est.)
country comparison to the world: 147

Telephone system: *general assessment:* competition from the mobile-cellular segment of the telecommunications market has led to a drop in fixed-line telephone subscriptions
domestic: combined fixed-line and mobile-cellular telephone subscribership about 120 per 100 persons
international: country code—389 (2017)

Broadcast media: public service TV broadcaster Macedonian Radio and Television operates 3 national terrestrial TV channels and 2 satellite TV channels; additionally, there are 5 privately owned TV channels that broadcast nationally using terrestrial transmitters, 4 TV channels with concession for cable TV, 5 satellite TV channels broadcasting on a national level, 47 local commercial TV channels, and a large number of cable operators that offer domestic and international programming; the public radio broadcaster operates over multiple stations; there are 3 privately owned radio stations that broadcast nationally and about 75 local commercial radio stations (2017)

Internet country code: .mk

Internet users: 1.475 million
70.4% (July 2016 est.)
country comparison to the world: 121

TRANSPORTATION

Civil aircraft registration country code prefix: Z3 (2016)

Airports: 10 (2013)
country comparison to the world: 155

Airports—with paved runways: *total:* 8
2,438 to 3,047 m: 2
under 914 m: 6 (2017)

Airports—with unpaved runways: *total:* 2
914 to 1,523 m: 1
under 914 m: 1 (2013)

Pipelines: gas 262 km; oil 120 km (2017)

Railways: *total:* 925 km
standard gauge: 925 km 1.435-m gauge (313 km electrified) (2017)
country comparison to the world: 100

Roadways: *total:* 14,182 km (includes 242 km of expressways)
paved: 9,633 km
unpaved: 4,549 km (2014)
country comparison to the world: 126

MILITARY AND SECURITY

Military expenditures: 1.1% of GDP (2017)
0.97% of GDP (2016)
1.05% of GDP (2015)
1.09% of GDP (2014)
1.17% of GDP (2013)
country comparison to the world: 92

Military branches: Army of the Republic of Macedonia (ARM; includes General Staff and subordinate Joint Operational Command, Logistic Support Command, Training and Doctrine Command, Special Ops Regiment, Electronic Surveillance Center, and Air Surveillance Center) (2017)

Military service age and obligation: 18 years of age for voluntary military service; conscription abolished in 2008 (2013)

TRANSNATIONAL ISSUES

Disputes—international: Kosovo and Macedonia completed demarcation of their boundary in September 2008; Greece continues to reject the use of the name Macedonia or Republic of Macedonia

Refugees and internally displaced persons: stateless persons: 600 (2016)
note: 478,651 estimated refugee and migrant arrivals (January 2015—February 2018); Macedonia is predominantly a transit country and hosts fewer than 50 refugees and asylum seekers as of October 2017

Illicit drugs: major transshipment point for Southwest Asian heroin and hashish; minor transit point for South American cocaine destined for Europe; although not a financial center and most criminal activity is thought to be domestic, money laundering is a problem due to a mostly cash-based economy and weak enforcement

MADAGASCAR

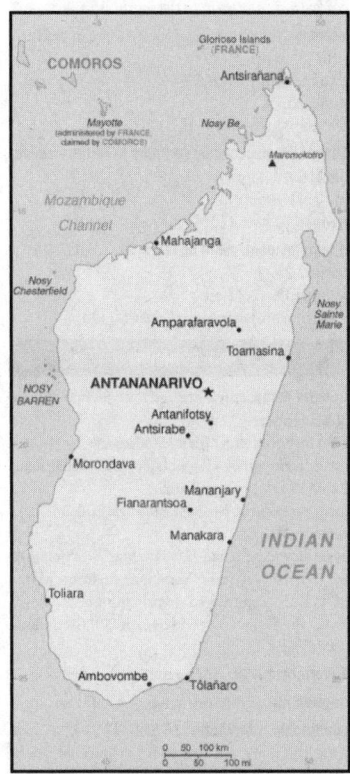

INTRODUCTION

Background: Madagascar was one of the last major landmasses on earth to be colonized by humans. The earliest settlers from present-day Indonesia arrived between A.D. 350 and 550. The island attracted Arab and Persian traders as early as the 7th century, and migrants from Africa arrived around A.D. 1000. Madagascar was a pirate stronghold during the late 17th and early 18th centuries, and served as a slave trading center into the 19th century. From the 16th to the late 19th century, a native Merina Kingdom dominated much of Madagascar. The island was conquered by the French in 1896 who made it a colony; independence was regained in 1960. During 1992-93, free presidential and National Assembly elections were held ending 17 years of single-party rule. In 1997, in the second presidential race, Didier RATSIRAKA, the leader during the 1970s and 1980s, was returned to the presidency. The 2001 presidential election was contested between the followers of Didier RATSIRAKA and Marc RAVALOMANANA, nearly causing secession of half of the country. In April 2002, the High Constitutional Court announced RAVALOMANANA the

winner. RAVALOMANANA won a second term in 2006 but, following protests in 2009, handed over power to the military, which then conferred the presidency on the mayor of Antananarivo, Andry RAJOELINA, in what amounted to a coup d'etat. Following a lengthy mediation process led by the Southern African Development Community, Madagascar held UN-supported presidential and parliamentary elections in 2013. Former de facto finance minister Hery RAJAONARIMAMPIANINA won a runoff election in December 2013 and was inaugurated in January 2014.

GEOGRAPHY

Location: Southern Africa, island in the Indian Ocean, east of Mozambique

Geographic coordinates: 20 00 S, 47 00 E

Map references: Africa

Area: *total:* 587,041 sq km
land: 581,540 sq km
water: 5,501 sq km
country comparison to the world: 48

Area—comparative: almost four times the size of Georgia; slightly less than twice the size of Arizona

Land boundaries: 0 km

Coastline: 4,828 km

Maritime claims: *territorial sea:* 12 nm
contiguous zone: 24 nm
exclusive economic zone: 200 nm
continental shelf: 200 nm or 100 nm from the 2,500-m isobath

Climate: tropical along coast, temperate inland, arid in south

Terrain: narrow coastal plain, high plateau and mountains in center

Elevation: *mean elevation:* 615 m

elevation extremes: *lowest point:* Indian Ocean 0 m
highest point: Maromokotro 2,876 m

Natural resources: graphite, chromite, coal, bauxite, rare earth elements, salt, quartz, tar sands, semiprecious stones, mica, fish, hydropower

Land use: *agricultural land:* 71.1%
arable land: 6%;
permanent crops: 1%;
permanent pasture: 64.1%
forest: 21.5%
other: 7.4% (2011 est.)
Irrigated land: 10,860 sq km (2012)

Population—distribution: most of population lives on the eastern half of the island; significant clustering is found in the central highlands and eastern coastline

Natural hazards: periodic cyclones; drought; and locust infestation
volcanism: Madagascar's volcanoes have not erupted in historical times

Environment—current issues: soil erosion results from deforestation and overgrazing; desertification; surface water contaminated with raw sewage and other organic wastes; several endangered species of flora and fauna unique to the island

Environment—international agreements: *party to:* Biodiversity, Climate Change, Climate Change-Kyoto Protocol, Desertification, Endangered Species, Hazardous Wastes, Law of the Sea, Marine Life Conservation, Ozone Layer Protection, Ship Pollution, Wetlands
signed, but not ratified: none of the selected agreements

Geography—note: world's fourth-largest island; strategic location along Mozambique Channel; despite Madagascar's close proximity to the African continent, ocean currents isolate the island resulting in high rates of endemic plant and animal species

PEOPLE AND SOCIETY

Population: 25,054,161 (July 2017 est.)
country comparison to the world: 52

Nationality: *noun:* Malagasy (singular and plural)
adjective: Malagasy

Ethnic groups: Malayo-Indonesian (Merina and related Betsileo), Cotiers (mixed African, Malayo-Indonesian, and Arab ancestry—Betsimisaraka, Tsimihety, Antaisaka, Sakalava), French, Indian, Creole, Comoran

Languages: French (official), Malagasy (official), English

Religions: Christian, indigenous religionist, Muslim

Demographic profile: Madagascar's youthful population—just over 60% are under the age of 25—and high total fertility rate of more than 4 children per women ensures that the Malagasy population will continue its rapid growth trajectory for the foreseeable future. The population is predominantly rural and poor; chronic malnutrition is prevalent, and large families are the norm. Many young Malagasy girls are withdrawn from school, marry early (often pressured to do so by their parents), and soon begin having children. Early childbearing, coupled with Madagascar's widespread poverty and lack of access to skilled health care providers during delivery, increases the risk of death and serious health problems for young mothers and their babies.

Child marriage perpetuates gender inequality and is prevalent among the poor, the uneducated, and rural households—as of 2013, of Malagasy women aged 20 to 24, more than 40% were married and more than a third had given birth by the age of 18. Although the legal age for marriage is 18, parental consent is often given for earlier marriages or the law is flouted, especially in rural areas that make up nearly 65% of the country. Forms of arranged marriage whereby young girls are married to older men in exchange for oxen or money are traditional. If a union does not work out, a girl can be placed in another marriage, but the dowry paid to her family diminishes with each unsuccessful marriage.

Madagascar's population consists of 18 main ethnic groups, all of whom speak the same Malagasy language. Most Malagasy are multi-ethnic, however, reflecting the island's diversity of settlers and historical contacts (see Background). Madagascar's legacy of hierarchical societies practicing domestic slavery (most notably the Merina Kingdom of the 16th to the 19th century) is evident today in persistent class tension, with some ethnic groups maintaining a caste system. Slave descendants are vulnerable to unequal access to education and jobs, despite Madagascar's constitutional guarantee of free compulsory primary education and its being party to several international conventions on human rights. Historical distinctions also remain between central highlanders and coastal people.

Age structure: *0-14 years:* 39.87% (male 5,035,160/female 4,952,909)
15-24 years: 20.34% (male 2,556,130/female 2,538,644)
25-54 years: 32.12% (male 4,022,698/female 4,025,038)
55-64 years: 4.38% (male 535,300/female 560,932)
65 years and over: 3.3% (male 374,770/female 452,580) (2017 est.)

Dependency ratios: *total dependency ratio:* 80.1
youth dependency ratio: 75
elderly dependency ratio: 5.1
potential support ratio: 19.6 (2015 est.)

Median age: *total:* 19.7 years
male: 19.5 years
female: 19.9 years (2017 est.)
country comparison to the world: 198

Population growth rate: 2.5% (2017 est.)
country comparison to the world: 18

Birth rate: 31.6 births/1,000 population (2017 est.)
country comparison to the world: 33

Death rate: 6.5 deaths/1,000 population (2017 est.)
country comparison to the world: 146

Net migration rate: 0 migrant(s)/1,000 population (2017 est.)
country comparison to the world: 89

Population distribution: most of population lives on the eastern half of the island; significant clustering is found in the central highlands and eastern coastline

Urbanization: *urban population:* 36.4% of total population (2017)
rate of urbanization: 4.47% annual rate of change (2015-20 est.)

Major urban areas—population: ANTANANARIVO (capital) 2.61 million (2015)

Sex ratio: *at birth:* 1.03 male(s)/female
0-14 years: 1.02 male(s)/female
15-24 years: 1.01 male(s)/female
25-54 years: 1 male(s)/female

55-64 years: 0.95 male(s)/female
65 years and over: 0.83 male(s)/female
total population: 1 male(s)/female (2016 est.)

Mother's mean age at first birth: 19.5 years
note: median age at first birth among women 25-29 (2008/09 est.)

Maternal mortality ratio: 353 deaths/100,000 live births (2015 est.)
country comparison to the world: 34

Infant mortality rate: *total:* 41.2 deaths/1,000 live births
male: 45 deaths/1,000 live births
female: 37.3 deaths/1,000 live births (2017 est.)
country comparison to the world: 45

Life expectancy at birth: *total population:* 66.3 years
male: 64.7 years
female: 67.8 years (2017 est.)
country comparison to the world: 175

Total fertility rate: 4.03 children born/woman (2017 est.)
country comparison to the world: 33

Contraceptive prevalence rate: 39.9% (2008/09)

Health expenditures: 3% of GDP (2014)
country comparison to the world: 181

Physicians density: 0.14 physicians/1,000 population (2012)

Hospital bed density: 0.2 beds/1,000 population (2010)

Drinking water source:
improved:
urban: 81.6% of population
rural: 35.3% of population
total: 51.5% of population
unimproved:
urban: 18.4% of population
rural: 64.7% of population
total: 48.5% of population (2015 est.)

Sanitation facility access:
improved:
urban: 18% of population
rural: 8.7% of population
total: 12% of population
unimproved:
urban: 82% of population
rural: 91.3% of population
total: 88% of population (2015 est.)

HIV/AIDS—adult prevalence rate: 0.2% (2016 est.)
country comparison to the world: 93

HIV/AIDS—people living with HIV/AIDS: 31,000 (2016 est.)
country comparison to the world: 66

HIV/AIDS—deaths: 1,600 (2016 est.)
country comparison to the world: 58

Major infectious diseases: *degree of risk:* very high
food or waterborne diseases: bacterial diarrhea, hepatitis A, and typhoid fever
vectorborne diseases: malaria and dengue fever
water contact disease: schistosomiasis
animal contact disease: rabies (2016)

Obesity—adult prevalence rate: 5.3% (2016)
country comparison to the world: 179

Education expenditures: 2.1% of GDP (2013)
country comparison to the world: 150

Literacy: *definition:* age 15 and over can read and write
total population: 64.7%
male: 66.7%
female: 62.6% (2015 est.)

School life expectancy (primary to tertiary education): *total:* 11 years
male: 11 years
female: 10 years (2014)

Unemployment, youth ages 15-24: *total:* 2.6%
male: 2.2%
female: 3% (2012 est.)
country comparison to the world: 133

GOVERNMENT

Country name: *conventional long form:* Republic of Madagascar
conventional short form: Madagascar
local long form: Republique de Madagascar/ Repoblikan'i Madagasikara
local short form: Madagascar/Madagasikara
former: Malagasy Republic
etymology: the name "Madageiscar" was first used by the 13th-century Venetian explorer Marco POLO, as a corrupted transliteration of Mogadishu, the Somali port with which POLO confused the island

Government type: semi-presidential republic

Capital: *name:* Antananarivo
geographic coordinates: 18 55 S, 47 31 E
time difference: UTC+3 (8 hours ahead of Washington, DC, during Standard Time)

Administrative divisions: 6 provinces (faritany); Antananarivo, Antsiranana, Fianarantsoa, Mahajanga, Toamasina, Toliara

Independence: 26 June 1960 (from France)

National holiday: Independence Day, 26 June (1960)

Constitution: *history:* previous 1992; latest passed by referendum 17 November 2010, promulgated 11 December 2010
amendments: proposed by the president of the republic in consultation with the cabinet or supported by a least two-thirds of both the Senate and National Assembly membership; passage requires at least three-fourths approval of both the Senate and National Assembly and approval in a referendum; constitutional articles including the form and powers of government, the sovereignty of the state, and the autonomy of Madagascar's collectivities cannot be amended (2017)

Legal system: civil law system based on the old French civil code and customary law in matters of marriage, family, and obligation

International law organization participation: accepts compulsory ICJ jurisdiction with reservations; accepts ICCt jurisdiction

Citizenship: *citizenship by birth:* no

citizenship by descent only: the father must be a citizen of Madagascar; in the case of a child born out of wedlock, the mother must be a citizen

dual citizenship recognized: no

residency requirement for naturalization: unknown

Suffrage: 18 years of age; universal

Executive branch: chief of state: President Hery Martial RAJAONARIMAMPIANINA Rakotoarimana (since 25 January 2014)

head of government: Prime Minister Olivier Mahafaly SOLONANDRASANA (since 13 April 2016); Prime Minister Jean RAVELONARIVO (since 17 January 2015) resigned 8 April 2016

cabinet: Council of Ministers appointed by the prime minister

elections/appointments: president directly elected by absolute majority popular vote in 2 rounds if needed for a 5-year term (eligible for a second term); election last held on 25 October and 20 December 2013 (next to be held in 2018); prime minister nominated by the National Assembly, appointed by the president

election results: Hery Martial RAJAONARIMAMPIANINA elected president in second round; percent of vote—Hery Martial RAJAONARIMAMPIANINA (HVM) 53.5%, Jean Louis ROBINSON (AVANA) 46.5%

note: on 17 March 2009, democratically elected President Marc RAVALOMANANA stepped down, handing the government over to the military, which in turn conferred the presidency on opposition leader and Antananarivo mayor Andry RAJOELINA; a power-sharing agreement established a 15-month transition period to conclude with a general election in 2010, which failed to occur; a subsequent agreement aimed for an early 2013 election—the first round was held on 25 October 2013 and the second on 20 December 2013

Legislative branch: description: bicameral; consists of the Senate or Antenimieran-Doholona (dissolved following the 2009 coup and reestablished in December 2015) (63 seats; 42 members indirectly elected by an electoral college of municipal, communal, regional, and provincial leaders and 21 appointed by the president of the republic; members serve 6-year terms)and the National Assembly or Antenimierampirenena (151 seats; 87 members directly elected in single-seat constituencies by simple majority vote and 64 directly elected in multi-seat constituencies by closed-list proportional representation vote; members serve 4-year terms)

elections: National Assembly—last held on 20 December 2013 (next to be held in 2017); Senate—last held 29 December 2015 (next to be held in 2021)

election results: National Assembly—percent of vote by party—MAPAR 17.3%, MR 10.8%, VPM MMM 8.2%, PHI 3.8%, AMHM 3.5%, LEADER-Fanilo 2.8%, FFF 1.6%, AIM 1.0%, SFN 0.3%, independent and other 50.6%; seats by party—MAPAR 49, MR 20, VPM MMM 13, PHI 5, AMHM 2, LEADER-Fanilo 5, FFF 2, AIM

2, SFN 2, other 22, independent 25, seats with delayed elections 4; Senate—percent of vote by party—NA; seats by party—TIM 3, MAPAR 2, LEADER-Fanilo 1, independent 2; appointed by the President 21

Judicial branch: highest court(s): Supreme Court or Cour Supreme (consists of 11 members; addresses judicial administration issues only); High Constitutional Court or Haute Cour Constitutionnelle (consists of 9 members); note—the judiciary includes a High Court of Justice responsible for adjudicating crimes and misdemeanors by government officials including the president

judge selection and term of office: Supreme Court heads elected by the president and judiciary officials to serve single-renewable, 3-year terms; High Constitutional Court members appointed—3 each by the president, by both legislative bodies, and by the Council of Magistrates; members serve single, 6-year terms

subordinate courts: Courts of Appeal; provincial and city tribunals

Political parties and leaders: AVANA Party [Jean-Louis ROBINSON]

Economic Liberalism and Democratic Action for National Recovery/LEADER-Fanilo [Manasse ESOAVELOMANDROSO]

Green Party/Parti Vert or AMHM [Sarah Georget RABEHARISOA]

I Love Madagascar (Tiako I Madagaskara) or TIM [Marc RAVALOMANANA]

National Unity, Freedom, and Development or FFF [Benjamin RADAVIDSON Andriamparany]

New Forces for Madagascar (Hery Vaovao ho an'i Madagaskara) or HVM [Hery RAJAONARIMAMPIANINA]

Parti Hiaraka Isika or PHI [Albert Camille VITAL]

Pillar of Madagascar or AIM [Andry RAKOTOVAO]

Ravalomanana Movement or MR

Sambo Fiaran'i Noe or SFN

Union Party or Tambatra [Pety RAKOTONIAINA]

Vondrona Politika Miara dia Malagasy Miara Miainga or VPM MMM [Milavonjy ANDRIASY]

With the President Andry RAJOELIN (Miaraka Amin'ny Prezida Andry Rajoelina) or MAPAR [Andry RAJOELIN]

Political pressure groups and leaders: Committee for the Defense of Truth and Justice or KMMR Committee for National Reconciliation or CRN National Council of Christian Churches or FFKM

International organization participation: ACP, AfDB, AU, CD, COMESA, EITI (candidate country), FAO, G-77, IAEA, IBRD, ICAO, ICC (NGOs), ICCt, ICRM, IDA, IFAD, IFC, IFRCS, ILO, IMF, IMO, InOC, Interpol, IOC, IOM, IPU, ISO (correspondent), ITSO, ITU, ITUC (NGOs), MIGA, NAM, OIF, OPCW, PCA, SADC, UN, UNCTAD, UNESCO, UNHCR, UNIDO, UNWTO, UPU, WCO, WFTU (NGOs), WHO, WIPO, WMO, WTO

Diplomatic representation in the US: chief of mission: Ambassador (vacant); Charge d'Affaires

Velotiana Rakotoanosy RAOBELINA (since 20 June 2011)

chancery: 2374 Massachusetts Avenue NW, Washington, DC 20008

telephone: [1] (202) 265-5525

FAX: [1] (202) 265-3034

consulate(s) general: New York

Diplomatic representation from the US: chief of mission: Ambassador Robert T. YAMATE (since 14 January 2015); note—also accredited to Comoros

embassy: Lot 207A, Point Liberty, Andranoro, Antehiroka, 105 Antananarivo

mailing address: B.P. 620, Antsahavola, Antananarivo

telephone: [261] 20 23 480 00

FAX: [261] 20 23 480 35 or [261] 33 44 328 17

Flag description: two equal horizontal bands of red (top) and green with a vertical white band of the same width on hoist side; by tradition, red stands for sovereignty, green for hope, white for purity

National symbol(s): traveller's palm, zebu; national colors: red, green, white

National anthem: name: "Ry Tanindraza nay malala o" (Oh, Our Beloved Fatherland)

lyrics/music: Pasteur RAHAJASON/Norbert RAHARISOA

note: adopted 1959

ECONOMY

Economy—overview: Madagascar is a mostly unregulated economy with many untapped natural resources, but no capital markets, a weak judicial system, poorly enforced contracts, and rampant government corruption. The country faces challenges to improve education, healthcare, and the environment to boost long-term economic growth. Agriculture, including fishing and forestry, is a mainstay of the economy, accounting for more than one-fourth of GDP and employing roughly 80% of the population. Deforestation and erosion, aggravated by bushfires, slash-and-burn clearing techniques, and the use of firewood as the primary source of fuel, are serious concerns to the agriculture dependent economy.

After discarding socialist economic policies in the mid-1990s, Madagascar followed a World Bank- and IMF-led policy of privatization and liberalization until the onset of a political crisis, which lasted from 2009 to 2013. The strategy had placed the country on a slow and steady growth path from an extremely low starting point. Exports of apparel boomed after gaining duty-free access to the US in 2000; however, Madagascar's failure to comply with the requirements of the African Growth and Opportunity Act (AGOA) led to the termination of the country's duty-free access in January 2010, a sharp fall in textile production, and a loss of more than 100,000 jobs.

Madagascar regained AGOA access in January 2015 following the democratic election of a new president the previous year. Madagascar produces around 80% of the world's vanilla supply; although supply was constrained by hurricane-related damage in 2017, international demand drove prices to record highs, increasing export earnings for Malagasy vanilla. Madagascar's financial sector remains weak, limiting the use of monetary policy to control inflation, but an ongoing IMF program aims to strengthen financial and investment management capacity.

GDP (purchasing power parity): $39.81 billion (2017 est.)
$38.15 billion (2016 est.)
$36.62 billion (2015 est.)
note: data are in 2017 dollars
country comparison to the world: 119

GDP (official exchange rate): $10.56 billion (2016 est.)

GDP—real growth rate: 4.3% (2017 est.)
4.2% (2016 est.)
3.1% (2015 est.)
country comparison to the world: 58

GDP—per capita (PPP): $1,600 (2017 est.)
$1,500 (2016 est.)
$1,500 (2015 est.)
note: data are in 2017 dollars
country comparison to the world: 218

Gross national saving: 14.5% of GDP (2017 est.)
16% of GDP (2016 est.)
11.2% of GDP (2015 est.)
country comparison to the world: 129

GDP—composition, by end use:
household consumption: 75.4%
government consumption: 12%
investment in fixed capital: 16.6%
investment in inventories: 0%
exports of goods and services: 32.1%
imports of goods and services: -36.1% (2017 est.)

GDP—composition, by sector of origin:
agriculture: 23.7%
industry: 16%
services: 60.3% (2017 est.)

Agriculture—products: coffee, vanilla, sugarcane, cloves, cocoa, rice, cassava (manioc, tapioca), beans, bananas, peanuts; livestock products

Industries: meat processing, seafood, soap, beer, leather, sugar, textiles, glassware, cement, automobile assembly plant, paper, petroleum, tourism, mining

Industrial production growth rate: 4.8% (2017 est.)
country comparison to the world: 50

Labor force: 13.4 million (2017 est.)
country comparison to the world: 43

Unemployment rate: 2.1% (2016 est.)
country comparison to the world: 15

Population below poverty line: 70.7% (2012 est.)

Household income or consumption by percentage share: *lowest 10%:* 2.2%
highest 10%: 34.7% (2010 est.)

Distribution of family income—Gini index: 41 (2012)
46.9 (2001)
country comparison to the world: 55

Budget: *revenues:* $1.292 billion
expenditures: $1.725 billion (2017 est.)

Taxes and other revenues: 12.2% of GDP (2017 est.)
country comparison to the world: 204

Budget surplus (+) or deficit (-): -4.1% of GDP (2017 est.)
country comparison to the world: 144

Public debt: 42.3% of GDP (2016 est.)
35.5% of GDP (2015 est.)
country comparison to the world: 129

Fiscal year: calendar year

Inflation rate (consumer prices): 7.8% (2017 est.)
6.7% (2016 est.)
country comparison to the world: 196

Central bank discount rate: 8.3% (31 December 2016)
8.7% (31 December 2015)
country comparison to the world: 38

Commercial bank prime lending rate: 64% (31 December 2017 est.)
62% (31 December 2016 est.)
country comparison to the world: 1

Stock of narrow money: $1.006 billion (31 December 2017 est.)
$849.1 million (31 December 2016 est.)
country comparison to the world: 156

Stock of broad money: $2.015 billion (31 December 2017 est.)
$1.793 billion (31 December 2016 est.)
country comparison to the world: 156

Stock of domestic credit: $1.957 billion (31 December 2017 est.)
$1.746 billion (31 December 2016 est.)
country comparison to the world: 151

Market value of publicly traded shares: $NA

Current account balance: -$494 million (2017 est.)
$75 million (2016 est.)
country comparison to the world: 104

Exports: $2.35 billion (2017 est.)
$2.196 billion (2016 est.)
country comparison to the world: 135

Exports—commodities: coffee, vanilla, shellfish, sugar, cotton cloth, clothing, chromite, petroleum products

Exports—partners: France 23.5%, US 12.8%, Germany 8.3%, China 6.3%, Japan 5%, Netherlands 4.3%, South Korea 4.2% (2016)

Imports: $3.235 billion (2017 est.)
$2.857 billion (2016 est.)
country comparison to the world: 141

Imports—commodities: capital goods, petroleum, consumer goods, food

Imports—partners: China 21.2%, France 6.9%, India 6.5%, UAE 5.6%, Saudi Arabia 5%, South Africa 5% (2016)

Reserves of foreign exchange and gold: $1.141 billion (31 December 2017 est.)
$1.184 billion (31 December 2016 est.)
country comparison to the world: 122

Debt—external: $3.914 billion (31 December 2017 est.)
$3.425 billion (31 December 2016 est.)

country comparison to the world: 140

Stock of direct foreign investment—at home: $6.461 billion (2014 est.)
$6.462 billion (2013 est.)
country comparison to the world: 100

Stock of direct foreign investment—abroad: $NA

Exchange rates: Malagasy ariary (MGA) per US dollar—
3,262.7 (2017 est.)
3,176.5 (2016 est.)
3,176.5 (2015 est.)
2,933.5 (2014 est.)
2,414.8 (2013 est.)

ENERGY

Electricity access: *population without electricity:* 19,500,000
electrification—*total population:* 15%
electrification—urban areas: 37%
electrification—rural areas: 4% (2013)

Electricity—production: 1.508 billion kWh (2015 est.)
country comparison to the world: 146

Electricity—consumption: 1.402 billion kWh (2015 est.)
country comparison to the world: 150

Electricity—exports: 0 kWh (2016 est.)
country comparison to the world: 163

Electricity—imports: 0 kWh (2016 est.)
country comparison to the world: 170

Electricity—installed generating capacity: m 668,200 kW (2015 est.)
country comparison to the world: 138

Electricity—from fossil fuels: 73.9% of total installed capacity (2015 est.)
country comparison to the world: 97

Electricity—from nuclear fuels: 0% of total installed capacity (2015 est.)
country comparison to the world: 133

Electricity—from hydroelectric plants: 24.5% of total installed capacity (2015 est.)
country comparison to the world: 80

Electricity—from other renewable sources: 1.8% of total installed capacity (2015 est.)
country comparison to the world: 126

Crude oil—production: 0 bbl/day (2016 est.)
country comparison to the world: 165

Crude oil—exports: 0 bbl/day (2014 est.)
country comparison to the world: 156

Crude oil—imports: 0 bbl/day (2014 est.)
country comparison to the world: 153

Crude oil—proved reserves: 0 bbl (1 January 2017 es)
country comparison to the world: 162

Refined petroleum products—production: 0 bbl/day (2014 est.)
country comparison to the world: 170

Refined petroleum products—consumption: 15,000 bbl/day (2015 est.)
country comparison to the world: 151

Refined petroleum products—exports: 0 bbl/day (2014 est.)
country comparison to the world: 174

Refined petroleum products—imports: 15,230 bbl/day (2014 est.)
country comparison to the world: 132

Natural gas—production: 0 cu m (2013 est.)
country comparison to the world: 162

Natural gas—consumption: 0 cu m (2013 est.)
country comparison to the world: 203

Natural gas—exports: 0 cu m (2013 est.)
country comparison to the world: 141

Natural gas—imports: 0 cu m (2013 est.)
country comparison to the world: 150

Natural gas—proved reserves: 2.01 billion cu m (1 January 2012 es)
country comparison to the world: 101

Carbon dioxide emissions from consumption of energy: 3 million Mt (2013 est.)
country comparison to the world: 143

COMMUNICATIONS

Telephones—fixed lines: *total subscriptions:* 148,585
subscriptions per 100 inhabitants: 1 (July 2016 est.)
country comparison to the world: 121

Telephones—mobile cellular: *total:* 10,411,721
subscriptions per 100 inhabitants: 43 (July 2016 est.)
country comparison to the world: 91

Telephone system: *general assessment:* system is above average for the region; competition among the three mobile service providers has spurred recent growth in the mobile market
domestic: combined fixed-line and mobile-cellular teledensity about 45 per 100 persons
international: country code—261; landing point for the EASSy, SEACOM, and LION fiber-optic submarine cable systems; satellite earth stations—2 (1 Intelsat—Indian Ocean, 1 Intersputnik—Atlantic Ocean region) (2016)

Broadcast media: state-owned Radio Nationale Malagasy (RNM) and Television Malagasy (TVM) have an extensive national network reach; privately owned radio and TV broadcasters in cities and major towns; state-run radio dominates in rural areas; relays of 2 international broadcasters are available in Antananarivo (2007)

Internet country code: .mg
Internet users: total: 1,151,563

percent of population: 4.7% (July 2016 est.)
country comparison to the world: 31

TRANSPORTATION

National air transport system: *number of registered air carriers:* 3
inventory of registered aircraft operated by air carriers: 11
annual passenger traffic on registered air carriers: 546,946
annual freight traffic on registered air carriers: 30,512,607 mt-km (2015)
Civil aircraft registration country code prefix: 5R (2016)

Airports: 83 (2013)
country comparison to the world: 65

Airports—with paved runways: *total:* 26
over 3,047 m: 1
2,438 to 3,047 m: 2
1,524 to 2,437 m: 6
914 to 1,523 m: 16
under 914 m: 1 (2017)

Airports—with unpaved runways: *total:* 57
1,524 to 2,437 m: 1
914 to 1,523 m: 38
under 914 m: 18 (2013)

Railways: *total:* 836 km
narrow gauge: 836 km 1.000-m gauge (2014)
country comparison to the world: 95

Roadways: *total:* 37,476 km
paved: 6,103 km
unpaved: 31,373 km (2010)
country comparison to the world: 92

Waterways: 600 km (432 km navigable) (2011)
country comparison to the world: 79

Merchant marine: *total:* 28
by type: general cargo 15, oil tanker 3, other 10 (2017)
country comparison to the world: 126

Ports and terminals: *major seaport(s):* Antsiranana (Diego Suarez), Mahajanga, Toamasina, Toliara (Tulear)

MILITARY AND SECURITY

Military expenditures: 0.59% of GDP (2016)
0.6% of GDP (2015)
0.65% of GDP (2014)
0.68% of GDP (2013)
0.69% of GDP (2012)
country comparison to the world: 119

Military branches: People's Armed Forces: Intervention Force, Development Force, Navy, Air Force (2014)

Military service age and obligation: 18-25 years of age for male-only mix of voluntary and conscripted military service; women are not conscripted but can volunteer for all services except the Navy; service obligation is 18 months for military or equivalent civil service; 20-30 years of age for National Gendarmerie recruits and 35 years of age for those with military experience (2017)

TRANSNATIONAL ISSUES

Disputes—international: claims Bassas da India, Europa Island, Glorioso Islands, and Juan de Nova Island (all administered by France); the vegetated drying cays of Banc du Geyser, which were claimed by Madagascar in 1976, also fall within the EEZ claims of the Comoros and France (Glorioso Islands, part of the French Southern and Antarctic Lands)
Refugees and internally displaced persons: IDPs: 246,842 (cyclone in 2017) (2017)

Illicit drugs: illicit producer of cannabis (cultivated and wild varieties) used mostly for domestic consumption; transshipment point for heroin

MALAWI

INTRODUCTION

Background: Established in 1891, the British protectorate of Nyasaland became the independent nation of Malawi in 1964. After three decades of one-party rule under President Hastings Kamuzu BANDA, the country held multiparty presidential and parliamentary elections in 1994, under a provisional constitution that came into full effect the following year. President Bingu wa MUTHARIKA, elected in 2004 after a failed attempt by the previous president to amend the constitution to permit another term, struggled to assert his authority against his predecessor and subsequently started his own party, the Democratic Progressive Party in 2005. MUTHARIKA was reelected to a second term in 2009. He oversaw some economic improvement in his first term, but was accused of economic mismanagement and poor governance in his second term. He died abruptly in 2012 and was succeeded by vice president, Joyce BANDA, who had earlier started her own party, the People's Party. MUTHARIKA's brother, Peter MUTHARIKA, defeated BANDA in the 2014 election. Population growth, increasing pressure on agricultural lands, corruption, and the scourge of HIV/AIDS pose major problems for Malawi.

GEOGRAPHY

Location: Southern Africa, east of Zambia, west and north of Mozambique

Geographic coordinates: 13 30 S, 34 00 E

Map references: Africa

Area: *total:* 118,484 sq km
land: 94,080 sq km
water: 24,404 sq km
country comparison to the world: 101

Area—comparative: slightly smaller than Pennsylvania

Land boundaries: *total:* 2,857 km

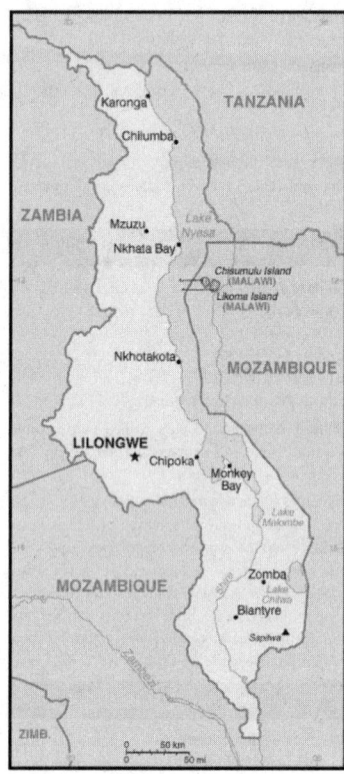

border countries (3): Mozambique 1,498 km, Tanzania 512 km, Zambia 847 km

Coastline: 0 km (landlocked)

Maritime claims: none (landlocked)

Climate: sub-tropical; rainy season (November to May); dry season (May to November)

Terrain: narrow elongated plateau with rolling plains, rounded hills, some mountains

Elevation: *mean elevation:* 779 m

elevation extremes: *lowest point:* junction of the Shire River and international boundary with Mozambique 37 m
highest point: Sapitwa (Mount Mlanje) 3,002 m

Natural resources: limestone, arable land, hydropower, unexploited deposits of uranium, coal, and bauxite

Land use: *agricultural land:* 59.2%
arable land: 38.2%;
permanent crops: 1.4%;
permanent pasture: 19.6%
forest: 34%
other: 6.8% (2011 est.)
Irrigated land: 740 sq km (2012)

Population—distribution: population density is highest south of Lake Nyasa

Natural hazards: flooding; droughts; earthquakes

Environment—current issues: deforestation; land degradation; water pollution from agricultural

runoff, sewage, industrial wastes; siltation of spawning grounds endangers fish populations

Environment—international agreements: *party to:* Biodiversity, Climate Change, Climate Change-Kyoto Protocol, Desertification, Endangered Species, Environmental Modification, Hazardous Wastes, Marine Life Conservation, Ozone Layer Protection, Ship Pollution, Wetlands
signed, but not ratified: Law of the Sea

Geography—note: landlocked; Lake Nyasa, some 580 km long, is the country's most prominent physical feature; it contains more fish species than any other lake on earth

PEOPLE AND SOCIETY

Population: 19,196,246
note: estimates for this country explicitly take into account the effects of excess mortality due to AIDS; this can result in lower life expectancy, higher infant mortality, higher death rates, lower population growth rates, and changes in the distribution of population by age and sex than would otherwise be expected (July 2017 est.)
country comparison to the world: 61

Nationality: *noun:* Malawian(s)
adjective: Malawian

Ethnic groups: Chewa 35.1%, Lomwe 18.9%, Yao 13.1%, Ngoni 12%, Tumbuka 9.4%, Sena 3.5%, Tonga 1.8%, Nyanja 1%, Nkhonde 0.9%, other 1.8% (2015-16 est.)

Languages: English (official), Chichewa (common), Chinyanja, Chiyao, Chitumbuka, Chilomwe, Chinkhonde, Chingoni, Chisena, Chitonga, Chinyakyusa, Chilambya

Religions: Protestant 27.2% (includes Church of Central Africa Presbyterian 17.7%, Seventh Day Adventist/Baptist 6.9%, Anglican 2.6%), Catholic 18.4%, other Christian 41%, Muslim 12.1%, other 0.3%, none 1% (2015-16 est.)

Demographic profile: Malawi has made great improvements in maternal and child health, but has made less progress in reducing its high fertility rate. In both rural and urban areas, very high proportions of mothers are receiving prenatal care and skilled birth assistance, and most children are being vaccinated. Malawi's fertility rate, however, has only declined slowly, decreasing from more than 7 children per woman in the 1980s to about 5.5 today. Nonetheless, Malawians prefer smaller families than in the past, and women are increasingly using contraceptives to prevent or space pregnancies. Rapid population growth and high population density is putting pressure on Malawi's land, water, and forest resources. Reduced plot sizes and increasing vulnerability to climate change, further threaten the sustainability of Malawi's agriculturally based economy and will worsen food shortages. About 80% of the population is employed in agriculture.

Historically, Malawians migrated abroad in search of work, primarily to South Africa and present-day Zimbabwe, but international migration became uncommon after the 1970s, and most migration in recent years has been internal. During

the colonial period, Malawians regularly migrated to southern Africa as contract farm laborers, miners, and domestic servants. In the decade and a half after independence in 1964, the Malawian Government sought to transform its economy from one dependent on small-scale farms to one based on estate agriculture. The resulting demand for wage labor induced more than 300,000 Malawians to return home between the mid-1960s and the mid-1970s. In recent times, internal migration has generally been local, motivated more by marriage than economic reasons.

Age structure: *0-14 years:* 46.34% (male 4,427,403/female 4,468,120)
15-24 years: 20.55% (male 1,956,360/female 1,988,123)
25-54 years: 27.41% (male 2,612,840/female 2,648,997)
55-64 years: 3.01% (male 275,998/female 302,286)
65 years and over: 2.69% (male 227,582/female 288,537) (2017 est.)

Dependency ratios: *total dependency ratio:* 91
youth dependency ratio: 85.3
elderly dependency ratio: 5.7
potential support ratio: 17.4 (2015 est.)

Median age: *total:* 16.5 years
male: 16.4 years
female: 16.7 years (2017 est.)
country comparison to the world: 226

Population growth rate: 3.31% (2017 est.)
country comparison to the world: 3

Birth rate: 41 births/1,000 population (2017 est.)
country comparison to the world: 8

Death rate: 7.9 deaths/1,000 population (2017 est.)
country comparison to the world: 94

Net migration rate: 0 migrant(s)/1,000 population (2017 est.)
country comparison to the world: 90

Population distribution: population density is highest south of Lake Nyasa

Urbanization: *urban population:* 16.6% of total population (2017)
rate of urbanization: 4.02% annual rate of change (2015-20 est.)

Major urban areas—population: LILONGWE (capital) 905,000; Blantyre-Limbe 808,000 (2015)

Sex ratio: *at birth:* 1.02 male(s)/female
0-14 years: 0.99 male(s)/female
15-24 years: 0.99 male(s)/female
25-54 years: 0.99 male(s)/female
55-64 years: 0.91 male(s)/female
65 years and over: 0.79 male(s)/female
total population: 0.98 male(s)/female (2016 est.)

Mother's mean age at first birth: 18.9 years
note: median age at first birth among women 25-29 (2015/16 est.)

Maternal mortality ratio: 634 deaths/100,000 live births (2015 est.)
country comparison to the world: 13

Infant mortality rate: *total:* 43.4 deaths/1,000 live births

male: 50 deaths/1,000 live births
female: 36.7 deaths/1,000 live births (2017 est.)
country comparison to the world: 43

Life expectancy at birth: *total population:* 61.7 years
male: 59.7 years
female: 63.8 years (2017 est.)
country comparison to the world: 200

Total fertility rate: 5.49 children born/woman (2017 est.)
country comparison to the world: 9

Contraceptive prevalence rate: 59.2% (2015/16)

Health expenditures: 11.4% of GDP (2014)
country comparison to the world: 9

Physicians density: 0.02 physicians/1,000 population (2009)

Hospital bed density: 1.3 beds/1,000 population (2011)

Drinking water source:
improved:
urban: 95.7% of population
rural: 89.1% of population
total: 90.2% of population
unimproved:
urban: 4.3% of population
rural: 10.9% of population
total: 9.8% of population (2015 est.)

Sanitation facility access:
improved:
urban: 47.3% of population
rural: 39.8% of population
total: 41% of population
unimproved:
urban: 52.7% of population
rural: 60.2% of population
total: 59% of population (2015 est.)

HIV/AIDS—adult prevalence rate: 9.2% (2016 est.)
country comparison to the world: 9

HIV/AIDS—people living with HIV/AIDS: 1 million (2016 est.)
country comparison to the world: 10

HIV/AIDS—deaths: 24,000 (2016 est.)
country comparison to the world: 12

Major infectious diseases: *degree of risk:* very high
food or waterborne diseases: bacterial and protozoal diarrhea, hepatitis A, and typhoid fever
vectorborne diseases: malaria and dengue fever
water contact disease: schistosomiasis
animal contact disease: rabies (2016)

Obesity—adult prevalence rate: 5.8% (2016)
country comparison to the world: 172

Children under the age of 5 years underweight: 16.7% (2014)
country comparison to the world: 52

Education expenditures: 5.6% of GDP (2015)
country comparison to the world: 60

Literacy: *definition:* age 15 and over can read and write
total population: 62.1%
male: 69.8%

female: 55.2% (2015 est.)

School life expectancy (primary to tertiary education): *total:* 11 years
male: 11 years
female: 11 years (2011)

Unemployment, youth ages 15-24: *total:* 8.6%
male: 9.1%
female: 8.2% (2013 est.)

GOVERNMENT

Country name: *conventional long form:* Republic of Malawi
conventional short form: Malawi
local long form: Dziko la Malawi
local short form: Malawi
former: British Central African Protectorate, Nyasaland Protectorate, Nyasaland
etymology: named for the East African Maravi Kingdom of the 16th century; the word "maravi" means "fire flames"

Government type: presidential republic

Capital: *name:* Lilongwe
geographic coordinates: 13 58 S, 33 47 E
time difference: UTC+2 (7 hours ahead of Washington, DC, during Standard Time)

Administrative divisions: 28 districts; Balaka, Blantyre, Chikwawa, Chiradzulu, Chitipa, Dedza, Dowa, Karonga, Kasungu, Likoma, Lilongwe, Machinga, Mangochi, Mchinji, Mulanje, Mwanza, Mzimba, Neno, Ntcheu, Nkhata Bay, Nkhotakota, Nsanje, Ntchisi, Phalombe, Rumphi, Salima, Thyolo, Zomba

Independence: 6 July 1964 (from the UK)

National holiday: Independence Day (Republic Day), 6 July (1964)

Constitution: history: previous 1953 (preindependence), 1966; latest drafted January to May 1994, approved 16 May 1994, entered into force 18 May 1995
amendments: proposed by the National Assembly; passage of amendments affecting constitutional articles including the sovereignty and territory of the state, fundamental constitutional principles, human rights, voting rights, and the judiciary requires majority approval in a referendum and majority approval by the Assembly; passage of other amendments requires at least two-thirds majority vote of the Assembly; amended several times, last in 2013 (2017)

Legal system: mixed legal system of English common law and customary law; judicial review of legislative acts in the Supreme Court of Appeal

International law organization participation: accepts compulsory ICJ jurisdiction with reservations; accepts ICCt jurisdiction

Citizenship: *citizenship by birth:* no
citizenship by descent only: at least one parent must be a citizen of Malawi
dual citizenship recognized: no
residency requirement for naturalization: 7 years

Suffrage: 18 years of age; universal

Executive branch: *chief of state:* President Arthur Peter MUTHARIKA (since 31 May 2014); Vice President Saulos CHILIMA (since 31 May 2014); note—the president is both chief of state and head of government

head of government: President Arthur Peter MUTHARIKA (since 31 May 2014); Vice President Saulos CHILIMA (since 31 May 2014)
cabinet: Cabinet named by the president
elections/appointments: president directly elected by simple majority popular vote for a 5-year term (eligible for a second term); election last held on 20 May 2014 (next to be held in May 2019)
election results: Peter MUTHARIKA elected president; percent of vote—Peter MUTHARIKA (DPP) 36.4%, Lazarus CHAKWERA (MCP) 27.8%, Joyce BANDA (PP) 20.2%, Atupele MULUZI (UDF) 13.7%, other 1.9%

Legislative branch: *description:* unicameral National Assembly (193 seats; members directly elected in single-seat constituencies by simple majority vote to serve 5-year terms)
elections: last held on 20-22 May 2014 (next to be held in May 2019)
election results: percent of vote by party—DPP 22.0%, MCP 17.4%, PP 18.5%, UDF 9.6%, other 2.8%, independent 29.7%; seats by party—DPP 51, MCP 48, PP 26, UDF 14, other 2, independent 52

Judicial branch: *highest court(s):* Supreme Court of Appeal (consists of the chief justice and at least 3 judges)
judge selection and term of office: Supreme Court chief justice appointed by the president and confirmed by the National Assembly; other judges appointed by the president upon recommendation of the Judicial Service Commission, which regulates judicial officers; judges serve until age 65
subordinate courts: High Court; magistrate courts; Industrial Relations Court; district and city traditional or local courts

Political parties and leaders: Alliance for Democracy or AFORD [Godfrey SHAWA]
Democratic Progressive Party or DPP [Peter MUTHARIKA]
Malawi Congress Party or MCP [Lazarus CHAKWERA]
People's Party or PP [Joyce BANDA]
United Democratic Front or UDF [Atupele MULUZI]

Political pressure groups and leaders: Council for NGOs in Malawi or CONGOMA (human rights, democracy, development)
Human Rights Consultative Committee or HRCC (human rights)
Malawi Economic Justice Network or MEJN (pro-economic growth, development, government accountability)
Malawi Law Society (an umbrella organization of all lawyers in Malawi)
Public Affairs Committee or PAC (promotes democracy, development, peace, unity)

International organization participation: ACP, AfDB, AU, C, CD, COMESA, FAO, G-77,

IAEA, IBRD, ICAO, ICCt, ICRM, IDA, IFAD, IFC, IFRCS, ILO, IMF, IMO, Interpol, IOC, IOM, IPU, ISO (correspondent), ITSO, ITU, ITUC (NGOs), MIGA, MINURSO, MONUSCO, NAM, OPCW, SADC, UN, UNCTAD, UNESCO, UNIDO, UNISFA, UNOCI, UNWTO, UPU, WCO, WFTU (NGOs), WHO, WIPO, WMO, WTO

Diplomatic representation in the US: *chief of mission:* Ambassador Edward Yakobe SAWERENGERA (since 16 September 2016) *chancery:* 2408 Massachusetts Avenue NW, Washington, DC 20008 *telephone:* [1] (202) 721-0270 *FAX:* [1] (202) 721-0288

Diplomatic representation from the US: *chief of mission:* Ambassador Virginia E. PALMER (since 5 February 2015) *embassy:* 16 Jomo Kenyatta Road, Lilongwe 3 *mailing address:* P.O. Box 30016, Lilongwe 3, Malawi *telephone:* [265] (1) 773-166 *FAX:* [265] (1) 770-471

Flag description: three equal horizontal bands of black (top), red, and green with a radiant, rising, red sun centered on the black band; black represents the native peoples, red the blood shed in their struggle for freedom, and green the color of nature; the rising sun represents the hope of freedom for the continent of Africa

National symbol(s): lion; national colors: black, red, green

National anthem: *name:* "Mulungu dalitsa Malawi" (Oh God Bless Our Land of Malawi) *lyrics/music:* Michael-Fredrick Paul SAUKA *note:* adopted 1964

ECONOMY

Economy—overview: Landlocked Malawi ranks among the world's most densely populated and least developed countries. The country's economic performance has historically been constrained by policy inconsistency, macroeconomic instability, poor infrastructure, rampant corruption, high population growth, and poor health and education outcomes that limit labor productivity. The economy is predominately agricultural with about 80% of the population living in rural areas. Agriculture accounts for about one-third of GDP and 80% of export revenues. The performance of the tobacco sector is key to short-term growth as tobacco accounts for more than half of exports, although Malawi is looking to diversify away from tobacco to other cash crops.

The economy depends on substantial inflows of economic assistance from the IMF, the World Bank, and individual donor nations. Donors halted aid from 2013 to 2016 because of concerns about corruption and fiscal carelessness, but the World Bank resumed budget support in May 2017. In 2006, Malawi was approved for relief under the Heavily Indebted Poor Countries (HIPC) program but recent increases in domestic borrowing mean that debt servicing in 2016 exceeded the levels prior to HIPC debt relief.

Heavily dependent on rain-fed agriculture, with corn being the staple crop, Malawi's economy was hit hard by the El Nino-driven drought in 2015 and 2016, and now faces threat from the fall armyworm. The drought also slowed economic activity, led to two consecutive years of declining economic growth, and contributed to high inflation rates. Because of concerns about subsequent droughts, the government banned maize exports from 2016 to late 2017, causing a market glut and depressing local prices.

GDP (purchasing power parity): $22.47 billion (2017 est.) $21.5 billion (2016 est.) $21.02 billion (2015 est.) *note:* data are in 2017 dollars *country comparison to the world:* 145

GDP (official exchange rate): $6.261 billion (2016 est.)

GDP—real growth rate: 4.5% (2017 est.) 2.3% (2016 est.) 3% (2015 est.) *country comparison to the world:* 56

GDP—per capita (PPP): $1,200 (2017 est.) $1,200 (2016 est.) $1,200 (2015 est.) *note:* data are in 2017 dollars *country comparison to the world:* 224

Gross national saving: 2.5% of GDP (2017 est.) -3.3% of GDP (2016 est.) 2.7% of GDP (2015 est.) *country comparison to the world:* 174

GDP—composition, by end use: *household consumption:* 82.8% *government consumption:* 16% *investment in fixed capital:* 11.6% *investment in inventories:* 2.7% *exports of goods and services:* 33.8% *imports of goods and services:* -46.8% (2017 est.)

GDP—composition, by sector of origin: *agriculture:* 28.6% *industry:* 15.6% *services:* 55.9% (2017 est.)

Agriculture—products: tobacco, sugarcane, tea, corn, potatoes, sweet potatoes, cassava (manioc, tapioca), sorghum, pulses, cotton, groundnuts, macadamia nuts, coffee; cattle, goats

Industries: tobacco, tea, sugar, sawmill products, cement, consumer goods

Industrial production growth rate: 1.2% (2017 est.) *country comparison to the world:* 157

Labor force: 7 million (2013 est.) *country comparison to the world:* 67

Labor force—by occupation: *agriculture:* 64.1% *industry:* 6.7% *services:* 29.2% (2013 est.)

Unemployment rate: 20.4% (2013 est.) *country comparison to the world:* 185

Population below poverty line: 50.7% (2010 est.)

Household income or consumption by percentage share: *lowest 10%:* 2.2% *highest 10%:* 37.5% (2010 est.)

Distribution of family income—Gini index: 46.1 (2010) 39.9 (2004) *country comparison to the world:* 32

Budget: *revenues:* $1.298 billion *expenditures:* $1.612 billion (2017 est.) *Taxes and other revenues:* 20.7% of GDP (2017 est.) *country comparison to the world:* 148

Budget surplus (+) or deficit (-): -5% of GDP (2017 est.) *country comparison to the world:* 162

Public debt: 54.6% of GDP (2017 est.) 56.1% of GDP (2016 est.) *country comparison to the world:* 87

Fiscal year: 1 July—30 June

Inflation rate (consumer prices): 13% (2017 est.) 21.7% (2016 est.) *country comparison to the world:* 211

Central bank discount rate: 24% (25 November 2016) 27% (July 2016) *country comparison to the world:* 3

Commercial bank prime lending rate: 42.3% (31 December 2017 est.) 44.1% (31 December 2016 est.) *country comparison to the world:* 3

Stock of narrow money: $638.1 million (31 December 2017 est.) $536.6 million (31 December 2016 est.) *country comparison to the world:* 165

Stock of broad money: $1.367 billion (31 December 2017 est.) $1.238 billion (31 December 2016 est.) *country comparison to the world:* 166

Stock of domestic credit: $1.181 billion (31 December 2017 est.) $1.054 billion (31 December 2016 est.) *country comparison to the world:* 166

Market value of publicly traded shares: $796.2 million (31 December 2016 est.) $936.3 million (31 December 2015 est.) $1.341 billion (31 December 2014 est.) *country comparison to the world:* 108

Current account balance: -$568 million (2017 est.) -$739 million (2016 est.) *country comparison to the world:* 107

Exports: $1.443 billion (2017 est.) $1.361 billion (2016 est.) *country comparison to the world:* 151

Exports—commodities: tobacco 55%, dried legumes (8.8%), sugar (6.7%), tea (5.7%), cotton (2%), peanuts, coffee, soy (2015 est.)

Exports—partners: Zimbabwe 12.9%, Mozambique 11%, Belgium 8.2%, South Africa 7.2%, US 6%, China 4.6%, Germany 4.3%, UK 4.2% (2016)

Imports: $2.388 billion (2017 est.) $2.318 billion (2016 est.) *country comparison to the world:* 154

Imports—commodities: food, petroleum products, semi-manufactures, consumer goods, transportation equipment

Imports—partners: South Africa 20.2%, China 13.8%, India 10.8%, UAE 9.7%, Zambia 5.7% (2016)

Reserves of foreign exchange and gold: $613.5 million (31 December 2017 est.) $563.1 million (31 December 2016 est.) *country comparison to the world:* 135

Debt—external: $2.184 billion (31 December 2017 est.)
$1.985 billion (31 December 2016 est.)
country comparison to the world: 151

Stock of direct foreign investment—at home: $800 million (2015)
country comparison to the world: 120

Stock of direct foreign investment—abroad: $NA

Exchange rates: Malawian kwachas (MWK) per US dollar—
729.1 (2017 est.)
713.85 (2016 est.)
713.85 (2015 est.)
499.6 (2014 est.)
424.9 (2013 est.)

ENERGY

Electricity access: *population without electricity:* 14,900,000
electrification—*total population:* 9%
electrification—urban areas: 32%
electrification—rural areas: 4% (2013)

Electricity—production: 2.12 billion kWh (2015 est.)
country comparison to the world: 139

Electricity—consumption: 1.972 billion kWh (2015 est.)
country comparison to the world: 144

Electricity—exports: 0 kWh (2016 est.)
country comparison to the world: 167

Electricity—imports: 0 kWh (2016 est.)
country comparison to the world: 172

Electricity—installed generating capacity: 353,100 kW (2017 est.)
country comparison to the world: 152

Electricity—from fossil fuels: 0.5% of total installed capacity (2015 est.)
country comparison to the world: 212

Electricity—from nuclear fuels: 0% of total installed capacity (2015 est.)
country comparison to the world: 138

Electricity—from hydroelectric plants: 93.3% of total installed capacity (2015 est.)
country comparison to the world: 8

Electricity—from other renewable sources: 6.1% of total installed capacity (2015 est.)
country comparison to the world: 88

Crude oil—production: 0 bbl/day (2016 est.)
country comparison to the world: 166

Crude oil—exports: 0 bbl/day (2014 est.)
country comparison to the world: 160

Crude oil—imports: 0 bbl/day (2014 est.)
country comparison to the world: 157

Crude oil—proved reserves: 0 bbl (1 January 2017 es)
country comparison to the world: 163

Refined petroleum products—production: 0 bbl/day (2014 est.)
country comparison to the world: 171

Refined petroleum products—consumption: 7,000 bbl/day (2015 est.)
country comparison to the world: 166

Refined petroleum products—exports: 0 bbl/day (2014 est.)
country comparison to the world: 178

Refined petroleum products—imports: 6,843 bbl/day (2014 est.)
country comparison to the world: 152

Natural gas—production: 0 cu m (2017 est.)
country comparison to the world: 166

Natural gas—consumption: 0 cu m (2017 est.)
country comparison to the world: 206

Natural gas—exports: 0 cu m (2017 est.)
country comparison to the world: 146

Natural gas—imports: 0 cu m (2017 est.)
country comparison to the world: 153

Natural gas—proved reserves: 0 cu m (2017 est.)
country comparison to the world: 169

Carbon dioxide emissions from consumption of energy: 1.9 million Mt (2013 est.)
country comparison to the world: 150

COMMUNICATIONS

Telephones—fixed lines: *total subscriptions:* 11,234
subscriptions per 100 inhabitants: less than 1 (July 2016 est.)
country comparison to the world: 153

Telephones—mobile cellular: *total:* 7,178,384
subscriptions per 100 inhabitants: 39 (July 2016 est.)
country comparison to the world: 117

Telephone system: *general assessment:* rudimentary; one fixed-line and two mobile-cellular operators govern the market
domestic: limited fixed-line subscribership of about 1 per 100 households; mobile-cellular services are expanding but network coverage is limited and is based around the main urban areas; mobile-cellular subscribership approaching 40 per 100 households
international: country code—265; satellite earth stations—2 Intelsat (1 Indian Ocean, 1 Atlantic Ocean) (2016)

Broadcast media: radio is the main broadcast medium; privately owned Zodiak radio has the widest national broadcasting reach, followed by state-run radio; numerous private and community radio stations broadcast in cities and towns around the country; the largest TV network is government-owned, but at least 4 private TV networks broadcast in urban areas; relays of multiple international broadcasters are available (2017)

Internet country code: .mw
Internet users: total: 1,785,369

percent of population: 9.6% (July 2016 est.)
country comparison to the world: 135

TRANSPORTATION

National air transport system: *number of registered air carriers:* 1
inventory of registered aircraft operated by air carriers: 2

annual passenger traffic on registered air carriers: 6,010
annual freight traffic on registered air carriers: 5,467 mt-km (2015)
Civil aircraft registration country code prefix: 7Q (2016)

Airports: 32 (2013)
country comparison to the world: 113

Airports—with paved runways: *total:* 7
over 3,047 m: 1
1,524 to 2,437 m: 2
914 to 1,523 m: 4 (2017)

Airports—with unpaved runways: *total:* 25
1,524 to 2,437 m: 1
914 to 1,523 m: 11
under 914 m: 13 (2013)

Railways: *total:* 767 km
narrow gauge: 767 km 1.067-m gauge (2014)
country comparison to the world: 98

Roadways: *total:* 15,450 km
paved: 6,951 km
unpaved: 8,499 km (2011)
country comparison to the world: 121

Waterways: 700 km (on Lake Nyasa [Lake Malawi] and Shire River) (2010)
country comparison to the world: 75

Ports and terminals: lake port(s): Chipoka, Monkey Bay, Nkhata Bay, Nkhotakota, Chilumba (Lake Nyasa)

MILITARY AND SECURITY

Military expenditures: 0.61% of GDP (2016)
0.7% of GDP (2015)
0.89% of GDP (2014)
1.24% of GDP (2013)
0.82% of GDP (2012)
country comparison to the world: 104

Military branches: Malawi Defense Forces (MDF): Army (includes Air Wing, Marine Unit) (2012)

Military service age and obligation: 18 years of age for voluntary military service; high school equivalent required for enlisted recruits and college equivalent for officer recruits; initial engagement is 7 years for enlisted personnel and 10 years for officers (2014)

TRANSNATIONAL ISSUES

Disputes—international: dispute with Tanzania over the boundary in Lake Nyasa (Lake Malawi) and the meandering Songwe River; Malawi contends that the entire lake up to the Tanzanian shoreline is its territory, while Tanzania claims the border is in the center of the lake; the conflict was reignited in 2012 when Malawi awarded a license to a British company for oil exploration in the lake

Refugees and internally displaced persons: refugees (country of origin): 5,444 (Democratic Republic of the Congo) (2016)
IDPs: 8,463 (floods in 2015) (2016)

575

MALAYSIA

INTRODUCTION

Background: During the late 18th and 19th centuries, Great Britain established colonies and protectorates in the area of current Malaysia; these were occupied by Japan from 1942 to 1945. In 1948, the British-ruled territories on the Malay Peninsula except Singapore formed the Federation of Malaya, which became independent in 1957. Malaysia was formed in 1963 when the former British colonies of Singapore, as well as Sabah and Sarawak on the northern coast of Borneo, joined the Federation. The first several years of the country's independence were marred by a communist insurgency, Indonesian confrontation with Malaysia, Philippine claims to Sabah, and Singapore's withdrawal in 1965. During the 22-year term of Prime Minister MAHATHIR bin Mohamad (1981-2003), Malaysia was successful in diversifying its economy from dependence on exports of raw materials to the development of manufacturing, services, and tourism. Prime Minister Mohamed NAJIB bin Abdul Razak (in office since April 2009) has continued these pro-business policies.

GEOGRAPHY

Location: Southeastern Asia, peninsula bordering Thailand and northern one-third of the island of Borneo, bordering Indonesia, Brunei, and the South China Sea, south of Vietnam

Geographic coordinates: 2 30 N, 112 30 E

Map references: Southeast Asia

Area: *total:* 329,847 sq km
land: 328,657 sq km
water: 1,190 sq km
country comparison to the world: 68

Area—comparative: slightly larger than New Mexico

Land boundaries: *total:* 2,742 km
border countries (3): Brunei 266 km, Indonesia 1,881 km, Thailand 595 km

Coastline: 4,675 km (Peninsular Malaysia 2,068 km, East Malaysia 2,607 km)

Maritime claims: *territorial sea:* 12 nm
exclusive economic zone: 200 nm
continental shelf: 200-m depth or to the depth of exploitation; specified boundary in the South China Sea

Climate: tropical; annual southwest (April to October) and northeast (October to February) monsoons

Terrain: coastal plains rising to hills and mountains

Elevation: *mean elevation:* 419 m

elevation extremes: *lowest point:* Indian Ocean 0 m
highest point: Gunung Kinabalu 4,095 m

Natural resources: tin, petroleum, timber, copper, iron ore, natural gas, bauxite

Land use: *agricultural land:* 23.2%
arable land: 2.9%;
permanent crops: 19.4%;
permanent pasture: 0.9%
forest: 62%
other: 14.8% (2011 est.)
Irrigated land: 3,800 sq km (2012)

Population—distribution: a highly uneven distribution with over 80% of the population residing on the Malay Peninsula

Natural hazards: flooding; landslides; forest fires

Environment—current issues: air pollution from industrial and vehicular emissions; water pollution from raw sewage; deforestation; smoke/haze from Indonesian forest fires

Environment—international agreements: *party to:* Biodiversity, Climate Change, Climate Change-Kyoto Protocol, Desertification, Endangered Species, Hazardous Wastes, Law of the Sea, Marine Life Conservation, Ozone Layer Protection, Ship Pollution, Tropical Timber 83, Tropical Timber 94, Wetlands
signed, but not ratified: none of the selected agreements

Geography—note: strategic location along Strait of Malacca and southern South China Sea

PEOPLE AND SOCIETY

Population: 31,381,992 (July 2017 est.)
country comparison to the world: 41

Nationality: *noun:* Malaysian(s)
adjective: Malaysian

Ethnic groups: Bumiputera 61.7% (Malays and indigenous peoples, including Orang Asli, Dayak, Anak Negeri), Chinese 20.8%, Indian 6.2%, other 0.9%, non-citizens 10.4% (2017 est.)

Languages: Bahasa Malaysia (official), English, Chinese (Cantonese, Mandarin, Hokkien, Hakka, Hainan, Foochow), Tamil, Telugu, Malayalam, Panjabi, Thai
note: Malaysia has 134 living languages—112 indigenous languages and 22 non-indigenous languages; in East Malaysia there are several indigenous languages; most widely spoken are Iban and Kadazan

Religions: Muslim (official) 61.3%, Buddhist 19.8%, Christian 9.2%, Hindu 6.3%, Confucianism, Taoism, other traditional Chinese religions 1.3%, other 0.4%, none 0.8%, unspecified 1% (2010 est.)

Age structure: *0-14 years:* 27.83% (male 4,493,084/female 4,238,991)
15-24 years: 16.81% (male 2,677,834/female 2,598,958)
25-54 years: 41% (male 6,507,499/female 6,358,762)
55-64 years: 8.27% (male 1,316,331/female 1,277,558)
65 years and over: 6.1% (male 907,850/female 1,005,125) (2017 est.)

Dependency ratios: *total dependency ratio:* 44.6
youth dependency ratio: 36.1
elderly dependency ratio: 8.5
potential support ratio: 11.8 (2015 est.)

Median age: *total:* 28.5 years
male: 28.2 years
female: 28.8 years (2017 est.)
country comparison to the world: 130

Population growth rate: 1.37% (2017 est.)
country comparison to the world: 82

Birth rate: 19.1 births/1,000 population (2017 est.)
country comparison to the world: 85

Death rate: 5.1 deaths/1,000 population (2017 est.)
country comparison to the world: 192

Net migration rate: -0.3 migrant(s)/1,000 population (2017 est.)
country comparison to the world: 117

Population distribution: a highly uneven distribution with over 80% of the population residing on the Malay Peninsula

Urbanization: *urban population:* 76% of total population (2017)
rate of urbanization: 2.19% annual rate of change (2015-20 est.)

Major urban areas—population: KUALA LUMPUR (capital) 6.837 million; Johor Bahru 912,000 (2015)

Sex ratio: *at birth:* 1.07 male(s)/female
0-14 years: 1.06 male(s)/female
15-24 years: 1.03 male(s)/female
25-54 years: 1.02 male(s)/female
55-64 years: 1.03 male(s)/female
65 years and over: 0.9 male(s)/female
total population: 1.03 male(s)/female (2016 est.)

Maternal mortality ratio: 40 deaths/100,000 live births (2015 est.)
country comparison to the world: 105

Infant mortality rate: *total:* 12.5 deaths/1,000 live births
male: 14.4 deaths/1,000 live births
female: 10.4 deaths/1,000 live births (2017 est.)
country comparison to the world: 115

Life expectancy at birth: *total population:* 75.2 years
male: 72.4 years

female: 78.2 years (2017 est.)
country comparison to the world: 109

Total fertility rate: 2.5 children born/woman (2017 est.)
country comparison to the world: 80

Contraceptive prevalence rate: 52.2% (2014)

Health expenditures: 4.2% of GDP (2014)
country comparison to the world: 163

Physicians density: 1.28 physicians/1,000 population (2011)

Hospital bed density: 1.9 beds/1,000 population (2012)

Drinking water source:
improved:
urban: 100% of population
rural: 93% of population
total: 98.2% of population
unimproved:
urban: 0% of population
rural: 7% of population
total: 1.8% of population (2015 est.)

Sanitation facility access:
improved:
urban: 96.1% of population
rural: 95.9% of population
total: 96% of population
unimproved:
urban: 3.9% of population
rural: 4.1% of population
total: 4% of population (2015 est.)

HIV/AIDS—adult prevalence rate: 0.4% (2016 est.)
country comparison to the world: 67

HIV/AIDS—people living with HIV/AIDS: 97,000 (2016 est.)
country comparison to the world: 43

HIV/AIDS—deaths: 7,000 (2016 est.)
country comparison to the world: 26

Major infectious diseases: *degree of risk:* intermediate
food or waterborne diseases: bacterial diarrhea
vectorborne diseases: dengue fever
water contact disease: leptospirosis (2016)

Obesity—adult prevalence rate: 15.6% (2016)
country comparison to the world: 125

Children under the age of 5 years underweight: 12.4% (2015)
country comparison to the world: 58

Education expenditures: 5% of GDP (2015)
country comparison to the world: 46

Literacy: *definition:* age 15 and over can read and write
total population: 94.6%
male: 96.2%
female: 93.2% (2015 est.)

School life expectancy (primary to tertiary education): *total:* 13 years
male: 12 years
female: 13 years (2015)

Unemployment, youth ages 15-24: *total:* 10.7%
male: 9.9%
female: 11.8% (2015 est.)

country comparison to the world: 100

GOVERNMENT

Country name: *conventional long form:* none
conventional short form: Malaysia
local long form: none
local short form: Malaysia
former: Federation of Malaya
etymology: the name means "Land of the Malays"

Government type: federal parliamentary constitutional monarchy
note: all Peninsular Malaysian states have hereditary rulers (commonly referred to as sultans) except Melaka (Malacca) and Pulau Pinang (Penang); those two states along with Sabah and Sarawak in East Malaysia have governors appointed by government; powers of state governments are limited by federal constitution; under terms of federation, Sabah and Sarawak retain certain constitutional prerogatives (e.g., right to maintain their own immigration controls)

Capital: *name:* Kuala Lumpur; note—nearby Putrajaya is referred to as a federal government administrative center but not the capital; Parliament meets in Kuala Lumpur

geographic coordinates: 3 10 N, 101 42 E
time difference: UTC+8 (13 hours ahead of Washington, DC, during Standard Time)

Administrative divisions: 13 states (negeri-negeri, singular—negeri); Johor, Kedah, Kelantan, Melaka, Negeri Sembilan, Pahang, Perak, Perlis, Pulau Pinang, Sabah, Sarawak, Selangor, Terengganu; and 1 federal territory (Wilayah Persekutuan) with 3 components, Kuala Lumpur, Labuan, and Putrajaya

Independence: 31 August 1957 (from the UK)

National holiday: Independence Day (or Merdeka Day), 31 August (1957) (independence of Malaya); Malaysia Day, 16 September (1963) (formation of Malaysia)

Constitution: previous 1948; latest drafted 21 February 1957, effective 27 August 1957; amended many times, last in 2010 (2016)

Legal system: mixed legal system of English common law, Islamic law, and customary law; judicial review of legislative acts in the Federal Court at request of supreme head of the federation

International law organization participation: has not submitted an ICJ jurisdiction declaration; non-party state to the ICCt

Citizenship: *citizenship by birth:* no
citizenship by descent only: at least one parent must be a citizen of Malaysia
dual citizenship recognized: no
residency requirement for naturalization: 10 out 12 years preceding application

Suffrage: 21 years of age; universal

Executive branch: *chief of state:* King MUHAMMAD V (formerly known as Tuanku Muhammad Faris Petra) (selected on 14 October 2016; installed on 13 December 2016); note—the position of the king is primarily ceremonial, but he is

the final arbiter on the appointment of the prime minister

head of government: Prime Minister Mohamed NAJIB bin Abdul Najib Razak (since 3 April 2009); Deputy Prime Minister Ahmad ZAHID Hamidi (since 29 July 2015)

cabinet: Cabinet appointed by the prime minister from among members of Parliament with the consent of the king

elections/appointments: king elected by and from the hereditary rulers of 9 states for a 5-year term; election is on a rotational basis among rulers of the 9 states; election last held on 14 October 2016 (next to be held in 2021); prime minister designated from among members of the House of Representatives; following legislative elections, the leader who commands support of the majority of members in the House becomes prime minister

election results: Mohamed NAJIB bin Abdul Najib Razak (UMNO) sworn in as prime minister for second term on 3 April 2009

Legislative branch: *description:* bicameral Parliament or Parlimen consists of the Senate or Dewan Negara (70 seats; 44 members appointed by the king and 26 indirectly elected by 13 state legislatures; members serve 3-year terms) and the House of Representatives or Dewan Rakyat (222 seats; members directly elected in single-seat constituencies by simple majority vote to serve 5-year terms)

elections: House of Representatives—last held on 5 May 2013 (next to be held by 24 August 2018)

election results: House of Representatives—percent of vote by party/coalition—BN 47.4%, People's Alliance (DAP, PAS, PKR) 50.9%, other 1.7%; seats by party/coalition—BN 133, People's Alliance (DAP, PAS, PKR) 89

note: seats by party/coalition as of October 2016—BN 132, PH 72 (DAP 37, PKR 28, AMANAH 6, PPBM 1), PAS 14, WARISAN 2, PSM 1, independent 1

Judicial branch: *highest court(s):* Federal Court (consists of the chief justice, president of the Court of Appeal, chief justice of the High Court of Malaya, chief judge of the High Court of Sabah and Sarawak and 7 judges); note—Malaysia has a dual judicial hierarchy of civil and religious (sharia) courts

judge selection and term of office: Federal Court justices appointed by the monarch on advice of the prime minister; judges serve until mandatory retirement at age 65

subordinate courts: Court of Appeal; High Court; Sessions Court; Magistrates' Court

Political parties and leaders: National Front (Barisan Nasional) or BN: Gerakan Rakyat Malaysia Party or GERAKAN [MAH Siew Keong]
Liberal Democratic Party (Parti Liberal Demokratik—Sabah) or LDP [TEO Chee Kang]
Malaysian Chinese Association (Persatuan China Malaysia) or MCA [LIOW Tiong Lai]
Malaysian Indian Congress (Kongres India Malaysia) or MIC [S. SUBRAMANIAM]
Parti Bersatu Sabah or PBS [Joseph PAIRIN Kitingan]

Sarawak United People's Party (Parti Bersatu Rakyat Sarawak) or SUPP [Dr. SIM Kui Hian]

United Malays National Organization or UMNO [NAJIB bin Abdul Razak]

United Pasokmomogun Kadazandusun Murut Organization (Pertubuhan Pasko Momogun Kadazan Dusun Bersatu) or UPKO [Wilfred Madius TANGAU]

Coalition of Hope (Pakatan Harapan) or PH (formerly the People's Alliance):: Democratic Action Party (Parti Tindakan Demokratik) or DAP [TAN Kok Wai, Acting National Chairman]

National Trust Party (Parti Amanah Negara) or AMANAH [Mohamad SABU]

People's Justice Party (Parti Keadilan Rakyat) or PKR [WAN AZIZAH Wan Ismail]

Parti Pribumi Bersatu Malaysia or PPBM [MAHATHIR Mohamad]

Other: Islamic Party of Malaysia (Parti Islam se Malaysia) or PAS [Abdul HADI Awang]

Sabah Heritage Party or WARISAN [Shafie APDAL]

Socialist Party of Malaysia (Parti Sosialis Malaysia) or PSM [Mohd Nasir HASHIM]

Political pressure groups and leaders: Bar Council

BERSIH (electoral reform coalition)

ISMA (Muslim NGO)

PERKASA (defense of Malay rights)

other: religious groups; women's groups; youth groups

International organization participation: ADB, APEC, ARF, ASEAN, BIS, C, CICA (observer), CP, D-8, EAS, FAO, G-15, G-77, IAEA, IBRD, ICAO, ICC (national committees), ICRM, IDA, IDB, IFAD, IFC, IFRCS, IHO, ILO, IMF, IMO, IMSO, Interpol, IOC, IPU, ISO, ITSO, ITU, ITUC (NGOs), MIGA, MINURSO, MONUSCO, NAM, OIC, OPCW, PCA, PIF (partner), UN, UNAMID, UNCTAD, UNESCO, UNIDO, UNIFIL, UNISFA, UNMIL, UNWTO, UPU, WCO, WFTU (NGOs), WHO, WIPO, WMO, WTO

Diplomatic representation in the US: *chief of mission*: Ambassador ZULHASNAN Rafique (since 9 January 2017)

chancery: 3516 International Court NW, Washington, DC 20008

telephone: [1] (202) 572-9700

FAX: [1] (202) 572-9882

consulate(s) general: Los Angeles, New York

Diplomatic representation from the US: *chief of mission*: Ambassador Kamala Shirin LAKHDIR (since 21 February 2017)

embassy: 376 Jalan Tun Razak, 50400 Kuala Lumpur

mailing address: US Embassy Kuala Lumpur, APO AP 96535-8152

telephone: [60] (3) 2168-5000

FAX: [60] (3) 2142-2207

Flag description: 14 equal horizontal stripes of red (top) alternating with white (bottom); there is a dark blue rectangle in the upper hoist-side corner bearing a yellow crescent and a yellow 14-pointed star; the flag is often referred to as Jalur Gemilang

(Stripes of Glory); the 14 stripes stand for the equal status in the federation of the 13 member states and the federal government; the 14 points on the star represent the unity between these entities; the crescent is a traditional symbol of Islam; blue symbolizes the unity of the Malay people and yellow is the royal color of Malay rulers

note: the design is based on the flag of the US

National symbol(s): tiger, hibiscus; national colors: red, white, blue, yellow

National anthem: *name*: "Negaraku" (My Country)

lyrics/music: collective, led by Tunku ABDUL RAHMAN/Pierre Jean DE BERANGER

note: adopted 1957; full version only performed in the presence of the king; the tune, which was adopted from a popular French melody titled "La Rosalie," was originally the anthem of Perak, one of Malaysia's 13 states

ECONOMY

Economy—overview: Malaysia, an upper middle-income country, has transformed itself since the 1970s from a producer of raw materials into a multi-sector economy. Under current Prime Minister NAJIB, Malaysia is attempting to achieve high-income status by 2020 and to move further up the value-added production chain by attracting investments in high technology, knowledge-based industries and services. NAJIB's Economic Transformation Program is a series of projects and policy measures intended to accelerate the country's economic growth. The government has also taken steps to liberalize some services sub-sectors. Malaysia is vulnerable to a fall in world commodity prices or a general slowdown in global economic activity.

The NAJIB administration is continuing efforts to boost domestic demand and reduce the economy's dependence on exports. Domestic demand continues to anchor economic growth, supported mainly by private consumption, which accounts for 53% of GDP. Nevertheless, exports—particularly of electronics, oil and gas, and palm oil—remain a significant driver of the economy. In 2015, gross exports of goods and services were equivalent to 73% of GDP. The oil and gas sector supplied about 22% of government revenue in 2015, down significantly from prior years amid a decline in commodity prices and diversification of government revenues. Malaysia has embarked on a fiscal reform program aimed at achieving a balanced budget by 2020, including rationalization of subsidies and the 2015 introduction of a 6% value added tax. Sustained low commodity prices throughout the period not only strained government finances, but also shrunk Malaysia's current account surplus and weighed heavily on the Malaysian ringgit, which was among the region's worst performing currencies during 2013-17. The ringgit hit new lows following the US presidential election amid a broader selloff of emerging market assets.

Bank Negara Malaysia (the central bank) maintains adequate foreign exchange reserves; a well-developed regulatory regime has limited

Malaysia's exposure to riskier financial instruments, although it remains vulnerable to volatile global capital flows. In order to increase Malaysia's competitiveness, Prime Minister NAJIB raised possible revisions to the special economic and social preferences accorded to ethnic Malays under the New Economic Policy of 1970, but retreated in 2013 after he encountered significant opposition from Malay nationalists and other vested interests. In September 2013 NAJIB launched the new Bumiputra Economic Empowerment Program, policies that favor and advance the economic condition of ethnic Malays.

Malaysia signed the 12-nation Trans-Pacific Partnership (TPP) free trade agreement in February 2016, although the future of the TPP remains unclear following the US withdrawal from the agreement. Along with nine other ASEAN members, Malaysia established the ASEAN Economic Community in 2015, which aims to advance regional economic integration.

GDP (purchasing power parity): $926.1 billion (2017 est.)

$878.4 billion (2016 est.)

$842.8 billion (2015 est.)

note: data are in 2017 dollars

country comparison to the world: 27

GDP (official exchange rate): $309.9 billion (2016 est.)

GDP—real growth rate: 5.4% (2017 est.)

4.2% (2016 est.)

5% (2015 est.)

country comparison to the world: 32

GDP—per capita (PPP): $28,900 (2017 est.)

$27,800 (2016 est.)

$27,000 (2015 est.)

note: data are in 2017 dollars

country comparison to the world: 70

Gross national saving: 28% of GDP (2017 est.)

28.2% of GDP (2016 est.)

28.2% of GDP (2015 est.)

country comparison to the world: 37

GDP—composition, by end use:

household consumption: 55.4%

government consumption: 12.5%

investment in fixed capital: 26.3%

investment in inventories: 0.1%

exports of goods and services: 75.2%

imports of goods and services: -69.5% (2017 est.)

GDP—composition, by sector of origin:

agriculture: 8.4%

industry: 36.9%

services: 54.7% (2017 est.)

Agriculture—products: Peninsular Malaysia—palm oil, rubber, cocoa, rice; Sabah—palm oil, subsistence crops; rubber, timber; Sarawak—palm oil, rubber, timber; pepper

Industries: Peninsular Malaysia—rubber and oil palm processing and manufacturing, petroleum and natural gas, light manufacturing, pharmaceuticals, medical technology, electronics and semiconductors, timber processing; Sabah—logging, petroleum and natural gas production;

Sarawak—agriculture processing, petroleum and natural gas production, logging

Industrial production growth rate: 4.6% (2017 est.)
country comparison to the world: 57

Labor force: 14.94 million (2017 est.)
country comparison to the world: 40

Labor force—by occupation: *agriculture:* 11%
industry: 36%
services: 53% (2012 est.)

Unemployment rate: 3.4% (2017 est.)
3.5% (2016 est.)
country comparison to the world: 38

Population below poverty line: 3.8% (2009 est.)

Household income or consumption by percentage share: *lowest 10%:* 1.8%
highest 10%: 34.7% (2009 est.)

Distribution of family income—Gini index: 46.2 (2009)
49.2 (1997)
country comparison to the world: 31

Budget: *revenues:* $51.23 billion
expenditures: $60.26 billion (2017 est.)
Taxes and other revenues: 16.5% of GDP (2017 est.)
country comparison to the world: 181

Budget surplus (+) or deficit (-): -2.9% of GDP (2017 est.)
country comparison to the world: 109

Public debt: 52.5% of GDP (2017 est.)
52.7% of GDP (2016 est.)
note: this figure is based on the amount of federal government debt, RM501.6 billion ($167.2 billion) in 2012; this includes Malaysian Treasury bills and other government securities, as well as loans raised externally and bonds and notes issued overseas; this figure excludes debt issued by non-financial public enterprises and guaranteed by the federal government, which was an additional $47.7 billion in 2012
country comparison to the world: 94

Fiscal year: calendar year

Inflation rate (consumer prices): 3.8% (2017 est.)
2.1% (2016 est.)
note: approximately 30% of goods are price-controlled
country comparison to the world: 149

Central bank discount rate: 3% (31 December 2011)
2.83% (31 December 2010)
country comparison to the world: 107

Commercial bank prime lending rate: 4.5% (31 December 2017 est.)
4.49% (31 December 2016 est.)
country comparison to the world: 151

Stock of narrow money: $95.12 billion (31 December 2017 est.)
$84.9 billion (31 December 2016 est.)
country comparison to the world: 42

Stock of broad money: $406.3 billion (31 December 2017 est.)
$365.1 billion (31 December 2016 est.)
country comparison to the world: 28

Stock of domestic credit: $447.9 billion (31 December 2017 est.)
$398.3 billion (31 December 2016 est.)
country comparison to the world: 27

Market value of publicly traded shares: $383 billion (31 December 2015 est.)
$459 billion (31 December 2014 est.)
$500.4 billion (31 December 2013 est.)
country comparison to the world: 27

Current account balance: $7.486 billion (2017 est.)
$6.996 billion (2016 est.)
country comparison to the world: 25

Exports: $188.2 billion (2017 est.)
$165.3 billion (2016 est.)
country comparison to the world: 29

Exports—commodities: semiconductors and electronic equipment, palm oil, petroleum and liquefied natural gas, wood and wood products, palm oil, rubber, textiles, chemicals, solar panels

Exports—partners: Singapore 14.7%, China 12.6%, US 10.3%, Japan 8.1%, Thailand 5.7%, Hong Kong 4.8%, India 4.1% (2016)

Imports: $163.4 billion (2017 est.)
$140.9 billion (2016 est.)
country comparison to the world: 27

Imports—commodities: electronics, machinery, petroleum products, plastics, vehicles, iron and steel products, chemicals

Imports—partners: China 19.4%, Singapore 9.8%, Japan 7.7%, US 7.6%, Thailand 5.8%, South Korea 5%, Indonesia 4% (2016)

Reserves of foreign exchange and gold: $97.44 billion (31 December 2017 est.)
$94.5 billion (31 December 2016 est.)
country comparison to the world: 27

Debt—external: $213 billion (31 December 2017 est.)
$195.3 billion (31 December 2016 est.)
country comparison to the world: 35

Stock of direct foreign investment—at home: $133.2 billion (31 December 2017 est.)
$121.6 billion (31 December 2016 est.)
country comparison to the world: 41

Stock of direct foreign investment—abroad: $137.9 billion (31 December 2017 est.)
$126.9 billion (31 December 2016 est.)
country comparison to the world: 32

Exchange rates: ringgits (MYR) per US dollar—
4.343 (2017 est.)
4.15 (2016 est.)
4.15 (2015 est.)
3.91 (2014 est.)
3.27 (2013 est.)

ENERGY

Electricity access: *population without electricity:* 100,000
electrification—*total population:* 99.5%
electrification—urban areas: 99.8%
electrification—rural areas: 98.7% (2013)

Electricity—production: 141.9 billion kWh (2015 est.)
country comparison to the world: 30

Electricity—consumption: 133 billion kWh (2015 est.)
country comparison to the world: 29

Electricity—exports: 3 million kWh (2015 est.)
country comparison to the world: 94

Electricity—imports: 13 million kWh (2015 est.)
country comparison to the world: 113

Electricity—installed generating capacity: 33.34 million kW (2015 est.)
country comparison to the world: 32

Electricity—from fossil fuels: 82.1% of total installed capacity (2015 est.)
country comparison to the world: 82

Electricity—from nuclear fuels: 0% of total installed capacity (2015 est.)
country comparison to the world: 148

Electricity—from hydroelectric plants: 14% of total installed capacity (2015 est.)
country comparison to the world: 107

Electricity—from other renewable sources: 4% of total installed capacity (2015 est.)
country comparison to the world: 105

Crude oil—production: 666,900 bbl/day (2016 est.)
country comparison to the world: 26

Crude oil—exports: 310,900 bbl/day (2014 est.)
country comparison to the world: 25

Crude oil—imports: 194,400 bbl/day (2014 est.)
country comparison to the world: 31

Crude oil—proved reserves: 3.6 billion bbl (1 January 2017 es)
country comparison to the world: 29

Refined petroleum products—production: 512,900 bbl/day (2014 est.)
country comparison to the world: 31

Refined petroleum products—consumption: 760,000 bbl/day (2015 est.)
country comparison to the world: 29

Refined petroleum products—exports: 231,400 bbl/day (2014 est.)
country comparison to the world: 32

Refined petroleum products—imports: 409,500 bbl/day (2014 est.)
country comparison to the world: 23

Natural gas—production: 63.43 billion cu m (2015 est.)
country comparison to the world: 14

Natural gas—consumption: 40.67 billion cu m (2015 est.)
country comparison to the world: 29

Natural gas—exports: 34.99 billion cu m (2015 est.)
country comparison to the world: 10

Natural gas—imports: 3.27 billion cu m (2015 est.)
country comparison to the world: 41

Natural gas—proved reserves: 1.183 trillion cu m (1 January 2017 es)

country comparison to the world: 25

Carbon dioxide emissions from consumption of energy: 208 million Mt (2013 est.)
country comparison to the world: 27

COMMUNICATIONS

Telephones—fixed lines: *total subscriptions:* 4,510,200
subscriptions per 100 inhabitants: 15 (July 2016 est.)
country comparison to the world: 37

Telephones—mobile cellular: *total:* 43,912,600
subscriptions per 100 inhabitants: 142 (July 2016 est.)
country comparison to the world: 31

Telephone system: *general assessment:* modern system featuring good intercity service on Peninsular Malaysia provided mainly by microwave radio relay and an adequate intercity microwave radio relay network between Sabah and Sarawak via Brunei; international service excellent
domestic: domestic satellite system with 2 earth stations; combined fixed-line and mobile-cellular teledensity exceeds 155 per 100 persons
international: country code—60; landing point for several major international submarine cable networks that provide connectivity to Asia, Middle East, and Europe; satellite earth stations—2 Intelsat (1 Indian Ocean, 1 Pacific Ocean) (2016)

Broadcast media: state-owned TV broadcaster operates 2 TV networks with relays throughout the country, and the leading private commercial media group operates 4 TV stations with numerous relays throughout the country; satellite TV subscription service is available; state-owned radio broadcaster operates multiple national networks, as well as regional and local stations; many private commercial radio broadcasters and some subscription satellite radio services are available; about 55 radio stations overall (2012)

Internet country code: .my
Internet users: total: 24,384,952
percent of population: 78.8% (July 2016 est.)
country comparison to the world: 40

TRANSPORTATION

National air transport system: *number of registered air carriers:* 12
inventory of registered aircraft operated by air carriers: 263
annual passenger traffic on registered air carriers: 50,347,149
annual freight traffic on registered air carriers: 2,005,979,379 mt-km (2015)
Civil aircraft registration country code prefix: 9M (2016)

Airports: 114 (2013)
country comparison to the world: 51

Airports—with paved runways: *total:* 39
over 3,047 m: 8
2,438 to 3,047 m: 8
1,524 to 2,437 m: 7
914 to 1,523 m: 8

under 914 m: 8 (2017)

Airports—with unpaved runways: *total:* 75
914 to 1,523 m: 6
under 914 m: 69 (2013)

Heliports: 4 (2013)

Pipelines: condensate 354 km; gas 6,439 km; liquid petroleum gas 155 km; oil 1,937 km; oil/gas/water 43 km; refined products 114 km; water 26 km (2013)

Railways: *total:* 1,851 km
standard gauge: 59 km 1.435-m gauge (59 km electrified)
narrow gauge: 1,792 km 1.000-m gauge (339 km electrified) (2014)
country comparison to the world: 75

Roadways: *total:* 144,403 km (excludes local roads)
paved: 116,169 km (includes 1,821 km of expressways)
unpaved: 28,234 km (2010)
country comparison to the world: 35

Waterways: 7,200 km (Peninsular Malaysia 3,200 km; Sabah 1,500 km; Sarawak 2,500 km) (2011)
country comparison to the world: 19

Merchant marine: *total:* 1,690
by type: bulk carrier 12, container ship 26, general cargo 188, oil tanker 129, other 1,335 (2017)
country comparison to the world: 14

Ports and terminals: *major seaport(s):* Bintulu, Johor Bahru, George Town (Penang), Port Kelang (Port Klang), Tanjung Pelepas
container port(s) (TEUs): George Town (Penang) (1,317,000), Port Kelang (Port Klang) (11,887,000), Tanjung Pelepas (8,797,000) (2015)
LNG terminal(s) (export): Bintulu (Sarawak)
LNG terminal(s) (import): Sungei Udang

MILITARY AND SECURITY

Military expenditures: 1.41% of GDP (2016)
1.53% of GDP (2015)
1.46% of GDP (2014)
1.52% of GDP (2013)
1.43% of GDP (2012)
country comparison to the world: 58

Military branches: Malaysian Armed Forces (Angkatan Tentera Malaysia, ATM): Malaysian Army (Tentera Darat Malaysia), Royal Malaysian Navy (Tentera Laut Diraja Malaysia, TLDM), Royal Malaysian Air Force (Tentera Udara Diraja Malaysia, TUDM) (2013)

Military service age and obligation: 17 years 6 months of age for voluntary military service (younger with parental consent and proof of age); mandatory retirement age 60; women serve in the Malaysian Armed Forces; no conscription (2013)

Maritime threats: the International Maritime Bureau reports that the territorial and offshore waters in the Strait of Malacca and South China Sea remain high risk for piracy and armed robbery against ships; in the past, commercial vessels have been attacked and hijacked both at anchor and while underway; hijacked vessels are often disguised and cargo diverted to ports in East Asia;

crews have been murdered or cast adrift; seven attacks were reported in 2016 including five ships boarded, two hijacked, and 47 crew taken hostage, this is down from 13 attacks in 2015; during the first half of 2017, three attacks were reported including two ships that were boarded and one that was hijacked

TERRORISM

Terrorist groups—foreign based: *Jemaah Islamiya (JI):* aim(s): enhance networks in Malaysia and, ultimately, overthrow the secular Malaysian Government and establish a pan-Islamic state across Southeast Asia
area(s) of operation: maintains a recruitment and operational presence, primarily in major cities; authorities have foiled several plots targeting densely populated sites for attack, including Kuala Lumpur City Centre, embassies, government buildings, and popular tourist attractions; prior to the government exerting intensive counterterrorism measures, JI was based in Malaysia until moving its headquarters to Indonesia in 1993; has established ties to the Malaysian Militant Movement (Kumpulan Mujahidin Malaysia, KMM), a home-grown Islamist extremist group; JI recruiters continue to target youths for fighting

Liberation Tigers of Tamil Eelam (LTTE): *aim(s):* enhance networks in Malaysia and, ultimately, revive the movement to establish a Tamil homeland
area(s) of operation: maintains safe havens, transit routes, human trafficking, and an operational presence in an effort to revive the movement and conduct attacks; authorities continue in 2017 to pursue leaders, operatives, and supporters for arrest

TRANSNATIONAL ISSUES

Disputes—international: while the 2002 "Declaration on the Conduct of Parties in the South China Sea" has eased tensions over the Spratly Islands, it is not the legally binding "code of conduct" sought by some parties; Malaysia was not party to the March 2005 joint accord among the national oil companies of China, the Philippines, and Vietnam on conducting marine seismic activities in the Spratly Islands; disputes continue over deliveries of fresh water to Singapore, Singapore's land reclamation, bridge construction, and maritime boundaries in the Johor and Singapore Straits; in 2008, ICJ awarded sovereignty of Pedra Branca (Pulau Batu Puteh/Horsburgh Island) to Singapore, and Middle Rocks to Malaysia, but did not rule on maritime regimes, boundaries, or disposition of South Ledge; land and maritime negotiations with Indonesia are ongoing, and disputed areas include the controversial Tanjung Datu and Camar Wulan border area in Borneo and the maritime boundary in the Ambalat oil block in the Celebes Sea; separatist violence in Thailand's predominantly Muslim southern provinces prompts measures to close and monitor border with Malaysia to stem terrorist activities; Philippines retains a dormant claim to Malaysia's Sabah State in northern Borneo; per Letters of Exchange signed in 2009, Malaysia in

2010 ceded two hydrocarbon concession blocks to Brunei in exchange for Brunei's sultan dropping claims to the Limbang corridor, which divides Brunei; piracy remains a problem in the Malacca Strait

Refugees and internally displaced persons: refugees (country of origin): 87,036 (Burma) (2016) *stateless persons:* 10,931 (2016); note—Malaysia's stateless population consists of Rohingya refugees from Burma, ethnic Indians, and the children of Filipino and Indonesian illegal migrants; Burma stripped the Rohingya of their nationality in 1982; Filipino and Indonesian children who have not been registered for birth certificates by their parents or who received birth certificates stamped "foreigner" are not eligible to attend government schools; these children are vulnerable to statelessness should they not be able to apply to their parents' country of origin for passports

Trafficking in persons: current situation: Malaysia is a destination and, to a lesser extent, a source and transit country for men, women, and children subjected to forced labor and women and children subjected to sex trafficking; Malaysia is mainly a destination country for foreign workers who migrate willingly from countries, including Indonesia, Bangladesh, the Philippines, Nepal, Burma, and other Southeast Asian countries, but subsequently encounter forced labor or debt bondage in agriculture, construction, factories, and domestic service at the hands of employers, employment agents, and labor recruiters; women from Southeast Asia and, to a much lesser extent, Africa, are recruited for legal work in restaurants, hotels, and salons but are forced into prostitution; refugees, including Rohingya adults and children, are not legally permitted to work and are vulnerable to trafficking; a small number of Malaysians are trafficked internally and subjected to sex trafficking abroad

tier rating: Tier 2 Watch list—Malaysia does not fully comply with the minimum standards for the elimination of trafficking; however, it is making significant efforts to do so; in 2014, amendments to strengthen existing anti-trafficking laws, including enabling victims to move freely and to work and for NGOs to run protective facilities, were drafted by the government and are pending approval from Parliament; authorities more than doubled investigations and prosecutions but convicted only three traffickers for forced labor and none for sex trafficking, a decline from 2013 and a disproportionately small number compared to the scale of the country's trafficking problem; NGOs provided the majority of victim rehabilitation and counseling services with no financial support from the government (2015)

Illicit drugs: drug trafficking prosecuted vigorously, including enforcement of the death penalty; heroin still primary drug of abuse, but synthetic drug demand remains strong; continued ecstasy and methamphetamine producer for domestic users and, to a lesser extent, the regional drug market

MALDIVES

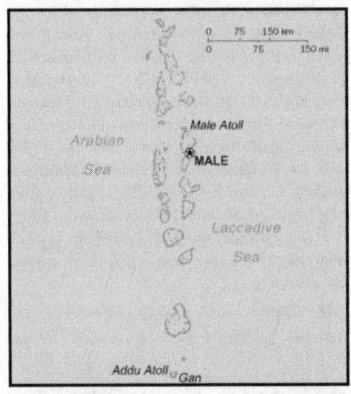

INTRODUCTION

Background: A sultanate since the 12th century, the Maldives became a British protectorate in 1887. It became a republic in 1968, three years after independence. President Maumoon Abdul GAYOOM dominated the islands' political scene for 30 years, elected to six successive terms by single-party referendums. Following political demonstrations in the capital Male in August 2003, GAYOOM and his government pledged to embark upon a process of liberalization and democratic reforms, including a more representative political system and expanded political freedoms. Political parties were legalized in 2005.

In June 2008, a constituent assembly—termed the "Special Majlis"—finalized a new constitution ratified by GAYOOM in August 2008. The first-ever presidential elections under a multi-candidate, multi-party system were held in October 2008. GAYOOM was defeated in a runoff poll by Mohamed NASHEED, a political activist who had been jailed several years earlier by the GAYOOM regime. NASHEED faced a number of challenges including strengthening democracy and combating poverty and drug abuse. In early February 2012, after several weeks of street protests in response to his ordering the arrest of a top judge, NASHEED resigned the presidency and handed over power to Vice President Mohammed WAHEED Hassan Maniku. In mid-2012, a Commission of National Inquiry was established by the government to probe events leading up to NASHEED's resignation. Though the commission found no evidence of a coup, the report recommended strengthening the country's democratic institutions to avert similar events in the future, and to investigate alleged police misconduct during the crisis. NASHEED, WAHEED, and Abdulla YAMEEN ran in the 2013 elections with YAMEEN ultimately winning the presidency after three rounds of voting. As president, YAMEEN has sought to weaken democratic institutions, jail his political opponents, restrict the press, and exert control over the judiciary to strengthen his hold on power and limit dissent. Maldivian officials have played a prominent role in international climate change discussions (due to the islands' vulnerability to rising sea-level).

GEOGRAPHY

Location: Southern Asia, group of atolls in the Indian Ocean, south-southwest of India

Geographic coordinates: 3 15 N, 73 00 E

Map references: Asia

Area: *total:* 298 sq km
land: 298 sq km

water: 0 sq km
country comparison to the world: 210

Area—comparative: about 1.7 times the size of Washington, DC

Land boundaries: 0 km

Coastline: 644 km

Maritime claims: measured from claimed archipelagic straight baselines
territorial sea: 12 nm
contiguous zone: 24 nm
exclusive economic zone: 200 nm

Climate: tropical; hot, humid; dry, northeast monsoon (November to March); rainy, southwest monsoon (June to August)

Terrain: flat, with white sandy beaches

Elevation: *mean elevation:* 1.8 m

elevation extremes: *lowest point:* Indian Ocean 0 m
highest point: 8th tee, golf course, Villingi Island 5 m

Natural resources: fish

Land use: *agricultural land:* 23.3%
arable land: 10%;
permanent crops: 10%;
permanent pasture: 3.3%
forest: 3%
other: 73.7% (2011 est.)
Irrigated land: 0 sq km (2012)

Population—distribution: about a third of the population lives in the centrally located capital city of Male and almost a tenth in southern Addu City; the remainder of the populace is spread over the 200 or so populated islands of the archipelago

Natural hazards: tsunamis; low elevation of islands makes them sensitive to sea level rise

Environment—current issues: depletion of fresh-water aquifers threatens water supplies; coral reef bleaching

Environment—international agreements: *party to:* Biodiversity, Climate Change, Climate Change-Kyoto Protocol, Desertification, Hazardous Wastes, Law of the Sea, Ozone Layer Protection, Ship Pollution
signed, but not ratified: none of the selected agreements

Geography—note: smallest Asian country; archipelago of 1,190 coral islands grouped into 26 atolls (200 inhabited islands, plus 80 islands with tourist resorts); strategic location astride and along major sea lanes in Indian Ocean

PEOPLE AND SOCIETY

Population: 392,709 (July 2017 est.)
country comparison to the world: 176

Nationality: *noun:* Maldivian(s)
adjective: Maldivian

Ethnic groups: South Indians, Sinhalese, Arabs

Languages: Dhivehi (official, dialect of Sinhala, script derived from Arabic), English (spoken by most government officials)

Religions: Sunni Muslim (official)

Age structure: *0-14 years:* 21.4% (male 42,871/female 41,162)
15-24 years: 20.21% (male 45,547/female 33,804)
25-54 years: 48.1% (male 106,701/female 82,187)
55-64 years: 5.85% (male 11,312/female 11,667)
65 years and over: 4.45% (male 8,042/female 9,416) (2017 est.)

Dependency ratios: *total dependency ratio:* 38
youth dependency ratio: 32.3
elderly dependency ratio: 5.7
potential support ratio: 17.7 (2015 est.)

Median age: *total:* 28.2 years
male: 28.1 years
female: 28.3 years (2017 est.)
country comparison to the world: 138

Population growth rate: -0.06% (2017 est.)
country comparison to the world: 203

Birth rate: 16.1 births/1,000 population (2017 est.)
country comparison to the world: 115

Death rate: 4 deaths/1,000 population (2017 est.)
country comparison to the world: 209

Net migration rate: -12.7 migrant(s)/1,000 population (2017 est.)
country comparison to the world: 213

Population distribution: about a third of the population lives in the centrally located capital city of Male and almost a tenth in southern Addu City; the remainder of the populace is spread over the 200 or so populated islands of the archipelago

Urbanization: *urban population:* 47.5% of total population (2017)
rate of urbanization: 3.52% annual rate of change (2015-20 est.)

Major urban areas—population: MALE (capital) 156,000 (2014)

Sex ratio: *at birth:* 1.05 male(s)/female

0-14 years: 1.04 male(s)/female
15-24 years: 1.37 male(s)/female
25-54 years: 1.34 male(s)/female
55-64 years: 1 male(s)/female
65 years and over: 0.89 male(s)/female
total population: 1.23 male(s)/female (2016 est.)

Mother's mean age at first birth: 23.9 years
note: median age at first birth among women 25-29 (2009 est.)

Maternal mortality ratio: 68 deaths/100,000 live births (2015 est.)
country comparison to the world: 84

Infant mortality rate: *total:* 22 deaths/1,000 live births
male: 24.4 deaths/1,000 live births
female: 19.6 deaths/1,000 live births (2017 est.)
country comparison to the world: 74

Life expectancy at birth: *total population:* 75.8 years
male: 73.5 years
female: 78.3 years (2017 est.)
country comparison to the world: 97

Total fertility rate: 1.73 children born/woman (2017 est.)
country comparison to the world: 168

Contraceptive prevalence rate: 34.7% (2009)

Health expenditures: 13.7% of GDP (2014)
country comparison to the world: 4

Physicians density: 1.58 physicians/1,000 population (2010)

Hospital bed density: 4.3 beds/1,000 population (2009)

Drinking water source:
improved:
urban: 99.5% of population
rural: 97.9% of population
total: 98.6% of population
unimproved:
urban: 0.5% of population
rural: 2.1% of population
total: 1.4% of population (2015 est.)

Sanitation facility access:
improved:
urban: 97.5% of population
rural: 98.3% of population
total: 97.9% of population
unimproved:
urban: 2.5% of population
rural: 1.7% of population
total: 2.1% of population (2015 est.)

HIV/AIDS—adult prevalence rate: NA

HIV/AIDS—people living with HIV/AIDS: NA

HIV/AIDS—deaths: NA

Obesity—adult prevalence rate: 8.6% (2016)
country comparison to the world: 148

Children under the age of 5 years underweight: 17.8% (2009)
country comparison to the world: 36

Education expenditures: 5.7% of GDP (2015)
country comparison to the world: 26

Literacy: *definition:* age 15 and over can read and write

total population: 99.3%
male: 99.8%
female: 98.8% (2015 est.)

Unemployment, youth ages 15-24: *total:* 25.4%
male: 29.1%
female: 21.4% (2010 est.)
country comparison to the world: 48

GOVERNMENT

Country name: *conventional long form:* Republic of Maldives
conventional short form: Maldives
local long form: Dhivehi Raajjeyge Jumhooriyyaa
local short form: Dhivehi Raajje
etymology: archipelago apparently named after the main island (and capital) of Male; the word "Maldives" means "the islands (dives) of Male"; alternatively, the name may derive from the Sanskrit word "maladvipa" meaning "garland of islands"; Dhivehi Raajje in Maldivian means "Kingdom of the Dhivehi people"

Government type: presidential republic

Capital: *name:* Male
geographic coordinates: 4 10 N, 73 30 E
time difference: UTC+5 (10 hours ahead of Washington, DC, during Standard Time)

Administrative divisions: 21 administrative atolls (atholhuthah, singular—atholhu); Addu, Ari-atholhu Dhekunuburi, Ariatholhu Uthuruburi, Faadhippolhu, Felidhuatholhu, Fuvammulah, Hahdhunmathi, Huvadhuatholhu Dhekunuburi, Huvadhuatholhu Uthuruburi, Kolhumadulu, Maale, Maaleatholhu, Maalhosmadulu Dhekunuburi, Maalhosmadulu Uthuruburi, Miladhunmadulu Dhekunuburi, Miladhunmadulu Uthuruburi, Mulakatholhu, Nilandheatholhu Dhekunuburi, Nilandheatholhu Uthuruburi, Thiladhunmathee Dhekunuburi, Thiladhunmathee Uthuruburi

Independence: 26 July 1965 (from the UK)

National holiday: Independence Day, 26 July (1965)

Constitution: *history:* many previous; latest ratified 7 August 2008
amendments: proposed by Parliament; passage requires at least three-quarters majority vote by its membership and the signature of the president of the republic; passage of amendments to constitutional articles on rights and freedoms and the terms of office of Parliament and of the president also requires a majority vote in a referendum; amended 2015 (2017)

Legal system: Islamic religious legal system with English common law influences, primarily in commercial matters

International law organization participation: has not submitted an ICJ jurisdiction declaration; accepts ICCt jurisdiction

Citizenship: *citizenship by birth:* no
citizenship by descent only: at least one parent must be a citizen of the Maldives
dual citizenship recognized: yes

residency requirement for naturalization: unknown

Suffrage: 18 years of age; universal

Executive branch: *chief of state:* President Abdulla YAMEEN Abdul Gayoom (since 17 November 2013); Vice President Abdulla JIHAD (since 21 June 2016); the president is both chief of state and head of government; note—Vice President Mohamed JAMEEL was removed from office 22 July 2015 and Vice President Ahmed ADEEB Abdul Ghafoor was removed from office 5 November 2015

head of government: President Abdulla YAMEEN Abdul Gayoom (since 17 November 2013); Vice President Abdulla JIHAD (since 21 June 2016); note—Vice President Mohamed JAMEEL was removed from office 22 July 2015 and Vice President Ahmed ADHEEB Abdul Ghafoor was removed from office 5 November 2015

cabinet: Cabinet of Ministers appointed by the president, approved by Parliament

elections/appointments: president directly elected by absolute majority popular vote in 2 rounds if needed for a 5-year term (eligible for a second term); the election held on 7 September 2013 was annulled by the Supreme Court; rerun of first round held on 9 November 2013 and a runoff held on 16 November 2013 (next election to be held in 2018)

election results: Abdulla YAMEEN Abdul Gayoom elected president in second round; percent of vote in first round—Mohamed NASHEED (MDP) 46.9%, Abdulla YAMEEN Abdul Gayoom (PPM) 29.7%, Qasim IBRAHIM (JP) 23.3%; percent of vote in second round—Abdulla YAMEEN Abdul Gayoom 51.4%, Mohamed NASHEED 48.6%

Legislative branch: *description:* unicameral Parliament or People's Majlis (85 seats; members directly elected in multi-seat constituencies by simple majority vote to serve 5-year terms)

elections: last held on 22 March 2014 (next to be held in 2019)

election results: percent of vote—MDP 40.8%, PPM 27.7%, JP 13.6%, MDA 4.0%, AP 2.7% other 0.3%, independent 10.9%; seats by party—PPM 33, MDP 26, JP 15, MDA 5, AP 1, independent 5

Judicial branch: *highest court(s):* Supreme Court (consists of the chief justice and 4 judges)

judge selection and term of office: Supreme Court judges appointed by the president in consultation with the Judicial Service Commission—a separate 10-member body of selected high government officials and the public—and upon confirmation by voting members of the People's Majlis; judges serve until mandatory retirement at age 70

subordinate courts: High Court; Criminal, Civil, Family, Juvenile, and Drug Courts; Magistrate Courts (on each of the inhabited islands)

Political parties and leaders: Adhaalath (Justice) Party or AP [Sheikh Imran ABDULLA]
Maldives Development Alliance or MDA [Ahmed Shiyam MOHAMED]
Maldivian Democratic Party or MDP [Hassan LATHEEF]

Progressive Party of Maldives or PPM [Abdulla YAMEEN]
Republican (Jumhooree) Party or JP [Qasim IBRAHIM]
Political pressure groups and leaders: other: various unregistered political parties

International organization participation: ADB, AOSIS, C, CP, FAO, G-77, IBRD, ICAO, ICC (NGOs), ICCt, IDA, IDB, IFAD, IFC, IFRCS, ILO, IMF, IMO, Interpol, IOC, IOM, IPU, ITU, MIGA, NAM, OIC, OPCW, SAARC, SACEP, UN, UNCTAD, UNESCO, UNIDO, UNWTO, UPU, WCO, WHO, WIPO, WMO, WTO

Diplomatic representation in the US: *chief of mission:* Ambassador Ali NASEER Mohamed (since 21 July 2017)
chancery: 801 Second Avenue, Suite 400E, New York, NY 10017
telephone: [1] (212) 599-6194 and 599-6195
FAX: [1] (212) 661-6405

Diplomatic representation from the US: the US does not have an embassy in Maldives; the US Ambassador to Sri Lanka is accredited to Maldives

Flag description: red with a large green rectangle in the center bearing a vertical white crescent moon; the closed side of the crescent is on the hoist side of the flag; red recalls those who have sacrificed their lives in defense of their country, the green rectangle represents peace and prosperity, and the white crescent signifies Islam

National symbol(s): coconut palm, yellowfin tuna; national colors: red, green, white

National anthem: name: "Gaumee Salaam" (National Salute)
lyrics/music: Mohamed Jameel DIDI/Wannaku-wattawaduge DON AMARADEVA
note: lyrics adopted 1948, music adopted 1972; between 1948 and 1972, the lyrics were sung to the tune of "Auld Lang Syne"

ECONOMY

Economy—overview: Maldives has quickly become a middle-income country, driven by the rapid growth of its tourism and fisheries sectors, but the country still contends with a large and growing fiscal deficit. Economic growth slowed to 2.8% in 2015, mainly because of a decline in tourists from China and Russia. Despite lower growth, tourism-related tax receipts increased by 13% in 2015 because of higher tax rates. This increase in tax receipts led to higher usable foreign exchange reserves that helped partially fund increases in construction related imports.

In 2015, Maldives' Parliament passed a constitutional amendment legalizing foreign ownership of land; foreign land-buyers must reclaim at least 70% of the desired land from the ocean and invest at least $1 billion in a construction project approved by Parliament.

Diversifying the economy beyond tourism and fishing, reforming public finance, increasing employment opportunities, and combating corruption, cronyism, and a growing drug problem are near-term challenges facing the government. Over

the longer term, Maldivian authorities worry about the impact of erosion and possible global warming on their low-lying country; 80% of the area is 1 meter or less above sea level.

GDP (purchasing power parity): $6.896 billion (2017 est.)
$6.596 billion (2016 est.)
$6.348 billion (2015 est.)
note: data are in 2017 dollars
country comparison to the world: 170

GDP (official exchange rate): $4.52 billion (2016 est.)

GDP—real growth rate: 4.6% (2017 est.)
3.9% (2016 est.)
3.3% (2015 est.)
country comparison to the world: 49

GDP—per capita (PPP): $19,200 (2017 est.)
$18,600 (2016 est.)
$18,200 (2015 est.)
note: data are in 2017 dollars
country comparison to the world: 93

Gross national saving: 2.8% of GDP (2017 est.)
0.4% of GDP (2016 est.)
12.7% of GDP (2015 est.)
country comparison to the world: 173

GDP—composition, by end use:
household consumption: NA%
government consumption: NA%
investment in fixed capital: NA%
investment in inventories: NA%
exports of goods and services: 108.2%
imports of goods and services: 89.3% (2014 est.)

GDP—composition, by sector of origin:
agriculture: 3%
industry: 16%
services: 81% (2015 est.)

Agriculture—products: coconuts, corn, sweet potatoes; fish

Industries: tourism, fish processing, shipping, boat building, coconut processing, woven mats, rope, handicrafts, coral and sand mining

Industrial production growth rate: 14% (2012 est.)
country comparison to the world: 4

Labor force: 195,100 (2014)
country comparison to the world: 176

Labor force—by occupation: *agriculture:* 15%
industry: 15%
services: 70% (2010 est.)

Unemployment rate: 11.6% (2013 est.)
11% (2012 est.)
country comparison to the world: 149

Population below poverty line: 16% (2008 est.)

Household income or consumption by percentage share: *lowest 10%:* 1.2%
highest 10%: 33.3% (FY09/10)

Distribution of family income—Gini index: 38.4 (2009 est.)
37.4 (2004 est.)
country comparison to the world: 71

Budget: *revenues:* $1.481 billion
expenditures: $1.7 billion (2016, est.)

Taxes and other revenues: 32.8% of GDP (2016, est.)
country comparison to the world: 69

Budget surplus (+) or deficit (-): -4.9% of GDP (2016, est.)
country comparison to the world: 159

Public debt: 81.5% of GDP (2016 est.)
72% of GDP (2015 est.)
country comparison to the world: 37

Fiscal year: calendar year

Inflation rate (consumer prices): 2.5% (2017 est.)
0.8% (2016 est.)
country comparison to the world: 116

Central bank discount rate: 7% (31 December 2013)
6.96% (31 December 2011)
country comparison to the world: 49

Commercial bank prime lending rate: 10.5% (31 December 2012 est.)
10.2% (31 December 2011 est.)
country comparison to the world: 76

Stock of narrow money: $338.5 million (31 December 2015 est.)
$623 million (31 December 2013 est.)
country comparison to the world: 175

Stock of broad money: $1.337 billion (31 December 2015)
$1.298 billion (31 December 2012 est.)
country comparison to the world: 167

Stock of domestic credit: $1.559 billion (31 December 2012 est.)
$1.601 billion (31 December 2011 est.)
country comparison to the world: 157

Market value of publicly traded shares: $555 million (31 December 2011 est.)
country comparison to the world: 113

Current account balance: -$779 million (2017 est.)
-$831 million (2016 est.)
country comparison to the world: 120

Exports: $239.7 million (2015 est.)
$300.9 million (2014 est.)
country comparison to the world: 186

Exports—commodities: fish

Exports—partners: Thailand 33.8%, Sri Lanka 10%, US 8.7%, France 8.6%, Germany 8.6%, Ireland 4.9%, Italy 4.8%, UK 4.1% (2016)

Imports: $1.896 billion (2015 est.)
$1.993 billion (2014 est.)
country comparison to the world: 162

Imports—commodities: petroleum products, clothing, intermediate and capital goods

Imports—partners: UAE 15.6%, Singapore 14.3%, China 13.4%, India 12.9%, Sri Lanka 6.3%, Malaysia 5.7%, Thailand 4.7% (2016)

Reserves of foreign exchange and gold: $565.5 million (31 December 2015 est.)
$627.4 million (31 December 2014 est.)
country comparison to the world: 141

Debt—external: $693.7 million (2015 est.)
$741.6 million (2014 est.)
country comparison to the world: 172

Stock of direct foreign investment—at home: $324 million (31 December 2015)
$256 million (31 December 2013)
country comparison to the world: 127

Exchange rates: rufiyaa (MVR) per US dollar—15.25 (2016)

ENERGY

Electricity access: electrification—*total population:* 100% (2016)

Electricity—production: 350 million kWh (2015 est.)
country comparison to the world: 175

Electricity—consumption: 325.5 million kWh (2015 est.)
country comparison to the world: 180

Electricity—exports: 0 kWh (2016 est.)
country comparison to the world: 173

Electricity—imports: 0 kWh (2016 est.)
country comparison to the world: 177

Electricity—installed generating capacity: 104,000 kW (2015 est.)
country comparison to the world: 178

Electricity—from fossil fuels: 96.2% of total installed capacity (2015 est.)
country comparison to the world: 48

Electricity—from nuclear fuels: 0% of total installed capacity (2015 est.)
country comparison to the world: 147

Electricity—from hydroelectric plants: 0% of total installed capacity (2015 est.)
country comparison to the world: 190

Electricity—from other renewable sources: 3.8% of total installed capacity (2015 est.)
country comparison to the world: 106

Crude oil—production: 0 bbl/day (2016 est.)
country comparison to the world: 167

Crude oil—exports: 0 bbl/day (2014 est.)
country comparison to the world: 166

Crude oil—imports: 0 bbl/day (2014 est.)
country comparison to the world: 164

Crude oil—proved reserves: 0 bbl (1 January 2017 es)
country comparison to the world: 164

Refined petroleum products—production: 0 bbl/day (2016 est.)
country comparison to the world: 172

Refined petroleum products—consumption: 11,000 bbl/day (2015 est.)
country comparison to the world: 160

Refined petroleum products—exports: 0 bbl/day (2014 est.)
country comparison to the world: 182

Refined petroleum products—imports: 10,760 bbl/day (2014 est.)
country comparison to the world: 142

Natural gas—production: 0 cu m (2016 est.)
country comparison to the world: 173

Natural gas—consumption: 0 cu m (2016 est.)
country comparison to the world: 212

Natural gas—exports: 0 cu m (2016 est.)

country comparison to the world: 154

Natural gas—imports: 0 cu m (2016 est.)
country comparison to the world: 159

Natural gas—proved reserves: 0 cu m (1 January 2016 es)
country comparison to the world: 175

Carbon dioxide emissions from consumption of energy: 1.2 million Mt (2013 est.)
country comparison to the world: 163

COMMUNICATIONS

Telephones—fixed lines: *total subscriptions:* 21,136
subscriptions per 100 inhabitants: 5 (July 2016 est.)
country comparison to the world: 183

Telephones—mobile cellular: *total:* 812,128
subscriptions per 100 inhabitants: 207 (July 2016 est.)
country comparison to the world: 164

Telephone system: *general assessment:* telephone services have improved; inter-atoll communication through microwave links; all inhabited islands and resorts are connected with telephone and fax service
domestic: each island now has at least 1 public telephone, and there are mobile-cellular networks with a rapidly expanding subscribership that has reached over 200 per 100 persons
international: country code—960; linked to international submarine cable Fiber-Optic Link Around the Globe (FLAG); satellite earth station—3 Intelsat (Indian Ocean) (2016)

Broadcast media: state-owned radio and TV monopoly until recently; state-owned TV operates 2 channels; 3 privately owned TV stations; state owns Voice of Maldives and operates both an entertainment and a music-based station; 5 privately owned radio stations (2012)

Internet country code: .mv
Internet users: total: 232,210

percent of population: 59.1% (July 2016 est.)
country comparison to the world: 201

TRANSPORTATION

National air transport system: *number of registered air carriers:* 3
inventory of registered aircraft operated by air carriers: 15 (2015)
Civil aircraft registration country code prefix: 8Q (2016)

Airports: 9 (2013)
country comparison to the world: 159

Airports—with paved runways: *total:* 7
over 3,047 m: 1
2,438 to 3,047 m: 1
1,524 to 2,437 m: 1
914 to 1,523 m: 4 (2017)

Airports—with unpaved runways: *total:* 2
914 to 1,523 m: 2 (2013)

Roadways: *total:* 88 km

paved roads: 88 km—60 km in Male; 14 km on Addu Atolis; 14 km on Laamu

note: island roads are mainly compacted coral (2013)

country comparison to the world: 216

Merchant marine: total: 66

by type: bulk carrier 1, container ship 1, general cargo 27, oil tanker 14, other 23 (2017)

country comparison to the world: 102

Ports and terminals: major seaport(s): Male

MILITARY AND SECURITY

Military branches: Maldives National Defense Force (MNDF): Marine Corps, Security Protection Group, Coast Guard (2010)

Military service age and obligation: 18-28 years of age for voluntary service; no conscription; 10th grade or equivalent education required; must not be a member of a political party (2012)

Military—note: the Maldives National Defense Force (MNDF), with its small size and with little serviceable equipment, is inadequate to prevent external aggression and is primarily tasked to reinforce the Maldives Police Service (MPS) and ensure security in the exclusive economic zone (2008)

TRANSNATIONAL ISSUES

Disputes—international: none

Trafficking in persons: current situation: Maldives is a destination country for men, women, and children subjected to forced labor and sex trafficking and a source country for women and children subjected to labor and sex trafficking; primarily Bangladeshi and Indian migrants working both legally and illegally in the construction and service sectors face conditions of forced labor, including fraudulent recruitment, confiscation of identity and travel documents, nonpayment and withholding of wages, and debt bondage; a small number of women from Asia, Eastern Europe, and former Soviet states are trafficked to Maldives for sexual exploitation; Maldivian women may be subjected to sex trafficking domestically or in Sri Lanka; some Maldivian children are transported to the capital for domestic service, where they may also be victims of sexual abuse and forced labor

tier rating: Tier 2 Watch List—Maldives does not fully comply with the minimum standards for the elimination of trafficking; however, it is making significant efforts to do so; the government adopted a national action plan for 2015-19 and is continuing to develop victim identification, protection, and referral procedures, but overall its anti-trafficking efforts did not increase; only five trafficking investigations were conducted, no new prosecutions were initiated for the second consecutive year, and no convictions were made, down from one in 2013; some officials warned businesses in advance of planned raids for suspected trafficking offenses; victim protection deteriorated when the state-run shelter for female victims barred access to victims shortly after opening in January 2014, in part because of bureaucratic disputes, which dissuaded victims from pursuing charges against perpetrators; the government did not prosecute or hold accountable any employers or government officials for withholding passports (2015)

MALI

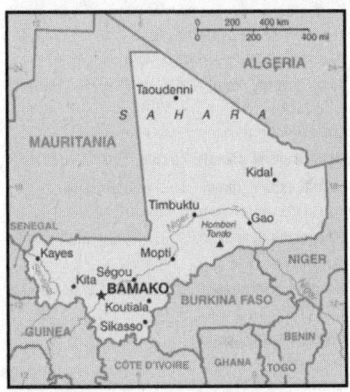

INTRODUCTION

Background: The Sudanese Republic and Senegal became independent of France in 1960 as the Mali Federation. When Senegal withdrew after only a few months, what formerly made up the Sudanese Republic was renamed Mali. Rule by dictatorship was brought to a close in 1991 by a military coup that ushered in a period of democratic rule. President Alpha KONARE won Mali's first two democratic presidential elections in 1992 and 1997. In keeping with Mali's two-term constitutional limit, he stepped down in 2002 and was succeeded by Amadou Toumani TOURE, who was elected to a second term in a 2007 election that was widely judged to be free and fair. Malian returnees from Libya in 2011 exacerbated tensions in northern Mali, and Tuareg ethnic militias rebelled in January 2012. Low- and mid-level soldiers, frustrated with the poor handling of the rebellion, overthrew TOURE on 22 March. Intensive mediation efforts led by the Economic Community of West African States (ECOWAS) returned power to a civilian administration in April with the appointment of Interim President Dioncounda TRAORE. The post-coup chaos led to rebels expelling the Malian military from the country's three northern regions and allowed Islamic militants to set up strongholds. Hundreds of thousands of northern Malians fled the violence to southern Mali and neighboring countries, exacerbating regional food shortages in host communities. An international military intervention to retake the three northern regions began in January 2013 and within a month most of the north had been retaken. In a democratic presidential election conducted in July and August of 2013, Ibrahim Boubacar KEITA was elected president. The Malian Government and northern armed groups signed an internationally-mediated peace accord in June 2015.

GEOGRAPHY

Location: interior Western Africa, southwest of Algeria, north of Guinea, Cote d'Ivoire, and Burkina Faso, west of Niger

Geographic coordinates: 17 00 N, 4 00 W

Map references: Africa

Area: total: 1,240,192 sq km

land: 1,220,190 sq km

water: 20,002 sq km

country comparison to the world: 25

Area—comparative: slightly less than twice the size of Texas

Land boundaries: total: 7,908 km

border countries (7): Algeria 1,359 km, Burkina Faso 1,325 km, Cote d'Ivoire 599 km, Guinea 1,062 km, Mauritania 2,236 km, Niger 838 km, Senegal 489 km

Coastline: 0 km (landlocked)

Maritime claims: none (landlocked)

Climate: subtropical to arid; hot and dry (February to June); rainy, humid, and mild (June to November); cool and dry (November to February)

Terrain: mostly flat to rolling northern plains covered by sand; savanna in south, rugged hills in northeast

Elevation: mean elevation: 343 m

elevation extremes: lowest point: Senegal River 23 m

highest point: Hombori Tondo 1,155 m

Natural resources: gold, phosphates, kaolin, salt, limestone, uranium, gypsum, granite, hydropower

note: bauxite, iron ore, manganese, tin, and copper deposits are known but not exploited

Land use: agricultural land: 34.1%

arable land: 5.6%;

permanent crops: 0.1%;

permanent pasture: 28.4%

forest: 10.2%

other: 55.7% (2011 est.)

Irrigated land: 3,780 sq km (2012)

Population—distribution: the overwhelming majority of the population lives in the southern half of the country, with greater density along the border with Burkina Faso

Natural hazards: hot, dust-laden harmattan haze common during dry seasons; recurring droughts; occasional Niger River flooding

Environment—current issues: deforestation; soil erosion; desertification; inadequate supplies of potable water

Environment—international agreements: *party to:* Biodiversity, Climate Change, Climate Change-Kyoto Protocol, Desertification, Endangered Species, Hazardous Wastes, Law of the Sea, Ozone Layer Protection, Wetlands, Whaling *signed, but not ratified:* none of the selected agreements

Geography—note: landlocked; divided into three natural zones: the southern, cultivated Sudanese; the central, semiarid Sahelian; and the northern, arid Saharan

PEOPLE AND SOCIETY

Population: 17,885,245 (July 2017 est.) *country comparison to the world:* 64

Nationality: *noun:* Malian(s) *adjective:* Malian

Ethnic groups: Bambara 34.1%, Fulani (Peul) 14.7%, Sarakole 10.8%, Senufo 10.5%, Dogon 8.9%, Malinke 8.7%, Bobo 2.9%, Songhai 1.6%, Tuareg 0.9%, other Malian 6.1%, from member of Economic Community of West African States 0.3%, other 0.4% (2012-13 est.)

Languages: French (official), Bambara 46.3%, Peul/Foulfoulbe 9.4%, Dogon 7.2%, Maraka/Soninke 6.4%, Malinke 5.6%, Sonrhai/Djerma 5.6%, Minianka 4.3%, Tamacheq 3.5%, Senoufo 2.6%, Bobo 2.1%, unspecified 0.7%, other 6.3% *note:* Mali has 13 national languages in addition to its official language (2009 est.)

Religions: Muslim 94.8%, Christian 2.4%, Animist 2%, none 0.5%, unspecified 0.3% (2009 est.)

Demographic profile: Mali's total population is expected to double by 2035; its capital Bamako is one of the fastest-growing cities in Africa. A young age structure, a declining mortality rate, and a sustained high total fertility rate of 6 children per woman—the third highest in the world—ensure continued rapid population growth for the foreseeable future. Significant outmigration only marginally tempers this growth. Despite decreases, Mali's infant, child, and maternal mortality rates remain among the highest in sub-Saharan Africa because of limited access to and adoption of family planning, early childbearing, short birth intervals, the prevalence of female genital cutting, infrequent use of skilled birth attendants, and a lack of emergency obstetrical and neonatal care.

Mali's high total fertility rate has been virtually unchanged for decades, as a result of the ongoing preference for large families, early childbearing, the lack of female education and empowerment, poverty, and extremely low contraceptive use. Slowing Mali's population growth by lowering its birth rate will be essential for poverty reduction, improving food security, and developing human capital and the economy.

Mali has a long history of seasonal migration and emigration driven by poverty, conflict, demographic pressure, unemployment, food insecurity, and droughts. Many Malians from rural areas migrate during the dry period to nearby villages and towns to do odd jobs or to adjoining countries to work in agriculture or mining. Pastoralists and nomads move seasonally to southern Mali or nearby coastal states. Others migrate long term to Mali's urban areas, Cote d'Ivoire, other neighboring countries, and in smaller numbers to France, Mali's former colonial ruler. Since the early 1990s, Mali's role has grown as a transit country for regional migration flows and illegal migration to Europe. Human smugglers and traffickers exploit the same regional routes used for moving contraband drugs, arms, and cigarettes.

Between early 2012 and 2013, renewed fighting in northern Mali between government forces and Tuareg secessionists and their Islamist allies, a French-led international military intervention, as well as chronic food shortages, caused the displacement of hundreds of thousands of Malians. Most of those displaced domestically sought shelter in urban areas of southern Mali, except for pastoralist and nomadic groups, who abandoned their traditional routes, gave away or sold their livestock, and dispersed into the deserts of northern Mali or crossed into neighboring countries. Almost all Malians who took refuge abroad (mostly Tuareg and Maure pastoralists) stayed in the region, largely in Mauritania, Niger, and Burkina Faso.

Age structure: *0-14 years:* 48.17% (male 4,330,370/female 4,285,171) *15-24 years:* 18.84% (male 1,604,914/female 1,765,479) *25-54 years:* 26.26% (male 2,171,171/female 2,525,109) *55-64 years:* 3.7% (male 335,023/female 326,910) *65 years and over:* 3.03% (male 270,856/female 270,242) (2017 est.)

Dependency ratios: *total dependency ratio:* 101.9 *youth dependency ratio:* 96.8 *elderly dependency ratio:* 5.1 *potential support ratio:* 19.5 (2015 est.)

Median age: *total:* 15.8 years *male:* 15.1 years *female:* 16.4 years (2017 est.) *country comparison to the world:* 227

Population growth rate: 3.02% (2017 est.) *country comparison to the world:* 7

Birth rate: 43.9 births/1,000 population (2017 est.) *country comparison to the world:* 3

Death rate: 9.8 deaths/1,000 population (2017 est.) *country comparison to the world:* 43

Net migration rate: -3.9 migrant(s)/1,000 population (2017 est.) *country comparison to the world:* 181

Population distribution: the overwhelming majority of the population lives in the southern half of the country, with greater density along the border with Burkina Faso

Urbanization: *urban population:* 41.4% of total population (2017) *rate of urbanization:* 4.97% annual rate of change (2015-20 est.)

Major urban areas—population: BAMAKO (capital) 2.515 million (2015)

Sex ratio: *at birth:* 1.03 male(s)/female *0-14 years:* 1.01 male(s)/female *15-24 years:* 0.91 male(s)/female *25-54 years:* 0.87 male(s)/female *55-64 years:* 1 male(s)/female *65 years and over:* 1 male(s)/female *total population:* 0.95 male(s)/female (2016 est.)

Mother's mean age at first birth: 18.8 years *note:* median age at first birth among women 25-29 (2012/13 est.)

Maternal mortality ratio: 587 deaths/100,000 live births (2015 est.) *country comparison to the world:* 16

Infant mortality rate: *total:* 69.5 deaths/1,000 live births *male:* 75.3 deaths/1,000 live births *female:* 63.5 deaths/1,000 live births (2017 est.) *country comparison to the world:* 9

Life expectancy at birth: *total population:* 60.3 years *male:* 58.2 years *female:* 62.5 years (2017 est.) *country comparison to the world:* 204

Total fertility rate: 6.01 children born/woman (2017 est.) *country comparison to the world:* 3

Contraceptive prevalence rate: 15.6% (2015)

Health expenditures: 6.9% of GDP (2014) *country comparison to the world:* 83

Physicians density: 0.09 physicians/1,000 population (2010)

Hospital bed density: 0.1 beds/1,000 population (2010)

Drinking water source: improved: *urban:* 96.5% of population *rural:* 64.1% of population *total:* 77% of population unimproved: *urban:* 3.5% of population *rural:* 35.9% of population *total:* 23% of population (2015 est.)

Sanitation facility access: improved: *urban:* 37.5% of population *rural:* 16.1% of population *total:* 24.7% of population unimproved: *urban:* 62.5% of population *rural:* 83.9% of population *total:* 75.3% of population (2015 est.)

HIV/AIDS—adult prevalence rate: 1% (2016 est.) *country comparison to the world:* 44

HIV/AIDS—people living with HIV/AIDS: 110,000 (2016 est.)
country comparison to the world: 40

HIV/AIDS—deaths: 6,100 (2016 est.)
country comparison to the world: 27

Major infectious diseases: *degree of risk:* very high
food or waterborne diseases: bacterial and protozoal diarrhea, hepatitis A, and typhoid fever
vectorborne diseases: malaria and dengue fever
water contact disease: schistosomiasis
respiratory disease: meningococcal meningitis
animal contact disease: rabies (2016)

Obesity—adult prevalence rate: 8.6% (2016)
country comparison to the world: 149

Education expenditures: 3.6% of GDP (2014)
country comparison to the world: 83

Literacy: *definition:* age 15 and over can read and write
total population: 33.1%
male: 45.1%
female: 22.2% (2015 est.)

School life expectancy (primary to tertiary education): *total:* 8 years
male: 9 years
female: 7 years (2011)

Unemployment, youth ages 15-24: *total:* 11.1%
male: NA
female: NA (2014 est.)

GOVERNMENT

Country name: *conventional long form:* Republic of Mali
conventional short form: Mali
local long form: Republique de Mali
local short form: Mali
former: French Sudan and Sudanese Republic
etymology: name derives from the West African Mali Empire of the 13th to 16th centuries A.D.

Government type: semi-presidential republic

Capital: *name:* Bamako
geographic coordinates: 12 39 N, 8 00 W
time difference: UTC 0 (5 hours ahead of Washington, DC, during Standard Time)

Administrative divisions: 8 regions (regions, singular—region), 1 district*; District de Bamako*, Gao, Kayes, Kidal, Koulikoro, Mopti, Segou, Sikasso, Tombouctou (Timbuktu); note—two new regions, Menaka and Taoudenni, were reportedly created in early 2016, but these have not yet been vetted by the US Board on Geographic Names

Independence: 22 September 1960 (from France)

National holiday: Independence Day, 22 September (1960)

Constitution: history: several previous; latest drafted August 1991, approved by referendum 12 January 1992, effective 25 February 1992, suspended briefly in 2012
amendments: roposed by the president of the republic or by members of the National Assembly; passage requires two-thirds majority vote by the Assembly and approval in a referendum;

constitutional sections on the integrity of the state, its republican and secular form of government, and its multiparty system cannot be amended; amended 1999 (2017)

Legal system: civil law system based on the French civil law model and influenced by customary law; judicial review of legislative acts in the Constitutional Court

International law organization participation: has not submitted an ICJ jurisdiction declaration; accepts ICCt jurisdiction

Citizenship: *citizenship by birth:* no
citizenship by descent only: at least one parent must be a citizen of Mali
dual citizenship recognized: yes
residency requirement for naturalization: 5 years

Suffrage: 18 years of age; universal

Executive branch: *chief of state:* President Ibrahim Boubacar KEITA (since 4 September 2013)
head of government: Prime Minister Soumeylou Boubeye MAIGA (since 31 December 2017)
cabinet: Council of Ministers appointed by the prime minister
elections/appointments: president directly elected by absolute majority popular vote in 2 rounds if needed for a 5-year term (eligible for a second term); election last held on 28 July 2013 with a runoff on 11 August 2013 (election delayed from April 2012 due to a coup in March 2012); prime minister appointed by the president
election results: Ibrahim Boubacar KEITA elected president in second round; percent of vote—Ibrahim Boubacar KEITA (RPM) 77.6%, Soumaila CISSE (URD) 22.4%

Legislative branch: *description:* unicameral National Assembly or Assemblee Nationale (147 seats; members directly elected in single-seat constituencies by absolute majority vote in 2 rounds if needed; 13 seats reserved for citizens living abroad; members serve 5-year terms)
elections: last held on 24 November and 15 December 2013 (next to be held in 2018); note—the scheduled July 2012 election was canceled due to a coup d'etat and the Tuareg Rebellion
election results: percent of vote by party—NA; seats by party—RPM 66, URD 17, ADEMA 16, FARE 6, CODEM 5, SADI 5, CNID 4, other 24, independent 4

Judicial branch: *highest court(s):* Supreme Court or Cour Supreme (consists of 19 members organized into 3 civil chambers and a criminal chamber); Constitutional Court (consists of 9 members)
judge selection and term of office: Supreme Court members appointed by the Ministry of Justice to serve 5-year terms; Constitutional Court members selected—3 each by the president, the National Assembly, and the Supreme Council of the Magistracy; members serve single renewable 7-year terms
subordinate courts: Court of Appeal; High Court of Justice (jurisdiction limited to cases of high treason or criminal offenses by the president or ministers while in office); magistrate courts; first

instance courts; labor dispute courts; special court of state security

Political parties and leaders: African Solidarity for Democracy and Independence or SADI [Oumar MARIKO]
Alliance for Democracy in Mali-Pan-African Party for Liberty, Solidarity, and Justice or ADEMA-PASJ [Tiemoko SANGARE]
Alliance for Democracy and Progress or ADP (coalition includes ADEMA and URD)
Alliance for the Solidarity of Mali-Convergence of Patriotic Forces or ASMA-CFP [Soumeylou Boubeye MAIGA]
Alternative Forces for Renewal and Emergence or FARE [Modibo SIDIBE]
Convergence for the Development of Mali or CODEM [Housseyni Amion GUINDO]
Economic and Social Development Party or PDES [Jamille BITTAR]
Front for Democracy and the Republic or FDR (coalition of smaller opposition parties)
National Congress for Democratic Initiative or CNID [Mountaga TALL]
Party for National Renewal or PARENA [Tiebile DRAME]
Patriotic Movement for Renewal or MPR [Choguel Kokalla MAIGA]
Rally for Mali or RPM [Ibrahim Boubacar KEITA]
Union for Republic and Democracy or URD [Younoussi TOURE]

Political pressure groups and leaders: Malian Company for Textile Development or CMDT
Malian Defence Force
other: Islamic authorities

International organization participation: ACP, AfDB, AU, CD, ECOWAS, EITI (compliant country), FAO, FZ, G-77, IAEA, IBRD, ICAO, ICCt, ICRM, IDA, IDB, IFAD, IFC, IFRCS, ILO, IMF, Interpol, IOC, IOM, IPU, ISO, ITSO, ITU, ITUC (NGOs), MIGA, MONUSCO, NAM, OIC, OIF, OPCW, UN, UNAMID, UNCTAD, UNESCO, UNIDO, UNISFA, UNMISS, UNWTO, UPU, WADB (regional), WAEMU, WCO, WFTU (NGOs), WHO, WIPO, WMO, WTO

Diplomatic representation in the US: *chief of mission:* Ambassador (vacant); Charge d'Affaires Mohamed CISSE (since 13 April 2017)
chancery: 2130 R Street NW, Washington, DC 20008
telephone: [1] (202) 332-2249, 939-8950
FAX: [1] (202) 332-6603

Diplomatic representation from the US: *chief of mission:* Ambassador Paul A. FOLMSBEE (since 3 June 2015)
embassy: located off the Roi Bin Fahad Aziz Bridge west of the Bamako central district
mailing address: ACI 2000, Rue 243, Porte 297, Bamako
telephone: [223] 2070-2300
FAX: [223] 2070-2479

Flag description: three equal vertical bands of green (hoist side), yellow, and red
note: uses the popular Pan-African colors of Ethiopia; the colors from left to right are the same as

587

those of neighboring Senegal (which has an additional green central star) and the reverse of those on the flag of neighboring Guinea

National symbol(s): Great Mosque of Djenne; national colors: green, yellow, red

National anthem: name: "Le Mali" (Mali)
lyrics/music: Seydou Badian KOUYATE/Banzoumana SISSOKO
note: adopted 1962; also known as "Pour L'Afrique et pour toi, Mali" (For Africa and for You, Mali) and "A ton appel Mali" (At Your Call, Mali)

ECONOMY

Economy—overview: Among the 25 poorest countries in the world, landlocked Mali depends on gold mining and agricultural exports for revenue. The country's fiscal status fluctuates with gold and agricultural commodity prices and the harvest; cotton and gold exports make up around 80% of export earnings. Mali remains dependent on foreign aid.

Economic activity is largely confined to the riverine area irrigated by the Niger River; about 65% of Mali's land area is desert or semidesert. About 10% of the population is nomadic and about 80% of the labor force is engaged in farming and fishing. Industrial activity is concentrated on processing farm commodities. The government subsidizes the production of cereals to decrease the country's dependence on imported foodstuffs and to reduce its vulnerability to food price shocks.

Mali is developing its iron ore extraction industry to diversify foreign exchange earnings away from gold, but the pace will depend on global price trends. Although the political coup in 2012 slowed Mali's growth, the economy has since bounced back, with GDP growth above 5% in 2014-17, although physical insecurity, high population growth, corruption, weak infrastructure, and low levels of human capital continue to constrain economic development. Higher rainfall helped to boost cotton output in 2017, and the country's 2017 budget increased spending more than 10%, much of which was devoted to infrastructure and agriculture. Corruption and political turmoil are strong downside risks in 2018 and beyond.

GDP (purchasing power parity): $40.98 billion (2017 est.)
$38.91 billion (2016 est.)
$36.78 billion (2015 est.)
note: data are in 2017 dollars
country comparison to the world: 117

GDP (official exchange rate): $15 billion (2016 est.)

GDP—real growth rate: 5.3% (2017 est.)
5.8% (2016 est.)
6% (2015 est.)
country comparison to the world: 33

GDP—per capita (PPP): $2,200 (2017 est.)
$2,100 (2016 est.)
$2,100 (2015 est.)
note: data are in 2017 dollars
country comparison to the world: 203

Gross national saving: 13% of GDP (2017 est.)

10.3% of GDP (2016 est.)
12.1% of GDP (2015 est.)
country comparison to the world: 139

GDP—composition, by end use:
household consumption: 71.9%
government consumption: 17%
investment in fixed capital: 18.8%
investment in inventories: 0.2%
exports of goods and services: 20.4%
imports of goods and services: -28.3% (2017 est.)

GDP—composition, by sector of origin:
agriculture: 40.9%
industry: 18.9%
services: 40.2% (2017 est.)

Agriculture—products: cotton, millet, rice, corn, vegetables, peanuts; cattle, sheep, goats

Industries: food processing; construction; phosphate and gold mining

Industrial production growth rate: 4.7% (2017 est.)
country comparison to the world: 56

Labor force: 6.447 million (2017 est.)
country comparison to the world: 72

Labor force—by occupation: *agriculture:* 80%
industry and services: 20% (2005 est.)

Unemployment rate: 8.1% (2016 est.)
8.1% (2016 est.)
country comparison to the world: 113

Population below poverty line: 36.1% (2005 est.)

Household income or consumption by percentage share: *lowest 10%:* 3.5%
highest 10%: 25.8% (2010 est.)

Distribution of family income—Gini index: 40.1 (2001)
50.5 (1994)
country comparison to the world: 61

Budget: *revenues:* $3.068 billion
expenditures: $3.584 billion (2017 est.)
Taxes and other revenues: 20.5% of GDP (2017 est.)
country comparison to the world: 150

Budget surplus (+) or deficit (-): -3.4% of GDP (2017 est.)
country comparison to the world: 130

Public debt: 28% of GDP (2017 est.)
29.7% of GDP (2016 est.)
country comparison to the world: 168

Fiscal year: calendar year

Inflation rate (consumer prices): 0.2% (2017 est.)
-1.8% (2016 est.)
country comparison to the world: 14

Central bank discount rate: 16% (31 December 2010)
4.25% (31 December 2009)
country comparison to the world: 7

Commercial bank prime lending rate: 9% (31 December 2017 est.)
5.3% (31 December 2016 est.)
country comparison to the world: 92

Stock of narrow money: $3.023 billion (31 December 2017 est.)
$2.687 billion (31 December 2016 est.)
country comparison to the world: 119

Stock of broad money: $4.439 billion (31 December 2017 est.)
$3.858 billion (31 December 2016 est.)
country comparison to the world: 134

Stock of domestic credit: $3.39 billion (31 December 2017 est.)
$2.931 billion (31 December 2016 est.)
country comparison to the world: 138

Market value of publicly traded shares: $NA

Current account balance: -$1.045 billion (2017 est.)
-$996 million (2016 est.)
country comparison to the world: 134

Exports: $3.036 billion (2017 est.)
$2.803 billion (2016 est.)
country comparison to the world: 125

Exports—commodities: cotton, gold, livestock

Exports—partners: Switzerland 30.4%, India 12.2%, Ukraine 5.1%, China 5.1%, Burkina Faso 4.9%, Senegal 4.3%, France 4%, South Africa 4% (2016)

Imports: $3.891 billion (2017 est.)
$3.443 billion (2016 est.)
country comparison to the world: 134

Imports—commodities: petroleum, machinery and equipment, construction materials, foodstuffs, textiles

Imports—partners: Senegal 12.2%, China 12.2%, France 10.3%, Benin 8.6%, Cote dIvoire 8.4% (2016)

Debt—external: $4.296 billion (31 December 2017 est.)
$3.981 billion (31 December 2016 est.)
country comparison to the world: 138

Stock of direct foreign investment—at home: $3.494 billion (31 December 2017 est.)
$3.266 billion (31 December 2016 est.)
country comparison to the world: 110

Stock of direct foreign investment—abroad: $72.2 million (31 December 2017 est.)
$62.2 million (31 December 2016 est.)
country comparison to the world: 104

Exchange rates: Communaute Financiere Africaine francs (XOF) per US dollar—
605.3 (2017 est.)
593.01 (2016 est.)
593.01 (2015 est.)
591.45 (2014 est.)
494.42 (2013 est.)

ENERGY

Electricity access: *population without electricity:* 11,400,000
electrification—*total population:* 26%
electrification—*urban areas:* 53%
electrification—*rural areas:* 9% (2013)

Electricity—production: 2.175 billion kWh (2015 est.)
country comparison to the world: 138

Electricity—consumption: 2.023 billion kWh (2015 est.)
country comparison to the world: 143

Electricity—exports: 0 kWh (2016 est.)
country comparison to the world: 168

Electricity—imports: 0 kWh (2016 est.)
country comparison to the world: 173

Electricity—installed generating capacity: 590,000 kW (2015 est.)
country comparison to the world: 140

Electricity—from fossil fuels: 67.8% of total installed capacity (2015 est.)
country comparison to the world: 107

Electricity—from nuclear fuels: 0% of total installed capacity (2015 est.)
country comparison to the world: 141

Electricity—from hydroelectric plants: 31.2% of total installed capacity (2015 est.)
country comparison to the world: 69

Electricity—from other renewable sources: 1% of total installed capacity (2015 est.)
country comparison to the world: 140

Crude oil—production: 0 bbl/day (2016 est.)
country comparison to the world: 168

Crude oil—exports: 0 bbl/day (2014 est.)
country comparison to the world: 162

Crude oil—imports: 0 bbl/day (2014 est.)
country comparison to the world: 160

Crude oil—proved reserves: 0 bbl (1 January 2017 es)
country comparison to the world: 165

Refined petroleum products—production: 0 bbl/day (2014 est.)
country comparison to the world: 173

Refined petroleum products—consumption: 7,500 bbl/day (2015 est.)
country comparison to the world: 162

Refined petroleum products—exports: 0 bbl/day (2014 est.)
country comparison to the world: 179

Refined petroleum products—imports: 7,486 bbl/day (2014 est.)
country comparison to the world: 150

Natural gas—production: 0 cu m (2013 est.)
country comparison to the world: 169

Natural gas—consumption: 0 cu m (2013 est.)
country comparison to the world: 208

Natural gas—exports: 0 cu m (2013 est.)
country comparison to the world: 149

Natural gas—imports: 0 cu m (2013 est.)
country comparison to the world: 155

Natural gas—proved reserves: 0 cu m (1 January 2014 es)
country comparison to the world: 172

Carbon dioxide emissions from consumption of energy: 800,000 Mt (2013 est.)
country comparison to the world: 170

COMMUNICATIONS

Telephones—fixed lines: *total subscriptions:* 200,812
subscriptions per 100 inhabitants: 1 (July 2016 est.)

country comparison to the world: 136

Telephones—mobile cellular: *total:* 20,182,160
subscriptions per 100 inhabitants: 116 (July 2016 est.)
country comparison to the world: 50

Telephone system: *general assessment:* domestic system improving; increasing use of local radio loops to extend network coverage to remote areas
domestic: fixed-line subscribership remains less than 1 per 100 persons; mobile-cellular subscribership has increased sharply to over 115 per 100 persons
international: country code—223; satellite communications center and fiber-optic links to neighboring countries; satellite earth stations—2 Intelsat (1 Atlantic Ocean, 1 Indian Ocean) (2016)

Broadcast media: national public TV broadcaster; 2 privately owned companies provide subscription services to foreign multi-channel TV packages; national public radio broadcaster supplemented by a large number of privately owned and community broadcast stations; transmissions of multiple international broadcasters are available (2007)

Internet country code: .ml
Internet users: total: 1,940,978

percent of population: 11.1% (July 2016 est.)
country comparison to the world: 38

TRANSPORTATION

National air transport system: *number of registered air carriers:* 1
inventory of registered aircraft operated by air carriers: 2 (2015)
Civil aircraft registration country code prefix: TZ, TT (2016)

Airports: 25 (2013)
country comparison to the world: 129

Airports—with paved runways: *total:* 8
over 3,047 m: 1
2,438 to 3,047 m: 4
1,524 to 2,437 m: 2
914 to 1,523 m: 1 (2017)

Airports—with unpaved runways: *total:* 17
1,524 to 2,437 m: 3
914 to 1,523 m: 9
under 914 m: 5 (2013)

Heliports: 2 (2013)

Railways: *total:* 593 km
narrow gauge: 593 km 1.000-m gauge (2014)
country comparison to the world: 111

Roadways: *total:* 22,474 km
paved: 5,522 km
unpaved: 16,952 km (2009)
country comparison to the world: 103

Waterways: 1,800 km (downstream of Koulikoro; low water levels on the River Niger cause problems in dry years; in the months before the rainy season the river is not navigable by commercial vessels) (2011)
country comparison to the world: 43

Ports and terminals: river port(s): Koulikoro (Niger)

MILITARY AND SECURITY

Military expenditures: 2.63% of GDP (2016)
2.43% of GDP (2015)
1.56% of GDP (2014)
1.2% of GDP (2013)
1.2% of GDP (2012)
country comparison to the world: 68

Military branches: Malian Armed Forces: Army (Armee de Terre), Republic of Mali Air Force (Force Aerienne de la Republique du Mali, FARM), National Guard (Garde National du Mali) (2013)

Military service age and obligation: 18 years of age for selective compulsory and voluntary military service; 2-year conscript service obligation (2012)

TERRORISM

Terrorist groups—home based: *al-Mulathamun Battalion:* aim(s): replace regional governments, including in Mali, with an Islamic state
area(s) of operation: headquartered in the north; targets primarily international interests, especially Westerners and Western entities; responsible for multiple lethal attacks across the country in 2016, including kidnappings in Tombouctou and along the border with Burkina Faso; affiliated with the Islamic State of Iraq and the Levant (ISIL); elements based in Mali are part of Jama'at Nusrat al-Islam wal-Muslimin (Group for the Support of Islam and Muslims, JNIM), an alliance umbrella of al-Qa'ida linked groups in Mali that announced its presence on 2 March 2017; JNIM is responsible for several attacks carried out in central Mali

Ansar al-Dine (AAD): *aim(s):* install Sharia throughout Mali; the Macina Liberation Front branch seeks to rebuild historic Islamic empires, primarily the Macina Empire
area(s) of operation: headquartered in the north, with its Macina Liberation Front branch based in Mopti in Central Mali increasing its operations in the south; launches attacks against Malian military and security forces, French troops, UN Multidimensional Integrated Stabilization Mission in Mali (MINUSMA), and other Westerners; AAD is a member group in Jama'at Nusrat al-Islam wal-Muslimin (Group for the support of Islam and Muslims, JNIM), an alliance umbrella of al-Qa'ida linked groups in Mali that announced its presence on 2 March 2017; AAD's overall leader and founder Iyad Ag GHALI leads JNIM, which is responsible for several attacks carried out in central Mali

Terrorist groups—foreign based: *al-Qa'ida (AQ):* aim(s): overthrow the Malian Government and, ultimately, establish a pan-Islamic caliphate under a strict Salafi Muslim interpretation of Sharia
area(s) of operation: maintains an operational presence and established networks, especially through its branch, Jama'at Nusrat al-Islam wal-Muslimin (Group for the Support of Islam and Muslims, JNIM), an alliance umbrella of al-Qa'ida linked groups in Mali that announced its presence

on 2 March 2017; JNIM is responsible for several attacks carried out in central Mali

al-Qaida in the Islamic Maghreb (AQIM): *aim(s):* replace the Malian Government with Sharia and, ultimately, create a regional Islamic caliphate across all of North and West Africa

area(s) of operation: maintains a heavy operational presence, especially in the northern half of the country; conducts attacks against foreigners and Malian, French Government, and UN forces and facilities; responsible for multiple attacks across the country in recent years; has engaged in numerous kidnappings for ransom in Tombouctou and along the border with Burkina Faso; on 20 November 2015, AQIM and al-Mulathamun Battalion operatives killed 20 foreigners at the Radisson Blu Hotel in Mali's capital, Bamako, when they stormed the hotel while shooting and lobbing handgrenades; AQIM's Sahara branch is a member group in Jama'ah Nusrah al-Islam wal-Muslimin (Group for the support of Islam and Muslims, JNIM), an alliance umbrella of al-Qa'ida linked groups in Mali that announced its presence on 2 March 2017; JNIM is responsible for several attacks carried out in central Mali

TRANSNATIONAL ISSUES

Disputes—international: demarcation is underway with Burkina Faso

Refugees and internally displaced persons: refugees (country of origin): 15,298 (Mauritania) (2016)

IDPs: 38,172 (Tuareg rebellion since 2012) (2017)

Trafficking in persons: current situation: Mali is a source, transit, and destination country for men, women, and children subjected to forced labor and sex trafficking; internal trafficking is more prevalent than transnational trafficking, but foreign women and girls are forced into domestic servitude, agricultural labor, and support roles in gold mines, as well as subjected to sex trafficking; Malian boys are forced to work in agricultural settings, gold mines, the informal commercial sector and to beg within Mali and neighboring countries; Malians and other Africans who travel through Mali to Mauritania, Algeria, or Libya in hopes of reaching Europe are particularly at risk of becoming victims of human trafficking; men and boys, primarily of Songhai ethnicity, are subjected to debt bondage in the salt mines of Taoudenni in northern Mali; some members of Mali's Tamachek

community are subjected to hereditary slavery-related practices; Malian women and girls are victims of sex trafficking in Gabon, Libya, Lebanon, and Tunisia; the recruitment of child soldiers by armed groups in northern Mali decreased

tier rating: Tier 2 Watch List—Mali does not fully comply with the minimum standards for the elimination of trafficking; however, it is making significant efforts to do so; in 2014, Mali was granted a waiver from an otherwise required downgrade to Tier 3 because its government has a written plan that, if implemented would constitute making significant efforts to bring itself into compliance with the minimum standards for the elimination of trafficking; officials failed to distribute the 2012 anti-trafficking law to judicial and law enforcement personnel, perpetuating a lack of understanding and awareness of the legislation; anti-trafficking law enforcement efforts decreased in 2014, with only one case investigated and no prosecutions or convictions; fewer victims were identified, and the government did not support the privately funded NGOs and international organizations it relied upon to provide victims with services; the government did not conduct any awareness-raising campaigns, workshops, or training sessions (2015)

MALTA

INTRODUCTION

Background: With a civilization that dates back thousands of years, Malta boasts some of the oldest megalithic sites in the world. Situated in the center of the Mediterranean, Malta's islands have long served as a strategic military asset, with the islands at various times having come under control of the Phoenicians, Carthaginians, Greeks, Romans,

GEOGRAPHY

Location: Southern Europe, islands in the Mediterranean Sea, south of Sicily (Italy)

Geographic coordinates: 35 50 N, 14 35 E

Map references: Europe

Area: *total:* 316 sq km
land: 316 sq km
water: 0 sq km
country comparison to the world: 209

Area—comparative: slightly less than twice the size of Washington, DC

Land boundaries: 0 km

Coastline: 196.8 km (excludes 56 km for the island of Gozo)

Maritime claims: *territorial sea:* 12 nm
contiguous zone: 24 nm
continental shelf: 200-m depth or to the depth of exploitation
exclusive fishing zone: 25 nm

Climate: Mediterranean; mild, rainy winters; hot, dry summers

Terrain: mostly low, rocky, flat to dissected plains; many coastal cliffs

Elevation: *mean elevation:* NA

elevation extremes: *lowest point:* Mediterranean Sea 0 m
highest point: Ta'Dmejrek on Dingli Cliffs 253 m

Natural resources: limestone, salt, arable land

Land use: *agricultural land:* 32.3%
arable land: 28.4%;
permanent crops: 3.9%;
permanent pasture: 0%
forest: 0.9%

other: 66.8% (2011 est.)
Irrigated land: 35 sq km (2012)

Population—distribution: most of the population lives on the eastern half of Malta, the largest of the three inhabited islands

Natural hazards: occasional droughts

Environment—current issues: limited natural freshwater resources; increasing reliance on desalination

Environment—international agreements: *party to:* Air Pollution, Biodiversity, Climate Change, Climate Change-Kyoto Protocol, Desertification, Endangered Species, Hazardous Wastes, Law of the Sea, Marine Dumping, Ozone Layer Protection, Ship Pollution, Wetlands
signed, but not ratified: none of the selected agreements

Geography—note: the country comprises an archipelago, with only the three largest islands (Malta, Ghawdex or Gozo, and Kemmuna or Comino) inhabited; numerous bays provide good harbors; Malta and Tunisia are discussing the commercial exploitation of the continental shelf between their countries, particularly for oil exploration

PEOPLE AND SOCIETY

Population: 416,338 (July 2017 est.)
country comparison to the world: 175

Nationality: *noun:* Maltese (singular and plural)
adjective: Maltese

Ethnic groups: Maltese (descendants of ancient Carthaginians and Phoenicians with strong elements of Italian and other Mediterranean stock)

Languages: Maltese (official) 90.1%, English (official) 6%, multilingual 3%, other 0.9% (2005 est.)

Religions: Roman Catholic (official) more than 90% (2006 est.)

Age structure: *0-14 years:* 15.04% (male 32,128/female 30,490)
15-24 years: 11.44% (male 24,471/female 23,142)
25-54 years: 39.98% (male 85,158/female 81,303)
55-64 years: 13.98% (male 28,919/female 29,298)
65 years and over: 19.56% (male 36,743/female 44,686) (2017 est.)

Dependency ratios: *total dependency ratio:* 48.8
youth dependency ratio: 21.4
elderly dependency ratio: 27.3
potential support ratio: 3.7 (2015 est.)

Median age: *total:* 41.8 years
male: 40.8 years
female: 43 years (2017 est.)

Population growth rate: 0.26% (2017 est.)
country comparison to the world: 176

Birth rate: 10.1 births/1,000 population (2017 est.)
country comparison to the world: 192

Death rate: 9.4 deaths/1,000 population (2017 est.)
country comparison to the world: 59

Net migration rate: 2 migrant(s)/1,000 population (2017 est.)
country comparison to the world: 47

Population distribution: most of the population lives on the eastern half of Malta, the largest of the three inhabited islands

Urbanization: *urban population:* 95.6% of total population (2017)
rate of urbanization: 0.32% annual rate of change (2015-20 est.)

Major urban areas—population: VALLETTA (capital) 197,000 (2014)

Sex ratio: *at birth:* 1.06 male(s)/female
0-14 years: 1.05 male(s)/female
15-24 years: 1.06 male(s)/female
25-54 years: 1.05 male(s)/female
55-64 years: 0.98 male(s)/female
65 years and over: 0.81 male(s)/female
total population: 0.99 male(s)/female (2016 est.)

Mother's mean age at first birth: 26.9 years
note: data refer to the average of the different childbearing ages of first-order births (2010 est.)

Maternal mortality ratio: 9 deaths/100,000 live births (2015 est.)
country comparison to the world: 155

Infant mortality rate: *total:* 3.5 deaths/1,000 live births
male: 3.9 deaths/1,000 live births
female: 3.1 deaths/1,000 live births (2017 est.)
country comparison to the world: 203

Life expectancy at birth: *total population:* 80.5 years
male: 78.1 years

female: 83 years (2017 est.)
country comparison to the world: 39

Total fertility rate: 1.55 children born/woman (2017 est.)
country comparison to the world: 190

Health expenditures: 9.7% of GDP (2014)
country comparison to the world: 28

Physicians density: 3.91 physicians/1,000 population (2015)

Hospital bed density: 4.8 beds/1,000 population (2012)

Drinking water source:
improved:
urban: 100% of population
rural: 100% of population
total: 100% of population
unimproved:
urban: 0% of population
rural: 0% of population
total: 0% of population (2015 est.)

Sanitation facility access:
improved:
urban: 100% of population
rural: 100% of population
total: 100% of population
unimproved:
urban: 0% of population
rural: 0% of population
total: 0% of population (2015 est.)

HIV/AIDS—adult prevalence rate: 0.1% (2016 est.)
country comparison to the world: 109

HIV/AIDS—people living with HIV/AIDS: <500 (2016 est.)

HIV/AIDS—deaths: <100 (2016 est.)

Obesity—adult prevalence rate: 28.9% (2016)
country comparison to the world: 28

Education expenditures: 8.3% of GDP (2013)
country comparison to the world: 23

Literacy: *definition:* age 15 and over can read and write
total population: 94.4%
male: 93.1%
female: 95.8% (2015 est.)

School life expectancy (primary to tertiary education): *total:* 15 years
male: 15 years
female: 15 years (2015)

Unemployment, youth ages 15-24: *total:* 11.8%
male: 13.9%
female: 9.4% (2015 est.)
country comparison to the world: 82

GOVERNMENT

Country name: *conventional long form:* Republic of Malta
conventional short form: Malta
local long form: Repubblika ta' Malta
local short form: Malta
etymology: the ancient Greeks called the island "Melite" meaning "honey-sweet" from the Greek

word "meli" meaning "honey" and referring to the island's honey production

Government type: parliamentary republic

Capital: *name:* Valletta
geographic coordinates: 35 53 N, 14 30 E
time difference: UTC+1 (6 hours ahead of Washington, DC, during Standard Time)
daylight saving time: +1hr, begins last Sunday in March; ends last Sunday in October

Administrative divisions: 68 localities (Il-lokalita); Attard, Balzan, Birgu, Birkirkara, Birzebbuga, Bormla, Dingli, Fgura, Floriana, Fontana, Ghajnsielem, Gharb, Gharghur, Ghasri, Ghaxaq, Gudja, Gzira, Hamrun, Iklin, Imdina, Imgarr, Imqabba, Imsida, Imtarfa, Isla, Kalkara, Kercem, Kirkop, Lija, Luqa, Marsa, Marsaskala, Marsaxlokk, Mellieha, Mosta, Munxar, Nadur, Naxxar, Paola, Pembroke, Pieta, Qala, Qormi, Qrendi, Rabat, Rabat (Ghawdex), Safi, San Giljan/Saint Julian, San Gwann/Saint John, San Lawrenz/Saint Lawrence, Sannat, San Pawl il-Bahar/Saint Paul's Bay, Santa Lucija/Saint Lucia, Santa Venera/Saint Venera, Siggiewi, Sliema, Swieqi, Tarxien, Ta' Xbiex, Valletta, Xaghra, Xewkija, Xghajra, Zabbar, Zebbug, Zebbug (Ghawdex), Zejtun, Zurrieq

Independence: 21 September 1964 (from the UK)

National holiday: Independence Day, 21 September (1964); Republic Day, 13 December (1974)

Constitution: history: many previous; latest adopted 21 September 1964
amendments: proposals (Acts of Parliament) require at least two-thirds majority vote by the House of Representatives; passage of "Acts" requires majority vote by referendum, followed by final majority vote by the House and assent by the president of the republic; amended many times, last in 2016 (2017)

Legal system: mixed legal system of English common law and civil law based on the Roman and Napoleonic civil codes

International law organization participation: accepts compulsory ICJ jurisdiction with reservations; accepts ICCt jurisdiction

Citizenship: *citizenship by birth:* no
citizenship by descent only: at least one parent must be a citizen of Malta
dual citizenship recognized: no
residency requirement for naturalization: 5 years

Suffrage: 18 years of age (16 in local council elections); universal

Executive branch: *chief of state:* President Marie-Louise Coleiro PRECA (since 4 April 2014)

head of government: Prime Minister Joseph MUSCAT (since 11 March 2013)
cabinet: Cabinet appointed by the president on the advice of the prime minister
elections/appointments: president indirectly elected by the House of Representatives for a 5-year term (1-term limit); election last held on 4 April 2014 (next to be held by April 2019); following legislative elections, the leader of the majority party or majority coalition usually appointed prime

minister by the president for a 5-year term; deputy prime minister appointed by the president on the advice of the prime minister

election results: Marie-Louise Coleiro PRECA (PL) elected president; House of Representatives vote—unanimous; Joseph MUSCAT (PL) reappointed prime minister

Legislative branch: *description:* unicameral House of Representatives or Il-Kamra Tad-Deputati, a component of the Parliament of Malta (normally 65 seats but can include at-large members; members directly elected in 5 multi-seat constituencies by proportional representation vote; members serve 5-year terms); note—the parliament elected in 2013 had 69 seats; an additional two seats were added in 2016 by the Constitutional Court to correct for mistakes made in the 2013 vote-counting process

elections: last held on 3 June 2017 (next to be held in 2022); note—Prime Minister MUSCAT called for early elections amid corruption allegations

election results: percent of vote by party—PL 55.0%, PN 43.7%, other 1.3%; seats by party—PL 37 PN 30; note—PN was awarded two additional seats for a total of 30 in accordance with the proportionality provisions specified in the constitution; PD candidates ran under the PN list

Judicial branch: *highest court(s):* Court of Appeal (consists of either 1 or 3 judges); Constitutional Court (consists of 3 judges); Court of Criminal Appeal (consists of either 1 or 3 judges)

judge selection and term of office: Court of Appeal and Constitutional Court judges appointed by the president, usually upon the advice of the prime minister; judges of both courts serve until age 65

subordinate courts: Civil Court (divided into the General Jurisdiction Section, Family Section, and Voluntary Section); Criminal Court; Court of Magistrates; Gozo Courts (for the islands of Gozo and Comino)

Political parties and leaders: Democratic Party or PD [Anthony BUTTIGIEG]
Labor Party or PL [Joseph MUSCAT]
Nationalist Party or PN [Adrian DELIA]

Political pressure groups and leaders: Alliance of Liberal Democrats Malta (Alleanza Liberali-Demokratika Malta) or ALDM (for divorce, abortion, gay marriage, women's rights)
Alliance for Change (Alleanza Bidla) (Euro-skeptic)
Together for a Better Environment (Flimkien Ghal-Ambjent Ahjar) or FAA
other: environmental groups

International organization participation: Australia Group, C, CD, CE, EAPC, EBRD, ECB, EIB, EMU, EU, FAO, IAEA, IBRD, ICAO, ICC (NGOs), ICCt, ICRM, IDA, IFAD, IFC, IFRCS, ILO, IMF, IMO, IMSO, Interpol, IOC, IOM, IPU, ISO, ITSO, ITU, ITUC (NGOs), MIGA, NSG, OAS (observer), OPCW, OSCE, PCA, PFP, Schengen Convention, UN, UNCTAD, UNESCO, UNIDO, Union Latina (observer), UNWTO, UPU, WCO, WHO, WIPO, WMO, WTO

Diplomatic representation in the US: *chief of mission:* Ambassador Pierre Clive AGIUS (since 2 March 2016)

chancery: 2017 Connecticut Avenue NW, Washington, DC 20008

telephone: [1] (202) 462-3611 through 3612

FAX: [1] (202) 387-5470

Diplomatic representation from the US: *chief of mission:* Ambassador G. Kathleen HILL (since 25 February 2016)

embassy: Ta' Qali National Park, Attard, ATD 4000

mailing address: 5800 Valletta Place, Dulles, VA 20189

telephone: [356] 2561 4000

FAX: [356] 2124 3229

Flag description: two equal vertical bands of white (hoist side) and red; in the upper hoist-side corner is a representation of the George Cross, edged in red; according to legend, the colors are taken from the red and white checkered banner of Count Roger of Sicily who removed a bi-colored corner and granted it to Malta in 1091; an uncontested explanation is that the colors are those of the Knights of Saint John who ruled Malta from 1530 to 1798; in 1942, King George VI of the UK awarded the George Cross to the islanders for their exceptional bravery and gallantry in World War II; since independence in 1964, the George Cross bordered in red has appeared directly on the white field

National symbol(s): Maltese eight-pointed cross; national colors: red, white

National anthem: name: "L-Innu Malti" (The Maltese Anthem)

lyrics/music: Dun Karm PSAILA/Robert SAMMUT

note: adopted 1945; written in the form of a prayer

ECONOMY

Economy—overview: Malta's free market economy—the smallest economy in the euro-zone—relies heavily on trade in both goods and services, principally with Europe. Malta produces less than a quarter of its food needs, has limited fresh water supplies, and has few domestic energy sources. Malta's economy is dependent on foreign trade, manufacturing, and tourism. Malta joined the EU in 2004 and adopted the euro on 1 January 2008.

Malta has weathered the euro-zone crisis better than most EU member states due to a low debt-to-GDP ratio and financially sound banking sector. It maintains one of the lowest unemployment rates in Europe, and growth has fully recovered since the 2009 recession. In 2014 through 2016, Malta led the euro zone in growth, expanding more than 4.5% per year.

Malta's services sector continues to grow, with sustained growth in the financial services and online gaming sectors. Advantageous tax schemes remained attractive to foreign investors, though EU discussions of anti-tax avoidance measures have raised concerns among Malta's financial services and insurance providers, as the measures could have a significant impact on those sectors.

The tourism sector also continued to grow, with 2016 showing record-breaking numbers of both air and cruise passenger arrivals.

Malta's GDP growth remains strong and is supported by a strong labor market. The government has implemented new programs, including free childcare, to encourage increased labor participation. The high cost of borrowing and small labor market remain potential constraints to future economic growth. Increasingly, other EU and European migrants are relocating to Malta for employment, though wages have remained low compared to other European countries. Inflation remains low.

GDP (purchasing power parity): $18.53 billion (2017 est.)
$17.62 billion (2016 est.)
$16.7 billion (2015 est.)
note: data are in 2017 dollars
country comparison to the world: 152

GDP (official exchange rate): $12.01 billion (2016 est.)

GDP—real growth rate: 5.1% (2017 est.)
5.5% (2016 est.)
7.1% (2015 est.)
country comparison to the world: 39

GDP—per capita (PPP): $42,500 (2017 est.)
$40,600 (2016 est.)
$38,900 (2015 est.)
note: data are in 2017 dollars
country comparison to the world: 42

Gross national saving: 31.1% of GDP (2017 est.)
31.6% of GDP (2016 est.)
29.9% of GDP (2015 est.)
country comparison to the world: 22

GDP—composition, by end use:
household consumption: 49.1%
government consumption: 16.8%
investment in fixed capital: 23.1%
investment in inventories: -0.8%
exports of goods and services: 145.4%
imports of goods and services: -133.5% (2017 est.)

GDP—composition, by sector of origin:
agriculture: 1.3%
industry: 10.6%
services: 88.1% (2016 est.)

Agriculture—products: potatoes, cauliflower, grapes, wheat, barley, tomatoes, citrus, cut flowers, green peppers; pork, milk, poultry, eggs

Industries: tourism, electronics, ship building and repair, construction, food and beverages, pharmaceuticals, footwear, clothing, tobacco, aviation services, financial services, information technology services

Industrial production growth rate: -3.3% (2016 est.)
country comparison to the world: 197

Labor force: 206,300 (2017 est.)
country comparison to the world: 169

Labor force—by occupation: *agriculture:* 1.6%
industry: 20.7%
services: 77.7% (2016 est.)

Unemployment rate: 4.4% (2017 est.)

4.7% (2016 est.)
country comparison to the world: 60

Population below poverty line: 16.3% (2015 est.)

Household income or consumption by percentage share: *lowest* 10%: NA%
highest 10%: NA%

Distribution of family income—Gini index: 28.1 (2015)
27.7 (2014)
country comparison to the world: 134

Budget: *revenues:* $4.295 billion
expenditures: $4.354 billion (2017 est.)
Taxes and other revenues: 35.8% of GDP (2017 est.)
country comparison to the world: 52

Budget surplus (+) or deficit (-): -0.5% of GDP (2017 est.)
country comparison to the world: 45

Public debt: 52.9% of GDP (2017 est.)
56% of GDP (2016 est.)
note: Malta reports public debt at nominal value outstanding at the end of the year, according to guidelines set out in the Maastricht Treaty for general government gross debt; the data include the following categories of government liabilities (as defined in ESA95): currency and deposits (AF.2), securities other than shares excluding financial derivatives (AF.3, excluding AF.34), and loans (AF.4); general government comprises the central government, state government, local government and social security funds
country comparison to the world: 91

Fiscal year: calendar year

Inflation rate (consumer prices): 1.3% (2017 est.)
0.9% (2016 est.)
country comparison to the world: 55

Central bank discount rate: -0.35% (31 December 2016 est.)
-0.2% (31 December 2015)
note: this is the European Central Bank's rate on the marginal lending facility, which offers overnight credit to banks in the euro area
country comparison to the world: 159

Commercial bank prime lending rate: 3% (31 December 2017 est.)
3.1% (31 December 2016 est.)
country comparison to the world: 168

Stock of narrow money: $14.69 billion (31 December 2017 est.)
$14.56 billion (31 December 2016 est.)
note: see entry for the EU for money supply for the entire euro area; the European Central Bank controls monetary policy for the 18 members of the Economic and Monetary Union (EMU); individual members of the EMU do not control the quantity of money circulating within their own borders
country comparison to the world: 75

Stock of broad money: $19.5 billion (31 December 2017 est.)
$19.2 billion (31 December 2016 est.)
country comparison to the world: 91

Stock of domestic credit: $20.02 billion (31 December 2017 est.)
$19.19 billion (31 December 2016 est.)
country comparison to the world: 91

Market value of publicly traded shares: $4.632 billion (31 December 2016 est.)
$4.468 billion (31 December 2015 est.)
$3.353 billion (31 December 2014 est.)
country comparison to the world: 87

Current account balance: $1.075 billion (2017 est.)
$867 million (2016 est.)
country comparison to the world: 37

Exports: $2.627 billion (2017 est.)
$2.493 billion (2016 est.)
country comparison to the world: 132

Exports—commodities: machinery and mechanical appliances; mineral fuels, oils and petroleum products; pharmaceutical products; books and newspapers; aircraft/spacecraft and parts; toys, games, and sports equipment

Exports—partners: US 27.3%, Germany 13.9%, France 8.3%, Singapore 5.6%, Japan 5.2%, Hong Kong 4.3%, Italy 4.2% (2016)

Imports: $5.191 billion (2017 est.)
$4.643 billion (2016 est.)
country comparison to the world: 122

Imports—commodities: mineral fuels, oils and products; electrical machinery; aircraft/spacecraft and parts thereof; machinery and mechanical appliances; plastic and other semi-manufactured goods; vehicles and parts

Imports—partners: Italy 20.9%, Canada 10.4%, Germany 6.3%, UK 5.9%, France 4.4% (2016)

Reserves of foreign exchange and gold: $671.1 million (31 December 2017 est.)
$677.1 million (31 December 2016 est.)
country comparison to the world: 133

Debt—external: $90.98 billion (September 2016 est.)
$99.02 billion (31 December 2015 est.)
country comparison to the world: 53

Stock of direct foreign investment—at home: $166.1 million (1 June 2016 est.)
$155.5 million (1 June 2015 est.)
country comparison to the world: 129

Stock of direct foreign investment—abroad: $65.49 million (June 2015 est.)
$64.77 million (June 2014 est.)
country comparison to the world: 106

Exchange rates: euros (EUR) per US dollar—
0.906 (2017 est.)
0.9214 (2016 est.)
0.9214 (2015 est.)
0.885 (2014 est.)
0.7634 (2013 est.)

ENERGY

Electricity access: electrification—*total population:* 100% (2016)

Electricity—production: 1.228 billion kWh (2015 est.)
country comparison to the world: 147

Electricity—consumption: 2.103 billion kWh (2015 est.)
country comparison to the world: 142

Electricity—exports: 0 kWh (2016 est.)
country comparison to the world: 171

Electricity—imports: 1.054 billion kWh (2015 est.)
country comparison to the world: 68

Electricity—installed generating capacity: 670,000 kW (2015 est.)
country comparison to the world: 136

Electricity—from fossil fuels: 88.5% of total installed capacity (2015 est.)
country comparison to the world: 63

Electricity—from nuclear fuels: 0% of total installed capacity (2015 est.)
country comparison to the world: 145

Electricity—from hydroelectric plants: 0% of total installed capacity (2015 est.)
country comparison to the world: 188

Electricity—from other renewable sources: 12.7% of total installed capacity (2015 est.)
country comparison to the world: 59

Crude oil—production: 0 bbl/day (2016 est.)
country comparison to the world: 169

Crude oil—exports: 0 bbl/day (2014 est.)
country comparison to the world: 165

Crude oil—imports: 0 bbl/day (2014 est.)
country comparison to the world: 163

Crude oil—proved reserves: 0 bbl (1 January 2017 es)
country comparison to the world: 166

Refined petroleum products—production: 0 bbl/day (2016 est.)
country comparison to the world: 174

Refined petroleum products—consumption: 42,000 bbl/day (2015 est.)
country comparison to the world: 113

Refined petroleum products—exports: 4,031 bbl/day (2014 est.)
country comparison to the world: 99

Refined petroleum products—imports: 43,950 bbl/day (2014 est.)
country comparison to the world: 90

Natural gas—production: 0 cu m (2016 est.)
country comparison to the world: 172

Natural gas—consumption: 0 cu m (2014 est.)
country comparison to the world: 211

Natural gas—exports: 0 cu m (2014 est.)
country comparison to the world: 153

Natural gas—imports: 0 cu m (2013 est.)
country comparison to the world: 158

Natural gas—proved reserves: 0 cu m (1 January 2014 es)
country comparison to the world: 174

Carbon dioxide emissions from consumption of energy: 887,700 Mt (2014 est.)
country comparison to the world: 168

COMMUNICATIONS

Telephones—fixed lines: *total subscriptions:* 234,383
subscriptions per 100 inhabitants: 56 (July 2016 est.)
country comparison to the world: 126

Telephones—mobile cellular: *total:* 539,589
subscriptions per 100 inhabitants: 130 (July 2016 est.)
country comparison to the world: 169

Telephone system: *general assessment:* automatic system featuring submarine cable and microwave radio relay between islands
domestic: combined fixed-line and mobile-cellular subscribership exceeds 185 per 100 persons
international: country code—356; submarine cable connects to Italy; satellite earth station—1 Intelsat (Atlantic Ocean) (2016)

Broadcast media: 2 publicly owned TV stations, Television Malta broadcasting nationally plus an educational channel; several privately owned national television stations, 2 of which are owned by political parties; Italian and British broadcast programs are available; multi-channel cable and satellite TV services are available; publicly owned radio broadcaster operates 3 stations; roughly 20 commercial radio stations (2017)

Internet country code: .mt
Internet users: total: 320,902
percent of population: 77.3% (July 2016 est.)
country comparison to the world: 160

TRANSPORTATION

National air transport system: *number of registered air carriers:* 9
inventory of registered aircraft operated by air carriers: 28
annual passenger traffic on registered air carriers: 1,583,046
annual freight traffic on registered air carriers: 3.352 million mt-km (2015)
Civil aircraft registration country code prefix: 9H (2016)

Airports: 1 (2013)
country comparison to the world: 225

Airports—with paved runways: *total:* 1
over 3,047 m: 1 (2017)

Heliports: 2 (2013)

Roadways: *total:* 3,096 km
paved: 2,704 km
unpaved: 392 km (2008)
country comparison to the world: 164

Merchant marine: *total:* 2,170
by type: bulk carrier 660, container ship 285, general cargo 317, oil tanker 330, other 578 (2017)
country comparison to the world: 11

Ports and terminals: *major seaport(s):* Marsaxlokk (Malta Freeport), Valletta
container port(s) (TEUs): Marsaxlokk (2,360,000)

MILITARY AND SECURITY

Military expenditures: 0.53% of GDP (2016)
0.5% of GDP (2015)
0.51% of GDP (2014)
0.53% of GDP (2013)
0.54% of GDP (2012)
country comparison to the world: 122

Military branches: Armed Forces of Malta (AFM, includes land, maritime, and air elements) (2017)

Military service age and obligation: 18 years of age for voluntary military service; no conscription (2017)

TRANSNATIONAL ISSUES

Disputes—international: none

Illicit drugs: minor transshipment point for hashish from North Africa to Western Europe

MARSHALL ISLANDS

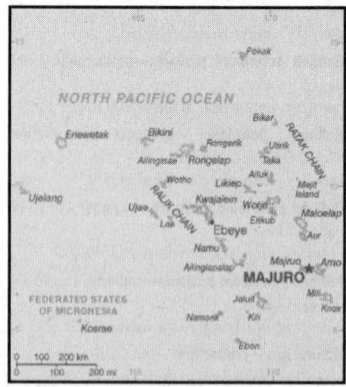

INTRODUCTION

Background: After almost four decades under US administration as the easternmost part of the UN Trust Territory of the Pacific Islands, the Marshall Islands attained independence in 1986 under a Compact of Free Association. Compensation claims continue as a result of US nuclear testing on some of the atolls between 1947 and 1962. The Marshall Islands hosts the US Army Kwajalein Atoll Reagan Missile Test Site, a key installation in the US missile defense network. Kwajalein also hosts one of four dedicated ground antennas (the others are on Ascension (Saint Helena, Ascension, and Tristan da Cunha), Diego Garcia (British Indian Ocean Territory), and at Cape Canaveral, Florida (US)) that assist in the operation of the Global Positioning System (GPS) navigation system.

GEOGRAPHY

Location: Oceania, two archipelagic island chains of 29 atolls, each made up of many small islets, and five single islands in the North Pacific Ocean, about halfway between Hawaii and Australia

Geographic coordinates: 9 00 N, 168 00 E

Map references: Oceania

Area: *total:* 181 sq km
land: 181 sq km
water: 0 sq km
note: the archipelago includes 11,673 sq km of lagoon waters and encompasses the atolls of Bikini, Enewetak, Kwajalein, Majuro, Rongelap, and Utirik
country comparison to the world: 217

Area—comparative: about the size of Washington, DC

Land boundaries: 0 km

Coastline: 370.4 km

Maritime claims: *territorial sea:* 12 nm
contiguous zone: 24 nm
exclusive economic zone: 200 nm

Climate: tropical; hot and humid; wet season May to November; islands border typhoon belt

Terrain: low coral limestone and sand islands

Elevation: *mean elevation:* 2 m

elevation extremes: *lowest point:* Pacific Ocean 0 m
highest point: East-central Airik Island, Maloelap Atoll 14 m

Natural resources: coconut products, marine products, deep seabed minerals

Land use: *agricultural land:* 50.7%
arable land: 7.8%;
permanent crops: 31.2%;
permanent pasture: 11.7%
forest: 49.3%
other: 0% (2011 est.)
Irrigated land: 0 sq km (2012)

Population—distribution: most people live in urban clusters found on many of the country's islands; more than two-thirds of the population lives on the atolls of Majuro and Ebeye

Natural hazards: infrequent typhoons

Environment—current issues: inadequate supplies of potable water; pollution of Majuro lagoon from household waste and discharges from fishing vessels

Environment—international agreements: *party to:* Biodiversity, Climate Change, Climate Change-Kyoto Protocol, Desertification, Hazardous Wastes, Law of the Sea, Ozone Layer Protection, Ship Pollution, Wetlands, Whaling
signed, but not ratified: none of the selected agreements

Geography—note: the islands of Bikini and Enewetak are former US nuclear test sites; Kwajalein atoll, famous as a World War II battleground, surrounds the world's largest lagoon and is used as a US missile test range; the island city of Ebeye is the second largest settlement in the Marshall Islands, after the capital of Majuro, and one of the most densely populated locations in the Pacific

PEOPLE AND SOCIETY

Population: 74,539 (July 2017 est.)
country comparison to the world: 201

Nationality: *noun:* Marshallese (singular and plural)
adjective: Marshallese

Ethnic groups: Marshallese 92.1%, mixed Marshallese 5.9%, other 2% (2006)

Languages: Marshallese (official) 98.2%, other languages 1.8% (1999 census)
note: English (official), widely spoken as a second language

Religions: Protestant 54.8%, Assembly of God 25.8%, Roman Catholic 8.4%, Bukot nan Jesus 2.8%, Mormon 2.1%, other Christian 3.6%, other 1%, none 1.5% (1999 census)

Age structure: *0-14 years:* 34.89% (male 13,261/female 12,743)
15-24 years: 18% (male 6,820/female 6,594)
25-54 years: 37.28% (male 14,147/female 13,642)
55-64 years: 5.82% (male 2,189/female 2,148)
65 years and over: 4.02% (male 1,475/female 1,520) (2017 est.)

Median age: *total:* 22.9 years
male: 22.8 years
female: 23 years (2017 est.)
country comparison to the world: 171

Population growth rate: 1.55% (2017 est.)
country comparison to the world: 73

Birth rate: 24.4 births/1,000 population (2017 est.)
country comparison to the world: 51

Death rate: 4.2 deaths/1,000 population (2017 est.)
country comparison to the world: 208

Net migration rate: -4.7 migrant(s)/1,000 population (2017 est.)
country comparison to the world: 187

Population distribution: most people live in urban clusters found on many of the country's islands; more than two-thirds of the population lives on the atolls of Majuro and Ebeye

Urbanization: *urban population:* 73.2% of total population (2017)
rate of urbanization: 1.07% annual rate of change (2015-20 est.)

Major urban areas—population: MAJURO (capital) 31,000 (2014)

Sex ratio: *at birth:* 1.05 male(s)/female
0-14 years: 1.04 male(s)/female
15-24 years: 1.03 male(s)/female
25-54 years: 1.04 male(s)/female
55-64 years: 1.04 male(s)/female
65 years and over: 0.97 male(s)/female
total population: 1.04 male(s)/female (2016 est.)

Mother's mean age at first birth: 20.7 years
note: median age at first birth among women 25-29 (2007 est.)

Infant mortality rate: *total:* 19.3 deaths/1,000 live births
male: 21.8 deaths/1,000 live births
female: 16.7 deaths/1,000 live births (2017 est.)
country comparison to the world: 83

Life expectancy at birth: *total population:* 73.4 years
male: 71.2 years
female: 75.7 years (2017 est.)
country comparison to the world: 137

Total fertility rate: 3.03 children born/woman (2017 est.)
country comparison to the world: 54

Contraceptive prevalence rate: 44.6% (2007)

Health expenditures: 17.1% of GDP (2014)
country comparison to the world: 2

Physicians density: 0.46 physicians/1,000 population (2012)

Hospital bed density: 2.7 beds/1,000 population (2010)

Drinking water source:
improved:
urban: 93.5% of population
rural: 97.6% of population
total: 94.6% of population
unimproved:
urban: 6.5% of population
rural: 2.4% of population
total: 5.4% of population (2015 est.)

Sanitation facility access:
improved:
urban: 84.5% of population
rural: 56.2% of population
total: 76.9% of population
unimproved:
urban: 15.5% of population
rural: 43.8% of population
total: 23.1% of population (2015 est.)

HIV/AIDS—adult prevalence rate: NA

HIV/AIDS—people living with HIV/AIDS: NA

HIV/AIDS—deaths: NA

Major infectious diseases: *note:* active local transmission of Zika virus by Aedes species mosquitoes has been identified in this country (as of August 2016); it poses an important risk (a large number of cases possible) among US citizens if bitten by an infective mosquito; other less common ways to get Zika are through sex, via blood transfusion, or during pregnancy, in which the pregnant woman passes Zika virus to her fetus (2016)

Obesity—adult prevalence rate: 52.9% (2016)
country comparison to the world: 4

Literacy: *definition:* age 15 and over can read and write
total population: 98.3%
male: 98.3%
female: 98.2% (2011 est.)

Unemployment, youth ages 15-24: *total:* 11%
male: 12.2%
female: 8.7% (2010 est.)

GOVERNMENT

Country name: *conventional long form:* Republic of the Marshall Islands
conventional short form: Marshall Islands
local long form: Republic of the Marshall Islands
local short form: Marshall Islands
abbreviation: RMI
former: Trust Territory of the Pacific Islands, Marshall Islands District
etymology: named after British Captain John MARSHALL, who charted many of the islands in 1788

Government type: presidential republic in free association with the US

Capital: *name:* Majuro; *note*—the capital is an atoll of 64 islands; governmental buildings are housed on three fused islands: Djarrit, Uliga, and Delap
geographic coordinates: 7 06 N, 171 23 E
time difference: UTC+12 (17 hours ahead of Washington, DC, during Standard Time)

Administrative divisions: 24 municipalities; Ailinglaplap, Ailuk, Arno, Aur, Bikini & Kili, Ebon, Enewetak & Ujelang, Jabat, Jaluit, Kwajalein, Lae, Lib, Likiep, Majuro, Maloelap, Mejit, Mili, Namdrik, Namu, Rongelap, Ujae, Utrik, Wotho, Wotje

Independence: 21 October 1986 (from the US-administered UN trusteeship)

National holiday: Constitution Day, 1 May (1979)

Constitution: effective 1 May 1979; amended several times, last in 1995 (2016)

Legal system: mixed legal system of US and English common law, customary law, and local statutes

International law organization participation: accepts compulsory ICJ jurisdiction with reservations; accepts ICCt jurisdiction

Citizenship: *citizenship by birth:* no
citizenship by descent only: at least one parent must be a citizen of the Marshall Islands
dual citizenship recognized: no
residency requirement for naturalization: 5 years

Suffrage: 18 years of age; universal

Executive branch: *chief of state:* President Hilda C. HEINE (since 28 January 2016); *note*—the president is both chief of state and head of government

head of government: President Hilda C. HEINE (since 28 January 2016)
cabinet: Cabinet nominated by the president from among members of the Nitijela, appointed by Nitijela speaker

elections/appointments: president indirectly elected by the Nitijela from among its members for a 4-year term (no term limits); election last held on 27 January 2016 (next to be held in 2020)

election results: Hilda C. HEINE elected president; Parliament vote—Hilda C. HEINE 24, she was the only candidate

note: Hilda C. HEINE is the first female elected head of state of any Pacific island nation

Legislative branch: *description:* bicameral legislature consists of the Council of Iroij (12 seats; consists of tribal chiefs chosen by holders of the chieftainship among the constituent islands) and the National Parliament or Nitijela (33 seats; members directly elected by simple majority vote to serve 4-year terms); note—the Council of Iroij advises the Presidential Cabinet and reviews legislation affecting customary law or any traditional practice)

elections: last held on 16 November 2015 (next to be held by November 2019)

election results: percent of vote by party—NA; seats by party—independent 33

Judicial branch: *highest court(s):* Supreme Court (consists of the chief justice and other judges as prescribed by law)

judge selection and term of office: judges appointed by the Cabinet on the recommendation of the Judicial Service Commission and upon the approval of the Nitijela; judges appointed until retirement, normally at age 72

subordinate courts: High Court; District Courts; Traditional Rights Court; Community Courts

Political parties and leaders: traditionally there have been no formally organized political parties; what has existed more closely resembles factions or interest groups because they do not have party headquarters, formal platforms, or party structures; the following two "groupings" have competed in legislative balloting in recent years—Aelon Kein Ad Party [Michael KABUA] and United Democratic Party or UDP [Litokwa TOMEING]

Political pressure groups and leaders: NA

International organization participation: ACP, ADB, AOSIS, FAO, G-77, IAEA, IBRD, ICAO, ICCt, IDA, IFAD, IFC, ILO, IMF, IMO, IMSO, Interpol, IOC, IOM, ITU, OPCW, PIF, Sparteca, SPC, UN, UNCTAD, UNESCO, WHO

Diplomatic representation in the US: *chief of mission:* Ambassador Gerald M. ZACKIOS (since 16 September 2016)

chancery: 2433 Massachusetts Avenue NW, 1st Floor, Washington, DC 20008

telephone: [1] (202) 234-5414

FAX: [1] (202) 232-3236

consulate(s) general: Honolulu, Springdale (AR)

consulate(s): Agana (Guam)

Diplomatic representation from the US: *chief of mission:* Ambassador Karen Brevard STEWART (since 25July 2016)

embassy: Oceanside, Mejen Weto, Long Island, Majuro

mailing address: P. O. Box 1379, Majuro, Republic of the Marshall Islands 96960-1379

telephone: [692] 247-4011

FAX: [692] 247-4012

Flag description: blue with two stripes radiating from the lower hoist-side corner—orange (top) and white; a white star with four large rays and 20 small rays appears on the hoist side above the two stripes; blue represents the Pacific Ocean, the orange stripe signifies the Ralik Chain or sunset and courage, while the white stripe signifies the Ratak Chain or sunrise and peace; the star symbolizes the cross of Christianity, each of the 24 rays designates one of the electoral districts in the country and the four larger rays highlight the principal cultural centers of Majuro, Jaluit, Wotje, and Ebeye; the rising diagonal band can also be interpreted as representing the equator, with the star showing the archipelago's position just to the north

National symbol(s): a 24-rayed star; national colors: blue, white, orange

National anthem: name: "Forever Marshall Islands"

lyrics/music: Amata KABUA

note: adopted 1981

ECONOMY

Economy—overview: US assistance and lease payments for the use of Kwajalein Atoll as a US military base are the mainstay of this small island country. Agricultural production, primarily subsistence, is concentrated on small farms; the most important commercial crops are coconuts and breadfruit. Industry is limited to handicrafts, tuna processing, and copra. Tourism holds some potential. The islands and atolls have few natural resources, and imports exceed exports.

The Marshall Islands received roughly $1 billion in aid from the US during the period 1986-2001 under the original Compact of Free Association (Compact). In 2002 and 2003, the US and the Marshall Islands renegotiated the Compact's financial package for a 20-year period, 2004 to 2024. Under the amended Compact, the Marshall Islands will receive roughly $1.5 billion in direct US assistance. Under the amended Compact, the US and Marshall Islands are also jointly funding a Trust Fund for the people of the Marshall Islands that will provide an income stream beyond 2024, when direct Compact aid ends.

GDP (purchasing power parity): $189 million (2017 est.)

$185.5 million (2016 est.)

$181.8 million (2015 est.)

note: data are in 2017 dollars

country comparison to the world: 222

GDP (official exchange rate): $199 million (2016 est.)

GDP—real growth rate: 1.9% (2017 est.)

2% (2016 est.)

1.9% (2015 est.)

country comparison to the world: 158

GDP—per capita (PPP): $3,400 (2017 est.)

$3,400 (2016 est.)

$3,400 (2015 est.)

note: data are in 2017 dollars

country comparison to the world: 189

GDP—composition, by sector of origin:

agriculture: 4.4%

industry: 9.9%

services: 85.7% (2013 est.)

Agriculture—products: coconuts, tomatoes, melons, taro, breadfruit, fruits; pigs, chickens

Industries: copra, tuna processing, tourism, craft items (from seashells, wood, and pearls)

Industrial production growth rate: NA%

Labor force: 10,670 (2013 est.)

country comparison to the world: 218

Labor force—by occupation: *agriculture:* 11%

industry: 16.3%

services: 72.7% (2011 est.)

Unemployment rate: 36% (2006 est.)

30.9% (2000 est.)

country comparison to the world: 210

Population below poverty line: NA%

Household income or consumption by percentage share: *lowest 10%:* NA%

highest 10%: NA%

Budget: *revenues:* $116.7 million

expenditures: $113.9 million (2013 est.)

Taxes and other revenues: 58.6% of GDP (2013 est.)

country comparison to the world: 8

Budget surplus (+) or deficit (-): 1.4% of GDP (2013 est.)

country comparison to the world: 11

Public debt: 32.2% of GDP (2016 est.)

34.7% of GDP (2015 est.)

country comparison to the world: 156

Fiscal year: 1 October—30 September

Inflation rate (consumer prices): 0.7% (2017 est.)

-1.5% (2016 est.)

country comparison to the world: 25

Current account balance: $12 million (2017 est.)

$17 million (2016 est.)

country comparison to the world: 58

Exports: $0 (2013 est.)

$47.21 million (2015 est.)

country comparison to the world: 224

Exports—commodities: copra cake, coconut oil, handicrafts, fish

Imports: $133.7 million (2013 est.)

$109 million (2015 est.)

country comparison to the world: 209

Imports—commodities: foodstuffs, machinery and equipment, fuels, beverages, tobacco

Debt—external: $97.96 million (2013 est.)

$87 million (2008 est.)

country comparison to the world: 194

Exchange rates: the US dollar is used

ENERGY

Electricity access: *population without electricity:* 30,084

electrification—total population: 59%

electrification—urban areas: 65%

electrification—rural areas: 45% (2012)

Electricity—production: 620 million kWh (2015 est.)
country comparison to the world: 164

Electricity—consumption: 576.6 million kWh (2015 est.)
country comparison to the world: 171

Electricity—exports: 0 kWh (2016 est.)
country comparison to the world: 187

Electricity—imports: 0 kWh (2016 est.)
country comparison to the world: 191

Electricity—installed generating capacity: 52,000 kW (2015 est.)
country comparison to the world: 190

Electricity—from fossil fuels: 80.8% of total installed capacity (2015 est.)
country comparison to the world: 86

Electricity—from nuclear fuels: 0% of total installed capacity (2015 est.)
country comparison to the world: 171

Electricity—from hydroelectric plants: 19.2% of total installed capacity (2015 est.)
country comparison to the world: 91

Electricity—from other renewable sources: 0% of total installed capacity (2015 est.)
country comparison to the world: 203

Crude oil—production: 0 bbl/day (2016 est.)
country comparison to the world: 170

Crude oil—exports: 0 bbl/day (2014 est.)
country comparison to the world: 180

Crude oil—imports: 0 bbl/day (2014 est.)
country comparison to the world: 180

Crude oil—proved reserves: 0 bbl (1 January 2017 es)
country comparison to the world: 167

Refined petroleum products—production: 0 bbl/day (2014 est.)
country comparison to the world: 175

Refined petroleum products—consumption: 2,000 bbl/day (2015 est.)
country comparison to the world: 194

Refined petroleum products—exports: 0 bbl/day (2014 est.)
country comparison to the world: 191

Refined petroleum products—imports: 2,060 bbl/day (2014 est.)
country comparison to the world: 188

Carbon dioxide emissions from consumption of energy: 300,000 Mt (2013 est.)
country comparison to the world: 191

COMMUNICATIONS

Telephones—fixed lines: *total subscriptions:* 2,361
subscriptions per 100 inhabitants: 3 (July 2016 est.)
country comparison to the world: 213

Telephones—mobile cellular: *total:* 16,000
subscriptions per 100 inhabitants: 21 (July 2016 est.)
country comparison to the world: 212

Telephone system: *general assessment:* some telecom infrastructure improvements made in recent years; modern services include telex, cellular, Internet, international calling, caller ID, and leased data circuits
domestic: Majuro Atoll and Ebeye and Kwajalein islands have regular, seven-digit, direct-dial telephones; other islands interconnected by high frequency radiotelephone (used mostly for government purposes) and mini-satellite telephones
international: country code—692; satellite earth stations—2 Intelsat (Pacific Ocean); US Government satellite communications system on Kwajalein (2016)

Broadcast media: no TV broadcast station; a cable network is available on Majuro with programming via videotape replay and satellite relays; 4 radio broadcast stations; American Armed Forces Radio and Television Service (AFRTS) provides satellite radio and television service to Kwajalein Atoll (2009)

Internet country code: .mh
Internet users: total: 21,857

percent of population: 29.8% (July 2016 est.)
country comparison to the world: 210

TRANSPORTATION

National air transport system: *number of registered air carriers:* 1
inventory of registered aircraft operated by air carriers: 1
annual passenger traffic on registered air carriers: 86,868
annual freight traffic on registered air carriers: 0 mt-km (2015)
Civil aircraft registration country code prefix: V7 (2016)

Airports: 15 (2013)
country comparison to the world: 146

Airports—with paved runways: *total:* 4

1,524 to 2,437 m: 3
914 to 1,523 m: 1 (2017)

Airports—with unpaved runways: *total:* 11
914 to 1,523 m: 10
under 914 m: 1 (2013)

Roadways: *total:* 2,028 km
paved: 75 km
note: roads are mostly unimproved (2007)
country comparison to the world: 175

Merchant marine: *total:* 3,199
by type: bulk carrier 1,263, container ship 260, general cargo 80, oil tanker 775, other 821 (2017)
country comparison to the world: 8

Ports and terminals: *major seaport(s):* Enitwetak Island, Kwajalein, Majuro

MILITARY AND SECURITY

Military branches: no regular military forces; Marshall Islands Police (2012)

Military—note: defense is the responsibility of the US

TRANSNATIONAL ISSUES

Disputes—international: claims US territory of Wake Island

Trafficking in persons: current situation: The Marshall Islands is a source and destination country for Marshallese women and girls and women from East Asia subjected to sex trafficking; Marshallese and foreign women are forced into prostitution in businesses frequented by crew members of fishing and transshipping vessels that dock in Majuro; some Chinese women are recruited to the Marshall Islands with promises of legitimate work and are subsequently forced into prostitution

tier rating: Tier 3—The Marshall Islands do not fully comply with the minimum standards for the elimination of trafficking and is not making significant efforts to do so; the government made no anti-trafficking law enforcement efforts, including developing a written plan to combat trafficking; no new trafficking investigations were opened in 2014, and no prosecutions or convictions were made for the fourth consecutive year; no efforts were made to identify trafficking victims, especially among women in prostitution or men working on foreign fishing vessels in Marshallese waters, and no attempt was made to ensure their access to protective services; limited awareness-raising events were conducted by an international organization (2015)

MAURITANIA

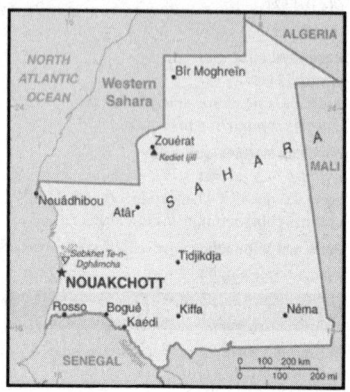

INTRODUCTION

Background: Independent from France in 1960, Mauritania annexed the southern third of the former Spanish Sahara (now Western Sahara) in 1976 but relinquished it after three years of raids by the Polisario guerrilla front seeking independence for the territory. Maaouya Ould Sid Ahmed TAYA seized power in a coup in 1984 and ruled Mauritania with a heavy hand for more than two decades. A series of presidential elections that he held were widely seen as flawed. A bloodless coup in August 2005 deposed President TAYA and ushered in a military council that oversaw a transition to democratic rule. Independent candidate Sidi Ould Cheikh ABDALLAHI was inaugurated in April 2007 as Mauritania's first freely and fairly elected president. His term ended prematurely in August 2008 when a military junta led by General Mohamed Ould Abdel AZIZ deposed him and installed a military council government. AZIZ was subsequently elected president in July 2009 and sworn in the following month. AZIZ sustained injuries from an accidental shooting by his own troops in October 2012 but has continued to maintain his authority. He was reelected in 2014 to a second and final term as president (according to the present constitution). The country continues to experience ethnic tensions among three major groups: Arabic-speaking descendants of slaves (Haratines), Arabic-speaking "White Moors" (Bidhan), and members of Sub-Saharan ethnic groups mostly originating in the Senegal River valley (Halpulaar, Soninke, and Wolof). Mauritania confronts a terrorism threat by al-Qa'ida in the Islamic Maghreb, which launched successful attacks between 2005 and 2011.

The activities of Al-Qaeda in the Islamic Maghreb (AQIM), and similar groups, pose a severe security threat to Mauritanians and foreign visitors. AQIM launched a series of attacks in Mauritania between 2005 and 2011, murdering American and foreign tourists and aid workers, attacking diplomatic and government facilities, and ambushing Mauritanian soldiers and gendarmes. A successful strategy against terrorism that combines dialogue with the terrorists and military actions has prevented the country from further terrorist attacks since 2011.

GEOGRAPHY

Location: Western Africa, bordering the North Atlantic Ocean, between Senegal and Western Sahara

Geographic coordinates: 20 00 N, 12 00 W

Map references: Africa

Area: *total:* 1,030,700 sq km
land: 1,030,700 sq km
water: 0 sq km
country comparison to the world: 30

Area—comparative: slightly larger than three times the size of New Mexico

Land boundaries: *total:* 5,002 km
border countries (4): Algeria 460 km, Mali 2,236 km, Senegal 742 km, Western Sahara 1,564 km

Coastline: 754 km

Maritime claims: *territorial sea:* 12 nm
contiguous zone: 24 nm
exclusive economic zone: 200 nm
continental shelf: 200 nm or to the edge of the continental margin

Climate: desert; constantly hot, dry, dusty

Terrain: mostly barren, flat plains of the Sahara; some central hills

Elevation: *mean elevation:* 276 m

elevation extremes: *lowest point:* Sebkhet Te-n-Dghamcha -5 m
highest point: Kediet Ijill 915 m

Natural resources: iron ore, gypsum, copper, phosphate, diamonds, gold, oil, fish

Land use: *agricultural land:* 38.5%
arable land: 0.4%;
permanent crops: 0%;
permanent pasture: 38.1%
forest: 0.2%
other: 61.3% (2011 est.)
Irrigated land: 450 sq km (2012)

Population—distribution: with most of the country being a desert, vast areas of the country, particularly in the central, northern, and eastern areas, are without sizeable population clusters; half the population lives in or around the coastal capital of Nouakchott; smaller clusters are found near the southern border with Mali and Senegal

Natural hazards: hot, dry, dust/sand-laden sirocco wind primarily in March and April; periodic droughts

Environment—current issues: overgrazing, deforestation, and soil erosion aggravated by drought are contributing to desertification; limited natural freshwater resources away from the Senegal, which is the only perennial river; locust infestation

Environment—international agreements: *party to:* Biodiversity, Climate Change, Climate Change-Kyoto Protocol, Desertification, Endangered Species, Hazardous Wastes, Law of the Sea, Ozone Layer Protection, Ship Pollution, Wetlands, Whaling
signed, but not ratified: none of the selected agreements

Geography—note: Mauritania is considered both a part of North Africa's Maghreb region and West Africa's Sahel region; most of the population is concentrated in the cities of Nouakchott and Nouadhibou and along the Senegal River in the southern part of the country

PEOPLE AND SOCIETY

Population: 3,758,571 (July 2017 est.)
country comparison to the world: 129

Nationality: *noun:* Mauritanian(s)
adjective: Mauritanian

Ethnic groups: black Moors (Haratines—Arab-speaking slaves, former slaves, and their descendants of African origin, enslaved by white Moors) 40%, white Moors (of Arab-Berber descent, known as Bidhan) 30%, Sub-Saharan Mauritanians (non-Arabic speaking, Halpulaar, Soninke, Wolof, and Bamara ethnic groups) 30%

Languages: Arabic (official and national), Pular, Soninke, Wolof (all national languages), French
note: the spoken Arabic in Mauritania differs considerably from the modern standard Arabic used for official written purposes or in the media; the Mauritanian dialect, which incorporates many Berber words, is referred to as Hassaniya

Religions: Muslim (official) 100%

Demographic profile: With a sustained total fertility rate of about 4 children per woman and almost 60% of the population under the age of 25, Mauritania's population is likely to continue growing for the foreseeable future. Mauritania's large youth cohort is vital to its development prospects, but available schooling does not adequately prepare students for the workplace. Girls continue to be underrepresented in the classroom, educational quality remains poor, and the dropout rate is high. The literacy rate is only about 50%, even though access to primary education has improved since the mid-2000s. Women's restricted access to education and discriminatory laws maintain gender inequality—worsened by early and forced marriages and female genital cutting.

The denial of education to black Moors also helps to perpetuate slavery. Although Mauritania abolished slavery in 1981 (the last country in the world to do so) and made it a criminal offense in 2007, the millenniums-old practice persists largely because anti-slavery laws are rarely enforced and the custom is so ingrained. Up to

20% of Mauritania's population is estimated to be enslaved, the highest rate worldwide.

Drought, poverty, and unemployment have driven outmigration from Mauritania since the 1970s. Early flows were directed toward other West African countries, including Senegal, Mali, Cote d'Ivoire, and Gambia. The 1989 Mauritania-Senegal conflict forced thousands of black Mauritanians to take refuge in Senegal and pushed labor migrants toward the Gulf, Libya, and Europe in the late 1980s and early 1990s. Mauritania has accepted migrants from neighboring countries to fill labor shortages since its independence in 1960 and more recently has received refugees escaping civil wars, including tens of thousands of Tuaregs who fled Mali in 2012.

Mauritania was an important transit point for sub-Saharan migrants moving illegally to North Africa and Europe. In the mid-2000s, as border patrols increased in the Strait of Gibraltar, security increased around Spain's North African enclaves (Ceuta and Melilla), and Moroccan border controls intensified, illegal migration flows shifted from the Western Mediterranean to Spain's Canary Islands. In 2006, departure points moved southward along the West African coast from Morocco and Western Sahara to Mauritania's two key ports (Nouadhibou and the capital Nouakchott), and illegal migration to the Canaries peaked at almost 32,000. The numbers fell dramatically in the following years because of joint patrolling off the West African coast by Frontex (the EU's border protection agency), Spain, Mauritania, and Senegal; the expansion of Spain's border surveillance system; and the 2008 European economic downturn.

Age structure: 0-14 years: 38.56% (male 727,855/female 721,508)
15-24 years: 19.81% (male 364,570/female 379,866)
25-54 years: 33.21% (male 578,422/female 669,628)
55-64 years: 4.67% (male 79,162/female 96,297)
65 years and over: 3.76% (male 59,928/female 81,335) (2017 est.)

Dependency ratios: total dependency ratio: 76.5
youth dependency ratio: 71
elderly dependency ratio: 5.5
potential support ratio: 18.3 (2015 est.)

Median age: total: 20.5 years
male: 19.5 years
female: 21.4 years (2017 est.)
country comparison to the world: 189

Population growth rate: 2.17% (2017 est.)
country comparison to the world: 37

Birth rate: 30.4 births/1,000 population (2017 est.)
country comparison to the world: 38

Death rate: 7.9 deaths/1,000 population (2017 est.)
country comparison to the world: 95

Net migration rate: -0.8 migrant(s)/1,000 population (2017 est.)
country comparison to the world: 132

Population distribution: with most of the country being a desert, vast areas of the country, particularly in the central, northern, and eastern areas, are without sizeable population clusters; half the population lives in or around the coastal capital of Nouakchott; smaller clusters are found near the southern border with Mali and Senegal

Urbanization: urban population: 61% of total population (2017)
rate of urbanization: 3.2% annual rate of change (2015-20 est.)

Major urban areas—population: NOUAKCHOTT (capital) 968,000 (2015)

Sex ratio: at birth: 1.03 male(s)/female
0-14 years: 1.01 male(s)/female
15-24 years: 0.96 male(s)/female
25-54 years: 0.86 male(s)/female
55-64 years: 0.82 male(s)/female
65 years and over: 0.74 male(s)/female
total population: 0.93 male(s)/female (2016 est.)

Maternal mortality ratio: 602 deaths/100,000 live births (2015 est.)
country comparison to the world: 14

Infant mortality rate: total: 51.9 deaths/1,000 live births
male: 56.7 deaths/1,000 live births
female: 46.9 deaths/1,000 live births (2017 est.)
country comparison to the world: 26

Life expectancy at birth: total population: 63.4 years
male: 61.1 years
female: 65.8 years (2017 est.)
country comparison to the world: 193

Total fertility rate: 3.86 children born/woman (2017 est.)
country comparison to the world: 39

Contraceptive prevalence rate: 17.8% (2015)

Health expenditures: 3.8% of GDP (2014)
country comparison to the world: 166

Physicians density: 0.13 physicians/1,000 population (2009)

Hospital bed density: 0.4 beds/1,000 population (2006)

Drinking water source:
improved:
urban: 58.4% of population
rural: 57.1% of population
total: 57.9% of population
unimproved:
urban: 41.6% of population
rural: 42.9% of population
total: 42.1% of population (2015 est.)

Sanitation facility access:
improved:
urban: 57.5% of population
rural: 13.8% of population
total: 40% of population
unimproved:
urban: 42.5% of population
rural: 86.2% of population
total: 60% of population (2015 est.)

HIV/AIDS—adult prevalence rate: 0.5% (2016 est.)

country comparison to the world: 62

HIV/AIDS—people living with HIV/AIDS: 11,000 (2016 est.)
country comparison to the world: 93

HIV/AIDS—deaths: <1000 (2016 est.)

Major infectious diseases: degree of risk: very high
food or waterborne diseases: bacterial and protozoal diarrhea, hepatitis A, and typhoid fever
vectorborne diseases: malaria and dengue fever
respiratory disease: meningococcal meningitis
animal contact disease: rabies (2016)

Obesity—adult prevalence rate: 12.7% (2016)
country comparison to the world: 132

Children under the age of 5 years underweight: 24.9% (2015)
country comparison to the world: 32

Education expenditures: 2.9% of GDP (2013)
country comparison to the world: 120

Literacy: definition: age 15 and over can read and write
total population: 52.1%
male: 62.6%
female: 41.6% (2015 est.)

School life expectancy (primary to tertiary education): total: 9 years
male: 9 years
female: 9 years (2015)

GOVERNMENT

Country name: conventional long form: Islamic Republic of Mauritania
conventional short form: Mauritania
local long form: Al Jumhuriyah al Islamiyah al Muritaniyah
local short form: Muritaniyah
etymology: named for the ancient kingdom of Mauretania (3rd century B.C. to 1st century A.D.), which existed further north in present-day Morocco; the name derives from the Mauri (Moors), the Berber-speaking peoples of northwest Africa

Government type: presidential republic

Capital: name: Nouakchott

geographic coordinates: 18 04 N, 15 58 W
time difference: UTC 0 (5 hours ahead of Washington, DC, during Standard Time)

Administrative divisions: 15 regions (wilayas, singular—wilaya); Adrar, Assaba, Brakna, Dakhlet Nouadhibou, Gorgol, Guidimaka, Hodh ech Chargui, Hodh El Gharbi, Inchiri, Nouakchott Nord, Nouakchott Ouest, Nouakchott Sud, Tagant, Tiris Zemmour, Trarza

Independence: 28 November 1960 (from France)

National holiday: Independence Day, 28 November (1960)

Constitution: history: previous 1964; latest adopted 12 July 1991
amendments: proposed by the president of the republic or by either house of Parliament; consideration of amendments by Parliament requires approval of at least one-third of the membership

599

THE CIA WORLD FACTBOOK

of either house; a referendum is held only if it is approved by two-thirds majority vote in both houses; passage by referendum requires simple majority vote by eligible voters; passage of amendments proposed by the president can bypass a referendum if approved by at least three-fifths majority vote by Parliament in joint session; amended 2004, 2006, 2017 (2017)

Legal system: mixed legal system of Islamic and French civil law

International law organization participation: has not submitted an ICJ jurisdiction declaration; non-party state to the ICCt

Citizenship: *citizenship by birth:* no
citizenship by descent only: at least one parent must be a citizen of Mauritania
dual citizenship recognized: no
residency requirement for naturalization: 5 years

Suffrage: 18 years of age; universal

Executive branch: *chief of state:* President Mohamed Ould Abdel AZIZ (since 5 August 2009); note—AZIZ deposed President Sidi Ould Cheikh ABDELLAHI in a coup and installed himself as president in August 2008; he subsequently retired from the military, stepped down from the appropriated presidency in April 2009 to run for the legitimate presidency; he was elected president in July 2009 and reelected in June 2014

head of government: Prime Minister Yahya Ould HADEMINE (since 21 August 2014)
cabinet: Council of Ministers appointed by the president
elections/appointments: president directly elected by absolute majority popular vote in 2 rounds if needed for a 5-year term (eligible for a second term); election last held on 21 June 2014 (next to be held by 2019); prime minister appointed by the president
election results: Mohamed Ould Abdel AZIZ elected president in first round; percent of vote—Mohamed Ould Abdel AZIZ (UPR) 81.9%, Biram Dah ABEID (IRA) 8.7%, Boidiel Ould HOUMEIT (El Wiam) 4.5%, Ibrahima Moctar SARR (SJD/MR) 4.4%, other 0.5%

Legislative branch: *description:* unicameral Parliament or Barlamane consists of the National Assembly or Al Jamiya Al Wataniya (147 seats; 107 members directly elected in single- and two-seat constituencies by absolute majority vote in 2 rounds if needed and 40 directly elected in constituencies with 3 or more seats by proportional representation vote; members serve a 5-year term); note—a referendum in August 2017 approved a constitutional amendment to change the Parliament structure from bicameral to unicameral by abolishing the Senate
elections: Senate—last held on 23 November 2013 (next election scheduled for 2015 but delayed because of opposition party threats to boycott election); National Assembly—first round last held on 23 November and second round on 21 December 2013 (next to be held in 2018)
election results: Senate—percent of vote by party—NA; seats by party—NA; National Assembly—percent of vote by party—NA; seats

by party—UPR 75, RNRD-TAWASSOUL 16, El Wiam 10, APP 7, El Karama Party 6, UDP 6, AJD/MR 4, Burst of Youth for the Nation 4, El Vadila Party 3, PRDR 3, PUD 3, Ravah Party 3, other 6; note—parties winning fewer than 3 seats sit as independents unless they join a coalition

Judicial branch: *highest court(s):* Supreme Court or Cour Supreme (subdivided into 1 criminal and 2 civil chambers, each with a president and 5 counselors); Constitutional Council (consists of 6 members)
judge selection and term of office: Supreme Court president appointed by the president of the republic to serve a 5-year renewable term; Constitutional Council members appointed—3 by the president of the republic, 2 by the president of the National Assembly, and 1 by the president of the Senate; members serve single, 9-year terms with one-third of membership renewed every 3 years
subordinate courts: High Court of Justice (cases involving treason and criminal acts of high government officials, including the president); courts of appeal; wilaya (regional) courts (located at the headquarters of each of the 13 regions); commercial and labor courts; criminal courts; moughataa (district) courts; informal/customary courts

Political parties and leaders: Alliance for Justice and Democracy/Movement for Renewal or AJD/MR [Ibrahima Moctar SARR]
Burst of Youth for the Nation [Lalla CHERIVA]
Coalition for Pacific Alternation or CAP (coalition of opposition parties, including APP, El Wiam)
Coalition of Majority Parties or CPM (includes UPR, UDP)
Coordination of Democratic Opposition or COD [Ahmed Ould DADDAH] (coalition includes RNRD-TAWASSOUL)
El Karama Party [Cheikhna Ould Mohamed Ould HAJBOU]
El Vadila Party [Ethmane Ould Ahmed ABOULMAALY]
El Wiam [Boidiel Ould HOUMEIT]
Initiative for the Resurgence of the Abolitionist Movement [Biram Dah ABEID]
National Rally for Reform and Development or RNRD-TAWASSOUL [Mohamed Mahmoud Ould SEYIDI]
Party for Liberty, Equality and Justice [Ba ALASSANE]
Party of Unity and Development or PUD [Mohamed BARO]
Popular Progressive Alliance or APP [Messaoud Ould BOULKHEIR]
Ravah Party
Republican Party for Democracy and Renewal or PRDR [Sidi Mohamed Ould Mohamed VALL]
Union for Democracy and Progress or UDP [Naha Mint MOUKNASS]
Union for Progress [Mohamed Ould MAOULOUD]
Union for the Republic or UPR [Sidi Mohamed Ould MAHAM]

Political pressure groups and leaders: Association of Women Heads of Household [Aminetou Mint ElMOCTAR]
General Confederation of Mauritanian Workers or CGTM [Abdallahi Ould MOHAMED]

Independent Confederation of Mauritanian Workers or CLTM and El Hor [Samory Ould BEYE] (civil society organization, anti-slavery)
Initiative for Resurgent Abolitionist Movement or IRA-Mauritania [Biram Dah ABEID] (US-based, anti-slavery group)
Mauritanian Human Rights Association or AMDH [Fatimata M'BAYE]
Mauritanian Workers Union or UTM [Mohamed Ely Ould BRAHIM]
National Forum for Democracy and Unity [Mohamed Jamil Ould MANSOUR]
SOS-Esclaves [Boubacar Ould MESSAOUD] (anti-slavery)
other: Arab nationalists; Ba'athists; Islamists; Nasserists

International organization participation: ABEDA, ACP, AfDB, AFESD, AMF, AMU, AU, CAEU (candidate), EITI (compliant country), FAO, G-77, IAEA, IBRD, ICAO, ICC (NGOs), ICRM, IDA, IDB, IFAD, IFC, IFRCS, IHO (pending member), ILO, IMF, IMO, Interpol, IOC, IOM, IPU, ISO (correspondent), ITSO, ITU, ITUC (NGOs), LAS, MIGA, MIUSMA, NAM, OIC, OIF, OPCW, UN, UNCTAD, UNESCO, UNIDO, UNWTO, UPU, WCO, WHO, WIPO, WMO, WTO

Diplomatic representation in the US: *chief of mission:* Ambassador Mohamedoun DADDAH (since 27 June 2016)
chancery: 2129 Leroy Place NW, Washington, DC 20008
telephone: [1] (202) 232-5700 through 5701
FAX: [1] (202) 319-2623

Diplomatic representation from the US: *chief of mission:* Ambassador Larry Edward ANDRE, Jr. (since 3 November 2014)
embassy: 288, rue 42-100 (rue Abdallaye), Nouakchott
mailing address: B.P. 222, Nouakchott
telephone: [222] 4525-2660 or [222] 2660-2663
FAX: [222] 4525-1592

Flag description: green with a yellow five-pointed star above a yellow, horizontal crescent; the closed side of the crescent is down; the crescent, star, and color green are traditional symbols of Islam; green also represents hope for a bright future; the yellow color stands for the sands of the Sahara

National symbol(s): star and crescent; national colors: green, yellow

National anthem: *name:* "Hymne National de la Republique Islamique de Mauritanie" (National Anthem of the Islamic Republic of Mauritania)
lyrics/music: Baba Ould CHEIKH/traditional, arranged by Tolia NIKIPROWETZKY
note: adopted 1960; the unique rhythm of the Mauritanian anthem makes it particularly challenging to sing

ECONOMY

Economy—overview: Mauritania's economy is dominated by extractive industries (oil and mines), fisheries and agriculture. Half the population still depends on farming and raising livestock, even though many nomads and subsistence farmers were forced into the cities by recurrent droughts in the 1970s, 1980s and 2000s. Recently, GDP growth has been driven largely by foreign investment in the mining and oil sectors.

Mauritania's extensive mineral resources include iron ore, gold, copper, gypsum, and phosphate rock, and exploration is ongoing for tantalum, uranium, crude oil, and natural gas. Extractive commodities make up about three-quarters of Mauritania's total exports, subjecting the economy to price swings in world commodity markets. Mining is also a growing source of government revenue, rising from 13% to 30% of total revenue from 2006 to 2016. The nation's coastal waters are among the richest fishing areas in the world, and fishing accounts for about 20% of budget revenues, 45% of foreign currency earnings. Mauritania processes a total of 1,800,000 tons of fish per year, but overexploitation by foreign and national fleets threaten the sustainability of this key source of revenue.

The economy is highly sensitive to international food and extractive commodity prices. Other risks to Mauritania's economy include its recurring droughts, dependence on foreign aid and investment, and insecurity in neighboring Mali, as well as significant shortages of infrastructure, institutional capacity, and human capital. Mauritania has sought additional IMF support by focusing efforts on poverty reduction. Investment in agriculture and infrastructure are the largest components of the country's public expenditures.

GDP (purchasing power parity): $17.37 billion (2017 est.)
$16.74 billion (2016 est.)
$16.45 billion (2015 est.)
note: data are in 2017 dollars
country comparison to the world: 155

GDP (official exchange rate): $4.985 billion (2016 est.)

GDP—real growth rate: 3.8% (2017 est.)
1.7% (2016 est.)
0.9% (2015 est.)
country comparison to the world: 79

GDP—per capita (PPP): $4,500 (2017 est.)
$4,400 (2016 est.)
$4,400 (2015 est.)
note: data are in 2017 dollars
country comparison to the world: 175

Gross national saving: 28.1% of GDP (2017 est.)
24.7% of GDP (2016 est.)
18.9% of GDP (2015 est.)
country comparison to the world: 35

GDP—composition, by end use:
household consumption: 56.9%
government consumption: 19.1%
investment in fixed capital: 48.6%
investment in inventories: 21.7%
exports of goods and services: 30.1%
imports of goods and services: -76.4% (2017 est.)

GDP—composition, by sector of origin:
agriculture: 22.5%
industry: 37.8%

services: 39.7% (2017 est.)

Agriculture—products: dates, millet, sorghum, rice, corn; cattle, camel and sheep

Industries: fish processing, oil production, mining (iron ore, gold, copper)
note: gypsum deposits have never been exploited

Industrial production growth rate: 0.7% (2017 est.)
country comparison to the world: 177

Labor force: 1.437 million (2017 est.)
country comparison to the world: 134

Labor force—by occupation: *agriculture:* 50%
industry: 1.9%
services: 48.1% (2014 est.)

Unemployment rate: 11.7% (2016 est.)
11.7% (2016 est.)
country comparison to the world: 151

Population below poverty line: 31% (2014 est.)

Household income or consumption by percentage share: *lowest 10%:* 2.5%
highest 10%: 29.5% (2000)

Distribution of family income—Gini index: 37 (2014)
39 (2006 est.)
country comparison to the world: 80

Budget: *revenues:* $1.248 billion
expenditures: $1.301 billion (2017 est.)
Taxes and other revenues: 25% of GDP (2017 est.)
country comparison to the world: 114

Budget surplus (+) or deficit (-): -1.1% of GDP (2017 est.)
country comparison to the world: 61

Public debt: 99.6% of GDP (2016 est.)
98.4% of GDP (2015 est.)
country comparison to the world: 17

Fiscal year: calendar year

Inflation rate (consumer prices): 2.1% (2017 est.)
1.5% (2016 est.)
country comparison to the world: 93

Central bank discount rate: 9% (31 December 2009)
12% (31 December 2007)
country comparison to the world: 32

Commercial bank prime lending rate: 17% (31 December 2017 est.)
17% (31 December 2016 est.)
country comparison to the world: 27

Stock of domestic credit: $1.451 billion (31 December 2017 est.)
$1.495 billion (31 December 2016 est.)
country comparison to the world: 158

Market value of publicly traded shares: $NA

Current account balance: -$709 million (2017 est.)
-$707 million (2016 est.)
country comparison to the world: 113

Exports: $1.606 billion (2017 est.)
$1.401 billion (2016 est.)
country comparison to the world: 149

Exports—commodities: iron ore, fish and fish products, livestock, gold, copper, crude oil

Exports—partners: China 36.9%, Switzerland 13.5%, Spain 8.9%, Japan 7.5%, Russia 4.8%, Nigeria 4.1%, Italy 4.1% (2016)

Imports: $2.097 billion (2017 est.)
$1.9 billion (2016 est.)
country comparison to the world: 157

Imports—commodities: machinery and equipment, petroleum products, capital goods, foodstuffs, consumer goods

Imports—partners: US 13.4%, UAE 11.9%, Belgium 9.2%, China 8.9%, Netherlands 7.1%, France 6.6%, Morocco 6.3%, Vanuatu 5% (2016)

Debt—external: $4.117 billion (31 December 2017 est.)
$3.899 billion (31 December 2016 est.)
country comparison to the world: 139

Exchange rates: ouguiyas (MRO) per US dollar—
363.6 (2017 est.)
352.37 (2016 est.)
352.37 (2015 est.)
319.7 (2014 est.)
299.5 (2013 est.)

ENERGY

Electricity access: *population without electricity:* 2,800,000
electrification—total population: 28%
electrification—urban areas: 47%
electrification—rural areas: 2% (2013)

Electricity—production: 1.191 billion kWh (2015 est.)
country comparison to the world: 148

Electricity—consumption: 1.108 billion kWh (2015 est.)
country comparison to the world: 154

Electricity—exports: 0 kWh (2016 est.)
country comparison to the world: 170

Electricity—imports: 0 kWh (2016 est.)
country comparison to the world: 175

Electricity—installed generating capacity: 412,000 kW (2015 est.)
country comparison to the world: 151

Electricity—from fossil fuels: 63.8% of total installed capacity (2015 est.)
country comparison to the world: 118

Electricity—from nuclear fuels: 0% of total installed capacity (2015 est.)
country comparison to the world: 144

Electricity—from hydroelectric plants: 23.5% of total installed capacity (2015 est.)
country comparison to the world: 82

Electricity—from other renewable sources: 16.7% of total installed capacity (2015 est.)
country comparison to the world: 40

Crude oil—production: 5,000 bbl/day (2016 est.)
country comparison to the world: 81

Crude oil—exports: 6,750 bbl/day (2014 est.)
country comparison to the world: 61

Crude oil—imports: 0 bbl/day (2014 est.)
country comparison to the world: 162

Crude oil—proved reserves: 20 million bbl (1 January 2017 es)
country comparison to the world: 86

Refined petroleum products—production: 0 bbl/day (2014 est.)
country comparison to the world: 176

Refined petroleum products—consumption: 16,000 bbl/day (2015 est.)
country comparison to the world: 147

Refined petroleum products—exports: 0 bbl/day (2014 est.)
country comparison to the world: 181

Refined petroleum products—imports: 16,390 bbl/day (2014 est.)
country comparison to the world: 124

Natural gas—production: 0 cu m (2013 est.)
country comparison to the world: 171

Natural gas—consumption: 0 cu m (2013 est.)
country comparison to the world: 210

Natural gas—exports: 0 cu m (2013 est.)
country comparison to the world: 152

Natural gas—imports: 0 cu m (2013 est.)
country comparison to the world: 157

Natural gas—proved reserves: 28.32 billion cu m (1 January 2017 es)
country comparison to the world: 72

Carbon dioxide emissions from consumption of energy: 2.4 million Mt (2013 est.)
country comparison to the world: 147

COMMUNICATIONS

Telephones—fixed lines: *total subscriptions:* 53,191
subscriptions per 100 inhabitants: 1 (July 2016 est.)
country comparison to the world: 160

Telephones—mobile cellular: *total:* 3,614,172
subscriptions per 100 inhabitants: 98 (July 2016 est.)
country comparison to the world: 126

Telephone system: *general assessment:* limited system of cable and open-wire lines, minor microwave radio relay links, and radiotelephone communications stations; mobile-cellular services expanding rapidly
domestic: fixed-line teledensity 1 per 100 persons; mobile-cellular network coverage extends mainly to urban areas with a teledensity of roughly 100 per 100 persons; mostly cable and open-wire lines; a domestic satellite telecommunications system links Nouakchott with regional capitals
international: country code—222; satellite earth stations—3 (1 Intelsat—Atlantic Ocean, 2 Arabsat); fiber-optic and asymmetric digital subscriber line cables for Internet access (2016)

Broadcast media: 1 state-run TV (Television de Mauritanie) and one state-run radio network (Radio de Mauritanie); Television de Mauritanie

has three channels, Al Mahadra station (for Islamic content) and Channels 1 and 2, which cover news, sports, and other programming; Radio de Mauritanie runs 12 regional stations, as well as a radio station for youth and the Holy Quran station; five private TV channels and five private radio stations also broadcast from Mauritania; six private international radio stations broadcast in Mauritania on the FM band; with satellite connections, Mauritanians also have access to hundreds of foreign TV channels (2013)

Internet country code: .mr
Internet users: total: 661,913

percent of population: 18.0% (July 2016 est.)
country comparison to the world: 134

TRANSPORTATION

National air transport system: *number of registered air carriers:* 1
inventory of registered aircraft operated by air carriers: 4
annual passenger traffic on registered air carriers: 248,158
annual freight traffic on registered air carriers: 0 mt-km (2015)
Civil aircraft registration country code prefix: 5T (2016)

Airports: 30 (2013)
country comparison to the world: 116

Airports—with paved runways: *total:* 9
2,438 to 3,047 m: 5
1,524 to 2,437 m: 4 (2017)

Airports—with unpaved runways: *total:* 21
2,438 to 3,047 m: 1
1,524 to 2,437 m: 10
914 to 1,523 m: 8
under 914 m: 2 (2013)

Railways: *total:* 728 km
standard gauge: 728 km 1.435-m gauge (2014)
country comparison to the world: 99

Roadways: *total:* 10,628 km
paved: 3,158 km
unpaved: 7,470 km (2010)
country comparison to the world: 133

Waterways: (some navigation possible on the Senegal River) (2011)

Merchant marine: *total:* 6
by type: bulk carrier 1, general cargo 2, other 3 (2017)
country comparison to the world: 154

Ports and terminals: *major seaport(s):* Nouadhibou, Nouakchott

MILITARY AND SECURITY

Military expenditures: 2.97% of GDP (2016)
2.75% of GDP (2015)
2.7% of GDP (2014)
2.56% of GDP (2013)
2.72% of GDP (2012)

Military branches: Mauritanian Armed Forces: Army, Mauritanian Navy (Marine Mauritanienne; includes naval infantry), Islamic Republic of Mauritania Air Group (Groupement Aerienne Islamique de Mauritanie, GAIM) (2013)

Military service age and obligation: 18 is the legal minimum age for voluntary military service; no conscription (2012)

TERRORISM

Terrorist groups—foreign based: *al-Qaida in the Islamic Maghreb (AQIM):* aim(s): replace the Mauritanian Government with Sharia and, ultimately, establish a regional Islamic caliphate across all of North and West Africa
area(s) of operation: maintains a heavy operational presence throughout the country, especially in the central and northwestern regions; AQIM is Mauritania's leading terrorist threat

TRANSNATIONAL ISSUES

Disputes—international: Mauritanian claims to Western Sahara remain dormant

Refugees and internally displaced persons: refugees (country of origin): 26,001 (Western Saharan—Sahrawis) (2016); 49,825 (Mali) (2017)

Trafficking in persons: current situation: Mauritania is a source and destination country for men, women, and children subjected to forced labor and sex trafficking; adults and children from traditional slave castes are subjected to slavery-related practices rooted in ancestral master-slave relationships; Mauritanian boy students called talibes are trafficked within the country by religious teachers for forced begging; Mauritanian girls, as well as girls from Mali, Senegal, The Gambia, and other West African countries, are forced into domestic servitude; Mauritanian women and girls are forced into prostitution domestically or transported to countries in the Middle East for the same purpose, sometimes through forced marriages

tier rating: Tier 3—Mauritania does not fully comply with the minimum standards for the elimination of trafficking and is not making significant efforts to do so; anti-trafficking law enforcement efforts were negligible; one slavery case identified by an NGO was investigated, but no prosecutions or convictions were made, including among the 4,000 child labor cases NGOs referred to the police; the 2007 anti-slavery law remains ineffective because it requires slaves, most of whom are illiterate, to file their own legal complaint, and the government agency that can submit claims on them did not file any in 2014; authorities arrested, prosecuted, and convicted several anti-slavery activists; NGOs continued to provide the majority of protective services to trafficking victims without support from the government; some steps were taken to raise public awareness about human trafficking (2015)

MAURITIUS

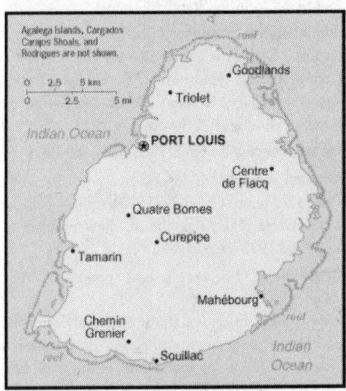

INTRODUCTION

Background: Although known to Arab and Malay sailors as early as the 10th century, Mauritius was first explored by the Portuguese in the 16th century and subsequently settled by the Dutch—who named it in honor of Prince Maurits van NASSAU—in the 17th century. The French assumed control in 1715, developing the island into an important naval base overseeing Indian Ocean trade, and establishing a plantation economy of sugar cane. The British captured the island in 1810, during the Napoleonic Wars. Mauritius remained a strategically important British naval base, and later an air station, playing an important role during World War II for anti-submarine and convoy operations, as well as the collection of signals intelligence. Independence from the UK was attained in 1968. A stable democracy with regular free elections and a positive human rights record, the country has attracted considerable foreign investment and has one of Africa's highest per capita incomes.

GEOGRAPHY

Location: Southern Africa, island in the Indian Ocean, about 800 km (500 mi) east of Madagascar

Geographic coordinates: 20 17 S, 57 33 E

Map references: Africa

Area: *total:* 2,040 sq km
land: 2,030 sq km
water: 10 sq km
note: includes Agalega Islands, Cargados Carajos Shoals (Saint Brandon), and Rodrigues
country comparison to the world: 181

Area—comparative: almost 11 times the size of Washington, DC

Land boundaries: 0 km

Coastline: 177 km

Maritime claims: measured from claimed archipelagic straight baselines
territorial sea: 12 nm

exclusive economic zone: 200 nm
continental shelf: 200 nm or to the edge of the continental margin

Climate: tropical, modified by southeast trade winds; warm, dry winter (May to November); hot, wet, humid summer (November to May)

Terrain: small coastal plain rising to discontinuous mountains encircling central plateau

Elevation: *mean elevation:* NA

elevation extremes: *lowest point:* Indian Ocean 0 m

highest point: Mont Piton 828 m

Natural resources: arable land, fish

Land use: *agricultural land:* 43.8%
arable land: 38.4%;
permanent crops: 2%;
permanent pasture: 3.4%
forest: 17.3%
other: 38.9% (2011 est.)
Irrigated land: 190 sq km (2012)

Population—distribution: population density is one of the highest in the world; urban cluster are found throught the main island, with a greater density in and around Port Luis; population on Rodrigues Island is spread across the island with a slightly denser cluster on the north coast

Natural hazards: cyclones (November to April); almost completely surrounded by reefs that may pose maritime hazards

Environment—current issues: water pollution, degradation of coral reefs

Environment—international agreements: *party to:* Antarctic-Marine Living Resources, Biodiversity, Climate Change, Climate Change-Kyoto Protocol, Desertification, Endangered Species, Environmental Modification, Hazardous Wastes, Law of the Sea, Marine Life Conservation, Ozone Layer Protection, Ship Pollution, Wetlands
signed, but not ratified: none of the selected agreements

Geography—note: the main island, from which the country derives its name, is of volcanic origin and is almost entirely surrounded by coral reefs; former home of the dodo, a large flightless bird related to pigeons, driven to extinction by the end of the 17th century through a combination of hunting and the introduction of predatory species

PEOPLE AND SOCIETY

Population: 1,356,388 (July 2017 est.)
country comparison to the world: 156

Nationality: *noun:* Mauritian(s)
adjective: Mauritian

Ethnic groups: Indo-Mauritian (compose approximately two thirds of the total population), Creole, Sino-Mauritian, Franco-Mauritian
note: Mauritius has not had a question on ethnicity on its national census since 1972

Languages: Creole 86.5%, Bhojpuri 5.3%, French 4.1%, two languages 1.4%, other 2.6% (includes English, the official language of the National Assembly, which is spoken by less than 1% of the population), unspecified 0.1% (2011 est.)

Religions: Hindu 48.5%, Roman Catholic 26.3%, Muslim 17.3%, other Christian 6.4%, other 0.6%, none 0.7%, unspecified 0.1% (2011 est.)

Demographic profile: Mauritius has transitioned from a country of high fertility and high mortality rates in the 1950s and mid-1960s to one with among the lowest population growth rates in the developing world today. After World War II, Mauritius' population began to expand quickly due to increased fertility and a dramatic drop in mortality rates as a result of improved health care and the eradication of malaria. This period of heightened population growth—reaching about 3% a year—was followed by one of the world's most rapid birth rate declines.

The total fertility rate fell from 6.2 children per women in 1963 to 3.2 in 1972—largely the result of improved educational attainment, especially among young women, accompanied by later marriage and the adoption of family planning methods. The family planning programs' success was due to support from the government and eventually the traditionally pronatalist religious communities, which both recognized that controlling population growth was necessary because of Mauritius' small size and limited resources. Mauritius' fertility rate has consistently been below replacement level since the late 1990s, a rate that is substantially lower than nearby countries in southern Africa.

With no indigenous population, Mauritius' ethnic mix is a product of more than two centuries of European colonialism and continued international labor migration. Sugar production relied on slave labor mainly from Madagascar, Mozambique, and East Africa from the early 18th century until its abolition in 1835, when slaves were replaced with indentured Indians. Most of the influx of indentured labor—peaking between the late 1830s and early 1860—settled permanently creating massive population growth of more than 7% a year and reshaping the island's social and cultural composition. While Indians represented about 12% of Mauritius' population in 1837, they and their descendants accounted for roughly two-thirds by the end of the 19th century. Most were Hindus, but the majority of the free Indian traders were Muslims.

Mauritius again turned to overseas labor when its success in clothing and textile exports led to a labor shortage in the mid-1980s. Clothing manufacturers brought in contract workers (increasingly women) from China, India, and, to a lesser extent Bangladesh and Madagascar, who worked longer hours for lower wages under poor conditions and were viewed as more productive than locals. Downturns in the sugar and textile industries in the mid-2000s and a lack of highly qualified domestic workers for Mauritius' growing services sector led to the emigration of low-skilled workers and a reliance on skilled foreign labor. Since 2007, Mauritius has pursued a circular migration program to enable citizens to acquire new skills and savings abroad and then return home to start businesses and to invest in the country's development.

Age structure: *0-14 years:* 20.16% (male 139,721/female 133,765)
15-24 years: 14.8% (male 101,453/female 99,288)
25-54 years: 43.74% (male 296,795/female 296,485)
55-64 years: 11.59% (male 74,650/female 82,585)
65 years and over: 9.71% (male 53,985/female 77,661) (2017 est.)

Dependency ratios: *total dependency ratio:* 41.6
youth dependency ratio: 27.5
elderly dependency ratio: 14.1
potential support ratio: 7.1 (2015 est.)

Median age: *total:* 35.3 years
male: 34.2 years
female: 36.3 years (2017 est.)
country comparison to the world: 77

Population growth rate: 0.59% (2017 est.)
country comparison to the world: 149

Birth rate: 13 births/1,000 population (2017 est.)
country comparison to the world: 153

Death rate: 7.1 deaths/1,000 population (2017 est.)
country comparison to the world: 127

Net migration rate: 0 migrant(s)/1,000 population (2017 est.)
country comparison to the world: 91

Population distribution: population density is one of the highest in the world; urban cluster are found throught the main island, with a greater density in and around Port Luis; population on Rodrigues Island is spread across the island with a slightly denser cluster on the north coast

Urbanization: *urban population:* 39.4% of total population (2017)
rate of urbanization: 0.07% annual rate of change (2015-20 est.)

Major urban areas—population: PORT LOUIS (capital) 135,000 (2014)

Sex ratio: *at birth:* 1.05 male(s)/female
0-14 years: 1.04 male(s)/female
15-24 years: 1.02 male(s)/female
25-54 years: 1 male(s)/female
55-64 years: 0.9 male(s)/female
65 years and over: 0.68 male(s)/female
total population: 0.97 male(s)/female (2016 est.)

Maternal mortality ratio: 53 deaths/100,000 live births (2015 est.)
country comparison to the world: 93

Infant mortality rate: *total:* 9.8 deaths/1,000 live births
male: 11.6 deaths/1,000 live births
female: 7.9 deaths/1,000 live births (2017 est.)
country comparison to the world: 140

Life expectancy at birth: *total population:* 75.8 years
male: 72.4 years
female: 79.5 years (2017 est.)
country comparison to the world: 98

Total fertility rate: 1.75 children born/woman (2017 est.)
country comparison to the world: 160

Contraceptive prevalence rate: 63.8% (2014)

Health expenditures: 4.8% of GDP (2014)
country comparison to the world: 148

Physicians density: 1.93 physicians/1,000 population (2014)

Hospital bed density: 3.4 beds/1,000 population (2011)

Drinking water source:
improved:
urban: 99.9% of population
rural: 99.8% of population
total: 99.9% of population
unimproved:
urban: 0.1% of population
rural: 0.2% of population
total: 0.1% of population (2015 est.)

Sanitation facility access:
improved:
urban: 93.9% of population
rural: 92.6% of population
total: 93.1% of population
unimproved:
urban: 6.1% of population
rural: 7.4% of population
total: 6.9% of population (2015 est.)

HIV/AIDS—adult prevalence rate: NA

HIV/AIDS—people living with HIV/AIDS: NA

HIV/AIDS—deaths: NA

Obesity—adult prevalence rate: 10.8% (2016)
country comparison to the world: 137

Education expenditures: 5% of GDP (2015)
country comparison to the world: 123

Literacy: *definition:* age 15 and over can read and write
total population: 92.7%
male: 94.9%
female: 90.7% (2015 est.)

School life expectancy (primary to tertiary education): *total:* 15 years
male: 14 years
female: 15 years (2015)

Unemployment, youth ages 15-24: *total:* 26.3%
male: 21.6%
female: 32.7% (2015 est.)
country comparison to the world: 41

GOVERNMENT

Country name: *conventional long form:* Republic of Mauritius
conventional short form: Mauritius
local long form: Republic of Mauritius
local short form: Mauritius
etymology: island named after Prince Maurice VAN NASSAU, stadtholder of the Dutch Republic, in 1598

Government type: parliamentary republic

Capital: *name:* Port Louis

geographic coordinates: 20 09 S, 57 29 E
time difference: UTC+4 (9 hours ahead of Washington, DC, during Standard Time)

Administrative divisions: 9 districts and 3 dependencies*; Agalega Islands*, Black River, Cargados Carajos Shoals*, Flacq, Grand Port, Moka, Pamplemousses, Plaines Wilhems, Port Louis, Riviere du Rempart, Rodrigues*, Savanne

Independence: 12 March 1968 (from the UK)

National holiday: Independence and Republic Day, 12 March (1968 & 1992); note—became independent and a republic on the same date in 1968 and 1992 respectively

Constitution: *history:* several previous; latest adopted 12 March 1968
amendments: proposed by the National Assembly; passage of amendments affecting constitutional articles including the sovereignty of the state, fundamental rights and freedoms, citizenship, or the branches of government requires approval in a referendum by at least three-fourths majority of voters followed by a unanimous vote by the Assembly; passage of other amendments requires only two-thirds majority vote by the Assembly; amended many times, last in 2016 (2017)

Legal system: civil legal system based on French civil law with some elements of English common law

International law organization participation: accepts compulsory ICJ jurisdiction with reservations; accepts ICCt jurisdiction

Citizenship: *citizenship by birth:* yes
citizenship by descent: yes
dual citizenship recognized: yes
residency requirement for naturalization: 5 out of the previous 7 years including the last 12 months

Suffrage: 18 years of age; universal

Executive branch: *chief of state:* President Ameenah GURIB-FAKIM (since 5 June 2015); Vice President Paramaslyum (aka Barlen) Pillay VYAPOORY (since 4 April 2016)

head of government: Prime Minister Pravind JUGNAUTH (since 23 January 2017); note—Prime Minister Sir Anerood JUGNAUTH (since 17 December 2014) stepped down on 23 January 2017 in favor of his son, Pravind Kumar JUGNAUTH who was then appointed prime minister; Anerood JUGNAUTH now holds the position of Mentor Minister, a position created when he stepped down
cabinet: Cabinet of Ministers (Council of Ministers) appointed by the president on the recommendation of the prime minister
elections/appointments: president and vice president indirectly elected by the National Assembly for 5-year renewable terms; election last held on 4 June 2015 (next to be held in 2020); prime minister and deputy prime minister appointed by the president, responsible to the National Assembly
election results: Ameenah GURIB-FAKIM (independent) elected president by the National Assembly—unanimous vote

Legislative branch: *description:* unicameral National Assembly or Assemblee Nationale (70 seats maximum; 62 members directly elected in single- and multi-seat constituencies by simple majority vote and up to 8 seats allocated to non-elected party candidates by the Electoral Commissioner's Office; members serve a 5-year term)
elections: last held on 10 December 2014 following dissolution of the Assembly on 6 October 2014 (next to be held by 2019)
election results: percent of vote by party—Alliance Lepep 49.8%, PTR-MMM 38.5%, FSM 2.1%, OPR 1.1%, other 8.5%; elected seats by party—Alliance Lepep 47, PTR-MMM 13, OPR 2; appointed seats Alliance Lepep 4, PTR-MMM 3

Judicial branch: *highest court(s):* Supreme Court of Mauritius (consists of the chief justice, a senior puisne judge, and 17 puisne judges); note—the Judicial Committee of the Privy Council (in London) serves as the final court of appeal
judge selection and term of office: chief justice appointed by the president after consultation with the prime minister; senior puisne judge appointed by the president with the advice of the chief justice; other puisne judges appointed by the president with the advice of the Judicial and Legal Commission, a 4-member body of judicial officials including the chief justice; all judges serve until retirement at age 67
subordinate courts: lower regional courts known as District Courts, Court of Civil Appeal; Court of Criminal Appeal; Public Bodies Appeal Tribunal

Political parties and leaders: Alliance Lepep (Alliance of the People) [Pravind JUGNAUTH] (coalition including MSM, PMSD, and ML)
Labor Party (Parti Travailliste) or PTR or MLP [Navinchandra RAMGOOLAM]
Mauritian Militant Movement (Mouvement Militant Mauricien) or MMM [Paul BERENGER]
Mauritian Social Democratic Party (Parti Mauricien Social Democrate) or PMSD [Xavier Luc DUVAL]
Mauritian Solidarity Front (Front Solidarite Mauricienne) or FSM [Cehl FAKEERMEEAH, known as Cehl MEEAH]
Militant Socialist Movement (Mouvement Socialist Mauricien) or MSM [Pravind JUGNAUTH]
Muvman Liberater or ML [Ivan COLLENDAVELLOO]
Rodrigues Peoples Organization (Organisation du Peuple Rodriguais) or OPR [Serge CLAIR]

Political pressure groups and leaders: Lalit Political Party
Resistance and Alternative (Rezistans ek Alternativ)
Say No to Coal!
other: various labor unions

International organization participation: ACP, AfDB, AOSIS, AU, C, CD, COMESA, CPLP (associate), FAO, G-77, IAEA, IBRD, ICAO, ICC (NGOs), ICCt, ICRM, IDA, IFAD, IFC, IFRCS, IHO, ILO, IMF, IMO, IMSO, InOC, Interpol, IOC, IOM, IPU, ISO, ITSO, ITU, ITUC (NGOs), MIGA, NAM, OIF, OPCW, PCA, SAARC (observer), SADC, UN, UNCTAD, UNESCO, UNIDO, UNWTO, UPU, WCO, WFTU (NGOs), WHO, WIPO, WMO, WTO

Diplomatic representation in the US: *chief of mission:* Ambassador Sooroojdev PHOKEER (since 3 August 2015)
chancery: 1709 N Street NW, Washington, DC 20036; administrative offices at 3201 Connecticut Avenue NW, Suite 441, Washington, DC 20036
telephone: [1] (202) 244-1491 through 1492
FAX: [1] (202) 966-0983

Diplomatic representation from the US: *chief of mission:* Ambassador (vacant); Charge d'Affaires Melanie ZIMMERMAN (since 2016); note—also accredited to Seychelles
embassy: 4th Floor, Rogers House, John Kennedy Avenue, Port Louis
mailing address: international mail: P.O. Box 544, Port Louis; US mail: American Embassy, Port Louis, US Department of State, Washington, DC 20521-2450
telephone: [230] 202-4400
FAX: [230] 208-9534

Flag description: four equal horizontal bands of red (top), blue, yellow, and green; red represents self-determination and independence, blue the Indian Ocean surrounding the island, yellow has been interpreted as the new light of independence, golden sunshine, or the bright future, and green can symbolize either agriculture or the lush vegetation of the island

National symbol(s): dodo bird, Trochetia Boutoniana flower; national colors: red, blue, yellow, green

National anthem: *name:* "Motherland"
lyrics/music: Jean Georges PROSPER/Philippe GENTIL
note: adopted 1968

ECONOMY

Economy—overview: Since independence in 1968, Mauritius has undergone a remarkable economic transformation from a low-income, agriculturally based economy to a diversified, upper middle-income economy with growing industrial, financial, and tourist sectors. Mauritius has achieved steady growth over the last several decades, resulting in more equitable income distribution, increased life expectancy, lowered infant mortality, and a much-improved infrastructure.

The economy currently depends on sugar, tourism, textiles and apparel, and financial services, but is expanding into fish processing, information and communications technology, and hospitality and property development. Sugarcane is grown on about 90% of the cultivated land area and accounts for 15% of export earnings. The government's development strategy centers on creating vertical and horizontal clusters of development in these sectors. Mauritius has attracted more than 32,000 offshore entities, many aimed at commerce in India, South Africa, and China. Investment in the banking sector alone has reached over $1 billion. Mauritius' textile sector has taken advantage of the Africa Growth and Opportunity Act, a preferential trade program that allows duty free access to the US market, with Mauritian exports to the US growing by 40% from 2000 to 2014.

Mauritius' sound economic policies and prudent banking practices helped mitigate negative effects of the global financial crisis in 2008-09. GDP grew in the 3-4% per year range in 2010-16, and the country continues to expand its trade and investment outreach around the globe. Growth in the US and Europe fostered goods and services exports, including tourism, while lower oil prices kept inflation low in 2016. Mauritius continues to rank first in sub-Saharan Africa on the World Bank's Doing Business Report.

GDP (purchasing power parity): $27.44 billion (2017 est.)
$26.41 billion (2016 est.)
$25.42 billion (2015 est.)
note: data are in 2017 dollars
country comparison to the world: 137

GDP (official exchange rate): $12.27 billion (2016 est.)

GDP—real growth rate: 3.9% (2017 est.)
3.9% (2016 est.)
3.5% (2015 est.)
country comparison to the world: 75

GDP—per capita (PPP): $21,600 (2017 est.)
$20,900 (2016 est.)
$20,100 (2015 est.)
note: data are in 2017 dollars
country comparison to the world: 86

Gross national saving: 13.7% of GDP (2017 est.)
16.3% of GDP (2016 est.)
16.3% of GDP (2015 est.)
country comparison to the world: 131

GDP—composition, by end use:
household consumption: 76.5%
government consumption: 16%
investment in fixed capital: 18.1%
investment in inventories: -0.5%
exports of goods and services: 46%
imports of goods and services: -56.1% (2017 est.)

GDP—composition, by sector of origin:
agriculture: 4%
industry: 21.8%
services: 74.2% (2017 est.)

Agriculture—products: sugarcane, tea, corn, potatoes, bananas, pulses; cattle, goats; fish

Industries: food processing (largely sugar milling), textiles, clothing, mining, chemicals, metal products, transport equipment, nonelectrical machinery, tourism

Industrial production growth rate: 3% (2017 est.)
country comparison to the world: 104

Labor force: 633,900 (2017 est.)
country comparison to the world: 154

Labor force—by occupation: agriculture and fishing: 8%
construction and industry: 29.8%
transportation and communication: 63.5%
trade, restaurants, hotels: 22%
finance: 6%
other services: 25% (2014 est.)

Unemployment rate: 6.9% (2017 est.)

7.2% (2016 est.)
country comparison to the world: 99

Population below poverty line: 8% (2006 est.)

Household income or consumption by percentage share: *lowest 10%:* NA%
highest 10%: NA%

Distribution of family income—Gini index: 35.9 (2012 est.)
39 (2006 est.)
country comparison to the world: 91

Budget: *revenues:* $2.912 billion
expenditures: $3.337 billion (2017 est.)
Taxes and other revenues: 23.7% of GDP (2017 est.)
country comparison to the world: 124

Budget surplus (+) or deficit (-): -3.5% of GDP (2017 est.)
country comparison to the world: 133

Public debt: 66% of GDP (2017 est.)
65% of GDP (2016 est.)
country comparison to the world: 59

Fiscal year: 1 July—30 June

Inflation rate (consumer prices): 4.2% (2017 est.)
1% (2016 est.)
country comparison to the world: 162

Central bank discount rate: 9% (31 December 2010)
country comparison to the world: 33

Commercial bank prime lending rate: 8.5% (31 December 2017 est.)
8.5% (31 December 2016 est.)
country comparison to the world: 101

Stock of narrow money: $3.096 billion (31 December 2017 est.)
$2.833 billion (31 December 2016 est.)
country comparison to the world: 117

Stock of broad money: $14.57 billion (31 December 2017 est.)
$13.27 billion (31 December 2016 est.)
country comparison to the world: 100

Stock of domestic credit: $15.41 billion (31 December 2017 est.)
$13.7 billion (31 December 2016 est.)
country comparison to the world: 98

Market value of publicly traded shares: $7.239 billion (31 December 2015 est.)
$8.751 billion (31 December 2014 est.)
$8.942 billion (31 December 2013 est.)
country comparison to the world: 78

Current account balance: -$710 million (2017 est.)
-$531 million (2016 est.)
country comparison to the world: 114

Exports: $2.329 billion (2017 est.)
$2.359 billion (2016 est.)
country comparison to the world: 136

Exports—commodities: clothing and textiles, sugar, cut flowers, molasses, fish, primates (for research)

Exports—partners: France 14.8%, UK 12%, US 11.4%, South Africa 8.2%, Madagascar 7.3%, Italy 6.8%, Spain 4.5% (2016)

Imports: $4.545 billion (2017 est.)
$4.408 billion (2016 est.)
country comparison to the world: 127

Imports—commodities: manufactured goods, capital equipment, foodstuffs, petroleum products, chemicals

Imports—partners: China 17.7%, India 16.5%, France 7.8%, South Africa 7.5% (2016)

Reserves of foreign exchange and gold: $5.068 billion (31 December 2017 est.)
$4.967 billion (31 December 2016 est.)
country comparison to the world: 92

Debt—external: $14.67 billion (31 December 2017 est.)
$14.34 billion (31 December 2016 est.)
country comparison to the world: 104

Stock of direct foreign investment—at home: NA

Stock of direct foreign investment—abroad: $NA

Exchange rates: Mauritian rupees (MUR) per US dollar—
35.17 (2017 est.)
35.542 (2016 est.)
35.542 (2015 est.)
35.057 (2014 est.)
30.622 (2013 est.)

ENERGY

Electricity access: electrification—*total population:* 100% (2016)

Electricity—production: 2.857 billion kWh (2015 est.)
country comparison to the world: 134

Electricity—consumption: 2.68 billion kWh (2015 est.)
country comparison to the world: 139

Electricity—exports: 0 kWh (2016 est.)
country comparison to the world: 169

Electricity—imports: 0 kWh (2016 est.)
country comparison to the world: 174

Electricity—installed generating capacity: 1.056 million kW (2015 est.)
country comparison to the world: 127

Electricity—from fossil fuels: 66.3% of total installed capacity (2015 est.)
country comparison to the world: 114

Electricity—from nuclear fuels: 0% of total installed capacity (2015 est.)
country comparison to the world: 143

Electricity—from hydroelectric plants: 5.8% of total installed capacity (2015 est.)
country comparison to the world: 128

Electricity—from other renewable sources: 29.4% of total installed capacity (2015 est.)
country comparison to the world: 17

Crude oil—production: 0 bbl/day (2016 est.)
country comparison to the world: 171

Crude oil—exports: 0 bbl/day (2014 est.)
country comparison to the world: 164

Crude oil—imports: 0 bbl/day (2014 est.)
country comparison to the world: 161

Crude oil—proved reserves: 0 bbl (1 January 2017 es)
country comparison to the world: 168

Refined petroleum products—production: 0 bbl/day (2014 est.)
country comparison to the world: 177

Refined petroleum products—consumption: 26,000 bbl/day (2015 est.)
country comparison to the world: 128

Refined petroleum products—exports: 0 bbl/day (2014 est.)
country comparison to the world: 180

Refined petroleum products—imports: 24,790 bbl/day (2014 est.)
country comparison to the world: 107

Natural gas—production: 0 cu m (2013 est.)
country comparison to the world: 170

Natural gas—consumption: 0 cu m (2013 est.)
country comparison to the world: 209

Natural gas—exports: 0 cu m (2013 est.)
country comparison to the world: 151

Natural gas—imports: 0 cu m (2013 est.)
country comparison to the world: 156

Natural gas—proved reserves: 0 cu m (1 January 2014 es)
country comparison to the world: 173

Carbon dioxide emissions from consumption of energy: 5.4 million Mt (2013 est.)
country comparison to the world: 124

COMMUNICATIONS

Telephones—fixed lines: *total subscriptions:* 385,500
subscriptions per 100 inhabitants: 29 (July 2016 est.)
country comparison to the world: 110

Telephones—mobile cellular: *total:* 1.814 million
subscriptions per 100 inhabitants: 135 (July 2016 est.)
country comparison to the world: 153

Telephone system: *general assessment:* small system with good service
domestic: monopoly over fixed-line services terminated in 2005; fixed-line teledensity roughly 30 per 100 persons; mobile-cellular services launched in 1989 with teledensity approaching 135 per 100 persons in 2016
international: country code—230; landing point for the SAFE submarine cable that provides links to Asia and South Africa where it connects to the SAT-3/WASC submarine cable that provides further links to parts of East Africa, and Europe; satellite earth station—1 Intelsat (Indian Ocean); new microwave link to Reunion; HF radiotelephone links to several countries (2016)

Broadcast media: the government maintains control over TV broadcasting through the Mauritius Broadcasting Corporation (MBC), which only operates digital TV stations since June 2015; MBC is a shareholder in a local company that operates 2 pay-TV stations; the state retains the largest radio broadcast network with multiple stations; several private radio broadcasters have entered the market since 2001; transmissions of at least 2 international broadcasters are available (2017)

Internet country code: .mu
Internet users: total: 717,618

percent of population: 53.2% (July 2016 est.)
country comparison to the world: 175

TRANSPORTATION

National air transport system: *number of registered air carriers:* 1
inventory of registered aircraft operated by air carriers: 13
annual passenger traffic on registered air carriers: 1,466,527
annual freight traffic on registered air carriers: 168.773 million mt-km (2015)
Civil aircraft registration country code prefix: 3B (2016)

Airports: 5 (2013)
country comparison to the world: 182

Airports—with paved runways: *total:* 2
over 3,047 m: 1
914 to 1,523 m: 1 (2017)

Airports—with unpaved runways: *total:* 3
914 to 1,523 m: 2
under 914 m: 1 (2013)

Roadways: *total:* 2,428 km
paved: 2,379 km (includes 99 km of expressways)
unpaved: 49 km (2015)
country comparison to the world: 173

Merchant marine: *total:* 28
by type: general cargo 2, oil tanker 3, other 23 (2017)
country comparison to the world: 125

Ports and terminals: *major seaport(s):* Port Louis

MILITARY AND SECURITY

Military expenditures: 0.19% of GDP (2016)
0.18% of GDP (2015)
0.15% of GDP (2014)
0.19% of GDP (2013)
0.14% of GDP (2012)
country comparison to the world: 130

Military branches: no regular military forces; Mauritius Police Force, Special Mobile Force, National Coast Guard (2014)

TRANSNATIONAL ISSUES

Disputes—international: Mauritius and Seychelles claim the Chagos Islands; claims French-administered Tromelin Island

Trafficking in persons: current situation: Mauritius is a source, transit, and destination country for men, women, and children subjected to forced labor and sex trafficking; Mauritian girls are induced or sold into prostitution, often by peers, family members, or businessmen offering other forms of employment; Mauritian adults have been identified as labor trafficking victims in the UK, Belgium, and Canada, while Mauritian women from Rodrigues Island are also subject to domestic servitude in Mauritius; Malagasy women transit Mauritius en route to the Middle East for jobs as domestic servants and subsequently are subjected to forced labor; Cambodian men are victims of forced labor on foreign fishing vessels in Mauritius' territorial waters; other migrant workers from East and South Asia and Madagascar are also subject to forced labor in Mauritius' manufacturing and construction sectors

tier rating: Tier 2 Watch List—Mauritius does not fully comply with the minimum standards for the elimination of trafficking; however, it is making significant efforts to do so; in 2014, the government made modest efforts to address child sex trafficking but none related to adult forced labor; law enforcement lacks an understanding of trafficking crimes outside of child sex trafficking, despite increasing evidence of other forms of human trafficking; authorities made no trafficking prosecutions or convictions and made modest efforts to assist a couple of child sex trafficking victims; officials sustained an extensive public awareness campaign to prevent child sex trafficking, but no efforts were made to raise awareness or reduce demand for forced adult or child labor (2015)

Illicit drugs: consumer and transshipment point for heroin from South Asia; small amounts of cannabis produced and consumed locally; significant offshore financial industry creates potential for money laundering, but corruption levels are relatively low and the government appears generally to be committed to regulating its banking industry

MEXICO

INTRODUCTION

Background: The site of several advanced Amerindian civilizations—including the Olmec, Toltec, Teotihuacan, Zapotec, Maya, and Aztec—Mexico was conquered and colonized by Spain in the early 16th century. Administered as the Viceroyalty of New Spain for three centuries, it achieved independence early in the 19th century. Elections held in 2000 marked the first time since the 1910 Mexican Revolution that an opposition candidate—Vicente FOX of the National Action Party (PAN)—defeated the party in government, the Institutional Revolutionary Party (PRI). He was succeeded in 2006 by another PAN candidate Felipe CALDERON, but Enrique PENA NIETO regained the presidency for the PRI in 2012, and

will serve as president until December 2018. The global financial crisis in late 2008 caused a massive economic downturn in Mexico the following year, although growth returned quickly in 2010. Ongoing economic and social concerns include low real wages, high underemployment, inequitable income distribution, and few advancement opportunities for the largely indigenous population in the impoverished southern states. Since 2007, Mexico's powerful drug-trafficking organizations have engaged in bloody feuding, resulting in tens of thousands of drug-related homicides.

GEOGRAPHY

Location: North America, bordering the Caribbean Sea and the Gulf of Mexico, between Belize and the United States and bordering the North Pacific Ocean, between Guatemala and the United States

Geographic coordinates: 23 00 N, 102 00 W

Map references: North America

Area: *total:* 1,964,375 sq km
land: 1,943,945 sq km
water: 20,430 sq km
country comparison to the world: 15

Area—comparative: slightly less than three times the size of Texas

Land boundaries: *total:* 4,389 km
border countries (3): Belize 276 km, Guatemala 958 km, US 3,155 km

Coastline: 9,330 km

Maritime claims: *territorial sea:* 12 nm
contiguous zone: 24 nm
exclusive economic zone: 200 nm
continental shelf: 200 nm or to the edge of the continental margin

Climate: varies from tropical to desert

Terrain: high, rugged mountains; low coastal plains; high plateaus; desert

Elevation: *mean elevation:* 1,111 m

elevation extremes: *lowest point:* Laguna Salada -10 m
highest point: Volcan Pico de Orizaba 5,636 m

Natural resources: petroleum, silver, copper, gold, lead, zinc, natural gas, timber

Land use: *agricultural land:* 54.9%
arable land: 11.8%;
permanent crops: 1.4%;
permanent pasture: 41.7%
forest: 33.3%

607

other: 11.8% (2011 est.)

Irrigated land: 65,000 sq km (2012)

Population—distribution: most of the population is found in the middle of the country between the states of Jalisco and Veracruz; approximately a quarter of the population lives in and around Mexico City

Natural hazards: tsunamis along the Pacific coast, volcanoes and destructive earthquakes in the center and south, and hurricanes on the Pacific, Gulf of Mexico, and Caribbean coasts

volcanism: volcanic activity in the central-southern part of the country; the volcanoes in Baja California are mostly dormant; Colima (3,850 m), which erupted in 2010, is Mexico's most active volcano and is responsible for causing periodic evacuations of nearby villagers; it has been deemed a Decade Volcano by the International Association of Volcanology and Chemistry of the Earth's Interior, worthy of study due to its explosive history and close proximity to human populations; Popocatepetl (5,426 m) poses a threat to Mexico City; other historically active volcanoes include Barcena, Ceboruco, El Chichon, Michoacan-Guanajuato, Pico de Orizaba, San Martin, Socorro, and Tacana

Environment—current issues: scarcity of hazardous waste disposal facilities; rural to urban migration; natural freshwater resources scarce and polluted in north, inaccessible and poor quality in center and extreme southeast; raw sewage and industrial effluents polluting rivers in urban areas; deforestation; widespread erosion; desertification; deteriorating agricultural lands; serious air and water pollution in the national capital and urban centers along US-Mexico border; land subsidence in Valley of Mexico caused by groundwater depletion

note: the government considers the lack of clean water and deforestation national security issues

Environment—international agreements: *party to:* Biodiversity, Climate Change, Climate Change-Kyoto Protocol, Desertification, Endangered Species, Hazardous Wastes, Law of the Sea, Marine Dumping, Marine Life Conservation, Ozone Layer Protection, Ship Pollution, Wetlands, Whaling

signed, but not ratified: none of the selected agreements

Geography—note: strategic location on southern border of US; corn (maize), one of the world's major grain crops, is thought to have originated in Mexico

PEOPLE AND SOCIETY

Population: 124,574,795 (July 2017 est.)

country comparison to the world: 11

Nationality: *noun:* Mexican(s)

adjective: Mexican

Ethnic groups: mestizo (Amerindian-Spanish) 62%, predominantly Amerindian 21%, Amerindian 7%, other 10% (mostly European)

note: Mexico does not collect census data on ethnicity (2012 est.)

Languages: Spanish only 92.7%, Spanish and indigenous languages 5.7%, indigenous only 0.8%, unspecified 0.8%

note: indigenous languages include various Mayan, Nahuatl, and other regional languages (2005)

Religions: Roman Catholic 82.7%, Pentecostal 1.6%, Jehovah's Witness 1.4%, other Evangelical Churches 5%, other 1.9%, none 4.7%, unspecified 2.7% (2010 est.)

Age structure: *0-14 years:* 26.93% (male 17,155,689/female 16,390,913)

15-24 years: 17.54% (male 11,065,927/female 10,778,382)

25-54 years: 40.81% (male 24,550,848/female 26,282,836)

55-64 years: 7.64% (male 4,362,868/female 5,160,514)

65 years and over: 7.09% (male 3,949,823/female 4,876,995) (2017 est.)

Dependency ratios: *total dependency ratio:* 51.4

youth dependency ratio: 41.6

elderly dependency ratio: 9.8

potential support ratio: 10.2 (2015 est.)

Median age: *total:* 28.3 years

male: 27.2 years

female: 29.4 years (2017 est.)

country comparison to the world: 133

Population growth rate: 1.12% (2017 est.)

country comparison to the world: 103

Birth rate: 18.3 births/1,000 population (2017 est.)

country comparison to the world: 94

Death rate: 5.3 deaths/1,000 population (2017 est.)

country comparison to the world: 182

Net migration rate: -1.8 migrant(s)/1,000 population (2017 est.)

country comparison to the world: 156

Population distribution: most of the population is found in the middle of the country between the states of Jalisco and Veracruz; approximately a quarter of the population lives in and around Mexico City

Urbanization: *urban population:* 79.8% of total population (2017)

rate of urbanization: 1.37% annual rate of change (2015-20 est.)

Major urban areas—population: MEXICO CITY (capital) 20.999 million; Guadalajara 4.843 million; Monterrey 4.513 million; Puebla 2.984 million; Toluca de Lerdo 2.164 million; Tijuana 1.987 million (2015)

Sex ratio: *at birth:* 1.05 male(s)/female

0-14 years: 1.05 male(s)/female

15-24 years: 1.03 male(s)/female

25-54 years: 0.93 male(s)/female

55-64 years: 0.85 male(s)/female

65 years and over: 0.82 male(s)/female

total population: 0.96 male(s)/female (2016 est.)

Mother's mean age at first birth: 21.3 years (2008 est.)

Maternal mortality ratio: 38 deaths/100,000 live births (2015 est.)

country comparison to the world: 107

Infant mortality rate: *total:* 11.6 deaths/1,000 live births

male: 13 deaths/1,000 live births

female: 10.1 deaths/1,000 live births (2017 est.)

country comparison to the world: 125

Life expectancy at birth: *total population:* 76.1 years

male: 73.3 years

female: 79 years (2017 est.)

country comparison to the world: 90

Total fertility rate: 2.24 children born/woman (2017 est.)

country comparison to the world: 95

Contraceptive prevalence rate: 66.9% (2015)

Health expenditures: 6.3% of GDP (2014)

country comparison to the world: 100

Physicians density: 2.07 physicians/1,000 population (2013)

Hospital bed density: 1.5 beds/1,000 population (2011)

Drinking water source:

improved:

urban: 97.2% of population

rural: 92.1% of population

total: 96.1% of population

unimproved:

urban: 2.8% of population

rural: 7.9% of population

total: 3.9% of population (2015 est.)

Sanitation facility access:

improved:

urban: 88% of population

rural: 74.5% of population

total: 85.2% of population

unimproved:

urban: 12% of population

rural: 25.5% of population

total: 14.8% of population (2015 est.)

HIV/AIDS—adult prevalence rate: 0.3% (2016 est.)

country comparison to the world: 87

HIV/AIDS—people living with HIV/AIDS: 220,000 (2016 est.)

country comparison to the world: 28

HIV/AIDS—deaths: 4,200 (2016 est.)

country comparison to the world: 33

Major infectious diseases: *degree of risk:* intermediate

food or waterborne diseases: bacterial diarrhea and hepatitis A

vectorborne disease: dengue fever

note: active local transmission of Zika virus by Aedes species mosquitoes has been identified in this country (as of August 2016); it poses an important risk (a large number of cases possible) among US citizens if bitten by an infective mosquito; other less common ways to get Zika are through sex, via blood transfusion, or during pregnancy, in which the pregnant woman passes Zika virus to her fetus (2016)

Obesity—adult prevalence rate: 28.9% (2016)

country comparison to the world: 29

Children under the age of 5 years underweight: 3.9% (2015)
country comparison to the world: 117

Education expenditures: 5.2% of GDP (2012)
country comparison to the world: 72

Literacy: *definition:* age 15 and over can read and write
total population: 94.5%
male: 95.5%
female: 93.5% (2015 est.)

School life expectancy (primary to tertiary education): *total:* 13 years
male: 13 years
female: 13 years (2014)

Unemployment, youth ages 15-24: *total:* 7.7%
male: 7.2%
female: 8.8% (2016 est.)
country comparison to the world: 104

GOVERNMENT

Country name: *conventional long form:* United Mexican States
conventional short form: Mexico
local long form: Estados Unidos Mexicanos
local short form: Mexico
etymology: named after the Mexica, the largest and most powerful branch of the Aztecs; the meaning of the name is uncertain

Government type: federal presidential republic

Capital: *name:* Mexico City (Ciudad de Mexico)
geographic coordinates: 19 26 N, 99 08 W
time difference: UTC-6 (1 hour behind Washington, DC, during Standard Time)
daylight saving time: +1hr, begins first Sunday in April; ends last Sunday in October
note: Mexico has four time zones

Administrative divisions: 31 states (estados, singular—estado) and 1 city* (ciudad); Aguascalientes, Baja California, Baja California Sur, Campeche, Chiapas, Chihuahua, Coahuila, Colima, Cuidad de Mexico*, Durango, Guanajuato, Guerrero, Hidalgo, Jalisco, Mexico, Michoacan, Morelos, Nayarit, Nuevo Leon, Oaxaca, Puebla, Queretaro, Quintana Roo, San Luis Potosi, Sinaloa, Sonora, Tabasco, Tamaulipas, Tlaxcala, Veracruz, Yucatan, Zacatecas

Independence: 16 September 1810 (declared independence from Spain); 27 September 1821 (recognized by Spain)

National holiday: Independence Day, 16 September (1810)

Constitution: several previous; latest approved 5 February 1917; amended many times, last in 2017 (2017)

Legal system: civil law system with US constitutional law influence; judicial review of legislative acts

International law organization participation: accepts compulsory ICJ jurisdiction with reservations; accepts ICCt jurisdiction

Citizenship: *citizenship by birth:* yes
citizenship by descent: yes

dual citizenship recognized: not specified
residency requirement for naturalization: 5 years

Suffrage: 18 years of age; universal and compulsory

Executive branch: *chief of state:* President Enrique PENA NIETO (since 1 December 2012); note—the president is both chief of state and head of government

head of government: President Enrique PENA NIETO (since 1 December 2012)
cabinet: Cabinet appointed by the president; note—appointment of attorney general, the head of the Bank of Mexico, and senior treasury officials require consent of the Senate
elections/appointments: president directly elected by simple majority popular vote for a single 6-year term; election last held on 1 July 2012 (next to be held in July 2018)
election results: Enrique PENA NIETO elected president; percent of vote—Enrique PENA NIETO (PRI) 38.2%, Andres Manuel LOPEZ OBRADOR (PRD) 31.6%, Josefina Eugenia VAZQUEZ Mota (PAN) 25.4%, other 4.8%

Legislative branch: *description:* bicameral National Congress or Congreso de la Union consists of the Senate or Camara de Senadores (128 seats; 96 members directly elected in multi-seat constituencies by simple majority vote and 32 directly elected in a single, nationwide constituency by proportional representation vote; members serve 6-year terms) and the Chamber of Deputies or Camara de Diputados (500 seats; 300 members directly elected in single-seat constituencies by simple majority vote and 200 directly elected in a single, nationwide constituency by proportional representation vote; members serve 3-year terms)
note: for the 2018 elections, senators will be eligible for a second term and deputies up to 4 consecutive terms
elections: Senate—last held on 1 July 2012 (next to be held on 1 July 2018); Chamber of Deputies—last held on 7 June 2015 (next to be held on 1 July 2018)
election results: Senate—percent of vote by party—NA; seats by party—PRI 52, PAN 38, PRD 22, PVEM 9, PT 4, MC 2, PANAL 1;
Chamber of Deputies—percent of vote by party—NA; seats by party—PRI 203, PAN 108, PRD 56, PVEM 47, MORENA 35, MC 26, PANAL 10, PES 8, PT 6, independent 1

Judicial branch: *highest court(s):* Supreme Court of Justice or Suprema Corte de Justicia de la Nacion (consists of the chief justice and 11 justices and organized into civil, criminal, administrative, and labor panels) and the Electoral Tribunal of the Federal Judiciary (organized into the superior court, with 7 judges including the court president and 5 regional courts, each with 3 judges)
judge selection and term of office: Supreme Court justices nominated by the president of the republic and approved by two-thirds vote of the members present in the Senate; justices serve for life; Electoral Tribunal superior and regional court judges nominated by the Supreme Court and elected by two-thirds vote of members present in the Senate;

superior court president elected from among its members to hold office for a 4-year term; other judges of the superior and regional courts serve staggered, 9-year terms
subordinate courts: federal level includes circuit, collegiate, and unitary courts; state and district level courts

Political parties and leaders: Citizen's Movement (Movimiento Ciudadano) or MC [Dante DELGADO Rannaoro]
Institutional Revolutionary Party (Partido Revolucionario Institucional) or PRI [Enrique OCHOA Reza]
Labor Party (Partido del Trabajo) or PT [Alberto ANAYA Gutierrez]
Mexican Green Ecological Party (Partido Verde Ecologista de Mexico) or PVEM [Carlos Alberto PUENTE Salas]
Movement for National Regeneration (Movimiento Regeneracion Nacional) or MORENA [Andres Manuel LOPEZ Obrador]
National Action Party (Partido Accion Nacional) or PAN [Damian ZEPEDA Vidales]
New Alliance Party (Partido Nueva Alianza) or PNA/PANAL [Luis CASTRO Obregon]
Party of the Democratic Revolution (Partido de la Revolucion Democratica) or PRD [Manuel GRANADOS]
Social Encounter Party (Partido Encuentro Social) or PES [Hugo Eric FLORES Cervantes]

Political pressure groups and leaders: Businessmen's Coordinating Council or CCE
Confederation of Employers of the Mexican Republic or COPARMEX
Confederation of Industrial Chambers or CONCAMIN
Confederation of Mexican Workers or CTM
Confederation of National Chambers of Commerce or CONCANACO
Coordinator for Foreign Trade Business Organizations or COECE
Federation of Unions Providing Goods and Services or FESEBES
National Chamber of Transformation Industries or CANACINTRA
National Confederation of Popular Organizations or CNOP
National Coordinator for Education Workers or CNTE
National Peasant Confederation or CNC
National Small Business Chamber or CANACOPE
National Syndicate of Education Workers or SNTE
National Union of Workers or UNT
Popular Assembly of the People of Oaxaca or APPO
Roman Catholic Church

International organization participation: APEC, Australia Group, BCIE, BIS, CAN (observer), Caricom (observer), CD, CDB, CE (observer), CELAC, CSN (observer), EBRD, FAO, FATF, G-3, G-15, G-20, G-24, G-5, IADB, IAEA, IBRD, ICAO, ICC (national committees), ICCt, ICRM, IDA, IFAD, IFC, IFRCS, IHO, ILO, IMF, IMO, IMSO, Interpol, IOC, IOM, IPU, ISO, ITSO,

ITU, ITUC (NGOs), LAES, LAIA, MIGA, NAFTA, NAM (observer), NEA, NSG, OAS, OECD, OPANAL, OPCW, Pacific Alliance, Paris Club (associate), PCA, SICA (observer), UN, UNASUR (observer), UNCTAD, UNESCO, UNHCR, UNIDO, Union Latina (observer), UNWTO, UPU, WCO, WFTU (NGOs), WHO, WIPO, WMO, WTO

Diplomatic representation in the US: *chief of mission:* Ambassador Geronimo GUTIERREZ Fernandez (since 24 April 2017)
chancery: 1911 Pennsylvania Avenue NW, Washington, DC 20006
telephone: [1] (202) 728-1600
FAX: [1] (202) 728-1698
consulate(s) general: Atlanta, Austin, Boston, Chicago, Dallas, Denver, El Paso (TX), Houston, Laredo (TX), Los Angeles, Miami, New York, Nogales (AZ), Phoenix, Sacramento (CA), San Antonio (TX), San Diego, San Francisco, San Jose (CA), San Juan (Puerto Rico), Saint Paul (MN)
consulate(s): Albuquerque (NM), Anchorage (AK), Boise (ID), Brownsville (TX), Calexico (CA), Del Rio (TX), Detroit, Douglas (AZ), Eagle Pass (TX), Fresno (CA), Indianapolis (IN), Kansas City (MO), Las Vegas, Little Rock (AR), McAllen (TX), Minneapolis (MN), New Orleans, Omaha (NE), Orlando (FL), Oxnard (CA), Philadelphia, Portland (OR), Presidio (TX), Raleigh (NC), Salt Lake City, San Bernardino (CA), Santa Ana (CA), Seattle, Tucson (AZ), Yuma (AZ); note—Washington DC Consular Section is located in a separate building from the Mexican Embassy and has jurisdiction over DC, parts of Virginia, Maryland, and West Virginia

Diplomatic representation from the US: *chief of mission:* Ambassador Roberta JACOBSON (since 20 June 2016)
embassy: Paseo de la Reforma 305, Colonia Cuauhtemoc, 06500 Mexico, Distrito Federal
mailing address: P. O. Box 9000, Brownsville, TX 78520-9000
telephone: (01-55) 5080-2000
FAX: (01-55) 5080-2005
consulate(s) general: Ciudad Juarez, Guadalajara, Hermosillo, Matamoros, Merida, Monterrey, Nogales, Nuevo Laredo, Tijuana

Flag description: three equal vertical bands of green (hoist side), white, and red; Mexico's coat of arms (an eagle with a snake in its beak perched on a cactus) is centered in the white band; green signifies hope, joy, and love; white represents peace and honesty; red stands for hardiness, bravery, strength, and valor; the coat of arms is derived from a legend that the wandering Aztec people were to settle at a location where they would see an eagle on a cactus eating a snake; the city they founded, Tenochtitlan, is now Mexico City
note: similar to the flag of Italy, which is shorter, uses lighter shades of red and green, and does not display anything in its white band

National symbol(s): golden eagle; national colors: green, white, red

National anthem: *name:* "Himno Nacional Mexicano" (National Anthem of Mexico)

lyrics/music: Francisco Gonzalez BOCANEGRA/ Jaime Nuno ROCA
note: adopted 1943, in use since 1854; also known as "Mexicanos, al grito de Guerra" (Mexicans, to the War Cry); according to tradition, Francisco Gonzalez BOCANEGRA, an accomplished poet, was uninterested in submitting lyrics to a national anthem contest; his fiancee locked him in a room and refused to release him until the lyrics were completed

ECONOMY

Economy—overview: Mexico's $2.2 trillion economy has become increasingly oriented toward manufacturing since the North American Free Trade Agreement (NAFTA) entered into force in 1994. Per capita income is roughly one-third that of the US; income distribution remains highly unequal.

Mexico has become the US' second-largest export market and third-largest source of imports. In 2016, two-way trade in goods and services exceeded $579 billion. Mexico has free trade agreements with 46 countries, putting more than 90% of trade under free trade agreements. In 2012, Mexico formed the Pacific Alliance with Peru, Colombia, and Chile.

Mexico's current government, led by President Enrique PENA NIETO, has emphasized economic reforms, passing and implementing sweeping energy, financial, fiscal, and telecommunications reform legislation, among others, with the long-term aim to improve competitiveness and economic growth across the Mexican economy. Mexico began holding public auctions of exploration and development rights to select oil and gas resources in 2015 as a part of reforms that allow for private investment in the oil, gas, and electricity sectors. Mexico held its fourth auction in December 2016 and allocated 8 of 10 deepwater fields, demonstrating Mexico's capacity to attract investment amid low oil prices. The government allocated additional fields in 2017.

Since 2013, Mexico's economic growth has averaged 2% annually, falling short of private-sector expectations that President PENA NIETO's sweeping reforms would bolster economic prospects. Growth is predicted to remain below potential given falling oil production, weak oil prices, structural issues such as low productivity, high inequality, a large informal sector employing over half of the workforce, weak rule of law, and corruption. Over the medium-term, the economy is vulnerable to global economic pressures, such as lower external demand, rising interest rates, and low oil prices—approximately 10% of government revenue comes from the state-owned oil company, PEMEX.

GDP (purchasing power parity): $2.406 trillion (2017 est.)
$2.356 trillion (2016 est.)
$2.303 trillion (2015 est.)
note: data are in 2017 dollars
country comparison to the world: 12

GDP (official exchange rate): $1.142 trillion (2016 est.)

GDP—real growth rate: 2.1% (2017 est.)
2.3% (2016 est.)
2.7% (2015 est.)
country comparison to the world: 150

GDP—per capita (PPP): $19,500 (2017 est.)
$19,300 (2016 est.)
$19,000 (2015 est.)
note: data are in 2017 dollars
country comparison to the world: 89

Gross national saving: 21.2% of GDP (2017 est.)
21.1% of GDP (2016 est.)
20.4% of GDP (2015 est.)
country comparison to the world: 81

GDP—composition, by end use:
household consumption: 68%
government consumption: 12.5%
investment in fixed capital: 22.1%
investment in inventories: -1.3%
exports of goods and services: 37.4%
imports of goods and services: -38.7% (2017 est.)

GDP—composition, by sector of origin:
agriculture: 3.9%
industry: 31.6%
services: 64% (2017 est.)

Agriculture—products: corn, wheat, soybeans, rice, beans, cotton, coffee, fruit, tomatoes; beef, poultry, dairy products; wood products

Industries: food and beverages, tobacco, chemicals, iron and steel, petroleum, mining, textiles, clothing, motor vehicles, consumer durables, tourism

Industrial production growth rate: 0% (2017 est.)
country comparison to the world: 186

Labor force: 54.51 million (2017 est.)
country comparison to the world: 13

Labor force—by occupation: *agriculture:* 13.4%
industry: 24.1%
services: 61.9% (2011)

Unemployment rate: 3.6% (2017 est.)
3.9% (2016 est.)
note: underemployment may be as high as 25%
country comparison to the world: 40

Population below poverty line: 46.2%
note: from a food-based definition of poverty; asset-based poverty amounted to more than 47% (2014 est.)

Household income or consumption by percentage share: *lowest 10%:* 2%
highest 10%: 40% (2014)

Distribution of family income—Gini index: 48.2 (2014)
48.3 (2008)
country comparison to the world: 24

Budget: *revenues:* $292.8 billion
expenditures: $314.9 billion (2017 est.)
Taxes and other revenues: 25.6% of GDP (2017 est.)
country comparison to the world: 109

Budget surplus (+) or deficit (-): -1.9% of GDP (2017 est.)

country comparison to the world: 82

Public debt: 51.5% of GDP (2017 est.)
50.2% of GDP (2016 est.)
country comparison to the world: 98

Fiscal year: calendar year

Inflation rate (consumer prices): 5.9% (2017 est.)
2.8% (2016 est.)
country comparison to the world: 181

Central bank discount rate: 6.25% (28 February 2017)
5.25% (28 February 2016)
country comparison to the world: 66

Commercial bank prime lending rate: 7.3% (31 December 2017 est.)
4.72% (31 December 2016 est.)
country comparison to the world: 115

Stock of narrow money: $235.5 billion (31 December 2017 est.)
$186.8 billion (31 December 2016 est.)
country comparison to the world: 24

Stock of broad money: $772.5 billion (31 December 2017 est.)
$603 billion (31 December 2016 est.)
country comparison to the world: 18

Stock of domestic credit: $510.2 billion (31 December 2017 est.)
$393.8 billion (31 December 2016 est.)
country comparison to the world: 29

Market value of publicly traded shares: $402.3 billion (31 December 2015 est.)
$480.2 billion (31 December 2014 est.)
$526 billion (31 December 2013 est.)
country comparison to the world: 26

Current account balance: -$19.81 billion (2017 est.)
-$22.97 billion (2016 est.)
country comparison to the world: 190

Exports: $406.5 billion (2017 est.)
$374.3 billion (2016 est.)
country comparison to the world: 13

Exports—commodities: manufactured goods, oil and oil products, silver, fruits, vegetables, coffee, cotton

Exports—partners: US 81% (2016)

Imports: $417.3 billion (2017 est.)
$387.4 billion (2016 est.)
country comparison to the world: 14

Imports—commodities: metalworking machines, steel mill products, agricultural machinery, electrical equipment, automobile parts for assembly and repair, aircraft, aircraft parts

Imports—partners: US 46.6%, China 18%, Japan 4.6% (2016)

Reserves of foreign exchange and gold: $189.2 billion (31 December 2017 est.)
$178.4 billion (31 December 2016 est.)
note: Mexico also maintains access to an $88 million Flexible Credit Line with the IMF
country comparison to the world: 14

Debt—external: $480.5 billion (31 December 2017 est.)
$450.2 billion (31 December 2016 est.)

country comparison to the world: 27

Stock of direct foreign investment—at home: $499.4 billion (31 December 2017 est.)
$473.5 billion (31 December 2016 est.)
country comparison to the world: 17

Stock of direct foreign investment—abroad: $160.1 billion (31 December 2017 est.)
$148.6 billion (31 December 2016 est.)
country comparison to the world: 30

Exchange rates: Mexican pesos (MXN) per US dollar—
18.26 (2017 est.)
18.664 (2016 est.)
18.664 (2015 est.)
15.848 (2014 est.)
13.292 (2013 est.)

ENERGY

Electricity access: *population without electricity:* 1,231,667
electrification—*total population:* 99%
electrification—urban areas: 100%
electrification—rural areas: 97% (2012)

Electricity—production: 292.7 billion kWh (2015 est.)
country comparison to the world: 14

Electricity—consumption: 245.2 billion kWh (2015 est.)
country comparison to the world: 16

Electricity—exports: 7.308 billion kWh (2016 est.)
country comparison to the world: 28

Electricity—imports: 392 million kWh (2016 est.)
country comparison to the world: 86

Electricity—installed generating capacity: 65.45 million kW (2016 est.)
country comparison to the world: 19

Electricity—from fossil fuels: 72.2% of total installed capacity (2015 est.)
country comparison to the world: 99

Electricity—from nuclear fuels: 2.1% of total installed capacity (2015 est.)
country comparison to the world: 27

Electricity—from hydroelectric plants: 18.1% of total installed capacity (2015 est.)
country comparison to the world: 96

Electricity—from other renewable sources: 8.5% of total installed capacity (2015 est.)
country comparison to the world: 76

Crude oil—production: 2.187 million bbl/day (2016 est.)
country comparison to the world: 12

Crude oil—exports: 1.224 million bbl/day (2016 est.)
country comparison to the world: 15

Crude oil—imports: 0 bbl/day (2016 est.)
country comparison to the world: 165

Crude oil—proved reserves: 7.64 billion bbl (1 January 2017 es)
country comparison to the world: 19

Refined petroleum products—production: 1.043 million bbl/day (2016 est.)
country comparison to the world: 19

Refined petroleum products—consumption: 2.027 million bbl/day (2016 est.)
country comparison to the world: 12

Refined petroleum products—exports: 181,600 bbl/day (2016 est.)
country comparison to the world: 34

Refined petroleum products—imports: 751,500 bbl/day (2016 est.)
country comparison to the world: 11

Natural gas—production: 40.37 billion cu m (2015 est.)
country comparison to the world: 21

Natural gas—consumption: 418.9 billion cu m (2015 est.)
country comparison to the world: 4

Natural gas—exports: 31 million cu m (2015 est.)
country comparison to the world: 52

Natural gas—imports: 36.47 billion cu m (2015 est.)
country comparison to the world: 12

Natural gas—proved reserves: 355.7 billion cu m (1 January 2017 es)
country comparison to the world: 36

Carbon dioxide emissions from consumption of energy: 455 million Mt (2013 est.)
country comparison to the world: 15

COMMUNICATIONS

Telephones—fixed lines: *total subscriptions:* 19,599,886
subscriptions per 100 inhabitants: 16 (July 2016 est.)
country comparison to the world: 14

Telephones—mobile cellular: *total:* 111,724,654
subscriptions per 100 inhabitants: 91 (July 2016 est.)
country comparison to the world: 14

Telephone system: *general assessment:* adequate telephone service for business and government; improving quality and increasing mobile cellular availability, with mobile subscribers far outnumbering fixed-line subscribers; domestic satellite system with 120 earth stations; extensive microwave radio relay network; considerable use of fiber-optic cable and coaxial cable
domestic: competition has spurred the mobile-cellular market; fixed-line teledensity exceeds 15 per 100 persons; mobile-cellular teledensity is about 90 per 100 persons
international: country code—52; Columbus-2 fiber-optic submarine cable with access to the US, Virgin Islands, Canary Islands, Spain, and Italy; the Americas Region Caribbean Ring System (ARCOS-1) and the MAYA-1 submarine cable system together provide access to Central America, parts of South America and the Caribbean, and the US; satellite earth stations—120 (32 Intelsat, 2 Solidaridad (giving Mexico improved access to South America, Central America, and much of the US as well as enhancing domestic

communications), 1 Panamsat, numerous Inmarsat mobile earth stations); linked to Central American Microwave System of trunk connections (2016)

Broadcast media: many TV stations and more than 1,400 radio stations with most privately owned; the Televisa group once had a virtual monopoly in TV broadcasting, but new broadcasting groups and foreign satellite and cable operators are now available (2012)

Internet country code: .mx

Internet users: total: 73,334,032

percent of population: 59.5% (July 2016 est.)
country comparison to the world: 12

TRANSPORTATION

National air transport system: *number of registered air carriers: 21*

inventory of registered aircraft operated by air carriers: 357

annual passenger traffic on registered air carriers: 45,560,063

annual freight traffic on registered air carriers: 713,985,467 mt-km (2015)

Civil aircraft registration country code prefix: XA (2016)

Airports: 1,714 (2013)
country comparison to the world: 3

Airports—with paved runways: *total:* 243
over 3,047 m: 12
2,438 to 3,047 m: 32
1,524 to 2,437 m: 80
914 to 1,523 m: 86
under 914 m: 33 (2017)

Airports—with unpaved runways: *total:* 1,471
over 3,047 m: 1
2,438 to 3,047 m: 1
1,524 to 2,437 m: 42
914 to 1,523 m: 281
under 914 m: 1,146 (2013)

Heliports: 1 (2013)

Pipelines: gas 18,074 km; liquid petroleum 2,102 km; oil 8,775 km; oil/gas/water 369 km; refined products 7,565 km; water 123 km (2013)

Railways: *total:* 15,389 km
standard gauge: 15,389 km 1.435-m gauge (27 km electrified) (2014)
country comparison to the world: 18

Roadways: *total:* 377,660 km
paved: 137,544 km (includes 7,176 km of expressways)
unpaved: 240,116 km (2012)
country comparison to the world: 20

Waterways: 2,900 km (navigable rivers and coastal canals mostly connected with ports on the country's east coast) (2012)
country comparison to the world: 33

Merchant marine: *total:* 622
by type: bulk carrier 5, general cargo 9, oil tanker 32, other 576 (2017)
country comparison to the world: 33

Ports and terminals: *major seaport(s):* Altamira, Coatzacoalcos, Lazaro Cardenas, Manzanillo, Veracruz
container port(s) (TEUs): Manzanillo (1,992,176), Lazaro Cardenas (1,242,777) (2012)
oil terminal(s): Cayo Arcas terminal, Dos Bocas terminal
LNG terminal(s) (import): Altamira, Ensenada
cruise port(s): Cancun, Cozumel, Ensenada

MILITARY AND SECURITY

Military expenditures: 0.58% of GDP (2016)
0.67% of GDP (2015)
0.67% of GDP (2014)
0.62% of GDP (2013)
0.59% of GDP (2012)
country comparison to the world: 124

Military branches: Secretariat of National Defense (Secretaria de Defensa Nacional, Sedena): Army (Ejercito), Mexican Air Force (Fuerza Aerea Mexicana, FAM); Secretariat of the Navy (Secretaria de Marina, Semar): Mexican Navy (Armada de Mexico (ARM); includes Naval Air Force (FAN), Mexican Naval Infantry Corps (Cuerpo de Infanteria de Marina, Mexmar or CIM)) (2013)

Military service age and obligation: 18 years of age for compulsory military service, conscript service

obligation is 12 months; 16 years of age with consent for voluntary enlistment; conscripts serve only in the Army; Navy and Air Force service is all voluntary; women are eligible for voluntary military service; cadets enrolled in military schools from the age of 15 are considered members of the armed forces (2012)

TRANSNATIONAL ISSUES

Disputes—international: abundant rainfall in recent years along much of the Mexico-US border region has ameliorated periodically strained water-sharing arrangements; the US has intensified security measures to monitor and control legal and illegal personnel, transport, and commodities across its border with Mexico; Mexico must deal with thousands of impoverished Guatemalans and other Central Americans who cross the porous border looking for work in Mexico and the US; Belize and Mexico are working to solve minor border demarcation discrepancies arising from inaccuracies in the 1898 border treaty

Refugees and internally displaced persons: IDPs: 311,000 (government's quashing of Zapatista uprising in 1994 in eastern Chiapas Region; drug cartel violence and government's military response since 2007; violence between and within indigenous groups) (2016)

stateless persons: 13 (2016)

Illicit drugs: major drug-producing and transit nation; Mexico is estimated to be the world's third largest producer of opium with poppy cultivation in 2015 estimated to be 28,000 hectares yielding a potential production of 475 metric tons of raw opium; government conducts the largest independent illicit-crop eradication program in the world; continues as the primary transshipment country for US-bound cocaine from South America, with an estimated 95% of annual cocaine movements toward the US stopping in Mexico; major drug syndicates control the majority of drug trafficking throughout the country; producer and distributor of ecstasy; significant money-laundering center; major supplier of heroin and largest foreign supplier of marijuana and methamphetamine to the US market

---

MICRONESIA, FEDERATED STATES OF

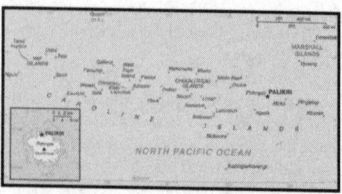

INTRODUCTION

Background: The Caroline Islands are a widely scattered archipelago in the western Pacific

Ocean; they became part of a UN Trust Territory under US administration following World War II. The eastern four island groups adopted a constitution in 1979 and chose to become the Federated States of Micronesia. (The westernmost island group became Palau.) Independence came in 1986 under a Compact of Free Association with the US, which was amended and renewed in 2004. Present concerns include large-scale unemployment, overfishing, overdependence on US foreign aid, and state perception of inequitable allocation of US aid.

GEOGRAPHY

Location: Oceania, island group in the North Pacific Ocean, about three-quarters of the way from Hawaii to Indonesia

Geographic coordinates: 6 55 N, 158 15 E

Map references: Oceania

Area: *total:* 702 sq km
land: 702 sq km
water: 0 sq km (fresh water only)
note: includes Pohnpei (Ponape), Chuuk (Truk) Islands, Yap Islands, and Kosrae (Kosaie)
country comparison to the world: 191

Area—comparative: four times the size of Washington, DC (land area only)

Land boundaries: 0 km

Coastline: 6,112 km

Maritime claims: *territorial sea:* 12 nm
exclusive economic zone: 200 nm

Climate: tropical; heavy year-round rainfall, especially in the eastern islands; located on southern edge of the typhoon belt with occasionally severe damage

Terrain: islands vary geologically from high mountainous islands to low, coral atolls; volcanic outcroppings on Pohnpei, Kosrae, and Chuuk

Elevation: *mean elevation:* NA

elevation extremes: *lowest point:* Pacific Ocean 0 m
highest point: Nanlaud on Pohnpei 782 m

Natural resources: timber, marine products, deep-seabed minerals, phosphate

Land use: *agricultural land:* 25.5%
arable land: 2.3%;
permanent crops: 19.7%;
permanent pasture: 3.5%
forest: 74.5%
other: 0% (2011 est.)
Irrigated land: 0 sq km NA (2012)

Population—distribution: the majority of the populaton lives in the coastal areas of the high islands; the mountainous interior is largely uninhabited; less than half of the population lives in urban areas

Natural hazards: typhoons (June to December)

Environment—current issues: overfishing, climate change, pollution

Environment—international agreements: *party to:* Biodiversity, Climate Change, Climate Change-Kyoto Protocol, Desertification, Hazardous Wastes, Law of the Sea, Ozone Layer Protection
signed, but not ratified: none of the selected agreements

Geography—note: composed of four major island groups totaling 607 islands

PEOPLE AND SOCIETY

Population: 104,196 (July 2017 est.)
country comparison to the world: 194

Nationality: *noun:* Micronesian(s)
adjective: Micronesian; Chuukese, Kosraen(s), Pohnpeian(s), Yapese

Ethnic groups: Chuukese/Mortlockese 49.3%, Pohnpeian 29.8%, Kosraean 6.3%, Yapese 5.7%, Yap outer islanders 5.1%, Polynesian 1.6%, Asian 1.4%, other 0.8% (2010 est.)

Languages: English (official and common language), Chuukese, Kosrean, Pohnpeian, Yapese, Ulithian, Woleaian, Nukuoro, Kapingamarangi

Religions: Roman Catholic 54.7%, Protestant 41.1% (includes Congregational 38.5%, Baptist 1.1%, Seventh Day Adventist 0.8%, Assembly of God 0.7%), Mormon 1.5%, other 1.9%, none 0.7%, unspecified 0.1% (2010 est.)

Age structure: *0-14 years:* 30.3% (male 16,050/female 15,520)
15-24 years: 19.59% (male 10,236/female 10,173)
25-54 years: 39.19% (male 19,737/female 21,094)
55-64 years: 6.99% (male 3,560/female 3,727)
65 years and over: 3.93% (male 1,849/female 2,250) (2017 est.)

Dependency ratios: *total dependency ratio:* 62.4
youth dependency ratio: 55.3
elderly dependency ratio: 7.1
potential support ratio: 14.1 (2015 est.)
Median age: 24*total:* 25.1 years
male: 24.4 years
female: 25.8 years (2017 est.)
country comparison to the world: 157

Population growth rate: -0.52% (2017 est.)
country comparison to the world: 224

Birth rate: 20 births/1,000 population (2017 est.)
country comparison to the world: 80

Death rate: 4.2 deaths/1,000 population (2017 est.)
country comparison to the world: 207

Net migration rate: -20.9 migrant(s)/1,000 population (2017 est.)
country comparison to the world: 220

Population distribution: the majority of the populaton lives in the coastal areas of the high islands; the mountainous interior is largely uninhabited; less than half of the population lives in urban areas

Urbanization: *urban population:* 22.5% of total population (2017)
rate of urbanization: 1.33% annual rate of change (2015-20 est.)

Major urban areas—population: PALIKIR (capital) 7,000 (2014)

Sex ratio: *at birth:* 1.05 male(s)/female
0-14 years: 1.03 male(s)/female
15-24 years: 1.01 male(s)/female
25-54 years: 0.94 male(s)/female
55-64 years: 0.97 male(s)/female
65 years and over: 0.81 male(s)/female
total population: 0.98 male(s)/female (2016 est.)

Maternal mortality ratio: 100 deaths/100,000 live births (2015 est.)
country comparison to the world: 72

Infant mortality rate: *total:* 19.8 deaths/1,000 live births
male: 21.9 deaths/1,000 live births
female: 17.5 deaths/1,000 live births (2017 est.)
country comparison to the world: 80

Life expectancy at birth: *total population:* 73.1 years
male: 71.1 years
female: 75.3 years (2017 est.)
country comparison to the world: 139

Total fertility rate: 2.41 children born/woman (2017 est.)
country comparison to the world: 82

Health expenditures: 13.7% of GDP (2014)
country comparison to the world: 5

Physicians density: 0.19 physicians/1,000 population (2009)

Hospital bed density: 3.2 beds/1,000 population (2009)

Drinking water source:
improved:
urban: 94.8% of population
rural: 87.4% of population
total: 89% of population
unimproved:
urban: 5.2% of population
rural: 12.6% of population
total: 11% of population (2015 est.)

Sanitation facility access:
improved:
urban: 85.1% of population
rural: 49% of population
total: 57.1% of population
unimproved:
urban: 14.9% of population
rural: 51% of population
total: 42.9% of population (2015 est.)

HIV/AIDS—adult prevalence rate: NA

HIV/AIDS—people living with HIV/AIDS: NA

HIV/AIDS—deaths: NA

Major infectious diseases: *note:* active local transmission of Zika virus by Aedes species mosquitoes has been identified in this country (as of August 2016); it poses an important risk (a large number of cases possible) among US citizens if bitten by an infective mosquito; other less common ways to get Zika are through sex, via blood transfusion, or during pregnancy, in which the pregnant woman passes Zika virus to her fetus (2016)

Obesity—adult prevalence rate: 45.8% (2016)
country comparison to the world: 10

Education expenditures: NA

GOVERNMENT

Country name: *conventional long form:* Federated States of Micronesia
conventional short form: none
local long form: Federated States of Micronesia
local short form: none
former: Trust Territory of the Pacific Islands, Ponape, Truk, and Yap Districts
abbreviation: FSM
etymology: the term "Micronesia" is a 19th-century construct of two Greek words, "micro" (small) and "nesoi" (islands), and refers to thousands of small islands in the western Pacific Ocean

Government type: federal republic in free association with the US

Capital: *name:* Palikir

geographic coordinates: 6 55 N, 158 09 E
time difference: UTC+11 (16 hours ahead of Washington, DC, during Standard Time)

Administrative divisions: 4 states; Chuuk (Truk), Kosrae (Kosaie), Pohnpei (Ponape), Yap

Independence: 3 November 1986 (from the US-administered UN trusteeship)

National holiday: Constitution Day, 10 May (1979)

613

Constitution: drafted June 1975, ratified 1 October 1978, entered into force 10 May 1979; amended 1990; note—in 2001, all 26 amendments proposed by the FSM constitutional convention were defeated in a national referendum (2016)

Legal system: mixed legal system of common and customary law

International law organization participation: has not submitted an ICJ jurisdiction declaration; non-party state to the ICCt

Citizenship: *citizenship by birth:* no
citizenship by descent only: at least one parent must be a citizen of FSM
dual citizenship recognized: no
residency requirement for naturalization: 5 years

Suffrage: 18 years of age; universal

Executive branch: *chief of state:* President Peter M. CHRISTIAN (since 11 May 2015); Vice President Yosiwo P. GEORGE (since 11 May 2015); note—the president is both chief of state and head of government

head of government: President Peter M. CHRISTIAN (since 11 May 2015); Vice President Yosiwo P. GEORGE (since 11 May 2015)
cabinet: Cabinet includes the vice president and the heads of the 8 executive departments
elections/appointments: president and vice president indirectly elected by Congress from among the 4 'at large' senators for a 4-year term (eligible for a second term); election last held on 11 May 2015 (next to be held in 2019)
election results: Peter M. CHRISTIAN elected president by Congress; Yosiwo P. GEORGE elected vice president

Legislative branch: *description:* unicameral Congress (14 seats; 10 members directly elected in single-seat constituencies by simple majority vote to serve 2-year terms and 4 directly elected from each of the 4 states by proportional representation vote to serve 4-year terms)
elections: last held on 7 March 2017 (next to be held in March 2019)
election results: percent of vote—NA; seats—independent 14

Judicial branch: *highest court(s):* Federated States of Micronesia (FSM) Supreme Court (consists of the chief justice and not more than 5 associate justices and organized into appellate and criminal divisions)
judge selection and term of office: justices appointed by the president of the Federated States of Micronesia with the approval of two-thirds of Congress; justices appointed for life
subordinate courts: the highest state-level courts are: Chuuk Supreme Court; Korsae State Court; Pohnpei State Court; Yap State Court

Political parties and leaders: no formal parties

Political pressure groups and leaders: NA

International organization participation: ACP, ADB, AOSIS, FAO, G-77, IBRD, ICAO, ICRM, IDA, IFC, IFRCS, IMF, IOC, IOM, IPU, ITSO, ITU, MIGA, OPCW, PIF, Sparteca, SPC, UN, UNCTAD, UNESCO, WHO, WMO

Diplomatic representation in the US: *chief of mission:* Ambassador Akillino Harris SUSAIA (since 24 April 2017)
chancery: 1725 N Street NW, Washington, DC 20036
telephone: [1] (202) 223-4383
FAX: [1] (202) 223-4391
consulate(s) general: Honolulu (HI), Tamuning (Guam)

Diplomatic representation from the US: *chief of mission:* Ambassador Robert Annan RILEY III (since 16 August 2016)
embassy: 101 Upper Pics Road, Kolonia
mailing address: P. O. Box 1286, Kolonia, Pohnpei, 96941; U.S. Embassy in Micronesia, 4120 Kolonia Place, Washington, D.C. 20521-4120
telephone: [691] 320-2187
FAX: [691] 320-2186

Flag description: light blue with four white five-pointed stars centered; the stars are arranged in a diamond pattern; blue symbolizes the Pacific Ocean, the stars represent the four island groups of Chuuk, Kosrae, Pohnpei, and Yap

National symbol(s): four, five-pointed, white stars on a light blue field; national colors: light blue, white

National anthem: *name:* "Patriots of Micronesia"
lyrics/music: unknown
note: adopted 1991; also known as "Across All Micronesia"; the music is based on the 1820 German patriotic song "Ich hab mich ergeben", which was the West German national anthem from 1949-1950; variants of this tune are used in Johannes Brahms' "Festival Overture" and Gustav Mahler's "Third Symphony"

ECONOMY

Economy—overview: Economic activity consists largely of subsistence farming and fishing, and government, which employs two-thirds of the adult working population and receives funding largely—58% in 2013—from Compact of Free Association assistance provided by the US. The islands have few commercially valuable mineral deposits. The potential for tourism is limited by isolation, lack of adequate facilities, and limited internal air and water transportation.

Under the terms of the original Compact, the US provided $1.3 billion in grants and aid from 1986 to 2001. The US and the Federated States of Micronesia (FSM) negotiated a second (amended) Compact agreement in 2002-03 that took effect in 2004. The amended Compact runs for a 20-year period to 2023; during which the US will provide roughly $2.1 billion to the FSM. The amended Compact also develops a trust fund for the FSM that will provide a comparable income stream beyond 2024 when Compact grants end.

The country's medium-term economic outlook appears fragile because of dependence on US assistance and lackluster performance of its small and stagnant private sector.

GDP (purchasing power parity): $347 million (2017 est.)
$340.1 million (2016 est.)
$330 million (2015 est.)
note: data are in 2017 dollars
country comparison to the world: 216

GDP (official exchange rate): $329 million (2016 est.)

GDP—real growth rate: 2% (2017 est.)
3% (2016 est.)
3.7% (2015 est.)
country comparison to the world: 154

GDP—per capita (PPP): $3,400 (2017 est.)
$3,300 (2016 est.)
$3,200 (2015 est.)
note: data are in 2017 dollars
country comparison to the world: 190

GDP—composition, by end use:
household consumption: 83.5%
government consumption: 41.8%
investment in fixed assets: 24.3%
investment in inventories: 0%
exports of goods and services: 26.6%
imports of goods and services: -76.2% (2013 est.)

GDP—composition, by sector of origin:
agriculture: 26.3%
industry: 18.9%
services: 54.8% (2013 est.)

Agriculture—products: taro, yams, coconuts, bananas, cassava (manioc, tapioca), sakau (kava), Kosraen citrus, betel nuts, black pepper, fish, pigs, chickens

Industries: tourism, construction; specialized aquaculture, craft items (shell and wood)

Industrial production growth rate: NA%

Labor force: 37,920 (2010 est.)
country comparison to the world: 201

Labor force—by occupation: *agriculture:* 0.9%
industry: 5.2%
services: 93.9%
note: two-thirds of the labor force are government employees (2013 est.)

Unemployment rate: 16.2% (2010 est.)
country comparison to the world: 175

Population below poverty line: 26.7% (2000 est.)

Household income or consumption by percentage share: *lowest 10%:* NA%
highest 10%: NA%

Distribution of family income—Gini index: 61.1 (2013 est.)
country comparison to the world: 4

Budget: *revenues:* $213.8 million
expenditures: $192.1 million (FY12/13 est.)
Taxes and other revenues: 65% of GDP (FY12/13 est.)
country comparison to the world: 6

Budget surplus (+) or deficit (-): 6.6% of GDP (FY12/13 est.)
country comparison to the world: 5

Public debt: 24.8% of GDP (2016 est.)
25.8% of GDP (2015 est.)
country comparison to the world: 178

Fiscal year: 1 October—30 September

Inflation rate (consumer prices): 0.9% (2017 est.)
0.5% (2016 est.)
country comparison to the world: 32

Commercial bank prime lending rate: 15.7% (31 December 2016 est.)
15.7% (31 December 2016 est.)
country comparison to the world: 36

Stock of narrow money: $196 million (31 December 2013 est.)
$44.07 million (31 December 2015 est.)
country comparison to the world: 184

Stock of broad money: $178.3 million (31 December 2015 est.)
$225.2 million (31 December 2013 est.)
country comparison to the world: 192

Stock of domestic credit: $56.98 million (31 December 2017 est.)
$-103 million (31 December 2015 est.)
country comparison to the world: 189

Market value of publicly traded shares: $NA

Current account balance: $11 million (2017 est.)
$10 million (2016 est.)
country comparison to the world: 59

Exports: $88.3 million (2013 est.)
$39.88 million (2015 est.)
country comparison to the world: 197

Exports—commodities: fish, sakau (kava), betel nuts, black pepper

Imports: $258.5 million (2013 est.)
$167.8 million (2015 est.)
country comparison to the world: 200

Imports—commodities: food, beverages, clothing, computers, household electronics, appliances, manufactured goods, automobiles, machinery and equipment, furniture, tools

Reserves of foreign exchange and gold: $157 million (31 December 2016 est.)
$135.1 million (31 December 2015 est.)
country comparison to the world: 161

Debt—external: $93.6 million (2013 est.)
$93.5 million (2012 est.)
country comparison to the world: 195

Stock of direct foreign investment—at home: $15.8 million (2013 est.)
$34.4 million (2012 est.)
country comparison to the world: 132

Exchange rates: the US dollar is used

ENERGY

Electricity access: *population without electricity:* 42,934
electrification—*total population:* 59%
electrification—urban areas: 100%

electrification—rural areas: 45% (2012)

Electricity—production: 192 million kWh (2002)
country comparison to the world: 191

Electricity—consumption: 178.6 million kWh (2002)
country comparison to the world: 193

Electricity—exports: 0 kWh (2013 est.)
country comparison to the world: 136

Electricity—imports: 0 kWh (2013 est.)
country comparison to the world: 150

Electricity—installed generating capacity: 18,000 kW (2015 est.)
country comparison to the world: 206

Electricity—from fossil fuels: 96% of total installed capacity (2015 est.)
country comparison to the world: 52

Electricity—from nuclear fuels: 0% of total installed capacity (2015 est.)
country comparison to the world: 91

Electricity—from hydroelectric plants: 1% of total installed capacity (2013 est.)
country comparison to the world: 146

Electricity—from other renewable sources: 3% of total installed capacity (2013 est.)
country comparison to the world: 112

Crude oil—production: 0 bbl/day (2014)
country comparison to the world: 172

Crude oil—exports: 0 bbl/day (2014)
country comparison to the world: 124

Crude oil—imports: 0 bbl/day (2014)
country comparison to the world: 127

Crude oil—proved reserves: 0 bbl (1 January 2014)
country comparison to the world: 169

Refined petroleum products—production: 0 bbl/day (2014)
country comparison to the world: 178

Refined petroleum products—exports: 0 bbl/day
country comparison to the world: 156

Natural gas—production: 0 cu m (2014)
country comparison to the world: 136

Natural gas—proved reserves: 0 cu m
country comparison to the world: 140

Carbon dioxide emissions from consumption of energy: 105 Mt (2010 est.)
country comparison to the world: 214

COMMUNICATIONS

Telephones—fixed lines: *total subscriptions:* 6,808
subscriptions per 100 inhabitants: 6 (July 2016 est.)
country comparison to the world: 204

Telephones—mobile cellular: *total:* 31,400
subscriptions per 100 inhabitants: 30 (July 2016 est.)
country comparison to the world: 208

Telephone system: *general assessment:* adequate system
domestic: islands interconnected by shortwave radiotelephone (used mostly for government purposes), satellite (Intelsat) ground stations, and some coaxial and fiber-optic cable; mobile-cellular service available on the major islands
international: country code—691; satellite earth stations—5 Intelsat (Pacific Ocean); in 2015, Fiber Optic was launched and is the primary communication path to the outside world (2016)

Broadcast media: no TV broadcast stations; each state has a multi-channel cable service with TV transmissions carrying roughly 95% imported programming and 5% local programming; about a half-dozen radio stations (2009)

Internet country code: .fm
Internet users: total: 33,000

percent of population: 31.5% (July 2016 est.)
country comparison to the world: 196

TRANSPORTATION

Civil aircraft registration country code prefix: V6 (2016)

Airports: 6 (2013)
country comparison to the world: 173

Airports—with paved runways: *total:* 6
1,524 to 2,437 m: 4
914 to 1,523 m: 2 (2017)

Roadways: *total:* 388 km
paved: 184 km
unpaved: 204 km (2015)
country comparison to the world: 201

Merchant marine: *total:* 88
by type: bulk carrier 2, general cargo 63, oil tanker 6, other 17 (2017)
country comparison to the world: 89

Ports and terminals: *major seaport(s):* Colonia (Tamil Harbor), Molsron Lele Harbor, Pohnepi Harbor

MILITARY AND SECURITY

Military branches: no regular military forces (2012)

Military—note: defense is the responsibility of the US

TRANSNATIONAL ISSUES

Disputes—international: none

Illicit drugs: major consumer of cannabis

MONACO

INTRODUCTION

Background: The Genoese built a fortress on the site of present day Monaco in 1215. The current ruling GRIMALDI family first seized control in 1297 but was not able to permanently secure its holding until 1419. Economic development was spurred in the late 19th century with a railroad linkup to France and the opening of a casino. Since then, the principality's mild climate, splendid scenery, and gambling facilities have made Monaco world famous as a tourist and recreation center.

GEOGRAPHY

Location: Western Europe, bordering the Mediterranean Sea on the southern coast of France, near the border with Italy

Geographic coordinates: 43 44 N, 7 24 E

Map references: Europe

Area: *total:* 2 sq km
land: 2 sq km
water: 0 sq km
country comparison to the world: 253

Area—comparative: about three times the size of the National Mall in Washington, DC

Land boundaries: *total:* 6 km
border countries (1): France 6 km

Coastline: 4.1 km

Maritime claims: *territorial sea:* 12 nm
exclusive economic zone: 12 nm

Climate: Mediterranean with mild, wet winters and hot, dry summers

Terrain: hilly, rugged, rocky

Elevation: *mean elevation:* NA

elevation extremes: *lowest point:* Mediterranean Sea 0 m
highest point: Chemin des Revoires on Mont Agel 162 m

Natural resources: none

Land use: *agricultural land:* 1%

arable land: 0%;
permanent crops: 1%;
permanent pasture: 0%
forest: 0%
other: 99% (2011 est.)
Irrigated land: 0 sq km (2012)

Population—distribution: the most densely populated country in the world; its entire population living on 2 square km

Natural hazards: none

Environment—current issues: NA no serious issues; actively monitors pollution levels in air and water

Environment—international agreements: *party to:* Air Pollution, Air Pollution-Sulfur 94, Air Pollution-Volatile Organic Compounds, Biodiversity, Climate Change, Climate Change-Kyoto Protocol, Desertification, Endangered Species, Hazardous Wastes, Law of the Sea, Marine Dumping, Ozone Layer Protection, Ship Pollution, Wetlands, Whaling
signed, but not ratified: none of the selected agreements

Geography—note: second-smallest independent state in the world (after the Holy See); smallest country with a coastline; almost entirely urban

PEOPLE AND SOCIETY

Population: 30,645 (July 2017 est.)
note: immigrants make up almost 55% of the total population, according to UN data (2017)
country comparison to the world: 217

Nationality: *noun:* Monegasque(s) or Monacan(s)
adjective: Monegasque or Monacan

Ethnic groups: French (official) 47%, Monegasque 16%, Italian 16%, other 21%

Languages: French (official), English, Italian, Monegasque

Religions: Roman Catholic 90% (official), other 10%

Age structure: *0-14 years:* 10.68% (male 1,685/female 1,587)
15-24 years: 9.27% (male 1,464/female 1,376)
25-54 years: 32.91% (male 5,067/female 5,018)
55-64 years: 14.94% (male 2,286/female 2,292)
65 years and over: 32.21% (male 4,387/female 5,483) (2017 est.)

Median age: *total:* 53.1 years
male: 51.7 years
female: 54.5 years (2017 est.)
country comparison to the world: 1

Population growth rate: 0.24% (2017 est.)
country comparison to the world: 179

Birth rate: 6.6 births/1,000 population (2017 est.)
country comparison to the world: 226

Death rate: 9.8 deaths/1,000 population (2017 est.)
country comparison to the world: 44

Net migration rate: 5.7 migrant(s)/1,000 population (2017 est.)
country comparison to the world: 19

Population distribution: the most densely populated country in the world; its entire population living on 2 square km

Urbanization: *urban population:* 100% of total population (2017)
rate of urbanization: 0.8% annual rate of change (2015-20 est.)

Major urban areas—population: MONACO (capital) 38,000 (2014)

Sex ratio: *at birth:* 1.04 male(s)/female
0-14 years: 1.06 male(s)/female
15-24 years: 1.06 male(s)/female
25-54 years: 1 male(s)/female
55-64 years: 0.99 male(s)/female
65 years and over: 0.81 male(s)/female
total population: 0.95 male(s)/female (2016 est.)

Infant mortality rate: *total:* 1.8 deaths/1,000 live births
male: 2.1 deaths/1,000 live births
female: 1.6 deaths/1,000 live births (2017 est.)
country comparison to the world: 225

Life expectancy at birth: *total population:* 89.4 years
male: 85.6 years
female: 93.5 years (2017 est.)
country comparison to the world: 1

Total fertility rate: 1.53 children born/woman (2017 est.)
country comparison to the world: 193

Health expenditures: 4.3% of GDP (2014)
country comparison to the world: 160

Physicians density: 6.65 physicians/1,000 population (2014)

Hospital bed density: 13.8 beds/1,000 population (2012)

Drinking water source:
improved:
urban: 100% of population
total: 100% of population
unimproved:
urban: 0% of population
total: 0% of population (2015 est.)

Sanitation facility access:
improved:
urban: 100% of population
rural: NA
total: 100% of population
unimproved:
urban: 0% of population
rural: NA
total: 0% of population (2015 est.)

HIV/AIDS—adult prevalence rate: NA

HIV/AIDS—people living with HIV/AIDS: NA

HIV/AIDS—deaths: NA

Education expenditures: 1% of GDP (2014)

country comparison to the world: 169

GOVERNMENT

Country name: *conventional long form:* Principality of Monaco
conventional short form: Monaco
local long form: Principaute de Monaco
local short form: Monaco
etymology: founded as a Greek colony in the 6th century B.C., the name derives from two Greek words "monos" (single, alone) and "oikos" (house) to convey the sense of a people "living apart" or in a "single habitation"

Government type: constitutional monarchy

Capital: *name:* Monaco
geographic coordinates: 43 44 N, 7 25 E
time difference: UTC+1 (6 hours ahead of Washington, DC, during Standard Time)
daylight saving time: +1hr, begins last Sunday in March; ends last Sunday in October

Administrative divisions: none; there are no first-order administrative divisions as defined by the US Government, but there are 4 quarters (quartiers, singular—quartier); Fontvieille, La Condamine, Monaco-Ville, Monte-Carlo; note—Moneghetti, a part of La Condamine, is sometimes called the 5th quarter of Monaco

Independence: 1419 (beginning of permanent rule by the House of GRIMALDI)

National holiday: National Day (Saint Rainier's Day), 19 November (1857)

Constitution: history: previous 1911 (suspended 1959); latest adopted 17 December 1962
amendments: proposed by joint agreement of the chief of state (the prince) and the National Council; passage requires two-thirds majority vote of National Council members; amended 2002 (2016)

Legal system: civil law system influenced by French legal tradition

International law organization participation: has not submitted an ICJ jurisdiction declaration; non-party state to the ICCt

Citizenship: *citizenship by birth:* no
citizenship by descent only: the father must be a citizen of Monaco; in the case of a child born out of wedlock, the mother must be a citizen and father unknown
dual citizenship recognized: no
residency requirement for naturalization: 10 years

Suffrage: 18 years of age; universal

Executive branch: *chief of state:* Prince ALBERT II (since 6 April 2005)
head of government: Minister of State Serge TELLE (since 1 February 2016)
cabinet: Council of Government under the authority of the monarch
elections/appointments: the monarchy is hereditary; minister of state appointed by the monarch from a list of three French national candidates presented by the French Government

Legislative branch: *description:* unicameral National Council or Conseil National (24 seats; 16 members directly elected in multi-seat constituencies by simple majority vote and 8 directly elected by proportional representation vote; members serve 5-year terms)
elections: last held on 11 February 2018 (next to be held in February 2023)
election results: percent of vote by party—Priorite Monaco 57.7%, Horizon Monaco 26.1%, Union Monegasque 16.2%; seats by party—Priorite Monaco 21, Horizon Monaco 2, Union Monegasque 1`

Judicial branch: *highest court(s):* Supreme Court (consists of 5 permanent members and 2 substitutes)
judge selection and term of office: Supreme Court members appointed by the monarch upon the proposals of the National Council, State Council, Crown Council, Court of Appeal, and Trial Court
subordinate courts: Court of Appeal; Civil Court of First Instance

Political parties and leaders: Horizon Monaco [Laurent NOUVION]
Priorite Monaco [Stephane VALERI]
Renaissance [SBM (public corporation)]
Union Monegasque [Jean-Francois ROBILLON]

Political pressure groups and leaders: NA

International organization participation: CD, CE, FAO, IAEA, ICAO, ICC (national committees), ICRM, IFRCS, IHO, IMO, IMSO, Interpol, IOC, IPU, ITSO, ITU, OAS (observer), OIF, OPCW, OSCE, Schengen Convention (de facto member), UN, UNCTAD, UNESCO, UNIDO, Union Latina, UNWTO, UPU, WHO, WIPO, WMO

Diplomatic representation in the US: *chief of mission:* Ambassador Maguy MACCARIO-DOYLE (since 3 December 2013)
chancery: 3400 International Drive NW, Suite 2K-100, Washington, DC 20008
telephone: (202) 234-1530
FAX: (202) 244-7656
consulate(s) general: New York

Diplomatic representation from the US: the US does not have an embassy in Monaco; the US Ambassador to France is accredited to Monaco; the US Consul General in Marseille (France), under the authority of the US Ambassador to France, handles diplomatic and consular matters concerning Monaco

Flag description: two equal horizontal bands of red (top) and white; the colors are those of the ruling House of Grimaldi and have been in use since 1339, making the flag one of the world's oldest national banners
note: similar to the flag of Indonesia which is longer and the flag of Poland which is white (top) and red

National symbol(s): red and white lozenges (diamond shapes); national colors: red, white

National anthem: name: "A Marcia de Muneghu" (The March of Monaco)
lyrics/music: Louis NOTARI/Charles ALBRECHT

note: music adopted 1867, lyrics adopted 1931; although French is commonly spoken, only the Monegasque lyrics are official; the French version is known as "Hymne Monegasque" (Monegasque Anthem); the words are generally only sung on official occasions

ECONOMY

Economy—overview: Monaco, bordering France on the Mediterranean coast, is a popular resort, attracting tourists to its casino and pleasant climate. The principality also is a banking center and has successfully sought to diversify into services and small, high-value-added, nonpolluting industries. The state retains monopolies in a number of sectors, including tobacco, the telephone network, and the postal service. Living standards are high, roughly comparable to those in prosperous French metropolitan areas.

The state has no income tax and low business taxes and thrives as a tax haven both for individuals who have established residence and for foreign companies that have set up businesses and offices. Monaco, however, is not a tax-free shelter; it charges nearly 20% value-added tax, collects stamp duties, and companies face a 33% tax on profits unless they can show that three-quarters of profits are generated within the principality. Monaco was formally removed from the OECD's "grey list" of uncooperative tax jurisdictions in late 2009, but continues to face international pressure to abandon its banking secrecy laws and help combat tax evasion. In October 2014, Monaco officially became the 84th jurisdiction participating in the OECD's Multilateral Convention on Mutual Administrative Assistance in Tax Matters, an effort to combat offshore tax avoidance and evasion.

Monaco's reliance on tourism and banking for its economic growth has left it vulnerable to downturns in France and other European economies which are the principality's main trade partners. In 2009, Monaco's GDP fell by 11.5% as the eurozone crisis precipitated a sharp drop in tourism and retail activity and home sales. A modest recovery ensued in 2010 and intensified in 2013, with GDP growth of more than 9%, but Monaco's economic prospects remain uncertain.

GDP (purchasing power parity): $7.672 billion (2015 est.)
$7.279 billion (2014 est.)
$6.79 billion (2013 est.)
note: data are in 2015 US dollars
country comparison to the world: 166

GDP (official exchange rate): $6.006 billion (2013 est.)

GDP—real growth rate: 5.4% (2015 est.)
7.2% (2014 est.)
9.6% (2013 est.)
country comparison to the world: 31

GDP—per capita (PPP): $115,700 (2015 est.)
$109,200 (2014 est.)
$101,900 (2013 est.)
country comparison to the world: 3

GDP—composition, by sector of origin:
agriculture: 0%
industry: 14%
services: 86% (2013)

Agriculture—products: none

Industries: banking, insurance, tourism, construction, small-scale industrial and consumer products

Industrial production growth rate: 6.8% (2015)
country comparison to the world: 28

Labor force: 52,000
note: includes all foreign workers (2014 est.)
country comparison to the world: 191

Labor force—by occupation: *agriculture:* 0%
industry: 16.1%
services: 83.9% (2012 est.)

Unemployment rate: 2% (2012)
country comparison to the world: 14

Population below poverty line: NA%

Household income or consumption by percentage share: *lowest 10%:* NA%
highest 10%: NA%

Budget: *revenues:* $878.4 million
expenditures: $934.6 million (2011 est.)
Taxes and other revenues: 14.6% of GDP (2011 est.)
country comparison to the world: 194

Budget surplus (+) or deficit (-): -0.9% of GDP (2011 est.)
country comparison to the world: 56

Fiscal year: calendar year

Inflation rate (consumer prices): 1.5% (2010)
country comparison to the world: 64

Market value of publicly traded shares: $NA

Exports: $964.6 million (2017 est.)
$1.115 billion (2011)

note: full customs integration with France, which collects and rebates Monegasque trade duties; also participates in EU market system through customs union with France
country comparison to the world: 159

Imports: $1.371 billion (2017 est.)
$1.162 billion (2011 est.)
note: full customs integration with France, which collects and rebates Monegasque trade duties; also participates in EU market system through customs union with France
country comparison to the world: 170

Debt—external: $NA

Exchange rates: euros (EUR) per US dollar—
0.906 (2017 est.)
0.9214 (2016 est.)
0.9214 (2015 est.)
0.885 (2014 est.)
0.7634 (2013 est.)

ENERGY

Electricity access: *electrification—total population:* 100% (2016)

COMMUNICATIONS

Telephones—fixed lines: *total subscriptions:* 46,575
subscriptions per 100 inhabitants: 152 (July 2016 est.)
country comparison to the world: 162

Telephones—mobile cellular: *total:* 33,297
subscriptions per 100 inhabitants: 109 (July 2016 est.)
country comparison to the world: 207

Telephone system: *general assessment:* modern automatic telephone system; the country's sole

fixed-line operator offers a full range of services to residential and business customers
domestic: combined fixed-line and mobile-cellular teledensity exceeds 250 per 100 persons
international: country code—377; no satellite earth stations; connected by cable into the French communications system (2016)

Broadcast media: TV Monte-Carlo operates a TV network; cable TV available; Radio Monte-Carlo has extensive radio networks in France and Italy with French-language broadcasts to France beginning in the 1960s and Italian-language broadcasts to Italy beginning in the 1970s; other radio stations include Riviera Radio and Radio Monaco (2012)

Internet country code: .mc
Internet users: total: 29,116

percent of population: 95.2% (July 2016 est.)
country comparison to the world: 199

TRANSPORTATION

Civil aircraft registration country code prefix: 3A (2016)

Heliports: 1 (2012)

Roadways: *total:* 77 km
paved: 77 km (2010)
country comparison to the world: 218

Ports and terminals: *major seaport(s):* Monaco

MILITARY AND SECURITY

Military branches: no regular military forces; Directorate of Public Security (2012)

Military—note: defense is the responsibility of France

TRANSNATIONAL ISSUES

Disputes—international: none

MONGOLIA

INTRODUCTION

Background: The Mongols gained fame in the 13th century when under Chinggis KHAAN they established a huge Eurasian empire through conquest. After his death the empire was divided into several powerful Mongol states, but these broke apart in the 14th century. The Mongols eventually retired to their original steppe homelands and in the late 17th century came under Chinese rule. Mongolia declared its independence from the Manchu-led

Qing Empire in 1911 and achieved limited autonomy until 1919, when it again came under Chinese control. The Mongolian Revolution of 1921 ended Chinese dominance, and a communist regime, the Mongolian People's Republic, took power in 1924.

The modern country of Mongolia, however, represents only part of the Mongols' historical homeland; today, more ethnic Mongolians live in the Inner Mongolia Autonomous Region in the People's Republic of China than in Mongolia. Since the country's peaceful democratic revolution in 1990, the ex-communist Mongolian People's Revolutionary Party (MPRP)—which took the name Mongolian People's Party (MPP) in 2010—has competed for political power with the Democratic Party (DP) and several other smaller parties, including a new party formed by former President ENKHBAYAR, which confusingly adopted for itself the MPRP name. In the country's most recent parliamentary elections in June

2016, Mongolians handed the MPP overwhelming control of Parliament, largely pushing out the DP, which had overseen a sharp decline in Mongolia's economy during its control of Parliament in the preceding years. Mongolians elected a DP member, Khaltmaa BATTULGA, as president in 2017.

GEOGRAPHY

Location: Northern Asia, between China and Russia

Geographic coordinates: 46 00 N, 105 00 E

Map references: Asia

Area: *total:* 1,564,116 sq km
land: 1,553,556 sq km
water: 10,560 sq km
country comparison to the world: 20

Area—comparative: slightly smaller than Alaska; more than twice the size of Texas

Land boundaries: *total:* 8,082 km
border countries (2): China 4,630 km, Russia 3,452 km

Coastline: 0 km (landlocked)

Maritime claims: none (landlocked)

Climate: desert; continental (large daily and seasonal temperature ranges)

Terrain: vast semidesert and desert plains, grassy steppe, mountains in west and southwest; Gobi Desert in south-central

Elevation: *mean elevation:* 1,528 m

elevation extremes: *lowest point:* Hoh Nuur 560 m
highest point: Nayramadlin Orgil (Khuiten Peak) 4,374 m

Natural resources: oil, coal, copper, molybdenum, tungsten, phosphates, tin, nickel, zinc, fluorspar, gold, silver, iron

Land use: *agricultural land:* 73%
arable land: 0.4%;
permanent crops: 0%;
permanent pasture: 72.6%
forest: 7%
other: 20% (2011 est.)
Irrigated land: 840 sq km (2012)

Population—distribution: sparsely distributed population throughout the country; the capital of Ulaanbaatar and the northern city of Darhan support the highest population densities

Natural hazards: dust storms; grassland and forest fires; drought; "zud," which is harsh winter conditions

Environment—current issues: limited natural freshwater resources in some areas; the policies of former Communist regimes promoted rapid urbanization and industrial growth that had negative effects on the environment; the burning of soft coal in power plants and the lack of enforcement of environmental laws severely polluted the air in Ulaanbaatar; deforestation, overgrazing, and the converting of virgin land to agricultural production increased soil erosion from wind and rain; desertification and mining activities had a deleterious effect on the environment

Environment—international agreements: *party to:* Biodiversity, Climate Change, Climate Change-Kyoto Protocol, Desertification, Endangered Species, Environmental Modification, Hazardous Wastes, Law of the Sea, Ozone Layer Protection, Ship Pollution, Wetlands, Whaling
signed, but not ratified: none of the selected agreements

Geography—note: landlocked; strategic location between China and Russia

PEOPLE AND SOCIETY

Population: 3,068,243
note: Mongolia is one of the least densely populated countries in the world (2 people per sq km); twice as many ethnic Mongols (some 6 million) live in Inner Mongolia (Nei Mongol) in neighboring China (July 2017 est.)

country comparison to the world: 135

Nationality: *noun:* Mongolian(s)
adjective: Mongolian

Ethnic groups: Khalkh 81.9%, Kazak 3.8%, Dorvod 2.7%, Bayad 2.1%, Buryat-Bouriates 1.7%, Zakhchin 1.2%, Dariganga 1%, Uriankhai 1%, other 4.6% (2010 est.)

Languages: Mongolian 90% (official) (Khalkha dialect is predominant), Turkic, Russian (1999)

Religions: Buddhist 53%, Muslim 3%, Shamanist 2.9%, Christian 2.2%, other 0.4%, none 38.6% (2010 est.)

Age structure: *0-14 years:* 26.95% (male 421,675/female 405,298)
15-24 years: 16.09% (male 249,805/female 243,784)
25-54 years: 45.6% (male 677,679/female 721,435)
55-64 years: 7.07% (male 99,099/female 117,818)
65 years and over: 4.29% (male 53,364/female 78,286) (2017 est.)

Dependency ratios: *total dependency ratio:* 48.5
youth dependency ratio: 42.7
elderly dependency ratio: 5.8
potential support ratio: 17.3 (2015 est.)

Median age: *total:* 28.3 years
male: 27.5 years
female: 29.2 years (2017 est.)
country comparison to the world: 134

Population growth rate: 1.18% (2017 est.)
country comparison to the world: 93

Birth rate: 18.9 births/1,000 population (2017 est.)
country comparison to the world: 88

Death rate: 6.3 deaths/1,000 population (2017 est.)
country comparison to the world: 152

Net migration rate: -0.8 migrant(s)/1,000 population (2017 est.)
country comparison to the world: 133

Population distribution: sparsely distributed population throughout the country; the capital of Ulaanbaatar and the northern city of Darhan support the highest population densities

Urbanization: *urban population:* 73.6% of total population (2017)
rate of urbanization: 2.23% annual rate of change (2015-20 est.)

Major urban areas—population: ULAANBAATAR (capital) 1.377 million (2015)

Sex ratio: *at birth:* 1.05 male(s)/female
0-14 years: 1.04 male(s)/female
15-24 years: 1.02 male(s)/female
25-54 years: 0.94 male(s)/female
55-64 years: 0.85 male(s)/female
65 years and over: 0.69 male(s)/female
total population: 0.96 male(s)/female (2016 est.)

Mother's mean age at first birth: 20.5 years
note: median age at first birth among women 20-24 (2008 est.)

Maternal mortality ratio: 44 deaths/100,000 live births (2015 est.)
country comparison to the world: 101

Infant mortality rate: *total:* 21.1 deaths/1,000 live births
male: 24.2 deaths/1,000 live births
female: 17.9 deaths/1,000 live births (2017 est.)
country comparison to the world: 79

Life expectancy at birth: *total population:* 69.9 years
male: 65.7 years
female: 74.4 years (2017 est.)
country comparison to the world: 160

Total fertility rate: 2.09 children born/woman (2017 est.)
country comparison to the world: 107

Contraceptive prevalence rate: 54.6% (2013)

Health expenditures: 4.7% of GDP (2014)
country comparison to the world: 153

Physicians density: 2.88 physicians/1,000 population (2011)

Hospital bed density: 6.8 beds/1,000 population (2012)

Drinking water source:
improved:
urban: 66.4% of population
rural: 59.2% of population
total: 64.4% of population
unimproved:
urban: 33.6% of population
rural: 40.8% of population
total: 35.6% of population (2015 est.)

Sanitation facility access:
improved:
urban: 66.4% of population
rural: 42.6% of population
total: 59.7% of population
unimproved:
urban: 33.6% of population
rural: 57.4% of population
total: 40.3% of population (2015 est.)

HIV/AIDS—adult prevalence rate: <.1% (2016 est.)

HIV/AIDS—people living with HIV/AIDS: <500 (2016 est.)

HIV/AIDS—deaths: <100 (2016 est.)

Obesity—adult prevalence rate: 20.6% (2016)
country comparison to the world: 96

Children under the age of 5 years underweight: 1.6% (2013)
country comparison to the world: 92

Education expenditures: 4.6% of GDP (2011)
country comparison to the world: 58

Literacy: *definition:* age 15 and over can read and write
total population: 98.4%
male: 98.2%
female: 98.6% (2015 est.)

School life expectancy (primary to tertiary education): *total:* 15 years
male: 14 years
female: 16 years (2015)

Unemployment, youth ages 15-24: *total:* 17.9%
male: 16.8%
female: 19.4% (2015 est.)

country comparison to the world: 92

GOVERNMENT

Country name: conventional long form: none
conventional short form: Mongolia
local long form: none
local short form: Mongol Uls
former: Outer Mongolia
etymology: the name means "Land of the Mongols" in Latin; the Mongolian name Mongol Uls translates as "Mongol State"

Government type: semi-presidential republic

Capital: name: Ulaanbaatar

geographic coordinates: 47 55 N, 106 55 E

time difference: UTC+8 (13 hours ahead of Washington, DC, during Standard Time)

daylight saving time: +1hr, begins last Saturday in March; ends last Saturday in September

note: Mongolia has two time zones—Ulaanbaatar Time (8 hours in advance of UTC) and Hovd Time (7 hours in advance of UTC)

Administrative divisions: 21 provinces (aymguud, singular—aymag) and 1 municipality* (singular—hot); Arhangay, Bayanhongor, Bayan-Olgiy, Bulgan, Darhan-Uul, Dornod, Dornogovi, Dundgovi, Dzavhan (Zavkhan), Govi-Altay, Govisumber, Hentiy, Hovd, Hovsgol, Omnogovi, Orhon, Ovorhangay, Selenge, Suhbaatar, Tov, Ulaanbaatar*, Uvs

Independence: 29 December 1911 (independence declared from China; in actuality, autonomy attained); 11 July 1921 (from China)

National holiday: Naadam (games) holiday (commemorates independence from China in the 1921 Revolution), 11-15 July; Constitution Day (marks the date that the Mongolian People's Republic was created under a new constitution), 26 November (1924)

Constitution: history: several previous; latest adopted 13 January 1992, effective 12 February 1992

amendments: proposed by the State Great Hural, by the president of the republic, by the government, or by petition submitted to the State Great Hural by the Constitutional Court; conducting referenda on proposed amendments requires at least two-thirds majority vote of the State Great Hural; passage of amendments by the State Great Hural requires at least three-quarters majority vote; passage by referendum requires majority participation of qualified voters and a majority of votes; amended 1999, 2001 (2017)

Legal system: civil law system influenced by Soviet and Romano-Germanic legal systems; constitution ambiguous on judicial review of legislative acts

International law organization participation: has not submitted an ICJ jurisdiction declaration; accepts ICCt jurisdiction

Citizenship: citizenship by birth: no
citizenship by descent only: both parents must be citizens of Mongolia; one parent if born within Mongolia

dual citizenship recognized: no
residency requirement for naturalization: 5 years

Suffrage: 18 years of age; universal

Executive branch: chief of state: President Khaltmaa BATTULGA (since 10 July 2017)

head of government: Prime Minister Ukhnaa KHURELSUKH (since 4 October 2017); Deputy Prime Minister Ulziisaikhan ENKHTUVSHUN (since 18 October 2017); note—Prime Minister Jargaltulga ERDENEBAT (since 8 July 2016) was voted out of office by the Parliament on 7 September 2017

cabinet: Cabinet nominated by the prime minister in consultation with the president, confirmed by the State Great Hural (parliament)

elections/appointments: presidential candidates nominated by political parties represented in the State Great Hural and directly elected by simple majority popular vote for a 4-year term (eligible for a second term); election last held on 26 June 2017 with a runoff held 9 July 2017 (next to be held in 2021); following legislative elections, the leader of the majority party or majority coalition usually elected prime minister by the State Great Hural

election results: Khaltmaa BATTULGA elected president in second round; percent of vote in first round—Khaltmaa BATTULGA (DP) 38.1%, Miyegombo ENKHBOLD (MPP) 30.3%, Sainkhuu GANBAATAR (MPRP) 30.2%, invalid 1.4%; percent of vote in second round Khaltmaa BATTULGA 55.2%, Miyegombo ENKHBOLD 44.8%

Legislative branch: description: unicameral State Great Hural or Ulsyn Ikh Khural (76 seats; members directly elected in single-seat constituencies by simple majority vote; each constituency requires at least 50% voter participation for the poll to be valid; members serve 4-year terms)

elections: last held on 29 June 2016 (next to be held in June 2020)

election results: percent of vote by party—MPP 45.1%, DP 33.1%, MPRP 8.0%, independent 4.8%, other 9.0%; seats by party—MPP 65, DP 9, MPRP 1, independent 1

Judicial branch: highest court(s): Supreme Court (consists of the Chief Justice and 24 judges organized into civil, criminal, and administrative chambers); Constitutional Court or Tsets (consists of a chairman and 8 members)

judge selection and term of office: Supreme Court chief justice and judges appointed by the president upon recommendation to the State Great Hural by the General Council of Courts, a 14-member body of judges and judicial officials; term of appointment is for life; chairman of the Constitutional Court elected from among its members; members appointed by the State Great Hural upon nominations—3 each by the president, the State Great Hural, and the Supreme Court; term of appointment is 6 years; chairmanship limited to a single renewable 3-year term

subordinate courts: aimag (provincial) and capital city appellate courts; soum, inter-soum, and district courts; Administrative Cases Courts

Political parties and leaders: Democratic Party or DP [Sodnomzundui ERDENE]
Mongolian National Democratic Party or MNDP [Bayanjargal TSOGTGEREL]
Mongolian People's Party or MPP [Miyegombo ENKHBOLD]
Mongolian People's Revolutionary Party or MPRP [Nambar ENKHBAYAR]

Political pressure groups and leaders: human rights groups; women's rights groups; disability rights groups

International organization participation: ADB, ARF, CD, CICA, CP, EBRD, EITI (compliant country), FAO, G-77, IAEA, IBRD, ICAO, ICC (NGOs), ICCt, ICRM, IDA, IFAD, IFC, IFRCS, ILO, IMF, IMO, IMSO, Interpol, IOC, IOM, IPU, ISO, ITSO, ITU, ITUC, MIGA, MINURSO, MONUSCO, NAM, OPCW, OSCE, SCO (observer), UN, UNAMID, UNCTAD, UNESCO, UNIDO, UNISFA, UNMISS, UNWTO, UPU, WCO, WHO, WIPO, WMO, WTO

Diplomatic representation in the US: chief of mission: Ambassador (vacant); Charge D'Affaires Bold BAT-OCHR (since 17 September 2017)

chancery: 2833 M Street NW, Washington, DC 20007

telephone: [1] (202) 333-7117

FAX: [1] (202) 298-9227

consulate(s) general: New York, San Francisco

Diplomatic representation from the US: chief of mission: embassy: Denver Street

mailing address: P.O. Box 341, Ulaanbaatar 14192

telephone: [976] 7007-6001

FAX: [976] 7007-6016

Flag description: three, equal vertical bands of red (hoist side), blue, and red; centered on the hoist-side red band in yellow is the national emblem ("soyombo"—a columnar arrangement of abstract and geometric representation for fire, sun, moon, earth, water, and the yin-yang symbol); blue represents the sky, red symbolizes progress and prosperity

National symbol(s): soyombo emblem; national colors: red, blue, yellow

National anthem: name: "Mongol ulsyn toriin duulal" (National Anthem of Mongolia)

lyrics/music: Tsendiin DAMDINSUREN/Bilegiin DAMDINSUREN and Luvsanjamts MURJORJ

note: music adopted 1950, lyrics adopted 2006; lyrics altered on numerous occasions

ECONOMY

Economy—overview: Foreign direct investment in Mongolia's extractive industries—which are based on extensive deposits of copper, gold, coal, molybdenum, fluorspar, uranium, tin, and tungsten—has transformed Mongolia's landlocked economy from its traditional dependence on herding and agriculture. Exports now account for more than 40% of GDP. Mongolia depends on China for more than 60% of its external trade—China receives some 90% of Mongolia's exports and supplies Mongolia with more than one-third of its imports. Mongolia also relies on Russia for 90% of its energy supplies, leaving it vulnerable to price increases. Remittances from Mongolians working abroad, particularly in South Korea, are significant.

Soviet assistance, at its height one-third of GDP, disappeared almost overnight in 1990 and 1991 at the time of the dismantlement of the USSR. The following decade saw Mongolia endure both deep recession, because of political inaction, and natural disasters, as well as strong economic growth, because of market reforms and extensive privatization of the formerly state-run economy. The country opened a fledgling stock exchange in 1991. Mongolia joined the WTO in 1997 and seeks to expand its participation in regional economic and trade regimes.

Growth averaged nearly 9% per year in 2004-08 largely because of high copper prices globally and new gold production. By late 2008, Mongolia was hit by the global financial crisis and Mongolia's real economy contracted 1.3% in 2009. In early 2009, the IMF reached a $236 million Stand-by Arrangement with Mongolia and it emerged from the crisis with a stronger banking sector and better fiscal management. In October 2009, Mongolia passed long-awaited legislation on an investment agreement to develop the Oyu Tolgoi (OT) mine, among the world's largest untapped copper-gold deposits. However, a dispute with foreign investors developing OT called into question the attractiveness of Mongolia as a destination for foreign investment. This caused a severe drop in FDI, and a slowing economy, leading to the dismissal of Prime Minister ALTANKHUYAG in November 2014. The economy had grown more than 10% per year between 2011 and 2013—largely on the strength of commodity exports and high government spending—before slowing to 7.8% in 2014, and falling to the 2% level in 2015. Growth rebounded from a brief 1.6% contraction in the third quarter of 2016 to 5.8% during the first three quarters of 2017, largely due to rising commodity prices.

The May 2015 agreement with Rio Tinto to restart the OT mine and the subsequent $4.4 billion finance package signing in December 2015 stemmed the loss of investor confidence. The current government has made restoring investor trust and reviving the economy its top priority, but has failed to invigorate the economy in the face of the large drop-off in foreign direct investment, mounting external debt, and a sizeable budget deficit. Mongolia secured a $5.5 billion financial assistance package from the IMF and a host of international creditors in May 2017, which is expected to improve Mongolia's long-term fiscal and economic stability as long as Ulaanbaatar can advance the agreement's difficult contingent reforms, such as consolidating the government's off-balance sheet liabilities and rehabilitating the Mongolian banking sector.

GDP (purchasing power parity): $38.4 billion (2017 est.)
$37.63 billion (2016 est.)
$37.27 billion (2015 est.)
note: data are in 2017 dollars

country comparison to the world: 122

GDP (official exchange rate): $10.87 billion (2016 est.)

GDP—real growth rate: 2% (2017 est.)
1% (2016 est.)
2.4% (2015 est.)
country comparison to the world: 153

GDP—per capita (PPP): $12,600 (2017 est.)
$12,500 (2016 est.)
$12,600 (2015 est.)
note: data are in 2017 dollars
country comparison to the world: 122

Gross national saving: 29.3% of GDP (2017 est.)
25.9% of GDP (2016 est.)
21.1% of GDP (2015 est.)
country comparison to the world: 27

GDP—composition, by end use:
household consumption: 51.9%
government consumption: 13.7%
investment in fixed capital: 21.7%
investment in inventories: 4.1%
exports of goods and services: 70.8%
imports of goods and services: -62.1% (2017 est.)

GDP—composition, by sector of origin:
agriculture: 13.2%
industry: 36.1%
services: 50.7% (2017 est.)

Agriculture—products: wheat, barley, vegetables, forage crops; sheep, goats, cattle, camels, horses

Industries: construction and construction materials; mining (coal, copper, molybdenum, fluorspar, tin, tungsten, gold); oil; food and beverages; processing of animal products, cashmere and natural fiber manufacturing

Industrial production growth rate: 6.1% (2017 est.)
country comparison to the world: 33

Labor force: 1.24 million (2016 est.)
country comparison to the world: 138

Labor force—by occupation: *agriculture:* 31.1%
industry: 18.5%
services: 50.5% (2016)

Unemployment rate: 8% (2017 est.)
7.9% (2016 est.)
country comparison to the world: 108

Population below poverty line: 21.6% (2014 est.)

Household income or consumption by percentage share: *lowest 10%:* 13.8%
highest 10%: 8.8% (2016)

Distribution of family income—Gini index: 36.5 (2008)
32.8 (2002)
country comparison to the world: 85

Budget: *revenues:* $2.623 billion
expenditures: $3.711 billion (2017 est.)
Taxes and other revenues: 24.1% of GDP (2017 est.)
country comparison to the world: 121

Budget surplus (+) or deficit (-): -10% of GDP (2017 est.)
country comparison to the world: 207

Public debt: 91.4% of GDP (2017 est.)
90% of GDP (2016 est.)

country comparison to the world: 25

Fiscal year: calendar year

Inflation rate (consumer prices): 4.4% (2017 est.)
0.6% (2016 est.)
country comparison to the world: 165

Central bank discount rate: 12% (14 January 2016)
13% (15 January 2015)
country comparison to the world: 15

Commercial bank prime lending rate: 19.9% (31 December 2017 est.)
19.74% (31 December 2016 est.)
country comparison to the world: 17

Stock of narrow money: $1.109 billion (31 December 2017 est.)
$839.6 million (31 December 2016 est.)
country comparison to the world: 154

Stock of broad money: $6.257 billion (31 December 2017 est.)
$4.851 billion (31 December 2016 est.)
country comparison to the world: 124

Stock of domestic credit: $9.406 billion (31 December 2017 est.)
$7.326 billion (31 December 2016 est.)
country comparison to the world: 115

Market value of publicly traded shares: $632.6 million (31 December 2015 est.)
$766.1 million (31 December 2014 est.)
$1.095 billion (31 December 2013 est.)
country comparison to the world: 110

Current account balance: -$532 million (2017 est.)
-$700 million (2016 est.)
country comparison to the world: 106

Exports: $5.676 billion (2017 est.)
$4.804 billion (2016 est.)
country comparison to the world: 104

Exports—commodities: copper, apparel, livestock, animal products, cashmere, wool, hides, fluorspar, other nonferrous metals, coal, crude oil

Exports—partners: China 84.1%, UK 6.8% (2016)

Imports: $4.196 billion (2017 est.)
$3.466 billion (2016 est.)
country comparison to the world: 131

Imports—commodities: machinery and equipment, fuel, cars, food products, industrial consumer goods, chemicals, building materials, cigarettes and tobacco, appliances, soap and detergent

Imports—partners: China 33.2%, Russia 25.6%, South Korea 8.6%, Japan 7% (2016)

Debt—external: $22.28 billion (31 December 2017 est.)
$19.79 billion (31 December 2016 est.)
country comparison to the world: 91

Stock of direct foreign investment—at home: $19.42 billion (31 December 2017 est.)
$16.28 billion (31 December 2016 est.)
country comparison to the world: 79

Stock of direct foreign investment—abroad: $475.2 million (31 December 2017 est.)
$455.2 million (31 December 2016 est.)
country comparison to the world: 93

THE CIA WORLD FACTBOOK

Exchange rates: togrog/tugriks (MNT) per US dollar—

2,378.1 (2017 est.)
2,140.3 (2016 est.)
2,140.3 (2015 est.)
1,970.3 (2014 est.)
1,817.9 (2013 est.)

ENERGY

Electricity access: *population without electricity:* 300,000

electrification—*total population:* 90%
electrification—*urban areas:* 98%
electrification—*rural areas:* 73% (2013)

Electricity—production: 5.192 billion kWh (2015 est.)
country comparison to the world: 121

Electricity—consumption: 5.785 billion kWh (2015 est.)
country comparison to the world: 116

Electricity—exports: 51 million kWh (2015 est.)
country comparison to the world: 86

Electricity—imports: 1.427 billion kWh (2015 est.)
country comparison to the world: 61

Electricity—installed generating capacity: 1.106 million kW (2015 est.)
country comparison to the world: 126

Electricity—from fossil fuels: 94.9% of total installed capacity (2015 est.)
country comparison to the world: 54

Electricity—from nuclear fuels: 0% of total installed capacity (2015 est.)
country comparison to the world: 136

Electricity—from hydroelectric plants: 0% of total installed capacity (2015 est.)
country comparison to the world: 186

Electricity—from other renewable sources: 5.1% of total installed capacity (2015 est.)
country comparison to the world: 97

Crude oil—production: 23,430 bbl/day (2016 est.)
country comparison to the world: 65

Crude oil—exports: 14,360 bbl/day (2014 est.)
country comparison to the world: 56

Crude oil—imports: 0 bbl/day (2014 est.)
country comparison to the world: 155

Crude oil—proved reserves: 0 bbl (1 January 2017)
country comparison to the world: 171

Refined petroleum products—production: 0 bbl/day (2014 est.)
country comparison to the world: 179

Refined petroleum products—consumption: 26,000 bbl/day (2015 est.)
country comparison to the world: 127

Refined petroleum products—exports: 0 bbl/day (2014 est.)
country comparison to the world: 176

Refined petroleum products—imports: 24,380 bbl/day (2014 est.)
country comparison to the world: 109

Natural gas—production: 0 cu m (2013 est.)
country comparison to the world: 164

Natural gas—consumption: 0 cu m (2013 est.)
country comparison to the world: 204

Natural gas—exports: 0 cu m (2013 est.)
country comparison to the world: 144

Natural gas—imports: 0 cu m (2013 est.)
country comparison to the world: 151

Natural gas—proved reserves: 0 cu m (1 January 2014 es)
country comparison to the world: 167

Carbon dioxide emissions from consumption of energy: 14 million Mt (2013 est.)
country comparison to the world: 94

COMMUNICATIONS

Telephones—fixed lines: *total subscriptions:* 225,287
subscriptions per 100 inhabitants: 7 (July 2016 est.)
country comparison to the world: 125

Telephones—mobile cellular: *total:* 3,367,573
subscriptions per 100 inhabitants: 111 (July 2016 est.)
country comparison to the world: 139

Telephone system: *general assessment:* network is improving with international direct dialing available in many areas; a fiber-optic network has been installed that is improving broadband and communication services between major urban centers with multiple companies providing inter-city fiber-optic cable services
domestic: very low fixed-line teledensity; there are four mobile-cellular providers and subscribership is increasing
international: country code—976; satellite earth stations—7 (2016)

Broadcast media: following a law passed in 2005, Mongolia's state-run radio and TV provider converted to a public service provider; also available are 69 radio and 131 TV stations, including multichannel satellite and cable TV providers; transmissions of multiple international broadcasters are available (2017)

Internet country code: .mn
Internet users: total: 674,949

percent of population: 22.3% (July 2016 est.)
country comparison to the world: 131

TRANSPORTATION

National air transport system: *number of registered air carriers:* 3
inventory of registered aircraft operated by air carriers: 12
annual passenger traffic on registered air carriers: 541,129
annual freight traffic on registered air carriers: 7,130,148 mt-km (2015)
Civil aircraft registration country code prefix: JU (2016)

Airports: 44 (2013)
country comparison to the world: 98

Airports—with paved runways: *total:* 15
over 3,047 m: 2
2,438 to 3,047 m: 10
1,524 to 2,437 m: 3 (2017)

Airports—with unpaved runways: *total:* 29
over 3,047 m: 2
2,438 to 3,047 m: 2
1,524 to 2,437 m: 24
under 914 m: 1 (2013)

Heliports: 1 (2013)

Railways: *total:* 1,815 km
broad gauge: 1,815 km 1.520-m gauge
note: national operator Ulaanbaatar Railway is jointly owned by the Mongolian Government and by the Russian State Railway (2016)
country comparison to the world: 76

Roadways: *total:* 49,249 km
paved: 4,800 km
unpaved: 44,449 km (2013)
country comparison to the world: 79

Waterways: 580 km (the only waterway in operation is Lake Hovsgol (135 km); Selenge River (270 km) and Orhon River (175 km) are navigable but carry little traffic; lakes and rivers ice free from May to September) (2010)
country comparison to the world: 81

Merchant marine: *total:* 261
by type: bulk carrier 8, container ship 5, general cargo 101, oil tanker 67, other 80 (2017)
country comparison to the world: 58

MILITARY AND SECURITY

Military expenditures: 0.92% of GDP (2016)
0.87% of GDP (2015)
0.86% of GDP (2014)
0.82% of GDP (2013)
0.92% of GDP (2012)
country comparison to the world: 90

Military branches: Mongolian Armed Forces (Mongol ulsyn zevsegt huchin): Mongolian Army, Mongolian Air Force

Military service age and obligation: 18-27 years of age for compulsory and voluntary military service; 1-year conscript service obligation in army or air forces or police for males only; after conscription, soldiers can contract into military service for 2 or 4 years; citizens can also voluntarily join the armed forces (2017)

TRANSNATIONAL ISSUES

Disputes—international: none
Refugees and internally displaced persons: stateless persons: 14 (2016)

MONTENEGRO

INTRODUCTION

Background: The use of the name Crna Gora or Black Mountain (Montenegro) began in the 13th century in reference to a highland region in the Serbian province of Zeta. The later medieval state of Zeta maintained its existence until 1496 when Montenegro finally fell under Ottoman rule. Over subsequent centuries, Montenegro managed to maintain a level of autonomy within the Ottoman Empire. From the 16th to 19th centuries, Montenegro was a theocracy ruled by a series of bishop princes; in 1852, it transformed into a secular principality. Montenegro was recognized as an independent sovereign principality at the Congress of Berlin in 1878. After World War I, during which Montenegro fought on the side of the Allies, Montenegro was absorbed by the Kingdom of Serbs, Croats, and Slovenes, which became the Kingdom of Yugoslavia in 1929. At the conclusion of World War II, it became a constituent republic of the Socialist Federal Republic of Yugoslavia. When the latter dissolved in 1992, Montenegro federated with Serbia, creating the Federal Republic of Yugoslavia and, after 2003, shifting to a looser State Union of Serbia and Montenegro. In May 2006, Montenegro invoked its right under the Constitutional Charter of Serbia and Montenegro to hold a referendum on independence from the state union. The vote for severing ties with Serbia barely exceeded 55%—the threshold set by the EU—allowing Montenegro to formally restore its independence on 3 June 2006. Montenegro is an EU candidate country, having officially applied to join in December 2008.

GEOGRAPHY

Location: Southeastern Europe, between the Adriatic Sea and Serbia

Geographic coordinates: 42 30 N, 19 18 E

Map references: Europe

Area: *total:* 13,812 sq km
land: 13,452 sq km

water: 360 sq km
country comparison to the world: 162

Area—comparative: slightly smaller than Connecticut

Land boundaries: *total:* 680 km
border countries (5): Albania 186 km, Bosnia and Herzegovina 242 km, Croatia 19 km, Kosovo 76 km, Serbia 157 km

Coastline: 293.5 km

Maritime claims: *territorial sea:* 12 nm
continental shelf: defined by treaty

Climate: Mediterranean climate, hot dry summers and autumns and relatively cold winters with heavy snowfalls inland

Terrain: highly indented coastline with narrow coastal plain backed by rugged high limestone mountains and plateaus

Elevation: *mean elevation:* 1,086 m

elevation extremes: *lowest point:* Adriatic Sea 0 m
highest point: Bobotov Kuk 2,522 m

Natural resources: bauxite, hydroelectricity

Land use: *agricultural land:* 38.2%
arable land: 12.9%;
permanent crops: 1.2%;
permanent pasture: 24.1%
forest: 40.4%
other: 21.4% (2011 est.)
Irrigated land: 24 sq km (2012)

Population—distribution: highest population density is concentrated in the south, southwest; the extreme eastern border is the least populated area

Natural hazards: destructive earthquakes

Environment—current issues: pollution of coastal waters from sewage outlets, especially in tourist-related areas such as Kotor

Environment—international agreements: *party to:* Air Pollution, Biodiversity, Climate Change, Climate Change-Kyoto Protocol, Desertification, Hazardous Wastes, Law of the Sea, Marine Dumping, Marine Life Conservation, Ozone Layer Protection, Ship Pollution
signed, but not ratified: none of the selected agreements

Geography—note: strategic location along the Adriatic coast

PEOPLE AND SOCIETY

Population: 642,550 (July 2017 est.)
country comparison to the world: 168

Nationality: *noun:* Montenegrin(s)
adjective: Montenegrin

Ethnic groups: Montenegrin 45%, Serbian 28.7%, Bosniak 8.7%, Albanian 4.9%, Muslim 3.3%, Romani 1%, Croat 1%, other 2.6%, unspecified 4.9% (2011 est.)

Languages: Serbian 42.9%, Montenegrin (official) 37%, Bosnian 5.3%, Albanian 5.3%, Serbo-Croat 2%, other 3.5%, unspecified 4% (2011 est.)

Religions: Orthodox 72.1%, Muslim 19.1%, Catholic 3.4%, atheist 1.2%, other 1.5%, unspecified 2.6% (2011 est.)

Age structure: *0-14 years:* 15.1% (male 47,937/female 49,102)
15-24 years: 9.58% (male 27,510/female 34,053)
25-54 years: 46.59% (male 161,842/female 137,549)
55-64 years: 13.58% (male 43,561/female 43,686)
65 years and over: 15.14% (male 39,164/female 58,146) (2017 est.)

Dependency ratios: *total dependency ratio:* 47.8
youth dependency ratio: 27.3
elderly dependency ratio: 20.5
potential support ratio: 4.9 (2015 est.)

Median age: *total:* 40.7 years
male: 39.9 years
female: 41.8 years (2017 est.)
country comparison to the world: 48

Population growth rate: -0.28% (2017 est.)
country comparison to the world: 216

Birth rate: 10 births/1,000 population (2017 est.)
country comparison to the world: 194

Death rate: 9.7 deaths/1,000 population (2017 est.)
country comparison to the world: 47

Population distribution: highest population density is concentrated in the south, southwest; the extreme eastern border is the least populated area

Urbanization: *urban population:* 64.4% of total population (2017)
rate of urbanization: 0.25% annual rate of change (2015-20 est.)

Major urban areas—population: PODGORICA (capital) 165,000 (2014)

Sex ratio: *at birth:* 1.06 male(s)/female
0-14 years: 0.97 male(s)/female
15-24 years: 0.83 male(s)/female
25-54 years: 1.17 male(s)/female
55-64 years: 1 male(s)/female
65 years and over: 0.66 male(s)/female
total population: 0.99 male(s)/female (2016 est.)

Mother's mean age at first birth: 26.3 years (2010 est.)

Maternal mortality ratio: 7 deaths/100,000 live births (2015 est.)
country comparison to the world: 163

Contraceptive prevalence rate: 23.3% (2013)

Health expenditures: 6.4% of GDP (2014)
country comparison to the world: 96

Physicians density: 2.34 physicians/1,000 population (2015)

Hospital bed density: 4 beds/1,000 population (2011)

Drinking water source:
improved:
urban: 100% of population
rural: 99.2% of population
total: 99.7% of population
unimproved:
urban: 0% of population
rural: 0.8% of population
total: 0.3% of population (2015 est.)

Sanitation facility access:
improved:
urban: 98% of population
rural: 92.2% of population
total: 95.9% of population
unimproved:
urban: 2% of population
rural: 7.8% of population
total: 4.1% of population (2015 est.)

HIV/AIDS—adult prevalence rate: 0.1% (2016 est.)
country comparison to the world: 105

HIV/AIDS—people living with HIV/AIDS: <500 (2016 est.)

HIV/AIDS—deaths: <100 (2016 est.)

Major infectious diseases: *degree of risk:* intermediate
food or waterborne diseases: bacterial diarrhea
vectorborne disease: Crimean-Congo hemorrhagic fever (2016)

Obesity—adult prevalence rate: 23.3% (2016)
country comparison to the world: 66

Children under the age of 5 years underweight: 1% (2013)
country comparison to the world: 133

Education expenditures: NA

Literacy: *definition:* age 15 and over can read and write
total population: 98.7%
male: 99.5%
female: 98% (2015 est.)

School life expectancy (primary to tertiary education): *total:* 15 years
male: 15 years
female: 15 years (2010)

Unemployment, youth ages 15-24: *total:* 37.7%
male: 39.9%
female: 34.5% (2015 est.)
country comparison to the world: 11

GOVERNMENT

Country name: *conventional long form:* none
conventional short form: Montenegro
local long form: none
local short form: Crna Gora
former: People's Republic of Montenegro, Socialist Republic of Montenegro, Republic of Montenegro
etymology: the country's name locally as well as in most Western European languages means "black mountain" and refers to the dark coniferous forests on Mount Lovcen and the surrounding area

Government type: parliamentary republic

Capital: *name:* Podgorica; note—Cetinje retains the status of "Old Royal Capital"

geographic coordinates: 42 26 N, 19 16 E
time difference: UTC+1 (6 hours ahead of Washington, DC, during Standard Time)
daylight saving time: +1 hr, begins last Sunday in March; ends last Sunday in October

Administrative divisions: 23 municipalities (opstine, singular—opstina); Andrijevica, Bar, Berane, Bijelo Polje, Budva, Cetinje, Danilovgrad, Gusinje, Herceg Novi, Kolasin, Kotor, Mojkovac, Niksic, Petnjica, Plav, Pljevlja, Pluzine, Podgorica, Rozaje, Savnik, Tivat, Ulcinj, Zabljak

Independence: 3 June 2006 (from the State Union of Serbia and Montenegro)

National holiday: National Day, 13 July (1878, the day the Berlin Congress recognized Montenegro as the 27th independent state in the world, and 1941, the day the Montenegrins staged an uprising against fascist occupiers and sided with the partisan communist movement)

Constitution: *history:* several previous; latest adopted 22 October 2007
amendments: proposed by the president of Montenegro, by the government, or by at least 25 members of the Assembly; passage of draft proposals requires two-thirds majority vote of the Assembly, followed by a public hearing; passage of draft amendments requires two-thirds majority vote of the Assembly; changes to certain constitutional articles such as sovereignty, state symbols, citizenship, and constitutional change procedures, require three-fifths majority vote in a referendum; amended 2013, 2014 (2016)

Legal system: civil law

International law organization participation: has not submitted an ICJ jurisdiction declaration; accepts ICCt jurisdiction

Citizenship: *citizenship by birth:* no
citizenship by descent only: at least one parent must be a citizen of Montenegro
dual citizenship recognized: no
residency requirement for naturalization: 10 years

Suffrage: 18 years of age; universal

Executive branch: *chief of state:* President Filip VUJANOVIC (since 6 April 2008)
head of government: Prime Minister Dusko MARKOVIC (since 28 November 2016); note—Prime Minister Milo DJUKANOVIC resigned 26 October 2016
cabinet: Ministers act as cabinet
elections/appointments: president directly elected by absolute majority popular vote in 2 rounds if needed for a 5-year term (eligible for a second term); election last held on 7 April 2013 (next to be held in 2018); prime minister nominated by the president, approved by the Assembly
election results: Filip VUJANOVIC reelected president in the first round; percent of vote—Filip VUJANOVIC (DPS) 51.2%, Miodrag LEKIC (independent) 48.8%

Legislative branch: *description:* unicameral Assembly or Skupstina (81 seats; members directly elected in a single nationwide constituency by proportional representation vote; members serve 4-year terms)

elections: last held on 16 October 2016 (next to be held by October 2020)
election results: percent of vote by party/coalition—DPS 41.4%, DF 20.3%, Key Coalition, 11.1%, DCG 10.0%, SDP 5.2%, SD 3.3%, BS, 3.2%, Albanians Decisively 1.3%, HGI .5%, other 3.7%; seats by party/coalition—DPS 36, DF 18, Key Coalition 9, DCG 8, SDP 4, SD 2, BS 2, Albanians Decisively 1, HGI 1

Judicial branch: *highest court(s):* Supreme Court or Vrhovni Sud (consists of the court president, deputy president, and 15 judges); Constitutional Court or Ustavni Sud (consists of the court president and 7 judges)
judge selection and term of office: Supreme Court president proposed by general session of the Supreme Court and elected by the Judicial Council, a 9-member body consisting of judges, lawyers designated by the Assembly, and the minister of judicial affairs; Supreme Court president elected for a single renewable, 5-year term; other judges elected by the Judicial Council for life; Constitutional Court judges—2 proposed by the president of Montenegro and 5 by the Assembly, and elected by the Assembly; court president elected from among the court members; court president elected for 3 years, other judges 9 years
subordinate courts: Administrative Courts; Appellate Court; Commercial Courts; High Courts; basic courts

Political parties and leaders: Albanians Decisively [Genci NIMANBEGU] (coalition includes FORCA, AA, DUA)
Albanian Alternative or AA [Nik DJELOSAJ]
Bosniak Party or BS [Rafet HUSOVIC]
Croatian Civic Initiative or HGI [Marija VUCINOVIC]
Democratic Alliance or DEMOS [Miodrag LEKIC]
Democratic Front or DF [collective leadership] (coalition includes NOVA, PZP, DNP, RP)
Democratic Montenegro or DCG [Aleksa BECIC]
Democratic Party of Socialists or DPS [Milo DJUKANOVIC]
Democratic People's Party or DNP [Milan KNEZEVIC]
Democratic Union of Albanians or DUA [Mehmet ZENKA]
Key Coalition [Miodrag LEKIC] (includes DEMOS, SNP, URA)
Liberal Party or LP [Andrija POPOVIC]
Movement for Change or PZP [Nebojsa MEDOJEVIC]
New Democratic Power or FORCA [Nazif CUNGU]
New Serb Democracy or NOVA [Andrija MANDIC]
Social Democratic Party or SDP [Ranko KRIVOKAPIC]
Social Democrats or SD [Ivan BRAJOVIC]
Socialist People's Party or SNP [Srdjan MILIC]
United Reform Action or URA [Dritan ABAZOVIC]
Workers' Party or RP [Janko VUCINIC]

Political pressure groups and leaders: NA

International organization participation: CE, CEI, EAPC, EBRD, FAO, IAEA, IBRD, ICAO, ICC (NGOs), ICCt, ICRM, IDA, IFC, IFRCS, IHO, ILO, IMF, IMO, IMSO, Interpol, IOC, IOM, IPU, ISO (correspondent), ITSO, ITU, ITUC (NGOs),

MIGA, OAS (observer), OIF (observer), OPCW, OSCE, PCA, PFP, SELEC, UN, UNCTAD, UNESCO, UNHCR, UNIDO, UNWTO, UPU, WCO, WHO, WIPO, WMO, WTO

Diplomatic representation in the US: *chief of mission:* Ambassador Nebojsa KALUDEROVIC (since 18 January 2017)
chancery: 1610 New Hampshire Avenue NW, Washington, DC, 20009
telephone: [1] (202) 234-6108
FAX: [1] (202) 234-6109
consulate(s) general: New York

Diplomatic representation from the US: *chief of mission:* Ambassador Margaret UYEHARA (since 19 February 2015)
embassy: Dzona Dzeksona 2, 81000 Podgorica, Montenegro
mailing address: use embassy street address
telephone: [382] (0) 20 410 500
FAX: [382] (0) 20 241 358

Flag description: a red field bordered by a narrow golden-yellow stripe with the Montenegrin coat of arms centered; the arms consist of a double-headed golden eagle—symbolizing the unity of church and state—surmounted by a crown; the eagle holds a golden scepter in its right claw and a blue orb in its left; the breast shield over the eagle shows a golden lion passant on a green field in front of a blue sky; the lion is a symbol of episcopal authority and harkens back to the three and a half centuries when Montenegro was ruled as a theocracy

National symbol(s): double-headed eagle; national colors: red, gold

National anthem: name: "Oj, svijetla majska zoro" (Oh, Bright Dawn of May)
lyrics/music: Sekula DRLJEVIC/unknown, arranged by Zarko MIKOVIC
note: adopted 2004; music based on a Montenegrin folk song

ECONOMY

Economy—overview: Montenegro's economy is transitioning to a market system. As of 2015, around 90% of Montenegrin state-owned companies have been privatized, including 100% of banking, telecommunications, and oil distribution. Tourism, which accounts for roughly 20% of Montenegro's GDP, brings in three times as many visitors as Montenegro's total population every year. Several new luxury tourism complexes are in various stages of development along the coast, and a number are being offered in connection with nearby boating and yachting facilities. In addition to tourism, energy and agriculture are considered two distinct pillars of the economy. Only 20% of Montenegro's hydropower potential is utilized. Montenegro plans to become a net energy exporter, and the construction of an underwater cable to Italy, which will be completed by 2018, will help meet its goal.

Montenegro uses the euro as its domestic currency, though it is not an official member of the euro zone. In January 2007, Montenegro joined the World Bank and IMF, and in December 2011, the WTO. Montenegro began negotiations to join the EU in 2012, having met the conditions set down by the European Council, which called on Montenegro to take steps to fight corruption and organized crime.

The government recognizes the need to remove impediments in order to remain competitive and open the economy to foreign investors. The biggest foreign investors in Montenegro are Russia, Italy, Cyprus, Denmark, Hungary and Serbia. Net foreign direct investment in 2016 reached $755 million and investment per capita is one of the highest in Europe, due to a low corporate tax rate.

Montenegro is currently planning major overhauls of its road and rail networks, and possible expansions of its air transportation system. In 2014, the Government of Montenegro selected two Chinese companies to construct a 41 km-long section of the country's highway system. Montenegro has recently explored further economic cooperation with China. Cheaper borrowing costs have stimulated Montenegro's growing debt, which currently sits at 71.3% of GDP. Montenegro first instituted a value-added tax (VAT) in April 2003, and introduced differentiated VAT rates of 17% and 7% (for tourism) in January 2006. The Montenegrin Government recently said it would increase the non-tourism rate to 21% as of January 2018, with the goal of reducing its public debt.

GDP (purchasing power parity): $10.86 billion (2017 est.)
$10.55 billion (2016 est.)
$10.3 billion (2015 est.)
note: data are in 2017 dollars
country comparison to the world: 159

GDP (official exchange rate): $4.405 billion (2016 est.)

GDP—real growth rate: 3% (2017 est.)
2.5% (2016 est.)
3.4% (2015 est.)
country comparison to the world: 117

GDP—per capita (PPP): $17,400 (2017 est.)
$16,900 (2016 est.)
$16,600 (2015 est.)
note: data are in 2017 dollars
country comparison to the world: 100

Gross national saving: 7.8% of GDP (2017 est.)
6.1% of GDP (2016 est.)
6.7% of GDP (2015 est.)
country comparison to the world: 168

GDP—composition, by end use:
household consumption: 81.8%
government consumption: 21.2%
investment in fixed capital: 19.5%
investment in inventories: -0.1%
exports of goods and services: 42.1%
imports of goods and services: -64.5% (2013 est.)

GDP—composition, by sector of origin:
agriculture: 8.3%
industry: 21.2%
services: 70.5% (2013 est.)

Agriculture—products: tobacco, potatoes, citrus fruits, olives, grapes; sheep

Industries: steelmaking, aluminum, agricultural processing, consumer goods, tourism

Industrial production growth rate: 4.5% (2013 est.)
country comparison to the world: 58

Labor force: 263,200 (2014 est.)
country comparison to the world: 168

Labor force—by occupation: *agriculture:* 5.3%
industry: 17.9%
services: 76.8% (2014 est.)

Unemployment rate: 17.1% (2016 est.)
17.6% (2015 est.)
country comparison to the world: 177

Population below poverty line: 8.6% (2013 est.)

Distribution of family income—Gini index: 26.2 (2013 est.)
24.3 (2010)
country comparison to the world: 142

Budget: *revenues:* $1.62 billion
expenditures: $1.95 billion (2016 est.)
Taxes and other revenues: 36.8% of GDP (2016 est.)
country comparison to the world: 47

Budget surplus (+) or deficit (-): -7.5% of GDP (2016 est.)
country comparison to the world: 194

Public debt: 71.3% of GDP (2016 est.)
69.3% of GDP (2015 est.)
note: data cover general government debt, and includes debt instruments issued (or owned) by government entities other than the treasury; the data include treasury debt held by foreign entities; the data include debt issued by subnational entities, as well as intra-governmental debt; intra-governmental debt consists of treasury borrowings from surpluses in the social funds, such as for retirement, medical care, and unemployment; debt instruments for the social funds are not sold at public auctions
country comparison to the world: 48

Fiscal year: calendar year

Inflation rate (consumer prices): 2.1% (2017 est.)
-0.3% (2016 est.)
country comparison to the world: 94

Commercial bank prime lending rate: 9.22% (31 December 2014 est.)
9.36% (31 December 2013 est.)
country comparison to the world: 89

Stock of narrow money: $749 million (31 December 2011 est.)
$783.3 million (31 December 2010 est.)
country comparison to the world: 161

Stock of broad money: $1.982 billion (31 December 2011 est.)
$2.01 billion (31 December 2010 est.)
country comparison to the world: 157

Stock of domestic credit: $2.63 billion (31 December 2014 est.)
$2.682 billion (31 December 2013 est.)
country comparison to the world: 140

Market value of publicly traded shares: $7.532 billion (31 December 2014 est.)
$3.827 billion (31 December 2012 est.)
$3.322 billion (31 December 2011 est.)
country comparison to the world: 76

Current account balance: -$889 million (2017 est.)
-$791 million (2016 est.)

country comparison to the world: 127

Exports: $370.2 million (2014 est.)
$489.2 million (2012 est.)
country comparison to the world: 180

Imports: $1.982 billion (2014 est.)
$2.4 billion (2012 est.)
country comparison to the world: 160

Reserves of foreign exchange and gold: $599.6 million (31 December 2014 est.)
country comparison to the world: 137

Debt—external: $1.576 billion (31 December 2014 est.)
$1.433 billion (31 December 2013 est.)
country comparison to the world: 157

Stock of direct foreign investment—at home: $483 million (31 December 2014 est.)
$446.5 million (31 December 2013 est.)
country comparison to the world: 124

Stock of direct foreign investment—abroad: $133 million (31 December 2014 est.)
country comparison to the world: 102

Exchange rates: euros (EUR) per US dollar—
0.906 (2017 est.)
0.9214 (2016 est.)
0.9214 (2015 est.)
0.885 (2014 est.)
0.7634 (2013 est.)

ENERGY

Electricity access: electrification—*total population:* 100% (2016)

Electricity—production: 2.897 billion kWh (2015 est.)
country comparison to the world: 133

Electricity—consumption: 2.834 billion kWh (2015 est.)
country comparison to the world: 137

Electricity—exports: 517 million kWh (2015 est.)
country comparison to the world: 68

Electricity—imports: 1.04 billion kWh (2015 est.)
country comparison to the world: 69

Electricity—installed generating capacity: 887,000 kW (2015 est.)
country comparison to the world: 131

Electricity—from fossil fuels: 24.8% of total installed capacity (2015 est.)
country comparison to the world: 190

Electricity—from nuclear fuels: 0% of total installed capacity (2015 est.)
country comparison to the world: 139

Electricity—from hydroelectric plants: 75.2% of total installed capacity (2015 est.)
country comparison to the world: 17

Electricity—from other renewable sources: 0% of total installed capacity (2015 est.)
country comparison to the world: 198

Crude oil—production: 0 bbl/day (2016 est.)
country comparison to the world: 174

Crude oil—exports: 0 bbl/day (2014 est.)
country comparison to the world: 161

Crude oil—imports: 0 bbl/day (2014 est.)
country comparison to the world: 158

Crude oil—proved reserves: 0 bbl (1 January 2017 es)
country comparison to the world: 172

Refined petroleum products—production: 0 bbl/day (2014 est.)
country comparison to the world: 180

Refined petroleum products—consumption: 6,000 bbl/day (2015 est.)
country comparison to the world: 172

Refined petroleum products—exports: 257.1 bbl/day (2014 est.)
country comparison to the world: 118

Refined petroleum products—imports: 6,244 bbl/day (2014 est.)
country comparison to the world: 157

Natural gas—production: 0 cu m (2013 est.)
country comparison to the world: 167

Natural gas—consumption: 0 cu m (2013 est.)
country comparison to the world: 207

Natural gas—exports: 0 cu m (2013 est.)
country comparison to the world: 147

Natural gas—imports: 0 cu m (2013 est.)
country comparison to the world: 154

Natural gas—proved reserves: 0 cu m (1 January 2014)
country comparison to the world: 170

Carbon dioxide emissions from consumption of energy: 18 million Mt (2013 est.)
country comparison to the world: 85

COMMUNICATIONS

Telephones—fixed lines: *total subscriptions:* 148,015
subscriptions per 100 inhabitants: 23 (July 2016 est.)
country comparison to the world: 135

Telephones—mobile cellular: *total:* 1,040,747
subscriptions per 100 inhabitants: 161 (July 2016 est.)
country comparison to the world: 158

Telephone system: *general assessment:* modern telecommunications system with access to European satellites
domestic: GSM mobile-cellular service, available through multiple providers with national coverage, is growing
international: country code—382; 2 international switches connect the national system (2015)

Broadcast media: state-funded national radio-TV broadcaster operates 2 terrestrial TV networks, 1 satellite TV channel, and 2 radio networks; 4 local public TV stations and over 20 private TV stations; 14 local public radio stations and more than 50 private radio stations (2017)

Internet country code: .me
Internet users: total: 450,442
percent of population: 69.9% (July 2016 est.)
country comparison to the world: 136

TRANSPORTATION

National air transport system: *number of registered air carriers:* 1

inventory of registered aircraft operated by air carriers: 6
annual passenger traffic on registered air carriers: 526,980
annual freight traffic on registered air carriers: 0 mt-km (2015)
Civil aircraft registration country code prefix: 4O (2016)

Airports: 5 (2013)
country comparison to the world: 181

Airports—with paved runways: *total:* 5
2,438 to 3,047 m: 2
1,524 to 2,437 m: 1
914 to 1,523 m: 1
under 914 m: 1 (2017)

Heliports: 1 (2012)

Railways: *total:* 250 km
standard gauge: 250 km 1.435-m gauge (224 km electrified) (2017)
country comparison to the world: 126

Roadways: *total:* 7,762 km
paved: 7,141 km
unpaved: 621 km (2010)
country comparison to the world: 143

Merchant marine: *total:* 12
by type: bulk carrier 4, other 8 (2017)
country comparison to the world: 140

Ports and terminals: *major seaport(s):* Bar

MILITARY AND SECURITY

Military expenditures: 1.66% of GDP (2017)
1.61% of GDP (2016)
1.38% of GDP (2015)
1.47% of GDP (2014)
1.45% of GDP (2013)
country comparison to the world: 46

Military branches: Armed Forces of the Republic of Montenegro: Army of Montenegro (includes Ground Troops (Kopnena Vojska), Montenegrin Navy (Mornarica Crne Gore, MCG)), Air Force (2016)

Military service age and obligation: 18 is the legal minimum age for voluntary military service; no conscription (2012)

TERRORISM

Terrorist groups—foreign based: *Aum Shinrikyo* (AUM): *aim(s):* enhance its networks in Montenegro for recruitment and fundraising
area(s) of operation: authorities expelled 58 foreign members in March 2016: four from Japan, seven from Belarus, three from Ukraine, one from Uzbekistan, and the rest from Russia

TRANSNATIONAL ISSUES

Disputes—international: none
Refugees and internally displaced persons: stateless persons: 3,237 (2016)

MONTSERRAT

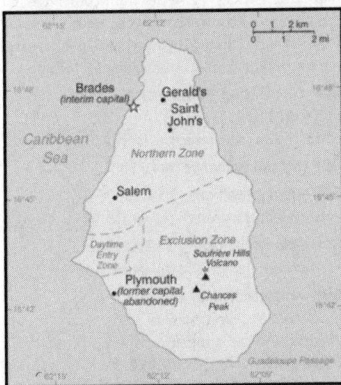

INTRODUCTION

Background: English and Irish colonists from St. Kitts first settled on Montserrat in 1632; the first African slaves arrived three decades later. The British and French fought for possession of the island for most of the 18th century, but it finally was confirmed as a British possession in 1783. The island's sugar plantation economy was converted to small farm landholdings in the mid-19th century. Much of this island was devastated and two-thirds of the population fled abroad because of the eruption of the Soufriere Hills Volcano that began on 18 July 1995. Montserrat has endured volcanic activity since, with the last eruption occurring in 2013.

GEOGRAPHY

Location: Caribbean, island in the Caribbean Sea, southeast of Puerto Rico

Geographic coordinates: 16 45 N, 62 12 W

Map references: Central America and the Caribbean

Area: *total:* 102 sq km
land: 102 sq km
water: 0 sq km
country comparison to the world: 226

Area—comparative: about 0.6 times the size of Washington, DC

Land boundaries: 0 km

Coastline: 40 km

Maritime claims: *territorial sea:* 12 nm
exclusive fishing zone: 200 nm

Climate: tropical; little daily or seasonal temperature variation

Terrain: volcanic island, mostly mountainous, with small coastal lowland

Elevation: *mean elevation:* NA

elevation extremes: *lowest point:* Caribbean Sea 0 m

highest point: Soufriere Hills volcano pre-eruption height was 915 m; current lava dome is subject to periodic build up and collapse; estimated dome height was 1050 m in 2015

Natural resources: NEGL

Land use: *agricultural land:* 30%
arable land: 20%;
permanent crops: 0%;
permanent pasture: 10%
forest: 25%
other: 45% (2011 est.)
Irrigated land: 0 sq km (2012)

Population—distribution: only the northern half of the island is populated, the southern portion is uninhabitable due to volcanic activity

Natural hazards: volcanic eruptions; severe hurricanes (June to November)
volcanism: Soufriere Hills volcano (915 m), has erupted continuously since 1995; a massive eruption in 1997 destroyed most of the capital, Plymouth, and resulted in approximately half of the island becoming uninhabitable; the island of Montserrat is part of the volcanic island arc of the Lesser Antilles that extends from Saba in the north to Grenada in the south

Environment—current issues: land erosion occurs on slopes that have been cleared for cultivation

Geography—note: the island is entirely volcanic in origin and comprised of three major volcanic centers of differing ages

PEOPLE AND SOCIETY

Population: 5,292
note: an estimated 8,000 refugees left the island following the resumption of volcanic activity in July 1995; some have returned (July 2017 est.)
country comparison to the world: 228

Nationality: *noun:* Montserratian(s)
adjective: Montserratian

Ethnic groups: African/black 88.4%, mixed 3.7%, hispanic/Spanish 3%, caucasian/white 2.7%, East Indian/Indian 1.5%, other 0.7% (2011 est.)

Languages: English

Religions: Protestant 67.1% (includes Anglican 21.8%, Methodist 17%, Pentecostal 14.1%, Seventh Day Adventist 10.5%, and Church of God 3.7%), Roman Catholic 11.6%, Rastafarian 1.4%, other 6.5%, none 2.6%, unspecified 10.8% (2001 est.)

Age structure: *0-14 years:* 16.5% (male 449/female 424)
15-24 years: 21.52% (male 599/female 540)
25-54 years: 47.43% (male 1,201/female 1,309)
55-64 years: 8.45% (male 194/female 253)
65 years and over: 6.1% (male 199/female 124) (2017 est.)

Median age: *total:* 33.2 years
male: 32.6 years

female: 33.7 years (2017 est.)
country comparison to the world: 94

Population growth rate: 0.45% (2017 est.)
country comparison to the world: 158

Birth rate: 10.8 births/1,000 population (2017 est.)
country comparison to the world: 183

Death rate: 6.2 deaths/1,000 population (2017 est.)
country comparison to the world: 154

Net migration rate: 0 migrant(s)/1,000 population (2017 est.)
country comparison to the world: 92

Population distribution: only the northern half of the island is populated, the southern portion is uninhabitable due to volcanic activity

Urbanization: *urban population:* 9% of total population (2017)
rate of urbanization: 0.7% annual rate of change (2015-20 est.)

Sex ratio: *at birth:* 1.03 male(s)/female
0-14 years: 1.07 male(s)/female
15-24 years: 1.08 male(s)/female
25-54 years: 0.92 male(s)/female
55-64 years: 0.83 male(s)/female
65 years and over: 1.6 male(s)/female
total population: 1 male(s)/female (2016 est.)

Infant mortality rate: *total:* 12.3 deaths/1,000 live births
male: 9.7 deaths/1,000 live births
female: 15.1 deaths/1,000 live births (2017 est.)
country comparison to the world: 116

Life expectancy at birth: *total population:* 74.6 years
male: 75.9 years
female: 73.2 years (2017 est.)
country comparison to the world: 122

Total fertility rate: 1.33 children born/woman (2017 est.)
country comparison to the world: 216

Drinking water source:
improved:
urban: 99% of population
rural: 99% of population
total: 99% of population
unimproved:
urban: 1% of population
rural: 1% of population
total: 1% of population (2015 est.)

Sanitation facility access:
improved:
urban: 82.9% of population
rural: 82.9% of population
total: 82.9% of population
unimproved:
urban: 17.1% of population
rural: 17.1% of population
total: 17.1% of population (2007 est.)

HIV/AIDS—adult prevalence rate: NA

HIV/AIDS—people living with HIV/AIDS: NA

HIV/AIDS—deaths: NA

Education expenditures: 5.1% of GDP (2009)

School life expectancy (primary to tertiary education): *total:* 15 years
male: 14 years
female: 17 years (2007)

GOVERNMENT

Country name: *conventional long form:* none
conventional short form: Montserrat
etymology: island named by explorer Christopher COLUMBUS in 1493 after the Benedictine abbey Santa Maria de Montserrat, near Barcelona, Spain

Dependency status: overseas territory of the UK

Government type: parliamentary democracy (Legislative Council); self-governing overseas territory of the UK

Capital: *name:* Plymouth; note—Plymouth was abandoned in 1997 because of volcanic activity; interim government buildings have been built at Brades Estate, the de facto capital, in the Carr's Bay/Little Bay vicinity at the northwest end of Montserrat

geographic coordinates: 16 42 N, 62 13 W
time difference: UTC-4 (1 hour ahead of Washington, DC, during Standard Time)

Administrative divisions: 3 parishes; Saint Anthony, Saint Georges, Saint Peter

Independence: none (overseas territory of the UK)

National holiday: birthday of Queen ELIZABETH II, second Saturday in June (1926)

Constitution: previous 1960; latest effective 1 September 2010; amended 2011 (2016)

Legal system: English common law

Citizenship: see United Kingdom

Suffrage: 18 years of age; universal

Executive branch: *chief of state:* Queen ELIZABETH II (since 6 February 1952); represented by Governor Andrew PEARCE (since 1 February 2018)

head of government: Premier Donaldson ROMERO (since 12 September 2014); note—effective with the new Constitution Order of October 2010, the office of premier replaced the office of chief minister
cabinet: Executive Council consists of the governor, the premier, 3 other ministers, the attorney general, and the finance secretary
elections/appointments: the monarchy is hereditary; governor appointed by the monarch; following legislative elections, the leader of the majority party usually becomes premier

Legislative branch: *description:* unicameral Legislative Assembly (11 seats; 9 members directly elected in a single constituency by absolute majority vote in 2 rounds to serve 5-year terms and 2 ex-officio members—the attorney general and financial secretary)
elections: last held on 11 September 2014 (next to be held by 2019)

election results: percent of vote by party—PDM 50.0%, MCAP 35.4%, other 14.6%; seats by party—PDM 7, MCAP 2

Judicial branch: *highest court(s):* the Eastern Caribbean Supreme Court (ECSC) is the superior court of the Organization of Eastern Caribbean States; the ECSC—headquartered on St. Lucia—consists of the Court of Appeal—headed by the chief justice and 4 judges—and the High Court with 18 judges; the Court of Appeal is itinerant, travelling to member states on a schedule to hear appeals from the High Court and subordinate courts; High Court judges reside at the member states with 1 assigned to Montserrat; Montserrat is also a member of the Caribbean Court of Justice
judge selection and term of office: chief justice of Eastern Caribbean Supreme Court appointed by the Her Majesty, Queen ELIZABETH II; other justices and judges appointed by the Judicial and Legal Services Commission, and independent body of judicial officials; Court of Appeal justices appointed for life with mandatory retirement at age 65; High Court judges appointed for life with mandatory retirement at age 62
subordinate courts: magistrate's court

Political parties and leaders: Movement for Change and Prosperity or MCAP [Reuben MEADE]
People's Democratic Movement or PDM [Shirley OSBORNE]

Political pressure groups and leaders: NA

International organization participation: Caricom, CDB, Interpol (subbureau), OECS, UPU

Diplomatic representation in the US: none (overseas territory of the UK)

Diplomatic representation from the US: none (overseas territory of the UK)

Flag description: blue with the flag of the UK in the upper hoist-side quadrant and the Montserratian coat of arms centered in the outer half of the flag; the arms feature a woman in green dress, Erin, the female personification of Ireland, standing beside a yellow harp and embracing a large dark cross with her right arm; Erin and the harp are symbols of Ireland reflecting the territory's Irish ancestry; blue represents awareness, trustworthiness, determination, and righteousness

National anthem: *note:* as a territory of the UK, "God Save the Queen" is official (see United Kingdom)

ECONOMY

Economy—overview: Severe volcanic activity, which began in July 1995, has put a damper on this small, open economy. A catastrophic eruption in June 1997 closed the airport and seaports, causing further economic and social dislocation. Two-thirds of the 12,000 inhabitants fled the island. Some began to return in 1998 but lack of housing limited the number. The agriculture sector continued to be affected by the lack of suitable land for farming and the destruction of crops.

Prospects for the economy depend largely on developments in relation to the volcanic activity

and on public sector construction activity. Half of the island remains uninhabitable. In January 2013, the EU announced the disbursement of a $55.2 million aid package to Montserrat in order to boost the country's economic recovery, with a specific focus on public finance management, public sector reform, and prudent economic management.

GDP (purchasing power parity): $43.78 million (2006 est.)
country comparison to the world: 226

GDP (official exchange rate): $NA

GDP—real growth rate: 3.5% (2008 est.)
country comparison to the world: 96

GDP—per capita (PPP): $8,500 (2006 est.)
country comparison to the world: 149

GDP—composition, by end use:
household consumption: 89.3%
government consumption: 53.4%
investment in fixed capital: 22.2%
investment in inventories: -0.1%
exports of goods and services: 25.7%
imports of goods and services: -90.5% (2017 est.)

GDP—composition, by sector of origin:
agriculture: 1.6%
industry: 21.8%
services: 76.6% (2017 est.)

Agriculture—products: cabbages, carrots, cucumbers, tomatoes, onions, peppers; livestock products

Industries: tourism, rum, textiles, electronic appliances

Industrial production growth rate: 2% (2017 est.)
country comparison to the world: 129

Labor force: 4,521 (2012)
country comparison to the world: 223

Unemployment rate: 6% (1998 est.)
country comparison to the world: 84

Population below poverty line: NA%

Household income or consumption by percentage share: *lowest 10%:* NA%
highest 10%: NA%

Budget: *revenues:* $37.04 million
expenditures: $37.04 million (2017 est.)

Fiscal year: 1 April–31 March

Inflation rate (consumer prices): 1.1% (2017 est.)
-0.2% (2016 est.)
country comparison to the world: 48

Central bank discount rate: 10.99% (31 December 2010)
6.5% (31 December 2009)
country comparison to the world: 20

Commercial bank prime lending rate: 7% (31 December 2017 est.)
7.26% (31 December 2016 est.)
country comparison to the world: 119

Stock of narrow money: $23.33 million (31 December 2017 est.)
$23.04 million (31 December 2016 est.)
country comparison to the world: 193

Stock of broad money: $100.7 million (31 December 2017 est.)
$91.6 million (31 December 2016 est.)

country comparison to the world: 195

Stock of domestic credit: $1.481 million (31 December 2017 est.)
$1.481 million (31 December 2016 est.)
country comparison to the world: 190

Exports: $5.7 million (2017 est.)
$5.2 million (2016 est.)
country comparison to the world: 217

Exports—commodities: electronic components, plastic bags, apparel; hot peppers, limes, live plants; cattle

Imports: $33.67 million (2017 est.)
$31.02 million (2016 est.)
country comparison to the world: 216

Imports—commodities: machinery and transportation equipment, foodstuffs, manufactured goods, fuels, lubricants

Reserves of foreign exchange and gold: $49.36 million (31 December 2016 est.)
$51.47 million (31 December 2015 est.)
country comparison to the world: 171

Debt—external: $8.9 million (1997)
country comparison to the world: 201

Exchange rates: East Caribbean dollars (XCD) per US dollar—
2.7 (2017 est.)
2.7 (2016 est.)
2.7 (2015 est.)
2.7 (2014 est.)
2.7 (2013 est.)

ENERGY

Electricity—production: 24 million kWh (2015 est.)
country comparison to the world: 213

Electricity—consumption: 22.32 million kWh (2015 est.)
country comparison to the world: 211

Electricity—exports: 0 kWh (2016 est.)
country comparison to the world: 166

Electricity—imports: 0 kWh (2016 est.)
country comparison to the world: 171

Electricity—installed generating capacity: 5,000 kW (2015 est.)
country comparison to the world: 214

Electricity—from fossil fuels: 100% of total installed capacity (2015 est.)
country comparison to the world: 12

Electricity—from nuclear fuels: 0% of total installed capacity (2015 est.)

country comparison to the world: 137

Electricity—from hydroelectric plants: 0% of total installed capacity (2015 est.)
country comparison to the world: 187

Electricity—from other renewable sources: 0% of total installed capacity (2015 est.)
country comparison to the world: 197

Crude oil—production: 0 bbl/day (2016 est.)
country comparison to the world: 175

Crude oil—exports: 0 bbl/day (2014 est.)
country comparison to the world: 159

Crude oil—imports: 0 bbl/day (2014 est.)
country comparison to the world: 156

Crude oil—proved reserves: 0 bbl (1 January 2017 es)
country comparison to the world: 173

Refined petroleum products—production: 0 bbl/day (2014 est.)
country comparison to the world: 181

Refined petroleum products—consumption: 570 bbl/day (2015 est.)
country comparison to the world: 209

Refined petroleum products—exports: 0 bbl/day (2014 est.)
country comparison to the world: 177

Refined petroleum products—imports: 416.4 bbl/day (2014 est.)
country comparison to the world: 207

Natural gas—production: 0 cu m (2013 est.)
country comparison to the world: 165

Natural gas—consumption: 0 cu m (2013 est.)
country comparison to the world: 205

Natural gas—exports: 0 cu m (2013 est.)
country comparison to the world: 145

Natural gas—imports: 0 cu m (2013 est.)
country comparison to the world: 152

Natural gas—proved reserves: 0 cu m (1 January 2014 es)
country comparison to the world: 168

Carbon dioxide emissions from consumption of energy: 88,010 Mt (2012 est.)
country comparison to the world: 209

COMMUNICATIONS

Telephones—fixed lines: *total subscriptions:* 3,000
subscriptions per 100 inhabitants: 57 (July 2016 est.)
country comparison to the world: 210

Telephones—mobile cellular: *total:* 5,000

subscriptions per 100 inhabitants: 95 (July 2016 est.)
country comparison to the world: 215

Telephone system: *general assessment:* modern and fully digitalized
domestic: combined fixed-line and mobile-cellular teledensity exceeds 150 per 100 persons
international: country code—1-664; landing point for the East Caribbean Fiber System (ECFS) optic submarine cable with links to 13 other islands in the eastern Caribbean extending from the British Virgin Islands to Trinidad (2016)

Broadcast media: Radio Montserrat, a public radio broadcaster, transmits on 1 station and has a repeater transmission to a second station; repeater transmissions from the GEM Radio Network of Trinidad and Tobago provide another 2 radio stations; cable and satellite TV available (2007)

Internet country code: .ms
Internet users: total: 2,860

percent of population: 54.6% (July 2016 est.)
country comparison to the world: 212

TRANSPORTATION

National air transport system: *number of registered air carriers:* 1
inventory of registered aircraft operated by air carriers: 3 (2015)
Civil aircraft registration country code prefix: VP-M (2016)

Airports: 1 (2013)
country comparison to the world: 226

Airports—with paved runways: *total:* 1
under 914 m: 1 (2017)
Roadways: note: volcanic eruptions that began in 1995 destroyed most of the 227 km road system; a new road infrastructure has been built on the north end of the island (2017)

Ports and terminals: *major seaport(s):* Little Bay, Plymouth

MILITARY AND SECURITY

Military branches: no regular military forces; Royal Montserrat Police Force (2011)

Military—note: defense is the responsibility of the UK

TRANSNATIONAL ISSUES

Disputes—international: none

Illicit drugs: transshipment point for South American narcotics destined for the US and Europe

MOROCCO

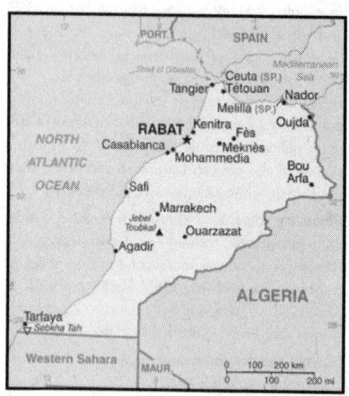

INTRODUCTION

Background: In 788, about a century after the Arab conquest of North Africa, a series of Moroccan Muslim dynasties began to rule in Morocco. In the 16th century, the Sa'adi monarchy, particularly under Ahmad al-MANSUR (1578-1603), repelled foreign invaders and inaugurated a golden age. The Alaouite Dynasty, to which the current Moroccan royal family belongs, dates from the 17th century. In 1860, Spain occupied northern Morocco and ushered in a half century of trade rivalry among European powers that saw Morocco's sovereignty steadily erode; in 1912, the French imposed a protectorate over the country. A protracted independence struggle with France ended successfully in 1956. The internationalized city of Tangier and most Spanish possessions were turned over to the new country that same year. Sultan MOHAMMED V, the current monarch's grandfather, organized the new state as a constitutional monarchy and in 1957 assumed the title of king. Since Spain's 1976 withdrawal from what is today called Western Sahara, Morocco has extended its de facto administrative control to roughly 80% of this territory; however, the UN does not recognize Morocco as the administering power for Western Sahara. The UN since 1991 has monitored a cease-fire between Morocco and the Polisario Front—Western Sahara's liberation movement—and leads ongoing negotiations over the status of the territory.

King MOHAMMED VI in early 2011 responded to the spread of pro-democracy protests in the region by implementing a reform program that included a new constitution, passed by popular referendum in July 2011, under which some new powers were extended to parliament and the prime minister but ultimate authority remains in the hands of the monarch. In November 2011, the Justice and Development Party (PJD)—a moderate Islamist party—won the largest number of seats in parliamentary elections, becoming the

first Islamist party to lead the Moroccan Government. In September 2015, Morocco held its first ever direct elections for regional councils, one of the reforms included in the 2011 constitution. The PJD again won the largest number of seats in nationwide parliamentary elections in October 2016.

GEOGRAPHY

Location: Northern Africa, bordering the North Atlantic Ocean and the Mediterranean Sea, between Algeria and Western Sahara

Geographic coordinates: 32 00 N, 5 00 W

Map references: Africa

Area: *total:* 446,550 sq km
land: 446,300 sq km
water: 250 sq km
country comparison to the world: 59

Area—comparative: slightly more than three times the size of New York; slightly larger than California

Land boundaries: *total:* 2,362.5 km
border countries (3): Algeria 1,900 km, Western Sahara 444 km, Spain (Ceuta) 8 km, Spain (Melilla) 10.5 km
note: an additional 75-meter border segment exists between Morocco and the Spanish exclave of Penon de Velez de la Gomera

Coastline: 1,835 km

Maritime claims: *territorial sea:* 12 nm
contiguous zone: 24 nm
exclusive economic zone: 200 nm
continental shelf: 200-m depth or to the depth of exploitation

Climate: Mediterranean, becoming more extreme in the interior

Terrain: mountainous northern coast (Rif Mountains) and interior (Atlas Mountains) bordered by large plateaus with intermontane valleys, and fertile coastal plains

Elevation: *mean elevation:* 909 m

elevation extremes: *lowest point:* Sebkha Tah -59 m
highest point: Jebel Toubkal 4,165 m

Natural resources: phosphates, iron ore, manganese, lead, zinc, fish, salt

Land use: *agricultural land:* 67.5%
arable land: 17.5%;
permanent crops: 2.9%;
permanent pasture: 47.1%
forest: 11.5%
other: 21% (2011 est.)
Irrigated land: 14,850 sq km (2012)

Population—distribution: the highest population density is found along the Atlantic and Mediterranean coasts; a number of densely populated agglomerations are found scattered through the Atlas Mountains

Natural hazards: northern mountains geologically unstable and subject to earthquakes; periodic droughts; windstorms; flash floods; landslides

Environment—current issues: land degradation/desertification (soil erosion resulting from farming of marginal areas, overgrazing, destruction of vegetation); water supplies contaminated by raw sewage; siltation of reservoirs; oil pollution of coastal waters

Environment—international agreements: *party to:* Biodiversity, Climate Change, Climate Change-Kyoto Protocol, Desertification, Endangered Species, Hazardous Wastes, Law of the Sea, Marine Dumping, Ozone Layer Protection, Ship Pollution, Wetlands, Whaling
signed, but not ratified: Environmental Modification

Geography—note: strategic location along Strait of Gibraltar; the only African nation to have both Atlantic and Mediterranean coastlines

PEOPLE AND SOCIETY

Population: 33,986,655 (July 2017 est.)
country comparison to the world: 40

Nationality: *noun:* Moroccan(s)
adjective: Moroccan

Ethnic groups: Arab-Berber 99%, other 1%

Languages: Arabic (official), Berber languages (Tamazight (official), Tachelhit, Tarifit), French (often the language of business, government, and diplomacy)

Religions: Muslim 99% (official; virtually all Sunni, <0.1% Shia), other 1% (includes Christian, Jewish, and Baha'i); note—Jewish about 6,000 (2010 est.)

Demographic profile: Morocco is undergoing a demographic transition. Its population is growing but at a declining rate, as people live longer and women have fewer children. Infant, child, and maternal mortality rates have been reduced through better health care, nutrition, hygiene, and vaccination coverage, although disparities between urban and rural and rich and poor households persist. Morocco's shrinking child cohort reflects the decline of its total fertility rate from 5 in mid-1980s to 2.2 in 2010, which is a result of increased female educational attainment, higher contraceptive use, delayed marriage, and the desire for smaller families. Young adults (persons aged 15-29) make up almost 26% of the total population and represent a potential economic asset if they can be gainfully employed. Currently, however, many youths are unemployed because Morocco's job creation rate has not kept pace with the growth of its working-age population. Most youths who have jobs work in the informal sector with little security or benefits.

During the second half of the 20th century, Morocco became one of the world's top emigration countries, creating large, widely dispersed migrant communities in Western Europe. The Moroccan Government has encouraged emigration since its independence in 1956, both to secure remittances for funding national development and as an outlet to prevent unrest in rebellious (often Berber) areas. Although Moroccan labor migrants earlier targeted Algeria and France, the flood of Moroccan "guest workers" from the mid-1960s to the early 1970s spread widely across northwestern Europe to fill unskilled jobs in the booming manufacturing, mining, construction, and agriculture industries. Host societies and most Moroccan migrants expected this migration to be temporary, but deteriorating economic conditions in Morocco related to the 1973 oil crisis and tighter European immigration policies resulted in these stays becoming permanent.

A wave of family migration followed in the 1970s and 1980s, with a growing number of second generation Moroccans opting to become naturalized citizens of their host countries. Spain and Italy emerged as new destination countries in the mid-1980s, but their introduction of visa restrictions in the early 1990s pushed Moroccans increasingly to migrate either legally by marrying Moroccans already in Europe or illegally to work in the underground economy. Women began to make up a growing share of these labor migrants. At the same time, some higher-skilled Moroccans went to the US and Quebec, Canada.

In the mid-1990s, Morocco developed into a transit country for asylum seekers from sub-Saharan Africa and illegal labor migrants from sub-Saharan Africa and South Asia trying to reach Europe via southern Spain, Spain's Canary Islands, or Spain's North African enclaves, Ceuta and Melilla. Forcible expulsions by Moroccan and Spanish security forces have not deterred these illegal migrants or calmed Europe's security concerns. Rabat remains unlikely to adopt an EU agreement to take back third-country nationals who have entered the EU illegally via Morocco. Thousands of other illegal migrants have chosen to stay in Morocco until they earn enough money for further travel or permanently as a "second-best" option. The launching of a regularization program in 2014 legalized the status of some migrants and granted them equal access to education, health care, and work, but xenophobia and racism remain obstacles.

Age structure: *0-14 years:* 25.77% (male 4,450,360/female 4,308,955)
15-24 years: 17.04% (male 2,879,828/female 2,910,029)
25-54 years: 42.32% (male 6,956,186/female 7,428,129)
55-64 years: 8.13% (male 1,365,611/female 1,398,553)
65 years and over: 6.74% (male 1,034,188/female 1,254,816) (2017 est.)

Dependency ratios: *total dependency ratio:* 51.6
youth dependency ratio: 41.9
elderly dependency ratio: 9.7
potential support ratio: 10.3 (2015 est.)

Median age: *total:* 29.3 years
male: 28.6 years
female: 29.9 years (2017 est.)
country comparison to the world: 124

Population growth rate: 0.97% (2017 est.)
country comparison to the world: 117

Birth rate: 17.7 births/1,000 population (2017 est.)
country comparison to the world: 105

Death rate: 4.9 deaths/1,000 population (2017 est.)
country comparison to the world: 195

Net migration rate: -3.2 migrant(s)/1,000 population (2017 est.)
country comparison to the world: 177

Population distribution: the highest population density is found along the Atlantic and Mediterranean coasts; a number of densely populated agglomerations are found scattered through the Atlas Mountains

Urbanization: *urban population:* 61.2% of total population (2017)
rate of urbanization: 1.92% annual rate of change (2015-20 est.)

Major urban areas—population: Casablanca 3.515 million; RABAT (capital) 1.967 million; Fes 1.172 million; Marrakech 1.134 million; Tangier 982,000 (2015)

Sex ratio: *at birth:* 1.05 male(s)/female
0-14 years: 1.03 male(s)/female
15-24 years: 0.99 male(s)/female
25-54 years: 0.94 male(s)/female
55-64 years: 0.99 male(s)/female
65 years and over: 0.82 male(s)/female
total population: 0.97 male(s)/female (2016 est.)

Maternal mortality ratio: 121 deaths/100,000 live births (2015 est.)
country comparison to the world: 69

Infant mortality rate: *total:* 21.9 deaths/1,000 live births
male: 26 deaths/1,000 live births
female: 17.6 deaths/1,000 live births (2017 est.)
country comparison to the world: 76

Life expectancy at birth: *total population:* 77.1 years
male: 74 years
female: 80.3 years (2017 est.)
country comparison to the world: 77

Total fertility rate: 2.11 children born/woman (2017 est.)
country comparison to the world: 104

Contraceptive prevalence rate: 67.4% (2010/11)

Health expenditures: 5.9% of GDP (2014)
country comparison to the world: 107

Physicians density: 0.62 physicians/1,000 population (2014)

Hospital bed density: 0.9 beds/1,000 population (2012)

Drinking water source:
improved:
urban: 98.7% of population
rural: 65.3% of population
total: 85.4% of population

unimproved:
urban: 1.3% of population
rural: 34.7% of population
total: 14.6% of population (2015 est.)

Sanitation facility access:
improved:
urban: 84.1% of population
rural: 65.5% of population
total: 76.7% of population
unimproved:
urban: 15.9% of population
rural: 34.5% of population
total: 23.3% of population (2015 est.)

HIV/AIDS—adult prevalence rate: 0.1% (2016 est.)
country comparison to the world: 106

HIV/AIDS—people living with HIV/AIDS: 22,000 (2016 est.)
country comparison to the world: 74

HIV/AIDS—deaths: <1000 (2016 est.)

Obesity—adult prevalence rate: 26.1% (2016)
country comparison to the world: 44

Children under the age of 5 years underweight: 3.1% (2011)
country comparison to the world: 113

Education expenditures: 5.3% of GDP (2009)
country comparison to the world: 59

Literacy: *definition:* age 15 and over can read and write
total population: 68.5%
male: 78.6%
female: 58.8% (2015 est.)

School life expectancy (primary to tertiary education): *total:* 12 years
male: 13 years
female: 12 years (2012)

Unemployment, youth ages 15-24: *total:* 19.9%
male: 20.8%
female: 17.7% (2014 est.)
country comparison to the world: 60

GOVERNMENT

Country name: *conventional long form:* Kingdom of Morocco
conventional short form: Morocco
local long form: Al Mamlakah al Maghribiyah
local short form: Al Maghrib
etymology: the English name "Morocco" derives from, respectively, the Spanish and Portuguese names "Marruecos" and "Marrocos," which stem from "Marrakesh" the Latin name for the former capital of ancient Morocco; the Arabic name "Al Maghrib" translates as "The West"

Government type: parliamentary constitutional monarchy

Capital: *name:* Rabat
geographic coordinates: 34 01 N, 6 49 W
time difference: UTC 0 (5 hours ahead of Washington, DC, during Standard Time)
daylight saving time: +1 hr, begins last Sunday in March; ends last Sunday in October

Administrative divisions: 11 regions (recognized); Beni Mellal-Khenifra, Casablanca-Settat, Draa-Tafilalet, Fes-Meknes, Guelmim-Oued Noun, Laayoune-Sakia al Hamra, Oriental, Marrakech-Safi, Rabat-Sale-Kenitra, Souss-Massa, Tanger-Tetouan-Al Hoceima

note: Morocco claims the territory of Western Sahara, the political status of which is considered undetermined by the US Government; portions of the regions Guelmim-Oued Noun and Laayoune-Sakia al Hamra as claimed by Morocco lie within Western Sahara; Morocco also claims a 12th region, Dakhla-Oued ed Dahab, that falls entirely within Western Sahara

Independence: 2 March 1956 (from France)

National holiday: Throne Day (accession of King MOHAMMED VI to the throne), 30 July (1999)

Constitution: history: several previous; latest drafted 17 June 2011, approved by referendum 1 July 2011; note—sources disagree on whether the 2011 referendum was for a new constitution or for reforms to the previous constitution

amendments: proposed by the king, by the prime minister, or by members in either chamber of Parliament; passage requires at least two-thirds majority vote by both chambers and approval in a referendum; the king can opt to submit self-initiated proposals directly to a referendum (2016)

Legal system: mixed legal system of civil law based on French law and Islamic law; judicial review of legislative acts by Constitutional Court

International law organization participation: has not submitted an ICJ jurisdiction declaration; non-party state to the ICCt

Citizenship: *citizenship by birth:* no

citizenship by descent only: the father must be a citizen of Morocco; if the father is unknown or stateless, the mother must be a citizen

dual citizenship recognized: yes

residency requirement for naturalization: 5 years

Suffrage: 18 years of age; universal

Executive branch: *chief of state:* King MOHAMMED VI (since 30 July 1999)

head of government: Prime Minister Saad-Eddine al-OTHMANI (since 17 March 2017)

cabinet: Council of Ministers chosen by the prime minister in consultation with Parliament and appointed by the monarch

elections/appointments: the monarchy is hereditary; prime minister appointed by the monarch from the majority party following legislative elections

Legislative branch: *description:* bicameral Parliament consists of the Chamber of Advisors (120 seats; members indirectly elected by an electoral college of local councils, professional organizations, and labor unions; members serve 6-year terms) and the Chamber of Representatives (395 seats; 305 members directly elected in multi-seat constituencies by proportional representation vote and 90 directly elected in a single nation-wide constituency by proportional representation vote; members serve 5-year terms); note—in the national constituency, 60 seats are reserved for women and 30 reserved for those under age 40

elections: Chamber of Advisors—last held on 2 October 2015 (next to be held in fall 2021); Chamber of Representatives—last held on 7 October 2016 (next to be held in fall 2021)

election results: Chamber of Advisors—percent of vote by party—NA; seats by party—NA; Chamber of Representatives—percent of vote by party NA; seats by party—PJD 125, PAM 102, PI 46, RNI 37, MP 27, USFP 20, UC 19, PPS 12, MDS 3, other 4

Judicial branch: *highest court(s):* Supreme Court or Court of Cassation (consists of 5-judge panels organized into civil, family matters, commercial, administrative, social, and criminal sections); Constitutional Court (consists of 12 members)

judge selection and term of office: Supreme Court judges appointed by the Superior Council of Judicial Power, a 20-member body presided by the monarch and including the Supreme Court president, the prosecutor general, representatives of the appeals and first instance courts—among them 1 woman magistrate, the president of the National Council of the Rights of Man, and 5 "notable persons" appointed by the monarch; judges appointed for life; Constitutional Court members—6 designated by the monarch and 6 elected by Parliament; court president appointed by the monarch from among the court members; members serve 9-year non-renewable terms

subordinate courts: courts of appeal; High Court of Justice; administrative and commercial courts; regional and sadad courts (for religious, civil and administrative, and penal adjudication); first instance courts

Political parties and leaders: Action Party or PA [Mohammed EL IDRISSI]

Amal (hope) Party [Mohamed BANI]

An-Nahj Ad-Dimocrati or An-Nahj [Mustapha BRAHMA]

Authenticity and Modernity Party or PAM [vacant]

Constitutional Union Party or UC [Mohamed SAJID]

Democratic and Social Movement or MDS [Abdessamad ARCHANE]

Democratic Forces Front or FFD [Mustapha BENALI]

Democratic Oath Party or SD

Democratic Socialist Vanguard Party or PADS [Abderrahman BENAMROU]

Democratic Society Party [Zhour CHAKKAFI]

Environment and Development Party or PED [Karim HRITAN]

Green Left Party [Mohamed FARES]

Istiqlal (Independence) Party or PI [Hamid CHABAT]

Ittihadi National Congress or CNI [Abdesalam EL AZIZ]

Labor Party or PT

Moroccan Liberal Party or PML [Mohammed ZIANE]

Moroccan Union for Democracy or UMD [Jamal MANDRI]

National Rally of Independents or RNI [Aziz AKHANNOUCH]

Neo-Democrats Party [Mohamed DARIF]

Party of Development Reform or PRD [Abderrahmane EL KOHEN]

Party of Justice and Development or PJD [Abdelillah BENKIRANE]

Party of Liberty and Social Justice [Miloud MOUSSAOUI]

Popular Movement or MP [Mohand LAENSER]

Progress and Socialism Party or PPS [Nabil BENABDELLAH]

Renaissance and Virtue Party [Mohamed KHALIDI]

Renaissance Party [Said EL GHENNIOUI]

Renewal and Equity Party or PRE [Chakir ACHEHABAR]

Shoura (consultation) and Istiqlal Party [Ahmed BELGHAZI]

Social Center Party or PCS [Lahcen MADIH]

Socialist Party [Abdelmajid BOUZOUBAA]

Socialist Union of Popular Forces or USFP [Driss LACHGAR]

Unified Socialist Party or GSU [Nabila MOUNIB]

Unity and Democracy Party [Ahmed FITRI]

Political pressure groups and leaders: Democratic Confederation of Labor or CDT [Noubir EL AMAOUI]

General Union of Moroccan Workers or UGTM [Mohamed KAFI CHERRAT]

Justice and Charity Organization or JCO [Mohammed ben Abdesslam ABBADI]

Moroccan Employers Association or CGEM [Miriem BENSALAH-CHAQROUN]

National Labor Union of Morocco or UNMT [Abdessalam MAATI]

Union of Moroccan Workers or UMT [Miloudi EL MOUKHARIK]

International organization participation: ABEDA, AfDB, AFESD, AMF, AMU, CAEU, CD, EBRD, FAO, G-11, G-77, IAEA, IBRD, ICAO, ICC (national committees), ICRM, IDA, IDB, IFAD, IFC, IFRCS, IHO, ILO, IMF, IMO, IMSO, Interpol, IOC, IOM, IPU, ISO, ITSO, ITU, ITUC (NGOs), LAS, MIGA, MONUSCO, NAM, OAS (observer), OIC, OIF, OPCW, OSCE (partner), Pacific Alliance (observer), Paris Club (associate), PCA, SICA (observer), UN, UNCTAD, UNESCO, UNHCR, UNIDO, UNOCI, UNSC (temporary), UNWTO, UPU, WCO, WHO, WIPO, WMO, WTO

Diplomatic representation in the US: *chief of mission:* Ambassador Lalla Joumala ALAOUI (since 24 April 2017)

chancery: 1601 21st Street NW, Washington, DC 20009

telephone: [1] (202) 462-7979

FAX: [1] (202) 462-7643

consulate(s) general: New York

Diplomatic representation from the US: *chief of mission:* Ambassador (vacant); Charge d'Affaires Stephanie MILEY (since 20 January 2017)

embassy: Km 5.7 Avenue Mohammed VI, Souissi, Rabat 10170

mailing address: Unit 9400, Box Front Office, DPO, AE 09718

telephone: [212] 537 637 200

FAX: [212] 537 637 201
consulate(s) general: Casablanca

Flag description: red with a green pentacle (five-pointed, linear star) known as Sulayman's (Solomon's) seal in the center of the flag; red and green are traditional colors in Arab flags, although the use of red is more commonly associated with the Arab states of the Persian Gulf; the pentacle represents the five pillars of Islam and signifies the association between God and the nation; design dates to 1912

National symbol(s): pentacle symbol, lion; national colors: red, green

National anthem: name: "Hymne Cherifien" (Hymn of the Sharif)
lyrics/music: Ali Squalli HOUSSAINI/Leo MORGAN
note: music adopted 1956, lyrics adopted 1970

ECONOMY

Economy—overview: Morocco has capitalized on its proximity to Europe and relatively low labor costs to work towards building a diverse, open, market-oriented economy. Key sectors of the economy include agriculture, tourism, aerospace, automotive, phosphates, textiles, apparel, and subcomponents. Morocco has increased investment in its port, transportation, and industrial infrastructure to position itself as a center and broker for business throughout Africa. Industrial development strategies and infrastructure improvements—most visibly illustrated by a new port and free trade zone near Tangier—are improving Morocco's competitiveness.

In the 1980s, Morocco was a heavily indebted country before pursuing austerity measures and pro-market reforms, overseen by the IMF. Since taking the throne in 1999, King MOHAMMED VI has presided over a stable economy marked by steady growth, low inflation, and gradually falling unemployment, although poor harvests and economic difficulties in Europe contributed to an economic slowdown. To boost exports, Morocco entered into a bilateral Free Trade Agreement with the US in 2006 and an Advanced Status agreement with the EU in 2008. In late 2014, Morocco eliminated subsidies for gasoline, diesel, and fuel oil, dramatically reducing outlays that weighted on the country's budget and current account. Subsidies on butane gas and certain food products remain in place. Morocco also seeks to expand its renewable energy capacity with a goal of making renewable more than 50% of installed electricity generation capacity by 2030.

Despite Morocco's economic progress, the country suffers from high unemployment, poverty, and illiteracy, particularly in rural areas. Key economic challenges for Morocco include reforming the education system and the judiciary.

GDP (purchasing power parity): $300.1 billion (2017 est.)
$286.3 billion (2016 est.)
$282.9 billion (2015 est.)
note: data are in 2017 dollars
country comparison to the world: 58

GDP (official exchange rate): $110.7 billion (2016 est.)

GDP—real growth rate: 4.8% (2017 est.)
1.2% (2016 est.)
4.6% (2015 est.)
country comparison to the world: 44

GDP—per capita (PPP): $8,600 (2017 est.)
$8,300 (2016 est.)
$8,300 (2015 est.)
note: data are in 2017 dollars
country comparison to the world: 148

Gross national saving: 29.2% of GDP (2017 est.)
28.2% of GDP (2016 est.)
28.7% of GDP (2015 est.)
country comparison to the world: 29

GDP—composition, by end use:
household consumption: 58%
government consumption: 18.8%
investment in fixed capital: 30.1%
investment in inventories: 2.8%
exports of goods and services: 35.7%
imports of goods and services: -45.5% (2017 est.)

GDP—composition, by sector of origin:
agriculture: 14.8%
industry: 29.1%
services: 56% (2017 est.)

Agriculture—products: barley, wheat, citrus fruits, grapes, vegetables, olives; livestock; wine

Industries: automotive parts, phosphate mining and processing, aerospace, food processing, leather goods, textiles, construction, energy, tourism

Industrial production growth rate: 2.6% (2017 est.)
country comparison to the world: 107

Labor force: 12 million (2017 est.)
country comparison to the world: 49

Labor force—by occupation: agriculture: 39.1%
industry: 20.3%
services: 40.5% (2014 est.)

Unemployment rate: 9.3% (2017 est.)
9.4% (2016 est.)
country comparison to the world: 128

Population below poverty line: 15% (2007 est.)

Household income or consumption by percentage share: lowest 10%: 2.7%
highest 10%: 33.2% (2007)

Distribution of family income—Gini index: 40.9 (2007 est.)
39.5 (1999 est.)
country comparison to the world: 57

Budget: revenues: $26.63 billion
expenditures: $30.71 billion (2017 est.)
Taxes and other revenues: 24.1% of GDP (2017 est.)
country comparison to the world: 120

Budget surplus (+) or deficit (-): -3.7% of GDP (2017 est.)
country comparison to the world: 138

Public debt: 77.2% of GDP (2017 est.)
77.5% of GDP (2016 est.)
country comparison to the world: 44

Fiscal year: calendar year

Inflation rate (consumer prices): 0.9% (2017 est.)

1.6% (2016 est.)
country comparison to the world: 36

Central bank discount rate: 6.5% (31 December 2010)
3.31% (31 December 2009)
country comparison to the world: 64

Commercial bank prime lending rate: 5.7% (31 December 2017 est.)
5.73% (31 December 2016 est.)
country comparison to the world: 132

Stock of narrow money: $83.8 billion (31 December 2017 est.)
$74.7 billion (31 December 2016 est.)
country comparison to the world: 45

Stock of broad money: $100 billion (31 December 2017 est.)
$89.22 billion (31 December 2016 est.)
country comparison to the world: 56

Stock of domestic credit: $118.4 billion (31 December 2017 est.)
$109.3 billion (31 December 2016 est.)
country comparison to the world: 54

Market value of publicly traded shares: $45.93 billion (31 December 2015 est.)
$52.75 billion (31 December 2014 est.)
$53.83 billion (31 December 2013 est.)
country comparison to the world: 54

Current account balance: -$4.442 billion (2017 est.)
-$4.537 billion (2016 est.)
country comparison to the world: 173

Exports: $19.64 billion (2017 est.)
$18.88 billion (2016 est.)
country comparison to the world: 71

Exports—commodities: clothing and textiles, automobiles, electric components, inorganic chemicals, transistors, crude minerals, fertilizers (including phosphates), petroleum products, citrus fruits, vegetables, fish

Exports—partners: Spain 23.4%, France 21.1%, Italy 4.6% (2016)

Imports: $39.64 billion (2017 est.)
$36.59 billion (2016 est.)
country comparison to the world: 56

Imports—commodities: crude petroleum, textile fabric, telecommunications equipment, wheat, gas and electricity, transistors, plastics

Imports—partners: Spain 15.7%, France 13.2%, China 9.1%, US 6.4%, Germany 5.9%, Italy 5.4%, Turkey 4.4% (2016)

Reserves of foreign exchange and gold: $22.97 billion (31 December 2017 est.)
$25.37 billion (31 December 2016 est.)
country comparison to the world: 57

Debt—external: $45.72 billion (31 December 2017 est.)
$44.65 billion (31 December 2016 est.)
country comparison to the world: 67

Stock of direct foreign investment—at home: $57.81 billion (31 December 2017 est.)
$54.78 billion (31 December 2016 est.)
country comparison to the world: 55

633

Stock of direct foreign investment—abroad:
$4.492 billion (31 December 2017 est.)
$5.203 billion (31 December 2016 est.)
country comparison to the world: 73

Exchange rates: Moroccan dirhams (MAD) per
US dollar—
9.639 (2017 est.)
9.7787 (2016 est.)
9.7787 (2015 est.)
9.7351 (2014 est.)
8.3798 (2013 est.)

ENERGY

Electricity access: *population without electricity:* 400,000
electrification—*total population:* 98.9%
electrification—urban areas: 100%
electrification—rural areas: 97.4% (2013)

Electricity—production: 27.37 billion kWh (2015 est.)
country comparison to the world: 67

Electricity—consumption: 26.83 billion kWh (2015 est.)
country comparison to the world: 64

Electricity—exports: 165 million kWh (2015 est.)
country comparison to the world: 78

Electricity—imports: 5.14 billion kWh (2015 est.)
country comparison to the world: 39

Electricity—installed generating capacity: 8.04 million kW (2015 est.)
country comparison to the world: 69

Electricity—from fossil fuels: 67.5% of total installed capacity (2015 est.)
country comparison to the world: 109

Electricity—from nuclear fuels: 0% of total installed capacity (2015 est.)
country comparison to the world: 142

Electricity—from hydroelectric plants: 16.2% of total installed capacity (2015 est.)
country comparison to the world: 98

Electricity—from other renewable sources: 12.5% of total installed capacity (2015 est.)
country comparison to the world: 61

Crude oil—production: 160 bbl/day (2016 est.)
country comparison to the world: 99

Crude oil—exports: 0 bbl/day (2014 est.)
country comparison to the world: 163

Crude oil—imports: 129,800 bbl/day (2014 est.)
country comparison to the world: 38

Crude oil—proved reserves: 684,000 bbl (1 January 2017 es)
country comparison to the world: 100

Refined petroleum products—production: 139,400 bbl/day (2014 est.)
country comparison to the world: 61

Refined petroleum products—consumption: 286,000 bbl/day (2015 est.)
country comparison to the world: 45

Refined petroleum products—exports: 24,830 bbl/day (2014 est.)
country comparison to the world: 67

Refined petroleum products—imports: 187,400 bbl/day (2014 est.)
country comparison to the world: 32

Natural gas—production: 94 million cu m (2015 est.)
country comparison to the world: 82

Natural gas—consumption: 1.48 billion cu m (2015 est.)
country comparison to the world: 91

Natural gas—exports: 0 cu m (2013 est.)
country comparison to the world: 150

Natural gas—imports: 1 billion cu m (2015 est.)
country comparison to the world: 60

Natural gas—proved reserves: 1.444 billion cu m (1 January 2017 es)
country comparison to the world: 102

Carbon dioxide emissions from consumption of energy: 39 million Mt (2013 est.)
country comparison to the world: 69

COMMUNICATIONS

Telephones—fixed lines: *total subscriptions:* 2,070,173
subscriptions per 100 inhabitants: 6 (July 2016 est.)
country comparison to the world: 54

Telephones—mobile cellular: *total:* 41,513,933
subscriptions per 100 inhabitants: 123 (July 2016 est.)
country comparison to the world: 32

Telephone system: *general assessment:* good system composed of open-wire lines, cables, and microwave radio relay links; principal switching centers are Casablanca and Rabat; national network nearly 100% digital using fiber-optic links; improved rural service employs microwave radio relay; Internet available but expensive
domestic: fixed-line teledensity is below 10 per 100 persons; mobile-cellular subscribership exceeds 120 per 100 persons
international: country code—212; landing point for the Atlas Offshore, Estepona-Tetouan, Euroafrica, Spain-Morocco, and SEA-ME-WE-3 fiber-optic telecommunications undersea cables that provide connectivity to Asia, the Middle East, and Europe; satellite earth stations—2 Intelsat (Atlantic Ocean) and 1 Arabsat; microwave radio relay to Gibraltar, Spain, and Western Sahara; coaxial cable and microwave radio relay to Algeria; participant in Medarabtel; fiber-optic cable link from Agadir to Algeria and Tunisia (2016)

Broadcast media: 2 TV broadcast networks with state-run Radio-Television Marocaine (RTM) operating one network and the state partially owning the other; foreign TV broadcasts are available via satellite dish; 3 radio broadcast networks with RTM operating one; the government-owned network includes 10 regional radio channels in addition to its national service (2007)

Internet country code: .ma
Internet users: total: 19,611,643

percent of population: 58.3% (July 2016 est.)
country comparison to the world: 29

TRANSPORTATION

National air transport system: *number of registered air carriers:* 4
inventory of registered aircraft operated by air carriers: 65
annual passenger traffic on registered air carriers: 6,786,850
annual freight traffic on registered air carriers: 47,828,227 mt-km (2015)
Civil aircraft registration country code prefix: CN (2016)

Airports: 55 (2013)
country comparison to the world: 86

Airports—with paved runways: *total:* 31
over 3,047 m: 11
2,438 to 3,047 m: 9
1,524 to 2,437 m: 7
914 to 1,523 m: 4 (2017)

Airports—with unpaved runways: *total:* 24
2,438 to 3,047 m: 1
1,524 to 2,437 m: 7
914 to 1,523 m: 11
under 914 m: 5 (2013)

Heliports: 1 (2013)

Pipelines: gas 944 km; oil 270 km; refined products 175 km (2013)

Railways: *total:* 2,067 km
standard gauge: 2,067 km 1.435-m gauge (1,022 km electrified) (2014)
country comparison to the world: 72

Roadways: *total:* 58,395 km
paved: 41,116 km (includes 1,080 km of expressways)
unpaved: 17,279 km (2010)
country comparison to the world: 74

Merchant marine: *total:* 82
by type: container ship 6, general cargo 6, oil tanker 1, other 69 (2017)
country comparison to the world: 93

Ports and terminals: *major seaport(s):* Casablanca, Jorf Lasfar, Mohammedia, Safi, Tangier
container port(s) (TEUs): Tangier (2,971,000) (2015)
LNG terminal(s) (import): Jorf Lasfar

MILITARY AND SECURITY

Military expenditures: 3.28% of GDP (2016)
3.25% of GDP (2015)
3.68% of GDP (2014)
3.81% of GDP (2013)
3.46% of GDP (2012)
country comparison to the world: 14

Military branches: Royal Armed Forces (Forces Armees Royales, FAR): Royal Moroccan Army (includes Air Defense), Royal Moroccan Navy (includes Coast Guard, Marines), Royal Moroccan Air Force (Al Quwwat al Jawyiya al Malakiya Marakishiya; Force Aerienne Royale Marocaine) (2010)

Military service age and obligation: 20 years of age for voluntary military service; no conscription; service obligation—18 months (2012)

TERRORISM

Terrorist groups—foreign based: *al-Qa'ida (AQ):*
aim(s): drive Westerners and Western influences
from Morocco and, ultimately, establish a pan-
Islamic caliphate under a strict Salafi Muslim
interpretation of Sharia
area(s) of operation: maintains a limited money
laundering presence; al-Qa'ida attacks over the
years galvanized the populace to protest against
group; authorities continue to pursue members and
supporters for arrest; on 16 May 2003, a team of
12 suicide bombers attacked five targets in Casablanca, killing 43 civilians and injuring at least
100; they attacked a Spanish restaurant, a Jewish
community, a Jewish cemetery, a hotel, and the
Belgian Consulate

Islamic State of Iraq and the Levant (ISIL): *aim(s):*
enhance its recruitment network and, ultimately,
replace the Moroccan Government with an
Islamic state and implement ISIL's strict interpretation of Sharia
area(s) of operation: maintains an operational
and recruitment presence across the country,
where authorities have taken members into custody in most of Morocco's major cities; authorities
have seized weapons and bombmaking materials
since 2014, foiling several ISIL attacks and plots
to assassinate military and security officers; hundreds of ISIL's fighters in Syria were recruited in
Morocco

TRANSNATIONAL ISSUES

Disputes—international: claims and administers
Western Sahara whose sovereignty remains unresolved; Morocco protests Spain's control over the
coastal enclaves of Ceuta, Melilla, and Penon
de Velez de la Gomera, the islands of Penon de
Alhucemas and Islas Chafarinas, and surrounding waters; both countries claim Isla Perejil (Leila
Island); discussions have not progressed on a
comprehensive maritime delimitation, setting
limits on resource exploration and refugee interdiction, since Morocco's 2002 rejection of Spain's
unilateral designation of a median line from the
Canary Islands; Morocco serves as one of the
primary launching areas of illegal migration into
Spain from North Africa; Algeria's border with
Morocco remains an irritant to bilateral relations,
each nation accusing the other of harboring militants and arms smuggling; the National Liberation
Front's assertions of a claim to Chirac Pastures in
southeastern Morocco is a dormant dispute

Illicit drugs: the world's largest producer and
exporter of cannabis; total production for 2015-
2016 growing season estimated to be 700 metric
tons; shipments of hashish mostly directed to
Western Europe; transit point for cocaine from
South America destined for Western Europe; significant consumer of cannabis

MOZAMBIQUE

INTRODUCTION

Background: Almost five centuries as a Portuguese
colony came to a close with independence in 1975.
Large-scale emigration, economic dependence on
South Africa, a severe drought, and a prolonged
civil war hindered the country's development until
the mid-1990s. The ruling Front for the Liberation
of Mozambique (FRELIMO) party formally abandoned Marxism in 1989, and a new constitution
the following year provided for multiparty elections and a free market economy. A UN-negoti-
ated peace agreement between FRELIMO and
rebel Mozambique National Resistance (REN-
AMO) forces ended the fighting in 1992. In 2004,
Mozambique underwent a delicate transition as
Joaquim CHISSANO stepped down after 18 years
in office. His elected successor, Armando GUE-
BUZA, served two terms and then passed executive power to Filipe NYUSI in 2014. RENAMO's
residual armed forces have intermittently engaged
in a low-level insurgency since 2012, although a
late December 2016 ceasefire held throughout
2017.

GEOGRAPHY

Location: Southeastern Africa, bordering the
Mozambique Channel, between South Africa and
Tanzania

Geographic coordinates: 18 15 S, 35 00 E

Map references: Africa

Area: *total:* 799,380 sq km
land: 786,380 sq km
water: 13,000 sq km
country comparison to the world: 36

Area—comparative: slightly more than five times
the size of Georgia; slightly less than twice the size
of California

Land boundaries: *total:* 4,783 km
border countries (6): Malawi 1,498 km, South
Africa 496 km, Swaziland 108 km, Tanzania 840
km, Zambia 439 km, Zimbabwe 1,402 km

Coastline: 2,470 km

Maritime claims: *territorial sea:* 12 nm
exclusive economic zone: 200 nm

Climate: tropical to subtropical

Terrain: mostly coastal lowlands, uplands in center,
high plateaus in northwest, mountains in west

Elevation: *mean elevation:* 345 m

elevation extremes: *lowest point:* Indian Ocean
0 m
highest point: Monte Binga 2,436 m

Natural resources: coal, titanium, natural gas,
hydropower, tantalum, graphite

Land use: *agricultural land:* 56.3%
arable land: 6.4%;
permanent crops: 0.3%;
permanent pasture: 49.6%
forest: 43.7%
other: 0% (2011 est.)
Irrigated land: 1,180 sq km (2012)

Population—distribution: three large populations clusters are found along the southern coast
between Maputo and Inhambane, in the central
area between Beira and Chimoio along the Zambezi River, and in and around the northern cities
of Nampula, Cidade de Nacala, and Pemba; the
northwest and southwest are the least populated
areas

Natural hazards: severe droughts; devastating cyclones and floods in central and southern
provinces

Environment—current issues: increased migration of the population to urban and coastal areas
with adverse environmental consequences; desertification; pollution of surface and coastal waters;
elephant poaching for ivory is a problem

Environment—international agreements: *party to:* Biodiversity, Climate Change, Climate Change-Kyoto Protocol, Desertification, Endangered Species, Hazardous Wastes, Law of the Sea, Ozone Layer Protection, Ship Pollution, Wetlands *signed, but not ratified:* none of the selected agreements

Geography—note: the Zambezi River flows through the north-central and most fertile part of the country

PEOPLE AND SOCIETY

Population: 26,573,706
note: estimates for this country explicitly take into account the effects of excess mortality due to AIDS; this can result in lower life expectancy, higher infant mortality, higher death rates, lower population growth rates, and changes in the distribution of population by age and sex than would otherwise be expected (July 2017 est.)
country comparison to the world: 50

Nationality: *noun:* Mozambican(s)
adjective: Mozambican

Ethnic groups: African 99.66% (Makhuwa, Tsonga, Lomwe, Sena, and others), Europeans 0.06%, Euro-Africans 0.2%, Indians 0.08%

Languages: Emakhuwa 25.3%, Portuguese (official) 10.7%, Xichangana 10.3%, Cisena 7.5%, Elomwe 7%, Echuwabo 5.1%, other Mozambican languages 30.1%, other 0.3%, unspecified 3.7% (2007 est.)

Religions: Roman Catholic 28.4%, Muslim 17.9%, Zionist Christian 15.5%, Protestant 12.2% (includes Pentecostal 10.9% and Anglican 1.3%), other 6.7%, none 18.7%, unspecified 0.7% (2007 est.)

Demographic profile: Mozambique is a poor, sparsely populated country with high fertility and mortality rates and a rapidly growing youthful population—45% of the population is younger than 15. Mozambique's high poverty rate is sustained by natural disasters, disease, high population growth, low agricultural productivity, and the unequal distribution of wealth. The country's birth rate is among the world's highest, averaging around more than 5 children per woman (and higher in rural areas) for at least the last three decades. The sustained high level of fertility reflects gender inequality, low contraceptive use, early marriages and childbearing, and a lack of education, particularly among women. The high population growth rate is somewhat restrained by the country's high HIV/AIDS and overall mortality rates. Mozambique ranks among the worst in the world for HIV/AIDS prevalence, HIV/AIDS deaths, and life expectancy at birth.

Mozambique is predominantly a country of emigration, but internal, rural-urban migration has begun to grow. Mozambicans, primarily from the country's southern region, have been migrating to South Africa for work for more than a century. Additionally, approximately 1.7 million Mozambicans fled to Malawi, South Africa, and other neighboring countries between 1979 and 1992 to escape from civil war. Labor migrants have usually been men from rural areas whose crops have failed or who are unemployed and have headed to South Africa to work as miners; multiple generations of the same family often become miners. Since the abolition of apartheid in South Africa in 1991, other job opportunities have opened to Mozambicans, including in the informal and manufacturing sectors, but mining remains their main source of employment.

Age structure: *0-14 years:* 44.72% (male 5,975,407/female 5,908,511)
15-24 years: 21.57% (male 2,824,012/female 2,907,033)
25-54 years: 27.42% (male 3,409,425/female 3,875,837)
55-64 years: 3.4% (male 435,203/female 468,939)
65 years and over: 2.9% (male 352,546/female 416,793) (2017 est.)

Dependency ratios: *total dependency ratio:* 93.5
youth dependency ratio: 87.5
elderly dependency ratio: 6.1
potential support ratio: 16.5 (2015 est.)

Median age: *total:* 17.2 years
male: 16.6 years
female: 17.8 years (2017 est.)
country comparison to the world: 222

Population growth rate: 2.46% (2017 est.)
country comparison to the world: 20

Birth rate: 38.1 births/1,000 population (2017 est.)
country comparison to the world: 11

Death rate: 11.6 deaths/1,000 population (2017 est.)
country comparison to the world: 25

Net migration rate: -1.9 migrant(s)/1,000 population (2017 est.)
country comparison to the world: 160

Population distribution: three large populations clusters are found along the southern coast between Maputo and Inhambane, in the central area between Beira and Chimoio along the Zambezi River, and in and around the northern cities of Nampula, Cidade de Nacala, and Pemba; the northwest and southwest are the least populated areas

Urbanization: *urban population:* 32.8% of total population (2017)
rate of urbanization: 3.36% annual rate of change (2015-20 est.)

Major urban areas—population: MAPUTO (capital) 1.187 million; Matola 937,000 (2015)

Sex ratio: *at birth:* 1.02 male(s)/female
0-14 years: 1.01 male(s)/female
15-24 years: 0.97 male(s)/female
25-54 years: 0.88 male(s)/female
55-64 years: 0.92 male(s)/female
65 years and over: 0.85 male(s)/female
total population: 0.96 male(s)/female (2016 est.)

Mother's mean age at first birth: 18.9 years
median age at first birth among women 25-29 (2011 est.)

Maternal mortality ratio: 489 deaths/100,000 live births (2015 est.)

country comparison to the world: 21

Infant mortality rate: *total:* 65.9 deaths/1,000 live births
male: 67.9 deaths/1,000 live births
female: 63.8 deaths/1,000 live births (2017 est.)
country comparison to the world: 13

Life expectancy at birth: *total population:* 53.7 years
male: 52.9 years
female: 54.5 years (2017 est.)
country comparison to the world: 215

Total fertility rate: 5.08 children born/woman (2017 est.)
country comparison to the world: 11

Contraceptive prevalence rate: 11.6% (2011)

Health expenditures: 7% of GDP (2014)
country comparison to the world: 82

Physicians density: 0.06 physicians/1,000 population (2013)

Hospital bed density: 0.7 beds/1,000 population (2011)

Drinking water source:
improved:
urban: 80.6% of population
rural: 37% of population
total: 51.1% of population
unimproved:
urban: 19.4% of population
rural: 63% of population
total: 48.9% of population (2015 est.)

Sanitation facility access:
improved:
urban: 42.4% of population
rural: 10.1% of population
total: 20.5% of population
unimproved:
urban: 57.6% of population
rural: 89.9% of population
total: 79.5% of population (2015 est.)

HIV/AIDS—adult prevalence rate: 12.3% (2016 est.)
country comparison to the world: 8

HIV/AIDS—people living with HIV/AIDS: 1.8 million (2016 est.)
country comparison to the world: 4

HIV/AIDS—deaths: 62,000 (2016 est.)
country comparison to the world: 4

Major infectious diseases: *degree of risk:* very high
food or waterborne diseases: bacterial and protozoal diarrhea, hepatitis A, and typhoid fever
vectorborne diseases: malaria and dengue fever
water contact disease: schistosomiasis
animal contact disease: rabies (2016)

Obesity—adult prevalence rate: 7.2% (2016)
country comparison to the world: 160

Children under the age of 5 years underweight: 15.6% (2011)
country comparison to the world: 44

Education expenditures: 6.5% of GDP (2013)
country comparison to the world: 78

Literacy: *definition:* age 15 and over can read and write
total population: 58.8%
male: 73.3%
female: 45.4% (2015 est.)

School life expectancy (primary to tertiary education): *total:* 10 years
male: 10 years
female: 9 years (2014)

Unemployment, youth ages 15-24: *total:* 39.3%
male: 40.2%
female: 38.7% (2012 est.)

GOVERNMENT

Country name: *conventional long form:* Republic of Mozambique
conventional short form: Mozambique
local long form: Republica de Mocambique
local short form: Mocambique
former: Portuguese East Africa
etymology: named for the offshore island of Mozambique; the island was apparently named after Mussa al-BIK, an influential Arab slave trader who set himself up as sultan on the island in the 15th century

Government type: presidential republic

Capital: *name:* Maputo

geographic coordinates: 25 57 S, 32 35 E
time difference: UTC+2 (7 hours ahead of Washington, DC, during Standard Time)

Administrative divisions: 10 provinces (provincias, singular—provincia), 1 city (cidade)*; Cabo Delgado, Gaza, Inhambane, Manica, Maputo, Cidade de Maputo*, Nampula, Niassa, Sofala, Tete, Zambezia

Independence: 25 June 1975 (from Portugal)

National holiday: Independence Day, 25 June (1975)

Constitution: history: previous 1975, 1990; latest adopted 16 November 2004, effective 21 December 2004
amendments: proposed by the president of the republic or supported by at least one-third of the Assembly of the Republic membership; passage of amendments affecting constitutional provisions including the independence and sovereignty of the state, the republican form of government, basic rights and freedoms, and universal suffrage requires at least a two-thirds majority vote by the Assembly and approval in a referendum; referenda not required for passage of other amendments; amended 2007 (2017)

Legal system: mixed legal system of Portuguese civil law, and customary law; note—in rural, predominantly Muslim villages with no formal legal system, Islamic law may be applied

International law organization participation: has not submitted an ICJ jurisdiction declaration; non-party state to the ICCt

Citizenship: *citizenship by birth:* no
citizenship by descent only: at least one parent must be a citizen of Mozambique
dual citizenship recognized: no

residency requirement for naturalization: 5 years

Suffrage: 18 years of age; universal

Executive branch: *chief of state:* President Filipe Jacinto NYUSI (since 15 January 2015)

head of government: President Filipe Jacinto NYUSI (since 15 January 2015); Prime Minister Carlos Agostinho DO ROSARIO (since 17 January 2015)
cabinet: Cabinet appointed by the president
elections/appointments: president elected directly elected by absolute majority popular vote in 2 rounds if needed for a 5-year term (eligible for 2 consecutive terms); election last held on 15 October 2014 (next to be held in October 2019); prime minister appointed by the president
election results: Filipe NYUSI elected president; percent of vote—Filipe NYUSI (FRELIMO) 57.0%, Afonso DHLAKAMA (RENAMO) 36.6%, Daviz SIMANGO (MDM) 6.4%

Legislative branch: *description:* unicameral Assembly of the Republic or Assembleia da Republica (250 seats; members directly elected in single- and multi-seat constituencies by proportional representation vote and 2 members representing Mozambicans abroad who are appointed by the elected party; members serve 5-year terms)
elections: last held on 15 October 2014 (next to be held in October 2019)
election results: percent of vote by party—FRELIMO 55.9%, RENAMO 32.5%, MDM 8.4%, other 3.3%; seats by party—FRELIMO 144, RENAMO 89, MDM 17

Judicial branch: *highest court(s):* Supreme Court (consists of the court president, vice president, and 5 judges); Constitutional Council (consists of 7 judges); note—the Higher Council of the Judiciary is responsible for judiciary management and discipline
judge selection and term of office: Supreme Court president and vice president appointed by Mozambique president in consultation with the Higher Council of the Judiciary (CSMJ) and with ratification by the legislature; other judges elected by the legislature; judges serve 5-year renewable terms; Constitutional Council judges appointed—1 by the president, 5 by the legislature, and 1 by the CSMJ; judges serve 5-year nonrenewable terms
subordinate courts: Administrative Court (capital city only); provincial courts or Tribunais Judicias de Provincia; District Courts or Tribunais Judicias de Districto; customs courts; maritime courts; courts marshal; labor courts; community courts

Political parties and leaders: Democratic Movement of Mozambique (Movimento Democratico de Mocambique) or MDM [Daviz SIMANGO]
Front for the Liberation of Mozambique (Frente de Liberatacao de Mocambique) or FRELIMO [Filipe NYUSI]
Mozambican National Resistance (Resistencia Nacional Mocambicana) or RENAMO [Afonso DHLAKAMA]

Political pressure groups and leaders: Mozambican League of Human Rights (Liga Mocambicana dos Direitos Humanos) or LDH [Alice MABOTA, president]
Youth Parliament (Parlamento Juvenil) [Salomao MUCHANGA]

International organization participation: ACP, AfDB, AU, C, CD, CPLP, EITI (compliant country), FAO, G-77, IAEA, IBRD, ICAO, ICC (NGOs), ICRM, IDA, IDB, IFAD, IFC, IFRCS, IHO, ILO, IMF, IMO, IMSO, Interpol, IOC, IOM, IPU, ISO (correspondent), ITSO, ITU, ITUC (NGOs), MIGA, NAM, OIC, OIF (observer), OPCW, SADC, UN, UNCTAD, UNESCO, UNHCR, UNIDO, Union Latina, UNISFA, UNWTO, UPU, WCO, WFTU (NGOs), WHO, WIPO, WMO, WTO

Diplomatic representation in the US: *chief of mission:* Ambassador Carlos DOS SANTOS (since 28 January 2016)
chancery: 1525 New Hampshire Avenue NW, Washington, DC 20036
telephone: [1] (202) 293-7146
FAX: [1] (202) 835-0245

Diplomatic representation from the US: *chief of mission:* Ambassador H. Dean PITTMAN (since 18 February 2016)
embassy: Avenida Kenneth Kuanda 193, Maputo
mailing address: P.O. Box 783, Maputo
telephone: [258] (21) 49 2797
FAX: [258] (21) 49 0114

Flag description: three equal horizontal bands of green (top), black, and yellow with a red isosceles triangle based on the hoist side; the black band is edged in white; centered in the triangle is a yellow five-pointed star bearing a crossed rifle and hoe in black superimposed on an open white book; green represents the riches of the land, white peace, black the African continent, yellow the country's minerals, and red the struggle for independence; the rifle symbolizes defense and vigilance, the hoe refers to the country's agriculture, the open book stresses the importance of education, and the star represents Marxism and internationalism
note: one of only two national flags featuring a firearm, the other is Guatemala

National symbol(s): national colors: green, black, yellow, white, red

National anthem: *name:* "Patria Amada" (Lovely Fatherland)
lyrics/music: Salomao J. MANHICA/unknown
note: adopted 2002

ECONOMY

Economy—overview: At independence in 1975, Mozambique was one of the world's poorest countries. Socialist policies, economic mismanagement, and a brutal civil war from 1977 to 1992 further impoverished the country. In 1987, the government embarked on a series of macroeconomic reforms designed to stabilize the economy. These steps, combined with donor assistance and with political stability since the multi-party elections in 1994, propelled the country's GDP from $4 billion in 1993, following the war, to about $37 billion in 2017. Fiscal reforms, including the introduction of a value-added tax and reform of the customs service, have improved the government's revenue collection abilities.

In spite of these gains, more than half the population remains below the poverty line. Subsistence agriculture continues to employ the vast majority of the country's work force. Citizens rioted in September 2010 after fuel, water, electricity, and bread price increases were announced. In an attempt to lessen the negative impact on the population, the government implemented subsidies, decreased taxes and tariffs, and instituted other fiscal measures.

A substantial trade imbalance persists, although aluminum production from the Mozal Aluminum Smelter has significantly boosted export earnings in recent years. In 2012, the Mozambican Government took over Portugal's last remaining share in the Cahora Bassa Hydroelectricity Company, a significant contributor to the Southern African Power Pool. The government has plans to expand the Cahora Bassa Dam and build additional dams to increase its electricity exports and fulfill the needs of its burgeoning domestic industries.

Mozambique's once substantial foreign debt was reduced through forgiveness and rescheduling under the IMF's Heavily Indebted Poor Countries (HIPC) and Enhanced HIPC initiatives. However, in 2016, information surfaced revealing that the Mozambican Government was responsible for over $2 billion in government-backed loans originally secured between 2012-14 by state-owned defense and security companies without parliamentary approval or national budget inclusion, which prompted the IMF and international donors to halt direct budget support to the Government of Mozambique. Mozambique grew at an average annual rate of 6%-8% in the decade leading up to 2015, one of Africa's strongest performances, but growth slowed in 2016. The sizable external debt burden, donor withdrawal, elevated inflation, and currency depreciation contributed to slower growth in 2016-17.

Two major international consortiums are seeking approval to develop massive natural gas deposits off the coast of Cabo Delgado province, in what has the potential to become the largest infrastructure project in Africa. The government predicts sales of liquefied natural gas from these projects could generate several billion dollars in revenues annually sometime after 2022.

GDP (purchasing power parity): $37.39 billion (2017 est.)
$35.69 billion (2016 est.)
$34.37 billion (2015 est.)
note: data are in 2017 dollars
country comparison to the world: 123

GDP (official exchange rate): $12.35 billion (2016 est.)

GDP—real growth rate: 4.7% (2017 est.)
3.8% (2016 est.)
6.6% (2015 est.)
country comparison to the world: 47

GDP—per capita (PPP): $1,300 (2017 est.)
$1,200 (2016 est.)
$1,200 (2015 est.)
note: data are in 2017 dollars
country comparison to the world: 222

Gross national saving: 18.7% of GDP (2017 est.)
5.6% of GDP (2016 est.)
5% of GDP (2015 est.)
country comparison to the world: 99

GDP—composition, by end use:
household consumption: 67.3%
government consumption: 24.5%
investment in fixed capital: 19.5%
investment in inventories: 24.9%
exports of goods and services: 42.6%
imports of goods and services: -78.8% (2017 est.)

GDP—composition, by sector of origin:
agriculture: 24.3%
industry: 23%
services: 52.8% (2017 est.)

Agriculture—products: cotton, cashew nuts, sugarcane, tea, cassava (manioc, tapioca), corn, coconuts, sisal, citrus and tropical fruits, potatoes, sunflowers; beef, poultry

Industries: aluminum, petroleum products, chemicals (fertilizer, soap, paints), textiles, cement, glass, asbestos, tobacco, food, beverages

Industrial production growth rate: 10.5% (2017 est.)
country comparison to the world: 8

Labor force: 12.98 million (2017 est.)
country comparison to the world: 44

Labor force—by occupation: *agriculture:* 81%
industry: 6%
services: 13% (1997 est.)

Unemployment rate: 22.4% (2014 est.)
17% (2007 est.)
country comparison to the world: 189

Population below poverty line: 46.1% (2015 est.)

Household income or consumption by percentage share: *lowest 10%:* 1.9%
highest 10%: 36.7% (2008)

Distribution of family income—Gini index: 45.6 (2008)
47.3 (2002)
country comparison to the world: 37

Budget: *revenues:* $2.758 billion
expenditures: $3.607 billion (2017 est.)
Taxes and other revenues: 22.3% of GDP (2017 est.)
country comparison to the world: 135

Budget surplus (+) or deficit (-): -6.9% of GDP (2017 est.)
country comparison to the world: 185

Public debt: 119.4% of GDP (2017 est.)
121.2% of GDP (2016 est.)
country comparison to the world: 8

Fiscal year: calendar year

Inflation rate (consumer prices): 17.5% (2017 est.)
19.2% (2016 est.)
country comparison to the world: 215

Central bank discount rate: 9.5% (17 January 2013)
3.25% (31 December 2010)
country comparison to the world: 27

Commercial bank prime lending rate: 27% (31 December 2017 est.)
21.18% (31 December 2016 est.)
country comparison to the world: 9

Stock of narrow money: $4.278 billion (31 December 2017 est.)
$3.411 billion (31 December 2016 est.)
country comparison to the world: 110

Stock of broad money: $6.496 billion (31 December 2017 est.)
$5.142 billion (31 December 2016 est.)
country comparison to the world: 123

Stock of domestic credit: $5.231 billion (31 December 2017 est.)
$4.242 billion (31 December 2016 est.)
country comparison to the world: 129

Market value of publicly traded shares: $NA

Current account balance: -$3.162 billion (2017 est.)
-$4.307 billion (2016 est.)
country comparison to the world: 167

Exports: $4.773 billion (2017 est.)
$3.328 billion (2016 est.)
country comparison to the world: 111

Exports—commodities: aluminum, prawns, cashews, cotton, sugar, citrus, timber; bulk electricity

Exports—partners: Netherlands 30.8%, India 15.2%, South Africa 14.6% (2016)

Imports: $5.021 billion (2017 est.)
$4.733 billion (2016 est.)
country comparison to the world: 123

Imports—commodities: machinery and equipment, vehicles, fuel, chemicals, metal products, foodstuffs, textiles

Imports—partners: South Africa 36.6%, China 10.9%, Netherlands 7.8%, Bahrain 5.2%, France 4.2%, Portugal 4.2%, UAE 4.1% (2016)

Reserves of foreign exchange and gold: $2.193 billion (31 December 2017 est.)
$2.081 billion (31 December 2016 est.)
country comparison to the world: 117

Debt—external: $10.27 billion (31 December 2017 est.)
$10.48 billion (31 December 2016 est.)
country comparison to the world: 114

Exchange rates: meticais (MZM) per US dollar—
64.4 (2017 est.)
63.067 (2016 est.)
63.067 (2015 est.)
39.983 (2014 est.)
31.367 (2013 est.)

ENERGY

Electricity access: *population without electricity:* 15,700,000
electrification—total population: 39%
electrification—urban areas: 66%
electrification—rural areas: 27% (2013)

Electricity—production: 19.58 billion kWh (2015 est.)
country comparison to the world: 76

Electricity—consumption: 13.86 billion kWh (2015 est.)
country comparison to the world: 82

Electricity—exports: 12.88 billion kWh (2015 est.)
country comparison to the world: 18

Electricity—imports: 10.55 billion kWh (2015 est.)
country comparison to the world: 25

Electricity—installed generating capacity: 2.556 million kW (2015 est.)
country comparison to the world: 104

Electricity—from fossil fuels: 14% of total installed capacity (2015 est.)
country comparison to the world: 198

Electricity—from nuclear fuels: 0% of total installed capacity (2015 est.)
country comparison to the world: 149

Electricity—from hydroelectric plants: 85.6% of total installed capacity (2015 est.)
country comparison to the world: 12

Electricity—from other renewable sources: 0.5% of total installed capacity (2015 est.)
country comparison to the world: 150

Crude oil—production: 0 bbl/day (2016 est.)
country comparison to the world: 176

Crude oil—exports: 0 bbl/day (2014 est.)
country comparison to the world: 167

Crude oil—imports: 0 bbl/day (2014 est.)
country comparison to the world: 166

Crude oil—proved reserves: 0 bbl (1 January 2017 es)
country comparison to the world: 174

Refined petroleum products—production: 0 bbl/day (2014 est.)
country comparison to the world: 182

Refined petroleum products—consumption: 23,000 bbl/day (2015 est.)
country comparison to the world: 131

Refined petroleum products—exports: 0 bbl/day (2014 est.)
country comparison to the world: 183

Refined petroleum products—imports: 21,890 bbl/day (2014 est.)
country comparison to the world: 115

Natural gas—production: 5.695 billion cu m (2015 est.)
country comparison to the world: 50

Natural gas—consumption: 2.726 billion cu m (2015 est.)
country comparison to the world: 81

Natural gas—exports: 3.8 billion cu m (2015 est.)
country comparison to the world: 34

Natural gas—imports: 0 cu m (2013 est.)
country comparison to the world: 160

Natural gas—proved reserves: 2.832 trillion cu m (1 January 2017 es)
country comparison to the world: 13

Carbon dioxide emissions from consumption of energy: 3.9 million Mt (2013 est.)
country comparison to the world: 135

COMMUNICATIONS

Telephones—fixed lines: *total subscriptions:* 84,310
subscriptions per 100 inhabitants: less than 1 (July 2016 est.)
country comparison to the world: 151

Telephones—mobile cellular: *total:* 18,404,857
subscriptions per 100 inhabitants: 71 (July 2016 est.)
country comparison to the world: 59

Telephone system: *general assessment:* the mobile segment has shown strong growth since the introduction of competition in 2003; poor fixed-line infrastructure means most Internet access is through mobile accounts
domestic: extremely low fixed-line teledensity contrasts with rapid growth in the mobile-cellular network; three mobile-cellular operators provide coverage that includes all the main cities and key roads; mobile-cellular teledensity now about 70 per 100 persons
international: country code—258; landing point for the EASSy and SEACOM fiber-optic submarine cable systems; satellite earth stations—5 Intelsat (2 Atlantic Ocean and 3 Indian Ocean) (2016)

Broadcast media: 1 state-run TV station supplemented by private TV station; Portuguese state TV's African service, RTP Africa, and Brazilian-owned TV Miramar are available; state-run radio provides nearly 100% territorial coverage and broadcasts in multiple languages; a number of privately owned and community-operated stations; transmissions of multiple international broadcasters are available (2007)

Internet country code: .mz
Internet users: total: 4,543,284
percent of population: 17.5% (July 2016 est.)
country comparison to the world: 111

TRANSPORTATION

National air transport system: *number of registered air carriers:* 3
inventory of registered aircraft operated by air carriers: 16
annual passenger traffic on registered air carriers: 686,892
annual freight traffic on registered air carriers: 5,138,916 mt-km (2015)
Civil aircraft registration country code prefix: C9 (2016)

Airports: 98 (2013)
country comparison to the world: 57

Airports—with paved runways: *total:* 21
over 3,047 m: 1
2,438 to 3,047 m: 2
1,524 to 2,437 m: 9
914 to 1,523 m: 5
under 914 m: 4 (2017)

Airports—with unpaved runways: *total:* 77
2,438 to 3,047 m: 1
1,524 to 2,437 m: 9
914 to 1,523 m: 29
under 914 m: 38 (2013)

Pipelines: gas 972 km; refined products 278 km (2013)

Railways: *total:* 4,787 km
narrow gauge: 4,787 km 1.067-m gauge (2014)
country comparison to the world: 39

Roadways: *total:* 31,083 km
paved: 7,365 km
unpaved: 23,718 km (2015)
country comparison to the world: 96

Waterways: 460 km (Zambezi River navigable to Tete and along Cahora Bassa Lake) (2010)
country comparison to the world: 85

Merchant marine: *total:* 27
by type: general cargo 10, other 17 (2017)
country comparison to the world: 127

Ports and terminals: *major seaport(s):* Beira, Maputo, Nacala

MILITARY AND SECURITY

Military expenditures: 1.03% of GDP (2016)
0.99% of GDP (2015)
1.02% of GDP (2014)
0.99% of GDP (2013)
0.91% of GDP (2012)

Military branches: Mozambique Armed Defense Forces (Forcas Armadas de Defesa de Mocambique, FADM): Mozambique Army, Mozambique Navy (Marinha de Guerra de Mocambique, MGM), Mozambique Air Force (Forca Aerea de Mocambique, FAM) (2012)

Military service age and obligation: registration for military service is mandatory for all males and females at 18 years of age; 18-35 years of age for selective compulsory military service; 18 years of age for voluntary service; 2-year service obligation; women may serve as officers or enlisted (2012)

TRANSNATIONAL ISSUES

Disputes—international: South Africa has placed military units to assist police operations along the border of Lesotho, Zimbabwe, and Mozambique to control smuggling, poaching, and illegal migration
Refugees and internally displaced persons: IDPs: 15,000 (2016)

Illicit drugs: southern African transit point for South Asian hashish and heroin, and South American cocaine probably destined for the European and South African markets; producer of cannabis (for local consumption) and methaqualone (for export to South Africa); corruption and poor regulatory capability make the banking system vulnerable to money laundering, but the lack of a well-developed financial infrastructure limits the country's utility as a money-laundering center

INTRODUCTION

Background: South Africa occupied the German colony of South-West Africa during World War I and administered it as a mandate until after World War II, when it annexed the territory. In 1966, the Marxist South-West Africa People's Organization (SWAPO) guerrilla group launched a war of independence for the area that became Namibia, but it was not until 1988 that South Africa agreed to end its administration in accordance with a UN peace plan for the entire region. Namibia has been governed by SWAPO since the country won independence in 1990, though the party has dropped much of its Marxist ideology. Prime Minister Hage GEINGOB was elected president in 2014 in a landslide victory, replacing Hifikepunye POHAMBA who stepped down after serving two terms. SWAPO retained its parliamentary super majority in the 2014 elections and established a system of gender parity in parliamentary positions.

GEOGRAPHY

Location: Southern Africa, bordering the South Atlantic Ocean, between Angola and South Africa

Geographic coordinates: 22 00 S, 17 00 E

Map references: Africa

Area: total: 824,292 sq km
land: 823,290 sq km
water: 1,002 sq km
country comparison to the world: 35

Area—comparative: slightly more than half the size of Alaska

Land boundaries: total: 4,220 km
border countries (4): Angola 1,427 km, Botswana 1,544 km, South Africa 1,005 km, Zambia 244 km

Coastline: 1,572 km

Maritime claims: territorial sea: 12 nm
contiguous zone: 24 nm
exclusive economic zone: 200 nm

Climate: desert; hot, dry; rainfall sparse and erratic

Terrain: mostly high plateau; Namib Desert along coast; Kalahari Desert in east

Elevation: mean elevation: 1,141 m

elevation extremes: lowest point: Atlantic Ocean 0 m
highest point: Konigstein on Brandberg 2,573 m

Natural resources: diamonds, copper, uranium, gold, silver, lead, tin, lithium, cadmium, tungsten, zinc, salt, hydropower, fish
note: suspected deposits of oil, coal, and iron ore

Land use: agricultural land: 47.2%
arable land: 1%;
permanent crops: 0%;
permanent pasture: 46.2%
forest: 8.8%
other: 44% (2011 est.)
Irrigated land: 80 sq km (2012)

Population—distribution: population density is very low, with the largest clustering found in the extreme north-central area along the border with Angola

Natural hazards: prolonged periods of drought

Environment—current issues: limited natural freshwater resources; desertification; wildlife poaching; land degradation has led to few conservation areas

Environment—international agreements: party to: Antarctic-Marine Living Resources, Biodiversity, Climate Change, Climate Change-Kyoto Protocol, Desertification, Endangered Species, Hazardous Wastes, Law of the Sea, Ozone Layer Protection, Wetlands
signed, but not ratified: none of the selected agreements

Geography—note: first country in the world to incorporate the protection of the environment into its constitution; some 14% of the land is protected, including virtually the entire Namib Desert coastal strip

PEOPLE AND SOCIETY

Population: 2,484,780
note: estimates for this country explicitly take into account the effects of excess mortality due to AIDS; this can result in lower life expectancy, higher infant mortality, higher death rates, lower population growth rates, and changes in the distribution of population by age and sex than would otherwise be expected (July 2017 est.)
country comparison to the world: 142

Nationality: noun: Namibian(s)
adjective: Namibian

Ethnic groups: black 87.5%, white 6%, mixed 6.5%
note: about 50% of the population belong to the Ovambo tribe and 9% to the Kavangos tribe; other indigenous ethnic groups include Herero 7%, Damara 7%, Nama 5%, Caprivian 4%, San 3%, Baster 2%, Tswana 0.5%

Languages: Oshivambo languages 48.9%, Nama/Damara 11.3%, Afrikaans 10.4% (common language of most of the population and about 60% of the white population), Otjiherero languages 8.6%, Kavango languages 8.5%, Caprivi languages 4.8%, English (official) 3.4%, other African languages 2.3%, other 1.7%
note: Namibia has 13 recognized national languages, including 10 indigenous African languages and 3 Indo-European languages (2011 est.)

Religions: Christian 80% to 90% (at least 50% Lutheran), indigenous beliefs 10% to 20%

Demographic profile: Planning officials view Namibia's reduced population growth rate as sustainable based on the country's economic growth over the past decade. Prior to independence in 1990, Namibia's relatively small population grew at about 3% annually, but declining fertility and the impact of HIV/AIDS slowed this growth to 1.4% by 2011, rebounding to close to 2% by 2016. Namibia's fertility rate has fallen over the last two decades—from about 4.5 children per woman in 1996 to 3.4 in 2016—due to increased contraceptive use, higher educational attainment among women, and greater female participation in the labor force. The average age at first birth has stayed fairly constant, but the age at first marriage continues to increase, indicating a rising incidence of premarital childbearing.

The majority of Namibians are rural dwellers (about 55%) and live in the better-watered north and northeast parts of the country. Migration, historically male-dominated, generally flows from northern communal areas—non-agricultural lands where blacks were sequestered under the apartheid system—to agricultural, mining, and manufacturing centers in the center and south. After independence from South Africa, restrictions on internal movement eased, and rural-urban migration increased, bolstering urban growth.

Some Namibians—usually persons who are better-educated, more affluent, and from urban areas—continue to legally migrate to South Africa temporarily to visit family and friends and, much less frequently, to pursue tertiary education or better economic opportunities. Namibians concentrated along the country's other borders make unauthorized visits to Angola, Zambia, Zimbabwe, or Botswana, to visit family and to trade agricultural goods. Few Namibians express interest in permanently settling in other countries; they prefer the safety of their homeland, have a strong national identity, and enjoy a well-supplied retail sector. Although Namibia is receptive to foreign investment and cross-border trade, intolerance toward non-citizens is widespread.

Age structure: 0-14 years: 36.97% (male 463,810/female 454,735)
15-24 years: 20.35% (male 251,838/female 253,823)
25-54 years: 34.37% (male 408,536/female 445,500)

55-64 years: 4.35% (male 48,529/female 59,543)
65 years and over: 3.96% (male 41,912/female 56,554) (2017 est.)

Dependency ratios: *total dependency ratio:* 68.1
youth dependency ratio: 62.2
elderly dependency ratio: 5.8
potential support ratio: 17.1 (2015 est.)

Median age: *total:* 21.2 years
male: 20.4 years
female: 21.9 years (2017 est.)
country comparison to the world: 183

Population growth rate: 1.95% (2017 est.)
country comparison to the world: 49

Birth rate: 27.3 births/1,000 population (2017 est.)
country comparison to the world: 46

Death rate: 7.9 deaths/1,000 population (2017 est.)
country comparison to the world: 96

Net migration rate: 0 migrant(s)/1,000 population (2017 est.)
country comparison to the world: 93

Population distribution: population density is very low, with the largest clustering found in the extreme north-central area along the border with Angola

Urbanization: *urban population:* 48.6% of total population (2017)
rate of urbanization: 3.63% annual rate of change (2015-20 est.)

Major urban areas—population: WINDHOEK (capital) 368,000 (2015)

Sex ratio: *at birth:* 1.03 male(s)/female
0-14 years: 1.02 male(s)/female
15-24 years: 0.99 male(s)/female
25-54 years: 0.91 male(s)/female
55-64 years: 0.82 male(s)/female
65 years and over: 0.75 male(s)/female
total population: 0.96 male(s)/female (2016 est.)

Mother's mean age at first birth: 21.5 years
note: median age at first birth among women 25-29 (2013 est.)

Maternal mortality ratio: 265 deaths/100,000 live births (2015 est.)
country comparison to the world: 44

Infant mortality rate: *total:* 35.1 deaths/1,000 live births
male: 37.3 deaths/1,000 live births
female: 32.8 deaths/1,000 live births (2017 est.)
country comparison to the world: 55

Life expectancy at birth: *total population:* 64 years
male: 62.4 years
female: 65.6 years (2017 est.)
country comparison to the world: 189

Total fertility rate: 3.29 children born/woman (2017 est.)
country comparison to the world: 47

Contraceptive prevalence rate: 56.1% (2013)

Health expenditures: 8.9% of GDP (2014)
country comparison to the world: 42

Physicians density: 0.37 physicians/1,000 population (2007)

Hospital bed density: 2.7 beds/1,000 population (2009)

Drinking water source:
improved:
urban: 98.2% of population
rural: 84.6% of population
total: 91% of population
unimproved:
urban: 1.8% of population
rural: 15.4% of population
total: 9% of population (2015 est.)

Sanitation facility access:
improved:
urban: 54.5% of population
rural: 16.8% of population
total: 34.4% of population
unimproved:
urban: 45.5% of population
rural: 83.2% of population
total: 65.6% of population (2015 est.)

HIV/AIDS—adult prevalence rate: 13.8% (2016 est.)
country comparison to the world: 5

HIV/AIDS—people living with HIV/AIDS: 230,000 (2016 est.)
country comparison to the world: 24

HIV/AIDS—deaths: 4,300 (2016 est.)
country comparison to the world: 32

Major infectious diseases: *degree of risk:* high
food or waterborne diseases: bacterial diarrhea, hepatitis A, and typhoid fever
vectorborne disease: malaria
water contact disease: schistosomiasis (2016)

Obesity—adult prevalence rate: 17.2% (2016)
country comparison to the world: 119

Children under the age of 5 years underweight: 13.2% (2013)
country comparison to the world: 37

Education expenditures: 8.3% of GDP (2010)
country comparison to the world: 9

Literacy: *definition:* age 15 and over can read and write
total population: 81.9%
male: 79.2%
female: 84.5% (2015 est.)

Unemployment, youth ages 15-24: *total:* 56.2%
male: 49.4%
female: 62.2% (2013 est.)
country comparison to the world: 19

GOVERNMENT

Country name: *conventional long form:* Republic of Namibia
conventional short form: Namibia
local long form: Republic of Namibia
local short form: Namibia
former: German South-West Africa (Deutsch Suedwest Afrika), South-West Africa
etymology: named for the coastal Namib Desert; the name "namib" means "vast place" in the Nama/Damara language

Government type: presidential republic

Capital: *name:* Windhoek
geographic coordinates: 22 34 S, 17 05 E
time difference: UTC+1 (6 hours ahead of Washington, DC, during Standard Time)
daylight saving time: +1hr, begins first Sunday in September; ends first Sunday in April

Administrative divisions: 14 regions; Erongo, Hardap, //Karas, Kavango East, Kavango West, Khomas, Kunene, Ohangwena, Omaheke, Omusati, Oshana, Oshikoto, Otjozondjupa, Zambezi; *note*—the Karas Region was renamed //Karas in September 2013 to include the alveolar lateral click of the Khoekhoegowab language

Independence: 21 March 1990 (from South African mandate)

National holiday: Independence Day, 21 March (1990)

Constitution: *history:* drafted 9 February 1990, signed 16 March 1990, entered into force 21 March 1990
amendments: proposed by Parliament; passage requires two-thirds majority vote of the National Assembly membership and of the National Council of Parliament and assent by the president of the republic; if the National Council fails to pass an amendment, the president can call for a referendum; passage by referendum requires two-thirds majority of votes cast; amendments that detract from or repeal constitutional articles on fundamental rights and freedoms cannot be amended, and the requisite majorities needed by Parliament to amend the constitution cannot be changed; amended 1998, 2010, 2014 (2017)

Legal system: mixed legal system of uncodified civil law based on Roman-Dutch law and customary law

International law organization participation: has not submitted an ICJ jurisdiction declaration; accepts ICCt jurisdiction

Citizenship: *citizenship by birth:* no
citizenship by descent only: at least one parent must be a citizen of Namibia
dual citizenship recognized: no
residency requirement for naturalization: 5 years

Suffrage: 18 years of age; universal

Executive branch: *chief of state:* President Hage GEINGOB (since 21 March 2015); *note*—the president is both chief of state and head of government

head of government: President Hage GEINGOB (since 21 March 2015); Prime Minister Saara KUUGONGELWA-AMADHILA (since 21 March 2015)
cabinet: Cabinet appointed by the president from among members of the National Assembly
elections/appointments: president elected by absolute majority popular vote in 2 rounds if needed for a 5-year term (eligible for a second term); election last held on 28 November 2014 (next to be held in November 2019)
election results: Hage GEINGOB elected president; percent of vote—Hage GEINGOB

(SWAPO) 86.7%, McHenry VENAANI (DTA) 5.0%, Hidipo HAMUTENYA (RDP) 3.4%, Asser MBAI (NUDO)1.9%, Henk MUDGE (RP) 1.0%, other 2.0%

Legislative branch: *description:* bicameral Parliament consists of the National Assembly (104 seats; 96 members directly elected in multi-seat constituencies by proportional representation vote to serve 5-year terms and 8 nonvoting members appointed by the president) and the National Council, which primarily reviews legislation passed and referred by the National Assembly (42 seats); members indirectly elected 3 each by the 14 regional councils to serve 5-year terms)

elections: National Council—elections for regional councils to determine members of the National Council held on 27 November 2015 (next to be held in November 2020); National Assembly—last held on 28 November 2014 (next to be held in November 2019)

election results: National Council—percent of vote by party—NA; seats by party—SWAPO 40, NUDO 1, DTA 1; National Assembly—percent of vote by party—SWAPO 80.0%, DTA 4.8%, RDP 3.5%, APP 2.3%, UDF 2.1%, NUDO 2.0%, CPN 1.5%, other 3.8%; seats by party—SWAPO 77, DTA 5, RDP 3, APP 2, UDF 2, NUDO 2, CPN 2, SWANU 1, UPM 1, RP 1

Judicial branch: *highest court(s):* Supreme Court (consists of the chief justice and at least 3 judges in quorum sessions)

judge selection and term of office: judges appointed by the president of Namibia upon the recommendation of the Judicial Service Commission; judges serve until age 65 but terms can be extended by the president until age 70

subordinate courts: High Court; Labor Court; regional and district magistrates' courts; community courts

Political parties and leaders: All People's Party or APP [Ignatius SHIXWAMENI]

Communist Party of Namibia or CPN (formerly known as Workers' Revolutionary Party or WRP) [Attie BEUKES and Harry BOESAK]

Democratic Turnhalle Alliance of Namibia or DTA [McHenry VENAANI]

National Unity Democratic Organization or NUDO [Asser MBAI]

Rally for Democracy and Progress or RDP [Jeremiah NAMBINGA]

Republican Party or RP [Henk MUDGE]

South West Africa National Union or SWANU [Usutuaije MAAMBERUA]

South West Africa People's Organization or SWAPO [Hage GEINGOB]

United Democratic Front or UDF [Apius AUCHAB]

United People's Movement or UPM [Jan J. VAN WYK]

Political pressure groups and leaders: National Society for Human Rights or NAMRIGHTS *other:* labor unions

International organization participation: ACP, AfDB, AU, C, CD, CPLP (associate observer), FAO, G-77, IAEA, IBRD, ICAO, ICCt, ICRM, IDA, IFAD, IFC, IFRCS, ILO, IMF, IMO, Interpol, IOC, IOM, IPU, ISO, ITSO, ITU, ITUC (NGOs), MIGA, NAM, OPCW, SACU, SADC, UN, UNAMID, UNCTAD, UNESCO, UNHCR, UNIDO, UNISFA, UNMIL, UNMISS, UNOCI, UNWTO, UPU, WCO, WHO, WIPO, WMO, WTO

Diplomatic representation in the US: *chief of mission:* Ambassador Martin ANDJABA (since 16 September 2010)

chancery: 1605 New Hampshire Avenue NW, Washington, DC 20009

telephone: [1] (202) 986-0540

FAX: [1] (202) 986-0443

Diplomatic representation from the US: *chief of mission:* Ambassador Thomas Frederick DAUGHTON (since 26 November 2014)

embassy: 14 Lossen Street, Windhoek

mailing address: Private Bag 12029 Ausspannplatz, Windhoek

telephone: [264] (61) 295-8500

FAX: [264] (61) 295-8603

Flag description: a wide red stripe edged by narrow white stripes divides the flag diagonally from lower hoist corner to upper fly corner; the upper hoist-side triangle is blue and charged with a golden-yellow, 12-rayed sunburst; the lower fly-side triangle is green; red signifies the heroism of the people and their determination to build a future of equal opportunity for all; white stands for peace, unity, tranquility, and harmony; blue represents the Namibian sky and the Atlantic Ocean, the country's precious water resources and rain; the golden-yellow sun denotes power and existence; green symbolizes vegetation and agricultural resources

National symbol(s): oryx (antelope); national colors: blue, red, green, white, yellow

National anthem: name: "Namibia, Land of the Brave"

lyrics/music: Axali DOESEB

note: adopted 1991

ECONOMY

Economy—overview: Namibia's economy is heavily dependent on the extraction and processing of minerals for export. Mining accounts for 11.5% of GDP, but provides more than 50% of foreign exchange earnings. Rich alluvial diamond deposits make Namibia a primary source for gem-quality diamonds. Marine diamond mining is increasingly important as the terrestrial diamond supply has dwindled. The rising cost of mining diamonds, especially from the sea, combined with increased diamond production in Russia and China, has reduced profit margins. Namibian authorities have emphasized the need to add value to raw materials, do more in-country manufacturing, and exploit the services market, especially in the logistics and transportation sectors.

Namibia is the world's fifth-largest producer of uranium. The Chinese-owned Husab uranium mine is expected to start producing uranium ore in 2017. Once the Husab mine reaches full production, Namibia is expected to become the world's second-largest producer of uranium. Namibia also produces large quantities of zinc and is a smaller producer of gold and copper. Namibia's economy remains vulnerable to world commodity price fluctuations and drought.

Namibia normally imports about 50% of its cereal requirements; in drought years, food shortages are problematic in rural areas. A high per capita GDP, relative to the region, obscures one of the world's most unequal income distributions. A priority of the current government is poverty eradication. Despite a drought, real GDP growth remained strong in 2015 because of construction in the mining and housing sectors, coupled with an expansionary fiscal policy. GDP growth in 2017 slowed to about 1%, however, due to contractions in both the construction and mining sectors, as well as the ongoing drought. Growth is expected to recover modestly in 2018.

A five-year Millennium Challenge Corporation compact ended in September 2014. As an upper middle income country, Namibia is ineligible for a second compact. The Namibian economy is closely linked to South Africa with the Namibian dollar pegged one-to-one to the South African rand. Namibia receives 30%-40% of its revenues from the Southern African Customs Union (SACU); volatility in the size of Namibia's annual SACU allotment and global mineral prices complicates budget planning.

GDP (purchasing power parity): $27.02 billion (2017 est.)

$26.81 billion (2016 est.)

$26.52 billion (2015 est.)

note: data are in 2017 dollars

country comparison to the world: 139

GDP (official exchange rate): $12.56 billion (2016 est.)

GDP—real growth rate: 0.8% (2017 est.)

1.1% (2016 est.)

6% (2015 est.)

country comparison to the world: 190

GDP—per capita (PPP): $11,500 (2017 est.)

$11,500 (2016 est.)

$11,600 (2015 est.)

note: data are in 2017 dollars

country comparison to the world: 134

Gross national saving: 18% of GDP (2017 est.)

11.6% of GDP (2016 est.)

20.9% of GDP (2015 est.)

country comparison to the world: 100

GDP—composition, by end use:

household consumption: 71.9%

government consumption: 23.3%

investment in fixed capital: 22.2%

investment in inventories: -0.1%

exports of goods and services: 41.7%

imports of goods and services: -59% (2017 est.)

GDP—composition, by sector of origin:

agriculture: 6.6%

industry: 25.8%

services: 67.6% (2017 est.)

Agriculture—products: millet, sorghum, peanuts, grapes; livestock; fish

Industries: meatpacking, fish processing, dairy products, pasta, beverages; mining (diamonds, lead, zinc, tin, silver, tungsten, uranium, copper)

Industrial production growth rate: 2.2% (2017 est.)
country comparison to the world: 122

Labor force: 956,800 (2017 est.)
country comparison to the world: 146

Labor force—by occupation: *agriculture:* 31%
industry: 14%
services: 54%
note: about half of Namibia's people are unemployed while about two-thirds live in rural areas; roughly two-thirds of rural dwellers rely on subsistence agriculture (2013 est.)

Unemployment rate: 28.1% (2014 est.)
29.6% (2013 est.)
country comparison to the world: 201

Population below poverty line: 28.7% (2010 est.)

Household income or consumption by percentage share: *lowest 10%:* 2.4%
highest 10%: 42% (2010)

Distribution of family income—Gini index: 59.7 (2010)
70.7 (2003)
country comparison to the world: 7

Budget: *revenues:* $3.967 billion
expenditures: $4.759 billion (2017 est.)
Taxes and other revenues: 31.6% of GDP (2017 est.)
country comparison to the world: 75

Budget surplus (+) or deficit (-): -6.3% of GDP (2017 est.)
country comparison to the world: 180

Public debt: 43% of GDP (2017 est.)
40.7% of GDP (2016 est.)
country comparison to the world: 125

Fiscal year: 1 April—31 March

Inflation rate (consumer prices): 6% (2017 est.)
6.7% (2016 est.)
country comparison to the world: 186

Central bank discount rate: 7% (12 April 2017)
6.5% (31 December 2015)
country comparison to the world: 47

Commercial bank prime lending rate: 9.9% (31 December 2017 est.)
9.87% (31 December 2016 est.)
country comparison to the world: 84

Stock of narrow money: $2.878 billion (31 December 2017 est.)
$2.898 billion (31 December 2016 est.)
country comparison to the world: 122

Stock of broad money: $6.03 billion (31 December 2017 est.)
$6.281 billion (31 December 2016 est.)
country comparison to the world: 126

Stock of domestic credit: $6.977 billion (31 December 2017 est.)
$7.006 billion (31 December 2016 est.)
country comparison to the world: 118

Market value of publicly traded shares: $1.305 billion (31 December 2012 est.)
$1.152 billion (31 December 2011 est.)

$1.176 billion (31 December 2010 est.)
country comparison to the world: 104

Current account balance: -$921 million (2017 est.)
-$1.529 billion (2016 est.)
country comparison to the world: 131

Exports: $4.71 billion (2017 est.)
$4.003 billion (2016 est.)
country comparison to the world: 112

Exports—commodities: diamonds, copper, gold, zinc, lead, uranium; cattle, white fish and mollusks

Exports—partners: Switzerland 20%, South Africa 17.1%, Botswana 15%, Zambia 6.7%, Spain 4.6%, Italy 4.2% (2016)

Imports: $6.846 billion (2017 est.)
$6.441 billion (2016 est.)
country comparison to the world: 110

Imports—commodities: foodstuffs; petroleum products and fuel, machinery and equipment, chemicals

Imports—partners: South Africa 57.1%, Botswana 6.8%, Zambia 4.1% (2016)

Reserves of foreign exchange and gold: $1.949 billion (31 December 2017 est.)
$1.834 billion (31 December 2016 est.)
country comparison to the world: 120

Debt—external: $7.489 billion (31 December 2017 est.)
$6.904 billion (31 December 2016 est.)
country comparison to the world: 124

Stock of direct foreign investment—at home: $NA

Stock of direct foreign investment—abroad: $NA

Exchange rates: Namibian dollars (NAD) per US dollar—
13.67 (2017 est.)
14.7096 (2016 est.)
14.7096 (2015 est.)
12.7589 (2014 est.)
10.8526 (2013 est.)

ENERGY

Electricity access: *population without electricity:* 1,600,000
electrification—total population: 32%
electrification—urban areas: 50%
electrification—rural areas: 17% (2013)

Electricity—production: 1.519 billion kWh (2015 est.)
country comparison to the world: 145

Electricity—consumption: 3.771 billion kWh (2015 est.)
country comparison to the world: 128

Electricity—exports: 88 million kWh (2015 est.)
country comparison to the world: 81

Electricity—imports: 2.623 billion kWh (2015 est.)
country comparison to the world: 51

Electricity—installed generating capacity: 514,200 kW (2015 est.)
country comparison to the world: 146

Electricity—from fossil fuels: 30.1% of total installed capacity (2015 est.)
country comparison to the world: 185

Electricity—from nuclear fuels: 0% of total installed capacity (2015 est.)
country comparison to the world: 208

Electricity—from hydroelectric plants: 64.6% of total installed capacity (2015 est.)
country comparison to the world: 23

Electricity—from other renewable sources: 5.9% of total installed capacity (2015 est.)
country comparison to the world: 89

Crude oil—production: 0 bbl/day (2016 est.)
country comparison to the world: 177

Crude oil—exports: 0 bbl/day (2014 est.)
country comparison to the world: 210

Crude oil—imports: 0 bbl/day (2014 est.)
country comparison to the world: 210

Crude oil—proved reserves: 0 bbl (1 January 2017 es)
country comparison to the world: 175

Refined petroleum products—production: 0 bbl/day (2014 est.)
country comparison to the world: 183

Refined petroleum products—consumption: 25,000 bbl/day (2015 est.)
country comparison to the world: 129

Refined petroleum products—exports: 79.56 bbl/day (2014 est.)
country comparison to the world: 123

Refined petroleum products—imports: 24,700 bbl/day (2014 est.)
country comparison to the world: 108

Natural gas—production: 0 cu m (2013 est.)
country comparison to the world: 211

Natural gas—consumption: 0 cu m (2013 est.)
country comparison to the world: 146

Natural gas—exports: 0 cu m (2013 est.)
country comparison to the world: 209

Natural gas—imports: 0 cu m (2013 est.)
country comparison to the world: 208

Natural gas—proved reserves: 62.29 billion cu m (1 January 2017 es)
country comparison to the world: 62

Carbon dioxide emissions from consumption of energy: 4 million Mt (2013 est.)
country comparison to the world: 133

COMMUNICATIONS

Telephones—fixed lines: *total subscriptions:* 187,812
subscriptions per 100 inhabitants: 8 (July 2016 est.)
country comparison to the world: 128

Telephones—mobile cellular: *total:* 2,659,951
subscriptions per 100 inhabitants: 109 (July 2016 est.)
country comparison to the world: 143

Telephone system: *general assessment:* good system; core fiber-optic network links most centers with digital connections *domestic:* multiple mobile-cellular providers with a combined subscribership of about 110 telephones per 100 persons

international: country code—264; fiber-optic cable to South Africa, microwave radio relay link to Botswana, direct links to other neighboring countries; connected to the South African Far East submarine cable through South Africa; connected to the West Africa Cable System, an ultra-high capacity fiber-optic submarine cable linking southern and western African countries to Europe; satellite earth stations—4 Intelsat (2016)

Broadcast media: 1 private and 1 state-run TV station; satellite and cable TV service available; state-run radio service broadcasts in multiple languages; about a dozen private radio stations; transmissions of multiple international broadcasters available (2007)

Internet country code: .na
Internet users: total: 756,118

percent of population: 31.0% (July 2016 est.)
country comparison to the world: 140

TRANSPORTATION

National air transport system: *number of registered air carriers:* 2
inventory of registered aircraft operated by air carriers: 12
annual passenger traffic on registered air carriers: 553,322
annual freight traffic on registered air carriers: 30,302,405 mt-km (2015)
Civil aircraft registration country code prefix: V5 (2016)

Airports: 112 (2013)
country comparison to the world: 52

Airports—with paved runways: *total:* 19
over 3,047 m: 4
2,438 to 3,047 m: 2
1,524 to 2,437 m: 12
914 to 1,523 m: 1 (2017)

Airports—with unpaved runways: *total:* 93
1,524 to 2,437 m: 25
914 to 1,523 m: 52
under 914 m: 16 (2013)

Railways: *total:* 2,628 km
narrow gauge: 2,628 km 1.067-m gauge (2014)
country comparison to the world: 63

Roadways: *total:* 44,138 km
paved: 6,387 km
unpaved: 37,751 km (2010)
country comparison to the world: 83

Merchant marine: *total:* 9
by type: general cargo 1, other 8 (2017)
country comparison to the world: 146

Ports and terminals: *major seaport(s):* Luderitz, Walvis Bay

MILITARY AND SECURITY

Military expenditures: 4.44% of GDP (2016)
4.7% of GDP (2015)
4.18% of GDP (2014)
3.07% of GDP (2013)
3.17% of GDP (2012)
country comparison to the world: 20

Military branches: Namibian Defense Force (NDF): Army, Navy, Air Force (2013)

Military service age and obligation: 18 years of age for voluntary military service; no conscription (2012)

TRANSNATIONAL ISSUES

Disputes—international: concerns from international experts and local populations over the Okavango Delta ecology in Botswana and human displacement scuttled Namibian plans to construct a hydroelectric dam on Popa Falls along the Angola-Namibia border; the governments of South Africa and Namibia have not signed or ratified the text of the 1994 Surveyor's General agreement placing the boundary in the middle of the Orange River;

Namibia has supported, and in 2004 Zimbabwe dropped objections to, plans between Botswana and Zambia to build a bridge over the Zambezi River, thereby de facto recognizing a short, but not clearly delimited, Botswana-Zambia boundary in the river

Trafficking in persons: *current situation:* Namibia is a country of origin and destination for children and, to a lesser extent, women subjected to forced labor and sex trafficking; victims, lured by promises of legitimate jobs, are forced to work in urban centers and on commercial farms; traffickers exploit Namibian children, as well as children from Angola, Zambia, and Zimbabwe, for forced labor in agriculture, cattle herding, domestic service, fishing, and street vending; children are also forced into prostitution, often catering to tourists from southern Africa and Europe; San and Zemba children are particularly vulnerable; foreign adults and Namibian adults and children are reportedly subjected to forced labor in Chinese-owned retail, construction, and fishing operations

tier rating: Tier 2 Watch List—Namibia does not fully comply with the minimum standards for the elimination of trafficking; however, it is making significant efforts to do so; Namibia was granted a waiver from an otherwise required downgrade to Tier 3 because its government has a written plan that, if implemented would constitute making significant efforts to bring itself into compliance with the minimum standards for the elimination of trafficking; in 2015, the Child Care and Protection Bill passed, criminalizing child trafficking; the government's first sex trafficking prosecution remained pending; no new prosecutions were initiated and no trafficking offenders have ever been convicted; accusations of forced labor at Chinese construction and mining companies continue to go uninvestigated; authorities failed to fully implement victim identification and referral processes, which led to the deportation of possible victims (2015)

NAVASSA ISLAND

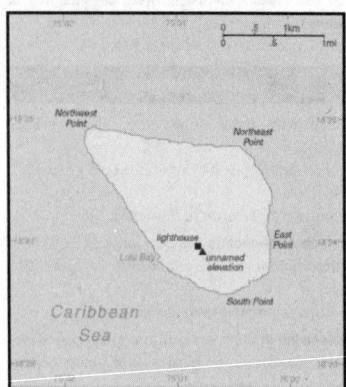

INTRODUCTION

Background: This uninhabited island was claimed by the US in 1857 for its guano. Mining took place between 1865 and 1898. The lighthouse, built in 1917, was shut down in 1996 and administration of Navassa Island transferred from the US Coast Guard to the Department of the Interior, Office of Insular Affairs. A 1998 scientific expedition to the island described it as a "unique preserve of Caribbean biodiversity." The following year it became a National Wildlife Refuge and annual scientific expeditions have continued.

GEOGRAPHY

Location: Caribbean, island in the Caribbean Sea, 30 nm west of Tiburon Peninsula of Haiti
Geographic coordinates: 18 25 N, 75 02 W

Map references: Central America and the Caribbean

Area: *total:* 5.4 sq km
land: 5.4 sq km
water: 0 sq km
country comparison to the world: 249

Area—comparative: about nine times the size of the National Mall in Washington, DC

Land boundaries: 0 km

Coastline: 8 km

Maritime claims: *territorial sea:* 12 nm
exclusive economic zone: 200 nm

Climate: marine, tropical

Terrain: raised flat to undulating coral and limestone plateau; ringed by vertical white cliffs (9 to 15 m high)

Elevation: *mean elevation:* NA

elevation extremes: *lowest point:* Caribbean Sea 0 m

highest point: 200 m NNW of lighthouse 85 m

Natural resources: guano (mining discontinued in 1898)

Land use: *agricultural land:* 0%
arable land: 0%;
permanent crops: 0%;
permanent pasture: 0%
forest: 0%
other: 100% (2011 est.)

Natural hazards: hurricanes

Environment—current issues: some coral bleaching

Geography—note: strategic location 160 km south of the US Naval Base at Guantanamo Bay, Cuba; mostly exposed rock with numerous solution holes (limestone sinkholes) but with enough grassland to support goat herds; dense stands of fig trees, scattered cactus

Population: uninhabited

note: transient Haitian fishermen and others camp on the island

GOVERNMENT

Country name: *conventional long form:* none
conventional short form: Navassa Island
etymology: the flat island was named "Navaza" by some of Christopher COLUMBUS' sailors in 1504; the name derives from the Spanish term "nava" meaning "flat land, plain, or field"

Dependency status: unorganized, unincorporated territory of the US; administered by the Fish and Wildlife Service, US Department of the Interior from the Caribbean Islands National Wildlife Refuge in Boqueron, Puerto Rico; in September 1996, the Coast Guard ceased operations and maintenance of Navassa Island Light, a 46-meter-tall lighthouse on the southern side of the island; Haiti has claimed the island since the 19th century

Legal system: the laws of the US, where applicable, apply

Diplomatic representation from the US: none (territory of the US)

Flag description: the flag of the US is used

ECONOMY

Economy—overview: Subsistence fishing and commercial trawling occur within refuge waters.

TRANSPORTATION

Ports and terminals: none; offshore anchorage only

MILITARY AND SECURITY

Military—note: defense is the responsibility of the US

TRANSNATIONAL ISSUES

Disputes—international: claimed by Haiti, source of subsistence fishing

NEPAL

INTRODUCTION

Background: During the late 18th-early 19th centuries, the principality of Gorkha united many of the other principalities and states of the sub-Himalayan region into a Nepalese Kingdom. Nepal retained its independence following the Anglo-Nepalese War of 1814-16 and the subsequent peace treaty laid the foundations for two centuries of amicable relations between Britain and Nepal. (The Brigade of Gurkhas continues to serve in the British Army to the present day.) In 1951, the Nepali monarch ended the century-old system of rule by hereditary premiers and instituted a cabinet system that brought political parties into the government. That arrangement lasted until 1960, when political parties were again banned, but was reinstated in 1990 with the establishment of a multiparty democracy within the framework of a constitutional monarchy.

An insurgency led by Maoists broke out in 1996. The ensuing 10-year civil war between Maoist and government forces witnessed the dissolution of the cabinet and parliament and the reassumption of absolute power by the king in 2002. A peace accord in 2006 led to the promulgation of an interim constitution in 2007. Following a nationwide Constituent Assembly (CA) election in 2008, the newly formed CA declared Nepal a federal democratic republic, abolished the monarchy, and elected the country's first president. After the CA failed to draft a constitution by a May 2012 deadline set by the Supreme Court, then-Prime Minister Baburam BHATTARAI dissolved the CA. Months of negotiations ensued until March 2013 when the major political parties agreed to create an interim government headed by then-Chief Justice Khil Raj REGMI with a mandate to hold elections for a new CA. Elections were held in November 2013, in which the Nepali Congress won the largest share of seats in the CA and in February 2014 formed a coalition government with the second place Communist Party of Nepal-Unified Marxist-Leninist and with Nepali Congress President Sushil KOIRALA as prime minister. Nepal's new constitution came into effect in September 2015, at which point the CA became the Parliament. Khagda Prasad Sharma OLI served as the first post-constitution prime minister from October 2015-August 2016, when a new coalition led by Maoist leader Pushpa Kamal DAHAL (aka "Prachanda") took over the premiership. The constitution provided for a transitional period during which three sets of elections—local, provincial, and national—needed to take place. The first local elections in 20 years occurred in three phases between May and September 2017, while state and federal elections proceeded in two phases in November and December 2017.

GEOGRAPHY

Location: Southern Asia, between China and India

Geographic coordinates: 28 00 N, 84 00 E

Map references: Asia

Area: *total:* 147,181 sq km
land: 143,351 sq km
water: 3,830 sq km
country comparison to the world: 96

Area—comparative: slightly larger than New York state

Land boundaries: *total:* 3,159 km
border countries (2): China 1,389 km, India 1,770 km

Coastline: 0 km (landlocked)

Maritime claims: none (landlocked)

Climate: varies from cool summers and severe winters in north to subtropical summers and mild winters in south

Terrain: Tarai or flat river plain of the Ganges in south; central hill region with rugged Himalayas in north

Elevation: *mean elevation:* 2,565 m

elevation extremes: *lowest point:* Kanchan Kalan 70 m

highest point: Mount Everest 8,848 m (highest peak in Asia and highest point on earth above sea level)

Natural resources: quartz, water, timber, hydropower, scenic beauty, small deposits of lignite, copper, cobalt, iron ore

Land use: *agricultural land:* 28.8%
arable land: 15.1%;
permanent crops: 1.2%;
permanent pasture: 12.5%
forest: 25.4%
other: 45.8% (2011 est.)
Irrigated land: 13,320 sq km (2012)

Population—distribution: most of the population is divided nearly equally between a concentration in the southern-most plains of the Tarai region and the central hilly region; overall density is quite low

Natural hazards: severe thunderstorms; flooding; landslides; drought and famine depending on the timing, intensity, and duration of the summer monsoons

Environment—current issues: deforestation (overuse of wood for fuel and lack of alternatives); contaminated water (with human and animal wastes, agricultural runoff, and industrial effluents); wildlife conservation; vehicular emissions

Environment—international agreements: *party to:* Biodiversity, Climate Change, Climate Change-Kyoto Protocol, Desertification, Endangered Species, Hazardous Wastes, Law of the Sea, Ozone Layer Protection, Tropical Timber 83, Tropical Timber 94, Wetlands
signed, but not ratified: Marine Life Conservation

Geography—note: landlocked; strategic location between China and India; contains eight of world's 10 highest peaks, including Mount Everest and Kanchenjunga—the world's tallest and third tallest mountains—on the borders with China and India respectively

PEOPLE AND SOCIETY

Population: 29,384,297 (July 2017 est.)
country comparison to the world: 45

Nationality: *noun:* Nepali (singular and plural)
adjective: Nepali

Ethnic groups: Chhettri 16.6%, Brahman-Hill 12.2%, Magar 7.1%, Tharu 6.6%, Tamang 5.8%, Newar 5%, Kami 4.8%, Muslim 4.4%, Yadav 4%, Rai 2.3%, Gurung 2%, Damai/Dholii 1.8%, Thakuri 1.6%, Limbu 1.5%, Sarki 1.4%, Teli 1.4%, Chamar/Harijan/Ram 1.3%, Koiri/Kushwaha 1.2%, other 19%
note: 125 caste/ethnic groups were reported in the 2011 national census (2011 est.)

Languages: Nepali (official) 44.6%, Maithali 11.7%, Bhojpuri 6%, Tharu 5.8%, Tamang 5.1%, Newar 3.2%, Magar 3%, Bajjika 3%, Urdu 2.6%, Avadhi 1.9%, Limbu 1.3%, Gurung 1.2%, other 10.4%, unspecified 0.2%
note: 123 languages reported as mother tongue in 2011 national census; many in government and business also speak English (2011 est.)

Religions: Hindu 81.3%, Buddhist 9%, Muslim 4.4%, Kirant 3.1%, Christian 1.4%, other 0.5%, unspecified 0.2% (2011 est.)

Age structure: *0-14 years:* 30.2% (male 4,610,861/female 4,264,580)
15-24 years: 21.73% (male 3,220,431/female 3,164,292)
25-54 years: 36.58% (male 4,847,427/female 5,900,442)
55-64 years: 6.32% (male 897,999/female 959,405)
65 years and over: 5.17% (male 753,771/female 765,089) (2017 est.)

Dependency ratios: *total dependency ratio:* 61.4

youth dependency ratio: 52.5
elderly dependency ratio: 8.8
potential support ratio: 11.3 (2015 est.)

Median age: *total:* 24.1 years
male: 22.8 years
female: 25.3 years (2017 est.)
country comparison to the world: 165

Population growth rate: 1.16% (2017 est.)
country comparison to the world: 97

Birth rate: 19.5 births/1,000 population (2017 est.)
country comparison to the world: 83

Death rate: 5.6 deaths/1,000 population (2017 est.)
country comparison to the world: 176

Net migration rate: -2.2 migrant(s)/1,000 population (2017 est.)
country comparison to the world: 167

Population distribution: most of the population is divided nearly equally between a concentration in the southern-most plains of the Tarai region and the central hilly region; overall density is quite low

Urbanization: *urban population:* 19.4% of total population (2017)
rate of urbanization: 3.08% annual rate of change (2015-20 est.)

Major urban areas—population: KATHMANDU (capital) 1.183 million (2015)

Sex ratio: *at birth:* 1.04 male(s)/female
0-14 years: 1.07 male(s)/female
15-24 years: 1 male(s)/female
25-54 years: 0.82 male(s)/female
55-64 years: 0.95 male(s)/female
65 years and over: 0.86 male(s)/female
total population: 0.95 male(s)/female (2016 est.)

Mother's mean age at first birth: 20.8 years
note: median age at first birth among women 25-29 (2016 est.)

Maternal mortality ratio: 258 deaths/100,000 live births (2015 est.)
country comparison to the world: 45

Infant mortality rate: *total:* 27.9 deaths/1,000 live births
male: 29.2 deaths/1,000 live births
female: 26.6 deaths/1,000 live births (2017 est.)
country comparison to the world: 67

Life expectancy at birth: *total population:* 71 years
male: 70.4 years
female: 71.6 years (2017 est.)
country comparison to the world: 153

Total fertility rate: 2.12 children born/woman (2017 est.)
country comparison to the world: 103

Contraceptive prevalence rate: 49.6% (2014)

Health expenditures: 5.8% of GDP (2014)
country comparison to the world: 110

Drinking water source:
improved:
urban: 90.9% of population
rural: 91.8% of population
total: 91.6% of population
unimproved:

urban: 9.1% of population
rural: 8.2% of population
total: 8.4% of population (2015 est.)

Sanitation facility access:
improved:
urban: 56% of population
rural: 43.5% of population
total: 45.8% of population
unimproved:
urban: 44% of population
rural: 56.5% of population
total: 54.2% of population (2015 est.)

HIV/AIDS—adult prevalence rate: 0.2% (2016 est.)
country comparison to the world: 94

HIV/AIDS—people living with HIV/AIDS: 32,000 (2016 est.)
country comparison to the world: 65

HIV/AIDS—deaths: 1,700 (2016 est.)
country comparison to the world: 56

Major infectious diseases: *degree of risk:* high
food or waterborne diseases: bacterial diarrhea, hepatitis A and E, and typhoid fever
vectorborne disease: Japanese encephalitis, malaria, and dengue fever (2016)

Obesity—adult prevalence rate: 4.1% (2016)
country comparison to the world: 187

Children under the age of 5 years underweight: 30.1% (2014)
country comparison to the world: 17

Education expenditures: 3.7% of GDP (2015)
country comparison to the world: 87

Literacy: *definition:* age 15 and over can read and write
total population: 63.9%
male: 76.4%
female: 53.1% (2015 est.)

School life expectancy (primary to tertiary education): *total:* 12 years
male: 12 years
female: 13 years (2015)

Unemployment, youth ages 15-24: *total:* 3.5%
male: 4.2%
female: 2.9% (2008 est.)

GOVERNMENT

Country name: *conventional long form:* Federal Democratic Republic of Nepal
conventional short form: Nepal
local long form: Sanghiya Loktantrik Ganatantra Nepal
local short form: Nepal
etymology: the Newar people of the Kathmandu Valley and surrounding areas apparently gave their name to the country; the terms "Nepal," "Newar," "Nepar," and "Newal" are phonetically different forms of the same word

Government type: federal parliamentary republic

Capital: *name:* Kathmandu

geographic coordinates: 27 43 N, 85 19 E
time difference: UTC+5.75 (10.75 hours ahead of Washington, DC, during Standard Time)

Administrative divisions: 14 zones (anchal, singular and plural); Bagmati, Bheri, Dhawalagiri, Gandaki, Janakpur, Karnali, Kosi, Lumbini, Mahakali, Mechi, Narayani, Rapti, Sagarmatha, Seti

Independence: 1768 (unified by Prithvi Narayan SHAH)

National holiday: Republic Day, 28 May (2008); note—marks the abdication of Gyanendra SHAH, the last Nepalese monarch, and the establishment of a federal republic

Constitution: history: several previous; latest approved by the Second Constituent Assembly 16 September 2015, signed by the president and effective 20 September 2015
amendments: proposed as a "bill" by either house of the Federal Parliament; bills affecting a state border or powers delegated to a state must be submitted to the affected state assembly; passage of such bills requires a majority vote of that state assembly membership; bills not requiring state assembly consent require at least two-thirds majority vote by the membership of both houses of the Federal Parliament; parts of the constitution on the sovereignty, territorial integrity, independence, and sovereignty vested in the people cannot be amended; amended January 2016 (2017)

Legal system: English common law and Hindu legal concepts

International law organization participation: has not submitted an ICJ jurisdiction declaration; non-party state to the ICCt

Citizenship: *citizenship by birth:* yes
citizenship by descent: yes
dual citizenship recognized: no
residency requirement for naturalization: 15 years

Suffrage: 18 years of age; universal

Executive branch: head of state: President Bidhya Devi BHANDARI (since 29 October 2015); Vice President Nanda Bahadar PUN (since 31 October 2015)

head of government: Prime Minister Khadga Prasad OLI (since 15 February 2018); Deputy Prime Ministers (vacant); note—Prime Minister Sher Bahadur DEUBA resigned on 15 February 2018
cabinet: Council of Ministers appointed by the prime minister; cabinet dominated by the CPN-MC and the NC
elections/appointments: president indirectly elected by an electoral college of the Federal Parliament and of the state assemblies for a 5-year term (eligible for a second term); prime minister indirectly elected by the Federal Parliament
election results: Bidhya Devi BHANDARI elected president; Constituent Assembly vote—Bidhya Devi BHANDARI (CPN-UML) 327, Kul Bahadur GURUNG (NC) 214; BHANDARI is Nepal's first woman president

Legislative branch: *description:* bicameral Federal Parliament consists of the National Assembly (59 seats; 56 members, including at least 3 women, 1 Dalit, 1 member with disabilities, or 1 minority indirectly elected by an electoral college of state and municipal government leaders, and 3 members, including 1 woman, nominated by the president of Nepal on the recommendation of the government; members serve 6-year terms with renewal of one-third of the membership every 2 years) and the House of Representatives (275 seats; 165 members directly elected in single-seat constituencies by simple majority vote and 110 members directly elected in a single nationwide constituency by party-list proportional representation vote; members serve 5-year terms)
elections: first election for the National Assembly held on 7 February 2018 (next to be held in 2024); first election for House of Representatives held on 26 November and 7 December 2017 (next to be held in 2019)
election results: National Assembly—percent of vote by party—NA; seats by party NA; House of Representatives—percent of vote by party—NA; seats by party—CPN-UML 121, NC 63, CPN-MC 53, RJPN 17, FSFN 16, other 4, independent 1

Judicial branch: *highest court(s):* Supreme Court (consists of the chief justice and up to 20 judges)
judge selection and term of office: the Supreme Court chief justice appointed by the president on the recommendation of the Constitutional Council, a 5-member, high-level advisory body headed by the prime minister; other judges appointed by the president on the recommendation of the Judicial Council, a 5-member advisory body headed by the chief justice; the chief justice term of office is 6 years; judges serve until age 65
subordinate courts: High Court; Court of Appeal; district courts
note: Nepal's judiciary was restructured under its 2007 Interim Constitution

Political parties and leaders: note: the Election Commission, Nepal, granted ballot access under the proportional system to 88 political parties for the November-December 2017 House of Representatives election to the Federal Parliament; of these, the following 9 parties and 1 independent won seats
Communist Party of Nepal (Maoist Centre) or CPN-MC [Pushpa Kamal DAHAL, also known as PRACHANDA]
Communist Party of Nepal-Unified Marxist-Leninist or CPN-UML [Khadga Prasad Sharma OLI]
Federal Socialist Forum Nepal or FSFN [Upendra YADAV]
Naya Shakti Party [Baburam BHATTARAI]
Nepali Congress or NC [Sher Bahadur DEUBA]
Nepal Workers Peasants Party [Narayan Man BIJUKCHHE]
Rastriya Janamorcha or RJM [Chitra BAHADUR]
Rastriya Janata Party Nepal or RJPN [Rajendra MAHATO]
Rastriya Prajatantra Party [Kamai THAPA]

Political pressure groups and leaders: National Federation of Indigenous Nationalities
Tharu Kalyankari Sabha (Tharus rights advocacy group)

International organization participation: ADB, BIMSTEC, CD, CP, FAO, G-77, IAEA, IBRD, ICAO, ICC (NGOs), ICRM, IDA, IFAD, IFC, IFRCS, ILO, IMF, IMO, Interpol, IOC, IOM, IPU, ISO, ITSO, ITU, ITUC (NGOs), MIGA, MINURSO, MINUSMA, MINUSTAH, MONUSCO, NAM, OPCW, SAARC, SACEP, UN, UNAMID, UNCTAD, UNDOF, UNESCO, UNIDO, UNIFIL, UNMIL, UNMISS, UNOCI, UNTSO, UNWTO, UPU, WCO, WFTU (NGOs), WHO, WIPO, WMO, WTO

Diplomatic representation in the US: *chief of mission:* Ambassador Arjun Kumar KARKI (since 18 May 2015)
chancery: 2131 Leroy Place NW, Washington, DC 20008
telephone: [1] (202) 667-4550
FAX: [1] (202) 667-5534
consulate(s) general: Cleveland (OH), New York

Diplomatic representation from the US: *chief of mission:* Ambassador Alaina B. TEPLITZ (since 7 October 2015)
embassy: Maharajgunj, Kathmandu
mailing address: use embassy street address
telephone: [977] (1) 423-4000
FAX: [977] (1) 400-7272

Flag description: crimson red with a blue border around the unique shape of two overlapping right triangles; the smaller, upper triangle bears a white stylized moon and the larger, lower triangle displays a white 12-pointed sun; the color red represents the rhododendron (Nepal's national flower) and is a sign of victory and bravery, the blue border signifies peace and harmony; the two right triangles are a combination of two single pennons (pennants) that originally symbolized the Himalaya Mountains while their charges represented the families of the king (upper) and the prime minister, but today they are understood to denote Hinduism and Buddhism, the country's two main religions; the moon represents the serenity of the Nepalese people and the shade and cool weather in the Himalayas, while the sun depicts the heat and higher temperatures of the lower parts of Nepal; the moon and the sun are also said to express the hope that the nation will endure as long as these heavenly bodies
note: Nepal is the only country in the world whose flag is not rectangular or square

National symbol(s): rhododendron blossom; national color: red

National anthem: name: "Sayaun Thunga Phool Ka" (Hundreds of Flowers)
lyrics/music: Pradeep Kumar RAI/Ambar GURUNG
note: adopted 2007; after the abolition of the monarchy in 2006, a new anthem was required because of the previous anthem's praise for the king

ECONOMY

Economy—overview: Nepal is among the least developed countries in the world, with about one-quarter of its population living below the poverty line. Nepal is heavily dependent on remittances, which amount to as much as 30% of GDP. Agriculture is the mainstay of the economy, providing a livelihood for almost two-thirds of the population but accounting for only one-third of GDP. Industrial activity mainly involves the processing of agricultural products, including pulses, jute, sugarcane, tobacco, and grain.

Nepal has considerable scope for exploiting its potential in hydropower, with an estimated 42,000 MW of commercially feasible capacity. Nepal and India signed trade and investment agreements in 2014 that increase Nepal's hydropower potential, but political uncertainty and a difficult business climate have hampered foreign investment.

Nepal was hit by massive earthquakes in early 2015, which damaged or destroyed infrastructure and homes and set back economic development. Political gridlock in the past several years and recent public protests, predominantly in the southern Tarai region, have hindered post-earthquake recovery and prevented much-needed economic reform. Additional challenges to Nepal's growth include its landlocked geographic location, persistent power shortages, and underdeveloped transportation infrastructure.

GDP (purchasing power parity): $78.55 billion (2017 est.)
$73.07 billion (2016 est.)
$72.77 billion (2015 est.)
note: data are in 2017 dollars
country comparison to the world: 95

GDP (official exchange rate): $24.07 billion (2016 est.)

GDP—real growth rate: 7.5% (2017 est.)
0.4% (2016 est.)
3.3% (2015 est.)
country comparison to the world: 6

GDP—per capita (PPP): $2,700 (2017 est.)
$2,500 (2016 est.)
$2,600 (2015 est.)
note: data are in 2017 dollars
country comparison to the world: 196

Gross national saving: 42.1% of GDP (2017 est.)
40% of GDP (2016 est.)
44% of GDP (2015 est.)
country comparison to the world: 6

GDP—composition, by end use:
household consumption: 76.2%
government consumption: 11.7%
investment in fixed capital: 33.8%
investment in inventories: 10.5%
exports of goods and services: 9.8%
imports of goods and services: -42% (2017 est.)

GDP—composition, by sector of origin:
agriculture: 27%
industry: 13.5%
services: 51.5% (2017 est.)

Agriculture—products: pulses, rice, corn, wheat, sugarcane, jute, root crops; milk, water buffalo meat

Industries: tourism, carpets, textiles; small rice, jute, sugar, and oilseed mills; cigarettes, cement and brick production

Industrial production growth rate: 10.9% (2017 est.)
country comparison to the world: 6

Labor force: 15.6 million
note: severe lack of skilled labor (2014 est.)
country comparison to the world: 39

Labor force—by occupation: agriculture: 69%
industry: 12%
services: 19% (2014 est.)

Unemployment rate: 3.3% (2013 est.)
2.7% (2008 est.)
country comparison to the world: 37

Population below poverty line: 25.2% (2011 est.)

Household income or consumption by percentage share: lowest 10%: 3.2%
highest 10%: 29.5% (2011)

Distribution of family income—Gini index: 32.8 (2010)
47.2 (2008 est.)
country comparison to the world: 109

Budget: revenues: $5.954 billion
expenditures: $5.974 billion (2017 est.)
Taxes and other revenues: 24.7% of GDP (FY2016 est.)
country comparison to the world: 117

Budget surplus (+) or deficit (-): -0.1% of GDP (FY2016 est.)
country comparison to the world: 38

Public debt: 27.3% of GDP (2016 est.)
25.2% of GDP (2015 est.)
country comparison to the world: 171

Fiscal year: 16 July—15 July

Inflation rate (consumer prices): 4.5% (2017 est.)
9.9% (2016 est.)
country comparison to the world: 170

Central bank discount rate: 7% (30 October 2016)
7% (30 October 2015)
country comparison to the world: 48

Commercial bank prime lending rate: 9% (31 December 2017 est.)
8.9% (31 December 2016 est.)
country comparison to the world: 93

Stock of narrow money: $5.834 billion (31 December 2017 est.)
$4.871 billion (31 December 2016 est.)
country comparison to the world: 98

Stock of broad money: $27.12 billion (31 December 2017 est.)
$22.19 billion (31 December 2016 est.)
country comparison to the world: 84

Stock of domestic credit: $21.93 billion (31 December 2017 est.)
$17.98 billion (31 December 2016 est.)
country comparison to the world: 92

Market value of publicly traded shares: $14.03 billion (30 April 2016 est.)
$11.81 billion (31 October 2015 est.)
$9.574 billion (31 October 2014 est.)
country comparison to the world: 68

Current account balance: -$88 million (2017 est.)
$1.339 billion (2016 est.)
country comparison to the world: 77

Exports: $818.7 million (2017 est.)
$761.6 million (2016 est.)
country comparison to the world: 167

Exports—commodities: clothing, pulses, carpets, textiles, juice, jute goods

Exports—partners: India 56.6%, US 11.5%, Turkey 4% (2016)

Imports: $11.03 billion (2017 est.)
$8.757 billion (2016 est.)
country comparison to the world: 93

Imports—commodities: petroleum products, machinery and equipment, gold, electrical goods, medicine

Imports—partners: India 70.1%, China 10.3% (2016)

Reserves of foreign exchange and gold: $8.668 billion (31 December 2017 est.)
$8.506 billion (31 December 2016 est.)
country comparison to the world: 76

Debt—external: $5.948 billion (31 December 2017 est.)
$4.321 billion (31 December 2016 est.)
country comparison to the world: 129

Stock of direct foreign investment—at home: $103 million (31 July 2013 est.)
country comparison to the world: 131

Stock of direct foreign investment—abroad: $NA

Exchange rates: Nepalese rupees (NPR) per US dollar—
104 (2017 est.)
107.38 (2016 est.)
107.38 (2015 est.)
102.41 (2014 est.)
99.53 (2013 est.)

ENERGY

Electricity access: population without electricity: 6,600,000

electrification—total population: 76%
electrification—urban areas: 97%
electrification—rural areas: 72% (2013)

Electricity—production: 3.342 billion kWh (FY 2016 est.)
country comparison to the world: 130

Electricity—consumption: 3.746 billion kWh (FY 2016 est.)
country comparison to the world: 129

Electricity—exports: 3.25 million kWh (FY 2016 est.)
country comparison to the world: 93

Electricity—imports: 1.758 billion kWh (FY 2016 est.)
country comparison to the world: 57

Electricity—installed generating capacity: 838,100 kW (2015 est.)
country comparison to the world: 134

Electricity—from fossil fuels: 6.3% of total installed capacity (2015 est.)
country comparison to the world: 203

Electricity—from nuclear fuels: 0% of total installed capacity (2015 est.)
country comparison to the world: 156

Electricity—from hydroelectric plants: 89.8% of total installed capacity (2015 est.)

country comparison to the world: 10

Electricity—from other renewable sources: 3.6% of total installed capacity (2015 est.)
country comparison to the world: 108

Crude oil—production: 0 bbl/day (2016 est.)
country comparison to the world: 179

Crude oil—exports: 2.016 million bbl/day (1)
country comparison to the world: 7

Crude oil—imports: 0 bbl/day (2016 est.)
country comparison to the world: 172

Crude oil—proved reserves: 0 bbl (1 January 2017 es)
country comparison to the world: 177

Refined petroleum products—production: 0 bbl/day (2014 est.)
country comparison to the world: 185

Refined petroleum products—consumption: 32,000 bbl/day (2015 est.)
country comparison to the world: 119

Refined petroleum products—exports: 0 bbl/day (2014 est.)
country comparison to the world: 186

Refined petroleum products—imports: 30,590 bbl/day (2014 est.)
country comparison to the world: 101

Natural gas—production: 0 cu m (2013 est.)
country comparison to the world: 178

Natural gas—consumption: 0 cu m (2013 est.)
country comparison to the world: 117

Natural gas—exports: 0 cu m (2013 est.)
country comparison to the world: 159

Natural gas—imports: 0 cu m (2013 est.)
country comparison to the world: 167

Natural gas—proved reserves: 0 cu m (1 January 2014 es)
country comparison to the world: 180

Carbon dioxide emissions from consumption of energy: 4.2 million Mt (2013 est.)
country comparison to the world: 131

COMMUNICATIONS

Telephones—fixed lines: *total subscriptions:* 858,237
subscriptions per 100 inhabitants: 3 (July 2016 est.)
country comparison to the world: 85

Telephones—mobile cellular: *total:* 32,120,305
subscriptions per 100 inhabitants: 111 (July 2016 est.)

country comparison to the world: 52

Telephone system: *general assessment:* mountainous topography hinders development of telecom infrastructure; fair radiotelephone communication service and mobile-cellular telephone network
domestic: mobile service has been extended to all 75 districts covering 90% of Nepal's land area; disparity between high coverage in cities and coverage available in underdeveloped rural regions
international: country code—977; radiotelephone communications; microwave and fiber landlines to India; satellite earth station—1 Intelsat (Indian Ocean) (2016)

Broadcast media: state operates 3 TV stations, as well as national and regional radio stations; 88 independent TV channels are registered with only 25 in regular operation; 672 FM radio stations are licensed with 588 operational (2016)

Internet country code: .np
Internet users: total: 5,716,419

percent of population: 19.7% (July 2016 est.)
country comparison to the world: 80

TRANSPORTATION

National air transport system: *number of registered air carriers:* 4
inventory of registered aircraft operated by air carriers: 15
annual passenger traffic on registered air carriers: 510,341
annual freight traffic on registered air carriers: 4,536,371 mt-km (2015)
Civil aircraft registration country code prefix: 9N (2016)

Airports: 47 (2013)
country comparison to the world: 95

Airports—with paved runways: *total:* 11
over 3,047 m: 1
1,524 to 2,437 m: 3
914 to 1,523 m: 6
under 914 m: 1 (2017)

Airports—with unpaved runways: *total:* 36
1,524 to 2,437 m: 1
914 to 1,523 m: 6
under 914 m: 29 (2013)

Railways: *total:* 53 km
narrow gauge: 53 km 0.762-m gauge (2014)
country comparison to the world: 131

Roadways: *total:* 27,990 km
paved: 11,890 km

unpaved: 16,100 km (2016)
country comparison to the world: 132

MILITARY AND SECURITY

Military expenditures: 1.52% of GDP (2016)
1.54% of GDP (2015)
1.63% of GDP (2014)
1.54% of GDP (2013)
1.43% of GDP (2012)

Military branches: Nepal Army (2012)

Military service age and obligation: 18 years of age for voluntary military service; no conscription (2014)

TERRORISM

Terrorist groups—foreign based: *Indian Mujahedeen (IM): aim(s):* enhance networks in Nepal to carry out attacks against Indians in Nepal and India
area(s) of operation: continues to have active hubs of small, loosely connected networks

TRANSNATIONAL ISSUES

Disputes—international: joint border commission continues to work on contested sections of boundary with India, including the 400 sq km dispute over the source of the Kalapani River; India has instituted a stricter border regime to restrict transit of illegal cross-border activities

Refugees and internally displaced persons: refugees (country of origin): 13,509 (Tibet/China) (2016); 9,804 (Bhutan) (2017)
IDPs: 50,000 (remaining from ten-year Maoist insurgency that officially ended in 2006; figure does not include people displaced since 2007 by inter-communal violence and insecurity in the Terai region; 2015 earthquakes) (2016)
stateless persons: undetermined (2016); note—the UNHCR is working with the Nepali Government to address the large number of individuals lacking citizenship certificates in Nepal; smaller numbers of Bhutanese Hindu refugees of Nepali origin (the Lhotshampa) who were stripped of Bhutanese nationality and forced to flee their country in the late 1980s and early 1990s—and undocumented Tibetan refugees who arrived in Nepal prior to the 1990s—are considered stateless

Illicit drugs: illicit producer of cannabis and hashish for the domestic and international drug markets; transit point for opiates from Southeast Asia to the West

NETHERLANDS

INTRODUCTION

Background: The Dutch United Provinces declared their independence from Spain in 1579; during the 17th century, they became a leading seafaring and commercial power, with settlements and colonies around the world. After a 20-year French occupation, a Kingdom of the Netherlands was formed in 1815. In 1830, Belgium seceded and formed a separate kingdom. The Netherlands remained neutral in World War I, but suffered German invasion and occupation in World War II. A modern, industrialized nation, the Netherlands is also a large exporter of agricultural products. The country was a founding member of NATO and the EEC (now the EU) and participated in the introduction of the euro in 1999. In October 2010, the former Netherlands Antilles was dissolved and the three smallest islands—Bonaire, Sint Eustatius,

649

and Saba—became special municipalities in the Netherlands administrative structure. The larger islands of Sint Maarten and Curacao joined the Netherlands and Aruba as constituent countries forming the Kingdom of the Netherlands.

In February 2018, the Sint Eustatius island council (governing body) was dissolved and replaced by a government commissioner to restore order on the island. Dutch Government neglect had brought on lawlessness and financial mismanagement necessitating the intervention, which was described as being as "short as possible and as long as needed."

GEOGRAPHY

Location: Western Europe, bordering the North Sea, between Belgium and Germany

Geographic coordinates: 52 30 N, 5 45 E

Map references: Europe

Area: *total:* 41,543 sq km
land: 33,893 sq km
water: 7,650 sq km
country comparison to the world: 135

Area—comparative: slightly less than twice the size of New Jersey

Land boundaries: *total:* 1,053 km
border countries (2): Belgium 478 km, Germany 575 km

Coastline: 451 km

Maritime claims: *territorial sea:* 12 nm
contiguous zone: 24 nm
exclusive fishing zone: 200 nm

Climate: temperate; marine; cool summers and mild winters

Terrain: mostly coastal lowland and reclaimed land (polders); some hills in southeast

Elevation: *mean elevation:* 30 m

elevation extremes: *lowest point:* Zuidplaspolder -7 m
highest point: Mount Scenery 862 m (on the island of Saba in the Caribbean, now considered an integral part of the Netherlands following the dissolution of the Netherlands Antilles)
note: the highest point on continental Netherlands is Vaalserberg at 322 m

Natural resources: natural gas, petroleum, peat, limestone, salt, sand and gravel, arable land

Land use: *agricultural land:* 55.1%
arable land: 29.8%;
permanent crops: 1.1%;
permanent pasture: 24.2%
forest: 10.8%
other: 34.1% (2011 est.)
Irrigated land: 4,860 sq km (2012)

Population—distribution: an area known as the Randstad, anchored by the cities of Amsterdam, Rotterdam, the Hague, and Utrecht, is the most densely populated region; the north tends to be less dense, though sizeable communities can be found throughout the entire country

Natural hazards: flooding
volcanism: Mount Scenery (887 m), located on the island of Saba in the Caribbean, last erupted in 1640; Round Hill (601 m), a dormant volcano also known as The Quill, is located on the island of St. Eustatius in the Caribbean; these islands are at the northern end of the volcanic island arc of the Lesser Antilles that extends south to Grenada

Environment—current issues: water pollution in the form of heavy metals, organic compounds, and nutrients such as nitrates and phosphates; air pollution from vehicles and refining activities; acid rain

Environment—international agreements: *party to:* Air Pollution, Air Pollution-Nitrogen Oxides, Air Pollution-Persistent Organic Pollutants, Air Pollution-Sulfur 85, Air Pollution-Sulfur 94, Air Pollution-Volatile Organic Compounds, Antarctic-Environmental Protocol, Antarctic-Marine Living Resources, Antarctic Treaty, Biodiversity, Climate Change, Climate Change-Kyoto Protocol, Desertification, Endangered Species, Environmental Modification, Hazardous Wastes, Law of the Sea, Marine Dumping, Marine Life Conservation, Ozone Layer Protection, Ship Pollution, Tropical Timber 83, Tropical Timber 94, Wetlands, Whaling
signed, but not ratified: none of the selected agreements

Geography—note: located at mouths of three major European rivers (Rhine, Maas or Meuse, and Schelde); about a quarter of the country lies below sea level and only about half of the land exceeds one meter above sea level

PEOPLE AND SOCIETY

Population: 17,084,719 (July 2017 est.)
country comparison to the world: 66

Nationality: *noun:* Dutchman(men), Dutchwoman(women)
adjective: Dutch

Ethnic groups: Dutch 77.4%, EU 6.2%, Turkish 2.3%, Moroccan 2.3%, Indonesian 2.1%, Surinamese 2%, other 7.7% (2017 est.)

Languages: Dutch (official)
note: Frisian is an official language in Fryslan province; Frisian, Low Saxon, Limburgish, Romani, and Yiddish have protected status under the

European Charter for Regional or Minority Languages; Dutch is the official language of the three special municipalities of the Caribbean Netherlands, English is a recognized regional language on Sint Eustatius and Saba, and Papiamento is a recognized regional language on Bonaire

Religions: Roman Catholic 23.7%, Protestant 15.5% (includes Dutch Reformed 6.5%, Protestant Church of The Netherlands 5.7%, Calvinist 3.3%), Islam 4.9%, other 5.7% (includes Hindu, Buddhist, Jewish), none 50.1% (2015 est.)

Age structure: *0-14 years:* 16.41% (male 1,434,919/female 1,368,437)
15-24 years: 12.07% (male 1,051,319/female 1,010,969)
25-54 years: 39.52% (male 3,387,716/female 3,364,010)
55-64 years: 13.28% (male 1,128,484/female 1,139,703)
65 years and over: 18.73% (male 1,449,752/ female 1,749,410) (2017 est.)

Dependency ratios: *total dependency ratio:* 53.1
youth dependency ratio: 25.6
elderly dependency ratio: 27.4
potential support ratio: 3.6 (2015 est.)

Median age: *total:* 42.6 years
male: 41.5 years
female: 43.6 years (2017 est.)
country comparison to the world: 22

Population growth rate: 0.39% (2017 est.)
country comparison to the world: 164

Birth rate: 10.9 births/1,000 population (2017 est.)
country comparison to the world: 182

Death rate: 8.9 deaths/1,000 population (2017 est.)
country comparison to the world: 67

Net migration rate: 1.9 migrant(s)/1,000 population (2017 est.)
country comparison to the world: 49

Population distribution: an area known as the Randstad, anchored by the cities of Amsterdam, Rotterdam, the Hague, and Utrecht, is the most densely populated region; the north tends to be less dense, though sizeable communities can be found throughout the entire country

Urbanization: *urban population:* 91.5% of total population (2017)
rate of urbanization: 0.72% annual rate of change (2015-20 est.)

Major urban areas—population: AMSTERDAM (capital) 1.091 million; Rotterdam 993,000; The Hague (seat of government) 650,000 (2015)

Sex ratio: *at birth:* 1.05 male(s)/female
0-14 years: 1.05 male(s)/female
15-24 years: 1.04 male(s)/female
25-54 years: 1.01 male(s)/female
55-64 years: 0.99 male(s)/female
65 years and over: 0.82 male(s)/female
total population: 0.98 male(s)/female (2016 est.)

Mother's mean age at first birth: 29.6 years (2015 est.)

Maternal mortality ratio: 7 deaths/100,000 live births (2015 est.)

country comparison to the world: 162

Infant mortality rate: *total:* 3.6 deaths/1,000 live births

male: 3.8 deaths/1,000 live births
female: 3.3 deaths/1,000 live births (2017 est.)
country comparison to the world: 201

Life expectancy at birth: *total population:* 81.4 years
male: 79.3 years
female: 83.7 years (2017 est.)
country comparison to the world: 25

Total fertility rate: 1.78 children born/woman (2017 est.)
country comparison to the world: 153

Contraceptive prevalence rate: 73%
note: percent of women aged 18-45 (2013)

Health expenditures: 10.9% of GDP (2014)
country comparison to the world: 15

Physicians density: 3.35 physicians/1,000 population (2014)

Hospital bed density: 4.7 beds/1,000 population (2009)

Drinking water source:
improved:
urban: 100% of population
rural: 100% of population
total: 100% of population
unimproved:
urban: 0% of population
rural: 0% of population
total: 0% of population (2015 est.)

Sanitation facility access:
improved:
urban: 97.5% of population
rural: 99.9% of population
total: 97.7% of population
unimproved:
urban: 2.5% of population
rural: 0.1% of population
total: 2.3% of population (2015 est.)

HIV/AIDS—adult prevalence rate: 0.2% (2016 est.)
country comparison to the world: 95

HIV/AIDS—people living with HIV/AIDS: 23,000 (2016 est.)
country comparison to the world: 73

HIV/AIDS—deaths: <200 (2016 est.)

Obesity—adult prevalence rate: 20.4% (2016)
country comparison to the world: 99

Education expenditures: 5.6% of GDP (2013)
country comparison to the world: 45

School life expectancy (primary to tertiary education): *total:* 18 years
male: 18 years
female: 18 years (2012)

Unemployment, youth ages 15-24: *total:* 11.3%
male: 11.3%
female: 11.2% (2015 est.)
country comparison to the world: 102

GOVERNMENT

Country name: *conventional long form:* Kingdom of the Netherlands
conventional short form: Netherlands
local long form: Koninkrijk der Nederlanden

local short form: Nederland
etymology: the country name literally means "the lowlands" and refers to the geographic features of the land being both flat and down river from higher areas (i.e., at the estuaries of the Scheldt, Meuse, and Rhine Rivers; only about half of the Netherlands is more than 1 meter above sea level)

Government type: parliamentary constitutional monarchy; part of the Kingdom of the Netherlands

Capital: *name:* Amsterdam; note—The Hague is the seat of government

geographic coordinates: 52 21 N, 4 55 E
time difference: UTC+1 (6 hours ahead of Washington, DC, during Standard Time)
daylight saving time: +1hr, begins last Sunday in March; ends last Sunday in October
note: time descriptions apply to the continental Netherlands only, not to the constituent countries in the Caribbean

Administrative divisions: 12 provinces (provincies, singular—provincie); Drenthe, Flevoland, Fryslan (Friesland), Gelderland, Groningen, Limburg, Noord-Brabant (North Brabant), Noord-Holland (North Holland), Overijssel, Utrecht, Zeeland (Zealand), Zuid-Holland (South Holland)
note 1: the Netherlands is one of four constituent countries of the Kingdom of the Netherlands; the other three, Aruba, Curacao, and Sint Maarten, are all islands in the Caribbean; while all four parts are considered equal partners, in practice, most of the Kingdom's affairs are administered by the Netherlands, which makes up about 98% of the Kingdom's total land area and population
note 2: three other Caribbean islands, Bonaire, Saint Eustatius, and Saba, are considered to be special municipalities of the Netherlands proper
Dependent areas: Aruba, Curacao, Sint Maarten

Independence: 23 January 1579 (the northern provinces of the Low Countries conclude the Union of Utrecht breaking with Spain; on 26 July 1581 they formally declared their independence with an Act of Abjuration; however, it was not until 30 January 1648 and the Peace of Westphalia that Spain recognized this independence)

National holiday: King's Day (birthday of King WILLEM-ALEXANDER), 27 April (1967); note—King's or Queen's Day are observed on the ruling monarch's birthday; celebrated on 26 April if 27 April is a Sunday

Constitution: history: previous 1597, 1798; latest adopted 24 August 1815 (substantially revised in 1848)
amendments: proposed as an "Act of Parliament" by or on behalf of the king or by the Second Chamber of the States General; the Second Chamber is dissolved after its first reading of the "Act"; passage requires a second reading by both the First Chamber and newly elected Second Chamber, followed by at least two-thirds majority vote of both chambers, and ratification by the king; amended many times, last in 2010 (2016)

Legal system: civil law system based on the French system; constitution does not permit judicial review of acts of the States General

International law organization participation: accepts compulsory ICJ jurisdiction with reservations; accepts ICCt jurisdiction

Citizenship: *citizenship by birth:* no
citizenship by descent only: at least one parent must be a citizen of the Netherlands
dual citizenship recognized: no
residency requirement for naturalization: 5 years

Suffrage: 18 years of age; universal

Executive branch: *chief of state:* King WILLEM-ALEXANDER (since 30 April 2013); Heir Apparent Princess Catharina-Amalia (since 30 April 2013)

head of government: Prime Minister Mark RUTTE (since 14 October 2010; Deputy Prime Ministers (since 26 October 2017) Hugo DE JONGE, Karin Kajsa OLLONGREN, and Carola SCHOUTEN (since 26 October 2017); note—Mark RUTTE heads his third cabinet since 26 October 2017
cabinet: Council of Ministers appointed by the monarch
elections/appointments: the monarchy is hereditary; following Second Chamber elections, the leader of the majority party or majority coalition usually appointed prime minister by the monarch; deputy prime ministers appointed by the monarch

Legislative branch: *description:* bicameral States General or Staten Generaal consists of the First Chamber or Eerste Kamer (75 seats; members indirectly elected by the country's 12 provincial council members by proportional representation vote; members serve 4-year terms) and the Second Chamber or Tweede Kamer (150 seats; members directly elected in multi-seat constituencies by proportional representation vote to serve up to 4-year terms)
elections: First Chamber—last held on 26 May 2015 (next to be held in May 2019); Second Chamber—last held on 15 March 2017 (next to be held 15 March 2021)
election results: First Chamber—percent of vote by party—NA; seats by party—VVD 13, CDA 12, D66 10, PVV 9, SP 9, PvdA 8, GL 4, CU 3, other 7; Second Chamber—percent of vote by party—VVD 21.3%, PVV 13.1%, CDA 12.4%, D66 12.2%, GL 9.1%, SP 9.1%, PvdA 5.7%, CU 3.4%, PvdD 3.2%, 50 Plus 3.1%, other 7.4%; seats by party—VVD 33, PVV 20, CDA 19, D66 19, GL 14, SP 14, PvdA 9, CU 5, PvdD 5, 50 Plus 4, other 8

Judicial branch: *highest court(s):* Supreme Court or Hoge Raad (consists of 41 judges: the president, 6 vice presidents, 31 justices or raadsheren, and 3 justices in exceptional service, referred to as buitengewone dienst); the court is divided into criminal, civil, tax, and ombuds chambers
judge selection and term of office: justices appointed by the monarch from a list provided by the Second Chamber of the States General; justices appointed for life or until mandatory retirement at age 70
subordinate courts: courts of appeal; district courts, each with up to 5 subdistrict courts; note in mid-July 2017, legislation was proposed to

establish a new commericial court for international trade disputes with the Netherlands

Political parties and leaders: Christian Democratic Appeal or CDA [Sybrand VAN HAERSMA BUMA]

Christian Union or CU [Gert-Jan SEGERS]

Democrats 66 or D66 [Alexander PECHTOLD]

Denk [Tunahan KUZU]

50 Plus [Henk KROL]

For the Netherlands or VNL [Jan ROOS]

Forum for Democracy or FvD [Thierry BAUDET]

Green Left or GL [Jesse KLAVER]

Labor Party or PvdA [Lodewijk ASSCHER]

Party for Freedom or PVV [Geert WILDERS]

Party for the Animals or PvdD [Marianne THIEME]

People's Party for Freedom and Democracy or VVD [Mark RUTTE]

Reformed Political Party or SGP [Kees VAN DER STAAIJ]

Socialist Party or SP [Emile ROEMER]

plus a few minor parties

Political pressure groups and leaders: Christian Trade Union Federation or CNV [Maurice LIMMEN]

Confederation of Netherlands Industry and Employers or VNO-NCW [Hans DE BOER]

Federation for Small and Medium-sized Businesses or MKB [Michael VAN STRAALEN]

Netherlands Trade Union Federation or FNV [Han BUSKER]

Social Economic Council or SER [Mariette HAMER]

Trade Union Professionals or VDP [Nic VAN HOLSTEIN]

International organization participation: ADB (nonregional member), AfDB (nonregional member), Arctic Council (observer), Australia Group, Benelux, BIS, CBSS (observer), CD, CE, CERN, EAPC, EBRD, ECB, EIB, EITI (implementing country), EMU, ESA, EU, FAO, FATF, G-10, IADB, IAEA, IBRD, ICAO, ICC (national committees), ICCt, ICRM, IDA, IEA, IFAD, IFC, IFRCS, IGAD (partners), IHO, ILO, IMF, IMO, IMSO, Interpol, IOC, IOM, IPU, ISO, ITSO, ITU, ITUC (NGOs), MIGA, MINUSMA, NATO, NEA, NSG, OAS (observer), OECD, OPCW, OSCE, Pacific Alliance (observer), Paris Club, PCA, Schengen Convention, SELEC (observer), UN, UNCTAD, UNDOF, UNESCO, UNHCR, UNIDO, UNMISS, UNRWA, UNTSO, UNWTO, UPU, WCO, WHO, WIPO, WMO, WTO, ZC

Diplomatic representation in the US: *chief of mission:* Ambassador Hendrik Jan Jurriaan SCHUWER (since 17 September 2015)

chancery: 4200 Linnean Avenue NW, Washington, DC 20008

telephone: [1] (202) 244-5300, [1] 877-388-2443

FAX: [1] (202) 362-3430

consulate(s) general: Chicago, Miami, New York, San Francisco

Diplomatic representation from the US: *chief of mission:* Ambassador Peter HOEKSTRA (since 10 January 2018)

embassy: Lange Voorhout 102, 2514 EJ, The Hague

mailing address: PSC 71, Box 1000, APO AE 09715

telephone: [31] (70) 310-2209

FAX: [31] (70) 310-2207

consulate(s) general: Amsterdam

Flag description: three equal horizontal bands of red (bright vermilion; top), white, and blue (cobalt); similar to the flag of Luxembourg, which uses a lighter blue and is longer; the colors were derived from those of WILLIAM I, Prince of Orange, who led the Dutch Revolt against Spanish sovereignty in the latter half of the 16th century; originally the upper band was orange, but because its dye tended to turn red over time, the red shade was eventually made the permanent color; the banner is perhaps the oldest tricolor in continuous use

National symbol(s): lion, tulip; national color: orange

National anthem: *name:* "Het Wilhelmus" (The William)

lyrics/music: Philips VAN MARNIX van Sint Aldegonde (presumed)/unknown

note: adopted 1932, in use since the 17th century, making it the oldest national anthem in the world; also known as "Wilhelmus van Nassouwe" (William of Nassau), it is in the form of an acrostic, where the first letter of each stanza spells the name of the leader of the Dutch Revolt

ECONOMY

Economy—overview: The Netherlands, the sixth-largest economy in the European Union, plays an important role as a European transportation hub, with a consistently high trade surplus, stable industrial relations, and low unemployment. Industry focuses on food processing, chemicals, petroleum refining, and electrical machinery. A highly mechanized agricultural sector employs only 2% of the labor force but provides large surpluses for food-processing and underpins the country's status as the world's second largest agricultural exporter.

The Netherlands is part of the euro zone, and as such, its monetary policy is controlled by the European Central Bank. The Dutch financial sector is highly concentrated, with four commercial banks possessing over 80% of banking assets, and is four times the size of Dutch GDP.

In 2008, during the financial crisis, the government budget deficit hit 5.3% of GDP. Following a protracted recession from 2009 to 2013, during which unemployment doubled to 7.4% and household consumption contracted for four consecutive years, economic growth began inching forward in 2014. Since 2010, Prime Minister Mark RUTTE's government has implemented significant austerity measures to improve public finances and has instituted broad structural reforms in key policy areas, including the labor market, the housing sector, the energy market, and the pension system. In 2017, the government budget returned to a surplus of 0.7% of GDP, with economic growth of 3.2%, and GDP per capita finally surpassed pre-crisis levels. The fiscal policy announced by the new government in the 2018-2021 coalition plans for increases in government consumption and public investment, fueling domestic demand and household consumption and investment. The new government's policy also plans to increase demand for workers in the public and private sector, forecasting a further decline in the unemployment rate, which hit 4.8% in 2017.

GDP (purchasing power parity): $915.2 billion (2017 est.)

$888 billion (2016 est.)

$868.8 billion (2015 est.)

note: data are in 2017 dollars

country comparison to the world: 28

GDP (official exchange rate): $824.5 billion (2016 est.)

GDP—real growth rate: 3.1% (2017 est.)

2.2% (2016 est.)

2.3% (2015 est.)

country comparison to the world: 113

GDP—per capita (PPP): $53,600 (2017 est.)

$52,100 (2016 est.)

$51,300 (2015 est.)

note: data are in 2017 dollars

country comparison to the world: 22

Gross national saving: 30.6% of GDP (2017 est.)

28.5% of GDP (2016 est.)

28.5% of GDP (2015 est.)

country comparison to the world: 23

GDP—composition, by end use:

household consumption: 44.4%

government consumption: 24.7%

investment in fixed capital: 20.5%

investment in inventories: 0.1%

exports of goods and services: 85.3%

imports of goods and services: -75% (2017 est.)

GDP—composition, by sector of origin:

agriculture: 1.6%

industry: 17.9%

services: 70.2% (2017 est.)

Agriculture—products: vegetables, ornamentals, dairy, poultry and livestock products; propagation materials

Industries: agroindustries, metal and engineering products, electrical machinery and equipment, chemicals, petroleum, construction, microelectronics, fishing

Industrial production growth rate: 2.5% (2017 est.)

country comparison to the world: 114

Labor force: 7.969 million (2017 est.)

country comparison to the world: 63

Labor force—by occupation: *agriculture:* 1.2%

industry: 17.2%

services: 81.6% (2015 est.)

Unemployment rate: 5.1% (2017 est.)

5.9% (2016 est.)

country comparison to the world: 70

Population below poverty line: 8.8% (2015 est.)

Household income or consumption by percentage share: *lowest 10%:* 2.3%

highest 10%: 24.9% (2014 est.)

Distribution of family income—Gini index: 30.3 (2015 est.)

25.1 (2013 est.)

country comparison to the world: 125

Budget: *revenues:* $344.8 billion

expenditures: $340.2 billion (2017 est.)

Taxes and other revenues: 41.8% of GDP (2017 est.)

country comparison to the world: 30

Budget surplus (+) or deficit (-): 0.6% of GDP (2017 est.)

country comparison to the world: 22

Public debt: 59% of GDP (2017 est.)

61.8% of GDP (2016 est.)

note: data cover general government debt, and includes debt instruments issued (or owned) by government entities other than the treasury; the data include treasury debt held by foreign entities; the data include debt issued by subnational entities, as well as intra-governmental debt; intra-governmental debt consists of treasury borrowings from surpluses in the social funds, such as for retirement, medical care, and unemployment, debt instruments for the social funds are not sold at public auctions

country comparison to the world: 77

Fiscal year: calendar year

Inflation rate (consumer prices): 1.3% (2017 est.)

0.1% (2016 est.)

country comparison to the world: 56

Central bank discount rate: 0% (31 December 2016)

0.05% (31 December 2015)

note: this is the European Central Bank's rate on the marginal lending facility, which offers overnight credit to banks in the euro area

country comparison to the world: 153

Commercial bank prime lending rate: 1.5% (31 December 2017 est.)

1.47% (31 December 2016 est.)

country comparison to the world: 183

Stock of narrow money: $452.7 billion (31 December 2017 est.)

$411.9 billion (31 December 2016 est.)

note: see entry for the European Union for money supply for the entire euro area; the European Central Bank (ECB) controls monetary policy for the 18 members of the Economic and Monetary Union (EMU); individual members of the EMU do not control the quantity of money circulating within their own borders

country comparison to the world: 13

Stock of broad money: $907.8 billion (31 December 2017 est.)

$827.6 billion (31 December 2016 est.)

country comparison to the world: 17

Stock of domestic credit: $1.636 trillion (31 December 2017 est.)

$1.507 trillion (31 December 2016 est.)

country comparison to the world: 15

Market value of publicly traded shares: $652.7 billion (31 December 2015 est.)

$735.1 billion (31 December 2014 est.)

$675 billion (31 December 2013 est.)

country comparison to the world: 18

Current account balance: $82.44 billion (2017 est.)

$65.71 billion (2016 est.)

country comparison to the world: 6

Exports: $526.4 billion (2017 est.)

$495.4 billion (2016 est.)

country comparison to the world: 9

Exports—commodities: machinery and transport equipment, chemicals, mineral fuels; food and livestock, manufactured goods

Exports—partners: Germany 24.1%, Belgium 10.7%, UK 9.4%, France 8.8%, Italy 4.2% (2016)

Imports: $435.4 billion (2017 est.)

$402.9 billion (2016 est.)

country comparison to the world: 11

Imports—commodities: machinery and transport equipment, chemicals, fuels, foodstuffs, clothing

Imports—partners: Germany 15.3%, China 14.1%, Belgium 8.4%, US 7.9%, UK 5.3%, Russia 4.1% (2016)

Reserves of foreign exchange and gold: $36.13 billion (31 December 2016 est.)

$38.21 billion (31 December 2015 est.)

country comparison to the world: 46

Debt—external: $4.063 trillion (31 December 2016 est.)

$4.054 trillion (31 December 2015 est.)

country comparison to the world: 6

Stock of direct foreign investment—at home: $4.888 trillion (31 December 2017 est.)

$4.759 trillion (31 December 2016 est.)

country comparison to the world: 2

Stock of direct foreign investment—abroad: $5.809 trillion (31 December 2017 est.)

$5.623 trillion (31 December 2016 est.)

country comparison to the world: 2

Exchange rates: euros (EUR) per US dollar—

0.906 (2017 est.)

0.9214 (2016 est.)

0.9214 (2015 est.)

0.885 (2014 est.)

0.7634 (2013 est.)

ENERGY

Electricity access: electrification—*total population:* 100% (2016)

Electricity—production: 102.5 billion kWh (2015 est.)

country comparison to the world: 35

Electricity—consumption: 106 billion kWh (2015 est.)

country comparison to the world: 33

Electricity—exports: 19.34 billion kWh (2016 est.)

country comparison to the world: 9

Electricity—imports: 24.26 billion kWh (2016 est.)

country comparison to the world: 8

Electricity—installed generating capacity: 33.86 million kW (2015 est.)

country comparison to the world: 30

Electricity—from fossil fuels: 80.4% of total installed capacity (2015 est.)

country comparison to the world: 87

Electricity—from nuclear fuels: 1.4% of total installed capacity (2015 est.)

country comparison to the world: 30

Electricity—from hydroelectric plants: 0.1% of total installed capacity (2015 est.)

country comparison to the world: 155

Electricity—from other renewable sources: 22% of total installed capacity (2015 est.)

country comparison to the world: 28

Crude oil—production: 18,090 bbl/day (2016 est.)

country comparison to the world: 72

Crude oil—exports: 6,335 bbl/day (2016 est.)

country comparison to the world: 62

Crude oil—imports: 1.09 million bbl/day (2016 est.)

country comparison to the world: 10

Crude oil—proved reserves: 113.2 million bbl (1 January 2017 es)

country comparison to the world: 72

Refined petroleum products—production: 1.28 million bbl/day (2016 est.)

country comparison to the world: 15

Refined petroleum products—consumption: 973,000 bbl/day (2016 est.)

country comparison to the world: 22

Refined petroleum products—exports: 2.331 million bbl/day (2016 est.)

country comparison to the world: 3

Refined petroleum products—imports: 2.1 million bbl/day (2016 est.)

country comparison to the world: 4

Natural gas—production: 47.46 billion cu m

note: the Netherlands has curbed gas production due to seismic activity in the province of Groningen, largest source of gas reserves (2016 est.)

country comparison to the world: 17

Natural gas—consumption: 39.96 billion cu m (2016 est.)

country comparison to the world: 30

Natural gas—exports: 53.65 billion cu m (2016 est.)

country comparison to the world: 6

Natural gas—imports: 39.57 billion cu m (2016 est.)

country comparison to the world: 11

Natural gas—proved reserves: 786.6 billion cu m (1 January 2017 es)

country comparison to the world: 28

Carbon dioxide emissions from consumption of energy: 184.8 million Mt (2015 est.)

country comparison to the world: 32

COMMUNICATIONS

Telephones—fixed lines: *total subscriptions:* 6,801,678

subscriptions per 100 inhabitants: 40 (July 2016 est.)

653

country comparison to the world: 25

Telephones—mobile cellular: *total:* 21,941,981
subscriptions per 100 inhabitants: 129 (July 2016 est.)
country comparison to the world: 58

Telephone system: *general assessment:* highly developed and well maintained
domestic: extensive fixed-line, fiber-optic network; large cellular telephone system with five major operators utilizing the third generation of the Global System for Mobile Communications technology; one in five households now use Voice over the Internet Protocol services
international: country code—31; submarine cables provide links to the US and Europe; satellite earth stations—5 (3 Intelsat—1 Indian Ocean and 2 Atlantic Ocean, 1 Eutelsat, and 1 Inmarsat (2011)

Broadcast media: more than 90% of households are connected to cable or satellite TV systems that provide a wide range of domestic and foreign channels; public service broadcast system includes multiple broadcasters, 3 with a national reach and the remainder operating in regional and local markets; 2 major nationwide commercial television companies, each with 3 or more stations, and many commercial TV stations in regional and local markets; nearly 600 radio stations with a mix of public and private stations providing national or regional coverage (2008)

Internet country code: .nl
Internet users: total: 15,385,203
percent of population: 90.4% (July 2016 est.)
country comparison to the world: 34

TRANSPORTATION

National air transport system: *number of registered air carriers:* 8

inventory of registered aircraft operated by air carriers: 244
annual passenger traffic on registered air carriers: 34,870,204
annual freight traffic on registered air carriers: 5,292,794,685 mt-km (2015)
Civil aircraft registration country code prefix: PH (2016)

Airports: 29 (2013)
country comparison to the world: 120

Airports—with paved runways: *total:* 23
over 3,047 m: 3
2,438 to 3,047 m: 11
1,524 to 2,437 m: 1
914 to 1,523 m: 6
under 914 m: 2 (2017)

Airports—with unpaved runways: *total:* 6
914 to 1,523 m: 4
under 914 m: 2 (2013)

Heliports: 1 (2013)

Pipelines: gas 14,000 km; oil and refined products 2,500 km; chemicals 3,000 km (2016)

Railways: *total:* 3,058 km
standard gauge: 3,058 km 1.435-m gauge (2,314 km electrified) (2016)
country comparison to the world: 56

Roadways: *total:* 139,124 km (includes 3,654 km of expressways) (2016)
country comparison to the world: 37

Waterways: 6,237 km (navigable by ships up to 50 tons) (2012)
country comparison to the world: 21

Merchant marine: *total:* 1,244
by type: bulk carrier 11, container ship 42, general cargo 597, oil tanker 15, other 579 (2017)
country comparison to the world: 23

Ports and terminals: *major seaport(s):* IJmuiden, Vlissingen

river port(s): Amsterdam (Nordsee Kanaal); Moerdijk (Hollands Diep River); Rotterdam (Rhine River); Terneuzen (Western Scheldt River)
container port(s) (TEUs): Rotterdam (12,235,000) (2015)
LNG terminal(s) (import): Rotterdam

MILITARY AND SECURITY

Military expenditures: 1.17% of GDP (2017)
1.17% of GDP (2016)
1.16% of GDP (2015)
1.15% of GDP (2014)
1.16% of GDP (2013)
country comparison to the world: 79

Military branches: Royal Netherlands Army, Royal Netherlands Navy (includes Naval Air Service and Marine Corps), Royal Netherlands Air Force (Koninklijke Luchtmacht, KLu), Royal Marechaussee (Military Police) (2015)

Military service age and obligation: 17 years of age for an all-volunteer force (2014)

TRANSNATIONAL ISSUES

Disputes—international: none

Refugees and internally displaced persons: refugees (country of origin): 28,394 (Syria); 16,512 (Somalia); 13,488 (Eritrea); 12,740 (Iraq); 5,791 (Afghanistan) (2016)
stateless persons: 1,951 (2016)

Illicit drugs: major European producer of synthetic drugs, including ecstasy, and cannabis cultivator; important gateway for cocaine, heroin, and hashish entering Europe; major source of US-bound ecstasy and a significant consumer of ecstasy; a large financial sector vulnerable to money laundering

NEW CALEDONIA

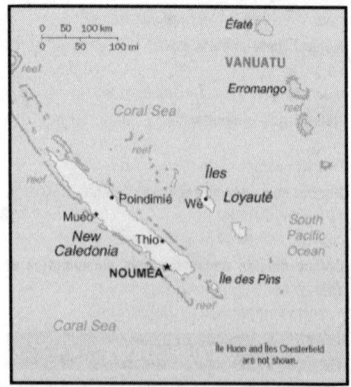

INTRODUCTION

Background: Settled by both Britain and France during the first half of the 19th century, the island

became a French possession in 1853. It served as a penal colony for four decades after 1864. Agitation for independence during the 1980s and early 1990s ended in the 1998 Noumea Accord, which over the past 20 years has transfered an increasing amount of governing responsibility from France to New Caledonia. The agreement also commits France to conduct a referendum by November 2018 for residents to decide whether New Caledonia should assume full sovereignty and independence.

GEOGRAPHY

Location: Oceania, islands in the South Pacific Ocean, east of Australia

Geographic coordinates: 21 30 S, 165 30 E

Map references: Oceania

Area: *total:* 18,575 sq km
land: 18,275 sq km
water: 300 sq km
country comparison to the world: 156

Area—comparative: slightly smaller than New Jersey

Land boundaries: 0 km

Coastline: 2,254 km

Maritime claims: *territorial sea:* 12 nm
exclusive economic zone: 200 nm

Climate: tropical; modified by southeast trade winds; hot, humid

Terrain: coastal plains with interior mountains

Elevation: *mean elevation:* NA

elevation extremes: *lowest point:* Pacific Ocean 0 m
highest point: Mont Panie 1,628 m

Natural resources: nickel, chrome, iron, cobalt, manganese, silver, gold, lead, copper

Land use: *agricultural land:* 10.4%
arable land: 0.4%;
permanent crops: 0.2%;
permanent pasture: 9.8%
forest: 45.9%

other: 43.7% (2011 est.)

Irrigated land: 100 sq km (2012)

Population—distribution: most of the populace lives in the southern part of the main island, in and around the capital of Noumea

Natural hazards: cyclones, most frequent from November to March

volcanism: Matthew and Hunter Islands are historically active

Environment—current issues: erosion caused by mining exploitation and forest fires

Geography—note: consists of the main island of New Caledonia (one of the largest in the Pacific Ocean), the archipelago of Iles Loyaute, and numerous small, sparsely populated islands and atolls

PEOPLE AND SOCIETY

Population: 279,070 (July 2017 est.)

country comparison to the world: 183

Nationality: *noun:* New Caledonian(s)

adjective: New Caledonian

Ethnic groups: Kanak 40.3%, European 29.2%, Wallisian, Futunian 8.7%, Tahitian 2%, Indonesian 1.6%, Vietnamese 1%, Ni-Vanuatu 0.9%, other 16.2% (2009 est.)

Languages: French (official), 33 Melanesian-Polynesian dialects

Religions: Roman Catholic 60%, Protestant 30%, other 10%

Age structure: *0-14 years:* 22.46% (male 32,025/ female 30,648)

15-24 years: 16.44% (male 23,438/female 22,438)

25-54 years: 43.5% (male 61,169/female 60,232)

55-64 years: 8.4% (male 11,352/female 12,097)

65 years and over: 9.2% (male 11,396/female 14,275) (2017 est.)

Dependency ratios: *total dependency ratio:* 48.3

youth dependency ratio: 33.9

elderly dependency ratio: 14.4

potential support ratio: 6.9 (2015 est.)

Median age: *total:* 32 years

male: 31.2 years

female: 32.7 years (2017 est.)

country comparison to the world: 101

Population growth rate: 1.33% (2017 est.)

country comparison to the world: 85

Birth rate: 15 births/1,000 population (2017 est.)

country comparison to the world: 129

Death rate: 5.7 deaths/1,000 population (2017 est.)

country comparison to the world: 174

Net migration rate: 3.9 migrant(s)/1,000 population

note: there has been steady emigration from Wallis and Futuna to New Caledonia (2017 est.)

country comparison to the world: 30

Population distribution: most of the populace lives in the southern part of the main island, in and around the capital of Noumea

Urbanization: *urban population:* 71.2% of total population (2017)

rate of urbanization: 1.91% annual rate of change (2015-20 est.)

Major urban areas—population: NOUMEA (capital) 181,000 (2014)

Sex ratio: *at birth:* 1.05 male(s)/female

0-14 years: 1.04 male(s)/female

15-24 years: 1.04 male(s)/female

25-54 years: 1.01 male(s)/female

55-64 years: 0.94 male(s)/female

65 years and over: 0.8 male(s)/female

total population: 1 male(s)/female (2016 est.)

Infant mortality rate: *total:* 5.2 deaths/1,000 live births

male: 6.1 deaths/1,000 live births

female: 4.3 deaths/1,000 live births (2017 est.)

country comparison to the world: 174

Life expectancy at birth: *total population:* 77.9 years

male: 73.9 years

female: 82 years (2017 est.)

country comparison to the world: 65

Total fertility rate: 1.93 children born/woman (2017 est.)

country comparison to the world: 130

Physicians density: 2.22 physicians/1,000 population (2009)

Drinking water source:

improved:

urban: 98.5% of population

rural: 98.5% of population

total: 98.5% of population

unimproved:

urban: 1.5% of population

rural: 1.5% of population

total: 1.5% of population (2015 est.)

Sanitation facility access:

improved:

urban: 100% of population

rural: 100% of population

total: 100% of population

unimproved:

urban: 0% of population

rural: 0% of population

total: 0% of population (2015 est.)

HIV/AIDS—adult prevalence rate: NA

HIV/AIDS—people living with HIV/AIDS: NA

HIV/AIDS—deaths: NA

Major infectious diseases: *note:* active local transmission of Zika virus by Aedes species mosquitoes has been identified in this country (as of August 2016); it poses an important risk (a large number of cases possible) among US citizens if bitten by an infective mosquito; other less common ways to get Zika are through sex, via blood transfusion, or during pregnancy, in which the pregnant woman passes Zika virus to her fetus (2016)

Literacy: *definition:* age 15 and over can read and write

total population: 96.9%

male: 97.3%

female: 96.5% (2015 est.)

GOVERNMENT

Country name: *conventional long form:* Territory of New Caledonia and Dependencies

conventional short form: New Caledonia

local long form: Territoire des Nouvelle-Caledonie et Dependances

local short form: Nouvelle-Caledonie

etymology: British explorer Captain James COOK discovered and named New Caledonia in 1774; he used the appellation because the northeast of the island reminded him of Scotland (Caledonia is the Latin designation for Scotland)

Dependency status: territorial collectivity (or a sui generis collectivity) of France since 1998; an independence referendum is to take place by November 2018

Government type: parliamentary democracy (Territorial Congress); an overseas collectivity of France

Capital: *name:* Noumea

geographic coordinates: 22 16 S, 166 27 E

time difference: UTC+11 (16 hours ahead of Washington, DC, during Standard Time)

Administrative divisions: 3 provinces; Province Iles (Islands Province), Province Nord (North Province), and Province Sud (South Province)

Independence: none none (overseas collectivity of France); note—a referendum on independence was held in 1998 but was rejected; a new referendum must be held by November 2018

National holiday: Fete de la Federation, 14 July (1790); note—the local holiday is New Caledonia Day, 24 September (1853)

Constitution: 4 October 1958 (French Constitution with changes as reflected in Noumea Accord of 5 May 1998) (2016)

Legal system: civil law system based on French law; the 1988 Matignon Accords (signed in the Matignon Hotel) set up a 10-year period of development during which the Kanak community received substantial autonomy but agreed not to raise the independence issue

Citizenship: see France

Suffrage: 18 years of age; universal

Executive branch: *chief of state:* President Emmanuel MACRON (since 14 May 2017); represented by High Commissioner Thierry LATASTE (since 20 June 2016)

head of government: President of the Government Philippe GERMAINE (since 1 April 2015); Vice President Jean-Louis D'ANGLEBERME (since 1 April 2015)

cabinet: Cabinet elected from and by the Territorial Congress

elections/appointments: French president directly elected by absolute majority popular vote in 2 rounds if needed for a 5-year term (eligible for a second term); high commissioner appointed by the French president on the advice of the French Ministry of Interior; president of New Caledonia elected by Territorial Congress for a 5-year term (no term limits); election last held on 1 December

2017 (next to be held in 2022); note—four rounds of voting were needed to elect the president (votes on 31 August, 12 October, and 24 October failed)
election results: Philippe GERMAINE (Caledonia Together) reelected president by Territorial Congress; vote NA

Legislative branch: unicameral Territorial Congress or Congres du Territoire (54 seats; members indirectly selected proportionally by the partisan makeup of the 3 Provincial Assemblies or Assemblees Provinciales; members of the 3 Provincial Assemblies directly elected by proportional representation vote; members serve 5-year terms)
note: the Customary Senate is the assembly of the various traditional councils of the Kanaks, the indigenous population, which rules on laws affecting the indigenous population; New Caledonia holds 2 seats in the French Senate; elections last held on 28 September 2014 (next to be held not later than September 2017); results—percent of vote by party—NA; seats by party—UMP 2; New Caledonia also elects 2 seats to the French National Assembly; elections last held on 11 and 18 June 2017 (next to be held by June 2022); results—percent of vote by party—NA; seats by party—CE 2
elections: last held on 11 May 2014 (next to be held in May 2019); note—the government that was elected on 11 May 2014 collapsed within 6 months leading to a new election on 31 December 2014, which reelected the same government
election results: percent of vote by party—N/A; seats by party—N/A
note: as of May 2014, seats by party—CE 13, FLNKS 9, UMP 7, Union for Caledonia in France 6, Build Our Rainbow Nation 6, UNI 6, other 7

Judicial branch: highest resident court(s): Court of Appeal in Noumea or Cour d'Appel; organized into civil, commercial, social, and pre-trial investigation chambers; court bench normally includes the court president and 2 counsilors); Administrative Court (number of judges NA); note—final appeals beyond the Court of Appeal are referred to the Court of Cassation or Cour de Cassation in Paris; final appeals beyond the Administrative Court are referred to the Administrative Court of Appeal (in Paris)
judge selection and term of office: judge appointment and tenure based on France's judicial system
subordinate courts: Courts of First Instance include: civil, juvenile, commercial, labor, police, criminal, assizes, and also a pre-trial investigation chamber; Joint Commerce Tribunal; administrative courts

Political parties and leaders: Build Our Rainbow Nation
Caledonia Together or CE [Philippe GERMAIN]
Caledonian Union or UC [Daniel GOA]
Future Together (l'Avenir Ensemble) [Harold MARTIN]
Kanak Socialist Front for National Liberation or FLNKS (alliance includes PALIKA, UNI, UC, and UPM) [Roch WAMYTAN]
Labor Party (Parti Travailliste) or PT [Louis Kotra UREGEI]

National Union for Independence (Union Nationale pour l'Independance) or UNI
Party of Kanak Liberation (Parti de Liberation Kanak) or PALIKA [Paul NEAOUTYINE]
Socialist Kanak Liberation or LKS [Nidoish NAISSELINE]
The Republicans (formerly The Rally or UMP) [Pierre FROGIER]
Union for Caledonia in France

Political pressure groups and leaders: NA

International organization participation: ITUC (NGOs), PIF (associate member), SPC, UPU, WFTU (NGOs), WMO

Diplomatic representation in the US: none (overseas territory of France)

Diplomatic representation from the US: none (overseas territory of France)

Flag description: New Caledonia has two official flags; alongside the flag of France, the Kanak (indigenous Melanesian) flag has equal status; the latter consists of three equal horizontal bands of blue (top), red, and green; a large yellow disk—diameter two-thirds the height of the flag—shifted slightly to the hoist side is edged in black and displays a black fleche faitiere symbol, a native rooftop adornment

National symbol(s): fleche faitiere (native rooftop adornment), kagu bird; national colors: blue, red, green, yellow, black

National anthem: name: "Soyons unis, devenons freres" (Let Us Be United, Let Us Become Brothers)
lyrics/music: Chorale Melodia (a local choir)
note: adopted 2008; contains a mixture of lyrics in both French and Nengone (an indigenous language); as a self-governing territory of France, in addition to the local anthem, "La Marseillaise" is official (see France)

ECONOMY

Economy—overview: New Caledonia has 11% of the world's nickel reserves, representing the second largest reserves on the planet. Only a small amount of the land is suitable for cultivation, and food accounts for about 20% of imports. In addition to nickel, substantial financial support from France—equal to more than 15% of GDP—and tourism are keys to the health of the economy.

During 2009-10, France sent more development assistance to New Caledonia than to any of its other overseas territories. In October 2014, French Prime Minister Manuel VALLS confirmed financial support to New Caledonia totaling $500 million for the period 2016-20. The new government, which inherited a $112 million deficit in 2013, is expected to focus on bringing the territory's budget back into balance.

With the gradual increase in the production of two new nickel plants in 2015, average production of metallurgical goods stood at a record level of 94 thousand tons. However, the sector is exposed to the high volatility of nickel prices. In April 2016, PM VALLS committed $180 million to support

New Caledonia's main nickel company, Societe Le Nickel.

GDP (purchasing power parity): $10.77 billion (2015 est.)
$10.62 billion (2014 est.)
$10.33 billion (2013 est.)
note: data in 2015 dollars
country comparison to the world: 160

GDP (official exchange rate): $15.54 billion (2014 est.)

GDP—real growth rate: 1.4% (2015 est.)
1.3% (2014 est.)
2.2% (2013)
country comparison to the world: 180

GDP—per capita (PPP): $31,100 (2015 est.)
$32,100 (2014 est.)
$29,800 (2012 est.)
country comparison to the world: 63

GDP—composition, by end use:
household consumption: 65%
government consumption: 24.6%
investment in fixed capital: 38.2%
investment in inventories: 0%
exports of goods and services: 18.6%
imports of goods and services: -46.5% (2017 est.)

GDP—composition, by sector of origin:
agriculture: 1.4%
industry: 26.5%
services: 72% (2017 est.)

Agriculture—products: vegetables; beef, venison, other livestock products; fish

Industries: nickel mining and smelting

Industrial production growth rate: 3.5% (2017 est.)
country comparison to the world: 85

Labor force: 119,500 (2016 est.)
country comparison to the world: 182

Labor force—by occupation: *agriculture:* 2.7%
industry: 22.4%
services: 74.9% (2010)

Unemployment rate: 14.7% (2014)
14% (2009)
country comparison to the world: 170

Population below poverty line: 17% (2008)

Household income or consumption by percentage share: *lowest 10%:* NA%
highest 10%: NA%

Budget: *revenues:* $1.995 billion
expenditures: $1.993 billion (2015 est.)
Taxes and other revenues: 12.8% of GDP (2015 est.)
country comparison to the world: 203

Budget surplus (+) or deficit (-): 0% of GDP (2015 est.)
country comparison to the world: 33

Public debt: 6.5% of GDP (2015 est.)
6.5% of GDP (2014 est.)
country comparison to the world: 201

Fiscal year: calendar year

Inflation rate (consumer prices): 1.9% (2017 est.)
0.6% (2016 est.)
country comparison to the world: 83

Stock of domestic credit: $9.522 billion (2015 est.)
country comparison to the world: 108

Market value of publicly traded shares: $NA

Current account balance: -$1.469 billion (2014 est.)
-$1.861 billion (2013 est.)
country comparison to the world: 144

Exports: $2.207 billion (2014 est.)
$1.314 billion (2015 est.)
country comparison to the world: 138

Exports—commodities: ferronickels, nickel ore, fish

Exports—partners: China 30.4%, Japan 15.7%, South Korea 14.7%, France 5%, Belgium 4.5% (2016)

Imports: $4.4 billion (2014 est.)
$2.715 billion (2015 est.)
country comparison to the world: 128

Imports—commodities: machinery and equipment, fuels, chemicals, foodstuffs

Imports—partners: France 25.1%, Singapore 10.1%, China 9.8%, Australia 6.2%, Malaysia 5.9%, South Korea 5.8%, NZ 4.6%, US 4.3% (2016)

Debt—external: $112 million (31 December 2013 est.)
$79 million (31 December 1998 est.)
country comparison to the world: 193

Stock of direct foreign investment—at home: $16.43 billion (2015 est.)
$14.55 billion (2014 est.)
country comparison to the world: 85

Stock of direct foreign investment—abroad: $658.2 million (2015 est.)
$593.8 million (2014 est.)
country comparison to the world: 89

Exchange rates: Comptoirs Francais du Pacifique francs (XPF) per US dollar—
110.2 (2017 est.)
107.84 (2016 est.)
107.84 (2015 est.)
89.85 (2013 est.)
90.56 (2012 est.)

ENERGY

Electricity access: *population without electricity:* 112,895
electrification—*total population:* 59%
electrification—urban areas: 68%
electrification—rural areas: 45% (2012)

Electricity—production: 2.807 billion kWh (2015 est.)
country comparison to the world: 135

Electricity—consumption: 2.611 billion kWh (2015 est.)
country comparison to the world: 140

Electricity—exports: 0 kWh (2016 est.)
country comparison to the world: 174

Electricity—imports: 0 kWh (2016 est.)
country comparison to the world: 178

Electricity—installed generating capacity: 557,200 kW (2015 est.)
country comparison to the world: 142

Electricity—from fossil fuels: 78.4% of total installed capacity (2015 est.)
country comparison to the world: 91

Electricity—from nuclear fuels: 0% of total installed capacity (2015 est.)
country comparison to the world: 150

Electricity—from hydroelectric plants: 14% of total installed capacity (2015 est.)
country comparison to the world: 106

Electricity—from other renewable sources: 7.8% of total installed capacity (2015 est.)
country comparison to the world: 80

Crude oil—production: 0 bbl/day (2016 est.)
country comparison to the world: 180

Crude oil—exports: 0 bbl/day (2014 est.)
country comparison to the world: 168

Crude oil—imports: 0 bbl/day (2014 est.)
country comparison to the world: 167

Crude oil—proved reserves: 0 bbl (1 January 2017 es)
country comparison to the world: 178

Refined petroleum products—production: 0 bbl/day (2014 est.)
country comparison to the world: 186

Refined petroleum products—consumption: 17,000 bbl/day (2015 est.)
country comparison to the world: 145

Refined petroleum products—exports: 116.8 bbl/day (2014 est.)
country comparison to the world: 121

Refined petroleum products—imports: 17,370 bbl/day (2014 est.)
country comparison to the world: 123

Natural gas—production: 0 cu m (2013 est.)
country comparison to the world: 174

Natural gas—consumption: 0 cu m (2013 est.)
country comparison to the world: 213

Natural gas—exports: 0 cu m (2013 est.)
country comparison to the world: 155

Natural gas—imports: 0 cu m (2013 est.)
country comparison to the world: 161

Natural gas—proved reserves: 0 cu m (1 January 2014 es)
country comparison to the world: 176

Carbon dioxide emissions from consumption of energy: 2.5 million Mt (2013 est.)
country comparison to the world: 145

COMMUNICATIONS

Telephones—fixed lines: *total subscriptions:* 92,000
subscriptions per 100 inhabitants: 34 (July 2016 est.)
country comparison to the world: 146

Telephones—mobile cellular: *total:* 246,000
subscriptions per 100 inhabitants: 91 (July 2016 est.)
country comparison to the world: 179

Telephone system: *general assessment:* a submarine cable network connection between New Caledonia and Australia, completed in 2007, increased network capacity and improved high-speed connectivity and access to international networks
domestic: combined fixed-line and mobile-cellular telephone subscribership exceeds 120 per 100 persons
international: country code—687; satellite earth station—1 Intelsat (Pacific Ocean) (2015)

Broadcast media: the publicly owned French Overseas Network (RFO), which operates in France's overseas departments and territories, broadcasts over the RFO Nouvelle Caledonie TV and radio stations; a small number of privately owned radio stations also broadcast (2008)

Internet country code: .nc
Internet users: total: 201,000

percent of population: 74% (July 2016 est.)
country comparison to the world: 159

TRANSPORTATION

National air transport system: *number of registered air carriers:* 2 (registered in France)
inventory of registered aircraft operated by air carriers: 10 (registered in France) (2015)

Airports: 25 (2013)
country comparison to the world: 128

Airports—with paved runways: *total:* 12
over 3,047 m: 1
914 to 1,523 m: 10
under 914 m: 1 (2017)

Airports—with unpaved runways: *total:* 13
914 to 1,523 m: 5
under 914 m: 8 (2013)

Heliports: 8 (2013)

Roadways: *total:* 5,622 km (2006)
country comparison to the world: 151

Merchant marine: *total:* 9
by type: general cargo 2, other 7 (2017)
country comparison to the world: 150

Ports and terminals: *major seaport(s):* Noumea

MILITARY AND SECURITY

Military branches: no regular military forces; French military, police, and gendarmerie (2012)

Military—note: defense is the responsibility of France

TRANSNATIONAL ISSUES

Disputes—international: Matthew and Hunter Islands east of New Caledonia claimed by France and Vanuatu

NEW ZEALAND

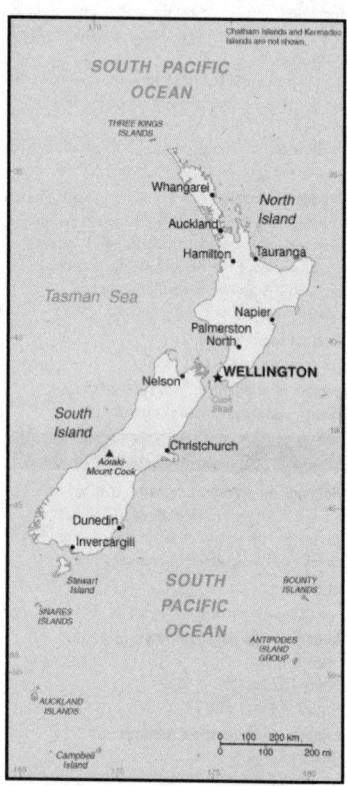

INTRODUCTION

Background: The Polynesian Maori reached New Zealand in about A.D. 800. In 1840, their chieftains entered into a compact with Britain, the Treaty of Waitangi, in which they ceded sovereignty to Queen Victoria while retaining territorial rights. That same year, the British began the first organized colonial settlement. A series of land wars between 1843 and 1872 ended with the defeat of the native peoples. The British colony of New Zealand became an independent dominion in 1907 and supported the UK militarily in both world wars. New Zealand's full participation in a number of defense alliances lapsed by the 1980s. In recent years, the government has sought to address longstanding Maori grievances.

GEOGRAPHY

Location: Oceania, islands in the South Pacific Ocean, southeast of Australia

Geographic coordinates: 41 00 S, 174 00 E

Map references: Oceania

Area: *total:* 268,838 sq km
land: 264,537 sq km

water: 4,301 sq km
note: includes Antipodes Islands, Auckland Islands, Bounty Islands, Campbell Island, Chatham Islands, and Kermadec Islands
country comparison to the world: 77

Area—comparative: almost twice the size of North Carolina; about the size of Colorado

Land boundaries: 0 km

Coastline: 15,134 km

Maritime claims: *territorial sea:* 12 nm
contiguous zone: 24 nm
exclusive economic zone: 200 nm
continental shelf: 200 nm or to the edge of the continental margin

Climate: temperate with sharp regional contrasts

Terrain: predominately mountainous with large coastal plains

Elevation: *mean elevation:* 388 m

elevation extremes: *lowest point:* Pacific Ocean 0 m
highest point: Aoraki-Mount Cook 3,724 m

Natural resources: natural gas, iron ore, sand, coal, timber, hydropower, gold, limestone

Land use: *agricultural land:* 43.2%
arable land: 1.8%;
permanent crops: 0.3%;
permanent pasture: 41.1%
forest: 31.4%
other: 25.4% (2011 est.)
Irrigated land: 7,210 sq km (2012)

Population—distribution: over three-quarters of New Zealanders, including the indigenous Maori, live on the North Island, primarily in urban areas

Natural hazards: earthquakes are common, though usually not severe; volcanic activity
volcanism: significant volcanism on North Island; Ruapehu (2,797 m), which last erupted in 2007, has a history of large eruptions in the past century; Taranaki has the potential to produce dangerous avalanches and lahars; other historically active volcanoes include Okataina, Raoul Island, Tongariro, and White Island

Environment—current issues: deforestation; soil erosion; native flora and fauna hard-hit by invasive species

Environment—international agreements: *party to:* Antarctic-Environmental Protocol, Antarctic-Marine Living Resources, Antarctic Treaty, Biodiversity, Climate Change, Climate Change-Kyoto Protocol, Desertification, Endangered Species, Environmental Modification, Hazardous Wastes, Law of the Sea, Marine Dumping, Ozone Layer Protection, Ship Pollution, Tropical Timber 83, Tropical Timber 94, Wetlands, Whaling
signed, but not ratified: Antarctic Seals, Marine Life Conservation

Geography—note: consists of two main islands and a number of smaller islands; South Island,

the larger main island, is the 12th largest island in the world and is divided along its length by the Southern Alps; North Island is the 14th largest island in the world and is not as mountainous, but it is marked by volcanism; almost 90% of the population lives in cities and over three-quarters on North Island; Wellington is the southernmost national capital in the world

PEOPLE AND SOCIETY

Population: 4,510,327 (July 2017 est.)
country comparison to the world: 126

Nationality: *noun:* New Zealander(s)
adjective: New Zealand

Ethnic groups: European 71.2%, Maori 14.1%, Asian 11.3%, Pacific peoples 7.6%, Middle Eastern, Latin American, African 1.1%, other 1.6%, not stated or unidentified 5.4%
note: based on the 2013 census of the usually resident population; percentages add up to more than 100% because respondents were able to identify more than one ethnic group (2013 est.)

Languages: English (de facto official) 89.8%, Maori (de jure official) 3.5%, Samoan 2%, Hindi 1.6%, French 1.2%, Northern Chinese 1.2%, Yue 1%, other or not stated 20.5%, New Zealand Sign Language (de jure official)
note: shares sum to 120.8% due to multiple responses on census (2013 est.)

Religions: Christian 44.3% (Catholic 11.6%, Anglican 10.8%, Presbyterian and Congregational 7.8%, Methodist 2.4%, Pentecostal 1.8%, other 9.9%), Hindu 2.1%, Buddhist 1.4%, Maori Christian 1.3%, Islam 1.1%, other religion 1.4% (includes Judaism, Spiritualism and New Age religions, Baha'i, Asian religions other than Buddhism), no religion 38.5%, not stated or unidentified 8.2%, objected to answering 4.1%
note: based on the 2013 census of the usually resident population; percentages add up to more than 100% because respondents were able to identify more than one religion (2013 est.)

Age structure: *0-14 years:* 19.69% (male 454,982/female 432,877)
15-24 years: 13.35% (male 309,707/female 292,586)
25-54 years: 39.82% (male 900,374/female 895,615)
55-64 years: 11.89% (male 261,097/female 275,151)
65 years and over: 15.25% (male 318,089/female 369,849) (2017 est.)

Dependency ratios: *total dependency ratio:* 52.9
youth dependency ratio: 30.5
elderly dependency ratio: 22.4
potential support ratio: 4.5 (2015 est.)

Median age: *total:* 37.9 years
male: 37.1 years
female: 38.8 years (2017 est.)
country comparison to the world: 63

Population growth rate: 0.79% (2017 est.)
country comparison to the world: 132

Birth rate: 13.2 births/1,000 population (2017 est.)
country comparison to the world: 150

Death rate: 7.5 deaths/1,000 population (2017 est.)
country comparison to the world: 111

Net migration rate: 2.2 migrant(s)/1,000 population (2017 est.)
country comparison to the world: 44

Population distribution: over three-quarters of New Zealanders, including the indigenous Maori, live on the North Island, primarily in urban areas

Urbanization: *urban population:* 86.4% of total population (2017)
rate of urbanization: 0.98% annual rate of change (2015-20 est.)

Major urban areas—population: Auckland 1.344 million; WELLINGTON (capital) 383,000 (2015)

Sex ratio: *at birth:* 1.05 male(s)/female
0-14 years: 1.05 male(s)/female
15-24 years: 1.06 male(s)/female
25-54 years: 1 male(s)/female
55-64 years: 0.95 male(s)/female
65 years and over: 0.86 male(s)/female
total population: 0.99 male(s)/female (2016 est.)

Mother's mean age at first birth: 27.8 years
note: median age at first birth (2009 est.)

Maternal mortality ratio: 11 deaths/100,000 live births (2015 est.)
country comparison to the world: 144

Infant mortality rate: *total:* 4.4 deaths/1,000 live births
male: 4.9 deaths/1,000 live births
female: 3.9 deaths/1,000 live births (2017 est.)
country comparison to the world: 183

Life expectancy at birth: *total population:* 81.3 years
male: 79.1 years
female: 83.5 years (2017 est.)
country comparison to the world: 27

Total fertility rate: 2.02 children born/woman (2017 est.)
country comparison to the world: 116

Health expenditures: 11% of GDP (2014)
country comparison to the world: 14

Physicians density: 2.85 physicians/1,000 population (2014)

Hospital bed density: 2.3 beds/1,000 population (2011)

Drinking water source:
improved:
urban: 100% of population
rural: 100% of population
total: 100% of population
unimproved:
urban: 0% of population
rural: 0% of population
total: 0% of population (2015 est.)

HIV/AIDS—adult prevalence rate: NA

HIV/AIDS—people living with HIV/AIDS: NA

HIV/AIDS—deaths: NA

Obesity—adult prevalence rate: 30.8% (2016)
country comparison to the world: 22

Education expenditures: 6.3% of GDP (2014)
country comparison to the world: 16

School life expectancy (primary to tertiary education): *total:* 19 years
male: 18 years
female: 20 years (2014)

Unemployment, youth ages 15-24: *total:* 13.2%
male: 13.1%
female: 13.4% (2016 est.)
country comparison to the world: 64

GOVERNMENT

Country name: *conventional long form:* none
conventional short form: New Zealand
abbreviation: NZ
etymology: Dutch explorer Abel TASMAN was the first European to reach New Zealand in 1642; he named it Staten Landt, but Dutch cartographers renamed it Nova Zeelandia in 1645 after the Dutch province of Zeeland; British explorer Captain James COOK subsequently anglicized the name to New Zealand when he mapped the islands in 1769

Government type: parliamentary democracy (New Zealand Parliament) under a constitutional monarchy; a Commonwealth realm

Capital: *name:* Wellington
geographic coordinates: 41 18 S, 174 47 E
time difference: UTC+12 (17 hours ahead of Washington, DC, during Standard Time)
daylight saving time: +1hr, begins last Sunday in September; ends first Sunday in April
note: New Zealand has two time zones—New Zealand standard time (12 hours in advance of UTC), and Chatham Islands time (45 minutes in advance of New Zealand standard time)

Administrative divisions: 16 regions and 1 territory*; Auckland, Bay of Plenty, Canterbury, Chatham Islands*, Gisborne, Hawke's Bay, Manawatu-Wanganui, Marlborough, Nelson, Northland, Otago, Southland, Taranaki, Tasman, Waikato, Wellington, West Coast

Dependent areas: Cook Islands, Niue, Tokelau

Independence: 26 September 1907 (from the UK)

National holiday: Waitangi Day (Treaty of Waitangi established British sovereignty over New Zealand), 6 February (1840); ANZAC Day (commemorated as the anniversary of the landing of troops of the Australian and New Zealand Army Corps during World War I at Gallipoli, Turkey), 25 April (1915)

Constitution: Constitution Act 1986 (the principal formal charter) adopted and effective 1 January 1987; amended 1999, 2005, 2014 (2016)

Legal system: common law system, based on English model, with special legislation and land courts for the Maori

International law organization participation: accepts compulsory ICJ jurisdiction with reservations; accepts ICCt jurisdiction

Citizenship: *citizenship by birth:* no
citizenship by descent only: at least one parent must be a citizen of New Zealand
dual citizenship recognized: yes
residency requirement for naturalization: 3 years

Suffrage: 18 years of age; universal

Executive branch: *chief of state:* Queen ELIZABETH II (since 6 February 1952); represented by Governor General Dame Patricia Lee REDDY (since 28 September 2016)

head of government: Prime Minister Jacinda ARDERN (since 26 October 2017); Deputy Prime Minister Winston PETERS (since 26 October 2017)

cabinet: Executive Council appointed by the governor general on the recommendation of the prime minister

elections/appointments: the monarchy is hereditary; governor general appointed by the monarch; following legislative elections, the leader of the majority party or majority coalition usually appointed prime minister by the governor general; deputy prime minister appointed by the governor general; note—Prime Minister ARDERN heads up a minority coalition government consisting of the Labor and New Zealand First parties with support from the Green Party

Legislative branch: *description:* unicameral House of Representatives—commonly called Parliament (usually 120 seats; 70 members directly elected in single-seat constituencies, including 7 Maori constituencies, by simple majority vote and 50 directly elected by proportional representation vote; members serve 3-year terms)
elections: last held on 23 September 2017 (next to be held in September 2020)
election results: percent of vote by party—National Party 46%, Labor Party 35.9%, NZ First 7.5%, Green Party 5.9%, ACT Party .5%; seats by party—National Party 56, Labor Party 46, NZ First 9, Green Party 8, ACT Party 1

Judicial branch: *highest court(s):* Supreme Court (consists of 5 justices including the chief justice); note—the Supreme Court in 2004 replaced the Judicial Committee of the Privy Council (in London) as the final appeals court
judge selection and term of office: justices appointed by the governor-general on the recommendation of the attorney-general; justices appointed for life
subordinate courts: Court of Appeal; High Court; tribunals and authorities; district courts; specialized courts for issues related to employment, environment, Maori lands, and military

Political parties and leaders: ACT New Zealand [David SEYMOUR]
Green Party [James SHAW]
Mana Movement [Hone HARAWIRA] (formerly Mana Party)
Maori Party [Marama FOX]
New Zealand First Party or NZ First [Winston PETERS]
New Zealand Labor Party [Jacinda ARDERN]
New Zealand National Party [Bill ENGLISH]

United Future New Zealand [Damian LIGHT]

Political pressure groups and leaders: Women's Electoral Lobby or WEL

other: apartheid groups; civil rights groups; farmers groups; Maori; nuclear weapons groups; women's rights groups

International organization participation: ADB, ANZUS (US suspended security obligations to NZ on 11 August 1986), APEC, ARF, ASEAN (dialogue partner), Australia Group, BIS, C, CD, CP, EAS, EBRD, FAO, FATF, IAEA, IBRD, ICAO, ICC (national committees), ICCt, ICRM, IDA, IEA, IFAD, IFC, IFRCS, IHO, ILO, IMF, IMO, IMSO, Interpol, IOC, IOM, IPU, ISO, ITSO, ITU, ITUC (NGOs), MIGA, NSG, OECD, OPCW, Pacific Alliance (observer), Paris Club (associate), PCA, PIF, SICA (observer), Sparteca, SPC, UN, UNCTAD, UNESCO, UNHCR, UNIDO, UNMISS, UNTSO, UPU, WCO, WFTU (NGOs), WHO, WIPO, WMO, WTO

Diplomatic representation in the US: *chief of mission:* Ambassador Timothy John GROSER (since 28 January 2016)

chancery: 37 Observatory Circle NW, Washington, DC 20008

telephone: [1] (202) 328-4800

FAX: [1] (202) 667-5227[1] (202) 667-5227

consulate(s) general: Honolulu (HI), Los Angeles, New York

Diplomatic representation from the US: *chief of mission:* Ambassador Scott P. BROWN (since 27 June 2017) note—also accredited to Samoa

embassy: 29 Fitzherbert Terrace, Thorndon, Wellington

mailing address: P. O. Box 1190, Wellington; PSC 467, Box 1, APO AP 96531-1034

telephone: [64] (4) 462-6000

FAX: [64] (4) 499-0490

consulate(s) general: Auckland

Flag description: blue with the flag of the UK in the upper hoist-side quadrant with four red five-pointed stars edged in white centered in the outer half of the flag; the stars represent the Southern Cross constellation

National symbol(s): Southern Cross constellation (four, five-pointed stars), kiwi (bird), silver fern; national colors: black, white, red (ochre)

National anthem: *name:* "God Defend New Zealand"

lyrics/music: Thomas BRACKEN [English], Thomas Henry SMITH [Maori]/John Joseph WOODS

note: adopted 1940 as national song, adopted 1977 as co-national anthem; New Zealand has two national anthems with equal status; as a commonwealth realm, in addition to "God Defend New Zealand," "God Save the Queen" serves as a national anthem (see United Kingdom); "God Save the Queen" normally played only when a member of the royal family or the governor-general is present; in all other cases, "God Defend New Zealand" is played

ECONOMY

Economy—overview: Over the past 40 years, the government has transformed New Zealand from an agrarian economy, dependent on concessionary British market access, to a more industrialized, free market economy that can compete globally. This dynamic growth has boosted real incomes, but left behind some at the bottom of the ladder and broadened and deepened the technological capabilities of the industrial sector.

Per capita income rose for 10 consecutive years until 2007 in purchasing power parity terms, but fell in 2008-09. Debt-driven consumer spending drove robust growth in the first half of the decade, fueling a large balance of payments deficit that posed a challenge for policymakers. Inflationary pressures caused the central bank to raise its key rate steadily from January 2004 until it was among the highest in the OECD in 2007 and 2008. The higher rate attracted international capital inflows, which strengthened the currency and housing market while aggravating the current account deficit. Rising house prices, especially in Auckland, have become a political issue in recent years, as well as a policy challenge in 2016 and 2017, as the ability to afford housing has declined for many.

Expanding New Zealand's network of free trade agreements remains a top foreign policy priority. New Zealand was an early promoter of the Trans-Pacific Partnership (TPP) and was the second country to ratify the agreement in May 2017. Following the United States' withdrawal from the TPP in January 2017, on 10 November 2017 the remaining 11 countries agreed on the core elements of a modified agreement, which they renamed the Comprehensive and Progressive Agreement for Trans-Pacific Partnership (CPTPP). In November 2016, New Zealand opened negotiations to \ upgrade its FTA with China; China is one of New Zealand's most important trading partners.

GDP (purchasing power parity): $185.7 billion (2017 est.)

$179.5 billion (2016 est.)

$173.3 billion (2015 est.)

note: data in 2017 dollars

country comparison to the world: 70

GDP (official exchange rate): $200.8 billion (2016 est.)

GDP—real growth rate: 3.5% (2017 est.)

3.6% (2016 est.)

3.2% (2015 est.)

country comparison to the world: 95

GDP—per capita (PPP): $38,500 (2017 est.)

$37,800 (2016 est.)

$37,300 (2015 est.)

note: data are in 2017 dollars

country comparison to the world: 47

Gross national saving: 21.1% of GDP (2017 est.)

20.5% of GDP (2016 est.)

20.1% of GDP (2015 est.)

country comparison to the world: 82

GDP—composition, by end use:

household consumption: 57.1%

government consumption: 18.4%

investment in fixed capital: 23.2%

investment in inventories: 0.3%

exports of goods and services: 27.4%

imports of goods and services: -26.4% (2017 est.)

GDP—composition, by sector of origin:

agriculture: 3.9%

industry: 26.2%

services: 69.9% (2017 est.)

Agriculture—products: dairy products, sheep, beef, poultry, fruit, vegetables, wine, seafood, wheat and barley

Industries: agriculture, forestry, fishing, logs and wood articles, manufacturing, mining, construction, financial services, real estate services, tourism

Industrial production growth rate: 2.5% (2017 est.)

country comparison to the world: 112

Labor force: 2.655 million (2017 est.)

country comparison to the world: 114

Labor force—by occupation: *agriculture:* 7%

industry: 19%

services: 74% (2006 est.)

Unemployment rate: 4.9% (2017 est.)

5.1% (2016 est.)

country comparison to the world: 67

Population below poverty line: NA%

Household income or consumption by percentage share: *lowest 10%:* NA%

highest 10%: NA%

Distribution of family income—Gini index: 36.2 (1997)

country comparison to the world: 87

Budget: *revenues:* $73.2 billion

expenditures: $71.9 billion (2017 est.)

Taxes and other revenues: 36.4% of GDP (2017 est.)

country comparison to the world: 49

Budget surplus (+) or deficit (-): 0.7% of GDP (2017 est.)

country comparison to the world: 21

Public debt: 32% of GDP (2017 est.)

33.3% of GDP (2016 est.)

country comparison to the world: 158

Fiscal year: 1 April—31 March

note: this is the fiscal year for tax purposes

Inflation rate (consumer prices): 2.2% (2017 est.)

0.6% (2016 est.)

country comparison to the world: 105

Central bank discount rate: 2.5% (31 December 2009)

5% (31 December 2008)

country comparison to the world: 113

Commercial bank prime lending rate: 4.9% (31 December 2017 est.)

5.02% (31 December 2016 est.)

country comparison to the world: 147

Stock of narrow money: $44.4 billion (31 December 2017 est.)

$42.01 billion (31 December 2016 est.)

country comparison to the world: 56

Stock of broad money: $199.9 billion (31 December 2017 est.)

$190 billion (31 December 2016 est.)

country comparison to the world: 40

Stock of domestic credit: $300.9 billion (31 December 2017 est.)

$284.7 billion (31 December 2016 est.)
country comparison to the world: 38

Market value of publicly traded shares: $74.35 billion (31 December 2015 est.)
$74.42 billion (31 December 2014 est.)
$65.96 billion (31 December 2013 est.)
country comparison to the world: 45

Current account balance: -$7.17 billion (2017 est.)
-$5.013 billion (2016 est.)
country comparison to the world: 181

Exports: $37.35 billion (2017 est.)
$33.61 billion (2016 est.)
country comparison to the world: 55

Exports—commodities: dairy products, meat and edible offal, logs and wood articles, fruit, crude oil, wine

Exports—partners: China 19.4%, Australia 17.1%, US 10.9%, Japan 6.2% (2016)

Imports: $38.74 billion (2017 est.)
$35.53 billion (2016 est.)
country comparison to the world: 58

Imports—commodities: petroleum and products, mechanical machinery, vehicles and parts, electrical machinery, textiles

Imports—partners: China 19.9%, Australia 12.6%, US 11.3%, Japan 7.1%, Germany 4.8%, Thailand 4.5%, South Korea 4.2% (2016)

Reserves of foreign exchange and gold: $18.32 billion (31 December 2017 est.)
$17.81 billion (31 December 2016 est.)
country comparison to the world: 63

Debt—external: $88.08 billion (31 December 2017 est.)
$84.03 billion (31 December 2016 est.)
country comparison to the world: 54

Stock of direct foreign investment—at home: $78.25 billion (31 December 2017 est.)
$77.31 billion (31 December 2016 est.)
country comparison to the world: 52

Stock of direct foreign investment—abroad: $59.08 billion (31 December 2009)
country comparison to the world: 41

Exchange rates: New Zealand dollars (NZD) per US dollar—
1.416 (2017 est.)
1.4341 (2016 est.)
1.4341 (2015 est.)
1.4279 (2014 est.)
1.2039 (2013 est.)

ENERGY

Electricity access: electrification—*total population:* 100% (2016)

Electricity—production: 42.77 billion kWh (2015 est.)
country comparison to the world: 58

Electricity—consumption: 39.93 billion kWh (2015 est.)
country comparison to the world: 57

Electricity—exports: 0 kWh (2016 est.)
country comparison to the world: 181

Electricity—imports: 0 kWh (2016 est.)
country comparison to the world: 184

Electricity—installed generating capacity: 9.454 million kW (2015 est.)
country comparison to the world: 65

Electricity—from fossil fuels: 24% of total installed capacity (2015 est.)
country comparison to the world: 191

Electricity—from nuclear fuels: 0% of total installed capacity (2015 est.)
country comparison to the world: 160

Electricity—from hydroelectric plants: 56.5% of total installed capacity (2015 est.)
country comparison to the world: 31

Electricity—from other renewable sources: 19.7% of total installed capacity (2015 est.)
country comparison to the world: 31

Crude oil—production: 34,730 bbl/day (2016 est.)
country comparison to the world: 60

Crude oil—exports: 30,560 bbl/day (2016 est.)
country comparison to the world: 49

Crude oil—imports: 109,200 bbl/day (2016 est.)
country comparison to the world: 42

Crude oil—proved reserves: 56.9 million bbl (1 January 2017 es)
country comparison to the world: 79

Refined petroleum products—production: 117,100 bbl/day (2016 est.)
country comparison to the world: 65

Refined petroleum products—consumption: 167,700 bbl/day (2016 est.)
country comparison to the world: 63

Refined petroleum products—exports: 3,863 bbl/day (2016 est.)
country comparison to the world: 102

Refined petroleum products—imports: 54,750 bbl/day (2016 est.)
country comparison to the world: 78

Natural gas—production: 4.954 billion cu m (2015 est.)
country comparison to the world: 51

Natural gas—consumption: 9.08 billion cu m (2015 est.)
country comparison to the world: 56

Natural gas—exports: 0 cu m (2014 est.)
country comparison to the world: 163

Natural gas—imports: 0 cu m (2014 est.)
country comparison to the world: 171

Natural gas—proved reserves: 35.88 billion cu m (1 January 2017 es)
country comparison to the world: 69

Carbon dioxide emissions from consumption of energy: 37 million Mt (2013 est.)
country comparison to the world: 72

COMMUNICATIONS

Telephones—fixed lines: *total subscriptions:* 1.82 million
subscriptions per 100 inhabitants: 41 (July 2016 est.)
country comparison to the world: 62

Telephones—mobile cellular: *total:* 5.8 million
subscriptions per 100 inhabitants: 130 (July 2016 est.)
country comparison to the world: 116

Telephone system: *general assessment:* excellent domestic and international systems
domestic: combined fixed-line and mobile-cellular telephone subscribership exceeds 170 per 100 persons
international: country code—64; the Southern Cross submarine cable system provides links to Australia, Fiji, and the US; satellite earth stations—8 (1 Inmarsat—Pacific Ocean, 7 other) (2016)

Broadcast media: state-owned Television New Zealand operates multiple TV networks and state-owned Radio New Zealand operates 3 radio networks and an external shortwave radio service to the South Pacific region; a small number of national commercial TV and radio stations and many regional commercial television and radio stations are available; cable and satellite TV systems are available (2008)

Internet country code: .nz
Internet users: total: 3,958,642

percent of population: 88.5% (July 2016 est.)
country comparison to the world: 77

TRANSPORTATION

National air transport system: *number of registered air carriers:* 6
inventory of registered aircraft operated by air carriers: 123
annual passenger traffic on registered air carriers: 15,304,409
annual freight traffic on registered air carriers: 999,384,961 mt-km (2015)
Civil aircraft registration country code prefix: ZK (2016)

Airports: 123 (2013)
country comparison to the world: 48

Airports—with paved runways: *total:* 39
over 3,047 m: 2
2,438 to 3,047 m: 1
1,524 to 2,437 m: 12
914 to 1,523 m: 23
under 914 m: 1 (2017)

Airports—with unpaved runways: *total:* 84
1,524 to 2,437 m: 3
914 to 1,523 m: 33
under 914 m: 48 (2013)

Pipelines: condensate 331 km; gas 1,936 km; liquid petroleum gas 172 km; oil 288 km; refined products 198 km (2013)

Railways: *total:* 4,128 km
narrow gauge: 4,128 km 1.067-m gauge (503 km electrified) (2014)
country comparison to the world: 42

Roadways: *total:* 94,902 km
paved: 62,759 km (includes 199 km of expressways)
unpaved: 32,143 km (2012)
country comparison to the world: 52

Merchant marine: *total:* 103

by type: general cargo 16, oil tanker 4, other 83 (2017)

country comparison to the world: 83

Ports and terminals: *major seaport(s):* Auckland, Lyttelton, Manukau Harbor, Marsden Point, Tauranga, Wellington

MILITARY AND SECURITY

Military expenditures: 1.13% of GDP (2016)
1.11% of GDP (2015)

1.13% of GDP (2014)
1.12% of GDP (2013)
1.19% of GDP (2012)
country comparison to the world: 87

Military branches: New Zealand Defense Force (NZDF): New Zealand Army, Royal New Zealand Navy, Royal New Zealand Air Force (Te Hokowhitu o Kahurangi, RNZAF) (2013)

Military service age and obligation: 17 years of age for voluntary military service; soldiers cannot be

deployed until the age of 18; no conscription; 3 years of secondary education required; must be a citizen of NZ, the UK, Australia, Canada, or the US, and resident of NZ for the previous 5 years (2013)

TRANSNATIONAL ISSUES

Disputes—international: asserts a territorial claim in Antarctica (Ross Dependency)

Illicit drugs: significant consumer of amphetamines

NICARAGUA

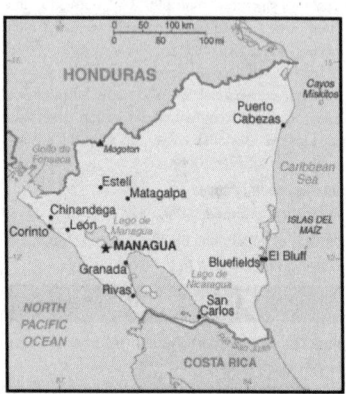

INTRODUCTION

Background: The Pacific coast of Nicaragua was settled as a Spanish colony from Panama in the early 16th century. Independence from Spain was declared in 1821 and the country became an independent republic in 1838. Britain occupied the Caribbean Coast in the first half of the 19th century, but gradually ceded control of the region in subsequent decades. Violent opposition to governmental manipulation and corruption spread to all classes by 1978 and resulted in a short-lived civil war that brought the Marxist Sandinista guerrillas led by Daniel ORTEGA Saavedra to power in 1979. Nicaraguan aid to leftist rebels in El Salvador prompted the US to sponsor anti-Sandinista contra guerrillas through much of the 1980s. After losing free and fair elections in 1990, 1996, and 2001, former Sandinista President Daniel ORTEGA was elected president in 2006, 2011, and most recently in 2016. Municipal, regional, and national-level elections since 2008 have been marred by widespread irregularities. Nicaragua's infrastructure and economy—hard hit by the earlier civil war and by Hurricane Mitch in 1998—are being rebuilt, but democratic institutions have weakened under the ORTEGA administration as the president has garnered full control over all four branches of government: the presidency, the judicial, the National Assembly, and the Supreme Electoral Council.

GEOGRAPHY

Location: Central America, bordering both the Caribbean Sea and the North Pacific Ocean, between Costa Rica and Honduras

Geographic coordinates: 13 00 N, 85 00 W

Map references: Central America and the Caribbean

Area: *total:* 130,370 sq km
land: 119,990 sq km
water: 10,380 sq km
country comparison to the world: 99

Area—comparative: slightly larger than Pennsylvania; slightly smaller than New York state

Land boundaries: *total:* 1,253 km
border countries (2): Costa Rica 313 km, Honduras 940 km

Coastline: 910 km

Maritime claims: *territorial sea:* 12 nm
contiguous zone: 24 nm
continental shelf: natural prolongation

Climate: tropical in lowlands, cooler in highlands

Terrain: extensive Atlantic coastal plains rising to central interior mountains; narrow Pacific coastal plain interrupted by volcanoes

Elevation: *mean elevation:* 298 m

elevation extremes: *lowest point:* Pacific Ocean 0 m
highest point: Mogoton 2,085 m

Natural resources: gold, silver, copper, tungsten, lead, zinc, timber, fish

Land use: *agricultural land:* 42.2%
arable land: 12.5%;
permanent crops: 2.5%;
permanent pasture: 27.2%
forest: 25.3%
other: 32.5% (2011 est.)
Irrigated land: 1,990 sq km (2012)

Population—distribution: the overwhelming majority of the population resides in the western half of the country, with much of the urban growth centered in the capital city of Managua; coastal areas also show large population clusters

Natural hazards: destructive earthquakes; volcanoes; landslides; extremely susceptible to hurricanes

volcanism: significant volcanic activity; Cerro Negro (728 m), which last erupted in 1999, is one of Nicaragua's most active volcanoes; its lava flows and ash have been known to cause significant damage to farmland and buildings; other historically active volcanoes include Concepcion, Cosiguina, Las Pilas, Masaya, Momotombo, San Cristobal, and Telica

Environment—current issues: deforestation; soil erosion; water pollution

Environment—international agreements: *party to:* Biodiversity, Climate Change, Climate Change-Kyoto Protocol, Desertification, Endangered Species, Environmental Modification, Hazardous Wastes, Law of the Sea, Ozone Layer Protection, Ship Pollution, Wetlands, Whaling
signed, but not ratified: none of the selected agreements

Geography—note: largest country in Central America; contains the largest freshwater body in Central America, Lago de Nicaragua

PEOPLE AND SOCIETY

Population: 6,025,951 (July 2017 est.)
country comparison to the world: 111

Nationality: *noun:* Nicaraguan(s)
adjective: Nicaraguan

Ethnic groups: mestizo (mixed Amerindian and white) 69%, white 17%, black 9%, Amerindian 5%

Languages: Spanish (official) 95.3%, Miskito 2.2%, Mestizo of the Caribbean coast 2%, other 0.5%
note: English and indigenous languages found on the Caribbean coast (2005 est.)

Religions: Roman Catholic 51.6%, Evangelical 33.9%, other 1.5%, unspecified 12.9%, none 0.2% (2016 est.)

Demographic profile: Despite being one of the poorest countries in Latin America, Nicaragua has improved its access to potable water and sanitation and has ameliorated its life expectancy, infant and child mortality, and immunization rates. However, income distribution is very uneven, and the poor, agriculturalists, and indigenous people continue to have less access to healthcare services. Nicaragua's total fertility rate has fallen from around 6 children per woman in 1980 to below replacement level today, but the high birth rate among adolescents perpetuates a cycle of poverty and low educational attainment.

Nicaraguans emigrate primarily to Costa Rica and to a lesser extent the United States. Nicaraguan men have been migrating seasonally to Costa Rica to harvest bananas and coffee since the early 20th century. Political turmoil, civil war, and natural disasters from the 1970s through the 1990s dramatically increased the flow of refugees and permanent migrants seeking jobs, higher wages, and better social and healthcare benefits. Since 2000, Nicaraguan emigration to Costa Rica has slowed and stabilized. Today roughly 300,000 Nicaraguans are permanent residents of Costa Rica—about 75% of the foreign population—and thousands more migrate seasonally for work, many illegally.

Age structure: *0-14 years:* 27.24% (male 837,465/female 803,985)
15-24 years: 21.26% (male 644,153/female 636,787)
25-54 years: 40.24% (male 1,149,747/female 1,274,818)
55-64 years: 5.98% (male 166,782/female 193,781)
65 years and over: 5.28% (male 141,816/female 176,617) (2017 est.)

Dependency ratios: *total dependency ratio:* 54.1
youth dependency ratio: 46.3
elderly dependency ratio: 7.8
potential support ratio: 12.8 (2015 est.)

Median age: *total:* 25.7 years
male: 24.8 years
female: 26.6 years (2017 est.)
country comparison to the world: 154

Population growth rate: 0.98% (2017 est.)
country comparison to the world: 116

Birth rate: 17.7 births/1,000 population (2017 est.)
country comparison to the world: 104

Death rate: 5.1 deaths/1,000 population (2017 est.)
country comparison to the world: 189

Net migration rate: -2.7 migrant(s)/1,000 population (2017 est.)
country comparison to the world: 171

Population distribution: the overwhelming majority of the population resides in the western half of the country, with much of the urban growth centered in the capital city of Managua; coastal areas also show large population clusters

Urbanization: *urban population:* 59.4% of total population (2017)
rate of urbanization: 1.84% annual rate of change (2015-20 est.)

Major urban areas—population: MANAGUA (capital) 956,000 (2015)

Sex ratio: *at birth:* 1.05 male(s)/female
0-14 years: 1.04 male(s)/female
15-24 years: 1.01 male(s)/female
25-54 years: 0.9 male(s)/female
55-64 years: 0.86 male(s)/female
65 years and over: 0.81 male(s)/female

total population: 0.95 male(s)/female (2016 est.)
Mother's mean age at first birth: 19.2 years
note: median age at first birth among women 25-29 (2011/12 est.)

Maternal mortality ratio: 150 deaths/100,000 live births (2015 est.)
country comparison to the world: 60

Infant mortality rate: *total:* 18.3 deaths/1,000 live births
male: 21.1 deaths/1,000 live births
female: 15.5 deaths/1,000 live births (2017 est.)
country comparison to the world: 89

Life expectancy at birth: *total population:* 73.5 years
male: 71.3 years
female: 75.8 years (2017 est.)
country comparison to the world: 133

Total fertility rate: 1.89 children born/woman (2017 est.)
country comparison to the world: 138

Contraceptive prevalence rate: 80.4% (2011/12)

Health expenditures: 9% of GDP (2014)
country comparison to the world: 41

Physicians density: 0.91 physicians/1,000 population (2014)

Hospital bed density: 0.9 beds/1,000 population (2012)

Drinking water source:
improved:
urban: 99.3% of population
rural: 69.4% of population
total: 87% of population
unimproved:
urban: 0.7% of population
rural: 30.6% of population
total: 13% of population (2015 est.)

Sanitation facility access:
improved:
urban: 76.5% of population
rural: 55.7% of population
total: 67.9% of population
unimproved:
urban: 23.5% of population
rural: 44.3% of population
total: 32.1% of population (2015 est.)

HIV/AIDS—adult prevalence rate: 0.2% (2016 est.)
country comparison to the world: 96

HIV/AIDS—people living with HIV/AIDS: 8,900 (2016 est.)
country comparison to the world: 97

HIV/AIDS—deaths: <500 (2016 est.)

Major infectious diseases: *degree of risk:* high
food or waterborne diseases: bacterial diarrhea, hepatitis A, and typhoid fever
vectorborne disease: dengue fever and malaria
note: active local transmission of Zika virus by Aedes species mosquitoes has been identified in this country (as of August 2016); it poses an important risk (a large number of cases possible) among US citizens if bitten by an infective mosquito; other less common ways to get Zika are

through sex, via blood transfusion, or during pregnancy, in which the pregnant woman passes Zika virus to her fetus (2016)

Obesity—adult prevalence rate: 23.7% (2016)
country comparison to the world: 63

Education expenditures: 4.5% of GDP (2010)
country comparison to the world: 88

Literacy: *definition:* age 15 and over can read and write
total population: 82.8%
male: 82.4%
female: 83.2% (2015 est.)

Unemployment, youth ages 15-24: *total:* 11.9%
male: 9.8%
female: 15.6% (2010 est.)
country comparison to the world: 110

GOVERNMENT

Country name: *conventional long form:* Republic of Nicaragua
conventional short form: Nicaragua
local long form: Republica de Nicaragua
local short form: Nicaragua
etymology: Nicarao was the name of the largest indigenous settlement at the time of Spanish arrival; conquistador Gil GONZALEZ Davila, who explored the area (1622-23), combined the name of the community with the Spanish word "agua" (water), referring to the two large lakes in the west of the country (Lake Managua and Lake Nicaragua)

Government type: presidential republic

Capital: *name:* Managua
geographic coordinates: 12 08 N, 86 15 W
time difference: UTC-6 (1 hour behind Washington, DC, during Standard Time)

Administrative divisions: 15 departments (departamentos, singular—departamento) and 2 autonomous regions* (regiones autonomistas, singular—region autonoma); Boaco, Carazo, Chinandega, Chontales, Costa Caribe Norte*, Costa Caribe Sur*, Esteli, Granada, Jinotega, Leon, Madriz, Managua, Masaya, Matagalpa, Nueva Segovia, Rio San Juan, Rivas

Independence: 15 September 1821 (from Spain)

National holiday: Independence Day, 15 September (1821)

Constitution: several previous; latest adopted 19 November 1986, effective 9 January 1987; amended several times, last in 2014 (2016)

Legal system: civil law system; Supreme Court may review administrative acts

International law organization participation: accepts compulsory ICJ jurisdiction with reservations; non-party state to the ICCt

Citizenship: *citizenship by birth:* yes
citizenship by descent: yes
dual citizenship recognized: no, except in cases where bilateral agreements exist
residency requirement for naturalization: 4 years

Suffrage: 16 years of age; universal

Executive branch: *chief of state:* President Jose Daniel ORTEGA Saavedra (since 10 January 2007); Vice President Rosario MURILLO Zambrana (since 10 January 2017); note—the president is both chief of state and head of government

head of government: President Jose Daniel ORTEGA Saavedra (since 10 January 2007); Vice President Rosario MURILLO Zambrana (since 10 January 2017)

cabinet: Council of Ministers appointed by the president

elections/appointments: president and vice president directly elected on the same ballot by simple majority popular vote for a 5-year term (no term limits); election last held on 6 November 2016 (next to be held by November 2021)

election results: Jose Daniel ORTEGA Saavedra reelected president; percent of vote—Jose Daniel ORTEGA Saavedra (FSLN) 72.4%, Maximino RODRIGUEZ (PLC) 15%, Jose del Carmen ALVARADO (PLI) 4.5%, Saturnino CERRATO Hodgson (ALN) 4.3%, other 3.7%

Legislative branch: *description:* unicameral National Assembly or Asamblea Nacional (92 seats; 70 members in multi-seat constituencies and 20 members in a single nationwide constituency directly elected by proportional representation vote; 2 seats reserved for the previous president and the runner-up candidate in the previous presidential election; members serve 5-year terms;)

elections: last held on 6 November 2016 (next to be held by November 2021)

election results: percent of vote by party—NA; seats by party—FSLN 70, PLC 13, ALN 2, PLI 2, APRE 1, PC 1, YATAMA 1

Judicial branch: *highest court(s):* Supreme Court or Corte Suprema de Justicia (consists of 16 judges organized into administrative, civil, criminal, and constitutional chambers)

judge selection and term of office: Supreme Court judges elected by the National Assembly to serve 5-year staggered terms

subordinate courts: Appeals Court; first instance civil, criminal, and military courts

Political parties and leaders: Alliance for the Republic or APRE [Carlos CANALES]
Conservative Party or PC [Alfredo CESAR]
Independent Liberal Party or PLI [Jose del Carmen ALVARADO]
Liberal Constitutionalist Party or PLC [Maria Haydee OSUNA]
Nicaraguan Liberal Alliance or ALN [Alejandro MEJIA Ferreti]
Sandinista National Liberation Front or FSLN [Jose Daniel ORTEGA Saavedra]
Sandinista Renovation Movement or MRS [Ana Margarita VIJIL]
Sons of Mother Earth or YATAMA [Brooklin RIVERA]

Political pressure groups and leaders: National Workers Front or FNT (a Sandinista umbrella group—includes Farm Workers Association or ATC, Health Workers Federation or FETASALUD, Heroes and Martyrs Confederation of Professional Associations or CONAPRO,

National Association of Educators of Nicaragua or –ANDEN, National Union of Employees or UNE, National Union of Farmers and Ranchers or UNAG, Sandinista Workers Central or CST, and Union of Journalists of Nicaragua or UPN)
Nicaraguan Workers' Central or CTN (independent labor union)
Permanent Congress of Workers or CPT (umbrella group of non-Sandinista labor unions—includes Autonomous Nicaraguan Workers Central or CTN-A, Confederation of Labor Unification or CUS, Independent General Confederation of Labor or CGT-I, Labor Action and Unity Central or CAUS)
Superior Council of Private Enterprise or COSEP (a confederation of business groups)

International organization participation: BCIE, CACM, CD, CELAC, FAO, G-77, IADB, IAEA, IBRD, ICAO, ICRM, IDA, IFAD, IFC, IFRCS, ILO, IMF, IMO, Interpol, IOC, IOM, IPU, ISO (correspondent), ITSO, ITU, ITUC (NGOs), LAES, LAIA (observer), MIGA, NAM, OAS, OPANAL, OPCW, PCA, Petrocaribe, SICA, UN, UNCTAD, UNESCO, UNHCR, UNIDO, Union Latina, UNWTO, UPU, WCO, WHO, WIPO, WMO, WTO

Diplomatic representation in the US: *chief of mission:* Ambassador Francisco Obadiah CAMPBELL Hooker (since 28 June 2010)
chancery: 1627 New Hampshire Avenue NW, Washington, DC 20009
telephone: [1] (202) 939-6570, 6573
FAX: [1] (202) 939-6545
consulate(s) general: Houston, Los Angeles, Miami, New York, San Francisco

Diplomatic representation from the US: *chief of mission:* Ambassador Laura Farnsworth DOGU (since 9 November 2015)
embassy: Kilometer 5.5 Carretera Sur, Managua
mailing address: American Embassy Managua, APO AA 34021
telephone: [505] 2252-7100, 2252-7888; 2252-7634 (after hours)
FAX: [505] 2252-7250

Flag description: three equal horizontal bands of blue (top), white, and blue with the national coat of arms centered in the white band; the coat of arms features a triangle encircled by the words REPUBLICA DE NICARAGUA on the top and AMERICA CENTRAL on the bottom; the banner is based on the former blue-white-blue flag of the Federal Republic of Central America; the blue bands symbolize the Pacific Ocean and the Caribbean Sea, while the white band represents the land between the two bodies of water
note: similar to the flag of El Salvador, which features a round emblem encircled by the words REPUBLICA DE EL SALVADOR EN LA AMERICA CENTRAL centered in the white band; also similar to the flag of Honduras, which has five blue stars arranged in an X pattern centered in the white band

National symbol(s): turquoise-browed motmot (bird); national colors: blue, white

National anthem: name: "Salve a ti, Nicaragua" (Hail to Thee, Nicaragua)
lyrics/music: Salomon Ibarra MAYORGA/traditional, arranged by Luis Abraham DELGADILLO
note: although only officially adopted in 1971, the music was approved in 1918 and the lyrics in 1939; the tune, originally from Spain, was used as an anthem for Nicaragua from the 1830s until 1876

ECONOMY

Economy—overview: Nicaragua, the poorest country in Central America and the second poorest in the Western Hemisphere, has widespread underemployment and poverty. GDP growth of 4.5% in 2017 was insufficient to make a significant difference. Textiles and agriculture combined account for nearly 50% of Nicaragua's exports. Beef, coffee, and gold are Nicaragua's top three export commodities.

The Dominican Republic-Central America-United States Free Trade Agreement has been in effect since April 2006 and has expanded export opportunities for many Nicaraguan agricultural and manufactured goods.

In 2013, the government granted a 50-year concession with the option for an additional 50 years to a newly formed Chinese-run company to finance and build an inter-oceanic canal and related projects, at an estimated cost of $50 billion. The canal construction has not started.

GDP (purchasing power parity): $36.22 billion (2017 est.)
$34.66 billion (2016 est.)
$33.11 billion (2015 est.)
note: data are in 2017 dollars
country comparison to the world: 125

GDP (official exchange rate): $13.69 billion (2016 est.)

GDP—real growth rate: 4.5% (2017 est.)
4.7% (2016 est.)
4.9% (2015 est.)
country comparison to the world: 55

GDP—per capita (PPP): $5,800 (2017 est.)
$5,600 (2016 est.)
$5,400 (2015 est.)
note: data are in 2017 dollars
country comparison to the world: 165

Gross national saving: 22.7% of GDP (2017 est.)
22.7% of GDP (2016 est.)
23.6% of GDP (2015 est.)
country comparison to the world: 69

GDP—composition, by end use:
household consumption: 70.8%
government consumption: 15.3%
investment in fixed capital: 29.8%
investment in inventories: 1.7%
exports of goods and services: 40.3%
imports of goods and services: -56.2% (2017 est.)

GDP—composition, by sector of origin:
agriculture: 15.5%
industry: 24.4%
services: 50.8% (2017 est.)

Agriculture—products: coffee, bananas, sugarcane, rice, corn, tobacco, cotton, sesame, soya, beans, beef, veal, pork, poultry, dairy products, shrimp, lobsters, peanuts

Industries: food processing, chemicals, machinery and metal products, knit and woven apparel, petroleum refining and distribution, beverages, footwear, wood, electric wire harness manufacturing, mining

Industrial production growth rate: 5.4% (2017 est.)
country comparison to the world: 40

Labor force: 3.046 million (2017 est.)
country comparison to the world: 103

Labor force—by occupation: *agriculture:* 31%
industry: 18%
services: 50% (2011 est.)

Unemployment rate: 6.5% (2017 est.)
6.2% (2016 est.)
note: underemployment was 46.5% in 2008
country comparison to the world: 89

Population below poverty line: 29.6% (2015 est.)

Household income or consumption by percentage share: *lowest 10%:* 1.8%
highest 10%: 47.1% (2014)

Distribution of family income—Gini index: 47.1 (2014)
45.8 (2009)
country comparison to the world: 26

Budget: *revenues:* $3.8 billion
expenditures: $4.074 billion (2017 est.)
Taxes and other revenues: 27.8% of GDP (2017 est.)
country comparison to the world: 98

Budget surplus (+) or deficit (-): -2% of GDP (2017 est.)
country comparison to the world: 83

Public debt: 46% of GDP (2017 est.)
45.2% of GDP (2016 est.)
note: official data; data cover general government debt, and includes debt instruments issued (or owned) by Government entities other than the treasury; the data include treasury debt held by foreign entities, as well as intra-governmental debt; intra-governmental debt consists of treasury borrowings from surpluses in the social funds, such as retirement, medical care, and unemployment, debt instruments for the social funds are not sold at public auctions; Nicaragua rebased its GDP figures in 2012, which reduced the figures for debt as a percentage of GDP
country comparison to the world: 115

Fiscal year: calendar year

Inflation rate (consumer prices): 4% (2017 est.)
3.5% (2016 est.)
country comparison to the world: 155

Central bank discount rate: 3% (31 December 2010)
country comparison to the world: 108

Commercial bank prime lending rate: 12.2% (31 December 2017 est.)
11.44% (31 December 2016 est.)
country comparison to the world: 66

Stock of narrow money: $1.161 billion (31 December 2017 est.)

$1.043 billion (31 December 2016 est.)
country comparison to the world: 153

Stock of broad money: $1.602 billion (31 December 2017 est.)
$1.445 billion (31 December 2016 est.)
country comparison to the world: 165

Stock of domestic credit: $6.39 billion (31 December 2017 est.)
$6.159 billion (31 December 2016 est.)
country comparison to the world: 119

Market value of publicly traded shares: $1.568 billion (31 December 2016)
$1.209 billion (31 December 2015)
$995 million (31 December 2014)
country comparison to the world: 103

Current account balance: -$1.154 billion (2017 est.)
-$1.133 billion (2016 est.)
country comparison to the world: 136

Exports: $3.611 billion (2017 est.)
$3.772 billion (2016 est.)
country comparison to the world: 120

Exports—commodities: coffee, beef, gold, sugar, peanuts, shrimp and lobster, tobacco, cigars, automobile wiring harnesses, textiles, apparel

Exports—partners: US 51.5%, Mexico 13.8%, El Salvador 6%, Venezuela 5.9% (2016)

Imports: $6.426 billion (2017 est.)
$6.384 billion (2016 est.)
country comparison to the world: 113

Imports—commodities: consumer goods, machinery and equipment, raw materials, petroleum products

Imports—partners: US 19.7%, China 12.9%, Mexico 9.7%, Costa Rica 7.8%, Guatemala 6.5%, Netherlands Antilles 5.7%, El Salvador 4.8% (2016)

Reserves of foreign exchange and gold: $2.521 billion (31 December 2017 est.)
$2.448 billion (31 December 2016 est.)
country comparison to the world: 111

Debt—external: $11.36 billion (31 December 2017 est.)
$10.87 billion (31 December 2016 est.)
country comparison to the world: 108

Exchange rates: cordobas (NIO) per US dollar—
30.11 (2017 est.)
28.678 (2016 est.)
28.678 (2015 est.)
27.257 (2014 est.)
26.01 (2013 est.)

ENERGY

Electricity access: *population without electricity:* 1,400,000
electrification—*total population:* 78%
electrification—urban areas: 100%
electrification—rural areas: 43% (2013)

Electricity—production: 3.218 billion kWh (2016 est.)
country comparison to the world: 132

Electricity—consumption: 3.177 billion kWh (2016 est.)
country comparison to the world: 134

Electricity—exports: 17.87 million kWh (2016 est.)
country comparison to the world: 91

Electricity—imports: 109 million kWh (2016 est.)
country comparison to the world: 96

Electricity—installed generating capacity: 1.395 million kW (2016 est.)
country comparison to the world: 124

Electricity—from fossil fuels: 59% of total installed capacity (2015 est.)
country comparison to the world: 132

Electricity—from nuclear fuels: 0% of total installed capacity (2015 est.)
country comparison to the world: 159

Electricity—from hydroelectric plants: 8.4% of total installed capacity (2015 est.)
country comparison to the world: 122

Electricity—from other renewable sources: 36.1% of total installed capacity (2015 est.)
country comparison to the world: 7

Crude oil—production: 0 bbl/day (2016 est.)
country comparison to the world: 181

Crude oil—exports: 0 bbl/day (2014 est.)
country comparison to the world: 174

Crude oil—imports: 14,180 bbl/day (2014 est.)
country comparison to the world: 69

Crude oil—proved reserves: 0 bbl (1 January 2017 es)
country comparison to the world: 179

Refined petroleum products—production: 14,260 bbl/day (2014 est.)
country comparison to the world: 99

Refined petroleum products—consumption: 30,000 bbl/day (2015 est.)
country comparison to the world: 121

Refined petroleum products—exports: 253.3 bbl/day (2014 est.)
country comparison to the world: 119

Refined petroleum products—imports: 16,130 bbl/day (2014 est.)
country comparison to the world: 126

Natural gas—production: 0 cu m (2016 est.)
country comparison to the world: 181

Natural gas—consumption: 0 cu m (2016 est.)
country comparison to the world: 120

Natural gas—exports: 0 cu m (2016 est.)
country comparison to the world: 162

Natural gas—imports: 0 cu m (2016 est.)
country comparison to the world: 170

Natural gas—proved reserves: 0 cu m (1 January 2015 es)
country comparison to the world: 183

Carbon dioxide emissions from consumption of energy: 5.2 million Mt (2013 est.)
country comparison to the world: 125

COMMUNICATIONS

Telephones—fixed lines: *total subscriptions:* 366,636

subscriptions per 100 inhabitants: 6 (July 2016 est.)
country comparison to the world: 111

Telephones—mobile cellular: *total:* 7,745,512
subscriptions per 100 inhabitants: 130 (July 2016 est.)
country comparison to the world: 105

Telephone system: *general assessment:* system being upgraded by foreign investment; nearly all installed telecommunications capacity now uses digital technology, owing to investments since privatization of the formerly state-owned telecommunications company
domestic: since privatization, access to fixed-line and mobile-cellular services has improved; fixed-line teledensity roughly 6 per 100 persons; mobile-cellular telephone subscribership has increased to almost 130 per 100 persons
international: country code—505; the Americas Region Caribbean Ring System (ARCOS-1) fiber-optic submarine cable provides connectivity to South and Central America, parts of the Caribbean, and the US; satellite earth stations—1 Intersputnik (Atlantic Ocean region) and 1 Intelsat (Atlantic Ocean) (2016)

Broadcast media: multiple terrestrial TV stations, supplemented by cable TV in most urban areas; nearly all are government-owned or affiliated; more than 300 radio stations, both government-affiliated and privately owned (2016)

Internet country code: .ni
Internet users: total: 1,466,152

percent of population: 24.6% (July 2016 est.)
country comparison to the world: 123

TRANSPORTATION

National air transport system: *number of registered air carriers:* 1
inventory of registered aircraft operated by air carriers: 2
annual passenger traffic on registered air carriers: 61,031

annual freight traffic on registered air carriers: 0 mt-km (2015)
Civil aircraft registration country code prefix: YN (2016)

Airports: 147 (2013)
country comparison to the world: 40

Airports—with paved runways: *total:* 12
2,438 to 3,047 m: 3
1,524 to 2,437 m: 2
914 to 1,523 m: 3
under 914 m: 4 (2017)

Airports—with unpaved runways: *total:* 135
1,524 to 2,437 m: 1
914 to 1,523 m: 15
under 914 m: 119 (2013)

Pipelines: oil 54 km (2013)

Roadways: *total:* 23,897 km
paved: 3,346 km
unpaved: 20,551 km (2014)
country comparison to the world: 101

Waterways: 2,220 km (navigable waterways as well as the use of the large Lake Managua and Lake Nicaragua; rivers serve only the sparsely populated eastern part of the country) (2011)
country comparison to the world: 39

Merchant marine: *total:* 5
by type: general cargo 1, oil tanker 1, other 3 (2017)
country comparison to the world: 157

Ports and terminals: *major seaport(s):* Bluefields, Corinto

MILITARY AND SECURITY

Military expenditures: 0.55% of GDP (2016)
0.78% of GDP (2015)
0.69% of GDP (2014)
0.68% of GDP (2013)
0.67% of GDP (2012)
country comparison to the world: 120

Military branches: National Army of Nicaragua (Ejercito Nacional de Nicaragua, ENN; includes Navy, Air Force) (2013)

Military service age and obligation: 18-30 years of age for voluntary military service; no conscription; tour of duty 18-36 months; requires Nicaraguan nationality and 6th-grade education (2012)

TRANSNATIONAL ISSUES

Disputes—international: the 1992 ICJ ruling for El Salvador and Honduras advised a tripartite resolution to establish a maritime boundary in the Gulf of Fonseca, which considers Honduran access to the Pacific; Nicaragua and Costa Rica regularly file border dispute cases over the delimitations of the San Juan River and the northern tip of Calero Island to the ICJ; there is an ongoing case in the ICJ to determine Pacific and Atlantic ocean maritime borders as well as land borders; in 2009, the ICJ ruled that Costa Rican vessels carrying out police activities could not use the river, but official Costa Rican vessels providing essential services to riverside inhabitants and Costa Rican tourists could travel freely on the river; in 2011, the ICJ provisionally ruled that both countries must remove personnel from the disputed area; in 2013, the ICJ rejected Nicaragua's 2012 suit to halt Costa Rica's construction of a highway paralleling the river on the grounds of irreparable environmental damage; in 2013, the ICJ, regarding the disputed territory, ordered that Nicaragua should refrain from dredging or canal construction and refill and repair damage caused by trenches connecting the river to the Caribbean and upheld its 2010 ruling that Nicaragua must remove all personnel; in early 2014, Costa Rica brought Nicaragua to the ICJ over offshore oil concessions in the disputed region; Nicaragua filed a case against Colombia in 2013 over the delimitation of the Continental shelf beyond the 200 nautical miles from the Nicaraguan coast, as well as over the alleged violation by Colombia of Nicaraguan maritime space in the Caribbean Sea

Illicit drugs: transshipment point for cocaine destined for the US and transshipment point for arms-for-drugs dealing

NIGER

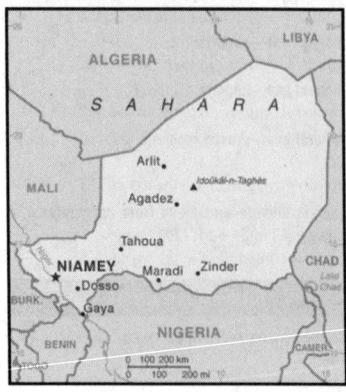

INTRODUCTION

Background: Niger became independent from France in 1960 and experienced single-party and military rule until 1991, when Gen. Ali SAIBOU was forced by public pressure to allow multiparty elections, which resulted in a democratic government in 1993. Political infighting brought the government to a standstill and in 1996 led to a coup by Col. Ibrahim BARE. In 1999, BARE was killed in a counter coup by military officers who restored democratic rule and held elections that brought Mamadou TANDJA to power in December of that year. TANDJA was reelected in 2004 and in 2009 spearheaded a constitutional amendment allowing him to extend his term as president. In February 2010, military officers led a coup that deposed TANDJA and suspended the constitution. ISSOUFOU Mahamadou was elected in April 2011 following the coup and reelected to a second term in early 2016. Niger is one of the poorest countries in the world with minimal government services and insufficient funds to develop its resource base. The largely agrarian and subsistence-based economy is frequently disrupted by extended droughts common to the Sahel region of Africa. A Tuareg rebellion emerged in 2007 and ended in 2009. Niger is facing increased security concerns on its borders from various external threats including insecurity in Libya, spillover from the conflict in Mali, and violent extremism in northeastern Nigeria.

GEOGRAPHY

Location: Western Africa, southeast of Algeria

Geographic coordinates: 16 00 N, 8 00 E

Map references: Africa

Area: *total:* 1.267 million sq km
land: 1,266,700 sq km
water: 300 sq km
country comparison to the world: 23

Area—comparative: slightly less than twice the size of Texas

Land boundaries: *total:* 5,834 km
border countries (7): Algeria 951 km, Benin 277 km, Burkina Faso 622 km, Chad 1,196 km, Libya 342 km, Mali 838 km, Nigeria 1,608 km

Coastline: 0 km (landlocked)

Maritime claims: none (landlocked)

Climate: desert; mostly hot, dry, dusty; tropical in extreme south

Terrain: predominately desert plains and sand dunes; flat to rolling plains in south; hills in north

Elevation: *mean elevation:* 474 m
elevation extremes: lowest point: Niger River 200 m
highest point: Idoukal-n-Taghes 2,022 m

Natural resources: uranium, coal, iron ore, tin, phosphates, gold, molybdenum, gypsum, salt, petroleum

Land use: *agricultural land:* 35.1%
arable land: 12.3%;
permanent crops: 0.1%;
permanent pasture: 22.7%;
forest: 1%
other: 63.9% (2011 est.)
Irrigated land: 1,000 sq km (2012)

Population—distribution: majority of the populace is located in the southernmost extreme of the country along the border with Nigeria and Benin

Natural hazards: recurring droughts

Environment—current issues: overgrazing; soil erosion; deforestation; desertification; wildlife populations (such as elephant, hippopotamus, giraffe, and lion) threatened because of poaching and habitat destruction

Environment—international agreements: *party to:* Biodiversity, Climate Change, Climate Change-Kyoto Protocol, Desertification, Endangered Species, Environmental Modification, Hazardous Wastes, Ozone Layer Protection, Wetlands
signed, but not ratified: Law of the Sea

Geography—note: landlocked; one of the hottest countries in the world; northern four-fifths is desert, southern one-fifth is savanna, suitable for livestock and limited agriculture

PEOPLE AND SOCIETY

Population: 19,245,344 (July 2017 est.)
country comparison to the world: 60

Nationality: *noun:* Nigerien(s)
adjective: Nigerien

Ethnic groups: Hausa 53.1%, Zarma/Songhai 21.2%, Tuareg 11%, Fulani (Peul) 6.5%, Kanuri 5.9%, Gurma 0.8%, Arab 0.4%, Tubu 0.4%, other/unavailable 0.9% (2006 est.)

Languages: French (official), Hausa, Djerma

Religions: Muslim 80%, other (includes indigenous beliefs and Christian) 20%

Demographic profile: Niger has the highest total fertility rate (TFR) of any country in the world, averaging close to 7 children per woman in 2016. A slight decline in fertility over the last few decades has stalled. This leveling off of the high fertility rate is in large part a product of the continued desire for large families. In Niger, the TFR is lower than the desired fertility rate, which makes it unlikely that contraceptive use will increase. The high TFR sustains rapid population growth and a large youth population—almost 70% of the populace is under the age of 25. Gender inequality, including a lack of educational opportunities for women and early marriage and childbirth, also contributes to high population growth.

Because of large family sizes, children are inheriting smaller and smaller parcels of land. The dependence of most Nigeriens on subsistence farming on increasingly small landholdings, coupled with declining rainfall and the resultant shrinkage of arable land, are all preventing food production from keeping up with population growth.

For more than half a century, Niger's lack of economic development has led to steady net out-migration. In the 1960s, Nigeriens mainly migrated to coastal West African countries to work on a seasonal basis. Some headed to Libya and Algeria in the 1970s to work in the booming oil industry until its decline in the 1980s. Since the 1990s, the principal destinations for Nigerien labor migrants have been West African countries, especially Burkina Faso and Cote d'Ivoire, while emigration to Europe and North America has remained modest. During the same period, Niger's desert trade route town Agadez became a hub for West African and other sub-Saharan migrants crossing the Sahara to North Africa and sometimes onward to Europe.

More than 60,000 Malian refugees have fled to Niger since violence between Malian government troops and armed rebels began in early 2012. Ongoing attacks by the Boko Haram Islamist insurgency, dating to 2013 in northern Nigeria and February 2015 in southeastern Niger, have pushed tens of thousands of Nigerian refugees and Nigerien returnees across the border to Niger and to displace thousands of locals in Niger's already impoverished Diffa region.

Age structure: *0-14 years:* 49.01% (male 4,757,806/female 4,674,437)
15-24 years: 19.1% (male 1,815,689/female 1,860,230)
25-54 years: 25.97% (male 2,495,927/female 2,501,362)
55-64 years: 3.28% (male 328,082/female 304,030)
65 years and over: 2.64% (male 259,046/female 248,735) (2017 est.)

Dependency ratios: *total dependency ratio:* 111.6

youth dependency ratio: 106.2
elderly dependency ratio: 5.4
potential support ratio: 18.6 (2015 est.)

Median age: *total:* 15.4 years
male: 15.3 years
female: 15.5 years (2017 est.)
country comparison to the world: 229

Population growth rate: 3.19% (2017 est.)
country comparison to the world: 6

Birth rate: 44.2 births/1,000 population (2017 est.)
country comparison to the world: 2

Death rate: 11.8 deaths/1,000 population (2017 est.)
country comparison to the world: 23

Net migration rate: -0.5 migrant(s)/1,000 population (2017 est.)
country comparison to the world: 127

Population distribution: majority of the populace is located in the southernmost extreme of the country along the border with Nigeria and Benin

Urbanization: *urban population:* 19.3% of total population (2017)
rate of urbanization: 5.49% annual rate of change (2015-20 est.)

Major urban areas—population: NIAMEY (capital) 1.09 million (2015)

Sex ratio: *at birth:* 1.03 male(s)/female
0-14 years: 1.02 male(s)/female
15-24 years: 0.98 male(s)/female
25-54 years: 1 male(s)/female
55-64 years: 1.08 male(s)/female
65 years and over: 1.04 male(s)/female
total population: 1.01 male(s)/female (2016 est.)

Mother's mean age at first birth: 18.1 years
note: median age at first birth among women 25-29 (2012 est.)

Maternal mortality ratio: 553 deaths/100,000 live births (2015 est.)
country comparison to the world: 17

Infant mortality rate: *total:* 81.1 deaths/1,000 live births
male: 85.5 deaths/1,000 live births
female: 76.6 deaths/1,000 live births (2017 est.)
country comparison to the world: 6

Life expectancy at birth: *total population:* 55.9 years
male: 54.7 years
female: 57.3 years (2017 est.)
country comparison to the world: 213

Total fertility rate: 6.49 children born/woman (2017 est.)
country comparison to the world: 1

Contraceptive prevalence rate: 16.9% (2016)

Health expenditures: 5.8% of GDP (2014)
country comparison to the world: 112

Physicians density: 0.02 physicians/1,000 population (2008)

Drinking water source:
improved:
urban: 100% of population
rural: 48.6% of population
total: 58.2% of population

unimproved:
urban: 0% of population
rural: 51.4% of population
total: 41.8% of population (2015 est.)

Sanitation facility access:
improved:
urban: 37.9% of population
rural: 4.6% of population
total: 10.9% of population
unimproved:
urban: 62.1% of population
rural: 95.4% of population
total: 89.1% of population (2015 est.)

HIV/AIDS—adult prevalence rate: 0.4% (2016 est.)
country comparison to the world: 66

HIV/AIDS—people living with HIV/AIDS: 48,000 (2016 est.)
country comparison to the world: 56

HIV/AIDS—deaths: 3,400 (2016 est.)
country comparison to the world: 38

Major infectious diseases: *degree of risk:* very high
food or waterborne diseases: bacterial and proto-zoal diarrhea, hepatitis A, and typhoid fever
vectorborne diseases: malaria and dengue fever
water contact disease: schistosomiasis
respiratory disease: meningococcal meningitis
animal contact disease: rabies (2016)

Obesity—adult prevalence rate: 5.5% (2016)
country comparison to the world: 176

Children under the age of 5 years underweight: 37.9% (2012)
country comparison to the world: 4

Education expenditures: 6.7% of GDP (2014)
country comparison to the world: 101

Literacy: *definition:* age 15 and over can read and write
total population: 19.1%
male: 27.3%
female: 11% (2015 est.)

School life expectancy (primary to tertiary education): *total:* 5 years
male: 6 years
female: 5 years (2012)

Unemployment, youth ages 15-24: *total:* 2.3%
male: 4.4%
female: 0.8% (2007 est.)

GOVERNMENT

Country name: *conventional long form:* Republic of Niger
conventional short form: Niger
local long form: Republique du Niger
local short form: Niger
etymology: named for the Niger River that passes through the southwest of the country; from a native term "Ni Gir" meaning "River Gir"

Government type: semi-presidential republic

Capital: *name:* Niamey

geographic coordinates: 13 31 N, 2 07 E

time difference: UTC+1 (6 hours ahead of Wash-ington, DC, during Standard Time)

Administrative divisions: 7 regions (regions, singu-lar—region) and 1 capital district* (communaute urbaine); Agadez, Diffa, Dosso, Maradi, Niamey*, Tahoua, Tillaberi, Zinder

Independence: 3 August 1960 (from France)

National holiday: Republic Day, 18 December (1958); note—commemorates the founding of the Republic of Niger which predated independence from France in 1960

Constitution: history: several previous; passed by referendum 31 October 2010, entered into force 25 November 2010
amendments: proposed by the president of the republic or by the National Assembly; considera-tion of amendments requires at least three-fourths majority vote by the Assembly; passage requires at least four-fifths majority vote; if disapproved, the proposed amendment is dropped or submitted to a referendum; constitutional articles on the form of government, the multiparty system, the separation of state and religion, disqualification of Assembly members, amendment procedures, and amnesty of participants in the 2010 coup d'Etat cannot be amended; amended 2011 (2017)

Legal system: mixed legal system of civil law (based on French civil law), Islamic law, and cus-tomary law

International law organization participation: has not submitted an ICJ jurisdiction declaration; accepts ICCt jurisdiction

Citizenship: *citizenship by birth:* no
citizenship by descent only: at least one parent must be a citizen of Niger
dual citizenship recognized: yes
residency requirement for naturalization: unknown

Suffrage: 18 years of age; universal

Executive branch: *chief of state:* President ISSOU-FOU Mahamadou (since 7 April 2011)
head of government: Prime Minister Brigi RAFINI (since 7 April 2011)
cabinet: Cabinet appointed by the president
elections/appointments: president directly elected by absolute majority popular vote in 2 rounds if needed for a 5-year term (eligible for a second term); election last held on 21 February 2016 with a runoff on 20 March 2016 (next to be held in 2021); prime minister appointed by the president, authorized by the National Assembly
election results: ISSOUFOU Mahamadou ree-lected president in second round; percent of vote in first round—ISSOUFOU Mahamadou (PNDS-Tarrayya) 48.6%, Hama AMADOU (MODEN/FA Lumana Africa) 17.8%, Seini OUMAROU (MNSD-Nassara) 11.3%, other 22.3%; percent of vote in second round—ISSOUFOU Mahamadou 92%, Hama AMADOU 8%

Legislative branch: *description:* unicameral National Assembly or Assemblee Nationale (171 seats; 158 members directly elected from 8 multi-member constituencies in 7 regions and

Niamey by party-list proportional representation, 8 reserved for minorities elected in special single-seat constituencies by simple majority vote, 5 seats reserved for Nigeriens living abroad—1 seat per continent—elected in single-seat constituencies by simple majority vote; members serve 5-year terms); note—the number of National Assembly seats increased from 113 to 171 in the February 2016 legislative election
elections: last held on 21 February 2016 (next to be held in 2021)
election results: percent of vote by party—PNDS-Tarrayya 44.1%, MODEN/FA Lumana 14.7%, MNSD-Nassara 11.8%, MPR-Jamhuriya 7.1%, MNRD Hankuri-PSDN Alheri 3.5%, MPN-Kishin Kassa 2.9%, ANDP-Zaman Lahiya 2.4%, RSD-Gaskiya 2.4%, CDS-Rahama 1.8%, CPR-Inganci 1.8%, RDP-Jama'a 1.8%, AMEN AMIN 1.8%, other 3.9%; seats by party—PNDS-Tarrayya 75, MODEN/FA Lumana 25, MNSD-Nassara 20, MPR-Jamhuriya 12, MNRD Hankuri-PSDN Alheri 6, MPN-Kishin Kassa 5, ANDP-Zaman Lahiya 4, RSD-Gaskiya 4, CDS-Rahama 3, CPR-Inganci 3, RDP-Jama'a 3, RDP-Jama'a 3, AMEN AMIN 3, other 8

Judicial branch: *highest court(s):* Constitutional Court (consists of 7 judges); High Court of Justice (consists of 7 members)
judge selection and term of office: Constitu-tional Court judges nominated/elected—1 by the president of the Republic, 1 by the president of the National Assembly, 2 by peer judges, 2 by peer lawyers, 1 law professor by peers, and 1 from within Nigerien society; all appointed by the presi-dent; judges serve 6-year nonrenewable terms with one-third of membership renewed every 2 years; High Judicial Court members selected from among the legislature and judiciary; members serve 5-year terms
subordinate courts: Court of Cassation; Council of State; Court of Finances; various specialized tri-bunals and customary courts

Political parties and leaders: Alliance of Move-ments for the Emergence of Niger or AMEN AMIN [Omar Hamidou TCHIANA]
Congress for the Republic or CPR-Inganci [Kas-soum MOCTAR]
Democratic Alliance for Niger or ADN-Fusaha [Habi Mahamadou SALISSOU]
Democratic and Social Convention-Rahama or CDS-Rahama [Abdou LABO]
National Movement for the Development of Society-Nassara or MNSD-Nassara [Seini OUMAROU]
Nigerien Alliance for Democracy and Progress-Zaman Lahiya or ANDP-Zaman Lahiya [Moussa Moumouni DJERMAKOYE]
Nigerien Democratic Movement for an Afri-can Federation or MODEN/FA Lumana [Hama AMADOU]
Nigerien Movement for Democratic Renewal or MNRD-Hankuri [Mahamane OUSMANE]
Nigerien Party for Democracy and Socialism or PNDS-Tarrayya [Mahamadou ISSOUFOU]
Nigerien Patriotic Movement or MPN-Kishin Kassa [Ibrahim YACOUBA]

Party for Socialism and Democracy in Niger or PSDN-Alheri

Patriotic Movement for the Republic or MPR-Jamhuriya [Albade ABOUBA]

Rally for Democracy and Progress-Jama'a or RDP-Jama'a [Hamid ALGABID]

Social and Democratic Rally or RSD-Gaskiyya [Amadou CHEIFFOU]

Social Democratic Party or PSD-Bassira [Mohamed BEN OMAR]

Union for Democracy and the Republic-Tabbat or UDR-Tabbat [Amadou Boubacar CISSE]

note: the SPLM and SPLM-DC are banned political parties

International organization participation: ACP, AfDB, AU, CD, ECOWAS, EITI (compliant country), Entente, FAO, FZ, G-77, IAEA, IBRD, ICAO, ICCt, ICRM, IDA, IDB, IFAD, IFC, IFRCS, ILO, IMF, Interpol, IOC, IOM, IPU, ISO (correspondent), ITSO, ITU, ITUC (NGOs), MIGA, MINUSMA, MONUSCO, NAM, OIC, OIF, OPCW, UN, UNCTAD, UNESCO, UNIDO, UNMIL, UNOCI, UNWTO, UPU, WADB (regional), WAEMU, WCO, WFTU (NGOs), WHO, WIPO, WMO, WTO

Diplomatic representation in the US: *chief of mission:* Ambassador Hassana ALIDOU (since 23 February 2015)

chancery: 2204 R Street NW, Washington, DC 20008

telephone: [1] (202) 483-4224 through 4227

FAX: [1] (202) 483-3169

Diplomatic representation from the US: *chief of mission:* Ambassador Eunice S. REDDICK (since 12 September 2014)

embassy: BP 11201, Rue Des Ambassades, Niamey

mailing address: 2420 Niamey Place, Washington DC 20521-2420

telephone: [227] 20-73-31-69 or [227] 20-72-39-41

FAX: [227] 20-73-55-60

Flag description: three equal horizontal bands of orange (top), white, and green with a small orange disk centered in the white band; the orange band denotes the drier northern regions of the Sahara; white stands for purity and innocence; green symbolizes hope and the fertile and productive southern and western areas, as well as the Niger River; the orange disc represents the sun and the sacrifices made by the people

note: similar to the flag of India, which has a blue spoked wheel centered in the white band

National symbol(s): zebu; national colors: orange, white, green

National anthem: name: "La Nigerienne" (The Nigerien)

lyrics/music: Maurice Albert THIRIET/Robert JACQUET and Nicolas Abel Francois FRIONNET

note: adopted 1961

ECONOMY

Economy—overview: Niger is a landlocked, sub-Saharan nation, whose economy centers on subsistence crops, livestock, and some of the world's

largest uranium deposits. Agriculture contributes approximately 25% of GDP and provides livelihood for 87% of the population. The UN ranked Niger as the second least developed country in the world in 2016 due to multiple factors such as food insecurity, lack of industry, high population growth, a weak educational sector, and few prospects for work outside of subsistence farming and herding.

Since 2011 public debt has increased due to efforts to scale-up public investment, particularly that related to infrastructure, as well as due to increased security spending. The government relies on foreign donor resources for a large portion of its fiscal budget. The economy in recent years has been hurt by terrorist activity and kidnappings near its uranium mines and by instability in Mali and in the Diffa region of the country; concerns about security have resulted in increased support from regional and international partners on defense. Low uranium prices, demographics, and security expenditures may continue to put pressure on the government's finances.

Future growth may be sustained by exploitation of oil, gold, coal, and other mineral resources. Although Niger has sizable reserves of oil, the prolonged drop in oil prices has reduced profitability. Food insecurity and drought remain perennial problems for Niger, and the government plans to invest more in irrigation. Niger's three-year $131 million IMF Extended Credit Facility (ECF) agreement for the years 2012-15 was extended until the end of 2016. In February 2017, the IMF approved a new 3-year $134 million ECF. A $437 million Millennium Challenge Account compact for Niger, commencing in FY17, will focus on large-scale irrigation infrastructure development and community-based, climate-resilient agriculture, while promoting sustainable increases in agricultural productivity and sales.

Formal private sector investment needed for economic diversification and growth remains a challenge, given the country's limited domestic markets, access to credit, and competitiveness. Although President ISSOUFOU is courting foreign investors, including those from the US, as of April 2017, there were no US firms operating in Niger.

GDP (purchasing power parity): $21.62 billion (2017 est.)

$20.75 billion (2016 est.)

$19.76 billion (2015 est.)

note: data are in 2017 dollars

country comparison to the world: 146

GDP (official exchange rate): $7.892 billion (2016 est.)

GDP—real growth rate: 4.2% (2017 est.)

5% (2016 est.)

4% (2015 est.)

country comparison to the world: 60

GDP—per capita (PPP): $1,200 (2017 est.)

$1,100 (2016 est.)

$1,100 (2015 est.)

note: data are in 2017 dollars

country comparison to the world: 223

Gross national saving: 23.7% of GDP (2017 est.)

24.1% of GDP (2016 est.)

24.4% of GDP (2015 est.)

country comparison to the world: 61

GDP—composition, by end use:

household consumption: 66.8%

government consumption: 14.4%

investment in fixed capital: 42.1%

investment in inventories: 0%

exports of goods and services: 16.4%

imports of goods and services: -39.7% (2017 est.)

GDP—composition, by sector of origin:

agriculture: 44.3%

industry: 14.9%

services: 40.8% (2017 est.)

Agriculture—products: cowpeas, cotton, peanuts, millet, sorghum, cassava (manioc, tapioca), rice; cattle, sheep, goats, camels, donkeys, horses, poultry

Industries: uranium mining, petroleum, cement, brick, soap, textiles, food processing, chemicals, slaughterhouses

Industrial production growth rate: 5% (2017 est.)

country comparison to the world: 44

Labor force: 6.5 million (2017 est.)

country comparison to the world: 71

Labor force—by occupation: *agriculture:* 87%

industry: 4%

services: 9% (2016 est.)

Unemployment rate: 2.6% (2016 est.)

2.6% (2016 est.)

country comparison to the world: 24

Population below poverty line: 45.4% (2014 est.)

Household income or consumption by percentage share: *lowest 10%:* 3.7%

highest 10%: 28.5% (2007)

Distribution of family income—Gini index: 34 (2007)

50.5 (1995)

country comparison to the world: 100

Budget: *revenues:* $1.68 billion

expenditures: $2.235 billion (2017 est.)

Taxes and other revenues: 21.3% of GDP (2017 est.)

country comparison to the world: 140

Budget surplus (+) or deficit (-): -7% of GDP (2017 est.)

country comparison to the world: 189

Public debt: 45.9% of GDP (2016 est.)

41.3% of GDP (2015 est.)

country comparison to the world: 117

Fiscal year: calendar year

Inflation rate (consumer prices): 1% (2017 est.)

0.3% (2016 est.)

country comparison to the world: 44

Central bank discount rate: 4.25% (31 December 2015)

4.25% (31 December 2014)

country comparison to the world: 94

Commercial bank prime lending rate: 5.4% (31 December 2017 est.)

5.3% (31 December 2016 est.)

country comparison to the world: 139

Stock of narrow money: $1.767 billion (31 December 2017 est.)
$1.535 billion (31 December 2016 est.)
country comparison to the world: 140

Stock of broad money: $2.322 billion (31 December 2017 est.)
$2.018 billion (31 December 2016 est.)
country comparison to the world: 151

Stock of domestic credit: $1.454 billion (31 December 2017 est.)
$1.267 billion (31 December 2016 est.)
country comparison to the world: 164

Market value of publicly traded shares: $NA

Current account balance: -$1.471 billion (2017 est.)
-$1.159 billion (2016 est.)
country comparison to the world: 146

Exports: $1.177 billion (2017 est.)
$1.101 billion (2016 est.)
country comparison to the world: 154

Exports—commodities: uranium ore, livestock, cowpeas, onions

Exports—partners: France 31.3%, Thailand 11.6%, Malaysia 11.1%, Nigeria 9.5%, Mali 5.6%, China 5.3% (2016)

Imports: $2.194 billion (2017 est.)
$2.031 billion (2016 est.)
country comparison to the world: 155

Imports—commodities: foodstuffs, machinery, vehicles and parts, petroleum, cereals

Imports—partners: France 28.3%, China 16.1%, US 7.8%, Nigeria 5.8%, Thailand 5.8% (2016)

Debt—external: $3.09 billion (31 December 2017 est.)
$2.926 billion (31 December 2016 est.)
country comparison to the world: 141

Exchange rates: Communaute Financiere Africaine francs (XOF) per US dollar—
605.3 (2017 est.)
593.01 (2016 est.)
593.01 (2015 est.)
591.45 (2014 est.)
494.42 (2013 est.)

ENERGY

Electricity access: *population without electricity:* 15,200,000
electrification—*total population:* 15%
electrification—urban areas: 62%
electrification—rural areas: 4% (2013)

Electricity—production: 499.4 million kWh (2015 est.)
country comparison to the world: 167

Electricity—consumption: 1.072 billion kWh (2015 est.)
country comparison to the world: 155

Electricity—exports: 0 kWh (2015 est.)
country comparison to the world: 176

Electricity—imports: 782 million kWh (2015 est.)
country comparison to the world: 72

Electricity—installed generating capacity: 179,000 kW (2015 est.)
country comparison to the world: 166

Electricity—from fossil fuels: 96.1% of total installed capacity (2015 est.)
country comparison to the world: 50

Electricity—from nuclear fuels: 0% of total installed capacity (2015 est.)
country comparison to the world: 152

Electricity—from hydroelectric plants: 0% of total installed capacity (2015 est.)
country comparison to the world: 192

Electricity—from other renewable sources: 4.5% of total installed capacity (2015 est.)
country comparison to the world: 101

Crude oil—production: 13,000 bbl/day (2016 est.)
country comparison to the world: 79

Crude oil—exports: 0 bbl/day (2014 est.)
country comparison to the world: 170

Crude oil—imports: 0 bbl/day (2014 est.)
country comparison to the world: 169

Crude oil—proved reserves: 150 million bbl (1 January 2017 es)
country comparison to the world: 63

Refined petroleum products—production: 16,570 bbl/day (2014 est.)
country comparison to the world: 94

Refined petroleum products—consumption: 13,000 bbl/day (2015 est.)
country comparison to the world: 155

Refined petroleum products—exports: 6,187 bbl/day (2014 est.)
country comparison to the world: 91

Refined petroleum products—imports: 2,465 bbl/day (2014 est.)
country comparison to the world: 182

Natural gas—production: 0 cu m (2016 est.)
country comparison to the world: 176

Natural gas—consumption: 0 cu m (2016 est.)
country comparison to the world: 215

Natural gas—exports: 0 cu m (2016 est.)
country comparison to the world: 157

Natural gas—imports: 0 cu m (2016 est.)
country comparison to the world: 163

Natural gas—proved reserves: 0 cu m (1 January 2016 es)
country comparison to the world: 178

Carbon dioxide emissions from consumption of energy: 900,000 Mt (2013 est.)
country comparison to the world: 167

COMMUNICATIONS

Telephones—fixed lines: *total subscriptions:* 113,000
subscriptions per 100 inhabitants: 1 (July 2016 est.)
country comparison to the world: 142

Telephones—mobile cellular: *total:* 9.791 million
subscriptions per 100 inhabitants: 53 (July 2016 est.)
country comparison to the world: 95

Telephone system: *general assessment:* inadequate; small system of wire, radio telephone communications, and microwave radio relay links concentrated in southwestern Niger
domestic: combined fixed-line and mobile-cellular teledensity remains only about 50 per 100 persons despite a rapidly increasing cellular subscribership base; domestic satellite system with 3 earth stations and 1 planned
international: country code—227; satellite earth stations—2 Intelsat (1 Atlantic Ocean and 1 Indian Ocean) (2016)

Broadcast media: state-run TV station; 3 private TV stations provide a mix of local and foreign programming; state-run radio has only radio station with national coverage; about 30 private radio stations operate locally; as many as 100 community radio stations broadcast; transmissions of multiple international broadcasters are available (2007)

Internet country code: .ne
Internet users: total: 805,702

percent of population: 4.3% (July 2016 est.)
country comparison to the world: 145

TRANSPORTATION

National air transport system: *number of registered air carriers:* 2
inventory of registered aircraft operated by air carriers: 2
annual passenger traffic on registered air carriers: 15,242
annual freight traffic on registered air carriers: 0 mt-km (2015)
Civil aircraft registration country code prefix: 5U (2016)

Airports: 30 (2013)
country comparison to the world: 115

Airports—with paved runways: *total:* 10
2,438 to 3,047 m: 3
1,524 to 2,437 m: 6
914 to 1,523 m: 1 (2017)

Airports—with unpaved runways: *total:* 20
1,524 to 2,437 m: 3
914 to 1,523 m: 15
under 914 m: 2 (2013)

Heliports: 1 (2013)

Roadways: *total:* 18,949 km
paved: 3,912 km
unpaved: 15,037 km (2010)
country comparison to the world: 114

Waterways: 300 km (the Niger, the only major river, is navigable to Gaya between September and March) (2012)
country comparison to the world: 93

Merchant marine: *total:* 2
by type: oil tanker 1, other 1 (2017)
country comparison to the world: 163

MILITARY AND SECURITY

Military expenditures: 4% of GDP (2016)
5.46% of GDP (2015)
3.45% of GDP (2014)
1.06% of GDP (2012)

1.31% of GDP (2011)
country comparison to the world: 95

Military branches: Nigerien Armed Forces (Forces Armees Nigeriennes, FAN): Army, Nigerien Air Force (Force Aerienne du Niger) (2012)

Military service age and obligation: 18 is the legal minimum age for compulsory or voluntary military service; enlistees must be Nigerien citizens and unmarried; 2-year service term; women may serve in health care (2017)

TERRORISM

Terrorist groups—foreign based: *al-Mulathamun Battalion: aim(s):* replace Niger's national regional governments with an Islamic state
area(s) of operation: conducts attacks against Nigerien military and security personnel; targets Westerners for kidnappings for ransom

al-Qaida in the Islamic Maghreb (AQIM): *aim(s):* replace the Niger Government with Sharia and, ultimately, establish a regional Islamic caliphate across all of North and West Africa

area(s) of operation: active throughout the country; conducts attacks against Nigerien military and security personnel; kidnaps Westerners for ransom

Boko Haram: *aim(s):* replace the Niger Government with an Islamic state and, ultimately, establish an Islamic caliphate across Africa; violently opposes any polical or social activity associated with Western society, including voting, attending secular schools, and wearing Western dress
area(s) of operation: conducts kidnappings, bombings, and assaults; responsible for displacing thousands of people and contributing to food insecurity, especially in the southeastern Diffa region; on 3 June 2016, the group conducted its deadliest attack in Niger, when operatives overran a military outpost in the Lake Chad Basin area in Bosso, killing 30 Nigerien soldiers, two Nigerian soldiers, and injuring 67; the group conducted its first known attack in Niger on 30 January 2015, when operatives tried to overrun Bosso and Diffa, resulting in the deaths of four Nigerien soldiers, one civilian, and approximately 109 Boko Haram fighters; Niger continues in 2017 to participate in the Joint Multinational Force's military offensives against Boko Haram

TRANSNATIONAL ISSUES

Disputes—international: Libya claims about 25,000 sq km in a currently dormant dispute in the Tommo region; location of Benin-Niger-Nigeria tripoint is unresolved; only Nigeria and Cameroon have heeded the Lake Chad Commission's admonition to ratify the delimitation treaty that also includes the Chad-Niger and Niger-Nigeria boundaries; the dispute with Burkina Faso was referred to the ICJ in 2010

Refugees and internally displaced persons: refugees (country of origin): 108,470 (Nigeria); 56,838 (Mali) (2017)
IDPs: 129,015 (unknown how many of the 11,000 people displaced by clashes between government forces and the Tuareg militant group, Niger Movement for Justice, in 2007 are still displaced; intercommunal violence; Boko Haram attacks in southern Niger, 2015) (2017)

NIGERIA

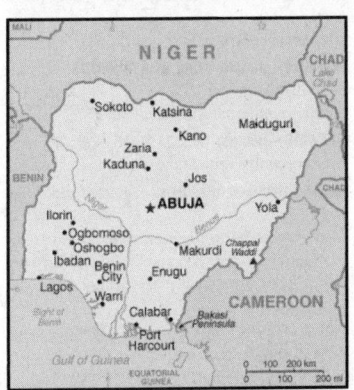

INTRODUCTION

Background: British influence and control over what would become Nigeria and Africa's most populous country grew through the 19th century. A series of constitutions after World War II granted Nigeria greater autonomy. After independence in 1960, politics were marked by coups and mostly military rule, until the death of a military head of state in 1998 allowed for a political transition. In 1999, a new constitution was adopted and a peaceful transition to civilian government was completed. The government continues to face the daunting task of institutionalizing democracy and reforming a petroleum-based economy, whose revenues have been squandered through corruption and mismanagement. In addition, Nigeria continues to experience longstanding ethnic and religious tensions. Although both the 2003 and 2007 presidential elections were marred by significant irregularities and violence, Nigeria is currently experiencing its longest period of civilian rule since independence. The general elections of April 2007 marked the first civilian-to-civilian transfer of power in the country's history and the elections of 2011 were generally regarded as credible. The 2015 election is considered the most well run in Nigeria since the return to civilian rule, with the umbrella opposition party, the All Progressives Congress, defeating the long-ruling People's Democratic Party that had governed since 1999.

GEOGRAPHY

Location: Western Africa, bordering the Gulf of Guinea, between Benin and Cameroon

Geographic coordinates: 10 00 N, 8 00 E

Map references: Africa

Area: *total:* 923,768 sq km
land: 910,768 sq km
water: 13,000 sq km
country comparison to the world: 33

Area—comparative: about six times the size of Georgia; slightly more than twice the size of California

Land boundaries: *total:* 4,477 km
border countries (4): Benin 809 km, Cameroon 1,975 km, Chad 85 km, Niger 1,608 km

Coastline: 853 km

Maritime claims: *territorial sea:* 12 nm
exclusive economic zone: 200 nm
continental shelf: 200-m depth or to the depth of exploitation

Climate: varies; equatorial in south, tropical in center, arid in north

Terrain: southern lowlands merge into central hills and plateaus; mountains in southeast, plains in north

Elevation: *mean elevation:* 380 m

elevation extremes: *lowest point:* Atlantic Ocean 0 m
highest point: Chappal Waddi 2,419 m

Natural resources: natural gas, petroleum, tin, iron ore, coal, limestone, niobium, lead, zinc, arable land

Land use: *agricultural land:* 78%
arable land: 37.3%;
permanent crops: 7.4%;
permanent pasture: 33.3%
forest: 9.5%
other: 12.5% (2011 est.)
Irrigated land: 2,930 sq km (2012)

Population—distribution: largest population of any African nation; significant population clusters are scattered throughout the country, with the highest density areas being in the south and southwest

Natural hazards: periodic droughts; flooding

Environment—current issues: soil degradation; rapid deforestation; urban air and water pollution; desertification; oil pollution—water, air, and soil; has suffered serious damage from oil spills; loss of arable land; rapid urbanization

Environment—international agreements: *party to:* Biodiversity, Climate Change, Climate Change-Kyoto Protocol, Desertification, Endangered Species, Hazardous Wastes, Law of the Sea, Marine Dumping, Marine Life Conservation, Ozone Layer Protection, Ship Pollution, Wetlands *signed, but not ratified:* none of the selected agreements

Geography—note: the Niger River enters the country in the northwest and flows southward through tropical rain forests and swamps to its delta in the Gulf of Guinea

PEOPLE AND SOCIETY

Population: 190,632,261

note: estimates for this country explicitly take into account the effects of excess mortality due to AIDS; this can result in lower life expectancy, higher infant mortality, higher death rates, lower population growth rates, and changes in the distribution of population by age and sex than would otherwise be expected (July 2017 est.)
country comparison to the world: 7

Nationality: *noun:* Nigerian(s)
adjective: Nigerian

Ethnic groups: Nigeria, Africa's most populous country, is composed of more than 250 ethnic groups; the most populous and politically influential are: Hausa and the Fulani 29%, Yoruba 21%, Igbo (Ibo) 18%, Ijaw 10%, Kanuri 4%, Ibibio 3.5%, Tiv 2.5%

Languages: English (official), Hausa, Yoruba, Igbo (Ibo), Fulani, over 500 additional indigenous languages

Religions: Muslim 50%, Christian 40%, indigenous beliefs 10%

Demographic profile: Nigeria's population is projected to grow from more than 186 million people in 2016 to 392 million in 2050, becoming the world's fourth most populous country. Nigeria's sustained high population growth rate will continue for the foreseeable future because of population momentum and its high birth rate. Abuja has not successfully implemented family planning programs to reduce and space births because of a lack of political will, government financing, and the availability and affordability of services and products, as well as a cultural preference for large families. Increased educational attainment, especially among women, and improvements in health care are needed to encourage and to better enable parents to opt for smaller families.

Nigeria needs to harness the potential of its burgeoning youth population in order to boost economic development, reduce widespread poverty, and channel large numbers of unemployed youth into productive activities and away from ongoing religious and ethnic violence. While most movement of Nigerians is internal, significant emigration regionally and to the West provides an outlet for Nigerians looking for economic opportunities, seeking asylum, and increasingly pursuing higher education. Immigration largely of West Africans continues to be insufficient to offset emigration and the loss of highly skilled workers. Nigeria also is a major source, transit, and destination country for forced labor and sex trafficking.

Age structure: *0-14 years:* 42.54% (male 41,506,288/female 39,595,720)

15-24 years: 19.61% (male 19,094,899/female 18,289,513)
25-54 years: 30.74% (male 30,066,196/female 28,537,846)
55-64 years: 3.97% (male 3,699,947/female 3,870,080)
65 years and over: 3.13% (male 2,825,134/female 3,146,638) (2017 est.)

Dependency ratios: *total dependency ratio:* 88.2
youth dependency ratio: 83
elderly dependency ratio: 5.1
potential support ratio: 19.4 (2015 est.)

Median age: *total:* 18.4 years
male: 18.3 years
female: 18.5 years (2017 est.)
country comparison to the world: 212

Population growth rate: 2.43% (2017 est.)
country comparison to the world: 24

Birth rate: 36.9 births/1,000 population (2017 est.)
country comparison to the world: 13

Death rate: 12.4 deaths/1,000 population (2017 est.)
country comparison to the world: 19

Net migration rate: -0.2 migrant(s)/1,000 population (2017 est.)
country comparison to the world: 106

Population distribution: largest population of any African nation; significant population clusters are scattered throughout the country, with the highest density areas being in the south and southwest

Urbanization: *urban population:* 49.4% of total population (2017)
rate of urbanization: 4.3% annual rate of change (2015-20 est.)

Major urban areas—population: Lagos 13.123 million; Kano 3.587 million; Ibadan 3.16 million; ABUJA (capital) 2.44 million; Port Harcourt 2.343 million; Benin City 1.496 million (2015)

Sex ratio: *at birth:* 1.06 male(s)/female
0-14 years: 1.05 male(s)/female
15-24 years: 1.04 male(s)/female
25-54 years: 1.05 male(s)/female
55-64 years: 0.95 male(s)/female
65 years and over: 0.91 male(s)/female
total population: 1.04 male(s)/female (2016 est.)

Mother's mean age at first birth: 20.3 years
note: median age at first birth among women 25-29 (2013 est.)

Maternal mortality ratio: 814 deaths/100,000 live births (2015 est.)
country comparison to the world: 4

Infant mortality rate: *total:* 69.8 deaths/1,000 live births
male: 74.5 deaths/1,000 live births
female: 64.8 deaths/1,000 live births (2017 est.)
country comparison to the world: 8

Life expectancy at birth: *total population:* 53.8 years
male: 52.8 years
female: 55 years (2017 est.)
country comparison to the world: 214

Total fertility rate: 5.07 children born/woman (2017 est.)
country comparison to the world: 13

Contraceptive prevalence rate: 20.4% (2016)

Health expenditures: 3.7% of GDP (2014)
country comparison to the world: 167

Physicians density: 0.38 physicians/1,000 population (2009)

Drinking water source:
improved:
urban: 80.8% of population
rural: 57.3% of population
total: 68.5% of population
unimproved:
urban: 19.2% of population
rural: 42.7% of population
total: 31.5% of population (2015 est.)

Sanitation facility access:
improved:
urban: 32.8% of population
rural: 25.4% of population
total: 29% of population
unimproved:
urban: 67.2% of population
rural: 74.6% of population
total: 71% of population (2015 est.)

HIV/AIDS—adult prevalence rate: 2.9% (2016 est.)
country comparison to the world: 21

HIV/AIDS—people living with HIV/AIDS: 3.2 million (2016 est.)
country comparison to the world: 2

HIV/AIDS—deaths: 160,000 (2016 est.)
country comparison to the world: 1

Major infectious diseases: *degree of risk:* very high
food or waterborne diseases: bacterial and protozoal diarrhea, hepatitis A and E, and typhoid fever
vectorborne diseases: malaria, dengue fever, and yellow fever
water contact diseases: leptospirosis and schistosomiasis
respiratory disease: meningococcal meningitis
aerosolized dust or soil contact disease: Lassa fever
animal contact disease: rabies (2016)

Obesity—adult prevalence rate: 8.9% (2016)
country comparison to the world: 145

Children under the age of 5 years underweight: 19.4% (2015)
country comparison to the world: 12

Education expenditures: NA

Literacy: *definition:* age 15 and over can read and write
total population: 59.6%
male: 69.2%
female: 49.7% (2015 est.)

School life expectancy (primary to tertiary education): *total:* 9 years
male: 9 years
female: 8 years (2011)

Unemployment, youth ages 15-24: *total:* 7.7%
male: NA

female: NA (2015 est.)

GOVERNMENT

Country name: *conventional long form:* Federal Republic of Nigeria
conventional short form: Nigeria
etymology: named for the Niger River that flows through the west of the country to the Atlantic Ocean; from a native term "Ni Gir" meaning "River Gir"

Government type: federal presidential republic

Capital: *name:* Abuja
geographic coordinates: 9 05 N, 7 32 E
time difference: UTC+1 (6 hours ahead of Washington, DC, during Standard Time)

Administrative divisions: 36 states and 1 territory*; Abia, Adamawa, Akwa Ibom, Anambra, Bauchi, Bayelsa, Benue, Borno, Cross River, Delta, Ebonyi, Edo, Ekiti, Enugu, Federal Capital Territory*, Gombe, Imo, Jigawa, Kaduna, Kano, Katsina, Kebbi, Kogi, Kwara, Lagos, Nasarawa, Niger, Ogun, Ondo, Osun, Oyo, Plateau, Rivers, Sokoto, Taraba, Yobe, Zamfara

Independence: 1 October 1960 (from the UK)

National holiday: Independence Day (National Day), 1 October (1960)

Constitution: history: several previous; latest adopted 5 May 1999, effective 29 May 1999
amendments: proposed by the National Assembly; passage requires at least two-thirds majority vote of both houses and approval by the Houses of Assembly of at least two-thirds of the states; amendments to constitutional articles on the creation of a new state, fundamental constitutional rights, or constitution-amending procedures requires at least four-fifths majority vote by both houses of the National Assembly and approval by the Houses of Assembly in at least two-thirds of the states; passage of amendments limited to the creation of a new state require at least two-thirds majority by the proposing National Assembly house and approval by the Houses of Assembly in two-thirds of the states; amended several times, last in 2012 (2017)

Legal system: mixed legal system of English common law, Islamic law (in 12 northern states), and traditional law

International law organization participation: accepts compulsory ICJ jurisdiction with reservations; accepts ICCt jurisdiction

Citizenship: *citizenship by birth:* no
citizenship by descent only: at least one parent must be a citizen of Nigeria
dual citizenship recognized: yes
residency requirement for naturalization: 15 years

Suffrage: 18 years of age; universal

Executive branch: *chief of state:* President Maj. Gen. (ret.) Muhammadu BUHARI (since 29 May 2015); Vice President Oluyemi "Yemi" OSINBAJO (since 29 May 2015); note—the president is both chief of state and head of government

head of government: President Maj.Gen. (ret.) Muhammadu BUHARI (since 29 May 2015); Vice President Oluyemi "Yemi" OSINBAJO (since 29 May 2015)
cabinet: Federal Executive Council appointed by the president
elections/appointments: president directly elected by 'qualified' majority popular vote and at least 25% of the votes cast in 24 of Nigeria's 36 states; president elected for a 4-year term (eligible for a second term); election last held on 28-29 March 2015 (next to be held on 19 February 2019)
election results: Muhammadu BUHARI elected president; percent of vote—Muhammadu BUHARI (APC) 54%, Goodluck JONATHAN (PDP) 45%, other 1%

Legislative branch: *description:* bicameral National Assembly consists of the Senate (109 seats—3 each for the 36 states and 1 for Abuja; members directly elected in single-seat constituencies by simple majority vote to serve 4-year terms) and the House of Representatives (360 seats; members directly elected in single-seat constituencies by simple majority vote to serve 4-year terms)
elections: Senate—last held on 28-29 March 2015 (next to be held in February 2019); House of Representatives—last held on 28-29 March 2015 (next to be held in 2019)
election results: Senate—percent of vote by party—NA; seats by party—APC 60, PDP 49; House of Representatives—percent of vote by party—NA; seats by party—APC 225, PDP 125, other 10
note: Senate—seats by party as of April 2017—APC 66, PDP 43 (with continuing defections to the APC)

Judicial branch: *highest court(s):* Supreme Court (consists of the chief justice and 15 justices)
judge selection and term of office: judges appointed by the president on the recommendation of the National Judicial Council, a 23-member independent body of federal and state judicial officials; judge appointments confirmed by the Senate; judges serve until age 70
subordinate courts: Court of Appeal; Federal High Court; High Court of the Federal Capital Territory; Sharia Court of Appeal of the Federal Capital Territory; Customary Court of Appeal of the Federal Capital Territory; state court system similar in structure to federal system

Political parties and leaders: Accord Party or ACC [Mohammad Lawal MALADO]
All Progressives Congress or APC [John Odigie OYEGUN]
All Progressives Grand Alliance or APGA [Victor C. UMEH]
Democratic Peoples Party or DPP [Biodun OGUNBIYI]
Labor Party or LP [Alhaj Abdulkadir ABDULSALAM]
Peoples Democratic Party or PDP [Ali Modu SHERIFF]

Political pressure groups and leaders: Academic Staff Union for Universities or ASUU
Campaign for Democracy or CD
Civil Liberties Organization or CLO
Committee for the Defense of Human Rights or CDHR
Constitutional Right Project or CRP
Human Right Africa
National Association of Democratic Lawyers or NADL
National Association of Nigerian Students or NANS
Nigerian Bar Association or NBA
Nigerian Labor Congress or NLC
Nigerian Medical Association or NMA
Universal Defenders of Democracy or UDD
other: media

International organization participation: ACP, AfDB, AU, C, CD, D-8, ECOWAS, EITI (compliant country), FAO, G-15, G-24, G-77, IAEA, IBRD, ICAO, ICC (national committees), ICCt, ICRM, IDA, IDB, IFAD, IFC, IFRCS, IHO, ILO, IMF, IMO, IMSO, Interpol, IOC, IOM, IPU, ISO, ITSO, ITU, ITUC (NGOs), MIGA, MINURSO, MINUSMA, MONUSCO, NAM, OAS (observer), OIC, OPCW, OPEC, PCA, UN, UNAMID, UNCTAD, UNESCO, UNHCR, UNIDO, UNIFIL, UNISFA, UNITAR, UNMIL, UNMISS, UNOCI, UNWTO, UPU, WCO, WFTU (NGOs), WHO, WIPO, WMO, WTO

Diplomatic representation in the US: *chief of mission:* Ambassador Sylvanus Adiewere NSOFOR (since 29 November 2017)
chancery: 3519 International Court NW, Washington, DC 20008
telephone: [1] (202) 986-8400
FAX: [1] (202) 362-6541
consulate(s) general: Atlanta, New York

Diplomatic representation from the US: *chief of mission:* Ambassador W. Stuart SYMINGTON (since 1 December 2016)
embassy: Plot 1075 Diplomatic Drive, Central District Area, Abuja
mailing address: P. O. Box 5760, Garki, Abuja
telephone: [234] (9) 461-4000
FAX: [234] (9) 461-4036
consulate(s): Lagos

Flag description: three equal vertical bands of green (hoist side), white, and green; the color green represents the forests and abundant natural wealth of the country, white stands for peace and unity

National symbol(s): eagle; national colors: green, white

National anthem: *name:* "Arise Oh Compatriots, Nigeria's Call Obey"
lyrics/music: John A. ILECHUKWU, Eme Etim AKPAN, B. A. OGUNNAIKE, Sotu OMOIGUI and P. O. ADERIBIGBE/Benedict Elide ODIASE
note: adopted 1978; lyrics are a mixture of the five top entries in a national contest

ECONOMY

Economy—overview: Nigeria is one of Sub Saharan Africa's largest economies and relies heavily on oil as its main source of foreign exchange earnings and government revenues. Following the

2008-09 global financial crises, the banking sector was effectively recapitalized and regulation enhanced. Since then, Nigeria's economic growth has been driven by growth in agriculture, telecommunications, and services. Economic diversification and strong growth have not translated into a significant decline in poverty levels; however, over 62% of Nigeria's 170 million people still live in extreme poverty.

Despite its strong fundamentals, oil-rich Nigeria has been hobbled by inadequate power supply, lack of infrastructure, delays in the passage of legislative reforms, an inefficient property registration system, restrictive trade policies, an inconsistent regulatory environment, a slow and ineffective judicial system, unreliable dispute resolution mechanisms, insecurity, and pervasive corruption. Regulatory constraints and security risks have limited new investment in oil and natural gas, and Nigeria's oil production had been contracting every year since 2012 until a slight rebound in 2017.

President BUHARI, elected in March 2015, has established a cabinet of economic ministers that includes several technocrats, and he has announced plans to increase transparency, diversify the economy away from oil, and improve fiscal management, but his reliance on the Central Bank governor has led to overwhelmingly protectionist policies aimed at defending the naira from further devaluation. President BUHARI ran on an anticorruption platform, and has made some headway in alleviating corruption, such as an implementation of a Treasury Single Account that allows the government to better manage its resources. The government also is working to develop stronger public-private partnerships for roads, agriculture, and power.

Partly because of lower oil prices, Nigeria entered a recession in 2016. However, GDP growth turned positive, with oil prices recovering and output stabilizing in 2017.

GDP (purchasing power parity): $1.118 trillion (2017 est.)
$1.109 trillion (2016 est.)
$1.127 trillion (2015 est.)
note: data are in 2017 dollars
country comparison to the world: 24

GDP (official exchange rate): $394.8 billion (2016 est.)

GDP—real growth rate: 0.8% (2017 est.)
-1.6% (2016 est.)
2.7% (2015 est.)
country comparison to the world: 191

GDP—per capita (PPP): $5,900 (2017 est.)
$6,000 (2016 est.)
$6,300 (2015 est.)
note: data are in 2017 dollars
country comparison to the world: 164

Gross national saving: 14.9% of GDP (2017 est.)
13.2% of GDP (2016 est.)
12.3% of GDP (2015 est.)
country comparison to the world: 126

GDP—composition, by end use:
household consumption: 79%

government consumption: 6.8%
investment in fixed capital: 14.4%
investment in inventories: 0.7%
exports of goods and services: 12.5%
imports of goods and services: -13.5% (2017 est.)

GDP—composition, by sector of origin:
agriculture: 21.6%
industry: 18.3%
services: 60.1% (2017 est.)

Agriculture—products: cocoa, peanuts, cotton, palm oil, corn, rice, sorghum, millet, cassava (manioc, tapioca), yams, rubber; cattle, sheep, goats, pigs; timber; fish

Industries: crude oil, coal, tin, columbite; rubber products, wood; hides and skins, textiles, cement and other construction materials, food products, footwear, chemicals, fertilizer, printing, ceramics, steel

Industrial production growth rate: 0.7% (2017 est.)
country comparison to the world: 176

Labor force: 60.08 million (2017 est.)
country comparison to the world: 11

Labor force—by occupation: *agriculture:* 70%
industry: 10%
services: 20% (1999 est.)

Unemployment rate: 13.4% (2017 est.)
13.4% (2017 est.)
country comparison to the world: 166

Population below poverty line: 70% (2010 est.)

Household income or consumption by percentage share: *lowest 10%:* 1.8%
highest 10%: 38.2% (2010 est.)

Distribution of family income—Gini index: 48.8 (2013)
50.6 (1997)
country comparison to the world: 21

Budget: *revenues:* $13.97 billion
expenditures: $22.15 billion (2017 est.)
Taxes and other revenues: 3.5% of GDP (2017 est.)
country comparison to the world: 219

Budget surplus (+) or deficit (-): -2.1% of GDP (2017 est.)
country comparison to the world: 92

Public debt: 15.3% of GDP (2017 est.)
14.3% of GDP (2016 est.)
country comparison to the world: 191

Fiscal year: calendar year

Inflation rate (consumer prices): 16.3% (2017 est.)
15.7% (2016 est.)
country comparison to the world: 213

Central bank discount rate: 4.25% (31 December 2010)
6% (31 December 2009)
country comparison to the world: 95

Commercial bank prime lending rate: 17.5% (31 December 2017 est.)
16.87% (31 December 2016 est.)
country comparison to the world: 26

Stock of narrow money: $32.99 billion (31 December 2017 est.)

$37.45 billion (31 December 2016 est.)
country comparison to the world: 62

Stock of broad money: $67.97 billion (31 December 2017 est.)
$77.91 billion (31 December 2016 est.)
country comparison to the world: 63

Stock of domestic credit: $79.26 billion (31 December 2017 est.)
$89.18 billion (31 December 2016 est.)
country comparison to the world: 57

Market value of publicly traded shares: $53.07 billion (31 December 2016 est.)
$63.47 billion (31 December 2014 est.)
$80.61 billion (31 December 2013 est.)
country comparison to the world: 50

Current account balance: $7.667 billion (2017 est.)
$2.722 billion (2016 est.)
country comparison to the world: 24

Exports: $40.81 billion (2017 est.)
$34.7 billion (2016 est.)
country comparison to the world: 54

Exports—commodities: petroleum and petroleum products 95%, cocoa, rubber (2012 est.)

Exports—partners: India 34%, US 9%, Spain 5.9%, France 5.8%, South Africa 5.5%, Canada 5.1% (2016)

Imports: $35.24 billion (2017 est.)
$35.24 billion (2016 est.)
country comparison to the world: 60

Imports—commodities: machinery, chemicals, transport equipment, manufactured goods, food and live animals

Imports—partners: China 20.3%, US 8.3%, Belgium 7.6%, UK 4.4%, Netherlands 4.1% (2016)

Reserves of foreign exchange and gold: $31.08 billion (31 December 2017 est.)
$25.84 billion (31 December 2016 est.)
country comparison to the world: 51

Debt—external: $35.23 billion (31 December 2017 est.)
$31.41 billion (31 December 2016 est.)
country comparison to the world: 77

Stock of direct foreign investment—at home: $118 billion (31 December 2017 est.)
$113.4 billion (31 December 2016 est.)
country comparison to the world: 44

Stock of direct foreign investment—abroad: $17.04 billion (31 December 2017 est.)
$15.65 billion (31 December 2016 est.)
country comparison to the world: 55

Exchange rates: nairas (NGN) per US dollar—323.5 (2017 est.)
253 (2016 est.)
253 (2015 est.)
192.73 (2014 est.)
158.55 (2013 est.)

ENERGY

Electricity access: *population without electricity:* 95,500,000
electrification—*total population:* 45%

electrification—urban areas: 55%
electrification—rural areas: 37% (2013)

Electricity—production: 29.83 billion kWh (2015 est.)
country comparison to the world: 65

Electricity—consumption: 24.57 billion kWh (2015 est.)
country comparison to the world: 68

Electricity—exports: 0 kWh (2016 est.)
country comparison to the world: 178

Electricity—imports: 0 kWh (2016 est.)
country comparison to the world: 181

Electricity—installed generating capacity: 10.48 million kW (2015 est.)
country comparison to the world: 59

Electricity—from fossil fuels: 80.3% of total installed capacity (2015 est.)
country comparison to the world: 88

Electricity—from nuclear fuels: 0% of total installed capacity (2015 est.)
country comparison to the world: 154

Electricity—from hydroelectric plants: 19.5% of total installed capacity (2015 est.)
country comparison to the world: 90

Electricity—from other renewable sources: 0.2% of total installed capacity (2015 est.)
country comparison to the world: 163

Crude oil—production: 1.871 million bbl/day (2016 est.)
country comparison to the world: 13

Crude oil—exports: 2.279 million bbl/day (2014 est.)
country comparison to the world: 6

Crude oil—imports: 0 bbl/day (2014 est.)
country comparison to the world: 171

Crude oil—proved reserves: 37.06 billion bbl (1 January 2017 es)
country comparison to the world: 10

Refined petroleum products—production: 70,140 bbl/day (2014 est.)
country comparison to the world: 72

Refined petroleum products—consumption: 316,000 bbl/day (2015 est.)
country comparison to the world: 43

Refined petroleum products—exports: 11,010 bbl/day (2014 est.)
country comparison to the world: 82

Refined petroleum products—imports: 180,100 bbl/day (2014 est.)
country comparison to the world: 35

Natural gas—production: 45.15 billion cu m (2015 est.)
country comparison to the world: 18

Natural gas—consumption: 26.86 billion cu m (2015 est.)
country comparison to the world: 38

Natural gas—exports: 26.33 billion cu m (2015 est.)
country comparison to the world: 14

Natural gas—imports: 0 cu m (2013 est.)
country comparison to the world: 165

Natural gas—proved reserves: 5.284 trillion cu m (1 January 2017 es)
country comparison to the world: 9

Carbon dioxide emissions from consumption of energy: 97 million Mt (2013 est.)
country comparison to the world: 40

COMMUNICATIONS

Telephones—fixed lines: *total subscriptions:* 154,513
subscriptions per 100 inhabitants: less than 1 (July 2016 est.)
country comparison to the world: 130

Telephones—mobile cellular: *total:* 154,342,168
subscriptions per 100 inhabitants: 83 (July 2016 est.)
country comparison to the world: 9

Telephone system: *general assessment:* further expansion and modernization of the fixed-line telephone network is needed; network quality remains a problem
domestic: fixed-line subscribership remains less than 1 per 100 persons; mobile-cellular services growing rapidly, in part responding to the shortcomings of the fixed-line network; multiple cellular providers operate nationally with subscribership base over 80 per 100 persons
international: country code—234; landing point for the SAT-3/WASC fiber-optic submarine cable that provides connectivity to Europe and Asia; satellite earth stations—3 Intelsat (2 Atlantic Ocean and 1 Indian Ocean) (2016)

Broadcast media: nearly 70 federal government-controlled national and regional TV stations; all 36 states operate TV stations; several private TV stations operational; cable and satellite TV subscription services are available; network of federal government-controlled national, regional, and state radio stations; roughly 40 state government-owned radio stations typically carry their own programs except for news broadcasts; about 20 private radio stations; transmissions of international broadcasters are available (2007)

Internet country code: .ng
Internet users: total: 47,759,904

percent of population: 25.7% (July 2016 est.)
country comparison to the world: 9

TRANSPORTATION

National air transport system: *number of registered air carriers:* 16
inventory of registered aircraft operated by air carriers: 73
annual passenger traffic on registered air carriers: 3,223,459
annual freight traffic on registered air carriers: 22,400,657 mt-km (2015)
Civil aircraft registration country code prefix: 5N (2016)

Airports: 54 (2013)
country comparison to the world: 88

Airports—with paved runways: *total:* 40
over 3,047 m: 10

2,438 to 3,047 m: 12
1,524 to 2,437 m: 9
914 to 1,523 m: 6
under 914 m: 3 (2017)

Airports—with unpaved runways: *total:* 14
1,524 to 2,437 m: 2
914 to 1,523 m: 9
under 914 m: 3 (2013)

Heliports: 5 (2013)

Pipelines: condensate 124 km; gas 4,045 km; liquid petroleum gas 164 km; oil 4,441 km; refined products 3,940 km (2013)

Railways: *total:* 3,798 km
standard gauge: 293 km 1.435-m gauge
narrow gauge: 3,505 km 1.067-m gauge (2014)
country comparison to the world: 47

Roadways: *total:* 193,200 km
paved: 28,980 km
unpaved: 164,220 km (2004)
country comparison to the world: 29

Waterways: 8,600 km (Niger and Benue Rivers and smaller rivers and creeks) (2011)
country comparison to the world: 15

Merchant marine: *total:* 583
by type: general cargo 14, oil tanker 83, other 486 (2017)
country comparison to the world: 36

Ports and terminals: *major seaport(s):* Bonny Inshore Terminal, Calabar, Lagos
LNG terminal(s) (export): Bonny Island

MILITARY AND SECURITYIA

Military expenditures: 0.43% of GDP (2016)
0.42% of GDP (2015)
0.41% of GDP (2014)
0.47% of GDP (2013)
0.5% of GDP (2012)
country comparison to the world: 108

Military branches: Nigerian Armed Forces: Army, Navy, Air Force (2013)

Military service age and obligation: 18 years of age for voluntary military service; no conscription (2012)

Maritime threats: the International Maritime Bureau reports the territorial and offshore waters in the Niger Delta and Gulf of Guinea as high risk for piracy and armed robbery of ships; in 2016, 36 commercial vessels were boarded or attacked compared with 14 attacks in 2015; in the first half of 2017, 31 crew members were abducted in five reported incidents; half of all reports of vessels being fired upon occur in Nigerian waters; Nigerian pirates have extended the range of their attacks to as far away as Cote d'Ivoire and as far as 100 nm offshore

TERRORISM

Terrorist groups—home based: *Ansaru: aim(s):* establish an Islamic state in Nigeria
area(s) of operation: headquartered in the north; formed in 2012 as a breakaway faction of Boko Haram; has a history of attacking Nigerian

Government officials and facilities and kidnapping and killing Westerners; activities have waned in recent years, especially since founder Khalid al-BARNAWI was arrested in Lokoja, Kogi State, in central Nigeria in April 2016; authorities arrested several commanders and fighters in Kogi State in mid-2016; kidnappings for ransom remain the group's primary revenue source; membership was assessed in 2017 to be much smaller than Boko Haram's estimated manpower strength of the low thousands

Boko Haram: *aim(s):* replace the Nigerian Government with an Islamic state under strict Sharia and, ultimately, establish an Islamic caliphate across Africa; avenge military offenses against the group and destroy any political or social activity associated with Western society, including voting, attending secular schools, and wearing shirts and trousers

area(s) of operation: headquartered in the northeast, where the group was founded under the late Muslim cleric Mohammed YUSUF; since 2011, fighters have killed over 26,000 Nigerians during hundreds of attacks and disrupted trade and farming in the northeast, causing a calamitous famine and internally displacing an estimated 2.6 million people; continues to carry out suicide bombings in heavily populated areas, especially in the north and northeast, and to deepen food insecurity; remains the country's largest jihadist group; Nigeria continues to participate in the Joint Multinational Force's military offensives combating Boko Haram; one of the group's deadliest attacks began on 3 January 2015, when fighters used petrol bombs and other explosives and burned buildings in a series of mass killings in the northeast in Borno State in Baga and several surrounding villages that ended

on 7 January 2015, with approximately 2,000 deaths and thousands of displaced civilians; lost its total control over the northeast in 2015, when the Nigerian military routed out cells from many of the group's longtime strongholds; conducted the largest recorded single kidnapping incident of women and children in Nigeria's history, when operatives abducted approximately 276 teenage female students in Chibok, Borno State, in April 2014; manpower strength was estimated in 2017 to be in the low thousands

Terrorist groups—foreign based: *Islamic State of Iraq and the Levant (ISIL):* *aim(s):* replace the Nigerian Government with an Islamic state and implement ISIL's strict interpretation of Sharia *area(s) of operation:* based in the north along the border with Niger, with its heaviest presence in the northeast; targets primarily regional military installations; in areas under its influence, members enforce its strict interpretation of Sharia, direct religious education, and collect taxes imposed on companies and individuals; operates under Abu Mus'ab al-BARNAWI, the branch's leader since July 2016; ISIL has referred to Nigeria since circa March 2015 as its Wilayat Gharb Afriqiya, which translates to West Africa; as an official branch of core ISIL, it is also known as Islamic State of Iraq and the Levant—West Africa (ISIL-WA), Islamic State of Iraq and ash-Sham—West Africa (ISIS-WA), and Islamic State West Africa; assessed in 2016 to have a fighter strength in the low thousands

TRANSNATIONAL ISSUESIA

Disputes—international: Joint Border Commission with Cameroon reviewed 2002 ICJ ruling

on the entire boundary and bilaterally resolved differences, including June 2006 Greentree Agreement that immediately cedes sovereignty of the Bakassi Peninsula to Cameroon with a phaseout of Nigerian control within two years while resolving patriation issues; the ICJ ruled on an equidistance settlement of Cameroon-Equatorial Guinea-Nigeria maritime boundary in the Gulf of Guinea, but imprecisely defined coordinates in the ICJ decision and a sovereignty dispute between Equatorial Guinea and Cameroon over an island at the mouth of the Ntem River all contribute to the delay in implementation; only Nigeria and Cameroon have heeded the Lake Chad Commission's admonition to ratify the delimitation treaty which also includes the Chad-Niger and Niger-Nigeria boundaries; location of Benin-Niger-Nigeria tripoint is unresolved

Refugees and internally displaced persons: IDPs: 1,782,940 (northeast Nigeria; Boko Haram attacks and counterinsurgency efforts in northern Nigeria; communal violence between Christians and Muslims in the middle belt region, political violence; flooding; forced evictions; cattle rustling; competition for resources) (2017)

Illicit drugs: a transit point for heroin and cocaine intended for European, East Asian, and North American markets; consumer of amphetamines; safe haven for Nigerian narcotraffickers operating worldwide; major money-laundering center; massive corruption and criminal activity; Nigeria has improved some anti-money-laundering controls, resulting in its removal from the Financial Action Task Force's (FATF's) Noncooperative Countries and Territories List in June 2006; Nigeria's anti-money-laundering regime continues to be monitored by FATF

NIUE

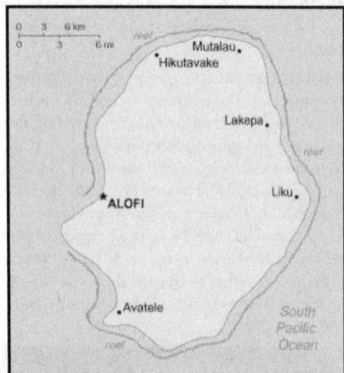

INTRODUCTION

Background: Niue's remoteness, as well as cultural and linguistic differences between its Polynesian

inhabitants and those of the adjacent Cook Islands, has caused it to be separately administered by New Zealand. The population of the island continues to drop (from a peak of 5,200 in 1966 to 1,618 in 2017) with substantial emigration to New Zealand 2,400 km to the southwest.

GEOGRAPHY

Location: Oceania, island in the South Pacific Ocean, east of Tonga

Geographic coordinates: 19 02 S, 169 52 W

Map references: Oceania

Area: *total:* 260 sq km
land: 260 sq km
water: 0 sq km
country comparison to the world: 213

Area—comparative: 1.5 times the size of Washington, DC

Land boundaries: 0 km

Coastline: 64 km

Maritime claims: *territorial sea:* 12 nm
exclusive economic zone: 200 nm

Climate: tropical; modified by southeast trade winds

Terrain: steep limestone cliffs along coast, central plateau

Elevation: *mean elevation:* NA

elevation extremes: *lowest point:* Pacific Ocean 0 m
highest point: unnamed elevation 1.4 km east of Hikutavake 80 m

Natural resources: fish, arable land

Land use: *agricultural land:* 19.1%
arable land: 3.8%;
permanent crops: 11.5%;
permanent pasture: 3.8%
forest: 71.2%
other: 9.7% (2011 est.)
Irrigated land: 0 sq km (2012)

Population—distribution: population distributed around the peripheral coastal areas of the island

Natural hazards: tropical cyclones

Environment—current issues: increasing attention to conservationist practices to counter loss of soil fertility from traditional slash and burn agriculture

Environment—international agreements: *party to:* Biodiversity, Climate Change, Climate Change-Kyoto Protocol, Desertification, Law of the Sea, Ozone Layer Protection

Geography—note: one of world's largest coral islands; the only major break in the surrounding coral reef occurs in the central western part of the coast

PEOPLE AND SOCIETY

Population: 1,618 (July 2017 est.)
country comparison to the world: 233

Nationality: *noun:* Niuean(s)
adjective: Niuean

Ethnic groups: Niuen 66.5%, part-Niuen 13.4%, non-Niuen 20.1% (includes 12% European and Asian and 8% Pacific Islanders) (2011 est.)

Languages: Niuean (official) 46% (a Polynesian language closely related to Tongan and Samoan), Niuean and English 32%, English (official) 11%, Niuean and others 5%, other 6% (2011 est.)

Religions: Ekalesia Niue (Congregational Christian Church of Niue—a Protestant church founded by missionaries from the London Missionary Society) 67%, other Protestant 3% (includes Seventh Day Adventist 1%, Presbyterian 1%, and Methodist 1%), Mormon 10%, Roman Catholic 10%, Jehovah's Witnesses 2%, other 6%, none 2% (2011 est.)

Population growth rate: -0.03% (2014 est.)
country comparison to the world: 201

Population distribution: population distributed around the peripheral coastal areas of the island

Urbanization: *urban population:* 44% of total population (2017)
rate of urbanization: -0.49% annual rate of change (2015-20 est.)

Major urban areas—population: ALOFI (capital) 1,000 (2014)

Sex ratio: NA

Infant mortality rate: *total:* NA
male: NA
female: NA

Life expectancy at birth: *total population:* NA
male: NA
female: NA (2017 est.)

Total fertility rate: NA

Health expenditures: 7.4% of GDP (2014)
country comparison to the world: 68

Physicians density: 1.84 physicians/1,000 population (2008)

Drinking water source:
improved:
urban: 98.4% of population
rural: 98.6% of population
total: 98.5% of population

unimproved:
urban: 1.6% of population
rural: 1.4% of population
total: 1.5% of population (2015 est.)

Sanitation facility access:
improved:
urban: 100% of population
rural: 100% of population
total: 100% of population
unimproved:
urban: 0% of population
rural: 0% of population
total: 0% of population (2015 est.)

HIV/AIDS—adult prevalence rate: NA

HIV/AIDS—people living with HIV/AIDS: NA

HIV/AIDS—deaths: NA

Obesity—adult prevalence rate: 50% (2016)
country comparison to the world: 6

Education expenditures: NA

GOVERNMENT

Country name: *conventional long form:* none
conventional short form: Niue
note: pronunciation falls between nyu-way and new-way, but not like new-wee
former: Savage Island
etymology: the origin of the name is obscure; in Niuean, the word supposedly translates as "behold the coconut"

Dependency status: self-governing in free association with New Zealand since 1974; Niue fully responsible for internal affairs; New Zealand retains responsibility for external affairs and defense; however, these responsibilities confer no rights of control and are only exercised at the request of the Government of Niue

Government type: self-governing parliamentary democracy (Fouo Ekepule) in free association with New Zealand

Capital: *name:* Alofi
geographic coordinates: 19 01 S, 169 55 W
time difference: UTC-11 (6 hours behind Washington, DC, during Standard Time)

Administrative divisions: none; note—there are no first-order administrative divisions as defined by the US Government, but there are 14 villages at the second order

Independence: 19 October 1974 (Niue became a self-governing state in free association with New Zealand)

National holiday: Waitangi Day (Treaty of Waitangi established British sovereignty over New Zealand), 6 February (1840)

Constitution: several previous (New Zealand colonial statutes); latest 19 October 1974 (Niue Constitution Act 1974); amended 1992, 2007 (2016)

Legal system: English common law

Suffrage: 18 years of age; universal

Executive branch: *chief of state:* Queen ELIZABETH II (since 6 February 1952); represented by Governor General of New Zealand Governor General Dame Patricia Lee REDDY (since 28

September 2016); the UK and New Zealand are represented by New Zealand High Commissioner Ross ARDEN (since February 2014)

head of government: Premier Toke TALAGI (since 18 June 2008)
cabinet: Cabinet chosen by the premier
elections/appointments: the monarchy is hereditary; premier indirectly elected by the Legislative Assembly for a 3-year term; election last held on 12 May 2017 (next to be held in 2020)
election results: Toke TALAGI reelected premier; Legislative Assembly vote—Toke TALAGI (independent) 15, O'Love JACOBSEN (independent) 5

Legislative branch: *description:* unicameral Assembly or Fono Ekepule (20 seats; 14 members directly elected in single-seat constituencies by simple majority vote and 6 directly elected from the National Register or "common roll" by majority vote; members serve 3-year terms)
elections: last held on 6 May 2017 (next to be held in 2020)
election results: percent of vote by party—NA; seats by party—independent 20

Judicial branch: highest resident court(s): Court of Appeal (consists of the chief justice and up to 3 judges); note—the Judicial Committee of the Privy Council (in London) is the final appeal court beyond the Niue Court of Appeal
judge selection and term of office: Niue chief justice appointed by the governor-general on the advice of the Cabinet and tendered by the premier; other judges appointed by the governor-general on the advice of the Cabinet and tendered by the chief justice and the minister of justice; judges serve until age 68
subordinate courts: High Court
note: Niue is a participant in the Pacific Judicial Development Program, which is designed to build governance and the rule of law in 15 Pacific island countries

Political parties and leaders: Alliance of Independents or AI
Niue People's Action Party or NPP [Young VIVIAN]

Political pressure groups and leaders: NA

International organization participation: ACP, AOSIS, FAO, IFAD, OPCW, PIF, Sparteca, SPC, UNESCO, UPU, WHO, WIPO, WMO

Diplomatic representation in the US: none (self-governing territory in free association with New Zealand)

Diplomatic representation from the US: none (self-governing territory in free association with New Zealand)

Flag description: yellow with the flag of the UK in the upper hoist-side quadrant; the flag of the UK bears five yellow five-pointed stars—a large star on a blue disk in the center and a smaller star on each arm of the bold red cross; the larger star stands for Niue, the smaller stars recall the Southern Cross constellation on the New Zealand flag and symbolize links with that country; yellow represents the bright sunshine of Niue and the warmth and friendship between Niue and New Zealand

National symbol(s): yellow, five-pointed star; national color: yellow

National anthem: name: "Ko e Iki he Lagi" (The Lord in Heaven)

lyrics/music: unknown/unknown, prepared by Sioeli FUSIKATA

note: adopted 1974

ECONOMY

Economy—overview: The economy suffers from the typical Pacific island problems of geographic isolation, few resources, and a small population. The agricultural sector consists mainly of subsistence gardening, although some cash crops are grown for export. Industry consists primarily of small factories for processing passion fruit, lime oil, honey, and coconut cream. The sale of postage stamps to foreign collectors is an important source of revenue.

Government expenditures regularly exceed revenues, and the shortfall is made up by critically needed grants from New Zealand that are used to pay wages to public employees. Economic aid allocation from New Zealand in FY13/14 was US$10.1 million. Niue has cut government expenditures by reducing the public service by almost half.

The island in recent years has suffered a serious loss of population because of emigration to New Zealand. Efforts to increase GDP include the promotion of tourism and financial services, although the International Banking Repeal Act of 2002 resulted in the termination of all offshore banking licenses.

GDP (purchasing power parity): $10.01 million (2003 est.)

country comparison to the world: 229

GDP (official exchange rate): $10.01 million (2003)

GDP—real growth rate: 6.2% (2003 est.)

country comparison to the world: 22

GDP—per capita (PPP): $5,800 (2003 est.)

country comparison to the world: 166

GDP—composition, by sector of origin:
agriculture: 23.5%
industry: 26.9%
services: 49.5% (2003)

Agriculture—products: coconuts, passion fruit, honey, limes, taro, yams, cassava (manioc, tapioca), sweet potatoes; pigs, poultry, beef cattle

Industries: handicrafts, food processing

Industrial production growth rate: NA%

Labor force: 663 (2001)

country comparison to the world: 231

Labor force—by occupation: note: most work on family plantations; paid work exists only in government service, small industry, and the Niue Development Board

Unemployment rate: 12% (2001)

country comparison to the world: 154

Population below poverty line: NA%

Household income or consumption by percentage share: lowest 10%: NA%
highest 10%: NA%

Budget: *revenues:* $15.07 million
expenditures: $16.33 million (FY04/05)

Budget surplus (+) or deficit (-): -12.6% of GDP (FY04/05)

country comparison to the world: 212

Fiscal year: 1 April—31 March

Inflation rate (consumer prices): 4% (2005)

country comparison to the world: 156

Exports: $201,400 (2004 est.)

country comparison to the world: 221

Exports—commodities: canned coconut cream, copra, honey, vanilla, passion fruit products, pawpaws, root crops, limes, footballs, stamps, handicrafts

Imports: $9.038 million (2004 est.)

country comparison to the world: 218

Imports—commodities: food, live animals, manufactured goods, machinery, fuels, lubricants, chemicals, drugs

Debt—external: $418,000 (2002 est.)

country comparison to the world: 203

Exchange rates: New Zealand dollars (NZD) per US dollar—
1.416 (2017)
1.4279 (2016)
1.4279 (2015)
1.4279 (2014 est.)
1.2039 (2013 est.)

ENERGY

Electricity—production: 3 million kWh (2015 est.)

country comparison to the world: 217

Electricity—consumption: 2.79 million kWh (2015 est.)

country comparison to the world: 215

Electricity—exports: 0 kWh (2016 est.)

country comparison to the world: 175

Electricity—imports: 0 kWh (2016 est.)

country comparison to the world: 179

Electricity—installed generating capacity: 1,000 kW (2015 est.)

country comparison to the world: 215

Electricity—from fossil fuels: 100% of total installed capacity (2015 est.)

country comparison to the world: 14

Electricity—from nuclear fuels: 0% of total installed capacity (2015 est.)

country comparison to the world: 151

Electricity—from hydroelectric plants: 0% of total installed capacity (2015 est.)

country comparison to the world: 191

Electricity—from other renewable sources: 0% of total installed capacity (2015 est.)

country comparison to the world: 200

Crude oil—production: 0 bbl/day (2016 est.)

country comparison to the world: 182

Crude oil—exports: 0 bbl/day (2014 est.)

country comparison to the world: 169

Crude oil—imports: 0 bbl/day (2014 est.)

country comparison to the world: 168

Crude oil—proved reserves: 0 bbl (1 January 2017 es)

country comparison to the world: 180

Refined petroleum products—production: 0 bbl/day (2014 est.)

country comparison to the world: 187

Refined petroleum products—consumption: 60 bbl/day (2015 est.)

country comparison to the world: 215

Refined petroleum products—exports: 0 bbl/day (2014 est.)

country comparison to the world: 184

Refined petroleum products—imports: 64.25 bbl/day (2014 est.)

country comparison to the world: 212

Natural gas—production: 0 cu m (2013 est.)

country comparison to the world: 175

Natural gas—consumption: 0 cu m (2013 est.)

country comparison to the world: 214

Natural gas—exports: 0 cu m (2015 est.)

country comparison to the world: 156

Natural gas—imports: 0 cu m (2013 est.)

country comparison to the world: 162

Natural gas—proved reserves: 0 cu m (1 January 2014 es)

country comparison to the world: 177

Carbon dioxide emissions from consumption of energy: 3,520 Mt (2012 est.)

country comparison to the world: 213

COMMUNICATIONS

Telephone system: *domestic:* single-line (fixed line) telephone system connects all villages (and virtually all households) on island
international: country code—683 (2015)

Broadcast media: 1 government-owned TV station with many of the programs supplied by Television New Zealand; 1 government-owned radio station broadcasting in AM and FM (2009)

Internet country code: .nu
Internet users: total: 1,090

percent of population: 91.6% (July 2016 est.)

country comparison to the world: 213

TRANSPORTATION

Airports: 1 (2013)

country comparison to the world: 228

Airports—with paved runways: *total:* 1
1,524 to 2,437 m: 1 (2017)

Airports—with unpaved runways: *total:* 1
1,524 to 2,437 m: 1 (2013)

Roadways: *total:* 234 km
paved: 210 km (2017)

country comparison to the world: 214

Ports and terminals: *major seaport(s):* Alofi

MILITARY AND SECURITY

Military branches: no regular indigenous military forces; Police Force

Military—note: defense is the responsibility of New Zealand

TRANSNATIONAL ISSUES

Disputes—international: none

NORFOLK ISLAND

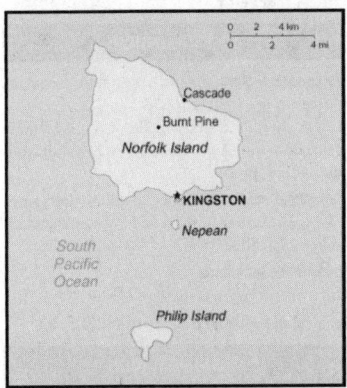

INTRODUCTION

Background: Two British attempts at establishing the island as a penal colony (1788-1814 and 1825-55) were ultimately abandoned. In 1856, the island was resettled by Pitcairn Islanders, descendants of the Bounty mutineers and their Tahitian companions.

GEOGRAPHY

Location: Oceania, island in the South Pacific Ocean, east of Australia

Geographic coordinates: 29 02 S, 167 57 E

Map references: Oceania

Area: *total:* 36 sq km
land: 36 sq km
water: 0 sq km
country comparison to the world: 236

Area—comparative: about 0.2 times the size of Washington, DC

Land boundaries: 0 km

Coastline: 32 km

Maritime claims: *territorial sea:* 12 nm
exclusive fishing zone: 200 nm

Climate: subtropical; mild, little seasonal temperature variation

Terrain: volcanic island with mostly rolling plains

Elevation: *mean elevation:* NA

elevation extremes: *lowest point:* Pacific Ocean 0 m
highest point: Mount Bates 319 m

Natural resources: fish

Land use: *agricultural land:* 25%
arable land: 0%;
permanent crops: 0%;
permanent pasture: 25%
forest: 11.5%
other: 63.5% (2011 est.)
Irrigated land: 0 sq km (2012)

Population—distribution: population concentrated around the capital of Kingston

Natural hazards: tropical cyclones (especially May to July)

Environment—current issues: inadequate solid waste management; freshwater obtained through rainwater catchment; deficient electrical network

Geography—note: most of the 32 km coastline consists of almost inaccessible cliffs, but the land slopes down to the sea in one small southern area on Sydney Bay, where the capital of Kingston is situated

PEOPLE AND SOCIETY

Population: 1,748 (2016 est.)
country comparison to the world: 231

Nationality: *noun:* Norfolk Islander(s)
adjective: Norfolk Islander(s)

Ethnic groups: Australian 79.5%, New Zealander 13.3%, Fijian 2.5%, Filipino 1.1%, English 1%, other 1.8%, unspecified 0.8% (2011 est.)

Languages: English (official) 67.6%, other 32.4% (includes Norfolk 23.7%—also known as Norfuk or Norf'k—which is a mixture of 18th century English and ancient Tahitian) (2011 est.)

Religions: Protestant 49.6% (Anglican 33.6%, Uniting Church in Australia 12.8%, Seventh Day Adventist 3.2%), Roman Catholic 11.7%, other 8.6%, none 23.5%, unspecified 6.6% (2011 est.)

Population growth rate: 0.01% (2014 est.)
country comparison to the world: 192

Population distribution: population concentrated around the capital of Kingston

Sex ratio: NA

Infant mortality rate: *total:* NA
male: NA
female: NA

Life expectancy at birth: *total population:* NA
male: NA
female: NA (2017 est.)

Total fertility rate: NA

HIV/AIDS—adult prevalence rate: NA

HIV/AIDS—people living with HIV/AIDS: NA

HIV/AIDS—deaths: NA

GOVERNMENT

Country name: *conventional long form:* Territory of Norfolk Island
conventional short form: Norfolk Island
etymology: named by British explorer Captain James COOK after Mary HOWARD, Duchess of Norfolk, in 1774

Dependency status: self-governing territory of Australia; administered from Canberra by the Department of Regional Australia, Local Government, Arts, and Sport

Government type: non-self-governing overseas territory of Australia; note—the Norfolk Island Regional Council, which began operations 1 July 2016, is responsible for planning and managing a variety of public services, including those funded by the Government of Australia

Capital: *name:* Kingston

geographic coordinates: 29 03 S, 167 58 E
time difference: UTC+11 (16 hours ahead of Washington, DC, during Standard Time)

Administrative divisions: none (territory of Australia)

Independence: none (territory of Australia)

National holiday: Bounty Day (commemorates the arrival of Pitcairn Islanders), 8 June (1856)

Constitution: previous 1913, 1957; latest effective 7 August 1979; amended many times, last in 2015 (2016)

Legal system: English common law and the laws of Australia

Citizenship: see Australia

Suffrage: 18 years of age; universal

Executive branch: *chief of state:* Queen ELIZABETH II (since 6 February 1952); represented by Governor General of the Commonwealth of Australia General Sir Peter COSGROVE (since 28 March 2014)

head of government: Administrator Eric HUTCHINSON (since 1 April 2017)
cabinet: Executive Council consists of 4 Legislative Assembly members
elections/appointments: the monarchy is hereditary; governor general appointed by the monarch; administrator appointed by the governor general of Australia for a 2-year term and represents the monarch and Australia

Legislative branch: *description:* unicameral Norfolk Island Regional Council (5 seats; councillors directly elected by simple majority vote to serve 4-year terms); mayor elected annually by the councillors
elections: elections last held 28 May 2016 (next to be held in 2020)
election results: seats by party—independent 5
note: following an administrative restructuring of local government, the Legislative Assembly was dissolved on 18 June 2015 and replaced by an interim Norfolk Island Advisory Council effective 1 July 2015; the Advisory Council consisted of 5 members appointed by the Norfolk Island administrator based on nominations from the community; following elections on 28 May 2016, the new Norfolk Island Regional Council commenced operations on 1 July 2016

Judicial branch: *highest court(s):* Supreme Court of Norfolk Island (consists of the chief justice and several justices); note—appeals beyond the Supreme Court of Norfolk Island are heard by the Federal Court and the High Court of Australia *judge selection and term of office:* justices appointed by the governor general of Australia from among justices of the Federal Court of Australia; justices serve until mandatory retirement at age 70

subordinate courts: Petty Court of Sessions; specialized courts including a Coroner's Court and the Employment Tribunal

Political parties and leaders: Norfolk Island Labor Party [Mike KELLY]
Norfolk Liberals [John BROWN]

Political pressure groups and leaders: none

International organization participation: UPU

Diplomatic representation in the US: none (territory of Australia)

Diplomatic representation from the US: none (territory of Australia)

Flag description: three vertical bands of green (hoist side), white, and green with a large green Norfolk Island pine tree centered in the slightly wider white band; green stands for the rich vegetation on the island, and the pine tree—endemic to the island—is a symbol of Norfolk Island
note: somewhat reminiscent of the flag of Canada with its use of only two colors and depiction of a prominent local floral symbol in the central white band; also resembles the green and white triband of Nigeria

National symbol(s): Norfolk Island pine

National anthem: *name:* "Come Ye Blessed"
lyrics/music: New Testament/John Prindle SCOTT
note: the local anthem, whose lyrics consist of the words from Matthew 25:34-36, 40, is also known as "The Pitcairn Anthem;" as a territory of Australia, "God Save the Queen" is official (see Australia);

however, the island does not recognize "Advance Australia Fair"

ECONOMY

Economy—overview: Norfolk Island is suffering from a severe economic downturn. Tourism, the primary economic activity, is the main driver of economic growth. The agricultural sector has become self-sufficient in the production of beef, poultry, and eggs.

GDP (purchasing power parity): $NA

Agriculture—products: Norfolk Island pine seed, Kentia palm seed, cereals, vegetables, fruit; cattle, poultry

Industries: tourism, light industry, ready mixed concrete

Labor force: 978 (2006)
country comparison to the world: 230

Labor force—by occupation: *agriculture:* 6%
industry: 14%
services: 80% (2006 est.)

Budget: *revenues:* $4.6 million
expenditures: $4.8 million (FY99/00)

Fiscal year: 1 July–30 June

Exports: $NA

Exports—commodities: postage stamps, seeds of the Norfolk Island pine and Kentia palm, small quantities of avocados

Imports: $NA

Imports—commodities: NA

Debt—external: $NA

Exchange rates: Australian dollars (AUD) per US dollar—
1.311 (2017)

1.3291 (2016)
1.3291 (2015)
1.3291 (2014 est.)
1.1094 (2013 est.)

COMMUNICATIONS

Telephone system: *general assessment:* adequate
domestic: free local calls
international: country code—672; submarine cable links with Australia and New Zealand; satellite earth station—1

Broadcast media: 1 local radio station; broadcasts of several Australian radio and TV stations available via satellite (2009)

Internet country code: .nf
Internet users: total: 765

percent of population: 34.6% (July 2016 est.)

TRANSPORTATION

Airports: 1 (2013)
country comparison to the world: 229

Airports—with paved runways: *total:* 1
1,524 to 2,437 m: 1 (2017)

Roadways: *total:* 80 km
paved: 53 km
unpaved: 27 km (2008)
country comparison to the world: 217

Ports and terminals: *major seaport(s):* Kingston

MILITARY AND SECURITY

Military—note: defense is the responsibility of Australia

TRANSNATIONAL ISSUES

Disputes—international: none

NORWAY

INTRODUCTION

Background: Two centuries of Viking raids into Europe tapered off following the adoption of Christianity by King Olav TRYGGVASON in 994; conversion of the Norwegian kingdom occurred over the next several decades. In 1397, Norway was absorbed into a union with Denmark that lasted more than four centuries. In 1814, Norwegians resisted the cession of their country to Sweden and adopted a new constitution. Sweden then invaded Norway but agreed to let Norway keep its constitution in return for accepting the union under a Swedish king. Rising nationalism throughout the 19th century led to a 1905 referendum granting Norway independence. Although Norway remained neutral in World War I, it suffered heavy losses to its shipping. Norway proclaimed its neutrality at the outset of World War II, but was nonetheless occupied for five years by Nazi Germany (1940-45). In 1949, Norway abandoned neutrality and became a member of NATO.

Discovery of oil and gas in adjacent waters in the late 1960s boosted Norway's economic fortunes. In referenda held in 1972 and 1994, Norway rejected joining the EU. Key domestic issues include immigration and integration of ethnic minorities, maintaining the country's extensive social safety net with an aging population, and preserving economic competitiveness.

GEOGRAPHY

Location: Northern Europe, bordering the North Sea and the North Atlantic Ocean, west of Sweden

Geographic coordinates: 62 00 N, 10 00 E

Map references: Europe

Area: *total:* 323,802 sq km
land: 304,282 sq km
water: 19,520 sq km
country comparison to the world: 69

Area—comparative: slightly larger than twice the size of Georgia; slightly larger than New Mexico

Land boundaries: *total:* 2,566 km
border countries (3): Finland 709 km, Sweden 1,666 km, Russia 191 km

Coastline: 25,148 km (includes mainland 2,650 km, as well as long fjords, numerous small islands, and minor indentations 22,498 km; length of island coastlines 58,133 km)

Maritime claims: *territorial sea:* 12 nm
contiguous zone: 10 nm
exclusive economic zone: 200 nm
continental shelf: 200 nm

Climate: temperate along coast, modified by North Atlantic Current; colder interior with increased precipitation and colder summers; rainy year-round on west coast

Terrain: glaciated; mostly high plateaus and rugged mountains broken by fertile valleys; small, scattered plains; coastline deeply indented by fjords; arctic tundra in north

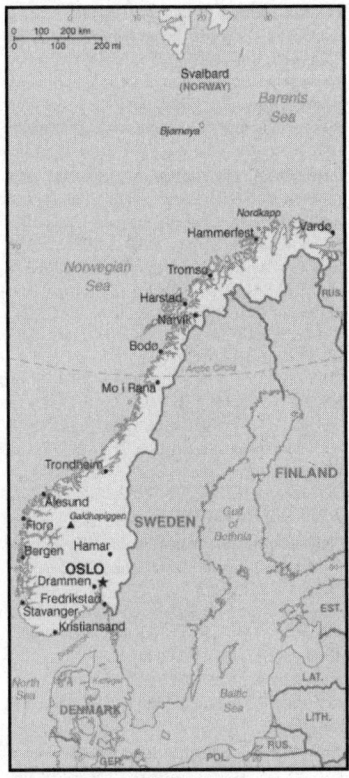

Elevation: *mean elevation:* 460 m
elevation extremes: *lowest point:* Norwegian Sea 0 m
highest point: Galdhopiggen 2,469 m

Natural resources: petroleum, natural gas, iron ore, copper, lead, zinc, titanium, pyrites, nickel, fish, timber, hydropower

Land use: *agricultural land:* 2.7%
arable land: 2.2%;
permanent crops: 0%;
permanent pasture: 0.5%
forest: 27.8%
other: 69.5% (2011 est.)
Irrigated land: 900 sq km (2012)

Population—distribution: most Norwegians live in the south where the climate is milder and there is better connectivity to mainland Europe; population clusters are found all along the North Sea coast in the southwest, and Skaggerak in the southeast; the interior areas of the north remain sparsely populated

Natural hazards: rockslides, avalanches
volcanism: Beerenberg (2,227 m) on Jan Mayen Island in the Norwegian Sea is the country's only active volcano

Environment—current issues: water pollution; acid rain damaging forests and adversely affecting lakes, threatening fish stocks; air pollution from vehicle emissions

Environment—international agreements: *party to:* Air Pollution, Air Pollution-Nitrogen Oxides, Air Pollution-Persistent Organic Pollutants, Air Pollution-Sulfur 85, Air Pollution-Sulfur 94, Air Pollution-Volatile Organic Compounds, Antarctic-Environmental Protocol, Antarctic-Marine Living Resources, Antarctic Seals, Antarctic Treaty, Biodiversity, Climate Change, Climate Change-Kyoto Protocol, Desertification, Endangered Species, Environmental Modification, Hazardous Wastes, Law of the Sea, Marine Dumping, Ozone Layer Protection, Ship Pollution, Tropical Timber 83, Tropical Timber 94, Wetlands, Whaling
signed, but not ratified: none of the selected agreements

Geography—note: about two-thirds mountains; some 50,000 islands off its much-indented coastline; strategic location adjacent to sea lanes and air routes in North Atlantic; one of the most rugged and longest coastlines in the world

PEOPLE AND SOCIETY

Population: 5,320,045 (July 2017 est.)
country comparison to the world: 120
Nationality: *noun:* Norwegian(s)
adjective: Norwegian

Ethnic groups: Norwegian 83.2% (includes about 60,000 Sami), other European 8.3%, other 8.5% (2017 est.)

Languages: Bokmal Norwegian (official), Nynorsk Norwegian (official), small Sami- and Finnish-speaking minorities
note: Sami is an official language in nine municipalities

Religions: Church of Norway (Evangelical Lutheran—official) 71.5%, Roman Catholic 2.8%, other Christian 3.9%, Muslim 2.8%, other 2%, unspecified 7.5% (2016 est.)

Age structure: *0-14 years:* 18% (male 490,915/female 466,515)
15-24 years: 12.58% (male 343,103/female 326,053)
25-54 years: 41.01% (male 1,125,334/female 1,056,330)
55-64 years: 11.71% (male 315,223/female 307,639)
65 years and over: 16.71% (male 409,057/female 479,876) (2017 est.)

Dependency ratios: *total dependency ratio:* 52.1
youth dependency ratio: 27.3
elderly dependency ratio: 24.8
potential support ratio: 4
note: data include Svalbard and Jan Mayen Islands (2015 est.)

Median age: *total:* 39.2 years
male: 38.4 years
female: 40 years (2017 est.)
country comparison to the world: 55

Population growth rate: 1.01% (2017 est.)
country comparison to the world: 113

Birth rate: 12.2 births/1,000 population (2017 est.)
country comparison to the world: 164

Death rate: 8.1 deaths/1,000 population (2017 est.)
country comparison to the world: 87

Net migration rate: 5.9 migrant(s)/1,000 population (2017 est.)
country comparison to the world: 17

Population distribution: most Norweigans live in the south where the climate is milder and there is better connectivity to mainland Europe; population clusters are found all along the North Sea coast in the southwest, and Skaggerak in the southeast; the interior areas of the north remain sparsely populated

Urbanization: *urban population:* 81% of total population (2017)
rate of urbanization: 1.31% annual rate of change (2015-20 est.)
note: data include Svalbard and Jan Mayen Islands

Major urban areas—population: OSLO (capital) 986,000 (2015)

Sex ratio: *at birth:* 1.06 male(s)/female
0-14 years: 1.05 male(s)/female
15-24 years: 1.05 male(s)/female
25-54 years: 1.06 male(s)/female
55-64 years: 1.02 male(s)/female
65 years and over: 0.84 male(s)/female
total population: 1.02 male(s)/female (2016 est.)

Mother's mean age at first birth: 28.9 years
note: data is calculated based on actual age at first births (2015 est.)

Maternal mortality ratio: 5 deaths/100,000 live births (2015 est.)
country comparison to the world: 174

Infant mortality rate: *total:* 2.5 deaths/1,000 live births
male: 2.8 deaths/1,000 live births
female: 2.2 deaths/1,000 live births (2017 est.)
country comparison to the world: 221

Life expectancy at birth: *total population:* 81.9 years
male: 79.8 years
female: 84 years (2017 est.)
country comparison to the world: 18

Total fertility rate: 1.85 children born/woman (2017 est.)
country comparison to the world: 145

Health expenditures: 9.7% of GDP (2014)
country comparison to the world: 27

Physicians density: 4.42 physicians/1,000 population (2014)

Hospital bed density: 3.85 beds/1,000 population (2014)

Drinking water source:
improved:
urban: 100% of population
rural: 100% of population
total: 100% of population
unimproved:
urban: 0% of population
rural: 0% of population
total: 0% of population (2015 est.)

Sanitation facility access:
improved:

urban: 98% of population
rural: 98.3% of population
total: 98.1% of population
unimproved:
urban: 2% of population
rural: 1.7% of population
total: 1.9% of population (2015 est.)

HIV/AIDS—adult prevalence rate: NA

HIV/AIDS—people living with HIV/AIDS: NA

HIV/AIDS—deaths: NA

Obesity—adult prevalence rate: 23.1% (2016)
country comparison to the world: 67

Education expenditures: 7.4% of GDP (2013)
country comparison to the world: 21

School life expectancy (primary to tertiary education): *total:* 18 years
male: 17 years
female: 18 years (2015)

Unemployment, youth ages 15-24: *total:* 11.1%
male: 13%
female: 9.3% (2016 est.)
country comparison to the world: 109

GOVERNMENT

Country name: *conventional long form:* Kingdom of Norway
conventional short form: Norway
local long form: Kongeriket Norge
local short form: Norge
etymology: derives from the Old Norse words "nordr" and "vegr" meaning "northern way" and refers to the long coastline of western Norway

Government type: parliamentary constitutional monarchy

Capital: *name:* Oslo

geographic coordinates: 59 55 N, 10 45 E
time difference: UTC+1 (6 hours ahead of Washington, DC, during Standard Time)
daylight saving time: +1hr, begins last Sunday in March; ends last Sunday in October

Administrative divisions: 19 counties (fylker, singular—fylke); Akershus, Aust-Agder, Buskerud, Finnmark, Hedmark, Hordaland, More og Romsdal, Nordland, Nord-Trondelag, Oppland, Oslo, Ostfold, Rogaland, Sogn og Fjordane, Sor-Trondelag, Telemark, Troms, Vest-Agder, Vestfold

Dependent areas: Bouvet Island, Jan Mayen, Svalbard

Independence: 7 June 1905 (declared the union with Sweden dissolved); 26 October 1905 (Sweden agreed to the repeal of the union)

National holiday: Constitution Day, 17 May (1814)

Constitution: history: drafted spring 1814, adopted 16 May 1814, signed by Constituent Assembly 17 May 1814
amendments: proposals submitted by members of Parliament or by the government within the first three years of Parliament's four-year term; passage requires two-thirds majority vote of a two-thirds quorum in the next elected Parliament; amended over 400 times, last in 2015 (2016)

Legal system: mixed legal system of civil, common, and customary law; Supreme Court can advise on legislative acts

International law organization participation: accepts compulsory ICJ jurisdiction with reservations; accepts ICCt jurisdiction

Citizenship: *citizenship by birth:* no
citizenship by descent only: at least one parent must be a citizen of Norway
dual citizenship recognized: no
residency requirement for naturalization: 7 years

Suffrage: 18 years of age; universal

Executive branch: *chief of state:* King HARALD V (since 17 January 1991); Heir Apparent Crown Prince HAAKON MAGNUS, son of the monarch (born 20 July 1973)

head of government: Prime Minister Erna SOLBERG (since 16 October 2013)
cabinet: State Council appointed by the monarch, approved by Parliament
elections/appointments: the monarchy is hereditary; following parliamentary elections, the leader of the majority party or majority coalition usually appointed prime minister by the monarch with the approval of the parliament

Legislative branch: *description:* unicameral Parliament or Storting (169 seats; members directly elected in multi-seat constituencies by proportional representation vote; members serve 4-year terms)
elections: last held on 11 September 2017 (next to be held in September 2021)
election results: percent of vote by party—Ap 27.4%, H 25%, FrP 15.2%, SP 10.3%, SV 6%, V 4.4%, KrF 4.2%, MDG 3.2%, R 2.4%, other/invalid 1.9%; seats by party—Ap 49, H 45, FrP 27, SP 19, SV 11, V 8, KrF 8, MDG 1, R 1

Judicial branch: *highest court(s):* Supreme Court or Hoyesterett (consists of the chief justice and 18 associate justices)
judge selection and term of office: justices appointed by the monarch (King in Council) upon the recommendation of the Judicial Appointments Board; justice retirement mandatory at age 70
subordinate courts: Courts of Appeal or Lagmensrett; regional and district courts; Conciliation Boards; ordinary and special courts; note—in addition to professionally trained judges, elected lay judges sit on the bench with professional judges in the Courts of Appeal and district courts

Political parties and leaders: Center Party or Sp [Trygve Slagsvold VEDUM]
Christian Democratic Party or KrF [Knut Arild HAREIDE]
Conservative Party or H [Erna SOLBERG]
Green Party or MDG [Rasmus HANSSON and Une Aina BASTHOLM]
Labor Party or Ap [Jonas Gahr STORE]
Liberal Party or V [Trine SKEI GRANDE]
Progress Party or FrP [Siv JENSEN]
Socialist Left Party or SV [Audun LYSBAKKEN]

Political pressure groups and leaders: Confederation of Norwegian Enterprise or NHO [Tore ULSTEIN, Kristin SKOGEN LUND]
Norwegian Confederation of Trade Unions or LO [Hans-Christian GABRIELSEN]
other: environmental groups; media; digital privacy movements

International organization participation: ADB (nonregional member), AfDB (nonregional member), Arctic Council, Australia Group, BIS, CBSS, CD, CE, CERN, EAPC, EBRD, EFTA, EITI (implementing country), ESA, FAO, FATF, IADB, IAEA, IBRD, ICAO, ICC (national committees), ICCt, ICRM, IDA, IEA, IFAD, IFC, IFRCS, IGAD (partners), IHO, ILO, IMF, IMO, IMSO, Interpol, IOC, IOM, IPU, ISO, ITSO, ITU, ITUC (NGOs), MIGA, MINUSMA, NATO, NC, NEA, NIB, NSG, OAS (observer), OECD, OPCW, OSCE, Paris Club, PCA, Schengen Convention, UN, UNCTAD, UNESCO, UNHCR, UNIDO, UNITAR, UNMISS, UNRWA, UNTSO, UNWTO, UPU, WCO, WHO, WIPO, WMO, WTO, ZC

Diplomatic representation in the US: *chief of mission:* Ambassador Kare Reidar AAS (since 17 September 2013)
chancery: 2720 34th Street NW, Washington, DC 20008
telephone: [1] (202) 333-6000
FAX: [1] (202) 459-3990
consulate(s) general: Houston, New York, San Francisco

Diplomatic representation from the US: *chief of mission:* Ambassador (vacant); Charge d'Affaires James P. DEHART (since 12 January 2017)
embassy: Morgedalsvegen 36, 0378 Oslo;
mailing address: PSC 69, Box 1000, APO AE 09707
telephone: [47] 21-30-85-40
FAX: [47] 22-44-33-63, 22-56-27-51

Flag description: red with a blue cross outlined in white that extends to the edges of the flag; the vertical part of the cross is shifted to the hoist side in the style of the Dannebrog (Danish flag); the colors recall Norway's past political unions with Denmark (red and white) and Sweden (blue)

National symbol(s): lion; national colors: red, white, blue

National anthem: name: "Ja, vi elsker dette landet" (Yes, We Love This Country)
lyrics/music: lyrics/music: Bjornstjerne BJORNSON/Rikard NORDRAAK
note: adopted 1864; in addition to the national anthem, "Kongesangen" (Song of the King), which uses the tune of "God Save the Queen," serves as the royal anthem

ECONOMY

Economy—overview: Norway has a stable economy with a vibrant private sector, a large state sector, and an extensive social safety net. Norway opted out of the EU during a referendum in November 1994; nonetheless, as a member of the

European Economic Area, it contributes sizably to the EU budget.

The country is richly endowed with natural resources in addition to oil and gas, including hydropower, fish, forests, and minerals. Norway is a leading producer and the world's second largest exporter of seafood, after China. The government manages the country's petroleum resources through extensive regulation. The petroleum sector provides about 9% of jobs, 12% of GDP, 13% of the state's revenue, and 37% of exports, according to official national estimates. Norway is one of the world's leading petroleum exporters, though oil production in 2016 was close to 50% below its peak in 2000; annual gas production, conversely, more than doubled over the same time period. After a continual decline from 2001 to 2013, oil production rose in 2016 for the third year running, due to the higher production of existing oil fields and to new fields coming on stream.

In anticipation of eventual declines in oil and gas production, Norway saves state revenue from petroleum sector activities in the world's largest sovereign wealth fund, valued at almost $900 billion as of early 2017. To help balance the federal budget each year, the government follows a "fiscal rule," which states that spending of revenues from petroleum and fund investments shall correspond to the expected real rate of return on the fund, an amount it estimates is sustainable over time. In February 2017, the government revised the expected rate of return for the fund downward from 4% to 3%.

After solid GDP growth in the 2004-07 period, the economy slowed in 2008, and contracted in 2009, before returning to modest, positive growth from 2010 to 2017. Lower oil prices in 2015 and 2016 caused growth to slow, increased unemployment, and weakened the Norwegian krone. The latter trend has mitigated the negative impact of lower oil and gas prices by making Norwegian exports cheaper for foreign buyers. The government has expressed willingness to increase public spending from the sovereign wealth fund to help prevent a recession.

GDP (purchasing power parity): $375.9 billion (2017 est.)
$370.9 billion (2016 est.)
$366.9 billion (2015 est.)
note: data are in 2017 dollars
country comparison to the world: 49

GDP (official exchange rate): $392.1 billion (2016 est.)

GDP—real growth rate: 1.4% (2017 est.)
1.1% (2016 est.)
1.6% (2015 est.)
country comparison to the world: 179

GDP—per capita (PPP): $70,600 (2017 est.)
$70,600 (2016 est.)
$70,500 (2015 est.)
note: data are in 2017 dollars
country comparison to the world: 12

Gross national saving: 34.4% of GDP (2017 est.)
34.1% of GDP (2016 est.)
36.9% of GDP (2015 est.)
country comparison to the world: 16

GDP—composition, by end use:
household consumption: 44.7%
government consumption: 24.6%
investment in fixed capital: 23.8%
investment in inventories: 4%
exports of goods and services: 36.4%
imports of goods and services: -33.5% (2017 est.)

GDP—composition, by sector of origin:
agriculture: 2.4%
industry: 31.1%
services: 66.5% (2017 est.)

Agriculture—products: barley, wheat, potatoes; pork, beef, veal, milk; fish

Industries: petroleum and gas, shipping, fishing, aquaculture, food processing, shipbuilding, pulp and paper products, metals, chemicals, timber, mining, textiles

Industrial production growth rate: 1% (2017 est.)
country comparison to the world: 169

Labor force: 2.797 million (2017 est.)
country comparison to the world: 108

Labor force—by occupation: *agriculture:* 2.1%
industry: 19.3%
services: 78.6% (2016 est.)

Unemployment rate: 4% (2017 est.)
4.7% (2016 est.)
country comparison to the world: 52

Population below poverty line: NA%

Household income or consumption by percentage share: *lowest 10%:* 3.8%
highest 10%: 21.2% (2014)

Distribution of family income—Gini index: 26.8 (2010)
25.8 (1995)
country comparison to the world: 139

Budget: *revenues:* $214.3 billion
expenditures: $198 billion (2017 est.)
Taxes and other revenues: 54.7% of GDP (2017 est.)
country comparison to the world: 9

Budget surplus (+) or deficit (-): 4.2% of GDP (2017 est.)
country comparison to the world: 8

Public debt: 37% of GDP (2017 est.)
35.7% of GDP (2016 est.)
note: data cover general government debt, and includes debt instruments issued (or owned) by government entities other than the treasury; the data exclude treasury debt held by foreign entities; the data exclude debt issued by subnational entities, as well as intra-governmental debt; intra-governmental debt consists of treasury borrowings from surpluses in the social funds, such as for retirement, medical care, and unemployment; debt instruments for the social funds are not sold at public auctions
country comparison to the world: 143

Fiscal year: calendar year

Inflation rate (consumer prices): 2.1% (2017 est.)
3.6% (2016 est.)
country comparison to the world: 95

Central bank discount rate: 6.25% (31 December 2010)
1.75% (31 December 2009)
country comparison to the world: 67

Commercial bank prime lending rate: 1.5% (31 December 2017 est.)
1.5% (31 December 2016 est.)
country comparison to the world: 184

Stock of narrow money: $236.7 billion (31 December 2017 est.)
$214 billion (31 December 2016 est.)
country comparison to the world: 23

Stock of broad money: $272.9 billion (31 December 2017 est.)
$234.3 billion (31 December 2016 est.)
country comparison to the world: 35

Stock of domestic credit: $650.5 billion (31 December 2017 est.)
$571.7 billion (31 December 2016 est.)
country comparison to the world: 23

Market value of publicly traded shares: $193.9 billion (31 December 2015 est.)
$219.4 billion (31 December 2014 est.)
$265.4 billion (31 December 2013 est.)
country comparison to the world: 34

Current account balance: $21.73 billion (2017 est.)
$18.43 billion (2016 est.)
country comparison to the world: 15

Exports: $102.8 billion (2017 est.)
$88.88 billion (2016 est.)
country comparison to the world: 36

Exports—commodities: petroleum and petroleum products, machinery and equipment, metals, chemicals, ships, fish

Exports—partners: UK 21%, Germany 14.4%, Netherlands 10.7%, France 6.9%, Sweden 6.5%, Belgium 4.4%, US 4.3%, Denmark 4% (2016)

Imports: $79.9 billion (2017 est.)
$73.62 billion (2016 est.)
country comparison to the world: 39

Imports—commodities: machinery and equipment, chemicals, metals, foodstuffs

Imports—partners: Germany 12.2%, Sweden 12.2%, China 11.2%, US 6.6%, Denmark 5.7%, UK 5.2%, Netherlands 4.1% (2016)

Reserves of foreign exchange and gold: $60.45 billion (31 December 2016 est.)
$57.46 billion (31 December 2015 est.)
country comparison to the world: 35

Debt—external: $642.3 billion (31 March 2016 est.)
$640.1 billion (31 March 2015 est.)
note: Norway is a net external creditor
country comparison to the world: 19

Stock of direct foreign investment—at home: $217.2 billion (31 December 2017 est.)
$219.1 billion (31 December 2016 est.)
country comparison to the world: 28

Stock of direct foreign investment—abroad: $205.9 billion (31 December 2017 est.)
$191.7 billion (31 December 2016 est.)
country comparison to the world: 26

Exchange rates: Norwegian kroner (NOK) per US dollar—
8.308 (2017 est.)
8.3978 (2016 est.)
8.3978 (2015 est.)
8.0646 (2014 est.)
6.3021 (2013 est.)

ENERGY

Electricity access: electrification—*total population:* 100% (2016)

Electricity—production: 149.5 billion kWh (2016 est.)
country comparison to the world: 28

Electricity—consumption: 133.1 billion kWh (2016 est.)
country comparison to the world: 28

Electricity—exports: 15.53 billion kWh (2016 est.)
country comparison to the world: 13

Electricity—imports: 5.7 billion kWh (2016 est.)
country comparison to the world: 36

Electricity—installed generating capacity: 33.85 million kW (2015 est.)
country comparison to the world: 31

Electricity—from fossil fuels: 4.1% of total installed capacity (2015 est.)
country comparison to the world: 207

Electricity—from nuclear fuels: 0% of total installed capacity (2015 est.)
country comparison to the world: 155

Electricity—from hydroelectric plants: 88.4% of total installed capacity (2015 est.)
country comparison to the world: 11

Electricity—from other renewable sources: 3.3% of total installed capacity (2015 est.)
country comparison to the world: 109

Crude oil—production: 1.648 million bbl/day (2016 est.)
country comparison to the world: 15

Crude oil—exports: 1.395 million bbl/day (2016 est.)
country comparison to the world: 11

Crude oil—imports: 10,630 bbl/day (2016 est.)
country comparison to the world: 74

Crude oil—proved reserves: 6.611 billion bbl (1 January 2017)
country comparison to the world: 21

Refined petroleum products—production: 282,400 bbl/day (2016 est.)
country comparison to the world: 42

Refined petroleum products—consumption: 227,700 bbl/day (2016 est.)
country comparison to the world: 53

Refined petroleum products—exports: 353,100 bbl/day (2016 est.)
country comparison to the world: 22

Refined petroleum products—imports: 124,500 bbl/day (2016 est.)
country comparison to the world: 53

Natural gas—production: 117.2 billion cu m (2015 est.)
country comparison to the world: 8

Natural gas—consumption: 9.428 billion cu m (2015 est.)
country comparison to the world: 55

Natural gas—exports: 112 billion cu m (2015 est.)
country comparison to the world: 3

Natural gas—imports: 0 cu m (2014 est.)
country comparison to the world: 166

Natural gas—proved reserves: 1.856 trillion cu m (1 January 2017 es)

country comparison to the world: 19

Carbon dioxide emissions from consumption of energy: 53.9 million Mt (2015 est.)
country comparison to the world: 58

COMMUNICATIONS

Telephones—fixed lines: *total subscriptions:* 863,855
subscriptions per 100 inhabitants: 16 (July 2016 est.)
country comparison to the world: 72

Telephones—mobile cellular: *total:* 5,718,740
subscriptions per 100 inhabitants: 109 (July 2016 est.)
country comparison to the world: 111

Telephone system: *general assessment:* modern in all respects; one of the most advanced telecommunications networks in Europe
domestic: Norway has a domestic satellite system; the prevalence of rural areas encourages the wide use of mobile-cellular systems
international: country code—47; 2 buried coaxial cable systems; submarine cables provide links to other Nordic countries and Europe; satellite earth stations—NA Eutelsat, NA Intelsat (Atlantic Ocean), and 1 Inmarsat (Atlantic and Indian Ocean regions); note—Norway shares the Inmarsat earth station with the other Nordic countries (Denmark, Finland, Iceland, and Sweden) (2016)

Broadcast media: state-owned public radio-TV broadcaster operates 3 nationwide TV stations, 3 nationwide radio stations, and 16 regional radio stations; roughly a dozen privately owned TV stations broadcast nationally and roughly another 25 local TV stations broadcasting; nearly 75% of households have access to multi-channel cable or satellite TV; 2 privately owned radio stations broadcast nationwide and another 240 stations operate locally; Norway is the first country in the world to phase out FM radio in favor of Digital Audio Broadcasting (DAB), a process scheduled for completion in late 2017 (2017)

Internet country code: .no
Internet users: total: 5,122,904

percent of population: 97.3% (July 2016 est.)
country comparison to the world: 70

TRANSPORTATION

National air transport system: *number of registered air carriers:* 3
inventory of registered aircraft operated by air carriers: 106
annual passenger traffic on registered air carriers: 12,277,220
annual freight traffic on registered air carriers: 0 mt-km (2015)
Civil aircraft registration country code prefix: LN (2016)

Airports: 95 (2013)
country comparison to the world: 61

Airports—with paved runways: *total:* 67
2,438 to 3,047 m: 14
1,524 to 2,437 m: 10
914 to 1,523 m: 22
under 914 m: 21 (2017)

Airports—with unpaved runways: *total:* 28
914 to 1,523 m: 6
under 914 m: 22 (2013)

Heliports: 1 (2013)

Pipelines: gas 8,520 km; oil/condensate 1,304 km (2017)

Railways: *total:* 4,250 km
standard gauge: 4,250 km 1.435-m gauge (2,518 km electrified) (2014)
country comparison to the world: 41

Roadways: *total:* 93,870 km (includes 393 km of expressways)
paved: 75,754 km
unpaved: 18,116 km (2013)
country comparison to the world: 53

Waterways: 1,577 km (2010)
country comparison to the world: 51

Merchant marine: *total:* 1,585
by type: bulk carrier 99, general cargo 240, oil tanker 80, other 1,166 (2017)
country comparison to the world: 16

Ports and terminals: *major seaport(s):* Bergen, Haugesund, Maaloy, Mongstad, Narvik, Sture
LNG terminal(s) (export): Kamoy, Kollsnes, Melkoya Island
LNG terminal(s) (import): Fredrikstad, Mosjoen

MILITARY AND SECURITY

Military expenditures: 1.62% of GDP (2016)
1.5% of GDP (2015)
1.47% of GDP (2014)
1.41% of GDP (2013)
1.4% of GDP (2012)
country comparison to the world: 72

Military branches: Norwegian Army (Haeren), Royal Norwegian Navy (Kongelige Norske Sjoeforsvaret; includes Coastal Rangers and Coast Guard (Kystvakt)), Royal Norwegian Air Force (Kongelige Norske Luftforsvaret), Home Guard (Heimevernet, HV) (2017)

Military service age and obligation: 19-35 years of age for male and female compulsory military service; 16 years of age in wartime; 17 years of age for male volunteers; 18 years of age for women; 19-month service obligation (2017)

TRANSNATIONAL ISSUES

Disputes—international: Norway asserts a territorial claim in Antarctica (Queen Maud Land and its continental shelf); Denmark (Greenland) and Norway have made submissions to the Commission on the Limits of the Continental Shelf (CLCS) and Russia is collecting additional data to augment its 2001 CLCS submission; Norway and Russia signed a comprehensive maritime boundary agreement in 2010

Refugees and internally displaced persons: refugees (country of origin): 15,062 (Eritrea); 11,537 (Syria); 8,379 (Somalia); 6,568 (Afghanistan) (2016)
stateless persons: 3,251 (2016)

OMAN

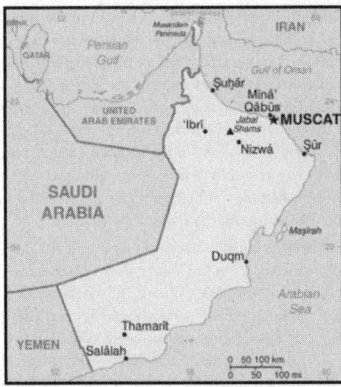

INTRODUCTION

Background: The inhabitants of the area of Oman have long prospered from Indian Ocean trade. In the late 18th century, the nascent sultanate in Muscat signed the first in a series of friendship treaties with Britain. Over time, Oman's dependence on British political and military advisors increased, although the Sultanate never became a British colony. In 1970, QABOOS bin Said Al-Said overthrew his father, and has since ruled as sultan, but he has not designated a successor. His extensive modernization program has opened the country to the outside world, while preserving the longstanding close ties with the UK and US. Oman's moderate, independent foreign policy has sought to maintain good relations with its neighbors and to avoid external entanglements. Inspired by the popular uprisings that swept the Middle East and North Africa beginning in January 2011, some Omanis staged demonstrations, calling for more jobs and economic benefits and an end to corruption. In response to those protester demands, QABOOS in 2011 pledged to implement economic and political reforms, such as granting legislative and regulatory powers to the Majlis al-Shura and increasing unemployment benefits. Additionally, in August 2012, the Sultan announced a royal directive mandating the speedy implementation of a national job creation plan for thousands of public and private sector Omani jobs. As part of the government's efforts to decentralize authority and allow greater citizen participation in local governance, Oman successfully conducted its first municipal council elections in December 2012. Announced by the Sultan in 2011, the municipal councils have the power to advise the Royal Court on the needs of local districts across Oman's 11 governorates. The Sultan returned to Oman in March 2015 after eight months in Germany, where he received medical treatment. He has since appeared publicly on a few occasions.

GEOGRAPHY

Location: Middle East, bordering the Arabian Sea, Gulf of Oman, and Persian Gulf, between Yemen and the UAE

Geographic coordinates: 21 00 N, 57 00 E

Map references: Middle East

Area: *total:* 309,500 sq km
land: 309,500 sq km
water: 0 sq km
country comparison to the world: 72

Area—comparative: twice the size of Georgia; slightly smaller than Kansas

Land boundaries: *total:* 1,561 km
border countries (3): Saudi Arabia 658 km, UAE 609 km, Yemen 294 km

Coastline: 2,092 km

Maritime claims: *territorial sea:* 12 nm
contiguous zone: 24 nm
exclusive economic zone: 200 nm

Climate: dry desert; hot, humid along coast; hot, dry interior; strong southwest summer monsoon (May to September) in far south

Terrain: central desert plain, rugged mountains in north and south

Elevation: *mean elevation:* 310 m
elevation extremes: *lowest point:* Arabian Sea 0 m
highest point: Jabal Shams 3,004 m

Natural resources: petroleum, copper, asbestos, some marble, limestone, chromium, gypsum, natural gas

Land use: *agricultural land:* 4.7%
arable land: 0.1%;
permanent crops: 0.1%;
permanent pasture: 4.5%
forest: 0%
other: 95.3% (2011 est.)
Irrigated land: 590 sq km (2012)

Population—distribution: the vast majority of the population is located in and around the Al Hagar Mountains in the north of the country; another smaller cluster is found around the city of Salalah in the far south; most of the country remains sparsely populated

Natural hazards: summer winds often raise large sandstorms and dust storms in interior; periodic droughts

Environment—current issues: rising soil salinity; beach pollution from oil spills; limited natural freshwater resources

Environment—international agreements: *party to:* Biodiversity, Climate Change, Climate Change-Kyoto Protocol, Desertification, Hazardous Wastes, Law of the Sea, Marine Dumping, Ozone Layer Protection, Ship Pollution, Whaling
signed, but not ratified: none of the selected agreements

Geography—note: consists of Oman proper and two northern exclaves, Musandam and Al Madhah; the former is a peninsula that occupies a strategic location adjacent to the Strait of Hormuz, a vital transit point for world crude oil

PEOPLE AND SOCIETY

Population: 3,424,386 (July 2017 est.)
note: immigrants make up almost 45% of the total population, according to UN data (2017)
country comparison to the world: 132

Nationality: *noun:* Omani(s)
adjective: Omani

Ethnic groups: Arab, Baluchi, South Asian (Indian, Pakistani, Sri Lankan, Bangladeshi), African

Languages: Arabic (official), English, Baluchi, Urdu, Indian dialects

Religions: Muslim 85.9%, Christian 6.5%, Hindu 5.5%, Buddhist 0.8%, Jewish <0.1%, other 1%, unaffiliated 0.2% (2010 est.)
note: Omani citizens represent approximately 60% of the population and are overwhelming Muslim (Ibadhi and Sunni sects each constitute about 45% and Shia about 5%); Christians, Hindus, and Buddhists accounting for roughly 5% of Omani citizens

Age structure: *0-14 years:* 30.1% (male 528,554/female 502,272)
15-24 years: 18.69% (male 335,764/female 304,207)
25-54 years: 43.8% (male 864,858/female 635,006)
55-64 years: 3.92% (male 71,477/female 62,793)
65 years and over: 3.49% (male 58,561/female 60,894) (2017 est.)

Dependency ratios: *total dependency ratio:* 32.4
youth dependency ratio: 29.4
elderly dependency ratio: 3.1
potential support ratio: 32.6 (2015 est.)

Median age: *total:* 25.6 years
male: 26.6 years
female: 24.2 years (2017 est.)
country comparison to the world: 153

Population growth rate: 2.03% (2017 est.)
country comparison to the world: 44

Birth rate: 24 births/1,000 population (2017 est.)
country comparison to the world: 54

Death rate: 3.3 deaths/1,000 population (2017 est.)
country comparison to the world: 220

Net migration rate: -0.4 migrant(s)/1,000 population (2017 est.)
country comparison to the world: 120

Population distribution: the vast majority of the population is located in and around the Al Hagar Mountains in the north of the country; another smaller cluster is found around the city of Salalah in the far south; most of the country remains sparsely poplulated

Urbanization: *urban population:* 78.5% of total population (2017)
rate of urbanization: 2.17% annual rate of change (2015-20 est.)

Major urban areas—population: MUSCAT (capital) 838,000 (2015)

Sex ratio: *at birth:* 1.05 male(s)/female
0-14 years: 1.05 male(s)/female
15-24 years: 1.1 male(s)/female
25-54 years: 1.38 male(s)/female
55-64 years: 1.14 male(s)/female
65 years and over: 0.99 male(s)/female
total population: 1.19 male(s)/female (2016 est.)

Maternal mortality ratio: 17 deaths/100,000 live births (2015 est.)
country comparison to the world: 133

Infant mortality rate: *total:* 12.8 deaths/1,000 live births
male: 13.1 deaths/1,000 live births
female: 12.5 deaths/1,000 live births (2017 est.)
country comparison to the world: 110

Life expectancy at birth: *total population:* 75.7 years
male: 73.7 years
female: 77.7 years (2017 est.)
country comparison to the world: 99

Total fertility rate: 2.82 children born/woman (2017 est.)
country comparison to the world: 60

Contraceptive prevalence rate: 29.7% (2014)

Health expenditures: 3.6% of GDP (2014)
country comparison to the world: 172

Physicians density: 1.54 physicians/1,000 population (2014)

Hospital bed density: 1.7 beds/1,000 population (2012)

Drinking water source:
improved:
urban: 95.5% of population
rural: 86.1% of population
total: 93.4% of population
unimproved:
urban: 4.5% of population
rural: 13.9% of population
total: 6.6% of population (2015 est.)

Sanitation facility access:
improved:
urban: 97.3% of population
rural: 94.7% of population
total: 96.7% of population
unimproved:
urban: 2.7% of population
rural: 5.3% of population
total: 3.3% of population (2015 est.)

HIV/AIDS—adult prevalence rate: NA

HIV/AIDS—people living with HIV/AIDS: NA

HIV/AIDS—deaths: NA

Obesity—adult prevalence rate: 27% (2016)
country comparison to the world: 39

Children under the age of 5 years underweight: 9.7% (2014)
country comparison to the world: 73

Education expenditures: 5% of GDP (2013)
country comparison to the world: 100

Literacy: *definition:* age 15 and over can read and write

total population: 93%
male: 96.6%
female: 86% (2015 est.)

School life expectancy (primary to tertiary education): *total:* 14 years
male: 13 years
female: 15 years (2015)

GOVERNMENT

Country name: *conventional long form:* Sultanate of Oman
conventional short form: Oman
local long form: Saltanat Uman
local short form: Uman
former: Sultanate of Muscat and Oman
etymology: the origin of the name is uncertain, but it apparently dates back at least 2,000 years since an "Omana" is mentioned by Pliny the Elder (1st century A.D.) and an "Omanon" by Ptolemy (2nd century A.D.)

Government type: absolute monarchy

Capital: *name:* Muscat
geographic coordinates: 23 37 N, 58 35 E
time difference: UTC+4 (9 hours ahead of Washington, DC, during Standard Time)

Administrative divisions: 11 governorates (muhafazat, singular—muhafaza); Ad Dakhiliyah, Al Buraymi, Al Wusta, Az Zahirah, Janub al Batinah (Al Batinah South), Janub ash Sharqiyah (Ash Sharqiyah South), Masqat (Muscat), Musandam, Shamal al Batinah (Al Batinah North), Shamal ash Sharqiyah (Ash Sharqiyah North), Zufar (Dhofar)

Independence: 1650 (expulsion of the Portuguese)

National holiday: National Day, 18 November; note—coincides with the birthday of Sultan QABOOS, 18 November (1940)

Constitution: history: promulgated by royal decree 6 November 1996 (the Basic Law of the Sultanate of Oman serves as the constitution); amended by royal decree in 2011
amendments: promulgated by the sultan or proposed by the Council of Oman and drafted by a technical committee as stipulated by royal decree and then promulgated through royal decree; amended 2011 (2016)

Legal system: mixed legal system of Anglo-Saxon law and Islamic law

International law organization participation: has not submitted an ICJ jurisdiction declaration; non-party state to the ICCt

Citizenship: *citizenship by birth:* no
citizenship by descent only: the father must be a citizen of Oman
dual citizenship recognized: no
residency requirement for naturalization: unknown

Suffrage: 21 years of age; universal; note—members of the military and security forces by law cannot vote

Executive branch: *chief of state:* Sultan and Prime Minister QABOOS bin Said Al-Said (sultan since

23 July 1970 and prime minister since 23 July 1972); note—the monarch is both chief of state and head of government

head of government: Sultan and Prime Minister QABOOS bin Said Al-Said (sultan since 23 July 1970 and prime minister since 23 July 1972)
cabinet: Cabinet appointed by the monarch
elections/appointments: members of the Ruling Family Council determine a successor from the sultan's extended family; if the Council cannot form a consensus within 3 days of the sultan's death or incapacitation, the Defense Council will relay a predetermined heir as chosen by the sultan

Legislative branch: *description:* bicameral Council of Oman or Majlis Oman consists of the Council of State or Majlis al-Dawla (85 seats including the chairman; members appointed by the sultan from among former government officials and prominent educators, businessmen, and citizens) and the Consultative Council or Majlis al-Shura (85 seats; members directly elected in single- and 2-seat constituencies by simple majority popular vote to serve renewable 4-year terms); note—since political reforms in 2011, legislation from the Consultative Council is submitted to the Council of State for review by the Royal Court
elections: Consultative Assembly—last held on 25 October 2015 (next to be held in October 2019)
election results: percent of vote by party—NA; seats by party—NA; note—organized political parties in Oman are legally banned

Judicial branch: *highest court(s):* Supreme Court (consists of 5 judges)
judge selection and term of office: judges nominated by the 9-member Supreme Judicial Council (chaired by the monarch) and appointed by the monarch; judges appointed for life
subordinate courts: Courts of Appeal; Administrative Court; Courts of First Instance; sharia courts; magistrates' courts; military courts

Political parties and leaders: none; note—organized political parties are legally banned in Oman, and loyalties tend to form around tribal affiliations

Political pressure groups and leaders: none

International organization participation: ABEDA, AFESD, AMF, CAEU, FAO, G-77, GCC, IAEA, IBRD, ICAO, ICC (NGOs), IDA, IDB, IFAD, IFC, IHO, ILO, IMF, IMO, IMSO, Interpol, IOC, IPU, ISO, ITSO, ITU, LAS, MIGA, NAM, OIC, OPCW, UN, UNCTAD, UNESCO, UNIDO, UNWTO, UPU, WCO, WFTU (NGOs), WHO, WIPO, WMO, WTO

Diplomatic representation in the US: *chief of mission:* Ambassador Hunaina bint Sultan bin Ahmad al-MUGHAIRI (since 2 December 2005)
chancery: 2535 Belmont Road, NW, Washington, DC 20008
telephone: [1] (202) 387-1980
FAX: [1] (202) 745-4933

Diplomatic representation from the US: *chief of mission:* Ambassador Marc J. SIEVERS (since 15 December 2016)
embassy: Jamait Ad Duwal Al Arabiyya Street, Al Khuwair area, Muscat

mailing address: P.O. Box 202, P.C. 115, Madinat Al Sultan Qaboos, Muscat
telephone: [968] 24-643-400
FAX: [968] 24-643-740

Flag description: three horizontal bands of white, red, and green of equal width with a broad, vertical, red band on the hoist side; the national emblem (a khanjar dagger in its sheath superimposed on two crossed swords in scabbards) in white is centered near the top of the vertical band; white represents peace and prosperity, red recalls battles against foreign invaders, and green symbolizes the Jebel al Akhdar (Green Mountains) and fertility

National symbol(s): khanjar dagger superimposed on two crossed swords; national colors: red, white, green

National anthem: name: "Nashid as-Salaam as-Sultani" (The Sultan's Anthem)
lyrics/music: Rashid bin Uzayyiz al KHUSAIDI/ James Frederick MILLS, arranged by Bernard EBBINGHAUS
note: adopted 1932; new lyrics written after QABOOS bin Said al Said gained power in 1970; first performed by the band of a British ship as a salute to the Sultan during a 1932 visit to Muscat; the bandmaster of the HMS Hawkins was asked to write a salutation to the Sultan on the occasion of his ship visit

ECONOMY

Economy—overview: Oman is heavily dependent on its dwindling oil resources, which generate 84% of government revenue. In 2016, low global oil prices drove Oman's budget deficit to $11.5 billion, or approximately 19% of GDP, but the budget deficit was reduced to 13% of GDP in 2017 as Oman reduced government subsidies. Oman has limited foreign assets and is issuing debt to cover its deficit.

Oman is using enhanced oil recovery techniques to boost production, but has simultaneously pursued a development plan that focuses on diversification, industrialization, and privatization, with the objective of reducing the oil sector's contribution to GDP from 46% at present to 9% by 2020 in accordance with Oman's ninth five-year development plan. Tourism and gas-based industries are key components of the government's diversification strategy.

Muscat also has notably focused on creating more Omani jobs to employ the rising number of nationals entering the workforce. However, high social welfare benefits — that had increased in the wake of the 2011 Arab Spring — have challenged the government's ability to effectively balance its budget in light of low export oil prices. In response, Omani officials imposed austerity measures to its gasoline and diesel subsidies in 2016, with further subsidy cuts planned for electricity and liquid petroleum gas. The spending cuts have faced some public opposition, which in 2017 prompted the Omani Government to announce a cap on fuel prices and a plan to provide 25,000 public-sector jobs for Omanis.

GDP (purchasing power parity): $187.9 billion (2017 est.)
$187.9 billion (2016 est.)
$182.4 billion (2015 est.)
note: data are in 2017 dollars
country comparison to the world: 68

GDP (official exchange rate): $71.93 billion (2016 est.)

GDP—real growth rate: 0% (2017 est.)
3% (2016 est.)
4.2% (2015 est.)
country comparison to the world: 202

GDP—per capita (PPP): $45,500 (2017 est.)
$46,900 (2016 est.)
$48,300 (2015 est.)
note: data are in 2017 dollars
country comparison to the world: 36

Gross national saving: 19.7% of GDP (2017 est.)
19.4% of GDP (2016 est.)
18.3% of GDP (2015 est.)
country comparison to the world: 92

GDP—composition, by end use:
household consumption: 34.5%
government consumption: 24.6%
investment in fixed capital: 35.3%
investment in inventories: 2.1%
exports of goods and services: 51%
imports of goods and services: -47.4% (2017 est.)

GDP—composition, by sector of origin:
agriculture: 1.7%
industry: 45.2%
services: 53% (2017 est.)

Agriculture—products: dates, limes, bananas, alfalfa, vegetables; camels, cattle; fish

Industries: crude oil production and refining, natural and liquefied natural gas production; construction, cement, copper, steel, chemicals, optic fiber

Industrial production growth rate: 0.3% (2017 est.)
country comparison to the world: 184

Labor force: 968,800
note: about 60% of the labor force is non-national (2007 est.)
country comparison to the world: 145

Labor force—by occupation: *agriculture:* NA%
industry: NA%
services: NA%

Unemployment rate: 15% (2004 est.)
country comparison to the world: 171

Population below poverty line: NA%

Household income or consumption by percentage share: *lowest 10%:* NA%
highest 10%: NA%

Budget: *revenues:* $22.68 billion
expenditures: $32.07 billion (2017 est.)
Taxes and other revenues: 31.5% of GDP (2017 est.)
country comparison to the world: 76

Budget surplus (+) or deficit (-): -13% of GDP (2017 est.)
country comparison to the world: 213

Public debt: 41.3% of GDP (2017 est.)

31.4% of GDP (2016 est.)
country comparison to the world: 132

Fiscal year: calendar year

Inflation rate (consumer prices): 3.2% (2017 est.)
1.1% (2016 est.)
country comparison to the world: 136

Central bank discount rate: 2% (31 December 2010)
0.05% (31 December 2009)
country comparison to the world: 116

Commercial bank prime lending rate: 5.4% (31 December 2017 est.)
5.08% (31 December 2016 est.)
country comparison to the world: 138

Stock of narrow money: $12.7 billion (31 December 2017 est.)
$12.95 billion (31 December 2016 est.)
country comparison to the world: 80

Stock of broad money: $41.44 billion (31 December 2017 est.)
$40.11 billion (31 December 2016 est.)
country comparison to the world: 74

Stock of domestic credit: $48.24 billion (31 December 2017 est.)
$46.47 billion (31 December 2016 est.)
country comparison to the world: 66

Market value of publicly traded shares: $41.12 billion (31 December 2015 est.)
$37.83 billion (31 December 2014 est.)
$36.77 billion (31 December 2013 est.)
country comparison to the world: 58

Current account balance: -$10.3 billion (2017 est.)
-$12.32 billion (2016 est.)
country comparison to the world: 185

Exports: $31.9 billion (2017 est.)
$27.54 billion (2016 est.)
country comparison to the world: 61

Exports—commodities: petroleum, reexports, fish, metals, textiles

Exports—partners: China 47.8%, UAE 8.3%, India 4.1% (2016)

Imports: $22.71 billion (2017 est.)
$21.29 billion (2016 est.)
country comparison to the world: 69

Imports—commodities: machinery and transport equipment, manufactured goods, food, livestock, lubricants

Imports—partners: UAE 44.9%, China 4.8%, India 4.8% (2016)

Reserves of foreign exchange and gold: $19.96 billion (31 December 2017 est.)
$20.26 billion (31 December 2016 est.)
country comparison to the world: 61

Debt—external: $39.17 billion (31 December 2017 est.)
$27.05 billion (31 December 2016 est.)
country comparison to the world: 74

Stock of direct foreign investment—at home: $NA

Stock of direct foreign investment—abroad: $NA

Exchange rates: Omani rials (OMR) per US dollar—
0.3845 (2017 est.)
0.3845 (2016 est.)
0.3845 (2015 est.)
0.3845 (2014 est.)
0.3845 (2013 est.)

ENERGY

Electricity access: *population without electricity:* 100,000
electrification—*total population:* 98%
electrification—*urban areas:* 99%
electrification—*rural areas:* 93% (2013)

Electricity—production: 30.79 billion kWh (2015 est.)
country comparison to the world: 64

Electricity—consumption: 27.62 billion kWh (2015 est.)
country comparison to the world: 63

Electricity—exports: 0 kWh (2016 est.)
country comparison to the world: 172

Electricity—imports: 0 kWh (2016 est.)
country comparison to the world: 176

Electricity—installed generating capacity: 7.869 million kW (2015 est.)
country comparison to the world: 70

Electricity—from fossil fuels: 100% of total installed capacity (2015 est.)
country comparison to the world: 13

Electricity—from nuclear fuels: 0% of total installed capacity (2015 est.)
country comparison to the world: 146

Electricity—from hydroelectric plants: 0% of total installed capacity (2015 est.)
country comparison to the world: 189

Electricity—from other renewable sources: 0% of total installed capacity (2015 est.)
country comparison to the world: 199

Crude oil—production: 1.007 million bbl/day (2016 est.)
country comparison to the world: 20

Crude oil—exports: 745,800 bbl/day (2014 est.)
country comparison to the world: 17

Crude oil—imports: 6,970 bbl/day (2014 est.)
country comparison to the world: 77

Crude oil—proved reserves: 5.373 billion bbl (1 January 2017 es)
country comparison to the world: 23

Refined petroleum products—production: 224,000 bbl/day (2014 est.)
country comparison to the world: 49

Refined petroleum products—consumption: 176,000 bbl/day (2015 est.)
country comparison to the world: 61

Refined petroleum products—exports: 33,240 bbl/day (2014 est.)
country comparison to the world: 59

Refined petroleum products—imports: 713.9 bbl/day (2014 est.)
country comparison to the world: 203

Natural gas—production: 29.93 billion cu m (2015 est.)
country comparison to the world: 26

Natural gas—consumption: 38.03 billion cu m (2015 est.)
country comparison to the world: 35

Natural gas—exports: 1.99 billion cu m (2015 est.)
country comparison to the world: 38

Natural gas—imports: 10 billion cu m (2015 est.)
country comparison to the world: 28

Natural gas—proved reserves: 651.3 billion cu m (1 January 2017 es)
country comparison to the world: 30

Carbon dioxide emissions from consumption of energy: 69 million Mt (2013 est.)
country comparison to the world: 51

COMMUNICATIONS

Telephones—fixed lines: *total subscriptions:* 422,518
subscriptions per 100 inhabitants: 13 (July 2016 est.)
country comparison to the world: 108

Telephones—mobile cellular: *total:* 6,866,260
subscriptions per 100 inhabitants: 205 (July 2016 est.)
country comparison to the world: 109

Telephone system: *general assessment:* modern system consisting of open-wire, microwave, and radiotelephone communication stations; limited coaxial cable; domestic satellite system with 8 earth stations
domestic: fixed-line and mobile-cellular subscribership both increasing with fixed-line phone service gradually being introduced to remote villages using wireless local loop systems
international: country code—968; the Fiber-Optic Link Around the Globe (FLAG) and the SEA-ME-WE-3 submarine cable provide connectivity to Asia, the Middle East, and Europe; satellite earth stations—2 Intelsat (Indian Ocean), 1 Arabsat (2016)

Broadcast media: 1 state-run TV broadcaster; TV stations transmitting from Saudi Arabia, the UAE, and Yemen available via satellite TV; state-run radio operates multiple stations; first private radio station began operating in 2007 and 2 additional stations now operating (2007)

Internet country code: .om
Internet users: total: 2,342,483
percent of population: 69.8% (July 2016 est.)
country comparison to the world: 96

TRANSPORTATION

National air transport system: *number of registered air carriers:* 1
inventory of registered aircraft operated by air carriers: 45
annual passenger traffic on registered air carriers: 6,365,784
annual freight traffic on registered air carriers: 412,234,008 mt-km (2015)

Civil aircraft registration country code prefix: A4O (2016)

Airports: 132 (2013)
country comparison to the world: 44

Airports—with paved runways: *total:* 13
over 3,047 m: 7
2,438 to 3,047 m: 5
914 to 1,523 m: 1 (2017)

Airports—with unpaved runways: *total:* 119
over 3,047 m: 2
2,438 to 3,047 m: 7
1,524 to 2,437 m: 51
914 to 1,523 m: 33
under 914 m: 26 (2013)

Heliports: 3 (2013)

Pipelines: condensate 106 km; gas 4,224 km; oil 3,558 km; oil/gas/water 33 km; refined products 264 km (2013)

Roadways: *total:* 60,230 km
paved: 29,685 km (includes 1,943 km of expressways)
unpaved: 30,545 km (2012)
country comparison to the world: 70

Merchant marine: *total:* 51
by type: general cargo 9, other 42 (2017)
country comparison to the world: 114

Ports and terminals: *major seaport(s):* Mina' Qabus, Salalah, Suhar
container port(s) (TEUs): Salalah (3,200,000)
LNG terminal(s) (export): Qalhat

MILITARY AND SECURITY

Military expenditures: 13.73% of GDP (2016)
14.38% of GDP (2015)
13.51% of GDP (2014)
14.81% of GDP (2013)
16.08% of GDP (2012)
country comparison to the world: 3

Military branches: Sultan's Armed Forces (SAF): Royal Army of Oman, Royal Navy of Oman, Royal Air Force of Oman (al-Quwwat al-Jawwiya al-Sultanat Oman) (2013)

Military service age and obligation: 18-30 years of age for voluntary military service; no conscription (2012)

TRANSNATIONAL ISSUES

Disputes—international: boundary agreement reportedly signed and ratified with UAE in 2003 for entire border, including Oman's Musandam Peninsula and Al Madha exclave, but details of the alignment have not been made public

Refugees and internally displaced persons: refugees (country of origin): 5,000 (Yemen) (2017)

PACIFIC OCEAN

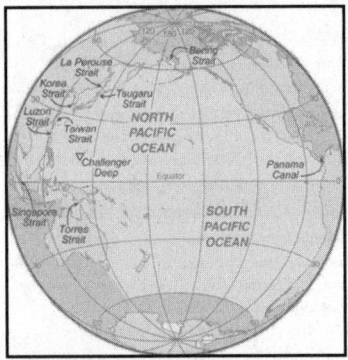

INTRODUCTION

Background: The Pacific Ocean is the largest of the world's five oceans (followed by the Atlantic Ocean, Indian Ocean, Southern Ocean, and Arctic Ocean). Strategically important access waterways include the La Perouse, Tsugaru, Tsushima, Taiwan, Singapore, and Torres Straits. The decision by the International Hydrographic Organization in the spring of 2000 to delimit a fifth ocean, the Southern Ocean, removed the portion of the Pacific Ocean south of 60 degrees south.

GEOGRAPHY

Location: body of water between the Southern Ocean, Asia, Australia, and the Western Hemisphere

Geographic coordinates: 0 00 N, 160 00 W

Map references: Political Map of the World

Area: *total:* 155.557 million sq km
note: includes Bali Sea, Bering Sea, Bering Strait, Coral Sea, East China Sea, Gulf of Alaska, Gulf of Tonkin, Philippine Sea, Sea of Japan, Sea of Okhotsk, South China Sea, Tasman Sea, and other tributary water bodies

Area—comparative: about 15 times the size of the US; covers about 28% of the global surface; almost equal to the total land area of the world

Coastline: 135,663 km

Climate: planetary air pressure systems and resultant wind patterns exhibit remarkable uniformity in the south and east; trade winds and westerly winds are well-developed patterns, modified by seasonal fluctuations; tropical cyclones (hurricanes) may form south of Mexico from June to October and affect Mexico and Central America; continental influences cause climatic uniformity to be much less pronounced in the eastern and western regions at the same latitude in the North Pacific Ocean; the western Pacific is monsoonal—a rainy season occurs during the summer months, when moisture-laden winds blow from the ocean over the land, and a dry season during the winter months, when dry winds blow from the Asian landmass back to

the ocean; tropical cyclones (typhoons) may strike southeast and east Asia from May to December

Terrain: surface dominated by two large gyres (broad, circular systems of currents), one in the northern Pacific and another in the southern Pacific; in the northern Pacific, sea ice forms in the Bering Sea and Sea of Okhotsk in winter; in the southern Pacific, sea ice from Antarctica reaches its northernmost extent in October; the ocean floor in the eastern Pacific is dominated by the East Pacific Rise, while the western Pacific is dissected by deep trenches, including the Mariana Trench, which is the world's deepest at 10,924 m
major surface currents: clockwise North Pacific Gyre formed by the warm Kuroshio Current in the west, the North Pacific Current in the north, the cold California Current in the east, and the North Equatorial Current in the south; the counterclockwise South Pacific Gyre composed of the warm East Australian Current in the west, the South Pacific Current in the south, the cold Peru (Humbolt) Current in the east, and the South Equatorial Current in the north

Elevation: mean depth: -3,970 m

elevation extremes: *lowest point:* Challenger Deep in the Mariana Trench -10,924 m
highest point: sea level 0 m

Natural resources: oil and gas fields, polymetallic nodules, sand and gravel aggregates, placer deposits, fish

Natural hazards: surrounded by a zone of violent volcanic and earthquake activity sometimes referred to as the "Pacific Ring of Fire"; subject to tropical cyclones (typhoons) in southeast and east Asia from May to December (most frequent from July to October); tropical cyclones (hurricanes) may form south of Mexico and strike Central America and Mexico from June to October (most common in August and September); cyclical El Nino/La Nina phenomenon occurs in the equatorial Pacific, influencing weather in the Western Hemisphere and the western Pacific; ships subject to superstructure icing in extreme north from October to May; persistent fog in the northern Pacific can be a maritime hazard from June to December

Environment—current issues: endangered marine species include the dugong, sea lion, sea otter, seals, turtles, and whales; oil pollution in Philippine Sea and South China Sea

Geography—note: the major chokepoints are the Bering Strait, Panama Canal, Luzon Strait, and the Singapore Strait; the Equator divides the Pacific Ocean into the North Pacific Ocean and the South Pacific Ocean; dotted with low coral islands and rugged volcanic islands in the southwestern Pacific Ocean

GOVERNMENT

Country name: etymology: named by Portuguese explorer Ferdinand MAGELLAN during the

Spanish circumnavigation of the world in 1521; encountering favorable winds upon reaching the ocean, he called it "Mar Pacifico," which means "peaceful sea" in both Portuguese and Spanish

ECONOMY

Economy—overview: The Pacific Ocean is a major contributor to the world economy and particularly to those nations its waters directly touch. It provides low-cost sea transportation between East and West, extensive fishing grounds, offshore oil and gas fields, minerals, and sand and gravel for the construction industry. In 1996, over 60% of the world's fish catch came from the Pacific Ocean. Exploitation of offshore oil and gas reserves is playing an ever-increasing role in the energy supplies of the US, Australia, NZ, China, and Peru. The high cost of recovering offshore oil and gas, combined with the wide swings in world prices for oil since 1985, has led to fluctuations in new drillings.

TRANSPORTATION

Ports and terminals: *major seaport(s):* Bangkok (Thailand), Hong Kong (China), Kao-hsiung (Taiwan), Los Angeles (US), Manila (Philippines), Pusan (South Korea), San Francisco (US), Seattle (US), Shanghai (China), Singapore, Sydney (Australia), Vladivostok (Russia), Wellington (NZ), Yokohama (Japan)

MILITARY AND SECURITY

Maritime threats: the Inside Passage offers protected waters from southeast Alaska to Puget Sound (Washington state); although the International Maritime Bureau reports the territorial waters of littoral states and offshore waters in the South China Sea as high risk for piracy and armed robbery against ships reports of attacks have generally declined from 2015 to 2016; an emerging threat area lies in the Celebes and Sulu Seas between the Philippines and Malaysia where 12 crew were kidnapped in three incidents during the last quarter of 2016; numerous commercial vessels have been attacked and hijacked both at anchor and while underway; hijacked vessels are often disguised and cargoes stolen; crew and passengers are often held for ransom, murdered, or cast adrift

TRANSNATIONAL ISSUES

Disputes—international: some maritime disputes (see littoral states)

PAKISTAN

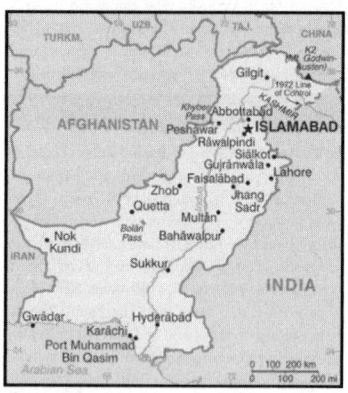

INTRODUCTION

Background: The Indus Valley civilization, one of the oldest in the world and dating back at least 5,000 years, spread over much of what is presently Pakistan. During the second millennium B.C., remnants of this culture fused with the migrating Indo-Aryan peoples. The area underwent successive invasions in subsequent centuries from the Persians, Greeks, Scythians, Arabs (who brought Islam), Afghans, and Turks. The Mughal Empire flourished in the 16th and 17th centuries; the British came to dominate the region in the 18th century. The separation in 1947 of British India into the Muslim state of Pakistan (with West and East sections) and largely Hindu India was never satisfactorily resolved, and India and Pakistan fought two wars and a limited conflict—in 1947-48, 1965, and 1999 respectively—over the disputed Kashmir territory. A third war between these countries in 1971—in which India capitalized on Islamabad's marginalization of Bengalis in Pakistani politics—resulted in East Pakistan becoming the separate nation of Bangladesh.

In response to Indian nuclear weapons testing, Pakistan conducted its own tests in mid-1998. India-Pakistan relations improved in the mid-2000s but have been rocky since the November 2008 Mumbai attacks and have been further strained by attacks in India by militants suspected of being based in Pakistan. Nawaz SHARIF took office as prime minister in 2013, marking the first time in Pakistani history that a democratically elected government completed a full term and transitioned to a successive democratically elected government. In July 2017, the Supreme Court disqualified SHARIF from public office, and Shahid Khaqan ABBASI replaced him as prime minister in August. Pakistan has been engaged in a decades-long armed conflict with militant groups that target government institutions and civilians, including the Tehrik-e-Taliban Pakistan (TTP) and other militant networks.

GEOGRAPHY

Location: Southern Asia, bordering the Arabian Sea, between India on the east and Iran and Afghanistan on the west and China in the north

Geographic coordinates: 30 00 N, 70 00 E

Map references: Asia

Area: *total:* 796,095 sq km
land: 770,875 sq km
water: 25,220 sq km
country comparison to the world: 37

Area—comparative: slightly more than five times the size of Georgia; slightly less than twice the size of California

Land boundaries: *total:* 7,257 km
border countries (4): Afghanistan 2,670 km, China 438 km, India 3,190 km, Iran 959 km

Coastline: 1,046 km

Maritime claims: *territorial sea:* 12 nm
contiguous zone: 24 nm
exclusive economic zone: 200 nm
continental shelf: 200 nm or to the edge of the continental margin

Climate: mostly hot, dry desert; temperate in northwest; arctic in north

Terrain: divided into three major geographic areas: the northern highlands, the Indus River plain in the center and east, and the Balochistan Plateau in the south and west

Elevation: *mean elevation:* 900 m

elevation extremes: *lowest point:* Arabian Sea 0 m
highest point: K2 (Mt. Godwin-Austen) 8,611 m

Natural resources: arable land, extensive natural gas reserves, limited petroleum, poor quality coal, iron ore, copper, salt, limestone

Land use: *agricultural land:* 35.2%
arable land: 27.6%;
permanent crops: 1.1%;
permanent pasture: 6.5%
forest: 2.1%
other: 62.7% (2011 est.)
Irrigated land: 202,000 sq km (2012)

Population—distribution: the Indus River and its tributaries attract most of the settlement, with Punjab province the most densely populated

Natural hazards: frequent earthquakes, occasionally severe especially in north and west; flooding along the Indus after heavy rains (July and August)

Environment—current issues: water pollution from raw sewage, industrial wastes, and agricultural runoff; limited natural freshwater resources; most of the population does not have access to potable water; deforestation; soil erosion; desertification

Environment—international agreements: *party to:* Biodiversity, Climate Change, Climate Change-Kyoto Protocol, Desertification, Endangered Species, Environmental Modification, Hazardous Wastes, Law of the Sea, Marine Dumping, Ozone Layer Protection, Ship Pollution, Wetlands
signed, but not ratified: Marine Life Conservation

Geography—note: controls Khyber Pass and Bolan Pass, traditional invasion routes between Central Asia and the Indian Subcontinent

PEOPLE AND SOCIETY

Population: 204,924,861 (July 2017 est.)
note: provisional results of Pakistan's 2017 national census estimate the country's total population to be 207,774,000
country comparison to the world: 6

Nationality: *noun:* Pakistani(s)
adjective: Pakistani

Ethnic groups: Punjabi 44.7%, Pashtun (Pathan) 15.4%, Sindhi 14.1%, Sariaki 8.4%, Muhajirs 7.6%, Balochi 3.6%, other 6.3%

Languages: Punjabi 48%, Sindhi 12%, Saraiki (a Punjabi variant) 10%, Pashto (alternate name, Pashtu) 8%, Urdu (official) 8%, Balochi 3%, Hindko 2%, Brahui 1%, English (official; lingua franca of Pakistani elite and most government ministries), Burushaski, and other 8%

Religions: Muslim (official) 96.4% (Sunni 85-90%, Shia 10-15%), other (includes Christian and Hindu) 3.6% (2010 est.)

Age structure: *0-14 years:* 31.36% (male 33,005,623/female 31,265,463)
15-24 years: 21.14% (male 22,337,897/female 20,980,455)
25-54 years: 37.45% (male 39,846,417/female 36,907,683)
55-64 years: 5.57% (male 5,739,817/female 5,669,495)
65 years and over: 4.48% (male 4,261,917/female 4,910,094) (2017 est.)

Dependency ratios: *total dependency ratio:* 65.3
youth dependency ratio: 57.9
elderly dependency ratio: 7.4
potential support ratio: 13.5 (2015 est.)

Median age: *total:* 23.8 years
male: 23.7 years
female: 23.8 years (2017 est.)
country comparison to the world: 167

Population growth rate: 1.43% (2017 est.)
country comparison to the world: 80

Birth rate: 21.9 births/1,000 population (2017 est.)
country comparison to the world: 74

Death rate: 6.3 deaths/1,000 population (2017 est.)
country comparison to the world: 150

Net migration rate: -1.3 migrant(s)/1,000 population (2017 est.)
country comparison to the world: 144

Population distribution: the Indus River and its tributaries attract most of the settlement, with Punjab province the most densely populated

Urbanization: *urban population:* 39.7% of total population (2017)
rate of urbanization: 2.77% annual rate of change (2015-20 est.)

Major urban areas—population: Karachi 16.618 million; Lahore 8.741 million; Faisalabad 3.567 million; Rawalpindi 2.506 million; Multan 1.921 million; ISLAMABAD (capital) 1.365 million (2015)

Sex ratio: *at birth:* 1.05 male(s)/female
0-14 years: 1.06 male(s)/female
15-24 years: 1.06 male(s)/female
25-54 years: 1.08 male(s)/female
55-64 years: 1.01 male(s)/female
65 years and over: 0.88 male(s)/female
total population: 1.06 male(s)/female (2016 est.)

Mother's mean age at first birth: 23.4 years
note: median age at first birth among women 25-29 (2012/13 est.)

Maternal mortality ratio: 178 deaths/100,000 live births (2015 est.)
country comparison to the world: 53

Infant mortality rate: *total:* 52.1 deaths/1,000 live births
male: 55.2 deaths/1,000 live births
female: 48.8 deaths/1,000 live births (2017 est.)
country comparison to the world: 25

Life expectancy at birth: *total population:* 68.1 years
male: 66.1 years
female: 70.1 years (2017 est.)
country comparison to the world: 168

Total fertility rate: 2.62 children born/woman (2017 est.)
country comparison to the world: 75

Contraceptive prevalence rate: 35.4% (2012/13)

Health expenditures: 2.6% of GDP (2014)
country comparison to the world: 187

Physicians density: 0.81 physicians/1,000 population (2014)

Hospital bed density: 0.6 beds/1,000 population (2012)

Drinking water source:
improved:
urban: 93.9% of population
rural: 89.9% of population
total: 91.4% of population
unimproved:
urban: 6.1% of population
rural: 10.1% of population
total: 8.6% of population (2015 est.)

Sanitation facility access:
improved:
urban: 83.1% of population
rural: 51.1% of population
total: 63.5% of population
unimproved:
urban: 16.9% of population
rural: 48.9% of population
total: 36.5% of population (2015 est.)

HIV/AIDS—adult prevalence rate: 0.1% (2016 est.)
country comparison to the world: 107

HIV/AIDS—people living with HIV/AIDS: 130,000 (2016 est.)
country comparison to the world: 35

HIV/AIDS—deaths: 5,500 (2016 est.)
country comparison to the world: 29

Major infectious diseases: *degree of risk:* high
food or waterborne diseases: bacterial diarrhea, hepatitis A and E, and typhoid fever
vectorborne diseases: dengue fever and malaria
animal contact disease: rabies (2016)

Obesity—adult prevalence rate: 8.6% (2016)
country comparison to the world: 150

Children under the age of 5 years underweight: 31.6% (2012)
country comparison to the world: 11

Education expenditures: 2.7% of GDP (2015)
country comparison to the world: 164

Literacy: *definition:* age 15 and over can read and write
total population: 57.9%
male: 69.5%
female: 45.8% (2015 est.)

School life expectancy (primary to tertiary education): *total:* 8 years
male: 9 years
female: 7 years (2015)

Unemployment, youth ages 15-24: *total:* 8.6%
male: 8%
female: 10.6% (2014 est.)
country comparison to the world: 115

GOVERNMENT

Country name: *conventional long form:* Islamic Republic of Pakistan
conventional short form: Pakistan
local long form: Jamhuryat Islami Pakistan
local short form: Pakistan
former: West Pakistan
etymology: the word "pak" means "pure" in Persian or Pashto, while the Persian suffix "-stan" means "place of" or "country," so the word Pakistan literally means "Land of the Pure"

Government type: federal parliamentary republic

Capital: *name:* Islamabad
geographic coordinates: 33 41 N, 73 03 E
time difference: UTC+5 (10 hours ahead of Washington, DC, during Standard Time)

Administrative divisions: 4 provinces, 1 territory*, and 1 capital territory**; Balochistan, Federally Administered Tribal Areas*, Islamabad Capital Territory**, Khyber Pakhtunkhwa (formerly North-West Frontier Province), Punjab, Sindh
note: the Pakistani-administered portion of the disputed Jammu and Kashmir region consists of 2 administrative entities: Azad Kashmir and Gilgit-Baltistan

Independence: 14 August 1947 (from British India)

National holiday: Pakistan Day (also referred to as Pakistan Resolution Day or Republic Day), 23 March (1940); note—commemorates both the adoption of the Lahore Resolution by the All-India Muslim League during its 22-24 March 1940 session, which called for the creation of independent Muslim states, and the adoption of the first constitution of Pakistan on 23 March 1956 during the transition to the Islamic Republic of Pakistan

Constitution: history: several previous; latest endorsed 12 April 1973, passed 19 April 1973, entered into force 14 August 1973 (suspended and restored several times)
amendments: proposed by the Senate or by the National Assembly; passage requires at least two-thirds majority vote of the membership of both houses; amended many times, last in 2015 (2017)

Legal system: common law system with Islamic law influence

International law organization participation: accepts compulsory ICJ jurisdiction with reservations; non-party state to the ICCt

Citizenship: *citizenship by birth:* yes
citizenship by descent: at least one parent must be a citizen of Pakistan
dual citizenship recognized: yes, but limited to select countries
residency requirement for naturalization: 4 out of the previous 7 years and including the 12 months preceding application

Suffrage: 18 years of age; universal; note—there are joint electorates and reserved parliamentary seats for women and non-Muslims

Executive branch: *chief of state:* President Mamnoon HUSSAIN (since 9 September 2013)

head of government: Prime Minister Shahid Khaqan ABBASI (since 1 August 2017); Prime Minister Mohammad Nawaz SHARIF resigned 7/28/17
cabinet: Cabinet appointed by the president upon the advice of the prime minister
elections/appointments: president indirectly elected by the Electoral College consisting of members of the Senate, National Assembly, and provincial assemblies for a 5-year term (limited to 2 consecutive terms); election last held on 9 September 2013 (next to be held in 2018); prime minister elected by the National Assembly
election results: Mamnoon HUSSAIN elected president; Mamnoon HUSSAIN (PML-N) 432 votes, Wajihuddin AHMED (PTI) 77 votes

Legislative branch: *description:* bicameral Parliament or Majlis-e-Shoora consists of the Senate (104 seats; members indirectly elected by the 4 provincial assemblies and the territories' representatives by proportional representation vote; members serve 6-year terms with one-half of the membership renewed every 3 years) and the National Assembly (342 seats; 272 members directly elected in single-seat constituencies by simple majority vote and 70 members—60 women and 10 non-Muslims—directly elected by proportional representation vote; all members serve 5-year terms)
elections: Senate—last held on 5 March 2015 (next to be held in March 2018); National

Assembly—last held on 11 May 2013 (next to be held by 2018)

election results: Senate—percent of vote by party—NA; seats by party—PPPP 27, PML-N 26, MQM 8, ANP 6, PTI 7, JUI-F 5, PML-Q 4, BNP-A 2, NP 1, PML-F 1, other 7, independent 10; National Assembly—percent of votes by party—NA; general seats by party—PML-N 126, PPPP 31, PTI 28, MQM 18, JUI-F 10, PML-F 5, other 22, independent 25, unfilled seats 7; 60 seats reserved for women, 10 seats reserved for non-Muslims; seats by party as of December 2017 (includes women and non-Muslim seats)—PML-N 188, PPPP 47, PTI 33, MQM 24, JUI-F 13, PML-F 5, other 20, independent 10

Judicial branch: *highest court(s):* Supreme Court of Pakistan (consists of the chief justice and 16 judges)

judge selection and term of office: justices nominated by an 8-member parliamentary committee upon the recommendation of the Judicial Commission (a 9-member body of judges and other judicial professionals), and appointed by the president of Pakistan; justices can serve until age 65

subordinate courts: High Courts; Federal Shariat Court; provincial and district civil and criminal courts; specialized courts for issues such as taxation, banking, customs, etc.

Political parties and leaders: Awami National Party or ANP [Mian Iftikhar HUSSAIN]
Balochistan National Party-Awami or BNP-A [Mir Israr Ullah ZEHRI]
Balochistan National Party-Mengal or BNP-M [Sardar Akhtar Jan MENGAL]
Jamaat-i Islami or JI [Sirajul HAQ]
Jamiat-i Ulema-i Islam Fazl-ur Rehman or JUI-F [Fazlur REHMAN]
Muttahida Quami Movement or MQM [Farooq SATTAR]
Muttahida Quami Movement-London or MQM-L [Nadeem NUSRAT]
Pakhtun khwa Milli Awami Party or PkMAP [Mahmood Khan ACHAKZAI]
Pakistan Muslim League-Functional or PML-F [Pir PAGARO or Syed Shah Mardan SHAH-II]
Pakistan Muslim League-Nawaz or PML-N [Nawaz SHARIF]
Pakistan Peoples Party Parliamentarians or PPPP [Bilawal Bhutto ZARDARI and Asif Ali ZARDARI]
Pakistan Tehrik-e Insaaf or PTI (Pakistan Movement for Justice) [Imran KHAN]
Pak Sarzameen Party or PSP [Mustafa KAMAL]
Quami Watan Party or QWP [Aftab Ahmed Khan SHERPAO]
note: political alliances in Pakistan shift frequently

Political pressure groups and leaders: Pakistan Ulema Council or PUC
other: military; landowners; industrialists; small merchants

International organization participation: ADB, ARF, ASEAN (dialogue partner), C, CICA, CP, D-8, ECO, FAO, G-11, G-24, G-77, IAEA, IBRD, ICAO, ICC (national committees), ICRM, IDA, IDB, IFAD, IFC, IFRCS, IHO, ILO, IMF,

IMO, IMSO, Interpol, IOC, IOM, IPU, ISO, ITSO, ITU, ITUC (NGOs), MIGA, MINURSO, MONUSCO, NAM, OAS (observer), OIC, OPCW, PCA, SAARC, SACEP, SCO (observer), UN, UNAMID, UNCTAD, UNESCO, UNHCR, UNIDO, UNMIL, UNOCI, UNWTO, UPU, WCO, WFTU (NGOs), WHO, WIPO, WMO, WTO

Diplomatic representation in the US: *chief of mission:* Ambassador Aizaz Ahmad CHAUDHRY (since 24 April 2017)
chancery: 3517 International Court NW, Washington, DC 20008
telephone: [1] (202) 243-6500
FAX: [1] (202) 686-1534
consulate(s) general: Chicago, Houston, Los Angeles, New York
consulate(s): Louisville (KY), San Francisco

Diplomatic representation from the US: *chief of mission:* Ambassador David M. HALE (since 3 December 2015)
embassy: Diplomatic Enclave, Ramna 5, Islamabad
mailing address: 8100 Islamabad Place, Washington, DC 20521-8100
telephone: [92] (51) 208-0000/[92] (51) 201-4000
FAX: [92] (51) 233-8071
consulate(s) general: Karachi, Lahore
consulate(s): Peshawar

Flag description: green with a vertical white band (symbolizing the role of religious minorities) on the hoist side; a large white crescent and star are centered in the green field; the crescent, star, and color green are traditional symbols of Islam

National symbol(s): star and crescent, jasmine; national colors: green, white

National anthem: *name:* "Qaumi Tarana" (National Anthem)
lyrics/music: Abu-Al-Asar Hafeez JULLAND-HURI/Ahmed Ghulamali CHAGLA
note: adopted 1954; also known as "Pak sarzamin shad bad" (Blessed Be the Sacred Land)

ECONOMY

Economy—overview: Decades of internal political disputes and low levels of foreign investment have led to underdevelopment in Pakistan. Pakistan has a large English-speaking population. A challenging security environment, electricity shortages, and a burdensome investment climate have deterred investors. Agriculture accounts for one-fifth of output and two-fifths of employment. Textiles and apparel account for more than half of Pakistan's export earnings; Pakistan's failure to diversify its exports has left the country vulnerable to shifts in world demand. Pakistan's GDP growth has gradually increased since 2012. Official unemployment was 6% in 2017, but this fails to capture the true picture, because much of the economy is informal and underemployment remains high. Human development continues to lag behind most of the region.

In 2013, Pakistan embarked on a $6.3 billion IMF Extended Fund Facility, which focused

on reducing energy shortages, stabilizing public finances, increasing revenue collection, and improving its balance of payments position. The program concluded in September 2016. Although Pakistan missed several structural reform criteria, it restored macroeconomic stability, improved its credit rating, and boosted growth. The Pakistani rupee, after heavy depreciation in 2013, remained relatively stable against the US dollar in 2015-17. Balance of payments concerns have reemerged, however, as a result of increased imports and declining remittances.

Pakistan must continue to address several long-standing issues, including expanding investment in education and healthcare, adapting to the effects of climate change and natural disasters, improving the country's business environment, reducing dependence on foreign donors, and widening the country's tax base. Given demographic challenges, Pakistan's leadership will be pressed to implement economic reforms, promote further development of the energy sector, and attract foreign investment to support sufficient economic growth necessary to employ its growing and rapidly urbanizing population, much of which is under the age of 25.

In an effort to boost development, Pakistan and China are implementing the "China-Pakistan Economic Corridor," with $60 billion in investments targeted towards energy and other infrastructure projects. Pakistan believes CPEC investments will enable growth rates of over 6% of GDP by laying the groundwork for increased exports. CPEC-related obligations, however, have raised IMF concern that capital outflows that will begin to increase in 2020.

GDP (purchasing power parity): $1.056 trillion (2017 est.)
$1.003 trillion (2016 est.)
$960.2 billion (2015 est.)
note: data are in 2017 dollars
data are for fiscal years
country comparison to the world: 26

GDP (official exchange rate): $278.9 billion (2015 est.)

GDP—real growth rate: 5.3% (2017 est.)
4.5% (2016 est.)
4.1% (2015 est.)
note: data are for fiscal years
country comparison to the world: 35

GDP—per capita (PPP): $5,400 (2017 est.)
$5,200 (2016 est.)
$5,100 (2015 est.)
note: data are in 2017 dollars
data are for fiscal years
country comparison to the world: 171

Gross national saving: 11.8% of GDP (2017 est.)
13.8% of GDP (2016 est.)
14.7% of GDP (2015 est.)
note: data are for fiscal years
country comparison to the world: 148

GDP—composition, by end use:
household consumption: 81.8%
government consumption: 11.9%
investment in fixed capital: 14.2%

investment in inventories: 1.6%
exports of goods and services: 8.3%
imports of goods and services: -17.8% (2017 est.)

GDP—composition, by sector of origin:
agriculture: 24.7%
industry: 19.1%
services: 56.3% (2017 est.)

Agriculture—products: cotton, wheat, rice, sugarcane, fruits, vegetables; milk, beef, mutton, eggs

Industries: textiles and apparel, food processing, pharmaceuticals, surgical instruments, construction materials, paper products, fertilizer, shrimp

Industrial production growth rate: 5% (2017 est.)
country comparison to the world: 45

Labor force: 63.89 million
note: extensive export of labor, mostly to the Middle East, and use of child labor (2017 est.)
country comparison to the world: 10

Labor force—by occupation: agriculture: 42.3%
industry: 22.6%
services: 35.1% (FY2015 est.)

Unemployment rate: 6% (2017 est.)
6% (2016 est.)
note: substantial underemployment exists
country comparison to the world: 85

Population below poverty line: 29.5% (FY2013 est.)

Household income or consumption by percentage share: lowest 10%: 4%
highest 10%: 26.1% (FY2013)

Distribution of family income—Gini index: 30.7 (FY2013)
30.9 (FY2011)
country comparison to the world: 123

Budget: revenues: $45.64 billion
expenditures: $59.28 billion
note: data are for fiscal years (2017 est.)
Taxes and other revenues: 14.9% of GDP (2016 est.)
country comparison to the world: 192

Budget surplus (+) or deficit (-): -4.5% of GDP (2016 est.)
country comparison to the world: 149

Public debt: 59.4% of GDP (2017 est.)
59.5% of GDP (2016 est.)
country comparison to the world: 76

Fiscal year: 1 July—30 June

Inflation rate (consumer prices): 4.1% (2017 est.)
2.9% (2016 est.)
country comparison to the world: 160

Central bank discount rate: 5.75% (15 November 2016)
6% (15 November 2015)
country comparison to the world: 71

Commercial bank prime lending rate: 7% (31 December 2017 est.)
6.94% (31 December 2016 est.)
country comparison to the world: 118

Stock of narrow money: $117.2 billion (31 December 2017 est.)
$103.5 billion (31 December 2016 est.)
country comparison to the world: 34

Stock of broad money: $142 billion (31 December 2017 est.)
$126.8 billion (31 December 2016 est.)
country comparison to the world: 51

Stock of domestic credit: $165.2 billion (31 December 2017 est.)
$145.2 billion (31 December 2016 est.)
country comparison to the world: 50

Market value of publicly traded shares: $43.68 billion (31 December 2012 est.)
$32.76 billion (31 December 2011 est.)
$38.17 billion (31 December 2010 est.)
country comparison to the world: 56

Current account balance: -$11.67 billion (2017 est.)
-$4.867 billion (2016 est.)
country comparison to the world: 186

Exports: $21.7 billion (2017 est.)
$21.71 billion (2016 est.)
country comparison to the world: 69

Exports—commodities: textiles (garments, bed linen, cotton cloth, yarn), rice, leather goods, sporting goods, chemicals, manufactures, surgical instruments, carpets and rugs

Exports—partners: US 16.3%, China 7.6%, UK 7.4%, Afghanistan 6.5%, Germany 5.7% (2016)

Imports: $48.21 billion (2017 est.)
$41.62 billion (2016 est.)
country comparison to the world: 52

Imports—commodities: petroleum, petroleum products, machinery, plastics, transportation equipment, edible oils, paper and paperboard, iron and steel, tea

Imports—partners: China 29.1%, UAE 13.2%, Indonesia 4.4%, US 4.3%, Japan 4.2% (2016)

Reserves of foreign exchange and gold: $20.02 billion (31 December 2017 est.)
$22.05 billion (31 December 2016 est.)
country comparison to the world: 60

Debt—external: $75.66 billion (31 December 2017 est.)
$70.45 billion (31 December 2016 est.)
country comparison to the world: 58

Stock of direct foreign investment—at home: $41.56 billion (31 December 2017 est.)
$39.06 billion (31 December 2016 est.)
country comparison to the world: 61

Stock of direct foreign investment—abroad: $2.175 billion (31 December 2017 est.)
$2.094 billion (31 December 2016 est.)
country comparison to the world: 80

Exchange rates: Pakistani rupees (PKR) per US dollar—
105.1 (2017 est.)
104.769 (2016 est.)
104.769 (2015 est.)
102.769 (FY2014 est.)
101.1 (FY2013 est.)

ENERGY

Electricity access: population without electricity: 49,500,000

electrification—total population: 73%
electrification—urban areas: 91%
electrification—rural areas: 62% (2013)

Electricity—production: 104.5 billion kWh (2015 est.)
country comparison to the world: 34

Electricity—consumption: 85.9 billion kWh (2015 est.)
country comparison to the world: 35

Electricity—exports: 0 kWh (2016 est.)
country comparison to the world: 183

Electricity—imports: 452 million kWh (2016 est.)
country comparison to the world: 83

Electricity—installed generating capacity: 22.83 million kW (2015 est.)
country comparison to the world: 38

Electricity—from fossil fuels: 61.8% of total installed capacity (2015 est.)
country comparison to the world: 124

Electricity—from nuclear fuels: 3% of total installed capacity (2015 est.)
country comparison to the world: 26

Electricity—from hydroelectric plants: 31.8% of total installed capacity (2015 est.)
country comparison to the world: 68

Electricity—from other renewable sources: 5.7% of total installed capacity (2015 est.)
country comparison to the world: 92

Crude oil—production: 85,500 bbl/day (2016 est.)
country comparison to the world: 46

Crude oil—exports: 493.2 bbl/day (2014 est.)
country comparison to the world: 76

Crude oil—imports: 166,000 bbl/day (2014 est.)
country comparison to the world: 32

Crude oil—proved reserves: 350.6 million bbl (1 January 2017 es)
country comparison to the world: 55

Refined petroleum products—production: 259,500 bbl/day (2014 est.)
country comparison to the world: 46

Refined petroleum products—consumption: 517,000 bbl/day (2015 est.)
country comparison to the world: 34

Refined petroleum products—exports: 20,720 bbl/day (2014 est.)
country comparison to the world: 71

Refined petroleum products—imports: 247,300 bbl/day (2014 est.)
country comparison to the world: 29

Natural gas—production: 39.3 billion cu m (2015 est.)
country comparison to the world: 23

Natural gas—consumption: 48.06 billion cu m (2015 est.)
country comparison to the world: 23

Natural gas—exports: 0 cu m (2016 est.)
country comparison to the world: 166

Natural gas—imports: 1.37 billion cu m (2015 est.)
country comparison to the world: 55

Natural gas—proved reserves: 542.5 billion cu m (1 January 2017 es)
country comparison to the world: 32

Carbon dioxide emissions from consumption of energy: 145 million Mt (2013 est.)
country comparison to the world: 33

COMMUNICATIONS

Telephones—fixed lines: *total subscriptions:* 3,067,911
subscriptions per 100 inhabitants: 2 (July 2016 est.)
country comparison to the world: 31

Telephones—mobile cellular: *total:* 136,489,014
subscriptions per 100 inhabitants: 68 (July 2016 est.)
country comparison to the world: 11

Telephone system: *general assessment:* the telecommunications infrastructure is improving, with investments in mobile-cellular networks increasing, but fixed-line subscriptions declining; system consists of microwave radio relay, coaxial cable, fiber-optic cable, cellular, and satellite networks; 3G and 4G mobile services introduced
domestic: mobile-cellular subscribership has skyrocketed; more than 90% of Pakistanis live within areas that have cell phone coverage; fiber-optic networks are being constructed throughout the country to increase broadband access, though broadband penetration in Pakistan is still relatively low
international: country code—92; landing point for the SEA-ME-WE-3 and SEA-ME-WE-4 submarine cable systems that provide links to Asia, the Middle East, and Europe; satellite earth stations—3 Intelsat (1 Atlantic Ocean and 2 Indian Ocean); 3 operational international gateway exchanges (1 at Karachi and 2 at Islamabad); microwave radio relay to neighboring countries (2015)

Broadcast media: media is government regulated; 1 dominant state-owned TV broadcaster, Pakistan Television Corporation (PTV), operates a network consisting of 8 channels; private TV broadcasters are permitted; to date 69 foreign satellite channels are operational; the state-owned radio network operates more than 30 stations; nearly 200 commercially licensed, privately owned radio stations provide programming mostly limited to music and talk shows (2017)

Internet country code: .pk

Internet users: *total:* 31,338,715
percent of population: 15.5% (July 2016 est.)
country comparison to the world: 27

TRANSPORTATION

National air transport system: *number of registered air carriers:* 4
inventory of registered aircraft operated by air carriers: 67
annual passenger traffic on registered air carriers: 8,467,827
annual freight traffic on registered air carriers: 183,177,313 mt-km (2015)

Civil aircraft registration country code prefix: AP (2016)

Airports: 151 (2013)
country comparison to the world: 37

Airports—with paved runways: *total:* 108
over 3,047 m: 15
2,438 to 3,047 m: 20
1,524 to 2,437 m: 43
914 to 1,523 m: 20
under 914 m: 10 (2017)

Airports—with unpaved runways: *total:* 43
2,438 to 3,047 m: 1
1,524 to 2,437 m: 9
914 to 1,523 m: 9
under 914 m: 24 (2013)

Heliports: 23 (2013)

Pipelines: gas 12,646 km; oil 2,576 km; refined products 1,087 km (2013)

Railways: *total:* 11,881 km
broad gauge: 11,492 km 1.676-m gauge (293 km electrified)
narrow gauge: 389 km 1.000-m gauge (2015)
country comparison to the world: 22

Roadways: *total:* 263,942 km
paved: 185,063 km (includes 708 km of expressways)
unpaved: 78,879 km (2014)
country comparison to the world: 21

Merchant marine: *total:* 52
by type: bulk carrier 5, oil tanker 6, other 41 (2017)
country comparison to the world: 112

Ports and terminals: *major seaport(s):* Karachi, Port Muhammad Bin Qasim
container port(s) (TEUs): Karachi (1,545,434)
LNG terminal(s) (import): Port Qasim

MILITARY AND SECURITY

Military expenditures: 3.56% of GDP (2016)
3.54% of GDP (2015)
3.48% of GDP (2014)
3.47% of GDP (2013)
3.48% of GDP (2012)
country comparison to the world: 21

Military branches: Pakistan Army (includes National Guard), Pakistan Navy (includes Maritime Security Agency), Pakistan Air Force (Pakistan Fiza'ya) (2015)

Military service age and obligation: 16-23 years of age for voluntary military service; soldiers cannot be deployed for combat until age 18; women serve in all three armed forces; reserve obligation to age 45 for enlisted men, age 50 for officers (2017)

TERRORISM

Terrorist groups—home based: *al-Qa'ida (AQ):*
aim(s): establish a pan-Islamic caliphate under a strict Salafi Muslim interpretation of Sharia through ridding the Muslim world of Western influence, expelling non-Muslims from the Arabian Peninsula, overthrowing Muslim governments it deems to be apostate, and attacking "far

enemy" (Western) interests and homelands with the intent to destabilize Western governments
area(s) of operation: headquartered in Pakistan, with its heaviest presence in the northwest and in northeastern Afghanistan near the Pakistan-Afghanistan border; maintains safehavens in North Waziristan Agency in Pakistan's Federally Administered Tribal Areas (FATA) region, a semi-autonomous region in the northwest consisting of seven tribal agencies (districts) and six frontier regions directly governed by Pakistan's federal government through a special set of laws called the Frontier Crimes Regulations; confronted with counterterrorism operations throughout the country; operates a blend of limited and well-established networks in Pakistan and across the globe, especially its affiliate al-Qa'ida organizations in the Middle East, Africa, and South Asia

al-Qa'ida in the Indian Subcontinent (AQIS):
aim(s): establish an Islamic caliphate in the Indian subcontinent
area(s) of operation: maintains a steady presence, where overall leader Asim UMAR is based; Pakistan is known to have been AQIS's original headquarters; operates safe havens in North Waziristan Agency and South Waziristan Agency in the country's Federally Administered Tribal Areas (FATA) region; FATA is a semi-autonomous region in the northwest consisting of seven tribal agencies (districts) and six frontier regions directly governed by Pakistan's federal government through a special set of laws called the Frontier Crimes Regulations; operational throughout the country, targeting military and security personnel and using machetes to attack university professors, bloggers, and others who oppose AQIS's ideology; responsible for numerous attacks in Karachi; stages attacks in Afghanistan, India, and Bangladesh, where the group is the most active; majority of members are Pakistanis; outlawed in Pakistan

Haqqani Network (HQN): *aim(s):* enhance its operational networks and capabilities for staging cross-border attacks in Afghanistan and, ultimately, replace the Afghan Government with a strict Salafi Muslim interpretation of Sharia
area(s) of operation: headquartered in the Federally Administered Tribal Areas (FATA) region in North Waziristan Agency (NWA); FATA is a semi-autonomous region in the northwest consisting of seven tribal agencies (districts) and six frontier regions directly governed by Pakistan's federal government through a special set of laws called the Frontier Crimes Regulations; NWA is located across from Afghanistan's southeastern border; fighters have staged numerous cross-border operations into Afghanistan, targeting Afghan, US, and NATO forces and other Afghan Government personnel and Westerners for attack or kidnappings for ransom

Harakat ul-Jihad-i-Islami (HUJI): *aim(s):* overthrow the Pakistan Government and install Sharia throughout the country
area(s) of operation: headquartered in Pakistan, where the group operates several camps; remains

heavily active in the southern area of Pakistan-controlled Azad Kashmir

Harakat ul-Mujahidin (HUM): *aim(s):* annex Kashmi into Pakistan and establish an Islamic state in Kashmir

area(s) of operation: headquartered in Islamabad, with a heavy operational presence in Muzaffarabad in Pakistan-administered Azad Kashmir, where operatives stage attacks against India; maintains training and paramilitary camps in the country's Federally Administered Tribal Areas (FATA) region; FATA is a semi-autonomous region in the northwest consisting of seven tribal agencies (districts) and six frontier regions directly governed by Pakistan's federal government through a special set of laws called the Frontier Crimes Regulations; outlawed in Pakistan since November 2003

Islamic Jihad Union (IJU): *aim(s):* secure its base in Pakistan's Federally Administered Tribal Areas (FATA) and, ultimately, overthrow the Government of Uzbekistan

area(s) of operation: headquartered in FATA, where fighters attack Pakistani security forces and stage attacks inside Afghanistan; FATA is a semi-autonomous region in the northwest consisting of seven tribal agencies (districts) and six frontier regions directly governed by Pakistan's federal government through a special set of laws called the Frontier Crimes Regulations; operates primarily against international and Afghan forces in Afghanistan, in collaboration with other armed groups; members are scattered throughout Central Asia and Europe; on 29 July 2004, an operative blew himself up next to a vehicle in Fateh Jhang, Attock District, Punjab Province, carrying Pakistan's then prime minister-designate, Shaukat AZIZ, killing at least nine people and injuring more than 25; membership was assessed in 2016 to be in the low hundreds

Islamic Movement of Uzbekistan (IMU): *aim(s):* enhance its networks and secure its territory in Pakistan to meet its historic goal of establishing an Islamic state in the Fergana Valley, a fertile valley spread across eastern Uzbekistan, southern Kyrgyzstan, and northern Tajikistan

area(s) of operation: leadership is based in Pakistan's Federally Administered Tribal Areas (FATA) region; FATA is a semi-autonomous region in country's northwest consisting of seven tribal agencies (districts) and six frontier regions directly governed by Pakistan's federal government through a special set of laws called the Frontier Crimes Regulations; IMU moved to Pakistan after the US-led invasion of Afghanistan in 2001; active along the Pakistan-Afghanistan border across from northern Afghanistan, where on the Pakistan side as of 2017, the group operates considerably fewer paramilitary training camps than during its peak in the late 1990s leading up to 2001

Jaish-e-Mohammed (JEM): *aim(s):* unite Kashmir with Pakistan, install Sharia in Pakistan, and drive foreign forces from Afghanistan

area(s) of operation: headquartered in Punjab Province; stages attacks against Indian forces, primarily in the Indian-administered state of Jammu and Kashmir; hundreds of members are active in the Kashmir Valley; outlawed in Pakistan

Jundallah: *aim(s):* seeks greater autonomy for Balochis in Pakistan and Iran

area(s) of operation: headquartered in Balochistan Province, where operatives stage attacks inside Iran against Shia Muslims, primarily Iranian soldiers and security personnel for murder or kidnapping; claimed responsibility for opening fire on a bus carrying Ismaili Shia Muslims on 13 May 2015 in Gulshan-e-Iqbal Park in Karachi, killing 43 passengers and wounding 30; outlawed in Pakistan since January 2017

Lashkar-e Tayyiba (LeT): *aim(s):* annex India's state of Jammu and Kashmir as part of Pakistan and, ultimately, install Islamic rule over parts of India and Pakistan

area(s) of operation: headquartered in Lahore, Punjab Province, with an operational presence throughout the country, especially in both the Pakistan-controlled and India-controlled Kashmir regions; stages attacks against Indian military and security forces; the Falah-e-Insaniat Foundation charity organization in Lahore is a JuD and LeT fundraising subsidiary; LeT has been outlawed in Pakistan since 2002; LeT changed its name to Kashmir Tehrik Azadi in early 2017

Terrorist groups—foreign based: *Indian Mujahedeen (IM):* aim(s): enhance networks in Pakistan to maintain safe havens and carry out attacks inside India

area(s) of operation: cofounders and brothers Mohammed Riyaz BHATKAL and Iqbal BHATKAL are reportedly leading IM from Karachi

Islamic State of Iraq and the Levant-Khorasan (ISIL-K): *aim(s):* establish an Islamic caliphate in the Afghanistan-Pakistan region

area(s) of operation: maintains a limited operational and recruitment presence throughout the country, primarily along the Pakistan-Afghanistan border to stage attacks inside Afghanistan; conducts small-scale shooting and bombing attacks against Pakistani Shia Muslims, military installations, and government buildings; claimed responsibility for the 13 May 2015 shooting of Shia Muslim bus passangers in Karachi, killing 45 people and injuring 13; assessed in early 2017 to have a few hundred fighters based in Pakistan; core ISIL refers to Pakistan and Afghanistan as its Wilayat al-Khorasan

Lashkar i Jhangvi (LJ): *aim(s):* exterminate Shia Muslims, rid the region of Western influence and, ultimately, establish an Islamic state under Sharia in Pakistan

area(s) of operation: has a growing presence in Karachi, the capital of Sindh Province; loosely coordinated cells are spread across the country, primarily in Punjab and Balochistan provinces, Karachi, and in the Federally Administered Tribal Areas (FATA) region; FATA is a semi-autonomous region in the northwest consisting of seven tribal agencies (districts) and six frontier regions directly governed by Pakistan's federal government through a special set of laws called the Frontier Crimes Regulations; majority of attacks are against local and foreign Shia Muslims and government personnel and facilities; LJ attacks in recent years have killed hundreds of Pakistanis, including the 21 January 2017 bombing at a vegetable market in the Shia Muslim section of Parachinar, Kurram Valley Agency, FATA, that killed at least 25 people and injured over 50; recruits travel to Afghanistan across from Pakistan's central FATA borders to attend paramilitary training in LJ camps; assessed in late 2015 to have a few hundred members; outlawed in Pakistan

Tehrik-e-Taliban Pakistan (TTP): *aim(s):* remove Pakistani forces from the Federally Administered Tribal Areas (FATA) and, ultimately, overthrow the Pakistan Government to install TTP's strict interpretation of Sharia throughout the country

area(s) of operation: maintains a large presence in Karachi, the capital of Sindh Province; trains and deploys fighters in the tribal belt in the Pashtun areas along the Pakistan-Afghanistan border, especially in Kunar Province where TTP has established sanctuaries; operationally active in the North Waziristan and Balochistan regions; targets Pakistan Government officials and military, security, and police personnel and Westerners, progovernment tribal elders, Shia Muslims, and education figures and advocates; formerly headquartered in Bajaur Agency in northern FATA, a semi-autonomous region in the northwestern consisting of seven tribal agencies (districts) and six frontier regions directly governed by Pakistan's federal government through a special set of laws called the Frontier Crimes Regulations; has carried out and claimed responsibility for numerous attacks against Pakistani and US interests throughout most of the country; killed approximately 543 people in Pakistan in 2014, including on 16 December 2014, when TTP gunmen entered the Army Public School in Khyber Pakhtunkhwa, Peshawar, and opened fire and detonated bombs, killing 157 and injuring 131 in the deadliest terrorist attack ever to occur in Pakistan; shot education rights activist Malala YOUSAFZAI in a failed assassination attempt on 9 October 2012; TTP has suspected involvement in the 2007 assassination of former Pakistani Prime Minister Benazir BHUTTO; outlawed in Pakistan

TRANSNATIONAL ISSUES

Disputes—international: various talks and confidence-building measures cautiously have begun to defuse tensions over Kashmir, particularly since the October 2005 earthquake in the region; Kashmir nevertheless remains the site of the world's largest and most militarized territorial dispute with portions under the de facto administration of China (Aksai Chin), India (Jammu and Kashmir), and Pakistan (Azad Kashmir and Northern Areas); UN Military Observer Group in India and Pakistan has maintained a small group of peacekeepers since 1949; India does not recognize Pakistan's ceding historic Kashmir lands to China in 1964; India and Pakistan have maintained their 2004 cease-fire in Kashmir and initiated discussions on defusing the armed standoff in the Siachen glacier region; Pakistan protests India's fencing the highly militarized Line of Control and construction of the Baglihar Dam on the Chenab River in Jammu and Kashmir, which is part of the larger dispute on water sharing of the Indus River and its tributaries; to defuse tensions and prepare for discussions on a maritime boundary, India and Pakistan seek technical resolution of the disputed boundary in Sir Creek estuary at the mouth of the Rann of Kutch in the Arabian Sea; Pakistani maps continue to show the Junagadh claim in India's Gujarat State; since 2002, with UN assistance, Pakistan has repatriated 3.8 million Afghan refugees, leaving about 2.6 million; Pakistan has sent troops across and built fences along some remote tribal areas of its treaty-defined Durand Line border with Afghanistan, which serve as bases for foreign terrorists and other illegal activities; Afghan, Coalition, and Pakistan military meet periodically to clarify the alignment of the boundary on the ground and on maps

Refugees and internally displaced persons: refugees (country of origin): 2—2.4 million (1.4 million registered, 600,000—1.0 million undocumented) (Afghanistan) (2017)

IDPs: 464,000 (primarily those who remain displaced by counter-terrorism and counter-insurgency operations and violent conflict between armed non-state groups in the Federally Administered Tribal Areas and Khyber-Paktunkwa

Province; more than 1 million displaced in northern Waziristan in 2014; individuals also have been displaced by repeated monsoon floods) (2016)

Trafficking in persons: current situation: Pakistan is a source, transit, and destination country for men, women, and children subjected to forced labor and sex trafficking; the largest human trafficking problem is bonded labor in agriculture, brickmaking and, to a lesser extent, fishing, mining and carpet-making; children are bought, sold, rented, and placed in forced begging rings, domestic service, small shops, brick-making factories, or prostitution; militant groups also force children to spy, fight, or die as suicide bombers, kidnapping the children or getting them from poor parents through sale or coercion; women and girls are forced into prostitution or marriages; Pakistani adults migrate to the Gulf States and African and European states for low-skilled jobs and sometimes become victims of forced labor, debt bondage, or prostitution; foreign adults and children, particularly from Afghanistan, Bangladesh, and Sri Lanka, may be subject to forced labor, and foreign women may be sex trafficked in Pakistan, with refugees and ethnic minorities being most vulnerable

tier rating: Tier 2 Watch List – Pakistan does not fully comply with the minimum standards for the elimination of trafficking; however, it is making significant efforts to do so; the government lacks political will and capacity to fully address

human trafficking, as evidenced by ineffective law enforcement efforts, official complicity, penalization of victims, and the continued conflation of migrant smuggling and human trafficking by many officials; not all forms of trafficking are prohibited; an anti-trafficking bill drafted in 2013 to address gaps in existing legislation remains pending, and a national action plan drafted in 2014 is not finalized; feudal landlords and brick kiln owners use their political influence to protect their involvement in bonded labor, while some police personnel have taken bribes to ignore prostitution that may have included sex trafficking; authorities began to use standard procedures for the identification and referral of trafficking victims, but it is not clear how widely these methods were practiced; in other instances, police were reluctant to assist NGOs with rescues and even punished victims for crimes committed as a direct result of being trafficked (2015)

Illicit drugs: significant transit area for Afghan drugs, including heroin, opium, morphine, and hashish, bound for Iran, Western markets, the Gulf States, Africa, and Asia; financial crimes related to drug trafficking, terrorism, corruption, and smuggling remain problems; opium poppy cultivation estimated to be 930 hectares in 2015; federal and provincial authorities continue to conduct anti-poppy campaigns that utilizes forced eradication, fines, and arrests

PALAU

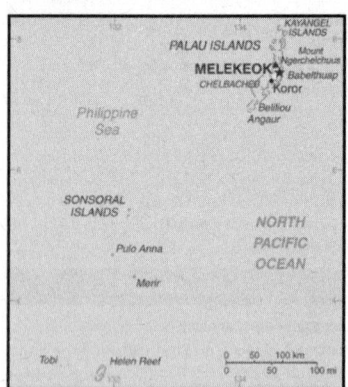

INTRODUCTION

Background: After three decades as part of the UN Trust Territory of the Pacific under US administration, this westernmost cluster of the Caroline Islands opted for independence in 1978 rather than join the Federated States of Micronesia. A Compact of Free Association with the US was approved in 1986 but not ratified until 1993. It entered into force the following year when the islands gained independence.

GEOGRAPHY

Location: Oceania, group of islands in the North Pacific Ocean, southeast of the Philippines

Geographic coordinates: 7 30 N, 134 30 E

Map references: Oceania

Area: *total:* 459 sq km
land: 459 sq km
water: 0 sq km
country comparison to the world: 198

Area—comparative: slightly more than 2.5 times the size of Washington, DC

Land boundaries: 0 km

Coastline: 1,519 km

Maritime claims: *territorial sea:* 12 nm
contiguous zone: 24 nm
exclusive economic zone: 200 nm
continental shelf: 200 nm

Climate: tropical; hot and humid; wet season May to November

Terrain: varying topography from the high, mountainous main island of Babelthuap to low, coral islands usually fringed by large barrier reefs

Elevation: *mean elevation:* NA

elevation extremes: *lowest point:* Pacific Ocean 0 m
highest point: Mount Ngerchelchuus 242 m

Natural resources: forests, minerals (especially gold), marine products, deep-seabed minerals

Land use: *agricultural land:* 10.8%
arable land: 2.2%;
permanent crops: 4.3%;
permanent pasture: 4.3%
forest: 87.6%
other: 1.6% (2011 est.)
Irrigated land: 0 sq km (2012)

Population—distribution: most of the population is located on the southern end of the main island of Babelthuap

Natural hazards: typhoons (June to December)

Environment—current issues: inadequate facilities for disposal of solid waste; threats to the marine ecosystem from sand and coral dredging, illegal fishing practices, and overfishing

Environment—international agreements: *party to:* Biodiversity, Climate Change, Climate Change-Kyoto Protocol, Desertification, Law of the Sea, Ozone Layer Protection, Wetlands, Whaling
signed, but not ratified: none of the selected agreements

Geography—note: westernmost archipelago in the Caroline chain, consists of six island groups totaling more than 300 islands; includes World War II battleground of Beliliou (Peleliu) and world-famous Rock Islands

PEOPLE AND SOCIETY

Population: 21,431 (July 2017 est.)
country comparison to the world: 219

Nationality: *noun:* Palauan(s)
adjective: Palauan

Ethnic groups: Palauan (Micronesian with Malayan and Melanesian admixtures) 73%, Carolinian 2%, Asian 21.7%, caucasian 1.2%, other 2.1% (2015 est.)

Languages: Palauan (official on most islands) 65.2%, other Micronesian 1.9%, English (official) 19.1%, Filipino 9.9%, Chinese 1.2%, other 2.8%
note: Sonsorolese is official in Sonsoral; Tobian is official in Tobi; Angaur and Japanese are official in Angaur (2015 est.)

Religions: Roman Catholic 45.3%, Protestant 34.9% (includes Evangelical 26.4%, Seventh Day Adventist 6.9%, Assembly of God .9%, Baptist .7%), Modekngei 5.7% (indigenous to Palau), Muslim 3%, Mormon 1.5%, other 9.7% (2015 est.)

Age structure: *0-14 years:* 19.69% (male 2,177/ female 2,043)
15-24 years: 16.68% (male 1,788/female 1,787)
25-54 years: 45.89% (male 6,005/female 3,830)
55-64 years: 9.65% (male 731/female 1,338)
65 years and over: 8.08% (male 446/female 1,286) (2017 est.)

Median age: *total:* 33.4 years
male: 32.7 years
female: 35 years (2017 est.)
country comparison to the world: 88

Population growth rate: 0.39% (2017 est.)
country comparison to the world: 162

Birth rate: 11.3 births/1,000 population (2017 est.)
country comparison to the world: 174

Death rate: 8.1 deaths/1,000 population (2017 est.)
country comparison to the world: 86

Net migration rate: 0.8 migrant(s)/1,000 population (2017 est.)
country comparison to the world: 59

Population distribution: most of the population is located on the southern end of the main island of Babelthuap

Urbanization: *urban population:* 88.2% of total population (2017)
rate of urbanization: 1.6% annual rate of change (2015-20 est.)

Major urban areas—population: MELEKEOK (capital) 299 (2012)

Sex ratio: *at birth:* 1.06 male(s)/female
0-14 years: 1.07 male(s)/female
15-24 years: 1 male(s)/female
25-54 years: 1.57 male(s)/female
55-64 years: 0.54 male(s)/female
65 years and over: 0.37 male(s)/female
total population: 1.09 male(s)/female (2016 est.)

Infant mortality rate: *total:* 10.6 deaths/1,000 live births
male: 12.1 deaths/1,000 live births
female: 9 deaths/1,000 live births (2017 est.)

country comparison to the world: 133

Life expectancy at birth: *total population:* 73.4 years
male: 70.2 years
female: 76.8 years (2017 est.)
country comparison to the world: 135

Total fertility rate: 1.71 children born/woman (2017 est.)
country comparison to the world: 170

Health expenditures: 9% of GDP (2014)
country comparison to the world: 39

Physicians density: 1.42 physicians/1,000 population (2010)

Hospital bed density: 4.8 beds/1,000 population (2010)

Drinking water source:
improved:
urban: 97% of population
rural: 86% of population
total: 95.3% of population
unimproved:
urban: 3% of population
rural: 14% of population
total: 4.7% of population (2011 est.)

Sanitation facility access:
improved:
urban: 100% of population
rural: 100% of population
total: 100% of population
unimproved:
urban: 0% of population
rural: 0% of population
total: 0% of population (2015 est.)

HIV/AIDS—adult prevalence rate: NA

HIV/AIDS—people living with HIV/AIDS: NA

HIV/AIDS—deaths: NA

Obesity—adult prevalence rate: 55.3% (2016)
country comparison to the world: 3

Literacy: *definition:* age 15 and over can read and write
total population: 96.6%
male: 96.8%
female: 86% (2015 est.)

School life expectancy (primary to tertiary education): *total:* 17 years
male: 16 years
female: 18 years (2013)

GOVERNMENT

Country name: *conventional long form:* Republic of Palau
conventional short form: Palau
local long form: Beluu er a Belau
local short form: Belau
former: Trust Territory of the Pacific Islands, Palau District
etymology: from the Palauan name for the islands, Belau, which likely derives from the Palauan word "beluu" meaning "village"

Government type: presidential republic in free association with the US

Capital: *name:* Ngerulmud

geographic coordinates: 7 30 N, 134 37 E
time difference: UTC+9 (14 hours ahead of Washington, DC, during Standard Time)

Administrative divisions: 16 states; Aimeliik, Airai, Angaur, Hatohobei, Kayangel, Koror, Melekeok, Ngaraard, Ngarchelong, Ngardmau, Ngatpang, Ngchesar, Ngeremlengui, Ngiwal, Peleliu, Sonsorol

Independence: 1 October 1994 (from the US-administered UN trusteeship)

National holiday: Constitution Day, 9 July (1981), day of a national referendum to pass the new constitution; Independence Day, 1 October (1994)

Constitution: ratified 9 July 1980, effective 1 January 1981; amended 1992, 2004, 2008 (2016)

Legal system: mixed legal system of civil, common, and customary law

International law organization participation: has not submitted an ICJ jurisdiction declaration; non-party state to the ICCt

Citizenship: *citizenship by birth:* no

citizenship by descent only: at least one parent must be a citizen of Palau
dual citizenship recognized: no
residency requirement for naturalization: note—no procedure for naturalization

Suffrage: 18 years of age; universal

Executive branch: *chief of state:* President Tommy REMENGESAU (since 17 January 2013); Vice President Antonio BELLS (since 17 January 2013); note—the president is both chief of state and head of government

head of government: President Tommy REMENGESAU (since 17 January 2013); Vice President Antonio BELLS (since 17 January 2013)
cabinet: Cabinet appointed by the president with the advice and consent of the Senate; also includes the vice president; the Council of Chiefs consists of chiefs from each of the states who advise the president on issues concerning traditional laws, customs, and their relationship to the constitution and laws of Palau
elections/appointments: president and vice president directly elected on separate ballots by absolute majority popular vote in 2 rounds if needed for a 4-year term (eligible for a second term); election last held on 1 November 2016 (next to be held in November 2020)
election results: Tommy REMENGESAU reelected president; percent of vote—Tommy REMENGESAU (independent) 51.3%, Surangel WHIPPS, Jr.(independent) 48.7%; Antonio BELLS elected vice president

Legislative branch: *description:* bicameral National Congress or Olbiil Era Kelulau consists of the Senate (13 seats; members directly elected in single-seat constituencies by majority vote to serve 4-year terms) and the House of Delegates (16 seats; members directly elected in single-seat constituencies by simple majority vote to serve 4-year terms)
elections: Senate—last held on 1 November 2016 (next to be held in November 2020); House of

697

Delegates—last held on 1 November 2016 (next to be held in November 2020)

election results: Senate—percent of vote—NA; seats—independent 13; House of Delegates—percent of vote—NA; seats—independent 16

Judicial branch: *highest court(s):* Supreme Court (consists of the chief justice and 3 associate justices organized into appellate trial divisions; also within the Supreme Court organization are the Common Pleas and Land Courts)

judge selection and term of office: justices nominated by a 7-member independent body consisting of judges, presidential appointees, and lawyers and appointed by the president; judges appointed until mandatory retirement at age 65

subordinate courts: National Court and other 'inferior' courts

Political parties and leaders: none

Political pressure groups and leaders: NA

International organization participation: ACP, ADB, AOSIS, FAO, IAEA, IBRD, ICAO, ICRM, IDA, IFC, IFRCS, ILO, IMF, IMO, IMSO, IOC, IPU, MIGA, OPCW, PIF, Sparteca, SPC, UN, UNAMID, UNCTAD, UNESCO, WHO

Diplomatic representation in the US: *chief of mission:* Ambassador Hersey KYOTA (since 12 November 1997)

chancery: 1701 Pennsylvania Avenue NW, Suite 300, Washington, DC 20036

telephone: [1] (202) 452-6814

FAX: [1] (202) 452-6281

consulate(s): Tamuning (Guam)

Diplomatic representation from the US: *chief of mission:* Ambassador Amy HYATT (since 9 March 2015)

embassy: Koror (no street address)

mailing address: P. O. Box 6028, Koror, Republic of Palau 96940

telephone: [680] 587-2920

FAX: [680] 587-2911

Flag description: light blue with a large yellow disk shifted slightly to the hoist side; the blue color represents the ocean, the disk represents the moon; Palauans consider the full moon to be the optimum time for human activity; it is also considered a symbol of peace, love, and tranquility

National symbol(s): bai (native meeting house); national colors: blue, yellow

National anthem: name: "Belau rekid" (Our Palau) *lyrics/music:* multiple/Ymesei O. EZEKIEL *note:* adopted 1980

ECONOMY

Economy—overview: The economy is dominated by tourism, fishing, and subsistence agriculture. Government is a major employer of the work force relying on financial assistance from the US under the Compact of Free Association (Compact) with the US that took effect after the end of the UN trusteeship on 1 October 1994. The US provided Palau with roughly $700 million in aid for the first 15 years following commencement of the Compact in 1994 in return for unrestricted access to its land

and waterways for strategic purposes. The population enjoys a per capita income roughly double that of the Philippines and much of Micronesia.

Business and leisure tourist arrivals reached a record 167,966 in 2015, a 14.4% increase over the previous year, but fell to 138,408 in 2016. Long-run prospects for tourism have been bolstered by the expansion of air travel in the Pacific, the rising prosperity of industrial East Asia, and the willingness of foreigners to finance infrastructure development. Proximity to Guam, the region's major destination for tourists from East Asia, and a regionally competitive tourist infrastructure enhance Palau's advantage as a destination.

GDP (purchasing power parity): $301 million (2017 est.)
$298 million (2016 est.)
$292.4 million (2015 est.)
note: data are in 2017 dollars
country comparison to the world: 217

GDP (official exchange rate): $321 million (2016 est.)

GDP—real growth rate: 1% (2017 est.)
1.9% (2016 est.)
11.4% (2015 est.)
country comparison to the world: 185

GDP—per capita (PPP): $16,700 (2017 est.)
$16,600 (2016 est.)
$16,200 (2015 est.)
note: data are in 2017 dollars
country comparison to the world: 105

GDP—composition, by end use:
household consumption: 60.6%
government consumption: 27.2%
investment in fixed capital: 22.6%
investment in inventories: 2%
exports of goods and services: 55.1%
imports of goods and services: -67.5% (2016)

GDP—composition, by sector of origin:
agriculture: 3%
industry: 19%
services: 78% (2016 est.)

Agriculture—products: coconuts, cassava (manioc, tapioca), sweet potatoes; fish, pigs, chickens, eggs, bananas, papaya, breadfruit, calamansi, soursop, Polynesian chestnuts, Polynesian almonds, mangoes, taro, guava, beans, cucumbers, squash/pumpkins (various), eggplant, green onions, kangkong (watercress), cabbages (various), radishes, betel nuts, melons, peppers, noni, okra

Industries: tourism, fishing, subsistence agriculture

Industrial production growth rate: NA%

Labor force: 11,610 (2016)
country comparison to the world: 217

Labor force—by occupation: *agriculture:* 1.2%
industry: 12.4%
services: 86.4% (2016)

Unemployment rate: 1.7% (2015 est.)
4.1% (2012)
country comparison to the world: 12

Population below poverty line: NA%

Household income or consumption by percentage share: *lowest 10%:* NA%

highest 10%: NA%

Budget: *revenues:* $212.2 million
expenditures: $183.9 million (2012 est.)
Taxes and other revenues: 66.1% of GDP (2016 est.)
country comparison to the world: 5

Budget surplus (+) or deficit (-): 8.8% of GDP (2016 est.)
country comparison to the world: 3

Public debt: 24.1% of GDP (2016 est.)
21.6% of GDP (2015)
country comparison to the world: 180

Fiscal year: 1 October—30 September

Inflation rate (consumer prices): 1.5% (2017 est.)
-1% (2016 est.)
country comparison to the world: 65

Market value of publicly traded shares: $NA

Current account balance: -$39 million (2017 est.)
-$32 million (2016 est.)
country comparison to the world: 69

Exports: $117.5 million (2016 est.)
$14.8 million (2015 est.)
country comparison to the world: 194

Exports—commodities: shellfish, tuna, other fish (many species)

Exports—partners: Greece 82.4%, US 6.9% (2016)

Imports: $179.3 million (2016 est.)
$156.8 million (2015 est.)
country comparison to the world: 206

Imports—commodities: machinery and equipment, fuels, metals; foodstuffs

Imports—partners: US 24.6%, Japan 19.8%, China 14.3%, Guam 14.2%, Philippines 4.4% (2016)

Reserves of foreign exchange and gold: $580.9 million (31 December 2015 est.)
country comparison to the world: 139

Debt—external: $18.38 billion (31 December 2014 est.)
$16.47 billion (31 December 2013 est.)
country comparison to the world: 94

Exchange rates: the US dollar is used

ENERGY

Electricity access: *population without electricity:* 8,752
electrification—*total population:* 59%
electrification—urban areas: 62%
electrification—rural areas: 45% (2012)

COMMUNICATIONS

Telephones—fixed lines: *total subscriptions:* 7,204
subscriptions per 100 inhabitants: 34 (July 2016 est.)
country comparison to the world: 203

Telephones—mobile cellular: *total:* 24,000
subscriptions per 100 inhabitants: 112 (July 2016 est.)
country comparison to the world: 210

Telephone system: *general assessment:* well-developed mobile sector recently boosted by satellite network capacity upgrades
domestic: fixed-line and mobile-cellular services available with a combined subscribership of over 140 per 100 persons
international: country code—680; satellite earth station—1 Intelsat (Pacific Ocean) (2016)

Broadcast media: no broadcast TV stations; a cable TV network covers the major islands and provides access to 4 local cable stations, rebroadcasts (on a delayed basis) of a number of US stations, as well as access to a number of real-time satellite TV channels; about a half dozen radio stations (1 government-owned) (2017)

Internet country code: .pw

Internet users: *total:* 7,650
percent of population: 36.0% (July 2016 est.)

TRANSPORTATION

National air transport system: *number of registered air carriers:* 1
inventory of registered aircraft operated by air carriers: 1 (2015)

Airports: 3 (2013)
country comparison to the world: 194

Airports—with paved runways: *total:* 1
1,524 to 2,437 m: 1 (2017)

Airports—with unpaved runways: *total:* 2
1,524 to 2,437 m: 2 (2013)

Ports and terminals: *major seaport(s):* Koror

MILITARY AND SECURITY

Military branches: no regular military forces; Palau National Police (2009)

Military—note: defense is the responsibility of the US; under a Compact of Free Association between Palau and the US, the US military is granted access to the islands for 50 years, but it has not stationed any military forces there (2008)

TRANSNATIONAL ISSUES

Disputes—international: maritime delineation negotiations continue with Philippines, Indonesia

PANAMA

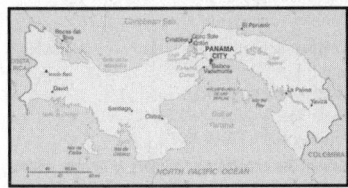

INTRODUCTION

Background: Explored and settled by the Spanish in the 16th century, Panama broke with Spain in 1821 and joined a union of Colombia, Ecuador, and Venezuela—named the Republic of Gran Colombia. When the latter dissolved in 1830, Panama remained part of Colombia. With US backing, Panama seceded from Colombia in 1903 and promptly signed a treaty with the US allowing for the construction of a canal and US sovereignty over a strip of land on either side of the structure (the Panama Canal Zone). The Panama Canal was built by the US Army Corps of Engineers between 1904 and 1914. In 1977, an agreement was signed for the complete transfer of the Canal from the US to Panama by the end of the century. Certain portions of the Zone and increasing responsibility over the Canal were turned over in the subsequent decades. With US help, dictator Manuel NORIEGA was deposed in 1989. The entire Panama Canal, the area supporting the Canal, and remaining US military bases were transferred to Panama by the end of 1999. An ambitious expansion project to more than double the Canal's capacity—by allowing for more Canal transits and larger ships—was carried out between 2007 and 2016.

GEOGRAPHY

Location: Central America, bordering both the Caribbean Sea and the North Pacific Ocean, between Colombia and Costa Rica

Geographic coordinates: 9 00 N, 80 00 W

Map references: Central America and the Caribbean

Area: *total:* 75,420 sq km
land: 74,340 sq km
water: 1,080 sq km
country comparison to the world: 119

Area—comparative: slightly smaller than South Carolina

Land boundaries: *total:* 687 km
border countries (2): Colombia 339 km, Costa Rica 348 km

Coastline: 2,490 km

Maritime claims: *territorial sea:* 12 nm
contiguous zone: 24 nm
exclusive economic zone: 200 nm or edge of continental margin

Climate: tropical maritime; hot, humid, cloudy; prolonged rainy season (May to January), short dry season (January to May)

Terrain: interior mostly steep, rugged mountains with dissected, upland plains; coastal plains with rolling hills

Elevation: *mean elevation:* 360 m

elevation extremes: *lowest point:* Pacific Ocean 0 m
highest point: Volcan Baru 3,475 m

Natural resources: copper, mahogany forests, shrimp, hydropower

Land use: *agricultural land:* 30.5%
arable land: 7.3%;
permanent crops: 2.5%;
permanent pasture: 20.7%
forest: 43.6%
other: 25.9% (2011 est.)
Irrigated land: 321 sq km (2012)

Population—distribution: population is concentrated towards the center of the country, particularly around the Canal, but a sizeable segment of the populace also lives in the far west around David; the eastern third of the country is sparsely inhabited

Natural hazards: occasional severe storms and forest fires in the Darien area

Environment—current issues: water pollution from agricultural runoff threatens fishery resources; deforestation of tropical rain forest; land degradation and soil erosion threatens siltation of Panama Canal; air pollution in urban areas; mining threatens natural resources

Environment—international agreements: *party to:* Biodiversity, Climate Change, Climate Change-Kyoto Protocol, Desertification, Endangered Species, Environmental Modification, Hazardous Wastes, Law of the Sea, Marine Dumping, Ozone Layer Protection, Ship Pollution, Tropical Timber 83, Tropical Timber 94, Wetlands, Whaling
signed, but not ratified: Marine Life Conservation

Geography—note: strategic location on eastern end of isthmus forming land bridge connecting North and South America; controls Panama Canal that links North Atlantic Ocean via Caribbean Sea with North Pacific Ocean

PEOPLE AND SOCIETY

Population: 3,753,142 (July 2017 est.)
country comparison to the world: 130

Nationality: *noun:* Panamanian(s)
adjective: Panamanian

Ethnic groups: mestizo (mixed Amerindian and white) 65%, Native American 12.3% (Ngabe 7.6%, Kuna 2.4%, Embera 0.9%, Bugle 0.8%, other 0.4%, unspecified 0.2%), black or African descent 9.2%, mulatto 6.8%, white 6.7% (2010 est.)

Languages: Spanish (official), indigenous languages (including Ngabere (or Guaymi), Buglere, Kuna, Embera, Wounaan, Naso (or Teribe), and Bri Bri), Panamanian English Creole (similar to Jamaican English Creole; a mixture of English and Spanish with elements of Ngabere; also known as Guari Guari and Colon Creole), English, Chinese (Yue and Hakka), Arabic, French Creole, other (Yiddish, Hebrew, Korean, Japanese) *note:* many Panamanians are bilingual

Religions: Roman Catholic 85%, Protestant 15%

Demographic profile: Panama is a country of demographic and economic contrasts. It is in the midst of a demographic transition, characterized by steadily declining rates of fertility, mortality, and population growth, but disparities persist based on wealth, geography, and ethnicity. Panama has one of the fastest growing economies in Latin America and dedicates substantial funding to social programs, yet poverty and inequality remain prevalent. The indigenous population accounts for a growing share of Panama's poor and extreme poor, while the non-indigenous rural poor have been more successful at rising out of poverty through rural-to-urban labor migration. The government's large expenditures on untargeted, indirect subsidies for water, electricity, and fuel have been ineffective, but its conditional cash transfer program has shown some promise in helping to decrease extreme poverty among the indigenous population.

Panama has expanded access to education and clean water, but the availability of sanitation and, to a lesser extent, electricity remains poor. The increase in secondary schooling—led by female enrollment—is spreading to rural and indigenous areas, which probably will help to alleviate poverty if educational quality and the availability of skilled jobs improve. Inadequate access to sanitation contributes to a high incidence of diarrhea in Panama's children, which is one of the main causes of Panama's elevated chronic malnutrition rate, especially among indigenous communities.

Age structure: *0-14 years:* 26.4% (male 505,711/female 484,980)
15-24 years: 16.99% (male 324,897/female 312,729)
25-54 years: 40.35% (male 766,747/female 747,472)
55-64 years: 7.91% (male 147,069/female 149,706)
65 years and over: 8.36% (male 144,086/female 169,745) (2017 est.)

Dependency ratios: *total dependency ratio:* 54.8
youth dependency ratio: 43.1
elderly dependency ratio: 11.7
potential support ratio: 8.5 (2015 est.)

Median age: *total:* 29.2 years
male: 28.8 years
female: 29.6 years (2017 est.)
country comparison to the world: 125

Population growth rate: 1.27% (2017 est.)
country comparison to the world: 89

Birth rate: 17.9 births/1,000 population (2017 est.)
country comparison to the world: 100

Death rate: 4.9 deaths/1,000 population (2017 est.)
country comparison to the world: 197

Net migration rate: -0.2 migrant(s)/1,000 population (2017 est.)
country comparison to the world: 108

Population distribution: population is concentrated towards the center of the country,

particularly around the Canal, but a sizeable segment of the populace also lives in the far west around David; the eastern third of the country is sparsely inhabited

Urbanization: *urban population:* 67.2% of total population (2017)
rate of urbanization: 1.94% annual rate of change (2015-20 est.)

Major urban areas—population: PANAMA CITY (capital) 1.673 million (2015)

Sex ratio: *at birth:* 1.05 male(s)/female
0-14 years: 1.04 male(s)/female
15-24 years: 1.04 male(s)/female
25-54 years: 1.03 male(s)/female
55-64 years: 0.98 male(s)/female
65 years and over: 0.85 male(s)/female
total population: 1.01 male(s)/female (2016 est.)

Maternal mortality ratio: 94 deaths/100,000 live births (2015 est.)
country comparison to the world: 74

Infant mortality rate: *total:* 9.9 deaths/1,000 live births
male: 10.6 deaths/1,000 live births
female: 9.1 deaths/1,000 live births (2017 est.)
country comparison to the world: 138

Life expectancy at birth: *total population:* 78.8 years
male: 76 years
female: 81.7 years (2017 est.)
country comparison to the world: 55

Total fertility rate: 2.3 children born/woman (2017 est.)
country comparison to the world: 90

Contraceptive prevalence rate: 62.8% (2013)

Health expenditures: 8% of GDP (2014)
country comparison to the world: 56

Physicians density: 1.59 physicians/1,000 population (2013)

Hospital bed density: 2.2 beds/1,000 population (2011)

Drinking water source:
improved:
urban: 97.7% of population
rural: 86.6% of population
total: 94.7% of population
unimproved:
urban: 2.3% of population
rural: 11.4% of population
total: 5.3% of population (2015 est.)

Sanitation facility access:
improved:
urban: 83.5% of population
rural: 58% of population
total: 75% of population
unimproved:
urban: 16.5% of population
rural: 42% of population
total: 25% of population (2015 est.)

HIV/AIDS—adult prevalence rate: 0.8% (2016 est.)
country comparison to the world: 49

HIV/AIDS—people living with HIV/AIDS: 21,000 (2016 est.)

country comparison to the world: 76

HIV/AIDS—deaths: <1000 (2016 est.)

Major infectious diseases: *degree of risk:* intermediate
food or waterborne diseases: bacterial diarrhea
vectorborne disease: dengue fever
note: active local transmission of Zika virus by Aedes species mosquitoes has been identified in this country (as of August 2016); it poses an important risk (a large number of cases possible) among US citizens if bitten by an infective mosquito; other less common ways to get Zika are through sex, via blood transfusion, or during pregnancy, in which the pregnant woman passes Zika virus to her fetus (2016)

Obesity—adult prevalence rate: 22.7% (2016)
country comparison to the world: 72

Children under the age of 5 years underweight: 3.9% (2008)
country comparison to the world: 99

Education expenditures: 3.3% of GDP (2011)
country comparison to the world: 122

Literacy: *definition:* age 15 and over can read and write
total population: 95%
male: 95.7%
female: 94.4% (2015 est.)

School life expectancy (primary to tertiary education): *total:* 13 years
male: 12 years
female: 13 years (2013)

Unemployment, youth ages 15-24: *total:* 11.5%
male: 9%
female: 16% (2016 est.)
country comparison to the world: 99

GOVERNMENT

Country name: *conventional long form:* Republic of Panama
conventional short form: Panama
local long form: Republica de Panama
local short form: Panama
etymology: according to tradition, the name derives from a former indigenous fishing village and its nearby beach that were called "Panama" meaning "an abundance of fish"

Government type: presidential republic

Capital: *name:* Panama City

geographic coordinates: 8 58 N, 79 32 W
time difference: UTC-5 (same time as Washington, DC, during Standard Time)

Administrative divisions: 10 provinces (provincias, singular—provincia) and 3 indigenous regions* (comarcas); Bocas del Toro, Chiriqui, Cocle, Colon, Darien, Embera-Wounaan*, Herrera, Guna Yala*, Los Santos, Ngobe-Bugle*, Panama, Panama Oeste, Veraguas

Independence: 3 November 1903 (from Colombia; became independent from Spain on 28 November 1821)

National holiday: Independence Day (Separation Day), 3 November (1903)

Constitution: several previous; latest effective 11 October 1972; amended several times, last in 2004 (2016)

Legal system: civil law system; judicial review of legislative acts in the Supreme Court of Justice

International law organization participation: accepts compulsory ICJ jurisdiction with reservations; accepts ICCt jurisdiction

Citizenship: *citizenship by birth:* yes
citizenship by descent: yes
dual citizenship recognized: no
residency requirement for naturalization: 5 years

Suffrage: 18 years of age; universal

Executive branch: *chief of state:* President Juan Carlos VARELA (since 1 July 2014); Vice President Isabel de SAINT MALO de Alvarado (since 1 July 2014); note—the president is both chief of state and head of government

head of government: President Juan Carlos VARELA (since 1 July 2014); Vice President Isabel de SAINT MALO de Alvarado (since 1 July 2014)
cabinet: Cabinet appointed by the president
elections/appointments: president and vice president directly elected on the same ballot by simple majority popular vote for a 5-year term; president eligible for a single non-consecutive term); election last held on 4 May 2014 (next to be held in 2019)
election results: Juan Carlos VARELA elected president; percent of vote—Juan Carlos VARELA (PP) 39.1%, Jose Domingo ARIAS (CD) 31.4%, Juan Carlos NAVARRO (PRD) 28.2%, other 1.3%

Legislative branch: *description:* unicameral National Assembly or Asamblea Nacional (71 seats; 45 members directly elected in multi-seat constituencies—populous towns and cities—by proportional representation vote and 26 directly elected in single-seat constituencies—outlying rural districts—by plurality vote; members serve 5-year terms)
elections: last held on 4 May 2014 (next to be held in May 2019)
election results: percent of vote by party—CD 33.7%, PRD 31.5%, Panamenista Party 20%, MOLIRENA 7.2%, PP 3.3%, other 1%, Independent 3%; seats by party—PRD 30, CD 25, Panamenista 12, MOLIRENA 2, PP 1, independent 1
note: an alliance between the Panamenista Party and Democratic Revolutionary Party (PRD) fractured after the 2014 election, but a loose coalition composed of Panamenista and moderate PRD and CD legislators generally work together to support the president's agenda

Judicial branch: *highest court(s):* Supreme Court of Justice or Corte Suprema de Justicia (consists of 9 magistrates and 9 alternates and divided into civil, criminal, administrative, and general business chambers)
judge selection and term of office: magistrates appointed by the president for staggered 10-year terms

subordinate courts: appellate courts or Tribunal Superior; Labor Supreme Courts; Court of Audit; circuit courts or Tribunal Circuital (2 each in 9 of the 10 provinces); municipal courts; electoral, family, maritime, and adolescent courts

Political parties and leaders: Democratic Change or CD [Ricardo MARTINELLI Berrocal]
Democratic Revolutionary Party or PRD [Benicio ROBINSON]
Nationalist Republican Liberal Movement or MOLIRENA [Francisco "Pancho" ALEMAN]
Panamenista Party [Jose Luis "Popi" VARELA Rodriguez] (formerly the Arnulfista Party)
Popular Party or PP [Milton C. HENRIQUEZ] (formerly Christian Democratic Party or PDC)

Political pressure groups and leaders: Chamber of Commerce
Concertacion Nacional (mechanism for Government of Panama to formally communicate with representatives of civil society)
National Council of Organized Workers or CONATO
National Council of Private Enterprise or CONEP
National Union of Construction and Similar Workers or SUNTRACS
Panamanian Association of Business Executives or APEDE
Panamanian Industrialists Society or SIP
Workers Confederation of the Republic of Panama or CTRP

International organization participation: BCIE, CAN (observer), CD, CELAC, FAO, G-77, IADB, IAEA, IBRD, ICAO, ICC (national committees), ICCt, ICRM, IDA, IFAD, IFC, IFRCS, ILO, IMF, IMO, IMSO, Interpol, IOC, IOM, IPU, ISO, ITSO, ITU, ITUC (NGOs), LAES, LAIA, MIGA, NAM, OAS, OPANAL, OPCW, Pacific Alliance (observer), PCA, SICA, UN, UNASUR (observer), UNCTAD, UNESCO, UNIDO, Union Latina, UNWTO, UPU, WCO, WFTU (NGOs), WHO, WIPO, WMO, WTO

Diplomatic representation in the US: *chief of mission:* Ambassador Emanuel Arturo GONZALEZ-REVILLA Lince (since 18 September 2014)
chancery: 2862 McGill Terrace NW, Washington, DC 20007
telephone: [1] (202) 483-1407
FAX: [1] (202) 483-8413
consulate(s) general: Atlanta, Houston, Miami, New Orleans, New York, Philadelphia, Tampa, Washington DC

Diplomatic representation from the US: *chief of mission:* Ambassador John D. FEELEY (since 16 February 2015)
embassy: Edificio 783, Avenida Demetrio Basilio Lakas Panama, Apartado Postal 0816-02561, Zona 5, Panama City
mailing address: American Embassy Panama, Unit 0945, APO AA 34002; American Embassy Panama, 9100 Panama City PL, Washington, DC 20521-9100
telephone: [507] 317-5000
FAX: [507] 317-5568

Flag description: divided into four, equal rectangles; the top quadrants are white (hoist side) with

a blue five-pointed star in the center and plain red; the bottom quadrants are plain blue (hoist side) and white with a red five-pointed star in the center; the blue and red colors are those of the main political parties (Conservatives and Liberals respectively) and the white denotes peace between them; the blue star stands for the civic virtues of purity and honesty, the red star signifies authority and law

National symbol(s): harpy eagle; national colors: blue, white, red

National anthem: *name:* "Himno Istmeno" (Isthmus Hymn)
lyrics/music: Jeronimo DE LA OSSA/Santos A. JORGE
note: adopted 1925

ECONOMY

Economy—overview: Panama's dollar-based economy rests primarily on a well-developed services sector that accounts for more than three-quarters of GDP. Services include operating the Panama Canal, logistics, banking, the Colon Free Trade Zone, insurance, container ports, flagship registry, and tourism and Panama is a center for offshore banking. Panama's transportation and logistics services sectors, along with infrastructure development projects, have boosted economic growth; however, public debt surpassed $37 billion in 2016 because of excessive government spending and public works projects. The US-Panama Trade Promotion Agreement was approved by Congress and signed into law in October 2011, and entered into force in October 2012.

Future growth will be bolstered by the Panama Canal expansion project that began in 2007 and was completed in 2016 at a cost of $5.3 billion—about 10-15% of current GDP. The expansion project more than doubled the Canal's capacity, enabling it to accommodate high-capacity vessels such as tankers and neopanamax vessels that are too large to traverse the existing canal. The US and China are the top users of the Canal.

Strong economic performance has not translated into broadly shared prosperity, as Panama has the second worst income distribution in Latin America. About one-fourth of the population lives in poverty; however, from 2006 to 2012 poverty was reduced by 10 percentage points.

GDP (purchasing power parity): $99.43 billion (2017 est.)
$94.43 billion (2016 est.)
$90.04 billion (2015 est.)
note: data are in 2017 dollars
country comparison to the world: 86

GDP (official exchange rate): $59.05 billion (2016 est.)

GDP—real growth rate: 5.3% (2017 est.)
4.9% (2016 est.)
5.8% (2015 est.)
country comparison to the world: 34

GDP—per capita (PPP): $24,300 (2017 est.)
$23,400 (2016 est.)
$22,700 (2015 est.)

note: data are in 2017 dollars
country comparison to the world: 81

Gross national saving: 40.2% of GDP (2017 est.)
40.6% of GDP (2016 est.)
39.3% of GDP (2015 est.)
country comparison to the world: 9

GDP—composition, by end use:
household consumption: 48.2%
government consumption: 10.1%
investment in fixed capital: 42.8%
investment in inventories: 3.2%
exports of goods and services: 49.4%
imports of goods and services: -53.7% (2017 est.)

GDP—composition, by sector of origin:
agriculture: 2.4%
industry: 15.7%
services: 77% (2017 est.)

Agriculture—products: bananas, rice, corn, coffee, sugarcane, vegetables; livestock; shrimp

Industries: construction, brewing, cement and other construction materials, sugar milling

Industrial production growth rate: 4.7% (2017 est.)
country comparison to the world: 55

Labor force: 1.633 million
note: shortage of skilled labor, but an oversupply of unskilled labor (2017 est.)
country comparison to the world: 129

Labor force—by occupation: *agriculture:* 17%
industry: 18.6%
services: 64.4% (2009 est.)

Unemployment rate: 5.5% (2017 est.)
5.5% (2016 est.)
country comparison to the world: 74

Population below poverty line: 23% (2015 est.)

Household income or consumption by percentage share: *lowest 10%:* 1.1%
highest 10%: 38.9% (2014 est.)

Distribution of family income—Gini index: 50.7 (2014 est.)
56.1 (2003)
country comparison to the world: 14

Budget: *revenues:* $12.6 billion
expenditures: $13.56 billion (2017 est.)
Taxes and other revenues: 21.3% of GDP (2017 est.)
country comparison to the world: 141

Budget surplus (+) or deficit (-): -1.6% of GDP (2017 est.)
country comparison to the world: 71

Public debt: 38.8% of GDP (2017 est.)
38.6% of GDP (2016 est.)
country comparison to the world: 140

Fiscal year: calendar year

Inflation rate (consumer prices): 1.6% (2017 est.)
0.7% (2016 est.)
country comparison to the world: 73

Commercial bank prime lending rate: 8.2% (31 December 2017 est.)
7.53% (31 December 2016 est.)
country comparison to the world: 106

Stock of narrow money: $8.911 billion (31 December 2017 est.)

$8.249 billion (31 December 2016 est.)
country comparison to the world: 88

Stock of broad money: $42.8 billion (31 December 2017 est.)
$38.14 billion (31 December 2016 est.)
country comparison to the world: 72

Stock of domestic credit: $49.89 billion (31 December 2017 est.)
$46.41 billion (31 December 2016 est.)
country comparison to the world: 67

Market value of publicly traded shares: $12.54 billion (31 December 2012 est.)
$10.68 billion (31 December 2011 est.)
$8.348 billion (31 December 2010 est.)
country comparison to the world: 70

Current account balance: -$2.99 billion (2017 est.)
-$3.151 billion (2016 est.)
country comparison to the world: 166

Exports: $15.48 billion (2017 est.)
$14.7 billion (2016 est.)
note: includes the Colon Free Zone
country comparison to the world: 75

Exports—commodities: fruit and nuts, fish, iron and steel waste, wood

Exports—partners: US 21.4%, Netherlands 15.2%, Costa Rica 6%, China 5.6% (2016)

Imports: $21.22 billion (2017 est.)
$22.48 billion (2016 est.)
note: includes the Colon Free Zone
country comparison to the world: 71

Imports—commodities: fuels, machinery, vehicles, iron and steel rods, pharmaceuticals

Imports—partners: US 25.7%, China 9.2%, Mexico 5.3% (2016)

Reserves of foreign exchange and gold: $3.888 billion (31 December 2017 est.)
$3.878 billion (31 December 2016 est.)
country comparison to the world: 99

Debt—external: $86.55 billion (31 December 2017 est.)
$83.81 billion (31 December 2016 est.)
country comparison to the world: 55

Stock of direct foreign investment—at home: $56.02 billion (31 December 2017 est.)
$50.62 billion (31 December 2016 est.)
country comparison to the world: 57

Stock of direct foreign investment—abroad: $11.59 billion (31 December 2017 est.)
$10.71 billion (31 December 2016 est.)
country comparison to the world: 60

Exchange rates: balboas (PAB) per US dollar—
1 (2017 est.)
1 (2016 est.)
1 (2015 est.)
1 (2014 est.)
1 (2013 est.)

ENERGY

Electricity access: *population without electricity:* 300,000
electrification—*total population:* 91%

electrification—urban areas: 94%
electrification—rural areas: 80% (2013)

Electricity—production: 9.724 billion kWh (2015 est.)
country comparison to the world: 102

Electricity—consumption: 8.202 billion kWh (2015 est.)
country comparison to the world: 101

Electricity—exports: 139 million kWh (2015 est.)
country comparison to the world: 79

Electricity—imports: 17 million kWh (2015 est.)
country comparison to the world: 111

Electricity—installed generating capacity: 3.203 million kW (2015 est.)
country comparison to the world: 96

Electricity—from fossil fuels: 35.8% of total installed capacity (2015 est.)
country comparison to the world: 175

Electricity—from nuclear fuels: 0% of total installed capacity (2015 est.)
country comparison to the world: 165

Electricity—from hydroelectric plants: 53.9% of total installed capacity (2015 est.)
country comparison to the world: 37

Electricity—from other renewable sources: 11.6% of total installed capacity (2015 est.)
country comparison to the world: 64

Crude oil—production: 0 bbl/day (2016 est.)
country comparison to the world: 183

Crude oil—exports: 0 bbl/day (2014 est.)
country comparison to the world: 176

Crude oil—imports: 0 bbl/day (2014 est.)
country comparison to the world: 177

Crude oil—proved reserves: 0 bbl (1 January 2017)
country comparison to the world: 181

Refined petroleum products—production: 0 bbl/day (2014 est.)
country comparison to the world: 188

Refined petroleum products—consumption: 144,000 bbl/day (2015 est.)
country comparison to the world: 70

Refined petroleum products—exports: 66.08 bbl/day (2014 est.)
country comparison to the world: 124

Refined petroleum products—imports: 131,000 bbl/day (2014 est.)
country comparison to the world: 50

Natural gas—production: 0 cu m (2013 est.)
country comparison to the world: 184

Natural gas—consumption: 0 cu m (2013 est.)
country comparison to the world: 123

Natural gas—exports: 0 cu m (2013 est.)
country comparison to the world: 167

Natural gas—imports: 0 cu m (2013 est.)
country comparison to the world: 175

Natural gas—proved reserves: 0 cu m (1 January 2014 es)
country comparison to the world: 185

Carbon dioxide emissions from consumption of energy: 17 million Mt (2013 est.)

country comparison to the world: 87

COMMUNICATIONS

Telephones—fixed lines: *total subscriptions:* 641,688
subscriptions per 100 inhabitants: 17 (July 2016 est.)
country comparison to the world: 92

Telephones—mobile cellular: *total:* 6,977,701
subscriptions per 100 inhabitants: 188 (July 2016 est.)
country comparison to the world: 110

Telephone system: *general assessment:* domestic and international facilities well-developed
domestic: mobile-cellular telephone subscribership has increased rapidly
international: country code—507; landing point for the Americas Region Caribbean Ring System (ARCOS-1), the MAYA-1, and PAN-AM submarine cable systems that together provide links to the US and parts of the Caribbean, Central America, and South America; satellite earth stations—2 Intelsat (Atlantic Ocean); connected to the Central American Microwave System (2015)

Broadcast media: multiple privately owned TV networks and a government-owned educational TV station; multi-channel cable and satellite TV subscription services are available; more than 100 commercial radio stations (2007)

Internet country code: .pa

Internet users: *total:* 2,000,833
percent of population: 54.0% (July 2016 est.)
country comparison to the world: 105

TRANSPORTATION

National air transport system: *number of registered air carriers:* 4

inventory of registered aircraft operated by air carriers: 103
annual passenger traffic on registered air carriers: 12,018,103
annual freight traffic on registered air carriers: 121,567,075 mt-km (2015)
Civil aircraft registration country code prefix: HP (2016)

Airports: 117 (2013)
country comparison to the world: 49

Airports—with paved runways: *total:* 57
over 3,047 m: 1
2,438 to 3,047 m: 3
1,524 to 2,437 m: 3
914 to 1,523 m: 20
under 914 m: 30 (2017)

Airports—with unpaved runways: *total:* 60
1,524 to 2,437 m: 1
914 to 1,523 m: 8
under 914 m: 51 (2013)

Heliports: 3 (2013)

Pipelines: oil 128 km (2013)

Railways: *total:* 77 km
standard gauge: 77 km 1.435-m gauge (2014)
country comparison to the world: 129

Roadways: *total:* 15,137 km
paved: 6,351 km
unpaved: 8,786 km (2010)
country comparison to the world: 123

Waterways: 800 km (includes the 82-km Panama Canal that is being widened) (2011)
country comparison to the world: 72

Ports and terminals: *major seaport(s):* Balboa, Colon, Cristobal
container port(s) (TEUs): Balboa (3,078,000), Colon (2,765,000), Manzanillo (1,821,000) (2015)

MILITARY AND SECURITY

Military branches: no regular military forces; Panamanian Public Security Forces (subordinate to the Ministry of Public Security), comprising the National Police (PNP), National Air-Naval Service (SENAN), National Border Service (SENAFRONT) (2013)

Military—note: on 10 February 1990, the government of then President ENDARA abolished Panama's military and reformed the security apparatus by creating the Panamanian Public Forces; in October 1994, Panama's Legislative Assembly approved a constitutional amendment prohibiting the creation of a standing military force but allowing the temporary establishment of special police units to counter acts of "external aggression"

TRANSNATIONAL ISSUES

Disputes—international: organized illegal narcotics operations in Colombia operate within the remote border region with Panama

Refugees and internally displaced persons: refugees (country of origin): 15,614 (Colombia) (2016)

Illicit drugs: major cocaine transshipment point and primary money-laundering center for narcotics revenue; money-laundering activity is especially heavy in the Colon Free Zone; offshore financial center; negligible signs of coca cultivation; monitoring of financial transactions is improving; official corruption remains a major problem

PAPUA NEW GUINEA

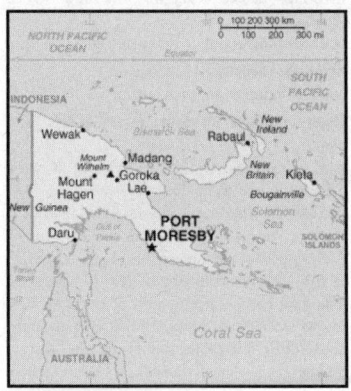

INTRODUCTION

Background: The eastern half of the island of New Guinea—second largest in the world—was divided between Germany (north) and the UK (south) in 1885. The latter area was transferred to Australia in 1902, which occupied the northern portion during World War I and continued to administer the combined areas until independence in 1975. A nine-year secessionist revolt on the island of Bougainville ended in 1997 after claiming some 20,000 lives. Since 2001, Bougainville has experienced autonomy. Under the terms of a peace accord, 2015 is the year that a five-year window opens for a referendum on the question of independence.

GEOGRAPHY

Location: Oceania, group of islands including the eastern half of the island of New Guinea between the Coral Sea and the South Pacific Ocean, east of Indonesia

Geographic coordinates: 6 00 S, 147 00 E

Map references: Oceania

Area: *total:* 462,840 sq km
land: 452,860 sq km
water: 9,980 sq km
country comparison to the world: 56

Area—comparative: slightly larger than California

Land boundaries: *total:* 824 km
border countries (1): Indonesia 824 km

Coastline: 5,152 km

Maritime claims: measured from claimed archipelagic baselines
territorial sea: 12 nm
continental shelf: 200-m depth or to the depth of exploitation
exclusive fishing zone: 200 nm

Climate: tropical; northwest monsoon (December to March), southeast monsoon (May to October); slight seasonal temperature variation

Terrain: mostly mountains with coastal lowlands and rolling foothills

Elevation: *mean elevation:* 667 m

elevation extremes: *lowest point:* Pacific Ocean 0 m
highest point: Mount Wilhelm 4,509 m

Natural resources: gold, copper, silver, natural gas, timber, oil, fisheries

Land use: *agricultural land:* 2.6%
arable land: 0.7%;
permanent crops: 1.5%;
permanent pasture: 0.4%
forest: 63.1%
other: 34.3% (2011 est.)
Irrigated land: 0 sq km (2012)

Population—distribution: population concentrated in the highlands and eastern coastal areas on the island of New Guinea; predominantly a rural distribution with only about one-fifth of the population residing in urban areas

Natural hazards: active volcanism; situated along the Pacific "Ring of Fire"; the country is subject to frequent and sometimes severe earthquakes; mud slides; tsunamis
volcanism: severe volcanic activity; Ulawun (2,334 m), one of Papua New Guinea's potentially most dangerous volcanoes, has been deemed a Decade Volcano by the International Association of Volcanology and Chemistry of the Earth's Interior, worthy of study due to its explosive history and close proximity to human populations; Rabaul (688 m) destroyed the city of Rabaul in 1937 and 1994; Lamington erupted in 1951 killing 3,000 people; Manam's 2004 eruption forced the island's abandonment; other historically active volcanoes include Bam, Bagana, Garbuna, Karkar, Langila, Lolobau, Long Island, Pago, St. Andrew Strait, Victory, and Waiowa

Environment—current issues: rain forest subject to deforestation as a result of growing commercial demand for tropical timber; pollution from mining projects; severe drought

Environment—international agreements: *party to:* Antarctic Treaty, Biodiversity, Climate Change, Climate Change-Kyoto Protocol, Desertification, Endangered Species, Environmental Modification, Hazardous Wastes, Law of the Sea, Marine Dumping, Ozone Layer Protection, Ship Pollution, Tropical Timber 83, Tropical Timber 94, Wetlands
signed, but not ratified: none of the selected agreements

Geography—note: shares island of New Guinea with Indonesia; generally east-west trending highlands break up New Guinea into diverse ecoregions; one of world's largest swamps along southwest coast

PEOPLE AND SOCIETY

Population: 6,909,701 (July 2017 est.)
country comparison to the world: 105

Nationality: *noun:* Papua New Guinean(s)
adjective: Papua New Guinean

Ethnic groups: Melanesian, Papuan, Negrito, Micronesian, Polynesian

Languages: Tok Pisin (official), English (official), Hiri Motu (official), some 839 indigenous languages spoken (about 12% of the world's total); many languages have fewer than 1,000 speakers
note: Tok Pisin, a creole language, is widely used and understood; English is spoken by 1%-2%; Hiri Motu is spoken by less than 2%

Religions: Roman Catholic 27%, Protestant 69.4% (Evangelical Lutheran 19.5%, United Church 11.5%, Seventh-Day Adventist 10%, Pentecostal 8.6%, Evangelical Alliance 5.2%, Anglican 3.2%, Baptist 2.5%, other Protestant 8.9%), Baha'i 0.3%, indigenous beliefs and other 3.3% (2000 census)

Age structure: *0-14 years:* 33.43% (male 1,175,934/female 1,133,882)
15-24 years: 19.92% (male 697,463/female 678,680)
25-54 years: 36.89% (male 1,309,843/female 1,238,972)
55-64 years: 5.49% (male 193,273/female 185,931)
65 years and over: 4.28% (male 148,802/female 146,921) (2017 est.)

Dependency ratios: *total dependency ratio:* 67.4
youth dependency ratio: 61.3
elderly dependency ratio: 6.1
potential support ratio: 16.4 (2015 est.)

Median age: *total:* 23.1 years
male: 23.2 years
female: 23.1 years (2017 est.)
country comparison to the world: 170

Population growth rate: 1.71% (2017 est.)
country comparison to the world: 61

Birth rate: 23.7 births/1,000 population (2017 est.)
country comparison to the world: 60

Death rate: 6.6 deaths/1,000 population (2017 est.)
country comparison to the world: 141

Net migration rate: 0 migrant(s)/1,000 population (2017 est.)
country comparison to the world: 94

Population distribution: population concentrated in the highlands and eastern coastal areas on the island of New Guinea; predominantly a rural distribution with only about one-fifth of the population residing in urban areas

Urbanization: *urban population:* 13.1% of total population (2017)
rate of urbanization: 2.42% annual rate of change (2015-20 est.)

Major urban areas—population: PORT MORESBY (capital) 345,000 (2015)

Sex ratio: *at birth:* 1.05 male(s)/female
0-14 years: 1.04 male(s)/female
15-24 years: 1.03 male(s)/female
25-54 years: 1.06 male(s)/female
55-64 years: 1.03 male(s)/female
65 years and over: 1.06 male(s)/female

total population: 1.04 male(s)/female (2016 est.)

Maternal mortality ratio: 215 deaths/100,000 live births (2015 est.)
country comparison to the world: 49

Infant mortality rate: *total:* 36.3 deaths/1,000 live births
male: 39.8 deaths/1,000 live births
female: 32.7 deaths/1,000 live births (2017 est.)
country comparison to the world: 50

Life expectancy at birth: *total population:* 67.3 years
male: 65.1 years
female: 69.7 years (2017 est.)
country comparison to the world: 171

Total fertility rate: 3.03 children born/woman (2017 est.)
country comparison to the world: 53

Health expenditures: 4.3% of GDP (2014)
country comparison to the world: 159

Physicians density: 0.06 physicians/1,000 population (2010)

Drinking water source:
improved:
urban: 88% of population
rural: 32.8% of population
total: 40% of population
unimproved:
urban: 12% of population
rural: 67.2% of population
total: 60% of population (2015 est.)

Sanitation facility access:
improved:
urban: 56.4% of population
rural: 13.3% of population
total: 18.9% of population
unimproved:
urban: 43.6% of population
rural: 86.7% of population
total: 81.1% of population (2015 est.)

HIV/AIDS—adult prevalence rate: 0.9% (2016 est.)
country comparison to the world: 47

HIV/AIDS—people living with HIV/AIDS: 46,000 (2016 est.)
country comparison to the world: 58

HIV/AIDS—deaths: 1,100 (2016 est.)
country comparison to the world: 62

Major infectious diseases: *degree of risk:* very high
food or waterborne diseases: bacterial diarrhea, hepatitis A, and typhoid fever
vectorborne diseases: dengue fever and malaria
note: active local transmission of Zika virus by Aedes species mosquitoes has been identified in this country (as of August 2016); it poses an important risk (a large number of cases possible) among US citizens if bitten by an infective mosquito; other less common ways to get Zika are through sex, via blood transfusion, or during pregnancy, in which the pregnant woman passes Zika virus to her fetus (2016)

Obesity—adult prevalence rate: 21.3% (2016)
country comparison to the world: 91

Children under the age of 5 years underweight: 27.9% (2010)
country comparison to the world: 19

Education expenditures: NA

Literacy: *definition:* age 15 and over can read and write
total population: 64.2%
male: 65.6%
female: 62.8% (2015 est.)

People—note: the indigenous population of Papua New Guinea (PNG) is one of the most heterogeneous in the world; PNG has several thousand separate communities, most with only a few hundred people; divided by language, customs, and tradition, some of these communities have engaged in low-scale tribal conflict with their neighbors for millennia; the advent of modern weapons and modern migrants into urban areas has greatly magnified the impact of this lawlessness

GOVERNMENT

Country name: *conventional long form:* Independent State of Papua New Guinea
conventional short form: Papua New Guinea
local short form: Papuaniugini
former: Territory of Papua and New Guinea
abbreviation: PNG
etymology: the word "papua" derives from the Malay "papuah" describing the frizzy hair of the Melanesians; Spanish explorer Ynigo ORTIZ de RETEZ applied the term "Nueva Guinea" to the island of New Guinea in 1545 after noting the resemblance of the locals to the peoples of the Guinea coast of Africa

Government type: parliamentary democracy (National Parliament) under a constitutional monarchy; a Commonwealth realm

Capital: *name:* Port Moresby
geographic coordinates: 9 27 S, 147 11 E
time difference: UTC+10 (15 hours ahead of Washington, DC, during Standard Time)

Administrative divisions: 20 provinces, 1 autonomous region*, and 1 district**; Bougainville*, Central, Chimbu, Eastern Highlands, East New Britain, East Sepik, Enga, Gulf, Hela, Jiwaka, Madang, Manus, Milne Bay, Morobe, National Capital**, New Ireland, Northern, Southern Highlands, Western, Western Highlands, West New Britain, West Sepik

Independence: 16 September 1975 (from the Australia-administered UN trusteeship)

National holiday: Independence Day, 16 September (1975)

Constitution: adopted 15 August 1975, effective at independence 16 September 1975; amended many times, last in 2013; note—in September 2015, the Supreme Court nullified the 2013 constitutional amendment that increased the grace period on motions of no confidence (2016)

Legal system: mixed legal system of English common law and customary law

International law organization participation: has not submitted an ICJ jurisdiction declaration; non-party state to the ICCt

Citizenship: *citizenship by birth:* no

citizenship by descent only: at least one parent must be a citizen of Papua New Guinea
dual citizenship recognized: no
residency requirement for naturalization: 8 years

Suffrage: 18 years of age; universal

Executive branch: *chief of state:* Queen ELIZABETH II (since 6 February 1952); represented by Governor General Grand Chief Sir Bob DADAE (since 28 February 2017)

head of government: Prime Minister Peter Paire O'NEILL (since 2 August 2011); Deputy Prime Minister Charles ABEL (since 4 August 2017)
cabinet: National Executive Council appointed by the governor general on the recommendation of the prime minister
elections/appointments: the monarchy is hereditary; governor general nominated by the National Parliament and appointed by the chief of state; following legislative elections, the leader of the majority party or majority coalition usually appointed prime minister by the governor general pending the outcome of a National Parliament vote
election results: Peter Paire O'NEILL (PNC) reelected prime minister; National Parliament vote—60 to 46

Legislative branch: *description:* unicameral National Parliament (111 seats; members directly elected in single-seat constituencies—91 local and 20 provincial—by majority preferential vote; members serve 5-year terms); note—the constitution allows up to 126 seats
elections: last held from 24 June 2017 to 8 July 2017 (next to be held in June 2022)
election results: results pending as of late October 2017; percent of vote by party—NA; seats by party—NA
note: 12 other parties won 2 or fewer seats; association with political parties is fluid

Judicial branch: *highest court(s):* Supreme Court (consists of the chief justice, deputy chief justice, and 28 judges); National Courts (13 courts located in the province capitals, with a total of 19 resident judges)
judge selection and term of office: Supreme Court chief justice appointed by the governor-general upon advice of the National Executive Council (cabinet) after consultation with the National Justice Administration Minister; deputy chief justice and other justices appointed by the Judicial and Legal Services Commission, a 5-member body to include the Supreme Court chief and deputy chief justices, the chief ombudsman, and a member of the National Parliament; full-time citizen judges appointed for 10-year renewable terms; non-citizen judges initially appointed for 3-year renewable terms and after first renewal until age 70; appointment and tenure of National Court resident judges NA

subordinate courts: district, village, and juvenile courts

Political parties and leaders: National Alliance Party or NAP [Patrick PRUAITCH]
Papua and Niugini Union Party or PANGU [Sam BASIL]
Papua New Guinea Party or PNGP [Belden NAMAH]
People's National Congress Party or PNC [Peter Paire O'NEILL]
People's Party or PP [Peter IPATAS]
People's Progress Party or PPP [Sir Julius CHAN]
Social Democratic Party or SDP [Powes PARKOP]
Triumph Heritage Empowerment Party or THE [Don POLYE]
United Resources Party or URP [William DUMA]
note: as of 8 July 2017, 45 political parties were registered

Political pressure groups and leaders: Centre for Environment Law and Community Rights or Celcor [Damien ASE]
Community Coalition Against Corruption
National Council of Women
Transparency International Papau New Guinea or TIPNG (chapter of Transparency International)

International organization participation: ACP, ADB, AOSIS, APEC, ARF, ASEAN (observer), C, CD, CP, EITI (candidate country), FAO, G-77, IAEA, IBRD, ICAO, ICRM, IDA, IFAD, IFC, IFRCS, IHO, ILO, IMF, IMO, Interpol, IOC, IOM, IPU, ISO (correspondent), ITSO, ITU, MIGA, NAM, OPCW, PIF, Sparteca, SPC, UN, UNCTAD, UNESCO, UNIDO, UNMISS, UNWTO, UPU, WCO, WFTU (NGOs), WHO, WIPO, WMO, WTO

Diplomatic representation in the US: *chief of mission:* Ambassador (vacant); Charge D'Affaires Elias Rahuromo WOHENGU (since 30 September 2017)
chancery: 1779 Massachusetts Avenue NW, Suite 805, Washington, DC 20036
telephone: [1] (202) 745-3680
FAX: [1] (202) 745-3679

Diplomatic representation from the US: *chief of mission:* Ambassador Catherine EBERT-GRAY (since 23 February 2016); note—also accredited to the Solomon Islands and Vanuatu
embassy: P.O. Box 1492, Port Moresby
mailing address: 4240 Port Moresby Place, US Department of State, Washington DC 20521-4240
telephone: [675] 321-1455
FAX: [675] 321-3423

Flag description: divided diagonally from upper hoist-side corner; the upper triangle is red with a soaring yellow bird of paradise centered; the lower triangle is black with five, white, five-pointed stars of the Southern Cross constellation centered; red, black, and yellow are traditional colors of Papua New Guinea; the bird of paradise—endemic to the island of New Guinea—is an emblem of regional tribal culture and represents the emergence of Papua New Guinea as a nation; the Southern Cross, visible in the night sky, symbolizes Papua New Guinea's connection with Australia and several other countries in the South Pacific

705

National symbol(s): bird of paradise; national colors: red, black

National anthem: name: "O Arise All You Sons" *lyrics/music:* Thomas SHACKLADY *note:* adopted 1975

ECONOMY

Economy—overview: Papua New Guinea (PNG) is richly endowed with natural resources, but exploitation has been hampered by rugged terrain, land tenure issues, and the high cost of developing infrastructure. The economy has a small formal sector, focused mainly on the export of those natural resources, and an informal sector, employing the majority of the population. Agriculture provides a subsistence livelihood for 85% of the people. The global financial crisis had little impact because of continued foreign demand for PNG's commodities.

Mineral deposits, including copper, gold, and oil, account for nearly two-thirds of export earnings. Natural gas reserves amount to an estimated 155 billion cubic meters. Following construction of a $19 billion liquefied natural gas (LNG) project, PNG LNG, a consortium led by ExxonMobil, began exporting liquefied natural gas to Asian markets in May 2014. The project was delivered on time and only slightly above budget. The success of the project has encouraged other companies to look at similar LNG projects. French supermajor Total is expected to begin construction on the Papua LNG project by 2020. Due to lower global commodity prices, resource revenues of all types have fallen dramatically. PNG's government has recently been forced to adjust spending levels downward.

Numerous challenges still face the government of Peter O'NEILL, including providing physical security for foreign investors, regaining investor confidence, restoring integrity to state institutions, promoting economic efficiency by privatizing moribund state institutions, and maintaining good relations with Australia, its former colonial ruler. Other socio-cultural challenges could upend the economy including chronic law and order and land tenure issues.

GDP (purchasing power parity): $30.84 billion (2017 est.)
$29.92 billion (2016 est.)
$29.22 billion (2015 est.)
note: data are in 2017 dollars
country comparison to the world: 132

GDP (official exchange rate): $21.81 billion (2016 est.)

GDP—real growth rate: 3.1% (2017 est.)
2.4% (2016 est.)
9.2% (2015 est.)
country comparison to the world: 108

GDP—per capita (PPP): $3,800 (2017 est.)
$3,800 (2016 est.)
$3,800 (2015 est.)
note: data are in 2017 dollars
country comparison to the world: 183

Gross national saving: 40.8% of GDP (2017 est.)
44.5% of GDP (2016 est.)
39.8% of GDP (2015 est.)
country comparison to the world: 8

GDP—composition, by end use:
household consumption: 45%
government consumption: 20.3%
investment in fixed capital: 10.4%
investment in inventories: -0.3%
exports of goods and services: 47.6%
imports of goods and services: -23% (2017 est.)

GDP—composition, by sector of origin:
agriculture: 22.1%
industry: 42.9%
services: 35% (2017 est.)

Agriculture—products: coffee, cocoa, copra, palm kernels, tea, sugar, rubber, sweet potatoes, fruit, vegetables, vanilla; poultry, pork; shellfish

Industries: copra crushing, palm oil processing, plywood production, wood chip production; mining (gold, silver, copper); crude oil and petroleum products; construction, tourism

Industrial production growth rate: 3.3% (2017 est.)
country comparison to the world: 90

Labor force: 3.681 million (2017 est.)
country comparison to the world: 98

Labor force—by occupation: *agriculture:* 85%
industry: NA%
services: NA% (2005 est.)

Unemployment rate: 2.5% (2017 est.)
2.5% (2016 est.)
country comparison to the world: 23

Population below poverty line: 37% (2002 est.)

Household income or consumption by percentage share: *lowest 10%:* 1.7%
highest 10%: 40.5% (1996)

Distribution of family income—Gini index: 50.9 (1996)
country comparison to the world: 13

Budget: *revenues:* $3.649 billion
expenditures: $4.763 billion (2017 est.)
Taxes and other revenues: 16.7% of GDP (2017 est.)
country comparison to the world: 179

Budget surplus (+) or deficit (-): -5.1% of GDP (2017 est.)
country comparison to the world: 163

Public debt: 39.8% of GDP (2017 est.)
39% of GDP (2016 est.)
country comparison to the world: 136

Fiscal year: calendar year

Inflation rate (consumer prices): 5.8% (2017 est.)
6.7% (2016 est.)
country comparison to the world: 179

Central bank discount rate: 14% (31 December 2010)
6.92% (31 December 2009)
country comparison to the world: 13

Commercial bank prime lending rate: 8.4% (31 December 2017 est.)
8.38% (31 December 2016 est.)
country comparison to the world: 102

Stock of narrow money: $5.495 billion (31 December 2017 est.)
$5.05 billion (31 December 2016 est.)
country comparison to the world: 102

Stock of broad money: $7.649 billion (31 December 2017 est.)
$7.061 billion (31 December 2016 est.)

country comparison to the world: 115

Stock of domestic credit: $7.859 billion (31 December 2017 est.)
$7.223 billion (31 December 2016 est.)
country comparison to the world: 116

Market value of publicly traded shares: $10.71 billion (31 December 2012 est.)
$8.999 billion (31 December 2011 est.)
$9.742 billion (31 December 2010 est.)
country comparison to the world: 74

Current account balance: $4.053 billion (2017 est.)
$4.119 billion (2016 est.)
country comparison to the world: 28

Exports: $9.526 billion (2017 est.)
$9.224 billion (2016 est.)
country comparison to the world: 93

Exports—commodities: oil, gold, copper ore, logs, palm oil, coffee, cocoa, crayfish, prawns

Exports—partners: Singapore 23.7%, Australia 22.9%, Japan 13.2%, China 11.9% (2016)

Imports: $1.878 billion (2017 est.)
$2.267 billion (2016 est.)
country comparison to the world: 163

Imports—commodities: machinery and transport equipment, manufactured goods, food, fuels, chemicals

Imports—partners: Australia 36%, China 14.9%, Singapore 8.5%, Malaysia 7.5% (2016)

Reserves of foreign exchange and gold: $1.8 billion (31 December 2017 est.)
$1.656 billion (31 December 2016 est.)
country comparison to the world: 121

Debt—external: $17.09 billion (31 December 2017 est.)
$18.28 billion (31 December 2016 est.)
country comparison to the world: 97

Stock of direct foreign investment—at home: $NA

Stock of direct foreign investment—abroad: $NA

Exchange rates: kina (PGK) per US dollar—
3.179 (2017 est.)
3.133 (2016 est.)
3.133 (2015 est.)
2.7684 (2014 est.)
2.4614 (2013 est.)

ENERGY

Electricity access: *population without electricity:* 5,568,879
electrification—total population: 18%
electrification—urban areas: 72%
electrification—rural areas: 10% (2012)

Electricity—production: 3.62 billion kWh (2015 est.)
country comparison to the world: 128

Electricity—consumption: 3.367 billion kWh (2015 est.)
country comparison to the world: 133

Electricity—exports: 0 kWh (2016 est.)
country comparison to the world: 184

Electricity—imports: 0 kWh (2016 est.)
country comparison to the world: 188

Electricity—installed generating capacity: 882,000 kW (2015 est.)

country comparison to the world: 132

Electricity—from fossil fuels: 62.1% of total installed capacity (2015 est.)
country comparison to the world: 123

Electricity—from nuclear fuels: 0% of total installed capacity (2015 est.)
country comparison to the world: 167

Electricity—from hydroelectric plants: 31.1% of total installed capacity (2015 est.)
country comparison to the world: 70

Electricity—from other renewable sources: 6.8% of total installed capacity (2015 est.)
country comparison to the world: 83

Crude oil—production: 55,990 bbl/day (2016 est.)
country comparison to the world: 51

Crude oil—exports: 17,400 bbl/day (2014 est.)
country comparison to the world: 53

Crude oil—imports: 14,880 bbl/day (2014 est.)
country comparison to the world: 68

Crude oil—proved reserves: 159.4 million bbl (1 January 2017 es)
country comparison to the world: 62

Refined petroleum products—production: 28,340 bbl/day (2014 est.)
country comparison to the world: 87

Refined petroleum products—consumption: 42,000 bbl/day (2015 est.)
country comparison to the world: 112

Refined petroleum products—exports: 8,062 bbl/day (2014 est.)
country comparison to the world: 87

Refined petroleum products—imports: 21,180 bbl/day (2014 est.)
country comparison to the world: 117

Natural gas—production: 9.8 billion cu m (2015 est.)
country comparison to the world: 42

Natural gas—consumption: 680 million cu m (2015 est.)
country comparison to the world: 106

Natural gas—exports: 9.7 billion cu m (2015 est.)
country comparison to the world: 22

Natural gas—imports: 0 cu m (2013 est.)
country comparison to the world: 176

Natural gas—proved reserves: 141.5 billion cu m (1 January 2017 es)
country comparison to the world: 49

Carbon dioxide emissions from consumption of energy: 3.7 million Mt (2013 est.)
country comparison to the world: 137

COMMUNICATIONS

Telephones—fixed lines: *total subscriptions:* 154,000
subscriptions per 100 inhabitants: 2 (July 2016 est.)
country comparison to the world: 137

Telephones—mobile cellular: *total:* 3.782 million
subscriptions per 100 inhabitants: 56 (July 2016 est.)
country comparison to the world: 132

Telephone system: *general assessment:* services are minimal; facilities provide radiotelephone and telegraph, coastal radio, aeronautical radio, and international radio communication services
domestic: access to telephone services is not widely available although combined fixed-line and mobile-cellular teledensity has increased to roughly 55 per 100 persons
international: country code—675; submarine cables to Australia and Guam; satellite earth station—1 Intelsat (Pacific Ocean); international radio communication service (2016)

Broadcast media: 2 TV stations, 1 commercial station operating since the late 1980s, and 1 state-run station launched in 2008; satellite and cable TV services are available; state-run National Broadcasting Corporation operates 3 radio networks with multiple repeaters and about 20 provincial stations; several commercial radio stations with multiple transmission points as well as several community stations; transmissions of several international broadcasters are accessible (2009)

Internet country code: .pg

Internet users: *total:* 652,071
percent of population: 9.6% (July 2016 est.)
country comparison to the world: 162

TRANSPORTATION

National air transport system: *number of registered air carriers:* 6
inventory of registered aircraft operated by air carriers: 47
annual passenger traffic on registered air carriers: 2,062,584
annual freight traffic on registered air carriers: 34,827,034 mt-km (2015)
Civil aircraft registration country code prefix: P2 (2016)

Airports: 561 (2013)
country comparison to the world: 12

Airports—with paved runways: *total:* 21
over 3,047 m: 1
2,438 to 3,047 m: 2
1,524 to 2,437 m: 12
914 to 1,523 m: 5
under 914 m: 1 (2017)

Airports—with unpaved runways: *total:* 540
1,524 to 2,437 m: 11
914 to 1,523 m: 53
under 914 m: 476 (2013)

Heliports: 2 (2013)

Pipelines: oil 264 km (2013)

Roadways: *total:* 9,349 km
paved: 3,000 km
unpaved: 6,349 km (2011)
country comparison to the world: 139

Waterways: 11,000 km (2011)
country comparison to the world: 11

Merchant marine: *total:* 173
by type: container ship 8, general cargo 80, oil tanker 3, other 82 (2017)
country comparison to the world: 66

Ports and terminals: *major seaport(s):* Kimbe, Lae, Madang, Rabaul, Wewak
LNG terminal(s) (export): Port Moresby

MILITARY AND SECURITY

Military expenditures: 0.66% of GDP (2014)
0.68% of GDP (2013)
0.72% of GDP (2012)
0.5% of GDP (2011)
country comparison to the world: 127

Military branches: Papua New Guinea Defense Force (PNGDF, includes Maritime Operations Element, Air Operations Element) (2013)

Military service age and obligation: 16 years of age for voluntary military service (with parental consent); no conscription; graduation from grade 12 required (2013)

TRANSNATIONAL ISSUES

Disputes—international: relies on assistance from Australia to keep out illegal cross-border activities from primarily Indonesia, including goods smuggling, illegal narcotics trafficking, and squatters and secessionists

Refugees and internally displaced persons: refugees (country of origin): 9,368 (Indonesia) (2016)
IDPs: 8,400 (natural disasters, tribal conflict, inter-communal violence, development projects) (2016)

Trafficking in persons: current situation: Papua New Guinea is a source and destination country for men, women, and children subjected to sex trafficking and forced labor; foreign and Papua New Guinean women and children are subjected to sex trafficking, domestic servitude, forced begging, and street vending; parents may sell girls into forced marriages to settle debts or as peace offerings or trade them to another tribe to forge a political alliance, leaving them vulnerable to forced domestic service, or, in urban areas, they may prostitute their children for income or to pay school fees; Chinese, Malaysian, and local men are forced to labor in logging and mining camps through debt bondage schemes; migrant women from Indonesia, Malaysia, Thailand, China, and the Philippines are subjected to sex trafficking and domestic servitude at logging and mining camps, fisheries, and entertainment sites

tier rating: Tier 2 Watch List—Papua New Guinea does not fully comply with the minimum standards for the elimination of trafficking; however, it is making significant efforts to do so; the Criminal Code Amendment of 2013, which prohibits all forms of trafficking was brought into force in 2014; the government also formed an anti-trafficking committee, which drafted a national action plan; despite corruption problems, trafficking-related crimes were prosecuted in village courts rather than criminal courts, resulting in restitution to the victim but no prison time for offenders; the government did not investigate, prosecute, or convict any officials or law enforcement personnel complicit in trafficking offenses; the government made no efforts to proactively identify trafficking victims, has no formal victim identification and referral mechanism, and does not provide care facilities to victims or funding to shelters run by NGOs or international organizations (2015)

Illicit drugs: major consumer of cannabis

PARACEL ISLANDS

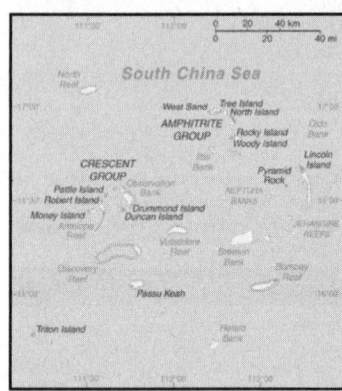

INTRODUCTION

Background: The Paracel Islands are surrounded by productive fishing grounds and by potential oil and gas reserves. In 1932, French Indochina annexed the islands and set up a weather station on Pattle Island; maintenance was continued by its successor, Vietnam. China has occupied all the Paracel Islands since 1974, when its troops seized a South Vietnamese garrison occupying the western islands. China built a military installation on Woody Island with an airfield and artificial harbor. The islands also are claimed by Taiwan and Vietnam.

GEOGRAPHY

Location: Southeastern Asia, group of small islands and reefs in the South China Sea, about one-third of the way from central Vietnam to the northern Philippines

Geographic coordinates: 16 30 N, 112 00 E

Map references: Southeast Asia

Area: *total:* ca. 7.75 sq km
land: ca. 7.75 sq km
water: 0 sq km
country comparison to the world: 245

Area—comparative: land area is about 13 times the size of the National Mall in Washington, DC

Land boundaries: 0 km

Coastline: 518 km

Maritime claims: NA

Climate: tropical

Terrain: mostly low and flat

Elevation: *mean elevation:* NA

elevation extremes: *lowest point:* South China Sea 0 m
highest point: unnamed location on Rocky Island 14 m

Natural resources: none

Land use: *agricultural land:* 0%
arable land: 0%;
permanent crops: 0%;
permanent pasture: 0%
forest: 0%
other: 100% (2011 est.)
Irrigated land: 0 sq km (2012)

Population—distribution: a population of over 1,000 Chinese resides on Woody Island, the largest of the Paracels; there are scattered Chinese garrisons on some other islands

Natural hazards: typhoons

Environment—current issues: China's use of dredged sand and coral to build artificial islands harms reef systems; ongoing human activities, including military operations, infrastructure construction, and tourism endangers local ecosystem including birds, fish, marine mammals, and marine reptiles

Geography—note: composed of 130 small coral islands and reefs divided into the northeast Amphitrite Group and the western Crescent Group

PEOPLE AND SOCIETY

Population: 1,440
note: Chinese activity has increased in recent years, particularly on Woody Island, where the population exceeds 1,000; there are scattered Chinese garrisons on some other islands (2014 est.)

Population distribution: a population of over 1,000 Chinese resides on Woody Island, the largest of the Paracels; there are scattered Chinese garrisons on some other islands

GOVERNMENT

Country name: *conventional long form:* none
conventional short form: Paracel Islands
etymology: Portuguese navigators began to refer to the "Ilhas do Pracel" in the 16th century as a designation of low lying islets, sandbanks, and reefs scattered over a wide area; over time the name changed to "parcel" and then "paracel"

ECONOMY

Economy—overview: The islands have the potential for oil and gas development. Waters around the islands support commercial fishing, but the islands themselves are not populated on a permanent basis.

TRANSPORTATION

Airports: 1 (2013)
country comparison to the world: 230

Airports—with paved runways: *total:* 1
1,524 to 2,437 m: 1 (2017)

Ports and terminals: small Chinese port facilities on Woody Island and Duncan Island

MILITARY AND SECURITY

Military—note: occupied by China

TRANSNATIONAL ISSUES

Disputes—international: occupied by China, also claimed by Taiwan and Vietnam

PERU

INTRODUCTION

Background: Ancient Peru was the seat of several prominent Andean civilizations, most notably that of the Incas whose empire was captured by Spanish conquistadors in 1533. Peru declared its independence in 1821, and remaining Spanish forces were defeated in 1824. After a dozen years of military rule, Peru returned to democratic leadership in 1980, but experienced economic problems and the growth of a violent insurgency. President Alberto FUJIMORI's election in 1990 ushered in a decade that saw a dramatic turnaround in the economy and significant progress in curtailing guerrilla activity. Nevertheless, the president's increasing reliance on authoritarian measures and an economic slump in the late 1990s generated mounting dissatisfaction with his regime, which led to his resignation in 2000. A caretaker government oversaw a new election in the spring of 2001, which installed Alejandro TOLEDO Manrique as the new head of government—Peru's first democratically elected president of indigenous ethnicity. The presidential election of 2006 saw the return of Alan GARCIA Perez who, after a disappointing presidential term from 1985 to 1990, oversaw a robust economic rebound. Former army officer Ollanta HUMALA Tasso was elected president in June 2011, and carried on the sound, market-oriented economic policies of the three preceding administrations. Poverty and unemployment levels have fallen dramatically in the last decade, and today Peru boasts one of the best performing economies in Latin America. Pedro Pablo KUCZYNSKI Godard won a very narrow presidential runoff election in June 2016.

GEOGRAPHY

Location: Western South America, bordering the South Pacific Ocean, between Chile and Ecuador

Geographic coordinates: 10 00 S, 76 00 W

Map references: South America

Area: *total:* 1,285,216 sq km
land: 1,279,996 sq km
water: 5,220 sq km
country comparison to the world: 21

Area—comparative: almost twice the size of Texas; slightly smaller than Alaska

Land boundaries: *total:* 7,062 km
border countries (5): Bolivia 1,212 km, Brazil 2,659 km, Chile 168 km, Colombia 1,494 km, Ecuador 1,529 km

Coastline: 2,414 km

Maritime claims: *territorial sea:* 200 nm
continental shelf: 200 nm

Climate: varies from tropical in east to dry desert in west; temperate to frigid in Andes

Terrain: western coastal plain (costa), high and rugged Andes in center (sierra), eastern lowland jungle of Amazon Basin (selva)

Elevation: *mean elevation:* 1,555 m

elevation extremes: *lowest point:* Pacific Ocean 0 m
highest point: Nevado Huascaran 6,746 m

Natural resources: copper, silver, gold, petroleum, timber, fish, iron ore, coal, phosphate, potash, hydropower, natural gas

Land use: *agricultural land:* 18.8%;
arable land: 3.1%;
permanent crops: 1.1%;
permanent pasture: 14.6%;
forest: 53%
other: 28.2% (2011 est.)
Irrigated land: 25,800 sq km (2012)

Population—distribution: approximately one-third of the population resides along the desert coastal belt in the west, with a strong focus on the capital city of Lima; the Andean highlands, or sierra, which is strongly identified with the country's Amerindian population, contains roughly half of the overall population; the eastern slopes of the Andes, and adjoining rainforest, are sparsely populated

Natural hazards: earthquakes, tsunamis, flooding, landslides, mild volcanic activity
volcanism: volcanic activity in the Andes Mountains; Ubinas (5,672 m), which last erupted in 2009, is the country's most active volcano; other historically active volcanoes include El Misti, Huaynaputina, Sabancaya, and Yucamane

Environment—current issues: deforestation (some the result of illegal logging); overgrazing of the slopes of the costa and sierra leading to soil erosion; desertification; air pollution in Lima; pollution of rivers and coastal waters from municipal and mining wastes

Environment—international agreements: *party to:* Antarctic-Environmental Protocol, Antarctic-Marine Living Resources, Antarctic Treaty, Biodiversity, Climate Change, Climate Change-Kyoto Protocol, Desertification, Endangered Species, Hazardous Wastes, Marine Dumping, Ozone Layer Protection, Ship Pollution, Tropical Timber 83, Tropical Timber 94, Wetlands, Whaling
signed, but not ratified: none of the selected agreements

Geography—note: shares control of Lago Titicaca, world's highest navigable lake, with Bolivia; a remote slope of Nevado Mismi, a 5,316 m peak, is the ultimate source of the Amazon River

PEOPLE AND SOCIETY

Population: 31,036,656 (July 2017 est.)
country comparison to the world: 43

Nationality: *noun:* Peruvian(s)
adjective: Peruvian

Ethnic groups: Amerindian 45%, mestizo (mixed Amerindian and white) 37%, white 15%, black, Japanese, Chinese, and other 3%

Languages: Spanish (official) 84.1%, Quechua (official) 13%, Aymara (official) 1.7%, Ashaninka 0.3%, other native languages (includes a large number of minor Amazonian languages) 0.7%, other (includes foreign languages and sign language) 0.2% (2007 est.)

Religions: Roman Catholic 81.3%, Evangelical 12.5%, other 3.3%, none 2.9% (2007 est.)

Demographic profile: Peru's urban and coastal communities have benefited much more from recent economic growth than rural, Afro-Peruvian, indigenous, and poor populations of the Amazon and mountain regions. The poverty rate has dropped substantially during the last decade but remains stubbornly high at about 30% (more than 55% in rural areas). After remaining almost static for about a decade, Peru's malnutrition rate began falling in 2005, when the government

introduced a coordinated strategy focusing on hygiene, sanitation, and clean water. School enrollment has improved, but achievement scores reflect ongoing problems with educational quality. Many poor children temporarily or permanently drop out of school to help support their families. About a quarter to a third of Peruvian children aged 6 to 14 work, often putting in long hours at hazardous mining or construction sites.

Peru was a country of immigration in the 19th and early 20th centuries, but has become a country of emigration in the last few decades. Beginning in the 19th century, Peru brought in Asian contract laborers mainly to work on coastal plantations. Populations of Chinese and Japanese descent—among the largest in Latin America—are economically and culturally influential in Peru today. Peruvian emigration began rising in the 1980s due to an economic crisis and a violent internal conflict, but outflows have stabilized in the last few years as economic conditions have improved. Nonetheless, more than 2 million Peruvians have emigrated in the last decade, principally to the US, Spain, and Argentina.

Age structure: *0-14 years:* 26.31% (male 4,155,672/female 4,009,888)
15-24 years: 18.31% (male 2,847,460/female 2,835,727)
25-54 years: 40.19% (male 5,985,354/female 6,487,232)
55-64 years: 7.78% (male 1,168,533/female 1,247,299)
65 years and over: 7.41% (male 1,086,790/female 1,212,701) (2017 est.)

Dependency ratios: *total dependency ratio:* 53.2
youth dependency ratio: 42.7
elderly dependency ratio: 10.5
potential support ratio: 9.6 (2015 est.)

Median age: *total:* 28 years
male: 27.2 years
female: 28.8 years (2017 est.)
country comparison to the world: 139

Population growth rate: 0.95% (2017 est.)
country comparison to the world: 118

Birth rate: 17.8 births/1,000 population (2017 est.)
country comparison to the world: 103

Death rate: 6.1 deaths/1,000 population (2017 est.)
country comparison to the world: 157

Net migration rate: -2.2 migrant(s)/1,000 population (2017 est.)
country comparison to the world: 166

Population distribution: approximately one-third of the population resides along the desert coastal belt in the west, with a strong focus on the capital city of Lima; the Andean highlands, or sierra, which is strongly identified with the country's Amerindian population, contains roughly half of the overall population; the eastern slopes of the Andes, and adjoining rainforest, are sparsely populated

Urbanization: *urban population:* 79.2% of total population (2017)

709

rate of urbanization: 1.57% annual rate of change (2015-20 est.)

Major urban areas—population: LIMA (capital) 9.897 million; Arequipa 850,000; Trujillo 798,000 (2015)

Sex ratio: *at birth:* 1.05 male(s)/female
0-14 years: 1.04 male(s)/female
15-24 years: 1 male(s)/female
25-54 years: 0.92 male(s)/female
55-64 years: 0.94 male(s)/female
65 years and over: 0.9 male(s)/female
total population: 0.97 male(s)/female (2016 est.)

Mother's mean age at first birth: 22.2 years
note: median age at first birth among women 25-29 (2013 est.)

Maternal mortality ratio: 68 deaths/100,000 live births (2015 est.)
country comparison to the world: 83

Infant mortality rate: *total:* 18.4 deaths/1,000 live births
male: 20.5 deaths/1,000 live births
female: 16.2 deaths/1,000 live births (2017 est.)
country comparison to the world: 88

Life expectancy at birth: *total population:* 74 years
male: 71.9 years
female: 76.1 years (2017 est.)
country comparison to the world: 126

Total fertility rate: 2.12 children born/woman (2017 est.)
country comparison to the world: 102

Contraceptive prevalence rate: 74.6% (2014)

Health expenditures: 5.5% of GDP (2014)
country comparison to the world: 128

Physicians density: 1.12 physicians/1,000 population (2012)

Hospital bed density: 1.5 beds/1,000 population (2012)

Drinking water source:
improved:
urban: 91.4% of population
rural: 69.2% of population
total: 86.7% of population
unimproved:
urban: 8.6% of population
rural: 30.8% of population
total: 13.3% of population (2015 est.)

Sanitation facility access:
improved:
urban: 82.5% of population
rural: 53.2% of population
total: 76.2% of population
unimproved:
urban: 17.5% of population
rural: 46.8% of population
total: 23.8% of population (2015 est.)

HIV/AIDS—adult prevalence rate: 0.3% (2016 est.)
country comparison to the world: 84

HIV/AIDS—people living with HIV/AIDS: 70,000 (2016 est.)
country comparison to the world: 48

HIV/AIDS—deaths: 2,200 (2016 est.)
country comparison to the world: 51

Major infectious diseases: *degree of risk:* very high
food or waterborne diseases: bacterial diarrhea, hepatitis A, and typhoid fever
vectorborne disease: dengue fever, malaria, and Bartonellosis (Oroya fever)
note: active local transmission of Zika virus by Aedes species mosquitoes has been identified in this country (as of August 2016); it poses an important risk (a large number of cases possible) among US citizens if bitten by an infective mosquito; other less common ways to get Zika are through sex, via blood transfusion, or during pregnancy, in which the pregnant woman passes Zika virus to her fetus (2016)

Obesity—adult prevalence rate: 19.7% (2016)
country comparison to the world: 109

Children under the age of 5 years underweight: 3.1% (2014)
country comparison to the world: 103

Education expenditures: 3.9% of GDP (2015)
country comparison to the world: 145

Literacy: *definition:* age 15 and over can read and write
total population: 94.2%
male: 97.2%
female: 94.3% (2016 est.)

School life expectancy (primary to tertiary education): *total:* 13 years
male: 13 years
female: 14 years (2010)

Unemployment, youth ages 15-24: *total:* 14.7%
male: 8.6%
female: 8.2% (2015 est.)
country comparison to the world: 101

GOVERNMENT

Country name: *conventional long form:* Republic of Peru
conventional short form: Peru
local long form: Republica del Peru
local short form: Peru
etymology: exact meaning is obscure, but the name may derive from a native word "biru" meaning "river"

Government type: presidential republic

Capital: *name:* Lima
geographic coordinates: 12 03 S, 77 03 W
time difference: UTC-5 (same time as Washington, DC, during Standard Time)

Administrative divisions: 25 regions (regiones, singular—region) and 1 province* (provincia); Amazonas, Ancash, Apurimac, Arequipa, Ayacucho, Cajamarca, Callao, Cusco, Huancavelica, Huanuco, Ica, Junin, La Libertad, Lambayeque, Lima, Lima*, Loreto, Madre de Dios, Moquegua, Pasco, Piura, Puno, San Martin, Tacna, Tumbes, Ucayali
note: Callao, the largest port in Peru, is also referred to as a constitutional province, the only province of the Callao region

Independence: 28 July 1821 (from Spain)

National holiday: Independence Day, 28-29 July (1821)

Constitution: several previous; latest promulgated 29 December 1993, enacted 31 December 1993; amended several times, last in 2015 (2016)

Legal system: civil law system

International law organization participation: accepts compulsory ICJ jurisdiction with reservations; accepts ICCt jurisdiction

Citizenship: *citizenship by birth:* yes
citizenship by descent: yes
dual citizenship recognized: yes
residency requirement for naturalization: 2 years

Suffrage: 18 years of age; universal and compulsory until the age of 70

Executive branch: *chief of state:* President Pedro Pablo KUCZYNSKI Godard (since 28 July 2016); First Vice President Martin Alberto VIZCARRA Cornejo (since 28 July 2016); Second Vice President Mercedes Rosalba ARAOZ Fernandez (since 28 July 2016); note—the president is both chief of state and head of government

head of government: President Pedro Pablo KUCZYNSKI Godard (since 28 July 2016); First Vice President Martin Alberto VIZCARRA Cornejo (since 28 July 2016); Second Vice President Mercedes Rosalba ARAOZ Fernandez (since 28 July 2016)
cabinet: Council of Ministers appointed by the president
elections/appointments: president directly elected by absolute majority popular vote in 2 rounds if needed for a 5-year term (eligible for nonconsecutive terms); election last held on 10 April 2016 with runoff on 5 June 2016 (next to be held in April 2021)
election results: Pedro Pablo KUCZYNSKI Godard elected president in second round; percent of vote in first round—Keiko FUJIMORI Higuchi (Fuerza Popular) 39.9%, Pedro Pablo KUCZYNSKI Godard (Peruanos Por el Kambio) 21.1%, Veronika MENDOZA (Broad Front) 18.7%, Alfredo BARNECHEA (Popular Action) 7%, Alan GARCIA (APRA) 5.8%, other 7.5%; percent of vote in second round—Pedro Pablo KUCZYNSKI Godard 50.1%, Keiko FUJIMORI Higuchi 49.9%
note: Prime Minister Mercedes Rosalba ARAOZ Fernandez (since 17 September 2017) does not exercise executive power; this power rests with the president

Legislative branch: *description:* unicameral Congress of the Republic of Peru or Congreso de la Republica del Peru (130 seats; members directly elected in multi-seat constituencies by closed party-list proportional representation vote to serve 5-year terms)
elections: last held on 10 April 2016 with run-off election on 6 June 2016 (next to be held in April 2021)
election results: percent of vote by party/coalition—Fuerza Popular 36.3%, PPK 16.5%, Frente Amplio 13.9%, APP 9.2%; APRA 8.3%; AP

7.2%, other 8.6%; seats by party/coalition—Fuerza Popular 73, Frente Amplio 20, PPK 18, APP 9; APRA 5; AP 5

Judicial branch: *highest court(s):* Supreme Court (consists of 16 judges and divided into civil, criminal, and constitutional-social sectors)

judge selection and term of office: justices proposed by the National Council of the Judiciary or National Judicial Council (a 7-member independent body), nominated by the president, and confirmed by the Congress (all appointments reviewed by the Council every 7 years); justices appointed for life or until age 70

subordinate courts: Court of Constitutional Guarantees; Superior Courts or Cortes Superiores; specialized civil, criminal, and mixed courts; 2 types of peace courts in which professional judges and selected members of the local communities preside

Political parties and leaders: Alliance for Progress (Alianza para el Progreso) or APP [Cesar ACUNA Peralta]

American Popular Revolutionary Alliance or APRA

Broad Front (Frente Amplio; also known as El Frente Amplio por Justicia, Vida y Libertad) (coalition includes Nuevo Peru [Veronika Mendoza], Tierra y Libertad [Marco ARANA Zegarra], and Fuerza Social [Susana VILLARAN de la Puente]

Fuerza Popular (formerly Fuerza 2011) [Keiko FUJIMORI Higuchi]

National Solidarity (Solidaridad Nacional) or SN [Luis CASTANEDA Lossio]

Peru Posible or PP (coalition includes Accion Popular and Somos Peru) [Alejandro TOLEDO Manrique]

Peruvian Aprista Party (Partido Aprista Peruano) or PAP [Javier VELASQUEZ Quesquen] (also referred to by its original name Alianza Popular Revolucionaria Americana or APRA]

Peruvian Nationalist Party [Ollanta HUMALA]

Peruvians for Change (Peruanos Por el Kambio) or PPK [Pedro Pablo KUCZYNSKI]

Popular Action (Accion Popular) or AP [Mesias GUEVARA Amasifuen]

Popular Christian Party (Partido Popular Cristiano) or PPC [Lourdes FLORES Nano]

Political pressure groups and leaders: General Workers Confederation of Peru (Confederacion General de Trabajadores del Peru) or CGTP [Geronimo LOPEZ]

Shining Path (Sendero Luminoso) or SL [Abimael GUZMAN Reynoso—imprisoned], Jorge and Victor QUISPE Palomino—indicted in US] (communist guerrilla group)

International organization participation: APEC, BIS, CAN, CD, CELAC, EITI (compliant country), FAO, G-24, G-77, IADB, IAEA, IBRD, ICAO, ICC (NGOs), ICCt, ICRM, IDA, IFAD, IFC, IFRCS, IHO, ILO, IMF, IMO, IMSO, Interpol, IOC, IOM, IPU, ISO, ITSO, ITU, ITUC (NGOs), LAES, LAIA, Mercosur (associate), MIGA, MINUSTAH, MONUSCO, NAM, OAS, OPANAL, OPCW, Pacific Alliance, PCA, SICA (observer), UN, UNAMID, UNASUR, UNCTAD, UNESCO, UNHCR, UNIDO, Union Latina, UNISFA, UNMISS, UNOCI, UNWTO, UPU, WCO, WFTU (NGOs), WHO, WIPO, WMO, WTO

Diplomatic representation in the US: *chief of mission:* Ambassador Carlos Jose PAREJA Rios (since 16 September 2016)

chancery: 1700 Massachusetts Avenue NW, Washington, DC 20036

telephone: [1] (202) 833-9860 through 9869

FAX: [1] (202) 659-8124

consulate(s) general: Atlanta, Boston, Chicago, Dallas, Denver, Hartford (CT), Houston, Los Angeles, Miami, New York, Paterson (NJ), San Francisco, Washington DC

Diplomatic representation from the US: *chief of mission:* Ambassador Krishna R. URS (since 18 October 2017)

embassy: Avenida La Encalada, Cuadra 17 s/n, Surco, Lima 33

mailing address: P. O. Box 1995, Lima 1; American Embassy (Lima), APO AA 34031-5000

telephone: [51] (1) 618-2000

FAX: [51] (1) 618-2397

Flag description: three equal, vertical bands of red (hoist side), white, and red with the coat of arms centered in the white band; the coat of arms features a shield bearing a vicuna (representing fauna), a cinchona tree (the source of quinine, signifying flora), and a yellow cornucopia spilling out coins (denoting mineral wealth); red recalls blood shed for independence, white symbolizes peace

National symbol(s): vicuna (a camelid related to the llama); national colors: red, white

National anthem: name: "Himno Nacional del Peru" (National Anthem of Peru)

lyrics/music: Jose DE LA TORRE Ugarte/Jose Bernardo ALZEDO

note: adopted 1822; the song won a national anthem contest

ECONOMY

Economy—overview: Peru's economy reflects its varied topography—an arid lowland coastal region, the central high sierra of the Andes, and the dense forest of the Amazon. A wide range of important mineral resources are found in the mountainous and coastal areas, and Peru's coastal waters provide excellent fishing grounds. Peru is the world's second largest producer of silver and copper.

The Peruvian economy grew by an average of 5.6% per year from 2009-13 with a stable exchange rate and low inflation. This growth was due partly to high international prices for Peru's metals and minerals exports, which account for 55% of the country's total exports. Growth slipped from 2014 to 2017, due to weaker world prices for these resources. Despite Peru's strong macroeconomic performance, dependence on minerals and metals exports and imported foodstuffs makes the economy vulnerable to fluctuations in world prices.

Peru's rapid expansion coupled with cash transfers and other programs have helped to reduce the national poverty rate by over 35 percentage points since 2004, but inequality persists and continued to pose a challenge for the Ollanta HUMALA administration, which championed a policy of social inclusion and a more equitable distribution of income. Poor infrastructure hinders the spread of growth to Peru's non-coastal areas. The HUMALA administration passed several economic stimulus packages in 2014 to bolster growth, including reforms to environmental regulations in order to spur investment in Peru's lucrative mining sector, a move that was opposed by some environmental groups. However, in 2015, mining investment fell as global commodity prices remained low and social conflicts plagued the sector.

Peru's free trade policy continued under the HUMALA administration; since 2006, Peru has signed trade deals with the US, Canada, Singapore, China, Korea, Mexico, Japan, the EU, the European Free Trade Association, Chile, Thailand, Costa Rica, Panama, Venezuela, Honduras, concluded negotiations with Guatemala and the Trans-Pacific Partnership, and begun trade talks with El Salvador, India, and Turkey. Peru also has signed a trade pact with Chile, Colombia, and Mexico, called the Pacific Alliance, that seeks integration of services, capital, investment and movement of people. Since the US-Peru Trade Promotion Agreement entered into force in February 2009, total trade between Peru and the US has doubled. President Pedro Pablo KUCZYNSKI succeeded HUMALA in July 2016 and is focusing on economic reforms and free market policies aimed at boosting investment in Peru. Mining output increased significantly in 2016-17, which helped Peru attain one of the highest GDP growth rates in Latin America, and Peru should maintain strong growth in 2018. However, economic performance was depressed by delays in infrastructure mega-projects and the start of a corruption scandal associated with a Brazilian firm. Massive flooding in early 2017 also was a drag on growth, offset somewhat by additional public spending aimed at recovery efforts.

GDP (purchasing power parity): $424.6 billion (2017 est.)

$413.6 billion (2016 est.)

$397.7 billion (2015 est.)

note: data are in 2017 dollars

country comparison to the world: 47

GDP (official exchange rate): $210 billion (2016 est.)

GDP—real growth rate: 2.7% (2017 est.)

4% (2016 est.)

3.3% (2015 est.)

country comparison to the world: 126

GDP—per capita (PPP): $13,300 (2017 est.)

$13,100 (2016 est.)

$12,800 (2015 est.)

note: data are in 2017 dollars

country comparison to the world: 118

Gross national saving: 20.5% of GDP (2017 est.)

20.1% of GDP (2016 est.)

19.7% of GDP (2015 est.)

country comparison to the world: 85

711

GDP—composition, by end use:
household consumption: 65.3%
government consumption: 11.7%
investment in fixed capital: 21.6%
investment in inventories: 0.2%
exports of goods and services: 23.1%
imports of goods and services: -22% (2017 est.)

GDP—composition, by sector of origin:
agriculture: 7.5%
industry: 36.3%
services: 56.1% (2017 est.)

Agriculture—products: artichokes, asparagus, avocados, blueberries, coffee, cocoa, cotton, sugarcane, rice, potatoes, corn, plantains, grapes, oranges, pineapples, guavas, bananas, apples, lemons, pears, coca, tomatoes, mangoes, barley, medicinal plants, quinoa, palm oil, marigolds, onions, wheat, dry beans; poultry, beef, pork, dairy products; guinea pigs; fish

Industries: mining and refining of minerals; steel, metal fabrication; petroleum extraction and refining, natural gas and natural gas liquefaction; fishing and fish processing, cement, glass, textiles, clothing, food processing, beer, soft drinks, rubber, machinery, electrical machinery, chemicals, furniture

Industrial production growth rate: 8% (2017 est.)
country comparison to the world: 18

Labor force: 17.03 million
note: individuals older than 14 years of age (2017 est.)
country comparison to the world: 38

Labor force—by occupation: *agriculture:* 25.8%
industry: 17.4%
services: 56.8% (2011)

Unemployment rate: 6.7% (2017 est.)
6.7% (2016 est.)
note: data are for metropolitan Lima; widespread underemployment
country comparison to the world: 94

Population below poverty line: 22.7% (2014 est.)

Household income or consumption by percentage share: *lowest 10%:* 1.4%
highest 10%: 36.1% (2010 est.)

Distribution of family income—Gini index: 45.3 (2012)
51 (2005)
country comparison to the world: 39

Budget: *revenues:* $59.66 billion
expenditures: $65.48 billion (2017 est.)
Taxes and other revenues: 28.4% of GDP (2017 est.)
country comparison to the world: 94

Budget surplus (+) or deficit (-): -2.8% of GDP (2017 est.)
country comparison to the world: 107

Public debt: 25.7% of GDP (2017 est.)
23.8% of GDP (2016 est.)
note: data cover general government debt, and includes debt instruments issued by government entities other than the treasury; the data exclude treasury debt held by foreign entities; the data include debt issued by subnational entities

country comparison to the world: 176

Fiscal year: calendar year

Inflation rate (consumer prices): 3.2% (2017 est.)
3.6% (2016 est.)
note: data are for metropolitan Lima, annual average
country comparison to the world: 135

Central bank discount rate: 4.25% (31 December 2016 est.)
5.05% (31 December 2012)
country comparison to the world: 93

Commercial bank prime lending rate: 16.5% (31 December 2017 est.)
16.47% (31 December 2016 est.)
note: domestic currency lending rate, 90 day maturity
country comparison to the world: 30

Stock of narrow money: $33.83 billion (31 December 2017 est.)
$31.08 billion (31 December 2016 est.)
country comparison to the world: 60

Stock of broad money: $96.27 billion (31 December 2017 est.)
$84.84 billion (31 December 2016 est.)
country comparison to the world: 57

Stock of domestic credit: $58.75 billion (31 December 2017 est.)
$52.8 billion (31 December 2016 est.)
country comparison to the world: 64

Market value of publicly traded shares: $56.56 billion (31 December 2015 est.)
$78.84 billion (31 December 2014 est.)
$80.98 billion (31 December 2013 est.)
country comparison to the world: 47

Current account balance: -$3.22 billion (2017 est.)
-$5.305 billion (2016 est.)
country comparison to the world: 168

Exports: $42.47 billion (2017 est.)
$37.02 billion (2016 est.)
country comparison to the world: 53

Exports—commodities: copper, gold, lead, zinc, tin, iron ore, molybdenum, silver; crude petroleum and petroleum products, natural gas; coffee, asparagus and other vegetables, fruit, apparel and textiles, fishmeal, fish, chemicals, fabricated metal products and machinery, alloys

Exports—partners: China 23.5%, US 17.3%, Switzerland 7.1%, Canada 4.7% (2016)

Imports: $38.8 billion (2017 est.)
$35.13 billion (2016 est.)
country comparison to the world: 57

Imports—commodities: petroleum and petroleum products, chemicals, plastics, machinery, vehicles, TV sets, power shovels, front-end loaders, telephones and telecommunication equipment, iron and steel, wheat, corn, soybean products, paper, cotton, vaccines and medicines

Imports—partners: China 22.8%, US 20.2%, Brazil 5.8%, Mexico 4.5% (2016)

Reserves of foreign exchange and gold: $61.34 billion (31 December 2017 est.)

$61.81 billion (31 December 2016 est.)
country comparison to the world: 34

Debt—external: $70.09 billion (31 December 2017 est.)
$66.76 billion (31 December 2016 est.)
country comparison to the world: 61

Stock of direct foreign investment—at home: $97.29 billion (31 December 2017 est.)
$91.48 billion (31 December 2016 est.)
country comparison to the world: 47

Stock of direct foreign investment—abroad: $4.362 billion (31 December 2017 est.)
$4.255 billion (31 December 2016 est.)
country comparison to the world: 74

Exchange rates: nuevo sol (PEN) per US dollar—
3.265 (2017 est.)
3.3751 (2016 est.)
3.3751 (2015 est.)
3.185 (2014 est.)
2.8383 (2013 est.)

ENERGY

Electricity access: *population without electricity:* 2,900,000
electrification—*total population:* 91%
electrification—*urban areas:* 98%
electrification—*rural areas:* 73% (2013)

Electricity—production: 46.31 billion kWh (2015 est.)
country comparison to the world: 56

Electricity—consumption: 40.93 billion kWh (2015 est.)
country comparison to the world: 56

Electricity—exports: 55 million kWh (2015 est.)
country comparison to the world: 85

Electricity—imports: 0 kWh (2016 est.)
country comparison to the world: 187

Electricity—installed generating capacity: 12.26 million kW (2015 est.)
country comparison to the world: 56

Electricity—from fossil fuels: 62.6% of total installed capacity (2015 est.)
country comparison to the world: 120

Electricity—from nuclear fuels: 0% of total installed capacity (2015 est.)
country comparison to the world: 163

Electricity—from hydroelectric plants: 33.9% of total installed capacity (2015 est.)
country comparison to the world: 61

Electricity—from other renewable sources: 4.3% of total installed capacity (2015 est.)
country comparison to the world: 103

Crude oil—production: 40,270 bbl/day (2016 est.)
country comparison to the world: 59

Crude oil—exports: 15,560 bbl/day (2014 est.)
country comparison to the world: 55

Crude oil—imports: 83,660 bbl/day (2014 est.)
country comparison to the world: 45

Crude oil—proved reserves: 473 million bbl (1 January 2017 es)
country comparison to the world: 50

Refined petroleum products—production: 187,200 bbl/day (2014 est.)
country comparison to the world: 54

Refined petroleum products—consumption: 240,000 bbl/day (2015 est.)
country comparison to the world: 51

Refined petroleum products—exports: 66,650 bbl/day (2014 est.)
country comparison to the world: 49

Refined petroleum products—imports: 52,880 bbl/day (2014 est.)
country comparison to the world: 81

Natural gas—production: 12.62 billion cu m (2015 est.)
country comparison to the world: 37

Natural gas—consumption: 10.88 billion cu m (2015 est.)
country comparison to the world: 53

Natural gas—exports: 4.83 billion cu m (2015 est.)
country comparison to the world: 33

Natural gas—imports: 0 cu m (2013 est.)
country comparison to the world: 174

Natural gas—proved reserves: 399 billion cu m (1 January 2017 es)
country comparison to the world: 35

Carbon dioxide emissions from consumption of energy: 41 million Mt (2013 est.)
country comparison to the world: 68

COMMUNICATIONS

Telephones—fixed lines: *total subscriptions:* 3,074,464
subscriptions per 100 inhabitants: 10 (July 2016 est.)
country comparison to the world: 48

Telephones—mobile cellular: *total:* 36,933,161
subscriptions per 100 inhabitants: 120 (July 2016 est.)
country comparison to the world: 38

Telephone system: *general assessment:* adequate for most requirements; nationwide microwave radio relay system and a domestic satellite system with 12 earth stations
domestic: fixed-line teledensity is only about 10 per 100 persons; mobile-cellular teledensity, spurred by competition among multiple providers, now 120 telephones per 100 persons
international: country code—51; the South America-1 (SAM-1) and Pan American (PAN-AM) submarine cable systems provide links to parts of Central and South America, the Caribbean, and US; satellite earth stations—2 Intelsat (Atlantic Ocean) (2016)

Broadcast media: 10 major TV networks of which only one, Television Nacional de Peru, is state owned; multi-channel cable TV services are available; in excess of 2,000 radio stations including a substantial number of indigenous language stations (2010)

Internet country code: .pe

Internet users: *total:* 13,975,422

percent of population: 45.5% (July 2016 est.)
country comparison to the world: 39

TRANSPORTATION

National air transport system: *number of registered air carriers:* 7
inventory of registered aircraft operated by air carriers: 35
annual passenger traffic on registered air carriers: 13,907,948
annual freight traffic on registered air carriers: 223,643,434 mt-km (2015)
Civil aircraft registration country code prefix: OB (2016)

Airports: 191 (2013)
country comparison to the world: 30

Airports—with paved runways: *total:* 59
over 3,047 m: 5
2,438 to 3,047 m: 21
1,524 to 2,437 m: 16
914 to 1,523 m: 12
under 914 m: 5 (2017)

Airports—with unpaved runways: *total:* 132
2,438 to 3,047 m: 1
1,524 to 2,437 m: 19
914 to 1,523 m: 30
under 914 m: 82 (2013)

Heliports: 5 (2013)

Pipelines: extra heavy crude 786 km; gas 1,526 km; liquid petroleum gas 679 km; oil 1,033 km; refined products 15 km (2013)

Railways: *total:* 1,854.4 km
standard gauge: 1,730.4 km 1.435-m gauge (34 km electrified)
narrow gauge: 124 km 0.914-m gauge (2014)
country comparison to the world: 74

Roadways: *total:* 140,672 km (18,699 km paved)
note: includes 24,593 km of national roads (14,748 km paved), 24,235 km of departmental roads (2,340 km paved), and 91,844 km of local roads (1,611 km paved) (2012)
country comparison to the world: 36

Waterways: 8,808 km (8,600 km of navigable tributaries on the Amazon River system and 208 km on Lago Titicaca) (2011)
country comparison to the world: 14

Merchant marine: *total:* 88
by type: container ship 2, oil tanker 12, other 74 (2017)
country comparison to the world: 88

Ports and terminals: *major seaport(s):* Callao, Matarani, Paita
river port(s): Iquitos, Pucallpa, Yurimaguas (Amazon)
oil terminal(s): Conchan oil terminal, La Pampilla oil terminal
container port(s) (TEUs): Callao (1,616,365)

MILITARY AND SECURITY

Military expenditures: 0.9% of GDP (2017)
1.29% of GDP (2016)
1.69% of GDP (2015)
1.46% of GDP (2014)
1.47% of GDP (2013)
1.33% of GDP (2012)
country comparison to the world: 78

Military branches: Peruvian Army (Ejercito Peruano), Peruvian Navy (Marina de Guerra del Peru, MGP, includes naval air, naval infantry, and Coast Guard), Air Force of Peru (Fuerza Aerea del Peru, FAP) (2013)

Military service age and obligation: 18-50 years of age for male and 18-45 years of age for female voluntary military service; no conscription (2012)

Maritime threats: the International Maritime Bureau reports the territorial waters of Peru are a risk for armed robbery against ships; in 2016, 11 attacks against commercial vessels were reported up from none in 2015; most of these occured in the main port of Callao

TERRORISM

Terrorist groups—home based: *Shining Path (Sendero Luminoso, SL):* aim(s): generate revenue by providing security for narcotics trafficking and growing coca to produce cocaine; historically, SL's goal was to replace Peruvian institutions with a peasant revolutionary regime
area(s) of operation: headquartered in the Valley of the Apurimac, Ene and Mantaro River Valleys (VRAEM) region; responsible for bombing and shooting attacks that have claimed over 70,000 deaths since SL's inception in the late 1960s; currently engages heavily in all aspects of narcotics trafficking activities, especially in the VRAEM and Upper Huallaga Valley (UHV) regions

TRANSNATIONAL ISSUES

Disputes—international: Chile and Ecuador rejected Peru's November 2005 unilateral legislation to shift the axis of their joint treaty-defined maritime boundaries along the parallels of latitude to equidistance lines which favor Peru; organized illegal narcotics operations in Colombia have penetrated Peru's shared border; Peru rejects Bolivia's claim to restore maritime access through a sovereign corridor through Chile along the Peruvian border

Refugees and internally displaced persons: *refugees (country of origin):* 9,518 (Venezuela) (economic and political crisis) (2017)
IDPs: 62,000 (civil war from 1980-2000; most IDPs are indigenous peasants in Andean and Amazonian regions; as of 2011, no new information on the situation of these IDPs) (2016)

Illicit drugs: until 1996 the world's largest coca leaf producer, Peru is now the world's second largest producer of coca leaf, though it lags far behind Colombia; cultivation of coca in Peru was estimated at 53,000 hectares in 2015, an increase of 14 per cent over 2014; second largest producer of cocaine, estimated at 380 metric tons of potential pure cocaine in 2015; finished cocaine is shipped out from Pacific ports to the international drug market; increasing amounts of base and finished cocaine, however, are being moved to Brazil, Chile, Argentina, and Bolivia for use in the Southern Cone or transshipment to Europe and Africa; increasing domestic drug consumption

PHILIPPINES

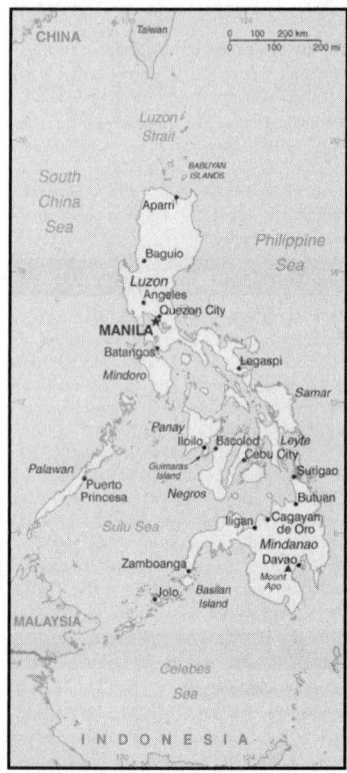

INTRODUCTION

Background: The Philippine Islands became a Spanish colony during the 16th century; they were ceded to the US in 1898 following the Spanish-American War. In 1935 the Philippines became a self-governing commonwealth. Manuel QUEZON was elected president and was tasked with preparing the country for independence after a 10-year transition. In 1942 the islands fell under Japanese occupation during World War II, and US forces and Filipinos fought together during 1944-45 to regain control. On 4 July 1946 the Republic of the Philippines attained its independence. A 20-year rule by Ferdinand MARCOS ended in 1986, when a "people power" movement in Manila ("EDSA 1") forced him into exile and installed Corazon AQUINO as president. Her presidency was hampered by several coup attempts that prevented a return to full political stability and economic development. Fidel RAMOS was elected president in 1992. His administration was marked by increased stability and by progress on economic reforms. In 1992, the US closed its last military bases on the islands. Joseph ESTRADA was elected president in 1998. He was succeeded by his vice-president,

Gloria MACAPAGAL-ARROYO, in January 2001 after ESTRADA's stormy impeachment trial on corruption charges broke down and another "people power" movement ("EDSA 2") demanded his resignation. MACAPAGAL-ARROYO was elected to a six-year term as president in May 2004. Her presidency was marred by several corruption allegations but the Philippine economy was one of the few to avoid contraction following the 2008 global financial crisis, expanding each year of her administration. Benigno AQUINO III was elected to a six-year term as president in May 2010 and was succeeded by Rodrigo DUTERTE in May 2016.

The Philippine Government faces threats from several groups, some of which are on the US Government's Foreign Terrorist Organization list. Manila has waged a decades-long struggle against ethnic Moro insurgencies in the southern Philippines, which has led to a peace accord with the Moro National Liberation Front and ongoing peace talks with the Moro Islamic Liberation Front. The decades-long Maoist-inspired New People's Army insurgency also operates through much of the country. In 2016, Philippine armed forces battled an ISIS-Philippines siege in Marawi City, driving DUTERTE to declare martial law in the region. The Philippines faces increased tension with China over disputed territorial and maritime claims in the South China Sea.

GEOGRAPHY

Location: Southeastern Asia, archipelago between the Philippine Sea and the South China Sea, east of Vietnam

Geographic coordinates: 13 00 N, 122 00 E

Map references: Southeast Asia

Area: *total:* 300,000 sq km
land: 298,170 sq km
water: 1,830 sq km
country comparison to the world: 74

Area—comparative: slightly less than twice the size of Georgia; slightly larger than Arizona

Land boundaries: 0 km

Coastline: 36,289 km

Maritime claims: *territorial sea:* irregular polygon extending up to 100 nm from coastline as defined by 1898 treaty; since late 1970s has also claimed polygonal-shaped area in South China Sea as wide as 285 nm
exclusive economic zone: 200 nm
continental shelf: to the depth of exploitation

Climate: tropical marine; northeast monsoon (November to April); southwest monsoon (May to October)

Terrain: mostly mountains with narrow to extensive coastal lowlands

Elevation: *mean elevation:* 442 m

elevation extremes: *lowest point:* Philippine Sea 0 m
highest point: Mount Apo 2,954 m

Natural resources: timber, petroleum, nickel, cobalt, silver, gold, salt, copper

Land use: *agricultural land:* 41%
arable land: 18.2%;
permanent crops: 17.8%;
permanent pasture: 5%
forest: 25.9%
other: 33.1% (2011 est.)
Irrigated land: 16,270 sq km (2012)

Population—distribution: population concentrated where good farmlands lie; highest concentrations are northwest and south-central Luzon, the southeastern extension of Luzon, and the islands of the Visayan Sea, particularly Cebu and Negros; Manila is home to one-eighth of the entire national population

Natural hazards: astride typhoon belt, usually affected by 15 and struck by five to six cyclonic storms each year; landslides; active volcanoes; destructive earthquakes; tsunamis
volcanism: significant volcanic activity; Taal (311 m), which has shown recent unrest and may erupt in the near future, has been deemed a Decade Volcano by the International Association of Volcanology and Chemistry of the Earth's Interior, worthy of study due to its explosive history and close proximity to human populations; Mayon (2,462 m), the country's most active volcano, erupted in 2009 forcing over 33,000 to be evacuated; other historically active volcanoes include Biliran, Babuyan Claro, Bulusan, Camiguin, Camiguin de Babuyanes, Didicas, Iraya, Jolo, Kanlaon, Makaturing, Musuan, Parker, Pinatubo, and Ragang

Environment—current issues: uncontrolled deforestation especially in watershed areas; soil erosion; air and water pollution in major urban centers; coral reef degradation; increasing pollution of coastal mangrove swamps that are important fish breeding grounds

Environment—international agreements: *party to:* Biodiversity, Climate Change, Climate Change-Kyoto Protocol, Desertification, Endangered Species, Hazardous Wastes, Law of the Sea, Marine Dumping, Ozone Layer Protection, Ship Pollution, Tropical Timber 83, Tropical Timber 94, Wetlands, Whaling
signed, but not ratified: Air Pollution-Persistent Organic Pollutants

Geography—note: note 1: favorably located in relation to many of Southeast Asia's main water bodies: the South China Sea, Philippine Sea, Sulu Sea, Celebes Sea, and Luzon Strait
note 2: for decades, the Philippine archipelago was reported as having 7,107 islands; in 2016, the national mapping authority reported that hundreds of new islands had been discovered and

increased the number of islands to 7,641—though not all of the new islands have been verified

PEOPLE AND SOCIETY

Population: 104,256,076 (July 2017 est.)
country comparison to the world: 13

Nationality: *noun:* Filipino(s)
adjective: Philippine

Ethnic groups: Tagalog 28.1%, Cebuano 13.1%, Ilocano 9%, Bisaya/Binisaya 7.6%, Hiligaynon Ilonggo 7.5%, Bikol 6%, Waray 3.4%, other 25.3% (2000 census)

Languages: Filipino (official; based on Tagalog) and English (official); eight major dialects—Tagalog, Cebuano, Ilocano, Hiligaynon or Ilonggo, Bicol, Waray, Pampango, and Pangasinan

Religions: Catholic 82.9% (Roman Catholic 80.9%, Aglipayan 2%), Muslim 5%, Evangelical 2.8%, Iglesia ni Kristo 2.3%, other Christian 4.5%, other 1.8%, unspecified 0.6%, none 0.1% (2000 census)

Age structure: *0-14 years:* 33.39% (male 17,764,826/female 17,050,168)
15-24 years: 19.16% (male 10,199,389/female 9,780,025)
25-54 years: 36.99% (male 19,597,675/female 18,964,900)
55-64 years: 5.97% (male 2,844,739/female 3,375,139)
65 years and over: 4.49% (male 1,930,273/female 2,748,942) (2017 est.)

Dependency ratios: *total dependency ratio:* 58.2
youth dependency ratio: 51
elderly dependency ratio: 7.2
potential support ratio: 13.8 (2015 est.)

Median age: *total:* 23.5 years
male: 23.1 years
female: 24 years (2017 est.)
country comparison to the world: 168

Population growth rate: 1.57% (2017 est.)
country comparison to the world: 70

Birth rate: 23.7 births/1,000 population (2017 est.)
country comparison to the world: 61

Death rate: 6.1 deaths/1,000 population (2017 est.)
country comparison to the world: 156

Net migration rate: -2 migrant(s)/1,000 population (2017 est.)
country comparison to the world: 162

Population distribution: population concentrated where good farmlands lie; highest concentrations are northwest and south-central Luzon, the southeastern extension of Luzon, and the islands of the Visayan Sea, particularly Cebu and Negros; Manila is home to one-eighth of the entire national population

Urbanization: *urban population:* 44.2% of total population (2017)
rate of urbanization: 1.57% annual rate of change (2015-20 est.)

Major urban areas—population: MANILA (capital) 12.946 million; Davao 1.63 million; Cebu City 951,000; Zamboanga 936,000 (2015)

Sex ratio: *at birth:* 1.05 male(s)/female
0-14 years: 1.04 male(s)/female
15-24 years: 1.04 male(s)/female
25-54 years: 1.03 male(s)/female
55-64 years: 0.84 male(s)/female
65 years and over: 0.72 male(s)/female
total population: 1.01 male(s)/female (2016 est.)

Mother's mean age at first birth: 23 years
note: median age at first birth among women 25-29 (2013 est.)

Maternal mortality ratio: 114 deaths/100,000 live births (2015 est.)
country comparison to the world: 71

Infant mortality rate: *total:* 21.4 deaths/1,000 live births
male: 24.3 deaths/1,000 live births
female: 18.3 deaths/1,000 live births (2017 est.)
country comparison to the world: 77

Life expectancy at birth: *total population:* 69.4 years
male: 65.9 years
female: 73.1 years (2017 est.)
country comparison to the world: 162

Total fertility rate: 3.02 children born/woman (2017 est.)
country comparison to the world: 55

Contraceptive prevalence rate: 55.1% (2013)

Health expenditures: 4.7% of GDP (2014)
country comparison to the world: 152

Hospital bed density: 1 beds/1,000 population (2011)

Drinking water source:
improved:
urban: 93.7% of population
rural: 90.3% of population
total: 91.8% of population
unimproved:
urban: 6.3% of population
rural: 9.7% of population
total: 8.2% of population (2015 est.)

Sanitation facility access:
improved:
urban: 77.9% of population
rural: 70.8% of population
total: 73.9% of population
unimproved:
urban: 22.1% of population
rural: 29.2% of population
total: 26.1% of population (2015 est.)

HIV/AIDS—adult prevalence rate: 0.1% (2016 est.)
country comparison to the world: 108

HIV/AIDS—people living with HIV/AIDS: 56,000 (2016 est.)
country comparison to the world: 54

HIV/AIDS—deaths: <1000 (2016 est.)

Major infectious diseases: *degree of risk:* high
food or waterborne diseases: bacterial diarrhea, hepatitis A, and typhoid fever
vectorborne diseases: dengue fever and malaria

water contact disease: leptospirosis (2016)

Obesity—adult prevalence rate: 6.4% (2016)
country comparison to the world: 168

Children under the age of 5 years underweight: 19.9% (2013)
country comparison to the world: 29

Education expenditures: 2.7% of GDP (2009)
country comparison to the world: 149

Literacy: *definition:* age 15 and over can read and write
total population: 96.3%
male: 95.8%
female: 96.8% (2015 est.)

School life expectancy (primary to tertiary education): *total:* 13 years
male: 12 years
female: 13 years (2013)

Unemployment, youth ages 15-24: *total:* 15%
male: 14.3%
female: 16% (2015 est.)
country comparison to the world: 74

GOVERNMENT

Country name: *conventional long form:* Republic of the Philippines
conventional short form: Philippines
local long form: Republika ng Pilipinas
local short form: Pilipinas
etymology: named in honor of King PHILLIP II of Spain by Spanish explorer Ruy LOPEZ de VILLALOBOS, who visited some of the islands in 1543

Government type: presidential republic

Capital: *name:* Manila

geographic coordinates: 14 36 N, 120 58 E
time difference: UTC+8 (13 hours ahead of Washington, DC, during Standard Time)

Administrative divisions: 80 provinces and 39 chartered cities
provinces: Abra, Agusan del Norte, Agusan del Sur, Aklan, Albay, Antique, Apayao, Aurora, Basilan, Bataan, Batanes, Batangas, Biliran, Benguet, Bohol, Bukidnon, Bulacan, Cagayan, Camarines Norte, Camarines Sur, Camiguin, Capiz, Catanduanes, Cavite, Cebu, Compostela, Cotabato, Davao del Norte, Davao del Sur, Davao Oriental, Dinagat Islands, Eastern Samar, Guimaras, Ifugao, Ilocos Norte, Ilocos Sur, Iloilo, Isabela, Kalinga, Laguna, Lanao del Norte, Lanao del Sur, La Union, Leyte, Maguindanao, Marinduque, Masbate, Mindoro Occidental, Mindoro Oriental, Misamis Occidental, Misamis Oriental, Mountain, Negros Occidental, Negros Oriental, Northern Samar, Nueva Ecija, Nueva Vizcaya, Palawan, Pampanga, Pangasinan, Quezon, Quirino, Rizal, Romblon, Samar, Sarangani, Siquijor, Sorsogon, South Cotabato, Southern Leyte, Sultan Kudarat, Sulu, Surigao del Norte, Surigao del Sur, Tarlac, Tawi-Tawi, Zambales, Zamboanga del Norte, Zamboanga del Sur, Zamboanga Sibugay
chartered cities: Angeles, Antipolo, Bacolod, Baguio, Butuan, Cagayan de Oro, Caloocan, Cebu, Cotabato, Dagupan, Davao, General Santos, Iligan, Iloilo, Lapu-Lapu, Las Pinas, Lucena, Makati,

Malabon, Mandaluyong, Mandaue, Manila, Marikina, Muntinlupa, Naga, Navotas, Olongapo, Ormoc, Paranaque, Pasay, Pasig, Puerto Princesa, Quezon, San Juan, Santiago, Tacloban, Taguig, Valenzuela, Zamboanga (2012)

Independence: 4 July 1946 (from the US)

National holiday: Independence Day, 12 June (1898); note—12 June 1898 was date of declaration of independence from Spain; 4 July 1946 was date of independence from the US

Constitution: several previous; latest ratified 2 February 1987, effective 11 February 1987 (2016)

Legal system: mixed legal system of civil, common, Islamic, and customary law

International law organization participation: accepts compulsory ICJ jurisdiction with reservations; accepts ICCt jurisdiction

Citizenship: *citizenship by birth:* no

citizenship by descent only: at least one parent must be a citizen of the Philippines
dual citizenship recognized: no
residency requirement for naturalization: 10 years

Suffrage: 18 years of age; universal

Executive branch: *chief of state:* President Rodrigo DUTERTE (since 30 June 2016); Vice President Leni ROBREDO (since 30 June 2016); note—the president is both chief of state and head of government

head of government: President Rodrigo DUTERTE (since 30 June 2016); Vice President Leni ROBREDO (since 30 June 2016)
cabinet: Cabinet appointed by the president with the consent of the Commission of Appointments, an independent body of 25 Congressional members including the Senate president (ex officio chairman), appointed by the president
elections/appointments: president and vice president directly elected on separate ballots by simple majority popular vote for a single 6-year term; election last held on 9 May 2016 (next to be held in May 2022)
election results: Rodrigo DUTERTE elected president; percent of vote—Rodrigo DUTERTE (PDP-Laban) 39%, Manuel "Mar" ROXAS (LP) 23.5%, Grace POE (independent) 21.4%, Jejomar BINAY (UNA) 12.7%, Miriam Defensor SANTIAGO (PRP) 3.4%; Leni ROBREDO elected vice president; percent of vote Leni ROBREDO (LP) 35.1%, Bongbong MARCOS (independent) 34.5%, Alan CAYETANO 14.4%, Francis ESCUDERO (independent) 12%, Antonio TRILLANES (independent) 2.1%, Gregorio HONASAN (UNA) 1.9%

Legislative branch: *description:* bicameral Congress or Kongreso consists of the Senate or Senado (24 seats; members directly elected in multi-seat constituencies by majority vote; members serve 6-year terms with one-half of the membership renewed every 3 years) and the House of Representatives or Kapulungan Ng Mga Kinatawan (297 seats; 238 members directly elected in single-seat constituencies by simple majority vote and 59

representing minorities directly elected by party-list proportional representation vote; members serve 3-year terms)
elections: Senate—elections last held on 9 May 2016 (next to be held in May 2019); House of Representatives—elections last held on 9 May 2016 (next to be held in May 2019)
election results: Senate—percent of vote by party—LP 31.3%, NPC 10.1%, UNA 7.6%, Akbayan 5.0%, other 30.9%, independent 15.1%; seats by party—LP 6, NPC 3, UNA 4, Akbayan 1, other 10; House of Representatives—percent of vote by party—LP 41.7%, NPC 17.0%, UNA 6.6%, NUP 9.7%, NP 9.4%, independent 6.0%, others 10.1%; seats by party—LP 115, NPC 42, NUP 23, NP 24, UNA 11, other 19, independent 4, party-list 59

Judicial branch: *highest court(s):* Supreme Court (consists of a chief justice and 14 associate justices)
judge selection and term of office: justices are appointed by the president on the recommendation of the Judicial and Bar Council, a constitutionally created, 6-member body that recommends Supreme Court nominees; justices serve until age 70
subordinate courts: Court of Appeals; Sandiganbayan (special court for corruption cases of government officials); Court of Tax Appeals; regional, metropolitan, and municipal trial courts; sharia courts

Political parties and leaders: Akbayon [Machris CABREROS]
Laban ng Demokratikong Pilipino (Struggle of Filipino Democrats) or LDP [Edgardo ANGARA]
Lakas ng EDSA-Christian Muslim Democrats or Lakas-CMD [Ferdinand Martin ROMUALDEZ]
Liberal Party or LP [Francis PANGILINAN]
Nacionalista Party or NP [Manuel "Manny" VILLAR]
Nationalist People's Coalition or NPC [Eduardo COJUNGCO, Jr.]
National Unity Party or NUP [Albert GARCIA]
PDP-Laban [Aquilino PIMENTEL III]
People's Reform Party or PRP [Narciso SANTIAGO]
Puwersa ng Masang Pilipino (Force of the Philippine Masses) or PMP [Joseph ESTRADA]
United Nationalist Alliance or UNA

Political pressure groups and leaders: Black and White Movement or BWM [Vicente ROMANO] People Action (Kilosbayan)

International organization participation: ADB, APEC, ARF, ASEAN, BIS, CD, CICA (observer), CP, EAS, FAO, G-24, G-77, IAEA, IBRD, ICAO, ICC (national committees), ICCt, ICRM, IDA, IFAD, IFC, IFRCS, IHO, ILO, IMF, IMO, IMSO, Interpol, IOC, IOM, IPU, ISO, ITSO, ITU, ITUC (NGOs), MIGA, MINUSTAH, NAM, OAS (observer), OPCW, PCA, PIF (partner), UN, UNCTAD, UNESCO, UNHCR, UNIDO, Union Latina, UNMIL, UNMOGIP, UNOCI, UNWTO, UPU, WCO, WFTU (NGOs), WHO, WIPO, WMO, WTO

Diplomatic representation in the US: *chief of mission:* Ambassador Jose Manuel del Gallego ROMUALDEZ (since 29 November 2017)

chancery: 1600 Massachusetts Avenue NW, Washington, DC 20036
telephone: [1] (202) 467-9300
FAX: [1] (202) 328-7614
consulate(s) general: Chicago, Honolulu, Los Angeles, New Yoek, Saipan (Northern Mariana Islands), San Francisco, Tamuning (Guam)

Diplomatic representation from the US: *chief of mission:* Ambassador Sung KIM (since 6 December 2016)
embassy: 1201 Roxas Boulevard, Manila 1000
mailing address: PSC 500, FPO AP 96515-1000
telephone: [63] (2) 301-2000
FAX: [63] (2) 301-2017

Flag description: two equal horizontal bands of blue (top) and red; a white equilateral triangle is based on the hoist side; the center of the triangle displays a yellow sun with eight primary rays; each corner of the triangle contains a small, yellow, five-pointed star; blue stands for peace and justice, red symbolizes courage, the white equal-sided triangle represents equality; the rays recall the first eight provinces that sought independence from Spain, while the stars represent the three major geographical divisions of the country: Luzon, Visayas, and Mindanao; the design of the flag dates to 1897
note: in wartime the flag is flown upside down with the red band at the top

National symbol(s): three stars and sun, Philippine eagle; national colors: red, white, blue, yellow

National anthem: *name:* "Lupang Hinirang" (Chosen Land)
lyrics/music: Jose PALMA (revised by Felipe PADILLA de Leon)/Julian FELIPE
note: music adopted 1898, original Spanish lyrics adopted 1899, Filipino (Tagalog) lyrics adopted 1956; although the original lyrics were written in Spanish, later English and Filipino versions were created; today, only the Filipino version is used

ECONOMY

Economy—overview: The economy has been relatively resilient to global economic shocks due to less exposure to troubled international securities, lower dependence on exports, relatively resilient domestic consumption, large remittances from about 10 million overseas Filipino workers and migrants, and a rapidly expanding services industry. During 2017, the current account balance fell into the negative range, the first time since the 2008 global financial crisis, in part due to an ambitious new infrastructure spending program announced this year. However, international reserves remain at comfortable levels and the banking system is stable.

Efforts to improve tax administration and expenditures management have helped ease the Philippines' debt burden and tight fiscal situation. The Philippines received investment-grade credit ratings on its sovereign debt under the former AQUINO administration and has had little difficulty financing its budget deficits. However, weak absorptive capacity and implementation bottlenecks have prevented the government from maximizing its expenditure plans. Although it has improved, the low tax-to-GDP ratio remains a constraint to supporting increasingly higher spending levels and sustaining high and inclusive growth over the longer term.

Economic growth has accelerated, averaging over 6% per year from 2011 to 2017, compared with 4.5% under the MACAPAGAL-ARROYO government; and competitiveness rankings have improved. Although 2016 saw a record year for net foreign direct investment inflows, FDI to the Philippines has continued to lag regional peers, in part because the Philippine constitution and other laws limit foreign investment and restrict foreign ownership in important activities/sectors—such as land ownership and public utilities.

Although the economy grew at a rapid pace under the AQUINO government, challenges to achieving more inclusive growth remain. Wealth is concentrated in the hands of the rich. The unemployment rate declined from 7.3% to 5.5% between 2010 and 2016, but underemployment hovers at around 18% to 19% of the employed population. At least 40% of the employed work in the informal sector. Poverty afflicts more than a fifth of the total population but is as high as 75% in some areas of the southern Philippines. More than 60% of the poor reside in rural areas, where the incidence of poverty (about 30%) is more severe—a challenge to raising rural farm and non-farm incomes. Continued efforts are needed to improve governance, the judicial system, the regulatory environment, the infrastructure, and the overall ease of doing business.

2016 saw the election of President Rodrigo DUTERTE, who has pledged to make inclusive growth and poverty reduction his top priority. DUTERTE believes that illegal drug use, crime and corruption are key barriers to economic development. The administration wants to reduce the poverty rate to 17% and graduate the economy to upper-middle income status by the end of President DUTERTE's term in 2022. Key themes under the government's Ten-Point Socioeconomic Agenda include continuity of macroeconomic policy, tax reform, higher investments in infrastructure and human capital development, and improving competitiveness and the overall ease of doing business. The administration sees infrastructure shortcomings as a key barrier to sustained economic growth and has pledged to spend $165 billion on infrastructure by 2022. However, the need to finance rehabilitation and reconstruction efforts in the southern region of Mindanao following the 2017 Marawi City siege probably will inhibit other spending on infrastructure.

GDP (purchasing power parity): $874.5 billion (2017 est.)
$820.4 billion (2016 est.)
$767.2 billion (2015 est.)
note: data are in 2017 dollars
country comparison to the world: 30

GDP (official exchange rate): $321.2 billion (2016 est.)

GDP—real growth rate: 6.6% (2017 est.)
6.9% (2016 est.)

6.1% (2015 est.)
country comparison to the world: 16

GDP—per capita (PPP): $8,200 (2017 est.)
$7,900 (2016 est.)
$7,500 (2015 est.)
note: data are in 2017 dollars
country comparison to the world: 153

Gross national saving: 25.8% of GDP (2017 est.)
24.5% of GDP (2016 est.)
23.7% of GDP (2015 est.)
country comparison to the world: 47

GDP—composition, by end use:
household consumption: 72.7%
government consumption: 10.9%
investment in fixed capital: 25.2%
investment in inventories: -0.2%
exports of goods and services: 32.1%
imports of goods and services: -40.7% (2017 est.)

GDP—composition, by sector of origin:
agriculture: 9.4%
industry: 30.8%
services: 59.8% (2017 est.)

Agriculture—products: rice, fish, livestock, poultry, bananas, coconut/copra, corn, sugarcane, mangoes, pineapple, cassava

Industries: semiconductors and electronics assembly, food and beverage manufacturing, construction, electric/gas/water supply, chemical products, radio/television/communications equipment and apparatus, petroleum and fuel, textile and garments, non-metallic minerals, basic metal industries, transport equipment

Industrial production growth rate: 6.5% (2017 est.)
country comparison to the world: 29

Labor force: 44.46 million (2017 est.)
country comparison to the world: 16

Labor force—by occupation: *agriculture:* 26.9%
industry: 17.5%
services: 55.6% (2016 est.)

Unemployment rate: 6% (2017 est.)
5.5% (2016 est.)
country comparison to the world: 86

Population below poverty line: 21.6% (2015 est.)

Household income or consumption by percentage share: *lowest 10%:* 3.2%
highest 10%: 29.5% (2015 est.)

Distribution of family income—Gini index: 44.4 (2015 est.)
46 (2012 est.)
country comparison to the world: 45

Budget: *revenues:* $44.74 billion
expenditures: $53.55 billion (2017 est.)
Taxes and other revenues: 13.9% of GDP (2017 est.)
country comparison to the world: 198

Budget surplus (+) or deficit (-): -2.7% of GDP (2017 est.)
country comparison to the world: 103

Public debt: 41.9% of GDP (2017 est.)
42.1% of GDP (2016 est.)
country comparison to the world: 130

Fiscal year: calendar year

Inflation rate (consumer prices): 3.1% (2017 est.)
1.8% (2016 est.)
country comparison to the world: 131

Central bank discount rate: 3.56% (31 December 2016)
6.19% (31 December 2015)
country comparison to the world: 100

Commercial bank prime lending rate: 6% (31 December 2017 est.)
5.64% (31 December 2016 est.)
country comparison to the world: 127

Stock of narrow money: $68.16 billion (31 December 2017 est.)
$61.62 billion (31 December 2016 est.)
country comparison to the world: 48

Stock of broad money: $199 billion (31 December 2017 est.)
$183.5 billion (31 December 2016 est.)
country comparison to the world: 41

Stock of domestic credit: $207.4 billion (31 December 2017 est.)
$184.6 billion (31 December 2016 est.)
country comparison to the world: 47

Market value of publicly traded shares: $290.4 billion (31 December 2016 est.)
$286.1 billion (31 December 2015 est.)
$318 billion (31 December 2014 est.)
country comparison to the world: 29

Current account balance: -$315 million (2017 est.)
$601 million (2016 est.)
country comparison to the world: 97

Exports: $53.22 billion (2017 est.)
$43.44 billion (2016 est.)
country comparison to the world: 51

Exports—commodities: semiconductors and electronic products, machinery and transport equipment, wood manufactures, chemicals, processed food and beverages, garments, coconut oil, copper concentrates, seafood, bananas/fruits

Exports—partners: Japan 20.9%, US 15.6%, Hong Kong 11.5%, China 11%, Singapore 6.6%, Germany 4.1% (2016)

Imports: $90.42 billion (2017 est.)
$77.52 billion (2016 est.)
country comparison to the world: 37

Imports—commodities: electronic products, mineral fuels, machinery and transport equipment, iron and steel, textile fabrics, grains, chemicals, plastic

Imports—partners: China 18.6%, Japan 11.8%, US 9%, Thailand 7.3%, South Korea 6.1%, Singapore 6.1%, Indonesia 5.1% (2016)

Reserves of foreign exchange and gold: $81.53 billion (31 December 2017 est.)
$80.69 billion (31 December 2016 est.)
country comparison to the world: 30

Debt—external: $80.88 billion (31 December 2017 est.)
$75.01 billion (31 December 2016 est.)
country comparison to the world: 56

Stock of direct foreign investment—at home:
$67.25 billion (31 December 2017 est.)
$64.25 billion (31 December 2016 est.)
country comparison to the world: 54

Stock of direct foreign investment—abroad:
$47.58 billion (31 December 2017 est.)
$45.38 billion (31 December 2016 est.)
country comparison to the world: 44

Exchange rates: Philippine pesos (PHP) per US dollar—
50.21 (2017 est.)
47.493 (2016 est.)
47.493 (2015 est.)
45.503 (2014 est.)
44.395 (2013 est.)

ENERGY

Electricity access: *population without electricity:* 20,600,000
electrification—*total population:* 88%
electrification—*urban areas:* 94%
electrification—*rural areas:* 82% (2013)

Electricity—production: 90.8 billion kWh (2016 est.)
country comparison to the world: 37

Electricity—consumption: 74.15 billion kWh (2016 est.)
country comparison to the world: 38

Electricity—exports: 0 kWh (2016 est.)
country comparison to the world: 188

Electricity—imports: 0 kWh (2016 est.)
country comparison to the world: 192

Electricity—installed generating capacity: 21.21 million kW (2015 est.)
country comparison to the world: 42

Electricity—from fossil fuels: 67.5% of total installed capacity (2016 est.)
country comparison to the world: 108

Electricity—from nuclear fuels: 0% of total installed capacity (2016 est.)
country comparison to the world: 172

Electricity—from hydroelectric plants: 16.9% of total installed capacity (2016 est.)
country comparison to the world: 97

Electricity—from other renewable sources: 15.6% of total installed capacity (2016 est.)
country comparison to the world: 46

Crude oil—production: 20,000 bbl/day (2016 est.)
country comparison to the world: 70

Crude oil—exports: 4,942 bbl/day (2016 est.)
country comparison to the world: 63

Crude oil—imports: 215,800 bbl/day (2016 est.)
country comparison to the world: 29

Crude oil—proved reserves: 138.5 million bbl (1 January 2017 es)
country comparison to the world: 68

Refined petroleum products—production: 169,000 bbl/day (2014 est.)
country comparison to the world: 56

Refined petroleum products—consumption: 390,000 bbl/day (2015 est.)
country comparison to the world: 38

Refined petroleum products—exports: 13,140 bbl/day (2014 est.)
country comparison to the world: 78

Refined petroleum products—imports: 186,100 bbl/day (2014 est.)
country comparison to the world: 33

Natural gas—production: 2.6 billion cu m (2015 est.)
country comparison to the world: 57

Natural gas—consumption: 3.196 billion cu m (2015 est.)
country comparison to the world: 77

Natural gas—exports: 0 cu m (2016 est.)
country comparison to the world: 171

Natural gas—imports: 0 cu m (2016 est.)
country comparison to the world: 179

Natural gas—proved reserves: 98.54 billion cu m (1 January 2017 es)
country comparison to the world: 53

Carbon dioxide emissions from consumption of energy: 88 million Mt (2013 est.)
country comparison to the world: 44

COMMUNICATIONS

Telephones—fixed lines: *total subscriptions:* 3,835,911
subscriptions per 100 inhabitants: 4 (July 2016 est.)
country comparison to the world: 47

Telephones—mobile cellular: *total:* 113 million
subscriptions per 100 inhabitants: 110 (July 2016 est.)
country comparison to the world: 13

Telephone system: *general assessment:* good international radiotelephone and submarine cable services; domestic and interisland service adequate
domestic: telecommunications infrastructure includes the following platforms: fixed line, mobile cellular, cable TV, over-the-air TV, radio and Very Small Aperture Terminal (VSAT), fiber-optic cable, and satellite for redundant international connectivity
international: country code—63; a series of submarine cables together provide connectivity to the US, and to countries like Hong Kong, Guam, Singapore, Taiwan, Japan, Brunei, and Malaysia, among others; multiple international gateways (2016)

Broadcast media: multiple national private TV and radio networks; multi-channel satellite and cable TV systems available; more than 400 TV stations; about 1,500 cable TV providers with more than 2 million subscribers, and some 1,400 radio stations; the Philippines adopted Japan's Integrated Service Digital Broadcast – Terrestrial standard for digital terrestrial television in November 2013 and is scheduled to complete the switch from analog to digital broadcasting by the end of 2023 (2016)

Internet country code: .ph

Internet users: *total:* 56,956,436
percent of population: 55.5% (July 2016 est.)
country comparison to the world: 17

TRANSPORTATION

National air transport system: *number of registered air carriers:* 11
inventory of registered aircraft operated by air carriers: 158
annual passenger traffic on registered air carriers: 32,230,986
annual freight traffic on registered air carriers: 484,190,968 mt-km (2015)
Civil aircraft registration country code prefix: RP (2016)

Airports: 247 (2013)
country comparison to the world: 24

Airports—with paved runways: *total:* 89
over 3,047 m: 4
2,438 to 3,047 m: 8
1,524 to 2,437 m: 33
914 to 1,523 m: 34
under 914 m: 10 (2017)

Airports—with unpaved runways: *total:* 158
1,524 to 2,437 m: 3
914 to 1,523 m: 56
under 914 m: 99 (2013)

Heliports: 2 (2013)

Pipelines: gas 530 km (2014); oil 138 km; refined products 185 km (2013)

Railways: *total:* 995 km
narrow gauge: 995 km 1.067-m gauge (484 km are in operation) (2015)
country comparison to the world: 88

Roadways: *total:* 216,387 km
paved: 61,093 km
unpaved: 155,294 km (2014)
country comparison to the world: 24

Waterways: 3,219 km (limited to vessels with draft less than 1.5 m) (2011)
country comparison to the world: 30

Merchant marine: *total:* 1,508
by type: bulk carrier 64, container ship 33, general cargo 627, oil tanker 184, other 600 (2017)
country comparison to the world: 18

Ports and terminals: *major seaport(s):* Batangas, Cagayan de Oro, Cebu, Davao, Liman, Manila
container port(s) (TEUs): Manila (3,976,000) (2015)

MILITARY AND SECURITY

Military expenditures: 1.28% of GDP (2016)
1.14% of GDP (2015)
1.09% of GDP (2014)
1.24% of GDP (2013)
1.16% of GDP (2012)
country comparison to the world: 83

Military branches: Armed Forces of the Philippines (AFP): Army, Navy (includes Marine Corps), Air Force (2013)

Military service age and obligation: 17-23 years of age (officers 20-24) for voluntary military service; no conscription; applicants must be single male or female Philippine citizens with either 72 college credit hours (enlisted) or a baccalaureate degree (officers) (2013)

Maritime threats: the International Maritime Bureau reports the territorial and offshore waters in the South China Sea as high risk for piracy and armed robbery against ships; during 2016, 10 attacks were reported in and around the Philippines including six ships that were boarded, one hijacked, one fired upon, and 18 crew were kidnapped for ransom; an emerging threat area lies in the Celebes and Sulu Seas between the Philippines and Malaysia where 12 crew were kidnapped in three incidents during the last quarter of 2016; it is believed the pirates involved are associated with the Abu Sayyaf Group (ASG) terrorist organization; during the first six months of 2017, 13 attacks were reported including 10 ships that were boarded, one was fired upon, 10 crew were kidnapped for ransom and two killed; numerous commercial vessels have been attacked and hijacked both at anchor and while underway; hijacked vessels are often disguised and cargo diverted to ports in East Asia; crews have been murdered or cast adrift

TERRORISM

Terrorist groups—home based: *Abu Sayyaf Group (ASG): aim(s):* establish an Islamic State in the Philippines' Mindanao Island and, ultimately, an Islamic caliphate across Southeast Asia *area(s) of operation:* headquartered in southern Philippines in Western Mindanao and active in Sulu, Basilan, and Tawi-Tawi provinces in the Sulu Archipalego; conducts bombings, shootings, beheadings, assassinations, and kidnappings; kills military and police personnel and bombs their facilities; as of mid-2017 supreme leader, Isnilon HAPILON, continued to lead ASG's and Maute Group's (a.k.a. Islamic State of Lanao) siege of Marawi that started on 23 May 2017, when government forces attempted to capture HAPILON in the Lanao de Sur Province's capital; the Maute Group is a fellow ISIL-affiliated organization; over 500 people had died in the conflict (89 security personnel and approximately 65 civilians and 353 militants) and over 471,224 others had been displaced by early July 2017; ASG engages heavily in kidnappings for ransom and kills hostages when ransoms are denied, such as beheading German hostage Jurgen KANTNER on 27 February 2017 and Canadian hostages Robert Hall on 13 June 2016 and John Ridsdel on 25 April 2016; reportedly, ASG was holding more than 20 foreign hostages as of February 2017; operatives bombed the 10,000-ton Superferry 14 on 27 February 2004 in the Philippines, killing 116 people; as of 2017, the ship's bombing remains the world's deadliest terrorist attack at sea; assessed in 2016 to have over 400 fighters, although several of them were reportedly killed in 2017 during clashes in Marawi

Communist Party of the Philippines/New People's Army (CPP/NPA): *aim(s):* destablize the Philippines' economy to inspire the populace to revolt against the government and, ultimately, overthrow the Philippine Government to install a communist regime

area(s) of operation: this decades-long Maoist-inspired armed group operates throughout most of the country, primarily in rural regions, with its strongest presence in the Sierra Madre Mountains, rural Luzon, Visayas, and parts of northern and eastern Mindanao; maintains cells in Manila, Davao City, and other metropolitan areas; before entering into formal peace talks with the Philippine Government on 19 January 2017—with the National Democratic Front representing the group—leaders deployed operatives to launch lethal attacks against Philippine military and security forces, government officials, government facilities, infrastructure (including power facilities, telecommunication towers, and bridges), foreign enterprises, and businesses that refused to pay extortion or "revolutionary taxes"; at least 30,000 people in the Philippines have been killed in its attacks since its inception in March 1969; killed four US military personnel in the Philippines during the 1980s and continues to oppose US military and commercial presence; estimated in late 2015 to have 4,000 male and female members, down from its peak strength of approximately 26,000 in the 1980s; in recent years, the Philippine Government has referred to the group as CNN, short for the Communist Party of the Philippines-New People's Army-National Democratic Front (CPP-NPA-NDF)

Terrorist groups—foreign based: *Islamic State of Iraq and the Levant (ISIL): aim(s):* establish a branch in Lanao de Sur Province

area(s) of operation: as of mid-2017, ISIL-affiliates Abu Sayyaf Group (ASG) and the Maute Group (a.k.a. Islamic State of Lanao) continued to control Marawi, Lanao de Sur Province's capitol; under ASG's supreme leader, Isnilon HAPILON, the two groups attacked Marawi on 23 May 2017, when government forces attempted to capture HAPILON; over 500 people had died in the conflict (89 security personnel and approximately 65 civilians and 353 militants) and over 471,224 others had been displaced by early July 2017

Jemaah Islamiya (JI): *aim(s):* enhance its networks in the Philippines and, ultimately, overthrow the Philippine Government and establish a pan-Islamic state across Southeast Asia

area(s) of operation: maintains an operational and recruitment presence, especially in the south; longstanding bases include JI's Camp Jabal Quba on Mount Cararao in Lanao del Sur Province in the Autonomous Region in Muslim Mindanao; 25 January 2015 members ambushed a police anti-terrorism squad conducting a raid in Maguindaneo Province's city of Mamasapano in the Philippines' southern island of Mindanao, killing 44 police officers and three civilians; incarcerated members radicalize and recruit fellow prisoners

TRANSNATIONAL ISSUES

Disputes—international: Philippines claims sovereignty over Scarborough Reef (also claimed by China together with Taiwan) and over certain of the Spratly Islands, known locally as the Kalayaan (Freedom) Islands, also claimed by China, Malaysia, Taiwan, and Vietnam; the 2002 "Declaration on the Conduct of Parties in the South China Sea," has eased tensions in the Spratly Islands but falls short of a legally binding "code of conduct" desired by several of the disputants; in March 2005, the national oil companies of China, the Philippines, and Vietnam signed a joint accord to conduct marine seismic activities in the Spratly Islands; Philippines retains a dormant claim to Malaysia's Sabah State in northern Borneo based on the Sultanate of Sulu's granting the Philippines Government power of attorney to pursue a sovereignty claim on his behalf; maritime delimitation negotiations continue with Palau

Refugees and internally displaced persons: IDPs: 359,680 (government troops fighting the Moro Islamic Liberation Front, the Abu Sayyaf Group, and the New People's Army; clan feuds; natural disasters) (2017)

stateless persons: 4,636 (2016); note—stateless persons are descendants of Indonesian migrants

Illicit drugs: domestic methamphetamine production has been a growing problem in recent years despite government crackdowns; major consumer of amphetamines; longstanding marijuana producer mainly in rural areas where Manila's control is limited

PITCAIRN ISLANDS

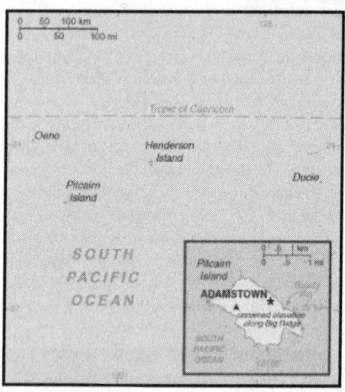

INTRODUCTION

Background: Pitcairn Island was discovered in 1767 by the British and settled in 1790 by the Bounty mutineers and their Tahitian companions. Pitcairn was the first Pacific island to become a British colony (in 1838) and today remains the last vestige of that empire in the South Pacific. Out-migration, primarily to New Zealand, has thinned the population from a peak of 233 in 1937 to less than 50 today.

GEOGRAPHY

Location: Oceania, islands in the South Pacific Ocean, about midway between Peru and New Zealand
Geographic coordinates: 25 04 S, 130 06 W
Map references: Oceania
Area: *total:* 47 sq km
land: 47 sq km
water: 0 sq km
country comparison to the world: 235
Area—comparative: about three-tenths the size of Washington, DC
Land boundaries: 0 km
Coastline: 51 km
Maritime claims: *territorial sea:* 12 nm
exclusive economic zone: 200 nm
Climate: tropical; hot and humid; modified by southeast trade winds; rainy season (November to March)
Terrain: rugged volcanic formation; rocky coastline with cliffs
Elevation: *mean elevation:* NA
elevation extremes: *lowest point:* Pacific Ocean 0 m
highest point: Palwala Valley Point on Big Ridge 347 m
Natural resources: miro trees (used for handicrafts), fish
note: manganese, iron, copper, gold, silver, and zinc have been discovered offshore

Land use: *agricultural land:* 0%
arable land: 0%;
permanent crops: 0%;
permanent pasture: 0%
forest: 74.5%
other: 25.5% (2011 est.)
Irrigated land: 0 sq km (2012)
Population—distribution: less than 50 inhabitants on Pitcairn Island, most reside near the village of Adamstown
Natural hazards: occasional tropical cyclones (especially November to March), but generally only heavy tropical storms; landslides
Environment—current issues: deforestation (only a small portion of the original forest remains because of burning and clearing for settlement)
Geography—note: Britain's most isolated dependency; only the larger island of Pitcairn is inhabited but it has no port or natural harbor; supplies must be transported by rowed longboat from larger ships stationed offshore

PEOPLE AND SOCIETY

Population: 54 (July 2016 est.)
country comparison to the world: 237
Nationality: *noun:* Pitcairn Islander(s)
adjective: Pitcairn Islander
Ethnic groups: descendants of the Bounty mutineers and their Tahitian wives
Languages: English (official), Pitkern (mixture of an 18th century English dialect and a Tahitian dialect)
Religions: Seventh-Day Adventist 100%
Population growth rate: 0% (2014 est.)
country comparison to the world: 194
Population distribution: less than 50 inhabitants on Pitcairn Island, most reside near the village of Adamstown
Urbanization: *urban population:* 0% of total population (2012)
rate of urbanization: NA
Sex ratio: NA
Infant mortality rate: *total:* NA
male: NA
female: NA
Life expectancy at birth: *total population:* NA
male: NA
female: NA (2017 est.)
Total fertility rate: NA
HIV/AIDS—adult prevalence rate: NA
HIV/AIDS—people living with HIV/AIDS: NA
HIV/AIDS—deaths: NA

GOVERNMENT

Country name: *conventional long form:* Pitcairn, Henderson, Ducie, and Oeno Islands
conventional short form: Pitcairn Islands

etymology: named after Midshipman Robert PITCAIRN who first sighted the island in 1767
Dependency status: overseas territory of the UK
Government type: parliamentary democracy (Island Council); overseas territory of the UK
Capital: *name:* Adamstown
geographic coordinates: 25 04 S, 130 05 W
time difference: UTC-9 (4 hours behind Washington, DC, during Standard Time)
Administrative divisions: none (overseas territory of the UK)
Independence: none (overseas territory of the UK)
National holiday: Birthday of Queen ELIZABETH II, second Saturday in June (1926); Discovery Day (Pitcairn Day), 2 July (1767)
Constitution: several previous; latest drafted 10 February 2010, presented 17 February 2010, effective 4 March 2010 (2016)
Legal system: local island by-laws
Citizenship: see United Kingdom
Suffrage: 18 years of age; universal with three years residency
Executive branch: *chief of state:* Queen ELIZABETH II (since 6 February 1952); represented by UK High Commissioner to New Zealand and Governor (nonresident) of the Pitcairn Islands Jonathan SINCLAIR (since August 2014); Commissioner (nonresident) Leslie JAQUES (since September 2003) serves as liaison between the governor and the Island Council
head of government: Mayor and Chairman of the Island Council Shawn CHRISTIAN (since 9 November 2016)
cabinet: none
elections/appointments: the monarchy is hereditary; governor and commissioner appointed by the monarch; island mayor directly elected by majority popular vote for a 3-year term; election last held on 9 November 2016 (next to be held not later than December 2019)
election results: Shawn CHRISTIAN reelected mayor and chairman of the Island Council; Island Council vote—NA
Legislative branch: *description:* unicameral Island Council (10 seats; 4 members directly elected by proportional representation vote, 1 nominated by the elected Council members, 2 appointed by the governor, and 3 ex-officio members—the governor, deputy governor, and commissioner; elected members serve 1-year terms)
elections: last held on 13 November 2013 (next to be held not later than December 2015)
election results: percent of vote—NA; seats—5 independent
Judicial branch: highest resident court(s): Pitcairn Court of Appeal (consists of the court president, 2 judges, and the Supreme Court chief justice (ex-officio member); Pitcairn Supreme Court (consists

of the chief justice and 2 judges); note—appeals beyond the Pitcairn Court of Appeal are referred to the Judicial Committee of the Privy Council (in London)

judge selection and term of office: all judges of both courts appointed by the governor of the Pitcairn Islands on the instructions of the Queen of England through the Secretary of State; all judges appointed until retirement, normally at age 75
subordinate courts: Magistrate's Court

Political parties and leaders: none

Political pressure groups and leaders: none

International organization participation: SPC, UPU

Diplomatic representation in the US: none (overseas territory of the UK)

Diplomatic representation from the US: none (overseas territory of the UK)

Flag description: blue with the flag of the UK in the upper hoist-side quadrant and the Pitcairn Islander coat of arms centered on the outer half of the flag; the green, yellow, and blue of the shield represents the island rising from the ocean; the green field features a yellow anchor surmounted by a bible (both the anchor and the bible were items found on the HMS Bounty); sitting on the crest is a Pitcairn Island wheelbarrow from which springs a slip of miro (a local plant)

National anthem: name: "We From Pitcairn Island"
lyrics/music: unknown/Frederick M. LEHMAN
note: serves as a local anthem; as a territory of the UK, "God Save the Queen" is official (see United Kingdom)

ECONOMY

Economy—overview: The inhabitants of this tiny isolated economy exist on fishing, subsistence farming, handicrafts, and postage stamps. The fertile soil of the valleys produces a wide variety of fruits and vegetables, including citrus, sugarcane, watermelons, bananas, yams, and beans. Bartering is an important part of the economy. The major sources of revenue are the sale of postage stamps to collectors and the sale of handicrafts to passing ships.

GDP (purchasing power parity): $NA

Agriculture—products: honey; wide variety of fruits and vegetables; goats, chickens; fish

Industries: postage stamps, handicrafts, beekeeping, honey

Labor force: 15 (2004)
country comparison to the world: 233
Labor force—by occupation: note: no business community in the usual sense; some public works; subsistence farming and fishing

Budget: *revenues:* $746,000
expenditures: $1.028 million (FY04/05)

Fiscal year: 1 April—31 March

Exports: $NA

Exports—commodities: honey, fruits, vegetables, curios, postage stamps

Imports: $NA

Imports—commodities: fuel oil, machinery, building materials, flour, sugar, other foodstuffs

Exchange rates: New Zealand dollars (NZD) per US dollar—

1.416 (2017)
1.4279 (2016)
1.4279 (2015)
1.4279 (2014 est.)
1.2039 (2013 est.)

COMMUNICATIONS

Telephone system: *general assessment:* satellite-based phone services
domestic: local phone service with international connections via Internet
international: country code—872; satellite earth station—1 (Inmarsat)

Broadcast media: satellite TV from Fiji-based Sky Pacific offering a wide range of international channels

Internet country code: .pn

Internet users: *total:* 54
percent of population: 100% (July 2016 est.)

Communications—note: satellite-based local phone service and broadband Internet connections available in all homes

TRANSPORTATION

Ports and terminals: *major seaport(s):* Adamstown (on Bounty Bay)

MILITARY AND SECURITY

Military—note: defense is the responsibility of the UK

TRANSNATIONAL ISSUES

Disputes—international: none

POLAND

INTRODUCTION

Background: Poland's history as a state began near the middle of the 10th century. By the mid-16th century, the Polish-Lithuanian Commonwealth ruled a vast tract of land in Central and Eastern Europe. During the 18th century, internal disorders weakened the nation, and in a series of agreements between 1772 and 1795, Russia, Prussia, and Austria partitioned Poland among themselves. Poland regained its independence in 1918 only to be overrun by Germany and the Soviet Union in World War II. It became a Soviet satellite state following the war, but its government was comparatively tolerant and progressive. Labor turmoil in 1980 led to the formation of the independent trade union "Solidarity" that over time became a political force with over 10 million members. Free elections in 1989 and 1990 won Solidarity control of the parliament and the presidency, bringing the communist era to a close. A "shock therapy" program during the early 1990s enabled the country to transform its economy into one of the most robust in Central Europe. Poland joined NATO in 1999 and the EU in 2004. With its transformation to a democratic, market-oriented country largely completed and with large investments in defense, energy, and other infrastructure, Poland is an increasingly active member of Euro-Atlantic organizations.

GEOGRAPHY

Location: Central Europe, east of Germany

Geographic coordinates: 52 00 N, 20 00 E

Map references: Europe

Area: *total:* 312,685 sq km
land: 304,255 sq km
water: 8,430 sq km
country comparison to the world: 71

Area—comparative: about twice the size of Georgia; slightly smaller than New Mexico

Land boundaries: *total:* 3,071 km
border countries (7): Belarus 418 km, Czech Republic 796 km, Germany 467 km, Lithuania 104 km, Russia (Kaliningrad Oblast) 210 km, Slovakia 541 km, Ukraine 535 km

Coastline: 440 km

Maritime claims: *territorial sea:* 12 nm
exclusive economic zone: defined by international treaties

Climate: temperate with cold, cloudy, moderately severe winters with frequent precipitation;

mild summers with frequent showers and thundershowers

Terrain: mostly flat plain; mountains along southern border

Elevation: *mean elevation:* 173 m

elevation extremes: *lowest point:* near Raczki Elblaskie -2 m
highest point: Rysy 2,499 m

Natural resources: coal, sulfur, copper, natural gas, silver, lead, salt, amber, arable land

Land use: *agricultural land:* 48.2%
arable land: 36.2%;
permanent crops: 1.3%;
permanent pasture: 10.7%
forest: 30.6%
other: 21.2% (2011 est.)
Irrigated land: 970 sq km (2012)

Population—distribution: population concentrated in the southern area around Krakow and the central area around Warsaw and Lodz, with an extension to the northern coastal city of Gdansk

Natural hazards: flooding

Environment—current issues: decreased emphasis on heavy industry and increased environmental concern by post-communist governments has improved environment; air pollution remains serious because of emissions from coal-fired power plants and the resulting acid rain has caused forest damage; water pollution from industrial and municipal sources is also a problem, as is disposal of hazardous wastes

Environment—international agreements: *party to:* Air Pollution, Antarctic-Environmental Protocol, Antarctic-Marine Living Resources, Antarctic Seals, Antarctic Treaty, Biodiversity, Climate Change, Climate Change-Kyoto Protocol, Desertification, Endangered Species, Environmental Modification, Hazardous Wastes, Law of the Sea, Marine Dumping, Ozone Layer Protection, Ship Pollution, Wetlands
signed, but not ratified: Air Pollution-Nitrogen Oxides, Air Pollution-Persistent Organic Pollutants, Air Pollution-Sulfur 94

Geography—note: historically, an area of conflict because of flat terrain and the lack of natural barriers on the North European Plain

PEOPLE AND SOCIETY

Population: 38,476,269 (July 2017 est.)
country comparison to the world: 36

Nationality: *noun:* Pole(s)
adjective: Polish

Ethnic groups: Polish 96.9%, Silesian 1.1%, German 0.2%, Ukrainian 0.1%, other and unspecified 1.7%
note: represents ethnicity declared first (2011 est.)

Languages: Polish (official) 98.2%, Silesian 1.4%, other 1.1%, unspecified 1.3%
note: data represents the language spoken at home; shares sum to more than 100% because some respondents gave more than one answer on the census; Poland ratified the European Charter for

Regional or Minority Languages in 2009 recognizing Kashub as a regional language, Czech, Hebrew, Yiddish, Belarusian, Lithuanian, German, Armenian, Russian, Slovak, and Ukrainian as national minority languages, and Karaim, Lemko, Romani (Polska Roma and Bergitka Roma), and Tatar as ethnic minority languages (2011 est.)

Religions: Catholic 87.2% (includes Roman Catholic 86.9% and Greek Catholic, Armenian Catholic, and Byzantine-Slavic Catholic .3%), Orthodox 1.3% (almost all are Polish Autocephalous Orthodox), Protestant 0.4% (mainly Augsburg Evangelical and Pentecostal), other 0.4% (includes Jehovah's Witness, Buddhist, Hare Krishna, Gaudiya Vaishnavism, Muslim, Jewish, Mormon), unspecified 10.8% (2012 est.)

Age structure: *0-14 years:* 14.76% (male 2,919,353/female 2,757,923)
15-24 years: 10.7% (male 2,113,358/female 2,003,033)
25-54 years: 43.48% (male 8,447,418/female 8,283,757)
55-64 years: 14.21% (male 2,586,097/female 2,880,031)
65 years and over: 16.86% (male 2,560,847/female 3,924,452) (2017 est.)

Dependency ratios: *total dependency ratio:* 43.9
youth dependency ratio: 21.4
elderly dependency ratio: 22.5
potential support ratio: 4.5 (2015 est.)

Median age: *total:* 40.7 years
male: 39 years
female: 42.4 years (2017 est.)
country comparison to the world: 46

Population growth rate: -0.13% (2017 est.)
country comparison to the world: 206

Birth rate: 9.5 births/1,000 population (2017 est.)
country comparison to the world: 202

Death rate: 10.4 deaths/1,000 population (2017 est.)
country comparison to the world: 33

Net migration rate: -0.4 migrant(s)/1,000 population (2017 est.)
country comparison to the world: 118

Population distribution: population concentrated in the southern area around Krakow and the central area around Warsaw and Lodz, with an extension to the northern coastal city of Gdansk

Urbanization: *urban population:* 60.5% of total population (2017)
rate of urbanization: 0.02% annual rate of change (2015-20 est.)

Major urban areas—population: WARSAW (capital) 1.722 million; Krakow 760,000 (2015)

Sex ratio: *at birth:* 1.06 male(s)/female
0-14 years: 1.06 male(s)/female
15-24 years: 1.05 male(s)/female
25-54 years: 1.02 male(s)/female
55-64 years: 0.9 male(s)/female
65 years and over: 0.64 male(s)/female
total population: 0.94 male(s)/female (2016 est.)

Mother's mean age at first birth: 27.4 years (2014 est.)

Maternal mortality ratio: 3 deaths/100,000 live births (2015 est.)
country comparison to the world: 182

Infant mortality rate: *total:* 4.4 deaths/1,000 live births
male: 4.8 deaths/1,000 live births
female: 4 deaths/1,000 live births (2017 est.)
country comparison to the world: 182

Life expectancy at birth: *total population:* 77.8 years
male: 73.9 years
female: 81.8 years (2017 est.)
country comparison to the world: 67

Total fertility rate: 1.35 children born/woman (2017 est.)
country comparison to the world: 215

Health expenditures: 6.4% of GDP (2014)
country comparison to the world: 97

Physicians density: 2.27 physicians/1,000 population (2014)

Hospital bed density: 6.5 beds/1,000 population (2011)

Drinking water source:
improved:
urban: 99.3% of population
rural: 96.9% of population
total: 98.3% of population
unimproved:
urban: 0.7% of population
rural: 3.1% of population
total: 1.7% of population (2015 est.)

Sanitation facility access:
improved:
urban: 97.5% of population
rural: 96.7% of population
total: 97.2% of population
unimproved:
urban: 2.5% of population
rural: 3.3% of population
total: 2.8% of population (2015 est.)

HIV/AIDS—adult prevalence rate: NA

HIV/AIDS—people living with HIV/AIDS: NA

HIV/AIDS—deaths: NA

Major infectious diseases: *degree of risk:* intermediate
vectorborne disease: tickborne encephalitis (2016)

Obesity—adult prevalence rate: 23.1% (2016)
country comparison to the world: 69

Education expenditures: 4.9% of GDP (2013)
country comparison to the world: 65

Literacy: *definition:* age 15 and over can read and write
total population: 99.8%
male: 99.9%
female: 99.7% (2015 est.)

School life expectancy (primary to tertiary education): *total:* 16 years
male: 16 years
female: 17 years (2013)

Unemployment, youth ages 15-24: *total:* 20.8%
male: 20.7%

female: 20.9% (2015 est.)
country comparison to the world: 34

GOVERNMENT

Country name: *conventional long form:* Republic of Poland
conventional short form: Poland
local long form: Rzeczpospolita Polska
local short form: Polska
etymology: name derives from the Polanians, a west Slavic tribe that united several surrounding Slavic groups (9th-10th centuries A.D.) and who passed on their name to the country; the name of the tribe likely comes from the Slavic "pole" (field or plain), indicating the flat nature of their country

Government type: parliamentary republic

Capital: *name:* Warsaw
geographic coordinates: 52 15 N, 21 00 E
time difference: UTC+1 (6 hours ahead of Washington, DC, during Standard Time)
daylight saving time: +1hr, begins last Sunday in March; ends last Sunday in October

Administrative divisions: 16 provinces (wojewodztwa, singular—wojewodztwo); Dolnoslaskie (Lower Silesia), Kujawsko-Pomorskie (Kuyavia-Pomerania), Lodzkie (Lodz), Lubelskie (Lublin), Lubuskie (Lubusz), Malopolskie (Lesser Poland), Mazowieckie (Masovia), Opolskie (Opole), Podkarpackie (Subcarpathia), Podlaskie, Pomorskie (Pomerania), Slaskie (Silesia), Swietokrzyskie (Holy Cross), Warminsko-Mazurskie (Warmia-Masuria), Wielkopolskie (Greater Poland), Zachodniopomorskie (West Pomerania)

Independence: 11 November 1918 (republic proclaimed); notable earlier dates: 966 (adoption of Christianity, traditional founding date), 1 July 1569 (Polish-Lithuanian Commonwealth created)

National holiday: Constitution Day, 3 May (1791)

Constitution: *history:* several previous; latest adopted 2 April 1997, approved by referendum 25 May 1997, effective 17 October 1997
amendments: proposed by at least one-fifth of Sejm deputies, by the Senate, or by the president of the republic; passage requires at least two-thirds majority vote in the Sejm and absolute majority vote in the Senate; amendments to articles relating to sovereignty, personal freedoms, and constitutional amendment procedures also require passage by majority vote in a referendum; amended 2006, 2009, 2015 (2016)

Legal system: civil law system; judicial review of legislative, administrative, and other governmental acts; constitutional law rulings of the Constitutional Tribunal are final

International law organization participation: accepts compulsory ICJ jurisdiction with reservations; accepts ICCt jurisdiction

Citizenship: *citizenship by birth:* no
citizenship by descent only: both parents must be citizens of Poland
dual citizenship recognized: no

residency requirement for naturalization: 5 years

Suffrage: 18 years of age; universal

Executive branch: *chief of state:* President Andrzej DUDA (since 6 August 2015)

head of government: Prime Minister Mateusz MORAWIECKI (since 11 December 2017); Deputy Prime Minister and Minister of Culture and National Heritage Piotr GLINSKI (since 16 November 2015), Deputy Prime Minister and Minister of Science and Higher Education Jaroslaw GOWIN (since 16 November 2015), Beata SZYDLO, Deputy Prime Minister and Minister of Social Policy (since 11 December 2017)
cabinet: Council of Ministers proposed by the prime minister, appointed by the president, and approved by the Sejm
elections/appointments: president directly elected by absolute majority popular vote in 2 rounds if needed for a 5-year term (eligible for a second term); election last held on 10 with a second round on 24 May 2015 (next to be held in 2020); prime minister, deputy prime ministers, and Council of Ministers appointed by the president and confirmed by the Sejm
election results: Andrzej DUDA elected president in second round; percent of vote—Andrzej DUDA (independent) 51.5%, Bronislaw KOMOROWSKI (independent) 48.5%

Legislative branch: *description:* bicameral legislature consists of the Senate or Senat (100 seats; members directly elected in single-seat constituencies by simple majority vote to serve 4-year terms) and the Sejm (460 seats; members directly elected in multi-seat constituencies by proportional representation vote to serve 4-year terms); note—the designation National Assembly or Zgromadzenie Narodowe is only used on those rare occasions when the 2 houses meet jointly
note: the German minority is exempt from the 5% threshold requirement for seats to the Sejm
elections: Senate—last held on 25 October 2015 (next to be held in October 2019); Sejm—last held on 25 October 2015 (next to be held in October 2019)
election results: Senate—percent of vote by party—NA; seats by party—PiS 61, PO 34, PSL 1, independent 4; Sejm—percent of vote by party—PiS 37.6%, PO 24.1%, K15 8.8%, N 7.6%, PSL 5.1% other 16.8%; seats by party—PiS 235, PO 138, K15 42, N 28, PSL 16, German minority 1

Judicial branch: *highest court(s):* Supreme Court or Sad Najwyzszy (consists of the president of the Supreme Court and 116 judges organized in criminal, civil, labor and social insurance, and military chambers)
judge selection and term of office: president of the Supreme Court nominated by the General Assembly of the Supreme Court and selected by the president of Poland; other judges nominated by the 25-member National Judiciary Council, and appointed by the president of Poland; judges appointed until retirement, usually at age 65, but tenure can be extended

subordinate courts: Constitutional Tribunal; State Tribunal; administrative courts; regional and appellate courts subdivided into military, civil, criminal, labor, and family courts

Political parties and leaders: Civic Platform or PO [Grzegorz SCHETYNA]
Democratic Left Alliance or SLD [Wlodzimierz CZARZASTY]
German Minority of Lower Silesia or MNSO [Ryszard GALLA]
Kukiz 15 or K15 [Pawel KUKIZ]
Law and Justice or PiS [Jaroslaw KACZYNSKI]
Liberty (formerly the Coalition for the Renewal of the Republic-Liberty and Hope or KORWiN) [Janusz KORWIN-MIKKE]
Nowoczesna ("Modern") or N [Katarzyna LUBNAUER]
Polish People's Party or PSL [Wladyslaw KOSINIAK-KAMYSZ]
Razem (Together) [collective leadership]

Political pressure groups and leaders: All Poland Trade Union Alliance or OPZZ [Jan GUZ] (trade union)
Independent Self-Governing Trade Union or Solidarity [Piotr DUDA]
Roman Catholic Church [Archbishop Wojciech POLAK, Archbishop Stanislaw GADECKI]

International organization participation: Arctic Council (observer), Australia Group, BIS, BSEC (observer), CBSS, CD, CE, CEI, CERN, EAPC, EBRD, ECB, EIB, ESA, EU, FAO, IAEA, IBRD, ICAO, ICC (national committees), ICCt, ICRM, IDA, IEA, IFC, IFRCS, IHO, ILO, IMF, IMO, IMSO, Interpol, IOC, IOM, IPU, ISO, ITSO, ITU, ITUC (NGOs), MIGA, MONUSCO, NATO, NEA, NSG, OAS (observer), OECD, OIF (observer), OPCW, OSCE, PCA, Schengen Convention, UN, UNCTAD, UNESCO, UNHCR, UNIDO, UNMIL, UNMISS, UNOCI, UNWTO, UPU, WCO, WFTU (NGOs), WHO, WIPO, WMO, WTO, ZC

Diplomatic representation in the US: *chief of mission:* Ambassador Piotr Antoni WILCZEK (since 18 January 2017)
chancery: 2640 16th Street NW, Washington, DC 20009
telephone: [1] (202) 499-1700
FAX: [1] (202) 328-6271
consulate(s) general: Chicago, Los Angeles, New York

Diplomatic representation from the US: *chief of mission:* Ambassador Paul Wayne JONES (since 7 October 2015)
embassy: Aleje Ujazdowskie 29/31 00-540 Warsaw
mailing address: American Embassy Warsaw, US Department of State, Washington, DC 20521-5010 (pouch)
telephone: [48] (22) 504-2000
FAX: [48] (22) 504-2688
consulate(s) general: Krakow

Flag description: two equal horizontal bands of white (top) and red; colors derive from the Polish emblem—a white eagle on a red field
note: similar to the flags of Indonesia and Monaco which are red (top) and white

National symbol(s): white crowned eagle; national colors: white, red

National anthem: name: "Mazurek Dabrowskiego" (Dabrowski's Mazurka)

lyrics/music: Jozef WYBICKI/traditional

note: adopted 1927; the anthem, commonly known as "Jeszcze Polska nie zginela" (Poland Has Not Yet Perished), was written in 1797; the lyrics resonate strongly with Poles because they reflect the numerous occasions in which the nation's lands have been occupied

ECONOMY

Economy—overview: Poland has the sixth-largest economy in the EU and has long had a reputation as a business-friendly country with largely sound macroeconomic policies. Since 1990, Poland has pursued a policy of economic liberalization. During the 2008-09 economic slowdown Poland was the only EU country to avoid a recession, in part because of the government's loose fiscal policy combined with a commitment to rein in spending in the medium-term Poland is the largest recipient of EU development funds and their cyclical allocation can significantly impact the rate of economic growth.

The Polish economy performed well during the 2014-17 period, with the real GDP growth rate generally exceeding 3%, in part because of increases in government social spending that have helped to accelerate consumer-driven growth. However, since 2015, Poland has implemented new business restrictions and taxes on foreign-dominated economic sectors, including banking and insurance, energy, and healthcare, that have dampened investor sentiment and has increased the government's ownership of some firms. The government reduced the retirement age in 2016 and has had mixed success in introducing new taxes and boosting tax compliance to offset the increased costs of social spending programs and relieve upward pressure on the budget deficit. Some credit ratings agencies estimate that Poland during the next few years is at risk of exceeding the EU's 3%-of-GDP limit on budget deficits, possibly impacting its access to future EU funds. Poland's economy is projected to perform well in the next few years in part because of an anticipated cyclical increase in the use of its EU development funds and continued, robust household spending.

Poland faces several systemic challenges, which include addressing some of the remaining deficiencies in its road and rail infrastructure, business environment, rigid labor code, commercial court system, government red tape, and burdensome tax system, especially for entrepreneurs. Additional long-term challenges include diversifying Poland's energy mix, strengthening investments in innovation, research, and development, as well as stemming the outflow of educated young Poles to other EU member states, especially in light of a coming demographic contraction due to emigration, persistently low fertility rates, and the aging of the Solidarity-era baby boom generation.

GDP (purchasing power parity): $1.111 trillion (2017 est.)
$1.07 trillion (2016 est.)
$1.042 trillion (2015 est.)
note: data are in 2017 dollars
country comparison to the world: 25

GDP (official exchange rate): $510 billion (2016 est.)

GDP—real growth rate: 3.8% (2017 est.)
2.6% (2016 est.)
3.9% (2015 est.)
country comparison to the world: 80

GDP—per capita (PPP): $29,300 (2017 est.)
$28,200 (2016 est.)
$27,400 (2015 est.)
note: data are in 2017 dollars
country comparison to the world: 66

Gross national saving: 19% of GDP (2017 est.)
19.4% of GDP (2016 est.)
19.9% of GDP (2015 est.)
country comparison to the world: 96

GDP—composition, by end use:
household consumption: 58.8%
government consumption: 18.1%
investment in fixed capital: 17.8%
investment in inventories: 0.8%
exports of goods and services: 56.2%
imports of goods and services: -51.8% (2017 est.)

GDP—composition, by sector of origin:
agriculture: 2.4%
industry: 40.2%
services: 64.3% (2017 est.)

Agriculture—products: potatoes, fruits, vegetables, wheat; poultry, eggs, pork, dairy

Industries: machine building, iron and steel, coal mining, chemicals, shipbuilding, food processing, glass, beverages, textiles

Industrial production growth rate: 4.2% (2017 est.)
country comparison to the world: 64

Labor force: 17.6 million (2017 est.)
country comparison to the world: 37

Labor force—by occupation: *agriculture:* 11.5%
industry: 30.4%
services: 57.6% (2015)

Unemployment rate: 4.8% (2017 est.)
6.2% (2016 est.)
country comparison to the world: 65

Population below poverty line: 17.6% (2015 est.)

Household income or consumption by percentage share: *lowest 10%:* 3%
highest 10%: 23.9% (2015 est.)

Distribution of family income—Gini index: 30.8 (2015)
33.7 (2008)
country comparison to the world: 122

Budget: *revenues:* $90.8 billion
expenditures: $102.2 billion (2017 est.)
Taxes and other revenues: 17.8% of GDP (2017 est.)
country comparison to the world: 171

Budget surplus (+) or deficit (-): -2.2% of GDP (2017 est.)

country comparison to the world: 93

Public debt: 46.2% of GDP (2017 est.)
48.4% of GDP (2016 est.)
note: data cover general government debt, and includes debt instruments issued (or owned) by government entities other than the treasury; the data include treasury debt held by foreign entities, the data include subnational entities, as well as intra-governmental debt; intra-governmental debt consists of treasury borrowings from surpluses in the social funds, such as for retirement, medical care, and unemployment; debt instruments for the social funds are not sold at public auctions
country comparison to the world: 114

Fiscal year: calendar year

Inflation rate (consumer prices): 1.9% (2017 est.)
-0.6% (2016 est.)
country comparison to the world: 86

Central bank discount rate: 1.5% (31 December 2016)
2% (31 December 2015)
country comparison to the world: 122

Commercial bank prime lending rate: 4.8% (31 December 2017 est.)
4.74% (31 December 2016 est.)
country comparison to the world: 148

Stock of narrow money: $255.1 billion (31 December 2017 est.)
$195.1 billion (31 December 2016 est.)
country comparison to the world: 21

Stock of broad money: $374.2 billion (31 December 2017 est.)
$300.6 billion (31 December 2016 est.)
country comparison to the world: 30

Stock of domestic credit: $413.8 billion (31 December 2017 est.)
$336.7 billion (31 December 2016 est.)
country comparison to the world: 34

Market value of publicly traded shares: $261.5 billion (31 December 2016 est.)
$277.4 billion (31 December 2015 est.)
$351.7 billion (31 December 2014 est.)
country comparison to the world: 30

Current account balance: -$4.958 billion (2017 est.)
-$959 million (2016 est.)
country comparison to the world: 175

Exports: $221.4 billion (2017 est.)
$195.7 billion (2016 est.)
country comparison to the world: 26

Exports—commodities: machinery and transport equipment 37.8%, intermediate manufactured goods 23.7%, miscellaneous manufactured goods 17.1%, food and live animals 7.6% (2012 est.)

Exports—partners: Germany 27.3%, UK 6.6%, Czech Republic 6.6%, France 5.4%, Italy 4.8%, Netherlands 4.5% (2016)

Imports: $221.8 billion (2017 est.)
$193.6 billion (2016 est.)
country comparison to the world: 21

Imports—commodities: machinery and transport equipment 38%, intermediate manufactured goods

21%, chemicals 15%, minerals, fuels, lubricants, and related materials 9% (2011 est.)

Imports—partners: Germany 28.3%, China 7.9%, Netherlands 6%, Russia 5.8%, Italy 5.3%, France 4.2%, Czech Republic 4.1% (2016)

Reserves of foreign exchange and gold: $115 billion (31 December 2017 est.)
$114.4 billion (31 December 2016 est.)
country comparison to the world: 23

Debt—external: $362 billion (31 December 2017 est.)
$347.8 billion (31 December 2016 est.)
country comparison to the world: 32

Stock of direct foreign investment—at home: $235.7 billion (31 December 2017 est.)
$224.5 billion (31 December 2016 est.)
country comparison to the world: 27

Stock of direct foreign investment—abroad: $68.22 billion (31 December 2017 est.)
$64.52 billion (31 December 2016 est.)
country comparison to the world: 39

Exchange rates: zlotych (PLN) per US dollar—
3.748 (2017 est.)
3.9459 (2016 est.)
3.9459 (2015 est.)
3.7721 (2014 est.)
3.1538 (2013 est.)

ENERGY

Electricity access: electrification—*total population:* 100% (2016)

Electricity—production: 152.1 billion kWh (2015 est.)
country comparison to the world: 27

Electricity—consumption: 141.3 billion kWh (2015 est.)
country comparison to the world: 25

Electricity—exports: 12.02 billion kWh (2016)
country comparison to the world: 19

Electricity—imports: 14.02 billion kWh (2016 est.)
country comparison to the world: 18

Electricity—installed generating capacity: 37.32 million kW (2015 est.)
country comparison to the world: 29

Electricity—from fossil fuels: 77.7% of total installed capacity (2015 est.)
country comparison to the world: 92

Electricity—from nuclear fuels: 0% of total installed capacity (2015 est.)
country comparison to the world: 164

Electricity—from hydroelectric plants: 1.6% of total installed capacity (2015 est.)
country comparison to the world: 142

Electricity—from other renewable sources: 18.8% of total installed capacity (2015 est.)
country comparison to the world: 34

Crude oil—production: 20,100 bbl/day (2016 est.)
country comparison to the world: 68

Crude oil—exports: 4,520 bbl/day (2016 est.)
country comparison to the world: 64

Crude oil—imports: 490,300 bbl/day (2016 est.)
country comparison to the world: 19

Crude oil—proved reserves: 137.8 million bbl (1 January 2017)
country comparison to the world: 69

Refined petroleum products—production: 557,700 bbl/day (2016 est.)
country comparison to the world: 30

Refined petroleum products—consumption: 578,200 bbl/day (2016 est.)
country comparison to the world: 33

Refined petroleum products—exports: 135,000 bbl/day (2016 est.)
country comparison to the world: 38

Refined petroleum products—imports: 173,500 bbl/day (2016 est.)
country comparison to the world: 37

Natural gas—production: 6.132 billion cu m (2015 est.)
country comparison to the world: 48

Natural gas—consumption: 26.78 billion cu m (2015 est.)
country comparison to the world: 39

Natural gas—exports: 56 million cu m (2015 est.)
country comparison to the world: 50

Natural gas—imports: 12.12 billion cu m (2015 est.)
country comparison to the world: 25

Natural gas—proved reserves: 81.66 billion cu m (1 January 2017 es)
country comparison to the world: 58

Carbon dioxide emissions from consumption of energy: 296 million Mt (2015 est.)
country comparison to the world: 22

COMMUNICATIONS

Telephones—fixed lines: *total subscriptions:* 9.345 million
subscriptions per 100 inhabitants: 24 (July 2016 est.)
country comparison to the world: 30

Telephones—mobile cellular: *total:* 55,878,845
subscriptions per 100 inhabitants: 145 (July 2016 est.)
country comparison to the world: 26

Telephone system: *general assessment:* modernization of the telecommunications network has accelerated with market-based competition; fixed-line service, dominated by the former state-owned company, is dwarfed by the growth in mobile-cellular services
domestic: several nation-wide networks provide mobile-cellular service; coverage is generally good; fixed-line service lags in rural areas
international: country code—48; international direct dialing with automated exchanges; satellite earth station—1 with access to Intelsat, Eutelsat, Inmarsat, and Intersputnik (2015)

Broadcast media: state-run public TV operates 2 national channels supplemented by 16 regional channels and several niche channels; privately owned entities operate several national TV networks and a number of special interest channels; many privately owned channels broadcasting locally; roughly half of all households are linked to either satellite or cable TV systems providing access to foreign television networks; state-run public radio operates 5 national networks and 17 regional radio stations; 2 privately owned national radio networks, several commercial stations broadcasting to multiple cities, and many privately owned local radio stations (2007)

Internet country code: .pl

Internet users: *total:* 28,237,820
percent of population: 73.3% (July 2016 est.)
country comparison to the world: 22

TRANSPORTATION

National air transport system: *number of registered air carriers:* 6
inventory of registered aircraft operated by air carriers: 92
annual passenger traffic on registered air carriers: 4,841,128
annual freight traffic on registered air carriers: 120,016,466 mt-km (2015)
Civil aircraft registration country code prefix: SP (2016)

Airports: 126 (2013)
country comparison to the world: 47

Airports—with paved runways: *total:* 87
over 3,047 m: 5
2,438 to 3,047 m: 30
1,524 to 2,437 m: 36
914 to 1,523 m: 10
under 914 m: 6 (2017)

Airports—with unpaved runways: *total:* 39
1,524 to 2,437 m: 1
914 to 1,523 m: 17
under 914 m: 21 (2013)

Heliports: 6 (2013)

Pipelines: gas 14,198 km; oil 1,374 km; refined products 777 km (2013)

Railways: *total:* 19,231 km
broad gauge: 395 km 1.524-m gauge
standard gauge: 18,836 km 1.435-m gauge (11,865 km electrified) (2015)
country comparison to the world: 15

Roadways: *total:* 417,026 km
paved: 287,650 km (includes 1,492 km of expressways)
unpaved: 129,376 km (2014)
country comparison to the world: 17

Waterways: 3,997 km (navigable rivers and canals) (2009)
country comparison to the world: 27

Merchant marine: *total:* 152
by type: container ship 1, general cargo 13, oil tanker 7, other 131 (2017)
country comparison to the world: 73

Ports and terminals: *major seaport(s):* Gdansk, Gdynia, Swinoujscie
river port(s): Szczecin (River Oder)
LNG terminal(s) (import): Swinoujscie

MILITARY AND SECURITY

Military expenditures: 1.99% of GDP (2016)
2.14% of GDP (2015)
1.9% of GDP (2014)
1.77% of GDP (2013)
1.8% of GDP (2012)
country comparison to the world: 44

Military branches: Polish Armed Forces: Land Forces, Navy, Air Force, Special Forces, Territorial Defense Force (2017)
note: Territorial Defense Force only began recruitment in winter 2016

Military service age and obligation: 18-28 years of age for male and female voluntary military service; conscription phased out in 2009-12; service obligation shortened from 12 to 9 months in 2005; women only allowed to serve as officers and non-commissioned officers (2013)

TRANSNATIONAL ISSUES

Disputes—international: as a member state that forms part of the EU's external border, Poland has implemented the strict Schengen border rules to restrict illegal immigration and trade along its eastern borders with Belarus and Ukraine

Refugees and internally displaced persons: refugees (country of origin): 71,302 applicants for forms of legal stay other than asylum (Ukraine) (2015); 9,864 (Russia) (2016)
stateless persons: 10,825 (2016)

Illicit drugs: despite diligent counternarcotics measures and international information sharing on cross-border crimes, a major illicit producer of synthetic drugs for the international market; minor transshipment point for Southwest Asian heroin and Latin American cocaine to Western Europe

PORTUGAL

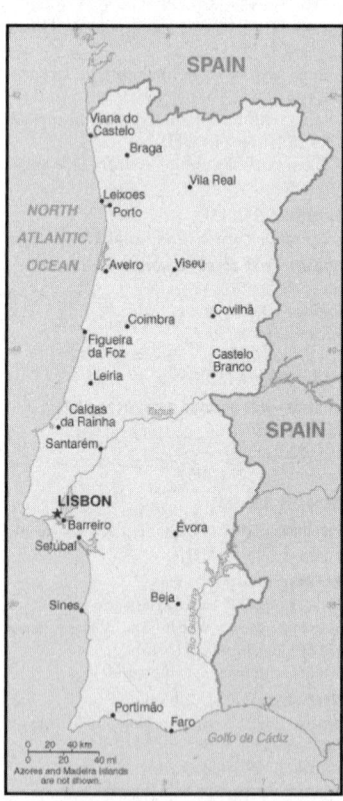

INTRODUCTION

Background: Following its heyday as a global maritime power during the 15th and 16th centuries, Portugal lost much of its wealth and status with the destruction of Lisbon in a 1755 earthquake, occupation during the Napoleonic Wars, and the independence of Brazil, its wealthiest colony, in 1822. A 1910 revolution deposed the monarchy; for most of the next six decades, repressive governments ran the country. In 1974, a left-wing military coup installed broad democratic reforms. The following year, Portugal granted independence to all of its African colonies. Portugal is a founding member of NATO and entered the EC (now the EU) in 1986.

GEOGRAPHY

Location: Southwestern Europe, bordering the North Atlantic Ocean, west of Spain

Geographic coordinates: 39 30 N, 8 00 W

Map references: Europe

Area: *total:* 92,090 sq km
land: 91,470 sq km
water: 620 sq km
note: includes Azores and Madeira Islands
country comparison to the world: 112

Area—comparative: slightly smaller than Virginia

Land boundaries: *total:* 1,224 km
border countries (1): Spain 1,224 km

Coastline: 1,793 km

Maritime claims: *territorial sea:* 12 nm
contiguous zone: 24 nm
exclusive economic zone: 200 nm
continental shelf: 200-m depth or to the depth of exploitation

Climate: maritime temperate; cool and rainy in north, warmer and drier in south

Terrain: the west-flowing Tagus River divides the country: the north is mountainous toward the interior, while the south is characterized by rolling plains

Elevation: *mean elevation:* 372 m

elevation extremes: *lowest point:* Atlantic Ocean 0 m
highest point: Ponta do Pico (Pico or Pico Alto) on Ilha do Pico in the Azores 2,351 m

Natural resources: fish, forests (cork), iron ore, copper, zinc, tin, tungsten, silver, gold, uranium, marble, clay, gypsum, salt, arable land, hydropower

Land use: *agricultural land:* 39.7%
arable land: 11.9%;
permanent crops: 7.8%;
permanent pasture: 20%
forest: 37.8%
other: 22.5% (2011 est.)
Irrigated land: 5,400 sq km (2012)

Population—distribution: concentrations are primarily along or near the Atlantic coast; both Lisbon and the second largest city, Porto, are coastal cities

Natural hazards: Azores subject to severe earthquakes
volcanism: limited volcanic activity in the Azores Islands; Fayal or Faial (1,043 m) last erupted in 1958; most volcanoes have not erupted in centuries; historically active volcanoes include Agua de Pau, Furnas, Pico, Picos Volcanic System, San Jorge, Sete Cidades, and Terceira

Environment—current issues: soil erosion; air pollution caused by industrial and vehicle emissions; water pollution, especially in coastal areas

Environment—international agreements: *party to:* Air Pollution, Biodiversity, Climate Change, Climate Change-Kyoto Protocol, Desertification, Endangered Species, Hazardous Wastes, Law of the Sea, Marine Dumping, Marine Life Conservation, Ozone Layer Protection, Ship Pollution, Tropical Timber 83, Tropical Timber 94, Wetlands, Whaling
signed, but not ratified: Air Pollution-Persistent Organic Pollutants, Air Pollution-Volatile Organic Compounds, Environmental Modification

Geography—note: Azores and Madeira Islands occupy strategic locations along western sea approaches to Strait of Gibraltar

PEOPLE AND SOCIETY

Population: 10,839,514 (July 2017 est.)
country comparison to the world: 84

Nationality: *noun:* Portuguese (singular and plural)
adjective: Portuguese

Ethnic groups: homogeneous Mediterranean population; citizens of black African descent who immigrated to mainland during decolonization number less than 100,000; since 1990, East Europeans have entered Portugal

Languages: Portuguese (official), Mirandese (official, but locally used)

Religions: Roman Catholic 81%, other Christian 3.3%, other (includes Jewish, Muslim, other) 0.6%, none 6.8%, unspecified 8.3%
note: represents population 15 years of age and older (2011 est.)

Age structure: *0-14 years:* 15.34% (male 866,004/female 797,004)
15-24 years: 11.36% (male 653,672/female 577,800)
25-54 years: 41.72% (male 2,298,920/female 2,223,184)
55-64 years: 12.18% (male 617,036/female 702,992)
65 years and over: 19.4% (male 861,270/female 1,241,632) (2017 est.)

Dependency ratios: *total dependency ratio:* 53.4
youth dependency ratio: 21.6
elderly dependency ratio: 31.8
potential support ratio: 3.1 (2015 est.)

Median age: *total:* 42.2 years
male: 40.2 years
female: 44.4 years (2017 est.)
country comparison to the world: 32

Population growth rate: 0.04% (2017 est.)
country comparison to the world: 189

Birth rate: 9 births/1,000 population (2017 est.)
country comparison to the world: 207

Death rate: 11.1 deaths/1,000 population (2017 est.)
country comparison to the world: 29

Net migration rate: 2.5 migrant(s)/1,000 population (2017 est.)
country comparison to the world: 38

Population distribution: concentrations are primarily along or near the Atlantic coast; both Lisbon and the second largest city, Porto, are coastal cities

Urbanization: *urban population:* 64.6% of total population (2017)
rate of urbanization: 0.76% annual rate of change (2015-20 est.)

Major urban areas—population: LISBON (capital) 2.884 million; Porto 1.299 million (2015)

Sex ratio: *at birth:* 1.07 male(s)/female
0-14 years: 1.09 male(s)/female
15-24 years: 1.13 male(s)/female
25-54 years: 1.03 male(s)/female
55-64 years: 0.88 male(s)/female
65 years and over: 0.69 male(s)/female
total population: 0.96 male(s)/female (2016 est.)

Mother's mean age at first birth: 30.2 years (2015 est.)

Maternal mortality ratio: 10 deaths/100,000 live births (2015 est.)
country comparison to the world: 149

Infant mortality rate: *total:* 4.3 deaths/1,000 live births
male: 4.8 deaths/1,000 live births

female: 3.9 deaths/1,000 live births (2017 est.)
country comparison to the world: 189

Life expectancy at birth: *total population:* 79.4 years
male: 76.2 years
female: 82.9 years (2017 est.)
country comparison to the world: 48

Total fertility rate: 1.53 children born/woman (2017 est.)
country comparison to the world: 192

Contraceptive prevalence rate: 73.9% (2014)

Health expenditures: 9.5% of GDP (2014)
country comparison to the world: 31

Physicians density: 4.43 physicians/1,000 population (2014)

Hospital bed density: 3.4 beds/1,000 population (2011)

Drinking water source:
improved:
urban: 100% of population
rural: 100% of population
total: 100% of population
unimproved:
urban: 0% of population
rural: 0% of population
total: 0% of population (2015 est.)

Sanitation facility access:
improved:
urban: 99.6% of population
rural: 99.8% of population
total: 99.7% of population
unimproved:
urban: 0.4% of population
rural: 0.2% of population
total: 0.3% of population (2015 est.)

HIV/AIDS—adult prevalence rate: NA

HIV/AIDS—people living with HIV/AIDS: NA

HIV/AIDS—deaths: NA

Obesity—adult prevalence rate: 20.8% (2016)
country comparison to the world: 95

Education expenditures: 5.3% of GDP (2013)
country comparison to the world: 55

Literacy: *definition:* age 15 and over can read and write
total population: 95.7%
male: 97.1%
female: 94.4% (2015 est.)

School life expectancy (primary to tertiary education): *total:* 17 years
male: 17 years
female: 17 years (2014)

Unemployment, youth ages 15-24: *total:* 28%
male: 27.2%
female: 28.8% (2016 est.)
country comparison to the world: 16

GOVERNMENT

Country name: *conventional long form:* Portuguese Republic
conventional short form: Portugal
local long form: Republica Portuguesa
local short form: Portugal

etymology: name derives from the Roman designation "Portus Cale" meaning "Port of Cale"; Cale was an ancient Celtic town and port in present-day northern Portugal

Government type: semi-presidential republic

Capital: *name:* Lisbon

geographic coordinates: 38 43 N, 9 08 W
time difference: UTC 0 (5 hours ahead of Washington, DC, during Standard Time)
daylight saving time: +1hr, begins last Sunday in March; ends last Sunday in October

Administrative divisions: 18 districts (distritos, singular—distrito) and 2 autonomous regions* (regioes autonomas, singular—regiao autonoma); Aveiro, Acores (Azores)*, Beja, Braga, Braganca, Castelo Branco, Coimbra, Evora, Faro, Guarda, Leiria, Lisboa (Lisbon), Madeira*, Portalegre, Porto, Santarem, Setubal, Viana do Castelo, Vila Real, Viseu

Independence: 1143 (Kingdom of Portugal recognized); 1640 (independence reestablished following 60-years of Spanish rule); 5 October 1910 (republic proclaimed)

National holiday: Portugal Day (Dia de Portugal), 10 June (1580); note—also called Camoes Day, the day that revered national poet Luis de Camoes (1524-80) died

Constitution: history: several previous; latest adopted 2 April 1976, effective 25 April 1976
amendments: proposed by the Assembly of the Republic; adoption requires two-thirds majority vote of Assembly members; amended several times, last in 2005 (2016)

Legal system: civil law system; Constitutional Court review of legislative acts

International law organization participation: accepts compulsory ICJ jurisdiction with reservations; accepts ICCt jurisdiction

Citizenship: *citizenship by birth:* no

citizenship by descent only: at least one parent must be a citizen of Portugal
dual citizenship recognized: yes
residency requirement for naturalization: 10 years; 6 years if from a Portuguese-speaking country

Suffrage: 18 years of age; universal

Executive branch: *chief of state:* President Marcelo REBELO DE SOUSA (since 9 March 2016)

head of government: Prime Minister Antonio Luis Santos da COSTA (since 24 November 2015)
cabinet: Council of Ministers appointed by the president on the recommendation of the prime minister
elections/appointments: president directly elected by absolute majority popular vote in 2 rounds if needed for a 5-year term (eligible for a second term); election last held on 24 January 2016 (next to be held in January 2021); following legislative elections last held in October 2015, the leader of the majority party or majority coalition was appointed prime minister by the president
election results: Marcelo REBELO DE SOUSA elected president; percent of vote—Marcelo REBELO DE SOUSA (PSD) 52%, Antonio

Sampaio da NOVA (independent) 22.9%, Marisa MATISA (BE) 10.1%, Maria de BELEM (independent) 4.2%, other 10.8%

note: there is also a Council of State that acts as a consultative body to the president

Legislative branch: description: unicameral Assembly of the Republic or Assembleia da Republica (230 seats; 226 members directly elected in multi-seat constituencies by proportional representation vote and 4 members—2 each in 2 constituencies representing Portuguese living abroad—directly elected by proportional representation vote; members serve 4-year terms)

elections: last held on 4 October 2015 (next to be held by October 2019)

election results: percent of vote by party—PaF 36.9%, PS 32.3%, B.E. 10.2%, CDU 8.3%, PPD/PSD (Azores and Madeira) 1.5%, PAN 1.4%, other 9.4%; seats by party—PaF 102, PS 86, B.E. 19, CDU 17, PPD/PSD (Azores and Madeira) 5, PAN 1

Judicial branch: highest court(s): Supreme Court or Supremo Tribunal de Justica (consists of 12 justices); Constitutional Court or Tribunal Constitucional (consists of 13 judges)

judge selection and term of office: Supreme Court justices nominated by the president and appointed by the Assembly of the Republic; judges appointed for life; Constitutional Court judges—10 elected by the Assembly and 3 elected by the other Constitutional Court judges; judges elected for 6-year non-renewable terms

subordinate courts: Supreme Administrative Court (Supremo Tribunal Administrativo); Audit Court (Tribunal de Contas); appellate, district, and municipal courts

Political parties and leaders: Democratic and Social Center/Popular Party or CDS-PP [Assuncao CRISTAS]
Ecologist Party "The Greens" or PEV [Heloisa APOLONiA]
People_Animals_Nature Party or PAN [Andre SILVA]
Portuguese Communist Party or PCP [Jeronimo DE SOUSA]
Social Democratic Party or PPD/PSD [Rui RIO]
Socialist Party or PS [Antonio COSTA]
The Left Bloc or BE or o Bloco [Catarina MARTINS]
Unitary Democratic Coalition or CDU [Jeronimo DE SOUSA] (includes PCP and PEV)

Political pressure groups and leaders: Armed Forces Officers' Association or AOFA [Lt. Col. Antonio Costa MOTA]
General Workers Union or UGT [Carlos SILVA]
General Confederation of Portuguesse Workers or CGTP-IN [Armenio CARLOS]
TugaLeaks (a website that has become a mouthpiece for publicizing diverse protest action)
other: media; labor unions

International organization participation: ADB (nonregional member), AfDB (nonregional member), Australia Group, BIS, CD, CE, CERN, CPLP, EAPC, EBRD, ECB, EIB, EMU, ESA, EU, FAO, FATF, IADB, IAEA, IBRD, ICAO, ICC

(national committees), ICCt, ICRM, IDA, IEA, IFAD, IFC, IFRCS, IHO, ILO, IMF, IMO, IMSO, Interpol, IOC, IOM, IPU, ISO, ITSO, ITU, ITUC (NGOs), LAIA (observer), MIGA, MINUSMA, NATO, NEA, NSG, OAS (observer), OECD, OPCW, OSCE, Pacific Alliance (observer), Paris Club (associate), PCA, Schengen Convention, SELEC (observer), UN, UNCTAD, UNESCO, UNHCR, UNIDO, Union Latina, UNWTO, UPU, WCO, WFTU (NGOs), WHO, WIPO, WMO, WTO, ZC

Diplomatic representation in the US: chief of mission: Ambassador Domingos T?eixeira de Abreu Fezas VITAL (since 28 January 2016)
chancery: 2012 Massachusetts Avenue NW, Washington, DC 20036
telephone: [1] (202) 328-8610
FAX: [1] (202) 462-3726
consulate(s) general: Boston, New York, San Francisco
consulate(s): New Bedford (MA), Newark (NJ), Providence (RI)

Diplomatic representation from the US: chief of mission: Ambassador George E. GLASS (since 25 August 2017)
embassy: Avenida das Forcas Armadas, 1600-081 Lisbon
mailing address: Apartado 43033, 1601-301 Lisboa; PSC 83, APO AE 09726
telephone: [351] (21) 727-3300
FAX: [351] (21) 726-9109
consulate(s): Ponta Delgada (Azores)

Flag description: two vertical bands of green (hoist side, two-fifths) and red (three-fifths) with the national coat of arms (armillary sphere and Portuguese shield) centered on the dividing line; explanations for the color meanings are ambiguous, but a popular interpretation has green symbolizing hope and red the blood of those defending the nation

National symbol(s): armillary sphere (a spherical astrolabe modeling objects in the sky and representing the Republic); national colors: red, green

National anthem: name: "A Portugesa" (The Song of the Portuguese)
lyrics/music: Henrique LOPES DE MENDOCA/Alfredo KEIL
note: adopted 1910; "A Portuguesa" was originally written to protest the Portuguese monarchy's acquiescence to the 1890 British ultimatum forcing Portugal to give up areas of Africa; the lyrics refer to the "insult" that resulted from the event

ECONOMY

Economy—overview: Portugal has become a diversified and increasingly service-based economy since joining the European Community—the EU's predecessor—in 1986. Over the following two decades, successive governments privatized many state-controlled firms and liberalized key areas of the economy, including the financial and telecommunications sectors. The country joined the Economic and Monetary Union in 1999 and began

circulating the euro on 1 January 2002 along with 11 other EU members.

The economy grew by more than the EU average for much of the 1990s, but the rate of growth slowed in 2001-08. After the global financial crisis in 2008, Portugal's economy contracted in 2009 and fell into recession from 2011 to 2013, as the government implemented spending cuts and tax increases to comply with conditions of an EU-IMF financial rescue package, signed in May 2011. Portugal successfully exited its EU-IMF program in May 2014, and its economic recovery gained traction in 2015 because of strong exports and a rebound in private consumption. GDP growth accelerated in 2016, and probably reached 2.5 % in 2017. Unemployment remained high, at 9.7% in 2017, but has improved steadily since peaking at 18% in 2013.

The center-left minority Socialist government has unwound some unpopular austerity measures while managing to remain within most EU fiscal targets. The budget deficit fell from 11.2% of GDP in 2010 to 1.8% in 2017, the country's lowest since democracy was restored in 1974, and surpassing the EU and IMF projections of 3%. Portugal exited the EU's excessive deficit procedure in mid-2017.

GDP (purchasing power parity): $311.3 billion (2017 est.)
$303.8 billion (2016 est.)
$299.6 billion (2015 est.)
note: data are in 2017 dollars
country comparison to the world: 56

GDP (official exchange rate): $211.7 billion (2016 est.)

GDP—real growth rate: 2.5% (2017 est.)
1.4% (2016 est.)
1.6% (2015 est.)
country comparison to the world: 136

GDP—per capita (PPP): $30,300 (2017 est.)
$29,400 (2016 est.)
$28,900 (2015 est.)
note: data are in 2017 dollars
country comparison to the world: 65

Gross national saving: 17% of GDP (2017 est.)
15.8% of GDP (2016 est.)
15.5% of GDP (2015 est.)
country comparison to the world: 109

GDP—composition, by end use:
household consumption: 65.7%
government consumption: 17.6%
investment in fixed capital: 15.4%
investment in inventories: -0.2%
exports of goods and services: 42.9%
imports of goods and services: -41.4% (2017 est.)

GDP—composition, by sector of origin:
agriculture: 2.2%
industry: 22.1%
services: 75.7% (2017 est.)

Agriculture—products: grain, potatoes, tomatoes, olives, grapes; sheep, cattle, goats, pigs, poultry, dairy products; fish

Industries: textiles, clothing, footwear, wood and cork, paper and pulp, chemicals, fuels and lubricants, automobiles and auto parts, base metals, minerals, porcelain and ceramics, glassware, technology, telecommunications; dairy products, wine, other foodstuffs; ship construction and refurbishment; tourism, plastics, financial services, optics

Industrial production growth rate: 1% (2017 est.)
country comparison to the world: 170

Labor force: 5.233 million (2017 est.)
country comparison to the world: 80

Labor force—by occupation: *agriculture:* 8.6%
industry: 23.9%
services: 67.5% (2014 est.)

Unemployment rate: 9.7% (2017 est.)
11.1% (2016 est.)
country comparison to the world: 134

Population below poverty line: 19% (2015 est.)

Household income or consumption by percentage share: *lowest 10%:* 2.6%
highest 10%: 25.9% (2015 est.)

Distribution of family income—Gini index: 33.9 (2015 est.)
34 (2014 est.)
country comparison to the world: 102

Budget: *revenues:* $92.99 billion
expenditures: $96.83 billion (2017 est.)
Taxes and other revenues: 43.9% of GDP (2017 est.)
country comparison to the world: 25

Budget surplus (+) or deficit (-): -1.8% of GDP (2017 est.)
country comparison to the world: 80

Public debt: 127.7% of GDP (2017 est.)
130.4% of GDP (2016 est.)
note: data cover general government debt, and includes debt instruments issued (or owned) by government entities other than the treasury; the data include treasury debt held by foreign entities; the data include debt issued by subnational entities, as well as intra-governmental debt; intra-governmental debt consists of treasury borrowings from surpluses in the social funds, such as for retirement, medical care, and unemployment; debt instruments for the social funds are not sold at public auctions
country comparison to the world: 6

Fiscal year: calendar year

Inflation rate (consumer prices): 1.6% (2017 est.)
0.6% (2016 est.)
country comparison to the world: 68

Central bank discount rate: 0% (2016)
0.05% (2015)
note: this is the European Central Bank's rate on the marginal lending facility, which offers overnight credit to banks in the euro area
country comparison to the world: 152

Commercial bank prime lending rate: 3.5% (31 December 2017 est.)
3.77% (31 December 2016 est.)
country comparison to the world: 164

Stock of narrow money: $106.5 billion (31 December 2017 est.)
$81.15 billion (31 December 2016 est.)
note: see entry for the European Union for money supply for the entire euro area; the European

Central Bank (ECB) controls monetary policy for the 18 members of the Economic and Monetary Union (EMU); individual members of the EMU do not control the quantity of money circulating within their own borders
country comparison to the world: 38

Stock of broad money: $216 billion (31 December 2017 est.)
$173.9 billion (31 December 2016 est.)
country comparison to the world: 38

Stock of domestic credit: $343.3 billion (31 December 2017 est.)
$311.5 billion (31 December 2016 est.)
country comparison to the world: 36

Market value of publicly traded shares: $59.84 billion (31 December 2015 est.)
$57.77 billion (31 December 2014 est.)
$79.18 billion (31 December 2013 est.)
country comparison to the world: 46

Current account balance: $888 million (2017 est.)
$1.462 billion (2016 est.)
country comparison to the world: 41

Exports: $62.6 billion (2017 est.)
$54.76 billion (2016 est.)
country comparison to the world: 45

Exports—commodities: agricultural products, foodstuffs, wine, oil products, chemical products, plastics and rubber, hides, leather, wood and cork, wood pulp and paper, textile materials, clothing, footwear, machinery and tools, base metals

Exports—partners: Spain 26.2%, France 12.6%, Germany 11.7%, UK 7%, US 4.9% (2016)

Imports: $74.32 billion (2017 est.)
$64.79 billion (2016 est.)
country comparison to the world: 42

Imports—commodities: agricultural products, chemical products, vehicles and other transport material, optical and precision instruments, computer accessories and parts, semiconductors and related devices, oil products, base metals, food products, textile materials

Imports—partners: Spain 32.8%, Germany 13.5%, France 7.8%, Italy 5.5%, Netherlands 5.1% (2016)

Reserves of foreign exchange and gold: $25.13 billion (31 December 2016 est.)
$19.4 billion (31 December 2015 est.)
country comparison to the world: 54

Debt—external: $449 billion (31 March 2016 est.)
$447 billion (31 March 2015 est.)
country comparison to the world: 29

Stock of direct foreign investment—at home: $158.9 billion (31 December 2017 est.)
$147.1 billion (31 December 2016 est.)
country comparison to the world: 34

Stock of direct foreign investment—abroad: $89.06 billion (31 December 2017 est.)
$84.73 billion (31 December 2016 est.)
country comparison to the world: 37

Exchange rates: euros (EUR) per US dollar—
0.906 (2017 est.)
0.9214 (2016 est.)
0.9214 (2015 est.)
0.7525 (2014 est.)

0.7634 (2013 est.)

ENERGY

Electricity access: electrification—*total population:* 100% (2016)

Electricity—production: 49.66 billion kWh (2015 est.)
country comparison to the world: 53

Electricity—consumption: 47.03 billion kWh (2015 est.)
country comparison to the world: 53

Electricity—exports: 9.701 billion kWh (2016 est.)
country comparison to the world: 24

Electricity—imports: 4.616 billion kWh (2016 est.)
country comparison to the world: 42

Electricity—installed generating capacity: 19.63 million kW (2015 est.)
country comparison to the world: 44

Electricity—from fossil fuels: 37.9% of total installed capacity (2015 est.)
country comparison to the world: 170

Electricity—from nuclear fuels: 0% of total installed capacity (2015 est.)
country comparison to the world: 166

Electricity—from hydroelectric plants: 22.3% of total installed capacity (2015 est.)
country comparison to the world: 84

Electricity—from other renewable sources: 32.5% of total installed capacity (2015 est.)
country comparison to the world: 10

Crude oil—production: 0 bbl/day (2016 est.)
country comparison to the world: 185

Crude oil—exports: 0 bbl/day (2016 est.)
country comparison to the world: 177

Crude oil—imports: 270,600 bbl/day (2016 est.)
country comparison to the world: 26

Crude oil—proved reserves: 0 bbl (1 January 2017 es)
country comparison to the world: 183

Refined petroleum products—production: 308,700 bbl/day (2016 est.)
country comparison to the world: 40

Refined petroleum products—consumption: 234,700 bbl/day (2016 est.)
country comparison to the world: 52

Refined petroleum products—exports: 128,800 bbl/day (2016 est.)
country comparison to the world: 40

Refined petroleum products—imports: 71,920 bbl/day (2016 est.)
country comparison to the world: 69

Natural gas—production: 0 cu m (2014 est.)
country comparison to the world: 185

Natural gas—consumption: 8.371 billion cu m (2015 est.)
country comparison to the world: 58

Natural gas—exports: 0 cu m (2014 est.)
country comparison to the world: 168

Natural gas—imports: 4.713 billion cu m (2015 est.)
country comparison to the world: 33

Natural gas—proved reserves: 0 cu m (1 January 2014 es)
country comparison to the world: 186

Carbon dioxide emissions from consumption of energy: 43.98 million Mt (2014 est.)
country comparison to the world: 65

COMMUNICATIONS

Telephones—fixed lines: *total subscriptions:* 4,787,677
subscriptions per 100 inhabitants: 44 (July 2016 est.)
country comparison to the world: 34

Telephones—mobile cellular: *total:* 11,572,085
subscriptions per 100 inhabitants: 107 (July 2016 est.)
country comparison to the world: 76

Telephone system: *general assessment:* Portugal's telephone system has a state-of-the-art network with broadband, high-speed capabilities
domestic: integrated network of coaxial cables, open-wire, microwave radio relay, and domestic satellite earth stations
international: country code—351; a combination of submarine cables provide connectivity to Europe, North and East Africa, South Africa, the Middle East, Asia, and the US; satellite earth stations—3 Intelsat (2 Atlantic Ocean and 1 Indian Ocean), NA Eutelsat; tropospheric scatter to Azores (2015)

Broadcast media: Radio e Televisao de Portugal (RTP), the publicly owned TV broadcaster, operates 4 domestic channels and external service channels to Africa; overall, roughly 40 domestic TV stations; viewers have widespread access to international broadcasters with more than half of all households connected to multi-channel cable or satellite TV systems; publicly owned radio operates 3 national networks and provides regional and external services; several privately owned national radio stations and some 300 regional and local commercial radio stations (2014)

Internet country code: .pt

Internet users: *total:* 7,629,560
percent of population: 70.4% (July 2016 est.)
country comparison to the world: 52

TRANSPORTATION

National air transport system: *number of registered air carriers:* 12
inventory of registered aircraft operated by air carriers: 122
annual passenger traffic on registered air carriers: 12,635,233
annual freight traffic on registered air carriers: 343,971,094 mt-km (2015)
Civil aircraft registration country code prefix: CR, CS (2016)

Airports: 64 (2013)
country comparison to the world: 77

Airports—with paved runways: *total:* 43
over 3,047 m: 5
2,438 to 3,047 m: 7
1,524 to 2,437 m: 8
914 to 1,523 m: 15
under 914 m: 8 (2017)

Airports—with unpaved runways: *total:* 21
914 to 1,523 m: 1
under 914 m: 20 (2013)

Pipelines: gas 1,344 km; oil 11 km; refined products 188 km (2013)

Railways: *total:* 3,075.1 km
broad gauge: 2,439 km 1.668-m gauge (1,633.4 km electrified)
narrow gauge: 108.1 km 1.000-m gauge
other: 528 km (gauge unspecified) (2014)
country comparison to the world: 58

Roadways: *total:* 82,900 km
paved: 71,294 km (includes 2,613 km of expressways)
unpaved: 11,606 km (2008)
country comparison to the world: 59

Waterways: 210 km (on Douro River from Porto) (2011)
country comparison to the world: 95

Merchant marine: *total:* 466
by type: bulk carrier 52, container ship 165, general cargo 57, oil tanker 7, other 185 (2017)
country comparison to the world: 41

Ports and terminals: *major seaport(s):* Leixoes, Lisbon, Setubal, Sines
LNG terminal(s) (import): Sines

MILITARY AND SECURITY

Military expenditures: 1.84% of GDP (2016)
1.79% of GDP (2015)
1.79% of GDP (2014)
2.09% of GDP (2013)
1.91% of GDP (2012)
country comparison to the world: 77

Military branches: Portuguese Army (Exercito Portuguesa), Portuguese Navy (Marinha Portuguesa; includes Marine Corps), Portuguese Air Force (Forca Aerea Portuguesa, FAP) (2013)

Military service age and obligation: 18-30 years of age for voluntary military service; no compulsory military service, but conscription possible if insufficient volunteers available; women serve in the armed forces, on naval ships since 1993, but are prohibited from serving in some combatant specialties; reserve obligation to age 35 (2012)

TRANSNATIONAL ISSUES

Disputes—international: Portugal does not recognize Spanish sovereignty over the territory of Olivenza based on a difference of interpretation of the 1815 Congress of Vienna and the 1801 Treaty of Badajoz

Refugees and internally displaced persons: *stateless persons:* 14 (2016)

Illicit drugs: seizing record amounts of Latin American cocaine destined for Europe; a European gateway for Southwest Asian heroin; transshipment point for hashish from North Africa to Europe; consumer of Southwest Asian heroin

PUERTO RICO

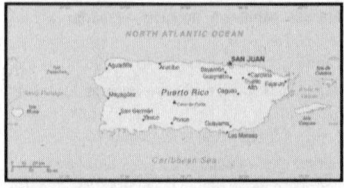

INTRODUCTION

Background: Populated for centuries by aboriginal peoples, the island was claimed by the Spanish Crown in 1493 following Christopher COLUMBUS' second voyage to the Americas. In 1898, after 400 years of colonial rule that saw the indigenous population nearly exterminated and African slave labor introduced, Puerto Rico was ceded to the US as a result of the Spanish-American War. Puerto Ricans were granted US citizenship in 1917. Popularly elected governors have served since 1948. In 1952, a constitution was enacted providing for internal self-government. In plebiscites held in 1967, 1993, and 1998, voters chose not to alter the existing political status with the US, but the results of a 2012 vote left open the possibility of American statehood. Economic recession on the island has led to a net population loss since about 2005, as large numbers of residents moved to the US mainland. The trend has accelerated since 2010; in 2014, Puerto Rico experienced a net population loss to the mainland of 64,000, more than double the net loss of 26,000 in 2010. Hurricane Maria struck the island on 20 September 2017 causing catastrophic damage, including destruction of the electrical grid that had been cripled by Hurricane Irma just two weeks before. It was the worst storm to hit the island in eight decades, and damage is estimated in the tens of billions of dollars.

GEOGRAPHY

Location: Caribbean, island between the Caribbean Sea and the North Atlantic Ocean, east of the Dominican Republic

Geographic coordinates: 18 15 N, 66 30 W

Map references: Central America and the Caribbean

Area: *total:* 9,104 sq km
land: 8,959 sq km
water: 145 sq km
country comparison to the world: 171

Area—comparative: slightly less than three times the size of Rhode Island

Land boundaries: 0 km

Coastline: 501 km

Maritime claims: *territorial sea:* 12 nm
exclusive economic zone: 200 nm

Climate: tropical marine, mild; little seasonal temperature variation

Terrain: mostly mountains with coastal plain in north; precipitous mountains to the sea on west coast; sandy beaches along most coastal areas

Elevation: *mean elevation:* 261 m

elevation extremes: *lowest point:* Caribbean Sea 0 m
highest point: Cerro de Punta 1,338 m

Natural resources: some copper and nickel; potential for onshore and offshore oil

Land use: *agricultural land:* 22%
arable land: 6.6%;
permanent crops: 5.6%;
permanent pasture: 9.8%
forest: 63.2%
other: 14.8% (2011 est.)
Irrigated land: 220 sq km (2012)

Population—distribution: population clusters tend to be found along the coast, the largest of these is found in and around San Juan; an exception to this is a sizeable population located in the interior of the island immediately south of the capital around Caguas; most of the interior, particularly in the western half of the island, is dominated by the Cordillera Central mountains, where population density is low

Natural hazards: periodic droughts; hurricanes

Environment—current issues: soil erosion; occasional drought causing water shortages

Geography—note: important location along the Mona Passage—a key shipping lane to the Panama Canal; San Juan is one of the biggest and best natural harbors in the Caribbean; many small rivers and high central mountains ensure land is well watered; south coast relatively dry; fertile coastal plain belt in north

PEOPLE AND SOCIETY

Population: 3,351,827 (July 2017 est.)
country comparison to the world: 134

Nationality: *noun:* Puerto Rican(s) (US citizens)
adjective: Puerto Rican

Ethnic groups: white 75.8%, black/African American 12.4%, other 8.5% (includes American Indian, Alaskan Native, Native Hawaiian, other Pacific Islander, and others), mixed 3.3%
note: 99% of the population is Latino (2010 est.)

Languages: Spanish, English

Religions: Roman Catholic 85%, Protestant and other 15%

Age structure: *0-14 years:* 15.77% (male 270,656/female 258,073)
15-24 years: 13.71% (male 233,667/female 225,812)
25-54 years: 38.1% (male 607,954/female 669,149)
55-64 years: 12.93% (male 198,720/female 234,713)
65 years and over: 19.48% (male 281,413/female 371,670) (2017 est.)

Dependency ratios: *total dependency ratio:* 49.6
youth dependency ratio: 27.9
elderly dependency ratio: 21.7
potential support ratio: 4.6 (2015 est.)

Median age: *total:* 41.5 years
male: 39.5 years
female: 43.2 years (2017 est.)
country comparison to the world: 52

Population growth rate: -1.74% (2017 est.)
country comparison to the world: 233

Birth rate: 8.1 births/1,000 population (2017 est.)
country comparison to the world: 222

Death rate: 8.6 deaths/1,000 population (2017 est.)
country comparison to the world: 76

Net migration rate: -16.9 migrant(s)/1,000 population (2017 est.)
country comparison to the world: 217

Population distribution: population clusters tend to be found along the coast, the largest of these is found in and around San Juan; an exception to this is a sizeable population located in the interior of the island immediately south of the capital around Caguas; most of the interior, particularly in the western half of the island, is dominated by the Cordillera Central mountains, where population density is low

Urbanization: *urban population:* 93.5% of total population (2017)
rate of urbanization: -0.03% annual rate of change (2015-20 est.)

Major urban areas—population: SAN JUAN (capital) 2.463 million (2015)

Sex ratio: *at birth:* 1.02 male(s)/female
0-14 years: 1.04 male(s)/female
15-24 years: 1.05 male(s)/female
25-54 years: 0.92 male(s)/female
55-64 years: 0.83 male(s)/female
65 years and over: 0.76 male(s)/female
total population: 0.91 male(s)/female (2016 est.)

Maternal mortality ratio: 14 deaths/100,000 live births (2015 est.)
country comparison to the world: 139

Infant mortality rate: *total:* 6.4 deaths/1,000 live births
male: 7 deaths/1,000 live births
female: 5.8 deaths/1,000 live births (2017 est.)
country comparison to the world: 166

Life expectancy at birth: *total population:* 80.9 years

male: 77.6 years
female: 84.4 years (2017 est.)
country comparison to the world: 32

Total fertility rate: 1.22 children born/woman (2017 est.)
country comparison to the world: 220

Drinking water source:
improved:
urban: 93.6% of population
rural: 93.6% of population
total: 93.6% of population
unimproved:
urban: 6.4% of population
rural: 6.4% of population
total: 6.4% of population (2001 est.)

Sanitation facility access:
improved:
urban: 99.3% of population
rural: 99.3% of population
total: 99.3% of population
unimproved:
urban: 0.7% of population
rural: 0.7% of population
total: 0.7% of population (2015 est.)

HIV/AIDS—adult prevalence rate: NA

HIV/AIDS—people living with HIV/AIDS: NA

HIV/AIDS—deaths: NA

Major infectious diseases: *note:* active local transmission of Zika virus by Aedes species mosquitoes has been identified in this country (as of August 2016); it poses an important risk (a large number of cases possible) among US citizens if bitten by an infective mosquito; other less common ways to get Zika are through sex, via blood transfusion, or during pregnancy, in which the pregnant woman passes Zika virus to her fetus (2016)

Education expenditures: 6.4% of GDP (2013)

Literacy: *definition:* age 15 and over can read and write
total population: 93.3%
male: 92.8%
female: 93.8% (2015 est.)

School life expectancy (primary to tertiary education): *total:* 14 years
male: 13 years
female: 15 years (2014)

Unemployment, youth ages 15-24: *total:* 26.6%
male: 28.9%
female: 23.1% (2012 est.)
country comparison to the world: 33

GOVERNMENT

Country name: *conventional long form:* Commonwealth of Puerto Rico
conventional short form: Puerto Rico
etymology: Christopher COLUMBUS named the island San Juan Bautista (Saint John the Baptist) and the capital city and main port Cuidad de Puerto Rico (Rich Port City); over time, however, the names were shortened and transposed and the island came to be called Puerto Rico and its capital San Juan

Dependency status: unincorporated, organized territory of the US with commonwealth status; policy relations between Puerto Rico and the US conducted under the jurisdiction of the Office of the President

Government type: presidential democracy; a self-governing commonwealth in political association with the US

Capital: *name:* San Juan

geographic coordinates: 18 28 N, 66 07 W

time difference: UTC-4 (1 hour ahead of Washington, DC, during Standard Time)

Administrative divisions: none (territory of the US with commonwealth status); there are no first-order administrative divisions as defined by the US Government, but there are 78 municipalities (municipios, singular—municipio) at the second order; Adjuntas, Aguada, Aguadilla, Aguas Buenas, Aibonito, Anasco, Arecibo, Arroyo, Barceloneta, Barranquitas, Bayamon, Cabo Rojo, Caguas, Camuy, Canovanas, Carolina, Catano, Cayey, Ceiba, Ciales, Cidra, Coamo, Comerio, Corozal, Culebra, Dorado, Fajardo, Florida, Guanica, Guayama, Guayanilla, Guaynabo, Gurabo, Hatillo, Hormigueros, Humacao, Isabela, Jayuya, Juana Diaz, Juncos, Lajas, Lares, Las Marias, Las Piedras, Loiza, Luquillo, Manati, Maricao, Maunabo, Mayaguez, Moca, Morovis, Naguabo, Naranjito, Orocovis, Patillas, Penuelas, Ponce, Quebradillas, Rincon, Rio Grande, Sabana Grande, Salinas, San German, San Juan, San Lorenzo, San Sebastian, Santa Isabel, Toa Alta, Toa Baja, Trujillo Alto, Utuado, Vega Alta, Vega Baja, Vieques, Villalba, Yabucoa, Yauco

Independence: none (territory of the US with commonwealth status)

National holiday: US Independence Day, 4 July (1776); Puerto Rico Constitution Day, 25 July (1952)

Constitution: previous 1900 (Organic Act, or Foraker Act); latest ratified 3 March 1952, approved 3 July 1952, effective 25 July 1952 (2016)

Legal system: civil law system based on the Spanish civil code and within the framework of the US federal system

Citizenship: see United States

Suffrage: 18 years of age; universal; note—island residents are US citizens but do not vote in US presidential elections

Executive branch: *chief of state:* President Donald J. TRUMP (since 20 January 2017); Vice President Michael R. PENCE (since 20 January 2017)

head of government: Governor Ricardo ROSSELLO (since 2 January 2017)

cabinet: Cabinet appointed by governor with the consent of the Legislative Assembly

elections/appointments: president and vice president indirectly elected on the same ballot by an Electoral College of 'electors' chosen from each state; president and vice president serve a 4-year term (eligible for a second term); under the US Constitution, residents of Puerto Rico do not

vote in elections for US president and vice president; however, they may vote in Democratic and Republican party presidential primary elections; governor directly elected by simple majority popular vote for a 4-year term (no term limits); election last held on 8 November 2016 (next to be held in November 2020)

election results: Ricardo ROSSELLO elected governor; percent of vote—Ricardo ROSSELLO (PNP) 41.8%, David BERNIER (PPD) 38.9%, Alexandra LUGARO (independent) 11.1%, Manuel CIDRE (independent) 5.7%

Legislative branch: *description:* bicameral Legislative Assembly or Asamblea Legislativa consists of the Senate or Senado (27 seats; 16 members directly elected in multi-seat constituencies by simple majority vote and 11 at-large members directly elected by simple majority vote to serve 4-year terms); the House of Representatives or Camara de Representantes (51 seats; members directly elected in single-seat constituencies by simple majority vote to serve 4-year terms)

elections: Senate—last held on 8 November 2016 (next to be held on 3 November 2020); House of Representatives—last held on 8 November 2016 (next to be held on 3 November 2020)

election results: Senate—percent of vote by party—NA; seats by party—PNP 21, PPD 7, PIP 1, Independent 1; House of Representatives—percent of vote by party—NA; seats by party—PNP 34, PPD 16, PIP 1

note: Puerto Rico directly elects 1 member by simple majority vote to serve a 4-year term as a commissioner to the US House of Representatives; the commissioner can vote when serving on a committee and when the House meets as the Committee of the Whole House but not when legislation is submitted for a "full floor" House vote; election of commissioner last held on 8 November 2016 (next to be held on 6 November 2018)

Judicial branch: *highest court(s):* Supreme Court (consists of the chief justice and 8 associate justices)

judge selection and term of office: justices appointed by the governor and confirmed by majority Senate vote; judges serve until compulsory retirement at age 70

subordinate courts: Court of Appeals; First Instance Court comprised of superior and municipal courts

Political parties and leaders: National Democratic Party [Charlie RODRIGUEZ]
National Republican Party of Puerto Rico [Jennifer GONZALEZ]
New Progressive Party or PNP [Ricardo ROSSELLO] (pro-US statehood)
Popular Democratic Party or PPD [Alejandro GARCIA Padilla] (pro-commonwealth)
Puerto Rican Independence Party or PIP [Ruben BERRIOS Martinez] (pro-independence)

Political pressure groups and leaders: Boricua Popular Army or EPB (a revolutionary group also known as Los Macheteros)

International organization participation: AOSIS (observer), Caricom (observer), Interpol

(subbureau), IOC, UNWTO (associate), UPU, WFTU (NGOs)

Diplomatic representation in the US: none (territory of the US)

Diplomatic representation from the US: none (territory of the US with commonwealth status)

Flag description: five equal horizontal bands of red (top, center, and bottom) alternating with white; a blue isosceles triangle based on the hoist side bears a large, white, five-pointed star in the center; the white star symbolizes Puerto Rico; the three sides of the triangle signify the executive, legislative and judicial parts of the government; blue stands for the sky and the coastal waters; red symbolizes the blood shed by warriors, while white represents liberty, victory, and peace

note: design initially influenced by the US flag, but similar to the Cuban flag, with the colors of the bands and triangle reversed

National symbol(s): Puerto Rican spindalis (bird), coqui (frog); national colors: red, white, blue

National anthem: *name:* "La Borinquena" (The Puerto Rican)

lyrics/music: Manuel Fernandez JUNCOS/Felix Astol ARTES

note: music adopted 1952, lyrics adopted 1977; the local anthem's name is a reference to the indigenous name of the island, Borinquen; the music was originally composed as a dance in 1867 and gained popularity in the early 20th century; there is some evidence that the music was written by Francisco RAMIREZ; as a commonwealth of the US, "The Star-Spangled Banner" is official (see United States)

ECONOMY

Economy—overview: Puerto Rico had one of the most dynamic economies in the Caribbean region until 2006; however, growth has been negative for each of the last 11 years. The downturn coincided with the phaseout of tax preferences that had led US firms to invest heavily in the Commonwealth since the 1950s, and a steep rise in the price of oil, which generates most of the island's electricity.

Diminished job opportunities prompted a sharp rise in outmigration, as many Puerto Ricans sought jobs on the US mainland. Unemployment reached 16% in 2011, but declined to 11.5% in December 2017. US minimum wage laws apply in Puerto Rico, hampering job expansion. Per capita income is about two-thirds that of the US mainland.

The industrial sector greatly exceeds agriculture as the locus of economic activity and income. Tourism has traditionally been an important source of income with estimated arrivals of more than 3.6 million tourists in 2008. Puerto Rico's merchandise trade surplus is exceptionally strong, with exports nearly 50% greater than imports, and its current account surplus about 10% of GDP.

Closing the budget deficit while restoring economic growth and employment remain the central concerns of the government. The gap between revenues and expenditures amounted to 0.6% of GDP in 2016, although analysts believe that not all expenditures have been accounted for in the budget and a better accounting of costs would yield an overall deficit of roughly 5% of GDP. Public debt remained steady at 92.5% of GDP in 2017, about $17,000 per person, or nearly three times the per capita debt of the State of Connecticut, the highest in the US. Much of that debt was issued by state-run schools and public corporations, including water and electric utilities. In June 2015, Governor Alejandro GARCIA Padilla announced that the island could not pay back at least $73 billion in debt and that it would seek a deal with its creditors.

Hurricane Maria hit Puerto Rico square on in September 2017, causing electrical power outages to 90% of the territory, as well as extensive loss of housing and infrastructure and contamination of potable water. Despite massive efforts, more than 40% of the territory remained without electricity as of yearend 2017. As a result of the destruction, many Puerto Ricans have emigrated to the US mainland.

GDP (purchasing power parity): $127.3 billion (2017 est.)
$131 billion (2016 est.)
$134.5 billion (2015 est.)
note: data are in 2017 dollars
country comparison to the world: 82

GDP (official exchange rate): $103.2 billion (2016 est.)

GDP—real growth rate: -2.8% (2017 est.)
-2.6% (2016 est.)
-1.1% (2015 est.)
country comparison to the world: 215

GDP—per capita (PPP): $37,900 (2017 est.)
$38,400 (2016 est.)
$38,700 (2015 est.)
note: data are in 2017 dollars
country comparison to the world: 50

GDP—composition, by end use:
household consumption: 87.7%
government consumption: 12.2%
investment in fixed capital: 11.7%
investment in inventories: 0.5%
exports of goods and services: 117.8%
imports of goods and services: -129.8% (2017 est.)

GDP—composition, by sector of origin:
agriculture: 0.8%
industry: 50.1%
services: 49.1% (2017 est.)

Agriculture—products: sugarcane, coffee, pineapples, plantains, bananas; livestock products, chickens

Industries: pharmaceuticals, electronics, apparel, food products, tourism

Industrial production growth rate: -2.1% (2017 est.)
country comparison to the world: 195

Labor force: 1.139 million (December 2014 est)
country comparison to the world: 142

Labor force—by occupation: *agriculture:* 2.1%
industry: 19%

services: 79% (2005 est.)

Unemployment rate: 11.5% (2017 est.)
11.8% (2016 est.)
country comparison to the world: 148

Population below poverty line: NA%

Household income or consumption by percentage share: *lowest 10%:* NA%
highest 10%: NA%

Budget: *revenues:* $9.268 billion
expenditures: $9.974 billion (2017 est.)
Taxes and other revenues: 9% of GDP (2017 est.)
country comparison to the world: 215

Budget surplus (+) or deficit (-): -0.7% of GDP (2017 est.)
country comparison to the world: 53

Public debt: 91.6% of GDP (2016 est.)
91.6% of GDP (2016 est.)
country comparison to the world: 24

Fiscal year: 1 July–30 June

Inflation rate (consumer prices): 1.1% (2017 est.)
-0.3% (2016 est.)
country comparison to the world: 46

Commercial bank prime lending rate: 5% (31 December 2017 est.)
4% (31 December 2016 est.)
country comparison to the world: 145

Market value of publicly traded shares: $NA

Exports: $73.16 billion (2017 est.)
$73.2 billion (2016 est.)
country comparison to the world: 41

Exports—commodities: chemicals, electronics, apparel, canned tuna, rum, beverage concentrates, medical equipment

Imports: $49.01 billion (2017 est.)
$48.86 billion (2016 est.)
country comparison to the world: 51

Imports—commodities: chemicals, machinery and equipment, clothing, food, fish, petroleum products

Debt—external: $56.82 billion (31 December 2010 est.)
$52.98 billion (31 December 2009 est.)
country comparison to the world: 62

Exchange rates: the US dollar is used

ENERGY

Electricity access: *population without electricity:* 357,805
electrification—total population: 91%
electrification—urban areas: 91%
electrification—rural areas: 80% (2012)

Electricity—production: 20.3 billion kWh (2015 est.)
country comparison to the world: 75

Electricity—consumption: 18.88 billion kWh (2015 est.)
country comparison to the world: 72

Electricity—exports: 0 kWh (2016 est.)
country comparison to the world: 189

Electricity—imports: 0 kWh (2016 est.)
country comparison to the world: 193

Electricity—installed generating capacity: 6.118 million kW (2015 est.)
country comparison to the world: 75

Electricity—from fossil fuels: 94.8% of total installed capacity (2015 est.)
country comparison to the world: 56

Electricity—from nuclear fuels: 0% of total installed capacity (2015 est.)
country comparison to the world: 173

Electricity—from hydroelectric plants: 1.6% of total installed capacity (2015 est.)
country comparison to the world: 141

Electricity—from other renewable sources: 4.2% of total installed capacity (2015 est.)
country comparison to the world: 104

Crude oil—production: 0 bbl/day (2016 est.)
country comparison to the world: 186

Crude oil—exports: 0 bbl/day (2014 est.)
country comparison to the world: 181

Crude oil—imports: 0 bbl/day (2014 est.)
country comparison to the world: 181

Crude oil—proved reserves: 0 bbl (1 January 2017 es)
country comparison to the world: 184

Refined petroleum products—production: 0 bbl/day (2014 est.)
country comparison to the world: 190

Refined petroleum products—consumption: 155,000 bbl/day (2015 est.)
country comparison to the world: 68

Refined petroleum products—exports: 6,274 bbl/day (2014 est.)
country comparison to the world: 90

Refined petroleum products—imports: 158,800 bbl/day (2014 est.)
country comparison to the world: 44

Natural gas—production: 0 cu m (2014 est.)
country comparison to the world: 187

Natural gas—consumption: 2.24 billion cu m (2015 est.)
country comparison to the world: 84

Natural gas—exports: 0 cu m (2014 est.)
country comparison to the world: 172

Natural gas—imports: 1.48 billion cu m (2015 est.)
country comparison to the world: 54

Natural gas—proved reserves: 0 cu m (1 January 2014 es)
country comparison to the world: 188

Carbon dioxide emissions from consumption of energy: 19 million Mt (2013 est.)
country comparison to the world: 82

COMMUNICATIONS

Telephones—fixed lines: *total subscriptions:* 813,546
subscriptions per 100 inhabitants: 23 (July 2016 est.)
country comparison to the world: 86

Telephones—mobile cellular: *total:* 3,227,281

733

subscriptions per 100 inhabitants: 90 (July 2016 est.)
country comparison to the world: 137

Telephone system: *general assessment:* modern system integrated with that of the US by high-capacity submarine cable and Intelsat with high-speed data capability
domestic: digital telephone system; mobile-cellular services
international: country code—1-787, 939; submarine cables provide connectivity to the US, Caribbean, Central and South America; satellite earth station—1 Intelsat (2016)

Broadcast media: more than 30 TV stations operating; cable TV subscription services are available; roughly 125 radio stations (2007)

Internet country code: .pr

Internet users: *total:* 2,873,895

percent of population: 80.3% (July 2016 est.)
country comparison to the world: 98

TRANSPORTATION

Airports: 29 (2013)
country comparison to the world: 119

Airports—with paved runways: *total:* 17
over 3,047 m: 2
2,438 to 3,047 m: 1
1,524 to 2,437 m: 2
914 to 1,523 m: 7
under 914 m: 5 (2017)

Airports—with unpaved runways: *total:* 12
1,524 to 2,437 m: 1
914 to 1,523 m: 1
under 914 m: 10 (2013)

Roadways: *total:* 26,862 km (includes 454 km of expressways) (2012)

country comparison to the world: 99

Ports and terminals: *major seaport(s):* Ensenada Honda, Mayaguez, Playa de Guayanilla, Playa de Ponce, San Juan
container port(s) (TEUs): San Juan (1,484,595)
LNG terminal(s) (import): Guayanilla Bay

MILITARY AND SECURITY

Military branches: no regular indigenous military forces; paramilitary National Guard, Police Force

Military—note: defense is the responsibility of the US

TRANSNATIONAL ISSUES

Disputes—international: increasing numbers of illegal migrants from the Dominican Republic cross the Mona Passage to Puerto Rico each year looking for work

QATAR

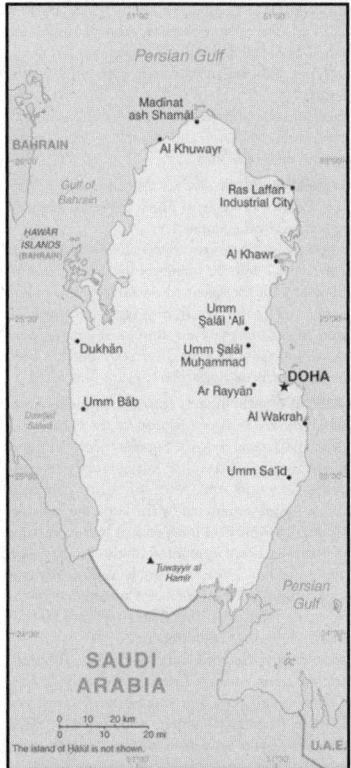

having prioritized improving the domestic welfare of Qataris, including establishing advanced healthcare and education systems and expanding the country's infrastructure in anticipation of Doha's hosting of the 2022 World Cup.

Recently, Qatar's relationships with its neighbors have been tense at times. Following the outbreak of regional unrest in 2011, Doha prided itself on its support for many popular revolutions, particularly in Libya and Syria. This stance was to the detriment of Qatar's relations with Bahrain, Saudi Arabia, and the United Arab Emirates (UAE), which temporarily recalled their respective ambassadors from Doha in March 2014. TAMIM later oversaw a warming of Qatar's relations with Bahrain, Saudi Arabia, and the UAE in November 2014 following Kuwaiti mediation and signing of the Riyadh Agreement. In June 2017, however, the Quartet—Bahrain, Egypt, Saudi Arabia, and the UAE—cut diplomatic and economic ties with Qatar in response to alleged violations of the agreement.

GEOGRAPHY

Location: Middle East, peninsula bordering the Persian Gulf and Saudi Arabia

Geographic coordinates: 25 30 N, 51 15 E

Map references: Middle East

Area: *total:* 11,586 sq km
land: 11,586 sq km
water: 0 sq km
country comparison to the world: 165

Area—comparative: almost twice the size of Delaware; slightly smaller than Connecticut

Land boundaries: *total:* 87 km
border countries (1): Saudi Arabia 87 km

Coastline: 563 km

Maritime claims: *territorial sea:* 12 nm
contiguous zone: 24 nm
exclusive economic zone: as determined by bilateral agreements or the median line

Climate: arid; mild, pleasant winters; very hot, humid summers

Terrain: mostly flat and barren desert

Elevation: *mean elevation:* 28 m

elevation extremes: *lowest point:* Persian Gulf 0 m
highest point: Tuwayyir al Hamir 103 m

Natural resources: petroleum, natural gas, fish

Land use: *agricultural land:* 5.6%
arable land: 1.1%;
permanent crops: 0.2%;
permanent pasture: 4.3%
forest: 0%
other: 94.4% (2011 est.)
Irrigated land: 130 sq km (2012)

Population—distribution: most of the population is clustered in or around the capital of Doha on the eastern side of the peninsula

Natural hazards: haze, dust storms, sandstorms common

Environment—current issues: limited natural freshwater resources are increasing dependence on large-scale desalination facilities

Environment—international agreements: *party to:* Biodiversity, Climate Change, Climate Change-Kyoto Protocol, Desertification, Endangered Species, Hazardous Wastes, Law of the Sea, Ozone Layer Protection, Ship Pollution
signed, but not ratified: none of the selected agreements

Geography—note: the peninsula occupies a strategic location in the central Persian Gulf near major petroleum deposits

PEOPLE AND SOCIETY

Population: 2,314,307 (July 2017 est.)
country comparison to the world: 143

Nationality: *noun:* Qatari(s)
adjective: Qatari

Ethnic groups: non-Qatari 88.4%, Qatari 11.6% (2015 est.)

Languages: Arabic (official), English commonly used as a second language

Religions: Muslim 67.7%, Christian 13.8%, Hindu 13.8%, Buddhist 3.1%, folk religion <.1%, Jewish <.1%, other 0.7%, unaffiliated 0.9% (2010 est.)

Age structure: *0-14 years:* 12.63% (male 148,021/female 144,252)
15-24 years: 12.35% (male 206,055/female 79,859)
25-54 years: 70.59% (male 1,359,383/female 274,334)
55-64 years: 3.42% (male 61,051/female 18,203)
65 years and over: 1% (male 14,932/female 8,217) (2017 est.)

Dependency ratios: *total dependency ratio:* 17.5
youth dependency ratio: 16.3
elderly dependency ratio: 1.3
potential support ratio: 78.1 (2015 est.)

Median age: *total:* 33.2 years
male: 34.3 years
female: 28.1 years (2017 est.)
country comparison to the world: 90

Population growth rate: 2.27% (2017 est.)
country comparison to the world: 33

Birth rate: 9.6 births/1,000 population (2017 est.)
country comparison to the world: 199

Death rate: 1.5 deaths/1,000 population (2017 est.)
country comparison to the world: 226

Net migration rate: 14.6 migrant(s)/1,000 population (2017 est.)
country comparison to the world: 3

Population distribution: most of the population is clustered in or around the capital of Doha on the eastern side of the peninsula

Urbanization: *urban population:* 99.4% of total population (2017)

INTRODUCTION

Background: Ruled by the Al Thani family since the mid-1800s, Qatar within the last 60 years transformed itself from a poor British protectorate noted mainly for pearling into an independent state with significant oil and natural gas revenues. The continuous siphoning off of petroleum revenue through the mid-1990s by Qatari amirs permanently residing in Europe had stunted Qatar's economic growth. Former amir HAMAD bin Khalifa Al Thani, who overthrew his father in a bloodless coup in 1995, ushered in wide-sweeping political and media reforms, unprecedented economic investment, and a growing Qatari regional leadership role, in part through the creation of the pan-Arab satellite news network Al-Jazeera and Qatar's mediation of some regional conflicts. In the 2000s, Qatar resolved its longstanding border disputes with both Bahrain and Saudi Arabia and by 2007 had attained the highest per capita income in the world. Qatar did not experience domestic unrest or violence like that seen in other Near Eastern and North African countries in 2010-11, due in part to its immense wealth. In mid-2013, HAMAD peacefully abdicated, transferring power to his son, the current Amir TAMIM bin Hamad. TAMIM remains popular with the Qatari public,

THE CIA WORLD FACTBOOK

rate of urbanization: 1.63% annual rate of change (2015-20 est.)

Major urban areas—population: DOHA (capital) 718,000 (2015)

Sex ratio: *at birth:* 1.02 male(s)/female
0-14 years: 1.03 male(s)/female
15-24 years: 2.64 male(s)/female
25-54 years: 4.91 male(s)/female
55-64 years: 3.38 male(s)/female
65 years and over: 1.71 male(s)/female
total population: 3.41 male(s)/female (2016 est.)

Maternal mortality ratio: 13 deaths/100,000 live births (2015 est.)
country comparison to the world: 140

Infant mortality rate: *total:* 6.2 deaths/1,000 live births
male: 6.4 deaths/1,000 live births
female: 5.9 deaths/1,000 live births (2017 est.)
country comparison to the world: 167

Life expectancy at birth: *total population:* 78.9 years
male: 76.8 years
female: 81 years (2017 est.)
country comparison to the world: 52

Total fertility rate: 1.9 children born/woman (2017 est.)
country comparison to the world: 133

Contraceptive prevalence rate: 37.5% (2012)

Health expenditures: 2.2% of GDP (2014)
country comparison to the world: 189

Physicians density: 1.96 physicians/1,000 population (2014)

Hospital bed density: 1.2 beds/1,000 population (2012)

Drinking water source:
improved:
urban: 100% of population
rural: 100% of population
total: 100% of population
unimproved:
urban: 0% of population
rural: 0% of population
total: 0% of population (2015 est.)

Sanitation facility access:
improved:
urban: 98% of population
rural: 98% of population
total: 98% of population
unimproved:
urban: 2% of population
rural: 2% of population
total: 2% of population (2015 est.)

HIV/AIDS—adult prevalence rate: <.1% (2016 est.)

HIV/AIDS—people living with HIV/AIDS: <100 (2016 est.)

HIV/AIDS—deaths: <100 (2016 est.)

Obesity—adult prevalence rate: 35.1% (2016)
country comparison to the world: 15

Education expenditures: 3.5% of GDP (2014)
country comparison to the world: 154

Literacy: *definition:* age 15 and over can read and write
total population: 97.3%
male: 97.4%
female: 96.8% (2015 est.)

School life expectancy (primary to tertiary education): *total:* 13 years
male: 13 years
female: 14 years (2011)

Unemployment, youth ages 15-24: *total:* 0.6%
male: 0.2%
female: 2.2% (2015 est.)
country comparison to the world: 134

GOVERNMENT

Country name: *conventional long form:* State of Qatar
conventional short form: Qatar
local long form: Dawlat Qatar
local short form: Qatar
note: closest approximation of the native pronunciation is gattar or cottar
etymology: the origin of the name is uncertain, but it dates back at least 2,000 years since a term "Catharrei" was used to describe the inhabitants of the peninsula by Pliny the Elder (1st century A.D.), and a "Catara" peninsula is depicted on a map by Ptolemy (2nd century A.D.)

Government type: absolute monarchy

Capital: *name:* Doha

geographic coordinates: 25 17 N, 51 32 E
time difference: UTC+3 (8 hours ahead of Washington, DC, during Standard Time)

Administrative divisions: 8 municipalities (baladiyat, singular—baladiyah); Ad Dawhah, Al Khawr wa adh Dhakhirah, Al Wakrah, Ar Rayyan, Ash Shamal, Ash Shihaniyah, Az Za'ayin, Umm Salal

Independence: 3 September 1971 (from the UK)

National holiday: National Day, 18 December (1878), anniversary of Al Thani family accession to the throne; Independence Day, 3 September (1971)

Constitution: history: previous 1972 (provisional); latest drafted 2 July 2002, approved by referendum 29 April 2003, endorsed 8 June 2004, effective 9 June 2005
amendments: proposed by the emir or by one-third of Advisory Council members; passage requires two-thirds majority vote of Advisory Council members and approval and promulgation by the emir; articles pertaining to the rule of state and its inheritance, functions of the emir, and citizen rights and liberties cannot be amended (2016)

Legal system: mixed legal system of civil law and Islamic law (in family and personal matters)

International law organization participation: has not submitted an ICJ jurisdiction declaration; non-party state to the ICCt

Citizenship: *citizenship by birth:* no
citizenship by descent only: the father must be a citizen of Qatar
dual citizenship recognized: no
residency requirement for naturalization: 20 years; 15 years if an Arab national

Suffrage: 18 years of age; universal

Executive branch: *chief of state:* Amir TAMIM bin Hamad Al Thani (since 25 June 2013)

head of government: Prime Minister ABDALLAH bin Nasir bin Khalifa Al Thani (since 26 June 2013); Deputy Prime Minister Ahmad bin Abdallah al-MAHMUD (since 20 September 2011)
cabinet: Council of Ministers appointed by the amir
elections/appointments: the monarchy is hereditary; prime minister and deputy prime minister appointed by the amir

Legislative branch: *description:* unicameral Advisory Council or Majlis al-Shura (35 seats; members appointed by the monarch)
note: the 2003 constitution calls for a 45-member council with 30 members directly elected by popular vote for 4-year re-electable terms and 15 appointed by the monarch to serve until resignation or until relieved; election for the new Council was initially scheduled for 2007 but has been extended several times, the latest to June 2019

Judicial branch: *highest court(s):* Supreme Court or Court of Cassation (consists of the court president and several judges); Supreme Constitutional Court (consists of the chief justice and 6 members)
judge selection and term of office: Supreme Court judges nominated by the Supreme Judiciary Council, a 9-member independent body consisting of judiciary heads appointed by the Amir; judges appointed for 3-year renewable terms; Supreme Constitutional Court members nominated by the Supreme Judiciary Council and appointed by the monarch; term of appointment NA
subordinate courts: Courts of Appeal; Administrative Court; courts of first instance; sharia courts; Courts of Justice; Qatar International Court and Dispute Resolution Center, established in 2009, provides dispute resolution services for institutions and bodies in Qatar, as well as internationally

Political parties and leaders: political parties are banned

Political pressure groups and leaders: none

International organization participation: ABEDA, AFESD, AMF, CAEU, CD, CICA (observer), EITI (implementing country), FAO, G-77, GCC, IAEA, IBRD, ICAO, ICC (national committees), ICRM, IDA, IDB, IFAD, IFC, IFRCS, IHO, ILO, IMF, IMO, IMSO, Interpol, IOC, IOM (observer), IPU, ISO, ITSO, ITU, LAS, MIGA, NAM, OAPEC, OAS (observer), OIC, OIF, OPCW, OPEC, PCA, UN, UNCTAD, UNESCO, UNIDO, UNIFIL, UNWTO, UPU, WCO, WHO, WIPO, WMO, WTO

Diplomatic representation in the US: *chief of mission:* Ambassador MISHAL bin Hamad bin Muhammad Al Thani (since 24 April 2017)
chancery: 2555 M Street NW, Washington, DC 20037
telephone: [1] (202) 274-1600
FAX: [1] (202) 237-0682
consulate(s) general: Houston, Los Angeles

Diplomatic representation from the US: *chief of mission:* Ambassador (vacant); Charge d'Affaires Ryan GLIHA (since 30 November 2017)
embassy: 22 February Street, Al Luqta District, Doha
mailing address: P. O. Box 2399, Doha
telephone: [974] 4496-6000

FAX: [974] 4488-4298

Flag description: maroon with a broad white serrated band (nine white points) on the hoist side; maroon represents the blood shed in Qatari wars, white stands for peace; the nine-pointed serrated edge signifies Qatar as the ninth member of the "reconciled emirates" in the wake of the Qatari-British treaty of 1916

note: the other eight emirates are the seven that compose the UAE and Bahrain; according to some sources, the dominant color was formerly red, but this darkened to maroon upon exposure to the sun and the new shade was eventually adopted

National symbol(s): a maroon field surmounted by a white serrated band with nine white points; national colors: maroon, white

National anthem: name: "Al-Salam Al-Amiri" (The Amiri Salute)
lyrics/music: Sheikh MUBARAK bin Saif al-Thani/Abdul Aziz Nasser OBAIDAN
note: adopted 1996; anthem first performed that year at a meeting of the Gulf Cooperative Council hosted by Qatar

ECONOMY

Economy—overview: Qatar's oil and natural gas resources are the country's main economic engine and government revenue source, driving Qatar's high economic growth and per capita income levels, robust state spending on public entitlements, and booming construction spending, particularly as Qatar prepares to host the World Cup in 2022. Although the government has maintained high capital spending levels for ongoing infrastructure projects, low oil and natural gas prices in recent years have led the Qatari Government to tighten some spending to help stem its budget deficit.

Qatar's reliance on oil and natural gas is likely to persist for the foreseeable future. Proved natural gas reserves exceed 25 trillion cubic meters—13% of the world total and, among countries, third largest in the world. Proved oil reserves exceed 25 billion barrels, allowing production to continue at current levels for about 56 years. Despite the dominance of oil and natural gas, Qatar has made significant gains in strengthening non-oil sectors, such as manufacturing, construction, and financial services, leading non-oil GDP to steadily rise in recent years to just over half the total.

Following trade restriction imposed by Saudi Arabia, the UAE, Bahrain, and Egypt in 2017, Qatar established new trade routes with other countries to maintain access to imports.

GDP (purchasing power parity): $341.7 billion (2017 est.)
$333.3 billion (2016 est.)
$326.1 billion (2015 est.)
note: data are in 2017 dollars
country comparison to the world: 53

GDP (official exchange rate): $166.3 billion (2016 est.)

GDP—real growth rate: 2.5% (2017 est.)
2.2% (2016 est.)
3.6% (2015 est.)
country comparison to the world: 137

GDP—per capita (PPP): $124,900 (2017 est.)
$127,300 (2016 est.)
$133,700 (2015 est.)

note: data are in 2017 dollars
country comparison to the world: 2

Gross national saving: 48.8% of GDP (2017 est.)
44% of GDP (2016 est.)
46.6% of GDP (2015 est.)
country comparison to the world: 2

GDP—composition, by end use:
household consumption: 24.8%
government consumption: 22.8%
investment in fixed capital: 40.1%
investment in inventories: 1.6%
exports of goods and services: 44.6%
imports of goods and services: -33.9% (2017 est.)

GDP—composition, by sector of origin:
agriculture: 0.2%
industry: 50.3%
services: 49.5% (2017 est.)

Agriculture—products: fruits, vegetables; poultry, dairy products, beef; fish

Industries: liquefied natural gas, crude oil production and refining, ammonia, fertilizer, petrochemicals, steel reinforcing bars, cement, commercial ship repair

Industrial production growth rate: -7% (2017 est.)
country comparison to the world: 201

Labor force: 1.953 million (2017 est.)
country comparison to the world: 126

Unemployment rate: 0.6% (2017 est.)
0.7% (2016 est.)
country comparison to the world: 3

Population below poverty line: NA%

Household income or consumption by percentage share: *lowest 10%:* 1.3%
highest 10%: 35.9% (2007)

Budget: *revenues:* $41.47 billion
expenditures: $54.97 billion (2017 est.)
Taxes and other revenues: 24.9% of GDP (2017 est.)
country comparison to the world: 116

Budget surplus (+) or deficit (-): -8.1% of GDP (2017 est.)
country comparison to the world: 198

Public debt: 56.8% of GDP (2017 est.)
55.4% of GDP (2016 est.)
country comparison to the world: 82

Fiscal year: 1 April—31 March

Inflation rate (consumer prices): 0.9% (2017 est.)
2.7% (2016 est.)
country comparison to the world: 35

Central bank discount rate: 4.5% (31 December 2012)
4.93% (31 December 2011)
country comparison to the world: 82

Commercial bank prime lending rate: 5% (31 December 2017 est.)
4.51% (31 December 2016 est.)
country comparison to the world: 146

Stock of narrow money: $35.54 billion (31 December 2017 est.)
$35.26 billion (31 December 2016 est.)
country comparison to the world: 59

Stock of broad money: $139.7 billion (31 December 2017 est.)
$136.7 billion (31 December 2016 est.)
country comparison to the world: 52

Stock of domestic credit: $228.7 billion (31 December 2017 est.)
$224.2 billion (31 December 2016 est.)
country comparison to the world: 43

Market value of publicly traded shares: $142.6 billion (31 December 2015 est.)
$185.9 billion (31 December 2014 est.)
$152.6 billion (31 December 2013 est.)
country comparison to the world: 37

Current account balance: $3.901 billion (2017 est.)
-$7.679 billion (2016 est.)
country comparison to the world: 29

Exports: $56.26 billion (2017 est.)
$57.25 billion (2016 est.)
country comparison to the world: 49

Exports—commodities: liquefied natural gas (LNG), petroleum products, fertilizers, steel

Exports—partners: Japan 20%, South Korea 15.5%, India 13.1%, China 8.2%, UAE 5.5%, Singapore 5.3% (2016)

Imports: $26.69 billion (2017 est.)
$31.93 billion (2016 est.)
country comparison to the world: 66

Imports—commodities: machinery and transport equipment, food, chemicals

Imports—partners: US 13.7%, Germany 9.8%, UAE 9.2%, China 8.6%, Japan 7.2%, UK 5.5%, Saudi Arabia 4.6%, Italy 4.4% (2016)

Reserves of foreign exchange and gold: $16.89 billion (31 December 2017 est.)
$31.89 billion (31 December 2016 est.)
country comparison to the world: 65

Debt—external: $168 billion (31 December 2017 est.)
$157.9 billion (31 December 2016 est.)
country comparison to the world: 39

Stock of direct foreign investment—at home: $36.04 billion (31 December 2017 est.)
$35.31 billion (31 December 2016 est.)
country comparison to the world: 65

Stock of direct foreign investment—abroad: $59.27 billion (31 December 2017 est.)
$57.63 billion (31 December 2016 est.)
country comparison to the world: 40

Exchange rates: Qatari rials (QAR) per US dollar—
3.64 (2017 est.)
3.64 (2016 est.)
3.64 (2015 est.)
3.64 (2014 est.)
3.64 (2013 est.)

ENERGY

Electricity access: *population without electricity:* 45,165
electrification—total population: 98%
electrification—urban areas: 98%
electrification—rural areas: 93% (2012)

Electricity—production: 39.01 billion kWh (2015 est.)
country comparison to the world: 59

Electricity—consumption: 36.53 billion kWh (2015 est.)
country comparison to the world: 59

737

Electricity—exports: 0 kWh (2016 est.)
country comparison to the world: 186

Electricity—imports: 0 kWh (2016 est.)
country comparison to the world: 190

Electricity—installed generating capacity: 8.836 million kW (2015 est.)
country comparison to the world: 67

Electricity—from fossil fuels: 99.5% of total installed capacity (2015 est.)
country comparison to the world: 30

Electricity—from nuclear fuels: 0% of total installed capacity (2015 est.)
country comparison to the world: 169

Electricity—from hydroelectric plants: 0% of total installed capacity (2015 est.)
country comparison to the world: 197

Electricity—from other renewable sources: 0.5% of total installed capacity (2015 est.)
country comparison to the world: 152

Crude oil—production: 1.523 million bbl/day (2016 est.)
country comparison to the world: 17

Crude oil—exports: 1.255 million bbl/day (2014 est.)
country comparison to the world: 14

Crude oil—imports: 0 bbl/day (2014 est.)
country comparison to the world: 179

Crude oil—proved reserves: 25.24 billion bbl (1 January 2017 es)
country comparison to the world: 14

Refined petroleum products—production: 278,300 bbl/day (2014 est.)
country comparison to the world: 43

Refined petroleum products—consumption: 280,000 bbl/day (2015 est.)
country comparison to the world: 46

Refined petroleum products—exports: 544,000 bbl/day (2014 est.)
country comparison to the world: 15

Refined petroleum products—imports: 245.3 bbl/day (2014 est.)
country comparison to the world: 210

Natural gas—production: 164 billion cu m (2015 est.)
country comparison to the world: 4

Natural gas—consumption: 49.64 billion cu m (2015 est.)
country comparison to the world: 22

Natural gas—exports: 123.9 billion cu m (2015 est.)
country comparison to the world: 2

Natural gas—imports: 0 cu m (2013 est.)
country comparison to the world: 178

Natural gas—proved reserves: 24.3 trillion cu m (1 January 2017 es)
country comparison to the world: 3

Carbon dioxide emissions from consumption of energy: 92 million Mt (2013 est.)
country comparison to the world: 42

COMMUNICATIONS

Telephones—fixed lines: *total subscriptions:* 467,148

subscriptions per 100 inhabitants: 21 (July 2016 est.)
country comparison to the world: 101

Telephones—mobile cellular: *total:* 3,552,579
subscriptions per 100 inhabitants: 157 (July 2016 est.)
country comparison to the world: 134

Telephone system: *general assessment:* modern system centered in Doha
domestic: combined fixed-line and mobile-cellular telephone subscribership exceeds 175 telephones per 100 persons
international: country code—974; landing point for the Fiber-Optic Link Around the Globe (FLAG) submarine cable network that provides links to Asia, Middle East, Europe, and the US; tropospheric scatter to Bahrain; microwave radio relay to Saudi Arabia and the UAE; satellite earth stations—2 Intelsat (1 Atlantic Ocean and 1 Indian Ocean) and 1 Arabsat (2016)

Broadcast media: TV and radio broadcast licensing and access to local media markets are state controlled; home of the satellite TV channel Al-Jazeera, which was originally owned and financed by the Qatari government but has evolved to independent corporate status; Al-Jazeera claims editorial independence in broadcasting; local radio transmissions include state, private, and international broadcasters on FM frequencies in Doha; in August 2013, Qatar's satellite company Es'hailSat launched its first communications satellite Es'hail 1 (manufactured in the US), which entered commercial service in December 2013 to provide improved television broadcasting capability and expand availability of voice and Internet; Es'hailSat expects to launch its second satellite in 2018 (2014)

Internet country code: .qa
Internet users: total: 2,129,360

percent of population: 94.3% (July 2016 est.)
country comparison to the world: 95

TRANSPORTATION

National air transport system: *number of registered air carriers:* 2
inventory of registered aircraft operated by air carriers: 199
annual passenger traffic on registered air carriers: 25,263,224
annual freight traffic on registered air carriers: 7,563,307,390 mt-km (2015)
Civil aircraft registration country code prefix: A7 (2016)

Airports: 6 (2013)
country comparison to the world: 178

Airports—with paved runways: *total:* 4
over 3,047 m: 3
1,524 to 2,437 m: 1 (2017)

Airports—with unpaved runways: *total:* 2
914 to 1,523 m: 1
under 914 m: 1 (2013)

Heliports: 1 (2013)

Pipelines: condensate 288 km; condensate/gas 221 km; gas 2,383 km; liquid petroleum gas 90 km; oil 745 km; refined products 103 km (2013)

Roadways: *total:* 9,830 km (2010)
country comparison to the world: 136

Merchant marine: *total:* 143
by type: bulk carrier 8, container ship 6, general cargo 5, oil tanker 6, other 118 (2017)
country comparison to the world: 74

Ports and terminals: *major seaport(s):* Doha, Mesaieed (Umaieed), Ra's Laffan
LNG terminal(s) (export): Ras Laffan

MILITARY AND SECURITY

Military branches: Qatari Emiri Land Force (QELF), Qatari Emiri Navy (QEN), Qatari Emiri Air Force (QEAF) (2013)

Military service age and obligation: conscription for males aged 18-35; 4-month general obligation, 3 months for graduates (2014)

TERRORISM

Terrorist groups—foreign based: HAMAS: *aim(s):* enhance its networks and support in Qatar *area(s) of operation:* maintains an official political bureau in Doha

TRANSNATIONAL ISSUES

Disputes—international: none

Refugees and internally displaced persons: *stateless persons:* 1,200 (2016)

Trafficking in persons: current situation: Qatar is a destination country for men, women, and children subjected to forced labor, and, to a much lesser extent, forced prostitution; the predominantly foreign workforce migrates to Qatar legally for low- and semi-skilled work but often experiences situations of forced labor, including debt bondage, delayed or nonpayment of salaries, confiscation of passports, abuse, hazardous working conditions, and squalid living arrangements; foreign female domestic workers are particularly vulnerable to trafficking because of their isolation in private homes and lack of protection under Qatari labor laws; some women who migrate for work are also forced into prostitution

tier rating: Tier 2 Watch List—Qatar does not fully comply with the minimum standards for the elimination of trafficking; however, it is making significant efforts to do so; the government investigated 11 trafficking cases but did not prosecute or convict any offenders, including exploitative employers and recruitment agencies; the primary solution for resolving labor violations was to transfer a worker's sponsorship to a new employer with minimal effort to investigate whether a forced labor violation had occurred; authorities increased their efforts to protect some trafficking victims, although many victims of forced labor, particularly domestic workers, remained unidentified and unprotected and were sometimes punished for immigration violations or running away from an employer or sponsor; authorities visited worksites throughout the country to meet and educate workers and employers on trafficking regulations, but the government failed to abolish or reform the sponsorship system, perpetuating Qatar's forced labor problem (2015)

INTRODUCTION

Background: The principalities of Wallachia and Moldavia—for centuries under the suzerainty of the Turkish Ottoman Empire—secured their autonomy in 1856; they were de facto linked in 1859 and formally united in 1862 under the new name of Romania. The country gained recognition of its independence in 1878. It joined the Allied Powers in World War I and acquired new territories—most notably Transylvania—following the conflict. In 1940, Romania allied with the Axis powers and participated in the 1941 German invasion of the USSR. Three years later, overrun by the Soviets, Romania signed an armistice. The post-war Soviet occupation led to the formation of a communist "people's republic" in 1947 and the abdication of the king. The decades-long rule of dictator Nicolae CEAUSESCU, who took power in 1965, and his Securitate police state became increasingly oppressive and draconian through the 1980s. CEAUSESCU was overthrown and executed in late 1989. Former communists dominated the government until 1996 when they were swept from power. Romania joined NATO in 2004 and the EU in 2007.

GEOGRAPHY

Location: Southeastern Europe, bordering the Black Sea, between Bulgaria and Ukraine

Geographic coordinates: 46 00 N, 25 00 E

Map references: Europe

Area: total: 238,391 sq km

land: 229,891 sq km

water: 8,500 sq km

country comparison to the world: 84

Area—comparative: twice the size of Pennsylvania; slightly smaller than Oregon

Land boundaries: *total:* 2,844 km

border countries (5): Bulgaria 605 km, Hungary 424 km, Moldova 683 km, Serbia 531 km, Ukraine 601 km

Coastline: 225 km

Maritime claims: *territorial sea:* 12 nm

contiguous zone: 24 nm

exclusive economic zone: 200 nm

continental shelf: 200-m depth or to the depth of exploitation

Climate: temperate; cold, cloudy winters with frequent snow and fog; sunny summers with frequent showers and thunderstorms

Terrain: central Transylvanian Basin is separated from the Moldavian Plateau on the east by the Eastern Carpathian Mountains and separated from the Walachian Plain on the south by the Transylvanian Alps

Elevation: *mean elevation:* 414 m

elevation extremes: *lowest point:* Black Sea 0 m

highest point: Moldoveanu 2,544 m

Natural resources: petroleum (reserves declining), timber, natural gas, coal, iron ore, salt, arable land, hydropower

Land use: *agricultural land:* 60.7%

arable land: 39.1%;

permanent crops: 1.9%;

permanent pasture: 19.7%

forest: 28.7%

other: 10.6% (2011 est.)

Irrigated land: 31,490 sq km (2012)

Population—distribution: urbanization is not particularly high, and a fairly even population distribution can be found throughout most of the country, with urban areas attracting larger and denser populations; Hungarians, the country's largest minority, have a particularly strong presence in eastern Transylvania

Natural hazards: earthquakes, most severe in south and southwest; geologic structure and climate promote landslides

Environment—current issues: soil erosion and degradation; water pollution; air pollution in south from industrial effluents; contamination of Danube delta wetlands

Environment—international agreements: *party to:* Air Pollution, Air Pollution-Persistent Organic Pollutants, Antarctic-Environmental Protocol, Antarctic Treaty, Biodiversity, Climate Change, Climate Change-Kyoto Protocol, Desertification, Endangered Species, Environmental Modification, Hazardous Wastes, Law of the Sea, Ozone Layer Protection, Ship Pollution, Wetlands

signed, but not ratified: none of the selected agreements

Geography—note: controls the most easily traversable land route between the Balkans, Moldova, and Ukraine; the Carpathian Mountains dominate the center of the country, while the Danube River forms much of the southern boundary with Serbia and Bulgaria

PEOPLE AND SOCIETY

Population: 21,529,967 (July 2017 est.)

country comparison to the world: 58

Nationality: *noun:* Romanian(s)

adjective: Romanian

Ethnic groups: Romanian 83.4%, Hungarian 6.1%, Romani 3.1%, Ukrainian 0.3%, German 0.2%, other 0.7%, unspecified 6.1% (2011 est.)

note: Romani populations are usually underestimated in official statistics and may represent 5–11% of Romania's population

Languages: Romanian (official) 85.4%, Hungarian 6.3%, Romani 1.2%, other 1%, unspecified 6.1% (2011 est.)

Religions: Eastern Orthodox (including all subdenominations) 81.9%, Protestant (various denominations including Reformed and Pentecostal) 6.4%, Roman Catholic 4.3%, other (includes Muslim) 0.9%, none or atheist 0.2%, unspecified 6.3% (2011 est.)

Age structure: *0-14 years:* 14.35% (male 1,586,976/female 1,502,864)

15-24 years: 10.6% (male 1,170,679/female 1,110,727)

25-54 years: 46.03% (male 5,016,529/female 4,893,792)

55-64 years: 12.61% (male 1,271,281/female 1,443,414)

65 years and over: 16.41% (male 1,428,599/female 2,105,106) (2017 est.)

Dependency ratios: *total dependency ratio:* 48

youth dependency ratio: 22.8

elderly dependency ratio: 25.2

potential support ratio: 4 (2015 est.)

Median age: *total:* 41.1 years

male: 39.7 years

female: 42.6 years (2017 est.)

country comparison to the world: 42

Population growth rate: -0.33% (2017 est.)

country comparison to the world: 219

Birth rate: 8.9 births/1,000 population (2017 est.)

country comparison to the world: 209

Death rate: 12 deaths/1,000 population (2017 est.)

country comparison to the world: 22

Net migration rate: -0.2 migrant(s)/1,000 population (2017 est.)

country comparison to the world: 109

Population distribution: urbanization is not particularly high, and a fairly even population distribution can be found throughout most of the country, with urban areas attracting larger and denser populations; Hungarians, the country's largest minority, have a particularly strong presence in eastern Transylvania

Urbanization: *urban population:* 54.9% of total population (2017)

rate of urbanization: 0.05% annual rate of change (2015-20 est.)

Major urban areas—population: BUCHAREST (capital) 1.868 million (2015)

Sex ratio: *at birth:* 1.06 male(s)/female

0-14 years: 1.06 male(s)/female

15-24 years: 1.05 male(s)/female

25-54 years: 1.02 male(s)/female
55-64 years: 0.88 male(s)/female
65 years and over: 0.68 male(s)/female
total population: 0.95 male(s)/female (2016 est.)

Mother's mean age at first birth: 26.7 years (2014 est.)

Maternal mortality ratio: 31 deaths/100,000 live births (2015 est.)
country comparison to the world: 112

Infant mortality rate: *total:* 9.4 deaths/1,000 live births
male: 10.7 deaths/1,000 live births
female: 8 deaths/1,000 live births (2017 est.)
country comparison to the world: 144

Life expectancy at birth: *total population:* 75.4 years
male: 71.9 years
female: 79 years (2017 est.)
country comparison to the world: 108

Total fertility rate: 1.35 children born/woman (2017 est.)
country comparison to the world: 214

Health expenditures: 5.6% of GDP (2014)
country comparison to the world: 122

Physicians density: 2.67 physicians/1,000 population (2013)

Hospital bed density: 6.1 beds/1,000 population (2011)

Drinking water source:
improved:
urban: 100% of population
rural: 100% of population
total: 100% of population
unimproved:
urban: 0% of population
rural: 0% of population
total: 0% of population (2015 est.)

Sanitation facility access:
improved:
urban: 92.2% of population
rural: 63.3% of population
total: 79.1% of population
unimproved:
urban: 7.8% of population
rural: 36.7% of population
total: 20.9% of population (2015 est.)

HIV/AIDS—adult prevalence rate: 0.1% (2016 est.)
country comparison to the world: 104

HIV/AIDS—people living with HIV/AIDS: 16,000 (2016 est.)
country comparison to the world: 81

HIV/AIDS—deaths: <200 (2016 est.)

Obesity—adult prevalence rate: 22.5% (2016)
country comparison to the world: 76

Education expenditures: 2.9% of GDP (2012)
country comparison to the world: 104

Literacy: *definition:* age 15 and over can read and write
total population: 98.8%
male: 99.1%
female: 98.5% (2015 est.)

School life expectancy (primary to tertiary education): *total:* 15 years
male: 15 years
female: 15 years (2015)

Unemployment, youth ages 15-24: *total:* 21.7%
male: 20.6%
female: 23.4% (2015 est.)
country comparison to the world: 45

GOVERNMENT

Country name: *conventional long form:* none
conventional short form: Romania
local long form: none
local short form: Romania
etymology: the name derives from the Latin "Romanus" meaning "citizen of Rome" and was used to stress the common ancient heritage of Romania's three main regions—Moldavia, Transylvania, and Wallachia—during their gradual unification between the mid-19th century and early 20th century

Government type: semi-presidential republic

Capital: *name:* Bucharest

geographic coordinates: 44 26 N, 26 06 E
time difference: UTC+2 (7 hours ahead of Washington, DC, during Standard Time)
daylight saving time: +1hr, begins last Sunday in March; ends last Sunday in October

Administrative divisions: 41 counties (judete, singular—judet) and 1 municipality* (municipiu); Alba, Arad, Arges, Bacau, Bihor, Bistrita-Nasaud, Botosani, Braila, Brasov, Bucuresti (Bucharest)*, Buzau, Calarasi, Caras-Severin, Cluj, Constanta, Covasna, Dambovita, Dolj, Galati, Gorj, Giurgiu, Harghita, Hunedoara, Ialomita, Iasi, Ilfov, Maramures, Mehedinti, Mures, Neamt, Olt, Prahova, Salaj, Satu Mare, Sibiu, Suceava, Teleorman, Timis, Tulcea, Vaslui, Valcea, Vrancea

Independence: 9 May 1877 (independence proclaimed from the Ottoman Empire; 13 July 1878 independence recognized by the Treaty of Berlin); 26 March 1881 (kingdom proclaimed); 30 December 1947 (republic proclaimed)

National holiday: Unification Day (unification of Romania and Transylvania), 1 December (1918)

Constitution: *history:* several previous; latest adopted 21 November 1991, approved by referendum and effective 8 December 1991
amendments: initiated by the president of Romania through a proposal by the government, by at least one-fourth of deputies or senators in Parliament, or by petition of eligible voters representing at least one-half of Romania's counties; passage requires at least two-thirds majority vote by both chambers or – if mediation is required—by three-fourths majority vote in a joint session, followed by approval in a referendum; articles including those on national sovereignty, form of government, political pluralism, and fundamental rights and freedoms cannot be amended; amended 2003 (2016)

Legal system: civil law system

International law organization participation: accepts compulsory ICJ jurisdiction with reservations; accepts ICCt jurisdiction

Citizenship: *citizenship by birth:* no

citizenship by descent only: at least one parent must be a citizen of Romania
dual citizenship recognized: yes
residency requirement for naturalization: 5 years

Suffrage: 18 years of age; universal

Executive branch: *chief of state:* President Klaus Werner IOHANNIS (since 21 December 2014)
head of government: Prime Minister Viorica DANCILA (since 29 January 2018); Deputy Prime Ministers Gratiela GAVRILESCU (since 29 June 2017), Paul STANESCU (17 October 2017), Viorel STEFAN (since 29 January 2018), Ana BIRCHALL (since 29 January 2018); note—Mihai TUDOSE resigned on 15 January 2018; DANCILA is Romania's first woman prime minister
cabinet: Council of Ministers appointed by the prime minister
elections/appointments: president directly elected by absolute majority popular vote in 2 rounds if needed for a 5-year term (eligible for a second term); election last held on 2 November 2014 with a runoff on 16 November 2014 (next to be held in November 2019); prime minister appointed by the president with consent of Parliament
election results: Klaus IOHANNIS elected president in second round; percent of vote—Klaus IOHANNIS (PNL) 54.4%, Victor PONTA (PSD) 45.6%; Mihai TUDOSE approved as prime minister 275-102

Legislative branch: *description:* bicameral Parliament or Parlament consists of the Senate or Senat (136 seats, 2 reserved for the diaspora; members serve 4-year terms) and the Chamber of Deputies or Camera Deputatilor (329 seats, 17 reserved for non-Hungarian national minorities and 4 for the diaspora; members serve 4-year terms); in 2016, the elections returned to a party list vote-proportional representation voting system
elections: Senate—last held on 11 December 2016 (next to be held by December 2020); Chamber of Deputies—last held on 11 December 2016 (next to be held by December 2020)
election results: Senate—percent of vote by party—PSD 45.7%, PNL 20.4%, USR 8.9%, UDMR 6.2%, ALDE 6%, PMP 5.7%, other 7.1%; seats by party—PSD 67, PNL 30, USR 13, UDMR 9, ALDE 9, PMP 8; Chamber of Deputies—percent of vote by party—PSD 45.5%, PNL 20%, USR 8.9%, UDMR 6.2%, ALDE 5.6%, PMP 5.4%, other 8.4%; seats by party—PSD 154, PNL 69, USR 30, UDMR 21, ALDE 20, PMP 18, minorities 17

Judicial branch: *highest court(s):* High Court of Cassation and Justice (consists of 111 judges organized into civil, penal, commercial, contentious administrative and fiscal business, and joint sections); Supreme Constitutional Court (consists of 9 members) *judge selection and term of office:* High Court of Cassation and Justice judges appointed by the president upon nomination by the Superior Council of Magistracy, a 19-member body of judges, prosecutors, and law specialists; judges appointed for 6-year renewable terms; Constitutional Court members—6 elected by Parliament and 3 appointed by the president; members serve 9-year, nonrenewable terms

subordinate courts: Courts of Appeal; regional tribunals; first instance courts; military and arbitration courts

Political parties and leaders: Christian-Democratic National Peasants' Party or PNT-CD [Aurelian PAVELESCU] Democratic Union of Hungarians in Romania or UDMR [Hunor KELEMEN] Civic Hungarian Party [Zsolt BIRO] Ecologist Party of Romania or PER [Danut POP] Greater Romania Party or PRM [Adrian POPESCU] M10 Party [Ioana CONSTANTIN] National Liberal Party or PNL [Ludovic ORBAN] New Romania Party or PNR [Sebastian POPESCU] Our Romania Alliance [Marian MUNTEANU] Party of the Alliance of Liberals and Democrats or ALDE [Calin POPESCU TARICEANU] Popular Movement Party or PMP [Traian BASESCU] Romanian Social Party or PSRo [Mircea GEOANA] Save Romania Union Party or Partidul USR [Dan BARNA] Social Democratic Party or PSD [Liviu DRAGNEA] United Romania Party or PRU [Robert BUGA]

Political pressure groups and leaders: various human rights and professional associations

International organization participation: Australia Group, BIS, BSEC, CBSS (observer), CD, CE, CEI, EAPC, EBRD, ECB, EIB, ESA, EU, FAO, G-9, IAEA, IBRD, ICAO, ICC (national committees), ICCt, ICRM, IDA, IFAD, IFC, IFRCS, IHO, ILO, IMF, IMO, IMSO, Interpol, IOC, IOM, IPU, ISO, ITSO, ITU, ITUC (NGOs), LAIA (observer), MIGA, MONUSCO, NATO, NSG, OAS (observer), OIF, OPCW, OSCE, PCA, SELEC, UN, UNCTAD, UNESCO, UNHCR, UNIDO, Union Latina, UNMIL, UNMISS, UNOCI, UNWTO, UPU, WCO, WFTU (NGOs), WHO, WIPO, WMO, WTO, ZC

Diplomatic representation in the US: chief of mission: Ambassador George Cristian MAIOR (since 17 September 2015)

chancery: 1607 23rd Street NW, Washington, DC 20008

telephone: [1] (202) 332-4846, 4848, 4851, 4852

FAX: [1] (202) 232-4748

consulate(s) general: Chicago, Los Angeles, New York

Diplomatic representation from the US: chief of mission: Ambassador Hans G. KLEMM (since 21 September 2015)

embassy: 4-6, Dr. Liviu Librescu Blvd., District 1, Bucharest, 015118

mailing address: American Embassy Bucharest, US Department of State, 5260 Bucharest Place, Washington, DC 20521-5260 (pouch)

telephone: [40] (21) 200-3300

FAX: [40] (21) 200-3442

Flag description: three equal vertical bands of cobalt blue (hoist side), chrome yellow, and vermilion red; modeled after the flag of France, the colors are those of the principalities of Walachia (red and yellow) and Moldavia (red and blue), which united in 1862 to form Romania; the national coat of arms that used to be centered in the yellow band has been removed

note: now similar to the flag of Chad, whose blue band is darker; also resembles the flags of Andorra and Moldova

National symbol(s): golden eagle; national colors: blue, yellow, red

National anthem: *name:* "Desteapta-te romane!" (Wake up, Romanian!)

lyrics/music: Andrei MURESIANU/Anton PANN

note: adopted 1990; the anthem was written during the 1848 Revolution

ECONOMY

Economy—overview: Romania, which joined the EU on 1 January 2007, began the transition from communism in 1989 with a largely obsolete industrial base and a pattern of output unsuited to the country's needs. Romania's macroeconomic gains have only recently started to spur creation of a middle class and to address Romania's widespread poverty. Corruption and red tape continue to permeate the business environment.

In the aftermath of the global financial crisis, Romania signed a $26 billion emergency assistance package from the IMF, the EU, and other international lenders, but GDP contracted until 2011. In March 2011, Romania and the IMF/EU/World Bank signed a 24-month precautionary standby agreement, worth $6.6 billion, to promote fiscal discipline, encourage progress on structural reforms, and strengthen financial sector stability; no funds were drawn. In September 2013, Romanian authorities and the IMF/EU agreed to a follow-on standby agreement, worth $5.4 billion, to continue with reforms. This agreement expired in September 2015, and no funds were drawn. Progress on structural reforms has been uneven, and the economy still is vulnerable to external shocks.

Economic growth rebounded in the 2013-17 period, driven by strong industrial exports, excellent agricultural harvests, and, more recently, expansionary fiscal policies in 2016-2017 that nearly quadrupled Bucharest's annual fiscal deficit, from +0.8% of GDP in 2015 to -3% of GDP in 2016 and an estimated -3.4% in 2017. Industry outperformed other sectors of the economy in 2017. Exports remained an engine of economic growth, led by trade with the EU, which accounts for roughly 70% of Romania trade. Domestic demand was the major driver, due to tax cuts and large wage increases that began last year and are set to continue in 2018.

An aging population, emigration of skilled labor, significant tax evasion, insufficient health care, and an aggressive loosening of the fiscal package compromise Romania's long-term growth and economic stability and are the economy's top vulnerabilities.

GDP (purchasing power parity): $474 billion (2017 est.)

$449.3 billion (2016 est.)

$428.7 billion (2015 est.)

note: data are in 2017 dollars

country comparison to the world: 43

GDP (official exchange rate): $204.9 billion (2016 est.)

GDP—real growth rate: 5.5% (2017 est.)

4.8% (2016 est.)

3.9% (2015 est.)

country comparison to the world: 28

GDP—per capita (PPP): $24,000 (2017 est.)

$22,700 (2016 est.)

$21,600 (2015 est.)

note: data are in 2017 dollars

country comparison to the world: 83

Gross national saving: 21.4% of GDP (2017 est.)

22.7% of GDP (2016 est.)

23.7% of GDP (2015 est.)

country comparison to the world: 80

GDP—composition, by end use: *household consumption:* 70.6%

government consumption: 7.9%

investment in fixed capital: 22.4%

investment in inventories: 1.2%

exports of goods and services: 43.9%

imports of goods and services: -46% (2017 est.)

GDP—composition, by sector of origin: *agriculture:* 4.2%

industry: 33.2%

services: 64.4% (2017 est.)

Agriculture—products: wheat, corn, barley, sugar beets, sunflower seed, potatoes, grapes; eggs, sheep

Industries: electric machinery and equipment, auto assembly, textiles and footwear, light machinery, metallurgy, chemicals, food processing, petroleum refining, mining, timber, construction materials

Industrial production growth rate: 2% (2017 est.)

country comparison to the world: 132

Labor force: 8.951 million (2017 est.)

country comparison to the world: 55

Labor force—by occupation: *agriculture:* 28.3%

industry: 28.9%

services: 42.8% (2014)

Unemployment rate: 5.3% (2017 est.)

5.9% (2016 est.)

country comparison to the world: 71

Population below poverty line: 22.4% (2012 est.)

Household income or consumption by percentage share: *lowest 10%:* 15.3%

highest 10%: 7.6% (2014 est.)

Distribution of family income—Gini index: 27.3 (2012)

28.2 (2010)

country comparison to the world: 136

Budget: *revenues:* $58.5 billion

expenditures: $65.54 billion (2017 est.)

Taxes and other revenues: 28.5% of GDP (2017 est.)
country comparison to the world: 92

Budget surplus (+) or deficit (-): -3.4% of GDP (2017 est.)
country comparison to the world: 129

Public debt: 38.5% of GDP (2017 est.)
37.6% of GDP (2016 est.)
note: defined by the EU's Maastricht Treaty as consolidated general government gross debt at nominal value, outstanding at the end of the year in the following categories of government liabilities: currency and deposits, securities other than shares excluding financial derivatives, and loans; general government sector comprises the subsectors: central government, state government, local government, and social security funds
country comparison to the world: 141

Fiscal year: calendar year

Inflation rate (consumer prices): 1.1% (2017 est.)
-1.6% (2016 est.)
country comparison to the world: 47

Central bank discount rate: 1.75% (31 December 2015)
2.75% (31 December 2014)
country comparison to the world: 119

Commercial bank prime lending rate: 5.7% (31 December 2017 est.)
5.71% (31 December 2016 est.)
country comparison to the world: 130

Stock of narrow money: $54.44 billion (31 December 2017 est.)
$41.82 billion (31 December 2016 est.)
country comparison to the world: 52

Stock of broad money: $90.36 billion (31 December 2017 est.)
$72.97 billion (31 December 2016 est.)
country comparison to the world: 58

Stock of domestic credit: $67.05 billion (31 December 2017 est.)
$60.3 billion (31 December 2016 est.)
country comparison to the world: 62

Market value of publicly traded shares: $36.5 billion (31 December 2015 est.)
$41.04 billion (31 December 2014 est.)
$42.59 billion (31 December 2013 est.)
country comparison to the world: 59

Current account balance: -$6.131 billion (2017 est.)
-$4.389 billion (2016 est.)
country comparison to the world: 178

Exports: $64.92 billion (2017 est.)
$57.72 billion (2016 est.)
country comparison to the world: 43

Exports—commodities: machinery and equipment, other manufactured goods, agricultural products and foodstuffs, metals and metal products, chemicals, minerals and fuels, raw materials

Exports—partners: Germany 21.5%, Italy 11.6%, France 7.2%, Hungary 5.2%, UK 4.3% (2016)

Imports: $78.12 billion (2017 est.)
$67.94 billion (2016 est.)

country comparison to the world: 40

Imports—commodities: machinery and equipment, other manufactured goods, chemicals, agricultural products and foodstuffs, fuels and minerals, metals and metal products, raw materials

Imports—partners: Germany 20.5%, Italy 10.3%, Hungary 7.5%, France 5.6%, Poland 5.1%, China 5.1%, Netherlands 4.1% (2016)

Reserves of foreign exchange and gold: $45.07 billion (31 December 2017 est.)
$40 billion (31 December 2016 est.)
country comparison to the world: 43

Debt—external: $94.17 billion (31 December 2017 est.)
$93.71 billion (31 December 2016 est.)
country comparison to the world: 50

Stock of direct foreign investment—at home: $81.53 billion (31 December 2017 est.)
$76.93 billion (31 December 2016 est.)
country comparison to the world: 50

Stock of direct foreign investment—abroad: $6.263 billion (31 December 2017 est.)
$5.963 billion (31 December 2016 est.)
country comparison to the world: 69

Exchange rates: lei (RON) per US dollar—
4.077 (2017 est.)
4.0592 (2016 est.)
4.0592 (2015 est.)
4.0057 (2014 est.)
3.3492 (2013 est.)

ENERGY

Electricity access: *electrification—total population:* 100% (2016)

Electricity—production: 62.16 billion kWh (2015 est.)
country comparison to the world: 47

Electricity—consumption: 48.28 billion kWh (2015 est.)
country comparison to the world: 51

Electricity—exports: 11.22 billion kWh (2015 est.)
country comparison to the world: 20

Electricity—imports: 4.492 billion kWh (2015 est.)
country comparison to the world: 43

Electricity—installed generating capacity: 24.03 million kW (2015 est.)
country comparison to the world: 37

Electricity—from fossil fuels: 46.7% of total installed capacity (2015 est.)
country comparison to the world: 155

Electricity—from nuclear fuels: 5.4% of total installed capacity (2015 est.)
country comparison to the world: 22

Electricity—from hydroelectric plants: 28% of total installed capacity (2015 est.)
country comparison to the world: 76

Electricity—from other renewable sources: 18.8% of total installed capacity (2015 est.)
country comparison to the world: 33

Crude oil—production: 77,910 bbl/day (2016 est.)
country comparison to the world: 47

Crude oil—exports: 1,049 bbl/day (2014 est.)
country comparison to the world: 71

Crude oil—imports: 145,500 bbl/day (2014 est.)
country comparison to the world: 37

Crude oil—proved reserves: 600 million bbl (1 January 2017 es)
country comparison to the world: 45

Refined petroleum products—production: 228,100 bbl/day (2014 est.)
country comparison to the world: 48

Refined petroleum products—consumption: 182,000 bbl/day (2015 est.)
country comparison to the world: 58

Refined petroleum products—exports: 80,400 bbl/day (2014 est.)
country comparison to the world: 47

Refined petroleum products—imports: 40,940 bbl/day (2014 est.)
country comparison to the world: 92

Natural gas—production: 11.17 billion cu m (2015 est.)
country comparison to the world: 41

Natural gas—consumption: 17.33 billion cu m (2015 est.)
country comparison to the world: 46

Natural gas—exports: 1.078 million cu m (2015 est.)
country comparison to the world: 55

Natural gas—imports: 728 million cu m (2015 est.)
country comparison to the world: 64

Natural gas—proved reserves: 105.5 billion cu m (1 January 2017 es)
country comparison to the world: 52

Carbon dioxide emissions from consumption of energy: 76 million Mt (2013 est.)
country comparison to the world: 48

COMMUNICATIONS

Telephones—fixed lines: *total subscriptions:* 4.11 million
subscriptions per 100 inhabitants: 19 (July 2016 est.)
country comparison to the world: 33

Telephones—mobile cellular: *total:* 22.9 million
subscriptions per 100 inhabitants: 106 (July 2016 est.)
country comparison to the world: 53

Telephone system: *general assessment:* the telecommunications sector is being expanded and modernized; domestic and international service improving rapidly, especially mobile-cellular services
domestic: fixed-line teledensity is about 20 telephones per 100 persons; mobile market served by five mobile network operators; mobile-cellular teledensity over 105 telephones per 100 persons
international: country code—40; the Black Sea Fiber-Optic Cable System provides connectivity to Bulgaria and Turkey; satellite earth stations—10;

digital, international, direct-dial exchanges operate in Bucharest (2016)

Broadcast media: a mixture of public and private TV stations; there are 7 public TV stations (2 national, 5 regional) using terrestrial broadcasting and 187 private TV stations (out of which 171 offer local coverage) using terrestrial broadcasting, plus 11 public TV stations using satellite broadcasting and 86 private TV stations using satellite broadcasting; state-owned public radio broadcaster operates 4 national networks and regional and local stations, having in total 20 public radio stations by terrestrial broadcasting plus 4 public radio stations by satellite broadcasting; there are 502 operational private radio stations using terrestrial broadcasting and 26 private radio stations using satellite broadcasting (2014)

Internet country code: .ro

Internet users: *total:* 12,852,696
percent of population: 59.5% (July 2016 est.)
country comparison to the world: 44

TRANSPORTATION

National air transport system: number of registered air carriers: 5
inventory of registered aircraft operated by air carriers: 51
annual passenger traffic on registered air carriers: 3,636,642
annual freight traffic on registered air carriers: 4,691,280 mt-km (2015)
Civil aircraft registration country code prefix: YR (2016)

Airports: 45 (2013)
country comparison to the world: 96

Airports—with paved runways: *total:* 26
over 3,047 m: 4
2,438 to 3,047 m: 10
1,524 to 2,437 m: 11
under 914 m: 1 (2017)

Airports—with unpaved runways: *total:* 19
914 to 1,523 m: 5
under 914 m: 14 (2013)

Heliports: 2 (2013)

Pipelines: gas 3,726 km; oil 2,451 km (2013)

Railways: *total:* 11,268 km
broad gauge: 60 km 1.524-m gauge
standard gauge: 10,781 km 1.435-m gauge (3,292 km electrified)
narrow gauge: 427 km 0.760-m gauge (2014)
country comparison to the world: 23

Roadways: *total:* 84,185 km
paved: 49,873 km (includes 337 km of expressways)
unpaved: 34,312 km (2012)
country comparison to the world: 57

Waterways: 1,731 km (includes 1,075 km on the Danube River, 524 km on secondary branches, and 132 km on canals) (2010)
country comparison to the world: 45

Merchant marine: *total:* 114
by type: general cargo 13, oil tanker 7, other 94 (2017)
country comparison to the world: 78

Ports and terminals: *major seaport(s):* Constanta, Midia
river port(s): Braila, Galati (Galatz), Mancanului (Giurgiu), Tulcea (Danube River)

MILITARY AND SECURITY

Military expenditures: 1.42% of GDP (2016)

1.45% of GDP (2015)
1.35% of GDP (2014)
1.28% of GDP (2013)
1.22% of GDP (2012)
country comparison to the world: 69

Military branches: Ground Forces, Navy, Air Force (2016)

Military service age and obligation: conscription ended 2006; 18 years of age for male and female voluntary service; all military inductees (including women) contract for an initial 5-year term of service, with subsequent successive 3-year terms until age 36 (2015)

TRANSNATIONAL ISSUES

Disputes—international: the ICJ ruled largely in favor of Romania in its dispute submitted in 2004 over Ukrainian-administered Zmiyinyy/Serpilor (Snake) Island and Black Sea maritime boundary delimitation; Romania opposes Ukraine's reopening of a navigation canal from the Danube border through Ukraine to the Black Sea

Refugees and internally displaced persons: stateless persons: 249 (2016)

Illicit drugs: major transshipment point for Southwest Asian heroin transiting the Balkan route and small amounts of Latin American cocaine bound for Western Europe; although not a significant financial center, role as a narcotics conduit leaves it vulnerable to laundering, which occurs via the banking system, currency exchange houses, and casinos

RUSSIA

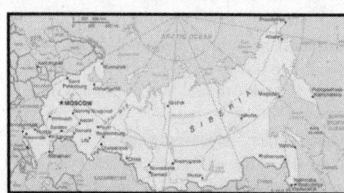

INTRODUCTION

Background: Founded in the 12th century, the Principality of Muscovy was able to emerge from over 200 years of Mongol domination (13th-15th centuries) and to gradually conquer and absorb surrounding principalities. In the early 17th century, a new ROMANOV Dynasty continued this policy of expansion across Siberia to the Pacific. Under PETER I (ruled 1682-1725), hegemony was extended to the Baltic Sea and the country was renamed the Russian Empire. During the 19th century, more territorial acquisitions were made in Europe and Asia. Defeat in the Russo-Japanese War of 1904-05 contributed to the Revolution of 1905, which resulted in the formation of a parliament and other reforms. Repeated devastating defeats of the Russian army in World War I led to widespread rioting in the major cities of the Russian Empire and to the overthrow in 1917 of the imperial household. The communists under Vladimir LENIN seized power soon after and formed the USSR. The brutal rule of Iosif STALIN (1928-53) strengthened communist rule and Russian dominance of the Soviet Union at a cost of tens of millions of lives. After defeating Germany in World War II as part of an alliance with the US (1939-1945), the USSR expanded its territory and influence in Eastern Europe and emerged as a global power. The USSR was the principal adversary of the US during the Cold War (1947-1991). The Soviet economy and society stagnated in the decades following Stalin's rule, until General Secretary Mikhail GORBACHEV (1985-91) introduced glasnost (openness) and perestroika (restructuring) in an attempt to modernize communism, but his initiatives inadvertently released forces that by December 1991 splintered the USSR into Russia and 14 other independent republics.

Following economic and political turmoil during President Boris YELTSIN's term (1991-99), Russia shifted toward a centralized authoritarian state under the leadership of President Vladimir PUTIN (2000-2008, 2012-present) in which the regime seeks to legitimize its rule through managed elections, populist appeals, a foreign policy focused on enhancing the country's geopolitical influence, and commodity-based economic growth. Russia faces a largely subdued rebel movement in Chechnya and some other surrounding regions, although violence still occurs throughout the North Caucasus.

GEOGRAPHY

Location: North Asia bordering the Arctic Ocean, extending from Europe (the portion west of the Urals) to the North Pacific Ocean

Geographic coordinates: 60 00 N, 100 00 E

Map references: Asia

Area: *total:* 17,098,242 sq km
land: 16,377,742 sq km
water: 720,500 sq km
country comparison to the world: 1

Area—comparative: approximately 1.8 times the size of the US

Land boundaries: *total:* 22,408 km
border countries (14): Azerbaijan 338 km, Belarus 1,312 km, China (southeast) 4,133 km, China (south) 46 km, Estonia 324 km, Finland 1,309 km, Georgia 894 km, Kazakhstan 7,644 km, North Korea 18 km, Latvia 332 km, Lithuania (Kaliningrad Oblast) 261 km, Mongolia 3,452 km, Norway 191 km, Poland (Kaliningrad Oblast) 210 km, Ukraine 1,944 km

Coastline: 37,653 km

Maritime claims: *territorial sea:* 12 nm
contiguous zone: 24 nm
exclusive economic zone: 200 nm
continental shelf: 200-m depth or to the depth of exploitation

Climate: ranges from steppes in the south through humid continental in much of European Russia; subarctic in Siberia to tundra climate in the polar north; winters vary from cool along Black Sea coast to frigid in Siberia; summers vary from warm in the steppes to cool along Arctic coast

Terrain: broad plain with low hills west of Urals; vast coniferous forest and tundra in Siberia; uplands and mountains along southern border regions

Elevation: *mean elevation:* 600 m
elevation extremes: *lowest point:* Caspian Sea -28 m
highest point: Gora El'brus 5,642 m (highest point in Europe)

Natural resources: wide natural resource base including major deposits of oil, natural gas, coal, and many strategic minerals, reserves of rare earth elements, timber
note: formidable obstacles of climate, terrain, and distance hinder exploitation of natural resources

Land use: *agricultural land:* 13.1%
arable land: 7.3%;
permanent crops: 0.1%;
permanent pasture: 5.7%
forest: 49.4%
other: 37.5% (2011 est.)
Irrigated land: 43,000 sq km (2012)

Population—distribution: population is heavily concentrated in the westernmost fifth of the country extending from the Baltic Sea, south to the Caspian Sea, and eastward parallel to the Kazakh border; elsewhere, sizeable pockets are isolated and generally found in the south

Natural hazards: permafrost over much of Siberia is a major impediment to development; volcanic activity in the Kuril Islands; volcanoes and earthquakes on the Kamchatka Peninsula; spring floods and summer/autumn forest fires throughout Siberia and parts of European Russia

volcanism: significant volcanic activity on the Kamchatka Peninsula and Kuril Islands; the peninsula alone is home to some 29 historically active volcanoes, with dozens more in the Kuril Islands; Kliuchevskoi (4,835 m), which erupted in 2007 and 2010, is Kamchatka's most active volcano; Avachinsky and Koryaksky volcanoes, which pose a threat to the city of Petropavlovsk-Kamchatsky, have been deemed Decade Volcanoes by the International Association of Volcanology and Chemistry of the Earth's Interior, worthy of study due to their explosive history and close proximity to human populations; other notable historically active volcanoes include Bezymianny, Chikurachki, Ebeko, Gorely, Grozny, Karymsky, Ketoi, Kronotsky, Ksudach, Medvezhia, Mutnovsky, Sarychev Peak, Shiveluch, Tiatia, Tolbachik, and Zheltovsky

Environment—current issues: air pollution from heavy industry, emissions of coal-fired electric plants, and transportation in major cities; industrial, municipal, and agricultural pollution of inland waterways and seacoasts; deforestation; soil erosion; soil contamination from improper application of agricultural chemicals; scattered areas of sometimes intense radioactive contamination; groundwater contamination from toxic waste; urban solid waste management; abandoned stocks of obsolete pesticides

Environment—international agreements: *party to:* Air Pollution, Air Pollution-Nitrogen Oxides, Air Pollution-Sulfur 85, Antarctic-Environmental Protocol, Antarctic-Marine Living Resources, Antarctic Seals, Antarctic Treaty, Biodiversity, Climate Change, Climate Change-Kyoto Protocol, Desertification, Endangered Species, Environmental Modification, Hazardous Wastes, Law of the Sea, Marine Dumping, Ozone Layer Protection, Ship Pollution, Tropical Timber 83, Wetlands, Whaling
signed, but not ratified: Air Pollution-Sulfur 94

Geography—note: largest country in the world in terms of area but unfavorably located in relation to major sea lanes of the world; despite its size, much of the country lacks proper soils and climates (either too cold or too dry) for agriculture; Mount El'brus is Europe's tallest peak; Lake Baikal, the deepest lake in the world, is estimated to hold one fifth of the world's fresh water

PEOPLE AND SOCIETY

Population: 142,257,519 (July 2017 est.)
country comparison to the world: 9

Nationality: *noun:* Russian(s)
adjective: Russian

Ethnic groups: Russian 77.7%, Tatar 3.7%, Ukrainian 1.4%, Bashkir 1.1%, Chuvash 1%, Chechen 1%, other 10.2%, unspecified 3.9%
note: nearly 200 national and/or ethnic groups are represented in Russia's 2010 census (2010 est.)

Languages: Russian (official) 85.7%, Tatar 3.2%, Chechen 1%, other 10.1%
note: data represent native language spoken (2010 est.)

Religions: Russian Orthodox 15-20%, Muslim 10-15%, other Christian 2% (2006 est.)
note: estimates are of practicing worshipers; Russia has large populations of non-practicing believers and non-believers, a legacy of over seven decades of Soviet rule; Russia officially recognizes Orthodox Christianity, Islam, Judaism, and Buddhism as traditional religions

Age structure: *0-14 years:* 17.12% (male 12,509,563/female 11,843,254)
15-24 years: 9.46% (male 6,881,880/female 6,572,191)
25-54 years: 44.71% (male 31,220,990/female 32,375,489)
55-64 years: 14.44% (male 8,849,707/female 11,693,131)
65 years and over: 14.28% (male 6,352,557/female 13,958,757) (2017 est.)

Dependency ratios: *total dependency ratio:* 43.5
youth dependency ratio: 24.2
elderly dependency ratio: 19.4
potential support ratio: 5.2 (2015 est.)

Median age: *total:* 39.6 years
male: 36.6 years
female: 42.5 years (2017 est.)
country comparison to the world: 53

Population growth rate: -0.08% (2017 est.)
country comparison to the world: 205

Birth rate: 11 births/1,000 population (2017 est.)
country comparison to the world: 178

Death rate: 13.5 deaths/1,000 population (2017 est.)
country comparison to the world: 9

Net migration rate: 1.7 migrant(s)/1,000 population (2017 est.)
country comparison to the world: 52

Population distribution: population is heavily concentrated in the westernmost fifth of the country extending from the Baltic Sea, south to the Caspian Sea, and eastward parallel to the Kazakh border; elsewhere, sizeable pockets are isolated and generally found in the south

Urbanization: *urban population:* 74.2% of total population (2017)
rate of urbanization: -0.15% annual rate of change (2015-20 est.)

Major urban areas—population: MOSCOW (capital) 12.166 million; Saint Petersburg 4.993 million; Novosibirsk 1.497 million; Yekaterinburg 1.379 million; Nizhniy Novgorod 1.212 million; Samara 1.164 million (2015)

Sex ratio: *at birth:* 1.06 male(s)/female
0-14 years: 1.06 male(s)/female
15-24 years: 1.05 male(s)/female
25-54 years: 0.96 male(s)/female
55-64 years: 0.75 male(s)/female
65 years and over: 0.45 male(s)/female
total population: 0.86 male(s)/female (2016 est.)

Mother's mean age at first birth: 24.6 years (2009 est.)

Maternal mortality ratio: 25 deaths/100,000 live births (2015 est.)
country comparison to the world: 122

Infant mortality rate: *total:* 6.8 deaths/1,000 live births
male: 7.6 deaths/1,000 live births
female: 5.9 deaths/1,000 live births (2017 est.)
country comparison to the world: 163

Life expectancy at birth: *total population:* 71 years
male: 65.3 years
female: 77.1 years (2017 est.)
country comparison to the world: 154

Total fertility rate: 1.61 children born/woman (2017 est.)
country comparison to the world: 179

Contraceptive prevalence rate: 68%
note: percent of women aged 15-44 (2011)

Health expenditures: 7.1% of GDP (2014)
country comparison to the world: 80

Physicians density: 3.31 physicians/1,000 population (2014)

Hospital bed density: 9.7 beds/1,000 population (2006)

Drinking water source:
improved:
urban: 98.9% of population
rural: 91.2% of population
total: 96.9% of population
unimproved:
urban: 1.1% of population
rural: 8.8% of population
total: 3.1% of population (2015 est.)

Sanitation facility access:
improved:
urban: 77% of population
rural: 58.7% of population
total: 72.2% of population
unimproved:
urban: 23% of population
rural: 41.3% of population
total: 27.8% of population (2015 est.)

HIV/AIDS—adult prevalence rate: NA

HIV/AIDS—people living with HIV/AIDS: NA

HIV/AIDS—deaths: NA

Major infectious diseases: degree of risk: intermediate
food or waterborne diseases: bacterial diarrhea
vectorborne disease: tickborne encephalitis (2016)

Obesity—adult prevalence rate: 23.1% (2016)
country comparison to the world: 70

Education expenditures: 3.9% of GDP (2012)
country comparison to the world: 110

Literacy: *definition:* age 15 and over can read and write
total population: 99.7%
male: 99.7%
female: 99.6% (2015 est.)

School life expectancy (primary to tertiary education): *total:* 15 years
male: 15 years
female: 15 years (2014)

Unemployment, youth ages 15-24: *total:* 16%
male: 15.3%

female: 16.9% (2015 est.)
country comparison to the world: 78

GOVERNMENT

Country name: *conventional long form:* Russian Federation
conventional short form: Russia
local long form: Rossiyskaya Federatsiya
local short form: Rossiya
former: Russian Empire, Russian Soviet Federative Socialist Republic
etymology: Russian lands were generally referred to as Muscovy until PETER I officially declared the Russian Empire in 1721; the new name sought to invoke the patrimony of the medieval eastern European Rus state centered on Kyiv in present-day Ukraine; the Rus were a Varangian (eastern Viking) elite that imposed their rule and eventually their name on their Slavic subjects

Government type: semi-presidential federation

Capital: *name:* Moscow
geographic coordinates: 55 45 N, 37 36 E
time difference: UTC+3 (8 hours ahead of Washington, DC, during Standard Time)
note: Russia has 11 time zones, the largest number of contiguous time zones of any country in the world; in 2014, two time zones were added and DST was dropped

Administrative divisions: 46 provinces (oblasti, singular—oblast), 21 republics (respubliki, singular—respublika), 4 autonomous okrugs (avtonomnyye okrugi, singular—avtonomnyy okrug), 9 krays (kraya, singular—kray), 2 federal cities (goroda, singular—gorod), and 1 autonomous oblast (avtonomnaya oblast')
oblasts: Amur (Blagoveshchensk), Arkhangel'sk, Astrakhan', Belgorod, Bryansk, Chelyabinsk, Irkutsk, Ivanovo, Kaliningrad, Kaluga, Kemerovo, Kirov, Kostroma, Kurgan, Kursk, Leningrad, Lipetsk, Magadan, Moscow, Murmansk, Nizhniy Novgorod, Novgorod, Novosibirsk, Omsk, Orenburg, Orel, Penza, Pskov, Rostov, Ryazan', Sakhalin (Yuzhno-Sakhalinsk), Samara, Saratov, Smolensk, Sverdlovsk (Yekaterinburg), Tambov, Tomsk, Tula, Tver', Tyumen', Ul'yanovsk, Vladimir, Volgograd, Vologda, Voronezh, Yaroslavl'
republics: Adygeya (Maykop), Altay (Gorno-Altaysk), Bashkortostan (Ufa), Buryatiya (Ulan-Ude), Chechnya (Groznyy), Chuvashiya (Cheboksary), Dagestan (Makhachkala), Ingushetiya (Magas), Kabardino-Balkariya (Nal'chik), Kalmykiya (Elista), Karachayevo-Cherkesiya (Cherkessk), Kareliya (Petrozavodsk), Khakasiya (Abakan), Komi (Syktyvkar), Mariy-El (Yoshkar-Ola), Mordoviya (Saransk), North Ossetia (Vladikavkaz), Sakha [Yakutiya] (Yakutsk), Tatarstan (Kazan'), Tyva (Kyzyl), Udmurtiya (Izhevsk)
autonomous okrugs: Chukotka (Anadyr'), Khanty-Mansi-Yugra (Khanty-Mansiysk), Nenets (Nar'yan-Mar), Yamalo-Nenets (Salekhard)
krays: Altay (Barnaul), Kamchatka (Petropavlovsk-Kamchatskiy), Khabarovsk, Krasnodar, Krasnoyarsk, Perm', Primorskiy [Maritime] (Vladivostok), Stavropol', Zabaykal'sk [Transbaikal] (Chita)

federal cities: Moscow [Moskva], Saint Petersburg [Sankt-Peterburg] autonomous oblast: Yevreyskaya [Jewish] (Birobidzhan)
note 1: administrative divisions have the same names as their administrative centers (exceptions have the administrative center name following in parentheses)
note 2: the United States does not recognize Russia's annexation of Ukraine's Autonomous Republic of Crimea and the municipality of Sevastopol, nor their redesignation as the Republic of Crimea and the Federal City of Sevastopol

Independence: 24 August 1991 (from the Soviet Union); notable earlier dates: 1157 (Principality of Vladimir-Suzdal created); 16 January 1547 (Tsardom of Muscovy established); 22 October 1721 (Russian Empire proclaimed); 30 December 1922 (Soviet Union established)

National holiday: Russia Day, 12 June (1990)

Constitution: *history:* several previous (during Russian Empire and Soviet era); latest drafted 12 July 1993, adopted by referendum 12 December 1993, effective 25 December 1993
amendments: proposed by the president of the Russian Federation, by either house of the Federal Assembly, by the government of the Russian Federation, or by legislative (representative) bodies of the Federation's constituent entities; proposals to amend the government's constitutional system, human and civil rights and freedoms, and procedures for amending or drafting a new constitution require formation of a Constitutional Assembly; passage of such amendments requires two-thirds majority vote of its total membership; passage in a referendum requires participation of an absolute majority of eligible voters and an absolute majority of valid votes; approval of proposed amendments to the government structure, authorities, and procedures requires approval by the legislative bodies of at least two-thirds of the Russian Federation's constituent entities; amended 2008, 2014 (2017)

Legal system: civil law system; judicial review of legislative acts

International law organization participation: has not submitted an ICJ jurisdiction declaration; non-party state to the ICCt

Citizenship: *citizenship by birth:* no
citizenship by descent only: at least one parent must be a citizen of Russia
dual citizenship recognized: yes
residency requirement for naturalization: 3-5 years

Suffrage: 18 years of age; universal

Executive branch: *chief of state:* President Vladimir Vladimirovich PUTIN (since 7 May 2012)
head of government: Premier Dmitriy Anatolyevich MEDVEDEV (since 8 May 2012); First Deputy Premier Igor Ivanovich SHUVALOV (since 12 May 2008); Deputy Premiers Arkadiy Vladimirovich DVORKOVICH (since 21 May 2012), Olga Yuryevna GOLODETS (since 21 May 2012), Aleksandr Gennadiyevich KHLOPONIN (since 19 January 2010), Dmitriy Nikolayevich

KOZAK (since 14 October 2008), Vitaliy Leontyevich MUTKO (since 19 October 2016), Dmitriy Olegovich ROGOZIN (since 23 December 2011), Sergey Eduardovich PRIKHODKO (since 22 May 2013); Yuriy Petrovich TRUTNEV (since 31 August 2013)

cabinet: the "Government" is composed of the premier, his deputies, and ministers, all appointed by the president; the premier is also confirmed by the Duma

elections/appointments: president directly elected by absolute majority popular vote in 2 rounds if needed for a 6-year term (eligible for a second term); election last held on 4 March 2012 (next to be held in March 2018); note—term length extended to 6 years from 4 years in late 2008, effective after the 2012 election; there is no vice president; premier appointed by the president with the approval of the Duma

election results: Vladimir PUTIN elected president; percent of vote—Vladimir PUTIN (United Russia) 63.6%, Gennadiy ZYUGANOV (CPRF) 17.2%, Mikhail PROKHOROV (CP) 8%, Vladimir ZHIRINOVSKIY (LDPR) 6.2%, Sergey MIRONOV (A Just Russia) 3.9%, other 1.1%; Dmitriy MEDVEDEV (United Russia) approved as premier by Duma; vote—299 to 144

note: there is also a Presidential Administration that provides staff and policy support to the president, drafts presidential decrees, and coordinates policy among government agencies; a Security Council also reports directly to the president

Legislative branch: *description:* bicameral Federal Assembly or Federalnoye Sobraniye consists of the Federation Council or Sovet Federatsii (170 seats; 2 members in each of the 83 federal administrative units (see note below)—oblasts, krays, republics, autonomous okrugs and oblasts, and the federal cities of Moscow and Saint Petersburg—appointed by the top executive and legislative officials; members serve 4-year terms) and the State Duma or Gosudarstvennaya Duma (450 seats; as of February 2014, the electoral system reverted to a mixed electoral system for the 2016 election, in which one-half of the members are directly elected by simple majority vote and one-half directly elected by proportional representation vote; members serve 5-year terms)

elections: State Duma—last held on 18 September 2016 (next to be held in fall 2021)

election results: State Duma—United Russia 54.2%, CPRF 13.3%, LDPR 13.1%, A Just Russia 6.2%, Rodina 1.5%, CP 0.2%; seats by party—United Russia 343, CPRF 42, LDPR 39, A Just Russia 23, Rodina 1, CP 1, independent 1

note: the State Duma now includes 3 representatives and the Federation Council 2 each from the Republic of Crimea and the Federal City of Sevastopol, two regions that Russia occupied and attempted to annex from Ukraine and that the US does not recognize as part of Russia

Judicial branch: *highest court(s):* Supreme Court of the Russian Federation (consists of 170 members organized into the Judicial Panel for Civil Affairs, the Judicial Panel for Criminal Affairs, and the Military Panel); Constitutional Court (consists of 19 members); note—in February 2014, Russia's Superior Court of Arbitration was abolished and its former authorities transferred to the Supreme Court, which in addition to being the country's highest judicial authority for appeals, civil, criminal, administrative, and military cases, and the disciplinary judicial board now has jurisdiction over economic disputes

judge selection and term of office: all members of Russia's 3 highest courts nominated by the president and appointed by the Federation Council (the upper house of the legislature); members of all 3 courts appointed for life

subordinate courts: Higher Arbitration Court; regional (kray) and provincial (oblast) courts; Moscow and St. Petersburg city courts; autonomous province and district courts; note—the 21 Russian Republics have court systems specified by their own constitutions

Political parties and leaders: A Just Russia [Sergey MIRONOV] Civic Platform or CP [Rifat SHAYKHUTDINOV] Communist Party of the Russian Federation or CPRF [Gennadiy ZYUGANOV] Liberal Democratic Party of Russia or LDPR [Vladimir ZHIRINOVSKIY] Rodina [Aleksei ZHURAVLYOV] United Russia [Dmitriy MEDVEDEV]

note: 72 political parties are registered with Russia's Ministry of Justice (as of August 2017), but only six parties maintain representation in Russia's national legislature, and two of these only have one deputy apiece

Political pressure groups and leaders: Committees of Soldiers' Mothers
Confederation of Labor of Russia or KTR
Federation of Independent Trade Unions of Russia
Golos Association in Defense of Voters' Rights
Memorial
Movement Against Illegal Migration
Russkiye
Solidarnost
The World Russian People's Congress
Union of Russian Writers
other: business associations; environmental organizations; religious groups (especially those with Orthodox or Muslim affiliation); veterans groups

International organization participation: APEC, Arctic Council, ARF, ASEAN (dialogue partner), BIS, BRICS, BSEC, CBSS, CD, CE, CERN (observer), CICA, CIS, CSTO, EAEC, EAEU, EAPC, EAS, EBRD, FAO, FATF, G-20, GCTU, IAEA, IBRD, ICAO, ICC (national committees), ICRM, IDA, IFAD, IFC, IFRCS, IHO, ILO, IMF, IMO, IMSO, Interpol, IOC, IOM (observer), IPU, ISO, ITSO, ITU, ITUC (NGOs), LAIA (observer), MIGA, MINURSO, MONUSCO, NEA, NSG, OAS (observer), OIC (observer), OPCW, OSCE, Paris Club, PCA, PFP, SCO, UN, UNCTAD, UNESCO, UNHCR, UNIDO, UNISFA, UNMIL, UNMISS, UNOCI, UNSC (permanent), UNTSO, UNWTO, UPU, WCO, WFTU (NGOs), WHO, WIPO, WMO, WTO, ZC

Diplomatic representation in the US: chief of mission: Ambassador Anatoliy Ivanovich ANTONOV (since 8 September 2017)

chancery: 2650 Wisconsin Avenue NW, Washington, DC 20007
telephone: [1] (202) 298-5700, 5701, 5704, 5708
FAX: [1] (202) 298-5735
consulate(s) general: Houston, New York, Seattle

Diplomatic representation from the US: *chief of mission:* Ambassador Jon HUNTSMAN (since 3 October 2017)
embassy: Bolshoy Deviatinskiy Pereulok No. 8, 121099 Moscow
mailing address: PSC-77, APO AE 09721
telephone: [7] (495) 728-5000
FAX: [7] (495) 728-5090
consulate(s) general: Saint Petersburg, Vladivostok, Yekaterinburg

Flag description: three equal horizontal bands of white (top), blue, and red
note: the colors may have been based on those of the Dutch flag; despite many popular interpretations, there is no official meaning assigned to the colors of the Russian flag; this flag inspired several other Slav countries to adopt horizontal tricolors of the same colors but in different arrangements, and so red, blue, and white became the Pan-Slav colors

National symbol(s): bear, double-headed eagle; national colors: white, blue, red

National anthem: *name:* "Gimn Rossiyskoy Federatsii" (National Anthem of the Russian Federation)
lyrics/music: Sergey Vladimirovich MIKHALKOV/Aleksandr Vasilyevich ALEKSANDROV
note: in 2000, Russia adopted the tune of the anthem of the former Soviet Union (composed in 1939); the lyrics, also adopted in 2000, were written by the same person who authored the Soviet lyrics in 1943

ECONOMY

Economy—overview: Russia has undergone significant changes since the collapse of the Soviet Union, moving from a centrally planned economy towards a more market-based system. Both economic growth and reform have stalled in recent years, however, and Russia remains a predominantly statist economy with a high concentration of wealth in officials' hands. Economic reforms in the 1990s privatized most industry, with notable exceptions in the energy, transportation, banking, and defense-related sectors. The protection of property rights is still weak, and the state continues to interfere in the free operation of the private sector.

Russia is one of the world's leading producers of oil and natural gas, and is also a top exporter of metals such as steel and primary aluminum. Russia is heavily dependent on the movement of world commodity prices as reliance on commodity exports makes it vulnerable to boom and bust cycles that follow the volatile swings in global prices. The economy, which had averaged 7% growth during the 1998-2008 period as oil prices rose rapidly, has seen diminishing growth rates since then due to the exhaustion of Russia's commodity-based growth model.

A combination of falling oil prices, international sanctions, and structural limitations pushed Russia into a deep recession in 2015, with GDP falling by close by 2.8%. The downturn continued through 2016, with GDP contracting another 0.2%, but was reversed in 2017 as world demand picked up. Government support for import substitution has increased recently in an effort to diversify the economy away from extractive industries.

GDP (purchasing power parity): $4 trillion (2017 est.)
$3.93 trillion (2016 est.)
$3.938 trillion (2015 est.)
note: data are in 2017 dollars
country comparison to the world: 7

GDP (official exchange rate): $1.469 trillion (2016 est.)

GDP—real growth rate: 1.8% (2017 est.)
-0.2% (2016 est.)
-2.8% (2015 est.)
country comparison to the world: 161

GDP—per capita (PPP): $27,900 (2017 est.)
$27,400 (2016 est.)
$27,500 (2015 est.)
note: data are in 2017 dollars
country comparison to the world: 71

Gross national saving: 26.6% of GDP (2017 est.)
27.3% of GDP (2016 est.)
27.2% of GDP (2015 est.)
country comparison to the world: 42

GDP—composition, by end use:
household consumption: 52.4%
government consumption: 17.8%
investment in fixed capital: 21.1%
investment in inventories: 2.5%
exports of goods and services: 25.6%
imports of goods and services: -19.4% (2017 est.)

GDP—composition, by sector of origin:
agriculture: 4.7%
industry: 32.4%
services: 62.3% (2017 est.)

Agriculture—products: grain, sugar beets, sunflower seeds, vegetables, fruits; beef, milk

Industries: complete range of mining and extractive industries producing coal, oil, gas, chemicals, and metals; all forms of machine building from rolling mills to high-performance aircraft and space vehicles; defense industries (including radar, missile production, advanced electronic components), shipbuilding; road and rail transportation equipment; communications equipment; agricultural machinery, tractors, and construction equipment; electric power generating and transmitting equipment; medical and scientific instruments; consumer durables, textiles, foodstuffs, handicrafts

Industrial production growth rate: 1.1% (2017 est.)
country comparison to the world: 160

Labor force: 76.53 million (2017 est.)
country comparison to the world: 7

Labor force—by occupation: *agriculture:* 9.4%
industry: 27.6%
services: 63% (2016 est.)

Unemployment rate: 5.5% (2017 est.)

5.5% (2016 est.)
country comparison to the world: 76

Population below poverty line: 13.3% (2015 est.)

Household income or consumption by percentage share: *lowest 10%:* 2.3%
highest 10%: 32.2% (2012 est.)

Distribution of family income—Gini index: 41.2 (2015)
41.9 (2013)
country comparison to the world: 54

Budget: *revenues:* $253.9 billion
expenditures: $287.5 billion (2017 est.)
Taxes and other revenues: 17.3% of GDP (2017 est.)
country comparison to the world: 175

Budget surplus (+) or deficit (-): -2.3% of GDP (2017 est.)
country comparison to the world: 95

Public debt: 11.8% of GDP (2017 est.)
10% of GDP (2016 est.)
note: data cover general government debt, and includes debt instruments issued (or owned) by government entities other than the treasury; the data include treasury debt held by foreign entities; the data include debt issued by subnational entities, as well as intra-governmental debt; intra-governmental debt consists of treasury borrowings from surpluses in the social funds, such as for retirement, medical care, and unemployment, debt instruments for the social funds are not sold at public auctions
country comparison to the world: 196

Fiscal year: calendar year

Inflation rate (consumer prices): 4.2% (2017 est.)
7% (2016 est.)
country comparison to the world: 161

Central bank discount rate: 10% (31 December 2016 est.)
11% (03 August 2015)
note: this is the so-called refinancing rate, but in Russia banks do not get refinancing at this rate; this is a reference rate used primarily for fiscal purposes
country comparison to the world: 21

Commercial bank prime lending rate: 10.3% (31 December 2017 est.)
12.59% (31 December 2016 est.)
country comparison to the world: 80

Stock of narrow money: $204.9 billion (31 December 2017 est.)
$195.9 billion (31 December 2016 est.)
country comparison to the world: 25

Stock of broad money: $688.4 billion (31 December 2017 est.)
$633.4 billion (31 December 2016 est.)
country comparison to the world: 20

Stock of domestic credit: $825.8 billion (31 December 2017 est.)
$770.1 billion (31 December 2016 est.)
country comparison to the world: 18

Market value of publicly traded shares: $635.9 billion (31 December 2016 est.)
$393.2 billion (31 December 2015 est.)

$385.9 billion (31 December 2014 est.)
country comparison to the world: 19

Current account balance: $41.46 billion (2017 est.)
$25.54 billion (2016 est.)
country comparison to the world: 12

Exports: $336.8 billion (2017 est.)
$281.9 billion (2016 est.)
country comparison to the world: 17

Exports—commodities: petroleum and petroleum products, natural gas, metals, wood and wood products, chemicals, and a wide variety of civilian and military manufactures

Exports—partners: Netherlands 10.5%, China 10.3%, Germany 7.8%, Turkey 5%, Italy 4.4%, Belarus 4.3% (2016)

Imports: $212.7 billion (2017 est.)
$191.6 billion (2016 est.)
country comparison to the world: 23

Imports—commodities: machinery, vehicles, pharmaceutical products, plastic, semi-finished metal products, meat, fruits and nuts, optical and medical instruments, iron, steel

Imports—partners: China 21.6%, Germany 11%, US 6.3%, France 4.8%, Italy 4.4%, Belarus 4.3% (2016)

Reserves of foreign exchange and gold: $418.5 billion (31 December 2017 est.)
$377.7 billion (31 December 2016 est.)
country comparison to the world: 7

Debt—external: $451.5 billion (31 December 2017 est.)
$434.8 billion (31 December 2016 est.)
country comparison to the world: 28

Stock of direct foreign investment—at home: $479.7 billion (31 December 2017 est.)
$461.7 billion (31 December 2016 est.)
country comparison to the world: 19

Stock of direct foreign investment—abroad: $443 billion (31 December 2017 est.)
$418 billion (31 December 2016 est.)
country comparison to the world: 19

Exchange rates: Russian rubles (RUB) per US dollar—
58.39 (2017 est.)
67.056 (2016 est.)
67.056 (2015 est.)
60.938 (2014 est.)
38.378 (2013 est.)

ENERGY

Electricity access: *electrification—total population:* 100% (2016)

Electricity—production: 1.008 trillion kWh (2015 est.)
country comparison to the world: 5

Electricity—consumption: 890.1 billion kWh (2015 est.)
country comparison to the world: 6

Electricity—exports: 13.13 billion kWh (2016 est.)
country comparison to the world: 16

Electricity—imports: 3.194 billion kWh (2016 est.)
country comparison to the world: 50

Electricity—installed generating capacity: 263.5 million kW (2015 est.)
country comparison to the world: 6

Electricity—from fossil fuels: 70.2% of total installed capacity (2015 est.)
country comparison to the world: 104

Electricity—from nuclear fuels: 9.7% of total installed capacity (2015 est.)
country comparison to the world: 16

Electricity—from hydroelectric plants: 19% of total installed capacity (2015 est.)
country comparison to the world: 92

Electricity—from other renewable sources: 0.6% of total installed capacity (2015 est.)
country comparison to the world: 148

Crude oil—production: 10.55 million bbl/day (2016 est.)
country comparison to the world: 1

Crude oil—exports: 5.116 million bbl/day (2016 est.)
country comparison to the world: 2

Crude oil—imports: 15,110 bbl/day (2016 est.)
country comparison to the world: 67

Crude oil—proved reserves: 80 billion bbl (1 January 2017 es)
country comparison to the world: 8

Refined petroleum products—production: 6.174 million bbl/day (2014 est.)
country comparison to the world: 4

Refined petroleum products—consumption: 3.594 million bbl/day (2015 est.)
country comparison to the world: 6

Refined petroleum products—exports: 3.133 million bbl/day (2014 est.)
country comparison to the world: 2

Refined petroleum products—imports: 47,770 bbl/day (2016 est.)
country comparison to the world: 84

Natural gas—production: 598.6 billion cu m (2015 est.)
country comparison to the world: 2

Natural gas—consumption: 418.9 billion cu m (2015 est.)
country comparison to the world: 3

Natural gas—exports: 197.7 billion cu m (2015 est.)
country comparison to the world: 1

Natural gas—imports: 18 billion cu m (2015 est.)
country comparison to the world: 20

Natural gas—proved reserves: 47.8 trillion cu m (1 January 2017 es)
country comparison to the world: 1

Carbon dioxide emissions from consumption of energy: 1.756 billion Mt (2014 est.)
country comparison to the world: 5

COMMUNICATIONS

Telephones—fixed lines: *total subscriptions:* 32,276,615

subscriptions per 100 inhabitants: 23 (July 2016 est.)
country comparison to the world: 7

Telephones—mobile cellular: *total:* 231,393,994
subscriptions per 100 inhabitants: 163 (July 2016 est.)
country comparison to the world: 7

Telephone system: *general assessment:* telecom sector impacted by sanctions related to the annexations in Ukraine; mobile market dominaed by four major operators; the estimated number of mobile subscribers jumped from fewer than 1 million in 1998 to 255 million in 2016; fixed-line service has improved but a large demand remains
domestic: cross-country digital trunk lines run from Saint Petersburg to Khabarovsk, and from Moscow to Novorossiysk; the telephone systems in 60 regional capitals have modern digital infrastructures; cellular services, both analog and digital, are available in many areas; in rural areas, telephone services are still outdated, inadequate, and low-density
international: country code—7; connected internationally by undersea fiber -optic cables; satellite earth stations provide access to Intelsat, Intersputnik, Eutelsat, Inmarsat, and Orbita systems (2016)

Broadcast media: 13 national TV stations with the federal government owning 1 and holding a controlling interest in a second; state-owned Gazprom maintains a controlling interest in 2 of the national channels; government-affiliated Bank Rossiya owns controlling interest in a fourth and fifth, while a sixth national channel is owned by the Moscow city administration; the Russian Orthodox Church and the Russian military, respectively, own 2 additional national channels; roughly 3,300 national, regional, and local TV stations with over two-thirds completely or partially controlled by the federal or local governments; satellite TV services are available; 2 state-run national radio networks with a third majority-owned by Gazprom; roughly 2,400 public and commercial radio stations (2016)

Internet country code: .ru; note—Russia also has responsibility for a legacy domain ".su" that was allocated to the Soviet Union and is being phased out

Internet users: *total:* 108,772,470

percent of population: 76.4% (July 2016 est.)
country comparison to the world: 7

TRANSPORTATION

National air transport system: number of registered air carriers: 32
inventory of registered aircraft operated by air carriers: 661
annual passenger traffic on registered air carriers: 76,846,126
annual freight traffic on registered air carriers: 4,761,047,070 mt-km (2015)
Civil aircraft registration country code prefix: RA (2016)

Airports: 1,218 (2013)
country comparison to the world: 5

Airports—with paved runways: *total:* 594
over 3,047 m: 54
2,438 to 3,047 m: 197
1,524 to 2,437 m: 123
914 to 1,523 m: 95
under 914 m: 125 (2017)

Airports—with unpaved runways: *total:* 624
over 3,047 m: 4
2,438 to 3,047 m: 13
1,524 to 2,437 m: 69
914 to 1,523 m: 81
under 914 m: 457 (2013)

Heliports: 49 (2013)

Pipelines: gas 177,700 km; oil 54,800 km; refined products 19,300 km (2016)

Railways: *total:* 87,157 km
broad gauge: 86,200 km 1.520-m gauge (40,300 km electrified)
narrow gauge: 957 km 1.067-m gauge (on Sakhalin Island)
note: an additional 30,000 km of non-common carrier lines serve industries (2014)
country comparison to the world: 3

Roadways: *total:* 1,283,387 km
paved: 927,721 km (includes 39,143 km of expressways)
unpaved: 355,666 km (2012)
country comparison to the world: 5

Waterways: 102,000 km (including 48,000 km with guaranteed depth; the 72,000-km system in European Russia links Baltic Sea, White Sea, Caspian Sea, Sea of Azov, and Black Sea) (2009)
country comparison to the world: 2

Merchant marine: *total:* 2,572
by type: bulk carrier 16, container ship 13, general cargo 874, oil tanker 411, other 1,258 (2017)
country comparison to the world: 10

Ports and terminals: *major seaport(s):* Kaliningrad, Nakhodka, Novorossiysk, Primorsk, Vostochnyy
river port(s): Saint Petersburg (Neva River)
oil terminal(s): Kavkaz oil terminal
container port(s) (TEUs): Saint Petersburg (2,365,174)
LNG terminal(s) (export): Sakhalin Island

MILITARY AND SECURITY

Military expenditures: 5.4% of GDP (2016)
4.86% of GDP (2015)
4.1% of GDP (2014)
3.96% of GDP (2013)
3.75% of GDP (2012)
country comparison to the world: 16

Military branches: Ground Troops (Sukhoputnyye Voyskia, SV), Navy (Voyenno-Morskoy Flot, VMF), Aerospace Forces (Vozdushno-Kosmicheskiye Sily, VKS); Airborne Troops (Vozdushno-Desantnyye Voyska, VDV) and Missile Troops of Strategic Purpose (Raketnyye Voyska Strategicheskogo Naznacheniya, RVSN) referred to commonly as Strategic Rocket Forces, are independent "combat arms," not subordinate to any of the three branches (2017)

Military service age and obligation: 18-27 years of age for compulsory or voluntary military service; males are registered for the draft at 17 years of age; 1-year service obligation (conscripts can only be sent to combat zones after 6 months of training); reserve obligation for non-officers to age 50; enrollment in military schools from the age of 16, cadets classified as members of the armed forces *note:* the chief of the General Staff Mobilization Directorate announced in March 2015 that for health reasons, only 76% of draftees called up during the spring 2015 draft campaign were fit for military service (2015)

TERRORISM

Terrorist groups—foreign based: Aum Shinrikyo (AUM): aim(s): attract new members seeking religious outlets and a willingness to commit an increasing amount of their assets to AUM
area(s) of operation: current membership is comprised largely of Russian nationals living in Russia, where the majority of members have lived since the group formed circa 1984, even during the group's peak in the 1990s of tens of thousands of members spread across the globe; according to Russian officials in 2016, there are between 1,500 and 30,000 Russian followers living in Russia; recruitment efforts have intensified in recent years; on 20 September 2016, the Russian Supreme Court declared the group to be a terrorist organization and outlawed its activity
Islamic State of Iraq and the Levant (ISIL): aim(s): implement its strict interpretation of Sharia in Dagestan, Chechnya, Ingushetia, and Kabardino-Balkariya
area(s) of operation: operational in the northern Caucasus's Dagestan, Chechnya, Ingushetia, and Kabardino-Balkariya (ISIL's Wilayat Kavkaz) regions, where the branch has been known as ISIL-Caucasus ISIL-C since 23 June 2015; ISIL-C claimed responsibility for attacking a Russian military base on 2 September 2015 in Magaramkent in southern Dagestan, killing and injuring several Russian citizens; ISIL-C was placed in the US Department of State's designated global terror category under Executive Order 13224 on 29 September 2015; overall leader Aslan Avgazarovich BYUTUKAEV (a.k.a. Emir Khamzat) commanded suicide battalions before assuming his current role in June 2015; BYUTUKAEV continues to direct suicide operations and is responsible for numerous lethal suicide bombings over the years, including the 24 January 2011 attack at Moscow's Domodedovo Airport that killed at least 37 people and injured over 100; comprises fighters from four Caucasus regions: Dagestan, Chechnya, Ingushetia, and Kabardino-Balkariya; as of early 2017, an estimated 2,400 Russian nationals were fighting alongside ISIL as foreign fighters

TRANSNATIONAL ISSUES

Disputes—international: Russia remains concerned about the smuggling of poppy derivatives from Afghanistan through Central Asian countries; China and Russia have demarcated the once disputed islands at the Amur and Ussuri confluence and in the Argun River in accordance with the 2004 Agreement, ending their centuries-long border disputes; the sovereignty dispute over the islands of Etorofu, Kunashiri, Shikotan, and the Habomai group, known in Japan as the "Northern Territories" and in Russia as the "Southern Kurils," occupied by the Soviet Union in 1945, now administered by Russia, and claimed by Japan, remains the primary sticking point to signing a peace treaty formally ending World War II hostilities; Russia's military support and subsequent recognition of Abkhazia and South Ossetia independence in 2008 continue to sour relations with Georgia; Azerbaijan, Kazakhstan, and Russia ratified Caspian seabed delimitation treaties based on equidistance, while Iran continues to insist on a one-fifth slice of the sea; Norway and Russia signed a comprehensive maritime boundary agreement in 2010; various groups in Finland advocate restoration of Karelia (Kareliya) and other areas ceded to the Soviet Union following World War II but the Finnish Government asserts no territorial demands; Russia and Estonia signed a technical border agreement in May 2005, but Russia recalled its signature in June 2005 after the Estonian parliament added to its domestic ratification act a historical preamble referencing the Soviet occupation and Estonia's pre-war borders under the 1920 Treaty of Tartu; Russia contends that the preamble allows Estonia to make territorial claims on Russia in the future, while Estonian officials deny that the preamble has any legal impact on the treaty text; Russia demands better treatment of the Russian-speaking population in Estonia and Latvia; Russia remains involved in the conflict in eastern Ukraine while also occupying Ukraine's territory of Crimea

Lithuania and Russia committed to demarcating their boundary in 2006 in accordance with the land and maritime treaty ratified by Russia in May 2003 and by Lithuania in 1999; Lithuania operates a simplified transit regime for Russian nationals traveling from the Kaliningrad coastal exclave into Russia, while still conforming, as an EU member state with an EU external border, where strict Schengen border rules apply; preparations for the demarcation delimitation of land boundary with Ukraine have commenced; the dispute over the boundary between Russia and Ukraine through the Kerch Strait and Sea of Azov is suspended due to the occupation of Crimea by Russia; Kazakhstan and Russia boundary delimitation was ratified on November 2005 and field demarcation should commence in 2007; Russian Duma has not yet ratified 1990 Bering Sea Maritime Boundary Agreement with the US; Denmark (Greenland) and Norway have made submissions to the Commission on the Limits of the Continental Shelf (CLCS) and Russia is collecting additional data to augment its 2001 CLCS submission

Refugees and internally displaced persons: refugees (country of origin): 427,240 (Ukraine) (2017)
IDPs: 19,000 (armed conflict, human rights violations, generalized violence in North Caucasus, particularly Chechnya and North Ossetia) (2016)

stateless persons: 90,771 (2016); note—Russia's stateless population consists of Roma, Meskhetian Turks, and ex-Soviet citizens from the former republics; between 2003 and 2010 more than 600,000 stateless people were naturalized; most Meskhetian Turks, followers of Islam with origins in Georgia, fled or were evacuated from Uzbekistan after a 1989 pogrom and have lived in Russia for more than the required five-year residency period; they continue to be denied registration for citizenship and basic rights by local Krasnodar Krai authorities on the grounds that they are temporary illegal migrants

Trafficking in persons: current situation: Russia is a source, transit, and destination country for men, women, and children who are subjected to forced labor and sex trafficking; with millions of foreign workers, forced labor is Russia's predominant human trafficking problem and sometimes involves organized crime syndicates; workers from Russia, other European countries, Central Asia, and East and Southeast Asia, including North Korea and Vietnam, are subjected to forced labor in the construction, manufacturing, agricultural, textile, grocery store, maritime, and domestic service industries, as well as in forced begging, waste sorting, and street sweeping; women and children from Europe, Southeast Asia, Africa, and Central Asia are subject to sex trafficking in Russia; Russian women and children are victims of sex trafficking domestically and in Northeast Asia, Europe, Central Asia, Africa, the US, and the Middle East
tier rating: Tier 3—Russia does not fully comply with the minimum standards for the elimination of trafficking and is not making a significant effort to do so; prosecutions of trafficking offenders remained low in comparison to the scope of Russia's trafficking problem; the government did not develop or employ a formal system for identifying trafficking victims or referring them to protective services, although authorities reportedly assisted a limited number of victims on an ad hoc basis; foreign victims, the largest group in Russia, were not entitled to state-provided rehabilitative services and were routinely detained and deported; the government has not reported investigating reports of slave-like conditions among North Korean workers in Russia; authorities have made no effort to reduce the demand for forced labor or to develop public awareness of forced labor or sex trafficking (2015)

Illicit drugs: limited cultivation of illicit cannabis and opium poppy and producer of methamphetamine, mostly for domestic consumption; government has active illicit crop eradication program; used as transshipment point for Asian opiates, cannabis, and Latin American cocaine bound for growing domestic markets, to a lesser extent Western and Central Europe, and occasionally to the US; major source of heroin precursor chemicals; corruption and organized crime are key concerns; major consumer of opiates

RWANDA

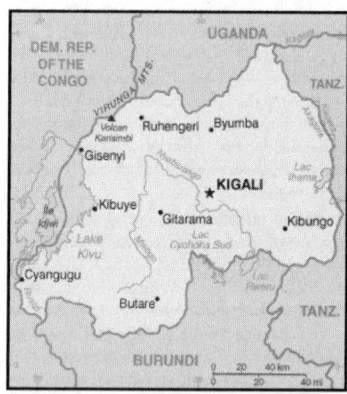

INTRODUCTION

Background: In 1959, three years before independence from Belgium, the majority ethnic group, the Hutus, overthrew the ruling Tutsi king. Over the next several years, thousands of Tutsis were killed, and some 150,000 driven into exile in neighboring countries. The children of these exiles later formed a rebel group, the Rwandan Patriotic Front (RPF), and began a civil war in 1990. The war, along with several political and economic upheavals, exacerbated ethnic tensions, culminating in April 1994 in a state-orchestrated genocide, in which Rwandans killed up to a million of their fellow citizens, including approximately three-quarters of the Tutsi population. The genocide ended later that same year when the predominantly Tutsi RPF, operating out of Uganda and northern Rwanda, defeated the national army and Hutu militias, and established an RPF-led government of national unity. Approximately 2 million Hutu refugees—many fearing Tutsi retribution—fled to neighboring Burundi, Tanzania, Uganda, and former Zaire. Since then, most of the refugees have returned to Rwanda, but several thousand remained in the neighboring Democratic Republic of the Congo (DRC, the former Zaire) and formed an extremist insurgency bent on retaking Rwanda, much as the RPF did in 1990. Rwanda held its first local elections in 1999 and its first post-genocide presidential and legislative elections in 2003. Rwanda in 2009 staged a joint military operation with the Congolese Army in DRC to rout out the Hutu extremist insurgency there, and Kigali and Kinshasa restored diplomatic relations. Rwanda also joined the Commonwealth in late 2009. President Paul KAGAME won the presidential election in August 2017 after changing the constitution in 2016 to allow him to run for a third term.

GEOGRAPHY

Location: Central Africa, east of the Democratic Republic of the Congo, north of Burundi

Geographic coordinates: 2 00 S, 30 00 E

Map references: Africa

Area: *total:* 26,338 sq km
land: 24,668 sq km
water: 1,670 sq km
country comparison to the world: 149

Area—comparative: slightly smaller than Maryland

Land boundaries: *total:* 930 km
border countries (4): Burundi 315 km, Democratic Republic of the Congo 221 km, Tanzania 222 km, Uganda 172 km

Coastline: 0 km (landlocked)

Maritime claims: none (landlocked)

Climate: temperate; two rainy seasons (February to April, November to January); mild in mountains with frost and snow possible

Terrain: mostly grassy uplands and hills; relief is mountainous with altitude declining from west to east

Elevation: *mean elevation:* 1,598 m

elevation extremes: *lowest point:* Rusizi River 950 m
highest point: Volcan Karisimbi 4,519 m

Natural resources: gold, cassiterite (tin ore), wolframite (tungsten ore), methane, hydropower, arable land

Land use: *agricultural land:* 74.5%
arable land: 47%;
permanent crops: 10.1%;
permanent pasture: 17.4%
forest: 18%
other: 7.5% (2011 est.)
Irrigated land: 96 sq km (2012)

Population—distribution: one of Africa's most densely populated countries; large concentrations tend to be in the central regions and along the shore of Lake Kivu in the west

Natural hazards: periodic droughts; the volcanic Virunga Mountains are in the northwest along the border with Democratic Republic of the Congo
volcanism: Visoke (3,711 m), located on the border with the Democratic Republic of the Congo, is the country's only historically active volcano

Environment—current issues: deforestation results from uncontrolled cutting of trees for fuel; overgrazing; soil exhaustion; soil erosion; widespread poaching

Environment—international agreements: *party to:* Biodiversity, Climate Change, Climate Change-Kyoto Protocol, Desertification, Endangered Species, Hazardous Wastes, Ozone Layer Protection, Wetlands
signed, but not ratified: Law of the Sea

Geography—note: landlocked; most of the country is savanna grassland with the population predominantly rural

PEOPLE AND SOCIETY

Population: 11,901,484
note: estimates for this country explicitly take into account the effects of excess mortality due to AIDS; this can result in lower life expectancy, higher infant mortality, higher death rates, lower population growth rates, and changes in the distribution of population by age and sex than would otherwise be expected (July 2017 est.)
country comparison to the world: 76

Nationality: *noun:* Rwandan(s)
adjective: Rwandan

Ethnic groups: Hutu (Bantu), Tutsi (Hamitic), Twa (Pygmy)

Languages: Kinyarwanda (official, universal Bantu vernacular) 93.2%, French (official) <.1, English (official) <.1, Swahili (or Kiswahili, used in commercial centers) <.1, more than one language, other 6.3%, unspecified 0.3% (2002 est.)

Religions: Protestant 50.2% (includes Adventist 12% and other Protestant 38.2%), Roman Catholic 44.3%, Muslim 2%, other 0.9% (includes traditionalist/animist), none 2.5%, unspecified <.1 (2002 est.)

Demographic profile: Rwanda's fertility rate declined sharply during the last decade, as a result of the government's commitment to family planning, the increased use of contraceptives, and a downward trend in ideal family size. Increases in educational attainment, particularly among girls, and exposure to social media also contributed to the reduction in the birth rate. The average number of births per woman decreased from a 5.6 in 2005 to 4.5 in 2016. Despite these significant strides in reducing fertility, Rwanda's birth rate remains very high and will continue to for an extended period of time because of its large population entering reproductive age. Because Rwanda is one of the most densely populated countries in Africa, its persistent high population growth and increasingly small agricultural landholdings will put additional strain on families' ability to raise foodstuffs and access potable water. These conditions will also hinder the government's efforts to reduce poverty and prevent environmental degradation.

The UNHCR recommended that effective 30 June 2013 countries invoke a cessation of refugee status for those Rwandans who fled their homeland between 1959 and 1998, including the 1994 genocide, on the grounds that the conditions that drove them to seek protection abroad no longer exist. The UNHCR's decision is controversial because many Rwandan refugees still fear persecution if they return home, concerns that are supported by the number of Rwandans granted asylum since 1998 and by the number exempted from the cessation. Rwandan refugees can still seek an exemption or local integration, but host countries are anxious to send the refugees back to Rwanda and are likely to avoid options that enable them to stay. Conversely, Rwanda itself hosts almost 160,000 refugees as of 2017; virtually all of them fleeing conflict in neighboring Burundi and the Democratic Republic of the Congo.

Age structure: *0-14 years:* 41.38% (male 2,485,386/female 2,439,101)
15-24 years: 19.34% (male 1,151,657/female 1,149,928)
25-54 years: 32.77% (male 1,845,501/female 2,054,410)
55-64 years: 4.09% (male 216,725/female 269,972)
65 years and over: 2.43% (male 113,822/female 174,982) (2017 est.)

Dependency ratios: *total dependency ratio:* 77.3
youth dependency ratio: 72.4
elderly dependency ratio: 5
potential support ratio: 20.1 (2015 est.)

Median age: *total:* 19 years
male: 18.3 years
female: 19.8 years (2017 est.)
country comparison to the world: 203

Population growth rate: 2.45% (2017 est.)
country comparison to the world: 21

Birth rate: 30.7 births/1,000 population (2017 est.)
country comparison to the world: 35

Death rate: 6.4 deaths/1,000 population (2017 est.)
country comparison to the world: 149

Net migration rate: 0.2 migrant(s)/1,000 population (2017 est.)
country comparison to the world: 68

Population distribution: one of Africa's most densely populated countries; large concentrations tend to be in the central regions and along the shore of Lake Kivu in the west

Urbanization: *urban population:* 30.7% of total population (2017)
rate of urbanization: 5.59% annual rate of change (2015-20 est.)

Major urban areas—population: KIGALI (capital) 1.257 million (2015)

Sex ratio: *at birth:* 1.03 male(s)/female
0-14 years: 1.02 male(s)/female
15-24 years: 1 male(s)/female
25-54 years: 1 male(s)/female
55-64 years: 0.88 male(s)/female
65 years and over: 0.7 male(s)/female
total population: 1 male(s)/female (2016 est.)

Mother's mean age at first birth: 23 years
note: median age at first birth among women 25-29 (2014/15 est.)

Maternal mortality ratio: 290 deaths/100,000 live births (2015 est.)
country comparison to the world: 43

Infant mortality rate: *total:* 29.7 deaths/1,000 live births
male: 32.7 deaths/1,000 live births
female: 26.7 deaths/1,000 live births (2017 est.)
country comparison to the world: 64

Life expectancy at birth: *total population:* 64.3 years

male: 62.3 years
female: 66.3 years (2017 est.)
country comparison to the world: 187

Total fertility rate: 3.87 children born/woman (2017 est.)
country comparison to the world: 38

Contraceptive prevalence rate: 53.2% (2014/15)

Health expenditures: 7.5% of GDP (2014)
country comparison to the world: 65

Physicians density: 0.06 physicians/1,000 population (2010)

Hospital bed density: 1.6 beds/1,000 population (2007)

Drinking water source:
improved:
urban: 86.6% of population
rural: 71.9% of population
total: 76.1% of population
unimproved:
urban: 13.4% of population
rural: 28.1% of population
total: 23.9% of population (2015 est.)

Sanitation facility access:
improved:
urban: 58.5% of population
rural: 62.9% of population
total: 61.6% of population
unimproved:
urban: 41.5% of population
rural: 37.1% of population
total: 38.4% of population (2015 est.)

HIV/AIDS—adult prevalence rate: 3.1% (2016 est.)
country comparison to the world: 18

HIV/AIDS—people living with HIV/AIDS: 220,000 (2016 est.)
country comparison to the world: 27

HIV/AIDS—deaths: 3,300 (2016 est.)
country comparison to the world: 39

Major infectious diseases: degree of risk: very high
food or waterborne diseases: bacterial diarrhea, hepatitis A, and typhoid fever
vectorborne diseases: malaria and dengue fever
animal contact disease: rabies (2016)

Obesity—adult prevalence rate: 5.8% (2016)
country comparison to the world: 174

Children under the age of 5 years underweight: 9.3% (2015)
country comparison to the world: 63

Education expenditures: 5% of GDP (2013)
country comparison to the world: 73

Literacy: *definition:* age 15 and over can read and write
total population: 70.5%
male: 73.2%
female: 68% (2015 est.)

School life expectancy (primary to tertiary education): *total:* 11 years
male: 11 years
female: 11 years (2013)

Unemployment, youth ages 15-24: *total:* 4.4%

male: 3.6%
female: 5.2% (2012 est.)

GOVERNMENT

Country name: *conventional long form:* Republic of Rwanda
conventional short form: Rwanda
local long form: Republika y'u Rwanda
local short form: Rwanda
former: Ruanda, German East Africa
etymology: the name translates as "domain" in the native Kinyarwanda language

Government type: presidential republic

Capital: *name:* Kigali
geographic coordinates: 1 57 S, 30 03 E
time difference: UTC+2 (7 hours ahead of Washington, DC, during Standard Time)

Administrative divisions: 4 provinces (in French—provinces, singular—province; in Kinyarwanda—intara for singular and plural) and 1 city* (in French—ville; in Kinyarwanda—umujyi; Est (Eastern), Kigali*, Nord (Northern), Ouest (Western), Sud (Southern)

Independence: 1 July 1962 (from Belgium-administered UN trusteeship)

National holiday: Independence Day, 1 July (1962)

Constitution: *history:* several previous; latest adopted by referendum 26 May 2003, effective 4 June 2003
amendments: proposed by the president of the republic (with Council of Ministers approval) or by two-thirds majority support of both houses of Parliament; passage requires at least three-quarters majority vote in both houses; changes to constitutional articles on national sovereignty, the presidential term, the form and system of government, and political pluralism also require approval in a referendum; amended 2008, 2010, 2015 (2017)

Legal system: mixed legal system of civil law, based on German and Belgian models, and customary law; judicial review of legislative acts in the Supreme Court

International law organization participation: has not submitted an ICJ jurisdiction declaration; non-party state to the ICCt

Citizenship: *citizenship by birth:* no
citizenship by descent only: the father must be a citizen of Rwanda; if the father is stateless or unknown, the mother must be a citizen
dual citizenship recognized: no
residency requirement for naturalization: 10 years

Suffrage: 18 years of age; universal

Executive branch: *chief of state:* President Paul KAGAME (since 22 April 2000)
head of government: Prime Minister Edouard NGIRENTE (since 30 August 2017)
cabinet: Council of Ministers appointed by the president
elections/appointments: president directly elected by simple majority vote for a 7-year term (eligible for a second term); note—constitutional amendments approved in December 2016,

included one that reduces the presidential term from 7 to 5 years but includes an exception that allowed President KAGAME to serve another 7-year term in 2017, potentially followed by two additional 5-year terms; election last held on 4 August 2017 (next to be held on 4 August 2024); prime minister appointed by the president

election results: Paul KAGAME reelected president; Paul KAGAME (RPF) 98.8%, Philippe MPAYIMANA (independent) 0.7%, Frank HABINEZA (DGP)0.5%

Legislative branch: *description:* bicameral Parliament consists of the Senate or Senat (26 seats; 12 members indirectly elected by local councils, 8 appointed by the president, 4 appointed by the Political Organizations Forum—a body of registered political parties, and 2 selected by institutions of higher learning; members serve 8-year terms) and the Chamber of Deputies or Chambre des Deputes (80 seats; 53 members directly elected by proportional representation vote, 24 women elected by special interest groups, and 3 selected by youth and disability organizations; members serve 5-year terms)

elections: Senate—NA; Chamber of Deputies—last held on 16-18 September 2013 (next to be held in 2018)

election results: Chamber of Deputies—percent of vote by party—Rwandan Patriotic Front Coalition 76.2%, PSD 13%, PL 9.3%, other 1.5%; seats by party—Rwandan Patriotic Front Coalition 41, PSD 7, PL 5, 27 indirectly elected members

Judicial branch: *highest court(s):* Supreme Court (consists of the chief and deputy chief justices and 15 judges; normally organized into 3-judge panels); High Court (consists of the court president, vice president, and a minimum of 24 judges and organized into 5 chambers

note: Supreme Court judges nominated by the president of the republic after consultation with the Cabinet and the Superior Council of the Judiciary or SCJ (a 27-member body of judges, other judicial officials, and legal professionals) and approved by the Senate; chief and deputy chief justices appointed for 8-year nonrenewable terms; tenure of judges NA; High Court president and vice president appointed by the president of the republic upon approval by the Senate; judges appointed by the Supreme Court chief justice upon approval of the SCJ; judge tenure NA

judge selection and term of office: High Court of the Republic; commercial courts including the High Commercial Court; intermediate courts; primary courts; Gacaca and military specialized courts

subordinate courts: High Court of the Republic; commercial courts including the High Commercial Court; intermediate courts; primary courts; Gacaca and military specialized courts

Political parties and leaders: Liberal Party or PL [Donatille MUKABALISA] Party for Progress and Concord or PPC [Dr. Alivera MUKABARAMBA] Rwandan Patriotic Front or RPF [Paul KAGAME] Rwandan Patriotic Front Coalition (includes RPF, PPC) [Paul KAGAME] Social Democratic Party or PSD [Vincent BIRUTA]

Political pressure groups and leaders: IBUKA (association of genocide survivors)

International organization participation: ACP, AfDB, AU, C, CEPGL, COMESA, EAC, EADB, FAO, G-77, IAEA, IBRD, ICAO, ICRM, IDA, IFAD, IFC, IFRCS, ILO, IMF, Interpol, IOC, IOM, IPU, ISO, ITSO, ITU, ITUC (NGOs), MIGA, MINUSMA, NAM, OIF, OPCW, PCA, UN, UNAMID, UNCTAD, UNESCO, UNHCR, UNIDO, UNISFA, UNMISS, UNWTO, UPU, WCO, WHO, WIPO, WMO, WTO

Diplomatic representation in the US: chief of mission: Ambassador Mathilde MUKANTABANA (since 18 July 2013)

chancery: 1875 Connecticut Avenue, NW, Suite 418, Washington, DC, 2000

telephone: [1] (202) 232-2882

FAX: [1] (202) 232-4544

Diplomatic representation from the US: *chief of mission:* Ambassador Erica BARKS-RUGGLES (since 26 January 2015)

embassy: 2657 Avenue de la Gendarmerie, Kigali

mailing address: B.P. 28, Kigali

telephone: [250] 252 596-400

FAX: [250] 252 580 325

Flag description: three horizontal bands of sky blue (top, double width), yellow, and green, with a golden sun with 24 rays near the fly end of the blue band; blue represents happiness and peace, yellow economic development and mineral wealth, green hope of prosperity and natural resources; the sun symbolizes unity, as well as enlightenment and transparency from ignorance

National symbol(s): traditional woven basket with peaked lid; national colors: blue, yellow, green

National anthem: *name:* "Rwanda nziza" (Rwanda, Our Beautiful Country)

lyrics/music: Faustin MURIGO/Jean-Bosco HASHAKAIMANA

note: adopted 2001

ECONOMY

Economy—overview: Rwanda is a rural, agrarian country with about 35% of the population engaged in subsistence agriculture, and with some mineral and agro-processing. Population density is high but not concentrated in large metropolises – its 13 million people are spread out on a small amount of land (about the size of Vermont and New Hampshire combined). Tourism, minerals, coffee, and tea are Rwanda's main sources of foreign exchange. Despite Rwanda's fertile ecosystem, food production often does not keep pace with demand, requiring food imports. Energy shortages, instability in neighboring states, and lack of adequate transportation linkages to other countries continue to handicap private sector growth.

The 1994 genocide decimated Rwanda's fragile economic base, severely impoverished the population, particularly women, and temporarily stalled the country's ability to attract private and external investment. However, Rwanda has made substantial progress in stabilizing and rehabilitating its economy beyond pre-1994 levels. GDP

has rebounded with an average annual growth of 6%-8% since 2003 and inflation has been reduced to single digits. In 2015, 39% of the population lived below the poverty line, according to government statistics, compared to 57% in 2006. Mining profits in 2015 were reduced by almost half, owing to the drop in global demand for minerals.

Africa's most densely populated country is trying to overcome the limitations of its small, landlocked economy by leveraging regional trade; Rwanda joined the East African Community and is aligning its budget, trade, and immigration policies with its regional partners. The government has embraced an expansionary fiscal policy to reduce poverty by improving education, infrastructure, and foreign and domestic investment. In recognition of Rwanda's successful management of its macro economy, the IMF graduated Rwanda to a Policy Support Instrument in 2010.

The Rwandan Government is seeking to become a regional leader in information and communication technologies. In 2012, Rwanda completed the first modern Special Economic Zone (SEZ) in Kigali. The SEZ seeks to attract investment in all sectors, but specifically in agribusiness, information and communications, trade and logistics, mining, and construction. In 2016, the government launched an online system to give investors information about public land and its suitability for agricultural development.

GDP (purchasing power parity): $24.61 billion (2017 est.)

$23.18 billion (2016 est.)

$21.89 billion (2015 est.)

note: data are in 2017 dollars

country comparison to the world: 143

GDP (official exchange rate): $8.918 billion (2016 est.)

GDP—real growth rate: 6.2% (2017 est.)

5.9% (2016 est.)

8.9% (2015 est.)

country comparison to the world: 21

GDP—per capita (PPP): $2,100 (2017 est.)

$2,000 (2016 est.)

$1,900 (2015 est.)

note: data are in 2017 dollars

country comparison to the world: 205

Gross national saving: 10.8% of GDP (2017 est.)

7.6% of GDP (2016 est.)

8.7% of GDP (2015 est.)

country comparison to the world: 153

GDP—composition, by end use:

household consumption: 78%

government consumption: 14.7%

investment in fixed capital: 26.5%

investment in inventories: 0.6%

exports of goods and services: 15.4%

imports of goods and services: -35.3% (2017 est.)

GDP—composition, by sector of origin:

agriculture: 30.9%

industry: 17.6%

services: 51.5% (2017 est.)

Agriculture—products: coffee, tea, pyrethrum (insecticide made from chrysanthemums), bananas, beans, sorghum, potatoes; livestock

Industries: cement, agricultural products, small-scale beverages, soap, furniture, shoes, plastic goods, textiles, cigarettes

Industrial production growth rate: 4.8% (2017 est.)
country comparison to the world: 53

Labor force: 6.227 million (2017 est.)
country comparison to the world: 73

Labor force—by occupation: *agriculture:* 75.3%
industry: 6.7%
services: 18% (2012 est.)

Unemployment rate: 2.7% (2014 est.)
country comparison to the world: 27

Population below poverty line: 39.1% (2015 est.)

Household income or consumption by percentage share: *lowest 10%:* 2.1%
highest 10%: 43.2% (2011 est.)

Distribution of family income—Gini index: 46.8 (2000)
28.9 (1985)
country comparison to the world: 29

Budget: *revenues:* $1.874 billion
expenditures: $2.255 billion (2017 est.)
Taxes and other revenues: 21% of GDP (2017 est.)
country comparison to the world: 144

Budget surplus (+) or deficit (-): -4.3% of GDP (2017 est.)
country comparison to the world: 146

Public debt: 47.2% of GDP (2017 est.)
43.4% of GDP (2016 est.)
country comparison to the world: 108

Fiscal year: calendar year

Inflation rate (consumer prices): 7.1% (2017 est.)
5.7% (2016 est.)
country comparison to the world: 193

Central bank discount rate: 7.75% (31 December 2010)
11.25% (31 December 2008)
country comparison to the world: 41

Commercial bank prime lending rate: 16.9% (31 December 2017 est.)
17.3% (31 December 2016 est.)
country comparison to the world: 28

Stock of narrow money: $941 million (31 December 2017 est.)
$940.6 million (31 December 2016 est.)
country comparison to the world: 158

Stock of broad money: $1.937 billion (31 December 2017 est.)
$1.903 billion (31 December 2016 est.)
country comparison to the world: 159

Stock of domestic credit: $2.054 billion (31 December 2017 est.)
$1.959 billion (31 December 2016 est.)
country comparison to the world: 146

Market value of publicly traded shares: $NA

Current account balance: -$905 million (2017 est.)
-$1.211 billion (2016 est.)

country comparison to the world: 128

Exports: $908.9 million (2017 est.)
$745 million (2016 est.)
country comparison to the world: 163

Exports—commodities: coffee, tea, hides, tin ore

Exports—partners: Democratic Republic of the Congo 31.3%, Kenya 15.7%, UAE 13.8%, Switzerland 8.7%, Burundi 5.7% (2016)

Imports: $2.007 billion (2017 est.)
$2.045 billion (2016 est.)
country comparison to the world: 159

Imports—commodities: foodstuffs, machinery and equipment, steel, petroleum products, cement and construction material

Imports—partners: China 21.2%, Uganda 11.2%, Kenya 7.8%, India 7.4%, UAE 5.8%, Tanzania 5.3% (2016)

Reserves of foreign exchange and gold: $1.026 billion (31 December 2017 est.)
$1.104 billion (31 December 2016 est.)
country comparison to the world: 123

Debt—external: $2.966 billion (31 December 2017 est.)
$2.611 billion (31 December 2016 est.)
country comparison to the world: 143

Stock of direct foreign investment—at home: $2.473 billion (31 December 2017 est.)
$2.072 billion (31 December 2016 est.)
country comparison to the world: 113

Stock of direct foreign investment—abroad: $26.8 million (31 December 2017 est.)
$26.8 million (31 December 2016 est.)
country comparison to the world: 108

Exchange rates: Rwandan francs (RWF) per US dollar—
839.1 (2017 est.)
787.25 (2016 est.)
787.25 (2015 est.)
720.54 (2014 est.)
680.95 (2013 est.)

ENERGY

Electricity access: population without electricity: 9,300,000

electrification—total population: *21%*
electrification—urban areas: 67%
electrification—rural areas: 5% (2013)

Electricity—production: 600 million kWh (2015 est.)
country comparison to the world: 165

Electricity—consumption: 644 million kWh (2015 est.)
country comparison to the world: 164

Electricity—exports: 4 million kWh (2015 est.)
country comparison to the world: 92

Electricity—imports: 90 million kWh (2015 est.)
country comparison to the world: 99

Electricity—installed generating capacity: 152,000 kW (2015 est.)
country comparison to the world: 169

Electricity—from fossil fuels: 27.6% of total installed capacity (2015 est.)

country comparison to the world: 187

Electricity—from nuclear fuels: 0% of total installed capacity (2015 est.)
country comparison to the world: 174

Electricity—from hydroelectric plants: 65.8% of total installed capacity (2015 est.)
country comparison to the world: 22

Electricity—from other renewable sources: 6.6% of total installed capacity (2015 est.)
country comparison to the world: 87

Crude oil—production: 0 bbl/day (2016 est.)
country comparison to the world: 187

Crude oil—exports: 0 bbl/day (2014 est.)
country comparison to the world: 182

Crude oil—imports: 0 bbl/day (2014 est.)
country comparison to the world: 182

Crude oil—proved reserves: 0 bbl (1 January 2017 es)
country comparison to the world: 185

Refined petroleum products—production: 0 bbl/day (2014 est.)
country comparison to the world: 191

Refined petroleum products—consumption: 6,000 bbl/day (2015 est.)
country comparison to the world: 169

Refined petroleum products—exports: 0 bbl/day (2014 est.)
country comparison to the world: 192

Refined petroleum products—imports: 5,979 bbl/day (2014 est.)
country comparison to the world: 159

Natural gas—production: 0 cu m (2013 est.)
country comparison to the world: 188

Natural gas—consumption: 0 cu m (2013 est.)
country comparison to the world: 125

Natural gas—exports: 0 cu m (2013 est.)
country comparison to the world: 173

Natural gas—imports: 0 cu m (2013 est.)
country comparison to the world: 180

Natural gas—proved reserves: 56.63 billion cu m (1 January 2017 es)
country comparison to the world: 63

Carbon dioxide emissions from consumption of energy: 800,000 Mt (2013 est.)
country comparison to the world: 172

COMMUNICATIONS

Telephones—fixed lines: *total subscriptions:* 13,403
subscriptions per 100 inhabitants: less than 1 (July 2016 est.)
country comparison to the world: 163

Telephones—mobile cellular: *total:* 8,921,533
subscriptions per 100 inhabitants: 69 (July 2016 est.)
country comparison to the world: 98

Telephone system: *general assessment:* small, inadequate telephone system primarily serves business, education, and government
domestic: the capital, Kigali, is connected to provincial centers by microwave radio relay and,

recently, by cellular telephone service; much of the network depends on wire and HF radiotelephone; combined fixed-line and mobile-cellular telephone density has increased and now exceeds 65 telephones per 100 persons

international: country code—250; international connections employ microwave radio relay to neighboring countries and satellite communications to more distant countries; satellite earth stations—1 Intelsat (Indian Ocean) in Kigali (includes telex and telefax service) (2015)

Broadcast media: government owns and operates the only TV station; government-owned and operated Radio Rwanda has a national reach; 9 private radio stations; transmissions of multiple international broadcasters are available (2007)

Internet country code: .rw

Internet users: *total:* 2,597,685
percent of population: 20.0% (July 2016 est.)
country comparison to the world: 120

TRANSPORTATION

National air transport system: number of registered air carriers: 1
inventory of registered aircraft operated by air carriers: 9
annual passenger traffic on registered air carriers: 645,815
annual freight traffic on registered air carriers: 21,382,897 mt-km (2015)
Civil aircraft registration country code prefix: 9XR (2016)

Airports: 7 (2013)
country comparison to the world: 167

Airports—with paved runways: *total:* 4
over 3,047 m: 1
914 to 1,523 m: 2
under 914 m: 1 (2017)

Airports—with unpaved runways: *total:* 3
914 to 1,523 m: 2
under 914 m: 1 (2013)

Roadways: *total:* 4,700 km
paved: 1,207 km
unpaved: 3,493 km (2012)
country comparison to the world: 152

Waterways: (Lac Kivu navigable by shallow-draft barges and native craft) (2011)

Ports and terminals: lake port(s): Cyangugu, Gisenyi, Kibuye (Lake Kivu)

MILITARY AND SECURITY

Military expenditures: 1.21% of GDP (2016)
1.25% of GDP (2015)
1.13% of GDP (2014)
1.08% of GDP (2013)
1.09% of GDP (2012)
country comparison to the world: 91

Military branches: Rwanda Defense Force (RDF): Rwanda Army (Rwanda Land Force), Rwanda Air Force (Force Aerienne Rwandaise, FAR) (2013)

Military service age and obligation: 18 years of age for voluntary military service; no conscription; Rwandan citizenship is required, as is a 9th-grade

education for enlisted recruits and an A-level certificate for officer candidates; enlistment is either as contract (5-years, renewable twice) or career; retirement (for officers and senior NCOs) after 20 years of service or at 40-60 years of age (2012)

TRANSNATIONAL ISSUES

Disputes—international: Burundi and Rwanda dispute two sq km (0.8 sq mi) of Sabanerwa, a farmed area in the Rukurazi Valley where the Akanyaru/Kanyaru River shifted its course southward after heavy rains in 1965; fighting among ethnic groups—loosely associated political rebels, armed gangs, and various government forces in Great Lakes region transcending the boundaries of Burundi, Democratic Republic of the Congo (DROC), Rwanda, and Uganda—abated substantially from a decade ago due largely to UN peacekeeping, international mediation, and efforts by local governments to create civil societies; nonetheless, 57,000 Rwandan refugees still reside in 21 African states, including Zambia, Gabon, and 20,000 who fled to Burundi in 2005 and 2006 to escape drought and recriminations from traditional courts investigating the 1994 massacres; the 2005 DROC and Rwanda border verification mechanism to stem rebel actions on both sides of the border remains in place

Refugees and internally displaced persons: refugees (country of origin): 89,171 (Burundi); 75,019 (Democratic Republic of the Congo) (2017)

SAINT HELENA, ASCENSION, AND TRISTAN DA CUNHA

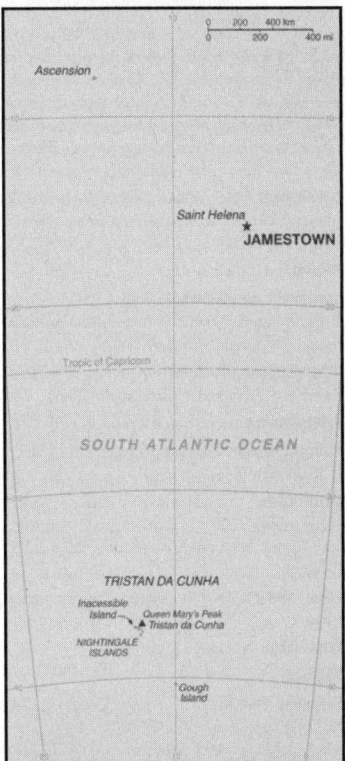

INTRODUCTION

Background: Saint Helena is a British Overseas Territory consisting of Saint Helena and Ascension Islands, and the island group of Tristan da Cunha.

Saint Helena: Uninhabited when first discovered by the Portuguese in 1502, Saint Helena was garrisoned by the British during the 17th century. It acquired fame as the place of Napoleon BONAPARTE's exile from 1815 until his death in 1821, but its importance as a port of call declined after the opening of the Suez Canal in 1869. During the Anglo-Boer War in South Africa, several thousand Boer prisoners were confined on the island between 1900 and 1903.

Saint Helena is one of the most remote populated places in the world. The British Government committed to building an airport on Saint Helena in 2005. After more than a decade of delays and construction, a commercial air service to South Africa via Namibia was inaugurated in October of 2017. The weekly service to Saint Helena from Johannesburg via Windhoek in Namibia takes just over six hours (including the refueling stop in Windhoek) and replaces the mail ship that had made a five-day journey to the island every three weeks.

Ascension Island: This barren and uninhabited island was discovered and named by the Portuguese in 1503. The British garrisoned the island in 1815 to prevent a rescue of Napoleon from Saint Helena. It served as a provisioning station for the Royal Navy's West Africa Squadron on anti-slavery patrol. The island remained under Admiralty control until 1922, when it became a dependency of Saint Helena. During World War II, the UK permitted the US to construct an airfield on Ascension in support of transatlantic flights to Africa and anti-submarine operations in the South Atlantic. In the 1960s the island became an important space tracking station for the US. In 1982, Ascension was an essential staging area for British forces during the Falklands War. It remains a critical refueling point in the air-bridge from the UK to the South Atlantic.

The island hosts one of four dedicated ground antennas (the others are on Diego Garcia (British Indian Ocean Territory), Kwajalein (Marshall Islands), and at Cape Canaveral, Florida (US)) that assist in the operation of the Global Positioning System (GPS) navigation system. NASA and the US Air Force also operate a Meter-Class Autonomous Telescope (MCAT) on Ascension as part of the deep space surveillance system for tracking orbital debris, which can be a hazard to spacecraft and astronauts.

Tristan da Cunha: The island group consists of Tristan da Cunha, Nightingale, Inaccessible, and Gough Islands. Tristan da Cunha, named after its Portuguese discoverer (1506), was garrisoned by the British in 1816 to prevent any attempt to rescue Napoleon from Saint Helena. Gough and Inaccessible Islands have been designated World Heritage Sites. South Africa leases a site for a meteorological station on Gough Island.

GEOGRAPHY

Location: islands in the South Atlantic Ocean, about midway between South America and Africa; Ascension Island lies 1,300 km (800 mi) northwest of Saint Helena; Tristan da Cunha lies 4,300 km (2,700 mi) southwest of Saint Helena

Geographic coordinates: Saint Helena: 15 57 S, 5 42 W
Ascension Island: 7 57 S, 14 22 W

Tristan da Cunha island group: 37 15 S, 12 30 W

Map references: Africa

Area: *total:* 394 sq km
land: Saint Helena Island 122 sq km; Ascension Island 88 sq km; Tristan da Cunha island group 184 sq km (includes Tristan (98 sq km), Inaccessible, Nightingale, and Gough islands)
water: 0 sq km
country comparison to the world: 204

Area—comparative: slightly more than twice the size of Washington, DC
Land boundaries: 0 km

Coastline: Saint Helena: 60 km

Ascension Island: NA
Tristan da Cunha (island only): 34 km

Maritime claims: *territorial sea:* 12 nm
exclusive fishing zone: 200 nm

Climate: Saint Helena: tropical marine; mild, tempered by trade winds
Ascension Island: tropical marine; mild, semi-arid
Tristan da Cunha: temperate marine; mild, tempered by trade winds (tends to be cooler than Saint Helena)

Terrain: the islands of this group are of volcanic origin associated with the Atlantic Mid-Ocean Ridge
Saint Helena: rugged, volcanic; small scattered plateaus and plains
Ascension: surface covered by lava flows and cinder cones of 44 dormant volcanoes; terrain rises to the east
Tristan da Cunha: sheer cliffs line the coastline of the nearly circular island; the flanks of the central volcanic peak are deeply dissected; narrow coastal plain lies between The Peak and the coastal cliffs

Elevation: *mean elevation:* NA

elevation extremes: *lowest point:* Atlantic Ocean 0 m
highest point: Queen Mary's Peak on Tristan da Cunha 2,060 m; Green Mountain on Ascension Island 859 m; Mount Actaeon on Saint Helena Island 818 m

Natural resources: fish, lobster

Land use: *agricultural land:* 30.8%
arable land: 10.3%;
permanent crops: 0%;
permanent pasture: 20.5%
forest: 5.1%
other: 64.1% (2011 est.)
Irrigated land: 0 sq km (2012)

Population—distribution: Saint Helena—population is concentrated in and around the capital Jamestown in the northwest, with another significant cluster in the interior Longwood area; Ascension—largest settlement, and location of most of the population, is Georgetown; Tristan da Cunha—most of the nearly 300 inhabitants live in the northern coastal town of Edinburgh of the Seven Seas

Natural hazards: active volcanism on Tristan da Cunha
volcanism: the island volcanoes of Tristan da Cunha (2,060 m) and Nightingale Island (365 m) experience volcanic activity; Tristan da Cunha erupted in 1962 and Nightingale in 2004

Environment—current issues: development threatens unique biota on Saint Helena

Geography—note: Saint Helena harbors at least 40 species of plants unknown elsewhere in the world; Ascension is a breeding ground for sea turtles and sooty terns; Queen Mary's Peak on Tristan da Cunha is the highest island mountain in the South Atlantic and a prominent landmark on the sea lanes around southern Africa

PEOPLE AND SOCIETY

Population: 7,828

note: Saint Helena's statistical agency estimated the enumerated national population (including Ascension Island and Tristan da Cuhna) to be 5,901 in 2016, according to the 2016 census; only Saint Helena, Ascension, and Tristan da Cunha islands are inhabited, none of the other nearby islands/islets (July 2017 est.)

country comparison to the world: 225

Nationality: *noun:* Saint Helenian(s)

adjective: Saint Helenian

note: referred to locally as "Saints"

Ethnic groups: African descent 50%, white 25%, Chinese 25%

Languages: English

Religions: Protestant 75.9% (includes Anglican 68.9, Baptist 2.1%, Seventh Day Adventist 1.8%, Salvation Army 1.7%, New Apostolic 1.4%), Jehovah's Witness 4.1%, Roman Catholic 1.2%, other 2.5% (includes Baha'i), unspecified 0.8%, none 6.1%, no response 9.4%

note: data represent Saint Helena only (2016 est.)

Demographic profile: The vast majority of the population of Saint Helena, Ascension, and Tristan da Cunha live on Saint Helena. Ascension has no indigenous or permanent residents and is inhabited only by persons contracted to work on the island (mainly with the UK and US military or in the space and communications industries) or their dependents, while Tristan da Cunha—the main island in a small archipelago—has fewer than 300 residents. The population of Saint Helena consists of the descendants of 17th century British sailors and settlers from the East India Company, African slaves, and indentured servants and laborers from India, Indonesia, and China. Most of the population of Ascension are Saint Helenians, Britons, and Americans, while that of Tristan da Cunha descends from shipwrecked sailors and Saint Helenians.

Change in Saint Helena's population size is driven by net outward migration. Since the 1980s, Saint Helena's population steadily has shrunk and aged as the birth rate has decreased and many working-age residents left for better opportunities elsewhere. The restoration of British citizenship in 2002 accelerated family emigration; from 1998 to 2008 alone, population declined by about 20%.

In the last few years, population has experienced some temporary growth, as foreigners and returning Saint Helenians, have come to build an international airport, but numbers are beginning to fade as the project reaches completion and workers depart. In the long term, once the airport is fully operational, increased access to the remote island has the potential to boost tourism and fishing, provide more jobs for Saint Helenians domestically, and could encourage some ex-patriots to return home. In the meantime, however, Saint Helena, Ascension, and Tristan da Cunha have to contend with the needs of an aging population. The elderly population of the islands has risen from an estimated 9.4% in 1998 to 20.4% in 2016.

Age structure: *0-14 years:* 15.97% (male 637/female 613)

15-24 years: 12.19% (male 486/female 468)

25-54 years: 43.89% (male 1,701/female 1,735)

55-64 years: 12.83% (male 517/female 487)

65 years and over: 15.13% (male 604/female 580) (2017 est.)

Median age: *total:* 41.9 years

male: 42 years

female: 41.9 years (2017 est.)

country comparison to the world: 35

Population growth rate: 0.18% (2017 est.)

country comparison to the world: 185

Birth rate: 9.6 births/1,000 population (2017 est.)

country comparison to the world: 200

Death rate: 7.8 deaths/1,000 population (2017 est.)

country comparison to the world: 100

Net migration rate: 0 migrant(s)/1,000 population (2017 est.)

country comparison to the world: 95

Population distribution: Saint Helena—population is concentrated in and around the capital Jamestown in the northwest, with another significant cluster in the interior Longwood area; Ascension—largest settlement, and location of most of the population, is Georgetown; Tristan da Cunha—most of the nearly 300 inhabitants live in the northern coastal town of Edinburgh of the Seven Seas

Urbanization: *urban population:* 39.5% of total population (2017)

rate of urbanization: 0.96% annual rate of change (2015-20 est.)

Major urban areas—population: JAMESTOWN (capital) 1,000 (2014)

Sex ratio: *at birth:* 1.05 male(s)/female

0-14 years: 1.04 male(s)/female

15-24 years: 1.05 male(s)/female

25-54 years: 0.98 male(s)/female

55-64 years: 1.09 male(s)/female

65 years and over: 1.04 male(s)/female

total population: 1.02 male(s)/female (2016 est.)

Infant mortality rate: *total:* 13.3 deaths/1,000 live births

male: 15.7 deaths/1,000 live births

female: 10.7 deaths/1,000 live births (2017 est.)

country comparison to the world: 107

Life expectancy at birth: *total population:* 79.6 years

male: 76.7 years

female: 82.7 years (2017 est.)

country comparison to the world: 45

Total fertility rate: 1.59 children born/woman (2017 est.)

country comparison to the world: 184

HIV/AIDS—adult prevalence rate: NA

HIV/AIDS—people living with HIV/AIDS: NA

HIV/AIDS—deaths: NA

GOVERNMENT

Country name: *conventional long form:* Saint Helena, Ascension, and Tristan da Cunha

conventional short form: none

etymology: Saint Helena was discovered in 1502 by Galician navigator Joao da NOVA, sailing in the service of the Kingdom of Portugal, who named it "Santa Helena"; Ascension was named in 1503 by Portuguese navigator Afonso de ALBUQUERQUE who sighted the island on the Feast Day of the Ascension; Tristan da Cunha was discovered in 1506 by Portuguese explorer Tristao da CUNHA who christened the main island after himself (the name was subsequently anglicized)

Dependency status: overseas territory of the UK

Government type: parliamentary democracy (Legislative Council); limited self-governing overseas territory of the UK

Capital: *name:* Jamestown

geographic coordinates: 15 56 S, 5 43 W

time difference: UTC 0 (5 hours ahead of Washington, DC, during Standard Time)

Administrative divisions: 3 administrative areas; Ascension, Saint Helena, Tristan da Cunha

Independence: none (overseas territory of the UK)

National holiday: Birthday of Queen ELIZABETH II, third Monday in April (1926)

Constitution: several previous; latest effective 1 September 2009 (The St. Helena, Ascension and Tristan da Cunha Constitution Order 2009) (2016)

Legal system: English common law and local statutes

Citizenship: see United Kingdom

Suffrage: 18 years of age

Executive branch: *chief of state:* Queen ELIZABETH II (since 6 February 1952)

head of government: Governor Lisa PHILLIPS (since 25 April 2016)

cabinet: Executive Council consists of the governor, 3 ex-officio officers, and 5 elected members of the Legislative Council

elections/appointments: none; the monarchy is hereditary; governor appointed by the monarch

note: the constitution order provides for an administrator for Ascension and Tristan da Cunha appointed by the governor

Legislative branch: *description:* unicameral Legislative Council (17 seats including the speaker and deputy speaker; 12 members directly elected in a single countrywide constituency by simple majority vote and 3 ex-officio members—the chief secretary, financial secretary, and attorney general; members serve 4-year terms)

note: the Constitution Order provides for separate Island Councils for both Ascension and Tristan da Cunha

elections: last held on 26 July 2017 (next to be held in 2021)

election results: percent of vote—NA; seats by party—independent 12

Judicial branch: highest resident court(s): Court of Appeal (consists of the court president and 2 justices); Supreme Court (consists of the chief justice—a non-resident—and NA judges); note—appeals beyond the Court of Appeal are heard by the Judicial Committee of the Privy Council (in London)

judge selection and term of office: Court of Appeal and Supreme Court justices appointed by the governor acting upon the instructions from a secretary of state acting on behalf of Queen ELIZABETH II; justices of both courts appointed until retirement at age 70 but terms can be extended

subordinate courts: Magistrate's Court; Small Claims Court; Juvenile Court

Political parties and leaders: none

Political pressure groups and leaders: private sector; unions

International organization participation: UPU

Diplomatic representation in the US: none (overseas territory of the UK)

Diplomatic representation from the US: none (overseas territory of the UK)

Flag description: blue with the flag of the UK in the upper hoist-side quadrant and the Saint Helenian shield centered on the outer half of the flag; the upper third of the shield depicts a white plover (wire bird) on a yellow field; the remainder of the shield depicts a rocky coastline on the left, offshore is a three-masted sailing ship with sails furled but flying an English flag

National symbol(s): Saint Helena plover (bird)
National anthem: note: as a territory of the UK, "God Save the Queen" is official (see United Kingdom)

ECONOMY

Economy—overview: The economy depends largely on financial assistance from the UK, which amounted to about $27 million in FY06/07 or more than twice the level of annual budgetary revenues. The local population earns income from fishing, raising livestock, and sales of handicrafts. Because there are few jobs, 25% of the work force has left to seek employment on Ascension Island, on the Falklands, and in the UK.

GDP (purchasing power parity): $31.1 million (FY09/10 est.)
country comparison to the world: 228

GDP (official exchange rate): $NA

GDP—real growth rate: NA%

GDP—per capita (PPP): $7,800 (FY09/10 est.)
country comparison to the world: 154

GDP—composition, by sector of origin:
agriculture: NA%
industry: NA%
services: NA%

Agriculture—products: coffee, corn, potatoes, vegetables; fish, lobster; livestock; timber

Industries: construction, crafts (furniture, lacework, fancy woodwork), fishing, collectible postage stamps

Industrial production growth rate: NA%

Labor force: 2,486 (1998 est.)
country comparison to the world: 227

Labor force—by occupation: *agriculture:* 6%
industry: 48%

services: 46% (1987 est.)

Unemployment rate: 14% (1998 est.)
country comparison to the world: 169

Population below poverty line: NA%

Household income or consumption by percentage share: *lowest 10%:* NA%
highest 10%: NA%

Budget: *revenues:* $8.342 million
expenditures: $20.49 million
note: revenue data reflect locally raised revenues only; the budget deficit is resolved by grant aid from the UK (FY06/07 est.)

Fiscal year: 1 April—31 March

Inflation rate (consumer prices): 4% (2012 est.)
country comparison to the world: 158

Exports: $19 million (2004 est.)
country comparison to the world: 212

Exports—commodities: fish (frozen, canned, and salt-dried skipjack, tuna), coffee, handicrafts

Imports: $20.53 million (2010 est.)
country comparison to the world: 217

Imports—commodities: food, beverages, tobacco, fuel oils, animal feed, building materials, motor vehicles and parts, machinery and parts

Debt—external: $NA

Exchange rates: Saint Helenian pounds (SHP) per US dollar—
0.7836 (2017)
0.6542 (2016)
0.6542 (2015)
0.607 (2014 est.)
0.6391 (2013 est.)

ENERGY

Electricity—production: 10 million kWh (2015 est.)
country comparison to the world: 216

Electricity—consumption: 9.3 million kWh (2015 est.)
country comparison to the world: 214

Electricity—exports: 0 kWh (2016 est.)
country comparison to the world: 195

Electricity—imports: 0 kWh (2016 est.)
country comparison to the world: 199

Electricity—installed generating capacity: 8,000 kW (2015 est.)
country comparison to the world: 211

Electricity—from fossil fuels: 100% of total installed capacity (2015 est.)
country comparison to the world: 18

Electricity—from nuclear fuels: 0% of total installed capacity (2015 est.)
country comparison to the world: 180

Electricity—from hydroelectric plants: 0% of total installed capacity (2015 est.)
country comparison to the world: 202

Electricity—from other renewable sources: 0% of total installed capacity (2015 est.)
country comparison to the world: 204

Crude oil—production: 0 bbl/day (2016 est.)
country comparison to the world: 188

Crude oil—exports: 0 bbl/day (2014 est.)
country comparison to the world: 188

Crude oil—imports: 0 bbl/day (2014 est.)
country comparison to the world: 187

Crude oil—proved reserves: 0 bbl (1 January 2017 es)
country comparison to the world: 186

Refined petroleum products—production: 0 bbl/day (2014 est.)
country comparison to the world: 192

Refined petroleum products—consumption: 80 bbl/day (2015 est.)
country comparison to the world: 214

Refined petroleum products—exports: 0 bbl/day (2014 est.)
country comparison to the world: 196

Refined petroleum products—imports: 84.68 bbl/day (2014 est.)
country comparison to the world: 211

Natural gas—production: 0 cu m (2013 est.)
country comparison to the world: 192

Natural gas—consumption: 0 cu m (2013 est.)
country comparison to the world: 129

Natural gas—exports: 0 cu m (2013 est.)
country comparison to the world: 180

Natural gas—imports: 0 cu m (2013 est.)
country comparison to the world: 186

Natural gas—proved reserves: 0 cu m (1 January 2014 es)
country comparison to the world: 192

Carbon dioxide emissions from consumption of energy: 12,080 Mt (2012 est.)
country comparison to the world: 212

COMMUNICATIONS

Telephones—fixed lines: *total:* 2,758
subscriptions per 100 inhabitants: 35 (July 2016 est.)
country comparison to the world: 211

Telephones—mobile cellular: *total:* 2,499
subscriptions per 100 inhabitants: 32 (July 2016 est.)

Telephone system: *general assessment:* can communicate worldwide
domestic: automatic digital network
international: country code (Saint Helena)—290, (Ascension Island)—247; international direct dialing; satellite voice and data communications; satellite earth stations—5 (Ascension Island—4, Saint Helena—1) (2010)

Broadcast media: Saint Helena has no local TV station; 2 local radio stations, one of which is relayed to Ascension Island; satellite TV stations rebroadcast terrestrially; Ascension Island has no local TV station but has 1 local radio station and receives relays of broadcasts from 1 radio station on Saint Helena; broadcasts from the British Forces Broadcasting Service (BFBS) are available, as well as TV services for the US military; Tristan da Cunha has 1 local radio station and receives BFBS TV and radio broadcasts (2007)

757

Internet country code: .sh; note—Ascension Island assigned .ac

Internet users: *total:* 1,800
percent of population: 23.1% (July 2016 est.)
country comparison to the world: 214

Communications—note: *South Africa maintains a meteorological station on Gough Island*

TRANSPORTATION

Civil aircraft registration country code prefix: VQ-H (2016)

Airports: 2 (2015)
country comparison to the world: 232

Airports—with paved runways: *total:* 2
over 3,047 m: 1 Ascension Island—Wideawake Field (ASI)

1,524 to 2,437 m: 1 Saint Helena (HLE); note—weekly commercial air service to South Africa via Namibia commenced on 14 October 2017 (2017)

Roadways: *total:* 198 km (Saint Helena 138 km, Ascension 40 km, Tristan da Cunha 20 km)
paved: 168 km (Saint Helena 118 km, Ascension 40 km, Tristan da Cunha 10 km)
unpaved: 30 km (Saint Helena 20 km, Tristan da Cunha 10 km) (2002)
country comparison to the world: 210

Ports and terminals: *major seaport(s):* Saint Helena: Jamestown
Ascension Island: Georgetown
Tristan da Cunha: Calshot Harbor (Edinburgh)
Transportation—note: the new airport on Saint Helena opened for limited operations in July 2016,

and the first commercial flight took place on 14 October 2017, marking the start of weekly air service between Saint Helena and South Africa via Namibia; the military airport on Ascension Island is closed to civilian traffic; there is no air connection to Tristan da Cunha and very limited sea connections making it one of the most isolated communities on the planet

MILITARY AND SECURITY

Military—note: defense is the responsibility of the UK

TRANSNATIONAL ISSUES

Disputes—international: none

SAINT KITTS AND NEVIS

Area: *total:* 261 sq km (Saint Kitts 168 sq km; Nevis 93 sq km)
land: 261 sq km
water: 0 sq km
country comparison to the world: 212

Area—comparative: 1.5 times the size of Washington, DC

Land boundaries: 0 km

Coastline: 135 km

Maritime claims: *territorial sea:* 12 nm
contiguous zone: 24 nm
exclusive economic zone: 200 nm
continental shelf: 200 nm or to the edge of the continental margin

Climate: tropical, tempered by constant sea breezes; little seasonal temperature variation; rainy season (May to November)

Terrain: volcanic with mountainous interiors

Elevation: *mean elevation:* NA

elevation extremes: *lowest point:* Caribbean Sea 0 m
highest point: Mount Liamuiga 1,156 m

Natural resources: arable land

Land use: *agricultural land:* 23.1%
arable land: 19.2%;
permanent crops: 0.4%;
permanent pasture: 3.5%
forest: 42.3%
other: 34.6% (2011 est.)
Irrigated land: 8 sq km (2012)

Population—distribution: population clusters are found in the small towns located on the periphery of both islands

Natural hazards: hurricanes (July to October)
volcanism: Mount Liamuiga (1,156 m) on Saint Kitts, and Nevis Peak (985 m) on Nevis, are both volcanoes that are part of the volcanic island arc of the Lesser Antilles, which extends from Saba in the north to Grenada in the south

Environment—current issues: deforestation; soil erosion and silting affects marine life on coral reefs; water pollution from uncontrolled dumping of sewage

Environment—international agreements: *party to:* Biodiversity, Climate Change, Climate Change-Kyoto Protocol, Desertification, Endangered Species, Hazardous Wastes, Law of the Sea, Marine Dumping, Ozone Layer Protection, Ship Pollution, Whaling
signed, but not ratified: none of the selected agreements

Geography—note: smallest country in the Americas and Western Hemisphere; with coastlines in the shape of a baseball bat and ball, the two volcanic islands are separated by a 3-km-wide channel called The Narrows; on the southern tip of long, baseball bat-shaped Saint Kitts lies the Great Salt Pond; Nevis Peak sits in the center of its almost circular namesake island and its ball shape complements that of its sister island

PEOPLE AND SOCIETY

Population: 52,715 (July 2017 est.)
country comparison to the world: 207

Nationality: *noun:* Kittitian(s), Nevisian(s)
adjective: Kittitian, Nevisian

Ethnic groups: predominantly black; some British, Portuguese, and Lebanese

Languages: English (official)

Religions: Anglican, other Protestant, Roman Catholic

Age structure: *0-14 years:* 20.32% (male 5,378/female 5,332)
15-24 years: 14.54% (male 3,689/female 3,978)
25-54 years: 44.6% (male 12,070/female 11,441)
55-64 years: 11.9% (male 3,130/female 3,142)
65 years and over: 8.64% (male 2,107/female 2,448) (2017 est.)

Median age: *total:* 35 years

INTRODUCTION

Background: Carib Indians occupied the islands of the West Indies for hundreds of years before the British began settlement in 1623. In 1967, the island territory of Saint Christopher-Nevis-Anguilla became an associated state of the UK with full internal autonomy. The island of Anguilla rebelled and was allowed to secede in 1971. The remaining islands achieved independence in 1983 as Saint Kitts and Nevis. In 1998, a referendum on Nevis to separate from Saint Kitts fell short of the two-thirds majority vote needed. Nevis continues in its efforts to separate from Saint Kitts.

GEOGRAPHY

Location: Caribbean, islands in the Caribbean Sea, about one-third of the way from Puerto Rico to Trinidad and Tobago

Geographic coordinates: 17 20 N, 62 45 W

Map references: Central America and the Caribbean

male: 35.2 years
female: 34.8 years (2017 est.)
country comparison to the world: 82

Population growth rate: 0.73% (2017 est.)
country comparison to the world: 142

Birth rate: 13.2 births/1,000 population (2017 est.)
country comparison to the world: 147

Death rate: 7.1 deaths/1,000 population (2017 est.)
country comparison to the world: 129

Net migration rate: 1.2 migrant(s)/1,000 population (2017 est.)
country comparison to the world: 55

Population distribution: population clusters are found in the small towns located on the periphery of both islands

Urbanization: *urban population:* 32.3% of total population (2017)
rate of urbanization: 1.42% annual rate of change (2015-20 est.)

Major urban areas—population: BASSETERRE (capital) 14,000 (2014)

Sex ratio: *at birth:* 1.02 male(s)/female
0-14 years: 1.01 male(s)/female
15-24 years: 0.94 male(s)/female
25-54 years: 1.05 male(s)/female
55-64 years: 1 male(s)/female
65 years and over: 0.83 male(s)/female
total population: 1 male(s)/female (2016 est.)

Infant mortality rate: *total:* 8.4 deaths/1,000 live births
male: 5.9 deaths/1,000 live births
female: 10.9 deaths/1,000 live births (2017 est.)
country comparison to the world: 151

Life expectancy at birth: *total population:* 75.9 years
male: 73.5 years
female: 78.4 years (2017 est.)
country comparison to the world: 95

Total fertility rate: 1.77 children born/woman (2017 est.)
country comparison to the world: 157

Health expenditures: 5.1% of GDP (2014)
country comparison to the world: 137

Hospital bed density: 2.3 beds/1,000 population (2012)

Drinking water source:
improved:
urban: 98.3% of population
rural: 98.3% of population
total: 98.3% of population
unimproved:
urban: 1.7% of population
rural: 1.7% of population
total: 1.7% of population (2015 est.)

Sanitation facility access:
improved:
urban: 87.3% of population
rural: 87.3% of population
total: 87.3% of population
unimproved:
urban: 12.7% of population

rural: 12.7% of population
total: 12.7% of population (2007 est.)

HIV/AIDS—adult prevalence rate: NA

HIV/AIDS—people living with HIV/AIDS: NA

HIV/AIDS—deaths: NA

Obesity—adult prevalence rate: 22.9% (2016)
country comparison to the world: 71

Education expenditures: 4.2% of GDP (2007)
country comparison to the world: 105

School life expectancy (primary to tertiary education): *total:* 14 years
male: 13 years
female: 16 years (2015)

GOVERNMENT

Country name: *conventional long form:* Federation of Saint Kitts and Nevis
conventional short form: Saint Kitts and Nevis
former: Federation of Saint Christopher and Nevis
etymology: Saint Kitts was, and still is, referred to as Saint Christopher and this name was well established by the 17th century (although who first applied the name is unclear); in the 17th century a common nickname for Christopher was Kit or Kitt, so the island began to be referred to as "Saint Kitt's Island" or just "Saint Kitts"; Nevis is derived from the original Spanish name "Nuestra Senora de las Nieves" (Our Lady of the Snows) and refers to the white halo of clouds that generally wreathes Nevis Peak

Government type: federal parliamentary democracy (National Assembly) under a constitutional monarchy; a Commonwealth realm

Capital: *name:* Basseterre

geographic coordinates: 17 18 N, 62 43 W
time difference: UTC-4 (1 hour ahead of Washington, DC, during Standard Time)

Administrative divisions: 14 parishes; Christ Church Nichola Town, Saint Anne Sandy Point, Saint George Basseterre, Saint George Gingerland, Saint James Windward, Saint John Capesterre, Saint John Figtree, Saint Mary Cayon, Saint Paul Capesterre, Saint Paul Charlestown, Saint Peter Basseterre, Saint Thomas Lowland, Saint Thomas Middle Island, Trinity Palmetto Point

Independence: 19 September 1983 (from the UK)

National holiday: Independence Day, 19 September (1983)

Constitution: several previous (preindependence); latest presented 23 June 1983, effective 19 September 1983 at independence (2016)

Legal system: English common law

International law organization participation: has not submitted an ICJ jurisdiction declaration; accepts ICCt jurisdiction

Citizenship: *citizenship by birth:* yes
citizenship by descent: yes
dual citizenship recognized: yes
residency requirement for naturalization: 14 years

Suffrage: 18 years of age; universal

Executive branch: *chief of state:* Queen ELIZABETH II (since 6 February 1952); represented by Governor General Samuel W.T. SEATON (since 2 September 2015); note—SEATON was acting Governor General from 20 May to 2 September 2015
head of government: Prime Minister Timothy HARRIS (since 18 February 2015); Deputy Prime Minister Shawn RICHARDS (since 22 February 2015)
cabinet: Cabinet appointed by governor general in consultation with prime minister
elections/appointments: the monarchy is hereditary; governor general appointed by the monarch; following legislative elections, the leader of the majority party or majority coalition usually appointed prime minister by governor general; deputy prime minister appointed by governor general

Legislative branch: *description:* unicameral National Assembly (14 seats; 11 members directly elected in single-seat constituencies by simple majority vote and 3 appointed by the governor general; members serve 5-year terms)
elections: last held on 16 February 2015 (next to be held by 2020)
election results: percent of vote by party—SKNLP 39.3%, PAM 27.9% CCM 13.0% NRP 10.8%, PLP 9.0%; seats by party—PAM 4, SKNLP 3, CCM 2, NRP 1, PLP 1

Judicial branch: *highest court(s):* the Eastern Caribbean Supreme Court (ECSC) is the superior court of the Organization of Eastern Caribbean States; the ECSC—headquartered on St. Lucia—consists of the Court of Appeal—headed by the chief justice and 4 judges—and the High Court with 18 judges; the Court of Appeal is itinerant, travelling to member states on a schedule to hear appeals from the High Court and subordinate courts; High Court judges reside at the member states with 2 assigned to Saint Kitts and Nevis; note—the ECSC in 2003 replaced the Judicial Committee of the Privy Council in London as the final court of appeal on Saint Kitts and Nevis; Saint Kitts and Nevis is also a member of the Caribbean Court of Justice
judge selection and term of office: chief justice of Eastern Caribbean Supreme Court appointed by Her Majesty, Queen ELIZABETH II; other justices and judges appointed by the Judicial and Legal Services Commission, an independent body of judicial officials; Court of Appeal justices appointed for life with mandatory retirement at age 65; High Court judges appointed for life with mandatory retirement at age 62
subordinate courts: magistrates' courts

Political parties and leaders: Concerned Citizens Movement or CCM [Mark BRANTLEY]
Nevis Reformation Party or NRP [Joseph PARRY]
People's Action Movement or PAM [Shawn RICHARDS]
People's Labour Party or PLP [Dr. Timothy HARRIS]

Saint Kitts and Nevis Labor Party or SKNLP [Dr. Denzil DOUGLAS]

Political pressure groups and leaders: NA

International organization participation: ACP, AOSIS, C, Caricom, CDB, CELAC, FAO, G-77, IBRD, ICAO, ICCt, ICRM, IDA, IFAD, IFC, IFRCS, ILO, IMF, IMO, Interpol, IOC, ITU, MIGA, OAS, OECS, OPANAL, OPCW, Petrocaribe, UN, UNCTAD, UNESCO, UNIDO, UPU, WHO, WIPO, WTO

Diplomatic representation in the US: chief of mission: Ambassador Dr. Thelma Patricia PHILLIP-BROWNE (since 28 January 2016)
chancery: 3216 New Mexico Avenue NW, Washington, DC 20016
telephone: [1] (202) 686-2636
FAX: [1] (202) 686-5740
consulate(s) general: Los Angeles, New York

Diplomatic representation from the US: the US does not have an embassy in Saint Kitts and Nevis; the US Ambassador to Barbados is accredited to Saint Kitts and Nevis

Flag description: divided diagonally from the lower hoist side by a broad black band bearing two white, five-pointed stars; the black band is edged in yellow; the upper triangle is green, the lower triangle is red; green signifies the island's fertility, red symbolizes the struggles of the people from slavery, yellow denotes year-round sunshine, and black represents the African heritage of the people; the white stars stand for the islands of Saint Kitts and Nevis, but can also express hope and liberty, or independence and optimism

National symbol(s): brown pelican, Royal Poinciana (Flamboyant) tree; national colors: green, yellow, red, black, white

National anthem: name: "Oh Land of Beauty!"
lyrics/music: Kenrick Anderson GEORGES
note: adopted 1983

ECONOMY

Economy—overview: The economy of Saint Kitts and Nevis depends on tourism; since the 1970s, tourism has replaced sugar as the economy's traditional mainstay. Roughly 200,000 tourists visited the islands in 2009, but reduced tourism arrivals and foreign investment led to an economic contraction in the 2009-2013 period, and the economy returned to growth only in 2014. Like other tourist destinations in the Caribbean, Saint Kitts and Nevis is vulnerable to damage from natural disasters and shifts in tourism demand.

Following the 2005 harvest, the government closed the sugar industry after several decades of losses. To compensate for lost jobs, the government has embarked on a program to diversify the agricultural sector and to stimulate other sectors of the economy, such as export-oriented manufacturing and offshore banking. The government has made notable progress in reducing its public debt, from 154% of GDP in 2011 to 83% in 2013, although it still faces one of the highest levels in the world, largely attributable to public enterprise losses. Saint Kitts and Nevis is among other

countries in the Caribbean that supplement their economic activity through economic citizenship programs, whereby foreigners can obtain citizenship from Saint Kitts and Nevis by investing there.

GDP (purchasing power parity): $1.528 billion (2017 est.)
$1.488 billion (2016 est.)
$1.443 billion (2015 est.)
note: data are in 2017 dollars
country comparison to the world: 200

GDP (official exchange rate): $939 million (2016 est.)

GDP—real growth rate: 2.7% (2017 est.)
3.1% (2016 est.)
4.9% (2015 est.)
country comparison to the world: 125

GDP—per capita (PPP): $26,800 (2017 est.)
$26,600 (2016 est.)
$25,800 (2015 est.)
note: data are in 2017 dollars
country comparison to the world: 74

Gross national saving: 17.2% of GDP (2017 est.)
18.6% of GDP (2016 est.)
16.5% of GDP (2015 est.)
country comparison to the world: 108

GDP—composition, by end use:
household consumption: 58.8%
government consumption: 20.4%
investment in fixed capital: 30.4%
investment in inventories: 0%
exports of goods and services: 33.3%
imports of goods and services: -43% (2017 est.)

GDP—composition, by sector of origin:
agriculture: 1.1%
industry: 30%
services: 68.9% (2017 est.)

Agriculture—products: sugarcane, rice, yams, vegetables, bananas; fish

Industries: tourism, cotton, salt, copra, clothing, footwear, beverages

Industrial production growth rate: 6% (2017 est.)
country comparison to the world: 35

Labor force: 18,170 (June 1995 est.)
country comparison to the world: 213

Unemployment rate: 4.5% (1997)
country comparison to the world: 64

Population below poverty line: NA%

Household income or consumption by percentage share: lowest 10%: NA%
highest 10%: NA%

Budget: revenues: $370.4 million
expenditures: $370.4 million (2017 est.)
Taxes and other revenues: 39.4% of GDP (2017 est.)
country comparison to the world: 38

Budget surplus (+) or deficit (-): 0% of GDP (2017 est.)
country comparison to the world: 36

Public debt: 65.8% of GDP (2016 est.)
70.6% of GDP (2015 est.)
country comparison to the world: 60

Fiscal year: calendar year

Inflation rate (consumer prices): 1.2% (2017 est.)
-0.4% (2016 est.)
country comparison to the world: 53

Central bank discount rate: 6.5% (31 December 2009)
6.5% (31 December 2008)
country comparison to the world: 63

Commercial bank prime lending rate: 9.1% (31 December 2017 est.)
9.24% (31 December 2016 est.)
country comparison to the world: 90

Stock of narrow money: $230.9 million (31 December 2017 est.)
$210.1 million (31 December 2016 est.)
country comparison to the world: 181

Stock of broad money: $1.122 billion (31 December 2017 est.)
$1.077 billion (31 December 2016 est.)
country comparison to the world: 171

Stock of domestic credit: $740.7 million (31 December 2017 est.)
$704.8 million (31 December 2016 est.)
country comparison to the world: 171

Market value of publicly traded shares: $598.4 million (31 December 2011 est.)
$598.4 million (31 December 2011 est.)
country comparison to the world: 112

Current account balance: -$120 million (2017 est.)
-$102 million (2016 est.)
country comparison to the world: 82

Exports: $58.4 million (2017 est.)
$53.9 million (2016 est.)
country comparison to the world: 201

Exports—commodities: machinery, food, electronics, beverages, tobacco

Exports—partners: US 49.6%, Poland 15.2%, Turkey 11.6% (2016)

Imports: $264.4 million (2017 est.)
$244.4 million (2016 est.)
country comparison to the world: 199

Imports—commodities: machinery, manufactures, food, fuels

Imports—partners: US 56.8%, Trinidad and Tobago 6.8%, Cyprus 6.2%, Japan 4% (2016)

Debt—external: $198 million (31 December 2017 est.)
$187.9 million (31 December 2016 est.)
country comparison to the world: 189

Exchange rates: East Caribbean dollars (XCD) per US dollar—
2.7 (2017 est.)
2.7 (2016 est.)
2.7 (2015 est.)
2.7 (2014 est.)
2.7 (2013 est.)

ENERGY

Electricity access: population without electricity: 5,232
electrification—total population: 91%
electrification—urban areas: 100%

electrification—rural areas: 80% (2012)

Electricity—production: 208 million kWh (2015 est.)
country comparison to the world: 188

Electricity—consumption: 193.4 million kWh (2015 est.)
country comparison to the world: 190

Electricity—exports: 0 kWh (2016 est.)
country comparison to the world: 192

Electricity—imports: 0 kWh (2016 est.)
country comparison to the world: 196

Electricity—installed generating capacity: 63,200 kW (2015 est.)
country comparison to the world: 188

Electricity—from fossil fuels: 94.9% of total installed capacity (2015 est.)
country comparison to the world: 55

Electricity—from nuclear fuels: 0% of total installed capacity (2015 est.)
country comparison to the world: 177

Electricity—from hydroelectric plants: 0% of total installed capacity (2015 est.)
country comparison to the world: 200

Electricity—from other renewable sources: 6.6% of total installed capacity (2015 est.)
country comparison to the world: 86

Crude oil—production: 0 bbl/day (2016 est.)
country comparison to the world: 189

Crude oil—exports: 0 bbl/day (2014 est.)
country comparison to the world: 184

Crude oil—imports: 0 bbl/day (2014 est.)
country comparison to the world: 185

Crude oil—proved reserves: 0 bbl (1 January 2017 es)
country comparison to the world: 187

Refined petroleum products—production: 0 bbl/day (2014 est.)
country comparison to the world: 193

Refined petroleum products—consumption: 1,900 bbl/day (2015 est.)
country comparison to the world: 195

Refined petroleum products—exports: 0 bbl/day (2014 est.)
country comparison to the world: 194

Refined petroleum products—imports: 1,907 bbl/day (2014 est.)

country comparison to the world: 189

Natural gas—production: 0 cu m (2013 est.)
country comparison to the world: 190

Natural gas—consumption: 0 cu m (2013 est.)
country comparison to the world: 127

Natural gas—exports: 0 cu m (2013 est.)
country comparison to the world: 176

Natural gas—imports: 0 cu m (2013 est.)
country comparison to the world: 183

Natural gas—proved reserves: 0 cu m (1 January 2014 es)
country comparison to the world: 190

Carbon dioxide emissions from consumption of energy: 300,000 Mt (2013 est.)
country comparison to the world: 190

COMMUNICATIONS

Telephones—fixed lines: *total subscriptions:* 17,433
subscriptions per 100 inhabitants: 33 (July 2016 est.)
country comparison to the world: 185

Telephones—mobile cellular: *total:* 76,583
subscriptions per 100 inhabitants: 146 (July 2016 est.)
country comparison to the world: 196

Telephone system: *general assessment:* good interisland and international connections
domestic: interisland links via ECFS; construction of enhanced wireless infrastructure launched in November 2004; fixed-line teledensity about 30 per 100 persons; mobile-cellular teledensity is roughly 145 per 100 persons
international: country code—1-869; connected internationally by the East ECFS and Southern Caribbean Fiber submarine cables (2016)

Broadcast media: the government operates a national TV network that broadcasts on 2 channels; cable subscription services provide access to local and international channels; the government operates a national radio network; a mix of government-owned and privately owned broadcasters operate roughly 15 radio stations (2007)

Internet country code: .kn

Internet users: *total:* 39,000
percent of population: 75.7% (July 2016 est.)

country comparison to the world: 203

TRANSPORTATION

Civil aircraft registration country code prefix: V4 (2016)

Airports: 2 (2013)
country comparison to the world: 209

Airports—with paved runways: *total:* 2
1,524 to 2,437 m: 1
914 to 1,523 m: 1 (2017)

Railways: *total:* 50 km
narrow gauge: 50 km 0.762-m gauge on Saint Kitts for tourists (2008)
country comparison to the world: 132

Roadways: *total:* 383 km
paved: 163 km
unpaved: 220 km (2002)
country comparison to the world: 202

Merchant marine: *total:* 274
by type: bulk carrier 6, container ship 5, general cargo 58, oil tanker 60, other 145 (2017)
country comparison to the world: 55

Ports and terminals: *major seaport(s):* Basseterre, Charlestown

MILITARY AND SECURITY

Military branches: Ministry of Foreign Affairs, National Security, Labour, Immigration, and Social Security: Royal Saint Kitts and Nevis Defense Force (includes Coast Guard), Royal Saint Kitts and Nevis Police Force (2013)

Military service age and obligation: 18 years of age for voluntary military service; no conscription (2012)

TRANSNATIONAL ISSUES

Disputes—international: joins other Caribbean states to counter Venezuela's claim that Aves Island sustains human habitation, a criterion under UN Convention on the Law of the Sea, which permits Venezuela to extend its EEZ/continental shelf over a large portion of the eastern Caribbean Sea

Illicit drugs: transshipment point for South American drugs destined for the US and Europe; some money-laundering activity

SAINT LUCIA

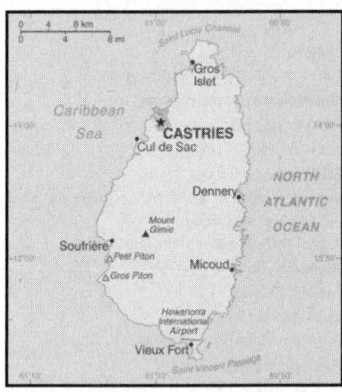

INTRODUCTION

Background: The island, with its fine natural harbor at Castries, was contested between England and France throughout the 17th and early 18th centuries (changing possession 14 times); it was finally ceded to the UK in 1814. Even after the abolition of slavery on its plantations in 1834, Saint Lucia remained an agricultural island, dedicated to producing tropical commodity crops. Self-government was granted in 1967 and independence in 1979.

GEOGRAPHY

Location: Caribbean, island between the Caribbean Sea and North Atlantic Ocean, north of Trinidad and Tobago

Geographic coordinates: 13 53 N, 60 58 W

Map references: Central America and the Caribbean

Area: *total:* 616 sq km
land: 606 sq km
water: 10 sq km
country comparison to the world: 193

Area—comparative: three and a half times the size of Washington, DC
Land boundaries: 0 km

Coastline: 158 km

Maritime claims: *territorial sea:* 12 nm
contiguous zone: 24 nm
exclusive economic zone: 200 nm
continental shelf: 200 nm or to the edge of the continental margin

Climate: tropical, moderated by northeast trade winds; dry season January to April, rainy season May to August

Terrain: volcanic and mountainous with broad, fertile valleys

Elevation: *mean elevation:* NA

elevation extremes: *lowest point:* Caribbean Sea 0 m
highest point: Mount Gimie 948 m

Natural resources: forests, sandy beaches, minerals (pumice), mineral springs, geothermal potential

Land use: *agricultural land:* 17.4%
arable land: 4.9%;
permanent crops: 11.5%;
permanent pasture: 1%
forest: 77%
other: 5.6% (2011 est.)
Irrigated land: 30 sq km (2012)

Population—distribution: most of the population is found on the periphery of the island, with a larger concentration in the north around the capital of Castries

Natural hazards: hurricanes
volcanism: Mount Gimie (948 m), also known as Qualibou, is a caldera on the west of the island; the iconic twin pyramidal peaks of Gros Piton (771 m) and Petit Piton (743 m) are lava dome remnants associated with the Soufriere volcano; there have been no historical magmatic eruptions, but a minor steam eruption in 1766 spread a thin layer of ash over a wide area; Saint Lucia is part of the volcanic island arc of the Lesser Antilles that extends from Saba in the north to Grenada in the south

Environment—current issues: deforestation; soil erosion, particularly in the northern region

Environment—international agreements: *party to:* Biodiversity, Climate Change, Climate Change-Kyoto Protocol, Desertification, Endangered Species, Environmental Modification, Hazardous Wastes, Law of the Sea, Marine Dumping, Ozone Layer Protection, Ship Pollution, Wetlands, Whaling
signed, but not ratified: none of the selected agreements

Geography—note: the twin Pitons (Gros Piton and Petit Piton), striking cone-shaped peaks south of Soufriere, are one of the scenic natural highlights of the Caribbean

PEOPLE AND SOCIETY

Population: 164,994 (July 2017 est.)
country comparison to the world: 187

Nationality: *noun:* Saint Lucian(s)
adjective: Saint Lucian

Ethnic groups: black/African descent 85.3%, mixed 10.9%, East Indian 2.2%, other 1.6%, unspecified 0.1% (2010 est.)

Languages: English (official), French patois

Religions: Roman Catholic 61.5%, Protestant 25.5% (includes Seventh Day Adventist 10.4%, Pentecostal 8.9%, Baptist 2.2%, Anglican 1.6%, Church of God 1.5%, other Protestant 0.9%), other Christian 3.4% (includes Evangelical 2.3% and Jehovah's Witness 1.1%), Rastafarian 1.9%, other 0.4%, none 5.9%, unspecified 1.4% (2010 est.)

Age structure: *0-14 years:* 20.02% (male 17,006/female 16,027)
15-24 years: 15.37% (male 12,870/female 12,492)
25-54 years: 42.97% (male 34,117/female 36,779)
55-64 years: 9.99% (male 7,608/female 8,881)
65 years and over: 11.65% (male 8,704/female 10,510) (2017 est.)

Dependency ratios: *total dependency ratio:* 41.1
youth dependency ratio: 27.9
elderly dependency ratio: 13.3
potential support ratio: 7.5 (2015 est.)

Median age: *total:* 34.8 years
male: 33.7 years
female: 36 years (2017 est.)
country comparison to the world: 84

Population growth rate: 0.32% (2017 est.)
country comparison to the world: 168

Birth rate: 13.3 births/1,000 population (2017 est.)
country comparison to the world: 144

Death rate: 7.7 deaths/1,000 population (2017 est.)
country comparison to the world: 103

Net migration rate: -2.5 migrant(s)/1,000 population (2017 est.)
country comparison to the world: 170

Population distribution: most of the population is found on the periphery of the island, with a larger concentration in the north around the capital of Castries

Urbanization: *urban population:* 18.6% of total population (2017)
rate of urbanization: 1.01% annual rate of change (2015-20 est.)

Major urban areas—population: CASTRIES (capital) 22,000 (2014)

Sex ratio: *at birth:* 1.06 male(s)/female
0-14 years: 1.06 male(s)/female
15-24 years: 1.03 male(s)/female
25-54 years: 0.93 male(s)/female
55-64 years: 0.86 male(s)/female
65 years and over: 0.83 male(s)/female
total population: 0.95 male(s)/female (2016 est.)

Maternal mortality ratio: 48 deaths/100,000 live births (2015 est.)
country comparison to the world: 97

Infant mortality rate: *total:* 10.9 deaths/1,000 live births
male: 10.4 deaths/1,000 live births
female: 11.4 deaths/1,000 live births (2017 est.)
country comparison to the world: 129

Life expectancy at birth: *total population:* 77.9 years
male: 75.2 years
female: 80.8 years (2017 est.)
country comparison to the world: 66

Total fertility rate: 1.75 children born/woman (2017 est.)
country comparison to the world: 161

Contraceptive prevalence rate: 55.5% (2011/12)

Health expenditures: 6.7% of GDP (2014)
country comparison to the world: 87

Physicians density: 0.1 physicians/1,000 population (2009)

Hospital bed density: 1.6 beds/1,000 population (2011)

Drinking water source:
improved:
urban: 99.5% of population
rural: 95.6% of population
total: 96.3% of population
unimproved:
urban: 0.5% of population
rural: 4.4% of population
total: 3.7% of population (2015 est.)

Sanitation facility access:
improved:
urban: 84.7% of population
rural: 91.9% of population
total: 90.5% of population
unimproved:
urban: 15.3% of population
rural: 8.1% of population
total: 9.5% of population (2015 est.)

HIV/AIDS—adult prevalence rate: NA

HIV/AIDS—people living with HIV/AIDS: NA

HIV/AIDS—deaths: NA

Major infectious diseases: *note:* active local transmission of Zika virus by Aedes species mosquitoes has been identified in this country (as of August 2016); it poses an important risk (a large number of cases possible) among US citizens if bitten by an infective mosquito; other less common ways to get Zika are through sex, via blood transfusion, or during pregnancy, in which the pregnant woman passes Zika virus to her fetus (2016)

Obesity—adult prevalence rate: 19.7% (2016)
country comparison to the world: 110

Children under the age of 5 years underweight: 2.8% (2012)
country comparison to the world: 116

Education expenditures: 4.8% of GDP (2015)
country comparison to the world: 107

School life expectancy (primary to tertiary education): *total:* 13 years
male: 12 years
female: 13 years (2007)

Unemployment, youth ages 15-24: *total:* 27.5%
male: 21.5%
female: 35.2% (2007 est.)
country comparison to the world: 12

GOVERNMENT

Country name: *conventional long form:* none
conventional short form: Saint Lucia
etymology: named after Saint LUCY of Syracuse by French sailors who were shipwrecked on the island on 13 December 1502, the saint's feast day

Government type: parliamentary democracy (Parliament) under a constitutional monarchy; a Commonwealth realm

Capital: *name:* Castries

geographic coordinates: 14 00 N, 61 00 W
time difference: UTC-4 (1 hour ahead of Washington, DC, during Standard Time)

Administrative divisions: 10 districts; Anse-la-Raye, Canaries, Castries, Choiseul, Dennery, Gros-Islet, Laborie, Micoud, Soufriere, Vieux-Fort

Independence: 22 February 1979 (from the UK)

National holiday: Independence Day, 22 February (1979)

Constitution: previous 1958, 1960 (preindependence); latest presented 20 December 1978, effective 22 February 1979; note—in mid-2015, an amendment was proposed to replace the London-based Privy Council with the Caribbean Court of Justice as the country's highest appellate court (2016)

Legal system: English common law

International law organization participation: has not submitted an ICJ jurisdiction declaration; accepts ICCt jurisdiction

Citizenship: *citizenship by birth:* yes

citizenship by descent: at least one parent must be a citizen of Saint Lucia
dual citizenship recognized: yes
residency requirement for naturalization: 8 years

Suffrage: 18 years of age; universal

Executive branch: *chief of state:* Queen ELIZABETH II (since 6 February 1952); represented by Governor General Neville CENAC (since 12 January 2018)
head of government: Prime Minister Allen CHASTANET (since 7 June 2016)
cabinet: Cabinet appointed by the governor general on the advice of the prime minister
elections/appointments: the monarchy is hereditary; governor general appointed by the monarch; following legislative elections, the leader of the majority party or majority coalition usually appointed prime minister by governor general; deputy prime minister appointed by governor general

Legislative branch: *description:* bicameral Parliament consists of the Senate (11 seats; 6 members appointed on the advice of the prime minister, 3 on the advice of the leader of the opposition, and 2 upon consultation with religious, economic, and social groups; members serve 5-year terms) and the House of Assembly (17 seats; members directly elected in single-seat constituencies by simple majority vote to serve 5-year terms)
elections: House of Assembly—last held on 6 June 2016 (next to be held in 2021)
election results: House of Assembly—percent of vote by party—UWP 54.8%, SLP 44.1%, other 1.1%; seats by party—UWP 11, SLP 6

Judicial branch: *highest court(s):* the Eastern Caribbean Supreme Court (ECSC) is the superior court of the Organization of Eastern Caribbean States; the ECSC—headquartered on St. Lucia—consists of the Court of Appeal—headed by the chief justice and 4 judges—and the High Court

with 18 judges; the Court of Appeal is itinerant, travelling to member states on a schedule to hears appeals from the High Court and subordinate courts; High Court judges reside at the member states with 4 on Saint Lucia; Saint Lucia is a member of the Caribbean Court of Justice
judge selection and term of office: chief justice of Eastern Caribbean Supreme Court appointed by Her Majesty, Queen ELIZABETH II; other justices and judges appointed by the Judicial and Legal Services Commission, an independent body of judicial officials; Court of Appeal justices appointed for life with mandatory retirement at age 65; High Court judges appointed for life with mandatory retirement at age 62
subordinate courts: magistrate's court

Political parties and leaders: Lucian People's Movement or LPM [Therold PRUDENT]
Saint Lucia Labor Party or SLP [Philip J. PIERRE]
United Workers Party or UWP [Allen CHASTANET]

Political pressure groups and leaders: NA

International organization participation: ACP, AOSIS, C, Caricom, CD, CDB, CELAC, FAO, G-77, IBRD, ICAO, ICCt, ICRM, IDA, IFAD, IFC, IFRCS, ILO, IMF, IMO, Interpol, IOC, ISO, ITU, ITUC (NGOs), MIGA, NAM, OAS, OECS, OIF, OPANAL, OPCW, Petrocaribe, UN, UNCTAD, UNESCO, UNIDO, UPU, WCO, WFTU (NGOs), WHO, WIPO, WMO, WTO

Diplomatic representation in the US: chief of mission: Ambassador Anton Edsel EDMUNDS (since 8 September 2017)
chancery: 3216 New Mexico Avenue NW, Washington, DC 20016
telephone: [1] (202) 364-6792 through 6795
FAX: [1] (202) 364-6723
consulate(s) general: New York

Diplomatic representation from the US: the US does not have an embassy in Saint Lucia; the US Ambassador to Barbados is accredited to Saint Lucia

Flag description: cerulean blue with a gold isosceles triangle below a black arrowhead; the upper edges of the arrowhead have a white border; the blue color represents the sky and sea, gold stands for sunshine and prosperity, and white and black the racial composition of the island (with the latter being dominant); the two major triangles invoke the twin Pitons (Gros Piton and Petit Piton), cone-shaped volcanic plugs that are a symbol of the island

National symbol(s): twin pitons (volcanic peaks), Saint Lucia parrot; national colors: cerulean blue, gold, black, white

National anthem: *name:* "Sons and Daughters of St. Lucia"
lyrics/music: Charles JESSE/Leton Felix THOMAS
note: adopted 1967

ECONOMY

Economy—overview: The island nation has been able to attract foreign business and investment, especially in its offshore banking and tourism industries. Tourism is Saint Lucia's main source of jobs and income—accounting for 65% of GDP—and the island's main source of foreign exchange earnings. The manufacturing sector is the most diverse in the Eastern Caribbean area. Crops such as bananas, mangos, and avocados continue to be grown for export, but St. Lucia's once solid banana industry has been devastated by strong competition.

Saint Lucia is vulnerable to a variety of external shocks, including volatile tourism receipts, natural disasters, and dependence on foreign oil. Furthermore, high public debt—77% of GDP in 2012—and high debt servicing obligations constrain the CHASTANET administration's ability to respond to adverse external shocks.

St. Lucia has experienced anemic growth since the onset of the global financial crisis in 2008, largely because of a slowdown in tourism—airlines cut back on their routes to St. Lucia in 2012. Also, St. Lucia introduced a value added tax in 2012 of 15%, becoming the last country in the Eastern Caribbean to do so. In 2013, the government introduced a National Competitiveness and Productivity Council to address St. Lucia's high public wages and lack of productivity.

GDP (purchasing power parity): $2.384 billion (2017 est.)
$2.346 billion (2016 est.)
$2.323 billion (2015 est.)
note: data are in 2017 dollars
country comparison to the world: 194

GDP (official exchange rate): $1.717 billion (2016 est.)

GDP—real growth rate: 1.6% (2017 est.)
1% (2016 est.)
2% (2015 est.)
country comparison to the world: 172

GDP—per capita (PPP): $13,500 (2017 est.)
$13,500 (2016 est.)
$13,400 (2015 est.)
note: data are in 2017 dollars
country comparison to the world: 115

Gross national saving: 17% of GDP (2017 est.)
21.3% of GDP (2016 est.)
29% of GDP (2015 est.)
country comparison to the world: 110

GDP—composition, by end use:
household consumption: 70.9%
government consumption: 14.8%
investment in fixed capital: 18.3%
investment in inventories: 0.1%
exports of goods and services: 41.3%
imports of goods and services: -45.3% (2017 est.)

GDP—composition, by sector of origin:
agriculture: 2.9%
industry: 14.2%
services: 82.8% (2017 est.)

Agriculture—products: bananas, coconuts, vegetables, citrus, root crops, cocoa

Industries: tourism; clothing, assembly of electronic components, beverages, corrugated cardboard boxes, lime processing, coconut processing

Industrial production growth rate: 4% (2017 est.)

country comparison to the world: 70

Labor force: 79,700 (2012 est.)
country comparison to the world: 184

Labor force—by occupation: *agriculture:* 21.7%
industry: 24.7%
services: 53.6% (2002 est.)

Unemployment rate: 20% (2003 est.)
country comparison to the world: 184

Population below poverty line: NA%

Household income or consumption by percentage share: *lowest 10%:* NA%
highest 10%: NA%

Budget: *revenues:* $402.3 million
expenditures: $430.7 million (2017 est.)
Taxes and other revenues: 23.4% of GDP (2017 est.)
country comparison to the world: 126

Budget surplus (+) or deficit (-): -1.7% of GDP (2017 est.)
country comparison to the world: 74

Public debt: 82.9% of GDP (2016 est.)
77.8% of GDP (2015 est.)
country comparison to the world: 33

Fiscal year: 1 April—31 March

Inflation rate (consumer prices): 0.2% (2017 est.)
-3.1% (2016 est.)
country comparison to the world: 13

Central bank discount rate: 6.5% (31 December 2010)
6.5% (31 December 2009)
country comparison to the world: 62

Commercial bank prime lending rate: 8.3% (31 December 2017 est.)
8.5% (31 December 2016 est.)
country comparison to the world: 104

Stock of narrow money: $321.1 million (31 December 2017 est.)
$318.4 million (31 December 2016 est.)
country comparison to the world: 177

Stock of broad money: $1.192 billion (31 December 2017 est.)
$1.157 billion (31 December 2016 est.)
country comparison to the world: 170

Stock of domestic credit: $1.363 billion (31 December 2017 est.)
$1.332 billion (31 December 2016 est.)
country comparison to the world: 161

Current account balance: -$8 million (2017 est.)
-$31 million (2016 est.)
country comparison to the world: 63

Exports: $204.2 million (2017 est.)
$188.2 million (2016 est.)
country comparison to the world: 187

Exports—commodities: bananas 41%, clothing, cocoa, avocados, mangoes, coconut oil (2010 est.)

Exports—partners: US 48.8%, Trinidad and Tobago 14.1%, UK 11.2%, Maldives 4.7% (2016)

Imports: $430.6 million (2017 est.)
$404.1 million (2016 est.)
country comparison to the world: 190

Imports—commodities: food, manufactured goods, machinery and transportation equipment, chemicals, fuels

Imports—partners: US 39.8%, Trinidad and Tobago 18%, UK 6.7%, Japan 4% (2016)

Debt—external: $523.2 million (31 December 2016 est.)
$529 million (31 December 2015 est.)
country comparison to the world: 178

Exchange rates: East Caribbean dollars (XCD) per US dollar—
2.7 (2017 est.)
2.7 (2016 est.)
2.7 (2015 est.)
2.7 (2014 est.)
2.7 (2013 est.)

ENERGY

Electricity access: population without electricity: 16,446
electrification—total population: 91%
electrification—urban areas: 100%
electrification—rural areas: 80% (2012)

Electricity—production: 358 million kWh (2015 est.)
country comparison to the world: 174

Electricity—consumption: 332.9 million kWh (2015 est.)
country comparison to the world: 178

Electricity—exports: 0 kWh (2016 est.)
country comparison to the world: 199

Electricity—imports: 0 kWh (2016 est.)
country comparison to the world: 203

Electricity—installed generating capacity: 89,000 kW (2015 est.)
country comparison to the world: 179

Electricity—from fossil fuels: 98.9% of total installed capacity (2015 est.)
country comparison to the world: 33

Electricity—from nuclear fuels: 0% of total installed capacity (2015 est.)
country comparison to the world: 184

Electricity—from hydroelectric plants: 0% of total installed capacity (2015 est.)
country comparison to the world: 205

Electricity—from other renewable sources: 1.1% of total installed capacity (2015 est.)
country comparison to the world: 137

Crude oil—production: 0 bbl/day (2016 est.)
country comparison to the world: 190

Crude oil—exports: 0 bbl/day (2014 est.)
country comparison to the world: 193

Crude oil—imports: 0 bbl/day (2014 est.)
country comparison to the world: 191

Crude oil—proved reserves: 0 bbl (1 January 2017 es)
country comparison to the world: 188

Refined petroleum products—production: 0 bbl/day (2014 est.)
country comparison to the world: 194

Refined petroleum products—consumption: 3,100 bbl/day (2015 est.)
country comparison to the world: 186

Refined petroleum products—exports: 0 bbl/day (2014 est.)
country comparison to the world: 199

Refined petroleum products—imports: 3,058 bbl/day (2014 est.)
country comparison to the world: 178

Natural gas—production: 0 cu m (2013 est.)
country comparison to the world: 196

Natural gas—consumption: 0 cu m (2013 est.)
country comparison to the world: 132

Natural gas—exports: 0 cu m (2013 est.)
country comparison to the world: 184

Natural gas—imports: 0 cu m (2013 est.)
country comparison to the world: 189

Natural gas—proved reserves: 0 cu m (1 January 2014 es)
country comparison to the world: 196

Carbon dioxide emissions from consumption of energy: 400,000 Mt (2013 est.)
country comparison to the world: 187

COMMUNICATIONS

Telephones—fixed lines: *total subscriptions:* 35,003
subscriptions per 100 inhabitants: 21 (July 2016 est.)
country comparison to the world: 171

Telephones—mobile cellular: *total:* 176,648
subscriptions per 100 inhabitants: 107 (July 2016 est.)
country comparison to the world: 181

Telephone system: *general assessment:* an adequate system that is automatically switched
domestic: fixed-line teledensity is 20 per 100 persons and mobile-cellular teledensity is roughly 105 per 100 persons
international: country code—1-758; the East Caribbean Fiber System and Southern Caribbean Fiber submarine cables, along with Intelsat from Martinique, carry calls internationally; direct microwave radio relay link with Martinique and Saint Vincent and the Grenadines; tropospheric scatter to Barbados (2016)

Broadcast media: 3 privately owned TV stations; 1 public TV station operating on a cable network; multi-channel cable TV service available; a mix of state-owned and privately owned broadcasters operate nearly 25 radio stations including repeater transmission stations (2007)

Internet country code: .lc

Internet users: *total:* 86,000
percent of population: 52.4% (July 2016 est.)
country comparison to the world: 166

TRANSPORTATION

Civil aircraft registration country code prefix: J6 (2016)

Airports: 2 (2013)
country comparison to the world: 204

Airports—with paved runways: *total:* 2
2,438 to 3,047 m: 1
1,524 to 2,437 m: 1 (2017)

Roadways: *total:* 1,210 km
paved: 847 km
unpaved: 363 km (2011)
country comparison to the world: 182

Ports and terminals: *major seaport(s):* Castries, Cul-de-Sac, Vieux-Fort

MILITARY AND SECURITY

Military branches: no regular military forces; Royal Saint Lucia Police Force (includes Special Service Unit, Marine Unit) (2012)

Military service age and obligation: 18 years of age for voluntary security service; no national army (2012)

TRANSNATIONAL ISSUES

Disputes—international: joins other Caribbean states to counter Venezuela's claim that Aves Island sustains human habitation, a criterion under UN Convention on the Law of the Sea, which permits Venezuela to extend its EEZ/continental shelf over a large portion of the eastern Caribbean Sea

Illicit drugs: transit point for South American drugs destined for the US and Europe

SAINT MARTIN

INTRODUCTION

Background: Although sighted by Christopher COLUMBUS in 1493 and claimed for Spain, it was the Dutch who occupied the island in 1631 and set about exploiting its salt deposits. The Spanish retook the island in 1633, but continued to be harassed by the Dutch. The Spanish finally relinquished Saint Martin to the French and Dutch, who divided it between themselves in 1648. Friction between the two sides caused the border to frequently fluctuate over the next two centuries, with the French eventually holding the greater portion of the island (about 57%). The cultivation of sugar cane introduced African slavery to the island in the late 18th century; the practice was not abolished until 1848. The island became a free port in 1939; the tourism industry was dramatically expanded during the 1970s and 1980s. In 2003, the populace of Saint Martin voted to secede from Guadeloupe and in 2007, the northern portion of the island became a French overseas collectivity. In 2010, the southern Dutch portion of the island became the independent nation of Sint Maarten within the Kingdom of the Netherlands. On 6 September 2017, Hurricane Irma passed over the island of Saint Martin causing extensive damage to roads, communications, electrical power, and housing; the UN estimated that 90% of the buildings were damaged or destroyed.

GEOGRAPHY

Location: Caribbean, located in the Leeward Islands (northern) group; French part of the island of Saint Martin in the Caribbean Sea; Saint Martin lies east of the US Virgin Islands

Geographic coordinates: 18 05 N, 63 57 W

Map references: Central America and the Caribbean

Area: *total:* 54.4 sq km
land: 54.4 sq km
water: negligible
country comparison to the world: 232

Area—comparative: more than one-third the size of Washington, DC
Land boundaries: total: 16 km
border countries (1): Sint Maarten 16 km

Coastline: 58.9 km (for entire island)

Climate: temperature averages 27-29 degrees Celsius all year long; low humidity, gentle trade winds, brief, intense rain showers; hurricane season stretches from July to November

Elevation: *mean elevation:* NA

elevation extremes: *lowest point:* Caribbean Ocean 0 m
highest point: Pic du Paradis 424 m

Natural resources: salt

Population—distribution: most of the population is found along the coast, with a largest concentrations

765

around the capital Marigot, Orleans, and Grand-Case

Natural hazards: subject to hurricanes from July to November

Environment—current issues: freshwater supply is dependent on desalination of sea water

Geography—note: the southern border is shared with Sint Maarten, a country within the Kingdom of the Netherlands; together, these two entities make up the smallest landmass in the world shared by two self-governing states

PEOPLE AND SOCIETY

Population: 32,125 (July 2017 est.)
country comparison to the world: 216

Ethnic groups: Creole (mulatto), black, Guadeloupe Mestizo (French-East Asia), white, East Indian

Languages: French (official), English, Dutch, French Patois, Spanish, Papiamento (dialect of Netherlands Antilles)

Religions: Roman Catholic, Jehovah's Witness, Protestant, Hindu

Age structure: *0-14 years:* 26.22% (male 4,192/female 4,231)
15-24 years: 10.35% (male 1,645/female 1,681)
25-54 years: 46.67% (male 7,160/female 7,832)
55-64 years: 8.74% (male 1,309/female 1,500)
65 years and over: 8.02% (male 1,138/female 1,437) (2017 est.)

Median age: *total:* 32.5 years
male: 31.6 years
female: 33.4 years (2017 est.)
country comparison to the world: 98

Population distribution: most of the population is found along the coast, with a largest concentrations around the capital Marigot, Orleans, and Grand-Case

Sex ratio: *at birth:* 1.04 male(s)/female
0-14 years: 0.99 male(s)/female
15-24 years: 0.99 male(s)/female
25-54 years: 0.91 male(s)/female
55-64 years: 0.87 male(s)/female
65 years and over: 0.81 male(s)/female
total population: 0.93 male(s)/female (2016 est.)

Major infectious diseases: *note:* active local transmission of Zika virus by Aedes species mosquitoes has been identified in this country (as of August 2016); it poses an important risk (a large number of cases possible) among US citizens if bitten by an infective mosquito; other less common ways to get Zika are through sex, via blood transfusion, or during pregnancy, in which the pregnant woman passes Zika virus to her fetus (2016)

GOVERNMENT

Country name: *conventional long form:* Overseas Collectivity of Saint Martin
conventional short form: Saint Martin
local long form: Collectivite d'outre mer de Saint-Martin
local short form: Saint-Martin

etymology: explorer Christopher COLUMBUS named the island after Saint MARTIN of Tours because the 11 November 1493 day of discovery was the saint's feast day

Dependency status: overseas collectivity of France
note: the only French overseas collectivity that is part of the EU

Capital: *name:* Marigot
geographical coordinates: 18 04 N, 63 05 W
time difference: UTC-4 (1 hour ahead of Washington, DC, during Standard Time)

Independence: none (overseas collectivity of France)

National holiday: Fete de la Federation, 14 July (1790); note—local holiday is Schoalcher Day (Slavery Abolition Day) 12 July (1848)

Constitution: 4 October 1958 (French Constitution)

Legal system: French civil law

Citizenship: see France

Suffrage: 18 years of age, universal

Executive branch: *chief of state:* President Emmanuel MACRON (since 14 May 2017); represented by Prefect Anne LAUBIES (since 8 June 2015)
head of government: President of Territorial Council Daniel GIBBS (since 2 April 2017)
cabinet: Executive Council; note—there is also an advisory economic, social, and cultural council
elections/appointments: French president directly elected by absolute majority popular vote in 2 rounds if needed for a 5-year term (eligible for a second term); prefect appointed by French president on the advice of French Ministry of Interior; president of Territorial Council elected by its members for a 5-year term; election last held on 17 April 2013 (next to be held in 2018)
election results: Aline HANSON elected president; Territorial Council vote—NA

Legislative branch: *description:* unicameral Territorial Council (23 seats; members directly elected by absolute majority vote in 2 rounds if needed to serve 5-year terms); Saint Martin elects 1 member to the French Senate and one member (shared with Saint Barthelemy) to the French National Assembly
elections: Territorial Council—last held on 18 and 25 March 2017 (next to be held in March 2022) French Senate—held on 28 September 2014 (next to be held not later than September 2020) French National Assembly—last held on 11 and 18 June 2017 (next to be held by June 2022)
election results: Territorial Council—percent of vote by party (first round)—TDG 49.1%, MJP 13.7%, MVP 12.3%, HOPE 8.7%, Continuons pour Saint-Martin 6.5%, other 9.7%; seats by party—NA; percent of vote by party (second round)—TDG 64.3%, MJP 24.2%, MVP 11.5.5%; seats by party—TDG 18, MJP 4, MVP 1 French Senate—1 seat: UMP 1 French National Assembly—1 seat: UMP 1

Political parties and leaders: Continuons pour St. Martin [Aline HANSON]

En marche vers le progres or MVP [Alain RICHARDSON]
Gereration Hope or HOPE [Jules CHARVILLE]
Movement for Justice and Prosperity or MJP [Louis MUSSINGTON]
New Direction [Jeanne VANTERPOOL]
Rally Responsibility Success (Rassemblement Responsabilite Reussite or RRR [Alain RICHARDSON]
Team Daniel Gibbs 2017 or TDG [Daniel GIBBS]
Union for Progress (Union Pour le Progres or UPP) [Louis-Constant FLEMING]; affiliated with UMP

Political pressure groups and leaders: NA

International organization participation: UPU

Diplomatic representation in the US: none (overseas collectivity of France)

Diplomatic representation from the US: none (overseas collectivity of France)

Flag description: the flag of France is used

National symbol(s): brown pelican

National anthem: *name:* "O Sweet Saint Martin's Land"
lyrics/music: Gerard KEMPS
note: the song, written in 1958, is used as an unofficial anthem for the entire island (both French and Dutch sides); as a collectivity of France, in addition to the local anthem, "La Marseillaise" remains official on the French side (see France); as a constituent part of the Kingdom of the Netherlands, in addition to the local anthem, "Het Wilhelmus" remains official on the Dutch side (see Netherlands)

ECONOMY

Economy—overview: The economy of Saint Martin centers on tourism with 85% of the labor force engaged in this sector. Over one million visitors come to the island each year with most arriving through the Princess Juliana International Airport in Sint Maarten. The financial sector is also important to Saint Martin's economy as it facilitates financial mediation for its thriving tourism sector. No significant agriculture and limited local fishing means that almost all food must be imported. Energy resources and manufactured goods are also imported, primarily from Mexico and the US. Saint Martin is reported to have one of the highest per capita income in the Caribbean. As with the rest of the Caribbean, Saint Martin's financial sector is having to deal with losing correspondent banking relationships.

GDP (purchasing power parity): $561.5 million (2005 est.)
country comparison to the world: 213

GDP (official exchange rate): $561.5 million (2005 est.)

GDP—per capita (PPP): $19,300 (2005 est.)
country comparison to the world: 92

GDP—composition, by sector of origin: *agriculture:* 1%
industry: 15%
services: 84% (2000)

Industries: tourism, light industry and manufacturing, heavy industry

Labor force: 17,300 (2008 est.)
country comparison to the world: 214

Labor force—by occupation: 85% directly or indirectly employed in tourist industry

Imports—commodities: crude petroleum, food, manufactured items

Exchange rates: euros (EUR) per US dollar—
0.906 (2017 est.)
0.9214 (2016 est.)
0.885 (2015 est.)
0.7489 (2014 est.)
0.7634 (2013 est.)

ENERGY

Electricity access: population without electricity: 3,194

electrification—*total population:* 91%
electrification—urban areas: 100%
electrification—rural areas: 80% (2012)

COMMUNICATIONS

Telephone system: *general assessment:* fully integrated access
domestic: direct dial capability with both fixed and wireless systems
international: country code—590; undersea fiber-optic cable provides voice and data connectivity to Puerto Rico and Guadeloupe (2009)

Broadcast media: 1 local TV station; access to about 20 radio stations, including RFO Guadeloupe radio broadcasts via repeater (2008)

Internet country code: .mf; note—.gp, the Internet country code for Guadeloupe, and .fr, the Internet country code for France, might also be encountered

Internet users: *total:* 1,100
percent of population: 3.5% (July 2016 est.)

TRANSPORTATION

Airports: 1 (2013)
country comparison to the world: 233

Airports—with paved runways: *total:* 1
914 to 1,523 m: 1 (2017)
Transportation—note: nearest airport for international flights is Princess Juliana International Airport (SXM) located on Sint Maarten

MILITARY AND SECURITY

Military—note: defense is the responsibility of France

SAINT VINCENT AND THE GRENADINES

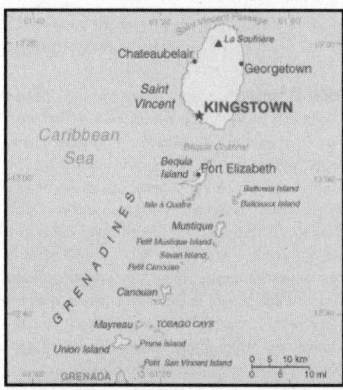

INTRODUCTION

Background: Resistance by native Caribs prevented colonization on Saint Vincent until 1719. Disputed between France and the UK for most of the 18th century, the island was ceded to the latter in 1783. Between 1960 and 1962, Saint Vincent and the Grenadines was a separate administrative unit of the Federation of the West Indies. Autonomy was granted in 1969 and independence in 1979.

GEOGRAPHY

Location: Caribbean, islands between the Caribbean Sea and North Atlantic Ocean, north of Trinidad and Tobago

Geographic coordinates: 13 15 N, 61 12 W

Map references: Central America and the Caribbean

Area: *total:* 389 sq km (Saint Vincent 344 sq km)
land: 389 sq km

water: 0 sq km
country comparison to the world: 205

Area—comparative: twice the size of Washington, DC

Land boundaries: 0 km

Coastline: 84 km

Maritime claims: *territorial sea:* 12 nm
contiguous zone: 24 nm
exclusive economic zone: 200 nm
continental shelf: 200 nm

Climate: tropical; little seasonal temperature variation; rainy season (May to November)

Terrain: volcanic, mountainous

Elevation: *mean elevation:* NA

elevation extremes: *lowest point:* Caribbean Sea 0 m
highest point: La Soufriere 1,234 m

Natural resources: hydropower, arable land

Land use: *agricultural land:* 25.6%
arable land: 12.8%;
permanent crops: 7.7%;
permanent pasture: 5.1%
forest: 68.7%
other: 5.7% (2011 est.)
Irrigated land: 10 sq km (2012)

Population—distribution: most of the population is concentrated in and around the capital of Kingstown

Natural hazards: hurricanes; La Soufriere volcano on the island of Saint Vincent is a constant threat
volcanism: La Soufriere (1,234 m) on the island of Saint Vincent last erupted in 1979; the island of Saint Vincent is part of the volcanic island arc of the Lesser Antilles that extends from Saba in the north to Grenada in the south

Environment—current issues: pollution of coastal waters and shorelines from discharges by pleasure yachts and other effluents; in some areas, pollution is severe enough to make swimming prohibitive

Environment—international agreements: *party to:* Biodiversity, Climate Change, Climate Change-Kyoto Protocol, Desertification, Endangered Species, Environmental Modification, Hazardous Wastes, Law of the Sea, Marine Dumping, Ozone Layer Protection, Ship Pollution, Whaling
signed, but not ratified: none of the selected agreements

Geography—note: the administration of the islands of the Grenadines group is divided between Saint Vincent and the Grenadines and Grenada; Saint Vincent and the Grenadines is comprised of 32 islands and cays

PEOPLE AND SOCIETY

Population: 102,089 (July 2017 est.)
country comparison to the world: 195

Nationality: *noun:* Saint Vincentian(s) or Vincentian(s)
adjective: Saint Vincentian or Vincentian

Ethnic groups: black 66%, mixed 19%, East Indian 6%, European 4%, Carib Amerindian 2%, other 3%

Languages: English, French patois

Religions: Protestant 75% (Anglican 47%, Methodist 28%), Roman Catholic 13%, other (includes Hindu, Seventh-Day Adventist, other Protestant) 12%

Age structure: *0-14 years:* 21.3% (male 10,970/female 10,779)
15-24 years: 15.97% (male 8,226/female 8,080)
25-54 years: 42.66% (male 22,608/female 20,939)
55-64 years: 10.64% (male 5,595/female 5,272)
65 years and over: 9.42% (male 4,515/female 5,105) (2017 est.)

Dependency ratios: *total dependency ratio:* 46.8

767

youth dependency ratio: 36
elderly dependency ratio: 10.8
potential support ratio: 9.3 (2015 est.)

Median age: *total:* 33.6 years
male: 33.8 years
female: 33.4 years (2017 est.)
country comparison to the world: 89

Population growth rate: -0.25% (2017 est.)
country comparison to the world: 213

Birth rate: 13.2 births/1,000 population (2017 est.)
country comparison to the world: 146

Death rate: 7.3 deaths/1,000 population (2017 est.)
country comparison to the world: 121

Net migration rate: -8.4 migrant(s)/1,000 population (2017 est.)
country comparison to the world: 208

Population distribution: most of the population is concentrated in and around the capital of Kingstown

Urbanization: *urban population:* 51.2% of total population (2017)
rate of urbanization: 0.7% annual rate of change (2015-20 est.)

Major urban areas—population: KINGSTOWN (capital) 27,000 (2014)

Sex ratio: *at birth:* 1.03 male(s)/female
0-14 years: 1.02 male(s)/female
15-24 years: 1.02 male(s)/female
25-54 years: 1.08 male(s)/female
55-64 years: 1.06 male(s)/female
65 years and over: 0.87 male(s)/female
total population: 1.03 male(s)/female (2016 est.)

Maternal mortality ratio: 45 deaths/100,000 live births (2015 est.)
country comparison to the world: 100

Infant mortality rate: *total:* 12 deaths/1,000 live births
male: 13.1 deaths/1,000 live births
female: 10.9 deaths/1,000 live births (2017 est.)
country comparison to the world: 121

Life expectancy at birth: *total population:* 75.5 years
male: 73.5 years
female: 77.6 years (2017 est.)
country comparison to the world: 104

Total fertility rate: 1.8 children born/woman (2017 est.)
country comparison to the world: 151

Health expenditures: 8.6% of GDP (2014)
country comparison to the world: 46

Hospital bed density: 5.2 beds/1,000 population (2012)

Drinking water source:
improved:
urban: 95.1% of population
rural: 95.1% of population
total: 95.1% of population
unimproved:
urban: 4.9% of population
rural: 4.9% of population
total: 4.9% of population (2015 est.)

Sanitation facility access:
improved:
urban: 76.1% of population
rural: 76.1% of population
total: 76.1% of population
unimproved:
urban: 23.9% of population
rural: 23.9% of population
total: 23.9% of population (2007 est.)

HIV/AIDS—adult prevalence rate: NA

HIV/AIDS—people living with HIV/AIDS: NA

HIV/AIDS—deaths: NA

Major infectious diseases: *note:* active local transmission of Zika virus by Aedes species mosquitoes has been identified in this country (as of August 2016); it poses an important risk (a large number of cases possible) among US citizens if bitten by an infective mosquito; other less common ways to get Zika are through sex, via blood transfusion, or during pregnancy, in which the pregnant woman passes Zika virus to her fetus (2016)

Obesity—adult prevalence rate: 23.7% (2016)
country comparison to the world: 64

Education expenditures: 5.1% of GDP (2010)
country comparison to the world: 69

Unemployment, youth ages 15-24: *total:* 33.8%
male: 27.8%
female: 41.4% (2008 est.)

GOVERNMENT

Country name: *conventional long form:* none
conventional short form: Saint Vincent and the Grenadines
etymology: Saint Vincent was named by explorer Christopher COLUMBUS after Saint VINCENT of Saragossa because the 22 January 1498 day of discovery was the saint's feast day

Government type: parliamentary democracy (House of Assembly) under a constitutional monarchy; a Commonwealth realm

Capital: *name:* Kingstown

geographic coordinates: 13 08 N, 61 13 W
time difference: UTC-4 (1 hour ahead of Washington, DC, during Standard Time)

Administrative divisions: 6 parishes; Charlotte, Grenadines, Saint Andrew, Saint David, Saint George, Saint Patrick

Independence: 27 October 1979 (from the UK)

National holiday: Independence Day, 27 October (1979)

Constitution: previous 1969, 1975; latest drafted 26 July 1979, effective 27 October 1979 (Saint Vincent Constitution Act 1979) (2017)

Legal system: English common law

International law organization participation: has not submitted an ICJ jurisdiction declaration; accepts ICCt jurisdiction

Citizenship: *citizenship by birth:* yes

citizenship by descent: at least one parent must be a citizen of Saint Vincent and the Grenadines
dual citizenship recognized: yes

residency requirement for naturalization: 7 years

Suffrage: 18 years of age; universal

Executive branch: *chief of state:* Queen ELIZABETH II (since 6 February 1952); represented by Governor General Sir Fredrick Nathaniel BALLANTYNE (since 2 September 2002)
head of government: Prime Minister Ralph E. GONSALVES (since 29 March 2001)
cabinet: Cabinet appointed by the governor general on the advice of the prime minister
elections/appointments: the monarchy is hereditary; governor general appointed by the monarch; following legislative elections, the leader of the majority party usually appointed prime minister by the governor general; deputy prime minister appointed by the governor general on the advice of the prime minister

Legislative branch: *description:* unicameral House of Assembly (21 seats; 15 members directly elected in single-seat constituencies by simple majority vote and 6 appointed by the governor general; members serve 5-year terms)
elections: last held on 9 December 2015 (next to be held in 2020)
election results: percent of vote by party—ULP 52.3%, NDP 47.4%, other 0.3%; seats by party—ULP 8, NDP 7

Judicial branch: *highest court(s):* the Eastern Caribbean Supreme Court (ECSC) is the superior court of the Organization of Eastern Caribbean States; the ECSC—headquartered on St. Lucia—consists of the Court of Appeal—headed by the chief justice and 4 judges—and the High Court with 18 judges; the Court of Appeal is itinerant, travelling to member states on a schedule to hear appeals from the High Court and subordinate courts; High Court judges reside at the member states with 2 assigned to Saint Vincent and the Grenadines; note—Saint Vincent and the Grenadines is also a member of the Caribbean Court of Justice
judge selection and term of office: chief justice of Eastern Caribbean Supreme Court appointed by Her Majesty, Queen ELIZABETH II; other justices and judges appointed by the Judicial and Legal Services Commission, an independent body of judicial officials; Court of Appeal justices appointed for life with mandatory retirement at age 65; High Court judges appointed for life with mandatory retirement at age 62
subordinate courts: magistrates' courts

Political parties and leaders: Democratic Republican Party or DRP [Anesia BAPTISTE]
New Democratic Party or NDP [Godwin L. FRIDAY]
Unity Labor Party or ULP [Dr. Ralph GONSALVES]
(formed by the coalition of Saint Vincent Labor Party or SVLP and the Movement for National Unity or MNU) SVG Green Party or SVGP [Ivan O'NEAL]

Political pressure groups and leaders: St. Vincent & the Grenadines Teachers' Union [Oswald CHAMBERS] *other:* several labor unions

International organization participation: ACP, AOSIS, C, Caricom, CDB, CELAC, FAO, G-77, IBRD, ICAO, ICCt, ICRM, IDA, IFAD, IFRCS, ILO, IMF, IMO, Interpol, IOC, IOM, ISO (subscriber), ITU, MIGA, NAM, OAS, OECS, OPANAL, OPCW, Petrocaribe, UN, UNCTAD, UNESCO, UNIDO, UPU, WFTU (NGOs), WHO, WIPO, WTO

Diplomatic representation in the US: chief of mission: Ambassador Lou-Anne Gaylene GILCHRIST (since 18 January 2017)
chancery: 3216 New Mexico Avenue NW, Washington, DC 20016
telephone: [1] (202) 364-6730
FAX: [1] (202) 364-6736
consulate(s) general: New York

Diplomatic representation from the US: the US does not have an embassy in Saint Vincent and the Grenadines; the US Ambassador to Barbados is accredited to Saint Vincent and the Grenadines

Flag description: three vertical bands of blue (hoist side), gold (double width), and green; the gold band bears three green diamonds arranged in a V pattern, which stands for Vincent; the diamonds recall the islands as "the Gems of the Antilles" and are set slightly lowered in the gold band to reflect the nation's position in the Antilles; blue conveys the colors of a tropical sky and crystal waters, yellow signifies the golden Grenadine sands, and green represents lush vegetation

National symbol(s): Saint Vincent parrot; national colors: blue, gold, green

National anthem: *name:* "St. Vincent! Land So Beautiful!"
lyrics/music: Phyllis Joyce MCCLEAN PUNNETT/Joel Bertram MIGUEL
note: adopted 1967

ECONOMY

Economy—overview: Success of the economy hinges upon seasonal variations in agriculture, tourism, and construction activity, as well as remittances. Much of the workforce is employed in banana production and tourism. Saint Vincent and the Grenadines is home to a small offshore banking sector and continues to fully adopt international regulatory standards.

This lower-middle-income country remains vulnerable to natural and external shocks. The economy has shown some signs of recovery due to increased tourist arrivals, falling oil prices and renewed growth in the construction sector. The much anticipated international airport opened in early 2017 with hopes for increased airlift and tourism activity. The government's ability to invest in social programs and respond to external shocks is constrained by its high public debt burden, which was 67% of GDP at the end of 2013.

GDP (purchasing power parity): $1.281 billion (2017 est.)
$1.253 billion (2016 est.)
$1.243 billion (2015 est.)
note: data are in 2017 dollars

country comparison to the world: 203

GDP (official exchange rate): $815 million (2016 est.)

GDP—real growth rate: 2.2% (2017 est.)
0.8% (2016 est.)
0.9% (2015 est.)
country comparison to the world: 146

GDP—per capita (PPP): $11,600 (2017 est.)
$11,400 (2016 est.)
$11,300 (2015 est.)
note: data are in 2017 dollars
country comparison to the world: 133

Gross national saving: -4.8% of GDP (2017 est.)
-5.1% of GDP (2016 est.)
-3.1% of GDP (2015 est.)
country comparison to the world: 180

GDP—composition, by end use:
household consumption: 87.4%
government consumption: 19.2%
investment in fixed capital: 20.3%
investment in inventories: -0.2%
exports of goods and services: 22.3%
imports of goods and services: -49.2% (2017 est.)

GDP—composition, by sector of origin:
agriculture: 7.1%
industry: 17.4%
services: 75.5% (2017 est.)

Agriculture—products: bananas, coconuts, sweet potatoes, spices; small numbers of cattle, sheep, pigs, goats; fish

Industries: tourism; food processing, cement, furniture, clothing, starch

Industrial production growth rate: 2% (2017 est.)
country comparison to the world: 134

Labor force: 57,520 (2007 est.)
country comparison to the world: 189

Labor force—by occupation:
agriculture: 26%
industry: 17%
services: 57% (1980 est.)

Unemployment rate: 18.8% (2008 est.)
country comparison to the world: 180

Population below poverty line: NA%

Household income or consumption by percentage share: *lowest 10%:* NA%
highest 10%: NA%

Budget: *revenues:* $222.2 million
expenditures: $259.3 million (2017 est.)
Taxes and other revenues: 27.3% of GDP (2017 est.)
country comparison to the world: 103

Budget surplus (+) or deficit (-): -4.5% of GDP (2017 est.)
country comparison to the world: 150

Public debt: 79.2% of GDP (2016 est.)
81.3% of GDP (2015 est.)
country comparison to the world: 40

Fiscal year: calendar year

Inflation rate (consumer prices): 1.7% (2017 est.)
-0.2% (2016 est.)
country comparison to the world: 74

Central bank discount rate: 6.5% (31 December 2010)
6.5% (31 December 2009)
country comparison to the world: 59

Commercial bank prime lending rate: 9% (31 December 2017 est.)
9.17% (31 December 2016 est.)
country comparison to the world: 95

Stock of narrow money: $182.7 million (31 December 2017 est.)
$177.7 million (31 December 2016 est.)
country comparison to the world: 186

Stock of broad money: $591.5 million (31 December 2017 est.)
$563.2 million (31 December 2016 est.)
country comparison to the world: 182

Stock of domestic credit: $432.8 million (31 December 2017 est.)
$424.6 million (31 December 2016 est.)
country comparison to the world: 179

Current account balance: -$120 million (2017 est.)
-$122 million (2016 est.)
country comparison to the world: 83

Exports: $51.3 million (2017 est.)
$47.3 million (2016 est.)
country comparison to the world: 203

Exports—commodities: bananas, eddoes and dasheen (taro), arrowroot starch; tennis racquets

Exports—partners: Barbados 18.3%, St. Lucia 17.6%, Antigua and Barbuda 14.8%, Trinidad and Tobago 12.3%, Dominica 9.5%, St. Kitts and Nevis 7.3%, Grenada 5.9% (2016)

Imports: $311.3 million (2017 est.)
$289.9 million (2016 est.)
country comparison to the world: 197

Imports—commodities: foodstuffs, machinery and equipment, chemicals and fertilizers, minerals and fuels

Imports—partners: US 44%, Trinidad and Tobago 14.1%, UK 6.5%, France 4.8% (2016)

Reserves of foreign exchange and gold: $160 million (31 December 2017 est.)
$192.3 million (31 December 2016 est.)
country comparison to the world: 160

Debt—external: $324.4 million (31 December 2017 est.)
$330.8 million (31 December 2016 est.)
country comparison to the world: 185

Exchange rates: East Caribbean dollars (XCD) per US dollar—
2.7 (2017 est.)
2.7 (2016 est.)
2.7 (2015 est.)
2.7 (2014 est.)
2.7 (2013 est.)

ENERGY

Electricity access: population without electricity: 25,587
electrification—*total population:* 76%
electrification—urban areas: 100%

electrification—rural areas: 32% (2012)

Electricity—production: 155 million kWh (2015 est.)
country comparison to the world: 195

Electricity—consumption: 144.2 million kWh (2015 est.)
country comparison to the world: 197

Electricity—exports: 0 kWh (2016 est.)
country comparison to the world: 211

Electricity—imports: 0 kWh (2016 est.)
country comparison to the world: 214

Electricity—installed generating capacity: 48,000 kW (2015 est.)
country comparison to the world: 192

Electricity—from fossil fuels: 83.3% of total installed capacity (2015 est.)
country comparison to the world: 79

Electricity—from nuclear fuels: 0% of total installed capacity (2015 est.)
country comparison to the world: 203

Electricity—from hydroelectric plants: 14.6% of total installed capacity (2015 est.)
country comparison to the world: 103

Electricity—from other renewable sources: 2.1% of total installed capacity (2015 est.)
country comparison to the world: 121

Crude oil—production: 0 bbl/day (2016 est.)
country comparison to the world: 192

Crude oil—exports: 0 bbl/day (2014 est.)
country comparison to the world: 207

Crude oil—imports: 0 bbl/day (2014 est.)
country comparison to the world: 205

Crude oil—proved reserves: 0 bbl (1 January 2017 es)
country comparison to the world: 190

Refined petroleum products—production: 0 bbl/day (2014 est.)
country comparison to the world: 196

Refined petroleum products—consumption: 1,600 bbl/day (2015 est.)
country comparison to the world: 197

Refined petroleum products—exports: 0 bbl/day (2014 est.)
country comparison to the world: 210

Refined petroleum products—imports: 1,519 bbl/day (2014 est.)
country comparison to the world: 194

Natural gas—production: 0 cu m (2013 est.)
country comparison to the world: 208

Natural gas—consumption: 0 cu m (2013 est.)
country comparison to the world: 143

Natural gas—exports: 0 cu m (2013 est.)
country comparison to the world: 204

Natural gas—imports: 0 cu m (2013 est.)

country comparison to the world: 204

Natural gas—proved reserves: 0 cu m (1 January 2014 es)
country comparison to the world: 204

Carbon dioxide emissions from consumption of energy: 300,000 Mt (2013 est.)
country comparison to the world: 189

COMMUNICATIONS

Telephones—fixed lines: *total subscriptions:* 20,550
subscriptions per 100 inhabitants: 20 (July 2016 est.)
country comparison to the world: 175

Telephones—mobile cellular: *total:* 112,649
subscriptions per 100 inhabitants: 110 (July 2016 est.)
country comparison to the world: 188

Telephone system: *general assessment:* adequate islandwide, fully automatic telephone system
domestic: fixed-line teledensity exceeds 20 per 100 persons and mobile-cellular teledensity is about 110 per 100 persons
international: country code—1-784; the East Caribbean Fiber System and Southern Caribbean Fiber submarine cables carry international calls; connectivity also provided by VHF/UHF radiotelephone from Saint Vincent to Barbados; SHF radiotelephone to Grenada and Saint Lucia; access to Intelsat earth station in Martinique through Saint Lucia (2016)

Broadcast media: St. Vincent and the Grenadines Broadcasting Corporation operates 1 TV station and 5 repeater stations that provide near total coverage to the multi-island state; multi-channel cable TV service available; a partially government-funded national radio service broadcasts on 1 station and has 2 repeater stations; about a dozen privately owned radio stations and repeater stations (2007)

Internet country code: .vc

Internet users: *total:* 53,000
percent of population: 51.8% (July 2016 est.)
country comparison to the world: 177

TRANSPORTATION

National air transport system: number of registered air carriers: 2
inventory of registered aircraft operated by air carriers: 11 (2015)
Civil aircraft registration country code prefix: J8 (2016)

Airports: 6 (2013)
country comparison to the world: 175

Airports—with paved runways: *total:* 5
1,524 to 2,437 m: 1

914 to 1,523 m: 3
under 914 m: 1 (2017)

Airports—with unpaved runways: *total:* 1
under 914 m: 1 (2013)

Roadways: *total:* 829 km
paved: 580 km
unpaved: 249 km (2003)
country comparison to the world: 189

Merchant marine: *total:* 882
by type: bulk carrier 22, container ship 12, general cargo 198, oil tanker 17, other 633 (2017)
country comparison to the world: 26

Ports and terminals: *major seaport(s):* Kingstown

MILITARY AND SECURITY

Military branches: no regular military forces; Royal Saint Vincent and the Grenadines Police Force (RSVPF) (2013)

TRANSNATIONAL ISSUES

Disputes—international: joins other Caribbean states to counter Venezuela's claim that Aves Island sustains human habitation, a criterion under UN Convention on the Law of the Sea, which permits Venezuela to extend its EEZ/continental shelf over a large portion of the eastern Caribbean Sea

Trafficking in persons: current situation: Saint Vincent and the Grenadines is a source, transit, and destination country for men, women, and children subjected to forced labor and sex trafficking; some children under 18 are pressured to engage in sex acts in exchange for money or gifts; foreign workers may experience forced labor and are particularly vulnerable when employed by small, foreign-owned companies; adults and children are vulnerable to forced labor domestically, especially in the agriculture sector

tier rating: Tier 2 Watch List—Saint Vincent and the Grenadines does not fully comply with the minimum standards for the elimination of trafficking; however, it is making significant efforts to do so; the government for the first time acknowledged a trafficking problem, launched an anti-trafficking public awareness campaign, and conducted anti-trafficking training for law enforcement, immigration, and labor officials; in 2014, authorities initiated three trafficking investigations, two of which were ultimately determined not to be trafficking cases, and did not prosecute or convict any trafficking offenders; the government did not identify or refer any potential trafficking victims to care (2015)

Illicit drugs: transshipment point for South American drugs destined for the US and Europe; small-scale cannabis cultivation

SAMOA

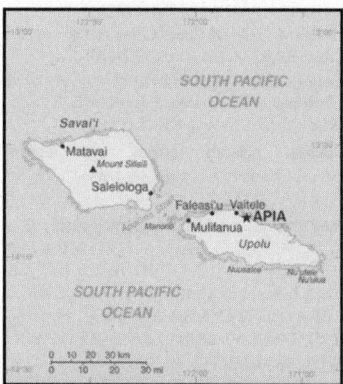

INTRODUCTION

Background: New Zealand occupied the German protectorate of Western Samoa at the outbreak of World War I in 1914. It continued to administer the islands as a mandate and then as a trust territory until 1962, when the islands became the first Polynesian nation to reestablish independence in the 20th century. The country dropped the "Western" from its name in 1997.

GEOGRAPHY

Location: Oceania, group of islands in the South Pacific Ocean, about halfway between Hawaii and New Zealand

Geographic coordinates: 13 35 S, 172 20 W

Map references: Oceania

Area: *total:* 2,831 sq km
land: 2,821 sq km
water: 10 sq km
country comparison to the world: 178

Area—comparative: slightly smaller than Rhode Island
Land boundaries: 0 km

Coastline: 403 km

Maritime claims: *territorial sea:* 12 nm
contiguous zone: 24 nm
exclusive economic zone: 200 nm

Climate: tropical; rainy season (November to April), dry season (May to October)

Terrain: two main islands (Savaii, Upolu) and several smaller islands and uninhabited islets; narrow coastal plain with volcanic, rugged mountains in interior

Elevation: *mean elevation:* NA

elevation extremes: *lowest point:* Pacific Ocean 0 m
highest point: Mount Silisili 1,857 m

Natural resources: hardwood forests, fish, hydropower

Land use: *agricultural land:* 12.4%
arable land: 2.8%;
permanent crops: 7.8%;
permanent pasture: 1.8%
forest: 60.4%
other: 27.2% (2011 est.)
Irrigated land: 0 sq km (2012)

Population—distribution: about three-quarters of the population lives on the island of Upolu

Natural hazards: occasional cyclones; active volcanism
volcanism: Savai'I Island (1,858 m), which last erupted in 1911, is historically active

Environment—current issues: soil erosion, deforestation, invasive species, overfishing

Environment—international agreements: *party to:* Biodiversity, Climate Change, Climate Change-Kyoto Protocol, Desertification, Hazardous Wastes, Law of the Sea, Ozone Layer Protection, Ship Pollution, Wetlands
signed, but not ratified: none of the selected agreements

Geography—note: occupies an almost central position within Polynesia

PEOPLE AND SOCIETY

Population: 200,108 (July 2017 est.)
country comparison to the world: 185

Nationality: *noun:* Samoan(s)
adjective: Samoan

Ethnic groups: Samoan 92.6%, Euronesians (persons of European and Polynesian blood) 7%, Europeans 0.4% (2001 census)

Languages: Samoan (Polynesian) (official), English

Religions: Protestant 57.4% (Congregationalist 31.8%, Methodist 13.7%, Assembly of God 8%, Seventh Day Adventist 3.9%), Roman Catholic 19.4%, Mormon 15.2%, Worship Centre 1.7%, other Christian 5.5%, other 0.7%, none 0.1%, unspecified 0.1% (2011 est.)

Age structure: *0-14 years:* 31.35% (male 32,372/female 30,359)
15-24 years: 19.82% (male 20,358/female 19,306)
25-54 years: 36.33% (male 37,423/female 35,273)
55-64 years: 6.78% (male 6,912/female 6,663)
65 years and over: 5.72% (male 4,976/female 6,466) (2017 est.)

Dependency ratios: *total dependency ratio:* 74.2
youth dependency ratio: 64.9
elderly dependency ratio: 9.3
potential support ratio: 10.8 (2015 est.)

Median age: *total:* 24.4 years
male: 24.1 years
female: 24.6 years (2017 est.)
country comparison to the world: 163

Population growth rate: 0.6% (2017 est.)
country comparison to the world: 147

Birth rate: 20.4 births/1,000 population (2017 est.)
country comparison to the world: 77

Death rate: 5.3 deaths/1,000 population (2017 est.)
country comparison to the world: 180

Net migration rate: -9.1 migrant(s)/1,000 population (2017 est.)
country comparison to the world: 210

Population distribution: about three-quarters of the population lives on the island of Upolu

Urbanization: *urban population:* 18.8% of total population (2017)
rate of urbanization: 0.06% annual rate of change (2015-20 est.)

Major urban areas—population: APIA (capital) 37,000 (2014)

Sex ratio: *at birth:* 1.05 male(s)/female
0-14 years: 1.07 male(s)/female
15-24 years: 1.05 male(s)/female
25-54 years: 1.07 male(s)/female
55-64 years: 1.04 male(s)/female
65 years and over: 0.77 male(s)/female
total population: 1.04 male(s)/female (2016 est.)

Mother's mean age at first birth: 23.6 years
note: median age at first birth among women 25-29 (2009 est.)

Maternal mortality ratio: 51 deaths/100,000 live births (2015 est.)
country comparison to the world: 95

Infant mortality rate: *total:* 18.6 deaths/1,000 live births
male: 22 deaths/1,000 live births
female: 15.1 deaths/1,000 live births (2017 est.)
country comparison to the world: 87

Life expectancy at birth: *total population:* 74 years
male: 71.1 years
female: 77 years (2017 est.)
country comparison to the world: 125

Total fertility rate: 2.7 children born/woman (2017 est.)
country comparison to the world: 65

Contraceptive prevalence rate: 26.9% (2014)

Health expenditures: 7.2% of GDP (2014)
country comparison to the world: 75

Physicians density: 0.46 physicians/1,000 population (2008)

Drinking water source:
improved:
urban: 97.5% of population
rural: 99.3% of population
total: 99% of population
unimproved:
urban: 2.5% of population
rural: 0.7% of population
total: 1% of population (2015 est.)

Sanitation facility access:
improved:

urban: 93.3% of population
rural: 91.1% of population
total: 91.5% of population
unimproved:
urban: 6.7% of population
rural: 8.9% of population
total: 8.5% of population (2015 est.)

HIV/AIDS—adult prevalence rate: NA

HIV/AIDS—people living with HIV/AIDS: NA

HIV/AIDS—deaths: NA

Major infectious diseases: *note:* active local transmission of Zika virus by Aedes species mosquitoes has been identified in this country (as of August 2016); it poses an important risk (a large number of cases possible) among US citizens if bitten by an infective mosquito; other less common ways to get Zika are through sex, via blood transfusion, or during pregnancy, in which the pregnant woman passes Zika virus to her fetus (2016)

Obesity—adult prevalence rate: 47.3% (2016)
country comparison to the world: 8

Education expenditures: 5.1% of GDP (2008)
country comparison to the world: 48

Literacy: *definition:* age 15 and over can read and write
total population: 99%
male: 99.1%
female: 98.8% (2015 est.)

Unemployment, youth ages 15-24: *total:* 19.1%
male: 15.6%
female: 25.3% (2014 est.)
country comparison to the world: 75

GOVERNMENT

Country name: *conventional long form:* Independent State of Samoa
conventional short form: Samoa
local long form: Malo Sa'oloto Tuto'atasi o Samoa
local short form: Samoa
former: Western Samoa
etymology: the name "Samoa" is composed of two parts, "sa" meaning sacred and "moa" meaning center, so the name can mean Holy Center; alternatively, it can mean "place of the sacred moa bird" of Polynesian mythology

Government type: parliamentary republic

Capital: *name:* Apia
geographic coordinates: 13 49 S, 171 46 W
time difference: UTC+13 (18 hours ahead of Washington, DC, during Standard Time)
+1hr, begins last Sunday in September; ends first Sunday in April

Administrative divisions: 11 districts; A'ana, Aiga-i-le-Tai, Atua, Fa'asaleleaga, Gaga'emauga, Gagai-fomauga, Palauli, Satupa'itea, Tuamasaga, Va'a-o-Fonoti, Vaisigano

Independence: 1 January 1962 (from New Zealand-administered UN trusteeship)

National holiday: Independence Day Celebration, 1 June (1962); note—1 January 1962 is the date of independence from the New Zealand-administered UN trusteeship, but it is observed in June

Constitution: several previous (preindependence); latest 1 January 1962; amended several times, last in 2017 (2017)

Legal system: mixed legal system of English common law and customary law; judicial review of legislative acts with respect to fundamental rights of the citizen

International law organization participation: has not submitted an ICJ jurisdiction declaration; accepts ICCt jurisdiction

Citizenship: *citizenship by birth:* no
citizenship by descent only: at least one parent must be a citizen of Samoa
dual citizenship recognized: no
residency requirement for naturalization: 5 years

Suffrage: 21 years of age; universal

Executive branch: *chief of state:* TUIMALEALI'IFANO Va'aletoa Sualauvi II (since 21 July 2017)
head of government: Prime Minister TUILA'EPA Lupesoliai Sailele Malielegaoi (since 23 November 1998); Deputy Prime Minister FONOTOE Pierre Lauofo (since 2011)
cabinet: Cabinet appointed by the chief of state on the prime minister's advice
elections/appointments: chief of state indirectly elected by the Legislative Assembly to serve a 5-year term (no term limits); election last held on 4 July 2017 (next to be held in 2022); following legislative elections, the leader of the majority party usually appointed prime minister by the chief of state, approved by the Legislative Assembly
election results: TUIMALEALI'IFANO Va'aletoa Sualauvi unanimously elected by the Legislative Assembly on 5 July 2017

Legislative branch: *description:* unicameral Legislative Assembly or Fono (50 seats; 47 members—traditional family chiefs or matai, 2 members—part-Samoan or non-Samoan, and 1 woman member—added following the 2016 election—directly elected by simple majority vote; members serve 5-year terms)
elections: election last held on 4 March 2016 (next election to be held no later than March 2021)
election results: percent of vote by party—HRPP 57.3%, Tautua Samoa 8%, independent 34.7%; seats by party—HRPP 35, Tautua Samoa 2, independents 3

Judicial branch: *highest court(s):* Court of Appeal (consists of the chief justice and 2 Supreme Court judges and meets once or twice a year); Supreme Court (consists of the chief justice and several judges)
judge selection and term of office: chief justice appointed by the head of state upon the advice of the prime minister; other Supreme Court judges appointed by the Judicial Service Commission, a 3-member body chaired by the chief justice and includes the attorney general and an appointee of the Minister of Justice; judges normally appointed until retirement at age 68

subordinate courts: District Court; Magistrates' Courts; Land and Titles Courts; village fono or village chief councils

Political parties and leaders: Human Rights Protection Party or HRPP [TUILA'EPA Sailele Malielegaoi] Samoa Christian Party or SCP [Tuala Falenaoti Tiresa MALIETOA]
Samoa Progressive Political Party or SPPP [Toalepaiali'i Toesulusulu S'iueva POSE II]
Tautua Samoa [Palasajue FA'APO II]

Political pressure groups and leaders: Samoa Workers Congress or SWC [Gatoloa'i AFAMASAGA]

International organization participation: ACP, ADB, AOSIS, C, FAO, G-77, IBRD, ICAO, ICCt, ICRM, IDA, IFAD, IFC, IFRCS, ILO, IMF, IMO, Interpol, IOC, IPU, ITU, ITUC (NGOs), MIGA, OPCW, PIF, Sparteca, SPC, UN, UNCTAD, UNESCO, UNIDO, UPU, WCO, WHO, WIPO, WMO, WTO

Diplomatic representation in the US: chief of mission: Ambassador Aliioaiga Feturi ELISAIA (since 4 December 2003)
chancery: 800 Second Avenue, Suite 400J, New York, NY 10017
telephone: [1] (212) 599-6196 through 6197
FAX: [1] (212) 599-0797
consulate(s) general: Pago Pago (American Samoa)

Diplomatic representation from the US: *chief of mission:* the US Ambassador to New Zealand is accredited to Samoa; Ambassador Scott BROWN (since 27 June 2017)
embassy: Accident Corporation Building, 5th Floor, Matafele, Apia
mailing address: P. O. Box 3430, Matafele, Apia
telephone: [685] 21436/21631/21452/22696
FAX: [685] 22030

Flag description: red with a blue rectangle in the upper hoist-side quadrant bearing five white five-pointed stars representing the Southern Cross constellation; red stands for courage, blue represents freedom, and white signifies purity
note: similar to the flag of Taiwan

National symbol(s): Southern Cross constellation (five, five-pointed stars); national colors: red, white, blue

National anthem: *name:* "O le Fu'a o le Sa'olotoga o Samoa" (The Banner of Freedom)
lyrics/music: Sauni Liga KURESA
note: adopted 1962; also known as "Samoa Tula'i" (Samoa Arise)

ECONOMY

Economy—overview: The economy of Samoa has traditionally been dependent on development aid, family remittances from overseas, tourism, agriculture, and fishing. It has a nominal GDP of $830 million. Agriculture, including fishing, employs roughly two-thirds of the labor force and furnishes 90% of exports, featuring fish, coconut oil, nonu products, and taro. The manufacturing sector mainly processes agricultural products. One factory in the Foreign Trade Zone employs over 700 people to make automobile electrical harnesses for an assembly plant in Australia, and accounts for 65% of total exports, but it is set to close by yearend 2017. Industry accounts for nearly 24% of GDP while employing less than 6% of the work force. The service sector accounts for nearly three-quarters of GDP and employs approximately 50% of the labor force. Tourism is an expanding sector accounting for 25% of GDP; 132,000 tourists visited the islands in 2013.

The country is vulnerable to devastating storms. In September 2009, an earthquake and the resulting tsunami severely damaged Samoa and nearby American Samoa, disrupting transportation and power generation, and resulting in about 200 deaths. In December 2012, extensive flooding and wind damage from Tropical Cyclone Evan killed four people, displaced over 6,000, and damaged or destroyed an estimated 1,500 homes on Samoa's Upolu Island.

The Samoan Government has called for deregulation of the country's financial sector, encouragement of investment, and continued fiscal discipline, while at the same time protecting the environment. Foreign reserves are relatively healthy and inflation is low, but external debt is approximately 45% of GDP. Samoa became the 155th member of the WTO in May 2012, and graduated from least developed country status in January 2014.

GDP (purchasing power parity): $1.13 billion (2017 est.)
$1.106 billion (2016 est.)
$1.033 billion (2015 est.)
note: data are in 2017 dollars
country comparison to the world: 204

GDP (official exchange rate): $844 million (2016 est.)

GDP—real growth rate: 2.1% (2017 est.)
7.1% (2016 est.)
1.6% (2015 est.)
country comparison to the world: 151

GDP—per capita (PPP): $5,700 (2017 est.)
$5,700 (2016 est.)
$5,300 (2015 est.)
note: data are in 2017 dollars
country comparison to the world: 168

GDP—composition, by sector of origin: *agriculture:* 10.4%
industry: 23.6%
services: 66% (2017 est.)

Agriculture—products: coconuts, nonu, bananas, taro, yams, coffee, cocoa

Industries: food processing, building materials, auto parts

Industrial production growth rate: 1.1% (2017 est.)
country comparison to the world: 159

Labor force: 50,700 (2016 est.)
country comparison to the world: 193

Labor force—by occupation: *agriculture:* 65%
industry: 6%
services: 29% (2015 est.)

Unemployment rate: NA%

Population below poverty line: NA%

Household income or consumption by percentage share: *lowest 10%:* NA%
highest 10%: NA%

Budget: *revenues:* $233.8 million
expenditures: $272.8 million (2017 est.)
Taxes and other revenues: 27.7% of GDP (2017 est.)
country comparison to the world: 100

Budget surplus (+) or deficit (-): -4.6% of GDP (2017 est.)
country comparison to the world: 153

Public debt: 52.6% of GDP (2016 est.)
57.8% of GDP (2015 est.)
country comparison to the world: 93

Fiscal year: June 1—May 31

Inflation rate (consumer prices): 1.8% (2017 est.)
0.1% (2016 est.)
country comparison to the world: 79

Commercial bank prime lending rate: 8.9% (31 December 2017 est.)
9.12% (31 December 2016 est.)
country comparison to the world: 96

Stock of narrow money: $137.5 million (31 December 2017 est.)
$131.7 million (31 December 2016 est.)
country comparison to the world: 188

Stock of broad money: $381.9 million (31 December 2017 est.)
$367 million (31 December 2016 est.)
country comparison to the world: 188

Stock of domestic credit: $383.7 million (31 December 2017 est.)
$380.2 million (31 December 2016 est.)
country comparison to the world: 180

Market value of publicly traded shares: $NA

Current account balance: -$48 million (2017 est.)
-$48 million (2016 est.)
country comparison to the world: 71

Exports: $27.5 million (2014 est.)
$33.8 million (2015 est.)
country comparison to the world: 207

Exports—commodities: fish, coconut oil and cream, nonu, copra, taro, automotive parts, garments, beer

Exports—partners: Australia 30.2%, American Samoa 21.7%, Afghanistan 11.2%, NZ 10.1%, US 5.6% (2016)

Imports: $341.3 million (2014 est.)
$297.7 million (2015 est.)
country comparison to the world: 194

Imports—commodities: machinery and equipment, industrial supplies, foodstuffs

Imports—partners: NZ 23%, Singapore 14%, China 13.5%, US 10.2%, Australia 9.9%, Fiji 6.3%, Japan 5% (2016)

Reserves of foreign exchange and gold: $99.31 million (31 December 2016 est.)
$122.5 million (31 December 2015 est.)
country comparison to the world: 166

Debt—external: $447.2 million (31 December 2013 est.)

$437.4 million (31 December 2015 est.)
country comparison to the world: 180

Exchange rates: tala (SAT) per US dollar—
2.566 (2017 est.)
2.565 (2016 est.)
2.565 (2015 est.)
2.5609 (2014 est.)
2.3318 (2013 est.)

ENERGY

Electricity access: population without electricity: 10,942
electrification—*total population:* 94%
electrification—urban areas: 100%
electrification—rural areas: 93% (2012)

Electricity—production: 127 million kWh (2015 est.)
country comparison to the world: 196

Electricity—consumption: 118.1 million kWh (2015 est.)
country comparison to the world: 198

Electricity—exports: 0 kWh (2016 est.)
country comparison to the world: 217

Electricity—imports: 0 kWh (2016 est.)
country comparison to the world: 219

Electricity—installed generating capacity: 45,000 kW (2015 est.)
country comparison to the world: 195

Electricity—from fossil fuels: 66.7% of total installed capacity (2015 est.)
country comparison to the world: 113

Electricity—from nuclear fuels: 0% of total installed capacity (2015 est.)
country comparison to the world: 211

Electricity—from hydroelectric plants: 26.7% of total installed capacity (2015 est.)
country comparison to the world: 77

Electricity—from other renewable sources: 15.6% of total installed capacity (2015 est.)
country comparison to the world: 47

Crude oil—production: 0 bbl/day (2016 est.)
country comparison to the world: 193

Crude oil—exports: 0 bbl/day (2014 est.)
country comparison to the world: 213

Crude oil—imports: 0 bbl/day (2014 est.)
country comparison to the world: 213

Crude oil—proved reserves: 0 bbl (1 January 2017 es)
country comparison to the world: 191

Refined petroleum products—production: 0 bbl/day (2014 est.)
country comparison to the world: 197

Refined petroleum products—consumption: 1,100 bbl/day (2015 est.)
country comparison to the world: 204

Refined petroleum products—exports: 0 bbl/day (2014 est.)
country comparison to the world: 215

Refined petroleum products—imports: 1,688 bbl/day (2014 est.)
country comparison to the world: 191

Natural gas—production: 0 cu m (2013 est.)
country comparison to the world: 214

Natural gas—consumption: 0 cu m (2013 est.)
country comparison to the world: 149

Natural gas—exports: 0 cu m (2013 est.)
country comparison to the world: 212

Natural gas—imports: 0 cu m (2013 est.)
country comparison to the world: 211

Natural gas—proved reserves: 0 cu m (1 January 2014 es)
country comparison to the world: 209

Carbon dioxide emissions from consumption of energy: 200,000 Mt (2013 est.)
country comparison to the world: 198

COMMUNICATIONS

Telephones—fixed lines: *total subscriptions:* 7,192
subscriptions per 100 inhabitants: 4 (July 2016 est.)
country comparison to the world: 196

Telephones—mobile cellular: *total:* 134,619
subscriptions per 100 inhabitants: 68 (July 2016 est.)
country comparison to the world: 190

Telephone system: *general assessment:* most households have at least one mobile phone; all businesses in the greater Apia area have access to broadband and Wi-Fi, which is reasonably reliable and fast, but relatively expensive; in rural Upolu and on Savaii Island there is limited availability of high speed Internet and Wi-Fi; Samoa recently completed the installation of a National Broadband Highway that will provide fiber optic data services and 4G LTE cellular data speeds to the entire country; 4G LTE data speeds are operative and commercially available to limited areas; 3G Internet accessibility from cellular devices is currently available nationwide (2017)
domestic: combined fixed-line and mobile-cellular teledensity roughly 70 telephones per 100 persons (2016)
international: country code—685; satellite earth station—1 Intelsat (Pacific Ocean) (2015)

Broadcast media: state-owned TV station privatized in 2008; 4 privately owned television broadcast stations; about a half-dozen privately owned radio stations and one state-owned radio station; TV and radio broadcasts of several stations from American Samoa are available (2009)

Internet country code: .ws

Internet users: *total:* 58,508
percent of population: 29.4% (July 2016 est.)
country comparison to the world: 198

TRANSPORTATION

National air transport system: number of registered air carriers: 1
inventory of registered aircraft operated by air carriers: 1
annual passenger traffic on registered air carriers: 270,908
annual freight traffic on registered air carriers: 0 mt-km (2015)
Civil aircraft registration country code prefix: 5W (2016)

Airports: 4 (2013)
country comparison to the world: 188

Airports—with paved runways: *total:* 1
2,438 to 3,047 m: 1 (2017)

Airports—with unpaved runways: *total:* 3
under 914 m: 3 (2013)

Roadways: *total:* 1,200 km
paved: 1,105 km
unpaved: 95 km (2017)
country comparison to the world: 172

Merchant marine: *total:* 10
by type: general cargo 4, other 6 (2017)
country comparison to the world: 142

Ports and terminals: *major seaport(s):* Apia

MILITARY AND SECURITY

Military branches: no regular military forces; Samoa Police Force

Military—note: Samoa has no formal defense structure or regular armed forces; informal defense ties exist with NZ, which is required to consider any Samoan request for assistance under the 1962 Treaty of Friendship

TRANSNATIONAL ISSUES

Disputes—international: none

SAO TOME AND PRINCIPE

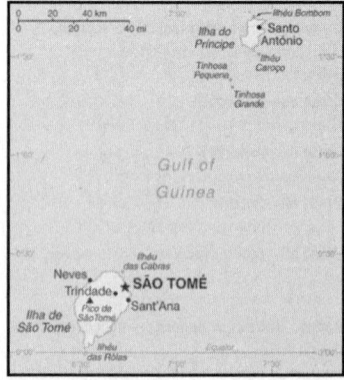

INTRODUCTION

Background: Discovered and claimed by Portugal in the late 15th century, the islands' sugar-based economy gave way to coffee and cocoa in the 19th century—all grown with African plantation slave labor, a form of which lingered into the 20th century. While independence was achieved in 1975, democratic reforms were not instituted until the late 1980s. The country held its first free elections in 1991, but frequent internal wrangling between the various political parties precipitated repeated changes in leadership and four failed, non-violent coup attempts in 1995, 1998, 2003, and 2009. In 2012, three opposition parties combined in a no confidence vote to bring down the majority government of former Prime Minister Patrice TROVOADA, but in 2014, legislative elections returned him to the office. President Evaristo CARVALHO, of the same political party as Prime Minister TROVOADA, was elected in September 2016, marking a rare instance in which the positions of president and prime minister are held by the same party. New oil discoveries in the Gulf of Guinea may attract increased attention to the small island nation.

GEOGRAPHY

Location: Central Africa, islands in the Gulf of Guinea, just north of the Equator, west of Gabon

Geographic coordinates: 1 00 N, 7 00 E

Map references: Africa

Area: *total:* 964 sq km
land: 964 sq km
water: 0 sq km
country comparison to the world: 185

Area—comparative: more than five times the size of Washington, DC
Land boundaries: 0 km

Coastline: 209 km

Maritime claims: measured from claimed archipelagic baselines
territorial sea: 12 nm
exclusive economic zone: 200 nm

Climate: tropical; hot, humid; one rainy season (October to May)

Terrain: volcanic, mountainous

Elevation: *mean elevation:* NA

elevation extremes: *lowest point:* Atlantic Ocean 0 m
highest point: Pico de Sao Tome 2,024 m

Natural resources: fish, hydropower

Land use: *agricultural land:* 50.7%
arable land: 9.1%;
permanent crops: 40.6%;
permanent pasture: 1%
forest: 28.1%
other: 21.2% (2011 est.)
Irrigated land: 100 sq km (2012)

Population—distribution: Sao Tome, the capital city, has roughly a quarter of the nation's population; Santo Antonio is the largest town on Principe; the northern areas of both islands have the highest population densities

Natural hazards: flooding

Environment—current issues: deforestation; soil erosion and exhaustion

Environment—international agreements: *party to:* Biodiversity, Climate Change, Climate Change-Kyoto Protocol, Desertification, Endangered Species, Environmental Modification, Law of the Sea, Ozone Layer Protection, Ship Pollution, Wetlands
signed, but not ratified: none of the selected agreements

Geography—note: the smallest country in Africa; the two main islands form part of a chain of extinct volcanoes and both are mountainous

PEOPLE AND SOCIETY

Population: 201,025 (July 2017 est.)
country comparison to the world: 184

Nationality: *noun:* Sao Tomean(s)
adjective: Sao Tomean

Ethnic groups: mestico, angolares (descendants of Angolan slaves), forros (descendants of freed slaves), servicais (contract laborers from Angola, Mozambique, and Cabo Verde), tongas (children of servicais born on the islands), Europeans (primarily Portuguese), Asians (mostly Chinese)

Languages: Portuguese 98.4% (official), Forro 36.2%, Cabo Verdian 8.5%, French 6.8%, Angolar 6.6%, English 4.9%, Lunguie 1%, other (including sign language) 2.4%
note: shares sum to more than 100% because some respondents gave more than one answer on the census (2012 est.)

Religions: Catholic 55.7%, Adventist 4.1%, Assembly of God 3.4%, New Apostolic 2.9%, Mana 2.3%, Universal Kingdom of God 2%, Jehovah's Witness 1.2%, other 6.2%, none 21.2%, unspecified 1% (2012 est.)

Demographic profile: Sao Tome and Principe's youthful age structure—more than 60% of the population is under the age of 25—and high fertility rate ensure future population growth. Although Sao Tome has a net negative international migration rate, emigration is not a sufficient safety valve to reduce already high levels of unemployment and poverty. While literacy and primary school attendance have improved in recent years, Sao Tome still struggles to improve its educational quality and to increase its secondary school completion rate. Despite some improvements in education and access to healthcare, Sao Tome and Principe has

much to do to decrease its high poverty rate, create jobs, and increase its economic growth.

The population of Sao Tome and Principe descends primarily from the islands' colonial Portuguese settlers, who first arrived in the late 15th century, and the much larger number of African slaves brought in for sugar production and the slave trade. For about 100 years after the abolition of slavery in 1876, the population was further shaped by the widespread use of imported unskilled contract laborers from Portugal's other African colonies, who worked on coffee and cocoa plantations. In the first decades after abolition, most workers were brought from Angola under a system similar to slavery. While Angolan laborers were technically free, they were forced or coerced into long contracts that were automatically renewed and extended to their children. Other contract workers from Mozambique and famine-stricken Cape Verde first arrived in the early 20th century under short-term contracts and had the option of repatriation, although some chose to remain in Sao Tome and Principe.

Today's Sao Tomean population consists of mesticos (creole descendants of the European immigrants and African slaves that first inhabited the islands), forros (descendants of freed African slaves), angolares (descendants of runaway African slaves that formed a community in the south of Sao Tome Island and today are fishermen), servicais (contract laborers from Angola, Mozambique, and Cape Verde), tongas (locally born children of contract laborers), and lesser numbers of Europeans and Asians.

Age structure: *0-14 years:* 41.85% (male 42,781/female 41,354)
15-24 years: 20.68% (male 21,070/female 20,507)
25-54 years: 30.82% (male 30,454/female 31,509)
55-64 years: 3.81% (male 3,515/female 4,140)
65 years and over: 2.83% (male 2,523/female 3,172) (2017 est.)

Dependency ratios: *total dependency ratio:* 86.7
youth dependency ratio: 81.1
elderly dependency ratio: 5.6
potential support ratio: 17.8 (2015 est.)

Median age: *total:* 18.4 years
male: 18 years
female: 18.8 years (2017 est.)
country comparison to the world: 214

Population growth rate: 1.72% (2017 est.)
country comparison to the world: 60

Birth rate: 32.4 births/1,000 population (2017 est.)
country comparison to the world: 31

Death rate: 6.8 deaths/1,000 population (2017 est.)
country comparison to the world: 138

Net migration rate: -8.3 migrant(s)/1,000 population (2017 est.)
country comparison to the world: 207

Population distribution: Sao Tome, the capital city, has roughly a quarter of the nation's population; Santo Antonio is the largest town on Principe; the northern areas of both islands have the highest population densities

Urbanization: *urban population:* 66.2% of total population (2017)
rate of urbanization: 3.03% annual rate of change (2015-20 est.)

Major urban areas—population: SAO TOME (capital) 71,000 (2014)

Sex ratio: *at birth:* 1.03 male(s)/female
0-14 years: 1.03 male(s)/female
15-24 years: 1.03 male(s)/female
25-54 years: 0.96 male(s)/female
55-64 years: 0.84 male(s)/female
65 years and over: 0.81 male(s)/female
total population: 1 male(s)/female (2016 est.)

Mother's mean age at first birth: 19.4 years
note: median age at first birth among women 25-29 (2008/09 est.)

Maternal mortality ratio: 156 deaths/100,000 live births (2015 est.)
country comparison to the world: 58

Infant mortality rate: *total:* 45.3 deaths/1,000 live births
male: 47.2 deaths/1,000 live births
female: 43.3 deaths/1,000 live births (2017 est.)
country comparison to the world: 40

Life expectancy at birth: *total population:* 65.3 years
male: 63.9 years
female: 66.7 years (2017 est.)
country comparison to the world: 178

Total fertility rate: 4.25 children born/woman (2017 est.)
country comparison to the world: 30

Contraceptive prevalence rate: 40.6% (2014)

Health expenditures: 8.4% of GDP (2014)
country comparison to the world: 49

Hospital bed density: 2.9 beds/1,000 population (2011)

Drinking water source:
improved:
urban: 98.9% of population
rural: 93.6% of population
total: 97.1% of population
unimproved:
urban: 1.1% of population
rural: 6.4% of population
total: 2.9% of population (2015 est.)

Sanitation facility access:
improved:
urban: 40.8% of population
rural: 23.3% of population
total: 34.7% of population
unimproved:
urban: 59.2% of population
rural: 76.7% of population
total: 65.3% of population (2015 est.)

HIV/AIDS—adult prevalence rate: NA

HIV/AIDS—people living with HIV/AIDS: NA

HIV/AIDS—deaths: NA

Major infectious diseases: *degree of risk:* high
food or waterborne diseases: bacterial diarrhea, hepatitis A, and typhoid fever
vectorborne diseases: malaria and dengue fever

775

water contact disease: schistosomiasis (2016)

Obesity—adult prevalence rate: 12.4% (2016)
country comparison to the world: 133

Children under the age of 5 years underweight: 8.8% (2014)
country comparison to the world: 50

Education expenditures: 3.9% of GDP (2014)
country comparison to the world: 6

Literacy: *definition:* age 15 and over can read and write
total population: 74.9%
male: 81.8%
female: 68.4% (2015 est.)

School life expectancy (primary to tertiary education): *total:* 13 years
male: 13 years
female: 13 years (2015)

Unemployment, youth ages 15-24: *total:* 20.8%
male: NA
female: NA (2012 est.)

GOVERNMENT

Country name: *conventional long form:* Democratic Republic of Sao Tome and Principe
conventional short form: Sao Tome and Principe
local long form: Republica Democratica de Sao Tome e Principe
local short form: Sao Tome e Principe
etymology: Sao Tome was named after Saint THOMAS the Apostle by the Portuguese who discovered the island on 21 December 1470 (or 1471), the saint's feast day; Principe is a shortening of the original Portuguese name of "Ilha do Principe" (Isle of the Prince) referring to the Prince of Portugal to whom duties on the island's sugar crop were paid

Government type: semi-presidential republic

Capital: *name:* Sao Tome

geographic coordinates: 0 20 N, 6 44 E
time difference: UTC 0 (5 hours ahead of Washington, DC, during Standard Time)

Administrative divisions: 2 provinces; Principe, Sao Tome

Independence: 12 July 1975 (from Portugal)

National holiday: Independence Day, 12 July (1975)

Constitution: *history:* approved 5 November 1975 *amendments:* proposed by the National Assembly; passage requires two-thirds majority vote by the Assembly; the Assembly can propose to the president of the republic that an amendment be submitted to a referendum; revised several times, last in 2006 (2017)

Legal system: mixed legal system of civil law base on the Portuguese model and customary law

International law organization participation: has not submitted an ICJ jurisdiction declaration; non-party state to the ICCt

Citizenship: *citizenship by birth:* no

citizenship by descent only: at least one parent must be a citizen of Sao Tome and Principe

dual citizenship recognized: no
residency requirement for naturalization: 5 years

Suffrage: 18 years of age; universal

Executive branch: *chief of state:* President Evaristo CARVALHO (since 3 September 2016)
head of government: Prime Minister Patrice Emery TROVOADA (since 29 November 2014)
cabinet: Council of Ministers proposed by the prime minister, appointed by the president
elections/appointments: president directly elected by absolute majority popular vote in 2 rounds if needed for a 5-year term (eligible for a second term); election last held on 7 July 2016 and 7 August 2016 (next to be held in July 2021); prime minister chosen by the National Assembly and approved by the president
election results: Evaristo CARVALHO elected president; percent of vote—Evaristo CARVALHO (ADI) 49.8%, Manuel Pinto DA COSTA (independent) 24.8%, Maria DAS NEVES (MLSTP-PSD) 24.1%; note—first round results for CARVALHO were revised downward from just over 50%, prompting the 7 August 2016 runoff; however, on 1 August 2016 DA COSTA withdrew from the runoff, citing voting irregularities, and CARVALHO was declared the winner

Legislative branch: *description:* unicameral National Assembly or Assembleia Nacional (55 seats; members directly elected in multi-seat constituencies by proportional representation vote to serve 4-year terms)
elections: last held on 12 October 2014 (next to be held in October 2018)
election results: percent of vote by party—ADI 52.6%, MLSTP-PSD 24.7%, PCD-GR 11%, other 11.7%; seats by party—ADI 33, MLSTP-PSD 16, PCD-GR 5, other 1

Judicial branch: *highest court(s):* Supreme Court or Supremo Tribunal Justica (consists of 5 judges); Constitutional Court or Tribunal Constitucional (consists of 5 judges, 3 of whom are from the Supreme Court)
judge selection and term of office: Supreme Court judges appointed by the National Assembly; judge tenure NA; Constitutional Court judges nominated by the president of the republic and elected by the National Assembly for 5-year terms
subordinate courts: Court of First Instance; Audit Court

Political parties and leaders: Force for Democratic Change Movement or MDFM [Fradique Bandeira Melo DE MENEZES]
Independent Democratic Action or ADI [Patrice TROVOADA]
Movement for the Liberation of Sao Tome and Principe-Social Democratic Party or MLSTP-PSD [Aurelio MARTINS]
Party for Democratic Convergence-Reflection Group or PCD-GR [Leonel Mario D'ALVA] other small parties

Political pressure groups and leaders: Association of Sao Tome and Principe NGOs or FONG
other: media

International organization participation: ACP, AfDB, AOSIS, AU, CD, CEMAC, CPLP, EITI (candidate country), FAO, G-77, IBRD, ICAO, ICRM, IDA, IFAD, IFC, IFRCS, ILO, IMF, IMO, Interpol, IOC, IOM (observer), IPU, ITU, ITUC (NGOs), MIGA, NAM, OIF, OPCW, PCA, UN, UNCTAD, UNESCO, UNIDO, Union Latina, UNWTO, UPU, WCO, WHO, WIPO, WMO, WTO (observer)

Diplomatic representation in the US: chief of mission: Ambassador Carlos Filomeno Azevedo Agostinho das NEVES (since 3 December 2013)
chancery: 675 Third Avenue, Suite 1807, New York, NY 10017
telephone: [1] (212) 651-8116
FAX: [1] (212) 651-8117

Diplomatic representation from the US: the US does not have an embassy in Sao Tome and Principe; the US Ambassador to Gabon is accredited to Sao Tome and Principe on a nonresident basis

Flag description: three horizontal bands of green (top), yellow (double width), and green with two black five-pointed stars placed side by side in the center of the yellow band and a red isosceles triangle based on the hoist side; green stands for the country's rich vegetation, red recalls the struggle for independence, and yellow represents cocoa, one of the country's main agricultural products; the two stars symbolize the two main islands
note: uses the popular Pan-African colors of Ethiopia

National symbol(s): palm tree; national colors: green, yellow, red, black

National anthem: *name:* "Independencia total" (Total Independence)
lyrics/music: Alda Neves DA GRACA do Espirito Santo/Manuel dos Santos Barreto de Sousa e ALMEIDA
note: adopted 1975

ECONOMY

Economy—overview: This small, poor island economy has become increasingly dependent on cocoa since independence in 1975. Cocoa production has substantially declined in recent years because of drought and mismanagement. Sao Tome and Principe has to import fuels, most manufactured goods, consumer goods, and food, making it vulnerable to fluctuations in global commodity prices. Maintaining control of inflation, fiscal discipline, and increasing flows of foreign direct investment into the nascent oil sector are major economic problems facing the country. The government also has attempted to reduce price controls and subsidies.

Over the years, Sao Tome and Principe has had difficulty servicing its external debt and has relied heavily on concessional aid and debt rescheduling. It benefited from $200 million in debt relief in December 2000 under the Highly Indebted Poor Countries program, which helped bring down the country's $300 million debt burden. In April 2011, the country completed a Threshold Country Program with The Millennium Challenge

Corporation to help increase tax revenues, reform customs, and improve the business environment. In 2016, Sao Tome and Portugal signed a five-year cooperation agreement worth approximately $64 million, some of which will be provided as loans.

Considerable potential exists for development of a tourist industry, and the government has taken steps to expand facilities in recent years. Potential also exists for the development of petroleum resources in Sao Tome and Principe's territorial waters in the oil-rich Gulf of Guinea, which are being jointly developed in a 60-40 split with Nigeria, but any actual production is at least several years off. Volatile aid and investment inflows, even with a growing tourism sector, have kept growth moderate at around 4% annually, which is insufficient to alleviate poverty. The IMF in late 2016 expressed concern about the country's banking sector vulnerabilities.

GDP (purchasing power parity): $682 million (2017 est.)
$649.5 million (2016 est.)
$623.9 million (2015 est.)
note: data are in 2017 dollars
country comparison to the world: 210

GDP (official exchange rate): $372 million (2016 est.)

GDP—real growth rate: 5% (2017 est.)
4.1% (2016 est.)
4% (2015 est.)
country comparison to the world: 42

GDP—per capita (PPP): $3,200 (2017 est.)
$3,100 (2016 est.)
$3,100 (2015 est.)
note: data are in 2017 dollars
country comparison to the world: 192

Gross national saving: 25.1% of GDP (2017 est.)
21.6% of GDP (2016 est.)
19.1% of GDP (2015 est.)
country comparison to the world: 50

GDP—composition, by end use: *household consumption:* 81.5%
government consumption: 20.6%
investment in fixed capital: 33.5%
investment in inventories: 0%
exports of goods and services: 7.9%
imports of goods and services: -43.4% (2017 est.)

GDP—composition, by sector of origin:
agriculture: 11.8%
industry: 14.8%
services: 73.4% (2017 est.)

Agriculture—products: cocoa, coconuts, palm kernels, copra, cinnamon, pepper, coffee, bananas, papayas, beans; poultry; fish

Industries: light construction, textiles, soap, beer, fish processing, timber

Industrial production growth rate: 4.7% (2017 est.)
country comparison to the world: 54

Labor force: 72,600 (2017 est.)
country comparison to the world: 186

Labor force—by occupation: *agriculture:* 26.1%
industry: 21.4%
services: 52.5% (2014 est.)

Unemployment rate: 12.2% (2017 est.)
12.6% (2016 est.)
country comparison to the world: 159

Population below poverty line: 66.2% (2009 est.)

Household income or consumption by percentage share: *lowest 10%:* NA%
highest 10%: NA%

Budget: *revenues:* $114.3 million
expenditures: $123.4 million (2017 est.)
Taxes and other revenues: 30.7% of GDP (2017 est.)
country comparison to the world: 78

Budget surplus (+) or deficit (-): -2.5% of GDP (2017 est.)
country comparison to the world: 101

Public debt: 60.2% of GDP (2017 est.)
58.8% of GDP (2016 est.)
country comparison to the world: 73

Fiscal year: calendar year

Inflation rate (consumer prices): 4.5% (2017 est.)
5.4% (2016 est.)
country comparison to the world: 169

Central bank discount rate: 16% (31 December 2009)
28% (31 December 2008)
country comparison to the world: 8

Commercial bank prime lending rate: 18.9% (31 December 2017 est.)
19.59% (31 December 2016 est.)
country comparison to the world: 21

Stock of narrow money: $71.48 million (31 December 2017 est.)
$65.47 million (31 December 2016 est.)
country comparison to the world: 190

Stock of broad money: $113 million (31 December 2017 est.)
$116.3 million (31 December 2016 est.)
country comparison to the world: 194

Stock of domestic credit: $66.4 million (31 December 2017 est.)
$72.19 million (31 December 2016 est.)
country comparison to the world: 188

Market value of publicly traded shares: $NA

Current account balance: -$38 million (2017 est.)
-$22 million (2016 est.)
country comparison to the world: 68

Exports: $11.3 million (2017 est.)
$13.6 million (2016 est.)
country comparison to the world: 215

Exports—commodities: cocoa 80%, copra, coffee, palm oil (2010 est.)

Exports—partners: Germany 23.3%, Netherlands 13.8%, Portugal 10%, Angola 6.4%, South Korea 5.2%, Peru 4.5%, Dominican Republic 4.1% (2016)

Imports: $125.4 million (2017 est.)
$119.1 million (2016 est.)
country comparison to the world: 210

Imports—commodities: machinery and electrical equipment, food products, petroleum products

Imports—partners: Portugal 58.8%, Angola 15.2%, China 5.3% (2016)

Reserves of foreign exchange and gold: $64 million (31 December 2017 est.)
$61.5 million (31 December 2016 est.)
country comparison to the world: 169

Debt—external: $343.4 million (31 December 2017 est.)
$308.5 million (31 December 2016 est.)
country comparison to the world: 184

Stock of direct foreign investment—at home: $453.3 million (31 December 2017 est.)
$430.3 million (31 December 2016 est.)
country comparison to the world: 125

Stock of direct foreign investment—abroad: $3.98 million (31 December 2017 est.)
$2.2 million (31 December 2016 est.)
country comparison to the world: 111

Exchange rates: dobras (STD) per US dollar—
22,608 (2017 est.)
22,149 (2016 est.)
22,149 (2015 est.)
22,091 (2014 est.)
18,466 (2013 est.)

ENERGY

Electricity access: population without electricity: 100,000
electrification—*total population:* 59%
electrification—urban areas: 70%
electrification—rural areas: 40% (2013)

Electricity—production: 66 million kWh (2015 est.)
country comparison to the world: 204

Electricity—consumption: 61.38 million kWh (2015 est.)
country comparison to the world: 202

Electricity—exports: 0 kWh (2016)
country comparison to the world: 205

Electricity—imports: 0 kWh (2016 est.)
country comparison to the world: 209

Electricity—installed generating capacity: 20,000 kW (2015 est.)
country comparison to the world: 205

Electricity—from fossil fuels: 80% of total installed capacity (2015 est.)
country comparison to the world: 90

Electricity—from nuclear fuels: 0% of total installed capacity (2015 est.)
country comparison to the world: 193

Electricity—from hydroelectric plants: 20% of total installed capacity (2015 est.)
country comparison to the world: 89

Electricity—from other renewable sources: 0% of total installed capacity (2015 est.)
country comparison to the world: 209

Crude oil—production: 0 bbl/day (2016 est.)
country comparison to the world: 194

Crude oil—exports: 0 bbl/day (2014 est.)
country comparison to the world: 199

Crude oil—imports: 0 bbl/day (2014 est.)
country comparison to the world: 198

Crude oil—proved reserves: 0 bbl (1 January 2017)
country comparison to the world: 192

Refined petroleum products—production: 0 bbl/day (2014 est.)
country comparison to the world: 198

Refined petroleum products—consumption: 1,000 bbl/day (2015 est.)
country comparison to the world: 205

Refined petroleum products—exports: 0 bbl/day (2014 est.)
country comparison to the world: 204

Refined petroleum products—imports: 1,001 bbl/day (2014 est.)
country comparison to the world: 201

Natural gas—production: 0 cu m (2013 est.)
country comparison to the world: 203

Natural gas—consumption: 0 cu m (2013 est.)
country comparison to the world: 138

Natural gas—exports: 0 cu m (2013 est.)
country comparison to the world: 195

Natural gas—imports: 0 cu m (2013 est.)
country comparison to the world: 196

Natural gas—proved reserves: 0 cu m (1 January 2014 es)
country comparison to the world: 201

Carbon dioxide emissions from consumption of energy: 100,000 Mt (2013 est.)
country comparison to the world: 208

COMMUNICATIONS

Telephones—fixed lines: *total subscriptions:* 5,733
subscriptions per 100 inhabitants: 3 (July 2016 est.)
country comparison to the world: 205

Telephones—mobile cellular: *total:* 132,000

subscriptions per 100 inhabitants: 68 (July 2016 est.)
country comparison to the world: 187

Telephone system: *general assessment:* local telephone network of adequate quality with most lines connected to digital switches
domestic: combined fixed-line and mobile-cellular teledensity roughly 70 telephones per 100 persons
international: country code—239; satellite earth station—1 Intelsat (Atlantic Ocean) (2016)

Broadcast media: 1 government-owned TV station; 1 government-owned radio station; 3 independent local radio stations authorized in 2005 with 2 operating at the end of 2006; transmissions of multiple international broadcasters are available (2007)

Internet country code: .st

Internet users: *total:* 50,000
percent of population: 25.8% (July 2016 est.)
country comparison to the world: 186

TRANSPORTATION

National air transport system: number of registered air carriers: 1
inventory of registered aircraft operated by air carriers: 1
annual passenger traffic on registered air carriers: 50,716
annual freight traffic on registered air carriers: 0 mt-km (2015)
Civil aircraft registration country code prefix: S9 (2016)

Airports: 2 (2013)
country comparison to the world: 206

Airports—with paved runways: *total:* 2
1,524 to 2,437 m: 1
914 to 1,523 m: 1 (2017)

Roadways: *total:* 320 km

paved: 218 km
unpaved: 102 km (2000)
country comparison to the world: 206

Merchant marine: *total:* 16
by type: general cargo 12, other 4 (2017)
country comparison to the world: 139

Ports and terminals: *major seaport(s):* Sao Tome

MILITARY AND SECURITY

Military branches: Armed Forces of Sao Tome and Principe (Forcas Armadas de Sao Tome e Principe, FASTP): Army, Coast Guard of Sao Tome e Principe (Guarda Costeira de Sao Tome e Principe, GCSTP; also called "Navy"), Presidential Guard, National Guard (2015)

Military service age and obligation: 18 is the legal minimum age for compulsory military service; 17 is the legal minimum age for voluntary service (2012)

Military—note: Sao Tome and Principe's army is a tiny force with almost no resources at its disposal and would be wholly ineffective operating unilaterally; infantry equipment is considered simple to operate and maintain but may require refurbishment or replacement after 25 years in tropical climates; poor pay, working conditions, and alleged nepotism in the promotion of officers have been problems in the past, as reflected in the 1995 and 2003 coups; these issues are being addressed with foreign assistance aimed at improving the army and its focus on realistic security concerns; command is exercised from the president, through the Minister of Defense, to the Chief of the Armed Forces (infantry, technical issues) and the Chief of the General Staff (logistics, administration, finances) (2012)

TRANSNATIONAL ISSUES

Disputes—international: none

SAUDI ARABIA

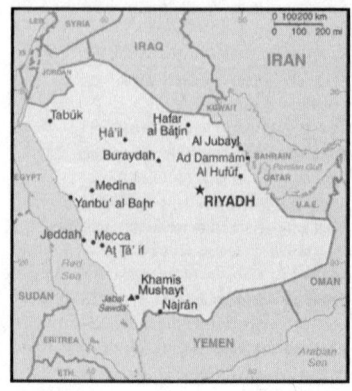

INTRODUCTION

Background: Saudi Arabia is the birthplace of Islam and home to Islam's two holiest shrines in Mecca and Medina. The king's official title is the Custodian of the Two Holy Mosques. The modern Saudi state was founded in 1932 by ABD AL-AZIZ bin Abd al-Rahman Al SAUD (Ibn Saud) after a 30-year campaign to unify most of the Arabian Peninsula. One of his male descendants rules the country today, as required by the country's 1992 Basic Law. Following Iraq's invasion of Kuwait in 1990, Saudi Arabia accepted the Kuwaiti royal family and 400,000 refugees while allowing Western and Arab troops to deploy on its soil for the liberation of Kuwait the following year. The continuing presence of foreign troops on Saudi soil after the liberation of Kuwait became a source of tension between the royal family and the public

until all operational US troops left the country in 2003. Major terrorist attacks in May and November 2003 spurred a strong ongoing campaign against domestic terrorism and extremism.

From 2005 to 2015, King ABDALLAH incrementally modernized the Kingdom. Driven by personal ideology and political pragmatism, he introduced a series of social and economic initiatives, including expanding employment and social opportunities for women, attracting foreign investment, increasing the role of the private sector in the economy, and discouraging businesses from hiring foreign workers. Saudi Arabia saw protests during the 2011 Arab Spring but not the level of bloodshed seen in protests elsewhere in the region. Shia Muslims in the Eastern Province protested primarily against the detention of political prisoners, endemic discrimination, and Bahraini and

Saudi Government actions in Bahrain. Riyadh took a cautious but firm approach by arresting some protesters but releasing most of them quickly and by using its state-sponsored clerics to counter political and Islamist activism.

The government held its first-ever elections in 2005 and 2011, when Saudis went to the polls to elect municipal councilors. In December 2015, women were allowed to vote and stand as candidates for the first time in municipal council elections, with 19 women winning seats. King SALMAN bin Abd al-Aziz Al Saud ascended to the throne in 2015 and placed the first next-generation prince, MUHAMMAD BIN NAIF bin Abd al-Aziz Al Saud, in the line of succession as Crown Prince. He designated his son, MUHAMMAD BIN SALMAN bin Abd al-Aziz Al Saud, as the Deputy Crown Prince. In March 2015, Saudi Arabia led a coalition of 10 countries in a military campaign to restore the government of Yemen, which had been ousted by Huthi forces allied with former president ALI ABDULLAH al-Salih. The war in Yemen has led to civilian casualties and shortages of basic supplies, which has drawn considerable international criticism. In December 2015, Deputy Crown Prince MUHAMMAD BIN SALMAN announced Saudi Arabia would lead a 34-nation Islamic Coalition to fight terrorism (it has since grown to 41 nations). In January 2016, Saudi Arabia executed 47 people on charges of terrorism, including Shia Muslim cleric NIMR al-Nimr. Iranian protesters overran Saudi diplomatic facilities in Iran to protest al-NIMR's execution and the Saudi government responded by cutting off diplomatic ties with Iran.

The country remains a leading producer of oil and natural gas and holds about 16% of the world's proven oil reserves as of 2015. The government continues to pursue economic reform and diversification, particularly since Saudi Arabia's accession to the WTO in 2005, and promotes foreign investment in the Kingdom. In April 2016, the Saudi government announced a broad set of socio-economic reforms, known as Vision 2030. Low global oil prices throughout 2015 and 2016 significantly lowered Saudi Arabia's governmental revenue. In response, the government cut subsidies on water, electricity, and gasoline; reduced government employee compensation packages; and announced limited new land taxes. In coordination with OPEC and some key non-OPEC countries, Saudi Arabia agreed cut oil output in early 2017 to regulate supply and help elevate global prices.

GEOGRAPHY

Location: Middle East, bordering the Persian Gulf and the Red Sea, north of Yemen

Geographic coordinates: 25 00 N, 45 00 E

Map references: Middle East

Area: total: 2,149,690 sq km
land: 2,149,690 sq km
water: 0 sq km
country comparison to the world: 14

Area—comparative: slightly more than one-fifth the size of the US

Land boundaries: total: 4,272 km
border countries (7): Iraq 811 km, Jordan 731 km, Kuwait 221 km, Oman 658 km, Qatar 87 km, UAE 457 km, Yemen 1,307 km

Coastline: 2,640 km

Maritime claims: territorial sea: 12 nm
contiguous zone: 18 nm
continental shelf: not specified

Climate: harsh, dry desert with great temperature extremes

Terrain: mostly sandy desert

Elevation: mean elevation: 665 m

elevation extremes: lowest point: Persian Gulf 0 m
highest point: Jabal Sawda' 3,133 m

Natural resources: petroleum, natural gas, iron ore, gold, copper

Land use: agricultural land: 80.7%
arable land: 1.5%;
permanent crops: 0.1%;
permanent pasture: 79.1%
forest: 0.5%
other: 18.8% (2011 est.)
Irrigated land: 16,200 sq km (2012)

Population—distribution: historically a population that was mostly nomadic or semi-nomadic, the Saudi population has become more settled since petroleum was discovered in the 1930s; most of the economic activities—and with it the country's population—is concentrated in a wide area across the middle of the peninsula, from Ad Dammam in the east, through Riyadh in the interior, to Mecca-Medina in the west near the Red Sea

Natural hazards: frequent sand and dust storms
volcanism: despite many volcanic formations, there has been little activity in the past few centuries; volcanoes include Harrat Rahat, Harrat Khaybar, Harrat Lunayyir, and Jabal Yar

Environment—current issues: desertification; depletion of underground water resources; the lack of perennial rivers or permanent water bodies has prompted the development of extensive seawater desalination facilities; coastal pollution from oil spills

Environment—international agreements: party to: Biodiversity, Climate Change, Climate Change-Kyoto Protocol, Desertification, Endangered Species, Hazardous Wastes, Law of the Sea, Marine Dumping, Ozone Layer Protection, Ship Pollution signed, but not ratified: none of the selected agreements

Geography—note: Saudi Arabia is the largest country in the world without a river; extensive coastlines on the Persian Gulf and Red Sea provide great leverage on shipping (especially crude oil) through the Persian Gulf and Suez Canal

PEOPLE AND SOCIETY

Population: 28,571,770 (July 2017 est.)
note: immigrants make up 37% of the total population, according to UN data (2017)
country comparison to the world: 47

Nationality: noun: Saudi(s)
adjective: Saudi or Saudi Arabian

Ethnic groups: Arab 90%, Afro-Asian 10%

Languages: Arabic (official)

Religions: Muslim (official; citizens are 85-90% Sunni and 10-15% Shia), other (includes Eastern Orthodox, Protestant, Roman Catholic, Jewish, Hindu, Buddhist, and Sikh) (2012 est.)
note: despite having a large expatriate community of various faiths (more than 30% of the population), most forms of public religious expression inconsistent with the government-sanctioned interpretation of Sunni Islam are restricted; non-Muslims are not allowed to have Saudi citizenship and non-Muslim places of worship are not permitted (2013)

Age structure: 0-14 years: 26.1% (male 3,825,242/female 3,631,967)
15-24 years: 18.57% (male 2,842,818/female 2,462,061)
25-54 years: 46.86% (male 7,559,248/female 5,829,656)
55-64 years: 5.03% (male 783,673/female 653,404)
65 years and over: 3.44% (male 498,830/female 484,871) (2017 est.)

Dependency ratios: total dependency ratio: 40.9
youth dependency ratio: 36.6
elderly dependency ratio: 4.3
potential support ratio: 23.2 (2015 est.)

Median age: total: 27.5 years
male: 28.2 years
female: 26.7 years (2017 est.)
country comparison to the world: 144

Population growth rate: 1.45% (2017 est.)
country comparison to the world: 79

Birth rate: 18.3 births/1,000 population (2017 est.)
country comparison to the world: 93

Death rate: 3.4 deaths/1,000 population (2017 est.)
country comparison to the world: 219

Net migration rate: -0.5 migrant(s)/1,000 population (2017 est.)
country comparison to the world: 125

Population distribution: historically a population that was mostly nomadic or semi-nomadic, the Saudi population has become more settled since petroleum was discovered in the 1930s; most of the economic activities—and with it the country's population—is concentrated in a wide area across the middle of the peninsula, from Ad Dammam in the east, through Riyadh in the interior, to Mecca-Medina in the west near the Red Sea

Urbanization: urban population: 83.5% of total population (2017)
rate of urbanization: 1.81% annual rate of change (2015-20 est.)

Major urban areas—population: RIYADH (capital) 6.195 million; Jeddah 4.076 million; Mecca 1.771 million; Medina 1.28 million; Ad Dammam 1.064 million (2015)

Sex ratio: at birth: 1.05 male(s)/female
0-14 years: 1.05 male(s)/female

15-24 years: 1.15 male(s)/female
25-54 years: 1.31 male(s)/female
55-64 years: 1.21 male(s)/female
65 years and over: 1.05 male(s)/female
total population: 1.19 male(s)/female (2016 est.)

Maternal mortality ratio: 12 deaths/100,000 live births (2015 est.)
country comparison to the world: 141

Infant mortality rate: *total:* 13.2 deaths/1,000 live births
male: 15.1 deaths/1,000 live births
female: 11.2 deaths/1,000 live births (2017 est.)
country comparison to the world: 108

Life expectancy at birth: *total population:* 75.5 years
male: 73.4 years
female: 77.7 years (2017 est.)
country comparison to the world: 105

Total fertility rate: 2.09 children born/woman (2017 est.)
country comparison to the world: 106

Contraceptive prevalence rate: 24.6% (2016)

Health expenditures: 4.7% of GDP (2014)
country comparison to the world: 151

Physicians density: 2.57 physicians/1,000 population (2014)

Hospital bed density: 2.1 beds/1,000 population (2012)

Drinking water source:
improved:
urban: 97% of population
rural: 97% of population
total: 97% of population
unimproved:
urban: 3% of population
rural: 3% of population
total: 3% of population (2015 est.)

Sanitation facility access:
improved:
urban: 100% of population
rural: 100% of population
total: 100% of population
unimproved:
urban: 0% of population
rural: 0% of population
total: 0% of population (2015 est.)

HIV/AIDS—adult prevalence rate: <.1% (2016 est.)

HIV/AIDS—people living with HIV/AIDS: 8,200 (2016 est.)
country comparison to the world: 102

HIV/AIDS—deaths: <500 (2016 est.)

Obesity—adult prevalence rate: 35.4% (2016)
country comparison to the world: 14

Education expenditures: 5.1% of GDP (2008)
country comparison to the world: 68

Literacy: *definition:* age 15 and over can read and write
total population: 94.7%
male: 97%
female: 91.1% (2015 est.)

School life expectancy (primary to tertiary education): *total:* 16 years
male: 17 years
female: 15 years (2014)

Unemployment, youth ages 15-24: *total:* 28.5%
male: 19.7%
female: 56% (2015 est.)
country comparison to the world: 29

GOVERNMENT

Country name: *conventional long form:* Kingdom of Saudi Arabia
conventional short form: Saudi Arabia
local long form: Al Mamlakah al Arabiyah as Suudiyah
local short form: Al Arabiyah as Suudiyah
etymology: named after the ruling dynasty of the country, the House of Saud; the name "Arabia" can be traced back many centuries B.C., the ancient Egyptians referred to the region as "Ar Rabi"

Government type: absolute monarchy

Capital: *name:* Riyadh
geographic coordinates: 24 39 N, 46 42 E
time difference: UTC+3 (8 hours ahead of Washington, DC, during Standard Time)

Administrative divisions: 13 provinces (mintaqat, singular—mintaqah); Al Bahah, Al Hudud ash Shamaliyah (Northern Border), Al Jawf, Al Madinah (Medina), Al Qasim, Ar Riyad (Riyadh), Ash Sharqiyah (Eastern), 'Asir, Ha'il, Jazan, Makkah (Mecca), Najran, Tabuk

Independence: 23 September 1932 (unification of the kingdom)

National holiday: Saudi National Day (Unification of the Kingdom), 23 September (1932)

Constitution: *history:* 1 March 1992—Basic Law of Government, issued by royal decree, serves as the constitutional framework and is based on the Qur'an and the life and traditions of the Prophet Muhammad
amendments: proposed by the king directly or proposed to the king by the Consultative Assembly or by the Council of Ministers; passage by the king through royal decree; Basic Law amended many times, last in 2005 (2016)

Legal system: Islamic (sharia) legal system with some elements of Egyptian, French, and customary law; note—several secular codes have been introduced; commercial disputes handled by special committees

International law organization participation: has not submitted an ICJ jurisdiction declaration; non-party state to the ICCt

Citizenship: *citizenship by birth:* no
citizenship by descent only: the father must be a citizen of Saudi Arabia; a child born out of wedlock in Saudi Arabia to a Saudi mother and unknown father
dual citizenship recognized: no
residency requirement for naturalization: 5 years

Suffrage: 18 years of age; restricted to male; universal for municipal elections

Executive branch: *chief of state:* King and Prime Minister SALMAN bin Abd al-Aziz Al Saud (since 23 January 2015); Crown Prince MUHAMMAD BIN SALMAN bin Abd al-Aziz Al Saud (born 31 August 1985); note—the monarch is both chief of state and head of government
head of government: King and Prime Minister SALMAN bin Abd al-Aziz Al Saud (since 23 January 2015); Crown Prince MUHAMMAD BIN SALMAN bin Abd al-Aziz Al Saud (born 31 August 1985)
cabinet: Council of Ministers appointed by the monarch every 4 years and includes many royal family members
elections/appointments: none; the monarchy is hereditary; an Allegiance Council created by royal decree in October 2006 established a committee of Saudi princes for a voice in selecting future Saudi kings

Legislative branch: *description:* unicameral Consultative Council or Majlis al-Shura (150 seats; members appointed by the monarch to serve 4-year terms); note—in early 2013, the monarch granted women 30 seats on the Council

Judicial branch: *highest court(s):* High Court (consists of the court chief and is organized into circuits with 3-judge panels, except for the criminal circuit, which has a 5-judge panel for cases involving major punishments)
judge selection and term of office: High Court chief and chiefs of the High Court Circuits appointed by royal decree following the recommendation of the Supreme Judiciary Council, a 10-member body of high-level judges and other judicial heads; new judges and assistant judges serve 1- and 2-year probations, respectively, before permanent assignment
subordinate courts: Court of Appeals; Specialized Criminal Court, first-degree courts composed of general, criminal, personal status, and commercial courts; Labor Court; a hierarchy of administrative courts

Political parties and leaders: none
Political pressure groups and leaders: other: gas companies; religious groups

International organization participation: ABEDA, AfDB (nonregional member), AFESD, AMF, BIS, CAEU, CP, FAO, G-20, G-77, GCC, IAEA, IBRD, ICAO, ICC (national committees), ICRM, IDA, IDB, IFAD, IFC, IFRCS, IHO, ILO, IMF, IMO, IMSO, Interpol, IOC, IOM (observer), IPU, ISO, ITSO, ITU, LAS, MIGA, NAM, OAPEC, OAS (observer), OIC, OPCW, OPEC, PCA, UN, UNCTAD, UNESCO, UNIDO, UNRWA, UNWTO, UPU, WCO, WFTU (NGOs), WHO, WIPO, WMO, WTO

Diplomatic representation in the US: chief of mission: Ambassador Khalid bin Salman bin Abdulaziz AL SAUD (since 21 July 2017)
chancery: 601 New Hampshire Avenue NW, Washington, DC 20037
telephone: [1] (202) 342-3800
FAX: [1] (202) 944-5983

consulate(s) general: Houston, Los Angeles, New York

Diplomatic representation from the US: *chief of mission:* Ambassador (vacant); Charge d'Affaires Christopher HENZEL (since 9 January 2017)
embassy: P.O. Box 94309, Riyadh 4693
mailing address: American Embassy, Unit 61307, APO AE 09803-1307; International Mail: P. O. Box 94309, Riyadh 11693
telephone: [966] (11) 488-3800
FAX: [966] (11) 488-7360
consulate(s) general: Dhahran, Jiddah (Jeddah)

Flag description: green, a traditional color in Islamic flags, with the Shahada or Muslim creed in large white Arabic script (translated as "There is no god but God; Muhammad is the Messenger of God") above a white horizontal saber (the tip points to the hoist side); design dates to the early twentieth century and is closely associated with the Al Saud family which established the kingdom in 1932; the flag is manufactured with differing obverse and reverse sides so that the Shahada reads—and the sword points—correctly from right to left on both sides
note: the only national flag to display an inscription as its principal design; one of only three national flags that differ on their obverse and reverse sides—the others are Moldova and Paraguay

National symbol(s): palm tree surmounting two crossed swords; national colors: green, white

National anthem: *name:* "Aash Al Maleek" (Long Live Our Beloved King)
lyrics/music: Ibrahim KHAFAJI/Abdul Rahman al-KHATEEB
note: music adopted 1947, lyrics adopted 1984

ECONOMY

Economy—overview: Saudi Arabia has an oil-based economy with strong government controls over major economic activities. It possesses about 16% of the world's proven petroleum reserves, ranks as the largest exporter of petroleum, and plays a leading role in OPEC. The petroleum sector accounts for roughly 87% of budget revenues, 42% of GDP, and 90% of export earnings.

Saudi Arabia is encouraging the growth of the private sector in order to diversify its economy and to employ more Saudi nationals. Over 6 million foreign workers play an important role in the Saudi economy, particularly in the oil and service sectors; at the same time, however, Riyadh is struggling to reduce unemployment among its own nationals. Saudi officials are particularly focused on employing its large youth population, which generally lacks the education and technical skills the private sector needs.

In 2017, the Kingdom incurred a budget deficit estimated at 8.3% of GDP, which was financed by bond sales and drawing down reserves. Although the Kingdom can finance high deficits for several years by drawing down its considerable foreign assets or by borrowing, it has cut capital spending and reduced subsidies on electricity, water, and petroleum products and plans to introduce a value-added tax. In January 2016, Crown Prince and Deputy Prime Minister MUHAMMAD BIN SALMAN announced that Saudi Arabia intends to list shares of its state-owned petroleum company, ARAMCO—another move to increase revenue and outside investment. The government has also looked at privatization and diversification of the economy more closely in the wake of a diminished oil market. Historically, Saudi Arabia has focused diversification efforts on power generation, telecommunications, natural gas exploration, and petrochemical sectors. More recently, the government has approached investors about expanding the role of the private sector in the health care, education and tourism industries. While Saudi Arabia has emphasized their goals of diversification for some time, current low oil prices may force the government to make more drastic changes ahead of their long-run timeline.

GDP (purchasing power parity): $1.789 trillion (2017 est.)
$1.787 trillion (2016 est.)
$1.756 trillion (2015 est.)
note: data are in 2017 dollars
country comparison to the world: 16

GDP (official exchange rate): $678.5 billion (2016 est.)

GDP—real growth rate: 0.1% (2017 est.)
1.7% (2016 est.)
4.1% (2015 est.)
country comparison to the world: 200

GDP—per capita (PPP): $55,300 (2017 est.)
$56,300 (2016 est.)
$56,600 (2015 est.)
note: data are in 2017 dollars
country comparison to the world: 21

Gross national saving: 28.8% of GDP (2017 est.)
25.2% of GDP (2016 est.)
26.1% of GDP (2015 est.)
country comparison to the world: 31

GDP—composition, by end use:
household consumption: 41.3%
government consumption: 24.6%
investment in fixed capital: 24.4%
investment in inventories: 4.4%
exports of goods and services: 35.6%
imports of goods and services: -30.3% (2017 est.)

GDP—composition, by sector of origin:
agriculture: 2.6%
industry: 44.2%
services: 53.2% (2017 est.)

Agriculture—products: wheat, barley, tomatoes, melons, dates, citrus; mutton, chickens, eggs, milk

Industries: crude oil production, petroleum refining, basic petrochemicals, ammonia, industrial gases, sodium hydroxide (caustic soda), cement, fertilizer, plastics, metals, commercial ship repair, commercial aircraft repair, construction

Industrial production growth rate: -0.3% (2017 est.)
country comparison to the world: 189

Labor force: 12.34 million

note: about 80% of the labor force is non-national (2017 est.)
country comparison to the world: 48

Labor force—by occupation: *agriculture:* 6.7%
industry: 21.4%
services: 71.9% (2005 est.)

Unemployment rate: 5.6% (2017 est.)
5.6% (2016 est.)
note: data are for Saudi males only (local bank estimates; some estimates are as high as 25%)
country comparison to the world: 79

Population below poverty line: NA%

Household income or consumption by percentage share: *lowest 10%:* NA%
highest 10%: NA%

Distribution of family income—Gini index: 45.9 (2013 est.)
country comparison to the world: 35

Budget: *revenues:* $171.6 billion
expenditures: $227.8 billion (2017 est.)
Taxes and other revenues: 25.3% of GDP (2017 est.)
country comparison to the world: 111

Budget surplus (+) or deficit (-): -8.3% of GDP (2017 est.)
country comparison to the world: 200

Public debt: 30% of GDP (2017 est.)
22.3% of GDP (2016 est.)
country comparison to the world: 162

Fiscal year: calendar year

Inflation rate (consumer prices): -0.2% (2017 est.)
3.5% (2016 est.)
country comparison to the world: 7

Central bank discount rate: 2.5% (31 December 2008)
country comparison to the world: 110

Commercial bank prime lending rate: 8.3% (31 December 2017 est.)
7.1% (31 December 2016 est.)
country comparison to the world: 103

Stock of narrow money: $311.2 billion (31 December 2017 est.)
$305.2 billion (31 December 2016 est.)
country comparison to the world: 16

Stock of broad money: $487.5 billion (31 December 2017 est.)
$476.6 billion (31 December 2016 est.)
country comparison to the world: 23

Stock of domestic credit: $250.1 billion (31 December 2017 est.)
$221.3 billion (31 December 2016 est.)
country comparison to the world: 44

Market value of publicly traded shares: $421.1 billion (31 December 2015 est.)
$483.1 billion (31 December 2014 est.)
$467.4 billion (31 December 2013 est.)
country comparison to the world: 24

Current account balance: $4.322 billion (2017 est.)
-$27.54 billion (2016 est.)
country comparison to the world: 27

Exports: $231.3 billion (2017 est.)
$183.6 billion (2016 est.)
country comparison to the world: 22

Exports—commodities: petroleum and petroleum products 90% (2012 est.)

Exports—partners: China 13.6%, Japan 11.3%, India 10.7%, US 9.8%, South Korea 9.1%, Singapore 4.7% (2016)

Imports: $136.8 billion (2017 est.)
$127.8 billion (2016 est.)
country comparison to the world: 33

Imports—commodities: machinery and equipment, foodstuffs, chemicals, motor vehicles, textiles

Imports—partners: China 16.2%, US 15%, Germany 6.3%, Japan 5.3%, UAE 5%, South Korea 4.3% (2016)

Reserves of foreign exchange and gold: $509 billion (31 December 2017 est.)
$535.8 billion (31 December 2016 est.)
country comparison to the world: 5

Debt—external: $212.9 billion (31 December 2017 est.)
$189.3 billion (31 December 2016 est.)
country comparison to the world: 36

Stock of direct foreign investment—at home: $264.6 billion (31 December 2017 est.)
$258.1 billion (31 December 2016 est.)
country comparison to the world: 24

Stock of direct foreign investment—abroad: $56.09 billion (31 December 2017 est.)
$46.45 billion (31 December 2016 est.)
country comparison to the world: 42

Exchange rates: Saudi riyals (SAR) per US dollar—
3.75 (2017 est.)
3.75 (2016 est.)
3.75 (2015 est.)
3.75 (2014 est.)
3.75 (2013 est.)

ENERGY

Electricity access: population without electricity: 200,000
electrification—total population: 98%
electrification—urban areas: 99%
electrification—rural areas: 93% (2013)

Electricity—production: 318 billion kWh (2015 est.)
country comparison to the world: 12

Electricity—consumption: 292.8 billion kWh (2015 est.)
country comparison to the world: 14

Electricity—exports: 0 kWh (2016 est.)
country comparison to the world: 190

Electricity—imports: 0 kWh (2016 est.)
country comparison to the world: 194

Electricity—installed generating capacity: 69.05 million kW (2015 est.)
country comparison to the world: 17

Electricity—from fossil fuels: 99.9% of total installed capacity (2015 est.)

country comparison to the world: 25

Electricity—from nuclear fuels: 0% of total installed capacity (2015 est.)
country comparison to the world: 175

Electricity—from hydroelectric plants: 0% of total installed capacity (2015 est.)
country comparison to the world: 198

Electricity—from other renewable sources: 0.1% of total installed capacity (2015 est.)
country comparison to the world: 165

Crude oil—production: 10.46 million bbl/day (2016 est.)
country comparison to the world: 2

Crude oil—exports: 7.273 million bbl/day (2014 est.)
country comparison to the world: 1

Crude oil—imports: 0 bbl/day (2014 est.)
country comparison to the world: 183

Crude oil—proved reserves: 266.5 billion bbl (1 January 2017 es)
country comparison to the world: 2

Refined petroleum products—production: 2.221 million bbl/day (2014 est.)
country comparison to the world: 9

Refined petroleum products—consumption: 3.237 million bbl/day (2015 est.)
country comparison to the world: 7

Refined petroleum products—exports: 1.621 million bbl/day (2014 est.)
country comparison to the world: 6

Refined petroleum products—imports: 486,900 bbl/day (2014 est.)
country comparison to the world: 17

Natural gas—production: 102.3 billion cu m (2015 est.)
country comparison to the world: 9

Natural gas—consumption: 102.3 billion cu m (2015 est.)
country comparison to the world: 13

Natural gas—exports: 0 cu m (2014 est.)
country comparison to the world: 174

Natural gas—imports: 0 cu m (2014 est.)
country comparison to the world: 181

Natural gas—proved reserves: 8.602 trillion cu m (1 January 2017 es)
country comparison to the world: 5

Carbon dioxide emissions from consumption of energy: 594 million Mt (2013 est.)
country comparison to the world: 10

COMMUNICATIONS

Telephones—fixed lines: *total subscriptions:* 3,637,442
subscriptions per 100 inhabitants: 13 (July 2016 est.)
country comparison to the world: 42

Telephones—mobile cellular: *total:* 47,932,521
subscriptions per 100 inhabitants: 170 (July 2016 est.)
country comparison to the world: 29

Telephone system: *general assessment:* modern system including a combination of extensive microwave radio relays, coaxial cables, and fiber-optic cables
domestic: mobile-cellular subscribership has been increasing rapidly
international: country code—966; landing point for the international submarine cable Fiber-Optic Link Around the Globe (FLAG) and for both the SEA-ME-WE-3 and SEA-ME-WE-4 submarine cable networks providing connectivity to Asia, Middle East, Europe, and US; microwave radio relay to Bahrain, Jordan, Kuwait, Qatar, UAE, Yemen, and Sudan; coaxial cable to Kuwait and Jordan; satellite earth stations—5 Intelsat (3 Atlantic Ocean and 2 Indian Ocean), 1 Arabsat, and 1 Inmarsat (Indian Ocean region) (2016)

Broadcast media: broadcast media are state-controlled; state-run TV operates 4 networks; Saudi Arabia is a major market for pan-Arab satellite TV broadcasters; state-run radio operates several networks; multiple international broadcasters are available (2007)

Internet country code: .sa

Internet users: *total:* 20,768,456
percent of population: 73.8% (July 2016 est.)
country comparison to the world: 35

TRANSPORTATION

National air transport system: number of registered air carriers: 12
inventory of registered aircraft operated by air carriers: 214
annual passenger traffic on registered air carriers: 32,778,827
annual freight traffic on registered air carriers: 1,783.086 million mt-km (2015)
Civil aircraft registration country code prefix: HZ (2016)

Airports: 214 (2013)
country comparison to the world: 26

Airports—with paved runways: *total:* 82
over 3,047 m: 33
2,438 to 3,047 m: 16
1,524 to 2,437 m: 27
914 to 1,523 m: 2
under 914 m: 4 (2017)

Airports—with unpaved runways: *total:* 132
2,438 to 3,047 m: 7
1,524 to 2,437 m: 72
914 to 1,523 m: 37
under 914 m: 16 (2013)

Heliports: 10 (2013)

Pipelines: condensate 209 km; gas 2,940 km; liquid petroleum gas 1,183 km; oil 5,117 km; refined products 1,151 km (2013)

Railways: *total:* 5,410 km
standard gauge: 5,410 km 1.435-m gauge (with branch lines and sidings) (2016)
country comparison to the world: 81

Roadways: *total:* 221,372 km
paved: 47,529 km (includes 3,891 km of expressways)

unpaved: 173,843 km (2006)
country comparison to the world: 23

Merchant marine: total: 357
by type: bulk carrier 5, container ship 1, general cargo 19, oil tanker 31, other 301 (2017)
country comparison to the world: 48

Ports and terminals: *major seaport(s):* Ad Dammam, Al Jubayl, Jeddah, Yanbu'
container port(s) (TEUs): Ad Dammam (1,954,000), Jeddah (5,417,000) (2015)

MILITARY AND SECURITY

Military expenditures: 9.85% of GDP (2016)
13.33% of GDP (2015)
10.68% of GDP (2014)
8.98% of GDP (2013)
7.68% of GDP (2012)
country comparison to the world: 4

Military branches: Ministry of Defense: Royal Saudi Land Forces, Royal Saudi Naval Forces (includes Marine Forces and Special Forces), Royal Saudi Air Force (Al-Quwwat al-Jawwiya al-Malakiya as-Sa'udiya), Royal Saudi Air Defense Forces, Royal Saudi Strategic Rocket Forces, Ministry of the National Guard (SANG) (2015)

Military service age and obligation: 17 is the legal minimum age for voluntary military service; no conscription (2012)

TERRORISM

Terrorist groups—foreign based: al-Qa'ida in the Arabian Peninsula (AQAP): aim(s): overthrow the Saudi Islamic monarchy and, ultimately, establish a regional Islamic caliphate; eradicate Western influence and presence from Saudi Arabia and the rest of the Arabian Peninsula
area(s) of operation: maintains a limited operational presence, targeting Saudi and Western interests; AQAP's senior bombmaker, Ibrahim Hassan Tali al-ASIRI, is among Saudi Arabia's most wanted for arrest
Islamic State of Iraq and the Levant (ISIL): aim(s): replace the Saudi Islamic monarchy with an Islamic state applying ISIL's strict interpretation of Sharia; target minority Shia Muslims, Saudi security personnel, and their interests

area(s) of operation: maintains a robust recruitment presence; conducts deadly strikes against Saudi security personnel and bombs Shia Muslim mosques, markets, and other places where Shia Muslims gather; suicide bombers conducted three bombings on 4 July 2016 in Jiddah, Medina, and al-Qatif, killing at least four Saudi security personnel and wounding several civilians; one bombing was close to Islam's second holiest site, the Prophet's Mosque in Medina where Muhammad is buried; ISIL's bombing and gunfire attacks in Saudi Arabia have killed dozens of people since 2014, primarily in Ash Sharquiyah Province, home to the majority of Shia Muslims living in Saudi Arabia; ISIL refers to Saudi Arabia as its Wilayat Haramayn; ISIL-Saudi Arabia was placed in the US State Department's designated global terror category under Executive Order 13224 on 19 May 2016

TRANSNATIONAL ISSUES

Disputes—international: Saudi Arabia has reinforced its concrete-filled security barrier along sections of the now fully demarcated border with Yemen to stem illegal cross-border activities; Kuwait and Saudi Arabia continue discussions on a maritime boundary with Iran; Saudi Arabia claims Egyptian-administered islands of Tiran and Sanafir

Refugees and internally displaced persons: refugees (country of origin): 30,000 (Yemen) (2017)
stateless persons: 70,000 (2016); note—thousands of biduns (stateless Arabs) are descendants of nomadic tribes who were not officially registered when national borders were established, while others migrated to Saudi Arabia in search of jobs; some have temporary identification cards that must be renewed every five years, but their rights remain restricted; most Palestinians have only legal resident status; some naturalized Yemenis were made stateless after being stripped of their passports when Yemen backed Iraq in its invasion of Kuwait in 1990; Saudi women cannot pass their citizenship on to their children, so if they marry a non-national, their children risk statelessness

Trafficking in persons: current situation: Saudi Arabia is a destination country for men and women subjected to forced labor and, to a lesser extent, forced prostitution; men and women from South and East Asia, the Middle East, and Africa who voluntarily travel to Saudi Arabia as domestic servants or low-skilled laborers subsequently face conditions of involuntary servitude, including nonpayment and withholding of passports; some migrant workers are forced to work indefinitely beyond the term of their contract because their employers will not grant them a required exit visa; female domestic workers are particularly vulnerable because of their isolation in private homes; women, primarily from Asian and African countries, are believed to be forced into prostitution in Saudi Arabia, while other foreign women were reportedly kidnapped and forced into prostitution after running away from abusive employers; children from South Asia, East Africa, and Yemen are subjected to forced labor as beggars and street vendors in Saudi Arabia, facilitated by criminal gangs

tier rating: Tier 2 Watch List—Saudi Arabia does not fully comply with the minimum standards for the elimination of trafficking; however, it is making significant efforts to do so; government officials and high-level religious leaders demonstrated greater political will to combat trafficking and publically acknowledged the problem—specifically forced labor; the government reported increased numbers of prosecutions and convictions of trafficking offenders; however, it did not proactively investigate and prosecute employers for potential labor trafficking crimes following their withholding of workers' wages and passports, which are illegal; authorities did not systematically use formal criteria to proactively identify victims, resulting in some unidentified victims being arrested, detained, deported, and sometimes prosecuted; more victims were identified and referred to protective services in 2014 than the previous year, but victims of sex trafficking and male trafficking victims were not provided with shelter and remained vulnerable to punishment (2015)

Illicit drugs: regularly enforces the death penalty for drug traffickers, with foreigners being convicted and executed disproportionately; improving anti-money-laundering legislation and enforcement

783

SENEGAL

INTRODUCTION

Background: The French colonies of Senegal and French Sudan were merged in 1959 and granted independence in 1960 as the Mali Federation. The union broke up after only a few months. Senegal joined with The Gambia to form the nominal confederation of Senegambia in 1982. The envisaged integration of the two countries was never implemented, and the union was dissolved in 1989. The Movement of Democratic Forces in the Casamance has led a low-level separatist insurgency in southern Senegal since the 1980s. Several peace deals have failed to resolve the conflict, but an unofficial cease-fire has remained largely in effect since 2012. Senegal remains one of the most stable democracies in Africa and has a long history of participating in international peacekeeping and regional mediation. Senegal was ruled by a Socialist Party for 40 years until Abdoulaye WADE was elected president in 2000. He was reelected in 2007 and during his two terms amended Senegal's constitution over a dozen times to increase executive power and weaken the opposition. His decision to run for a third presidential term sparked a large public backlash that led to his defeat in a March 2012 runoff with Macky SALL, whose term runs until 2019. A 2016 constitutional referendum reduced the term to five years with a maximum of two consecutive terms for future presidents.

GEOGRAPHY

Location: Western Africa, bordering the North Atlantic Ocean, between Guinea-Bissau and Mauritania

Geographic coordinates: 14 00 N, 14 00 W

Map references: Africa

Area: *total:* 196,722 sq km
land: 192,530 sq km
water: 4,192 sq km
country comparison to the world: 89

Area—comparative: slightly smaller than South Dakota
Land boundaries: total: 2,684 km
border countries (5): The Gambia 749 km, Guinea 363 km, Guinea-Bissau 341 km, Mali 489 km, Mauritania 742 km

Coastline: 531 km

Maritime claims: *territorial sea:* 12 nm
contiguous zone: 24 nm
exclusive economic zone: 200 nm
continental shelf: 200 nm or to the edge of the continental margin

Climate: tropical; hot, humid; rainy season (May to November) has strong southeast winds; dry season (December to April) dominated by hot, dry, harmattan wind

Terrain: generally low, rolling, plains rising to foothills in southeast

Elevation: *mean elevation:* 69 m

elevation extremes: *lowest point:* Atlantic Ocean 0 m
highest point: unnamed elevation 2.8 km southeast of Nepen Diaka 648 m

Natural resources: fish, phosphates, iron ore

Land use: *agricultural land:* 46.8%
arable land: 17.4%;
permanent crops: 0.3%;
permanent pasture: 29.1%
forest: 43.8%
other: 9.4% (2011 est.)
Irrigated land: 1,200 sq km (2012)

Population—distribution: the population is concentrated in the west, with Dakar anchoring a well-defined core area; approximately 70% of the population is rural

Natural hazards: lowlands seasonally flooded; periodic droughts

Environment—current issues: wildlife populations threatened by poaching; deforestation; overgrazing; soil erosion; desertification; overfishing

Environment—international agreements: *party to:* Biodiversity, Climate Change, Climate Change-Kyoto Protocol, Desertification, Endangered Species, Hazardous Wastes, Law of the Sea, Marine Life Conservation, Ozone Layer Protection, Ship Pollution, Wetlands, Whaling
signed, but not ratified: none of the selected agreements

Geography—note: westernmost country on the African continent; The Gambia is almost an enclave within Senegal

PEOPLE AND SOCIETY

Population: 14,668,522 (July 2017 est.)
country comparison to the world: 71

Nationality: *noun:* Senegalese (singular and plural)
adjective: Senegalese

Ethnic groups: Wolof 41.6%, Pular 28.1%, Serer 15.3%, Mandinka 5.4%, Jola 3.4%, Soninke 0.8%, other 5.4% (includes Europeans and persons of Lebanese descent) (2016 est.)

Languages: French (official), Wolof, Pular, Jola, Mandinka, Serer, Soninke

Religions: Muslim 96.1% (most adhere to one of the four main Sufi brotherhoods), Christian 3.6% (mostly Roman Catholic), animist 0.3% (2016 est.)

Demographic profile: Senegal has a large and growing youth population but has not been successful in developing its potential human capital. Senegal's high total fertility rate of almost 4.5 children per woman continues to bolster the country's large youth cohort—more than 60% of the population is under the age of 25. Fertility remains high because of the continued desire for large families, the low use of family planning, and early childbearing. Because of the country's high illiteracy rate (more than 40%), high unemployment (even among university graduates), and widespread poverty, Senegalese youths face dim prospects; women are especially disadvantaged.

Senegal historically was a destination country for economic migrants, but in recent years West African migrants more often use Senegal as a transit point to North Africa—and sometimes illegally onward to Europe. The country also has been host to several thousand black Mauritanian refugees since they were expelled from their homeland during its 1989 border conflict with Senegal. The country's economic crisis in the 1970s stimulated emigration; departures accelerated in the 1990s. Destinations shifted from neighboring countries, which were experiencing economic decline, civil wars, and increasing xenophobia, to Libya and Mauritania because of their booming oil industries and to developed countries (most notably former colonial ruler France, as well as Italy and Spain). The latter became attractive in the 1990s because of job opportunities and their periodic regularization programs (legalizing the status of illegal migrants).

Additionally, about 16,000 Senegalese refugees still remain in The Gambia and Guinea-Bissau as a result of more than 30 years of fighting between government forces and rebel separatists in southern Senegal's Casamance region.

Age structure: *0-14 years:* 41.51% (male 3,060,118/female 3,028,975)
15-24 years: 20.33% (male 1,486,393/female 1,496,393)
25-54 years: 31.19% (male 2,102,757/female 2,472,683)
55-64 years: 3.98% (male 251,673/female 332,113)
65 years and over: 2.98% (male 194,491/female 242,926) (2017 est.)

Dependency ratios: *total dependency ratio:* 85.4
youth dependency ratio: 79.8

elderly dependency ratio: 5.6
potential support ratio: 18 (2015 est.)

Median age: *total:* 18.8 years
male: 18 years
female: 19.7 years (2017 est.)
country comparison to the world: 206

Population growth rate: 2.39% (2017 est.)
country comparison to the world: 25

Birth rate: 33.4 births/1,000 population (2017 est.)
country comparison to the world: 28

Death rate: 8.1 deaths/1,000 population (2017 est.)
country comparison to the world: 90

Net migration rate: -1.5 migrant(s)/1,000 population (2017 est.)
country comparison to the world: 149

Population distribution: the population is concentrated in the west, with Dakar anchoring a well-defined core area; approximately 70% of the population is rural

Urbanization: *urban population:* 44.4% of total population (2017)
rate of urbanization: 3.53% annual rate of change (2015-20 est.)

Major urban areas—population: DAKAR (capital) 3.52 million (2015)

Sex ratio: *at birth:* 1.03 male(s)/female
0-14 years: 1.01 male(s)/female
15-24 years: 0.99 male(s)/female
25-54 years: 0.85 male(s)/female
55-64 years: 0.76 male(s)/female
65 years and over: 0.82 male(s)/female
total population: 0.94 male(s)/female (2016 est.)

Mother's mean age at first birth: 21.5 years
note: median age at first birth among women 25-29 (2016 est.)

Maternal mortality ratio: 315 deaths/100,000 live births (2015 est.)
country comparison to the world: 40

Infant mortality rate: *total:* 49.1 deaths/1,000 live births
male: 55 deaths/1,000 live births
female: 43.1 deaths/1,000 live births (2017 est.)
country comparison to the world: 32

Life expectancy at birth: *total population:* 62.1 years
male: 60 years
female: 64.3 years (2017 est.)
country comparison to the world: 199

Total fertility rate: 4.28 children born/woman (2017 est.)
country comparison to the world: 29

Contraceptive prevalence rate: 23.3% (2015)

Health expenditures: 4.7% of GDP (2014)
country comparison to the world: 150

Physicians density: 0.06 physicians/1,000 population (2008)

Hospital bed density: 0.3 beds/1,000 population (2008)

Drinking water source:
improved:
urban: 92.9% of population

rural: 67.3% of population
total: 78.5% of population
unimproved:
urban: 7.1% of population
rural: 32.7% of population
total: 21.5% of population (2015 est.)

Sanitation facility access:
improved:
urban: 65.4% of population
rural: 33.8% of population
total: 47.6% of population
unimproved:
urban: 34.6% of population
rural: 66.2% of population
total: 52.4% of population (2015 est.)

HIV/AIDS—adult prevalence rate: 0.4% (2016 est.)
country comparison to the world: 79

HIV/AIDS—people living with HIV/AIDS: 41,000 (2016 est.)
country comparison to the world: 61

HIV/AIDS—deaths: 1,900 (2016 est.)
country comparison to the world: 53

Major infectious diseases: *degree of risk:* very high
food or waterborne diseases: bacterial and protozoal diarrhea, hepatitis A, and typhoid fever
vectorborne diseases: malaria and dengue fever
water contact disease: schistosomiasis
respiratory disease: meningococcal meningitis
animal contact disease: rabies (2016)

Obesity—adult prevalence rate: 8.8% (2016)
country comparison to the world: 146

Children under the age of 5 years underweight: 15.5% (2015)
country comparison to the world: 40

Education expenditures: 7.2% of GDP (2014)
country comparison to the world: 53

Literacy: *definition:* age 15 and over can read and write
total population: 57.7%
male: 69.7%
female: 46.6% (2015 est.)

School life expectancy (primary to tertiary education): *total:* 9 years
male: 9 years
female: 9 years (2015)

Unemployment, youth ages 15-24: *total:* 12.7%
male: 8.3%
female: 19% (2011 est.)
country comparison to the world: 77

GOVERNMENT

Country name: *conventional long form:* Republic of Senegal
conventional short form: Senegal
local long form: Republique du Senegal
local short form: Senegal
former: Senegambia (along with The Gambia), Mali Federation
etymology: named for the Senegal River that forms the northern border of the country; many theories exist for the origin of the river name;

perhaps the most widely cited derives the name from "Azenegue," the Portuguese appellation for the Berber Zenaga people who lived north of the river

Government type: presidential republic

Capital: *name:* Dakar

geographic coordinates: 14 44 N, 17 38 W
time difference: UTC 0 (5 hours ahead of Washington, DC, during Standard Time)

Administrative divisions: 14 regions (regions, singular—region); Dakar, Diourbel, Fatick, Kaffrine, Kaolack, Kedougou, Kolda, Louga, Matam, Saint-Louis, Sedhiou, Tambacounda, Thies, Ziguinchor

Independence: 4 April 1960 (from France); note—complete independence achieved upon dissolution of federation with Mali on 20 August 1960

National holiday: Independence Day, 4 April (1960)

Constitution: *history:* previous 1959 (preindependence), 1963; latest adopted by referendum 7 January 2001, promulgated 22 January 2001
amendments: proposed by the president of the republic, by the prime minister through the president, or by the National Assembly; passage requires Assembly approval and approval in a referendum; the president can bypass a referendum and submit an amendment directly to the Assembly, which requires at least three-fifths majority vote; the republican form of government is not amendable; amended several times, last in 2016 (2017)

Legal system: civil law system based on French law; judicial review of legislative acts in Constitutional Court

International law organization participation: accepts compulsory ICJ jurisdiction with reservations; accepts ICCt jurisdiction

Citizenship: *citizenship by birth:* no
citizenship by descent only: at least one parent must be a citizen of Senegal
dual citizenship recognized: no, but Senegalese citizens do not automatically lose their citizenship if they acquire citizenship in another state
residency requirement for naturalization: 5 years

Suffrage: 18 years of age; universal

Executive branch: *chief of state:* President Macky SALL (since 2 April 2012)
head of government: Prime Minister Mohammed Abdallah Boun DIONNE (since 4 July 2014)
cabinet: Council of Ministers appointed by the prime minister in consultation with the president
elections/appointments: president directly elected by absolute majority popular vote in 2 rounds if needed for a 5-year term (eligible for a second consecutive term); election last held on 26 February 2012 with a runoff on 25 March 2012 (next to be held in 2019); prime minister appointed by the president
election results: Macky SALL elected president in second round; percent of vote—Macky SALL (APR) 65.8%, Abdoulaye WADE (PDS) 34.2%

Legislative branch: *description:* unicameral National Assembly or Assemblee Nationale (165 seats; 105 members including 15 representing Senegalese diaspora directly elected by plurality vote in single- and multi-seat constituencies and 60 members directly elected by proportional representation vote in single- and multi-seat constituencies)
elections: National Assembly—last held on 2 July 2017 (next to be held in July 2022)
election results: National Assembly results—percent of vote by party/coalition—BBK 49.5%, CGWS 16.7%, MTS 11.7%, PUR 4.7%, CP-Kaddu Askan Wi 2%, other 15.4%; seats by party/coalition—BBY 125, CGWS 19, MTS 7, PUR 3, CP-Kaddu Askan Wi 2, other 9

Judicial branch: *highest court(s):* Supreme Court or Cour Supreme (consists of the president and 12 judges and organized into civil and commercial, criminal, administrative, and social chambers); Constitutional Council or Conseil Constitutionel (consists of 7 members including the court president, vice president, and 5 judges)
judge selection and term of office: Supreme Court judges' appointed by the president of the republic upon recommendation of the Higher Council of the Judiciary, a body chaired by the president; judge tenure NA; Constitutional Council members appointed—5 by the president and 2 by the National Assembly speaker to serve 6-year terms with the renewal of 2 members every 2 years
subordinate courts: High Court of Justice (for crimes of high treason by the president); Courts of Appeal; Court of Auditors; assize courts; regional and district courts; Labor Court; note—in early 2013, the Extraordinary African Chambers were established by agreement of the African Union and the Government of Senegal to try cases of high-level officials involved in crimes committed in Chad during the period 1982-1990

Political parties and leaders: Alliance for the Republic-Yakaar or APR-Yakaar [Macky SALL]
Alliance of Forces of Progress or AFP [Moustapha NIASSE]
And-Jef/African Party for Democracy and Socialism or AJ/PADS [Mamadou DIOP Decriox]
And-Jef/African Party for Democracy and Socialism or AJ/PADS-A [Landing SAVANE]
Benno Bokk Yakaar or BBY (United in Hope) [Macky SALL] (coalition includes AFP, APR, LD-MPT, PIT, PS, UNP)
Bokk Gis Gis coalition [Pape DIOP]
Citizen Movement for National Reform or MCRN-Bes Du Nakk [Mansour Sy DJAMIL]
Democratic League-Labor Party Movement or LD-MPT [Mamadou NDOYE]
Front for Socialism and Democracy/Benno Jubel or FSD/BJ [Cheikh Abdoulaye Bamba DIEYE]
Gainde Centrist Bloc or BGC [Jean-Paul DIAS]
Grand Party or GP [Malick GAKOU]
Independence and Labor Party or PIT [Magatte THIAM]
Manko Taxawu Senegaal or MTS [Khalifa SALL] (coalition includes BGC, Du Nakk, FSD/BJ, GP, MCRN/Bes, Rewmi)

National Union for the People or UNP [Souleymane Ndene NDIAYE]
Party for Truth and Development or PVD [Cheikh Ahmadou Kara MBAKE]
Party of Unity and Rally or PUR [El Hadji SALL]
Patriotic Convergence Kaddu Askan Wi or CP-Kaddu Askan Wi [Abdoulaye BALDE]
Reform Party or PR [Abdourahim AGNE]
Rewmi Party [Idrissa SECK]
Senegalese Democratic Party or PDS [Abdoulaye WADE]
Socialist Party or PS [Ousmane Tanor DIENG]
Tekki Movement [Mamadou Lamine DIALLO]
Union for Democratic Renewal or URD [Djibo Leyti KA]
Winning Coalition Wattu Senegal or CGWS [Abdoulaye WADE] (includes AJ/PADS, AJ/PADS-A, Bokk Gis Gis, PDS, Tekki Movement)

Political pressure groups and leaders: Catholic clergy; labor; religious groups; students; Sufi brotherhoods, including the Mourides and Tidjanes; teachers

International organization participation: ACP, AfDB, AU, CD, CPLP (associate), ECOWAS, EITI (candidate country), FAO, FZ, G-15, G-77, IAEA, IBRD, ICAO, ICC (national committees), ICCt, ICRM, IDA, IDB, IFAD, IFC, IFRCS, ILO, IMF, IMO, IMSO, Interpol, IOC, IOM, IPU, ISO, ITSO, ITU, ITUC (NGOs), MIGA, MINUSMA, MONUSCO, NAM, OIC, OIF, OPCW, PCA, UN, UN Security Council (temporary), UNA-MID, UNCTAD, UNESCO, UNHCR, UNIDO, UNMIL, UNMISS, UNOCI, UNWTO, UPU, WADB (regional), WAEMU, WCO, WFTU (NGOs), WHO, WIPO, WMO, WTO

Diplomatic representation in the US: chief of mission: Ambassador Babacar DIAGNE (since 18 November 2014)
chancery: 2215 M Street, NW, Washington, DC 20007
telephone: [1] (202) 234-0540
FAX: [1] (202) 629-2961
consulate(s) general: Houston, New York

Diplomatic representation from the US: *chief of mission:* ambassador Tulinabo S. MUSHINGI (since August 2017); note—also accredited to Guinea-Bissau
embassy: Route des Almadies, Dakar
mailing address: B.P. 49, Dakar
telephone: [221] 33-879-4000
FAX: [221] 33-822-2991

Flag description: three equal vertical bands of green (hoist side), yellow, and red with a small green five-pointed star centered in the yellow band; green represents Islam, progress, and hope; yellow signifies natural wealth and progress; red symbolizes sacrifice and determination; the star denotes unity and hope
note: uses the popular Pan-African colors of Ethiopia; the colors from left to right are the same as those of neighboring Mali and the reverse of those on the flag of neighboring Guinea

National symbol(s): lion; national colors: green, yellow, red

National anthem: *name:* "Pincez Tous vos Koras, Frappez les Balafons" (Pluck Your Koras, Strike the Balafons)
lyrics/music: Leopold Sedar SENGHOR/Herbert PEPPER
note: adopted 1960; lyrics written by Leopold Sedar SENGHOR, Senegal's first president; the anthem sometimes played incorporating the Koras (harp-like stringed instruments) and Balafons (types of xylophones) mentioned in the title

ECONOMY

Economy—overview: Senegal's economy is driven by mining, construction, tourism, fisheries and agriculture, which are the primary sources of employment in rural areas. The country's key export industries include phosphate mining, fertilizer production, agricultural products and commercial fishing and it is also working on oil exploration projects. Senegal relies heavily on donor assistance, remittances and foreign direct investment. Senegal reached a growth rate of 6.5% in 2015 and surpassed that in 2016-17, due in part to a buoyant performance in agriculture because of higher rainfall and productivity in the sector.

President Macky SALL, who was elected in March 2012 under a reformist policy agenda, inherited an economy with high energy costs, a challenging business environment, and a culture of overspending. President SALL unveiled an ambitious economic plan, the Emerging Senegal Plan (ESP), which aims to implement priority economic reforms and investment projects to increase economic growth while preserving macroeconomic stability and debt sustainability. Bureaucratic bottlenecks and a challenging business climate are among the perennial challenges that may slow the implementation of this plan.

Senegal is receiving technical support from the IMF during 2015-17 under a Policy Support Instrument (PSI) to assist with implementation of the ESP. The PSI implementation continues to be satisfactory as concluded by the IMF's second review mission in March 2016. Investors have signaled confidence in the country through Senegal's successful Eurobond issuances in recent years, including in 2014.

The government is focusing on 19 projects under the ESP to continue the structural transformation of the economy. These 19 projects include the Thies-Touba Highway, including the new airport- Mbour-Thies Highway. Senegal increased the national family allowances program and the community development emergency program in 2016. Electricity supply is a chief constraint for Senegal's development. Electricity prices in Senegal are among the highest in the world. Power Africa, a program led by USAID and OPIC, plans to increase the current 500 MW of generating capacity to over 1,000 mW in the next three to five years. Recent gas discoveries on the Senegal-Mauritanian border, as well as just south of Dakar, will help alleviate some of the energy shortages.

GDP (purchasing power parity): $43.07 billion (2017 est.)

$40.33 billion (2016 est.)
$37.78 billion (2015 est.)
note: data are in 2017 dollars
country comparison to the world: 114

GDP (official exchange rate): $16.06 billion (2016 est.)

GDP—real growth rate: 6.8% (2017 est.)
6.7% (2016 est.)
6.5% (2015 est.)
country comparison to the world: 12

GDP—per capita (PPP): $2,700 (2017 est.)
$2,600 (2016 est.)
$2,500 (2015 est.)
note: data are in 2017 dollars
country comparison to the world: 197

Gross national saving: 22% of GDP (2017 est.)
21.5% of GDP (2016 est.)
17.7% of GDP (2015 est.)
country comparison to the world: 76

GDP—composition, by end use: household consumption: 76.5%
government consumption: 16.1%
investment in fixed capital: 26.2%
investment in inventories: -2%
exports of goods and services: 28.9%
imports of goods and services: -45.7% (2017 est.)

GDP—composition, by sector of origin: agriculture: 16.9%
industry: 24.3%
services: 58.8% (2017 est.)

Agriculture—products: peanuts, millet, corn, sorghum, rice, cotton, tomatoes, green vegetables; cattle, poultry, pigs; fish

Industries: agricultural and fish processing, phosphate mining, fertilizer production, petroleum refining, zircon, and gold mining, construction materials, ship construction and repair

Industrial production growth rate: 8.4% (2017 est.)
country comparison to the world: 14

Labor force: 6.966 million (2017 est.)
country comparison to the world: 68

Labor force—by occupation: agriculture: 77.5%
industry and services: 22.5% (2007 est.)

Unemployment rate: 48% (2007 est.)
country comparison to the world: 213

Population below poverty line: 46.7% (2011 est.)

Household income or consumption by percentage share: lowest 10%: 2.5%
highest 10%: 31.1% (2011)

Distribution of family income—Gini index: 40.3 (2011)
country comparison to the world: 59

Budget: revenues: $3.863 billion
expenditures: $4.474 billion (2017 est.)
Taxes and other revenues: 24.1% of GDP (2017 est.)
country comparison to the world: 122

Budget surplus (+) or deficit (-): -3.8% of GDP (2017 est.)
country comparison to the world: 140

Public debt: 61.3% of GDP (2017 est.)
58.6% of GDP (2016 est.)

country comparison to the world: 70

Fiscal year: calendar year

Inflation rate (consumer prices): 2.1% (2017 est.)
0.9% (2016 est.)
country comparison to the world: 98

Central bank discount rate: 0.25% (31 December 2010)
4.25% (31 December 2009)
country comparison to the world: 141

Commercial bank prime lending rate: 16.3% (31 December 2017 est.)
16.4% (31 December 2016 est.)
country comparison to the world: 32

Stock of narrow money: $5.305 billion (31 December 2017 est.)
$4.736 billion (31 December 2016 est.)
country comparison to the world: 103

Stock of broad money: $8.035 billion (31 December 2017 est.)
$7.244 billion (31 December 2016 est.)
country comparison to the world: 113

Stock of domestic credit: $5.55 billion (31 December 2017 est.)
$5.15 billion (31 December 2016 est.)
country comparison to the world: 126

Market value of publicly traded shares: $NA

Current account balance: -$817 million (2017 est.)
-$783 million (2016 est.)
country comparison to the world: 124

Exports: $2.546 billion (2017 est.)
$2.498 billion (2016 est.)
country comparison to the world: 133

Exports—commodities: fish, groundnuts (peanuts), petroleum products, phosphates, cotton

Exports—partners: Mali 18.2%, Switzerland 10.6%, India 8.2%, Cote dIvoire 5.3%, China 5% (2016)

Imports: $5.227 billion (2017 est.)
$4.993 billion (2016 est.)
country comparison to the world: 121

Imports—commodities: food and beverages, capital goods, fuels

Imports—partners: France 15.9%, China 10.3%, Nigeria 7.8%, India 7.6%, Netherlands 5.3%, Spain 4.9% (2016)

Reserves of foreign exchange and gold: $151.8 million (31 December 2017 est.)
$116.9 million (31 December 2016 est.)
country comparison to the world: 162

Debt—external: $6.745 billion (31 December 2017 est.)
$6.327 billion (31 December 2016 est.)
country comparison to the world: 127

Exchange rates: Communaute Financiere Africaine francs (XOF) per US dollar—
617.4 (2017 est.)
593.01 (2016 est.)
593.01 (2015 est.)
591.45 (2014 est.)
494.42 (2013 est.)

ENERGY

Electricity access: population without electricity: 6,400,000
electrification—total population: 55%
electrification—urban areas: 90%
electrification—rural areas: 28% (2013)

Electricity—production: 3.673 billion kWh (2015 est.)
country comparison to the world: 127

Electricity—consumption: 3.014 billion kWh (2015 est.)
country comparison to the world: 135

Electricity—exports: 0 kWh (2016 est.)
country comparison to the world: 194

Electricity—imports: 0 kWh (2016 est.)
country comparison to the world: 198

Electricity—installed generating capacity: 965,000 kW (2015 est.)
country comparison to the world: 129

Electricity—from fossil fuels: 88.5% of total installed capacity (2015 est.)
country comparison to the world: 64

Electricity—from nuclear fuels: 0% of total installed capacity (2015 est.)
country comparison to the world: 179

Electricity—from hydroelectric plants: 7.8% of total installed capacity (2015 est.)
country comparison to the world: 123

Electricity—from other renewable sources: 8.2% of total installed capacity (2015 est.)
country comparison to the world: 77

Crude oil—production: 0 bbl/day (2016 est.)
country comparison to the world: 195

Crude oil—exports: 0 bbl/day (2014 est.)
country comparison to the world: 187

Crude oil—imports: 18,060 bbl/day (2014 est.)
country comparison to the world: 65

Crude oil—proved reserves: 0 bbl (1 January 2017 es)
country comparison to the world: 193

Refined petroleum products—production: 16,850 bbl/day (2014 est.)
country comparison to the world: 92

Refined petroleum products—consumption: 44,000 bbl/day (2015 est.)
country comparison to the world: 109

Refined petroleum products—exports: 3,892 bbl/day (2014 est.)
country comparison to the world: 101

Refined petroleum products—imports: 30,120 bbl/day (2014 est.)
country comparison to the world: 102

Natural gas—production: 62 million cu m (2015 est.)
country comparison to the world: 86

Natural gas—consumption: 497 million cu m (2015 est.)
country comparison to the world: 107

Natural gas—exports: 0 cu m (2013 est.)
country comparison to the world: 179

Natural gas—imports: 0 cu m (2013 est.)
country comparison to the world: 185

Natural gas—proved reserves: 9.911 billion cu m (1 January 2012 es)
country comparison to the world: 83

Carbon dioxide emissions from consumption of energy: 7.3 million Mt (2013 est.)
country comparison to the world: 117

COMMUNICATIONS

Telephones—fixed lines: *total subscriptions:* 285,933
subscriptions per 100 inhabitants: 2 (July 2016 est.)
country comparison to the world: 115

Telephones—mobile cellular: *total:* 15,186,485
subscriptions per 100 inhabitants: 106 (July 2016 est.)
country comparison to the world: 67

Telephone system: *general assessment:* good system with microwave radio relay, coaxial cable and fiber-optic cable in trunk system
domestic: generally reliable urban system with a fiber-optic network; about two-thirds of all fixed-line connections are in Dakar; mobile-cellular service is steadily displacing fixed-line service, even in urban areas
international: country code—221; the ACE fiber-optic cable connects Senegal to Europe, the SAT-3/WASC provides fiber-optic connectivity to Europe and Asia, and Atlantis-2 provides connectivity to South America; satellite earth station—1 Intelsat (Atlantic Ocean) (2017)

Broadcast media: state-run Radiodiffusion Television Senegalaise (RTS) broadcasts TV programs from five cities in Senegal; in most regions of the country, viewers can receive TV programming from at least 7 private broadcasters; a wide range of independent TV programming is available via satellite; RTS operates a national radio network and a number of regional FM stations; at least 7 community radio stations and 18 private-broadcast radio stations are available; transmissions of at least 5 international broadcasters are accessible on FM in Dakar (2017)

Internet country code: .sn

Internet users: *total:* 3,675,209
percent of population: 25.7% (July 2016 est.)
country comparison to the world: 84

TRANSPORTATION

National air transport system: number of registered air carriers: inventory of registered aircraft operated by air carriers: annual passenger traffic on registered air carriers: 115,355
annual freight traffic on registered air carriers: 3,095,523 mt-km (2015)
Civil aircraft registration country code prefix: 6V (2016)

Airports: 20 (2013)
country comparison to the world: 136

Airports—with paved runways: *total:* 9
over 3,047 m: 2
1,524 to 2,437 m: 6
914 to 1,523 m: 1 (2017)

Airports—with unpaved runways: *total:* 11
1,524 to 2,437 m: 7
914 to 1,523 m: 3
under 914 m: 1 (2013)

Pipelines: gas 43 km; refined products 8 km (2017)

Railways: *total:* 906 km (713 km operational in 2017)
narrow gauge: 906 km 1.000-m gauge (2017)
country comparison to the world: 93

Roadways: *total:* 16,496 km
paved: 5,957 km (includes 72 km of expressways)
unpaved: 10,539 km (2017)
country comparison to the world: 124

Waterways: 1,000 km (primarily on the Senegal, Saloum, and Casamance Rivers) (2012)
country comparison to the world: 64

Merchant marine: *total:* 26
by type: general cargo 3, oil tanker 1, other 22 (2017)
country comparison to the world: 129

Ports and terminals: *major seaport(s):* Dakar

MILITARY AND SECURITY

Military expenditures: 1.89% of GDP (2017 est.)
1.73% of GDP (2016)
1.58% of GDP (2015)
1.57% of GDP (2014)
1.6% of GDP (2013)

Military branches: Senegalese Armed Forces: Army, Senegalese National Navy (Marine Senegalaise, MNS), Senegalese Air Force (Armee de l'Air du Senegal) (2017)

Military service age and obligation: 18 years of age for voluntary military service; 20 years of age for selective conscript service; 2-year service obligation; women have been accepted into military service since 2008 (2013)

TRANSNATIONAL ISSUES

Disputes—international: cross-border trafficking in persons, timber, wildlife, and cannabis; rebels from the Movement of Democratic Forces in the Casamance find refuge in Guinea-Bissau

Refugees and internally displaced persons: refugees (country of origin): 13,683 (Mauritania) (2017)
IDPs: 24,000 (clashes between government troops and separatists in Casamance region) (2016)

Illicit drugs: transshipment point for Southwest and Southeast Asian heroin and South American cocaine moving to Europe and North America; illicit cultivator of cannabis

SERBIA

INTRODUCTION

Background: The Kingdom of Serbs, Croats, and Slovenes was formed in 1918; its name was changed to Yugoslavia in 1929. Communist Partisans resisted the Axis occupation and division of Yugoslavia from 1941 to 1945 and fought nationalist opponents and collaborators as well. The military and political movement headed by Josip Broz "TITO" (Partisans) took full control of Yugoslavia when their domestic rivals and the occupiers were defeated in 1945. Although communists, TITO and his successors (Tito died in 1980) managed to steer their own path between the Warsaw Pact nations and the West for the next four and a half decades. In 1989, Slobodan MILOSEVIC became president of the Republic of Serbia and his ultra-nationalist calls for Serbian domination led to the violent breakup of Yugoslavia along ethnic lines. In 1991, Croatia, Slovenia, and Macedonia declared independence, followed by Bosnia in 1992. The remaining republics of Serbia and Montenegro declared a new Federal Republic of Yugoslavia (FRY) in April 1992 and under MILOSEVIC's leadership, Serbia led various military campaigns to unite ethnic Serbs in neighboring republics into a "Greater Serbia." These actions ultimately failed and, after international intervention, led to the signing of the Dayton Peace Accords in 1995.

MILOSEVIC retained control over Serbia and eventually became president of the FRY in 1997. In 1998, an ethnic Albanian insurgency in the formerly autonomous Serbian province of Kosovo provoked a Serbian counterinsurgency campaign that resulted in massacres and massive expulsions of ethnic Albanians living in Kosovo. The

MILOSEVIC government's rejection of a proposed international settlement led to NATO's bombing of Serbia in the spring of 1999. Serbian military and police forces withdrew from Kosovo in June 1999, and the UN Security Council authorized an interim UN administration and a NATO-led security force in Kosovo. FRY elections in late 2000 led to the ouster of MILOSEVIC and the installation of democratic government. In 2003, the FRY became the State Union of Serbia and Montenegro, a loose federation of the two republics. Widespread violence predominantly targeting ethnic Serbs in Kosovo in March 2004 led to more intense calls to address Kosovo's status, and the UN began facilitating status talks in 2006. In June 2006, Montenegro seceded from the federation and declared itself an independent nation. Serbia subsequently gave notice that it was the successor state to the union of Serbia and Montenegro.

In February 2008, after nearly two years of inconclusive negotiations, Kosovo declared itself independent of Serbia—an action Serbia refuses to recognize. At Serbia's request, the UN General Assembly (UNGA) in October 2008 sought an advisory opinion from the International Court of Justice (ICJ) on whether Kosovo's unilateral declaration of independence was in accordance with international law. In a ruling considered unfavorable to Serbia, the ICJ issued an advisory opinion in July 2010 stating that international law did not prohibit declarations of independence. In late 2010, Serbia agreed to an EU-drafted UNGA Resolution acknowledging the ICJ's decision and calling for a new round of talks between Serbia and Kosovo, this time on practical issues rather than Kosovo's status. Serbia and Kosovo signed the first agreement of principles governing the normalization of relations between the two countries in April 2013 and are in the process of implementing its provisions. In 2015, Serbia and Kosovo reached four additional agreements within the Brussels Dialogue framework. These included agreements on the Community of Serb-Majority Municipalities; telecommunications; energy production and distribution; and freedom of movement. President Aleksandar VUCIC has promoted an ambitious goal of Serbia joining the EU by 2020. Under his leadership as prime minister, in January 2014 Serbia opened formal negotiations for accession.

GEOGRAPHY

Location: Southeastern Europe, between Macedonia and Hungary

Geographic coordinates: 44 00 N, 21 00 E

Map references: Europe

Area: *total:* 77,474 sq km
land: 77,474 sq km
water: 0 sq km
country comparison to the world: 118

Area—comparative: slightly smaller than South Carolina
Land boundaries: total: 2,322 km
border countries (8): Bosnia and Herzegovina 345 km, Bulgaria 344 km, Croatia 314 km, Hungary 164 km, Kosovo 366 km, Macedonia 101 km, Montenegro 157 km, Romania 531 km

Coastline: 0 km (landlocked)

Maritime claims: none (landlocked)

Climate: in the north, continental climate (cold winters and hot, humid summers with well-distributed rainfall); in other parts, continental and Mediterranean climate (relatively cold winters with heavy snowfall and hot, dry summers and autumns)

Terrain: extremely varied; to the north, rich fertile plains; to the east, limestone ranges and basins; to the southeast, ancient mountains and hills

Elevation: *mean elevation:* 442 m

elevation extremes: *lowest point:* Danube and Timok Rivers 35 m
highest point: Midzor 2,169 m

Natural resources: oil, gas, coal, iron ore, copper, zinc, antimony, chromite, gold, silver, magnesium, pyrite, limestone, marble, salt, arable land

Land use: *agricultural land:* 57.9%
arable land: 37.7%;
permanent crops: 3.4%;
permanent pasture: 16.8%
forest: 31.6%
other: 10.5% (2011 est.)
Irrigated land: 950 sq km (2012)

Population—distribution: a fairly even distribution throughout most of the country, with urban areas attracting larger and denser populations

Natural hazards: destructive earthquakes

Environment—current issues: air pollution around Belgrade and other industrial cities; water pollution from industrial wastes dumped into the Sava which flows into the Danube

Environment—international agreements: *party to:* Air Pollution, Biodiversity, Climate Change, Climate Change-Kyoto Protocol, Desertification, Endangered Species, Hazardous Wastes, Law of the Sea, Marine Dumping, Marine Life Conservation, Ozone Layer Protection, Ship Pollution, Wetlands
signed, but not ratified: none of the selected agreements

Geography—note: landlocked; controls one of the major land routes from Western Europe to Turkey and the Near East

PEOPLE AND SOCIETY

Population: 7,111,024
note: does not include the population of Kosovo (July 2017 est.)
country comparison to the world: 102

Nationality: *noun:* Serb(s)
adjective: Serbian

Ethnic groups: Serb 83.3%, Hungarian 3.5%, Romani 2.1%, Bosniak 2%, other 5.7%, undeclared or unknown 3.4% (2011 est.)
note: Romani populations are usually underestimated in official statistics and may represent 5–11% of Serbia's population

Languages: Serbian (official) 88.1%, Hungarian 3.4%, Bosnian 1.9%, Romani 1.4%, other 3.4%, undeclared or unknown 1.8%
note: Serbian, Hungarian, Slovak, Romanian, Croatian, and Ruthenian (Rusyn) are official in the Autonomous Province of Vojvodina (2011 est.)

Religions: Orthodox 84.6%, Catholic 5%, Muslim 3.1%, Protestant 1%, atheist 1.1%, other 0.8% (includes agnostics, other Christians, Eastern religionists, Jewish), undeclared or unknown 4.5% (2011 est.)

Age structure: *0-14 years:* 14.5% (male 531,524/ female 499,715)
15-24 years: 11.26% (male 413,046/female 387,697)
25-54 years: 41.32% (male 1,483,392/female 1,454,931)
55-64 years: 14.49% (male 496,944/female 533,329)
65 years and over: 18.43% (male 541,569/female 768,877) (2017 est.)

Dependency ratios: *total dependency ratio:* 49.2
youth dependency ratio: 24.9
elderly dependency ratio: 24.3
potential support ratio: 4.1
note: data include Kosovo (2015 est.)

Median age: *total:* 42.6 years
male: 40.9 years
female: 44.3 years (2017 est.)
country comparison to the world: 26

Population growth rate: -0.46% (2017 est.)
country comparison to the world: 221

Birth rate: 9 births/1,000 population (2017 est.)
country comparison to the world: 206

Death rate: 13.6 deaths/1,000 population (2017 est.)
country comparison to the world: 8

Net migration rate: 0 migrant(s)/1,000 population (2017 est.)
country comparison to the world: 96

Population distribution: a fairly even distribution throughout most of the country, with urban areas attracting larger and denser populations

Urbanization: *urban population:* 55.8% of total population (2017)
rate of urbanization: -0.29% annual rate of change (2015-20 est.)
note: data include Kosovo

Major urban areas—population: BELGRADE (capital) 1.182 million (2015)

Sex ratio: *at birth:* 1.07 male(s)/female
0-14 years: 1.06 male(s)/female
15-24 years: 1.06 male(s)/female
25-54 years: 1.02 male(s)/female
55-64 years: 0.93 male(s)/female
65 years and over: 0.7 male(s)/female
total population: 0.95 male(s)/female (2016 est.)

Mother's mean age at first birth: 27.9 years
note: data do not cover Kosovo or Metohija (2014 est.)

Maternal mortality ratio: 17 deaths/100,000 live births (2015 est.)

country comparison to the world: 132

Infant mortality rate: *total:* 5.8 deaths/1,000 live births

male: 6.7 deaths/1,000 live births

female: 4.9 deaths/1,000 live births (2017 est.)

country comparison to the world: 171

Life expectancy at birth: *total population:* 75.7 years

male: 72.8 years

female: 78.8 years (2017 est.)

country comparison to the world: 100

Total fertility rate: 1.44 children born/woman (2017 est.)

country comparison to the world: 207

Contraceptive prevalence rate: 58.4% (2014)

Health expenditures: 10.4% of GDP (2014)

country comparison to the world: 21

Physicians density: 2.46 physicians/1,000 population (2014)

Hospital bed density: 5.4 beds/1,000 population (2009)

Drinking water source:

improved:

urban: 99.4% of population

rural: 98.9% of population

total: 99.2% of population

unimproved:

urban: 0.6% of population

rural: 1.1% of population

total: 0.8% of population (2015 est.)

Sanitation facility access:

improved:

urban: 98.2% of population

rural: 94.2% of population

total: 96.4% of population

unimproved:

urban: 1.8% of population

rural: 5.8% of population

total: 3.6% of population (2015 est.)

HIV/AIDS—adult prevalence rate: <.1% (2016 est.)

HIV/AIDS—people living with HIV/AIDS: 2,700 (2016 est.)

country comparison to the world: 115

HIV/AIDS—deaths: <100 (2016 est.)

Major infectious diseases: *degree of risk:* intermediate

food or waterborne diseases: bacterial diarrhea (2016)

Obesity—adult prevalence rate: 21.5% (2016)

country comparison to the world: 88

Children under the age of 5 years underweight: 1.8% (2014)

country comparison to the world: 125

Education expenditures: 4.2% of GDP (2014)

country comparison to the world: 82

Literacy: *definition:* age 15 and over can read and write

total population: 98.8%

male: 99.5%

female: 98.2% (2016 est.)

School life expectancy (primary to tertiary education): *total:* 15 years

male: 14 years

female: 15 years (2015)

Unemployment, youth ages 15-24: *total:* 43.2%

male: 40.1%

female: 48.2% (2015 est.)

country comparison to the world: 7

GOVERNMENT

Country name: *conventional long form:* Republic of Serbia

conventional short form: Serbia

local long form: Republika Srbija

local short form: Srbija

former: People's Republic of Serbia, Socialist Republic of Serbia

etymology: the origin of the name in uncertain, but seems to be related to the name of the West Slavic Sorbs who reside in the Lusatian region in present-day eastern Germany; by tradition, the Serbs migrated from that region to the Balkans in about the 6th century A.D.

Government type: parliamentary republic

Capital: *name:* Belgrade (Beograd)

geographic coordinates: 44 50 N, 20 30 E

time difference: UTC+1 (6 hours ahead of Washington, DC, during Standard Time)

daylight saving time: +1hr, begins last Sunday in March; ends last Sunday in October

Administrative divisions: 119 municipalities (opstine, singular—opstina) and 26 cities (gradovi, singular—grad)

municipalities: Ada*, Aleksandrovac, Aleksinac, Alibunar*, Apatin*, Arandelovac, Arilje, Babusnica, Bac*, Backa Palanka*, Backa Topola*, Backi Petrovac*, Bajina Basta, Batocina, Becej*, Bela Crkva*, Bela Palanka, Beocin*, Blace, Bogatic, Bojnik, Boljevac, Bor, Bosilegrad, Brus, Bujanovac, Cajetina, Cicevac, Coka*, Crna Trava, Cuprija, Despotovac, Dimitrov, Doljevac, Gadzin Han, Golubac, Gornji Milanovac, Indija*, Irig*, Ivanjica, Kanjiza*, Kladovo, Knic, Knjazevac, Koceljeva, Kosjeric, Kovacica*, Kovin*, Krupanj, Kucevo, Kula*, Kursumlija, Lajkovac, Lapovo, Lebane, Ljig, Ljubovija, Lucani, Majdanpek, Mali Idos*, Mali Zvornik, Malo Crnice, Medveda, Merosina, Mionica, Negotin, Nova Crnja*, Nova Varos, Novi Becej*, Novi Knezevac*, Odzaci*, Opovo*, Osecina, Paracin, Pecinci*, Petrovac na Mlavi, Plandiste*, Pozega, Presevo, Priboj, Prijepolje, Prokuplje, Raca, Raska, Razanj, Rekovac, Ruma*, Secanj*, Senta*, Sid*, Sjenica, Smederevska Palanka, Sokobanja, Srbobran*, Sremski Karlovci*, Stara Pazova*, Surdulica, Svilajnac, Svrljig, Temerin*, Titel*, Topola, Trgoviste, Trstenik, Tutin, Ub, Varvarin, Velika Plana, Veliko Gradiste, Vladicin Han, Vladimirci, Vlasotince, Vrbas*, Vrnjacka Banja, Zabalj*, Zabari, Zagubica, Zitiste*, Zitorada

cities: Beograd, Cacak, Jagodina, Kikinda*, Kragujevac, Kraljevo, Krusevac, Leskovac, Loznica, Nis, Novi Pazar, Novi Sad*, Pancevo*, Pirot, Pozarevac, Sabac, Smederevo, Sombor*, Sremska

Mitrovica*, Subotica*, Uzice, Valjevo, Vranje, Vrsac, Zajecar, Zrenjanin*

note: the northern 39 municipalities and 6 cities—about 28% of Serbia's area—compose the Autonomous Province of Vojvodina and are indicated with *

Independence: 5 June 2006 (from the State Union of Serbia and Montenegro)

National holiday: National Day (Statehood Day), 15 February (1835), the day the first constitution of the country was adopted

Constitution: *history:* many previous; latest adopted 30 September 2006, approved by referendum 28-29 October 2006, effective 8 November 2006

amendments: proposed by at least one-third of deputies in the National Assembly, by the president of the republic, by the government, or by petition of at least 150,000 voters; passage of proposals and draft amendments each requires at least two-thirds majority vote in the Assembly; amendments to constitutional articles including the preamble, constitutional principles, and human and minority rights and freedoms also require a referendum with passage by simple majority vote (2016)

Legal system: civil law system

International law organization participation: has not submitted an ICJ jurisdiction declaration; accepts ICCt jurisdiction

Citizenship: *citizenship by birth:* no

citizenship by descent only: at least one parent must be a citizen of Serbia

dual citizenship recognized: yes

residency requirement for naturalization: 3 years

Suffrage: 18 years of age, 16 if employed; universal

Executive branch: *chief of state:* President Aleksandar VUCIC (since 31 May 2017)

head of government: Prime Minister Ana BRNABIC (since 29 June 2017)

cabinet: Cabinet elected by the National Assembly

elections/appointments: president directly elected by absolute majority popular vote in 2 rounds if needed for a 5-year term (eligible for a second term); election last held on 2 April 2017 (next to be held in 2022); prime minister elected by the National Assembly

election results: Aleksandar VUCIC elected president; percent of vote—Aleksandar VUCIC (SNS) 55.1%, Sasa JANKOVIC (independent) 16.4%, Luka MAKSIMOVIC (independent) 9.4%, Vuk JEREMIC (independent) 5.7%, Vojislav SESELJ (SRS) 4.5%, Bosko OBRADOVIC (Dveri) 2.3%, other 5.0%, invalid/blank 1.6%

Legislative branch: *description:* unicameral National Assembly or Narodna Skupstina (250 seats; members directly elected by party list proportional representation vote in a single nationwide constituency to serve 4-year terms)

elections: last held on 24 April 2016 (next to be held by April 2020)

election results: percent of vote by party/coalition—Serbia is Winning 48.3%, SPS-JS-ZS-KP

11.0%, SRS 8.1%, For a Just Serbia 6.0%, Enough is Enough 6.0%, Alliance for a Better Serbia 5.0%, Dveri-DSS 5.0%, SVM 1.5%, other 9.1%; seats by party/coalition Serbia is Winning 131, SPS-JS-ZS-KP 29, SRS 22, For a Just Serbia 16, Enough is Enough 16, Alliance for a Better Serbia 13, Dveri-DSS 13, SVM 4, other 6

Judicial branch: *highest court(s):* Supreme Court of Cassation (consists of more than 60 judges organized into 3- and 5-member panels for criminal, civil, and administrative cases); Constitutional Court (consists of 15 judges)
judge selection and term of office: Supreme Court justices proposed by the High Judicial Council (HJC), an 11-member body of which 7 are judges, and elected by the National Assembly; Constitutional Court judges appointed—5 each by the National Assembly, the president, and the Supreme Court of Cassation; judges of both courts appointed to permanent tenure by the HJC
subordinate courts: appellate courts, higher courts, and municipal and district courts; courts of special jurisdiction include the Administrative Court, Appellate Commercial Court, and 2 levels of misdemeanor courts
note: in 2003, specialized panels on war crimes were established within the Serbian court system; the panels have jurisdiction over alleged violations of the Basic Criminal Code and crimes against humanity, international law, and criminal acts as defined by the Statute of the International Criminal Tribunal for the former Yugoslavia

Political parties and leaders: Alliance for a Better Serbia (coalition includes LDP, LSV, SDS)
Alliance of Vojvodina Hungarians or SVM [Istvan PASZTOR]
Bosniak Democratic Union of Sandzak or BDZS [Jahja FEHRATOVIC]
Communist Party or KP [Josip Joska BROZ]
Democratic Party or DS [Dragan SUTANOVAC]
Democratic Party of Serbia or DSS [Milos JOVANOVIC]
Dveri [Bosko OBRADOVIC]
Enough of Enough [Sasa RADULOVIC]
For a Just Serbia (coalition includes DS, NS, DSVH, VVS)
Greens of Serbia or ZS [Ivan KARIC]
League of Social Democrats of Vojvodina or LSV [Nenad CANAK]
Liberal Democratic Party or LDP [Cedomir JOVANOVIC]
Movement of Socialists or PS [Aleksandar VULIN]
New Serbia or NS [Velimir ILIC]
Party for Democratic Action or PDD [Riza HALIMI]
Party of Democratic Action of the Sandzak or SDA [Sulejman UGLJANIN]
Party of United Pensioners of Serbia or PUPS [Milan KRKOBABIC]
Serbia is Winning (coalition includes NDSS, NS, PS, PSS, PUPS, SDPS, SNP, SNS, SPO)
Serbian People's Party or SNP [Nenad POPOVIC]
Serbian Progressive Party or SNS [Aleksandar VUCIC]
Serbian Radical Party or SRS [Vojislav SESELJ]

Serbian Renewal Movement or SPO [Vuk DRASKOVIC]
Social Democratic Party or SDS [Boris TADIC]
Social Democratic Party of Serbia or SDPS [Rasim LJAJIC]
Socialist Party of Serbia or SPS [Ivica DACIC]
Strength of Serbia or PSS [Bogoljub KARIC]
Together for Serbia or ZZS [Dusan PETROVIC]
United Serbia or JS [Dragan MARKOVIC]
note: as of April 2016, Serbia had 111 registered political parties and citizens' associations

Political pressure groups and leaders: Independent Association of Journalists of Serbia or NUNS
Journalists Association of Serbia (Udruzenje novinara Srbije) or UNS
Obraz (Orthodox clero-fascist organization)
SNP 1389 (Serbian nationalist movement)
SNP NASI 1389 (Serbian National Movement NASI)
Eastern Alternative (pro-Russian association)

International organization participation: BIS, BSEC, CD, CE, CEI, EAPC, EBRD, EU (candidate country), FAO, G-9, IAEA, IBRD, ICAO, ICC (national committees), ICCt, ICRM, IDA, IFC, IFRCS, IHO, ILO, IMF, IMO, IMSO, Interpol, IOC, IOM, IPU, ISO, ITSO, ITU, ITUC (NGOs), MIGA, MONUSCO, NAM (observer), NSG, OAS (observer), OIF (observer), OPCW, OSCE, PCA, PFP, SELEC, UN, UNCTAD, UNESCO, UNFICYP, UNHCR, UNIDO, UNIFIL, UNMIL, UNOCI, UNTSO, UNWTO, UPU, WCO, WHO, WIPO, WMO, WTO (observer)

Diplomatic representation in the US: *chief of mission:* Ambassador Djerdj MATKOVIC (since 23 February 2015)
chancery: 2233 Wisconsin Ave NW
telephone: [1] (202) 332-0333
FAX: [1] (202) 332-3933
consulate(s) general: Chicago, New York

Diplomatic representation from the US: *chief of mission:* Ambassador Kyle SCOTT (since 5 February 2016)
embassy: 92 Bulevar kneza Aleksandra Karadjordjevica, 11040 Belgrade, Serbia
mailing address: 5070 Belgrade Place, Washington, DC 20521-5070
telephone: [381] (11) 706-4000
FAX: [381] (11) 706-4005

Flag description: three equal horizontal stripes of red (top), blue, and white—the Pan-Slav colors representing freedom and revolutionary ideals; charged with the coat of arms of Serbia shifted slightly to the hoist side; the principal field of the coat of arms represents the Serbian state and displays a white two-headed eagle on a red shield; a smaller red shield on the eagle represents the Serbian nation, and is divided into four quarters by a white cross; interpretations vary as to the meaning and origin of the white, curved symbols resembling firesteels or Cyrillic "C's" in each quarter; a royal crown surmounts the coat of arms
note: the Pan-Slav colors were inspired by the 19th-century flag of Russia

National symbol(s): white double-headed eagle; national colors: red, blue, white

National anthem: *name:* "Boze pravde" (God of Justice)
lyrics/music: Jovan DORDEVIC/Davorin JENKO
note: adopted 1904; song originally written as part of a play in 1872 and has been used as an anthem by the Serbian people throughout the 20th and 21st centuries

ECONOMY

Economy—overview: Serbia has a transitional economy largely dominated by market forces, but the state sector remains significant in certain areas. The economy relies on manufacturing and exports, driven largely by foreign investment. MILOSEVIC-era mismanagement of the economy, an extended period of international economic sanctions, civil war, and the damage to Yugoslavia's infrastructure and industry during the NATO airstrikes in 1999 left the economy worse off than it was in 1990. In 2015, Serbia's GDP was 27.5% below where it was in 1989.

After former Federal Yugoslav President MILOSEVIC was ousted in September 2000, the Democratic Opposition of Serbia (DOS) coalition government implemented stabilization measures and embarked on a market reform program. Serbia renewed its membership in the IMF in December 2000 and rejoined the World Bank and the European Bank for Reconstruction and Development. Serbia has made progress in trade liberalization and enterprise restructuring and privatization, but many large enterprises—including the power utilities, telecommunications company, natural gas company, and others—remain state-owned. Serbia has made some progress towards EU membership, gaining candidate status in March 2012. In January 2014, Serbia's EU accession talks officially opened and, as of December 2017, Serbia had opened 12 negotiating chapters including one on foreign trade. Serbia's negotiations with the WTO are advanced, with the country's complete ban on the trade and cultivation of agricultural biotechnology products representing the primary remaining obstacle to accession. Serbia maintains a three-year Stand-by Arrangement with the IMF worth approximately $1.3 billion that is scheduled to end in February 2018. The government has shown progress implementing economic reforms, such as fiscal consolidation, privatization, and reducing public spending.

Unemployment in Serbia, while relatively low (16% in 2017) compared with its Balkan neighbors, remains significantly above the European average. Serbia is slowly implementing structural economic reforms needed to ensure the country's long-term prosperity. Serbia reduced its budget deficit to 1.7% of GDP and its public debt to 71% of GDP in 2017. Public debt had more than doubled between 2008 and 2015. Serbia's concerns about inflation and exchange-rate stability preclude the use of expansionary monetary policy.

Major economic challenges ahead include: stagnant household incomes; the need for private sector job creation; structural reforms of state-owned companies; strategic public sector reforms; and the need for new foreign direct investment. Other serious longer-term challenges include an inefficient judicial system, high levels of corruption, and an aging population. Factors favorable to Serbia's economic growth include the economic reforms it is undergoing as part of its EU accession process and IMF agreement, its strategic location, a relatively inexpensive and skilled labor force, and free trade agreements with the EU, Russia, Turkey, and countries that are members of the Central European Free Trade Agreement.

GDP (purchasing power parity): $106.6 billion (2017 est.)
$103.5 billion (2016 est.)
$100.7 billion (2015 est.)
note: data are in 2017 dollars
country comparison to the world: 83

GDP (official exchange rate): $39.37 billion (2016 est.)

GDP—real growth rate: 3% (2017 est.)
2.8% (2016 est.)
0.8% (2015 est.)
country comparison to the world: 119

GDP—per capita (PPP): $15,200 (2017 est.)
$14,700 (2016 est.)
$14,200 (2015 est.)
note: data are in 2017 dollars
country comparison to the world: 108

Gross national saving: 14.5% of GDP (2017 est.)
14% of GDP (2016 est.)
14.1% of GDP (2015 est.)
country comparison to the world: 128

GDP—composition, by end use:
household consumption: 78.2%
government consumption: 10.1%
investment in fixed capital: 18.4%
investment in inventories: 0.5%
exports of goods and services: 49.4%
imports of goods and services: -56.6% (2017 est.)

GDP—composition, by sector of origin:
agriculture: 9.8%
industry: 41.1%
services: 49.1% (2017 est.)

Agriculture—products: wheat, maize, sunflower, sugar beets, grapes/wine, fruits (raspberries, apples, sour cherries), vegetables (tomatoes, peppers, potatoes), beef, pork, and meat products, milk and dairy products

Industries: automobiles, base metals, furniture, food processing, machinery, chemicals, sugar, tires, clothes, pharmaceuticals

Industrial production growth rate: 3.3% (2017 est.)
country comparison to the world: 89

Labor force: 2.92 million (2017 est.)
country comparison to the world: 106

Labor force—by occupation: *agriculture:* 17.8%
industry: 25.6%
services: 56.6% (2016 est.)

Unemployment rate: 16% (2017 est.)
15.9% (2016 est.)
country comparison to the world: 174

Population below poverty line: 8.9% (2014 est.)

Distribution of family income—Gini index: 38.7 (2014 est.)
28.2 (2008 est.)
country comparison to the world: 70

Budget: *revenues:* $16.25 billion
expenditures: $16.93 billion
note: this is the consolidated budget, including both central government and local goverment budgets (2017 est.)
Taxes and other revenues: 41.3% of GDP (2017 est.)
country comparison to the world: 31

Budget surplus (+) or deficit (-): -1.7% of GDP (2017 est.)
country comparison to the world: 75

Public debt: 71% of GDP (2017 est.)
74% of GDP (2016 est.)
country comparison to the world: 50

Inflation rate (consumer prices): 3.4% (2017 est.)
1.1% (2016 est.)
country comparison to the world: 139

Central bank discount rate: 4% (31 December 2016)
7.5% (12 March 2015)
country comparison to the world: 96

Commercial bank prime lending rate: 7.6% (31 December 2017 est.)
8.45% (31 December 2016 est.)
country comparison to the world: 112

Stock of narrow money: $6.161 billion (31 December 2017 est.)
$5.189 billion (31 December 2016 est.)
country comparison to the world: 96

Stock of broad money: $21.27 billion (31 December 2017 est.)
$18.76 billion (31 December 2016 est.)
country comparison to the world: 89

Stock of domestic credit: $22.51 billion (31 December 2017 est.)
$20.22 billion (31 December 2016 est.)
country comparison to the world: 89

Market value of publicly traded shares: $5.064 billion (31 December 2016 est.)
$5.841 billion (31 December 2015 est.)
$4.525 billion (31 December 2014 est.)
country comparison to the world: 86

Current account balance: -$1.586 billion (2017 est.)
-$1.516 billion (2016 est.)
country comparison to the world: 149

Exports: $14.69 billion (2017 est.)
$13.99 billion (2016 est.)
country comparison to the world: 76

Exports—commodities: automobiles, iron and steel, rubber, clothes, wheat, fruit and vegetables, nonferrous metals, electric appliances, metal products, weapons and ammunition

Exports—partners: Italy 14.6%, Germany 13.1%, Bosnia and Herzegovina 8.3%, Romania 5.7%, Russia 5.4% (2016)

Imports: $19.24 billion (2017 est.)
$17.99 billion (2016 est.)
country comparison to the world: 75

Imports—commodities: machinery and transport equipment, fuels and lubricants, manufactured goods, chemicals, food and live animals, raw materials

Imports—partners: Germany 12.9%, Italy 10.4%, China 8.4%, Russia 7.9%, Hungary 4.6%, Poland 4.4% (2016)

Reserves of foreign exchange and gold: $10.79 billion (31 December 2017 est.)
$10.76 billion (31 December 2016 est.)
country comparison to the world: 73

Debt—external: $30.6 billion (31 December 2017 est.)
$30.38 billion (31 December 2016 est.)
country comparison to the world: 80

Stock of direct foreign investment—at home: $41.52 billion (31 December 2016 est.)
$11.95 billion (31 December 2015 est.)
country comparison to the world: 62

Stock of direct foreign investment—abroad: $NA

Exchange rates: Serbian dinars (RSD) per US dollar—
112.4 (2017 est.)
111.278 (2016 est.)
111.278 (2015 est.)
108.811 (2014 est.)
88.405 (2013 est.)

ENERGY

Electricity access: *electrification—total population:* 100% (2016)

Electricity—production: 38.11 billion kWh (2016 est.)
country comparison to the world: 60

Electricity—consumption: 26.78 billion kWh (2016 est.)
country comparison to the world: 65

Electricity—exports: 6.428 billion kWh (2016 est.)
country comparison to the world: 30

Electricity—imports: 5.065 billion kWh (2016 est.)
country comparison to the world: 40

Electricity—installed generating capacity: 7.594 million kW (2016 est.)
country comparison to the world: 71

Electricity—from fossil fuels: 59% of total installed capacity (2016 est.)
country comparison to the world: 131

Electricity—from nuclear fuels: 0% of total installed capacity (2016 est.)
country comparison to the world: 170

Electricity—from hydroelectric plants: 38.8% of total installed capacity (2016 est.)
country comparison to the world: 54

Electricity—from other renewable sources: 2.2% of total installed capacity (2016 est.)
country comparison to the world: 119

Crude oil—production: 20,000 bbl/day (2016 est.)
country comparison to the world: 69

Crude oil—exports: 0 bbl/day (2016 est.)
country comparison to the world: 179

Crude oil—imports: 45,790 bbl/day (2016 est.)
country comparison to the world: 55

Crude oil—proved reserves: 77.5 million bbl (1 January 2017 es)
country comparison to the world: 76

Refined petroleum products—production: 67,360 bbl/day (2016 est.)
country comparison to the world: 73

Refined petroleum products—consumption: 66,230 bbl/day (2016 est.)
country comparison to the world: 94

Refined petroleum products—exports: 12,050 bbl/day (2016 est.)
country comparison to the world: 80

Refined petroleum products—imports: 16,070 bbl/day (2016 est.)
country comparison to the world: 127

Natural gas—production: 586.3 million cu m (2016 est.)
country comparison to the world: 71

Natural gas—consumption: 2.25 billion cu m (2016 est.)
country comparison to the world: 83

Natural gas—exports: 0 cu m (2016 est.)
country comparison to the world: 170

Natural gas—imports: 1.664 billion cu m (2016 est.)
country comparison to the world: 53

Natural gas—proved reserves: 48.14 billion cu m (1 January 2017 es)
country comparison to the world: 66

Carbon dioxide emissions from consumption of energy: 56.55 million Mt (2015 est.)
country comparison to the world: 57

COMMUNICATIONS

Telephones—fixed lines: *total subscriptions:* 2,711,725
subscriptions per 100 inhabitants: 38 (July 2016 est.)
country comparison to the world: 51

Telephones—mobile cellular: *total:* 9,094,447
subscriptions per 100 inhabitants: 127 (July 2016 est.)
country comparison to the world: 89

Telephone system: *general assessment:* replacements of, and upgrades to, telecommunications equipment damaged during the 1999 war resulted in a modern digitalized telecommunications system
domestic: wireless service, available through multiple providers with national coverage, is growing very rapidly; best telecommunications services are centered in urban centers; 4G/LTE mobile network launched in March 2015
international: country code—381 (2016)

Internet country code: .rs

Internet users: *total:* 4,790,488
percent of population: 67.1% (July 2016 est.)
country comparison to the world: 83

TRANSPORTATION

National air transport system: *number of registered air carriers:* 2
inventory of registered aircraft operated by air carriers: 21
annual passenger traffic on registered air carriers: 2,424,886
annual freight traffic on registered air carriers: 2.748 million mt-km (2015)
Civil aircraft registration country code prefix: YU (2016)

Airports: 26 (2013)
country comparison to the world: 127

Airports—with paved runways: *total:* 10
over 3,047 m: 2
2,438 to 3,047 m: 3
1,524 to 2,437 m: 3
914 to 1,523 m: 2 (2017)

Airports—with unpaved runways: *total:* 16
1,524 to 2,437 m: 1
914 to 1,523 m: 10
under 914 m: 5 (2013)

Heliports: 2 (2012)

Railways: *total:* 3,809 km
standard gauge: 3,809 km 1.435-m gauge (3,526 km one-track lines and 283 km double-track lines) out of which 1,279 km electrified (1,000 km one-track lines and 279 km double-track lines) (2015)
country comparison to the world: 46

Roadways: *total:* 44,248 km
paved: 28,000 km (16,162 km state roads, out of which 741 km highways)
unpaved: 16,248 km (2016)
country comparison to the world: 82

Waterways: 587 km (primarily on the Danube and Sava Rivers) (2009)
country comparison to the world: 80

Ports and terminals: river port(s): Belgrade (Danube)

MILITARY AND SECURITY

Military expenditures: 1.34% of GDP (2017 est.)
1.25% of GDP (2016)
1.41% of GDP (2015)
1.49% of GDP (2014)
1.48% of GDP (2013)
country comparison to the world: 36

Military branches: Serbian Armed Forces (Vojska Srbije, VS): Land Forces (includes Riverine Component, consisting of a river flotilla on the Danube) and Air and Air Defense Forces (2016)

Military service age and obligation: 18 years of age for voluntary military service; conscription abolished December 2010; reserve obligation to age 60 for men and age 50 for women (2013)

TRANSNATIONAL ISSUES

Disputes—international: Serbia with several other states protest the US and other states' recognition of Kosovo's declaration of its status as a sovereign and independent state in February 2008; ethnic Serbian municipalities along Kosovo's northern border challenge final status of Kosovo-Serbia boundary; several thousand NATO-led Kosovo Force peacekeepers under UN Interim Administration Mission in Kosovo authority continue to keep the peace within Kosovo between the ethnic Albanian majority and the Serb minority in Kosovo; Serbia delimited about half of the boundary with Bosnia and Herzegovina, but sections along the Drina River remain in dispute

Refugees and internally displaced persons: refugees (country of origin): 20,346 (Croatia); 9,081 (Bosnia and Herzegovina) (2016)
IDPs: 219,633 (most are Kosovar Serbs, some are Roma, Ashkalis, and Egyptian (RAE); some RAE IDPs are unregistered) (2016)
stateless persons: 2,373 (includes stateless persons in Kosovo) (2016)
note: 678,493 estimated refugee and migrant arrivals (January 2015—December 2016); Serbia is predominantly a transit country and hosts an estimated 4,400 migrants, refugees, and asylum seekers as of the end of November 2017

Illicit drugs: transshipment point for Southwest Asian heroin moving to Western Europe on the Balkan route; economy vulnerable to money laundering

SEYCHELLES

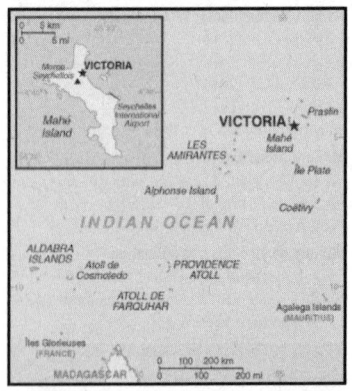

INTRODUCTION

Background: A lengthy struggle between France and Great Britain for the islands ended in 1814, when they were ceded to the latter. During colonial rule, a plantation-based economy developed that relied on imported labor, primarily from European colonies in Africa. Independence came in 1976. Single-party rule was brought to a close with a new constitution and free elections in 1993. President France-Albert RENE, who had served since 1977, was reelected in 2001, but stepped down in 2004. Vice President James Alix MICHEL took over the presidency and in 2006 was elected to a new five-year term; he was reelected in 2011 and again in 2015. In 2016, James MICHEL resigned and handed over the presidency to his Vice-President Danny FAURE.

GEOGRAPHY

Location: archipelago in the Indian Ocean, northeast of Madagascar

Geographic coordinates: 4 35 S, 55 40 E

Map references: Africa

Area: *total:* 455 sq km
land: 455 sq km
water: 0 sq km
country comparison to the world: 199

Area—comparative: 2.5 times the size of Washington, DC
Land boundaries: 0 km

Coastline: 491 km

Maritime claims: *territorial sea:* 12 nm
contiguous zone: 24 nm
exclusive economic zone: 200 nm
continental shelf: 200 nm or to the edge of the continental margin

Climate: tropical marine; humid; cooler season during southeast monsoon (late May to September); warmer season during northwest monsoon (March to May)

Terrain: Mahe Group is volcanic with a narrow coastal strip and rocky, hilly interior; others are coral, flat, elevated reefs

Elevation: *mean elevation:* NA

elevation extremes: *lowest point:* Indian Ocean 0 m
highest point: Morne Seychellois 905 m

Natural resources: fish, coconuts (copra), cinnamon trees

Land use: *agricultural land:* 6.5%
arable land: 2.2%;
permanent crops: 4.3%;
permanent pasture: 0%
forest: 88.5%
other: 5% (2011 est.)
Irrigated land: 3 sq km (2012)

Population—distribution: more than three-quarters of the population lives on the main island of Mahe; Praslin contains less than 10%; a smaller percent on La Digue and the outer islands

Natural hazards: lies outside the cyclone belt, so severe storms are rare; occasional short droughts

Environment—current issues: water supply depends on catchments to collect rainwater

Environment—international agreements: *party to:* Biodiversity, Climate Change, Climate Change-Kyoto Protocol, Desertification, Endangered Species, Hazardous Wastes, Law of the Sea, Marine Dumping, Ozone Layer Protection, Ship Pollution, Wetlands
signed, but not ratified: none of the selected agreements

Geography—note: smallest African country; the constitution of the Republic of Seychelles lists 155 islands: 42 granitic and 113 coralline; by far the largest island is Mahe, which is home to about 90% of the population and the site of the capital city of Victoria

PEOPLE AND SOCIETY

Population: 93,920 (July 2017 est.)
country comparison to the world: 198

Nationality: *noun:* Seychellois (singular and plural)
adjective: Seychellois

Ethnic groups: mixed French, African, Indian, Chinese, and Arab

Languages: Seychellois Creole (official) 89.1%, English (official) 5.1%, French (official) 0.7%, other 3.8%, unspecified 1.4% (2010 est.)

Religions: Roman Catholic 76.2%, Protestant 10.5% (Anglican 6.1%, Pentecostal Assembly 1.5%, Seventh Day Adventist 1.2%, other Protestant 1.7%), other Christian 2.4%, Hindu 2.4%, Muslim 1.6%, other non-Christian 1.1%, unspecified 4.8%, none 0.9% (2010 est.)

Demographic profile: Seychelles has no indigenous population and was first permanently settled by a small group of French planters, African slaves, and South Indians in 1770. Seychelles' modern population is composed of the descendants of French and later British settlers, Africans, and Indian, Chinese, and Middle Eastern traders and is concentrated on three of its 155 islands—the vast majority on Mahe and lesser numbers on Praslin and La Digue. Seychelles' population grew rapidly during the second half of the 20th century, largely due to natural increase, but the pace has slowed because of fertility decline. The total fertility rate dropped sharply from 4.0 children per woman in 1980 to 1.9 in 2015, mainly as a result of a family planning program, free education and health care, and increased female labor force participation. Life expectancy has increased steadily, but women on average live 9 years longer than men, a difference that is higher than that typical of developed countries.

The combination of reduced fertility and increased longevity has resulted in an aging population, which will put pressure on the government's provision of pensions and health care. Seychelles' sustained investment in social welfare services, such as free primary health care and education up to the post-secondary level, have enabled the country to achieve a high human development index score—among the highest in Africa. Despite some of its health and education indicators being nearly on par with Western countries, Seychelles has a high level of income inequality.

An increasing number of migrant workers—mainly young men—have been coming to Seychelles in recent years to work in the construction and tourism industries. As of 2011, foreign workers made up nearly a quarter of the workforce. Indians are the largest non-Seychellois population—representing half of the country's foreigners—followed by Malagasy.

Age structure: *0-14 years:* 19.88% (male 9,578/female 9,089)
15-24 years: 13.24% (male 6,536/female 5,898)
25-54 years: 49.36% (male 24,585/female 21,775)
55-64 years: 9.88% (male 4,758/female 4,522)
65 years and over: 7.64% (male 2,868/female 4,311) (2017 est.)

Dependency ratios: *total dependency ratio:* 42.8
youth dependency ratio: 31
elderly dependency ratio: 11.7
potential support ratio: 8.5 (2015 est.)

Median age: *total:* 35.4 years
male: 34.9 years
female: 36 years (2017 est.)
country comparison to the world: 76

Population growth rate: 0.77% (2017 est.)
country comparison to the world: 136

Birth rate: 13.7 births/1,000 population (2017 est.)
country comparison to the world: 142

Death rate: 7 deaths/1,000 population (2017 est.)
country comparison to the world: 132

Net migration rate: 1 migrant(s)/1,000 population (2017 est.)
country comparison to the world: 57

Population distribution: more than three-quarters of the population lives on the main island of Mahe; Praslin contains less than 10%; a smaller percent on La Digue and the outer islands

Urbanization: *urban population:* 54.5% of total population (2017)
rate of urbanization: 1.02% annual rate of change (2015-20 est.)

Major urban areas—population: VICTORIA (capital) 26,000 (2014)

Sex ratio: *at birth:* 1.03 male(s)/female
0-14 years: 1.05 male(s)/female
15-24 years: 1.1 male(s)/female
25-54 years: 1.12 male(s)/female
55-64 years: 1.06 male(s)/female
65 years and over: 0.64 male(s)/female
total population: 1.06 male(s)/female (2016 est.)

Infant mortality rate: *total:* 10 deaths/1,000 live births
male: 12.5 deaths/1,000 live births
female: 7.4 deaths/1,000 live births (2017 est.)
country comparison to the world: 136

Life expectancy at birth: *total population:* 74.9 years
male: 70.4 years
female: 79.6 years (2017 est.)
country comparison to the world: 118

Total fertility rate: 1.85 children born/woman (2017 est.)
country comparison to the world: 146

Health expenditures: 3.4% of GDP (2014)
country comparison to the world: 176

Physicians density: 0.98 physicians/1,000 population (2012)

Hospital bed density: 3.6 beds/1,000 population (2011)

Drinking water source:
improved:
 urban: 95.7% of population
rural: 95.7% of population
total: 95.7% of population
unimproved:
urban: 4.3% of population
rural: 4.3% of population
total: 4.3% of population (2015 est.)

Sanitation facility access:
improved:
urban: 98.4% of population
rural: 98.4% of population
total: 98.4% of population
unimproved:
urban: 1.6% of population
rural: 1.6% of population
total: 1.6% of population (2015 est.)

HIV/AIDS—adult prevalence rate: NA

HIV/AIDS—people living with HIV/AIDS: NA

HIV/AIDS—deaths: NA

Obesity—adult prevalence rate: 14% (2016)
country comparison to the world: 130

Children under the age of 5 years underweight: 3.6% (2012)

Education expenditures: 3.6% of GDP (2011)
country comparison to the world: 121

Literacy: *definition:* age 15 and over can read and write
total population: 91.8%
male: 91.4%
female: 92.3% (2012 est.)

School life expectancy (primary to tertiary education): *total:* 14 years
male: 13 years
female: 15 years (2015)

Unemployment, youth ages 15-24: *total:* 14%
male: 12.1%
female: 16.2% (2015 est.)

GOVERNMENT

Country name: *conventional long form:* Republic of Seychelles
conventional short form: Seychelles
local long form: Republic of Seychelles
local short form: Seychelles
etymology: named by French Captain Corneille Nicholas MORPHEY after Jean Moreau de SECHELLES, the finance minister of France, in 1756

Government type: presidential republic

Capital: *name:* Victoria

geographic coordinates: 4 37 S, 55 27 E
time difference: UTC+4 (9 hours ahead of Washington, DC, during Standard Time)

Administrative divisions: 25 administrative districts; Anse aux Pins, Anse Boileau, Anse Etoile, Anse Royale, Au Cap, Baie Lazare, Baie Sainte Anne, Beau Vallon, Bel Air, Bel Ombre, Cascade, Glacis, Grand Anse Mahe, Grand Anse Praslin, Inner Islands, La Riviere Anglaise, Les Mamalles, Mont Buxton, Mont Fleuri, Plaisance, Pointe Larue, Port Glaud, Roche Caiman, Saint Louis, Takamaka

Independence: 29 June 1976 (from the UK)

National holiday: Constitution Day, 18 June (1993); Independence Day (National Day), 29 June (1976)

Constitution: *history:* previous 1970, 1979; latest drafted May 1993, approved by referendum 18 June 1993, effective 23 June 1993
amendments: proposed by the National Assembly; passage requires at least two-thirds majority vote by the National Assembly; passage of amendments affecting the country's sovereignty, symbols and languages, the supremacy of the constitution, fundamental rights and freedoms, amendment procedures, and dissolution of the Assembly also requires approval by at least 60% of voters in a referendum; amended several times, last in 2017 (2017)

Legal system: mixed legal system of English common law, French civil law, and customary law

International law organization participation: has not submitted an ICJ jurisdiction declaration; accepts ICCt jurisdiction

Citizenship: *citizenship by birth:* no

citizenship by descent only: at least one parent must be a citizen of the Seychelles
dual citizenship recognized: no
residency requirement for naturalization: 5 years

Suffrage: 18 years of age; universal

Executive branch: *chief of state:* President Danny FAURE (since 16 October 2016); Vice President Vincent MERITON (since 28 October 2016); note—James Alix MICHEL resigned the presidency effective 16 October 2016; the president is both chief of state and head of government
head of government: President Danny FAURE (since 16 October 2016); Vice President Vincent MERITON (since 28 October 2016); note—James Alix MICHEL resigned the presidency effective 16 October 2016
cabinet: Council of Ministers appointed by the president
elections/appointments: president directly elected by absolute majority popular vote in 2 rounds if needed for a 5-year term (eligible for 1 additional term); election last held on 3-5 December 2015 with runoff on 16-18 December 2015 (next to be held in December 2020)
election results: President James Alix MICHEL reelected president in second round; percent of vote in—James Alix MICHEL (PL) 50.2%, Wavel RAMKALAWAN (SNP) 49.8%

Legislative branch: *description:* unicameral National Assembly or Assemblee Nationale (up to 35 seats—the Assembly elected in September 2016 has 33 members; 25 members directly elected in single-seat constituencies by simple majority vote and up to 10 members elected by proportional representation vote; members serve 5-year terms)
elections: last held on 8-10 September 2016 (next to be held in 2021); note—the National Assembly was dissolved in July 2011 resulting in early elections
election results: percent of vote by party—LDS 49.6%, PL 49.2%, other 1.2%; seats by party—LDS 19, PL 14

Judicial branch: *highest court(s):* Seychelles Court of Appeal (consists of the court president and 4 justices); Supreme Court of Seychelles (consists of the chief justice and 9 puisne judges); Constitutional Court (consists of 3 Supreme Court judges)
judge selection and term of office: all judges appointed by the president of the republic upon the recommendation of the Constitutional Appointments Authority, a 3-member body, with 1 member appointed by the president of the republic, 1 by the opposition leader in the National Assembly, and 1 by the other 2 appointees; judges appointed until retirement at age 70
subordinate courts: Magistrates' Courts of Seychelles; Family Tribunal for issues such as domestic violence, child custody, and maintenance; Employment Tribunal for labor-related disputes

795

Political parties and leaders: Lafors Demokratik Seselwa or LSD (Martin AGLAE)

People's Party (Parti Lepep) or PL [James Alix MICHEL] (formerly SPPF)

Seselwa (Seychelles) United Party or SUP [Robert ERNESTA] (formerly the New Democratic Party or NDP)

Seychelles National Party or SNP [Wavel RAM-KALAWAN] (formerly the United Opposition or UO)

Seychelles Party for Social Justice and Democracy or SPSD

Seychelles Patriotic Movement or SPM [Regis FRANCOURT]

Seychelloise Alliance (Lalyans Seselwa) [Patrick PILLAY]

Seychellois Democratic Alliance (Linyon Demokratik Seselwa) or LDS [Roger MANCI-ENNE] (includes SNP, Seychelloise Alliance, SPSD, SUP)

International organization participation: ACP, AfDB, AOSIS, AU, C, CD, COMESA, EITI (candidate country), FAO, G-77, IAEA, IBRD, ICAO, ICC (NGOs), ICCt, ICRM, IDA, IFAD, IFC, IFRCS, ILO, IMF, IMO, InOC, Interpol, IOC, IOM, IPU, ISO (correspondent), ITU, MIGA, NAM, OIF, OPCW, SADC, UN, UNCTAD, UNESCO, UNIDO, UNWTO, UPU, WCO, WHO, WIPO, WMO, WTO (observer)

Diplomatic representation in the US: chief of mission: Ambassador Ronald Jean JUMEAU (since 8 September 2017)

chancery: 800 Second Avenue, Suite 400C, New York, NY 10017

telephone: [1] (212) 972-1785

FAX: [1] (212) 972-1786

consulate(s) general: New York

Diplomatic representation from the US: the US does not have an embassy in Seychelles; the US Ambassador to Mauritius is accredited to Seychelles

Flag description: five oblique bands of blue (hoist side), yellow, red, white, and green (bottom) radiating from the bottom of the hoist side; the oblique bands are meant to symbolize a dynamic new country moving into the future; blue represents sky and sea, yellow the sun giving light and life, red the peoples' determination to work for the future in unity and love, white social justice and harmony, green the land and natural environment

National symbol(s): coco de mer (sea coconut); national colors: blue, yellow, red, white, green

National anthem: *name:* "Koste Seselwa" (Seychellois Unite)

lyrics/music: David Francois Marc ANDRE and George Charles Robert PAYET

note: adopted 1996

ECONOMY

Economy—overview: Since independence in 1976, per capita output in this Indian Ocean archipelago has expanded to roughly seven times the pre-independence, near-subsistence level, moving the island into the upper-middle-income group of countries. Growth has been led by the tourist sector, which employs about 30% of the labor force and provides more than 70% of hard currency earnings, and by tuna fishing.

In recent years, the government has encouraged foreign investment to upgrade hotels and other services. At the same time, the government has moved to reduce the dependence on tourism by promoting the development of farming, fishing, and small-scale manufacturing.

In 2008, having depleted its foreign exchange reserves, Seychelles defaulted on interest payments due on a $230 million Eurobond, requested assistance from the IMF, and immediately enacted a number of significant structural reforms, including liberalization of the exchange rate, reform of the public sector to include layoffs, and the sale of some state assets. In December 2013, the IMF declared that Seychelles had successfully transitioned to a market-based economy with full employment and a fiscal surplus. Effective 1 January 2017, Seychelles was no longer be eligible for trade benefits under the US African Growth and Opportunities Act after having gained developed country status. Seychelles grew at 4.1% in 2017 because of a strong tourist sector and low commodity prices. The Seychellois Government met the IMF's performance criteria for 2017 but recognizes a need to make additional progress to combat high poverty levels, estimated at 39% in 2013.

GDP (purchasing power parity): $2.712 billion (2017 est.)

$2.606 billion (2016 est.)

$2.494 billion (2015 est.)

note: data are in 2017 dollars

country comparison to the world: 190

GDP (official exchange rate): $1.479 billion (2016 est.)

GDP—real growth rate: 4.1% (2017 est.)

4.5% (2016 est.)

5% (2015 est.)

country comparison to the world: 63

GDP—per capita (PPP): $28,900 (2017 est.)

$27,700 (2016 est.)

$26,800 (2015 est.)

note: data are in 2017 dollars

country comparison to the world: 68

Gross national saving: 16.6% of GDP (2017 est.)

11.8% of GDP (2016 est.)

15.2% of GDP (2015 est.)

country comparison to the world: 112

GDP—composition, by end use: *household consumption:* 47.7%

government consumption: 28.1%

investment in fixed capital: 33.2%

investment in inventories: 1.6%

exports of goods and services: 71.5%

imports of goods and services: -82.1% (2017 est.)

GDP—composition, by sector of origin: *agriculture:* 2.5%

industry: 13.8%

services: 83.7% (2017 est.)

Agriculture—products: coconuts, cinnamon, vanilla, sweet potatoes, cassava (manioc, tapioca), copra, bananas; tuna

Industries: fishing, tourism, beverages

Industrial production growth rate: 2.5% (2017 est.)

country comparison to the world: 111

Labor force: 39,560 (2006 est.)

country comparison to the world: 197

Labor force—by occupation: *agriculture:* 3%

industry: 23%

services: 74% (2006)

Unemployment rate: 3% (2017 est.)

2.7% (2016 est.)

country comparison to the world: 34

Population below poverty line: 39.3% (2013 est.)

Household income or consumption by percentage share: *lowest 10%:* 4.7%

highest 10%: 15.4% (2007)

Budget: *revenues:* $571.8 million

expenditures: $557.2 million (2017 est.)

Taxes and other revenues: 38.7% of GDP (2017 est.)

country comparison to the world: 42

Budget surplus (+) or deficit (-): 1% of GDP (2017 est.)

country comparison to the world: 16

Public debt: 56.8% of GDP (2017 est.)

57.6% of GDP (2016 est.)

country comparison to the world: 81

Fiscal year: calendar year

Inflation rate (consumer prices): 2.8% (2017 est.)

-1% (2016 est.)

country comparison to the world: 124

Central bank discount rate: 11.17% (31 December 2010)

country comparison to the world: 18

Commercial bank prime lending rate: 12.4% (31 December 2017 est.)

12.36% (31 December 2016 est.)

country comparison to the world: 65

Stock of narrow money: $587.7 million (31 December 2017 est.)

$556.5 million (31 December 2016 est.)

country comparison to the world: 166

Stock of broad money: $702.4 million (31 December 2017 est.)

$638.2 million (31 December 2016 est.)

country comparison to the world: 179

Stock of domestic credit: $610.3 million (31 December 2017 est.)

$565.9 million (31 December 2016 est.)

country comparison to the world: 174

Market value of publicly traded shares: $NA

Current account balance: -$230 million (2017 est.)

-$263 million (2016 est.)

country comparison to the world: 90

Exports: $495.4 million (2017 est.)

$477.6 million (2016 est.)

country comparison to the world: 175

Exports—commodities: canned tuna, frozen fish, petroleum products (reexports)

Exports—partners: UAE 28.8%, France 21%, UK 14.7%, Italy 9.2%, Spain 8.8% (2016)

Imports: $1.044 billion (2017 est.)
$962.4 million (2016 est.)
country comparison to the world: 178

Imports—commodities: machinery and equipment, foodstuffs, petroleum products, chemicals, other manufactured goods

Imports—partners: UAE 21.6%, France 9.9%, South Africa 8.4%, Mauritius 7.8%, Spain 7.2%, India 4.9%, China 4.8%, UK 4.7% (2016)

Reserves of foreign exchange and gold: $538.8 million (31 December 2017 est.)
$523.5 million (31 December 2016 est.)
country comparison to the world: 142

Debt—external: $2.729 billion (31 December 2017 est.)
$2.651 billion (31 December 2016 est.)
country comparison to the world: 145

Exchange rates: Seychelles rupees (SCR) per US dollar—
13.64 (2017 est.)
13.319 (2016 est.)
13.319 (2015 est.)
13.314 (2014 est.)
12.747 (2013 est.)

ENERGY

Electricity access: population without electricity: 2,795
electrification—*total population:* 97%
electrification—urban areas: 97%
electrification—rural areas: 97% (2012)

Electricity—production: 347 million kWh (2015 est.)
country comparison to the world: 176

Electricity—consumption: 322.7 million kWh (2015 est.)
country comparison to the world: 181

Electricity—exports: 0 kWh (2016 est.)
country comparison to the world: 193

Electricity—imports: 0 kWh (2016 est.)
country comparison to the world: 197

Electricity—installed generating capacity: 87,000 kW (2015 est.)
country comparison to the world: 181

Electricity—from fossil fuels: 92% of total installed capacity (2015 est.)
country comparison to the world: 59

Electricity—from nuclear fuels: 0% of total installed capacity (2015 est.)
country comparison to the world: 178

Electricity—from hydroelectric plants: 0% of total installed capacity (2015 est.)
country comparison to the world: 201

Electricity—from other renewable sources: 9.2% of total installed capacity (2015 est.)
country comparison to the world: 74

Crude oil—production: 0 bbl/day (2016 est.)
country comparison to the world: 196

Crude oil—exports: 0 bbl/day (2014 est.)
country comparison to the world: 185

Crude oil—imports: 0 bbl/day (2014 est.)
country comparison to the world: 186

Crude oil—proved reserves: 0 bbl (1 January 2017 es)
country comparison to the world: 194

Refined petroleum products—production: 0 bbl/day (2014 est.)
country comparison to the world: 199

Refined petroleum products—consumption: 6,500 bbl/day (2015 est.)
country comparison to the world: 168

Refined petroleum products—exports: 0 bbl/day (2014 est.)
country comparison to the world: 195

Refined petroleum products—imports: 5,956 bbl/day (2014 est.)
country comparison to the world: 162

Natural gas—production: 0 cu m (2013 est.)
country comparison to the world: 191

Natural gas—consumption: 0 cu m (2013 est.)
country comparison to the world: 128

Natural gas—exports: 0 cu m (2013 est.)
country comparison to the world: 177

Natural gas—imports: 0 cu m (2013 est.)
country comparison to the world: 184

Natural gas—proved reserves: 0 cu m (1 January 2014 es)
country comparison to the world: 191

Carbon dioxide emissions from consumption of energy: 1.4 million Mt (2013 est.)
country comparison to the world: 161

COMMUNICATIONS

Telephones—fixed lines: *total subscriptions:* 20,836
subscriptions per 100 inhabitants: 22 (July 2016 est.)
country comparison to the world: 184

Telephones—mobile cellular: *total:* 151,857
subscriptions per 100 inhabitants: 163 (July 2016 est.)
country comparison to the world: 184

Telephone system: *general assessment:* effective system
domestic: combined fixed-line and mobile-cellular teledensity is approximately 185 telephones per 100 persons; radiotelephone communications between islands in the archipelago
international: country code—248; direct radiotelephone communications with adjacent island countries and African coastal countries; satellite earth station—1 Intelsat (Indian Ocean) (2016)

Broadcast media: the government operates the only terrestrial TV station, which provides local programming and airs broadcasts from international services; multi-channel cable and satellite TV are available through 2 providers; the government operates 1 AM and 1 FM radio station; there is 1 privately operated radio station; transmissions of 2 international broadcasters are accessible in Victoria (2016)

Internet country code: .sc

Internet users: *total:* 52,664
percent of population: 56.5% (July 2016 est.)
country comparison to the world: 184

TRANSPORTATION

National air transport system: *number of registered air carriers:* 1
inventory of registered aircraft operated by air carriers: 3
annual passenger traffic on registered air carriers: 497,496
annual freight traffic on registered air carriers: 19,234,992 mt-km (2015)
Civil aircraft registration country code prefix: S7 (2016)

Airports: 14 (2013)
country comparison to the world: 150

Airports—with paved runways: *total:* 7
2,438 to 3,047 m: 1
914 to 1,523 m: 5
under 914 m: 1 (2017)

Airports—with unpaved runways: *total:* 7
914 to 1,523 m: 2
under 914 m: 5 (2013)

Heliports: 1 (2013)

Roadways: *total:* 526 km
paved: 514 km
unpaved: 12 km (2015)
country comparison to the world: 196

Merchant marine: *total:* 24
by type: general cargo 4, oil tanker 6, other 14 (2017)
country comparison to the world: 130

Ports and terminals: *major seaport(s):* Victoria

MILITARY AND SECURITY

Military expenditures: 1.29% of GDP (2016)
1.21% of GDP (2015)
2.17% of GDP (2014)
0.98% of GDP (2013)
0.87% of GDP (2012)
country comparison to the world: 109

Military branches: Seychelles People's Defense Forces (SPDF): Army (includes infantry, Special Forces (Tazar)), Coast Guard (includes Naval Wing, Air Wing) (2015)

Military service age and obligation: 18 years of age for voluntary military service (younger with parental consent); no conscription (2012)

TRANSNATIONAL ISSUES

Disputes—international: Mauritius and Seychelles claim the Chagos Islands (UK-administered British Indian Ocean Territory)

SIERRA LEONE

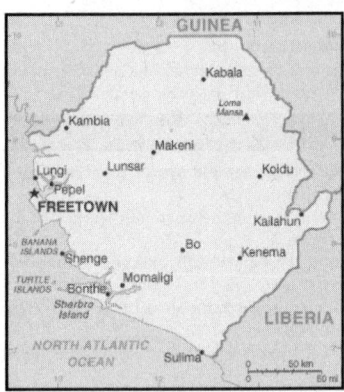

INTRODUCTION

Background: The British set up a trading post near present-day Freetown in the 17th century. Originally the trade involved timber and ivory, but later it expanded into slaves. Following the American Revolution, a colony was established in 1787 and Sierra Leone became a destination for resettling black loyalists who had originally been resettled in Nova Scotia. After the abolition of the slave trade in 1807, British crews delivered thousands of Africans liberated from illegal slave ships to Sierra Leone, particularly Freetown. The colony gradually expanded inland during the course of the 19th century; independence was attained in 1961. Democracy is slowly being reestablished after the civil war (1991-2002) that resulted in tens of thousands of deaths and the displacement of more than 2 million people (about one third of the population). The military, which took over full responsibility for security following the departure of UN peacekeepers at the end of 2005, has developed as a guarantor of the country's stability; the armed forces remained on the sideline during the 2007 and 2012 national elections. In March 2014, the closure of the UN Integrated Peacebuilding Office in Sierra Leone marked the end of more than 15 years of peacekeeping and political operations in Sierra Leone. The government's stated priorities include furthering development—including recovering from the Ebola epidemic—creating jobs, and stamping out endemic corruption.

GEOGRAPHY

Location: Western Africa, bordering the North Atlantic Ocean, between Guinea and Liberia

Geographic coordinates: 8 30 N, 11 30 W

Map references: Africa

Area: *total:* 71,740 sq km
land: 71,620 sq km
water: 120 sq km
country comparison to the world: 120

Area—comparative: slightly smaller than South Carolina
Land boundaries: total: 1,093 km
border countries (2): Guinea 794 km, Liberia 299 km

Coastline: 402 km

Maritime claims: *territorial sea:* 12 nm
contiguous zone: 24 nm
exclusive economic zone: 200 nm
continental shelf: 200 nm

Climate: tropical; hot, humid; summer rainy season (May to December); winter dry season (December to April)

Terrain: coastal belt of mangrove swamps, wooded hill country, upland plateau, mountains in east

Elevation: *mean elevation:* 279 m

elevation extremes: *lowest point:* Atlantic Ocean 0 m
highest point: Loma Mansa (Bintimani) 1,948 m

Natural resources: diamonds, titanium ore, bauxite, iron ore, gold, chromite

Land use: *agricultural land:* 56.2%
arable land: 23.4%;
permanent crops: 2.3%;
permanent pasture: 30.5%
forest: 37.5%
other: 6.3% (2011 est.)
Irrigated land: 300 sq km (2012)

Population—distribution: population clusters are found in the lower elevations of the south and west; the northern third of the country is less populated

Natural hazards: dry, sand-laden harmattan winds blow from the Sahara (December to February); sandstorms, dust storms

Environment—current issues: rapid population growth pressuring the environment; overharvesting of timber, expansion of cattle grazing, and slash-and-burn agriculture have resulted in deforestation and soil exhaustion; civil war depleted natural resources; overfishing

Environment—international agreements: *party to:* Biodiversity, Climate Change, Climate Change-Kyoto Protocol, Desertification, Endangered Species, Law of the Sea, Marine Life Conservation, Ozone Layer Protection, Ship Pollution, Wetlands *signed, but not ratified:* Environmental Modification

Geography—note: rainfall along the coast can reach 495 cm (195 inches) a year, making it one of the wettest places along coastal, western Africa

PEOPLE AND SOCIETY

Population: 6,163,195 (July 2017 est.)
country comparison to the world: 109

Nationality: *noun:* Sierra Leonean(s)
adjective: Sierra Leonean

Ethnic groups: Temne 35.5%, Mende 33.2%, Limba 6.4%, Kono 4.4%, Fullah 3.4%, Loko 2.9%, Koranko 2.8%, Sherbro 2.6%, Mandingo 2.4%, Creole 1.2% (descendants of freed Jamaican slaves who were settled in the Freetown area in the late-18th century; also known as Krio), other Sierra Leone 4.7%, other foreign 0.3% (includes refugees from Liberia's recent civil war, and small numbers of Europeans, Lebanese, Pakistanis, and Indians), unspecified 0.2% (2013 est.)

Languages: English (official, regular use limited to literate minority), Mende (principal vernacular in the south), Temne (principal vernacular in the north), Krio (English-based Creole, spoken by the descendants of freed Jamaican slaves who were settled in the Freetown area, a lingua franca and a first language for 10% of the population but understood by 95%)

Religions: Muslim 78.6%, Christian 20.8%, other 0.3%, unspecified 0.2% (2013 est.)

Demographic profile: Sierra Leone's youthful and growing population is driven by its high total fertility rate (TFR) of almost 5 children per woman, which has declined little over the last two decades. Its elevated TFR is sustained by the continued desire for large families, the low level of contraceptive use, and the early start of childbearing. Despite its high TFR, Sierra Leone's population growth is somewhat tempered by high infant, child, and maternal mortality rates that are among the world's highest and are a result of poverty, a lack of potable water and sanitation, poor nutrition, limited access to quality health care services, and the prevalence of female genital cutting.

Sierra Leone's large youth cohort—about 60% of the population is under the age of 25—continues to struggle with high levels of unemployment, which was one of the major causes of the country's 1991-2002 civil war and remains a threat to stability today. Its estimated 60% youth unemployment rate is attributed to high levels of illiteracy and unskilled labor, a lack of private sector jobs, and low pay.

Sierra Leone has been a source of and destination for refugees. Sierra Leone's civil war internally displaced as many as 2 million people, or almost half the population, and forced almost another half million to seek refuge in neighboring countries (370,000 Sierra Leoneans fled to Guinea and 120,000 to Liberia). The UNHCR has helped almost 180,000 Sierra Leoneans to return home, while more than 90,000 others have repatriated on their own. Of the more than 65,000 Liberians who took refuge in Sierra Leone during their country's civil war (1989-2003), about 50,000 have been voluntarily repatriated by the UNHCR and others have returned home independently. As of 2015, less than 1,000 Liberians still reside in Sierra Leone.

Age structure: *0-14 years:* 41.82% (male 1,286,681/female 1,290,924)

15-24 years: 18.56% (male 556,478/female 587,454)
25-54 years: 32.16% (male 949,264/female 1,032,783)
55-64 years: 3.7% (male 106,706/female 121,111)
65 years and over: 3.76% (male 96,285/female 135,509) (2017 est.)

Dependency ratios: *total dependency ratio:* 82.6
youth dependency ratio: 78
elderly dependency ratio: 4.6
potential support ratio: 21.9 (2015 est.)

Median age: *total:* 19 years
male: 18.4 years
female: 19.6 years (2017 est.)
country comparison to the world: 202

Population growth rate: 2.38% (2017 est.)
country comparison to the world: 26

Birth rate: 36.3 births/1,000 population (2017 est.)
country comparison to the world: 15

Death rate: 10.4 deaths/1,000 population (2017 est.)
country comparison to the world: 34

Net migration rate: -2.1 migrant(s)/1,000 population (2017 est.)
country comparison to the world: 164

Population distribution: population clusters are found in the lower elevations of the south and west; the northern third of the country is less populated

Urbanization: *urban population:* 40.7% of total population (2017)
rate of urbanization: 2.72% annual rate of change (2015-20 est.)

Major urban areas—population: FREETOWN (capital) 1.007 million (2015)

Sex ratio: *at birth:* 1.03 male(s)/female
0-14 years: 1 male(s)/female
15-24 years: 0.94 male(s)/female
25-54 years: 0.92 male(s)/female
55-64 years: 0.86 male(s)/female
65 years and over: 0.73 male(s)/female
total population: 0.95 male(s)/female (2016 est.)

Mother's mean age at first birth: 19.2 years
note: median age at first birth among women 25-29 (2013 est.)

Maternal mortality ratio: 1,360 deaths/100,000 live births (2015 est.)
country comparison to the world: 1

Infant mortality rate: *total:* 68.4 deaths/1,000 live births
male: 76.6 deaths/1,000 live births
female: 59.8 deaths/1,000 live births (2017 est.)
country comparison to the world: 10

Life expectancy at birth: *total population:* 58.6 years
male: 56 years
female: 61.3 years (2017 est.)
country comparison to the world: 209

Total fertility rate: 4.73 children born/woman (2017 est.)
country comparison to the world: 20

Contraceptive prevalence rate: 16.6% (2013)

Health expenditures: 11.1% of GDP (2014)
country comparison to the world: 13

Physicians density: 0.02 physicians/1,000 population (2010)

Hospital bed density: 0.4 beds/1,000 population (2006)

Drinking water source:
improved:
urban: 84.9% of population
rural: 47.8% of population
total: 62.6% of population
unimproved:
urban: 15.1% of population
rural: 52.2% of population
total: 37.4% of population (2015 est.)

Sanitation facility access:
improved:
urban: 22.8% of population
rural: 6.9% of population
total: 13.3% of population
unimproved:
urban: 77.2% of population
rural: 93.1% of population
total: 86.7% of population (2015 est.)

HIV/AIDS—adult prevalence rate: 1.7% (2016 est.)
country comparison to the world: 28

HIV/AIDS—people living with HIV/AIDS: 67,000 (2016 est.)
country comparison to the world: 51

HIV/AIDS—deaths: 2,800 (2016 est.)
country comparison to the world: 46

Major infectious diseases: *degree of risk:* very high
food or waterborne diseases: bacterial and protozoal diarrhea, hepatitis A, and typhoid fever
vectorborne diseases: malaria, dengue fever, and yellow fever
water contact disease: schistosomiasis
animal contact disease: rabies
aerosolized dust or soil contact disease: Lassa fever (2016)

Obesity—adult prevalence rate: 8.7% (2016)
country comparison to the world: 147

Children under the age of 5 years underweight: 18.1% (2013)
country comparison to the world: 34

Education expenditures: 2.7% of GDP (2014)
country comparison to the world: 141

Literacy: *definition:* age 15 and over can read and write English, Mende, Temne, or Arabic
total population: 48.1%
male: 58.7%
female: 37.7% (2015 est.)

GOVERNMENT

Country name: *conventional long form:* Republic of Sierra Leone
conventional short form: Sierra Leone
local long form: Republic of Sierra Leone
local short form: Sierra Leone
etymology: the Portuguese explorer Pedro de SINTRA named the country "Serra Leoa" (Lion Mountains) for the impressive mountains he saw while sailing the West African coast in 1462

Government type: presidential republic

Capital: *name:* Freetown
geographic coordinates: 8 29 N, 13 14 W
time difference: UTC 0 (5 hours ahead of Washington, DC, during Standard Time)

Administrative divisions: 3 provinces and 1 area*; Eastern, Northern, Southern, Western*

Independence: 27 April 1961 (from the UK)

National holiday: Independence Day, 27 April (1961)

Constitution: *history:* several previous; latest effective 1 October 1991
amendments: proposed by Parliament; passage of amendments requires at least two-thirds majority vote of Parliament in two successive readings and assent by the president of the republic; passage of amendments affecting fundamental rights and freedoms and many other constitutional sections also requires approval in a referendum with participation of at least one-half of qualified voters and at least two-thirds of votes cast; amended several times, last in 2013 (2017)

Legal system: mixed legal system of English common law and customary law

International law organization participation: has not submitted an ICJ jurisdiction declaration; accepts ICCt jurisdiction

Citizenship: *citizenship by birth:* no
citizenship by descent only: at least one parent or grandparent must be a citizen of Sierra Leone
dual citizenship recognized: yes
residency requirement for naturalization: 5 years

Suffrage: 18 years of age; universal

Executive branch: *chief of state:* President Ernest Bai KOROMA (since 17 September 2007); note—the president is both chief of state and head of government
head of government: President Ernest Bai KOROMA (since 17 September 2007)
cabinet: Ministers of State appointed by the president, approved by Parliament; the cabinet is responsible to the president
elections/appointments: president directly elected by absolute majority popular vote in 2 rounds if needed for a 5-year term (eligible for a second term); election last held on 17 November 2012 (next to be on 7 March 2018)
election results: Ernest Bai KOROMA reelected president; percent of vote—Ernest Bai KOROMA (APC) 58.7%, Julius Maada BIO (SLPP) 37.4%, other 3.9%

Legislative branch: *description:* unicameral Parliament (124 seats; 112 members directly elected in single-seat constituencies by simple majority vote and 12 seats filled in separate elections by non-partisan members of Parliament called "paramount chiefs;" members serve 5-year terms)
elections: last held on 17 November 2012 (next to be held on 7 March 2018)

election results: percent of vote by party—APC 53.7%, SLPP 38.3%, other 8.0%; seats by party—APC 67, SLPP 42

Judicial branch: *highest court(s):* Superior Court of Judicature (consists of the Supreme Court—at the apex—with the chief justice and 4 other judges, the Court of Appeal with the chief justice and 7 other judges, and the High Court of Justice with the chief justice and 9 other judges; note—the Judicature has jurisdiction in all civil, criminal, and constitutional matters
judge selection and term of office: Supreme Court chief justice and other judges of the Judicature appointed by the president on the advice of the Judicial and Legal Service Commission (a 7-member independent body of judges, presidential appointees, and the Commission chairman) and are subject to the approval of Parliament; all Judicature judges appointed until retirement at age 65
subordinate courts: magistrates' courts; District Appeals Court; local courts

Political parties and leaders: All People's Congress or APC [Ernest Bai KOROMA]
Sierra Leone People's Party or SLPP [Sumanoh KAPEN]
numerous other parties

Political pressure groups and leaders: student unions; trade unions

International organization participation: ACP, AfDB, AU, C, ECOWAS, EITI (compliant country), FAO, G-77, IAEA, IBRD, ICAO, ICCt, ICRM, IDA, IDB, IFAD, IFC, IFRCS, IHO (pending member), ILO, IMF, IMO, Interpol, IOC, IOM, IPU, ISO (correspondent), ITU, ITUC (NGOs), MIGA, MINUSMA, NAM, OIC, OPCW, UN, UNAMID, UNCTAD, UNESCO, UNIDO, UNIFIL, UNISFA, UNWTO, UPU, WCO, WFTU (NGOs), WHO, WIPO, WMO, WTO

Diplomatic representation in the US: chief of mission: Ambassador Bockari Kortu STEVENS (since 4 April 2008)
chancery: 1701 19th Street NW, Washington, DC 20009
telephone: [1] (202) 939-9261 through 9263
FAX: [1] (202) 483-1793

Diplomatic representation from the US: *chief of mission:* Ambassador Maria E. BREWER (since 20 December 2017)
embassy: Southridge-Hill Station, Freetown
mailing address: use embassy street address
telephone: [232] 99 1055 00
FAX: [232] 99 515 355

Flag description: three equal horizontal bands of light green (top), white, and light blue; green symbolizes agriculture, mountains, and natural resources, white represents unity and justice, and blue the sea and the natural harbor in Freetown

National symbol(s): lion; national colors: green, white, blue

National anthem: *name:* "High We Exalt Thee, Realm of the Free"
lyrics/music: Clifford Nelson FYLE/John Joseph AKA
note: adopted 1961

ECONOMY

Economy—overview: Sierra Leone is extremely poor and nearly half of the working-age population engages in subsistence agriculture. The country possesses substantial mineral, agricultural, and fishery resources, but it is still recovering from a civil war that destroyed most institutions before ending in the early 2000s.

In recent years, economic growth has been driven by mining—particularly iron ore. The country's principal exports are iron ore, diamonds, and rutile, and the economy is vulnerable to fluctuations in international prices. Until 2014, the government had relied on external assistance to support its budget, but it was gradually becoming more independent. The Ebola outbreak of 2014 and 2015, combined with falling global commodities prices, caused a significant contraction of economic activity in all areas. While the World Health Organization declared an end to the Ebola outbreak in Sierra Leone in November 2015, low commodity prices in 2015-2016 contributed to the country's biggest fiscal shortfall since 2001. In 2017, increased iron ore exports, together with the end of the Ebola epidemic, supported a resumption of economic growth.

Continued economic growth will depend on rising commodities prices and increased efforts to diversify the sources of growth. Non-mining activities will remain constrained by inadequate infrastructure, such as power and roads, even though power sector projects may provide some additional electricity capacity in the near term. Pervasive corruption and undeveloped human capital will continue to deter foreign investors. Sustained international donor support in the near future will partially offset these fiscal constraints.

GDP (purchasing power parity): $11.75 billion (2017 est.)
$11.08 billion (2016 est.)
$10.45 billion (2015 est.)
note: data are in 2017 dollars
country comparison to the world: 157

GDP (official exchange rate): $3.897 billion (2016 est.)

GDP—real growth rate: 6% (2017 est.)
6.1% (2016 est.)
-20.5% (2015 est.)
country comparison to the world: 23

GDP—per capita (PPP): $1,800 (2017 est.)
$1,700 (2016 est.)
$1,700 (2015 est.)
note: data are in 2017 dollars
country comparison to the world: 212

Gross national saving: -1.9% of GDP (2017 est.)
-9.3% of GDP (2016 est.)
-5.9% of GDP (2015 est.)
country comparison to the world: 179

GDP—composition, by end use:
household consumption: 102.1%
government consumption: 10.7%
investment in fixed capital: 16.8%
investment in inventories: 0.4%

exports of goods and services: 26.7%
imports of goods and services: -56.7% (2017 est.)

GDP—composition, by sector of origin:
agriculture: 60.7%
industry: 6.5%
services: 32.9% (2017 est.)

Agriculture—products: rice, coffee, cocoa, palm kernels, palm oil, peanuts, cashews; poultry, cattle, sheep, pigs; fish

Industries: diamond mining; iron ore, rutile and bauxite mining; small-scale manufacturing (beverages, textiles, footwear)

Industrial production growth rate: 15.5% (2017 est.)
country comparison to the world: 3

Labor force: 2.972 million (2017 est.)
country comparison to the world: 105

Labor force—by occupation: *agriculture:* 61.1%
industry: 5.5%
services: 33.4% (2014 est.)

Unemployment rate: 9.1% (2014 est.)
country comparison to the world: 125

Population below poverty line: 70.2% (2004 est.)

Household income or consumption by percentage share: *lowest 10%:* 2.6%
highest 10%: 33.6% (2003)

Distribution of family income—Gini index: 34 (2011)
62.9 (1989)
country comparison to the world: 101

Budget: *revenues:* $684.3 million
expenditures: $962.6 million (2017 est.)
Taxes and other revenues: 17.6% of GDP (2017 est.)
country comparison to the world: 172

Budget surplus (+) or deficit (-): -7.1% of GDP (2017 est.)
country comparison to the world: 190

Public debt: 57.6% of GDP (2017 est.)
54.9% of GDP (2016 est.)
country comparison to the world: 80

Fiscal year: calendar year

Inflation rate (consumer prices): 16.9% (2017 est.)
11.5% (2016 est.)
country comparison to the world: 214

Central bank discount rate: NA%

Commercial bank prime lending rate: 18.6% (31 December 2017 est.)
18% (31 December 2016 est.)
country comparison to the world: 22

Stock of narrow money: $378.7 million (31 December 2017 est.)
$381.8 million (31 December 2016 est.)
country comparison to the world: 174

Stock of broad money: $910.1 million (31 December 2017 est.)
$847.2 million (31 December 2016 est.)
country comparison to the world: 174

Stock of domestic credit: $567.7 million (31 December 2017 est.)

$527.6 million (31 December 2016 est.)
country comparison to the world: 175

Market value of publicly traded shares: $NA

Current account balance: -$822 million (2017 est.)
-$733 million (2016 est.)
country comparison to the world: 125

Exports: $836.8 million (2017 est.)
$670 million (2016 est.)
country comparison to the world: 164

Exports—commodities: iron ore, diamonds, rutile, cocoa, coffee, fish

Exports—partners: Cote dIvoire 31.7%, US 28.3%, Belgium 17.7%, China 6.6% (2016)

Imports: $1.564 billion (2017 est.)
$1.316 billion (2016 est.)
country comparison to the world: 168

Imports—commodities: foodstuffs, machinery and equipment, fuels and lubricants, chemicals

Imports—partners: China 12.5%, US 9.7%, India 7.8%, UAE 7.2%, Senegal 6.2%, Belgium 5.5%, Turkey 5.5%, UK 4.7% (2016)

Debt—external: $1.707 billion (31 December 2017 est.)
$1.503 billion (31 December 2016 est.)
country comparison to the world: 154

Stock of direct foreign investment—at home:
$2.254 billion (31 December 2017 est.)
$1.832 billion (31 December 2016 est.)
country comparison to the world: 115

Stock of direct foreign investment—abroad: $9.7 million (31 December 2015 est.)
$6.7 million (31 December 2014 est.)
country comparison to the world: 110

Exchange rates: leones (SLL) per US dollar—
7,396.3 (2017 est.)
6,289.9 (2016 est.)
6,289.9 (2015 est.)
5,080.8 (2014 est.)
4,524.2 (2013 est.)

ENERGY

Electricity access: population without electricity: 5,800,000
electrification—*total population:* 5%
electrification—urban areas: 11%
electrification—rural areas: 1% (2013)

Electricity—production: 175 million kWh (2015 est.)
country comparison to the world: 192

Electricity—consumption: 162.8 million kWh (2015 est.)
country comparison to the world: 194

Electricity—exports: 0 kWh (2016 est.)
country comparison to the world: 196

Electricity—imports: 0 kWh (2016 est.)
country comparison to the world: 200

Electricity—installed generating capacity: 81,000 kW (2015 est.)
country comparison to the world: 183

Electricity—from fossil fuels: 33.3% of total installed capacity (2015 est.)
country comparison to the world: 182

Electricity—from nuclear fuels: 0% of total installed capacity (2015 est.)
country comparison to the world: 181

Electricity—from hydroelectric plants: 66.7% of total installed capacity (2015 est.)
country comparison to the world: 20

Electricity—from other renewable sources: 0% of total installed capacity (2015 est.)
country comparison to the world: 205

Crude oil—production: 0 bbl/day (2016 est.)
country comparison to the world: 197

Crude oil—exports: 0 bbl/day (2014 est.)
country comparison to the world: 190

Crude oil—imports: 0 bbl/day (2014 est.)
country comparison to the world: 189

Crude oil—proved reserves: 0 bbl (1 January 2017 es)
country comparison to the world: 195

Refined petroleum products—production: 0 bbl/day (2014 est.)
country comparison to the world: 200

Refined petroleum products—consumption: 7,500 bbl/day (2015 est.)
country comparison to the world: 163

Refined petroleum products—exports: 0 bbl/day (2014 est.)
country comparison to the world: 197

Refined petroleum products—imports: 7,354 bbl/day (2014 est.)
country comparison to the world: 151

Natural gas—production: 0 cu m (2013 est.)
country comparison to the world: 193

Natural gas—consumption: 0 cu m (2013 est.)
country comparison to the world: 130

Natural gas—exports: 0 cu m (2013 est.)
country comparison to the world: 182

Natural gas—imports: 0 cu m (2013 est.)
country comparison to the world: 187

Natural gas—proved reserves: 0 cu m (1 January 2014 es)
country comparison to the world: 194

Carbon dioxide emissions from consumption of energy: 1.4 million Mt (2013 est.)
country comparison to the world: 157

COMMUNICATIONS

Telephones—fixed lines: *total subscriptions:* 17,000
subscriptions per 100 inhabitants: less than 1 (July 2016 est.)
country comparison to the world: 192

Telephones—mobile cellular: *total:* 6,279,270
subscriptions per 100 inhabitants: 104 (July 2016 est.)
country comparison to the world: 120

Telephone system: *general assessment:* telephone service improving with the expansion of the mobile sector

domestic: the national microwave radio relay trunk system connects Freetown to Bo and Kenema; mobile-cellular service has grown rapidly from a small base, overcoming the deficiencies of the fixed-line sector
international: country code—232; satellite earth station—1 Intelsat (Atlantic Ocean) (2016)

Broadcast media: 1 government-owned TV station; 3 private TV stations; a pay-TV service began operations in late 2007; 1 government-owned national radio station; about two-dozen private radio stations primarily clustered in major cities; transmissions of several international broadcasters are available (2016)

Internet country code: .sl

Internet users: total: 708,615
percent of population: 11.8% (July 2016 est.)
country comparison to the world: 173

TRANSPORTATION

National air transport system: number of registered air carriers: inventory of registered aircraft operated by air carriers: annual passenger traffic on registered air carriers: 50,193
annual freight traffic on registered air carriers: 0 mt-km (2015)
Civil aircraft registration country code prefix: 9L (2016)

Airports: 8 (2013)
country comparison to the world: 164

Airports—with paved runways: total: 1
over 3,047 m: 1 (2017)

Airports—with unpaved runways: total: 7
914 to 1,523 m: 7 (2013)

Heliports: 2 (2013)

Roadways: total: 11,300 km
paved: 904 km
unpaved: 10,396 km (2002)
country comparison to the world: 131

Waterways: 800 km (600 km navigable year-round) (2011)
country comparison to the world: 71

Merchant marine: total: 451
by type: bulk carrier 20, container ship 10, general cargo 252, oil tanker 59, other 110 (2017)
country comparison to the world: 42

Ports and terminals: *major seaport(s):* Freetown, Pepel, Sherbro Islands

MILITARY AND SECURITY

Military expenditures: 0.81% of GDP (2016)
0.92% of GDP (2015)
0.97% of GDP (2014)
0.64% of GDP (2013)
0.78% of GDP (2012)
country comparison to the world: 118

Military branches: Republic of Sierra Leone Armed Forces (RSLAF): Army (includes Maritime Wing and Air Wing) (2013)

Military service age and obligation: 18 is the legal minimum age for voluntary military service (younger with parental consent); women are eligible to serve; no conscription; candidates must be HIV negative (2012)

TRANSNATIONAL ISSUES

Disputes—international: Sierra Leone opposes Guinean troops' continued occupation of Yenga, a small village on the Makona River that serves as a border with Guinea; Guinea's forces came to Yenga in the mid-1990s to help the Sierra Leonean military to suppress rebels and to secure their common border but have remained there even after both countries signed a 2005 agreement acknowledging that Yenga belonged to Sierra Leone; in 2012, the two sides signed a declaration to demilitarize the area

SINGAPORE

INTRODUCTION

Background: A Malay trading port known as Temasek existed on the island of Singapore by the 14th century. The settlement changed hands several times in the ensuing centuries and was eventually burned in the 17th century and fell into obscurity. The British founded Singapore as a trading colony on the site in 1819. It joined the Malaysian Federation in 1963 but was ousted two years later and became independent. Singapore subsequently became one of the world's most prosperous countries with strong international trading links (its port is one of the world's busiest in terms of tonnage handled) and with per capita GDP equal to that of the leading nations of Western Europe.

GEOGRAPHY

Location: Southeastern Asia, islands between Malaysia and Indonesia

Geographic coordinates: 1 22 N, 103 48 E

Map references: Southeast Asia

Area: *total:* 719.2 sq km
land: 709.2 sq km
water: 10 sq km
country comparison to the world: 192

Area—comparative: slightly more than 3.5 times the size of Washington, DC
Land boundaries: 0 km

Coastline: 193 km

Maritime claims: *territorial sea:* 3 nm

exclusive fishing zone: within and beyond territorial sea, as defined in treaties and practice

Climate: tropical; hot, humid, rainy; two distinct monsoon seasons—northeastern monsoon (December to March) and southwestern monsoon (June to September); inter-monsoon—frequent afternoon and early evening thunderstorms

Terrain: lowlying, gently undulating central plateau

Elevation: *mean elevation:* NA

elevation extremes: *lowest point:* Singapore Strait 0 m
highest point: Bukit Timah 166 m

Natural resources: fish, deepwater ports

Land use: *agricultural land:* 1%
arable land: 0.9%;
permanent crops: 0.1%;
permanent pasture: 0%
forest: 3.3%
other: 95.7% (2011 est.)
Irrigated land: 0 sq km (2012)

Population—distribution: most of the urbanization is along the southern coast, with relatively dense population clusters found in the central areas

Natural hazards: flash floods

Environment—current issues: industrial pollution; limited natural freshwater resources; limited land availability presents waste disposal problems; seasonal smoke/haze resulting from forest fires in Indonesia

Environment—international agreements: *party to:* Biodiversity, Climate Change, Climate Change-Kyoto Protocol, Desertification, Endangered Species, Hazardous Wastes, Law of the Sea, Ozone Layer Protection, Ship Pollution
signed, but not ratified: none of the selected agreements

Geography—note: focal point for Southeast Asian sea routes; consists of about 60 islands, by far the largest of which is Pulau Ujong; land reclamation has removed many former islands and created a number of new ones

PEOPLE AND SOCIETY

Population: 5,888,926 (July 2017 est.)
country comparison to the world: 113

Nationality: *noun:* Singaporean(s)
adjective: Singapore

Ethnic groups: Chinese 74.3%, Malay 13.4%, Indian 9.1% (includes Sri Lankan), other 3.2% (2016 est.)

Languages: Mandarin (official) 36.3%, English (official) 29.8%, Malay (official) 11.9%, Hokkien 8.1%, Cantonese 4.1%, Tamil (official) 3.2%, Teochew 3.2%, other Indian languages 1.2%, other Chinese dialects 1.1%, other 1.1% (2010 est.)

Religions: Buddhist 33.9%, Muslim 14.3%, Taoist 11.3%, Catholic 7.1%, Hindu 5.2%, other Christian 11%, other 0.7%, none 16.4% (2010 est.)

Age structure: *0-14 years:* 12.82% (male 386,139/female 368,874)
15-24 years: 16.56% (male 479,683/female 495,649)
25-54 years: 50.53% (male 1,448,463/female 1,527,038)
55-64 years: 10.46% (male 308,477/female 307,557)
65 years and over: 9.63% (male 258,597/female 308,449) (2017 est.)

Dependency ratios: *total dependency ratio:* 37.3
youth dependency ratio: 21.3
elderly dependency ratio: 16
potential support ratio: 6.2 (2015 est.)

Median age: *total:* 34.6 years
male: 34.5 years
female: 34.7 years (2017 est.)
country comparison to the world: 83

Population growth rate: 1.82% (2017 est.)
country comparison to the world: 57

Birth rate: 8.6 births/1,000 population (2017 est.)
country comparison to the world: 214

Death rate: 3.5 deaths/1,000 population (2017 est.)
country comparison to the world: 217

Net migration rate: 13.1 migrant(s)/1,000 population (2017 est.)
country comparison to the world: 5

Population distribution: most of the urbanization is along the southern coast, with relatively dense population clusters found in the central areas

Urbanization: *urban population:* 100% of total population (2017)
rate of urbanization: 1.5% annual rate of change (2015-20 est.)

Major urban areas—population: SINGAPORE (capital) 5.619 million (2015)

Sex ratio: *at birth:* 1.07 male(s)/female
0-14 years: 1.05 male(s)/female

15-24 years: 0.97 male(s)/female
25-54 years: 0.95 male(s)/female
55-64 years: 1 male(s)/female
65 years and over: 0.83 male(s)/female
total population: 0.96 male(s)/female (2016 est.)

Mother's mean age at first birth: 30.5 years
median age (2015 est.)

Maternal mortality ratio: 10 deaths/100,000 live
births (2015 est.)
country comparison to the world: 148

Infant mortality rate: *total:* 2.4 deaths/1,000 live
births
male: 2.6 deaths/1,000 live births
female: 2.2 deaths/1,000 live births (2017 est.)
country comparison to the world: 222

Life expectancy at birth: *total population:* 85.2
years
male: 82.6 years
female: 88.1 years (2017 est.)
country comparison to the world: 3

Total fertility rate: 0.83 children born/woman
(2017 est.)
country comparison to the world: 224

Health expenditures: 4.9% of GDP (2014)
country comparison to the world: 144

Physicians density: 1.91 physicians/1,000 population (2013)

Hospital bed density: 2 beds/1,000 population
(2011)

Drinking water source:
improved:
urban: 100% of population
total: 100% of population
unimproved:
urban: 0% of population
total: 0% of population (2015 est.)

Sanitation facility access:
improved:
urban: 100% of population
total: 100% of population
unimproved:
urban: 0% of population
total: 0% of population (2015 est.)

HIV/AIDS—adult prevalence rate: NA

HIV/AIDS—people living with HIV/AIDS: NA

HIV/AIDS—deaths: NA

Major infectious diseases: *note:* active local transmission of Zika virus by Aedes species mosquitoes
has been identified in this country (as of August
2016); it poses an important risk (a large number
of cases possible) among US citizens if bitten by
an infective mosquito; other less common ways to
get Zika are through sex, via blood transfusion, or
during pregnancy, in which the pregnant woman
passes Zika virus to her fetus (2016)

Obesity—adult prevalence rate: 6.1% (2016)
country comparison to the world: 170

Education expenditures: 2.9% of GDP (2013)
country comparison to the world: 140

Literacy: *definition:* age 15 and over can read and
write
total population: 97%

male: 98.7%
female: 98.2% (2016 est.)

**School life expectancy (primary to tertiary educa-
tion):** *total:* 13 years
male: 13 years
female: 13 years (2009)

Unemployment, youth ages 15-24: *total:* 6.6%
male: 5.6%
female: 7.7% (2015 est.)
country comparison to the world: 121

GOVERNMENT

Country name: *conventional long form:* Republic
of Singapore
conventional short form: Singapore
local long form: Republic of Singapore
local short form: Singapore
etymology: name derives from the Sanskrit words
"singa" (lion) and "pura" (city) to describe the
city-state's leonine symbol

Government type: parliamentary republic

Capital: *name:* Singapore

geographic coordinates: 1 17 N, 103 51 E
time difference: UTC+8 (13 hours ahead of
Washington, DC, during Standard Time)

Administrative divisions: none

Independence: 9 August 1965 (from Malaysian
Federation)

National holiday: National Day, 9 August (1965)

Constitution: several previous; latest adopted 22
December 1965; amended many times, last in
2015 (2016)

Legal system: English common law

International law organization participation: has
not submitted an ICJ jurisdiction declaration;
non-party state to the ICCt

Citizenship: *citizenship by birth:* no

citizenship by descent only: at least one parent
must be a citizen of Singapore
dual citizenship recognized: no
residency requirement for naturalization: 10
years

Suffrage: 21 years of age; universal and compulsory

Executive branch: *chief of state:* President Halimah YACOB (since 14 September 2017); note—
President TAN's term ended on 31 August 2017;
YACOB is Singapore's first female president; the
head of the Council of Presidential Advisors, J.Y.
PILLAY, served as acting president until YACOB
was sworn in as president on 14 September 2017
head of government: Prime Minister LEE Hsien
Loong (since 12 August 2004); Deputy Prime
Ministers TEO Chee Hean (since 1 April 2009)
and Tharman SHANMUGARATNAM (since 21
May 2011)
cabinet: Cabinet appointed by the president on
the advice of the prime minister; Cabinet responsible to Parliament
elections/appointments: president directly
elected by simple majority popular vote for a
single 6-year term; election last held on 13 September 2017 (next to be held in 2023); following

legislative elections, leader of majority party or
majority coalition usually appointed prime minister by president; deputy prime ministers appointed
by the president
election results: Halimah YACOB was declared
president on 13 September 2017, being the only
eligible candidate; Tony TAN Keng Yam elected
president in the previous contested election on 27
August 2011; percent of vote—Tony TAN Keng
Yam (independent) 35.2% , TAN Cheng Bock
(independent) 34.9%, TAN Jee Say (independent) 25%, TAN Kin Lian (PP) 4.9%

Legislative branch: *description:* unicameral Parliament (101 seats; 89 members directly elected
by popular vote, 9 nominated by the president,
and up to 9—but currently 3—non-constituency
members from opposition parties to ensure political diversity; members serve 5-year terms)
elections: last held on 11 September 2015 (next to
be held in 2020)
election results: percent of vote by party—PAP
69.9%, WP 12.5%, other 17.6%; seats by party—
PAP 83, WP 6

Judicial branch: *highest court(s):* Supreme Court
(consists of the president or chief justice and 16
justices and is organized into an upper tier Appeal
Court and a lower tier High Court)
judge selection and term of office: all judges
appointed by the president from candidates recommended by the prime minister after consultation
with the chief justice; justices appointed for life
subordinate courts: district, magistrates', juvenile, family, community, and coroners' courts;
small claims tribunals

Political parties and leaders: National Solidarity
Party or NSP
People's Action Party or PAP [LEE Hsien Loong]
Singapore Democratic Party or SDP [Dr. CHEE
Soon Juan]
Workers' Party or WP [LOW Thia Khiang]

Political pressure groups and leaders: none

International organization participation: ADB,
AOSIS, APEC, Arctic Council (observer), ARF,
ASEAN, BIS, C, CP, EAS, FAO, FATF, G-77,
IAEA, IBRD, ICAO, ICC (national committees),
ICCt, ICRM, IDA, IFC, IFRCS, IHO, ILO, IMF,
IMO, IMSO, Interpol, IOC, IPU, ISO, ITSO,
ITU, ITUC (NGOs), MIGA, NAM, OPCW,
Pacific Alliance (observer), PCA, UN, UNC-
TAD, UNESCO, UNHCR, UPU, WCO, WHO,
WIPO, WMO, WTO

Diplomatic representation in the US: chief of mission: Ambassador Ashok Kumar MIRPURI (since
30 July 2012)
chancery: 3501 International Place NW, Washington, DC 20008
telephone: [1] (202) 537-3100
FAX: [1] (202) 537-0876
consulate(s) general: San Francisco
consulate(s): New York

Diplomatic representation from the US: *chief of
mission:* Ambassador (vacant); Charge d'Affaires
Stephanie SYPTAK-RAMNATH (since 20 January 2017)

embassy: 27 Napier Road, Singapore 258508
mailing address: FPO AP 96507-0001
telephone: [65] 6476-9100
FAX: [65] 6476-9340

Flag description: two equal horizontal bands of red (top) and white; near the hoist side of the red band, there is a vertical, white crescent (closed portion is toward the hoist side) partially enclosing five white five-pointed stars arranged in a circle; red denotes brotherhood and equality; white signifies purity and virtue; the waxing crescent moon symbolizes a young nation on the ascendancy; the five stars represent the nation's ideals of democracy, peace, progress, justice, and equality

National symbol(s): lion, merlion (mythical half lion-half fish creature), orchid; national colors: red, white

National anthem: *name:* "Majulah Singapura" (Onward Singapore)
lyrics/music: ZUBIR Said
note: adopted 1965; first performed in 1958 at the Victoria Theatre, the anthem is sung only in Malay

ECONOMY

Economy—overview: Singapore has a highly developed and successful free-market economy. It enjoys a remarkably open and corruption-free environment, stable prices, and a per capita GDP higher than that of most developed countries. Unemployment is very low. The economy depends heavily on exports, particularly of consumer electronics, information technology products, medical and optical devices, pharmaceuticals, and on its vibrant transportation, business, and financial services sectors.

The economy contracted 0.6% in 2009 as a result of the global financial crisis, but has continued to grow since 2010. Growth in 2014-17 was slower than during the previous decade, at under 3% annually, largely a result of soft demand for exports amid a sluggish global economy and weak growth in Singapore's manufacturing sector.

The government is attempting to restructure Singapore's economy by weaning its dependence on foreign labor, addressing weak productivity growth, and increasing Singaporean wages. Singapore has attracted major investments in advanced manufacturing, pharmaceuticals, and medical technology production and will continue efforts to strengthen its position as Southeast Asia's leading financial and technology hub. Singapore is a member of the Regional Comprehensive Economic Partnership negotiations with the nine other ASEAN members plus Australia, China, India, Japan, South Korea, and New Zealand. In 2015, Singapore formed, with the other ASEAN members, the ASEAN Economic Community.

GDP (purchasing power parity): $513.7 billion (2017 est.)
$501.1 billion (2016 est.)
$491.3 billion (2015 est.)
note: data are in 2017 dollars
country comparison to the world: 41

GDP (official exchange rate): $305.8 billion (2016 est.)

GDP—real growth rate: 2.5% (2017 est.)
2% (2016 est.)
1.9% (2015 est.)
country comparison to the world: 138

GDP—per capita (PPP): $90,500 (2017 est.)
$89,400 (2016 est.)
$88,800 (2015 est.)
note: data are in 2017 dollars
country comparison to the world: 7

Gross national saving: 45% of GDP (2017 est.)
44.4% of GDP (2016 est.)
44.9% of GDP (2015 est.)
country comparison to the world: 5

GDP—composition, by end use:
household consumption: 34.7%
government consumption: 11.4%
investment in fixed capital: 23.5%
investment in inventories: 1.9%
exports of goods and services: 179.2%
imports of goods and services: -150.6% (2017 est.)

GDP—composition, by sector of origin:
agriculture: 0%
industry: 26%
services: 74% (2017 est.)

Agriculture—products: orchids, vegetables; poultry, eggs; fish, ornamental fish

Industries: electronics, chemicals, financial services, oil drilling equipment, petroleum refining, rubber processing and rubber products, processed food and beverages, ship repair, offshore platform construction, life sciences, entrepot trade

Industrial production growth rate: 3% (2017 est.)
country comparison to the world: 93

Labor force: 3.668 million
note: excludes non-residents (2017 est.)
country comparison to the world: 99

Labor force—by occupation: *agriculture:* 0.96%
industry: 15.5%
services: 83.5%
note: excludes non-residents (2016)

Unemployment rate: 2.2% (2017 est.)
2.1% (2016 est.)
country comparison to the world: 17

Population below poverty line: NA%

Household income or consumption by percentage share: *lowest 10%:* 1.7%
highest 10%: 26% (2016)

Distribution of family income—Gini index: 45.8 (2016)
46.3 (2015)
country comparison to the world: 36

Budget: *revenues:* $53.4 billion
expenditures: $56.49 billion
note: expenditures include both operational and development expenditures (2017 est.)
Taxes and other revenues: 17.5% of GDP (2017 est.)
country comparison to the world: 174

Budget surplus (+) or deficit (-): -1% of GDP (2017 est.)
country comparison to the world: 57

Public debt: 114.6% of GDP (2017 est.)
112.9% of GDP (2016 est.)
note: Singapore's public debt consists largely of Singapore Government Securities (SGS) issued to assist the Central Provident Fund (CPF), which administers Singapore's defined contribution pension fund; special issues of SGS are held by the CPF, and are non-tradable; the government has not borrowed to finance deficit expenditures since the 1980s; Singapore has no external public debt
country comparison to the world: 11

Fiscal year: 1 April—31 March

Inflation rate (consumer prices): 0.9% (2017 est.)
-0.5% (2016 est.)
country comparison to the world: 34

Central bank discount rate: 1.17% (2016 est.)
1.21% (2015 est.)
country comparison to the world: 126

Commercial bank prime lending rate: 5.4% (31 December 2017 est.)
5.35% (31 December 2016 est.)
country comparison to the world: 136

Stock of narrow money: $134.3 billion (31 December 2017 est.)
$119.4 billion (31 December 2016 est.)
country comparison to the world: 32

Stock of broad money: $437.6 billion (31 December 2017 est.)
$388.6 billion (31 December 2016 est.)
country comparison to the world: 25

Stock of domestic credit: $455.4 billion (31 December 2017 est.)
$383.3 billion (31 December 2016 est.)
country comparison to the world: 31

Market value of publicly traded shares: $654.8 billion (31 December 2016 est.)
$640 billion (31 December 2015 est.)
$752.8 billion (31 December 2014 est.)
country comparison to the world: 17

Current account balance: $59.79 billion (2017 est.)
$56.5 billion (2016 est.)
country comparison to the world: 9

Exports: $396.4 billion (2017 est.)
$361.6 billion (2016 est.)
country comparison to the world: 14

Exports—commodities: machinery and equipment (including electronics and telecommunications), pharmaceuticals and other chemicals, refined petroleum products, foodstuffs and beverages

Exports—partners: China 12.8%, Hong Kong 12.6%, Malaysia 10.5%, Indonesia 7.8%, US 6.8%, Japan 4.5%, South Korea 4.4% (2016)

Imports: $309.7 billion (2017 est.)
$278.8 billion (2016 est.)
country comparison to the world: 16

Imports—commodities: machinery and equipment, mineral fuels, chemicals, foodstuffs, consumer goods

Imports—partners: China 14.3%, Malaysia 11.4%, US 10.8%, Japan 7%, South Korea 6.1%, Indonesia 4.8% (2016)

Reserves of foreign exchange and gold: $266.3 billion (31 December 2017 est.)
$246.6 billion (31 December 2016 est.)
country comparison to the world: 12

Debt—external: $482.8 billion (31 December 2017 est.)
$504.2 billion (31 December 2016 est.)
country comparison to the world: 26

Stock of direct foreign investment—at home: $1.158 trillion (31 December 2017 est.)
$1.096 trillion (31 December 2016 est.)
country comparison to the world: 10

Stock of direct foreign investment—abroad: $725.9 billion (31 December 2017 est.)
$682.4 billion (31 December 2016 est.)
country comparison to the world: 15

Exchange rates: Singapore dollars (SGD) per US dollar—
1.392 (2017 est.)
1.3815 (2016 est.)
1.3815 (2015 est.)
1.3748 (2014 est.)
1.2671 (2013 est.)

ENERGY

Electricity access: *electrification—total population:* 100% (2016)

Electricity—production: 47.48 billion kWh (2015 est.)
country comparison to the world: 55

Electricity—consumption: 46.6 billion kWh (2015 est.)
country comparison to the world: 54

Electricity—exports: 0 kWh (2016 est.)
country comparison to the world: 197

Electricity—imports: 0 kWh (2016 est.)
country comparison to the world: 201

Electricity—installed generating capacity: 13.28 million kW (2015 est.)
country comparison to the world: 53

Electricity—from fossil fuels: 98.6% of total installed capacity (2015 est.)
country comparison to the world: 36

Electricity—from nuclear fuels: 0% of total installed capacity (2015 est.)
country comparison to the world: 182

Electricity—from hydroelectric plants: 0% of total installed capacity (2015 est.)
country comparison to the world: 203

Electricity—from other renewable sources: 1.9% of total installed capacity (2015 est.)
country comparison to the world: 124

Crude oil—production: 0 bbl/day (2016 est.)
country comparison to the world: 198

Crude oil—exports: 11,460 bbl/day (2014 est.)
country comparison to the world: 59

Crude oil—imports: 831,300 bbl/day (2014 est.)
country comparison to the world: 13

Crude oil—proved reserves: 0 bbl (1 January 2017 es)
country comparison to the world: 196

Refined petroleum products—production: 955,500 bbl/day (2014 est.)
country comparison to the world: 22

Refined petroleum products—consumption: 1.34 million bbl/day (2015 est.)
country comparison to the world: 17

Refined petroleum products—exports: 1.718 million bbl/day (2014 est.)
country comparison to the world: 5

Refined petroleum products—imports: 2.153 million bbl/day (2014 est.)
country comparison to the world: 3

Natural gas—production: 0 cu m (2014 est.)
country comparison to the world: 194

Natural gas—consumption: 19.73 billion cu m (2015 est.)
country comparison to the world: 43

Natural gas—exports: 250 million cu m (2015 est.)
country comparison to the world: 47

Natural gas—imports: 12.37 billion cu m (2015 est.)
country comparison to the world: 24

Natural gas—proved reserves: 0 cu m (1 January 2015 es)
country comparison to the world: 195

Carbon dioxide emissions from consumption of energy: 205 million Mt (2015 est.)
country comparison to the world: 29

COMMUNICATIONS

Telephones—fixed lines: *total subscriptions:* 2,003,200
subscriptions per 100 inhabitants: 35 (July 2016 est.)
country comparison to the world: 58

Telephones—mobile cellular: *total:* 8,399,700
subscriptions per 100 inhabitants: 145 (July 2016 est.)
country comparison to the world: 92

Telephone system: *general assessment:* excellent service
domestic: excellent domestic facilities; combined fixed-line and mobile-cellular teledensity more than 180 telephones per 100 persons; multiple providers of high-speed Internet connectivity
international: country code—65; numerous submarine cables provide links throughout Asia, Australia, the Middle East, Europe, and US; satellite earth stations—4; supplemented by VSAT coverage (2016)

Broadcast media: state controls broadcast media; 8 domestic TV stations operated by MediaCorp which is wholly owned by a state investment company; broadcasts from Malaysian and Indonesian stations available; satellite dishes banned; multichannel cable TV service available; a total of 18 domestic radio stations broadcasting with MediaCorp operating more than a dozen and another

4 stations are closely linked to the ruling party or controlled by the Singapore Armed Forces Reservists Association; many Malaysian and Indonesian radio stations are available

Internet country code: .sg

Internet users: *total:* 4,683,200
percent of population: 81.0% (July 2016 est.)
country comparison to the world: 73

TRANSPORTATION

National air transport system: *number of registered air carriers:* 5
inventory of registered aircraft operated by air carriers: 197
annual passenger traffic on registered air carriers: 33,290,544
annual freight traffic on registered air carriers: 6,154,365,275 mt-km (2015)
Civil aircraft registration country code prefix: 9V (2016)

Airports: 9 (2013)
country comparison to the world: 158

Airports—with paved runways: *total:* 9
over 3,047 m: 2
2,438 to 3,047 m: 2
1,524 to 2,437 m: 3
914 to 1,523 m: 1
under 914 m: 1 (2017)

Pipelines: gas 122 km; refined products 8 km (2013)

Roadways: *total:* 3,425 km
paved: 3,425 km (includes 161 km of expressways) (2012)
country comparison to the world: 163

Merchant marine: *total:* 3,558
by type: bulk carrier 592, container ship 504, general cargo 134, oil tanker 722, other 1,606 (2017)
country comparison to the world: 6

Ports and terminals: *major seaport(s):* Singapore
container port(s) (TEUs): Singapore (30,922,000) (2015)
LNG terminal(s) (import): Singapore

MILITARY AND SECURITY

Military expenditures: 3.35% of GDP (2016)
3.16% of GDP (2015)
3.11% of GDP (2014)
3.09% of GDP (2013)
3.17% of GDP (2012)
country comparison to the world: 15

Military branches: Singapore Armed Forces: Army, Navy, Air Force (includes Air Defense) (2013)

Military service age and obligation: 18-21 years of age for male compulsory military service; 16 1/2 years of age for volunteers; 2-year conscript service obligation, with a reserve obligation to age 40 (enlisted) or age 50 (officers) (2012)

Maritime threats: the International Maritime Bureau reports the territorial and offshore waters in the South China Sea as high risk for piracy and armed robbery against ships; numerous commercial vessels have been attacked and hijacked both at anchor and while underway; hijacked vessels are often disguised and cargo diverted to ports in East Asia; crews have been murdered or cast adrift; in the Singapore Straits there were nine attacks against commercial vessels in 2015, declining to only two attacks in 2016

TERRORISM

Terrorist groups—foreign based: Islamic State of Iraq and the Levant (ISIL): aim(s): enhance its networks in Singapore and, ultimately, implement ISIL's strict interpretation of Sharia

area(s) of operation: attacks in Bangladesh are staged in Singapore; operates under the name the Islamic State in Bangladesh; Singapore's

authorities have arrested several Bangladeshi members and supporters since 2015, who were subsequently deported to Bangladesh

Jemaah Islamiya (JI): aim(s): enhance its networks in Singapore and, ultimately, overthrow the Singapore Government and establish a pan-Islamic state across Southeast Asia

area(s) of operation: maintains a limited presence, primarily recruitment efforts in large cities; authorities have exercised intense counterterrorism measures against the group since at least 2000

TRANSNATIONAL ISSUES

Disputes—international: disputes persist with Malaysia over deliveries of fresh water to Singapore, Singapore's extensive land reclamation

works, bridge construction, and maritime boundaries in the Johor and Singapore Straits; in 2008, ICJ awarded sovereignty of Pedra Branca (Pulau Batu Puteh/Horsburgh Island) to Singapore, and Middle Rocks to Malaysia, but did not rule on maritime regimes, boundaries, or disposition of South Ledge; Indonesia and Singapore continue to work on finalization of their 1973 maritime boundary agreement by defining unresolved areas north of Indonesia's Batam Island; piracy remains a problem in the Malacca Strait

Illicit drugs: drug abuse limited because of aggressive law enforcement efforts, including carrying out death sentences; as a transportation and financial services hub, Singapore is vulnerable, despite strict laws and enforcement, as a venue for money laundering

SINT MAARTEN

INTRODUCTION

Background: Although sighted by Christopher COLUMBUS in 1493 and claimed for Spain, it was the Dutch who occupied the island in 1631 and began exploiting its salt deposits. The Spanish retook the island in 1633, but continued to be harassed by the Dutch. The Spanish finally relinquished the island of Saint Martin to the French and Dutch, who divided it amongst themselves in 1648. The establishment of cotton, tobacco, and sugar plantations dramatically expanded African slavery on the island in the 18th and 19th centuries; the practice was not abolished in the Dutch half until 1863. The island's economy declined until 1939 when it became a free port; the tourism industry was dramatically expanded beginning in the 1950s. In 1954, Sint Maarten and several other Dutch Caribbean possessions became part of the Kingdom of the Netherlands as the Netherlands Antilles. In a 2000 referendum, the citizens of Sint Maarten voted to become a self-governing country within the Kingdom of the Netherlands. The change in status became effective in October of 2010 with the dissolution of the

Netherlands Antilles. On 6 September 2017, Hurricane Irma passed over the island of Saint Martin/Sint Maarten causing extensive damage to roads, communications, electrical power, and housing; the UN estimated that 90% of the buildings were damaged or destroyed. Princess Juliana International Airport was heavily damaged and forced to close to commercial air traffic for five weeks.

GEOGRAPHY

Location: Caribbean, located in the Leeward Islands (northern) group; Dutch part of the island of Saint Martin in the Caribbean Sea; Sint Maarten lies east of the US Virgin Islands

Geographic coordinates: 18 4 N, 63 4 W

Map references: Central America and the Caribbean

Area: *total:* 34 sq km
land: 34 sq km
water: 0 sq km
note: Dutch part of the island of Saint Martin
country comparison to the world: 237

Area—comparative: one-fifth the size of Washington, DC

Land boundaries: total: 16 km
border countries (1): Saint Martin (France) 16 km

Coastline: 58.9 km (for entire island)

Maritime claims: *territorial sea:* 12 nm
exclusive economic zone: 200 nm

Climate: tropical marine climate, ameliorated by northeast trade winds, results in moderate temperatures; average rainfall of 150 cm/year; hurricane season stretches from July to November

Terrain: low, hilly terrain, volcanic origin

Elevation: *mean elevation:* NA

elevation extremes: *lowest point:* Caribbean Sea 0 m
highest point: Mount Flagstaff 383 m

Natural resources: fish, salt

Population—distribution: most populous areas are Lower Prince's Quarter (north of Philipsburg), followed closely by Cul de Sac

Natural hazards: subject to hurricanes from July to November

Environment—current issues: scarcity of potable water (increasing percentage provided by desalination); inadequate solid waste management; pollution from construction, chemical runoff, and sewage harms reefs

Geography—note: the northern border is shared with the French overseas collectivity of Saint Martin; together, these two entities make up the smallest landmass in the world shared by two self-governing states

PEOPLE AND SOCIETY

Population: 42,083 (July 2017 est.)
country comparison to the world: 212

Languages: English (official) 67.5%, Spanish 12.9%, Creole 8.2%, Dutch (official) 4.2%, Papiamento (a Spanish-Portuguese-Dutch-English dialect) 2.2%, French 1.5%, other 3.5% (2001 census)

Religions: Protestant 41.9% (Pentecostal 14.7%, Methodist 10.0%, Seventh Day Adventist 6.6%, Baptist 4.7%, Anglican 3.1%, other Protestant 2.8%), Roman Catholic 33.1%, Hindu 5.2%, Christian 4.1%, Jehovah's Witness 1.7%, Evangelical 1.4%, Muslim/Jewish 1.1%, other 1.3% (includes Buddhist, Sikh, Rastafarian), none 7.9%, no response 2.4% (2011 est.)

Age structure: *0-14 years:* 18.43% (male 4,045/female 3,709)
15-24 years: 14.59% (male 3,066/female 3,073)
25-54 years: 41.99% (male 8,624/female 9,048)
55-64 years: 15.92% (male 3,204/female 3,495)
65 years and over: 9.07% (male 1,837/female 1,982) (2017 est.)

Median age: *total:* 41 years
male: 39.9 years

female: 42 years (2017 est.)
country comparison to the world: 43

Population growth rate: 1.42% (2017 est.)
country comparison to the world: 81

Birth rate: 13.1 births/1,000 population (2017 est.)
country comparison to the world: 151

Death rate: 5.2 deaths/1,000 population (2017 est.)
country comparison to the world: 188

Net migration rate: 6.3 migrant(s)/1,000 population (2017 est.)
country comparison to the world: 15

Population distribution: most populous areas are Lower Prince's Quarter (north of Philipsburg), followed closely by Cul de Sac

Urbanization: *urban population:* 100% of total population (2017)
rate of urbanization: 1.56% annual rate of change (2015-20 est.)

Major urban areas—population: PHILIPSBURG (capital) 1,327 (2011)

Sex ratio: *at birth:* 1.05 male(s)/female
0-14 years: 1.09 male(s)/female
15-24 years: 0.98 male(s)/female
25-54 years: 0.95 male(s)/female
55-64 years: 0.92 male(s)/female
65 years and over: 0.92 male(s)/female
total population: 0.98 male(s)/female (2016 est.)

Infant mortality rate: *total:* 8.1 deaths/1,000 live births
male: 8.8 deaths/1,000 live births
female: 7.4 deaths/1,000 live births (2017 est.)
country comparison to the world: 153

Life expectancy at birth: *total population:* 78.3 years
male: 76 years
female: 80.8 years (2017 est.)
country comparison to the world: 63

Total fertility rate: 2.05 children born/woman (2017 est.)
country comparison to the world: 112

HIV/AIDS—adult prevalence rate: NA

HIV/AIDS—people living with HIV/AIDS: NA

HIV/AIDS—deaths: NA

Major infectious diseases: *note:* active local transmission of Zika virus by Aedes species mosquitoes has been identified in this country (as of August 2016); it poses an important risk (a large number of cases possible) among US citizens if bitten by an infective mosquito; other less common ways to get Zika are through sex, via blood transfusion, or during pregnancy, in which the pregnant woman passes Zika virus to her fetus (2016)

GOVERNMENT

Country name: *conventional long form:* none
conventional short form: Sint Maarten
local long form: Land Sint Maarten (Dutch); Country of Sint Maarten (English)
local short form: Sint Maarten (Dutch and English)

former: Netherlands Antilles; Curacao and Dependencies
etymology: explorer Christopher COLUMBUS named the island after Saint MARTIN of Tours because the 11 November 1493 day of discovery was the saint's feast day

Dependency status: constituent country within the Kingdom of the Netherlands; full autonomy in internal affairs granted in 2010; Dutch Government responsible for defense and foreign affairs

Government type: parliamentary democracy (Estates of Sint Maarten) under a constitutional monarchy

Capital: *name:* Philipsburg
geographic coordinates: 18 1 N, 63 2 W
time difference: UTC-4 (1 hour ahead of Washington, DC, during Standard Time)

Administrative divisions: none (part of the Kingdom of the Netherlands)
note: Sint Maarten is one of four constituent countries of the Kingdom of the Netherlands; the other three are the Netherlands, Aruba, and Curacao

Independence: none (part of the Kingdom of the Netherlands)

National holiday: King's Day (birthday of King WILLEM-ALEXANDER), 27 April (1967); note—King's or Queen's Day are observed on the ruling monarch's birthday; celebrated on 26 April if 27 April is a Sunday

Constitution: Staatsregeling, 10 October 2010; revised Kingdom Charter pending previous 1947, 1955; latest adopted 21 July 2010, entered into force 10 October 2010 (regulates governance of Sint Maarten but is subordinate to the Charter for the Kingdom of the Netherlands); note—in October 2010, with the dissolution of the Netherlands Antilles, Sint Maarten became a constituent country within the Kingdom of the Netherlands

Legal system: based on Dutch civil law system with some English common law influence

Citizenship: see the Netherlands

Suffrage: 18 years of age; universal

Executive branch: *chief of state:* Queen BEATRIX of the Netherlands (since 30 April 1980); represented by Governor General Eugene HOLIDAY (since 10 October 2010)
head of government: Prime Minister Leona MARLIN-ROMEO (since 15 January 2018)
cabinet: Cabinet nominated by the prime minister and appointed by the governor-general
elections/appointments: the monarch is hereditary; governor general appointed by the monarch for a 6-year term; following legislative elections, the leader of the majority party is usually elected prime minister by the legislature

Legislative branch: *description:* unicameral Estates of Sint Maarten or Staten (15 seats; members directly elected by proportional representation vote to serve 4-year terms)
elections: last held 26 September 2016 (next to be held in 2020)
election results: percent of vote by party—UPP 29.1%, NA 26.6%, US Party 19.6%, DP 12.8%,

other 11.9%; seats by party—NA 5, UPP 5, US Party 3, DP 2

Judicial branch: *highest court(s):* Joint Court of Justice of Aruba, Curacao, Sint Maarten, and of Bonaire, Sint Eustatius and Saba or "Joint Court of Justice" (consists of the presiding judge, other members, and their substitutes); final appeals heard by the Supreme Court, in The Hague, Netherlands; note—prior to 2010, the Joint Court of Justice was the Common Court of Justice of the Netherlands Antilles and Aruba
judge selection and term of office: Joint Court judges appointed by the monarch for life
subordinate courts: Courts in First Instance

Political parties and leaders: Concordia Political Alliance or CPA [Jeffery RICHARDSON]
Democratic Party or DP [Sarah WESCOTT-WILLIAMS]
National Alliance or NA [William MARLIN]
United People's Party or UPP [Theodore HEYLIGER]
United Sint Maarten Party or US Party [Frans RICHARDSON]

Diplomatic representation in the US: none (represented by the Kingdom of the Netherlands)

Diplomatic representation from the US: the US does not have an embassy in Sint Maarten; the Consul General to Curacao is accredited to Sint Maarten

Flag description: two equal horizontal bands of red (top) and blue with a white isosceles triangle based on the hoist side; the center of the triangle displays the Sint Maarten coat of arms; the arms consist of an orange-bordered blue shield prominently displaying the white court house in Philipsburg, as well as a bouquet of yellow sage (the national flower) in the upper left, and the silhouette of a Dutch-French friendship monument in the upper right; the shield is surmounted by a yellow rising sun in front of which is a brown pelican in flight; a yellow scroll below the shield bears the motto: SEMPER PROGREDIENS (Always Progressing); the three main colors are identical to those on the Dutch flag
note: the flag somewhat resembles that of the Philippines, but with the main red and blue bands reversed; the banner more closely evokes the wartime Philippine flag

National symbol(s): brown pelican, yellow sage (flower); national colors: red, white, blue

National anthem: *name:* "O Sweet Saint Martin's Land"
lyrics/music: Gerard KEMPS
note: the song, written in 1958, is used as an unofficial anthem for the entire island (both French and Dutch sides); as a collectivity of France, in addition to the local anthem, "La Marseillaise" is official on the French side (see France); as a constituent part of the Kingdom of the Netherlands, in addition to the local anthem, "Het Wilhelmus" is official on the Dutch side (see Netherlands)

ECONOMY

Economy—overview: The economy of Sint Maarten centers around tourism with nearly four-fifths of the labor force engaged in this sector. Nearly 1.8 million visitors came to the island by cruise ship and roughly 500,000 visitors arrived through Princess Juliana International Airport in 2013. Cruise ships and yachts also call on Sint Maarten's numerous ports and harbors. Limited agriculture and local fishing means that almost all food must be imported. Energy resources and manufactured goods are also imported. Sint Maarten had the highest per capita income among the five islands that formerly comprised the Netherlands Antilles.

GDP (purchasing power parity): $365.8 million (2014 est.)
$353.5 million (2013 est.)
$339.6 million (2012 est.)
note: datar are in 2014 US dollars
country comparison to the world: 215

GDP (official exchange rate): $304.1 million (2014 est.)

GDP—real growth rate: 3.6% (2014 est.)
4.1% (2013 est.)
1.9% (2012 est.)
country comparison to the world: 87

GDP—per capita (PPP): $66,800 (2014 est.)
$65,500 (2013 est.)
$63,900 (2012 est.)
note: data are in 2015 US dollars
country comparison to the world: 15

GDP—composition, by sector of origin:
agriculture: 0.4%
industry: 18.3%
services: 81.3% (2008 est.)

Agriculture—products: sugar

Industries: tourism, light industry

Labor force: 23,200 (2008 est.)
country comparison to the world: 211

Labor force—by occupation: *agriculture:* 1.1%
industry: 15.2%
services: 83.7% (2008 est.)

Unemployment rate: 12% (2012 est.)
10.6% (2008 est.)
country comparison to the world: 155

Inflation rate (consumer prices): 4% (2012 est.)
0.7% (2009 est.)
country comparison to the world: 159

Exports—commodities: sugar

Exchange rates: Netherlands Antillean guilders (ANG) per US dollar—
1.79 (2016)
1.79 (2016)
1.79 (2013)
1.79 (2012)
1.79 (2011)

Electricity—production: 304.3 million kWh (2008 est.)
country comparison to the world: 182

Telephone system: *general assessment:* generally adequate facilities
domestic: extensive interisland microwave radio relay links

international: country code—1-721; the Americas Region Caribbean Ring System (ARCOS-1) and the Americas-2 submarine cable systems provide connectivity to Central America, parts of South America and the Caribbean, and the US; satellite earth stations—2 Intelsat (Atlantic Ocean) (2010)

Internet country code: .sx; note—IANA has designated .sx for Sint Maarten, but has not yet assigned it to a sponsoring organization

Airports: 1 (2013)
country comparison to the world: 234

Airports—with paved runways: *total:* 1
1,524 to 2,437 m: 1
note: Princess Juliana International Airport (SXM) was severely damaged on 6 September 2017 by hurricane Irma, but resumed commercial operations on 10 October 2017 (2017)

Roadways: *total:* 53 km
country comparison to the world: 219

Ports and terminals: *major seaport(s):* Philipsburg
oil terminal(s): Coles Bay oil terminal

Military branches: no regular military forces (2012)

Military—note: defense is the responsibility of the Kingdom of the Netherlands

Background: Slovakia traces its roots to the 9th century state of Great Moravia. Subsequently, the Slovaks became part of the Hungarian Kingdom, where they remained for the next 1,000 years. Following the formation of the dual Austro-Hungarian monarchy in 1867, language and education policies favoring the use of Hungarian (Magyarization) resulted in a strengthening of Slovak nationalism and a cultivation of cultural ties with the closely related Czechs, who were under Austrian rule. After the dissolution of the Austro-Hungarian Empire at the close of World War I, the

Slovaks joined the Czechs to form Czechoslovakia. During the interwar period, Slovak nationalist leaders pushed for autonomy within Czechoslovakia, and in 1939 Slovakia became an independent state allied with Nazi Germany. Following World War II, Czechoslovakia was reconstituted and came under communist rule within Soviet-dominated Eastern Europe. In 1968, an invasion by Warsaw Pact troops ended the efforts of the country's leaders to liberalize communist rule and create "socialism with a human face," ushering in a period of repression known as "normalization." The peaceful "Velvet Revolution" swept the Communist Party from power at the end of 1989 and inaugurated a return to democratic rule and a market economy. On 1 January 1993, the country underwent a nonviolent "velvet divorce" into its two national components, Slovakia and the Czech Republic. Slovakia joined both NATO and the EU in the spring of 2004 and the euro zone on 1 January 2009.

Location: Central Europe, south of Poland

Geographic coordinates: 48 40 N, 19 30 E

Map references: Europe

Area: *total:* 49,035 sq km
land: 48,105 sq km
water: 930 sq km
country comparison to the world: 131

Area—comparative: about one and a half times the size of Maryland; about twice the size of New Hampshire
Land boundaries: total: 1,611 km
border countries (5): Austria 105 km, Czech Republic 241 km, Hungary 627 km, Poland 541 km, Ukraine 97 km

Coastline: 0 km (landlocked)

Maritime claims: none (landlocked)

Climate: temperate; cool summers; cold, cloudy, humid winters

Terrain: rugged mountains in the central and northern part and lowlands in the south

Elevation: *mean elevation:* 458 m

elevation extremes: *lowest point:* Bodrok River 94 m
highest point: Gerlachovsky Stit 2,655 m

Natural resources: lignite, small amounts of iron ore, copper and manganese ore; salt; arable land

Land use: *agricultural land:* 40.1%
arable land: 28.9%;
permanent crops: 0.4%;
permanent pasture: 10.8%
forest: 40.2%
other: 19.7% (2011 est.)
Irrigated land: 869 sq km (2012)

Population—distribution: a fairly even distribution throughout most of the country; slightly larger concentration in the west in proximity to the Czech border

Natural hazards: flooding

Environment—current issues: air pollution from metallurgical plants presents human health risks; acid rain damaging forests

Environment—international agreements: *party to:* Air Pollution, Air Pollution-Nitrogen Oxides, Air Pollution-Persistent Organic Pollutants, Air Pollution-Sulfur 85, Air Pollution-Sulfur 94, Air Pollution-Volatile Organic Compounds, Antarctic Treaty, Biodiversity, Climate Change, Climate Change-Kyoto Protocol, Desertification, Endangered Species, Environmental Modification, Hazardous Wastes, Law of the Sea, Ozone Layer Protection, Ship Pollution, Wetlands, Whaling
signed, but not ratified: none of the selected agreements

Geography—note: landlocked; most of the country is rugged and mountainous; the Tatra Mountains in the north are interspersed with many scenic lakes and valleys

PEOPLE AND SOCIETY

Population: 5,445,829 (July 2017 est.)
country comparison to the world: 118

Nationality: *noun:* Slovak(s)
adjective: Slovak

Ethnic groups: Slovak 80.7%, Hungarian 8.5%, Romani 2%, other and unspecified 8.8% (2011 est.)
note: Romani populations are usually underestimated in official statistics and may represent 7–11% of Slovakia's population

Languages: Slovak (official) 78.6%, Hungarian 9.4%, Roma 2.3%, Ruthenian 1%, other or unspecified 8.8% (2011 est.)

Religions: Roman Catholic 62%, Protestant 8.2%, Greek Catholic 3.8%, other or unspecified 12.5%, none 13.4% (2011 est.)

Age structure: *0-14 years:* 15.17% (male 424,039/ female 402,284)
15-24 years: 10.87% (male 305,058/female 286,902)
25-54 years: 45.1% (male 1,240,943/female 1,215,260)
55-64 years: 13.42% (male 347,221/female 383,852)
65 years and over: 15.43% (male 325,738/female 514,532) (2017 est.)

Dependency ratios: *total dependency ratio:* 41.5
youth dependency ratio: 21.6

elderly dependency ratio: 26.8
potential support ratio: 3.7 (2015 est.)

Median age: *total:* 40.5 years
male: 38.8 years
female: 42.3 years (2017 est.)
country comparison to the world: 49

Population growth rate: -0.01% (2017 est.)
country comparison to the world: 196

Birth rate: 9.7 births/1,000 population (2017 est.)
country comparison to the world: 197

Death rate: 9.9 deaths/1,000 population (2017 est.)
country comparison to the world: 41

Net migration rate: 0.1 migrant(s)/1,000 population (2017 est.)
country comparison to the world: 69

Population distribution: a fairly even distribution throughout most of the country; slightly larger concentration in the west in proximity to the Czech border

Urbanization: *urban population:* 53.4% of total population (2017)
rate of urbanization: -0.09% annual rate of change (2015-20 est.)

Major urban areas—population: BRATISLAVA (capital) 401,000 (2015)

Sex ratio: *at birth:* 1.07 male(s)/female
0-14 years: 1.05 male(s)/female
15-24 years: 1.06 male(s)/female
25-54 years: 1.02 male(s)/female
55-64 years: 0.9 male(s)/female
65 years and over: 0.62 male(s)/female
total population: 0.94 male(s)/female (2016 est.)

Mother's mean age at first birth: 27.6 years (2014 est.)

Maternal mortality ratio: 6 deaths/100,000 live births (2015 est.)
country comparison to the world: 167

Infant mortality rate: *total:* 5.1 deaths/1,000 live births
male: 5.7 deaths/1,000 live births
female: 4.5 deaths/1,000 live births (2017 est.)
country comparison to the world: 176

Life expectancy at birth: *total population:* 77.3 years
male: 73.7 years
female: 81.1 years (2017 est.)
country comparison to the world: 75

Total fertility rate: 1.41 children born/woman (2017 est.)
country comparison to the world: 210

Health expenditures: 8.1% of GDP (2014)
country comparison to the world: 54

Physicians density: 3.39 physicians/1,000 population (2013)

Hospital bed density: 6 beds/1,000 population (2011)

Drinking water source:
improved:
urban: 100% of population
rural: 100% of population
total: 100% of population

unimproved:
urban: 0% of population
rural: 0% of population
total: 0% of population (2015 est.)

Sanitation facility access:
improved:
urban: 99.4% of population
rural: 98.2% of population
total: 98.8% of population
unimproved:
urban: 0.6% of population
rural: 1.8% of population
total: 1.2% of population (2015 est.)

HIV/AIDS—adult prevalence rate: <.1% (2016 est.)

HIV/AIDS—people living with HIV/AIDS: <1000 (2016 est.)

HIV/AIDS—deaths: <100 (2016 est.)

Obesity—adult prevalence rate: 20.5% (2016)
country comparison to the world: 98

Education expenditures: 4.1% of GDP (2013)
country comparison to the world: 103

School life expectancy (primary to tertiary education): *total:* 15 years
male: 14 years
female: 16 years (2014)

Unemployment, youth ages 15-24: *total:* 26.5%
male: 25.8%
female: 27.5% (2015 est.)
country comparison to the world: 21

GOVERNMENT

Country name: *conventional long form:* Slovak Republic
conventional short form: Slovakia
local long form: Slovenska republika
local short form: Slovensko
etymology: related to the Slavic autonym (self-designation) "Slovenin," a derivation from "slovo" (word), denoting "people who speak (the same language)" (i.e., people who understand each other)

Government type: parliamentary republic

Capital: *name:* Bratislava

geographic coordinates: 48 09 N, 17 07 E
time difference: UTC+1 (6 hours ahead of Washington, DC, during Standard Time)
daylight saving time: +1hr, begins last Sunday in March; ends last Sunday in October

Administrative divisions: 8 regions (kraje, singular—kraj); Banskobystricky, Bratislavsky, Kosicky, Nitriansky, Presovsky, Trenciansky, Trnavsky, Zilinsky

Independence: 1 January 1993 (Czechoslovakia split into the Czech Republic and Slovakia)

National holiday: Constitution Day, 1 September (1992)

Constitution: *history:* several previous (preindependence); latest passed by the National Council 1 September 1992, signed 3 September 1992, effective 1 October 1992

amendments: proposed by the National Council; passage requires at least three-fifths majority vote of Council members; amended many times, last in 2017 (2017)

Legal system: civil law system based on Austro-Hungarian codes; note—legal code modified to comply with the obligations of Organization on Security and Cooperation in Europe

International law organization participation: accepts compulsory ICJ jurisdiction with reservations; accepts ICCt jurisdiction

Citizenship: *citizenship by birth:* no

citizenship by descent only: at least one parent must be a citizen of Slovakia

dual citizenship recognized: no

residency requirement for naturalization: 5 years

Suffrage: 18 years of age; universal

Executive branch: *chief of state:* President Andrej KISKA (since 15 June 2014)

head of government: Prime Minister Robert FICO (since 4 April 2012); Deputy Prime Ministers Robert KALINAK (since 4 April 2012), Lucia ZITNANSKA (since 23 March 2016), Gabriela MATECNA (since 29 November 2017)

cabinet: Cabinet appointed by the president on the recommendation of the prime minister

elections/appointments: president directly elected by absolute majority popular vote in 2 rounds if needed for a 5-year term (eligible for a second term); election last held on 15 and 29 March 2014 (next to be held in March 2019); following National Council elections, the leader of the majority party or majority coalition usually appointed prime minister by the president

election results: Andrej KISKA elected president in second round; percent of vote—Andrej KISKA (independent) 59.4%, Robert FICO (Smer-SD) 40.6%

Legislative branch: *description:* unicameral National Council or Narodna Rada (150 seats; members directly elected in a single national constituency by proportional representation vote; members serve 4-year terms)

elections: last held on 5 March 2016 (next to be held in March 2020)

election results: percent of vote by party—Smer-SD 28.3%, SaS 12.1%, OLaNO-NOVA 11%, SNS 8.6%, LSNS 8%, Sme-Rodina 6.6%, Most-Hid 6.5%, Siet 5.6%, other 13.3%; seats by party—Smer-SD 49, SaS 21, OLaNO-NOVA 19, SNS 15, LSNS 14, Sme-Rodina 11, Most-Hid 11, Siet 10

Judicial branch: *highest court(s):* Supreme Court of the Slovak Republic (consists of the court president, vice president, and 79 judges organized into criminal, civil, commercial, and administrative divisions with 3- and 5-judge panels); Constitutional Court (consists of 13 judges)

judge selection and term of office: Supreme Court judge candidates proposed by the Judicial Council of the Slovak Republic, an 18-member independent body to include the Supreme Court chief justice and presidential, governmental, parliamentary, and judiciary appointees; judges appointed by

the president for life with mandatory retirement at age 65; Constitutional Court judges nominated by the National Council of the Republic and appointed by the president; judges appointed for 12-year terms

subordinate courts: regional and district civil courts; Higher Military Court; military district courts; Court of Audit

Political parties and leaders: Christian Democratic Movement or KDH [Alojz HLINA]
Bridge or Most-Hid [Bela BUGAR]
Direction-Social Democracy or Smer-SD [Robert FICO]
Freedom and Solidarity or SaS [Richard SULIK]
Kotleba-People's Party Our Slovakia or LSNS [Marian KOTLEBA]
Network or Siet [Marek CEPKO, acting]
Ordinary People and Independent Personalities—New Majority or OLaNO-NOVA [Igor MATOVIC]
Party of the Hungarian Coalition or SMK [Jozsef MENYHART]
Slovak National Party or SNS [Andrej DANKO]
We Are Family or Sme-Rodina [Boris KOLLAR]

Political pressure groups and leaders: Alliance of Companies Employing 500 or More Employees or Klub500
Association of Towns and Villages or ZMOS
Confederation of Trade Unions or KOZ
Entrepreneurs Association of Slovakia or ZPS
Federation of Employers' Associations of the Slovak Republic or AZZZ
Medical Trade Association or LOZ
National Union of Employers or RUZ
Slovak Chamber of Commerce and Industry or SOPK
The Business Alliance of Slovakia or PAS

International organization participation: Australia Group, BIS, BSEC (observer), CBSS (observer), CD, CE, CEI, CERN, EAPC, EBRD, ECB, EIB, EMU, EU, FAO, IAEA, IBRD, ICAO, ICC (national committees), ICRM, IDA, IEA, IFC, IFRCS, ILO, IMF, IMO, IMSO, Interpol, IOC, IOM, IPU, ISO, ITU, ITUC (NGOs), MIGA, NATO, NEA, NSG, OAS (observer), OECD, OIF (observer), OPCW, OSCE, PCA, Schengen Convention, SELEC (observer), UN, UNCTAD, UNESCO, UNFICYP, UNIDO, UNTSO, UNWTO, UPU, WCO, WFTU (NGOs), WHO, WIPO, WMO, WTO, ZC

Diplomatic representation in the US: chief of mission: Ambassador Peter KMEC (since 19 September 2012)

chancery: 3523 International Court NW, Washington, DC 20008

telephone: [1] (202) 237-1054

FAX: [1] (202) 237-6438

consulate(s) general: Los Angeles, New York

Diplomatic representation from the US: *chief of mission:* Ambassador Adam H. Sterling (since August 2016)

embassy: Hviezdoslavovo Namestie 4, 81102 Bratislava

mailing address: P.O. Box 309, 814 99 Bratislava

telephone: [421] (2) 5443-3338

FAX: [421] (2) 5441-8861

Flag description: three equal horizontal bands of white (top), blue, and red derive from the Pan-Slav colors; the Slovakian coat of arms (consisting of a red shield bordered in white and bearing a white double-barred cross of St. Cyril and St. Methodius surmounting three blue hills) is centered over the bands but offset slightly to the hoist side

note: the Pan-Slav colors were inspired by the 19th-century flag of Russia

National symbol(s): double-barred cross (Cross of St. Cyril and St. Methodius) surmounting three peaks; national colors: white, blue, red

National anthem: *name:* "Nad Tatrou sa blyska" (Lightning Over the Tatras)

lyrics/music: Janko MATUSKA/traditional

note: adopted 1993, in use since 1844; music based on the Slovak folk song "Kopala studienku"

ECONOMY

Economy—overview: Slovakia's economy suffered from a slow start in the first years after its separation from the Czech Republic in 1993, due to the country's authoritarian leadership and high levels of corruption, but economic reforms implemented after 1998 have placed Slovakia on a path of strong growth. With a population of 5.4 million, the Slovak Republic has a small, open economy driven mainly by automobile and electronics exports, which account for more than 80% of GDP. Slovakia joined the EU in 2004 and the euro zone in 2009. The country's banking sector is sound and predominantly foreign owned.

Slovakia has been a regional FDI champion for several years, attractive due to a relatively low-cost yet skilled labor force, and a favorable geographic location in the heart of Central Europe. Exports and investment have been key drivers of Slovakia's robust growth in recent years. The unemployment rate fell to historical lows in 2017, and rising wages fueled increased consumption, which played a more prominent role in 2017 GDP growth. A favorable outlook for the Eurozone suggests continued strong growth prospects for Slovakia during the next few years, although inflation is also expected to pick up.

Among the most pressing domestic issues potentially threatening the attractiveness of the Slovak market are shortages in the qualified labor force, persistent corruption issues, and an inadequate judiciary, as well as a slow transition to an innovation-based economy. The energy sector in particular is characterized by unpredictable regulatory oversight and high costs, in part driven by government interference in regulated tariffs. Moreover, the government's attempts to maintain low household energy prices could harm the profitability of domestic energy firms while undercutting energy efficiency initiatives.

GDP (purchasing power parity): $178.7 billion (2017 est.)
$173 billion (2016 est.)
$167.5 billion (2015 est.)
note: data are in 2017 dollars
country comparison to the world: 71

GDP (official exchange rate): $95 billion (2016 est.)

GDP—real growth rate: 3.3% (2017 est.)
3.3% (2016 est.)
3.8% (2015 est.)
country comparison to the world: 104

GDP—per capita (PPP): $32,900 (2017 est.)
$31,900 (2016 est.)
$30,900 (2015 est.)
note: data are in 2017 dollars
country comparison to the world: 59

Gross national saving: 22.9% of GDP (2017 est.)
20.8% of GDP (2016 est.)
23.4% of GDP (2015 est.)
country comparison to the world: 65

GDP—composition, by end use:
household consumption: 55.2%
government consumption: 19.2%
investment in fixed capital: 20.9%
investment in inventories: 1.2%
exports of goods and services: 96.4%
imports of goods and services: -93% (2017 est.)

GDP—composition, by sector of origin:
agriculture: 3.8%
industry: 35%
services: 61.2% (2017 est.)

Agriculture—products: grains, potatoes, sugar beets, hops, fruit; pigs, cattle, poultry; forest products

Industries: automobiles; metal and metal products; electricity, gas, coke, oil, nuclear fuel; chemicals, synthetic fibers, wood and paper products; machinery; earthenware and ceramics; textiles; electrical and optical apparatus; rubber products; food and beverages; pharmaceutical

Industrial production growth rate: 3.5% (2017 est.)
country comparison to the world: 84

Labor force: 2.758 million (2017 est.)
country comparison to the world: 110

Labor force—by occupation: *agriculture:* 3.9%
industry: 22.7%
services: 73.4% (2015)

Unemployment rate: 8.1% (2017 est.)
9.6% (2016 est.)
country comparison to the world: 110

Population below poverty line: 12.3% (2015 est.)

Household income or consumption by percentage share: *lowest 10%:* 3.3%
highest 10%: 19.3% (2015 est.)

Distribution of family income—Gini index: 23.7 (2015)
26.1 (2014)
country comparison to the world: 148

Budget: *revenues:* $37.09 billion
expenditures: $38.52 billion (2017 est.)
Taxes and other revenues: 39% of GDP (2017 est.)
country comparison to the world: 39

Budget surplus (+) or deficit (-): -1.5% of GDP (2017 est.)
country comparison to the world: 69

Public debt: 51.6% of GDP (2017 est.)

51.9% of GDP (2016 est.)
note: data cover general Government Gross Debt, and includes debt instruments issued (or owned) by Government entities, including sub-sectors of central government, state government, local government, and social security funds
country comparison to the world: 97

Fiscal year: calendar year

Inflation rate (consumer prices): 1.2% (2017 est.)
-0.5% (2016 est.)
country comparison to the world: 51

Central bank discount rate: 0% (31 December 2016 est.)
0.05% (31 December 2015 est.)
note: this is the European Central Bank's rate on the marginal lending facility, which offers overnight credit to banks from the euro area; Slovakia became a member of the Economic and Monetary Union (EMU) on 1 January 2009
country comparison to the world: 154

Commercial bank prime lending rate: 2.6% (31 December 2017 est.)
2.55% (31 December 2016 est.)
country comparison to the world: 174

Stock of narrow money: $53.06 billion (31 December 2017 est.)
$45.63 billion (31 December 2016 est.)
note: see entry for the European Union for money supply for the entire euro area; the European Central Bank (ECB) controls monetary policy for the 18 members of the Economic and Monetary Union (EMU); individual members of the EMU do not control the quantity of money circulating within their own borders
country comparison to the world: 53

Stock of broad money: $66.55 billion (31 December 2017 est.)
$59.48 billion (31 December 2016 est.)
country comparison to the world: 64

Stock of domestic credit: $80.45 billion (31 December 2017 est.)
$70.84 billion (31 December 2016 est.)
country comparison to the world: 59

Market value of publicly traded shares: $4.492 billion (30 November 2016 est.)
$4.634 billion (31 December 2015 est.)
$4.732 billion (31 December 2014 est.)
country comparison to the world: 90

Current account balance: $282 million (2017 est.)
-$653 million (2016 est.)
country comparison to the world: 52

Exports: $80.57 billion (2017 est.)
$75.53 billion (2016 est.)
country comparison to the world: 39

Exports—commodities: vehicles and related parts 27%, machinery and electrical equipment 20%, nuclear reactors and furnaces 12%, iron and steel 4%, mineral oils and fuels 5% (2015 est.)

Exports—partners: Germany 21.9%, Czech Republic 11.9%, Poland 7.7%, France 6.1%, UK 5.9%, Austria 5.7%, Hungary 5.7%, Italy 4.8% (2016)

Imports: $77.96 billion (2017 est.)

$73.01 billion (2016 est.)
country comparison to the world: 41

Imports—commodities: machinery and electrical equipment 20%, vehicles and related parts 14%, nuclear reactors and furnaces 12%, fuel and mineral oils 9% (2015 est.)

Imports—partners: Germany 20.2%, Czech Republic 16.9%, Austria 9.8%, Poland 6.5%, Hungary 6.1%, South Korea 4.7%, China 4.6%, France 4.4% (2016)

Reserves of foreign exchange and gold: $3.133 billion (31 December 2017 est.)
$2.892 billion (31 December 2016 est.)
country comparison to the world: 104

Debt—external: $75.04 billion (31 March 2016 est.)
$74.19 billion (31 March 2015 est.)
country comparison to the world: 59

Stock of direct foreign investment—at home: $57.23 billion (31 December 2017 est.)
$54.03 billion (31 December 2016 est.)
country comparison to the world: 56

Stock of direct foreign investment—abroad: $16.26 billion (31 December 2017 est.)
$15.06 billion (31 December 2016 est.)
country comparison to the world: 58

Exchange rates: euros (EUR) per US dollar—
0.906 (2017 est.)
0.9214 (2016 est.)
0.9214 (2015 est.)
0.885 (2014 est.)
0.7634 (2013 est.)

ENERGY

Electricity access: *electrification—total population:* 100% (2016)

Electricity—production: 24.85 billion kWh (2015 est.)
country comparison to the world: 72

Electricity—consumption: 25.87 billion kWh (2015 est.)
country comparison to the world: 67

Electricity—exports: 10.6 billion kWh (2016 est.)
country comparison to the world: 21

Electricity—imports: 13.25 billion kWh (2016 est.)
country comparison to the world: 20

Electricity—installed generating capacity: 7.11 million kW (2015 est.)
country comparison to the world: 73

Electricity—from fossil fuels: 35.1% of total installed capacity (2015 est.)
country comparison to the world: 177

Electricity—from nuclear fuels: 25.5% of total installed capacity (2015 est.)
country comparison to the world: 4

Electricity—from hydroelectric plants: 14.9% of total installed capacity (2015 est.)
country comparison to the world: 101

Electricity—from other renewable sources: 11.8% of total installed capacity (2015 est.)
country comparison to the world: 63

Crude oil—production: 200 bbl/day (2016 est.)
country comparison to the world: 96

Crude oil—exports: 129.7 bbl/day (2016 est.)
country comparison to the world: 81

Crude oil—imports: 115,600 bbl/day (2016 est.)
country comparison to the world: 41

Crude oil—proved reserves: 9 million bbl (1 January 2017 es)
country comparison to the world: 94

Refined petroleum products—production: 137,400 bbl/day (2016 est.)
country comparison to the world: 62

Refined petroleum products—consumption: 84,290 bbl/day (2016 est.)
country comparison to the world: 88

Refined petroleum products—exports: 83,030 bbl/day (2016 est.)
country comparison to the world: 46

Refined petroleum products—imports: 36,470 bbl/day (2016 est.)
country comparison to the world: 95

Natural gas—production: 94 million cu m (2015 est.)
country comparison to the world: 81

Natural gas—consumption: 7.868 billion cu m (2015 est.)
country comparison to the world: 59

Natural gas—exports: 3 million cu m (2014 est.)
country comparison to the world: 54

Natural gas—imports: 4.407 billion cu m (2015 est.)
country comparison to the world: 35

Natural gas—proved reserves: 14.16 billion cu m (1 January 2017 es)
country comparison to the world: 80

Carbon dioxide emissions from consumption of energy: 31.1 million Mt (2015 est.)
country comparison to the world: 76

COMMUNICATIONS

Telephones—fixed lines: *total subscriptions:* 823,594
subscriptions per 100 inhabitants: 15 (July 2016 est.)
country comparison to the world: 80

Telephones—mobile cellular: *total:* 6,989,902
subscriptions per 100 inhabitants: 128 (July 2016 est.)
country comparison to the world: 108

Telephone system: *general assessment:* a modern telecommunications system that has expanded dramatically in recent years with the growth of cellular services
domestic: Slovak Telecom maintains a near monopoly on fixed-line service; four companies provide nationwide cellular services
international: country code—421; 3 international exchanges (1 in Bratislava and 2 in Banska Bystrica) are available; Slovakia is participating in several international telecommunications projects that will increase the availability of external services (2017)

Broadcast media: state-owned public broadcaster, Radio and Television of Slovakia (RTVS), operates 2 national TV stations and multiple national and regional radio networks; roughly 50 privately owned TV stations operating nationally, regionally, and locally; about 40% of households are connected to multi-channel cable or satellite TV; 32 privately owned radio stations (2016)

Internet country code: .sk

Internet users: *total:* 4,382,558
percent of population: 80.5% (July 2016 est.)
country comparison to the world: 72

TRANSPORTATION

National air transport system: number of registered air carriers: 4
inventory of registered aircraft operated by air carriers: 23
annual passenger traffic on registered air carriers: 11,100
annual freight traffic on registered air carriers: 0 mt-km (2015)
Civil aircraft registration country code prefix: OM (2016)

Airports: 35 (2013)
country comparison to the world: 111

Airports—with paved runways: *total:* 21
over 3,047 m: 2
2,438 to 3,047 m: 2
1,524 to 2,437 m: 3
914 to 1,523 m: 3
under 914 m: 11 (2013)

Airports—with unpaved runways: *total:* 14
914 to 1,523 m: 9
under 914 m: 5 (2013)

Heliports: 1 (2013)

Pipelines: gas transmission pipelines 2,270 km; high-pressure gas distribution pipelines 6,278 km; mid- and low-pressure gas distribution pipelines 27,023 km (2016); oil 510 km (2015)

Railways: *total:* 3,626 km
broad gauge: 99 km 1.520-m gauge
standard gauge: 3,477 km 1.435-m gauge (1,587 km electrified)
narrow gauge: 50 km 1.000-m or 0.750-m gauge (2016)
country comparison to the world: 49

Roadways: *total:* 54,869 km (includes local roads, national roads, and 420 km of highways) (2012)
country comparison to the world: 75

Waterways: 172 km (on Danube River) (2012)
country comparison to the world: 99
Ports and terminals: river port(s): Bratislava, Komarno (Danube)

MILITARY AND SECURITY

Military expenditures: 1.16% of GDP (2016)
1.15% of GDP (2015)
1.01% of GDP (2014)
1% of GDP (2013)
1.2% of GDP (2012)
country comparison to the world: 89

Military branches: Armed Forces of the Slovak Republic (Ozbrojene Sily Slovenskej Republiky): Land Forces (Pozemne Sily), Air Forces (Vzdusne Sily) (2010)

Military service age and obligation: 18-30 years of age for voluntary military service; conscription in peacetime suspended in 2006; women are eligible to serve (2012)

TRANSNATIONAL ISSUES

Disputes—international: bilateral government, legal, technical and economic working group negotiations continued between Slovakia and Hungary over Hungary's completion of its portion of the Gabcikovo-Nagymaros hydroelectric dam project along the Danube; as a member state that forms part of the EU's external border, Slovakia has implemented strict Schengen border rules

Refugees and internally displaced persons: stateless persons: 1,523 (2016)

Illicit drugs: transshipment point for Southwest Asian heroin bound for Western Europe; producer of synthetic drugs for regional market; consumer of ecstasy

SLOVENIA

INTRODUCTION

Background: The Slovene lands were part of the Austro-Hungarian Empire until the latter's dissolution at the end of World War I. In 1918, the Slovenes joined the Serbs and Croats in forming a new multinational state, which was named Yugoslavia in 1929. After World War II, Slovenia became a republic of the renewed Yugoslavia, which though communist, distanced itself from Moscow's rule. Dissatisfied with the exercise of power by the majority Serbs, the Slovenes succeeded in establishing their independence in 1991 after a short 10-day war. Historical ties to Western Europe, a strong economy, and a stable democracy have assisted in Slovenia's transformation to a modern state. Slovenia acceded to both NATO and the EU in the spring of 2004; it joined the euro zone and the Schengen zone in 2007.

GEOGRAPHY

Location: south Central Europe, Julian Alps between Austria and Croatia

Geographic coordinates: 46 07 N, 14 49 E

Map references: Europe

Area: *total:* 20,273 sq km
land: 20,151 sq km
water: 122 sq km
country comparison to the world: 155

Area—comparative: slightly smaller than New Jersey
Land boundaries: total: 1,211 km
border countries (4): Austria 299 km, Croatia 600 km, Hungary 94 km, Italy 218 km

Coastline: 46.6 km

Maritime claims: *territorial sea:* 12 nm

Climate: Mediterranean climate on the coast, continental climate with mild to hot summers and cold winters in the plateaus and valleys to the east

Terrain: a short southwestern coastal strip of Karst topography on the Adriatic; an alpine mountain region lies adjacent to Italy and Austria in the north; mixed mountains and valleys with numerous rivers to the east

Elevation: *mean elevation:* 492 m

elevation extremes: *lowest point:* Adriatic Sea 0 m
highest point: Triglav 2,864 m

Natural resources: lignite, lead, zinc, building stone, hydropower, forests

Land use: *agricultural land:* 22.8%
arable land: 8.4%;
permanent crops: 1.3%;
permanent pasture: 13.1%
forest: 62.3%
other: 14.9% (2011 est.)
Irrigated land: 60 sq km (2012)

Population—distribution: a fairly even distribution throughout most of the country, with urban areas attracting larger and denser populations; pockets in the mountainous northwest exhibit less density than elsewhere

Natural hazards: flooding; earthquakes

Environment—current issues: Sava River polluted with domestic and industrial waste; pollution of coastal waters with heavy metals and toxic chemicals; forest damage from urban air pollution and resulting acid rain

Environment—international agreements: *party to:* Air Pollution, Air Pollution-Nitrogen Oxides, Air Pollution-Persistent Organic Pollutants, Air Pollution-Sulfur 94, Biodiversity, Climate Change, Climate Change-Kyoto Protocol, Desertification, Endangered Species, Environmental Modification, Hazardous Wastes, Law of the Sea, Marine Dumping, Ozone Layer Protection, Ship Pollution, Wetlands, Whaling
signed, but not ratified: none of the selected agreements

Geography—note: despite its small size, this eastern Alpine country controls some of Europe's major transit routes

PEOPLE AND SOCIETY

Population: 1,972,126 (July 2017 est.)
country comparison to the world: 147

Nationality: *noun:* Slovene(s)
adjective: Slovenian

Ethnic groups: Slovene 83.1%, Serb 2%, Croat 1.8%, Bosniak 1.1%, other or unspecified 12% (2002 census)

Languages: Slovenian (official) 91.1%, Serbo-Croatian 4.5%, other or unspecified 4.4%, Italian (official, only in municipalities where Italian national communities reside), Hungarian (official, only in municipalities where Hungarian national communities reside) (2002 census)

Religions: Catholic 57.8%, Muslim 2.4%, Orthodox 2.3%, other Christian 0.9%, unaffiliated 3.5%, other or unspecified 23%, none 10.1% (2002 census)

Age structure: *0-14 years:* 13.32% (male 135,371/female 127,246)
15-24 years: 9.45% (male 95,546/female 90,744)
25-54 years: 42.9% (male 427,723/female 418,349)
55-64 years: 14.83% (male 143,642/female 148,821)
65 years and over: 19.51% (male 157,794/female 226,890) (2017 est.)

Dependency ratios: *total dependency ratio:* 48.7
youth dependency ratio: 21.9
elderly dependency ratio: 26.8
potential support ratio: 3.7 (2015 est.)

Median age: *total:* 44.5 years
male: 42.8 years
female: 46.2 years (2017 est.)
country comparison to the world: 9

Population growth rate: -0.31% (2017 est.)
country comparison to the world: 218

Birth rate: 8.2 births/1,000 population (2017 est.)
country comparison to the world: 221

Death rate: 11.6 deaths/1,000 population (2017 est.)
country comparison to the world: 26

Net migration rate: 0.4 migrant(s)/1,000 population (2017 est.)
country comparison to the world: 65

Population distribution: a fairly even distribution throughout most of the country, with urban areas attracting larger and denser populations; pockets in the mountainous northwest exhibit less density than elsewhere

Urbanization: *urban population:* 49.6% of total population (2017)
rate of urbanization: 0.18% annual rate of change (2015-20 est.)

Major urban areas—population: LJUBLJANA (capital) 279,000 (2014)

Sex ratio: *at birth:* 1.07 male(s)/female
0-14 years: 1.06 male(s)/female
15-24 years: 1.05 male(s)/female
25-54 years: 1.02 male(s)/female
55-64 years: 0.97 male(s)/female
65 years and over: 0.68 male(s)/female
total population: 0.95 male(s)/female (2016 est.)

Mother's mean age at first birth: 29.1 years (2014 est.)

Maternal mortality ratio: 9 deaths/100,000 live births (2015 est.)
country comparison to the world: 154

Infant mortality rate: *total:* 3.9 deaths/1,000 live births
male: 4.4 deaths/1,000 live births
female: 3.4 deaths/1,000 live births (2017 est.)

country comparison to the world: 194

Life expectancy at birth: *total population:* 78.3 years
male: 74.8 years
female: 82.2 years (2017 est.)
country comparison to the world: 62

Total fertility rate: 1.36 children born/woman (2017 est.)
country comparison to the world: 213

Health expenditures: 9.2% of GDP (2014)
country comparison to the world: 37

Physicians density: 2.77 physicians/1,000 population (2014)

Hospital bed density: 4.6 beds/1,000 population (2013)

Drinking water source:
improved:
urban: 99.7% of population
rural: 99.4% of population
total: 99.5% of population
unimproved:
urban: 0.3% of population
rural: 0.6% of population
total: 0.5% of population (2015 est.)

Sanitation facility access:
improved:
urban: 99.1% of population
rural: 99.1% of population
total: 99.1% of population
unimproved:
urban: 0.9% of population
rural: 0.9% of population
total: 0.9% of population (2015 est.)

HIV/AIDS—adult prevalence rate: <.1% (2016 est.)

HIV/AIDS—people living with HIV/AIDS: <1000 (2016 est.)

HIV/AIDS—deaths: <100 (2016 est.)

Obesity—adult prevalence rate: 20.2% (2016)
country comparison to the world: 102

Education expenditures: 5.5% of GDP (2013)
country comparison to the world: 51

Literacy: *definition:* NA
total population: 99.7%
male: 99.7%
female: 99.7% (2015 est.)

School life expectancy (primary to tertiary education): *total:* 17 years
male: 17 years
female: 18 years (2014)

Unemployment, youth ages 15-24: *total:* 16.3%
male: 17.6%
female: 14.6% (2015 est.)
country comparison to the world: 54

GOVERNMENT

Country name: *conventional long form:* Republic of Slovenia
conventional short form: Slovenia
local long form: Republika Slovenija
local short form: Slovenija

former: People's Republic of Slovenia, Socialist Republic of Slovenia
etymology: related to the Slavic autonym (self-designation) "Slovenin," a derivation from "slovo" (word), denoting "people who speak (the same language)" (i.e., people who understand each other)

Government type: parliamentary republic

Capital: *name:* Ljubljana

geographic coordinates: 46 03 N, 14 31 E
time difference: UTC+1 (6 hours ahead of Washington, DC, during Standard Time)
daylight saving time: +1hr, begins last Sunday in March; ends last Sunday in October

Administrative divisions: 201 municipalities (obcine, singular—obcina) and 11 urban municipalities (mestne obcine, singular—mestna obcina)
municipalities: Ajdovscina, Ankaran, Apace, Beltinci, Benedikt, Bistrica ob Sotli, Bled, Bloke, Bohinj, Borovnica, Bovec, Braslovce, Brda, Brezice, Brezovica, Cankova, Cerklje na Gorenjskem, Cerknica, Cerkno, Cerkvenjak, Cirkulane, Crensovci, Crna na Koroskem, Crnomelj, Destrnik, Divaca, Dobje, Dobrepolje, Dobrna, Dobrova-Polhov Gradec, Dobrovnik/Dobronak, Dolenjske Toplice, Dol pri Ljubljani, Domzale, Dornava, Dravograd, Duplek, Gorenja Vas-Poljane, Gorisnica, Gorje, Gornja Radgona, Gornji Grad, Gornji Petrovci, Grad, Grosuplje, Hajdina, Hoce-Slivnica, Hodos, Horjul, Hrastnik, Hrpelje-Kozina, Idrija, Ig, Ilirska Bistrica, Ivancna Gorica, Izola/Isola, Jesenice, Jezersko, Jursinci, Kamnik, Kanal, Kidricevo, Kobarid, Kobilje, Kocevje, Komen, Komenda, Kosanjevica na Krki, Kostel, Kozje, Kranjska Gora, Krizevci, Krsko, Kungota, Kuzma, Lasko, Lenart, Lendava/Lendva, Litija, Ljubno, Ljutomer, Log-Dragomer, Logatec, Loska Dolina, Loski Potok, Lovrenc na Pohorju, Luce, Lukovica,
Majsperk, Makole, Markovci, Medvode, Menges, Metlika, Mezica, Miklavz na Dravskem Polju, Miren-Kostanjevica, Mirna, Mirna Pec, Mislinja, Mokronog-Trebelno, Moravce, Moravske Toplice, Mozirje, Muta, Naklo, Nazarje, Odranci, Oplotnica, Ormoz, Osilnica, Pesnica, Piran/Pirano, Pivka, Podcetrtek, Podlehnik, Podvelka, Poljcane, Polzela, Postojna, Prebold, Preddvor, Prevalje, Puconci, Race-Fram, Radece, Radenci, Radlje ob Dravi, Radovljica, Ravne na Koroskem, Razkrizje, Recica ob Savinji, Rence-Vogrsko, Ribnica, Ribnica na Pohorju, Rogaska Slatina, Rogasovci, Rogatec, Ruse, Selnica ob Dravi, Semic, Sevnica, Sezana, Slovenska Bistrica, Slovenske Konjice, Sodrazica, Solcava, Sredisce ob Dravi, Starse, Straza, Sveta Ana, Sveta Trojica v Slovenskih Goricah, Sveti Andraz v Slovenskih Goricah, Sveti Jurij ob Scavnici, Sveti Jurij v Slovenskih Goricah, Sveti Tomaz, Salovci, Sempeter-Vrtojba, Sencur, Sentilj, Sentjernej, Sentjur, Sentrupert, Skocjan, Skofja Loka, Skofljica, Smarje pri Jelsah, Smarjeske Toplice, Smartno ob Paki, Smartno pri Litiji, Sostanj, Store, Tabor, Tisina, Tolmin, Trbovlje, Trebnje, Trnovska Vas, Trzic, Trzin, Turnisce, Velika Polana, Velike Lasce, Verzej, Videm, Vipava, Vitanje, Vodice, Vojnik,

Vransko, Vrhnika, Vuzenica, Zagorje ob Savi, Zalec, Zavrc, Zelezniki, Zetale, Ziri, Zirovnica, Zrece, Zuzemberk
urban municipalities: Celje, Koper-Capodistria, Kranj, Ljubljana, Maribor, Murska Sobota, Nova Gorica, Novo Mesto, Ptuj, Slovenj Gradec, Velenje

Independence: 25 June 1991 (from Yugoslavia)

National holiday: Independence Day/Statehood Day, 25 June (1991)

Constitution: *history:* previous 1974 (preindependence); latest passed by Parliament 23 December 1991
amendments: proposed by at least 20 National Assembly members, by the government, or by petition of at least 30,000 voters; passage requires at least two-thirds majority vote by the Assembly; referendum required if agreed upon by at least 30 Assembly members; passage in a referendum requires participation of a majority of eligible voters and a simple majority of votes cast; amended several times, last in 2015 (2016)

Legal system: civil law system

International law organization participation: has not submitted an ICJ jurisdiction declaration; accepts ICCt jurisdiction

Citizenship: *citizenship by birth:* no
citizenship by descent only: at least one parent must be a citizen of Slovenia; both parents if the child is born outside of Slovenia
dual citizenship recognized: yes, for select cases
residency requirement for naturalization: 10 years, the last 5 of which have been continuous

Suffrage: 18 years of age, 16 if employed; universal

Executive branch: *chief of state:* President Borut PAHOR (since 22 December 2012)
head of government: Prime Minister Miro CERAR (since 18 September 2014)
cabinet: Council of Ministers nominated by the prime minister, elected by the National Assembly
elections/appointments: president directly elected by absolute majority popular vote in 2 rounds if needed for a 5-year term (eligible for a second term); election last held on 22 October with a runoff on 12 November 2017 (next election to be held by November 2022); following National Assembly elections, the leader of the majority party or majority coalition usually nominated prime minister by the president and elected by the National Assembly
election results: Borut PAHOR is reelected president in second round; percent of vote in first round—Borut PAHOR (independent) 47.1%, Marjan SAREC (Marjan Sarec List) 25%, Romana TOMC (SDS) 13.7%, Ljudmila NOVAK (NSi) 7.2%, other 7%; percent of vote in second round—Borut PAHOR 52.9%, Marjan SAREC 47.1%; note—a snap election was held on 13 July 2014 following the resignation of Prime Minister Alenka BRATUSEK on 5 May 2014; Miro CERAR (SMC) elected prime minister; National Assembly vote—57 to 11

Legislative branch: *description:* bicameral Parliament consists of the National Council or Drzavni

Svet (40 seats; members indirectly elected by an electoral college to serve 5-year terms) and the National Assembly or Drzavni Zbor (90 seats; 88 members directly elected in single-seat constituencies by proportional representation vote and 2 directly elected in special constituencies for Italian and Hungarian minorities by simple majority vote; members serve 4-year terms); note—the National Council is primarily an advisory body with limited legislative powers

elections: National Assembly—last held on 13 July 2014 (next to be held by July 2018)

election results: percent of vote by party—SMC 34.5%, SDS 20.7%, DeSUS 10.2%, ZL 6%, SD 6%, NSi 5.6%, ZaAB 4.4%, other 12.6%; seats by party—SMC 36, SDS 21, DeSUS 10, ZL 6, SD 6, NSi, 5, ZaAB 4, Hungarian minority 1, Italian minority 1

note: as of January 2017, seats by party—SMC 35, SDS 19, DeSUS 11, ZL 6, SD 6, NSi 5, Hungarian minority 1, Italian minority 1, unaffiliated 6

Judicial branch: *highest court(s):* Supreme Court (consists of the court president and 37 judges organized into civil, criminal, commercial, labor and social security, administrative, and registry departments); Constitutional Court (consists of the court president, vice president, and 7 judges)

judge selection and term of office: Supreme Court president and vice president appointed by the National Assembly upon the proposal of the Minister of Justice based on the opinions of the Judicial Council; Constitutional Court judges appointed by the National Assembly from nominations by the president of the republic; Constitutional Court president selected from among their own for a 3-year term; other judges elected for single 9-year terms

subordinate courts: county, district, regional, and high courts; specialized labor-related and social courts; Court of Audit; Administrative Court

Political parties and leaders: Alliance of Social Liberal Democrats or ZSD (formerly Alliance of Alenka Bratusek or ZaAB) [Alenka BRATUSEK]
Democratic Party of Pensioners of Slovenia or DeSUS [Karl ERJAVEC]
Marjan Sarej List [Marjan SAREC]
Modern Center Party or SMC [Miro CERAR]
New Slovenia or NSi [Ljudmila NOVAK]
Slovenian Democratic Party or SDS [Janez JANSA]
Social Democrats or SD [Dejan ZIDAN]
United Left or ZL (collective leadership)
inactive: Alliance for the Re-liberation of Somalia; reportedly inactive since 2009

Political pressure groups and leaders: Roman Catholic Church
other: various trade and public sector employee unions

International organization participation: Australia Group, BIS, CD, CE, CEI, EAPC, EBRD, ECB, EIB, EMU, ESA (cooperating state), EU, FAO, IADB, IAEA, IBRD, ICAO, ICC (national committees), ICCt, ICRM, IDA, IFC, IFRCS, IHO, ILO, IMF, IMO, Interpol, IOC, IOM, IPU, ISO, ITU, MIGA, NATO, NEA, NSG, OAS (observer), OECD, OIF (observer), OPCW, OSCE, PCA, Schengen Convention, SELEC, UN, UNCTAD, UNESCO, UNHCR, UNIDO, UNIFIL, UNTSO, UNWTO, UPU, WCO, WHO, WIPO, WMO, WTO, ZC

Diplomatic representation in the US: chief of mission: Ambassador Stanislav VIDOVIC (since 21 July 2017)

chancery: 2410 California Street N.W., Washington, DC 20008

telephone: [1] (202) 386-6601

FAX: [1] (202) 386-6633

consulate(s) general: Cleveland (OH)

Diplomatic representation from the US: *chief of mission:* Ambassador Brent Robert HARTLEY (since 12 February 2015)

embassy: Presernova 31, 1000 Ljubljana

mailing address: American Embassy Ljubljana, US Department of State, 7140 Ljubljana Place, Washington, DC 20521-7140

telephone: [386] (1) 200-5500

FAX: [386] (1) 200-5555

Flag description: three equal horizontal bands of white (top), blue, and red, derive from the medieval coat of arms of the Duchy of Carniola; the Slovenian seal (a shield with the image of Triglav, Slovenia's highest peak, in white against a blue background at the center; beneath it are two wavy blue lines depicting seas and rivers, and above it are three six-pointed stars arranged in an inverted triangle, which are taken from the coat of arms of the Counts of Celje, the prominent Slovene dynastic house of the late 14th and early 15th centuries) appears in the upper hoist side of the flag centered on the white and blue bands

National symbol(s): Mount Triglav; national colors: white, blue, red

National anthem: *name:* "Zdravljica" (A Toast)
lyrics/music: France PRESEREN/Stanko PREMRL
note: adopted 1989; originally written in 1848; the full poem, whose seventh verse is used as the anthem, speaks of pan-Slavic nationalism

ECONOMY

Economy—overview: With excellent infrastructure, a well-educated work force, and a strategic location between the Balkans and Western Europe, Slovenia has one of the highest per capita GDPs in Central Europe, despite having suffered a protracted recession in the 2008-09 period in the wake of the global financial crisis. Slovenia became the first 2004 EU entrant to adopt the euro (on 1 January 2007) and has experienced a stable political and economic transition.

In March 2004, Slovenia became the first transition country to graduate from borrower status to

donor partner at the World Bank. In 2007, Slovenia was invited to begin the process for joining the OECD; it became a member in 2012. However, long-delayed privatizations, particularly within Slovenia's largely state-owned and increasingly indebted banking sector, have fueled investor concerns since 2012 that the country would need EU-IMF financial assistance. In 2013, the European Commission granted Slovenia permission to begin recapitalizing ailing lenders and transferring their nonperforming assets into a "bad bank" established to restore bank balance sheets. From 2014 to 2017, export-led growth, fueled by demand in larger European markets, pushed GDP growth above 2.3% in each year from 2014-2016, and probably reached 4.6% in 2017. What had been stubbornly high unemployment fell below 7% in 2017, driven by strong exports and increasing consumption that boosted labor demand. Continued fiscal consolidation through increased tax collection and social security contributions is set to have a positive impact in 2018 as the government plans a balanced budget.

Prime Minister CERAR's government took office in September 2014, pledging to press ahead with commitments to privatize a select group of state-run companies, rationalize public spending, and further stabilize the banking sector.

GDP (purchasing power parity): $70.36 billion (2017 est.)
$67.66 billion (2016 est.)
$65.59 billion (2015 est.)
note: data are in 2017 dollars
country comparison to the world: 98

GDP (official exchange rate): $48.08 billion (2016 est.)

GDP—real growth rate: 4% (2017 est.)
3.1% (2016 est.)
2.3% (2015 est.)
country comparison to the world: 66

GDP—per capita (PPP): $34,100 (2017 est.)
$32,800 (2016 est.)
$31,800 (2015 est.)
note: data are in 2017 dollars
country comparison to the world: 58

Gross national saving: 24.5% of GDP (2017 est.)
23.9% of GDP (2016 est.)
23.7% of GDP (2015 est.)
country comparison to the world: 55

GDP—composition, by end use:
household consumption: 52%
government consumption: 18.8%
investment in fixed capital: 18.9%
investment in inventories: 1.1%
exports of goods and services: 82.3%
imports of goods and services: -73.2% (2017 est.)

GDP—composition, by sector of origin:
agriculture: 2.3%
industry: 32%
services: 65.8% (2017 est.)

Agriculture—products: hops, wheat, coffee, corn, apples, pears; cattle, sheep, poultry

Industries: ferrous metallurgy and aluminum products, lead and zinc smelting; electronics (including military electronics), trucks, automobiles, electric power equipment, wood products, textiles, chemicals, machine tools

Industrial production growth rate: 2.5% (2017 est.)
country comparison to the world: 110

Labor force: 931,200 (2017 est.)
country comparison to the world: 148

Labor force—by occupation: *agriculture:* 3.7%
industry: 31.7%
services: 64.6% (2015 est.)

Unemployment rate: 6.8% (2017 est.)
8% (2016 est.)
country comparison to the world: 95

Population below poverty line: 14.3% (2015 est.)

Household income or consumption by percentage share: *lowest 10%:* 3.8%
highest 10%: 20.2% (2015)

Distribution of family income—Gini index: 24.5 (2015)
25 (2014)
country comparison to the world: 147

Budget: *revenues:* $20.2 billion
expenditures: $20.97 billion (2017 est.)
Taxes and other revenues: 42% of GDP (2017 est.)
country comparison to the world: 29

Budget surplus (+) or deficit (-): -1.6% of GDP (2017 est.)
country comparison to the world: 70

Public debt: 78.6% of GDP (2017 est.)
79.7% of GDP (2016 est.)
note: defined by the EU's Maastricht Treaty as consolidated general government gross debt at nominal value, outstanding at the end of the year in the following categories of government liabilities: currency and deposits, securities other than shares excluding financial derivatives, and loans; general government sector comprises the subsectors: central government, state government, local government, and social security funds
country comparison to the world: 41

Fiscal year: calendar year

Inflation rate (consumer prices): 1.6% (2017 est.)
-0.1% (2016 est.)
country comparison to the world: 66

Central bank discount rate: 0% (16 March 2016)
0.05% (4 Sept 2014)
note: this is the European Central Bank's rate on the marginal lending facility, which offers overnight credit to banks in the euro area
country comparison to the world: 151

Commercial bank prime lending rate: 2.9% (31 December 2017 est.)
2.81% (31 December 2016 est.)
country comparison to the world: 171

Stock of narrow money: $20.79 billion (31 December 2017 est.)
$16.54 billion (31 December 2016 est.)
note: see entry for the European Union for money supply for the entire euro area; the European Central Bank (ECB) controls monetary policy for the 18 members of the Economic and Monetary Union (EMU); individual members of the EMU do not control the quantity of money circulating within their own borders

country comparison to the world: 69

Stock of broad money: $27.88 billion (31 December 2017 est.)
$24.3 billion (31 December 2016 est.)
country comparison to the world: 82

Stock of domestic credit: $33.33 billion (31 December 2017 est.)
$30.23 billion (31 December 2016 est.)
country comparison to the world: 77

Market value of publicly traded shares: $5.6 billion (31 December 2016 est.)
$5.94 billion (31 December 2015 est.)
$6.2 billion (31 December 2014 est.)
country comparison to the world: 84

Current account balance: $2.415 billion (2017 est.)
$2.332 billion (2016 est.)
country comparison to the world: 32

Exports: $30.23 billion (2017 est.)
$27.65 billion (2016 est.)
country comparison to the world: 62

Exports—commodities: manufactured goods, machinery and transport equipment, chemicals, food

Exports—partners: Germany 19.3%, Italy 10.4%, Austria 7.5%, Croatia 7.3%, Hungary 4.4%, France 4.1% (2016)

Imports: $28.7 billion (2017 est.)
$25.95 billion (2016 est.)
country comparison to the world: 65

Imports—commodities: machinery and transport equipment, manufactured goods, chemicals, fuels and lubricants, food

Imports—partners: Germany 16.8%, Italy 13.5%, Austria 9.9%, Croatia 5.5%, China 4.8%, Turkey 4.4% (2016)

Reserves of foreign exchange and gold: $911.2 million (31 December 2017 est.)
$743.2 million (31 December 2016 est.)
country comparison to the world: 129

Debt—external: $46.3 billion (31 January 2017 est.)
$48.2 billion (31 January 2016 est.)
country comparison to the world: 66

Stock of direct foreign investment—at home: $16 billion (31 December 2017 est.)
$14.83 billion (31 December 2016 est.)
country comparison to the world: 88

Stock of direct foreign investment—abroad: $8.137 billion (31 December 2017 est.)
$7.837 billion (31 December 2016 est.)
country comparison to the world: 65

Exchange rates: euros (EUR) per US dollar—
0.906 (2017 est.)
0.9214 (2016 est.)
0.9214 (2015 est.)
0.885 (2014 est.)
0.7634 (2013 est.)

ENERGY

Electricity access: *electrification—total population:* 100% (2016)

Electricity—production: 16.53 billion kWh (2016 est.)
country comparison to the world: 84

Electricity—consumption: 14.57 billion kWh (2016 est.)
country comparison to the world: 80

Electricity—exports: 10.28 billion kWh (2016 est.)
country comparison to the world: 22

Electricity—imports: 8.325 billion kWh (2016 est.)
country comparison to the world: 30

Electricity—installed generating capacity: 3.37 million kW (2016 est.)
country comparison to the world: 95

Electricity—from fossil fuels: 31.8% of total installed capacity (2016 est.)
country comparison to the world: 184

Electricity—from nuclear fuels: 34.4% of total installed capacity (2016 est.)
country comparison to the world: 2

Electricity—from hydroelectric plants: 31.9% of total installed capacity (2016 est.)
country comparison to the world: 66

Electricity—from other renewable sources: 1.7% of total installed capacity (2016 est.)
country comparison to the world: 128

Crude oil—production: 5 bbl/day (2016 est.)
country comparison to the world: 101

Crude oil—exports: 0 bbl/day (2016 est.)
country comparison to the world: 189

Crude oil—imports: 0 bbl/day (2016 est.)
country comparison to the world: 188

Crude oil—proved reserves: 0 bbl (1 January 2017 es)
country comparison to the world: 197

Refined petroleum products—production: 0 bbl/day (2016 est.)
country comparison to the world: 201

Refined petroleum products—consumption: 52,300 bbl/day (2016 est.)
country comparison to the world: 104

Refined petroleum products—exports: 28,400 bbl/day (2016 est.)
country comparison to the world: 63

Refined petroleum products—imports: 87,530 bbl/day (2016 est.)
country comparison to the world: 61

Natural gas—production: 4.5 million cu m (2016 est.)
country comparison to the world: 99

Natural gas—consumption: 836.5 million cu m (2016 est.)
country comparison to the world: 103

Natural gas—exports: 0 cu m (2016 est.)
country comparison to the world: 181

Natural gas—imports: 832 million cu m (2016 est.)
country comparison to the world: 62

Natural gas—proved reserves: 0 cu m (2016 est.)
country comparison to the world: 193

Carbon dioxide emissions from consumption of energy: 14.3 million Mt (2013 est.)
country comparison to the world: 92

COMMUNICATIONS

Telephones—fixed lines: *total subscriptions:* 731,320
subscriptions per 100 inhabitants: 37 (July 2016 est.)
country comparison to the world: 88

Telephones—mobile cellular: *total:* 2,385,757
subscriptions per 100 inhabitants: 121 (July 2016 est.)
country comparison to the world: 149

Telephone system: *general assessment:* well-developed telecommunications infrastructure
domestic: combined fixed-line and mobile-cellular teledensity roughly 155 telephones per 100 persons
international: country code—386 (2016)

Broadcast media: public TV broadcaster, Radiotelevizija Slovenija (RTV), operates a system of national and regional TV stations; 35 domestic commercial TV stations operating nationally, regionally, and locally; about 60% of households are connected to multi-channel cable TV; public radio broadcaster operates 3 national and 4 regional stations; more than 75 regional and local commercial and non-commercial radio stations (2007)

Internet country code: .si

Internet users: *total:* 1,493,382
percent of population: 75.5% (July 2016 est.)
country comparison to the world: 115

TRANSPORTATION

National air transport system: number of registered air carriers: 2
inventory of registered aircraft operated by air carriers: 35

annual passenger traffic on registered air carriers: 1,130,637
annual freight traffic on registered air carriers: 1,349,442 mt-km (2015)
Civil aircraft registration country code prefix: S5 (2016)

Airports: 16 (2013)
country comparison to the world: 143

Airports—with paved runways: *total:* 7
over 3,047 m: 1
2,438 to 3,047 m: 1
1,524 to 2,437 m: 1
914 to 1,523 m: 3
under 914 m: 1 (2013)

Airports—with unpaved runways: *total:* 9
1,524 to 2,437 m: 1
914 to 1,523 m: 3
under 914 m: 5 (2013)

Pipelines: gas 844 km; oil 5 km (2013)

Railways: *total:* 1,229 km
standard gauge: 1,229 km 1.435-m gauge (503 km electrified) (2014)
country comparison to the world: 85

Roadways: *total:* 38,985 km
paved: 38,985 km (includes 769 km of expressways) (2012)
country comparison to the world: 91

Waterways: (some transport on the Drava River) (2012)

Merchant marine: *total:* 7
by type: other 7 (2017)
country comparison to the world: 152

Ports and terminals: *major seaport(s):* Koper

MILITARY AND SECURITY

Military expenditures: 0.92% of GDP (2016)
0.94% of GDP (2015)
0.98% of GDP (2014)
1.06% of GDP (2013)

1.17% of GDP (2012)
country comparison to the world: 85

Military branches: Slovenian Armed Forces (Slovenska Vojska, SV): Forces Command (with ground units, naval element, air and air defense brigade); Administration for Civil Protection and Disaster Relief (ACPDR) (2013)

Military service age and obligation: 18-25 years of age for voluntary military service; conscription abolished in 2003 (2012)

TRANSNATIONAL ISSUES

Disputes—international: since the breakup of Yugoslavia in the early 1990s, Croatia and Slovenia have each claimed sovereignty over Piranski Bay and four villages, and Slovenia has objected to Croatia's claim of an exclusive economic zone in the Adriatic Sea; in 2009, however Croatia and Slovenia signed a binding international arbitration agreement to define their disputed land and maritime borders, which led Slovenia to lift its objections to Croatia joining the EU; as a member state that forms part of the EU's external border, Slovenia has implemented the strict Schengen border rules to curb illegal migration and commerce through southeastern Europe while encouraging close cross-border ties with Croatia; Slovenia continues to impose a hard border Schengen regime with Croatia, which joined the EU in 2013 but has not yet fulfilled Schengen requirements
Refugees and internally displaced persons: note: 477,791 estimated refugee and migrant arrivals (January 2015—December 2016); migration through the Western Balkans has decreased significantly since March 2016; Slovenia is predominantly a transit country and hosts fewer than 250 asylum seekers as of September 2017

Illicit drugs: minor transit point for cocaine and Southwest Asian heroin bound for Western Europe, and for precursor chemicals

SOLOMON ISLANDS

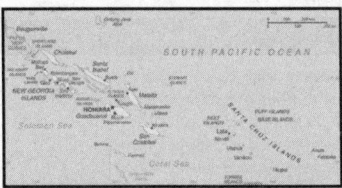

INTRODUCTION

Background: The UK established a protectorate over the Solomon Islands in the 1890s. Some of the bitterest fighting of World War II occurred on this archipelago. Self-government was achieved in 1976 and independence two years later. Ethnic violence, government malfeasance, endemic

crime, and a narrow economic base have undermined stability and civil society. In June 2003, then Prime Minister Sir Allan KEMAKEZA sought the assistance of Australia in reestablishing law and order; the following month, an Australian-led multinational force arrived to restore peace and disarm ethnic militias. The Regional Assistance Mission to the Solomon Islands (RAMSI) has generally been effective in restoring law and order and rebuilding government institutions.

GEOGRAPHY

Location: Oceania, group of islands in the South Pacific Ocean, east of Papua New Guinea
Geographic coordinates: 8 00 S, 159 00 E
Map references: Oceania

Area: *total:* 28,896 sq km
land: 27,986 sq km
water: 910 sq km
country comparison to the world: 144

Area—comparative: slightly smaller than Maryland
Land boundaries: 0 km

Coastline: 5,313 km

Maritime claims: measured from claimed archipelagic baselines
territorial sea: 12 nm
exclusive economic zone: 200 nm
continental shelf: 200 nm

Climate: tropical monsoon; few temperature and weather extremes

Terrain: mostly rugged mountains with some low coral atolls

Elevation: *mean elevation:* NA

elevation extremes: *lowest point:* Pacific Ocean 0 m

highest point: Mount Popomanaseu 2,335 m

Natural resources: fish, forests, gold, bauxite, phosphates, lead, zinc, nickel

Land use: *agricultural land:* 3.9%
arable land: 0.7%;
permanent crops: 2.9%;
permanent pasture: 0.3%
forest: 78.9%
other: 17.2% (2011 est.)
Irrigated land: 0 sq km NA (2012)

Population—distribution: most of the population lives along the coastal regions; about one in five live in urban areas, and of these some two-thirds reside in Honiara, the largest town and chief port

Natural hazards: tropical cyclones, but rarely destructive; geologically active region with frequent earthquakes, tremors, and volcanic activity; tsunamis

volcanism: Tinakula (851 m) has frequent eruption activity, while an eruption of Savo (485 m) could affect the capital Honiara on nearby Guadalcanal

Environment—current issues: deforestation; soil erosion; many of the surrounding coral reefs are dead or dying

Environment—international agreements: *party to:* Biodiversity, Climate Change, Climate Change-Kyoto Protocol, Desertification, Environmental Modification, Law of the Sea, Marine Dumping, Marine Life Conservation, Ozone Layer Protection, Whaling

signed, but not ratified: none of the selected agreements

Geography—note: strategic location on sea routes between the South Pacific Ocean, the Solomon Sea, and the Coral Sea; on 2 April 2007 an undersea earthquake measuring 8.1 on the Richter scale occurred 345 km WNW of the capital Honiara; the resulting tsunami devastated coastal areas of Western and Choiseul provinces with dozens of deaths and thousands dislocated; the provincial capital of Gizo was especially hard hit

PEOPLE AND SOCIETY

Population: 647,581 (July 2017 est.)
country comparison to the world: 167

Nationality: *noun:* Solomon Islander(s)
adjective: Solomon Islander

Ethnic groups: Melanesian 95.3%, Polynesian 3.1%, Micronesian 1.2%, other 0.3% (2009 est.)

Languages: Melanesian pidgin (in much of the country is lingua franca), English (official but spoken by only 1%-2% of the population), 120 indigenous languages

Religions: Protestant 73.4% (Church of Melanesia 31.9%, South Sea Evangelical 17.1%, Seventh Day Adventist 11.7%, United Church 10.1%,

Christian Fellowship Church 2.5%), Roman Catholic 19.6%, other Christian 2.9%, other 4%, none 0.03%, unspecified 0.1% (2009 est.)

Age structure: *0-14 years:* 34.59% (male 115,329/female 108,645)
15-24 years: 19.99% (male 66,608/female 62,843)
25-54 years: 36.5% (male 120,339/female 116,048)
55-64 years: 4.65% (male 15,316/female 14,828)
65 years and over: 4.27% (male 13,096/female 14,529) (2017 est.)

Dependency ratios: *total dependency ratio:* 75.4
youth dependency ratio: 69.4
elderly dependency ratio: 6
potential support ratio: 16.6 (2015 est.)

Median age: *total:* 22.5 years
male: 22.3 years
female: 22.8 years (2017 est.)
country comparison to the world: 178

Population growth rate: 1.94% (2017 est.)
country comparison to the world: 50

Birth rate: 24.9 births/1,000 population (2017 est.)
country comparison to the world: 49

Death rate: 3.8 deaths/1,000 population (2017 est.)
country comparison to the world: 213

Net migration rate: -1.7 migrant(s)/1,000 population (2017 est.)
country comparison to the world: 153

Population distribution: most of the population lives along the coastal regions; about one in five live in urban areas, and of these some two-thirds reside in Honiara, the largest town and chief port

Urbanization: *urban population:* 23.2% of total population (2017)
rate of urbanization: 3.79% annual rate of change (2015-20 est.)

Major urban areas—population: HONIARA (capital) 73,000 (2014)

Sex ratio: *at birth:* 1.05 male(s)/female
0-14 years: 1.06 male(s)/female
15-24 years: 1.06 male(s)/female
25-54 years: 1.04 male(s)/female
55-64 years: 1.02 male(s)/female
65 years and over: 0.92 male(s)/female
total population: 1.04 male(s)/female (2016 est.)

Mother's mean age at first birth: 21.6 years
note: median age at first birth among women 25-29 (2006/07 est.)

Maternal mortality ratio: 114 deaths/100,000 live births (2015 est.)
country comparison to the world: 70

Infant mortality rate: *total:* 14.7 deaths/1,000 live births
male: 16.8 deaths/1,000 live births
female: 12.5 deaths/1,000 live births (2017 est.)
country comparison to the world: 102

Life expectancy at birth: *total population:* 75.6 years
male: 72.9 years
female: 78.3 years (2017 est.)
country comparison to the world: 103

Total fertility rate: 3.16 children born/woman (2017 est.)
country comparison to the world: 50

Health expenditures: 5.1% of GDP (2014)
country comparison to the world: 138

Physicians density: 0.2 physicians/1,000 population (2011)

Hospital bed density: 1.3 beds/1,000 population (2012)

Drinking water source:
improved:
 urban: 93.2% of population
rural: 77.2% of population
total: 80.8% of population
unimproved:
urban: 6.8% of population
rural: 22.8% of population
total: 19.2% of population (2015 est.)

Sanitation facility access:
improved:
urban: 81.4% of population
rural: 15% of population
total: 29.8% of population
unimproved:
urban: 18.6% of population
rural: 85% of population
total: 70.2% of population (2015 est.)

HIV/AIDS—adult prevalence rate: NA

HIV/AIDS—people living with HIV/AIDS: NA

HIV/AIDS—deaths: NA

Obesity—adult prevalence rate: 22.5% (2016)
country comparison to the world: 75

Children under the age of 5 years underweight: 11.5% (2007)
country comparison to the world: 65

Education expenditures: 10% of GDP (2010)
country comparison to the world: 18

Literacy: *definition:* age 15 and over can read and write
total population: 84.1%
male: 88.9%
female: 79.2% (2009 est.)

School life expectancy (primary to tertiary education): *total:* 9 years
male: 10 years
female: 9 years (2007)

GOVERNMENT

Country name: *conventional long form:* none
conventional short form: Solomon Islands
local long form: none
local short form: Solomon Islands
former: British Solomon Islands
etymology: Spanish explorer Alvaro de MENDANA named the isles in 1568 after the wealthy biblical King SOLOMON in the mistaken belief that the islands contained great riches

Government type: parliamentary democracy (National Parliament) under a constitutional monarchy; a Commonwealth realm

Capital: *name:* Honiara

geographic coordinates: 9 26 S, 159 57 E

time difference: UTC+11 (16 hours ahead of Washington, DC, during Standard Time)

Administrative divisions: 9 provinces and 1 city*; Central, Choiseul, Guadalcanal, Honiara*, Isabel, Makira and Ulawa, Malaita, Rennell and Bellona, Temotu, Western

Independence: 7 July 1978 (from the UK)

National holiday: Independence Day, 7 July (1978)

Constitution: adopted 31 May 1978, effective 7 July 1978; new constitution drafted in 2014 (2016)

Legal system: mixed legal system of English common law and customary law

International law organization participation: has not submitted an ICJ jurisdiction declaration; non-party state to the ICCt

Citizenship: *citizenship by birth:* no

citizenship by descent only: at least one parent must be a citizen of the Solomon Islands
dual citizenship recognized: no
residency requirement for naturalization: 7 years

Suffrage: 21 years of age; universal

Executive branch: *chief of state:* Queen ELIZABETH II (since 6 February 1952); represented by Governor General Frank KABUI (since 7 July 2009)
head of government: Prime Minister Rick HOU (since 16 November 2017)
cabinet: Cabinet appointed by the governor general on the advice of the prime minister
elections/appointments: the monarchy is hereditary; governor general appointed by the monarch on the advice of the National Parliament for up to 5 years (eligible for a second term); following legislative elections, the leader of the majority party or majority coalition usually elected prime minister by the National Parliament; deputy prime minister appointed by the governor general on the advice of the prime minister from among members of the National Parliament
election results: Manasseh SOGAVARE (independent) defeated in no-confidence vote on 6 November 2017; Rick HOU elected prime minister on 15 November 2017

Legislative branch: *description:* unicameral National Parliament (50 seats; members directly elected in single-seat constituencies by simple majority vote to serve 4-year terms)
elections: last held on 19 November 2014 (next to be held in 2018)
election results: percent of vote by party—UDP 10.7%, DAP 7.8%, PAP 4.4%, other 20.8%, independent 56.3%; seats by party—DAP 7, UDP 5, PAP 3, KPSI 1, SIPFP 1, SIPRA 1, independent 32

Judicial branch: *highest court(s):* Court of Appeal (consists of the court president, and ex officio members to include the High Court chief justice and its puisne judges); High Court (consists of the chief justice and puisne judges as prescribed by the National Parliament)
judge selection and term of office: Court of Appeal and High Court president, chief justices, and puisne judges appointed by the governor-general upon recommendation of the Judicial and Legal Service Commission, chaired by the chief justice to include 5 members, mostly judicial officials and legal professionals; all judges appointed until retirement at age 60

subordinate courts: Magistrates' Courts; Customary Land Appeal Court; local courts

Political parties and leaders: Democratic Alliance Party or DAP [Steve ABANA]
Kadere Party of Solomon Islands or KPSI [Peter BOYERS]
People's Alliance Party or PAP [Nathaniel WAENA]
Solomon Islands People First Party or SIPFP [Dr. Jimmie RODGERS]
Solomon Islands Party for Rural Advancement or SIPRA [Manasseh MAELANGA]
United Democratic Party or UDP [Sir Thomas Ko CHAN]
note: in general, Solomon Islands politics is characterized by fluid coalitions

Political pressure groups and leaders: Isatabu Freedom Movement or IFM
Malaita Eagle Force or MEF
note: these rival armed ethnic factions crippled the Solomon Islands in a wave of violence from 1999 to 2003

International organization participation: ACP, ADB, AOSIS, C, EITI (candidate country), ESCAP, FAO, G-77, IBRD, ICAO, ICRM, IDA, IFAD, IFC, IFRCS, ILO, IMF, IMO, IOC, ITU, MIGA, OPCW, PIF, Sparteca, SPC, UN, UNCTAD, UNESCO, UPU, WFTU, WHO, WMO, WTO

Diplomatic representation in the US: chief of mission: Ambassador Robert SISILO (since 21 July 2017)
chancery: 800 Second Avenue, Suite 400L, New York, NY 10017
telephone: [1] (212) 599-6192, 6193
FAX: [1] (212) 661-8925

Diplomatic representation from the US: the US does not have an embassy in the Solomon Islands; the US Ambassador to Papua New Guinea is accredited to the Solomon Islands

Flag description: divided diagonally by a thin yellow stripe from the lower hoist-side corner; the upper triangle (hoist side) is blue with five white five-pointed stars arranged in an X pattern; the lower triangle is green; blue represents the ocean; green the land; and yellow sunshine; the five stars stand for the five main island groups of the Solomon Islands

National symbol(s): national colors: blue, yellow, green, white

National anthem: *name:* "God Save Our Solomon Islands"
lyrics/music: Panapasa BALEKANA and Matila BALEKANA/Panapasa BALEKANA
note: adopted 1978

ECONOMY

Economy—overview: The bulk of the population depends on agriculture, fishing, and forestry for at least part of its livelihood. Most manufactured goods and petroleum products must be imported. The islands are rich in undeveloped mineral resources such as lead, zinc, nickel, and gold. Prior to the arrival of The Regional Assistance Mission to the Solomon Islands (RAMSI), severe ethnic violence, the closure of key businesses, and an empty government treasury culminated in economic collapse. RAMSI's efforts to restore law and order and economic stability have led to modest growth as the economy rebuilds.

GDP (purchasing power parity): $1.317 billion (2017 est.)
$1.279 billion (2016 est.)
$1.239 billion (2015 est.)
note: data are in 2017 dollars
country comparison to the world: 202

GDP (official exchange rate): $1.273 billion (2016 est.)

GDP—real growth rate: 3% (2017 est.)
3.3% (2016 est.)
2.5% (2015 est.)
country comparison to the world: 116

GDP—per capita (PPP): $2,100 (2017 est.)
$2,100 (2016 est.)
$2,100 (2015 est.)
note: data are in 2017 dollars
country comparison to the world: 207

Gross national saving: 16.1% of GDP (2017 est.)
14% of GDP (2016 est.)
14.5% of GDP (2015 est.)
country comparison to the world: 120

GDP—composition, by sector of origin:
agriculture: 34.3%
industry: 7.6%
services: 58.1% (2017 est.)

Agriculture—products: cocoa, coconuts, palm kernels, rice, fruit; cattle, pigs; fish; timber

Industries: fish (tuna), mining, timber

Industrial production growth rate: 3.7% (2017 est.)
country comparison to the world: 77

Labor force: 202,500 (2007 est.)
country comparison to the world: 171

Labor force—by occupation: *agriculture:* 75%
industry: 5%
services: 20% (2000 est.)

Unemployment rate: NA%

Population below poverty line: NA%

Household income or consumption by percentage share: *lowest 10%:* NA%
highest 10%: NA%

Budget: *revenues:* $434.6 million
expenditures: $471.9 million (2017 est.)
Taxes and other revenues: 34.1% of GDP (2017 est.)
country comparison to the world: 60

Budget surplus (+) or deficit (-): -2.9% of GDP (2017 est.)
country comparison to the world: 112

Public debt: 9% of GDP (2016 est.)
10.5% of GDP (2015 est.)
country comparison to the world: 198

Fiscal year: calendar year

Inflation rate (consumer prices): -0.5% (2017 est.)
0.5% (2016 est.)
country comparison to the world: 3

Commercial bank prime lending rate: 10.2% (31 December 2017 est.)
10.1% (31 December 2016 est.)
country comparison to the world: 82

Stock of narrow money: $510 million (31 December 2017 est.)
$461 million (31 December 2016 est.)
country comparison to the world: 168

Stock of broad money: $520.5 million (31 December 2017 est.)
$476.3 million (31 December 2016 est.)
country comparison to the world: 186

Stock of domestic credit: $174.7 million (31 December 2017 est.)
$150.7 million (31 December 2016 est.)
country comparison to the world: 186

Current account balance: -$64 million (2017 est.)
-$49 million (2016 est.)
country comparison to the world: 74

Exports: $419.9 million (2015 est.)
$420.7 million (2015 est.)
country comparison to the world: 178

Exports—commodities: timber, fish, copra, palm oil, cocoa

Exports—partners: China 62.4%, Italy 7%, UK 4.4% (2016)

Imports: $425.7 million (2015 est.)
country comparison to the world: 191

Imports—commodities: food, plant and equipment, manufactured goods, fuels, chemicals

Imports—partners: China 25.3%, Australia 15.5%, Singapore 9.6%, Malaysia 9.5%, Japan 5.2%, South Korea 5%, NZ 5%, Papua New Guinea 4.4% (2016)

Debt—external: $491.5 million (31 December 2013 est.)
$207.4 million (31 December 2015 est.)
country comparison to the world: 179

Stock of direct foreign investment—at home: $608.1 million (31 December 2017 est.)
$571.2 million (31 December 2016 est.)
country comparison to the world: 121

Stock of direct foreign investment—abroad: $50.1 million (31 December 2017 est.)
$50.1 million (31 December 2016 est.)
country comparison to the world: 107

Exchange rates: Solomon Islands dollars (SBD) per US dollar—
8.053 (2017 est.)
7.94 (2016 est.)
7.94 (2015 est.)
7.9147 (2014 est.)
7.3754 (2013 est.)

ENERGY

Electricity access: population without electricity: 495,321

electrification—*total population:* 23%
electrification—urban areas: 62%
electrification—rural areas: 13% (2012)

Electricity—production: 90 million kWh (2015 est.)
country comparison to the world: 200

Electricity—consumption: 83.7 million kWh (2015 est.)
country comparison to the world: 201

Electricity—exports: 0 kWh (2016 est.)
country comparison to the world: 112

Electricity—imports: 0 kWh (2016 est.)
country comparison to the world: 128

Electricity—installed generating capacity: 37,000 kW (2015 est.)
country comparison to the world: 199

Electricity—from fossil fuels: 97.3% of total installed capacity (2015 est.)
country comparison to the world: 41

Electricity—from nuclear fuels: 0% of total installed capacity (2015 est.)
country comparison to the world: 57

Electricity—from hydroelectric plants: 0% of total installed capacity (2015 est.)
country comparison to the world: 165

Electricity—from other renewable sources: 5.4% of total installed capacity (2015 est.)
country comparison to the world: 94

Crude oil—production: 0 bbl/day (2016 est.)
country comparison to the world: 199

Crude oil—exports: 0 bbl/day (2014 est.)
country comparison to the world: 99

Crude oil—imports: 0 bbl/day (2014 est.)
country comparison to the world: 102

Crude oil—proved reserves: 0 bbl (1 January 2017 es)
country comparison to the world: 198

Refined petroleum products—production: 0 bbl/day (2014 est.)
country comparison to the world: 202

Refined petroleum products—consumption: 1,600 bbl/day (2015 est.)
country comparison to the world: 198

Refined petroleum products—exports: 0 bbl/day (2014 est.)
country comparison to the world: 136

Refined petroleum products—imports: 1,554 bbl/day (2014 est.)
country comparison to the world: 193

Natural gas—production: 0 cu m (2013 est.)
country comparison to the world: 113

Natural gas—consumption: 0 cu m (2013 est.)
country comparison to the world: 161

Natural gas—exports: 0 cu m (2013 est.)
country comparison to the world: 74

Natural gas—imports: 0 cu m (2013 est.)
country comparison to the world: 97

Natural gas—proved reserves: 0 cu m (1 January 2014 es)
country comparison to the world: 119

Carbon dioxide emissions from consumption of energy: 300,000 Mt (2013 est.)
country comparison to the world: 194

COMMUNICATIONS

Telephones—fixed lines: *total subscriptions:* 7,405
subscriptions per 100 inhabitants: 1 (July 2016 est.)
country comparison to the world: 201

Telephones—mobile cellular: *total:* 416,572
subscriptions per 100 inhabitants: 66 (July 2016 est.)
country comparison to the world: 174
Telephone system: domestic: mobile-cellular telephone density is about 65 per 100 persons
international: country code—677; satellite earth station—1 Intelsat (Pacific Ocean) (2016)

Broadcast media: Solomon Islands Broadcasting Corporation (SIBC) is the sole TV broadcaster with 1 station; multi-channel pay-TV is available; SIBC operates 2 national radio stations and 2 provincial stations; 2 local commercial radio stations; Radio Australia is available via satellite feed (2009)

Internet country code: .sb

Internet users: *total:* 69,859
percent of population: 11.0% (July 2016 est.)
country comparison to the world: 187

TRANSPORTATION

National air transport system: number of registered air carriers: 1
inventory of registered aircraft operated by air carriers: 3
annual passenger traffic on registered air carriers: 373,738
annual freight traffic on registered air carriers: 3,691,584 mt-km (2015)
Civil aircraft registration country code prefix: H4 (2016)

Airports: 36 (2013)
country comparison to the world: 109

Airports—with paved runways: *total:* 1
1,524 to 2,437 m: 1 (2013)

Airports—with unpaved runways: *total:* 35
1,524 to 2,437 m: 1
914 to 1,523 m: 10
under 914 m: 24 (2013)

Heliports: 3 (2013)

Roadways: *total:* 1,390 km
paved: 34 km
unpaved: 1,356 km
note: includes 920 km of private plantation roads (2011)
country comparison to the world: 179

Merchant marine: *total:* 22
by type: general cargo 6, other 16 (2017)
country comparison to the world: 132

Ports and terminals: *major seaport(s):* Honiara, Malloco Bay, Viru Harbor, Tulaghi

MILITARY AND SECURITY

Military branches: no regular military forces; Royal Solomon Islands Police Force (2013)

SOMALIA

TRANSNATIONAL ISSUES

Disputes—international: since 2003, the Regional Assistance Mission to Solomon Islands, consisting of police, military, and civilian advisors drawn from 15 countries, has assisted in reestablishing and maintaining civil and political order while reinforcing regional stability and security

Trafficking in persons: current situation: the Solomon Islands is a source and destination country for local adults and children and Southeast Asian men and women subjected to forced labor and forced prostitution; women from China, Indonesia, Malaysia, and the Philippines are recruited for legitimate work and upon arrival are forced into prostitution; men from Indonesia and Malaysia recruited to work in the Solomon Islands' mining and logging industries may be subjected to forced labor; local children are forced into prostitution near foreign logging camps, on fishing vessels, at hotels, and entertainment venues; some local children are also sold by their parents for marriage to foreign workers or put up for "informal adoption" to pay off debts and then find themselves forced into domestic servitude or forced prostitution

tier rating: Tier 2 Watch List—the Solomon Islands does not fully comply with the minimum standards for the elimination of trafficking; however, it is making significant efforts to do so; in 2014, the Solomon Islands was granted a waiver from an otherwise required downgrade to Tier 3 because its government has a written plan that, if implemented, would constitute making significant efforts to bring itself into compliance with the minimum standards for the elimination of trafficking; the government gazetted implementing regulations for the 2012 immigration act prohibiting transnational trafficking, but the penalties are not sufficiently stringent because they allow the option of paying a fine; a new draft law to address these weaknesses awaits parliamentary review; no new trafficking investigations were conducted, even after labor inspections at logging and fishing companies, no existing cases led to prosecutions or convictions, and no funding was allocated for national anti-trafficking efforts; authorities did not identify or protect any victims and lack any procedures or shelters to do so; civil society and religious organizations provide most of the limited services available; a lack of understanding of the crime of trafficking remains a serious challenge (2015)

SOMALIA

INTRODUCTION

Background: Britain withdrew from British Somaliland in 1960 to allow its protectorate to join with Italian Somaliland and form the new nation of Somalia. In 1969, a coup headed by Mohamed SIAD Barre ushered in an authoritarian socialist rule characterized by the persecution, jailing, and torture of political opponents and dissidents. After the regime's collapse early in 1991, Somalia descended into turmoil, factional fighting, and anarchy. In May 1991, northern clans declared an independent Republic of Somaliland that now includes the administrative regions of Awdal, Woqooyi Galbeed, Togdheer, Sanaag, and Sool. Although not recognized by any government, this entity has maintained a stable existence and continues efforts to establish a constitutional democracy, including holding municipal, parliamentary, and presidential elections. The regions of Bari, Nugaal, and northern Mudug comprise a neighboring semi-autonomous state of Puntland,

which has been self-governing since 1998 but does not aim at independence; it has also made strides toward reconstructing a legitimate, representative government but has suffered some civil strife. Puntland disputes its border with Somaliland as it also claims the regions of Sool and Sanaag, and portions of Togdheer. Beginning in 1993, a two-year UN humanitarian effort (primarily in south-central Somalia) was able to alleviate famine conditions, but when the UN withdrew in 1995, having suffered significant casualties, order still had not been restored.

In 2000, the Somalia National Peace Conference (SNPC) held in Djibouti resulted in the formation of an interim government, known as the Transitional National Government (TNG). When the TNG failed to establish adequate security or governing institutions, the Government of Kenya, under the auspices of the Intergovernmental Authority on Development (IGAD), led a subsequent peace process that concluded in October 2004 with the election of Abdullahi YUSUF Ahmed as President of a second interim government, known as the Transitional Federal Government (TFG) of the Somali Republic. The TFG included a 275-member parliamentary body, known as the Transitional Federal Parliament (TFP). President YUSUF resigned late in 2008 while UN-sponsored talks between the TFG and the opposition Alliance for the Re-Liberation of Somalia (ARS) were underway in Djibouti. In January 2009, following the creation of a TFG-ARS unity government, Ethiopian military forces, which had entered Somalia in December 2006 to support the TFG in the face of advances by the opposition Islamic Courts Union (ICU), withdrew from the country. The TFP was doubled in size to 550 seats with the addition of 200 ARS and 75 civil society members of parliament. The expanded parliament elected Sheikh SHARIF Sheikh Ahmed, the former ICU and ARS chairman as president in January 2009. The creation of the TFG was

based on the Transitional Federal Charter (TFC), which outlined a five-year mandate leading to the establishment of a new Somali constitution and a transition to a representative government following national elections. In 2009, the TFP amended the TFC to extend TFG's mandate until 2011 and in 2011 Somali principals agreed to institute political transition by August 2012. The transition process ended in September 2012 when clan elders replaced the TFP by appointing 275 members to a new parliament who subsequently elected a new president.

GEOGRAPHY

Location: Eastern Africa, bordering the Gulf of Aden and the Indian Ocean, east of Ethiopia

Geographic coordinates: 10 00 N, 49 00 E

Map references: Africa

Area: *total:* 637,657 sq km
land: 627,337 sq km
water: 10,320 sq km
country comparison to the world: 45

Area—comparative: almost five times the size of Alabama; slightly smaller than Texas
Land boundaries: total: 2,385 km
border countries (3): Djibouti 61 km, Ethiopia 1,640 km, Kenya 684 km

Coastline: 3,025 km

Maritime claims: *territorial sea:* 200 nm

Climate: principally desert; northeast monsoon (December to February), moderate temperatures in north and hot in south; southwest monsoon (May to October), torrid in the north and hot in the south, irregular rainfall, hot and humid periods (tangambili) between monsoons

Terrain: mostly flat to undulating plateau rising to hills in north

Elevation: *mean elevation:* 410 m

elevation extremes: *lowest point:* Indian Ocean 0 m
highest point: Shimbiris 2,416 m

Natural resources: uranium and largely unexploited reserves of iron ore, tin, gypsum, bauxite, copper, salt, natural gas, likely oil reserves

Land use: *agricultural land:* 70.3%
arable land: 1.8%;
permanent crops: 0%;
permanent pasture: 68.5%
forest: 10.6%
other: 19.1% (2011 est.)
Irrigated land: 2,000 sq km (2012)

Population—distribution: distribution varies greatly throughout the country; least densely populated areas are in the northeast and central regions, as well as areas along the Kenyan border; most populated areas are in and around the cities of Mogadishu, Marka, Boorama, Hargeysa, and Baidoa

Natural hazards: recurring droughts; frequent dust storms over eastern plains in summer; floods during rainy season

Environment—current issues: famine; use of contaminated water contributes to human health problems; deforestation; overgrazing; soil erosion; desertification

Environment—international agreements: *party to:* Biodiversity, Desertification, Endangered Species, Law of the Sea, Ozone Layer Protection
signed, but not ratified: none of the selected agreementsGeography—note: strategic location on Horn of Africa along southern approaches to Bab el Mandeb and route through Red Sea and Suez Canal

PEOPLE AND SOCIETY

Population: 11,031,386
note: this estimate was derived from an official census taken in 1975 by the Somali Government; population counting in Somalia is complicated by the large number of nomads and by refugee movements in response to famine and clan warfare (July 2017 est.)
country comparison to the world: 83

Nationality: *noun:* Somali(s)
adjective: Somali

Ethnic groups: Somali 85%, Bantu and other non-Somali 15% (including 30,000 Arabs)

Languages: Somali (official, according to the 2012 Transitional Federal Charter), Arabic (official, according to the 2012 Transitional Federal Charter), Italian, English

Religions: Sunni Muslim (Islam) (official, according to the 2012 Transitional Federal Charter)

Demographic profile: Somalia scores very low for most humanitarian indicators, suffering from poor governance, protracted internal conflict, underdevelopment, economic decline, poverty, social and gender inequality, and environmental degradation. Despite civil war and famine raising its mortality rate, Somalia's high fertility rate and large proportion of people of reproductive age maintain rapid population growth, with each generation being larger than the prior one. More than 60% of Somalia's population is younger than 25, and the fertility rate is among the world's highest at almost 6 children per woman—a rate that has decreased little since the 1970s.

A lack of educational and job opportunities is a major source of tension for Somalia's large youth cohort, making them vulnerable to recruitment by extremist and pirate groups. Somalia has one of the world's lowest primary school enrollment rates— just over 40% of children are in school—and one of world's highest youth unemployment rates. Life expectancy is low as a result of high infant and maternal mortality rates, the spread of preventable diseases, poor sanitation, chronic malnutrition, and inadequate health services.

During the two decades of conflict that followed the fall of the SIAD regime in 1991, hundreds of thousands of Somalis fled their homes. Today Somalia is the world's third highest source country for refugees, after Syria and Afghanistan. Insecurity, drought, floods, food shortages, and a lack of economic opportunities are the driving factors.

As of 2016, more than 1.1 million Somali refugees were hosted in the region, mainly in Kenya, Yemen, Egypt, Ethiopia, Djibouti, and Uganda, while more than 1.1 million Somalis were internally displaced. Since the implementation of a tripartite voluntary repatriation agreement among Kenya, Somalia, and the UNHCR in 2013, nearly 40,000 Somali refugees have returned home from Kenya's Dadaab refugee camp—still houses to approximately 260,000 Somalis. The flow sped up rapidly after the Kenyan Government in May 2016 announced its intention to close the camp, worsening security and humanitarian conditions in receiving communities in south-central Somalia. Despite the conflict in Yemen, thousands of Somalis and other refugees and asylum seekers from the Horn of Africa risk their lives crossing the Gulf of Aden to reach Yemen and beyond (often Saudi Arabia). Bossaso in Puntland overtook Obock, Djibouti, as the primary departure point in mid-2014.

Age structure: *0-14 years:* 43.15% (male 2,376,526/female 2,383,060)
15-24 years: 19.04% (male 1,059,608/female 1,040,343)
25-54 years: 31.43% (male 1,795,355/female 1,671,421)
55-64 years: 4.2% (male 230,027/female 233,257)
65 years and over: 2.19% (male 93,736/female 148,053) (2017 est.)

Dependency ratios: *total dependency ratio:* 97.4
youth dependency ratio: 92.1
elderly dependency ratio: 5.3
potential support ratio: 18.8 (2015 est.)

Median age: *total:* 18.1 years
male: 18.3 years
female: 17.9 years (2017 est.)
country comparison to the world: 216

Population growth rate: 2% (2017 est.)
country comparison to the world: 46

Birth rate: 39.6 births/1,000 population (2017 est.)
country comparison to the world: 9

Death rate: 13.1 deaths/1,000 population (2017 est.)
country comparison to the world: 14

Net migration rate: -6.5 migrant(s)/1,000 population (2017 est.)
country comparison to the world: 201

Population distribution: distribution varies greatly throughout the country; least densely populated areas are in the northeast and central regions, as well as areas along the Kenyan border; most populated areas are in and around the cities of Mogadishu, Marka, Boorama, Hargeysa, and Baidoa

Urbanization: *urban population:* 40.5% of total population (2017)
rate of urbanization: 4.05% annual rate of change (2015-20 est.)

Major urban areas—population: MOGADISHU (capital) 2.138 million; Hargeysa 760,000 (2015)

Sex ratio: *at birth:* 1.03 male(s)/female
0-14 years: 1 male(s)/female
15-24 years: 1.02 male(s)/female
25-54 years: 1.07 male(s)/female
55-64 years: 0.96 male(s)/female
65 years and over: 0.64 male(s)/female
total population: 1.01 male(s)/female (2016 est.)

Maternal mortality ratio: 732 deaths/100,000 live births (2015 est.)
country comparison to the world: 6

Infant mortality rate: *total:* 94.8 deaths/1,000 live births
male: 103.3 deaths/1,000 live births
female: 86 deaths/1,000 live births (2017 est.)
country comparison to the world: 2

Life expectancy at birth: *total population:* 52.8 years
male: 50.7 years
female: 54.9 years (2017 est.)
country comparison to the world: 218

Total fertility rate: 5.8 children born/woman (2017 est.)
country comparison to the world: 5

Physicians density: 0.03 physicians/1,000 population (2014)

Drinking water source:
improved:
urban: 69.6% of population
rural: 8.8% of population
total: 31.7% of population
unimproved:
urban: 30.4% of population
rural: 91.2% of population
total: 68.3% of population (2011 est.)

Sanitation facility access:
improved:
urban: 52% of population
rural: 6.3% of population
total: 23.6% of population
unimproved:
urban: 48% of population
rural: 93.7% of population
total: 76.4% of population (2011 est.)

HIV/AIDS—adult prevalence rate: 0.4% (2016 est.)
country comparison to the world: 78

HIV/AIDS—people living with HIV/AIDS: 24,000 (2016 est.)
country comparison to the world: 72

HIV/AIDS—deaths: 1,700 (2016 est.)
country comparison to the world: 55

Major infectious diseases: *degree of risk:* very high
food or waterborne diseases: bacterial and protozoal diarrhea, hepatitis A and E, and typhoid fever
vectorborne diseases: dengue fever, malaria, and Rift Valley fever
water contact disease: schistosomiasis
animal contact disease: rabies (2016)

Obesity—adult prevalence rate: 8.3% (2016)
country comparison to the world: 153

Children under the age of 5 years underweight: 23% (2009)
country comparison to the world: 9

Education expenditures: NA

GOVERNMENT

Country name: *conventional long form:* Federal Republic of Somalia
conventional short form: Somalia
local long form: Jamhuuriyadda Federaalkaa Soomaaliya
local short form: Soomaaliya
former: Somali Republic, Somali Democratic Republic
etymology: "Land of the Somali" (ethnic group)

Government type: federal parliamentary republic

Capital: *name:* Mogadishu
geographic coordinates: 2 04 N, 45 20 E
time difference: UTC+3 (8 hours ahead of Washington, DC, during Standard Time)

Administrative divisions: 18 regions (plural—NA, singular—gobolka); Awdal, Bakool, Banaadir, Bari, Bay, Galguduud, Gedo, Hiiraan, Jubbada Dhexe (Middle Jubba), Jubbada Hoose (Lower Jubba), Mudug, Nugaal, Sanaag, Shabeellaha Dhexe (Middle Shabeelle), Shabeellaha Hoose (Lower Shabeelle), Sool, Togdheer, Woqooyi Galbeed

Independence: 1 July 1960 (from a merger of British Somaliland that became independent from the UK on 26 June 1960 and Italian Somaliland that became independent from the Italian-administered UN trusteeship on 1 July 1960 to form the Somali Republic)

National holiday: Foundation of the Somali Republic, 1 July (1960); note—26 June (1960) in Somaliland

Constitution: *history:* previous 1961, 1979; latest drafted 12 June 2012, approved 1 August 2012 (provisional)
amendments: proposed by the federal government, by members of the state governments, the Federal Parliament, or by public petition; proposals require review by a joint committee of Parliament with inclusion of public comments and state legislatures' comments; passage requires at least two-thirds majority vote in both houses of Parliament and approval by a majority of votes cast in a referendum; constitutional clauses on Islamic principles, the federal system, human rights and freedoms, powers and authorities of the government branches, and inclusion of women in national institutions cannot be amended

Legal system: mixed legal system of civil law, Islamic law, and customary law (referred to as Xeer)

International law organization participation: accepts compulsory ICJ jurisdiction with reservations; non-party state to the ICCt

Citizenship: *citizenship by birth:* no
citizenship by descent only: the father must be a citizen of Somalia
dual citizenship recognized: no
residency requirement for naturalization: 7 years

Suffrage: 18 years of age; universal

Executive branch: *chief of state:* President Mohamed ABDULLAHI Mohamed "Farmaajo" (since 8 February 2017)
head of government: Prime Minister Hassan Ali KHAYRE (since 1 March 2017)
cabinet: Cabinet appointed by the prime minister, approved by the House of the People
elections/appointments: president indirectly elected by the Federal Parliament by two-thirds majority vote in 2 rounds if needed for a single 4-year term; election last held on 8 February 2017 (previously scheduled for 30 September 2016 but postponed repeatedly); prime minister appointed by the president, approved by the House of the People
election results: Mohamed ABDULLAHI Mohamed "Farmaajo" elected president; Federal Parliament second round vote—Mohamed ABDULLAHI Mohamed "Farmaajo" (TPP) 184, HASSAN SHEIKH Mohamud (PDP) 97, Sheikh SHARIF Sheikh Ahmed (ARS) 46

Legislative branch: *description:* bicameral Federal Parliament to consist of an Upper House (54 seats; senators elected by state assemblies to serve 4-year terms) and the House of the People (275 seats; members elected by regional delegates to serve 4-year terms)
note: the inaugural House of the People was appointed in September 2012 by clan elders; in elections in 2016 and 2017, the Federal Parliament became bicameral with elections scheduled for 10 October 2016 for the Upper House and 23 October to 10 November 2016 for the House of the People; while the elections were delayed, they were eventually held in most regions despite voting irregularities; on 27 December 2016, 41 Upper House senators and 242 House of the People members were sworn in

Judicial branch: *highest court(s):* the provisional constitution stipulates the establishment of the Constitutional Court (consists of 5 judges including the chief judge and deputy chief judge); note—under the terms of the 2004 Transitional National Charter, a Supreme Court based in Mogadishu and an Appeal Court were established; yet most regions have reverted to local forms of conflict resolution, either secular, traditional Somali customary law, or sharia Islamic law
judge selection and term of office: judges appointed by the president upon proposal of the Judicial Service Commission, a 9-member judicial and administrative body; judge tenure NA
subordinate courts: federal courts; federal member state-level courts; military courts; sharia courts

Political parties and leaders: Cosmopolitan Democratic Party [Yarow Sharef ADEN]
Daljir Party or DP [Hassan MOALIM]
Democratic Green Party of Somalia or DGPS [Abdullahi Y. MAHAMOUD]
Democratic Party of Somalia or DPS [Maslah Mohamed SIAD]
Green Leaf for Democracy or GLED
Hiil Qaran
Justice and Communist Party [Mohamed NUR]
Justice and Development of Democracy and Self-Respectfulness Party or CAHDI [Abdirahman Abdigani IBRAHIM Bile]
Liberal Party of Somalia
National Unity Party (Xisbiga MIdnimo-Quaran) [Abdurahman BAADIYOW]
Peace and Development Party or PDP
Somali National Party or SNP [Mohammed Ameen Saeed AHMED]
Somali People's Party [Mahamud Hassan RAGE]
Somali Green Party (local chapter of Federation of Green Parties of Africa)
Tayo or TPP [Mohamed Abdullahi MOHAMED]
Tiir Party [Fadhil Sheik MOHAMUD]
United and Democratic Party [Salad Ali JELLE]
United Somali Parliamentarians
inactive: Alliance for the Reliberation of Somalia; reportedly inactive since 2009

Political pressure groups and leaders: numerous political associations and clan and sub-clan factions exist in support of and against political leaders from clans, Federal Member State presidents, and others, including the former and current presidents

International organization participation: ACP, AfDB, AFESD, AMF, AU, CAEU (candidate), FAO, G-77, IBRD, ICAO, ICRM, IDA, IDB, IFAD, IFC, IFRCS, IGAD, ILO, IMF, IMO, Interpol, IOC, IOM, IPU, ITSO, ITU, LAS, NAM, OIC, OPCW, OPCW (signatory), UN, UNCTAD, UNESCO, UNHCR, UNIDO, UPU, WFTU (NGOs), WHO, WIPO, WMO

Diplomatic representation in the US: chief of mission: Ambassador Ahmed Issa AWAD (since 17 September 2015)
chancery: 425 East 61st Street, Suite 702, New York City, NY 10021
telephone: [1] (212) 688-9410, 688-5046
FAX: [1] (212) 759-0651

Diplomatic representation from the US: the US Mission to Somalia, operating out of the US Embassy in Nairobi, Kenya, is headed by Acting Head of Mission Martin DALE (since July 2017)

Flag description: light blue with a large white five-pointed star in the center; the blue field was originally influenced by the flag of the UN, but today is said to denote the sky and the neighboring Indian Ocean; the five points of the star represent the five regions in the horn of Africa that are inhabited by Somali people: the former British Somaliland and Italian Somaliland (which together make up Somalia), Djibouti, Ogaden (Ethiopia), and the North East Province (Kenya)

National symbol(s): leopard; national colors: blue, white

National anthem: name: "Qolobaa Calankeed" (Every Nation Has its own Flag)
lyrics/music: lyrics/music: Abdullahi QARSHE
note: adopted 2012; written in 1959
Government—note: regional and local governing bodies continue to exist and control various areas of the country, including the self-declared Republic of Somaliland in northwestern Somalia

ECONOMY

Economy—overview: Despite the lack of effective national governance, Somalia maintains an informal economy largely based on livestock, remittance/money transfer companies, and telecommunications. Somalia's government lacks the ability to collect domestic revenue and external debt—mostly in arrears—was estimated at about 77% of GDP in 2017.

Agriculture is the most important sector, with livestock normally accounting for about 40% of GDP and more than 50% of export earnings. Nomads and semi-pastoralists, who are dependent upon livestock for their livelihood, make up a large portion of the population. Economic activity is estimated to have increased by 2.4% in 2017 because of growth in the agriculture, construction and telecommunications sector. Somalia's small industrial sector, based on the processing of agricultural products, has largely been looted and the machinery sold as scrap metal.

In recent years, Somalia's capital city, Mogadishu, has witnessed the development of the city's first gas stations, supermarkets, and airline flights to Turkey since the collapse of central authority in 1991. Mogadishu's main market offers a variety of goods from food to electronic gadgets. Hotels continue to operate and are supported with private-security militias. Formalized economic growth has yet to expand outside of Mogadishu and a few regional capitals, and within the city, security concerns dominate business. Telecommunication firms provide wireless services in most major cities and offer the lowest international call rates on the continent. In the absence of a formal banking sector, money transfer/remittance services have sprouted throughout the country, handling up to $1.6 billion in remittances annually, although international concerns over the money transfers into Somalia continues to threaten these services' ability to operate in Western nations. In 2017, Somalia elected a new president and collected a record amount of foreign aid and investment, a positive sign for economic recovery.

GDP (purchasing power parity): $17.47 billion (2017 est.)
$17.06 billion (2016 est.)
$16.53 billion (2015 est.)
note: data are in 2016 US dollars
country comparison to the world: 154

GDP (official exchange rate): $6.522 billion (2015 est.)

GDP—real growth rate: 2.4% (2017 est.)
3.2% (2016 est.)
3.6% (2015 est.)
country comparison to the world: 140

GDP—per capita (PPP): $NA (2017 est.)
$NA (2016 est.)
$NA (2015 est.)

GDP—composition, by end use:
household consumption: 72.1%
government consumption: 8.7%
investment in fixed capital: 19.8%
investment in inventories: 0.8%
exports of goods and services: 0.3%
imports of goods and services: -1.7% (2014 est.)

GDP—composition, by sector of origin:
agriculture: 60.2%
industry: 7.4%
services: 32.5% (2013 est.)

Agriculture—products: bananas, sorghum, corn, coconuts, rice, sugarcane, mangoes, sesame seeds, beans; cattle, sheep, goats; fish

Industries: light industries, including sugar refining, textiles, wireless communication

Industrial production growth rate: 3.5% (2014 est.)
country comparison to the world: 83

Labor force: 4.154 million (2016 est.)
country comparison to the world: 91

Labor force—by occupation: agriculture: 71%
industry and services: 29% (1975)

Unemployment rate: NA%

Population below poverty line: NA%

Household income or consumption by percentage share: lowest 10%: NA%
highest 10%: NA%

Budget: revenues: $145.3 million
expenditures: $151.1 million (2014 est.)
Taxes and other revenues: 2.2% of GDP (2014 est.)
country comparison to the world: 220

Budget surplus (+) or deficit (-): -0.1% of GDP (2014 est.)
country comparison to the world: 37

Fiscal year: NA

Inflation rate (consumer prices): 1.5% (2017 est.)
-71.1% (2016 est.)
country comparison to the world: 60

Central bank discount rate: NA%

Commercial bank prime lending rate: NA%

Current account balance: -$722 million (2017 est.)
-$640 million (2016 est.)
country comparison to the world: 116

Exports: $819 million (2014 est.)

$779 million (2013 est.)
country comparison to the world: 166

Exports—commodities: livestock, bananas, hides, fish, charcoal, scrap metal

Exports—partners: Saudi Arabia 37.2%, Oman 22.7%, UAE 16.3% (2016)

Imports: $3.482 billion (2014 est.)
$3.322 billion (2013 est.)
country comparison to the world: 138

Imports—commodities: manufactures, petroleum products, foodstuffs, construction materials, qat

Imports—partners: India 26.3%, China 20.8%, Oman 9.1%, Kenya 8.3%, Turkey 6%, Malaysia 4.3%, Brazil 4.2% (2016)

Reserves of foreign exchange and gold: $30.45 million (2014 est.)
country comparison to the world: 173

Debt—external: $5.3 billion (31 December 2014 est.)
$2.892 billion (31 December 2015 est.)
country comparison to the world: 134

Stock of direct foreign investment—at home: $NA

Exchange rates: Somali shillings (SOS) per US dollar—
23,960 (2016 est.)

ENERGY

Electricity access: population without electricity: 8,900,000
electrification—total population: 15%
electrification—urban areas: 33%
electrification—rural areas: 4% (2013)

Electricity—production: 344 million kWh (2015 est.)
country comparison to the world: 177

Electricity—consumption: 319.9 million kWh (2015 est.)
country comparison to the world: 182

Electricity—exports: 0 kWh (2016 est.)
country comparison to the world: 198

Electricity—imports: 0 kWh (2016 est.)
country comparison to the world: 202

Electricity—installed generating capacity: 81,000 kW (2015 est.)
country comparison to the world: 182

Electricity—from fossil fuels: 98.8% of total installed capacity (2015 est.)
country comparison to the world: 34

Electricity—from nuclear fuels: 0% of total installed capacity (2015 est.)
country comparison to the world: 183

Electricity—from hydroelectric plants: 0% of total installed capacity (2015 est.)
country comparison to the world: 204

Electricity—from other renewable sources: 1.2% of total installed capacity (2015 est.)
country comparison to the world: 135

Crude oil—production: 0 bbl/day (2016 est.)
country comparison to the world: 200

Crude oil—exports: 0 bbl/day (2014 est.)

Crude oil—imports: 0 bbl/day (2014 est.)
country comparison to the world: 190

Crude oil—proved reserves: 0 bbl (1 January 2017 es)
country comparison to the world: 199

Refined petroleum products—production: 0 bbl/day (2014 est.)
country comparison to the world: 203

Refined petroleum products—consumption: 5,700 bbl/day (2015 est.)
country comparison to the world: 174

Refined petroleum products—exports: 0 bbl/day (2014 est.)
country comparison to the world: 198

Refined petroleum products—imports: 5,679 bbl/day (2014 est.)
country comparison to the world: 163

Natural gas—production: 0 cu m (2013 est.)
country comparison to the world: 195

Natural gas—consumption: 0 cu m (2013 est.)
country comparison to the world: 131

Natural gas—exports: 0 cu m (2013 est.)
country comparison to the world: 183

Natural gas—imports: 0 cu m (2013 est.)
country comparison to the world: 188

Natural gas—proved reserves: 5.663 billion cu m (1 January 2017 es)
country comparison to the world: 94

Carbon dioxide emissions from consumption of energy: 900,000 Mt (2013 est.)
country comparison to the world: 166

COMMUNICATIONS

Telephones—fixed lines: *total subscriptions:* 48,000
subscriptions per 100 inhabitants: less than 1 (July 2016 est.)
country comparison to the world: 157

Telephones—mobile cellular: *total:* 6,653,040
subscriptions per 100 inhabitants: 62 (July 2016 est.)
country comparison to the world: 113

Telephone system: *general assessment:* the public telecom system was almost completely destroyed or dismantled during the civil war; private companies offer limited local fixed-line service, and private wireless companies offer service in most major cities, while charging some of the lowest rates on the continent
domestic: seven networks compete for customers in the mobile sector; some of these mobile-service providers offer fixed-line and Internet services
international: country code—252; Mogadishu is a landing point for the EASSy fiber-optic submarine cable system linking East Africa with Europe and North America; this connection ended the country's expensive satellite-dependent Internet access (2016)

Broadcast media: 2 private TV stations rebroadcast Al-Jazeera and CNN; Somaliland has 1 government-operated TV station and Puntland has 1 private TV station; the transitional government operates Radio Mogadishu; 1 SW and roughly 10 private FM radio stations broadcast in Mogadishu; several radio stations operate in central and southern regions; Somaliland has 1 government-operated radio station; Puntland has roughly a half-dozen private radio stations; transmissions of at least 2 international broadcasters are available (2007)

Internet country code: .so

Internet users: *total:* 203,366
percent of population: 1.9% (July 2016 est.)
country comparison to the world: 164

TRANSPORTATION

National air transport system: number of registered air carriers: 1
inventory of registered aircraft operated by air carriers: 1
annual passenger traffic on registered air carriers: 251,652
annual freight traffic on registered air carriers: 0 mt-km (2015)
Civil aircraft registration country code prefix: 6O (2016)

Airports: 61 (2013)
country comparison to the world: 81

Airports—with paved runways: *total:* 6
over 3,047 m: 4
2,438 to 3,047 m: 1
1,524 to 2,437 m: 1 (2013)

Airports—with unpaved runways: *total:* 55
over 3,047 m: 1
2,438 to 3,047 m: 5
1,524 to 2,437 m: 20
914 to 1,523 m: 23
under 914 m: 6 (2013)

Roadways: *total:* 22,100 km
paved: 2,608 km
unpaved: 19,492 km (2000)
country comparison to the world: 105

Merchant marine: *total:* 5
by type: general cargo 2, other 3 (2017)
country comparison to the world: 156

Ports and terminals: *major seaport(s):* Berbera, Kismaayo

MILITARY AND SECURITY

Military branches: National Security Force (NSF): Somali National Army (2017)

Military service age and obligation: 18 is the legal minimum age for compulsory and voluntary military service (2012)

Maritime threats: despite a dramatic drop in the number of attacks in 2016, the International Maritime Bureau continues to report the territorial and offshore waters in the Gulf of Aden and Indian Ocean as a region of significant risk for piracy and armed robbery against ships; during the first half of 2017, nine vessels were attacked or hijacked compared with two in 2016; Operation Ocean Shield, the NATO naval task force established in 2009 to combat Somali piracy, concluded its operations in December 2016 as a result of the drop in reported incidents over the last few years; additional anti-piracy measures on the part of ship operators, including the use of on-board armed security teams, have reduced piracy incidents in that body of water; Somali pirates tend to be heavily armed with automatic weapons and rocket propelled grenades; the use of "mother ships" from which skiffs can be launched to attack vessels allows these pirates to extend the range of their operations hundreds of nautical miles offshore

TERRORISM

Terrorist groups—home based: al-Shabaab:
aim(s): discredit and destabilize the Federal Government of Somalia and target any countries' interests that supports Somalia's fight against al-Shabaab; establish Islamic rule in Somalia and Kenya's border regions
area(s) of operation: a core al-Qa'ida affiliate that maintains strongholds in rural areas in the south, where it controls a large swathe of the Lower and Middle Juba regions, and has increased its attacks in 2017 in the northeast in Puntland State; responsible for numerous high-profile bombings and shootings throughout Somalia targeting African Union Mission for Somalia (AMISOM) troops, Somali military and police personnel, and civilian-populated areas, especially where Westerners and other foreigners are present, such as shopping malls, hotels, and restaurants; AMISOM is a regional peacekeeping force operated by the African Union with the approval of the UN; fighters have increasingly targeted peacekeeping forces since early 2016; assassins have killed scores of civil society figures, government officials, international aid workers, members of NGOs, and journalists; assessed to have less than 10,000 combatants; The death toll from two truck bombs in Somalia's capital soared to an estimated 280 on 14 October 2017 as the deadliest attack in the country's decade-long war with Islamist extremists. Also, more than 300 people were reported wounded.

Terrorist groups—foreign based: al-Qa'ida (AQ):
aim(s): bolster networks and, ultimately, establish a pan-Islamic caliphate under a strict Salafi Muslim interpretation of Sharia
area(s) of operation: operates primarily in the south alongside al-Shabaab, an al-Qa'ida affiliate whose aim is to discredit and destabilize the Federal Government of Somalia
Islamic State of Iraq and the Levant (ISIL):
aim(s): replace the Federal Government of Somalia with an Islamic state and implement ISIL's strict interpretation of Sharia
area(s) of operation: increasing its operations, recruitment efforts, and training camps in 2017 in the northeast in Puntland State; uses its growing presence to conduct attacks against African Union Mission for Somalia personnel, a regional peacekeeping force operated by the African Union with the UN's approval; leadership includes former al-Shabaab cleric Abdulkadir MUMIN

TRANSNATIONAL ISSUES

Disputes—international: Ethiopian forces invaded southern Somalia and routed Islamist Courts from

825

Mogadishu in January 2007; "Somaliland" secessionists provide port facilities in Berbera to landlocked Ethiopia and have established commercial ties with other regional states; "Puntland" and "Somaliland" "governments" seek international support in their secessionist aspirations and overlapping border claims; the undemarcated former British administrative line has little meaning as a political separation to rival clans within Ethiopia's Ogaden and southern Somalia's Oromo region; Kenya works hard to prevent the clan and militia fighting in Somalia from spreading south across the border, which has long been open to nomadic pastoralists

Refugees and internally displaced persons: refugees (country of origin): 10,970 (Yemen) (2018) *IDPs:* 2.1 million (civil war since 1988, clan-based competition for resources; 2011 famine; insecurity because of fighting between al-Shabaab and the Transitional Federal Government's allied forces) (2017)

SOUTH AFRICA

INTRODUCTION

Background: Dutch traders landed at the southern tip of modern day South Africa in 1652 and established a stopover point on the spice route between the Netherlands and the Far East, founding the city of Cape Town. After the British seized the Cape of Good Hope area in 1806, many of the Dutch settlers (Afrikaners, called "Boers" (farmers) by the British) trekked north to found their own republics, Transvaal and Orange Free State. The discovery of diamonds (1867) and gold (1886) spurred wealth and immigration and intensified the subjugation of the native inhabitants. The Afrikaners resisted British encroachments but were defeated in the Second South African War (1899-1902); however, the British and the Afrikaners, ruled together beginning in 1910 under the Union of South Africa, which became a republic in 1961 after a whites-only referendum. In 1948, the Afrikaner-dominated National Party was voted into power and instituted a policy of apartheid—the separate development of the races—which favored the white minority at the expense of the black majority. The African National Congress (ANC) led the opposition to apartheid and many top ANC leaders, such as Nelson MANDELA, spent decades in South Africa's prisons. Internal protests and insurgency, as well as boycotts by some Western nations and institutions, led to the regime's eventual willingness to negotiate a peaceful transition to majority rule.

The first multi-racial elections in 1994 following the end of apartheid ushered in majority rule under an ANC-led government. South Africa has since struggled to address apartheid-era imbalances in decent housing, education, and health care. ANC infighting came to a head in 2008 when President Thabo MBEKI was recalled by Parliament, and Deputy President Kgalema MOTLANTHE, succeeded him as interim president. Jacob ZUMA became president after the ANC won general elections in 2009; he was reelected in 2014. His government has been plagued by numerous scandals, leading to gains by opposition parties at the municipal level in 2016.

GEOGRAPHY

Location: Southern Africa, at the southern tip of the continent of Africa

Geographic coordinates: 29 00 S, 24 00 E

Map references: Africa

Area: *total:* 1,219,090 sq km
land: 1,214,470 sq km
water: 4,620 sq km
note: includes Prince Edward Islands (Marion Island and Prince Edward Island)
country comparison to the world: 26

Area—comparative: slightly less than twice the size of Texas
Land boundaries: total: 5,244 km
border countries (6): Botswana 1,969 km, Lesotho 1,106 km, Mozambique 496 km, Namibia 1,005 km, Swaziland 438 km, Zimbabwe 230 km

Coastline: 2,798 km

Maritime claims: *territorial sea:* 12 nm
contiguous zone: 24 nm
exclusive economic zone: 200 nm
continental shelf: 200 nm or to edge of the continental margin

Climate: mostly semiarid; subtropical along east coast; sunny days, cool nights

Terrain: vast interior plateau rimmed by rugged hills and narrow coastal plain

Elevation: *mean elevation:* 1,034 m
elevation extremes: lowest point: Atlantic Ocean 0 m
highest point: Njesuthi 3,408 m

Natural resources: gold, chromium, antimony, coal, iron ore, manganese, nickel, phosphates, tin, rare earth elements, uranium, gem diamonds, platinum, copper, vanadium, salt, natural gas

Land use: *agricultural land:* 79.4%
arable land: 9.9%;
permanent crops: 0.3%;

permanent pasture: 69.2%
forest: 7.6%
other: 13% (2011 est.)
Irrigated land: 16,700 sq km (2012)

Population—distribution: the population concentrated along the southern and southeastern coast, and inland around Petoria; the eastern half of the country is more densly populated than the west

Natural hazards: prolonged droughts
volcanism: the volcano forming Marion Island in the Prince Edward Islands, which last erupted in 2004, is South Africa's only active volcano

Environment—current issues: lack of important arterial rivers or lakes requires extensive water conservation and control measures; growth in water usage outpacing supply; pollution of rivers from agricultural runoff and urban discharge; air pollution resulting in acid rain; soil erosion; desertification

Environment—international agreements: *party to:* Antarctic-Environmental Protocol, Antarctic-Marine Living Resources, Antarctic Seals, Antarctic Treaty, Biodiversity, Climate Change, Climate Change-Kyoto Protocol, Desertification, Endangered Species, Hazardous Wastes, Law of the Sea, Marine Dumping, Marine Life Conservation, Ozone Layer Protection, Ship Pollution, Wetlands, Whaling
signed, but not ratified: none of the selected agreementsGeography—note: South Africa completely surrounds Lesotho and almost completely surrounds Swaziland

PEOPLE AND SOCIETY

Population: 54,841,552
note: estimates for this country explicitly take into account the effects of excess mortality due to AIDS; this can result in lower life expectancy, higher infant mortality, higher death rates, lower population growth rates, and changes in the distribution of population by age and sex than would otherwise be expected (July 2017 est.)
country comparison to the world: 25

Nationality: *noun:* South African(s)
adjective: South African

Ethnic groups: black African 80.2%, white 8.4%, colored 8.8%, Indian/Asian 2.5%
note: colored is a term used in South Africa, including on the national census, for persons of mixed race ancestry (2014 est.)

Languages: isiZulu (official) 22.7%, isiXhosa (official) 16%, Afrikaans (official) 13.5%, English (official) 9.6%, Sepedi (official) 9.1%, Setswana (official) 8%, Sesotho (official) 7.6%, Xitsonga (official) 4.5%, siSwati (official) 2.5%, Tshivenda (official) 2.4%, isiNdebele (official) 2.1%, sign language 0.5%, other 1.6% (2011 est.)

Religions: Protestant 36.6% (Zionist Christian 11.1%, Pentecostal/Charismatic 8.2%, Methodist 6.8%, Dutch Reformed 6.7%, Anglican 3.8%), Catholic 7.1%, Muslim 1.5%, other Christian 36%, other 2.3%, unspecified 1.4%, none 15.1% (2001 est.)

Demographic profile: South Africa's youthful population is gradually aging, as the country's total fertility rate (TFR) has declined dramatically from about 6 children per woman in the 1960s to roughly 2.2 in 2014. This pattern is similar to fertility trends in South Asia, the Middle East, and North Africa, and sets South Africa apart from the rest of sub-Saharan Africa, where the average TFR remains higher than other regions of the world. Today, South Africa's decreasing number of reproductive age women is having fewer children, as women increase their educational attainment, workforce participation, and use of family planning methods; delay marriage; and opt for smaller families.

As the proportion of working-age South Africans has grown relative to children and the elderly, South Africa has been unable to achieve a demographic dividend because persistent high unemployment and the prevalence of HIV/AIDs have created a larger-than-normal dependent population. HIV/AIDS was also responsible for South Africa's average life expectancy plunging to less than 43 years in 2008; it has rebounded to 63 years as of 2017. HIV/AIDS continues to be a serious public health threat, although awareness-raising campaigns and the wider availability of anti-retroviral drugs is stabilizing the number of new cases, enabling infected individuals to live longer, healthier lives, and reducing mother-child transmissions.

Migration to South Africa began in the second half of the 17th century when traders from the Dutch East India Company settled in the Cape and started using slaves from South and southeast Asia (mainly from India but also from present-day Indonesia, Bangladesh, Sri Lanka, and Malaysia) and southeast Africa (Madagascar and Mozambique) as farm laborers and, to a lesser extent, as domestic servants. The Indian subcontinent remained the Cape Colony's main source of slaves in the early 18th century, while slaves were increasingly obtained from southeast Africa in the latter part of the 18th century and into the 19th century under British rule.

After slavery was completely abolished in the British Empire in 1838, South Africa's colonists turned to temporary African migrants and indentured labor through agreements with India and later China, countries that were anxious to export workers to alleviate domestic poverty and overpopulation. Of the more than 150,000 indentured Indian laborers hired to work in Natal's sugar plantations between 1860 and 1911, most exercised the right as British subjects to remain permanently (a small number of Indian immigrants came freely as merchants). Because of growing resentment toward Indian workers, the 63,000 indentured Chinese workers who mined gold in Transvaal between 1904 and 1911 were under more restrictive contracts and generally were forced to return to their homeland.

In the late 19th century and nearly the entire 20th century, South Africa's then British colonies' and Dutch states' enforced selective immigration policies that welcomed "assimilable" white Europeans as permanent residents but excluded or restricted other immigrants. Following the Union of South Africa's passage of a law in 1913 prohibiting Asian and other non-white immigrants and its elimination of the indenture system in 1917, temporary African contract laborers from neighboring countries became the dominant source of labor in the burgeoning mining industries. Others worked in agriculture and smaller numbers in manufacturing, domestic service, transportation, and construction. Throughout the 20th century, at least 40% of South Africa's miners were foreigners; the numbers peaked at over 80% in the late 1960s. Mozambique, Lesotho, Botswana, and Swaziland were the primary sources of miners, and Malawi and Zimbabwe were periodic suppliers.

Under apartheid, a "two gates" migration policy focused on policing and deporting illegal migrants rather than on managing migration to meet South Africa's development needs. The exclusionary 1991 Aliens Control Act limited labor recruitment to the highly skilled as defined by the ruling white minority, while bilateral labor agreements provided exemptions that enabled the influential mining industry and, to a lesser extent, commercial farms, to hire temporary, low-paid workers from neighboring states. Illegal African migrants were often tacitly allowed to work for low pay in other sectors but were always under threat of deportation.

The abolishment of apartheid in 1994 led to the development of a new inclusive national identity and the strengthening of the country's restrictive immigration policy. Despite South Africa's protectionist approach to immigration, the downsizing and closing of mines, and rising unemployment, migrants from across the continent believed that the country held work opportunities. Fewer African labor migrants were issued temporary work permits and, instead, increasingly entered South Africa with visitors' permits or came illegally, which drove growth in cross-border trade and the informal job market. A new wave of Asian immigrants has also arrived over the last two decades, many operating small retail businesses.

In the post-apartheid period, increasing numbers of highly skilled white workers emigrated, citing dissatisfaction with the political situation, crime, poor services, and a reduced quality of life. The 2002 Immigration Act and later amendments were intended to facilitate the temporary migration of skilled foreign labor to fill labor shortages, but instead the legislation continues to create regulatory obstacles. Although the education system has improved and brain drain has slowed in the wake of the 2008 global financial crisis, South Africa continues to face skills shortages in several key sectors, such as health care and technology.

South Africa's stability and economic growth has acted as a magnet for refugees and asylum seekers from nearby countries, despite the prevalence of discrimination and xenophobic violence. Refugees have included an estimated 350,000 Mozambicans during its 1980s civil war and, more recently, several thousand Somalis, Congolese, and Ethiopians. Nearly all of the tens of thousands of Zimbabweans who have applied for asylum in South Africa have been categorized as economic migrants and denied refuge.

Age structure: *0-14 years:* 28.27% (male 7,768,960/female 7,733,706)
15-24 years: 17.61% (male 4,776,096/female 4,881,962)
25-54 years: 41.78% (male 11,589,099/female 11,323,869)
55-64 years: 6.66% (male 1,694,904/female 1,955,391)
65 years and over: 5.68% (male 1,309,597/female 1,807,968) (2017 est.)

Dependency ratios: *total dependency ratio:* 52.5
youth dependency ratio: 44.8
elderly dependency ratio: 7.7
potential support ratio: 12.9 (2015 est.)

Median age: *total:* 27.1 years
male: 26.9 years
female: 27.3 years (2017 est.)
country comparison to the world: 145

Population growth rate: 0.99% (2017 est.)
country comparison to the world: 114

Birth rate: 20.2 births/1,000 population (2017 est.)
country comparison to the world: 78

Death rate: 9.4 deaths/1,000 population (2017 est.)
country comparison to the world: 58

Net migration rate: -0.9 migrant(s)/1,000 population (2017 est.)
country comparison to the world: 136

Population distribution: the population concentrated along the southern and southeastern coast, and inland around Petoria; the eastern half of the country is more densly populated than the west

Urbanization: *urban population:* 65.8% of total population (2017)
rate of urbanization: 1.33% annual rate of change (2015-20 est.)

Major urban areas—population: Johannesburg (includes Ekurhuleni) 9.399 million; Cape Town (legislative capital) 3.66 million; Durban 2.901 million; PRETORIA (capital) 2.059 million; Port Elizabeth 1.179 million; Vereeniging 1.155 million (2015)

Sex ratio: *at birth:* 1.02 male(s)/female
0-14 years: 1.01 male(s)/female
15-24 years: 0.98 male(s)/female
25-54 years: 1.02 male(s)/female
55-64 years: 0.87 male(s)/female

65 years and over: 0.73 male(s)/female
total population: 0.98 male(s)/female (2016 est.)

Maternal mortality ratio: 138 deaths/100,000 live births (2015 est.)
country comparison to the world: 63

Infant mortality rate: *total:* 31 deaths/1,000 live births
male: 34.4 deaths/1,000 live births
female: 27.5 deaths/1,000 live births (2017 est.)
country comparison to the world: 62

Life expectancy at birth: *total population:* 63.8 years
male: 62.4 years
female: 65.3 years (2017 est.)
country comparison to the world: 190

Total fertility rate: 2.29 children born/woman (2017 est.)
country comparison to the world: 91

Health expenditures: 8.8% of GDP (2014)
country comparison to the world: 44

Physicians density: 0.77 physicians/1,000 population (2015)

Drinking water source:
improved:
 urban: 99.6% of population
rural: 81.4% of population
total: 93.2% of population
unimproved:
urban: 0.4% of population
rural: 18.6% of population
total: 6.8% of population (2015 est.)

Sanitation facility access:
improved:
urban: 69.6% of population
rural: 60.5% of population
total: 66.4% of population
unimproved:
urban: 30.4% of population
rural: 39.5% of population
total: 33.6% of population (2015 est.)

HIV/AIDS—adult prevalence rate: 18.9% (2016 est.)
country comparison to the world: 4

HIV/AIDS—people living with HIV/AIDS: 7.1 million (2016 est.)
country comparison to the world: 1

HIV/AIDS—deaths: 110,000 (2016 est.)
country comparison to the world: 2

Major infectious diseases: *degree of risk:* intermediate
food or waterborne diseases: bacterial diarrhea, hepatitis A, and typhoid fever
water contact disease: schistosomiasis (2016)

Obesity—adult prevalence rate: 28.3% (2016)
country comparison to the world: 30

Children under the age of 5 years underweight: 8.7% (2008)
country comparison to the world: 72

Education expenditures: 6.1% of GDP (2014)
country comparison to the world: 42

Literacy: *definition:* age 15 and over can read and write

total population: 94.4%
male: 95.4%
female: 93.4% (2015 est.)

School life expectancy (primary to tertiary education): *total:* 13 years
male: 12 years
female: 13 years (2012)

Unemployment, youth ages 15-24: *total:* 50.1%
male: 46.3%
female: 54.9% (2015 est.)
country comparison to the world: 6

GOVERNMENT

Country name: *conventional long form:* Republic of South Africa
conventional short form: South Africa
former: Union of South Africa
abbreviation: RSA
etymology: self-descriptive name from the country's location on the continent; "Africa" is derived from the Roman designation of the area corresponding to present-day Tunisia "Africa terra," which meant "Land of the Afri" (the tribe resident in that area), but which eventually came to mean the entire continent

Government type: parliamentary republic

Capital: *name:* Pretoria (administrative capital); Cape Town (legislative capital); Bloemfontein (judicial capital)

geographic coordinates: 25 42 S, 28 13 E
time difference: UTC+2 (7 hours ahead of Washington, DC, during Standard Time)

Administrative divisions: 9 provinces; Eastern Cape, Free State, Gauteng, KwaZulu-Natal, Limpopo, Mpumalanga, Northern Cape, North West, Western Cape

Independence: 31 May 1910 (Union of South Africa formed from four British colonies: Cape Colony, Natal, Transvaal, and Orange Free State); 31 May 1961 (republic declared); 27 April 1994 (majority rule)

National holiday: Freedom Day, 27 April (1994)

Constitution: *history:* several previous; latest drafted 8 May 1996, approved by Constitutional Court 4 December 1996, effective 4 February 1997
amendments: proposed by the National Assembly of Parliament; passage of amendments affecting constitutional sections on human rights and freedoms, non-racism and non-sexism, supremacy of the constitution, suffrage, the multi-party system of democratic government, and amendment procedures requires at least 75% majority vote of the Assembly, approval by at least six of the nine provinces represented in the National Council of Provinces, and assent by the president of the republic; passage of amendments affecting the Bill of Rights, and those related to provincial boundaries, powers, and authorities requires at least two-thirds majority vote of the Assembly, approval by at least six of the nine provinces represented in the National Council, and assent by the president; amended many times, last in 2013 (2017)

Legal system: mixed legal system of Roman-Dutch civil law, English common law, and customary law

International law organization participation: has not submitted an ICJ jurisdiction declaration; accepts ICCt jurisdiction

Citizenship: *citizenship by birth:* no
citizenship by descent only: at least one parent must be a citizen of South Africa
dual citizenship recognized: yes, but requires prior permission of the government
residency requirement for naturalization: 1 year

Suffrage: 18 years of age; universal

Executive branch: *chief of state:* Acting President Matamela Cyril RAMAPHOSA (since 14 February 2018); note—the president is both chief of state and head of government; Jacob ZUMA resigned the presidency on 14 February 2018
head of government: Acting President Matamela Cyril RAMAPHOSA (since 14 February 2018); note—Jacob ZUMA resigned the presidency on 14 February 2018
cabinet: Cabinet appointed by the president
elections/appointments: president indirectly elected by the National Assembly for a 5-year term (eligible for a second term); election last held on 15 February 2018 to elect an acting president to replace ZUMA for the remainder of his term (next to be held in May 2019)
election results: Jacob ZUMA (ANC) reelected president by the National Assembly unopposed

Legislative branch: *description:* bicameral Parliament consists of the National Council of Provinces (90 seats; 10-member delegations appointed by each of the 9 provincial legislatures to serve 5-year terms; note—this council has special powers to protect regional interests, including safeguarding cultural and linguistic traditions among ethnic minorities) and the National Assembly (400 seats; members directly elected in multi-seat constituencies by proportional representation vote to serve 5-year terms)
elections: National Council of Provinces and National Assembly—last held on 7 May 2014 (next to be held in 2019)
election results: National Council of Provinces—percent of vote by party—NA; seats by party—ANC 60, DA 20, EFF 7, IFP 1, NFP 1, UDM 1; National Assembly—percent of vote by party—ANC 62.2%, DA 22.2%, EFF 6.4%, IFP 2.4%, NFP 1.6%, UDM 1.0%, other 4.2%; seats by party—ANC 249, DA 89, EFF 25, IFP 10, NFP 6, UDM 4, other 17

Judicial branch: *highest court(s):* Supreme Court of Appeals (consists of the court president, deputy president, and 21 judges); Constitutional Court (consists of the chief and deputy chief justices and 9 judges)
judge selection and term of office: Supreme Court of Appeals president and vice president appointed by the national president after consultation with the Judicial Services Commission (JSC), a 23-member body chaired by the chief justice and includes other judges and judicial executives,

members of parliament, practicing lawyers and advocates, a teacher of law, and several members designated by the national president; other Supreme Court judges appointed by the national president on the advice of the JSC and hold office until discharged from active service by an Act of Parliament; Constitutional Court chief and deputy chief justices appointed by the national president after consultation with the JSC and with heads of the National Assembly; other Constitutional Court judges appointed by the national president after consultation with the chief justice and leaders of the National Assembly; Constitutional Court judges appointed for 12-year non-renewable terms or until age 70

subordinate courts: High Courts; Magistrates' Courts; labor courts; land claims courts

Political parties and leaders: African Christian Democratic Party or ACDP [Kenneth MESHOE] African Independent Congress or AIC [Mandla GALO] African National Congress or ANC [Cyril RAMAPHOSA] African People's Convention or APC [Themba GODI] Agang SA [Mike TSHISHONGA] Congress of the People or COPE [Mosiuoa LEKOTA] Democratic Alliance or DA [Mmusi MAIMANE] Economic Freedom Fighters or EFF [Julius Sello MALEMA] Freedom Front Plus or FF+ [Pieter GROENEWALD] Inkatha Freedom Party or IFP [Mangosuthu BUTHELEZI] National Freedom Party or NFP [Zanele kaMAGWAZA-MSIBI] Pan-Africanist Congress of Azania or PAC [Luthanado MBINDA] United Christian Democratic Party or UCDP [Isaac Sipho MFUNDISI] United Democratic Movement or UDM [Bantu HOLOMISA]

Political pressure groups and leaders: Congress of South African Trade Unions or COSATU [Sdumo DLAMINI] South African Communist Party or SACP [Blade NZIMANDE] South African National Civic Organization or SANCO [Richard MDAKANE] *note:* COSATU and SACP are in a formal alliance with the African National Congress

International organization participation: ACP, AfDB, AU, BIS, BRICS, C, CD, FAO, FATF, G-20, G-24, G-5, G-77, IAEA, IBRD, ICAO, ICC (national committees), ICCt, ICRM, IDA, IFAD, IFC, IFRCS, IHO, ILO, IMF, IMO, IMSO, Interpol, IOC, IOM, IPU, ISO, ITSO, ITU, ITUC (NGOs), MIGA, MONUSCO, NAM, NSG, OECD (enhanced engagement), OPCW, Paris Club (associate), PCA, SACU, SADC, UN, UNAMID, UNCTAD, UNESCO, UNHCR, UNIDO, UNITAR, UNWTO, UPU, WCO, WFTU (NGOs), WHO, WIPO, WMO, WTO, ZC

Diplomatic representation in the US: chief of mission: Ambassador Mninwa Johannes MAHLANGU (since 23 February 2015) *chancery:* 3051 Massachusetts Avenue NW, Washington, DC 20008 *telephone:* [1] (202) 232-4400 [1] (202) 232-4400 *FAX:* [1] (202) 265-1607 *consulate(s) general:* Chicago, Los Angeles, New York

Diplomatic representation from the US: *chief of mission:* Ambassador (vacant); Charge d'Affaires Jessica "Jessye" LAPENN (since 16 December 2016) *embassy:* 877 Pretorius Street, Arcadia, Pretoria *mailing address:* P.O. Box 9536, Pretoria 0001 *telephone:* [27] (12) 431-4000 *FAX:* [27] (12) 342-2299 *consulate(s) general:* Cape Town, Durban, Johannesburg

Flag description: two equal width horizontal bands of red (top) and blue separated by a central green band that splits into a horizontal Y, the arms of which end at the corners of the hoist side; the Y embraces a black isosceles triangle from which the arms are separated by narrow yellow bands; the red and blue bands are separated from the green band and its arms by narrow white stripes; the flag colors do not have any official symbolism, but the Y stands for the "convergence of diverse elements within South African society, taking the road ahead in unity"; black, yellow, and green are found on the flag of the African National Congress, while red, white, and blue are the colors in the flags of the Netherlands and the UK, whose settlers ruled South Africa during the colonial era *note:* the South African flag is one of only two national flags to display six colors as part of its primary design, the other is South Sudan's

National symbol(s): springbok (antelope), king protea flower; national colors: red, green, blue, yellow, black, white

National anthem: *name:* "National Anthem of South Africa" *lyrics/music:* Enoch SONTONGA and Cornelius Jacob LANGENHOVEN/Enoch SONTONGA and Marthinus LOURENS de Villiers *note:* adopted 1994; a combination of "N'kosi Sikelel' iAfrica" (God Bless Africa) and "Die Stem van Suid Afrika" (The Call of South Africa), which were respectively the anthems of the non-white and white communities under apartheid; official lyrics contain a mixture of Xhosa, Zulu, Sesotho, Afrikaans, and English (i.e., the five most widely spoken of South Africa's 11 official languages); music incorporates the melody used in the Tanzanian and Zambian anthems

ECONOMY

Economy—overview: South Africa is a middle-income emerging market with an abundant supply of natural resources; well-developed financial, legal, communications, energy, and transport sectors; and a stock exchange that is Africa's largest and among the top 20 in the world.

Economic growth has decelerated in recent years, slowing to an estimated 0.7% in 2017. Unemployment, poverty, and inequality—among the highest in the world—remain a challenge. Official unemployment is roughly 27% of the workforce, and runs significantly higher among black youth. Even though the country's modern infrastructure supports a relatively efficient distribution of goods to major urban centers throughout the region, unstable electricity supplies retard growth. Eskom, the state-run power company, is building three new power stations and is installing new power demand management programs to improve power grid reliability; in late 2016 they issued a request for bids to revamp South Africa's nuclear power generating capabilities. Load shedding and resulting rolling blackouts gripped many parts of South Africa in late 2014 and early 2015 because of electricity supply constraints due to technical problems at some generation units, unavoidable planned maintenance, and an accident at a power station.

South Africa's economic policy has focused on controlling inflation; however, the country faces structural constraints that also limit economic growth, such as skills shortages, declining global competitiveness, and frequent work stoppages due to strike action. The government faces growing pressure from urban constituencies to improve the delivery of basic services to low-income areas, to increase job growth, and to provide university level-education at affordable prices. Political infighting among South Africa's ruling party and the volatility of the rand risks economic growth. International investors are concerned about the country's long-term economic stability; as of December 2016, most major international credit ratings agencies placed South Africa only one level above junk bond status.

GDP (purchasing power parity): $757.3 billion (2017 est.) $752.1 billion (2016 est.) $750 billion (2015 est.) *note:* data are in 2017 dollars *country comparison to the world:* 31

GDP (official exchange rate): $344.1 billion (2016 est.)

GDP—real growth rate: 0.7% (2017 est.) 0.3% (2016 est.) 1.3% (2015 est.) *country comparison to the world:* 194

GDP—per capita (PPP): $13,400 (2017 est.) $13,500 (2016 est.) $13,700 (2015 est.) *note:* data are in 2017 dollars *country comparison to the world:* 116

Gross national saving: 16.2% of GDP (2017 est.) 16.1% of GDP (2016 est.) 16.3% of GDP (2015 est.) *country comparison to the world:* 116

GDP—composition, by end use: *household consumption:* 59.8% *government consumption:* 20.7% *investment in fixed capital:* 20% *investment in inventories:* -0.4%

829

exports of goods and services: 26.9%
imports of goods and services: -27% (2017 est.)

GDP—composition, by sector of origin:
agriculture: 2.8%
industry: 29.7%
services: 67.5% (2017 est.)

Agriculture—products: corn, wheat, sugarcane, fruits, vegetables; beef, poultry, mutton, wool, dairy products

Industries: mining (world's largest producer of platinum, gold, chromium), automobile assembly, metalworking, machinery, textiles, iron and steel, chemicals, fertilizer, foodstuffs, commercial ship repair

Industrial production growth rate: 0.5% (2017 est.)
country comparison to the world: 183

Labor force: 22.19 million (2017 est.)
country comparison to the world: 30

Labor force—by occupation: *agriculture:* 4.6%
industry: 23.5%
services: 71.9% (2014 est.)

Unemployment rate: 27.6% (2017 est.)
26.7% (2016 est.)
country comparison to the world: 198

Population below poverty line: 16.6% (2016 est.)

Household income or consumption by percentage share: *lowest 10%:* 1.2%
highest 10%: 51.3% (2011 est.)

Distribution of family income—Gini index: 62.5 (2013 est.)
63.4 (2011 est.)
country comparison to the world: 2

Budget: *revenues:* $92.38 billion
expenditures: $103.3 billion (2017 est.)
Taxes and other revenues: 26.9% of GDP (2017 est.)
country comparison to the world: 104

Budget surplus (+) or deficit (-): -3.2% of GDP (2017 est.)
country comparison to the world: 121

Public debt: 50.1% of GDP (2017 est.)
50.1% of GDP (2016 est.)
country comparison to the world: 103

Fiscal year: 1 April—31 March

Inflation rate (consumer prices): 5.4% (2017 est.)
6.3% (2016 est.)
country comparison to the world: 175

Central bank discount rate: 5.75% (31 December 2014)
7% (31 December 2009)
country comparison to the world: 72

Commercial bank prime lending rate: 10.4% (31 December 2017 est.)
10.46% (31 December 2016 est.)
country comparison to the world: 78

Stock of narrow money: $116.5 billion (31 December 2017 est.)
$117.3 billion (31 December 2016 est.)
country comparison to the world: 35

Stock of broad money: $183.8 billion (31 December 2017 est.)
$189.9 billion (31 December 2016 est.)

country comparison to the world: 44

Stock of domestic credit: $237.6 billion (31 December 2017 est.)
$244.8 billion (31 December 2016 est.)
country comparison to the world: 41

Market value of publicly traded shares: $735.9 billion (31 December 2015 est.)
$933.9 billion (31 December 2014 est.)
$942.8 billion (31 December 2013 est.)
country comparison to the world: 16

Current account balance: -$9.81 billion (2017 est.)
-$9.624 billion (2016 est.)
country comparison to the world: 184

Exports: $78.25 billion (2017 est.)
$75.16 billion (2016 est.)
country comparison to the world: 40

Exports—commodities: gold, diamonds, platinum, other metals and minerals, machinery and equipment

Exports—partners: China 9.2%, Germany 7.5%, US 7.4%, Botswana 5%, Namibia 4.8%, Japan 4.6%, India 4.3%, UK 4.2% (2016)

Imports: $80.22 billion (2017 est.)
$74.17 billion (2016 est.)
country comparison to the world: 38

Imports—commodities: machinery and equipment, chemicals, petroleum products, scientific instruments, foodstuffs

Imports—partners: China 18.1%, Germany 11.8%, US 6.7%, India 4.2% (2016)

Reserves of foreign exchange and gold: $48.18 billion (31 December 2017 est.)
$47.23 billion (31 December 2016 est.)
country comparison to the world: 40

Debt—external: $144.1 billion (31 December 2017 est.)
$144.6 billion (31 December 2016 est.)
country comparison to the world: 43

Stock of direct foreign investment—at home: $139.2 billion (31 December 2017 est.)
$136.8 billion (31 December 2016 est.)
country comparison to the world: 40

Stock of direct foreign investment—abroad: $176.3 billion (31 December 2017 est.)
$172.8 billion (31 December 2016 est.)
country comparison to the world: 28

Exchange rates: rand (ZAR) per US dollar—
13.67 (2017 est.)
14.6924 (2016 est.)
14.6924 (2015 est.)
12.7581 (2014 est.)
10.8469 (2013 est.)

ENERGY

Electricity access: population without electricity: 7,700,000
electrification—*total population:* 85%
electrification—urban areas: 90%
electrification—rural areas: 77% (2013)

Electricity—production: 229.2 billion kWh (2015 est.)

country comparison to the world: 21

Electricity—consumption: 207.7 billion kWh (2015 est.)
country comparison to the world: 21

Electricity—exports: 16.55 billion kWh (2016 est.)
country comparison to the world: 12

Electricity—imports: 10.56 billion kWh (2016 est.)
country comparison to the world: 24

Electricity—installed generating capacity: 47.28 million kW (2015 est.)
country comparison to the world: 23

Electricity—from fossil fuels: 86.7% of total installed capacity (2015 est.)
country comparison to the world: 72

Electricity—from nuclear fuels: 3.9% of total installed capacity (2015 est.)
country comparison to the world: 25

Electricity—from hydroelectric plants: 1.4% of total installed capacity (2015 est.)
country comparison to the world: 144

Electricity—from other renewable sources: 7.1% of total installed capacity (2015 est.)
country comparison to the world: 82

Crude oil—production: 2,000 bbl/day (2016 est.)
country comparison to the world: 88

Crude oil—exports: 0 bbl/day (2014 est.)
country comparison to the world: 186

Crude oil—imports: 434,500 bbl/day (2014 est.)
country comparison to the world: 22

Crude oil—proved reserves: 15 million bbl (1 January 2017 es)
country comparison to the world: 88

Refined petroleum products—production: 431,000 bbl/day (2014 est.)
country comparison to the world: 37

Refined petroleum products—consumption: 660,000 bbl/day (2015 est.)
country comparison to the world: 32

Refined petroleum products—exports: 78,110 bbl/day (2014 est.)
country comparison to the world: 48

Refined petroleum products—imports: 164,700 bbl/day (2014 est.)
country comparison to the world: 41

Natural gas—production: 1.1 billion cu m (2015 est.)
country comparison to the world: 66

Natural gas—consumption: 8.66 billion cu m (2015 est.)
country comparison to the world: 57

Natural gas—exports: 0 cu m (2013 est.)
country comparison to the world: 178

Natural gas—imports: 3.8 billion cu m (2015 est.)
country comparison to the world: 38

Natural gas—proved reserves: 15.01 billion cu m (1 January 2012 es)
country comparison to the world: 79

Carbon dioxide emissions from consumption of energy: 482 million Mt (2013 est.)

country comparison to the world: 14

COMMUNICATIONS

Telephones—fixed lines: *total subscriptions:* 3,562,982
subscriptions per 100 inhabitants: 7 (July 2016 est.)
country comparison to the world: 40

Telephones—mobile cellular: *total:* 76,653,421
subscriptions per 100 inhabitants: 141 (July 2016 est.)
country comparison to the world: 19

Telephone system: *general assessment:* the system is the best-developed and most modern in Africa
domestic: combined fixed-line and mobile-cellular teledensity exceeds 145 telephones per 100 persons; consists of carrier-equipped open-wire lines, coaxial cables, microwave radio relay links, fiber-optic cable, radiotelephone communication stations, and wireless local loops; key centers are Bloemfontein, Cape Town, Durban, Johannesburg, Port Elizabeth, and Pretoria
international: country code—27; the SAT-3/WASC and SAFE fiber-optic submarine cable systems connect South Africa to Europe and Asia; the EASSy fiber-optic cable system connects with Europe and North America; satellite earth stations—3 Intelsat (1 Indian Ocean and 2 Atlantic Ocean) (2016)

Broadcast media: the South African Broadcasting Corporation (SABC) operates 4 TV stations, 3 are free-to-air and 1 is pay TV; e.tv, a private station, is accessible to more than half the population; multiple subscription TV services provide a mix of local and international channels; well-developed mix of public and private radio stations at the national, regional, and local levels; the SABC radio network, state-owned and controlled but nominally independent, operates 18 stations, one for each of the 11 official languages, 4 community stations, and 3 commercial stations; more than 100 community-based stations extend coverage to rural areas (2007)

Internet country code: .za

Internet users: *total:* 29,322,380
percent of population: 54.0% (July 2016 est.)
country comparison to the world: 24

TRANSPORTATION

National air transport system: number of registered air carriers: 23
inventory of registered aircraft operated by air carriers: 216
annual passenger traffic on registered air carriers: 17,188,887
annual freight traffic on registered air carriers: 885,277,991 mt-km (2015)
Civil aircraft registration country code prefix: ZS (2016)

Airports: 566 (2013)
country comparison to the world: 11

Airports—with paved runways: *total:* 144
over 3,047 m: 11
2,438 to 3,047 m: 7
1,524 to 2,437 m: 52
914 to 1,523 m: 65
under 914 m: 9 (2013)

Airports—with unpaved runways: *total:* 422
2,438 to 3,047 m: 1
1,524 to 2,437 m: 31
914 to 1,523 m: 258
under 914 m: 132 (2013)

Heliports: 1 (2013)

Pipelines: condensate 94 km; gas 1,293 km; oil 992 km; refined products 1,460 km (2013)

Railways: *total:* 20,986 km
standard gauge: 80 km 1.435-m gauge (80 km electrified)
narrow gauge: 19,756 km 1.065-m gauge (8,271 km electrified)
other: 1,150 km (passenger rail, gauge unspecified, 1,115.5 km electrified) (2014)
country comparison to the world: 13

Roadways: *total:* 747,014 km
paved: 158,952 km
unpaved: 588,062 km (2014)
country comparison to the world: 10

Merchant marine: *total:* 82
by type: bulk carrier 2, general cargo 1, oil tanker 5, other 74 (2017)
country comparison to the world: 92

Ports and terminals: *major seaport(s):* Cape Town, Durban, Port Elizabeth, Richards Bay, Saldanha Bay

container port(s) (TEUs): Durban (2,770,000) (2015)
LNG terminal(s) (import): Mossel Bay

MILITARY AND SECURITY

Military expenditures: 1.07% of GDP (2016)
1.09% of GDP (2015)
1.11% of GDP (2014)
1.12% of GDP (2013)
1.13% of GDP (2012)
country comparison to the world: 100

Military branches: South African National Defense Force (SANDF): South African Army, South African Navy (SAN), South African Air Force (SAAF), South African Military Health Services (2013)

Military service age and obligation: 18 years of age for voluntary military service; women are eligible to serve in noncombat roles; 2-year service obligation (2012)

TRANSNATIONAL ISSUES

Disputes—international: South Africa has placed military units to assist police operations along the border of Lesotho, Zimbabwe, and Mozambique to control smuggling, poaching, and illegal migration; the governments of South Africa and Namibia have not signed or ratified the text of the 1994 Surveyor's General agreement placing the boundary in the middle of the Orange River

Refugees and internally displaced persons: refugees (country of origin): 28,695 (Somalia); 26,156 (Democratic Republic of the Congo); 17,776 (Ethiopia); 5,394 (Republic of the Congo) (2016)

Illicit drugs: transshipment center for heroin, hashish, and cocaine, as well as a major cultivator of marijuana in its own right; cocaine and heroin consumption on the rise; world's largest market for illicit methaqualone, usually imported illegally from India through various east African countries, but increasingly producing its own synthetic drugs for domestic consumption; attractive venue for money launderers given the increasing level of organized criminal and narcotics activity in the region and the size of the South African economy

831

SOUTHERN OCEAN

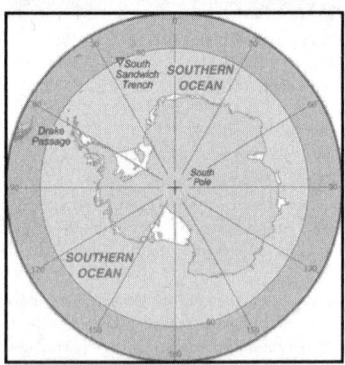

INTRODUCTION

Background: A large body of recent oceanographic research has shown that the Antarctic Circumpolar Current (ACC), an ocean current that flows from west to east around Antarctica, plays a crucial role in global ocean circulation. The region where the cold waters of the ACC meet and mingle with the warmer waters of the north defines a distinct border—the Antarctic Convergence—which fluctuates with the seasons, but which encompasses a discrete body of water and a unique ecologic region. The Convergence concentrates nutrients, which promotes marine plant life, and which, in turn, allows for a greater abundance of animal life. In 2000, the International Hydrographic Organization delimited the waters within the Convergence as a fifth world ocean—the Southern Ocean—by combining the southern portions of the Atlantic Ocean, Indian Ocean, and Pacific Ocean. The Southern Ocean extends from the coast of Antarctica north to 60 degrees south latitude, which coincides with the Antarctic Treaty region and which approximates the extent of the Antarctic Convergence. As such, the Southern Ocean is now the fourth largest of the world's five oceans (after the Pacific Ocean, Atlantic Ocean, and Indian Ocean, but larger than the Arctic Ocean). It should be noted that inclusion of the Southern Ocean does not imply recognition of this feature as one of the world's primary oceans by the US Government.

GEOGRAPHY

Location: body of water between 60 degrees south latitude and Antarctica

Geographic coordinates: 60 00 S, 90 00 E (nominally), but the Southern Ocean has the unique distinction of being a large circumpolar body of water totally encircling the continent of Antarctica; this ring of water lies between 60 degrees south latitude and the coast of Antarctica and encompasses 360 degrees of longitude

Map references: Antarctic Region

Area: *total:* 20.327 million sq km
note: includes Amundsen Sea, Bellingshausen Sea, part of the Drake Passage, Ross Sea, a small part of the Scotia Sea, Weddell Sea, and other tributary water bodies

Area—comparative: slightly more than twice the size of the US

Coastline: 17,968 km

Climate: sea temperatures vary from about 10 degrees Celsius to -2 degrees Celsius; cyclonic storms travel eastward around the continent and frequently are intense because of the temperature contrast between ice and open ocean; the ocean area from about latitude 40 south to the Antarctic Circle has the strongest average winds found anywhere on Earth; in winter the ocean freezes outward to 65 degrees south latitude in the Pacific sector and 55 degrees south latitude in the Atlantic sector, lowering surface temperatures well below 0 degrees Celsius; at some coastal points intense persistent drainage winds from the interior keep the shoreline ice-free throughout the winter

Terrain: the Southern Ocean is 4,000 to 5,000-m deep over most of its extent with only limited areas of shallow water; the Antarctic continental shelf is generally narrow and unusually deep, its edge lying at depths of 400 to 800 m (the global mean is 133 m); the Antarctic icepack grows from an average minimum of 2.6 million sq km in March to about 18.8 million sq km in September, better than a six-fold increase in area
major surface currents: the cold, clockwise-flowing Antarctic Circumpolar Current (West Wind Drift; 21,000 km long) moves perpetually eastward around the continent and is the world's largest and strongest ocean current, transporting 130 million cubic meters of water per second—100 times the flow of all the world's rivers; it is also the only current that flows all the way around the planet and connects the Atlantic, Pacific, and Indian Oceans; the cold Antarctic Coastal Current (East Wind Drift) is the southernmost current in the world, flowing westward and parallel to the Antarctic coastline

Elevation: mean depth: -3,270 m

elevation extremes: *lowest point:* southern end of the South Sandwich Trench -7,235 m
highest point: sea level 0 m

Natural resources: probable large oil and gas fields on the continental margin; manganese nodules, possible placer deposits, sand and gravel, fresh water as icebergs; squid, whales, and seals—none exploited; krill, fish

Natural hazards: huge icebergs with drafts up to several hundred meters; smaller bergs and iceberg fragments; sea ice (generally 0.5 to 1 m thick) with sometimes dynamic short-term variations and with large annual and interannual variations; deep continental shelf floored by glacial deposits varying

widely over short distances; high winds and large waves much of the year; ship icing, especially May-October; most of region is remote from sources of search and rescue

Environment—current issues: increased solar ultraviolet radiation resulting from the Antarctic ozone hole in recent years, reducing marine primary productivity (phytoplankton), damaging the DNA of some fish, and causing sun damage to some mammals; large amount of mortality of seabirds resulting from long-line fishing for toothfish; ocean acidification
note: the now-protected fur seal population is making a strong comeback after severe overexploitation in the 18th and 19th centuries

Environment—international agreements: the Southern Ocean is subject to all international agreements regarding the world's oceans; in addition, it is subject to these agreements specific to the Antarctic region: International Whaling Commission (prohibits commercial whaling south of 40 degrees south [south of 60 degrees south between 50 degrees and 130 degrees west]); Convention on the Conservation of Antarctic Seals (limits sealing); Convention on the Conservation of Antarctic Marine Living Resources (regulates fishing)
note: many nations (including the US) prohibit mineral resource exploration and exploitation south of the fluctuating Polar Front (Antarctic Convergence), which is in the middle of the Antarctic Circumpolar Current and serves as the dividing line between the cold polar surface waters to the south and the warmer waters to the northGeography—note: the major chokepoint is the Drake Passage between South America and Antarctica; the Polar Front (Antarctic Convergence) is the best natural definition of the northern extent of the Southern Ocean; it is a distinct region at the middle of the Antarctic Circumpolar Current that separates the cold polar surface waters to the south from the warmer waters to the north; the Front and the Current extend entirely around Antarctica, reaching south of 60 degrees south near New Zealand and near 48 degrees south in the far South Atlantic coinciding with the path of the maximum westerly winds

GOVERNMENT

Country name: *etymology:* the International Hydrographic Organization (IHO) included the ocean and its definition as the waters south of 60 degrees south in its year 2000 revision, but this has not formally been adopted; the 2000 IHO definition, however, was circulated in a draft edition in 2002 and has acquired de facto usage by many nations and organizations, including the CIA

ECONOMY

Economy—overview: Fisheries in 2013-14 landed 302,960 metric tons, of which 96% (291,370

tons-the highest reported catch since 1991) was krill and 4% (11,590 tons) Patagonian toothfish (also known as Chilean sea bass), compared to 15,330 tons in 2012-13 (estimated fishing from the area covered by the Convention of the Conservation of Antarctic Marine Living Resources, which extends slightly beyond the Southern Ocean area). International agreements were adopted in late 1999 to reduce illegal, unreported, and unregulated fishing, which in the 2000-01 season landed, by one estimate, 8,376 metric tons of Patagonian and Antarctic toothfish. In the 2014-15 Antarctic summer, 36,702 tourists visited the Southern Ocean, slightly lower than the 37,405 visitors in 2013-14 (estimates provided to the Antarctic Treaty by the International Association of Antarctica Tour Operators, and does not include passengers on overflights and those flying directly in and out of Antarctica).

TRANSPORTATION

Ports and terminals: *major seaport(s):* McMurdo, Palmer, and offshore anchorages in Antarctica
note: few ports or harbors exist on the southern side of the Southern Ocean; ice conditions limit use of most to short periods in midsummer; even then some cannot be entered without icebreaker escort; most Antarctic ports are operated by government research stations and, except in an emergency, are not open to commercial or private vessels

Transportation—note: Drake Passage offers alternative to transit through the Panama Canal

TRANSNATIONAL ISSUES

Disputes—international: Antarctic Treaty defers claims (see Antarctica entry), but Argentina, Australia, Chile, France, NZ, Norway, and UK assert claims (some overlapping), including the continental shelf in the Southern Ocean; several states have expressed an interest in extending those continental shelf claims under the UN Convention on the Law of the Sea to include undersea ridges; the US and most other states do not recognize the land or maritime claims of other states and have made no claims themselves (the US and Russia have reserved the right to do so); no formal claims exist in the waters in the sector between 90 degrees west and 150 degrees west

SOUTH SUDAN

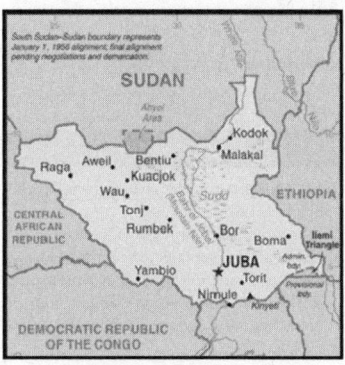

INTRODUCTION

Background: Egypt attempted to colonize the region of southern Sudan by establishing the province of Equatoria in the 1870s. Islamic Mahdist revolutionaries overran the region in 1885, but in 1898 a British force was able to overthrow the Mahdist regime. An Anglo-Egyptian Sudan was established the following year with Equatoria being the southernmost of its eight provinces. The isolated region was largely left to itself over the following decades, but Christian missionaries converted much of the population and facilitated the spread of English. When Sudan gained its independence in 1956, it was with the understanding that the southerners would be able to participate fully in the political system. When the Arab Khartoum government reneged on its promises, a mutiny began that led to two prolonged periods of conflict (1955-1972 and 1983-2005) in which perhaps 2.5 million people died—mostly civilians—due to starvation and drought. Ongoing peace talks finally resulted in a Comprehensive Peace Agreement, signed in January 2005. As part of this agreement, the south was granted a six-year period of autonomy to be followed by a referendum on final status. The result of this referendum, held in January 2011, was a vote of 98% in favor of secession.

Since independence on 9 July 2011, South Sudan has struggled with good governance and nation building and has attempted to control rebel militia groups operating in its territory. Economic conditions have deteriorated since January 2012 when the government decided to shut down oil production following bilateral disagreements with Sudan. In December 2013, conflict between government and opposition forces led to a humanitarian crisis with millions of South Sudanese displaced and food insecure. The warring parties signed a peace agreement in August 2015 that created a transitional government of national unity in April 2016. However, in July 2016, fighting broke out between the two principal signatories plunging the country back into conflict.

GEOGRAPHY

Location: East-Central Africa; south of Sudan, north of Uganda and Kenya, west of Ethiopia

Geographic coordinates: 8 00 N, 30 00 E

Map references: Africa

Area: *total:* 644,329 sq km
land: NA
water: NA
country comparison to the world: 43

Area—comparative: more than four times the size of Georgia; slightly smaller than Texas
Land boundaries: total: 6,018 km
border countries (6): Central African Republic 1,055 km, Democratic Republic of the Congo 714 km, Ethiopia 1,299 km, Kenya 317 km, Sudan 2,158 km, Uganda 475 km
note: South Sudan-Sudan boundary represents 1 January 1956 alignment; final alignment pending negotiations and demarcation; final sovereignty status of Abyei Area pending negotiations between South Sudan and Sudan

Coastline: 0 km (landlocked)

Maritime claims: none (landlocked)

Climate: hot with seasonal rainfall influenced by the annual shift of the Inter-Tropical Convergence Zone; rainfall heaviest in upland areas of the south and diminishes to the north

Terrain: plains in the north and center rise to southern highlands along the border with Uganda and Kenya; the White Nile, flowing north out of the uplands of Central Africa, is the major geographic feature of the country; The Sudd (a name derived from floating vegetation that hinders navigation) is a large swampy area of more than 100,000 sq km fed by the waters of the White Nile that dominates the center of the country

Elevation: *mean elevation:* NA

elevation extremes: *lowest point:* White Nile 381 m
highest point: Kinyeti 3,187 m

Natural resources: hydropower, fertile agricultural land, gold, diamonds, petroleum, hardwoods, limestone, iron ore, copper, chromium ore, zinc, tungsten, mica, silver

Land use: *agricultural land:* 100%
arable land: 0%;
permanent crops: 0%;
permanent pasture: 100%
forest: 0%
other: 0%
Irrigated land: 1,000 sq km (2012)

Population—distribution: clusters found in urban areas, particularly in the western interior and around the White NileGeography—note: landlocked; The Sudd is a vast swamp in South Sudan, formed by the White Nile, comprising more than

15% of the country's total area; it is one of the world's largest wetlands

PEOPLE AND SOCIETY

Population: 13,026,129 (July 2017 est.)
country comparison to the world: 73

Nationality: *noun:* South Sudanese (singular and plural)
adjective: South Sudanese

Ethnic groups: Dinka 35.8%, Nuer 15.6%, Shilluk, Azande, Bari, Kakwa, Kuku, Murle, Mandari, Didinga, Ndogo, Bviri, Lndi, Anuak, Bongo, Lango, Dungotona, Acholi, Baka, Fertit (2011 est.)

Languages: English (official), Arabic (includes Juba and Sudanese variants), regional languages include Dinka, Nuer, Bari, Zande, Shilluk

Religions: animist, Christian

Demographic profile: South Sudan, independent from Sudan since July 2011 after decades of civil war, is one of the world's poorest countries and ranks among the lowest in many socioeconomic categories. Problems are exacerbated by ongoing tensions with Sudan over oil revenues and land borders, fighting between government forces and rebel groups, and inter-communal violence. Most of the population lives off of farming, while smaller numbers rely on animal husbandry; more than 80% of the populace lives in rural areas. The maternal mortality rate is among the world's highest for a variety of reasons, including a shortage of health care workers, facilities, and supplies; poor roads and a lack of transport; and cultural beliefs that prevent women from seeking obstetric care. Most women marry and start having children early, giving birth at home with the assistance of traditional birth attendants, who are unable to handle complications.

Educational attainment is extremely poor due to the lack of schools, qualified teachers, and materials. Less than a third of the population is literate (the rate is even lower among women), and half live below the poverty line. Teachers and students are also struggling with the switch from Arabic to English as the language of instruction. Many adults missed out on schooling because of warfare and displacement.

Almost 2 million South Sudanese have sought refuge in neighboring countries since the current conflict began in December 2013. Another 1.96 million South Sudanese are internally displaced as of August 2017. Despite South Sudan's instability and lack of infrastructure and social services, more than 240,000 people have fled to South Sudan to escape fighting in Sudan.

Age structure: *0-14 years:* 44.37% (male 2,947,277/female 2,831,822)
15-24 years: 20.56% (male 1,402,746/female 1,275,276)
25-54 years: 29.58% (male 1,869,480/female 1,983,504)
55-64 years: 3.39% (male 235,546/female 206,304)
65 years and over: 2.1% (male 151,166/female 123,008) (2017 est.)

Dependency ratios: *total dependency ratio:* 83.7
youth dependency ratio: 77.3
elderly dependency ratio: 6.4
potential support ratio: 15.7 (2015 est.)

Median age: *total:* 17.3 years
male: 17.2 years
female: 17.5 years (2017 est.)
country comparison to the world: 221

Population growth rate: 3.83% (2017 est.)
country comparison to the world: 1

Birth rate: 35.5 births/1,000 population (2017 est.)
country comparison to the world: 18

Death rate: 7.7 deaths/1,000 population (2017 est.)
country comparison to the world: 104

Net migration rate: 10.6 migrant(s)/1,000 population (2017 est.)
country comparison to the world: 8

Population distribution: clusters found in urban areas, particularly in the western interior and around the White Nile

Urbanization: *urban population:* 19.3% of total population (2017)
rate of urbanization: 3.91% annual rate of change (2015-20 est.)

Major urban areas—population: JUBA (capital) 321,000 (2015)

Maternal mortality ratio: 789 deaths/100,000 live births (2015 est.)
country comparison to the world: 5

Infant mortality rate: *total:* 62.8 deaths/1,000 live births
male: 67.3 deaths/1,000 live births
female: 58.1 deaths/1,000 live births (2017 est.)
country comparison to the world: 15

Total fertility rate: 5.07 children born/woman (2017 est.)
country comparison to the world: 12

Contraceptive prevalence rate: 4% (2010)

Health expenditures: 2.7% of GDP (2014)
country comparison to the world: 185

Drinking water source:
improved:
urban: 66.7% of population
rural: 56.9% of population
total: 58.7% of population
unimproved:
urban: 33.3% of population
rural: 43.1% of population
total: 41.3% of population (2015 est.)

Sanitation facility access:
improved:
urban: 16.4% of population
rural: 4.5% of population
total: 6.7% of population
unimproved:
urban: 83.6% of population
rural: 95.5% of population
total: 93.3% of population (2015 est.)

HIV/AIDS—adult prevalence rate: 2.7% (2016 est.)
country comparison to the world: 23

HIV/AIDS—people living with HIV/AIDS: 200,000 (2016 est.)
country comparison to the world: 29

HIV/AIDS—deaths: 13,000 (2016 est.)
country comparison to the world: 19

Major infectious diseases: *degree of risk:* very high
food or waterborne disease: bacterial and protozoal diarrhea, hepatitis A and E, and typhoid fever
vectorborne disease: malaria, dengue fever, trypanosomiasis-Gambiense (African sleeping sickness)
water contact disease: schistosomiasis
respiratory disease: meningococcal meningitis
animal contact disease: rabies (2016)

Obesity—adult prevalence rate: 6.6% (2014)
country comparison to the world: 166

Children under the age of 5 years underweight: 27.6% (2010)
country comparison to the world: 10

Education expenditures: 0.8% of GDP (2011)

Literacy: *definition:* age 15 and over can read and write
total population: 27%
male: 40%
female: 16% (2009 est.)

Unemployment, youth ages 15-24: *total:* 18.5%
male: 20%
female: 17% (2008 est.)

GOVERNMENT

Country name: *conventional long form:* Republic of South Sudan
conventional short form: South Sudan
etymology: self-descriptive name from the country's former position within Sudan prior to independence; the name "Sudan" derives from the Arabic "bilad-as-sudan" meaning "Land of the Black [peoples]"

Government type: presidential republic

Capital: *name:* Juba
geographic coordinates: 04 51 N 31 37 E
time difference: UTC+3 (8 hours ahead of Washington, DC, during Standard Time)

Administrative divisions: 10 states; Central Equatoria, Eastern Equatoria, Jonglei, Lakes, Northern Bahr el Ghazal, Unity, Upper Nile, Warrap, Western Bahr el Ghazal, Western Equatoria

Independence: 9 July 2011 (from Sudan)

National holiday: Independence Day, 9 July (2011)

Constitution: *history:* previous 2005 (preindependence); latest signed 7 July 2011, effective 9 July 2011 (Transitional Constitution of the Republic of South Sudan, 2011)
amendments: proposed by the National Legislature or by the president of the republic; passage requires submission of the proposal to the Legislature at least one month prior to consideration, approval by at least two-thirds majority vote in both houses of the Legislature, and assent by the president; amended 2013, 2015 (2017)

Citizenship: *citizenship by birth:* no

citizenship by descent only: at least one parent must be a citizen of South Sudan

dual citizenship recognized: yes

residency requirement for naturalization: 10 years

Suffrage: 18 years of age; universal

Executive branch: *chief of state:* President Salva KIIR Mayardit (since 9 July 2011); First Vice President Taban Deng GAI (since 26 July 2016); Second Vice President James Wani IGGA (since 26 April 2016); note—the president is both chief of state and head of government

head of government: President Salva KIIR Mayardit (since 9 July 2011); First Vice President Taban Deng GAI (since 26 July 2016); Second Vice President James Wani IGGA (since 26 April 2016)

cabinet: National Council of Ministers appointed by the president, approved by the Transitional National Legislative Assembly

elections/appointments: president directly elected by simple majority popular vote for a 4-year term (eligible for a second term); election last held on 11-15 April 2010 (the next election has been postponed from 2015 to 2018 due to instability and violence)

election results: Salva KIIR Mayardit elected president; percent of vote—Salva KIIR Mayardit (SPLM) 93%, Lam AKOL (SPLM-DC) 7%

Legislative branch: *description:* bicameral National Legislature consists of the Council of States, established by presidential decree in August 2011 (50 seats; 20 former members of the Council of States and 30 appointed representatives) and the Transitional National Legislative Assembly, established on 4 August 2016, in accordance with the August 2015 Agreement on the Resolution of the Conflict in the Republic of South Sudan (400 seats; 170 members elected in April 2010, 96 members of the former National Assembly, 66 members appointed after independence, and 68 members added as a result of the 2016 Agreement)

elections: National Legislative Assembly—last held 11-15 April 2010 but did not take office until July 2011; because of political instability, current parliamentary term extended until next election on 9 July 2018; Council of States—established and members appointed 1 August 2011

election results: Council of States—percent of vote by party—NA; seats by party—SPLM 20, unknown 30; National Legislative Assembly—percent of vote by party—NA; seats by party—SPLM 251, SPLM-DC 6, DCP 4, independent 6, unknown 65

Judicial branch: *highest court(s):* Supreme Court of South Sudan (consists of the chief and deputy chief justices, 9 other justices and normally organized into panels of 3 justices except when sitting as a Constitutional panel of all 9 justices chaired by the chief justice)

judge selection and term of office: justices appointed by the president upon proposal of the Judicial Service Council, a 9-member judicial and administrative body; justice tenure set by the National Legislature

subordinate courts: national level—Courts of Appeal; High Courts; County Courts; state level—High Courts; County Courts; customary courts; other specialized courts and tribunals

Political parties and leaders: Sudan People's Liberation Movement or SPLM [Salva KIIR Mayardit] Sudan People's Liberation Movement-Democratic Movement or SPLM-DC [Lam AKOL, chairman] Sudan People's Liberation Movement-In Opposition or SPLM-IO [Riek MACHAR Teny Dhurgon] Democratic Change or DC [Onyoti Adigo NYIK-WEC] (formerly SPLM-DC)

International organization participation: AU, FAO, G-77, IBRD, ICAO, ICRM, IDA, IFAD, IFC, IFRCS, ILO, IMF, Interpol, IOM, IPU, ITU, MIGA, UN, UNCTAD, UNESCO, UPU, WCO, WHO, WMO

Diplomatic representation in the US: chief of mission: Ambassador Garang Diing AKUONG (since 23 February 2015)

chancery: 1015 31st St., NW, Third Floor, Washington, DC, 20007

telephone: [1] (202) 293-7940

FAX: [1] (202) 293-7941

Diplomatic representation from the US: *chief of mission:* Ambassador (vacant); Charge d'Affaires Michael K. MORROW (since 22 August 2017)

embassy: Kololo Road adjacent to the EU's compound, Juba

telephone: [211] (0) 912-105-188

Flag description: three equal horizontal bands of black (top), red, and green; the red band is edged in white; a blue isosceles triangle based on the hoist side contains a gold, five-pointed star; black represents the people of South Sudan, red the blood shed in the struggle for freedom, green the verdant land, and blue the waters of the Nile; the gold star represents the unity of the states making up South Sudan

note: resembles the flag of Kenya; one of only two national flags to display six colors as part of its primary design, the other is South Africa's

National symbol(s): African fish eagle; national colors: red, green, blue, yellow, black, white

National anthem: *name:* South Sudan Oyee! (Hooray!)

lyrics/music: collective of 49 poets/Juba University students and teachers

note: adopted 2011; anthem selected in a national contest

ECONOMY

Economy—overview: Following several decades of civil war with Sudan, industry and infrastructure in landlocked South Sudan are severely underdeveloped and poverty is widespread. Subsistence agriculture provides a living for the vast majority of the population. Property rights are insecure and price signals are weak, because markets are not well organized. After independence, South Sudan's central bank issued a new currency, the South Sudanese pound, allowing a short grace period for turning in the old currency.

South Sudan has little infrastructure—approximately 200 kilometers of paved roads. Electricity is produced mostly by costly diesel generators, and indoor plumbing and potable water are scarce. South Sudan depends largely on imports of goods, services, and capital—mainly from Uganda, Kenya and Sudan.

Nevertheless, South Sudan does have abundant natural resources. At independence in 2011, South Sudan produced nearly three-fourths of former Sudan's total oil output of nearly a half million barrels per day. The Government of South Sudan used to rely on oil for the vast majority of its budget revenues before oil production fell sharply. Oil is exported through a pipeline that runs to refineries and shipping facilities at Port Sudan on the Red Sea. The economy of South Sudan will remain linked to Sudan for some time, given the long lead time and great expense required to build another pipeline, should the government decide to do so. In January 2012, South Sudan suspended production of oil because of its dispute with Sudan over transshipment fees. This suspension lasted 15 months and had a devastating impact on GDP, which declined by 48% in 2012. With the resumption of oil flows the economy rebounded during the second half of calendar year 2013. GDP grew by nearly 30% for the year. This occurred in spite of the fact that oil production, at an average level of 222,000 barrels per day, was 40% lower compared with 2011, prior to the shutdown. However, the outbreak of conflict in December 2013 combined with a further reduction of oil production and exports, meant that GDP fell significantly from 2014 to 2017, and poverty and food insecurity rose. South Sudan holds one of the richest agricultural areas in Africa with fertile soils and abundant water supplies. Currently the region supports 10-20 million head of cattle.

South Sudan is currently burdened by considerable debt because of increased military spending and revenue shortfalls due to low oil prices and decreased production. South Sudan has received more than $4 billion in foreign aid since 2005, largely from the UK, the US, Norway, and the Netherlands. Annual inflation peaked at over 800% in October 2016. The government has relied on borrowing from the central bank to fund budget expenses. The decision in December 2015 by the central bank to abandon a fixed exchange rate and allow the South Sudanese Pound to float has not reduced inflation in the short term. Long-term challenges include diversifying the formal economy, alleviating poverty, maintaining macroeconomic stability, improving tax collection and financial management and improving the business environment.

GDP (purchasing power parity): $19.75 billion (2017 est.)

$21.07 billion (2016 est.)

$24.45 billion (2015 est.)

note: data are in 2017 dollars

country comparison to the world: 150

GDP (official exchange rate): $2.915 billion (2016 est.)

GDP—real growth rate: -6.3% (2017 est.)
-13.8% (2016 est.)
-0.2% (2015 est.)
country comparison to the world: 219

GDP—per capita (PPP): $1,500 (2017 est.)
$1,700 (2016 est.)
$2,100 (2015 est.)
note: data are in 2017 dollars
country comparison to the world: 220

Gross national saving: 9.9% of GDP (2017 est.)
20% of GDP (2016 est.)
7.3% of GDP (2015 est.)
country comparison to the world: 160

GDP—composition, by end use:
household consumption: 34.9%
government consumption: 17.1%
investment in fixed capital: 10.4%
exports of goods and services: 64.9%
imports of goods and services: -27.2% (2011 est.)

Agriculture—products: sorghum, maize, rice, millet, wheat, gum arabic, sugarcane, mangoes, papayas, bananas, sweet potatoes, sunflower seeds, cotton, sesame seeds, cassava (manioc, tapioca), beans, peanuts; cattle, sheep

Population below poverty line: 50.6% (2009 est.)

Distribution of family income—Gini index: 46 (2010 est.)
country comparison to the world: 33

Budget: *revenues:* $437 million
expenditures: $2.259 billion (FY2013 est.)
Taxes and other revenues: 15% of GDP (FY2013 est.)
country comparison to the world: 188

Budget surplus (+) or deficit (-): -62.5% of GDP (FY2013 est.)
country comparison to the world: 220

Public debt: 33% of GDP (2016 est.)
65.7% of GDP (2015 est.)
country comparison to the world: 152

Inflation rate (consumer prices): 182.2% (2017 est.)
379.8% (2016 est.)
country comparison to the world: 226

Stock of narrow money: $1.873 billion (31 December 2013)
$2.032 billion (31 December 2012)
country comparison to the world: 136

Stock of broad money: $2.194 billion (31 December 2013 est.)
$2.23 billion (31 December 2012 est.)
country comparison to the world: 153

Current account balance: $49 million (2017 est.)
$142 million (2016 est.)
country comparison to the world: 54

Exchange rates: South Sudanese pounds (SSP) per US dollar—
0.906 (2017 est.)
0.9214 (2016 est.)
0.9214 (2015 est.)
0.885 (2014 est.)
0.7634 (2013 est.)

ENERGY

Electricity access: population without electricity: 11,200,000

electrification—total population: 1%
electrification—urban areas: 4%
electrification—rural areas: 0% (2013)

Electricity—production: 310.3 million kWh (2015 est.)
country comparison to the world: 181

Electricity—consumption: 0 kWh (2015 est.)
country comparison to the world: 218

Electricity—exports: 0 kWh (2016 est.)
country comparison to the world: 182

Electricity—imports: 0 kWh (2016 est.)
country comparison to the world: 185

Electricity—installed generating capacity: 80,000 kW (2015 est.)
country comparison to the world: 185

Electricity—from fossil fuels: 100% of total installed capacity (2015 est.)
country comparison to the world: 16

Electricity—from nuclear fuels: 0% of total installed capacity (2015 est.)
country comparison to the world: 161

Electricity—from hydroelectric plants: 0% of total installed capacity (2015 est.)
country comparison to the world: 195

Electricity—from other renewable sources: 0% of total installed capacity (2015 est.)
country comparison to the world: 201

Crude oil—production: 152,500 bbl/day (2016 est.)
country comparison to the world: 39

Crude oil—exports: 155,200 bbl/day (2014 est.)
country comparison to the world: 33

Crude oil—imports: 0 bbl/day (2014 est.)
country comparison to the world: 175

Crude oil—proved reserves: 3.75 billion bbl (1 January 2017 es)
country comparison to the world: 28

Refined petroleum products—production: 0 bbl/day (2014 est.)
country comparison to the world: 204

Refined petroleum products—consumption: 11,000 bbl/day (2015 est.)
country comparison to the world: 159

Refined petroleum products—exports: 0 bbl/day (2014 est.)
country comparison to the world: 188

Refined petroleum products—imports: 10,630 bbl/day (2014 est.)
country comparison to the world: 143

Natural gas—production: 0 cu m (2013 est.)
country comparison to the world: 182

Natural gas—consumption: 0 cu m (2013 est.)
country comparison to the world: 121

Natural gas—exports: 0 cu m (2013 est.)
country comparison to the world: 164

Natural gas—imports: 0 cu m (2013 est.)
country comparison to the world: 172

Natural gas—proved reserves: 63.71 billion cu m (1 January 2016 es)
country comparison to the world: 61

Carbon dioxide emissions from consumption of energy: 2.016 million Mt (2011 est.)
country comparison to the world: 149

COMMUNICATIONS

Telephones—fixed lines: *total subscriptions:* 150 *subscriptions per 100 inhabitants:* less than 1 (July 2016 est.)

Telephones—mobile cellular: *total:* 2.899 million *subscriptions per 100 inhabitants:* 24 (July 2016 est.)
country comparison to the world: 141

Telephone system: *general assessment:* one of the least developed telecommunications and Internet systems in the world; domestic mobile providers are waiting for a political settlement and the return of social stability in order to expand their networks
international: country code—211 (2016)

Broadcast media: TV is controlled by the government; several private FM stations are operational in South Sudan; some foreign radio broadcasts are available

Internet country code: .ss

TRANSPORTATION

Civil aircraft registration country code prefix: Z8 (2016)

Airports: 85 (2013)
country comparison to the world: 64

Airports—with paved runways: *total:* 3
2,438 to 3,047 m: 1
1,524 to 2,437 m: 2 (2013)

Airports—with unpaved runways: *total:* 82
2,438 to 3,047 m: 1
1,524 to 2,437 m: 12
914 to 1,523 m: 35
under 914 m: 34 (2013)

Heliports: 1 (2013)

Railways: *total:* 248 km
note: a narrow gauge, single-track railroad between Babonosa (Sudan) and Wau, the only existing rail system, was repaired in 2010 with $250 million in UN funds (2014)
country comparison to the world: 127

Roadways: *total:* 7,000 km
note: most of the road network is unpaved and much of it is in disrepair; a 192-km paved road between the capital, Juba, and Nimule on the Ugandan border was constructed with USAID funds in 2012 (2012)
country comparison to the world: 145

Waterways: see entry for Sudan

MILITARY AND SECURITY

Military expenditures: 10.93% of GDP (2015)
9.77% of GDP (2014)
7.41% of GDP (2013)
9.53% of GDP (2012)
5.91% of GDP (2011)
country comparison to the world: 1

Military branches: South Sudan Defense Force (SSDF): ground force, navy, air force and air defense units (2017)

Military service age and obligation: 18 is the legal minimum age for compulsory and voluntary military service; the Government of South Sudan signed agreements in March 2012 and August 2015 that included the demobilization of all child soldiers within the armed forces and opposition, but the recruitment of child soldiers by the warring parties continues; as of the end of 2016, UNICEF estimates that more than 17,000 child soldiers had been used in the country's civil war since it began in December 2013 (2016)

TRANSNATIONAL ISSUES

Disputes—international: South Sudan-Sudan boundary represents 1 January 1956 alignment, final alignment pending negotiations and demarcation; final sovereignty status of Abyei Area pending negotiations between South Sudan and Sudan; periodic violent skirmishes with South Sudanese residents over water and grazing rights persist among related pastoral populations along the border with the Central African Republic; the boundary that separates Kenya and South Sudan's sovereignty is unclear in the "Ilemi Triangle," which Kenya has administered since colonial times

Refugees and internally displaced persons: refugees (country of origin): 264,730 (Sudan) (refugees and asylum seekers); 14,975 (Democratic Republic of the Congo) (refugees and asylum seekers) (2018)

IDPs: 1.87 million (alleged coup attempt and ethnic conflict beginning in December 2013; information is lacking on those displaced in earlier years by: fighting in Abyei between the Sudanese Armed Forces and the Sudan People's Liberation Army (SPLA) in May 2011; clashes between the SPLA and dissident militia groups in South Sudan; inter-ethnic conflicts over resources and cattle; attacks from the Lord's Resistance Army; floods and drought) (2017)

Trafficking in persons: current situation: South Sudan is a source and destination country for men, women, and children subjected to forced labor and sex trafficking; South Sudanese women and girls, particularly those who are internally displaced, orphaned, refugees, or from rural areas, are vulnerable to forced labor and sexual exploitation, often in urban centers; children may be victims of forced labor in construction, market vending, shoe shining, car washing, rock breaking, brick making, delivery cart pulling, and begging; girls are also forced into marriages and subsequently subjected to sexual slavery or domestic servitude; women and girls migrate willingly from Uganda, Kenya,

Ethiopia, Eritrea, and the Democratic Republic of the Congo to South Sudan with the promise of legitimate jobs and are forced into the sex trade; inter-ethnic abductions and abductions by criminal groups continue, with abductees subsequently forced into domestic servitude, herding, or sex trafficking; in 2014, the recruitment and use of child soldiers increased significantly within government security forces and was also prevalent among opposition forces

tier rating: Tier 3—South Sudan does not fully comply with the minimum standards for the elimination of trafficking and is not making significant efforts to do so; despite the government's formal recommitment to an action plan to eliminate the recruitment and use of child soldiers by 2016, the practice expanded during 2014, and the government did not hold any officers criminally responsible; government officials reportedly are complicit in trafficking offenses but these activities continue to go uninvestigated; authorities reportedly identified five trafficking victims but did not transfer them to care facilities; law enforcement continued to arrest and imprison individuals for prostitution, including trafficking victims; no known steps were taken to address the exploitation of South Sudanese nationals working abroad or foreign workers in South Sudan (2015)

SPAIN

INTRODUCTION

Background: Spain's powerful world empire of the 16th and 17th centuries ultimately yielded command of the seas to England. Subsequent failure to embrace the mercantile and industrial revolutions caused the country to fall behind Britain, France, and Germany in economic and political power. Spain remained neutral in World War I and II but suffered through a devastating civil war (1936-39). A peaceful transition to democracy following the death of dictator Francisco FRANCO in 1975,

and rapid economic modernization (Spain joined the EU in 1986) gave Spain a dynamic and rapidly growing economy and made it a global champion of freedom and human rights. More recently Spain has emerged from a severe economic recession that began in mid-2008, posting three straight years of GDP growth above the EU average. Unemployment has fallen, but remains high especially among youth. Spain is the Eurozone's fourth largest economy.

GEOGRAPHY

Location: Southwestern Europe, bordering the Mediterranean Sea, North Atlantic Ocean, Bay of Biscay, and Pyrenees Mountains; southwest of France

Geographic coordinates: 40 00 N, 4 00 W

Map references: Europe

Area: *total:* 505,370 sq km

land: 498,980 sq km

water: 6,390 sq km

note: there are two autonomous cities—Ceuta and Melilla—and 17 autonomous communities including Balearic Islands and Canary Islands, and three small Spanish possessions off the coast of Morocco—Islas Chafarinas, Penon de Alhucemas, and Penon de Velez de la Gomera

country comparison to the world: 53

Area—comparative: almost five times the size of Kentucky; slightly more than twice the size of Oregon

Land boundaries: total: 1,952.7 km

border countries (5): Andorra 63 km, France 646 km, Gibraltar 1.2 km, Portugal 1,224 km, Morocco (Ceuta) 8 km, Morocco (Melilla) 10.5 km

note: an additional 75-meter border segment exists between Morocco and the Spanish exclave of Penon de Velez de la Gomera

Coastline: 4,964 km

Maritime claims: *territorial sea:* 12 nm

contiguous zone: 24 nm

exclusive economic zone: 200 nm (applies only to the Atlantic Ocean)

Climate: temperate; clear, hot summers in interior, more moderate and cloudy along coast; cloudy, cold winters in interior, partly cloudy and cool along coast

Terrain: large, flat to dissected plateau surrounded by rugged hills; Pyrenees Mountains in north

Elevation: *mean elevation:* 660 m

elevation extremes: lowest point: Atlantic Ocean 0 m

highest point: Pico de Teide (Tenerife) on Canary Islands 3,718 m

Natural resources: coal, lignite, iron ore, copper, lead, zinc, uranium, tungsten, mercury, pyrites, magnesite, fluorspar, gypsum, sepiolite, kaolin, potash, hydropower, arable land

Land use: *agricultural land:* 54.1%
arable land: 24.9%;
permanent crops: 9.1%;
permanent pasture: 20.1%
forest: 36.8%
other: 9.1% (2011 est.)
Irrigated land: 38,000 sq km (2012)

Population—distribution: with the notable exception of Madrid, Sevilla, and Zaragoza, the largest urban agglomerations are found along the Mediterranean and Atlantic coasts; numerous smaller cities are spread throughout the interior reflecting Spain's agrarian heritage; dense settlement is found around the capital of Madrid, as well as the port city of Barcelona

Natural hazards: periodic droughts, occasional flooding
volcanism: volcanic activity in the Canary Islands, located off Africa's northwest coast; Teide (3,715 m) has been deemed a Decade Volcano by the International Association of Volcanology and Chemistry of the Earth's Interior, worthy of study due to its explosive history and close proximity to human populations; La Palma (2,426 m), which last erupted in 1971, is the most active of the Canary Islands volcanoes; Lanzarote is the only other historically active volcano

Environment—current issues: pollution of the Mediterranean Sea from raw sewage and effluents from the offshore production of oil and gas; water quality and quantity nationwide; air pollution; deforestation; desertification

Environment—international agreements: *party to:* Air Pollution, Air Pollution-Nitrogen Oxides, Air Pollution-Sulfur 94, Air Pollution-Volatile Organic Compounds, Antarctic-Environmental Protocol, Antarctic-Marine Living Resources, Antarctic Treaty, Biodiversity, Climate Change, Climate Change-Kyoto Protocol, Desertification, Endangered Species, Environmental Modification, Hazardous Wastes, Law of the Sea, Marine Dumping, Marine Life Conservation, Ozone Layer Protection, Ship Pollution, Tropical Timber 83, Tropical Timber 94, Wetlands, Whaling
signed, but not ratified: Air Pollution-Persistent Organic PollutantsGeography—note: strategic location along approaches to Strait of Gibraltar; Spain controls a number of territories in northern Morocco including the enclaves of Ceuta and Melilla, and the islands of Penon de Velez de la Gomera, Penon de Alhucemas, and Islas Chafarinas

PEOPLE AND SOCIETY

Population: 48,958,159 (July 2017 est.)
country comparison to the world: 28

Nationality: *noun:* Spaniard(s)
adjective: Spanish

Ethnic groups: composite of Mediterranean and Nordic types

Languages: Castilian Spanish (official nationwide) 74%, Catalan (official in Catalonia, the Balearic Islands, and the Valencian Community (where it is known as Valencian)) 17%, Galician (official in Galicia) 7%, Basque (official in the Basque Country and in the Basque-speaking area of Navarre) 2%, Aranese (official in the northwest corner of Catalonia (Vall d'Aran) along with Catalan, <5,000 speakers)
note: Aragonese, Aranese Asturian, Basque, Calo, Catalan, Galician, and Valencian are recognized as regional languages under the European Charter for Regional or Minority Languages

Religions: Roman Catholic 67.8%, atheist 9.1%, other 2.2%, non-believer 18.4%, unspecified 2.5% (2016 est.)

Age structure: *0-14 years:* 15.38% (male 3,872,763/female 3,656,549)
15-24 years: 9.58% (male 2,424,352/female 2,267,429)
25-54 years: 44.91%' (male 11,214,102/female 10,775,039)
55-64 years: 12.14% (male 2,899,088/female 3,044,111)
65 years and over: 17.98% (male 3,763,989/female 5,040,737) (2017 est.)

Dependency ratios: *total dependency ratio:* 51
youth dependency ratio: 22.5
elderly dependency ratio: 28.5
potential support ratio: 3.5 (2015 est.)

Median age: *total:* 42.7 years
male: 41.5 years
female: 43.9 years (2017 est.)
country comparison to the world: 27

Population growth rate: 0.78% (2017 est.)
country comparison to the world: 134

Birth rate: 9.2 births/1,000 population (2017 est.)
country comparison to the world: 204

Death rate: 9.1 deaths/1,000 population (2017 est.)
country comparison to the world: 64

Net migration rate: 7.8 migrant(s)/1,000 population (2017 est.)
country comparison to the world: 13

Population distribution: with the notable exception of Madrid, Sevilla, and Zaragoza, the largest urban agglomerations are found along the Mediterranean and Atlantic coasts; numerous smaller cities are spread throughout the interior reflecting Spain's agrarian heritage; dense settlement is found around the capital of Madrid, as well as the port city of Barcelona

Urbanization: *urban population:* 80% of total population (2017)
rate of urbanization: 0.52% annual rate of change (2015-20 est.)
note: data include Canary Islands, Ceuta, and Melilla

Major urban areas—population: MADRID (capital) 6.199 million; Barcelona 5.258 million; Valencia 810,000 (2015)

Sex ratio: *at birth:* 1.07 male(s)/female
0-14 years: 1.06 male(s)/female
15-24 years: 1.07 male(s)/female
25-54 years: 1.04 male(s)/female
55-64 years: 0.95 male(s)/female
65 years and over: 0.74 male(s)/female
total population: 0.98 male(s)/female (2016 est.)

Mother's mean age at first birth: 30.7 years (2015 est.)

Maternal mortality ratio: 5 deaths/100,000 live births (2015 est.)
country comparison to the world: 173

Infant mortality rate: *total:* 3.3 deaths/1,000 live births
male: 3.6 deaths/1,000 live births
female: 2.9 deaths/1,000 live births (2017 est.)
country comparison to the world: 212

Life expectancy at birth: *total population:* 81.8 years
male: 78.8 years
female: 84.9 years (2017 est.)
country comparison to the world: 22

Total fertility rate: 1.5 children born/woman (2017 est.)
country comparison to the world: 197

Health expenditures: 9% of GDP (2014)
country comparison to the world: 40

Physicians density: 3.82 physicians/1,000 population (2014)

Hospital bed density: 3.1 beds/1,000 population (2011)

Drinking water source:
improved:
 urban: 100% of population
 rural: 100% of population
 total: 100% of population
unimproved:
 urban: 0% of population
 rural: 0% of population
 total: 0% of population (2015 est.)

Sanitation facility access:
improved:
 urban: 99.8% of population
 rural: 100% of population
 total: 99.9% of population
unimproved:
 urban: 0.2% of population
 rural: 0% of population
 total: 0.1% of population (2015 est.)

HIV/AIDS—adult prevalence rate: 0.4% (2016 est.)
country comparison to the world: 77

HIV/AIDS—people living with HIV/AIDS: 140,000 (2016 est.)
country comparison to the world: 32

HIV/AIDS—deaths: NA

Obesity—adult prevalence rate: 23.8% (2016)
country comparison to the world: 62

Education expenditures: 4.3% of GDP (2013)
country comparison to the world: 80

Literacy: *definition:* age 15 and over can read and write
total population: 98.3%
male: 98.8%
female: 97.7% (2016 est.)

School life expectancy (primary to tertiary education): total: 18 years
male: 18 years
female: 18 years (2015)

Unemployment, youth ages 15-24: total: 44.4%
male: 44%
female: 44.9% (2016 est.)
country comparison to the world: 5

GOVERNMENT

Country name: *conventional long form:* Kingdom of Spain
conventional short form: Spain
local long form: Reino de Espana
local short form: Espana
etymology: derivation of the name "Espana" is uncertain, but may come from the Phoenician term "span," related to the word "spy," meaning "to forge metals," so, "i-spn-ya" would mean "place where metals are forged"; the ancient Phoenicians long exploited the Iberian Peninsula for its mineral wealth

Government type: parliamentary constitutional monarchy

Capital: *name:* Madrid
geographic coordinates: 40 24 N, 3 41 W
time difference: UTC+1 (6 hours ahead of Washington, DC, during Standard Time)
daylight saving time: +1hr, begins last Sunday in March; ends last Sunday in October
note: Spain has two time zones, including the Canary Islands

Administrative divisions: 17 autonomous communities (comunidades autonomas, singular—comunidad autonoma) and 2 autonomous cities* (ciudades autonomas, singular—ciudad autonoma); Andalucia; Aragon; Asturias; Canarias (Canary Islands); Cantabria; Castilla-La Mancha; Castilla-Leon; Cataluna (Castilian), Catalunya (Catalan), Catalonha (Aranese) [Catalonia]; Ceuta*; Comunidad Valenciana (Castilian), Comunitat Valenciana (Valencian) [Valencian Community]; Extremadura; Galicia; Illes Baleares (Balearic Islands); La Rioja; Madrid; Melilla*; Murcia; Navarra (Castilian), Nafarroa (Basque) [Navarre]; Pais Vasco (Castilian), Euskadi (Basque) [Basque Country]
note: the autonomous cities of Ceuta and Melilla plus three small islands of Islas Chafarinas, Penon de Alhucemas, and Penon de Velez de la Gomera, administered directly by the Spanish central government, are all along the coast of Morocco and are collectively referred to as Places of Sovereignty (Plazas de Soberania)

Independence: 1492; the Iberian peninsula was characterized by a variety of independent kingdoms prior to the Muslim occupation that began in the early 8th century A.D. and lasted nearly seven centuries; the small Christian redoubts of the north began the reconquest almost immediately, culminating in the seizure of Granada in 1492; this event completed the unification of several kingdoms and is traditionally considered the forging of present-day Spain

National holiday: National Day (Hispanic Day), 12 October (1492); note—commemorates COLUMBUS' arrival in the Americas

Constitution: *history:* previous 1812; latest approved by the General Courts 31 October 1978, passed by referendum 6 December 1978, signed by the king 27 December 1978, effective 29 December 1978
amendments: proposed by the government, by the General Courts (the Congress or the Senate), or by the self-governing communities submitted through the government; passage requires three-fifths majority vote by both houses and passage by referendum if requested by one-tenth of members of either house; proposals disapproved by both houses are submitted to a joint committee, which submits an agreed upon text for another vote; passage requires two-thirds vote in Congress and simple majority vote in the Senate; amended 1992, 2007, 2011 (2016)

Legal system: civil law system with regional variations

International law organization participation: accepts compulsory ICJ jurisdiction with reservations; accepts ICCt jurisdiction

Citizenship: *citizenship by birth:* no
citizenship by descent only: at least one parent must be a citizen of Spain
dual citizenship recognized: only with select Latin American countries
residency requirement for naturalization: 10 years for persons with no ties to Spain

Suffrage: 18 years of age; universal

Executive branch: *chief of state:* King FELIPE VI (since 19 June 2014); Heir Apparent Princess LEONOR, Princess of Asturias, daughter of the monarch (born 31 October 2005)
head of government: President of the Government or Prime Minister Mariano RAJOY (since 20 December 2011); Vice President (and Minister of the President's Office) Soraya SAENZ DE SANTAMARIA (since 22 December 2011)
cabinet: Council of Ministers designated by the president
elections/appointments: the monarchy is hereditary; following legislative elections, the monarch usually proposes at president the leader of the party or coalition with the largest majority of seats, who is then indirectly elected by the Congress of Deputies; election last held on 26 June 2016 (next to be held in June 2020); vice president and Council of Ministers appointed by the president
election results: percent of National Assembly vote—NA
note: there is also a Council of State that is the supreme consultative organ of the government, but its recommendations are non-binding

Legislative branch: *description:* bicameral General Courts or Las Cortes Generales consists of the Senate or Senado (266 seats; 208 members directly elected in multi-seat constituencies by simple majority vote and 58 appointed by the regional legislatures; members serve 4-year terms) and the Congress of Deputies or Congreso de los

Diputados (350 seats; 348 members directly elected in 50 multi-seat constituencies by proportional representation vote and 2 directly elected from the North African Ceuta and Melilla enclaves by proportional representation vote; members serve 4-year terms or until the government is dissolved)
elections: Senate—last held on 26 June 2016 (next to be held no later than June 2020); Congress of Deputies—last held on 26 June 2016 (next to be held no later than June 2020)
election results: Senate—percent of vote by party—NA; seats by party—PP 149, PSOE 62, Podemos 20, ERC 12, EAJ/PNV 6, other 17; Congress of Deputies—percent of vote by party—PP 33.0%, PSOE 22.7%, Podemos 21.1%, C's 13.0%, ERC-CatSi 2.6%, EAJ/PNV 1.2%, other 6.4%; seats by party—PP 134, PSOE 84, Podemos 67, C's 32, ERC-CatSi 9, EAJ/PNV 5, other 19

Judicial branch: *highest court(s):* Supreme Court or Tribunal Supremo (consists of the court president and organized into the Civil Room with a president and 9 judges, the Penal Room with a president and 14 judges, the Administrative Room with a president and 32 judges, the Social Room with a president and 12 judges, and the Military Room with a president and 7 judges); Constitutional Court or Tribunal Constitucional de Espana (consists of 12 judges)
judge selection and term of office: Supreme Court judges appointed by the monarch from candidates proposed by the General Council of the Judiciary Power, a 20-member governing board chaired by the monarch that includes presidential appointees, and lawyers and jurists confirmed by the National Assembly; judges can serve until age 70; Constitutional Court judges nominated by the National Assembly, executive branch, and the General Council of the Judiciary, and appointed by the monarch for 9-year terms
subordinate courts: National High Court; High Courts of Justice (in each of the autonomous communities); provincial courts; courts of first instance

Political parties and leaders: Asturias Forum or FAC [Cristina COTO]
Basque Country Unite (Euskal Herria Bildu) or EH Bildu [Arnaldo OTEGI Mondragon] (coalition of 4 Basque pro-independence parties)
Basque Nationalist Party or PNV or EAJ [Andoni ORTUZAR]
Canarian Coalition or CC [Claudina MORALES Rodriguez] (coalition of 5 parties)
Canarian Nationalist Party or PNC [Juan Manuel GARCIA Ramos]
Catalan European Democratic Party or PDeCat [Artur MAS] (formerly Democratic Convergence of Catalonia)
Ciudadanos Party or C's [Albert RIVERA]
Compromis [Eric MORERA i Catala]
Galician Nationalist Bloc or BNG [Ana PONTON Mondelo]
Gomera Socialist Group or ASG [Casimiro CURBELO]
Initiative for Catalonia Greens or ICV [Joan HERRERA i Torres and Dolors CAMATS]

Unidos Podemos [Pablo IGLESIAS Turrion] (formerly Podemos IU; electoral coalition formed for May 2016 election)

Popular Party or PP [Mariano RAJOY Brey]

Republican Left of Catalonia or ERC [Oriol JUNQUERAS i Vies]

Spanish Socialist Workers Party or PSOE [Pedro SANCHEZ]

Union of People of Navarra or UPN [Javier ESPARZA]

Union, Progress and Democracy or UPyD [Cristiano BROWN]

United Left or IU [Alberto GARZON] (coalition includes Communist Party of Spain or PCE and other small parties; ran as Popular Unity or UP in 2016 election)

Yes to the Future or Geroa Bai [Uxue BARKOS] (coalition include 4 Navarran parties)

Political pressure groups and leaders: Association for Victims of Terrorism or AVT (grassroots organization devoted primarily to supporting victims of the Basque Fatherland and Liberty (ETA) terrorist organization)

Roman Catholic Church

Socialist General Union of Workers or UGT (includes the smaller independent Workers Syndical Union or USO)

Trade Union Confederation of Workers' Commissions or CC.OO.

Spanish Confederation of Employers' Organizations or CEOE

other: business and landowning interests; free labor unions (authorized in April 1977); university students

International organization participation: ADB (nonregional member), AfDB (nonregional member), Arctic Council (observer), Australia Group, BCIE, BIS, CAN (observer), CBSS (observer), CD, CE, CERN, EAPC, EBRD, ECB, EIB, EITI (implementing country), EMU, ESA, EU, FAO, FATF, IADB, IAEA, IBRD, ICAO, ICC (national committees), ICCt, ICRM, IDA, IEA, IFAD, IFC, IFRCS, IHO, ILO, IMF, IMO, IMSO, Interpol, IOC, IOM, IPU, ISO, ITSO, ITU, ITUC (NGOs), LAIA (observer), MIGA, NATO, NEA, NSG, OAS (observer), OECD, OPCW, OSCE, Pacific Alliance (observer), Paris Club, PCA, PIF (partner), Schengen Convention, SELEC (observer), SICA (observer), UN, UNCTAD, UNESCO, UNHCR, UNIDO, UNIFIL, Union Latina, UNOCI, UNRWA, UNWTO, UPU, WCO, WHO, WIPO, WMO, WTO, ZC

Diplomatic representation in the US: chief of mission: Ambassador Pedro MORENES Eulate (since 24 April 2017)

chancery: 2375 Pennsylvania Avenue NW, Washington, DC 20037

telephone: [1] (202) 452-0100, 728-2340

FAX: [1] (202) 833-5670

consulate(s) general: Boston, Chicago, Houston, Los Angeles, Miami, New York, San Francisco, San Juan (Puerto Rico)

consulate(s): Kansas City (MO)

Diplomatic representation from the US: *chief of mission:* Ambassador Richard BUCHAN (since December 2017) note—also accredited to Andorra

embassy: Serrano 75, 28006 Madrid

mailing address: PSC 61, APO AE 09642

telephone: [34] (91) 587-2200

FAX: [34] (91) 587-2303

consulate(s) general: Barcelona

Flag description: three horizontal bands of red (top), yellow (double width), and red with the national coat of arms on the hoist side of the yellow band; the coat of arms is quartered to display the emblems of the traditional kingdoms of Spain (clockwise from upper left, Castile, Leon, Navarre, and Aragon) while Granada is represented by the stylized pomegranate at the bottom of the shield; the arms are framed by two columns representing the Pillars of Hercules, which are the two promontories (Gibraltar and Ceuta) on either side of the eastern end of the Strait of Gibraltar; the red scroll across the two columns bears the imperial motto of "Plus Ultra" (further beyond) referring to Spanish lands beyond Europe; the triband arrangement with the center stripe twice the width of the outer dates to the 18th century

note: the red and yellow colors are related to those of the oldest Spanish kingdoms: Aragon, Castile, Leon, and Navarre

National symbol(s): Pillars of Hercules; national colors: red, yellow

National anthem: *name:* "Himno Nacional Espanol" (National Anthem of Spain)

lyrics/music: no lyrics/unknown

note: officially in use between 1770 and 1931, restored in 1939; the Spanish anthem is the first anthem to be officially adopted, but it has no lyrics; in the years prior to 1931 it became known as "Marcha Real" (The Royal March); it first appeared in a 1761 military bugle call book and was replaced by "Himno de Riego" in the years between 1931 and 1939; the long version of the anthem is used for the king, while the short version is used for the prince, prime minister, and occasions such as sporting events

ECONOMY

Economy—overview: After experiencing a prolonged recession in the wake of the global financial crisis that began in 2008, in 2017 Spain marked the fourth full year of positive economic growth in ten years, largely due to increased private consumption. At the onset of the financial crisis, Spain's GDP contracted by 3.7% in 2009, ending a 16-year growth trend, and continued contracting through most of 2013. In that year, the government successfully shored up struggling banks—exposed to the collapse of Spain's depressed real estate and construction sectors—and in January 2014 completed an EU-funded restructuring and recapitalization program for its financial sector.

Until 2014, credit contraction in the private sector, fiscal austerity, and high unemployment weighed on domestic consumption and investment. The unemployment rate rose from a low of about 8% in 2007 to more than 26% in 2013, but labor reforms prompted a modest reduction to 17% in 2017. High unemployment has strained Spain's public finances, as spending on social

benefits increased while tax revenues fell. Spain's budget deficit peaked at 11.4% of GDP in 2010, but Spain gradually reduced the deficit to about 3.3% of GDP in 2017. Public debt has increased substantially—from 60.1% of GDP in 2010 to nearly 96.7% in 2017.

Exports were resilient throughout the economic downturn and helped to bring Spain's current account into surplus in 2013 for the first time since 1986, where it remained through 2016. Rising labor productivity and an internal devaluation resulting from moderating labor costs and lower inflation have helped to improve foreign investor interest in the economy and positive FDI flows have been restored.

Political gridlock after the national elections in December 2015 and June 2016 and ensuing government formation process constrained the caretaker government's ability to implement needed labor, pension, health care, tax, and education reforms— in 2016. The European Commission criticized Spain's 2016 budget for easing austerity measures and for its alleged overly optimistic growth and deficit projections. Spain's borrowing costs are dramatically lower since their peak in mid-2012, and with the recent uptick in economic activity, inflation has reappeared, at 2% per year.

GDP (purchasing power parity): $1.769 trillion (2017 est.)

$1.716 trillion (2016 est.)

$1.662 trillion (2015 est.)

note: data are in 2017 dollars

country comparison to the world: 17

GDP (official exchange rate): $1.307 trillion (2016 est.)

GDP—real growth rate: 3.1% (2017 est.)

3.2% (2016 est.)

3.2% (2015 est.)

country comparison to the world: 109

GDP—per capita (PPP): $38,200 (2017 est.)

$37,000 (2016 est.)

$35,800 (2015 est.)

note: data are in 2017 dollars

country comparison to the world: 48

Gross national saving: 22.5% of GDP (2017 est.)

22.3% of GDP (2016 est.)

21.4% of GDP (2015 est.)

country comparison to the world: 71

GDP—composition, by end use:

household consumption: 57.3%

government consumption: 18.5%

investment in fixed capital: 19.8%

investment in inventories: 0.4%

exports of goods and services: 34.2%

imports of goods and services: -30.2% (2017 est.)

GDP—composition, by sector of origin:

agriculture: 2.6%

industry: 23.2%

services: 74.2% (2017 est.)

Agriculture—products: grain, vegetables, olives, wine grapes, sugar beets, citrus; beef, pork, poultry, dairy products; fish

Industries: textiles and apparel (including footwear), food and beverages, metals and metal manufactures, chemicals, shipbuilding, automobiles, machine tools, tourism, clay and refractory products, footwear, pharmaceuticals, medical equipment

Industrial production growth rate: 2.6% (2017 est.)
country comparison to the world: 108

Labor force: 22.75 million (2017 est.)
country comparison to the world: 28

Labor force—by occupation: *agriculture:* 4.2%
industry: 24%
services: 71.7% (2009)

Unemployment rate: 17.1% (2017 est.)
19.6% (2016 est.)
country comparison to the world: 178

Population below poverty line: 21.1% (2012 est.)

Household income or consumption by percentage share: *lowest 10%:* 2.5%
highest 10%: 24% (2011)

Distribution of family income—Gini index: 35.9 (2012)
32 (2005)
country comparison to the world: 90

Budget: *revenues:* $492.4 billion
expenditures: $535.9 billion (2017 est.)
Taxes and other revenues: 37.7% of GDP (2017 est.)
country comparison to the world: 46

Budget surplus (+) or deficit (-): -3.3% of GDP (2017 est.)
country comparison to the world: 123

Public debt: 96.7% of GDP (2017 est.)
99.4% of GDP (2016 est.)
country comparison to the world: 19

Fiscal year: calendar year

Inflation rate (consumer prices): 2% (2017 est.)
-0.2% (2016 est.)
country comparison to the world: 89

Central bank discount rate: 0.05% (10 September 2014)
0.25% (13 November 2013)
note: this is the European Central Bank's rate on the marginal lending facility, which offers overnight credit to banks in the euro area
country comparison to the world: 147

Commercial bank prime lending rate: 2.2% (31 December 2017 est.)
2.19% (31 December 2016 est.)
country comparison to the world: 176

Stock of narrow money: $1.082 trillion (31 December 2017 est.)
$841.6 billion (31 December 2016 est.)
note: see entry for the European Union for money supply for the entire euro area; the European Central Bank (ECB) controls monetary policy for the 18 members of the Economic and Monetary Union (EMU); individual members of the EMU do not control the quantity of money circulating within their own borders
country comparison to the world: 8

Stock of broad money: $1.337 trillion (31 December 2017 est.)
$1.189 trillion (31 December 2016 est.)

country comparison to the world: 15

Stock of domestic credit: $2.455 trillion (31 December 2017 est.)
$2.21 trillion (31 December 2016 est.)
country comparison to the world: 11

Market value of publicly traded shares: $787.2 billion (31 December 2015 est.)
$992.9 billion (31 December 2014 est.)
$1.117 trillion (31 December 2013 est.)
country comparison to the world: 15

Current account balance: $24.3 billion (2017 est.)
$23.76 billion (2016 est.)
country comparison to the world: 13

Exports: $301.5 billion (2017 est.)
$280.5 billion (2016 est.)
country comparison to the world: 20

Exports—commodities: machinery, motor vehicles; foodstuffs, pharmaceuticals, medicines, other consumer goods

Exports—partners: France 15.2%, Germany 11.4%, Italy 7.8%, UK 7.6%, Portugal 7%, US 4.4% (2016)

Imports: $333.4 billion (2017 est.)
$300.3 billion (2016 est.)
country comparison to the world: 15

Imports—commodities: machinery and equipment, fuels, chemicals, semi-finished goods, foodstuffs, consumer goods, measuring and medical control instruments

Imports—partners: Germany 14.7%, France 12%, China 7.1%, Italy 6.7%, Netherlands 5.2%, UK 4.4% (2016)

Reserves of foreign exchange and gold: $63.14 billion (31 December 2016 est.)
$63.14 billion (31 December 2016 est.)
country comparison to the world: 33

Debt—external: $2.094 trillion (31 March 2016 est.)
$1.963 trillion (31 March 2015 est.)
country comparison to the world: 11

Stock of direct foreign investment—at home: $772.1 billion (31 December 2017 est.)
$739.7 billion (31 December 2016 est.)
country comparison to the world: 15

Stock of direct foreign investment—abroad: $752.4 billion (31 December 2017 est.)
$696.9 billion (31 December 2016 est.)
country comparison to the world: 14

Exchange rates: euros (EUR) per US dollar—0.906 (2017 est.)
0.9214 (2016 est.)
0.9214 (2015 est.)
0.7525 (2014 est.)
0.7634 (2013 est.)

ENERGY

Electricity access: *electrification—total population:* 100% (2016)

Electricity—production: 267.1 billion kWh (2015 est.)
country comparison to the world: 16

Electricity—consumption: 240.4 billion kWh (2015 est.)
country comparison to the world: 17

Electricity—exports: 14.18 billion kWh (2016 est.)
country comparison to the world: 15

Electricity—imports: 21.85 billion kWh (2016 est.)
country comparison to the world: 10

Electricity—installed generating capacity: 106.7 million kW (2015 est.)
country comparison to the world: 12

Electricity—from fossil fuels: 45.1% of total installed capacity (2015 est.)
country comparison to the world: 159

Electricity—from nuclear fuels: 6.7% of total installed capacity (2015 est.)
country comparison to the world: 21

Electricity—from hydroelectric plants: 13.2% of total installed capacity (2015 est.)
country comparison to the world: 113

Electricity—from other renewable sources: 29.5% of total installed capacity (2015 est.)
country comparison to the world: 16

Crude oil—production: 2,667 bbl/day (2016 est.)
country comparison to the world: 86

Crude oil—exports: 0 bbl/day (2016 est.)
country comparison to the world: 192

Crude oil—imports: 1.285 million bbl/day (2016 est.)
country comparison to the world: 7

Crude oil—proved reserves: 150 million bbl (1 January 2017 es)
country comparison to the world: 65

Refined petroleum products—production: 1.342 million bbl/day (2016 est.)
country comparison to the world: 14

Refined petroleum products—consumption: 1.287 million bbl/day (2016 est.)
country comparison to the world: 18

Refined petroleum products—exports: 501,100 bbl/day (2016 est.)
country comparison to the world: 16

Refined petroleum products—imports: 421,000 bbl/day (2016 est.)
country comparison to the world: 20

Natural gas—production: 62 million cu m (2015 est.)
country comparison to the world: 85

Natural gas—consumption: 39.84 billion cu m (2015 est.)
country comparison to the world: 32

Natural gas—exports: 5.065 billion cu m (2015 est.)
country comparison to the world: 31

Natural gas—imports: 32.39 billion cu m (2015 est.)
country comparison to the world: 13

Natural gas—proved reserves: 2.548 billion cu m (1 January 2017 es)
country comparison to the world: 100

Carbon dioxide emissions from consumption of energy: 276 million Mt (2013 est.)
country comparison to the world: 24

COMMUNICATIONS

Telephones—fixed lines: *total subscriptions:* 19,557,141
subscriptions per 100 inhabitants: 40 (July 2016 est.)
country comparison to the world: 16

Telephones—mobile cellular: *total:* 51,943,202
subscriptions per 100 inhabitants: 107 (July 2016 est.)
country comparison to the world: 30

Telephone system: *general assessment:* well-developed, modern facilities
domestic: combined fixed-line and mobile-cellular teledensity exceeds 145 telephones per 100 persons
international: country code—34; submarine cables provide connectivity to Europe, Middle East, Asia, and US; satellite earth stations—2 Intelsat (1 Atlantic Ocean and 1 Indian Ocean), NA Eutelsat; tropospheric scatter to adjacent countries (2016)

Broadcast media: a mixture of both publicly operated and privately owned TV and radio stations; overall, hundreds of TV channels are available including national, regional, local, public, and international channels; satellite and cable TV systems available; multiple national radio networks, a large number of regional radio networks, and a larger number of local radio stations; overall, hundreds of radio stations (2008)

Internet country code: .es

Internet users: *total:* 39,123,384
percent of population: 80.6% (July 2016 est.)
country comparison to the world: 20

TRANSPORTATION

National air transport system: number of registered air carriers: 20
inventory of registered aircraft operated by air carriers: 414
annual passenger traffic on registered air carriers: 60,809,228
annual freight traffic on registered air carriers: 1,040,913,279 mt-km (2015)
Civil aircraft registration country code prefix: EC (2016)

Airports: 150 (2013)
country comparison to the world: 38

Airports—with paved runways: *total:* 99
over 3,047 m: 18
2,438 to 3,047 m: 14
1,524 to 2,437 m: 19
914 to 1,523 m: 24
under 914 m: 24 (2013)

Airports—with unpaved runways: *total:* 51
1,524 to 2,437 m: 2
914 to 1,523 m: 13
under 914 m: 36 (2013)

Heliports: 10 (2013)

Pipelines: gas 10,481 km; oil 616 km; refined products 3,461 km (2013)

Railways: *total:* 16,101.5 km
broad gauge: 11,873 km 1.668-m gauge (6,488 km electrified)
standard gauge: 2,312 km 1.435-m gauge (2,312 km electrified)
narrow gauge: 1,884.9 km 1.000-m gauge (807 km electrified); 28 km 0.914-m gauge (28 km electrified); 3.6 km 0.600-m gauge (2014)
country comparison to the world: 17

Roadways: *total:* 683,175 km
paved: 683,175 km (includes 16,205 km of expressways) (2011)
country comparison to the world: 11

Waterways: 1,000 km (2012)
country comparison to the world: 63

Merchant marine: *total:* 472
by type: bulk carrier 1, general cargo 44, oil tanker 28, other 399 (2017)
country comparison to the world: 40

Ports and terminals: *major seaport(s):* Algeciras, Barcelona, Bilbao, Cartagena, Huelva, Tarragona, Valencia (all in Spain); Las Palmas, Santa Cruz de Tenerife (in the Canary Islands)
container port(s) (TEUs): Algeciras (4,516,000), Barcelona (1,965,000), Valencia (4,615,000) (2015)
LNG terminal(s) (import): Barcelona, Bilbao, Cartagena, Huelva, Mugardos, Sagunto

MILITARY AND SECURITY

Military expenditures: 0.91% of GDP (2017)
1.21% of GDP (2016)
1.18% of GDP (2015)
1.23% of GDP (2014)
1.26% of GDP (2013)
1.41% of GDP (2012)
country comparison to the world: 110

Military branches: Spanish Armed Forces: Army (Ejercito de Tierra), Spanish Navy (Armada Espanola, AE, includes Marine Corps), Spanish Air Force (Ejercito del Aire Espanola, EdA) (2013)

Military service age and obligation: 18-26 years of age for voluntary military service by a Spanish citizen or legal immigrant, 2-3 year obligation; women allowed to serve in all SAF branches, including combat units; no conscription, but Spanish Government retains right to mobilize citizens 19-25 years of age in a national emergency; mandatory retirement of non-NCO enlisted personnel at age 45 or 58, depending on service length (2013)

TERRORISM

Terrorist groups—home based: Basque Fatherland and Liberty (ETA): aim(s): establish an independent Basque homeland based on Marxist principles in what is now northern Spain and southwestern France
area(s) of operation: headquartered in northern Spain, where the Spanish and French Governments collaborate to arrest members and demand

disarmament before engaging in negotiations; ETA has refrained from conducting attacks since its 20 October 2011 communique declaring a permanent cessation of violence, but had neither formally disbanded nor given up its weapons arsenal by early 2017; 279 members are currently in Spain's prisons, with an unknown number present in the country; on 14 January 2017, tens of thousands of supporters gathered in Bilbao in northern Spain at the annual ETA prisoner amnesty rally to demand at a minimum that members be released who have served their court-imposed sentences and for others to be transfered to jails close to their families; the group marked its 50th anniversary in 2009 with a series of high-profile and lethal car bombings, including the 29-30 July 2009 attacks on Civil Guard Barracks in Burgos and Calvia that killed two guards and injured more than 65 civilians; responsible for hundreds of deaths in Spain since its inception in 1959; outlawed in Spain

TRANSNATIONAL ISSUES

Disputes—international: in 2002, Gibraltar residents voted overwhelmingly by referendum to reject any "shared sovereignty" arrangement; the Government of Gibraltar insists on equal participation in talks between the UK and Spain; Spain disapproves of UK plans to grant Gibraltar greater autonomy; after voters in the UK chose to leave the EU in a June 2016 referendum, Spain again proposed shared sovereignty of Gibraltar; UK officials rejected Spain's joint sovereignty proposal; Morocco protests Spain's control over the coastal enclaves of Ceuta, Melilla, and the islands of Penon de Velez de la Gomera, Penon de Alhucemas, and Islas Chafarinas, and surrounding waters; both countries claim Isla Perejil (Leila Island); Morocco serves as the primary launching site of illegal migration into Spain from North Africa; Portugal does not recognize Spanish sovereignty over the territory of Olivenza based on a difference of interpretation of the 1815 Congress of Vienna and the 1801 Treaty of Badajoz
Refugees and internally displaced persons: refugees (country of origin): 8,205 (Afghanistan) (2016); 12,036 (Venezuela) (economic and political crisis) (2017); 8,100 (Ukraine) (2017); note: estimate represents asylum applicants since Ukraine crisis began in 2014 until September 2017
stateless persons: 1,011 (2016)
note: 64,272 estimated refugee and migrant arrivals (January 2015—February 2018); 28,349 migrant arrivals in 2017

Illicit drugs: despite rigorous law enforcement efforts, North African, Latin American, Galician, and other European traffickers take advantage of Spain's long coastline to land large shipments of cocaine and hashish for distribution to the European market; consumer for Latin American cocaine and North African hashish; destination and minor transshipment point for Southwest Asian heroin; money-laundering site for Colombian narcotics trafficking organizations and organized crime

SPRATLY ISLANDS

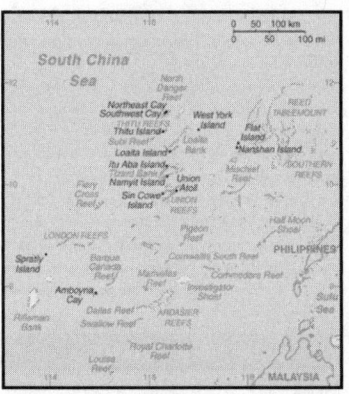

INTRODUCTION

Background: The Spratly Islands consist of more than 100 small islands or reefs surrounded by rich fishing grounds—and potentially by gas and oil deposits. They are claimed in their entirety by China, Taiwan, and Vietnam, while portions are claimed by Malaysia and the Philippines. About 45 islands are occupied by relatively small numbers of military forces from China, Malaysia, the Philippines, Taiwan, and Vietnam. Since 1985 Brunei has claimed a continental shelf that overlaps a southern reef but has not made any formal claim to the reef. Brunei claims an exclusive economic zone over this area.

GEOGRAPHY

Location: Southeastern Asia, group of reefs and islands in the South China Sea, about two-thirds of the way from southern Vietnam to the southern Philippines

Geographic coordinates: 8 38 N, 111 55 E

Map references: Southeast Asia

Area: *total:* less than 5 sq km
land: less than 5 sq km
water: 0 sq km
note: includes 100 or so islets, coral reefs, and sea mounts scattered over an area of nearly 410,000

sq km (158,000 sq mi) of the central South China Sea
country comparison to the world: 250

Area—comparative: land area is about seven times the size of the National Mall in Washington, DC
Land boundaries: 0 km

Coastline: 926 km

Maritime claims: NA

Climate: tropical

Terrain: small, flat islands, islets, cays, and reefs

Elevation: *mean elevation:* NA

elevation extremes: *lowest point:* South China Sea 0 m
highest point: unnamed location on Southwest Cay 6 m

Natural resources: fish, guano, undetermined oil and natural gas potential

Land use: *agricultural land:* 0%
arable land: 0%;
permanent crops: 0%;
permanent pasture: 0%
forest: 0%
other: 100% (2011 est.)

Natural hazards: typhoons; numerous reefs and shoals pose a serious maritime hazard

Environment—current issues: China's use of dredged sand and coral to build artificial islands harms reef systems; illegal fishing practices indiscriminately harvest endangered species, including sea turtles and giant clamsGeography—note: strategically located near several primary shipping lanes in the central South China Sea; includes numerous small islands, atolls, shoals, and coral reefs

PEOPLE AND SOCIETY

Population: no indigenous inhabitants
note: there are scattered garrisons occupied by military personnel of several claimant states

GOVERNMENT

Country name: *conventional long form:* none
conventional short form: Spratly Islands
etymology: named after a British whaling captain Richard SPRATLY, who sighted Spratly Island in

1843; the name of the island eventually passed to the entire archipelago

ECONOMY

Economy—overview: Economic activity is limited to commercial fishing. The proximity to nearby oil- and gas-producing sedimentary basins indicate potential oil and gas deposits, but the region is largely unexplored. No reliable estimates of potential reserves are available. Commercial exploitation has yet to be developed.

TRANSPORTATION

Airports: 4 (2013)
country comparison to the world: 189

Airports—with paved runways: *total:* 3
914 to 1,523 m: 2
under 914 m: 1 (2013)

Airports—with unpaved runways: *total:* 1
914 to 1,523 m: 1 (2013)

Heliports: 3 (2013)
Ports and terminals: none; offshore anchorage only

MILITARY AND SECURITY

Military—note: Spratly Islands consist of more than 100 small islands or reefs of which about 45 are claimed and occupied by China, Malaysia, the Philippines, Taiwan, and Vietnam

TRANSNATIONAL ISSUES

Disputes—international: all of the Spratly Islands are claimed by China (including Taiwan) and Vietnam; parts of them are claimed by Brunei, Malaysia and the Philippines; despite no public territorial claim to Louisa Reef, Brunei implicitly lays claim by including it within the natural prolongation of its continental shelf and basis for a seabed median with Vietnam; claimants in November 2002 signed the "Declaration on the Conduct of Parties in the South China Sea," which has eased tensions but falls short of a legally binding "code of conduct"; in March 2005, the national oil companies of China, the Philippines, and Vietnam signed a joint accord to conduct marine seismic activities in the Spratly Islands

SRI LANKA

INTRODUCTION

Background: The first Sinhalese arrived in Sri Lanka late in the 6th century B.C., probably from northern India. Buddhism was introduced circa 250 B.C., and the first kingdoms developed at the cities of Anuradhapura (from circa 200 B.C. to circa A.D. 1000) and Polonnaruwa (from about 1070 to 1200). In the 14th century, a south Indian dynasty established a Tamil kingdom in northern Sri Lanka. The Portuguese controlled the coastal areas of the island in the 16th century and the Dutch in the 17th century. The island was ceded to the British in 1796, became a crown colony in 1802, and was formally united under British rule by 1815. As Ceylon, it became independent in 1948; its name was changed to Sri Lanka in 1972. Prevailing tensions between the Sinhalese majority and Tamil separatists erupted into war in 1983. After two decades of fighting, the government and Liberation Tigers of Tamil Eelam (LTTE) formalized a cease-fire in February 2002 with Norway brokering peace negotiations. Both the LTTE and the government unofficially abrogated the cease-fire and violence between the LTTE and government forces intensified in 2006, but the government regained control of the Eastern Province in 2007. The government officially withdrew from the cease-fire agreement in January 2008 and by May 2009, the remnants of the LTTE had been defeated.

Since the end of the conflict, the government has enacted an ambitious program of economic development projects, many of which are financed by loans from the Government of China. In addition to efforts at reconstructing its economy, the government has resettled more than 95% of those civilians displaced during the final phase of the conflict and released the vast majority of former LTTE combatants captured by Government Security Forces. Slow progress continues on more contentious and politically difficult issues such as reaching a political settlement with Tamil elected

representatives and holding accountable those alleged to have been involved in human rights violations and other abuses during the conflict.

GEOGRAPHY

Location: Southern Asia, island in the Indian Ocean, south of India

Geographic coordinates: 7 00 N, 81 00 E

Map references: Asia

Area: *total:* 65,610 sq km
land: 64,630 sq km
water: 980 sq km
country comparison to the world: 123

Area—comparative: slightly larger than West Virginia
Land boundaries: 0 km

Coastline: 1,340 km

Maritime claims: *territorial sea:* 12 nm
contiguous zone: 24 nm
exclusive economic zone: 200 nm
continental shelf: 200 nm or to the edge of the continental margin

Climate: tropical monsoon; northeast monsoon (December to March); southwest monsoon (June to October)

Terrain: mostly low, flat to rolling plain; mountains in south-central interior

Elevation: *mean elevation:* 228 m

elevation extremes: *lowest point:* Indian Ocean 0 m
highest point: Pidurutalagala 2,524 m

Natural resources: limestone, graphite, mineral sands, gems, phosphates, clay, hydropower, arable land

Land use: *agricultural land:* 43.5%
arable land: 20.7%;
permanent crops: 15.8%;
permanent pasture: 7%
forest: 29.4%
other: 27.1% (2011 est.)
Irrigated land: 5,700 sq km (2012)

Population—distribution: the population is primarily concentrated within a broad wet zone in the southwest, urban centers along the eastern coast, and on the Jaffna Peninsula in the north

Natural hazards: occasional cyclones and tornadoes

Environment—current issues: deforestation; soil erosion; wildlife populations threatened by poaching and urbanization; coastal degradation from mining activities and increased pollution; freshwater resources being polluted by industrial wastes and sewage runoff; waste disposal; air pollution in Colombo

Environment—international agreements: *party to:* Biodiversity, Climate Change, Climate Change-Kyoto Protocol, Desertification, Endangered

Species, Environmental Modification, Hazardous Wastes, Law of the Sea, Ozone Layer Protection, Ship Pollution, Wetlands
signed, but not ratified: Marine Life Conservation Geography—note: strategic location near major Indian Ocean sea lanes; Adam's Bridge is a chain of limestone shoals between the southeastern coast of India and the northwestern coast of Sri Lanka; geological evidence suggests that this 50-km long bridge once connected India and Sri Lanka; ancient records seem to indicate that a foot passage was possible between the two land masses until the 15th century when the land bridge broke up in a cyclone

PEOPLE AND SOCIETY

Population: 22,409,381 (July 2017 est.)
country comparison to the world: 57

Nationality: *noun:* Sri Lankan(s)
adjective: Sri Lankan

Ethnic groups: Sinhalese 74.9%, Sri Lankan Tamil 11.2%, Sri Lankan Moors 9.2%, Indian Tamil 4.2%, other 0.5% (2012 est.)

Languages: Sinhala (official and national language) 74%, Tamil (official and national language) 18%, other 8%
note: English, spoken competently by about 10% of the population, is commonly used in government and is referred to as the link language in the constitution

Religions: Buddhist (official) 70.2%, Hindu 12.6%, Muslim 9.7%, Roman Catholic 6.1%, other Christian 1.3%, other 0.05% (2012 est.)

Age structure: *0-14 years:* 24.06% (male 2,750,004/female 2,642,606)
15-24 years: 14.63% (male 1,666,859/female 1,611,379)
25-54 years: 41.58% (male 4,571,200/female 4,747,119)
55-64 years: 10.06% (male 1,043,199/female 1,210,930)
65 years and over: 9.67% (male 917,014/female 1,249,071) (2017 est.)

Dependency ratios: *total dependency ratio:* 51.2
youth dependency ratio: 37.2
elderly dependency ratio: 14.1
potential support ratio: 7.1 (2015 est.)

Median age: *total:* 32.8 years
male: 31.5 years
female: 34 years (2017 est.)
country comparison to the world: 95

Population growth rate: 0.76% (2017 est.)
country comparison to the world: 137

Birth rate: 15.2 births/1,000 population (2017 est.)
country comparison to the world: 126

Death rate: 6.2 deaths/1,000 population (2017 est.)
country comparison to the world: 153

Net migration rate: -1.3 migrant(s)/1,000 population (2017 est.)
country comparison to the world: 145

Population distribution: the population is primarily concentrated within a broad wet zone in the southwest, urban centers along the eastern coast, and on the Jaffna Peninsula in the north

Urbanization: *urban population:* 18.5% of total population (2017)
rate of urbanization: 1.11% annual rate of change (2015-20 est.)

Major urban areas—population: Sri Jayewardenepura Kotte (legislative capital) 128,000 (2014); COLOMBO (capital) 707,000 (2015)

Sex ratio: *at birth:* 1.04 male(s)/female
0-14 years: 1.04 male(s)/female
15-24 years: 1.03 male(s)/female
25-54 years: 0.96 male(s)/female
55-64 years: 0.86 male(s)/female
65 years and over: 0.74 male(s)/female
total population: 0.96 male(s)/female (2016 est.)

Mother's mean age at first birth: 25.4 years
note: median age at first birth among women 30-34 (2006/07 est.)

Maternal mortality ratio: 30 deaths/100,000 live births (2015 est.)
country comparison to the world: 114

Infant mortality rate: *total:* 8.4 deaths/1,000 live births
male: 9.3 deaths/1,000 live births
female: 7.4 deaths/1,000 live births (2017 est.)
country comparison to the world: 150

Life expectancy at birth: *total population:* 76.9 years
male: 73.5 years
female: 80.6 years (2017 est.)
country comparison to the world: 82

Total fertility rate: 2.07 children born/woman (2017 est.)
country comparison to the world: 111

Health expenditures: 3.5% of GDP (2014)
country comparison to the world: 173

Physicians density: 0.73 physicians/1,000 population (2010)

Hospital bed density: 3.6 beds/1,000 population (2012)

Drinking water source:
improved:
urban: 98.5% of population
rural: 95% of population
total: 95.6% of population
unimproved:
urban: 1.5% of population
rural: 5% of population
total: 4.4% of population (2015 est.)

Sanitation facility access:
improved:
urban: 88.1% of population
rural: 96.7% of population
total: 95.1% of population
unimproved:
urban: 11.9% of population
rural: 3.3% of population

total: 4.9% of population (2015 est.)

HIV/AIDS—adult prevalence rate: <.1% (2016 est.)

HIV/AIDS—people living with HIV/AIDS: 4,000 (2016 est.)
country comparison to the world: 108

HIV/AIDS—deaths: <200 (2016 est.)

Major infectious diseases: *degree of risk:* high
food or waterborne diseases: bacterial diarrhea and hepatitis A
vectorborne disease: dengue fever
water contact disease: leptospirosis
animal contact disease: rabies (2016)

Obesity—adult prevalence rate: 5.2% (2016)
country comparison to the world: 182

Children under the age of 5 years underweight: 26.3% (2012)
country comparison to the world: 23

Education expenditures: 2.2% of GDP (2015)
country comparison to the world: 168

Literacy: *definition:* age 15 and over can read and write
total population: 92.6%
male: 93.6%
female: 91.7% (2015 est.)

School life expectancy (primary to tertiary education): *total:* 14 years
male: 14 years
female: 14 years (2013)

Unemployment, youth ages 15-24: *total:* 20.7%
male: 16.5%
female: 27.3% (2015 est.)
country comparison to the world: 69

GOVERNMENT

Country name: *conventional long form:* Democratic Socialist Republic of Sri Lanka
conventional short form: Sri Lanka
local long form: Shri Lanka Prajatantrika Samajavadi Janarajaya/Ilankai Jananayaka Choshalichak Kutiyarachu
local short form: Shri Lanka/Ilankai
former: Serendib, Ceylon
etymology: the name means "resplendent island" in Sanskrit

Government type: presidential republic

Capital: *name:* Colombo (commercial capital); Sri Jayewardenepura Kotte (administrative capital)
geographic coordinates: 6 55 N, 79 50 E
time difference: UTC+5.5 (10.5 hours ahead of Washington, DC, during Standard Time)

Administrative divisions: 9 provinces; Central, Eastern, North Central, Northern, North Western, Sabaragamuwa, Southern, Uva, Western

Independence: 4 February 1948 (from the UK)

National holiday: Independence Day (National Day), 4 February (1948)

Constitution: *history:* several previous; latest adopted 16 August 1978, certified 31 August 1978
amendments: proposed by Parliament; passage requires at least two-thirds majority vote of its

total membership, certification by the president of the republic or the Parliament speaker, and approval in a referendum by an absolute majority of valid votes; amended many times, last in 2015; note—in September 2017, the Steering Committee of the Constitutional Assembly released its interim report on constitutional reforms (2017)

Legal system: mixed legal system of Roman-Dutch civil law, English common law, and Jaffna Tamil customary law

International law organization participation: has not submitted an ICJ jurisdiction declaration; non-party state to the ICCt

Citizenship: *citizenship by birth:* no
citizenship by descent only: at least one parent must be a citizen of Sri Lanka
dual citizenship recognized: no, except in cases where the government rules it is to the benefit of Sri Lanka
residency requirement for naturalization: 7 years

Suffrage: 18 years of age; universal

Executive branch: *chief of state:* President Maithripala SIRISENA (since 9 January 2015); note—the president is both chief of state and head of government; Ranil WICKREMESINGHE (since 9 January 2015) holds the title of prime minister
head of government: President Maithripala SIRISENA (since 9 January 2015)
cabinet: Cabinet appointed by the president in consultation with the prime minister
elections/appointments: president directly elected by preferential majority popular vote for a 5-year term (eligible for a second term); election last held on 8 January 2015 (next to be held by January 2020); note—the January 2015 election was held nearly 2 years ahead of schedule
election results: Maithripala SIRISENA elected president; percent of vote—Maithripala SIRISENA (SLFP) 51.3%, Mahinda RAJAPAKSA (SLFP) 47.6%, other 1.1%

Legislative branch: *description:* unicameral Parliament (225 seats; 196 members directly elected in multi-seat constituencies by proportional representation vote using a preferential method in which voters select 3 candidates in order of preference; remaining 29 seats allocated to other political parties and groups in proportion to share of national vote; members serve 5-year terms)
elections: last held on 17 August 2015 following President SIRISENA's dissolution of Parliament in late June 2015 in an effort to consolidate power and pass reforms (next to be held in 2020)
election results: percent of vote by coalition/party—EYJP 45.7%, UPFA 42.4%, JVP 4.9%, TNA 4.6%, SLMC 0.4%, EPDP 0.3% other 1.7%; seats by coalition/party EYJP 106, UPFA 95, TNA 16, JVP 6, SLMC 1, EPDP 1

Judicial branch: *highest court(s):* Supreme Court of the Republic (consists of the chief justice and 9 justices); note—the court has exclusive jurisdiction to review legislation
judge selection and term of office: chief justice nominated by the Constitutional Council (CC), a

9-member high-level advisory body, and appointed by the president; other justices nominated by the CC and appointed by the president on the advice of the chief justice; all justices can serve until age 65

subordinate courts: Court of Appeals; High Courts; Magistrates' Courts; municipal and primary courts

Political parties and leaders: Eelam People's Democratic Party or EPDP [Douglas DEVANANDA] Janatha Vimukthi Peramuna or JVP [Anura Kumara DISSANAYAKE] Jathika Hela Urumaya or JHU [Karunarathna PARANAWITHANA and Ven Hadigalle WIMALASARA THERO] New Democratic Front or NDF [Shalila MOONESINGHE] Sri Lanka Freedom Party or SLFP [Maithripala SIRISENA] Sri Lanka Muslim Congress or SLMC [Rauff HAKEEM] Tamil National Alliance or TNA [Rajavarothiam SAMPANTHAN] (alliance includes Eelam People's Revolutionary Liberation Front [Suresh PREMACHANDRAN], Illankai Tamil Arasu Kachchi Mavai SENATHIRAJAH], People's Liberation Organisation of Tamil Eelam [D. SIDDARTHAN], Tamil Eelam Liberation Organization Selvam ADAIKALANATHAN]) United National Front for Good Governance or EYJP [Ranil WICKREMESINGHE] (coalition includes JHU, UNP) United National Party or UNP [Ranil WICKREMESINGHE] United People's Freedom Alliance or UPFA [Maithripala SIRISENA] (coalition includes SLFP)

Political pressure groups and leaders: Buddhist clergy
Sinhalese Buddhist lay groups
diaspora groups
other: labor unions; hardline nationalist Sinhalese groups, such as the National Movement Against Terrorism

International organization participation: ABEDA, ADB, ARF, BIMSTEC, C, CD, CICA (observer), CP, FAO, G-11, G-15, G-24, G-77, IAEA, IBRD, ICAO, ICC (national committees), ICRM, IDA, IFAD, IFC, IFRCS, IHO, ILO, IMF, IMO, IMSO, Interpol, IOC, IOM, IPU, ISO, ITSO, ITU, ITUC (NGOs), MIGA, MINURSO, MINUSTAH, MONUSCO, NAM, OAS (observer), OPCW, PCA, SAARC, SACEP, SCO (dialogue member), UN, UNCTAD, UNESCO, UNIDO, UNIFIL, UNISFA, UNMISS, UNWTO, UPU, WCO, WFTU (NGOs), WHO, WIPO, WMO, WTO

Diplomatic representation in the US: chief of mission: Ambassador Prasad KARIYAWASAM (since 14 July 2014)
chancery: 3025 Whitehaven Street NW, Washington, DC 20008
telephone: [1] (202) 483-4025 through 4028
FAX: [1] (202) 232-7181
consulate(s) general: Los Angeles, New York

Diplomatic representation from the US: *chief of mission:* Ambassador Atul KESHAP (since 21 August 2015); note—also accredited to Maldives
embassy: 210 Galle Road, Colombo 3
mailing address: P. O. Box 106, Colombo
telephone: [94] (11) 249-8500
FAX: [94] (11) 243-7345

Flag description: yellow with two panels; the smaller hoist-side panel has two equal vertical bands of green (hoist side) and orange; the other larger panel depicts a yellow lion holding a sword on a maroon rectangular field that also displays a yellow bo leaf in each corner; the yellow field appears as a border around the entire flag and extends between the two panels; the lion represents Sinhalese ethnicity, the strength of the nation, and bravery; the sword demonstrates the sovereignty of the nation; the four bo leaves—symbolizing Buddhism and its influence on the country—stand for the four virtues of kindness, friendliness, happiness, and equanimity; orange signifies Sri Lankan Tamils, green Sri Lankan Moors, and maroon the Sinhalese majority; yellow denotes other ethnic groups; also referred to as the Lion Flag

National symbol(s): lion, water lily; national colors: maroon, yellow

National anthem: *name:* "Sri Lanka Matha" (Mother Sri Lanka)
lyrics/music: Ananda SAMARKONE
note: adopted 1951

ECONOMY

Economy—overview: Sri Lanka is attempting to sustain economic growth while maintaining macroeconomic stability under its IMF program that it began in 2016. The government's high debt payments and bloated civil service cadre, which have contributed to historically high budget deficits and low tax revenues, remain a concern. Government debt is about 75% of GDP and remains among the highest of the emerging markets. Sri Lanka will need to balance its elevated debt repayment schedule with its requirement to maintain adequate foreign exchange reserve levels in the coming years.

In May 2016, Sri Lanka regained its preferential trade preferences under the European Union's Generalized System of Preferences Plus (GSP+), enabling many of its firms to export products, including it top export garments, tax free to the EU. Also in 2016, the government reformed elements of the country's tax regime to increase some tax rates and broaden the tax net in response to recommendations made under its IMF program. Tourism has experienced strong growth during recent years following the resolution of the government's 26-year conflict with the Liberation Tigers of Tamil Eelam. The government has been pursuing large-scale reconstruction and development projects in its efforts to spur growth.

GDP (purchasing power parity): $278.2 billion (2017 est.)
$265.6 billion (2016 est.)
$254.5 billion (2015 est.)
note: data are in 2017 dollars

country comparison to the world: 62

GDP (official exchange rate): $83.57 billion (2016 est.)

GDP—real growth rate: 4.7% (2017 est.)
4.4% (2016 est.)
4.8% (2015 est.)
country comparison to the world: 46

GDP—per capita (PPP): $13,000 (2017 est.)
$12,500 (2016 est.)
$12,100 (2015 est.)
note: data are in 2017 dollars
country comparison to the world: 121

Gross national saving: 29.3% of GDP (2017 est.)
29% of GDP (2016 est.)
26.1% of GDP (2015 est.)
country comparison to the world: 28

GDP—composition, by end use:
household consumption: 67.9%
government consumption: 8.6%
investment in fixed capital: 28.9%
investment in inventories: 3.3%
exports of goods and services: 21.3%
imports of goods and services: -30% (2017 est.)

GDP—composition, by sector of origin:
agriculture: 7.8%
industry: 30.5%
services: 61.7% (2017 est.)

Agriculture—products: rice, sugarcane, grains, pulses, oilseed, spices, vegetables, fruit, tea, rubber, coconuts; milk, eggs, hides, beef; fish

Industries: processing of rubber, tea, coconuts, tobacco and other agricultural commodities; telecommunications, insurance, banking; tourism, shipping; clothing, textiles; cement, petroleum refining, information technology services, construction

Industrial production growth rate: 5.4% (2017 est.)
country comparison to the world: 38

Labor force: 8.937 million (2017 est.)
country comparison to the world: 56

Labor force—by occupation: *agriculture:* 28.4%
industry: 25.7%
services: 45.9% (30 Jun 2015)

Unemployment rate: 4% (2017 est.)
4% (2016 est.)
country comparison to the world: 50

Population below poverty line: 6.7% (2012 est.)

Household income or consumption by percentage share: *lowest 10%:* 1.6%
highest 10%: 39.5% (2009)

Distribution of family income—Gini index: 49 (2010)
46 (1995)
country comparison to the world: 20

Budget: *revenues:* $12.64 billion
expenditures: $16.66 billion (2017 est.)
Taxes and other revenues: 15.1% of GDP (2017 est.)
country comparison to the world: 187

Budget surplus (+) or deficit (-): -4.8% of GDP (2017 est.)
country comparison to the world: 157

Public debt: 79.6% of GDP (2017 est.)
79.3% of GDP (2016 est.)
note: covers central government debt, and excludes debt instruments directly owned by government entities other than the treasury (e.g. commercial bank borrowings of a government corporation); the data includes treasury debt held by foreign entities as well as intra-governmental debt; intra-governmental debt consists of treasury borrowings from surpluses in the social funds, such as for retirement; sub-national entities are usually not permitted to sell debt instruments
country comparison to the world: 39

Fiscal year: calendar year

Inflation rate (consumer prices): 6% (2017 est.)
4% (2016 est.)
country comparison to the world: 185

Central bank discount rate: 7% (30 September 2016)
6% (31 December 2015)
country comparison to the world: 50

Commercial bank prime lending rate: 11.8% (31 December 2017 est.)
10.49% (31 December 2016 est.)
country comparison to the world: 68

Stock of narrow money: $5.213 billion (31 December 2017 est.)
$5.184 billion (31 December 2016 est.)
country comparison to the world: 104

Stock of broad money: $36.83 billion (31 December 2017 est.)
$32.2 billion (31 December 2016 est.)
country comparison to the world: 76

Stock of domestic credit: $51.72 billion (31 December 2017 est.)
$46.21 billion (31 December 2016 est.)
country comparison to the world: 68

Market value of publicly traded shares: $20.8 billion (31 December 2015 est.)
$23.67 billion (31 December 2014 est.)
$18.81 billion (31 December 2013 est.)
country comparison to the world: 65

Current account balance: -$2.094 billion (2017 est.)
-$1.942 billion (2016 est.)
country comparison to the world: 158

Exports: $10.93 billion (2017 est.)
$10.31 billion (2016 est.)
country comparison to the world: 86

Exports—commodities: textiles and apparel, tea and spices; rubber manufactures; precious stones; coconut products, fish

Exports—partners: US 27.3%, UK 10.2%, India 5%, Germany 5%, Italy 4% (2016)

Imports: $21.14 billion (2017 est.)
$19.4 billion (2016 est.)
country comparison to the world: 73

Imports—commodities: petroleum, textiles, machinery and transportation equipment, building materials, mineral products, foodstuffs

Imports—partners: China 22%, India 20%, UAE 6.1%, Singapore 5.9%, Japan 5.4% (2016)

Reserves of foreign exchange and gold: $6.632 billion (31 December 2017 est.)
$6.019 billion (31 December 2016 est.)
country comparison to the world: 86

Debt—external: $47.8 billion (31 December 2017 est.)
$45.26 billion (31 December 2016 est.)
country comparison to the world: 65

Stock of direct foreign investment—at home: $NA

Stock of direct foreign investment—abroad: $NA

Exchange rates: Sri Lankan rupees (LKR) per US dollar—
154.1 (2017 est.)
145.58 (2016 est.)
145.58 (2015 est.)
135.86 (2014 est.)
130.57 (2013 est.)

ENERGY

Electricity access: population without electricity: 1,334,100
electrification—total population: 94%
electrification—urban areas: 99%
electrification—rural areas: 93% (2013)

Electricity—production: 12.64 billion kWh (2015 est.)
country comparison to the world: 92

Electricity—consumption: 11.72 billion kWh (2015 est.)
country comparison to the world: 87

Electricity—exports: 0 kWh (2016 est.)
country comparison to the world: 118

Electricity—imports: 0 kWh (2016 est.)
country comparison to the world: 132

Electricity—installed generating capacity: 4.056 million kW (2015 est.)
country comparison to the world: 88

Electricity—from fossil fuels: 55.3% of total installed capacity (2015 est.)
country comparison to the world: 141

Electricity—from nuclear fuels: 0% of total installed capacity (2015 est.)
country comparison to the world: 63

Electricity—from hydroelectric plants: 41.1% of total installed capacity (2015 est.)
country comparison to the world: 48

Electricity—from other renewable sources: 3.6% of total installed capacity (2015 est.)
country comparison to the world: 107

Crude oil—production: 0 bbl/day (2016 est.)
country comparison to the world: 201

Crude oil—exports: 0 bbl/day (2014 est.)
country comparison to the world: 104

Crude oil—imports: 36,480 bbl/day (2014 est.)
country comparison to the world: 58

Crude oil—proved reserves: 0 bbl (1 January 2017 es)
country comparison to the world: 200

Refined petroleum products—production: 35,650 bbl/day (2014 est.)

country comparison to the world: 85

Refined petroleum products—consumption: 103,000 bbl/day (2015 est.)
country comparison to the world: 80

Refined petroleum products—exports: 472.9 bbl/day (2014 est.)
country comparison to the world: 112

Refined petroleum products—imports: 60,840 bbl/day (2014 est.)
country comparison to the world: 74

Natural gas—production: 0 cu m (2013 est.)
country comparison to the world: 119

Natural gas—consumption: 0 cu m (2013 est.)
country comparison to the world: 167

Natural gas—exports: 0 cu m (2013 est.)
country comparison to the world: 81

Natural gas—imports: 0 cu m (2013 est.)
country comparison to the world: 104

Natural gas—proved reserves: 0 cu m (1 January 2014 es)
country comparison to the world: 125

Carbon dioxide emissions from consumption of energy: 16 million Mt (2013 est.)
country comparison to the world: 88

COMMUNICATIONS

lines: *total subscriptions:* 2,479,802
subscriptions per 100 inhabitants: 11 (July 2016 est.)
country comparison to the world: 52

Telephones—mobile cellular: *total:* 25,797,199
subscriptions per 100 inhabitants: 116 (July 2016 est.)
country comparison to the world: 55

Telephone system: *general assessment:* telephone services have improved significantly and are available in most parts of the country
domestic: national trunk network consists mostly of digital microwave radio relay; fiber-optic links now in use in Colombo area and fixed wireless local loops have been installed; competition is strong in mobile cellular systems and mobile cellular subscribership is increasing
international: country code—94; the SEA-ME-WE-3 and SEA-ME-WE-4 submarine cables provide connectivity to Asia, Australia, Middle East, Europe, US; satellite earth stations—2 Intelsat (Indian Ocean) (2016)

Broadcast media: government operates 5 TV channels and 19 radio channels; multi-channel satellite and cable TV subscription services available; 25 private TV stations and about 43 radio stations; 6 non-profit TV stations and 4 radio stations (2017)

Internet country code: .lk

Internet users: *total:* 7,126,540
percent of population: 32.1% (July 2016 est.)
country comparison to the world: 74

TRANSPORTATION

National air transport system: number of registered air carriers: 3

inventory of registered aircraft operated by air carriers: 25
annual passenger traffic on registered air carriers: 4,911,730
annual freight traffic on registered air carriers: 381,381,300 mt-km (2015)
Civil aircraft registration country code prefix: 4R (2016)

Airports: 19 (2013)
country comparison to the world: 137

Airports—with paved runways: *total:* 15
over 3,047 m: 2
1,524 to 2,437 m: 6
914 to 1,523 m: 7 (2013)

Airports—with unpaved runways: *total:* 4
914 to 1,523 m: 1
under 914 m: 3 (2013)

Heliports: 1 (2013)

Railways: *total:* 1,447 km
broad gauge: 1,447 km 1.676-m gauge (2014)
country comparison to the world: 80

Roadways: *total:* 114,093 km
paved: 16,977 km
unpaved: 97,116 km (2010)
country comparison to the world: 42

Waterways: 160 km (primarily on rivers in southwest) (2012)
country comparison to the world: 100

Merchant marine: *total:* 82
by type: bulk carrier 8, container ship 1, general cargo 9, oil tanker 10, other 54 (2017)
country comparison to the world: 94
Ports and terminals: major seaport(s): Colombo
container port(s) (TEUs): Colombo (3,651,963)

MILITARY AND SECURITY

Military expenditures: 2.44% of GDP (2016)
2.55% of GDP (2015)
2.41% of GDP (2014)
2.15% of GDP (2013)

2.16% of GDP (2012)
country comparison to the world: 29

Military branches: Sri Lanka Army, Sri Lanka Navy (includes Marine Corps), Sri Lanka Air Force, Sri Lanka Coast Guard (2016)

Military service age and obligation: 18-22 years of age for voluntary military service; no conscription; 5-year service obligation (Air Force) (2012)

TERRORISM

Terrorist groups—home based: Liberation Tigers of Tamil Eelam (LTTE): aim(s): revive the movement to establish a Tamil homeland
area(s) of operation: sustains efforts primarily in the east to revive the movement and, occasionally, to plot attacks; despite LTTE's military defeat at the hands of the Sri Lankan Government in 2009, LTTE remains capable of raising funds, mostly from the global Tamil diaspora; members remain operational, such as the LTTE operatives who were arrested in India in 2014 for plotting imminent attacks; authorities continue in 2017 to pursue leaders, operatives, and supporters for arrest; prior to its 2009 defeat, LTTE employed an integrated battlefield insurgent strategy targeting Sri Lanka's key installations and senior political and military leaders; since LTTE began its armed campaign in Sri Lanka in 1983, clashes between government forces and LTTE have resulted in an estimated 300,000 internally displaced persons, a million Tamils leaving the country, and 100,000 deaths, including an estimated 200 Tamil political leaders that LTTE has assassinated over the years

TRANSNATIONAL ISSUES

Disputes—international: none
Refugees and internally displaced persons: IDPs: 44,000 (civil war; more than half displaced prior to 2008; many of the more than 480,000 IDPs registered as returnees have not reached durable solutions) (2016)

Trafficking in persons: current situation: Sri Lanka is primarily a source and, to a lesser extent, a destination country for men, women, and children subjected to forced labor and sex trafficking; some Sri Lankan adults and children who migrate willingly to the Middle East, Southeast Asia, and Afghanistan to work in the construction, garment, and domestic service sectors are subsequently subjected to forced labor or debt bondage (incurred through high recruitment fees or money advances); some Sri Lankan women are forced into prostitution in Jordan, Maldives, Malaysia, Singapore, and other countries; within Sri Lanka, women and children are subjected to sex trafficking, and children are also forced to beg and work in the agriculture, fireworks, and fish-drying industries; a small number of women from Asia, Central Asia, Europe, and the Middle East have been forced into prostitution in Sri Lanka in recent years

tier rating: Tier 2 Watch List—Sri Lanka does not fully comply with the minimum standards for the elimination of trafficking; however, it is making significant efforts to do so; in 2014, Sri Lanka was granted a waiver from an otherwise required downgrade to Tier 3 because its government has a written plan that, if implemented, would constitute making significant efforts to bring itself into compliance with the minimum standards for the elimination of trafficking; law enforcement continues to demonstrate a lack of understanding of trafficking crimes and inadequate investigations, relying on trafficking cases to be prosecuted under the procurement statute rather than the trafficking statute, which carries more stringent penalties; authorities convicted only one offender under the procurement statute, a decrease from 2013; the government approved guidelines for the identification of victims and their referral to protective services but failed to ensure that victims were not jailed and charged for crimes committed as a direct result of being trafficked; no government employees were investigated or prosecuted, despite allegations of complicity (2015)

SUDAN

INTRODUCTION

Background: Military regimes favoring Islamic-oriented governments have dominated national politics since independence from Anglo-Egyptian co-rule in 1956. Sudan was embroiled in two prolonged civil wars during most of the remainder of the 20th century. These conflicts were rooted in northern economic, political, and social domination of largely non-Muslim, non-Arab southern Sudanese. The first civil war ended in 1972 but another broke out in 1983. Peace talks gained momentum in 2002-04 with the signing of several accords. The final North/South Comprehensive Peace Agreement (CPA), signed in January 2005, granted the southern rebels autonomy for six years

followed by a referendum on independence for Southern Sudan. The referendum was held in January 2011 and indicated overwhelming support for independence. South Sudan became independent on 9 July 2011. Sudan and South Sudan have yet to fully implement security and economic agreements signed in September 2012 relating to the normalization of relations between the two countries. The final disposition of the contested Abyei region has also to be decided.

Following South Sudan's independence, conflict broke out between the government and the Sudan People's Liberation Movement-North in Southern Kordofan and Blue Nile states (together known as the Two Areas), and has resulted in 1.1 million internally displaced persons or severely affected persons needing humanitarian assistance. A separate conflict broke out in the western region of Darfur in 2003, displacing nearly 2 million people and causing thousands of deaths. Fighting in both the Two Areas and Darfur between government forces and opposition has largely subsided, however the civilian populations are affected by low-level violence including inter-tribal conflict and banditry, largely a result of weak rule of law. The UN and the African Union have jointly commanded a Darfur peacekeeping operation (UNAMID) since 2007. Peacekeeping troops have struggled to address insecurity in Darfur and have increasingly become targets for attacks by armed groups. Sudan also has faced refugee influxes from neighboring countries, primarily Ethiopia, Eritrea, Chad, Central African Republic, and South Sudan. Armed conflict, poor transport infrastructure, and denial of access by both the government and armed opposition have impeded the provision of humanitarian assistance to affected populations.

GEOGRAPHY

Location: north-eastern Africa, bordering the Red Sea, between Egypt and Eritrea

Geographic coordinates: 15 00 N, 30 00 E

Map references: Africa

Area: *total:* 1,861,484 sq km
land: NA
water: NA
country comparison to the world: 17

Area—comparative: slightly less than one-fifth the size of the US
Land boundaries: total: 6,819 km

border countries (7): Central African Republic 174 km, Chad 1,403 km, Egypt 1,276 km, Eritrea 682 km, Ethiopia 744 km, Libya 382 km, South Sudan 2,158 km
note: Sudan-South Sudan boundary represents 1 January 1956 alignment; final alignment pending negotiations and demarcation; final sovereignty status of Abyei region pending negotiations between Sudan and South Sudan

Coastline: 853 km

Maritime claims: *territorial sea:* 12 nm
contiguous zone: 18 nm
continental shelf: 200-m depth or to the depth of exploitation

Climate: hot and dry; arid desert; rainy season varies by region (April to November)

Terrain: generally flat, featureless plain; desert dominates the north

Elevation: *mean elevation:* 568 m

elevation extremes: *lowest point:* Red Sea 0 m
highest point: Jabal Marrah 3,042 m

Natural resources: petroleum; small reserves of iron ore, copper, chromium ore, zinc, tungsten, mica, silver, gold; hydropower

Land use: *agricultural land:* 100%
arable land: 15.7%;
permanent crops: 0.2%;
permanent pasture: 84.2%

forest: 0%
other: 0% (2011 est.)
Irrigated land: 18,900 sq km (2012)

Population—distribution: with the exception of a ribbon of settlement that corresponds to the banks of the Nile, northern Sudan, which extends into the dry Sahara, is sparsely populated; more abundant vegetation and broader access to water increases population distribution in the south extending habitable range along nearly the entire border with South Sudan; sizeable areas of population are found around Khartoum, southeast between the Blue and White Nile Rivers, and throughout South Darfur

Natural hazards: dust storms and periodic persistent droughts

Environment—current issues: inadequate supplies of potable water; wildlife populations threatened by excessive hunting; soil erosion; desertification; periodic drought

Environment—international agreements: *party to:* Biodiversity, Climate Change, Climate Change-Kyoto Protocol, Desertification, Endangered Species, Hazardous Wastes, Law of the Sea, Ozone Layer Protection, Wetlands
signed, but not ratified: none of the selected agreementsGeography—note: the Nile is Sudan's primary water source; its major tributaries, the White Nile and the Blue Nile, meet at Khartoum to form the River Nile which flows northward through Egypt to the Mediterranean Sea

PEOPLE AND SOCIETY

Population: 37,345,935 (July 2017 est.)
country comparison to the world: 37

Nationality: *noun:* Sudanese (singular and plural)
adjective: Sudanese

Ethnic groups: Sudanese Arab (approximately 70%), Fur, Beja, Nuba, Fallata

Languages: Arabic (official), English (official), Nubian, Ta Bedawie, Fur

Religions: Sunni Muslim, small Christian minority

Age structure: *0-14 years:* 38.68% (male 7,335,613/female 7,111,552)
15-24 years: 21.04% (male 4,033,787/female 3,823,098)
25-54 years: 32.77% (male 5,943,906/female 6,293,921)
55-64 years: 4.24% (male 824,577/female 760,014)
65 years and over: 3.27% (male 655,795/female 563,672) (2017 est.)

Dependency ratios: *total dependency ratio:* 81.6
youth dependency ratio: 75.4
elderly dependency ratio: 6.3
potential support ratio: 15.9 (2015 est.)

Median age: *total:* 19.9 years
male: 19.7 years
female: 20.1 years (2017 est.)
country comparison to the world: 197

Population growth rate: 1.64% (2017 est.)
country comparison to the world: 65

Birth rate: 27.9 births/1,000 population (2017 est.)
country comparison to the world: 44

Death rate: 7.3 deaths/1,000 population (2017 est.)
country comparison to the world: 122

Net migration rate: -4.1 migrant(s)/1,000 population (2017 est.)
country comparison to the world: 183

Population distribution: with the exception of a ribbon of settlement that corresponds to the banks of the Nile, northern Sudan, which extends into the dry Sahara, is sparsely populated; more abundant vegetation and broader access to water increases population distribution in the south extending habitable range along nearly the entire border with South Sudan; sizeable areas of population are found around Khartoum, southeast between the Blue and White Nile Rivers, and througout South Darfur

Urbanization: *urban population:* 34.2% of total population (2017)
rate of urbanization: 3.02% annual rate of change (2015-20 est.)

Major urban areas—population: KHARTOUM (capital) 5.129 million (2015)

Sex ratio: *at birth:* 1.05 male(s)/female
0-14 years: 1.03 male(s)/female
15-24 years: 1.06 male(s)/female
25-54 years: 0.94 male(s)/female
55-64 years: 1.1 male(s)/female
65 years and over: 1.19 male(s)/female
total population: 1.02 male(s)/female (2016 est.)

Maternal mortality ratio: 311 deaths/100,000 live births (2015 est.)
country comparison to the world: 41

Infant mortality rate: *total:* 48.8 deaths/1,000 live births
male: 54 deaths/1,000 live births
female: 43.4 deaths/1,000 live births (2017 est.)
country comparison to the world: 33

Life expectancy at birth: *total population:* 64.4 years
male: 62.3 years
female: 66.7 years (2017 est.)
country comparison to the world: 185

Total fertility rate: 3.57 children born/woman (2017 est.)
country comparison to the world: 42

Contraceptive prevalence rate: 12.2% (2014)

Health expenditures: 8.4% of GDP (2014)
country comparison to the world: 48

Physicians density: 3.06 physicians/1,000 population (2014)

Hospital bed density: 0.8 beds/1,000 population (2012)

Drinking water source:
improved:
urban: 66% of population
rural: 50.2% of population
total: 55.5% of population
unimproved:
urban: 34% of population
rural: 49.8% of population

total: 44.5% of population (2012 est.)

Sanitation facility access:
improved:
urban: 43.9% of population
rural: 13.4% of population
total: 23.6% of population
unimproved:
urban: 56.1% of population
rural: 86.6% of population
total: 76.4% of population (2012 est.)

HIV/AIDS—adult prevalence rate: 0.2% (2016 est.)
country comparison to the world: 97

HIV/AIDS—people living with HIV/AIDS: 56,000 (2016 est.)
country comparison to the world: 55

HIV/AIDS—deaths: 3,000 (2016 est.)
country comparison to the world: 41

Major infectious diseases: *degree of risk:* very high
food or waterborne diseases: bacterial and protozoal diarrhea, hepatitis A and E, and typhoid fever
vectorborne diseases: malaria, dengue fever, and Rift Valley fever
water contact disease: schistosomiasis
respiratory disease: meningococcal meningitis
animal contact disease: rabies (2016)

Obesity—adult prevalence rate: 6.6% (2014)
country comparison to the world: 165

Children under the age of 5 years underweight: 33% (2014)
country comparison to the world: 21

Education expenditures: 2.2% of GDP (2009)

Literacy: *definition:* age 15 and over can read and write
total population: 75.9%
male: 83.3%
female: 68.6% (2015 est.)

School life expectancy (primary to tertiary education): *total:* 7 years
male: 7 years
female: 7 years (2013)

Unemployment, youth ages 15-24: *total:* 20%
male: 16%
female: 32% (2009 est.)

GOVERNMENT

Country name: *conventional long form:* Republic of the Sudan
conventional short form: Sudan
local long form: Jumhuriyat as-Sudan
local short form: As-Sudan
former: Anglo-Egyptian Sudan
etymology: the name "Sudan" derives from the Arabic "bilad-as-sudan" meaning "Land of the Black [peoples]"

Government type: presidential republic

Capital: *name:* Khartoum

geographic coordinates: 15 36 N, 32 32 E
time difference: UTC+3 (8 hours ahead of Washington, DC, during Standard Time)

Administrative divisions: 18 states (wilayat, singular—wilayah); Blue Nile, Central Darfur, East Darfur, Gedaref, Gezira, Kassala, Khartoum, North Darfur, North Kordofan, Northern, Red Sea, River Nile, Sennar, South Darfur, South Kordofan, West Darfur, West Kordofan, White Nile

Independence: 1 January 1956 (from Egypt and the UK)

National holiday: Independence Day, 1 January (1956)

Constitution: *history:* previous 1998; latest adopted 6 July 2005, effective 9 July 2005 (interim constitution)
amendments: proposed by the National Legislature or by the president of the republic; passage requires submission of the proposal to the Legislature at least two months prior to consideration, approval by at least three-quarters majority vote in both houses of the Legislature, and assent by the president; amended 2015 (2017)

Legal system: mixed legal system of Islamic law and English common law

International law organization participation: accepts compulsory ICJ jurisdiction with reservations; withdrew acceptance of ICCt jurisdiction in 2008

Citizenship: *citizenship by birth:* no
citizenship by descent only: the father must be a citizen of Sudan
dual citizenship recognized: no
residency requirement for naturalization: 10 years

Suffrage: 17 years of age; universal

Executive branch: *chief of state:* President Umar Hassan Ahmad al-BASHIR (since 16 October 1993); First Vice President BAKRI Hassan Salih (since 3 December 2013) and prime minister (since 2 March 2017); Second Vice President Hasabu Mohamed ABDEL RAHMIN (since 3 December 2013); note—the president is both chief of state and head of government
head of government: President Umar Hassan Ahmad al-BASHIR (since 16 October 1993); First Vice President BAKRI Hassan Salih (since 3 December 2013) and prime minister (since 2 March 2017); Second Vice President Hasabu Mohamed ABDEL RAHMIN (since 3 December 2013)
cabinet: Council of Ministers appointed by the president; note—the NCP dominates al-BASHIR's cabinet
elections/appointments: president directly elected by absolute majority popular vote in 2 rounds if needed; last held on 13-16 April 2015 (next to be held in 2020); prime minister appointed by the president; note—the position of prime minister was reinstated in December 2016 as a result of the 2015-16 national dialogue process, and President al-BASHIR appointed BAKRI Hassan Salih to the position on 2 March 2017
election results: Umar Hassan Ahmad al-BASHIR reelected president; percent of vote—Umar Hassan Ahmad al-BASHIR (NCP) 94.1%, other (15 candidates) 5.9%

Legislative branch: *description:* bicameral National Legislature consists of the Council of States or Majlis al-Wilayat (50 seats; members indirectly elected—2 each by the 25 state legislatures to serve 6-year terms) and the National Assembly or Majlis Watani (426 seats; 213 members directly elected in single-seat constituencies by simple majority vote, 128 for women only directly elected by proportional representation vote, and 85 directly elected by proportional representation vote; members serve 6-year terms)
elections: last held on 13-15 April 2015 (next to be held in 2021)
election results: National Assembly—percent of vote by party—NA; seats by party—NCP 323, DUP 25, Democratic Unionist Party 15, other 44, independent 19

Judicial branch: *highest court(s):* National Supreme Court (consists of 70 judges organized into panels of 3 judges and includes 4 circuits that operate outside the capital); Constitutional Court (consists of 9 justices including the court president); note—the Constitutional Court resides outside the national judiciary
judge selection and term of office: National Supreme Court and Constitutional Court judges appointed by the president of the republic upon the recommendation of the National Judicial Service Commission, an independent body chaired by the chief justice of the republic and members including other judges and judicial and legal officials; Supreme Court judge tenure NA; Constitutional Court judges appointed for 7 years
subordinate courts: Court of Appeal; other national courts; public courts; district, town, and rural courts

Political parties and leaders: Democratic Unionist Party or DUP [Jalal al-DIGAIR]
Democratic Unionist Party [Muhammad Uthman al-MIRGHANI]
Federal Umma Party [Dr. Ahmed Babikir NAHAR]
Muslim Brotherhood or MB
National Congress Party or NCP [Umar Hassan al-BASHIR]
National Umma Party or NUP [Saddiq al-MAHDI]
Popular Congress Party or PCP [Hassan al-TURABI]
Reform Movement Now [Dr. Ghazi Salahuddin al-ATABANI]
Sudan National Front [Ali Mahmud HASANAYN]
Sudanese Communist Party or SCP [Mohammed Moktar Al-KHATEEB]
Sudanese Congress Party or SCoP [Ibrahim Al-SHEIKH]
Umma Party for Reform and Development
Unionist Movement Party or UMP

Political pressure groups and leaders: Darfur rebel groups including the Justice and Equality Movement or JEM [Gibril Fidail IBRAHIM], Sudan Liberation Movement or SLM-AW [Abdel Wahid al-NUR, various factional leaders], Sudan

Liberation Movement or SLM-MM [Minni Arkou MINAWI]

National Consensus Front or NCF [Farouq ABU ISSA]

Sudan People's Liberation Movement-North or SPLM-N [Yasir ARMAN]

International organization participation: ABEDA, ACP, AfDB, AFESD, AMF, AU, CAEU, COMESA, FAO, G-77, IAEA, IBRD, ICAO, ICC (NGOs), ICRM, IDA, IDB, IFAD, IFC, IFRCS, IGAD, ILO, IMF, IMO, Interpol, IOC, IOM, IPU, ISO, ITSO, ITU, LAS, MIGA, NAM, OIC, OPCW, PCA, UN, UNCTAD, UNESCO, UNHCR, UNIDO, UNWTO, UPU, WCO, WFTU (NGOs), WHO, WIPO, WMO, WTO (observer)

Diplomatic representation in the US: chief of mission: Ambassador (vacant); Charge d'Affaires MAOWIA Osman Khalid Mohammed (since 31 January 2014)

chancery: 2210 Massachusetts Avenue NW, Washington, DC 20008

telephone: [1] (202) 338-8565

FAX: [1] (202) 667-2406

Diplomatic representation from the US: chief of mission: Ambassador (vacant); Charge d'Affaires Steven KOUTSIS (since July 2016)

embassy: Sharia Ali Abdul Latif Street, Khartoum

mailing address: P.O. Box 699, Kilo 10, Soba, Khartoum; APO AE 09829

telephone: [249] (187)-0-(22000)

FAX: [249] (183) 774-137

Flag description: three equal horizontal bands of red (top), white, and black with a green isosceles triangle based on the hoist side; colors and design based on the Arab Revolt flag of World War I, but the meanings of the colors are expressed as follows: red signifies the struggle for freedom, white is the color of peace, light, and love, black represents the people of Sudan (in Arabic 'Sudan' means black), green is the color of Islam, agriculture, and prosperity

National symbol(s): secretary bird; national colors: red, white, black, green

National anthem: name: "Nahnu Djundulla Djundulwatan" (We Are the Army of God and of Our Land)

lyrics/music: Sayed Ahmad Muhammad SALIH/ Ahmad MURJAN

note: adopted 1956; originally served as the anthem of the Sudanese military

ECONOMY

Economy—overview: Sudan has experienced protracted social conflict, civil war, and, in July 2011, the loss of three-quarters of its oil production due to the secession of South Sudan. The oil sector had driven much of Sudan's GDP growth since 1999. For nearly a decade, the economy boomed on the back of rising oil production, high oil prices, and significant inflows of foreign direct investment. Since the economic shock of South Sudan's secession, Sudan has struggled to stabilize its economy and make up for the loss of foreign exchange earnings. The interruption of oil production in South Sudan in 2012 for over a year and the consequent loss of oil transit fees further exacerbated the fragile state of Sudan's economy. Ongoing conflicts in Southern Kordofan, Darfur, and the Blue Nile states, lack of basic infrastructure in large areas, and reliance by much of the population on subsistence agriculture, keep close to half of the population at or below the poverty line.

Sudan was subject to comprehensive US sanctions, which were lifted in October 2017. Sudan is attempting to develop non-oil sources of revenues, such as gold mining and agriculture, while carrying out an austerity program to reduce expenditures. The world's largest exporter of gum Arabic, Sudan produces 75-80% of the world's total output. Agriculture continues to employ 80% of the work force.

Sudan introduced a new currency, still called the Sudanese pound, following South Sudan's secession, but the value of the currency has fallen since its introduction. Khartoum formally devalued the currency in June 2012, when it passed austerity measures that included gradually repealing fuel subsidies. Sudan also faces high inflation, which reached 47% on an annual basis in November 2012 but fell to about 35% per year in 2017.

GDP (purchasing power parity): $186.8 billion (2017 est.)

$180.1 billion (2016 est.)

$174.7 billion (2015 est.)

note: data are in 2017 dollars

country comparison to the world: 69

GDP (official exchange rate): $119 billion (2016 est.)

GDP—real growth rate: 3.7% (2017 est.)

3.1% (2016 est.)

4.9% (2015 est.)

country comparison to the world: 84

GDP—per capita (PPP): $4,600 (2017 est.)

$4,500 (2016 est.)

$4,500 (2015 est.)

note: data are in 2017 dollars

country comparison to the world: 174

Gross national saving: 12.1% of GDP (2017 est.)

11.5% of GDP (2016 est.)

9.1% of GDP (2015 est.)

country comparison to the world: 145

GDP—composition, by end use:

household consumption: 77.3%

government consumption: 6.1%

investment in fixed capital: 18.5%

investment in inventories: 0.9%

exports of goods and services: 8.9%

imports of goods and services: -11.7% (2017 est.)

GDP—composition, by sector of origin:

agriculture: 39.6%

industry: 2.6%

services: 57.8% (2017 est.)

Agriculture—products: cotton, groundnuts (peanuts), sorghum, millet, wheat, gum Arabic, sugarcane, cassava (manioc, tapioca), mangoes, papaya, bananas, sweet potatoes, sesame seeds; animal feed, sheep and other livestock

Industries: oil, cotton ginning, textiles, cement, edible oils, sugar, soap distilling, shoes, petroleum refining, pharmaceuticals, armaments, automobile/light truck assembly, milling

Industrial production growth rate: 2.5% (2017 est.)

country comparison to the world: 109

Labor force: 11.92 million (2007 est.)

country comparison to the world: 50

Labor force—by occupation: agriculture: 80%

industry: 7%

services: 13% (1998 est.)

Unemployment rate: 19.6% (2017 est.)

20.6% (2016 est.)

country comparison to the world: 182

Population below poverty line: 46.5% (2009 est.)

Household income or consumption by percentage share: lowest 10%: 2.7%

highest 10%: 26.7% (2009 est.)

Budget: revenues: $8.198 billion

expenditures: $13.4 billion (2017 est.)

Taxes and other revenues: 6.9% of GDP (2017 est.)

country comparison to the world: 217

Budget surplus (+) or deficit (-): -4.4% of GDP (2017 est.)

country comparison to the world: 147

Public debt: 54.8% of GDP (2017 est.)

65.4% of GDP (2016 est.)

country comparison to the world: 86

Fiscal year: calendar year

Inflation rate (consumer prices): 26.9% (2017 est.)

17.8% (2016 est.)

country comparison to the world: 222

Stock of narrow money: $13.64 billion (31 December 2017 est.)

$12.51 billion (31 December 2016 est.)

country comparison to the world: 76

Stock of broad money: $20.96 billion (31 December 2017 est.)

$19.53 billion (31 December 2016 est.)

country comparison to the world: 90

Stock of domestic credit: $21.63 billion (31 December 2017 est.)

$21.61 billion (31 December 2016 est.)

country comparison to the world: 85

Market value of publicly traded shares: $NA

Current account balance: -$2.317 billion (2017 est.)

-$5.126 billion (2016 est.)

country comparison to the world: 162

Exports: $3.808 billion (2017 est.)

$3.094 billion (2016 est.)

country comparison to the world: 118

Exports—commodities: gold; oil and petroleum products; cotton, sesame, livestock, peanuts, gum Arabic, sugar

Exports—partners: UAE 42.9%, Saudi Arabia 19.5%, Egypt 15.9% (2016)

Imports: $8.649 billion (2017 est.)

$7.325 billion (2016 est.)

851

country comparison to the world: 104

Imports—commodities: foodstuffs, manufactured goods, refinery and transport equipment, medicines, chemicals, textiles, wheat

Imports—partners: UAE 15.4%, India 11.2%, Egypt 10.4%, Saudi Arabia 9.2%, Turkey 8.9%, Japan 5% (2016)

Reserves of foreign exchange and gold: $504.9 million (31 December 2017 est.)
$168.3 million (31 December 2016 est.)
country comparison to the world: 143

Debt—external: $53.35 billion (31 December 2017 est.)
$51.26 billion (31 December 2016 est.)
country comparison to the world: 63

Stock of direct foreign investment—at home:
$25.47 billion (31 December 2016 est.)
$25.47 billion (31 December 2016 est.)
country comparison to the world: 73

Exchange rates: Sudanese pounds (SDG) per US dollar—
6.72 (2017 est.)
6.14 (2016 est.)
6.14 (2015 est.)
6.03 (2014 est.)
5.74 (2013 est.)

ENERGY

Electricity access: population without electricity: 24,700,000
electrification—total population: 35%
electrification—urban areas: 63%
electrification—rural areas: 21% (2013)

Electricity—production: 12.69 billion kWh (2015 est.)
country comparison to the world: 91

Electricity—consumption: 10.26 billion kWh (2015 est.)
country comparison to the world: 93

Electricity—exports: 0 kWh (2016 est.)
country comparison to the world: 200

Electricity—imports: 0 kWh (2016 est.)
country comparison to the world: 204

Electricity—installed generating capacity: 3.736 million kW (2015 est.)
country comparison to the world: 92

Electricity—from fossil fuels: 34.4% of total installed capacity (2015 est.)
country comparison to the world: 180

Electricity—from nuclear fuels: 0% of total installed capacity (2015 est.)
country comparison to the world: 185

Electricity—from hydroelectric plants: 60.2% of total installed capacity (2015 est.)
country comparison to the world: 28

Electricity—from other renewable sources: 5.4% of total installed capacity (2015 est.)
country comparison to the world: 95

Crude oil—production: 104,900 bbl/day (2016 est.)
country comparison to the world: 43

Crude oil—exports: 152,100 bbl/day (2014 est.)
country comparison to the world: 34

Crude oil—imports: 0 bbl/day (2014 est.)
country comparison to the world: 192

Crude oil—proved reserves: 5 billion bbl (1 January 2017 es)
country comparison to the world: 24

Refined petroleum products—production: 89,300 bbl/day (2014 est.)
country comparison to the world: 70

Refined petroleum products—consumption: 110,000 bbl/day (2015 est.)
country comparison to the world: 78

Refined petroleum products—exports: 7,396 bbl/day (2014 est.)
country comparison to the world: 88

Refined petroleum products—imports: 23,920 bbl/day (2014 est.)
country comparison to the world: 110

Natural gas—production: 0 cu m (2013 est.)
country comparison to the world: 197

Natural gas—consumption: 0 cu m (2013 est.)
country comparison to the world: 133

Natural gas—exports: 0 cu m (2013 est.)
country comparison to the world: 185

Natural gas—imports: 0 cu m (2013 est.)
country comparison to the world: 190

Natural gas—proved reserves: 84.95 billion cu m (1 January 2017 es)
country comparison to the world: 57

Carbon dioxide emissions from consumption of energy: 14 million Mt (2013 est.)
country comparison to the world: 93

COMMUNICATIONS

Telephones—fixed lines: *total subscriptions:* 136,472
subscriptions per 100 inhabitants: less than 1 (July 2016 est.)
country comparison to the world: 102

Telephones—mobile cellular: *total:* 27,807,293
subscriptions per 100 inhabitants: 76 (July 2016 est.)
country comparison to the world: 46

Telephone system: *general assessment:* well-equipped system by regional standards and being upgraded; cellular communications started in 1996 and have expanded substantially with wide coverage of most major cities
domestic: consists of microwave radio relay, cable, fiber optic, radiotelephone communications, tropospheric scatter, and a domestic satellite system with 14 earth stations; teledensity exceeeds 75 telephones per 100 persons
international: country code—249; linked to the EASSy and FLAG fiber-optic submarine cable systems; satellite earth stations—1 Intelsat (Atlantic Ocean), 1 Arabsat (2016)

Broadcast media: the Sudanese Government directly controls TV and radio, requiring that both media reflect government policies; TV has a permanent military censor; a private radio station is in operation (2007)

Internet country code: .sd

Internet users: *total:* 10,284,260
percent of population: 28.0% (July 2016 est.)
country comparison to the world: 48

TRANSPORTATION

National air transport system: number of registered air carriers: 6
inventory of registered aircraft operated by air carriers: 25
annual passenger traffic on registered air carriers: 496,178
annual freight traffic on registered air carriers: 13,161,592 mt-km (2015)
Civil aircraft registration country code prefix: ST (2016)

Airports: 74 (2013)
country comparison to the world: 71

Airports—with paved runways: *total:* 16
over 3,047 m: 2
2,438 to 3,047 m: 10
1,524 to 2,437 m: 2
under 914 m: 2 (2013)

Airports—with unpaved runways: *total:* 58
2,438 to 3,047 m: 1
1,524 to 2,437 m: 17
914 to 1,523 m: 28
under 914 m: 12 (2013)

Heliports: 6 (2013)

Pipelines: gas 156 km; oil 4,070 km; refined products 1,613 km (2013)

Railways: *total:* 7,251 km
narrow gauge: 5,851 km 1.067-m gauge; 1,400 km 0.600-m gauge for cotton plantations (20014)
country comparison to the world: 31

Roadways: *total:* 11,900 km
paved: 4,320 km
unpaved: 7,580 km (2000)
country comparison to the world: 129

Waterways: 4,068 km (1,723 km open year-round on White and Blue Nile Rivers) (2011)
country comparison to the world: 24

Merchant marine: *total:* 17
by type: general cargo 1, other 16 (2017)
country comparison to the world: 137

Ports and terminals: *major seaport(s):* Port Sudan

MILITARY AND SECURITY

Military branches: Sudanese Armed Forces (SAF): Land Forces, Navy (includes Marines), Sudanese Air Force (Sikakh al-Jawwiya as-Sudaniya), Rapid Support Forces, Popular Defense Forces (2016)

Military service age and obligation: 18-33 years of age for male and female compulsory or voluntary military service; 1-2 year service obligation; a requirement that completion of national service was mandatory before entering public or private sector employment has been cancelled (2012)

TRANSNATIONAL ISSUES

Disputes—international: the effects of Sudan's ethnic and rebel militia fighting since the mid-20th century have penetrated all of the neighboring states; Chad wishes to be a helpful mediator in resolving the Darfur conflict, and in 2010 established a joint border monitoring force with Sudan, which has helped to reduce cross-border banditry and violence; as of April 2017, more than 610,000 Sudanese refugees are being hosted in the Central African Republic, Chad, Egypt, Ethiopia, Kenya, and South Sudan; Sudan, in turn, is hosting about 507,000 refugees, including more than 375,000 from South Sudan; Sudan accuses South Sudan of supporting Sudanese rebel groups; Sudan claims but Egypt de facto administers security and economic development of the Halaib region north of the 22nd parallel boundary; periodic violent skirmishes with Sudanese residents over water and grazing rights persist among related pastoral populations along the border with the Central African Republic; South Sudan-Sudan boundary represents 1 January 1956 alignment, final alignment pending negotiations and demarcation; final sovereignty status of Abyei Area pending negotiations between South Sudan and Sudan

Refugees and internally displaced persons: refugees (country of origin): 103,176 (Eritrea); 8,502 (Chad); 6,997 (Syria) (2016); 770,110 (South Sudan) (refugees and asylum seekers) (2018)
IDPs: 3.3 million (civil war 1983-2005; ongoing conflict in Darfur region; government and rebel fighting along South Sudan border; inter-tribal clashes) (2016)

Trafficking in persons: current situation: Sudan is a source, transit, and destination country for men, women, and children who are subjected to forced labor and sex trafficking; Sudanese women and girls, particularly those from rural areas or who are internally displaced, or refugees are vulnerable to domestic servitude in country, as well as domestic servitude and sex trafficking abroad; migrants from East and West Africa, South Sudan, Syria, and Nigeria smuggled into or through Sudan are vulnerable to exploitation; Ethiopian, Eritrean, and Filipina women are subjected to domestic servitude in Sudanese homes, and East African and possibly Thai women are forced into prostitution in Sudan; Sudanese children continue to be

recruited and used as combatants by government forces and armed groups

tier rating: Tier 2 Watch List—Sudan does not fully comply with the minimum standards for the elimination of trafficking; however, it is making significant efforts to do so; the government increased its efforts to publically address and prevent trafficking, established a national anti-trafficking council, and began drafting a national action plan against trafficking; the government acknowledges cross-border trafficking but still denies the existence of forced labor, sex trafficking, and the recruitment of child soldiers domestically; law enforcement and judicial officials struggled to apply the national anti-trafficking law, often relying on other statutes with lesser penalties; authorities did not use systematic procedure to identify victims or refer them to care and relied on international organizations and domestic groups to provide protective services; some foreign victims were penalized for unlawful acts committed as a direct result of being trafficked, such as immigration or prostitution violations (2015)

SURINAME

INTRODUCTION

Background: First explored by the Spaniards in the 16th century and then settled by the English in the mid-17th century, Suriname became a Dutch colony in 1667. With the abolition of African slavery in 1863, workers were brought in from India and Java. The Netherlands granted the colony independence in 1975. Five years later the civilian government was replaced by a military regime that soon declared Suriname a socialist republic. It continued to exert control through a succession of nominally civilian administrations until 1987, when international pressure finally forced a democratic election. In 1990, the military overthrew the civilian leadership, but a democratically elected government—a four-party coalition—returned to power in 1991. The coalition expanded to eight

parties in 2005 and ruled until August 2010, when voters returned former military leader Desire BOUTERSE and his opposition coalition to power. President BOUTERSE was reelected unopposed in 2015.

GEOGRAPHY

Location: Northern South America, bordering the North Atlantic Ocean, between French Guiana and Guyana

Geographic coordinates: 4 00 N, 56 00 W

Map references: South America

Area: *total:* 163,820 sq km
land: 156,000 sq km
water: 7,820 sq km
country comparison to the world: 93

Area—comparative: slightly larger than Georgia
Land boundaries: total: 1,907 km
border countries (3): Brazil 515 km, French Guiana 556 km, Guyana 836 km

Coastline: 386 km

Maritime claims: *territorial sea:* 12 nm
exclusive economic zone: 200 nm

Climate: tropical; moderated by trade winds

Terrain: mostly rolling hills; narrow coastal plain with swamps

Elevation: *mean elevation:* 246 m

elevation extremes: *lowest point:* unnamed location in the coastal plain -2 m
highest point: Juliana Top 1,230 m

Natural resources: timber, hydropower, fish, kaolin, shrimp, bauxite, gold, and small amounts of nickel, copper, platinum, iron ore

Land use: *agricultural land:* 0.5%
arable land: 0.4%;
permanent crops: 0%;
permanent pasture: 0.1%
forest: 94.6%
other: 4.9% (2011 est.)
Irrigated land: 570 sq km (2012)

Population—distribution: population concentrated along the northern coastal strip; the remainder of the country is sparsely populated

Natural hazards: flooding

Environment—current issues: deforestation as timber is cut for export; pollution of inland waterways by small-scale mining activities

Environment—international agreements: *party to:* Biodiversity, Climate Change, Climate Change-Kyoto Protocol, Desertification, Endangered Species, Law of the Sea, Marine Dumping, Ozone Layer Protection, Ship Pollution, Tropical Timber 94, Wetlands, Whaling
signed, but not ratified: none of the selected agreementsGeography—note: smallest independent country on South American continent; mostly tropical rain forest; great diversity of flora and fauna that, for the most part, is increasingly threatened by new development; relatively small population, mostly along the coast

PEOPLE AND SOCIETY

Population: 591,919 (July 2017 est.)
country comparison to the world: 172

Nationality: *noun:* Surinamer(s)
adjective: Surinamese

Ethnic groups: Hindustani (also known locally as "East Indians"; their ancestors emigrated from northern India in the latter part of the 19th century) 27.4%, "Maroon" (their African ancestors were brought to the country in the 17th and 18th centuries as slaves and escaped to the interior) 21.7%, Creole (mixed white and black) 15.7%, Javanese 13.7%, mixed 13.4%, other 7.6%, unspecified 0.6% (2012 est.)

Languages: Dutch (official), English (widely spoken), Sranang Tongo (Surinamese, sometimes called Taki-Taki, is the native language of Creoles and much of the younger population and is lingua franca among others), Caribbean Hindustani (a dialect of Hindi), Javanese

Religions: Protestant 23.6% (includes Evangelical 11.2%, Moravian 11.2%, Reformed .7%, Lutheran .5%), Hindu 22.3%, Roman Catholic 21.6%, Muslim 13.8%, other Christian 3.2%, Winti 1.8%, Jehovah's Witness 1.2%, other 1.7%, none 7.5%, unspecified 3.2% (2012 est.)

Demographic profile: Suriname is a pluralistic society consisting primarily of Creoles (persons of mixed African and European heritage), the descendants of escaped African slaves known as Maroons, and the descendants of Indian and Javanese (Indonesian) contract workers. The country overall is in full, post-industrial demographic transition, with a low fertility rate, a moderate mortality rate, and a rising life expectancy. However, the Maroon population of the rural interior lags behind because of lower educational attainment and contraceptive use, higher malnutrition, and significantly less access to electricity, potable water, sanitation, infrastructure, and health care.

Some 350,000 people of Surinamese descent live in the Netherlands, Suriname's former colonial ruler. In the 19th century, better-educated, largely Dutch-speaking Surinamese began emigrating to the Netherlands. World War II interrupted the outflow, but it resumed after the war when Dutch labor demands grew—emigrants included all segments of the Creole population. Suriname still is strongly influenced by the Netherlands because most Surinamese have relatives living there and it is the largest supplier of development aid. Other emigration destinations include French Guiana and the United States. Suriname's immigration rules are flexible, and the country is easy to enter illegally because rainforests obscure its borders. Since the mid-1980s, Brazilians have settled in Suriname's capital, Paramaribo, or eastern Suriname, where they mine gold. This immigration is likely to slowly re-orient Suriname toward its Latin American roots.

Age structure: 0-14 years: 24.62% (male 74,247/female 71,456)
15-24 years: 17.44% (male 52,599/female 50,618)
25-54 years: 44.4% (male 133,835/female 128,980)
55-64 years: 7.54% (male 21,940/female 22,697)
65 years and over: 6.01% (male 15,394/female 20,153) (2017 est.)

Dependency ratios: total dependency ratio: 50.7
youth dependency ratio: 40.6

elderly dependency ratio: 10.1
potential support ratio: 9.9 (2015 est.)

Median age: total: 29.8 years
male: 29.4 years
female: 30.2 years (2017 est.)
country comparison to the world: 120

Population growth rate: 1.02% (2017 est.)
country comparison to the world: 111

Birth rate: 15.8 births/1,000 population (2017 est.)
country comparison to the world: 117

Death rate: 6.1 deaths/1,000 population (2017 est.)
country comparison to the world: 158

Net migration rate: 0.6 migrant(s)/1,000 population (2017 est.)
country comparison to the world: 62

Population distribution: population concentrated along the nothern coastal strip; the remainder of the country is sparsely populated

Urbanization: urban population: 66% of total population (2017)
rate of urbanization: 0.75% annual rate of change (2015-20 est.)

Major urban areas—population: PARAMARIBO (capital) 234,000 (2014)

Sex ratio: at birth: 1.05 male(s)/female
0-14 years: 1.04 male(s)/female
15-24 years: 1.04 male(s)/female
25-54 years: 1.04 male(s)/female
55-64 years: 0.96 male(s)/female
65 years and over: 0.76 male(s)/female
total population: 1.01 male(s)/female (2016 est.)

Maternal mortality ratio: 155 deaths/100,000 live births (2015 est.)
country comparison to the world: 59

Infant mortality rate: total: 24.5 deaths/1,000 live births
male: 28.5 deaths/1,000 live births
female: 20.2 deaths/1,000 live births (2017 est.)
country comparison to the world: 69

Life expectancy at birth: total population: 72.5 years
male: 70.1 years
female: 75.1 years (2017 est.)
country comparison to the world: 148

Total fertility rate: 1.93 children born/woman (2017 est.)
country comparison to the world: 131

Contraceptive prevalence rate: 47.6% (2010)

Health expenditures: 5.7% of GDP (2014)
country comparison to the world: 116

Hospital bed density: 3.1 beds/1,000 population (2010)

Drinking water source:
improved:
urban: 98.1% of population
rural: 88.4% of population
total: 94.8% of population
unimproved:
urban: 1.9% of population
rural: 11.6% of population
total: 5.2% of population (2015 est.)

Sanitation facility access:
improved:
urban: 88.4% of population
rural: 61.4% of population
total: 79.2% of population
unimproved:
urban: 11.6% of population
rural: 38.6% of population
total: 20.8% of population (2015 est.)

HIV/AIDS—adult prevalence rate: 1.4% (2016 est.)
country comparison to the world: 35

HIV/AIDS—people living with HIV/AIDS: 4,900 (2016 est.)
country comparison to the world: 106

HIV/AIDS—deaths: <200 (2016 est.)

Major infectious diseases: degree of risk: very high
food or waterborne diseases: bacterial and protozoal diarrhea, hepatitis A, and typhoid fever
vectorborne disease: dengue fever and malaria
note: active local transmission of Zika virus by Aedes species mosquitoes has been identified in this country (as of August 2016); it poses an important risk (a large number of cases possible) among US citizens if bitten by an infective mosquito; other less common ways to get Zika are through sex, via blood transfusion, or during pregnancy, in which the pregnant woman passes Zika virus to her fetus (2016)

Obesity—adult prevalence rate: 26.4% (2016)
country comparison to the world: 41

Children under the age of 5 years underweight: 5.8% (2010)
country comparison to the world: 83

Education expenditures: NA

Literacy: definition: age 15 and over can read and write
total population: 95.6%
male: 96.1%
female: 95% (2015 est.)

Unemployment, youth ages 15-24: total: 16.4%
male: 7.8%
female: 30.7% (2014 est.)
country comparison to the world: 51

GOVERNMENT

Country name: conventional long form: Republic of Suriname
conventional short form: Suriname
local long form: Republiek Suriname
local short form: Suriname
former: Netherlands Guiana, Dutch Guiana
etymology: name may derive from the indigenous "Surinen" people who inhabited the area at the time of European contact

Government type: presidential republic

Capital: name: Paramaribo
geographic coordinates: 5 50 N, 55 10 W
time difference: UTC-3 (2 hours ahead of Washington, DC, during Standard Time)

Administrative divisions: 10 districts (distrikten, singular—distrikt); Brokopondo, Commewijne, Coronie, Marowijne, Nickerie, Para, Paramaribo, Saramacca, Sipaliwini, Wanica

Independence: 25 November 1975 (from the Netherlands)

National holiday: Independence Day, 25 November (1975)

Constitution: previous 1975; latest ratified 30 September 1987, effective 30 October 1987; amended 1992 (2016)

Legal system: civil law system influenced by Dutch civil law; note—the Commissie Nieuw Surinaamse Burgerlijk Wetboek completed drafting a new civil code in February 2009

International law organization participation: accepts compulsory ICJ jurisdiction with reservations; accepts ICCt jurisdiction

Citizenship: *citizenship by birth:* no

citizenship by descent only: at least one parent must be a citizen of Suriname

dual citizenship recognized: no

residency requirement for naturalization: 5 years

Suffrage: 18 years of age; universal

Executive branch: *chief of state:* President Desire Delano BOUTERSE (since 12 August 2010); Vice President Ashwin ADHIN (since 12 August 2015); note—the president is both chief of state and head of government

head of government: President Desire Delano BOUTERSE (since 12 August 2010); Vice President Ashwin ADHIN (since 12 August 2015)

cabinet: Cabinet of Ministers appointed by the president

elections/appointments: president and vice president indirectly elected by the National Assembly; president and vice president serve a 5-year term (no term limits); election last held on 25 May 2015 (next to be held in May 2020)

election results: Desire Delano BOUTERSE reelected president unopposed; National Assembly vote—NA

Legislative branch: *description:* unicameral National Assembly or Nationale Assemblee (51 seats; members directly elected in multi-seat constituencies by proportional representation vote to serve 5-year terms)

elections: last held on 25 May 2015 (next to be held in May 2020)

election results: percent of vote by party—NDP 45.5%, V7 37.2%, A-Com 10.5%, DOE 4.3%, PALU .7%, other 1.7%; seats by party—NDP 26, V7 18, A-Com 5, DOE 1, PALU 1

note: seats by party as of April 2017—seats by party—NDP 26, VHP 9, ABOP 5, PL 3, NPS 2, BEP 2, DOE 1, PALU 1, independent 2

Judicial branch: *highest resident court(s):* High Court of Justice of Suriname (consists of the court president, vice president, and 4 judges); note—appeals beyond the High Court are referred to the Caribbean Court of Justice; human rights violations can be appealed to the Inter-American

Commission on Human Rights with judgments issued by the Inter-American Court on Human Rights

judge selection and term of office: court judges appointed by the national president in consultation with the National Assembly, the State Advisory Council, and the Order of Private Attorneys; judges appointed for life

subordinate courts: cantonal courts

Political parties and leaders: Alternative Combination or A-Com (coalition includes ABOP, KTPI, Party for Democracy and Development)

Brotherhood and Unity in Politics or BEP [Celsius WATERBERG]

Democratic Alternative '91 or DA91 [Angelique DEL CASTILLO]

General Liberation and Development Party or ABOP [Ronnie BRUNSWIJK]

National Democratic Party or NDP [Desire Delano BOUTERSE]

National Party of Suriname or NPS [Gregory RUSLAND]

Party for Democracy and Development in Unity or DOE [Carl BREEVELD]

Party for National Unity and Solidarity or KTPI [Willy SOEMITA]

People's Alliance, Pertjaja Luhur or PL [Paul SOMOHARDJO]

Progressive Worker and Farmer's Union or PALU [Jim HOK]

Surinamese Labor Party or SPA [Guno CASTELEN]

Progressive Reform Party or VHP [Chandrikapersad SANTOKHI]

Victory 7 or V7 [Chandrikapresad SANTOKHI] (formerly the New Front for Democracy and Development or NF; an electoral coalition of NPS, VHP, DA91, PL, SPA formed only for the May 2015 election)

Political pressure groups and leaders: Association of Indigenous Village Chiefs [Lesley ARTIST]

Association of Saramaccan Authorities or Maroons [Stiefen PETRUSI]

Women's Parliament Forum or WPF (Vrouwen Parlement Forum or VPF) [Iris GILLIAD]

International organization participation: ACP, AOSIS, Caricom, CD, CDB, CELAC, FAO, G-77, IADB, IBRD, ICAO, ICCt, ICRM, IDA, IDB, IFAD, IFC, IFRCS, IHO, ILO, IMF, IMO, Interpol, IOC, IOM, IPU, ISO (correspondent), ITU, ITUC (NGOs), LAES, MIGA, NAM, OAS, OIC, OPANAL, OPCW, PCA, Petrocaribe, UN, UNASUR, UNCTAD, UNESCO, UNIDO, UPU, WHO, WIPO, WMO, WTO

Diplomatic representation in the US: chief of mission: Ambassador Niermala Sakoentala BADRISING (since 21 July 2017)

chancery: Suite 460, 4301 Connecticut Avenue NW, Washington, DC 20008

telephone: [1] (202) 244-7488

FAX: [1] (202) 244-5878

consulate(s) general: Miami

Diplomatic representation from the US: *chief of mission:* Ambassador Edwin "Ned" Richard NOLAN, Jr.(since 11 January 2016)

embassy: 165 Kristalstraat, Paramaribo

mailing address: US Department of State, PO Box 1821, Paramaribo

telephone: [597] 472-900

FAX: [597] 410-972

Flag description: five horizontal bands of green (top, double width), white, red (quadruple width), white, and green (double width); a large, yellow, five-pointed star is centered in the red band; red stands for progress and love; green symbolizes hope and fertility; white signifies peace, justice, and freedom; the star represents the unity of all ethnic groups; from its yellow light the nation draws strength to bear sacrifices patiently while working toward a golden future

National symbol(s): royal palm, faya lobi (flower); national colors: green, white, red, yellow

National anthem: *name:* "God zij met ons Suriname!" (God Be With Our Suriname)

lyrics/music: Cornelis Atses HOEKSTRA and Henry DE ZIEL/Johannes Corstianus DE PUY

note: adopted 1959; originally adapted from a Sunday school song written in 1893 and contains lyrics in both Dutch and Sranang Tongo

ECONOMY

Economy—overview: Suriname's economy is dominated by the mining industry, with exports of oil and gold accounting for approximately 85% of exports and 27% of government revenues. This makes the economy highly vulnerable to mineral price volatility. The worldwide drop in international commodity prices and the cessation of alumina mining in Suriname significantly reduced government revenue and national income during the past few years. After 99 years of operations, a major US aluminum company recently discontinued its activities in Suriname. Public sector revenues fell, together with exports, international reserves, employment, and private sector investment.

Economic growth declined annually from just under 5% in 2012 to -10.4% in 2016. In January 2011, the government devalued the currency by 20% and raised taxes to reduce the budget deficit. Suriname began instituting macro adjustments between September 2015 and 2016; these included another 20% currency devaluation in November 2015 and foreign currency interventions by the Central Bank until March 2016, after which time the Bank allowed the Surinamese dollar (SRD) to float. By December 2016, the SRD had lost 46% of its value against the dollar. High import price pass-through from depreciation and electricity tariff increases caused inflation to increase 55.5% year-over-year in December 2016.

Suriname's economic prospects for the medium-term will depend on continued commitment to responsible monetary and fiscal policies and on the introduction of structural reforms to liberalize markets and promote competition. The government's over-reliance on revenue from the extractive sector colors Suriname's economic outlook. One credit bureau forecasted that the economy would contract 2% in 2017. Rising international

855

oil prices and higher production by Suriname's oil company, Staatsolie's, will lift oil exports. Two new offshore oil exploration wells will draw 100 million dollars in foreign direct investment inflows. Higher gold prices and increased production from the Merian gold mine also will lift exports. However, investment overall is slowing and unemployment is rising, reflecting government spending cuts, weak business confidence, and the completion of large mining infrastructure projects. Fiscal problems, such as a failure to secure sufficient external financing, could result in additional pressure on the exchange rate and inflation.

GDP (purchasing power parity): $7.928 billion (2017 est.)
$8.023 billion (2016 est.)
$8.964 billion (2015 est.)
note: data are in 2017 dollars
country comparison to the world: 165

GDP (official exchange rate): $3.665 billion (2016 est.)

GDP—real growth rate: -1.2% (2017 est.)
-10.5% (2016 est.)
-2.7% (2015 est.)
country comparison to the world: 209

GDP—per capita (PPP): $13,900 (2017 est.)
$14,200 (2016 est.)
$16,100 (2015 est.)
note: data are in 2017 dollars
country comparison to the world: 114

Gross national saving: 50.5% of GDP (2017 est.)
57.1% of GDP (2016 est.)
51.6% of GDP (2015 est.)
country comparison to the world: 1

GDP—composition, by end use:
household consumption: 32.8%
government consumption: 16.1%
investment in fixed capital: 64.1%
investment in inventories: 26.5%
exports of goods and services: 50.6%
imports of goods and services: -63.7% (2017 est.)

GDP—composition, by sector of origin:
agriculture: 11.6%
industry: 31.1%
services: 57.4% (2017 est.)

Agriculture—products: rice, bananas, palm kernels, coconuts, plantains, peanuts; beef, chickens; shrimp; forest products

Industries: bauxite and gold mining, alumina production; oil, lumbering, food processing, fishing

Industrial production growth rate: 1.5% (2017 est.)
country comparison to the world: 151

Labor force: 144,000 (2014 est.)
country comparison to the world: 177

Labor force—by occupation: *agriculture:* 11.2%
industry: 19.5%
services: 69.3% (2010)

Unemployment rate: 9.1% (2017 est.)
11% (2016 est.)
country comparison to the world: 126

Population below poverty line: 70% (2002 est.)

Household income or consumption by percentage share: *lowest 10%:* NA%

highest 10%: NA%

Budget: *revenues:* $545.7 million
expenditures: $805.5 million (2017 est.)
Taxes and other revenues: 14.9% of GDP (2017 est.)
country comparison to the world: 189

Budget surplus (+) or deficit (-): -7.1% of GDP (2017 est.)
country comparison to the world: 191

Public debt: 64.6% of GDP (2016 est.)
45.7% of GDP (2015 est.)
country comparison to the world: 64

Fiscal year: calendar year

Inflation rate (consumer prices): 22.3% (2017 est.)
55.5% (2016 est.)
country comparison to the world: 218

Central bank discount rate: 10% (2013)
9% (2012)
country comparison to the world: 22

Commercial bank prime lending rate: 20.5% (31 December 2017 est.)
13.5% (31 December 2016 est.)
country comparison to the world: 14

Stock of narrow money: $1.08 billion (31 December 2017 est.)
$921.8 million (31 December 2016 est.)
country comparison to the world: 155

Stock of broad money: $2.355 billion (31 December 2017 est.)
$2.182 billion (31 December 2016 est.)
country comparison to the world: 149

Stock of domestic credit: $1.513 billion (31 December 2017 est.)
$1.402 billion (31 December 2016 est.)
country comparison to the world: 160

Market value of publicly traded shares: $NA

Current account balance: $344 million (2017 est.)
-$102 million (2016 est.)
country comparison to the world: 50

Exports: $1.976 billion (2017 est.)
$1.449 billion (2016 est.)
country comparison to the world: 140

Exports—commodities: alumina, gold, crude oil, lumber, shrimp and fish, rice, bananas

Exports—partners: Switzerland 28.3%, UAE 27.1%, Belgium 9.1%, Guyana 9%, US 4.7%, Trinidad and Tobago 4.5% (2016)

Imports: $1.57 billion (2017 est.)
$1.197 billion (2016 est.)
country comparison to the world: 167

Imports—commodities: capital equipment, petroleum, foodstuffs, cotton, consumer goods

Imports—partners: US 21.2%, Netherlands 10.9%, China 10.5%, Trinidad and Tobago 10.1%, St. Lucia 7% (2016)

Reserves of foreign exchange and gold: $381.1 million (31 December 2016 est.)
$330.2 million (31 December 2015 est.)
country comparison to the world: 150

Debt—external: $1.7 billion (31 December 2017 est.)
$1.625 billion (31 December 2016 est.)
country comparison to the world: 155

Exchange rates: Surinamese dollars (SRD) per US dollar—
7.697 (2017 est.)
6.229 (2016 est.)
6.229 (2015 est.)
3.4167 (2014 est.)
3.3 (2013 est.)

ENERGY

Electricity access: *electrification—total population:* 100% (2016)

Electricity—production: 2.19 billion kWh (2015 est.)
country comparison to the world: 137

Electricity—consumption: 1.948 billion kWh (2015 est.)
country comparison to the world: 145

Electricity—exports: 0 kWh (2016 est.)
country comparison to the world: 180

Electricity—imports: 0 kWh (2016 est.)
country comparison to the world: 183

Electricity—installed generating capacity: 435,000 kW (2015 est.)
country comparison to the world: 150

Electricity—from fossil fuels: 54.7% of total installed capacity (2015 est.)
country comparison to the world: 143

Electricity—from nuclear fuels: 0% of total installed capacity (2015 est.)
country comparison to the world: 158

Electricity—from hydroelectric plants: 43.4% of total installed capacity (2015 est.)
country comparison to the world: 47

Electricity—from other renewable sources: 1.8% of total installed capacity (2015 est.)
country comparison to the world: 125

Crude oil—production: 17,000 bbl/day (2016 est.)
country comparison to the world: 73

Crude oil—exports: 0 bbl/day (2014 est.)
country comparison to the world: 173

Crude oil—imports: 0 bbl/day (2014 est.)
country comparison to the world: 174

Crude oil—proved reserves: 83.98 million bbl (1 January 2017 es)
country comparison to the world: 74

Refined petroleum products—production: 7,632 bbl/day (2014 est.)
country comparison to the world: 102

Refined petroleum products—consumption: 14,000 bbl/day (2015 est.)
country comparison to the world: 152

Refined petroleum products—exports: 10,620 bbl/day (2014 est.)
country comparison to the world: 83

Refined petroleum products—imports: 9,938 bbl/day (2014 est.)
country comparison to the world: 144

Natural gas—production: 0 cu m (2013 est.)
country comparison to the world: 180

Natural gas—consumption: 0 cu m (2013 est.)
country comparison to the world: 119

Natural gas—exports: 0 cu m (2013 est.)
country comparison to the world: 161

Natural gas—imports: 0 cu m (2013 est.)
country comparison to the world: 169

Natural gas—proved reserves: 0 cu m (1 January 2011 es)
country comparison to the world: 182

Carbon dioxide emissions from consumption of energy: 2.4 million Mt (2013 est.)
country comparison to the world: 146

COMMUNICATIONS

Telephones—fixed lines: *total subscriptions:* 89,030
subscriptions per 100 inhabitants: 15 (July 2016 est.)
country comparison to the world: 147

Telephones—mobile cellular: *total:* 806,881
subscriptions per 100 inhabitants: 138 (July 2016 est.)
country comparison to the world: 159

Telephone system: *general assessment:* international facilities are good
domestic: combined fixed-line and mobile-cellular teledensity exceeds 150 telephones per 100 persons; microwave radio relay network is in place
international: country code—597; satellite earth stations—2 Intelsat (Atlantic Ocean) (2017)

Broadcast media: 2 state-owned TV stations; 1 state-owned radio station; multiple private radio and TV stations (2007)

Internet country code: .sr

Internet users: *total:* 265,964
percent of population: 45.4% (July 2016 est.)
country comparison to the world: 154

TRANSPORTATION

National air transport system: number of registered air carriers: 2

inventory of registered aircraft operated by air carriers: 5
annual passenger traffic on registered air carriers: 259,682
annual freight traffic on registered air carriers: 29,324,319 mt-km (2015)
Civil aircraft registration country code prefix: PZ (2016)

Airports: 55 (2013)
country comparison to the world: 85

Airports—with paved runways: *total:* 6
over 3,047 m: 1
under 914 m: 5 (2013)

Airports—with unpaved runways: *total:* 49
914 to 1,523 m: 4
under 914 m: 45 (2013)

Pipelines: oil 50 km (2013)

Roadways: *total:* 4,304 km
paved: 1,130 km
unpaved: 3,174 km (2003)
country comparison to the world: 154

Waterways: 1,200 km (most navigable by ships with drafts up to 7 m) (2011)
country comparison to the world: 58

Merchant marine: *total:* 10
by type: general cargo 5, oil tanker 3, other 2 (2017)
country comparison to the world: 143

Ports and terminals: *major seaport(s):* Paramaribo, Wageningen

MILITARY AND SECURITY

Military branches: Suriname Army (National Leger, NL): Army, Coast Guard, Air Force (2017)

Military service age and obligation: 18 is the legal minimum age for voluntary military service; no conscription; personnel drawn almost exclusively from the Creole community (2012)

TRANSNATIONAL ISSUES

Disputes—international: area claimed by French Guiana between Riviere Litani and Riviere Marouini (both headwaters of the Lawa); Suriname claims a triangle of land between the New and Kutari/Koetari rivers in a historic dispute over the headwaters of the Courantyne; Guyana seeks UN Convention on the Law of the Sea arbitration to resolve the longstanding dispute with Suriname over the axis of the territorial sea boundary in potentially oil-rich waters

Trafficking in persons: current situation: Suriname is a source, transit, and destination country for women and children subjected to sex trafficking and men, women, and children subjected to forced labor; women and girls from Suriname, Guyana, Brazil, and the Dominican Republic are subjected to sex trafficking in the country, sometimes in interior mining camps; migrant workers in agriculture and on fishing boats and children working in informal urban sectors and gold mines are vulnerable to forced labor; traffickers from Suriname exploit victims in the Netherlands

tier rating: Tier 2 Watch List—Suriname does not fully comply with the minimum standards for the elimination of trafficking; however, it is making significant efforts to do so; in 2014, Suriname was granted a waiver from an otherwise required downgrade to Tier 3 because its government has a written plan that, if implemented, would constitute making significant efforts to bring itself into compliance with the minimum standards for the elimination of trafficking; authorities increased the number of trafficking investigations, prosecutions, and convictions as compared to 2013, but resources were insufficient to conduct investigations in the country's interior; more trafficking victims were identified in 2014 than in 2013, but protective services for adults and children were inadequate, with a proposed government shelter for women and child trafficking victims remaining unopened (2015)

Illicit drugs: growing transshipment point for South American drugs destined for Europe via the Netherlands and Brazil; transshipment point for arms-for-drugs dealing

SVALBARD

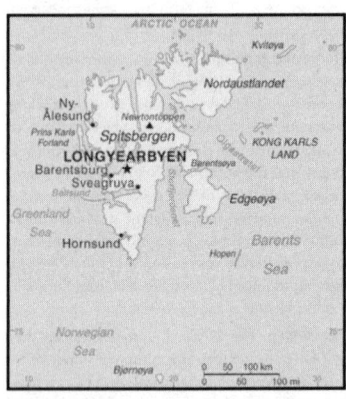

INTRODUCTION

Background: The archipelago may have been first discovered by Norse explorers in the 12th century; the islands served as an international whaling base during the 17th and 18th centuries. Norway's sovereignty was internationally recognized by treaty in 1920, and five years later it officially took over the territory. In the 20th century coal mining started and today a Norwegian and a Russian company are still functioning. Travel between the settlements is accomplished with snowmobiles, aircraft, and boats.

GEOGRAPHY

Location: Northern Europe, islands between the Arctic Ocean, Barents Sea, Greenland Sea, and Norwegian Sea, north of Norway

Geographic coordinates: 78 00 N, 20 00 E

Map references: Arctic Region

Area: *total:* 62,045 sq km
land: 62,045 sq km
water: 0 sq km
note: includes Spitsbergen and Bjornoya (Bear Island)
country comparison to the world: 126

Area—comparative: slightly smaller than West Virginia
Land boundaries: 0 km

Coastline: 3,587 km

Maritime claims: *territorial sea:* 12 nm
contiguous zone: 24 nm

exclusive fishing zone: 200 nm
continental shelf: extends to depth of exploitation

Climate: arctic, tempered by warm North Atlantic Current; cool summers, cold winters; North Atlantic Current flows along west and north coasts of Spitsbergen, keeping water open and navigable most of the year

Terrain: rugged mountains; much of the upland areas are ice covered; west coast clear of ice about half the year; fjords along west and north coasts

Elevation: *mean elevation:* NA

elevation extremes: *lowest point:* Arctic Ocean 0 m
highest point: Newtontoppen 1,717 m

Natural resources: coal, iron ore, copper, zinc, phosphate, wildlife, fish

Land use: *agricultural land:* 0%
arable land: 0%;
permanent crops: 0%;
permanent pasture: 0%
forest: 0%
other: 100% (2011 est.)

Population—distribution: the small population is primarily concentrated on the island of Spitsbergen in a handful of settlements on the south side of the Isfjorden, with Longyearbyen being the largest

Natural hazards: ice floes often block the entrance to Bellsund (a transit point for coal export) on the west coast and occasionally make parts of the northeastern coast inaccessible to maritime traffic

Environment—current issues: ice floes are a maritime hazard; past exploitation of mammal species (whale, seal, walrus, and polar bear) severely depleted the populations, but a gradual recovery seems to be occurringGeography—note: northernmost part of the Kingdom of Norway; consists of nine main islands; glaciers and snowfields cover 60% of the total area; Spitsbergen Island is the site of the Svalbard Global Seed Vault, a seed repository established by the Global Crop Diversity Trust and the Norwegian Government

PEOPLE AND SOCIETY

Population: 2,583 (July 2017 est.)
country comparison to the world: 230

Ethnic groups: Norwegian 59.8%, Russian and Ukrainian 20.4%, other 19.4% (primarily Swedish, Thai, and Philippine) (2016 est.)

Languages: Norwegian, Russian

Population growth rate: -0.03% (2014 est.)
country comparison to the world: 199

Population distribution: the small population is primarily concentrated on the island of Spitsbergen in a handful of settlements on the south side of the Isfjorden, with Longyearbyen being the largest

Sex ratio: NA

Infant mortality rate: *total:* NA
male: NA
female: NA

Life expectancy at birth: *total population:* NA
male: NA
female: NA (2017 est.)

Total fertility rate: NA

GOVERNMENT

Country name: *conventional long form:* none

conventional short form: Svalbard (sometimes referred to as Spitsbergen, the largest island in the archipelago)
etymology: 12th century Norse accounts speak of the discovery of a "Svalbard"—literally "cold shores"—but they may have referred to Jan Mayen Island or eastern Greenland; the archipelago was traditionally known as Spitsbergen, but Norway renamed it Svalbard in the 1920s when it assumed sovereignty of the islands

Dependency status: territory of Norway; administered by the Polar Department of the Ministry of Justice, through a governor (sysselmann) residing in Longyearbyen, Spitsbergen; by treaty (9 February 1920), sovereignty was awarded to Norway

Government type: non-self-governing territory of Norway

Capital: *name:* Longyearbyen
geographic coordinates: 78 13 N, 15 38 E
time difference: UTC+1 (6 hours ahead of Washington, DC, during Standard Time)
daylight saving time: +1hr, begins last Sunday in March; ends last Sunday in October

Independence: none (territory of Norway)

Legal system: the laws of Norway where applicable apply; only the laws of Norway made explicitly applicable to Svalbard have effect there; the Svalbard Act and the Svalbard Environmental Protection Act, and certain regulations, apply only to Svalbard; the Spitsbergen Treaty and the Svalbard Treaty grant certain rights to citizens and corporations of signatory nations; as of June 2017, 45 nations had ratified the Svalbard Treaty

Citizenship: see Norway

Executive branch: *chief of state:* King HARALD V of Norway (since 17 January 1991); Heir Apparent Crown Prince Haakon MAGNUS, son of the king (born 20 July 1973)
head of government: Governor Kjerstin ASKHOLT (since 1 October 2015); Assistant Governor Berit SAGFOSSEN (since 1 April 2016)
elections/appointments: none; the monarchy is hereditary; governor and assistant governor responsible to the Polar Department of the Ministry of Justice

Legislative branch: *description:* unicameral Longyearben Community Council (15 seats; members elected by direct vote to serve 4-year-terms); note—the Council acts very much like a Norwegian municipality, responsible for infrastructure and utilities, including power, land-use and community planning, education, and child welfare; however, healthcare services are provided by the state
elections: last held on 6 October 2015 (next to be held in October 2019)
election results: seats by party—Conservatives 5, Labor Party 5, Liberals 3, Green Party 2

Judicial branch: *highest court(s):* none; note—Svalbard is subordinate to Norway's Nord-Troms

District Court and Halogaland Court of Appeal, both located in Tromso

Political parties and leaders: Svalbard Conservative Party [Kjetil FIGENSCHOU]
Svalbard Green Party [Helga Bardsdatter KRISTIANSEN and Espen Klungseth ROTEVATN]
Svalbard Labor Party [Arild OLSEN]
Svalbard Liberal Party [Erik BERGER]

Political pressure groups and leaders: NA

International organization participation: none

Flag description: the flag of Norway is used
National anthem: note: as a territory of Norway, "Ja, vi elsker dette landet" is official (see Norway)

ECONOMY

Economy—overview: Coal mining, tourism, and international research are Svalbard's major industries. Coal mining has historically been the dominant economic activity, and the Treaty of 9 February 1920 gives the 45 countries that so far have ratified the treaty equal rights to exploit mineral deposits, subject to Norwegian regulation. Although US, UK, Dutch, and Swedish coal companies have mined in the past, the only companies still engaging in this are Norwegian and Russian. Low coal prices have forced the Norwegian coal company, Store Norske Spitsbergen Kulkompani, to close one of its two mines and to considerably reduce the activity of the other. Since the 1990s, the tourism and hospitality industry has grown rapidly, and Svalbard now receives 60,000 visitors annually.

The settlements on Svalbard were established as company towns, and at their height in the 1950s, the Norwegian state-owned coal company supported nearly 1,000 jobs. Today, only about 300 people work in the mining industry.

Goods such as alcohol, tobacco, and vehicles, normally highly taxed on mainland Norway, are considerably cheaper in Svalbard in an effort by the Norwegian government to entice more people to live on the Arctic archipelago. By law, Norway collects only enough taxes to pay for the needs of the local government; none of tax proceeds go to the central government.

GDP—real growth rate: NA%

Labor force: 1,590 (2013)
country comparison to the world: 229

Budget: *revenues:* $NA
expenditures: $NA
Taxes and other revenues: NA% of GDP

Budget surplus (+) or deficit (-): NA% of GDP

Exports: $NA

Imports: $NA

Exchange rates: Norwegian kroner (NOK) per US dollar—
8.308 (2017)
8.0646 (2016)
8.0646 (2015)
8.0646 (2014 est.)
6.3021 (2013 est.)

ENERGY

Crude oil—production: 194,300 bbl/day (2014 est.)
country comparison to the world: 38

Crude oil—exports: 16,070 bbl/day (2012 est.)
country comparison to the world: 54

Crude oil—imports: 0 bbl/day (2012 est.)
country comparison to the world: 193

Refined petroleum products—consumption: 80,250 bbl/day (2013 est.)
country comparison to the world: 89

Refined petroleum products—exports: 4,488 bbl/day (2012 est.)
country comparison to the world: 97

Refined petroleum products—imports: 18,600 bbl/day (2012 est.)
country comparison to the world: 122

Natural gas—production: 0 cu m (2013 est.)
country comparison to the world: 198

Natural gas—consumption: 0 cu m (2013 est.)
country comparison to the world: 134

Natural gas—exports: 0 cu m (2013 est.)
country comparison to the world: 186

Natural gas—imports: 0 cu m (2013 est.)
country comparison to the world: 191

COMMUNICATIONS

Telephone system: *general assessment:* modern, well-developed
domestic: the Svalbard Satellite Station—connected to the mainland via the Svalbard Undersea Cable System—is the only Arctic ground station that can see low-altitude, polar-orbiting satellites; it provides ground services to more satellites than any other facility in the world
international: country code—47-790; the Svalbard Undersea Cable System is a twin communications cable that connects Svalbard to mainland Norway; the system is the sole telecommunications link to the archipelago (2017)

Broadcast media: the Norwegian Broadcasting Corporation (NRK) began direct TV transmission to Svalbard via satellite in 1984; Longyearbyen households have access to 3 NRK radio and 2 TV stations (2008)

Internet country code: .sj

TRANSPORTATION

Airports: 4 (2013)
country comparison to the world: 190

Airports—with paved runways: total: 1
2,438 to 3,047 m: 1 (2013)

Airports—with unpaved runways: total: 3
under 914 m: 3 (2013)

Heliports: 1 (2013)

Ports and terminals: *major seaport(s):* Barentsburg, Longyearbyen, Ny-Alesund, Pyramiden

MILITARY AND SECURITY

Military branches: no regular military forces

Military—note: Svalbard is a territory of Norway, demilitarized by treaty on 9 February 1920; Norwegian military activity is limited to fisheries surveillance by the Norwegian Coast Guard

TRANSNATIONAL ISSUES

Disputes—international: despite recent discussions, Russia and Norway dispute their maritime limits in the Barents Sea and Russia's fishing rights beyond Svalbard's territorial limits within the Svalbard Treaty zone

SWAZILAND

INTRODUCTION

Background: Autonomy for the Swazis of southern Africa was guaranteed by the British in the late 19th century; independence was granted in 1968. Student and labor unrest during the 1990s pressured King MSWATI III, Africa's last absolute monarch, to grudgingly allow political reform and greater democracy, although he has backslid on these promises in recent years. A constitution came into effect in 2006, but the legal status of political parties was not defined and their status remains unclear. Swaziland has surpassed Botswana as the country with the world's highest known HIV/AIDS prevalence rate.

GEOGRAPHY

Location: Southern Africa, between Mozambique and South Africa

Geographic coordinates: 26 30 S, 31 30 E

Map references: Africa

Area: *total:* 17,364 sq km
land: 17,204 sq km
water: 160 sq km
country comparison to the world: 159

Area—comparative: slightly smaller than New Jersey
Land boundaries: total: 546 km
border countries (2): Mozambique 108 km, South Africa 438 km

Coastline: 0 km (landlocked)

Maritime claims: none (landlocked)

Climate: varies from tropical to near temperate

Terrain: mostly mountains and hills; some moderately sloping plains

Elevation: *mean elevation:* 305 m

elevation extremes: *lowest point:* Great Usutu River 21 m
highest point: Emlembe 1,862 m

Natural resources: asbestos, coal, clay, cassiterite, hydropower, forests, small gold and diamond deposits, quarry stone, and talc

Land use: *agricultural land:* 68.3%
arable land: 9.8%;
permanent crops: 0.8%;
permanent pasture: 57.7%
forest: 31.7%
other: 0% (2011 est.)
Irrigated land: 500 sq km (2012)

Population—distribution: because of its mountainous terrain, the population distribution is uneven throughout the country, concentrating primarily in valleys and plains

Natural hazards: drought

Environment—current issues: limited supplies of potable water; wildlife populations being depleted because of excessive hunting; overgrazing; soil degradation; soil erosion

Environment—international agreements: *party to:* Biodiversity, Climate Change, Climate Change-Kyoto Protocol, Desertification, Endangered Species, Hazardous Wastes, Ozone Layer Protection *signed, but not ratified:* Law of the SeaGeography—*note:* landlocked; almost completely surrounded by South Africa

PEOPLE AND SOCIETY

Population: 1,467,152
note: estimates for this country explicitly take into account the effects of excess mortality due to AIDS; this can result in lower life expectancy, higher infant mortality, higher death rates, lower population growth rates, and changes in the distribution of population by age and sex than would otherwise be expected (July 2017 est.)
country comparison to the world: 154

Nationality: *noun:* Swazi(s)
adjective: Swazi

Ethnic groups: African 97%, European 3%

Languages: English (official, used for government business), siSwati (official)

Religions: Christian 90% (Zionist—a blend of Christianity and indigenous ancestral worship—40%, Roman Catholic 20%, other 30%—includes Anglican, Methodist, Mormon, Jehovah's Witness), Muslim 2%, other 8% (includes Baha'i, Buddhist, Hindu, indigenous religionist, Jewish) (2015 est.)

Demographic profile: Swaziland, a small, predominantly rural, landlocked country surrounded by South Africa and Mozambique, suffers from severe poverty and the world's highest HIV/AIDS prevalence rate. A weak and deteriorating economy, high unemployment, rapid population growth, and an uneven distribution of resources all combine to worsen already persistent poverty and food insecurity, especially in rural areas. Erratic weather (frequent droughts and intermittent heavy rains and flooding), overuse of small plots, the overgrazing of cattle, and outdated agricultural practices reduce crop yields and further degrade the environment, exacerbating Swaziland's poverty and subsistence problems. Swaziland's extremely high HIV/AIDS prevalence rate—more than 28% of adults have the disease—compounds these issues. Agricultural production has declined due to HIV/AIDS, as the illness causes households to lose manpower and to sell livestock and other assets to pay for medicine and funerals.

Swazis, mainly men from the country's rural south, have been migrating to South Africa to work in coal, and later gold, mines since the late 19th century. Although the number of miners abroad has never been high in absolute terms because of Swaziland's small population, the outflow has had important social and economic repercussions. The peak of mining employment in South Africa occurred during the 1980s. Cross-border movement has accelerated since the 1990s, as increasing unemployment has pushed more Swazis to look for work in South Africa (creating a "brain drain" in the health and educational sectors); southern Swazi men have continued to pursue mining, although the industry has downsized. Women now make up an increasing share of migrants and dominate cross-border trading in handicrafts, using the proceeds to purchase goods back in Swaziland. Much of today's migration, however, is not work-related but focuses on visits to family and friends, tourism, and shopping.

Age structure: *0-14 years:* 35.01% (male 259,646/female 253,976)
15-24 years: 22.12% (male 164,117/female 160,478)
25-54 years: 34.6% (male 264,262/female 243,362)
55-64 years: 4.3% (male 25,319/female 37,763)
65 years and over: 3.97% (male 22,113/female 36,116) (2017 est.)

Dependency ratios: *total dependency ratio:* 68.8
youth dependency ratio: 63.5
elderly dependency ratio: 5.2
potential support ratio: 19.1 (2015 est.)

Median age: *total:* 21.7 years
male: 21.5 years
female: 21.9 years (2017 est.)
country comparison to the world: 181

Population growth rate: 1.08% (2017 est.)
country comparison to the world: 105

Birth rate: 24 births/1,000 population (2017 est.)
country comparison to the world: 55

Death rate: 13.2 deaths/1,000 population (2017 est.)
country comparison to the world: 13

Net migration rate: 0 migrant(s)/1,000 population (2017 est.)
country comparison to the world: 97

Population distribution: because of its mountainous terrain, the population distribution is uneven throughout the country, concentrating primarily in valleys and plains

Urbanization: *urban population:* 21.3% of total population (2017)

rate of urbanization: 1.41% annual rate of change (2015-20 est.)

Major urban areas—population: MBABANE (capital) 66,000 (2014)

Sex ratio: *at birth:* 1.03 male(s)/female
0-14 years: 1.02 male(s)/female
15-24 years: 1.02 male(s)/female
25-54 years: 1.08 male(s)/female
55-64 years: 0.66 male(s)/female
65 years and over: 0.64 male(s)/female
total population: 1 male(s)/female (2016 est.)

Mother's mean age at first birth: 19.5 years
note: median age at first birth among women 25-29 (2006/07 est.)

Maternal mortality ratio: 389 deaths/100,000 live births (2015 est.)
country comparison to the world: 29

Infant mortality rate: *total:* 48.4 deaths/1,000 live births
male: 52.2 deaths/1,000 live births
female: 44.4 deaths/1,000 live births (2017 est.)
country comparison to the world: 34

Life expectancy at birth: *total population:* 52.1 years
male: 52.7 years
female: 51.5 years (2017 est.)
country comparison to the world: 220

Total fertility rate: 2.69 children born/woman (2017 est.)
country comparison to the world: 68

Contraceptive prevalence rate: 66.1% (2014)

Health expenditures: 9.3% of GDP (2014)
country comparison to the world: 34

Physicians density: 0.15 physicians/1,000 population (2009)

Hospital bed density: 2.1 beds/1,000 population (2011)

Drinking water source:
improved:
urban: 93.6% of population
rural: 68.9% of population
total: 74.1% of population
unimproved:
urban: 6.4% of population
rural: 31.1% of population
total: 25.9% of population (2015 est.)

Sanitation facility access:
improved:
urban: 63.1% of population
rural: 56% of population
total: 57.5% of population
unimproved:
urban: 36.9% of population
rural: 44% of population
total: 42.5% of population (2015 est.)

HIV/AIDS—adult prevalence rate: 27.2% (2016 est.)
country comparison to the world: 1

HIV/AIDS—people living with HIV/AIDS: 220,000 (2016 est.)
country comparison to the world: 26

HIV/AIDS—deaths: 3,900 (2016 est.)
country comparison to the world: 35

Major infectious diseases: *degree of risk:* intermediate

food or waterborne diseases: bacterial diarrhea, hepatitis A, and typhoid fever

vectorborne disease: malaria
water contact disease: schistosomiasis (2016)

Obesity—adult prevalence rate: 16.5% (2016)
country comparison to the world: 124

Children under the age of 5 years underweight: 5.8% (2014)
country comparison to the world: 84

Education expenditures: 7.1% of GDP (2014)
country comparison to the world: 12

Literacy: *definition:* age 15 and over can read and write
total population: 87.5%
male: 87.4%
female: 87.5% (2015 est.)

School life expectancy (primary to tertiary education): *total:* 11 years
male: 12 years
female: 11 years (2013)

GOVERNMENT

Country name: *conventional long form:* Kingdom of Swaziland
conventional short form: Swaziland
local long form: Umbuso weSwatini
local short form: eSwatini
etymology: "Land of the Swazi" people; the name "Swazi" derives from 19th century King MSWATI II, under whose rule Swazi territory was expanded and unified

Government type: absolute monarchy

Capital: *name:* Mbabane (administrative capital); Lobamba (royal and legislative capital)
geographic coordinates: 26 19 S, 31 08 E
time difference: UTC+2 (7 hours ahead of Washington, DC, during Standard Time)

Administrative divisions: 4 regions; Hhohho, Lubombo, Manzini, Shiselweni

Independence: 6 September 1968 (from the UK)

National holiday: Independence Day (Somhlolo Day), 6 September (1968)

Constitution: *history:* previous 1968, 1978; latest signed by the king 26 July 2005, effective 8 February 2006
amendments: proposed at a joint sitting of both houses of Parliament; passage requires majority vote by both houses and/or majority vote in a referendum, and assent by the king; passage of amendments affecting "specially entrenched" constitutional provisions requires at least three-fourths majority vote by both houses, passage by simple majority vote in a referendum, and assent by the king; passage of "entrenched" provisions requires at least two-thirds majority vote of both houses, passage in a referendum, and assent by the king (2017)

Legal system: mixed legal system of civil, common, and customary law

International law organization participation: accepts compulsory ICJ jurisdiction with reservations; non-party state to the ICCt

Citizenship: *citizenship by birth:* no

citizenship by descent only: both parents must be citizens of Swaziland

dual citizenship recognized: no
residency requirement for naturalization: 5 years

Suffrage: 18 years of age

Executive branch: *chief of state:* King MSWATI III (since 25 April 1986)
head of government: Prime Minister Barnabas Sibusiso DLAMINI (since 23 October 2008); Deputy Prime Minister Paul DLAMINI (since 2013)
cabinet: Cabinet recommended by the prime minister, confirmed by the monarch
elections/appointments: the monarchy is hereditary; prime minister appointed by the monarch from among elected members of the House of Assembly

Legislative branch: *description:* bicameral Parliament or Libandla consists of the Senate (30 seats; 20 members appointed by the monarch and 10 indirectly elected by simple majority vote by the House of Assembly; members serve 5-year terms) and the House of Assembly (65 seats; 55 members directly elected in single-seat constituencies by absolute majority vote in 2 rounds if needed and 10 members appointed by the monarch; members serve 5-year terms)
elections: House of Assembly—last held on 24 August 2013 with a runoff on 20 September 2013 (next scheduled for September 2018)
election results: House of Assembly—percent of vote by party—NA; seats by party—independent 55

Judicial branch: *highest court(s):* the Supreme Court of the Judicature comprising the Supreme Court (consists of the chief justice and at least 6 justices) and the High Court (consists of chief justice—ex officio—and at least 12 justices); note—the Supreme Court has jurisdiction in all constitutional matters
judge selection and term of office: justices of the Supreme Court of the Judicature appointed by the monarch on the advice of the Judicial Service Commission or JSC, a judicial advisory body consisting of the Supreme Court Chief Justice, 4 members appointed by the monarch, and the JSC head; justices of both courts eligible for retirement at age 65 with mandatory retirement at age 75 for Supreme Court justices and at age 70 for High Court justices
subordinate courts: magistrates' courts; National Swazi Courts for administering customary/traditional laws (jurisdiction restricted to customary law for Swazi citizens)
note: the national constitution as amended in 2006 shifted judicial power from the monarch and vested it exclusively in the judiciary

Political parties and leaders: the status of political parties, previously banned, is unclear under the 2006 Constitution; the following are considered political associations: African United Democratic Party or AUDP [Sibusiso DLAMINI]
Ngwane National Liberatory Congress or NNLC [Dr. Alvit DLAMINI]
People's United Democratic Movement or PUDEMO [Mario MASUKU]
Swaziland Democratic Party or SWADEPA [Jan SITHOLE]

Political pressure groups and leaders: Swaziland United Democratic Front or SUDF

Trade Union Congress of Swaziland or TUCOSWA
Swaziland Solidarity Network or SSN

International organization participation: ACP, AfDB, AU, C, COMESA, FAO, G-77, IAEA, IBRD, ICAO, ICRM, IDA, IFAD, IFC, IFRCS, ILO, IMF, IMO, Interpol, IOC, IOM, ISO (correspondent), ITSO, ITU, ITUC (NGOs), MIGA, NAM, OPCW, PCA, SACU, SADC, UN, UNCTAD, UNESCO, UNIDO, UNWTO, UPU, WCO, WHO, WIPO, WMO, WTO

Diplomatic representation in the US: chief of mission: Ambassador Njabuliso Busisiwe Sikhulile GWEBU (since 24 April 2017)
chancery: 1712 New Hampshire Avenue, NW, Washington, DC 20009
telephone: [1] (202) 234-5002
FAX: [1] (202) 234-8254

Diplomatic representation from the US: *chief of mission:* Ambassador Lisa J. PETERSON (since February 2016)
embassy: corner of MR 103 and Cultural Center Drive, Ezulwini
mailing address: P.O. Box D202, The Gables, H106
telephone: [268] 2417-9000
FAX: [268] 2416-3344

Flag description: three horizontal bands of blue (top), red (triple width), and blue; the red band is edged in yellow; centered in the red band is a large black and white shield covering two spears and a staff decorated with feather tassels, all placed horizontally; blue stands for peace and stability, red represents past struggles, and yellow the mineral resources of the country; the shield, spears, and staff symbolize protection from the country's enemies, while the black and white of the shield are meant to portray black and white people living in peaceful coexistence

National symbol(s): lion, elephant; national colors: blue, yellow, red

National anthem: *name:* "Nkulunkulu Mnikati wetibusiso temaSwati" (Oh God, Bestower of the Blessings of the Swazi)
lyrics/music: Andrease Enoke Fanyana SIMELANE/David Kenneth RYCROFT
note: adopted 1968; uses elements of both ethnic Swazi and Western music styles

ECONOMY

Economy—overview: A small, landlocked kingdom, Swaziland is bordered in the north, west and south by the Republic of South Africa and by Mozambique in the east. Swaziland depends on South Africa for 60% of its exports and for more than 90% of its imports. Swaziland's currency is pegged to the South African rand, effectively relinquishing Swaziland's monetary policy to South Africa. The government is dependent on customs duties from the Southern African Customs Union (SACU) for 49% of revenue; income tax accounts for 27% and a valued added tax for 19% of revenues. Swaziland is a lower middle income country, but its income distribution is highly skewed, with an estimated 20% of the population controlling 80% of the nation's wealth. As of 2017, more than one-quarter of the adult population was infected by HIV/AIDS; Swaziland has the world's highest HIV prevalence rate.

Subsistence agriculture employs approximately 70% of the population. The manufacturing sector diversified in the 1980s and 1990s, but manufacturing has grown little in the last decade. Sugar and soft drink concentrate are the largest foreign exchange earners. Mining has declined in importance in recent years. Coal, gold, diamond, and quarry stone mines are small scale, and the only iron ore mine closed in 2014.

With an estimated 28% unemployment rate, Swaziland's need to increase the number and size of small and medium enterprises and to attract foreign direct investment is acute. On 1 January 2015, Swaziland lost its eligibility for benefits under the US African Growth and Opportunity Act after failing to meet benchmarks relating to workers' rights.

The IMF forecasted that Swaziland's economy will grow at a slower pace in 2017 because of a region-wide drought, which is likely to hurt Swaziland's revenue from sugar exports and other agricultural products; tourism and transport sectors will also decline. Overgrazing, soil depletion, drought, and floods are persistent problems. Swaziland's revenue from SACU receipts also are projected to decline in 2017, making it harder for the government to maintain fiscal balance.

GDP (purchasing power parity): $11.34 billion (2017 est.)
$11.31 billion (2016 est.)
$11.31 billion (2015 est.)
note: data are in 2017 dollars
country comparison to the world: 158

GDP (official exchange rate): $4.03 billion (2016 est.)

GDP—real growth rate: 0.3% (2017 est.)
0% (2016 est.)
1.1% (2015 est.)
country comparison to the world: 198

GDP—per capita (PPP): $9,900 (2017 est.)
$10,000 (2016 est.)
$10,100 (2015 est.)
note: data are in 2017 dollars
country comparison to the world: 140

Gross national saving: 11.1% of GDP (2017 est.)
12.8% of GDP (2016 est.)
23% of GDP (2015 est.)
country comparison to the world: 151

GDP—composition, by end use:
household consumption: 65.7%
government consumption: 14.5%
investment in fixed capital: 14.5%
investment in inventories: -0.1%
exports of goods and services: 34.9%
imports of goods and services: -29.7% (2017 est.)

GDP—composition, by sector of origin:
agriculture: 6.5%
industry: 45%
services: 48.6% (2017 est.)

Agriculture—products: sugarcane, corn, cotton, citrus, pineapples, cattle, goats

Industries: soft drink concentrates, coal, forestry, sugar processing, textiles, and apparel

Industrial production growth rate: 1.1% (2017 est.)
country comparison to the world: 158

Labor force: 427,900 (2016 est.)
country comparison to the world: 158

Labor force—by occupation: agriculture: 10.7%
industry: 30.4%
services: 58.9% (2014 est.)

Unemployment rate: 28% (2014 est.)
28% (2013 est.)
country comparison to the world: 200

Population below poverty line: 63% (2010 est.)

Household income or consumption by percentage share: *lowest 10%:* 1.7%
highest 10%: 40.1% (2010 est.)

Distribution of family income—Gini index: 50.4 (2001)
country comparison to the world: 16

Budget: *revenues:* $1.15 billion
expenditures: $1.475 billion (2017 est.)
Taxes and other revenues: 28.5% of GDP (2017 est.)
country comparison to the world: 93

Budget surplus (+) or deficit (-): -8.1% of GDP (2017 est.)
country comparison to the world: 199

Public debt: 27.5% of GDP (2016 est.)
18.6% of GDP (2015 est.)
country comparison to the world: 169

Fiscal year: 1 April–31 March

Inflation rate (consumer prices): 7% (2017 est.)
8% (2016 est.)
country comparison to the world: 192

Central bank discount rate: 7.25% (31 December 2016)
6.5% (31 December 2015)
country comparison to the world: 45

Commercial bank prime lending rate: 11.7% (31 December 2017 est.)
10.3% (31 December 2016 est.)
country comparison to the world: 70

Stock of narrow money: $290.3 million (31 December 2017 est.)
$316.6 million (31 December 2016 est.)
country comparison to the world: 180

Stock of broad money: $973.5 million (31 December 2017 est.)
$1.015 billion (31 December 2016 est.)
country comparison to the world: 173

Stock of domestic credit: $983.6 million (31 December 2017 est.)
$890.5 million (31 December 2016 est.)
country comparison to the world: 169

Market value of publicly traded shares: $NA
$203.1 million (31 December 2007)
$199.9 million (31 December 2006)

Current account balance: -$44 million (2017 est.)
$26 million (2016 est.)
country comparison to the world: 70

Exports: $1.631 billion (2017 est.)

$1.377 billion (2016 est.)
country comparison to the world: 147

Exports—commodities: soft drink concentrates, sugar, timber, cotton yarn, refrigerators, citrus, and canned fruit

Exports—partners: South Africa 87.1%, Namibia 4% (2016)

Imports: $1.467 billion (2017 est.)
$1.405 billion (2016 est.)
country comparison to the world: 169

Imports—commodities: motor vehicles, machinery, transport equipment, foodstuffs, petroleum products, chemicals

Imports—partners: South Africa 60.3%, China 5.3%, Mozambique 5.1% (2016)

Reserves of foreign exchange and gold: $576.6 million (31 December 2017 est.)
$564.4 million (31 December 2016 est.)
country comparison to the world: 140

Debt—external: $548.2 million (31 December 2017 est.)
$468.9 million (31 December 2016 est.)
country comparison to the world: 177

Stock of direct foreign investment—at home: $NA

Stock of direct foreign investment—abroad: $NA

Exchange rates: emalangeni per US dollar—
14.44 (2017 est.)
14.6924 (2016 est.)
14.6924 (2015 est.)
12.7581 (2014 est.)
10.8469 (2013 est.)

ENERGY

Electricity access: population without electricity: 900,000
electrification—*total population:* 27%
electrification—urban areas: 40%
electrification—rural areas: 24% (2013)

Electricity—production: 431 million kWh (2015 est.)
country comparison to the world: 170

Electricity—consumption: 1.481 billion kWh (2015 est.)
country comparison to the world: 149

Electricity—exports: 0 kWh (2016)
country comparison to the world: 218

Electricity—imports: 1.08 billion kWh (2015 est.)
country comparison to the world: 65

Electricity—installed generating capacity: 281,000 kW (2015 est.)
country comparison to the world: 159

Electricity—from fossil fuels: 35.6% of total installed capacity (2015 est.)
country comparison to the world: 176

Electricity—from nuclear fuels: 0% of total installed capacity (2015 est.)
country comparison to the world: 212

Electricity—from hydroelectric plants: 21.4% of total installed capacity (2015 est.)
country comparison to the world: 85

Electricity—from other renewable sources: 43.1% of total installed capacity (2015 est.)
country comparison to the world: 4

Crude oil—production: 0 bbl/day (2016 est.)
country comparison to the world: 202

Crude oil—exports: 0 bbl/day (2014 est.)
country comparison to the world: 214

Crude oil—imports: 0 bbl/day (2014 est.)
country comparison to the world: 214

Crude oil—proved reserves: 0 bbl (1 January 2017)
country comparison to the world: 201

Refined petroleum products—production: 0 bbl/day (2014 est.)
country comparison to the world: 205

Refined petroleum products—consumption: 5,000 bbl/day (2015 est.)
country comparison to the world: 176

Refined petroleum products—exports: 0 bbl/day (2014 est.)
country comparison to the world: 216

Refined petroleum products—imports: 5,029 bbl/day (2014 est.)
country comparison to the world: 167

Natural gas—production: 0 cu m (2013 est.)
country comparison to the world: 215

Natural gas—consumption: 0 cu m (2013 est.)
country comparison to the world: 150

Natural gas—exports: 0 cu m (2013 est.)
country comparison to the world: 213

Natural gas—imports: 0 cu m (2013 est.)
country comparison to the world: 212

Natural gas—proved reserves: 0 cu m (1 January 2014 es)
country comparison to the world: 210

Carbon dioxide emissions from consumption of energy: 600,000 Mt (2013 est.)
country comparison to the world: 176

COMMUNICATIONS

Telephones—fixed lines: *total subscriptions:* 42,000
subscriptions per 100 inhabitants: 3 (July 2016 est.)
country comparison to the world: 166

Telephones—mobile cellular: *total:* 995,000
subscriptions per 100 inhabitants: 69 (July 2016 est.)
country comparison to the world: 160

Telephone system: *general assessment:* a somewhat modern but not an advanced system
domestic: Swaziland recently awarded a second mobile-cellular service; communication infrastructure has a geographic coverage of about 90% and a rising subscriber base; combined fixed-line and mobile cellular teledensity roughly 70 telephones per 100 persons; telephone system consists of carrier-equipped, open-wire lines and low-capacity, microwave radio relay
international: country code—268; satellite earth station—1 Intelsat (Atlantic Ocean) (2017)

Broadcast media: 1 state-owned TV station; satellite dishes are able to access South African providers; state-owned radio network with 3 channels; 1 private radio station (2017)

Internet country code: .sz

Internet users: *total:* 414,724
percent of population: 28.6% (July 2016 est.)
country comparison to the world: 137

TRANSPORTATION

National air transport system: number of registered air carriers: 1
inventory of registered aircraft operated by air carriers: 1
annual passenger traffic on registered air carriers: 89,791
annual freight traffic on registered air carriers: 0 mt-km (2015)
Civil aircraft registration country code prefix: 3D (2016)

Airports: 14 (2013)
country comparison to the world: 149

Airports—with paved runways: *total:* 2
over 3,047 m: 1
2,438 to 3,047 m: 1 (2013)

Airports—with unpaved runways: *total:* 12
914 to 1,523 m: 5
under 914 m: 7 (2013)

Railways: *total:* 301 km
narrow gauge: 301 km 1.067-m gauge (2014)
country comparison to the world: 123

Roadways: *total:* 3,594 km
paved: 1,078 km
unpaved: 2,516 km (2002)
country comparison to the world: 160
Merchant marine: total: by type: (2017)
country comparison to the world: 2

MILITARY AND SECURITY

Military expenditures: 1.81% of GDP (2016)
1.78% of GDP (2015)
1.81% of GDP (2014)
1.88% of GDP (2013)
1.89% of GDP (2012)
country comparison to the world: 18

Military branches: Umbutfo Swaziland Defense Force (USDF): Ground Force (includes Air Wing (no operational aircraft)) (2013)

Military service age and obligation: 18-30 years of age for male and female voluntary military service; no conscription; compulsory HIV testing required, only HIV-negative applicants accepted (2012)

TRANSNATIONAL ISSUES

Disputes—international: in 2006, Swazi king advocated resorting to ICJ to claim parts of Mpumalanga and KwaZulu-Natal from South Africa

SWEDEN

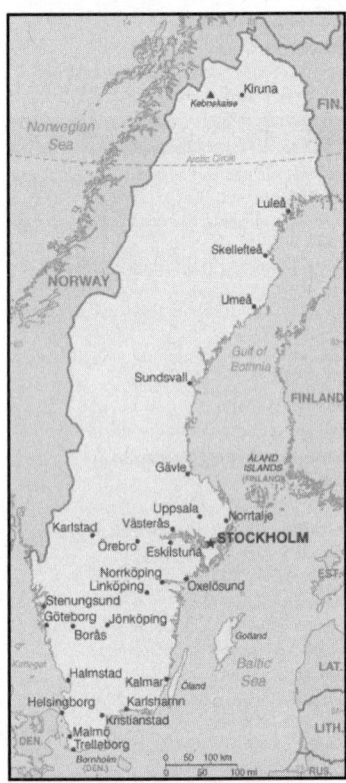

INTRODUCTION

Background: A military power during the 17th century, Sweden has not participated in any war for two centuries. An armed neutrality was preserved in both world wars. Sweden's long-successful economic formula of a capitalist system intermixed with substantial welfare elements was challenged in the 1990s by high unemployment and in 2000-02 and 2009 by the global economic downturns, but fiscal discipline over the past several years has allowed the country to weather economic vagaries. Sweden joined the EU in 1995, but the public rejected the introduction of the euro in a 2003 referendum.

GEOGRAPHY

Location: Northern Europe, bordering the Baltic Sea, Gulf of Bothnia, Kattegat, and Skagerrak, between Finland and Norway

Geographic coordinates: 62 00 N, 15 00 E

Map references: Europe

Area: *total:* 450,295 sq km
land: 410,335 sq km
water: 39,960 sq km

country comparison to the world: 57
Area—comparative: almost three times the size of Georgia; slightly larger than California
Land boundaries: total: 2,211 km
border countries (2): Finland 545 km, Norway 1,666 km

Coastline: 3,218 km

Maritime claims: *territorial sea:* 12 nm (adjustments made to return a portion of straits to high seas)
exclusive economic zone: agreed boundaries or midlines
continental shelf: 200-m depth or to the depth of exploitation

Climate: temperate in south with cold, cloudy winters and cool, partly cloudy summers; subarctic in north

Terrain: mostly flat or gently rolling lowlands; mountains in west

Elevation: *mean elevation:* 320 m

elevation extremes: *lowest point:* reclaimed bay of Lake Hammarsjön, near Kristianstad -2.4 m
highest point: Kebnekaise 2,111 m

Natural resources: iron ore, copper, lead, zinc, gold, silver, tungsten, uranium, arsenic, feldspar, timber, hydropower

Land use: *agricultural land:* 7.5%
arable land: 6.4%;
permanent crops: 0%;
permanent pasture: 1.1%
forest: 68.7%
other: 23.8% (2011 est.)
Irrigated land: 1,640 sq km (2012)

Population—distribution: most Swedes live in the south where the climate is milder and there is better connectivity to mainland Europe; population clusters are found all along the Baltic coast in the east; the interior areas of the north remain sparsely populated

Natural hazards: ice floes in the surrounding waters, especially in the Gulf of Bothnia, can interfere with maritime traffic

Environment—current issues: acid rain damage to soils and lakes; pollution of the North Sea and the Baltic Sea

Environment—international agreements: *party to:* Air Pollution, Air Pollution-Nitrogen Oxides, Air Pollution-Persistent Organic Pollutants, Air Pollution-Sulfur 85, Air Pollution-Sulfur 94, Air Pollution-Volatile Organic Compounds, Antarctic-Environmental Protocol, Antarctic-Marine Living Resources, Antarctic Treaty, Biodiversity, Climate Change, Climate Change-Kyoto Protocol, Desertification, Endangered Species, Environmental Modification, Hazardous Wastes, Law of the Sea, Marine Dumping, Ozone Layer Protection, Ship Pollution, Tropical Timber 83, Tropical Timber 94, Wetlands, Whaling

signed, but not ratified: none of the selected agreementsGeography—note: strategic location along Danish Straits linking Baltic and North Seas; Sweden has almost 100,000 lakes, the largest of which, Vanern, is the third largest in Europe

PEOPLE AND SOCIETY

Population: 9,960,487 (July 2017 est.)
country comparison to the world: 91

Nationality: *noun:* Swede(s)
adjective: Swedish

Ethnic groups: indigenous population: Swedes with Finnish and Sami minorities; most common countries of origin among immigrants: Finland, Syria, Iraq, Poland, Iran

Languages: Swedish (official)
note: Finnish, Sami, Romani, Yiddish, and Meankieli are official minority languages

Religions: Church of Sweden (Lutheran) 63%, other (includes Roman Catholic, Orthodox, Baptist, Muslim, Jewish, and Buddhist) 17% (2016 est.)

Age structure: *0-14 years:* 17.43% (male 892,462/female 843,375)
15-24 years: 11.31% (male 581,025/female 545,971)
25-54 years: 39.42% (male 1,993,590/female 1,933,080)
55-64 years: 11.58% (male 578,942/female 574,479)
65 years and over: 20.26% (male 931,593/female 1,085,970) (2017 est.)

Dependency ratios: *total dependency ratio:* 58.5
youth dependency ratio: 27.4
elderly dependency ratio: 31.1
potential support ratio: 3.2 (2015 est.)

Median age: *total:* 41.2 years
male: 40.2 years
female: 42.2 years (2017 est.)
country comparison to the world: 38

Population growth rate: 0.81% (2017 est.)
country comparison to the world: 128

Birth rate: 12.1 births/1,000 population (2017 est.)
country comparison to the world: 167

Death rate: 9.4 deaths/1,000 population (2017 est.)
country comparison to the world: 57

Net migration rate: 5.3 migrant(s)/1,000 population (2017 est.)
country comparison to the world: 23

Population distribution: most Swedes live in the south where the climate is milder and there is better connectivity to mainland Europe; population clusters are found all along the Baltic coast in the east; the interior areas of the north remain sparsely populated

Urbanization: *urban population:* 86.1% of total population (2017)

rate of urbanization: 0.86% annual rate of change (2015-20 est.)

Major urban areas—population: STOCKHOLM (capital) 1.486 million (2015)

Sex ratio: *at birth:* 1.06 male(s)/female
0-14 years: 1.06 male(s)/female
15-24 years: 1.06 male(s)/female
25-54 years: 1.03 male(s)/female
55-64 years: 1.01 male(s)/female
65 years and over: 0.85 male(s)/female
total population: 1 male(s)/female (2016 est.)

Mother's mean age at first birth: 29.1 years (2015 est.)

Maternal mortality ratio: 4 deaths/100,000 live births (2015 est.)
country comparison to the world: 177

Infant mortality rate: *total:* 2.6 deaths/1,000 live births
male: 2.9 deaths/1,000 live births
female: 2.3 deaths/1,000 live births (2017 est.)
country comparison to the world: 218

Life expectancy at birth: *total population:* 82.1 years
male: 80.2 years
female: 84.2 years (2017 est.)
country comparison to the world: 16

Total fertility rate: 1.88 children born/woman (2017 est.)
country comparison to the world: 141

Health expenditures: 11.9% of GDP (2014)
country comparison to the world: 6

Physicians density: 4.11 physicians/1,000 population (2013)

Hospital bed density: 2.54 beds/1,000 population (2014)

Drinking water source:
improved:
urban: 100% of population
rural: 100% of population
total: 100% of population
unimproved:
urban: 0% of population
rural: 0% of population
total: 0% of population (2015 est.)

Sanitation facility access:
improved:
urban: 99.3% of population
rural: 99.6% of population
total: 99.3% of population
unimproved:
urban: 0.7% of population
rural: 0.4% of population
total: 0.7% of population (2015 est.)

HIV/AIDS—adult prevalence rate: 0.2% (2016 est.)
country comparison to the world: 98

HIV/AIDS—people living with HIV/AIDS: 11,000 (2016 est.)
country comparison to the world: 92

HIV/AIDS—deaths: <100 (2016 est.)

Obesity—adult prevalence rate: 20.6% (2016)
country comparison to the world: 97

Education expenditures: 7.7% of GDP (2013)
country comparison to the world: 20

School life expectancy (primary to tertiary education): *total:* 18 years
male: 17 years
female: 20 years (2014)

Unemployment, youth ages 15-24: *total:* 20.4%
male: 21.2%
female: 19.6% (2015 est.)
country comparison to the world: 40

GOVERNMENT

Country name: *conventional long form:* Kingdom of Sweden
conventional short form: Sweden
local long form: Konungariket Sverige
local short form: Sverige
etymology: name ultimately derives from the North Germanic Svear tribe, which inhabited central Sweden and is first mentioned in the first centuries A.D.

Government type: parliamentary constitutional monarchy

Capital: *name:* Stockholm
geographic coordinates: 59 20 N, 18 03 E
time difference: UTC+1 (6 hours ahead of Washington, DC, during Standard Time)
daylight saving time: +1hr, begins last Sunday in March; ends last Sunday in October

Administrative divisions: 21 counties (lan, singular and plural); Blekinge, Dalarna, Gavleborg, Gotland, Halland, Jamtland, Jonkoping, Kalmar, Kronoberg, Norrbotten, Orebro, Ostergotland, Skane, Sodermanland, Stockholm, Uppsala, Varmland, Vasterbotten, Vasternorrland, Vastmanland, Vastra Gotaland

Independence: 6 June 1523 (Gustav VASA elected king of Sweden, marking the abolishment of the Kalmar Union between Denmark, Norway, and Sweden)

National holiday: National Day, 6 June (1983); note—from 1916 to 1982 this date was celebrated as Swedish Flag Day

Constitution: *history:* several previous; latest adopted 1 January 1975
amendments: proposed by Parliament; passage requires simple majority vote in two consecutive parliamentary terms with an intervening general election; passage also requires approval by simple majority vote in a referendum if Parliament approves a motion for a referendum by one-third of its members; amended several times, last in 2014 (changes to the "Instrument of Government") (2016)

Legal system: civil law system influenced by Roman-Germanic law and customary law

International law organization participation: accepts compulsory ICJ jurisdiction with reservations; accepts ICCt jurisdiction

Citizenship: *citizenship by birth:* no

citizenship by descent only: the father must be a citizen of Sweden; in the case of a child born out of wedlock, the mother must be a citizen of Sweden and the father unknown
dual citizenship recognized: no, unless the other citizenship was acquired involuntarily
residency requirement for naturalization: 5 years

Suffrage: 18 years of age; universal

Executive branch: *chief of state:* King CARL XVI GUSTAF (since 19 September 1973); Heir Apparent Princess VICTORIA Ingrid Alice Desiree, daughter of the monarch (born 14 July 1977)
head of government: Prime Minister Stefan LOFVEN (since 3 October 2014); Deputy Prime Minister Isabella LOVIN (since 25 May 2016)
cabinet: Cabinet appointed by the prime minister
elections/appointments: the monarchy is hereditary; following legislative elections, the leader of the majority party or majority coalition usually becomes the prime minister

Legislative branch: *description:* unicameral Parliament or Riksdag (349 seats; 310 members directly elected in multi-seat constituencies by proportional representation vote and 39 members in "at-large" seats directly elected by proportional representation vote; members serve 4-year terms)
elections: last held on 14 September 2014 (next to be held on or before 9 September 2018)
election results: percent of vote by party—SAP 31.0%, M 23.3%, SD 12.9%, MP 6.9%, C 6.1%, V 5.7%, L 5.4%, KD 4.6%, other 4.1%; seats by party—SAP 113, M 84, SD 49, MP 25, C 22, V 21, L 19, KD 16

Judicial branch: *highest court(s):* Supreme Court of Sweden (consists of 16 justices including the court chairman); Supreme Administrative Court (consists of 18 justices including the court president)
judge selection and term of office: Supreme Court and Supreme Administrative Court justices nominated by the Board of Judges, a 9-member nominating body consisting of high-level judges, prosecutors, and members of Parliament; justices appointed by the Government; following a probationary period, justices' appointments are permanent
subordinate courts: first instance, appellate, general, and administrative courts; specialized courts that handle cases such as land and environment, immigration, labor, markets, and patents

Political parties and leaders: Center Party (Centerpartiet) or C [Annie LOOF]
Christian Democrats (Kristdemokraterna) or KD [Ebba Busch THOR]
Green Party (Miljopartiet de Grona) or MP [Isabella LOVIN and Gustav FRIDOLIN]
Left Party (Vansterpartiet) or V [Jonas SJOSTEDT]
Liberal Party (Liberalerna) or L [Jan BJORKLUND]
Moderate Party (Moderaterna) or M [Ulf KRISTERSSON]
Swedish Social Democratic Party (Socialdemokraterna) or SAP [Stefan LOFVEN]
Sweden Democrats (Sverigedemokraterna) or SD [Jimmie AKESSON]

Political pressure groups and leaders: Confederation of Swedish Enterprise (Svenskt Naringsliv) [Carola LEMNE]

Swedish Confederation of Professional Associations or SACO [Goran ARRIUS]

Swedish Confederation of Professional Employees or TCO [Eva NORDMARK]

Swedish Trade Union Confederation (Landsorganisationen) or LO [Karl-Petter THORWALDSSON]

other: environmental groups; media

International organization participation: ADB (nonregional member), AfDB (nonregional member), Arctic Council, Australia Group, BIS, CBSS, CD, CE, CERN, EAPC, EBRD, ECB, EIB, EITI (implementing country), EMU, ESA, EU, FAO, FATF, G-9, G-10, IADB, IAEA, IBRD, ICAO, ICC (national committees), ICCt, ICRM, IDA, IEA, IFAD, IFC, IFRCS, IGAD (partners), IHO, ILO, IMF, IMO, IMSO, Interpol, IOC, IOM, IPU, ISO, ITSO, ITU, ITUC (NGOs), MIGA, MINUSMA, MONUSCO, NC, NEA, NIB, NSG, OAS (observer), OECD, OPCW, OSCE, Paris Club, PCA, PFP, Schengen Convention, UN, UN Security Council (temporary), UNCTAD, UNESCO, UNHCR, UNIDO, UNMISS, UNMOGIP, UNRWA, UNTSO, UPU, WCO, WFTU (NGOs), WHO, WIPO, WMO, WTO, ZC

Diplomatic representation in the US: chief of mission: Ambassador Karin Ulrika OLOFSDOTTER (since 17 September 2017)

chancery: The House of Sweden, 2900 K Street NW, Washington, DC 20007

telephone: [1] (202) 467-2600

FAX: [1] (202) 467-2699

consulate(s) general: New York

Diplomatic representation from the US: *chief of mission:* Ambassador (vacant); Charge d'Affaires David E. LINDWALL (since 20 January 2017)

embassy: Dag Hammarskjolds Vag 31, SE-11589 Stockholm

mailing address: American Embassy Stockholm, US Department of State, 5750 Stockholm Place, Washington, DC 20521-5750

telephone: [46] (08) 783 53 00

FAX: [46] (08) 661 19 64

Flag description: blue with a golden yellow cross extending to the edges of the flag; the vertical part of the cross is shifted to the hoist side in the style of the Dannebrog (Danish flag); the colors reflect those of the Swedish coat of arms—three gold crowns on a blue field

National symbol(s): three crowns, lion; national colors: blue, yellow

National anthem: *name:* "Du Gamla, Du Fria" (Thou Ancient, Thou Free)

lyrics/music: Richard DYBECK/traditional

note: in use since 1844; also known as "Sang till Norden" (Song of the North), is based on a Swedish folk tune; it has never been officially adopted by the government; "Kungssangen" (The King's Song) serves as the royal anthem and is played in the presence of the royal family and during certain state ceremonies

ECONOMY

Economy—overview: Sweden has achieved an enviable standard of living with its combination of free-market capitalism and extensive welfare benefits. Sweden remains outside the euro zone largely out of concern that joining the European Economic and Monetary Union would diminish the country's sovereignty over its welfare system. Timber, hydropower, and iron ore constitute the resource base of an economy heavily oriented toward foreign trade.

Sweden's economy experienced modest growth in 2014-17, with real GDP growth above 3%, but continues to struggle with deflationary pressure.

GDP (purchasing power parity): $521.7 billion (2017 est.)

$506 billion (2016 est.)

$490.4 billion (2015 est.)

note: data are in 2017 dollars

country comparison to the world: 39

GDP (official exchange rate): $541.9 billion (2016 est.)

GDP—real growth rate: 3.1% (2017 est.)

3.2% (2016 est.)

4.1% (2015 est.)

country comparison to the world: 110

GDP—per capita (PPP): $51,300 (2017 est.)

$50,600 (2016 est.)

$49,800 (2015 est.)

note: data are in 2017 dollars

country comparison to the world: 26

Gross national saving: 29.9% of GDP (2017 est.)

29.2% of GDP (2016 est.)

28.9% of GDP (2015 est.)

country comparison to the world: 24

GDP—composition, by end use:

household consumption: 44.2%

government consumption: 25.4%

investment in fixed capital: 25.3%

investment in inventories: 0.3%

exports of goods and services: 45.5%

imports of goods and services: -40.7% (2017 est.)

GDP—composition, by sector of origin:

agriculture: 1.6%

industry: 33%

services: 65.4% (2017 est.)

Agriculture—products: barley, wheat, sugar beets; meat, milk

Industries: iron and steel, precision equipment (bearings, radio and telephone parts, armaments), wood pulp and paper products, processed foods, motor vehicles

Industrial production growth rate: 2.5% (2017 est.)

country comparison to the world: 113

Labor force: 5.361 million (2017 est.)

country comparison to the world: 77

Labor force—by occupation: *agriculture:* 2%

industry: 12%

services: 86% (2014 est.)

Unemployment rate: 6.6% (2017 est.)

7% (2016 est.)

country comparison to the world: 93

Population below poverty line: 15% (2014 est.)

Household income or consumption by percentage share: *lowest 10%:* 3.4%

highest 10%: 24% (2012)

Distribution of family income—Gini index: 24.9 (2013)

25 (1992)

country comparison to the world: 145

Budget: *revenues:* $274.8 billion

expenditures: $269.9 billion (2017 est.)

Taxes and other revenues: 50.7% of GDP (2017 est.)

country comparison to the world: 15

Budget surplus (+) or deficit (-): 0.9% of GDP (2017 est.)

country comparison to the world: 18

Public debt: 39% of GDP (2017 est.)

41.7% of GDP (2016 est.)

note: data cover general government debt, and includes debt instruments issued (or owned) by government entities other than the treasury; the data include treasury debt held by foreign entities; the data include debt issued by subnational entities, as well as intra-governmental debt; intra-governmental debt consists of treasury borrowings from surpluses in the social funds, such as for retirement, medical care, and unemployment; debt instruments for the social funds are not sold at public auctions

country comparison to the world: 137

Fiscal year: calendar year

Inflation rate (consumer prices): 1.6% (2017 est.)

1.1% (2016 est.)

country comparison to the world: 72

Central bank discount rate: -0.5% (31 December 2016)

-0.35% (31 December 2015)

note: the Discount rate was abolished in 2002, and replaced by a "Reference rate" with no bearing on monetary policy; the rate quoted here is the Reference rate

country comparison to the world: 160

Commercial bank prime lending rate: 2% (31 December 2017 est.)

1.85% (31 December 2016 est.)

country comparison to the world: 177

Stock of narrow money: $339.9 billion (31 December 2017 est.)

$273.5 billion (31 December 2016 est.)

country comparison to the world: 15

Stock of broad money: $395.8 billion (31 December 2017 est.)

$321.3 billion (31 December 2016 est.)

country comparison to the world: 29

Stock of domestic credit: $953.1 billion (31 December 2017 est.)

$748.6 billion (31 December 2016 est.)

country comparison to the world: 19

Market value of publicly traded shares: $560.5 billion (31 December 2012 est.)

$470.1 billion (31 December 2011 est.)

$581.2 billion (31 December 2010 est.)

country comparison to the world: 21

Current account balance: $21.4 billion (2017 est.)
$23.07 billion (2016 est.)
country comparison to the world: 17

Exports: $169.7 billion (2017 est.)
$151.4 billion (2016 est.)
country comparison to the world: 30

Exports—commodities: machinery 35%, motor vehicles, paper products, pulp and wood, iron and steel products, chemicals (2012 est.)

Exports—partners: Germany 10.6%, Norway 10.4%, US 7.3%, Denmark 7%, Finland 6.8%, UK 6%, Netherlands 5.4%, Belgium 4.7%, France 4.4% (2016)

Imports: $154.8 billion (2017 est.)
$139.9 billion (2016 est.)
country comparison to the world: 29

Imports—commodities: machinery, petroleum and petroleum products, chemicals, motor vehicles, iron and steel; foodstuffs, clothing

Imports—partners: Germany 18.8%, Netherlands 8.2%, Norway 7.8%, Denmark 7.6%, China 5.6%, UK 5.2%, Belgium 4.6%, Finland 4.5%, France 4.1% (2016)

Reserves of foreign exchange and gold: $59.39 billion (31 December 2016 est.)
$59.39 billion (31 December 2016 est.)
country comparison to the world: 37

Debt—external: $939.9 billion (31 March 2016 est.)
$929.4 billion (31 March 2015 est.)
country comparison to the world: 17

Stock of direct foreign investment—at home: $405.1 billion (31 December 2017 est.)
$390.5 billion (31 December 2016 est.)
country comparison to the world: 20

Stock of direct foreign investment—abroad: $495.7 billion (31 December 2017 est.)
$479.3 billion (31 December 2016 est.)
country comparison to the world: 17

Exchange rates: Swedish kronor (SEK) per US dollar—
8.442 (2017 est.)
8.5605 (2016 est.)
8.5605 (2015 est.)
8.4335 (2014 est.)
6.8612 (2013 est.)

ENERGY

Electricity access: *electrification—total population:* 100% (2016)

Electricity—production: 154.3 billion kWh (2015 est.)
country comparison to the world: 25

Electricity—consumption: 125.4 billion kWh (2015 est.)
country comparison to the world: 30

Electricity—exports: 26.02 billion kWh (2016 est.)
country comparison to the world: 7

Electricity—imports: 14.29 billion kWh (2016 est.)
country comparison to the world: 17

Electricity—installed generating capacity: 39.67 million kW (2015 est.)
country comparison to the world: 26

Electricity—from fossil fuels: 6.3% of total installed capacity (2015 est.)
country comparison to the world: 204

Electricity—from nuclear fuels: 24.3% of total installed capacity (2015 est.)
country comparison to the world: 5

Electricity—from hydroelectric plants: 40.9% of total installed capacity (2015 est.)
country comparison to the world: 50

Electricity—from other renewable sources: 30% of total installed capacity (2015 est.)
country comparison to the world: 13

Crude oil—production: 0 bbl/day (2016 est.)
country comparison to the world: 203

Crude oil—exports: 0 bbl/day (2016 est.)
country comparison to the world: 194

Crude oil—imports: 393,900 bbl/day (2016 est.)
country comparison to the world: 23

Crude oil—proved reserves: 0 bbl (1 January 2017 es)
country comparison to the world: 202

Refined petroleum products—production: 418,700 bbl/day (2016 est.)
country comparison to the world: 38

Refined petroleum products—consumption: 320,200 bbl/day (2016 est.)
country comparison to the world: 42

Refined petroleum products—exports: 336,300 bbl/day (2016 est.)
country comparison to the world: 25

Refined petroleum products—imports: 220,300 bbl/day (2016 est.)
country comparison to the world: 30

Natural gas—production: 0 cu m (2015 est.)
country comparison to the world: 199

Natural gas—consumption: 1.25 billion cu m (2015 est.)
country comparison to the world: 94

Natural gas—exports: 0 cu m (2015 est.)
country comparison to the world: 187

Natural gas—imports: 812 million cu m (2015 est.)
country comparison to the world: 63

Natural gas—proved reserves: 0 cu m (1 January 2014 es)
country comparison to the world: 197

Carbon dioxide emissions from consumption of energy: 62 million Mt (2015 est.)
country comparison to the world: 55

COMMUNICATIONS

Telephones—fixed lines: *total subscriptions:* 3,328,371
subscriptions per 100 inhabitants: 34 (July 2016 est.)
country comparison to the world: 43

Telephones—mobile cellular: *total:* 12,362,191

subscriptions per 100 inhabitants: 125 (July 2016 est.)
country comparison to the world: 75

Telephone system: *general assessment:* highly developed telecommunications infrastructure; ranked among leading countries for fixed-line, mobile-cellular, Internet, and broadband penetration
domestic: coaxial and multiconductor cables carry most of the voice traffic; parallel microwave radio relay systems carry some additional telephone channels
international: country code—46; submarine cables provide links to other Nordic countries and Europe; satellite earth stations—1 Intelsat (Atlantic Ocean), 1 Eutelsat, and 1 Inmarsat (Atlantic and Indian Ocean regions); note—Sweden shares the Inmarsat earth station with the other Nordic countries (Denmark, Finland, Iceland, and Norway) (2016)

Broadcast media: publicly owned TV broadcaster operates 2 terrestrial networks plus regional stations; multiple privately owned TV broadcasters operating nationally, regionally, and locally; about 50 local TV stations; widespread access to pan-Nordic and international broadcasters through multi-channel cable and satellite TV; publicly owned radio broadcaster operates 3 national stations and a network of 25 regional channels; roughly 100 privately owned local radio stations with some consolidating into near national networks; an estimated 900 community and neighborhood radio stations broadcast intermittently (2008)

Internet country code: .se

Internet users: *total:* 9,041,427
percent of population: 91.5% (July 2016 est.)
country comparison to the world: 47

TRANSPORTATION

National air transport system: number of registered air carriers: 8
inventory of registered aircraft operated by air carriers: 219
annual passenger traffic on registered air carriers: 11,623,930
annual freight traffic on registered air carriers: 0 mt-km (2015)
Civil aircraft registration country code prefix: SE (2016)

Airports: 231 (2013)
country comparison to the world: 25

Airports—with paved runways: *total:* 149
over 3,047 m: 3
2,438 to 3,047 m: 12
1,524 to 2,437 m: 75
914 to 1,523 m: 22
under 914 m: 37 (2013)

Airports—with unpaved runways: *total:* 82
914 to 1,523 m: 5
under 914 m: 77 (2013)

Heliports: 2 (2013)

Pipelines: gas 1,626 km (2013)

Railways: *total:* 14,127 km
standard gauge: 14,062 km 1.435-m gauge (12,322 km electrified)
narrow gauge: 65 km 0.891-m gauge (65 km electrified) (2016)
country comparison to the world: 21

Roadways: *total:* 573,134 km (includes 2,050 km of expressways)
paved: 140,100 km
unpaved: 433,034 km
note: includes 98,500 km of state roads, 433,034 km of private roads, and 41,600 km of municipal roads (2016)
country comparison to the world: 13

Waterways: 2,052 km (2010)
country comparison to the world: 40

Merchant marine: *total:* 368
by type: general cargo 71, oil tanker 23, other 274 (2017)

country comparison to the world: 47

Ports and terminals: *major seaport(s):* Brofjorden, Goteborg, Helsingborg, Karlshamn, Lulea, Malmo, Stockholm, Trelleborg, Visby
LNG terminal(s) (import): Brunnsviksholme, Lysekil

MILITARY AND SECURITY

Military expenditures: 1.04% of GDP (2016)
1.09% of GDP (2015)
1.14% of GDP (2014)
1.13% of GDP (2013)
1.15% of GDP (2012)
country comparison to the world: 84

Military branches: Swedish Armed Forces (Forsvarsmakten): Army (Armen), Royal Swedish Navy (Marinen), Swedish Air Force (Svenska Flygvapnet) (2016)

Military service age and obligation: 18-47 years of age for male and female voluntary military service; Swedish citizenship required; service obligation: 7.5 months (Army), 7-15 months (Navy), 8-12 months (Air Force); after completing initial service, soldiers have a reserve commitment until age 47; compulsory military service, abolished in 2010, is due to be reinstated in 2018 (2017)

TRANSNATIONAL ISSUES

Disputes—international: none

Refugees and internally displaced persons: refugees (country of origin): 96,914 (Syria); 25,968 (Eritrea); 21,693 (Iraq); 22,548 (Somalia); 16,558 (Afghanistan) (2016)
stateless persons: 36,036 (2016); note—the majority of stateless people are from the Middle East and Somalia

SWITZERLAND

INTRODUCTION

Background: The Swiss Confederation was founded in 1291 as a defensive alliance among three cantons. In succeeding years, other localities joined the original three. The Swiss Confederation secured its independence from the Holy Roman Empire in 1499. A constitution of 1848, subsequently modified in 1874, replaced the confederation with a centralized federal government. Switzerland's sovereignty and neutrality have long been honored by the major European powers, and the country was not involved in either of the two world wars. The political and economic integration of Europe over the past half century, as well as Switzerland's role in many UN and international organizations, has strengthened Switzerland's ties with its neighbors. However, the country did not officially become a UN member until 2002. Switzerland remains active in many UN and international organizations but retains a strong commitment to neutrality.

GEOGRAPHY

Location: Central Europe, east of France, north of Italy

Geographic coordinates: 47 00 N, 8 00 E

Map references: Europe

Area: *total:* 41,277 sq km
land: 39,997 sq km
water: 1,280 sq km
country comparison to the world: 136

Area—comparative: slightly less than twice the size of New Jersey

Land boundaries: total: 1,770 km
border countries (5): Austria 158 km, France 525 km, Italy 698 km, Liechtenstein 41 km, Germany 348 km

Coastline: 0 km (landlocked)

Maritime claims: none (landlocked)

Climate: temperate, but varies with altitude; cold, cloudy, rainy/snowy winters; cool to warm, cloudy, humid summers with occasional showers

Terrain: mostly mountains (Alps in south, Jura in northwest) with a central plateau of rolling hills, plains, and large lakes

Elevation: *mean elevation:* 1,350 m

elevation extremes: *lowest point:* Lake Maggiore 195 m
highest point: Dufourspitze 4,634 m

Natural resources: hydropower potential, timber, salt

Land use: *agricultural land:* 38.7%
arable land: 10.2%;
permanent crops: 0.6%;
permanent pasture: 27.9%
forest: 31.5%
other: 29.8% (2011 est.)
Irrigated land: 630 sq km (2012)

Population—distribution: population distribution corresponds to elevation with the northern and western areas far more heavily populated; the higher Alps of the south limit settlement

Natural hazards: avalanches, landslides; flash floods

Environment—current issues: air pollution from vehicle emissions and open-air burning; acid rain; water pollution from increased use of agricultural fertilizers; loss of biodiversity

Environment—international agreements: *party to:* Air Pollution, Air Pollution-Nitrogen Oxides, Air Pollution-Persistent Organic Pollutants, Air Pollution-Sulfur 85, Air Pollution-Sulfur 94, Air Pollution-Volatile Organic Compounds, Antarctic Treaty, Biodiversity, Climate Change, Climate Change-Kyoto Protocol, Desertification, Endangered Species, Environmental Modification, Hazardous Wastes, Marine Dumping, Marine Life Conservation, Ozone Layer Protection, Ship Pollution, Tropical Timber 83, Tropical Timber 94, Wetlands, Whaling
signed, but not ratified: Law of the SeaGeography—note: landlocked; crossroads of northern and southern Europe; along with southeastern France, northern Italy, and southwestern Austria, has the highest elevations in the Alps

PEOPLE AND SOCIETY

Population: 8,236,303 (July 2017 est.)
country comparison to the world: 98

Nationality: *noun:* Swiss (singular and plural)
adjective: Swiss

Ethnic groups: German 65%, French 18%, Italian 10%, Romansch 1%, other 6%

Languages: German (or Swiss German) (official) 63%, French (official) 22.7%, Italian (official) 8.1%, English 4.9%, Portuguese 3.7%, Albanian 3%, Serbo-Croatian 2.4%, Spanish 2.2%, Romansch (official) 0.5%, other 7.1%
note: German, French, Italian, and Romansch are all national and official languages; totals more than 100% because some respondents indicated more than one main language (2015 est.)

Religions: Roman Catholic 37.3%, Protestant 24.9%, other Christian 5.8%, Muslim 5.1%, other 1.4%, Jewish 0.2%, none 23.9%, unspecified 1.3% (2015 est.)

Age structure: 0-14 years: 15.16% (male 642,814/female 605,689)

15-24 years: 10.88% (male 458,044/female 438,373)

25-54 years: 43.21% (male 1,784,051/female 1,774,494)

55-64 years: 12.6% (male 519,709/female 518,421)

65 years and over: 18.15% (male 658,673/female 836,035) (2017 est.)

Dependency ratios: total dependency ratio: 48.8
youth dependency ratio: 22
elderly dependency ratio: 26.8
potential support ratio: 3.7 (2015 est.)

Median age: total: 42.4 years
male: 41.4 years
female: 43.4 years (2017 est.)
country comparison to the world: 28

Population growth rate: 0.69% (2017 est.)
country comparison to the world: 144

Birth rate: 10.5 births/1,000 population (2017 est.)
country comparison to the world: 187

Death rate: 8.3 deaths/1,000 population (2017 est.)
country comparison to the world: 83

Net migration rate: 4.7 migrant(s)/1,000 population (2017 est.)
country comparison to the world: 26

Population distribution: population distribution corresponds to elevation with the northern and western areas far more heavily populated; the higher Alps of the south limit settlement

Urbanization: urban population: 74.1% of total population (2017)
rate of urbanization: 1.1% annual rate of change (2015-20 est.)

Major urban areas—population: Zurich 1.246 million; BERN (capital) 358,000 (2015)

Sex ratio: at birth: 1.06 male(s)/female
0-14 years: 1.06 male(s)/female
15-24 years: 1.04 male(s)/female
25-54 years: 1.01 male(s)/female
55-64 years: 1 male(s)/female
65 years and over: 0.78 male(s)/female
total population: 0.97 male(s)/female (2016 est.)

Mother's mean age at first birth: 30.7 years (2014 est.)

Maternal mortality ratio: 5 deaths/100,000 live births (2015 est.)
country comparison to the world: 172

Infant mortality rate: total: 3.6 deaths/1,000 live births
male: 4 deaths/1,000 live births
female: 3.2 deaths/1,000 live births (2017 est.)
country comparison to the world: 202

Life expectancy at birth: total population: 82.6 years
male: 80.3 years
female: 85.1 years (2017 est.)

country comparison to the world: 10

Total fertility rate: 1.56 children born/woman (2017 est.)
country comparison to the world: 189

Contraceptive prevalence rate: 72.9% (2012)

Health expenditures: 11.7% of GDP (2014)
country comparison to the world: 7

Physicians density: 4.11 physicians/1,000 population (2014)

Hospital bed density: 5 beds/1,000 population (2011)

Drinking water source:
improved:
 urban: 100% of population
rural: 100% of population
total: 100% of population
unimproved:
urban: 0% of population
rural: 0% of population
total: 0% of population (2015 est.)

Sanitation facility access:
improved:
urban: 99.9% of population
rural: 99.8% of population
total: 99.9% of population
unimproved:
urban: 0.1% of population
rural: 0.2% of population
total: 0.1% of population (2015 est.)

HIV/AIDS—adult prevalence rate: NA

HIV/AIDS—people living with HIV/AIDS: NA

HIV/AIDS—deaths: NA

Obesity—adult prevalence rate: 19.5% (2016)
country comparison to the world: 112

Education expenditures: 5.1% of GDP (2013)
country comparison to the world: 66

School life expectancy (primary to tertiary education): total: 16 years
male: 16 years
female: 16 years (2014)

Unemployment, youth ages 15-24: total: 8.4%
male: 8.7%
female: 8.1% (2016 est.)
country comparison to the world: 111

GOVERNMENT

Country name: conventional long form: Swiss Confederation
conventional short form: Switzerland
local long form: Schweizerische Eidgenossenschaft (German); Confederation Suisse (French); Confederazione Svizzera (Italian); Confederaziun Svizra (Romansh)
local short form: Schweiz (German); Suisse (French); Svizzera (Italian); Svizra (Romansh)
etymology: name derives from the canton of Schwyz, one of the founding cantons of the Old Swiss Confederacy that formed in the 14th century

Government type: federal republic (formally a confederation)

Capital: name: Bern

geographic coordinates: 46 55 N, 7 28 E
time difference: UTC+1 (6 hours ahead of Washington, DC, during Standard Time)
daylight saving time: +1hr, begins last Sunday in March; ends last Sunday in October

Administrative divisions: 26 cantons (cantons, singular—canton in French; cantoni, singular—cantone in Italian; Kantone, singular—Kanton in German); Aargau, Appenzell Ausserrhoden, Appenzell Innerrhoden, Basel-Landschaft, Basel-Stadt, Berne/Bern, Fribourg/Freiburg, Geneve, Glarus, Graubuenden/Grigioni/Grischun, Jura, Luzern, Neuchatel, Nidwalden, Obwalden, Sankt Gallen, Schaffhausen, Schwyz, Solothurn, Thurgau, Ticino, Uri, Valais/Wallis, Vaud, Zug, Zuerich
note: 6 of the cantons—Appenzell Ausserrhoden, Appenzell Innerrhoden, Basel-Landschaft, Basel-Stadt, Nidwalden, Obwalden—are referred to as half cantons because they elect only one member to the Council of States and, in popular referendums where a majority of popular votes and a majority of cantonal votes are required, these 6 cantons only have a half vote

Independence: 1 August 1291 (founding of the Swiss Confederation)

National holiday: Founding of the Swiss Confederation in 1291; note—since 1 August 1891 celebrated as Swiss National Day

Constitution: history: previous 1848, 1874; latest adopted by referendum 18 April 1999, effective 1 January 2000
amendments: proposed by the two houses of the Federal Assembly or by petition of at least one million voters (called the "federal popular initiative"); passage of proposals requires majority vote in a referendum; following drafting of an amendment by the Assembly, its passage requires approval by majority vote in a referendum and approval by the majority of cantons; amended many times, last in 2016 (2016)

Legal system: civil law system; judicial review of legislative acts, except for federal decrees of a general obligatory character

International law organization participation: accepts compulsory ICJ jurisdiction with reservations; accepts ICCt jurisdiction

Citizenship: citizenship by birth: no
citizenship by descent only: at least one parent must be a citizen of Switzerland
dual citizenship recognized: yes
residency requirement for naturalization: 12 years including at least 3 of the last 5 years prior to application

Suffrage: 18 years of age; universal

Executive branch: chief of state: President of the Swiss Confederation Alain BERSET (since 1 January 2018); Vice President Ueli MAURER (since 1 January 2018); note—the Federal Council, which is comprised of 7 federal councillors, constitutes the federal government of Switzerland; council members rotate in a 1-year term as federal president (chief of state and head of government)
head of government: President of the Swiss Confederation Alain BERSET (since 1 January 2018);

Vice President Ueli MAURER (since 1 January 2018)

cabinet: Federal Council or Bundesrat (in German), Conseil Federal (in French), Consiglio Federale (in Italian) indirectly elected usually from among its members by the Federal Assembly for a 4-year term

elections/appointments: president and vice president elected by the Federal Assembly from among members of the Federal Council for a 1-year, nonconsecutive term; election last held on December 2017 (next to be held in December 2018)

election results: Alain BERSET elected president; Federal Assembly vote—190 of 210; Ueli MAURER elected vice president; Federal Assembly vote—178 of 192

Legislative branch: *description:* bicameral Federal Assembly or Bundesversammlung (in German), Assemblee Federale (in French), Assemblea Federale (in Italian) consists of the Council of States or Staenderat (in German), Conseil des Etats (in French), Consiglio degli Stati (in Italian) (46 seats; members in multi-seat constituencies representing cantons and single-seat constituencies representing half cantons directly elected by simple majority vote; members serve 4-year terms) and the National Council or Nationalrat (in German), Conseil National (in French), Consiglio Nazionale (in Italian) (200 seats; 195 members in cantons directly elected by proportional representation vote and 6 in half cantons directly elected by simple majority vote; members serve 4-year terms)

elections: Council of States—last held in most cantons on 18 October 2015 (each canton determines when the next election will be held); National Council—last held on 18 October 2015 (next to be held in October 2019)

election results: Council of States—percent of vote by party—NA; seats by party as of 18 October 2015—CVP 13, FDP 13, SDP 12, SVP 5, other 3; National Council—percent of vote by party—SVP 29.4%, SPS 18.8%, FDP 16.4%, CVP 11.6%, Green Party 7.1%, GLP 4.6%, BDP 4.1%, other 8.0%; seats by party—SVP 68, SPS 43, FDP 33, CVP 30, Green Party 12, GLP 7, BDP 7

Judicial branch: *highest court(s):* Federal Supreme Court (consists of 38 judges and 31 substitutes and organized into 5 sections)

judge selection and term of office: judges elected by the Federal Assembly for 6-year terms; note—judges are affiliated with political parties and are elected according to linguistic and regional criteria in approximate proportion to the level of party representation in the Federal Assembly

subordinate courts: Federal Criminal Court (began in 2004); Federal Administrative Court (began in 2007); note—each of Switzerland's 26 cantons has its own courts

Political parties and leaders: Christian Democratic People's Party (Christlichdemokratische Volkspartei der Schweiz or CVP, Parti Democrate-Chretien Suisse or PDC, Partito Popolare Democratico Svizzero or PPD, Partida Cristiandemocratica dalla Svizra or PCD) [Gerhard PFISTER]

Conservative Democratic Party (Buergerlich-Demokratische Partei Schweiz or BDP, Parti Bourgeois Democratique Suisse or PBD, Partito Borghese Democratico Svizzero or PBD, Partido burgais democratica Svizera or PBD) [Martin LANDOLT]

Free Democratic Party or FDP.The Liberals (FDP. Die Liberalen, PLR.Les Liberaux-Radicaux, PLR.I Liberali, Ils Liberals) [Petra GOESSI]

Green Liberal Party (Grunliberale or GLP, Parti vert liberale or PVL, Partito Verde-Liberale or PVL, Partida Verde Liberale or PVL) [Jurge GROSSEN]

Green Party (Gruene Partei der Schweiz or Gruene, Parti Ecologiste Suisse or Les Verts, Partito Ecologista Svizzero or I Verdi, Partida Ecologica Svizra or La Verda) [Regula RYTZ]

Social Democratic Party (Sozialdemokratische Partei der Schweiz or SPS, Parti Socialiste Suisse or PSS, Partito Socialista Svizzero or PSS, Partida Socialdemocratica de la Svizra or PSS) [Christian LEVRAT]

Swiss People's Party (Schweizerische Volkspartei or SVP, Union Democratique du Centre or UDC, Unione Democratica di Centro or UDC, Uniun Democratica dal Center or UDC) [Albert ROESTI]

other minor parties

Political pressure groups and leaders: NA

International organization participation: ADB (nonregional member), AfDB (nonregional member), Australia Group, BIS, CD, CE, CERN, EAPC, EBRD, EFTA, EITI (implementing country), ESA, FAO, FATF, G-10, IADB, IAEA, IBRD, ICAO, ICC (national committees), ICCt, ICRM, IDA, IEA, IFAD, IFC, IFRCS, IGAD (partners), ILO, IMF, IMO, IMSO, Interpol, IOC, IOM, IPU, ISO, ITSO, ITU, ITUC (NGOs), LAIA (observer), MIGA, MINUSMA, MONUSCO, NEA, NSG, OAS (observer), OECD, OIF, OPCW, OSCE, Pacific Alliance (observer), Paris Club, PCA, PFP, Schengen Convention, UN, UNCTAD, UNESCO, UNHCR, UNIDO, UNITAR, UNMISS, UNMOGIP, UNRWA, UNTSO, UNWTO, UPU, WCO, WHO, WIPO, WMO, WTO, ZC

Diplomatic representation in the US: chief of mission: Ambassador Martin Werner DAHINDEN (since 18 November 2014)

chancery: 2900 Cathedral Avenue NW, Washington, DC 20008

telephone: [1] (202) 745-7900

FAX: [1] (202) 387-2564

consulate(s) general: Atlanta, Chicago, Los Angeles, New York, San Francisco

Diplomatic representation from the US: *chief of mission:* Ambassador Edward "Ed" MCMULLEN (since 21 November 2017) note—also accredited to Liechtenstein

embassy: Sulgeneckstrasse 19, CH-3007 Bern

mailing address: use embassy street address

telephone: [41] (031) 357-70-11

FAX: [41] (031) 357-73-20

Flag description: red square with a bold, equilateral white cross in the center that does not extend to the edges of the flag; various medieval legends purport to describe the origin of the flag; a white cross used as identification for troops of the Swiss Confederation is first attested at the Battle of Laupen (1339)

National symbol(s): Swiss cross (white cross on red field, arms equal length); national colors: red, white

National anthem: the Swiss anthem has four names: "Schweizerpsalm" [German] "Cantique Suisse" [French] "Salmo svizzero," [Italian] "Psalm svizzer" [Romansch] (Swiss Psalm)

lyrics/music: Leonhard WIDMER [German], Charles CHATELANAT [French], Camillo VALSANGIACOMO [Italian], and Flurin CAMATHIAS [Romansch]/Alberik ZWYSSIG

note: unofficially adopted 1961, officially 1981; the anthem has been popular in a number of Swiss cantons since its composition (in German) in 1841; translated into the other three official languages of the country (French, Italian, and Romansch), it is official in each of those languages

ECONOMY

Economy—overview: Switzerland, a country that espouses neutrality, is a prosperous and modern market economy with low unemployment, a highly skilled labor force, and a per capita GDP among the highest in the world. Switzerland's economy benefits from a highly developed service sector, led by financial services, and a manufacturing industry that specializes in high-technology, knowledge-based production. Its economic and political stability, transparent legal system, exceptional infrastructure, efficient capital markets, and low corporate tax rates also make Switzerland one of the world's most competitive economies.

The Swiss have brought their economic practices largely into conformity with the EU's to enhance their international competitiveness, but some trade protectionism remains, particularly for its small agricultural sector. The fate of the Swiss economy is tightly linked to that of its neighbors in the euro zone, which purchases half of Swiss exports. The global financial crisis of 2008 and resulting economic downturn in 2009 stalled demand for Swiss exports and put Switzerland into a recession. During this period, the Swiss National Bank (SNB) implemented a zero-interest rate policy to boost the economy, as well as to prevent appreciation of the franc, and Switzerland's economy began to recover in 2010.

The sovereign debt crises unfolding in neighboring euro-zone countries, however, coupled with ongoing economic instability in Russia and other eastern European economies continue to pose a significant risk to the Swiss economy, driving up demand for the Swiss franc by investors seeking a safe-haven currency. In January 2015, the SNB abandoned the Swiss franc's peg to the euro, roiling global currency markets and making active SNB intervention a necessary hallmark of present-day Swiss monetary policy. The independent SNB has upheld its zero interest rate policy and conducted major market interventions to prevent further appreciation of the Swiss franc, but parliamentarians have urged it to do more to weaken the currency. The franc's strength has made Swiss exports less competitive and weakened the country's growth outlook; GDP growth fell below 2% per year from 2011-17.

In recent years, Switzerland has responded to increasing pressure from neighboring countries and trading partners to reform its banking secrecy laws, by agreeing to conform to OECD regulations on administrative assistance in tax matters, including tax evasion. The Swiss government has also renegotiated its double taxation agreements with numerous countries, including the US, to incorporate OECD standards, and is openly considering the possibility of imposing taxes on bank deposits held by foreigners.

GDP (purchasing power parity): $516.7 billion (2017 est.)
$511.5 billion (2016 est.)
$504.5 billion (2015 est.)
note: data are in 2017 dollars
country comparison to the world: 40

GDP (official exchange rate): $680.6 billion (2016 est.)

GDP—real growth rate: 1% (2017 est.)
1.4% (2016 est.)
1.2% (2015 est.)
country comparison to the world: 187

GDP—per capita (PPP): $61,400 (2017 est.)
$61,400 (2016 est.)
$61,200 (2015 est.)
note: data are in 2017 dollars
country comparison to the world: 17

Gross national saving: 33.5% of GDP (2017 est.)
33.6% of GDP (2016 est.)
34.5% of GDP (2015 est.)
country comparison to the world: 18

GDP—composition, by end use:
household consumption: 53.7%
government consumption: 11.5%
investment in fixed capital: 24%
investment in inventories: -0.7%
exports of goods and services: 67.5%
imports of goods and services: -56% (2017 est.)

GDP—composition, by sector of origin:
agriculture: 0.7%
industry: 25.6%
services: 73.7% (2017 est.)

Agriculture—products: grains, fruits, vegetables; meat, eggs, dairy products

Industries: machinery, chemicals, watches, textiles, precision instruments, tourism, banking, insurance, pharmaceuticals

Industrial production growth rate: 2% (2017 est.)
country comparison to the world: 133

Labor force: 5.159 million (2017 est.)
country comparison to the world: 81

Labor force—by occupation: *agriculture:* 3.3%
industry: 19.8%
services: 76.9% (2015)

Unemployment rate: 3% (2017 est.)
3.3% (2016 est.)

country comparison to the world: 35

Population below poverty line: 6.6% (2014 est.)

Household income or consumption by percentage share: *lowest 10%:* 7.5%
highest 10%: 19% (2007)

Distribution of family income—Gini index: 29.5 (2014 est.)
33.1 (1992)
country comparison to the world: 128

Budget: *revenues:* $223.5 billion
expenditures: $222.1 billion
note: includes federal, cantonal, and municipal budgets (2017 est.)
Taxes and other revenues: 32.8% of GDP (2017 est.)
country comparison to the world: 70

Budget surplus (+) or deficit (-): 0.2% of GDP (2017 est.)
country comparison to the world: 29

Public debt: 32.9% of GDP (2017 est.)
32.6% of GDP (2016 est.)
note: general government gross debt; gross debt consists of all liabilities that require payment or payments of interest and/or principal by the debtor to the creditor at a date or dates in the future; includes debt liabilities in the form of Special Drawing Rights (SDRs), currency and deposits, debt securities, loans, insurance, pensions and standardized guarantee schemes, and other accounts payable; all liabilities in the GFSM 2001 system are debt, except for equity and investment fund shares and financial derivatives and employee stock options
country comparison to the world: 153

Fiscal year: calendar year

Inflation rate (consumer prices): 0.5% (2017 est.)
-0.4% (2016 est.)
country comparison to the world: 20

Central bank discount rate: 0.5% (31 December 2016)
0.75% (31 December 2009)
country comparison to the world: 133

Commercial bank prime lending rate: 2.6% (31 December 2017 est.)
2.65% (31 December 2016 est.)
country comparison to the world: 175

Stock of narrow money: $619.4 billion (31 December 2017 est.)
$555.7 billion (31 December 2016 est.)
country comparison to the world: 11

Stock of broad money: $1.335 trillion (31 December 2017 est.)
$1.232 trillion (31 December 2016 est.)
country comparison to the world: 16

Stock of domestic credit: $1.267 trillion (31 December 2017 est.)
$1.166 trillion (31 December 2016 est.)
country comparison to the world: 16

Market value of publicly traded shares: $1.519 trillion (31 December 2015 est.)
$1.495 trillion (31 December 2014 est.)
$1.541 trillion (31 December 2013 est.)
country comparison to the world: 10

Current account balance: $67.33 billion (2017 est.)
$70.54 billion (2016 est.)
country comparison to the world: 8

Exports: $336.8 billion (2017 est.)
$318.1 billion (2016 est.)
note: trade data exclude trade with Switzerland
country comparison to the world: 16

Exports—commodities: machinery, chemicals, metals, watches, agricultural products

Exports—partners: Germany 14.4%, US 12.1%, UK 10.7%, China 9%, Hong Kong 6.1%, France 5.8%, Italy 4.9%, India 4.8% (2016)

Imports: $286.7 billion (2017 est.)
$264.9 billion (2016 est.)
country comparison to the world: 18

Imports—commodities: machinery, chemicals, vehicles, metals; agricultural products, textiles

Imports—partners: Germany 19.4%, US 9%, Italy 7.4%, UK 7.1%, UAE 6.2%, France 6.1%, China 4.7% (2016)

Reserves of foreign exchange and gold: $679.3 billion (31 December 2016 est.)
$679.3 billion (31 December 2016 est.)
country comparison to the world: 4

Debt—external: $1.664 trillion (31 March 2016 est.)
$1.663 trillion (31 March 2015 est.)
country comparison to the world: 13

Stock of direct foreign investment—at home: $1.23 trillion (31 December 2017 est.)
$1.217 trillion (31 December 2016 est.)
country comparison to the world: 9

Stock of direct foreign investment—abroad: $1.556 trillion (31 December 2017 est.)
$1.528 trillion (31 December 2016 est.)
country comparison to the world: 7

Exchange rates: Swiss francs (CHF) per US dollar—
0.9875 (2017 est.)
0.9852 (2016 est.)
0.9852 (2015 est.)
0.9627 (2014 est.)
0.9152 (2013 est.)

ENERGY

Electricity access: *electrification—total population:* 100% (2016)

Electricity—production: 64.06 billion kWh (2015 est.)
country comparison to the world: 45

Electricity—consumption: 58.45 billion kWh (2015 est.)
country comparison to the world: 44

Electricity—exports: 30.17 billion kWh (2016 est.)
country comparison to the world: 6

Electricity—imports: 34.1 billion kWh (2016 est.)
country comparison to the world: 5

Electricity—installed generating capacity: 19.62 million kW (2015 est.)
country comparison to the world: 45

Electricity—from fossil fuels: 2.9% of total installed capacity (2015 est.)
country comparison to the world: 208

Electricity—from nuclear fuels: 17% of total installed capacity (2015 est.)
country comparison to the world: 12

Electricity—from hydroelectric plants: 61% of total installed capacity (2015 est.)
country comparison to the world: 26

Electricity—from other renewable sources: 11.1% of total installed capacity (2015 est.)
country comparison to the world: 67

Crude oil—production: 0 bbl/day (2016 est.)
country comparison to the world: 204

Crude oil—exports: 319.1 bbl/day (2016 est.)
country comparison to the world: 77

Crude oil—imports: 58,400 bbl/day (2016 est.)
country comparison to the world: 53

Crude oil—proved reserves: 0 bbl (1 January 2017 es)
country comparison to the world: 203

Refined petroleum products—production: 63,400 bbl/day (2016 est.)
country comparison to the world: 79

Refined petroleum products—consumption: 217,400 bbl/day (2016 est.)
country comparison to the world: 54

Refined petroleum products—exports: 8,894 bbl/day (2016 est.)
country comparison to the world: 85

Refined petroleum products—imports: 166,300 bbl/day (2016 est.)
country comparison to the world: 39

Natural gas—production: 25 million cu m (2015 est.)
country comparison to the world: 91

Natural gas—consumption: 4.639 billion cu m (2015 est.)
country comparison to the world: 67

Natural gas—exports: 0 cu m (2016 est.)
country comparison to the world: 189

Natural gas—imports: 3.484 billion cu m (2015 est.)
country comparison to the world: 40

Natural gas—proved reserves: NA cu m (1 January 2011 es)

Carbon dioxide emissions from consumption of energy: 45 million Mt (2013 est.)
country comparison to the world: 63

COMMUNICATIONS

Telephones—fixed lines: *total subscriptions:* 4.029 million
subscriptions per 100 inhabitants: 49 (July 2016 est.)
country comparison to the world: 38

Telephones—mobile cellular: *total:* 11,283,400
subscriptions per 100 inhabitants: 138 (July 2016 est.)
country comparison to the world: 79

Telephone system: *general assessment:* highly developed telecommunications infrastructure with excellent domestic and international services
domestic: ranked among leading countries for fixed-line teledensity and infrastructure; mobile-cellular subscribership roughly 140 per 100 persons; extensive cable and microwave radio relay networks
international: country code—41; satellite earth stations—2 Intelsat (Atlantic Ocean and Indian Ocean) (2016)

Broadcast media: the publicly owned radio and TV broadcaster, Swiss Broadcasting Corporation (SRG/SSR), operates 7 national TV networks, 3 broadcasting in German, 2 in Italian, and 2 in French; private commercial TV stations broadcast regionally and locally; TV broadcasts from stations in Germany, Italy, and France are widely available via multi-channel cable and satellite TV services; SRG/SSR operates 17 radio stations that, along with private broadcasters, provide national to local coverage (2015)

Internet country code: .ch

Internet users: *total:* 7,312,744
percent of population: 89.4% (July 2016 est.)
country comparison to the world: 54

TRANSPORTATION

National air transport system: number of registered air carriers: 12
inventory of registered aircraft operated by air carriers: 163
annual passenger traffic on registered air carriers: 26,843,991
annual freight traffic on registered air carriers: 1,322,379,468 mt-km (2015)
Civil aircraft registration country code prefix: HB (2016)

Airports: 63 (2013)
country comparison to the world: 78

Airports—with paved runways: *total:* 40
over 3,047 m: 3
2,438 to 3,047 m: 2
1,524 to 2,437 m: 12
914 to 1,523 m: 6
under 914 m: 17 (2013)

Airports—with unpaved runways: *total:* 23
under 914 m: 23 (2013)

Heliports: 2 (2013)

Pipelines: gas 1,800 km; oil 94 km; refined products 7 km (2013)

Railways: *total:* 5,651.5 km
standard gauge: 4,424.8 km 1.435-m gauge (3,634.1 km electrified)

narrow gauge: 2 km 1.200-m gauge (2 km electrified); 1,188.3 km 1.000-m gauge (1,167.3 km electrified); 36.4 km 0.800-m gauge (36.4 km electrified) (2014)
country comparison to the world: 33

Roadways: *total:* 71,464 km
paved: 71,464 km (includes 1,415 of expressways) (2011)
country comparison to the world: 66

Waterways: 1,292 km (there are 1,227 km of waterways on lakes and rivers for public transport and 65 km on the Rhine River between Basel-Rheinfelden and Schaffhausen-Bodensee for commercial goods transport) (2010)
country comparison to the world: 57

Merchant marine: *total:* 51
by type: bulk carrier 30, general cargo 12, oil tanker 1, other 8 (2017)
country comparison to the world: 113
Ports and terminals: river port(s): Basel (Rhine)

MILITARY AND SECURITY

Military expenditures: 0.71% of GDP (2016)
0.67% of GDP (2015)
0.66% of GDP (2014)
0.73% of GDP (2013)
0.69% of GDP (2012)
country comparison to the world: 117

Military branches: Swiss Armed Forces: Land Forces, Swiss Air Force (Schweizer Luftwaffe) (2013)

Military service age and obligation: 19-26 years of age for male compulsory military service; 18 years of age for voluntary male and female military service; every Swiss male has to serve at least 260 days in the armed forces; conscripts receive 18 weeks of mandatory training, followed by seven 3-week intermittent recalls for training during the next 10 years (2012)

TRANSNATIONAL ISSUES

Disputes—international: none
Refugees and internally displaced persons: refugees (country of origin): 26,264 (Eritrea); 11,159 (Syria); 5,675 (Afghanistan); 5,458 (Sri Lanka) (2016)
stateless persons: 66 (2016)

Illicit drugs: a major international financial center vulnerable to the layering and integration stages of money laundering; despite significant legislation and reporting requirements, secrecy rules persist and nonresidents are permitted to conduct business through offshore entities and various intermediaries; transit country for and consumer of South American cocaine, Southwest Asian heroin, and Western European synthetics; domestic cannabis cultivation and limited ecstasy production

SYRIA

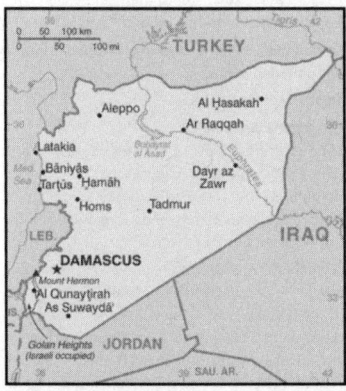

INTRODUCTION

Background: Following World War I, France acquired a mandate over the northern portion of the former Ottoman Empire province of Syria. The French administered the area as Syria until granting it independence in 1946. The new country lacked political stability and experienced a series of military coups. Syria united with Egypt in February 1958 to form the United Arab Republic. In September 1961, the two entities separated, and the Syrian Arab Republic was reestablished. In the 1967 Arab-Israeli War, Syria lost the Golan Heights region to Israel. During the 1990s, Syria and Israel held occasional, albeit unsuccessful, peace talks over its return. In November 1970, Hafiz al-ASAD, a member of the socialist Ba'th Party and the minority Alawi sect, seized power in a bloodless coup and brought political stability to the country. Following the death of President Hafiz al-ASAD, his son, Bashar al-ASAD, was approved as president by popular referendum in July 2000. Syrian troops—stationed in Lebanon since 1976 in an ostensible peacekeeping role—were withdrawn in April 2005. During the July-August 2006 conflict between Israel and Hizballah, Syria placed its military forces on alert but did not intervene directly on behalf of its ally Hizballah. In May 2007, Bashar al-ASAD's second term as president was approved by popular referendum.

Influenced by major uprisings that began elsewhere in the region, and compounded by additional social and economic factors, antigovernment protests broke out first in the southern province of Dar'a in March 2011 with protesters calling for the repeal of the restrictive Emergency Law allowing arrests without charge, the legalization of political parties, and the removal of corrupt local officials. Demonstrations and violent unrest spread across Syria with the size and intensity of protests fluctuating. The government responded to unrest with a mix of concessions—including the repeal of the Emergency Law, new laws

permitting new political parties, and liberalizing local and national elections—and with military force and detentions. The government's efforts to quell unrest and armed opposition activity led to extended clashes between government forces, their allies, and oppositionists.

International pressure on the ASAD regime intensified after late 2011, as the Arab League, the EU, Turkey, and the US expanded economic sanctions against the regime and those entities that support it. In December 2012, the Syrian National Coalition, was recognized by more than 130 countries as the sole legitimate representative of the Syrian people. In September 2015, Russia launched a military intervention on behalf of the ASAD regime, and government-aligned forces recaptured Aleppo city in December 2016, shifting the conflict in the regime's favor. Political negotiations between the government and opposition delegations at UN-sponsored Geneva conferences since 2014 have failed to produce a resolution of the conflict. Russia, Iran, and Turkey since early 2017 have held negotiations in Astana to establish de-escalation zones to reduce violence in Syria, and Russia has also begun pushing for political negotiations in Sochi. Unrest continues in Syria, and according to an April 2016 UN estimate, the death toll among Syrian Government forces, opposition forces, and civilians was over 400,000. As of December 2017, approximately 13.1 million people were in need of humanitarian assistance in Syria, with 6.3 million people displaced internally, and an additional 5.4 million registered Syrian refugees, making the Syrian situation among the largest humanitarian crises worldwide

GEOGRAPHY

Location: Middle East, bordering the Mediterranean Sea, between Lebanon and Turkey

Geographic coordinates: 35 00 N, 38 00 E

Map references: Middle East

Area: *total:* 185,180 sq km
land: 183,630 sq km
water: 1,550 sq km
note: includes 1,295 sq km of Israeli-occupied territory
country comparison to the world: 90

Area—comparative: slightly more than 1.5 times the size of Pennsylvania
Land boundaries: total: 2,363 km
border countries (5): Iraq 599 km, Israel 83 km, Jordan 379 km, Lebanon 403 km, Turkey 899 km

Coastline: 193 km

Maritime claims: *territorial sea:* 12 nm
contiguous zone: 24 nm

Climate: mostly desert; hot, dry, sunny summers (June to August) and mild, rainy winters (December to February) along coast; cold weather with snow or sleet periodically in Damascus

Terrain: primarily semiarid and desert plateau; narrow coastal plain; mountains in west

Elevation: *mean elevation:* 514 m

elevation extremes: *lowest point:* unnamed location near Lake Tiberias -208 m
highest point: Mount Hermon (Jabal a-Shayk) 2,814 m

Natural resources: petroleum, phosphates, chrome and manganese ores, asphalt, iron ore, rock salt, marble, gypsum, hydropower

Land use: *agricultural land:* 75.8%
arable land: 25.4%;
permanent crops: 5.8%;
permanent pasture: 44.6%
forest: 2.7%
other: 21.5% (2011 est.)
Irrigated land: 14,280 sq km (2012)

Population—distribution: significant population density along the Mediterranean coast; larger concentrations found in the major cities of Damascus, Aleppo (the country's largest city), and Hims (Homs); more than half of the population lives in the coastal plain, the province of Halab, and the Euphrates River valley
note: the ongoing civil war has altered the population distribution

Natural hazards: dust storms, sandstorms
volcanism: Syria's two historically active volcanoes, Es Safa and an unnamed volcano near the Turkish border have not erupted in centuries

Environment—current issues: deforestation; overgrazing; soil erosion; desertification; water pollution from raw sewage and petroleum refining wastes; inadequate potable water

Environment—international agreements: *party to:* Biodiversity, Climate Change, Climate Change-Kyoto Protocol, Desertification, Endangered Species, Hazardous Wastes, Ozone Layer Protection, Ship Pollution, Wetlands
signed, but not ratified: Environmental ModificationGeography—note: the capital of Damascus—located at an oasis fed by the Barada River—is thought to be one of the world's oldest continuously inhabited cities; there are 42 Israeli settlements and civilian land use sites in the Israeli-occupied Golan Heights (2017)

PEOPLE AND SOCIETY

Population: 18,028,549 (July 2017 est.)
note: approximately 20,500 Israeli settlers live in the Golan Heights (2014)
country comparison to the world: 63

Nationality: *noun:* Syrian(s)
adjective: Syrian

Ethnic groups: Arab 90.3%, Kurdish, Armenian, and other 9.7%

Languages: Arabic (official), Kurdish, Armenian, Aramaic, Circassian, French, English

Religions: Muslim 87% (official; includes Sunni 74% and Alawi, Ismaili, and Shia 13%), Christian 10% (includes Orthodox, Uniate, and Nestorian), Druze 3%, Jewish (few remaining in Damascus and Aleppo)

Age structure: *0-14 years:* 31.62% (male 2,923,814/female 2,777,073)
15-24 years: 19.54% (male 1,790,360/female 1,732,694)
25-54 years: 39.22% (male 3,522,653/female 3,547,540)
55-64 years: 5.41% (male 482,576/female 493,085)
65 years and over: 4.21% (male 342,407/female 416,347) (2017 est.)

Dependency ratios: *total dependency ratio:* 72.8
youth dependency ratio: 65.8
elderly dependency ratio: 7
potential support ratio: 14.3 (2015 est.)

Median age: *total:* 24.3 years
male: 23.9 years
female: 24.8 years (2017 est.)
country comparison to the world: 160

Population growth rate: NA

Birth rate: 21.2 births/1,000 population (2017 est.)
country comparison to the world: 75

Death rate: 4 deaths/1,000 population (2017 est.)
country comparison to the world: 211

Net migration rate: NA

Population distribution: significant population density along the Mediterranean coast; larger concentrations found in the major cities of Damascus, Aleppo (the country's largest city), and Hims (Homs); more than half of the population lives in the coastal plain, the province of Halab, and the Euphrates River valley
note: the ongoing civil war has altered the population distribution

Urbanization: *urban population:* 58.5% of total population (2017)
rate of urbanization: 3.59% annual rate of change (2015-20 est.)

Major urban areas—population: Aleppo 3.562 million; DAMASCUS (capital) 2.566 million; Hims (Homs) 1.641 million; Hamah 1.237 million; Lattakia 781,000 (2015)

Sex ratio: *at birth:* 1.06 male(s)/female
0-14 years: 1.05 male(s)/female
15-24 years: 1.03 male(s)/female
25-54 years: 0.99 male(s)/female
55-64 years: 0.98 male(s)/female
65 years and over: 0.82 male(s)/female
total population: 1.01 male(s)/female (2016 est.)

Maternal mortality ratio: 68 deaths/100,000 live births (2015 est.)
country comparison to the world: 85

Infant mortality rate: *total:* 14.8 deaths/1,000 live births
male: 17 deaths/1,000 live births
female: 12.5 deaths/1,000 live births (2017 est.)
country comparison to the world: 101

Life expectancy at birth: *total population:* 75.1 years
male: 72.7 years
female: 77.6 years (2017 est.)
country comparison to the world: 111

Total fertility rate: 2.5 children born/woman (2017 est.)
country comparison to the world: 79

Contraceptive prevalence rate: 53.9% (2009/10)

Health expenditures: 3.3% of GDP (2014)
country comparison to the world: 180

Physicians density: 1.55 physicians/1,000 population (2014)

Hospital bed density: 1.5 beds/1,000 population (2012)

Drinking water source:
improved:
 urban: 92.3% of population
 rural: 87.2% of population
 total: 90.1% of population
unimproved:
 urban: 7.7% of population
 rural: 12.8% of population
 total: 9.9% of population (2015 est.)

Sanitation facility access:
improved:
 urban: 96.2% of population
 rural: 95.1% of population
 total: 95.7% of population
unimproved:
 urban: 3.8% of population
 rural: 4.9% of population
 total: 4.3% of population (2015 est.)

HIV/AIDS—adult prevalence rate: NA

HIV/AIDS—people living with HIV/AIDS: NA

HIV/AIDS—deaths: NA (2016 est.)

Obesity—adult prevalence rate: 27.8% (2016)
country comparison to the world: 35

Children under the age of 5 years underweight: 10.1% (2009)
country comparison to the world: 70

Education expenditures: 5.1% of GDP (2009)
country comparison to the world: 70

Literacy: *definition:* age 15 and over can read and write
total population: 86.4%
male: 91.7%
female: 81% (2015 est.)

School life expectancy (primary to tertiary education): *total:* 9 years
male: 9 years
female: 9 years (2013)

Unemployment, youth ages 15-24: *total:* 35.8%
male: 26.6%
female: 71.1% (2011 est.)
country comparison to the world: 58

GOVERNMENT

Country name: *conventional long form:* Syrian Arab Republic
conventional short form: Syria
local long form: Al Jumhuriyah al Arabiyah as Suriyah
local short form: Suriyah

former: United Arab Republic (with Egypt)
etymology: name ultimately derived from the ancient Assyrians who dominated northern Mesopotamia, but whose reach also extended westward to the Levant; over time, the name came to be associated more with the western area

Government type: presidential republic; highly authoritarian regime

Capital: *name:* Damascus
geographic coordinates: 33 30 N, 36 18 E
time difference: UTC+2 (7 hours ahead of Washington, DC, during Standard Time)
daylight saving time: +1hr, begins midnight on the last Friday in March; ends at midnight on the last Friday in October

Administrative divisions: 14 provinces (muhafazat, singular—muhafazah); Al Hasakah, Al Ladhiqiyah (Latakia), Al Qunaytirah, Ar Raqqah, As Suwayda', Dar'a, Dayr az Zawr, Dimashq (Damascus), Halab, Hamah, Hims (Homs), Idlib, Rif Dimashq (Damascus Countryside), Tartus

Independence: 17 April 1946 (from League of Nations mandate under French administration)

National holiday: Independence Day (Evacuation Day), 17 April (1946); note—celebrates the leaving of the last French troops and the proclamation of full independence

Constitution: *history:* several previous; latest issued 15 February 2012, passed by referendum and effective 27 February 2012
amendments: proposed by the president of the republic or by one-third of the People's Assembly members; following review by a special Assembly committee, passage requires at least three-quarters majority vote by the Assembly and approval by the president (2016)

Legal system: mixed legal system of civil and Islamic law (for family courts)

International law organization participation: has not submitted an ICJ jurisdiction declaration; non-party state to the ICCt

Citizenship: *citizenship by birth:* no
citizenship by descent only: the father must be a citizen of Syria; if the father is unknown or stateless, the mother must be a citizen of Syria
dual citizenship recognized: yes
residency requirement for naturalization: 10 years

Suffrage: 18 years of age; universal

Executive branch: *chief of state:* President Bashar al-ASAD (since 17 July 2000); Vice President Najah al-ATTAR (since 23 March 2006)
head of government: Prime Minister Imad Muhammad Dib KHAMIS (since 22 June 2016); Deputy Prime Ministers Fahd Jasim al-FURAYJ, Lt. Gen.(since 23 June 2012) and Walid al-MUALEM (since 23 June 2012)
cabinet: Council of Ministers appointed by the president
elections/appointments: president directly elected by simple majority popular vote for a 7-year term (eligible for a second term); election last held on 3 June 2014 (next to be held in June

2021); the president appoints the vice presidents, prime minister, and deputy prime ministers

election results: Bashar al-ASAD elected president; percent of vote—Bashar al-ASAD (Ba'th Party) 88.7%, Hassan al-NOURI (independent) 4.3%, Maher HAJJER (independent) 3.2%, other/invalid 3.8%

Legislative branch: *description:* unicameral People's Assembly or Majlis al-Shaab (250 seats; members directly elected in multi-seat constituencies by proportional representation vote to serve 4-year terms)

elections: last held on 13 April 2016 (next to be held in 2020)

election results: percent of vote by party—NPF 80%, other 20%; seats by party—NPF 200, other 50

Judicial branch: highest court(s): Court of Cassation (organized into civil, criminal, religious, and military divisions, each with 3 judges); Supreme Constitutional Court (consists of 7 members)

judge selection and term of office: Court of Cassation judges appointed by the Supreme Judicial Council or SJC, a judicial management body headed by the minister of justice with 7 members including the national president; judge tenure NA; Supreme Constitutional Court judges nominated by the president and appointed by the SJC; judges appointed for 4-year renewable terms

subordinate courts: courts of first instance; magistrates' courts; religious and military courts; Economic Security Court; Counterterrorism Court (established June 2012)

Political parties and leaders: legal parties/alliances: Arab Socialist Ba'ath Party [Bashar al-ASAD, regional secretary)

Arab Socialist Union of Syria or ASU [Safwan al-QUDSI]

National Progressive Front or NPF [Bashar al-ASAD, Suleiman QADDAH] (alliance includes Arab Socialist Renaissance (Ba'th) Party [President Bashar al-ASAD], Socialist Unionist Democratic Party [Fadlallah Nasr al-DIN])

Syrian Communist Party (two branches) [Wissal Farha BAKDASH, Yusuf Rashid FAYSAL]

Syrian Social Nationalist Party or SSNP [Ali HAIDAR]

Unionist Socialist Party [Fayez ISMAIL]

Kurdish parties (considered illegal): Kurdish Azadi Party

Kurdish Democratic Accord Party (al Wifaq) [Fowzi SHINKALI]

Kurdish Democratic Left Party [Saleh KIDDO]

Kurdish Democratic Party (al Parti-Ibrahim wing) [Nasr al-Din IBRAHIM]

Kurdish Democratic Party (al Parti-Mustafa wing)

Kurdish Democratic Party in Syria or KDP-S [Saud AL-MALA]

Kurdish Democratic Patriotic/National Party

Kurdish Democratic Peace Party [Talal MOHAMMED]

Kurdish Democratic Progressive Party or KDPP-Darwish

Kurdish Democratic Progressive Party or KDPP-Muhammad

Kurdish Democratic Union Party or PYD [Salih Muslim MOHAMMAD]

Kurdish Democratic Unity Party [Kamiron Haj ABDU]

Kurdish Democratic Yekiti Party [Mahi al-Din Sheikh ALI]

Kurdish Equality Party [Namet DAOUD]

Kurdish Future Party [Rezan HASSAN]

Kurdish Green Party [Laqman AHMI]

Kurdish Left Party [Shallal KIDDO]

Kurdish National Democratic Rally in Syria

Kurdish Reform Movement in Syria [Amjad OTHMAN]

Kurdish Reform Movement Party [Feisal AL-YUSSEF]

Kurdish Yekiti (Union) Party

Kurdistan Communist Party [Nejm al-Sin MALA'AMIR]

Kurdistan Democratic Party in Syria [Abdul Karim SAKKO]

Kurdistan Liberal Union [Farhad TILO]

Syrian Kurdish Democratic Party

Tiyar al-Mustaqbal [Narin MATINI]

other: Syrian Democratic Party [Mustafa QALAAJI]

Political pressure groups and leaders: note: as of December 2017,there were hundreds of political and armed opposition groups that organize protests, provide civilian services, and stage armed attacks

International organization participation: ABEDA, AFESD, AMF, CAEU, FAO, G-24, G-77, IAEA, IBRD, ICAO, ICC (national committees), ICRM, IDA, IDB, IFAD, IFC, IFRCS, IHO, ILO, IMF, IMO, Interpol, IOC, IPU, ISO, ITSO, ITU, LAS, MIGA, NAM, OAPEC, OIC, OPCW, UN, UNCTAD, UNESCO, UNIDO, UNRWA, UNWTO, UPU, WCO, WFTU (NGOs), WHO, WIPO, WMO, WTO (observer)

Diplomatic representation in the US: *note:* Embassy ceased operations and closed on 18 March 2014

chief of mission: Ambassador (vacant); Charge d'Affaires Mounir KOUDMANI (since 1 June 2012)

chancery: 2215 Wyoming Avenue NW, Washington, DC 20008

telephone: [1] (202) 232-6313

FAX: [1] (202) 234-9548

Diplomatic representation from the US: *chief of mission:* ambassador (vacant); US Senior Advisor for Syria Stephanie WILLIAMS (since 2017); note—on 6 February 2012, the US closed its embassy in Damascus; Czechia serves as protecting power for US interests in Syria

embassy: Abou Roumaneh, 2 Al Mansour Street, Damascus

mailing address: P. O. Box 29, Damascus

telephone: [963] (11) 3391-4444

FAX: [963] (11) 3391-3999

Flag description: three equal horizontal bands of red (top), white, and black; two small, green, five-pointed stars in a horizontal line centered in the white band; the band colors derive from the Arab Liberation flag and represent oppression

(black), overcome through bloody struggle (red), to be replaced by a bright future (white); identical to the former flag of the United Arab Republic (1958-1961) where the two stars represented the constituent states of Syria and Egypt; the current design dates to 1980

note: similar to the flag of Yemen, which has a plain white band, Iraq, which has an Arabic inscription centered in the white band, and that of Egypt, which has a gold Eagle of Saladin centered in the white band

National symbol(s): hawk; national colors: red, white, black, green

National anthem: *name:* "Humat ad-Diyar" (Guardians of the Homeland)

lyrics/music: Khalil Mardam BEY/Mohammad Salim FLAYFEL and Ahmad Salim FLAYFEL

note: adopted 1936, restored 1961; between 1958 and 1961, while Syria was a member of the United Arab Republic with Egypt, the country had a different anthem

ECONOMY

Economy—overview: Syria's economy continues to deteriorate amid the ongoing conflict that began in 2011, declining by more than 70% from 2010 to 2017. The government has struggled to address the effects of international sanctions, widespread infrastructure damage, diminished domestic consumption and production, reduced subsidies, and high inflation, which have caused dwindling foreign exchange reserves, rising budget and trade deficits, a decreasing value of the Syrian pound, and falling household purchasing power.

During 2014, the ongoing conflict and continued unrest and economic decline worsened the humanitarian crisis and elicited a greater need for international assistance, as the number of people in need inside Syria increased from 9.3 million to 12.2 million, and the number of Syrian refugees increased from 2.2 million to more than 3.3 million.

Prior to the turmoil, Damascus had begun liberalizing economic policies, including cutting lending interest rates, opening private banks, consolidating multiple exchange rates, raising prices on some subsidized items, and establishing the Damascus Stock Exchange, but the economy remains highly regulated. Long-run economic constraints include foreign trade barriers, declining oil production, high unemployment, rising budget deficits, increasing pressure on water supplies caused by heavy use in agriculture, rapid population growth, industrial expansion, water pollution, and widespread infrastructure damage.

GDP (purchasing power parity): $50.28 billion (2015 est.)

$55.8 billion (2014 est.)

$61.9 billion (2013 est.)

notes: data are in 2015 US dollars

the war-driven deterioration of the economy resulted in a disappearance of quality national level statistics in the 2012-13 period

country comparison to the world: 110

GDP (official exchange rate): $24.6 billion (2014 est.)

GDP—real growth rate: NA% (2017 est.)
-36.5% (2014 est.)
-30.9% (2013 est.)
note: data are in 2015 dollars

GDP—per capita (PPP): $2,900 (2015 est.)
$3,300 (2014 est.)
$2,800 (2013 est.)
note: data are in 2015 US dollars
country comparison to the world: 194

Gross national saving: 20.3% of GDP (2017 est.)
19.1% of GDP (2016 est.)
20.1% of GDP (2015 est.)
country comparison to the world: 86

GDP—composition, by end use:
household consumption: 63.9%
government consumption: 22.9%
investment in fixed capital: 18.1%
investment in inventories: 10.9%
exports of goods and services: 9.4%
imports of goods and services: -25.1% (2017 est.)

GDP—composition, by sector of origin:
agriculture: 20%
industry: 19.6%
services: 60.4% (2017 est.)

Agriculture—products: wheat, barley, cotton, lentils, chickpeas, olives, sugar beets; beef, mutton, eggs, poultry, milk

Industries: petroleum, textiles, food processing, beverages, tobacco, phosphate rock mining, cement, oil seeds crushing, automobile assembly

Industrial production growth rate: 4.4% (2017 est.)
country comparison to the world: 62

Labor force: 3.767 million (2017 est.)
country comparison to the world: 96

Labor force—by occupation: *agriculture:* 17%
industry: 16%
services: 67% (2008 est.)

Unemployment rate: 50% (2017 est.)
50% (2016 est.)
country comparison to the world: 214

Population below poverty line: 82.5% (2014 est.)

Household income or consumption by percentage share: *lowest 10%:* NA%
highest 10%: NA%

Budget: *revenues:* $1.033 billion
expenditures: $3.177 billion
note: government projections for FY2016 (2017 est.)
Taxes and other revenues: 4.2% of GDP (2017 est.)
country comparison to the world: 218

Budget surplus (+) or deficit (-): -8.7% of GDP (2017 est.)
country comparison to the world: 202

Public debt: 58.4% of GDP (2017 est.)
55.7% of GDP (2016 est.)
country comparison to the world: 78

Fiscal year: calendar year

Inflation rate (consumer prices): 25.5% (2017 est.)
43.9% (2016 est.)
country comparison to the world: 220

Central bank discount rate: 0.75% (31 December 2017)
5% (31 December 2016)
country comparison to the world: 130

Commercial bank prime lending rate: 33.3% (31 December 2017 est.)
32% (31 December 2016 est.)
country comparison to the world: 5

Stock of narrow money: $5.795 billion (31 December 2017 est.)
$4.488 billion (31 December 2016 est.)
country comparison to the world: 99

Stock of broad money: $6.696 billion (31 December 2017 est.)
$5.522 billion (31 December 2016 est.)
country comparison to the world: 120

Stock of domestic credit: $6.816 billion (31 December 2017 est.)
$5.993 billion (31 December 2016 est.)
country comparison to the world: 120

Market value of publicly traded shares: $NA

Current account balance: -$2.123 billion (2017 est.)
-$2.077 billion (2016 est.)
country comparison to the world: 159

Exports: $1.786 billion (2017 est.)
$1.705 billion (2016 est.)
country comparison to the world: 143

Exports—commodities: crude oil, minerals, petroleum products, fruits and vegetables, cotton fiber, textiles, clothing, meat and live animals, wheat

Exports—partners: Lebanon 34.6%, Jordan 11.6%, China 9.4%, Turkey 8.2%, Iraq 7.7%, Tunisia 4.9% (2016)

Imports: $5.649 billion (2017 est.)
$5.496 billion (2016 est.)
country comparison to the world: 118

Imports—commodities: machinery and transport equipment, electric power machinery, food and livestock, metal and metal products, chemicals and chemical products, plastics, yarn, paper

Imports—partners: Russia 22%, Turkey 20%, China 11.3% (2016)

Reserves of foreign exchange and gold: $407.3 million (31 December 2017 est.)
$504.6 million (31 December 2016 est.)
country comparison to the world: 147

Debt—external: $5.699 billion (31 December 2017 est.)
$5.085 billion (31 December 2016 est.)
country comparison to the world: 131

Exchange rates: Syrian pounds (SYP) per US dollar—
514.6 (2017 est.)
459.2 (2016 est.)
459.2 (2015 est.)
236.41 (2014 est.)

153.695 (2013 est.)

ENERGY

Electricity access: population without electricity: 1,600,000
electrification—*total population:* 96%
electrification—urban areas: 100%
electrification—rural areas: 81% (2013)

Electricity—production: 16.83 billion kWh (2015 est.)
country comparison to the world: 83

Electricity—consumption: 13.96 billion kWh (2015 est.)
country comparison to the world: 81

Electricity—exports: 262 million kWh (2015 est.)
country comparison to the world: 73

Electricity—imports: 0 kWh (2016 est.)
country comparison to the world: 205

Electricity—installed generating capacity: 9.61 million kW (2015 est.)
country comparison to the world: 62

Electricity—from fossil fuels: 84.4% of total installed capacity (2015 est.)
country comparison to the world: 78

Electricity—from nuclear fuels: 0% of total installed capacity (2015 est.)
country comparison to the world: 186

Electricity—from hydroelectric plants: 15.6% of total installed capacity (2015 est.)
country comparison to the world: 100

Electricity—from other renewable sources: 0% of total installed capacity (2015 est.)
country comparison to the world: 206

Crude oil—production: 28,670 bbl/day (2016 est.)
country comparison to the world: 64

Crude oil—exports: 0 bbl/day (2014 est.)
country comparison to the world: 195

Crude oil—imports: 83,140 bbl/day (2014 est.)
country comparison to the world: 46

Crude oil—proved reserves: 2.5 billion bbl (1 January 2017 es)
country comparison to the world: 33

Refined petroleum products—production: 111,600 bbl/day (2014 est.)
country comparison to the world: 66

Refined petroleum products—consumption: 140,000 bbl/day (2015 est.)
country comparison to the world: 74

Refined petroleum products—exports: 12,500 bbl/day (2014 est.)
country comparison to the world: 79

Refined petroleum products—imports: 41,120 bbl/day (2014 est.)
country comparison to the world: 91

Natural gas—production: 4.3 billion cu m (2015 est.)
country comparison to the world: 54

Natural gas—consumption: 4.9 billion cu m (2015 est.)
country comparison to the world: 65

Natural gas—exports: 0 cu m (2013 est.)
country comparison to the world: 188

Natural gas—imports: 249.2 million cu m (2011 est.)
country comparison to the world: 69

Natural gas—proved reserves: 240.7 billion cu m (1 January 2017 es)
country comparison to the world: 42

Carbon dioxide emissions from consumption of energy: 49 million Mt (2013 est.)
country comparison to the world: 61

COMMUNICATIONS

Telephones—fixed lines: *total subscriptions:* 3,464,846
subscriptions per 100 inhabitants: 20 (July 2016 est.)
country comparison to the world: 41

Telephones—mobile cellular: *total:* 12,350,927
subscriptions per 100 inhabitants: 72 (July 2016 est.)
country comparison to the world: 66

Telephone system: *general assessment:* the armed insurgency that began in 2011 has led to major disruptions to the network and has caused telephone and Internet outages throughout the country
domestic: the number of fixed-line connections increased markedly prior to the civil war in 2011; mobile-cellular service stands at about 70 per 100 persons
international: country code—963; submarine cable connection to Egypt, Lebanon, and Cyprus; satellite earth stations—1 Intelsat (Indian Ocean) and 1 Intersputnik (Atlantic Ocean region); coaxial cable and microwave radio relay to Iraq, Jordan, Lebanon, and Turkey; participant in Medarabtel (2016)

Broadcast media: state-run TV and radio broadcast networks; state operates 2 TV networks and a satellite channel; roughly two-thirds of Syrian homes have a satellite dish providing access to foreign TV broadcasts; 3 state-run radio channels; first private radio station launched in 2005; private radio broadcasters prohibited from transmitting news or political content (2007)

Internet country code: .sy

Internet users: *total:* 5,476,850
percent of population: 31.9% (July 2016 est.)
country comparison to the world: 71

TRANSPORTATION

National air transport system: number of registered air carriers: 2
inventory of registered aircraft operated by air carriers: 11
annual passenger traffic on registered air carriers: 475,932
annual freight traffic on registered air carriers: 1,517,388 mt-km (2015)
Civil aircraft registration country code prefix: YK (2016)

Airports: 90 (2013)
country comparison to the world: 62

Airports—with paved runways: *total:* 29
over 3,047 m: 5
2,438 to 3,047 m: 16
914 to 1,523 m: 3
under 914 m: 5 (2013)

Airports—with unpaved runways: *total:* 61
1,524 to 2,437 m: 1
914 to 1,523 m: 12
under 914 m: 48 (2013)

Heliports: 6 (2013)

Pipelines: gas 3,170 km; oil 2,029 km (2013)

Railways: *total:* 2,052 km
standard gauge: 1,801 km 1.435-m gauge
narrow gauge: 251 km 1.050-m gauge (2014)
country comparison to the world: 73

Roadways: *total:* 69,873 km
paved: 63,060 km
unpaved: 6,813 km (2010)
country comparison to the world: 68

Waterways: 900 km (navigable but not economically significant) (2011)
country comparison to the world: 68

Merchant marine: *total:* 21
by type: bulk carrier 1, general cargo 7, other 13 (2017)
country comparison to the world: 133

Ports and terminals: *major seaport(s):* Baniyas, Latakia, Tartus

MILITARY AND SECURITY

Military branches: Syrian Armed Forces: Land Forces, Naval Forces, Air Forces (includes Air Defense Forces), Intelligence Services (Air Force Intelligence, Military Intelligence)

Ministry of Interior: Political Security Directorate, General Intelligence Directorate, National Police Force (2017)

Military service age and obligation: 18 years of age for compulsory and voluntary military service; conscript service obligation is 18 months; women are not conscripted but may volunteer to serve (2017)

TERRORISM

Terrorist groups—home based: al-Nusrah Front: aim(s): overthrow Syrian President Bashar al-ASAD's regime, absorb like-minded Syrian rebel groups and, ultimately, establish a regional Islamic caliphate
area(s) of operation: headquartered in the northwestern Idlib Governorate, with a minor in Halab Governorate; operational primarily in northern, western, and southern Syria; al-Nusrah's subunit Jund al-Aqsa operates in Idlib and Hama governorates; installs Sharia in areas under its control; targets primarily Syrian regime and proregime forces, some minorities, occasionally other Syrian insurgent groups, and Western interests; openly collaborated with core al-Qa'ida veteran and senior figures until supreme leader Fateh al-JAWLANI announced publicly in mid-2016 that formal ties with al-Qa'ida had been cut and al-Nusrah would henceforth operate under the name Jabhat Fateh

al-Sham (Front for the Conquest of the Levant); JAWLANI's disaffiliation claim remained unsubstantiated as of early 2017, according to the US Government; engages in effective online and in-person recruitment campaigns in Syria; majority of members are Syrian, with many al-Qa'ida veterans from other jihad theaters; assessed in mid-2016 to have at least 6,000 active fighters

Islamic State of Iraq and the Levant (ISIL): *aim(s):* replace the Syrian Government with an Sunni Islamic state and implement ISIL's strict interpretation of Sharia
area(s) of operation: maintains extensive networks and an operational presence throughout the country, despite losing large swathes of territory since early 2016; ISIL had lost most of its control in its defacto capital, the city of Ar Raqqah, by mid-2017; continues to operate bases in the Ar Raqqah area and along the Syria-Iraq border; thousands of combatants target Syrian and Russian Government interests, religious and ethnic minorities, and all groups or governments that oppose ISIL's hardline Sunni jihadist ideology, including perceived Sunni rivals; exploits natural resources, especially oil and wheat, and levies taxes and fees on companies and individuals in areas under its control; responsible for millions of Syrians fleeing their homes, including the estimated 5 million who had left Syria by early 2017; fighters have ransacked and demolished numerous ancient sites that pre-date Islam, denouncing them as idolatrous; in May 2015, ISIL overran the ancient city of Palmyra, a UNESCO World Heritage site famed for its well-preserved Graeco-Roman ruins, and went on to destroy its best known structures; has used mustard and chlorine gas against civilian and military targets in Syria, where allies continue to work together to dismantle its chemical weapons production plants; dozens of key leaders have been killed since early 2016, putting ISIL's highly decentralized structure and spawling network of regional affiliates to the test; senior leader Gulmurod KHALIMOV, a former Tajik military officer serving as ISIL's chief recruiter, remains based in Syria; ISIL's chief cleric, Turki al-BINALI, was killed on 31 May 2017 during an airstrike in Al Mayadin, Dayr az Zawr Governorate, near the border with Iraq; al-BINALI's recorded lectures and other propaganda were central in recruiting foreign fighters

Terrorist groups—foreign based: Abdallah Azzam Brigades (AAB): aim(s): disrupt and attack Shia Muslim and Western interests in Syria
area(s) of operation: remains operational; conducts attacks against primarily Shia Muslim organizations and individuals, including Hizballah members, and Westerners and their interests
al-Qa'ida (AQ): aim(s): support al-Nusrah Front's efforts to overthrow President Bashar al-ASAD's regime and, ultimately, establish a regional Islamic caliphate
area(s) of operation: operational primarily in Idlib Governorate, with established networks and operating paramilitary training camps; likely continues to collaborate closely with al-Nusrah Front

leaders, despite public claims of severing ties; majority of members are not Syrian nationals

Ansar al-Islam (AAI): *aim(s):* remove Syrian President Bashar al-ASAD from power and install Sharia

area(s) of operation: operationally active in Syria since 2011; remained operational in Aleppo as of late 2016; launches attacks on Syrian Government and security forces and pro-Syrian Government militias; some AAI factions combat ISIL, while others are aligned with ISIL

Hizballah: *aim(s):* preserve Syrian President Bashar al-ASAD's regime

area(s) of operation: operational activity throughout the country since 2012; centered on providing paramilitary support to President Bashar al-ASAD's regime against armed insurgents; tens of thousands of fighters remained active in Syria as of 2017; thousands of fighters have died on the Syrian battlefield

Kata'ib Hizballah (KH): *aim(s):* preserve Syrian President Bashar al-ASAD's regime

area(s) of operation: deploys combatants to Syria to fight alongside Syrian Government and Lebanese Hizballah forces

Kurdistan Workers Party (PKK) (Kongra-Gel): *aim(s):* establish Kurdistan, which comprises territory in northern Syria

area(s) of operation: operational in the north combating ISIL, primarily in the Kurdish-populated region known as Rojava and Syrian Kurdistan; Salih MUSLIM Muhammad leads Kurdistan Workers Party's Syrian wing, the Syrian Kurdish Democratic Union Party (PYD); majority of fighters inside Syria are Syrian Kurds, along with Kurds from Iran, Turkey, and Iraq

Mujahidin Shura Council in the Environs of Jerusalem (MSC): *aim(s):* enhance its networks in Syria and, ultimately, destroy the state of Israel

area(s) of operation: maintains limited networks for operational planning against Israel, logistics, transferring funds, and smuggling fighters and arms through Syria from the Gaza Strip and Libya to be used against Israel; by 2017, the majority of veteran members had defected to join other groups

Palestine Liberation Front (PLF): *aim(s):* enhances its networks and, ultimately, destroy the state of Israel and establish a secular, Marxist Palestinian state with Jerusalem as its capital

area(s) of operation: maintains a recruitment and limited training presence in many refugee camps

PFLP-General Command (PFLP-GC): *aim(s):* preserve Syrian President Bashar al-ASAD's regime

area(s) of operation: maintains a political base in Damascus; fighting since early 2012 alongside President al-ASAD's forces and Hizballah in areas where anti-regime paramilitary groups are active; currently, preserving al-ASAD's government is the group's most pressing priority; receives funds and training from the regime

Popular Front for the Liberation of Palestine (PFLP): *aim(s):* enhance its recruitment networks in Syria

area(s) of operation: maintains a recruitment and limited training presence in several refugee camps

TRANSNATIONAL ISSUES

Disputes—international: Golan Heights is Israeli-occupied with the almost 1,000-strong UN Disengagement Observer Force patrolling a buffer zone since 1964; lacking a treaty or other documentation describing the boundary, portions of the Lebanon-Syria boundary are unclear with several sections in dispute; since 2000, Lebanon has claimed Shab'a Farms in the Golan Heights; 2004 Agreement and pending demarcation would settle border dispute with Jordan

Refugees and internally displaced persons: refugees (country of origin): 438,000 (Palestinian Refugees) (2017); 16,879 (Iraq)

note: the ongoing civil war has resulted almost 5.6 million Syrian refugees—dispersed in Egypt, Iraq, Jordan, Lebanon, and Turkey—as of February 2018

IDPs: 6.3 million (ongoing civil war since 2011) (2017)

stateless persons: 160,000 (2016); note—Syria's stateless population consists of Kurds and Palestinians; stateless persons are prevented from voting, owning land, holding certain jobs, receiving food subsidies or public healthcare, enrolling in public

schools, or being legally married to Syrian citizens; in 1962, some 120,000 Syrian Kurds were stripped of their Syrian citizenship, rendering them and their descendants stateless; in 2011, the Syrian Government granted citizenship to thousands of Syrian Kurds as a means of appeasement; however, resolving the question of statelessness is not a priority given Syria's ongoing civil war

Trafficking in persons: current situation: as conditions continue to deteriorate due to Syria's civil war, human trafficking has increased; Syrians remaining in the country and those that are refugees abroad are vulnerable to trafficking; Syria is a source and destination country for men, women and children subjected to forced labor and sex trafficking; Syrian children continue to be forcibly recruited by government forces, pro-regime militias, armed opposition groups, and terrorist organizations to serve as soldiers, human shields, and executioners; ISIL forces Syrian women and girls and Yazidi women and girls taken from Iraq to marry its fighters, where they experience domestic servitude and sexual violence; Syrian refugee women and girls are forced into exploitive marriages or prostitution in neighboring countries, while displaced children are forced into street begging domestically and abroad

tier rating: Tier 3—the government does not fully comply with the minimum standards for the elimination of trafficking and is not making significant efforts to do so; in 2014, Syria's violent conditions enabled human trafficking to flourish; the government made no effort to investigate, prosecute, or convict trafficking offenders or complicit government officials, including those who forcibly recruited child soldiers; authorities did not identify victims and failed to ensure victims, including child soldiers, were protected from arrest, detention, and severe abuse as a result of being trafficked (2015)

Illicit drugs: a transit point for opiates, hashish, and cocaine bound for regional and Western markets; weak anti-money-laundering controls and bank privatization may leave it vulnerable to money laundering

INTRODUCTION

Background: First inhabited by Austronesian people, Taiwan became home to Han immigrants beginning in the late Ming Dynasty (17th century). In 1895, military defeat forced China's Qing Dynasty to cede Taiwan to Japan, which then governed Taiwan for 50 years. Taiwan came under Chinese Nationalist (Kuomintang, KMT) control after World War II. With the communist victory in the Chinese civil war in 1949, the Nationalist-controlled Republic of China government and 2 million Nationalists fled to Taiwan and continued to claim to be the legitimate government for mainland China and Taiwan based on a 1947 Constitution drawn up for all of China. Until 1987, however, the Nationalist government ruled Taiwan under a civil war martial law declaration dating to 1948. Beginning in the 1970s, Nationalist authorities gradually began to incorporate the native population into the governing structure beyond the local level. The democratization process expanded rapidly in the 1980s, leading to the then illegal founding of Taiwan's first opposition party (the Democratic Progressive Party or DPP) in 1986 and the lifting of martial law the following year. Taiwan held legislative elections in 1992, the first in over forty years, and its first direct presidential election in 1996. In the 2000 presidential elections, Taiwan underwent its first peaceful transfer of power with the KMT loss to the DPP and afterwards experienced two additional democratic transfers of power in 2008 and 2016. Throughout this period, the island prospered, became one of East Asia's economic "Tigers," and after 2000 became a major investor in mainland China as cross-Strait ties matured. The dominant political issues continue to be economic reform and growth as well as management of sensitive relations between Taiwan and China.

GEOGRAPHY

Location: Eastern Asia, islands bordering the East China Sea, Philippine Sea, South China Sea, and Taiwan Strait, north of the Philippines, off the southeastern coast of China

Geographic coordinates: 23 30 N, 121 00 E

Map references: Southeast Asia

Area: *total:* 35,980 sq km
land: 32,260 sq km
water: 3,720 sq km
note: includes the Pescadores, Matsu, and Quemoy islands
country comparison to the world: 139

Area—comparative: slightly smaller than Maryland and Delaware combined
Land boundaries: 0 km

Coastline: 1,566.3 km

Maritime claims: *territorial sea:* 12 nm
exclusive economic zone: 200 nm

Climate: tropical; marine; rainy season during southwest monsoon (June to August); persistent and extensive cloudiness all year

Terrain: eastern two-thirds mostly rugged mountains; flat to gently rolling plains in west

Elevation: *mean elevation:* 1,150 m

elevation extremes: *lowest point:* South China Sea 0 m
highest point: Yu Shan 3,952 m

Natural resources: small deposits of coal, natural gas, limestone, marble, asbestos, arable land

Land use: *agricultural land:* 22.7%
arable land: 16.9%;
permanent crops: 5.8%;
permanent pasture: NA
forest: NA
other: 77.3% (2011 est.)
Irrigated land: 3,820 sq km (2012)

Population—distribution: distribution exhibits a peripheral coastal settlement pattern, with the largest populations on the north and west coasts

Natural hazards: earthquakes; typhoons
volcanism: Kueishantao Island (401 m), east of Taiwan, is its only historically active volcano, although it has not erupted in centuries

Environment—current issues: air pollution; water pollution from industrial emissions, raw sewage; contamination of drinking water supplies; trade in endangered species; low-level radioactive waste disposal

Environment—international agreements: *party to:* none of the selected agreements because of Taiwan's international status

Geography—note: strategic location adjacent to both the Taiwan Strait and the Luzon Strait

PEOPLE AND SOCIETY

Population: 23,508,428 (July 2017 est.)
country comparison to the world: 55

Nationality: *noun:* Taiwan (singular and plural)
note: example—he or she is from Taiwan; they are from Taiwan

adjective: Taiwan (or Taiwanese)

Ethnic groups: more than 95% Han Chinese (including Hoklo, who compose approximately 70% of Taiwan's population, Hakka, and other groups originating in mainland China), 2.3% indigenous Malayo-Polynesian peoples
note: there are 16 officially recognized indigenous groups: Amis, Atayal, Bunun, Hla'alua, Kanakaravu, Kavalan, Paiwan, Puyuma, Rukai, Saisiyat, Sakizaya, Seediq, Thao, Truku, Tsou, and Yami; Amis, Paiwan, and Atayal are the largest and account for roughly 70% of the indigenous population

Languages: Mandarin Chinese (official), Taiwanese (Min), Hakka dialects

Religions: Buddhist 35.3%, Taoist 33.2%, Christian 3.9%, Taoist or Confucian folk religionist approximately 10%, none or unspecified 18.2% (2005 est.)

Age structure: *0-14 years:* 12.88% (male 1,559,074/female 1,468,319)
15-24 years: 12.88% (male 1,551,228/female 1,476,660)
25-54 years: 46.41% (male 5,445,338/female 5,463,804)
55-64 years: 14.12% (male 1,622,111/female 1,696,564)
65 years and over: 13.72% (male 1,475,534/female 1,749,796) (2017 est.)

Dependency ratios: *total dependency ratio:* 35.2
youth dependency ratio: 18.6
elderly dependency ratio: 16.6
potential support ratio: 6 (2015 est.)

Median age: *total:* 40.7 years
male: 40 years
female: 41.5 years (2017 est.)
country comparison to the world: 47

Population growth rate: 0.17% (2017 est.)
country comparison to the world: 186

Birth rate: 8.3 births/1,000 population (2017 est.)
country comparison to the world: 219

Death rate: 7.4 deaths/1,000 population (2017 est.)
country comparison to the world: 113

Net migration rate: 0.9 migrant(s)/1,000 population (2017 est.)
country comparison to the world: 58

Population distribution: distribution exhibits a peripheral coastal settlement pattern, with the largest populations on the north and west coasts

Major urban areas—population: TAIPEI (capital) 2.666 million; Kaohsiung 1.523 million; Taichung 1.225 million; Tainan 815,000 (2015)

Sex ratio: *at birth:* 1.07 male(s)/female
0-14 years: 1.06 male(s)/female
15-24 years: 1.05 male(s)/female
25-54 years: 1 male(s)/female
55-64 years: 0.96 male(s)/female
65 years and over: 0.86 male(s)/female
total population: 0.99 male(s)/female (2016 est.)

Infant mortality rate: *total:* 4.3 deaths/1,000 live births

male: 4.7 deaths/1,000 live births

female: 3.9 deaths/1,000 live births (2017 est.)

country comparison to the world: 187

Life expectancy at birth: *total population:* 80.2 years

male: 77.1 years

female: 83.6 years (2017 est.)

country comparison to the world: 40

Total fertility rate: 1.13 children born/woman (2017 est.)

country comparison to the world: 222

HIV/AIDS—adult prevalence rate: NA

HIV/AIDS—people living with HIV/AIDS: NA

HIV/AIDS—deaths: NA

Literacy: *definition:* age 15 and over can read and write

total population: 98.5%

male: 99.7%

female: 97.3% (2014 est.)

GOVERNMENT

Country name: *conventional long form:* none

conventional short form: Taiwan

local long form: none

local short form: Taiwan

former: Formosa

etymology: "Tayowan" was the name of the coastal sandbank where the Dutch erected their colonial headquarters on the island in the 17th century; the former name "Formosa" means "beautiful" in Portuguese

Government type: semi-presidential republic

Capital: *name:* Taipei

geographic coordinates: 25 02 N, 121 31 E

time difference: UTC+8 (13 hours ahead of Washington, DC, during Standard Time)

Administrative divisions: includes main island of Taiwan plus smaller islands nearby and off coast of China's Fujian Province; Taiwan is divided into 13 counties (xian, singular and plural), 3 cities (shi, singular and plural), and 6 special municipalities directly under the jurisdiction of the Executive Yuan

counties: Changhua, Chiayi, Hsinchu, Hualien, Kinmen, Lienchiang, Miaoli, Nantou, Penghu, Pingtung, Taitung, Yilan, Yunlin

cities: Chiayi, Hsinchu, Keelung

special municipalities: Kaohsiung (city), New Taipei (city), Taichung (city), Tainan (city), Taipei (city), Taoyuan (city)

note: Taiwan uses a variety of romanization systems; while a modified Wade-Giles system still dominates, the city of Taipei has adopted a Pinyin romanization for street and place names within its boundaries; other local authorities use different romanization systems

National holiday: Republic Day (National Day), 10 October (1911); note—celebrates the anniversary of the Chinese Revolution, also known as Double Ten (10-10) Day

Constitution: previous 1912, 1931; latest adopted 25 December 1946, promulgated 1 January 1947, effective 25 December 1947; amended/revised several times, last in 2005 (2016)

Legal system: civil law system

International law organization participation: has not submitted an ICJ jurisdiction declaration; non-party state to the ICCt

Citizenship: *citizenship by birth:* no

citizenship by descent only: at least one parent must be a citizen of Taiwan

dual citizenship recognized: yes, except that citizens of Taiwan are not recognized as dual citizens of the People's Republic of China

residency requirement for naturalization: 5 years

Suffrage: 20 years of age; universal; note—in mid-2016, the Legislative Yuan drafted a constitutional amendment to reduce the voting age to 18, but it has not passed as of December 2017

Executive branch: *chief of state:* President TSAI Ing-wen (since 20 May 2016); Vice President CHEN Chien-jen (since 20 May 2016)

head of government: Premier LAI Ching-te (President of the Executive Yuan) (since 8 September 2017); Vice Premier LIN Hsi-yao, Vice President of the Executive Yuan (since 20 May 2016)

cabinet: Executive Yuan—ministers appointed by president on recommendation of premier

elections/appointments: president and vice president directly elected on the same ballot by simple majority popular vote for a 4-year term (eligible for a second term); election last held on 16 January 2016 (next to be held in 2020); premier appointed by the president; vice premiers appointed by the president on the recommendation of the premier

election results: TSAI Ing-wen elected president; percent of vote—TSAI Ing-wen (DPP) 56.1%, Eric CHU Li-lun (KMT) 31.0%, James SOONG Chu-yu (PFP) 12.8%; note—TSAI is the first woman elected president of Taiwan

Legislative branch: *description:* unicameral Legislative Yuan (113 seats; 73 members directly elected in single-seat constituencies by simple majority vote, 34 directly elected in a single island-wide constituency by proportional representation vote, and 6 directly elected in multi-seat aboriginal constituencies by proportional representation vote; members serve 4-year terms)

elections: last held on 16 January 2016 (next to be held in January 2020)

election results: percent of vote by party—NA; seats by party—DPP 68, KMT 35, NPP 5, PFP 3, NPSU 1, independent 1; note—this is the first non-KMT-led legislature in Taiwan's history

Judicial branch: *highest court(s):* Supreme Court (consists of the court president, vice president, and approximately 100 judges organized into 8 civil and 12 criminal divisions, each with a division chief justice and 4 associate justices); Constitutional Court (consists of the court president, vice president, and 13 justices)

judge selection and term of office: Supreme Court justices appointed by the president; Constitutional

Court justices appointed by the president with approval of the Legislative Yuan; Supreme Court justices appointed for life; Constitutional Court justices appointed for 8-year terms with half the membership renewed every 4 years

subordinate courts: high courts; district courts; hierarchy of administrative courts

Political parties and leaders: Democratic Progressive Party or DPP [TSAI Ing-wen]

Kuomintang or KMT (Nationalist Party) [WU Den-yih]

New Power Party or NPP [HUANG Kuo-chang]

Non-Partisan Solidarity Union or NPSU [LIN Pin-kuan]

People First Party or PFP [James SOONG Chu-yu]

Political pressure groups and leaders: environmental groups; independence movement; various business groups

note: public opinion polls consistently show most Taiwanese conclude the Republic of China—Taiwan's official name for itself—is a sovereign state and support maintaining Taiwan's status quo rather than seeking unification with or permanent separation from the China mainland; advocates of Taiwan independence oppose steps toward future unification with mainland China; most advocates of eventual unification predicate their goal on the democratic transformation of the mainland

International organization participation: ADB (Taipei, China), APEC (Chinese Taipei), BCIE, ICC (national committees), IOC, ITUC (NGOs), SICA (observer), WTO (Taipei, China)

Diplomatic representation in the US: none; commercial and cultural relations with iats citizens in the US are maintained through an unofficial instrumentality, the Taipei Economic and Cultural Representative Office in the United States (TECRO), a private nonprofit corporation that performs citizen and consular services similar to those at diplomatic posts

representative: Stanley KAO (since 5 June 2016)

office: 4201 Wisconsin Avenue NW, Washington, DC 20016

telephone: [1] 202 895-1800

Taipei Economic and Cultural Offices (branch offices): Atlanta, Boston, Chicago, Denver (CO), Hagatna (Guam), Houston, Honolulu (HI), Los Angeles, Miami, New York, San Francisco, Seattle

Diplomatic representation from the US: none; commercial and cultural relations with the people of Taiwan are maintained through an unofficial instrumentality, the American Institute in Taiwan (AIT), a private nonprofit corporation that forms citizen and consular services similar to those at diplomatic posts; Director Kin W. MOY (since June 2015)

office: telephone: [1] [886] (02) 2162-2000

FAX: [1] [886] (02) 2162-2251

other offices: Kaohsiung (Branch Office)

Flag description: red field with a dark blue rectangle in the upper hoist-side corner bearing a white sun with 12 triangular rays; the blue and white design of the canton (symbolizing the sun of progress) dates to 1895; it was later adopted as the flag of the Kuomintang Party; blue signifies liberty, justice, and democracy; red stands for fraternity, sacrifice, and nationalism, white represents equality, frankness, and the people's livelihood; the 12 rays of the sun are those of the months and the twelve traditional Chinese hours (each ray equals two hours)

note: similar to the flag of Samoa

National symbol(s): white, 12-rayed sun on blue field; national colors: blue, white, red

National anthem: *name:* "Zhonghua Minguo guoge" (National Anthem of the Republic of China)

lyrics/music: HU Han-min, TAI Chi-t'ao, and LIAO Chung-k'ai/CHENG Mao-Yun

note: adopted 1930; also the song of the Kuomintang Party; it is informally known as "San Min Chu I" or "San Min Zhu Yi" (Three Principles of the People); because of political pressure from China, "Guo Qi Ge" (National Banner Song) is used at international events rather than the official anthem of Taiwan; the "National Banner Song" has gained popularity in Taiwan and is commonly used during flag raisings

ECONOMY

Economy—overview: Taiwan has a dynamic capitalist economy that is driven largely by industrial manufacturing, and especially exports of electronics, machinery, and petrochemicals. This heavy dependence on exports exposes the economy to fluctuations in global demand. Taiwan's diplomatic isolation, low birth rate, rapidly aging population, and increasing competition from China and other Asia Pacific markets are other major long-term challenges.

Following the landmark Economic Cooperation Framework Agreement (ECFA) signed with China in June 2010, Taiwan in July 2013 signed a free trade deal with New Zealand—Taipei's first-ever with a country with which it does not maintain diplomatic relations—and, in November of that year, inked a trade pact with Singapore. However, follow-on components of the ECFA, including a signed agreement on trade in services and negotiations on trade in goods and dispute resolution, have stalled. In early 2014, the government bowed to public demand and proposed a new law governing the oversight of cross-Strait agreements, before any additional deals with China are implemented; the legislature has yet to vote on such legislation, leaving the future of ECFA uncertain. President TSAI since taking office in May 2016 has promoted greater economic integration with South and Southeast Asia through the New Southbound Policy initiative and has also expressed interest in Taiwan joining the Trans-Pacific Partnership as well as bilateral trade deals with partners such as the US. These overtures have likely played a role in increasing Taiwan's total exports, which rose 11% during the first half of 2017, buoyed by strong demand for semiconductors.

Taiwan's total fertility rate of just over one child per woman is among the lowest in the world, raising the prospect of future labor shortages,

falling domestic demand, and declining tax revenues. Taiwan's population is aging quickly, with the number of people over 65 expected to account for nearly 20% of the island's total population by 2025.

The island runs a trade surplus with many economies, including China and the US, and its foreign reserves are the world's fifth largest, behind those of China, Japan, Saudi Arabia, and Switzerland. In 2006, China overtook the US to become Taiwan's second-largest source of imports after Japan. China is also the island's number one destination for foreign direct investment. Taiwan since 2009 has gradually loosened rules governing Chinese investment and has also secured greater market access for its investors on the mainland. In August 2012, the Taiwan Central Bank signed a memorandum of understanding (MOU) on cross-Strait currency settlement with its Chinese counterpart. The MOU allows for the direct settlement of Chinese renminbi (RMB) and the New Taiwan dollar across the Strait, which has helped Taiwan develop into a local RMB hub.

Closer economic links with the mainland bring opportunities for Taiwan's economy but also pose challenges as political differences remain unresolved and China's economic growth is slowing. President TSAI's administration has made little progress on the domestic economic issues that loomed large when she was elected, including concerns about stagnant wages, high housing prices, youth unemployment, job security, and financial security in retirement. TSAI has made more progress on boosting trade with South and Southeast Asia, however, which may help insulate Taiwan's economy from a fall in mainland demand should China's growth slow in 2018.

GDP (purchasing power parity): $1.175 trillion (2017 est.)
$1.152 trillion (2016 est.)
$1.136 trillion (2015 est.)
note: data are in 2017 dollars
country comparison to the world: 23

GDP (official exchange rate): $571.5 billion (2016 est.)

GDP—real growth rate: 2% (2017 est.)
1.5% (2016 est.)
0.7% (2015 est.)
country comparison to the world: 156

GDP—per capita (PPP): $49,800 (2017 est.)
$49,000 (2016 est.)
$48,300 (2015 est.)
note: data are in 2017 dollars
country comparison to the world: 30

Gross national saving: 34.8% of GDP (2017 est.)
35.6% of GDP (2016 est.)
36.4% of GDP (2015 est.)
country comparison to the world: 14

GDP—composition, by end use:
household consumption: 52.4%
government consumption: 14.1%
investment in fixed capital: 21.4%
investment in inventories: 0%
exports of goods and services: 64.8%
imports of goods and services: -52.7% (2017 est.)

GDP—composition, by sector of origin:
agriculture: 1.8%
industry: 36%
services: 62.1% (2017 est.)

Agriculture—products: rice, vegetables, fruit, tea, flowers; pigs, poultry; fish

Industries: electronics, communications and information technology products, petroleum refining, chemicals, textiles, iron and steel, machinery, cement, food processing, vehicles, consumer products, pharmaceuticals

Industrial production growth rate: 2% (2017 est.)
country comparison to the world: 131

Labor force: 11.78 million (2017 est.)
country comparison to the world: 52

Labor force—by occupation: *agriculture:* 4.9%
industry: 35.9%
services: 59.2% (2016 est.)

Unemployment rate: 3.8% (2017 est.)
3.9% (2016 est.)
country comparison to the world: 43

Population below poverty line: 1.5% (2012 est.)

Household income or consumption by percentage share: *lowest 10%:* 6.4%
highest 10%: 40.3% (2010)

Distribution of family income—Gini index: 33.6 (2014)
32.6 (2000)
country comparison to the world: 106

Budget: *revenues:* $93 billion
expenditures: $91.67 billion (2017 est.)
Taxes and other revenues: 16.3% of GDP (2017 est.)
country comparison to the world: 182

Budget surplus (+) or deficit (-): 0.2% of GDP (2017 est.)
country comparison to the world: 30

Public debt: 29.9% of GDP (2017 est.)
31.2% of GDP (2016 est.)
note: data for central government
country comparison to the world: 163

Fiscal year: calendar year

Inflation rate (consumer prices): 1% (2017 est.)
1.4% (2016 est.)
country comparison to the world: 39

Central bank discount rate: 1.38% (31 December 2016)
1.63% (31 December 2015)
country comparison to the world: 123

Commercial bank prime lending rate: 2.7% (31 December 2017 est.)
2.63% (31 December 2016 est.)
country comparison to the world: 173

Stock of narrow money: $535.1 billion (31 December 2017 est.)
$501.2 billion (31 December 2016 est.)
country comparison to the world: 12

Stock of broad money: $1.374 trillion (31 December 2017 est.)
$1.28 trillion (31 December 2016 est.)
country comparison to the world: 14

Stock of domestic credit: $835.8 billion (31 December 2017 est.)
$778.3 billion (31 December 2016 est.)
country comparison to the world: 17

Market value of publicly traded shares: $851.2 billion (31 December 2016)
$742.5 billion (31 December 2015)
$848.3 billion (31 December 2014)
country comparison to the world: 14

Current account balance: $79 billion (2017 est.)
$74.28 billion (2016 est.)
country comparison to the world: 7

Exports: $344.6 billion (2017 est.)
$310.4 billion (2016 est.)
country comparison to the world: 15

Exports—commodities: semiconductors, petrochemicals, automobile/auto parts, ships, wireless communication equipment, flat display displays, steel, electronics, plastics, computers

Imports: $272.6 billion (2017 est.)
$239.7 billion (2016 est.)
country comparison to the world: 19

Imports—commodities: oil/petroleum, semiconductors, natural gas, coal, steel, computers, wireless communication equipment, automobiles, fine chemicals, textiles

Reserves of foreign exchange and gold: $468.1 billion (31 December 2017 est.)
$439 billion (31 December 2016 est.)
country comparison to the world: 6

Debt—external: $204.7 billion (31 December 2017 est.)
$172.2 billion (31 December 2016 est.)
country comparison to the world: 38

Stock of direct foreign investment—at home: $85.58 billion (31 December 2017 est.)
$80.68 billion (31 December 2016 est.)
country comparison to the world: 48

Stock of direct foreign investment—abroad: $367.2 billion (31 December 2017 est.)
$354 billion (31 December 2016 est.)
country comparison to the world: 20

Exchange rates: New Taiwan dollars (TWD) per US dollar—
30.68 (2017 est.)
32.325 (2016 est.)
32.325 (2016 est.)
31.911 (2014 est.)
30.363 (2013 est.)

ENERGY

Electricity—production: 264.1 billion kWh (2016 est.)
country comparison to the world: 18

Electricity—consumption: 255.3 billion kWh (2016 est.)
country comparison to the world: 15

Electricity—exports: 0 kWh (2016 est.)
country comparison to the world: 208

Electricity—imports: 0 kWh (2016 est.)
country comparison to the world: 212

Electricity—installed generating capacity: 48.61 million kW (2015 est.)
country comparison to the world: 22

Electricity—from fossil fuels: 75.4% of total installed capacity (2015 est.)
country comparison to the world: 96

Electricity—from nuclear fuels: 10.4% of total installed capacity (2015 est.)
country comparison to the world: 15

Electricity—from hydroelectric plants: 4.3% of total installed capacity (2015 est.)
country comparison to the world: 130

Electricity—from other renewable sources: 5.4% of total installed capacity (2015 est.)
country comparison to the world: 96

Crude oil—production: 196 bbl/day (2016 est.)
country comparison to the world: 97

Crude oil—exports: 0 bbl/day (2016 est.)
country comparison to the world: 202

Crude oil—imports: 858,700 bbl/day (2016 est.)
country comparison to the world: 12

Crude oil—proved reserves: 2.38 million bbl (1 January 2017 es)
country comparison to the world: 97

Refined petroleum products—production: 917,500 bbl/day (2014 est.)
country comparison to the world: 24

Refined petroleum products—consumption: 955,300 bbl/day (2015 est.)
country comparison to the world: 23

Refined petroleum products—exports: 350,300 bbl/day (2014 est.)
country comparison to the world: 24

Refined petroleum products—imports: 416,200 bbl/day (2014 est.)
country comparison to the world: 21

Natural gas—production: 340 million cu m (2015 est.)
country comparison to the world: 75

Natural gas—consumption: 31.71 billion cu m (2015 est.)
country comparison to the world: 37

Natural gas—exports: 0 cu m (2016 est.)
country comparison to the world: 198

Natural gas—imports: 19.39 billion cu m (2015 est.)
country comparison to the world: 16

Natural gas—proved reserves: 6.229 billion cu m (1 January 2017 es)
country comparison to the world: 91

Carbon dioxide emissions from consumption of energy: 25.05 million Mt (2015 est.)
country comparison to the world: 78

COMMUNICATIONS

Telephones—fixed lines: *total subscriptions:* 13,770,996
subscriptions per 100 inhabitants: 59 (July 2016 est.)
country comparison to the world: 18

Telephones—mobile cellular: *total:* 29.681 million
subscriptions per 100 inhabitants: 127 (July 2016 est.)
country comparison to the world: 43

Telephone system: *general assessment:* provides telecommunications service for every business and private need
domestic: thoroughly modern; completely digitalized
international: country code—886; roughly 15 submarine fiber cables provide links throughout Asia, Australia, the Middle East, Europe, and the US; satellite earth stations—2 (2016)

Broadcast media: 5 nationwide television networks operating roughly 75 TV stations; about 60% of households utilize multi-channel cable TV; national and regional radio networks with about 170 radio stations (2016)

Internet country code: .tw

Internet users: *total:* 20.601 million
percent of population: 88% (July 2016 est.)
country comparison to the world: 36

TRANSPORTATION

National air transport system: number of registered air carriers: 8
inventory of registered aircraft operated by air carriers: 221 (2015)
Civil aircraft registration country code prefix: B (2016)

Airports: 37 (2013)
country comparison to the world: 107

Airports—with paved runways: *total:* 35
over 3,047 m: 8
2,438 to 3,047 m: 7
1,524 to 2,437 m: 10
914 to 1,523 m: 8
under 914 m: 2 (2013)

Airports—with unpaved runways: *total:* 2
1,524 to 2,437 m: 1
under 914 m: 1 (2013)

Heliports: 31 (2013)

Pipelines: condensate 25 km; gas 802 km; oil 241 km (2013)

Railways: *total:* 1,597 km
standard gauge: 345 km 1.435-m gauge (345 km electrified)
narrow gauge: 1,102 km 1.067-m gauge (692 km electrified); 150 km 0.762-m gauge
note: the 0.762-gauge track belongs to three entities: the Forestry Bureau, Taiwan Cement, and TaiPower (2014)
country comparison to the world: 79

Roadways: *total:* 42,520 km
paved: 42,078 km (includes 1,348 km of highways and 737 km of expressways)
unpaved: 442 km (2013)
country comparison to the world: 85

Merchant marine: *total:* 350
by type: bulk carrier 26, container ship 38, general cargo 59, oil tanker 24, other 203 (2017)
country comparison to the world: 49

Ports and terminals: *major seaport(s):* Keelung (Chi-lung), Kaohsiung, Hualian, Taichung
container port(s) (TEUs): Keelung (Chi-lung) (2,666,000), Kaohsiung (10,264,000), Taichung (1,447,000) (2015)
LNG terminal(s) (import): Yung An (Kaohsiung), Taichung

MILITARY AND SECURITY

Military branches: Army, Navy (includes Marine Corps), Air Force, Military Police Command, Armed Forces Reserve Command, Coast Guard Administration (2016)

Military service age and obligation: starting with those born in 1994, males 18-36 years of age may volunteer for military service or must complete 4 months of compulsory military training (or substitute civil service in some cases); men born before December 1993 are required to complete compulsory service for 1 year (military or civil); men are subject to training recalls up to four times for periods not to exceed 20 days for 8 years after discharge; women may enlist, but are restricted to noncombat roles in most cases; Taiwan is planning to implement an all-volunteer military in 2018 (2017) (2016)

TRANSNATIONAL ISSUES

Disputes—international: involved in complex dispute with Brunei, China, Malaysia, the Philippines, and Vietnam over the Spratly Islands, and with China and the Philippines over Scarborough Reef; the 2002 "Declaration on the Conduct of Parties in the South China Sea" has eased tensions but falls short of a legally binding "code of conduct" desired by several of the disputants; Paracel Islands are occupied by China, but claimed by Taiwan and Vietnam; in 2003, China and Taiwan became more vocal in rejecting both Japan's claims to the uninhabited islands of the Senkaku-shoto (Diaoyu Tai) and Japan's unilaterally declared exclusive economic zone in the East China Sea where all parties engage in hydrocarbon prospecting

Illicit drugs: regional transit point for heroin, methamphetamine, and precursor chemicals; transshipment point for drugs to Japan; major problem with domestic consumption of methamphetamine and heroin; rising problems with use of ketamine and club drugs

TAJIKISTAN

INTRODUCTION

Background: The Tajik people came under Russian rule in the 1860s and 1870s, but Russia's hold on Central Asia weakened following the Revolution of 1917. Bands of indigenous guerrillas (called "basmachi") fiercely contested Bolshevik control of the area, which was not fully reestablished until 1925. Tajikistan was first created as an autonomous republic within Uzbekistan in 1924, but the USSR designated Tajikistan a separate republic in 1929 and transferred to it much of present-day Sughd province. Ethnic Uzbeks form a substantial minority in Tajikistan, and ethnic Tajiks an even larger minority in Uzbekistan. Tajikistan became independent in 1991 following the breakup of the Soviet Union, and experienced a civil war between regional factions from 1992 to 1997. Tajikistan has endured several domestic security incidents since 2010, including armed conflict between government forces and local strongmen in the Rasht Valley and between government forces and criminal groups in Gorno-Badakhshan Autonomous Oblast. In September 2015, government security forces rebuffed attacks led by a former high-ranking official in the Ministry of Defense. President Emomali RAHMON, who came to power during the civil war, used the attacks to ban the main opposition political party in Tajikistan. In May 2016, RAHMON further strengthened his position by having himself designated "Leader of the Nation" with limitless terms and lifelong immunity through constitutional amendments ratified in a referendum. The referendum also lowered the minimum age required to run for president from 35 to 30, which would make RAHMON's son Rustam EMOMALI, eligible to run for president in 2020. The country remains the poorest in the former Soviet sphere. Tajikistan became a member of the WTO in March 2013. However, its economy continues to face major challenges, including dependence on remittances from Tajiks working in Russia, pervasive corruption, and the opiate trade emanating from neighboring Afghanistan.

GEOGRAPHY

Location: Central Asia, west of China, south of Kyrgyzstan

Geographic coordinates: 39 00 N, 71 00 E

Map references: Asia

Area: *total:* 144,100 sq km
land: 141,510 sq km
water: 2,590 sq km
country comparison to the world: 97

Area—comparative: slightly smaller than Wisconsin
Land boundaries: total: 4,130 km
border countries (4): Afghanistan 1,357 km, China 477 km, Kyrgyzstan 984 km, Uzbekistan 1,312 km

Coastline: 0 km (landlocked)

Maritime claims: none (landlocked)

Climate: mid-latitude continental, hot summers, mild winters; semiarid to polar in Pamir Mountains

Terrain: mountainous region dominated by the Trans-Alay Range in the north and the Pamirs in the southeast; western Fergana Valley in north, Kofarnihon and Vakhsh Valleys in southwest

Elevation: *mean elevation:* 3,186 m

elevation extremes: *lowest point:* Syr Darya (Sirdaryo) 300 m
highest point: Qullai Ismoili Somoni 7,495 m

Natural resources: hydropower, some petroleum, uranium, mercury, brown coal, lead, zinc, antimony, tungsten, silver, gold

Land use: *agricultural land:* 34.7%
arable land: 6.1%;
permanent crops: 0.9%;
permanent pasture: 27.7%
forest: 2.9%
other: 62.4% (2011 est.)
Irrigated land: 7,420 sq km (2012)

Population—distribution: the country's population is concentrated at lower elevations, with perhaps as much as 90% of the people living in valleys; overall density increases from east to west

Natural hazards: earthquakes; floods

Environment—current issues: inadequate sanitation facilities; increasing levels of soil salinity; industrial pollution; excessive pesticides

Environment—international agreements: *party to:* Biodiversity, Climate Change, Climate Change-Kyoto Protocol, Desertification, Environmental Modification, Ozone Layer Protection, Wetlands
signed, but not ratified: none of the selected agreements

Geography—note: landlocked; highest point, Qullai Ismoili Somoni (formerly Communism Peak), was the tallest mountain in the former USSR

PEOPLE AND SOCIETY

Population: 8,468,555 (July 2017 est.)
country comparison to the world: 96

Nationality: *noun:* Tajikistani(s)
adjective: Tajikistani

Ethnic groups: Tajik 84.3%, Uzbek 13.8% (includes Lakai, Kongrat, Katagan, Barlos, Yuz), other 2% (includes Kyrgyz, Russian, Turkmen, Tatar, Arab) (2010 est.)

Languages: Tajik (official), Russian widely used in government and business *note:* different ethnic groups speak Uzbek, Kyrgyz, and Pashto

Religions: Sunni Muslim 85%, Shia Muslim 5%, other 10% (2003 est.)

Age structure: *0-14 years:* 32.33% (male 1,393,804/female 1,343,825)
15-24 years: 18.61% (male 799,736/female 776,417)
25-54 years: 40.12% (male 1,683,228/female 1,714,507)
55-64 years: 5.62% (male 219,043/female 257,066)
65 years and over: 3.32% (male 116,511/female 164,418) (2017 est.)

Dependency ratios: *total dependency ratio:* 62.5
youth dependency ratio: 57.1
elderly dependency ratio: 5.4
potential support ratio: 18.5 (2015 est.)

Median age: *total:* 24.5 years
male: 23.9 years
female: 25.1 years (2017 est.)
country comparison to the world: 159

Population growth rate: 1.62% (2017 est.)
country comparison to the world: 66

Birth rate: 23.3 births/1,000 population (2017 est.)
country comparison to the world: 65

Death rate: 6 deaths/1,000 population (2017 est.)
country comparison to the world: 161

Net migration rate: -1.1 migrant(s)/1,000 population (2017 est.)
country comparison to the world: 140

Population distribution: the country's population is concentrated at lower elevations, with perhaps as much as 90% of the people living in valleys; overall density increases from east to west

Urbanization: *urban population:* 27% of total population (2017)
rate of urbanization: 2.72% annual rate of change (2015-20 est.)

Major urban areas—population: DUSHANBE (capital) 822,000 (2015)

Sex ratio: *at birth:* 1.05 male(s)/female
0-14 years: 1.04 male(s)/female
15-24 years: 1.03 male(s)/female
25-54 years: 0.98 male(s)/female
55-64 years: 0.85 male(s)/female
65 years and over: 0.72 male(s)/female
total population: 0.99 male(s)/female (2016 est.)

Mother's mean age at first birth: 22.9 years (2014 est.)

Maternal mortality ratio: 32 deaths/100,000 live births (2015 est.)
country comparison to the world: 111

Infant mortality rate: *total:* 31.8 deaths/1,000 live births
male: 35.9 deaths/1,000 live births
female: 27.5 deaths/1,000 live births (2017 est.)
country comparison to the world: 60

Life expectancy at birth: *total population:* 68.1 years
male: 64.9 years
female: 71.4 years (2017 est.)
country comparison to the world: 169

Total fertility rate: 2.63 children born/woman (2017 est.)

country comparison to the world: 72

Contraceptive prevalence rate: 27.9% (2012)
Health expenditures: 6.9% of GDP (2014)
country comparison to the world: 85

Physicians density: 1.71 physicians/1,000 population (2014)

Hospital bed density: 5.5 beds/1,000 population (2011)

Drinking water source:
improved:
urban: 93.1% of population
rural: 66.7% of population
total: 73.8% of population
unimproved:
urban: 6.9% of population
rural: 33.3% of population
total: 26.2% of population (2015 est.)

Sanitation facility access:
improved:
urban: 93.8% of population
rural: 95.5% of population
total: 95% of population
unimproved:
urban: 6.2% of population
rural: 4.5% of population
total: 5% of population (2015 est.)

HIV/AIDS—adult prevalence rate: 0.3% (2016 est.)
country comparison to the world: 83

HIV/AIDS—people living with HIV/AIDS: 14,000 (2016 est.)
country comparison to the world: 84

HIV/AIDS—deaths: <1000 (2016 est.)

Major infectious diseases: *degree of risk:* high
food or waterborne diseases: bacterial diarrhea, hepatitis A, and typhoid fever
vectorborne disease: malaria (2016)

Obesity—adult prevalence rate: 14.2% (2016)
country comparison to the world: 128

Children under the age of 5 years underweight: 13.3% (2012)
country comparison to the world: 56
Education expenditures: 5.2% of GDP (2015)
country comparison to the world: 114

Literacy: *definition:* age 15 and over can read and write
total population: 99.8%
male: 99.8%
female: 99.7% (2015 est.)

School life expectancy (primary to tertiary education): *total:* 11 years
male: 12 years
female: 11 years (2013)

Unemployment, youth ages 15-24: *total:* 16.7%
male: 19.2%
female: 13.7% (2009 est.)
country comparison to the world: 72

GOVERNMENT

Country name: *conventional long form:* Republic of Tajikistan
conventional short form: Tajikistan

local long form: Jumhurii Tojikiston
local short form: Tojikiston
former: Tajik Soviet Socialist Republic
etymology: the Persian suffix "-stan" means "place of" or "country," so the word Tajikistan literally means "Land of the Tajik [people]"

Government type: presidential republic

Capital: *name:* Dushanbe

geographic coordinates: 38 33 N, 68 46 E
time difference: UTC+5 (10 hours ahead of Washington, DC, during Standard Time)

Administrative divisions: 2 provinces (viloyatho, singular—viloyat), 1 autonomous province* (viloyati mukhtor), 1 capital region** (viloyati poytakht), and 1 area referred to as Districts Under Republic Administration***; Dushanbe**, Khatlon (Qurghonteppa), Kuhistoni Badakhshon [Gorno-Badakhshon]* (Khorugh), Nohiyahoi Tobei Jumhuri*** (Sughd (Khujand)
note: the administrative center name follows in parentheses

Independence: 9 September 1991 (from the Soviet Union)

National holiday: Independence Day (or National Day), 9 September (1991)

Constitution: *history:* several previous; latest adopted 6 November 1994
amendments: proposed by the president of the republic or by at least one-third of the total membership of both houses of the Supreme Assembly; adoption of any amendment requires a referendum, which includes approval by the president or approval by at least two-thirds of the Assembly of Representatives membership; passage in a referendum requires participation of an absolute majority of eligible voters and an absolute majority of votes; note – constitutional articles including Tajikistan's form of government, its territory, and its democratic nature cannot be amended; amended several times, last in 2016 (2017)

Legal system: civil law system

International law organization participation: has not submitted an ICJ jurisdiction declaration; accepts ICCt jurisdiction

Citizenship: *citizenship by birth:* no
citizenship by descent only: at least one parent must be a citizen of Tajikistan
dual citizenship recognized: no
residency requirement for naturalization: 5 years or 3 years of continuous residence prior to application

Suffrage: 18 years of age; universal

Executive branch: *chief of state:* President Emomali RAHMON (since 6 November 1994; head of state and Supreme Assembly chairman since 19 November 1992)

head of government: Prime Minister Qohir RASULZODA (since 23 November 2013)
cabinet: Council of Ministers appointed by the president, approved by the Supreme Assembly
elections/appointments: president directly elected by simple majority popular vote for a 7-year

term (unlimited terms); election last held on 6 November 2013 (next to be held in November 2020); prime minister appointed by the president

election results: Emomali RAHMON reelected president; percent of vote—Emomali RAHMON (PDPT) 83.9%, Ismoil TALBAKOV (CPT) 5%, other 11.1%

Legislative branch: *description:* bicameral Supreme Assembly or Majlisi Oli consists of the National Assembly or Majlisi Milli (34 seats; 25 members indirectly elected by local representative assemblies or majlisi, 8 appointed by the president, and 1 reserved for the former president; members serve 5-year terms) and the Assembly of Representatives or Majlisi Namoyandagon (63 seats; 41 members directly elected in single-seat constituencies by 2-round absolute majority vote and 22 directly elected in a single nationwide constituency by proportional representation vote; members serve 5-year terms)

elections: National Assembly—last held on 1 March 2015 (next to be held in 2020); Assembly of Representatives—last held on 1 March 2015 (next to be held in 2020)

election results: National Assembly—percent of vote by party—NA; seats by party—NA; Assembly of Representatives—percent of vote by party—PDPT 65.4%, APT 11.7%, PERT 7.5%, SPT 5.5%, CPT 2.2%, DPT 1.7%, other 6%; seats by party—PDPT 51, APT 5, PERT 3, CPT 2, SPT 1, DPT 1

Judicial branch: *highest court(s):* Supreme Court (consists of the chairman, deputy chairmen, and 34 judges organized into civil, criminal, and military chambers); Constitutional Court (consists of the court chairman, vice president, and 5 judges); High Economic Court (consists of 16 judicial positions)

judge selection and term of office: Supreme Court, Constitutional Court, and High Economic Court judges nominated by the president of the republic and approved by the National Assembly; judges of all 3 courts appointed for 10-year renewable terms with no limit on terms, but last appointment must occur before the age of 65

subordinate courts: regional and district courts; Dushanbe City Court; viloyat (province level) courts; Court of Gorno-Badakhshan Autonomous Region

Political parties and leaders: Agrarian Party of Tajikistan or APT [Rustam LATIFZODA]
Communist Party of Tajikistan or CPT [Miroj ABDULLOYEV]
Democratic Party of Tajikistan or DPT [SaidjafFar USMONZODA]
Party of Economic Reform or PERT [Olimjon BOBOEV]
Party of Industrialists and Entrepreneurs [Ovezmammed MAMMEDOV]
People's Democratic Party of Tajikistan or PDPT [Emomali RAHMON]
Social Democratic Party of Tajikistan or SDPT [Rahmatullo ZOIROV]
Socialist Party of Tajikistan or SPT [Abduhalim GHAFFOROV]

Political pressure groups and leaders: Group 24 [Suhrob ZAFAR] (banned)
New Tajikistan Party [Zayd SAIDOV (jailed since 2013)] (unregistered)
Vatandor (Patriot) Movement [Dodojon ATOVULLOEV]
Youth for the Revival of Tajikistan [Maqsud IBROHIMOV—jailed in 2015] (banned)
Youth Party of Tajikistan [Izzat AMON] (unregistered)
Islamic Renaissance Party of Tajikistan or IRPT [Muhiddin KABIRI—in exile] (banned)

International organization participation: ADB, CICA, CIS, CSTO, EAEC, EAPC, EBRD, ECO, EITI (candidate country), FAO, G-77, GCTU, IAEA, IBRD, ICAO, ICC (NGOs), ICCt, ICRM, IDA, IDB, IFAD, IFC, IFRCS, ILO, IMF, Interpol, IOC, IOM, IPU, ISO (correspondent), ITSO, ITU, MIGA, NAM (observer), OIC, OPCW, OSCE, PFP, SCO, UN, UNCTAD, UNESCO, UNIDO, UNWTO, UPU, WCO, WFTU (NGOs), WHO, WIPO, WMO, WTO

Diplomatic representation in the US: chief of mission: Ambassador Farhod SALIM (since 21 May 2014)
chancery: 1005 New Hampshire Avenue NW, Washington, DC 20037
telephone: [1] (202) 223-6090
FAX: [1] (202) 223-6091

Diplomatic representation from the US: *chief of mission:* Ambassador (vacant); Charge d'Affaires Kevin COVERT (since 31 August 2017)
embassy: 109-A Ismoili Somoni Avenue, Dushanbe 734019
mailing address: 7090 Dushanbe Place, Dulles, VA 20189
telephone: [992] (37) 229-20-00
FAX: [992] (37) 229-20-50

Flag description: three horizontal stripes of red (top), a wider stripe of white, and green; a gold crown surmounted by seven gold, five-pointed stars is located in the center of the white stripe; red represents the sun, victory, and the unity of the nation, white stands for purity, cotton, and mountain snows, while green is the color of Islam and the bounty of nature; the crown symbolizes the Tajik people; the seven stars signify the Tajik magic number "seven"—a symbol of perfection and the embodiment of happiness

National symbol(s): crown surmounted by an arc of seven, five-pointed stars; snow leopard; national colors: red, white, green

National anthem: *name:* "Surudi milli" (National Anthem)
lyrics/music: Gulnazar KELDI/Sulaimon YUDAKOV
note: adopted 1991; after the fall of the Soviet Union, Tajikistan kept the music of the anthem from its time as a Soviet republic but adopted new lyrics

ECONOMY

Economy—overview: Tajikistan is a poor, mountainous country with an economy dominated by minerals extraction, metals processing, agriculture, and reliance on remittances from citizens working abroad. The 1992-97 civil war severely damaged an already weak economic infrastructure and caused a sharp decline in industrial and agricultural production. Today, Tajikistan has one of the lowest per capita GDPs among the 15 former Soviet republics. Less than 7% of the land area is arable and cotton is the most important crop. Tajikistan imports approximately 70% of its food. Mineral resources include silver, gold, uranium, antimony, and tungsten. Industry consists mainly of small obsolete factories in food processing and light industry, substantial hydropower facilities, and a large aluminum plant—currently operating well below its capacity.

Because of a lack of employment opportunities in Tajikistan, more than one million Tajik citizens work abroad—roughly 90% in Russia—supporting families back home through remittances that in 2014 were equivalent to nearly 50% of GDP. Some experts estimate the value of narcotics transiting Tajikistan is equivalent to 30%-50% of GDP.

Since the end of the civil war, the country has pursued half-hearted reforms and privatizations in the economic sphere, but the poor business climate remains a hurdle to attracting foreign investment. Tajikistan has sought to develop its substantial hydroelectricity potential through partnership with Russian, Iranian and Chinese investors, and is pursuing completion of the Roghun Dam—which, if built according to plan, would be the tallest dam in the world. However, the project is a sensitive issue for downstream neighbors and faces large financing shortfalls. In 2016, Tajikistan contracted with the Italian firm Salini Impregilo to build the dam over a 13-year period for $3.9 billion, and has yet to finance most of the project.

Recent slowdowns in the Russian and Chinese economies, low commodity prices, and currency fluctuations are hampering economic growth in Tajikistan. The dollar value of remittances from Russia to Tajikistan started showing small increases in 2017 after dropping by almost 65% in 2015. The government spent almost $500 million in 2016 to bail out the country's banking sector, which is still troubled, and the government is facing challenges financing a public debt that is equivalent to approximately 50% of GDP. The National Bank of Tajikistan has aggressively spent its reserves to bolster the weakening somoni, leaving little space for fiscal or monetary measures to counter additional economic shocks.

GDP (purchasing power parity): $27.67 billion (2017 est.)
$26.48 billion (2016 est.)
$24.77 billion (2015 est.)
note: data are in 2017 dollars
country comparison to the world: 136

GDP (official exchange rate): $7.234 billion (2016 est.)

GDP—real growth rate: 4.5% (2017 est.)
6.9% (2016 est.)
6% (2015 est.)
country comparison to the world: 53

GDP—per capita (PPP): $3,100 (2017 est.)

$3,100 (2016 est.)
$2,900 (2015 est.)
note: data are in 2017 dollars
country comparison to the world: 193

Gross national saving: 11.7% of GDP (2017 est.)
17.6% of GDP (2016 est.)
12.9% of GDP (2015 est.)
country comparison to the world: 149

GDP—composition, by end use:
household consumption: 103.2%
government consumption: 16.8%
investment in fixed capital: 12.3%
investment in inventories: 3%
exports of goods and services: 13.4%
imports of goods and services: -48.7% (2017 est.)

GDP—composition, by sector of origin:
agriculture: 28.6%
industry: 25.5%
services: 45.9% (2017 est.)

Agriculture—products: cotton, grain, fruits, grapes, vegetables; cattle, sheep, goats

Industries: aluminum, cement, vegetable oil

Industrial production growth rate: 1% (2017 est.)
country comparison to the world: 168

Labor force: 2.295 million (2016 est.)
country comparison to the world: 119

Labor force—by occupation: *agriculture:* 43%
industry: 10.6%
services: 46.4% (2016 est.)

Unemployment rate: 2.4% (2016 est.)
2.5% (2015 est.)
note: official rates; actual unemployment is much higher
country comparison to the world: 22

Population below poverty line: 31.5% (2016 est.)

Household income or consumption by percentage share: *lowest 10%:* NA%
highest 10%: NA% (2009 est.)

Distribution of family income—Gini index: 32.6 (2006)
34.7 (1998)
country comparison to the world: 110

Budget: *revenues:* $2.214 billion
expenditures: $2.316 billion (2017 est.)
Taxes and other revenues: 30.6% of GDP (2017 est.)
country comparison to the world: 79

Budget surplus (+) or deficit (-): -1.4% of GDP (2017 est.)
country comparison to the world: 66

Public debt: 41.5% of GDP (2017 est.)
43.5% of GDP (2016 est.)
country comparison to the world: 131

Fiscal year: calendar year

Inflation rate (consumer prices): 8.9% (2017 est.)
5.9% (2016 est.)
country comparison to the world: 202

Central bank discount rate: 16% (20 March 2017)
6.5% (31 December 2012)
country comparison to the world: 9

Commercial bank prime lending rate: 30% (31 December 2017 est.)

25.6% (31 December 2016 est.)
country comparison to the world: 7

Stock of narrow money: $936 million (31 December 2017 est.)
$1.108 billion (31 December 2016 est.)
country comparison to the world: 159

Stock of broad money: $1.065 billion (31 December 2017 est.)
$1.3 billion (31 December 2016 est.)
country comparison to the world: 172

Stock of domestic credit: $1.301 billion (31 December 2017 est.)
$1.711 billion (31 December 2016 est.)
country comparison to the world: 154

Market value of publicly traded shares: $NA

Current account balance: -$458 million (2017 est.)
-$265 million (2016 est.)
country comparison to the world: 103

Exports: $794.7 million (2017 est.)
$691.1 million (2016 est.)
country comparison to the world: 168

Exports—commodities: aluminum, electricity, cotton, fruits, vegetable oil, textiles

Exports—partners: Turkey 27.8%, Russia 15.6%, China 14.7%, Switzerland 9.8%, Iran 6.5%, Algeria 6.5%, Italy 5.8% (2016)

Imports: $2.725 billion (2017 est.)
$2.604 billion (2016 est.)
country comparison to the world: 146

Imports—commodities: petroleum products, aluminum oxide, machinery and equipment, foodstuffs

Imports—partners: Russia 31.2%, China 13.9%, Kazakhstan 12.8%, Uzbekistan 5.2%, Iran 5.1% (2016)

Reserves of foreign exchange and gold: $642.4 million (31 December 2017 est.)
$652.8 million (31 December 2016 est.)
country comparison to the world: 134

Debt—external: $5.77 billion (31 December 2017 est.)
$5.495 billion (31 December 2016 est.)
country comparison to the world: 130

Stock of direct foreign investment—at home: $2.272 billion (31 December 2013 est.)
country comparison to the world: 114

Stock of direct foreign investment—abroad: $16.3 billion (31 December 2009)
country comparison to the world: 57

Exchange rates: Tajikistani somoni (TJS) per US dollar—
8.764 (2017 est.)
7.8358 (2016 est.)
7.8358 (2015 est.)
6.1631 (2014 est.)
4.9348 (2013 est.)

ENERGY

Electricity access: *electrification—total population:* 100% (2016)

Electricity—production: 16.98 billion kWh (2015 est.)

country comparison to the world: 82

Electricity—consumption: 12.94 billion kWh (2015 est.)
country comparison to the world: 84

Electricity—exports: NA kWh (2015 est.)

Electricity—imports: 63 million kWh (2015 est.)
country comparison to the world: 103

Electricity—installed generating capacity: 5.5 million kW (2016 est.)
country comparison to the world: 77

Electricity—from fossil fuels: 7% of total installed capacity (2016 est.)
country comparison to the world: 202

Electricity—from nuclear fuels: 0% of total installed capacity (2013 est.)
country comparison to the world: 189

Electricity—from hydroelectric plants: 93% of total installed capacity (2016 est.)
country comparison to the world: 9

Electricity—from other renewable sources: 0% of total installed capacity (2013 est.)
country comparison to the world: 207

Crude oil—production: 180 bbl/day (2016 est.)
country comparison to the world: 98

Crude oil—exports: 78.6 bbl/day (2014 est.)
country comparison to the world: 82

Crude oil—imports: 0 bbl/day (2014 est.)
country comparison to the world: 194

Crude oil—proved reserves: 12 million bbl (1 January 2017 es)
country comparison to the world: 92

Refined petroleum products—production: 445.8 bbl/day (2014 est.)
country comparison to the world: 107

Refined petroleum products—consumption: 23,000 bbl/day (2015 est.)
country comparison to the world: 132

Refined petroleum products—exports: 0 bbl/day (2014 est.)
country comparison to the world: 200

Refined petroleum products—imports: 21,980 bbl/day (2014 est.)
country comparison to the world: 114

Natural gas—production: 20 million cu m (2015 est.)
country comparison to the world: 92

Natural gas—consumption: 189 million cu m (2015 est.)
country comparison to the world: 111

Natural gas—exports: 0 cu m (2013 est.)
country comparison to the world: 191

Natural gas—imports: 212 million cu m (2014 est.)
country comparison to the world: 70

Natural gas—proved reserves: 5.663 billion cu m (1 January 2017 es)
country comparison to the world: 96

Carbon dioxide emissions from consumption of energy: 3.7 million Mt (2013 est.)
country comparison to the world: 138

COMMUNICATIONS

Telephones—fixed lines: *total subscriptions:* 468,000
subscriptions per 100 inhabitants: 6 (July 2016 est.)
country comparison to the world: 98

Telephones—mobile cellular: *total:* 9.4 million
subscriptions per 100 inhabitants: 113 (July 2016 est.)
country comparison to the world: 96

Telephone system: *general assessment:* foreign investment in the telephone system has resulted in major improvements; conversion of the existing fixed network from analogue to digital was completed in 2012
domestic: fixed line availability has not changed significantly since 1998, while mobile cellular subscribership, aided by competition among multiple operators, has expanded rapidly; coverage now extends to all major cities and towns
international: country code—992; linked by cable and microwave radio relay to other CIS republics and by leased connections to the Moscow international gateway switch; Dushanbe linked by Intelsat to international gateway switch in Ankara (Turkey); satellite earth stations—3 (2 Intelsat and 1 Orbita); established a single gateway for Internet traffic in December 2015, which is expected to limit the connectivity of nonstate-owned telecom, Internet, and mobile companies (2016)

Broadcast media: state-run TV broadcasters transmit nationally on 9 TV and 10 radio stations, and regionally on 4 stations; 31 independent TV and 20 radio stations broadcast locally and regionally; many households are able to receive Russian and other foreign stations via cable and satellite (2016)

Internet country code: .tj

Internet users: *total:* 1,705,345

percent of population: 20.5% (July 2016 est.)
country comparison to the world: 118

TRANSPORTATION

National air transport system: number of registered air carriers: 2
inventory of registered aircraft operated by air carriers: 10
annual passenger traffic on registered air carriers: 802,470
annual freight traffic on registered air carriers: 105,376 mt-km (2015)
Civil aircraft registration country code prefix: EY (2016)

Airports: 24 (2013)
country comparison to the world: 131

Airports—with paved runways: *total:* 17
over 3,047 m: 2
2,438 to 3,047 m: 4
1,524 to 2,437 m: 5
914 to 1,523 m: 3
under 914 m: 3 (2013)

Airports—with unpaved runways: *total:* 7
1,524 to 2,437 m: 1
914 to 1,523 m: 1
under 914 m: 5 (2013)

Pipelines: gas 549 km; oil 38 km (2013)

Railways: *total:* 680 km
broad gauge: 680 km 1.520-m gauge (2014)
country comparison to the world: 103

Roadways: *total:* 27,767 km (2000)

country comparison to the world: 97

Waterways: 200 km (along Vakhsh River) (2011)
country comparison to the world: 98

MILITARY AND SECURITY

Military expenditures: 1.19% of GDP (2017)
1.25% of GDP (2016)
1.22% of GDP (2015)
1.13% of GDP (2014)
1% of GDP (2012)

Military branches: Ground Forces, Air and Air Defense Forces, Mobile Forces (2013)

Military service age and obligation: 18-27 years of age for compulsory or voluntary military service; 2-year conscript service obligation; males required to undergo compulsory military training between ages 16 and 55; males can enroll in military schools from at least age 15 (2012)

TRANSNATIONAL ISSUES

Disputes—international: in 2006, China and Tajikistan pledged to commence demarcation of the revised boundary agreed to in the delimitation of 2002; talks continue with Uzbekistan to delimit border and remove minefields; disputes in Isfara Valley delay delimitation with Kyrgyzstan

Refugees and internally displaced persons: *stateless persons:* 17,002 (2016)

Illicit drugs: Tajikistan sits on one of the world's highest volume illicit drug trafficking routes, between Afghan opiate production to the south and the illicit drug markets of Russia and Eastern Europe to the north; limited illicit cultivation of opium poppy for domestic consumption; significant consumer of opiates

TANZANIA

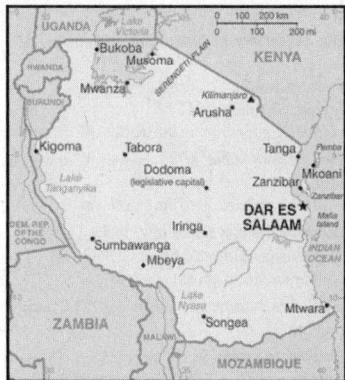

INTRODUCTION

Background: Shortly after achieving independence from Britain in the early 1960s, Tanganyika and Zanzibar merged to form the United Republic of Tanzania in 1964. One-party rule ended in 1995 with the first democratic elections held in the country since the 1970s. Zanzibar's semi-autonomous status and popular opposition led to four contentious elections since 1995, which the ruling party won despite international observers' claims of voting irregularities.

GEOGRAPHY

Location: Eastern Africa, bordering the Indian Ocean, between Kenya and Mozambique

Geographic coordinates: 6 00 S, 35 00 E

Map references: Africa

Area: *total:* 947,300 sq km
land: 885,800 sq km
water: 61,500 sq km
note: includes the islands of Mafia, Pemba, and Zanzibar
country comparison to the world: 32

Area—comparative: more than six times the size of Georgia; slightly larger than twice the size of California
Land boundaries: total: 4,161 km
border countries (8): Burundi 589 km, Democratic Republic of the Congo 479 km, Kenya 775 km, Malawi 512 km, Mozambique 840 km, Rwanda 222 km, Uganda 391 km, Zambia 353 km

Coastline: 1,424 km

Maritime claims: *territorial sea:* 12 nm
exclusive economic zone: 200 nm

Climate: varies from tropical along coast to temperate in highlands

Terrain: plains along coast; central plateau; highlands in north, south

Elevation: *mean elevation:* 1,018 m

elevation extremes: *lowest point:* Indian Ocean 0 m
highest point: Kilimanjaro 5,895 m (highest point in Africa)

Natural resources: hydropower, tin, phosphates, iron ore, coal, diamonds, gemstones, gold, natural gas, nickel

Land use: *agricultural land:* 43.7%
arable land: 14.3%;
permanent crops: 2.3%;
permanent pasture: 27.1%
forest: 37.3%
other: 19% (2011 est.)
Irrigated land: 1,840 sq km (2012)

Population—distribution: the largest and most populous East African country; population distribution is extremely uneven, but greater population clusters occur in the northern half of country and along the east coast

Natural hazards: flooding on the central plateau during the rainy season; drought
volcanism: limited volcanic activity; Ol Doinyo Lengai (2,962 m) has emitted lava in recent years; other historically active volcanoes include Kieyo and Meru

Environment—current issues: soil degradation; deforestation; desertification; destruction of coral reefs threatens marine habitats; recent droughts affected marginal agriculture; wildlife threatened by illegal hunting and trade, especially for ivory

Environment—international agreements: *party to:* Biodiversity, Climate Change, Climate Change-Kyoto Protocol, Desertification, Endangered Species, Hazardous Wastes, Law of the Sea, Ozone Layer Protection, Wetlands
signed, but not ratified: none of the selected agreements

Geography—note: Kilimanjaro is the highest point in Africa and one of only two mountains on the continent that has glaciers (the other is Mount Kenya); bordered by three of the largest lakes on the continent: Lake Victoria (the world's second-largest freshwater lake) in the north, Lake Tanganyika (the world's second deepest) in the west, and Lake Nyasa (Lake Malawi) in the southwest

PEOPLE AND SOCIETY

Population: 53,950,935
note: estimates for this country explicitly take into account the effects of excess mortality due to AIDS; this can result in lower life expectancy, higher infant mortality, higher death rates, lower population growth rates, and changes in the distribution of population by age and sex than would otherwise be expected (July 2017 est.)
country comparison to the world: 26

Nationality: *noun:* Tanzanian(s)
adjective: Tanzanian

Ethnic groups: mainland—African 99% (of which 95% are Bantu consisting of more than 130 tribes), other 1% (consisting of Asian, European, and Arab); Zanzibar—Arab, African, mixed Arab and African

Languages: Kiswahili or Swahili (official), Kiunguja (name for Swahili in Zanzibar), English (official, primary language of commerce, administration, and higher education), Arabic (widely spoken in Zanzibar), many local languages
note: Kiswahili (Swahili) is the mother tongue of the Bantu people living in Zanzibar and nearby coastal Tanzania; although Kiswahili is Bantu in structure and origin, its vocabulary draws on a variety of sources including Arabic and English; it has become the lingua franca of central and eastern Africa; the first language of most people is one of the local languages

Religions: Christian 61.4%, Muslim 35.2%, folk religion 1.8%, other 0.2%, unaffiliated 1.4%
note: Zanzibar is almost entirely Muslim (2010 est.)

Demographic profile: Tanzania has the largest population in East Africa and the lowest population density; almost a third of the population is urban. Tanzania's youthful population – about two-thirds of the population is under 25 – is growing rapidly because of the high total fertility rate of 4.8 children per woman. Progress in reducing the birth rate has stalled, sustaining the country's nearly 3% annual growth. The maternal mortality rate has improved since 2000, yet it remains very high because of early and frequent pregnancies, inadequate maternal health services, and a lack of skilled birth attendants – problems that are worse among poor and rural women. Tanzania has made strides in reducing under-5 and infant mortality rates, but a recent drop in immunization threatens to undermine gains in child health. Malaria is a leading killer of children under 5, while HIV is the main source of adult mortality.

For Tanzania, most migration is internal, rural to urban movement, while some temporary labor migration from towns to plantations takes place seasonally for harvests. Tanzania was Africa's largest refugee-hosting country for decades, hosting hundreds of thousands of refugees from the Great Lakes region, primarily Burundi, over the last fifty years. However, the assisted repatriation and naturalization of tens of thousands of Burundian refugees between 2002 and 2014 dramatically reduced the refugee population. Tanzania is increasingly a transit country for illegal migrants from the Horn of Africa and the Great Lakes region who are heading to southern Africa for security reasons and/or economic opportunities. Some of these migrants choose to settle in Tanzania.

Age structure: *0-14 years:* 43.74% (male 11,921,393/female 11,678,536)
15-24 years: 19.86% (male 5,361,747/female 5,351,794)
25-54 years: 29.88% (male 8,098,183/female 8,020,289)
55-64 years: 3.51% (male 836,313/female 1,055,347)
65 years and over: 3.02% (male 687,118/female 940,215) (2017 est.)

Dependency ratios: *total dependency ratio:* 93.4
youth dependency ratio: 87.4
elderly dependency ratio: 6
potential support ratio: 16.6 (2015 est.)

Median age: *total:* 17.7 years
male: 17.5 years

female: 18 years (2017 est.)
country comparison to the world: 219

Population growth rate: 2.75% (2017 est.)
country comparison to the world: 11

Birth rate: 35.6 births/1,000 population (2017 est.)
country comparison to the world: 16

Death rate: 7.6 deaths/1,000 population (2017 est.)
country comparison to the world: 107

Net migration rate: -0.5 migrant(s)/1,000 population (2017 est.)
country comparison to the world: 124

Population distribution: the largest and most populous East African country; population distribution is extremely uneven, but greater population clusters occur in the northern half of country and along the east coast

Urbanization: *urban population:* 33% of total population (2017)
rate of urbanization: 5% annual rate of change (2015-20 est.)

Major urban areas—population: DAR ES SALAAM (capital) 5.116 million; Mwanza 838,000 (2015)

Sex ratio: *at birth:* 1.03 male(s)/female
0-14 years: 1.02 male(s)/female
15-24 years: 1 male(s)/female
25-54 years: 1.01 male(s)/female
55-64 years: 0.78 male(s)/female
65 years and over: 0.75 male(s)/female
total population: 0.99 male(s)/female (2016 est.)

Mother's mean age at first birth: 19.8 years
note: median age at first birth among women 25-29 (2015/16 est.)

Maternal mortality ratio: 398 deaths/100,000 live births (2015 est.)
country comparison to the world: 27

Infant mortality rate: *total:* 39.9 deaths/1,000 live births
male: 42 deaths/1,000 live births
female: 37.8 deaths/1,000 live births (2017 est.)
country comparison to the world: 46

Life expectancy at birth: *total population:* 62.6 years
male: 61.2 years
female: 64.1 years (2017 est.)
country comparison to the world: 197

Total fertility rate: 4.77 children born/woman (2017 est.)
country comparison to the world: 18

Contraceptive prevalence rate: 38.4% (2015/16)
Health expenditures: 5.6% of GDP (2014)
country comparison to the world: 121

Physicians density: 0.03 physicians/1,000 population (2012)

Hospital bed density: 0.7 beds/1,000 population (2010)

Drinking water source:
improved:
urban: 77.2% of population
rural: 45.5% of population
total: 55.6% of population

unimproved:

urban: 22.1% of population

rural: 56% of population

total: 46.8% of population (2015 est.)

Sanitation facility access:

improved:

urban: 31.3% of population

rural: 8.3% of population

total: 15.6% of population

unimproved:

urban: 68.7% of population

rural: 91.7% of population

total: 84.4% of population (2015 est.)

HIV/AIDS—adult prevalence rate: 4.7% (2016 est.)

country comparison to the world: 13

HIV/AIDS—people living with HIV/AIDS: 1.4 million (2016 est.)

country comparison to the world: 6

HIV/AIDS—deaths: 33,000 (2016 est.)

country comparison to the world: 7

Major infectious diseases: *degree of risk:* very high

food or waterborne diseases: bacterial diarrhea, hepatitis A, and typhoid fever

vectorborne diseases: malaria, dengue fever, and Rift Valley fever

water contact diseases: schistosomiasis and leptospirosis

animal contact disease: rabies (2016)

Obesity—adult prevalence rate: 8.4% (2016)

country comparison to the world: 152

Children under the age of 5 years underweight: 13.7% (2015)

country comparison to the world: 53

Education expenditures: 3.5% of GDP (2014)

country comparison to the world: 37

Literacy: *definition:* age 15 and over can read and write Kiswahili (Swahili), English, or Arabic

total population: 77.9%

male: 83.2%

female: 73.1% (2015 est.)

School life expectancy (primary to tertiary education): *total:* 8 years

male: 8 years

female: 8 years (2013)

Unemployment, youth ages 15-24: *total:* 9.4%

male: 7%

female: 11.7% (2014 est.)

country comparison to the world: 120

GOVERNMENT

Country name: *conventional long form:* United Republic of Tanzania

conventional short form: Tanzania

local long form: Jamhuri ya Muungano wa Tanzania

local short form: Tanzania

former: United Republic of Tanganyika and Zanzibar

etymology: the country's name is a combination of the first letters of Tanganyika and Zanzibar, the two states that merged to form Tanzania in 1964

Government type: presidential republic

Capital: *name:* Dodoma (legislative capital), Dar es Salaam (administrative capital); note—Dodoma was designated the national capital in 1996 and serves as the meeting place for the National Assembly; Dar es Salaam remains the de facto capital, the country's largest city and commercial center, and the site of the executive branch offices and diplomatic representation; the government contends that it will complete the transfer of the executive branch to Dodoma by 2020

geographic coordinates: 6 48 S, 39 17 E

time difference: UTC+3 (8 hours ahead of Washington, DC, during Standard Time)

Administrative divisions: 30 regions; Arusha, Dar es Salaam, Dodoma, Geita, Iringa, Kagera, Kaskazini Pemba (Pemba North), Kaskazini Unguja (Zanzibar North), Katavi, Kigoma, Kilimanjaro, Kusini Pemba (Pemba South), Kusini Unguja (Zanzibar Central/South), Lindi, Manyara, Mara, Mbeya, Mjini Magharibi (Zanzibar Urban/West), Morogoro, Mtwara, Mwanza, Njombe, Pwani (Coast), Rukwa, Ruvuma, Shinyanga, Simiyu, Singida, Tabora, Tanga

Independence: 26 April 1964 (Tanganyika united with Zanzibar to form the United Republic of Tanganyika and Zanzibar); 29 October 1964 (renamed United Republic of Tanzania); notable earlier dates: 9 December 1961 (Tanganyika became independent from UK-administered UN trusteeship); 10 December 1963 (Zanzibar became independent from UK)

National holiday: Union Day (Tanganyika and Zanzibar), 26 April (1964)

Constitution: *history:* several previous; latest adopted 25 April 1977; note—progress enacting a new constitution drafted in 2014 by the Constituent Assembly has been stalled

amendments: proposed by the National Assembly; passage of amendments to constitutional articles including those on sovereignty of the United Republic, the authorities and powers of the government, the president, the Assembly, and the High Court requires two-thirds majority vote of the mainland Assembly membership and of the Zanzibar House of Representatives membership; House of Representatives approval of other amendments is not required (2017)

Legal system: English common law; judicial review of legislative acts limited to matters of interpretation

International law organization participation: has not submitted an ICJ jurisdiction declaration; accepts ICCt jurisdiction

Citizenship: *citizenship by birth:* no

citizenship by descent only: at least one parent must be a citizen of Tanzania; if a child is born abroad, the father must be a citizen of Tanzania

dual citizenship recognized: no

residency requirement for naturalization: 5 years

Suffrage: 18 years of age; universal

Executive branch: *chief of state:* President John MAGUFULI (since 5 November 2015); Vice President Samia SULUHU (since 5 November 2015); note—the president is both chief of state and head of government

head of government: President John MAGUFULI, Dr. (since 5 November 2015); Vice President Samia SULUHU (since 5 November 2015); note—Prime Minister Kassim Majaliwa MAJALIWA (since 20 November 2015) has authority over the day-to-day functions of the government, is the leader of government business in the National Assembly, and is head of the Cabinet

cabinet: Cabinet appointed by the president from among members of the National Assembly

elections/appointments: president and vice president directly elected on the same ballot by simple majority popular vote for a 5-year term (eligible for a second term); election last held on 25 October 2015 (next to be held in October 2020); prime minister appointed by the president

election results: John MAGUFULI elected president; percent of vote—John MAGUFULI (CCM) 58.5%, Edward LOWASSA (CHADEMA) 40%, other 1.5%

note: Zanzibar elects a president as head of government for matters internal to Zanzibar; election held on 25 October 2015 was annulled by the Zanzibar Electoral Commission and rerun on 20 March 2016; President Ali Mohamed SHEIN reelected; percent of vote—Ali Mohamed SHEIN (CCM) 91.4%, Hamad Rashid MOHAMED (ADC) 3%, other 5.6%

Legislative branch: *description:* unicameral National Assembly or Parliament (Bunge) (393 seats; 264 members directly elected in single-seat constituencies by simple majority vote, 113 women directly elected by proportional representation vote, 5 indirectly elected by simple majority vote by the Zanzibar House of Representatives, 10 appointed by the president, and 1 seat reserved for the attorney general; members serve a 5-year term); note—in addition to enacting laws that apply to the entire United Republic of Tanzania, the National Assembly enacts laws that apply only to the mainland; Zanzibar has its own House of Representatives or Baraza La Wawakilishi (82 seats; 50 members directly elected in single-seat constituencies by simple majority vote, 20 women directly elected by proportional representation vote, 10 appointed by the Zanzibar president, 1 seat for the House speaker, and 1 ex-officio seat for the attorney general; elected members serve a 5-year term)

elections: Tanzania National Assembly and Zanzibar House of Representatives elections last held on 25 October 2015 (next National Assembly election to be held in October 2020; next Zanzibar election NA; note the Zanzibar Electoral Commission annulled the 2015 election; repoll held on 20 March 2016

election results: National Assembly—percent of vote by party—CCM 55%, Chadema 31.8%, CUF 8.6%, other 2.2%; seats by party—CCM 253, Chadema 70%, CUF 42%, other 2

Zanzibar House of Representatives—percent of vote by party—NA; seats by party—NA

Judicial branch: *highest court(s):* Court of Appeal of the United Republic of Tanzania (consists of the chief justice and 14 justices); High Court of the United Republic for Mainland Tanzania (consists of the principal judge and 30 judges organized into commercial, land, and labor courts); High Court of Zanzibar (consists of the chief justice and 10 justices)

judge selection and term of office: Court of Appeal and High Court justices appointed by the national president after consultation with the Judicial Service Commission for Tanzania, a judicial body of high level judges and 2 members appointed by the national president; Court of Appeal and High Court judges appointed until mandatory retirement at age 60 but terms can be extended; High Court of Zanzibar judges appointed by the national president after consultation with the Judicial Commission of Zanzibar; judges may serve until mandatory retirement at age 65

subordinate courts: Resident Magistrates Courts; Kadhi courts (for Islamic family matters); district and primary courts

Political parties and leaders: Alliance for Change and Transparency or ACT [Zitto KABWE]
Alliance for Democratic Change or ADC [Miraji ABDALLAH]
Civic United Front or CUF (Chama Cha Wananchi [Seif Shariff HAMAD, Secretary General]
National Convention for Construction and Reform—Mageuzi or NCCR-M [James Francis MBATCA]
Party of Democracy and Development or CHADEMA (Chama Cha Demokrasia na Maendeleo) [Freeman MBOWE]
Revolutionary Party or CCM (Chama Cha Mapinduzi) [John MAGUFULI]
Tanzania Labor Party or TLP [Augustine MREMA]
United Democratic Party or UDP [John Momose CHEYO]
note: in March 2014, four opposition parties (CUF, CHADEMA, NCCR-Mageuzi, and the National League for Democracy) united to form Umoja wa Katiba ya Wananchi (Coalition for the People's Constitution) or UKAWA; during local elections held in October, 2014, UKAWA entered one candidate representing the three parties united in the coalition

Political pressure groups and leaders: Economic and Social Research Foundation or ESRF
Free Zanzibar
Tanzania Media Women's Association or TAMWA
Tanzania Private Sector Foundation or TPSF
Twaweza

International organization participation: ACP, AfDB, AU, C, CD, EAC, EADB, EITI, FAO, G-77, IAEA, IBRD, ICAO, ICC (NGOs), ICCt, ICRM, IDA, IFAD, IFC, IFRCS, ILO, IMF, IMO, IMSO, Interpol, IOC, IOM, IPU, ISO, ITSO, ITU, ITUC (NGOs), MIGA, MONUSCO, NAM, OPCW, SADC, UN, UNAMID, UNCTAD, UNESCO, UNHCR, UNIDO, UNIFIL, UNISFA, UNMISS, UNWTO, UPU, WCO, WFTU (NGOs), WHO, WIPO, WMO, WTO

Diplomatic representation in the US: chief of mission: Ambassador Wilson Mutagaywa MASILINGI (since 17 September 2015)
chancery: 1232 22nd Street NW, Washington, DC 20037
telephone: [1] (202) 939-6125
FAX: [1] (202) 797-7408

Diplomatic representation from the US: *chief of mission:* Ambassador (vacant); Charge d'Affaires Inmi PATTERSON (since 5 July 2017)
embassy: 686 Old Bagamoyo Road, Msasani, Dar es Salaam
mailing address: P.O. Box 9123, Dar es Salaam
telephone: [255] (22) 229-4000
FAX: [255] (22) 229-4970 or 4971

Flag description: divided diagonally by a yellow-edged black band from the lower hoist-side corner; the upper triangle (hoist side) is green and the lower triangle is blue; the banner combines colors found on the flags of Tanganyika and Zanzibar; green represents the natural vegetation of the country, gold its rich mineral deposits, black the native Swahili people, and blue the country's many lakes and rivers, as well as the Indian Ocean

National symbol(s): Uhuru (Freedom) torch, giraffe; national colors: green, yellow, blue, black

National anthem: *name:* "Mungu ibariki Afrika" (God Bless Africa)
lyrics/music: collective/Enoch Mankayi SONTONGA
note: adopted 1961; the anthem, which is also a popular song in Africa, shares the same melody with that of Zambia, but has different lyrics; the melody is also incorporated into South Africa's anthem

ECONOMY

Economy—overview: Tanzania is one of the world's poorest economies in terms of per capita income, but has achieved high growth rates based on its vast natural resource wealth and tourism. GDP growth in 2009-17 averaged 6%-7% per year. Dar es Salaam used fiscal stimulus measures and easier monetary policies to lessen the impact of the global recession. Tanzania has largely completed its transition to a market economy, though the government retains a presence in sectors such as telecommunications, banking, energy, and mining.

The economy depends on agriculture, which accounts for more than one-quarter of GDP, provides 85% of exports, and employs about 65% of the work force. All land in Tanzania is owned by the government, which can lease land for up to 99 years. Proposed reforms to allow for land ownership, particularly foreign land ownership, remain unpopular.

The financial sector in Tanzania has expanded in recent years and foreign-owned banks account for about 48% of the banking industry's total assets. Competition among foreign commercial banks has resulted in significant improvements in the efficiency and quality of financial services, though interest rates are still relatively high, reflecting high fraud risk. Recent banking reforms have helped increase private-sector growth and investment.

The World Bank, the IMF, and bilateral donors have provided funds to rehabilitate Tanzania's aging infrastructure, including rail and port, which provide important trade links for inland countries. In 2013, Tanzania completed the world's largest Millennium Challenge Compact (MCC) grant, worth $698 million, but in late 2015, the MCC Board of Directors deferred a decision to renew Tanzania's eligibility because of irregularities in voting in Zanzibar and concerns over the government's use of a controversial cybercrime bill.

Under the new government elected in 2015, Tanzania has developed an ambitious development agenda focused on creating a better business environment through improved infrastructure, access to financing, and education progress, but implementing budgets remains challenging for the government.

GDP (purchasing power parity): $162.8 billion (2017 est.)
$152.9 billion (2016 est.)
$143 billion (2015 est.)
note: data are in 2017 dollars
country comparison to the world: 76

GDP (official exchange rate): $51.61 billion (2016 est.)

GDP—real growth rate: 6.5% (2017 est.)
7% (2016 est.)
7% (2015 est.)
country comparison to the world: 17

GDP—per capita (PPP): $3,300 (2017 est.)
$3,100 (2016 est.)
$3,000 (2015 est.)
note: data are in 2017 dollars
country comparison to the world: 191

Gross national saving: 19.7% of GDP (2017 est.)
23% of GDP (2016 est.)
24.7% of GDP (2015 est.)
country comparison to the world: 93

GDP—composition, by end use:
household consumption: 65%
government consumption: 13.4%
investment in fixed capital: 34.3%
investment in inventories: -8.6%
exports of goods and services: 17.9%
imports of goods and services: -22% (2017 est.)

GDP—composition, by sector of origin:
agriculture: 23.4%
industry: 28.6%
services: 47.6% (2017 est.)

Agriculture—products: coffee, sisal, tea, cotton, pyrethrum (insecticide made from chrysanthemums), cashew nuts, tobacco, cloves, corn, wheat, cassava (manioc, tapioca), bananas, fruits, vegetables; cattle, sheep, goats

Industries: agricultural processing (sugar, beer, cigarettes, sisal twine); mining (diamonds, gold, and iron), salt, soda ash; cement, oil refining, shoes, apparel, wood products, fertilizer

Industrial production growth rate: 8.8% (2017 est.)

country comparison to the world: 13

Labor force: 24.89 million (2017 est.)
country comparison to the world: 26

Labor force—by occupation: *agriculture:* 66.9%
industry: 6.4%
services: 26.6% (2014 est.)

Unemployment rate: 10.3% (2014 est.)
country comparison to the world: 140

Population below poverty line: 22.8% (2015 est.)

Household income or consumption by percentage share: *lowest 10%:* 2.8%
highest 10%: 29.6% (2007)

Distribution of family income—Gini index: 37.6 (2007)
34.6 (2000)
country comparison to the world: 77

Budget: *revenues:* $7.872 billion
expenditures: $9.271 billion (2017 est.)
Taxes and other revenues: 15.3% of GDP (2017 est.)
country comparison to the world: 184

Budget surplus (+) or deficit (-): -2.7% of GDP (2017 est.)
country comparison to the world: 102

Public debt: 35.2% of GDP (2017 est.)
34% of GDP (2016 est.)
country comparison to the world: 145

Fiscal year: 1 July—30 June

Inflation rate (consumer prices): 5.4% (2017 est.)
5.2% (2016 est.)
country comparison to the world: 176

Central bank discount rate: 8.25% (31 December 2010)
3.7% (31 December 2009)
country comparison to the world: 39

Commercial bank prime lending rate: 15% (31 December 2017 est.)
15.96% (31 December 2016 est.)
country comparison to the world: 44

Stock of narrow money: $4.869 billion (31 December 2017 est.)
$4.601 billion (31 December 2016 est.)
country comparison to the world: 105

Stock of broad money: $8.291 billion (31 December 2017 est.)
$7.613 billion (31 December 2016 est.)
country comparison to the world: 112

Stock of domestic credit: $9.77 billion (31 December 2017 est.)
$9.625 billion (31 December 2016 est.)
country comparison to the world: 107

Market value of publicly traded shares: $1.803 billion (31 December 2012 est.)
$1.539 billion (31 December 2011 est.)
$1.264 billion (31 December 2010 est.)
country comparison to the world: 102

Current account balance: -$2.907 billion (2017 est.)
-$2.677 billion (2016 est.)
country comparison to the world: 165

Exports: $5.194 billion (2017 est.)
$5.697 billion (2016 est.)

country comparison to the world: 107

Exports—commodities: gold, coffee, cashew nuts, manufactures, cotton

Exports—partners: Switzerland 15.1%, India 13.8%, South Africa 12.4%, China 7%, Kenya 6.2%, Democratic Republic of the Congo 5.7%, Belgium 5.6% (2016)

Imports: $8.61 billion (2017 est.)
$8.464 billion (2016 est.)
country comparison to the world: 105

Imports—commodities: consumer goods, machinery and transportation equipment, industrial raw materials, crude oil

Imports—partners: China 20.7%, India 18.1%, UAE 7.5%, South Africa 6%, Japan 4.7% (2016)

Reserves of foreign exchange and gold: $4.174 billion (31 December 2017 est.)
$4.067 billion (31 December 2016 est.)
note: excludes gold
country comparison to the world: 97

Debt—external: $15.88 billion (31 December 2017 est.)
$15.21 billion (31 December 2016 est.)
country comparison to the world: 101

Stock of direct foreign investment—at home: $NA

Stock of direct foreign investment—abroad: $NA

Exchange rates: Tanzanian shillings (TZS) per US dollar—
2,243.8 (2017 est.)
2,177.1 (2016 est.)
2,177.1 (2015 est.)
1,989.7 (2014 est.)
1,654 (2013 est.)

ENERGY

Electricity access: population without electricity: 37,400,000
electrification—*total population:* 24%
electrification—urban areas: 71%
electrification—rural areas: 4% (2013)

Electricity—production: 6.025 billion kWh (2015 est.)
country comparison to the world: 115

Electricity—consumption: 4.976 billion kWh (2015 est.)
country comparison to the world: 120

Electricity—exports: 0 kWh (2016 est.)
country comparison to the world: 209

Electricity—imports: 71 million kWh (2015 est.)
country comparison to the world: 101

Electricity—installed generating capacity: 1.187 million kW (2015 est.)
country comparison to the world: 125

Electricity—from fossil fuels: 46% of total installed capacity (2015 est.)
country comparison to the world: 156

Electricity—from nuclear fuels: 0% of total installed capacity (2015 est.)
country comparison to the world: 198

Electricity—from hydroelectric plants: 47.3% of total installed capacity (2015 est.)
country comparison to the world: 43

Electricity—from other renewable sources: 6.8% of total installed capacity (2015 est.)
country comparison to the world: 84

Crude oil—production: 0 bbl/day (2016 est.)
country comparison to the world: 205

Crude oil—exports: 0 bbl/day (2014 est.)
country comparison to the world: 203

Crude oil—imports: 0 bbl/day (2014 est.)
country comparison to the world: 202

Crude oil—proved reserves: 0 bbl (1 January 2017 es)
country comparison to the world: 204

Refined petroleum products—production: 0 bbl/day (2014 est.)
country comparison to the world: 206

Refined petroleum products—consumption: 60,000 bbl/day (2015 est.)
country comparison to the world: 97

Refined petroleum products—exports: 0 bbl/day (2014 est.)
country comparison to the world: 207

Refined petroleum products—imports: 58,700 bbl/day (2014 est.)
country comparison to the world: 75

Natural gas—production: 1.1 billion cu m (2015 est.)
country comparison to the world: 65

Natural gas—consumption: 1.5 billion cu m (2015 est.)
country comparison to the world: 90

Natural gas—exports: 0 cu m (2013 est.)
country comparison to the world: 199

Natural gas—imports: 0 cu m (2013 est.)
country comparison to the world: 200

Natural gas—proved reserves: 6.513 billion cu m (1 January 2017 es)
country comparison to the world: 90

Carbon dioxide emissions from consumption of energy: 10 million Mt (2013 est.)
country comparison to the world: 104

COMMUNICATIONS

Telephones—fixed lines: *total subscriptions:* 129,597
subscriptions per 100 inhabitants: less than 1 (July 2016 est.)
country comparison to the world: 139

Telephones—mobile cellular: *total:* 40,044,186
subscriptions per 100 inhabitants: 76 (July 2016 est.)
country comparison to the world: 37

Telephone system: *general assessment:* telecommunications services are marginal; system operating below capacity and being modernized for better service
domestic: fixed-line telephone network inadequate with less than 1 connection per 100 persons; mobile-cellular service, aided by multiple providers, is increasing rapidly and exceeds 75

telephones per 100 persons; trunk service provided by open-wire, microwave radio relay, tropospheric scatter, and fiber-optic cable; some links being made digital

international: country code—255; landing point for the EASSy fiber-optic submarine cable system linking East Africa with Europe and North America; satellite earth stations—2 Intelsat (1 Indian Ocean, 1 Atlantic Ocean) (2016)

Broadcast media: a state-owned TV station and multiple privately owned TV stations; state-owned national radio station supplemented by more than 40 privately owned radio stations; transmissions of several international broadcasters are available (2007)

Internet country code: .tz

Internet users: total: 6,822,754

percent of population: 13.0% (July 2016 est.)
country comparison to the world: 51

TRANSPORTATION

National air transport system: number of registered air carriers: 5
inventory of registered aircraft operated by air carriers: 17
annual passenger traffic on registered air carriers: 1,239,707
annual freight traffic on registered air carriers: 2,337,440 mt-km (2015)
Civil aircraft registration country code prefix: 5H (2016)

Airports: 166 (2013)
country comparison to the world: 34

Airports—with paved runways: *total:* 10
over 3,047 m: 2
2,438 to 3,047 m: 2
1,524 to 2,437 m: 4
914 to 1,523 m: 2 (2013)

Airports—with unpaved runways: *total:* 156
over 3,047 m: 1
1,524 to 2,437 m: 24
914 to 1,523 m: 98
under 914 m: 33 (2013)

Pipelines: gas 311 km; oil 891 km; refined products 8 km (2013)

Railways: *total:* 4,567 km
narrow gauge: 1,860 km 1.067-m gauge; 2,707 km 1.000-m gauge (2014)
country comparison to the world: 40

Roadways: *total:* 86,472 km
paved: 7,092 km
unpaved: 79,380 km (2010)
country comparison to the world: 55

Waterways: (Lake Tanganyika, Lake Victoria, and Lake Nyasa (Lake Malawi) are the principal avenues of commerce with neighboring countries; the rivers are not navigable) (2011)

Merchant marine: *total:* 279
by type: bulk carrier 10, container ship 9, general cargo 147, oil tanker 29, other 84 (2017)
country comparison to the world: 54

Ports and terminals: *major seaport(s):* Dar es Salaam, Zanzibar

MILITARY AND SECURITY

Military expenditures: 1.14% of GDP (2016)
1.13% of GDP (2015)
1.05% of GDP (2014)
1% of GDP (2013)
0.93% of GDP (2012)
country comparison to the world: 88

Military branches: Tanzania People's Defense Force (Jeshi la Wananchi la Tanzania, JWTZ): Army, Naval Wing (includes Coast Guard), Air Defense Command (includes Air Wing), National Service (2007)

Military service age and obligation: 18 years of age for voluntary military service; no conscription (2012)

Maritime threats: the International Maritime Bureau reports that shipping in territorial and offshore waters in the Indian Ocean remain at risk for piracy and armed robbery against ships, especially as Somali-based pirates extend their activities south; numerous commercial vessels have been attacked and hijacked both at anchor and while underway; crews have been robbed and stores or cargoes stolen

TERRORISM

Terrorist groups—foreign based: al-Qa'ida (AQ): aim(s): drive US Government personnel, US business people, and other US influences out of Tanzania and, ultimately, establish a pan-Islamic caliphate under a strict Salafi Muslim interpretation *area(s) of operation:* maintains a limited presence; on 7 August 1998, operatives detonated truck bombs that exploded and killed and injured scores of workers and severely damaged the US Embassy in Dar es Salaam, killing approximately 11 people and injuring a few thousand others; almost all of the dead and injured were Tanzanians

TRANSNATIONAL ISSUES

Disputes—international: dispute with Tanzania over the boundary in Lake Nyasa (Lake Malawi) and the meandering Songwe River; Malawi contends that the entire lake up to the Tanzanian

shoreline is its territory, while Tanzania claims the border is in the center of the lake; the conflict was reignited in 2012 when Malawi awarded a license to a British company for oil exploration in the lake
Refugees and internally displaced persons:
refugees (country of origin): 278,801 (Burundi); 80,176 (Democratic Republic of the Congo) (2017)

Trafficking in persons: current situation: Tanzania is a source, transit, and destination country for men, women, and children subjected to forced labor and sex trafficking; the exploitation of young girls in domestic servitude continues to be Tanzania's largest human trafficking problem; Tanzanian boys are subject to forced labor mainly on farms but also in mines and quarries, in the informal commercial sector, in factories, in the sex trade, and possibly on small fishing boats; Tanzanian children and adults are subjected to domestic servitude, other forms of forced labor, and sex trafficking in other African countries, the Middle East, Europe, and the US; internal trafficking is more prevalent than transnational trafficking and is usually facilitated by friends, family members, or intermediaries with false offers of education or legitimate jobs; trafficking victims from Burundi, Kenya, South Asia, and Yemen are forced to work in Tanzania's agricultural, mining, and domestic service sectors or may be sex trafficked

tier rating: Tier 2 Watch List – Tanzania does not fully comply with the minimum standards for the elimination of trafficking; however, it is making significant efforts to do so; in 2014, Tanzania was granted a waiver from an otherwise required downgrade to Tier 3 because its government has a written plan that, if implemented, would constitute making significant efforts to bring itself into compliance with the minimum standards for the elimination of trafficking; the government adopted a three-year national action plan and implementing regulations for the 2008 anti-trafficking law; authorities somewhat increased their number of trafficking investigations and prosecutions and convicted one offender, but the penalty was a fine in lieu of prison, which was inadequate given the severity of the crime; the government did not operate any shelters for victims and relied on NGOs to provide protective services (2015)

Illicit drugs: targeted by traffickers moving hashish, Afghan heroin, and South American cocaine transported down the East African coastline, through airports, or overland through Central Africa; Zanzibar likely used by traffickers for drug smuggling; traffickers in the past have recruited Tanzanian couriers to move drugs through Iran into East Asia

THAILAND

INTRODUCTION

Background: A unified Thai kingdom was established in the mid-14th century. Known as Siam until 1939, Thailand is the only Southeast Asian country never to have been colonized by a European power. A bloodless revolution in 1932 led to the establishment of a constitutional monarchy. In alliance with Japan during World War II, Thailand became a US treaty ally in 1954 after sending troops to Korea and later fighting alongside the US in Vietnam. Thailand since 2005 has experienced several rounds of political turmoil including a military coup in 2006 that ousted then Prime Minister THAKSIN Chinnawat, followed by large-scale street protests by competing political factions in 2008, 2009, and 2010. THAKSIN's youngest sister, YINGLAK Chinnawat, in 2011 led the Puea Thai Party to an electoral win and assumed control of the government. A blanket amnesty bill for individuals involved in street protests, altered at the last minute to include all political crimes—including all convictions against THAKSIN—triggered months of large-scale anti-government protests in Bangkok beginning in November 2013.

In early May 2014, YINGLAK was removed from office by the Constitutional Court and in late May 2014 the Royal Thai Army, led by Royal Thai Army Gen. PRAYUT Chan-ocha, staged a coup against the caretaker government. PRAYUT was appointed prime minister in August 2014. The interim military government created several interim institutions to promote reform and draft a new constitution, which was passed in a national referendum in August 2016. Elections are tentatively set for late-2018. King PHUMIPHON Adunyadet passed away in October 2016 after 70 years on the throne; his only son, WACHIRALONGKON Bodinthrathepphayawarangkun, ascended the throne in December 2016. He signed the new constitution in April 2017. Thailand has also experienced violence associated with the ethno-nationalist insurgency in its southern Malay-Muslim majority provinces. Since January 2004, thousands have been killed and wounded in the insurgency.

GEOGRAPHY

Location: Southeastern Asia, bordering the Andaman Sea and the Gulf of Thailand, southeast of Burma

Geographic coordinates: 15 00 N, 100 00 E

Map references: Southeast Asia

Area: *total:* 513,120 sq km
land: 510,890 sq km
water: 2,230 sq km
country comparison to the world: 52

Area—comparative: about three times the size of Florida; slightly more than twice the size of Wyoming
Land boundaries: total: 5,673 km
border countries (4): Burma 2,416 km, Cambodia 817 km, Laos 1,845 km, Malaysia 595 km

Coastline: 3,219 km

Maritime claims: *territorial sea:* 12 nm
exclusive economic zone: 200 nm
continental shelf: 200-m depth or to the depth of exploitation

Climate: tropical; rainy, warm, cloudy southwest monsoon (mid-May to September); dry, cool northeast monsoon (November to mid-March); southern isthmus always hot and humid

Terrain: central plain; Khorat Plateau in the east; mountains elsewhere

Elevation: *mean elevation:* 287 m

elevation extremes: *lowest point:* Gulf of Thailand 0 m
highest point: Doi Inthanon 2,565 m

Natural resources: tin, rubber, natural gas, tungsten, tantalum, timber, lead, fish, gypsum, lignite, fluorite, arable land

Land use: *agricultural land:* 41.2%
arable land: 30.8%;

permanent crops: 8.8%;
permanent pasture: 1.6%
forest: 37.2%
other: 21.6% (2011 est.)
Irrigated land: 64,150 sq km (2012)

Population—distribution: highest population density is found in and around Bangkok; significant population clusters found throughout large parts of the country, particularly north and northeast of Bangkok and in the extreme southern region of the country

Natural hazards: land subsidence in Bangkok area resulting from the depletion of the water table; droughts

Environment—current issues: air pollution from vehicle emissions; water pollution from organic and factory wastes; deforestation; soil erosion; wildlife populations threatened by illegal hunting

Environment—international agreements: *party to:* Biodiversity, Climate Change, Climate Change-Kyoto Protocol, Desertification, Endangered Species, Hazardous Wastes, Marine Life Conservation, Ozone Layer Protection, Tropical Timber 83, Tropical Timber 94, Wetlands
signed, but not ratified: Law of the Sea

Geography—note: controls only land route from Asia to Malaysia and Singapore; ideas for the construction of a canal across the Kra Isthmus that would create a bypass to the Strait of Malacca and shorten shipping times around Asia continue to be discussed

PEOPLE AND SOCIETY

Population: 68,414,135
note: estimates for this country explicitly take into account the effects of excess mortality due to AIDS; this can result in lower life expectancy, higher infant mortality, higher death rates, lower population growth rates, and changes in the distribution of population by age and sex than would otherwise be expected (July 2017 est.)
country comparison to the world: 20

Nationality: *noun:* Thai (singular and plural)
adjective: Thai

Ethnic groups: Thai 97.5%, Burmese 1.3%, other 1.1%, unspecified <.1% (2015 est.)

Languages: Thai (official) 90.7%, Burmese 1.3%, other 8%
note: English is a secondary language of the elite (2010 est.)

Religions: Buddhist 94.6%, Muslim 4.3%, Christian 1%, other <.1%, none <.1% (2015 est.)

Age structure: *0-14 years:* 16.93% (male 5,933,269/female 5,649,864)
15-24 years: 14.17% (male 4,943,583/female 4,752,038)
25-54 years: 46.32% (male 15,677,322/female 16,009,399)

55-64 years: 12% (male 3,851,575/female 4,358,837)
65 years and over: 10.58% (male 3,165,799/female 4,072,449) (2017 est.)

Dependency ratios: *total dependency ratio:* 40
youth dependency ratio: 25.2
elderly dependency ratio: 14.8
potential support ratio: 6.8 (2015 est.)

Median age: *total:* 37.7 years
male: 36.6 years
female: 38.7 years (2017 est.)
country comparison to the world: 66

Population growth rate: 0.3% (2017 est.)
country comparison to the world: 171

Birth rate: 11 births/1,000 population (2017 est.)
country comparison to the world: 179

Death rate: 8 deaths/1,000 population (2017 est.)
country comparison to the world: 91

Net migration rate: 0 migrant(s)/1,000 population (2017 est.)
country comparison to the world: 98

Population distribution: highest population density is found in and around Bangkok; significant population clusters found throuogut large parts of the country, particularly north and northeast of Bangkok and in the extreme southern region of the country

Urbanization: *urban population:* 52.7% of total population (2017)
rate of urbanization: 2.2% annual rate of change (2015-20 est.)

Major urban areas—population: BANGKOK (capital) 9.27 million; Samut Prakan 1.814 million (2015)

Sex ratio: *at birth:* 1.05 male(s)/female
0-14 years: 1.05 male(s)/female
15-24 years: 1.04 male(s)/female
25-54 years: 0.98 male(s)/female
55-64 years: 0.89 male(s)/female
65 years and over: 0.78 male(s)/female
total population: 0.97 male(s)/female (2016 est.)

Mother's mean age at first birth: 23.3 years (2009 est.)

Maternal mortality ratio: 20 deaths/100,000 live births (2015 est.)
country comparison to the world: 129

Infant mortality rate: *total:* 9.2 deaths/1,000 live births
male: 10.1 deaths/1,000 live births
female: 8.2 deaths/1,000 live births (2017 est.)
country comparison to the world: 146

Life expectancy at birth: *total population:* 74.9 years
male: 71.7 years
female: 78.3 years (2017 est.)
country comparison to the world: 116

Total fertility rate: 1.52 children born/woman (2017 est.)
country comparison to the world: 194

Contraceptive prevalence rate: 79.3% (2012)
Health expenditures: 6.5% of GDP (2014)
country comparison to the world: 92

Physicians density: 0.39 physicians/1,000 population (2010)

Hospital bed density: 2.1 beds/1,000 population (2010)

Drinking water source:
improved:
urban: 97.6% of population
rural: 98% of population
total: 97.8% of population
unimproved:
urban: 2.4% of population
rural: 2% of population
total: 2.2% of population (2015 est.)

Sanitation facility access:
improved:
urban: 89.9% of population
rural: 96.1% of population
total: 93% of population
unimproved:
urban: 10.1% of population
rural: 3.9% of population
total: 7% of population (2015 est.)

HIV/AIDS—adult prevalence rate: 1.1% (2016 est.)
country comparison to the world: 40

HIV/AIDS—people living with HIV/AIDS: 450,000 (2016 est.)
country comparison to the world: 16

HIV/AIDS—deaths: 16,000 (2016 est.)
country comparison to the world: 16

Major infectious diseases: *degree of risk:* very high
food or waterborne diseases: bacterial diarrhea
vectorborne diseases: dengue fever, Japanese encephalitis, and malaria (2016)

Obesity—adult prevalence rate: 10% (2016)
country comparison to the world: 140

Children under the age of 5 years underweight: 9.2% (2012)
country comparison to the world: 71
Education expenditures: 4.1% of GDP (2013)
country comparison to the world: 47

Literacy: *definition:* age 15 and over can read and write
total population: 92.9%
male: 94.7%
female: 91.2% (2015 est.)

School life expectancy (primary to tertiary education): *total:* 16 years
male: 16 years
female: 16 years (2015)

Unemployment, youth ages 15-24: *total:* 0.9%
male: 0.8%
female: 1.1% (2015 est.)
country comparison to the world: 132

GOVERNMENT

Country name: *conventional long form:* Kingdom of Thailand
conventional short form: Thailand
local long form: Ratcha Anachak Thai
local short form: Prathet Thai
former: Siam

etymology: "Land of the Tai [People]"; the meaning of "tai" is uncertain, but may originally have meant "human beings," "people," or "free people"

Government type: constitutional monarchy; note—interim military-affiliated government since May 2014

Capital: *name:* Bangkok
geographic coordinates: 13 45 N, 100 31 E
time difference: UTC+7 (12 hours ahead of Washington, DC, during Standard Time)

Administrative divisions: 76 provinces (changwat, singular and plural) and 1 municipality* (maha nakhon); Amnat Charoen, Ang Thong, Bueng Kan, Buri Ram, Chachoengsao, Chai Nat, Chaiyaphum, Chanthaburi, Chiang Mai, Chiang Rai, Chon Buri, Chumphon, Kalasin, Kamphaeng Phet, Kanchanaburi, Khon Kaen, Krabi, Krung Thep* (Bangkok), Lampang, Lamphun, Loei, Lop Buri, Mae Hong Son, Maha Sarakham, Mukdahan, Nakhon Nayok, Nakhon Pathom, Nakhon Phanom, Nakhon Ratchasima, Nakhon Sawan, Nakhon Si Thammarat, Nan, Narathiwat, Nong Bua Lamphu, Nong Khai, Nonthaburi, Pathum Thani, Pattani, Phangnga, Phatthalung, Phayao, Phetchabun, Phetchaburi, Phichit, Phitsanulok, Phra Nakhon Si Ayutthaya, Phrae, Phuket, Prachin Buri, Prachuap Khiri Khan, Ranong, Ratchaburi, Rayong, Roi Et, Sa Kaeo, Sakon Nakhon, Samut Prakan, Samut Sakhon, Samut Songkhram, Saraburi, Satun, Sing Buri, Si Sa Ket, Songkhla, Sukhothai, Suphan Buri, Surat Thani, Surin, Tak, Trang, Trat, Ubon Ratchathani, Udon Thani, Uthai Thani, Uttaradit, Yala, Yasothon

Independence: 1238 (traditional founding date; never colonized)

National holiday: Birthday of King Maha VAJIRALONGKORN, 28 July (1952)

Constitution: many previous; draft of latest completed 29 March 2016, approved by referendum 7 August 2016, signed by the king 6 April 2017; note—the final version has several changes not reflected in the one passed by referendum (2016)

Legal system: civil law system with common law influences

International law organization participation: has not submitted an ICJ jurisdiction declaration; non-party state to the ICCt

Citizenship: *citizenship by birth:* no
citizenship by descent only: at least one parent must be a citizen of Thailand
dual citizenship recognized: no
residency requirement for naturalization: 5 years

Suffrage: 18 years of age; universal and compulsory

Executive branch: *chief of state:* King WACHIRALONGKON Bodinthrathepphayawarangkun, also spelled Vajiralongkorn Bodindradebayavarangkun (since 1 December 2016); note—King PHUMIPHON Adunyadet, also spelled BHUMIBOL Adulyadej (since 9 June 1946) died 13 October 2016

head of government: Interim Prime Minister Gen. PRAYUT Chan-ocha (since 25 August 2014);

Deputy Prime Ministers PRAWIT Wongsuwan, Gen. (since 31 August 2014), WISSANU Krueangam (since 31 August 2014), SOMKHIT Chatusiphithak (since 20 August 2015), PRACHIN Chantong, Air Chief Mar. (since 20 August 2015), CHATCHAI Sarikan, Gen. (since 23 November 2017)

cabinet: Council of Ministers nominated by the prime minister, appointed by the king; a Privy Council advises the king

elections/appointments: the monarchy is hereditary; the House of Representatives approves a person for Prime Minister who must then be appointed by the King (as stated in the transitory provision of the 2017 constitution); the office of prime minister can be held for up to a total of 8 years

note: Gen. Prayut Chan-ocha was appointed interim prime minister in August 2014, three months after he staged the coup that removed the previously elected government of Prime Minister YINGLUCK Chinnawat, also spelled YINGLUCK Shinawatra

Legislative branch: description: in transition; following the May 2014 military coup, a National Legislative Assembly or Sapha Nitibanyat Haeng Chat of no more than 220 members replaced the bicameral National Assembly; expanded to 250 members in September 2016; elections for a permanent legislative body are scheduled for November 2018; the 2017 constitution calls for a 250-member military-appointed Senate with 5-year terms and a 500-member elected House of Representatives with 4-year terms

elections: Senate—last held on 30 March 2014 but invalidated by the coup (in future, members will be appointed); House of Representatives—last held on 2 February 2014 but later declared invalid by the Constitutional Court (next to be held in November 2018)

election results: Senate—percent of vote by party—NA; seats by party—NA; House of Representatives—percent of vote by party—NA; seats by party—NA

Judicial branch: highest court(s): Supreme Court of Justice (consists of court president, 6 vice-presidents, and 60-70 judges, and organized into 10 divisions); Constitutional Court (consists of court president and 8 judges); Supreme Administrative Court (number of judges determined by Judicial Commission of the Administrative Courts)

judge selection and term of office: Supreme Court judges selected by the Judicial Commission of the Courts of Justice and approved by the monarch; judge term determined by the monarch; Constitutional Court justices—3 judges drawn from the Supreme Court, 2 judges drawn from the Administrative Court, and 4 judge candidates selected by the Selective Committee for Judges of the Constitutional Court and confirmed by the Senate; judges appointed by the monarch to serve single 9-year terms; Supreme Administrative Court judges selected by the Judicial Commission of the Administrative Courts and appointed by the monarch; judges appointed for life

subordinate courts: courts of first instance and appeals courts within both the judicial and administrative systems; military courts

Political parties and leaders: Chat Thai Phatthana Party or CTP (Thai Nation Development Party)

Phumchai (Bhumjai) Thai Party or PJT (Thai Pride) [ANUTHIN Chanwirakun]

Prachathipat Party or DP (Democrat Party) [ABHISIT Wechachiwa, also spelled ABHISIT Vejjajiva]

Puea Thai Party (For Thais Party) or PTP [acting leader WIROT Paoin]

Political pressure groups and leaders: New Democracy Movement

People's Democratic Reform Committee or PDRC
United Front for Democracy Against Dictatorship or UDD

International organization participation: ADB, APEC, ARF, ASEAN, BIMSTEC, BIS, CD, CICA, CP, EAS, FAO, G-77, IAEA, IBRD, ICAO, ICC (national committees), ICRM, IDA, IFAD, IFC, IFRCS, IHO, ILO, IMF, IMO, IMSO, Interpol, IOC, IOM, IPU, ISO, ITSO, ITU, ITUC (NGOs), MIGA, NAM, OAS (observer), OIC (observer), OIF (observer), OPCW, OSCE (partner), PCA, PIF (partner), UN, UNAMID, UNCTAD, UNESCO, UNHCR, UNIDO, UNMOGIP, UNOCI, UNWTO, UPU, WCO, WFTU (NGOs), WHO, WIPO, WMO, WTO

Diplomatic representation in the US: chief of mission: Ambassador (vacant); Charge d'Affaires PHATTHARAWAN Wetchasat (since 27 October 2017)

chancery: 1024 Wisconsin Avenue NW, Suite 401, Washington, DC 20007

telephone: [1] (202) 944-3600

FAX: [1] (202) 944-3611

consulate(s) general: Chicago, Los Angeles, New York

Diplomatic representation from the US: chief of mission: Ambassador Glyn T. DAVIES (since 28 November 2015)

embassy: 95 Wireless Road, Bangkok 10330

mailing address: APO AP 96546

telephone: [66] (2) 205-4000

FAX: [66] (2) 254-2990, 205-4131

consulate(s) general: Chiang Mai

Flag description: five horizontal bands of red (top), white, blue (double width), white, and red; the red color symbolizes the nation and the blood of life; white represents religion and the purity of Buddhism; blue stands for the monarchy

note: similar to the flag of Costa Rica but with the blue and red colors reversed

National symbol(s): garuda (mythical half-man, half-bird figure), elephant; national colors: red, white, blue

National anthem: name: "Phleng Chat Thai" (National Anthem of Thailand)

lyrics/music: Luang SARANUPRAPAN/Phra JENDURIYANG

note: music adopted 1932, lyrics adopted 1939; by law, people are required to stand for the national

anthem at 0800 and 1800 every day; the anthem is played in schools, offices, theaters, and on television and radio during this time; "Phleng Sanlasoen Phra Barami" (A Salute to the Monarch) serves as the royal anthem and is played in the presence of the royal family and during certain state ceremonies

ECONOMY

Economy—overview: With a relatively well-developed infrastructure, a free-enterprise economy, and generally pro-investment policies, Thailand is highly dependent on international trade, with exports accounting for about two-thirds of GDP. Thailand's exports include electronics, agricultural commodities, automobiles and parts, and processed foods. The industry and service sectors produce about 90% of GDP. The agricultural sector, comprised mostly of small-scale farms, contributes only 10% of GDP but employs about one-third of the labor force. Thailand has attracted an estimated 3.0-4.5 million migrant workers, mostly from neighboring countries.

Over the last few decades, Thailand has reduced poverty substantially. In 2013, the Thai Government implemented a nationwide 300 baht (roughly \$10) per day minimum wage policy and deployed new tax reforms designed to lower rates on middle-income earners.

Thailand's economy is recovering from slow growth during the years since the 2014 coup. Thailand's economic fundamentals are sound, with low inflation, low unemployment, and reasonable public and external debt levels. Tourism and government spending—mostly on infrastructure and short-term stimulus measures – have helped to boost the economy, and The Bank of Thailand has been supportive, with several interest rate reductions.

Over the longer-term, household debt levels, political uncertainty, and an aging population pose risks to growth.

GDP (purchasing power parity): \$1.229 trillion (2017 est.)
\$1.185 trillion (2016 est.)
\$1.148 trillion (2015 est.)
note: data are in 2017 dollars
country comparison to the world: 21

GDP (official exchange rate): \$437.8 billion (2016 est.)

GDP—real growth rate: 3.7% (2017 est.)
3.2% (2016 est.)
2.9% (2015 est.)
country comparison to the world: 85

GDP—per capita (PPP): \$17,800 (2017 est.)
\$17,200 (2016 est.)
\$16,700 (2015 est.)
note: data are in 2017 dollars
country comparison to the world: 97

Gross national saving: 32.8% of GDP (2017 est.)
33.5% of GDP (2016 est.)
30.3% of GDP (2015 est.)
country comparison to the world: 19

GDP—composition, by end use:
household consumption: 50.1%
government consumption: 17%

investment in fixed capital: 24.2%
investment in inventories: -7%
exports of goods and services: 70.4%
imports of goods and services: -54.7% (2017 est.)

GDP—composition, by sector of origin:
agriculture: 8.2%
industry: 36.2%
services: 55.6% (2017 est.)

Agriculture—products: rice, cassava (manioc, tapioca), rubber, corn, sugarcane, coconuts, palm oil, pineapple, livestock, fish products

Industries: tourism, textiles and garments, agricultural processing, beverages, tobacco, cement, light manufacturing such as jewelry and electric appliances, computers and parts, integrated circuits, furniture, plastics, automobiles and automotive parts, agricultural machinery, air conditioning and refrigeration, ceramics, aluminum, chemical, environmental management, glass, granite and marble, leather, machinery and metal work, petrochemical, petroleum refining, pharmaceuticals, printing, pulp and paper, rubber, sugar, rice, fishing, cassava, world's second-largest tungsten producer and third-largest tin producer

Industrial production growth rate: 3.6% (2017 est.)
country comparison to the world: 78

Labor force: 38.37 million (2017 est.)
country comparison to the world: 17

Labor force—by occupation: agriculture: 31.8%
industry: 16.7%
services: 51.5% (2015 est.)

Unemployment rate: 0.7% (2017 est.)
0.8% (2016 est.)
country comparison to the world: 4

Population below poverty line: 7.2% (2015 est.)

Household income or consumption by percentage share: lowest 10%: 2.8%
highest 10%: 31.5% (2009 est.)

Distribution of family income—Gini index: 44.5 (2015)
48.4 (2011)
country comparison to the world: 43

Budget: revenues: $79.6 billion
expenditures: $90.56 billion (2017 est.)
Taxes and other revenues: 18.2% of GDP (2017 est.)
country comparison to the world: 166

Budget surplus (+) or deficit (-): -2.5% of GDP (2017 est.)
country comparison to the world: 99

Public debt: 44.1% of GDP (2017 est.)
41.2% of GDP (2016 est.)
note: data cover general government debt, and includes debt instruments issued (or owned) by government entities other than the treasury; the data include treasury debt held by foreign entities; the data include debt issued by subnational entities, as well as intra-governmental debt; intra-governmental debt consists of treasury borrowings from surpluses in the social funds, such as for retirement, medical care, and unemployment; debt instruments for the social funds are sold at public auctions

country comparison to the world: 120

Fiscal year: 1 October—30 September

Inflation rate (consumer prices): 0.6% (2017 est.)
0.2% (2016 est.)
country comparison to the world: 22

Central bank discount rate: 1.5% (31 December 2016)
1.5% (31 December 2015)
country comparison to the world: 121

Commercial bank prime lending rate: 6.2% (31 December 2017 est.)
6.31% (31 December 2016 est.)
country comparison to the world: 125

Stock of narrow money: $56.36 billion (31 December 2017 est.)
$52.03 billion (31 December 2016 est.)
country comparison to the world: 51

Stock of broad money: $546.1 billion (31 December 2017 est.)
$510.4 billion (31 December 2016 est.)
country comparison to the world: 22

Stock of domestic credit: $537.2 billion (31 December 2017 est.)
$507.5 billion (31 December 2016 est.)
country comparison to the world: 25

Market value of publicly traded shares: $348.8 billion (31 December 2015 est.)
$430.4 billion (31 December 2014 est.)
$354.4 billion (31 December 2013 est.)
country comparison to the world: 28

Current account balance: $44 billion (2017 est.)
$46.83 billion (2016 est.)
country comparison to the world: 11

Exports: $228.2 billion (2017 est.)
$214.3 billion (2016 est.)
country comparison to the world: 23

Exports—commodities: automobiles and parts, computer and parts, jewelry and precious stones, polymers of ethylene in primary forms, refine fuels, electronic integrated circuits, chemical products, rice, fish products, rubber products, sugar, cassava, poultry, machinery and parts, iron and steel and their products

Exports—partners: US 11.4%, China 11.1%, Japan 9.6%, Hong Kong 5.3%, Australia 4.8%, Malaysia 4.5%, Vietnam 4.4% (2016)

Imports: $190 billion (2017 est.)
$177.7 billion (2016 est.)
country comparison to the world: 26

Imports—commodities: machinery and parts, crude oil, electrical machinery and parts, chemicals, iron & steel and product, electronic integrated circuit, automobile's parts, jewelry including silver bars and gold, computers and parts, electrical household appliances, soybean, soybean meal, wheat, cotton, dairy products

Imports—partners: China 21.6%, Japan 15.8%, US 6.2%, Malaysia 5.6% (2016)

Reserves of foreign exchange and gold: $193.5 billion (31 December 2017 est.)
$171.9 billion (31 December 2016 est.)
country comparison to the world: 13

Debt—external: $135.5 billion (31 December 2017 est.)
$130.6 billion (31 December 2016 est.)
country comparison to the world: 44

Stock of direct foreign investment—at home: $205.5 billion (31 December 2017 est.)
$193.5 billion (31 December 2016 est.)
country comparison to the world: 30

Stock of direct foreign investment—abroad: $112.3 billion (31 December 2017 est.)
$96.27 billion (31 December 2016 est.)
country comparison to the world: 34

Exchange rates: baht per US dollar—
34.34 (2017 est.)
35.296 (2016 est.)
35.296 (2015 est.)
34.248 (2014 est.)
32.48 (2013 est.)

ENERGY

Electricity access: population without electricity: 700,000
electrification—total population: 99%
electrification—urban areas: 99.7%
electrification—rural areas: 98.3% (2013)

Electricity—production: 167.9 billion kWh (2015 est.)
country comparison to the world: 24

Electricity—consumption: 168.3 billion kWh (2015 est.)
country comparison to the world: 23

Electricity—exports: 2.267 billion kWh (2015 est.)
country comparison to the world: 43

Electricity—imports: 14.41 billion kWh (2015 est.)
country comparison to the world: 16

Electricity—installed generating capacity: 40.97 million kW (2015 est.)
country comparison to the world: 24

Electricity—from fossil fuels: 76.7% of total installed capacity (2015 est.)
country comparison to the world: 94

Electricity—from nuclear fuels: 0% of total installed capacity (2015 est.)
country comparison to the world: 188

Electricity—from hydroelectric plants: 8.9% of total installed capacity (2015 est.)
country comparison to the world: 121

Electricity—from other renewable sources: 14.2% of total installed capacity (2015 est.)
country comparison to the world: 51

Crude oil—production: 257,500 bbl/day (2016 est.)
country comparison to the world: 34

Crude oil—exports: 12,200 bbl/day (2014 est.)
country comparison to the world: 57

Crude oil—imports: 830,500 bbl/day (2014 est.)
country comparison to the world: 14

Crude oil—proved reserves: 396.4 million bbl (1 January 2017 es)
country comparison to the world: 52

Refined petroleum products—production: 1.213 million bbl/day (2014 est.)
country comparison to the world: 18

Refined petroleum products—consumption: 1.272 million bbl/day (2015 est.)
country comparison to the world: 19

Refined petroleum products—exports: 238,800 bbl/day (2014 est.)
country comparison to the world: 31

Refined petroleum products—imports: 162,800 bbl/day (2014 est.)
country comparison to the world: 42

Natural gas—production: 39.82 billion cu m (2015 est.)
country comparison to the world: 22

Natural gas—consumption: 114.8 billion cu m (2015 est.)
country comparison to the world: 11

Natural gas—exports: 0 cu m (2013 est.)
country comparison to the world: 190

Natural gas—imports: 13.33 billion cu m (2015 est.)
country comparison to the world: 23

Natural gas—proved reserves: 206.8 billion cu m (1 January 2017 es)
country comparison to the world: 44

Carbon dioxide emissions from consumption of energy: 301 million Mt (2013 est.)
country comparison to the world: 21

COMMUNICATIONS

Telephones—fixed lines: *total subscriptions:* 4.706 million
subscriptions per 100 inhabitants: 7 (July 2016 est.)
country comparison to the world: 27

Telephones—mobile cellular: *total:* 116.606 million
subscriptions per 100 inhabitants: 171 (July 2016 est.)
country comparison to the world: 16

Telephone system: *general assessment:* high quality system, especially in urban areas like Bangkok
domestic: fixed-line system provided by both a government-owned and commercial provider; wireless service expanding rapidly
international: country code—66; connected to major submarine cable systems providing links throughout Asia, Australia, Middle East, Europe, and US; satellite earth stations—2 Intelsat (1 Indian Ocean, 1 Pacific Ocean) (2016)

Broadcast media: 26 digital TV stations in Bangkok broadcast nationally, 6 terrestrial TV stations in Bangkok broadcast nationally via relay stations—2 of the stations are owned by the military, the other 4 are government-owned or controlled, leased to private enterprise, and all are required to broadcast government-produced news programs twice a day; multi-channel satellite and cable TV subscription services are available; radio frequencies have been allotted for more than 500 government and commercial radio stations; many small community radio stations operate with low-power transmitters (2017)

Internet country code: .th

Internet users: *total:* 32,398,778

percent of population: 47.5% (July 2016 est.)
country comparison to the world: 30

TRANSPORTATION

National air transport system: number of registered air carriers: 19
inventory of registered aircraft operated by air carriers: 276
annual passenger traffic on registered air carriers: 54,259,629
annual freight traffic on registered air carriers: 2,134,149,001 mt-km (2015)
Civil aircraft registration country code prefix: HS (2016)

Airports: 101 (2013)
country comparison to the world: 56

Airports—with paved runways: *total:* 63
over 3,047 m: 8
2,438 to 3,047 m: 12
1,524 to 2,437 m: 23
914 to 1,523 m: 14
under 914 m: 6 (2013)

Airports—with unpaved runways: *total:* 38
2,438 to 3,047 m: 1
1,524 to 2,437 m: 1
914 to 1,523 m: 10
under 914 m: 26 (2013)

Heliports: 7 (2013)

Pipelines: condensate 2 km; gas 5,900 km; liquid petroleum gas 85 km; oil 1 km; refined products 1,097 km (2013)

Railways: *total:* 4,127 km
standard gauge: 84 km 1.435-m gauge (84 km electrified)
narrow gauge: 4,043 km 1.000-m gauge (2017)
country comparison to the world: 43

Roadways: *total:* 180,053 km (includes 450 km of expressways) (2006)
country comparison to the world: 30

Waterways: 4,000 km (3,701 km navigable by boats with drafts up to 0.9 m) (2011)
country comparison to the world: 26

Merchant marine: *total:* 781
by type: bulk carrier 25, container ship 23, general cargo 94, oil tanker 240, other 399 (2017)
country comparison to the world: 27

Ports and terminals: *major seaport(s):* Bangkok, Laem Chabang, Map Ta Phut, Prachuap Port, Si Racha

container port(s) (TEUs): Bangkok (1,559,000), Laem Chabang (6,780,000) (2015)
LNG terminal(s) (import): Map Ta Phut

MILITARY AND SECURITY

Military expenditures: 1.5% of GDP (2017)
1.45% of GDP (2016)
1.44% of GDP (2015)
1.41% of GDP (2014)
1.4% of GDP (2013)
country comparison to the world: 63

Military branches: Royal Thai Armed Forces (Kongthap Thai, RTARF): Royal Thai Army (Kongthap Bok Thai, RTA), Royal Thai Navy (Kongthap Ruea Thai, RTN, includes Royal Thai Marine Corps), Royal Thai Air Force (Kongthap Agard Thai, RTAF) (2017)

Military service age and obligation: 21 years of age for compulsory military service; 18 years of age for voluntary military service; males register at 18 years of age; 2-year conscript service obligation (2012)

TRANSNATIONAL ISSUES

Disputes—international: separatist violence in Thailand's predominantly Malay-Muslim southern provinces prompt border closures and controls with Malaysia to stem insurgent activities; Southeast Asian states have enhanced border surveillance to check the spread of avian flu; talks continue on completion of demarcation with Laos but disputes remain over several islands in the Mekong River; despite continuing border committee talks, Thailand must deal with Karen and other ethnic rebels, refugees, and illegal cross-border activities; Cambodia and Thailand dispute sections of boundary; in 2011, Thailand and Cambodia resorted to arms in the dispute over the location of the boundary on the precipice surmounted by Preah Vihear temple ruins, awarded to Cambodia by ICJ decision in 1962 and part of a planned UN World Heritage site; Thailand is studying the feasibility of jointly constructing the Hatgyi Dam on the Salween river near the border with Burma; in 2004, international environmentalist pressure prompted China to halt construction of 13 dams on the Salween River that flows through China, Burma, and Thailand; approximately 105,000 mostly Karen refugees fleeing civil strife, political upheaval and economic stagnation in Burma live in remote camps in Thailand near the border

Refugees and internally displaced persons: refugees (country of origin): 102,633 (Burma) (2016)
IDPs: 35,000 (resurgence in ethno-nationalist violence in south of country since 2004) (2016)
stateless persons: 487,741 (2016); note—about half of Thailand's northern hill tribe people do not have citizenship and make up the bulk of Thailand's stateless population; most lack documentation showing they or one of their parents were born in Thailand; children born to Burmese refugees are not eligible for Burmese or Thai citizenship and are stateless; most Chao Lay, maritime nomadic peoples, who travel from island to island in the Andaman Sea west of Thailand are also stateless; stateless Rohingya refugees from Burma are considered illegal migrants by Thai authorities and are detained in inhumane conditions or expelled; stateless persons are denied access to voting, property, education, employment, healthcare, and driving
note: Thai nationality was granted to more than 18,000 stateless persons in the last 3 years (2015)

Trafficking in persons: current situation: Thailand is a source, transit, and destination country for men, women, and children subjected to forced labor and sex trafficking; victims from Burma, Cambodia, Laos, China, Vietnam, Uzbekistan, and India, migrate to Thailand in search of jobs but are forced, coerced, or defrauded into labor in commercial fishing, fishing-related industries, factories, domestic work, street begging, or the sex trade; some Thai, Burmese, Cambodian, and Indonesian men forced to work on fishing boats are kept at sea for years; sex trafficking of adults and children from Thailand, Laos, Vietnam, and Burma remains a significant problem; Thailand is a transit country for victims from China, Vietnam, Bangladesh, and Burma subjected to sex trafficking and forced labor in Malaysia, Indonesia, Singapore, Russia, South Korea, the US, and countries in Western Europe; Thai victims are also trafficked in North America, Europe, Africa, Asia, and the Middle East

tier rating: Tier 2 Watch List—Thailand does not fully comply with the minimum standards for the elimination of trafficking, and is not making significant efforts to do so; in 2014, authorities investigated, prosecuted, and convicted fewer traffickers and identified fewer victims; some cases of official complicity were investigated and prosecuted, but trafficking-related corruption continues to hinder progress in combatting trafficking; authorities' efforts to screen for victims among vulnerable populations remained inadequate due to a poor understanding of trafficking indicators, a failure to recognize non-physical forms of coercion, and a shortage of language interpreters; the government passed new labor laws increasing the minimum age in the fishing industry to 18 years old, guaranteeing the minimum wage, and requiring work contracts, but weak law enforcement and poor coordination among regulatory agencies enabled exploitive labor practices to continue; the government increased efforts to raise public awareness to the dangers of human trafficking and to deny entry to foreign sex tourists (2015)

Illicit drugs: a minor producer of opium, heroin, and marijuana; transit point for illicit heroin en route to the international drug market from Burma and Laos; eradication efforts have reduced the area of cannabis cultivation and shifted some production to neighboring countries; opium poppy cultivation has been reduced by eradication efforts; also a drug money-laundering center; minor role in methamphetamine production for regional consumption; major consumer of methamphetamine since the 1990s despite a series of government crackdowns

TIMOR-LESTE

INTRODUCTION

Background: The Portuguese began to trade with the island of Timor in the early 16th century and colonized it in mid-century. Skirmishing with the Dutch in the region eventually resulted in an 1859 treaty in which Portugal ceded the western portion of the island. Imperial Japan occupied Portuguese Timor from 1942 to 1945, but Portugal resumed colonial authority after the Japanese defeat in World War II. East Timor declared itself independent from Portugal on 28 November 1975 and was invaded and occupied by Indonesian forces nine days later. It was incorporated into Indonesia in July 1976 as the province of Timor Timur (East Timor). An unsuccessful campaign of pacification followed over the next two decades, during which an estimated 100,000 to 250,000 people died. In an August 1999 UN-supervised popular referendum, an overwhelming majority of the people of Timor-Leste voted for independence from Indonesia. However, in the next three weeks, anti-independence Timorese militias—organized and supported by the Indonesian military—commenced a large-scale, scorched-earth campaign of retribution. The militias killed approximately 1,400 Timorese and forced 300,000 people into western Timor as refugees. Most of the country's infrastructure, including homes, irrigation systems, water supply systems, and schools, and nearly all of the country's electrical grid were destroyed. On 20 September 1999, Australian-led peacekeeping troops deployed to the country and brought the violence to an end. On 20 May 2002, Timor-Leste was internationally recognized as an independent state.

In 2006, internal tensions threatened the new nation's security when a military strike led to violence and a breakdown of law and order. At Dili's request, an Australian-led International Stabilization Force (ISF) deployed to Timor-Leste, and the UN Security Council established the UN Integrated Mission in Timor-Leste (UNMIT), which included an authorized police presence of over 1,600 personnel. The ISF and UNMIT restored stability, allowing for presidential and parliamentary elections in 2007 in a largely peaceful atmosphere. In February 2008, a rebel group staged an unsuccessful attack against the president and prime minister. The ringleader was killed in the attack, and most of the rebels surrendered in April 2008. Since the attack, the government has enjoyed one of its longest periods of post-independence stability, including successful 2012 elections for both the parliament and president and a successful transition of power in February 2015. In late 2012, the UN Security Council ended its peacekeeping mission in Timor-Leste and both the ISF and UNMIT departed the country.

GEOGRAPHY

Location: Southeastern Asia, northwest of Australia in the Lesser Sunda Islands at the eastern end of the Indonesian archipelago; note—Timor-Leste includes the eastern half of the island of Timor, the Oecussi (Ambeno) region on the northwest portion of the island of Timor, and the islands of Pulau Atauro and Pulau Jaco

Geographic coordinates: 8 50 S, 125 55 E

Map references: Southeast Asia

Area: *total:* 14,874 sq km
land: 14,874 sq km
water: 0 sq km
country comparison to the world: 160

Area—comparative: slightly larger than Connecticut
Land boundaries: total: 253 km
border countries (1): Indonesia 253 km

Coastline: 706 km

Maritime claims: *territorial sea:* 12 nm
contiguous zone: 24 nm
exclusive fishing zone: 200 nm

Climate: tropical; hot, humid; distinct rainy and dry seasons

Terrain: mountainous

Elevation: *mean elevation:* NA

elevation extremes: *lowest point:* Timor Sea, Savu Sea, and Banda Sea 0 m
highest point: Foho Tatamailau 2,963 m

Natural resources: gold, petroleum, natural gas, manganese, marble

Land use: *agricultural land:* 25.1%
arable land: 10.1%;
permanent crops: 4.9%;
permanent pasture: 10.1%
forest: 49.1%

Other: 25.8% (2011 est.)
Irrigated land: 350 sq km (2012)

Population—distribution: most of the population concentrated in the western third of the country, particularly around Dili

Natural hazards: floods and landslides are common; earthquakes; tsunamis; tropical cyclones

Environment—current issues: widespread use of slash and burn agriculture has led to deforestation and soil erosion

Environment—international agreements: *party to:* Biodiversity, Climate Change, Climate Change-Kyoto Protocol, Desertification
signed, but not ratified: none of the selected agreements

Geography—note: Timor comes from the Malay word for "east"; the island of Timor is part of the Malay Archipelago and is the largest and easternmost of the Lesser Sunda Islands

PEOPLE AND SOCIETY

Population: 1,291,358 (July 2017 est.)
country comparison to the world: 157

Nationality: *noun:* Timorese
adjective: Timorese

Ethnic groups: Austronesian (Malayo-Polynesian) (includes Tetun, Mambai, Tokodede, Galoli, Kemak, Baikeno), Melanesian-Papuan (includes Bunak, Fataluku, Bakasai), small Chinese minority

Languages: Tetun Prasa 30.6%, Mambai 16.6%, Makasai 10.5%, Tetun Terik 6.1%, Baikenu 5.9%, Kemak 5.8%, Bunak 5.5%, Tokodede 4%, Fataluku 3.5%, Waima'a 1.8%, Galoli 1.4%, Naueti 1.4%, Idate 1.2%, Midiki 1.2%, other 4.5%
note: data represent population by mother tongue; Tetun and Portuguese are official languages; Indonesian and English are working languages; there are about 32 indigenous languages

Religions: Roman Catholic 97.6%, Protestant/Evangelical 2%, Muslim 0.2%, other 0.2% (2015 est.)

Age structure: *0-14 years:* 40.91% (male 271,623/female 256,733)
15-24 years: 20.32% (male 133,254/female 129,166)
25-54 years: 29.95% (male 185,911/female 200,903)
55-64 years: 4.94% (male 32,168/female 31,680)
65 years and over: 3.87% (male 23,924/female 25,996) (2017 est.)

Dependency ratios: *total dependency ratio:* 90.3
youth dependency ratio: 83.7
elderly dependency ratio: 6.6
potential support ratio: 15.2 (2015 est.)

Median age: *total:* 18.9 years
male: 18.3 years
female: 19.6 years (2017 est.)
country comparison to the world: 205

Population growth rate: 2.36% (2017 est.)
country comparison to the world: 30

Birth rate: 33.4 births/1,000 population (2017 est.)
country comparison to the world: 27

Death rate: 5.9 deaths/1,000 population (2017 est.)
country comparison to the world: 171

Net migration rate: -3.9 migrant(s)/1,000 population (2017 est.)
country comparison to the world: 182

Population distribution: most of the population concentrated in the western third of the country, particularly around Dili

Urbanization: *urban population:* 34% of total population (2017)
rate of urbanization: 3.63% annual rate of change (2015-20 est.)

Major urban areas—population: DILI (capital) 228,000 (2015)

Sex ratio: *at birth:* 1.07 male(s)/female
0-14 years: 1.06 male(s)/female
15-24 years: 1.03 male(s)/female
25-54 years: 0.93 male(s)/female
55-64 years: 1.04 male(s)/female
65 years and over: 0.91 male(s)/female
total population: 1.01 male(s)/female (2016 est.)

Mother's mean age at first birth: 22.1 years
note: median age at first birth among women 25-29 (2009/10 est.)

Maternal mortality ratio: 215 deaths/100,000 live births (2015 est.)
country comparison to the world: 50

Infant mortality rate: *total:* 35.1 deaths/1,000 live births
male: 37.9 deaths/1,000 live births
female: 32.1 deaths/1,000 live births (2017 est.)
country comparison to the world: 54

Life expectancy at birth: *total population:* 68.4 years
male: 66.8 years
female: 70.1 years (2017 est.)
country comparison to the world: 166

Total fertility rate: 4.79 children born/woman (2017 est.)
country comparison to the world: 16

Contraceptive prevalence rate: 22.3% (2009/10)
Health expenditures: 1.5% of GDP (2014)
country comparison to the world: 192

Physicians density: 0.08 physicians/1,000 population (2011)

Hospital bed density: 5.9 beds/1,000 population (2010)

Drinking water source:
improved:
urban: 95.2% of population
rural: 60.5% of population
total: 71.9% of population
unimproved:
urban: 4.8% of population
rural: 39.5% of population
total: 28.1% of population (2015 est.)

Sanitation facility access:
improved:
urban: 69% of population
rural: 26.8% of population
total: 40.6% of population
unimproved:

urban: 31% of population
rural: 73.2% of population
total: 59.4% of population (2015 est.)

HIV/AIDS—adult prevalence rate: NA

HIV/AIDS—people living with HIV/AIDS: NA

HIV/AIDS—deaths: NA

Major infectious diseases: *degree of risk:* very high
food or waterborne diseases: bacterial diarrhea, hepatitis A, and typhoid fever
vectorborne diseases: dengue fever and malaria (2016)

Obesity—adult prevalence rate: 3.8% (2016)
country comparison to the world: 190

Children under the age of 5 years underweight: 37.7% (2013)
country comparison to the world: 1
Education expenditures: 7.9% of GDP (2014)
country comparison to the world: 7

Literacy: *definition:* age 15 and over can read and write
total population: 67.5%
male: 71.5%
female: 63.4% (2015 est.)

School life expectancy (primary to tertiary education): *total:* 13 years
male: 14 years
female: 13 years (2010)

Unemployment, youth ages 15-24: *total:* 11.1%
male: 11.1%
female: 20% (2010 est.)
country comparison to the world: 79

GOVERNMENT

Country name: *conventional long form:* Democratic Republic of Timor-Leste
conventional short form: Timor-Leste
note: pronounced TEE-mor LESS-tay
local long form: Republika Demokratika Timor Lorosa'e [Tetum]; Republica Democratica de Timor-Leste [Portuguese]
local short form: Timor Lorosa'e [Tetum]; Timor-Leste [Portuguese]
former: East Timor, Portuguese Timor
etymology: "timor" derives from the Indonesian and Malay word "timur" meaning "east"; "leste" is the Portuguese word for "east", so "Timor-Leste" literally means "Eastern-East"; the local [Tetum] name "Timor Lorosa'e" translates as "East Rising Sun"

Government type: semi-presidential republic

Capital: *name:* Dili

geographic coordinates: 8 35 S, 125 36 E
time difference: UTC+9 (14 hours ahead of Washington, DC, during Standard Time)

Administrative divisions: 13 administrative districts; Aileu, Ainaro, Baucau, Bobonaro (Maliana), Cova-Lima (Suai), Dili, Ermera (Gleno), Lautem (Los Palos), Liquica, Manatuto, Manufahi (Same), Oecussi (Ambeno), Viqueque
note: administrative divisions have the same names as their administrative centers (exceptions

899

have the administrative center name following in parentheses)

Independence: 20 May 2002 (from Indonesia); note—28 November 1975 was the date independence was proclaimed from Portugal; 20 May 2002 was the date of international recognition of Timor-Leste's independence from Indonesia

National holiday: Restoration of Independence Day, 20 May (2002); Proclamation of Independence Day, 28 November (1975)

Constitution: drafted 2001, approved 22 March 2002, entered into force 20 May 2002 (2016)

Legal system: civil law system based on the Portuguese model; note—penal and civil law codes to replace the Indonesian codes were passed by Parliament and promulgated in 2009 and 2011, respectively

International law organization participation: accepts compulsory ICJ jurisdiction with reservations; accepts ICCt jurisdiction

Citizenship: *citizenship by birth:* no
citizenship by descent only: at least one parent must be a citizen of Timor-Leste
dual citizenship recognized: no
residency requirement for naturalization: 10 years

Suffrage: 17 years of age; universal

Executive branch: *chief of state:* President Francisco GUTERRES (since 20 May 2017); note—the president plays a largely symbolic role but is the commander in chief of the military and is able to veto legislation, dissolve parliament, and call national elections

head of government: Prime Minister Mari ALKATIRI (since 15 September 2017)
cabinet: Council of Ministers proposed by the prime minister and appointed by the president
elections/appointments: president directly elected by absolute majority popular vote in 2 rounds if needed for a 5-year term (eligible for a second term); election last held on 20 March 2017 (next to be held in 2022); following parliamentary elections, the president appoints the leader of the majority party or majority coalition as the prime minister
election results: Francisco GUTERRES elected president; percent of vote—Francisco GUTERRES (FRETILIN) 57.1%, Antonio DA CONCEICAO (PD) 32.5%, Jose Luis GUTERRES (Frenti-Mudanca) 2.6%, Jose NEVES (independent) 2.3%, Luis Alves TILMAN (independent) 2.2%, other 3.4%

Legislative branch: *description:* unicameral National Parliament (65 seats; members directly elected in a single nationwide constituency by proportional representation vote to serve 5-year terms)
elections: elections were held on 22 July 2017 (next to be held in July 2022)
election results: percent of vote by party—FRETILIN 29.7%, CNRT 29.5%, PLP 10.6%, PD 9.8%, KHUNTO 6.4%, other 14%; seats by party—FRETILIN 23, CNRT 22, PLP 8, PD 7, KHUNTO 5

Judicial branch: *highest court(s):* Supreme Court of Justice (consists of the court president and NA judges)
judge selection and term of office: Supreme Court president appointed by the president of the republic from among the other court judges to serve a 4-year term; other Supreme Court judges appointed—1 by the Parliament and the others by the Supreme Council for the Judiciary, a body presided by the Supreme Court president and includes mostly presidential and parliamentary appointees; other Supreme Court judges appointed for life
subordinate courts: Court of Appeal; High Administrative, Tax, and Audit Court; district courts; magistrates' courts; military courts
note: the UN Justice System Programme, launched in 2003 in 4 phases through 2018, is helping strengthen the country's justice system; the Programme is aligned with the country's long-range Justice Sector Strategic Plan, which includes legal reform

Political parties and leaders: Democratic Party or PD
Frenti-Mudanca [Jose Luis GUTERRES]
Kmanek Haburas Unidade Nasional Timor Oan or KHUNTO
National Congress for Timorese Reconstruction or CNRT [Kay Rala Xanana GUSMAO]
People's Liberation Party or PLP [Taur Matan RUAK]
Revolutionary Front of Independent Timor-Leste or FRETILIN [Mari ALKATIRI]

Political pressure groups and leaders: NA

International organization participation: ACP, ADB, AOSIS, ARF, ASEAN (observer), CPLP, EITI (compliant country), FAO, G-77, IBRD, ICAO, ICCt, ICRM, IDA, IFAD, IFC, IFRCS, ILO, IMF, IMO, Interpol, IOC, IOM, IPU, ITU, MIGA, NAM, OPCW, PIF (observer), UN, UNCTAD, UNESCO, UNIDO, Union Latina, UNWTO, UPU, WCO, WHO, WMO

Diplomatic representation in the US: chief of mission: Ambassador Domingos Sarmento ALVES (since 21 May 2014)
chancery: 4201 Connecticut Avenue NW, Suite 504, Washington, DC 20008
telephone: [1] (202) 966-3202
FAX: [1] (202) 966-3205

Diplomatic representation from the US: *chief of mission:* Ambassador Karen STANTON (since 16 January 2015)
embassy: Avenida de Portugal, Praia dos Coqueiros, Dili
mailing address: US Department of State, 8250 Dili Place, Washington, DC 20521-8250
telephone: (670) 332-4684
FAX: (670) 331-3206

Flag description: red with a black isosceles triangle (based on the hoist side) superimposed on a slightly longer yellow arrowhead that extends to the center of the flag; a white star—pointing to the upper hoist-side corner of the flag—is in the center of the black triangle; yellow denotes the colonialism in Timor-Leste's past; black represents the obscurantism that needs to be overcome; red

stands for the national liberation struggle; the white star symbolizes peace and serves as a guiding light

National symbol(s): Mount Ramelau; national colors: red, yellow, black, white

National anthem: *name:* "Patria" (Fatherland)
lyrics/music: Fransisco Borja DA COSTA/Afonso DE ARAUJO
note: adopted 2002; the song was first used as an anthem when Timor-Leste declared its independence from Portugal in 1975; the lyricist, Fransisco Borja DA COSTA, was killed in the Indonesian invasion just days after independence was declared

ECONOMY

Economy—overview: Since independence in 1999, Timor-Leste has faced great challenges in rebuilding its infrastructure, strengthening the civil administration, and generating jobs for young people entering the work force. The development of offshore oil and gas resources has greatly supplemented government revenues. This technology-intensive industry, however, has done little to create jobs in part because there are no production facilities in Timor-Leste. Gas is currently piped to Australia for processing, but Timor-Leste has expressed interest in developing a domestic processing capacity.

In June 2005, the National Parliament unanimously approved the creation of the Timor-Leste Petroleum Fund to serve as a repository for all petroleum revenues and to preserve the value of Timor-Leste's petroleum wealth for future generations. The Fund held assets of $16 billion, as of mid-2016. Oil accounts for over 90% of government revenues, and the drop in the price of oil in 2014-16 has led to concerns about the long-term sustainability of government spending. Timor-Leste compensated for the decline in price by exporting more oil. The Ministry of Finance maintains that the Petroleum Fund is sufficient to sustain government operations for the foreseeable future.

Annual government budget expenditures increased markedly between 2009 and 2012 but dropped significantly through 2016. Historically, the government failed to spend as much as its budget allowed. The government has focused significant resources on basic infrastructure, including electricity and roads, but limited experience in procurement and infrastructure building has hampered these projects. The underlying economic policy challenge the country faces remains how best to use oil-and-gas wealth to lift the non-oil economy onto a higher growth path and to reduce poverty.

GDP (purchasing power parity): $6.211 billion (2017 est.)
$5.972 billion (2016 est.)
$5.688 billion (2015 est.)
note: data are in 2017 dollars
country comparison to the world: 172

GDP (official exchange rate): $2.716 billion (2016 est.)
note: non-oil GDP

GDP—real growth rate: 4% (2017 est.)
5% (2016 est.)
4% (2015 est.)
country comparison to the world: 67

GDP—per capita (PPP): $5,000 (2017 est.)
$4,900 (2016 est.)
$4,800 (2015 est.)
note: data are in 2017 dollars
country comparison to the world: 172

GDP—composition, by end use:
household consumption: 19.7%
government consumption: 30.7%
investment in fixed capital: 21.2%
investment in inventories: 0%
exports of goods and services: 79.6%
imports of goods and services: -51.2% (2017 est.)

GDP—composition, by sector of origin:
agriculture: 9.4%
industry: 57.8%
services: 31.3% (2017 est.)

Agriculture—products: coffee, rice, corn, cassava (manioc, tapioca), sweet potatoes, soybeans, cabbage, mangoes, bananas, vanilla

Industries: printing, soap manufacturing, handicrafts, woven cloth

Industrial production growth rate: 2% (2017 est.)
country comparison to the world: 128

Labor force: 286,700 (2016 est.)
country comparison to the world: 165

Labor force—by occupation: *agriculture:* 64%
industry: 10%
services: 26% (2010)

Unemployment rate: 4.4% (2014 est.)
3.9% (2010 est.)
country comparison to the world: 61

Population below poverty line: 41.8% (2014 est.)

Household income or consumption by percentage share: *lowest 10%:* 4%
highest 10%: 27% (2007)

Distribution of family income—Gini index: 31.9 (2007 est.)
38 (2002 est.)
country comparison to the world: 117

Budget: *revenues:* $300 million
expenditures: $2.2 billion (2017 est.)
Taxes and other revenues: 11% of GDP (2017 est.)
country comparison to the world: 210

Budget surplus (+) or deficit (-): -70% of GDP (2017 est.)
country comparison to the world: 221

Public debt: 0% of GDP (2016)
0% of GDP (2015)
country comparison to the world: 205

Fiscal year: calendar year

Inflation rate (consumer prices): 1% (2017 est.)
-1.3% (2016 est.)
country comparison to the world: 40

Commercial bank prime lending rate: 14.9% (31 December 2017 est.)
14.22% (31 December 2016 est.)
country comparison to the world: 46

Stock of narrow money: $559.5 million (31 December 2017 est.)
$464.1 million (31 December 2016 est.)
country comparison to the world: 167

Stock of broad money: $788.9 million (31 December 2017 est.)
$733.9 million (31 December 2016 est.)
country comparison to the world: 176

Stock of domestic credit: $-300 million (31 December 2017 est.)
$-200 million (31 December 2016 est.)
country comparison to the world: 191

Market value of publicly traded shares: $NA

Current account balance: -$153 million (2017 est.)
-$523 million (2016 est.)
country comparison to the world: 86

Exports: $20 million (2016 est.)
$18 million (2015 est.)
country comparison to the world: 210

Exports—commodities: oil, coffee, sandalwood, marble
note: potential for vanilla exports

Imports: $558.6 million (2016 est.)
$652.9 million (2015 est.)
country comparison to the world: 188

Imports—commodities: food, gasoline, kerosene, machinery

Debt—external: $311.5 million (31 December 2014 est.)
$687 million (31 December 2013 est.)
country comparison to the world: 186

Exchange rates: the US dollar is used

ENERGY

ectricity access: population without electricity: 744,032

electrification—total population: 42%
electrification—urban areas: 78%
electrification—rural areas: 27% (2012)

Electricity—production: 0 kWh (2015 est.)
country comparison to the world: 221

Electricity—consumption: 0 kWh (2015 est.)
country comparison to the world: 220

Electricity—exports: 0 kWh (2015 est.)
country comparison to the world: 206

Electricity—imports: 0 kWh (2015 est.)
country comparison to the world: 210

Electricity—installed generating capacity: NA kW (2015 est.)

Crude oil—production: 49,240 bbl/day (2016 est.)
country comparison to the world: 56

Crude oil—exports: 74,230 bbl/day (2014 est.)
country comparison to the world: 39

Crude oil—imports: 0 bbl/day (2014 est.)
country comparison to the world: 199

Crude oil—proved reserves: 0 bbl (1 January 2017 es)
country comparison to the world: 205

Refined petroleum products—production: 0 bbl/day (2014 est.)
country comparison to the world: 207

Refined petroleum products—consumption: 3,100 bbl/day (2015 est.)
country comparison to the world: 187

Refined petroleum products—exports: 0 bbl/day (2014 est.)
country comparison to the world: 205

Refined petroleum products—imports: 3,055 bbl/day (2014 est.)
country comparison to the world: 179

Natural gas—production: 7.7 billion cu m (2015 est.)
country comparison to the world: 46

Natural gas—consumption: 0 cu m (2013 est.)
country comparison to the world: 139

Natural gas—exports: 7.7 billion cu m (2015 est.)
country comparison to the world: 26

Natural gas—imports: 0 cu m (2013 est.)
country comparison to the world: 197

Natural gas—proved reserves: 200 billion cu m (1 January 2006 es)
country comparison to the world: 46

Carbon dioxide emissions from consumption of energy: 500,000 Mt (2013 est.)
country comparison to the world: 183

COMMUNICATIONS

Telephones—fixed lines: *total subscriptions:* 2,720
subscriptions per 100 inhabitants: less than 1 (July 2016 est.)
country comparison to the world: 212

Telephones—mobile cellular: *total:* 1,492,124
subscriptions per 100 inhabitants: 118 (July 2016 est.)
country comparison to the world: 163

Telephone system: *general assessment:* rudimentary service in urban and some rural areas, which is expanding with the entrance of new competitors
domestic: system suffered significant damage during the violence associated with independence; limited fixed-line services; mobile-cellular services have been expanding and are now available in urban and most rural areas
international: country code—670; international service is available (2016)

Broadcast media: 7 TV stations (2 nationwide satellite coverage; 3 terrestrial coverage, mostly in Dili; 2 cable) and 21 radio stations (3 nationwide coverage) (2017)

Internet country code: .tl

Internet users: *total:* 318,373

percent of population: 25.2% (July 2016 est.)
country comparison to the world: 205

TRANSPORTATION

Civil aircraft registration country code prefix: 4W (2016)

Airports: 6 (2013)

country comparison to the world: 176

Airports—with paved runways: *total:* 2
2,438 to 3,047 m: 1
1,524 to 2,437 m: 1 (2013)

Airports—with unpaved runways: *total:* 4
914 to 1,523 m: 2
under 914 m: 2 (2013)

Heliports: 8 (2013)

Roadways: *total:* 6,040 km
paved: 2,600 km
unpaved: 3,440 km (2005)
country comparison to the world: 149

Ports and terminals: *major seaport(s):* Dili

MILITARY AND SECURITY

Military expenditures: 2.56% of GDP (2015)
2.12% of GDP (2014)
2.42% of GDP (2013)
2.58% of GDP (2012)
1.79% of GDP (2011)
country comparison to the world: 23

Military branches: Timor-Leste Defense Force
(Falintil-Forcas de Defesa de Timor-L'este, Falintil
(F-FDTL)): Army, Navy (Armada) (2013)

Military service age and obligation: 18 years of age
for voluntary military service; 18-month service
obligation; no conscription but, as of May 2013,
introduction of conscription was under discussion
(2013)

TRANSNATIONAL ISSUES

Disputes—international: three stretches of land
borders with Timor-Leste have yet to be delimited,
two of which are in the Oecussi exclave area, and
no maritime or Economic Exclusion Zone boundaries have been established between the countries;
maritime boundaries with Indonesia remain unresolved; in 2007, Australia and Timor-Leste signed
a 50-year development zone and revenue sharing
agreement in lieu of a maritime boundary

Trafficking in persons: current situation: Timor-
Leste is a source and destination country for men,
women, and children subjected to forced labor and
sex trafficking; Timorese women and girls from
rural areas are lured to the capital with promises of

legitimate jobs or education prospects and are then
forced into prostitution or domestic servitude, and
other women and girls may be sent to Indonesia
for domestic servitude; Timorese family members
force children into bonded domestic or agricultural
labor to repay debts; foreign migrant women are
vulnerable to sex trafficking in Timor-Leste, while
men and boys from Burma, Cambodia, and Thailand are forced to work on fishing boats in Timorese waters under inhumane conditions

tier rating: Tier 2 Watch List – Timor-Leste does
not fully comply with the minimum standards for
the elimination of trafficking; however, it is making significant efforts to do so; in 2014, legislation
was drafted but not finalized or implemented that
outlines procedures for screening potential trafficking victims; law enforcement made modest
progress, including one conviction for sex trafficking, but efforts are hindered by prosecutors' and
judges' lack of expertise in applying anti-trafficking laws effectively; the government rescued two
child victims with support from an NGO but did
not provide protective services (2015)

Illicit drugs: NA

TOGO

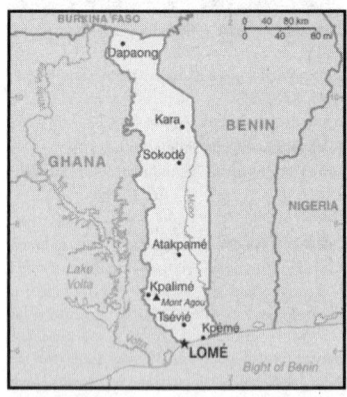

INTRODUCTION

Background: French Togoland became Togo in
1960. Gen. Gnassingbe EYADEMA, installed as
military ruler in 1967, ruled Togo with a heavy
hand for almost four decades. Despite the facade
of multi-party elections instituted in the early
1990s, the government was largely dominated
by President EYADEMA, whose Rally of the
Togolese People (RPT) party has been in power
almost continually since 1967 and its successor,
the Union for the Republic, maintains a majority
of seats in today's legislature. Upon EYADEMA's
death in February 2005, the military installed the
president's son, Faure GNASSINGBE, and then
engineered his formal election two months later.

Democratic gains since then allowed Togo to hold
its first relatively free and fair legislative elections
in October 2007. Since 2007, President GNASS-
INGBE has started the country along a gradual
path to political reconciliation and democratic
reform, and Togo has held multiple presidential
and legislative elections that were deemed generally free and fair by international observers.
Despite those positive moves, political reconciliation has moved slowly and many Togolese
complain that important political measures such
as presidential term limits and electoral reforms
remain undone, leaving the country's politics in a
lethargic state. Internationally, Togo is still known
as a country where the same family has been in
power for five decades.

GEOGRAPHY

Location: Western Africa, bordering the Bight of
Benin, between Benin and Ghana

Geographic coordinates: 8 00 N, 1 10 E

Map references: Africa

Area: *total:* 56,785 sq km
land: 54,385 sq km
water: 2,400 sq km
country comparison to the world: 127

Area—comparative: slightly smaller than West
Virginia
Land boundaries: total: 1,880 km
border countries (3): Benin 651 km, Burkina Faso
131 km, Ghana 1,098 km

Coastline: 56 km

Maritime claims: *territorial sea:* 30 nm

exclusive economic zone: 200 nm

Climate: tropical; hot, humid in south; semiarid
in north

Terrain: gently rolling savanna in north; central
hills; southern plateau; low coastal plain with
extensive lagoons and marshes

Elevation: *mean elevation:* 236 m

elevation extremes: *lowest point:* Atlantic Ocean
0 m
highest point: Mont Agou 986 m

Natural resources: phosphates, limestone, marble,
arable land

Land use: *agricultural land:* 67.4%
arable land: 45.2%;
permanent crops: 3.8%;
permanent pasture: 18.4%
forest: 4.9%
other: 27.7% (2011 est.)
Irrigated land: 70 sq km (2012)

Population—distribution: one of the more densely
populated African nations with most of the population residing in rural communities, density is
highest in the south on or near the Atlantic coast

Natural hazards: hot, dry harmattan wind can
reduce visibility in north during winter; periodic
droughts

Environment—current issues: deforestation
attributable to slash-and-burn agriculture and
the use of wood for fuel; water pollution presents
health hazards and hinders the fishing industry; air
pollution increasing in urban areas

Environment—international agreements: *party
to:* Biodiversity, Climate Change, Climate

Change-Kyoto Protocol, Desertification, Endangered Species, Law of the Sea, Ozone Layer Protection, Ship Pollution, Tropical Timber 83, Tropical Timber 94, Wetlands, Whaling
signed, but not ratified: none of the selected agreements

Geography—note: the country's length allows it to stretch through six distinct geographic regions; climate varies from tropical to savanna

PEOPLE AND SOCIETY

Population: 7,965,055
note: estimates for this country explicitly take into account the effects of excess mortality due to AIDS; this can result in lower life expectancy, higher infant mortality, higher death rates, lower population growth rates, and changes in the distribution of population by age and sex than would otherwise be expected (July 2017 est.)
country comparison to the world: 99

Nationality: *noun:* Togolese (singular and plural)
adjective: Togolese

Ethnic groups: African (37 tribes; largest and most important are Ewe, Mina, and Kabre) 99%, European and Syrian-Lebanese less than 1%

Languages: French (official, the language of commerce), Ewe and Mina (the two major African languages in the south), Kabye (sometimes spelled Kabiye) and Dagomba (the two major African languages in the north)

Religions: Christian 29%, Muslim 20%, indigenous beliefs 51%

Demographic profile: Togo's population is estimated to have grown to four times its size between 1960 and 2010. With nearly 60% of its populace under the age of 25 and a high annual growth rate attributed largely to high fertility, Togo's population is likely to continue to expand for the foreseeable future. Reducing fertility, boosting job creation, and improving education will be essential to reducing the country's high poverty rate. In 2008, Togo eliminated primary school enrollment fees, leading to higher enrollment but increased pressure on limited classroom space, teachers, and materials. Togo has a good chance of achieving universal primary education, but educational quality, the underrepresentation of girls, and the low rate of enrollment in secondary and tertiary schools remain concerns.

Togo is both a country of emigration and asylum. In the early 1990s, southern Togo suffered from the economic decline of the phosphate sector and ethnic and political repression at the hands of dictator Gnassingbe EYADEMA and his northern, Kabye-dominated administration. The turmoil led 300,000 to 350,000 predominantly southern Togolese to flee to Benin and Ghana, with most not returning home until relative stability was restored in 1997. In 2005, another outflow of 40,000 Togolese to Benin and Ghana occurred when violence broke out between the opposition and security forces over the disputed election of EYADEMA's son Faure GNASSINGBE to the presidency. About half of the refugees reluctantly returned

home in 2006, many still fearing for their safety. Despite ethnic tensions and periods of political unrest, Togo in September 2017 was home to more than 9,600 refugees from Ghana.

Age structure: *0-14 years:* 40.29% (male 1,610,020/female 1,599,105)
15-24 years: 19.2% (male 763,507/female 765,884)
25-54 years: 32.79% (male 1,297,489/female 1,314,130)
55-64 years: 4.31% (male 161,809/female 181,180)
65 years and over: 3.41% (male 117,409/female 154,522) (2017 est.)

Dependency ratios: *total dependency ratio:* 81.2
youth dependency ratio: 76.2
elderly dependency ratio: 5.1
potential support ratio: 19.8 (2015 est.)

Median age: *total:* 19.8 years
male: 19.5 years
female: 20.1 years (2017 est.)
country comparison to the world: 193

Population growth rate: 2.64% (2017 est.)
country comparison to the world: 14

Birth rate: 33.3 births/1,000 population (2017 est.)
country comparison to the world: 29

Death rate: 6.9 deaths/1,000 population (2017 est.)
country comparison to the world: 134

Net migration rate: 0 migrant(s)/1,000 population (2017 est.)
country comparison to the world: 99

Population distribution: one of the more densely populated African nations with most of the population residing in rural communities, density is highest in the south on or near the Atlantic coast

Urbanization: *urban population:* 41% of total population (2017)
rate of urbanization: 3.6% annual rate of change (2015-20 est.)

Major urban areas—population: LOME (capital) 956,000 (2015)

Sex ratio: *at birth:* 1.03 male(s)/female
0-14 years: 1.01 male(s)/female
15-24 years: 1 male(s)/female
25-54 years: 0.99 male(s)/female
55-64 years: 0.89 male(s)/female
65 years and over: 0.76 male(s)/female
total population: 0.98 male(s)/female (2016 est.)

Mother's mean age at first birth: 21 years
note: median age at first birth among women 25-29 (2013/14 est.)

Maternal mortality ratio: 368 deaths/100,000 live births (2015 est.)
country comparison to the world: 32

Infant mortality rate: *total:* 42.2 deaths/1,000 live births
male: 48.5 deaths/1,000 live births
female: 35.7 deaths/1,000 live births (2017 est.)
country comparison to the world: 44

Life expectancy at birth: *total population:* 65.4 years
male: 62.8 years
female: 68.1 years (2017 est.)

country comparison to the world: 177

Total fertility rate: 4.38 children born/woman (2017 est.)
country comparison to the world: 26

Contraceptive prevalence rate: 19.9% (2013/14)
Health expenditures: 5.2% of GDP (2014)
country comparison to the world: 136

Physicians density: 0.06 physicians/1,000 population (2008)

Hospital bed density: 0.7 beds/1,000 population (2011)

Drinking water source:
improved:
urban: 91.4% of population
rural: 44.2% of population
total: 63.1% of population
unimproved:
urban: 8.6% of population
rural: 55.8% of population
total: 36.9% of population (2015 est.)

Sanitation facility access:
improved:
urban: 24.7% of population
rural: 2.9% of population
total: 11.6% of population
unimproved:
urban: 75.3% of population
rural: 97.1% of population
total: 88.4% of population (2015 est.)

HIV/AIDS—adult prevalence rate: 2.1% (2016 est.)
country comparison to the world: 25

HIV/AIDS—people living with HIV/AIDS: 100,000 (2016 est.)
country comparison to the world: 42

HIV/AIDS—deaths: 5,100 (2016 est.)
country comparison to the world: 30

Major infectious diseases: *degree of risk:* very high
food or waterborne diseases: bacterial and protozoal diarrhea, hepatitis A, and typhoid fever
vectorborne diseases: malaria, dengue fever, and yellow fever
respiratory disease: meningococcal meningitis
water contact disease: schistosomiasis
animal contact disease: rabies (2016)

Obesity—adult prevalence rate: 8.4% (2016)
country comparison to the world: 151

Children under the age of 5 years underweight: 16.2% (2014)
country comparison to the world: 41
Education expenditures: 5.3% of GDP (2015)
country comparison to the world: 91

Literacy: *definition:* age 15 and over can read and write
total population: 63.7%
male: 77.3%
female: 51.2% (2015 est.)

School life expectancy (primary to tertiary education): *total:* 12 years
male: NA
female: NA (2011)

GOVERNMENT

Country name: *conventional long form:* Togolese Republic
conventional short form: Togo
local long form: Republique Togolaise
local short form: none
former: French Togoland
etymology: derived from the Ewe words "to" (water) and "go" (shore) to give the sense of "by the water"; originally, this designation applied to the town of Togo (now Togoville) on the northern shore of Lake Togo, but the name was eventually extended to the entire nation

Government type: presidential republic

Capital: *name:* Lome

geographic coordinates: 6 07 N, 1 13 E
time difference: UTC 0 (5 hours ahead of Washington, DC, during Standard Time)

Administrative divisions: 5 regions (regions, singular—region); Centrale, Kara, Maritime, Plateaux, Savanes

Independence: 27 April 1960 (from French-administered UN trusteeship)

National holiday: Independence Day, 27 April (1960)

Constitution: *history:* several previous; latest adopted 27 September 1992, effective 14 October 1992
amendments: proposed by the president of the republic or supported by at least one-fifth of the National Assembly membership; passage requires four-fifths majority vote by the Assembly; a referendum is required if approved by only two-thirds majority of the Assembly or if requested by the president; constitutional articles on the republican and secular form of government cannot be amended; amended 2002, 2007; note—a September 2017 Assembly vote on a package of amendments failed the four-fifths majority vote required for passage but met the two-thirds majority vote required for holding a referendeum (2017)

Legal system: customary law system

International law organization participation: accepts compulsory ICJ jurisdiction with reservations; non-party state to the ICCt

Citizenship: *citizenship by birth:* no
citizenship by descent only: at least one parent must be a citizen of Togo
dual citizenship recognized: yes
residency requirement for naturalization: 5 years

Suffrage: 18 years of age; universal

Executive branch: *chief of state:* President Faure GNASSINGBE (since 4 May 2005)

head of government: Prime Minister Komi KLAS-SOU (since 5 June 2015)
cabinet: Council of Ministers appointed by the president on the advice of the prime minister
elections/appointments: president directly elected by simple majority popular vote for a 5-year term (no term limits); election last held on

25 April 2015 (next to be held in 2020); prime minister appointed by the president
election results: Faure GNASSINGBE reelected president; percent of vote—Faure GNASSINGBE (UNIR) 58.8%, Jean-Pierre FABRE (ANC) 35.2%, Tchaboure GOGUE (ADDI) 4%, other 2%

Legislative branch: *description:* unicameral National Assembly or Assemblee Nationale (91 seats; members directly elected in multi-seat constituencies by proportional representation vote to serve 5-year terms)
elections: last held on 25 July 2013 (next to be held in 2018)
election results: percent of vote by coalition/party—UNIR 46.7%, CST 28.9%, Rainbow Alliance 10.8%, UFC 7.7%, independent 0.8%, other 5.1%; seats by coalition/party—UNIR 62, CST 19, Rainbow Alliance 6, UFC 3, independent 1

Judicial branch: *highest court(s):* Supreme Court or Cour Supreme (organized into criminal and administrative chambers, each with a chamber president and advisors); Constitutional Court (consists of 9 judges including the court president)
judge selection and term of office: Supreme Court president appointed by decree of the president of the republic upon the proposal of the Supreme Council of the Magistracy, a 9-member judicial, advisory, and disciplinary body; other judge appointments and judge tenure NA; Constitutional Court judges appointed by the National Assembly; judge tenure NA
subordinate courts: Court of Assizes (sessions court); Appeal Court; tribunals of first instance (divided into civil, commercial, and correctional chambers; Court of State Security; military tribunal

Political parties and leaders: Action Committee for Renewal or CAR [Yaovi AGBOYIBO]
Alliance of Democrats for Integral Development or ADDI [Tchaboure GOGUE]
Combat for Political Change in 2015 or CAP 2015 [Jean-Pierre FABRE]
Democratic Convention of African Peoples or CDPA [Brigitte ADJAMAGBO-JOHNSON]
Democrastic Forces for the Republic or FDR [Dodji APEVON]
National Alliance for Change or ANC [Jean-Pierre FABRE]
New Togolese Commitment [Gerry TAAMA]
Pan-African National Party or PNP [Tikpi ATCHADAM]
Pan-African Patriotic Convergence or CPP [Edem KODJO]
Rainbow Alliance (a coalition including CAR and CDPA) [Brigitte ADJAMAGBO-JOHNSON]
Socialist Pact for Renewal or PSR [Abi TCHESSA]
The Togolese Party [Nathaniel OLYMPIO]
Union of Forces for Change or UFC [Gilchrist OLYMPIO]
Union for the Republic or UNIR [Faure GNASSINGBE]

Political pressure groups and leaders: NA

International organization participation: ACP, AfDB, AU, ECOWAS, EITI (compliant country), Entente, FAO, FZ, G-77, IAEA, IBRD, ICAO, ICRM, IDA, IDB, IFAD, IFC, IFRCS, ILO, IMF, IMO, Interpol, IOC, IOM, IPU, ISO (correspondent), ITSO, ITU, ITUC (NGOs), MIGA, MINURSO, MINUSMA, NAM, OIC, OIF, OPCW, PCA, UN, UNAMID, UNCTAD, UNESCO, UNHCR, UNIDO, UNMIL, UNOCI, UNWTO, UPU, WADB (regional), WAEMU, WCO, WFTU (NGOs), WHO, WIPO, WMO, WTO

Diplomatic representation in the US: chief of mission: Ambassador Frederic Edem HEGBE (since 24 April 2017)
chancery: 2208 Massachusetts Avenue NW, Washington, DC 20008
telephone: [1] (202) 234-4212
FAX: [1] (202) 232-3190

Diplomatic representation from the US: *chief of mission:* Ambassador David R. GILMOUR (20 December 2015)
embassy: 4332 Blvd. Gnassingbe Eyadema, Cite OUA, Lome
mailing address: B.P. 852, Lome; 2300 Lome Place, Washington, DC 20521-2300
telephone: [228] 2261-5470
FAX: [228] 2261-5501

Flag description: five equal horizontal bands of green (top and bottom) alternating with yellow; a white five-pointed star on a red square is in the upper hoist-side corner; the five horizontal stripes stand for the five different regions of the country; the red square is meant to express the loyalty and patriotism of the people; green symbolizes hope, fertility, and agriculture; yellow represents mineral wealth and faith that hard work and strength will bring prosperity; the star symbolizes life, purity, peace, dignity, and Togo's independence
note: uses the popular Pan-African colors of Ethiopia

National symbol(s): lion; national colors: green, yellow, red, white

National anthem: *name:* "Salut a toi, pays de nos aieux" (Hail to Thee, Land of Our Forefathers)
lyrics/music: Alex CASIMIR-DOSSEH
note: adopted 1960, restored 1992; this anthem was replaced by another during one-party rule between 1979 and 1992

ECONOMY

Economy—overview: Togo has enjoyed a period of steady economic growth fueled by political stability and a concerted effort by the government to modernize the country's commercial infrastructure, but discontent with President Faure GNASSINGBE has led to a rapid rise in protests, creating downside risks. The country completed an ambitious large-scale infrastructure improvement program, including two new principal roads, a new airport terminal, and a new sea-port. The economy depends heavily on both commercial and subsistence agriculture, which provides employment for around 60% of the labor force. Some basic foodstuffs must still be imported. Cocoa, coffee, and cotton and other agricultural products generate about 20% of export earnings with cotton being the most important cash crop. Togo is among the world's largest producers of phosphate and seeks to develop its carbonate phosphate reserves, which provide more than 20% of export earnings.

The government's decade-long effort, supported by the World Bank and the IMF, to implement economic reform measures, encourage foreign investment, and bring revenues in line with expenditures has moved slowly. Togo completed its IMF Extended Credit Facility in 2011 and reached a Heavily Indebted Poor Country debt relief completion point in 2010 at which 95% of the country's debt was forgiven. Togo continues to work with the IMF on structural reforms, and in January 2017, the IMF signed an Extended Credit Facility arrangement consisting of a three-year $238 million loan package. Progress depends on follow through on privatization, increased openness in government financial operations, progress toward legislative elections, and continued support from foreign donors.

Togo's 2017 economic growth probably remained steady at 5.0%, largely driven by infusions of foreign aid, infrastructure investment in the port and mineral sectors, and improvements in the business climate. Foreign direct investment inflows have slowed in recent years.

GDP (purchasing power parity): $12.43 billion (2017 est.)
$11.84 billion (2016 est.)
$11.28 billion (2015 est.)
note: data are in 2017 dollars
country comparison to the world: 156

GDP (official exchange rate): $4.797 billion (2016 est.)

GDP—real growth rate: 5% (2017 est.)
5% (2016 est.)
5.3% (2015 est.)
country comparison to the world: 40

GDP—per capita (PPP): $1,600 (2017 est.)
$1,600 (2016 est.)
$1,500 (2015 est.)
note: data are in 2017 dollars
country comparison to the world: 217

Gross national saving: 17.7% of GDP (2017 est.)
17.6% of GDP (2016 est.)
15.9% of GDP (2015 est.)
country comparison to the world: 104

GDP—composition, by end use:
household consumption: 79.2%
government consumption: 18.2%
investment in fixed capital: 24.2%
investment in inventories: -1.7%
exports of goods and services: 39.1%
imports of goods and services: -59% (2017 est.)

GDP—composition, by sector of origin:
agriculture: 28.1%
industry: 21.6%
services: 50.3% (2017 est.)

Agriculture—products: coffee, cocoa, cotton, yams, cassava (manioc, tapioca), corn, beans, rice, millet, sorghum; livestock; fish

Industries: phosphate mining, agricultural processing, cement, handicrafts, textiles, beverages

Industrial production growth rate: 7.5% (2017 est.)
country comparison to the world: 22

Labor force: 2.595 million (2007 est.)
country comparison to the world: 115

Labor force—by occupation: *agriculture:* 65%
industry: 5%
services: 30% (1998 est.)

Unemployment rate: 6.9% (2016 est.)
country comparison to the world: 96

Population below poverty line: 55.1% (2015 est.)

Household income or consumption by percentage share: *lowest 10%:* 3.3%
highest 10%: 27.1% (2006)

Distribution of family income—Gini index: 46 (2011)
country comparison to the world: 34

Budget: *revenues:* $1.469 billion
expenditures: $1.7 billion (2017 est.)
Taxes and other revenues: 30.6% of GDP (2017 est.)
country comparison to the world: 80

Budget surplus (+) or deficit (-): -4.8% of GDP (2017 est.)
country comparison to the world: 156

Public debt: 68.6% of GDP (2017 est.)
71.6% of GDP (2016 est.)
country comparison to the world: 52

Fiscal year: calendar year

Inflation rate (consumer prices): 0.8% (2017 est.)
0.9% (2016 est.)
country comparison to the world: 29

Central bank discount rate: 2.5% (31 December 2010)
4.25% (31 December 2009)
country comparison to the world: 112

Commercial bank prime lending rate: 8.29% (31 December 2015 est.)
country comparison to the world: 105

Stock of narrow money: $1.202 billion (31 December 2017 est.)
$1.118 billion (31 December 2016 est.)
country comparison to the world: 152

Stock of broad money: $2.519 billion (31 December 2017 est.)
$2.239 billion (31 December 2016 est.)
country comparison to the world: 146

Stock of domestic credit: $1.814 billion (31 December 2017 est.)
$1.62 billion (31 December 2016 est.)
country comparison to the world: 156

Market value of publicly traded shares: $NA

Current account balance: -$396 million (2017 est.)
-$431 million (2016 est.)
country comparison to the world: 99

Exports: $1.002 billion (2017 est.)

$967.4 million (2016 est.)
country comparison to the world: 158

Exports—commodities: reexports, cotton, phosphates, coffee, cocoa

Exports—partners: Benin 17.5%, Burkina Faso 15.9%, India 7.6%, Mali 7.2%, Niger 7%, Cote dIvoire 6.1%, Ghana 4.8%, Nigeria 4.3% (2016)

Imports: $2.009 billion (2017 est.)
$1.981 billion (2016 est.)
country comparison to the world: 158

Imports—commodities: machinery and equipment, foodstuffs, petroleum products

Imports—partners: China 28.7%, France 8.9%, Netherlands 4.3%, Japan 4.2% (2016)

Reserves of foreign exchange and gold: $215.1 million (31 December 2017 est.)
$42.6 million (31 December 2016 est.)
country comparison to the world: 158

Debt—external: $1.387 billion (31 December 2017 est.)
$1.22 billion (31 December 2016 est.)
country comparison to the world: 161

Exchange rates: Communaute Financiere Africaine francs (XOF) per US dollar—
617.4 (2017 est.)
593.01 (2016 est.)
593.01 (2015 est.)
591.45 (2014 est.)
494.42 (2013 est.)

ENERGY

Electricity access: population without electricity: 5,000,000
electrification—total population: 27%
electrification—urban areas: 35%
electrification—rural areas: 21% (2013)

Electricity—production: 78.8 million kWh (2015 est.)
country comparison to the world: 201

Electricity—consumption: 1.213 billion kWh (2015 est.)
country comparison to the world: 152

Electricity—exports: 0 kWh (2016 est.)
country comparison to the world: 204

Electricity—imports: 1.242 billion kWh (2015 est.)
country comparison to the world: 63

Electricity—installed generating capacity: 229,000 kW (2015 est.)
country comparison to the world: 162

Electricity—from fossil fuels: 69.9% of total installed capacity (2015 est.)
country comparison to the world: 105

Electricity—from nuclear fuels: 0% of total installed capacity (2015 est.)
country comparison to the world: 192

Electricity—from hydroelectric plants: 29.3% of total installed capacity (2015 est.)
country comparison to the world: 73

Electricity—from other renewable sources: 0.9% of total installed capacity (2015 est.)
country comparison to the world: 144

Crude oil—production: 0 bbl/day (2016 est.)
country comparison to the world: 206

Crude oil—exports: 0 bbl/day (2014 est.)
country comparison to the world: 198

Crude oil—imports: 0 bbl/day (2014 est.)
country comparison to the world: 197

Crude oil—proved reserves: 0 bbl (1 January 2017 es)
country comparison to the world: 206

Refined petroleum products—production: 0 bbl/day (2014 est.)
country comparison to the world: 208

Refined petroleum products—consumption: 14,000 bbl/day (2015 est.)
country comparison to the world: 153

Refined petroleum products—exports: 0 bbl/day (2014 est.)
country comparison to the world: 203

Refined petroleum products—imports: 12,700 bbl/day (2014 est.)
country comparison to the world: 136

Natural gas—production: 0 cu m (2013 est.)
country comparison to the world: 202

Natural gas—consumption: 0 cu m (2013 est.)
country comparison to the world: 137

Natural gas—exports: 0 cu m (2013 est.)
country comparison to the world: 194

Natural gas—imports: 0 cu m (2013 est.)
country comparison to the world: 195

Natural gas—proved reserves: 0 cu m (1 January 2014 es)
country comparison to the world: 200

Carbon dioxide emissions from consumption of energy: 1.8 million Mt (2013 est.)
country comparison to the world: 154

COMMUNICATIONS

Telephones—fixed lines: *total subscriptions:* 33,817
subscriptions per 100 inhabitants: 0 (July 2016 est.)
country comparison to the world: 155

Telephones—mobile cellular: *total:* 5,505,424

subscriptions per 100 inhabitants: 71 (July 2016 est.)
country comparison to the world: 121

Telephone system: *general assessment:* fair system based on a network of microwave radio relay routes supplemented by open-wire lines and a mobile-cellular system
domestic: microwave radio relay and open-wire lines for conventional system; combined fixed-line and mobile-cellular teledensity roughly 70 telephones per 100 persons with mobile-cellular use predominating
international: country code—228; satellite earth stations—1 Intelsat (Atlantic Ocean), 1 Symphonie (2016)

Broadcast media: 1 state-owned TV station with multiple transmission sites; 5 private TV stations broadcast locally; cable TV service is available; state-owned radio network with multiple stations; several dozen private radio stations and a few community radio stations; transmissions of multiple international broadcasters available (2017)

Internet country code: .tg

Internet users: *total:* 877,310

percent of population: 11.3% (July 2016 est.)
country comparison to the world: 138

TRANSPORTATION

National air transport system: number of registered air carriers: 1
inventory of registered aircraft operated by air carriers: 8
annual passenger traffic on registered air carriers: 769,904
annual freight traffic on registered air carriers: 0 mt-km (2015)
Civil aircraft registration country code prefix: 5V (2016)

Airports: 8 (2013)
country comparison to the world: 163

Airports—with paved runways: *total:* 2
2,438 to 3,047 m: 2 (2013)

Airports—with unpaved runways: *total:* 6
914 to 1,523 m: 4
under 914 m: 2 (2013)

Railways: *total:* 568 km

narrow gauge: 568 km 1.000-m gauge (2014)
country comparison to the world: 112

Roadways: *total:* 11,652 km
paved: 2,447 km
unpaved: 9,205 km (2007)
country comparison to the world: 130

Waterways: 50 km (seasonally navigable by small craft on the Mono River depending on rainfall) (2011)
country comparison to the world: 102

Merchant marine: *total:* 308
by type: bulk carrier 11, container ship 3, general cargo 199, oil tanker 44, other 51 (2017)
country comparison to the world: 51

Ports and terminals: *major seaport(s):* Kpeme, Lome

MILITARY AND SECURITY

Military expenditures: 1.86% of GDP (2016)
1.71% of GDP (2015)
1.85% of GDP (2014)
1.77% of GDP (2013)
1.63% of GDP (2012)

Military branches: Togolese Armed Forces (Forces Armees Togolaise, FAT): Togolese Army (l'Armee de Terre); update State, April 2017, Togolese Navy (Forces Naval Togolaises), Togolese Air Force (Force Aerienne Togolaise, TAF), National Gendarmerie (2017)

Military service age and obligation: 18 years of age for military service; 2-year service obligation; currently the military is only an all-volunteer force (2017)

TRANSNATIONAL ISSUES

Disputes—international: in 2001, Benin claimed Togo moved boundary monuments—joint commission continues to resurvey the boundary; talks continue between Benin and Togo on funding the Adjrala hydroelectric dam on the Mona River

Refugees and internally displaced persons: refugees (country of origin): 9,677 (Ghana) (2017)

Illicit drugs: transit hub for Nigerian heroin and cocaine traffickers; money laundering not a significant problem

TONGA

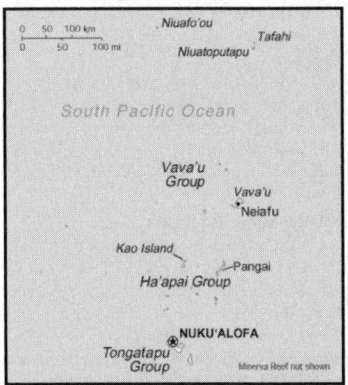

INTRODUCTION

Background: Tonga—unique among Pacific nations—never completely lost its indigenous governance. The archipelagos of "The Friendly Islands" were united into a Polynesian kingdom in 1845. Tonga became a constitutional monarchy in 1875 and a British protectorate in 1900; it withdrew from the protectorate and joined the Commonwealth of Nations in 1970. Tonga remains the only monarchy in the Pacific; in 2010 it began implementing steps to conduct more representative elections. Tropical Cyclone Gita, the strongest-ever recorded storm to impact Tonga, hit the islands in February 2018 causing extensive damage.

GEOGRAPHY

Location: Oceania, archipelago in the South Pacific Ocean, about two-thirds of the way from Hawaii to New Zealand

Geographic coordinates: 20 00 S, 175 00 W

Map references: Oceania

Area: *total:* 747 sq km
land: 717 sq km
water: 30 sq km
country comparison to the world: 190

Area—comparative: four times the size of Washington, DC
Land boundaries: 0 km

Coastline: 419 km

Maritime claims: *territorial sea:* 12 nm
exclusive economic zone: 200 nm
continental shelf: 200-m depth or to the depth of exploitation

Climate: tropical; modified by trade winds; warm season (December to May), cool season (May to December)

Terrain: mostly flat islands with limestone bedrock formed from uplifted coral formation; others have limestone overlying volcanic rock

Elevation: *mean elevation:* NA

elevation extremes: *lowest point:* Pacific Ocean 0 m
highest point: Kao Volcano on Kao Island 1,046 m

Natural resources: fish, arable land

Land use: *agricultural land:* 43.1%
arable land: 22.2%;
permanent crops: 15.3%;
permanent pasture: 5.6%
forest: 12.5%
other: 44.4% (2011 est.)
Irrigated land: 0 sq km (2012)

Population—distribution: over two-thirds of the population lives on the island of Tongatapu; only 45 of the nation's 171 islands are occupied

Natural hazards: cyclones (October to April); earthquakes and volcanic activity on Fonuafo'ou
volcanism: moderate volcanic activity; Fonualei (180 m) has shown frequent activity in recent years, while Niuafo'ou (260 m), which last erupted in 1985, has forced evacuations; other historically active volcanoes include Late and Tofua

Environment—current issues: deforestation results as more and more land is being cleared for agriculture and settlement; some damage to coral reefs from starfish and indiscriminate coral and shell collectors; overhunting threatens native sea turtle populations

Environment—international agreements: *party to:* Biodiversity, Climate Change, Climate Change-Kyoto Protocol, Desertification, Law of the Sea, Marine Dumping, Marine Life Conservation, Ozone Layer Protection, Ship Pollution
signed, but not ratified: none of the selected agreements

Geography—note: archipelago of 171 islands (45 inhabited)

PEOPLE AND SOCIETY

Population: 106,479 (July 2017 est.)
country comparison to the world: 193

Nationality: *noun:* Tongan(s)
adjective: Tongan

Ethnic groups: Tongan 96.6%, part-Tongan 1.7%, other 1.7%, unspecified 0.03% (2006 est.)

Languages: English and Tongan 87%, Tongan (official) 10.7%, English (official) 1.2%, other 1.1%, unspecified 0.03% (2006 est.)

Religions: Protestant 64.9% (includes Free Wesleyan Church 37.3%, Free Church of Tonga 11.4%, Church of Tonga 7.2%, Tokaikolo Christian Church 2.6%, Assembly of God 2.3%, Seventh Day Adventist 2.2%, Constitutional Church of Tonga 0.9%, Anglican 0.8% and Full Gospel Church 0.2%), Mormon 16.8%, Roman Catholic 15.6%, other 1.1%, none 0.03%, unspecified 1.7% (2006 est.)

Age structure: *0-14 years:* 33.87% (male 18,323/female 17,741)
15-24 years: 19.65% (male 10,715/female 10,209)
25-54 years: 34.3% (male 18,243/female 18,278)
55-64 years: 5.76% (male 3,048/female 3,083)
65 years and over: 6.42% (male 3,090/female 3,749) (2017 est.)

Dependency ratios: *total dependency ratio:* 74.2
youth dependency ratio: 63.9
elderly dependency ratio: 10.2
potential support ratio: 9.8 (2015 est.)

Median age: *total:* 23 years
male: 22.5 years
female: 23.4 years (2017 est.)
country comparison to the world: 175

Population growth rate: -0.05% (2017 est.)
country comparison to the world: 202

Birth rate: 22.2 births/1,000 population (2017 est.)
country comparison to the world: 70

Death rate: 4.9 deaths/1,000 population (2017 est.)
country comparison to the world: 196

Net migration rate: -17.8 migrant(s)/1,000 population (2017 est.)
country comparison to the world: 218

Population distribution: over two-thirds of the population lives on the island of Tongatapu; only 45 of the nation's 171 islands are occupied

Urbanization: *urban population:* 23.9% of total population (2017)
rate of urbanization: 1.3% annual rate of change (2015-20 est.)

Major urban areas—population: NUKU'ALOFA 25,000 (2014)

Sex ratio: *at birth:* 1.03 male(s)/female
0-14 years: 1.03 male(s)/female
15-24 years: 1.05 male(s)/female
25-54 years: 1 male(s)/female
55-64 years: 0.98 male(s)/female
65 years and over: 0.84 male(s)/female
total population: 1.01 male(s)/female (2016 est.)

Mother's mean age at first birth: 24.9 years
note: median age at first birth among women 25-49 (2012 est.)

Maternal mortality ratio: 124 deaths/100,000 live births (2015 est.)
country comparison to the world: 68

Infant mortality rate: *total:* 11.3 deaths/1,000 live births
male: 11.7 deaths/1,000 live births
female: 10.8 deaths/1,000 live births (2017 est.)
country comparison to the world: 126

Life expectancy at birth: *total population:* 76.4 years
male: 74.9 years
female: 78.1 years (2017 est.)
country comparison to the world: 87

Total fertility rate: 3.1 children born/woman (2017 est.)
country comparison to the world: 51

Contraceptive prevalence rate: 34.1% (2012)
Health expenditures: 5.2% of GDP (2014)
country comparison to the world: 133

Physicians density: 0.56 physicians/1,000 population (2010)

Hospital bed density: 2.6 beds/1,000 population (2010)

Drinking water source:
improved:
urban: 99.7% of population
rural: 99.6% of population
total: 99.6% of population
unimproved:
urban: 0.3% of population
rural: 0.4% of population
total: 0.4% of population (2015 est.)

Sanitation facility access:
improved:
urban: 97.6% of population
rural: 89% of population
total: 91% of population
unimproved:
urban: 2.4% of population
rural: 11% of population
total: 9% of population (2015 est.)

HIV/AIDS—adult prevalence rate: NA

HIV/AIDS—people living with HIV/AIDS: NA

HIV/AIDS—deaths: NA
Major infectious diseases: note: active local transmission of Zika virus by Aedes species mosquitoes has been identified in this country (as of August 2016); it poses an important risk (a large number of cases possible) among US citizens if bitten by an infective mosquito; other less common ways to get Zika are through sex, via blood transfusion, or during pregnancy, in which the pregnant woman passes Zika virus to her fetus (2016)

Obesity—adult prevalence rate: 48.2% (2016)
country comparison to the world: 7

Children under the age of 5 years underweight: 1.9% (2012)

Literacy: *definition:* can read and write Tongan and/or English
total population: 99.4%
male: 99.3%
female: 99.4% (2015 est.)

GOVERNMENT

Country name: *conventional long form:* Kingdom of Tonga
conventional short form: Tonga
local long form: Pule'anga Fakatu'i 'o Tonga
local short form: Tonga
former: Friendly Islands
etymology: "tonga" means "south" in the Tongan language and refers to the country's geographic position in relation to central Polynesia

Government type: constitutional monarchy

Capital: *name:* Nuku'alofa

geographic coordinates: 21 08 S, 175 12 W

time difference: UTC+13 (18 hours ahead of Washington, DC, during Standard Time)
daylight saving time: +1hr, begins first Sunday in November; ends second Sunday in January

Administrative divisions: 5 island divisions; 'Eua, Ha'apai, Ongo Niua, Tongatapu, Vava'u

Independence: 4 June 1970 (from UK protectorate)

National holiday: Official Birthday of King TUPOU VI, 4 July (1959); note—actual birthday of the monarch is 12 July 1959; 4 July (2015) is the day the king was crowned; Constitution Day (National Day), 4 November (1875)

Constitution: adopted 4 November 1875, revised 1988; amended many times, last in 2014 (2016)

Legal system: English common law

International law organization participation: has not submitted an ICJ jurisdiction declaration; non-party state to the ICCt

Citizenship: *citizenship by birth:* no
citizenship by descent only: the father must be a citizen of Tonga; if a child is born out of wedlock, the mother must be a citizen of Tonga
dual citizenship recognized: yes
residency requirement for naturalization: 5 years

Suffrage: 21 years of age; universal

Executive branch: *chief of state:* King TUPOU VI (since 18 March 2012); Heir Apparent Crown Prince Siaosi Manumataogo 'Alaivahamama'o 'Ahoeitu Konstantin Tuku'aho, son of the king (born 17 September 1985); note—on 18 March 2012, King George TUPOU V died and his brother, Crown Prince TUPOUTO'A Lavaka, assumed the throne as TUPOU VI
head of government: Interim Prime Minister 'Akilisi POHIVA (since 30 December 2014); note—King TUPOU VI dissolved the parliament on 26 August 2017
cabinet: Cabinet nominated by the prime minister and appointed by the monarch
elections/appointments: the monarchy is hereditary; prime minister and deputy prime minister indirectly elected by the Legislative Assembly and appointed by the monarch; election last held on 18 December 2017 (next to be held in November 2021); note—King TUPOU VI's dissolution of parliament in August 2017 triggered an early election
election results: 'Akilisi POHIVA (Democratic Party of the Friendly Islands) reelected prime minister by parliament receiving 14 of 26 votes
note: a Privy Council advises the monarch

Legislative branch: *description:* unicameral Legislative Assembly or Fale Alea (26 seats; 17 people's representatives directly elected in single-seat constituencies by simple majority vote and 9 indirectly elected by hereditary leaders; members serve 3-year terms)
elections: last held on 16 November 2017 (next to be held in 2020)
election results: percent of vote—NA; seats by party—Democratic Party 14, nobles' representatives 9, independent 3

Judicial branch: *highest court(s):* Court of Appeal (consists of the court president and a number of judges determined by the monarch); note—appeals beyond the Court of Appeal are brought before the King in Privy Council, the monarch's advisory organ that has both judicial and legislative powers
judge selection and term of office: judge appointments and tenures made by the King in Privy Council, judge appointments subject to consent of the Legislative Assembly
subordinate courts: Supreme Court; Magistrate's Courts; Land Courts

Political parties and leaders: Democratic Party of the Friendly Islands [Samuela 'Akilisi POHIVA]
People's Democratic Party or PDP [Tesina FUKO]
Sustainable Nation-Building Party [Sione FONUA]
Tonga Democratic Labor Party
Tonga Human Rights and Democracy Movement or THRDM
Political pressure groups and leaders: Human Rights and Democracy Movement Tonga or HRDMT [Rev. Simote VEA]
Public Service Association or PSA [Finau TUTONE]

International organization participation: ACP, ADB, AOSIS, C, FAO, G-77, IBRD, ICAO, ICRM, IDA, IFAD, IFC, IFRCS, IHO, IMF, IMO, IMSO, Interpol, IOC, IPU, ITU, ITUC (NGOs), OPCW, PIF, Sparteca, SPC, UN, UNCTAD, UNESCO, UNIDO, UPU, WCO, WHO, WIPO, WMO, WTO

Diplomatic representation in the US: chief of mission: Ambassador Mahe'uli'uli Sandhurst TUPOUNIUA (since 17 September 2013)
chancery: 250 E. 51st Street, New York, NY, 10022
telephone: [1] (917) 369-1025
FAX: [1] (917) 369-1024
consulate(s) general: San Francisco

Diplomatic representation from the US: the US does not have an embassy in Tonga; the US Ambassador to Fiji is accredited to Tonga

Flag description: red with a bold red cross on a white rectangle in the upper hoist-side corner; the cross reflects the deep-rooted Christianity in Tonga; red represents the blood of Christ and his sacrifice; white signifies purity

National symbol(s): red cross on white field, arms equal length; national colors: red, white

National anthem: *name:* "Ko e fasi 'o e tu"i 'o e 'Otu Tonga" (Song of the King of the Tonga Islands)
lyrics/music: Uelingatoni Ngu TUPOUMALOHI/Karl Gustavus SCHMITT
note: in use since 1875; more commonly known as "Fasi Fakafonua" (National Song)

ECONOMY

Economy—overview: Tonga has a small, open island economy and is the last constitutional monarchy among the Pacific Island countries. It has a narrow export base in agricultural goods. Squash, vanilla beans, and yams are the main crops. Agricultural exports, including fish, make up two-thirds of total exports. Tourism is the second-largest source of hard currency earnings following remittances. Tonga had 53,800 visitors in 2015. The country must import a high proportion of its food, mainly from New Zealand.

The country remains dependent on external aid and remittances from overseas Tongans to off-set its trade deficit. The government is emphasiz-ing the development of the private sector, encour-aging investment, and is committing increased funds for health care and education. Tonga's Eng-lish-speaking and educated workforce offer a viable labor market, and the tropical climate provides fertile soil. Renewable energy and deep-sea mining also offer opportunities for investment.

Tonga has a reasonably sound basic infra-structure and well developed social services. The government faces high unemployment among the young, moderate inflation, pressures for demo-cratic reform, and rising civil service expenditures.

GDP (purchasing power parity): $587 million (2017 est.)
$569.6 million (2016 est.)
$552.7 million (2015 est.)
note: data are in 2017 dollars
country comparison to the world: 212

GDP (official exchange rate): $437 million (2016 est.)

GDP—real growth rate: 3.1% (2017 est.)
3.1% (2016 est.)
3.5% (2015 est.)
country comparison to the world: 112

GDP—per capita (PPP): $5,600 (2017 est.)
$5,500 (2016 est.)
$5,300 (2015 est.)
note: data are in 2017 dollars
country comparison to the world: 169

GDP—composition, by end use:
household consumption: 99.2%
government consumption: 20%
investment in fixed capital: 26.3%
investment in inventories: -2.7%
exports of goods and services: 18.7%
imports of goods and services: -61.5% (2017 est.)

GDP—composition, by sector of origin:
agriculture: 19.5%
industry: 20.8%
services: 59.8% (2017 est.)

Agriculture—products: squash, coconuts, copra, bananas, vanilla beans, cocoa, coffee, sweet pota-toes, cassava, taro and kava

Industries: tourism, construction, fishing

Industrial production growth rate: 5% (2017 est.)
country comparison to the world: 48

Labor force: 33,800 (2011 est.)
country comparison to the world: 202

Labor force—by occupation: agriculture: 27.5%
industry: 27.5%
services: 2,006% (2006 est.)

Unemployment rate: 1.1% (2011 est.)
1.1% (2006)

country comparison to the world: 8

Population below poverty line: 24% (FY03/04 est.)

Household income or consumption by percentage share: lowest 10%: NA%
highest 10%: NA%

Budget: revenues: $134.6 million
expenditures: $134.6 million (2017 est.)
Taxes and other revenues: 30.8% of GDP (2017 est.)
country comparison to the world: 77

Budget surplus (+) or deficit (-): 0% of GDP (2017 est.)
country comparison to the world: 35

Public debt: 45.1% of GDP (2013)
46.5% of GDP (2012)
country comparison to the world: 118

Fiscal year: 1 July–30 June

Inflation rate (consumer prices): 7.5% (2017 est.)
2.6% (2016 est.)
country comparison to the world: 195

Commercial bank prime lending rate: 8.1% (31 December 2017 est.)
7.9% (31 December 2016 est.)
country comparison to the world: 107

Stock of narrow money: $137.7 million (31 December 2017 est.)
$112.8 million (31 December 2016 est.)
country comparison to the world: 187

Stock of broad money: $263.9 million (31 December 2017 est.)
$227.7 million (31 December 2016 est.)
country comparison to the world: 191

Stock of domestic credit: $166.7 million (31 December 2017 est.)
$135.2 million (31 December 2016 est.)
country comparison to the world: 187

Market value of publicly traded shares: $NA

Current account balance: -$59 million (2017 est.)
-$53 million (2016 est.)
country comparison to the world: 72

Exports: $18.2 million (2017 est.)
$19.4 million (2016 est.)
country comparison to the world: 214

Exports—commodities: squash, fish, vanilla beans, root crops

Exports—partners: Hong Kong 25.6%, Japan 15.1%, NZ 14.3%, US 13.5%, Australia 10%, Philippines 9.4% (2016)

Imports: $320.7 million (2017 est.)
$266.6 million (2016 est.)
country comparison to the world: 195

Imports—commodities: foodstuffs, machinery and transport equipment, fuels, chemicals

Imports—partners: NZ 35.3%, Fiji 12.1%, Singa-pore 9.3%, China 8.4%, US 8%, Australia 7.6%, Japan 4.3% (2016)

Reserves of foreign exchange and gold: $131.9 million (31 December 2017 est.)
$176.5 million (31 December 2016 est.)
country comparison to the world: 165

Debt—external: $233.5 million (31 December 2017 est.)
$198.2 million (31 December 2016 est.)
country comparison to the world: 188

Stock of direct foreign investment—at home:
$127.2 million (31 December 2017 est.)
$117.2 million (31 December 2016 est.)
country comparison to the world: 130

Exchange rates: pa'anga (TOP) per US dollar—
2.228 (2017 est.)
2.216 (2016 est.)
2.216 (2015 est.)
2.106 (2014 est.)
1.847 (2013 est.)

ENERGY

Electricity access: population without electricity: 5,325
electrification—total population: 96%
electrification—urban areas: 100%
electrification—rural areas: 83% (2012)

Electricity—production: 50 million kWh (2015 est.)
country comparison to the world: 207

Electricity—consumption: 46.5 million kWh (2015 est.)
country comparison to the world: 205

Electricity—exports: 0 kWh (2016)
country comparison to the world: 203

Electricity—imports: 0 kWh (2016 est.)
country comparison to the world: 208

Electricity—installed generating capacity: 17,000 kW (2015 est.)
country comparison to the world: 207

Electricity—from fossil fuels: 82.4% of total installed capacity (2015 est.)
country comparison to the world: 81

Electricity—from nuclear fuels: 0% of total installed capacity (2015 est.)
country comparison to the world: 191

Electricity—from hydroelectric plants: 0% of total installed capacity (2015 est.)
country comparison to the world: 208

Electricity—from other renewable sources: 17.6% of total installed capacity (2015 est.)
country comparison to the world: 37

Crude oil—production: 0 bbl/day (2016 est.)
country comparison to the world: 207

Crude oil—exports: 0 bbl/day (2014 est.)
country comparison to the world: 197

Crude oil—imports: 0 bbl/day (2014 est.)
country comparison to the world: 196

Crude oil—proved reserves: 0 bbl (1 January 2017 es)
country comparison to the world: 208

Refined petroleum products—production: 0 bbl/day (2014 est.)
country comparison to the world: 209

Refined petroleum products—consumption: 1,500 bbl/day (2015 est.)
country comparison to the world: 199

Refined petroleum products—exports: 0 bbl/day (2014 est.)
country comparison to the world: 202

Refined petroleum products—imports: 1,457 bbl/day (2014 est.)
country comparison to the world: 196

Natural gas—production: 0 cu m (2013 est.)
country comparison to the world: 201

Natural gas—consumption: 0 cu m (2013 est.)
country comparison to the world: 136

Natural gas—exports: 0 cu m (2013 est.)
country comparison to the world: 193

Natural gas—imports: 0 cu m (2013 est.)
country comparison to the world: 194

Natural gas—proved reserves: 0 cu m (1 January 2014 es)
country comparison to the world: 199

Carbon dioxide emissions from consumption of energy: 200,000 Mt (2013 est.)
country comparison to the world: 206

COMMUNICATIONS

Telephones—fixed lines: *total subscriptions:* 11,000
subscriptions per 100 inhabitants: 10 (July 2016 est.)
country comparison to the world: 195

Telephones—mobile cellular: *total:* 80,000
subscriptions per 100 inhabitants: 75 (July 2016 est.)
country comparison to the world: 197

Telephone system: *general assessment:* competition between Tonga Telecommunications Corporation (TCC) and Digicel Tonga Limited is accelerating expansion of telecommunications; both parties provide high speed Internet, mobile telephone networks, and international telecom services; Digicel also holds a telecommunication license after its acquisition of TonFon (a subsidiary of former Shoreline Communications Tonga); submarine cable infrastructure, managed by Tonga Cable Limited, has also been brought to the country by Asian Development Bank and World Bank aid
domestic: combined fixed-line and mobile-cellular teledensity about 85 telephones per 100 persons; fully automatic switched network
international: country code—676; satellite earth station—1 Intelsat (Pacific Ocean) (2016)

Broadcast media: 1 state-owned TV station and 3 privately owned TV stations; satellite and cable TV services are available; 1 state-owned and 3 privately owned radio stations; Radio Australia broadcasts available via satellite (2015)

Internet country code: .to

Internet users: *total:* 42,552

percent of population: 40.0% (July 2016 est.)
country comparison to the world: 191

TRANSPORTATION

National air transport system: number of registered air carriers: 1
inventory of registered aircraft operated by air carriers: 1
annual passenger traffic on registered air carriers: 75,416
annual freight traffic on registered air carriers: 0 mt-km (2015)

Civil aircraft registration country code prefix: A3 (2016)

Airports: 6 (2013)
country comparison to the world: 177

Airports—with paved runways: *total:* 1
2,438 to 3,047 m: 1 (2013)

Airports—with unpaved runways: *total:* 5
1,524 to 2,437 m: 1
914 to 1,523 m: 3
under 914 m: 1 (2013)

Roadways: *total:* 680 km
paved: 184 km
unpaved: 496 km (2011)
country comparison to the world: 191

Merchant marine: *total:* 34
by type: bulk carrier 1, container ship 1, general cargo 14, oil tanker 1, other 17 (2017)
country comparison to the world: 120

Ports and terminals: *major seaport(s):* Nuku'alofa, Neiafu, Pangai

MILITARY AND SECURITY

Military branches: Tonga Defense Services (TDS): Land Force (Royal Guard), Maritime Force (includes Royal Marines, Air Wing) (2013)

Military service age and obligation: 16 years of age for voluntary enlistment (with parental consent); no conscription; the king retains the right to call up "all those capable of bearing arms" in wartime (2012)

TRANSNATIONAL ISSUES

Disputes—international: none

TRINIDAD AND TOBAGO

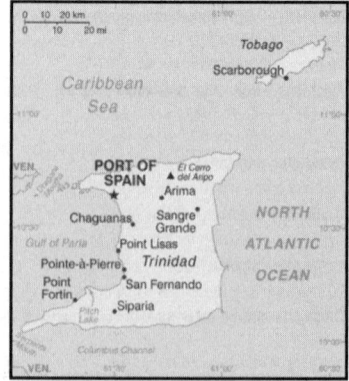

INTRODUCTION

Background: First colonized by the Spanish, the islands came under British control in the early 19th century. The islands' sugar industry was hurt by the emancipation of the slaves in 1834. Manpower was replaced with the importation of contract laborers from India between 1845 and 1917, which boosted sugar production as well as the cocoa industry. The discovery of oil on Trinidad in 1910 added another important export. Independence was attained in 1962. The country is one of the most prosperous in the Caribbean thanks largely to petroleum and natural gas production and processing. Tourism, mostly in Tobago, is targeted for expansion and is growing. The government is struggling to reverse a surge in violent crime.

GEOGRAPHY

Location: Caribbean, islands between the Caribbean Sea and the North Atlantic Ocean, northeast of Venezuela

Geographic coordinates: 11 00 N, 61 00 W

Map references: Central America and the Caribbean

Area: *total:* 5,128 sq km
land: 5,128 sq km
water: 0 sq km
country comparison to the world: 174

Area—comparative: slightly smaller than Delaware
Land boundaries: 0 km

Coastline: 362 km

Maritime claims: measured from claimed archipelagic baselines
territorial sea: 12 nm
contiguous zone: 24 nm
exclusive economic zone: 200 nm
continental shelf: 200 nm or to the outer edge of the continental margin

Climate: tropical; rainy season (June to December)

Terrain: mostly plains with some hills and low mountains

Elevation: *mean elevation:* 83 m

elevation extremes: *lowest point:* Caribbean Sea 0 m
highest point: El Cerro del Aripo 940 m

Natural resources: petroleum, natural gas, asphalt

Land use: *agricultural land:* 10.6%
arable land: 4.9%;
permanent crops: 4.3%;
permanent pasture: 1.4%
forest: 44%
other: 45.4% (2011 est.)
Irrigated land: 70 sq km (2012)

Population—distribution: population on Trinidad concentrated in the western half of the island; on Tobago in the southern half

Natural hazards: outside usual path of hurricanes and other tropical storms

Environment—current issues: water pollution from agricultural chemicals, industrial wastes, and raw sewage; oil pollution of beaches; deforestation; soil erosion

Environment—international agreements: *party to:* Biodiversity, Climate Change, Climate Change-Kyoto Protocol, Desertification, Endangered Species, Hazardous Wastes, Law of the Sea, Marine Dumping, Marine Life Conservation, Ozone Layer Protection, Ship Pollution, Tropical Timber 83, Tropical Timber 94, Wetlands
signed, but not ratified: none of the selected agreements

Geography—note: Pitch Lake, on Trinidad's southwestern coast, is the world's largest natural reservoir of asphalt

PEOPLE AND SOCIETYTOBAGO

Population: 1,218,208 (July 2017 est.)
country comparison to the world: 160

Nationality: *noun:* Trinidadian(s), Tobagonian(s)
adjective: Trinidadian, Tobagonian

Ethnic groups: East Indian 35.4%, African 34.2%, mixed—other 15.3%, mixed African/East Indian 7.7%, other 1.3%, unspecified 6.2% (2011 est.)

Languages: English (official), Trinidadian Creole English, Tobagonian Creole English, Caribbean Hindustani (a dialect of Hindi), Trinidadian Creole French, Spanish, Chinese

Religions: Protestant 32.1% (Pentecostal/Evangelical/Full Gospel 12%, Baptist 6.9%, Anglican 5.7%, Seventh-Day Adventist 4.1%, Presbyterian/Congretational 2.5%, other Protestant 0.9%), Roman Catholic 21.6%, Hindu 18.2%, Muslim 5%, Jehovah's Witness 1.5%, other 8.4%, none 2.2%, unspecified 11.1% (2011 est.)

Age structure: *0-14 years:* 19.29% (male 119,651/female 115,348)
15-24 years: 11.88% (male 75,402/female 69,333)
25-54 years: 45.56% (male 289,244/female 265,808)
55-64 years: 12.61% (male 76,601/female 77,056)
65 years and over: 10.65% (male 56,550/female 73,215) (2017 est.)

Dependency ratios: *total dependency ratio:* 43.2
youth dependency ratio: 29.8
elderly dependency ratio: 13.5
potential support ratio: 7.4 (2015 est.)

Median age: *total:* 36 years
male: 35.6 years
female: 36.6 years (2017 est.)

country comparison to the world: 75

Population growth rate: -0.2% (2017 est.)
country comparison to the world: 209

Birth rate: 12.7 births/1,000 population (2017 est.)
country comparison to the world: 156

Death rate: 8.8 deaths/1,000 population (2017 est.)
country comparison to the world: 70

Net migration rate: -5.9 migrant(s)/1,000 population (2017 est.)
country comparison to the world: 196

Population distribution: population on Trinidad is concentrated in the western half of the island, on Tobago in the southern half

Urbanization: *urban population:* 8.3% of total population (2017)
rate of urbanization: -83% annual rate of change (2015-20 est.)
Major urban areas—population: PORT-OF-SPAIN (capital) 34,000 (2014)

Sex ratio: *at birth:* 1.03 male(s)/female
0-14 years: 1.04 male(s)/female
15-24 years: 1.09 male(s)/female
25-54 years: 1.09 male(s)/female
55-64 years: 0.99 male(s)/female
65 years and over: 0.77 male(s)/female
total population: 1.03 male(s)/female (2016 est.)

Maternal mortality ratio: 63 deaths/100,000 live births (2015 est.)
country comparison to the world: 88

Infant mortality rate: *total:* 22.3 deaths/1,000 live births
male: 23.6 deaths/1,000 live births
female: 20.9 deaths/1,000 live births (2017 est.)
country comparison to the world: 72

Life expectancy at birth: *total population:* 73.1 years
male: 70.2 years
female: 76.2 years (2017 est.)
country comparison to the world: 138

Total fertility rate: 1.71 children born/woman (2017 est.)
country comparison to the world: 172
Health expenditures: 5.9% of GDP (2014)
country comparison to the world: 108

Physicians density: 1.18 physicians/1,000 population (2007)

Hospital bed density: 2.7 beds/1,000 population (2012)

Drinking water source:
improved:
urban: 95.1% of population
rural: 95.1% of population
total: 95.1% of population
unimproved:
urban: 4.9% of population
rural: 4.9% of population
total: 4.9% of population (2015 est.)

Sanitation facility access:
improved:
urban: 91.5% of population
rural: 91.5% of population

total: 91.5% of population
unimproved:
urban: 8.5% of population
rural: 8.5% of population
total: 8.5% of population (2015 est.)

HIV/AIDS—adult prevalence rate: 1.2% (2016 est.)
country comparison to the world: 39

HIV/AIDS—people living with HIV/AIDS: 11,000 (2016 est.)
country comparison to the world: 91

HIV/AIDS—deaths: <500 (2016 est.)
Major infectious diseases: note: active local transmission of Zika virus by Aedes species mosquitoes has been identified in this country (as of August 2016); it poses an important risk (a large number of cases possible) among US citizens if bitten by an infective mosquito; other less common ways to get Zika are through sex, via blood transfusion, or during pregnancy, in which the pregnant woman passes Zika virus to her fetus (2016)

Obesity—adult prevalence rate: 18.6% (2016)
country comparison to the world: 116

Literacy: *definition:* age 15 and over can read and write
total population: 99%
male: 99.2%
female: 98.7% (2015 est.)

Unemployment, youth ages 15-24: *total:* 8.4%
male: 7.4%
female: 9.9% (2015 est.)
country comparison to the world: 98

GOVERNMENT

Country name: *conventional long form:* Republic of Trinidad and Tobago
conventional short form: Trinidad and Tobago
etymology: explorer Christopher COLUMBUS named the larger island "La Isla de la Trinidad" (The Island of the Trinity) on 31 July 1498 on his third voyage; the tobacco grown and smoked by the natives of the smaller island or its elongated cigar shape may account for the "tobago" name, which is spelled "tobaco" in Spanish

Government type: parliamentary republic

Capital: *name:* Port of Spain
geographic coordinates: 10 39 N, 61 31 W
time difference: UTC-4 (1 hour ahead of Washington, DC, during Standard Time)

Administrative divisions: 9 regions, 3 boroughs, 2 cities, 1 ward
regions: Couva/Tabaquite/Talparo, Diego Martin, Mayaro/Rio Claro, Penal/Debe, Princes Town, Sangre Grande, San Juan/Laventille, Siparia, Tunapuna/Piarco
borough: Arima, Chaguanas, Point Fortin
cities: Port of Spain, San Fernando
ward: Tobago

Independence: 31 August 1962 (from the UK)

National holiday: Independence Day, 31 August (1962)

Constitution: previous 1962; latest 1976; amended many times, last in 2007 (2016)

Legal system: English common law; judicial review of legislative acts in the Supreme Court

International law organization participation: has not submitted an ICJ jurisdiction declaration; accepts ICCt jurisdiction

Citizenship: *citizenship by birth:* yes

citizenship by descent: yes

dual citizenship recognized: yes

residency requirement for naturalization: 8 years

Suffrage: 18 years of age; universal

Executive branch: *chief of state:* President Anthony CARMONA (since 18 March 2013)

head of government: Prime Minister Keith ROW-LEY (since 9 September 2015)

cabinet: Cabinet appointed from among members of Parliament

elections/appointments: president indirectly elected by an electoral college of selected Senate and House of Representatives members for a 5-year term (eligible for a second term); election last held on 19 January 2018 (next to be held by February 2023); the president usually appoints the leader of the majority party in the House of Representatives as prime minister

election results: Paula-Mae WEEKES (independent) elected president; ran unopposed and was elected without a vote; when she takes office in March 2018, she will be Trinidad and Tabago's first female head of state

Legislative branch: *description:* bicameral Parliament consists of the Senate (31 seats; 16 members appointed by the ruling party, 9 by the president, and 6 by the opposition party; members serve 5-year terms;) and the House of Representatives (41 seats; members directly elected in single-seat constituencies by simple majority vote to serve 5-year terms)

note: Tobago has a unicameral House of Assembly (16 seats; 12 assemblymen directly elected by simple majority vote and 4 appointed councillors—3 on the advice of the chief secretary and 1 on the advice of the minority leader; members serve 4-year terms)

elections: House of Representatives—last held on 7 September 2015 (next to be held in 2020)

election results: House of Representatives—percent of vote—PNM 51.7%, People's Partnership coalition 46.6% (UNC 39.6%, COP 6.0%, other 1.0%), other 1.7%; seats by party—PNM 23, UNC 17, COP 1

Judicial branch: highest resident court(s): Supreme Court of the Judicature (consists of a chief justice for both the Court of Appeal with 12 judges and the High Court with 24 judges); note—Trinidad and Tobago can file appeals beyond its Supreme Court to the Caribbean Court of Justice, with final appeal to the Judicial Committee of the Privy Council (in London)

judge selection and term of office: Supreme Court chief justice appointed by the president after consultation with the prime minister and

the parliamentary leader of the opposition; other judges appointed by the Judicial Legal Services Commission, headed by the chief justice and 5 members with judicial experience; all judges appointed for life with mandatory retirement normally at age 65

subordinate courts: Courts of Summary Criminal Jurisdiction; Petty Civil Courts; Family Court

Political parties and leaders: Congress of the People or COP

People's National Movement or PNM [Keith ROWLEY]

People's Partnrship [Kamla PERSAD-BISSES-SAR] (coalition includes UNC, COP, TOP, National Joint Action Committee)

National Joint Action Committee or NJAC [Kwasi MUTEMA]

Tobago Organization of the People or TOP [Ashworth JACK]

United National Congress or UNC [Kamla PERSAD-BISSESSAR]

Political pressure groups and leaders: Jamaat al-Muslimeen [Yasin ABU BAKR]

International organization participation: ACP, AOSIS, C, Caricom, CDB, CELAC, EITI (compliant country), FAO, G-24, G-77, IADB, IAEA, IBRD, ICAO, ICC (NGOs), ICCt, ICRM, IDA, IFAD, IFC, IFRCS, IHO, ILO, IMF, IMO, Interpol, IOC, IOM, IPU, ISO, ITSO, ITU, ITUC (NGOs), LAES, MIGA, NAM, OAS, OPANAL, OPCW, Pacific Alliance (observer), Paris Club (associate), UN, UNCTAD, UNESCO, UNIDO, UPU, WCO, WFTU (NGOs), WHO, WIPO, WMO, WTO

Diplomatic representation in the US: chief of mission: Ambassador Anthony Wayne Jerome PHIL-LIPS-SPENCER (since 27 June 2016)

chancery: 1708 Massachusetts Avenue NW, Washington, DC 20036

telephone: [1] (202) 467-6490

FAX: [1] (202) 785-3130

consulate(s) general: Miami, New York

Diplomatic representation from the US: *chief of mission:* Ambassador (vacant); Charge d'Affaires John W. MCINTYRE (since 20 January 2017)

embassy: 15 Queen's Park West, Port of Spain

mailing address: P. O. Box 752, Port of Spain

telephone: [1] (868) 622-6371 through 6376

FAX: [1] (868) 822-5905

Flag description: red with a white-edged black diagonal band from the upper hoist side to the lower fly side; the colors represent the elements of earth, water, and fire; black stands for the wealth of the land and the dedication of the people; white symbolizes the sea surrounding the islands, the purity of the country's aspirations, and equality; red symbolizes the warmth and energy of the sun, the vitality of the land, and the courage and friendliness of its people

National symbol(s): scarlet ibis (bird of Trinidad), cocrico (bird of Tobago), Chaconia flower; national colors: red, white, black

National anthem: *name:* "Forged From the Love of Liberty"

lyrics/music: Patrick Stanislaus CASTAGNE

note: adopted 1962; song originally created to serve as an anthem for the West Indies Federation; adopted by Trinidad and Tobago following the Federation's dissolution in 1962

ECONOMY

Economy—overview: Trinidad and Tobago relies on its energy sector for much of its economic activity, and has one of the highest per capita incomes in Latin America. Economic growth between 2000 and 2007 averaged slightly over 8% per year, significantly above the regional average of about 3.7% for that same period; however, GDP has slowed down since then, contracting during 2009-12, making small gains in 2013 and contracting again in 2014-17. Trinidad and Tobago is buffered by considerable foreign reserves and a sovereign wealth fund that equals about one-and-a-half times the national budget, but the country is in a recession and the government faces the dual challenge of gas shortages and a low price environment.

Energy production and downstream industrial use dominate the economy. Oil and gas typically account for about 40% of GDP and 80% of exports but less than 5% of employment. Trinidad and Tobago is home to one of the largest natural gas liquefaction facilities in the Western Hemisphere. Trinidad and Tobago produces about nine times more natural gas than crude oil on an energy equivalent basis with gas contributing about two-thirds of energy sector government revenue. The US is the country's largest trading partner, accounting for 28% of its total imports and taking 48% of its exports.

Economic diversification is a longstanding government talking point, and Trinidad and Tobago has much potential due to its stable, democratic government and its educated, English speaking workforce. The country is also a regional financial center with a well-regulated and stable financial system. Other sectors the Government of Trinidad and Tobago has targeted for increased investment and projected growth include tourism, agriculture, information and communications technology, and shipping. Unfortunately, a host of other factors, including low labor productivity, inefficient government bureaucracy, and corruption, have hampered economic development.

GDP (purchasing power parity): $42.78 billion (2017 est.)

$44.18 billion (2016 est.)

$46.69 billion (2015 est.)

note: data are in 2017 dollars

country comparison to the world: 115

GDP (official exchange rate): $20.3 billion (2016 est.)

GDP—real growth rate: -3.2% (2017 est.)

-5.4% (2016 est.)

-0.6% (2015 est.)

country comparison to the world: 216

GDP—per capita (PPP): $31,200 (2017 est.)

$32,300 (2016 est.)

$34,300 (2015 est.)

note: data are in 2017 dollars
country comparison to the world: 62

Gross national saving: 10.4% of GDP (2017 est.)
9.5% of GDP (2016 est.)
12.4% of GDP (2015 est.)
country comparison to the world: 156

GDP—composition, by end use:
household consumption: 77.9%
government consumption: 17.8%
investment in fixed capital: 9%
investment in inventories: 0.6%
exports of goods and services: 47.5%
imports of goods and services: -52.2% (2017 est.)

GDP—composition, by sector of origin:
agriculture: 0.4%
industry: 48.8%
services: 50.8% (2017 est.)

Agriculture—products: cocoa, dasheen, pumpkin, cassava, tomatoes, cucumbers, eggplant, hot pepper, pommecythere, coconut water, poultry

Industries: petroleum and petroleum products, liquefied natural gas, methanol, ammonia, urea, steel products, beverages, food processing, cement, cotton textiles

Industrial production growth rate: 2% (2017 est.)
country comparison to the world: 135

Labor force: 629,400 (2017 est.)
country comparison to the world: 155

Labor force—by occupation: *agriculture:* 3.4%
industry: 11.5%
services: 84.7% (2015 est.)

Unemployment rate: 4.1% (2017 est.)
4.1% (2016 est.)
country comparison to the world: 53

Population below poverty line: 20% (2014 est.)

Household income or consumption by percentage share: *lowest 10%:* NA%
highest 10%: NA%

Budget: *revenues:* $6.916 billion
expenditures: $7.838 billion (2017 est.)
Taxes and other revenues: 34.1% of GDP (2017 est.)
country comparison to the world: 61

Budget surplus (+) or deficit (-): -4.5% of GDP (2017 est.)
country comparison to the world: 151

Public debt: 65.3% of GDP (2017 est.)
62.5% of GDP (2016 est.)
country comparison to the world: 62

Fiscal year: 1 October—30 September

Inflation rate (consumer prices): 3.2% (2017 est.)
3.1% (2016 est.)
country comparison to the world: 134

Central bank discount rate: 6.75% (04 March 2016 est.)
6.75% (31 December 2015 est.)
country comparison to the world: 54

Commercial bank prime lending rate: 9% (31 December 2017 est.)
9% (31 December 2016 est.)
country comparison to the world: 94

Stock of narrow money: $7.238 billion (31 December 2017 est.)
$6.72 billion (31 December 2016 est.)
country comparison to the world: 90

Stock of broad money: $18.54 billion (31 December 2017 est.)
$16.66 billion (31 December 2016 est.)
country comparison to the world: 92

Stock of domestic credit: $10.08 billion (31 December 2017 est.)
$9.718 billion (31 December 2016 est.)
country comparison to the world: 106

Market value of publicly traded shares: $177.4 million (31 December 2015 est.)
$171.6 million (31 December 2014 est.)
$170 million (31 December 2013 est.)
country comparison to the world: 118

Current account balance: -$1.835 billion (2017 est.)
-$2.395 billion (2016 est.)
country comparison to the world: 155

Exports: $9.668 billion (2017 est.)
$8.714 billion (2016 est.)
country comparison to the world: 92

Exports—commodities: petroleum and petroleum products, liquefied natural gas, methanol, ammonia, urea, steel products, beverages, cereal and cereal products, cocoa, fish, preserved fruits, cosmetics, household cleaners, plastic packaging

Exports—partners: US 39.2%, Argentina 9.3% (2016)

Imports: $10.19 billion (2017 est.)
$9.485 billion (2016 est.)
country comparison to the world: 97

Imports—commodities: mineral fuels, lubricants, machinery, transportation equipment, manufactured goods, food, chemicals, live animals

Imports—partners: US 33.4%, Russia 13.3%, Gabon 12.4%, China 6.1% (2016)

Reserves of foreign exchange and gold: $8.66 billion (31 December 2017 est.)
$9.995 billion (31 December 2016 est.)
country comparison to the world: 77

Debt—external: $10.07 billion (31 December 2017 est.)
$8.746 billion (31 December 2016 est.)
country comparison to the world: 115

Stock of direct foreign investment—at home: $382.9 million (31 December 2014 est.)
$311.7 million (31 December 2013 est.)
country comparison to the world: 126

Stock of direct foreign investment—abroad: $1.266 billion (2014 est.)
$2.061 billion (2013 est.)
country comparison to the world: 83

Exchange rates: Trinidad and Tobago dollars (TTD) per US dollar—
6.762 (2017 est.)
6.669 (2016 est.)
6.669 (2015 est.)
6.4041 (2014 est.)
6.4041 (2013 est.)

ENERGY

Electricity access: population without electricity: 12,452
electrification—*total population:* 99.8%
electrification—urban areas: 100%
electrification—rural areas: 99% (2012)

Electricity—production: 9.682 billion kWh (2015 est.)
country comparison to the world: 103

Electricity—consumption: 9.461 billion kWh (2015 est.)
country comparison to the world: 96

Electricity—exports: 0 kWh (2016 est.)
country comparison to the world: 201

Electricity—imports: 0 kWh (2016 est.)
country comparison to the world: 206

Electricity—installed generating capacity: 2.117 million kW (2015 est.)
country comparison to the world: 111

Electricity—from fossil fuels: 99.6% of total installed capacity (2015 est.)
country comparison to the world: 28

Electricity—from nuclear fuels: 0% of total installed capacity (2015 est.)
country comparison to the world: 187

Electricity—from hydroelectric plants: 0% of total installed capacity (2015 est.)
country comparison to the world: 206

Electricity—from other renewable sources: 0.4% of total installed capacity (2015 est.)
country comparison to the world: 154

Crude oil—production: 71,570 bbl/day (2016 est.)
country comparison to the world: 48

Crude oil—exports: 32,620 bbl/day (2014 est.)
country comparison to the world: 46

Crude oil—imports: 58,460 bbl/day (2014 est.)
country comparison to the world: 52

Crude oil—proved reserves: 243 million bbl (1 January 2017 es)
country comparison to the world: 56

Refined petroleum products—production: 109,300 bbl/day (2014 est.)
country comparison to the world: 67

Refined petroleum products—consumption: 46,000 bbl/day (2015 est.)
country comparison to the world: 107

Refined petroleum products—exports: 97,960 bbl/day (2014 est.)
country comparison to the world: 43

Refined petroleum products—imports: 1,498 bbl/day (2014 est.)
country comparison to the world: 195

Natural gas—production: 40.87 billion cu m (2015 est.)
country comparison to the world: 20

Natural gas—consumption: 39.39 billion cu m (2015 est.)
country comparison to the world: 34

Natural gas—exports: 17.86 billion cu m (2015 est.)

country comparison to the world: 15

Natural gas—imports: 0 cu m (2015 est.)
country comparison to the world: 192

Natural gas—proved reserves: 300.1 billion cu m (1 January 2017 es)
country comparison to the world: 40

Carbon dioxide emissions from consumption of energy: 48 million Mt (2013 est.)
country comparison to the world: 62

COMMUNICATIONS

Telephones—fixed lines: *total subscriptions:* 272,072
subscriptions per 100 inhabitants: 22 (July 2016 est.)
country comparison to the world: 116

Telephones—mobile cellular: *total:* 2.123 million
subscriptions per 100 inhabitants: 174 (July 2016 est.)
country comparison to the world: 152

Telephone system: *general assessment:* excellent international service; good local service
domestic: combined fixed-line and mobile-cellular teledensity over 190 telephones per 100 persons
international: country code—1-868; submarine cable systems provide connectivity to US and parts of the Caribbean and South America; satellite earth station—1 Intelsat (Atlantic Ocean); tropospheric scatter to Barbados and Guyana (2016)

Broadcast media: 16 TV networks (11 commercial, 5 non-commercial), 2 of which are state-owned that broadcast on multiple stations; 9 TV subscription service providers (cable and satellite); 19 radio networks, 1 state-owned, broadcast over about 35 stations (2016)

Internet country code: .tt

Internet users: *total:* 846,000

percent of population: 69.2% (July 2016 est.)
country comparison to the world: 126

TRANSPORTATION

National air transport system: number of registered air carriers: 1
inventory of registered aircraft operated by air carriers: 17

annual passenger traffic on registered air carriers: 2,617,842
annual freight traffic on registered air carriers: 43,198,176 mt-km (2015)
Civil aircraft registration country code prefix: 9Y (2016)

Airports: 4 (2013)
country comparison to the world: 187

Airports—with paved runways: *total:* 2
over 3,047 m: 1
2,438 to 3,047 m: 1 (2013)

Airports—with unpaved runways: *total:* 2
914 to 1,523 m: 1
under 914 m: 1 (2013)

Pipelines: condensate 257 km; condensate/gas 11 km; gas 1,567 km; oil 587 km (2013)

Roadways: *total:* 9,592 km
paved: 5,524 km
unpaved: 4,068 km (2015)
country comparison to the world: 137

Merchant marine: *total:* 105
by type: general cargo 1, other 104 (2017)
country comparison to the world: 81

Ports and terminals: *major seaport(s):* Point Fortin, Point Lisas, Port of Spain, Scarborough
oil terminal(s): Galeota Point terminal
LNG terminal(s) (export): Port Fortin

MILITARY AND SECURITY

Military expenditures: 1.12% of GDP (2016)
0.88% of GDP (2015)
0.72% of GDP (2014)
0.8% of GDP (2013)
0.66% of GDP (2012)

Military branches: Trinidad and Tobago Defense Force (TTDF): Trinidad and Tobago Army, Coast Guard, Air Guard, Defense Force Reserves (2010)

Military service age and obligation: 18-25 years of age for voluntary military service (16 years of age with parental consent); no conscription; Trinidad and Tobago citizenship and completion of secondary school required (2012)

TRANSNATIONAL ISSUES

Disputes—international: Barbados and Trinidad and Tobago abide by the April 2006 Permanent Court of Arbitration decision delimiting a maritime boundary and limiting catches of flying fish in Trinidad and Tobago's EEZ; in 2005, Barbados and Trinidad and Tobago agreed to compulsory international arbitration under UN Convention on the Law of the Sea challenging whether the northern limit of Trinidad and Tobago's and Venezuela's maritime boundary extends into Barbadian waters; Guyana has expressed its intention to include itself in the arbitration, as the Trinidad and Tobago-Venezuela maritime boundary may also extend into its waters

Trafficking in persons: current situation: Trinidad and Tobago is a destination, transit, and possible source country for adults and children subjected to sex trafficking and forced labor; women and girls from Venezuela, the Dominican Republic, Guyana, and Colombia have been subjected to sex trafficking in Trinidad and Tobago's brothels and clubs; some economic migrants from the Caribbean region and Asia are vulnerable to forced labor in domestic service and the retail sector; the steady flow of vessels transiting Trinidad and Tobago's territorial waters may also increase opportunities for forced labor for fishing; international crime organizations are increasingly involved in trafficking, and boys are coerced to sell drugs and guns; corruption among police and immigration officials impedes anti-trafficking efforts

tier rating: Tier 2 Watch List – Trinidad and Tobago does not fully comply with the minimum standards for the elimination of trafficking; however, it is making significant efforts to do so; anti-trafficking law enforcement efforts decreased from the initiation of 12 prosecutions in 2013 to 1 in 2014; the government has yet to convict anyone under its 2011 anti-trafficking law, and all prosecutions from previous years remain pending; the government sustained efforts to identify victims and to refer them for care at NGO facilities, which it provided with funding; the government failed to draft a national action plan as mandated under the 2011 anti-trafficking law and did not launch a sufficiently robust awareness campaign to educate the public and officials (2015)

Illicit drugs: transshipment point for South American drugs destined for the US and Europe; producer of cannabis

TUNISIA

INTRODUCTION

Background: Rivalry between French and Italian interests in Tunisia culminated in a French invasion in 1881 and the creation of a protectorate. Agitation for independence in the decades following World War I was finally successful in convincing the French to recognize Tunisia as an independent state in 1956. The country's first president, Habib BOURGUIBA, established a strict one-party state. He dominated the country for 31 years, repressing Islamic fundamentalism and establishing rights for women unmatched by any other Arab nation. In November 1987, BOURGUIBA was removed from office and replaced by Zine el Abidine BEN ALI in a bloodless coup. Street protests that began in Tunis in December 2010 over high unemployment, corruption, widespread poverty, and high food prices escalated in January 2011, culminating in rioting that led to hundreds of deaths. On 14 January 2011, the same day BEN ALI dismissed the government, he fled the country, and by late January 2011, a "national unity government" was formed. Elections for the new Constituent Assembly were held in late October 2011, and in December, it elected human

rights activist Moncef MARZOUKI as interim president. The Assembly began drafting a new constitution in February 2012 and, after several iterations and a months-long political crisis that stalled the transition, ratified the document in January 2014. Parliamentary and presidential elections for a permanent government were held at the end of 2014. Beji CAID ESSEBSI was elected as the first president under the country's new constitution. In 2016, the new unity government continued to seek to balance political cohesion with economic and social pressures.

GEOGRAPHY

Location: Northern Africa, bordering the Mediterranean Sea, between Algeria and Libya

Geographic coordinates: 34 00 N, 9 00 E

Map references: Africa

Area: *total:* 163,610 sq km
land: 155,360 sq km
water: 8,250 sq km
country comparison to the world: 94

Area—comparative: slightly larger than Georgia
Land boundaries: total: 1,495 km
border countries (2): Algeria 1,034 km, Libya 461 km

Coastline: 1,148 km

Maritime claims: *territorial sea:* 12 nm
contiguous zone: 24 nm
exclusive economic zone: 12 nm

Climate: temperate in north with mild, rainy winters and hot, dry summers; desert in south

Terrain: mountains in north; hot, dry central plain; semiarid south merges into the Sahara

Elevation: *mean elevation:* 246 m

elevation extremes: *lowest point:* Shatt al Gharsah -17 m
highest point: Jebel ech Chambi 1,544 m

Natural resources: petroleum, phosphates, iron ore, lead, zinc, salt

Land use: *agricultural land:* 64.8%
arable land: 18.3%;
permanent crops: 15.4%;
permanent pasture: 31.1%
forest: 6.6%
other: 28.6% (2011 est.)
Irrigated land: 4,590 sq km (2012)

Population—distribution: the overwhelming majority of the population is located in the northern half of the country; the south remains largely underpopulated

Natural hazards: flooding; earthquakes; droughts

Environment—current issues: toxic and hazardous waste disposal is ineffective and poses health risks; water pollution from raw sewage; limited natural freshwater resources; deforestation; overgrazing; soil erosion; desertification

Environment—international agreements: *party to:* Biodiversity, Climate Change, Climate Change-Kyoto Protocol, Desertification, Endangered Species, Environmental Modification, Hazardous Wastes, Law of the Sea, Marine Dumping, Ozone Layer Protection, Ship Pollution, Wetlands
signed, but not ratified: Marine Life Conservation

Geography—note: strategic location in central Mediterranean; Malta and Tunisia are discussing the commercial exploitation of the continental shelf between their countries, particularly for oil exploration

PEOPLE AND SOCIETY

Population: 11,403,800 (July 2017 est.)
country comparison to the world: 79

Nationality: *noun:* Tunisian(s)
adjective: Tunisian

Ethnic groups: Arab 98%, European 1%, Jewish and other 1%

Languages: Arabic (official, one of the languages of commerce), French (commerce), Berber (Tamazight)
note: despite having no official status, French plays a major role in the country and is spoken by about two-thirds of the population

Religions: Muslim (official; Sunni) 99.1%, other (includes Christian, Jewish, Shia Muslim, and Baha'i) 1%

Demographic profile: The Tunisian Government took steps in the 1960s to decrease population growth and gender inequality in order to improve socioeconomic development. Through its introduction of a national family planning program (the first in Africa) and by raising the legal age of marriage, Tunisia rapidly reduced its total fertility rate from about 7 children per woman in 1960 to 2 today. Unlike many of its North African and Middle Eastern neighbors, Tunisia will soon be shifting from being a youth-bulge country to having a transitional age structure, characterized by lower fertility and mortality rates, a slower population growth rate, a rising median age, and a longer average life expectancy.

Currently, the sizable young working-age population is straining Tunisia's labor market and education and health care systems. Persistent high unemployment among Tunisia's growing workforce, particularly its increasing number of university graduates and women, was a key factor in the uprisings that led to the overthrow of the BEN ALI regime in 2011. In the near term, Tunisia's large number of jobless young, working-age adults; deficiencies in primary and secondary education; and the ongoing lack of job creation and skills mismatches could contribute to future unrest. In the longer term, a sustained low fertility rate will shrink future youth cohorts and alleviate demographic pressure on Tunisia's labor market, but employment and education hurdles will still need to be addressed.

Tunisia has a history of labor emigration. In the 1960s, workers migrated to European countries to escape poor economic conditions and to fill Europe's need for low-skilled labor in construction and manufacturing. The Tunisian Government signed bilateral labor agreements with France, Germany, Belgium, Hungary, and the Netherlands, with the expectation that Tunisian workers would eventually return home. At the same time, growing numbers of Tunisians headed to Libya, often illegally, to work in the expanding oil industry. In the mid-1970s, with European countries beginning to restrict immigration and Tunisian-Libyan tensions brewing, Tunisian economic migrants turned toward the Gulf countries. After mass expulsions from Libya in 1983, Tunisian migrants increasingly sought family reunification in Europe or moved illegally to southern Europe, while Tunisia itself developed into a transit point for sub-Saharan migrants heading to Europe.

Following the ousting of BEN ALI in 2011, the illegal migration of unemployed Tunisian youths to Italy and onward to France soared into the tens of thousands. Thousands more Tunisian and foreign workers escaping civil war in Libya flooded into Tunisia and joined the exodus. A readmission agreement signed by Italy and Tunisia in April 2011 helped stem the outflow, leaving Tunisia and international organizations to repatriate, resettle, or accommodate some 1 million Libyans and third-country nationals.

Age structure: *0-14 years:* 25.15% (male 1,482,303/female 1,385,407)
15-24 years: 13.99% (male 805,376/female 790,119)
25-54 years: 43.38% (male 2,410,724/female 2,536,015)
55-64 years: 9.54% (male 543,865/female 543,642)
65 years and over: 7.95% (male 429,681/female 476,668) (2017 est.)

Dependency ratios: *total dependency ratio:* 45.6
youth dependency ratio: 34.5
elderly dependency ratio: 11.1
potential support ratio: 9 (2015 est.)

Median age: *total:* 31.6 years
male: 31 years
female: 32.2 years (2017 est.)
country comparison to the world: 97

Population growth rate: 1.01% (2017 est.)
country comparison to the world: 112

Birth rate: 18.2 births/1,000 population (2017 est.)
country comparison to the world: 95

Death rate: 6.3 deaths/1,000 population (2017 est.)
country comparison to the world: 151

Net migration rate: -1.7 migrant(s)/1,000 population (2017 est.)
country comparison to the world: 152

Population distribution: the overwhelming majority of the population is located in the northern

half of the country; the south remains largely underpopulated

Urbanization: *urban population:* 67.3% of total population (2017)
rate of urbanization: 1.28% annual rate of change (2015-20 est.)

Major urban areas—population: TUNIS (capital) 1.993 million (2015)

Sex ratio: *at birth:* 1.07 male(s)/female
0-14 years: 1.06 male(s)/female
15-24 years: 1.01 male(s)/female
25-54 years: 0.94 male(s)/female
55-64 years: 1.03 male(s)/female
65 years and over: 0.97 male(s)/female
total population: 0.99 male(s)/female (2016 est.)

Maternal mortality ratio: 62 deaths/100,000 live births (2015 est.)
country comparison to the world: 89

Infant mortality rate: *total:* 12.1 deaths/1,000 live births
male: 13.3 deaths/1,000 live births
female: 10.8 deaths/1,000 live births (2017 est.)
country comparison to the world: 119

Life expectancy at birth: *total population:* 75.7 years
male: 74.1 years
female: 77.4 years (2017 est.)
country comparison to the world: 101

Total fertility rate: 2.23 children born/woman (2017 est.)
country comparison to the world: 97

Contraceptive prevalence rate: 62.5% (2011/12)
Health expenditures: 7% of GDP (2014)
country comparison to the world: 81

Physicians density: 1.65 physicians/1,000 population (2014)

Hospital bed density: 2.1 beds/1,000 population (2012)

Drinking water source:
improved:
urban: 100% of population
rural: 93.2% of population
total: 97.7% of population
unimproved:
urban: 0% of population
rural: 6.8% of population
total: 2.3% of population (2015 est.)

Sanitation facility access:
improved:
urban: 97.4% of population
rural: 79.8% of population
total: 91.6% of population
unimproved:
urban: 2.6% of population
rural: 20.2% of population
total: 8.4% of population (2015 est.)

HIV/AIDS—adult prevalence rate: <.1% (2016 est.)

HIV/AIDS—people living with HIV/AIDS: 2,900 (2016 est.)
country comparison to the world: 112

HIV/AIDS—deaths: <100 (2016 est.)

Obesity—adult prevalence rate: 26.9% (2016)
country comparison to the world: 40

Children under the age of 5 years underweight: 2.3% (2012)
country comparison to the world: 118
Education expenditures: 6.3% of GDP (2012)
country comparison to the world: 38

Literacy: *definition:* age 15 and over can read and write
total population: 81.8%
male: 89.6%
female: 74.2% (2015 est.)

School life expectancy (primary to tertiary education): *total:* 15 years
male: NA
female: NA (2015)

Unemployment, youth ages 15-24: *total:* 37.6%
male: 35.7%
female: 41.8% (2012 est.)
country comparison to the world: 10

GOVERNMENT

Country name: *conventional long form:* Republic of Tunisia
conventional short form: Tunisia
local long form: Al Jumhuriyah at Tunisiyah
local short form: Tunis
etymology: the country name derives from the capital city of Tunis

Government type: parliamentary republic

Capital: *name:* Tunis
geographic coordinates: 36 48 N, 10 11 E
time difference: UTC+1 (6 hours ahead of Washington, DC, during Standard Time)

Administrative divisions: 24 governorates (wilayat, singular—wilayah); Beja (Bajah), Ben Arous (Bin 'Arus), Bizerte (Banzart), Gabes (Qabis), Gafsa (Qafsah), Jendouba (Jundubah), Kairouan (Al Qayrawan), Kasserine (Al Qasrayn), Kebili (Qibili), Kef (Al Kaf), L'Ariana (Aryanah), Mahdia (Al Mahdiyah), Manouba (Manubah), Medenine (Madanin), Monastir (Al Munastir), Nabeul (Nabul), Sfax (Safaqis), Sidi Bouzid (Sidi Bu Zayd), Siliana (Silyanah), Sousse (Susah), Tataouine (Tatawin), Tozeur (Tawzar), Tunis, Zaghouan (Zaghwan)

Independence: 20 March 1956 (from France)

National holiday: Independence Day, 20 March (1956); Revolution and Youth Day, 14 January (2011)

Constitution: *history:* several previous; latest approved by Constituent Assembly 26 January 2014, signed by the president, prime minister, and Constituent Assembly speaker 27 January 2014
amendments: proposed by the president of the republic or by one-third of members of the Assembly of the Representatives of the People; following review by the Constitutional Court, approval to proceed requires an absolute majority vote by the Assembly and final passage requires a two-thirds majority vote by the Assembly; the president can opt to submit an amendment to a referendum,

which requires an absolute majority of votes cast for passage (2017)

Legal system: mixed legal system of civil law, based on the French civil code, and Islamic law; some judicial review of legislative acts in the Supreme Court in joint session

International law organization participation: has not submitted an ICJ jurisdiction declaration; accepts ICCt jurisdiction

Citizenship: *citizenship by birth:* no
citizenship by descent only: at least one parent must be a citizen of Tunisia
dual citizenship recognized: yes
residency requirement for naturalization: 5 years

Suffrage: 18 years of age; universal except for active government security forces (including the police and the military), people with mental disabilities, people who have served more than three months in prison (criminal cases only), and people given a suspended sentence of more than six months

Executive branch: *chief of state:* President Beji CAID ESSEBSI (since 31 December 2014)

head of government: Prime Minister Youssef CHAHED (since 27 August 2016)
cabinet: selected by the prime minister and approved by the Assembly of the Representatives of the People
elections/appointments: president directly elected by absolute majority popular vote in 2 rounds if needed for a 5-year term (eligible for a second term); election last held on 23 November and 21 December 2014 (next to be held in 2019); following legislative elections, the prime minister is selected by the majority party or majority coalition and appointed by the president
election results: Beji CAID ESSEBSI elected president in second round; percent of vote—Beji CAID ESSEBSI (Call for Tunisia) 55.7%, Moncef MARZOUKI (CPR) 44.3%

Legislative branch: *description:* unicameral Assembly of the Representatives of the People or Nuwwab ash-Sha'b (Assemblee des representants du peuple) (217 seats; members directly elected in multi-seat constituencies by proportional representation vote; members serve 5-year terms)
elections: initial election held on 26 October 2014 (next to be held in 2019)
election results: percent of vote by party—Call for Tunisia 37.6%, Ennahdha 27.8%, UPL 4.1%, Popular Front 3.6%, Afek Tounes 3.0%, CPR 2.1%, other 21.8%; seats by party—Call to Tunisia 86, Nahda 69, UPL 16, Popular Front 15, Afek Tounes 8, CPR 4, other 17, independent 2

Judicial branch: *highest court(s):* Court of Cassation or Cour de Cassation (organized into 1 civil and 3 criminal chambers); Constitutional Court (consists of 12 members)
note: the new Tunisian constitution of January 2014 called for the creation of a constitutional court by the end of 2015; the court will consist of 12 members—4 each appointed by the president, the Supreme Judicial Council or SJC (an independent 4-part body consisting mainly of elected judges and the remainder legal specialists), and the Chamber of the People's Deputies (parliament); members will serve 9-year terms with one-third of the membership renewed every 3 years; in late 2015, the International Commission of Jurists called on Tunisia's parliament to revise the draft on the Constitutional Court to ensure compliance with international standards; as of spring 2017 the court had not been appointed
judge selection and term of office: Supreme Court judges nominated by the SJC; judge tenure based on terms of appointment; Constitutional Court members appointed 3 each by the president of the republic, the Chamber of the People's Deputies, and the SJC; members serve 9-year terms with one-third of the membership renewed every 3 years
subordinate courts: Courts of Appeal; administrative courts; Court of Audit; Housing Court; courts of first instance; lower district courts; military courts

Political parties and leaders: Afek Tounes [Yassine BRAHIM]
Al Badil Al-Tounisi (The Tunisian Alternative) [Mehdi JOMAA]
Call for Tunisia (Nidaa Tounes) [Hafedh CAID ESSEBSI]
Congress for the Republic or CPR [Imed DAIMI]
Current of Love [Hachemi HAMDI] (formerly the Popular Petition party)
Democratic Alliance Party [Mohamed HAMDI]
Democratic Current [Mohamed ABBOU]
Democratic Patriots' Unified Party [Zied LAKHDHAR]
Free Patriotic Union or UPL (Union patriotique libre) [Slim RIAHI]
Green Tunisia Party [Abdelkader ZITOUNI]
Machrou Tounes (Tunisia Project) [Mohsen MARZOUK]
Movement of Socialist Democrats or MDS [Ahmed KHASKHOUSSI]
Nahda Movement (The Renaissance) [Rachid GHANNOUCHI]
National Destourian Initiative or El Moubadra [Kamel MORJANE]
Party of the Democratic Arab Vanguard [Ahmed JEDDICK, Kheireddine SOUABNI]
People's Movement [Zouheir MAGHZAOUI]
Popular Front (coalition includes Democratic Patriots' Unified Party, Workers' Party, Green Tunisia, Tunisian Ba'ath Movement, and Party of the Democratic Arab Vanguard)
Republican Party [Maya JRIBI]
Tunisian Ba'ath Movement [OMAR Othman BELHADJ]
Workers' Party [Hamma HAMMAMI]

Political pressure groups and leaders: Tunisian Association of Women Democrats or ATFD
Tunisian League for Human Rights or LTDH [Jamel MSALLEM]
Tunisian General Labor Union or UGTT [Noureddine TABOUBI]
Tunisian Women's Association for Research and Development or AFTURD

International organization participation: ABEDA, AfDB, AFESD, AMF, AMU, AU, BSEC (observer), CAEU, CD, EBRD, FAO, G-11, G-77, IAEA, IBRD, ICAO, ICC (national committees), ICCt, ICRM, IDA, IDB, IFAD, IFC, IFRCS, IHO, ILO, IMF, IMO, IMSO, Interpol, IOC, IOM, IPU, ISO, ITSO, ITU, ITUC (NGOs), LAS, MIGA, MONUSCO, NAM, OAS (observer), OIC, OIF, OPCW, OSCE (partner), UN, UNCTAD, UNESCO, UNHCR, UNIDO, UNOCI, UNWTO, UPU, WCO, WFTU (NGOs), WHO, WIPO, WMO, WTO

Diplomatic representation in the US: *chief of mission:* Ambassador Faycal GOUIA (since 18 May 2015)
chancery: 1515 Massachusetts Avenue NW, Washington, DC 20005
telephone: [1] (202) 862-1850
FAX: [1] (202) 862-1858

Diplomatic representation from the US: *chief of mission:* Ambassador Daniel H. RUBINSTEIN (since 26 October 2015)
embassy: Zone Nord-Est des Berges du Lac Nord de Tunis 1053
mailing address: Zone Nord-Est des Berges du Lac Nord de Tunis 1053
telephone: [216] 71 107-000
FAX: [216] 71 963-263

Flag description: red with a white disk in the center bearing a red crescent nearly encircling a red five-pointed star; resembles the Ottoman flag (red banner with white crescent and star) and recalls Tunisia's history as part of the Ottoman Empire; red represents the blood shed by martyrs in the struggle against oppression, white stands for peace; the crescent and star are traditional symbols of Islam
note: the flag is based on that of Turkey, itself a successor state to the Ottoman Empire

National symbol(s): encircled red star and crescent; national colors: red, white

National anthem: *name:* "Humat Al Hima" (Defenders of the Homeland)
lyrics/music: Mustafa Sadik AL-RAFII and Aboul-Qacem ECHEBBI/Mohamad Abdel WAHAB
note: adopted 1957, replaced 1958, restored 1987; Mohamad Abdel WAHAB also composed the music for the anthem of the United Arab Emirates

ECONOMY

Economy—overview: Tunisia's diverse, market-oriented economy has long been cited as a success story in Africa and the Middle East, but it faces an array of challenges following the 2011 Arab Spring revolution, including slow economic growth and high unemployment. Following an ill-fated experiment with socialist economic policies in the 1960s, Tunisia embarked on a successful strategy focused on bolstering exports, foreign investment, and tourism, all of which have become central to the country's economy. Key exports now include textiles and apparel, food products, petroleum products, chemicals, and phosphates, with about

80% of exports bound for Tunisia's main economic partner, the EU.

Tunisia's liberal strategy, coupled with investments in education and infrastructure, fueled decades of 4-5% annual GDP growth and improved living standards. Former President Zine el Abidine BEN ALI (1987-2011) continued these policies, but as his reign wore on cronyism and corruption stymied economic performance, and unemployment rose among the country's growing ranks of university graduates. These grievances contributed to the January 2011 overthrow of BEN ALI, sending Tunisia's economy into a tailspin as tourism and investment declined sharply.

Tunisia's government remains under pressure to boost economic growth quickly to mitigate chronic socio-economic challenges, especially high levels of youth unemployment, which has persisted since the revolution in 2011. Successive terrorist attacks against the tourism sector and worker strikes in the phosphate sector, which combined account for nearly 15% of GDP, slowed growth from 2015 to 2017. Tunis is seeking increased foreign investment and working with labor unions to limit labor disruption.

GDP (purchasing power parity): $135.9 billion (2017 est.)
$132.8 billion (2016 est.)
$131.5 billion (2015 est.)
note: data are in 2017 dollars
country comparison to the world: 79

GDP (official exchange rate): $39.88 billion (2016 est.)

GDP—real growth rate: 2.3% (2017 est.)
1% (2016 est.)
1.1% (2015 est.)
country comparison to the world: 143

GDP—per capita (PPP): $12,000 (2017 est.)
$11,800 (2016 est.)
$11,800 (2015 est.)
note: data are in 2017 dollars
country comparison to the world: 131

Gross national saving: 13.8% of GDP (2017 est.)
13.5% of GDP (2016 est.)
12.5% of GDP (2015 est.)
country comparison to the world: 130

GDP—composition, by end use:
household consumption: 72.2%
government consumption: 21.2%
investment in fixed capital: 18%
investment in inventories: 0.7%
exports of goods and services: 44.7%
imports of goods and services: -56.8% (2017 est.)

GDP—composition, by sector of origin:
agriculture: 10%
industry: 25.9%
services: 63.5% (2017 est.)

Agriculture—products: olives, olive oil, grain, tomatoes, citrus fruit, sugar beets, dates, almonds; beef, dairy products

Industries: petroleum, mining (particularly phosphate, iron ore), tourism, textiles, footwear, agribusiness, beverages

Industrial production growth rate: 0.5% (2017 est.)

country comparison to the world: 182

Labor force: 4.054 million (2017 est.)
country comparison to the world: 92

Labor force—by occupation: *agriculture:* 14.8%
industry: 33.2%
services: 51.7% (2014 est.)

Unemployment rate: 13% (2017 est.)
14% (2016 est.)
country comparison to the world: 162

Population below poverty line: 15.5% (2010 est.)

Household income or consumption by percentage share: *lowest 10%:* 2.6%
highest 10%: 27% (2010 est.)

Distribution of family income—Gini index: 40 (2005 est.)
41.7 (1995 est.)
country comparison to the world: 63

Budget: *revenues:* $9.397 billion
expenditures: $11.61 billion (2017 est.)
Taxes and other revenues: 23.6% of GDP (2017 est.)
country comparison to the world: 125

Budget surplus (+) or deficit (-): -5.6% of GDP (2017 est.)
country comparison to the world: 172

Public debt: 66.5% of GDP (2017 est.)
62.4% of GDP (2016 est.)
country comparison to the world: 57

Fiscal year: calendar year

Inflation rate (consumer prices): 4.5% (2017 est.)
3.7% (2016 est.)
country comparison to the world: 168

Central bank discount rate: 5.75% (31 December 2010)
country comparison to the world: 73

Commercial bank prime lending rate: 7.31% (31 December 2016 est.)
6.76% (31 December 2013 est.)
country comparison to the world: 114

Stock of narrow money: $11.78 billion (31 December 2017 est.)
$11.86 billion (31 December 2016 est.)
country comparison to the world: 82

Stock of broad money: $26.91 billion (31 December 2017 est.)
$26.73 billion (31 December 2016 est.)
country comparison to the world: 85

Stock of domestic credit: $35.41 billion (31 December 2017 est.)
$34.18 billion (31 December 2016 est.)
country comparison to the world: 73

Market value of publicly traded shares: $8.887 billion (31 December 2012 est.)
$9.662 billion (31 December 2011 est.)
$10.68 billion (31 December 2010 est.)
country comparison to the world: 75

Current account balance: -$3.487 billion (2017 est.)
-$3.776 billion (2016 est.)
country comparison to the world: 171

Exports: $14.22 billion (2017 est.)
$13.57 billion (2016 est.)

country comparison to the world: 78

Exports—commodities: clothing, semi-finished goods and textiles, agricultural products, mechanical goods, phosphates and chemicals, hydrocarbons, electrical equipment

Exports—partners: France 30.1%, Italy 19.3%, Germany 10.7%, Spain 5.2%, Libya 4.3% (2016)

Imports: $19.57 billion (2017 est.)
$18.37 billion (2016 est.)
country comparison to the world: 74

Imports—commodities: textiles, machinery and equipment, hydrocarbons, chemicals, foodstuffs

Imports—partners: France 18%, Italy 14.8%, China 8%, Germany 7.3%, Spain 4.3%, Algeria 4.1% (2016)

Reserves of foreign exchange and gold: $5.699 billion (31 December 2017 est.)
$5.941 billion (31 December 2016 est.)
country comparison to the world: 90

Debt—external: $31.05 billion (31 December 2017 est.)
$28.93 billion (31 December 2016 est.)
country comparison to the world: 79

Stock of direct foreign investment—at home: $38.33 billion (31 December 2017 est.)
$37.34 billion (31 December 2016 est.)
country comparison to the world: 63

Stock of direct foreign investment—abroad: $285 million (31 December 2017 est.)
$285 million (31 December 2016 est.)
country comparison to the world: 97

Exchange rates: Tunisian dinars (TND) per US dollar—
2.422 (2017 est.)
2.148 (2016 est.)
2.148 (2015 est.)
1.9617 (2014 est.)
1.6976 (2013 est.)

ENERGY

Electricity access: *electrification—total population:* 100% (2016)

Electricity—production: 18.39 billion kWh (2015 est.)
country comparison to the world: 79

Electricity—consumption: 15.12 billion kWh (2015 est.)
country comparison to the world: 78

Electricity—exports: 500 million kWh (2015 est.)
country comparison to the world: 69

Electricity—imports: 403 million kWh (2015 est.)
country comparison to the world: 85

Electricity—installed generating capacity: 5.028 million kW (2015 est.)
country comparison to the world: 78

Electricity—from fossil fuels: 93.4% of total installed capacity (2015 est.)
country comparison to the world: 57

Electricity—from nuclear fuels: 0% of total installed capacity (2015 est.)
country comparison to the world: 194

Electricity—from hydroelectric plants: 1.3% of total installed capacity (2015 est.)
country comparison to the world: 145

Electricity—from other renewable sources: 5.6% of total installed capacity (2015 est.)
country comparison to the world: 93

Crude oil—production: 48,670 bbl/day (2016 est.)
country comparison to the world: 57

Crude oil—exports: 46,370 bbl/day (2014 est.)
country comparison to the world: 43

Crude oil—imports: 23,600 bbl/day (2014 est.)
country comparison to the world: 62

Crude oil—proved reserves: 425 million bbl (1 January 2017 es)
country comparison to the world: 51

Refined petroleum products—production: 34,760 bbl/day (2014 est.)
country comparison to the world: 86

Refined petroleum products—consumption: 98,000 bbl/day (2015 est.)
country comparison to the world: 82

Refined petroleum products—exports: 16,710 bbl/day (2014 est.)
country comparison to the world: 73

Refined petroleum products—imports: 72,610 bbl/day (2014 est.)
country comparison to the world: 68

Natural gas—production: 1.575 billion cu m (2015 est.)
country comparison to the world: 61

Natural gas—consumption: 7.67 billion cu m (2015 est.)
country comparison to the world: 60

Natural gas—exports: 0 cu m (2013 est.)
country comparison to the world: 196

Natural gas—imports: 2.97 billion cu m (2015 est.)
country comparison to the world: 45

Natural gas—proved reserves: 65.13 billion cu m (1 January 2017 es)
country comparison to the world: 60

Carbon dioxide emissions from consumption of energy: 21 million Mt (2013 est.)
country comparison to the world: 81

COMMUNICATIONS

Telephones—fixed lines: *total subscriptions:* 974,975
subscriptions per 100 inhabitants: 9 (July 2016 est.)
country comparison to the world: 78

Telephones—mobile cellular: *total:* 14,282,078
subscriptions per 100 inhabitants: 128 (July 2016 est.)
country comparison to the world: 68

Telephone system: *general assessment:* above the African average and continuing to be upgraded; key centers are Sfax, Sousse, Bizerte, and Tunis; telephone network is completely digitized; Internet access available throughout the country
domestic: in an effort to jumpstart expansion of the fixed-line network, the government awarded a concession to build and operate a VSAT network with international connectivity; rural areas are served by wireless local loops; competition between several mobile-cellular service providers has resulted in lower activation and usage charges and a strong surge in subscribership; overall fixed-line and mobile-cellular teledensity has reached about 135 telephones per 100 persons
international: country code—216; a landing point for the SEA-ME-WE-4 submarine cable system that provides links to Europe, Middle East, and Asia; satellite earth stations—1 Intelsat (Atlantic Ocean) and 1 Arabsat; coaxial cable and microwave radio relay to Algeria and Libya; participant in Medarabtel; 2 international gateway digital switches (2016)

Broadcast media: broadcast media is mainly government-controlled; the state-run Tunisian Radio and Television Establishment (ERTT) operates 2 national TV networks, several national radio networks, and a number of regional radio stations; 1 TV and 3 radio stations are privately owned and report domestic news stories directly from the official Tunisian news agency; the state retains control of broadcast facilities and transmitters through L'Office National de la Telediffusion; Tunisians also have access to Egyptian, pan-Arab, and European satellite TV channels (2007)

Internet country code: .tn

Internet users: *total:* 5,665,242

percent of population: 50.9% (July 2016 est.)
country comparison to the world: 65

TRANSPORTATION

National air transport system: number of registered air carriers: 3
inventory of registered aircraft operated by air carriers: 41
annual passenger traffic on registered air carriers: 3,496,190
annual freight traffic on registered air carriers: 10,354,241 mt-km (2015)
Civil aircraft registration country code prefix: TS (2016)

Airports: 29 (2013)
country comparison to the world: 118

Airports—with paved runways: *total:* 15
over 3,047 m: 4
2,438 to 3,047 m: 6
1,524 to 2,437 m: 2
914 to 1,523 m: 3 (2013)

Airports—with unpaved runways: *total:* 14
1,524 to 2,437 m: 1
914 to 1,523 m: 5
under 914 m: 8 (2013)

Pipelines: condensate 68 km; gas 3,111 km; oil 1,381 km; refined products 453 km (2013)

Railways: *total:* 2,173 km (1,991 in use)
standard gauge: 471 km 1.435-m gauge
dual gauge: 8 km 1.435-1.000-m gauge
narrow gauge: 1,694 km 1.000-m gauge (65 km electrified) (2014)
country comparison to the world: 69

Roadways: *total:* 19,418 km
paved: 14,756 km (includes 357 km of expressways)
unpaved: 4,662 km (2010)
country comparison to the world: 112

Merchant marine: *total:* 62
by type: general cargo 13, oil tanker 1, other 48 (2017)
country comparison to the world: 104

Ports and terminals: *major seaport(s):* Bizerte, Gabes, Rades, Sfax, Skhira

MILITARY AND SECURITY

Military expenditures: 2.32% of GDP (2016)
2.27% of GDP (2015)
1.91% of GDP (2014)
1.64% of GDP (2013)
1.51% of GDP (2012)
country comparison to the world: 57

Military branches: Tunisian Armed Forces (Forces Armees Tunisiens, FAT): Tunisian Army (includes Tunisian Air Defense Force), Tunisian Navy, Republic of Tunisia Air Force (Al-Quwwat al-Jawwiya al-Jamahiriyah At'Tunisia) (2012)

Military service age and obligation: 20-23 years of age for compulsory service, 1-year service obligation; 18-23 years of age for voluntary service; Tunisian nationality required (2012)

TERRORISM

Terrorist groups—home based: Ansar al-Shari'a in Tunisia (AAS-T): aim(s): expand its influence in Tunisia and, ultimately, replace the Tunisian Government with Sharia
area(s) of operations: headquartered in Tunisia, where members instigate riots and violent demonstrations, engage in attacks, and teach religious classes to locals; assassins and suicide bombers target Tunisian military and security personnel, Tunisian politicans, religious sites, and groups and places representing Western influence such as tourists and places they frequent; in February and July 2013, members were implicated in the assassination of Tunisian politicians Chokri BELAID and Mohamed BRAHMI; on 14 September 2012, members overran and ransacked the US Embassy and a nearby school in Tunis, causing millions of dollars in damage; manpower strength was unknown as of early 2017; majority of fighters are Tunisian; in recent years, some of the fighters have either left the country or defected to join other armed groups; outlawed in Tunisia

Terrorist groups—foreign based: al-Qa'ida (AQ): aim(s): overthrow the Tunisian Government and, ultimately, establish a pan-Islamic caliphate under a strict Salafi Muslim interpretation of Sharia
area(s) of operation: maintains a longtime operational presence and established networks

al-Qaida in the Islamic Maghreb (AQIM): aim(s): replace the Tunisian Government with Sharia and, ultimately, establish a regional Islamic caliphate across all of North and West Africa
area(s) of operation: operationally active, primarily in the south near the borders with Algeria; Uqba bin Nafi Battalion, AQIM's branch in

Tunisia, has claimed several lethal assaults in recent years against Tunisian military and security forces; AQIM's most deadliest attack on Tunisian forces happened in the Mount Chaambi region of Kasserine Governorate in July 2014, when operatives killed 15 soldiers and wounded at least 20

Islamic State of Iraq and the Levant (ISIL): *aim(s):* replace the Tunisian Government with an Islamic state and implement ISIL's strict interpretation of Sharia

area(s) of operation: Tunisian ISIL fighters stage attacks just across the border in Libya against government facilities and personnel and foreign tourists in Tunisia; bolstering its operational and recruitment presence throughout the country; operatives armed with AK-47 assault rifles and rocket-propelled grenades killed 12 Tunisian security officials and seven civilians during attacks on Army and police posts on 7 March 2016 in the southeastern border town of Ben Guerdane, Medenine Governorate; assessed in 2016 to have recruited 4,000-6,000 Tunisians from all walks of

life in person and online to fight in Syria and Iraq but primarily in Libya, where some have become key ISIL figures; Tunisia is a top source country for ISIL recruits

TRANSNATIONAL ISSUES

Disputes—international: none

Trafficking in persons: current situation: Tunisia is a source, destination, and possible transit country for men, women, and children subjected to forced labor and sex trafficking; Tunisia's increased number of street children, rural children working to support their families, and migrants who have fled unrest in neighboring countries are vulnerable to human trafficking; organized gangs force street children to serve as thieves, beggars, and drug transporters; Tunisian women have been forced into prostitution domestically and elsewhere in the region under false promises of legitimate work; East and West African women may be subjected to forced labor as domestic workers

tier rating: Tier 2 Watch List – Tunisia does not fully comply with the minimum standards for the elimination of trafficking; however, it is making significant efforts to do so; in 2014, Tunisia was granted a waiver from an otherwise required downgrade to Tier 3 because its government has a written plan that, if implemented would constitute making significant efforts to bring itself into compliance with the minimum standards for the elimination of trafficking; in early 2015, the government drafted a national anti-trafficking action plan outlining proposals to raise awareness and enact draft anti-trafficking legislation; authorities did not provide data on the prosecution and conviction of offenders but reportedly identified 24 victims, as opposed to none in 2013, and operated facilities specifically dedicated to trafficking victims, regardless of nationality and gender; the government did not fully implement its national victim referral mechanism; some unidentified victims were not protected from punishment for unlawful acts directly resulting from being trafficked (2015)

TURKEY

INTRODUCTION

Background: Modern Turkey was founded in 1923 from the remnants of the defeated Ottoman Empire by national hero Mustafa KEMAL, who was later honored with the title Ataturk or "Father of the Turks." Under his leadership, the country adopted radical social, legal, and political reforms. After a period of one-party rule, an experiment with multi-party politics led to the 1950 election victory of the opposition Democrat Party and the peaceful transfer of power. Since then, Turkish political parties have multiplied, but democracy has been fractured by periods of instability and military coups (1960, 1971, 1980), which in each case eventually resulted in a return of formal political power to civilians. In 1997, the military again helped engineer the ouster—popularly dubbed a "post-modern coup"—of the then Islamic-oriented government. A coup attempt was made in July 2016 by a faction of the Turkish Armed Forces.

Turkey intervened militarily on Cyprus in 1974 to prevent a Greek takeover of the island and has since acted as patron state to the "Turkish Republic of Northern Cyprus," which only Turkey recognizes. A separatist insurgency begun in 1984 by the Kurdistan Workers' Party (PKK), a US-designated terrorist organization, has long dominated the

attention of Turkish security forces and claimed more than 40,000 lives. In 2013, the Turkish Government and the PKK conducted negotiations aimed at ending the violence, however intense fighting resumed in 2015. Turkey joined the UN in 1945 and in 1952 it became a member of NATO. In 1963, Turkey became an associate member of the European Community; it began accession talks with the EU in 2005. Over the past decade, economic reforms, coupled with some political reforms, have contributed to a growing economy, although economic growth slowed in recent years.

From 2015 and continuing through 2016, Turkey witnessed an uptick in terrorist violence, including major attacks in Ankara, Istanbul, and throughout the predominantly Kurdish southeastern region of Turkey. On 15 July 2016, elements of the Turkish Armed forces attempted a coup that ultimately failed following widespread popular resistance. More than 240 people were killed and over 2,000 injured when Turkish citizens took to the streets en masse to confront the coup forces. In response, Turkish Government authorities arrested, suspended, or dismissed more than 100,000 security personnel, journalists, judges, academics, and civil servants due to their alleged connection with the attempted coup. The government accused followers of an Islamic transnational religious and social movement for allegedly instigating the failed coup and designates the followers as terrorists. Following the failed coup, the Turkish Government instituted a State of Emergency in July 2016 that has been extended to July 2017. The Turkish Government conducted a referendum on 16 April 2017 that will, when implemented, change Turkey from a parliamentary to a presidential system.

GEOGRAPHY

Location: Southeastern Europe and Southwestern Asia (that portion of Turkey west of the Bosporus is geographically part of Europe), bordering the Black Sea, between Bulgaria and Georgia, and bordering the Aegean Sea and the Mediterranean Sea, between Greece and Syria

Geographic coordinates: 39 00 N, 35 00 E

Map references: Middle East

Area: *total:* 783,562 sq km
land: 769,632 sq km
water: 13,930 sq km
country comparison to the world: 38

Area—comparative: slightly larger than Texas
Land boundaries: total: 2,816 km
border countries (8): Armenia 311 km, Azerbaijan 17 km, Bulgaria 223 km, Georgia 273 km, Greece 192 km, Iran 534 km, Iraq 367 km, Syria 899 km

Coastline: 7,200 km

Maritime claims: *territorial sea:* 6 nm in the Aegean Sea; 12 nm in Black Sea and in Mediterranean Sea
exclusive economic zone: in Black Sea only: to the maritime boundary agreed upon with the former USSR

Climate: temperate; hot, dry summers with mild, wet winters; harsher in interior

Terrain: high central plateau (Anatolia); narrow coastal plain; several mountain ranges

Elevation: *mean elevation:* 1,132 m

elevation extremes: *lowest point:* Mediterranean Sea 0 m
highest point: Mount Ararat 5,137 m

Natural resources: coal, iron ore, copper, chromium, antimony, mercury, gold, barite, borate, celestite (strontium), emery, feldspar, limestone, magnesite, marble, perlite, pumice, pyrites (sulfur), clay, arable land, hydropower

Land use: *agricultural land:* 49.7%
arable land: 26.7%;
permanent crops: 4%;
permanent pasture: 19%
forest: 14.9%
other: 35.4% (2011 est.)
Irrigated land: 52,150 sq km (2012)

Population—distribution: the most densely populated area is found around the Bosporus in the northwest where 20% of the population lives in Istanbul; with the exception of Ankara, urban centers remain small and scattered throughout the interior of Anatolia; an overall pattern of peripheral development exists, particularly along the Aegean Sea coast in the west, and the Tigris and Euphrates River systems in the southeast

Natural hazards: severe earthquakes, especially in northern Turkey, along an arc extending from the Sea of Marmara to Lake Van; landslides; flooding
volcanism: limited volcanic activity; its three historically active volcanoes, Ararat, Nemrut Dagi, and Tendurek Dagi have not erupted since the 19th century or earlier

Environment—current issues: water pollution from dumping of chemicals and detergents; air pollution, particularly in urban areas; deforestation; concern for oil spills from increasing Bosporus ship traffic

Environment—international agreements: *party to:* Air Pollution, Antarctic Treaty, Biodiversity, Climate Change, Desertification, Endangered Species, Hazardous Wastes, Ozone Layer Protection, Ship Pollution, Wetlands
signed, but not ratified: Environmental Modification

Geography—note: strategic location controlling the Turkish Straits (Bosporus, Sea of Marmara, Dardanelles) that link the Black and Aegean Seas; the 3% of Turkish territory north of the Straits lies in Europe and goes by the names of European Turkey, Eastern Thrace, or Turkish Thrace; the 97% of the country in Asia is referred to as Anatolia; Mount Ararat, the legendary landing place of Noah's ark, is in the far eastern portion of the country

PEOPLE AND SOCIETY

Population: 80,845,215 (July 2017 est.)
country comparison to the world: 18

Nationality: *noun:* Turk(s)
adjective: Turkish

Ethnic groups: Turkish 70-75%, Kurdish 19%, other minorities 7-12% (2016 est.)

Languages: Turkish (official), Kurdish, other minority languages

Religions: Muslim 99.8% (mostly Sunni), other 0.2% (mostly Christians and Jews)

Age structure: *0-14 years:* 24.68% (male 10,209,284/female 9,745,057)
15-24 years: 15.99% (male 6,601,471/female 6,324,277)
25-54 years: 43.21% (male 17,691,703/female 17,243,428)
55-64 years: 8.58% (male 3,448,232/female 3,492,199)
65 years and over: 7.53% (male 2,712,323/female 3,377,241) (2017 est.)

Dependency ratios: *total dependency ratio:* 50.1
youth dependency ratio: 38.4
elderly dependency ratio: 11.7
potential support ratio: 8.5 (2015 est.)

Median age: *total:* 30.9 years
male: 30.5 years
female: 31.4 years (2017 est.)
country comparison to the world: 110

Population growth rate: 0.52% (2017 est.)
country comparison to the world: 153

Birth rate: 15.7 births/1,000 population (2017 est.)
country comparison to the world: 119

Death rate: 6 deaths/1,000 population (2017 est.)
country comparison to the world: 165

Net migration rate: -4.5 migrant(s)/1,000 population (2017 est.)
country comparison to the world: 185

Population distribution: the most densely populated area is found around the Bosporus in the northwest where 20% of the population lives in Istanbul; with the exception of Ankara, urban centers remain small and scattered throughout the interior of Anatolia; an overall pattern of peripheral development exists, particularly along the Aegean Sea coast in the west, and the Tigris and Euphrates River systems in the southeast

Urbanization: *urban population:* 74.4% of total population (2017)
rate of urbanization: 1.54% annual rate of change (2015-20 est.)

Major urban areas—population: Istanbul 14.164 million; ANKARA (capital) 4.75 million; Izmir 3.04 million; Bursa 1.923 million; Adana 1.83 million; Gaziantep 1.528 million (2015)

Sex ratio: *at birth:* 1.05 male(s)/female
0-14 years: 1.05 male(s)/female
15-24 years: 1.04 male(s)/female
25-54 years: 1.03 male(s)/female
55-64 years: 0.99 male(s)/female
65 years and over: 0.8 male(s)/female
total population: 1.01 male(s)/female (2016 est.)

Mother's mean age at first birth: 22.3 years (2010 est.)

Maternal mortality ratio: 16 deaths/100,000 live births (2015 est.)
country comparison to the world: 134

Infant mortality rate: *total:* 17.6 deaths/1,000 live births
male: 18.8 deaths/1,000 live births
female: 16.3 deaths/1,000 live births (2017 est.)
country comparison to the world: 91

Life expectancy at birth: *total population:* 75 years

male: 72.7 years
female: 77.5 years (2017 est.)
country comparison to the world: 113

Total fertility rate: 2.01 children born/woman (2017 est.)
country comparison to the world: 118

Contraceptive prevalence rate: 73.5% (2013)
Health expenditures: 5.4% of GDP (2014)
country comparison to the world: 131

Physicians density: 1.75 physicians/1,000 population (2014)

Hospital bed density: 2.5 beds/1,000 population (2011)

Drinking water source:
improved:
urban: 100% of population
rural: 100% of population
total: 100% of population
unimproved:
urban: 0% of population
rural: 0% of population
total: 0% of population (2015 est.)

Sanitation facility access:
improved:
urban: 98.3% of population
rural: 85.5% of population
total: 94.9% of population
unimproved:
urban: 1.7% of population
rural: 14.5% of population
total: 5.1% of population (2015 est.)

HIV/AIDS—adult prevalence rate: NA

HIV/AIDS—people living with HIV/AIDS: NA

HIV/AIDS—deaths: NA

Obesity—adult prevalence rate: 32.1% (2016)
country comparison to the world: 17

Children under the age of 5 years underweight: 1.9% (2013)
country comparison to the world: 123
Education expenditures: 4.8% of GDP (2013)
country comparison to the world: 142

Literacy: *definition:* age 15 and over can read and write
total population: 95.6%
male: 98.6%
female: 92.6% (2015 est.)

School life expectancy (primary to tertiary education): *total:* 16 years
male: 17 years
female: 16 years (2013)

Unemployment, youth ages 15-24: *total:* 18.5%
male: 16.5%
female: 22.2% (2015 est.)
country comparison to the world: 66

GOVERNMENT

Country name: *conventional long form:* Republic of Turkey
conventional short form: Turkey
local long form: Turkiye Cumhuriyeti
local short form: Turkiye
etymology: the name means "Land of the Turks"

Government type: parliamentary republic

Capital: *name:* Ankara

geographic coordinates: 39 56 N, 32 52 E

time difference: UTC+2 (7 hours ahead of Washington, DC, during Standard Time)

Administrative divisions: 81 provinces (iller, singular—ili); Adana, Adiyaman, Afyonkarahisar, Agri, Aksaray, Amasya, Ankara, Antalya, Ardahan, Artvin, Aydin, Balikesir, Bartin, Batman, Bayburt, Bilecik, Bingol, Bitlis, Bolu, Burdur, Bursa, Canakkale, Cankiri, Corum, Denizli, Diyarbakir, Duzce, Edirne, Elazig, Erzincan, Erzurum, Eskisehir, Gaziantep, Giresun, Gumushane, Hakkari, Hatay, Igdir, Isparta, Istanbul, Izmir (Smyrna), Kahramanmaras, Karabuk, Karaman, Kars, Kastamonu, Kayseri, Kilis, Kirikkale, Kirklareli, Kirsehir, Kocaeli, Konya, Kutahya, Malatya, Manisa, Mardin, Mersin, Mugla, Mus, Nevsehir, Nigde, Ordu, Osmaniye, Rize, Sakarya, Samsun, Sanliurfa, Siirt, Sinop, Sirnak, Sivas, Tekirdag, Tokat, Trabzon (Trebizond), Tunceli, Usak, Van, Yalova, Yozgat, Zonguldak

Independence: 29 October 1923 (republic proclaimed succeeding the Ottoman Empire)

National holiday: Republic Day, 29 October (1923)

Constitution: *history:* several previous; latest ratified 9 November 1982

amendments: proposed by written consent of at least one-third of Grand National Assembly (GNA) members; adoption of draft amendments requires two debates in plenary GNA session and three-fifths majority vote of all GNA members; the president of the republic can request GNA reconsideration of the amendment and, if readopted by two-thirds majority GNA vote, the president may submit the amendment to a referendum; passage by referendum requires absolute majority vote; amended several times, last in 2017 (2017)

Legal system: civil law system based on various European legal systems, notably the Swiss civil code

International law organization participation: has not submitted an ICJ jurisdiction declaration; non-party state to the ICCt

Citizenship: *citizenship by birth:* no

citizenship by descent only: at least one parent must be a citizen of Turkey

dual citizenship recognized: yes, but requires prior permission from the government

residency requirement for naturalization: 5 years

Suffrage: 18 years of age; universal

Executive branch: *chief of state:* President Recep Tayyip ERDOGAN (since 10 August 2014)

head of government: Prime Minister Binali YILDIRIM (since 22 May 2016); Deputy Prime Ministers Recep AKDAG (since 20 July 2017), Bekir BOZDAG (since 20 July 2017), Hakan CAVUSOGLU (since 20 July 2017), Fikri ISIK (since 20 July 2017), Mehmet SIMSEK (since 24 November 2015)

cabinet: Council of Ministers nominated by the prime minister, appointed by the president (until the next parliamentary or presidential election following the April 2017 referendum)

elections/appointments: president directly elected by absolute majority popular vote in 2 rounds if needed for a 5-year term (eligible for a second term); prime minister appointed by the president from among members of parliament; note—a 2007 constitutional amendment changed the presidential electoral process to direct popular vote; prime minister appointed by the president from among members of the Grand National Assembly of Turkey

election results: Recep Tayyip ERDOGAN elected president; Recep Tayyip ERDOGAN (AKP) 51.8%, Ekmeleddin IHSANOGLU (independent) 38.4%, Selahattin DEMIRTAS (HDP) 9.8%

Legislative branch: *description:* unicameral Grand National Assembly of Turkey or Turkiye Buyuk Millet Meclisi (550 seats (will increase to 600 with next election following the April 2017 referendum); members directly elected in multiseat constituencies by proportional representation vote to serve 4-year terms)

elections: last held on 1 November 2015 (next to be held on 3 November 2019)

election results: percent of vote by party—AKP 49.5%, CHP 25.3%, MHP 11.9%, HDP 10.8%, other 2.5%; seats by party—AKP 317, CHP 134, HDP 59, MHP 40, ; note—only parties surpassing the 10% threshold can win parliamentary seats

Judicial branch: highest court: Constitutional Court or Anayasa Mahkemesi (consists of 15 members); Court of Cassation (consists of about 390 judges and is organized into civil and penal chambers); Council of State (organized into 15 divisions—14 judicial and 1 consultative—each with a division head and at least 5 members)

judge selection and term of office: Constitutional Court members—3 appointed by the Grand National Assembly and 12 by the president of the republic; court president and 2 deputy presidents appointed from among its members for 4-year terms; judges appointed for 12-year, nonrenewable terms with mandatory retirement at age 65; Court of Cassation judges appointed by the Council of Judges and Prosecutors (HSK), a 13-member body of judicial officials; Court of Cassation judges appointed until retirement at age 65; Council of State members appointed by the HSK and by the president of the republic; members appointed for renewable, 4-year terms

subordinate courts: regional appeals courts; basic (first instance) courts, peace courts; military courts; state security courts; specialized courts, including administrative and audit

Political parties and leaders: Democrat Party or DP [Gultekin UYSAL]

Democratic Left Party or DSP [Onder AKSAKAL]

Felicity Party or SP [Temel KARAMOLLAOGLU]

Good Party or IYI [Meral AKSENER]

Grand Unity Party or BBP [Mustafa DESTICI]

Justice and Development Party or AKP [Recep Tayyip ERDOGAN]

Nationalist Movement Party or MHP [Devlet BAHCELI]

Patriotic Party or VP [Dogu PERINCEK]

People's Democratic Party or HDP [Selahattin DEMIRTAS and Serpil KEMALBAY]; note—DEMIRTAS was detained by Turkish authorities in November 2016 over his alleged links to the PKK

Republican People's Party or CHP [Kemal KILICDAROGLU]

True Path Party or DYP [Cetin OZACIRGOZ]

Political pressure groups and leaders: Confederation of Public Sector Unions or KESK [Mehmet BOZGEYIK, Aysun GEZEN, cochairs]

Confederation of Revolutionary Workers Unions or DISK [Kani BEKO]

Independent Industrialists' and Businessmen's Association or MUSIAD [Abfuttahman KAAN]

Moral Rights Workers Union or Hak-Is [Mahmut ARSLAN]

Turkish Confederation of Employer Associations or TISK [Kudret ONEN]

Turkish Confederation of Labor Unions or Turk-Is [Ergun ATALAY]

Turkish Confederation of Tradesmen and Craftsmen or TESK [Bendevi PALANDOKEN]

Turkish Industrialists' and Businessmen's Association or TUSIAD [Erol BILECIK]

Turkish Union of Chambers of Commerce and Commodity Exchanges or TOBB [M. Rifat HISARCIKLIOGLU]

International organization participation: ADB (nonregional member), Australia Group, BIS, BSEC, CBSS (observer), CD, CE, CERN (observer), CICA, CPLP (associate observer), D-8, EAPC, EBRD, ECO, EU (candidate country), FAO, FATF, G-20, IAEA, IBRD, ICAO, ICC (national committees), ICRM, IDA, IDB, IEA, IFAD, IFC, IFRCS, IHO, ILO, IMF, IMO, IMSO, Interpol, IOC, IOM, IPU, ISO, ITSO, ITU, ITUC (NGOs), MIGA, NATO, NEA, NSG, OAS (observer), OECD, OIC, OPCW, OSCE, Pacific Alliance (observer), Paris Club (associate), PCA, PIF (partner), SCO (dialogue member), SELEC, UN, UNCTAD, UNESCO, UNHCR, UNIDO, UNIFIL, UNRWA, UNWTO, UPU, WCO, WFTU (NGOs), WHO, WIPO, WMO, WTO, ZC

Diplomatic representation in the US: chief of mission: Ambassador Serdar KILIC (since 21 May 2014)

chancery: 2525 Massachusetts Avenue NW, Washington, DC 20008

telephone: [1] (202) 612-6700

FAX: [1] (202) 612-6744

consulate(s) general: Boston, Chicago, Houston, Los Angeles, Miami, New York

Diplomatic representation from the US: *chief of mission:* Ambassador (vacant); Charge d'Affaires Philip KOSNETT (since 16 October 2017)

embassy: 110 Ataturk Boulevard, Kavaklidere, 06100 Ankara

mailing address: PSC 93, Box 5000, APO AE 09823
telephone: [90] (312) 455-5555
FAX: [90] (312) 467-0019
consulate(s) general: Istanbul
consulate(s): Adana

Flag description: red with a vertical white crescent moon (the closed portion is toward the hoist side) and white five-pointed star centered just outside the crescent opening; the flag colors and designs closely resemble those on the banner of the Ottoman Empire, which preceded modern-day Turkey; the crescent moon and star serve as insignia for Turkic peoples; according to one interpretation, the flag represents the reflection of the moon and a star in a pool of blood of Turkish warriors

National symbol(s): star and crescent; national colors: red, white

National anthem: *name:* "Istiklal Marsi" (Independence March)
lyrics/music: Mehmet Akif ERSOY/Zeki UNGOR
note: lyrics adopted 1921, music adopted 1932; the anthem's original music was adopted in 1924; a new composition was agreed upon in 1932

ECONOMY

Economy—overview: Turkey's largely free-market economy is driven by its industry and, increasingly, service sectors, although its traditional agriculture sector still accounts for about 25% of employment. The automotive, petrochemical, and electronics industries have risen in importance and surpassed the traditional textiles and clothing sectors within Turkey's export mix. However, the recent period of political stability and economic dynamism has given way to domestic uncertainty and security concerns, which are generating financial market volatility and weighing on Turkey's economic outlook.

Current government policies emphasize populist spending measures and credit breaks, while implementation of structural economic reforms has slowed. The government is playing a more active role in some strategic sectors and has used economic institutions and regulators to target political opponents, undermining private sector confidence in the judicial system. Between July 2016 and March 2017, three credit ratings agencies downgraded Turkey's sovereign credit ratings, citing concerns about the rule of law and the pace of economic reforms.

Turkey remains highly dependent on imported oil and gas but is pursuing energy relationships with a broader set of international partners and taking steps to increase use of domestic energy sources including renewables, nuclear, and coal. The joint Turkish-Azerbaijani Trans-Anatolian Natural Gas Pipeline is moving forward to increase transport of Caspian gas to Turkey and Europe, and when completed will help diversify Turkey's sources of imported gas.

After Turkey experienced a severe financial crisis in 2001, Ankara adopted financial and fiscal reforms as part of an IMF program. The reforms strengthened the country's economic fundamentals and ushered in an era of strong growth averaging more than 6% annually until 2008. An aggressive privatization program also reduced state involvement in basic industry, banking, transport, power generation, and communication. Global economic conditions and tighter fiscal policy caused GDP to contract in 2009, but Turkey's well-regulated financial markets and banking system helped the country weather the global financial crisis, and GDP growth rebounded to around 9% in 2010 and 2011, as exports and investment recovered following the crisis.

Since 2014, productivity and growth has slowed to reveal persistent underlying imbalances in the Turkish economy. In particular, Turkey's large current account deficit means it must rely on external investment inflows to finance growth, leaving the economy vulnerable to destabilizing shifts in investor confidence. Other troublesome trends include rising unemployment and inflation, which increased in 2017, given the Turkish lira's continuing depreciation against the dollar. Although government debt remains low at about 30% of GDP, bank and corporate borrowing has almost tripled as a percent of GDP during the past decade, outpacing its emerging-market peers and prompting investor concerns about its long-term sustainability.

GDP (purchasing power parity): $2.133 trillion (2017 est.)
$2.029 trillion (2016 est.)
$1.966 trillion (2015 est.)
note: data are in 2017 dollars
country comparison to the world: 14

GDP (official exchange rate): $841.2 billion (2016 est.)

GDP—real growth rate: 5.1% (2017 est.)
3.2% (2016 est.)
6.1% (2015 est.)
country comparison to the world: 38

GDP—per capita (PPP): $26,500 (2017 est.)
$25,400 (2016 est.)
$25,000 (2015 est.)
note: data are in 2017 dollars
country comparison to the world: 75

Gross national saving: 25.1% of GDP (2017 est.)
24.5% of GDP (2016 est.)
24.8% of GDP (2015 est.)
country comparison to the world: 49

GDP—composition, by end use:
household consumption: 59.8%
government consumption: 15.3%
investment in fixed capital: 28.6%
investment in inventories: -0.9%
exports of goods and services: 24%
imports of goods and services: -26.8% (2017 est.)

GDP—composition, by sector of origin:
agriculture: 6.7%
industry: 31.8%
services: 61.4% (2017 est.)

Agriculture—products: tobacco, cotton, grain, olives, sugar beets, hazelnuts, pulses, citrus; livestock

Industries: textiles, food processing, automobiles, electronics, mining (coal, chromate, copper, boron), steel, petroleum, construction, lumber, paper

Industrial production growth rate: 3% (2017 est.)
country comparison to the world: 94

Labor force: 31.3 million
note: this number is for the domestic labor force only; number does not include about 1.2 million Turks working abroad, nor refugees (2017 est.)
country comparison to the world: 20

Labor force—by occupation: *agriculture:* 18.4%
industry: 26.6%
services: 54.9% (2016)

Unemployment rate: 11.2% (2017 est.)
10.9% (2016 est.)
country comparison to the world: 145

Population below poverty line: 21.9% (2015 est.)

Household income or consumption by percentage share: *lowest 10%:* 2.1%
highest 10%: 30.3% (2008)

Distribution of family income—Gini index: 40.2 (2010)
43.6 (2003)
country comparison to the world: 60

Budget: *revenues:* $173.9 billion
expenditures: $190.4 billion (2017 est.)
Taxes and other revenues: 20.7% of GDP (2017 est.)
country comparison to the world: 147

Budget surplus (+) or deficit (-): -2% of GDP (2017 est.)
country comparison to the world: 84

Public debt: 29.6% of GDP (2017 est.)
29.4% of GDP (2016 est.)
country comparison to the world: 164

Fiscal year: calendar year

Inflation rate (consumer prices): 10.9% (2017 est.)
7.8% (2016 est.)
country comparison to the world: 205

Central bank discount rate: 5.25% (31 December 2011)
15% (22 December 2009)
country comparison to the world: 78

Commercial bank prime lending rate: 15.2% (31 December 2017 est.)
14.74% (31 December 2016 est.)
country comparison to the world: 42

Stock of narrow money: $122 billion (31 December 2017 est.)
$108.7 billion (31 December 2016 est.)
country comparison to the world: 33

Stock of broad money: $445 billion (31 December 2017 est.)
$399.4 billion (31 December 2016 est.)
country comparison to the world: 24

Stock of domestic credit: $612.6 billion (31 December 2017 est.)
$549.9 billion (31 December 2016 est.)
country comparison to the world: 24

Market value of publicly traded shares: $188.9 billion (31 December 2015 est.)
$219.8 billion (31 December 2014 est.)
$195.7 billion (31 December 2013 est.)
country comparison to the world: 36

Current account balance: -$38.95 billion (2017 est.)
-$32.61 billion (2016 est.)
country comparison to the world: 198

Exports: $157.3 billion (2017 est.)
$150.2 billion (2016 est.)
country comparison to the world: 34

Exports—commodities: apparel, foodstuffs, textiles, metal manufactures, transport equipment

Exports—partners: Germany 9.8%, UK 8.2%, Iraq 5.4%, Italy 5.3%, US 4.7%, France 4.2% (2016)

Imports: $196.8 billion (2017 est.)
$191 billion (2016 est.)
country comparison to the world: 24

Imports—commodities: machinery, chemicals, semi-finished goods, fuels, transport equipment

Imports—partners: China 12.8%, Germany 10.8%, Russia 7.6%, US 5.5%, Italy 5.2% (2016)

Reserves of foreign exchange and gold: $107.5 billion (31 December 2017 est.)
$106.1 billion (31 December 2016 est.)
country comparison to the world: 25

Debt—external: $429.6 billion (31 December 2017 est.)
$404.9 billion (31 December 2016 est.)
country comparison to the world: 30

Stock of direct foreign investment—at home: $143.7 billion (31 December 2017 est.)
$133.2 billion (31 December 2016 est.)
country comparison to the world: 39

Stock of direct foreign investment—abroad: $41.81 billion (31 December 2017 est.)
$38.31 billion (31 December 2016 est.)
country comparison to the world: 46

Exchange rates: Turkish liras (TRY) per US dollar—
3.628 (2017 est.)
3.0201 (2016 est.)
3.0201 (2015 est.)
2.72 (2014 est.)
2.1885 (2013 est.)

ENERGY

Electricity access: *electrification—total population:* 100% (2016)

Electricity—production: 245.8 billion kWh (2015 est.)
country comparison to the world: 19

Electricity—consumption: 213.2 billion kWh (2015 est.)
country comparison to the world: 20

Electricity—exports: 1.442 billion kWh (2016 est.)
country comparison to the world: 49

Electricity—imports: 6.4 billion kWh (2016 est.)
country comparison to the world: 33

Electricity—installed generating capacity: 73.15 million kW (2015 est.)
country comparison to the world: 15

Electricity—from fossil fuels: 56.8% of total installed capacity (2015 est.)
country comparison to the world: 138

Electricity—from nuclear fuels: 0% of total installed capacity (2015 est.)
country comparison to the world: 195

Electricity—from hydroelectric plants: 35.4% of total installed capacity (2015 est.)
country comparison to the world: 59

Electricity—from other renewable sources: 11.2% of total installed capacity (2015 est.)
country comparison to the world: 66

Crude oil—production: 49,500 bbl/day (2016 est.)
country comparison to the world: 55

Crude oil—exports: 0 bbl/day (2016 est.)
country comparison to the world: 200

Crude oil—imports: 506,300 bbl/day (2016 est.)
country comparison to the world: 18

Crude oil—proved reserves: 388.5 million bbl (1 January 2017 es)
country comparison to the world: 54

Refined petroleum products—production: 618,300 bbl/day (2016 est.)
country comparison to the world: 29

Refined petroleum products—consumption: 943,700 bbl/day (2016 est.)
country comparison to the world: 24

Refined petroleum products—exports: 134,900 bbl/day (2016 est.)
country comparison to the world: 39

Refined petroleum products—imports: 527,700 bbl/day (2016 est.)
country comparison to the world: 16

Natural gas—production: 381 million cu m (2015 est.)
country comparison to the world: 73

Natural gas—consumption: 81.35 billion cu m (2015 est.)
country comparison to the world: 15

Natural gas—exports: 624 million cu m (2015 est.)
country comparison to the world: 41

Natural gas—imports: 48.43 billion cu m (2015 est.)
country comparison to the world: 7

Natural gas—proved reserves: 18.49 billion cu m (1 January 2017 es)
country comparison to the world: 77

Carbon dioxide emissions from consumption of energy: 319 million Mt (2013 est.)
country comparison to the world: 20

COMMUNICATIONS

Telephones—fixed lines: *total subscriptions:* 11,077,559
subscriptions per 100 inhabitants: 14 (July 2016 est.)
country comparison to the world: 19

Telephones—mobile cellular: *total:* 75,061,699
subscriptions per 100 inhabitants: 94 (July 2016 est.)
country comparison to the world: 21

Telephone system: *general assessment:* comprehensive telecommunications network undergoing rapid modernization and expansion, especially in mobile-cellular services
domestic: additional digital exchanges are permitting a rapid increase in subscribers; the construction of a network of technologically advanced intercity trunk lines, using both fiber-optic cable and digital microwave radio relay, is facilitating communication between urban centers; remote areas are reached by a domestic satellite system; combined fixed-line and mobile-cellular teledensity is roughly 105 telephones per 100 persons
international: country code—90; international service is provided by the SEA-ME-WE-3 submarine cable and by submarine fiber-optic cables in the Mediterranean and Black Seas that link Turkey with Italy, Greece, Israel, Bulgaria, Romania, and Russia; satellite earth stations—12 Intelsat; mobile satellite terminals—328 in the Inmarsat and Eutelsat systems (2016)

Broadcast media: Turkish Radio and Television Corporation (TRT) operates multiple TV and radio networks and stations; multiple privately owned national television stations and up to 300 private regional and local television stations; multi-channel cable TV subscriptions available; more than 1,000 private radio broadcast stations (2009)

Internet country code: .tr

Internet users: *total:* 46,838,412

percent of population: 58.3% (July 2016 est.)
country comparison to the world: 19

TRANSPORTATION

National air transport system: number of registered air carriers: 15
inventory of registered aircraft operated by air carriers: 531
annual passenger traffic on registered air carriers: 96,604,665
annual freight traffic on registered air carriers: 2,882.162 million mt-km (2015)
Civil aircraft registration country code prefix: TC (2016)

Airports: 98 (2013)
country comparison to the world: 58

Airports—with paved runways: *total:* 91
over 3,047 m: 16
2,438 to 3,047 m: 38
1,524 to 2,437 m: 17
914 to 1,523 m: 16
under 914 m: 4 (2013)

Airports—with unpaved runways: *total:* 7
1,524 to 2,437 m: 1
914 to 1,523 m: 4
under 914 m: 2 (2013)

Heliports: 20 (2013)

Pipelines: gas 12,603 km; oil 3,038 km (2016)

Railways: *total:* 12,008 km
standard gauge: 12,008 km 1.435-m gauge (3,216 km electrified) (2014)
country comparison to the world: 20

Roadways: *total:* 385,754 km
paved: 352,268 km (includes 2,127 km of expressways)
unpaved: 33,486 km (2012)
country comparison to the world: 19

Waterways: 1,200 km (2010)
country comparison to the world: 59

Merchant marine: *total:* 1,285
by type: bulk carrier 78, container ship 50, general cargo 432, oil tanker 121, other 604 (2017)
country comparison to the world: 22

Ports and terminals: *major seaport(s):* Aliaga, Ambarli, Diliskelesi, Eregli, Izmir, Kocaeli (Izmit), Mersin (Icel), Limani, Yarimca
container port(s) (TEUs): Ambarli (3,062,000), Mersin (Icel) (1,428,000) (2015)
LNG terminal(s) (import): Izmir Aliaga, Marmara Ereglisi

MILITARY AND SECURITY

Military expenditures: 1.73% of GDP (2016)
1.85% of GDP (2015)
1.9% of GDP (2014)
1.96% of GDP (2013)
2.05% of GDP (2012)
country comparison to the world: 35

Military branches: Turkish Armed Forces (TSK): Turkish Land Forces (Turk Kara Kuvvetleri), Turkish Naval Forces (Turk Deniz Kuvvetleri; includes naval air and naval infantry), Turkish Air Forces (Turk Hava Kuvvetleri) (2013)

Military service age and obligation: 21-41 years of age for male compulsory military service (in case of mobilization, up to 65 years of age); 18 years of age for voluntary service; 12-month conscript obligation for non-university graduates, 6-12 months for university graduates (graduates of higher education may perform 6 months of military service as short-term privates, or 12 months as reserve officers); conscripts are called to register at age 20, for service at 21; women serve in the Turkish Armed Forces only as officers; reserve obligation to age 41; Turkish citizens with a residence or work permit who have worked abroad for at least 3 years (1095 days) can be exempt from military service in exchange for 6,000 EUR or its equivalent in foreign currencies; a law passed in December 2014 introduced a one-time payment scheme which exempted Turkish citizens 27 and older from conscription in exchange for a payment of $8,150 (2013)

Military—note: the ruling Justice and Development Party (AKP) has actively pursued the goal of asserting civilian control over the military since first taking power in 2002; the Turkish Armed Forces (TSK) role in internal security has been significantly reduced; the TSK leadership continues to be an influential institution within Turkey, but plays a much smaller role in politics; the Turkish military remains focused on the threats

emanating from the Syrian civil war, Russia's actions in Ukraine, and the PKK insurgency; primary domestic threats are listed as fundamentalism (with the definition in some dispute with the civilian government), separatism (Kurdish discontent), and the extreme left wing; Ankara strongly opposed establishment of an autonomous Kurdish region in Iraq; an overhaul of the Turkish Land Forces Command (TLFC) taking place under the "Force 2014" program is to produce 20-30% smaller, more highly trained forces characterized by greater mobility and firepower and capable of joint and combined operations; the TLFC has taken on increasing international peacekeeping responsibilities including in Afghanistan; the Turkish Navy is a regional naval power that wants to develop the capability to project power beyond Turkey's coastal waters; the Navy is heavily involved in NATO, multinational, and UN operations; its roles include control of territorial waters and security for sea lines of communications; the Turkish Air Force adopted an "Aerospace and Missile Defense Concept" in 2002 and has initiated project work on an integrated missile defense system; Air Force priorities include attaining a modern deployable, survivable, and sustainable force structure, and establishing a sustainable command and control system; Turkey is a NATO ally and hosts NATO's Land Forces Command in Izmir, as well as the AN/TPY-2 radar as part of NATO Missile Defense (2014)

TERRORISM

Terrorist groups—home based: Revolutionary People's Liberation Party/Front (DHKP/C): aim(s): install a Marxist-Leninist government in Turkey
area(s) of operation: headquartered in Turkey, where the group has assassinated numerous Turkish businessmen, security officers, judiciary personnel, and attacked US personnel and facilities in Turkey over the years; has revived its attacks, primarily in Istanbul, against Turkish Government elements in recent years; launched rocket attacks on police and government buildings in Istanbul as recently as 21 January 2017; known for employing youths sympathetic to the group's cause to participate in violent riots; participates in terrorist acts with other armed groups, such as in August 2015, when a female member and a female from another group shot at the US Consulate in Istanbul, resulting in no fatalities; DHKP/C's central leadership directs the group's affairs in Turkey and abroad; senior leaders' whereabouts are unknown; numerous senior leaders and operatives have been arrested in recent years; assessed to have several dozen members operating in Turkey; outlawed in Turkey

Terrorist groups—foreign based: *Islamic State of Iraq and the Levant (ISIL): aim(s):* replace the Turkish Government with an Islamic state and implement ISIL's strict interpretation of Sharia
area(s) of operation: launches rocket attacks into southern Turkey from northern Syria; moves fighters and supplies across the Turkey-Syria

border; responsible for suicide bombings and gunfire attacks on 28 June 2016 at Ataturk Aiport in Istanbul, killing 44 locals and foreigners and injuring at least 240; suicide bombers killed 102 people at a peace rally in Ankara on 10 October 2015, marking the deadliest attack in modern Turkish history; actively recruits fighters

Kurdistan Workers Party (PKK) (Kongra-Gel): *aim(s):* establish Kurdistan, which includes land in eastern and southeastern Turkey
area(s) of operation: PKK attacks have surged since 2016 in the southeast and spilled over to the country's western cities; targets primarily tourist locations and government, military, and security personnel and facilities; in October 2016, the Turkish Government reported thousands of PKK fighters had been killed and over 600 Turkish security force members had lost their lives and Human Rights groups reported hundreds of civilian deaths since the conflict between the Turkish Government and PKK resumed in July 2015, following a 2-1/2-year ceasefire; outlawed in Turkey

TRANSNATIONAL ISSUES

Disputes—international: complex maritime, air, and territorial disputes with Greece in the Aegean Sea; status of north Cyprus question remains; Turkey has expressed concern over the status of Kurds in Iraq; in 2009, Swiss mediators facilitated an accord reestablishing diplomatic ties between Armenia and Turkey, but neither side has ratified the agreement and the rapprochement effort has faltered; Turkish authorities have complained that blasting from quarries in Armenia might be damaging the medieval ruins of Ani, on the other side of the Arpacay valley

Refugees and internally displaced persons: *refugees (country of origin):* 157,000 (Afghanistan); 152,000 (Iraq); 33,000 (Iran) (2017); 3,506,532 (Syria) (2018)
IDPs: 1.108 million (displaced from 1984-2005 because of fighting between the Kurdish PKK and Turkish military; most IDPs are Kurds from eastern and southeastern provinces; no information available on persons displaced by development projects) (2016)
stateless persons: 780 (2016)

Illicit drugs: key transit route for Southwest Asian heroin to Western Europe and, to a lesser extent, the US—via air, land, and sea routes; major Turkish and other international trafficking organizations operate out of Istanbul; laboratories to convert imported morphine base into heroin exist in remote regions of Turkey and near Istanbul; government maintains strict controls over areas of legal opium poppy cultivation and over output of poppy straw concentrate; lax enforcement of money-laundering controls

925

TURKMENISTAN

INTRODUCTION

Background: Present-day Turkmenistan covers territory that has been at the crossroads of civilizations for centuries. The area was ruled in antiquity by various Persian empires, and was conquered by Alexander the Great, Muslim armies, the Mongols, Turkic warriors, and eventually the Russians. In medieval times, Merv (located in present-day Mary province) was one of the great cities of the Islamic world and an important stop on the Silk Road. Annexed by Russia in the late 1800s, Turkmenistan later figured prominently in the anti-Bolshevik movement in Central Asia. In 1924, Turkmenistan became a Soviet republic; it achieved independence upon the dissolution of the USSR in 1991. Extensive hydrocarbon/natural gas reserves, which have yet to be fully exploited, have begun to transform the country. The Government of Turkmenistan is moving to expand its extraction and delivery projects and has attempted to diversify its gas export routes beyond Russia's pipeline network. In 2010, new gas export pipelines that carry Turkmen gas to China and to northern Iran began operating, effectively ending the Russian monopoly on Turkmen gas exports. In 2016, Russia and Iran halted their purchase of gas from Turkmenistan making China the only buyer of Turkmen gas. President for Life Saparmurat NYYAZOW died in December 2006, and Turkmenistan held its first multi-candidate presidential election in February 2007. Gurbanguly BERDIMUHAMEDOW, a deputy cabinet chairman under NYYAZOW, emerged as the country's new president. He was reelected in 2012 and again in 2017 with over 97% of the vote in both instances, in elections widely regarded as undemocratic.

GEOGRAPHY

Location: Central Asia, bordering the Caspian Sea, between Iran and Kazakhstan

Geographic coordinates: 40 00 N, 60 00 E

Map references: Asia

Area: *total:* 488,100 sq km
land: 469,930 sq km
water: 18,170 sq km
country comparison to the world: 54

Area—comparative: slightly more than three times the size of Georgia; slightly larger than California
Land boundaries: total: 4,158 km
border countries (4): Afghanistan 804 km, Iran 1,148 km, Kazakhstan 413 km, Uzbekistan 1,793 km

Coastline: 0 km (landlocked); note—Turkmenistan borders the Caspian Sea (1,768 km)

Maritime claims: none (landlocked)

Climate: subtropical desert

Terrain: flat-to-rolling sandy desert with dunes rising to mountains in the south; low mountains along border with Iran; borders Caspian Sea in west

Elevation: *mean elevation:* 230 m

elevation extremes: *lowest point:* Vpadina Akchanaya -81 m (Sarygamysh Koli is a lake in northern Turkmenistan with a water level that fluctuates above and below the elevation of Vpadina Akchanaya, the lake has dropped as low as -110 m)
highest point: Gora Ayriraba 3,139 m

Natural resources: petroleum, natural gas, sulfur, salt

Land use: *agricultural land:* 72%
arable land: 4.1%;
permanent crops: 0.1%;
permanent pasture: 67.8%
forest: 8.8%
other: 19.2% (2011 est.)
Irrigated land: 19,950 sq km (2012)

Population—distribution: the most densely populated areas are the southern, eastern, and northeastern oases; approximately 50% of the population lives in and around the capital of Ashgabat

Natural hazards: earthquakes; mudslides; droughts; dust storms; floods

Environment—current issues: contamination of soil and groundwater with agricultural chemicals, pesticides; salination, water logging of soil due to poor irrigation methods; Caspian Sea pollution; diversion of a large share of the flow of the Amu Darya into irrigation contributes to that river's inability to replenish the Aral Sea; desertification

Environment—international agreements: *party to:* Biodiversity, Climate Change, Climate Change-Kyoto Protocol, Desertification, Hazardous Wastes, Ozone Layer Protection
signed, but not ratified: none of the selected agreements

Geography—note: landlocked; the western and central low-lying desolate portions of the country make up the great Garagum (Kara-Kum) desert, which occupies over 80% of the country; eastern part is plateau

PEOPLE AND SOCIETY

Population: 5,351,277 (July 2017 est.)
country comparison to the world: 119

Nationality: *noun:* Turkmen(s)
adjective: Turkmen

Ethnic groups: Turkmen 85%, Uzbek 5%, Russian 4%, other 6% (2003)

Languages: Turkmen (official) 72%, Russian 12%, Uzbek 9%, other 7%

Religions: Muslim 89%, Eastern Orthodox 9%, unknown 2%

Age structure: *0-14 years:* 25.79% (male 699,612/female 680,583)
15-24 years: 18.39% (male 495,025/female 488,930)
25-54 years: 43.18% (male 1,147,044/female 1,163,762)
55-64 years: 7.9% (male 199,363/female 223,443)
65 years and over: 4.74% (male 110,505/female 143,010) (2017 est.)

Dependency ratios: *total dependency ratio:* 52.7
youth dependency ratio: 46.5
elderly dependency ratio: 6.2
potential support ratio: 16.1 (2015 est.)

Median age: *total:* 27.9 years
male: 27.5 years
female: 28.4 years (2017 est.)
country comparison to the world: 141

Population growth rate: 1.12% (2017 est.)
country comparison to the world: 102

Birth rate: 19.1 births/1,000 population (2017 est.)
country comparison to the world: 86

Death rate: 6.1 deaths/1,000 population (2017 est.)
country comparison to the world: 160

Net migration rate: -1.8 migrant(s)/1,000 population (2017 est.)
country comparison to the world: 154

Population distribution: the most densely populated areas are the southern, eastern, and northeastern oases; approximately 50% of the population lives in and around the capital of Ashgabat

Urbanization: *urban population:* 50.8% of total population (2017)
rate of urbanization: 1.87% annual rate of change (2015-20 est.)

Major urban areas—population: ASHGABAT (capital) 746,000 (2015)

Sex ratio: *at birth:* 1.05 male(s)/female
0-14 years: 1.03 male(s)/female
15-24 years: 1.01 male(s)/female
25-54 years: 0.98 male(s)/female
55-64 years: 0.89 male(s)/female
65 years and over: 0.77 male(s)/female
total population: 0.98 male(s)/female (2016 est.)

Mother's mean age at first birth: 24.6 years (2006 est.)

Maternal mortality ratio: 42 deaths/100,000 live births (2015 est.)
country comparison to the world: 104

Infant mortality rate: *total:* 34.3 deaths/1,000 live births
male: 41.2 deaths/1,000 live births
female: 27 deaths/1,000 live births (2017 est.)
country comparison to the world: 56

Life expectancy at birth: *total population:* 70.4 years
male: 67.4 years
female: 73.6 years (2017 est.)
country comparison to the world: 159

Total fertility rate: 2.07 children born/woman (2017 est.)
country comparison to the world: 110

Contraceptive prevalence rate: 50.2% (2015/16)
Health expenditures: 2.1% of GDP (2014)
country comparison to the world: 190

Physicians density: 2.29 physicians/1,000 population (2014)

Hospital bed density: 4 beds/1,000 population (2012)

Drinking water source:
improved:
urban: 89.1% of population
rural: 53.7% of population
total: 71.1% of population
unimproved:
urban: 10.9% of population
rural: 46.3% of population
total: 28.9% of population (2012 est.)

Sanitation facility access:
improved:
urban: 100% of population
rural: 98.2% of population
total: 99.1% of population
unimproved:
urban: 0% of population
rural: 1.8% of population
total: 0.9% of population (2012 est.)

HIV/AIDS—adult prevalence rate: NA

HIV/AIDS—people living with HIV/AIDS: NA

HIV/AIDS—deaths: NA

Obesity—adult prevalence rate: 18.6% (2016)
country comparison to the world: 117

Children under the age of 5 years underweight: 3.2% (2015)
country comparison to the world: 68
Education expenditures: 3% of GDP (2012)

Literacy: *definition:* age 15 and over can read and write
total population: 99.7%
male: 99.8%
female: 99.6% (2015 est.)

School life expectancy (primary to tertiary education): *total:* 11 years
male: 11 years
female: 11 years (2014)

GOVERNMENT

Country name: *conventional long form:* none
conventional short form: Turkmenistan
local long form: none
local short form: Turkmenistan
former: Turkmen Soviet Socialist Republic
etymology: the suffix "-stan" means "place of" or "country," so Turkmenistan literally means the "Land of the Turkmen [people]"

Government type: presidential republic; authoritarian

Capital: *name:* Ashgabat (Ashkhabad)
geographic coordinates: 37 57 N, 58 23 E
time difference: UTC+5 (10 hours ahead of Washington, DC, during Standard Time)

Administrative divisions: 5 provinces (welayatlar, singular—welayat) and 1 independent city*: Ahal Welayaty (Anew), Ashgabat*, Balkan Welayaty (Balkanabat), Dasoguz Welayaty, Lebap Welayaty (Turkmenabat), Mary Welayaty
note: administrative divisions have the same names as their administrative centers (exceptions have the administrative center name following in parentheses)

Independence: 27 October 1991 (from the Soviet Union)

National holiday: Independence Day, 27 October (1991)

Constitution: *history:* adopted 18 May 1992
amendments: proposed by the National Assembly; passage requires two-thirds majority vote of the total Assembly membership or absolute majority approval in a referendum; amended several times, last in 2016; note—in mid-2014, the president established a Constitutional Commission to initiate a process for developing constitutional reforms (2017)

Legal system: civil law system with Islamic law influences

International law organization participation: has not submitted an ICJ jurisdiction declaration; non-party state to the ICCt

Citizenship: *citizenship by birth:* no
citizenship by descent only: at least one parent must be a citizen of Turkmenistan
dual citizenship recognized: yes
residency requirement for naturalization: 7 years

Suffrage: 18 years of age; universal

Executive branch: *chief of state:* President Gurbanguly BERDIMUHAMEDOW (since 14 February 2007); note—the president is both chief of state and head of government

head of government: President Gurbanguly BERDIMUHAMEDOW (since 14 February 2007)
cabinet: Cabinet of Ministers appointed by the president
elections/appointments: president directly elected by absolute majority popular vote in 2 rounds if needed for a 7-year term (no term limits); election last held on 12 February 2017 (next to be held in February 2024)

election results: Gurbanguly BERDIMUHAMEDOW reelected president; percent of vote—Gurbanguly BERDIMUHAMEDOW (DPT) 97.7%, other 2.3%

Legislative branch: *description:* unicameral National Assembly or Mejlis (125 seats; members directly elected from single-seat constituencies by absolute majority vote; members serve 5-year terms)
elections: last held on 15 December 2013 (next to be held in December 2018), although interim elections are held on an ad hoc basis to fill vacant sets
election results: percent of vote by party—NA; seats by party—DPT 47, Organization of Trade Unions of Turkmenistan 33, Women's Union of Turkmenistan 16, PIE 14, Magtymguly Youth Organization 8, independent 7; note—all of these parties support President BERDIMUHAMEDOW

Judicial branch: *highest court(s):* Supreme Court of Turkmenistan (consists of the court president and 21 associate judges and organized into civil, criminal, and military chambers)
judge selection and term of office: judges appointed by the president for 5-year terms
subordinate courts: High Commercial Court; appellate courts; provincial, district, and city courts; military courts

Political parties and leaders: Agrarian Party of Turkmenistan or APT [Ovezmyrat ENERMYRADOW]
Democratic Party of Turkmenistan or DPT [Kasymguly BABAYEW]
Organization of Trade Unions of Turkmenistan
Magtymguly Youth Organization
Party of Industrialists and Entrepreneurs or PIE [Ovezmammed MAMMEDOW]
Women's Union of Turkmenistan
note: a law authorizing the registration of political parties went into effect in January 2012; unofficial, small opposition movements exist abroad

Political pressure groups and leaders: none

International organization participation: ADB, CIS (associate member, has not ratified the 1993 CIS charter although it participates in meetings and held the chairmanship of the CIS in 2012), EAPC, EBRD, ECO, FAO, G-77, IBRD, ICAO, ICRM, IDA, IDB, IFC, IFRCS, ILO, IMF, IMO, Interpol, IOC, IOM (observer), ISO (correspondent), ITU, MIGA, NAM, OIC, OPCW, OSCE, PFP, UN, UNCTAD, UNESCO, UNHCR, UNIDO, UNWTO, UPU, WCO, WFTU (NGOs), WHO, WIPO, WMO

Diplomatic representation in the US: chief of mission: Ambassador Mered Bairamovich ORAZOW (since 14 February 2001)
chancery: 2207 Massachusetts Avenue NW, Washington, DC 20008
telephone: [1] (202) 588-1500
FAX: [1] (202) 588-0697

Diplomatic representation from the US: *chief of mission:* Ambassador Allan MUSTARD (since 20 January 2015)
embassy: No. 9 1984 Street (formerly Pushkin Street), Ashgabat, Turkmenistan 744000

927

mailing address: 7070 Ashgabat Place, Washington, DC 20521-7070
telephone: [993] (12) 94-00-45
FAX: [993] (12) 94-26-14

Flag description: green field with a vertical red stripe near the hoist side, containing five tribal guls (designs used in producing carpets) stacked above two crossed olive branches; five white stars and a white crescent moon appear in the upper corner of the field just to the fly side of the red stripe; the green color and crescent moon represent Islam; the five stars symbolize the regions or welayats of Turkmenistan; the guls reflect the national identity of Turkmenistan where carpet-making has long been a part of traditional nomadic life
note: the flag of Turkmenistan is the most intricate of all national flags

National symbol(s): Akhal-Teke horse; national colors: green, white

National anthem: *name:* "Garassyz, Bitarap Turkmenistanyn" (Independent, Neutral, Turkmenistan State Anthem)
lyrics/music: collective/Veli MUKHATOV
note: adopted 1997, lyrics revised in 2008, following the death of President Saparmurat NYYAZOW, to eliminate references to him

ECONOMY

Economy—overview: Turkmenistan is largely a desert country with intensive agriculture in irrigated oases and significant natural gas and oil resources. The two largest crops are cotton, most of which is produced for export, and wheat, which is domestically consumed. Although agriculture accounts for almost 8% of GDP, it continues to employ nearly half of the country's workforce. Hydrocarbon exports, the bulk of which is natural gas going to China, make up 25% of Turkmenistan's GDP. Ashgabat has explored two initiatives to bring gas to new markets: a trans-Caspian pipeline that would carry gas to Europe and the Turkmenistan-Afghanistan-Pakistan-India gas pipeline. Both face major financing and security hurdles and are unlikely to be completed soon.

Turkmenistan's autocratic governments under presidents NIYAZOW (1991-2006) and BERDIMUHAMEDOW (since 2007) have made little progress improving the business climate, privatizing state-owned industries, and combating corruption, limiting economic development outside the energy sector. High energy prices in the mid-2000s allowed the government to undertake extensive development and social spending, including providing heavy utility subsidies.

Low energy prices since mid-2014 are hampering Turkmenistan's economic growth and reducing government revenues. The government has cut subsidies in several areas, and wage arrears have increased. In January 2014, the Central Bank of Turkmenistan devalued the manat by 19%, and downward pressure on the currency continues. There is a widening spread between the official exchange rate (4.1 TMM per US dollar) and the black market exchange rate (approximately 7 TMM per US dollar). Currency depreciation, corruption, isolationist policies, and limited spending on public services has resulted in a stagnate economy that is nearing crisis. Turkmenistan claims substantial foreign currency reserves, but non-transparent data limit international institutions' ability to verify this information.

GDP (purchasing power parity): $103.5 billion (2017 est.)
$97.16 billion (2016 est.)
$91.48 billion (2015 est.)
note: data are in 2017 dollars
country comparison to the world: 84

GDP (official exchange rate): $41.67 billion (2016 est.)

GDP—real growth rate: 6.5% (2017 est.)
6.2% (2016 est.)
6.5% (2015 est.)
country comparison to the world: 18

GDP—per capita (PPP): $18,700 (2017 est.)
$17,800 (2016 est.)
$17,000 (2015 est.)
note: data are in 2017 dollars
country comparison to the world: 94

Gross national saving: 23.9% of GDP (2017 est.)
23.5% of GDP (2016 est.)
19.1% of GDP (2015 est.)
country comparison to the world: 60

GDP—composition, by end use:
household consumption: 50%
government consumption: 8.2%
investment in fixed capital: 29%
investment in inventories: 0%
exports of goods and services: 29.7%
imports of goods and services: -16.9% (2017 est.)

GDP—composition, by sector of origin:
agriculture: 7.5%
industry: 44.9%
services: 47.7% (2017 est.)

Agriculture—products: cotton, grain, melons; livestock

Industries: natural gas, oil, petroleum products, textiles, food processing

Industrial production growth rate: 1% (2017 est.)
country comparison to the world: 167

Labor force: 2.305 million (2013 est.)
country comparison to the world: 117

Labor force—by occupation: *agriculture:* 48.2%
industry: 14%
services: 37.8% (2004 est.)

Unemployment rate: 11% (2014 est.)
10.6% (2013)
country comparison to the world: 142

Population below poverty line: 0.2% (2012 est.)

Household income or consumption by percentage share: *lowest 10%:* 2.6%
highest 10%: 31.7% (1998)

Distribution of family income—Gini index: 40.8 (1998)
country comparison to the world: 58

Budget: *revenues:* $4.436 billion
expenditures: $4.703 billion (2017 est.)

Taxes and other revenues: 10.6% of GDP (2017 est.)
country comparison to the world: 212

Budget surplus (+) or deficit (-): -0.6% of GDP (2017 est.)
country comparison to the world: 52

Public debt: 23.9% of GDP (2016 est.)
19.4% of GDP (2015 est.)
country comparison to the world: 181

Fiscal year: calendar year

Inflation rate (consumer prices): 6% (2017 est.)
3.6% (2016 est.)
country comparison to the world: 182

Central bank discount rate: 5% (31 December 2014)
5% (31 December 2013)
country comparison to the world: 81

Stock of narrow money: $1.326 billion (31 December 2015 est.)
$1.255 billion (31 December 2014 est.)
country comparison to the world: 148

Stock of broad money: $12.23 billion (31 December 2015 est.)
$5.632 billion (31 December 2014 est.)
country comparison to the world: 103

Stock of domestic credit: $28.4 billion (31 December 2015 est.)
$13.09 billion (31 December 2014 est.)
country comparison to the world: 81

Market value of publicly traded shares: $NA

Current account balance: -$6.417 billion (2017 est.)
-$7.605 billion (2016 est.)
country comparison to the world: 179

Exports: $7.394 billion (2017 est.)
$6.987 billion (2016 est.)
country comparison to the world: 101

Exports—commodities: gas, crude oil, petrochemicals, textiles, cotton fiber

Exports—partners: China 70%, Turkey 5.3%, Italy 5.3%, Afghanistan 4.5%, Russia 4.1% (2016)

Imports: $4.801 billion (2017 est.)
$5.001 billion (2016 est.)
country comparison to the world: 124

Imports—commodities: machinery and equipment, chemicals, foodstuffs

Imports—partners: Turkey 26.4%, Russia 10.5%, Japan 8.6%, Germany 8.2%, South Korea 7.8%, China 7.2%, Italy 5.2% (2016)

Reserves of foreign exchange and gold: $20.6 billion (31 December 2017 est.)
$25.05 billion (31 December 2016 est.)
country comparison to the world: 59

Debt—external: $443.4 million (31 December 2017 est.)
$425.3 million (31 December 2016 est.)
country comparison to the world: 181

Stock of direct foreign investment—at home: $3.061 billion (2013 est.)
$3.117 billion (2012 est.)
country comparison to the world: 111

Exchange rates: Turkmen manat (TMM) per US dollar—
4.125 (2017 est.)
3.5 (2016 est.)
3.5 (2015 est.)
3.5 (2014 est.)
2.85 (2013 est.)

ENERGY

Electricity access: *electrification—total population:* 100% (2016)

Electricity—production: 21.18 billion kWh (2015 est.)
country comparison to the world: 74

Electricity—consumption: 15.09 billion kWh (2015 est.)
country comparison to the world: 79

Electricity—exports: 3.201 billion kWh (2015 est.)
country comparison to the world: 41

Electricity—imports: 0 kWh (2016 est.)
country comparison to the world: 213

Electricity—installed generating capacity: 4.001 million kW (2015 est.)
country comparison to the world: 89

Electricity—from fossil fuels: 100% of total installed capacity (2015 est.)
country comparison to the world: 20

Electricity—from nuclear fuels: 0% of total installed capacity (2015 est.)
country comparison to the world: 197

Electricity—from hydroelectric plants: 0% of total installed capacity (2015 est.)
country comparison to the world: 210

Electricity—from other renewable sources: 0% of total installed capacity (2015 est.)
country comparison to the world: 210

Crude oil—production: 230,800 bbl/day (2016 est.)
country comparison to the world: 35

Crude oil—exports: 62,880 bbl/day (2014 est.)
country comparison to the world: 41

Crude oil—imports: 0 bbl/day (2014 est.)
country comparison to the world: 201

Crude oil—proved reserves: 600 million bbl (1 January 2017 es)
country comparison to the world: 46

Refined petroleum products—production: 191,100 bbl/day (2014 est.)
country comparison to the world: 51

Refined petroleum products—consumption: 158,000 bbl/day (2015 est.)
country comparison to the world: 66

Refined petroleum products—exports: 53,780 bbl/day (2014 est.)
country comparison to the world: 51

Refined petroleum products—imports: 0 bbl/day (2014 est.)
country comparison to the world: 213

Natural gas—production: 83.7 billion cu m (2015 est.)
country comparison to the world: 10

Natural gas—consumption: 67.52 billion cu m (2015 est.)
country comparison to the world: 20

Natural gas—exports: 40.3 billion cu m (2015 est.)
country comparison to the world: 9

Natural gas—imports: 0 cu m (2014 est.)
country comparison to the world: 199

Natural gas—proved reserves: 7.504 trillion cu m (1 January 2017 es)
country comparison to the world: 6

Carbon dioxide emissions from consumption of energy: 67 million Mt (2013 est.)
country comparison to the world: 52

COMMUNICATIONS

Telephones—fixed lines: *total subscriptions:* 665,000
subscriptions per 100 inhabitants: 13 (July 2016 est.)
country comparison to the world: 91

Telephones—mobile cellular: *total:* 8.575 million
subscriptions per 100 inhabitants: 162 (July 2016 est.)
country comparison to the world: 103

Telephone system: *general assessment:* telecommunications network is gradually improving
domestic: Turkmentelekom, in cooperation with foreign partners, has installed high-speed fiber-optic lines and has upgraded most of the country's telephone exchanges and switching centers with new digital technology; combined fixed-line and mobile teledensity is about 170 per 100 persons; Russia's Mobile Telesystems, the only foreign mobile-cellular service provider in Turkmenistan, had its operating license suspended in December 2010 but was able to resume operations in September 2012; Turkmenistan's first telecommunication satellite was launched in 2015 and is expected to greatly improve connectivity in the country
international: country code—993; linked by fiber-optic cable and microwave radio relay to other CIS republics and to other countries by leased connections to the Moscow international gateway switch; an exchange in Ashgabat switches international traffic through Turkey via Intelsat; satellite earth stations—1 Orbita and 1 Intelsat (2016)

Broadcast media: broadcast media is government controlled and censored; 7 state-owned TV and 4 state-owned radio networks; satellite dishes and programming provide an alternative to the state-run media; officials sometimes limit access to satellite TV by removing satellite dishes (2007)

Internet country code: .tm

Internet users: *total:* 951,925

percent of population: 18.0% (July 2016 est.)
country comparison to the world: 133

TRANSPORTATION

National air transport system: number of registered air carriers: 1

inventory of registered aircraft operated by air carriers: 23
annual passenger traffic on registered air carriers: 2,138,389
annual freight traffic on registered air carriers: 0 mt-km (2015)
Civil aircraft registration country code prefix: EZ (2016)

Airports: 26 (2013)
country comparison to the world: 126

Airports—with paved runways: *total:* 21
over 3,047 m: 1
2,438 to 3,047 m: 9
1,524 to 2,437 m: 9
914 to 1,523 m: 2 (2013)

Airports—with unpaved runways: *total:* 5
1,524 to 2,437 m: 1
under 914 m: 4 (2013)

Heliports: 1 (2013)

Pipelines: gas 7,500 km; oil 1,501 km (2013)

Railways: *total:* 2,980 km
broad gauge: 2,980 km 1.520-m gauge (2014)
country comparison to the world: 59

Roadways: *total:* 58,592 km
paved: 47,577 km
unpaved: 11,015 km (2002)
country comparison to the world: 72

Waterways: 1,300 km (Amu Darya River and Kara Kum Canal are important inland waterways) (2011)
country comparison to the world: 55

Merchant marine: *total:* 73
by type: general cargo 8, oil tanker 8, other 57 (2017)
country comparison to the world: 100

Ports and terminals: *major seaport(s):* Caspian Sea—Turkmenbasy

MILITARY AND SECURITY

Military branches: Turkmen Armed Forces: Ground Forces, Navy, Air and Air Defense Forces (2013)

Military service age and obligation: 18-27 years of age for compulsory male military service; 2-year conscript service obligation; 20 years of age for voluntary service; males may enroll in military schools from age 15 (2015)

TRANSNATIONAL ISSUES

Disputes—international: cotton monoculture in Uzbekistan and Turkmenistan creates water-sharing difficulties for Amu Darya river states; field demarcation of the boundaries with Kazakhstan commenced in 2005, but Caspian seabed delimitation remains stalled with Azerbaijan, Iran, and Kazakhstan due to Turkmenistan's indecision over how to allocate the sea's waters and seabed; bilateral talks continue with Azerbaijan on dividing the seabed and contested oilfields in the middle of the Caspian

Refugees and internally displaced persons: stateless persons: 5,744 (2016)

Trafficking in persons: current situation: Turkmenistan is a source country for men, women, and children subjected to forced labor and sex trafficking; Turkmen who migrate abroad are forced to work in the textile, agriculture, construction, and domestic service industries, while women and girls may also be sex trafficked; in 2014, men surpassed women as victims; Turkey and Russia are primary trafficking destinations, followed by the Middle East, South and Central Asia, and other parts of Europe; Turkmen also experience forced labor domestically in the informal construction industry; participation

in the cotton harvest is still mandatory for some public sector employees

tier rating: Tier 2 Watch List – Turkmenistan does not fully comply with the minimum standards for the elimination of trafficking; however, it is making significant efforts to do so; in 2014, Turkmenistan was granted a waiver from an otherwise required downgrade to Tier 3 because its government has a written plan that, if implemented, would constitute making significant efforts to bring itself into compliance with the minimum standards for the elimination of trafficking; the

government made some progress in its law enforcement efforts in 2014, convicting more offenders than in 2013; authorities did not make adequate efforts to identify and protect victims and did not fund international organizations or NGOs that offered protective services; some victims were punished for crimes as a result of being trafficked (2015)

Illicit drugs: transit country for Afghan narcotics bound for Russian and Western European markets; transit point for heroin precursor chemicals bound for Afghanistan

TURKS AND CAICOS ISLANDS

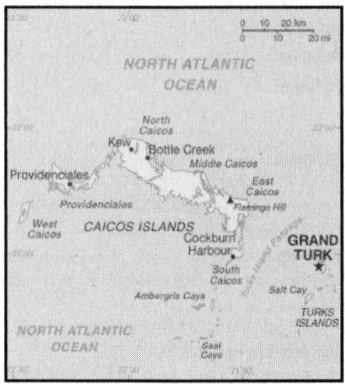

INTRODUCTION

Background: The islands were part of the UK's Jamaican colony until 1962, when they assumed the status of a separate crown colony upon Jamaica's independence. The governor of The Bahamas oversaw affairs from 1965 to 1973. With Bahamian independence, the islands received a separate governor in 1973. Although independence was agreed upon for 1982, the policy was reversed and the islands remain a British overseas territory. Grand Turk island suffered extensive damage from Hurricane Maria on 22 September 2017 resulting in loss of power and communications as well as damage to housing and businesses.

GEOGRAPHY

Location: two island groups in the North Atlantic Ocean, southeast of The Bahamas, north of Haiti

Geographic coordinates: 21 45 N, 71 35 W

Map references: Central America and the Caribbean

Area: total: 948 sq km
land: 948 sq km
water: 0 sq km
country comparison to the world: 186

Area—comparative: 2.5 times the size of Washington, DC

Land boundaries: 0 km

Coastline: 389 km

Maritime claims: territorial sea: 12 nm
exclusive fishing zone: 200 nm

Climate: tropical; marine; moderated by trade winds; sunny and relatively dry

Terrain: low, flat limestone; extensive marshes and mangrove swamps

Elevation: mean elevation: NA

elevation extremes: lowest point: Caribbean Sea 0 m
highest point: Blue Hill on Providenciales and Flamingo Hill on East Caicos 48 m

Natural resources: spiny lobster, conch

Land use: agricultural land: 1.1%
arable land: 1.1%;
permanent crops: 0%;
permanent pasture: 0%
forest: 36.2%
other: 62.7% (2011 est.)
Irrigated land: 0 sq km (2012)

Population—distribution: eight of the thirty islands are inhabited; the island of Providenciales is the most populated, but the most densely populated is Grand Turk

Natural hazards: frequent hurricanes

Environment—current issues: limited natural freshwater resources, private cisterns collect rainwater

Geography—note: include eight large islands and numerous smaller cays, islets, and reefs; only two of the Caicos Islands and six of the Turks group are inhabited

PEOPLE AND SOCIETY

Population: 52,570 (July 2017 est.)
country comparison to the world: 208

Nationality: noun: none
adjective: none

Ethnic groups: black 87.6%, white 7.9%, mixed 2.5%, East Indian 1.3%, other 0.7% (2006)

Languages: English (official)

Religions: Protestant 72.8% (Baptist 35.8%, Church of God 11.7%, Anglican 10%, Methodist

9.3%, Seventh-Day Adventist 6%), Roman Catholic 11.4%, Jehovah's Witnesses 1.8%, other 14%

Age structure: 0-14 years: 21.74% (male 5,826/female 5,604)
15-24 years: 13.99% (male 3,641/female 3,711)
25-54 years: 53.17% (male 14,097/female 13,855)
55-64 years: 6.54% (male 1,839/female 1,597)
65 years and over: 4.57% (male 1,096/female 1,304) (2017 est.)

Median age: total: 33.3 years
male: 33.6 years
female: 33 years (2017 est.)
country comparison to the world: 92

Population growth rate: 2.16% (2017 est.)
country comparison to the world: 38

Birth rate: 15.3 births/1,000 population (2017 est.)
country comparison to the world: 124

Death rate: 3.2 deaths/1,000 population (2017 est.)
country comparison to the world: 221

Net migration rate: 9.5 migrant(s)/1,000 population (2017 est.)
country comparison to the world: 10

Population distribution: eight of the thirty islands are inhabited; the island of Providenciales is the most populated, but the most densely populated is Grand Turk

Urbanization: urban population: 92.8% of total population (2017)
rate of urbanization: 1.71% annual rate of change (2015-20 est.)

Major urban areas—population: GRAND TURK (capital) 5,000 (2014)

Sex ratio: at birth: 1.05 male(s)/female
0-14 years: 1.04 male(s)/female
15-24 years: 0.97 male(s)/female
25-54 years: 1.02 male(s)/female
55-64 years: 1.18 male(s)/female
65 years and over: 0.8 male(s)/female
total population: 1.02 male(s)/female (2016 est.)

Infant mortality rate: total: 10.1 deaths/1,000 live births
male: 12.5 deaths/1,000 live births
female: 7.5 deaths/1,000 live births (2017 est.)
country comparison to the world: 135

Life expectancy at birth: *total population:* 80 years
male: 77.2 years
female: 82.9 years (2017 est.)
country comparison to the world: 42

Total fertility rate: 1.7 children born/woman (2017 est.)
country comparison to the world: 173

Sanitation facility access:
improved:
urban: 81.4% of population
rural: 81.4% of population
total: 81.4% of population
unimproved:
urban: 18.6% of population
rural: 18.6% of population
total: 18.6% of population (2007 est.)

HIV/AIDS—adult prevalence rate: NA

HIV/AIDS—people living with HIV/AIDS: NA

HIV/AIDS—deaths: NA

Major infectious diseases: note: active local transmission of Zika virus by Aedes species mosquitoes has been identified in this country (as of August 2016); it poses an important risk (a large number of cases possible) among US citizens if bitten by an infective mosquito; other less common ways to get Zika are through sex, via blood transfusion, or during pregnancy, in which the pregnant woman passes Zika virus to her fetus (2016)
Education expenditures: 3.3% of GDP (2015)
People—note: destination and transit point for illegal Haitian immigrants bound for the Turks and Caicos Islands, The Bahamas, and the US

GOVERNMENT

Country name: *conventional long form:* none
conventional short form: Turks and Caicos Islands
abbreviation: TCI
etymology: the Turks Islands are named after the Turk's cap cactus (native to the islands and appearing on the flag and coat of arms), while the Caicos Islands derive from the native term "caya hico" meaning "string of islands"
Dependency status: overseas territory of the UK

Government type: parliamentary democracy (House of Assembly); self-governing overseas territory of the UK

Capital: *name:* Grand Turk (Cockburn Town)
geographic coordinates: 21 28 N, 71 08 W
time difference: UTC-5 (same time as Washington, DC, during Standard Time)

Administrative divisions: none (overseas territory of the UK)

Independence: none (overseas territory of the UK)

National holiday: Birthday of Queen ELIZABETH II, usually celebrated the Monday after the second Saturday in June

Constitution: several previous; latest signed 7 August 2012, effective 15 October 2012 (Turks and Caicos Constitution Order 2011) (2016)

Legal system: mixed legal system of English common law and civil law

Citizenship: see United Kingdom

Suffrage: 18 years of age; universal

Executive branch: *chief of state:* Queen ELIZABETH II (since 6 February 1952); represented by Governor John FREEMAN (since 17 October 2016)

head of government: Premier Sharlene CARTWRIGHT-ROBINSON (since 20 December 2016); first female Premier of Turks and Caicos
cabinet: Cabinet appointed by the governor from among members of the House of Assembly
elections/appointments: the monarch is hereditary; governor appointed by the monarch; following legislative elections, the leader of the majority party is appointed premier by the governor

Legislative branch: *description:* unicameral House of Assembly (19 seats; 15 members in multi-seat constituencies and a single all-islands constituency directly elected by simple majority vote, 1 member nominated by the premier and appointed by the governor, 1 nominated by the opposition party leader and appointed by the governor, and 2 from the Turks and Caicos Islands Civic Society directly appointed by the governor; members serve 4-year terms)
elections: last held on 15 December 2016 (next to be held in 2020)
election results: percent of vote—NA; seats by party—PDM 10, PNP 5

Judicial branch: highest resident court(s): Supreme Court (consists of the chief justice and such number of other judges as determined by the governor); Court of Appeal (consists of the court president and 2 justices); note—appeals beyond the Supreme Court are referred to the Judicial Committee of the Privy Council (in London)
judge selection and term of office: Supreme Court and Appeals Court judges appointed by the governor in accordance with the Judicial Service Commission, a 3-member body of high level judicial officials; Supreme Court judges appointed until mandatory retirement at age 65, but terms can be extended to age 70; Appeals Court judge tenure determined by individual terms of appointment
subordinate courts: magistrates' courts

Political parties and leaders: People's Democratic Movement or PDM [Sharlene CARTWRIGHT-ROBINSON]
Progressive National Party or PNP [Washington MISICK]

Political pressure groups and leaders: NA

International organization participation: Caricom (associate), CDB, Interpol (subbureau), UPU

Diplomatic representation in the US: none (overseas territory of the UK)

Diplomatic representation from the US: none (overseas territory of the UK)

Flag description: blue with the flag of the UK in the upper hoist-side quadrant and the colonial shield centered on the outer half of the flag; the shield is yellow and displays a conch shell, a spiny

lobster, and Turk's cap cactus—three common elements of the islands' biota

National symbol(s): conch shell, Turk's cap cactus

National anthem: *name:* "This Land of Ours"
lyrics/music: Conrad HOWELL
note: serves as a local anthem; as a territory of the UK, "God Save the Queen" is the official anthem (see United Kingdom)

ECONOMY

Economy—overview: The Turks and Caicos economy is based on tourism, offshore financial services, and fishing. Most capital goods and food for domestic consumption are imported. The US is the leading source of tourists, accounting for more than three-quarters of the more than 1 million visitors that arrived in 2013. Three-quarters of the visitors came by ship. Major sources of government revenue also include fees from offshore financial activities and customs receipts.

GDP (purchasing power parity): $632 million (2007 est.)
$568.3 million (2006 est.)
country comparison to the world: 211

GDP (official exchange rate): $NA

GDP—real growth rate: 11.2% (2007 est.)
country comparison to the world: 3

GDP—per capita (PPP): $29,100 (2007 est.)
country comparison to the world: 67

GDP—composition, by end use:
household consumption: 48.8%
government consumption: 21.3%
investment in fixed capital: 16.3%
investment in inventories: -0.1%
exports of goods and services: 69.5%
imports of goods and services: -55.9% (2017 est.)

GDP—composition, by sector of origin:
agriculture: 0.5%
industry: 8.9%
services: 90.6% (2017 est.)

Agriculture—products: corn, beans, cassava (manioc, tapioca), citrus fruits; fish

Industries: tourism, offshore financial services

Industrial production growth rate: 3% (2017 est.)
country comparison to the world: 95

Labor force: 4,848 (1990 est.)
country comparison to the world: 221
Labor force—by occupation: note: about 33% in government and 20% in agriculture and fishing; significant numbers in tourism, financial, and other services

Unemployment rate: 10% (1997 est.)
country comparison to the world: 138

Population below poverty line: NA%

Household income or consumption by percentage share: *lowest 10%:* NA%
highest 10%: NA%

Budget: *revenues:* $232.8 million
expenditures: $190.9 million (2017 est.)

Fiscal year: calendar year

Inflation rate (consumer prices): 1.5% (2017 est.)

1.1% (2016 est.)
country comparison to the world: 61

Exports: $24.77 million (2008 est.)
country comparison to the world: 208

Exports—commodities: lobster, dried and fresh conch, conch shells

Imports: $591.3 million (2008 est.)
country comparison to the world: 185

Imports—commodities: food and beverages, tobacco, clothing, manufactures, construction materials

Debt—external: $NA

Exchange rates: the US dollar is used

ENERGY

Electricity access: population without electricity: 5,143
electrification—*total population:* 91%
electrification—urban areas: 92%
electrification—rural areas: 80% (2012)

Electricity—production: 220 million kWh (2015 est.)
country comparison to the world: 186

Electricity—consumption: 204.6 million kWh (2015 est.)
country comparison to the world: 188

Electricity—exports: 0 kWh (2016 est.)
country comparison to the world: 202

Electricity—imports: 0 kWh (2016 est.)
country comparison to the world: 207

Electricity—installed generating capacity: 79,000 kW (2015 est.)
country comparison to the world: 186

Electricity—from fossil fuels: 100% of total installed capacity (2015 est.)
country comparison to the world: 19

Electricity—from nuclear fuels: 0% of total installed capacity (2015 est.)
country comparison to the world: 190

Electricity—from hydroelectric plants: 0% of total installed capacity (2015 est.)
country comparison to the world: 207

Electricity—from other renewable sources: 0% of total installed capacity (2015 est.)
country comparison to the world: 208

Crude oil—production: 0 bbl/day (2016 est.)
country comparison to the world: 208

Crude oil—exports: 0 bbl/day (2014 est.)
country comparison to the world: 196

Crude oil—imports: 0 bbl/day (2014 est.)
country comparison to the world: 195

Crude oil—proved reserves: 0 bbl (1 January 2017 es)
country comparison to the world: 209

Refined petroleum products—production: 0 bbl/day (2014 est.)
country comparison to the world: 210

Refined petroleum products—consumption: 1,340 bbl/day (2015 est.)
country comparison to the world: 201

Refined petroleum products—exports: 0 bbl/day (2014 est.)
country comparison to the world: 201

Refined petroleum products—imports: 1,328 bbl/day (2014 est.)
country comparison to the world: 198

Natural gas—production: 0 cu m (2013 est.)
country comparison to the world: 200

Natural gas—consumption: 0 cu m (2013 est.)
country comparison to the world: 135

Natural gas—exports: 0 cu m (2013 est.)
country comparison to the world: 192

Natural gas—imports: 0 cu m (2013 est.)
country comparison to the world: 193

Natural gas—proved reserves: 0 cu m (1 January 2014 es)
country comparison to the world: 198

Carbon dioxide emissions from consumption of energy: 200,000 Mt (2013 est.)
country comparison to the world: 205

COMMUNICATIONS

Telephone system: *general assessment:* fully digital system with international direct dialing
domestic: full range of services available; GSM wireless service available
international: country code—1-649; the Americas Region Caribbean Ring System (ARCOS-1) fiber-optic telecommunications submarine cable provides connectivity to South and Central America, parts of the Caribbean, and the US; satellite earth station—1 Intelsat (Atlantic Ocean) (2015)

Broadcast media: no local terrestrial TV stations, broadcasts from the Bahamas can be received and multi-channel cable and satellite TV services are available; government-run radio network operates alongside private broadcasters with a total of about 15 stations (2007)

Internet country code: .tc

TRANSPORTATION

National air transport system: number of registered air carriers: 1
inventory of registered aircraft operated by air carriers: 16 (2015)
Civil aircraft registration country code prefix: VQ-T (2016)

Airports: 8 (2013)
country comparison to the world: 162

Airports—with paved runways: *total:* 6
2,438 to 3,047 m: 1
1,524 to 2,437 m: 3
914 to 1,523 m: 1
under 914 m: 1 (2013)

Airports—with unpaved runways: *total:* 2
under 914 m: 2 (2013)

Roadways: *total:* 121 km
paved: 24 km
unpaved: 97 km (2003)
country comparison to the world: 213

Merchant marine: *total:* 4
by type: general cargo 1, other 3 (2017)
country comparison to the world: 159

Ports and terminals: *major seaport(s):* Cockburn Harbour, Grand Turk, Providenciales

MILITARY AND SECURITY

Military—note: defense is the responsibility of the UK

TRANSNATIONAL ISSUES

Disputes—international: have received Haitians fleeing economic and civil disorder

Illicit drugs: transshipment point for South American narcotics destined for the US and Europe

TUVALU

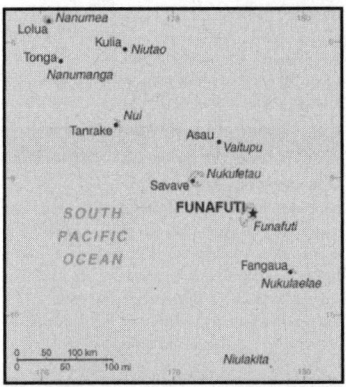

INTRODUCTION

Background: In 1974, ethnic differences within the British colony of the Gilbert and Ellice Islands caused the Polynesians of the Ellice Islands to vote for separation from the Micronesians of the Gilbert Islands. The following year, the Ellice Islands became the separate British colony of Tuvalu. Independence was granted in 1978. In 2000, Tuvalu negotiated a contract leasing its Internet domain name ".tv" for $50 million in royalties over a 12-year period. The agreement was subsequently renegotiated but details were not disclosed.

GEOGRAPHY

Location: Oceania, island group consisting of nine coral atolls in the South Pacific Ocean, about half way from Hawaii to Australia

Geographic coordinates: 8 00 S, 178 00 E

Map references: Oceania

Area: *total:* 26 sq km
land: 26 sq km
water: 0 sq km
country comparison to the world: 239

Area—comparative: 0.1 times the size of Washington, DC
Land boundaries: 0 km

Coastline: 24 km

Maritime claims: *territorial sea:* 12 nm
contiguous zone: 24 nm
exclusive economic zone: 200 nm

Climate: tropical; moderated by easterly trade winds (March to November); westerly gales and heavy rain (November to March)

Terrain: low-lying and narrow coral atolls

Elevation: *mean elevation:* 2 m

elevation extremes: *lowest point:* Pacific Ocean 0 m
highest point: unnamed location 5 m

Natural resources: fish, coconut (copra)

Land use: *agricultural land:* 60%
arable land: 0%;
permanent crops: 60%;
permanent pasture: 0%
forest: 33.3%
other: 6.7% (2011 est.)
Irrigated land: 0 sq km (2012)

Population—distribution: over half of the population resides on the atoll of Funafuti

Natural hazards: severe tropical storms are usually rare, but in 1997 there were three cyclones; low levels of islands make them sensitive to changes in sea level

Environment—current issues: water needs met by catchment systems; the use of sand as a building material has led to beachhead erosion; excessive clearance of forest undergrowth for use as fuel; damage to coral reefs from increasing ocean temperatures and acidification; rising sea levels threaten water table; in 2000, the government appealed to Australia and New Zealand to take in Tuvaluans if rising sea levels should make evacuation necessary

Environment—international agreements: *party to:* Biodiversity, Climate Change, Climate Change-Kyoto Protocol, Desertification, Law of the Sea, Ozone Layer Protection, Ship Pollution, Whaling
signed, but not ratified: none of the selected agreements

Geography—note: one of the smallest and most remote countries on Earth; six of the nine coral atolls—Nanumea, Nui, Vaitupu, Nukufetau, Funafuti, and Nukulaelae—have lagoons open to the ocean; Nanumaya and Niutao have landlocked lagoons; Niulakita does not have a lagoon

PEOPLE AND SOCIETY

Population: 11,052 (July 2017 est.)
country comparison to the world: 222

Nationality: *noun:* Tuvaluan(s)
adjective: Tuvaluan

Ethnic groups: Polynesian 96%, Micronesian 4%

Languages: Tuvaluan (official), English (official), Samoan, Kiribati (on the island of Nui)

Religions: Protestant 98.4% (Church of Tuvalu (Congregationalist) 97%, Seventh-Day Adventist 1.4%), Baha'i 1%, other 0.6%

Age structure: *0-14 years:* 29.29% (male 1,659/female 1,578)
15-24 years: 19.26% (male 1,106/female 1,023)
25-54 years: 36.66% (male 2,036/female 2,016)
55-64 years: 8.77% (male 396/female 573)
65 years and over: 6.02% (male 263/female 402) (2017 est.)

Median age: *total:* 25.7 years
male: 24.7 years
female: 26.9 years (2017 est.)
country comparison to the world: 152

Population growth rate: 0.85% (2017 est.)
country comparison to the world: 127

Birth rate: 23.7 births/1,000 population (2017 est.)
country comparison to the world: 62

Death rate: 8.5 deaths/1,000 population (2017 est.)
country comparison to the world: 79

Net migration rate: -6.7 migrant(s)/1,000 population (2017 est.)
country comparison to the world: 202

Population distribution: over half of the population resides on the atoll of Funafuti

Urbanization: *urban population:* 61.5% of total population (2017)
rate of urbanization: 1.71% annual rate of change (2015-20 est.)

Major urban areas—population: FUNAFUTI (capital) 6,000 (2014)

Sex ratio: *at birth:* 1.05 male(s)/female
0-14 years: 1.05 male(s)/female
15-24 years: 1.1 male(s)/female
25-54 years: 0.99 male(s)/female
55-64 years: 0.69 male(s)/female
65 years and over: 0.69 male(s)/female
total population: 0.98 male(s)/female (2016 est.)

Mother's mean age at first birth: 23.5 years
note: median age at first birth among women 25-29 (2007 est.)

Infant mortality rate: *total:* 29 deaths/1,000 live births
male: 31.5 deaths/1,000 live births
female: 26.4 deaths/1,000 live births (2017 est.)
country comparison to the world: 66

Life expectancy at birth: *total population:* 66.9 years
male: 64.7 years
female: 69.2 years (2017 est.)
country comparison to the world: 173

Total fertility rate: 2.95 children born/woman (2017 est.)
country comparison to the world: 58

Contraceptive prevalence rate: 30.5% (2007)
Health expenditures: 16.5% of GDP (2014)
country comparison to the world: 3

Physicians density: 1.22 physicians/1,000 population (2009)

Drinking water source:
improved:
urban: 98.3% of population
rural: 97% of population
total: 97.7% of population
unimproved:
urban: 1.7% of population
rural: 3% of population
total: 2.3% of population (2015 est.)

Sanitation facility access:
improved:
urban: 86.3% of population

933

rural: 80.2% of population
total: 83.3% of population
unimproved:
urban: 13.7% of population
rural: 19.8% of population
total: 16.7% of population (2012 est.)

HIV/AIDS—adult prevalence rate: NA

HIV/AIDS—people living with HIV/AIDS: NA

HIV/AIDS—deaths: NA

Obesity—adult prevalence rate: 51.6% (2016)
country comparison to the world: 5

Children under the age of 5 years underweight: 1.6% (2007)
country comparison to the world: 126
Education expenditures: NA

GOVERNMENT

Country name: *conventional long form:* none
conventional short form: Tuvalu
local long form: none
local short form: Tuvalu
former: Ellice Islands
etymology: "tuvalu" means "group of eight" or "eight standing together" referring to the country's eight traditionally inhabited islands

Government type: parliamentary democracy (House of Assembly) under a constitutional monarchy; a Commonwealth realm

Capital: *name:* Funafuti; *note*—the capital is an atoll of some 29 islets; administrative offices are in Vaiaku Village on Fongafale Islet

geographic coordinates: 8 31 S, 179 13 E
time difference: UTC+12 (17 hours ahead of Washington, DC, during Standard Time)

Administrative divisions: 7 island councils and 1 town council*; Funafuti*, Nanumaga, Nanumea, Niutao, Nui, Nukufetau, Nukulaelae, Vaitupu

Independence: 1 October 1978 (from the UK)

National holiday: Independence Day, 1 October (1978)

Constitution: previous 1978 (at independence); latest effective 1 October 1986; amended 2007, 2010, 2013 (2016)

Legal system: mixed legal system of English common law and local customary law

International law organization participation: has not submitted an ICJ jurisdiction declaration; non-party state to the ICCt

Citizenship: *citizenship by birth:* yes

citizenship by descent: yes; for a child born abroad, at least one parent must be a citizen of Tuvalu
dual citizenship recognized: yes
residency requirement for naturalization: na

Suffrage: 18 years of age; universal

Executive branch: *chief of state:* Queen ELIZABETH II (since 6 February 1952); represented by Governor General Iakoba TAEIA Italeli (since 16 April 2010)

head of government: Prime Minister Enele SOPOAGA (since 5 August 2013)

cabinet: Cabinet appointed by the governor general on recommendation of the prime minister
elections/appointments: the monarchy is hereditary; governor general appointed by the monarch on recommendation of the prime minister; prime minister and deputy prime minister elected by and from members of House of Assembly following parliamentary elections
election results: Enele SOPOAGA elected prime minister by House of Assembly; House of Assembly vote count on 4 August 2013—8 to 5; note—Willie TELAVI removed as prime minister by the governor general on 1 August 2013

Legislative branch: *description:* unicameral House of Assembly or Fale I Fono (15 seats; members directly elected in single- and multi-seat constituencies by simple majority vote to serve 4-year terms)
elections: last held on 31 March 2015 (next to be held in 2019)
election results: percent of vote—NA; seats—independent 15; 12 members reelected

Judicial branch: *highest court(s):* Court of Appeal (consists of the chief justice and not less than 3 appeals judges); High Court (consists of the chief justice); appeals beyond the Court of Appeal are heard by the Judicial Committee of the Privy Council (in London)
judge selection and term of office: Appeal Court judges appointed by the governor general on the advice of the Cabinet; judges' tenure based on terms of appointment; High Court chief justice appointed by the governor general on the advice of the Cabinet; chief justice appointed for life; other judges appointed by the governor-general on the advice of the Cabinet after consultation with chief justice; tenure of judges set by terms of appointment
subordinate courts: magistrates' courts; island courts; land courts

Political parties and leaders: there are no political parties but members of parliament usually align themselves in informal groupings

Political pressure groups and leaders: none

International organization participation: ACP, ADB, AOSIS, C, FAO, IBRD, IDA, IFAD, IFRCS (observer), ILO, IMF, IMO, IOC, ITU, OPCW, PIF, Sparteca, SPC, UN, UNCTAD, UNESCO, UNIDO, UPU, WHO, WIPO, WMO

Diplomatic representation in the US: chief of mission: Ambassador Samuelu LALONIU (since 21 July 2017)
chancery: note—Tuvalu does not have an embassy in Washington, D.C.; UN office located at 800 2nd Avenue, Suite 400D, New York, NY 10017
telephone: [1] (212) 490-0534
FAX: [1] (212) 937-0692

Diplomatic representation from the US: the US does not have an embassy in Tuvalu; the US Ambassador to Fiji is accredited to Tuvalu

Flag description: light blue with the flag of the UK in the upper hoist-side quadrant; the outer half of the flag represents a map of the country with nine

yellow, five-pointed stars on a blue field symbolizing the nine atolls in the ocean

National symbol(s): maneapa (native meeting house); national colors: light blue, yellow

National anthem: *name:* "Tuvalu mo te Atua" (Tuvalu for the Almighty)
lyrics/music: Afaese MANOA
note: adopted 1978; the anthem's name is also the nation's motto

ECONOMY

Economy—overview: Tuvalu consists of a densely populated, scattered group of nine coral atolls with poor soil. Only eight of the atolls are inhabited. It is one of the smallest countries in the world, with its highest point at 4.6 meters above sea level. The country is isolated, almost entirely dependent on imports, particularly of food and fuel, and vulnerable to climate change and rising sea levels, which pose significant challenges to development.

The public sector dominates economic activity. Tuvalu has few natural resources, except for its fisheries. Earnings from fish exports and fishing licenses for Tuvalu's territorial waters are a significant source of government revenue. In 2013, revenue from fishing licenses doubled and totaled more than 45% of GDP.

Official aid from foreign development partners has also increased. Tuvalu has substantial assets abroad. The Tuvalu Trust Fund, an international trust fund established in 1987 by development partners, has grown to $104 million (A$141 million) in 2014 and is an important cushion for meeting shortfalls in the government's budget. While remittances are another substantial source of income, the value of remittances has declined since the 2008-09 global financial crisis, but has stabilized at nearly $4 million per year. The financial impact of climate change and the cost of climate related adaptation projects is one of many concerns for the nation.

GDP (purchasing power parity): $42 million (2017 est.)
$40.68 million (2016 est.)
$39.48 million (2015 est.)
note: data are in 2017 dollars
country comparison to the world: 227

GDP (official exchange rate): $40 million (2016 est.)

GDP—real growth rate: 3.2% (2017 est.)
3% (2016 est.)
9.1% (2015 est.)
country comparison to the world: 105

GDP—per capita (PPP): $3,800 (2017 est.)
$3,700 (2016 est.)
$3,600 (2015 est.)
note: data are in 2017 dollars
country comparison to the world: 182

GDP—composition, by sector of origin:
agriculture: 24.5%
industry: 5.6%
services: 70% (2012 est.)

Agriculture—products: coconuts; fish

Industries: fishing

Industrial production growth rate: -26.1% (2012 est.)
country comparison to the world: 202

Labor force: 3,615 (2004 est.)
country comparison to the world: 224
Labor force—by occupation: note: people make a living mainly through exploitation of the sea, reefs, and atolls and through overseas remittances (mostly from workers in the phosphate industry and sailors)

Unemployment rate: NA%

Population below poverty line: 26.3% (2010 est.)

Household income or consumption by percentage share: *lowest 10%:* NA%
highest 10%: NA%

Budget: *revenues:* $42.68 million
expenditures: $32.46 million (2013 est.)
Taxes and other revenues: 106.7% of GDP (2013 est.)
country comparison to the world: 1

Budget surplus (+) or deficit (-): 25.6% of GDP (2013 est.)
country comparison to the world: 1

Public debt: 53.7% of GDP (2016 est.)
58.2% of GDP (2015 est.)
country comparison to the world: 88

Fiscal year: calendar year

Inflation rate (consumer prices): 2.9% (2017 est.)
3.5% (2016 est.)
country comparison to the world: 126

Commercial bank prime lending rate: 10.6% (31 December 2013 est.)
10.6% (31 December 2012 est.)
country comparison to the world: 75

Market value of publicly traded shares: $0 (2014)
country comparison to the world: 123

Current account balance: -$15 million (2017 est.)
-$12 million (2016 est.)
country comparison to the world: 65

Exports: $600,000 (2010 est.)
$1 million (2004 est.)
country comparison to the world: 220

Exports—commodities: copra, fish

Exports—partners: Bosnia and Herzegovina 24.8%, Singapore 18.8%, Nigeria 17.3%, Fiji 14.5%, US 6% (2016)

Imports: $136.5 million (2013 est.)
$238.6 million (2012 est.)
country comparison to the world: 208

Imports—commodities: food, animals, mineral fuels, machinery, manufactured goods

Imports—partners: Singapore 51.3%, NZ 9.4%, Australia 8.6%, US 6.8%, Japan 6.1%, Fiji 5.9% (2016)

Debt—external: $NA

Exchange rates: Tuvaluan dollars or Australian dollars (AUD) per US dollar—
1.67 (2014 est.)
1.352 (2013 est.)

ENERGY

Electricity access: population without electricity: 6,137
electrification—total population: 45%
electrification—urban areas: 57%
electrification—rural areas: 32% (2012)

Electricity—production: 11.8 million kWh (2011)
country comparison to the world: 215

Electricity—exports: 0 kWh (2014 est.)
country comparison to the world: 207

Electricity—imports: 0 kWh (2014)
country comparison to the world: 211

Electricity—installed generating capacity: 5,100 kW (2011)
country comparison to the world: 212

Electricity—from fossil fuels: 96% of total installed capacity (2015 est.)
country comparison to the world: 51

Electricity—from nuclear fuels: 0% of total installed capacity (2014)
country comparison to the world: 196

Electricity—from hydroelectric plants: 0% of total installed capacity (2014)
country comparison to the world: 209

Crude oil—production: 0 bbl/day (2014)
country comparison to the world: 209

Crude oil—exports: 0 bbl/day (2014)
country comparison to the world: 201

Crude oil—imports: 0 bbl/day (2014)
country comparison to the world: 200

Crude oil—proved reserves: 0 bbl (2014 est.)
country comparison to the world: 210

Refined petroleum products—production: 0 bbl/day (2014 est.)
country comparison to the world: 211

Refined petroleum products—exports: 0 bbl/day
country comparison to the world: 206

Natural gas—production: 0 cu m (2014)
country comparison to the world: 204

Natural gas—consumption: 0 cu m (2014)
country comparison to the world: 140

Natural gas—exports: 0 cu m (2014)
country comparison to the world: 197

Natural gas—imports: 0 cu m (2014)
country comparison to the world: 198

COMMUNICATIONS

Telephones—fixed lines: *total subscriptions:* 2,000
subscriptions per 100 inhabitants: 18 (July 2016 est.)
country comparison to the world: 215

Telephones—mobile cellular: *total:* 7,600
subscriptions per 100 inhabitants: 69 (July 2016 est.)
country comparison to the world: 217

Telephone system: *general assessment:* serves particular needs for internal communications
domestic: radiotelephone communications between islands
international: country code—688; international calls can be made by satellite (2015)

Broadcast media: no TV stations; many households use satellite dishes to watch foreign TV stations; 1 government-owned radio station, Radio Tuvalu, includes relays of programming from international broadcasters (2009)

Internet country code: .tv

Internet users: *total:* 5,042

percent of population: 46.0% (July 2016 est.)
country comparison to the world: 206

TRANSPORTATION

Civil aircraft registration country code prefix: T2 (2016)

Airports: 1 (2013)
country comparison to the world: 235

Airports—with unpaved runways: *total:* 1
1,524 to 2,437 m: 1 (2013)

Roadways: *total:* 8 km
paved: 8 km (2011)
country comparison to the world: 223

Merchant marine: *total:* 245
by type: bulk carrier 18, container ship 2, general cargo 36, oil tanker 27, other 162 (2017)
country comparison to the world: 61

Ports and terminals: *major seaport(s):* Funafuti

MILITARY AND SECURITY

Military branches: no regular military forces; Tuvalu Police Force (2012)

TRANSNATIONAL ISSUES

Disputes—international: none

INTRODUCTION

Background: Ukraine was the center of the first eastern Slavic state, Kyivan Rus, which during the 10th and 11th centuries was the largest and most powerful state in Europe. Weakened by internecine quarrels and Mongol invasions, Kyivan Rus was incorporated into the Grand Duchy of Lithuania and eventually into the Polish-Lithuanian Commonwealth. The cultural and religious legacy of Kyivan Rus laid the foundation for Ukrainian nationalism through subsequent centuries. A new Ukrainian state, the Cossack Hetmanate, was established during the mid-17th century after an uprising against the Poles. Despite continuous Muscovite pressure, the Hetmanate managed to remain autonomous for well over 100 years. During the latter part of the 18th century, most Ukrainian ethnographic territory was absorbed by the Russian Empire. Following the collapse of czarist Russia in 1917, Ukraine achieved a short-lived period of independence (1917-20), but was reconquered and endured a brutal Soviet rule that engineered two forced famines (1921-22 and 1932-33) in which over 8 million died. In World War II, German and Soviet armies were responsible for 7 to 8 million more deaths. Although Ukraine achieved independence in 1991 with the dissolution of the USSR, democracy and prosperity remained elusive as the legacy of state control and endemic corruption stalled efforts at economic reform, privatization, and civil liberties.

A peaceful mass protest referred to as the "Orange Revolution" in the closing months of 2004 forced the authorities to overturn a rigged presidential election and to allow a new internationally monitored vote that swept into power a reformist slate under Viktor YUSHCHENKO. Subsequent internal squabbles in the YUSHCHENKO camp allowed his rival Viktor YANUKOVYCH to stage a comeback in parliamentary (Rada) elections, become prime minister in August 2006, and be elected president in February 2010. In October 2012, Ukraine held Rada elections, widely criticized by Western observers as flawed due to use of government resources to favor ruling party candidates, interference with media access, and harassment of opposition candidates. President YANUKOVYCH's backtracking on a trade and cooperation agreement with the EU in November 2013—in favor of closer economic ties with Russia—and subsequent use of force against students, civil society activists, and other civilians in favor of the agreement led to a three-month

protest occupation of Kyiv's central square. The government's use of violence to break up the protest camp in February 2014 led to all out pitched battles, scores of deaths, international condemnation, and the president's abrupt departure for Russia. New elections in the spring allowed pro-West president Petro POROSHENKO to assume office on 7 June 2014.

Shortly after YANUKOVYCH's departure in late February 2014, Russian President PUTIN ordered the invasion of Ukraine's Crimean Peninsula claiming the action was to protect ethnic Russians living there. Two weeks later, a "referendum" was held regarding the integration of Crimea into the Russian Federation. The "referendum" was condemned as illegitimate by the Ukrainian Government, the EU, the US, and the UN General Assembly (UNGA). In response to Russia's purported annexation of Crimea, 100 members of the UN passed UNGA resolution 68/262, rejecting the "referendum" as baseless and invalid and confirming the sovereignty, political independence, unity, and territorial integrity of Ukraine. Russia also continues to supply so-called separatists in two of Ukraine's eastern provinces with manpower, funding, and materiel resulting in an armed conflict with the Ukrainian Government. Representatives from Ukraine, Russia, and the unrecognized separatist republics signed the Minsk Protocol and Memorandum in September 2014 to end the conflict. However, this agreement failed to stop the fighting. In a renewed attempt to alleviate ongoing clashes, leaders of Ukraine, Russia, France, and Germany negotiated a follow-on package of measures in February 2015 to implement the Minsk Agreements. Representatives from Ukraine, Russia, and the Organization for Security and Cooperation in Europe also meet regularly to facilitate implementation of the peace deal. More than 33,000 civilians have been killed or wounded in the fighting resulting from Russian aggression in eastern Ukraine.

GEOGRAPHY

Location: Eastern Europe, bordering the Black Sea, between Poland, Romania, and Moldova in the west and Russia in the east

Geographic coordinates: 49 00 N, 32 00 E

Map references: Asia, Europe

Area: *total:* 603,550 sq km
land: 579,330 sq km
water: 24,220 sq km
note: approximately 43,133 sq km, or about 7.1% of Ukraine's area, is Russian occupied; the seized area includes all of Crimea and about one-third of both Luhans'k and Donets'k oblasts
country comparison to the world: 47

Area—comparative: almost four times the size of Georgia; slightly smaller than Texas

Land boundaries: *total:* 5,618 km

border countries (7): Belarus 1,111 km, Hungary 128 km, Moldova 1,202 km, Poland 535 km, Romania 601 km, Russia 1,944 km, Slovakia 97 km

Coastline: 2,782 km

Maritime claims: *territorial sea:* 12 nm
exclusive economic zone: 200 nm
continental shelf: 200 m or to the depth of exploitation

Climate: temperate continental; Mediterranean only on the southern Crimean coast; precipitation disproportionately distributed, highest in west and north, lesser in east and southeast; winters vary from cool along the Black Sea to cold farther inland; warm summers across the greater part of the country, hot in the south

Terrain: mostly fertile plains (steppes) and plateaus, with mountains found only in the west (the Carpathians) or in the extreme south of the Crimean Peninsula

Elevation: *mean elevation:* 175 m

elevation extremes: *lowest point:* Black Sea 0 m
highest point: Hora Hoverla 2,061 m

Natural resources: iron ore, coal, manganese, natural gas, oil, salt, sulfur, graphite, titanium, magnesium, kaolin, nickel, mercury, timber, arable land

Land use: *agricultural land:* 71.2%
arable land: 56.1%;
permanent crops: 1.5%;
permanent pasture: 13.6%
forest: 16.8%
other: 12% (2011 est.)
Irrigated land: 21,670 sq km (2012)

Population—distribution: densest settlement in the eastern (Donbas) and western regions; notable concentrations in and around major urban areas of Kyiv, Kharkiv, Donets'k, Dnipropetrovs'k, and Odesa

Natural hazards: occasional floods; occasional droughts

Environment—current issues: inadequate supplies of potable water; air and water pollution; deforestation; radiation contamination in the northeast from 1986 accident at Chornobyl' Nuclear Power Plant

Environment—international agreements: *party to:* Air Pollution, Air Pollution-Nitrogen Oxides, Air Pollution-Sulfur 85, Antarctic-Environmental Protocol, Antarctic-Marine Living Resources, Antarctic Treaty, Biodiversity, Climate Change, Climate Change-Kyoto Protocol, Desertification, Endangered Species, Environmental Modification, Hazardous Wastes, Law of the Sea, Marine Dumping, Ozone Layer Protection, Ship Pollution, Wetlands
signed, but not ratified: Air Pollution-Persistent Organic Pollutants, Air Pollution-Sulfur 94, Air Pollution-Volatile Organic Compounds

Geography—note: strategic position at the cross-roads between Europe and Asia; second-largest country in Europe after Russia

PEOPLE AND SOCIETY

Population: 44,033,874 (July 2017 est.)
country comparison to the world: 32

Nationality: *noun:* Ukrainian(s)
adjective: Ukrainian

Ethnic groups: Ukrainian 77.8%, Russian 17.3%, Belarusian 0.6%, Moldovan 0.5%, Crimean Tatar 0.5%, Bulgarian 0.4%, Hungarian 0.3%, Romanian 0.3%, Polish 0.3%, Jewish 0.2%, other 1.8% (2001 est.)

Languages: Ukrainian (official) 67.5%, Russian (regional language) 29.6%, ther (includes small Crimean Tatar-, Moldovan/Romanian-, and Hungarian-speaking minorities) 2.9% (2001 est.)
note: 2012 legislation enables a language spoken by at least 10% of an oblast's population to be given the status of "regional language," allowing for its use in courts, schools, and other government institutions; Ukrainian remains the country's only official nationwide language

Religions: Orthodox (includes Ukrainian Autocephalous Orthodox (UAOC), Ukrainian Orthodox—Kyiv Patriarchate (UOC-KP), Ukrainian Orthodox—Moscow Patriarchate (UOC-MP)), Ukrainian Greek Catholic, Roman Catholic, Protestant, Muslim, Jewish
note: Ukraine's population is overwhelmingly Christian; the vast majority—up to two-thirds—identify themselves as Orthodox, but many do not specify a particular branch; the UOC-KP and the UOC-MP each represent less than a quarter of the country's population, the Ukrainian Greek Catholic Church accounts for 8-10%, and the UAOC accounts for 1-2%; Muslim and Jewish adherents each compose less than 1% of the total population (2013 est.)

Age structure: *0-14 years:* 15.76% (male 3,571,358/female 3,366,380)
15-24 years: 9.86% (male 2,226,142/female 2,114,853)
25-54 years: 44.29% (male 9,579,149/female 9,921,387)
55-64 years: 13.8% (male 2,605,849/female 3,469,246)
65 years and over: 16.3% (male 2,409,049/female 4,770,461) (2017 est.)

Dependency ratios: *total dependency ratio:* 44.8
youth dependency ratio: 21.8
elderly dependency ratio: 23
potential support ratio: 4.3
note: data include Crimea (2015 est.)

Median age: *total:* 40.6 years
male: 37.4 years
female: 43.7 years (2017 est.)
country comparison to the world: 45

Population growth rate: -0.41% (2017 est.)
country comparison to the world: 220

Birth rate: 10.3 births/1,000 population (2017 est.)
country comparison to the world: 189

Death rate: 14.4 deaths/1,000 population (2017 est.)
country comparison to the world: 5

Net migration rate: 0 migrant(s)/1,000 population (2017 est.)
country comparison to the world: 100

Population distribution: densest settlement in the eastern (Donbas) and western regions; noteable concentrations in and around major urban areas of Kyiv, Kharkiv, Donets'k, Dnipropetrovs'k, and Odesa

Urbanization: *urban population:* 70.1% of total population (2017)
rate of urbanization: -0.35% annual rate of change (2015-20 est.)

Major urban areas—population: KYIV (capital) 2.942 million; Kharkiv 1.441 million; Odesa 1.01 million; Dnipropetrovsk 957,000; Donetsk 934,000; Zaporizhzhya 753,000 (2015)

Sex ratio: *at birth:* 1.06 male(s)/female
0-14 years: 1.06 male(s)/female
15-24 years: 1.05 male(s)/female
25-54 years: 0.96 male(s)/female
55-64 years: 0.75 male(s)/female
65 years and over: 0.5 male(s)/female
total population: 0.86 male(s)/female (2016 est.)

Mother's mean age at first birth: 24.9 years (2014 est.)

Maternal mortality ratio: 24 deaths/100,000 live births (2015 est.)
country comparison to the world: 125

Infant mortality rate: *total:* 7.8 deaths/1,000 live births
male: 8.7 deaths/1,000 live births
female: 6.9 deaths/1,000 live births (2017 est.)
country comparison to the world: 158

Life expectancy at birth: *total population:* 72.1 years
male: 67.4 years
female: 77.1 years (2017 est.)
country comparison to the world: 150

Total fertility rate: 1.54 children born/woman (2017 est.)
country comparison to the world: 191

Contraceptive prevalence rate: 65.4% (2012)

Health expenditures: 7.1% of GDP (2014)
country comparison to the world: 78

Physicians density: 3 physicians/1,000 population (2014)

Hospital bed density: 9 beds/1,000 population (2012)

Drinking water source:
improved:
urban: 95.5% of population
rural: 97.8% of population
total: 96.2% of population
unimproved:
urban: 4.5% of population
rural: 2.2% of population
total: 3.8% of population (2015 est.)

Sanitation facility access:
improved:

urban: 97.4% of population
rural: 92.6% of population
total: 95.9% of population
unimproved:
urban: 2.6% of population
rural: 7.4% of population
total: 4.1% of population (2015 est.)

HIV/AIDS—adult prevalence rate: 0.9% (2016 est.)
country comparison to the world: 46

HIV/AIDS—people living with HIV/AIDS: 240,000 (2016 est.)
country comparison to the world: 23

HIV/AIDS—deaths: 8,500 (2016 est.)
country comparison to the world: 22

Obesity—adult prevalence rate: 24.1% (2016)
country comparison to the world: 61

Education expenditures: 6% of GDP (2014)
country comparison to the world: 35

Literacy: *definition:* age 15 and over can read and write
total population: 99.8%
male: 99.8%
female: 99.7% (2015 est.)

School life expectancy (primary to tertiary education): *total:* 15 years
male: 15 years
female: 16 years (2014)

Unemployment, youth ages 15-24: *total:* 22.4%
male: 22.7%
female: 21.9% (2015 est.)
country comparison to the world: 67

GOVERNMENT

Country name: *conventional long form:* none
conventional short form: Ukraine
local long form: none
local short form: Ukrayina
former: Ukrainian National Republic, Ukrainian State, Ukrainian Soviet Socialist Republic
etymology: name derives from the Old East Slavic word "ukraina" meaning "borderland or march (militarized border region)" and began to be used extensively in the 19th century; originally Ukrainians referred to themselves as Rusyny (Rusyns, Ruthenians, or Ruthenes), an endonym derived from the medieval Rus state (Kyivan Rus)

Government type: semi-presidential republic

Capital: *name:* Kyiv (Kiev)
note: pronounced KAY-yiv

geographic coordinates: 50 26 N, 30 31 E
time difference: UTC+2 (7 hours ahead of Washington, DC, during Standard Time)
daylight saving time: +1hr, begins last Sunday in March; ends last Sunday in October

Administrative divisions: 24 provinces (oblasti, singular—oblast'), 1 autonomous republic* (avtonomna respublika), and 2 municipalities** (mista, singular—misto) with oblast status; Cherkasy, Chernihiv, Chernivtsi, Crimea or Avtonomna Respublika Krym* (Simferopol'), Dnipropetrovs'k (Dnipro), Donets'k, Ivano-Frankivs'k, Kharkiv, Kherson, Khmel'nyts'kyy,

Kirovohrad (Kropyvnyts'kyy), Kyiv**, Kyiv, Luhans'k, L'viv, Mykolayiv, Odesa, Poltava, Rivne, Sevastopol'**, Sumy, Ternopil', Vinnytsya, Volyn' (Luts'k), Zakarpattya (Uzhhorod), Zaporizhzhya, Zhytomyr

note 1: administrative divisions have the same names as their administrative centers (exceptions have the administrative center name following in parentheses); plans include the eventual renaming of Dnipropetrovsk and Kirovohrad oblasts, but because these names are mentioned in the Constitution of Ukraine, the change will require a constitutional amendment

note 2: the US Government does not recognize Russia's annexation of Ukraine's Autonomous Republic of Crimea and the municipality of Sevastopol, nor their redesignation as the Republic of Crimea and the Federal City of Sevastopol

Independence: 24 August 1991 (from the Soviet Union); notable earlier dates: ca. 982 (VOLODYMYR I consolidates Kyivan Rus); 1648 (establishment of the Cossack Hetmanate)

National holiday: Independence Day, 24 August (1991); note—22 January 1918, the day Ukraine first declared its independence from Soviet Russia, and the date the short-lived Western and Greater (Eastern) Ukrainian republics united (1919), is now celebrated as Unity Day

Constitution: history: several previous; latest adopted and ratified 28 June 1996

amendments: proposed by the president of Ukraine or by at least one-third of the Supreme Council members; adoption requires simple majority vote by the Council and at least two-thirds majority vote in its next regular session; adoption of proposals relating to general constitutional principles, elections, and amendment procedures requires two-thirds majority vote by the Council and approval in a referendum; constitutional articles on personal rights and freedoms, national independence, and territorial integrity cannot be amended; amended 2004, 2010, 2015 (2016)

Legal system: civil law system; judicial review of legislative acts

International law organization participation: has not submitted an ICJ jurisdiction declaration; non-party state to the ICCt

Citizenship: citizenship by birth: no

citizenship by descent only: at least one parent must be a citizen of Ukraine

dual citizenship recognized: no

residency requirement for naturalization: 5 years

Suffrage: 18 years of age; universal

Executive branch: chief of state: President Petro POROSHENKO (since 7 June 2014)

head of government: Prime Minister Volodymyr HROYSMAN (since 14 April 2016); First Deputy Prime Minister Stepan KUBIV (since 14 April 2016)

cabinet: Cabinet of Ministers nominated by the prime minister, approved by the Verkhovna Rada

elections/appointments: president directly elected by absolute majority popular vote in 2

rounds if needed for a 5-year term (eligible for a second term); election last held on 25 May 2014 (next to be held in 2019); prime minister nominated by the president, confirmed by the Verkhovna Rada

election results: Petro POROSHENKO elected president; percent of vote—Petro POROSHENKO (independent) 54.5%, Yuliya TYMOSHENKO (Fatherland) 12.9%, Oleh LYASHKO (Radical Party) 8.4%, other 24.2%; Volodymyr HROYSMAN (BPP) elected prime minister; Verkhovna Rada vote 257-50

note: there is also a National Security and Defense Council or NSDC originally created in 1992 as the National Security Council; the NSDC staff is tasked with developing national security policy on domestic and international matters and advising the president; a presidential administration helps draft presidential edicts and provides policy support to the president

Legislative branch: description: unicameral Supreme Council or Verkhovna Rada (450 seats; 225 members directly elected in single-seat constituencies by simple majority vote and 225 directly elected in a single nationwide constituency by proportional representation vote; members serve 5-year terms)

elections: last held on 26 October 2014 (next to be held fall of 2019)

election results: percent of vote by party/coalition—NF 22.1%, BPP 21.8%, Samopomich 11.0%, OB 9.4%, Radical 7.4%, Batkivshchyna 5.7%, Svoboda 4.7%, CPU 3.9%, other 14%; seats by party/coalition—BPP 132, NF 82, Samopomich 33, OB 29, Radical 22, Batkivshchyna 19, Svoboda 6, other 4, independent 96, vacant 27; note—voting not held in Crimea and parts of two Russian-occupied eastern oblasts leaving 27 seats vacant

note: as of December 2017, seats by party/coalition—BPP 138, NF 81, OB 43, Samopomich 25, Vidrozhennya 26, Radical 21, Batkivshchyna 20, VN 18, independent 51, vacant 27

Judicial branch: highest court(s): Supreme Court of Ukraine or SCU (consists of 95 judges organized into civil, criminal, commercial, and administrative chambers, and a military panel); Constitutional Court (consists of 18 justices)

judge selection and term of office: Supreme Court judges proposed by the Supreme Council of Justice or SCJ (a 20-member independent body of judicial officials and other appointees) and appointed by presidential decree; judges initially appointed for 5 years and, if approved by the SCJ, serve until mandatory retirement at age 65; Constitutional Court justices appointed—6 each by the president, by the SCU, and by the Verkhovna Rada; justices appointed for 9-year nonrenewable terms

subordinate courts: specialized high courts; Courts of Cassation; Courts of Appeal; regional, district, city, and town courts

Political parties and leaders: Batkivshchyna ("Fatherland") [Yuliya TYMOSHENKO]

Bloc of Petro Poroshenko—Solidarnist or BPP [Vitaliy KLYCHKO] (formed from the merger of Solidarnist and UDAR)

Hromadyanska Positsiya ("Civic Position") [Anatoliy HRYTSENKO]

Narodnyy Front ("People's Front") or NF [Arseniy YATSENIUK]

Opposition Bloc or OB [Yuriy BOYKO]

Radical Party [Oleh LYASHKO]

Rukh Novykh Syl ("Movement of New Forces") [Mikheil SAAKASHVILI]

Samopomich ("Self Reliance") [Andriy SADOVYY]

Svoboda ("Freedom") [Oleh TYAHNYBOK]

Ukrainian Association of Patriots or UKROP [Taras BATENKO]

Vidrozhennya ("Revival") [Vitaliy KHOMUTYNNIK]

Volya Narodu ("People's Will") or VN [Yaroslav MOSKALENKO] (parliamentary group)

Za Zhyttya ("For Life") [Vadym RABYNOVICH]

Political pressure groups and leaders: Centre UA [Oleh RYBACHUK]

OPORA Civic Network [Olha AIVAZOVSKA]

International organization participation: Australia Group, BSEC, CBSS (observer), CD, CE, CEI, CICA (observer), CIS (participating member, has not signed the 1993 CIS charter), EAEC (observer), EAPC, EBRD, FAO, GCTU, GUAM, IAEA, IBRD, ICAO, ICC (national committees), ICRM, IDA, IFC, IFRCS, IHO, ILO, IMF, IMO, IMSO, Interpol, IOC, IOM, IPU, ISO, ITU, ITUC (NGOs), LAIA (observer), MIGA, MONUSCO, NAM (observer), NSG, OAS (observer), OIF (observer), OPCW, OSCE, PCA, PFP, SELEC (observer), UN, UN Security Council (temporary), UNCTAD, UNESCO, UNFICYP, UNIDO, UNISFA, UNMIL, UNMISS, UNOCI, UNWTO, UPU, WCO, WFTU (NGOs), WHO, WIPO, WMO, WTO, ZC

Diplomatic representation in the US: chief of mission: Ambassador Valeriy CHALYY (since 3 August 2015)

chancery: 3350 M Street NW, Washington, DC 20007

telephone: [1] (202) 349-2920

FAX: [1] (202) 333-0817

consulate(s) general: Chicago, New York, San Francisco

Diplomatic representation from the US: chief of mission: Ambassador Marie YOVANOVITCH (since 29 August 2016)

embassy: 4 Igor Sikorsky Street, 04112 Kyiv

mailing address: 5850 Kyiv Place, Washington, DC 20521-5850

telephone: [380] (44) 521-5000

FAX: [380] (44) 521-5155

Flag description: two equal horizontal bands of azure (top) and golden yellow represent grain fields under a blue sky

National symbol(s): tryzub (trident); national colors: blue, yellow

National anthem: name: "Shche ne vmerla Ukraina" (Ukraine Has Not Yet Perished)

lyrics/music: Paul CHUBYNSKYI/Mikhail VERBYTSKYI

note: music adopted 1991, lyrics adopted 2003; song first performed in 1864 at the Ukraine Theatre in Lviv; the lyrics, originally written in 1862, were revised in 2003

ECONOMY

Economy—overview: After Russia, the Ukrainian Republic was the most important economic component of the former Soviet Union, producing about four times the output of the next-ranking republic. Its fertile black soil generated more than one-fourth of Soviet agricultural output, and its farms provided substantial quantities of meat, milk, grain, and vegetables to other republics. Likewise, its diversified heavy industry supplied unique equipment, such as, large diameter pipes and vertical drilling apparatus, and raw materials to industrial and mining sites in other regions of the former USSR.

Shortly after independence in August 1991, the Ukrainian Government liberalized most prices and erected a legal framework for privatization, but widespread resistance to reform within the government and the legislature soon stalled reform efforts and led to some backtracking. Output by 1999 had fallen to less than 40% of the 1991 level. Outside institutions—particularly the IMF encouraged Ukraine to quicken the pace and scope of reforms to foster economic growth. Ukrainian Government officials eliminated most tax and customs privileges in a March 2005 budget law, bringing more economic activity out of Ukraine's large shadow economy. From 2000 until mid-2008, Ukraine's economy was buoyant despite political turmoil between the prime minister and president. The economy contracted nearly 15% in 2009, among the worst economic performances in the world. In April 2010, Ukraine negotiated a price discount on Russian gas imports in exchange for extending Russia's lease on its naval base in Crimea.

Ukraine's oligarch-dominated economy grew slowly from 2010 to 2013. After former President YANUKOVYCH fled the country during the Revolution of Dignity, the international community began efforts to stabilize the Ukrainian economy, including a March 2014 IMF assistance package of $17.5 billion, of which Ukraine has received four disbursements, most recently in April 2017, bringing the total disbursed as of that date to approximately $8.4 billion. Ukraine has made significant progress on reforms designed to make the country prosperous, democratic, and transparent. But more improvements are needed, including fighting corruption, developing capital markets, and improving the legislative framework.

Russia's occupation of Crimea in March 2014 and ongoing aggression in eastern Ukraine have hurt economic growth. With the loss of a major portion of Ukraine's heavy industry in Donbas and ongoing violence, Ukraine's economy contracted by 6.6% in 2014 and by 9.8% in 2015, but grew by 2.3% in 2016 and 2.0% in 2017 as key reforms

took hold. After the EU and Ukraine enacted the Deep and Comprehensive Free Trade Area and Russia imposed a series of trade restrictions, the EU replaced Russia as Ukraine's largest trading partner. A new prohibition on commercial trade with separatist-controlled territories has had an uncertain effect on Ukraine's key industrial sectors.

GDP (purchasing power parity): $366.4 billion (2017 est.)
$359 billion (2016 est.)
$350.9 billion (2015 est.)
note: data are in 2017 dollars
country comparison to the world: 51

GDP (official exchange rate): $104.1 billion (2016 est.)

GDP—real growth rate: 2% (2017 est.)
2.3% (2016 est.)
-9.8% (2015 est.)
country comparison to the world: 152

GDP—per capita (PPP): $8,700 (2017 est.)
$8,500 (2016 est.)
$8,200 (2015 est.)
note: data are in 2017 dollars
country comparison to the world: 146

Gross national saving: 17.7% of GDP (2017 est.)
17.5% of GDP (2016 est.)
15.7% of GDP (2015 est.)
country comparison to the world: 103

GDP—composition, by end use:
household consumption: 65%
government consumption: 18.7%
investment in fixed capital: 14%
investment in inventories: 2%
exports of goods and services: 47.9%
imports of goods and services: -47.4% (2017 est.)

GDP—composition, by sector of origin:
agriculture: 14%
industry: 27.8%
services: 58.7%
(2017 est.)

Agriculture—products: grain, sugar beets, sunflower seeds, vegetables; beef, milk

Industries: coal, electric power, ferrous and nonferrous metals, machinery and transport equipment, chemicals, food processing

Industrial production growth rate: 3.6% (2017 est.)
country comparison to the world: 79

Labor force: 17.99 million (2017 est.)
country comparison to the world: 36
Labor force—by occupation: agriculture: 5.8%
industry: 26.5%
services: 67.8%
(2014)

Unemployment rate: 9.5% (2017 est.)
9.3% (2016 est.)
note: officially registered workers; large number of unregistered or underemployed workers
country comparison to the world: 132

Population below poverty line: 24.1% (2010 est.)

Household income or consumption by percentage share: *lowest 10%:* 3.8%
highest 10%: 22.5% (2011 est.)

Distribution of family income—Gini index: 24.6 (2013)
28.2 (2009)
country comparison to the world: 146

Budget: *revenues:* $35.6 billion
expenditures: $38.91 billion
note: this is the planned, consolidated budget (2017 est.)

Taxes and other revenues: 34.2% of GDP (2017 est.)
country comparison to the world: 59

Budget surplus (+) or deficit (-): -3.2% of GDP (2017 est.)
country comparison to the world: 118

Public debt: 89% of GDP (2017 est.)
81% of GDP (2016 est.)
note: the total public debt of $64.5 billion consists of: domestic public debt ($23.8 billion); external public debt ($26.1 billion); and sovereign guarantees ($14.6 billion)
country comparison to the world: 27

Fiscal year: calendar year

Inflation rate (consumer prices): 12.8% (2017 est.)
13.9% (2016 est.)
note: Excluding the temporarily occupied territories of the Autonomous Republic of Crimea, the city of Sevastopol and part of the anti-terrorist operation zone
country comparison to the world: 208

Central bank discount rate: 22% (23 December 2015)
7.5% (31 January 2012)
country comparison to the world: 5

Commercial bank prime lending rate: 16.5% (31 December 2017 est.)
19.24% (31 December 2016 est.)
country comparison to the world: 31

Stock of narrow money: $22.43 billion (31 December 2017 est.)
$19.49 billion (31 December 2016 est.)
country comparison to the world: 68

Stock of broad money: $45.55 billion (31 December 2017 est.)
$40.54 billion (31 December 2016 est.)
country comparison to the world: 71

Stock of domestic credit: $69.99 billion (31 December 2017 est.)
$61.65 billion (31 December 2016 est.)
country comparison to the world: 61

Market value of publicly traded shares: $20.71 billion (31 December 2012 est.)
$25.56 billion (31 December 2011 est.)
$39.46 billion (31 December 2010 est.)
country comparison to the world: 66

Current account balance: -$3.409 billion (2017 est.)
-$3.779 billion (2016 est.)
country comparison to the world: 169

Exports: $36.85 billion (2017 est.)
$33.56 billion (2016 est.)
country comparison to the world: 56

Exports—commodities: ferrous and nonferrous metals, fuel and petroleum products, chemicals, machinery and transport equipment, foodstuffs

Exports—partners: Russia 9.9%, Egypt 6.2%, Poland 6.1%, Turkey 5.7%, Italy 5.3%, India 5.2%, China 5.1% (2016)

Imports: $44.42 billion (2017 est.)
$40.57 billion (2016 est.)
country comparison to the world: 54

Imports—commodities: energy, machinery and equipment, chemicals

Imports—partners: Russia 13.1%, China 12%, Germany 11%, Belarus 7.1%, Poland 6.9%, US 4.3% (2016)

Reserves of foreign exchange and gold: $21.8 billion (31 December 2017 est.)
$15.54 billion (31 December 2016 est.)
country comparison to the world: 58

Debt—external: $125.3 billion (31 December 2017 est.)
$121.1 billion (31 December 2016 est.)
country comparison to the world: 46

Stock of direct foreign investment—at home: $71.15 billion (31 December 2017 est.)
$64.95 billion (31 December 2016 est.)
country comparison to the world: 53

Stock of direct foreign investment—abroad: $8.983 billion (31 December 2017 est.)
$7.983 billion (31 December 2016 est.)
country comparison to the world: 63

Exchange rates: hryvnia (UAH) per US dollar—
26.71 (2017 est.)
25.5513 (2016 est.)
25.5513 (2015 est.)
21.8447 (2014 est.)
11.8867 (2013 est.)

ENERGY

Electricity access: *electrification—total population:* 100% (2016)

Electricity—production: 152.2 billion kWh (2015 est.)
country comparison to the world: 26

Electricity—consumption: 133.4 billion kWh (2015 est.)
country comparison to the world: 27

Electricity—exports: 3.591 billion kWh (2015 est.)
country comparison to the world: 39

Electricity—imports: 2.241 billion kWh (2015 est.)
country comparison to the world: 53

Electricity—installed generating capacity: 56.92 million kW (2015 est.)
country comparison to the world: 21

Electricity—from fossil fuels: 62.1% of total installed capacity (2015 est.)
country comparison to the world: 122

Electricity—from nuclear fuels: 23% of total installed capacity (2015 est.)
country comparison to the world: 6

Electricity—from hydroelectric plants: 10.3% of total installed capacity (2015 est.)
country comparison to the world: 119

Electricity—from other renewable sources: 2.7% of total installed capacity (2015 est.)
country comparison to the world: 114

Crude oil—production: 32,070 bbl/day (2016 est.)
country comparison to the world: 62

Crude oil—exports: 1,336 bbl/day (2014 est.)
country comparison to the world: 69

Crude oil—imports: 7,840 bbl/day (2014 est.)
country comparison to the world: 76

Crude oil—proved reserves: 395 million bbl (1 January 2017 es)
country comparison to the world: 53

Refined petroleum products—production: 78,030 bbl/day (2014 est.)
country comparison to the world: 71

Refined petroleum products—consumption: 248,000 bbl/day (2015 est.)
country comparison to the world: 50

Refined petroleum products—exports: 15,210 bbl/day (2014 est.)
country comparison to the world: 76

Refined petroleum products—imports: 177,700 bbl/day (2014 est.)
country comparison to the world: 36

Natural gas—production: 19 billion cu m (2015 est.)
country comparison to the world: 33

Natural gas—consumption: 41.1 billion cu m (2015 est.)
country comparison to the world: 28

Natural gas—exports: 0 cu m (2015 est.)
country comparison to the world: 201

Natural gas—imports: 14.18 billion cu m (2015 est.)
country comparison to the world: 22

Natural gas—proved reserves: 1.104 trillion cu m (1 January 2017 es)
country comparison to the world: 26

Carbon dioxide emissions from consumption of energy: 291 million Mt (2013 est.)
country comparison to the world: 23

COMMUNICATIONS

Telephones—fixed lines: *total subscriptions:* 8,451,229
subscriptions per 100 inhabitants: 19 (July 2016 est.)
country comparison to the world: 20

Telephones—mobile cellular: *total:* 56,717,856
subscriptions per 100 inhabitants: 128 (July 2016 est.)
country comparison to the world: 25

Telephone system: *general assessment:* Ukraine's telecommunication development plan emphasizes improving domestic trunk lines, international connections, and the mobile-cellular system
domestic: the country's former sole telephone provider, Ukrtelecom, was successfully privatized 2011 and independent foreign-invested private

companies now provide substantial telecommunications services; the mobile-cellular telephone system's expansion has slowed, largely due to saturation of the market that is now about 130 mobile phones per 100 persons
international: country code—380; 2 new domestic trunk lines are a part of the fiber-optic Trans-Asia-Europe (TAE) system and 3 Ukrainian links have been installed in the fiber-optic Trans-European Lines (TEL) project that connects 18 countries; additional international service is provided by the Italy-Turkey-Ukraine-Russia (ITUR) fiber-optic submarine cable and by an unknown number of earth stations in the Intelsat, Inmarsat, and Intersputnik satellite systems (2016)

Broadcast media: state-controlled nationwide TV broadcast channel (UT1) and a number of privately owned TV networks provide basic TV coverage; multi-channel cable and satellite TV services are available; Russian television broadcasts have a small audience nationwide, but larger audiences in the eastern and southern regions; the radio broadcast market, a mix of independent and state-owned networks, is comprised of some 300 stations (2007)

Internet country code: .ua

Internet users: *total:* 23,202,067

percent of population: 52.5% (July 2016 est.)
country comparison to the world: 32

TRANSPORTATION

National air transport system: *number of registered air carriers:* 17
inventory of registered aircraft operated by air carriers: 92
annual passenger traffic on registered air carriers: 4,613,224
annual freight traffic on registered air carriers: 37,721,565 mt-km (2015)
Civil aircraft registration country code prefix: UR (2016)

Airports: 187 (2013)
country comparison to the world: 31

Airports—with paved runways: *total:* 108
over 3,047 m: 13
2,438 to 3,047 m: 42
1,524 to 2,437 m: 22
914 to 1,523 m: 3
under 914 m: 28 (2013)

Airports—with unpaved runways: *total:* 79
1,524 to 2,437 m: 5
914 to 1,523 m: 5
under 914 m: 69 (2013)

Heliports: 9 (2013)

Pipelines: gas 36,720 km; oil 4,514 km; refined products 4,363 km (2013)

Railways: *total:* 21,733 km
broad gauge: 21,684 km 1.524-m gauge (9,250 km electrified)
standard gauge: 49 km 1.435-m gauge (49 km electrified) (2014)
country comparison to the world: 12

Roadways: *total:* 169,694 km

paved: 166,095 km (includes 17 km of expressways)
unpaved: 3,599 km (2012)
country comparison to the world: 31

Waterways: 1,672 km (most on Dnieper River) (2012)
country comparison to the world: 46

Merchant marine: *total:* 419
by type: general cargo 91, oil tanker 15, other 313 (2017)
country comparison to the world: 45

Ports and terminals: *major seaport(s):* Feodosiya (Theodosia), Illichivsk, Mariupol', Mykolayiv, Odesa, Yuzhnyy

MILITARY AND SECURITY

Military expenditures: 3.5% of GDP (2017)
3.67% of GDP (2016)
3.97% of GDP (2015)
3.02% of GDP (2014)
2.39% of GDP (2013)
country comparison to the world: 26

Military branches: Ground Forces, High Mobility Assault Troops, Naval Forces, Air Forces (2017)

Military service age and obligation: 20-27 years of age for compulsory military service; conscript service obligation is 18 months (2015)

TRANSNATIONAL ISSUES

Disputes—international: 1997 boundary delimitation treaty with Belarus remains unratified due to unresolved financial claims, stalling demarcation and reducing border security; delimitation of land boundary with Russia is complete and demarcation began in 2012; the dispute over the boundary between Russia and Ukraine through the Kerch Strait and Sea of Azov is suspended due to the occupation of Crimea by Russia; Ukraine and Moldova signed an agreement officially delimiting their border in 1999, but the border has not been demarcated due to Moldova's difficulties with the break-away region of Transnistria; Moldova and Ukraine operate joint customs posts to monitor transit of people and commodities through Moldova's Transnistria Region, which remains under the auspices of an Organization for Security and Cooperation in Europe-mandated peacekeeping mission comprised of Moldovan, Transnistrian, Russian, and Ukrainian troops; the ICJ ruled largely in favor of Romania in its dispute submitted in 2004 over Ukrainian-administered Zmiyinyy/Serpilor (Snake) Island and Black Sea maritime boundary delimitation; Romania opposes Ukraine's reopening of a navigation canal from the Danube border through Ukraine to the Black Sea

Refugees and internally displaced persons: IDPs: 1,494,806 (Russian-sponsored separatist violence in Crimea and eastern Ukraine) (2017)
stateless persons: 35,363 (2016); note—citizens of the former USSR who were permanently resident in Ukraine were granted citizenship upon Ukraine's independence in 1991, but some missed this window of opportunity; people arriving after 1991, Crimean Tatars, ethnic Koreans, people with expired Soviet passports, and people with no documents have difficulty acquiring Ukrainian citizenship; following the fall of the Soviet Union in 1989, thousands of Crimean Tatars and their descendants deported from Ukraine under the STALIN regime returned to their homeland, some being stateless and others holding the citizenship of Uzbekistan or other former Soviet republics; a 1998 bilateral agreement between Ukraine and Uzbekistan simplified the process of renouncing Uzbek citizenship and obtaining Ukrainian citizenship

Trafficking in persons: current situation: Ukraine is a source, transit, and destination country for men, women, and children subjected to forced labor and sex trafficking; Ukrainian victims are sex trafficked within Ukraine as well as in Russia, Poland, Iraq, Spain, Turkey, Cyprus, Greece, Seychelles, Portugal, the Czech Republic, Israel, Italy, South Korea, Moldova, China, the United Arab Emirates, Montenegro, UK, Kazakhstan, Tunisia, and other countries; small numbers of foreigners from Moldova, Russia, Vietnam, Uzbekistan, Pakistan, Cameroon, and Azerbaijan were victims of labor trafficking in Ukraine; Ukrainian recruiters most often target Ukrainians from rural areas with limited job prospects using fraud, coercion, and debt bondage

tier rating: Tier 2 Watch List—Ukraine does not fully comply with the minimum standards for the elimination of trafficking; however, it is making significant efforts to do so; the government's focus on its security situation constrained its anti-trafficking capabilities; law enforcement efforts to pursue trafficking cases weakened in 2014, continuing a multi-year decline, and no investigations, prosecutions, or convictions of government officials were made, despite reports of official complicity in the sex and labor trafficking of children living in state-run institutions; fewer victims were identified and referred to NGOs, which continued to provide and to fund the majority of victims' services (2015)

Illicit drugs: limited cultivation of cannabis and opium poppy, mostly for CIS consumption; some synthetic drug production for export to the West; limited government eradication program; used as transshipment point for opiates and other illicit drugs from Africa, Latin America, and Turkey to Europe and Russia; Ukraine has improved anti-money-laundering controls, resulting in its removal from the Financial Action Task Force's (FATF's) Noncooperative Countries and Territories List in February 2004; Ukraine's anti-money-laundering regime continues to be monitored by FATF

UNITED ARAB EMIRATES

INTRODUCTION

Background: The Trucial States of the Persian Gulf coast granted the UK control of their defense and foreign affairs in 19th century treaties. In 1971, six of these states—Abu Dhabi, 'Ajman, Al Fujayrah, Ash Shariqah, Dubayy, and Umm al Qaywayn—merged to form the United Arab Emirates (UAE). They were joined in 1972 by Ra's al Khaymah. The UAE's per capita GDP is on par with those of leading West European nations. For more than three decades, oil and global finance drove the UAE's economy. However, in 2008-09, the confluence of falling oil prices, collapsing real estate prices, and the international banking crisis hit the UAE especially hard. The UAE essentially avoided the "Arab Spring" unrest seen elsewhere in the Middle East in 2010-11 and in an effort to stem potential unrest, the government announced a multi-year, $1.6-billion infrastructure investment plan for the poorer northern emirates and aggressively pursued advocates of political reform. The UAE in recent years has played a vital role in regional affairs. In addition to donating billions of dollars in economic aid to help stabilize Egypt, the UAE is a member of a US-led global coalition to defeat the Islamic State in Iraq and the Levant (ISIL) and a coalition partner in a Saudi-led military campaign to restore the Government of Yemen.

GEOGRAPHY

Location: Middle East, bordering the Gulf of Oman and the Persian Gulf, between Oman and Saudi Arabia

Geographic coordinates: 24 00 N, 54 00 E

Map references: Middle East

Area: *total:* 83,600 sq km
land: 83,600 sq km
water: 0 sq km
country comparison to the world: 116

Area—comparative: slightly larger than South Carolina; slightly smaller than Maine

Land boundaries: *total:* 1,066 km

941

border countries (2): Oman 609 km, Saudi Arabia 457 km

Coastline: 1,318 km

Maritime claims: *territorial sea:* 12 nm
contiguous zone: 24 nm
exclusive economic zone: 200 nm
continental shelf: 200 nm or to the edge of the continental margin

Climate: desert; cooler in eastern mountains

Terrain: flat, barren coastal plain merging into rolling sand dunes of vast desert; mountains in east

Elevation: *mean elevation:* 149 m

elevation extremes: *lowest point:* Persian Gulf 0 m
highest point: Jabal Yibir 1,527 m

Natural resources: petroleum, natural gas

Land use: *agricultural land:* 4.6%
arable land: 0.5%;
permanent crops: 0.5%;
permanent pasture: 3.6%
forest: 3.8%
other: 91.6% (2011 est.)
Irrigated land: 923 sq km (2012)

Population—distribution: population is heavily concentrated to the northeast on the Musandam Peninsula; the three largest emirates—Abu Dhabi, Dubai, and Sharjah—are home to nearly 85% of the population

Natural hazards: frequent sand and dust storms

Environment—current issues: lack of natural freshwater resources compensated by desalination plants; desertification; beach pollution from oil spills

Environment—international agreements: *party to:* Biodiversity, Climate Change, Climate Change-Kyoto Protocol, Desertification, Endangered Species, Hazardous Wastes, Marine Dumping, Ozone Layer Protection
signed, but not ratified: Law of the Sea

Geography—note: strategic location along southern approaches to Strait of Hormuz, a vital transit point for world crude oil

PEOPLE AND SOCIETY

Population: 6,072,475 (July 2017 est.)
note: the UN estimated the country's total population was 9,400,145 as of mid-year 2017; immigrants make up more than 88% of the total population, according to 2015 UN data (2017)
country comparison to the world: 110

Nationality: *noun:* Emirati(s)
adjective: Emirati

Ethnic groups: Emirati 11.6%, South Asian 59.4% (includes Indian 38.2%, Bangladeshi 9.5%, Pakistani 9.4%, other 2.3%), Egyptian 10.2%, Philippine 6.1%, other 12.8% (2015 est.)

Languages: Arabic (official), Persian, English, Hindi, Urdu

Religions: Muslim (official) 76%, Christian 9%, other (primarily Hindu and Buddhist, less than 5% of the population consists of Parsi, Baha'i, Druze,

Sikh, Ahmadi, Ismaili, Dawoodi Bohra Muslim, and Jewish) 15%
note: represents the total population; about 85% of the population consists of noncitizens (2005 est.)

Age structure: *0-14 years:* 21.01% (male 652,718/female 622,850)
15-24 years: 13.51% (male 487,558/female 332,829)
25-54 years: 61.14% (male 2,828,731/female 884,233)
55-64 years: 3.27% (male 147,429/female 51,097)
65 years and over: 1.07% (male 40,226/female 24,804) (2017 est.)

Dependency ratios: *total dependency ratio:* 17.4
youth dependency ratio: 16.2
elderly dependency ratio: 1.2
potential support ratio: 83.4 (2015 est.)

Median age: *total:* 30.3 years
male: 32.1 years
female: 25 years (2017 est.)
country comparison to the world: 112

Population growth rate: 2.37% (2017 est.)
country comparison to the world: 28

Birth rate: 15.1 births/1,000 population (2017 est.)
country comparison to the world: 128

Death rate: 1.9 deaths/1,000 population (2017 est.)
country comparison to the world: 225

Net migration rate: 10.5 migrant(s)/1,000 population (2017 est.)
country comparison to the world: 9

Population distribution: population is heavily concentrated to the northeast on the Musandam Peninsula; the three largest emirates—Abu Dhabi, Dubai, and Sharjah—are home to nearly 85% of the population

Urbanization: *urban population:* 86.1% of total population (2017)
rate of urbanization: 2.32% annual rate of change (2015-20 est.)

Major urban areas—population: Dubai 2.415 million; Sharjah 1.279 million; ABU DHABI (capital) 1.145 million (2015)

Sex ratio: *at birth:* 1.05 male(s)/female
0-14 years: 1.05 male(s)/female
15-24 years: 1.47 male(s)/female
25-54 years: 3.2 male(s)/female
55-64 years: 2.93 male(s)/female
65 years and over: 1.69 male(s)/female
total population: 2.18 male(s)/female (2016 est.)

Maternal mortality ratio: 6 deaths/100,000 live births (2015 est.)
country comparison to the world: 165

Infant mortality rate: *total:* 10 deaths/1,000 live births
male: 11.6 deaths/1,000 live births
female: 8.3 deaths/1,000 live births (2017 est.)
country comparison to the world: 137

Life expectancy at birth: *total population:* 77.7 years
male: 75 years
female: 80.4 years (2017 est.)
country comparison to the world: 69

Total fertility rate: 2.32 children born/woman (2017 est.)
country comparison to the world: 87

Health expenditures: 3.6% of GDP (2014)
country comparison to the world: 171

Physicians density: 1.56 physicians/1,000 population (2014)

Hospital bed density: 1.1 beds/1,000 population (2012)

Drinking water source:
improved:
urban: 99.6% of population
rural: 100% of population
total: 99.6% of population
unimproved:
urban: 0.4% of population
rural: 0% of population
total: 0.4% of population (2015 est.)

Sanitation facility access:
improved:
urban: 98% of population
rural: 95.2% of population
total: 97.6% of population
unimproved:
urban: 2% of population
rural: 4.8% of population
total: 2.4% of population (2015 est.)

HIV/AIDS—adult prevalence rate: NA

HIV/AIDS—people living with HIV/AIDS: NA

HIV/AIDS—deaths: NA

Obesity—adult prevalence rate: 31.7% (2016)
country comparison to the world: 20

Education expenditures: NA

Literacy: *definition:* age 15 and over can read and write
total population: 93.8%
male: 93.1%
female: 95.8% (2015 est.)

Unemployment, youth ages 15-24: *total:* 12.1%
male: 7.9%
female: 21.8% (2008 est.)
country comparison to the world: 91

GOVERNMENT

Country name: *conventional long form:* United Arab Emirates
conventional short form: none
local long form: Al Imarat al Arabiyah al Muttahidah
local short form: none
former: Trucial Oman, Trucial States
abbreviation: UAE
etymology: self-descriptive country name; the name "Arabia" can be traced back many centuries B.C., the ancient Egyptians referred to the region as "Ar Rabi"; "emirates" derives from "amir" the Arabic word for "commander," "lord," or "prince"

Government type: federation of monarchies

Capital: *name:* Abu Dhabi
geographic coordinates: 24 28 N, 54 22 E
time difference: UTC+4 (9 hours ahead of Washington, DC, during Standard Time)

Administrative divisions: 7 emirates (imarat, singular—imarah); Abu Zaby (Abu Dhabi), 'Ajman, Al Fujayrah, Ash Shariqah (Sharjah), Dubayy (Dubai), Ra's al Khaymah, Umm al Qaywayn

Independence: 2 December 1971 (from the UK)

National holiday: Independence Day (National Day), 2 December (1971)

Constitution: *history:* previous 1971 (provisional); latest drafted in 1979, became permanent May 1996
amendments: proposed by the Supreme Council and submitted to the Federal National Council; passage requires at least a two-thirds majority vote of Federal National Council members present, and approval by the Supreme Council president; amended 2009 (2016)

Legal system: mixed legal system of Islamic law and civil law

International law organization participation: has not submitted an ICJ jurisdiction declaration; non-party state to the ICCt

Citizenship: *citizenship by birth:* no
citizenship by descent only: the father must be a citizen of the United Arab Emirates; if the father is unknown, the mother must be a citizen
dual citizenship recognized: no
residency requirement for naturalization: 30 years

Suffrage: limited; note—rulers of the seven emirates each select a proportion of voters for the Federal National Council (FNC) that together account for about 12 percent of Emirati citizens

Executive branch: *chief of state:* President KHALIFA bin Zayid Al-Nuhayyan (since 3 November 2004), ruler of Abu Zaby (Abu Dhabi) (since 4 November 2004); Vice President and Prime Minister MUHAMMAD BIN RASHID Al-Maktum (since 5 January 2006)

head of government: Prime Minister Vice President MUHAMMAD BIN RASHID Al-Maktum (since 5 January 2006); Deputy Prime Ministers SAIF bin Zayid Al-Nuhayyan, MANSUR bin Zayid Al-Nuhayyan (both since 11 May 2009)
cabinet: Council of Ministers announced by the prime minister and approved by the president
elections/appointments: president and vice president indirectly elected by the Federal Supreme Council—composed of the rulers of the 7 emirates—for a 5-year term (no term limits); election last held 3 November 2009 (next election NA); prime minister and deputy prime minister appointed by the president
election results: KHALIFA bin Zayid Al-Nuhayyan reelected president; FSC vote NA
note: there is also a Federal Supreme Council (FSC) composed of the 7 emirate rulers; the FSC is the highest constitutional authority in the UAE; establishes general policies and sanctions federal legislation; meets 4 times a year; Abu Zaby (Abu Dhabi) and Dubayy (Dubai) rulers have effective veto power

Legislative branch: *description:* unicameral Federal National Council (FNC) or Majlis al-Ittihad al-Watani (40 seats; 20 members indirectly elected by an electoral college whose members are selected by each emirate ruler proportional to its FNC membership, and 20 members appointed by the rulers of the 7 constituent states; members serve 4-year terms)
elections: last held on 3 October 2015 (next to be held in 2019); note—the electoral college was expanded from 129,274 electors in the December 2011 election to 224,279 in the October 2015 election; 347 candidates including 78 women ran for 20 contested seats in the 40-member FNC
election results: 19 men and 1 woman were elected; seats by emirate—Abu Dhabi 4, Dubai 4, Sharjah 3, Ras al-Khaimah 3, Ajman 2, Fujairah 2, Umm al-Quwain 2; note—only 1 woman (from Ras Al Khaimah) won an FNC seat

Judicial branch: *highest court(s):* Federal Supreme Court (consists of the court president and 4 judges; jurisdiction limited to federal cases)
judge selection and term of office: judges appointed by the federal president following approval by the Federal Supreme Council, the highest executive and legislative authority consisting of the 7 emirate rulers; judges serve until retirement age or the expiry of their appointment terms
subordinate courts: Federal Court of Cassation (determines the constitutionality of laws promulgated at the federal and emirate level; federal level courts of first instance and appeals courts; the emirates of Abu Dhabi, Dubai, and Ra's al Khaymah have parallel court systems; the other 4 emirates have incorporated their courts into the federal system; note—the Abu Dhabi Global Market (ADGM) Courts and the Dubai International Financial Center (DIFC) Courts both adjudicate civil and commercial disputes.

Political parties and leaders: none; political parties are banned

Political pressure groups and leaders: NA

International organization participation: ABEDA, AfDB (nonregional member), AFESD, AMF, BIS, CAEU, CICA, FAO, G-77, GCC, IAEA, IBRD, ICAO, ICC (national committees), ICRM, IDA, IDB, IFAD, IFC, IFRCS, IHO, ILO, IMF, IMO, IMSO, Interpol, IOC, IPU, ISO, ITSO, ITU, LAS, MIGA, NAM, OAPEC, OIC, OIF (observer), OPCW, OPEC, PCA, UN, UNCTAD, UNESCO, UNIDO, UNRWA, UNWTO, UPU, WCO, WHO, WIPO, WMO, WTO

Diplomatic representation in the US: *chief of mission:* Ambassador Yusif bin Mani bin Said al-UTAYBA (since 28 July 2008)
chancery: 3522 International Court NW, Suite 400, Washington, DC 20008
telephone: [1] (202) 243-2400
FAX: [1] (202) 243-2432
consulate(s) general: Boston, Los Angeles, New York

Diplomatic representation from the US: *chief of mission:* Ambassador Barbara A. LEAF (since 17 November 2014)
embassy: Embassies District, Plot 38 Sector W59-02, Street No. 4, Abu Dhabi
mailing address: P. O. Box 4009, Abu Dhabi
telephone: [971] (2) 414-2200

FAX: [971] (2) 414-2603
consulate(s) general: Dubai

Flag description: three equal horizontal bands of green (top), white, and black with a wider vertical red band on the hoist side; the flag incorporates all four Pan-Arab colors, which in this case represent fertility (green), neutrality (white), petroleum resources (black), and unity (red); red was the traditional color incorporated into all flags of the emirates before their unification

National symbol(s): golden falcon; national colors: green, white, black, red

National anthem: name: "Nashid al-watani al-imarati" (National Anthem of the UAE)
lyrics/music: AREF Al Sheikh Abdullah Al Hassan/Mohamad Abdel WAHAB
note: music adopted 1971, lyrics adopted 1996; Mohamad Abdel WAHAB also composed the music for the anthem of Tunisia

ECONOMY

Economy—overview: The UAE has an open economy with a high per capita income and a sizable annual trade surplus. Successful efforts at economic diversification have reduced the portion of GDP from the oil and gas sector to 30%.

Since the discovery of oil in the UAE nearly 60 years ago, the country has undergone a profound transformation from an impoverished region of small desert principalities to a modern state with a high standard of living. The government has increased spending on job creation and infrastructure expansion and is opening up utilities to greater private sector involvement. The country's free trade zones—offering 100% foreign ownership and zero taxes—are helping to attract foreign investors.

The global financial crisis of 2008-09, tight international credit, and deflated asset prices constricted the economy in 2009. UAE authorities tried to blunt the crisis by increasing spending and boosting liquidity in the banking sector. The crisis hit Dubai hardest, as it was heavily exposed to depressed real estate prices. Dubai lacked sufficient cash to meet its debt obligations, prompting global concern about its solvency and ultimately a $20 billion bailout from the UAE Central Bank and Abu Dhabi Government that was refinanced in March 2014.

The UAE's dependence on oil is a significant long-term challenge. Low oil prices have prompted the UAE to cut expenditures, including on some social programs, but the UAE has sufficient assets in its sovereign investment funds to cover its deficits. The government reduced fuel subsidies in August 2015, and has announced plans to introduce excise and value-added taxes by January 1, 2018. The UAE's strategic plan for the next few years focuses on economic diversification, promoting the UAE as a global trade and tourism hub, developing industry, and creating more job opportunities for nationals through improved education and increased private sector employment.

GDP (purchasing power parity): $691.9 billion (2017 est.)

$682.8 billion (2016 est.)
$662.7 billion (2015 est.)
note: data are in 2017 dollars
country comparison to the world: 33

GDP (official exchange rate): $378.7 billion (2016 est.)

GDP—real growth rate: 1.3% (2017 est.)
3% (2016 est.)
3.8% (2015 est.)
country comparison to the world: 182

GDP—per capita (PPP): $68,200 (2017 est.)
$69,300 (2016 est.)
$69,200 (2015 est.)
note: data are in 2017 dollars
country comparison to the world: 14

Gross national saving: 24.8% of GDP (2017 est.)
27.5% of GDP (2016 est.)
29.7% of GDP (2015 est.)
country comparison to the world: 53

GDP—composition, by end use:
household consumption: 50.5%
government consumption: 12.1%
investment in fixed capital: 20.4%
investment in inventories: 1.3%
exports of goods and services: 94.9%
imports of goods and services: -79.2% (2017 est.)

GDP—composition, by sector of origin:
agriculture: 0.9%
industry: 49.8%
services: 49.2% (2017 est.)

Agriculture—products: dates, vegetables, watermelons; poultry, eggs, dairy products; fish

Industries: petroleum and petrochemicals; fishing, aluminum, cement, fertilizer, commercial ship repair, construction materials, handicrafts, textiles

Industrial production growth rate: -0.1% (2017 est.)
country comparison to the world: 188

Labor force: 5.344 million
note: expatriates account for about 85% of the workforce (2017 est.)
country comparison to the world: 78
Labor force—by occupation: agriculture: 7%
industry: 15%
services: 78% (2000 est.)

Unemployment rate: 3.6% (2014 est.)
2.4% (2001 est.)
country comparison to the world: 39

Population below poverty line: 19.5% (2003 est.)

Household income or consumption by percentage share: *lowest 10%:* NA%
highest 10%: NA%

Budget: *revenues:* $83.44 billion
expenditures: $112.4 billion
note: the UAE federal budget does not account for emirate-level spending in Abu Dhabi and Dubai (2017 est.)

Taxes and other revenues: 22% of GDP (2017 est.)
country comparison to the world: 136

Budget surplus (+) or deficit (-): -7.6% of GDP (2017 est.)

country comparison to the world: 195

Public debt: 60.3% of GDP (2017 est.)
62.7% of GDP (2016 est.)
country comparison to the world: 72

Fiscal year: calendar year

Inflation rate (consumer prices): 2.1% (2017 est.)
1.8% (2016 est.)
country comparison to the world: 99

Central bank discount rate: NA%

Stock of narrow money: $134.8 billion (31 December 2017 est.)
$129 billion (31 December 2016 est.)
country comparison to the world: 31

Stock of broad money: $355.8 billion (31 December 2017 est.)
$333.6 billion (31 December 2016 est.)
country comparison to the world: 32

Stock of domestic credit: $412.5 billion (31 December 2017 est.)
$389.9 billion (31 December 2016 est.)
country comparison to the world: 30

Market value of publicly traded shares: $195.9 billion (31 December 2015 est.)
$201.6 billion (31 December 2014 est.)
$180.3 billion (31 December 2013 est.)
country comparison to the world: 33

Current account balance: $7.878 billion (2017 est.)
$8.412 billion (2016 est.)
country comparison to the world: 23

Exports: $314.7 billion (2017 est.)
$298.6 billion (2016 est.)
country comparison to the world: 18

Exports—commodities: crude oil 45%, natural gas, reexports, dried fish, dates (2012 est.)

Exports—partners: India 9.9%, Iran 8.9%, Japan 8.8%, Switzerland 8.5%, Oman 5.4%, China 5.1% (2016)

Imports: $241.3 billion (2017 est.)
$230.3 billion (2016 est.)
country comparison to the world: 20

Imports—commodities: machinery and transport equipment, chemicals, food

Imports—partners: China 7.4%, US 6.9%, India 6.8%, Germany 4.4% (2016)

Reserves of foreign exchange and gold: $89.79 billion (31 December 2017 est.)
$85.39 billion (31 December 2016 est.)
country comparison to the world: 28

Debt—external: $239.7 billion (31 December 2017 est.)
$218.7 billion (31 December 2016 est.)
country comparison to the world: 34

Stock of direct foreign investment—at home: $144.3 billion (31 December 2017 est.)
$134.8 billion (31 December 2016 est.)
country comparison to the world: 38

Stock of direct foreign investment—abroad: $124.9 billion (31 December 2017 est.)
$114.6 billion (31 December 2016 est.)
country comparison to the world: 33

Exchange rates: Emirati dirhams (AED) per US dollar—
3.673 (2017 est.)
3.673 (2016 est.)
3.673 (2015 est.)
3.673 (2014 est.)
3.673 (2013 est.)

ENERGY

Electricity access: *population without electricity:* 177,824
electrification—*total population:* 98%
electrification—urban areas: 99%
electrification—rural areas: 93% (2012)

Electricity—production: 119.7 billion kWh (2015 est.)
country comparison to the world: 32

Electricity—consumption: 110.6 billion kWh (2015 est.)
country comparison to the world: 32

Electricity—exports: 0 kWh (2016 est.)
country comparison to the world: 98

Electricity—imports: 0 kWh (2016 est.)
country comparison to the world: 118

Electricity—installed generating capacity: 28.9 million kW (2015 est.)
country comparison to the world: 34

Electricity—from fossil fuels: 99.5% of total installed capacity (2015 est.)
country comparison to the world: 29

Electricity—from nuclear fuels: 0% of total installed capacity (2015 est.)
country comparison to the world: 35

Electricity—from hydroelectric plants: 0% of total installed capacity (2015 est.)
country comparison to the world: 158

Electricity—from other renewable sources: 0.5% of total installed capacity (2015 est.)
country comparison to the world: 151

Crude oil—production: 3.106 million bbl/day (2016 est.)
country comparison to the world: 8

Crude oil—exports: 2.684 million bbl/day (2014 est.)
country comparison to the world: 4

Crude oil—imports: 0 bbl/day (2014 est.)
country comparison to the world: 88

Crude oil—proved reserves: 97.8 billion bbl (1 January 2017 es)
country comparison to the world: 7

Refined petroleum products—production: 479,400 bbl/day (2014 est.)
country comparison to the world: 33

Refined petroleum products—consumption: 901,000 bbl/day (2015 est.)
country comparison to the world: 25

Refined petroleum products—exports: 334,900 bbl/day (2014 est.)
country comparison to the world: 26

Refined petroleum products—imports: 413,700 bbl/day (2014 est.)
country comparison to the world: 22

Natural gas—production: 60.18 billion cu m (2015 est.)
country comparison to the world: 15

Natural gas—consumption: 186 billion cu m (2015 est.)
country comparison to the world: 8

Natural gas—exports: 11.08 billion cu m (2015 est.)
country comparison to the world: 21

Natural gas—imports: 20.53 billion cu m (2015 est.)
country comparison to the world: 14

Natural gas—proved reserves: 6.091 trillion cu m (1 January 2017 es)
country comparison to the world: 7

Carbon dioxide emissions from consumption of energy: 245 million Mt (2013 est.)
country comparison to the world: 26

COMMUNICATIONS

Telephones—fixed lines: *total subscriptions:* 2,285,809
subscriptions per 100 inhabitants: 39 (July 2016 est.)
country comparison to the world: 56

Telephones—mobile cellular: *total:* 19,905,093
subscriptions per 100 inhabitants: 336 (July 2016 est.)
country comparison to the world: 64

Telephone system: *general assessment:* modern fiber-optic integrated services; digital network with rapidly growing use of mobile-cellular telephones; key centers are Abu Dhabi and Dubai
domestic: microwave radio relay, fiber-optic and coaxial cable
international: country code—971; linked to the international submarine cable FLAG (Fiber-Optic Link Around the Globe); landing point for both the SEA-ME-WE-3 and SEA-ME-WE-4 submarine cable networks; satellite earth stations—3 Intelsat (1 Atlantic Ocean and 2 Indian (2016)

Broadcast media: except for the many organizations now operating in media free zones in Abu Dhabi and Dubai, most TV and radio stations remain government-owned; widespread use of satellite dishes provides access to pan-Arab and other international broadcasts (2017)

Internet country code: .ae

Internet users: *total:* 5,370,299

percent of population: 90.6% (July 2016 est.)
country comparison to the world: 63

TRANSPORTATION

National air transport system: *number of registered air carriers:* 12
inventory of registered aircraft operated by air carriers: 498
annual passenger traffic on registered air carriers: 84,738,479
annual freight traffic on registered air carriers: 16.647 billion mt-km (2015)
Civil aircraft registration country code prefix: A6 (2016)

Airports: 43 (2013)
country comparison to the world: 100

Airports—with paved runways: *total:* 25
over 3,047 m: 12
2,438 to 3,047 m: 3
1,524 to 2,437 m: 5
914 to 1,523 m: 3
under 914 m: 2 (2013)

Airports—with unpaved runways: *total:* 18
over 3,047 m: 1
2,438 to 3,047 m: 1
1,524 to 2,437 m: 4
914 to 1,523 m: 6
under 914 m: 6 (2013)

Heliports: 5 (2013)

Pipelines: condensate 533 km; gas 3,277 km; liquid petroleum gas 300 km; oil 3,287 km; oil/gas/water 24 km; refined products 218 km; water 99 km (2013)

Roadways: *total:* 4,080 km
paved: 4,080 km (includes 253 km of expressways) (2008)
country comparison to the world: 157

Merchant marine: *total:* 618
by type: general cargo 97, oil tanker 26, other 495 (2017)

country comparison to the world: 34

Ports and terminals: *major seaport(s):* Al Fujayrah, Mina' Jabal 'Ali (Dubai), Khor Fakkan (Khawr Fakkan) (Sharjah), Mubarraz Island (Abu Dhabi), Mina' Rashid (Dubai), Mina' Saqr (Ra's al Khaymah)
container port(s) (TEUs): Dubai Port (15,585,000), Khor Fakkan (Khawr Fakkan) (Sharjah) (4,414,000) (2015)
LNG terminal(s) (export): Das Island

MILITARY AND SECURITY

Military expenditures: 5.66% of GDP (2014)
6.06% of GDP (2013)
5.09% of GDP (2012)
5.5% of GDP (2011)

Military branches: United Arab Emirates Armed Forces: Critical Infrastructure Coastal Patrol Agency (CICPA), Land Forces, Navy, Air Force and Air Defense, Presidential Guard (2015)

Military service age and obligation: 18-30 years of age for compulsory military service for men, optional service for women; 17 years of age for male volunteers with parental approval; 2-year general obligation, 9 months for secondary school graduates; women may train for 9 months regardless of education (2014)

TRANSNATIONAL ISSUES

Disputes—international: boundary agreement was signed and ratified with Oman in 2003 for entire border, including Oman's Musandam Peninsula and Al Madhah enclaves, but contents of the agreement and detailed maps showing the alignment have not been published; Iran and UAE dispute Tunb Islands and Abu Musa Island, which Iran occupies

Illicit drugs: the UAE is a drug transshipment point for traffickers given its proximity to Southwest Asian drug-producing countries; the UAE's position as a major financial center makes it vulnerable to money laundering; anti-money-laundering controls improving, but informal banking remains unregulated

UNITED KINGDOM

INTRODUCTION

Background: The United Kingdom has historically played a leading role in developing parliamentary democracy and in advancing literature and science. At its zenith in the 19th century, the British Empire stretched over one-fourth of the earth's surface. The first half of the 20th century saw the UK's strength seriously depleted in two world wars and the Irish Republic's withdrawal from the union. The second half witnessed the dismantling of the Empire and the UK rebuilding itself into a modern and prosperous European nation. As one of five permanent members of the UN Security Council and a founding member of NATO and the Commonwealth, the UK pursues a global approach to foreign policy. The Scottish Parliament, the National Assembly for Wales, and the Northern Ireland Assembly were established in 1998.

The UK has been an active member of the EU since its accession in 1973, although it chose to remain outside the Economic and Monetary Union. However, motivated in part by frustration at a remote bureaucracy in Brussels and massive migration into the country, UK citizens on 23 June 2016 narrowly voted to leave the EU. The UK and the EU are currently negotiating the terms of the UK's withdrawal and will discuss a framework for their future relationship ahead of the UK's scheduled departure from the bloc on 29 March 2019.

GEOGRAPHY

Location: Western Europe, islands—including the northern one-sixth of the island of Ireland—between the North Atlantic Ocean and the North Sea; northwest of France

Geographic coordinates: 54 00 N, 2 00 W

Map references: Europe

Area: *total:* 243,610 sq km
land: 241,930 sq km
water: 1,680 sq km
note: includes Rockall and Shetland Islands
country comparison to the world: 81

Area—comparative: twice the size of Pennsylvania; slightly smaller than Oregon

Land boundaries: *total:* 443 km
border countries (1): Ireland 443 km

Coastline: 12,429 km

Maritime claims: *territorial sea:* 12 nm
exclusive fishing zone: 200 nm
continental shelf: as defined in continental shelf orders or in accordance with agreed upon boundaries

Climate: temperate; moderated by prevailing southwest winds over the North Atlantic Current; more than one-half of the days are overcast

Terrain: mostly rugged hills and low mountains; level to rolling plains in east and southeast

Elevation: *mean elevation:* 162 m

elevation extremes: *lowest point:* The Fens -4 m
highest point: Ben Nevis 1,343 m

Natural resources: coal, petroleum, natural gas, iron ore, lead, zinc, gold, tin, limestone, salt, clay, chalk, gypsum, potash, silica sand, slate, arable land

Land use: *agricultural land:* 71%
arable land: 25.1%;
permanent crops: 0.2%;
permanent pasture: 45.7%
forest: 11.9%
other: 17.1% (2011 est.)
Irrigated land: 950 sq km (2012)

Population—distribution: the core of the population lies in and around London, with significant clusters found in central Britain around Manchester and Liverpool, in the Scottish lowlands between Edinburgh and Glasgow, southern Wales in and around Cardiff, and far eastern Northern Ireland centered on Belfast

Natural hazards: winter windstorms; floods

Environment—current issues: continues to reduce greenhouse gas emissions, but air pollution remains a concern, particularly in the London region; soil pollution from pesticides and heavy metals; decline in marine and coastal habitats brought on by pressures from housing, tourism, and industry

Environment—international agreements: *party to:* Air Pollution, Air Pollution-Nitrogen Oxides, Air Pollution-Persistent Organic Pollutants, Air Pollution-Sulfur 94, Air Pollution-Volatile Organic Compounds, Antarctic-Environmental Protocol, Antarctic-Marine Living Resources, Antarctic Seals, Antarctic Treaty, Biodiversity, Climate Change, Climate Change-Kyoto Protocol, Desertification, Endangered Species, Environmental Modification, Hazardous Wastes, Law of the Sea, Marine Dumping, Marine Life Conservation, Ozone Layer Protection, Ship Pollution, Tropical Timber 83, Tropical Timber 94, Wetlands, Whaling
signed, but not ratified: none of the selected agreements

Geography—note: lies near vital North Atlantic sea lanes; only 35 km from France and linked by tunnel under the English Channel (the Channel Tunnel or Chunnel); because of heavily indented coastline, no location is more than 125 km from tidal waters

PEOPLE AND SOCIETY

Population: 64,769,452 (July 2017 est.)
country comparison to the world: 22

Nationality: *noun:* Briton(s), British (collective plural)
adjective: British

Ethnic groups: white 87.2%, black/African/Caribbean/black British 3%, Asian/Asian British: Indian 2.3%, Asian/Asian British: Pakistani 1.9%, mixed 2%, other 3.7% (2011 est.)

Languages: English
note: the following are recognized regional languages: Scots (about 30% of the population of Scotland), Scottish Gaelic (about 60,000 in Scotland), Welsh (about 20% of the population of Wales), Irish (about 10% of the population of Northern Ireland), Cornish (some 2,000 to 3,000 in Cornwall) (2012 est.)

Religions: Christian (includes Anglican, Roman Catholic, Presbyterian, Methodist) 59.5%, Muslim 4.4%, Hindu 1.3%, other 2%, unspecified 7.2%, none 25.7% (2011 est.)

Age structure: *0-14 years:* 17.53% (male 5,819,363/female 5,532,123)
15-24 years: 11.9% (male 3,938,643/female 3,770,511)
25-54 years: 40.55% (male 13,387,903/female 12,873,090)
55-64 years: 11.98% (male 3,843,268/female 3,918,244)
65 years and over: 18.04% (male 5,246,475/female 6,439,832) (2017 est.)

Dependency ratios: *total dependency ratio:* 55.5
youth dependency ratio: 27.4
elderly dependency ratio: 28.2
potential support ratio: 3.5 (2015 est.)

Median age: *total:* 40.5 years
male: 39.3 years
female: 41.7 years (2017 est.)
country comparison to the world: 44

Population growth rate: 0.52% (2017 est.)
country comparison to the world: 154

Birth rate: 12.1 births/1,000 population (2017 est.)
country comparison to the world: 166

Death rate: 9.4 deaths/1,000 population (2017 est.)
country comparison to the world: 55

Net migration rate: 2.5 migrant(s)/1,000 population (2017 est.)
country comparison to the world: 37

Population distribution: the core of the population lies in and around London, with significant clusters found in central Britain around Manchester and Liverpool, in the Scottish lowlands between Endinburgh and Glasgow, southern Wales in and around Cardiff, and far eastern Northern Ireland centered on Belfast

Urbanization: *urban population:* 83.1% of total population (2017)
rate of urbanization: 0.82% annual rate of change (2015-20 est.)

Major urban areas—population: LONDON (capital) 10.313 million; Manchester 2.646 million; Birmingham 2.515 million; Glasgow 1.223 million; Southampton/Portsmouth 882,000; Liverpool 870,000 (2015)

Sex ratio: *at birth:* 1.05 male(s)/female
0-14 years: 1.05 male(s)/female
15-24 years: 1.04 male(s)/female
25-54 years: 1.04 male(s)/female
55-64 years: 0.98 male(s)/female
65 years and over: 0.81 male(s)/female
total population: 0.99 male(s)/female (2016 est.)

Mother's mean age at first birth: 28.5 years
note: data represent England and Wales only (2014 est.)

Maternal mortality ratio: 9 deaths/100,000 live births (2015 est.)
country comparison to the world: 153

Infant mortality rate: *total:* 4.3 deaths/1,000 live births
male: 4.7 deaths/1,000 live births
female: 3.9 deaths/1,000 live births (2017 est.)
country comparison to the world: 185

Life expectancy at birth: *total population:* 80.8 years
male: 78.6 years
female: 83.1 years (2017 est.)
country comparison to the world: 35

Total fertility rate: 1.88 children born/woman (2017 est.)
country comparison to the world: 142

Contraceptive prevalence rate: 84%
note: percent of women aged 16-49 (2008/09)

Health expenditures: 9.1% of GDP (2014)
country comparison to the world: 38

Physicians density: 2.81 physicians/1,000 population (2015)

Hospital bed density: 2.9 beds/1,000 population (2011)

Drinking water source:
improved:
urban: 100% of population
rural: 100% of population
total: 100% of population
unimproved:
urban: 0% of population
rural: 0% of population
total: 0% of population (2015 est.)

Sanitation facility access:
improved:
urban: 99.1% of population
rural: 99.6% of population
total: 99.2% of population
unimproved:
urban: 0.9% of population
rural: 0.4% of population
total: 0.8% of population (2015 est.)

HIV/AIDS—adult prevalence rate: NA

HIV/AIDS—people living with HIV/AIDS: NA

HIV/AIDS—deaths: NA

Obesity—adult prevalence rate: 27.8% (2016)
country comparison to the world: 36

Education expenditures: 5.8% of GDP (2014)
country comparison to the world: 36

School life expectancy (primary to tertiary education): *total:* 18 years
male: 17 years
female: 18 years (2014)

Unemployment, youth ages 15-24: *total:* 14.6%
male: 16.2%
female: 12.9% (2015 est.)
country comparison to the world: 52

GOVERNMENT

Country name: *conventional long form:* United Kingdom of Great Britain and Northern Ireland; *note*—the island of Great Britain includes England, Scotland, and Wales
conventional short form: United Kingdom
abbreviation: UK
etymology: self-descriptive country name; the designation "Great Britain," in the sense of "Larger Britain," dates back to medieval times and was used to distinguish the island from "Little Britain," or Brittany in modern France; the name Ireland derives from the Gaelic "Eriu," the matron goddess of Ireland (goddess of the land)

Government type: parliamentary constitutional monarchy; a Commonwealth realm

Capital: *name:* London
geographic coordinates: 51 30 N, 0 05 W
time difference: UTC 0 (5 hours ahead of Washington, DC, during Standard Time)
daylight saving time: +1hr, begins last Sunday in March; ends last Sunday in October

note: applies to the United Kingdom proper, not to its Crown dependencies or overseas territories

Administrative divisions: England: 27 two-tier counties, 32 London boroughs and 1 City of London or Greater London, 36 metropolitan districts, 56 unitary authorities (including 4 single-tier counties*)
two-tier counties: Buckinghamshire, Cambridgeshire, Cumbria, Derbyshire, Devon, Dorset, East Sussex, Essex, Gloucestershire, Hampshire, Hertfordshire, Kent, Lancashire, Leicestershire, Lincolnshire, Norfolk, North Yorkshire, Northamptonshire, Nottinghamshire, Oxfordshire, Somerset, Staffordshire, Suffolk, Surrey, Warwickshire, West Sussex, Worcestershire
London boroughs and City of London or Greater London: Barking and Dagenham, Barnet, Bexley, Brent, Bromley, Camden, Croydon, Ealing, Enfield, Greenwich, Hackney, Hammersmith and Fulham, Haringey, Harrow, Havering, Hillingdon, Hounslow, Islington, Kensington and Chelsea, Kingston upon Thames, Lambeth, Lewisham, City of London, Merton, Newham, Redbridge, Richmond upon Thames, Southwark, Sutton, Tower Hamlets, Waltham Forest, Wandsworth, Westminster
metropolitan districts: Barnsley, Birmingham, Bolton, Bradford, Bury, Calderdale, Coventry, Doncaster, Dudley, Gateshead, Kirklees, Knowlsey, Leeds, Liverpool, Manchester, Newcastle upon Tyne, North Tyneside, Oldham, Rochdale, Rotherham, Salford, Sandwell, Sefton, Sheffield, Solihull, South Tyneside, St. Helens, Stockport, Sunderland, Tameside, Trafford, Wakefield, Walsall, Wigan, Wirral, Wolverhampton
unitary authorities: Bath and North East Somerset, Blackburn with Darwen, Bedford, Blackpool, Bournemouth, Bracknell Forest, Brighton and Hove, City of Bristol, Central Bedfordshire, Cheshire East, Cheshire West and Chester, Cornwall, Darlington, Derby, Durham County*, East Riding of Yorkshire, Halton, Hartlepool, Herefordshire*, Isle of Wight*, Isles of Scilly, City of Kingston upon Hull, Leicester, Luton, Medway, Middlesbrough, Milton Keynes, North East Lincolnshire, North Lincolnshire, North Somerset, Northumberland*, Nottingham, Peterborough, Plymouth, Poole, Portsmouth, Reading, Redcar and Cleveland, Rutland, Shropshire, Slough, South Gloucestershire, Southampton, Southend-on-Sea, Stockton-on-Tees, Stoke-on-Trent, Swindon, Telford and Wrekin, Thurrock, Torbay, Warrington, West Berkshire, Wiltshire, Windsor and Maidenhead, Wokingham, York
Northern Ireland: 5 borough councils, 4 district councils, 2 city councils
borough councils: Antrim and Newtownabbey; Ards and North Down; Armagh, Banbridge, and Craigavon; Causeway Coast and Glens; Mid and East Antrim
district councils: Derry and Strabane; Fermanagh and Omagh; Mid Ulster; Newry, Murne, and Down
city councils: Belfast; Lisburn and Castlereagh
Scotland: 32 council areas
council areas: Aberdeen City, Aberdeenshire, Angus, Argyll and Bute, Clackmannanshire,

Dumfries and Galloway, Dundee City, East Ayrshire, East Dunbartonshire, East Lothian, East Renfrewshire, City of Edinburgh, Eilean Siar (Western Isles), Falkirk, Fife, Glasgow City, Highland, Inverclyde, Midlothian, Moray, North Ayrshire, North Lanarkshire, Orkney Islands, Perth and Kinross, Renfrewshire, Shetland Islands, South Ayrshire, South Lanarkshire, Stirling, The Scottish Borders, West Dunbartonshire, West Lothian

Wales: 22 unitary authorities

unitary authorities: Blaenau Gwent, Bridgend, Caerphilly, Cardiff, Carmarthenshire, Ceredigion, Conwy, Denbighshire, Flintshire, Gwynedd, Isle of Anglesey, Merthyr Tydfil, Monmouthshire, Neath Port Talbot, Newport, Pembrokeshire, Powys, Rhondda Cynon Taff, Swansea, The Vale of Glamorgan, Torfaen, Wrexham

Dependent areas: Anguilla, Bermuda, British Indian Ocean Territory, British Virgin Islands, Cayman Islands, Falkland Islands, Gibraltar, Montserrat, Pitcairn Islands, Saint Helena, Ascension, and Tristan da Cunha, South Georgia and the South Sandwich Islands, Turks and Caicos Islands

Independence: 12 April 1927 (Royal and Parliamentary Titles Act establishes current name of the United Kingdom of Great Britain and Northern Ireland); notable earlier dates: 927 (minor English kingdoms united); 3 March 1284 (enactment of the Statute of Rhuddlan uniting England and Wales); 1536 (Act of Union formally incorporates England and Wales); 1 May 1707 (Acts of Union formally unite England, Scotland, and Wales as Great Britain); 1 January 1801 (Acts of Union formally unite Great Britain and Ireland as the United Kingdom of Great Britain and Ireland); 6 December 1921 (Anglo-Irish Treaty formalizes partition of Ireland; six counties remain part of the United Kingdom and Northern Ireland)

National holiday: the UK does not celebrate one particular national holiday

Constitution: *history:* unwritten; partly statutes, partly common law and practice

amendments: proposed as a "bill" for an "Act of Parliament" by the government, by the House of Commons, or by the House of Lords; passage requires agreement by both houses and by the monarch (Royal Assent); note—recent additions include the Human Rights Act of 1998, the Constitutional Reform and Governance Act 2010, the Parliamentary Voting System and Constituencies Act 2011, the Fixed-term Parliaments Act 2011, and the House of Lords (Expulsion and Suspension) Act 2015 (2016)

Legal system: common law system; has nonbinding judicial review of Acts of Parliament under the Human Rights Act of 1998

International law organization participation: accepts compulsory ICJ jurisdiction with reservations; accepts ICCt jurisdiction

Citizenship: *citizenship by birth:* no

citizenship by descent only: at least one parent must be a citizen of the United Kingdom

dual citizenship recognized: yes

residency requirement for naturalization: 5 years

Suffrage: 18 years of age; universal

Executive branch: *chief of state:* Queen ELIZABETH II (since 6 February 1952); Heir Apparent Prince CHARLES, son of the queen (born 14 November 1948)

head of government: Prime Minister Theresa MAY (Conservative) (since 13 July 2016)

cabinet: Cabinet appointed by the prime minister

elections/appointments: the monarchy is hereditary; following legislative elections, the leader of the majority party or majority coalition usually becomes the prime minister; election last held on 8 June 2017 (next to be held by 5 May 2022)

Legislative branch: description: bicameral Parliament consists of the House of Lords (membership not fixed; as of December 2016, 809 lords were eligible to participate in the work of the House of Lords—692 life peers, 91 hereditary peers, and 26 clergy; members are appointed by the monarch on the advice of the prime minister and non-party political members recommended by the House of Lords Appointments Commission), and the House of Commons (650 seats; members directly elected in single-seat constituencies by simple majority popular vote to serve 5-year terms unless the House is dissolved earlier)

elections: House of Lords—no elections; note—in 1999, as provided by the House of Lords Act, elections were held in the House of Lords to determine the 92 hereditary peers who would remain; elections held only as vacancies in the hereditary peerage arise; House of Commons—last held on 8 June 2017 (next to be held by 5 May 2022)

election results: House of Commons—percent of vote by party—Conservative 42.3%, Labor 40.0%, SNP 43.0%, Lib Dems 7.4%, DUP 0.9%, Sinn Fein 0.7%, Plaid Cymru 0.5%,other 0.6%; seats by party—Conservative 317, Labor 262, SNP 35, Lib Dems 12, DUP 10, Sinn Fein 7, Plaid Cymru 4, other 3

Judicial branch: *highest court(s):* Supreme Court (consists of 12 justices including the court president and deputy president); note—the Supreme Court was established by the Constitutional Reform Act 2005 and implemented in October 2009, replacing the Appellate Committee of the House of Lords as the highest court in the United Kingdom

judge selection and term of office: judge candidates selected by an independent committee of several judicial commissions, followed by their recommendations to the prime minister, and appointed by the monarch; justices appointed for life

subordinate courts: England and Wales—Court of Appeal (civil and criminal divisions); High Court; Crown Court; County Courts; Magistrates' Courts; Scotland—Court of Sessions; Sheriff Courts; High Court of Justiciary; tribunals; Northern Ireland—Court of Appeal in Northern Ireland; High Court; county courts; magistrates' courts; specialized tribunals

Political parties and leaders: Alliance Party (Northern Ireland) [Naomi LONG]
Conservative and Unionist Party [Theresa MAY]
Democratic Unionist Party or DUP (Northern Ireland) [Arlene FOSTER]
Green Party of England and Wales or Greens [Caroline LUCAS and Jonathan BARTLEY]
Labor (Labour) Party [Jeremy CORBYN]
Liberal Democrats (Lib Dems) [Sir Vince CABLE]
Party of Wales (Plaid Cymru) [Leanne WOOD]
Scottish National Party or SNP [Nicola STURGEON]
Sinn Fein (Northern Ireland) [Gerry ADAMS]
Social Democratic and Labor Party or SDLP (Northern Ireland) [Colum EASTWOOD]
Ulster Unionist Party or UUP (Northern Ireland) [Robin SWANN]
UK Independence Party or UKIP [Henry BOLTON]

Political pressure groups and leaders: Campaign for Nuclear Disarmament
Confederation of British Industry
National Farmers' Union
Trades Union Congress

International organization participation: ADB (nonregional member), AfDB (nonregional member), Arctic Council (observer), Australia Group, BIS, C, CBSS (observer), CD, CDB, CE, CERN, EAPC, EBRD, ECB, EIB, EITI (implementing country), ESA, EU, FAO, FATF, G-5, G-7, G-8, G-10, G-20, IADB, IAEA, IBRD, ICAO, ICC (national committees), ICCt, ICRM, IDA, IEA, IFAD, IFC, IFRCS, IGAD (partners), IHO, ILO, IMF, IMO, IMSO, Interpol, IOC, IOM, IPU, ISO, ITSO, ITU, ITUC (NGOs), MIGA, MINUSMA, MONUSCO, NATO, NEA, NSG, OAS (observer), OECD, OPCW, OSCE, Pacific Alliance (observer), Paris Club, PCA, PIF (partner), SELEC (observer), SICA (observer), UN, UNCTAD, UNESCO, UNFICYP, UNHCR, UNMISS, UNRWA, UNSC (permanent), UPU, WCO, WHO, WIPO, WMO, WTO, ZC

Diplomatic representation in the US: *chief of mission:* Ambassador Sir Nigel Kim DARROCH (since 28 January 2016)

chancery: 3100 Massachusetts Avenue NW, Washington, DC 20008

telephone: [1] (202) 588-6500

FAX: [1] (202) 588-7870

consulate(s) general: Atlanta, Boston, Chicago, Denver, Houston, Los Angeles, Miami, New York, San Francisco

consulate(s): Orlando (FL), San Juan (Puerto Rico)

Diplomatic representation from the US: *chief of mission:* Ambassador Robert Wood (Woody) JOHNSON IV (since 29 August 2017)

embassy: 24 Grosvenor Square, London, W1K 6AH; note—a new embassy is scheduled to open in early 2018 in the Nine Elms area of Wandsworth

mailing address: PSC 801, Box 40, FPO AE 09498-4040

telephone: [44] (0) 20 7499-9000

FAX: [44] (0) 20 7629-9124

consulate(s) general: Belfast, Edinburgh

Flag description: blue field with the red cross of Saint George (patron saint of England) edged in white superimposed on the diagonal red cross of Saint Patrick (patron saint of Ireland), which is superimposed on the diagonal white cross of Saint Andrew (patron saint of Scotland); properly known as the Union Flag, but commonly called the Union Jack; the design and colors (especially the Blue Ensign) have been the basis for a number of other flags including other Commonwealth countries and their constituent states or provinces, and British overseas territories

National symbol(s): lion (Britain in general); lion, Tudor rose, oak (England); lion, unicorn, thistle (Scotland); dragon, daffodil, leek (Wales); shamrock, flax (Northern Ireland); national colors: red, white, blue (Britain in general); red, white (England); blue, white (Scotland); red, white, green (Wales)

National anthem: name: "God Save the Queen"
lyrics/music: unknown
note: in use since 1745; by tradition, the song serves as both the national and royal anthem of the UK; it is known as either "God Save the Queen" or "God Save the King," depending on the gender of the reigning monarch; it also serves as the royal anthem of many Commonwealth nations

ECONOMY

Economy—overview: The UK, a leading trading power and financial center, is the third largest economy in Europe after Germany and France. Agriculture is intensive, highly mechanized, and efficient by European standards, producing about 60% of food needs with less than 2% of the labor force. The UK has large coal, natural gas, and oil resources, but its oil and natural gas reserves are declining; the UK has been a net importer of energy since 2005. Services, particularly banking, insurance, and business services, are key drivers of British GDP growth. Manufacturing, meanwhile, has declined in importance but still accounts for about 10% of economic output.

In 2008, the global financial crisis hit the economy particularly hard, due to the importance of its financial sector. Falling home prices, high consumer debt, and the global economic slowdown compounded the UK's economic problems, pushing the economy into recession in the latter half of 2008 and prompting the then BROWN (Labour) government to implement a number of measures to stimulate the economy and stabilize the financial markets. Facing burgeoning public deficits and debt levels, in 2010 the then CAMERON-led coalition government (between Conservatives and Liberal Democrats) initiated an austerity program, which has continued under the Conservative government. However, the deficit still remains one of the highest in the G7, standing at 3.6% of GDP as of 2017, and the UK has pledged to lower its corporation tax from 20% to 17% by 2020. The UK had a debt burden of 90.4% GDP at the end of 2017.

The UK's economy has begun to slow since the referendum vote to leave the EU in June 2016. A sustained depreciation of the British pound has increased consumer and producer prices, weighing on consumer spending without spurring a meaningful increase in exports. The UK has an extensive trade relationship with other EU members through its single market membership and economic observers have warned the exit will jeopardize its position as the central location for European financial services. Prime Minister MAY is seeking a new "deep and special" trade relationship with the EU following the UK's exit. However, economists doubt that the UK will be able to preserve the benefits of EU membership without the obligations.

GDP (purchasing power parity): $2.88 trillion (2017 est.)
$2.833 trillion (2016 est.)
$2.783 trillion (2015 est.)
note: data are in 2017 dollars
country comparison to the world: 10

GDP (official exchange rate): $2.565 trillion (2016 est.)

GDP—real growth rate: 1.7% (2017 est.)
1.8% (2016 est.)
2.2% (2015 est.)
country comparison to the world: 169

GDP—per capita (PPP): $43,600 (2017 est.)
$43,200 (2016 est.)
$42,700 (2015 est.)
note: data are in 2017 dollars
country comparison to the world: 40

Gross national saving: 13.4% of GDP (2017 est.)
12.6% of GDP (2016 est.)
13% of GDP (2015 est.)
country comparison to the world: 136

GDP—composition, by end use:
household consumption: 65.3%
government consumption: 19%
investment in fixed capital: 16.6%
investment in inventories: 0.7%
exports of goods and services: 30.1%
imports of goods and services: -31.7% (2017 est.)

GDP—composition, by sector of origin:
agriculture: 0.6%
industry: 19%
services: 80.4%
(2017 est.)

Agriculture—products: cereals, oilseed, potatoes, vegetables; cattle, sheep, poultry; fish

Industries: machine tools, electric power equipment, automation equipment, railroad equipment, shipbuilding, aircraft, motor vehicles and parts, electronics and communications equipment, metals, chemicals, coal, petroleum, paper and paper products, food processing, textiles, clothing, other consumer goods

Industrial production growth rate: 0.7% (2017 est.)
country comparison to the world: 175

Labor force: 33.5 million (2017 est.)
country comparison to the world: 18
Labor force—by occupation: agriculture: 1.3%
industry: 15.2%
services: 83.5% (2014 est.)

Unemployment rate: 4.4% (2017 est.)
4.9% (2016 est.)
country comparison to the world: 62

Population below poverty line: 15% (2013 est.)

Household income or consumption by percentage share: *lowest 10%:* 1.7%
highest 10%: 31.1% (2012)

Distribution of family income—Gini index: 32.4 (2012)
33.4 (2010)
country comparison to the world: 111

Budget: *revenues:* $984.4 billion
expenditures: $1.076 trillion (2017 est.)

Taxes and other revenues: 38.4% of GDP (2017 est.)
country comparison to the world: 43

Budget surplus (+) or deficit (-): -3.6% of GDP (2017 est.)
country comparison to the world: 134

Public debt: 90.4% of GDP (2017 est.)
89.3% of GDP (2016 est.)
note: data cover general government debt, and include debt instruments issued (or owned) by government entities other than the treasury; the data include treasury debt held by foreign entities; the data include debt issued by subnational entities, as well as intra-governmental debt; intra-governmental debt consists of treasury borrowings from surpluses in the social funds, such as for retirement, medical care, and unemployment; debt instruments for the social funds are not sold at public auctions
country comparison to the world: 26

Fiscal year: 6 April—5 April

Inflation rate (consumer prices): 2.6% (2017 est.)
0.7% (2016 est.)
country comparison to the world: 119

Central bank discount rate: 0.25% (31 December 2016)
0.5% (31 December 2015)
country comparison to the world: 138

Commercial bank prime lending rate: 4.3% (31 December 2017 est.)
4.44% (31 December 2016 est.)
country comparison to the world: 155

Stock of narrow money: $104.8 billion (31 December 2017 est.)
$96.15 billion (31 December 2016 est.)
country comparison to the world: 39

Stock of broad money: $3.066 trillion (31 December 2017 est.)
$2.778 trillion (31 December 2016 est.)
country comparison to the world: 6

Stock of domestic credit: $3.042 trillion (31 December 2017 est.)
$2.785 trillion (31 December 2016 est.)
country comparison to the world: 9

Market value of publicly traded shares: $3.019 trillion (31 December 2012 est.)
$2.903 trillion (31 December 2011 est.)
$3.107 trillion (31 December 2010 est.)
country comparison to the world: 6

Current account balance: -$91.42 billion (2017 est.)
-$114.5 billion (2016 est.)
country comparison to the world: 200

Exports: $436.5 billion (2017 est.)
$407.3 billion (2016 est.)
country comparison to the world: 11

Exports—commodities: manufactured goods, fuels, chemicals; food, beverages, tobacco

Exports—partners: US 14.8%, Germany 10.7%, France 6.4%, Netherlands 6.2%, Ireland 5.6%, Switzerland 4.6%, China 4.4% (2016)

Imports: $602.5 billion (2017 est.)
$588.4 billion (2016 est.)
country comparison to the world: 6

Imports—commodities: manufactured goods, machinery, fuels; foodstuffs

Imports—partners: Germany 13.6%, US 9.3%, China 9.2%, Netherlands 7.4%, France 5.2%, Belgium 4.9%, Switzerland 4.5% (2016)

Reserves of foreign exchange and gold: $135 billion (31 December 2017 est.)
$129.6 billion (31 December 2015 est.)
country comparison to the world: 19

Debt—external: $8.126 trillion (31 March 2016 est.)
$8.642 trillion (31 March 2015 est.)
country comparison to the world: 3

Stock of direct foreign investment—at home: $2.027 trillion (31 December 2017 est.)
$1.858 trillion (31 December 2016 est.)
country comparison to the world: 4

Stock of direct foreign investment—abroad: $1.634 trillion (31 December 2017 est.)
$1.611 trillion (31 December 2016 est.)
country comparison to the world: 6

Exchange rates: British pounds (GBP) per US dollar—
0.7836 (2017 est.)
0.738 (2016 est.)
0.738 (2015 est.)
0.607 (2014 est.)
0.6391 (2013 est.)

ENERGY

Electricity access: *electrification—total population:* 100% (2016)

Electricity—production: 309.8 billion kWh (2015 est.)
country comparison to the world: 13

Electricity—consumption: 301.6 billion kWh (2015 est.)
country comparison to the world: 12

Electricity—exports: 2.153 billion kWh (2016 est.)
country comparison to the world: 44

Electricity—imports: 19.7 billion kWh (2016 est.)
country comparison to the world: 12

Electricity—installed generating capacity: 94.64 million kW (2015 est.)
country comparison to the world: 14

Electricity—from fossil fuels: 55.6% of total installed capacity (2015 est.)
country comparison to the world: 140

Electricity—from nuclear fuels: 9.4% of total installed capacity (2015 est.)
country comparison to the world: 17

Electricity—from hydroelectric plants: 1.9% of total installed capacity (2015 est.)
country comparison to the world: 138

Electricity—from other renewable sources: 33.4% of total installed capacity (2015 est.)
country comparison to the world: 9

Crude oil—production: 933,000 bbl/day (2016 est.)
country comparison to the world: 21

Crude oil—exports: 636,200 bbl/day (2016 est.)
country comparison to the world: 20

Crude oil—imports: 808,800 bbl/day (2016 est.)
country comparison to the world: 15

Crude oil—proved reserves: 2.564 billion bbl (1 January 2017 es)
country comparison to the world: 32

Refined petroleum products—production: 1.28 million bbl/day (2016 est.)
country comparison to the world: 16

Refined petroleum products—consumption: 1.586 million bbl/day (2016 est.)
country comparison to the world: 16

Refined petroleum products—exports: 632,200 bbl/day (2016 est.)
country comparison to the world: 11

Refined petroleum products—imports: 941,200 bbl/day (2016 est.)
country comparison to the world: 7

Natural gas—production: 41.34 billion cu m (2015 est.)
country comparison to the world: 19

Natural gas—consumption: 186.2 billion cu m (2015 est.)
country comparison to the world: 7

Natural gas—exports: 14.22 billion cu m (2015 est.)
country comparison to the world: 18

Natural gas—imports: 44.5 billion cu m (2015 est.)
country comparison to the world: 8

Natural gas—proved reserves: 207.2 billion cu m (1 January 2017 es)
country comparison to the world: 43

Carbon dioxide emissions from consumption of energy: 568.3 million Mt (2013 est.)
country comparison to the world: 11

COMMUNICATIONS

Telephones—fixed lines: *total subscriptions:* 33,510,796
subscriptions per 100 inhabitants: 52 (July 2016 est.)
country comparison to the world: 9

Telephones—mobile cellular: *total:* 78,529,373

subscriptions per 100 inhabitants: 122 (July 2016 est.)
country comparison to the world: 20

Telephone system: *general assessment:* technologically advanced domestic and international system
domestic: equal mix of buried cables, microwave radio relay, and fiber-optic systems
international: country code—44; numerous submarine cables provide links throughout Europe, Asia, Australia, the Middle East, and US; satellite earth stations—10 Intelsat (7 Atlantic Ocean and 3 Indian Ocean), 1 Inmarsat (Atlantic Ocean region), and 1 Eutelsat; at least 8 large international switching centers (2016)

Broadcast media: public service broadcaster, British Broadcasting Corporation (BBC), is the largest broadcasting corporation in the world; BBC operates multiple TV networks with regional and local TV service; a mixed system of public and commercial TV broadcasters along with satellite and cable systems provide access to hundreds of TV stations throughout the world; BBC operates multiple national, regional, and local radio networks with multiple transmission sites; a large number of commercial radio stations, as well as satellite radio services are available (2008)

Internet country code: .uk

Internet users: *total:* 61,064,454

percent of population: 94.8% (July 2016 est.)
country comparison to the world: 10

TRANSPORTATION

National air transport system: *number of registered air carriers:* 28
inventory of registered aircraft operated by air carriers: 1,242
annual passenger traffic on registered air carriers: 131,449,680
annual freight traffic on registered air carriers: 5,466,504,676 mt-km (2015)
Civil aircraft registration country code prefix: G (2016)

Airports: 460 (2013)
country comparison to the world: 18

Airports—with paved runways: *total:* 271
over 3,047 m: 7
2,438 to 3,047 m: 29
1,524 to 2,437 m: 89
914 to 1,523 m: 80
under 914 m: 66 (2013)

Airports—with unpaved runways: *total:* 189
1,524 to 2,437 m: 3
914 to 1,523 m: 26
under 914 m: 160 (2013)

Heliports: 9 (2013)

Pipelines: condensate 502 km; condensate/gas 9 km; gas 28,603 km; liquid petroleum gas 59 km; oil 5,256 km; oil/gas/water 175 km; refined products 4,919 km; water 255 km (2013)

Railways: *total:* 16,837 km
broad gauge: 303 km 1.600-m gauge (in Northern Ireland)

standard gauge: 16,534 km 1.435-m gauge (5,357 km electrified) (2015)
country comparison to the world: 16

Roadways: *total*: 394,428 km
paved: 394,428 km (includes 3,519 km of expressways) (2009)
country comparison to the world: 18

Waterways: 3,200 km (620 km used for commerce) (2009)
country comparison to the world: 31

Merchant marine: *total*: 1,551
by type: bulk carrier 117, container ship 112, general cargo 175, oil tanker 173, other 974 (2017)
country comparison to the world: 17

Ports and terminals: *major seaport(s)*: Dover, Felixstowe, Immingham, Liverpool, London, Southampton, Teesport (England); Forth Ports (Scotland); Milford Haven (Wales)
oil terminal(s): Fawley Marine terminal, Liverpool Bay terminal (England); Braefoot Bay terminal, Finnart oil terminal, Hound Point terminal (Scotland)
container port(s) (TEUs): Felixstowe (3,676,000), London (1,185,000), Southampton (2,349,000) (2015)
LNG terminal(s) (import): Isle of Grain, Milford Haven, Teesside

MILITARY AND SECURITY

Military expenditures: 2.2% of GDP (2016)
2.05% of GDP (2015)
2.22% of GDP (2014)
2.25% of GDP (2013)
2.51% of GDP (2012)
country comparison to the world: 28

Military branches: Army, Royal Navy (includes Royal Marines), Royal Air Force (2013)

Military service age and obligation: 16-33 years of age (officers 17-28) for voluntary military service (with parental consent under 18); no conscription; women serve in military services including ground combat roles; must be citizen of the UK, Commonwealth, or Republic of Ireland; reservists serve a minimum of 3 years, to age 45 or 55; 17 years 6 months of age for voluntary military service by Nepalese citizens in the Brigade of Gurkhas; 16-34 years of age for voluntary military service by Papua New Guinean citizens (2016)

TERRORISM

Terrorist groups—home based: Continuity Irish Republican Army (CIRA): aim(s): disrupt the Northern Ireland peace process, remove British rule in Northern Ireland and, ultimately, unify Ireland
area(s) of operation: based and operationally active primarily in Belfast and along the border areas of Northern Ireland, where operatives have carried out bombings, assassinations, kidnappings, hijackings, extortion, and robberies over the years; articulates its intent to target drug dealers and other criminals, especially those who harm any Republican, including RIRA members; remains sporadically operational targeting primarily the British military, Northern Ireland security forces, and Loyalist paramilitary groups; attacks in recent years involve shootings and small-scale bombings; does not have an established presence on the UK mainland; accused in 1996 of directing operatives to park a vehicle with 1,500 pounds of homemade explosives at the Killyhelvin Hotel in Enniskillen, County Fermanagh, Northern Ireland; on 15 July 1996, at least 11 people were injured and most of the immensely popular and newly refurbished hotel was demolished; the attack occurred during the original IRA's first ceasefire; estimated in 2016 to have 50-100 members

Real Irish Republican Army (RIRA): *aim(s)*: committed to using violence to remove British rule in Northern Ireland, disupt the Northern Ireland peace process, and unify Ireland
area(s) of operation: based and operationally active in Northern Ireland, where operatives continue to conduct occasional shootings and small-scale bombings; RIRA claimed responsibility for the 2 April 2011 murder of the Police Services of Northern Ireland's Constable Ronan Kerr, who was killed when a booby-trap bomb exploded under his car in Omagh; RIRA conducted its deadliest attack in the UK on 15 August 1998, when operatives detonated a vehicle-borne improvised explosive device with 500 pounds of explosives on a busy street in Omagh, killing 29 people and injuring at least 220; maintains a limited presence in Great Britain; estimated in 2015 to have a 100 active members

Terrorist groups—foreign based: *Islamic State of Iraq and the Levant (ISIL)*: *aim(s)*: bolster its support and recruitment networks in the UK and, ultimately, destabilize the UK economy
area(s) of operation: maintains support and recruitment networks; Anjem CHOUDARY and associate Mizanur RAHMAN pled guilty on 16 August 2016 to inviting support for ISIL; CHOUDARY founded the banned UK-based extremist movement known as al-Muhajiroun, which UK authorities accuse of recruiting and facilitating activities on ISIL's behalf; the UK is a top source country in Europe for ISIL recruits; as of early 2017, approximately 750 to 850 British citizens were fighting in Syria or Iraq alongside ISIL, planning to go to fight, or had returned from the fight

TRANSNATIONAL ISSUES

Disputes—international: in 2002, Gibraltar residents voted overwhelmingly by referendum to reject any "shared sovereignty" arrangement between the UK and Spain; the Government of Gibraltar insisted on equal participation in talks between the two countries; Spain disapproved of UK plans to grant Gibraltar greater autonomy; Mauritius and Seychelles claim the Chagos Archipelago (British Indian Ocean Territory); in 2001, the former inhabitants of the archipelago, evicted 1967—1973, were granted UK citizenship and the right of return, followed by Orders in Council in 2004 that banned rehabitation, a High Court ruling reversed the ban, a Court of Appeal refusal to hear the case, and a Law Lords' decision in 2008 denied the right of return; in addition, the UK created the world's largest marine protection area around the Chagos islands prohibiting the extraction of any natural resources therein; UK rejects sovereignty talks requested by Argentina, which still claims the Falkland Islands (Islas Malvinas) and South Georgia and the South Sandwich Islands; territorial claim in Antarctica (British Antarctic Territory) overlaps Argentine claim and partially overlaps Chilean claim; Iceland, the UK, and Ireland dispute Denmark's claim that the Faroe Islands' continental shelf extends beyond 200 nm

Refugees and internally displaced persons: refugees (country of origin): 14,363 (Iran); 13,720 (Eritrea); 9,752 (Afghanistan); 8,790 (Zimbabwe); 8,269 (Syria); 7,326 (Sudan); 6,814 (Pakistan); 5,954 (Somalia); 5,809 (Sri Lanka) (2016)
stateless persons: 64 (2016)

Illicit drugs: producer of limited amounts of synthetic drugs and synthetic precursor chemicals; major consumer of Southwest Asian heroin, Latin American cocaine, and synthetic drugs; money-laundering center

UNITED STATES

INTRODUCTION

Background: Britain's American colonies broke with the mother country in 1776 and were recognized as the new nation of the United States of America following the Treaty of Paris in 1783. During the 19th and 20th centuries, 37 new states were added to the original 13 as the nation expanded across the North American continent and acquired a number of overseas possessions. The two most traumatic experiences in the nation's history were the Civil War (1861-65), in which a northern Union of states defeated a secessionist Confederacy of 11 southern slave states, and the Great Depression of the 1930s, an economic downturn during which about a quarter of the labor force lost its jobs. Buoyed by victories in World Wars I and II and the end of the Cold War in 1991, the US remains the world's most powerful nation state. Since the end of World War II, the economy has achieved relatively steady growth, low unemployment and inflation, and rapid advances in technology.

GEOGRAPHY

Location: North America, bordering both the North Atlantic Ocean and the North Pacific Ocean, between Canada and Mexico

Geographic coordinates: 38 00 N, 97 00 W

Map references: North America

Area: *total:* 9,833,517 sq km
land: 9,147,593 sq km
water: 685,924 sq km
note: includes only the 50 states and District of Columbia, no overseas territories (2010)
country comparison to the world: 4

Area—comparative: about half the size of Russia; about three-tenths the size of Africa; about half the size of South America (or slightly larger than Brazil); slightly larger than China; more than twice the size of the European Union

Land boundaries: *total:* 12,048 km
border countries (2): Canada 8,893 km (including 2,477 km with Alaska), Mexico 3,155 km
note: US Naval Base at Guantanamo Bay, Cuba is leased by the US and is part of Cuba; the base boundary is 28.5 km

Coastline: 19,924 km

Maritime claims: *territorial sea:* 12 nm
contiguous zone: 24 nm

exclusive economic zone: 200 nm
continental shelf: not specified

Climate: mostly temperate, but tropical in Hawaii and Florida, arctic in Alaska, semiarid in the great plains west of the Mississippi River, and arid in the Great Basin of the southwest; low winter temperatures in the northwest are ameliorated occasionally in January and February by warm chinook winds from the eastern slopes of the Rocky Mountains

Terrain: vast central plain, mountains in west, hills and low mountains in east; rugged mountains and broad river valleys in Alaska; rugged, volcanic topography in Hawaii

Elevation: *mean elevation:* 760 m

elevation extremes: *lowest point:* Death Valley -86 m (lowest point in North America)
highest point: Denali (Mount McKinley) 6,190 m (highest point in North America)
note: the peak of Mauna Kea (4,205 m above sea level) on the island of Hawaii rises about 10,200 m above the Pacific Ocean floor; by this measurement, it is the world's tallest mountain—higher than Mount Everest (8,850 m), which is recognized as the tallest mountain above sea level

Natural resources: coal, copper, lead, molybdenum, phosphates, rare earth elements, uranium, bauxite, gold, iron, mercury, nickel, potash, silver, tungsten, zinc, petroleum, natural gas, timber, arable land
note: the US has the world's largest coal reserves with 491 billion short tons accounting for 27% of the world's total

Land use: *agricultural land:* 44.5%
arable land: 16.8%;
permanent crops: 0.3%;
permanent pasture: 27.4%
forest: 33.3%
other: 22.2% (2011 est.)
Irrigated land: 264,000 sq km (2012)

Population—distribution: large urban clusters are spread throughout the eastern half of the US (particularly the Great Lakes area, northeast, east, and southeast) and the western tier states; mountainous areas, principally the Rocky Mountains and Appalachian chain, deserts in the southwest, the dense boreal forests in the extreme north, and the central prairie states are less densely populated; Alaska's population is concentrated along its southern coast—with particular emphasis on the city of Anchorage—and Hawaii's is centered on the island of Oahu

Natural hazards: tsunamis; volcanoes; earthquake activity around Pacific Basin; hurricanes along the Atlantic and Gulf of Mexico coasts; tornadoes in the Midwest and Southeast; mud slides in California; forest fires in the west; flooding; permafrost in northern Alaska, a major impediment to development
volcanism: volcanic activity in the Hawaiian Islands, Western Alaska, the Pacific Northwest,

and in the Northern Mariana Islands; both Mauna Loa (4,170 m) in Hawaii and Mount Rainier (4,392 m) in Washington have been deemed Decade Volcanoes by the International Association of Volcanology and Chemistry of the Earth's Interior, worthy of study due to their explosive history and close proximity to human populations; Pavlof (2,519 m) is the most active volcano in Alaska's Aleutian Arc and poses a significant threat to air travel since the area constitutes a major flight path between North America and East Asia; St. Helens (2,549 m), famous for the devastating 1980 eruption, remains active today; numerous other historically active volcanoes exist, mostly concentrated in the Aleutian arc and Hawaii; they include: in Alaska: Aniakchak, Augustine, Chiginagak, Fourpeaked, Iliamna, Katmai, Kupreanof, Martin, Novarupta, Redoubt, Spurr, Wrangell; in Hawaii: Trident, Ugashik-Peulik, Ukinrek Maars, Veniaminof; in the Northern Mariana Islands: Anatahan; and in the Pacific Northwest: Mount Baker, Mount Hood

Environment—current issues: large emitter of carbon dioxide from the burning of fossil fuels; air pollution resulting in acid rain in both the US and Canada; water pollution from runoff of pesticides and fertilizers; limited natural freshwater resources in much of the western part of the country require careful management; desertification

Environment—international agreements: *party to:* Air Pollution, Air Pollution-Nitrogen Oxides, Antarctic-Environmental Protocol, Antarctic-Marine Living Resources, Antarctic Seals, Antarctic Treaty, Climate Change, Desertification, Endangered Species, Environmental Modification, Marine Dumping, Marine Life Conservation, Ozone Layer Protection, Ship Pollution, Tropical Timber 83, Tropical Timber 94, Wetlands, Whaling
signed, but not ratified: Air Pollution-Persistent Organic Pollutants, Air Pollution-Volatile Organic Compounds, Biodiversity, Climate Change-Kyoto Protocol, Hazardous Wastes

Geography—note: world's third-largest country by size (after Russia and Canada) and by population (after China and India); Denali (Mt. McKinley) is the highest point in North America and Death Valley the lowest point on the continent

PEOPLE AND SOCIETY

Population: 326,625,791 (July 2017 est.)
country comparison to the world: 3

Nationality: *noun:* American(s)
adjective: American

Ethnic groups: white 72.4%, black 12.6%, Asian 4.8%, Amerindian and Alaska native 0.9%, native Hawaiian and other Pacific islander 0.2%, other 6.2%, two or more races 2.9% (2010 estimate)
note: a separate listing for Hispanic is not included because the US Census Bureau considers Hispanic

to mean persons of Spanish/Hispanic/Latino origin including those of Mexican, Cuban, Puerto Rican, Dominican Republic, Spanish, and Central or South American origin living in the US who may be of any race or ethnic group (white, black, Asian, etc.); an estimated 16.3% of the total US population is Hispanic as of 2010

Languages: English 79%, Spanish 13%, other Indo-European 3.7%, Asian and Pacific island 3.4%, other 1% (2015 est.)

note: data represent the language spoken at home; the US has no official national language, but English has acquired official status in 32 of the 50 states; Hawaiian is an official language in the state of Hawaii, and 20 indigenous languages are official in Alaska

Religions: Protestant 46.5%, Roman Catholic 20.8%, Jewish 1.9%, Mormon 1.6%, other Christian 0.9%, Muslim 0.9%, Jehovah's Witness 0.8%, Buddhist 0.7%, Hindu 0.7%, other 1.8%, unaffiliated 22.8%, don't know/refused 0.6% (2014 est.)

Age structure: *0-14 years:* 18.73% (male 31,255,995/female 29,919,938)

15-24 years: 13.27% (male 22,213,952/female 21,137,826)

25-54 years: 39.45% (male 64,528,673/female 64,334,499)

55-64 years: 12.91% (male 20,357,880/female 21,821,976)

65 years and over: 15.63% (male 22,678,235/female 28,376,817) (2017 est.)

Dependency ratios: *total dependency ratio:* 51.2
youth dependency ratio: 29
elderly dependency ratio: 22.1
potential support ratio: 4.5 (2015 est.)

Median age: *total:* 38.1 years
male: 36.8 years
female: 39.4 years (2017 est.)
country comparison to the world: 62

Population growth rate: 0.81% (2017 est.)
country comparison to the world: 129

Birth rate: 12.5 births/1,000 population (2017 est.)
country comparison to the world: 158

Death rate: 8.2 deaths/1,000 population (2017 est.)
country comparison to the world: 85

Net migration rate: 3.9 migrant(s)/1,000 population (2017 est.)
country comparison to the world: 29

Population distribution: large urban clusters are spread throughout the eastern half of the US (particularly the Great Lakes area, northeast, east, and southeast) and the western tier states; mountainous areas, principally the Rocky Mountains and Appalachian chain, deserts in the southwest, the dense boreal forests in the extreme north, and the central prairie states are less densely populated; Alaska's population is concentrated along its southern coast—with particular emphasis on the city of Anchorage—and Hawaii's is centered on the island of Oahu

Urbanization: *urban population:* 82% of total population (2017)

rate of urbanization: 0.99% annual rate of change (2015-20 est.)

Major urban areas—population: New York-Newark 18.593 million; Los Angeles-Long Beach-Santa Ana 12.31 million; Chicago 8.745 million; Miami 5.817 million; Dallas-Fort Worth 5.703 million; WASHINGTON, D.C. (capital) 4.955 million (2015)

Sex ratio: *at birth:* NA
0-14 years: 1.04 male(s)/female
15-24 years: 1.05 male(s)/female
25-54 years: 1 male(s)/female
55-64 years: 0.93 male(s)/female
65 years and over: 0.79 male(s)/female
total population: 0.97 male(s)/female (2016 est.)

Mother's mean age at first birth: 26.4 years (2015 est.)

Maternal mortality ratio: 14 deaths/100,000 live births (2015 est.)
country comparison to the world: 138

Infant mortality rate: *total:* 5.8 deaths/1,000 live births
male: 6.3 deaths/1,000 live births
female: 5.3 deaths/1,000 live births (2017 est.)
country comparison to the world: 170

Life expectancy at birth: *total population:* 80 years
male: 77.7 years
female: 82.2 years (2017 est.)
country comparison to the world: 43

Total fertility rate: 1.87 children born/woman (2017 est.)
country comparison to the world: 143

Contraceptive prevalence rate: 74.1%
note: percent of women aged 15-44 (2011/13)

Health expenditures: 17.1% of GDP (2014)
country comparison to the world: 1

Physicians density: 2.55 physicians/1,000 population (2013)

Hospital bed density: 2.9 beds/1,000 population (2011)

Drinking water source:
improved:
urban: 99.4% of population
rural: 98.2% of population
total: 99.2% of population
unimproved:
urban: 0.6% of population
rural: 1.8% of population
total: 0.8% of population (2015 est.)

Sanitation facility access:
improved:
urban: 100% of population
rural: 100% of population
total: 100% of population
unimproved:
urban: 0% of population
rural: 0% of population
total: 0% of population (2015 est.)

HIV/AIDS—adult prevalence rate: NA

HIV/AIDS—people living with HIV/AIDS: NA

HIV/AIDS—deaths: NA

Obesity—adult prevalence rate: 36.2% (2016)
country comparison to the world: 12

Children under the age of 5 years underweight: 0.5% (2012)
country comparison to the world: 136

Education expenditures: 4.9% of GDP (2013)
country comparison to the world: 63

School life expectancy (primary to tertiary education): *total:* 17 years
male: 16 years
female: 17 years (2014)

Unemployment, youth ages 15-24: *total:* 10.4%
male: 11.4%
female: 9.3% (2016 est.)
country comparison to the world: 68

GOVERNMENT

Country name: *conventional long form:* United States of America
conventional short form: United States
abbreviation: US or USA
etymology: the name America is derived from that of Amerigo VESPUCCI (1454-1512)—Italian explorer, navigator, and cartographer—using the Latin form of his name, Americus, feminized to America

Government type: constitutional federal republic

Capital: name: Washington, DC

geographic coordinates: 38 53 N, 77 02 W
time difference: UTC-5 (during Standard Time)
daylight saving time: +1hr, begins second Sunday in March; ends first Sunday in November
note: the 50 United States cover six time zones

Administrative divisions: 50 states and 1 district*; Alabama, Alaska, Arizona, Arkansas, California, Colorado, Connecticut, Delaware, District of Columbia*, Florida, Georgia, Hawaii, Idaho, Illinois, Indiana, Iowa, Kansas, Kentucky, Louisiana, Maine, Maryland, Massachusetts, Michigan, Minnesota, Mississippi, Missouri, Montana, Nebraska, Nevada, New Hampshire, New Jersey, New Mexico, New York, North Carolina, North Dakota, Ohio, Oklahoma, Oregon, Pennsylvania, Rhode Island, South Carolina, South Dakota, Tennessee, Texas, Utah, Vermont, Virginia, Washington, West Virginia, Wisconsin, Wyoming

Dependent areas: American Samoa, Baker Island, Guam, Howland Island, Jarvis Island, Johnston Atoll, Kingman Reef, Midway Islands, Navassa Island, Northern Mariana Islands, Palmyra Atoll, Puerto Rico, Virgin Islands, Wake Island
note: from 18 July 1947 until 1 October 1994, the US administered the Trust Territory of the Pacific Islands; it entered into a political relationship with all four political entities: the Northern Mariana Islands is a commonwealth in political union with the US (effective 3 November 1986); the Republic of the Marshall Islands signed a Compact of Free Association with the US (effective 21 October 1986); the Federated States of Micronesia signed a Compact of Free Association with the US (effective 3 November 1986); Palau concluded a

Compact of Free Association with the US (effective 1 October 1994)

Independence: 4 July 1776 (declared independence from Great Britain); 3 September 1783 (recognized by Great Britain)

National holiday: Independence Day, 4 July (1776)

Constitution: previous 1781 (Articles of Confederation and Perpetual Union); latest drafted July–September 1787, submitted to the Congress of the Confederation 20 September 1787, submitted for states' ratification 28 September 1787, ratification completed by nine states 21 June 1788, effective 4 March 1789; amended many times, last in 1992 (2016)

Legal system: common law system based on English common law at the federal level; state legal systems based on common law except Louisiana, which is based on Napoleonic civil code; judicial review of legislative acts

International law organization participation: withdrew acceptance of compulsory ICJ jurisdiction in 2005; withdrew acceptance of ICCt jurisdiction in 2002

Citizenship: *citizenship by birth:* yes
citizenship by descent: yes
dual citizenship recognized: no, but the US government acknowledges such situtations exist; US citizens are not encouraged to seek dual citizenship since it limits protection by the US
residency requirement for naturalization: 5 years

Suffrage: 18 years of age; universal

Executive branch: *chief of state:* President Donald J. TRUMP (since 20 January 2017); Vice President Michael R. PENCE (since 20 January 2017); note—the president is both chief of state and head of government

head of government: President Donald J. TRUMP (since 20 January 2017); Vice President Michael R. PENCE (since 20 January 2017)
cabinet: Cabinet appointed by the president, approved by the Senate
elections/appointments: president and vice president indirectly elected on the same ballot by the Electoral College of 'electors' chosen from each state; president and vice president serve a 4-year term (eligible for a second term); election last held on 8 November 2016 (next to be held on 10 November 2020)
election results: Donald J. TRUMP elected president; electoral vote—Donald J. TRUMP (Republican Party) 304, Hillary D. CLINTON (Democratic Party) 227, other 7; percent of direct popular vote—Hillary D. CLINTON 48.2%, Donald J. TRUMP 46.1%, other 5.7%

Legislative branch: description: bicameral Congress consists of the Senate (100 seats; 2 members directly elected in each of the 50 state constituencies by simple majority vote except in Georgia and Louisiana which require an absolute majority vote with a second round if needed; members serve 6-year terms with one-third of membership renewed every 2 years) and the House of Representatives (435 seats; members directly elected

in single-seat constituencies by simple majority vote except in Georgia which requires an absolute majority vote with a second round if needed; members serve 2-year terms)
elections: Senate—last held on 8 November 2016 (next to be held on 6 November 2018); House of Representatives—last held on 8 November 2016 (next to be held on 6 November 2018)
election results: Senate—percent of vote by party—NA; seats by party—Republican Party 24, Democratic Party 10; House of Representatives—percent of vote by party—NA; seats by party—Republican Party 241, Democratic Party 194,
note: in addition to the regular members of the House of Representatives there are 6 non-voting delegates elected from the District of Columbia and the US territories of American Samoa, Guam, Puerto Rico, the Northern Mariana Islands, and the Virgin Islands; these are single seat constituencies directly elected by simple majority vote to serve a 2-year term (except for the resident commissioner of Puerto Rico who serves a 4-year term); the delegate can vote when serving on a committee and when the House meets as the Committee of the Whole House, but not when legislation is submitted for a "full floor" House vote; election of delegates last held on 8 November 2016 (next to be held on 6 November 2018)

Judicial branch: *highest court(s):* US Supreme Court (consists of 9 justices—the chief justice and 8 associate justices)
judge selection and term of office: president nominates and, with the advice and consent of the Senate, appoints Supreme Court justices; justices appointed for life
subordinate courts: Courts of Appeal (includes the US Court of Appeal for the Federal District and 12 regional appeals courts); 94 federal district courts in 50 states and territories
note: the US court system consists of the federal court system and the state court systems; although each court system is responsible for hearing certain types of cases, neither is completely independent of the other, and the systems often interact

Political parties and leaders: Democratic Party [Tom PEREZ]
Green Party [collective leadership]
Libertarian Party [Nicholas SARWARK]
Republican Party [Ronna Romney MCDANIEL]

Political pressure groups and leaders: environmentalists; business groups; labor unions; churches; ethnic groups; political action committees or PACs; health groups; education groups; civic groups; youth groups; transportation groups; agricultural groups; veterans groups; women's groups; reform lobbies

International organization participation: ADB (nonregional member), AfDB (nonregional member), ANZUS, APEC, Arctic Council, ARF, ASEAN (dialogue partner), Australia Group, BIS, BSEC (observer), CBSS (observer), CD, CE (observer), CERN (observer), CICA (observer), CP, EAPC, EAS, EBRD, EITI (implementing country), FAO, FATF, G-5, G-7, G-8, G-10, G-20, IADB, IAEA, IBRD, ICAO, ICC

(national committees), ICRM, IDA, IEA, IFAD, IFC, IFRCS, IGAD (partners), IHO, ILO, IMF, IMO, IMSO, Interpol, IOC, IOM, ISO, ITSO, ITU, ITUC (NGOs), MIGA, MINUSMA, MINUSTAH, MONUSCO, NAFTA, NATO, NEA, NSG, OAS, OECD, OPCW, OSCE, Pacific Alliance (observer), Paris Club, PCA, PIF (partner), SAARC (observer), SELEC (observer), SICA (observer), SPC, UN, UNCTAD, UNESCO, UNHCR, UNITAR, UNMIL, UNMISS, UNRWA, UNSC (permanent), UNTSO, UPU, WCO, WHO, WIPO, WMO, WTO, ZC

Flag description: 13 equal horizontal stripes of red (top and bottom) alternating with white; there is a blue rectangle in the upper hoist-side corner bearing 50 small, white, five-pointed stars arranged in nine offset horizontal rows of six stars (top and bottom) alternating with rows of five stars; the 50 stars represent the 50 states, the 13 stripes represent the 13 original colonies; the blue stands for loyalty, devotion, truth, justice, and friendship; red symbolizes courage, zeal, and fervency, while white denotes purity and rectitude of conduct; commonly referred to by its nickname of Old Glory
note: the design and colors have been the basis for a number of other flags, including Chile, Liberia, Malaysia, and Puerto Rico

National symbol(s): bald eagle; national colors: red, white, blue

National anthem: *name:* "The Star-Spangled Banner"
lyrics/music: Francis Scott KEY/John Stafford SMITH
note: adopted 1931; during the War of 1812, after witnessing the successful American defense of Fort McHenry in Baltimore following British naval bombardment, Francis Scott KEY wrote the lyrics to what would become the national anthem; the lyrics were set to the tune of "The Anacreontic Song"; only the first verse is sung

ECONOMY

Economy—overview: The US has the most technologically powerful economy in the world, with a per capita GDP of $57,300. US firms are at or near the forefront in technological advances, especially in computers, pharmaceuticals, and medical, aerospace, and military equipment; however, their advantage has narrowed since the end of World War II. Based on a comparison of GDP measured at purchasing power parity conversion rates, the US economy in 2014, having stood as the largest in the world for more than a century, slipped into second place behind China, which has more than tripled the US growth rate for each year of the past four decades.

In the US, private individuals and business firms make most of the decisions, and the federal and state governments buy needed goods and services predominantly in the private marketplace. US business firms enjoy greater flexibility than their counterparts in Western Europe and Japan in decisions to expand capital plant, to lay off surplus workers, and to develop new products. At the same time, businesses face higher barriers to enter their rivals' home markets than foreign firms face entering US markets.

Long-term problems for the US include stagnation of wages for lower-income families, inadequate investment in deteriorating infrastructure, rapidly rising medical and pension costs of an aging population, energy shortages, and sizable current account and budget deficits.

The onrush of technology has been a driving factor in the gradual development of a "two-tier" labor market in which those at the bottom lack the education and the professional/technical skills of those at the top and, more and more, fail to get comparable pay raises, health insurance coverage, and other benefits. But the globalization of trade, and especially the rise of low-wage producers such as China, has put additional downward pressure on wages and upward pressure on the return to capital. Since 1975, practically all the gains in household income have gone to the top 20% of households. Since 1996, dividends and capital gains have grown faster than wages or any other category of after-tax income.

Imported oil accounts for nearly 55% of US consumption and oil has a major impact on the overall health of the economy. Crude oil prices doubled between 2001 and 2006, the year home prices peaked; higher gasoline prices ate into consumers' budgets and many individuals fell behind in their mortgage payments. Oil prices climbed another 50% between 2006 and 2008, and bank foreclosures more than doubled in the same period. Besides dampening the housing market, soaring oil prices caused a drop in the value of the dollar and a deterioration in the US merchandise trade deficit, which peaked at $840 billion in 2008. Because the US economy is energy-intensive, falling oil prices since 2013 have alleviated many of the problems the earlier increases had created.

The sub-prime mortgage crisis, falling home prices, investment bank failures, tight credit, and the global economic downturn pushed the US into a recession by mid-2008. GDP contracted until the third quarter of 2009, making this the deepest and longest downturn since the Great Depression. To help stabilize financial markets, the US Congress established a $700 billion Troubled Asset Relief Program (TARP) in October 2008. The government used some of these funds to purchase equity in US banks and industrial corporations, much of which had been returned to the government by early 2011. In January 2009, Congress passed and President Barack OBAMA signed a bill providing an additional $787 billion fiscal stimulus to be used over 10 years—two-thirds on additional spending and one-third on tax cuts—to create jobs and to help the economy recover. In 2010 and 2011, the federal budget deficit reached nearly 9% of GDP. In 2012, the Federal Government reduced the growth of spending and the deficit shrank to 7.6% of GDP. US revenues from taxes and other sources are lower, as a percentage of GDP, than those of most other countries.

Wars in Iraq and Afghanistan required major shifts in national resources from civilian to military purposes and contributed to the growth of the budget deficit and public debt. Through 2014, the direct costs of the wars totaled more than $1.5 trillion, according to US Government figures.

In March 2010, President OBAMA signed into law the Patient Protection and Affordable Care Act, a health insurance reform that was designed to extend coverage to an additional 32 million Americans by 2016, through private health insurance for the general population and Medicaid for the impoverished. Total spending on healthcare—public plus private—rose from 9.0% of GDP in 1980 to 17.9% in 2010.

In July 2010, the president signed the DODD-FRANK Wall Street Reform and Consumer Protection Act, a law designed to promote financial stability by protecting consumers from financial abuses, ending taxpayer bailouts of financial firms, dealing with troubled banks that are "too big to fail," and improving accountability and transparency in the financial system—in particular, by requiring certain financial derivatives to be traded in markets that are subject to government regulation and oversight.

In December 2012, the Federal Reserve Board (Fed) announced plans to purchase $85 billion per month of mortgage-backed and Treasury securities in an effort to hold down long-term interest rates, and to keep short-term rates near zero until unemployment dropped below 6.5% or inflation rose above 2.5%. In late 2013, the Fed announced that it would begin scaling back long-term bond purchases to $75 billion per month in January 2014 and further reduce them as conditions warranted; the Fed ended the purchases during the summer of 2014. In 2014, the unemployment rate dropped to 6.2%, and continued to fall to 5.5% by mid-2015, the lowest rate of joblessness since before the global recession began; inflation stood at 1.7%, and public debt as a share of GDP continued to decline, following several years of increases. In December 2015, the Fed raised its target for the benchmark federal funds rate by 0.25%, the first increase since the recession began. With US GDP growth below 2%, the Fed opted to raise rates three times since then, and in mid-June 2017, the range for the target rate stood at 1% to 1.25%.

GDP (purchasing power parity): $19.36 trillion (2017 est.)
$18.95 trillion (2016 est.)
$18.67 trillion (2015 est.)
note: data are in 2017 dollars
country comparison to the world: 3

GDP (official exchange rate): $19.36 trillion (2016 est.)

GDP—real growth rate: 2.2% (2017 est.)
1.5% (2016 est.)
2.9% (2015 est.)
country comparison to the world: 145

GDP—per capita (PPP): $59,500 (2017 est.)
$58,600 (2016 est.)
$58,200 (2015 est.)
note: data are in 2017 dollars
country comparison to the world: 20

Gross national saving: 17.5% of GDP (2017 est.)
18% of GDP (2016 est.)

19.4% of GDP (2015 est.)
country comparison to the world: 105

GDP—composition, by end use:
household consumption: 69.1%
government consumption: 17.2%
investment in fixed capital: 16.3%
investment in inventories: 0.3%
exports of goods and services: 12.2%
imports of goods and services: -15.1% (2017 est.)

GDP—composition, by sector of origin:
agriculture: 0.9%
industry: 18.9%
services: 80.2%
(2017 est.)

Agriculture—products: wheat, corn, other grains, fruits, vegetables, cotton; beef, pork, poultry, dairy products; fish; forest products

Industries: highly diversified, world leading, high-technology innovator, second-largest industrial output in the world; petroleum, steel, motor vehicles, aerospace, telecommunications, chemicals, electronics, food processing, consumer goods, lumber, mining

Industrial production growth rate: 1.8% (2017 est.)
country comparison to the world: 144

Labor force: 160.4 million
note: includes unemployed (2017 est.)
country comparison to the world: 4

Labor force—by occupation: farming, forestry, and fishing: 0.7%
manufacturing, extraction, transportation, and crafts: 20.3%
managerial, professional, and technical: 37.3%
sales and office: 24.2%
other services: 17.6%
note: figures exclude the unemployed (2009)

Unemployment rate: 4.4% (2017 est.)
4.9% (2016 est.)
country comparison to the world: 63

Population below poverty line: 15.1% (2010 est.)

Household income or consumption by percentage share: *lowest 10%:* 2%
highest 10%: 30% (2007 est.)

Distribution of family income—Gini index: 45 (2007)
40.8 (1997)
country comparison to the world: 40

Budget: *revenues:* $3.336 trillion
expenditures: $3.991 trillion
note: for the US, revenues exclude social contributions of approximately $1.0 trillion; expenditures exclude social benefits of approximately $2.3 trillion (2017 est.)

Taxes and other revenues: 17.2% of GDP
note: excludes contributions for social security and other programs; if social contributions were added, taxes and other revenues would amount to approximately 22% of GDP (2017 est.)
country comparison to the world: 176

Budget surplus (+) or deficit (-): -3.4% of GDP (2017 est.)
country comparison to the world: 127

Public debt: 77.4% of GDP (2017 est.)
76.5% of GDP (2016 est.)

note: data cover only what the United States Treasury denotes as "Debt Held by the Public," which includes all debt instruments issued by the Treasury that are owned by non-US Government entities; the data include Treasury debt held by foreign entities; the data exclude debt issued by individual US states, as well as intra-governmental debt; intra-governmental debt consists of Treasury borrowings from surpluses in the trusts for Federal Social Security, Federal Employees, Hospital and Supplemental Medical Insurance (Medicare), Disability and Unemployment, and several other smaller trusts; if data for intra-government debt were added, "gross debt" would increase by about one-third of GDP
country comparison to the world: 43

Fiscal year: 1 October—30 September

Inflation rate (consumer prices): 2.1% (2017 est.)
1.3% (2016 est.)
country comparison to the world: 96

Central bank discount rate: 0.5% (31 December 2010)
0.5% (31 December 2009)
country comparison to the world: 131

Commercial bank prime lending rate: 4.3% (31 December 2017 est.)
3.51% (31 December 2016 est.)
country comparison to the world: 156

Stock of narrow money: $3.627 trillion (31 December 2017 est.)
$3.25 trillion (31 December 2016 est.)
country comparison to the world: 4

Stock of broad money: $14 trillion (31 December 2017 est.)
$12.84 trillion (31 December 2016 est.)
country comparison to the world: 2

Stock of domestic credit: $21.59 trillion (31 December 2017 est.)
$20.24 trillion (31 December 2016 est.)
country comparison to the world: 2

Market value of publicly traded shares: $25.07 trillion (31 December 2015 est.)
$26.33 trillion (31 December 2014 est.)
$24.03 trillion (31 December 2013 est.)
country comparison to the world: 1

Current account balance: -$462 billion (2017 est.)
-$451.7 billion (2016 est.)
country comparison to the world: 201

Exports: $1.576 trillion (2017 est.)
$1.456 trillion (2016 est.)
country comparison to the world: 3

Exports—commodities: agricultural products (soybeans, fruit, corn) 9.2%, industrial supplies (organic chemicals) 26.8%, capital goods (transistors, aircraft, motor vehicle parts, computers, telecommunications equipment) 49.0%, consumer goods (automobiles, medicines) 15.0% (2008 est.)

Exports—partners: Canada 18.3%, Mexico 15.9%, China 8%, Japan 4.4% (2016)

Imports: $2.352 trillion (2017 est.)
$2.208 trillion (2016 est.)
country comparison to the world: 1

Imports—commodities: agricultural products 4.9%, industrial supplies 32.9% (crude oil 8.2%), capital goods 30.4% (computers, telecommunications equipment, motor vehicle parts, office machines, electric power machinery), consumer goods 31.8% (automobiles, clothing, medicines, furniture, toys) (2008 est.)

Imports—partners: China 21.1%, Mexico 13.4%, Canada 12.7%, Japan 6%, Germany 5.2% (2016)

Reserves of foreign exchange and gold: $117.3 billion (31 December 2016 est.)
$117.6 billion (31 December 2015 est.)
country comparison to the world: 22

Debt—external: $17.91 trillion (31 March 2016 est.)
$17.85 trillion (31 March 2015 est.)
note: approximately 4/5ths of US external debt is denominated in US dollars; foreign lenders have been willing to hold US dollar denominated debt instruments because they view the dollar as the world's reserve currency
country comparison to the world: 1

Stock of direct foreign investment—at home: $4.084 trillion (31 December 2017 est.)
$3.614 trillion (31 December 2016 est.)
country comparison to the world: 3

Stock of direct foreign investment—abroad: $5.644 trillion (31 December 2017 est.)
$5.352 trillion (31 December 2016 est.)
country comparison to the world: 3

Exchange rates: British pounds per US dollar: 0.7836 (2017 est.), 0.738 (2016 est.), 0.738 (2015 est.), 0.607 (2014 est), 0.6391 (2013 est.)
Canadian dollars per US dollar: 1, 1.308 (2017 est.), 1.3256 (2016 est.), 1.3256 (2015 est.), 1.2788 (2014 est.), 1.0298 (2013 est.)
Chinese yuan per US dollar: 1, 6.7588 (2017 est.), 6.6445 (2016 est.), 6.2275 (2015 est.), 6.1434 (2014 est.), 6.1958 (2013 est.)
euros per US dollar: 0.906 (2017 est.), 0.9214 (2016 est.), 0.9214(2015 est.), 0.885 (2014 est.), 0.7634 (2013 est.)
Japanese yen per US dollar: 111.10 (2017 est.), 108.76 (2016 est.), 108.76 (2015 est.), 121.02 (2014 est.), 97.44 (2013 est.)

ENERGY

Electricity access: *electrification—total population:* 100% (2016)

Electricity—production: 4.088 trillion kWh (2015 est.)
country comparison to the world: 2

Electricity—consumption: 3.911 trillion kWh (2015 est.)
country comparison to the world: 2

Electricity—exports: 9.695 billion kWh (2016 est.)
country comparison to the world: 25

Electricity—imports: 80.66 billion kWh (2016 est.)
country comparison to the world: 2

Electricity—installed generating capacity: 1.074 billion kW (2015 est.)
country comparison to the world: 3

Electricity—from fossil fuels: 70.6% of total installed capacity (2015 est.)
country comparison to the world: 103

Electricity—from nuclear fuels: 9.2% of total installed capacity (2015 est.)
country comparison to the world: 18

Electricity—from hydroelectric plants: 7.4% of total installed capacity (2015 est.)
country comparison to the world: 124

Electricity—from other renewable sources: 10.7% of total installed capacity (2015 est.)
country comparison to the world: 69

Crude oil—production: 8.853 million bbl/day (2016 est.)
country comparison to the world: 3

Crude oil—exports: 590,900 bbl/day (2016 est.)
country comparison to the world: 21

Crude oil—imports: 7.85 million bbl/day (2016 est.)
country comparison to the world: 1

Crude oil—proved reserves: 36.52 billion bbl (1 January 2017 es)
country comparison to the world: 11

Refined petroleum products—production: 20.08 million bbl/day (2016 est.)
country comparison to the world: 1

Refined petroleum products—consumption: 19.69 million bbl/day (2015 est.)
country comparison to the world: 1

Refined petroleum products—exports: 4.67 million bbl/day (2016 est.)
country comparison to the world: 1

Refined petroleum products—imports: 2.205 million bbl/day (2016 est.)
country comparison to the world: 2

Natural gas—production: 766.2 billion cu m (2015 est.)
country comparison to the world: 1

Natural gas—consumption: 773.2 billion cu m (2015 est.)
country comparison to the world: 1

Natural gas—exports: 50.52 billion cu m (2015 est.)
country comparison to the world: 7

Natural gas—imports: 76.96 billion cu m (2015 est.)
country comparison to the world: 4

Natural gas—proved reserves: 8.714 trillion cu m (1 January 2016 es)
country comparison to the world: 4

Carbon dioxide emissions from consumption of energy: 5.402 billion Mt (2013 est.)
country comparison to the world: 2

COMMUNICATIONS

Telephones—fixed lines: *total subscriptions:* 121.53 million
subscriptions per 100 inhabitants: 38 (July 2016 est.)
country comparison to the world: 3

Telephones—mobile cellular: *total:* 416.684 million
subscriptions per 100 inhabitants: 129 (July 2016 est.)
country comparison to the world: 5

Telephone system: *general assessment:* a large, technologically advanced, multipurpose communications system

domestic: a large system of fiber-optic cable, microwave radio relay, coaxial cable, and domestic satellites carries every form of telephone traffic; a rapidly growing cellular system carries mobile telephone traffic throughout the country
international: country code—1; multiple ocean cable systems provide international connectivity; satellite earth stations—61 Intelsat (45 Atlantic Ocean and 16 Pacific Ocean), 5 Intersputnik (Atlantic Ocean region), and 4 Inmarsat (Pacific and Atlantic Ocean regions) (2016)

Broadcast media: 4 major terrestrial TV networks with affiliate stations throughout the country, plus cable and satellite networks, independent stations, and a limited public broadcasting sector that is largely supported by private grants; overall, thousands of TV stations broadcasting; multiple national radio networks with many affiliate stations; while most stations are commercial, National Public Radio (NPR) has a network of some 600 member stations; satellite radio available; overall, nearly 15,000 radio stations operating (2008)

Internet country code: .us

Internet users: total: 246,809,221

percent of population: 76.2% (July 2016 est.)
country comparison to the world: 3

TRANSPORTATION

National air transport system: *number of registered air carriers:* 92
inventory of registered aircraft operated by air carriers: 6,817
annual passenger traffic on registered air carriers: 798.23 million
annual freight traffic on registered air carriers: 37.219 billion mt-km (2015)
Civil aircraft registration country code prefix: N (2016)

Airports: 13,513 (2013)
country comparison to the world: 1

Airports—with paved runways: total: 5,054
over 3,047 m: 189
2,438 to 3,047 m: 235
1,524 to 2,437 m: 1,478
914 to 1,523 m: 2,249
under 914 m: 903 (2013)

Airports—with unpaved runways: total: 8,459
over 3,047 m: 1
2,438 to 3,047 m: 6
1,524 to 2,437 m: 140
914 to 1,523 m: 1,552
under 914 m: 6,760 (2013)

Heliports: 5,287 (2013)

Pipelines: natural gas 1,984,321 km; petroleum products 240,711 km (2013)

Railways: total: 293,564.2 km
standard gauge: 293,564.2 km 1.435-m gauge (2014)
country comparison to the world: 1

Roadways: total: 6,586,610 km
paved: 4,304,715 km (includes 76,334 km of expressways)

unpaved: 2,281,895 km (2012)
country comparison to the world: 1

Waterways: 41,009 km (19,312 km used for commerce; Saint Lawrence Seaway of 3,769 km, including the Saint Lawrence River of 3,058 km, is shared with Canada) (2012)
country comparison to the world: 5

Merchant marine: *total:* 3,611
by type: bulk carrier 5, container ship 61, general cargo 114, oil tanker 66, other 3,365 (2017)
country comparison to the world: 5

Ports and terminals: cargo ports: Baton Rouge, Corpus Christi, Hampton Roads, Houston, Long Beach, Los Angeles, New Orleans, New York, Plaquemines (LA), Tampa, Texas City
container port(s) (TEUs): Hampton Roads (2,549,000), Houston (2,131,000), Long Beach (7,192,000), Los Angeles (8,160,000), New York/New Jersey (6,372,000), Oakland (2,278,000), Savannah (3,737,000), Seattle (3,531,000) (2015)
cruise departure ports (passengers): Miami (2,032,000), Port Everglades (1,277,000), Port Canaveral (1,189,000), Seattle (430,000), Long Beach (415,000) (2009)
oil terminal(s): LOOP terminal, Haymark terminal
LNG terminal(s) (import): Cove Point (MD), Elba Island (GA), Everett (MA), Freeport (TX), Golden Pass (TX), Hackberry (LA), Lake Charles (LA), Neptune (offshore), Northeast Gateway (offshore), Pascagoula (MS), Sabine Pass (TX)
LNG terminal(s) (export): Kenai (AK)

MILITARY AND SECURITY

Military expenditures: 3.29% of GDP (2016)
3.3% of GDP (2015)
3.51% of GDP (2014)
3.83% of GDP (2013)
4.24% of GDP (2012)
country comparison to the world: 9

Military branches: United States Armed Forces: US Army, US Navy (includes Marine Corps), US Air Force, US Coast Guard; note—Coast Guard administered in peacetime by the Department of Homeland Security, but in wartime reports to the Department of the Navy (2017)

Military service age and obligation: 18 years of age (17 years of age with parental consent) for male and female voluntary service; no conscription; maximum enlistment age 42 (Army), 27 (Air Force), 34 (Navy), 28 (Marines); 8-year service obligation, including 2-5 years active duty (Army), 2 years active (Navy), 4 years active (Air Force, Marines); all military occupations and positions open to women (2016)

TERRORISM

Terrorist groups—foreign based: *al-Qa'ida (AQ):*
aim(s): drive the US and US influence out of Muslim countries, destabilize the US economy and, ultimately, destroy the US
area(s) of operation: maintains a limited presence; authorities continue to pursue operatives and supporters; on 11 September 2001, 19

operatives hijacked four commercial airliners in the US and took control of the cockpits; the hijackers crashed two planes into the World Trade Center's twin towers in New York City, one plane into the Pentagon in Arlington County, Virginia, and the fourth hijacked plane is thought to have been intended to crash into either the White House or Capitol Building; passengers overpowered the hijackers on the fourth plane that crashed in Stonycreek Township, Somerset County, Pennsylvania; approximately 2,993 people died and over 8,900 more were injured; these coordinated hijackings marked the deadliest terrorist attack to date in the US; on 26 February 1993, operatives detonated a massive VBIED inside the World Trade Center's North Tower in New York City in the US, killing six people and injuring 1,000

TRANSNATIONAL ISSUES

Disputes—international: the US has intensified domestic security measures and is collaborating closely with its neighbors, Canada and Mexico, to monitor and control legal and illegal personnel, transport, and commodities across the international borders; abundant rainfall in recent years along much of the Mexico-US border region has ameliorated periodically strained water-sharing arrangements; 1990 Maritime Boundary Agreement in the Bering Sea still awaits Russian Duma ratification; Canada and the United States dispute how to divide the Beaufort Sea and the status of the Northwest Passage but continue to work cooperatively to survey the Arctic continental shelf; The Bahamas and US have not been able to agree on a maritime boundary; US Naval Base at Guantanamo Bay is leased from Cuba and only mutual agreement or US abandonment of the area can terminate the lease; Haiti claims US-administered Navassa Island; US has made no territorial claim in Antarctica (but has reserved the right to do so) and does not recognize the claims of any other states; Marshall Islands claims Wake Island; Tokelau included American Samoa's Swains Island among the islands listed in its 2006 draft constitution

Refugees and internally displaced persons: *refugees (country of origin):* the US admitted 84,994 refugees during FY2016 including: 16,370 (Democratic Republic of the Congo); 12,587 (Syria); 12,347 (Burma); 9,880 (Iraq); 9,020 (Somalia); 5,817 (Bhutan); 3,750 (Iran)
note: more than 46,000 Venezuelans have claimed asylum since 2014 because of the economic and political crisis (2017)

Illicit drugs: world's largest consumer of cocaine (shipped from Colombia through Mexico and the Caribbean), Colombian heroin, and Mexican heroin and marijuana; major consumer of ecstasy and Mexican methamphetamine; minor consumer of high-quality Southeast Asian heroin; illicit producer of cannabis, marijuana, depressants, stimulants, hallucinogens, and methamphetamine; money-laundering center

UNITED STATES PACIFIC ISLAND WILDLIFE REFUGES

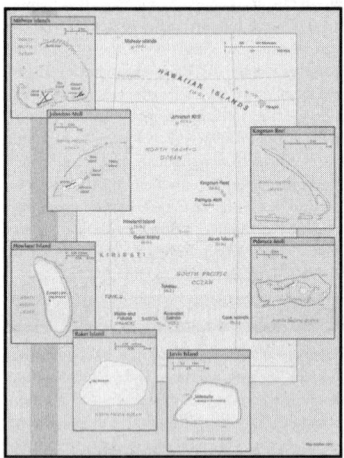

INTRODUCTION

Background: All of the following US Pacific island territories except Midway Atoll constitute the Pacific Remote Islands National Wildlife Refuge (NWR) Complex and as such are managed by the Fish and Wildlife Service of the US Department of the Interior. Midway Atoll NWR has been included in a Refuge Complex with the Hawaiian Islands NWR and also designated as part of Papahanaumokuakea Marine National Monument. These remote refuges are the most widespread collection of marine- and terrestrial-life protected areas on the planet under a single country's jurisdiction. They sustain many endemic species including corals, fish, shellfish, marine mammals, seabirds, water birds, land birds, insects, and vegetation not found elsewhere.

Baker Island: The US took possession of the island in 1857. Its guano deposits were mined by US and British companies during the second half of the 19th century. In 1935, a short-lived attempt at colonization began on this island but was disrupted by World War II and thereafter abandoned. The island was established as a NWR in 1974.

Howland Island: Discovered by the US early in the 19th century, the uninhabited atoll was officially claimed by the US in 1857. Both US and British companies mined for guano deposits until about 1890. In 1935, a short-lived attempt at colonization began on this island, similar to the effort on nearby Baker Island, but was disrupted by World War II and thereafter abandoned. The famed American aviatrix Amelia EARHART disappeared while seeking out Howland Island as a refueling stop during her 1937 round-the-world flight; Earhart Light, a day beacon near the middle of the west coast, was named in her memory. The island was established as a NWR in 1974.

Jarvis Island: First discovered by the British in 1821, the uninhabited island was annexed by the US in 1858 but abandoned in 1879 after tons of guano had been removed. The UK annexed the island in 1889 but never carried out plans for further exploitation. The US occupied and reclaimed the island in 1935. It was abandoned in 1942 during World War II. The island was established as a NWR in 1974.

Johnston Atoll: Both the US and the Kingdom of Hawaii annexed Johnston Atoll in 1858, but it was the US that mined the guano deposits until the late 1880s. Johnston and Sand Islands were designated wildlife refuges in 1926. The US Navy took over the atoll in 1934. Subsequently, the US Air Force assumed control in 1948. The site was used for high-altitude nuclear tests in the 1950s and 1960s. Until late in 2000 the atoll was maintained as a storage and disposal site for chemical weapons. Munitions destruction, cleanup, and closure of the facility were completed by May 2005. The Fish and Wildlife Service and the US Air Force are currently discussing future management options; in the interim, Johnston Atoll and the three-mile Naval Defensive Sea around it remain under the jurisdiction and administrative control of the US Air Force.

Kingman Reef: The US annexed the reef in 1922. Its sheltered lagoon served as a way station for flying boats on Hawaii-to-American Samoa flights during the late 1930s. There are no terrestrial plants on the reef, which is frequently awash, but it does support abundant and diverse marine fauna and flora. In 2001, the waters surrounding the reef out to 12 nm were designated a NWR.

Midway Islands: The US took formal possession of the islands in 1867. The laying of the transpacific cable, which passed through the islands, brought the first residents in 1903. Between 1935 and 1947, Midway was used as a refueling stop for transpacific flights. The US naval victory over a Japanese fleet off Midway in 1942 was one of the turning points of World War II. The islands continued to serve as a naval station until closed in 1993. Today the islands are a NWR and are the site of the world's largest Laysan albatross colony.

Palmyra Atoll: The Kingdom of Hawaii claimed the atoll in 1862, and the US included it among the Hawaiian Islands when it annexed the archipelago in 1898. The Hawaii Statehood Act of 1959 did not include Palmyra Atoll, which is now partly privately owned by the Nature Conservancy with the rest owned by the Federal government and managed by the US Fish and Wildlife Service. These organizations are managing the atoll as a wildlife refuge. The lagoons and surrounding waters within the 12-nm US territorial seas were transferred to the US Fish and Wildlife Service and designated a NWR in January 2001.

GEOGRAPHY

Location: Oceania

Baker Island: atoll in the North Pacific Ocean 3,390 km southwest of Honolulu, about halfway between Hawaii and Australia

Howland Island: island in the North Pacific Ocean 3,360 km southwest of Honolulu, about halfway between Hawaii and Australia

Jarvis Island: island in the South Pacific Ocean 2,415 km south of Honolulu, about halfway between Hawaii and Cook Islands

Johnston Atoll: atoll in the North Pacific Ocean 1,330 km southwest of Honolulu, about one-third of the way from Hawaii to the Marshall Islands

Kingman Reef: reef in the North Pacific Ocean 1,720 km south of Honolulu, about halfway between Hawaii and American Samoa

Midway Islands: atoll in the North Pacific Ocean 2,335 km northwest of Honolulu near the end of the Hawaiian Archipelago, about one-third of the way from Honolulu to Tokyo

Palmyra Atoll: atoll in the North Pacific Ocean 1,780 km south of Honolulu, about halfway between Hawaii and American Samoa

Geographic coordinates: Baker Island: 0 13 N, 176 28 W

Howland Island: 0 48 N, 176 38 W

Jarvis Island: 0 23 S, 160 01 W

Johnston Atoll: 16 45 N, 169 31 W

Kingman Reef: 6 23 N, 162 25 W

Midway Islands: 28 12 N, 177 22 W

Palmyra Atoll: 5 53 N, 162 05 W

Map references: Oceania

Area: total—6,959.41 sq km; emergent land—22.41 sq km; submerged—6,937 sq km

Baker Island: total—129.1 sq km; emergent land—2.1 sq km; submerged—127 sq km

Howland Island: total—138.6 sq km; emergent land—2.6 sq km; submerged—136 sq km

Jarvis Island: total—152 sq km; emergent land—5 sq km; submerged—147 sq km

Johnston Atoll: total—276.6 sq km; emergent land—2.6 sq km; submerged—274 sq km

Kingman Reef: total—1,958.01 sq km; emergent land—0.01 sq km; submerged—1,958 sq km

Midway Islands: total—2,355.2 sq km; emergent land—6.2 sq km; submerged—2,349 sq km

Palmyra Atoll: total—1,949.9 sq km; emergent land—3.9 sq km; submerged—1,946 sq km

country comparison to the world: 241

Area—comparative: Baker Island: about 2.5 times the size of the National Mall in Washington, DC

Howland Island: about three times the size of the National Mall in Washington, DC

Jarvis Island: about eight times the size of the National Mall in Washington, DC

Johnston Atoll: about 4.5 times the size of the National Mall in Washington, DC

Kingman Reef: a little more than 1.5 times the size of the National Mall in Washington, DC

Midway Islands: about nine times the size of the National Mall in Washington, DC

Palmyra Atoll: about 20 times the size of the National Mall in Washington, DC

Land boundaries: 0 km
Coastline: Baker Island: 4.8 km
Howland Island: 6.4 km
Jarvis Island: 8 km
Johnston Atoll: 34 km
Kingman Reef: 3 km
Midway Islands: 15 km
Palmyra Atoll: 14.5 km

Maritime claims: *territorial sea:* 12 nm
exclusive economic zone: 200 nm

Climate: Baker, Howland, and Jarvis Islands: equatorial; scant rainfall, constant wind, burning sun
Johnston Atoll and Kingman Reef: tropical, but generally dry; consistent northeast trade winds with little seasonal temperature variation
Midway Islands: subtropical with cool, moist winters (December to February) and warm, dry summers (May to October); moderated by prevailing easterly winds; most of the 107 cm of annual rainfall occurs during the winter
Palmyra Atoll: equatorial, hot; located within the low pressure area of the Intertropical Convergence Zone (ITCZ) where the northeast and southeast trade winds meet, it is extremely wet with between 400-500 cm of rainfall each year

Terrain: low and nearly flat sandy coral islands with narrow fringing reefs that have developed at the top of submerged volcanic mountains, which in most cases rise steeply from the ocean floor

Elevation: *elevation extremes:* lowest point: Pacific Ocean 0 m
highest point: Baker Island, unnamed location—8 m; Howland Island, unnamed location—3 m; Jarvis Island, unnamed location—7 m; Johnston Atoll, Sand Island—10 m; Kingman Reef, unnamed location—less than 2 m; Midway Islands, unnamed location—13 m; Palmyra Atoll, unnamed location—3 m

Natural resources: terrestrial and aquatic wildlife

Land use: *agricultural land:* 0%
arable land: 0%;
permanent crops: 0%;
permanent pasture: 0%
forest: 0%
other: 100% (2011 est.)

Natural hazards: Baker, Howland, and Jarvis Islands: the narrow fringing reef surrounding the island poses a maritime hazard
Kingman Reef: wet or awash most of the time, maximum elevation of less than 2 m makes Kingman Reef a maritime hazard
Midway Islands, Johnston, and Palmyra Atolls: NA

Environment—current issues: Baker, Howland, and Jarvis Islands, and Johnston Atoll: no natural freshwater resources
Kingman Reef: none
Midway Islands and Palmyra Atoll: NA

Geography—note: Baker, Howland, and Jarvis Islands: scattered vegetation consisting of grasses, prostrate vines, and low growing shrubs; primarily a nesting, roosting, and foraging habitat for seabirds, shorebirds, and marine wildlife; closed to the public
Johnston Atoll: Johnston Island and Sand Island are natural islands, which have been expanded by coral dredging; North Island (Akau) and East Island (Hikina) are manmade islands formed from coral dredging; the egg-shaped reef is 34 km in circumference; closed to the public
Kingman Reef: barren coral atoll with deep interior lagoon; closed to the public
Midway Islands: a coral atoll managed as a National Wildlife Refuge and open to the public for wildlife-related recreation in the form of wildlife observation and photography
Palmyra Atoll: the high rainfall and resulting lush vegetation make the environment of this atoll unique among the US Pacific Island territories; supports a large undisturbed stand of Pisonia beach forest

PEOPLE AND SOCIETY

Population: no indigenous inhabitants
note: public entry is only by special-use permit from US Fish and Wildlife Service and generally restricted to scientists and educators; visited annually by US Fish and Wildlife Service
Jarvis Island: Millersville settlement on western side of island occasionally used as a weather station from 1935 until World War II, when it was abandoned; reoccupied in 1957 during the International Geophysical Year by scientists who left in 1958; currently unoccupied
Johnston Atoll: in previous years, an average of 1,100 US military and civilian contractor personnel were present; as of May 2005, all US Government personnel had left the island
Midway Islands: approximately 40 people make up the staff of US Fish and Wildlife Service and their services contractor living at the atoll
Palmyra Atoll: four to 20 Nature Conservancy, US Fish and Wildlife staff, and researchers

GOVERNMENT

Country name: *conventional long form:* none
conventional short form: Baker Island; Howland Island; Jarvis Island; Johnston Atoll; Kingman Reef; Midway Islands; Palmyra Atoll
etymology: self-descriptive name specifying the territories' affiliation and location

Dependency status: unincorporated territories of the US; administered from Washington, DC, by the Fish and Wildlife Service of the US Department of the Interior as part of the National Wildlife Refuge System

note on Palmyra Atoll: incorporated territory of the US; partly privately owned and partly federally owned; administered from Washington, DC, by the Fish and Wildlife Service of the US Department of the Interior; the Office of Insular Affairs of the US Department of the Interior continues to administer nine excluded areas comprising certain tidal and submerged lands within the 12 nm territorial sea or within the lagoon

Legal system: the laws of the US, where applicable, apply

Diplomatic representation from the US: none (territories of the US)

Flag description: the flag of the US is used

ECONOMY

Economy—overview: no economic activity

TRANSPORTATION

Airports: *Baker Island:* one abandoned World War II runway of 1,665 m covered with vegetation and unusable
Howland Island: airstrip constructed in 1937 for scheduled refueling stop on the round-the-world flight of Amelia EARHART and Fred NOONAN; the aviators left Lae, New Guinea, for Howland Island but were never seen again; the airstrip is no longer serviceable
Johnston Atoll: one closed and not maintained
Kingman Reef: lagoon was used as a halfway station between Hawaii and American Samoa by Pan American Airways for flying boats in 1937 and 1938
Midway Islands: 3—one operational (2,377 m paved); no fuel for sale except emergencies
Palmyra Atoll: 1—1,846 m unpaved runway; privately owned (2013)

Airports—with paved runways: 2,438 to 3,047 m: 1—Johnston Atoll; note—abandoned but usable (2016)

Airports—with unpaved runways: 1,524 to 2,437 m: 1—Palmyra Atoll (2016)

Ports and terminals: *major seaport(s):* Baker, Howland, and Jarvis Islands, and Kingman Reef: none; offshore anchorage only
Johnston Atoll: Johnston Island
Midway Islands: Sand Island
Palmyra Atoll: West Lagoon

MILITARY AND SECURITY

Military—note: defense is the responsibility of the US

TRANSNATIONAL ISSUES

Disputes—international: none

URUGUAY

INTRODUCTION

Background: Montevideo, founded by the Spanish in 1726 as a military stronghold, soon took advantage of its natural harbor to become an important commercial center. Claimed by Argentina but annexed by Brazil in 1821, Uruguay declared its independence four years later and secured its freedom in 1828 after a three-year struggle. The administrations of President Jose BATLLE in the early 20th century launched widespread political, social, and economic reforms that established a statist tradition. A violent Marxist urban guerrilla movement named the Tupamaros, launched in the late 1960s, led Uruguay's president to cede control of the government to the military in 1973. By yearend, the rebels had been crushed, but the military continued to expand its hold over the government. Civilian rule was restored in 1985. In 2004, the left-of-center Frente Amplio Coalition won national elections that effectively ended 170 years of political control previously held by the Colorado and National (Blanco) parties. Uruguay's political and labor conditions are among the freest on the continent.

GEOGRAPHY

Location: Southern South America, bordering the South Atlantic Ocean, between Argentina and Brazil

Geographic coordinates: 33 00 S, 56 00 W

Map references: South America

Area: *total:* 176,215 sq km
land: 175,015 sq km
water: 1,200 sq km
country comparison to the world: 92

Area—comparative: about the size of Virginia and West Virginia combined; slightly smaller than the state of Washington

Land boundaries: *total:* 1,591 km
border countries (2): Argentina 541 km, Brazil 1,050 km

Coastline: 660 km

Maritime claims: *territorial sea:* 12 nm
contiguous zone: 24 nm
exclusive economic zone: 200 nm
continental shelf: 200 nm or the edge of continental margin

Climate: warm temperate; freezing temperatures almost unknown

Terrain: mostly rolling plains and low hills; fertile coastal lowland

Elevation: *mean elevation:* 109 m

elevation extremes: *lowest point:* Atlantic Ocean 0 m
highest point: Cerro Catedral 514 m

Natural resources: arable land, hydropower, minor minerals, fish

Land use: *agricultural land:* 87.2%
arable land: 10.1%;
permanent crops: 0.2%;
permanent pasture: 76.9%
forest: 10.2%
other: 2.6% (2011 est.)
Irrigated land: 2,380 sq km (2012)

Population—distribution: most of the country's population resides in the southern half of the country; approximately 80% of the populace is urban, living in towns or cities; nearly half of the population lives in and around the capital of Montevideo

Natural hazards: seasonally high winds (the pampero is a chilly and occasional violent wind that blows north from the Argentine pampas), droughts, floods; because of the absence of mountains, which act as weather barriers, all locations are particularly vulnerable to rapid changes from weather fronts

Environment—current issues: water pollution from meat packing/tannery industry; inadequate solid/hazardous waste disposal

Environment—international agreements: *party to:* Antarctic-Environmental Protocol, Antarctic-Marine Living Resources, Antarctic Treaty, Biodiversity, Climate Change, Climate Change-Kyoto Protocol, Desertification, Endangered Species, Environmental Modification, Hazardous Wastes, Law of the Sea, Ozone Layer Protection, Ship Pollution, Wetlands
signed, but not ratified: Marine Dumping, Marine Life Conservation

Geography—note: second-smallest South American country (after Suriname); most of the low-lying landscape (three-quarters of the country) is grassland, ideal for cattle and sheep raising

PEOPLE AND SOCIETY

Population: 3,360,148 (July 2017 est.)
country comparison to the world: 133

Nationality: *noun:* Uruguayan(s)

adjective: Uruguayan

Ethnic groups: white 88%, mestizo 8%, black 4%, Amerindian (practically nonexistent)

Languages: Spanish (official), Portunol, Brazilero (Portuguese-Spanish mix on the Brazilian frontier)

Religions: Roman Catholic 47.1%, non-Catholic Christians 11.1%, nondenominational 23.2%, Jewish 0.3%, atheist or agnostic 17.2%, other 1.1% (2006 est.)

Demographic profile: Uruguay rates high for most development indicators and is known for its secularism, liberal social laws, and well-developed social security, health, and educational systems. It is one of the few countries in Latin America and the Caribbean where the entire population has access to clean water. Uruguay's provision of free primary through university education has contributed to the country's high levels of literacy and educational attainment. However, the emigration of human capital has diminished the state's return on its investment in education. Remittances from the roughly 18% of Uruguayans abroad amount to less than 1 percent of national GDP. The emigration of young adults and a low birth rate are causing Uruguay's population to age rapidly.

In the 1960s, Uruguayans for the first time emigrated en masse—primarily to Argentina and Brazil—because of economic decline and the onset of more than a decade of military dictatorship. Economic crises in the early 1980s and 2002 also triggered waves of emigration, but since 2002 more than 70% of Uruguayan emigrants have selected the US and Spain as destinations because of better job prospects. Uruguay had a tiny population upon its independence in 1828 and welcomed thousands of predominantly Italian and Spanish immigrants, but the country has not experienced large influxes of new arrivals since the aftermath of World War II. More recent immigrants include Peruvians and Arabs.

Age structure: *0-14 years:* 20.17% (male 344,810/female 332,791)
15-24 years: 15.69% (male 267,000/female 260,135)
25-54 years: 39.34% (male 654,036/female 667,780)
55-64 years: 10.56% (male 167,002/female 187,865)
65 years and over: 14.25% (male 191,597/female 287,132) (2017 est.)

Dependency ratios: *total dependency ratio:* 55.9
youth dependency ratio: 33.4
elderly dependency ratio: 22.5
potential support ratio: 4.4 (2015 est.)

Median age: *total:* 35 years
male: 33.1 years
female: 36.7 years (2017 est.)
country comparison to the world: 78

Population growth rate: 0.27% (2017 est.)
country comparison to the world: 175

Birth rate: 13 births/1,000 population (2017 est.)
country comparison to the world: 152

Death rate: 9.4 deaths/1,000 population (2017 est.)
country comparison to the world: 56

Net migration rate: -0.9 migrant(s)/1,000 population (2017 est.)
country comparison to the world: 137

Population distribution: most of the country's population resides in the southern half of the country; approximately 80% of the populace is urban, living in towns or cities; nearly half of the population lives in and around the capital of Montevideo

Urbanization: *urban population:* 95.6% of total population (2017)
rate of urbanization: 0.44% annual rate of change (2015-20 est.)

Major urban areas—population: MONTEVIDEO (capital) 1.707 million (2015)

Sex ratio: *at birth:* 1.04 male(s)/female
0-14 years: 1.04 male(s)/female
15-24 years: 1.03 male(s)/female
25-54 years: 0.98 male(s)/female
55-64 years: 0.89 male(s)/female
65 years and over: 0.66 male(s)/female
total population: 0.94 male(s)/female (2016 est.)

Maternal mortality ratio: 15 deaths/100,000 live births (2015 est.)
country comparison to the world: 136

Infant mortality rate: *total:* 8.3 deaths/1,000 live births
male: 9.3 deaths/1,000 live births
female: 7.4 deaths/1,000 live births (2017 est.)
country comparison to the world: 152

Life expectancy at birth: *total population:* 77.4 years
male: 74.2 years
female: 80.6 years (2017 est.)
country comparison to the world: 70

Total fertility rate: 1.8 children born/woman (2017 est.)
country comparison to the world: 150

Health expenditures: 8.6% of GDP (2014)
country comparison to the world: 47

Physicians density: 3.94 physicians/1,000 population (2008)

Hospital bed density: 2.5 beds/1,000 population (2012)

Drinking water source:
improved:
urban: 100% of population
rural: 93.9% of population
total: 99.7% of population
unimproved:
urban: 0% of population
rural: 6.1% of population
total: 0.3% of population (2015 est.)

Sanitation facility access:
improved:
urban: 96.6% of population
rural: 92.6% of population
total: 96.4% of population
unimproved:

urban: 3.4% of population
rural: 7.4% of population
total: 3.6% of population (2015 est.)

HIV/AIDS—adult prevalence rate: 0.6% (2016 est.)
country comparison to the world: 59

HIV/AIDS—people living with HIV/AIDS: 12,000 (2016 est.)
country comparison to the world: 88

HIV/AIDS—deaths: <500 (2016 est.)

Obesity—adult prevalence rate: 27.9% (2016)
country comparison to the world: 34

Children under the age of 5 years underweight: 4% (2011)
country comparison to the world: 94

Education expenditures: 4.4% of GDP (2011)
country comparison to the world: 92

Literacy: *definition:* age 15 and over can read and write
total population: 98.5%
male: 98.1%
female: 98.9% (2015 est.)

School life expectancy (primary to tertiary education): *total:* 16 years
male: 14 years
female: 17 years (2010)

Unemployment, youth ages 15-24: *total:* 22.5%
male: 19.9%
female: 26.2% (2015 est.)
country comparison to the world: 61

GOVERNMENT

Country name: *conventional long form:* Oriental Republic of Uruguay
conventional short form: Uruguay
local long form: Republica Oriental del Uruguay
local short form: Uruguay
former: Banda Oriental, Cisplatine Province
etymology: name derives from the Spanish pronunciation of the Guarani Indian designation of the Uruguay River, which makes up the western border of the country and whose name later came to be applied to the entire country

Government type: presidential republic

Capital: name: Montevideo
geographic coordinates: 34 51 S, 56 10 W
time difference: UTC-3 (2 hours ahead of Washington, DC, during Standard Time)

Administrative divisions: 19 departments (departamentos, singular—departamento); Artigas, Canelones, Cerro Largo, Colonia, Durazno, Flores, Florida, Lavalleja, Maldonado, Montevideo, Paysandu, Rio Negro, Rivera, Rocha, Salto, San Jose, Soriano, Tacuarembo, Treinta y Tres

Independence: 25 August 1825 (from Brazil)

National holiday: Independence Day, 25 August (1825)

Constitution: several previous; latest approved by plebiscite 27 November 1966, effective 15 February 1967; amended several times, last in 2004 (2016)

Legal system: civil law system based on the Spanish civil code

International law organization participation: accepts compulsory ICJ jurisdiction; accepts ICCt jurisdiction

Citizenship: *citizenship by birth:* yes
citizenship by descent: yes
dual citizenship recognized: yes
residency requirement for naturalization: 3-5 years

Suffrage: 18 years of age; universal and compulsory

Executive branch: *chief of state:* President Tabare VAZQUEZ (since 1 March 2015); Vice President Lucia TOPOLANSKY (since 13 September 2017); note—note—Vice President Raul Fernando SENDIC Rodriguez (since 1 March 2015) stepped down on 9 September amid accusations of misuse of public funds; the president is both chief of state and head of government

head of government: President Tabare VAZQUEZ (since 1 March 2015); Vice President Lucia TOPOLANSKY (since 13 September 2017); note—Vice President Raul Fernando SENDIC Rodriguez (since 1 March 2015) stepped down on 9 September amid accusations of misuse of public funds

cabinet: Council of Ministers appointed by the president with approval of the General Assembly
elections/appointments: president and vice president directly elected on the same ballot by absolute majority vote in 2 rounds if needed for a 5-year term (eligible for nonconsecutive terms); election last held on 26 October 2014, with a runoff election on 30 November 2014 (next to be held on 27 October 2019, and a runoff if needed on 24 November 2019)

election results: Tabare VAZQUEZ elected president in second round; percent of vote—Tabare VAZQUEZ (Socialist Party) 56.5%, Luis Alberto LACALLE Pou (Blanco) 43.4%

Legislative branch: description: bicameral General Assembly or Asamblea General consists of the Chamber of Senators or Camara de Senadores (31 seats; members directly elected in a single nationwide constituency by proportional representation vote; the vice-president serves as the presiding ex-officio member; elected members serve 5-year terms) and the Chamber of Representatives or Camara de Representantes (99 seats; members directly elected in multi-seat constituencies by proportional representation vote to serve 5-year terms)

elections: Chamber of Senators—last held on 26 October 2014 (next to be held in October 2019); Chamber of Representatives—last held on 26 October 2014 (next to be held in October 2019)

election results: Chamber of Senators—percent of vote by coalition/party—Frente Amplio 49.5%, National Party 31.9%, Colorado Party 13.3%, Independent Party 3.2%, other 2.1%; seats by coalition/party—Frente Amplio 15, National Party 10, Colorado Party 4, Independent Party 1

Chamber of Representatives—percent of vote by coalition/party—Frente Amplio 49.5%, National Party 31.9%, Colorado Party 13.3%, Independent

961

Party 3.2%, AP 1.2%, other 0.9%; seats by coalition/party—Frente Amplio 50, National Party 32, Colorado Party 13, Independent Party 3, AP 1

Judicial branch: *highest court(s):* Supreme Court of Justice (consists of 5 judges)
judge selection and term of office: judges nominated by the president and appointed in joint conference of the General Assembly; judges appointed for 10-year terms, with reelection after a lapse of 5 years following the previous term
subordinate courts: Courts of Appeal; District Courts (Juzgados Letrados); Peace Courts (Juzgados de Paz); Rural Courts (Juzgados Rurales)

Political parties and leaders: Broad Front or FA (Frente Amplio)—(a broad governing coalition that includes Uruguay Assembly [Danilo ASTORI], Progressive Alliance [Rodolfo NIN NOVOA], New Space [Rafael MICHELINI], Socialist Party [Monica XAVIER], Vertiente Artiguista [Enrique RUBIO], Christian Democratic Party [Juan Andres ROBALLO], For the People's Victory [Luis PUIG], Popular Participation Movement (MPP) [Jose MUJICA], Broad Front Commitment [Raul SENDIC], Big House [Constanza MOREIRA], Communist Party [Marcos CARAMBULA], The Federal League [Dario PEREZ]
Colorado Party (including Vamos Uruguay (or Let's Go Uruguay) [Pedro BORDABERRY], Open Space [Tabare VIERA], and Open Batllism [Ope PASQUET])
Independent Party [Pablo MIERES]
National Party or Blanco (including All Forward [Luis LACALLE POU] and National Alliance [Jorge LARRANAGA])
Popular Assembly [Gonzalo ABELLA]

Political pressure groups and leaders: B'nai B'rith Catholic Church
Chamber of Commerce and Export of Agriproducts
Chamber of Industries (manufacturers' association)
Exporters Union of Uruguay
National Chamber of Commerce and Services
PIT/CNT (powerful federation of Uruguayan Unions—umbrella labor organization)
Rural Association of Uruguay (ranchers' association)
Uruguayan Network of Political Women
other: students

International organization participation: CAN (associate), CD, CELAC, FAO, G-77, IADB, IAEA, IBRD, ICAO, ICC (national committees), ICCt, ICRM, IDA, IFAD, IFC, IFRCS, IHO, ILO, IMF, IMO, Interpol, IOC, IOM, IPU, ISO, ITSO, ITU, LAES, LAIA, Mercosur, MIGA, MINUSTAH, MONUSCO, NAM (observer), OAS, OIF (observer), OPANAL, OPCW, Pacific Alliance (observer), PCA, SICA (observer), UN, UN Security Council (temporary), UNASUR, UNCTAD, UNESCO, UNIDO, Union Latina, UNMOGIP, UNOCI, UNWTO, UPU, WCO, WFTU (NGOs), WHO, WIPO, WMO, WTO

Diplomatic representation in the US: *chief of mission:* Ambassador Carlos Alberto GIANELLI Derois (since 3 August 2015)
chancery: 1913 I Street NW, Washington, DC 20006

telephone: [1] (202) 331-1313
FAX: [1] (202) 331-8142
consulate(s) general: Chicago, Los Angeles, Miami, New York

Diplomatic representation from the US: *chief of mission:* Ambassador Kelly Ann KEIDERLING-FRANZ (since 23 June 2016)
embassy: Lauro Muller 1776, Montevideo 11200
mailing address: APO AA 34035
telephone: [598] (2) 1770-2000
FAX: [598] (2) 1770-2128

Flag description: nine equal horizontal stripes of white (top and bottom) alternating with blue; a white square in the upper hoist-side corner with a yellow sun bearing a human face (delineated in black) known as the Sun of May with 16 rays that alternate between triangular and wavy; the stripes represent the nine original departments of Uruguay; the sun symbol evokes the legend of the sun breaking through the clouds on 25 May 1810 as independence was first declared from Spain (Uruguay subsequently won its independence from Brazil); the sun features are said to represent those of Inti, the Inca god of the sun
note: the banner was inspired by the national colors of Argentina and by the design of the US flag

National symbol(s): Sun of May (a sun-with-face symbol); national colors: blue, white, yellow

National anthem: *name:* "Himno Nacional" (National Anthem of Uruguay)
lyrics/music: Francisco Esteban ACUNA de Figueroa/Francisco Jose DEBALI
note: adopted 1848; the anthem is also known as "Orientales, la Patria o la tumba!" ("Uruguayans, the Fatherland or Death!"); it is the world's longest national anthem in terms of music (105 bars; almost five minutes); generally only the first verse and chorus are sung

ECONOMY

Economy—overview: Uruguay has a free market economy characterized by an export-oriented agricultural sector, a well-educated workforce, and high levels of social spending. Uruguay has sought to expand trade within the Common Market of the South (Mercosur) and with non-Mercosur members, and President VAZQUEZ has maintained his predecessor's mix of pro-market policies and a strong social safety net.

Following financial difficulties in the late 1990s and early 2000s, Uruguay's economic growth averaged 8% annually during the period 2004-08. The 2008-09 global financial crisis put a brake on Uruguay's vigorous growth, which decelerated to 2.6% in 2009. Nevertheless, the country managed to avoid a recession and keep positive growth rates, mainly through higher public expenditure and investment; GDP growth reached 8.9% in 2010 but slowed markedly in the period 2012-16 as a result of a renewed slowdown in the global economy and in Uruguay's main trade partners and Mercosur counterparts, Argentina and Brazil. Reforms in those countries should give Uruguay an economic boost. Growth picked up in 2017.

GDP (purchasing power parity): $78.41 billion (2017 est.)
$75.76 billion (2016 est.)
$74.67 billion (2015 est.)
note: data are in 2017 dollars
country comparison to the world: 96

GDP (official exchange rate): $60.27 billion (2016 est.)

GDP—real growth rate: 3.5% (2017 est.)
1.5% (2016 est.)
0.4% (2015 est.)
country comparison to the world: 93

GDP—per capita (PPP): $22,400 (2017 est.)
$21,800 (2016 est.)
$21,500 (2015 est.)
note: data are in 2017 dollars
country comparison to the world: 84

Gross national saving: 17.3% of GDP (2017 est.)
18.6% of GDP (2016 est.)
17.6% of GDP (2015 est.)
country comparison to the world: 107

GDP—composition, by end use:
household consumption: 65.3%
government consumption: 14.1%
investment in fixed capital: 18.6%
investment in inventories: -0.2%
exports of goods and services: 22.3%
imports of goods and services: -20.1% (2017 est.)

GDP—composition, by sector of origin:
agriculture: 6.2%
industry: 25%
services: 68.8% (2017 est.)

Agriculture—products: Cellulose, beef, soybeans, rice, wheat; dairy products; fish; lumber, tobacco, wine

Industries: food processing, electrical machinery, transportation equipment, petroleum products, textiles, chemicals, beverages

Industrial production growth rate: 1.6% (2017 est.)
country comparison to the world: 149

Labor force: 1.748 million (2017 est.)
country comparison to the world: 127
Labor force—by occupation: agriculture: 13%
industry: 14%
services: 73% (2010 est.)

Unemployment rate: 7.3% (2017 est.)
7.9% (2016 est.)
country comparison to the world: 103

Population below poverty line: 9.7% (2015 est.)

Household income or consumption by percentage share: *lowest 10%:* 1.9%
highest 10%: 30.8% (2014 est.)

Distribution of family income—Gini index: 41.6 (2014)
41.9 (2013)
country comparison to the world: 52

Budget: *revenues:* $17.69 billion
expenditures: $19.9 billion (2017 est.)

Taxes and other revenues: 29.3% of GDP (2017 est.)
country comparison to the world: 86

Budget surplus (+) or deficit (-): -3.7% of GDP (2017 est.)
country comparison to the world: 137

Public debt: 62.5% of GDP (2017 est.)
62.7% of GDP (2016 est.)
note: data cover general government debt, and include debt instruments issued (or owned) by government entities other than the treasury; the data include treasury debt held by foreign entities; the data include debt issued by subnational entities, as well as intra-governmental debt; intra-governmental debt consists of treasury borrowings from surpluses in the social funds, such as for retirement, medical care, and unemployment; debt instruments for the social funds are not sold at public auctions.
country comparison to the world: 68

Fiscal year: calendar year

Inflation rate (consumer prices): 6.1% (2017 est.)
9.6% (2016 est.)
country comparison to the world: 187

Central bank discount rate: 9% (31 December 2012)
8.75% (31 December 2011)
note: Uruguay's central bank uses the benchmark interest rate, rather than the discount rate, to conduct monetary policy; the rates shown here are the benchmark rates
country comparison to the world: 31

Commercial bank prime lending rate: 13.6% (31 December 2017 est.)
16.17% (31 December 2016 est.)
country comparison to the world: 57

Stock of narrow money: $4.859 billion (31 December 2017 est.)
$4.582 billion (31 December 2016 est.)
country comparison to the world: 106

Stock of broad money: $9.329 billion (31 December 2017 est.)
$8.781 billion (31 December 2016 est.)
country comparison to the world: 108

Stock of domestic credit: $20.98 billion (31 December 2017 est.)
$19.61 billion (31 December 2016 est.)
country comparison to the world: 90

Market value of publicly traded shares: $175.4 million (31 December 2012 est.)
$174.6 million (31 December 2011 est.)
$156.9 million (31 December 2010 est.)
country comparison to the world: 119

Current account balance: -$268 million (2017 est.)
-$36 million (2016 est.)
country comparison to the world: 95

Exports: $8.976 billion (2017 est.)
$8.387 billion (2016 est.)
country comparison to the world: 94

Exports—commodities: beef, soybeans, cellulose, rice, wheat, wood, dairy products, wool

Exports—partners: Brazil 16.4%, China 12.2%, US 6.2%, Argentina 5% (2016)

Imports: $8.74 billion (2017 est.)
$8.037 billion (2016 est.)

country comparison to the world: 102

Imports—commodities: refined oil, crude oil, passenger and other transportation vehicles, vehicle parts, cellular phones

Imports—partners: China 18.8%, Brazil 17.9%, Argentina 13.3%, US 6.9%, Germany 4.7% (2016)

Reserves of foreign exchange and gold: $14.28 billion (31 December 2017 est.)
$13.47 billion (31 December 2016 est.)
country comparison to the world: 69

Debt—external: $28.27 billion (31 December 2017 est.)
$27.9 billion (31 December 2016 est.)
country comparison to the world: 83

Stock of direct foreign investment—at home: $24.35 billion (31 December 2017 est.)
$22.81 billion (31 December 2016 est.)
country comparison to the world: 74

Stock of direct foreign investment—abroad: $228.9 million (31 December 2017 est.)
$136.1 million (31 December 2016 est.)
country comparison to the world: 98

Exchange rates: Uruguayan pesos (UYU) per US dollar—
28.77 (2017 est.)
30.163 (2016 est.)
30.163 (2015 est.)
27.52 (2014 est.)
23.246 (2013 est.)

ENERGY

Electricity access: population without electricity: 20,106
electrification—*total population:* 99.4%
electrification—urban areas: 99.7%
electrification—rural areas: 93.8% (2012)

Electricity—production: 12.23 billion kWh (2015 est.)
country comparison to the world: 93

Electricity—consumption: 9.42 billion kWh (2015 est.)
country comparison to the world: 97

Electricity—exports: 1.321 billion kWh (2015 est.)
country comparison to the world: 53

Electricity—imports: 2 million kWh (2015 est.)
country comparison to the world: 114

Electricity—installed generating capacity: 4.408 million kW (2015 est.)
country comparison to the world: 82

Electricity—from fossil fuels: 34.7% of total installed capacity (2015 est.)
country comparison to the world: 179

Electricity—from nuclear fuels: 0% of total installed capacity (2015 est.)
country comparison to the world: 201

Electricity—from hydroelectric plants: 34.9% of total installed capacity (2015 est.)
country comparison to the world: 60

Electricity—from other renewable sources: 39% of total installed capacity (2015 est.)

country comparison to the world: 5

Crude oil—production: 0 bbl/day (2016 est.)
country comparison to the world: 211

Crude oil—exports: 0 bbl/day (2014 est.)
country comparison to the world: 206

Crude oil—imports: 37,900 bbl/day (2014 est.)
country comparison to the world: 57

Crude oil—proved reserves: 0 bbl (1 January 2017 es)
country comparison to the world: 211

Refined petroleum products—production: 42,440 bbl/day (2014 est.)
country comparison to the world: 84

Refined petroleum products—consumption: 54,000 bbl/day (2015 est.)
country comparison to the world: 100

Refined petroleum products—exports: 537.5 bbl/day (2014 est.)
country comparison to the world: 111

Refined petroleum products—imports: 10,870 bbl/day (2014 est.)
country comparison to the world: 140

Natural gas—production: 0 cu m (2013 est.)
country comparison to the world: 207

Natural gas—consumption: 378 million cu m (2015 est.)
country comparison to the world: 109

Natural gas—exports: 0 cu m (2013 est.)
country comparison to the world: 203

Natural gas—imports: 40 million cu m (2015 est.)
country comparison to the world: 77

Natural gas—proved reserves: 0 cu m (1 January 2014 es)
country comparison to the world: 203

Carbon dioxide emissions from consumption of energy: 7.4 million Mt (2013 est.)
country comparison to the world: 116

COMMUNICATIONS

Telephones—fixed lines: *total subscriptions:* 1,113,566
subscriptions per 100 inhabitants: 33 (July 2016 est.)
country comparison to the world: 75

Telephones—mobile cellular: *total:* 5,116,736
subscriptions per 100 inhabitants: 153 (July 2016 est.)
country comparison to the world: 112

Telephone system: *general assessment:* fully digitalized
domestic: most modern facilities concentrated in Montevideo; nationwide microwave radio relay network; overall fixed-line and mobile-cellular teledensity over 185 telephones per 100 persons
international: country code—598; the UNISOR submarine cable system provides direct connectivity to Brazil and Argentina; satellite earth stations—2 Intelsat (Atlantic Ocean) (2016)

Broadcast media: mixture of privately owned and state-run broadcast media; more than 100 commercial radio stations and about 20 TV channels;

963

cable TV is available; many community radio and TV stations; adopted the hybrid Japanese/Brazilian HDTV standard (ISDB-T) in December 2010 (2010)

Internet country code: .uy

Internet users: *total:* 2,225,075

percent of population: 66.4% (July 2016 est.) *country comparison to the world:* 99

TRANSPORTATION

National air transport system: *number of registered air carriers:* 2
inventory of registered aircraft operated by air carriers: 3 (2015)
Civil aircraft registration country code prefix: CX (2016)

Airports: 133 (2013)
country comparison to the world: 42

Airports—with paved runways: *total:* 11
over 3,047 m: 1
1,524 to 2,437 m: 4
914 to 1,523 m: 4
under 914 m: 2 (2013)

Airports—with unpaved runways: *total:* 122
1,524 to 2,437 m: 3
914 to 1,523 m: 40
under 914 m: 79 (2013)

Pipelines: gas 257 km; oil 160 km (2013)

Railways: *total:* 1,673 km (operational; government claims overall length is 2,961 km)
standard gauge: 1,673 km 1.435-m gauge (2016)
country comparison to the world: 78

Roadways: *total:* 77,732 km
paved: 7,743 km
unpaved: 69,989 km (2010)
country comparison to the world: 63

Waterways: 1,600 km (2011)
country comparison to the world: 48

Merchant marine: *total:* 56
by type: container ship 1, general cargo 6, oil tanker 4, other 45 (2017)
country comparison to the world: 107

Ports and terminals: *major seaport(s):* Montevideo

MILITARY AND SECURITY

Military expenditures: 1.85% of GDP (2016)
1.82% of GDP (2015)
1.81% of GDP (2014)
1.82% of GDP (2013)
1.8% of GDP (2012)
country comparison to the world: 42

Military branches: Uruguayan Armed Forces: Uruguayan National Army (Ejercito Nacional Uruguaya, ENU), Uruguayan National Navy (Armada Nacional del Uruguay, includes naval air arm, Naval Rifle Corps (Cuerpo de Fusileros Navales, Fusna), Maritime Prefecture in wartime), Uruguayan Air Force (Fuerza Aerea Uruguaya, FAU) (2012)

Military service age and obligation: 18-30 years of age (18-22 years of age for navy) for male or female voluntary military service; up to 40 years of age for specialists; enlistment is voluntary in peacetime, but the government has the authority to conscript in emergencies; minimum 6-year education (2013)

TRANSNATIONAL ISSUES

Disputes—international: in 2010, the ICJ ruled in favor of Uruguay's operation of two paper mills on the Uruguay River, which forms the border with Argentina; the two countries formed a joint pollution monitoring regime; uncontested boundary dispute between Brazil and Uruguay over Braziliera/Brasiliera Island in the Quarai/Cuareim River leaves the tripoint with Argentina in question; smuggling of firearms and narcotics continues to be an issue along the Uruguay-Brazil border

Illicit drugs: small-scale transit country for drugs mainly bound for Europe, often through sea-borne containers; law enforcement corruption; money laundering because of strict banking secrecy laws; weak border control along Brazilian frontier; increasing consumption of cocaine base and synthetic drugs

UZBEKISTAN

INTRODUCTION

Background: Russia conquered the territory of present-day Uzbekistan in the late 19th century. Stiff resistance to the Red Army after the Bolshevik Revolution was eventually suppressed and a socialist republic established in 1924. During the Soviet era, intensive production of "white gold" (cotton) and grain led to overuse of agrochemicals and the depletion of water supplies, which have left the land degraded and the Aral Sea and certain rivers half dry. Independent since 1991 upon the dissolution of the USSR, the country has reduced its dependence on the cotton monoculture by diversifying agricultural production while developing its mineral and petroleum export capacity and increasing its manufacturing base. Uzbekistan's first president, Islom KARIMOV, led Uzbekistan for 25 years until his death in September 2016. The political transition to his successor,

then-Prime Minister Shavkat MIRZIYOYEV was peaceful, but sidelined the constitutional process where the chairman of the Senate would have served as the acting president. MIRZIYOYEV, who won the presidential election in December 2016, has improved relations with Uzbekistan's neighbors and introduced wide-ranging economic and judicial reforms.

GEOGRAPHY

Location: Central Asia, north of Turkmenistan, south of Kazakhstan

Geographic coordinates: 41 00 N, 64 00 E

Map references: Asia

Area: *total:* 447,400 sq km
land: 425,400 sq km
water: 22,000 sq km
country comparison to the world: 58

Area—comparative: about four times the size of Virginia; slightly larger than California

Land boundaries: *total:* 6,893 km
border countries (5): Afghanistan 144 km, Kazakhstan 2,330 km, Kyrgyzstan 1,314 km, Tajikistan 1,312 km, Turkmenistan 1,793 km

Coastline: 0 km (doubly landlocked); note—Uzbekistan includes the southern portion of the Aral Sea with a 420 km shoreline

Maritime claims: none (doubly landlocked)

Climate: mostly mid-latitude desert, long, hot summers, mild winters; semiarid grassland in east

Terrain: mostly flat-to-rolling sandy desert with dunes; broad, flat intensely irrigated river valleys along course of Amu Darya, Syr Darya (Sirdaryo), and Zarafshon; Fergana Valley in east surrounded by mountainous Tajikistan and Kyrgyzstan; shrinking Aral Sea in west

Elevation: *mean elevation:* NA

elevation extremes: *lowest point:* Sariqamish Kuli -12 m
highest point: Adelunga Toghi 4,301 m

Natural resources: natural gas, petroleum, coal, gold, uranium, silver, copper, lead and zinc, tungsten, molybdenum

Land use: *agricultural land:* 62.6%
arable land: 10.1%;
permanent crops: 0.8%;
permanent pasture: 51.7%
forest: 7.7%
other: 29.7% (2011 est.)
Irrigated land: 42,150 sq km (2012)

Population—distribution: most of the population is concentrated in the fertile Fergana Valley in the easternmost arm of the country; the south has significant clusters of people, while the central and western deserts are sparsely populated

Natural hazards: earthquakes; floods; landslides or mudslides; avalanches; droughts

Environment—current issues: shrinkage of the Aral Sea has resulted in growing concentrations of chemical pesticides and natural salts; these substances are then blown from the increasingly exposed lake bed and contribute to desertification and respiratory health problems; water pollution from industrial wastes and the heavy use of fertilizers and pesticides is the cause of many human health disorders; increasing soil salination; soil contamination from buried nuclear processing and agricultural chemicals, including DDT

Environment—international agreements: *party to:* Biodiversity, Climate Change, Climate Change-Kyoto Protocol, Desertification, Endangered Species, Environmental Modification, Hazardous Wastes, Ozone Layer Protection, Wetlands
signed, but not ratified: none of the selected agreements

Geography—note: along with Liechtenstein, one of the only two doubly landlocked countries in the world

PEOPLE AND SOCIETY

Population: 29,748,859 (July 2017 est.)
country comparison to the world: 44

Nationality: *noun:* Uzbekistani
adjective: Uzbekistani

Ethnic groups: Uzbek 80%, Russian 5.5%, Tajik 5%, Kazakh 3%, Karakalpak 2.5%, Tatar 1.5%, other 2.5% (1996 est.)

Languages: Uzbek (official) 74.3%, Russian 14.2%, Tajik 4.4%, other 7.1%
note: in the Karakalpak Republic, both the Karakalpak language and Uzbek have official status

Religions: Muslim 88% (mostly Sunni), Eastern Orthodox 9%, other 3%

Age structure: *0-14 years:* 23.88% (male 3,640,914/female 3,464,304)
15-24 years: 18.52% (male 2,804,516/female 2,706,399)
25-54 years: 44.49% (male 6,583,745/female 6,651,261)
55-64 years: 7.85% (male 1,105,034/female 1,231,714)
65 years and over: 5.25% (male 667,109/female 893,863) (2017 est.)

Dependency ratios: *total dependency ratio:* 47.7
youth dependency ratio: 41.4
elderly dependency ratio: 6.2
potential support ratio: 16 (2015 est.)

Median age: *total:* 28.6 years
male: 28 years
female: 29.2 years (2017 est.)
country comparison to the world: 131

Population growth rate: 0.93% (2017 est.)
country comparison to the world: 119

Birth rate: 16.8 births/1,000 population (2017 est.)
country comparison to the world: 109

Death rate: 5.3 deaths/1,000 population (2017 est.)
country comparison to the world: 181

Net migration rate: -2.2 migrant(s)/1,000 population (2017 est.)
country comparison to the world: 165

Population distribution: most of the population is concentrated in the fertile Fergana Valley in the easternmost arm of the country; the south has significant clusters of people, while the central and western deserts are sparsely populated

Urbanization: *urban population:* 36.6% of total population (2017)
rate of urbanization: 1.62% annual rate of change (2015-20 est.)

Major urban areas—population: TASHKENT (capital) 2.251 million (2015)

Sex ratio: *at birth:* 1.06 male(s)/female
0-14 years: 1.05 male(s)/female
15-24 years: 1.03 male(s)/female
25-54 years: 0.99 male(s)/female
55-64 years: 0.9 male(s)/female
65 years and over: 0.74 male(s)/female
total population: 0.99 male(s)/female (2016 est.)

Mother's mean age at first birth: 23.4 years (2014 est.)

Maternal mortality ratio: 36 deaths/100,000 live births (2015 est.)
country comparison to the world: 109

Infant mortality rate: *total:* 18 deaths/1,000 live births
male: 21.4 deaths/1,000 live births
female: 14.4 deaths/1,000 live births (2017 est.)
country comparison to the world: 90

Life expectancy at birth: *total population:* 74 years
male: 71 years
female: 77.3 years (2017 est.)
country comparison to the world: 127

Total fertility rate: 1.76 children born/woman (2017 est.)
country comparison to the world: 159

Health expenditures: 5.8% of GDP (2014)
country comparison to the world: 111

Physicians density: 2.45 physicians/1,000 population (2014)

Hospital bed density: 4.4 beds/1,000 population (2010)

Drinking water source:
improved:
urban: 98.5% of population
rural: 80.9% of population
total: 87.3% of population
unimproved:
urban: 1.5% of population
rural: 19.1% of population
total: 12.7% of population (2012 est.)

Sanitation facility access:
improved:
urban: 100% of population
rural: 100% of population
total: 100% of population
unimproved:

urban: 0% of population
rural: 0% of population
total: 0% of population (2015 est.)

HIV/AIDS—adult prevalence rate: NA

HIV/AIDS—people living with HIV/AIDS: NA

HIV/AIDS—deaths: NA

Obesity—adult prevalence rate: 16.6% (2016)
country comparison to the world: 123

Education expenditures: NA

Literacy: *definition:* age 15 and over can read and write
total population: 100%
male: 100%
female: 100% (2015 est.)

School life expectancy (primary to tertiary education): *total:* 12 years
male: 13 years
female: 12 years (2016)

GOVERNMENT

Country name: *conventional long form:* Republic of Uzbekistan
conventional short form: Uzbekistan
local long form: O'zbekiston Respublikasi
local short form: O'zbekiston
former: Uzbek Soviet Socialist Republic
etymology: a combination of the Turkic words "uz" (self) and "bek" (master) with the Persian suffix "-stan" (country) to give the meaning "Land of the Free"

Government type: presidential republic; highly authoritarian

Capital: *name:* Tashkent (Toshkent)
geographic coordinates: 41 19 N, 69 15 E
time difference: UTC+5 (10 hours ahead of Washington, DC, during Standard Time)

Administrative divisions: 12 provinces (viloyatlar, singular—viloyat), 1 autonomous republic* (avtonom respublikasi), and 1 city** (shahar); Andijon Viloyati, Buxoro Viloyati, Farg'ona Viloyati, Jizzax Viloyati, Namangan Viloyati, Navoiy Viloyati, Qashqadaryo Viloyati (Qarshi), Qoraqalpog'iston Respublikasi [Karakalpakstan Republic]* (Nukus), Samarqand Viloyati, Sirdaryo Viloyati (Guliston), Surxondaryo Viloyati (Termiz), Toshkent Shahri [Tashkent City]**, Toshkent Viloyati [Tashkent province], Xorazm Viloyati (Urganch)
note: administrative divisions have the same names as their administrative centers (exceptions have the administrative center name following in parentheses)

Independence: 1 September 1991 (from the Soviet Union)

National holiday: Independence Day, 1 September (1991)

Constitution: *history:* several previous; latest adopted 8 December 1992
amendments: proposed by the Supreme Assembly or by referendum; passage requires two-thirds majority vote of both houses of the Assembly or

passage in a referendum; amended several times, last in 2014 (2017)

Legal system: civil law system

International law organization participation: has not submitted an ICJ jurisdiction declaration; non-party state to the ICCt

Citizenship: *citizenship by birth:* no
citizenship by descent only: at least one parent must be a citizen of Uzbekistan
dual citizenship recognized: no
residency requirement for naturalization: 5 years

Suffrage: 18 years of age; universal

Executive branch: *chief of state:* President Shavkat MIRZIYOYEV (interim president from 8 September 2016; formally elected president on 4 December 2016 to succeed longtime President Islom KARIMOV, who died on 2 September 2016)

head of government: Prime Minister Abdulla ARIPOV (since 14 December 2016); First Deputy Prime Minister Achilbay RAMATOV (since 15 December 2016)

cabinet: Cabinet of Ministers appointed by the president with most requiring approval of the Senate chamber of the Supreme Assembly (Oliy Majlis)

elections/appointments: president directly elected by absolute majority popular vote in 2 rounds if needed for a 5-year term (eligible for a second term; previously a 5-year term, extended by a 2002 constitutional amendment to 7 years, and reverted to 5 years in 2011); election last held on 4 December 2016 (next to be held in 2021); prime minister nominated by majority party in legislature since 2011, but appointed along with the ministers and deputy ministers by the president

election results: Shavkat MIRZIYOYEV elected president; percent of vote—Shavkat MIRZI-YOYEV (LDPU) 88.6%, Khatamjon KET-MONOV (NDP) 3.7%, Narimon UMAROV (Adolat) 3.5%, Sarvar OTAMURADOV (Milliy Tiklanish/National Revival) 2.4%, other 1.8%

Legislative branch: description: bicameral Supreme Assembly or Oliy Majlis consists of the Senate (100 seats; 84 members indirectly elected by regional governing councils and 16 appointed by the president; members serve 5-year terms) and the Legislative Chamber or Qonunchilik Palatasi (150 seats; 135 members directly elected in single-seat constituencies by absolute majority vote with a second round, if needed, and 15 indirectly elected by the Ecological Movement of Uzbekistan; members serve 5-year terms)

note: all parties in the Supreme Assembly support President Shavkat MIRZIYOYEV

elections: last held on 21 December 2014 and 4 January 2015 (next to be held in December 2019)

election results: Senate—percent of vote by party—NA; seats by party—NA; Legislative Chamber—percent of vote by party—NA; seats by party—LDPU 52, National Revival Democratic Party 36, NDP 27, Adolat 20, Ecological Movement 15

Judicial branch: *highest court(s):* Supreme Court (consists of 67 judges organized into administrative, civil, criminal, economic, and military sections); Constitutional Court (consists of 7 judges)

judge selection and term of office: judges of the highest courts nominated by the president and confirmed by the Oliy Majlis; judges appointed for initial 5-year term, subsequent 10-year term, and lifetime term subject to reappointment

subordinate courts: regional, district, city, and town courts; economic courts

Political parties and leaders: Ecological Movement of Uzbekistan (O'zbekiston Ekologik Harakati) [Boriy ALIKHANOV]
Justice (Adolat) Social Democratic Party of Uzbekistan [Narimon UMAROV]
Liberal Democratic Party of Uzbekistan (O'zbekiston Liberal-Demokratik Partiyasi) or LDPU [Shavkat MIRZIYOYEV]
National Revival Democratic Party of Uzbekistan (O'zbekiston Milliy Tiklanish Demokratik Partiyasi) [Sarvar OTAMURADOV]
People's Democratic Party of Uzbekistan (Xalq Demokratik Partiyas) or NDP [Hotamjon KET-MONOV] (formerly Communist Party)

Political pressure groups and leaders: no significant opposition political parties or pressure groups in Uzbekistan

International organization participation: ADB, CICA, CIS, EAPC, EBRD, ECO, FAO, IAEA, IBRD, ICAO, ICC (national committees), ICCt, ICRM, IDA, IDB, IFAD, IFC, IFRCS, ILO, IMF, Interpol, IOC, ISO, ITSO, ITU, MIGA, NAM, OIC, OPCW, OSCE, PFP, SCO, UN, UN Security Council (temporary), UNCTAD, UNESCO, UNIDO, UNWTO, UPU, WCO, WFTU (NGOs), WHO, WIPO, WMO, WTO (observer)

Diplomatic representation in the US: *chief of mission:* Ambassador Javlon VAHOBOV (since 1 December 2017)
chancery: 1746 Massachusetts Avenue NW, Washington, DC 20036
telephone: [1] (202) 887-5300
FAX: [1] (202) 293-6804
consulate(s) general: New York

Diplomatic representation from the US: *chief of mission:* Ambassador Pamela L. SPRATLEN (since 27 January 2015)
embassy: 3 Moyqo'rq'on, 5th Block, Yunusobod District, Tashkent 100093
mailing address: use embassy street address
telephone: [998] (71) 120-5450
FAX: [998] (71) 120-6335

Flag description: three equal horizontal bands of blue (top), white, and green separated by red fimbriations with a white crescent moon (closed side to the hoist) and 12 white stars shifted to the hoist on the top band; blue is the color of the Turkic peoples and of the sky, white signifies peace and the striving for purity in thoughts and deeds, while green represents nature and is the color of Islam; the red stripes are the vital force of all living organisms that links good and pure ideas with the eternal sky and with deeds on earth; the crescent

represents Islam and the 12 stars the months and constellations of the Uzbek calendar

National symbol(s): khumo (mythical bird); national colors: blue, white, red, green

National anthem: name: "O'zbekiston Respublikasining Davlat Madhiyasi" (National Anthem of the Republic of Uzbekistan)
lyrics/music: Abdulla ARIPOV/Mutal BURHANOV
note: adopted 1992; after the fall of the Soviet Union, Uzbekistan kept the music of the anthem from its time as a Soviet Republic but adopted new lyrics

ECONOMY

Economy—overview: Uzbekistan is a doubly landlocked country in which 51% of the population lives in urban settlements; the agriculture-rich Fergana Valley, in which Uzbekistan's eastern borders are situated, has been counted among the most densely populated parts of Central Asia. Since its independence in September 1991, the government has largely maintained its Soviet-style command economy with subsidies and tight controls on production, prices, and access to foreign currency. Despite ongoing efforts to diversify crops, Uzbek agriculture remains largely centered on cotton; Uzbekistan is the world's fifth-largest cotton exporter and seventh-largest producer. Uzbekistan's growth has been driven primarily by state-led investments, and export of natural gas, gold, and cotton provides a significant share of foreign exchange earnings.

Recently, lower global commodity prices and economic slowdowns in neighboring Russia and China have hurt Uzbekistan's trade and investment and worsened its foreign currency shortage. Aware of the need to improve the investment climate, the government is taking incremental steps to reform the business sector and address impediments to foreign investment in the country. Since the death of first President Islam KARIMOV and election of President Shavkat MIRZIYOYEV, emphasis on such initiatives and government efforts to improve the private sector have increased. In the past, Uzbek authorities accused US and other foreign companies operating in Uzbekistan of violating Uzbek laws and have frozen and seized their assets.

As a part of its economic reform efforts, the Uzbek Government is looking to expand opportunities for small and medium enterprises and prioritizes increasing foreign direct investment. In September 2017, the government devalued the official currency rate by almost 50% and announced the loosening of currency restrictions to eliminate the currency black market, increase access to hard currency, and boost investment.

GDP (purchasing power parity): $221.7 billion (2017 est.)
$209.2 billion (2016 est.)
$194.1 billion (2015 est.)
note: data are in 2017 dollars
country comparison to the world: 64

GDP (official exchange rate): $67.51 billion (2016 est.)

GDP—real growth rate: 6% (2017 est.)
7.8% (2016 est.)
8% (2015 est.)
country comparison to the world: 24

GDP—per capita (PPP): $7,000 (2017 est.)
$6,700 (2016 est.)
$6,300 (2015 est.)
note: data are in 2017 dollars
country comparison to the world: 158

Gross national saving: 31.8% of GDP (2017 est.)
31.6% of GDP (2016 est.)
31.6% of GDP (2015 est.)
country comparison to the world: 21

GDP—composition, by end use:
household consumption: 58.4%
government consumption: 16.9%
investment in fixed capital: 25.2%
investment in inventories: 3%
exports of goods and services: 20%
imports of goods and services: -20.5% (2017 est.)

GDP—composition, by sector of origin:
agriculture: 18.5%
industry: 34.4%
services: 47% (2017 est.)

Agriculture—products: cotton, vegetables, fruits, grain; livestock

Industries: textiles, food processing, machine building, metallurgy, mining, hydrocarbon extraction, chemicals

Industrial production growth rate: 4.5% (2017 est.)
country comparison to the world: 59

Labor force: 18.12 million (2017 est.)
country comparison to the world: 34
Labor force—by occupation: agriculture: 25.9%
industry: 13.2%
services: 60.9% (2012 est.)

Unemployment rate: 4.9% (2017 est.)
4.9% (2016 est.)
note: official data; another 20% are underemployed
country comparison to the world: 66

Population below poverty line: 14% (2016 est.)

Household income or consumption by percentage share: *lowest 10%:* 2.8%
highest 10%: 29.6% (2003)

Distribution of family income—Gini index: 36.8 (2003)
44.7 (1998)
country comparison to the world: 82

Budget: *revenues:* $20.11 billion
expenditures: $19.92 billion (2017 est.)

Taxes and other revenues: 29.8% of GDP (2017 est.)
country comparison to the world: 83

Budget surplus (+) or deficit (-): 0.3% of GDP (2017 est.)
country comparison to the world: 27

Public debt: 15.1% of GDP (2017 est.)
15.4% of GDP (2016 est.)
country comparison to the world: 192

Fiscal year: calendar year

Inflation rate (consumer prices): 13% (2017 est.)
8% (2016 est.)
note: official data; based on independent analysis of consumer prices, inflation reached 22% in 2012
country comparison to the world: 210

Central bank discount rate: 9% (2016)
9% (2015)
country comparison to the world: 30

Commercial bank prime lending rate: 16% (31 December 2016 est.)
11.2% (31 December 2012 est.)
country comparison to the world: 33

Stock of narrow money: $6.456 billion (31 December 2017 est.)
$7.555 billion (31 December 2016 est.)
country comparison to the world: 94

Stock of broad money: $15.47 billion (31 December 2017 est.)
$17.47 billion (31 December 2016 est.)
country comparison to the world: 97

Stock of domestic credit: $9.506 billion (31 December 2017 est.)
$11.63 billion (31 December 2016 est.)
country comparison to the world: 104

Market value of publicly traded shares: $NA (31 December 2012)
$715.3 million (31 December 2006)

Current account balance: $632 million (2017 est.)
$498 million (2016 est.)
country comparison to the world: 44

Exports: $11.38 billion (2017 est.)
$11.2 billion (2016 est.)
country comparison to the world: 84

Exports—commodities: energy products, cotton, gold, mineral fertilizers, ferrous and nonferrous metals, textiles, foodstuffs, machinery, automobiles

Exports—partners: Switzerland 35.1%, China 19.7%, Russia 9.3%, Turkey 8.7%, Kazakhstan 7.2%, Bangladesh 5.4%, Afghanistan 4.9% (2016)

Imports: $11.44 billion (2017 est.)
$10.91 billion (2016 est.)
country comparison to the world: 92

Imports—commodities: machinery and equipment, foodstuffs, chemicals, ferrous and nonferrous metals

Imports—partners: China 22.2%, Russia 18%, South Korea 10.5%, Kazakhstan 10%, Turkey 5.8%, Germany 5.2% (2016)

Reserves of foreign exchange and gold: $16 billion (31 December 2017 est.)
$14 billion (31 December 2016 est.)
country comparison to the world: 66

Debt—external: $16.86 billion (31 December 2017 est.)
$16.76 billion (31 December 2016 est.)
country comparison to the world: 98

Stock of direct foreign investment—at home: $NA

Stock of direct foreign investment—abroad: $NA

Exchange rates: Uzbekistani soum (UZS) per US dollar—
3,906.1 (2017 est.)
2,966.6 (2016 est.)
2,966.6 (2015 est.)
2,569.6 (2014 est.)
2,311.4 (2013 est.)

ENERGY

Electricity access: *electrification—total population:* 100% (2016)

Electricity—production: 59 billion kWh (2016 est.)
country comparison to the world: 49

Electricity—consumption: 48 billion kWh (2014 est.)
country comparison to the world: 52

Electricity—exports: 13 billion kWh (2014 est.)
country comparison to the world: 17

Electricity—imports: 13 billion kWh (2014 est.)
country comparison to the world: 21

Electricity—installed generating capacity: 12.93 million kW (2015 est.)
country comparison to the world: 54

Electricity—from fossil fuels: 86.4% of total installed capacity (2015 est.)
country comparison to the world: 73

Electricity—from nuclear fuels: 0% of total installed capacity (2015 est.)
country comparison to the world: 202

Electricity—from hydroelectric plants: 13.6% of total installed capacity (2015 est.)
country comparison to the world: 110

Electricity—from other renewable sources: 0% of total installed capacity (2015 est.)
country comparison to the world: 211

Crude oil—production: 52,910 bbl/day (2016 est.)
country comparison to the world: 52

Crude oil—exports: 27,000 bbl/day (2014 est.)
country comparison to the world: 50

Crude oil—imports: 380 bbl/day (2014 est.)
country comparison to the world: 80

Crude oil—proved reserves: 594 million bbl (1 January 2017 es)
country comparison to the world: 47

Refined petroleum products—production: 63,650 bbl/day (2014 est.)
country comparison to the world: 78

Refined petroleum products—consumption: 61,000 bbl/day (2015 est.)
country comparison to the world: 96

Refined petroleum products—exports: 4,102 bbl/day (2014 est.)
country comparison to the world: 98

Refined petroleum products—imports: 0 bbl/day (2014 est.)
country comparison to the world: 215

Natural gas—production: 55.7 billion cu m (2015 est.)
country comparison to the world: 16

Natural gas—consumption: 10.44 billion cu m (2015 est.)
country comparison to the world: 54

Natural gas—exports: 14.7 billion cu m (2014 est.)
country comparison to the world: 17

Natural gas—imports: 0 cu m (2013 est.)
country comparison to the world: 203

Natural gas—proved reserves: 1.841 trillion cu m (1 January 2017 es)
country comparison to the world: 20

Carbon dioxide emissions from consumption of energy: 109 million Mt (2013 est.)
country comparison to the world: 37

COMMUNICATIONS

Telephones—fixed lines: *total subscriptions:* 3,412,921
subscriptions per 100 inhabitants: 12 (July 2016 est.)
country comparison to the world: 53

Telephones—mobile cellular: *total:* 23,265,389
subscriptions per 100 inhabitants: 79 (July 2016 est.)
country comparison to the world: 56

Telephone system: *general assessment:* digital exchanges in large cities and in rural areas
domestic: the state-owned telecommunications company, Uzbektelecom, owner of the fixed-line telecommunications system, has used loans from the Japanese government and the China Development Bank to upgrade fixed-line services including conversion to digital exchanges; mobile-cellular services are provided by three private and two state-owned operators with a total subscriber base of 23 million as of mid-2016
international: country code—998; linked by fiber-optic cable or microwave radio relay with CIS member states and to other countries by leased connection via the Moscow international gateway switch; the country also has a link to the Trans-Asia-Europe (TAE) fiber-optic cable; Uzbekistan has supported the national fiber- optic backbone project of Afghanistan since 2008 (2016)

Broadcast media: government controls media; 18 state-owned broadcasters—14 TV and 4 radio—provide service to virtually the entire country; about 20 privately owned TV stations, overseen by local officials, broadcast to local markets; privately owned TV stations are required to lease transmitters from the government-owned Republic TV and Radio Industry Corporation; in 2013, the government closed TV and radio broadcasters affiliated with the National Association of Electronic Mass Media (NAEMM) of Uzbekistan, a government-sponsored NGO for private broadcast media; in 2015, the NAEMM relaunched its TV channel under a different name (2017)

Internet country code: .uz

Internet users: *total:* 13,791,083
percent of population: 46.8% (July 2016 est.)
country comparison to the world: 41

TRANSPORTATION

National air transport system: *number of registered air carriers:* 2
inventory of registered aircraft operated by air carriers: 29

annual passenger traffic on registered air carriers: 2,486,673
annual freight traffic on registered air carriers: 114,334,520 mt-km (2015)
Civil aircraft registration country code prefix: UK (2016)

Airports: 53 (2013)
country comparison to the world: 89

Airports—with paved runways: *total:* 33
over 3,047 m: 6
2,438 to 3,047 m: 13
1,524 to 2,437 m: 6
914 to 1,523 m: 4
under 914 m: 4 (2013)

Airports—with unpaved runways: *total:* 20
2,438 to 3,047 m: 2
under 914 m: 18 (2013)

Pipelines: gas 13,700 km; oil 944 km (2016)

Railways: *total:* 4,304 km
broad gauge: 4,304 km 1.520-m gauge (1,354 km electrified) (2016)
country comparison to the world: 48

Roadways: *total:* 86,496 km
paved: 75,511 km
unpaved: 10,985 km (2000)
country comparison to the world: 54

Waterways: 1,100 km (2012)
country comparison to the world: 62

Ports and terminals: river port(s): Termiz (Amu Darya)

MILITARY AND SECURITY

Military branches: Armed Forces: Army, Air and Air Defense Forces, National Guard (2017)

Military service age and obligation: 18 years of age for compulsory military service; 1-month or 1-year conscript service obligation for males; moving toward a professional military, but conscription in some form will continue; the military cannot accommodate everyone who wishes to enlist, and competition for entrance into the military is similar to the competition for admission to universities; note—widely considered to have one of the strongest militaries in Central Asia, although it is untested (2016)

TERRORISM

Terrorist groups—foreign based: Islamic Jihad Union (IJU): aim(s): overthrow the Government of Uzbekistan
area(s) of operation: maintains a limited operational presence; IJU's attack tempo diminished after suicide bombers conducted three simultaneous lethal explosions in Tashkent on 30 July 2004 aimed at the US and Israeli embassies and the Uzbek chief prosecutor's headquarters; two Uzbek security guards at the Israeli Embassy were killed; the bombings occurred as the trial began for 15 IJU operatives accused in a wave of attacks in the spring of 2004 that killed approximately 50 people in the first known cases of suicide bombings in Central Asia

Islamic Movement of Uzbekistan (IMU): *aim(s):* overthrow the Uzbekistan and Kyrgyzstan

Governments and establish an Islamic state in the Fergana Valley, a fertile valley in eastern Uzbekistan, southern Kyrgyzstan, and northern Tajikistan
area(s) of operation: maintains a limited operational presence; attack tempo against government personnel and facilities has diminished dramatically since 2015

TRANSNATIONAL ISSUES

Disputes—international: prolonged drought and cotton monoculture in Uzbekistan and Turkmenistan created water-sharing difficulties for Amu Darya river states; field demarcation of the boundaries with Kazakhstan commenced in 2004; border delimitation of 130 km of border with Kyrgyzstan is hampered by serious disputes around enclaves and other areas

Refugees and internally displaced persons: stateless persons: 86,524 (2016)

Trafficking in persons: current situation: Uzbekistan is a source country for men, women, and children subjected to forced labor and women and children subjected to sex trafficking; government-compelled forced labor of adults remained endemic during the 2014 cotton harvest; despite a decree banning the use of persons under 18, children were mobilized to harvest cotton by local officials in some districts; in some regions, local officials forced teachers, students, private business employees, and others to work in construction, agriculture, and cleaning parks; Uzbekistani women and children are victims of sex trafficking domestically and in the Middle East, Eurasia, and Asia; Uzbekistani men and, to a lesser extent, women are subjected to forced labor in Kazakhstan, Russia, and Ukraine in the construction, oil, agriculture, retail, and food sectors

tier rating: Tier 2 Watch List—Uzbekistan does not fully comply with the minimum standards for the elimination of trafficking; however, it is making significant efforts to do so; law enforcement efforts in 2014 were mixed; the government made efforts to combat sex and transnational labor trafficking, but government-compelled forced labor of adults in the cotton harvest went unaddressed, and the decree prohibiting forced child labor was not applied universally; official complicity in human trafficking in the cotton harvest remained prevalent; authorities made efforts to identify and protect sex and transnational labor victims, although a systematic process is still lacking; minimal efforts were made to assist victims of forced labor in the cotton harvest, as the government does not openly acknowledge the existence of this forced labor; the ILO did not have permission or funding to monitor the 2014 harvest, but the government authorized the UN's International Labour Organization to conduct a survey on recruitment practices and working conditions in agriculture, particularly the cotton sector, and to monitor the 2015-17 cotton harvests for child and forced labor in project areas (2015)

Illicit drugs: transit country for Afghan narcotics bound for Russian and, to a lesser extent, Western European markets; limited illicit cultivation of cannabis and small amounts of opium poppy for domestic consumption; poppy cultivation almost wiped out by government crop eradication program; transit point for heroin precursor chemicals bound for Afghanistan

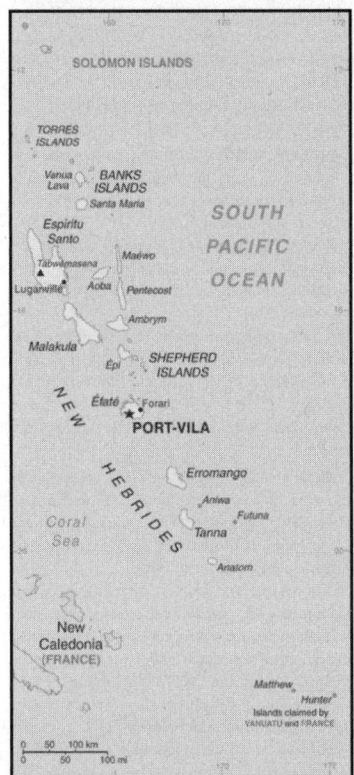

INTRODUCTION

Background: Multiple waves of colonizers, each speaking a distinct language, migrated to the New Hebrides in the millennia preceding European exploration in the 18th century. This settlement pattern accounts for the complex linguistic diversity found on the archipelago to this day. The British and French, who settled the New Hebrides in the 19th century, agreed in 1906 to an Anglo-French Condominium, which administered the islands until independence in 1980, when the new name of Vanuatu was adopted.

GEOGRAPHY

Location: Oceania, group of islands in the South Pacific Ocean, about three-quarters of the way from Hawaii to Australia

Geographic coordinates: 16 00 S, 167 00 E

Map references: Oceania

Area: *total:* 12,189 sq km
land: 12,189 sq km
water: 0 sq km
note: includes more than 80 islands, about 65 of which are inhabited

country comparison to the world: 163

Area—comparative: slightly larger than Connecticut

Land boundaries: 0 km

Coastline: 2,528 km

Maritime claims: measured from claimed archipelagic baselines
territorial sea: 12 nm
contiguous zone: 24 nm
exclusive economic zone: 200 nm
continental shelf: 200 nm or to the edge of the continental margin

Climate: tropical; moderated by southeast trade winds from May to October; moderate rainfall from November to April; may be affected by cyclones from December to April

Terrain: mostly mountainous islands of volcanic origin; narrow coastal plains

Elevation: *mean elevation:* NA

elevation extremes: *lowest point:* Pacific Ocean 0 m
highest point: Tabwemasana 1,877 m

Natural resources: manganese, hardwood forests, fish

Land use: *agricultural land:* 15.3%
arable land: 1.6%;
permanent crops: 10.3%;
permanent pasture: 3.4%
forest: 36.1%
other: 48.6% (2011 est.)
Irrigated land: 0 sq km (2012)

Population—distribution: three-quarters of the population lives in rural areas; the urban populace lives primarily in two cities, Port-Vila and Lugenville; three largest islands—Espiritu Santo, Malakula, and Efate—accomodate over half of the populace

Natural hazards: tropical cyclones (January to April); volcanic eruption on Aoba (Ambae) island began on 27 November 2005, volcanism also causes minor earthquakes; tsunamis
volcanism: significant volcanic activity with multiple eruptions in recent years; Yasur (361 m), one of the world's most active volcanoes, has experienced continuous activity in recent centuries; other historically active volcanoes include, Aoba, Ambrym, Epi, Gaua, Kuwae, Lopevi, Suretamatai, and Traitor's Head

Environment—current issues: most of the population does not have access to a reliable supply of potable water; deforestation

Environment—international agreements: *party to:* Antarctic-Marine Living Resources, Biodiversity, Climate Change, Climate Change-Kyoto Protocol, Desertification, Endangered Species, Law of the Sea, Marine Dumping, Ozone Layer Protection, Ship Pollution, Tropical Timber 94

signed, but not ratified: none of the selected agreements

Geography—note: a Y-shaped chain of four main islands and 80 smaller islands; several of the islands have active volcanoes and there are several underwater volcanoes as well

PEOPLE AND SOCIETY

Population: 282,814 (July 2017 est.)
country comparison to the world: 182

Nationality: *noun:* Ni-Vanuatu (singular and plural)
adjective: Ni-Vanuatu

Ethnic groups: Ni-Vanuatu 97.6%, part Ni-Vanuatu 1.1%, other 1.3% (2009 est.)

Languages: local languages (more than 100) 63.2%, Bislama (official; creole) 33.7%, English (official) 2%, French (official) 0.6%, other 0.5% (2009 est.)

Religions: Protestant 70% (includes Presbyterian 27.9%, Anglican 15.1%, Seventh Day Adventist 12.5%, Assemblies of God 4.7%, Church of Christ 4.5%, Neil Thomas Ministry 3.1%, and Apostolic 2.2%), Roman Catholic 12.4%, customary beliefs 3.7% (including Jon Frum cargo cult), other 12.6%, none 1.1%, unspecified 0.2% (2009 est.)

Age structure: *0-14 years:* 35.51% (male 51,261/female 49,157)
15-24 years: 20.02% (male 28,110/female 28,514)
25-54 years: 35.06% (male 48,476/female 50,675)
55-64 years: 5.42% (male 7,646/female 7,677)
65 years and over: 3.99% (male 5,713/female 5,585) (2017 est.)

Dependency ratios: *total dependency ratio:* 68.7
youth dependency ratio: 61.6
elderly dependency ratio: 7.1
potential support ratio: 14.1 (2015 est.)

Median age: *total:* 22 years
male: 21.6 years
female: 22.4 years (2017 est.)
country comparison to the world: 179

Population growth rate: 1.85% (2017 est.)
country comparison to the world: 54

Birth rate: 24 births/1,000 population (2017 est.)
country comparison to the world: 57

Death rate: 4 deaths/1,000 population (2017 est.)
country comparison to the world: 210

Net migration rate: -1.4 migrant(s)/1,000 population (2017 est.)
country comparison to the world: 147

Population distribution: three-quarters of the population lives in rural areas; the urban populace lives primarily in two cities, Port-Vila and Lugenville; three largest islands—Espiritu Santo, Malakula, and Efate—accomodate over half of the populace

Urbanization: *urban population:* 26.8% of total population (2017)

rate of urbanization: 3.23% annual rate of change (2015-20 est.)

Major urban areas—population: PORT-VILA (capital) 53,000 (2014)

Sex ratio: *at birth:* 1.05 male(s)/female
0-14 years: 1.04 male(s)/female
15-24 years: 0.99 male(s)/female
25-54 years: 0.96 male(s)/female
55-64 years: 1 male(s)/female
65 years and over: 1.04 male(s)/female
total population: 1 male(s)/female (2016 est.)

Maternal mortality ratio: 78 deaths/100,000 live births (2015 est.)
country comparison to the world: 81

Infant mortality rate: *total:* 14.4 deaths/1,000 live births
male: 15.4 deaths/1,000 live births
female: 13.4 deaths/1,000 live births (2017 est.)
country comparison to the world: 103

Life expectancy at birth: *total population:* 73.7 years
male: 72.1 years
female: 75.4 years (2017 est.)
country comparison to the world: 131

Total fertility rate: 3.07 children born/woman (2017 est.)
country comparison to the world: 52

Contraceptive prevalence rate: 49% (2013)

Health expenditures: 5% of GDP (2014)
country comparison to the world: 139

Physicians density: 0.19 physicians/1,000 population (2012)

Hospital bed density: 1.8 beds/1,000 population (2008)

Drinking water source:
improved:
urban: 98.9% of population
rural: 92.9% of population
total: 94.5% of population
unimproved:
urban: 1.1% of population
rural: 7.1% of population
total: 5.5% of population (2015 est.)

Sanitation facility access:
improved:
urban: 65.1% of population
rural: 55.4% of population
total: 57.9% of population
unimproved:
urban: 34.9% of population
rural: 44.6% of population
total: 42.1% of population (2015 est.)

HIV/AIDS—adult prevalence rate: NA

HIV/AIDS—people living with HIV/AIDS: NA

HIV/AIDS—deaths: NA

Obesity—adult prevalence rate: 25.2% (2016)
country comparison to the world: 52

Children under the age of 5 years underweight: 10.7% (2013)
country comparison to the world: 62

Education expenditures: 4.9% of GDP (2014)
country comparison to the world: 79

Literacy: *definition:* age 15 and over can read and write
total population: 85.2%
male: 86.6%
female: 83.8% (2015 est.)

Unemployment, youth ages 15-24: *total:* 10.6%
male: 10.2%
female: 11.2% (2009 est.)

GOVERNMENT

Country name: *conventional long form:* Republic of Vanuatu
conventional short form: Vanuatu
local long form: Ripablik blong Vanuatu
local short form: Vanuatu
former: New Hebrides
etymology: derived from the words "vanua" (home or land) and "tu" (stand) that occur in several of the Austonesian languages spoken on the islands and which provide a meaning of "the land remains" but which also convey a sense of "independence" or "our land"

Government type: parliamentary republic

Capital: name: Port-Vila (on Efate)
geographic coordinates: 17 44 S, 168 19 E
time difference: UTC+11 (16 hours ahead of Washington, DC, during Standard Time)

Administrative divisions: 6 provinces; Malampa, Penama, Sanma, Shefa, Tafea, Torba

Independence: 30 July 1980 (from France and the UK)

National holiday: Independence Day, 30 July (1980)

Constitution: effective 30 July 1980; amended several times, last in 2013 (2016)

Legal system: mixed legal system of English common law, French law, and customary law

International law organization participation: has not submitted an ICJ jurisdiction declaration; accepts ICCt jurisdiction

Citizenship: *citizenship by birth:* no
citizenship by descent only: both parents must be citizens of Vanuatu; in the case of only one parent, it must be the father who is a citizen
dual citizenship recognized: no
residency requirement for naturalization: 10 years

Suffrage: 18 years of age; universal

Executive branch: *chief of state:* President Tallis Obed MOSES (since 6 July 2017)

head of government: Prime Minister Charlot SAL-WAI (since 11 February 2016)
cabinet: Council of Ministers appointed by the prime minister, responsible to parliament
elections/appointments: president indirectly elected by an electoral college consisting of Parliament and presidents of the 6 provinces; Vanuatu president serves a 5-year term; election last held on 17 June 2017 (next to be held in 2022); following legislative elections, the leader of the majority party or majority coalition usually elected prime minister by parliament from among its members;

election for prime minister last held on 11 February 2016 (next to be held following general elections in 2020)
election results: Baldwin LONSDALE (independent) died suddenly on 17 June 2017; Parliament elected Tallis Obed MOSES on 6 July 2017 with a 39 to 17 vote in the fourth round; Charlot SAL-WAI elected prime minister on 11 February 2016 with 46 votes

Legislative branch: description: unicameral Parliament (52 seats; members directly elected in multi-seat constituencies by simple majority vote to serve 4-year terms)
note: the National Council of Chiefs advises on matters of culture and language
elections: last held on 22 January 2016 (next to be held in 2020)
election results: percent of vote by party—NA; seats by party—VP 8, PPP 6, UMP 5, GJP 4, NUP 4, IG 3, GC 3, NAG 3, RMC 3, MPP 2, NIPDP 2, PSP 1, VLDP 1, VNP 1, VPDP 1, VRP 1, and independent 4; note—political party associations are fluid

Judicial branch: *highest court(s):* Court of Appeal (consists of 2 or more judges of the Supreme Court designated by the chief justice); Supreme Court (consists of the chief justice and 6 puisne judges—3 local and 3 expatriate)
judge selection and term of office: Supreme Court chief justice appointed by the president after consultation with the prime minister and the leader of the opposition; other judges are appointed by the president on the advice of the Judicial Service Commission, a 4-member advisory body; judges appointed until age of retirement
subordinate courts: Magistrates Courts; Island Courts

Political parties and leaders: Greens Confederation or GC [Moana CARCASSES Kalosil]
Iauko Group or IG [Tony NARI]
Land and Justice Party (Graon mo Jastis Pati) or GJP [Ralph REGENVANU]
Melanesian Progressive Party or MPP [Barak SOPE]
Nagriamel movement or NAG [Frankie STEVENS]
Natatok Indigenous People's Democratic Party or (NATATOK) or NIPDP [Alfred Roland CARLOT]
National United Party or NUP [Ham LINI]
People's Progressive Party or PPP [Sato KILMAN]
People's Service Party or PSP [Don KEN]
Reunification of Movement for Change or RMC [Charlot SALWAI]
Union of Moderate Parties or UMP [Serge VOHOR]
Vanua'aku Pati (Our Land Party) or VP [Edward NATAPEI]
Vanuatu Democratic Party [Maxime Carlot KORMAN]
Vanuatu Liberal Democratic Party or VLDP [Tapangararua WILLIE]
Vanuatu National Party or VNP [Issac HAMARILIU]

Vanuatu National Development Party or VNDP
[Robert Bohn SIKOL]

Vanuatu Republican Party or VRP [Marcellino
PIPITE]

Political pressure groups and leaders: NA

International organization participation: ACP,
ADB, AOSIS, C, FAO, G-77, IBRD, ICAO,
ICRM, IDA, IFC, IFRCS, ILO, IMF, IMO, IMSO,
IOC, IOM, ITU, ITUC (NGOs), MIGA, NAM,
OAS (observer), OIF, OPCW, PIF, Sparteca, SPC,
UN, UNCTAD, UNESCO, UNIDO, UNWTO,
UPU, WCO, WFTU (NGOs), WHO, WIPO,
WMO, WTO

Diplomatic representation in the US: Vanuatu
does not have an embassy in the US; it does, however, have a Permanent Mission to the UN

Diplomatic representation from the US: the US
does not have an embassy in Vanuatu; the US
Ambassador to Papua New Guinea is accredited
to Vanuatu

Flag description: two equal horizontal bands of
red (top) and green with a black isosceles triangle
(based on the hoist side) all separated by a black-
edged yellow stripe in the shape of a horizontal Y
(the two points of the Y face the hoist side and
enclose the triangle); centered in the triangle is
a boar's tusk encircling two crossed namele fern
fronds, all in yellow; red represents the blood of
boars and men, as well as unity, green the richness
of the islands, and black the ni-Vanuatu people;
the yellow Y-shape—which reflects the pattern of
the islands in the Pacific Ocean—symbolizes the
light of the Gospel spreading through the islands;
the boar's tusk is a symbol of prosperity frequently
worn as a pendant on the islands; the fern fronds
represent peace
note: one of several flags where a prominent
component of the design reflects the shape of the
country; other such flags are those of Bosnia and
Herzegovina, Brazil, and Eritrea

National symbol(s): boar's tusk with crossed fern
fronds; national colors: red, black, green, yellow

National anthem: name: "Yumi, Yumi, Yumi" (We,
We, We)
lyrics/music: Francois Vincent AYSSAV
note: adopted 1980; the anthem is written in Bislama, a Creole language that mixes Pidgin English
and French

ECONOMY

Economy—overview: This South Pacific island
economy is based primarily on small-scale agriculture, which provides a living for about two-thirds
of the population. Fishing, offshore financial services, and tourism, with nearly 350,000 visitors in
2016, are other mainstays of the economy. Tourism
has struggled after Efate, the most populous and
popular island for tourists, was damaged by Tropical Cyclone Pam in 2015. Ongoing infrastructure
difficulties at Port Vila's Bauerfield Airport have
caused air travel disruptions, further hampering
tourism numbers. Australia and New Zealand are
the main source of tourists and foreign aid. A small
light industry sector caters to the local market. Tax

revenues come mainly from import duties. Mineral
deposits are negligible; the country has no known
petroleum deposits.

Economic development is hindered by dependence on relatively few commodity exports, vulnerability to natural disasters, and long distances from
main markets and between constituent islands.
In response to foreign concerns, the government
has promised to tighten regulation of its offshore
financial center.

Since 2002, the government has stepped up
efforts to boost tourism through improved air
connections, resort development, and cruise ship
facilities. Agriculture, especially livestock farming,
is a second target for growth.

GDP (purchasing power parity): $787 million
(2017 est.)
$753.1 million (2016 est.)
$724.1 million (2015 est.)
note: data are in 2017 dollars
country comparison to the world: 207

GDP (official exchange rate): $837 million (2016
est.)

GDP—real growth rate: 4.5% (2017 est.)
4% (2016 est.)
1.6% (2015 est.)
country comparison to the world: 52

GDP—per capita (PPP): $2,800 (2017 est.)
$2,700 (2016 est.)
$2,700 (2015 est.)
note: data are in 2017 dollars
country comparison to the world: 195

GDP—composition, by end use:
household consumption: 59.4%
government consumption: 17.9%
investment in fixed capital: 29.1%
investment in inventories: 0%
exports of goods and services: 41.8%
imports of goods and services: -48.2% (2017 est.)

GDP—composition, by sector of origin:
agriculture: 27%
industry: 9.1%
services: 63.9% (2017 est.)

Agriculture—products: copra, coconuts, cocoa,
coffee, taro, yams, fruits, vegetables; beef; fish

Industries: food and fish freezing, wood processing,
meat canning

Industrial production growth rate: 4.5% (2017 est.)
country comparison to the world: 60

Labor force: 115,900 (2007 est.)
country comparison to the world: 183
Labor force—by occupation: agriculture: 65%
industry: 5%
services: 30% (2000 est.)

Unemployment rate: 1.7% (1999 est.)
country comparison to the world: 11

Population below poverty line: NA%

**Household income or consumption by percentage
share:** *lowest 10%:* NA%
highest 10%: NA%

Budget: *revenues:* $202.4 million
expenditures: $206.9 million (2017 est.)

Taxes and other revenues: 24.2% of GDP (2017
est.)
country comparison to the world: 119

Budget surplus (+) or deficit (-): -0.5% of GDP
(2017 est.)
country comparison to the world: 46

Public debt: 31.3% of GDP (2016 est.)
25.6% of GDP (2015 est.)
country comparison to the world: 160

Fiscal year: calendar year

Inflation rate (consumer prices): 2.6% (2017 est.)
0.9% (2016 est.)
country comparison to the world: 122

Central bank discount rate: 20% (31 December
2010)
6% (31 December 2009)
country comparison to the world: 6

Commercial bank prime lending rate: 3.7% (31
December 2017 est.)
2.95% (31 December 2016 est.)
country comparison to the world: 163

Stock of narrow money: $457.4 million (31
December 2017 est.)
$379.9 million (31 December 2016 est.)
country comparison to the world: 170

Stock of broad money: $716.4 million (31 Decem-
ber 2017 est.)
$641 million (31 December 2016 est.)
country comparison to the world: 177

Stock of domestic credit: $509.1 million (31
December 2017 est.)
$463.4 million (31 December 2016 est.)
country comparison to the world: 177

Market value of publicly traded shares: $NA

Current account balance: -$120 million (2017
est.)
-$30 million (2016 est.)
country comparison to the world: 84

Exports: $43.9 million (2017 est.)
$53.5 million (2016 est.)
country comparison to the world: 205

Exports—commodities: copra, beef, cocoa, timber,
kava, coffee

Exports—partners: Ecuador 18.4%, Australia
13.8%, Venezuela 10.1%, US 9.8%, Japan 8.2%,
UK 6.7%, France 5.7%, Hong Kong 5.2% (2016)

Imports: $249.9 million (2017 est.)
$308.5 million (2016 est.)
country comparison to the world: 201

Imports—commodities: machinery and equipment, foodstuffs, fuels

Imports—partners: Australia 27.8%, NZ 17.6%,
China 10.5%, France 10%, Singapore 6.1%, Thailand 4.8% (2016)

Reserves of foreign exchange and gold: $288.9
million (31 December 2017 est.)
$267.4 million (31 December 2016 est.)
country comparison to the world: 155

Debt—external: $185.4 million (31 December
2017 est.)
$182.5 million (31 December 2016 est.)
country comparison to the world: 190

Stock of direct foreign investment—at home:
$590.9 million (31 December 2017 est.)
$535.9 million (31 December 2016 est.)
country comparison to the world: 122

Stock of direct foreign investment—abroad: $22.3 million (31 December 2017 est.)
$22.4 million (31 December 2016 est.)
country comparison to the world: 109

Exchange rates: vatu (VUV) per US dollar—
109.7 (2017 est.)
108.48 (2016 est.)
108.48 (2015 est.)
108.99 (2014 est.)
97.07 (2013 est.)

ENERGY

Electricity access: *population without electricity:* 202,614
electrification—*total population:* 27%
electrification—urban areas: 55%
electrification—rural areas: 18% (2012)

Electricity—production: 55 million kWh (2015 est.)
country comparison to the world: 205

Electricity—consumption: 51.15 million kWh (2015 est.)
country comparison to the world: 203

Electricity—exports: 0 kWh (2016 est.)
country comparison to the world: 177

Electricity—imports: 0 kWh (2016 est.)
country comparison to the world: 180

Electricity—installed generating capacity: 33,000 kW (2015 est.)
country comparison to the world: 201

Electricity—from fossil fuels: 81.8% of total installed capacity (2015 est.)
country comparison to the world: 83

Electricity—from nuclear fuels: 0% of total installed capacity (2015 est.)
country comparison to the world: 153

Electricity—from hydroelectric plants: 0% of total installed capacity (2015 est.)
country comparison to the world: 193

Electricity—from other renewable sources: 18.2% of total installed capacity (2015 est.)
country comparison to the world: 36

Crude oil—production: 0 bbl/day (2016 est.)
country comparison to the world: 212

Crude oil—exports: 0 bbl/day (2014 est.)
country comparison to the world: 171

Crude oil—imports: 0 bbl/day (2014 est.)
country comparison to the world: 170

Crude oil—proved reserves: 0 bbl (1 January 2017 es)
country comparison to the world: 212

Refined petroleum products—production: 0 bbl/day (2014 est.)
country comparison to the world: 213

Refined petroleum products—consumption: 1,000 bbl/day (2015 est.)
country comparison to the world: 207

Refined petroleum products—exports: 0 bbl/day (2014 est.)
country comparison to the world: 185

Refined petroleum products—imports: 1,008 bbl/day (2014 est.)
country comparison to the world: 200

Natural gas—production: 0 cu m (2013 est.)
country comparison to the world: 177

Natural gas—consumption: 0 cu m (2013 est.)
country comparison to the world: 216

Natural gas—exports: 0 cu m (2013 est.)
country comparison to the world: 158

Natural gas—imports: 0 cu m (2013 est.)
country comparison to the world: 164

Natural gas—proved reserves: 0 cu m (1 January 2014 es)
country comparison to the world: 179

Carbon dioxide emissions from consumption of energy: 200,000 Mt (2013 est.)
country comparison to the world: 204

COMMUNICATIONS

Telephones—fixed lines: *total subscriptions:* 4,267
subscriptions per 100 inhabitants: 2 (July 2016 est.)
country comparison to the world: 207

Telephones—mobile cellular: *total:* 192,167
subscriptions per 100 inhabitants: 69 (July 2016 est.)
country comparison to the world: 183

Telephone system: *general assessment:* telecom services have progressed significantly in recent years; mobile phones are now the primary means of communication and more than 90% of the population is covered by a mobile network
domestic: 2016 saw the launch of LTE services by Digicel and the introduction of rural satellite broadband services by Kacific; mobile phone use in some rural areas is constrained by electricity shortages
international: country code—678; satellite earth station—1 Intelsat (Pacific Ocean) (2016)

Broadcast media: 1 state-owned TV station; multi-channel pay TV is available; state-owned Radio Vanuatu operates 2 radio stations; 2 privately owned radio broadcasters; programming from multiple international broadcasters is available (2008)

Internet country code: .vu

Internet users: *total:* 66,613

percent of population: 24.0% (July 2016 est.)
country comparison to the world: 194

TRANSPORTATION

National air transport system: *number of registered air carriers:* 1
inventory of registered aircraft operated by air carriers: 6
annual passenger traffic on registered air carriers: 287,526
annual freight traffic on registered air carriers: 1,510,732 mt-km (2015)
Civil aircraft registration country code prefix: YJ (2016)

Airports: 31 (2013)
country comparison to the world: 114

Airports—with paved runways: *total:* 3
2,438 to 3,047 m: 1
1,524 to 2,437 m: 1
914 to 1,523 m: 1 (2013)

Airports—with unpaved runways: *total:* 28
914 to 1,523 m: 7
under 914 m: 21 (2013)

Roadways: *total:* 1,070 km
paved: 256 km
unpaved: 814 km (2000)
country comparison to the world: 185

Merchant marine: *total:* 421
by type: bulk carrier 22, container ship 1, general cargo 27, other 371 (2017)
country comparison to the world: 44

Ports and terminals: *major seaport(s):* Forari Bay, Luganville (Santo, Espiritu Santo), Port-Vila

MILITARY AND SECURITY

Military branches: no regular military forces; Vanuatu Police Force (VPF), Vanuatu Mobile Force (VMF; includes Police Maritime Wing (PMW)) (2013)

TRANSNATIONAL ISSUES

Disputes—international: Matthew and Hunter Islands east of New Caledonia claimed by Vanuatu and France

VENEZUELA

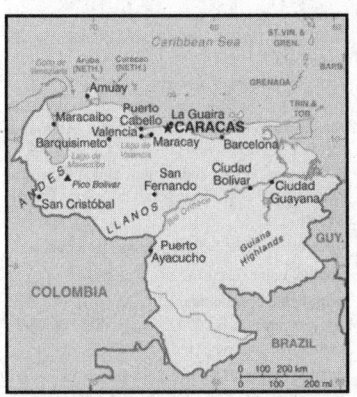

INTRODUCTION

Background: Venezuela was one of three countries that emerged from the collapse of Gran Colombia in 1830 (the others being Ecuador and New Granada, which became Colombia). For most of the first half of the 20th century, Venezuela was ruled by generally benevolent military strongmen who promoted the oil industry and allowed for some social reforms. Democratically elected governments have held sway since 1959. Under Hugo CHAVEZ, president from 1999 to 2013, and his hand-picked successor, President Nicolas MADURO, the executive branch has exercised increasingly authoritarian control over other branches of government. At the same time, democratic institutions have deteriorated, freedoms of expression and the press have been curtailed, and political polarization has grown. The ruling party's economic policies have expanded the state's role in the economy through expropriations of major enterprises, strict currency exchange and price controls that discourage private sector investment and production, and overdependence on the petroleum industry for revenues, among others. Current concerns include: human rights abuses, rampant violent crime, high inflation, and widespread shortages of basic consumer goods, medicine, and medical supplies.

GEOGRAPHY

Location: Northern South America, bordering the Caribbean Sea and the North Atlantic Ocean, between Colombia and Guyana

Geographic coordinates: 8 00 N, 66 00 W

Map references: South America

Area: *total:* 912,050 sq km
land: 882,050 sq km
water: 30,000 sq km
country comparison to the world: 34

Area—comparative: almost six times the size of Georgia; slightly more than twice the size of California

Land boundaries: *total:* 5,267 km
border countries (3): Brazil 2,137 km, Colombia 2,341 km, Guyana 789 km

Coastline: 2,800 km

Maritime claims: *territorial sea:* 12 nm
contiguous zone: 15 nm
exclusive economic zone: 200 nm
continental shelf: 200-m depth or to the depth of exploitation

Climate: tropical; hot, humid; more moderate in highlands

Terrain: Andes Mountains and Maracaibo Lowlands in northwest; central plains (llanos); Guiana Highlands in southeast

Elevation: *mean elevation:* 450 m

elevation extremes: *lowest point:* Caribbean Sea 0 m
highest point: Pico Bolivar 4,978 m

Natural resources: petroleum, natural gas, iron ore, gold, bauxite, other minerals, hydropower, diamonds

Land use: *agricultural land:* 24.5%
arable land: 3.1%;
permanent crops: 0.8%;
permanent pasture: 20.6%
forest: 52.1%
other: 23.4% (2011 est.)
Irrigated land: 10,550 sq km (2012)

Population—distribution: most of the population is concentrated in the northern and western highlands along an eastern spur at the northern end of the Andes, an area that includes the capital of Caracas

Natural hazards: subject to floods, rockslides, mudslides; periodic droughts

Environment—current issues: sewage pollution of Lago de Valencia; oil and urban pollution of Lago de Maracaibo; deforestation; soil degradation; urban and industrial pollution, especially along the Caribbean coast; threat to the rainforest ecosystem from irresponsible mining operations

Environment—international agreements: *party to:* Antarctic Treaty, Biodiversity, Climate Change, Climate Change-Kyoto Protocol, Desertification, Endangered Species, Hazardous Wastes, Marine Life Conservation, Ozone Layer Protection, Ship Pollution, Tropical Timber 83, Tropical Timber 94, Wetlands
signed but not ratified: none of the selected agreements

Geography—note: on major sea and air routes linking North and South America; Angel Falls in the Guiana Highlands is the world's highest waterfall (979 m)

PEOPLE AND SOCIETY

Population: 31,304,016 (July 2017 est.)
country comparison to the world: 42

Nationality: *noun:* Venezuelan(s)

adjective: Venezuelan

Ethnic groups: Spanish, Italian, Portuguese, Arab, German, African, indigenous people

Languages: Spanish (official), numerous indigenous dialects

Religions: nominally Roman Catholic 96%, Protestant 2%, other 2%

Demographic profile: Social investment in Venezuela during the CHAVEZ administration reduced poverty from nearly 50% in 1999 to about 27% in 2011, increased school enrollment, substantially decreased infant and child mortality, and improved access to potable water and sanitation through social investment. "Missions" dedicated to education, nutrition, healthcare, and sanitation were funded through petroleum revenues. The sustainability of this progress remains questionable, however, as the continuation of these social programs depends on the prosperity of Venezuela's oil industry. In the long-term, education and health care spending may increase economic growth and reduce income inequality, but rising costs and the staffing of new health care jobs with foreigners are slowing development.

While CHAVEZ was in power, more than one million predominantly middle- and upper-class Venezuelans are estimated to have emigrated. The brain drain is attributed to a repressive political system, lack of economic opportunities, steep inflation, a high crime rate, and corruption. Thousands of oil engineers emigrated to Canada, Colombia, and the United States following CHAVEZ's firing of over 20,000 employees of the state-owned petroleum company during a 2002-03 oil strike. Additionally, thousands of Venezuelans of European descent have taken up residence in their ancestral homelands. Nevertheless, Venezuela has attracted hundreds of thousands of immigrants from South America and southern Europe because of its lenient migration policy and the availability of education and health care. Venezuela also has been a fairly accommodating host to Colombian refugees, numbering about 170,000 as of year-end 2016. However, since 2014, falling oil prices have driven a major economic crisis that has pushed Venezuelans from all walks of life to migrate or to seek asylum abroad to escape severe shortages of food, water, and medicine; soaring inflation; unemployment; and violence. Tens of thousands of Venezuelans have migrated, often illegally, to Colombia, Brazil, Mexico, Panama, Chile, Guyana, the Dominican Republic, or taken perilous journeys by raft to Aruba and Curacao. Asylum applications increased significantly in the US and Brazil in 2016 and 2017. Although several receiving countries are making efforts to increase immigration restrictions and to deport illegal Venezuelan migrants, Venezuelans continue to migrate to avoid economic collapse at home.

Age structure: *0-14 years:* 27.36% (male 4,390,773/female 4,175,080)

973

15-24 years: 17.03% (male 2,707,934/female 2,624,031)

25-54 years: 40.53% (male 6,289,673/female 6,398,217)

55-64 years: 7.98% (male 1,198,525/female 1,299,498)

65 years and over: 7.09% (male 1,003,534/female 1,216,751) (2017 est.)

Dependency ratios: *total dependency ratio:* 52.6
youth dependency ratio: 43
elderly dependency ratio: 9.5
potential support ratio: 10.5 (2015 est.)

Median age: *total:* 28.3 years
male: 27.6 years
female: 29 years (2017 est.)
country comparison to the world: 132

Population growth rate: 1.24% (2017 est.)
country comparison to the world: 91

Birth rate: 18.8 births/1,000 population (2017 est.)
country comparison to the world: 90

Death rate: 5.3 deaths/1,000 population (2017 est.)
country comparison to the world: 185

Net migration rate: -1.2 migrant(s)/1,000 population (2017 est.)
country comparison to the world: 143

Population distribution: most of the population is concentrated in the northern and western highlands along an eastern spur at the northern end of the Andes, an area that includes the capital of Caracas

Urbanization: *urban population:* 89.1% of total population (2017)
rate of urbanization: 1.38% annual rate of change (2015-20 est.)

Major urban areas—population: CARACAS (capital) 2.916 million; Maracaibo 2.196 million; Valencia 1.734 million; Maracay 1.166 million; Barquisimeto 1.039 million (2015)

Sex ratio: *at birth:* 1.05 male(s)/female
0-14 years: 1.05 male(s)/female
15-24 years: 1.03 male(s)/female
25-54 years: 0.98 male(s)/female
55-64 years: 0.92 male(s)/female
65 years and over: 0.79 male(s)/female
total population: 0.99 male(s)/female (2016 est.)

Maternal mortality ratio: 95 deaths/100,000 live births (2015 est.)
country comparison to the world: 73

Infant mortality rate: *total:* 12.2 deaths/1,000 live births
male: 12.8 deaths/1,000 live births
female: 11.6 deaths/1,000 live births (2017 est.)
country comparison to the world: 117

Life expectancy at birth: *total population:* 76 years
male: 73 years
female: 79.1 years (2017 est.)
country comparison to the world: 92

Total fertility rate: 2.32 children born/woman (2017 est.)
country comparison to the world: 88

Contraceptive prevalence rate: 75% (2010)

Health expenditures: 5.3% of GDP (2014)
country comparison to the world: 132

Hospital bed density: 0.9 beds/1,000 population (2011)

Drinking water source:
improved:
urban: 95% of population
rural: 77.9% of population
total: 93.1% of population
unimproved:
urban: 5% of population
rural: 22.1% of population
total: 6.9% of population (2015 est.)

Sanitation facility access:
improved:
urban: 97.5% of population
rural: 69.9% of population
total: 94.4% of population
unimproved:
urban: 2.5% of population
rural: 30.1% of population
total: 5.6% of population (2015 est.)

HIV/AIDS—adult prevalence rate: 0.6% (2016 est.)
country comparison to the world: 55

HIV/AIDS—people living with HIV/AIDS: 120,000 (2016 est.)
country comparison to the world: 39

HIV/AIDS—deaths: 2,500 (2016 est.)
country comparison to the world: 47

Major infectious diseases: *degree of risk:* high
food or waterborne diseases: bacterial diarrhea and hepatitis A
vectorborne diseases: dengue fever and malaria
note: active local transmission of Zika virus by Aedes species mosquitoes has been identified in this country (as of August 2016); it poses an important risk (a large number of cases possible) among US citizens if bitten by an infective mosquito; other less common ways to get Zika are through sex, via blood transfusion, or during pregnancy, in which the pregnant woman passes Zika virus to her fetus (2016)

Obesity—adult prevalence rate: 25.6% (2016)
country comparison to the world: 50

Children under the age of 5 years underweight: 2.9% (2009)
country comparison to the world: 115

Education expenditures: 6.9% of GDP (2009)
country comparison to the world: 22

Literacy: *definition:* age 15 and over can read and write
total population: 97.1%
male: 97%
female: 97.2% (2016 est.)

School life expectancy (primary to tertiary education): *total:* 14 years
male: NA
female: NA (2009)

Unemployment, youth ages 15-24: *total:* 14.6%
male: NA
female: NA (2015 est.)
country comparison to the world: 70

GOVERNMENT

Country name: *conventional long form:* Bolivarian Republic of Venezuela
conventional short form: Venezuela
local long form: Republica Bolivariana de Venezuela
local short form: Venezuela
etymology: native stilt-houses built on Lake Maracaibo reminded early explorers Alonso de OJEDA and Amerigo VESPUCCI in 1499 of buildings in Venice and so they named the region "Venezuela," which in Italian means "Little Venice"

Government type: federal presidential republic

Capital: *name:* Caracas
geographic coordinates: 10 29 N, 66 52 W
time difference: UTC-4 (1 hour ahead of Washington, DC, during Standard Time)

Administrative divisions: 23 states (estados, singular—estado), 1 capital district* (distrito capital), and 1 federal dependency** (dependencia federal); Amazonas, Anzoategui, Apure, Aragua, Barinas, Bolivar, Carabobo, Cojedes, Delta Amacuro, Dependencias Federales (Federal Dependencies)**, Distrito Capital (Capital District)*, Falcon, Guarico, Lara, Merida, Miranda, Monagas, Nueva Esparta, Portuguesa, Sucre, Tachira, Trujillo, Vargas, Yaracuy, Zulia
note: the federal dependency consists of 11 federally controlled island groups with a total of 72 individual islands

Independence: 5 July 1811 (from Spain)

National holiday: Independence Day, 5 July (1811)

Constitution: many previous; latest adopted 15 December 1999, effective 30 December 1999; amended 2009 (2016)

Legal system: civil law system based on the Spanish civil code

International law organization participation: has not submitted an ICJ jurisdiction declaration; accepts ICCt jurisdiction

Citizenship: *citizenship by birth:* yes
citizenship by descent: yes
dual citizenship recognized: no
residency requirement for naturalization: 5 years

Suffrage: 18 years of age; universal

Executive branch: *chief of state:* President Nicolas MADURO Moros (since 19 April 2013); Executive Vice President Tareck EL AISSAMI (since 4 January 2017); note—the president is both chief of state and head of government

head of government: President Nicolas MADURO Moros (since 19 April 2013); Executive Vice President Tareck EL AISSAMI (since 4 January 2017)
cabinet: Council of Ministers appointed by the president
elections/appointments: president directly elected by simple majority popular vote for a 6-year term (no term limits); election last held on 14 April 2013—a special election held following the death of President Hugo CHAVEZ Frias on 5 March 2013 (next election expected in late 2018

or early 2019 pending official convocation by the country's electoral body)

election results: Nicolas MADURO Moros elected president; percent of vote—Nicolas MADURO Moros (PSUV) 50.6%, Henrique CAPRILES Radonski (PJ) 49.1%, other 0.3%

Legislative branch: description: unicameral National Assembly or Asamblea Nacional (167 seats; 113 members directly elected in single- and multi-seat constituencies by simple majority vote, 51 directly elected in multi-seat constituencies by proportional representation vote, and 3 seats reserved for indigenous peoples of Venezuela; members serve 5-year terms)

elections: last held on 6 December 2015 (next expected to be held in 2020)

election results: percent of vote by party—MUD (opposition coalition) 56.2%, PSUV (pro-government) 40.9%, other 2.9%; seats by party—MUD 109, PSUV 55, indigenous peoples 3

note: amid months of protests and clashes beginning in latter 2016, President MADURO issued a decree to hold an election to form a Constituent Assembly; the 30 July 2017 poll approved the formation of a 545-member Constituent Assembly, which is empowered to change the constitution and dismiss government institutions and officials

Judicial branch: *highest court(s):* Supreme Tribunal of Justice (consists of 32 judges organized into 6 divisions—constitutional, political administrative, electoral, civil appeals, criminal appeals, and social (mainly agrarian and labor issues)

judge selection and term of office: judges proposed by the Committee of Judicial Postulation (an independent body of organizations dealing with legal issues and of the organs of citizen power) and appointed by the National Assembly; judges serve nonrenewable 12-year terms

subordinate courts: Superior or Appeals Courts (Tribunales Superiores); District Tribunals (Tribunales de Distrito); Courts of First Instance (Tribunales de Primera Instancia); Parish Courts (Tribunales de Parroquia); Justices of the Peace (Justicia de Paz) Network

Political parties and leaders: A New Time or UNT [Manuel ROSALES]

Brave People's Alliance or ABP [Richard BLANCO]

Christian Democrats or COPEI [Roberto ENRIQUEZ]

Coalition of opposition parties -- The Democratic Unity Table or MUD [Jose Luis CARTAYA]

Communist Party of Venezuela or PCV [Oscar FIGUERA]

Democratic Action or AD [Henry RAMOS ALLUP]

Fatherland for All or PPT [Rafael UZCATEGUI]

For Social Democracy or PODEMOS [Didalco Antonio BOLIVAR GRATEROL]

Justice First or PJ [Julio BORGES]

Movement Toward Socialism or MAS [Segundo MELENDEZ]

Popular Will or VP [Leopoldo LOPEZ]

Progressive Wave or AP [Henri FALCON]

The Radical Cause or La Causa R [Americo DE GRAZIA]

United Socialist Party of Venezuela or PSUV [Nicolas MADURO]

Venezuelan Progressive Movement or MPV [Simon CALZADILLA]

Venezuela Project or PV [Henrique Fernando SALAS FEO]

Political pressure groups and leaders: Bolivarian and Socialist Workers' Union (a ruling-party-oriented organized labor union)

Confederacion Venezolana de Industriales or Coindustria (a conservative business group)

Consejos Comunales (pro-government local communal councils)

Federation of Chambers and Associations of Commerce and Production of Venezuela or FEDECAMARAS (a conservative business group)

Union of Oil Workers of Venezuela or FUTPV

Venezuelan Confederation of Workers or CTV (opposition-oriented labor organization)

other: various civil society groups and human rights organizations

International organization participation: Caricom (observer), CD, CDB, CELAC, FAO, G-15, G-24, G-77, IADB, IAEA, IBRD, ICAO, ICC (national committees), ICCt (signatory), ICRM, IDA, IFAD, IFC, IFRCS, IHO, ILO, IMF, IMO, IMSO, Interpol, IOC, IOM, IPU, ITSO, ITU, ITUC (NGOs), LAES, LAIA, LAS (observer), MIGA, NAM, OAS, OPANAL, OPCW, OPEC, PCA, Petrocaribe, UN, UNASUR, UNCTAD, UNESCO, UNHCR, UNIDO, Union Latina, UNWTO, UPU, WCO, WFTU (NGOs), WHO, WIPO, WMO, WTO

Diplomatic representation in the US: *chief of mission:* Ambassador (vacant); Charge d'Affaires Carlos Julio RON Martinez (since February 2017)

chancery: 1099 30th Street NW, Washington, DC 20007

telephone: [1] (202) 342-2214

FAX: [1] (202) 342-6820

consulate(s) general: Boston, Chicago, Houston, New Orleans, New York, San Francisco, San Juan (Puerto Rico)

Diplomatic representation from the US: *chief of mission:* Ambassador (vacant); Charge d'Affaires Todd ROBINSON (December 2017)

embassy: Calle F con Calle Suapure, Urbanizacion Colinas de Valle Arriba, Caracas 1080

mailing address: P. O. Box 62291, Caracas 1060-A; APO AA 34037

telephone: [58] (212) 975-6411, 907-8400 (after hours)

FAX: [58] (212) 907-8199

Flag description: three equal horizontal bands of yellow (top), blue, and red with the coat of arms on the hoist side of the yellow band and an arc of eight white five-pointed stars centered in the blue band; the flag retains the three equal horizontal bands and three main colors of the banner of Gran Colombia, the South American republic that broke up in 1830; yellow is interpreted as standing for the riches of the land, blue for the courage of its people, and red for the blood shed in attaining independence; the seven stars on the original flag represented the seven provinces in Venezuela that united in the war of independence; in 2006, then President Hugo CHAVEZ ordered an eighth star added to the star arc—a decision that sparked much controversy—to conform with the flag proclaimed by Simon Bolivar in 1827 and to represent the historic province of Guayana

National symbol(s): troupial (bird); national colors: yellow, blue, red

National anthem: name: "Gloria al bravo pueblo" (Glory to the Brave People)

lyrics/music: Vicente SALIAS/Juan Jose LANDAETA

note: adopted 1881; lyrics written in 1810, the music some years later; both SALIAS and LANDAETA were executed in 1814 during Venezuela's struggle for independence

ECONOMY

Economy—overview: Venezuela remains highly dependent on oil revenues, which account for almost all export earnings and nearly half of the government's revenue. In 2017, GDP contracted 12%, inflation exceeded 650%, people faced widespread shortages of consumer goods, the exchange rate tumbled, and central bank international reserves dwindled. On the other hand, Venezuela managed to pay down its external debt and narrow its current account deficit. Domestic production and industry continues to severely underperform and the Venezuelan government continues to rely on imports to meet its basic food and consumer goods needs.

Falling oil prices since 2014 have aggravated Venezuela's economic crisis. Insufficient access to dollars, price controls, and rigid labor regulations have led some US and multinational firms to reduce or shut down their Venezuelan operations. Market uncertainty and state oil company PDVSA's poor cash flow have slowed investment in the petroleum sector, resulting in a decline in oil production.

Under President Nicolas MADURO, the Venezuelan Government's response to the economic crisis has been to increase state control over the economy and blame the private sector for the shortages. MADURO has ceded increasing authority for the production and distribution of scarce goods to the military and to local socialist party member committees. The Venezuelan Government has maintained strict currency controls since 2003. On 17 February 2016, the Venezuelan Government announced a change from three official currency exchange mechanisms to only two official rates for the sale of dollars to private-sector firms and individuals, with rates based on the government's import priorities. The official exchange rate used for food and medicine imports was devalued to 10 bolivars per dollar from 6.3 bolivars per dollar. The second rate moved to a managed float. These currency controls present significant obstacles to trade with Venezuela because importers cannot obtain sufficient dollars to purchase goods needed to maintain their operations. Meting out access to the multiple exchange rates has created opportunities for arbitrage and corruption. MADURO has used decree powers to enact legislation to deepen the state's role as the primary buyer and distributor of imports, further tighten currency controls, cap business profits, and extend price controls.

GDP (purchasing power parity): $389.4 billion (2017 est.)
$442.5 billion (2016 est.)
$529.6 billion (2015 est.)
note: data are in 2017 dollars
country comparison to the world: 48

GDP (official exchange rate): $215.3 billion (2016 est.)

GDP—real growth rate: -12% (2017 est.)
-16.5% (2016 est.)
-6.2% (2015 est.)
country comparison to the world: 222

GDP—per capita (PPP): $12,400 (2017 est.)
$14,300 (2016 est.)
$17,300 (2015 est.)
note: data are in 2017 dollars
country comparison to the world: 126

Gross national saving: 8.8% of GDP (2017 est.)
7.6% of GDP (2016 est.)
31.8% of GDP (2015 est.)
country comparison to the world: 163

GDP—composition, by end use:
household consumption: 73.8%
government consumption: 17.8%
investment in fixed capital: 15%
investment in inventories: 1.6%
exports of goods and services: 8.6%
imports of goods and services: -16.7% (2017 est.)

GDP—composition, by sector of origin:
agriculture: 4.4%
industry: 38.2%
services: 57.4% (2017 est.)

Agriculture—products: corn, sorghum, sugarcane, rice, bananas, vegetables, coffee; beef, pork, milk, eggs; fish

Industries: agricultural products, livestock, raw materials, machinery and equipment, transport equipment, construction materials, medical equipment, pharmaceuticals, chemicals, iron and steel products, crude oil and petroleum products

Industrial production growth rate: -2% (2017 est.)
country comparison to the world: 194

Labor force: 14.21 million (2017 est.)
country comparison to the world: 41
Labor force—by occupation: agriculture: 7.3%
industry: 21.8%
services: 70.9% (4th quarter, 2011)

Unemployment rate: 26.4% (2017 est.)
20.6% (2016 est.)
country comparison to the world: 194

Population below poverty line: 19.7% (2015 est.)

Household income or consumption by percentage share: lowest 10%: 1.7%
highest 10%: 32.7% (2006)

Distribution of family income—Gini index: 39 (2011)

49.5 (1998)
country comparison to the world: 68

Budget: revenues: $77.89 billion
expenditures: $160 billion (2017 est.)

Taxes and other revenues: 36.2% of GDP (2017 est.)
country comparison to the world: 51

Budget surplus (+) or deficit (-): -38.1% of GDP (2017 est.)
country comparison to the world: 219

Public debt: 25.8% of GDP (2017 est.)
39.3% of GDP (2016 est.)
note: data cover central government debt, as well as the debt of state-owned oil company PDVSA; the data include treasury debt held by foreign entities; the data include some debt issued by subnational entities, as well as intra-governmental debt; intra-governmental debt consists of treasury borrowings from surpluses in the social funds, such as for retirement, medical care, and unemployment; some debt instruments for the social funds are sold at public auctions
country comparison to the world: 175

Fiscal year: calendar year

Inflation rate (consumer prices): 652.7% (2017 est.)
254.4% (2016 est.)
country comparison to the world: 227

Central bank discount rate: 29.5% (2015)
country comparison to the world: 1

Commercial bank prime lending rate: 23.8% (31 December 2017 est.)
20.78% (31 December 2016 est.)
country comparison to the world: 12

Stock of narrow money: $145.3 billion (31 December 2017 est.)
$163.3 billion (31 December 2016 est.)
country comparison to the world: 30

Stock of broad money: $159.5 billion (31 December 2017 est.)
$165.4 billion (31 December 2016 est.)
country comparison to the world: 49

Stock of domestic credit: $194.8 billion (31 December 2017 est.)
$339.6 billion (31 December 2016 est.)
country comparison to the world: 33

Market value of publicly traded shares: $25.3 billion (31 December 2012 est.)
$5.143 billion (31 December 2011 est.)
$3.991 billion (31 December 2011 est.)
country comparison to the world: 62

Current account balance: -$947 million (2017 est.)
-$3.87 billion (2016 est.)
country comparison to the world: 133

Exports: $29.16 billion (2017 est.)
$27.2 billion (2016 est.)
country comparison to the world: 64

Exports—commodities: petroleum and petroleum products, bauxite and aluminum, minerals, chemicals, agricultural products

Exports—partners: US 35.1%, India 17.2%, China 14.1%, Netherlands Antilles 8%, Singapore 5.3%, Cuba 4.1% (2016)

Imports: $17.75 billion (2017 est.)
$20.19 billion (2016 est.)
country comparison to the world: 78

Imports—commodities: agricultural products, livestock, raw materials, machinery and equipment, transport equipment, construction materials, medical equipment, petroleum products, pharmaceuticals, chemicals, iron and steel products

Imports—partners: US 22.1%, China 14.3%, Brazil 7.4%, Colombia 4.2% (2016)

Reserves of foreign exchange and gold: $6.696 billion (31 December 2017 est.)
$10.99 billion (31 December 2016 est.)
country comparison to the world: 85

Debt—external: $103.1 billion (31 December 2017 est.)
$109.8 billion (31 December 2016 est.)
country comparison to the world: 48

Stock of direct foreign investment—at home: $36.36 billion (31 December 2017 est.)
$33.78 billion (31 December 2016 est.)
country comparison to the world: 64

Stock of direct foreign investment—abroad: $32.47 billion (31 December 2017 est.)
$31.12 billion (31 December 2016 est.)
country comparison to the world: 50

Exchange rates: bolivars (VEB) per US dollar—
437.1 (2017 est.)
48.07 (2016 est.)
48.07 (2015 est.)
13.72 (2014 est.)
6.28 (2013 est.)

ENERGY

Electricity access: population without electricity: 100,000
electrification—total population: 99.7%
electrification—urban areas: 99.8%
electrification—rural areas: 98.6% (2013)

Electricity—production: 114.4 billion kWh (2015 est.)
country comparison to the world: 33

Electricity—consumption: 73.99 billion kWh (2015 est.)
country comparison to the world: 39

Electricity—exports: 0 kWh (2015 est.)
country comparison to the world: 212

Electricity—imports: 0 kWh (2015 est.)
country comparison to the world: 215

Electricity—installed generating capacity: 32.17 million kW (2015 est.)
country comparison to the world: 33

Electricity—from fossil fuels: 52.8% of total installed capacity (2015 est.)
country comparison to the world: 145

Electricity—from nuclear fuels: 0% of total installed capacity (2015 est.)
country comparison to the world: 204

Electricity—from hydroelectric plants: 47.1% of total installed capacity (2015 est.)
country comparison to the world: 44

Electricity—from other renewable sources: 0.1% of total installed capacity (2015 est.)
country comparison to the world: 169

Crude oil—production: 2.277 million bbl/day (2016 est.)
country comparison to the world: 11

Crude oil—exports: 1.514 million bbl/day (2014 est.)
country comparison to the world: 10

Crude oil—imports: 0 bbl/day (2014 est.)
country comparison to the world: 206

Crude oil—proved reserves: 300.9 billion bbl (1 January 2017 es)
country comparison to the world: 1

Refined petroleum products—production: 1.028 million bbl/day (2014 est.)
country comparison to the world: 20

Refined petroleum products—consumption: 747,000 bbl/day (2015 est.)
country comparison to the world: 30

Refined petroleum products—exports: 402,300 bbl/day (2014 est.)
country comparison to the world: 19

Refined petroleum products—imports: 0 bbl/day (2014 est.)
country comparison to the world: 214

Natural gas—production: 26 billion cu m (2015 est.)
country comparison to the world: 29

Natural gas—consumption: 39.62 billion cu m (2015 est.)
country comparison to the world: 33

Natural gas—exports: 0 cu m (2014 est.)
country comparison to the world: 205

Natural gas—imports: 500 million cu m (2015 est.)
country comparison to the world: 67

Natural gas—proved reserves: 5.701 trillion cu m (1 January 2017 es)
country comparison to the world: 8

Carbon dioxide emissions from consumption of energy: 188 million Mt (2013 est.)
country comparison to the world: 31

COMMUNICATIONS

Telephones—fixed lines: *total subscriptions:* 7,752,232
subscriptions per 100 inhabitants: 25 (July 2016 est.)
country comparison to the world: 23

Telephones—mobile cellular: *total:* 27,600,893
subscriptions per 100 inhabitants: 89 (July 2016 est.)
country comparison to the world: 40

Telephone system: *general assessment:* modern and expanding
domestic: two domestic satellite systems with three earth stations; recent substantial improvement in telephone service in rural areas; installation of a

national interurban fiber-optic network capable of digital multimedia services; three major providers operate the mobile market; combined fixed-line and mobile-cellular telephone subscribership about 115 per 100 persons
international: country code—58; submarine cable systems provide connectivity to Cuba and the Caribbean, Central and South America, and US; satellite earth stations—1 Intelsat (Atlantic Ocean) and 1 PanAmSat; participating with Colombia, Ecuador, Peru, and Bolivia in the construction of an international fiber-optic network (2016)

Broadcast media: government supervises a mixture of state-run and private broadcast media; 13 public service networks, 61 privately owned TV networks, a privately owned news channel with limited national coverage, and a government-backed Pan-American channel; state-run radio network includes roughly 65 news stations and another 30 stations targeted at specific audiences; state-sponsored community broadcasters include 235 radio stations and 44 TV stations; the number of private broadcast radio stations has been declining, but many still remain in operation (2014)

Internet country code: .ve

Internet users: *total:* 18,547,381

percent of population: 60.0% (July 2016 est.)
country comparison to the world: 37

TRANSPORTATION

National air transport system: *number of registered air carriers:* 17
inventory of registered aircraft operated by air carriers: 122
annual passenger traffic on registered air carriers: 6,456,853
annual freight traffic on registered air carriers: 6,204,085 mt-km (2015)
Civil aircraft registration country code prefix: YV (2016)

Airports: 444 (2013)
country comparison to the world: 19

Airports—with paved runways: *total:* 127
over 3,047 m: 6
2,438 to 3,047 m: 9
1,524 to 2,437 m: 33
914 to 1,523 m: 62
under 914 m: 17 (2013)

Airports—with unpaved runways: *total:* 317
2,438 to 3,047 m: 3
1,524 to 2,437 m: 57
914 to 1,523 m: 127
under 914 m: 130 (2013)

Heliports: 3 (2013)

Pipelines: extra heavy crude 981 km; gas 5,941 km; oil 7,588 km; refined products 1,778 km (2013)

Railways: *total:* 447 km
standard gauge: 447 km 1.435-m gauge (41.4 km electrified) (2014)
country comparison to the world: 117

Roadways: *total:* 96,189 km (2014)

country comparison to the world: 50

Waterways: 7,100 km (Orinoco River (400 km) and Lake de Maracaibo navigable by oceangoing vessels) (2011)
country comparison to the world: 20

Merchant marine: *total:* 267
by type: bulk carrier 4, container ship 1, general cargo 31, oil tanker 24, other 207 (2017)
country comparison to the world: 57

Ports and terminals: *major seaport(s):* La Guaira, Maracaibo, Puerto Cabello, Punta Cardon
oil terminal(s): Jose terminal

MILITARY AND SECURITY

Military expenditures: 1% of GDP (2015)
1.16% of GDP (2014)
1.43% of GDP (2013)
1.3% of GDP (2012)
0.75% of GDP (2011)
country comparison to the world: 98

Military branches: Bolivarian National Armed Forces (Fuerza Armada Nacional Bolivariana, FANB): Bolivarian Army (Ejercito Bolivariano, EB), Bolivarian Navy (Armada Bolivariana, AB; includes Naval Infantry, Coast Guard, Naval Aviation), Bolivarian Military Aviation (Aviacion Militar Bolivariana, AMB; includes Air National Guard), Bolivarian National Guard (Guardia Nacional Bolivaria, GNB), Bolivarian Militia (Milicia Bolivariana, NMB) (2016)

Military service age and obligation: all citizens of military service age (18-60 years old) are obligated to register for military service, though mandatory recruitment is forbidden; the minimum service obligation is 12 months (2016)
Maritime threats: the International Maritime Bureau continues to report the territorial and offshore waters in the Caribbean Sea as at risk for piracy and armed robbery against ships; numerous vessels, including commercial shipping and pleasure craft, have been attacked and hijacked both at anchor and while underway; crews have been robbed and stores or cargoes stolen; in 2016, there were five attacks reported and this increased to six attacks in the first half of 2017 making Venezuela the fourth most dangerous area in the World

TERRORISM

Terrorist groups—foreign based: National Liberation Army (Ejercito de Liberacion Nacional, ELN): aim(s): enhance its narcotics trafficking networks in Venezuela
area(s) of operation: maintains a narcotics trafficking presence, facilitating the transshipment of narcotics through the country; has a history of transporting and holding hostages in Venezuela who were abducted in Colombia

TRANSNATIONAL ISSUES

Disputes—international: claims all of the area west of the Essequibo River in Guyana, preventing any discussion of a maritime boundary; Guyana has expressed its intention to join Barbados in asserting claims before the UN Convention on the Law of the Sea that Trinidad and Tobago's maritime boundary with Venezuela extends into their waters; dispute with Colombia over maritime boundary and Venezuelan administered Los Monjes Islands near the Gulf of Venezuela; Colombian organized illegal narcotics and paramilitary activities penetrate Venezuela's shared border region; US, France, and the Netherlands recognize Venezuela's granting full effect to Aves Island, thereby claiming a Venezuelan Economic Exclusion Zone/continental shelf extending over a large portion of the eastern Caribbean Sea; Dominica, Saint Kitts and Nevis, Saint Lucia, and Saint Vincent and the Grenadines protest Venezuela's full effect claim

Refugees and internally displaced persons: refugees (country of origin): 171,920 (Colombia) (2016)

Trafficking in persons: current situation: Venezuela is a source and destination country for men, women, and children subjected to sex trafficking

and forced labor; Venezuelan women and girls, sometimes lured from poor interior regions to urban and tourist areas, are trafficked for sexual exploitation within the country, as well as in the Caribbean; Venezuelan children are exploited, frequently by their families, in domestic servitude; people from South America, the Caribbean, Asia, and Africa are sex and labor trafficking victims in Venezuela; thousands of Cuban citizens, particularly doctors, who work in Venezuela on government social programs in exchange for the provision of resources to the Cuban Government experience conditions of forced labor

tier rating: Tier 3—Venezuela does not fully comply with the minimum standards for the elimination of trafficking and is not making significant efforts to do so; in 2014, the government appeared to increase efforts to hold traffickers criminally accountable, but a lack of government data made anti-trafficking law enforcement efforts difficult to assess; publically available information indicated many cases pursued under anti-trafficking law involved illegal adoption rather than sex and labor

trafficking; authorities identified a small number of trafficking victims, and victim referrals to limited government services were made on an ad hoc basis; because no specialized facilities are available for trafficking victims, women and child victims accessed centers for victims of domestic violence or at-risk youth, and services for men were virtually non-existent; NGOs provided some services to sex and labor trafficking victims; Venezuela has no permanent anti-trafficking interagency body, no national anti-trafficking plan, and still has not passed anti-trafficking legislation drafted in 2010 (2015)

Illicit drugs: small-scale illicit producer of opium and coca for the processing of opiates and coca derivatives; however, large quantities of cocaine, heroin, and marijuana transit the country from Colombia bound for US and Europe; significant narcotics-related money-laundering activity, especially along the border with Colombia and on Margarita Island; active eradication program primarily targeting opium; increasing signs of drug-related activities by Colombian insurgents on border

VIETNAM

INTRODUCTION

Background: The conquest of Vietnam by France began in 1858 and was completed by 1884. It became part of French Indochina in 1887. Vietnam declared independence after World War II, but France continued to rule until its 1954 defeat by communist forces under Ho Chi MINH. Under the Geneva Accords of 1954, Vietnam was divided into the communist North and anti-communist South. US economic and military aid to South Vietnam grew through the 1960s in an attempt to bolster the government, but US armed forces were withdrawn following a cease-fire agreement in 1973. Two years later, North Vietnamese forces overran the South reuniting the country under communist rule. Despite the return of peace, for over a decade the country experienced little economic growth because of conservative leadership policies, the persecution and mass exodus of individuals—many of them successful South Vietnamese merchants—and growing international isolation. However, since the enactment of Vietnam's "doi moi" (renovation) policy in 1986, Vietnamese authorities have committed to increased economic liberalization and enacted structural reforms needed to modernize the economy and to produce more competitive, export-driven industries. The communist leaders maintain tight control on political expression but have demonstrated some modest steps toward better protection of human rights. The country continues to experience small-scale protests, the vast majority connected to either land-use issues, calls for increased political space, or the lack of equitable mechanisms for resolving disputes. The small-scale protests in the urban areas are often organized by human rights

activists, but many occur in rural areas and involve various ethnic minorities such as the Montagnards of the Central Highlands, Hmong in the Northwest Highlands, and the Khmer Krom in the southern delta region.

GEOGRAPHY

Location: Southeastern Asia, bordering the Gulf of Thailand, Gulf of Tonkin, and South China Sea, as well as China, Laos, and Cambodia

Geographic coordinates: 16 10 N, 107 50 E

Map references: Southeast Asia

Area: *total:* 331,210 sq km
land: 310,070 sq km
water: 21,140 sq km
country comparison to the world: 67

Area—comparative: about three times the size of Tennessee; slightly larger than New Mexico

Land boundaries: *total:* 4,616 km
border countries (3): Cambodia 1,158 km, China 1,297 km, Laos 2,161 km

Coastline: 3,444 km (excludes islands)

Maritime claims: *territorial sea:* 12 nm
contiguous zone: 24 nm
exclusive economic zone: 200 nm
continental shelf: 200 nm or to the edge of the continental margin

Climate: tropical in south; monsoonal in north with hot, rainy season (May to September) and warm, dry season (October to March)

Terrain: low, flat delta in south and north; central highlands; hilly, mountainous in far north and northwest

Elevation: *mean elevation:* 398 m

elevation extremes: *lowest point:* South China Sea 0 m
highest point: Fan Si Pan 3,144 m

Natural resources: phosphates, coal, manganese, rare earth elements, bauxite, chromate, offshore oil and gas deposits, timber, hydropower, arable land

Land use: *agricultural land:* 34.8%
arable land: 20.6%;
permanent crops: 12.1%;
permanent pasture: 2.1%
forest: 45%
other: 20.2% (2011 est.)
Irrigated land: 46,000 sq km (2012)

Population—distribution: though it has one of the highest population densities in the world, the population is not evenly dispersed; clustering is heaviest along the South China Sea and Gulf of Tonkin, with the Mekong Delta (in the south) and the Red River Valley (in the north) having the largest concentrations of people

Natural hazards: occasional typhoons (May to January) with extensive flooding, especially in the Mekong River delta

Environment—current issues: logging and slash-and-burn agricultural practices contribute to deforestation and soil degradation; water pollution and overfishing threaten marine life populations; groundwater contamination limits potable water supply; growing urban industrialization and population migration are rapidly degrading environment in Hanoi and Ho Chi Minh City

Environment—international agreements: *party to:* Biodiversity, Climate Change, Climate Change-Kyoto Protocol, Desertification, Endangered Species, Environmental Modification, Hazardous Wastes, Law of the Sea, Ozone Layer Protection, Ship Pollution, Wetlands
signed, but not ratified: none of the selected agreements

Geography—note: extending 1,650 km north to south, the country is only 50 km across at its narrowest point

PEOPLE AND SOCIETY

Population: 96,160,163 (July 2017 est.)
country comparison to the world: 15

Nationality: *noun:* Vietnamese (singular and plural)
adjective: Vietnamese

Ethnic groups: Kinh (Viet) 85.7%, Tay 1.9%, Thai 1.8%, Muong 1.5%, Khmer 1.5%, Mong 1.2%, Nung 1.1%, Hoa 1% other 4.3%
note: 54 ethnic groups are recognized by the Vietnamese Government (2009 est.)

Languages: Vietnamese (official), English (increasingly favored as a second language), some French, Chinese, and Khmer, mountain area languages (Mon-Khmer and Malayo-Polynesian)

Religions: Buddhist 7.9%, Catholic 6.6%, Hoa Hao 1.7%, Cao Dai 0.9%, Protestant 0.9%, Muslim 0.1%, none 81.8% (2009 est.)

Age structure: *0-14 years:* 23.55% (male 11,909,326/female 10,735,324)
15-24 years: 16.23% (male 8,098,019/female 7,509,021)
25-54 years: 45.56% (male 22,087,095/female 21,719,615)
55-64 years: 8.55% (male 3,798,928/female 4,419,837)
65 years and over: 6.12% (male 2,281,923/female 3,601,075) (2017 est.)

Dependency ratios: *total dependency ratio:* 42.5
youth dependency ratio: 32.9
elderly dependency ratio: 9.6
potential support ratio: 10.4 (2015 est.)

Median age: *total:* 30.5 years
male: 29.4 years
female: 31.7 years (2017 est.)
country comparison to the world: 114

Population growth rate: 0.93% (2017 est.)
country comparison to the world: 120

Birth rate: 15.5 births/1,000 population (2017 est.)
country comparison to the world: 122

Death rate: 5.9 deaths/1,000 population (2017 est.)
country comparison to the world: 170

Net migration rate: -0.3 migrant(s)/1,000 population (2017 est.)
country comparison to the world: 115

Population distribution: though it has one of the highest population densities in the world, the population is not evenly dispersed; clustering is heaviest along the South China Sea and Gulf of Tonkin, with the Mekong Delta (in the south) and the Red River Valley (in the north) having the largest concentrations of people

Urbanization: *urban population:* 34.9% of total population (2017)
rate of urbanization: 2.59% annual rate of change (2015-20 est.)

Major urban areas—population: Ho Chi Minh City 7.298 million; HANOI (capital) 3.629 million; Can Tho 1.175 million; Haiphong 1.075 million; Da Nang 952,000; Bien Hoa 834,000 (2015)

Sex ratio: *at birth:* 1.11 male(s)/female
0-14 years: 1.11 male(s)/female
15-24 years: 1.08 male(s)/female
25-54 years: 1.01 male(s)/female
55-64 years: 0.85 male(s)/female
65 years and over: 0.63 male(s)/female
total population: 1 male(s)/female (2016 est.)

Maternal mortality ratio: 54 deaths/100,000 live births (2015 est.)
country comparison to the world: 91

Infant mortality rate: *total:* 17.3 deaths/1,000 live births
male: 17.6 deaths/1,000 live births
female: 16.9 deaths/1,000 live births (2017 est.)
country comparison to the world: 94

Life expectancy at birth: *total population:* 73.7 years
male: 71.2 years
female: 76.4 years (2017 est.)
country comparison to the world: 132

Total fertility rate: 1.81 children born/woman (2017 est.)
country comparison to the world: 149

Contraceptive prevalence rate: 75.7% (2015)

Health expenditures: 7.1% of GDP (2014)
country comparison to the world: 79

Physicians density: 1.18 physicians/1,000 population (2013)

Hospital bed density: 2 beds/1,000 population (2010)

Drinking water source:
improved:
urban: 99.1% of population
rural: 96.9% of population
total: 97.6% of population
unimproved:
urban: 0.9% of population
rural: 3.1% of population
total: 2.4% of population (2015 est.)

Sanitation facility access:
improved:
urban: 94.4% of population
rural: 69.7% of population
total: 78% of population
unimproved:
urban: 5.6% of population
rural: 30.3% of population
total: 22% of population (2015 est.)

HIV/AIDS—adult prevalence rate: 0.4% (2016 est.)
country comparison to the world: 74

HIV/AIDS—people living with HIV/AIDS: 250,000 (2016 est.)
country comparison to the world: 22

HIV/AIDS—deaths: 8,000 (2016 est.)
country comparison to the world: 23

Major infectious diseases: *degree of risk:* very high
food or waterborne diseases: bacterial diarrhea, hepatitis A, and typhoid fever
vectorborne diseases: dengue fever, malaria, and Japanese encephalitis (2016)

Obesity—adult prevalence rate: 2.1% (2016)
country comparison to the world: 192

Children under the age of 5 years underweight: 14.1% (2015)
country comparison to the world: 60

Education expenditures: 5.7% of GDP (2013)
country comparison to the world: 33

Literacy: *definition:* age 15 and over can read and write
total population: 94.5%
male: 96.3%
female: 92.8% (2015 est.)

Unemployment, youth ages 15-24: *total:* 7%
male: 6.8%
female: 7.3% (2015 est.)
country comparison to the world: 124

GOVERNMENT

Country name: *conventional long form:* Socialist Republic of Vietnam

conventional short form: Vietnam
local long form: Cong Hoa Xa Hoi Chu Nghia Viet Nam
local short form: Viet Nam
abbreviation: SRV
etymology: "Viet nam" translates as "Viet south," where "Viet" is an ethnic self identification dating to a second century B.C. kingdom and "nam" refers to its location in relation to other Viet kingdoms

Government type: communist state

Capital: name: Hanoi (Ha Noi)

geographic coordinates: 21 02 N, 105 51 E
time difference: UTC+7 (12 hours ahead of Washington, DC, during Standard Time)

Administrative divisions: 58 provinces (tinh, singular and plural) and 5 municipalities (thanh pho, singular and plural)
provinces: An Giang, Bac Giang, Bac Kan, Bac Lieu, Bac Ninh, Ba Ria-Vung Tau, Ben Tre, Binh Dinh, Binh Duong, Binh Phuoc, Binh Thuan, Ca Mau, Cao Bang, Dak Lak, Dak Nong, Dien Bien, Dong Nai, Dong Thap, Gia Lai, Ha Giang, Ha Nam, Ha Tinh, Hai Duong, Hau Giang, Hoa Binh, Hung Yen, Khanh Hoa, Kien Giang, Kon Tum, Lai Chau, Lam Dong, Lang Son, Lao Cai, Long An, Nam Dinh, Nghe An, Ninh Binh, Ninh Thuan, Phu Tho, Phu Yen, Quang Binh, Quang Nam, Quang Ngai, Quang Ninh, Quang Tri, Soc Trang, Son La, Tay Ninh, Thai Binh, Thai Nguyen, Thanh Hoa, Thua Thien-Hue, Tien Giang, Tra Vinh, Tuyen Quang, Vinh Long, Vinh Phuc, Yen Bai
municipalities: Can Tho, Da Nang, Ha Noi, Hai Phong, Ho Chi Minh City (Saigon)

Independence: 2 September 1945 (from France)

National holiday: Independence Day (National Day), 2 September (1945)

Constitution: several previous; latest adopted 15 April 1992, effective 1 January 1995; amended 2001, 2013 (2016)

Legal system: civil law system; note—the civil code of 2005 reflects a European-style civil law

International law organization participation: has not submitted an ICJ jurisdiction declaration; non-party state to the ICCt

Citizenship: *citizenship by birth:* no
citizenship by descent only: at least one parent must be a citizen of Vietnam
dual citizenship recognized: no
residency requirement for naturalization: 5 years

Suffrage: 18 years of age; universal

Executive branch: *chief of state:* President Tran Dai QUANG (since 2 April 2016); Vice President Dang Thi Ngoc THINH (since 7 April 2016)

head of government: Prime Minister Nguyen Xuan PHUC (since 7 April 2016); Deputy Prime Ministers Truong Hoa BINH (since 9 April 2016), Vuong Dinh HUE (since 9 April 2016), Vu Duc DAM (since 13 November 2013), Trinh Dinh DUNG (since 9 April 2016), Pham Binh MINH (since 13 November 2013)

cabinet: Cabinet proposed by prime minister, appointed by the president, and confirmed by the National Assembly
elections/appointments: president indirectly elected by National Assembly from among its members for a single 5-year term; election last held on 2 April 2016 (next to be held in spring 2021); prime minister appointed by the president from among members of the National Assembly, confirmed by National Assembly; deputy prime ministers appointed by the prime minister, confirmed by National Assembly
election results: Tran Dai QUANG (CPV) elected president; percent of National Assembly vote—98.9%; Nguyen Xuan PHUC elected prime minister; percent of National Assembly vote—91.0%

Legislative branch: description: unicameral National Assembly or Quoc Hoi (500 seats; members directly elected by absolute majority vote with a second round if needed; members serve 5-year terms)
elections: last held on 22 May 2016 (next to be held in May 2021)
election results: percent of vote by party—CPV 95.8%, non-party members 4.2%; seats by party—CPV 473, non-party CPV-approved 19, self-nominated 2; note—496 candidates elected, 2 CPV candidates-elect were disqualified

Judicial branch: *highest court(s):* Supreme People's Court (consists of the chief justice and 13 judges)
judge selection and term of office: chief justice elected by the National Assembly on the recommendation of the president for a 5-year, renewable term; other judges appointed by the president for 5-year terms
subordinate courts: Court of Appeals; administrative, civil, criminal, economic, and labor courts; Central Military Court; People's Special Courts; note—the National Assembly can establish special tribunals

Political parties and leaders: Communist Party of Vietnam or CPV [Nguyen Phu TRONG]
note: other parties proscribed

Political pressure groups and leaders: 8406 Bloc
Democratic Party of Vietnam or DPV
People's Democratic Party Vietnam or PDP-VN
Alliance for Democracy
note: these groups advocate democracy but are not recognized by the government

International organization participation: ADB, APEC, ARF, ASEAN, CICA, CP, EAS, FAO, G-77, IAEA, IBRD, ICAO, ICC (NGOs), ICRM, IDA, IFAD, IFC, IFRCS, ILO, IMF, IMO, IMSO, Interpol, IOC, IOM, IPU, ISO, ITSO, ITU, MIGA, NAM, OIF, OPCW, PCA, UN, UNCTAD, UNESCO, UNIDO, UNWTO, UPU, WCO, WFTU (NGOs), WHO, WIPO, WMO, WTO

Diplomatic representation in the US: *chief of mission:* Ambassador Pham Quang VINH (since 23 February 2015)
chancery: 1233 20th Street NW, Suite 400, Washington, DC 20036

telephone: [1] (202) 861-0737
FAX: [1] (202) 861-0917
consulate(s) general: Houston, San Francisco
consulate: New York

Diplomatic representation from the US: *chief of mission:* Ambassador Daniel KRITENBRINK (since 6 November 2017)
embassy: 7 Lang Ha Street, Hanoi
mailing address: 7 Lang Ha Street, Ba Dinh District, Hanoi; 4550 Hanoi Place, Washington, DC 20521-4550
telephone: [84] (4) 3850-5000
FAX: [84] (4) 3850-5010
consulate(s) general: Ho Chi Minh City

Flag description: red field with a large yellow five-pointed star in the center; red symbolizes revolution and blood, the five-pointed star represents the five elements of the populace—peasants, workers, intellectuals, traders, and soldiers—that unite to build socialism

National symbol(s): yellow, five-pointed star on red field; lotus blossom; national colors: red, yellow

National anthem: name: "Tien quan ca" (The Song of the Marching Troops)
lyrics/music: Nguyen Van CAO
note: adopted as the national anthem of the Democratic Republic of Vietnam in 1945; it became the national anthem of the unified Socialist Republic of Vietnam in 1976; although it consists of two verses, only the first is used as the official anthem

ECONOMY

Economy—overview: Vietnam is a densely populated developing country that has been transitioning since 1986 from the rigidities of a centrally planned, highly agrarian economy to a more industrial and market based economy, and it has raised incomes substantially. In 2016 and 2017, Vietnam missed its yearly growth target of 6.7% due to environmental issues—drought and salinization—impacting the agricultural sector, and low oil prices affecting the extractive sector. However, annual GDP growth reached 6.3%, reflecting strengthening domestic demand and strong manufacturing exports.

Vietnam has a young population, stable political system, commitment to sustainable growth, relatively low inflation, stable currency, strong FDI inflows, and strong manufacturing sector. In addition, the country is committed to continuing its global economic integration. Vietnam joined the WTO in January 2007 and concluded several free trade agreements in 2015-16, including the EU-Vietnam Free Trade Agreement, the Korean Free Trade Agreement, and the Eurasian Economic Union Free Trade Agreement. In 2017, Vietnam successfully chaired the Asia-Pacific Economic Cooperation (APEC) Conference with its key priorities including inclusive growth, innovation, strengthening small and medium enterprises, food security and climate change. Seeking to diversify its opportunities, Vietnam also continued to pursue other multilateral relationships, including the Comprehensive and Progressive Agreement for the Transpacific Partnership and the Regional Comprehensive Economic Partnership.

To continue its trajectory of strong economic growth, the government acknowledges the need to spark a second wave' of reforms, including reforming state-owned-enterprises, reducing red tape, increasing business sector transparency, reducing the level of non-performing loans in the banking sector, and increasing financial sector transparency. Vietnam's public debt to GDP ratio is nearing the government mandated ceiling of 65%.

In 2016, Vietnam cancelled its civilian nuclear energy development program, citing public concerns about safety and the high cost of the program; it faces growing pressure on energy infrastructure. Overall, the country's infrastructure fails to meet the needs of an expanding middle class. Vietnam has demonstrated a commitment to sustainable growth over the last several years, but the recent slowdown in economic growth could test the government's resolve.

GDP (purchasing power parity): $643.9 billion (2017 est.)
$605.7 billion (2016 est.)
$570.3 billion (2015 est.)
note: data are in 2017 dollars
country comparison to the world: 36

GDP (official exchange rate): $216 billion (2016 est.)

GDP—real growth rate: 6.3% (2017 est.)
6.2% (2016 est.)
6.7% (2015 est.)
country comparison to the world: 20

GDP—per capita (PPP): $6,900 (2017 est.)
$6,500 (2016 est.)
$6,200 (2015 est.)
note: data are in 2017 dollars
country comparison to the world: 159

Gross national saving: 28% of GDP (2017 est.)
30.7% of GDP (2016 est.)
27.5% of GDP (2015 est.)
country comparison to the world: 36

GDP—composition, by end use:
household consumption: 68.5%
government consumption: 6.6%
investment in fixed capital: 24.8%
investment in inventories: 2.9%
exports of goods and services: 98.6%
imports of goods and services: -101.4% (2017 est.)

GDP—composition, by sector of origin:
agriculture: 15.9%
industry: 32.7%
services: 41.3% (2017 est.)

Agriculture—products: rice, coffee, rubber, tea, pepper, soybeans, cashews, sugar cane, peanuts, bananas; pork; poultry; seafood

Industries: food processing, garments, shoes, machine-building; mining, coal, steel; cement, chemical fertilizer, glass, tires, oil, mobile phones

Industrial production growth rate: 6.4% (2017 est.)
country comparison to the world: 31

Labor force: 56.46 million (2017 est.)

country comparison to the world: 12
Labor force—by occupation: agriculture: 48%
industry: 21%
services: 31% (2012)

Unemployment rate: 2.3% (2017 est.)
2.3% (2016 est.)
country comparison to the world: 19

Population below poverty line: 11.3% (2012 est.)

Household income or consumption by percentage share: *lowest 10%:* 3.2%
highest 10%: 30.2% (2008)

Distribution of family income—Gini index: 37.6 (2008)
36.1 (1998)
country comparison to the world: 76

Budget: *revenues:* $49.41 billion
expenditures: $61.14 billion (2017 est.)

Taxes and other revenues: 22.9% of GDP (2017 est.)
country comparison to the world: 131

Budget surplus (+) or deficit (-): -5.4% of GDP (2017 est.)
country comparison to the world: 168

Public debt: 62.3% of GDP (2017 est.)
61.6% of GDP (2016 est.)
note: official data; data cover general government debt, and includes debt instruments issued (or owned) by government entities other than the treasury; the data include treasury debt held by foreign entities; the data include debt issued by subnational entities, as well as intra-governmental debt; intra-governmental debt consists of treasury borrowings from surpluses in the social funds, such as for retirement, medical care, and unemployment; debt instruments for the social funds are not sold at public auctions
country comparison to the world: 69

Fiscal year: calendar year

Inflation rate (consumer prices): 4.4% (2017 est.)
2.7% (2016 est.)
country comparison to the world: 164

Central bank discount rate: 9% (31 December 2012)
15% (31 December 2011)
country comparison to the world: 29

Commercial bank prime lending rate: 6.8% (31 December 2017 est.)
6.96% (31 December 2016 est.)
country comparison to the world: 120

Stock of narrow money: $84.22 billion (31 December 2017 est.)
$73.48 billion (31 December 2016 est.)
country comparison to the world: 44

Stock of broad money: $341.4 billion (31 December 2017 est.)
$299.2 billion (31 December 2016 est.)
country comparison to the world: 33

Stock of domestic credit: $320.1 billion (31 December 2017 est.)
$277.3 billion (31 December 2016 est.)
country comparison to the world: 39

Market value of publicly traded shares: $51.88 billion (31 December 2015 est.)
$46.07 billion (31 December 2014 est.)
$40.06 billion (31 December 2013 est.)
country comparison to the world: 51

Current account balance: $2.794 billion (2017 est.)
$8.235 billion (2016 est.)
country comparison to the world: 31

Exports: $194.6 billion (2017 est.)
$176.6 billion (2016 est.)
country comparison to the world: 28

Exports—commodities: clothes, shoes, electronics, seafood, crude oil, rice, coffee, wooden products, machinery

Exports—partners: US 20.2%, China 14.2%, Japan 8.2%, South Korea 6.2% (2016)

Imports: $190.1 billion (2017 est.)
$162.6 billion (2016 est.)
country comparison to the world: 25

Imports—commodities: machinery and equipment, petroleum products, steel products, raw materials for the clothing and shoe industries, electronics, plastics, automobiles

Imports—partners: China 25.1%, South Korea 17.5%, Japan 7.9%, US 6%, Thailand 4.7% (2016)

Reserves of foreign exchange and gold: $38.75 billion (31 December 2017 est.)
$36.91 billion (31 December 2016 est.)
country comparison to the world: 45

Debt—external: $91.79 billion (31 December 2017 est.)
$84.34 billion (31 December 2016 est.)
country comparison to the world: 52

Stock of direct foreign investment—at home: $128.3 billion (31 December 2017 est.)
$115.4 billion (31 December 2016 est.)
country comparison to the world: 42

Stock of direct foreign investment—abroad: $7.7 billion (31 December 2009 est.)
$5.3 billion (31 December 2008 est.)
country comparison to the world: 66

Exchange rates: dong (VND) per US dollar—
22,784 (2017 est.)
22,355 (2016 est.)
22,355 (2015 est.)
21,909 (2014 est.)
21,189 (2013 est.)

ENERGY

Electricity access: population without electricity: 2,600,000
electrification—*total population:* 99%
electrification—urban areas: 100%
electrification—rural areas: 98% (2013)

Electricity—production: 146.9 billion kWh (2015 est.)
country comparison to the world: 29

Electricity—consumption: 134.3 billion kWh (2015 est.)
country comparison to the world: 26

Electricity—exports: 811 million kWh (2015 est.)

country comparison to the world: 60

Electricity—imports: 2.393 billion kWh (2015 est.)
country comparison to the world: 52

Electricity—installed generating capacity: 40.49 million kW (2015 est.)
country comparison to the world: 25

Electricity—from fossil fuels: 58% of total installed capacity (2015 est.)
country comparison to the world: 134

Electricity—from nuclear fuels: 0% of total installed capacity (2015 est.)
country comparison to the world: 206

Electricity—from hydroelectric plants: 41% of total installed capacity (2015 est.)
country comparison to the world: 49

Electricity—from other renewable sources: 1% of total installed capacity (2015 est.)
country comparison to the world: 141

Crude oil—production: 301,800 bbl/day (2016 est.)
country comparison to the world: 32

Crude oil—exports: 183,600 bbl/day (2014 est.)
country comparison to the world: 32

Crude oil—imports: 0 bbl/day (2014 est.)
country comparison to the world: 208

Crude oil—proved reserves: 4.4 billion bbl (1 January 2017 es)
country comparison to the world: 26

Refined petroleum products—production: 156,900 bbl/day (2014 est.)
country comparison to the world: 57

Refined petroleum products—consumption: 422,000 bbl/day (2015 est.)
country comparison to the world: 37

Refined petroleum products—exports: 28,860 bbl/day (2014 est.)
country comparison to the world: 62

Refined petroleum products—imports: 256,600 bbl/day (2014 est.)
country comparison to the world: 28

Natural gas—production: 9.08 billion cu m (2015 est.)
country comparison to the world: 43

Natural gas—consumption: 15.5 billion cu m (2015 est.)
country comparison to the world: 48

Natural gas—exports: 0 cu m (2013 est.)
country comparison to the world: 207

Natural gas—imports: 0 cu m (2013 est.)
country comparison to the world: 206

Natural gas—proved reserves: 699.4 billion cu m (1 January 2017 es)
country comparison to the world: 29

Carbon dioxide emissions from consumption of energy: 142 million Mt (2013 est.)
country comparison to the world: 34

COMMUNICATIONS

Telephones—fixed lines: *total subscriptions:* 5,598,017

subscriptions per 100 inhabitants: 6 (July 2016 est.)
country comparison to the world: 28

Telephones—mobile cellular: *total:* 122 million
subscriptions per 100 inhabitants: 129 (July 2016 est.)
country comparison to the world: 10

Telephone system: *general assessment:* Vietnam is putting considerable effort into modernization and expansion of its telecommunication system
domestic: all provincial exchanges are digitalized and connected to Hanoi, Da Nang, and Ho Chi Minh City by fiber-optic cable or microwave radio relay networks; main lines have been increased, and the use of mobile telephones is growing rapidly
international: country code—84; a landing point for the SEA-ME-WE-3, the C2C, and Thailand-Vietnam-Hong Kong submarine cable systems; the Asia-America Gateway submarine cable system, completed in 2009, provided new access links to Asia and the US; satellite earth stations—2 Intersputnik (Indian Ocean region) (2016)

Broadcast media: government controls all broadcast media exercising oversight through the Ministry of Information and Communication (MIC); government-controlled national TV provider, Vietnam Television (VTV), operates a network of 9 channels with several regional broadcasting centers; programming is relayed nationwide via a network of provincial and municipal TV stations; law limits access to satellite TV but many households are able to access foreign programming via home satellite equipment; government-controlled Voice of Vietnam, the national radio broadcaster, broadcasts on 6 channels and is repeated on AM, FM, and shortwave stations throughout Vietnam (2008)

Internet country code: .vn

Internet users: *total:* 49.741 million

percent of population: 52.7% (July 2016 est.)
country comparison to the world: 16

TRANSPORTATION

National air transport system: *number of registered air carriers:* 4
inventory of registered aircraft operated by air carriers: 140
annual passenger traffic on registered air carriers: 29,944,771
annual freight traffic on registered air carriers: 384,470,240 mt-km (2015)
Civil aircraft registration country code prefix: VN (2016)

Airports: 45 (2013)
country comparison to the world: 97

Airports—with paved runways: *total:* 38
over 3,047 m: 10
2,438 to 3,047 m: 6
1,524 to 2,437 m: 13
914 to 1,523 m: 9 (2013)

Airports—with unpaved runways: *total:* 7
1,524 to 2,437 m: 1
914 to 1,523 m: 3
under 914 m: 3 (2013)

Heliports: 1 (2013)

Pipelines: condensate 72 km; condensate/gas 398 km; gas 955 km; oil 128 km; oil/gas/water 33 km; refined products 206 km; water 13 km (2013)

Railways: *total:* 2,600 km
standard gauge: 178 km 1.435-m gauge; 253 km mixed gauge
narrow gauge: 2,169 km 1.000-m gauge (2014)
country comparison to the world: 64

Roadways: *total:* 195,468 km
paved: 148,338 km
unpaved: 47,130 km (2013)
country comparison to the world: 28

Waterways: 47,130 km (30,831 km weight under 50 tons) (2011)
country comparison to the world: 4

Merchant marine: *total:* 1,818
by type: bulk carrier 81, container ship 34, general cargo 1,259, oil tanker 109, other 335 (2017)
country comparison to the world: 13

Ports and terminals: *major seaport(s):* Cam Pha Port, Da Nang, Haiphong, Phu My, Quy Nhon
river port(s): Ho Chi Minh (Mekong)
container port(s) (TEUs): Saigon (6,556,000), Saigon New Port (5,026,000) (2015)

MILITARY AND SECURITY

Military expenditures: 2.44% of GDP (2016)
2.36% of GDP (2015)
2.29% of GDP (2014)
2.18% of GDP (2013)
2.16% of GDP (2012)
country comparison to the world: 33

Military branches: People's Armed Forces: People's Army of Vietnam (PAVN, includes Vietnam People's Navy (with Naval Infantry), Vietnam People's Air and Air Defense Force, Border Defense Command, Coast Guard) (2013)

Military service age and obligation: 18-25 years of age for male compulsory and voluntary military service; females may volunteer for active duty military service; conscription typically takes place twice annually and service obligation is 18 months (Army, Air Defense), 2 years (Navy and Air Force); 18-45 years of age (male) or 18-40 years of age (female) for Militia Force or Self Defense Force service; males may enroll in military schools at age 17 (2013)
Maritime threats: the International Maritime Bureau reports the territorial and offshore waters in the South China Sea as high risk for piracy and armed robbery against ships; numerous commercial vessels have been attacked and hijacked both at anchor and while underway; hijacked vessels are often disguised and cargo diverted to ports in East Asia; crews have been murdered or cast adrift; the number of reported incidents declined from 15 in 2015 to seven in 2016, primarily near the port of Vung Tau

TRANSNATIONAL ISSUES

Disputes—international: southeast Asian states have enhanced border surveillance to check the spread of avian flu; Cambodia and Laos protest

Vietnamese squatters and armed encroachments along border; Cambodia accuses Vietnam of a wide variety of illicit cross-border activities; progress on a joint development area with Cambodia is hampered by an unresolved dispute over sovereignty of offshore islands; an estimated 300,000 Vietnamese refugees reside in China; establishment of a maritime boundary with Cambodia is hampered by unresolved dispute over the sovereignty of offshore islands; the decade-long demarcation of the China-Vietnam land boundary was completed in 2009; China occupies the Paracel Islands also claimed by Vietnam and Taiwan; Brunei claims a maritime boundary extending beyond as far as a median with Vietnam, thus asserting an implicit claim to Lousia Reef; the 2002 "Declaration on the Conduct of Parties in the South China Sea" has eased tensions but falls short of a legally binding "code of conduct" desired by several of the disputants; Vietnam continues to expand construction of facilities in the Spratly Islands; in March 2005, the national oil companies of China, the Philippines, and Vietnam signed a joint accord to conduct marine seismic activities in the Spratly Islands; Economic Exclusion Zone negotiations with Indonesia are ongoing, and the two countries in Fall 2011 agreed to work together to reduce illegal fishing along their maritime boundary

Refugees and internally displaced persons: *stateless persons:* 11,000 (2016); note—Vietnam's stateless ethnic Chinese Cambodian population dates to the 1970s when thousands of Cambodians fled to Vietnam to escape the Khmer Rouge and were no longer recognized as Cambodian citizens; Vietnamese women who gave up their citizenship to marry foreign men have found themselves stateless after divorcing and returning home to Vietnam; the government addressed this problem in 2009, and Vietnamese women are beginning to reclaim their citizenship

Illicit drugs: minor producer of opium poppy; probable minor transit point for Southeast Asian heroin; government continues to face domestic opium/heroin/methamphetamine addiction problems despite longstanding crackdowns; enforces the death penalty for drug trafficking

VIRGIN ISLANDS

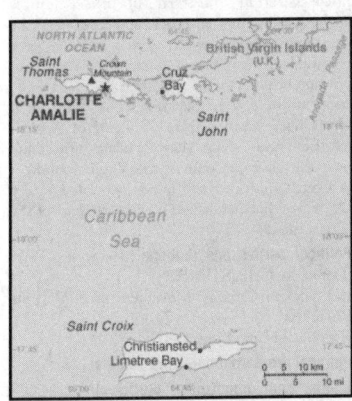

INTRODUCTION

Background: The Danes secured control over the southern Virgin Islands of Saint Thomas, Saint John, and Saint Croix during the 17th and early 18th centuries. Sugarcane, produced by African slave labor, drove the islands' economy during the 18th and early 19th centuries. In 1917, the US purchased the Danish holdings, which had been in economic decline since the abolition of slavery in 1848. On 6 September 2017, Hurricane Irma passed over the northern Virgin Islands of Saint Thomas and Saint John and inflicted severe damage to structures, roads, the airport on Saint Thomas, communications, and electricity. Less than two weeks later, Hurricane Maria passed over the island of Saint Croix in the southern Virgin Islands, inflicting considerable damage with heavy winds and flooding rains.

GEOGRAPHY

Location: Caribbean, islands between the Caribbean Sea and the North Atlantic Ocean, east of Puerto Rico

Geographic coordinates: 18 20 N, 64 50 W

Map references: Central America and the Caribbean

Area: *total:* 1,910 sq km
land: 346 sq km
water: 1,564 sq km
country comparison to the world: 182

Area—comparative: twice the size of Washington, DC

Land boundaries: 0 km

Coastline: 188 km

Maritime claims: *territorial sea:* 12 nm
exclusive economic zone: 200 nm

Climate: subtropical, tempered by easterly trade winds, relatively low humidity, little seasonal temperature variation; rainy season September to November

Terrain: mostly hilly to rugged and mountainous with little flat land

Elevation: *mean elevation:* NA

elevation extremes: *lowest point:* Caribbean Sea 0 m
highest point: Crown Mountain 474 m

Natural resources: pleasant climate, beaches foster tourism

Land use: *agricultural land:* 11.5%
arable land: 2.9%;
permanent crops: 2.9%;
permanent pasture: 5.7%;
forest: 57.4%
other: 31.1% (2011 est.)
Irrigated land: 1 sq km (2012)

Population—distribution: while overall population density throughout the islands is relatively low, concentrations appear around Charlotte Amalie on St. Thomas and Christiansted on St. Croix

Natural hazards: several hurricanes in recent years; frequent and severe droughts and floods; occasional earthquakes

Environment—current issues: lack of natural freshwater resources

Geography—note: important location along the Anegada Passage—a key shipping lane for the Panama Canal; Saint Thomas has one of the best natural deepwater harbors in the Caribbean

PEOPLE AND SOCIETY

Population: 107,268 (July 2017 est.)
country comparison to the world: 192

Nationality: *noun:* Virgin Islander(s) (US citizens)
adjective: Virgin Islander

Ethnic groups: black 76%, white 15.6%, Asian 1.4%, other 4.9%, mixed 2.1%
note: 17.4% self-identify as latino (2010 est.)

Languages: English 71.6%, Spanish or Spanish Creole 17.2%, French or French Creole 8.6%, other 2.5% (2010 est.)

Religions: Protestant 59% (Baptist 42%, Episcopalian 17%), Roman Catholic 34%, other 7%

Age structure: *0-14 years:* 20.41% (male 11,220/female 10,671)
15-24 years: 11.19% (male 5,853/female 6,154)
25-54 years: 37.07% (male 18,587/female 21,182)
55-64 years: 13.78% (male 6,967/female 7,812)
65 years and over: 17.55% (male 8,618/female 10,204) (2017 est.)

Dependency ratios: *total dependency ratio:* 60.8
youth dependency ratio: 32.8
elderly dependency ratio: 28
potential support ratio: 3.6 (2015 est.)

Median age: *total:* 41 years
male: 39.9 years
female: 41.9 years (2017 est.)
country comparison to the world: 5

Population growth rate: -0.25% (2017 est.)
country comparison to the world: 215

Birth rate: 12.8 births/1,000 population (2017 est.)
country comparison to the world: 155

Death rate: 7.8 deaths/1,000 population (2017 est.)
country comparison to the world: 99

Net migration rate: -7.5 migrant(s)/1,000 population (2017 est.)
country comparison to the world: 204

Population distribution: while overall population density throughout the islands is relatively low, concentrations appear around Charlotte Amalie on St. Thomas and Christiansted on St. Croix

Urbanization: *urban population:* 95.6% of total population (2017)
rate of urbanization: 0.08% annual rate of change (2015-20 est.)

Major urban areas—population: CHARLOTTE AMALIE (capital) 52,000 (2014)

Sex ratio: *at birth:* 1.06 male(s)/female
0-14 years: 1.02 male(s)/female
15-24 years: 0.82 male(s)/female
25-54 years: 0.82 male(s)/female
55-64 years: 0.93 male(s)/female
65 years and over: 0.83 male(s)/female
total population: 0.87 male(s)/female (2016 est.)

Infant mortality rate: *total:* 7.9 deaths/1,000 live births
male: 9 deaths/1,000 live births
female: 6.8 deaths/1,000 live births (2017 est.)
country comparison to the world: 156

Life expectancy at birth: *total population:* 79.4 years
male: 76.2 years
female: 82.8 years (2017 est.)
country comparison to the world: 49

Total fertility rate: 2.08 children born/woman (2017 est.)
country comparison to the world: 108

Drinking water source:
improved:
urban: 100% of population
rural: 100% of population
total: 100% of population
unimproved:
urban: 0% of population
rural: 0% of population
total: 0% of population (2015 est.)

Sanitation facility access:
improved:
urban: 96.4% of population
rural: 96.4% of population
total: 96.4% of population
unimproved:
urban: 3.6% of population
rural: 3.6% of population
total: 3.6% of population (2015 est.)

HIV/AIDS—adult prevalence rate: NA

HIV/AIDS—people living with HIV/AIDS: NA

HIV/AIDS—deaths: NA

Major infectious diseases: note: active local transmission of Zika virus by Aedes species mosquitoes has been identified in this country (as of August 2016); it poses an important risk (a large number of cases possible) among US citizens if bitten by an infective mosquito; other less common ways to get Zika are through sex, via blood transfusion, or during pregnancy, in which the pregnant woman passes Zika virus to her fetus (2016)

GOVERNMENT

Country name: *conventional long form:* United States Virgin Islands
conventional short form: Virgin Islands
former: Danish West Indies
abbreviation: USVI
etymology: the myriad islets, cays, and rocks surrounding the major islands reminded Christopher COLUMBUS in 1493 of Saint Ursula and her 11,000 virgin followers (Santa Ursula y las Once Mil Virgenes), which over time shortened to the Virgins (las Virgenes)

Dependency status: organized, unincorporated territory of the US with policy relations between the Virgin Islands and the US under the jurisdiction of the Office of Insular Affairs, US Department of the Interior

Government type: presidential democracy; a self-governing territory of the US

Capital: *name:* Charlotte Amalie
geographic coordinates: 18 21 N, 64 56 W
time difference: UTC-4 (1 hour ahead of Washington, DC, during Standard Time)

Administrative divisions: none (territory of the US); there are no first-order administrative divisions as defined by the US Government, but there are 3 islands at the second order; Saint Croix, Saint John, Saint Thomas

Independence: none (territory of the US)

National holiday: Transfer Day (from Denmark to the US), 31 March (1917)

Constitution: 22 July 1954—the Revised Organic Act of the Virgin Islands functions as a constitution for this territory of the US; revised 1962, 2000 (2016)

Legal system: US common law

Citizenship: see United States

Suffrage: 18 years of age; universal; note—island residents are US citizens but do not vote in US presidential elections

Executive branch: *chief of state:* President Donald J. TRUMP (since 20 January 2017); Vice President Michael R. PENCE (since 20 January 2017)
head of government: Governor Kenneth MAPP (since 5 January 2015), Lieutenant Governor Osbert POTTER (since 5 January 2015)
cabinet: Territorial Cabinet appointed by the governor and confirmed by the Senate
elections/appointments: president and vice president indirectly elected on the same ballot by an Electoral College of 'electors' chosen from each state; president and vice president serve a 4-year term (eligible for a second term); under the US Constitution, residents of the Virgin Islands do not vote in elections for US president and vice president; however, they may vote in the Democratic and Republican presidential primary elections; governor and lieutenant governor directly elected on the same ballot by absolute majority vote in 2 rounds if needed for a 4-year term (eligible for a second term); election last held on 4 November 2014 (next to be held in November 2018)
election results: Kenneth MAPP elected governor in second round; percent of vote—Kenneth MAPP (independent) 63.9%, Donna CHRISTIAN-CHRISTIANSEN (Democratic Party) 36.1%

Legislative branch: *description:* unicameral Senate (15 seats; members directly elected in single- and multi-seat constituencies by simple majority popular vote to serve 2-year terms)
elections: last held on 8 November 2016 (next to be held on 6 November 2018)
election results: percent of vote by party—NA; seats by party—Democratic Party 10, ICM 1, independent 4
note: the Virgin Islands directly elects 1 member by simple majority vote to serve a 2-year term as a delegate to the US House of Representatives; the delegate can vote when serving on a committee and when the House meets as the Committee of the Whole House, but not when legislation is submitted for a "full floor" House vote; election of delegate last held on 8 November 2016 (next to be held on 6 November 2018)

Judicial branch: *highest court(s):* Supreme Court of the Virgin Islands (consists of the chief justice and 2 associate justices); note—court established by US Congress in 2004 and assumed appellate jurisdiction in 2007
judge selection and term of office: justices appointed by the governor and confirmed by the Virgin Islands Senate; justices initially serve renewable 10-year terms; chief justice elected to position by peers for a 3-year term
subordinate courts: Superior Court (Territorial Court renamed in 2004); US Court of Appeals for the Third Circuit (has appellate jurisdiction over the District Court of the Virgin Islands; it is a territorial court and is not associated with a US federal judicial district); District Court of the Virgin Islands

Political parties and leaders: Democratic Party [Donna M. CHRISTENSEN]
Independent Citizens' Movement or ICM [Dale BLYDEN]
Republican Party [John CANEGATA]

Political pressure groups and leaders: NA

International organization participation: AOSIS (observer), Interpol (subbureau), IOC, UPU, WFTU (NGOs)

Diplomatic representation in the US: none (territory of the US)

Diplomatic representation from the US: none (territory of the US)

Flag description: white field with a modified US coat of arms in the center between the large blue initials V and I; the coat of arms shows a yellow eagle holding an olive branch in its right talon and three arrows in the left with a superimposed shield of seven red and six white vertical stripes below a blue panel; white is a symbol of purity, the letters stand for the Virgin Islands

National anthem: *name:* "Virgin Islands March"
lyrics/music: multiple/Alton Augustus ADAMS, Sr.
note: adopted 1963; serves as a local anthem; as a territory of the US, "The Star-Spangled Banner" is official (see United States)

ECONOMY

Economy—overview: Tourism, trade, and other services are the primary economic activities, accounting for nearly 60% of the Virgin Island's GDP and about half of total civilian employment. The islands host nearly 3 million tourists per year, mostly from visiting cruise ships. The islands are vulnerable to damage from storms. The agriculture sector is small, with most food being imported. Industry and government each account for about one-fifth of GDP. The manufacturing sector consists of rum distilling, electronics, pharmaceuticals, and watch assembly. A refinery on St. Croix, one of the world's largest, processed 350,000 barrels of crude oil a day until it was shut down in February 2012, after operating for 45 years.

Federal programs and grants, totaling $241.4 million in 2013, contributed 19.7% of the territory's total revenues. The economy declined in 2013, due to decreases in exports resulting from the loss of refined oil products. Nevertheless, the economy remains relatively diversified. Along with a vibrant tourism industry, rum exports, trade, and services will be major income sources in future years.

GDP (purchasing power parity): $3.792 billion (2013 est.)
$4.143 billion (2012 est.)
$4.288 billion (2011 est.)
note: data are in 2013 dollars
country comparison to the world: 180

GDP (official exchange rate): $5.075 billion (2013)

GDP—real growth rate: -5.4% (2013 est.)
-13.8% (2012 est.)
-7.5% (2011 est.)
country comparison to the world: 218

GDP—per capita (PPP): $36,100 (2013 est.)
$39,300 (2012 est.)

$40,500 (2011 est.)
country comparison to the world: 54

GDP—composition, by end use:
household consumption: 63.6%
government consumption: 28%

investment in fixed assets: 6.1%
investment in inventories: NA%
exports of goods and services: 69.3%
imports of goods and services: -66.9% (2013)

GDP—composition, by sector of origin:
agriculture: 2%
industry: 20%
services: 78% (2012 est.)

Agriculture—products: fruit, vegetables, sorghum; Senepol cattle

Industries: tourism, watch assembly, rum distilling, construction, pharmaceuticals, electronics

Industrial production growth rate: NA%

Labor force: 50,580 (2012 est.)
country comparison to the world: 194
Labor force—by occupation: agriculture: 1%
industry: 19%
services: 80% (2003 est.)

Unemployment rate: 13% (2014)
country comparison to the world: 163

Population below poverty line: 28.9% (2002 est.)

Household income or consumption by percentage share: *lowest 10%:* NA%
highest 10%: NA%

Budget: *revenues:* $1.223 billion
expenditures: $1.551 billion (2013)

Taxes and other revenues: 24.1% of GDP (2013)
country comparison to the world: 123

Budget surplus (+) or deficit (-): -6.5% of GDP (2013)

country comparison to the world: 183

Public debt: 45.9% of GDP (2014)
country comparison to the world: 116

Fiscal year: 1 October—30 September

Inflation rate (consumer prices): 3.1% (2012)
country comparison to the world: 132

Exports: $2.627 billion (2013)
$3.339 billion (2012)
country comparison to the world: 131

Exports—commodities: rum

Imports: $2.694 billion (2013)
$3.056 billion (2012)
country comparison to the world: 147

Imports—commodities: foodstuffs, consumer goods, building materials

Debt—external: $NA

Exchange rates: the US dollar is used

ENERGY

Electricity access: population without electricity: 10,295
electrification—*total population:* 91%
electrification—urban areas: 91%
electrification—rural areas: 80% (2012)

Electricity—production: 679 million kWh (2015 est.)
country comparison to the world: 159

Electricity—consumption: 117.2 million kWh (2015 est.)
country comparison to the world: 199

Electricity—exports: 0 kWh (2016 est.)
country comparison to the world: 214

Electricity—imports: 0 kWh (2016 est.)
country comparison to the world: 217

Electricity—installed generating capacity: 316,000 kW (2015 est.)
country comparison to the world: 155

Electricity—from fossil fuels: 13.9% of total installed capacity (2015 est.)
country comparison to the world: 199

Electricity—from nuclear fuels: 0% of total installed capacity (2015 est.)
country comparison to the world: 207

Electricity—from hydroelectric plants: 0% of total installed capacity (2015 est.)
country comparison to the world: 211

Electricity—from other renewable sources: 1.3% of total installed capacity (2015 est.)
country comparison to the world: 134

Crude oil—production: 0 bbl/day (2016 est.)
country comparison to the world: 213

Crude oil—exports: 0 bbl/day (2014 est.)
country comparison to the world: 209

Crude oil—imports: 0 bbl/day (2014 est.)
country comparison to the world: 209

Crude oil—proved reserves: 0 bbl (1 January 2017 es)
country comparison to the world: 213

Refined petroleum products—production: 0 bbl/day (2014 est.)
country comparison to the world: 214

Refined petroleum products—consumption: 132,000 bbl/day (2015 est.)
country comparison to the world: 75

Refined petroleum products—exports: 0 bbl/day (2014 est.)

country comparison to the world: 212

Refined petroleum products—imports: 130,000 bbl/day (2014 est.)
country comparison to the world: 51

Natural gas—production: 0 cu m (2014 est.)
country comparison to the world: 210

Natural gas—consumption: 0 cu m (2014 est.)
country comparison to the world: 145

Natural gas—exports: 0 cu m (2014 est.)
country comparison to the world: 208

Natural gas—imports: 0 cu m (2014 est.)
country comparison to the world: 207

Natural gas—proved reserves: 0 cu m (1 January 2014 es)
country comparison to the world: 206

Carbon dioxide emissions from consumption of energy: 9.4 million Mt (2013 est.)
country comparison to the world: 105

COMMUNICATIONS

Telephones—fixed lines: *total subscriptions:* 76,000
subscriptions per 100 inhabitants: 73 (July 2016 est.)
country comparison to the world: 149

Telephone system: *general assessment:* modern system with total digital switching, uses fiber-optic cable and microwave radio relay
domestic: full range of services available
international: country code—1-340; submarine cable connections to US, the Caribbean, Central and South America; satellite earth stations—NA (2016)

Broadcast media: about a dozen TV broadcast stations including 1 public TV station; multi-channel cable and satellite TV services are available; 24 radio stations (2009)

Internet country code: .vi

Internet users: *total:* 57,000

percent of population: 54.8% (July 2016 est.)
country comparison to the world: 195

TRANSPORTATION

Airports: 2 (2013)
country comparison to the world: 207

Airports—with paved runways: *total:* 2
over 3,047 m: 1
1,524 to 2,437 m: 1 (2013)

Roadways: *total:* 1,260 km (2008)
country comparison to the world: 181

Ports and terminals: *major seaport(s):* Charlotte Amalie, Christiansted, Cruz Bay, Frederiksted, Limetree Bay

MILITARY AND SECURITY

Military—note: defense is the responsibility of the US

TRANSNATIONAL ISSUES

Disputes—international: none

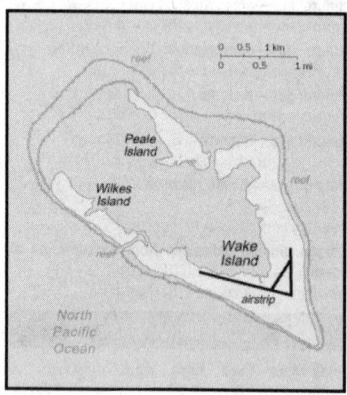

INTRODUCTION

Background: The US annexed Wake Island in 1899 for a cable station. An important air and naval base was constructed in 1940-41. In December 1941, the island was captured by the Japanese and held until the end of World War II. In subsequent years, Wake became a stopover and refueling site for military and commercial aircraft transiting the Pacific. Since 1974, the island's airstrip has been used by the US military, as well as for emergency landings. Operations on the island were temporarily suspended and all personnel evacuated in 2006 with the approach of super typhoon IOKE (category 5), but resultant damage was comparatively minor. A US Air Force repair team restored full capability to the airfield and facilities, and the island remains a vital strategic link in the Pacific region.

GEOGRAPHY

Location: Oceania, atoll in the North Pacific Ocean, about two-thirds of the way from Hawaii to the Northern Mariana Islands

Geographic coordinates: 19 17 N, 166 39 E

Map references: Oceania

Area: *total:* 6.5 sq km
land: 6.5 sq km
water: 0 sq km
country comparison to the world: 247

Area—comparative: about 11 times the size of the National Mall in Washington, DC

Land boundaries: 0 km

Coastline: 19.3 km

Maritime claims: *territorial sea:* 12 nm
exclusive economic zone: 200 nm

Climate: tropical

Terrain: atoll of three low coral islands, Peale, Wake, and Wilkes, built up on an underwater volcano; central lagoon is former crater, islands are part of the rim

Elevation: *mean elevation:* NA

elevation extremes: *lowest point:* Pacific Ocean 0 m
highest point: unnamed location 8 m

Natural resources: none

Land use: *agricultural land:* 0%
arable land: 0%;
permanent crops: 0%;
permanent pasture: 0%
forest: 0%
other: 100% (2011 est.)
Irrigated land: 0 sq km (2012)

Natural hazards: subject to occasional typhoons

Environment—current issues: potable water obtained through a catchment rainwater system and a desalinization plant for brackish ground water; hazardous wastes moved to an accumulation site for storage and eventual transport off site via barge

Geography—note: strategic location in the North Pacific Ocean; emergency landing location for transpacific flights

PEOPLE AND SOCIETY

Population: no indigenous inhabitants
note: approximately 150 military personnel and civilian contractors maintain and operate the airfield and communications facilities (2009)

GOVERNMENT

Country name: *conventional long form:* none
conventional short form: Wake Island
etymology: although first discovered by British Captain William WAKE in 1792, the island is named after British Captain Samuel WAKE who rediscovered the island in 1796

Dependency status: unorganized, unincorporated territory of the US; administered from Washington, DC, by the Department of the Interior; activities in the atoll are currently conducted by the US Air Force

Legal system: US common law

Citizenship: see United States

Flag description: the flag of the US is used

ECONOMY

Economy—overview: Economic activity is limited to providing services to military personnel and contractors located on the island. All food and manufactured goods must be imported.

COMMUNICATIONS

Telephone system: *general assessment:* satellite communications; 2 Defense Switched Network circuits off the Overseas Telephone System (OTS); located in the Hawaii area code—808

Broadcast media: American Armed Forces Radio and Television Service (AFRTS) provides satellite radio/TV broadcasts (2009)

TRANSPORTATION

Airports: 1 (2013)
country comparison to the world: 211

Airports—with paved runways: *total:* 1
2,438 to 3,047 m: 1 (2013)

Ports and terminals: none; two offshore anchorages for large ships

Transportation—note: there are no commercial or civilian flights to and from Wake Island, except in direct support of island missions; emergency landing is available

MILITARY AND SECURITY

Military—note: defense is the responsibility of the US; the US Air Force is responsible for overall administration and operation of the island facilities; the launch support facility is administered by the US Missile Defense Agency (MDA)

TRANSNATIONAL ISSUES

Disputes—international: claimed by Marshall Islands

WALLIS AND FUTUNA

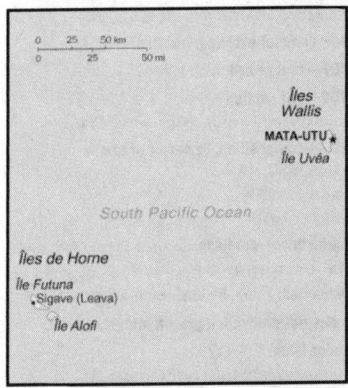

INTRODUCTION

Background: The Futuna island group was discovered by the Dutch in 1616 and Wallis by the British in 1767, but it was the French who declared a protectorate over the islands in 1842, and took official control of them between 1886 and 1888. Notably, Wallis and Futuna was the only French colony to side with the Vichy regime during World War II, a phase that ended in May of 1942 with the arrival of 2,000 American troops. In 1959, the inhabitants of the islands voted to become a French overseas territory and officially assumed that status in 1961. In 2003, Wallis and Futuna's designation changed to that of an overseas collectivity.

GEOGRAPHY

Location: Oceania, islands in the South Pacific Ocean, about two-thirds of the way from Hawaii to New Zealand

Geographic coordinates: 13 18 S, 176 12 W

Map references: Oceania

Area: *total:* 142 sq km
land: 142 sq km
water: 0 sq km
note: includes Ile Uvea (Wallis Island), Ile Futuna (Futuna Island), Ile Alofi, and 20 islets
country comparison to the world: 221

Area—comparative: 1.5 times the size of Washington, DC

Land boundaries: 0 km

Coastline: 129 km

Maritime claims: *territorial sea:* 12 nm
exclusive economic zone: 200 nm

Climate: tropical; hot, rainy season (November to April); cool, dry season (May to October); rains 250-300 cm per year (80% humidity); average temperature 26.6 degrees Celsius

Terrain: volcanic origin; low hills

Elevation: *mean elevation:* NA

elevation extremes: *lowest point:* Pacific Ocean 0 m
highest point: Mont Singavi (on Futuna) 522 m

Natural resources: NEGL

Land use: *agricultural land:* 42.8%
arable land: 7.1%;
permanent crops: 35.7%;
permanent pasture: 0%
forest: 41.9%
other: 15.3% (2011 est.)
Irrigated land: 0 sq km (2012)

Natural hazards: cyclones; tsunamis

Environment—current issues: deforestation (only small portions of the original forests remain) largely as a result of the continued use of wood as the main fuel source; as a consequence of cutting down the forests, the mountainous terrain of Futuna is particularly prone to erosion; there are no permanent settlements on Alofi because of the lack of natural freshwater resources

Geography—note: both island groups have fringing reefs; Wallis contains several prominent crater lakes

PEOPLE AND SOCIETY

Population: 15,714 (July 2017 est.)
country comparison to the world: 221

Nationality: *noun:* Wallisian(s), Futunan(s), or Wallis and Futuna Islanders
adjective: Wallisian, Futunan, or Wallis and Futuna Islander

Ethnic groups: Polynesian

Languages: Wallisian (indigenous Polynesian language) 58.9%, Futunian 30.1%, French (official) 10.8%, other 0.2% (2003 census)

Religions: Roman Catholic 99%, other 1%

Age structure: *0-14 years:* 21.83% (male 1,789/female 1,641)
15-24 years: 16.3% (male 1,358/female 1,203)
25-54 years: 42.08% (male 3,336/female 3,276)
55-64 years: 9.79% (male 744/female 794)
65 years and over: 10.01% (male 752/female 821) (2017 est.)

Median age: *total:* 32.2 years
male: 31.3 years
female: 33.4 years (2017 est.)
country comparison to the world: 102

Population growth rate: 0.32% (2017 est.)
country comparison to the world: 169

Birth rate: 13.2 births/1,000 population (2017 est.)
country comparison to the world: 148

Death rate: 5.4 deaths/1,000 population (2017 est.)
country comparison to the world: 179

Net migration rate: -4.7 migrant(s)/1,000 population

note: there has been steady emigration from Wallis and Futuna to New Caledonia (2017 est.)
country comparison to the world: 188

Urbanization: *urban population:* 0% of total population (2017)
rate of urbanization: 0% annual rate of change (2015-20 est.)

Major urban areas—population: MATA-UTU (capital) 1,000 (2014)

Sex ratio: *at birth:* 1.05 male(s)/female
0-14 years: 1.09 male(s)/female
15-24 years: 1.11 male(s)/female
25-54 years: 1.01 male(s)/female
55-64 years: 0.97 male(s)/female
65 years and over: 0.92 male(s)/female
total population: 1.03 male(s)/female (2016 est.)

Infant mortality rate: *total:* 4.3 deaths/1,000 live births
male: 4.6 deaths/1,000 live births
female: 4.1 deaths/1,000 live births (2017 est.)
country comparison to the world: 186

Life expectancy at birth: *total population:* 79.8 years
male: 76.8 years
female: 83 years (2017 est.)
country comparison to the world: 44

Total fertility rate: 1.73 children born/woman (2017 est.)
country comparison to the world: 166

Physicians density: 1.1 physicians/1,000 population (2008)
Sanitation facility access:
improved:
rural: 96% of population
total: 96% of population
unimproved:
rural: 4% of population
total: 4% of population (2008 est.)

HIV/AIDS—adult prevalence rate: NA

HIV/AIDS—people living with HIV/AIDS: NA

HIV/AIDS—deaths: NA

GOVERNMENT

Country name: *conventional long form:* Territory of the Wallis and Futuna Islands
conventional short form: Wallis and Futuna
local long form: Territoire des Iles Wallis et Futuna
local short form: Wallis et Futuna
etymology: Wallis Island is named after British Captain Samuel WALLIS who discovered it in 1767; Futuna is derived from the native word "futu," which is the name of the fish-poison tree found on the island

Dependency status: overseas collectivity of France

Government type: parliamentary democracy (Territorial Assembly); overseas collectivity of France

Capital: *name:* Mata-Utu (on Ile Uvea)

geographic coordinates: 13 57 S, 171 56 W

time difference: UTC+12 (17 hours ahead of Washington, DC, during Standard Time)

Administrative divisions: 3 administrative precincts (circonscriptions, singular—circonscription) Alo, Sigave, Uvea

Independence: none (overseas colectivity of France)

National holiday: Bastille Day, 14 July (1789)

Constitution: 4 October 1958 (French Constitution)

Legal system: French civil law

Citizenship: see France

Suffrage: 18 years of age; universal

Executive branch: *chief of state:* President Emmanuel MACRON (since 14 May 2017); represented by High Administrator Jean-Francis TREFFEL (since 6 February 2017)

head of government: President of the Territorial Assembly David VERGE (since 4 April 2017)

cabinet: Council of the Territory appointed by the high administrator on the advice of the Territorial Assembly

elections/appointments: French president elected by absolute majority popular vote in 2 rounds if needed for a 5-year term (eligible for a second term); high administrator appointed by the French president on the advice of the French Ministry of the Interior; the presidents of the Territorial Government and the Territorial Assembly elected by assembly members

note: there are 3 traditional kings with limited powers

Legislative branch: description: unicameral Territorial Assembly or Assemblee Territoriale (20 seats—Wallis 13, Futuna 7; members directly elected in multi-seat constituencies by party-list proportional representation vote to serve 5-year terms); Wallis and Futuna indirectly elects 1 member to the French Senate via an electoral college by absolute majority vote in 2 rounds if needed for a 6-year term, and 1 member directly elected to the French National Assembly by absolute majority vote for a 5-year term

elections: Territorial Assembly—last held on 26 March 2017 (next to be held in March 2022)
French Senate—last held on 28 September 2014 (next to be held by September 2020)
French National Assembly—last held on 11 June 2017 (next to be held in June 2022)

election results: Territorial Assembly—percent of vote by party—NA; seats by party—2 members are elected from the list Fia gaue fakatahi kihe kaha'u e lelei and 1 each from 18 other lists
French Senate—1 seat: LR 1
French National Assembly—1 seat: independent 1

Judicial branch: highest resident court(s): Court of Assizes or Cour d'Assizes (consists of 1 judge; court hears primarily serious criminal cases); note—appeals beyond the Court of Assizes are heard before the Court of Appeal or Cour d'Appel, located in Noumea, New Caledonia
judge selection and term of office: NA

subordinate courts: courts of first instance; labor court; note—justice generally administered under French law by the high administrator, but the 3 traditional kings administer customary law, and there is a magistrate in Mata-Utu

Political parties and leaders: Left Radical Party or PRG [Sylvia PINEL] (formerly Radical Socialist Party or PRS and the Left Radical Movement or MRG)
Lua Kae Tahi (Giscardians)
Rally for Wallis and Futuna-The Republicans (Rassemblement pour Wallis and Futuna) or RPWF-LR [Clovis LOGOLOGOFOLAU]
Socialist Party or PS
Taumu'a Lelei [Soane Muni UHILA]
Union Pour la Democratie Francaise or UDF

Political pressure groups and leaders: NA

International organization participation: PIF (observer), SPC, UPU

Diplomatic representation in the US: none (overseas territory of France)

Diplomatic representation from the US: none (overseas collectivity of France);;;

Flag description: unofficial, local flag has a red field with four white isosceles triangles in the middle, representing the three native kings of the islands and the French administrator; the apexes of the triangles are oriented inward and at right angles to each other; the flag of France, outlined in white on two sides, is in the upper hoist quadrant
note: the design is derived from an original red banner with a white cross pattee that was introduced in the 19th century by French missionaries; the flag of France is used for official occasions

National symbol(s): red saltire (Saint Andrew's Cross) on a white square on a red field; national colors: red, white
National anthem: note: as a territory of France, "La Marseillaise" is official (see France)

ECONOMY

Economy—overview: The economy is limited to traditional subsistence agriculture, with 80% of labor force earnings coming from agriculture (coconuts and vegetables), livestock (mostly pigs), and fishing. However, roughly 70% of the labor force is employed in the public sector, although only about 20% of the population is in salaried employment.

Revenues come from French Government subsidies, licensing of fishing rights to Japan and South Korea, import taxes, and remittances from expatriate workers in New Caledonia. France directly finances the public sector and healthcare and education services. It also provides funding for key development projects in a range of areas, including infrastructure, economic development, environmental management, and healthcare facilities.

A key concern for Wallis and Futuna is an aging population with consequent economic development issues. Very few people aged 18-30 live on the islands due to the limited formal employment opportunities. Improving job creation is a current priority for the territorial government.

GDP (purchasing power parity): $60 million (2004 est.)
country comparison to the world: 225

GDP (official exchange rate): $NA

GDP—real growth rate: NA%

GDP—per capita (PPP): $3,800 (2004 est.)
country comparison to the world: 184

GDP—composition, by sector of origin:
agriculture: NA%
industry: NA%
services: NA%

Agriculture—products: coconuts, breadfruit, yams, taro, bananas; pigs, goats; fish

Industries: copra, handicrafts, fishing, lumber

Industrial production growth rate: NA%

Labor force: 3,104 (2003)
country comparison to the world: 226
Labor force—by occupation: agriculture: 80%
industry: 4%
services: 16% (2001)

Unemployment rate: 12.2% (2008 est.)
country comparison to the world: 158

Population below poverty line: NA%

Household income or consumption by percentage share: *lowest 10%:* NA%
highest 10%: NA%

Budget: *revenues:* NA
expenditures: NA

Taxes and other revenues: NA%

Budget surplus (+) or deficit (-): NA% of GDP

Public debt: 5.6% of GDP (2004 est.)
note: official data; data cover general government debt, and includes debt instruments issued (or owned) by government entities other than the treasury; the data include treasury debt held by foreign entities; the data include debt issued by subnational entities, as well as intra-governmental debt; intra-governmental debt consists of treasury borrowings from surpluses in the social funds, such as for retirement, medical care, and unemployment; debt instruments for the social funds are not sold at public auctions
country comparison to the world: 202

Fiscal year: calendar year

Inflation rate (consumer prices): 2.8% (2005)
country comparison to the world: 123

Exports: $47,450 (2004 est.)
country comparison to the world: 222

Exports—commodities: copra, chemicals, construction materials

Imports: $61.17 million (2004)
country comparison to the world: 215

Imports—commodities: chemicals, machinery, consumer goods

Debt—external: $3.67 million (2004)
country comparison to the world: 202

Exchange rates: Comptoirs Francais du Pacifique francs (XPF) per US dollar—

110.2 (2015 est.)
89.8 (2014 est.)
89.85 (2013 est.)
90.56 (2012 est.)

COMMUNICATIONS

Telephones—fixed lines: *total subscriptions:* 3,132
subscriptions per 100 inhabitants: 20 (July 2016 est.)
Telephone system: international: country code—681

Broadcast media: the publicly owned French Overseas Network (RFO), which broadcasts to France's overseas departments, collectivites, and territories, is carried on the RFO Wallis and Fortuna TV and radio stations (2008)

Internet country code: .wf

Internet users: *total:* 3,450

percent of population: 22.1% (July 2016 est.)
country comparison to the world: 211

TRANSPORTATION

Airports: 2 (2013)
country comparison to the world: 208

Airports—with paved runways: *total:* 2
1,524 to 2,437 m: 1
914 to 1,523 m: 1 (2013)

Ports and terminals: *major seaport(s):* Leava, Mata-Utu

MILITARY AND SECURITY

Military—note: defense is the responsibility of France

TRANSNATIONAL ISSUES

Disputes—international: none

WEST BANK

West Bank is Israeli-occupied with current status subject to the Israeli-Palestinian Interim Agreement; permanent status to be determined through further negotiation.

INTRODUCTION

Background: From the early 16th century through 1917, the area now known as the West Bank fell under Ottoman rule. Following World War I, the Allied powers (France, UK, Russia) allocated the area to the British Mandate of Palestine. After World War II, the UN passed a resolution to establish two states within the Mandate, and designated a territory including what is now known as the West Bank as part of the proposed Arab

state. During the 1948 Arab-Israeli War, the area was captured by Transjordan (later renamed Jordan). Jordan annexed the West Bank in 1950. In June 1967, Israel captured the West Bank and East Jerusalem during the 1967 Six-Day War. With the exception of East Jerusalem, roughly 60% of the West Bank remains under Israeli military control. Israel transferred security and civilian responsibility for a number of Palestinian-populated areas of the West Bank and Gaza Strip to the Palestinian Authority (PA) under a series of agreements signed between 1993 and 1999, the so-called "Oslo Accords." Negotiations to determine the permanent status of the West Bank and Gaza Strip stalled after the outbreak of an intifada in mid-2000. In early 2003, the "Quartet" of the US, EU, UN, and Russia, presented a roadmap to a final peace settlement by 2005, calling for two states—Israel and a democratic Palestine.

Following Palestinian leader Yassir ARAFAT's death in late 2004 and the subsequent election of Mahmud ABBAS (head of the Fatah political faction) as PA president, Israel and the Palestinians agreed to move the peace process forward. Israel in late 2005 unilaterally withdrew all of its settlers and soldiers, dismantled its military facilities in the Gaza Strip, and redeployed its military from several West Bank settlements, but it continues to control maritime, airspace, and other access. In early 2006, the Islamic Resistance Movement, HAMAS, won the Palestinian Legislative Council election and took control of the PA government. Attempts to form a unity government failed, and violent clashes between Fatah and HAMAS supporters ensued, culminating in HAMAS's violent seizure of all military and governmental institutions in the Gaza Strip. Fatah and HAMAS have made several attempts at reconciliation, but the factions have been unable to implement details on governance and security. In an attempt to reenergize peace talks between the Israelis and Palestinians, France in June 2016 hosted a ministerial meeting that included participants from 29 countries, although not Israel or the Palestinians, to lay the groundwork for an envisioned "multilateral peace conference" later in the year.

GEOGRAPHY

Location: Middle East, west of Jordan, east of Israel

Geographic coordinates: 32 00 N, 35 15 E

Map references: Middle East

Area: *total:* 5,860 sq km
land: 5,640 sq km
water: 220 sq km
note: includes West Bank, Latrun Salient, and the northwest quarter of the Dead Sea, but excludes Mt. Scopus; East Jerusalem and Jerusalem No Man's Land are also included only as a means of depicting the entire area occupied by Israel in 1967
country comparison to the world: 172

Area—comparative: slightly smaller than Delaware

Land boundaries: *total:* 478 km
border countries (2): Israel 330 km, Jordan 148 km

Coastline: 0 km (landlocked)

Maritime claims: none (landlocked)

Climate: temperate; temperature and precipitation vary with altitude, warm to hot summers, cool to mild winters

Terrain: mostly rugged, dissected upland in west, flat plains descending to Jordan River Valley to the east

Elevation: *mean elevation:* NA
elevation extremes: *lowest point:* Dead Sea -431 m
highest point: Khallat al Batrakh 1,020 m

Natural resources: arable land

Land use: *agricultural land:* 43.3%
arable land: 7.4%;
permanent crops: 11%;
permanent pasture: 24.9%;
forest: 1.5%
other: 55.2%
note: includes Gaza Strip (2011 est.)
Irrigated land: 240 sq km; note—includes Gaza Strip (2012)

Population—distribution: Palestinian settlements are primarily located in the central to western half of the territory; Jewish settlements are found in

989

pockets throughout, particularly in the northeast, north-central, and around Jerusalem

Natural hazards: droughts

Environment—current issues: adequacy of freshwater supply; sewage treatment

Geography—note: landlocked; highlands are main recharge area for Israel's coastal aquifers; there are about 380 Israeli civilian sites, including about 213 settlements and 132 small outpost communities in the West Bank and 35 sites in East Jerusalem (2017)

PEOPLE AND SOCIETY

Population: 2,747,943 (July 2017 est.)
note: approximately 391,000 Israeli settlers live in the West Bank (2016); approximately 201,200 Israeli settlers live in East Jerusalem (2014)
country comparison to the world: 141

Nationality: *noun:* NA
adjective: NA

Ethnic groups: Palestinian Arab, Jewish, other

Languages: Arabic, Hebrew (spoken by Israeli settlers and many Palestinians), English (widely understood)

Religions: Muslim 80-85% (predominantly Sunni), Jewish 12-14%, Christian 1-2.5% (mainly Greek Orthodox), other, unaffiliated, unspecified <1% (2012 est.)

Age structure: *0-14 years:* 36.5% (male 514,691/female 488,233)
15-24 years: 21.37% (male 299,859/female 287,367)
25-54 years: 34.1% (male 475,860/female 461,252)
55-64 years: 4.54% (male 64,275/female 60,507)
65 years and over: 3.49% (male 43,060/female 52,839) (2017 est.)

Dependency ratios: *total dependency ratio:* 75.8
youth dependency ratio: 70.5
elderly dependency ratio: 5.2
potential support ratio: 19.1
note: data represent Gaza Strip and the West Bank (2015 est.)

Median age: *total:* 21.1 years
male: 20.9 years
female: 21.3 years (2017 est.)
country comparison to the world: 185

Population growth rate: 1.84% (2017 est.)
country comparison to the world: 56

Birth rate: 26.3 births/1,000 population (2017 est.)
country comparison to the world: 47

Death rate: 3.5 deaths/1,000 population (2017 est.)
country comparison to the world: 216

Net migration rate: -4.5 migrant(s)/1,000 population (2017 est.)
country comparison to the world: 186

Population distribution: Palestinian settlements are primarily located in the central to western half of the territory; Jewish settlements are found in pockets throughout, particularly in the northeast, north-central, and around Jerusalem

Urbanization: *urban population:* 75.7% of total population (2017)
rate of urbanization: 2.75% annual rate of change (2015-20 est.)
note: data represent Gaza Strip and the West Bank

Sex ratio: *at birth:* 1.06 male(s)/female
0-14 years: 1.05 male(s)/female
15-24 years: 1.04 male(s)/female
25-54 years: 1.03 male(s)/female
55-64 years: 1.06 male(s)/female
65 years and over: 0.73 male(s)/female
total population: 1.04 male(s)/female (2016 est.)

Maternal mortality ratio: 45 deaths/100,000 live births
note: data represent Gaza Strip and the West Bank (2015 est.)
country comparison to the world: 99

Infant mortality rate: *total:* 14.1 deaths/1,000 live births
male: 15.8 deaths/1,000 live births
female: 12.3 deaths/1,000 live births (2017 est.)
country comparison to the world: 105

Life expectancy at birth: *total population:* 75.2 years
male: 73.2 years
female: 77.4 years (2017 est.)
country comparison to the world: 110

Total fertility rate: 3.27 children born/woman (2017 est.)
country comparison to the world: 48

Contraceptive prevalence rate: 57.2% (includes Gaza Strip and West Bank) (2014)

Physicians density: 1.3 physicians/1,000 population (2013)

Hospital bed density: 1.2 beds/1,000 population (2010)

Drinking water source:
improved:
urban: 50.7% of population
rural: 81.5% of population
total: 58.4% of population
unimproved:
urban: 49.3% of population
rural: 18.5% of population
total: 41.6% of population
note: includes Gaza Strip and the West Bank (2015 est.)

Sanitation facility access:
improved:
urban: 93% of population
rural: 90.2% of population
total: 92.3% of population
unimproved:
urban: 7% of population
rural: 9.8% of population
total: 7.7% of population
note: includes Gaza Strip and the West Bank (2015 est.)

HIV/AIDS—adult prevalence rate: NA

HIV/AIDS—people living with HIV/AIDS: NA

HIV/AIDS—deaths: NA

Children under the age of 5 years underweight: 1.4%

note: estimate are for Gaza and the West Bank (2014)

Education expenditures: 1.3% of GDP
note: includes Gaza Strip (2015)

Literacy: *definition:* age 15 and over can read and write
total population: 96.9%
male: 98.6%
female: 95.2%
note: estimates are for Gaza and the West Bank (2016 est.)

School life expectancy (primary to tertiary education): *total:* 13 years
male: 12 years
female: 14 years
note: data represent Gaza and the West Bank (2015)

Unemployment, youth ages 15-24: *total:* 40.7%
male: 36.4%
female: 60.8%
note: includes Gaza Strip (2015 est.)
country comparison to the world: 15

GOVERNMENT

Country name: *conventional long form:* none
conventional short form: West Bank
etymology: name refers to the location of the region—occupied and administered by Jordan after 1948—that fell on the far side (west bank) of the Jordan River in relation to Jordan proper; the designation was retained following the 1967 Six-Day War and the subsequent changes in government

ECONOMY

Economy—overview: In 2017, the economic outlook in the West Bank—the larger of the two areas comprising the Palestinian Territories—remained fragile, as security concerns and political friction slowed economic growth. Unemployment in the West Bank remained high at 19.0% in the third quarter of 2017, only slightly better than 19.6% at the same point in the previous year, while the labor force participation rate remained flat, year-on-year.

Longstanding Israeli restrictions on imports, exports, and movement continue to disrupt labor and trade flows and the territory's industrial capacity, and constrain private sector development. The PA's budget benefited from an effort to improve tax collection, coupled with lower spending in 2017, but the PA for the foreseeable future will continue to rely heavily on donor aid for its budgetary needs and infrastructure development.

GDP (purchasing power parity): $21.22 billion (2014 est.)
$20.15 billion (2013 est.)
$19.95 billion (2012 est.)
note: data are in 2014 US dollars; includes Gaza Strip
country comparison to the world: 147

GDP (official exchange rate): $9.828 billion (2014 est.)
note: excludes Gaza Strip

GDP—real growth rate: 5.3% (2014 est.)
1% (2013 est.)
6% (2012 est.)
note: excludes Gaza Strip
country comparison to the world: 36

GDP—per capita (PPP): $4,300 (2014 est.)
$4,400 (2013 est.)
$4,600 (2012 est.)
note: includes Gaza Strip
country comparison to the world: 176

Gross national saving: 7.8% of GDP (2014 est.)
9.5% of GDP (2013 est.)
5% of GDP (2012 est.)
note: includes Gaza Strip
country comparison to the world: 167

GDP—composition, by end use:
household consumption: 91.3%
government consumption: 26.7%
investment in fixed capital: 23%
investment in inventories: 0%
exports of goods and services: 20%
imports of goods and services: -61%
note: excludes Gaza Strip (2017 est.)

GDP—composition, by sector of origin:
agriculture: 3%
industry: 21.1%
services: 62.5%
note: excludes Gaza Strip (2017 est.)

Agriculture—products: olives, citrus fruit, vegetables; beef, dairy products

Industries: small-scale manufacturing, quarrying, textiles, soap, olive-wood carvings, and mother-of-pearl souvenirs

Industrial production growth rate: 4%
note: includes Gaza Strip (2017 est.)
country comparison to the world: 71

Labor force: 1.24 million
note: excludes Gaza Strip (2017 est.)
country comparison to the world: 139
Labor force—by occupation: agriculture: 11.5%
industry: 34.4%
services: 54.1%
note: excludes Gaza Strip (2013 est.)

Unemployment rate: 26.7% (2017 est.)
26.9% (2016 est.)
note: excludes Gaza Strip
country comparison to the world: 195

Population below poverty line: 18% (2011 est.)

Household income or consumption by percentage share: lowest 10%: 3.2%
highest 10%: 28.2%
note: includes Gaza Strip (2009 est.)

Distribution of family income—Gini index: 34.5 (2009 est.)
38.7 (2007 est.)
note: includes Gaza Strip
country comparison to the world: 98

Budget: revenues: $1.314 billion
expenditures: $1.278 billion
note: includes Palestinian Authority expenditures in the Gaza Strip (2017 est.)

Taxes and other revenues: 13.4% of GDP (2017 est.)

country comparison to the world: 201

Budget surplus (+) or deficit (-): 0.4% of GDP (2017 est.)
country comparison to the world: 24

Public debt: 24.4% of GDP (2014 est.)
23.8% of GDP (2013 est.)
country comparison to the world: 179

Fiscal year: calendar year

Inflation rate (consumer prices): 0.8% (2017 est.)
-0.2% (2016 est.)
note: excludes Gaza Strip
country comparison to the world: 26

Commercial bank prime lending rate: 6.7% (31 December 2017 est.)
6.5% (31 December 2016 est.)
country comparison to the world: 121

Stock of narrow money: $382 million (31 December 2017 est.)
$317 million (31 December 2016 est.)
country comparison to the world: 173

Stock of broad money: $2.901 billion (31 December 2017 est.)
$2.538 billion (31 December 2016 est.)
country comparison to the world: 143

Stock of domestic credit: $2.041 billion (31 December 2017 est.)
$1.712 billion (31 December 2016 est.)
country comparison to the world: 153

Market value of publicly traded shares: $3.339 billion (31 December 2015 est.)
$3.187 billion (31 December 2014 est.)
$3.247 billion (31 December 2013 est.)
country comparison to the world: 94

Current account balance: -$1.444 billion (2017 est.)
-$1.348 billion (2016 est.)
country comparison to the world: 143

Exports: $1.955 billion (2017 est.)
$1.827 billion (2016 est.)
note: excludes Gaza Strip
country comparison to the world: 141

Exports—commodities: stone, olives, fruit, vegetables, limestone

Imports: $6.476 billion (2017 est.)
$6.11 billion (2016 est.)
note: data include the Gaza Strip
country comparison to the world: 111

Imports—commodities: food, consumer goods, construction materials, petroleum, chemicals

Reserves of foreign exchange and gold: $312.8 million (31 December 2016 est.)
$583 million (31 December 2015 est.)
country comparison to the world: 154

Debt—external: $1.662 billion (31 March 2016 est.)

$1.467 billion (31 March 2015 est.)
note: data include the Gaza Strip
country comparison to the world: 156

Exchange rates: new Israeli shekels (ILS) per US dollar—
3.606 (2017 est.)
3.841 (2016 est.)

3.841 (2015 est.)
3.8869 (2014 est.)
3.5779 (2013 est.)

Electricity access: population without electricity: 80,930
electrification—total population: 98%
electrification—urban areas: 99%
electrification—rural areas: 93%
note: data for West Bank and Gaza Strip combined (2012)

Electricity—production: 475 million kWh (2015 est.)
country comparison to the world: 168

Electricity—consumption: 5.845 billion kWh (2015 est.)
country comparison to the world: 115

Electricity—exports: 0 kWh (2016)
country comparison to the world: 215

Electricity—imports: 5.403 billion kWh (2015 est.)
country comparison to the world: 37

Electricity—installed generating capacity: 152,000 kW
note: includes Gaza Strip (2015 est.)
country comparison to the world: 170

Electricity—from fossil fuels: 92.1% of total installed capacity (2015 est.)
country comparison to the world: 58

Electricity—from nuclear fuels: 0% of total installed capacity (2015 est.)
country comparison to the world: 209

Electricity—from hydroelectric plants: 0% of total installed capacity (2015 est.)
country comparison to the world: 213

Electricity—from other renewable sources: 9.2% of total installed capacity (2015 est.)
country comparison to the world: 73

Crude oil—production: 0 bbl/day (2016 est.)
country comparison to the world: 214

Crude oil—exports: 0 bbl/day (2014 est.)
country comparison to the world: 211

Crude oil—imports: 0 bbl/day (2014 est.)
country comparison to the world: 211

Crude oil—proved reserves: 0 bbl (1 January 2017)
country comparison to the world: 214

Refined petroleum products—production: 0 bbl/day (2014 est.)
country comparison to the world: 215

Refined petroleum products—consumption: 19,000 bbl/day (2015 est.)
country comparison to the world: 141

Refined petroleum products—exports: 0 bbl/day (2014 est.)
country comparison to the world: 213

Refined petroleum products—imports: 18,690 bbl/day (2014 est.)
country comparison to the world: 121

Natural gas—production: 0 cu m (2013 est.)

country comparison to the world: 212

Natural gas—consumption: 0 cu m (2013 est.)
country comparison to the world: 147

Natural gas—exports: 0 cu m (2013 est.)
country comparison to the world: 210

Natural gas—imports: 0 cu m (2013 est.)
country comparison to the world: 209

Natural gas—proved reserves: 0 cu m (1 January 2014 es)
country comparison to the world: 207

Carbon dioxide emissions from consumption of energy: 3 million Mt (2013 est.)
country comparison to the world: 142

COMMUNICATIONS

Telephones—fixed lines: *total subscriptions:* 406,500 (includes Gaza Strip)
subscriptions per 100 inhabitants: 9 (July 2016 est.)
country comparison to the world: 104

Telephones—mobile cellular: *total:* 3.531 million (includes Gaza Strip)
subscriptions per 100 inhabitants: 76 (includes Gaza Strip) (July 2016 est.)
country comparison to the world: 135

Telephone system: *general assessment:* continuing political and economic instability has impeded liberalization of the telecommunications industry
domestic: Israeli company BEZEK and the Palestinian company PALTEL are responsible for fixed-line services; two Palestinian cellular providers, JAWWAL and WATANIYA MOBILE, launched 3G mobile networks in the West Bank in January 2018 after Israel lifted its ban; Israel had witheld frequencies for Palestinians for 12 years (2004-2015)
international: country code—970; 1 international switch in Ramallah (2018)

Broadcast media: the Palestinian Authority operates 1 TV and 1 radio station; about 20 private TV and 40 radio stations; both Jordanian TV and satellite TV are accessible (2013)

Internet country code: .ps; note—same as Gaza Strip

Internet users: *total:* 2.673 million (includes Gaza Strip)

percent of population: 57.4% (includes Gaza Strip) (July 2016 est.)

country comparison to the world: 112

TRANSPORTATION

Airports: 2 (2013)
country comparison to the world: 203

Airports—with paved runways: *total:* 2
1,524 to 2,437 m: 1
under 914 m: 1 (2013)

Heliports: 1 (2013)

Roadways: *total:* 4,686 km
paved: 4,686 km
note: includes Gaza Strip (2010)
country comparison to the world: 153

TERRORISM

Terrorist groups—home based: Al-Aqsa Martyrs Brigade (AAMB): *aim(s):* drive the Israeli military and Jewish settlers from the West Bank, impel Israelis to leave Jerusalem and, ultimately, establish a Palestinian state comprising the West Bank, Gaza Strip, and Jerusalem
area(s) of operation: headquartered in the West Bank, where AAMB is operationally active targeting Israeli soldiers and Israeli civilians living in Jewish settlements in the West Bank; estimated in 2015 to have a few hundred members, who operate in small decentralized cells, with each cell reporting to a local leader

Terrorist groups—foreign based: Army of Islam (AOI): *aim(s):* enhance its networks in the West Bank and, ultimately, establish an Islamic caliphate
area(s) of operation: maintains a limited operational presence
HAMAS: *aim(s):* bolster recruitment networks in the West Bank and, ultimately, destroy the state of Israel
area(s) of operation: actively recruits youths and grooms young school children to embrace the group's ideology; in late 2016, an Islamic faction identified with HAMAS was known to recruit at the al-Quds University in Abu Dis, a Palestinian town in the Jerusalem Governorate bordering Israeli-controlled Jerusalem

Kahane Chai (Kach): *aim(s):* expel Arabs from Israel's biblical lands and, ultimately, restore the biblical state of Israel
area(s) of operation: present in West Bank Jewish settlements, especially the Qiryat Arba' settlement

in Hebron, where operatives have previously conducted bombings and shootings against Muslim and Christian Palestinians; considered to be operationally inactive in recent years

Palestinian Islamic Jihad (PIJ): *aim(s):* create an Islamic state in all of historic Palestine as defined by the British Mandate, which includes the West Bank
area(s) of operation: maintains a limited operational presence

Palestine Liberation Front (PLF): *aim(s):* enhance its networks in the West Bank and, ultimately, destroy the state of Israel and establish a secular, Marxist Palestinian state with Jerusalem as its capital
area(s) of operation: maintains a recruitment and limited training presence in some of the West Bank's refugee camps

Popular Front for the Liberation of Palestine (PFLP): *aim(s):* bolster its recruitment networks in the West Bank
area(s) of operation: maintains a recruitment presence targeting youths

TRANSNATIONAL ISSUES

Disputes—international: the current status of the West Bank is subject to the Israeli-Palestinian Interim Agreement—permanent status to be determined through further negotiation; Israel continues construction of a "seam line" separation barrier along parts of the Green Line and within the West Bank; Israel withdrew from Gaza and four settlements in the northern West Bank in August 2005; since 1948, about 350 peacekeepers from the UN Truce Supervision Organization (UNTSO), headquartered in Jerusalem, monitor ceasefires, supervise armistice agreements, prevent isolated incidents from escalating, and assist other UN personnel in the region

Refugees and internally displaced persons: refugees (country of origin): 809,738 (Palestinian refugees) (2017)
IDPs: 193,000 (includes persons displaced within the Gaza strip due to the intensification of the Israeli-Palestinian conflict since June 2014 and other Palestinian IDPs in the Gaza Strip and West Bank who fled as long ago as 1967, although confirmed cumulative data do not go back beyond 2006) (2016)

WESTERN SAHARA

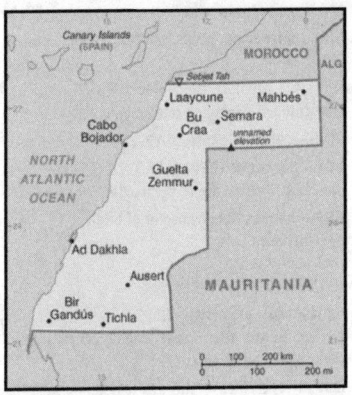

INTRODUCTION

Background: Western Sahara is a disputed territory on the northwest coast of Africa bordered by Morocco, Mauritania, and Algeria. After Spain withdrew from its former colony of Spanish Sahara in 1976, Morocco annexed the northern two-thirds of Western Sahara and claimed the rest of the territory in 1979, following Mauritania's withdrawal. A guerrilla war with the Polisario Front contesting Morocco's sovereignty ended in a 1991 cease-fire and the establishment of a UN peace-keeping operation. As part of this effort, the UN sought to offer a choice to the peoples of Western Sahara between independence (favored by the Polisario Front) or integration into Morocco. A proposed referendum never took place due to lack of agreement on voter eligibility. The 2,700 km- (1,700 mi-) long defensive sand berm, built by the Moroccans from 1980 to 1987 and running the length of the territory, continues to separate the opposing forces with Morocco controlling the roughly 80 percent of the territory west of the berm. Local demonstrations criticizing the Moroccan authorities occur regularly, and there are periodic ethnic tensions between the native Sahrawi population and Moroccan immigrants. Morocco maintains a heavy security presence in the territory.

GEOGRAPHY

Location: Northern Africa, bordering the North Atlantic Ocean, between Mauritania and Morocco

Geographic coordinates: 24 30 N, 13 00 W

Map references: Africa

Area: *total:* 266,000 sq km
land: 266,000 sq km
water: 0 sq km
country comparison to the world: 79

Area—comparative: about the size of Colorado

Land boundaries: *total:* 2,049 km

border countries (3): Algeria 41 km, Mauritania 1,564 km, Morocco 444 km

Coastline: 1,110 km

Maritime claims: contingent upon resolution of sovereignty issue

Climate: hot, dry desert; rain is rare; cold offshore air currents produce fog and heavy dew

Terrain: mostly low, flat desert with large areas of rocky or sandy surfaces rising to small mountains in south and northeast

Elevation: *mean elevation:* 256 m

elevation extremes: *lowest point:* Sebjet Tah -55 m
highest point: unnamed elevation 805 m

Natural resources: phosphates, iron ore

Land use: *agricultural land:* 18.8%
arable land: 0%;
permanent crops: 0%;
permanent pasture: 18.8%
forest: 2.7%
other: 78.5% (2011 est.)
Irrigated land: 0 sq km (2012)

Population—distribution: most of the population lives in the two-thirds of the area west of the berm (Moroccan-occupied) that divides the territory; about 40% of that populace resides in Laayoune

Natural hazards: hot, dry, dust/sand-laden sirocco wind can occur during winter and spring; widespread harmattan haze exists 60% of time, often severely restricting visibility

Environment—current issues: sparse water and lack of arable land

Geography—note: the waters off the coast are particularly rich fishing areas

PEOPLE AND SOCIETY

Population: 603,253
note: estimate is based on projections by age, sex, fertility, mortality, and migration; fertility and mortality are based on data from neighboring countries (July 2017 est.)
country comparison to the world: 169

Nationality: *noun:* Sahrawi(s), Sahraoui(s)
adjective: Sahrawi, Sahrawian, Sahraouian

Ethnic groups: Arab, Berber

Languages: Standard Arabic (national), Hassaniya Arabic, Moroccan Arabic

Religions: Muslim

Demographic profile: Western Sahara is a disputed territory; 85% is under Moroccan control. It was inhabited almost entirely by Sahrawi pastoral nomads until the mid-20th century. Their traditional vast migratory ranges, based on following unpredictable rainfall, did not coincide with colonial and later international borders. Since the 1930s, most Sahrawis have been compelled to adopt a sedentary lifestyle and to live in urban settings as a result of fighting, the presence of minefields, job opportunities in the phosphate industry, prolonged drought, the closure of Western Sahara's border with Mauritania from 1979-2002, and the construction of the defensive berm separating Moroccan- and Polisario-controlled (Sahrawi liberalization movement) areas. Morocco supported rapid urbanization to facilitate surveillance and security.

Today more than 80% of Western Sahara's population lives in urban areas; more than 40% live in the administrative center Laayoune. Moroccan immigration has altered the composition and dramatically increased the size of Western Sahara's population. Morocco maintains a large military presence in Western Sahara and has encouraged its citizens to settle there, offering bonuses, pay raises, and food subsidies to civil servants and a tax exemption, in order to integrate Western Sahara into the Moroccan Kingdom and, Sahrawis contend, to marginalize the native population.

Western Saharan Sahrawis have been migrating to Europe, principally to former colonial ruler Spain, since the 1950s. Many who moved to refugee camps in Tindouf, Algeria, also have migrated to Spain and Italy, usually alternating between living in cities abroad with periods back at the camps. The Polisario claims that the population of the Tindouf camps is about 155,000, but this figure may include thousands of Arabs and Tuaregs from neighboring countries. Because international organizations have been unable to conduct an independent census in Tindouf, the UNHCR bases its aid on a figure of 90,000 refugees. Western Saharan coastal towns emerged as key migration transit points (for reaching Spain's Canary Islands) in the mid-1990s, when Spain's and Italy's tightening of visa restrictions and EU pressure on Morocco and other North African countries to control illegal migration pushed sub-Saharan African migrants to shift their routes to the south.

Age structure: *0-14 years:* 37.24% (male 113,581/ female 111,077)
15-24 years: 19.53% (male 59,309/female 58,478)
25-54 years: 34.33% (male 102,031/female 105,093)
55-64 years: 5.03% (male 14,153/female 16,178)
65 years and over: 3.87% (male 10,287/female 13,066) (2017 est.)

Dependency ratios: *total dependency ratio:* 45
youth dependency ratio: 41.4
elderly dependency ratio: 3.7
potential support ratio: 27.1 (2015 est.)

Median age: *total:* 21.3 years
male: 20.8 years
female: 21.8 years (2017 est.)
country comparison to the world: 182

Population growth rate: 2.7% (2017 est.)
country comparison to the world: 13

Birth rate: 29.3 births/1,000 population (2017 est.)
country comparison to the world: 42

993

Death rate: 8.1 deaths/1,000 population (2017 est.)

country comparison to the world: 89

Population distribution: most of the population lives in the two-thirds of the area west of the berm (Moroccan-occupied) that divides the territory; about 40% of that populace resides in Laayoune

Urbanization: *urban population:* 81.1% of total population (2017)

rate of urbanization: 2.87% annual rate of change (2015-20 est.)

Major urban areas—population: Laayoune 262,000 (2014)

Sex ratio: *at birth:* 1.04 male(s)/female

0-14 years: 1.02 male(s)/female

15-24 years: 1.01 male(s)/female

25-54 years: 0.97 male(s)/female

55-64 years: 0.87 male(s)/female

65 years and over: 0.78 male(s)/female

total population: 0.99 male(s)/female (2016 est.)

Infant mortality rate: *total:* 51.9 deaths/1,000 live births

male: 56.7 deaths/1,000 live births

female: 46.9 deaths/1,000 live births (2017 est.)

country comparison to the world: 27

Life expectancy at birth: *total population:* 63.4 years

male: 61.1 years

female: 65.8 years (2017 est.)

country comparison to the world: 192

Total fertility rate: 3.86 children born/woman (2017 est.)

country comparison to the world: 40

HIV/AIDS—adult prevalence rate: NA

HIV/AIDS—people living with HIV/AIDS: NA

HIV/AIDS—deaths: NA

GOVERNMENT

Country name: *conventional long form:* none

conventional short form: Western Sahara

former: Rio de Oro, Saguia el Hamra, Spanish Sahara

etymology: self-descriptive name specifying the territory's western location on the African continent's vast desert

Government type: legal status of territory and issue of sovereignty unresolved—territory contested by Morocco and Polisario Front (Popular Front for the Liberation of the Saguia el Hamra and Rio de Oro), which in February 1976 formally proclaimed a government-in-exile of the Sahrawi Arab Democratic Republic (SADR), near Tindouf, Algeria, was led by President Mohamed ABDELAZIZ until his death in May 2016; current President Brahim GHALI elected in July 2016; territory partitioned between Morocco and Mauritania in April 1976 when Spain withdrew, with Morocco acquiring northern two-thirds; Mauritania, under pressure from Polisario guerrillas, abandoned all claims to its portion in August 1979; Morocco moved to occupy that sector shortly thereafter and has since asserted administrative control; the Polisario's government-in-exile was seated as an Organization of

African Unity (OAU) member in 1984—Morocco between 1980 and 1987 built a fortified sand berm delineating the roughly 80 percent of Western Sahara west of the barrier that currently is controlled by Morocco; guerrilla activities continued sporadically until a UN-monitored cease-fire was implemented on 6 September 1991 (Security Council Resolution 690) by the United Nations Mission for the Referendum in Western Sahara (MINURSO)

Capital: Laayoune (administrative center)

time difference: UTC 0 (5 hours ahead of Washington, DC, during Standard Time)

daylight saving time: +1hr, begins last Sunday in March; ends last Sunday in October

Administrative divisions: none officially; the territory west of the Moroccan berm falls under de facto Moroccan control; Morocco claims the territory of Western Sahara, the political status of which is considered undetermined by the US Government; portions of the regions Guelmim-Es Smara and Laayoune-Boujdour-Sakia El Hamra, as claimed by Morocco, lie within Western Sahara; Morocco also claims Oued Eddahab-Lagouira, another region that falls entirely within Western Sahara

Suffrage: none; (residents of Moroccan-controlled Western Sahara participate in Moroccan elections)

Executive branch: none

Political pressure groups and leaders: Polisario Front

International organization participation: AU, CAN (observer), WFTU (NGOs)

Diplomatic representation in the US: none

Diplomatic representation from the US: none

ECONOMY

Economy—overview: Western Sahara has a small market-based economy whose main industries are fishing, phosphate mining, and pastoral nomadism. The territory's arid desert climate makes sedentary agriculture difficult, and Western Sahara imports much of its food. The Moroccan Government administers Western Sahara's economy and is a key source of employment, infrastructure development, and social spending in the territory.

Western Sahara's unresolved legal status makes the exploitation of its natural resources a contentious issue between Morocco and the Polisario. Morocco and the EU in December 2013 finalized a four-year agreement allowing European vessels to fish off the coast of Morocco, including disputed waters off the coast of Western Sahara.

Oil has never been found in Western Sahara in commercially significant quantities, but Morocco and the Polisario have quarreled over who has the right to authorize and benefit from oil exploration in the territory. Western Sahara's main long-term economic challenge is the development of a more diverse set of industries capable of providing greater employment and income to the territory. However, following King MOHAMMED VI's November 2015 visit to Western Sahara, the

Government of Morocco announced a series of investments aimed at spurring economic activity in the region, while the General Confederation of Moroccan Enterprises announced a $609 million investment initiative in the region in March 2015.

GDP (purchasing power parity): $906.5 million (2007 est.)

country comparison to the world: 205

GDP (official exchange rate): $NA

GDP—real growth rate: NA%

GDP—per capita (PPP): $2,500 (2007 est.)

country comparison to the world: 198

GDP—composition, by sector of origin:

agriculture: NA%

industry: NA%

services: 40% (2007 est.)

Agriculture—products: fruits and vegetables (grown in the few oases); camels, sheep, goats (kept by nomads); fish

Industries: phosphate mining, handicrafts

Industrial production growth rate: NA%

Labor force: 144,000 (2010 est.)

country comparison to the world: 178

Labor force—by occupation: agriculture: 50%

industry and services: 50% (2005 est.)

Unemployment rate: NA%

Population below poverty line: NA%

Household income or consumption by percentage share: *lowest 10%:* NA%

highest 10%: NA%

Budget: *revenues:* $NA

expenditures: $NA

Taxes and other revenues: NA%

Budget surplus (+) or deficit (-): NA%

Fiscal year: calendar year

Inflation rate (consumer prices): NA%

Exports: $NA

Exports—commodities: phosphates 62% (2012 est.)

Imports: $NA

Imports—commodities: fuel for fishing fleet, foodstuffs

Debt—external: $NA

Exchange rates: Moroccan dirhams (MAD) per US dollar—

9.639 (2017)

9.7351 (2016)

9.7351 (2015)

9.7351 (2014 est.)

8.3798 (2013 est.)

ENERGY

Electricity—production: 0 kWh (2015 est.)

country comparison to the world: 220

Electricity—consumption: 0 kWh (2015 est.)

country comparison to the world: 219

Electricity—exports: 0 kWh (2016 est.)

country comparison to the world: 216

Electricity—imports: 0 kWh (2016 est.)

country comparison to the world: 218

Electricity—installed generating capacity: 58,000 kW (2015 est.)
country comparison to the world: 189

Electricity—from fossil fuels: 100% of total installed capacity (2015 est.)
country comparison to the world: 2

Electricity—from nuclear fuels: 0% of total installed capacity (2015 est.)
country comparison to the world: 210

Electricity—from hydroelectric plants: 0% of total installed capacity (2015 est.)
country comparison to the world: 214

Electricity—from other renewable sources: 0% of total installed capacity (2015 est.)
country comparison to the world: 171

Crude oil—production: 0 bbl/day (2016 est.)
country comparison to the world: 215

Crude oil—exports: 0 bbl/day (2014 est.)
country comparison to the world: 212

Crude oil—imports: 0 bbl/day (2014 est.)
country comparison to the world: 212

Crude oil—proved reserves: 0 bbl (1 January 2017 es)
country comparison to the world: 215

Refined petroleum products—production: 0 bbl/day (2014 est.)
country comparison to the world: 216

Refined petroleum products—consumption: 1,700 bbl/day (2015 est.)

country comparison to the world: 196

Refined petroleum products—exports: 0 bbl/day (2014 est.)
country comparison to the world: 214

Refined petroleum products—imports: 1,702 bbl/day (2014 est.)
country comparison to the world: 190

Natural gas—production: 0 cu m (2013 est.)
country comparison to the world: 213

Natural gas—consumption: 0 cu m (2013 est.)
country comparison to the world: 148

Natural gas—exports: 0 cu m (2013 est.)
country comparison to the world: 211

Natural gas—imports: 0 cu m (2013 est.)
country comparison to the world: 210

Natural gas—proved reserves: 0 cu m (1 January 2014 es)
country comparison to the world: 208

Carbon dioxide emissions from consumption of energy: 300,000 Mt (2013 est.)
country comparison to the world: 195

COMMUNICATIONS

Telephone system: *general assessment:* sparse and limited system
international: country code—212; tied into Morocco's system by microwave radio relay, tropospheric scatter, and satellite; satellite earth stations—2 Intelsat (Atlantic Ocean) linked to Rabat, Morocco (2015)

Broadcast media: Morocco's state-owned broadcaster, Radio-Television Marocaine (RTM), operates a radio service from Laayoune and relays TV service; a Polisario-backed radio station also broadcasts (2008)

Internet country code: .eh

TRANSPORTATION

Airports: 6 (2013)
country comparison to the world: 174

Airports—with paved runways: *total:* 3
2,438 to 3,047 m: 3 (2013)

Airports—with unpaved runways: *total:* 3
1,524 to 2,437 m: 1
914 to 1,523 m: 1
under 914 m: 1 (2013)

Ports and terminals: *major seaport(s):* Ad Dakhla, Laayoune (El Aaiun)

TRANSNATIONAL ISSUES

Disputes—international: many neighboring states reject Moroccan administration of Western Sahara; several states have extended diplomatic relations to the "Sahrawi Arab Democratic Republic" represented by the Polisario Front in exile in Algeria, while others recognize Moroccan sovereignty over Western Sahara; approximately 90,000 Sahrawi refugees continue to be sheltered in camps in Tindouf, Algeria, which has hosted Sahrawi refugees since the 1980s

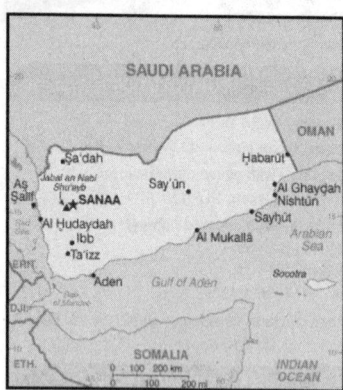

INTRODUCTION

Background: North Yemen became independent from the Ottoman Empire in 1918. The British, who had set up a protectorate area around the southern port of Aden in the 19th century, withdrew in 1967 from what became South Yemen. Three years later, the southern government adopted a Marxist orientation. The massive exodus of hundreds of thousands of Yemenis from the south to the north contributed to two decades of hostility between the states. The two countries were formally unified as the Republic of Yemen in 1990. A southern secessionist movement and brief civil war in 1994 was quickly subdued. In 2000, Saudi Arabia and Yemen agreed to delineate their border. Fighting in the northwest between the government and the Huthis, a Zaydi Shia Muslim minority, continued intermittently from 2004 to 2010. The southern secessionist movement was revitalized in 2007.

Public rallies in Sana'a against then President SALIH—inspired by similar demonstrations in Tunisia and Egypt—slowly built momentum starting in late January 2011 fueled by complaints over high unemployment, poor economic conditions, and corruption. By the following month, some protests had resulted in violence, and the demonstrations had spread to other major cities. By March the opposition had hardened its demands and was unifying behind calls for SALIH's immediate ouster. In April 2011, the Gulf Cooperation Council (GCC), in an attempt to mediate the crisis in Yemen, proposed the GGC Initiative, an agreement in which the president would step down in exchange for immunity from prosecution. SALIH's refusal to sign an agreement led to further violence. The UN Security Council passed Resolution 2014 in October 2011 calling for an end to the violence and completing a power transfer deal. In November 2011, SALIH signed the GCC Initiative to step down and to transfer some of his powers to Vice President Abd Rabuh Mansur HADI. Following

HADI's uncontested election victory in February 2012, SALIH formally transferred his powers. In accordance with the GCC initiative, Yemen launched a National Dialogue Conference (NDC) in March 2013 to discuss key constitutional, political, and social issues. HADI concluded the NDC in January 2014 and planned to begin implementing subsequent steps in the transition process, including constitutional drafting, a constitutional referendum, and national elections.

The Huthis, perceiving their grievances not addressed in the NDC, joined forces with SALIH and expanded their influence in northwestern Yemen, culminating in a major offensive against military units and rival tribes and enabling their forces to overrun the capital, Sanaa, in September 2014. In January 2015, the Huthis surrounded the presidential palace, HADI's residence, and key government facilities, prompting HADI and the cabinet to submit their resignations. HADI fled to Aden in February 2015 and rescinded his resignation. He subsequently escaped to Oman and then moved to Saudi Arabia and asked the GCC to intervene militarily in Yemen to protect the legitimate government from the Huthis. In March, Saudi Arabia assembled a coalition of Arab militaries and began airstrikes against the Huthis and Huthi-affiliated forces. Ground fighting between Huthi-aligned forces and resistance groups backed by the Saudi-led coalition continued through 2016. In 2016, the UN brokered a months-long cessation of hostilities that reduced airstrikes and fighting, and initiated peace talks in Kuwait. However, the talks ended without agreement. The Huthis and SALIH's political party announced a Supreme Political Council in August 2016 and a National Salvation Government, including a prime minister and several dozen cabinet members, in November 2016, to govern in Sanaa and further challenge the legitimacy of HADI's government. Further attempts at peace have failed while neither side has made decisive battlefield gains, perpetuating the conflict and deepening the divisions between northern and southern Yemen. Amid rising tensions between the Huthis and SALIH, sporadic clashes erupted in mid-2017, and Huthi forces killed SALIH in early December 2017.

GEOGRAPHY

Location: Middle East, bordering the Arabian Sea, Gulf of Aden, and Red Sea, between Oman and Saudi Arabia

Geographic coordinates: 15 00 N, 48 00 E

Map references: Middle East

Area: *total:* 527,968 sq km
land: 527,968 sq km
water: 0 sq km
note: includes Perim, Socotra, the former Yemen Arab Republic (YAR or North Yemen), and the

former People's Democratic Republic of Yemen (PDRY or South Yemen)
country comparison to the world: 51

Area—comparative: almost four times the size of Alabama; slightly larger than twice the size of Wyoming

Land boundaries: *total:* 1,601 km
border countries (2): Oman 294 km, Saudi Arabia 1,307 km

Coastline: 1,906 km

Maritime claims: *territorial sea:* 12 nm
contiguous zone: 24 nm
exclusive economic zone: 200 nm
continental shelf: 200 nm or to the edge of the continental margin

Climate: mostly desert; hot and humid along west coast; temperate in western mountains affected by seasonal monsoon; extraordinarily hot, dry, harsh desert in east

Terrain: narrow coastal plain backed by flat-topped hills and rugged mountains; dissected upland desert plains in center slope into the desert interior of the Arabian Peninsula

Elevation: *mean elevation:* 999 m

elevation extremes: *lowest point:* Arabian Sea 0 m
highest point: Jabal an Nabi Shu'ayb 3,666 m

Natural resources: petroleum, fish, rock salt, marble; small deposits of coal, gold, lead, nickel, and copper; fertile soil in west

Land use: *agricultural land:* 44.5%
arable land: 2.2%;
permanent crops: 0.6%;
permanent pasture: 41.7%
forest: 1%
other: 54.5% (2011 est.)
Irrigated land: 6,800 sq km (2012)

Population—distribution: the vast majority of the population is found in the Asir Mountains (part of the larger Sarawat Mountain system), located in the far western region of the country

Natural hazards: sandstorms and dust storms in summer
volcanism: limited volcanic activity; Jebel at Tair (Jabal al-Tair, Jebel Teir, Jabal al-Tayr, Jazirat at-Tair) (244 m), which forms an island in the Red Sea, erupted in 2007 after awakening from dormancy; other historically active volcanoes include Harra of Arhab, Harras of Dhamar, Harra es-Sawad, and Jebel Zubair, although many of these have not erupted in over a century

Environment—current issues: limited natural freshwater resources; inadequate supplies of potable water; overgrazing; soil erosion; desertification

Environment—international agreements: *party to:* Biodiversity, Climate Change, Climate Change-Kyoto Protocol, Desertification, Endangered

Species, Environmental Modification, Hazardous Wastes, Law of the Sea, Ozone Layer Protection *signed, but not ratified:* none of the selected agreements

Geography—note: strategic location on Bab el Mandeb, the strait linking the Red Sea and the Gulf of Aden, one of world's most active shipping lanes

PEOPLE AND SOCIETY

Population: 28,036,829 (July 2017 est.)
country comparison to the world: 48

Nationality: *noun:* Yemeni(s)
adjective: Yemeni

Ethnic groups: predominantly Arab; but also Afro-Arab, South Asians, Europeans

Languages: Arabic (official)
note: a distinct Socotri language is widely used on Socotra Island and Archipelago; Mahri is still fairly widely spoken in eastern Yemen

Religions: Muslim 99.1% (official; virtually all are citizens, an estimated 65% are Sunni and 35% are Shia), other 0.9% (includes Jewish, Baha'i, Hindu, and Christian; many are refugees or temporary foreign residents) (2010 est.)

Age structure: *0-14 years:* 39.83% (male 5,681,084/female 5,485,959)
15-24 years: 21.21% (male 3,015,232/female 2,930,329)
25-54 years: 32.27% (male 4,625,967/female 4,422,418)
55-64 years: 3.94% (male 506,759/female 598,973)
65 years and over: 2.75% (male 353,953/female 416,155) (2017 est.)

Dependency ratios: *total dependency ratio:* 76.8
youth dependency ratio: 71.7
elderly dependency ratio: 5.1
potential support ratio: 19.8 (2015 est.)

Median age: *total:* 19.5 years
male: 19.3 years
female: 19.6 years (2017 est.)
country comparison to the world: 201

Population growth rate: 2.28% (2017 est.)
country comparison to the world: 32

Birth rate: 28.4 births/1,000 population (2017 est.)
country comparison to the world: 43

Death rate: 6 deaths/1,000 population (2017 est.)
country comparison to the world: 166

Net migration rate: 0.4 migrant(s)/1,000 population (2017 est.)
country comparison to the world: 64

Population distribution: the vast majority of the population is found in the Asir Mountains (part of the larger Sarawat Mountain system), located in the far western region of the country

Urbanization: *urban population:* 35.8% of total population (2017)
rate of urbanization: 3.76% annual rate of change (2015-20 est.)

Major urban areas—population: SANAA (capital) 2.962 million; Aden 882,000 (2015)

Sex ratio: *at birth:* 1.05 male(s)/female
0-14 years: 1.04 male(s)/female
15-24 years: 1.03 male(s)/female
25-54 years: 1.05 male(s)/female
55-64 years: 0.85 male(s)/female
65 years and over: 0.87 male(s)/female
total population: 1.02 male(s)/female (2016 est.)
Mother's mean age at first birth: 21.4 years
median age at first birth among women 25-29 (2013 est.)

Maternal mortality ratio: 385 deaths/100,000 live births (2015 est.)
country comparison to the world: 30

Infant mortality rate: *total:* 46 deaths/1,000 live births
male: 50.1 deaths/1,000 live births
female: 41.7 deaths/1,000 live births (2017 est.)
country comparison to the world: 38

Life expectancy at birth: *total population:* 65.9 years
male: 63.7 years
female: 68.2 years (2017 est.)
country comparison to the world: 176

Total fertility rate: 3.63 children born/woman (2017 est.)
country comparison to the world: 41

Contraceptive prevalence rate: 33.5% (2013)

Health expenditures: 5.6% of GDP (2014)
country comparison to the world: 120

Physicians density: 0.31 physicians/1,000 population (2014)

Hospital bed density: 0.7 beds/1,000 population (2012)

Drinking water source:
improved:
urban: 72% of population
rural: 46.5% of population
total: 54.9% of population
unimproved:
urban: 28% of population
rural: 53.5% of population
total: 45.1% of population (2012 est.)

Sanitation facility access:
improved:
urban: 92.5% of population
rural: 34.1% of population
total: 53.3% of population
unimproved:
urban: 7.5% of population
rural: 65.9% of population
total: 46.7% of population (2012 est.)

HIV/AIDS—adult prevalence rate: <.1% (2016 est.)

HIV/AIDS—people living with HIV/AIDS: 9,900 (2016 est.)
country comparison to the world: 95

HIV/AIDS—deaths: <500 (2016 est.)

Major infectious diseases: *degree of risk:* high
food or waterborne diseases: bacterial diarrhea, hepatitis A, and typhoid fever
vectorborne diseases: dengue fever and malaria
water contact disease: schistosomiasis (2016)

Obesity—adult prevalence rate: 17.1% (2016)

country comparison to the world: 120

Children under the age of 5 years underweight: 39.9% (2013)
country comparison to the world: 3

Education expenditures: 4.6% of GDP (2008)
country comparison to the world: 67

Literacy: *definition:* age 15 and over can read and write
total population: 70.1%
male: 85.1%
female: 55% (2015 est.)

School life expectancy (primary to tertiary education): *total:* 9 years
male: 10 years
female: 8 years (2011)

Unemployment, youth ages 15-24: *total:* 33.7%
male: 26%
female: 74% (2010 est.)
country comparison to the world: 22

GOVERNMENT

Country name: *conventional long form:* Republic of Yemen
conventional short form: Yemen
local long form: Al Jumhuriyah al Yamaniyah
local short form: Al Yaman
former: Yemen Arab Republic [Yemen (Sanaa) or North Yemen] and People's Democratic Republic of Yemen [Yemen (Aden) or South Yemen]
etymology: name derivation remains unclear but may come from the Arab term "yumn" (happiness) and be related to the region's classical name "Arabia Felix" (Fertile or Happy Arabia); the Romans referred to the rest of the peninsula as "Arabia Deserta" (Deserted Arabia)

Government type: in transition

Capital: name: Sanaa

geographic coordinates: 15 21 N, 44 12 E
time difference: UTC+3 (8 hours ahead of Washington, DC, during Standard Time)

Administrative divisions: 22 governorates (muhafazat, singular—muhafazah); Abyan, 'Adan (Aden), Ad Dali', Al Bayda', Al Hudaydah, Al Jawf, Al Mahrah, Al Mahwit, Amanat al 'Asimah (Sanaa City), 'Amran, Arkhabil Suqutra (Socotra Archipelago), Dhamar, Hadramawt, Hajjah, Ibb, Lahij, Ma'rib, Raymah, Sa'dah, San'a' (Sanaa), Shabwah, Ta'izz

Independence: 22 May 1990 (Republic of Yemen was established with the merger of the Yemen Arab Republic [Yemen (Sanaa) or North Yemen] and the Marxist-dominated People's Democratic Republic of Yemen [Yemen (Aden) or South Yemen]); notable earlier dates: North Yemen became independent on 1 November 1918 (from the Ottoman Empire) and became a republic with the overthrow of the theocratic Imamate on 27 September 1962; South Yemen became independent on 30 November 1967 (from the UK)

National holiday: Unification Day, 22 May (1990)

Constitution: *history:* adopted by referendum 16 May 1991 (following unification); amended several times, last in 2009; note—after the National

Dialogue ended in January 2015, a presidentially appointed Constitutional Drafting Committee worked to prepare a new draft constitution that was expected to be put to a national referendum before being adopted; however, the president's resignation in January 2015 and subsequent conflict have interrupted the process (2016)

Legal system: mixed legal system of Islamic law, Napoleonic law, English common law, and customary law

International law organization participation: has not submitted an ICJ jurisdiction declaration; non-party state to the ICCt

Citizenship: *citizenship by birth:* no
citizenship by descent only: the father must be a citizen of Yemen; if the father is unknown, the mother must be a citizen
dual citizenship recognized: no
residency requirement for naturalization: 10 years

Suffrage: 18 years of age; universal

Executive branch: *chief of state:* President Abd Rabuh Mansur HADI (since 21 February 2012); Vice President Ali Mohsin al-AHMAR, Gen. (since 3 April 2016)

head of government: Prime Minister Ahmad Obaid bin DAGHIR (since 3 April 2016)
cabinet: appointed by the president
elections/appointments: president directly elected by absolute majority popular vote in 2 rounds if needed for a 7-year term (eligible for a second term); election last held on 21 February 2012 (next election NA); note—a special election was held on 21 February 2012 to remove Ali Abdallah SALIH under the terms of a Gulf Cooperation Council-mediated deal during the political crisis of 2011; vice president appointed by the president; prime minister appointed by the president
election results: Abd Rabuh Mansur HADI (GPC) elected as a consensus president with about 50% popular participation; no other candidates

Legislative branch: description: bicameral Parliament or Majlis consists of the Shura Council or Majlis Alshoora (111 seats; members appointed by the president; member tenure NA) and the House of Representatives or Majlis al Nuwaab (301 seats; members directly elected in single-seat constituencies by simple majority vote to serve 6-year terms)
elections: last held on 27 April 2003 (next scheduled for April 2009 but postponed indefinitely)
election results: House of Representatives percent of vote by party—GPC 58.0%, Islah 22.6%, YSP 3.8%, Unionist Party 1.9%, other 13.7%; seats by party—GPC 238, Islah 46, YSP 8, Nasserist Unionist Party 3, National Arab Socialist Ba'ath Party 2, independent 4

Judicial branch: *highest court(s):* Supreme Court (consists of the president of the Court, 2 deputies, and nearly 50 judges; court organized into constitutional, civil, commercial, family, administrative, criminal, military, and appeals scrutiny divisions)
judge selection and term of office: judges appointed by the Supreme Judicial Council, chaired by the president of the republic and

consisting of 10 high-ranking judicial officers; judges appointed for life with mandatory retirement at age 65
subordinate courts: appeal courts; district or first instance courts; commercial courts

Political parties and leaders: General People's Congress or GPC [Sadiq Abu RAS]
National Arab Socialist Ba'ath Party [Qassem Salam SAID]
Nasserist Unionist People's Organization [Abdulmalik al-MEKHLAFI]
Yemeni Reform Grouping or Islah [Muhammed Abdallah al-YADUMI]
Yemeni Socialist Party or YSP [Dr. Abd al-Rahman Umar al-SAQQAF]

Political pressure groups and leaders: Huthis
Muslim Brotherhood
Women National Committee
other: conservative tribal groups; southern secessionist groups; al-Qa'ida in the Arabian Peninsula (AQAP)

International organization participation: AFESD, AMF, CAEU, CD, EITI (temporarily suspended), FAO, G-77, IAEA, IBRD, ICAO, ICRM, IDA, IDB, IFAD, IFC, IFRCS, ILO, IMF, IMO, IMSO, Interpol, IOC, IOM, IPU, ISO, ITSO, ITU, ITUC (NGOs), LAS, MIGA, MINURSO, MINUSMA, MONUSCO, NAM, OAS (observer), OIC, OPCW, UN, UNAMID, UNCTAD, UNESCO, UNHCR, UNIDO, UNISFA, UNMIL, UNMISS, UNOCI, UNWTO, UPU, WCO, WFTU (NGOs), WHO, WIPO, WMO, WTO

Diplomatic representation in the US: *chief of mission:* Ambassador Ahmad Awadh BIN MUBARAK (since 3 August 2015)
chancery: 2319 Wyoming Avenue NW, Washington, DC 20008
telephone: [1] (202) 965-4760
FAX: [1] (202) 337-2017

Diplomatic representation from the US: *chief of mission:* Ambassador Matthew H. TUELLER (since 10 June 2014)
embassy: Sa'awan Street, Sanaa; note—Embassy closed in March 2015; relocated to Jeddah, Saudia Arabia
mailing address: P. O. Box 22347, Sanaa
telephone: [967] (1) 755-2000 ext. 2153 or 2266
FAX: [967] (1) 303-182

Flag description: three equal horizontal bands of red (top), white, and black; the band colors derive from the Arab Liberation flag and represent oppression (black), overcome through bloody struggle (red), to be replaced by a bright future (white)
note: similar to the flag of Syria, which has two green stars in the white band, and of Iraq, which has an Arabic inscription centered in the white band; also similar to the flag of Egypt, which has a heraldic eagle centered in the white band

National symbol(s): golden eagle; national colors: red, white, black

National anthem: name: "al-qumhuriyatu l-muttahida" (United Republic)

lyrics/music: Abdullah Abdulwahab NOA'MAN/ Ayyoab Tarish ABSI
note: adopted 1990; the music first served as the anthem for South Yemen before unification with North Yemen in 1990

ECONOMY

Economy—overview: Yemen is a low-income country that faces difficult long-term challenges to stabilizing and growing its economy, and the current conflict has only exacerbated those issues. The ongoing war has halted Yemen's exports, pressured the currency's exchange rate, accelerated inflation, severely limited food and fuel imports, and caused widespread damage to infrastructure. The conflict has also created a severe humanitarian crisis—the world's largest cholera outbreak currently at nearly 1 million cases, more than 7 million people at risk of famine, and more than 80% of the population in need of humanitarian assistance.

Prior to the start of the conflict in 2014, Yemen was highly dependent on declining oil and gas resources for revenue. Oil and gas earnings accounted for roughly 25% of GDP and 65% of government revenue. The Yemeni Government regularly faced annual budget shortfalls and tried to diversify the Yemeni economy through a reform program designed to bolster non-oil sectors of the economy and foreign investment. In July 2014, the government continued reform efforts by eliminating some fuel subsidies and in August 2014, the IMF approved a three-year, $570 million Extended Credit Facility for Yemen.

However, the conflict that began in 2014 stalled these reform efforts and ongoing fighting continues to accelerate the country's economic decline. In September 2016, President HADI announced the move of the main branch of Central Bank of Yemen from Sanaa to Aden where his government could exert greater control over the central bank's dwindling resources. Regardless of which group controls the main branch, the central bank system is struggling to function. Yemen's Central Bank's foreign reserves, which stood at roughly $5.2 billion prior to the conflict, have declined to negligible amounts. The Central Bank can no longer fully support imports of critical goods or the country's exchange rate. The country also is facing a growing liquidity crisis and rising inflation. The private sector is hemorrhaging, with almost all businesses making substantial layoffs. Access to food and other critical commodities such as medical equipment is limited across the country due to security issues on the ground. The Social Welfare Fund, a cash transfer program for Yemen's neediest, is no longer operational and has not made any disbursements since late 2014.

Yemen will require significant international assistance during and after the protracted conflict to stabilize its economy. Long-term challenges include a high population growth rate, high unemployment, declining water resources, and severe food scarcity.

GDP (purchasing power parity): $68.95 billion (2017 est.)

$70.37 billion (2016 est.)
$78 billion (2015 est.)
note: data are in 2017 dollars
country comparison to the world: 101

GDP (official exchange rate): $25.67 billion (2016 est.)

GDP—real growth rate: -2% (2017 est.)
-9.8% (2016 est.)
-28.1% (2015 est.)
country comparison to the world: 211

GDP—per capita (PPP): $2,300 (2017 est.)
$2,400 (2016 est.)
$2,800 (2015 est.)
note: data are in 2017 dollars
country comparison to the world: 202

Gross national saving: 0.1% of GDP (2017 est.)
-4.1% of GDP (2016 est.)
-3.7% of GDP (2015 est.)
country comparison to the world: 177

GDP—composition, by end use:
household consumption: 121.3%
government consumption: 13.5%
investment in fixed capital: 3.7%
investment in inventories: -7.8%
exports of goods and services: 4.2%
imports of goods and services: -34.8% (2017 est.)

GDP—composition, by sector of origin:
agriculture: 24.1%
industry: 14.3%
services: 61.6% (2017 est.)

Agriculture—products: grain, fruits, vegetables, pulses, qat, coffee, cotton; dairy products, livestock (sheep, goats, cattle, camels), poultry; fish

Industries: crude oil production and petroleum refining; small-scale production of cotton textiles, leather goods; food processing; handicrafts; aluminum products; cement; commercial ship repair; natural gas production

Industrial production growth rate: 13.7% (2017 est.)
country comparison to the world: 5

Labor force: 7.425 million (2017 est.)
country comparison to the world: 66
Labor force—by occupation: note: most people are employed in agriculture and herding; services, construction, industry, and commerce account for less than one-fourth of the labor force

Unemployment rate: 27% (2014 est.)
35% (2003 est.)
country comparison to the world: 197

Population below poverty line: 54% (2014 est.)

Household income or consumption by percentage share: *lowest 10%*: 2.6%
highest 10%: 30.3% (2008 est.)

Distribution of family income—Gini index: 37.9 (2009 est.)
37.3 (1999 est.)
country comparison to the world: 74

Budget: *revenues*: $3.467 billion
expenditures: $5.232 billion (2017 est.)

Taxes and other revenues: 13.5% of GDP (2017 est.)

country comparison to the world: 200

Budget surplus (+) or deficit (-): -6.9% of GDP (2017 est.)
country comparison to the world: 187

Public debt: 135.5% of GDP (2017 est.)
119.1% of GDP (2016 est.)
country comparison to the world: 4

Fiscal year: calendar year

Inflation rate (consumer prices): 20% (2017 est.)
5% (2016 est.)
country comparison to the world: 217

Central bank discount rate: NA%

Commercial bank prime lending rate: 26% (31 December 2017 est.)
27% (31 December 2016 est.)
country comparison to the world: 10

Stock of narrow money: $5.542 billion (31 December 2017 est.)
$6.718 billion (31 December 2016 est.)
country comparison to the world: 101

Stock of broad money: $9.338 billion (31 December 2017 est.)
$11.95 billion (31 December 2016 est.)
country comparison to the world: 106

Stock of domestic credit: $3.706 billion (31 December 2017 est.)
$4.515 billion (31 December 2016 est.)
country comparison to the world: 128

Market value of publicly traded shares: $NA

Current account balance: -$579 million (2017 est.)
-$1.532 billion (2016 est.)
country comparison to the world: 109

Exports: $501.2 million (2017 est.)
$163.6 million (2016 est.)
country comparison to the world: 174

Exports—commodities: crude oil, coffee, dried and salted fish, liquefied natural gas

Exports—partners: Egypt 26%, Saudi Arabia 15.4%, Oman 11.3%, Malaysia 9.8%, Thailand 5.8%, UAE 4.9% (2016)

Imports: $4.573 billion (2017 est.)
$3.117 billion (2016 est.)
country comparison to the world: 126

Imports—commodities: food and live animals, machinery and equipment, chemicals

Imports—partners: UAE 12.8%, China 12%, Turkey 8%, Saudi Arabia 8%, Indonesia 6.8%, Brazil 6.6%, India 4.8% (2016)

Reserves of foreign exchange and gold: $245.1 million (31 December 2017 est.)
$592.6 million (31 December 2016 est.)
country comparison to the world: 156

Debt—external: $7.252 billion (31 December 2017 est.)
$7.181 billion (31 December 2016 est.)
country comparison to the world: 125

Stock of direct foreign investment—at home: $NA

Exchange rates: Yemeni rials (YER) per US dollar—

275 (2017 est.)
214.9 (2016 est.)
214.9 (2015 est.)
228 (2014 est.)
214.89 (2013 est.)

ENERGY

Electricity access: population without electricity: 13,300,000
electrification—total population: 48%
electrification—urban areas: 79%
electrification—rural areas: 33% (2013)

Electricity—production: 5.006 billion kWh (2015 est.)
country comparison to the world: 122

Electricity—consumption: 3.634 billion kWh (2015 est.)
country comparison to the world: 132

Electricity—exports: 0 kWh (2016 est.)
country comparison to the world: 219

Electricity—imports: 0 kWh (2016 est.)
country comparison to the world: 220

Electricity—installed generating capacity: 1.534 million kW (2015 est.)
country comparison to the world: 123

Electricity—from fossil fuels: 99% of total installed capacity (2015 est.)
country comparison to the world: 32

Electricity—from nuclear fuels: 0% of total installed capacity (2015 est.)
country comparison to the world: 213

Electricity—from hydroelectric plants: 0% of total installed capacity (2015 est.)
country comparison to the world: 157

Electricity—from other renewable sources: 2% of total installed capacity (2015 est.)
country comparison to the world: 123

Crude oil—production: 21,670 bbl/day (2016 est.)
country comparison to the world: 67

Crude oil—exports: 49,590 bbl/day (2014 est.)
country comparison to the world: 42

Crude oil—imports: 0 bbl/day (2014 est.)
country comparison to the world: 215

Crude oil—proved reserves: 3 billion bbl (1 January 2017 es)
country comparison to the world: 31

Refined petroleum products—production: 56,840 bbl/day (2014 est.)
country comparison to the world: 81

Refined petroleum products—consumption: 140,000 bbl/day (2015 est.)
country comparison to the world: 73

Refined petroleum products—exports: 27,290 bbl/day (2014 est.)
country comparison to the world: 64

Refined petroleum products—imports: 84,340 bbl/day (2014 est.)
country comparison to the world: 64

Natural gas—production: 2.85 billion cu m (2015 est.)
country comparison to the world: 56

Natural gas—consumption: 1.19 billion cu m (2015 est.)
country comparison to the world: 95

Natural gas—exports: 8.8 billion cu m (2014 est.)
country comparison to the world: 23

Natural gas—imports: 0 cu m (2013 est.)
country comparison to the world: 213

Natural gas—proved reserves: 478.5 billion cu m (1 January 2017 es)
country comparison to the world: 33

Carbon dioxide emissions from consumption of energy: 22 million Mt (2013 est.)
country comparison to the world: 80

COMMUNICATIONS

Telephones—fixed lines: *total subscriptions:* 1.213 million
subscriptions per 100 inhabitants: 4 (July 2016 est.)
country comparison to the world: 71

Telephones—mobile cellular: *total:* 17.536 million
subscriptions per 100 inhabitants: 64 (July 2016 est.)
country comparison to the world: 62

Telephone system: *general assessment:* cell phone penetration growing rapidly
domestic: the national network consists of microwave radio relay, cable, tropospheric scatter, GSM and CDMA mobile-cellular telephone systems; fixed-line teledensity remains low by regional standards but mobile cellular use expanding apace
international: country code—967; landing point for the international submarine cable Fiber-Optic Link Around the Globe (FLAG); satellite earth stations—3 Intelsat (2 Indian Ocean and 1 Atlantic Ocean), 1 Intersputnik (Atlantic Ocean region), and 2 Arabsat; microwave radio relay to Saudi Arabia and Djibouti (2016)

Broadcast media: state-run TV with 2 stations; state-run radio with 2 national radio stations and 5 local stations; stations from Oman and Saudi Arabia can be accessed (2007)

Internet country code: .ye

Internet users: *total:* 6,732,928
percent of population: 24.6% (July 2016 est.)
country comparison to the world: 67

TRANSPORTATION

National air transport system: *number of registered air carriers:* 2
inventory of registered aircraft operated by air carriers: 10
annual passenger traffic on registered air carriers: 1,387,999
annual freight traffic on registered air carriers: 0 mt-km (2015)
Civil aircraft registration country code prefix: 7O (2016)

Airports: 57 (2013)
country comparison to the world: 84

Airports—with paved runways: *total:* 17

over 3,047 m: 4
2,438 to 3,047 m: 9
1,524 to 2,437 m: 3
914 to 1,523 m: 1 (2013)

Airports—with unpaved runways: *total:* 40
over 3,047 m: 3
2,438 to 3,047 m: 5
1,524 to 2,437 m: 7
914 to 1,523 m: 16
under 914 m: 9 (2013)

Pipelines: gas 641 km; liquid petroleum gas 22 km; oil 1,370 km (2013)

Roadways: *total:* 71,300 km
paved: 6,200 km
unpaved: 65,100 km (2005)
country comparison to the world: 67

Merchant marine: *total:* 31
by type: general cargo 3, oil tanker 4, other 24 (2017)
country comparison to the world: 124

Ports and terminals: *major seaport(s):* Aden, Al Hudaydah, Al Mukalla

MILITARY AND SECURITY

Military expenditures: 3.97% of GDP (2014)
4.08% of GDP (2013)
4.57% of GDP (2012)
4.93% of GDP (2011)
country comparison to the world: 12

Military branches: Land Forces, Naval and Coastal Defense Forces (includes Marines), Air and Air Defense Force (al-Quwwat al-Jawwiya al-Yemeniya), Border Guards, Strategic Reserve Forces (2013)

Military service age and obligation: 18 is the legal minimum age for voluntary military service; no conscription; 2-year service obligation (2012)
Maritime threats: the International Maritime Bureau reports offshore waters in the Gulf of Aden are high risk for piracy; numerous vessels, including commercial shipping and pleasure craft, have been attacked and hijacked both at anchor and while underway; crew, passengers, and cargo are held for ransom; the presence of several naval task forces in the Gulf of Aden and additional anti-piracy measures on the part of ship operators reduced the incidence of piracy in that body of water; one attack was reported in 2016 and one reported during the first half of 2017
Military—note:

TERRORISM

Terrorist groups—home based: al-Qa'ida in the Arabian Peninsula (AQAP): *aim(s):* overthrow the Yemen Government and, ultimately, establish a regional Islamic caliphate; eradicate Western influence and presence from Yemen and the rest of the Arabian Peninsula
area(s) of operation: a core al-Qa'ida affiliate that was headquartered in Al Mukalla, Hadramawt Governorate, until Yemeni forces and their allies drove AQAP from the city in April 2016; most active in southern, eastern, and central Yemen,

especially in Abyan, Al Baydah, Hadramawt, Sabwah, and Ma'rib governorates; conducts ongoing attacks against Yemeni Government forces, officials, and facilities and Western embassies, diplomats, tourists, and Shia Muslims, oil facilities, and merchant ships, as well as Western and Saudi Arabian interests; assessed in 2015 to have up to 4,000 members

Terrorist groups—foreign based: al-Qa'ida (AQ): *aim(s):* overthrow the Yemen Government and, ultimately, establish a pan-Islamic caliphate under a strict Salafi Muslim interpretation of Sharia
area(s) of operation: operational throughout Yemen, in collaboration with its affiliate organization, al-Qa'ida in the Arabian Peninsula (AQAP)

Islamic State of Iraq and the Levant (ISIL): *aim(s):* replace the Yemen Government with an Islamic state and implement ISIL's strict interpretation of Sharia
area(s) of operation: operational primarily in 'Adan and the capital, Sanaa, where operatives conduct attacks against Shia Muslims and government facilities and personnel; claimed responsibility for the deadliest attack in to 'Adan, where a suicide bomber detonated a vehicle-borne improvised explosive device on 29 August 2016, killing approximately 70 new recruits standing in line to register to join the military; suicide bombers detonated explosives on 20 March 2015 inside two Shia Muslim mosques in Sanaa, killing at least 137 worshippers and injuring over 300, which marked the first attack ISIL had claimed in Yemen; actively recruits Sunni Muslim youths; ISIL refers to Yemen as its Wilayat Sanaa; ISIL-Yemen was placed in the US State Department's designated global terror category under Executive Order 13224 on 19 May 2016

TRANSNATIONAL ISSUES

Disputes—international: Saudi Arabia has reinforced its concrete-filled security barrier along sections of the fully demarcated border with Yemen to stem illegal cross-border activities

Refugees and internally displaced persons: refugees (country of origin): 5,877 (Ethiopia) (2016); 256,283 (Somalia) (2017)
IDPs: 2,014,026 (conflict in Sa'ada Governorate; clashes between al-Qa'ida in the Arabian Peninsula and government forces) (2017)

Trafficking in persons: current situation: Yemen is a source and, to a lesser extent, transit and destination country for men, women, and children subjected to forced labor and women and children subjected to sex trafficking; trafficking activities grew in Yemen in 2014, as the country's security situation deteriorated and poverty worsened; armed groups increased their recruitment of Yemeni children as combatants or checkpoint guards, and the Yemeni military and security forces continue to use child soldiers; some other Yemeni children, mostly boys, migrate to Yemeni cities or Saudi Arabia and, less frequently Oman, where they end up as beggars, drug smugglers, prostitutes, or forced laborers in domestic service or small shops; Yemeni children increasingly are also subjected to sex trafficking in country and in Saudi Arabia; tens of thousands of Yemeni migrant workers deported from Saudi Arabia and thousands of Syrian refugees are vulnerable to trafficking; additionally, Yemen is a destination and transit country for women and children from the Horn of Africa who are looking for work or receive fraudulent job offers in the Gulf states but are subjected to sexual exploitation or forced labor upon arrival; reports indicate that adults and children are still sold or inherited as slaves in Yemen

tier rating: Tier 3—Yemen does not fully comply with the minimum standards for the elimination of trafficking and is not making significant efforts to do so; weak government institutions, corruption, economic problems, security threats, and poor law enforcement capabilities impeded the government's ability to combat human trafficking; not all forms of trafficking are criminalized, and officials continue to conflate trafficking and smuggling; the status of an anti-trafficking law drafted with assistance from an international organization remains unknown following the dissolution of the government in January 2015; the government did not report efforts to investigate, prosecute, or convict anyone of trafficking or slavery offenses, including complicit officials, despite reports of officials willfully ignoring trafficking crimes and using child soldiers in the government's armed forces; the government acknowledged the use of child soldiers and signed a UN action plan to end the practice in 2014 but made no efforts to release child soldiers from the military and provide them with rehabilitative services; authorities failed to identify victims and refer them to protective services; the status of a draft national anti-trafficking strategy remains unknown (2015)

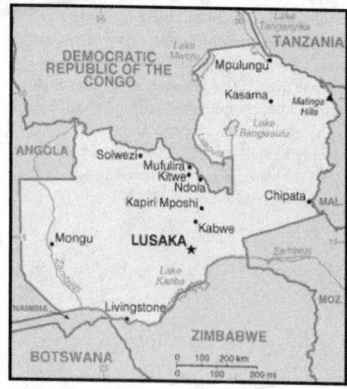

Background: The territory of Northern Rhodesia was administered by the former British South Africa Company from 1891 until it was taken over by the UK in 1923. During the 1920s and 1930s, advances in mining spurred development and immigration. The name was changed to Zambia upon independence in 1964. In the 1980s and 1990s, declining copper prices, economic mismanagement, and a prolonged drought hurt the economy. Elections in 1991 brought an end to one-party rule and propelled the Movement for Multiparty Democracy (MMD) to govern-ment. The subsequent vote in 1996, however, saw increasing harassment of opposition parties and abuse of state media and other resources. The election in 2001 was marked by administrative problems, with three parties filing a legal petition challenging the election of ruling party candidate Levy MWANAWASA. MWANAWASA was reelected in 2006 in an election that was deemed free and fair. Upon his death in August 2008, he was succeeded by his vice president, Rupiah BANDA, who won a special presidential byelection later that year. The MMD and BANDA lost to the Patriotic Front (PF) and Michael SATA in the 2011 general elections. SATA, however, presided over a period of haphazard economic management and attempted to silence opposition to PF policies. SATA died in October 2014 and was succeeded by his vice president, Guy SCOTT, who served as interim president until January 2015, when Edgar LUNGU won the presidential byelection and completed SATA's term. LUNGU then won a full term in August 2016 presidential elections.

Location: Southern Africa, east of Angola, south of the Democratic Republic of the Congo

Geographic coordinates: 15 00 S, 30 00 E

Map references: Africa

Area: *total:* 752,618 sq km
land: 743,398 sq km
water: 9,220 sq km
country comparison to the world: 40

Area—comparative: almost five times the size of Georgia; slightly larger than Texas

Land boundaries: *total:* 6,043.15 km
border countries (8): Angola 1,065 km, Botswana 0.15 km, Democratic Republic of the Congo 2,332 km, Malawi 847 km, Mozambique 439 km, Namibia 244 km, Tanzania 353 km, Zimbabwe 763 km

Coastline: 0 km (landlocked)

Maritime claims: none (landlocked)

Climate: tropical; modified by altitude; rainy season (October to April)

Terrain: mostly high plateau with some hills and mountains

Elevation: *mean elevation:* 1,138 m

elevation extremes: *lowest point:* Zambezi river 329 m
highest point: unnamed elevation in Mafinga Hills 2,301 m

Natural resources: copper, cobalt, zinc, lead, coal, emeralds, gold, silver, uranium, hydropower

Land use: *agricultural land:* 31.7%
arable land: 4.8%;
permanent crops: 0%;
permanent pasture: 26.9%
forest: 66.3%
other: 2% (2011 est.)
Irrigated land: 1,560 sq km (2012)

Population—distribution: one of the highest levels of urbanization in Africa; high density in the central area, particularly around the cities of Lusaka, Ndola, Kitwe, and Mufulira

Natural hazards: periodic drought; tropical storms (November to April)

Environment—current issues: air pollution and resulting acid rain in the mineral extraction and refining region; chemical runoff into watersheds; poaching seriously threatens rhinoceros, elephant, antelope, and large cat populations; deforestation; soil erosion; desertification; lack of adequate water treatment presents human health risks

Environment—international agreements: *party to:* Biodiversity, Climate Change, Climate Change-Kyoto Protocol, Desertification, Endangered Species, Hazardous Wastes, Law of the Sea, Ozone Layer Protection, Wetlands
signed, but not ratified: none of the selected agreements

Geography—note: landlocked; the Zambezi forms a natural riverine boundary with Zimbabwe; Lake Kariba on the Zambia-Zimbabwe border forms the world's largest reservoir by volume (180 cu km; 43 cu mi)

Population: 15.972 million
note: estimates for this country explicitly take into account the effects of excess mortality due to AIDS; this can result in lower life expectancy, higher infant mortality, higher death rates, lower population growth rates, and changes in the distribution of population by age and sex than would otherwise be expected (July 2017 est.)
country comparison to the world: 69

Nationality: *noun:* Zambian(s)
adjective: Zambian

Ethnic groups: Bemba 21%, Tonga 13.6%, Chewa 7.4%, Lozi 5.7%, Nsenga 5.3%, Tumbuka 4.4%, Ngoni 4%, Lala 3.1%, Kaonde 2.9%, Namwanga 2.8%, Lunda (north Western) 2.6%, Mambwe 2.5%, Luvale 2.2%, Lamba 2.1%, Ushi 1.9%, Lenje 1.6%, Bisa 1.6%, Mbunda 1.2%, other 13.8%, unspecified 0.4% (2010 est.)

Languages: Bembe 33.4%, Nyanja 14.7%, Tonga 11.4%, Lozi 5.5%, Chewa 4.5%, Nsenga 2.9%, Tumbuka 2.5%, Lunda (North Western) 1.9%, Kaonde 1.8%, Lala 1.8%, Lamba 1.8%, English (official) 1.7%, Luvale 1.5%, Mambwe 1.3%, Namwanga 1.2%, Lenje 1.1%, Bisa 1%, other 9.7%, unspecified 0.2%
note: Zambia is said to have over 70 languages, although many of these may be considered dialects; all of Zambia's major languages are members of the Bantu family (2010 est.)

Religions: Protestant 75.3%, Roman Catholic 20.2%, other 2.7% (includes Muslim Buddhist, Hindu, and Baha'i), none 1.8% (2010 est.)

Demographic profile: Zambia's poor, youthful population consists primarily of Bantu-speaking people representing nearly 70 different ethnicities. Zambia's high fertility rate continues to drive rapid population growth, averaging almost 3 percent annually between 2000 and 2010. The country's total fertility rate has fallen by less than 1.5 children per woman during the last 30 years and still averages among the world's highest, almost 6 children per woman, largely because of the country's lack of access to family planning services, education for girls, and employment for women. Zambia also exhibits wide fertility disparities based on rural or urban location, education, and income. Poor, uneducated women from rural areas are more likely to marry young, to give birth early, and to have more children, viewing children as a sign of prestige and recognizing that not all of their children will live to adulthood. HIV/AIDS is prevalent in Zambia and contributes to its low life expectancy.

Zambian emigration is low compared to many other African countries and is comprised predominantly of the well-educated. The small amount of brain drain, however, has a major impact in Zambia because of its limited human capital and lack of educational infrastructure for developing skilled professionals in key fields. For example, Zambia has few schools for training doctors, nurses, and other health care workers. Its spending on education is low compared to other sub-Saharan countries.

Age structure: *0-14 years:* 46.03% (male 3,693,255/female 3,657,890)
15-24 years: 20% (male 1,595,628/female 1,598,065)
25-54 years: 28.72% (male 2,310,961/female 2,276,018)
55-64 years: 2.93% (male 217,954/female 250,134)
65 years and over: 2.33% (male 162,605/female 209,490) (2017 est.)

Dependency ratios: *total dependency ratio:* 91.9
youth dependency ratio: 87.1
elderly dependency ratio: 4.8
potential support ratio: 20.8 (2015 est.)

Median age: *total:* 16.8 years
male: 16.6 years
female: 16.9 years (2017 est.)
country comparison to the world: 225

Population growth rate: 2.93% (2017 est.)
country comparison to the world: 9

Birth rate: 41.5 births/1,000 population (2017 est.)
country comparison to the world: 5

Death rate: 12.2 deaths/1,000 population (2017 est.)
country comparison to the world: 20

Net migration rate: 0 migrant(s)/1,000 population (2017 est.)
country comparison to the world: 71

Population distribution: one of the highest levels of urbanization in Africa; high density in the central area, particularly around the cities of Lusaka, Ndola, Kitwe, and Mufulira

Urbanization: *urban population:* 41.8% of total population (2017)
rate of urbanization: 4.35% annual rate of change (2015-20 est.)

Major urban areas—population: LUSAKA (capital) 2.179 million (2015)

Sex ratio: *at birth:* 1.03 male(s)/female
0-14 years: 1.01 male(s)/female
15-24 years: 1 male(s)/female
25-54 years: 1.02 male(s)/female
55-64 years: 0.88 male(s)/female
65 years and over: 0.76 male(s)/female
total population: 1 male(s)/female (2016 est.)

Mother's mean age at first birth: 19.2 years
note: median age at first birth among women 25-29 (2013/14 est.)

Maternal mortality ratio: 224 deaths/100,000 live births (2015 est.)
country comparison to the world: 48

Infant mortality rate: *total:* 61.1 deaths/1,000 live births
male: 66.4 deaths/1,000 live births
female: 55.6 deaths/1,000 live births (2017 est.)
country comparison to the world: 16

Life expectancy at birth: *total population:* 52.7 years
male: 51.1 years
female: 54.4 years (2017 est.)
country comparison to the world: 219

Total fertility rate: 5.63 children born/woman (2017 est.)
country comparison to the world: 8

Contraceptive prevalence rate: 49% (2013/14)

Health expenditures: 5% of GDP (2014)
country comparison to the world: 141

Physicians density: 0.16 physicians/1,000 population (2012)

Hospital bed density: 2 beds/1,000 population (2010)

Drinking water source:
improved:
urban: 85.6% of population
rural: 51.3% of population
total: 65.4% of population
unimproved:
urban: 14.4% of population
rural: 48.7% of population
total: 34.6% of population (2015 est.)

Sanitation facility access:
improved:
urban: 55.6% of population
rural: 35.7% of population
total: 43.9% of population
unimproved:
urban: 44.4% of population
rural: 64.3% of population
total: 56.1% of population (2015 est.)

HIV/AIDS—adult prevalence rate: 12.4% (2016 est.)
country comparison to the world: 7

HIV/AIDS—people living with HIV/AIDS: 1.2 million (2016 est.)
country comparison to the world: 9

HIV/AIDS—deaths: 21,000 (2016 est.)
country comparison to the world: 13

Major infectious diseases: *degree of risk:* very high
food or waterborne diseases: bacterial and protozoal diarrhea, hepatitis A, and typhoid fever
vectorborne diseases: malaria and dengue fever
water contact disease: schistosomiasis
animal contact disease: rabies (2016)

Obesity—adult prevalence rate: 8.1% (2016)
country comparison to the world: 155

Children under the age of 5 years underweight: 14.8% (2013)
country comparison to the world: 49

Education expenditures: 1.1% of GDP (2008)
country comparison to the world: 170

Literacy: *definition:* age 15 and over can read and write English
total population: 63.4%
male: 70.9%
female: 56% (2015 est.)

Unemployment, youth ages 15-24: *total:* 15.2%
male: 14.6%
female: 15.8% (2012 est.)
country comparison to the world: 42

GOVERNMENT

Country name: *conventional long form:* Republic of Zambia
conventional short form: Zambia
former: Northern Rhodesia
etymology: name derived from the Zambezi River, which flows through the western part of the country and forms its southern border with neighboring Zimbabwe

Government type: presidential republic

Capital: name: Lusaka; note—a proposal to build a new capital city in Ngabwe was announced in May 2017
geographic coordinates: 15 25 S, 28 17 E
time difference: UTC+2 (7 hours ahead of Washington, DC, during Standard Time)

Administrative divisions: 10 provinces; Central, Copperbelt, Eastern, Luapula, Lusaka, Muchinga, Northern, North-Western, Southern, Western

Independence: 24 October 1964 (from the UK)

National holiday: Independence Day, 24 October (1964)

Constitution: *history:* several previous; latest adopted 24 August 1991, promulgated 30 August 1991
amendments: proposed by the National Assembly; passage requires two-thirds majority vote by the Assembly in two separate readings at least 30 days apart; passage of amendments affecting fundamental rights and freedoms requires approval by at least one-half of votes cast in a referendum prior to consideration and voting by the Assembly; amended 1996, 2015, last in 2016 (2017)

Legal system: mixed legal system of English common law and customary law

International law organization participation: has not submitted an ICJ jurisdiction declaration; accepts ICCt jurisdiction

Citizenship: *citizenship by birth:* only if at least one parent is a citizen of Zambia
citizenship by descent: yes, if at least one parent was a citizen of Zambia
dual citizenship recognized: yes
residency requirement for naturalization: 5 years for those with an ancestor who was a citizen of Zambia, otherwise 10 years residency is required

Suffrage: 18 years of age; universal

Executive branch: *chief of state:* President Edgar LUNGU (since 25 January 2015); Vice President Inonge WINA (since 26 January 2015); note—the president is both chief of state and head of government
head of government: President Edgar LUNGU (since 25 January 2015); Vice President Inonge WINA (since 26 January 2015)
cabinet: Cabinet appointed by president from among members of the National Assembly
elections/appointments: president directly elected by absolute majority popular vote in 2 rounds if needed for a 5-year term (eligible for a second term); last held on 11 August 2016 (next to be held in 2021)

election results: Edgar LUNGU reelected president; percent of vote—Edgar LUNGU (PF) 50.4%, Hakainde HICHILEMA (UPND) 47.6%, other 2.0%

Legislative branch: description: unicameral National Assembly (164 seats; 156 members directly elected in single-seat constituencies by simple majority vote, and 8 appointed by the president; members serve 5-year terms); note—6 additional electoral seats were added for the 11 August 2016 election, up from 150 electoral seats in the 2011 election

elections: last held on 11 August 2016 (next to be held in 2021)

election results: percent of vote by party—PF 42%, UPND 41.7%, MMD 2.7%, FDD 2.2%, other 1.9%, independent 9.5%; seats by party—PF 80, UPND 58, MMD 3, FDD 1, independent 14

Judicial branch: *highest court(s):* Supreme Court (consists of the chief justice and deputy chief justices, and at least 11 judges); Constitutional Court (consists of the court president, vice-president, and 11 judges); note—the Constitutional Court began operation in June 2016

judge selection and term of office: Supreme Court and Constitutional Court judges appointed by the president upon the advice of the 9-member Judicial Service Commission headed by the chief justice, and ratified by the National Assembly; judges normally serve until age 65

subordinate courts: Court of Appeal; High Court; Industrial Relations Court; subordinate courts 3 levels, based on upper limit of money involved); Small Claims Court; local courts (2 grades, based on upper limit of money involved)

Political parties and leaders: Alliance for Democracy and Development or ADD [Charles MILUPI] Forum for Democracy and Development or FDD [Edith NAWAKWI] Movement for Multiparty Democracy or MMD [Nevers MUMBA] Patriotic Front or PF [Edgar LUNGU] United Party for National Development or UPND [Hakainde HICHILEMA]

Political pressure groups and leaders: Congress of Trade Unions or ZCTU; Federation of Free Trade Unions in Zambia *other:* other labor and trade unions

International organization participation: ACP, AfDB, AU, C, COMESA, EITI (compliant country), FAO, G-77, IAEA, IBRD, ICAO, ICCt, ICRM, IDA, IFAD, IFC, IFRCS, ILO, IMF, Interpol, IOC, IOM, IPU, ISO (correspondent), ITSO, ITU, ITUC (NGOs), MIGA, MONUSCO, NAM, OPCW, PCA, SADC, UN, UNAMID, UNCTAD, UNESCO, UNHCR, UNIDO, UNISFA, UNMIL, UNMISS, UNOCI, UNWTO, UPU, WCO, WHO, WIPO, WMO, WTO

Diplomatic representation in the US: *chief of mission:* Ambassador Ngosa SIMBYAKULA (since 29 November 2017)

chancery: 2419 Massachusetts Avenue NW, Washington, DC 20008

telephone: [1] (202) 265-9717 through 9719

FAX: [1] (202) 332-0826

Diplomatic representation from the US: *chief of mission:* Ambassador Eric T. SCHULTZ (since 12 December 2014)

embassy: Eastern end of Kabulonga Road, Ibex Hill, Lusaka

mailing address: P. O. Box 320065, Lusaka

telephone: [260] (211) 357-000

FAX: [260]) (211) 357-224

Flag description: green field with a panel of three vertical bands of red (hoist side), black, and orange below a soaring orange eagle, on the outer edge of the flag; green stands for the country's natural resources and vegetation, red symbolizes the struggle for freedom, black the people of Zambia, and orange the country's mineral wealth; the eagle represents the people's ability to rise above the nation's problems

National symbol(s): African fish eagle; national colors: green, red, black, orange

National anthem: name: "Lumbanyeni Zambia" (Stand and Sing of Zambia, Proud and Free) *lyrics/music:* multiple/Enoch Mankayi SONTONGA

note: adopted 1964; the melody, from the popular song "God Bless Africa," is the same as that of Tanzania but with different lyrics; the melody is also incorporated into South Africa's anthem

ECONOMY

Economy—overview: Zambia had one of the world's fastest growing economies for the ten years up to 2014, with real GDP growth averaging roughly 6.7% per annum, though growth slowed during the period 2015 to 2017, due to falling copper prices, reduced power generation, and depreciation of the kwacha. Zambia's lack of economic diversification and dependency on copper as its sole major export makes it vulnerable to fluctuations in the world commodities market and prices turned downward in 2015 due to declining demand from China; Zambia was overtaken by the Democratic Republic of Congo as Africa's largest copper producer.

Despite recent strong economic growth and its status as a lower middle-income country, widespread and extreme rural poverty and high unemployment levels remain significant problems, made worse by a high birth rate, a relatively high HIV/AIDS burden, and by market-distorting agricultural and energy policies. Zambia has raised $7 billion from international investors by issuing separate sovereign bonds in 2012, 2014, and 2015, significantly increasing the country's public debt burden to 56% of GDP; the government plan refinanced $2.8 billion worth of Eurobonds in 2017 to cut debt servicing costs.

Poor management of water resources has also contributed to a power generation shortage, which has hampered industrial productivity and contributed to an increase in year-on-year inflation to more than 20% in 2016. Zambia's currency, the kwacha, also depreciated sharply against the dollar through 2016, leading the central bank to restrict lending. Rampant spending in recent years has increased the fiscal deficit to over 8% in 2017 and may encourage the government to seek external financing from the IMF to fund the shortfall.

GDP (purchasing power parity): $68.9 billion (2017 est.)
$66.27 billion (2016 est.)
$64.08 billion (2015 est.)
note: data are in 2017 dollars
country comparison to the world: 102

GDP (official exchange rate): $25.58 billion (2016 est.)

GDP—real growth rate: 4% (2017 est.)
3.4% (2016 est.)
2.9% (2015 est.)
country comparison to the world: 69

GDP—per capita (PPP): $4,000 (2017 est.)
$4,000 (2016 est.)
$4,000 (2015 est.)
note: data are in 2017 dollars
country comparison to the world: 179

Gross national saving: 38.3% of GDP (2017 est.)
37.3% of GDP (2016 est.)
38.9% of GDP (2015 est.)
country comparison to the world: 10

GDP—composition, by end use:
household consumption: 53.8%
government consumption: 21.2%
investment in fixed capital: 27.8%
investment in inventories: 1.2%
exports of goods and services: 45.3%
imports of goods and services: -49.2% (2017 est.)

GDP—composition, by sector of origin:
agriculture: 5.4%
industry: 35.6%
services: 59% (2017 est.)

Agriculture—products: corn, sorghum, rice, peanuts, sunflower seeds, vegetables, flowers, tobacco, cotton, sugarcane, cassava (manioc, tapioca), coffee; cattle, goats, pigs, poultry, milk, eggs, hides

Industries: copper mining and processing, emerald mining, construction, foodstuffs, beverages, chemicals, textiles, fertilizer, horticulture

Industrial production growth rate: 5.1% (2017 est.)
country comparison to the world: 43

Labor force: 6.898 million (2017 est.)
country comparison to the world: 69
Labor force—by occupation: agriculture: 85%
industry: 6%
services: 9% (2004)

Unemployment rate: 15% (2008 est.)
50% (2000 est.)
country comparison to the world: 172

Population below poverty line: 60.5% (2010 est.)

Household income or consumption by percentage share: *lowest 10%:* 1.5%
highest 10%: 47.4% (2010)

Distribution of family income—Gini index: 57.5 (2013)
50.8 (2004)
country comparison to the world: 8

Budget: *revenues:* $4.895 billion
expenditures: $7.05 billion (2017 est.)

Taxes and other revenues: 19.1% of GDP (2017 est.)
country comparison to the world: 161

Budget surplus (+) or deficit (-): -8.4% of GDP (2017 est.)
country comparison to the world: 201

Public debt: 62.8% of GDP (2017 est.)
58.6% of GDP (2016 est.)
country comparison to the world: 67

Fiscal year: calendar year

Inflation rate (consumer prices): 6.8% (2017 est.)
17.9% (2016 est.)
country comparison to the world: 191

Central bank discount rate: 9.1% (31 December 2012)
19% (31 December 2011)
country comparison to the world: 28

Commercial bank prime lending rate: 15.5% (31 December 2017 est.)
15.5% (31 December 2016 est.)
country comparison to the world: 40

Stock of narrow money: $1.816 billion (31 December 2017 est.)
$1.582 billion (31 December 2016 est.)
country comparison to the world: 138

Stock of broad money: $4.904 billion (31 December 2017 est.)
$4.145 billion (31 December 2016 est.)
country comparison to the world: 129

Stock of domestic credit: $5.207 billion (31 December 2017 est.)
$4.167 billion (31 December 2016 est.)
country comparison to the world: 130

Market value of publicly traded shares: $3.004 billion (31 December 2012 est.)
$4.009 billion (31 December 2011 est.)
$2.817 billion (31 December 2010 est.)
country comparison to the world: 95

Current account balance: -$918 million (2017 est.)
-$934 million (2016 est.)
country comparison to the world: 130

Exports: $8.106 billion (2017 est.)
$6.514 billion (2016 est.)
country comparison to the world: 97

Exports—commodities: copper/cobalt, cobalt, electricity; tobacco, flowers, cotton

Exports—partners: Switzerland 39.4%, China 18%, Democratic Republic of the Congo 6.7%, South Africa 6.4%, UAE 6%, Singapore 5.6% (2016)

Imports: $7.336 billion (2017 est.)
$6.539 billion (2016 est.)
country comparison to the world: 109

Imports—commodities: machinery, transportation equipment, petroleum products, electricity, fertilizer, foodstuffs, clothing

Imports—partners: South Africa 31.2%, Democratic Republic of the Congo 12.3%, Kuwait 8.1%, China 7.6%, Mauritius 4.4%, UAE 4.2%, India 4% (2016)

Reserves of foreign exchange and gold: $2.426 billion (31 December 2017 est.)
$2.353 billion (31 December 2016 est.)
country comparison to the world: 112

Debt—external: $10.79 billion (31 December 2017 est.)
$9.562 billion (31 December 2016 est.)
country comparison to the world: 111

Stock of direct foreign investment—at home: $NA

Stock of direct foreign investment—abroad: $NA

Exchange rates: Zambian kwacha (ZMK) per US dollar—
9.2 (2017 est.)
10.3 (2016 est.)
10.3 (2015 est.)
8.6 (2014 est.)
6.2 (2013 est.)

ENERGY

Electricity access: population without electricity: 10,700,000
electrification—*total population:* 26%
electrification—urban areas: 45%
electrification—rural areas: 14% (2013)

Electricity—production: 13.28 billion kWh (2015 est.)
country comparison to the world: 89

Electricity—consumption: 11.62 billion kWh (2015 est.)
country comparison to the world: 88

Electricity—exports: 1.176 billion kWh (2015 est.)
country comparison to the world: 56

Electricity—imports: 785 million kWh (2015 est.)
country comparison to the world: 71

Electricity—installed generating capacity: 2.37 million kW (2015 est.)
country comparison to the world: 106

Electricity—from fossil fuels: 0.3% of total installed capacity (2015 est.)
country comparison to the world: 213

Electricity—from nuclear fuels: 0% of total installed capacity (2015 est.)
country comparison to the world: 214

Electricity—from hydroelectric plants: 97.9% of total installed capacity (2015 est.)
country comparison to the world: 6

Electricity—from other renewable sources: 1.8% of total installed capacity (2015 est.)
country comparison to the world: 127

Crude oil—production: 0 bbl/day (2016 est.)
country comparison to the world: 216

Crude oil—exports: 0 bbl/day (2014 est.)
country comparison to the world: 215

Crude oil—imports: 11,200 bbl/day (2014 est.)
country comparison to the world: 72

Crude oil—proved reserves: 0 bbl (1 January 2017 es)
country comparison to the world: 216

Refined petroleum products—production: 14,290 bbl/day (2014 est.)
country comparison to the world: 98

Refined petroleum products—consumption: 23,000 bbl/day (2015 est.)
country comparison to the world: 133

Refined petroleum products—exports: 937.4 bbl/day (2014 est.)
country comparison to the world: 107

Refined petroleum products—imports: 7,917 bbl/day (2014 est.)
country comparison to the world: 147

Natural gas—production: 0 cu m (2013 est.)
country comparison to the world: 216

Natural gas—consumption: 0 cu m (2014 est.)
country comparison to the world: 151

Natural gas—exports: 0 cu m (2013 est.)
country comparison to the world: 214

Natural gas—imports: 0 cu m (2013 est.)
country comparison to the world: 214

Natural gas—proved reserves: 0 cu m (1 January 2014 es)
country comparison to the world: 211

Carbon dioxide emissions from consumption of energy: 3.5 million Mt (2013 est.)
country comparison to the world: 140

COMMUNICATIONS

Telephones—fixed lines: *total subscriptions:* 101,407
subscriptions per 100 inhabitants: 1 (July 2016 est.)
country comparison to the world: 144

Telephones—mobile cellular: *total:* 12,017,034
subscriptions per 100 inhabitants: 77 (July 2016 est.)
country comparison to the world: 86

Telephone system: *general assessment:* among the best in sub-Saharan Africa
domestic: high-capacity microwave radio relay connects most larger towns and cities; several cellular telephone services in operation and network coverage is improving; domestic satellite system being installed to improve telephone service in rural areas; Internet service is widely available; very small aperture terminal (VSAT) networks are operated by private firms
international: country code—260; satellite earth stations—2 Intelsat (1 Indian Ocean and 1 Atlantic Ocean), 3 owned by Zamtel (2015)

Broadcast media: state-owned Zambia National Broadcasting Corporation (ZNBC) operates 3 TV stations, is the principal local-content provider, and owns about 45% of multi-channel Zambia shares; several private TV stations and multi-channel subscription TV services are available; ZNBC operates 4 radio networks; 64 private radio stations are available (most regionally) and relays of at least 2 international broadcasters — including BBC and Radio France International—are accessible in Lusaka and Kitwe (2015)

Internet country code: .zm

Internet users: *total:* 3,956,252
percent of population: 25.5% (July 2016 est.)
country comparison to the world: 94

TRANSPORTATION

National air transport system: *number of registered air carriers:* 1
inventory of registered aircraft operated by air carriers: 1
annual passenger traffic on registered air carriers: 11,796
annual freight traffic on registered air carriers: 79,092,826 mt-km (2015)
Civil aircraft registration country code prefix: 9J (2016)

Airports: 88 (2013)
country comparison to the world: 63

Airports—with paved runways: *total:* 8
over 3,047 m: 1
2,438 to 3,047 m: 3
1,524 to 2,437 m: 3
914 to 1,523 m: 1 (2013)

Airports—with unpaved runways: *total:* 80
2,438 to 3,047 m: 1
1,524 to 2,437 m: 5
914 to 1,523 m: 53
under 914 m: 21 (2013)

Pipelines: oil 771 km (2013)

Railways: *total:* 3,126 km
narrow gauge: 3,126 km 1.067-m gauge
note: includes 1,860 km of the Tanzania-Zambia Railway Authority (TAZARA) (2014)
country comparison to the world: 57

Roadways: *total:* 40,454 km
paved: 9,403 km
unpaved: 31,051 km (2005)
country comparison to the world: 87

Waterways: 2,250 km (includes Lake Tanganyika and the Zambezi and Luapula Rivers) (2010)
country comparison to the world: 37

Merchant marine: *total:* 1
by type: other 1 (2017)
country comparison to the world: 166

Ports and terminals: river port(s): Mpulungu (Zambezi)

MILITARY AND SECURITY

Military expenditures: 1.53% of GDP (2016)
1.75% of GDP (2015)
1.63% of GDP (2014)
1.36% of GDP (2013)
1.36% of GDP (2012)
country comparison to the world: 59

Military branches: Zambian Defense Force (ZDF): Zambia Army, Zambia Air Force, Zambia National Service (support organization) (2015)

Military service age and obligation: national registration required at age 16; 18-25 years of age for male and female voluntary military service (16 years of age with parental consent); no conscription; Zambian citizenship required; grade 12 certification required; mandatory HIV testing on enlistment; mandatory retirement for officers at age 65 (Army, Air Force) (2012)

TRANSNATIONAL ISSUES

Disputes—international: in 2004, Zimbabwe dropped objections to plans between Botswana and Zambia to build a bridge over the Zambezi River, thereby de facto recognizing a short, but not clearly delimited, Botswana-Zambia boundary in the river

Refugees and internally displaced persons: refugees (country of origin): 33,000 (Democratic Republic of the Congo) (2017)

Illicit drugs: transshipment point for moderate amounts of methaqualone, small amounts of heroin, and cocaine bound for southern Africa and possibly Europe; a poorly developed financial infrastructure coupled with a government commitment to combating money laundering make it an unattractive venue for money launderers; major consumer of cannabis

ZIMBABWE

INTRODUCTION

Background: The UK annexed Southern Rhodesia from the former British South Africa Company in 1923. A 1961 constitution was formulated that favored whites in power. In 1965 the government unilaterally declared its independence, but the UK did not recognize the act and demanded more complete voting rights for the black African majority in the country (then called Rhodesia). UN sanctions and a guerrilla uprising finally led to free elections in 1979 and independence (as Zimbabwe) in 1980. Robert MUGABE, the nation's first prime minister, has been the country's only ruler (as president since 1987) and has dominated the country's political system since independence. His chaotic land redistribution campaign, which began in 1997 and intensified after 2000, caused an exodus of white farmers, crippled the economy, and ushered in widespread shortages of basic commodities. Ignoring international condemnation, MUGABE rigged the 2002 presidential election to ensure his reelection. In 2005, the capital city of Harare embarked on Operation Restore Order, ostensibly an urban rationalization program, which resulted in the destruction of the homes or businesses of 700,000 mostly poor supporters of the opposition. MUGABE in 2007 instituted price controls on all basic commodities causing panic buying and leaving store shelves empty for months. General elections held in March 2008 contained irregularities but still amounted to a censure of the ZANU-PF-led government with the opposition winning a majority of seats in parliament. Movement for Democratic Change—Tsvangirai opposition leader Morgan TSVANGIRAI won the most votes in the presidential poll, but not enough to win outright. In the lead up to a run-off election in June 2008, considerable violence against opposition party members led to the withdrawal of TSVANGIRAI from the ballot. Extensive evidence of violence and intimidation resulted in international condemnation of the process. Difficult negotiations over a power-sharing "government of national unity," in which MUGABE remained president and TSVANGIRAI became prime minister, were finally settled in February 2009, although the leaders failed to agree upon many key outstanding governmental issues. MUGABE was reelected president in 2013 in balloting that was severely flawed and internationally condemned. As a prerequisite to holding the election, Zimbabwe enacted a new constitution by referendum, although many provisions in the new constitution have yet to be codified in law. In November 2017, Vice President Emmerson MNANGAGWA took over following a military intervention that forced MUGABE to resign. MNANGAGWA was inaugurated president days later, promising to hold presidential elections in 2018.

GEOGRAPHY

Location: Southern Africa, between South Africa and Zambia

Geographic coordinates: 20 00 S, 30 00 E

Map references: Africa

Area: *total:* 390,757 sq km
land: 386,847 sq km
water: 3,910 sq km
country comparison to the world: 62

Area—comparative: about four times the size of Indiana; slightly larger than Montana

Land boundaries: *total:* 3,229 km
border countries (4): Botswana 834 km, Mozambique 1,402 km, South Africa 230 km, Zambia 763 km

Coastline: 0 km (landlocked)

Maritime claims: none (landlocked)

Climate: tropical; moderated by altitude; rainy season (November to March)

Terrain: mostly high plateau with higher central plateau (high veld); mountains in east

Elevation: *mean elevation:* 961 m

elevation extremes: *lowest point:* junction of the Runde and Save Rivers 162 m
highest point: Inyangani 2,592 m

Natural resources: coal, chromium ore, asbestos, gold, nickel, copper, iron ore, vanadium, lithium, tin, platinum group metals

Land use: *agricultural land:* 42.5%
arable land: 10.9%;
permanent crops: 0.3%;
permanent pasture: 31.3%
forest: 39.5%
other: 18% (2011 est.)
Irrigated land: 1,740 sq km (2012)

Population—distribution: Aside from major urban agglomerations in Harare and Bulawayo, population distribution is fairly even, with slightly greater overall numbers in the eastern half

Natural hazards: recurring droughts; floods and severe storms are rare

Environment—current issues: deforestation; soil erosion; land degradation; air and water pollution; the black rhinoceros herd—once the largest concentration of the species in the world—has been significantly reduced by poaching; poor mining practices have led to toxic waste and heavy metal pollution

Environment—international agreements: *party to:* Biodiversity, Climate Change, Desertification, Endangered Species, Law of the Sea, Ozone Layer Protection
signed, but not ratified: none of the selected agreements

Geography—note: landlocked; the Zambezi forms a natural riverine boundary with Zambia; in full flood (February-April) the massive Victoria Falls on the river forms the world's largest curtain of falling water; Lake Kariba on the Zambia-Zimbabwe border forms the world's largest reservoir by volume (180 cu km; 43 cu mi)

PEOPLE AND SOCIETY

Population: 13,805,084
note: estimates for this country explicitly take into account the effects of excess mortality due to AIDS; this can result in lower life expectancy, higher infant mortality, higher death rates, lower population growth rates, and changes in the distribution of population by age and sex than would otherwise be expected (July 2017 est.)

country comparison to the world: 72

Nationality: *noun:* Zimbabwean(s)
adjective: Zimbabwean

Ethnic groups: African 99.4% (predominantly Shona; Ndebele is the second largest ethnic group), other 0.4%, unspecified 0.2% (2012 est.)

Languages: Shona (official; most widely spoken), Ndebele (official, second most widely spoken), English (official; traditionally used for official business), 13 minority languages (official; includes Chewa, Chibarwe, Kalanga, Koisan, Nambya, Ndau, Shangani, sign language, Sotho, Tonga, Tswana, Venda, and Xhosa)

Religions: Protestant 74.8% (includes Apostolic 37.5%, Pentecostal 21.8%, other 15.5%), Roman Catholic 7.3%, other Christian 5.3%, traditional 1.5%, Muslim 0.5%, other 0.1%, none 10.5% (2015 est.)

Demographic profile: Zimbabwe's progress in reproductive, maternal, and child health has stagnated in recent years. According to a 2010 Demographic and Health Survey, contraceptive use, the number of births attended by skilled practitioners, and child mortality have either stalled or somewhat deteriorated since the mid-2000s. Zimbabwe's total fertility rate has remained fairly stable at about 4 children per woman for the last two decades, although an uptick in the urban birth rate in recent years has caused a slight rise in the country's overall fertility rate. Zimbabwe's HIV prevalence rate dropped from approximately 29% to 15% since 1997 but remains among the world's highest and continues to suppress the country's life expectancy rate. The proliferation of HIV/AIDS information and prevention programs and personal experience with those suffering or dying from the disease have helped to change sexual behavior and reduce the epidemic.

Historically, the vast majority of Zimbabwe's migration has been internal—a rural-urban flow. In terms of international migration, over the last 40 years Zimbabwe has gradually shifted from being a destination country to one of emigration and, to a lesser degree, one of transit (for East African illegal migrants traveling to South Africa). As a British colony, Zimbabwe attracted significant numbers of permanent immigrants from the UK and other European countries, as well as temporary economic migrants from Malawi, Mozambique, and Zambia. Although Zimbabweans have migrated to South Africa since the beginning of the 20th century to work as miners, the first major exodus from the country occurred in the years before and after independence in 1980. The outward migration was politically and racially influenced; a large share of the white population of European origin chose to leave rather than live under a new black-majority government.

In the 1990s and 2000s, economic mismanagement and hyperinflation sparked a second, more diverse wave of emigration. This massive out migration—primarily to other southern African countries, the UK, and the US—has created a variety of challenges, including brain drain, illegal migration, and human smuggling and trafficking.

Several factors have pushed highly skilled workers to go abroad, including unemployment, lower wages, a lack of resources, and few opportunities for career growth.

Age structure: *0-14 years:* 38.9% (male 2,658,563/ female 2,711,017)
15-24 years: 20.47% (male 1,383,337/female 1,442,738)
25-54 years: 31.9% (male 2,207,012/female 2,196,996)
55-64 years: 4.27% (male 233,771/female 355,738)
65 years and over: 4.46% (male 251,968/female 363,944) (2017 est.)

Dependency ratios: *total dependency ratio:* 79.5
youth dependency ratio: 74.4
elderly dependency ratio: 5.1
potential support ratio: 19.7 (2015 est.)

Median age: *total:* 20 years
male: 19.6 years
female: 20.4 years (2017 est.)
country comparison to the world: 188

Population growth rate: 1.56% (2017 est.)
country comparison to the world: 71

Birth rate: 34.2 births/1,000 population (2017 est.)
country comparison to the world: 25

Death rate: 10.2 deaths/1,000 population (2017 est.)
country comparison to the world: 36

Net migration rate: -8.5 migrant(s)/1,000 population (2017 est.)
country comparison to the world: 209

Population distribution: Aside from major urban agglomerations in Harare and Bulawayo, population distribution is fairly even, with slightly greater overall numbers in the eastern half

Urbanization: *urban population:* 32.2% of total population (2017)
rate of urbanization: 2.44% annual rate of change (2015-20 est.)

Major urban areas—population: HARARE (capital) 1.501 million (2015)

Sex ratio: *at birth:* 1.03 male(s)/female
0-14 years: 1.02 male(s)/female
15-24 years: 1.02 male(s)/female
25-54 years: 1.1 male(s)/female
55-64 years: 0.58 male(s)/female
65 years and over: 0.64 male(s)/female
total population: 1.01 male(s)/female (2016 est.)

Mother's mean age at first birth: 20 years
note: median age at first birth among women 25-29 (2015 est.)

Maternal mortality ratio: 443 deaths/100,000 live births (2015 est.)
country comparison to the world: 24

Infant mortality rate: *total:* 32.7 deaths/1,000 live births
male: 36.8 deaths/1,000 live births
female: 28.5 deaths/1,000 live births (2017 est.)
country comparison to the world: 57

Life expectancy at birth: *total population:* 60.4 years
male: 58.3 years

female: 62.5 years (2017 est.)
country comparison to the world: 203

Total fertility rate: 3.98 children born/woman (2017 est.)
country comparison to the world: 37

Contraceptive prevalence rate: 66.8% (2015)

Health expenditures: 6.4% of GDP (2014)
country comparison to the world: 98

Physicians density: 0.07 physicians/1,000 population (2011)

Hospital bed density: 1.7 beds/1,000 population (2011)

Drinking water source:
improved:
urban: 97% of population
rural: 67.3% of population
total: 76.9% of population
unimproved:
urban: 3% of population
rural: 32.7% of population
total: 23.1% of population (2015 est.)

Sanitation facility access:
improved:
urban: 49.3% of population
rural: 30.8% of population
total: 36.8% of population
unimproved:
urban: 50.7% of population
rural: 69.2% of population
total: 63.2% of population (2015 est.)

HIV/AIDS—adult prevalence rate: 13.5% (2016 est.)
country comparison to the world: 6

HIV/AIDS—people living with HIV/AIDS: 1.3 million (2016 est.)
country comparison to the world: 8

HIV/AIDS—deaths: 30,000 (2016 est.)
country comparison to the world: 8

Major infectious diseases: *degree of risk:* high
food or waterborne diseases: bacterial and protozoal diarrhea, hepatitis A, and typhoid fever
vectorborne diseases: malaria and dengue fever
water contact disease: schistosomiasis
animal contact disease: rabies (2016)

Obesity—adult prevalence rate: 15.5% (2016)
country comparison to the world: 126

Children under the age of 5 years underweight: 11.2% (2014)
country comparison to the world: 69

Education expenditures: 8.4% of GDP (2014)
country comparison to the world: 155

Literacy: *definition:* age 15 and over can read and write English
total population: 86.5%
male: 88.5%
female: 84.6% (2015 est.)

School life expectancy (primary to tertiary education): *total:* 10 years
male: 10 years
female: 10 years (2013)

Unemployment, youth ages 15-24: *total:* 16.5%
male: 11.7%

female: 21.1% (2014 est.)
country comparison to the world: 116

GOVERNMENT

Country name: *conventional long form:* Republic of Zimbabwe
conventional short form: Zimbabwe
former: Southern Rhodesia, Rhodesia
etymology: takes its name from the Kingdom of Zimbabwe (13th-15th century) and its capital of Great Zimbabwe, the largest stone structure in precolonial southern Africa

Government type: semi-presidential republic

Capital: name: Harare

geographic coordinates: 17 49 S, 31 02 E
time difference: UTC+2 (7 hours ahead of Washington, DC, during Standard Time)

Administrative divisions: 8 provinces and 2 cities* with provincial status; Bulawayo*, Harare*, Manicaland, Mashonaland Central, Mashonaland East, Mashonaland West, Masvingo, Matabeleland North, Matabeleland South, Midlands

Independence: 18 April 1980 (from the UK)

National holiday: Independence Day, 18 April (1980)

Constitution: *history:* previous 1965 (at Rhodesian independence), 1979 (Lancaster House Agreement), 1980 (at Zimbabwean independence); latest final draft completed January 2013, approved by referendum 16 March 2013, approved by Parliament 9 May 2013, effective 22 May 2013
amendments: proposed by the Senate or by the House of Assembly; passage requires two-thirds majority vote by the membership of both houses of Parliament and assent by the president of the republic; amendments to constitutional chapters on fundamental human rights and freedoms and on agricultural lands also require approval by a majority of votes cast in a referendum; amended many times, last in 2017 (2017)

Legal system: mixed legal system of English common law, Roman-Dutch civil law, and customary law

International law organization participation: has not submitted an ICJ jurisdiction declaration; non-party state to the ICCt

Citizenship: *citizenship by birth:* no
citizenship by descent only: the father must be a citizen of Zimbabwe; in the case of a child born out of wedlock, the mother must be a citizen
dual citizenship recognized: no
residency requirement for naturalization: 5 years

Suffrage: 18 years of age; universal

Executive branch: *chief of state:* President Emmerson Dambudzo MNANGAGWA (since 24 November 2017); note—Robert Gabriel MUGABE resigned on 21 November 2017, after ruling for 37 years

head of government: President Emmerson Dambudzo MNANGAGWA (since 24 November 2017)

cabinet: Cabinet appointed by president, responsible to House of Assembly
elections/appointments: each presidential candidate nominated with a nomination paper signed by at least 10 registered voters (at least 1 candidate from each province) and directly elected by absolute majority popular vote in 2 rounds if needed for a 5-year term (no term limits); election last held on 31 July 2013 (next to be held in 2018); co-vice presidents drawn from party leadership
election results: Robert Gabriel MUGABE reelected president; percent of vote—Robert Gabriel MUGABE (ZANU-PF) 61.1%, Morgan TSVANGIRAI (MDC-T) 34.4%, Welshman NCUBE (MDC-N) 2.7%, other 1.8%; note—the election process was considered flawed and roundly criticized by election monitors and international bodies; both the African Union and the South African Development Community endorsed the results of the election with some concerns

Legislative branch: description: bicameral Parliament consists of the Senate (80 seats; 60 members directly elected in multi-seat constituencies—6 seats in each of the 10 provinces—by proportional representation vote, 16 indirectly elected by the regional governing councils, 2 reserved for the National Council Chiefs, and 2 reserved for members with disabilities; members serve 5-year terms) and the House of Assembly (270 seats; 210 members directly elected in single-seat constituencies by simple majority vote and 60 seats reserved for women directly elected by proportional representation vote; members serve 5-year terms)
elections: last held on 31 July 2013 (next to be held in 2018)
election results: Senate—percent of vote by party—NA; seats by party—ZANU-PF 37, MDC-T 21, MDC-N 2, chiefs 18, people with disabilities 2; House of Assembly—percent of vote by party—ZANU-PF 62.4%, MDC-T 30.3%, MDC-N 4.7%, other 0.7%, independent 1.9%; seats by party—ZANU-PF 196, MDC-T 70, MDC-N 2, independent 2

Judicial branch: *highest court(s):* Supreme Court (consists of the chief justice and 4 judges); Constitutional Court (consists of the chief and deputy chief justices and 9 judges)
judge selection and term of office: Supreme Court judges appointed by the president upon recommendation of the Judicial Service Commission, an independent body consisting of the chief justice, Public Service Commission chairman, attorney general, and 2-3 members appointed by the president; judges normally serve until age 65 but can elect to serve until age 70; Constitutional Court judge appointment NA; judges serve nonrenewable 15-year terms
subordinate courts: High Court; Labor Court; Administrative Court; regional magistrate courts; customary law courts; special courts

Political parties and leaders: Freedom Front [Cosmas MPONDA]
Movement for Democratic Change—Ncube or MDC-N [Welshman NCUBE]

Movement for Democratic Change—Tsvangirai or MDC-T (vacant)

National People's Party or NPP [Joyce MUJURU] formerly Zimbabwe People First or ZimPF)

Peoples Democratic Party or PDP [Tendai BITI]

Transform Zimbabwe or TZ [Jacob NGARIVHUME]

Zimbabwe African National Union-Patriotic Front or ZANU-PF [Emmerson Dambudzo MNANGAGWA]

Zimbabwe African Peoples Union or ZAPU [Dumiso DABENGWA]

Zimbabwe People First or ZimFirst [Maxwell SHUMBA]

Political pressure groups and leaders: Crisis in Zimbabwe Coalition

National Constitutional Assembly or NCA [Lovemore MADHUKU]

Women of Zimbabwe Arise or WOZA [Jenni WILLIAMS]

Zimbabwe Congress of Trade Unions or ZCTU [Peter MUTASA]

Zimbabwe Human Rights Association or Zim-Rights [Okay MACHISA]

Zimbabwe Human Rights NGO Forum [Jestina MUKOKO]

Zimbabwe Lawyers for Human Rights or ZLHR [Roselyn HANZI]

International organization participation: ACP, AfDB, AU, COMESA, FAO, G-15, G-77, IAEA, IBRD, ICAO, ICRM, IDA, IFAD, IFC, IFRCS, ILO, IMF, IMO, Interpol, IOC, IOM, IPU, ISO, ITSO, ITU, ITUC (NGOs), MIGA, NAM, OPCW, PCA, SADC, UN, UNAMID, UNC-TAD, UNESCO, UNIDO, UNMIL, UNMISS, UNOCI, UNWTO, UPU, WCO, WFTU (NGOs), WHO, WIPO, WMO, WTO

Diplomatic representation in the US: *chief of mission:* Ambassador Ammon MUTEMBWA (since 18 November 2014)

chancery: 1608 New Hampshire Avenue NW, Washington, DC 20009

telephone: [1] (202) 332-7100

FAX: [1] (202) 483-9326

Diplomatic representation from the US: *chief of mission:* Ambassador Harry K. THOMAS, Jr. (since 25 February 2016)

embassy: 172 Herbert Chitepo Avenue, Harare

mailing address: P.O. Box 3340, Harare

telephone: [263] (4) 250-593 through 250-594

FAX: [263] (4) 796-488, or 722-618

Flag description: seven equal horizontal bands of green, yellow, red, black, red, yellow, and green with a white isosceles triangle edged in black with its base on the hoist side; a yellow Zimbabwe bird representing the long history of the country is superimposed on a red five-pointed star in the center of the triangle, which symbolizes peace; green represents agriculture, yellow mineral wealth, red the blood shed to achieve independence, and black stands for the native people

National symbol(s): Zimbabwe bird symbol, African fish eagle, flame lily; national colors: green, yellow, red, black, white

National anthem: name: "Kalibusiswe Ilizwe leZimbabwe" [Northern Ndebele language] "Simudzai Mureza WeZimbabwe" [Shona] (Blessed Be the Land of Zimbabwe)

lyrics/music: Solomon MUTSWAIRO/Fred Lecture CHANGUNDEGA

note: adopted 1994

ECONOMY

Economy—overview: Zimbabwe's economy depends heavily on its mining and agriculture sectors. Following a decade of contraction from 1998 to 2008, the economy recorded real growth of more than 10% per year in the period 2010-13, before falling below 3% in the period 2014-17, due to poor harvests, low diamond revenues, and decreased investment. Lower mineral prices, infrastructure and regulatory deficiencies, a poor investment climate, a large public and external debt burden, and extremely high government wage expenses impede the country's economic performance.

Until early 2009, the Reserve Bank of Zimbabwe (RBZ) routinely printed money to fund the budget deficit, causing hyperinflation. Adoption of a multi-currency basket in early 2009—which allowed currencies such as the Botswana pula, the South Africa rand, and the US dollar to be used locally—reduced inflation below 10% per year. In January 2015, as part of the government's effort to boost trade and attract foreign investment, the RBZ announced that the Chinese renmimbi, Indian rupee, Australian dollar, and Japanese yen would be accepted as legal tender in Zimbabwe, though transactions were predominantly carried out in US dollars and South African rand until 2016, when the rand's devaluation and instability led to near-exclusive use of the US dollar. The government in November 2016 began releasing bond notes, a parallel currency legal only in Zimbabwe which the government claims will have a one-to-one exchange ratio with the US dollar, to ease cash shortages. Bond notes began trading at a discount of up to 10% in the black market by the end of 2016.

Zimbabwe's government entered a second Staff Monitored Program with the IMF in 2014 and undertook other measures to reengage with international financial institutions. Zimbabwe repaid roughly $108 million in arrears to the IMF in October 2016, but financial observers note that Zimbabwe is unlikely to gain new financing because the government has not disclosed how it plans to repay more than $1.7 billion in arrears to the World Bank and African Development Bank. International financial institutions want Zimbabwe to implement significant fiscal and structural reforms before granting new loans. Foreign and domestic investment continues to be hindered by the lack of land tenure and titling, the inability to repatriate dividends to investors overseas, and the lack of clarity regarding the government's Indigenization and Economic Empowerment Act.

GDP (purchasing power parity): $33.87 billion (2017 est.)

$32.94 billion (2016 est.)

$32.73 billion (2015 est.)

note: data are in 2017 dollars

country comparison to the world: 128

GDP (official exchange rate): $17.11 billion (2016 est.)

GDP—real growth rate: 2.8% (2017 est.)

0.7% (2016 est.)

1.4% (2015 est.)

country comparison to the world: 123

GDP—per capita (PPP): $2,300 (2017 est.)

$2,300 (2016 est.)

$2,300 (2015 est.)

note: data are in 2017 dollars

country comparison to the world: 201

Gross national saving: 15.4% of GDP (2017 est.)

15.5% of GDP (2016 est.)

4.9% of GDP (2015 est.)

country comparison to the world: 124

GDP—composition, by end use:

household consumption: 84%

government consumption: 20.5%

investment in fixed capital: 13.8%

investment in inventories: 0%

exports of goods and services: 26.4%

imports of goods and services: -44.9% (2017 est.)

GDP—composition, by sector of origin:

agriculture: 12.5%

industry: 26.9%

services: 60.6% (2017 est.)

Agriculture—products: tobacco, corn, cotton, wheat, coffee, sugarcane, peanuts; sheep, goats, pigs

Industries: mining (coal, gold, platinum, copper, nickel, tin, diamonds, clay, numerous metallic and nonmetallic ores), steel; wood products, cement, chemicals, fertilizer, clothing and footwear, foodstuffs, beverages

Industrial production growth rate: 2.1% (2017 est.)

country comparison to the world: 126

Labor force: 7.907 million (2017 est.)

country comparison to the world: 64

Labor force—by occupation: agriculture: 66%

industry: 10%

services: 24% (1996)

Unemployment rate: 95% (2009 est.)

80% (2005 est.)

note: data include both unemployment and under-employment; true unemployment is unknown and, under current economic conditions, unknowable

country comparison to the world: 217

Population below poverty line: 72.3% (2012 est.)

Household income or consumption by percentage share: *lowest 10%:* 2%

highest 10%: 40.4% (1995)

Distribution of family income—Gini index: 50.1 (2006)

50.1 (1995)

country comparison to the world: 18

Budget: *revenues:* $3.6 billion

expenditures: $4.8 billion (2017 est.)

Taxes and other revenues: 21% of GDP (2017 est.)
country comparison to the world: 143

Budget surplus (+) or deficit (-): -7% of GDP (2017 est.)
country comparison to the world: 188

Public debt: 75.5% of GDP (2017 est.)
69.9% of GDP (2016 est.)
country comparison to the world: 46

Fiscal year: calendar year

Inflation rate (consumer prices): 2.5% (2017 est.)
-1.6% (2016 est.)
country comparison to the world: 118

Central bank discount rate: 7.17% (31 December 2010)
975% (31 December 2007)
country comparison to the world: 46

Commercial bank prime lending rate: 18% (31 December 2017 est.)
15% (31 December 2016 est.)
country comparison to the world: 25

Stock of narrow money: $2.395 billion (31 December 2017 est.)
$2.274 billion (31 December 2016 est.)
note: Zimbabwe's central bank no longer publishes data on monetary aggregates, except for bank deposits, which amounted to $2.1 billion in November 2010; the Zimbabwe dollar stopped circulating in early 2009; since then, the US dollar and South African rand have been the most frequently used currencies; there are no reliable estimates of the amount of foreign currency circulating in Zimbabwe
country comparison to the world: 128

Stock of broad money: $3.753 billion (31 December 2016 est.)
$3.949 billion (31 December 2017 est.)
country comparison to the world: 139

Stock of domestic credit: $5.68 billion (31 December 2017 est.)
$5.398 billion (31 December 2016 est.)
country comparison to the world: 124

Market value of publicly traded shares: $4.073 billion (13 April 2015 est.)
$11.82 billion (31 December 2012 est.)
$10.9 billion (31 December 2011 est.)
country comparison to the world: 92

Current account balance: -$617 million (2017 est.)
-$662 million (2016 est.)
country comparison to the world: 110

Exports: $3.763 billion (2017 est.)
$3.366 billion (2016 est.)
country comparison to the world: 119

Exports—commodities: platinum, cotton, tobacco, gold, ferroalloys, textiles/clothing

Exports—partners: South Africa 79.5%, Mozambique 9.5%, UAE 4.1% (2016)

Imports: $5.605 billion (2017 est.)
$5.351 billion (2016 est.)
country comparison to the world: 119

Imports—commodities: machinery and transport equipment, other manufactures, chemicals, fuels, food products

Imports—partners: South Africa 46.6%, Zambia 24% (2016)

Reserves of foreign exchange and gold: $374 million (31 December 2017 est.)
$407.2 million (31 December 2016 est.)
country comparison to the world: 151

Debt—external: $10.97 billion (31 December 2017 est.)
$10.14 billion (31 December 2016 est.)
country comparison to the world: 110

Stock of direct foreign investment—at home: $3.918 billion (31 December 2017 est.)
$3.518 billion (31 December 2016 est.)
country comparison to the world: 108

Stock of direct foreign investment—abroad: $294.8 million (31 December 2017 est.)
$271.6 million (31 December 2016 est.)
country comparison to the world: 96

Exchange rates: Zimbabwean dollars (ZWD) per US dollar—
1 (2017 est.)
1 (2016 est.)
NA (2013)
234.25 (2010)
note: the dollar was adopted as a legal currency in 2009; since then the Zimbabwean dollar has experienced hyperinflation and is essentially worthless

ENERGY

Electricity access: population without electricity: 8,500,000
electrification—*total population:* 40%
electrification—urban areas: 80%
electrification—rural areas: 21% (2013)

Electricity—production: 9.384 billion kWh (2015 est.)
country comparison to the world: 106

Electricity—consumption: 7.63 billion kWh (2015 est.)
country comparison to the world: 106

Electricity—exports: 1.239 billion kWh (2015 est.)
country comparison to the world: 54

Electricity—imports: 1.139 billion kWh (2015 est.)
country comparison to the world: 64

Electricity—installed generating capacity: 2.129 million kW (2015 est.)
country comparison to the world: 110

Electricity—from fossil fuels: 58% of total installed capacity (2015 est.)
country comparison to the world: 135

Electricity—from nuclear fuels: 0% of total installed capacity (2015 est.)
country comparison to the world: 215

Electricity—from hydroelectric plants: 37.1% of total installed capacity (2015 est.)
country comparison to the world: 56

Electricity—from other renewable sources: 5% of total installed capacity (2015 est.)
country comparison to the world: 98

Crude oil—production: 0 bbl/day (2016 est.)
country comparison to the world: 217

Crude oil—exports: 0 bbl/day (2014 est.)
country comparison to the world: 216

Crude oil—imports: 0 bbl/day (2014 est.)
country comparison to the world: 216

Crude oil—proved reserves: 0 bbl (1 January 2017 es)
country comparison to the world: 217

Refined petroleum products—production: 0 bbl/day (2014 est.)
country comparison to the world: 217

Refined petroleum products—consumption: 29,000 bbl/day (2015 est.)
country comparison to the world: 124

Refined petroleum products—exports: 0 bbl/day (2014 est.)
country comparison to the world: 217

Refined petroleum products—imports: 26,390 bbl/day (2014 est.)
country comparison to the world: 104

Natural gas—production: 0 cu m (2013 est.)
country comparison to the world: 217

Natural gas—consumption: 0 cu m (2014 est.)
country comparison to the world: 152

Natural gas—exports: 0 cu m (2013 est.)
country comparison to the world: 215

Natural gas—imports: 0 cu m (2013 est.)
country comparison to the world: 215

Natural gas—proved reserves: 0 cu m (1 January 2014 es)
country comparison to the world: 212

Carbon dioxide emissions from consumption of energy: 11 million Mt (2013 est.)
country comparison to the world: 101

COMMUNICATIONS

Telephones—fixed lines: *total subscriptions:* 305,720
subscriptions per 100 inhabitants: 2 (July 2016 est.)
country comparison to the world: 113

Telephones—mobile cellular: *total:* 12,878,926
subscriptions per 100 inhabitants: 89 (July 2016 est.)
country comparison to the world: 77

Telephone system: *general assessment:* competition has driven rapid expansion of telecommunications, particularly cellular voice and mobile broadband, in recent years; continued economic instability and infrastructure limitations, such as reliable power, hinder progress
domestic: consists of microwave radio relay links, open-wire lines, radiotelephone communication stations, fixed wireless local loop installations, fiber-optic cable, VSAT terminals, and a substantial mobile-cellular network; Internet connection is most readily available in Harare and major towns; two government owned and two private

cellular providers; 3G and VoIP services are widely available with 4G/LTE service being deployed *international:* country code—263; satellite earth stations—2 Intelsat; 5 international digital gateway exchanges; fiber-optic connections to neighboring states provide access to international networks via undersea cable (2017)

Broadcast media: government owns all local radio and TV stations; foreign shortwave broadcasts and satellite TV are available to those who can afford antennas and receivers; in rural areas, access to TV broadcasts is extremely limited; analog TV only, no digital service (2017)

Internet country code: .zw

Internet users: *total:* 3,363,256

percent of population: 23.1% (July 2016 est.)
country comparison to the world: 88

TRANSPORTATION

National air transport system: *number of registered air carriers:* 2
inventory of registered aircraft operated by air carriers: 4
annual passenger traffic on registered air carriers: 370,164
annual freight traffic on registered air carriers: 962,642 mt-km (2015)
Civil aircraft registration country code prefix: Z (2016)

Airports: 196 (2013)
country comparison to the world: 29

Airports—with paved runways: *total:* 17
over 3,047 m: 3
2,438 to 3,047 m: 2
1,524 to 2,437 m: 5
914 to 1,523 m: 7 (2013)

Airports—with unpaved runways: *total:* 179
1,524 to 2,437 m: 3
914 to 1,523 m: 104
under 914 m: 72 (2013)

Pipelines: refined products 270 km (2013)

Railways: *total:* 3,427 km
narrow gauge: 3,427 km 1.067-m gauge (313 km electrified) (2014)

country comparison to the world: 53

Roadways: *total:* 97,267 km
paved: 18,481 km
unpaved: 78,786 km (2002)
country comparison to the world: 49

Waterways: (some navigation possible on Lake Kariba) (2011)

Ports and terminals: river port(s): Binga, Kariba (Zambezi)

MILITARY AND SECURITY

Military expenditures: 2.2% of GDP (2016)
2.34% of GDP (2015)
2.32% of GDP (2014)
2.34% of GDP (2013)
2.26% of GDP (2012)
country comparison to the world: 22

Military branches: Zimbabwe Defense Forces (ZDF): Zimbabwe National Army (ZNA), Air Force of Zimbabwe (AFZ) (2012)

Military service age and obligation: 18-24 years of age for voluntary military service; no conscription; women are eligible to serve (2012)

TRANSNATIONAL ISSUES

Disputes—international: Namibia has supported, and in 2004 Zimbabwe dropped objections to, plans between Botswana and Zambia to build a bridge over the Zambezi River, thereby de facto recognizing a short, but not clearly delimited, Botswana-Zambia boundary in the river; South Africa has placed military units to assist police operations along the border of Lesotho, Zimbabwe, and Mozambique to control smuggling, poaching, and illegal migration

Refugees and internally displaced persons: refugees (country of origin): 5,925 (Democratic Republic of Congo) (2016)
IDPs: undetermined (political violence, violence in association with the 2008 election, human rights violations, land reform, and economic collapse) (2015)
stateless persons: 300,000 (2016)

Trafficking in persons: current situation: Zimbabwe is a source, transit, and destination country for men, women, and children subjected to forced labor and sex trafficking; Zimbabwean women and girls from towns bordering South Africa, Mozambique, and Zambia are subjected to forced labor, including domestic servitude, and prostitution catering to long-distance truck drivers; Zimbabwean men, women, and children experience forced labor in agriculture and domestic servitude in rural areas; family members may recruit children and other relatives from rural areas with promises of work or education in cities and towns where they end up in domestic servitude and sex trafficking; Zimbabwean women and men are lured into exploitative labor situations in South Africa and other neighboring countries

tier rating: Tier 3—Zimbabwe does not fully comply with the minimum standards for the elimination of trafficking and is not making significant efforts to do so; the government passed an anti-trafficking law in 2014 defining trafficking in persons as a crime of transportation and failing to capture the key element of the international definition of human trafficking—the purpose of exploitation—which prevents the law from being comprehensive or consistent with the 2000 UN TIP Protocol that Zimbabwe acceded to in 2013; the government did not report on anti-trafficking law enforcement efforts during 2014, and corruption in law enforcement and the judiciary remain a concern; authorities made minimal efforts to identify and protect trafficking victims, relying on NGOs to identify and assist victims; Zimbabwe's 2014 anti-trafficking law required the opening of 10 centers for trafficking victims, but none were established during the year; five existing shelters for vulnerable children and orphans may have accommodated child victims; in January 2015, an inter-ministerial anti-trafficking committee was established, but it is unclear if the committee ever met or initiated any activities (2015)

Illicit drugs: transit point for cannabis and South Asian heroin, mandrax, and methamphetamines en route to South Africa

ABBREVIATIONS

ABEDA	Arab Bank for Economic Development in Africa
ACP Group	African, Caribbean, and Pacific Group of States
ADB	Asian Development Bank
AfDB	African Development Bank
AFESD	Arab Fund for Economic and Social Development
AG	Australia Group
Air Pollution	Convention on Long-Range Transboundary Air Pollution
Air Pollution-Nitrogen Oxides	Protocol to the 1979 Convention on Long-Range Transboundary Air Pollution Concerning the Control of Emissions of Nitrogen Oxides or Their Transboundary Fluxes
Air Pollution-Persistent Organic Pollutants	Protocol to the 1979 Convention on Long-Range Transboundary Air Pollution on Persistent Organic Pollutants
Air Pollution-Sulphur 85	Protocol to the 1979 Convention on Long-Range Transboundary Air Pollution on the Reduction of Sulphur Emissions or Their Transboundary Fluxes by at Least 30%
Air Pollution-Sulphur 94	Protocol to the 1979 Convention on Long-Range Transboundary Air Pollution on Further Reduction of Sulphur Emissions
Air Pollution-Volatile Organic Compounds	Protocol to the 1979 Convention on Long-Range Transboundary Air Pollution Concerning the Control of Emissions of Volatile Organic Compounds or Their Transboundary Fluxes
AMF	Arab Monetary Fund
AMU	Arab Maghreb Union
Antarctic Marine Living Resources	Convention on the Conservation of Antarctic Marine Living Resources
Antarctic Seals	Convention for the Conservation of Antarctic Seals
Antarctic-Environmental Protocol	Protocol on Environmental Protection to the Antarctic Treaty
ANZUS	Australia-New Zealand-United States Security Treaty
AOSIS	Alliance of Small Island States
APEC	Asia-Pacific Economic Cooperation
Arabsat	Arab Satellite Communications Organization
ARF	ASEAN Regional Forum
ASEAN	Association of Southeast Asian Nations
AU	African Union
Autodin	Automatic Digital Network
BA	Baltic Assembly
bbl/day	barrels per day
BCIE	Central American Bank for Economic Integration
BDEAC	Central African States Development Bank
Benelux	Benelux Union
BGN	United States Board on Geographic Names
BIMSTEC	Bay of Bengal Initiative for Multi-sectoral Technical and Economic Cooperation
Biodiversity	Convention on Biological Diversity
BIS	Bank for International Settlements
BRICS	(Brazil, Russia, India, China, and South Africa)
BSEC	Black Sea Economic Cooperation Zone
C	Commonwealth
CD	Community of Democracies
c.i.f.	cost, insurance, and freight
CACM	Central American Common Market
CAEU	Council of Arab Economic Unity
CAN	Andean Community
Caricom	Caribbean Community and Common Market
CB	citizen's band mobile radio communications
CBSS	Council of the Baltic Sea States
CCC	Customs Cooperation Council

CDB	Caribbean Development Bank
CE	Council of Europe
CEI	Central European Initiative
CELAC	Community of Latin America and Caribbean States
CEMA	Council for Mutual Economic Assistance
CEMAC	Economic and Monetary Community of Central Africa
CEPGL	Economic Community of the Great Lakes Countries
CERN	European Organization for Nuclear Research
CIA	Central Intelligence Agency
CICA	Conference of Interaction and Confidence-Building Measures in Asia
CIS	Commonwealth of Independent States
CITES	see Endangered Species
Climate Change	United Nations Framework Convention on Climate Change
Climate Change-Kyoto Protocol	Kyoto Protocol to the United Nations Framework Convention on Climate Change
COCOM	Coordinating Committee on Export Controls
COMESA	Common Market for Eastern and Southern Africa
Comsat	Communications Satellite Corporation
CP	Colombo Plan
CPLP	Comunidade dos Paises de Lingua Portuguesa
CSN	South American Community of Nations became UNASUL—Union of South American Nations
CSTO	Collective Security Treaty Organization
CTBTO	Preparatory Commission for the Nuclear-Test-Ban Treaty Organization
CY	calendar year
D-8	Developing Eight
DC	developed country
DDT	dichloro-diphenyl-trichloro-ethane
Desertification	United Nations Convention to Combat Desertification in Those Countries Experiencing Serious Drought and/or Desertification, Particularly in Africa
DIA	United States Defense Intelligence Agency
DSN	Defense Switched Network
DST	daylight savings time
DWT	deadweight ton
EAC	East African Community
EADB	East African Development Bank
EAEC	Eurasian Economic Community
EAPC	Euro-Atlantic Partnership Council
EAS	East Asia Summit
EBRD	European Bank for Reconstruction and Development
EC	European Community or European Commission
ECA	Economic Commission for Africa
ECB	European Central Bank
ECE	Economic Commission for Europe
ECLAC	Economic Commission for Latin America and the Caribbean
ECO	Economic Cooperation Organization
ECOSOC	Economic and Social Council
ECOWAS	Economic Community of West African States
ECSC	European Coal and Steel Community
EE	Eastern Europe
EEC	European Economic Community
EEZ	exclusive economic zone
EFTA	European Free Trade Association
EIB	European Investment Bank
EITI	Extractive Industry Trnsparency Iniative
EMU	European Monetary Union
Endangered Species	Convention on the International Trade in Endangered Species of Wild Flora and Fauna (CITES)

Entente	Council of the Entente
Environmental Modification	Convention on the Prohibition of Military or Any Other Hostile Use of Environmental Modification Techniques
ESA	European Space Agency
ESCAP	Economic and Social Commission for Asia and the Pacific
ESCWA	Economic and Social Commission for Western Asia
est.	estimate
EU	European Union
Euratom	European Atomic Energy Community
Eutelsat	European Telecommunications Satellite Organization
Ex-Im	Export-Import Bank of the United States
f.o.b.	free on board
FAO	Food and Agriculture Organization
FATF	Financial Action Task Force
FAX	facsimile
FLS	Front Line States
FOC	flags of convenience
FSU	former Soviet Union
FY	fiscal year
FZ	Franc Zone
G-3	Group of 3
G-5	Group of 5
G-6	Group of 6
G-7	Group of 7
G-8	Group of 8
G-9	Group of 9
G-10	Group of 10
G-15	Group of 15
G-11	Group of 11
G-20	Group of 20
G-24	Group of 24
G-77	Group of 77
GATT	General Agreement on Tariffs and Trade; now WTO
GCC	Gulf Cooperation Council
GCN	Global Caribbean Network
GCTU	General Confederation of Trade Unions
GDP	gross domestic product
GMT	Greenwich Mean Time
GNP	gross national product
GRT	gross register ton
GSM	global system for mobile cellular communications
GUAM	Organization for Democracy and Economic Development; acronym for member states— Georgia, Ukraine, Azerbaijan, Moldova
GWP	gross world product
Hazardous Wastes	Basel Convention on the Control of Transboundary Movements of Hazardous Wastes and Their Disposal
HF	high-frequency
HIV/AIDS	human immunodeficiency virus/acquired immune deficiency syndrome
IADB	Inter-American Development Bank
IAEA	International Atomic Energy Agency
IANA	Internet Assigned Numbers Authority
IBRD	International Bank for Reconstruction and Development (World Bank)
ICAO	International Civil Aviation Organization
ICC	International Chamber of Commerce
ICCt	International Criminal Court
ICJ	International Court of Justice (World Court)
ICRC	International Committee of the Red Cross

ICRM	International Red Cross and Red Crescent Movement
ICSID	International Center for Settlement of Investment Disputes
ICTR	International Criminal Tribunal for Rwanda
ICTY	International Criminal Tribunal for the former Yugoslavia
IDA	International Development Association
IDB	Islamic Development Bank
IDP	Internally Displaced Person
IEA	International Energy Agency
IFAD	International Fund for Agricultural Development
IFC	International Finance Corporation
IFRCS	International Federation of Red Cross and Red Crescent Societies
IGAD	Inter-Governmental Authority on Development
IHO	International Hydrographic Organization
ILO	International Labor Organization
IMF	International Monetary Fund
IMO	International Maritime Organization
IMSO	International Mobile Satellite Organization
Inmarsat	International Maritime Satellite Organization
InOC	Indian Ocean Commission
Intelsat	International Telecommunications Satellite Organization
Interpol	International Criminal Police Organization
Intersputnik	International Organization of Space Communications
IOC	International Olympic Committee
IOM	International Organization for Migration
IPU	Inter-Parliamentary Union
ISO	International Organization for Standardization
ISP	Internet Service Provider
ITC	International Trade Center
ITSO	International Telecommunications Satellite Organization
ITU	International Telecommunication Union
ITUC	International Trade Union Confederation, the successor to ICFTU (International Confederation of Free Trade Unions) and the WCL (World Confederation of Labor)
kHz	kilohertz
km	kilometer
kW	kilowatt
kWh	kilowatt-hour
LAES	Latin American and Caribbean Economic System
LAIA	Latin American Integration Association
LAS	League of Arab States
Law of the Sea	United Nations Convention on the Law of the Sea (LOS)
LDC	less developed country
LLDC	least developed country
London Convention	see Marine Dumping
LOS	see Law of the Sea
m	meter
Marecs	Maritime European Communications Satellite
Marine Dumping	Convention on the Prevention of Marine Pollution by Dumping Wastes and Other Matter
Marine Life Conservation	Convention on Fishing and Conservation of Living Resources of the High Seas
MARPOL	see Ship Pollution
Medarabtel	Middle East Telecommunications Project of the International Telecommunications Union
Mercosur	Southern Cone Common Market
MHz	megahertz
MICAH	International Civilian Support Mission in Haiti
MIGA	Multilateral Investment Guarantee Agency
MINURCAT	United Nations Mission in the Central African Republic and Chad

MINURSO	United Nations Mission for the Referendum in Western Sahara
MINUSTAH	United Nations Stabilization Mission in Haiti
MONUSCO	United Nations Organization Stabilization Mission in the Democratic Republic of the Congo
NA	not available
NAFTA	North American Free Trade Agreement
NAM	Nonaligned Movement
NATO	North Atlantic Treaty Organization
NC	Nordic Council
NEA	Nuclear Energy Agency
NEGL	negligible
NGA	National Geospatial-Intelligence Agency
NGO	nongovernmental organization
NIB	Nordic Investment Bank
NIC	newly industrializing country
NIE	newly industrializing economy
NIS	new independent states
nm	nautical mile
NMT	Nordic Mobile Telephone
NSG	Nuclear Suppliers Group
Nuclear Test Ban	Treaty Banning Nuclear Weapons Tests in the Atmosphere, in Outer Space, and Under Water
NZ	New Zealand
OAPEC	Organization of Arab Petroleum Exporting Countries
OAS	Organization of American States
OAU	Organization of African Unity; see African Union
ODA	official development assistance
OECD	Organization for Economic Cooperation and Development
OECS	Organization of Eastern Caribbean States
OHCHR	Office of the United Nations High Commissioner for Human Rights
OIC	Organization of the Islamic Conference
OIF	International Organization of the French-speaking World
OOF	other official flows
OPANAL	Agency for the Prohibition of Nuclear Weapons in Latin America and the Caribbean
OPCW	Organization for the Prohibition of Chemical Weapons
OPEC	Organization of Petroleum Exporting Countries
OSCE	Organization for Security and Cooperation in Europe
Ozone Layer Protection	Montreal Protocol on Substances That Deplete the Ozone Layer
PCA	Permanent Court of Arbitration
PFP	Partnership for Peace
PIF	Pacific Islands Forum
PPP	purchasing power parity
Ramsar	see Wetlands
RG	Rio Group
SAARC	South Asian Association for Regional Cooperation
SACEP	South Asia Co-operative Environment Program
SACU	Southern African Customs Union
SADC	Southern African Development Community
SAFE	South African Far East Cable
SCO	Shanghai Cooperation Organization
SECI	Southeast European Cooperative Initiative
SELEC	Convention of the Southeast European Law Enforcement Centers (successor to SECI)
SHF	super-high-frequency
Ship Pollution	Protocol of 1978 Relating to the International Convention for the Prevention of Pollution From Ships, 1973 (MARPOL)
SICA	Central American Integration System
Sparteca	South Pacific Regional Trade and Economic Cooperation Agreement

SPC	Secretariat of the Pacific Communities
SPF	South Pacific Forum
sq km	square kilometer
sq mi	square mile
TAT	Trans-Atlantic Telephone
TEU	Twenty-Foot Equivalent Unit, a unit of measure for containerized cargo capacity
Tropical Timber 83	International Tropical Timber Agreement, 1983
Tropical Timber 94	International Tropical Timber Agreement, 1994
UAE	United Arab Emirates
UDEAC	Central African Customs and Economic Union
UHF	ultra-high-frequency
UK	United Kingdom
UN	United Nations
UN-AIDS	Joint United Nations Program on HIV/AIDS
UNAMA	United Nations Assistance Mission in Afghanistan
UNAMID	African Union/United Nations Hybrid Operation in Darfur
UNASUR	Union of South American Nations
UNCLOS	United Nations Convention on the Law of the Sea, also know as LOS
UNCTAD	United Nations Conference on Trade and Development
UNDCP	United Nations Drug Control Program
UNDEF	United Nations Democracy Fund
UNDOF	United Nations Disengagement Observer Force
UNDP	United Nations Development Program
UNEP	United Nations Environment Program
UNESCO	United Nations Educational, Scientific, and Cultural Organization
UNFICYP	United Nations Peace-keeping Force in Cyprus
UNFPA	United Nations Population Fund
UN-Habitat	United Nations Center for Human Settlements
UNHCR	United Nations High Commissioner for Refugees
UNICEF	United Nations Children's Fund
UNICRI	United Nations Interregional Crime and Justice Research Institute
UNIDIR	United Nations Institute for Disarmament Research
UNIDO	United Nations Industrial Development Organization
UNIFIL	United Nations Interim Force in Lebanon
UNISFA	United Nations Interim Force for Abyei
UNITAR	United Nations Institute for Training and Research
UNMIK	United Nations Interim Administration Mission in Kosovo
UNMIL	United Nations Mission in Liberia
UNMIS	United Nations Mission in the Sudan
UNMISS	United Nations Mission in South Sudan
UNMIT	United Nations Integrated Mission in Timor-Leste
UNMOGIP	United Nations Military Observer Group in India and Pakistan
UNOCI	United Nations Operation in Cote d'Ivoire
UNODC	United Nations Office of Drugs and Crime
UNOPS	United Nations Office of Project Services
UNRISD	United Nations Research Institute for Social Development
UNRWA	United Nations Relief and Works Agency for Palestine Refugees in the Near East
UNSC	United Nations Security Council
UNSSC	Untied Nations System Staff College
UNTSO	United Nations Truce Supervision Organization
UNU	United Nations University
UNWTO	World Tourism Organization
UPU	Universal Postal Union
US	United States
USSR	Union of Soviet Socialist Republics (Soviet Union); used for information dated before 25 December 1991

UTC	Coordinated Universal Time
UV	ultra violet
VHF	very-high-frequency
VSAT	very small aperture terminal
WADB	West African Development Bank
WAEMU	West African Economic and Monetary Union
WCL	World Confederation of Labor
WCO	World Customs Organization
Wetlands	Convention on Wetlands of International Importance Especially As Waterfowl Habitat
WEU	Western European Union
WFP	World Food Program
WFTU	World Federation of Trade Unions
Whaling	International Convention for the Regulation of Whaling
WHO	World Health Organization
WIPO	World Intellectual Property Organization
WMO	World Meteorological Organization
WP	Warsaw Pact
WTO	World Trade Organization
ZC	Zangger Committee

INTERNATIONAL ORGANIZATIONS AND GROUPS

advanced developing countries
another term for those less developed countries (LDCs) with particularly rapid industrial development; see newly industrializing economies (NIEs)

advanced economies
a term used by the International Monetary FUND (IMF) for the top group in its hierarchy of advanced economies, countries in transition, and developing countries; it includes the following 33 advanced economies: Australia, Austria, Belgium, Canada, Cyprus, Czech Republic, Denmark, Finland, France, Germany, Greece, Hong Kong, Iceland, Ireland, Israel, Italy, Japan, South Korea, Luxembourg, Malta, Netherlands, NZ, Norway, Portugal, Singapore, Slovak Republic, Slovenia, Spain, Sweden, Switzerland, Taiwan, UK, US; note—this group would presumably also cover the following nine smaller countries of Andorra, Bermuda, Faroe Islands, Guernsey, Holy See, Jersey, Liechtenstein, Monaco, and San Marino that are included in the more comprehensive group of "developed countries"

African Development Bank Group (AfDB)
note—regional multilateral development finance institution temporarily located in Tunis, Tunisia; the Bank Group consists of the African Development Bank, the African Development Fund, and the Nigerian Trust Fund
established—10 September 1964
aim—to promote economic development and social progress
regional members—(53) Algeria, Angola, Benin, Botswana, Burkina Faso, Burundi, Cameroon, cabo Verde, Central African Republic, Chad, Comoros, Democratic Republic of the Congo, Republic of the Congo, Cote d'Ivoire, Djibouti, Egypt, Equatorial Guinea, Eritrea, Ethiopia, Gabon, The Gambia, Ghana, Guinea, Guinea-Bissau, Kenya, Lesotho, Liberia, Libya, Madagascar, Malawi, Mali, Mauritania, Mauritius, Morocco, Mozambique, Namibia, Niger, Nigeria, Rwanda, Sao Tome and Principe, Senegal, Seychelles, Sierra Leone, Somalia, South Africa, Sudan, Swaziland, Tanzania, Togo, Tunisia, Uganda, Zambia, Zimbabwe
nonregional members—(25) Argentina, Austria, Belgium, Brazil, Canada, China, Denmark, Finland, France, Germany, India, Italy, Japan, South Korea, Kuwait, Netherlands, Norway, Portugal, Saudi Arabia, Spain, Sweden, Switzerland, UAE (ADF members only), UK, US

African Union (AU)
note—replaces Organization of African Unity (OAU)
established—8 July 2001
aim—to achieve greater unity among African States; to defend states' integrity and independence; to accelerate political, social, and economic integration; to encourage international cooperation; to promote democratic principles and institutions
members—(54) Algeria, Angola, Benin, Botswana, Burkina Faso, Burundi, Cabo Verde, Cameroon, Central African Republic, Chad, Comoros, Democratic Republic of the Congo, Republic of the Congo, Cote d'Ivoire, Djibouti, Egypt, Equatorial Guinea, Eritrea, Ethiopia, Gabon, The Gambia, Ghana, Guinea (suspended), Guinea-Bissau, Kenya, Lesotho, Liberia, Libya, Madagascar, Malawi, Mali, Mauritania, Mauritius, Mozambique, Namibia, Niger, Nigeria, Rwanda, Sahrawi Arab Democratic Republic (Western Sahara), Sao Tome and Principe, Senegal, Seychelles, Sierra Leone, Somalia, South Africa, South Sudan, Sudan, Swaziland, Tanzania, Togo, Tunisia, Uganda, Zambia, Zimbabwe

African Union/United Nations Hybrid Operation in Darfur (UNAMID)
established—31 July 2007
aim—to contribute to the restoration of security conditions which will allow safe humanitarian assistance throughout Darfur, to contribute to the protection of civilian populations under imminent threat of physical attack, to monitor, observe compliance with, and verify the implementation of various ceasefire agreements
members—(47) Bangladesh, Benin, Bolivia, Burkina Faso, Burundi, Cambodia, Cabo Verde, Cameroon, Djibouti, Ecuador, Egypt, Ethiopia, The Gambia, Germany, Ghana, Indonesia, Iran, Jordan, Kenya, South Korea,Kyrgyzstan, Lesotho, Malawi, Malaysia, Mali, Mongolia, Namibia, Nepal, Nigeria, Pakistan, Palau, Peru, Rwanda,Senegal, Sierra Leone, South Africa, Tajikistan, Tanzania, Thailand, Togo, Tunisia, Turkey, Uganda, Yemen, Zambia, Zimbabwe

African, Caribbean, and Pacific Group of States (ACP Group)
established—6 June 1975
aim—to manage their preferential economic and aid relationship with the EU
members—(79) Angola, Antigua and Barbuda, The Bahamas, Barbados, Belize, Benin, Botswana, Burkina Faso, Burundi, Cabo Verde, Cameroon, Central African Republic, Chad, Comoros, Democratic Republic of the Congo, Republic of the Congo, Cook Islands, Cote d'Ivoire, Cuba, Djibouti, Dominica, Dominican Republic, Equatorial Guinea, Eritrea, Ethiopia, Fiji, Gabon, The Gambia, Ghana, Grenada, Guinea, Guinea-Bissau, Guyana, Haiti, Jamaica, Kenya, Kiribati, Lesotho, Liberia, Madagascar, Malawi, Mali, Marshall Islands, Mauritania, Mauritius, Federated States of Micronesia, Mozambique, Namibia, Nauru, Niger, Nigeria, Niue, Palau, Papua New Guinea, Rwanda, Saint Kitts and Nevis, Saint Lucia, Saint Vincent and the Grenadines, Samoa, Sao Tome and Principe, Senegal, Seychelles, Sierra Leone, Solomon Islands, Somalia, South Africa, Sudan, Suriname, Swaziland, Tanzania, Timor-Leste, Togo, Tonga, Trinidad and Tobago, Tuvalu, Uganda, Vanuatu, Zambia, Zimbabwe

Agency for the Prohibition of Nuclear Weapons in Latin America and the Caribbean (OPANAL)
note—acronym from Organismo para la Proscripcion de las Armas Nucleares en la America Latina y el Caribe (OPANAL)
established—14 February 1967 under the Treaty of Tlatelolco; effective—25 April 1969 on the 11th ratification

aim—to encourage the peaceful uses of atomic energy and prohibit nuclear weapons
members—(33) Antigua and Barbuda, Argentina, The Bahamas, Barbados, Belize, Bolivia, Brazil, Chile, Colombia, Costa Rica, Cuba, Dominica, Dominican Republic, Ecuador, El Salvador, Grenada, Guatemala, Guyana, Haiti, Honduras, Jamaica, Mexico, Nicaragua, Panama, Paraguay, Peru, Saint Kitts and Nevis, Saint Lucia, Saint Vincent and the Grenadines, Suriname, Trinidad and Tobago, Uruguay, Venezuela

Alliance of Small Island States (AOSIS)

established—November 1990
aim—to call attention to threats of sea-level rise and coral bleaching to small islands and lowlying coastal developing states from global warming; to emphasize the importance of information and information technology in the process of achieving sustainable development
members—(39) Antigua and Barbuda, The Bahamas, Barbados, Belize, Cabo Verde, Comoros, Cook Islands, Cuba, Dominica, Dominican Republic, Fiji, Grenada, Guinea-Bissau, Guyana, Haiti, Jamaica, Kiribati, Maldives, Marshall Islands, Mauritius, Federated States of Micronesia, Nauru, Niue, Palau, Papua New Guinea, St. Kitts and Nevis, St. Lucia, St. Vincent and the Grenadines, Samoa, Sao Tome and Principe, Seychelles, Singapore, Solomon Islands, Suriname, Timor-Leste, Tonga, Trinidad and Tobago, Tuvalu, Vanuatu
observers—(5) American Samoa, Guam, Netherlands Antilles, Puerto Rico, U.S. Virgin Islands

Andean Community (CAN)

note—formerly known as the Andean Group (AG) and the Andean Common Market (Ancom)
established—26 May 1969; present name established 1 October 1992; effective—16 October 1969
aim—to promote harmonious development through economic integration
members—(4) Bolivia, Colombia, Ecuador, Peru
associate members—(5) Argentina, Brazil, Chile, Paraguay, Uruguay
observers—(1) Spain

Arab Bank for Economic Development in Africa (ABEDA)

note—also known as Banque Arabe de Developpement Economique en Afrique (BADEA)
established—18 February 1974; effective—16 September 1974
aim—to promote economic development
members—(17 plus the Palestine Liberation Organization) Algeria, Bahrain, Egypt, Iraq, Jordan, Kuwait, Lebanon, Libya, Mauritania, Morocco, Oman, Qatar, Saudi Arabia, Sudan, Syria, Tunisia, UAE, Palestine Liberation Organization; note—these are all the members of the Arab League excluding Comoros, Djibouti, Somalia, Yemen

Arab Fund for Economic and Social Development (AFESD)

established—16 May 1968
aim—to promote economic and social development
members—(20 plus the Palestine Liberation Organization) Algeria, Bahrain, Djibouti, Egypt, Iraq, Jordan, Kuwait, Lebanon, Libya, Mauritania, Morocco, Oman, Qatar, Saudi Arabia, Somalia (suspended 1993), Sudan, Syria, Tunisia, UAE, Yemen, Palestine Liberation Organization

Arab Maghreb Union (AMU)

established—17 February 1989
aim—to promote cooperation and integration among the Arab states of northern Africa
members—(5) Algeria, Libya, Mauritania, Morocco, Tunisia

Arab Monetary Fund (AMF)

established—27 April 1976; effective—2 February 1977
aim—to promote Arab cooperation, development, and integration in monetary and economic affairs
members—(21 plus the Palestine Liberation Organization) Algeria, Bahrain, Comoros, Djibouti, Egypt, Iraq, Jordan, Kuwait, Lebanon, Libya, Mauritania, Morocco, Oman, Qatar, Saudi Arabia, Somalia, Sudan, Syria, Tunisia, UAE, Yemen, Palestine Liberation Organization

Arctic Council

established—18 September 1996
aim—to address the common concerns and challenges faced by Arctic governments and the people of the Arctic; to protect the Arctic environment
members—(8) Canada, Denmark (Greenland, Faroe Islands), Finland, Iceland, Norway, Russia, Sweden, US
permanent participants—(6) Aleut International Association, Arctic Athabaskan Council, Gwich'in Council International, Inuit Circumpolar Conference, Russian Association of Indigenous People of the North, Saami Council
observers—(12) China, France, Germany, India, Italy, Japan, South Korea, Netherlands, Poland, Singapore, Spain, UK

ASEAN Regional Forum (ARF)

established—25 July 1994
aim—to foster constructive dialogue and consultation on political and security issues of common interest and concern
members—(27) Australia, Bangladesh, Brunei, Burma, Cambodia, Canada, China, EU, India, Indonesia, Japan, North Korea, South Korea, Laos, Malaysia, Mongolia, NZ, Pakistan, Papua New Guinea, Philippines, Russia, Singapore, Sri Lanka, Thailand, Timor-Leste, US, Vietnam

Asia-Pacific Economic Cooperation (APEC)

established—7 November 1989
aim—to promote trade and investment in the Pacific basin

members—(21) Australia, Brunei, Canada, Chile, China, Hong Kong, Indonesia, Japan, South Korea, Malaysia, Mexico, NZ, Papua New Guinea, Peru, Philippines, Russia, Singapore, Taiwan, Thailand, US, Vietnam
observers—(3) Association of Southeast Asian Nations, Pacific Economic Cooperation Council, Pacific Islands Forum Secretariat

Asian Development Bank (ADB)
established—19 December 1966
aim—to promote regional economic cooperation
members—(48) Afghanistan, Armenia, Australia, Azerbaijan, Bangladesh, Bhutan, Brunei, Burma, Cambodia, China, Cook Islands, Fiji, Georgia, Hong Kong, India, Indonesia, Japan, Kazakhstan, Kiribati, South Korea, Kyrgyzstan, Laos, Malaysia, Maldives, Marshall Islands, Federated States of Micronesia, Mongolia, Nauru, Nepal, NZ, Pakistan, Palau, Papua New Guinea, Philippines, Samoa, Singapore, Solomon Islands, Sri Lanka, Taiwan, Tajikistan, Thailand, Timor- Leste, Tonga, Turkmenistan, Tuvalu, Uzbekistan, Vanuatu, Vietnam
nonregional members—(19) Austria, Belgium, Canada, Denmark, Finland, France, Germany, Ireland, Italy, Luxembourg, Netherlands, Norway, Portugal, Spain, Sweden, Switzerland, Turkey, UK, US

Association of Southeast Asian Nations (ASEAN)
established—8 August 1967
aim—to encourage regional economic, social, and cultural cooperation among the non-Communist countries of Southeast Asia
members—(10) Brunei, Burma, Cambodia, Indonesia, Laos, Malaysia, Philippines, Singapore, Thailand, Vietnam
dialogue partners—(10) Australia, Canada, China, EU, India, Japan, South Korea, NZ, Russia, US
observers—(2) Papua New Guinea, Timor-Leste

Australia Group (AG)
established—June 1985
aim—to consult on and coordinate export controls related to chemical and biological weapons
members—(42) Argentina, Australia, Austria, Belgium, Bulgaria, Canada, Croatia, Cyprus, Czech Republic, Denmark, Estonia, European Commission, Finland, France, Germany, Greece, Hungary, Iceland, Ireland, Italy, Japan, South Korea, Latvia, Lithuania, Luxembourg, Malta, Mexico, Netherlands, NZ, Norway, Poland, Portugal, Romania, Slovakia, Slovenia, Spain, Sweden, Switzerland, Turkey, Ukraine, UK, US

Australia-New Zealand-United States Security Treaty (ANZUS)
established—1 September 1951; effective—29 April 1952
aim—to implement a trilateral mutual security agreement, although the US suspended security obligations to NZ on 11 August 1986; Australia and the US continue to hold annual meetings
members—(3) Australia, NZ, US

Baltic Assembly (BA)
established—12 May 1990
aim—to thoroughly discuss various cooperation issues between Baltic states
members—(3) Estonia, Latvia, Lithuania

Bank for International Settlements (BIS)
established—20 January 1930; effective—17 March 1930
aim—to promote cooperation among central banks in international financial settlements
members—(60) Algeria, Argentina, Australia, Austria, Belgium, Bosnia and Herzegovina, Brazil, Bulgaria, Canada, Chile, China, Colombia, Croatia, Czech Republic, Denmark, European Central Bank, Estonia, Finland, France, Germany, Greece, Hong Kong, Hungary, Iceland, India, Indonesia, Ireland, Israel, Italy, Japan, South Korea, Latvia, Lithuania, Luxembourg, Macedonia, Malaysia, Mexico, Netherlands, NZ, Norway, Peru, Philippines, Poland, Portugal, Romania, Russia, Saudi Arabia, Serbia, Singapore, Slovakia, Slovenia, South Africa, Spain, Sweden, Switzerland, Thailand, Turkey, UAE, UK, US; note—Montenegro has a separate central bank; its links with BIS are currently under review

Bay of Bengal Initiative for Multi-Sectoral Technical and Economic Cooperation (BIMSTEC)
established—June 1997
aim—to foster socio-economic cooperation among members
members—(7) Bangladesh, Bhutan, Burma, India, Nepal, Sri Lanka, Thailand

Benelux Union (Benelux)
note—acronym from Belgium, Netherlands, and Luxembourg; was formerly known as Benelux Economic Union
established—3 February 1958; effective—1 November 1960; changed names 17 June 2008
aim—to develop closer economic and legal cooperation and integration
members—(3) Belgium, Luxembourg, Netherlands

Big Seven
note—membership is the same as the Group of 7
established—1975
aim—to discuss and coordinate major economic policies
members—(7) Big Six (Canada, France, Germany, Italy, Japan, UK) plus the US

Black Sea Economic Cooperation Zone (BSEC)
established—25 June 1992

aim—to enhance regional stability through economic cooperation
members—(12) Albania, Armenia, Azerbaijan, Bulgaria, Georgia, Greece, Moldova, Romania, Russia, Serbia, Turkey, Ukraine; note—Macedonia is in the process of joining
observers—(17) Austria, Belarus, Black Sea Commission, EU, Croatia, Czech Republic, Egypt, Energy Charter Secretariat, France, Germany, International Black Sea Club, Israel, Italy, Poland, Slovakia, Tunisia, US; note—Bosnia and Herzegovina and Slovenia have applied for observer status

BRICS
note—the name of the organization stands for the first letter of each of the five members' names
established—BRIC established 16 June 2009; BRICS established 24 December 2011
aim—to seek common ground in political and economic venues; to achieve peace, security, development, and cooperation; to contribute significantly to the development of humanity and to establish a more equitable world
members—(5) Brazil, Russia, India, China, South Africa

Caribbean Community and Common Market (Caricom)
established—4 July 1973; effective—1 August 1973
aim—to promote economic integration and development, especially among the less developed countries
members—(15) Antigua and Barbuda, The Bahamas, Barbados, Belize, Dominica, Grenada, Guyana, Haiti, Jamaica, Montserrat, Saint Kitts and Nevis, Saint Lucia, Saint Vincent and the Grenadines, Suriname, Trinidad and Tobago
associate members—(5) Anguilla, Bermuda, British Virgin Islands, Cayman Islands, Turks and Caicos Islands
observers—(8) Aruba, Colombia, Curacao, Dominican Republic, Mexico, Puerto Rico, Sint Maarten, Venezuela

Caribbean Development Bank (CDB)
established—18 October 1969; effective—26 January 1970
aim—to promote economic development and cooperation
regional members—(21) Anguilla, Antigua and Barbuda, The Bahamas, Barbados, Belize, British Virgin Islands, Cayman Islands, Colombia, Dominica, Grenada, Guyana, Haiti, Jamaica, Mexico, Montserrat, Saint Kitts and Nevis, Saint Lucia, Saint Vincent and the Grenadines, Trinidad and Tobago, Turks and Caicos Islands, Venezuela
nonregional members—(5) Canada, China, Germany, Italy, UK

Central African Customs and Economic Union (UDEAC)
see *Economic and Monetary Community of Central Africa (CEMAC)*

Central African States Development Bank (BDEAC)
note—acronym from Banque de Developpement des Etats de l'Afrique Centrale
established—3 December 1975
aim—to provide loans for economic development
members—(11) African Development Bank (AfDB), Cameroon, Central African States Bank (BEAC), Central African Republic, Chad, Republic of the Congo, Equatorial Guinea, France, Gabon, Kuwait, Libya

Central American Bank for Economic Integration (BCIE)
note—acronym from Banco Centroamericano de Integracion Economico
established—13 December 1960 signature of Articles of Agreement; 31 May 1961 began operations
aim—to promote economic integration and development
members—(5) Costa Rica, El Salvador, Guatemala, Honduras, Nicaragua
nonregional members—(7) Argentina, Colombia, Dominican Republic, Mexico, Panama, Spain, Taiwan

Central American Common Market (CACM)
established—13 December 1960, collapsed in 1969, reinstated in 1991
aim—to promote establishment of a Central American Common Market
members—(5) Costa Rica, El Salvador, Guatemala, Honduras, Nicaragua

Central American Integration System (SICA)
established—13 December 1991; operational 1 February 1993
aim—to strengthen democracy; to set up a new model of regional security; to promote freedom; to achieve a regional system of welfare and economic and social justice; to attain economic unity and strengthen the area as an economic bloc; to act as a bloc in international matters
members—(7) Belize, Costa Rica, El Salvador, Guatemala, Honduras, Nicaragua, Panama
associated member—(1) Dominican Republic
observers—(15) Argentina, Australia, Brazil, Chile, China, France, Germany, Holy See, Italy, Japan, South Korea, Mexico, Peru, Spain, US

Central European Initiative (CEI)
note—evolved from the Quadrilateral Initiative and the Hexagonal Initiative
established—11 November 1989 as the Quadrilateral Initiative, 27 July 1991 became the Hexagonal Initiative, July 1992 its present name was adopted
aim—to form an economic and political cooperation group for the region between the Adriatic and the Baltic Seas
members—(18) Albania, Austria, Belarus, Bosnia and Herzegovina, Bulgaria, Croatia, Czech Republic, Hungary, Italy, Macedonia, Moldova, Montenegro, Poland, Romania, Serbia, Slovakia, Slovenia, Ukraine

centrally planned economies

a term applied mainly to the traditionally Communist states that looked to the former USSR for leadership; most are now evolving toward more democratic and market-oriented systems; also known formerly as the Second World or as the Communist countries; through the 1980s, this group included Albania, Bulgaria, Cambodia, China, Cuba, Czechoslovakia, German Democratic Republic, Hungary, North Korea, Laos, Mongolia, Poland, Romania, USSR, Vietnam, Yugoslavia, but now is limited to Cuba and North Korea, and less so to China

Collective Security Treaty Organization (CSTO)

established—7 October 2002
aim—to coordinate military and political cooperation, to develop multilateral structures and mechanisms of cooperation for ensuring national security of the member states
members—(7) Armenia, Belarus, Kazakhstan, Kyrgyzstan, Russia, Tajikistan, Uzbekistan

Colombo Plan (CP)

established—May 1950 proposal was adopted; 1 July 1951 commenced full operations
aim—to promote economic and social development in Asia and the Pacific
members—(27) Afghanistan, Australia, Bangladesh, Bhutan, Brunei, Burma, Fiji, India, Indonesia, Iran, Japan, South Korea, Laos, Malaysia, Maldives, Mongolia, Nepal, NZ, Pakistan, Papua New Guinea, Philippines, Saudi Arabia, Singapore, Sri Lanka, Thailand, US, Vietnam

Common Market for Eastern and Southern Africa (COMESA)

note—formerly known as Preferential Trade Area for Eastern and Southern Africa (PTA)
established—treaty signed 5 November 1993; treaty ratified 8 December 1994
aim—recognizing, promoting and protecting fundamental human rights, commitment to the principles of liberty and rule of law, maintaining peace and stability through the promotion and strengthening of good neighborliness, commitment to peaceful settlement of disputes among member states
members—(19) Burundi, Comoros, Democratic Republic of the Congo, Djibouti, Egypt, Eritrea, Ethiopia, Kenya, Libya, Madagascar, Malawi, Mauritius, Rwanda, Seychelles, Sudan, Swaziland, Uganda, Zambia, Zimbabwe

Commonwealth (C)

note—also known as Commonwealth of Nations
established—31 December 1931
aim—to foster multinational cooperation and assistance, as a voluntary association that evolved from the British Empire
members—(53) Antigua and Barbuda, Australia, The Bahamas, Bangladesh, Barbados, Belize, Botswana, Brunei, Cameroon, Canada, Cyprus, Dominica, Fiji (suspended), Ghana, Grenada, Guyana, India, Jamaica, Kenya, Kiribati, Lesotho, Malawi, Malaysia, Maldives, Malta, Mauritius, Mozambique, Namibia, Nauru, NZ, Nigeria, Pakistan (reinstated 2004), Papua New Guinea, Rwanda, Saint Kitts and Nevis, Saint Lucia, Saint Vincent and the Grenadines, Samoa, Seychelles, Sierra Leone, Singapore, Solomon Islands, South Africa, Sri Lanka, Swaziland, Tanzania, Tonga, Trinidad and Tobago, Tuvalu, Uganda, UK, Vanuatu, Zambia; note—on 7 December 2003 Zimbabwe withdrew its membership from the Commonwealth

Commonwealth of Independent States (CIS)

established—8 December 1991; effective—21 December 1991
aim—to coordinate intercommonwealth relations and to provide a mechanism for the orderly dissolution of the USSR
members—(11) Armenia, Azerbaijan, Belarus, Kazakhstan, Kyrgyzstan, Moldova, Russia, Tajikistan, Turkmenistan (unofficial), Ukraine (unofficial), Uzbekistan; note—neither Ukraine as a participating member nor Turkmenistan as an associate member have signed the 1993 CIS charter, although both participate in meetings; Georgia left the organization in August 2009

Communist countries

traditionally the Marxist-Leninist states with authoritarian governments and command economies based on the Soviet model; most of the original and the successor states are no longer Communist; see centrally planned economies

Community of Democracies (CD)

established—27 June 2000
aim—"to respect and uphold core democratic principles and practices" including free and fair elections, freedom of speech and expression, equal access to education, rule of law, and freedom of peaceful assembly
signatories of the Warsaw Declaration—(110) Albania, Algeria, Argentina, Armenia, Australia, Austria, Azerbaijan, Bangladesh, Belgium, Belize, Benin, Bolivia, Bosnia and Herzegovina, Botswana, Brazil, Bulgaria, Burkina Faso, Cabo Verde, Canada, Chile, Colombia, Costa Rica, Croatia, Cyprus, Czech Republic, Denmark, Dominica, Dominican Republic, Ecuador, Egypt, El Salvador, Estonia, Finland, Georgia, Germany, Greece, Guatemala, Guyana, Haiti, Honduras, Hungary, Iceland, India, Indonesia, Ireland, Israel, Italy, Japan, Jordan, Kenya, South Korea, Kuwait, Latvia, Lesotho, Liechtenstein, Lithuania, Luxembourg, Macedonia, Madagascar, Malawi, Mali, Malta, Mauritius, Mexico, Moldova, Monaco, Mongolia, Morocco, Mozambique, Namibia, Nepal, Netherlands, NZ, Nicaragua, Niger, Nigeria, Norway, Panama, Papua New Guinea, Paraguay, Peru, Philippines, Poland, Portugal, Qatar, Romania, Russia, Saint Lucia, Sao Tome and Principe, Senegal, Seychelles, Slovakia, Slovenia, South Africa, Spain, Sri Lanka, Suriname, Sweden, Switzerland, Tanzania, Thailand, Tunisia, Turkey, Ukraine, UK, US, Uruguay, Venezuela, Yemen, Yugoslavia

Community of Latin American and Caribbean States (CELAC)

note—successor to the Rio Group and the Latin America and Caribbean Summit on Integration and Development
established—created 23 February 2010; established July 2011

aim—to deepen the integration within Latin American and to reduce the influence of the US in the politics and economics of that part of the world

members—(33) Antigua and Barbuda, Argentina, The Bahamas, Barbados, Belize, Bolivia, Brazil, Chile, Colombia, Costa Rica, Cuba, Dominica, Dominican Republic, Ecuador, El Salvador, Grenada, Guatemala, Guyana, Haiti, Honduras, Jamaica, Mexico, Nicaragua, Panama, Paraguay, Peru, St. Kitts and Nevis, St. Lucia, St. Vincent and the Grenadines, Suriname, Trinidad and Tobago, Uruguay, Venezuela

Comuinidade dos Paises de Lingua Portuguesa (CPLP)

established—1996
aim—to establish a forum for friendship among Portuguese-speaking nations where Portuguese is an official language
members—(8) Angola, Brazil, Cabo Verde, Guinea-Bissau, Mozambique, Portugal, Sao Tome and Principe, Timor-Leste
associate observers—(3) Equatorial Guinea, Mauritius, Senegal

Conference of Interaction and Confidence-Building Measures in Asia (CICA)

established—proposed 5 October 1992; established 14 September 1999
aim—promoting a multi-national forum for enhancing cooperation towards promoting peace, security, and stability in Asia
members—(23 and the Palestine Liberation Organization) Afghanistan, Azerbaijan, Bahrain, Cambodia, China, Egypt, India, Iraq, Iran, Israel, Jordan, Kazakhstan, Kyrgyzstan, Mongolia, Pakistan, South Korea, Russia, Tajikistan, Thailand, Turkey, UAE, Uzbekistan, Vietnam, and the Palestine Liberation Organization
observers—(13) Bangladesh, Indonesia, Japan, League of Arab States, Malaysia, OSCE, Parliamentary Assembly of the Turkic Speaking Countries, Philippines, Qatar, Sri Lanka, Ukraine, UN, US

Convention of the Southeast European Law Enforcement Center (SELEC)

note—successor to Southeast European Cooperative Initiative (SECI) formed in 1996 to help the Southeast European countries rebuild and stabilize through access to resources
established—7 October 2011
aim—to provide support for Member States and enhance coordination in preventing and combating crime in trans-border activity
members—(13) Albania, Bosnia and Herzegovina, Bulgaria, Croatia, Greece, Hungary, Macedonia, Moldova, Montenegro, Romania, Serbia, Slovenia, Turkey
observers—(15) Austria, Azerbaijan, Belgium, Canada, France, Georgia, Germany, Italy, Japan, The Netherlands, Portugal, Spain, Ukraine, UK, US

Coordinating Committee on Export Controls (COCOM)

established in 1949 to control the export of strategic products and technical data from member countries to proscribed destinations; members were: Australia, Belgium, Canada, Denmark, France, Germany, Greece, Italy, Japan, Luxembourg, Netherlands, Norway, Portugal, Spain, Turkey, UK, US; abolished 31 March 1994; COCOM members established a new organization, the Wassenaar Arrangement, with expanded membership on 12 July 1996 that focuses on nonproliferation export controls as opposed to East-West control of advanced technology

Council for Mutual Economic Assistance (CEMA)

note—also known as CMEA or Comecon
established 25 January 1949 to promote the development of socialist economies and abolished 1 January 1991; members included Afghanistan (observer), Albania (had not participated since 1961 break with USSR), Angola (observer), Bulgaria, Cuba, Czechoslovakia, Ethiopia (observer), GDR, Hungary, Laos (observer), Mongolia, Mozambique (observer), Nicaragua (observer), Poland, Romania, USSR, Vietnam, Yemen (observer), Yugoslavia (associate)

Council of Arab Economic Unity (CAEU)

established—3 June 1957; effective—30 May 1964
aim—to promote economic integration among Arab nations
members—(17 plus the Palestine Liberation Organization) Algeria, Bahrain, Egypt, Iraq, Jordan, Kuwait, Lebanon, Libya, Morocco, Oman, Qatar, Saudi Arabia, Sudan, Syria, Tunisia, UAE, Yemen, Palestine Liberation Organization
candidates—(4) Comoros, Djibouti, Mauritania, Somalia

Council of Europe (CE)

established—5 May 1949; effective—3 August 1949
aim—to promote increased unity and quality of life in Europe
members—(47) Albania, Andorra, Armenia, Austria, Azerbaijan, Belgium, Bosnia and Herzegovina, Bulgaria, Croatia, Cyprus, Czech Republic, Denmark, Estonia, Finland, France, Georgia, Germany, Greece, Hungary, Iceland, Ireland, Italy, Latvia, Liechtenstein, Lithuania, Luxembourg, Macedonia, Malta, Moldova, Monaco, Montenegro, Netherlands, Norway, Poland, Portugal, Romania, Russia, San Marino, Serbia, Slovakia, Slovenia, Spain, Sweden, Switzerland, Turkey, Ukraine, UK
observers—(6) Canada, Holy See, Israel, Japan, Mexico, US

Council of the Baltic Sea States (CBSS)

established—6 March 1992
aim—to promote cooperation among the Baltic Sea states in the areas of aid to new democratic institutions, economic development, humanitarian aid, energy and the environment, cultural programs and education, and transportation and communication
members—(12) Denmark, Estonia, EC, Finland, Germany, Iceland, Latvia, Lithuania, Norway, Poland, Russia, Sweden
observers—(10) Belarus, France, Italy, Netherlands, Romania, Spain, Slovakia, Ukraine, UK, US

Council of the Entente (Entente)

established—29 May 1959
aim—to promote economic, social, and political coordination
members—(5) Benin, Burkina Faso, Cote d'Ivoire, Niger, Togo

countries in transition

a term used by the International Monetary Fund (IMF) for the middle group in its hierarchy of formerly centrally planned economies; IMF statistics include the following 28 countries in transition: Albania, Armenia, Azerbaijan, Belarus, Bosnia and Herzegovina, Bulgaria, Croatia, Czech Republic, Estonia, Georgia, Hungary, Kazakhstan, Kyrgyzstan, Latvia, Lithuania, Macedonia, Moldova, Mongolia, Montenegro, Poland, Romania, Russia, Serbia, Slovakia, Slovenia, Tajikistan, Turkmenistan, Ukraine, Uzbekistan; note—this group is identical to the group traditionally referred to as the "former USSR/Eastern Europe" except for the addition of Mongolia

Customs Cooperation Council (CCC)

note—see World Customs Organization (WCO)

developed countries (DCs)

the top group in the hierarchy of developed countries (DCs), former USSR/Eastern Europe (former USSR/EE), and less developed countries (LDCs); includes the market-oriented economies of the mainly democratic nations in the Organization for Economic Cooperation and Development (OECD), Bermuda, Israel, South Africa, and the European ministates; also known as the First World, high- income countries, the North, industrial countries; generally have a per capita GDP in excess of $15,000 although four OECD countries and South Africa have figures well under $15,000 and eight of the excluded OPEC countries have figures of more than $20,000; the DCs include: Andorra, Australia, Austria, Belgium, Bermuda, Canada, Denmark, Faroe Islands, Finland, France, Germany, Greece, Holy See, Iceland, Ireland, Israel, Italy, Japan, Liechtenstein, Luxembourg, Malta, Monaco, Netherlands, NZ, Norway, Portugal, San Marino, South Africa, Spain, Sweden, Switzerland, Turkey, UK, US; note—similar to the new International Monetary Fund (IMF) term "advanced economies" that adds Hong Kong, South Korea, Singapore, and Taiwan but drops Malta, Mexico, South Africa, and Turkey

developing countries

a term used by the International Monetary Fund (IMF) for the bottom group in its hierarchy of advanced economies, countries in transition, and developing countries; IMF statistics include the following 126 developing countries: Afghanistan, Algeria, Angola, Antigua and Barbuda, Argentina, Aruba, The Bahamas, Bahrain, Bangladesh, Barbados, Belize, Benin, Bhutan, Bolivia, Botswana, Brazil, Burkina Faso, Burma, Burundi, Cambodia, Cabo Verde, Cameroon, Central African Republic, Chad, Chile, China, Colombia, Comoros, Democratic Republic of the Congo, Republic of the Congo, Costa Rica, Cote d'Ivoire, Cyprus, Djibouti, Dominica, Dominican Republic, Ecuador, Egypt, El Salvador, Equatorial Guinea, Ethiopia, Fiji, Gabon, The Gambia, Ghana, Grenada, Guatemala, Guinea, Guinea-Bissau, Guyana, Haiti, Honduras, India, Indonesia, Iran, Iraq, Jamaica, Jordan, Kenya, Kiribati, Kuwait, Laos, Lebanon, Lesotho, Liberia, Libya, Madagascar, Malawi, Malaysia, Maldives, Mali, Malta, Marshall Islands, Mauritania, Mauritius, Mexico, Federated States of Micronesia, Morocco, Mozambique, Namibia, Nepal, Netherlands Antilles, Nicaragua, Niger, Nigeria, Oman, Pakistan, Panama, Papua New Guinea, Paraguay, Peru, Philippines, Qatar, Rwanda, Saint Kitts and Nevis, Saint Lucia, Saint Vincent and the Grenadines, Samoa, Sao Tome and Principe, Saudi Arabia, Senegal, Seychelles, Sierra Leone, Solomon Islands, Somalia, South Africa, Sri Lanka, Sudan, Suriname, Swaziland, Syria, Tanzania, Thailand, Togo, Trinidad and Tobago, Tunisia, Turkey, UAE, Uganda, Uruguay, Vanuatu, Venezuela, Vietnam, Yemen, Zambia, Zimbabwe; note—this category would presumably also cover the following 46 other countries that are traditionally included in the more comprehensive group of "less developed countries": American Samoa, Anguilla, British Virgin Islands, Brunei, Cayman Islands, Christmas Island, Cocos Islands, Cook Islands, Cuba, Eritrea, Falkland Islands, French Guiana, French Polynesia, Gaza Strip, Gibraltar, Greenland, Grenada, Guadeloupe, Guam, Guernsey, Isle of Man, Jersey, North Korea, Macau, Martinique, Mayotte, Montserrat, Nauru, New Caledonia, Niue, Norfolk Island, Northern Mariana Islands, Palau, Pitcairn Islands, Puerto Rico, Reunion, Saint Helena, Ascension, and Tristan da Cunha, Saint Pierre and Miquelon, Tokelau, Tonga, Turks and Caicos Islands, Tuvalu, Virgin Islands, Wallis and Futuna, West Bank, Western Sahara

Developing Eight (D-8)

established—15 June 1997
aim—to improve developing countries' positions in the world economy, diversify and create new opportunities in trade relations, enhance participation in decision-making at the international level, provide better standards of living
member—(8) Bangladesh, Egypt, Indonesia, Iran, Malaysia, Nigeria, Pakistan, Turkey

East African Community (EAC)

note—originally established in 1967, it was disbanded in 1977
established—January 2001
aim—to establish a political and economic union among the countries
members—(5) Burundi, Kenya, Rwanda, Tanzania, Uganda

East African Development Bank (EADB)

established—6 June 1967; effective—1 December 1967
aim—to promote economic development
members—(4) Kenya, Rwanda, Tanzania, Uganda

East Asia Summit (EAS)

established—14 December 2005
aim—to promote cooperation in political and security issues; to promote development, financial stability, energy security, economic integration and growth; to eradicate poverty and narrow the development gap in East Asia, and to promote deeper cultural understanding

members—(18) Australia, Brunei, Burma, Cambodia, China, India, Indonesia, Japan, South Korea, Laos, Malaysia, NZ, Philippines, Russia, Singapore, Thailand, US, Vietnam

Economic and Monetary Community of Central Africa (CEMAC)
note—was formerly the Central African Customs and Economic Union (UDEAC)
established—8 December 1964; effective—1 January 1966
aim—to promote the establishment of a Central African Common Market
members—(7) Cameroon, Central African Republic, Chad, Democratic Republic of the Congo, Equatorial Guinea, Gabon, The Gambia

Economic and Monetary Union (EMU)
note—an integral part of the European Union; also known as the European Economic and Monetary Union
established—1-2 December 1969 (proposed at summit conference of heads of government; 7 February 1992 (Maastricht Treaty signed)
aim—to promote a single market by creating a single currency, the euro; timetable—2 May 1998: European exchange rates fixed for 1 January 1999; 1 January 1999: all banks and stock exchanges begin using euros; 1 January 2002: the euro goes into circulation; 1 July 2002 local currencies no longer accepted
members—(18) Austria, Belgium, Cyprus, Estonia, Finland, France, Germany, Greece, Ireland, Italy, Latvia, Luxembourg, Malta, Netherlands, Portugal, Slovakia, Slovenia, Spain

Economic and Social Council (ECOSOC)
established—26 June 1945; effective—24 October 1945
aim—to coordinate the economic and social work of the UN; includes five regional commissions (Economic Commission for Africa, Economic Commission for Europe, Economic Commission for Latin America and the Caribbean, Economic and Social Commission for Asia and the Pacific, Economic and Social Commission for Western Asia) and nine functional commissions (Commission for Social Development, Commission on Human Rights, Commission on Narcotic Drugs, Commission on the Status of Women, Commission on Population and Development, Statistical Commission, Commission on Science and Technology for Development, Commission on Sustainable Development, and Commission on Crime Prevention and Criminal Justice)
members—(54) selected on a rotating basis from all regions

Economic Community of the Great Lakes Countries (CEPGL)
note—acronym from Communaute Economique des Pays des Grands Lacs
established—20 September 1976
aim—to promote regional economic cooperation and integration
members—(3) Burundi, Democratic Republic of the Congo, Rwanda; note—organization collapsed because of fighting in 1998; reactivated in 2006

Economic Community of West African States (ECOWAS)
established—28 May 1975
aim—to promote regional economic cooperation
members—(15) Benin, Burkina Faso, Cabo Verde, Cote d'Ivoire, The Gambia, Ghana, Guinea, Guinea-Bissau, Liberia, Mali, Niger, Nigeria, Senegal, Sierra Leone, Togo

Economic Cooperation Organization (ECO)
established—27-29 January 1985
aim—to promote regional cooperation in trade, transportation, communications, tourism, cultural affairs, and economic development
members—(10) Afghanistan, Azerbaijan, Iran, Kazakhstan, Kyrgyzstan, Pakistan, Tajikistan, Turkey, Turkmenistan, Uzbekistan

Eurasian Economic Community (EAEC or EurasEC)
note—merged with Central Asian Cooperation Organization (CACO) in 2005
established—May 2001
aim—to create a common economic and energy policy
members—(6) Belarus, Kazakhstan, Kyrgyzstan, Russia, Tajikistan, Uzbekistan
observers—(3) Armenia, Moldova, Ukraine

Euro-Atlantic Partnership Council (EAPC)
note—began as the North Atlantic Cooperation Council (NACC); an extension of NATO
established—8 November 1991; effective—20 December 1991
aim—to discuss cooperation on mutual political and security issues
members—(50) Albania, Armenia, Austria, Azerbaijan, Belarus, Belgium, Bosnia and Herzegovina, Bulgaria, Canada, Croatia, Czech Republic, Denmark, Estonia, Finland, France, Georgia, Germany, Greece, Hungary, Iceland, Ireland, Italy, Kazakhstan, Kyrgyzstan, Latvia, Lithuania, Luxembourg, Macedonia, Malta, Moldova, Montenegro, Netherlands, Norway, Poland, Portugal, Romania, Russia, Serbia, Slovakia, Slovenia, Spain, Sweden, Switzerland, Tajikistan, Turkey, Turkmenistan, Ukraine, UK, US, Uzbekistan

European Bank for Reconstruction and Development (EBRD)
established—8-9 January 1990 (proposals made); 15 April 1991 (bank inaugurated)
aim—to facilitate the transition of seven centrally planned economies in Europe (Bulgaria, former Czechoslovakia, Hungary, Poland, Romania, former USSR, and former Yugoslavia) to market economies by committing 60% of its loans to privatization
members—(66) Albania, Armenia, Australia, Austria, Azerbaijan, Belarus, Belgium, Bosnia and Herzegovina, Bulgaria, Canada, Croatia, Cyprus, Czech Republic, Denmark, Egypt, EU, European Investment Bank (EIB), Estonia, Finland, France, Georgia, Germany, Greece,

Hungary, Iceland, Ireland, Israel, Italy, Japan, Jordan, Kazakhstan, South Korea, Kosovo, Kyrgyzstan, Latvia, Liechtenstein, Lithuania, Luxembourg, Macedonia, Malta, Mexico, Moldova, Mongolia, Montenegro, Morocco, Netherlands, NZ, Norway, Poland, Portugal, Romania, Russia, Serbia, Slovakia, Slovenia, Spain, Sweden, Switzerland, Tajikistan, Tunisia, Turkey, Turkmenistan, Ukraine, UK, US, Uzbekistan

European Central Bank (ECB)
established—1 June 1998
aim—to administer the monetary policy of the EU Eurozone member states
members—(18) Austria, Belgium, Cyprus, Estonia, Finland, France, Germany, Greece, Ireland, Italy, Latvia, Luxembourg, Malta, Netherlands, Portugal, Slovakia, Slovenia, Spain

European Community (or European Communities, EC)
established 8 April 1965 to integrate the European Atomic Energy Community (Euratom), the European Coal and Steel Community (ECSC), the European Economic Community (EEC or Common Market), and to establish a completely integrated common market and an eventual federation of Europe; merged into the European Union (EU) on 7 February 1992; member states at the time of merger were Belgium, Denmark, France, Germany, Greece, Ireland, Italy, Luxembourg, Netherlands, Portugal, Spain, UK

European Free Trade Association (EFTA)
established—4 January 1960; effective—3 May 1960
aim—to promote expansion of free trade
members—(4) Iceland, Liechtenstein, Norway, Switzerland

European Investment Bank (EIB)
established—25 March 1957; effective—1 January 1958
aim—to promote economic development of the EU and its predecessors, the EEC and the EC
members—(28) Austria, Belgium, Bulgaria, Croatia, Cyprus, Czech Republic, Denmark, Estonia, Finland, France, Germany, Greece, Hungary, Ireland, Italy, Latvia, Lithuania, Luxembourg, Malta, Netherlands, Poland, Portugal, Romania, Slovakia, Slovenia, Spain, Sweden, UK

European Organization for Nuclear Research (CERN)
note—acronym retained from the predecessor organization Conseil Europeenne pour la Recherche Nucleaire
established—1 July 1953; effective—29 September 1954
aim—to foster nuclear research for peaceful purposes only
members—(20) Austria, Belgium, Bulgaria, Czech Republic, Denmark, Finland, France, Germany, Greece, Hungary, Italy, Netherlands, Norway, Poland, Portugal, Slovakia, Spain, Sweden, Switzerland, UK
observers—(7) EC, India, Japan, Russia, Turkey, United Nations Educational, Scientific, and Cultural Organization (UNESCO), US

European Space Agency (ESA)
established—31 May 1975
aim—to promote peaceful cooperation in space research and technology
members—(20) Austria, Belgium, Czech Republic, Denmark, Finland, France, Germany, Greece, Ireland, Italy, Luxembourg, Netherlands, Norway, Poland, Portugal, Romania, Spain, Sweden, Switzerland, UK
cooperating states—(3) Estonia, Hungary, Slovenia

European Union (EU)
note—see European Union entry at the end of the "country" listings

Extractive Industry Transparency Initiative (EITI)
established—October 2002 Initiative announced; June 2003 first EITC Plenary Conference
aim—to set a global standard for transparency in the extractive industries in an effort to make natural resources benefit all
stake holders or implementing countries—(17) Australia, Belgium, Canada, Denmark, Finland, France, Germany, Italy, Japan, Netherlands, Norway, Qatar, Spain, Sweden, Switzerland, UK, US
compliant countries—(23) Albania, Azerbaijan, Burkina Faso, Cameroon, Congo, Cote d'Ivoire, Ghana, Iraq, Kazakhstan, Kyrgyzstan, Liberia, Mali, Mauritania, Mongolia, Mozambique, Niger, Nigeria, Peru, Tanzania, Timor-Leste, Togo, Yemen, Zambia; note—Central African Republic is suspended
candidate countries—(13) Afghanistan, Chad, Guatemala, Guinea, Honduras, Indonesia, Philippines, Sao Tome and Principe, Senegal, Solomon Islands, Tajikistan, Trinidad and Tobago, Ukraine; note—Democratic Republic of the Congo, Madagascar, and Sierra Leone are suspended

Financial Action Task Force (FATF)
established—by G-7 Summit in Paris in 1989
aim—to develop and promote policies to combat money laundering and terrorist financing
members—(36) Argentina, Australia, Austria, Belgium, Brazil, Canada, China, Denmark, EC, Finland, France, Germany, Greece, Gulf Cooperation Council, Hong Kong, Iceland, India, Ireland, Italy, Japan, South Korea, Luxembourg, Mexico, Netherlands (Aruba, Curacao, Sint Maarten), NZ, Norway, Portugal, Russia, Singapore, South Africa, Spain, Sweden, Switzerland, Turkey, UK, US

First World
another term for countries with advanced, industrialized economies; this term is fading from use; see developed countries (DCs)

Food and Agriculture Organization (FAO)
established—16 October 1945
aim—to raise living standards and increase availability of agricultural products; a UN specialized agency
members—(195) includes all UN member countries except Liechtenstein (192 total); plus Cook Islands, EU, and Niue
associate members—(2) Faroe Islands, Tokelau

former Soviet Union (FSU)
former term often used to identify as a group the successor nations to the Soviet Union or USSR; this group of 15 countries consists of: Armenia, Azerbaijan, Belarus, Estonia, Georgia, Kazakhstan, Kyrgyzstan, Latvia, Lithuania, Moldova, Russia, Tajikistan, Turkmenistan, Ukraine, Uzbekistan

former USSR/Eastern Europe (former USSR/EE)
the middle group in the hierarchy of developed countries (DCs), former USSR/Eastern Europe (former USSR/EE), and less developed countries (LDCs); these countries are in political and economic transition and may well be grouped differently in the near future; this group of 27 countries consists of: Albania, Armenia, Azerbaijan, Belarus, Bosnia and Herzegovina, Bulgaria, Croatia, Czech Republic, Estonia, Georgia, Hungary, Kazakhstan, Kyrgyzstan, Latvia, Lithuania, Macedonia, Moldova, Poland, Romania, Russia, Slovakia, Slovenia, Tajikistan, Turkmenistan, Ukraine, Uzbekistan, Yugoslavia; this group is identical to the IMF group "countries in transition" except for the IMF's inclusion of Mongolia

Four Dragons
the four small Asian less developed countries (LDCs) that have experienced unusually rapid economic growth; also known as the Four Tigers; this group consists of Hong Kong, South Korea, Singapore, Taiwan; these countries are included in the IMF's "advanced economies" group

Franc Zone (FZ)
note—also known as Conference des Ministres des Finances des Pays de la Zone Franc
established—1964
aim—to form a monetary union among countries whose currencies were linked to the French franc
members—(16) Benin, Burkina Faso, Cameroon, Central African Republic, Chad, Comoros, Republic of the Congo, Cote d'Ivoire, Equatorial Guinea, France, Gabon, Guinea-Bissau, Mali, Niger, Senegal, Togo

Front Line States (FLS)
established to achieve black majority rule in South Africa; has since gone out of existence; members included Angola, Botswana, Mozambique, Namibia, Tanzania, Zambia, Zimbabwe

General Agreement on Tariffs and Trade (GATT)
see the World Trade Organization (WTO)

General Confederation of Trade Unions (GCTU)
established—16 April 1992
aim—to consolidate trade union actions to protect citizens' social and labor rights and interests, to help secure trade unions' rights and guarantees, and to strengthen international trade union solidarity
members—(10) Armenia, Azerbaijan, Belarus, Georgia, Kazakhstan, Kyrgyzstan, Moldova, Russia, Tajikistan, Ukraine

Group of 10 (G-10)
note—also known as the Paris Club; includes the wealthiest members of the IMF who provide most of the money to be loaned and act as the informal steering committee; name persists despite increased membership
established—October 1962
aim—to coordinate credit policy
members—(11) Belgium, Canada, France, Germany, Italy, Japan, Netherlands, Sweden, Switzerland, UK, US
observers—(4) BIS, EC, IMF, OECD

Group of 11 (G-11)
established—2006
aim—to narrow the income gap with the world's richest nations
members—(11) Croatia, Ecuador, El Salvador, Georgia, Honduras, Indonesia, Jordan, Morocco, Pakistan, Paraguay, Sri Lanka

Group of 15 (G-15)
note—byproduct of the Nonaligned Movement; name persists despite increased membership
established—September 1989
aim—to promote economic cooperation among developing nations; to act as the main political organ for the Nonaligned Movement
members—(17) Algeria, Argentina, Brazil, Chile, Egypt, India, Indonesia, Iran, Jamaica, Kenya, Malaysia, Mexico, Nigeria, Senegal, Sri Lanka, Venezuela, Zimbabwe

Group of 20 (G-20)
established—created 1999; inaugurated 15-16 December 1999
aim—to promote open and constructive discussion between industrial and emerging-market countries on any issues related to global economic stability; helps to support growth and development across the globe

members—(20) Argentina, Australia, Brazil, Canada, China, EU, France, Germany, India, Indonesia, Italy, Japan, South Korea, Mexico, Russia, Saudi Arabia, South Africa, Turkey, UK, US

Group of 24 (G-24)
established—1 August 1989
aim—to promote the interests of developing countries in Africa, Asia, and Latin America within the IMF
members—(24) Algeria, Argentina, Brazil, Colombia, Democratic Republic of the Congo, Cote d'Ivoire, Egypt, Ethiopia, Gabon, Ghana, Guatemala, India, Iran, Lebanon, Mexico, Nigeria, Pakistan, Peru, Philippines, South Africa, Sri Lanka, Syria, Trinidad and Tobago, Venezuela
observers—(1) China

Group of 3 (G-3)
established—September 1990
aim—mechanism for policy coordination
members—(2) Colombia, Mexico; note—Panama shows interest in joining

Group of 5 (G-5)
note—with the addition of Italy, Canada, and Russia, it is now known as the Group of 8 or G-8; meanwhile the Group of 5 now refers to Brazil, China, India, Mexico, and South Africa
established—22 September 1985
aim—to coordinate the economic policies of five major noncommunist economic powers
members—(5) France, Germany, Japan, UK, US

Group of 6 (G-6)
also known as Groupe des Six Sur le Desarmement (not to be confused with the Big Six) was established in 22 May 1984 with the aim of achieving nuclear disarmament; its members were Argentina, Greece, India, Mexico, Sweden, Tanzania

Group of 7 (G-7)
note—membership is the same as the Big Seven
established—22 September 1985
aim—to facilitate economic cooperation among the seven major noncommunist economic powers
members—(7) Group of 5 (France, Germany, Japan, UK, US) plus Canada and Italy

Group of 77 (G-77)
established—15 June1964; October 1967 first ministerial meeting
aim—to promote economic cooperation among developing countries; name persists in spite of increased membership
members—(132 plus the Palestine Liberation Organization) Afghanistan, Algeria, Angola, Antigua and Barbuda, Argentina, The Bahamas, Bahrain, Bangladesh, Barbados, Belize, Benin, Bhutan, Bolivia, Bosnia and Herzegovina, Botswana, Brazil, Brunei, Burkina Faso, Burma, Burundi, Cambodia, Cabo Verde, Cameroon, Central African Republic, Chad, Chile, China, Colombia, Comoros, Democratic Republic of the Congo, Republic of the Congo, Costa Rica, Cote d'Ivoire, Cuba, Djibouti, Dominica, Dominican Republic, Ecuador, Egypt, El Salvador, Equatorial Guinea, Eritrea, Ethiopia, Fiji, Gabon, The Gambia, Ghana, Grenada, Guatemala, Guinea, Guinea-Bissau, Guyana, Haiti, Honduras, India, Indonesia, Iran, Iraq, Jamaica, Jordan, Kenya, Kiribati, North Korea, Kuwait, Laos, Lebanon, Lesotho, Liberia, Libya, Madagascar, Malawi, Malaysia, Maldives, Mali, Marshall Islands, Mauritania, Mauritius, Federated States of Micronesia, Mongolia, Morocco, Mozambique, Namibia, Nauru, Nepal, Nicaragua, Niger, Nigeria, Oman, Pakistan, Panama, Papua New Guinea, Paraguay, Peru, Philippines, Qatar, Rwanda, Saint Kitts and Nevis, Saint Lucia, Saint Vincent and the Grenadines, Samoa, Sao Tome and Principe, Saudi Arabia, Senegal, Seychelles, Sierra Leone, Singapore, Solomon Islands, Somalia, South Africa, Sri Lanka, Sudan, Suriname, Swaziland, Syria, Tajikistan, Tanzania, Thailand, Timor-Leste, Togo, Tonga, Trinidad and Tobago, Tunisia, Turkmenistan, Uganda, UAE, Uruguay, Vanuatu, Venezuela, Vietnam, Yemen, Zambia, Zimbabwe, Palestine Liberation Organization

Group of 8 (G-8)
established—October 1975
aim—to facilitate economic cooperation among the developed countries (DCs) that participated in the Conference on International Economic Cooperation (CIEC), held in several sessions between December 1975 and 3 June 1977
members—(8) Canada, EU, France, Germany, Italy, Japan, UK, US

Group of 9 (G-9)
established—NA
aim—to discuss matters of mutual interest on an informal basis
members—(9) Austria, Belgium, Bulgaria, Denmark, Finland, Hungary, Romania, Serbia, Sweden

Gulf Cooperation Council (GCC)
note—also known as the Cooperation Council for the Arab States of the Gulf
established—25 May 1981
aim—to promote regional cooperation in economic, social, political, and military affairs
members—(6) Bahrain, Kuwait, Oman, Qatar, Saudi Arabia, UAE

high income countries
another term for the industrialized countries with high per capita GDPs; see developed countries (DCs)

Indian Ocean Commission (InOC)
established—21 December 1982
aim—to organize and promote regional cooperation in all sectors, especially economic
members—(5) Comoros, France (for Reunion), Madagascar, Mauritius, Seychelles

industrial countries
another term for the developed countries; see developed countries (DCs)

Inter-American Development Bank (IADB)
note—also known as Banco Interamericano de Desarrollo (BID)
established—8 April 1959; effective—30 December 1959
aim—to promote economic and social development in Latin America
members—(48) Argentina, Austria, The Bahamas, Barbados, Belgium, Belize, Bolivia, Brazil, Canada, Chile, China, Colombia, Costa Rica, Croatia, Denmark, Dominican Republic, Ecuador, El Salvador, Finland, France, Germany, Guatemala, Guyana, Haiti, Honduras, Israel, Italy, Jamaica, Japan, South Korea, Mexico, Netherlands, Nicaragua, Norway, Panama, Paraguay, Peru, Portugal, Slovenia, Spain, Suriname, Sweden, Switzerland, Trinidad and Tobago, UK, US, Uruguay, Venezuela

Inter-Governmental Authority on Development (IGAD)
note—formerly known as Inter-Governmental Authority on Drought and Development (IGADD)
established—15-16 January 1986 as the Inter-Governmental Authority on Drought and Development; revitalized—21 March 1996 as the Inter-Governmental Authority on Development
aim—to promote a social, economic, and scientific community among its members
members—(6) Djibouti, Ethiopia, Kenya, Somalia, Sudan, Uganda; note—Eritrea declared its suspension in 2007
partners—(20) Austria, Belgium, Canada, Denmark, EC, France, Germany, Greece, International Organization for Migration, Ireland, Italy, Japan, Netherlands, Norway, Sweden, Switzerland, UK, UN Development Program, US, World Bank

Inter-Parliamentary Union (IPU)
established—1889
aim—fosters contacts among parliamentarians, considers and expresses views of international interest and concern with the purpose of bringing about action by parliaments and parliamentarians, contributes to the defense and promotion of human rights, contributes to better knowledge of representative institutions
members—(162 and the Palestine Liberation Organization) Afghanistan, Albania, Algeria, Andorra, Angola, Argentina, Armenia, Australia, Austria, Azerbaijan, Bahrain, Bangladesh, Belarus, Belgium, Benin, Bhutan, Bolivia, Bosnia and Herzegovina, Botswana, Brazil, Bulgaria, Burkina Faso, Burma, Burundi, Cabo Verde, Cameroon, Canada, Chad, Chile, China, Colombia, Democratic Republic of the Congo, Republic of the Congo, Costa Rica, Cote d'Ivoire, Croatia, Cuba, Cyprus, Czech Republic, Denmark, Djibouti, Dominican Republic, Ecuador, El Salvador, Equatorial Guinea, Estonia, Ethiopia, Finland, France, Gabon, The Gambia, Georgia, Germany, Ghana, Greece, Guatemala, Guinea-Bissau, Haiti, Honduras, Hungary, Iceland, India, Indonesia, Iran, Iraq, Ireland, Israel, Italy, Japan, Jordan, Kazakhstan, Kenya, North Korea, South Korea, Kuwait, Kyrgyzstan, Laos, Latvia, Lebanon, Lesotho, Libya, Liechtenstein, Lithuania, Luxembourg, Macedonia, Malawi, Malaysia, Maldives, Mali, Malta, Mauritania, Mauritius, Mexico, Federated States of Micronesia, Moldova, Monaco, Mongolia, Montenegro, Morocco, Mozambique, Namibia, Nepal, Netherlands, NZ, Nicaragua, Niger, Nigeria, Norway, Oman, Pakistan, Palau, Panama, Papua New Guinea, Paraguay, Peru, Philippines, Poland, Portugal, Qatar, Romania, Russia, Rwanda, Samoa, San Marino, Sao Tome and Principe, Saudi Arabia, Senegal, Serbia, Seychelles, Sierra Leone, Singapore, Slovakia, Slovenia, Somalia, South Africa, South Sudan, Spain, Sri Lanka, Sudan, Suriname, Sweden, Switzerland, Syria, Tanzania, Tajikistan, Thailand, Timor-Leste, Togo, Trinidad and Tobago, Tunisia, Turkey, Uganda, Ukraine, UAE, UK, Uruguay, Venezuela, Vietnam, Yemen, Zambia, Zimbabwe, Palestine Liberation Organization
associate members—(10) Andean Parliament, Central American Parliament, East African Legislative Assembly, European Parliament, Inter-Parliamentary Committee of the West African Economic and Monetary Union, Latin American Parliament, Parliament of the Economic Community of West African States, Parliament of the Economic and Monetary Community of Central Africa, Parliamentary Assembly of the Council of Europe, Transitional Arab Parliament

International Atomic Energy Agency (IAEA)
established—26 October 1956; effective—29 July 1957
aim—to promote peaceful uses of atomic energy
members—(162) Afghanistan, Albania, Algeria, Angola, Argentina, Armenia, Australia, Austria, Azerbaijan, The Bahamas, Bahrain, Bangladesh, Belarus, Belgium, Belize, Benin, Bolivia, Bosnia and Herzegovina, Botswana, Brazil, Brunei, Bulgaria, Burkina Faso, Burma, Burundi, Cabo Verde, Cambodia, Cameroon, Canada, Central African Republic, Chad, Chile, China, Colombia, Democratic Republic of the Congo, Republic of the Congo, Costa Rica, Cote d'Ivoire, Croatia, Cuba, Cyprus, Czech Republic, Denmark, Dominica, Dominican Republic, Ecuador, Egypt, El Salvador, Eritrea, Estonia, Ethiopia, Fiji, Finland, France, Gabon, Georgia, Germany, Ghana, Greece, Guatemala, Haiti, Holy See, Honduras, Hungary, Iceland, India, Indonesia, Iran, Iraq, Ireland, Israel, Italy, Jamaica, Japan, Jordan, Kazakhstan, Kenya, South Korea, Kuwait, Kyrgyzstan, Laos, Latvia, Lebanon, Lesotho, Liberia, Libya, Liechtenstein, Lithuania, Luxembourg, Macedonia, Madagascar, Malawi, Malaysia, Mali, Malta, Marshall Islands, Mauritania, Mauritius, Mexico, Moldova, Monaco, Mongolia, Montenegro, Morocco, Mozambique, Namibia, Nepal, Netherlands, NZ, Nicaragua, Niger, Nigeria, Norway, Oman, Pakistan, Palau, Panama, Papua New Guinea, Paraguay, Peru, Philippines, Poland, Portugal, Qatar, Romania, Russia, Rwanda, San Marino, Saudi Arabia, Senegal, Serbia,

Seychelles, Sierra Leone, Singapore, Slovakia, Slovenia, South Africa, Spain, Sri Lanka, Sudan, Swaziland, Sweden, Switzerland, Syria, Tajikistan, Tanzania, Thailand, Togo, Tonga, Trinidad and Tobago, Tunisia, Turkey, Uganda, Ukraine, UAE, UK, US, Uruguay, Uzbekistan, Venezuela, Vietnam, Yemen, Zambia, Zimbabwe

International Bank for Reconstruction and Development (IBRD)
note—also known as the World Bank
established—22 July 1944; effective—27 December 1945
aim—to provide economic development loans; a UN specialized agency
members—(188) includes all UN member countries except Andorra, Cuba, North Korea, Liechtenstein, Monaco, Nauru; plus Kosovo

International Chamber of Commerce (ICC)
established—1919
aim—to promote free trade and private enterprise and to represent business interests at national and international levels
members—128 plus the Palestine Liberation Organization
countries with national committees—(93 and the Palestine Liberation Organization) Albania, Algeria, Argentina, Australia, Austria, Bahrain, Bangladesh, Belgium, Bolivia, Brazil, Bulgaria, Burkina Faso, Cameroon, Canada, Caribbean, Chile, China, Colombia, Costa Rica, Croatia, Cuba, Cyprus, Czech Republic, Denmark, Dominican Republic, Ecuador, Egypt, El Salvador, Estonia, Finland, France, Georgia, Germany, Ghana, Greece, Guatemala, Hong Kong, Hungary, Iceland, India, Indonesia, Iran, Ireland, Israel, Italy, Japan, Jordan, Kenya, South Korea, Kuwait, Lebanon, Lithuania, Luxembourg, Macao, Madagascar, Malaysia, Mexico, Monaco, Morocco, Netherlands, NZ, Nigeria, Norway, Pakistan, Panama, Philippines, Poland, Portugal, Qatar, Romania, Russia, Saudi Arabia, Senegal, Serbia, Singapore, Slovakia, Slovenia, South Africa, Spain, Sri Lanka, Sweden, Switzerland, Syria, Taiwan, Thailand, Togo, Tunisia, Turkey, Ukraine, UAE, UK, US, Uruguay, Palestine Liberation Organization; note—Peru is restructuring
countries with no national committees having direct members—(35) Afghanistan, Andorra, Armenia, Azerbaijan, Belarus, Bermuda, Bosnia and Herzegovina, Botswana, Democratic Republic of the Congo, Burma, Cote d'Ivoire, Eritrea, Ethiopia, Gibraltar, Haiti, Honduras, Iraq, North Korea, Latvia, Liberia, Macedonia, Malta, Mauritania, Mauritius, Moldova, Mongolia, Montenegro, Mozambique, Oman, Peru, Sudan, Tajikistan, Tanzania, Uganda, Vietnam

International Civil Aviation Organization (ICAO)
established—7 December 1944; effective—4 April 1947
aim—to promote international cooperation in civil aviation; a UN specialized agency
members—(191) includes all UN member countries except Dominica, Liechtenstein, and Tuvalu (190 total); plus Cook Islands

International Civilian Support Mission in Haiti (MICAH)
established 17 December 1999 to promote respect for human rights; members included Argentina, Benin, Canada, France, India, Mali, Niger, Senegal, Togo, Tunisia, US; closed 2001

International Committee of the Red Cross (ICRC)
established—17 February 1863
aim—to provide humanitarian aid in wartime
members—(15-25 individuals) all Swiss nationals

International Court of Justice (ICJ)
also known as the World Court; primary judicial organ of the UN
established—26 June 1945 with the signing of the UN Charter (inaugural sitting of the Court was on 18 April 1946); superseded Permanent Court of International Justice (attached to the League of Nations)
aim—to settle disputes submitted by member states and to provide advice to UN organs and other international agencies
members—(15 judges) elected by the UN General Assembly and Security Council to represent all principal legal systems; judges elected to nine-year terms (eligible for two additional terms); elections held every three years for one-third of the judges
jurisdiction—based on the principle of consent in contentious issues; consent to compulsory jurisdiction is outlined in Statute 36 of the ICJ; states provide declarations of consent to compulsory jurisdiction of the ICJ either with or without reservations (date in parens after each state is when the declaration was deposited with the UN Secretary-General); Haiti, Luxembourg, Nicaragua, and Uruguay deposited declarations with the Permanent Court of International Justice prior to 1945 and these were later transferred to the ICJ)
states accepting compulsory jurisdiction with reservations—(57) Australia (22 March 2002), Barbados (1 August 1980), Belgium (17 June 1958), Botswana (16 March 1970), Bulgaria (21 June 1992), Cambodia (19 September 1957), Canada (10 May 1994), Democratic Republic of the Congo (8 February 1989), Cote d'Ivoire (29 September 2001), Cyprus (3 September 2002), Denmark (10 December 1956), Djibouti (2 September 2005), Egypt (22 July 1957), Estonia (31 October 1991), Finland (25 June 1958), The Gambia (22 June 1966), Germany (30 April 2008), Greece (10 January 1994), Guinea (4 December 1998), Honduras (6 June 1986), Hungary (22 October 1992), India (18 September 1974), Japan (9 July 2007), Kenya (19 April 1965), Lesotho (6 September 2000), Liberia (20 March 1952), Liechtenstein (29 March 1950), Lithuania (26 September 2012), Madagascar (2 July 1992), Malawi (12 December 1966), Malta (2 September 1983), Marshall Islands (23 April 2013), Mauritius (23 September 1968), Mexico (28 October 1947), Netherlands (1 August 1956), New Zealand (23 September 1977), Nicaragua (24 September 1929), Nigeria (30 April 1998), Norway (25 June 1996), Pakistan (13 September 1960), Panama (25 October 1921), Peru (7 July 2003), Philippines (18 January 1972), Poland (25 March 1996), Portugal (25 February 2005), Senegal (2 December 1985), Slovakia (28 May 2004), Somalia (11 April 1963), Spain (20 October 1990), Sudan (2 January 1958), Suriname (31 August 1987), Swaziland (26 May 1969), Sweden (6 April 1957), Switzerland (28 July 1948), Togo (25 October 1979), Uganda (3 October 1963), United Kingdom (5 July 2004)

states accepting compulsory jurisdiction without reservations—(13) Austria (19 May 1971), Cameroon (3 March 1994), Costa Rica (20 February 1973), Dominica (31 March 2006), Dominican Republic (30 September 1924), Georgia (20 June 1995), Guinea-Bissau (7 August 1989), Haiti (4 October 1921), Ireland (15 December 2011), Luxembourg (15 September 1930), Paraguay (25 September 1996), Timor-Leste (21 September 2012), Uruguay (28 January 1921)

International Criminal Court (ICCt)
established—1 July 2002
aim—to hold all individuals and countries accountable to international laws of conduct; to specify international standards of conduct; to provide an important mechanism for implementing these standards; to ensure that perpetrators are brought to justice
members—21 judges (three judges form the Presidency) and six judges each in the Pre-trial, Trial, and Appeals Divisions; judges elected by secret ballot by the Assembly of States Parties to the Rome Statute for nine-year terms (not eligible for reelection) governed by the Statute of the International Criminal Court treaty (or Rome Statute), adopted 17 July 1998 at the UN Conference of Plenipotentiaries in Rome and entered into force 1 July 2002
states accepting jurisdiction—(122) Afghanistan, Albania, Andorra, Antigua and Barbuda, Argentina, Australia, Austria, Bangladesh, Barbados, Belgium, Belize, Benin, Bolivia, Bosnia and Herzegovina, Botswana, Brazil, Bulgaria, Burkina Faso, Burundi, Cambodia, Canada, Cabo Verde, Central African Republic, Chad, Chile, Colombia, Comoros, Cook Islands, Democratic Republic of the Congo, Republic of the Congo, Costa Rica, Cote d'Ivoire, Croatia, Cyprus, Czech Republic, Denmark, Djibouti, Dominica, Dominican Republic, Ecuador, Estonia, Fiji, Finland, France, Gabon, The Gambia, Georgia, Germany, Ghana, Greece, Grenada, Guatemala, Guinea, Guyana, Honduras, Hungary, Iceland, Ireland, Italy, Japan, Jordan, Kenya, South Korea, Latvia, Lesotho, Liberia, Liechtenstein, Lithuania, Luxembourg, Macedonia, Madagascar, Malawi, Maldives, Mali, Malta, Marshall Islands, Mauritius, Mexico, Moldova, Mongolia, Montenegro, Namibia, Nauru, Netherlands, NZ, Niger, Nigeria, Norway, Panama, Paraguay, Peru, Philippines, Poland, Portugal, Romania, Saint Kitts and Nevis, Saint Lucia, Saint Vincent and the Grenadines, Samoa, San Marino, Senegal, Serbia, Seychelles, Sierra Leone, Slovakia, Slovenia, South Africa, Spain, Suriname, Sweden, Switzerland, Tajikistan, Tanzania, Timor-Leste, Trinidad and Tobago, Tunisia, Uganda, UK, Uruguay, Vanuatu, Venezuela, Zambia

International Criminal Police Organization (Interpol)
established—September 1923 set up as the International Criminal Police Commission; 13 June 1956 constitution modified and present name adopted
aim—to promote international cooperation among police authorities in fighting crime
members—(190) Afghanistan, Albania, Algeria, Andorra, Angola, Antigua and Barbuda, Argentina, Armenia, Aruba, Australia, Austria, Azerbaijan, The Bahamas, Bahrain, Bangladesh, Barbados, Belarus, Belgium, Belize, Benin, Bhutan, Bolivia, Bosnia and Herzegovina, Botswana, Brazil, Brunei, Bulgaria, Burkina Faso, Burma, Burundi, Cabo Verde, Cambodia, Cameroon, Canada, Central African Republic, Chad, Chile, China, Colombia, Comoros, Democratic Republic of the Congo, Republic of the Congo, Costa Rica, Cote d'Ivoire, Croatia, Cuba, Curacao, Cyprus, Czech Republic, Denmark, Djibouti, Dominica, Dominican Republic, Ecuador, Egypt, El Salvador, Equatorial Guinea, Eritrea, Estonia, Ethiopia, Fiji, Finland, France, Gabon, The Gambia, Georgia, Germany, Ghana, Greece, Grenada, Guatemala, Guinea, Guinea-Bissau, Guyana, Haiti, Holy See, Honduras, Hungary, Iceland, India, Indonesia, Iran, Iraq, Ireland, Israel, Italy, Jamaica, Japan, Jordan, Kazakhstan, Kenya, South Korea, Kuwait, Kyrgyzstan, Laos, Latvia, Lebanon, Lesotho, Liberia, Libya, Liechtenstein, Lithuania, Luxembourg, Macedonia, Madagascar, Malawi, Malaysia, Maldives, Mali, Malta, Marshall Islands, Mauritania, Mauritius, Mexico, Moldova, Monaco, Mongolia, Montenegro, Morocco, Mozambique, Namibia, Nauru, Nepal, Netherlands, NZ, Nicaragua, Niger, Nigeria, Norway, Oman, Pakistan, Panama, Papua New Guinea, Paraguay, Peru, Philippines, Poland, Portugal, Qatar, Romania, Russia, Rwanda, Saint Kitts and Nevis, Saint Lucia, Saint Vincent and the Grenadines, Samoa, San Marino, Sao Tome and Principe, Saudi Arabia, Senegal, Serbia, Seychelles, Sierra Leone, Singapore, Sint Maarten, Slovakia, Slovenia, Somalia, South Africa, South Sudan, Spain, Sri Lanka, Sudan, Suriname, Swaziland, Sweden, Switzerland, Syria, Tajikistan, Tanzania, Thailand, Timor-Leste, Togo, Tonga, Trinidad and Tobago, Tunisia, Turkey, Turkmenistan, Uganda, Ukraine, UAE, UK, US, Uruguay, Uzbekistan, Venezuela, Vietnam, Yemen, Zambia, Zimbabwe
subbureaus—(11) American Samoa, Anguilla, Bermuda, British Virgin Islands, Cayman Islands, Gibraltar, Hong Kong, Macau, Montserrat, Puerto Rico, Turks and Caicos Islands

International Development Association (IDA)
established—26 January 1960; effective—24 September 1960
aim—to provide economic loans for low-income countries; UN specialized agency and IBRD affiliate
members—(173) Afghanistan, Albania, Algeria, Angola, Argentina, Armenia, Australia, Austria, Azerbaijan, The Bahamas, Bangladesh, Barbados, Belgium, Belize, Benin, Bhutan, Bolivia, Bosnia and Herzegovina, Botswana, Brazil, Burkina Faso, Burma, Burundi, Cabo Verde, Cambodia, Cameroon, Canada, Central African Republic, Chad, Chile, China, Colombia, Comoros, Democratic Republic of the Congo, Republic of the Congo, Costa Rica, Cote d'Ivoire, Croatia, Cyprus, Czech Republic, Denmark, Djibouti, Dominica, Dominican Republic, Ecuador, Egypt, El Salvador, Equatorial Guinea, Eritrea, Estonia, Ethiopia, EU, Fiji, Finland, France, Gabon, The Gambia, Georgia, Germany, Ghana, Greece, Grenada, Guatemala, Guinea, Guinea-Bissau, Guyana, Haiti, Honduras, Hungary, Iceland, India, Indonesia, Iran, Iraq, Ireland, Israel, Italy, Japan, Jordan, Kazakhstan, Kenya, Kiribati, South Korea, Kosovo, Kuwait, Kyrgyzstan, Laos, Latvia, Lebanon, Lesotho, Liberia, Libya, Lithuania, Luxembourg, Macedonia, Madagascar, Malawi, Malaysia, Maldives, Mali, Marshall Islands, Mauritania, Mauritius, Mexico, Federated States of Micronesia, Moldova, Mongolia, Montenegro, Morocco, Mozambique, Nepal, Netherlands, NZ, Nicaragua, Niger, Nigeria, Norway, Oman, Pakistan, Palau, Panama, Papua New Guinea, Paraguay, Peru, Philippines, Poland, Portugal, Russia, Rwanda, Saint Kitts and Nevis, Saint Lucia, Saint Vincent and the Grenadines, Samoa, Sao Tome and Principe, Saudi Arabia, Senegal, Serbia, Sierra Leone, Singapore, Slovakia, Slovenia, Solomon Islands, Somalia, South Africa, South Sudan, Spain, Sri Lanka, Sudan, Swaziland, Sweden, Switzerland, Syria, Tajikistan, Tanzania, Thailand, Timor-Leste, Togo, Tonga, Trinidad and Tobago, Tunisia, Turkey, Tuvalu, Uganda, Ukraine, UAE, UK, US, Uzbekistan, Vanuatu, Vietnam, Yemen, Zambia, Zimbabwe

International Energy Agency (IEA)

established—15 November 1974

aim—to promote cooperation on energy matters, especially emergency oil sharing and relations between oil consumers and oil producers; established by the OECD

members—(29) Australia, Austria, Belgium, Canada, Czech Republic, Denmark, EC, Finland, France, Germany, Greece, Hungary, Ireland, Italy, Japan, South Korea, Luxembourg, Netherlands, NZ, Norway, Poland, Portugal, Slovakia, Spain, Sweden, Switzerland, Turkey, UK, US

International Federation of Red Cross and Red Crescent Societies (IFRCS)

note—formerly known as League of Red Cross and Red Crescent Societies (LORCS)

established—5 May 1919

aim—to organize, coordinate, and direct international relief actions; to promote humanitarian activities; to represent and encourage the development of National Societies; to bring help to victims of armed conflicts, refugees, and displaced people; to reduce the vulnerability of people through development programs

members—(187 plus the Palestine Liberation Organization) Afghanistan, Albania, Algeria, Andorra, Angola, Antigua and Barbuda, Argentina, Armenia, Australia, Austria, Azerbaijan, The Bahamas, Bahrain, Bangladesh, Barbados, Belarus, Belgium, Belize, Benin, Bolivia, Bosnia and Herzegovina, Botswana, Brazil, Brunei, Bulgaria, Burkina Faso, Burma, Burundi, Cabo Verde, Cambodia, Cameroon, Canada, Central African Republic, Chad, Chile, China, Colombia, Comoros, Democratic Republic of the Congo, Republic of the Congo, Cook Islands, Costa Rica, Cote d'Ivoire, Croatia, Cuba, Czech Republic, Denmark, Djibouti, Dominica, Dominican Republic, Ecuador, Egypt, El Salvador, Equatorial Guinea, Estonia, Ethiopia, Fiji, Finland, France, Gabon, The Gambia, Georgia, Germany, Ghana, Greece, Grenada, Guatemala, Guinea, Guinea-Bissau, Guyana, Haiti, Honduras, Hungary, Iceland, India, Indonesia, Iran, Iraq, Ireland, Israel, Italy, Jamaica, Japan, Jordan, Kazakhstan, Kenya, Kiribati, North Korea, South Korea, Kuwait, Kyrgyzstan, Laos, Latvia, Lebanon, Lesotho, Liberia, Libya, Liechtenstein, Lithuania, Luxembourg, Macedonia, Madagascar, Malawi, Malaysia, Maldives, Mali, Malta, Mauritania, Mauritius, Mexico, Federated States of Micronesia, Moldova, Monaco, Mongolia, Montenegro, Morocco, Mozambique, Namibia, Nepal, Netherlands, NZ, Nicaragua, Niger, Nigeria, Norway, Pakistan, Palau, Panama, Papua New Guinea, Paraguay, Peru, Philippines, Poland, Portugal, Qatar, Romania, Russia, Rwanda, Saint Kitts and Nevis, Saint Lucia, Saint Vincent and the Grenadines, Samoa, San Marino, Sao Tome and Principe, Saudi Arabia, Senegal, Serbia, Seychelles, Sierra Leone, Singapore, Slovakia, Slovenia, Solomon Islands, Somalia, South Africa, South Sudan, Spain, Sri Lanka, Sudan, Suriname, Swaziland, Sweden, Switzerland, Syria, Tajikistan, Tanzania, Thailand, Timor-Leste, Togo, Tonga, Trinidad and Tobago, Tunisia, Turkey, Turkmenistan, Uganda, Ukraine, UAE, UK, US, Uruguay, Uzbekistan, Vanuatu, Venezuela, V

observers—(3) Cyprus, Eritrea, and Tuvalu

International Finance Corporation (IFC)

established—25 May 1955; effective—24 July 1956

aim—to support private enterprise in international economic development; a UN specialized agency and IBRD affiliate

members—(183) includes all UN member countries except Andorra, Brunei, Cuba, North Korea, Liechtenstein, Monaco, Nauru, Saint Vincent and the Grenadines, San Marino, Tuvalu; plus Kosovo

International Fund for Agricultural Development (IFAD)

established—November 1974

aim—to promote agricultural development; a UN specialized agency

members—(171)

List A—(23 industrialized aid contributors) Belgium, Canada, Denmark, Estonia, Finland, France, Germany, Greece, Hungary, Iceland, Ireland, Italy, Japan, Luxembourg, Netherlands, NZ, Norway, Portugal, Spain, Sweden, Switzerland, UK, US

List B—(12 petroleum-exporting aid contributors) Algeria, Gabon, Indonesia, Iran, Iraq, Kuwait, Libya, Nigeria, Qatar, Saudi Arabia, UAE, Venezuela

List C—(133 aid recipients) Afghanistan, Albania, Angola, Antigua and Barbuda, Argentina, Armenia, Azerbaijan, The Bahamas, Bangladesh, Barbados, Belize, Benin, Bhutan, Bolivia, Bosnia and Herzegovina, Botswana, Brazil, Burkina Faso, Burma, Burundi, Cabo Verde, Cambodia, Cameroon, Central African Republic, Chad, Chile, China, Colombia, Comoros, Democratic Republic of the Congo, Republic of the Congo, Cook Islands, Costa Rica, Cote d'Ivoire, Croatia, Cuba, Cyprus, Djibouti, Dominica, Dominican Republic, Ecuador, Egypt, El Salvador, Equatorial Guinea, Eritrea, Ethiopia, Fiji, The Gambia, Georgia, Ghana, Grenada, Guatemala, Guinea, Guinea-Bissau, Guyana, Haiti, Honduras, India, Israel, Jamaica, Jordan, Kazakhstan, Kenya, Kiribati, North Korea, South Korea, Kyrgyzstan, Laos, Lebanon, Lesotho, Liberia, Macedonia, Madagascar, Malawi, Malaysia, Maldives, Mali, Malta, Marshall Islands, Mauritania, Mauritius, Mexico, Moldova, Mongolia, Morocco, Mozambique, Namibia, Nauru, Nepal, Nicaragua, Niger, Niue, Oman, Pakistan, Panama, Papua New Guinea, Paraguay, Peru, Philippines, Romania, Rwanda, Saint Kitts and Nevis, Saint Lucia, Saint Vincent and the Grenadines, Samoa, Sao Tome and Principe, Senegal, Seychelles, Sierra Leone, Solomon Islands, Somalia, South Africa, South Sudan, Sri Lanka, Sudan, Suriname, Swaziland, Syria, Tajikistan, Tanzania, Thailand, Timor-Leste, Togo, Tonga, Trinidad and Tobago, Tunisia, Turkey, Tuvalu, Uganda, Uruguay, Uzbekistan, Vanuatu, Vietnam, Yemen, Zambia, Zimbabwe

International Hydrographic Organization (IHO)

note—name changed from International Hydrographic Bureau on 22 September 1970

established—June 1919; effective—June 1921

aim—to train hydrographic surveyors and nautical cartographers to achieve standardization in nautical charts and electronic chart displays; to provide advice on nautical cartography and hydrography; to develop the sciences in the field of hydrography and techniques used for descriptive oceanography

members—(81) Algeria, Argentina, Australia, Bahrain, Bangladesh, Belgium, Brazil, Burma, Cameroon, Canada, Chile, China (including Hong Kong and Macau), Colombia, Democratic Republic of the Congo, Croatia, Cuba, Cyprus, Denmark, Dominican Republic, Ecuador, Egypt, Estonia, Fiji, Finland, France, Germany, Greece, Guatemala, Iceland, India, Indonesia, Iran, Ireland, Italy, Jamaica, Japan, North

Korea, South Korea, Kuwait, Latvia, Malaysia, Mauritius, Mexico, Monaco, Morocco, Mozambique, Netherlands, NZ, Nigeria, Norway, Oman, Pakistan, Papua New Guinea, Peru, Philippines, Poland, Portugal, Qatar, Romania, Russia, Saudi Arabia, Serbia, Singapore, Slovenia, South Africa, Spain, Sri Lanka, Suriname, Sweden, Syria, Thailand, Tonga, Trinidad and Tobago, Tunisia, Turkey, Ukraine, UAE, UK, US, Uruguay, Venezuela; note—members approved but waiting for Instrument of Accession: Bulgaria, Mauritania, Montenegro, Sierra Leone

International Labor Organization (ILO)
established—28 June 1919 set up as part of Treaty of Versailles; 11 April 1919 became operative; 14 December 1946 affiliated with the UN
aim—to deal with world labor issues; a UN specialized agency
members—(185) includes all UN member countries except Andorra, Bhutan, North Korea, Liechtenstein, Federated States of Micronesia, Monaco, Nauru, Tonga; note—includes the following dependencies: Netherlands (Aruba, Curacao, Sint Maarten)

International Maritime Organization (IMO)
note—name changed from Intergovernmental Maritime Consultative Organization (IMCO) on 22 May 1982
established—6 March 1948 set up as the Inter-Governmental Maritime Consultative Organization; effective—17 March 1958
aim—to deal with international maritime affairs; a UN specialized agency
members—(170) includes all UN member countries except Afghanistan, Andorra, Armenia, Belarus, Bhutan, Botswana, Burkina Faso, Burundi, Central African Republic, Chad, Kyrgyzstan, Laos, Lesotho, Liechtenstein, Mali, Federated States of Micronesia, Nauru, Niger, Rwanda, South Sudan, Swaziland, Tajikistan, Uzbekistan, Zambia; and Cook Islands
associate members—(3) Faroe Islands, Hong Kong, Macau

International Mobile Satellite Organization (IMSO)
established—15 April 1999
aim—acts as watchdog over Inmarsat (International Maritime Satellite Organization), a private company, to make sure it follows ICAO standards and recommended practices; plays an active role in the development of international telecommunications policies
members—(98) Algeria, Antigua and Barbuda, Argentina, Australia, The Bahamas, Bahrain, Bangladesh, Belarus, Belgium, Bosnia and Herzegovina, Brazil, Brunei, Bulgaria, Cameroon, Canada, Chile, China, Colombia, Comoros, Cook Islands, Costa Rica, Croatia, Cuba, Cyprus, Czech Republic, Denmark, Egypt, Finland, France, Gabon, Germany, Ghana, Greece, Hungary, Iceland, India, Indonesia, Iran, Iraq, Israel, Italy, Japan, Kenya, North Korea, South Korea, Kuwait, Latvia, Lebanon, Liberia, Libya, Malaysia, Malta, Marshall Islands, Mauritius, Mexico, Monaco, Mongolia, Montenegro, Morocco, Mozambique, Netherlands, NZ, Nigeria, Norway, Oman, Pakistan, Palau, Panama, Peru, Philippines, Poland, Portugal, Qatar, Romania, Russia, Saudi Arabia, Senegal, Serbia, Singapore, Slovakia, South Africa, Spain, Sri Lanka, Sweden, Switzerland, Tanzania, Thailand, Tonga, Tunisia, Turkey, Ukraine, UAE, UK, US, Vanuatu, Venezuela, Vietnam, Yemen

International Monetary Fund (IMF)
established—22 July 1944; effective—27 December 1945
aim—to promote world monetary stability and economic development; a UN specialized agency
members—(188) includes all UN member countries except Andorra, Cuba, North Korea, Liechtenstein, Monaco, Nauru; plus Kosovo; note—includes the following dependencies or areas of special interest: China (Hong Kong and Macau), Netherlands (Aruba, Curacao, Sint Maarten)

International Olympic Committee (IOC)
established—23 June 1894
aim—to promote the Olympic ideals and administer the Olympic games: 2012 Summer Olympics in London, UK; 2014 Winter Olympics in Sochi, Russia
National Olympic Committees—(204 and the Palestine Liberation Organization) Afghanistan, Albania, Algeria, American Samoa, Andorra, Angola, Antigua and Barbuda, Argentina, Armenia, Aruba, Australia, Austria, Azerbaijan, The Bahamas, Bahrain, Bangladesh, Barbados, Belarus, Belgium, Belize, Benin, Bermuda, Bhutan, Bolivia, Bosnia and Herzegovina, Botswana, Brazil, British Virgin Islands, Brunei, Bulgaria, Burkina Faso, Burma, Burundi, Cabo Verde, Cambodia, Cameroon, Canada, Cayman Islands, Central African Republic, Chad, Chile, China, Colombia, Comoros, Democratic Republic of the Congo, Republic of the Congo, Cook Islands, Costa Rica, Cote d'Ivoire, Croatia, Cuba, Cyprus, Czech Republic, Denmark, Djibouti, Dominica, Dominican Republic, Ecuador, Egypt, El Salvador, Equatorial Guinea, Eritrea, Estonia, Ethiopia, Fiji, Finland, France, Gabon, The Gambia, Georgia, Germany, Ghana, Greece, Grenada, Guam, Guatemala, Guinea, Guinea-Bissau, Guyana, Haiti, Honduras, Hong Kong, Hungary, Iceland, India, Indonesia, Iran, Iraq, Ireland, Israel, Italy, Jamaica, Japan, Jordan, Kazakhstan, Kenya, Kiribati, North Korea, South Korea, Kuwait, Kyrgyzstan, Laos, Latvia, Lebanon, Lesotho, Liberia, Libya, Liechtenstein, Lithuania, Luxembourg, Macedonia, Madagascar, Malawi, Malaysia, Maldives, Mali, Malta, Marshall Islands, Mauritania, Mauritius, Mexico, Federated States of Micronesia, Moldova, Monaco, Mongolia, Montenegro, Morocco, Mozambique, Namibia, Nauru, Nepal, Netherlands, NZ, Nicaragua, Niger, Nigeria, Norway, Oman, Pakistan, Palau, Panama, Papua New Guinea, Paraguay, Peru, Philippines, Poland, Portugal, Puerto Rico, Qatar, Romania, Russia, Rwanda, Saint Kitts and Nevis, Saint Lucia, Saint Vincent and the Grenadines, Samoa, San Marino, Sao Tome and Principe, Saudi Arabia, Senegal, Serbia, Seychelles, Sierra Leone, Singapore, Slovakia, Slovenia, Solomon Islands, Somalia, South Africa, Spain, Sri Lanka, Sudan, Suriname, Swaziland, Sweden, Switzerland, Syria, Taiwan, Tajikistan, Tanzania, Thailand, Timor-Leste, Togo, Tonga, Trinidad and Tobago, Tunisia, Turkey, Turkmenistan, Tuvalu, Uganda, Ukraine, UAE, UK, US, Uruguay, Uzbekistan, Vanuatu, Venezuela, Vietnam, Virgin Islands, Yemen, Zambia, Zimbabwe, Palestine Liberation Organization

International Organization for Migration (IOM)

note—established as Provisional Intergovernmental Committee for the Movement of Migrants from Europe; renamed Intergovernmental Committee for European Migration (ICEM) on 15 November 1952; renamed Intergovernmental Committee for Migration (ICM) in November 1980; current name adopted 14 November 1989

established—5 December 1951

aim—to facilitate orderly international emigration and immigration

members—(151) Afghanistan, Albania, Algeria, Angola, Antigua and Barbuda, Argentina, Armenia, Australia, Austria, Azerbaijan, The Bahamas, Bangladesh, Belarus, Belgium, Belize, Benin, Bolivia, Bosnia and Herzegovina, Botswana, Brazil, Bulgaria, Burkina Faso, Burma, Burundi, Cabo Verde, Cambodia, Cameroon, Canada, Central African Republic, Chad, Chile, Colombia, Comoros, Democratic Republic of the Congo, Republic of the Congo, Costa Rica, Cote d'Ivoire, Croatia, Cyprus, Czech Republic, Denmark, Djibouti, Dominican Republic, Ecuador, Egypt, El Salvador, Estonia, Ethiopia, Finland, France, Gabon, The Gambia, Georgia, Germany, Ghana, Greece, Guatemala, Guinea, Guinea-Bissau, Guyana, Haiti, Holy See, Honduras, Hungary, India, Iran, Ireland, Israel, Italy, Jamaica, Japan, Jordan, Kazakhstan, Kenya, South Korea, Kyrgyzstan, Latvia, Lesotho, Liberia, Libya, Lithuania, Luxembourg, Madagascar, Malawi, Maldives, Mali, Malta, Mauritania, Mauritius, Mexico, Federation of Micronesia, Moldova, Mongolia, Montenegro, Morocco, Mozambique, Namibia, Nauru, Nepal, Netherlands, NZ, Nicaragua, Niger, Nigeria, Norway, Pakistan, Panama, Papua New Guinea, Paraguay, Peru, Philippines, Poland, Portugal, Romania, Rwanda, Saint Vincent and the Grenadines, Senegal, Serbia, Seychelles, Sierra Leone, Slovakia, Slovenia, Somalia, South Africa, South Sudan, Spain, Sri Lanka, Sudan, Suriname, Swaziland, Sweden, Switzerland, Tajikistan, Tanzania, Thailand, Timor-Leste, Togo, Trinidad and Tobago, Tunisia, Turkey, Uganda, Ukraine, UK, US, Uruguay, Vanuatu, Venezuela, Vietnam, Yemen, Zambia, Zimbabwe

observers—(12) Bahrain, Bhutan, China, Cuba, Indonesia, Macedonia, Qatar, Russia, San Marino, Sao Tome and Principe, Saudi Arabia, Turkmenistan

International Organization for Standardization (ISO)

established—February 1947

aim—to promote the development of international standards with a view to facilitating international exchange of goods and services and to developing cooperation in the sphere of intellectual, scientific, technological and economic activity

members—(114 national standards organizations) Algeria, Argentina, Armenia, Australia, Austria, Azerbaijan, Bahrain, Bangladesh, Barbados, Belarus, Belgium, Bosnia and Herzegovina, Botswana, Brazil, Bulgaria, Cameroon, Canada, Chile, China, Colombia, Democratic Republic of the Congo, Costa Rica, Cote d'Ivoire, Croatia, Cuba, Cyprus, Czech Republic, Denmark, Ecuador, Egypt, El Salvador, Estonia, Ethiopia, Fiji, Finland, France, Gabon, Germany, Ghana, Greece, Hungary, Iceland, India, Indonesia, Iran, Iraq, Ireland, Israel, Italy, Jamaica, Japan, Jordan, Kazakhstan, Kenya, North Korea, South Korea, Kuwait, Lebanon, Libya, Lithuania, Luxembourg, Macedonia, Malaysia, Mali, Malta, Mauritius, Mexico, Mongolia, Morocco, Namibia, Netherlands, NZ, Nigeria, Norway, Oman, Pakistan, Panama, Peru, Philippines, Poland, Portugal, Qatar, Romania, Russia, Rwanda, Saint Lucia, Saudi Arabia, Senegal, Serbia, Singapore, Slovakia, Slovenia, South Africa, Spain, Sri Lanka, Sudan, Sweden, Switzerland, Syria, Tanzania, Thailand, Trinidad and Tobago, Tunisia, Turkey, Uganda, Ukraine, UAE, UK, US, Uruguay, Uzbekistan, Vietnam, Yemen, Zimbabwe

correspondent members—(45 plus the Palestine Liberation Organization) Afghanistan, Albania, Angola, Benin, Bhutan, Bolivia, Brunei, Burkina Faso, Burma, Burundi, Cambodia, Republic of the Congo, Dominica, Dominican Republic, Eritrea, Gabon, The Gambia, Georgia, Guatemala, Guinea, Guyana, Hong Kong, Kyrgyzstan, Latvia, Lesotho, Liberia, Macau, Madagascar, Malawi, Mauritania, Moldova, Montenegro, Mozambique, Nepal, Nicaragua, Niger, Papua New Guinea, Paraguay, Seychelles, Sierra Leone, Suriname, Swaziland, Tajikistan, Togo, Turkmenistan, Zambia, Palestine Liberation Organization

subscriber members—(4) Antigua and Barbuda, Honduras, Laos, Saint Vincent and the Grenadines

International Organization of the French-speaking World (OIF)

note—name changed from Agency of Cultural and Technical Cooperation (ACCT) in 1997; also known as Organisation Internationale de la Francophonie

established—20 March 1970

aim—founded around a common language to promote and spread the cultures of its members and to reinforce cultural and technical cooperation between them

members—(57) Albania, Andorra, Armenia, Belgium, Benin, Bulgaria, Burkina Faso, Burundi, Cabo Verde, Cambodia, Cameroon, Canada, Canada - New Brunswick, Canada - Quebec, Central African Republic, Chad, Comoros, Democratic Republic of Congo, Republic of Congo, Cote d'Ivoire, Cyprus, Djibouti, Dominica, Egypt, Equatorial Guinea, France, French Community of Belgium, Gabon, Ghana, Greece, Guinea, Guinea-Bissau, Haiti, Laos, Lebanon, Luxembourg, Macedonia, Madagascar, Mali, Mauritania, Mauritius, Moldova, Monaco, Morocco, Niger, Qatar, Romania, Rwanda, Saint Lucia, Sao Tome and Principe, Senegal, Seychelles, Switzerland, Togo, Tunisia, Vanuatu, Vietnam

observers—(20) Austria, Bosnia and Herzegovina, Croatia, Czech Republic, Dominican Republic, Estonia, Georgia, Hungary, Latvia, Lithuania, Montenegro, Mozambique, Poland, Serbia, Slovakia, Slovenia, Thailand, Ukraine, UAE, Uruguay

International Red Cross and Red Crescent Movement (ICRM)

established—1928

aim—to promote worldwide humanitarian aid through the International Committee of the Red Cross (ICRC) in wartime, and International Federation of Red Cross and Red Crescent Societies (IFRCS; formerly League of Red Cross and Red Crescent Societies or LORCS) in peacetime

National Societies—(187 countries and the Palestine Liberation Organization); note—same as membership for International Federation of Red Cross and Red Crescent Societies (IFRCS)

International Telecommunication Satellite Organization (ITSO)

established—August 1964

aim—to act as a watchdog over Intelsat, Ltd., a private company, to make sure it provides on a global and non-discriminatory basis public telecommunication services

members—(150) Afghanistan, Algeria, Angola, Argentina, Armenia, Australia, Austria, Azerbaijan, The Bahamas, Bahrain, Bangladesh, Barbados, Belgium, Benin, Bhutan, Bolivia, Bosnia and Herzegovina, Botswana, Brazil, Brunei, Bulgaria, Burkina Faso, Cabo Verde, Cameroon, Canada, Central African Republic, Chad, Chile, China, Colombia, Comoros, Democratic Republic of the Congo, Republic of the Congo, Costa Rica, Cote d'Ivoire, Croatia, Cuba, Cyprus, Czech Republic, Denmark, Dominican Republic, Ecuador, Egypt, El Salvador, Equatorial Guinea, Estonia, Ethiopia, Fiji, Finland, France, Gabon, The Gambia, Georgia, Germany, Ghana, Greece, Guatemala, Guinea, Guinea-Bissau, Haiti, Holy See, Honduras, Hungary, Iceland, India, Indonesia, Iran, Iraq, Ireland, Israel, Italy, Jamaica, Japan, Jordan, Kazakhstan, Kenya, North Korea, South Korea, Kuwait, Kyrgyzstan, Lebanon, Libya, Liechtenstein, Luxembourg, Madagascar, Malawi, Malaysia, Mali, Malta, Mauritania, Mauritius, Mexico, the Federated States of Micronesia, Monaco, Mongolia, Montenegro, Morocco, Mozambique, Namibia, Nepal, Netherlands, NZ, Nicaragua, Niger, Nigeria, Norway, Oman, Pakistan, Panama, Papua New Guinea, Paraguay, Peru, Philippines, Poland, Portugal, Qatar, Romania, Russia, Rwanda, Saudi Arabia, Senegal, Serbia, Singapore, Somalia, South Africa, Spain, Sri Lanka, Sudan, Swaziland, Sweden, Switzerland, Syria, Tajikistan, Tanzania, Thailand, Togo, Trinidad and Tobago, Tunisia, Turkey, Uganda, UAE, UK, US, Uruguay, Uzbekistan, Venezuela, Vietnam, Yemen, Zambia, Zimbabwe

International Telecommunication Union (ITU)

established—17 May 1865 set up as the International Telegraph Union; 9 December 1932 adopted present name; effective—1 January 1934; affiliated with the UN—15 November 1947

aim—to deal with world telecommunications issues; a UN specialized agency

members—(193) includes all UN member countries except Palau (192 total); plus Holy See

International Trade Union Confederation (ITUC)

note—its predecessors were the International Confederation of Free Trade Unions (ICFTU) and the World Confederation of Labor (WCL)

established—3 November 2006

aim—to promote the trade union movement

members—(325 affiliated organizations in 156 countries or territories and the Palestine Liberation Organization as of 2013) Albania, Algeria, Angola, Antigua and Barbuda, Aruba, Argentina, Australia, Austria, Azerbaijan, Bahrain, Bangladesh, Barbados, Belarus, Belgium, Belize, Benin, Bermuda, Bonaire, Bosnia and Herzegovina, Botswana, Brazil, Bulgaria, Burkina Faso, Burma, Burundi, Cabo Verde, Cambodia, Cameroon, Canada, Central African Republic, Chad, Chile, Colombia, Comoros, Democratic Republic of the Congo, Republic of the Congo, Cook Islands, Costa Rica, Cote d'Ivoire, Croatia, Curacao, Cyprus, Czech Republic, Denmark, Djibouti, Dominica, Dominican Republic, Ecuador, El Salvador, Eritrea, Estonia, Ethiopia, Fiji, Finland, France, French Polynesia, Gabon, The Gambia, Georgia, Germany, Ghana, Greece, Grenada, Guatemala, Guinea, Guinea-Bissau, Haiti, Holy See, Honduras, Hong Kong, Hungary, Iceland, India, Indonesia, Ireland, Israel, Italy, Japan, Jordan, Kenya, Kiribati, South Korea, Kosovo, Kuwait, Latvia, Liberia, Liechtenstein, Lithuania, Luxembourg, Macedonia, Madagascar, Malawi, Malaysia, Mali, Malta, Mauritania, Mauritius, Mexico, Moldova, Mongolia, Montenegro, Morocco, Mozambique, Namibia, Nepal, Netherlands, New Caledonia, NZ, Nicaragua, Niger, Nigeria, Norway, Pakistan, Panama, Paraguay, Peru, Philippines, Poland, Portugal, Romania, Russia, Rwanda, Saint Lucia, Samoa, San Marino, Sao Tome and Principe, Senegal, Serbia, Sierra Leone, Singapore, Slovakia, South Africa, Spain, Sri Lanka, Suriname, Swaziland, Sweden, Switzerland, Taiwan, Tanzania, Thailand, Togo, Tonga, Trinidad and Tobago, Tunisia, Turkey, Uganda, Ukraine, UK, US, Vanuatu, Venezuela, Yemen, Zambia, Zimbabwe, and the Palestine Liberation Organization

Islamic Development Bank (IDB)

established—15 December 1973 by declaration of intent; effective—12 August 1974

aim—to promote Islamic economic aid and social development

members—(55 plus the Palestine Liberation Organization) Afghanistan, Albania, Algeria, Azerbaijan, Bahrain, Bangladesh, Benin, Brunei, Burkina Faso, Cameroon, Chad, Comoros, Cote d'Ivoire, Djibouti, Egypt, Gabon, The Gambia, Guinea, Guinea-Bissau, Indonesia, Iran, Iraq, Jordan, Kazakhstan, Kuwait, Kyrgyzstan, Lebanon, Libya, Malaysia, Maldives, Mali, Mauritania, Morocco, Mozambique, Niger, Nigeria, Oman, Pakistan, Qatar, Saudi Arabia, Senegal, Sierra Leone, Somalia, Sudan, Suriname, Syria, Tajikistan, Togo, Tunisia, Turkey, Turkmenistan, Uganda, UAE, Uzbekistan, Yemen, Palestine Liberation Organization

Latin American and Caribbean Economic System (LAES)

note—also known as Sistema Economico Latinoamericana (SELA)

established—17 October 1975

aim—to promote economic and social development through regional cooperation

members—(28) Argentina, the Bahamas, Barbados, Belize, Bolivia, Brazil, Chile, Colombia, Costa Rica, Cuba, Dominican Republic, Ecuador, El Salvador, Grenada, Guatemala, Guyana, Haiti, Honduras, Jamaica, Mexico, Nicaragua, Panama, Paraguay, Peru, Suriname, Trinidad and Tobago, Uruguay, Venezuela

Latin American Integration Association (LAIA)

note—also known as Asociacion Latinoamericana de Integracion (ALADI)

established—12 August 1980; effective—18 March 1981

aim—to promote freer regional trade

members—(14) Argentina, Bolivia, Brazil, Chile, Colombia, Cuba, Ecuador, Mexico, Nicaragua, Panama, Paraguay, Peru, Uruguay, Venezuela *observers*—(29) China, Corporacion Andina de Fomento, Costa Rica, Dominican Republic, EC, El Salvador, Guatemala, Honduras, Inter-American Development Bank, Inter-American Institute for Cooperation on Agriculture, Italy, Japan, South Korea, Latin America Economic System, Nicaragua, Organizacion Panamericana de la Salud, Organizacion Mundial de la Salud, Organization of American States, Pakistan, Portugal, Romania, Russia, San Marino, Secretaria General Iberoamericana, Spain, Switzerland, Ukraine, United Nations Development Program, United Nations Economic Commission for Latin America and the Caribbean

League of Arab States (LAS)

note—also known as Arab League (AL)

established—22 March 1945

aim—to promote economic, social, political, and military cooperation

members—(20 plus the Palestine Liberation Organization) Algeria, Bahrain, Comoros, Djibouti, Egypt, Iraq, Jordan, Kuwait, Lebanon, Libya, Mauritania, Morocco, Oman, Qatar, Saudi Arabia, Somalia, Sudan, Tunisia, UAE, Yemen, Palestine Liberation Organization

observers—(4) Brazil, Eritrea, India, Venezuela

least developed countries (LLDCs)

that subgroup of the less developed countries (LDCs) initially identified by the UN General Assembly in 1971 as having no significant economic growth, per capita GDPs normally less than $1,000, and low literacy rates; also known as the undeveloped countries; the 44 LLDCs are: Afghanistan, Bangladesh, Benin, Bhutan, Burkina Faso, Burma, Burundi, Cambodia, Cameroon, Central African Republic, Chad, Comoros, Democratic Republic of the Congo, Cote d'Ivoire, Equatorial Guinea, Eritrea, Ethiopia, The Gambia, Ghana, Guinea, Guinea-Bissau, Haiti, Kenya, Lesotho, Liberia, Malawi, Mali, Moldova, Mozambique, Nepal, Niger, Rwanda, Sao Tome and Principe, Senegal, Sierra Leone, Somalia, Sudan, Tajikistan, Tanzania, Togo, Tokelau, Tuvalu, Uganda, Zambia

less developed countries (LDCs)

the bottom group in the hierarchy of developed countries (DCs), former USSR/Eastern Europe (former USSR/EE), and less developed countries (LDCs); mainly countries and dependent areas with low levels of output, living standards, and technology; per capita GDPs are generally below $5,000 and often less than $1,500; however, the group also includes a number of countries with high per capita incomes, areas of advanced technology, and rapid rates of growth; includes the advanced developing countries, developing countries, Four Dragons (Four Tigers), least developed countries (LLDCs), low-income countries, middle-income countries, newly industrializing economies (NIEs), the South, Third World, underdeveloped countries, undeveloped countries; the 172 LDCs are: Afghanistan, Algeria, American Samoa, Angola, Anguilla, Antigua and Barbuda, Argentina, Aruba, The Bahamas, Bahrain, Bangladesh, Barbados, Belize, Benin, Bhutan, Bolivia, Botswana, Brazil, British Virgin Islands, Brunei, Burkina Faso, Burma, Burundi, Cabo Verde, Cambodia, Cameroon, Cayman Islands, Central African Republic, Chad, Chile, China, Christmas Island, Cocos Islands, Colombia, Comoros, Democratic Republic of the Congo, Republic of the Congo, Cook Islands, Costa Rica, Cote d'Ivoire, Cuba, Cyprus, Djibouti, Dominica, Dominican Republic, Ecuador, Egypt, El Salvador, Equatorial Guinea, Eritrea, Ethiopia, Falkland Islands, Fiji, French Guiana, French Polynesia, Gabon, The Gambia, Gaza Strip, Ghana, Gibraltar, Greenland, Grenada, Guadeloupe, Guam, Guatemala, Guernsey, Guinea, Guinea-Bissau, Guyana, Haiti, Honduras, Hong Kong, India, Indonesia, Iran, Iraq, Isle of Man, Jamaica, Jersey, Jordan, Kenya, Kiribati, North Korea, South Korea, Kuwait, Laos, Lebanon, Lesotho, Liberia, Libya, Macau, Madagascar, Malawi, Malaysia, Maldives, Mali, Marshall Islands, Martinique, Mauritania, Mauritius, Mayotte, Federated States of Micronesia, Mongolia, Montserrat, Morocco, Mozambique, Namibia, Nauru, Nepal, Netherlands Antilles, New Caledonia, Nicaragua, Niger, Nigeria, Niue, Norfolk Island, Northern Mariana Islands, Oman, Palau, Pakistan, Panama, Papua New Guinea, Paraguay, Peru, Philippines, Pitcairn Islands, Puerto Rico, Qatar, Reunion, Rwanda, Saint Helena, Ascension, and Tristan da Cunha, Saint Kitts and Nevis, Saint Lucia, Saint Pierre and Miquelon, Saint Vincent and the Grenadines, Samoa, Sao Tome and Principe, Saudi Arabia, Senegal, Seychelles, Sierra Leone, Singapore, Solomon Islands, Somalia, Sri Lanka, Sudan, Suriname, Swaziland, Syria, Taiwan, Tanzania, Thailand, Togo, Tokelau, Tonga, Trinidad and Tobago, Tunisia, Turks and Caicos Islands, Tuvalu, UAE, Uganda, Uruguay, Vanuatu, Venezuela, Vietnam, Virgin Islands, Wallis and Futuna, West Bank, Western Sahara, Yemen, Zambia, Zimbabwe; note—similar to the new International Monetary Fund (IMF) term "developing countries" which adds Malta, Mexico, South Africa, and Turkey but omits in its recently published statistics American Samoa, Anguilla, British Virgin Islands, Brunei, Cayman Islands, Christmas Island, Cocos Islands, Cook Islands, Cuba, Eritrea, Falkland Islands, French Guiana, French Polynesia, Gaza Strip, Gibraltar, Greenland, Grenada, Guadeloupe, Guam, Guernsey, Isle of Man, Jersey, North Korea, Macau, Martinique, Mayotte, Montserrat, Nauru, New Caledonia, Niue, Norfolk Island, Northern Mariana Islands, Palau, Pitcairn Islands, Puerto Rico, Reunion, Saint Helena, Ascension, and Tristan da Cunha, Saint Pierre and Miquelon, Tokelau, Tonga, Turks and Caicos Islands, Tuvalu, Virgin Islands, Wallis and Futuna, West Bank, Western Sahara

low-income countries

another term for those less developed countries with below-average per capita GDPs; see less developed countries (LDCs)

middle-income countries

another term for those less developed countries with above-average per capita GDPs; see less developed countries (LDCs)

Multilateral Investment Guarantee Agency (MIGA)

established—12 April 1988

aim—encourages flow of foreign direct investment among member countries by offering investment insurance, consultation, and negotiation on conditions for foreign investment and technical assistance; a UN specialized agency

members—(179) includes all UN member countries except Andorra, Bhutan, Brunei, Burma, Cuba, Kiribati, North Korea, Liechtenstein, Marshall Islands, Monaco, Nauru, San Marino, Somalia, Tonga, Tuvalu; plus Kosovo

Near Abroad
Russian term for the 14 non-Russian successor states of the USSR, in which 25 million ethnic Russians live and in which Moscow has expressed a strong national security interest; the 14 countries are Armenia, Azerbaijan, Belarus, Estonia, Georgia, Kazakhstan, Kyrgyzstan, Latvia, Lithuania, Moldova, Tajikistan, Turkmenistan, Ukraine, Uzbekistan

new independent states (NIS)
a term referring to all the countries of the FSU except the Baltic countries (Estonia, Latvia, Lithuania)

newly industrializing countries (NICs)
former term for the newly industrializing economies; see newly industrializing economies (NIEs)

newly industrializing economies (NIEs)
that subgroup of the less developed countries (LDCs) that has experienced particularly rapid industrialization of their economies; formerly known as the newly industrializing countries (NICs); also known as advanced developing countries; usually includes the Four Dragons (Hong Kong, South Korea, Singapore, Taiwan), and Brazil

Nonaligned Movement (NAM)
established—1-6 September 1961
aim—to establish political and military cooperation apart from the traditional East or West blocs
members—(119 plus the Palestine Liberation Organization) Afghanistan, Algeria, Angola, Antigua and Barbuda, Azerbaijan, The Bahamas, Bahrain, Bangladesh, Barbados, Belarus, Belize, Benin, Bhutan, Bolivia, Botswana, Brunei, Burkina Faso, Burma, Burundi, Cabo Verde, Cambodia, Cameroon, Central African Republic, Chad, Chile, Colombia, Comoros, Democratic Republic of the Congo, Republic of the Congo, Cote d'Ivoire, Cuba, Djibouti, Dominica, Dominican Republic, Ecuador, Egypt, Equatorial Guinea, Eritrea, Ethiopia, Fiji, Gabon, The Gambia, Ghana, Grenada, Guatemala, Guinea, Guinea-Bissau, Guyana, Haiti, Honduras, India, Indonesia, Iran, Iraq, Jamaica, Jordan, Kenya, North Korea, Kuwait, Laos, Lebanon, Lesotho, Liberia, Libya, Madagascar, Malawi, Malaysia, Maldives, Mali, Mauritania, Mauritius, Mongolia, Morocco, Mozambique, Namibia, Nepal, Nicaragua, Niger, Nigeria, Oman, Pakistan, Panama, Papua New Guinea, Peru, Philippines, Qatar, Rwanda, Saint Kitts and Nevis, Saint Lucia, Saint Vincent and the Grenadines, Sao Tome and Principe, Saudi Arabia, Senegal, Seychelles, Sierra Leone, Singapore, Somalia, South Africa, Sri Lanka, Sudan, Suriname, Swaziland, Syria, Tanzania, Thailand, Timor-Leste, Togo, Trinidad and Tobago, Tunisia, Turkmenistan, Uganda, UAE, Uzbekistan, Vanuatu, Venezuela, Vietnam, Yemen, Zambia, Zimbabwe, Palestine Liberation Organization
observers—(17) Argentina, Armenia, Bosnia and Herzegovina, Brazil, China, Costa Rica, Croatia, El Salvador, Kazakhstan, Kyrgyzstan, Mexico, Montenegro, Paraguay, Serbia, Tajikistan, Ukraine, Uruguay

Nordic Council (NC)
established—16 March 1952; effective—12 February 1953
aim—to promote regional economic, cultural, and environmental cooperation
members—(5) Denmark (including Faroe Islands and Greenland), Finland (including Aland Islands), Iceland, Norway, Sweden
observers—(6) Estonia, Latvia, Lithuania, and the Sami (Lapp) local parliaments of Finland, Norway, and Sweden

Nordic Investment Bank (NIB)
established—4 December 1975; effective—1 June 1976
aim—to promote economic cooperation and development
members—(8) Denmark (including Faroe Islands and Greenland), Estonia, Finland (including Aland Islands), Iceland, Latvia, Lithuania, Norway, Sweden

North
a popular term for the rich industrialized countries generally located in the northern portion of the Northern Hemisphere; the counterpart of the South; see developed countries (DCs)

North American Free Trade Agreement (NAFTA)
established—17 December 1992
aim—to eliminate trade barriers, promote fair competition, increase investment opportunities, provide protection of intellectual property rights, and create procedures to settle disputes
members—(3) Canada, Mexico, US

North Atlantic Treaty Organization (NATO)
established—4 April 1949
aim—to promote mutual defense and cooperation
members—(28) Albania, Belgium, Bulgaria, Canada, Croatia, Czech Republic, Denmark, Estonia, France, Germany, Greece, Hungary, Iceland, Italy, Latvia, Lithuania, Luxembourg, Netherlands, Norway, Poland, Portugal, Romania, Slovakia, Slovenia, Spain, Turkey, UK, US

Nuclear Energy Agency (NEA)
note—also known as OECD Nuclear Energy Agency
established—1 February 1958
aim—to promote the peaceful uses of nuclear energy; associated with OECD

members—(31) Australia, Austria, Belgium, Canada, Czech Republic, Denmark, Finland, France, Germany, Greece, Hungary, Iceland, Ireland, Italy, Japan, South Korea, Luxembourg, Mexico, Netherlands, Norway, Poland, Portugal, Russia, Slovakia, Slovenia, Spain, Sweden, Switzerland, Turkey, UK, US

Nuclear Suppliers Group (NSG)
note—also known as the London Suppliers Group or the London Group
established—1974; effective—1975
aim—to establish guidelines for exports of nuclear materials, processing equipment for uranium enrichment, and technical information to countries of proliferation concern and regions of conflict and instability
members—(48) Argentina, Australia, Austria, Belarus, Belgium, Brazil, Bulgaria, Canada, China, Croatia, Cyprus, Czech Republic, Denmark, Estonia, Finland, France, Germany, Greece, Hungary, Iceland, Ireland, Italy, Japan, Kazakhstan, South Korea, Latvia, Lithuania, Luxembourg, Malta, Mexico, Netherlands, NZ, Norway, Poland, Portugal, Romania, Russia, Serbia, Slovakia, Slovenia, South Africa, Spain, Sweden, Switzerland, Turkey, Ukraine, UK, US
observer—(2) Chairman of the Zangger Committee, European Commission (a policy-planning body for the EU)

Organization for Democracy and Economic Development (GUAM)
note—acronym standing for the member countries, Georgia, Ukraine, Azerbaijan, Moldova; formerly known as GUUAM before Uzbekistan withdrew in 5 May 2005
established—7 June 2001
aim—commits the countries to cooperation and assistance in social and economic development, the strengthening and broadening of trade and economic relations, and the development and effective use of transport and communications, highways, and related infrastructure crossing the boundaries of the member states
members—(4) Azerbaijan, Georgia, Moldova, Ukraine

Organization for Economic Cooperation and Development (OECD)
established—14 December 1960; effective—30 September 1961
aim—to promote economic cooperation and development
members—(34) Australia, Austria, Belgium, Canada, Chile, Czech Republic, Denmark, Estonia, Finland, France, Germany, Greece, Hungary, Iceland, Ireland, Israel, Italy, Japan, South Korea, Luxembourg, Mexico, Netherlands, NZ, Norway, Poland, Portugal, Slovakia, Slovenia, Spain, Sweden, Switzerland, Turkey, UK, US
special member—(1) EC

Organization for Security and Cooperation in Europe (OSCE)
note—formerly the Conference on Security and Cooperation in Europe (CSCE) established 3 July 1975
established—1 January 1995
aim—to foster the implementation of human rights, fundamental freedoms, democracy, and the rule of law; to act as an instrument of early warning, conflict prevention, and crisis management; and to serve as a framework for conventional arms control and confidence building measures
members—(57) Albania, Andorra, Armenia, Austria, Azerbaijan, Belarus, Belgium, Bosnia and Herzegovina, Bulgaria, Canada, Croatia, Cyprus, Czech Republic, Denmark, Estonia, Finland, France, Georgia, Germany, Greece, Holy See, Hungary, Iceland, Ireland, Italy, Kazakhstan, Kyrgyzstan, Latvia, Liechtenstein, Lithuania, Luxembourg, Macedonia, Malta, Moldova, Monaco, Mongolia, Montenegro, Netherlands, Norway, Poland, Portugal, Romania, Russia, San Marino, Serbia, Slovakia, Slovenia, Spain, Sweden, Switzerland, Tajikistan, Turkey, Turkmenistan, Ukraine, UK, US, Uzbekistan
partners for cooperation—(11) Afghanistan, Algeria, Australia, Egypt, Israel, Japan, Jordan, South Korea, Morocco, Thailand, Tunisia

Organization for the Prohibition of Chemical Weapons (OPCW)
established—29 April 1997
aim—to enforce the Convention on the Prohibition of the Development, Production, Stockpiling, and Use of Chemical Weapons and on Their Destruction; to provide a forum for consultation and cooperation among the signatories of the Convention
members (countries that have ratified the Convention)—(190) Afghanistan, Albania, Algeria, Andorra, Antigua and Barbuda, Argentina, Armenia, Australia, Austria, Azerbaijan, The Bahamas, Bahrain, Bangladesh, Barbados, Belarus, Belgium, Belize, Benin, Bhutan, Bolivia, Bosnia and Herzegovina, Botswana, Brazil, Brunei, Bulgaria, Burkina Faso, Burundi, Cabo Verde, Cambodia, Cameroon, Canada, Central African Republic, Chad, Chile, China, Colombia, Comoros, Democratic Republic of the Congo, Republic of the Congo, Cook Islands, Costa Rica, Cote d'Ivoire, Croatia, Cuba, Cyprus, Czech Republic, Denmark, Dominica, Dominican Republic, Djibouti, Ecuador, El Salvador, Equatorial Guinea, Eritrea, Estonia, Ethiopia, Fiji, Finland, France, Gabon, The Gambia, Georgia, Germany, Ghana, Greece, Grenada, Guatemala, Guinea, Guinea-Bissau, Guyana, Haiti, Holy See, Honduras, Hungary, Iceland, India, Indonesia, Iran, Iraq, Ireland, Italy, Jamaica, Japan, Jordan, Kazakhstan, Kenya, Kiribati, South Korea, Kuwait, Kyrgyzstan, Laos, Latvia, Lebanon, Lesotho, Liberia, Libya, Liechtenstein, Lithuania, Luxembourg, Macedonia, Madagascar, Malawi, Malaysia, Maldives, Mali, Malta, Marshall Islands, Mauritania, Mauritius, Mexico, Federated States of Micronesia, Moldova, Monaco, Mongolia, Montenegro, Morocco, Mozambique, Namibia, Nauru, Nepal, Netherlands, NZ, Nicaragua, Niger, Nigeria, Niue, Norway, Oman, Pakistan, Palau, Panama, Papua New Guinea, Paraguay, Peru, Philippines, Poland, Portugal, Qatar, Romania, Russia, Rwanda, Saint Kitts and Nevis, Saint Lucia, Saint Vincent and the Grenadines, Samoa, San Marino, Sao Tome and Principe, Saudi Arabia, Senegal, Serbia, Seychelles, Sierra Leone, Singapore, Slovakia, Slovenia, Solomon Islands, Somalia, South Africa, Spain, Sri Lanka, Sudan, Suriname, Swaziland, Sweden, Switzerland, Syria, Tajikistan, Tanzania, Thailand, Timor-Leste, Togo, Tonga, Trinidad and Tobago, Tunisia, Turkey, Turkmenistan, Tuvalu, Uganda, Ukraine, UAE, UK, US, Uruguay, Uzbekis
signatory states (countries that have signed, but not ratified, the Convention)—(2) Burma, Israel

Organization of African Unity (OAU)
see African Union

Organization of American States (OAS)
established—14 April 1890 as the International Union of American Republics; 30 April 1948 adopted present charter; effective—13 December 1951
aim—to promote regional peace and security as well as economic and social development
members—(35) Antigua and Barbuda, Argentina, The Bahamas, Barbados, Belize, Bolivia, Brazil, Canada, Chile, Colombia, Costa Rica, Cuba (suspended), Dominica, Dominican Republic, Ecuador, El Salvador, Grenada, Guatemala, Guyana, Haiti, Honduras, Jamaica, Mexico, Nicaragua, Panama, Paraguay, Peru, Saint Kitts and Nevis, Saint Lucia, Saint Vincent and the Grenadines, Suriname, Trinidad and Tobago, US, Uruguay, Venezuela
observers—(68) Albania, Algeria, Angola, Armenia, Austria, Azerbaijan, Belgium, Benin, Bosnia and Herzegovina, Bulgaria, China, Croatia, Cyprus, Czech Republic, Denmark, Egypt, Equatorial Guinea, Estonia, EU, Finland, France, Georgia, Germany, Ghana, Greece, Holy See, Hungary, Iceland, India, Ireland, Israel, Italy, Japan, Kazakhstan, South Korea, Latvia, Lebanon, Lithuania, Luxembourg, Macedonia, Malta, Monaco, Morocco, Netherlands, Nigeria, Norway, Pakistan, Philippines, Poland, Portugal, Qatar, Romania, Russia, Saudi Arabia, Serbia, Slovakia, Slovenia, Spain, Sri Lanka, Sweden, Switzerland, Thailand, Tunisia, Turkey, Ukraine, UK, Vanuatu, Yemen

Organization of Arab Petroleum Exporting Countries (OAPEC)
established—9 January 1968
aim—to promote cooperation in the petroleum industry
members—(11) Algeria, Bahrain, Egypt, Iraq, Kuwait, Libya, Qatar, Saudi Arabia, Syria, Tunisia (suspended), UAE

Organization of Eastern Caribbean States (OECS)
established—18 June 1981; effective—4 July 1981
aim—to promote political, economic, and defense cooperation
members—(9) Anguilla, Antigua and Barbuda, British Virgin Islands, Dominica, Grenada, Montserrat, Saint Kitts and Nevis, Saint Lucia, Saint Vincent and the Grenadines

Organization of Islamic Cooperation (OIC)
note—formerly the Organization of the Islamic Conference
established—22-25 September 1969
aim—to promote Islamic solidarity in economic, social, cultural, and political affairs
members—(56 plus the Palestine Liberation Organization) Afghanistan, Albania, Algeria, Azerbaijan, Bahrain, Bangladesh, Benin, Brunei, Burkina Faso, Cameroon, Chad, Comoros, Cote d'Ivoire, Djibouti, Egypt, Gabon, The Gambia, Guinea, Guinea-Bissau, Guyana, Indonesia, Iran, Iraq, Jordan, Kazakhstan, Kuwait, Kyrgyzstan, Lebanon, Libya, Malaysia, Maldives, Mali, Mauritania, Morocco, Mozambique, Niger, Nigeria, Oman, Pakistan, Qatar, Saudi Arabia, Senegal, Sierra Leone, Somalia, Sudan, Suriname, Syria, Tajikistan, Togo, Tunisia, Turkey, Turkmenistan, Uganda, UAE, Uzbekistan, Yemen, Palestine Liberation Organization
observers—(12) AU, Bosnia and Herzegovina, Central African Republic, ECO, LAS, Moro National Liberation Front, NAM, Parliamentary Union of the OIC Member States, Russia, Thailand, Turkish Muslim Community of Kibris, UN

Organization of Petroleum Exporting Countries (OPEC)
established—14 September 1960
aim—to coordinate petroleum policies
members—(12) Algeria, Angola, Ecuador, Iran, Iraq, Kuwait, Libya, Nigeria, Qatar, Saudi Arabia, UAE, Venezuela; note—Indonesia left OPEC in 2008

Pacific Alliance
established—28 April 2011
aim—to reduce trade barriers between member countries, to install visa-free travel, to install a common stock exchange, and to set up joint embassies in some countries
members—(5) Chile, Columbia, Costa Rica, Mexico, Peru
observers—(29) Australia, Canada, China, Dominican Republic, Ecuador, El Salvador , Finland, France, Germany, Guatemala, Honduras, India, Israel, Italy, Japan, Morocco, Netherlands, New Zealand, Panama, Paraguay, Portugal, Singapore, South Korea, Spain, Switzerland, Turkey, United Kingdom, United States, Uruguay

Pacific Community (SPC)
local name of the Secretariat of the Pacific Community

Pacific Islands Forum (PIF)
note—formerly known as South Pacific Forum (SPF)
established—5 August 1971
aim—to promote regional cooperation in political matters
members—(16) Australia, Cook Islands, Fiji, Kiribati, Marshall Islands, Federated States of Micronesia, Nauru, NZ, Niue, Palau, Papua New Guinea, Samoa, Solomon Islands, Tonga, Tuvalu, Vanuatu
associate members—(2) French Polynesia, New Caledonia
partners—(14) Canada, China, EU, France, India, Indonesia, Italy, Japan, South Korea, Malaysia, Philippines, Thailand, UK, US

observers—(12) ACP Group, American Samoa, Asia Development Bank, The Commonwealth, Commonwealth of the Northern Marianas, Guam, Timor-Leste (special observer), Tokelau, UN, Wallis and Futuna, Western and Central Pacific Fisheries Commission, the World Bank

Paris Club

established—1956

aim—to provide a forum for debtor countries to negotiate rescheduling of debt service payments or loans extended by governments or official agencies of participating countries; to help restore normal trade and project finance to debtor countries

members—(19) Australia, Austria, Belgium, Canada, Denmark, Finland, France, Germany, Ireland, Italy, Japan, Netherlands, Norway, Russia, Spain, Sweden, Switzerland, UK, US

associate members—(13) Abu Dhabi, Argentina, Brazil, Israel, South Korea, Kuwait, Mexico, Morocco, NZ, Portugal, South Africa, Trinidad and Tobago, Turkey

Partnership for Peace (PFP)

established—10-11 January 1994

aim—to expand and intensify political and military cooperation throughout Europe, increase stability, diminish threats to peace, and build relationships by promoting the spirit of practical cooperation and commitment to democratic principles that underpin NATO; program under the auspices of NATO

members—(22) Armenia, Austria, Azerbaijan, Belarus, Bosnia and Herzegovina, Finland, Georgia, Ireland, Kazakhstan, Kyrgyzstan, Macedonia, Malta, Moldova, Montenegro, Russia, Serbia, Sweden, Switzerland, Tajikistan, Turkmenistan, Ukraine, Uzbekistan; note—a nation that becomes a member of NATO is no longer a member of PFP

Permanent Court of Arbitration (PCA)

established—29 July 1899

aim—to facilitate the settlement of international disputes

members—(115) Albania, Argentina, Australia, Austria, Bahrain, Bangladesh, Belarus, Belgium, Belize, Benin, Bolivia, Brazil, Bulgaria, Burkina Faso, Cambodia, Cameroon, Canada, Chile, China, Colombia, Democratic Republic of the Congo, Costa Rica, Croatia, Cuba, Cyprus, Czech Republic, Denmark, Dominican Republic, Ecuador, Egypt, El Salvador, Eritrea, Estonia, Ethiopia, Fiji, Finland, France, Germany, Greece, Guatemala, Guyana, Haiti, Honduras, Hungary, Iceland, India, Iran, Iraq, Ireland, Israel, Italy, Japan, Jordan, Kenya, South Korea, Kuwait, Kyrgyzstan, Laos, Latvia, Lebanon, Libya, Liechtenstein, Lithuania, Luxembourg, Macedonia, Madagascar, Malaysia, Malta, Mauritius, Mexico, Montenegro, Morocco, Netherlands, NZ, Nicaragua, Nigeria, Norway, Pakistan, Panama, Paraguay, Peru, Philippines, Poland, Portugal, Qatar, Romania, Russia, Rwanda, Saudi Arabia, Senegal, Serbia, Singapore, Slovakia, Slovenia, South Africa, Spain, Sri Lanka, Sudan, Suriname, Swaziland, Sweden, Switzerland, Thailand, Togo, Turkey, Uganda, Ukraine, UAE, UK, US, Uruguay, Venezuela, Vietnam, Zambia, Zimbabwe

Petrocaribe

established—29 June 2005

aim—to eliminate existing social inequities, to foster high standards of living, to promote effective people's participation in shaping their own destiny

members—(18) Antigua and Barbuda, The Bahamas, Belize, Cuba, Dominica, Dominican Republic, Grenada, Guatemala, Guyana, Haiti, Honduras, Jamaica, Nicaragua, St. Kitts and Nevis, St. Lucia, St. Vincent and the Grenadines, Suriname, Venezuela

Rio Group (RG)

note—formerly known as Grupo de los Ocho, established NA December 1986; composed of the Contadora Group and the Lima Group established in 1988 to consult on regional Latin American issues; its members were Argentina, Belize, Bolivia, Brazil, Chile, Colombia, Costa Rica, Cuba, Dominican Republic, Ecuador, El Salvador, Guatemala, Guyana, Haiti, Honduras, Jamaica (representing CARICOM), Mexico, Nicaragua, Panama, Paraguay, Peru, Uruguay, Venezuela; in 2010 joined with the Caribbean Summit on Integration and Development (CALC) to form the Community of Latin American and Caribbean States (CELAC)

Schengen Convention

established—signed June 1990; effective March 1995

aim—to allow free movement within an area without internal border controls

members—(26) Austria, Belgium, Czech Republic, Denmark, Estonia, Finland, France, Germany, Greece, Hungary, Iceland, Italy, Latvia, Liechtenstein, Lithuania, Luxembourg, Malta, Netherlands, Norway, Poland, Portugal, Slovakia, Slovenia, Spain, Sweden, Switzerland; note- UK and Ireland have not joined; Cyprus will probably join in the near future; Bulgaria and Romania are still not fully implemented

De Facto members (microstates within or between Schengen states)—(5) Andorra, Holy See, Liechtenstein, Monaco, San Marino

Second World

another term for the traditionally Marxist-Leninist states of the USSR and Eastern Europe, with authoritarian governments and command economies based on the Soviet model; the term is fading from use; see centrally planned economies

Secretariat of the Pacific Community (SPC)

established—6 February 1947; effective 29 July 1948

aim—to serve island development in 22 Pacific countries; to develop technical assistance and professional, scientific, and research support; to build planning and management capability *members*—(26) America Samoa, Australia, Cook Islands, Fiji, France, French Polynesia, Guam, Kiribati, Marshall Islands, Federated States of Micronesia, Nauru, New Caledonia, Niue, Northern Mariana Islands, NZ, Palau, Papua New Guinea, Pitcairn Islands, Samoa, Solomon Islands, Tokelau, Tonga, Tuvalu, Vanuatu, US, Wallis and Futuna

Shanghai Cooperation Organization (SCO)
established—15 June 2001
aim—to combat terrorism, extremism, and separatism; to safeguard regional security through mutual trust, disarmament, and cooperative security; and to increase cooperation in political, trade, economic, scientific and technological, cultural, and educational fields
members—(6) China, Kazakhstan, Kyrgyzstan, Russia, Tajikistan, Uzbekistan
dialogue members—(3) Belarus, Sri Lanka Turkey
observers—(5) Afghanistan, India, Iran, Mongolia, Pakistan

socialist countries
in general, countries in which the government owns and plans the use of the major factors of production; note—the term is sometimes used incorrectly as a synonym for Communist countries

South
a popular term for the poorer, less industrialized countries generally located south of the developed countries; the counterpart of the North; see less developed countries (LDCs)

South American Community of Nations (CSN)
established on 9 December 2004; its aim was to coordinate common policies regarding multilateral organizations, to integrate physical infrastructure, and to consolidate the merger of CAN and Mercosur; the members were Argentina, Bolivia, Brazil, Chile, Colombia, Ecuador, Guyana, Paraguay, Peru, Surinam, Uruguay, Venezuela; in 2008 it became Union of South American Nations (UNASUR)

South Asia Co-operative Environment Program (SACEP)
established—January 1983
aim—to promote regional cooperation in South Asia in the field of environment, both natural and human, and on issues of economic and social development; to support conservation and management of natural resources of the region
members—(8) Afghanistan, Bangladesh, Bhutan, India, Maldives, Nepal, Pakistan, Sri Lanka

South Asian Association for Regional Cooperation (SAARC)
established—8 December 1985
aim—to promote economic, social, and cultural cooperation
members—(8) Afghanistan, Bangladesh, Bhutan, India, Maldives, Nepal, Pakistan, Sri Lanka
observers—(9) Australia, Burma, China, EU, Iran, Japan, South Korea, Mauritius, US

South Pacific Forum (SPF)
note—see Pacific Island Forum

South Pacific Regional Trade and Economic Cooperation Agreement (Sparteca)
established—1981
aim—to redress unequal trade relationships of Australia and New Zealand with small island economies in the Pacific region
members—(16) Australia, Cook Islands, Fiji (suspended), Kiribati, Marshall Islands, Federated States of Micronesia, Nauru, NZ, Niue, Palau, Papua New Guinea, Samoa, Solomon Islands, Tonga, Tuvalu, Vanuatu

Southern African Customs Union (SACU)
established—11 December 1969
aim—to promote free trade and cooperation in customs matters
members—(5) Botswana, Lesotho, Namibia, South Africa, Swaziland

Southern African Development Community (SADC)
note—evolved from the Southern African Development Coordination Conference (SADCC)
established—17 August 1992
aim—to promote regional economic development and integration
members—(15) Angola, Botswana, Democratic Republic of the Congo, Lesotho, Madagascar, Malawi, Mauritius, Mozambique, Namibia, Seychelles, South Africa, Swaziland, Tanzania, Zambia, Zimbabwe

Southern Cone Common Market (Mercosur) or Southern Common Market
note—also known as Mercado Comun del Cono Sur (Mercosur)
established—26 March 1991
aim—to increase regional economic cooperation
members—(6) Argentina, Bolivia, Brazil, Paraguay (suspended), Uruguay, Venezuela
associate members—(6) Chile, Colombia, Ecuador, Guyana, Peru, Surinam

Third World
another term for the less developed countries; the term is obsolescent; see less developed countries (LDCs)

underdeveloped countries

refers to those less developed countries with the potential for above-average economic growth; see less developed countries (LDCs)

undeveloped countries

refers to those extremely poor less developed countries (LDCs) with little prospect for economic growth; see least developed countries (LLDCs)

Union Latina

established—15 May 1954; became functional 1983
aim—to project, protect, and promote the common heritage and unifying identities of the Latin, and Latin-influenced, world
members—(36) Andorra, Angola, Bolivia, Brazil, Cabo Verde, Chile, Colombia, Cote d'Ivoire, Costa Rica, Cuba, Dominican Republic, Ecuador, El Salvador, France, Guatemala, Guinea-Bissau, Haiti, Honduras, Italy, Moldova, Monaco, Mozambique, Nicaragua, Panama, Paraguay, Peru, Philippines, Portugal, Romania, San Marino, Sao Tome and Principe, Senegal, Spain, Timor-Leste, Uruguay, Venezuela
observers—(4) Argentina, Holy See, Mexico, Order of Malta

Union of South American Nations (UNASUR—Spanish; UNASUL—Portuguese)

formerly South American Community of Nations (CSN) which terminated on 16 April 2007
established—23 May 2008
aim—to model a community after the European Union which will include a common currency, parliament, passport, and defense policy
members—(12) Argentina, Bolivia, Brazil, Chile, Colombia, Ecuador, Guyana, Paraguay, Peru, Suriname, Uruguay, Venezuela
observers—(2) Mexico, Panama

United Nations (UN)

established—26 June 1945; effective—24 October 1945
aim—to maintain international peace and security and to promote cooperation involving economic, social, cultural, and humanitarian problems
constituent organizations—the UN is composed of six principal organs and numerous subordinate agencies and bodies as follows:
1) *Secretariat*
2) *General Assembly*: International Computing Center (ICC), International Trade Center (ITC), Joint United Nations Program on HIV/AIDS (UN-AIDS), Office of the United Nations High Commissioner for Refugees (UNHCR), United Nations Center for Human Settlements (UN-Habitat), United Nations Children's Fund (UNICEF), United Nations Conference on Trade and Development (UNCTAD), United Nations Development Program (UNDP), United Nations Environment Program (UNEP), United Nations Institute for Disarmament Research (UNIDIR), United Nations Institute for Training and Research (UNITAR), United Nations Interregional Crime and Justice Research Institute (UNICRI), United Nations Office on Drugs and Crime (UNODC), United Nations Population Fund (UNFPA), United Nations Office of Project Services (UNOPS), United Nations Relief and Works Agency for Palestine Refugees in the Near East (UNRWA), United Nations Research Institute for Social Development (UNRISD), United Nations System Staff College (UNSSC), United Nations University (UNU), United Nations Women, World Food Program (WFP)
3) *Security Council*: International Criminal Tribunal for the Former Yugoslavia (ICTY), International Criminal Tribunal for Rwanda (ICTR), United Nations Compensation Commission, United Nations Disengagement Observer Force (UNDOF), African Union/United Nations Hybrid Operation in Darfur (UNAMID), United Nations Assistance Mission in Afghanistan (UNAMA), United Nations Interim Administration Mission in Kosovo (UNMIK), United Nations Interim Force for Abyei (UNIFSA), United Nations Interim Force in Lebanon (UNIFIL), United Nations Mission in Liberia (UNMIL), United Nations Military Observer Group in India and Pakistan (UNMOGIP), United Nations Multidimensional Integrated Stabilization Mission in Mali (MINUSMA), United Nations Operation in Cote d'Ivoire (UNOCI), United Nations Mission for the Referendum in Western Sahara (MINURSO), United Nations Mission in South Sudan (UNMISS), United Nations Organization Stabilization Mission in the Democratic Republic of the Congo (MONUSCO), United Nations Peace-Keeping Force in Cyprus (UNFICYP), United Nations Stabilization Mission in Haiti (MINUSTAH), and United Nations Truce Supervision Organization (UNTSO)
4) *Economic and Social Council (ECOSOC)*: Commission for Social Development, Commission on Crime Prevention and Criminal Justice, Commission on Narcotics Drugs, Commission on Population and Development, Commission on Science and Technology for Development, Commission on Sustainable Development, Commission on the Status of Women, Economic and Social Commission for Asia and the Pacific (ESCAP), Economic and Social Commission for Western Asia (ESCWA), Economic Commission for Africa (ECA), Economic Commission for Europe (ECE), Economic Commission for Latin America and the Caribbean (ECLAC), Statistical Commission, Food and Agriculture Organization of the United Nations (FAO), International Atomic Energy Agency (IAEA), Preparatory Commission for the Nuclear-Test-Ban Treaty Organization (CTBTO), International Bank for Reconstruction and Development (IBRD), International Center for Secretariat of Investment Disputes (ICSID), International Civil Aviation Organization (ICAO), International Development Association (IDA), International Finance Corporation (IFC), International Fund for Agricultural Development (IFAD), International Labor Organization (ILO), International Maritime Organization (IMO), International Monetary Fund (IMF), International Telecommunication Union (ITU), Multilateral Investment Guarantee Agency (MIGA), Statistical Commission, United Nations Educational, Scientific, and Cultural Organization (UNESCO), United Nations Forum on Forests, United Nations Industrial Development Organization (UNIDO), Universal Postal Union (UPU), World Health Organization (WHO), World Intellectual Property Organization (WIPO), World Meteorological Organization (WMO), World Tourism Organization (UNWTO), and World Trade Organization (WTO), Statistical Commission, UN Forum on Forests
5) *Trusteeship Council* (inactive; no trusteeships at this time)
6) *International Court of Justice (ICJ)*
UN members—(193) Afghanistan, Albania, Algeria, Andorra, Angola, Antigua and Barbuda, Argentina, Armenia, Australia, Austria, Azerbaijan, The Bahamas, Bahrain, Bangladesh, Barbados, Belarus, Belgium, Belize, Benin, Bhutan, Bolivia, Bosnia and Herzegovina,

Botswana, Brazil, Brunei, Bulgaria, Burkina Faso, Burma, Burundi, Cabo Verde, Cambodia, Cameroon, Canada, Central African Republic, Chad, Chile, China, Colombia, Comoros, Democratic Republic of the Congo, Republic of the Congo, Costa Rica, Cote d'Ivoire, Croatia, Cuba, Cyprus, Czech Republic, Denmark, Djibouti, Dominica, Dominican Republic, Ecuador, Egypt, El Salvador, Equatorial Guinea, Eritrea, Estonia, Ethiopia, Fiji, Finland, France, Gabon, The Gambia, Georgia, Germany, Ghana, Greece, Grenada, Guatemala, Guinea, Guinea-Bissau, Guyana, Haiti, Honduras, Hungary, Iceland, India, Indonesia, Iran, Iraq, Ireland, Israel, Italy, Jamaica, Japan, Jordan, Kazakhstan, Kenya, Kiribati, North Korea, South Korea, Kuwait, Kyrgyzstan, Laos, Latvia, Lebanon, Lesotho, Liberia, Libya, Liechtenstein, Lithuania, Luxembourg, Macedonia, Madagascar, Malawi, Malaysia, Maldives, Mali, Malta, Marshall Islands, Mauritania, Mauritius, Mexico, Federated States of Micronesia, Moldova, Monaco, Mongolia, Montenegro, Morocco, Mozambique, Namibia, Nauru, Nepal, Netherlands, NZ, Nicaragua, Niger, Nigeria, Norway, Oman, Pakistan, Palau, Panama, Papua New Guinea, Paraguay, Peru, Philippines, Poland, Portugal, Qatar, Romania, Russia, Rwanda, Saint Kitts and Nevis, Saint Lucia, Saint Vincent and the Grenadines, Samoa, San Marino, Sao Tome and Principe, Saudi Arabia, Senegal, Serbia, Seychelles, Sierra Leone, Singapore, Slovakia, Slovenia, Solomon Islands, Somalia, South Africa, South Sudan, Spain, Sri Lanka, Sudan, Suriname, Swaziland, Sweden, Switzerland, Syria, Tajikistan, Tanzania, Thailand, Timor-Leste, Togo, Tonga, Trinidad and Tobago, Tunisia, Turkey, Turkmenistan, Tuvalu, Uganda, Ukraine, UAE, UK, US, Uruguay, Uzbekistan, Vanuatu, Venezuela, Vietnam, Yemen, Zambia, Zimbabwe; note—all UN members are represented in the General Assembly
observers—(1 plus the Palestine Liberation Organization) Holy See, Palestine Liberation Organization

United Nations Assistance Mission in Afghanistan (UNAMA)
established—January 2010
aim—to support the government of Afghanistan, in its attempt to improve security, governance, and economic development and regional cooperation; protect civilians and support efforts to support human rights
note—gives civilian support only

United Nations Children's Fund (UNICEF)
note—acronym retained from the predecessor organization, UN International Children's Emergency Fund
established—11 December 1946
aim—to help establish child health and welfare services
executive board members—(36) selected on a rotating basis from all regions

United Nations Conference on Trade and Development (UNCTAD)
established—30 December 1964
aim—to promote international
trade members—(194) all UN members plus Holy See

United Nations Development Program (UNDP)
established—22 November 1965
aim—to provide technical assistance to stimulate economic and social development
members (executive board)—(36) selected on a rotating basis from all regions

United Nations Disengagement Observer Force (UNDOF)
established—31 May 1974
aim—to observe the 1973 Arab-Israeli cease-fire; established by the UN Security Council
members—(6) Fiji, India, Ireland, Nepal, Netherlands, Philippines

United Nations Educational, Scientific, and Cultural Organization (UNESCO)
established—16 November 1945; effective—4 November 1946
aim—to promote cooperation in education, science, and culture
members—(194 plus the Palestine Liberation Organization) includes all UN member countries except Liechtenstein (192 total); plus Cook Islands, Niue, and the Palestine Liberation Organization
associate members—(9) Anguilla, Aruba, British Virgin Islands, Cayman Islands, Curacao, Faroe Islands, Macau, Sint Maarten, Tokelau

United Nations Environment Program (UNEP)
established—15 December 1972
aim—to promote international cooperation on all environmental matters
members—(58) selected on a rotating basis from all regions

United Nations General Assembly
established—26 June 1945; effective—24 October 1945
aim—to function as the primary deliberative organ of the UN
members—(193) all UN members are represented in the General Assembly

United Nations High Commissioner for Refugees (UNHCR)
established—3 December 1949; effective—1 January 1951
aim—to ensure the humanitarian treatment of refugees and find permanent solutions to refugee problems
members (executive committee)—(87) Algeria, Argentina, Australia, Austria, Azerbaijan, Bangladesh, Belgium, Benin, Brazil, Bulgaria, Cameroon, Canada, Chile, China, Colombia, Democratic Republic of the Congo, Republic of the Congo, Costa Rica, Cote d'Ivoire, Croatia, Cyprus, Denmark, Djibouti, Ecuador, Egypt, Estonia, Ethiopia, Finland, France, Germany, Ghana, Greece, Guinea, Holy See,

Hungary, India, Iran, Ireland, Israel, Italy, Japan, Jordan, Kenya, South Korea, Lebanon, Lesotho, Luxembourg, Macedonia, Madagascar, Mexico, Moldova, Montenegro, Morocco, Mozambique, Namibia, Netherlands, NZ, Nicaragua, Nigeria, Norway, Pakistan, Philippines, Poland, Portugal, Romania, Russia, Rwanda, Serbia, Slovenia, Somalia, South Africa, Spain, Sudan, Sweden, Switzerland, Tanzania, Thailand, Togo, Tunisia, Turkey, Turkmenistan, Uganda, UK, US, Venezuela, Yemen, Zambia

United Nations Industrial Development Organization (UNIDO)
established—17 November 1966; effective—1 January 1967
aim—UN specialized agency that promotes industrial development especially among the members
members—(174) includes all UN member countries except Andorra, Antigua and Barbuda, Australia, Brunei, Canada, Estonia, Iceland, Kiribati, Latvia, Liechtenstein, Marshall Islands, Federated States of Micronesia, Nauru, Palau, San Marino, Singapore, Solomon Islands, South Sudan, US

United Nations Institute for Training and Research (UNITAR)
established—11 December 1963 adoption of the resolution establishing the Institute; effective—24 March 1965
aim—to help the UN become more effective through training and research
members (Board of Trustees)—(12) Algeria, Brazil, Republic of the Congo, Guatemala, India, Iran, Jamaica, Nigeria, Norway, Russia, South Africa, Switzerland; note - the UN Secretary General can appoint up to 30 members

United Nations Integrated Mission in Timor-Leste (UNMIT)
established—25 August 2006
aim—to support the Government, to support the electoral process, to ensure the restoration and maintenance of public security
members—(15) Australia, Bangladesh, Brazil, China, Fiji, Japan, India, Malaysia, Nepal, NZ, Pakistan, Philippines, Portugal, Sierra Leone, Singapore

United Nations Interim Administration Mission in Kosovo (UNMIK)
established—10 June 1999
aim—to promote the establishment of substantial autonomy and self-government in Kosovo; to perform basic civilian administrative functions; to support the reconstruction of key infrastructure and humanitarian and disaster relief
note—gives civilian support only; works closely with NATO Kosovo Force (KFOR)

United Nations Interim Force in Lebanon (UNIFIL)
established—19 March 1978
aim—to confirm the withdrawal of Israeli forces, and assist in reestablishing Lebanese authority in southern Lebanon; established by the UN Security Council
members—(37) Armenia, Austria, Bangladesh, Belarus, Belgium, Brazil, Brunei, Cambodia, China, Croatia, Cyprus, El Salvador, Finland, France, Germany, Ghana, Greece, Guatemala, Hungary, India, Indonesia, Ireland, Italy, Kenya, South Korea, Macedonia, Malaysia, Nepal, Nigeria, Qatar, Serbia, Sierra Leone, Slovenia, Spain, Sri Lanka, Tanzania, Turkey

United Nations Interim Security Force for Abyei (UNISFA)
established—27 June 2011
aim—to protect civilians and humanitarian workers in Abyei
members—(28) Benin, Bolivia, Brazil, Burundi, Cambodia, Ecuador, Ethiopia, Ghana, Guatemala, Guinea, India, Mongolia, Namibia, Nepal, Nigeria, Paraguay, Peru, Philippines, Russia, Rwanda, Sierra Leone, Sri Lanka, Tanzania, Ukraine, Uruguay, Yemen, Zambia, Zimbabwe

United Nations Military Observer Group in India and Pakistan (UNMOGIP)
established—24 January 1949
aim—to observe the 1949 India-Pakistan cease-fire; established by the UN Security Council
members—(9) Chile, Croatia, Finland, Italy, South Korea, Philippines, Sweden, Thailand, Uruguay

United Nations Mission for the Referendum in Western Sahara (MINURSO)
established—29 April 1991
aim—to supervise the cease-fire and conduct a referendum in Western Sahara; established by the UN Security Council
members—(30) Argentina, Austria, Bangladesh, Brazil, China, Croatia, Egypt, El Salvador, France, Ghana, Guinea, Honduras, Hungary, Ireland, Italy, South Korea, Malawi, Malaysia, Mongolia, Nepal, Nigeria, Pakistan, Paraguay, Peru, Poland, Russia, Sri Lanka, Togo, Uruguay, Yemen

United Nations Mission in Liberia (UNMIL)
established—19 September 2003
aim—to support the cease-fire agreement and peace process, protect UN facilities and people, support humanitarian activities, and assist in national security reform
members—(43) Bangladesh, Benin, Bolivia, Brazil, Bulgaria, China, Croatia, Denmark, Ecuador, Egypt, El Salvador, Ethiopia, Finland, France, The Gambia, Ghana, Indonesia, Jordan, Kenya, South Korea, Kyrgyzstan, Malaysia, Moldova, Montenegro, Namibia, Nepal, Niger, Nigeria, Pakistan, Paraguay, Peru, Philippines, Poland, Romania, Russia, Senegal, Serbia, Togo, Ukraine, US, Yemen, Zambia, Zimbabwe

United Nations Mission in the Central African Republic and Chad (MINURCAT)

established on 25 September 2007; to create the security and conditions which will to contribute to the protection of refugees, displaced persons, and citizens in danger, to facilitate the provision of humanitarian assistance in eastern Chad and the northeastern Central African Republic, to create favorable conditions for the reconstruction and economic and social development of these areas; members were Bangladesh, Benin, Burkina Faso, Democratic Republic of the Congo, Egypt, Ethiopia, Ghana, Ireland, Kenya, Mali, Mongolia, Namibia, Nepal, Nigeria, Norway, Pakistan, Poland, Russia, Rwanda, Senegal, Serbia, Sri Lanka, Togo, Tunisia, US; MINURCAT was dissolved in December 2010

United Nations Mission in the Republic of South Sudan (UNMISS)

established—8 July 2011
aim—to consolidate peace and security and to establish the conditions in South Sudan which will strengthen its ability to govern effectively and democratically and establish good relations with its neighbors
members—(54) Australia, Bangladesh, Belarus, Benin, Bolivia, Brazil, Cambodia, Canada, China, Denmark, Ecuador, Egypt, El Salvador, Fiji, Germany, Ghana, Guatemala, Guinea, India, Indonesia, Italy, Japan, Jordan, Kenya, South Korea, Kyrgyzstan, Moldova, Mongolia, Namibia, Nepal, Netherlands, NZ, Nigeria, Norway, Papua New Guinea, Paraguay, Peru, Poland, Romania, Russia, Rwanda, Senegal, Sri Lanka, Sweden, Switzerland, Tanzania, Timor-Leste, Togo, Uganda, Ukraine, UK, US, Yemen, Zambia

United Nations Mission in the Sudan (UNMIS)

established in March 2005 to support implementation of the comprehensive Peace Agreement by monitoring and verifying the implementation of the Cease Fire Agreement, by observing and monitoring movements of armed groups, and by helping disarm, demobilizing and reintegrating armed bands; members were Australia, Bangladesh, Belgium, Benin, Bolivia, Brazil, Burkina Faso, Cambodia, Canada, China, Croatia, Denmark, Ecuador, Egypt, El Salvador, Fiji, Finland, Germany, Greece, Guatemala, Guinea, India, Indonesia, Iran, Japan, Jordan, Kenya, Kyrgyzstan, Malaysia, Moldova, Mongolia, Morocco, Namibia, Nepal, Netherland, NZ, Niger, Norway, Pakistan, Paraguay, Peru, Philippines, Poland, Qatar, Romania, Russia, Rwanda, Sierra Leone, Spain, Sweden, Switzerland, Tanzania, Thailand, Turkey, Uganda, Ukraine, UK, Yemen, Zambia, Zimbabwe; UNMIS was dissolved on 9 July 2011

United Nations Multidimensional Integrated Stabilization Mission in Mali, MINUSMA

established—25 April 2013
aim—to support political processes and carry out a number of security-related tasks
members—(36) Bangladesh, Benin, Burkina Faso, Cambodia, Chad, China, Cote d'Ivoire, Denmark, Dominican Republic, Estonia, Finland, France, The Gambia, Germany, Ghana, Guinea, Guinea-Bissau, Italy, Jordan, Kenya, Liberia, Mauritania, Nepal, Netherlands, Niger, Nigeria, Norway, Rwanda, Senegal, Sierra Leone, Sweden, Switzerland, Togo, UK, US, Yemen

United Nations Operation in Cote d'Ivoire (UNOCI)

established—27 February 2004
aim—to facilitate the implementation by the Ivorian parties of the peace agreement signed by them in January 2003
members—(44) Bangladesh, Benin, Bolivia, Brazil, Chad, China, Ecuador, Egypt, El Salvador, Ethiopia, France, The Gambia, Ghana, Guatemala, Guinea, India, Ireland, Jordan, South Korea, Malawi, Moldova, Morocco, Namibia, Nepal, Niger, Nigeria, Pakistan, Paraguay, Peru, Philippines, Poland, Romania, Russia, Senegal, Serbia, Tanzania, Togo, Tunisia, Uganda, Ukraine, Uruguay, Yemen, Zambia, Zimbabwe

United Nations Organization Stabilization Mission in the Democratic Republic of the Congo (MONUSCO)

established—28 May 2010
aim—to protect the civilians; to assist the government in the areas of stabilization and peace consolidation
members—(49) Algeria, Bangladesh, Belgium, Benin, Bolivia, Bosnia and Herzegovina, Burkina Faso, Cameroon, Canada, China, Czech Republic, Egypt, France, Ghana, Guatemala, Guinea, India, Indonesia, Ireland, Jordan, Kenya, Malawi, Malaysia, Mali, Mongolia, Morocco, Nepal, Niger, Nigeria, Pakistan, Paraguay, Peru, Poland, Romania, Russia, Senegal, Serbia, South Africa, Sri Lanka, Sweden, Switzerland, Tanzania, Tunisia, Ukraine, UK, US, Uruguay, Yemen, Zambia

United Nations Peacekeeping Force in Cyprus (UNFICYP)

established—4 March 1964
aim—to serve as a peacekeeping force between Greek Cypriots and Turkish Cypriots in Cyprus; established by the UN Security Council
members—(13) Argentina, Austria, Brazil, Canada, Chile, China, Croatia, Hungary, Paraguay, Serbia, Slovakia, Ukraine, UK

United Nations Population Fund (UNFPA)

note—acronym retained from predecessor organization UN Fund for Population Activities
established—July 1967
aim—to assist both developed and developing countries to deal with their population problems
members (executive board)—(36) selected on a rotating basis from all regions

United Nations Relief and Works Agency for Palestine Refugees in the Near East (UNRWA)

established—8 December 1949
aim—to provide assistance to Palestinian refugees
members (advisory commission)—(25) Australia, Belgium, Canada, Denmark, Egypt, Finland, France, Germany, Ireland, Italy, Japan, Jordan, Kuwait, Lebanon, Luxembourg, Netherlands, Norway, Saudi Arabia, Spain, Sweden, Switzerland, Syria, Turkey, UK, US
observers—(3) EC, LAS, Palestine Liberation Organization

United Nations Research Institute for Social Development (UNRISD)

established—1963

aim—to conduct research into the problems of economic development during different phases of economic growth

members—no country members, but a Board of Directors consisting of a chairman appointed by the UN Secretary General and 10 members confirmed by ECOSOC and a representative of the Secretary General

United Nations Secretariat

established—26 June 1945; effective—24 October 1945

aim—to serve as the primary administrative organ of the UN; a Secretary General is appointed for a five-year term by the General Assembly on the recommendation of the Security Council

members—the UN Secretary General and staff

United Nations Security Council (UNSC)

established—26 June 1945; effective—24 October 1945

aim—to maintain international peace and security

permanent members—(5) China, France, Russia, UK, US

nonpermanent members— (10) elected for two-year terms by the UN General Assembly; Argentina (2013-14), Australia (2013-14), Chad (2014-15), Chile (2014-15), Jordan (2014-15), Lithuania (2014-15), Luxembourg (2013-14), South Korea (2013-14), Nigeria (2014-15), Rwanda (2013-14)

United Nations Truce Supervision Organization (UNTSO)

established—June 1948

aim—to supervise the 1948 Arab-Israeli cease-fire; currently supports timely deployment of reinforcements to other peacekeeping operations in the region as needed; initially established by the UN Security Council

members—(24) Argentina, Australia, Austria, Belgium, Canada, Chile, China, Denmark, Estonia, Finland, France, Ireland, Italy, Nepal, Netherlands, NZ, Norway, Russia, Serbia, Slovakia, Slovenia, Sweden, Switzerland, US

United Nations Trusteeship Council

established on 26 June 1945, effective on 24 October 1945, to supervise the administration of the 11 UN trust territories; members were China, France, Russia, UK, US; it formally suspended operations 1 November 1994 after the Trust Territory of the Pacific Islands (Palau) became the Republic of Palau, a constitutional government in free association with the US; the Trusteeship Council was not dissolved

United Nations University (UNU)

established—3 December 1973

aim—to conduct research in development, welfare, and human survival and to train scholars

members—(16 members of UNU Council and the Rector are appointed by the Secretary General of the United Nations and the Director General of UNESCO)

Universal Postal Union (UPU)

established—9 October 1874, affiliated with the UN 15 November 1947; effective—1 July 1948

aim—to promote international postal cooperation; a UN specialized agency

members—(192) includes all UN member countries except Andorra, Marshall Islands, Federated States of Micronesia, Palau (189 total); plus Aruba, Curacao, and Sint Maarten; and Holy See; and Overseas Territories of the UK; note—includes the following dependencies or areas of special interest: Australia (Norfolk Island), China (Hong Kong, Macau), Denmark (Faroe Islands, Greenland), France (French Guiana, French Polynesia including Clipperton Island, French Southern and Antarctic Lands, Guadeloupe, Martinique, Mayotte, New Caledonia, Reunion, Saint Barthelemy, Saint Martin, Saint Pierre and Miquelon, Scattered Islands [Bassas da India, Europe, Juan de Nova, Glorioso Islands, Tromelin], Wallis and Futuna), Netherlands (Aruba, Curacao, Sint Maarten), NZ (Cook Island, Niue, Tokelau), UK (Guernsey, Isle of Man, Jersey; Anguilla, Bermuda, British Indian Ocean Territory, British Virgin Islands, Cayman Islands, Falkland Islands, Gibraltar, Montserrat, Pitcairn Islands, Saint Helena, Ascension, and Tristan da Cunha, South Georgia and South Sandwich Islands, Turks and Caicos), US (American Samoa, Guam, Northern Mariana Islands, Puerto Rico, Virgin Islands)

Warsaw Pact (WP)

established 14 May 1955 to promote mutual defense; members met 1 July 1991 to dissolve the alliance; member states at the time of dissolution were: Bulgaria, Czechoslovakia, Hungary, Poland, Romania, and the USSR; earlier members included German Democratic Republic (GDR) and Albania

West African Development Bank (WADB)

note—also known as Banque Ouest-Africaine de Developpement (BOAD); is a financial institution of WAEMU

established—14 November 1973

aim—to promote regional economic development and integration

regional members—(8) Benin, Burkina Faso, Cote d'Ivoire, Guinea-Bissau, Mali, Niger, Senegal, Togo

West African Economic and Monetary Union (WAEMU)

note—also known as Union Economique et Monetaire Ouest Africaine (UEMOA)

established—1 August 1994

aim—to increase competitiveness of members' economic markets; to create a common market

members—(8) Benin, Burkina Faso, Cote d'Ivoire, Guinea-Bissau, Mali, Niger, Senegal, Togo

Western European Union (WEU)

established 23 October 1954; effective—6 May 1955; aim to provide mutual defense and to move toward political unification; 10 members: Belgium, France, Germany, Greece, Italy, Luxembourg, Netherlands, Portugal, Spain, UK; 6 associate members: Czech Republic, Hungary, Iceland, Norway, Poland, Turkey; 7 associate partners: Bulgaria, Estonia, Latvia, Lithuania, Romania, Slovakia, Slovenia; 5 observers: Austria, Denmark, Finland, Ireland, Sweden; note—to cease existence completely by June 2011

World Bank Group

includes International Bank for Reconstruction and Development (IBRD), International Development Association (IDA), International Finance Corporation (IFC), and Multilateral Investment Guarantee Agency (MIGA)

World Confederation of Labor (WCL)

established 19 June 1920 as the International Federation of Christian Trade Unions (IFCTU), renamed 4 October 1968; aim was to promote the trade union movement; on 31 October 2006 it merged with the International Confederation of Free Trade Unions (ICFTU) to form the International Trade Union Confederation (ITUC); members were (105 national organizations) Antigua and Barbuda, Argentina, Aruba, Austria, Bangladesh, Belgium, Belize, Benin, Bolivia, Brazil, Bulgaria, Burkina Faso, Cameroon, Canada, Central African Republic, Chad, Chile, Colombia, Democratic Republic of the Congo, Republic of the Congo, Costa Rica, Cote d'Ivoire, Cuba, Cyprus, Czech Republic, Denmark, Dominica, Dominican Republic, Ecuador, El Salvador, France, French Guiana, Gabon, The Gambia, Ghana, Guadeloupe, Guatemala, Guinea, Guyana, Haiti, Honduras, Hong Kong, Hungary, India, Indonesia, Iran, Italy, Japan, Kazakhstan, South Korea, Liberia, Libya, Liechtenstein, Lithuania, Luxembourg, Macedonia, Madagascar, Malawi, Malaysia, Malta, Martinique, Mauritania, Mauritius, Mexico, Morocco, Namibia, Nepal, Netherlands, Nicaragua, Niger, Pakistan, Panama, Paraguay, Peru, Philippines, Poland, Portugal, Puerto Rico, Romania, Rwanda, Saint Lucia, Saint Vincent and the Grenadines, Sao Tome and Principe, Senegal, Serbia, Sierra Leone, Singapore, Slovakia, South Africa, Spain, Sri Lanka, Suriname, Switzerland, Taiwan, Thailand, Togo, Trinidad and Tobago, Ukraine, US, Uruguay, Venezuela, Vietnam, Zambia, Zimbabwe

World Customs Organization (WCO)

note—began as the Customs Cooperation Council (CCC)
established—15 December 1950
aim—to promote international cooperation in customs matters
members—(180) Afghanistan, Albania, Algeria, Andorra, Angola, Argentina, Armenia, Australia, Austria, Azerbaijan, The Bahamas, Bahrain, Bangladesh, Barbados, Belarus, Belgium, Belize, Benin, Bermuda, Bhutan, Bolivia, Bosnia and Herzegovina, Botswana, Brazil, Brunei, Bulgaria, Burkina Faso, Burma, Burundi, Cabo Verde, Cambodia, Cameroon, Canada, Central African Republic, Chad, Chile, China, Colombia, Comoros, Democratic Republic of the Congo, Republic of the Congo, Costa Rica, Cote d'Ivoire, Croatia, Cuba, Curacao, Cyprus, Czech Republic, Denmark, Djibouti, Dominican Republic, EU, Ecuador, Egypt, El Salvador, Eritrea, Estonia, Ethiopia, Fiji, Finland, France, Gabon, The Gambia, Georgia, Germany, Ghana, Greece, Guatemala, Guinea, Guinea-Bissau, Guyana, Haiti, Honduras, Hong Kong, Hungary, Iceland, India, Indonesia, Iran, Iraq, Ireland, Israel, Italy, Jamaica, Japan, Jordan, Kazakhstan, Kenya, South Korea, Kuwait, Kyrgyzstan, Laos, Latvia, Lebanon, Lesotho, Liberia, Libya, Lithuania, Luxembourg, Macau, Macedonia, Madagascar, Malawi, Malaysia, Maldives, Mali, Malta, Mauritania, Mauritius, Mexico, Moldova, Mongolia, Montenegro, Morocco, Mozambique, Namibia, Nepal, Netherlands, NZ, Nicaragua, Niger, Nigeria, Norway, Oman, Pakistan, Panama, Papua New Guinea, Paraguay, Peru, Philippines, Poland, Portugal, Qatar, Romania, Russia, Rwanda, Saint Lucia, Samoa, Sao Tome and Principe, Saudi Arabia, Senegal, Serbia, Seychelles, Sierra Leone, Singapore, Slovakia, Slovenia, Somalia, South Africa, South Sudan, Spain, Sri Lanka, Sudan, Swaziland, Sweden, Switzerland, Syria, Tajikistan, Tanzania, Thailand, Timor-Leste, Togo, Tonga, Trinidad and Tobago, Tunisia, Turkey, Turkmenistan, Uganda, Ukraine, UAE, UK, US, Uruguay, Uzbekistan, Vanuatu, Venezuela, Vietnam, Yemen, Zambia, Zimbabwe

World Federation of Trade Unions (WFTU)

established—3 October 1945
aim—to promote the trade union movement
members—(in 2013 there were 126 participating nations and territories and the Palestine Liberation Organization); (in 2009 there were 125 nations and the Palestine Liberation Organization) Afghanistan, Albania, Angola, Antigua and Barbuda, Argentina, Armenia, Australia, Austria, Azerbaijan, Bahrain, Bangladesh, Barbados, Belarus, Benin, Bolivia, Botswana, Brazil, Bulgaria, Burkina Faso, Cambodia, Cameroon, Canada, Chile, Colombia, Democratic Republic of the Congo, Republic of the Congo, Costa Rica, Cote d'Ivoire, Cuba, Cyprus, Czech Republic, Djibouti, Dominican Republic, Ecuador, Egypt, El Salvador, Eritrea, Ethiopia, Fiji, Finland, France, French Guiana, The Gambia, Ghana, Greece, Guadeloupe, Guatemala, Guinea, Guinea-Bissau, Guyana, Haiti, Honduras, Hungary, India, Indonesia, Iran, Iraq, Jamaica, Japan, Jordan, Kazakhstan, North Korea, Kuwait, Kyrgyzstan, Laos, Lebanon, Lesotho, Liberia, Libya, Madagascar, Malawi, Malaysia, Mali, Martinique, Mauritius, Mexico, Mozambique, Nepal, New Caledonia, NZ, Niger, Nigeria, Oman, Pakistan, Panama, Papua New Guinea, Peru, Philippines, Poland, Portugal, Puerto Rico, Reunion, Romania, Russia, Saint Lucia, Saint Pierre and Miquelon, Saint Vincent and the Grenadines, Saudi Arabia, Senegal, Sierra Leone, Slovakia, Solomon Islands, Somalia, South Africa, Sri Lanka, Sudan, Sweden, Syria, Tajikistan, Tanzania, Thailand, Togo, Trinidad and Tobago, Tunisia, Turkey, Turkmenistan, Uganda, Ukraine, Uruguay, Uzbekistan, Vanuatu, Venezuela, Vietnam, Yemen, Zimbabwe, Palestine Liberation Organization

World Food Program (WFP)

established—24 November 1961
aim—to provide food aid in support of economic development or disaster relief; an ECOSOC organization
members (Executive Board)—(36) selected on a rotating basis from all regions

World Health Organization (WHO)

established—22 July 1946; effective—7 April 1948
aim—to deal with health matters worldwide; a UN specialized agency
members—(194) includes all UN member countries except Liechtenstein (192 total); plus Cook Islands and Niue

World Intellectual Property Organization (WIPO)

established—14 July 1967; effective—26 April 1970
aim—to furnish protection for literary, artistic, and scientific works; a UN specialized agency
members—(185) includes all UN member countries except Marshall Islands, Federated States of Micronesia, Nauru, Palau, Solomon Islands, South Sudan, Timor-Leste, Tuvalu (185 total); plus Holy See

World Meteorological Organization (WMO)

established—11 October 1947; effective—4 April 1951
aim—to sponsor meteorological cooperation; a UN specialized agency
members—(185) includes all UN member countries except Andorra, Equatorial Guinea, Grenada, Liechtenstein, Marshall Islands, Nauru, Palau, Saint Kitts and Nevis, Saint Vincent and the Grenadines, San Marino (183 total); plus Cook Islands and Niue

World Tourism Organization (UNWTO)

established—2 January 1975
aim—to promote tourism as a means of contributing to economic development, international understanding, and peace
members—(156) Afghanistan, Albania, Algeria, Andorra, Angola, Argentina, Armenia, Australia, Austria, Azerbaijan, The Bahamas, Bahrain, Bangladesh, Belarus, Benin, Bhutan, Bolivia, Bosnia and Herzegovina, Botswana, Brazil, Brunei, Bulgaria, Burkina Faso, Burma, Burundi, Cabo Verde, Cambodia, Cameroon, Central African Republic, Chad, Chile, China, Colombia, Democratic Republic of the Congo, Republic of the Congo, Costa Rica, Cote d'Ivoire, Croatia, Cuba, Cyprus, Czech Republic, Djibouti, Dominican Republic, Ecuador, Egypt, El Salvador, Equatorial Guinea, Eritrea, Ethiopia, Fiji, France, Gabon, The Gambia, Georgia, Germany, Ghana, Greece, Guatemala, Guinea, Guinea-Bissau, Haiti, Honduras, Hungary, India, Indonesia, Iran, Iraq, Israel, Italy, Jamaica, Japan, Jordan, Kazakhstan, Kenya, North Korea, South Korea, Kuwait, Kyrgyzstan, Laos, Lebanon, Lesotho, Liberia, Libya, Lithuania, Macedonia, Madagascar, Malawi, Malaysia, Maldives, Mali, Malta, Mauritania, Mauritius, Mexico, Moldova, Monaco, Mongolia, Montenegro, Morocco, Mozambique, Namibia, Nepal, Netherlands, Nicaragua, Niger, Nigeria, Norway, Oman, Pakistan, Panama, Papua New Guinea, Paraguay, Peru, Philippines, Poland, Portugal, Qatar, Romania, Russia, Rwanda, San Marino, Sao Tome and Principe, Saudi Arabia, Senegal, Serbia, Seychelles, Sierra Leone, Slovakia, Slovenia, South Africa, Spain, Sri Lanka, Sudan, Swaziland, Switzerland, Syria, Tajikistan, Tanzania, Thailand, Timor-Leste, Togo, Trinidad and Tobago, Tunisia, Turkey, Turkmenistan, Uganda, Ukraine, UAE, Uruguay, Uzbekistan, Vanuatu, Venezuela, Vietnam, Yemen, Zambia, Zimbabwe
associate members—(6) Aruba, Flemish Community of Belgium, Hong Kong, Macau, Madeira Islands, Puerto Rico
observers—(1 plus Palestine Liberation Organization) Holy See, Palestine Liberation Organization

World Trade Organization (WTO)

note—succeeded General Agreement on Tariff and Trade (GATT)
established—15 April 1994; effective—1 January 1995
aim—to provide a forum to resolve trade conflicts between members and to carry on negotiations with the goal of further lowering and/or eliminating tariffs and other trade barriers
members—(159) Albania, Angola, Antigua and Barbuda, Argentina, Armenia, Australia, Austria, Bahrain, Bangladesh, Barbados, Belgium, Belize, Benin, Bolivia, Botswana, Brazil, Brunei, Bulgaria, Burkina Faso, Burma, Burundi, Cabo Verde, Cambodia, Cameroon, Canada, Central African Republic, Chad, Chile, China, Colombia, Democratic Republic of the Congo, Republic of the Congo, Costa Rica, Cote d'Ivoire, Croatia, Cuba, Cyprus, Czech Republic, Denmark, Djibouti, Dominica, Dominican Republic, Ecuador, Egypt, El Salvador, Estonia, EU, Fiji, Finland, France, Gabon, The Gambia, Georgia, Germany, Ghana, Greece, Grenada, Guatemala, Guinea, Guinea-Bissau, Guyana, Haiti, Honduras, Hong Kong, Hungary, Iceland, India, Indonesia, Ireland, Israel, Italy, Jamaica, Japan, Jordan, Kenya, South Korea, Kuwait, Kyrgyzstan, Laos, Latvia, Lesotho, Liechtenstein, Lithuania, Luxembourg, Macau, Macedonia, Madagascar, Malawi, Malaysia, Maldives, Mali, Malta, Mauritania, Mauritius, Mexico, Moldova, Mongolia, Montenegro, Morocco, Mozambique, Namibia, Nepal, Netherlands, NZ, Nicaragua, Niger, Nigeria, Norway, Oman, Pakistan, Panama, Papua New Guinea, Paraguay, Peru, Philippines, Poland, Portugal, Qatar, Romania, Russia, Rwanda, Saint Kitts and Nevis, Saint Lucia, Saint Vincent and the Grenadines, Samoa, Saudi Arabia, Senegal, Sierra Leone, Singapore, Slovakia, Slovenia, Solomon Islands, South Africa, Spain, Sri Lanka, Suriname, Swaziland, Sweden, Switzerland, Taiwan, Tajikistan, Tanzania, Thailand, Togo, Tonga, Trinidad and Tobago, Tunisia, Turkey, Uganda, Ukraine, UAE, UK, US, Uruguay, Vanuatu, Venezuela, Vietnam, Zambia, Zimbabwe
observers—(25) Afghanistan, Algeria, Andorra, Azerbaijan, The Bahamas, Belarus, Bhutan, Bosnia and Herzegovina, Comoros, Equatorial Guinea, Ethiopia, Holy See, Iran, Iraq, Kazakhstan, Lebanon, Liberia, Libya, Sao Tome and Principe, Serbia, Seychelles, Sudan, Syria, Uzbekistan, Yemen; note - with the exception of the Holy See, an observer must start accession negotiations within five years of becoming observers

Zangger Committee (ZC)

established—early 1970s
aim—to establish guidelines for the export control provisions of the Nonproliferation of Nuclear Weapons Treaty (NPT)
members—(39) Argentina, Australia, Austria, Belarus, Belgium, Bulgaria, Canada, China, Croatia, Czech Republic, Denmark, Finland, France, Germany, Greece, Hungary, Ireland, Italy, Japan, Kazakhstan, South Korea, Luxembourg, Netherlands, NZ, Norway, Poland, Portugal, Romania, Russia, Slovakia, Slovenia, South Africa, Spain, Sweden, Switzerland, Turkey, Ukraine, UK, US
observers—(1) European Commission

APPENDIX C

Air Pollution

see Convention on Long-Range Transboundary Air Pollution

Air Pollution-Nitrogen Oxides

see Protocol to the 1979 Convention on Long-Range Transboundary Air Pollution Concerning the Control of Emissions of Nitrogen Oxides or Their Transboundary Fluxes

Air Pollution-Persistent Organic Pollutants

see Protocol to the 1979 Convention on Long-Range Transboundary Air Pollution on Persistent Organic Pollutants

Air Pollution-Sulphur 85

see Protocol to the 1979 Convention on Long-Range Transboundary Air Pollution on the Reduction of Sulphur Emissions or Their Transboundary Fluxes by at least 30%

Air Pollution-Sulphur 94

see Protocol to the 1979 Convention on Long-Range Transboundary Air Pollution on Further Reduction of Sulphur Emissions

Air Pollution-Volatile Organic Compounds

see Protocol to the 1979 Convention on Long-Range Transboundary Air Pollution Concerning the Control of Emissions of Volatile Organic Compounds or Their Transboundary Fluxes

Antarctic—Environmental Protocol

see Protocol on Environmental Protection to the Antarctic Treaty

Antarctic Treaty

opened for signature—1 December 1959
entered into force—23 June 1961
objective—to ensure that Antarctica is used for peaceful purposes only (such as international cooperation in scientific research); to defer the question of territorial claims asserted by some nations and not recognized by others; to provide an international forum for management of the region; applies to land and ice shelves south of 60 degrees south latitude
parties—(50) Argentina, Australia, Austria, Belarus, Belgium, Brazil, Bulgaria, Canada, Chile, China, Colombia, Cuba, Czech Republic, Denmark, Ecuador, Estonia, Finland, France, Germany, Greece, Guatemala, Hungary, India, Italy, Japan, North Korea, South Korea, Malaysia, Monaco, Netherlands, NZ, Norway, Pakistan, Papua New Guinea, Peru, Poland, Portugal, Romania, Russia, Slovakia, South Africa, Spain, Sweden, Switzerland, Turkey, Ukraine, UK, US, Uruguay, Venezuela

Basel Convention on the Control of Transboundary Movements of Hazardous Wastes and Their Disposal

note—abbreviated as Hazardous Wastes
opened for signature—22 March 1989
entered into force—5 May 1992
objective—to reduce transboundary movements of wastes subject to the Convention to a minimum consistent with the environmentally sound and efficient management of such wastes; to minimize the amount and toxicity of wastes generated and ensure their environmentally sound management as closely as possible to the source of generation; and to assist LDCs in environmentally sound management of the hazardous and other wastes they generate
parties—(171) Albania, Algeria, Andorra, Antigua and Barbuda, Argentina, Armenia, Australia, Austria, Azerbaijan, The Bahamas, Bahrain, Bangladesh, Barbados, Belarus, Belgium, Belize, Benin, Bhutan, Bolivia, Bosnia and Herzegovina, Botswana, Brazil, Brunei, Bulgaria, Burkina Faso, Burundi, Cambodia, Cameroon, Canada, Cape Verde, Central African Republic, Chad, Chile, China, Colombia, Comoros, Democratic Republic of the Congo, Republic of the Congo, Cook Islands, Costa Rica, Cote d'Ivoire, Croatia, Cuba, Cyprus, Czech Republic, Denmark, Djibouti, Dominica, Dominican Republic, Ecuador, Egypt, El Salvador, Equatorial Guinea, Eritrea, Estonia, Ethiopia, EU, Finland, France, Gabon, The Gambia, Georgia, Germany, Ghana, Greece, Guatemala, Guinea, Guinea-Bissau, Guyana, Honduras, Hungary, Iceland, India, Indonesia, Iran, Ireland, Israel, Italy, Jamaica, Japan, Jordan, Kazakhstan, Kenya, Kiribati, North Korea, South Korea, Kuwait, Kyrgyzstan, Latvia, Lebanon, Lesotho, Liberia, Libya, Liechtenstein, Lithuania, Luxembourg, Macedonia, Madagascar, Malawi, Malaysia, Maldives, Mali, Malta, Marshall Islands, Mauritania, Mauritius, Mexico, Federated States of Micronesia, Moldova, Monaco, Mongolia, Montenegro, Morocco, Mozambique, Namibia, Nauru, Nepal, Netherlands, NZ, Nicaragua, Niger, Nigeria, Norway, Oman, Pakistan, Panama, Papua New Guinea, Paraguay, Peru, Philippines, Poland, Portugal, Qatar, Romania, Russia, Rwanda, Saint Kitts and Nevis, Saint Lucia, Saint Vincent and the Grenadines, Samoa, Saudi Arabia, Senegal, Serbia, Seychelles, Singapore, Slovakia, Slovenia, South Africa, Spain, Sri Lanka, Sudan, Swaziland, Sweden, Switzerland, Syria, Tanzania, Thailand, Trinidad and Tobago, Tunisia, Turkey, Turkmenistan, Uganda, Ukraine, UAE, UK, Uruguay, Uzbekistan, Venezuela, Vietnam, Yemen, Zambia
countries that have signed, but not yet ratified—(3) Afghanistan, Haiti, US

Biodiversity

see Convention on Biological Diversity

Climate Change
see United Nations Framework Convention on Climate Change

Climate Change-Kyoto Protocol
see Kyoto Protocol to the United Nations Framework Convention on Climate Change

Convention for the Conservation of Antarctic Seals
note—abbreviated as Antarctic Seals
opened for signature—1 June 1972
entered into force—11 March 1978
objective—to promote and achieve the protection, scientific study, and rational use of Antarctic seals, and to maintain a satisfactory balance within the ecological system of Antarctica
parties—(16) Argentina, Australia, Belgium, Brazil, Canada, Chile, France, Germany, Italy, Japan, Norway, Poland, Russia, South Africa, UK, US
countries that have signed, but not yet ratified—(1) NZ

Convention on Biological Diversity
note—abbreviated as Biodiversity
opened for signature—5 June 1992
entered into force—29 December 1993
objective—to develop national strategies for the conservation and sustainable use of biological diversity and to address the fair and equitable sharing of benefits arising out of the utilization of genetic resources
parties—(191) Afghanistan, Albania, Algeria, Andorra, Angola, Antigua and Barbuda, Argentina, Armenia, Australia, Austria, Azerbaijan, The Bahamas, Bahrain, Bangladesh, Barbados, Belarus, Belgium, Belize, Benin, Bhutan, Bolivia, Bosnia and Herzegovina, Botswana, Brazil, Brunei, Bulgaria, Burkina Faso, Burma, Burundi, Cambodia, Cameroon, Canada, Cape Verde, Central African Republic, Chad, Chile, China, Colombia, Comoros, Democratic Republic of the Congo, Republic of the Congo, Cook Islands, Costa Rica, Cote d'Ivoire, Croatia, Cuba, Cyprus, Czech Republic, Denmark, Djibouti, Dominica, Dominican Republic, Ecuador, Egypt, El Salvador, Equatorial Guinea, Eritrea, Estonia, Ethiopia, EU, Fiji, Finland, France, Gabon, The Gambia, Georgia, Germany, Ghana, Greece, Grenada, Guatemala, Guinea, Guinea-Bissau, Guyana, Haiti, Honduras, Hungary, Iceland, India, Indonesia, Iran, Iraq, Ireland, Israel, Italy, Jamaica, Japan, Jordan, Kazakhstan, Kenya, Kiribati, North Korea, South Korea, Kuwait, Kyrgyzstan, Laos, Latvia, Lebanon, Lesotho, Liberia, Libya, Liechtenstein, Lithuania, Luxembourg, Macedonia, Madagascar, Malawi, Malaysia, Maldives, Mali, Malta, Marshall Islands, Mauritania, Mauritius, Mexico, Federated States of Micronesia, Moldova, Monaco, Mongolia, Montenegro, Morocco, Mozambique, Namibia, Nauru, Nepal, Netherlands, NZ, Nicaragua, Niger, Nigeria, Niue, Norway, Oman, Pakistan, Palau, Panama, Papua New Guinea, Paraguay, Peru, Philippines, Poland, Portugal, Qatar, Romania, Russia, Rwanda, Saint Kitts and Nevis, Saint Lucia, Saint Vincent and the Grenadines, Samoa, San Marino, Sao Tome and Principe, Saudi Arabia, Senegal, Serbia, Seychelles, Sierra Leone, Singapore, Slovakia, Slovenia, Solomon Islands, Somalia, South Africa, Spain, Sri Lanka, Sudan, Suriname, Swaziland, Sweden, Switzerland, Syria, Tajikistan, Tanzania, Thailand, Timor-Leste, Togo, Tonga, Trinidad and Tobago, Tunisia, Turkey, Turkmenistan, Tuvalu, Uganda, Ukraine, UAE, UK, Uruguay, Uzbekistan, Vanuatu, Venezuela, Vietnam, Yemen, Zambia, Zimbabwe
countries that have signed, but not yet ratified—(1) US

Convention on Fishing and Conservation of Living Resources of the High Seas
note—abbreviated as Marine Life Conservation
opened for signature—29 April 1958
entered into force—20 March 1966
objective—to solve through international cooperation the problems involved in the conservation of living resources of the high seas, considering that because of the development of modern technology some of these resources are in danger of being overexploited
parties—(39) Australia, Belgium, Bosnia and Herzegovina, Burkina Faso, Cambodia, Colombia, Republic of the Congo, Denmark, Dominican Republic, Fiji, Finland, France, Haiti, Jamaica, Kenya, Lesotho, Madagascar, Malawi, Malaysia, Mauritius, Mexico, Montenegro, Netherlands, Nigeria, Portugal, Senegal, Serbia, Sierra Leone, Solomon Islands, South Africa, Spain, Switzerland, Thailand, Tonga, Trinidad and Tobago, Uganda, UK, US, Venezuela
countries that have signed, but not yet ratified—(21) Afghanistan, Argentina, Bolivia, Canada, Costa Rica, Cuba, Ghana, Iceland, Indonesia, Iran, Ireland, Israel, Lebanon, Liberia, Nepal, NZ, Pakistan, Panama, Sri Lanka, Tunisia, Uruguay

Convention on Long-Range Transboundary Air Pollution
note—abbreviated as Air Pollution
opened for signature—13 November 1979
entered into force—16 March 1983
objective—to protect the human environment against air pollution and, as far as possible, to gradually reduce and prevent air pollution, including long-range transboundary air pollution
parties—(51) Albania, Armenia, Austria, Azerbaijan, Belarus, Belgium, Bosnia and Herzegovina, Bulgaria, Canada, Croatia, Cyprus, Czech Republic, Denmark, Estonia, EU, Finland, France, Georgia, Germany, Greece, Hungary, Iceland, Ireland, Italy, Kazakhstan, Kyrgyzstan, Latvia, Liechtenstein, Lithuania, Luxembourg, Macedonia, Malta, Moldova, Monaco, Montenegro, Netherlands, Norway, Poland, Portugal, Romania, Russia, Serbia, Slovakia, Slovenia, Spain, Sweden, Switzerland, Turkey, Ukraine, UK, US
countries that have signed, but not yet ratified—(2) Holy See, San Marino

Convention on Wetlands of International Importance Especially as Waterfowl Habitat (Ramsar)

note—abbreviated as Wetlands
opened for signature—2 February 1971
entered into force—21 December 1975
objective—to stem the progressive encroachment on and loss of wetlands now and in the future
parties—(168) Albania, Algeria, Andorra, Antigua and Barbuda, Argentina, Armenia, Australia, Austria, Azerbaijan, The Bahamas, Bahrain, Bangladesh, Barbados, Belarus, Belgium, Belize, Benin, Bhutan, Bolivia, Bosnia and Herzegovina, Botswana, Brazil, Bulgaria, Burkina Faso, Burma, Burundi, Cambodia, Cameroon, Canada, Cape Verde, Central African Republic, Chad, Chile, China, Colombia, Comoros, Democratic Republic of the Congo, Republic of the Congo, Costa Rica, Cote d'Ivoire, Croatia, Cuba, Cyprus, Czech Republic, Denmark, Djibouti, Dominican Republic, Ecuador, Egypt, El Salvador, Equatorial Guinea, Estonia, Fiji, Finland, France, Gabon, The Gambia, Georgia, Germany, Ghana, Greece, Grenada, Guatemala, Guinea, Guinea-Bissau, Honduras, Hungary, Gambia, Georgia, Germany, Ghana, Greece, Grenada, Guatemala, Guinea, Guinea-Bissau, Honduras, Hungary, Iceland, India, Indonesia, Iran, Iraq, Ireland, Israel, Italy, Jamaica, Japan, Jordan, Kazakhstan, Kenya, Kiribati, South Korea, Kyrgyzstan, Laos, Latvia, Lebanon, Lesotho, Liberia, Libya, Liechtenstein, Lithuania, Luxembourg, Macedonia, Madagascar, Malawi, Malaysia, Mali, Malta, Marshall Islands, Mauritania, Mauritius, Mexico, Moldova, Monaco, Mongolia, Montenegro, Morocco, Mozambique, Namibia, Nepal, Netherlands, NZ, Nicaragua, Niger, Nigeria, Norway, Oman, Pakistan, Palau, Panama, Papua New Guinea, Paraguay, Peru, Philippines, Poland, Portugal, Romania, Russia, Rwanda, Saint Lucia, Samoa, Sao Tome and Principe, Senegal, Serbia, Seychelles, Sierra Leone, Slovakia, Slovenia, South Africa, South Sudan, Spain, Sri Lanka, Sudan, Suriname, Swaziland, Sweden, Switzerland, Syria, Tanzania, Tajikistan, Thailand, Togo, Trinidad and Tobago, Tunisia, Turkey, Turkmenistan, Uganda, Ukraine, UAE, UK, US, Uruguay, Uzbekistan, Venezuela, Vietnam, Yemen, Zambia, Zimbabwe

Convention on the Conservation of Antarctic Marine Living Resources

note—abbreviated as Antarctic-Marine Living Resources
opened for signature—5 May 1980
entered into force—7 April 1982
objective—to safeguard the environment and protect the integrity of the ecosystem of the seas surrounding Antarctica, and to conserve Antarctic marine living resources
parties—(34) Argentina, Australia, Belgium, Brazil, Bulgaria, Canada, Chile, China, Cook Islands, EU, Finland, France, Germany, Greece, India, Italy, Japan, South Korea, Mauritius, Namibia, Netherlands, NZ, Norway, Peru, Poland, Russia, South Africa, Spain, Sweden, Ukraine, UK, US, Uruguay, Vanuatu

Convention on the International Trade in Endangered Species of Wild Flora and Fauna (CITES)

note—abbreviated as Endangered Species
opened for signature—3 March 1973
entered into force—1 July 1975
objective—to protect certain endangered species from overexploitation by means of a system of import/export permits
parties—(179) Afghanistan, Albania, Algeria, Angola, Antigua and Barbuda, Argentina, Armenia, Australia, Austria, Azerbaijan, The Bahamas, Bahrain, Bangladesh, Barbados, Belarus, Belgium, Belize, Benin, Bhutan, Bolivia, Bosnia and Herzegovina, Botswana, Brazil, Brunei, Bulgaria, Burkina Faso, Burma, Burundi, Cambodia, Cameroon, Canada, Cape Verde, Central African Republic, Chad, Chile, China, Colombia, Comoros, Democratic Republic of the Congo, Republic of the Congo, Costa Rica, Cote d'Ivoire, Croatia, Cuba, Cyprus, Czech Republic, Denmark, Djibouti, Dominica, Dominican Republic, Ecuador, Egypt, El Salvador, Equatorial Guinea, Eritrea, Estonia, Ethiopia, Fiji, Finland, France, Gabon, The Gambia, Georgia, Germany, Ghana, Greece, Grenada, Guatemala, Guinea, Guinea-Bissau, Guyana, Honduras, Hungary, Iceland, India, Indonesia, Iran, Ireland, Israel, Italy, Jamaica, Japan, Jordan, Kazakhstan, Kenya, South Korea, Kuwait, Kyrgyzstan, Laos, Latvia, Lebanon, Liberia, Libya, Liechtenstein, Lithuania, Luxembourg, Macedonia, Madagascar, Malawi, Malaysia, Maldives, Mali, Malta, Mauritania, Mauritius, Mexico, Moldova, Monaco, Mongolia, Montenegro, Morocco, Mozambique, Namibia, Nepal, Netherlands, NZ, Nicaragua, Niger, Nigeria, Norway, Oman, Palau, Pakistan, Panama, Papua New Guinea, Paraguay, Peru, Philippines, Poland, Portugal, Qatar, Romania, Russia, Rwanda, Saint Kitts and Nevis, Saint Lucia, Saint Vincent and the Grenadines, Samoa, San Marino, Sao Tome and Principe, Saudi Arabia, Senegal, Serbia, Seychelles, Sierra Leone, Singapore, Slovakia, Slovenia, Solomon Islands, Somalia, South Africa, Spain, Sri Lanka, Sudan, Suriname, Swaziland, Sweden, Switzerland, Syria, Tanzania, Thailand, Togo, Trinidad and Tobago, Tunisia, Turkey, Uganda, Ukraine, UAE, UK, US, Uruguay, Uzbekistan, Vanuatu, Venezuela, Vietnam, Yemen, Zambia, Zimbabwe

Convention on the Prevention of Marine Pollution by Dumping Wastes and Other Matter (London Convention)

note—abbreviated as Marine Dumping
opened for signature—29 December 1972
entered into force—30 August 1975
objective—to promote effective control of all sources of marine pollution and to take all practicable steps to prevent pollution of the sea by dumping and to encourage regional agreements supplementary to the Convention
parties—(87) Afghanistan, Antigua and Barbuda, Argentina, Australia, Azerbaijan, Barbados, Belarus, Belgium, Benin, Bolivia, Brazil, Bulgaria, Canada, Cape Verde, Chile, China, Democratic Republic of the Congo, Costa Rica, Cote d'Ivoire, Croatia, Cuba, Cyprus, Denmark, Dominican Republic, Egypt, Equatorial Guinea, Finland, France, Gabon, Germany, Greece, Guatemala, Haiti, Honduras, Hong Kong (associate member), Hungary, Iceland, Iran, Ireland, Italy, Jamaica, Japan, Jordan, Kenya, Kiribati, South Korea, Libya, Luxembourg, Malta, Mexico, Monaco, Montenegro, Morocco, Nauru, Netherlands, NZ, Nigeria, Norway, Oman, Pakistan, Panama, Papua New Guinea, Peru, Philippines, Poland, Portugal, Russia, Saint Lucia, Saint Vincent and the Grenadines, Serbia, Seychelles, Sierra Leon, Slovenia, Solomon Islands, South Africa, Spain, Suriname, Sweden, Switzerland, Syria, Tanzania, Tonga, Tunisia, Ukraine, UAE, UK, US, Vanuatu
associate members to the London Convention—(2) Faroe Islands, Macau
countries that have signed, but not yet ratified—(3) Chad, Kuwait, Uruguay

Convention on the Prohibition of Military or Any Other Hostile Use of Environmental Modification Techniques

note—abbreviated as Environmental Modification
opened for signature—18 May 1977
entered into force—5 October 1978
objective—to prohibit the military or other hostile use of environmental modification techniques in order to further world peace and trust among nations
parties—(76) Afghanistan, Algeria, Antigua and Barbuda, Argentina, Armenia, Australia, Austria, Bangladesh, Belarus, Belgium, Benin, Brazil, Bulgaria, Canada, Cameroon, Cape Verde, Chile, China, Costa Rica, Cuba, Cyprus, Czech Republic, Denmark, Dominica, Egypt, Estonia, Finland, Germany, Ghana, Greece, Guatemala, Honduras, Hungary, India, Ireland, Italy, Japan, Kazakhstan, North Korea, South Korea, Kuwait, Laos, Lithuania, Malawi, Mauritius, Mongolia, Netherlands, NZ, Nicaragua, Niger, Norway, Pakistan, Panama, Papua New Guinea, Poland, Romania, Russia, Saint Lucia, Saint Vincent and the Grenadines, Sao Tome and Principe, Slovakia, Slovenia, Solomon Islands, Spain, Sri Lanka, Sweden, Switzerland, Tajikistan, Tunisia, Ukraine, UK, US, Uruguay, Uzbekistan, Vietnam, Yemen
countries that have signed, but not yet ratified—(16) Bolivia, Democratic Republic of the Congo, Ethiopia, Holy See, Iceland, Iran, Iraq, Lebanon, Liberia, Luxembourg, Morocco, Portugal, Sierra Leone, Syria, Turkey, Uganda

Desertification

see United Nations Convention to Combat Desertification in those Countries Experiencing Serious Drought and/or Desertification, Particularly in Africa

Endangered Species

see Convention on the International Trade in Endangered Species of Wild Flora and Fauna (CITES)

Environmental Modification

see Convention on the Prohibition of Military or Any Other Hostile Use of Environmental Modification Techniques

Hazardous Wastes

see Basel Convention on the Control of Transboundary Movements of Hazardous Wastes and Their Disposal

International Convention for the Regulation of Whaling

note—abbreviated as Whaling
opened for signature—2 December 1946
entered into force—10 November 1948
objective—to protect all species of whales from overhunting; to establish a system of international regulation for the whale fisheries to ensure proper conservation and development of whale stocks; and to safeguard for future generations the great natural resources represented by whale stocks
parties—(88) Antigua and Barbuda, Argentina, Australia, Austria, Belgium, Belize, Benin, Brazil, Bulgaria, Cambodia, Cameroon, Chile, China, Colombia, Republic of the Congo, Costa Rica, Cote D'Ivoire, Croatia, Cyprus, Czech Republic, Denmark, Dominica, Dominican Republic, Ecuador, Eritrea, Estonia, Finland, France, Gabon, The Gambia, Germany, Ghana, Greece, Grenada, Guatemala, Guinea, Guinea-Bissau, Hungary, Iceland, India, Ireland, Israel, Italy, Japan, Kenya, Kiribati, South Korea, Laos, Lithuania, Luxembourg, Mali, Marshall Islands, Mauritania, Mexico, Monaco, Mongolia, Morocco, Nauru, Netherlands, NZ, Nicaragua, Norway, Oman, Palau, Panama, Peru, Poland, Portugal, Romania, Russia, Saint Kitts and Nevis, Saint Lucia, Saint Vincent and the Grenadines, San Marino, Senegal, Slovakia, Slovenia, Solomon Islands, South Africa, Spain, Suriname, Sweden, Switzerland, Tanzania, Togo, Tuvalu, UK, US, Uruguay

International Tropical Timber Agreement, 1983

note—abbreviated as Tropical Timber 83
opened for signature—18 November 1983
entered into force—1 April 1985; this agreement was superseded by the International Tropical Timber Agreement, 1994
objective—to provide an effective framework for cooperation between tropical timber producers and consumers and to encourage the development of national policies aimed at sustainable utilization and conservation of tropical forests and their genetic resources
parties—(59) Australia, Austria, Belgium, Bolivia, Brazil, Burma, Cambodia, Cameroon, Canada, Central African Republic, China, Colombia, Democratic Republic of the Congo, Republic of the Congo, Cote d'Ivoire, Denmark, Ecuador, Egypt, EU, Fiji, Finland, France, Gabon, Germany, Ghana, Greece, Guatemala, Guyana, Honduras, India, Indonesia, Ireland, Italy, Japan, South Korea, Liberia, Luxembourg, Malaysia, Mexico, Nepal, Netherlands, NZ, Nigeria, Norway, Panama, Papua New Guinea, Peru, Philippines, Portugal, Russia, Spain, Suriname, Sweden, Switzerland, Thailand, Togo, Trinidad and Tobago, UK, US, Vanuatu, Venezuela

International Tropical Timber Agreement, 1994

note—abbreviated as Tropical Timber 94
opened for signature—1 April 1994
entered into force—1 January 1997 (provisional application)
objective—to provide a framework for international cooperation on conservation and sustainable development of tropical timber and enhance the capacity of members to implement a strategy for achieving exports of tropical timber and timber products from sustainably managed sources by the year 2000; to establish a fund to assist tropical timper producers in obtaining the resources necessary to reach this objective
parties—(61) Australia, Austria, Belgium, Bolivia, Brazil, Burma, Cambodia, Cameroon, Canada, Central African Republic, China, Colombia, Democratic Republic of the Congo, Republic of the Congo, Cote d'Ivoire, Denmark, Ecuador, Egypt, EU, Fiji, Finland, France, Gabon, Germany, Ghana, Greece, Guatemala, Guyana, Honduras, India, Indonesia, Ireland, Italy, Japan, South Korea, Liberia, Luxembourg,

Malaysia, Mexico, Nepal, Netherlands, NZ, Nigeria, Norway, Panama, Papua New Guinea, Peru, Philippines, Poland, Portugal, Spain, Suriname, Sweden, Switzerland, Thailand, Togo, Trinidad and Tobago, UK, US, Vanuatu, Venezuela

Kyoto Protocol to the United Nations Framework Convention on Climate Change
note—abbreviated as Climate Change-Kyoto Protocol
opened for signature—16 March 1998
entered into force—23 February 2005
objective—to further reduce greenhouse gas emissions by enhancing the national programs of developed countries aimed at this goal and by establishing percentage reduction targets for the developed countries
parties—(192) Albania, Algeria, Angola, Antigua and Barbuda, Argentina, Armenia, Australia, Austria, Azerbaijan, The Bahamas, Bahrain, Bangladesh, Barbados, Belarus, Belgium, Belize, Benin, Bhutan, Bolivia, Bosnia and Herzegovina, Botswana, Brazil, Brunei, Bulgaria, Burkina Faso, Burma, Burundi, Cambodia, Cameroon, Cape Verde, Central African Republic, Chad, Chile, China, Colombia, Comoros, Democratic Republic of the Congo, Republic of the Congo, Cook Island, Costa Rica, Cote d'Ivoire, Croatia, Cuba, Cyprus, Czech Republic, Denmark, Djibouti, Dominica, Dominican Republic, Ecuador, Egypt, El Salvador, Equatorial Guinea, Eritrea, Estonia, Ethiopia, EU, Fiji, Finland, France, Gabon, The Gambia, Georgia, Germany, Ghana, Greece, Grenada, Guatemala, Guinea, Guinea-Bissau, Guyana, Haiti, Honduras, Hungary, Iceland, India, Indonesia, Iran, Iraq, Ireland, Israel, Italy, Jamaica, Japan, Jordan, Kazakhstan, Kenya, Kiribati, North Korea, South Korea, Kuwait, Kyrgyzstan, Laos, Latvia, Lebanon, Lesotho, Liberia, Libya, Liechtenstein, Lithuania, Luxembourg, Macedonia, Madagascar, Malawi, Malaysia, Maldives, Mali, Malta, Marshall Islands, Mauritania, Mauritius, Mexico, Federated States of Micronesia, Moldova, Monaco, Mongolia, Montenegro, Morocco, Mozambique, Namibia, Nauru, Nepal, Netherlands, NZ, Nicaragua, Niger, Nigeria, Niue, Norway, Oman, Pakistan, Palau, Panama, Papua New Guinea, Paraguay, Peru, Philippines, Poland, Portugal, Qatar, Romania, Russia, Rwanda, Saint Kitts and Nevis, Saint Lucia, Saint Vincent and the Grenadines, Samoa, San Marino, Sao Tome and Principe, Saudi Arabia, Senegal, Serbia, Seychelles, Sierra Leone, Singapore, Slovakia, Slovenia, Solomon Islands, Somalia, South Africa, Spain, Sri Lanka, Sudan, Suriname, Swaziland, Sweden, Switzerland, Syria, Tajikistan, Tanzania, Thailand, Timor-Leste, Togo, Tonga, Trinidad and Tobago, Tunisia, Turkey, Turkmenistan, Tuvalu, Uganda, Ukraine, UAE, UK, Uruguay, Uzbekistan, Vanuatu, Venezuela, Vietnam, Yemen, Zam ia, Zimbabwe
countries that have signed, but not yet ratified—(1) US

Law of the Sea
see United Nations Convention on the Law of the Sea (LOS)

Marine Dumping
see Convention on the Prevention of Marine Pollution by Dumping Wastes and Other Matter (London Convention)

Marine Life Conservation
see Convention on Fishing and Conservation of Living Resources of the High Seas

Montreal Protocol on Substances That Deplete the Ozone Layer
note—abbreviated as Ozone Layer Protection
opened for signature—16 September 1987
entered into force—1 January 1989
objective—to protect the ozone layer by controlling emissions of substances that deplete it
parties—(197) Afghanistan, Albania, Algeria, Andorra, Angola, Antigua and Barbuda, Argentina, Armenia, Australia, Austria, Azerbaijan, The Bahamas, Bahrain, Bangladesh, Barbados, Belarus, Belgium, Belize, Benin, Bhutan, Bolivia, Bosnia and Herzegovina, Botswana, Brazil, Brunei, Bulgaria, Burkina Faso, Burma, Burundi, Cambodia, Cameroon, Canada, Cape Verde, Central African Republic, Chad, Chile, China, Colombia, Comoros, Democratic Republic of the Congo, Republic of the Congo, Cook Islands, Costa Rica, Cote d'Ivoire, Croatia, Cuba, Cyprus, Czech Republic, Denmark, Djibouti, Dominica, Dominican Republic, Ecuador, Egypt, El Salvador, Equatorial Guinea, Eritrea, Estonia, Ethiopia, EU, Fiji, Finland, France, Gabon, The Gambia, Georgia, Germany, Ghana, Greece, Grenada, Guatemala, Guinea, Guinea-Bissau, Guyana, Haiti, Holy See, Honduras, Hungary, Iceland, India, Indonesia, Iran, Iraq, Ireland, Israel, Italy, Jamaica, Japan, Jordan, Kazakhstan, Kenya, Kiribati, North Korea, South Korea, Kuwait, Kyrgyzstan, Laos, Latvia, Lebanon, Lesotho, Liberia, Libya, Liechtenstein, Lithuania, Luxembourg, Macedonia, Madagascar, Malawi, Malaysia, Maldives, Mali, Malta, Marshall Islands, Mauritania, Mauritius, Mexico, Federated States of Micronesia, Moldova, Monaco, Mongolia, Montenegro, Morocco, Mozambique, Namibia, Nauru, Nepal, Netherlands, NZ, Nicaragua, Niger, Nigeria, Niue, Norway, Oman, Pakistan, Palau, Panama, Papua New Guinea, Paraguay, Peru, Philippines, Poland, Portugal, Qatar, Romania, Russia, Rwanda, Saint Kitts and Nevis, Saint Lucia, Saint Vincent and the Grenadines, Samoa, San Marino, Sao Tome and Principe, Saudi Arabia, Senegal, Serbia, Seychelles, Sierra Leone, Singapore, Slovakia, Slovenia, Solomon Islands, Somalia, South Africa, South Sudan, Spain, Sri Lanka, Sudan, Suriname, Swaziland, Sweden, Switzerland, Syria, Tajikistan, Tanzania, Thailand, Timor-Leste, Togo, Tonga, Trinidad and Tobago, Tunisia, Turkey, Turkmenistan, Tuvalu, Uganda, Ukraine, UAE, UK, US, Ur guay, Uzbekistan, Vanuatu, Venezuela, Vietnam, Yemen, Zambia, Zimbabwe

Nuclear Test Ban
see Treaty Banning Nuclear Weapons Tests in the Atmosphere, in Outer Space, and Under Water

Ozone Layer Protection
see Montreal Protocol on Substances That Deplete the Ozone Layer

Protocol of 1978 Relating to the International Convention for the Prevention of Pollution From Ships, 1973 (MARPOL)
note—abbreviated as Ship Pollution
opened for signature—1 June 1978
entered into force—2 October 1983
objective—to modify the International Convention for the Prevention of Pollution from Ships, 1973, including by extending the period of compliance under the Convention by three years
parties—(152) Albania, Algeria, Angola, Antigua and Barbuda, Argentina, Australia, Austria, Azerbaijan, The Bahamas, Bahrain, Bangladesh, Barbados, Belarus, Belgium, Belize, Benin, Bolivia, Brazil, Brunei, Bulgaria, Burma, Cambodia, Canada, Cape Verde, Chile, China, Colombia, Comoros, Republic of Congo, Cote d'Ivoire, Croatia, Cuba, Cyprus, Czech Republic, Denmark, Djibouti, Dominica, Dominican Republic, Ecuador, Egypt, El Salvador, Equatorial Guinea, Estonia, Faroe Islands, Finland, France, Gabon, The Gambia, Georgia, Germany, Ghana, Greece, Guatemala, Guinea, Guyana, Honduras, Hong Kong, Hungary, Iceland, India, Indonesia, Iran, Ireland, Israel, Italy, Jamaica, Japan, Jordan, Kazakhstan, Kenya, Kiribati, North Korea, South Korea, Kuwait, Latvia, Lebanon, Liberia, Lithuania, Luxembourg, Libya, Macau, Madagascar, Malawi, Malaysia, Maldives, Malta, Marshall Islands, Mauritania, Mauritius, Mexico, Moldova, Monaco, Mongolia, Montenegro, Morocco, Mozambique, Namibia, Netherlands, NZ, Nicaragua, Nigeria, Norway, Nuie, Oman, Pakistan, Palau, Panama, Papua New Guinea, Peru, Philippines, Poland, Portugal, Qatar Romania, Russia, Saint Kitts and Nevis, Saint Lucia, Saint Vincent and the Grenadines, Samoa, Sao Tome and Principe, Saudi Arabia, Senegal, Serbia, Seychelles, Sierra Leone, Singapore, Slovakia, Slovenia, Solomon Islands, South Africa, Spain, Sri Lanka, Suriname, Sweden, Switzerland, Syria, Tanzania, Togo, Tonga, Trinidad and Tobago, Tunisia, Turkey, Turkmenistan, Tuvalu, Ukraine, UAE, UK, US, Uruguay, Vanuatu, Venezuela, Vietnam

Protocol on Environmental Protection to the Antarctic Treaty
note—abbreviated as Antarctic-Environmental Protocol
opened for signature—4 October 1991
entered into force—14 January 1998
objective—to provide for comprehensive protection of the Antarctic environment and dependent and associated ecosystems; applies to the area covered by the Antarctic Treaty
consultative parties—(28) Argentina, Australia, Belgium, Brazil, Bulgaria, Chile, China, Ecuador, Finland, France, Germany, India, Italy, Japan, South Korea, Netherlands, NZ, Norway, Peru, Poland, Russia, South Africa, Spain, Sweden, Ukraine, UK, US, Uruguay
non consultative parties—(22) Austria, Belarus, Canada, Colombia, Cuba, Czech Republic, Denmark, Estonia, Greece, Guatemala, Hungary, North Korea, Malaysia, Monaco, Pakistan, Papua New Guinea, Romania, Slovakia, Switzerland, Turkey, Venezuela

Protocol to the 1979 Convention on Long-Range Transboundary Air Pollution Concerning the Control of Emissions of Nitrogen Oxides or Their Transboundary Fluxes
note—abbreviated as Air Pollution-Nitrogen Oxides
opened for signature—31 October 1988
entered into force—14 February 1991
objective—to provide for the control or reduction national of nitrogen oxide emissions and their transboundary fluxes
parties—(35) Albania, Austria, Belarus, Belgium, Bulgaria, Canada, Croatia, Cyprus, Czech Republic, Denmark, Estonia, EU, Finland, France, Germany, Greece, Hungary, Ireland, Italy, Liechtenstein, Lithuania, Luxembourg, Macedonia, Netherlands, Norway, Poland, Russia, Slovakia, Slovenia, Spain, Sweden, Switzerland, Ukraine, UK, US

Protocol to the 1979 Convention on Long-Range Transboundary Air Pollution Concerning the Control of Emissions of Volatile Organic Compounds or Their Transboundary Fluxes
note—abbreviated as Air Pollution-Volatile Organic Compounds
opened for signature—18 November 1991
entered into force—29 September 1997
objective—to provide for the control and reduction of national emissions of volatile organic compounds in order to reduce their transboundary fluxes
parties—(23) (24) Austria, Belgium, Bulgaria, Croatia, Czech Republic, Denmark, Estonia, Finland, France, Germany, Hungary, Italy, Liechtenstein, Lithuania, Luxembourg, Macedonia, Monaco, Netherlands, Norway, Slovakia, Spain, Sweden, Switzerland, UK Sweden, Switzerland, UK
countries that have signed, but not yet ratified—(6) Canada, EU, Greece, Portugal, Ukraine, US

Protocol to the 1979 Convention on Long-Range Transboundary Air Pollution on Further Reduction of Sulphur Emissions
note—abbreviated as Air Pollution-Sulphur 94
opened for signature—14 June 1994
entered into force—5 August 1998
objective—to provide for a further reduction in national sulfur emissions or transboundary fluxes on a regional basis within Europe
parties—(29) Austria, Belgium, Bulgaria, Canada, Croatia, Cyprus, Czech Republic, Denmark, EU, Finland, France, Germany, Greece, Hungary, Ireland, Italy, Liechtenstein, Lithuania, Luxembourg, Macedonia, Monaco, Netherlands, Norway, Slovakia, Slovenia, Spain, Sweden, Switzerland, UK
countries that have signed, but not yet ratified—(3) Poland, Russia, Ukraine

Protocol to the 1979 Convention on Long-Range Transboundary Air Pollution on Persistent Organic Pollutants
note—abbreviated as Air Pollution-Persistent Organic Pollutants
opened for signature—24 June 1998
entered into force—23 October 2003
objective—to provide for the control, reduction, or elimination of discharges, emissions of persistent organic pollutants

parties—(33) Austria, Belgium, Bulgaria, Canada, Croatia, Cyprus, Czech Republic, Denmark, Estonia, EU, Finland, France, Germany, Hungary, Iceland, Italy, Latvia, Liechtenstein, Lithuania, Luxembourg, Macedonia, Moldova, Montenegro, Netherlands, Norway, Romania, Serbia, Slovakia, Slovenia, Spain, Sweden, Switzerland, UK
countries that have signed, but not yet ratified—(8) Armenia, Greece, Ireland, Poland, Portugal, Spain, Ukraine, US

Protocol to the 1979 Convention on Long-Range Transboundary Air Pollution on the Reduction of Sulphur Emissions or Their Transboundary Fluxes by at Least 30%
note—abbreviated as Air Pollution-Sulphur 85
opened for signature—8 July 1985
entered into force—2 September 1987
objective—to provide for national reductions in sulfur emissions or transboundary fluxes by 30% of 1980 emission or transboundary flux levels by no later than 1993
parties—(25) Albania, Austria, Belarus, Belgium, Bulgaria, Canada, Czech Republic, Denmark, Estonia, Finland, France, Germany, Hungary, Italy, Liechtenstein, Lithuania, Luxembourg, Macedonia, Netherlands, Norway, Russia, Slovakia, Sweden, Switzerland, Ukraine

Ship Pollution
see Protocol of 1978 Relating to the International Convention for the Prevention of Pollution From Ships, 1973 (MARPOL)

Treaty Banning Nuclear Weapon Tests in the Atmosphere, in Outer Space, and Under Water
note—abbreviated as Nuclear Test Ban
opened for signature—5 August 1963
entered into force—10 October 1963
objective—to ban nuclear weapons testing in the atmosphere, outer space, or under water
parties—(124) Afghanistan, Antigua and Barbuda, Argentina, Armenia, Australia, Austria, The Bahamas, Bangladesh, Belarus, Belgium, Benin, Bhutan, Bolivia, Bosnia and Herzegovina, Botswana, Brazil, Bulgaria, Burma, Canada, Cape Verde, Central African Republic, Chad, Chile, China, Colombia, Costa Rica, Cote d'Ivoire, Croatia, Cyprus, Czech Republic, Democratic Republic of the Congo, Denmark, Dominican Republic, Ecuador, Egypt, El Salvador, Fiji, Finland, Gabon, The Gambia, Germany, Ghana, Greece, Guatemala, Honduras, Hungary, Iceland, India, Indonesia, Iran, Iraq, Ireland, Israel, Italy, Jamaica, Japan, Jordan, Kenya, South Korea, Kuwait, Laos, Lebanon, Liberia, Libya, Luxembourg, Madagascar, Malawi, Malaysia, Malta, Mauritania, Mauritius, Mexico, Mongolia, Montenegro, Morocco, Nepal, Netherlands, New Zealand, Nicaragua, Niger, Nigeria, Norway, Panama, Pakistan, Papua New Guinea, Peru, Philippines, Poland, Romania, Russia, Rwanda, Samoa, San Marino, Senegal, Serbia, Seychelles, Sierra Leone, Singapore, Slovakia, Slovenia, South Africa, Spain, Sri Lanka, Sudan, Suriname, Swaziland, Sweden, Switzerland, Syria, Tanzania, Thailand, Togo, Tonga, Trinidad and Tobago, Tunisia, Turkey, Uganda, Ukraine, UK, US, Uruguay, Venezuela, Yemen, Zambia
countries that have signed, but not yet ratified—(11) Algeria, Burkina Faso, Burundi, Cameroon, Ethiopia, Haiti, Mali, Paraguay, Portugal, Somalia, Vietnam

Tropical Timber 83
see International Tropical Timber Agreement, 1983

Tropical Timber 94
see International Tropical Timber Agreement, 1994

United Nations Convention on the Law of the Sea (LOS)
note—abbreviated as Law of the Sea
opened for signature—10 December 1982
entered into force—16 November 1994
objective—to provide a comprehensive legal regime for the sea and oceans
parties—(164) Albania, Algeria, Angola, Antigua and Barbuda, Argentina, Armenia, Australia, Austria, The Bahamas, Bahrain, Bangladesh, Barbados, Belarus, Belgium, Belize, Benin, Bolivia, Bosnia and Herzegovina, Botswana, Brazil, Brunei, Bulgaria, Burkina Faso, Burma, Cameroon, Canada, Cape Verde, Chad, Chile, China, Comoros, Democratic Republic of the Congo, Republic of the Congo, Cook Islands, Costa Rica, Cote d'Ivoire, Croatia, Cuba, Cyprus, Czech Republic, Denmark, Djibouti, Dominica, Dominican Republic, Egypt, Equatorial Guinea, Estonia, EU, Fiji, Finland, France, Gabon, The Gambia, Georgia, Germany, Ghana, Greece, Grenada, Guatemala, Guinea, Guinea-Bissau, Guyana, Haiti, Honduras, Hungary, Iceland, India, Indonesia, Iraq, Ireland, Italy, Jamaica, Japan, Jordan, Kenya, Kiribati, South Korea, Kuwait, Laos, Latvia, Lebanon, Lesotho, Liberia, Lithuania, Luxembourg, Macedonia, Madagascar, Malawi, Malaysia, Mali, Malta, Marshall Islands, Mauritania, Mauritius, Mexico, Federated States of Micronesia, Moldova, Monaco, Mongolia, Montenegro, Morocco, Mozambique, Namibia, Nauru, Nepal, Netherlands, NZ, Nicaragua, Nigeria, Niue, Norway, Oman, Pakistan, Palau, Panama, Papua New Guinea, Paraguay, Philippines, Poland, Portugal, Qatar, Romania, Russia, Saint Kitts and Nevis, Saint Lucia, Saint Vincent and the Grenadines, Samoa, Sao Tome and Principe, Saudi Arabia, Senegal, Serbia, Seychelles, Sierra Leone, Singapore, Slovakia, Slovenia, Solomon Islands, Somalia, South Africa, Spain, Sri Lanka, Sudan, Suriname, Swaziland, Sweden, Switzerland, Tanzania, Thailand, Timor-Liste, Togo, Tonga, Trinidad and Tobago, Tunisia, Tuvalu, Uganda, Ukraine, UK, Uruguay, Vanuatu, Vietnam, Yemen, Zambia, Zimbabwe
countries that have signed, but not yet ratified—(15) Afghanistan, Bhutan, Burundi, Cambodia, Central African Republic, Colombia, El Salvador, Ethiopia, Iran, North Korea, Libya, Liechtenstein, Niger, Rwanda, UAE

United Nations Convention to Combat Desertification in Those Countries Experiencing Serious Drought and/or Desertification, Particularly in Africa
note—abbreviated as Desertification
opened for signature—14 October 1994
entered into force—26 December 1996
objective—to combat desertification and mitigate the effects of drought through an integrated framework that is consistent with Agenda 21, employing international cooperation and partnership arrangements, and effective action at all levels
parties—(195) Afghanistan, Albania, Algeria, Andorra, Angola, Antigua and Barbuda, Argentina, Armenia, Australia, Austria, Azerbaijan, The Bahamas, Bahrain, Bangladesh, Barbados, Belarus, Belgium, Belize, Benin, Bhutan, Bolivia, Bosnia and Herzegovina, Botswana, Brazil, Brunei, Bulgaria, Burkina Faso, Burma, Burundi, Cambodia, Cameroon, Canada, Cape Verde, Central African

Republic, Chad, Chile, China, Colombia, Comoros, Democratic Republic of the Congo, Republic of the Congo, Cook Islands, Costa Rica, Cote d'Ivoire, Croatia, Cuba, Cyprus, Czech Republic, Denmark, Djibouti, Dominica, Dominican Republic, Ecuador, Egypt, El Salvador, Equatorial Guinea, Eritrea, Estonia, Ethiopia, EU, Fiji, Finland, France, Gabon, The Gambia, Georgia, Germany, Ghana, Greece, Grenada, Guatemala, Guinea, Guinea-Bissau, Guyana, Haiti, Honduras, Hungary, Iceland, India, Indonesia, Iran, Iraq, Ireland, Israel, Italy, Jamaica, Japan, Jordan, Kazakhstan, Kenya, Kiribati, North Korea, South Korea, Kuwait, Kyrgyzstan, Laos, Latvia, Lebanon, Lesotho, Liberia, Libya, Liechtenstein, Lithuania, Luxembourg, Macedonia, Madagascar, Malawi, Malaysia, Maldives, Mali, Malta, Marshall Islands, Mauritania, Mauritius, Mexico, Federated States of Micronesia, Moldova, Monaco, Mongolia, Montenegro, Morocco, Mozambique, Namibia, Nauru, Nepal, Netherlands, NZ, Nicaragua, Niger, Nigeria, Niue, Norway, Oman, Pakistan, Palau, Panama, Papua New Guinea, Paraguay, Peru, Philippines, Poland, Portugal, Qatar, Romania, Russia, Rwanda, Saint Kitts and Nevis, Saint Lucia, Saint Vincent and the Grenadines, Samoa, San Marino, Sao Tome and Principe, Saudi Arabia, Senegal, Serbia, Seychelles, Sierra Leone, Singapore, Slovakia, Slovenia, Solomon Islands, Somalia, South Africa, Spain, Sri Lanka, Sudan, Suriname, Swaziland, Sweden, Switzerland, Syria, Tajikistan, Thailand, Tanzania, Timor-Leste, Togo, Tonga, Trinidad and Tobago, Tunisia, Turkey, Turkmenistan, Tuvalu, Uganda, Ukraine, UAE, UK, US, Uruguay, Uzbekistan Vanu tu, Venezuela, Vietnam, Yemen, Zambia, Zimbabwe

United Nations Framework Convention on Climate Change

note—abbreviated as Climate Change
opened for signature—9 May 1992
entered into force—21 March 1994
objective—to achieve stabilization of greenhouse gas concentrations in the atmosphere at a low enough level to prevent dangerous anthropogenic interference with the climate system
parties—(195) Afghanistan, Albania, Algeria, Andorra, Angola, Antigua and Barbuda, Argentina, Armenia, Australia, Austria, Azerbaijan, The Bahamas, Bahrain, Bangladesh, Barbados, Belarus, Belgium, Belize, Benin, Bhutan, Bolivia, Bosnia and Herzegovina, Botswana, Brazil, Brunei, Bulgaria, Burkina Faso, Burma, Burundi, Cambodia, Cameroon, Canada, Cape Verde, Central African Republic, Chad, Chile, China, Colombia, Comoros, Democratic Republic of the Congo, Republic of the Congo, Cook Islands, Costa Rica, Cote d'Ivoire, Croatia, Cuba, Cyprus, Czech Republic, Denmark, Djibouti, Dominica, Dominican Republic, Ecuador, Egypt, El Salvador, Equatorial Guinea, Eritrea, Estonia, Ethiopia, EU, Fiji, Finland, France, Gabon, The Gambia, Georgia, Germany, Ghana, Greece, Grenada, Guatemala, Guinea, Guinea-Bissau, Guyana, Haiti, Honduras, Hungary, Iceland, India, Indonesia, Iran, Iraq, Ireland, Israel, Italy, Jamaica, Japan, Jordan, Kazakhstan, Kenya, Kiribati, North Korea, South Korea, Kuwait, Kyrgyzstan, Laos, Latvia, Lebanon, Lesotho, Liberia, Libya, Liechtenstein, Lithuania, Luxembourg, Macedonia, Madagascar, Malawi, Malaysia, Maldives, Mali, Malta, Marshall Islands, Mauritius, Mexico, Federated States of Micronesia, Moldova, Monaco, Mongolia, Montenegro, Morocco, Mozambique, Namibia, Nauru, Nepal, Netherlands, NZ, Nicaragua, Niger, Nigeria, Niue, Norway, Oman, Pakistan, Palau, Panama, Papua New Guinea, Paraguay, Peru, Philippines, Poland, Portugal, Qatar, Romania, Russia, Rwanda, Saint Kitts and Nevis, Saint Lucia, Saint Vincent and the Grenadines, Samoa, San Marino, Sao Tome and Principe, Saudi Arabia, Senegal, Serbia, Seychelles, Sierra Leone, Singapore, Slovakia, Slovenia, Solomon Islands, Somalia, South Africa, Spain, Sri Lanka, Sudan, Suriname, Swaziland, Sweden, Switzerland, Syria, Tajikistan, Tanzania, Thailand, Timor-Leste, Togo, Tonga, Trinidad and Tobago, Tunisia, Turkey, Turkmenistan, Tuvalu, Uganda, Ukraine, UAE, UK, US, Uruguay, Uzbekistan, Vanu tu, Venezuela, Vietnam, Yemen, Zambia, Zimbabwe

Wetlands

see Convention on Wetlands of International Importance Especially As Waterfowl Habitat (Ramsar)

Whaling

see International Convention for the Regulation of Whaling

CROSS-REFERENCE LIST OF COUNTRY DATA CODES

GEOPOLITICAL ENTITIES and CODES (formerly FIPS PUB 10-4): FIPS PUB 10-4 was withdrawn by the National Institute of Standards and Technology on September 2, 2008 based on Public Law 104-113 (codified OMB Circular A-119 and the National Technology Transfer and Advancement Act of 1995). The National Geospatial-Intelligence Agency (NGA), as the maintenance authority for FIPS PUB 10-4, has continued to maintain and provide regular updates to its content in a document known as Geopolitical Entities and Codes (GEC) (Formerly FIPS 1PUB 10-4).

ISO 3166: Codes for the Representation of Names of Countries (ISO 3166) is prepared by the International Organization for Standardization. ISO 3166 includes two- and three-character alphabetic codes and three-digit numeric codes that may be needed for activities involving exchange of data with international organizations that have adopted that standard. Except for the numeric codes, ISO 3166 codes have been adopted in the US as FIPS 104-1: American National Standard Codes for the Representation of Names of Countries, Dependencies, and Areas of Special Sovereignty for Information Interchange.

STANAG 1059: Letter Codes for Geographical Entities (8th edition, 2004) is a Standardization Agreement (STANAG) established and maintained by the North Atlantic Treaty Organization (NATO/OTAN) for the purpose of providing a common set of geo-spatial identifiers for countries, territories, and possessions. The 8th edition established trigraph codes for each country based upon the ISO 3166-1 alpha-3 character sets. These codes are used throughout NATO.

Internet: The Internet country code is the two-letter digraph maintained by the International Organization for Standardization (ISO) in the ISO 3166 Alpha-2 list and used by the Internet Assigned Numbers Authority (IANA) to establish country-coded top-level domains (ccTLDs).

Entity	GEC		ISO 3166		Stanag	Internet	Comment
Afghanistan	AF	AF	AFG	004	AFG	.af	
Akrotiri	AX	–	–	–	–	–	
Albania	AL	AL	ALB	008	ALB	.al	
Algeria	AG	DZ	DZA	012	DZA	.dz	
American Samoa	AQ	AS	ASM	016	ASM	.as	
Andorra	AN	AD	AND	020	AND	.ad	
Angola	AO	AO	AGO	024	AGO	.ao	
Anguilla	AV	AI	AIA	660	AIA	.ai	
Antarctica	AY	AQ	ATA	010	ATA	.aq	ISO defines as the territory south of 60 degrees south latitude
Antigua and Barbuda	AC	AG	ATG	028	ATG	.ag	
Argentina	AR	AR	ARG	032	ARG	.ar	
Armenia	AM	AM	ARM	051	ARM	.am	
Aruba	AA	AW	ABW	533	ABW	.aw	
Ashmore and Cartier Islands	AT	–	–	–	AUS	–	ISO includes with Australia
Australia	AS	AU	AUS	036	AUS	.au	ISO includes Ashmore and Cartier Islands, Coral Sea Islands
Austria	AU	AT	AUT	040	AUT	.at	
Azerbaijan	AJ	AZ	AZE	031	AZE	.az	
Bahamas, The	BF	BS	BHS	044	BHS	.bs	
Bahrain	BA	BH	BHR	048	BHR	.bh	
Baker Island	FQ	–	–	–	UMI	–	ISO includes with the US Minor Outlying Islands
Bangladesh	BG	BD	BGD	050	BGD	.bd	
Barbados	BB	BB	BRB	052	BRB	.bb	

Entity	GEC	ISO 3166			Stanag	Internet	Comment
Bassas da India	BS	–	–	–	–	–	administered as part of French Southern and Antarctic Lands; no ISO codes assigned
Belarus	BO	BY	BLR	112	BLR	.by	
Belgium	BE	BE	BEL	056	BEL	.be	
Belize	BH	BZ	BLZ	084	BLZ	.bz	
Benin	BN	BJ	BEN	204	BEN	.bj	
Bermuda	BD	BM	BMU	060	BMU	.bm	
Bhutan	BT	BT	BTN	064	BTN	.bt	
Bolivia	BL	BO	BOL	068	BOL	.bo	
Bosnia and Herzegovina	BK	BA	BIH	070	BIH	.ba	
Botswana	BC	BW	BWA	072	BWA	.bw	
Bouvet Island	BV	BV	BVT	074	BVT	.bv	
Brazil	BR	BR	BRA	076	BRA	.br	
British Indian Ocean Territory	IO	IO	IOT	086	IOT	.io	
British Virgin Islands	VI	VG	VGB	092	VGB	.vg	
Brunei	BX	BN	BRN	096	BRN	.bn	
Bulgaria	BU	BG	BGR	100	BGR	.bg	
Burkina Faso	UV	BF	BFA	854	BFA	.bf	
Burma	BM	MM	MMR	104	MMR	.mm	ISO uses the name Myanmar
Burundi	BY	BI	BDI	108	BDI	.bi	
Cabo Verde	CV	CV	CPV	132	CPV	.cv	
Cambodia	CB	KH	KHM	116	KHM	.kh	
Cameroon	CM	CM	CMR	120	CMR	.cm	
Canada	CA	CA	CAN	124	CAN	.ca	
Cayman Islands	CJ	KY	CYM	136	CYM	.ky	
Central African Republic	CT	CF	CAF	140	CAF	.cf	
Chad	CD	TD	TCD	148	TCD	.td	
Chile	CI	CL	CHL	152	CHL	.cl	
China	CH	CN	CHN	156	CHN	.cn	see also Taiwan
Christmas Island	KT	CX	CXR	162	CXR	.cx	
Clipperton Island	IP	–	–	–	FYP	–	ISO includes with France
Cocos (Keeling) Islands	CK	CC	CCK	166	AUS	.cc	
Colombia	CO	CO	COL	170	COL	.co	
Comoros	CN	KM	COM	174	COM	.km	
Congo, Democratic Republic of the	CG	CD	COD	180	COD	.cd	formerly Zaire
Congo, Republic of the	CF	CG	COG	178	COG	.cg	
Cook Islands	CW	CK	COK	184	COK	.ck	
Coral Sea Islands	CR	–	–	–	AUS	–	ISO includes with Australia

Entity	GEC	ISO 3166			Stanag	Internet	Comment
Costa Rica	CS	CR	CRI	188	CRI	.cr	
Cote d'Ivoire	IV	CI	CIV	384	CIV	.ci	
Croatia	HR	HR	HRV	191	HRV	.hr	
Cuba	CU	CU	CUB	192	CUB	.cu	
Curacao	UC	CW	CUW	531	–	.cw	
Cyprus	CY	CY	CYP	196	CYP	.cy	
Czech Republic	EZ	CZ	CZE	203	CZE	.cz	
Denmark	DA	DK	DNK	208	DNK	.dk	
Dhekelia	DX	–	–	–	–	–	
Djibouti	DJ	DJ	DJI	262	DJI	.dj	
Dominica	DO	DM	DMA	212	DMA	.dm	
Dominican Republic	DR	DO	DOM	214	DOM	.do	
Ecuador	EC	EC	ECU	218	ECU	.ec	
Egypt	EG	EG	EGY	818	EGY	.eg	
El Salvador	ES	SV	SLV	222	SLV	.sv	
Equatorial Guinea	EK	GQ	GNQ	226	GNQ	.gq	
Eritrea	ER	ER	ERI	232	ERI	.er	
Estonia	EN	EE	EST	233	EST	.ee	
Ethiopia	ET	ET	ETH	231	ETH	.et	
Europa Island	EU	–	–	–	–	–	administered as part of French Southern and Antarctic Lands; no ISO codes assigned
Falkland Islands (Islas Malvinas)	FK	FK	FLK	238	FLK	.fk	
Faroe Islands	FO	FO	FRO	234	FRO	.fo	
Fiji	FJ	FJ	FJI	242	FJI	.fj	
Finland	FI	FI	FIN	246	FIN	.fi	
France	FR	FR	FRA	250	FRA	.fr	ISO includes metropolitan France along with the dependencies of Clipperton Island, French Guiana, French Polynesia, French Southern and Antarctic Lands, Guadeloupe, Martinique, Mayotte, New Caledonia, Reunion, Saint Pierre and Miquelon, Wallis and Futuna
France, Metropolitan	–	FX	FXX	249	–	.fx	ISO limits to the European part of France
French Guiana	FG	GF	GUF	254	GUF	.gf	
French Polynesia	FP	PF	PYF	258	PYF	.pf	
French Southern and Antarctic Lands	FS	TF	ATF	260	ATF	.tf	FIPS 10-4 does not include the French-claimed portion of Antarctica (Terre Adelie)
Gabon	GB	GA	GAB	266	GAB	.ga	

Entity	GEC	ISO 3166			Stanag	Internet	Comment
Gambia, The	GA	GM	GMB	270	GMB	.gm	
Gaza Strip	GZ	PS	PSE	275	PSE	.ps	ISO identifies as Occupied Palestinian Territory
Georgia	GG	GE	GEO	268	GEO	.ge	
Germany	GM	DE	DEU	276	DEU	.de	
Ghana	GH	GH	GHA	288	GHA	.gh	
Gibraltar	GI	GI	GIB	292	GIB	.gi	
Glorioso Islands	GO	–	–	–	–	–	administered as part of French Southern and Antarctic Lands; no ISO codes assigned
Greece	GR	GR	GRC	300	GRC	.gr	For its internal communications, the European Union recommends the use of the code EL in lieu of the ISO 3166-2 code of GR
Greenland	GL	GL	GRL	304	GRL	.gl	
Grenada	GJ	GD	GRD	308	GRD	.gd	
Guadeloupe	GP	GP	GLP	312	GLP	.gp	
Guam	GQ	GU	GUM	316	GUM	.gu	
Guatemala	GT	GT	GTM	320	GTM	.gt	
Guernsey	GK	GG	GGY	831	UK	.gg	
Guinea	GV	GN	GIN	324	GIN	.gn	
Guinea-Bissau	PU	GW	GNB	624	GNB	.gw	
Guyana	GY	GY	GUY	328	GUY	.gy	
Haiti	HA	HT	HTI	332	HTI	.ht	
Heard Island and McDonald Islands	HM	HM	HMD	334	HMD	.hm	
Holy See (Vatican City)	VT	VA	VAT	336	VAT	.va	
Honduras	HO	HN	HND	340	HND	.hn	
Hong Kong	HK	HK	HKG	344	HKG	.hk	
Howland Island	HQ	–	–	–	UMI	–	ISO includes with the US Minor Outlying Islands
Hungary	HU	HU	HUN	348	HUN	.hu	
Iceland	IC	IS	ISL	352	ISL	.is	
India	IN	IN	IND	356	IND	.in	
Indonesia	ID	ID	IDN	360	IDN	.id	
Iran	IR	IR	IRN	364	IRN	.ir	
Iraq	IZ	IQ	IRQ	368	IRQ	.iq	
Ireland	EI	IE	IRL	372	IRL	.ie	
Isle of Man	IM	IM	IMN	833	UK	.im	
Israel	IS	IL	ISR	376	ISR	.il	
Italy	IT	IT	ITA	380	ITA	.it	
Jamaica	JM	JM	JAM	388	JAM	.jm	

Entity	GEC	ISO 3166		Stanag	Internet	Comment
Jan Mayen	JN	–	–	–	SJM	–	ISO includes with Svalbard
Japan	JA	JP	JPN	392	JPN	.jp	
Jarvis Island	DQ	–	–	–	UMI	–	ISO includes with the US Minor Outlying Islands
Jersey	JE	JE	JEY	832	UK	.je	
Johnston Atoll	JQ	–	–	–	UMI	–	ISO includes with the US Minor Outlying Islands
Jordan	JO	JO	JOR	400	JOR	.jo	
Juan de Nova Island	JU	–	–	–	–	–	administered as part of French Southern and Antarctic Lands; no ISO codes assigned
Kazakhstan	KZ	KZ	KAZ	398	KAZ	.kz	
Kenya	KE	KE	KEN	404	KEN	.ke	
Kingman Reef	KQ	–	–	–	UMI	–	ISO includes with the US Minor Outlying Islands
Kiribati	KR	KI	KIR	296	KIR	.ki	
Korea, North	KN	KP	PRK	408	PRK	.kp	
Korea, South	KS	KR	KOR	410	KOR	.kr	
Kosovo	KV	XK	XKS	–	–	–	XK and XKS are ISO 3166 user assigned codes; ISO 3166 Maintenace Authority has not assigned codes
Kuwait	KU	KW	KWT	414	KWT	.kw	
Kyrgyzstan	KG	KG	KGZ	417	KGZ	.kg	
Laos	LA	LA	LAO	418	LAO	.la	
Latvia	LG	LV	LVA	428	LVA	.lv	
Lebanon	LE	LB	LBN	422	LBN	.lb	
Lesotho	LT	LS	LSO	426	LSO	.ls	
Liberia	LI	LR	LBR	430	LBR	.lr	
Libya	LY	LY	LBY	434	LBY	.ly	
Liechtenstein	LS	LI	LIE	438	LIE	.li	
Lithuania	LH	LT	LTU	440	LTU	.lt	
Luxembourg	LU	LU	LUX	442	LUX	.lu	
Macau	MC	MO	MAC	446	MAC	.mo	
Macedonia	MK	MK	MKD	807	FYR	.mk	
Madagascar	MA	MG	MDG	450	MDG	.mg	
Malawi	MI	MW	MWI	454	MWI	.mw	
Malaysia	MY	MY	MYS	458	MYS	.my	
Maldives	MV	MV	MDV	462	MDV	.mv	
Mali	ML	ML	MLI	466	MLI	.ml	
Malta	MT	MT	MLT	470	MLT	.mt	
Marshall Islands	RM	MH	MHL	584	MHL	.mh	

Entity	GEC	ISO 3166			Stanag	Internet	Comment
Martinique	MB	MQ	MTQ	474	MTQ	.mq	
Mauritania	MR	MR	MRT	478	MRT	.mr	
Mauritius	MP	MU	MUS	480	MUS	.mu	
Mayotte	MF	YT	MYT	175	FRA	.yt	
Mexico	MX	MX	MEX	484	MEX	.mx	
Micronesia, Federated States of	FM	FM	FSM	583	FSM	.fm	
Midway Islands	MQ	–	–	–	UMI	–	ISO includes with the US Minor Outlying Islands
Moldova	MD	MD	MDA	498	MDA	.md	
Monaco	MN	MC	MCO	492	MCO	.mc	
Mongolia	MG	MN	MNG	496	MNG	.mn	
Montenegro	MJ	ME	MNE	499	MNE	.me	
Montserrat	MH	MS	MSR	500	MSR	.ms	
Morocco	MO	MA	MAR	504	MAR	.ma	
Mozambique	MZ	MZ	MOZ	508	MOZ	.mz	
Myanmar	–	–	–	–	–	–	see Burma
Namibia	WA	NA	NAM	516	NAM	.na	
Nauru	NR	NR	NRU	520	NRU	.nr	
Navassa Island	BQ	–	–	–	UMI	–	ISO includes with the US Minor Outlying Islands
Nepal	NP	NP	NPL	524	NPL	.np	
Netherlands	NL	NL	NLD	528	NLD	.nl	
Netherlands Antilles	NT				ANT	.an	disestablished in October 2010 this entity no longer exists; ISO deleted the codes in December 2010
New Caledonia	NC	NC	NCL	540	NCL	.nc	
New Zealand	NZ	NZ	NZL	554	NZL	.nz	
Nicaragua	NU	NI	NIC	558	NIC	.ni	
Niger	NG	NE	NER	562	NER	.ne	
Nigeria	NI	NG	NGA	566	NGA	.ng	
Niue	NE	NU	NIU	570	NIU	.nu	
Norfolk Island	NF	NF	NFK	574	NFK	.nf	
Northern Mariana Islands	CQ	MP	MNP	580	MNP	.mp	
Norway	NO	NO	NOR	578	NOR	.no	
Oman	MU	OM	OMN	512	OMN	.om	
Pakistan	PK	PK	PAK	586	PAK	.pk	
Palau	PS	PW	PLW	585	PLW	.pw	
Palmyra Atoll	LQ	–	–	–	UMI	–	ISO includes with the US Minor Outlying Islands
Panama	PM	PA	PAN	591	PAN	.pa	

Entity	GEC	ISO 3166		Stanag	Internet	Comment
Papua New Guinea	PP	PG	PNG	598	PNG	.pg	
Paracel Islands	PF	–	–	–	–	–	
Paraguay	PA	PY	PRY	600	PRY	.py	
Peru	PE	PE	PER	604	PER	.pe	
Philippines	RP	PH	PHL	608	PHL	.ph	
Pitcairn Islands	PC	PN	PCN	612	PCN	.pn	
Poland	PL	PL	POL	616	POL	.pl	
Portugal	PO	PT	PRT	620	PRT	.pt	
Puerto Rico	RQ	PR	PRI	630	PRI	.pr	
Qatar	QA	QA	QAT	634	QAT	.qa	
Reunion	RE	RE	REU	638	REU	.re	
Romania	RO	RO	ROU	642	ROU	.ro	
Russia	RS	RU	RUS	643	RUS	.ru	
Rwanda	RW	RW	RWA	646	RWA	.rw	
Saint Barthelemy	TB	BL	BLM	652	–	.bl	ccTLD .fr and .gp may also be used
Saint Helena, Ascension, and Tristan da Cunha	SH	SH	SHN	654	SHN	.sh	includes Saint Helena Island, Ascension Island, and the Tristan da Cunha archipelago
Saint Kitts and Nevis	SC	KN	KNA	659	KNA	.kn	
Saint Lucia	ST	LC	LCA	662	LCA	.lc	
Saint Martin	RN	MF	MAF	663	–	.mf	ccTLD .fr and .gp may also be used
Saint Pierre and Miquelon	SB	PM	SPM	666	SPM	.pm	
Saint Vincent and the Grenadines	VC	VC	VCT	670	VCT	.vc	
Samoa	WS	WS	WSM	882	WSM	.ws	
San Marino	SM	SM	SMR	674	SMR	.sm	
Sao Tome and Principe	TP	ST	STP	678	STP	.st	
Saudi Arabia	SA	SA	SAU	682	SAU	.sa	
Senegal	SG	SN	SEN	686	SEN	.sn	
Serbia	RI	RS	SRB	688	–	.rs	
Seychelles	SE	SC	SYC	690	SYC	.sc	
Sierra Leone	SL	SL	SLE	694	SLE	.sl	
Singapore	SN	SG	SGP	702	SGP	.sg	
Sint Maarten	NN	SX	SXM	534	–	.sx	
Slovakia	LO	SK	SVK	703	SVK	.sk	
Slovenia	SI	SI	SVN	705	SVN	.si	
Solomon Islands	BP	SB	SLB	090	SLB	.sb	
Somalia	SO	SO	SOM	706	SOM	.so	
South Africa	SF	ZA	ZAF	710	ZAF	.za	

Entity	GEC	ISO 3166			Stanag	Internet	Comment
South Georgia and the Islands	SX	GS	SGS	239	SGS	.gs	
South Sudan	OD	SS	SSD	728	–	–	IANA has designated .ss as the ccTLD for South Sudan, however it has not been activated in DNS root zone
Spain	SP	ES	ESP	724	ESP	.es	
Spratly Islands	PG	–	–	–	–	–	
Sri Lanka	CE	LK	LKA	144	LKA	.lk	
Sudan	SU	SD	SDN	729	SDN	.sd	
Suriname	NS	SR	SUR	740	SUR	.sr	
Svalbard	SV	SJ	SJM	744	SJM	.sj	ISO includes Jan Mayen
Swaziland	WZ	SZ	SWZ	748	SWZ	.sz	
Sweden	SW	SE	SWE	752	SWE	.se	
Switzerland	SZ	CH	CHE	756	CHE	.ch	
Syria	SY	SY	SYR	760	SYR	.sy	
Taiwan	TW	TW	TWN	158	TWN	.tw	
Tajikistan	TI	TJ	TJK	762	TJK	.tj	
Tanzania	TZ	TZ	TZA	834	TZA	.tz	
Thailand	TH	TH	THA	764	THA	.th	
Timor-Leste	TT	TL	TLS	626	TLS	.tl	
Togo	TO	TG	TGO	768	TGO	.tg	
Tokelau	TL	TK	TKL	772	TKL	.tk	
Tonga	TN	TO	TON	776	TON	.to	
Trinidad and Tobago	TD	TT	TTO	780	TTO	.tt	
Tromelin Island	TE	–	–	–	–	–	administered as part of French Southern and Antarctic Lands; no ISO codes assigned
Tunisia	TS	TN	TUN	788	TUN	.tn	
Turkey	TU	TR	TUR	792	TUR	.tr	
Turkmenistan	TX	TM	TKM	795	TKM	.tm	
Turks and Caicos Islands	TK	TC	TCA	796	TCA	.tc	
Tuvalu	TV	TV	TUV	798	TUV	.tv	
Uganda	UG	UG	UGA	800	UGA	.ug	
Ukraine	UP	UA	UKR	804	UKR	.ua	
United Arab Emirates	AE	AE	ARE	784	ARE	.ae	
United Kingdom	UK	GB	GBR	826	GBR	.uk	for its internal communications, the European Union recommends the use of the code UK in lieu of the ISO 3166-2 code of GB
United States	US	US	USA	840	USA	.us	

Entity	GEC	ISO 3166		Stanag	Internet	Comment
United States Minor Outlying Islands	–	UM	UMI	581	–	.um	ISO includes Baker Island, Howland Island, Jarvis Island, Johnston Atoll, Kingman Reef, Midway Islands, Navassa Island, Palmyra Atoll, Wake Island
Uruguay	UY	UY	URY	858	URY	.uy	
Uzbekistan	UZ	UZ	UZB	860	UZB	.uz	
Vanuatu	NH	VU	VUT	548	VUT	.vu	
Venezuela	VE	VE	VEN	862	VEN	.ve	
Vietnam	VM	VN	VNM	704	VNM	.vn	
Virgin Islands	VQ	VI	VIR	850	VIR	.vi	
Virgin Islands (UK)	–	–	–	–	–	.vg	see British Virgin Islands
Virgin Islands (US)	–	–	–	–	–	.vi	see Virgin Islands
Wake Island	WQ	–	–	–	UMI	–	ISO includes with the US Minor Outlying Islands
Wallis and Futuna	WF	WF	WLF	876	WLF	.wf	
West Bank	WE	PS	PSE	275	PSE	.ps	ISO identifies as Occupied Palestinian Territory
Western Sahara	WI	EH	ESH	732	ESH	.eh	
Western Samoa	–	–	–	–	–	.ws	see Samoa
World	–	–	–	–	–	–	the Factbook uses the W data code from DIAM 65-18 Geopolitical Data Elements and Related Features, Data Standard No. 3, December 1994, published by the Defense Intelligence Agency
Yemen	YM	YE	YEM	887	YEM	.ye	
Zaire	–	–	–	–	–	–	see Democratic Republic of the Congo
Zambia	ZA	ZM	ZMB	894	ZMB	.zm	
Zimbabwe	ZI	ZW	ZWE	716	ZWE	.zw	

CROSS-REFERENCE LIST OF HYDROGRAPHIC DATA CODES

IHO 23-4th: *Limits of Oceans and Seas,* Special Publication 23, Draft 4th Edition 1986, published by the International Hydrographic Bureau of the International Hydrographic Organization.

IHO 23-3rd: *Limits of Oceans and Seas,* Special Publication 23, 3rd Edition 1953, published by the International Hydrographic Organization.

ACIC M 49-1: *Chart of Limits of Seas and Oceans,* revised January 1958, published by the Aeronautical Chart and Information Center (ACIC), United States Air Force.

DIAM 65-18: *Geopolitical Data Elements and Related Features,* Data Standard No. 4, Defense Intelligence Agency Manual 65-18, December 1994, published by the Defense Intelligence Agency. The US Government has not yet adopted a standard for hydrographic codes similar to the Federal Information Processing Standards (FIPS) 10-4 country codes. The names and limits of the following oceans and seas are not always directly comparable because of differences in the customers, needs, and requirements of the individual organizations. Even the number of principal water bodies varies from organization to organization. *Factbook* users, for example, find the Atlantic Ocean and Pacific Ocean entries useful, but none of the following standards include those oceans in their entirety. Nor is there any provision for combining codes or overcodes to aggregate water bodies. The recently delimited Southern Ocean is not included.

Principal Oceans and Seas of the World With Hydrographic Codes by Institution

	IHO 23-4th	IHO 23-3rd*	ACIC M 49-1	DIAM 65-18
Arctic Ocean	9	17	A	5A
Atlantic Ocean	–	–	–	–
Baltic Sea	2	1	B26	7B
Eastern Mediterranean	3.1.2	28 B	–	8E
Indian Ocean	5	45	F	6A
Mediterranean Sea	3.1	28	B11	–
North Atlantic Ocean	1	23	B	1A
North Pacific Ocean	7	57	D	3A
Pacific Ocean	–	–	–	–
South Atlantic Ocean	4	32	C	2A
South China and Eastern Archipelagic Seas	6	49, 48	D18 plus others	3U plus others
South Pacific Ocean	8	61	E	4A
Western Mediterranean	3.1.1	28 A	–	8W

*The letters after the numbers are subdivisions, not footnotes.

APPENDIX F

CROSS-REFERENCE LIST OF GEOGRAPHIC NAMES

Name	Entry in *The World Factbook*	Latitude (deg min)	Longitude (deg min)
Abidjan (capital)	Cote d'Ivoire	5 19 N	4 02 W
Abkhazia (region)	Georgia	43 00 N	41 00 E
Abu Dhabi (capital)	United Arab Emirates	24 28 N	54 22 E
Abu Musa (island)	Iran	25 52 N	55 03 E
Abuja (capital)	Nigeria	9 12 N	7 11 E
Abyssinia (former name for Ethiopia)	Ethiopia	8 00 N	38 00 E
Acapulco (city)	Mexico	16 51 N	99 55 W
Accra (capital)	Ghana	5 33 N	0 13 W
Adamstown (capital)	Pitcairn Islands	25 04 S	130 05 W
Addis Ababa (capital)	Ethiopia	9 02 N	38 42 E
Adelie Land (claimed by France; also Terre Adelie)	Antarctica	66 30 S	139 00 E
Aden (city)	Yemen	12 46 N	45 01 E
Aden, Gulf of	Indian Ocean	12 30 N	48 00 E
Admiralty Island	United States (Alaska)	57 44 N	134 20 W
Admiralty Islands	Papua New Guinea	2 10 S	147 00 E
Adriatic Sea	Atlantic Ocean	42 30 N	16 00 E
Adygey (region)	Russia	44 30 N	40 10 E
Aegean Islands	Greece	38 00 N	25 00 E
Aegean Sea	Atlantic Ocean	38 30 N	25 00 E
Afars and Issas, French Territory of the (or FTAI; former name for Djibouti)	Djibouti	11 30 N	43 00 E
Afghanestan (local name for Afghanistan)	Afghanistan	33 00 N	65 00 E
Agalega Islands	Mauritius	10 25 S	56 40 E
Agana (city; former name for Hagatna)	Guam	13 28 N	144 45 E
Ajaccio (city)	France (Corsica)	41 55 N	8 44 E
Ajaria (region)	Georgia	41 45 N	42 10 E
Akmola (city; former name for Astana)	Kazakhstan	51 10 N	71 30 E
Aksai Chin (region)	China (de facto), India (claimed)	35 00 N	79 00 E
Al Arabiyah as Suudiyah (local name for Saudi Arabia)	Saudi Arabia	25 00 N	45 00 E
Al Bahrayn (local name for Bahrain)	Bahrain	26 00 N	50 33 E
Al Imarat al Arabiyah al Muttahidah (local name for the United Arab Emirates)	United Arab Emirates	24 00 N	54 00 E
Al Iraq (local name for Iraq)	Iraq	33 00 N	44 00 E
Al Jaza'ir (local name for Algeria)	Algeria	28 00 N	3 00 E
Al Kuwayt (local name for Kuwait)	Kuwait	29 30 N	45 45 E
Al Maghrib (local name for Morocco)	Morocco	32 00 N	5 00 W
Al Urdun (local name for Jordan)	Jordan	31 00 N	36 00 E
Al Yaman (local name for Yemen)	Yemen	15 00 N	48 00 E
Aland Islands	Finland	60 15 N	20 00 E
Alaska (state)	United States	65 00 N	153 00 W

Name	Entry in *The World Factbook*	Latitude (deg min)	Longitude (deg min)
Alaska, Gulf of	Pacific Ocean	58 00 N	145 00 W
Alboran Sea	Atlantic Ocean	36 00 N	2 30 W
Aldabra Islands (Groupe d'Aldabra)	Seychelles	9 25 S	46 22 E
Alderney (island)	Guernsey	49 43 N	2 12 W
Aleutian Islands	United States (Alaska)	52 00 N	176 00 W
Alexander Archipelago (island group)	United States (Alaska)	57 00 N	134 00 W
Alexander Island	Antarctica	71 00 S	70 00 W
Alexandretta (region; former name for Iskenderun)	Turkey	36 34 N	36 08 E
Alexandria (city)	Egypt	31 12 N	29 54 E
Algiers (capital)	Algeria	36 47 N	2 03 E
Alhucemas, Penon de (island group)	Spain	35 13 N	3 53 W
Alma-Ata (city; former name for Almaty)	Kazakhstan	43 15 N	76 57 E
Almaty (former capital)	Kazakhstan	43 15 N	76 57 E
Alofi (capital)	Niue	19 01 S	169 55 W
Alphonse Island	Seychelles	7 01 S	52 45 E
Alsace (region)	France	48 30 N	7 20 E
Amami Strait	Pacific Ocean	28 40 N	129 30 E
Amindivi Islands (former name for Laccadive Islands)	India	11 30 N	72 30 E
Amirante Isles (island group; also Les Amirantes)	Seychelles	6 00 S	53 10 E
Amman (capital)	Jordan	31 57 N	35 56 E
Amsterdam (capital)	Netherlands	52 23 N	4 54 E
Amsterdam Island (Ile Amsterdam)	French Southern and Antarctic Lands	37 52 S	77 32 E
Amundsen Sea	Southern Ocean	72 30 S	112 00 W
Amur River	China, Russia	52 56 N	141 10 E
Amurskiy Liman (strait)	Pacific Ocean	53 00 N	141 30 E
Anadyrskiy Zaliv (gulf)	Pacific Ocean	64 00 N	177 00 E
Anatolia (region)	Turkey	39 00 N	35 00 E
Andaman Islands	India	12 00 N	92 45 E
Andaman Sea	Indian Ocean	10 00 N	95 00 E
Andorra la Vella (capital)	Andorra	42 30 N	1 30 E
Andros (island)	Greece	37 45 N	24 42 E
Andros Island	The Bahamas	24 26 N	77 57 W
Anegada Passage	Atlantic Ocean	18 30 N	63 40 W
Angkor Wat (ruins)	Cambodia	13 26 N	103 50 E
Anglo-Egyptian Sudan (former name for Sudan)	Sudan	15 00 N	30 00 E
Anjouan (island)	Comoros	12 15 S	44 25 E
Ankara (capital)	Turkey	39 56 N	32 52 E
Annobon (island)	Equatorial Guinea	1 25 S	5 36 E
Antananarivo (capital)	Madagascar	18 52 S	47 30 E
Antigua (island)	Antigua and Barbuda	14 34 N	90 44 W
Antipodes Islands	New Zealand	49 41 S	178 43 E
Antwerp (city)	Belgium	51 13 N	4 25 E
Aomen (local Chinese short-form name for Macau)	Macau	22 10 N	113 33 E
Aozou Strip (region)	Chad	22 00 N	18 00 E
Apia (capital)	Samoa	13 50 S	171 44 W

Name	Entry in *The World Factbook*	Latitude (deg min)	Longitude (deg min)
Aqaba, Gulf of	Indian Ocean	29 00 N	34 30 E
Arab, Shatt al (river)	Iran, Iraq	29 57 N	48 34 E
Arabian Sea	Indian Ocean	15 00 N	65 00 E
Arafura Sea	Pacific Ocean	9 00 S	133 00 E
Aral Sea	Kazakhstan, Uzbekistan	45 00 N	60 00 E
Argun River	China, Russia	53 20 N	121 28 E
Aru Sea	Pacific Ocean	6 15 S	135 00 E
As-Sudan (local name for Sudan)	Sudan	15 00 N	30 00 E
Ascension Island	Saint Helena, Ascension, and Tristan da Cunha	7 57 S	14 22 W
Ashgabat, Ashkhabad (capital)	Turkmenistan	37 57 N	58 23 E
Asmara, Asmera (capital)	Eritrea	15 20 N	38 53 E
Assumption Island	Seychelles	9 46 S	46 34 E
Astana (capital; formerly Akmola)	Kazakhstan	51 10 N	71 30 E
Asuncion (capital)	Paraguay	25 16 S	57 40 W
Asuncion Island	Northern Mariana Islands	19 40 N	145 24 E
Atacama (desert)	Chile	23 00 S	70 10 W
Atacama (region)	Chile	24 30 S	69 15 W
Athens (capital)	Greece	37 59 N	23 44 E
Attu Island	United States	52 55 N	172 57 E
Auckland (city)	New Zealand	36 52 S	174 46 E
Auckland Islands	New Zealand	51 00 S	166 30 E
Australes, Iles (island group; also Iles Tubuai)	French Polynesia	23 20 S	151 00 W
Avarua (capital)	Cook Islands	21 12 S	159 46 W
Axel Heiberg Island	Canada	79 30 N	90 00 W
Azad Kashmir (region)	Pakistan	34 30 N	74 00 E
Azarbaycan, Azerbaidzhan (local name for Azerbaijan)	Azerbaijan	40 30 N	47 30 E
Azores (islands)	Portugal	38 30 N	28 00 W
Azov, Sea of	Atlantic Ocean	49 00 N	36 00 E
Bab el Mandeb (strait)	Indian Ocean	12 40 N	43 20 E
Babuyan Channel	Pacific Ocean	18 44 N	121 40 E
Babuyan Islands	Philippines	19 10 N	121 40 E
Baffin Bay	Arctic Ocean	73 00 N	66 00 W
Baffin Island	Canada	68 00 N	70 00 W
Baghdad (capital)	Iraq	33 21 N	44 25 E
Baku (capital; also Baki, Baky)	Azerbaijan	40 23 N	49 51 E
Balabac Strait	Pacific Ocean	7 35 N	117 00 E
Balearic Islands	Spain	39 30 N	3 00 E
Balearic Sea (Iberian Sea)	Atlantic Ocean (Mediterranean Sea)	40 30 N	2 00 E
Bali (island)	Indonesia	8 20 S	115 00 E
Bali Sea	Indian Ocean	7 45 S	115 30 E
Balintang Channel	Pacific Ocean	19 49 N	121 40 E
Balintang Islands	Philippines	19 55 N	122 10 E

Name	Entry in *The World Factbook*	Latitude (deg min)	Longitude (deg min)
Balkan Peninsula	Albania, Bosnia and Herzegovina, Bulgaria, Croatia, Greece, Kosovo, Macedonia, Montenegro, Romania, Serbia, Slovenia, Turkey (European part)	42 00 N	23 00 E
Balleny Islands	Antarctica	67 00 S	163 00 E
Balochistan (region)	Pakistan	28 00 N	63 00 E
Baltic Sea	Atlantic Ocean	57 00 N	19 00 E
Bamako (capital)	Mali	12 39 N	8 00 W
Banaba (Ocean Island)	Kiribati	0 52 S	169 35 E
Banat (region)	Hungary, Romania, Serbia	45 30 N	21 00 E
Banda Sea	Pacific Ocean	5 00 S	128 00 E
Bandar Seri Begawan (capital)	Brunei	4 53 N	114 56 E
Bangka (island)	Indonesia	2 30 S	106 00 E
Bangkok (capital)	Thailand	13 45 N	100 31 E
Bangui (capital)	Central African Republic	4 22 N	18 35 E
Banjul (capital)	The Gambia	13 28 N	16 39 W
Banks Island	Canada	75 15 N	121 30 W
Banks Island	Australia	10 12 S	142 16 E
Banks Islands (Iles Banks)	Vanuatu	14 00 S	167 30 E
Barbuda (island)	Antigua and Barbuda	17 38 N	61 48 W
Barcelona (city)	Spain	41 25 N	2 13 E
Barents Sea	Arctic Ocean	74 00 N	36 00 E
Barranquilla (city)	Colombia	10 59 N	74 48 W
Bashi Channel	Pacific Ocean	22 00 N	121 00 E
Basilan Strait	Pacific Ocean	6 49 N	122 05 E
Basque Provinces	Spain	43 00 N	2 30 W
Bass Strait	Pacific Ocean	39 20 S	145 30 E
Bassas da India	Indian Ocean	21 30 S	39 50 E
Basse-Terre (capital)	France (Guadeloupe)	16 00 N	61 44 W
Basseterre (capital)	Saint Kitts and Nevis	17 18 N	62 43 W
Bastia (city)	France (Corsica)	42 42 N	9 27 E
Basutoland (former name for Lesotho)	Lesotho	29 30 S	28 30 E
Batan Islands	Philippines	20 30 N	121 50 E
Bavaria (region; also Bayern)	Germany	48 30 N	11 30 E
Beagle Channel	Atlantic Ocean	54 53 S	68 10 W
Bear Island (see Bjornoya)	Svalbard	74 26 N	19 05 E
Beaufort Sea	Arctic Ocean	73 00 N	140 00 W
Bechuanaland (former name for Botswana)	Botswana	22 00 S	24 00 E
Beijing (capital)	China	39 56 N	116 24 E
Beirut (capital)	Lebanon	33 53 N	35 30 E
Bekaa Valley	Lebanon	34 00 N	36 05 E
Belau (Palau Islands)	Palau	7 30 N	134 30 E
Belep Islands (Iles Belep)	New Caledonia	19 45 S	163 40 E
Belfast (city)	United Kingdom	54 36 N	5 55 W
Belgian Congo (former name for Democratic Republic of the Congo)	Democratic Republic of the Congo	0 00 N	25 00 E

Name	Entry in *The World Factbook*	Latitude (deg min)	Longitude (deg min)
Belgie, Belgique (local name for Belgium)	Belgium	50 50 N	4 00 E
Belgrade (capital)	Serbia	44 50 N	20 30 E
Belize City	Belize	17 30 N	88 12 W
Belle Isle, Strait of	Atlantic Ocean	51 35 N	56 30 W
Bellingshausen Sea	Southern Ocean	71 00 S	85 00 W
Belmopan (capital)	Belize	17 15 N	88 46 W
Belorussia (former name for Belarus)	Belarus	53 00 N	28 00 E
Benadir (region; former name of Italian Somaliland)	Somalia	4 00 N	46 00 E
Bengal (region)	Bangladesh, India	24 30 N	88 15 E
Bengal, Bay of	Indian Ocean	15 00 N	90 00 E
Berau, Gulf of	Pacific Ocean	2 30 S	132 30 E
Bering Island	Russia	55 00 N	166 30 E
Bering Sea	Pacific Ocean	60 00 N	175 00 W
Bering Strait	Pacific Ocean	65 30 N	169 00 W
Berkner Island	Antarctica	79 30 S	49 30 W
Berlin (capital)	Germany	52 31 N	13 24 E
Berlin, East (former name for eastern sector of Berlin)	Germany	52 30 N	13 33 E
Berlin, West (former name for western sector of Berlin)	Germany	52 30 N	13 20 E
Bern (capital)	Switzerland	46 57 N	7 26 E
Bessarabia (region)	Moldova, Romania, Ukraine	47 00 N	28 30 E
Bharat (local name for India)	India	20 00 N	77 00 E
Bhopal (city)	India	23 16 N	77 24 E
Biafra (region)	Nigeria	5 30 N	7 30 E
Big Diomede Island	Russia	65 46 N	169 06 W
Bijagos, Arquipelago dos (island group)	Guinea-Bissau	11 25 N	16 20 W
Bikini Atoll	Marshall Islands	11 35 N	165 23 E
Bilbao (city)	Spain	43 15 N	2 58 W
Bioko (island)	Equatorial Guinea	3 30 N	8 42 E
Biscay, Bay of	Atlantic Ocean	44 00 N	4 00 W
Bishkek (capital)	Kyrgyzstan	42 54 N	74 36 E
Bishop Rock	United Kingdom	49 52 N	6 27 W
Bismarck Archipelago (island group)	Papua New Guinea	5 00 S	150 00 E
Bismarck Sea	Pacific Ocean	4 00 S	148 00 E
Bissau (capital)	Guinea-Bissau	11 51 N	15 35 W
Bjornoya (Bear Island)	Svalbard	74 26 N	19 05 E
Black Forest (region)	Germany	48 00 N	8 15 E
Black Rock (island)	South Georgia and the South Sandwich Islands	53 39 S	41 48 W
Black Sea	Atlantic Ocean	43 00 N	35 00 E
Bloemfontein (judicial capital)	South Africa	29 12 S	26 07 E
Bo Hai (gulf)	Pacific Ocean	38 00 N	120 00 E
Boa Vista (island)	Cabo Verde	16 05 N	22 50 W
Bogota (capital)	Colombia	4 36 N	74 05 W
Bohemia (region)	Czech Republic	50 00 N	14 30 E
Bombay (city; see Mumbai)	India	18 58 N	72 50 E
Bonaire (island)	Netherlands	12 10 N	68 15 W

Name	Entry in *The World Factbook*	Latitude (deg min)	Longitude (deg min)
Bonifacio, Strait of	Atlantic Ocean (Mediterranean Sea)	41 01 N	14 00 E
Bonin Islands	Japan	27 00 N	142 10 E
Bonn (former capital)	Germany	50 44 N	7 05 E
Bophuthatswana (region; enclave)	South Africa	26 30 S	25 30 E
Bora-Bora (island)	French Polynesia	16 30 S	151 45 W
Bordeaux (city)	France	44 50 N	0 34 W
Borneo (island)	Brunei, Indonesia, Malaysia	0 30 N	114 00 E
Bornholm (island)	Denmark	55 10 N	15 00 E
Bosna i Hercegovina (local name for Bosnia and Herzegovina)	Bosnia and Herzegovina	44 00 N	18 00 E
Bosnia (political region)	Bosnia and Herzegovina	44 00 N	18 00 E
Bosporus (strait)	Atlantic Ocean	41 00 N	29 00 E
Bothnia, Gulf of	Atlantic Ocean	63 00 N	20 00 E
Bougainville (island)	Papua New Guinea	6 00 S	155 00 E
Bougainville Strait	Pacific Ocean	6 40 S	156 10 E
Bounty Islands	New Zealand	47 43 S	174 00 E
Bourbon Island (former name of Reunion)	Reunion	21 06 S	55 36 E
Brasilia (capital)	Brazil	15 47 S	47 55 W
Bratislava (capital)	Slovakia	48 09 N	17 07 E
Brazzaville (capital)	Republic of the Congo	4 16 S	15 17 E
Bridgetown (capital)	Barbados	13 06 N	59 37 W
Brisbane (city)	Australia	27 28 S	153 02 E
Bristol Bay	Pacific Ocean	57 00 N	160 00 W
Bristol Channel	Atlantic Ocean	51 18 N	3 30 W
Britain (see Great Britain)	United Kingdom	54 00 N	2 00 W
British Bechuanaland (region; former name for northwest South Africa)	South Africa	27 30 S	23 30 E
British Central African Protectorate (former name of Nyasaland)	Malawi	13 30 S	34 00 E
British East Africa (former name for British possessions in eastern Africa)	Kenya, Tanzania, Uganda	1 00 N	38 00 E
British Guiana (former name for Guyana)	Guyana	5 00 N	59 00 W
British Honduras (former name for Belize)	Belize	17 15 N	88 45 W
British Solomon Islands (former name for Solomon Islands)	Solomon Islands	8 00 S	159 00 E
British Somaliland (former name for northern Somalia)	Somalia	10 00 N	49 00 E
Brussels (capital)	Belgium	50 50 N	4 20 E
Bubiyan (island)	Kuwait	29 47 N	48 10 E
Bucharest (capital)	Romania	44 26 N	26 06 E
Budapest (capital)	Hungary	47 30 N	19 05 E
Buenos Aires (capital)	Argentina	34 36 S	58 27 W
Bujumbura (capital)	Burundi	3 23 S	29 22 E
Bukovina (region)	Romania, Ukraine	48 00 N	26 00 E
Byelarus (local name for Belarus)	Belarus	53 00 N	28 00 E
Byelorussia (former name for Belarus)	Belarus	53 00 N	28 00 E
Cabinda (province)	Angola	5 33 S	12 12 E
Cabot Strait	Atlantic Ocean	47 20 N	59 30 W
Caicos Islands	Turks and Caicos Islands	21 56 N	71 58 W
Cairo (capital)	Egypt	30 03 N	31 15 E

Name	Entry in *The World Factbook*	Latitude (deg min)	Longitude (deg min)
Calcutta (city)	India	22 32 N	88 21 E
Calgary (city)	Canada	51 02 N	114 04 W
California, Gulf of	Pacific Ocean	28 00 N	112 00 W
Cameroun (local name for Cameroon)	Cameroon	6 00 N	12 00 E
Campbell Island	New Zealand	52 33 S	169 09 E
Campeche, Bay of	Atlantic Ocean (Gulf of Mexico)	20 00 N	94 00 W
Canal Zone (former name for US possessions in Panama)	Panama	9 00 N	79 45 W
Canarias Sea	Atlantic Ocean	28 00 N	16 00 W
Canary Islands	Spain	28 00 N	15 30 W
Canberra (capital)	Australia	35 17 S	149 08 E
Cancun (city)	Mexico	21 10 N	86 50 W
Canton (city; now Guangzhou)	China	23 06 N	113 16 E
Canton Island (Kanton Island)	Kiribati	2 49 S	171 40 W
Cape Juby (region; former name for Southern Morocco)	Morocco	27 53 N	12 58 W
Cape Province (region; former name for Northern, Western, and Eastern Cape Provinces of South Africa)	South Africa	31 30 S	22 30 E
Cape Town (legislative capital)	South Africa	33 57 S	18 25 E
Cape of Good Hope (cape; also alternate name for Cape Province of South Africa)	South Africa	34 15 S	18 20 E
Caracas (capital)	Venezuela	10 30 N	66 56 W
Cargados Carajos Shoals	Mauritius	16 25 S	59 38 E
Caribbean Sea	Atlantic Ocean	15 00 N	73 00 W
Caroline Islands	Federated States of Micronesia, Palau	7 30 N	148 00 E
Carpatho-Ukraine (region; former name for Zakarpattya oblast')	Ukraine	48 22 N	23 32 E
Carpentaria, Gulf of	Pacific Ocean	14 00 S	139 00 E
Casablanca (city)	Morocco	33 35 N	7 34 W
Castries (capital)	Saint Lucia	14 01 N	61 00 W
Catalonia (region)	Spain	42 00 N	2 00 E
Cato Island	Australia	23 15 S	155 32 E
Caucasus (region)	Russia	42 00 N	45 00 E
Cayenne (capital)	French Guiana	4 56 N	52 20 W
Celebes (island)	Indonesia	2 00 S	121 00 E
Celebes Sea	Pacific Ocean	3 00 N	122 00 E
Celtic Sea	Atlantic Ocean	51 00 N	6 30 W
Central African Empire (former name for Central African Republic)	Central African Republic	7 00 N	21 00 E
Ceram (Seram) Sea	Pacific Ocean	2 30 S	129 30 E
Ceska Republika (local name for Czech Republic)	Czech Republic	49 45 N	15 30 E
Ceskoslovensko (former local name for Czechoslovakia)	Czech Republic, Slovakia	49 00 N	17 30 E
Cetinje (capital city)	Montenegro	42 24 N	18 55 E
Ceuta (city)	Spain	35 53 N	5 19 W
Ceylon (former name for Sri Lanka)	Sri Lanka	7 00 N	81 00 E
Chafarinas, Islas (island)	Spain	35 12 N	2 26 W
Chagos Archipelago (Oil Islands)	British Indian Ocean Territory	6 00 S	71 30 E
Challenger Deep (Mariana Trench)	Pacific Ocean	11 22 N	142 36 E

Name	Entry in *The World Factbook*	Latitude (deg min)	Longitude (deg min)
Channel Islands	Guernsey, Jersey	49 20 N	2 20 W
Charlotte Amalie (capital)	Virgin Islands	18 21 N	64 56 W
Chatham Islands	New Zealand	44 00 S	176 30 W
Chechnya (region; also Chechnia)	Russia	43 15 N	45 40 E
Cheju Strait	Pacific Ocean	34 00 N	126 30 E
Cheju-do (island)	Korea, South	33 20 N	126 30 E
Chengdu (city)	China	30 43 N	104 04 E
Chennai (city; also Madras)	India	13 04 N	80 16 E
Chesterfield Islands (Iles Chesterfield)	New Caledonia	19 52 S	158 15 E
Chihli, Gulf of (see Bo Hai)	Pacific Ocean	38 30 N	120 00 E
Chiloe (island)	Chile	42 50 S	74 00 W
China, People's Republic of	China	35 00 N	105 00 E
China, Republic of	Taiwan	23 30 N	121 00 E
Chisinau (capital; also Kishinev)	Moldova	47 00 N	28 50 E
Choiseul (island)	Solomon Islands	7 05 S	121 00 E
Choson (local name for North Korea)	North Korea	40 00 N	127 00 E
Christmas Island (Indian Ocean)	Australia	10 25 S	105 39 E
Christmas Island (Pacific Ocean; also Kiritimati)	Kiribati	1 52 N	157 20 W
Chukchi Sea	Arctic Ocean	69 00 N	171 00 W
Chuuk Islands (Truk Islands)	Federated States of Micronesia	7 25 N	151 47 W
Cilicia (region)	Turkey	36 50 N	34 30 E
Ciskei (enclave)	South Africa	33 00 S	27 00 E
Citta del Vaticano (local name for Vatican City)	Holy See	41 54 N	12 27 E
Cochin China (region)	Vietnam	11 00 N	107 00 E
Coco, Isla del (island)	Costa Rica	5 32 N	87 04 W
Cocos Islands	Cocos (Keeling) Islands	12 30 S	96 50 E
Colombo (capital)	Sri Lanka	6 56 N	79 51 E
Colon, Archipielago de (Galapagos Islands)	Ecuador	0 00 N	90 30 W
Commander Islands (Komandorskiye Ostrova)	Russia	55 00 N	167 00 E
Comores (local name for Comoros)	Comoros	12 10 S	44 15 E
Con Son (islands)	Vietnam	8 43 N	106 36 E
Conakry (capital)	Guinea	9 31 N	13 43 W
Confederatio Helvetica (local name for Switzerland)	Switzerland	47 00 N	8 00 E
Congo (Brazzaville) (former name for Republic of the Congo)	Republic of the Congo	1 00 S	15 00 E
Congo (Leopoldville) (former name for the Democratic Republic of the Congo)	Democratic Republic of the Congo	0 00 N	25 00 E
Constantinople (city; former name for Istanbul)	Turkey	41 01 N	28 58 E
Cook Strait	Pacific Ocean	41 15 S	174 30 E
Copenhagen (capital)	Denmark	55 40 N	12 35 E
Coral Sea	Pacific Ocean	15 00 S	150 00 E
Corfu (island)	Greece	39 40 N	19 45 E
Corinth (region)	Greece	37 56 N	22 56 E
Corisco (island)	Equatorial Guinea	0 55 N	9 19 E
Corn Islands (Islas del Maiz)	Nicaragua	12 15 N	83 00 W
Corocoro Island	Guyana, Venezuela	3 38 N	66 50 W
Corsica (island; also Corse)	France	42 00 N	9 00 E

Name	Entry in *The World Factbook*	Latitude (deg min)	Longitude (deg min)
Cosmoledo Group (island group; also Atoll de Cosmoledo)	Seychelles	9 43 S	47 35 E
Cotonou (former capital)	Benin	6 21 N	2 26 E
Cotopaxi (volcano)	Ecuador	0 39 S	78 26 W
Courantyne River	Guyana, Suriname	5 57 N	57 06 W
Cozumel (island)	Mexico	20 30 N	86 55 W
Crete (island)	Greece	35 15 N	24 45 E
Crimea (region)	Ukraine	45 00 N	34 00 E
Crimean Peninsula	Ukraine	45 00 N	34 00 E
Crooked Island Passage	Atlantic Ocean	22 55 N	74 35 W
Crozet Islands (Iles Crozet)	French Southern and Antarctic Lands	46 30 S	51 00 E
Cyclades (island group)	Greece	37 00 N	25 10 E
Cyrenaica (region)	Libya	31 00 N	22 00 E
Czechoslovakia (former name for the entity that subsequently split into the Czech Republic and Slovakia)	Czech Republic, Slovakia	49 00 N	18 00 E
D'Entrecasteaux Islands	Papua New Guinea	9 30 S	150 40 E
Dagestan (region)	Russia	43 00 N	47 00 E
Dahomey (former name for Benin)	Benin	9 30 N	2 15 E
Daito Islands	Japan	43 00 N	17 00 E
Dakar (capital)	Senegal	14 40 N	17 26 W
Dalmatia (region)	Croatia	43 00 N	17 00 E
Daman (city; also Damao)	India	20 10 N	73 00 E
Damascus (capital)	Syria	33 30 N	36 18 E
Danger Islands (see Pukapuka Atoll)	Cook Islands	10 53 S	165 49 W
Danish Straits	Atlantic Ocean	58 00 N	11 00 E
Danish West Indies (former name for the Virgin Islands)	Virgin Islands	18 20 N	64 50 W
Danmark (local name)	Denmark	56 00 N	10 00 E
Danzig (city; former name for Gdansk)	Poland	54 23 N	18 40 E
Dao Bach Long Vi (island)	Vietnam	20 08 N	107 44 E
Dar es Salaam (capital)	Tanzania	6 48 S	39 17 E
Dardanelles (strait)	Atlantic Ocean	40 15 N	26 25 E
Davis Strait	Atlantic Ocean	67 00 N	57 00 W
Dead Sea	Israel, Jordan, West Bank	32 30 N	35 30 E
Deception Island	Antarctica	62 56 S	60 34 W
Denmark Strait	Atlantic Ocean	67 00 N	24 00 W
Desolation Islands (Isles Kerguelen)	French Southern and Antarctic Lands	49 30 S	69 30 E
Deutschland (local name for Germany)	Germany	51 00 N	9 00 E
Devils Island (Ile du Diable)	French Guiana	5 17 N	52 35 W
Devon Island	Canada	76 00 N	87 00 W
Dhaka (capital)	Bangladesh	23 43 N	90 25 E
Dhivehi Raajje (local name for Maldives)	Maldives	3 15 N	73 00 E
Dhofar (region)	Oman	17 00 N	54 10 E
Diego Garcia (island)	British Indian Ocean Territory	7 20 S	72 25 E
Diego Ramirez (islands)	Chile	56 30 S	68 43 W
Dili (capital)	Timor-Leste	8 35 S	125 36 E
Dilmun (former name for Bahrain)	Bahrain	7 00 N	81 00 E

Name	Entry in *The World Factbook*	Latitude (deg min)	Longitude (deg min)
Diomede Islands	Russia (Big Diomede), United States (Little Diomede)	65 47 N	169 00 W
Diu (region)	India	20 42 N	70 59 E
Djibouti (capital)	Djibouti	11 30 N	43 15 E
Dnieper (river)	Belarus, Russia, Ukraine (Dnyapro, Dnepr, Dnipro)	46 30 N	32 18 E
Dniester (river)	Moldova, Ukraine (Nistru, Dnister)	46 18 N	30 17 E
Dobruja (region)	Bulgaria, Romania	43 30 N	28 00 E
Dodecanese (island group)	Greece	36 00 N	27 05 E
Dodoma (city)	Tanzania	6 11 S	35 45 E
Doha (capital)	Qatar	25 17 N	51 32 E
Donets Basin	Russia, Ukraine	48 15 N	38 30 E
Douala (city)	Cameroon	4 03 N	9 42 E
Douglas (capital)	Man, Isle of	54 09 N	4 28 W
Dover, Strait of	Atlantic Ocean	51 00 N	1 30 E
Drake Passage	Atlantic Ocean, Southern Ocean	60 00 S	60 00 W
Druk Yul (local name for Bhutan)	Bhutan	27 30 N	90 30 E
Dubai, Dubayy (city)	United Arab Emirates	25 18 N	55 18 E
Dublin (capital)	Ireland	53 20 N	6 15 W
Duesseldorf (city)	Germany	51 13 N	6 47 E
Durban (city)	South Africa	29 51 S	31 02 E
Dushanbe (capital)	Tajikistan	38 35 N	68 48 E
Dutch Antilles (former name for the Netherlands Antilles)	Aruba, Curacao, Sint Maarten	12 10 N	68 30 W
Dutch East Indies (former name for Indonesia)	Indonesia	5 00 S	120 00 E
Dutch Guiana (former name for Suriname)	Suriname	4 00 N	56 00 W
Dutch West Indies (former name for the Netherlands Antilles)	Aruba, Curacao, Sint Maarten	12 10 N	68 30 W
Dzungarian Gate (valley)	China, Kazakhstan	45 25 N	82 25 E
East China Sea	Pacific Ocean	30 00 N	126 00 E
East Frisian Islands	Germany	53 44 N	7 25 E
East Germany (German Democratic Republic; former name for eastern portion of Germany)	Germany	52 00 N	13 00 E
East Korea Strait (Eastern Channel or Tsushima Strait)	Pacific Ocean	34 00 N	129 00 E
East Pakistan (former name for Bangladesh)	Bangladesh	24 00 N	90 00 E
East Siberian Sea	Arctic Ocean	74 00 N	166 00 E
Easter Island (Isla de Pascua)	Chile	27 07 S	109 22 W
Eastern Channel (East Korea Strait or Tsushima Strait)	Pacific Ocean	34 00 N	129 00 E
Eastern Samoa (former name for American Samoa)	American Samoa	14 20 S	170 00 W
Edinburgh (city)	United Kingdom	55 57 N	3 11 W
Eesti (local name for Estonia)	Estonia	59 00 N	26 00 E
Eire (local name for Ireland)	Ireland	53 00 N	8 00 W
Elba (island)	Italy	42 46 N	10 17 E
Elemi Triangle (region)	Ethiopia (claimed), Kenya (de facto), Sudan (claimed)	5 00 N	35 30 E
Ellada, Ellas (local name for Greece)	Greece	39 00 N	22 00 E
Ellef Ringnes Island	Canada	78 00 N	103 00 W
Ellesmere Island	Canada	81 00 N	80 00 W

Name	Entry in *The World Factbook*	Latitude (deg min)	Longitude (deg min)
Ellice Islands	Tuvalu	8 00 S	178 00 E
Ellsworth Land (region)	Antarctica	75 00 S	92 00 W
Elobey, Islas de (island group)	Equatorial Guinea	0 59 N	9 33 E
Enderbury Island	Kiribati	3 08 S	171 05 W
Enewetak Atoll (Eniwetok Atoll)	Marshall Islands	11 30 N	162 15 E
England (region)	United Kingdom	52 30 N	1 30 W
English Channel	Atlantic Ocean	50 20 N	1 00 W
Eniwetok Atoll (see Enewetak Atoll)	Marshall Islands	11 30 N	162 15 E
Eolie, Isole (island group)	Italy	38 30 N	15 00 E
Epirus, Northern (region)	Albania, Greece	40 00 N	20 30 E
Episkopi Cantonment (capital)	Akrotiri, Dhekelia	34 40 N	32 51 E
Ertra (local name for Eritrea)	Eritrea	15 00 N	39 00 E
Espana	Spain	40 00 N	4 00 W
Essequibo (region; claimed by Venezuela)	Guyana	6 59 N	58 23 W
Etorofu (island; also Iturup)	Russia (de facto)	44 55 N	147 40 E
Europa Island	Indian Ocean	22 20 S	40 22 E
Farquhar Group (island group; also Atoll de Farquhar)	Seychelles	10 10 S	51 10 E
Fashoda (town; also Kodok)	South Sudan	9 53 N	32 7 E
Fergana Valley	Kyrgyzstan, Tajikistan, Uzbekistan	41 00 N	72 00 E
Fernando Po (island; see Bioko)	Equatorial Guinea	3 30 N	8 42 E
Fernando de Noronha (island group)	Brazil	3 51 S	32 25 W
Filipinas (local name for the Philippines; also Pilipinas)	Philippines	13 00 N	122 00 E
Finland, Gulf of	Atlantic Ocean (Baltic Sea)	60 00 N	27 00 E
Fiume (city; former name for Rijeka)	Croatia	45 19 N	14 25 E
Florence (city)	Italy	43 46 N	11 16 E
Flores (island)	Indonesia	8 45 S	121 00 E
Flores Sea	Pacific Ocean	7 40 S	119 45 E
Florida, Straits of	Atlantic Ocean	25 00 N	79 45 W
Fongafale (largest island of Funafuti)	Tuvalu	8 30 S	179 12 E
Former Soviet Union (FSU)	Armenia, Azerbaijan, Belarus, Estonia, Georgia, Kazakhstan, Kyrgyzstan, Latvia, Lithuania, Moldova, Russia, Tajikistan, Turkmenistan, Ukraine, Uzbekistan		
Formosa (island)	Taiwan	23 30 N	121 00 E
Formosa Strait (see Taiwan Strait)	Pacific Ocean	24 00 N	119 00 E
Foroyar (local name for Faroe Islands)	Faroe Islands	62 00 N	7 00 W
Fort-de-France (capital)	Martinique	14 36 N	61 05 W
Frankfurt am Main (city)	Germany	50 07 N	8 41 E
Franz Josef Land (island group)	Russia	81 00 N	55 00 E
Freetown (capital)	Sierra Leone	8 30 N	13 15 W
French Cameroon (former name for Cameroon)	Cameroon	6 00 N	12 00 E
French Guinea (former name for Guinea)	Guinea	11 00 N	10 00 W
French Indochina (former name for French possessions in southeast Asia)	Cambodia, Laos, Vietnam	15 00 N	107 00 E
French Morocco (former name for Morocco)	Morocco	32 00 N	5 00 W

Name	Entry in *The World Factbook*	Latitude (deg min)	Longitude (deg min)
French Somaliland (former name for Djibouti)	Djibouti	11 30 N	43 00 E
French Sudan (former name for Mali)	Mali	17 00 N	4 00 W
French Territory of the Afars and Issas (or FTAI; former name for Djibouti)	Djibouti	11 30 N	43 00 E
French Togoland (former name for Togo)	Togo	8 00 N	1 10 E
French West Indies (former name for French possessions in the West Indies)	Guadeloupe, Martinique	16 30 N	62 00 W
Friendly Islands	Tonga	20 00 S	175 00 W
Frisian Islands	Denmark, Germany, Netherlands	53 35 N	6 40 E
Frunze (city; former name for Bishkek)	Kyrgyzstan	42 54 N	74 36 E
Funafuti (capital, atoll)	Tuvalu	8 30 S	179 12 E
Fundy, Bay of	Atlantic Ocean	45 00 N	66 00 W
Futuna Islands (Hoorn Islands/Iles de Horne)	Wallis and Futuna	14 19 S	178 05 W
Fyn (island)	Denmark	55 20 N	10 25 E
Gaborone (capital)	Botswana	24 45 S	25 55 E
Galapagos Islands (Archipielago de Colon)	Ecuador	0 00 N	90 30 W
Galicia (region)	Spain	42 45 N	8 10 E
Galicia (region)	Poland, Ukraine	49 30 N	23 00 E
Galilee (region)	Israel	32 54 N	35 20 E
Galleons Passage	Atlantic Ocean	11 00 N	60 55 W
Gambier Islands (Iles Gambier)	French Polynesia	23 09 S	134 58 W
Gaspar Strait	Pacific Ocean	3 00 S	107 00 E
Gdansk (city; formerly Danzig)	Poland	54 23 N	18 40 E
Geneva (city)	Switzerland	46 12 N	6 10 E
Genoa (city)	Italy	44 25 N	8 57 E
George Town (capital)	Cayman Islands	19 20 N	81 23 W
George Town (city)	Malaysia	5 26 N	100 16 E
George Town (city)	The Bahamas	23 30 N	75 46 W
Georgetown (capital)	Guyana	6 48 N	58 10 W
Georgetown (city)	The Gambia	13 30 N	14 47 W
German Democratic Republic (East Germany; former name for eastern portion of Germany)	Germany	52 00 N	13 00 E
German Southwest Africa (former name for Namibia)	Namibia	22 00 S	17 00 E
Germany, Federal Republic of	Germany	51 00 N	9 00 E
Gibraltar (city, peninsula)	Gibraltar	36 11 N	5 22 W
Gibraltar, Strait of	Atlantic Ocean	35 57 N	5 36 W
Gidi Pass	Egypt	30 13 N	33 09 E
Gilbert Islands	Kiribati	1 25 N	173 00 E
Glorioso Islands	Indian Ocean	11 30 S	47 20 E
Goa (state)	India	15 20 N	74 00 E
Gobi (desert)	China, Mongolia	42 30 N	107 00 E
Godthab (capital; also Nuuk)	Greenland	64 11 N	51 44 W
Golan Heights (region)	Syria	33 00 N	35 45 E
Gold Coast (former name for Ghana)	Ghana	8 00 N	2 00 W
Golfo San Jorge (gulf)	Atlantic Ocean	46 00 S	66 00 W
Golfo San Matias (gulf)	Atlantic Ocean	41 30 S	64 00 W

Name	Entry in *The World Factbook*	Latitude (deg min)	Longitude (deg min)
Good Hope, Cape of	South Africa	34 24 S	18 30 E
Goteborg (city)	Sweden	57 43 N	11 58 E
Gotland (island)	Sweden	57 30 N	18 33 E
Gough Island	Saint Helena, Ascension, and Tristan da Cunha	40 20 S	9 55 W
Graham Land (region)	Antarctica	65 00 S	64 00 W
Gran Chaco (region)	Argentina, Paraguay	24 00 S	60 00 W
Grand Bahama (island)	The Bahamas	26 40 N	78 35 W
Grand Banks (fishing ground)	Atlantic Ocean	47 06 N	55 48 W
Grand Cayman (island)	Cayman Islands	19 20 N	81 20 W
Grand Turk (capital; also Cockburn Town)	Turks and Caicos Islands	21 28 N	71 08 W
Great Australian Bight	Indian Ocean	35 00 S	130 00 E
Great Belt (strait; also Store Baelt)	Atlantic Ocean	55 30 N	11 00 E
Great Bitter Lake	Egypt	30 20 N	32 23 E
Great Britain (island)	United Kingdom	54 00 N	2 00 W
Great Channel	Indian Ocean	6 25 N	94 20 E
Great Inagua (island)	The Bahamas	21 00 N	73 20 W
Great Rift Valley	Ethiopia, Kenya	0 30 N	36 00 E
Greater Sunda Islands	Brunei, Indonesia, Malaysia	2 00 S	110 00 E
Green Islands	Papua New Guinea	4 30 S	154 10 E
Greenland Sea	Arctic Ocean	79 00 N	5 00 W
Grenadines, Northern (island group)	Saint Vincent and the Grenadines	13 15 N	61 12 W
Grenadines, Southern (island group)	Grenada	12 07 N	61 40 W
Grytviken (town; on South Georgia)	South Georgia and the South Sandwich Islands	54 15 S	36 45 W
Guadalahara (city)	Mexico	20 40 N	103 24 W
Guadalcanal (island)	Solomon Islands	9 32 S	160 12 E
Guadalupe, Isla de (island)	Mexico	29 11 N	118 17 W
Guangzhou (city; also Canton)	China	23 09 N	113 21 E
Guantanamo Bay (US Naval Base)	Cuba	20 00 N	75 08 W
Guatemala (capital)	Guatemala	14 38 N	90 31 W
Guine-Bissau (local name for Guinea-Bissau)	Guinea-Bissau	12 00 N	15 00 W
Guinea Ecuatorial (local name for Equatorial Guinea)	Equatorial Guinea	2 00 N	10 00 E
Guinea, Gulf of	Atlantic Ocean	3 00 N	2 30 E
Guinee (local name for Guinea)	Guinea	11 00 N	10 00 W
Gustavia (capital)	Saint Barthelemy	17 53 N	62 51 W
Guyane Francaise (local name for French Guiana)	French Guiana	4 00 N	53 00 W
Ha'apai Group (island group)	Tonga	19 42 S	174 29 W
Habomai Islands	Russia (de facto)	43 30 N	146 10 E
Hadramaut (region)	Yemen	15 00 N	50 00 E
Hagatna (capital; formerly Agana)	Guam	13 28 N	144 45 E
Hague, The (seat of government)	Netherlands	52 05 N	4 18 E
Haifa (city)	Israel	32 50 N	35 00 E
Hainan Dao (island)	China	19 00 N	109 30 E
Haiphong (city)	Vietnam	20 52 N	106 41 E

Name	Entry in *The World Factbook*	Latitude (deg min)	Longitude (deg min)
Hala'ib Triangle (region)	Egypt (claimed), Sudan (de facto)	22 30 N	35 00 E
Halifax (city)	Canada	44 39 N	63 36 W
Halmahera (island)	Indonesia	1 00 N	128 00 E
Halmahera Sea	Pacific Ocean	0 30 S	129 00 E
Hamburg (city)	Germany	53 34 N	9 59 E
Hamilton (capital)	Bermuda	32 17 N	64 46 W
Han-guk (local name for South Korea	South Korea	37 00 N	127 30 E
Hanoi (capital)	Vietnam	21 02 N	105 51 E
Harare (capital)	Zimbabwe	17 50 S	31 03 E
Harvey Islands (former name for Cook Islands)	Cook Islands	21 14 S	159 46 W
Hatay (province)	Turkey	36 30 N	36 15 E
Havana (capital)	Cuba	23 08 N	82 22 W
Hawaii (island)	United States	19 45 N	155 45 W
Hawaiian Islands	United States	21 00 N	157 45 W
Hawar (island)	Bahrain	25 40 N	50 47 E
Hayastan (local name for Armenia)	Armenia	40 00 N	45 00 E
Heard Island	Heard Island and McDonald Islands	53 06 S	73 30 E
Hejaz (region)	Saudi Arabia	24 30 N	38 30 E
Helsinki (capital)	Finland	60 10 N	24 58 E
Herzegovina (political region)	Bosnia and Herzegovina	44 00 N	18 00 E
Hiiumaa (island)	Estonia	58 50 N	22 30 E
Hispaniola (island)	Dominican Republic, Haiti	18 45 N	71 00 W
Ho Chi Minh City (formerly Saigon)	Vietnam	10 45 N	106 40 E
Hokkaido (island)	Japan	44 00 N	143 00 E
Holland (region)	Netherlands	52 30 N	5 45 E
Hong Kong (special administrative region)	Hong Kong	22 15 N	114 10 E
Honiara (capital)	Solomon Islands	9 26 S	159 57 E
Honshu (island)	Japan	36 00 N	138 00 E
Hormuz, Strait of	Indian Ocean	26 34 N	56 15 E
Horn of Africa (region)	Djibouti, Eritrea, Ethiopia, Somalia	8 00 N	48 00 E
Horn, Cape (Cabo de Hornos)	Chile	55 59 S	67 16 W
Horne, Iles de (island group)	Wallis and Futuna	14 19 S	178 05 W
Hrvatska (local name for Croatia)	Croatia	45 10 N	15 30 E
Hudson Bay	Arctic Ocean	60 00 N	86 00 W
Hudson Strait	Arctic Ocean	62 00 N	71 00 W
Hunter Island	New Caledonia, Vanuatu	22 24 S	172 06 E
Iberian Peninsula	Portugal, Spain	40 00 N	5 00 W
Iceland Sea	Arctic Ocean	68 00 N	20 00 W
Ifni (region; former name of part of Spanish West Africa)	Morocco	29 22 N	10 09 W
Inaccessible Island	Saint Helena, Ascension, and Tristan da Cunha	37 17 S	12 40 W
Indochina (region)	Cambodia, Laos, Vietnam	15 00 N	107 00 E
Ingushetia (region)	Russia	43 15 N	45 00 E
Inhambane (region)	Mozambique	22 30 S	34 30 E

Name	Entry in *The World Factbook*	Latitude (deg min)	Longitude (deg min)
Inini (former name for French Guiana)	French Guiana	4 00 N	53 00 W
Inland Sea	Japan	34 20 N	133 30 E
Inner Hebrides (islands)	United Kingdom	56 30 N	6 20 W
Inner Mongolia (region; also Nei Mongol)	China	42 00 N	113 00 E
Ionian Islands	Greece	38 30 N	20 30 E
Ionian Sea	Atlantic Ocean	38 30 N	18 00 E
Irian Jaya (province)	Indonesia	5 00 S	138 00 E
Irish Sea	Atlantic Ocean	53 30 N	5 20 W
Iron Gate (river gorge)	Romania, Serbia	44 41 N	22 31 E
Iskenderun (region; formerly Alexandretta)	Turkey	36 34 N	36 08 E
Islamabad (capital)	Pakistan	33 42 N	73 10 E
Island (local name for Iceland)	Iceland	65 00 N	18 00 W
Islas Malvinas (island group)	Falkland Islands (Islas Malvinas)	51 45 S	59 00 W
Istanbul (city)	Turkey	41 01 N	28 58 E
Istrian Peninsula	Croatia, Slovenia	45 00 N	14 00 E
Italia (local name for Italy)	Italy	42 50 N	12 50 E
Italian East Africa (former name for Italian possessions in eastern Africa)	Eritrea, Ethiopia, Somalia	8 00 N	38 00 E
Italian Somaliland (former name for southern Somalia)	Somalia	10 00 N	49 00 E
Ittihad al-Imarat al-Arabiyah (local name for the United Arab Emirates)	United Arab Emirates	24 00 N	54 00 E
Iturup (island; see Etorofu)	Russia (de facto)	44 55 N	147 40 E
Ityop'iya (local name for Ethiopia)	Ethiopia	8 00 N	38 00 E
Ivory Coast (former name for Cote d'Ivoire)	Cote d'Ivoire	8 00 N	5 00 W
Iwo Jima (island)	Japan	24 47 N	141 20 E
Izmir (region)	Turkey	38 25 N	27 10 E
Jakarta (capital)	Indonesia	6 10 S	106 48 E
James Bay	Arctic Ocean	54 00 N	80 00 W
Jamestown (capital)	Saint Helena, Ascension, and Tristan da Cunha	15 56 S	5 44 W
Jammu (city)	India	32 42 N	74 52 E
Jammu and Kashmir (region)	India, Pakistan	34 00 N	76 00 E
Japan, Sea of	Pacific Ocean	40 00 N	135 00 E
Jars, Plain of	Laos	19 27 N	103 10 E
Java (island)	Indonesia	7 30 S	110 00 E
Java Sea	Pacific Ocean	5 00 S	110 00 E
Jerusalem (capital, proclaimed)	Israel, West Bank	31 47 N	35 14 E
Jiddah, Jeddah (city)	Saudi Arabia	21 30 N	39 12 E
Johannesburg (city)	South Africa	26 15 S	28 00 E
Joseph Bonaparte Gulf	Pacific Ocean	14 00 S	128 45 E
Juan Fernandez, Islas de (island group)	Chile	33 00 S	80 00 W
Juan de Fuca, Strait of	Pacific Ocean	48 18 N	124 00 W
Juan de Nova Island	Indian Ocean	17 03 S	42 45 E
Juba (capital)	South Sudan	04 51 N	31 37 E
Jubal, Strait of	Indian Ocean	27 40 N	33 55 E
Judaea (region)	Israel, West Bank	31 35 N	35 00 E

Name	Entry in *The World Factbook*	Latitude (deg min)	Longitude (deg min)
Jugoslavia, Jugoslavija (local names for Yugoslavia, a former Balkan federation)	Bosnia and Herzegovina, Croatia, Macedonia, Montenegro, Serbia, Slovenia	43 00 N	21 00 E
Jutland (region)	Denmark	56 00 N	9 15 E
Juventud, Isla de la (Isle of Youth)	Cuba	21 40 N	82 50 W
Kabardino-Balkaria (region)	Russia	43 30 N	43 30 E
Kabul (capital)	Afghanistan	34 31 N	69 12 E
Kaduna (city)	Nigeria	10 33 N	7 27 E
Kailas Range	China, India	30 00 N	82 00 E
Kalaallit Nunaat (local name for Greenland)	Greenland	72 00 N	40 00 W
Kalahari (desert)	Botswana, Namibia	24 30 S	21 00 E
Kalimantan (region)	Indonesia	0 00 N	115 00 E
Kaliningrad (region; formerly part of East Prussia)	Russia	54 30 N	21 00 E
Kamaran (island)	Yemen	15 21 N	42 34 E
Kamchatka Peninsula (Poluostrov Kamchatka)	Russia	56 00 N	160 00 E
Kampala (capital)	Uganda	0 19 N	32 25 E
Kampuchea (former name for Cambodia)	Cambodia	13 00 N	105 00 E
Kane Basin (portion of channel)	Arctic Ocean	79 30 N	68 00 W
Kanton Island	Kiribati	2 49 S	171 40 W
Kara Sea	Arctic Ocean	76 00 N	80 00 E
Karachevo-Cherkessia (region)	Russia	43 40 N	41 50 E
Karachi (city)	Pakistan	24 51 N	67 03 E
Karafuto (island; former name for southern Sakhalin Island)	Russia	50 00 N	143 00 E
Karakoram Pass	China, India	35 30 N	77 50 E
Karelia, Kareliya (region)	Finland, Russia	63 15 N	30 48 E
Karelian Isthmus	Russia	60 25 N	30 00 E
Karimata Strait	Pacific Ocean	2 05 S	108 40 E
Kashmir (region)	India, Pakistan	34 00 N	76 00 E
Katanga (region)	Democratic Republic of the Congo	10 00 S	26 00 E
Kathmandu (capital)	Nepal	27 43 N	85 19 E
Kattegat (strait)	Atlantic Ocean	57 00 N	11 00 E
Kauai Channel	Pacific Ocean	21 45 N	158 50 W
Kazakstan (former name for Kazakhstan)	Kazakhstan	48 00 N	68 00 E
Keeling Islands	Cocos (Keeling) Islands	12 30 S	96 50 E
Kerguelen, Iles (island group)	French Southern and Antarctic Lands	49 30 S	69 30 E
Kermadec Islands	New Zealand	29 50 S	178 15 W
Kerulen River	China, Mongolia	48 48 N	117 00 E
Khabarovsk (city)	Russia	48 27 N	135 06 E
Khanka, Lake	China, Russia	45 00 N	132 24 E
Khartoum (capital)	Sudan	15 36 N	32 32 E
Khios (island)	Greece	38 22 N	26 04 E
Khmer Republic (former name for Cambodia)	Cambodia	13 00 N	105 00 E
Khuriya Muriya Islands (Kuria Muria Islands)	Oman	17 30 N	56 00 E
Khyber Pass	Afghanistan, Pakistan	34 05 N	71 10 E
Kibris (Turkish local name for Cyprus)	Cyprus	35 00 N	33 00 E

Name	Entry in *The World Factbook*	Latitude (deg min)	Longitude (deg min)
Kiel Canal (Nord-Ostsee Kanal)	Atlantic Ocean	53 53 N	9 08 E
Kiev (city; former name for Kyiv)	Ukraine	50 26 N	30 31 E
Kigali (capital)	Rwanda	1 57 S	30 04 E
Kingston (capital)	Jamaica	18 00 N	76 48 W
Kingston (capital)	Norfolk Island	29 03 S	167 58 E
Kingstown (capital)	Saint Vincent and the Grenadines	13 09 N	61 14 W
Kinshasa (capital)	Democratic Republic of the Congo	4 18 S	15 18 E
Kipros (Greek local name for Cyprus)	Cyprus	35 00 N	33 00 E
Kirghiziya, Kirgizia (former name for Kyrgyzstan)	Kyrgyzstan	41 00 N	75 00 E
Kirguizstan (local name for Kyrgyzstan)	Kyrgyzstan	41 00 N	75 00 E
Kiritimati (Christmas Island)	Kiribati	1 52 N	157 20 W
Kishinev (see Chisinau)	Moldova	47 00 N	28 50 E
Kithira Strait	Atlantic Ocean	36 00 N	23 00 E
Kobe (city)	Japan	34 41 N	135 10 E
Kodiak Island	United States	57 49 N	152 23 W
Kodok (town; also Fashoda)	South Sudan	9 53 N	32 7 E
Kola Peninsula (Kol'skiy Poluostrov)	Russia	67 20 N	37 00 E
Kolonia (town; former capital; changed to Palikir)	Federated States of Micronesia	6 58 N	158 13 E
Korea Bay	Pacific Ocean	39 00 N	124 00 E
Korea Strait	Pacific Ocean	34 00 N	129 00 E
Korea, Democratic People's Republic of	North Korea	40 00 N	127 00 E
Korea, Republic of	South Korea	37 00 N	127 30 E
Koror (capital)	Palau	7 20 N	134 29 E
Kosovo (region)	Kosovo	42 30 N	21 00 E
Kosrae (island)	Federated States of Micronesia	5 20 N	163 00 E
Kowloon (city)	Hong Kong	22 18 N	114 10 E
Kra, Isthmus of	Burma, Thailand	10 20 N	99 00 E
Krakatoa (volcano)	Indonesia	6 07 S	105 24 E
Krakow (city)	Poland	50 03 N	19 56 E
Kuala Lumpur (capital)	Malaysia	3 10 N	101 42 E
Kunashiri (island; also Kunashir)	Russia (de facto)	44 20 N	146 00 E
Kunlun Mountains	China	36 00 N	84 00 E
Kuril Islands	Russia (de facto)	46 10 N	152 00 E
Kuwait (capital)	Kuwait	29 20 N	47 59 E
Kuznetsk Basin	Russia	54 00 N	86 00 E
Kwajalein Atoll	Marshall Islands	9 05 N	167 20 E
Kyiv (capital)	Ukraine	50 26 N	30 31 E
Kyushu (island)	Japan	33 00 N	131 00 E
La Paz (administrative capital)	Bolivia	16 30 S	68 09 W
La Perouse Strait	Pacific Ocean	45 45 N	142 00 E
Labrador (peninsula, region)	Canada	54 00 N	62 00 W
Labrador Sea	Atlantic Ocean	60 00 N	55 00 W
Laccadive Islands	India	10 00 N	73 00 E
Laccadive Sea	Indian Ocean	7 00 N	76 00 E
Lagos (former capital)	Nigeria	6 27 N	3 24 E

Name	Entry in *The World Factbook*	Latitude (deg min)	Longitude (deg min)
Lahore (city)	Pakistan	31 33 N	74 23 E
Lake Erie	Atlantic Ocean	42 30 N	81 00 W
Lake Huron	Atlantic Ocean	45 00 N	83 00 W
Lake Michigan	Atlantic Ocean	43 30 N	87 30 W
Lake Ontario	Atlantic Ocean	43 30 N	78 00 W
Lake Superior	Atlantic Ocean	48 00 N	88 00 W
Lakshadweep (Laccadive Islands)	India	10 00 N	73 00 E
Lantau Island	Hong Kong	22 15 N	113 55 E
Lao (local name for Laos)	Laos	18 00 N	105 00 E
Laptev Sea	Arctic Ocean	76 00 N	126 00 E
Las Palmas (city)	Spain (Canary Islands)	28 06 N	15 24 W
Latakia (region)	Syria	36 00 N	35 50 E
Latvija (local name for Latvia)	Latvia	57 00 N	25 00 E
Lau Group (island group)	Fiji	18 20 S	178 30 E
Lefkosa (see Nicosia)	Cyprus	35 10 N	33 22 E
Leipzig (city)	Germany	51 21 N	12 23 E
Lemnos (island)	Greece	39 54 N	25 21 E
Leningrad (city; former name for Saint Petersburg)	Russia	59 55 N	30 15 E
Lesser Sunda Islands	Indonesia	9 00 S	120 00 E
Lesvos (island)	Greece	39 15 N	26 15 E
Leyte (island)	Philippines	10 50 N	124 50 E
Liancourt Rocks (claimed by Japan)	South Korea	37 15 N	131 50 E
Liaodong Wan (gulf)	Pacific Ocean	40 30 N	121 20 E
Liban (local name for Lebanon)	Lebanon	33 50 N	36 50 E
Libreville (capital)	Gabon	0 23 N	9 27 E
Lietuva (local name for Lithuania)	Lithuania	56 00 N	24 00 E
Ligurian Sea	Atlantic Ocean	43 30 N	9 00 E
Lilongwe (capital)	Malawi	13 59 S	33 44 E
Lima (capital)	Peru	12 03 S	77 03 W
Lincoln Sea	Arctic Ocean	83 00 N	56 00 W
Line Islands	Jarvis Island, Kingman Reef, Kiribati, Palmyra Atoll	0 05 N	157 00 W
Lion, Gulf of	Atlantic Ocean	43 20 N	4 00 E
Lisbon (capital)	Portugal	38 43 N	9 08 W
Little Belt (strait; also Lille Baelt)	Atlantic Ocean	55 05 N	9 55 E
Ljubljana (capital)	Slovenia	46 03 N	14 31 E
Llanos (region)	Venezuela	8 00 N	68 00 W
Lobamba (city)	Swaziland	26 27 S	31 12 E
Lombok (island)	Indonesia	8 28 S	116 40 E
Lombok Strait	Indian Ocean	8 30 S	115 50 E
Lome (capital)	Togo	6 08 N	1 13 E
London (capital)	United Kingdom	51 30 N	0 10 W
Longyearbyen (capital)	Svalbard	78 13 N	15 33 E
Lord Howe Island	Australia	31 30 S	159 00 E
Lorraine (region)	France	48 42 N	6 11 E
Louisiade Archipelago	Papua New Guinea	11 00 S	153 00 E

Name	Entry in *The World Factbook*	Latitude (deg min)	Longitude (deg min)
Lourenco Marques (city; former name for Maputo)	Mozambique	25 56 S	32 34 E
Loyalty Islands (Iles Loyaute)	New Caledonia	21 00 S	167 00 E
Luanda (capital)	Angola	8 48 S	13 14 E
Lubnan (local name for Lebanon)	Lebanon	33 50 N	36 50 E
Lubumbashi (city)	Democratic Republic of the Congo	11 40 S	27 28 E
Lusaka (capital)	Zambia	15 25 S	28 17 E
Luxembourg (capital)	Luxembourg	49 45 N	6 10 E
Luzon (island)	Philippines	16 00 N	121 00 E
Luzon Strait	Pacific Ocean	20 30 N	121 00 E
Lyakhov Islands	Russia	73 45 N	138 00 E
Macao	Macau	22 10 N	113 33 E
Macau (special administrative region)	China	22 10 N	113 33 E
Macquarie Island	Australia	54 36 S	158 54 E
Madagasikara (local name for Madagascar)	Madagascar	20 00 S	47 00 E
Maddalena, Isola	Italy	41 13 N	09 24 E
Madeira Islands	Portugal	32 40 N	16 45 W
Madras (city; see Chennai)	India	13 04 N	80 16 E
Madrid (capital)	Spain	40 24 N	3 41 W
Magellan, Strait of	Atlantic Ocean	54 00 S	71 00 W
Maghreb (region)	Algeria, Libya, Mauritania, Morocco, Tunisia	34 00 N	3 00 E
Magreb (local name for Morocco)	Morocco	32 00 N	5 00 W
Magyarorszag (local name for Hungary)	Hungary	47 00 N	20 00 E
Mahe Island	Seychelles	4 41 S	55 30 E
Maiz, Islas del (Corn Islands)	Nicaragua	12 15 N	83 00 W
Majorca Island (Isla de Mallorca)	Spain	39 30 N	3 00 E
Majuro (capital)	Marshall Islands	7 05 N	171 08 E
Makassar Strait	Pacific Ocean	2 00 S	117 30 E
Makedonija (local name for Macedonia)	Macedonia	41 50 N	22 00 E
Malabo (capital)	Equatorial Guinea	3 45 N	8 47 E
Malacca, Strait of	Indian Ocean	2 30 N	101 20 E
Malagasy Republic	Madagascar	20 00 S	47 00 E
Malay Archipelago	Brunei, Indonesia, Malaysia, Papua New Guinea, Philippines	2 30 N	120 00 E
Malay Peninsula	Malaysia, Thailand	7 10 N	100 35 E
Male (capital)	Maldives	4 10 N	73 31 E
Mallorca, Isla de (island; also Majorca)	Spain	39 30 N	3 00 E
Malmady (region)	Belgium	50 26 N	6 02 E
Malpelo, Isla de (island)	Colombia	4 00 N	90 30 W
Malta Channel	Atlantic Ocean	56 44 N	26 53 E
Malvinas, Islas (island group)	Falkland Islands (Islas Malvinas)	51 45 S	59 00 W
Mamoutzou (capital)	Mayotte	12 47 S	45 14 E
Managua (capital)	Nicaragua	12 09 N	86 17 W
Manama (capital)	Bahrain	26 13 N	50 35 E

Name	Entry in *The World Factbook*	Latitude (deg min)	Longitude (deg min)
Manchukuo (former state)	China	44 00 N	124 00 E
Manchuria (region)	China	44 00 N	124 00 E
Manila (capital)	Philippines	14 35 N	121 00 E
Manipa Strait	Pacific Ocean	3 20 S	127 23 E
Mannar, Gulf of	Indian Ocean	8 30 N	79 00 E
Manua Islands	American Samoa	14 13 S	169 35 W
Maputo (capital)	Mozambique	25 58 S	32 35 E
Marcus Island (Minami-tori-shima)	Japan	24 16 N	154 00 E
Margarita, Isla (island)	Venezuela	10 00 N	64 00 W
Mariana Islands	Guam, Northern Mariana Islands	16 00 N	145 30 E
Marie Byrd Land (region)	Antarctica	77 00 S	130 00 W
Marigot (capital)	Saint Martin	18 04 N	63 05 W
Marion Island	South Africa	46 51 S	37 52 E
Marmara, Sea of	Atlantic Ocean	40 40 N	28 15 E
Marquesas Islands (Iles Marquises)	French Polynesia	9 00 S	139 30 W
Marseille (city)	France	43 18 N	5 23 E
Martin Vaz, Ilhas (island group)	Brazil	20 30 S	28 51 W
Mas a Tierra (Robinson Crusoe Island)	Chile	33 38 S	78 52 W
Mascarene Islands	Mauritius, Reunion	21 00 S	57 00 E
Maseru (capital)	Lesotho	29 28 S	27 30 E
Mata-Utu (capital)	Wallis and Futuna	13 57 S	171 56 W
Matsu (island)	Taiwan	26 13 N	119 56 E
Matthew Island	New Caledonia, Vanuatu	22 20 S	171 20 E
Mauritanie (local name for Mauritania)	Mauritania	20 00 N	12 00 W
Mazatlan (city)	Mexico	23 13 N	106 25 W
Mbabane (capital)	Swaziland	26 18 S	31 06 E
McDonald Islands	Heard Island and McDonald Islands	53 06 S	73 30 E
Mecca (city)	Saudi Arabia	21 27 N	39 49 E
Mediterranean Sea	Atlantic Ocean	36 00 N	15 00 E
Melbourne (city)	Australia	37 49 S	144 58 E
Melilla (exclave)	Spain	35 19 N	2 58 W
Memel (region)	Lithuania	55 43 N	21 30 E
Mesopotamia (region)	Iraq	33 00 N	44 00 E
Messina, Strait of	Atlantic Ocean	38 15 N	15 35 E
Mexico City (capital)	Mexico	19 24 N	99 09 W
Mexico, Gulf of	Atlantic Ocean	25 00 N	90 00 W
Middle Congo (former name for Republic of the Congo)	Republic of the Congo	1 00 S	15 00 E
Milan (city)	Italy	45 28 N	9 11 E
Milwaukee Deep (Puerto Rico Trench)	Atlantic Ocean	19 55 N	65 27 W
Minami-tori-shima (Marcus Island)	Japan	24 16 N	154 00 E
Mindanao (island)	Philippines	8 00 N	125 00 E
Mindanao Sea	Pacific Ocean	9 15 N	124 30 E
Mindoro (island)	Philippines	12 50 N	121 05 E
Mindoro Strait	Pacific Ocean	12 20 N	120 40 E
Mingrelia (region)	Georgia	42 30 N	41 52 E

Name	Entry in *The World Factbook*	Latitude (deg min)	Longitude (deg min)
Minicoy Island	India	8 17 N	73 02 E
Minorca Island (Isla de Menorca)	Spain	40 00 N	4 00 E
Minsk (capital)	Belarus	53 54 N	27 34 E
Misr (local name for Egypt)	Egypt	27 00 N	30 00 E
Mitla Pass	Egypt	30 02 N	32 54 E
Mocambique (local name for Mozambique)	Mozambique	18 15 S	35 00 E
Mogadishu (capital)	Somalia	2 04 N	45 22 E
Moldavia (region)	Moldova, Romania	47 00 N	29 00 E
Molucca Sea	Pacific Ocean	2 00 N	127 00 E
Moluccas (Spice Islands)	Indonesia	2 00 S	128 00 E
Mombasa (city)	Kenya	4 03 S	39 40 E
Mona Passage	Atlantic Ocean	18 30 N	67 45 W
Monaco (capital)	Monaco	43 44 N	7 25 E
Mongol Uls (local name for Mongolia)	Mongolia	46 00 N	105 00 E
Monrovia (capital)	Liberia	6 18 N	10 47 W
Monterrey (city)	Mexico	25 40 N	100 19 W
Montevideo (capital)	Uruguay	34 53 S	56 11 W
Montreal (city)	Canada	45 31 N	73 34 W
Moravia (region)	Czech Republic	49 30 N	17 00 E
Moravian Gate (pass)	Czech Republic	49 35 N	17 50 E
Moroni (capital)	Comoros	11 41 S	43 16 E
Mortlock Islands (Nomoi Islands)	Federated States of Micronesia	5 30 N	153 40 E
Moscow (capital)	Russia	55 45 N	37 35 E
Mount Pinatubo (volcano)	Philippines	15 08 N	120 21 E
Mozambique Channel	Indian Ocean	19 00 S	41 00 E
Mumbai (city; also Bombay)	India	18 58 N	72 50 E
Munich, Muenchen (city)	Germany	48 08 N	11 35 E
Muritaniyah (local name for Mauritania)	Mauritania	20 00 N	12 00 W
Musandam Peninsula	Oman, United Arab Emirates	26 18 N	56 24 E
Muscat (capital)	Oman	23 37 N	58 35 E
Muscat and Oman (former name for Oman)	Oman	21 00 N	57 00 E
Myanma, Myanmar	Burma	22 00 N	98 00 E
N'Djamena (capital)	Chad	12 07 N	15 03 E
Nagorno-Karabakh (region)	Azerbaijan	40 00 N	46 40 E
Nairobi (capital)	Kenya	1 17 S	36 49 E
Namib (desert)	Namibia	24 00 S	15 00 E
Nampo-shoto (island group)	Japan	30 00 N	140 00 E
Nan Madol (ruins)	Federated States of Micronesia	6 85 N	158 35 E
Naples (city)	Italy	40 51 N	14 15 E
Nassau (capital)	The Bahamas	25 05 N	77 21 W
Natal (region)	South Africa	29 00 S	30 25 E
Natuna Besar Islands	Indonesia	3 30 N	102 30 E
Natuna Sea	Pacific Ocean	3 30 N	108 00 E
Naxcivan (region)	Azerbaijan	39 20 N	45 20 E
Naxos (island)	Greece	37 05 N	25 30 E
Nederland (local name for the Netherlands)	Netherlands	52 30 N	5 45 E

Name	Entry in *The World Factbook*	Latitude (deg min)	Longitude (deg min)
Nederlandse Antillen (local name for the former Netherlands Antilles)	Curacao, Sint Maarten	12 15 N	68 45 W
Negev (region)	Israel	30 30 N	34 55 E
Negros (island)	Philippines	10 00 N	123 00 E
Nejd (region)	Saudi Arabia	24 05 N	45 15 E
Netherlands Antilles (former name of Dutch Caribbean dependencies)	Curacao, Sint Maarten	12 15 N	68 45 W
Netherlands East Indies (former name for Indonesia)	Indonesia	5 00 S	120 00 E
Netherlands Guiana (former name for Suriname)	Suriname	4 00 N	56 00 W
Nevis (island)	Saint Kitts and Nevis	17 09 N	62 35 W
New Britain (island)	Papua New Guinea	6 00 S	150 00 E
New Delhi (capital)	India	28 36 N	77 12 E
New Guinea (island)	Indonesia, Papua New Guinea	5 00 S	140 00 E
New Hebrides (island group)	Vanuatu	16 00 S	167 00 E
New Ireland (island)	Papua New Guinea	3 20 N	152 00 E
New Siberian Islands	Russia	75 00 N	142 00 E
New Territories (mainland region)	Hong Kong	22 24 N	114 10 E
Newfoundland (island, with mainland area, and a province)	Canada	52 00 N	56 00 W
Niamey (capital)	Niger	13 31 N	2 07 E
Nicobar Islands	India	8 00 N	93 30 E
Nicosia (capital; also Lefkosia)	Cyprus	35 10 N	33 22 E
Nightingale Island	Saint Helena, Ascension, and Tristan da Cunha	37 25 S	12 30 W
Nihon, Nippon (local name for Japan)	Japan	36 00 N	138 00 E
Nomoi Islands (Mortlock Islands)	Federated States of Micronesia	5 30 N	153 40 E
Norge (local name for Norway)	Norway	62 00 N	10 00 E
Norman Isles (Channel Islands)	Guernsey, Jersey	49 20 N	2 20 W
North Atlantic Ocean	Atlantic Ocean	30 00 N	45 00 W
North Channel	Atlantic Ocean	55 10 N	5 40 W
North Frisian Islands	Denmark, Germany	54 50 N	8 12 E
North Greenland Sea	Arctic Ocean	78 00 N	5 00 W
North Island	New Zealand	39 00 S	176 00 E
North Ossetia (region)	Russia	43 00 N	44 10 E
North Pacific Ocean	Pacific Ocean	30 00 N	165 00 W
North Sea	Atlantic Ocean	56 00 N	4 00 E
North Vietnam (former name for northern portion of Vietnam)	Vietnam	23 00 N	106 00 E
North Yemen (Yemen Arab Republic; now part of Yemen)	Yemen	15 00 N	44 00 E
Northeast Providence Channel	Atlantic Ocean	25 40 N	77 09 W
Northern Areas	Pakistan	36 0 N	75 0 E
Northern Cyprus (region)	Cyprus	35 15 N	33 44 E
Northern Epirus (region)	Albania, Greece	40 00 N	20 30 E
Northern Grenadines (political region)	Saint Vincent and the Grenadines	12 45 N	61 15 W
Northern Ireland	United Kingdom	54 40 N	6 45 W
Northern Rhodesia (former name for Zambia)	Zambia	15 00 S	30 00 E
Northwest Passages	Arctic Ocean	74 40 N	100 00 W
Norwegian Sea	Atlantic Ocean	66 00 N	6 00 E

Name	Entry in *The World Factbook*	Latitude (deg min)	Longitude (deg min)
Nouakchott (capital)	Mauritania	18 06 N	15 57 W
Noumea (capital)	New Caledonia	22 16 S	166 27 E
Nouvelle-Caledonie (local name for New Caledonia)	New Caledonia	21 30 S	165 30 E
Nouvelles Hebrides (former name for Vanuatu)	Vanuatu	16 00 S	167 00 E
Novaya Zemlya (islands)	Russia	74 00 N	57 00 E
Nubia (region)	Egypt, Sudan	20 30 N	33 00 E
Nuku'alofa (capital)	Tonga	21 08 S	175 12 W
Nunavut (region)	Canada	72 00 N	90 00 W
Nuuk (capital; also Godthab)	Greenland	64 11 N	51 44 W
Nyasaland (former name for Malawi)	Malawi	13 30 S	34 00 E
Nyassa (region)	Mozambique	13 30 S	37 00 E
Oahu (island)	United States (Hawaii)	21 30 N	158 00 W
Ocean Island (Banaba)	Kiribati	0 52 S	169 35 E
Ocean Island (Kure Island)	United States	28 25 N	178 20 W
Oesterreich (local name for Austria)	Austria	47 20 N	13 20 E
Ogaden (region)	Ethiopia, Somalia	7 00 N	46 00 E
Oil Islands (Chagos Archipelago)	British Indian Ocean Territory	6 00 S	71 30 E
Okhotsk, Sea of	Pacific Ocean	53 00 N	150 00 E
Okinawa (island group)	Japan	26 30 N	128 00 E
Oland (island)	Sweden	56 45 N	16 40 E
Oman, Gulf of	Indian Ocean	24 30 N	58 30 E
Ombai Strait	Pacific Ocean	8 30 S	125 00 E
Oran (city)	Algeria	35 43 N	0 43 W
Orange River Colony (region; former name of Free State Province of South Africa)	South Africa	28 20 S	26 40 E
Oranjestad (capital)	Aruba	12 33 N	70 06 W
Oresund (The Sound) (strait)	Atlantic Ocean	55 50 N	12 40 E
Orkney Islands	United Kingdom	59 00 N	3 00 W
Osaka (city)	Japan	34 42 N	135 30 E
Oslo (capital)	Norway	59 55 N	10 45 E
Osumi Strait (Van Diemen Strait)	Pacific Ocean	31 00 N	131 00 E
Otranto, Strait of	Atlantic Ocean	40 00 N	19 00 E
Ottawa (capital)	Canada	45 25 N	75 40 W
Ouagadougou (capital)	Burkina Faso	12 22 N	1 31 W
Outer Hebrides (islands)	United Kingdom	57 45 N	7 00 W
Outer Mongolia (region)	Mongolia	46 00 N	105 00 E
P'yongyang (capital)	North Korea	39 01 N	125 45 E
Pacific Islands, Trust Territory of the (former name of a large area of the western North Pacific Ocean)	Marshall Islands, Federated States of Micronesia, Northern Mariana Islands, Palau	10 00 N	155 00 E
Pagan (island)	Northern Mariana Islands	18 08 N	145 47 E
Pago Pago (capital)	American Samoa	14 16 S	170 42 W
Palawan (island)	Philippines	9 30 N	118 30 E
Palermo (city)	Italy	38 07 N	13 21 E
Palestine (region)	Israel, West Bank	32 00 N	35 15 E
Palikir (capital)	Federated States of Micronesia	6 55 N	158 08 E
Palk Strait	Indian Ocean	10 00 N	79 45 E

Name	Entry in *The World Factbook*	Latitude (deg min)	Longitude (deg min)
Pamirs (mountains)	China, Tajikistan	38 00 N	73 00 E
Pampas (region)	Argentina	35 00 S	63 00 W
Panama (capital)	Panama	8 58 N	79 32 W
Panama Canal	Panama	9 00 N	79 45 W
Panama, Gulf of	Pacific Ocean	8 00 N	79 30 W
Panay (island)	Philippines	11 15 N	122 30 E
Pantelleria, Isola di (island)	Italy	36 47 N	12 00 E
Papeete (capital)	French Polynesia	17 32 S	149 34 W
Paramaribo (capital)	Suriname	5 50 N	55 10 W
Parece Vela (island)	Japan	20 20 N	136 00 E
Paris (capital)	France	48 52 N	2 20 E
Pascua, Isla de (Easter Island)	Chile	27 07 S	109 22 W
Pashtunistan (region)	Afghanistan, Pakistan	32 00 N	69 00 E
Passion, Ile de la (island)	Clipperton Island	10 17 N	109 13 W
Patagonia (region)	Argentina	48 00 S	61 00 W
Peking (see Beijing)	China	39 56 N	116 24 E
Pelagian Islands (Isole Pelagie)	Italy	35 40 N	12 40 E
Peleliu (Beliliou) (island)	Palau	7 01 N	134 15 E
Peloponnese (peninsula)	Greece	37 30 N	22 25 E
Pemba Island	Tanzania	5 20 S	39 45 E
Penang Island	Malaysia	5 23 N	100 15 E
Pentland Firth (channel)	Atlantic Ocean	58 44 N	3 13 W
Perim (island)	Yemen	12 39 N	43 25 E
Perouse Strait, La	Pacific Ocean	44 45 N	142 00 E
Persia (former name for Iran)	Iran	32 00 N	53 00 E
Persian Gulf	Indian Ocean	27 00 N	51 00 E
Perth (city)	Australia	31 56 S	115 50 E
Pescadores (islands)	Taiwan	23 30 N	119 30 E
Peshawar (city)	Pakistan	34 01 N	71 40 E
Peter I Island	Antarctica	68 48 S	90 35 W
Petrograd (city; former name for Saint Petersburg)	Russia	59 55 N	30 15 E
Philip Island	Norfolk Island	29 08 S	167 57 E
Philippine Sea	Pacific Ocean	20 00 N	134 00 E
Philipsburg (capital)	Sint Maarten	18 1 N	63 2 W
Phnom Penh (capital)	Cambodia	11 33 N	104 55 E
Phoenix Islands	Kiribati	3 30 S	172 00 W
Pinatubo, Mount (volcano)	Philippines	15 08 N	120 21 E
Pines, Isle of (island; former name for Isla de la Juventud)	Cuba	21 40 N	82 50 W
Pleasant Island	Nauru	0 32 S	166 55 E
Plymouth (capital)	Montserrat	16 44 N	62 14 W
Podgorica (administrative capital)	Montenegro	42 26 N	19 16 E
Polska (local name)	Poland	52 00 N	20 00 E
Polynesie Francaise (local name for French Polynesia)	French Polynesia	15 00 S	140 00 W
Pomerania (region)	Germany, Poland	53 40 N	15 35 E
Ponape (Pohnpei) (island)	Federated States of Micronesia	6 55 N	158 15 E
Port Louis (capital)	Mauritius	20 10 S	57 30 E

Name	Entry in *The World Factbook*	Latitude (deg min)	Longitude (deg min)
Port Moresby (capital)	Papua New Guinea	9 30 S	147 10 E
Port-Vila (capital)	Vanuatu	17 44 S	168 19 E
Port-au-Prince (capital)	Haiti	18 32 N	72 20 W
Port-of-Spain (capital)	Trinidad and Tobago	10 39 N	61 31 W
Porto-Novo (capital)	Benin	6 29 N	2 37 E
Portuguese East Africa (former name for Mozambique)	Mozambique	18 15 S	35 00 E
Portuguese Guinea (former name for Guinea-Bissau)	Guinea-Bissau	12 00 N	15 00 W
Portuguese Timor (former name for Timor-Leste)	Timor-Leste	9 00 S	126 00 E
Poznan (city)	Poland	52 25 N	16 55 E
Prague (capital)	Czech Republic	50 05 N	14 28 E
Praia (capital)	Cabo Verde	14 55 N	23 31 W
Prathet Thai (local name for Thailand)	Thailand	15 00 N	100 00 E
Pretoria (administrative capital)	South Africa	25 42 S	28 13 E
Prevlaka peninsula	Croatia	42 24 N	18 31 E
Pribilof Islands	United States	57 00 N	170 00 W
Prince Edward Island	Canada	46 20 N	63 20 W
Prince Edward Islands	South Africa	46 35 S	38 00 E
Prince Patrick Island	Canada	76 30 N	119 00 W
Principe (island)	Sao Tome and Principe	1 38 N	7 25 E
Pristina, Prishtina, Prishtine (capital)	Kosovo	42 40 N	21 10 E
Prussia (region)	Germany, Poland, Russia	53 00 N	14 00 E
Pukapuka Atoll	Cook Islands	10 53 S	165 49 W
Punjab (region)	India, Pakistan	30 50 N	73 30 E
Puntland (region)	Somalia	8 21 N	49 08 E
Qazaqstan (local name for Kazakhstan)	Kazakhstan	48 00 N	68 00 E
Qita Ghazzah (local name Gaza Strip)	Gaza Strip	31 25 N	34 20 E
Quebec (city)	Canada	46 48 N	71 15 W
Queen Charlotte Islands	Canada	53 00 N	132 00 W
Queen Elizabeth Islands	Canada	78 00 N	95 00 W
Queen Maud Land (claimed by Norway)	Antarctica	73 30 S	12 00 E
Quemoy (island)	Taiwan	24 27 N	118 23 E
Quito (capital)	Ecuador	0 13 S	78 30 W
Rabat (capital)	Morocco	34 02 N	6 51 W
Ralik Chain (island group)	Marshall Islands	8 00 N	167 00 E
Rangoon (capital; also Yangon)	Burma	16 47 N	96 10 E
Rapa Nui (Easter Island)	Chile	27 07 S	109 22 W
Ratak Chain (island group)	Marshall Islands	9 00 N	171 00 E
Red Sea	Indian Ocean	20 00 N	38 00 E
Redonda (island)	Antigua and Barbuda	16 55 N	62 19 W
Republica Dominicana (local name for Dominican Republic)	Dominican Republic	19 00 N	70 40 W
Republique Centrafricain (local name for Central African Republic)	Central African Republic	7 00 N	21 00 E
Republique Francaise (local name for France)	France	46 00 N	2 00 E
Republique Gabonaise (local name for Gabon)	Gabon	1 00 S	11 45 E
Republique Rwandaise (local name for Rwanda)	Rwanda	2 00 S	30 00 E
Republique Togolaise (local name for Togo)	Togo	8 00 N	1 10 E

Name	Entry in *The World Factbook*	Latitude (deg min)	Longitude (deg min)
Revillagigedo Island	United States (Alaska)	55 35 N	131 06 W
Revillagigedo Islands	Mexico	19 00 N	112 45 W
Reykjavik (capital)	Iceland	64 09 N	21 57 W
Rhodes (island)	Greece	36 10 N	28 00 E
Rhodesia, Northern (former name for Zambia)	Zambia	15 00 S	30 00 E
Rhodesia, Southern (former name for Zimbabwe)	Zimbabwe	20 00 S	30 00 E
Riga (capital)	Latvia	56 57 N	24 06 E
Riga, Gulf of	Atlantic Ocean	57 30 N	23 30 E
Rio Muni (mainland region)	Equatorial Guinea	1 30 N	10 00 E
Rio de Janiero (city)	Brazil	22 55 S	43 17 W
Rio de Oro (region)	Western Sahara	23 45 N	15 45 W
Rio de la Plata (gulf)	Atlantic Ocean	35 00 S	59 00 W
Riyadh (capital)	Saudi Arabia	24 38 N	46 43 E
Road Town (capital)	British Virgin Islands	18 27 N	64 37 W
Robinson Crusoe Island (Mas a Tierra)	Chile	33 38 S	78 52 W
Rocas, Atol das (island)	Brazil	3 51 S	33 49 W
Rockall (island)	United Kingdom	57 35 N	13 48 W
Rodrigues (island)	Mauritius	19 42 S	63 25 E
Rome (capital)	Italy	41 54 N	12 29 E
Roncador Cay (island)	Colombia	13 32 N	80 03 W
Roosevelt Island	Antarctica	79 30 S	162 00 W
Roseau (capital)	Dominica	15 18 N	61 24 W
Ross Dependency (claimed by New Zealand)	Antarctica	80 00 S	180 00 E
Ross Island	Antarctica	81 30 S	175 00 W
Ross Sea	Antarctica, Southern Ocean	76 00 S	175 00 W
Rossiya (local name for Russia)	Russia	60 00 N	100 00 E
Rota (island)	Northern Mariana Islands	14 10 N	145 12 E
Rotuma (island)	Fiji	12 30 S	177 05 E
Ruanda (former name for Rwanda)	Rwanda	2 00 S	30 00 E
Rub al Khali (desert)	Saudi Arabia	19 30 N	49 00 E
Rumelia (region)	Albania, Bulgaria, Macedonia	42 00 N	22 30 E
Ruthenia (region; former name for Carpatho-Ukraine)	Ukraine	48 22 N	23 32 E
Ryukyu Islands	Japan	26 30 N	128 00 E
Saar (region)	Germany	49 25 N	7 00 E
Saaremaa (island)	Estonia	58 25 N	22 30 E
Saba (island)	Netherlands	17 38 N	63 10 W
Sabah (state)	Malaysia	5 20 N	117 10 E
Sable Island	Canada	43 55 N	59 50 W
Safety Islands (Iles du Salut)	French Guiana	5 20 N	52 37 W
Sahara Occidental (former name for Western Sahara)	Western Sahara	24 30 N	13 00 W
Sahel (region)	Burkina Faso, Chad, The Gambia, Guinea- Bissau, Mali, Mauritania, Niger, Senegal	15 00 N	8 00 W
Saigon (city; former name for Ho Chi Minh City)	Vietnam	10 45 N	106 40 E
Saint Brandon (Cargados Carajos Shoals)	Mauritius	16 25 S	59 38 E
Saint Christopher (island)	Saint Kitts and Nevis	17 20 N	62 45 W
Saint Christopher and Nevis	Saint Kitts and Nevis	17 20 N	62 45 W

Name	Entry in *The World Factbook*	Latitude (deg min)	Longitude (deg min)
Saint Eustatius (island)	Netherlands	17 30 N	63 00 W
Saint George's (capital)	Grenada	12 03 N	61 45 W
Saint George's Channel	Atlantic Ocean	52 00 N	6 00 W
Saint Helena Island	Saint Helena, Ascension, and Tristan da Cunha	15 57 S	5 42 W
Saint Helens, Mount (volcano)	United States	46 15 N	122 12 W
Saint Helier (capital)	Jersey	49 12 N	2 07 W
Saint John (city)	Canada (New Brunswick)	45 16 N	66 04 W
Saint John's (capital)	Antigua and Barbuda	17 06 N	61 51 W
Saint Lawrence Island	United States	49 30 N	67 00 W
Saint Lawrence Seaway	Atlantic Ocean	49 15 N	67 00 W
Saint Lawrence, Gulf of	Atlantic Ocean	48 00 N	62 00 W
Saint Paul Island	Canada	47 12 N	60 09 W
Saint Paul Island	United States	57 11 N	170 16 W
Saint Paul Island (Ile Saint-Paul)	French Southern and Antarctic Lands	38 43 S	77 29 E
Saint Peter Port (capital)	Guernsey	49 27 N	2 32 W
Saint Peter and Saint Paul Rocks (Penedos de Sao Pedro e Sao Paulo)	Brazil	0 23 N	29 23 W
Saint Petersburg (city; former capital)	Russia	59 55 N	30 15 E
Saint Thomas (island)	Virgin Islands	18 21 N	64 55 W
Saint Vincent Passage	Atlantic Ocean	13 30 N	61 00 W
Saint-Denis (capital)	Reunion	20 52 S	55 28 E
Saint-Pierre (capital)	Saint Pierre and Miquelon	46 46 N	56 11 W
Saipan (island)	Northern Mariana Islands	15 12 N	145 45 E
Sak'art'velo (local name for Georgia)	Georgia	42 00 N	43 30 E
Sakhalin Island (Ostrov Sakhalin)	Russia	51 00 N	143 00 E
Sakishima Islands	Japan	24 30 N	124 00 E
Sala y Gomez, Isla (island)	Chile	26 28 S	105 00 W
Salisbury (city; former name for Harare)	Zimbabwe	17 50 S	105 00 W
Salzburg (city)	Austria	47 48 N	13 02 E
Samar (island)	Philippines	12 00 N	125 00 E
Samaria (region)	West Bank	32 15 N	35 10 E
Samoa Islands	American Samoa, Samoa	14 00 S	171 00 W
Samos (island)	Greece	37 48 N	26 44 E
San Ambrosio, Isla (island)	Chile	26 21 S	79 52 W
San Andres y Providencia, Archipielago (island group)	Colombia	13 00 N	81 30 W
San Bernardino Strait	Pacific Ocean	12 32 N	124 10 E
San Felix, Isla (island)	Chile	26 17 S	80 05 W
San Jose (capital)	Costa Rica	9 56 N	84 05 W
San Juan (capital)	Puerto Rico	18 28 N	66 07 W
San Marino (capital)	San Marino	43 56 N	12 25 E
San Salvador (capital)	El Salvador	13 42 N	89 12 W
Sanaa (capital)	Yemen	15 21 N	44 12 E
Sandzak (region)	Montenegro, Serbia	43 05 N	19 45 E
Santa Cruz (city)	Bolivia	17 48 S	63 10 W
Santa Cruz Islands	Solomon Islands	11 00 S	166 15 E

Name	Entry in *The World Factbook*	Latitude (deg min)	Longitude (deg min)
Santa Sede (local name for the Holy See)	Holy See	41 54 N	12 27 E
Santiago (capital)	Chile	33 27 S	70 40 W
Santo Antao (island)	Cabo Verde	17 05 N	25 10 W
Santo Domingo (capital)	Dominican Republic	18 28 N	69 54 W
Sao Paulo (city)	Brazil	23 35 S	46 43 W
Sao Pedro e Sao Paulo, Penedos de (rocks)	Brazil	0 23 N	29 23 W
Sao Tiago (island)	Cabo Verde	15 05 N	23 40 W
Sao Tome (island)	Sao Tome and Principe	0 12 N	6 39 E
Sapporo (city)	Japan	43 04 N	141 20 E
Sapudi Strait	Pacific Ocean	7 05 S	114 10 E
Sarajevo (capital)	Bosnia and Herzegovina	43 52 N	18 25 E
Sarawak (state)	Malaysia	2 30 N	113 30 E
Sardinia (island)	Italy	40 00 N	9 00 E
Sargasso Sea (region)	Atlantic Ocean	30 00 N	55 00 W
Sark (island)	Guernsey	49 26 N	2 21 W
Savage Island (former name for Niue)	Niue	19 02 S	169 52 W
Savu Sea	Pacific Ocean	9 30 S	122 00 E
Saxony (region)	Germany	51 00 N	13 00 E
Schleswig-Holstein (region)	Germany	54 31 N	9 33 E
Schweiz (local German name for Switzerland)	Switzerland	47 00 N	8 00 E
Scopus, Mount	Israel, West Bank	31 48 N	35 14 E
Scotia Sea	Atlantic Ocean, Southern Ocean	56 00 S	40 00 W
Scotland (region)	United Kingdom	57 00 N	4 00 W
Scott Island	Antarctica	67 24 S	179 55 W
Senegambia (region; former name of confederation of Senegal and The Gambia)	The Gambia, Senegal	13 50 N	15 25 W
Senyavin Islands	Federated States of Micronesia	6 55 N	158 00 E
Seoul (capital)	South Korea	37 34 N	127 00 E
Serendib (former name for Sri Lanka)	Sri Lanka	7 00 N	81 00 E
Serrana Bank (shoal)	Colombia	14 25 N	80 16 W
Serranilla Bank (shoal)	Colombia	15 51 N	79 46 W
Settlement, The (capital)	Christmas Island	10 25 S	105 43 E
Severnaya Zemlya (island group; also Northland)	Russia	79 30 N	98 00 E
Shaba (region)	Democratic Republic of the Congo	8 00 S	27 00 E
Shag Island	Heard Island and McDonald Islands	53 00 S	72 30 E
Shag Rocks	South Georgia and the South Sandwich Islands	53 33 S	42 02 W
Shanghai (city)	China	31 14 N	121 30 E
Shenyang (city; also Mukden)	China	41 46 N	123 24 E
Shetland Islands	United Kingdom	60 30 N	1 30 W
Shikoku (island)	Japan	33 45 N	133 30 E
Shikotan (island)	Russia (de facto)	43 47 N	146 45 E
Shqiperia (local name for Albania)	Albania	41 00 N	20 00 E
Siam (former name for Thailand)	Thailand	15 00 N	100 00 E

Name	Entry in *The World Factbook*	Latitude (deg min)	Longitude (deg min)
Siberia (region)	Russia	60 00 N	100 00 E
Sibutu Passage	Pacific Ocean	4 50 N	119 35 E
Sicily (island)	Italy	37 30 N	14 00 E
Sicily, Strait of	Atlantic Ocean	37 20 N	11 20 E
Sidra, Gulf of	Atlantic Ocean	31 30 N	18 00 E
Sikkim (state)	India	27 50 N	88 30 E
Silesia (region)	Czech Republic, Germany, Poland	51 00 N	17 00 E
Sinai Peninsula	Egypt	29 30 N	34 00 E
Singapore (capital)	Singapore	1 17 N	103 51 E
Singapore Strait	Pacific Ocean	1 15 N	104 00 E
Sinkiang (autonomous region; also Xinjiang)	China	42 00 N	86 00 E
Sint Eustatius (island)	Netherlands	17 29 N	62 58 W
Sint Maarten (island; also Saint-Martin)	Sint Maarten, Saint Martin	18 04 N	63 04 W
Sjaelland (island)	Denmark	55 30 N	12 00 E
Skagerrak (strait)	Atlantic Ocean	57 45 N	9 00 E
Skopje (capital)	Macedonia	41 59 N	21 26 E
Slavonia (region)	Croatia	45 27 N	18 00 E
Slovenija (local name for Slovenia)	Slovenia	46 00 N	15 00 E
Slovensko (local name for Slovakia)	Slovakia	48 40 N	19 30 E
Smyrna (region; former name for Izmir)	Turkey	38 25 N	27 10 E
Society Islands (Iles de la Societe)	French Polynesia	17 00 S	150 00 W
Socotra (island)	Yemen	12 30 N	54 00 E
Sofia (capital)	Bulgaria	42 41 N	23 19 E
Solomon Islands, northern	Papua New Guinea	6 00 S	155 00 E
Solomon Islands, southern	Solomon Islands	8 00 S	159 00 E
Solomon Sea	Pacific Ocean	8 00 S	153 00 E
Somaliland (region)	Somalia	9 30 N	46 00 E
Somers Islands (former name for Bermuda)	Bermuda	32 20 N	64 45 W
Songkhla (city)	Thailand	7 12 N	100 36 E
Sound, The (strait; also Oresund)	Atlantic Ocean	55 50 N	12 40 E
South Atlantic Ocean	Atlantic Ocean	30 00 S	15 00 W
South China Sea	Pacific Ocean	10 00 N	113 00 E
South Georgia (island)	South Georgia and the South Sandwich Islands	54 15 S	36 45 W
South Island	New Zealand	43 00 S	171 00 E
South Korea	South Korea	37 00 N	127 30 E
South Orkney Islands	Antarctica	61 00 S	45 00 W
South Ossetia (region)	Georgia	42 20 N	44 00 E
South Pacific Ocean	Pacific Ocean	30 00 S	130 00 W
South Sandwich Islands	South Georgia and the South Sandwich Islands	57 45 S	26 30 W
South Shetland Islands	Antarctica	62 00 S	59 00 W
South Tyrol (region)	Italy	46 30 N	10 30 E
South Vietnam (former name for the southern portion of Vietnam)	Vietnam	12 00 N	108 00 E

Name	Entry in *The World Factbook*	Latitude (deg min)	Longitude (deg min)
South Yemen (People's Democratic Republic of Yemen; now part of Yemen)	Yemen	14 00 N	48 00 E
South-West Africa (former name for Namibia)	Namibia	22 00 S	17 00 E
Southern Grenadines (island group)	Grenada	12 20 N	61 30 W
Southern Rhodesia (former name for Zimbabwe)	Zimbabwe	20 00 S	30 00 E
Soviet Union (former name of a large Eurasian empire, roughly coequal with the former Russian Empire)	Armenia, Azerbaijan, Belarus, Estonia, Georgia, Kazakhstan, Kyrgyzstan, Latvia, Lithuania, Moldova, Russia, Tajikistan, Turkmenistan, Ukraine, Uzbekistan		
Spanish Guinea (former name for Equatorial Guinea)	Equatorial Guinea	2 00 N	10 00 E
Spanish Morocco (former name for northern Morocco)	Morocco	32 00 N	7 00 W
Spanish North Africa (exclaves)	Spain (Ceuta, Islas Chafarinas, Melilla, Penon de Alhucemas, Penon de Velez de la Gomera)	35 15 N	4 00 W
Spanish Sahara (former name)	Western Sahara	24 30 N	13 00 W
Spanish West Africa (former name for Ifni and Spanish Sahara)	Morocco, Western Sahara	25 00 N	13 00 W
Spice Islands (Moluccas)	Indonesia	2 00 S	28 00 E
Spitsbergen (island)	Svalbard	78 00 N	20 00 E
Srbija (local name for Serbia)	Serbia	44 00 N	21 00 E
St. John's (city)	Canada (Newfoundland)	47 34 N	52 43 W
Stanley (capital)	Falkland Islands (Islas Malvinas)	51 42 S	57 41 W
Stockholm (capital)	Sweden	59 20 N	18 03 E
Strasbourg (city)	France	48 35 N	7 44 E
Stuttgart (city)	Germany	48 46 N	9 11 E
Sucre (constitutional capital)	Bolivia	19 02 S	65 17 W
Suez Canal	Egypt	29 55 N	32 33 E
Suez, Gulf of	Indian Ocean	28 10 N	33 27 E
Suisse (local French name for Switzerland)	Switzerland	47 00 N	8 00 E
Sulawesi (island; Celebes)	Indonesia	2 00 S	121 00 E
Sulawesi Sea	Pacific Ocean	3 00 N	122 00 E
Sulu Archipelago (island group)	Philippines	6 00 N	121 00 E
Sulu Sea	Pacific Ocean	8 00 N	120 00 E
Sumatra (island)	Indonesia	0 00 N	102 00 E
Sumba (island)	Indonesia	10 00 S	120 00 E
Sumba Strait	Pacific Ocean	9 10 S	120 00 E
Sumbawa (island)	Indonesia	8 30 S	118 00 E
Sunda Islands (Soenda Isles)	Indonesia, Malaysia	2 00 S	110 00 E
Sunda Strait	Indian Ocean	6 00 S	105 45 E
Suomi (local name for Finland)	Finland	64 00 N	26 00 E
Surabaya (city)	Indonesia	7 13 S	112 45 E
Surigao Strait	Pacific Ocean	10 15 N	125 23 E
Surinam (former name for Suriname)	Suriname	4 00 N	56 00 W
Suriyah (local name for Syria)	Syria	35 00 N	38 00 E
Surtsey (volcanic island)	Iceland	63 17 N	20 40 W
Suva (capital)	Fiji	18 08 S	178 25 E

Name	Entry in *The World Factbook*	Latitude (deg min)	Longitude (deg min)
Sverdlovsk (city; also Yekaterinburg)	Russia	56 50 N	60 39 E
Sverige (local name for Sweden)	Sweden	62 00 N	15 00 E
Svizzera (local Italian name for Switzerland)	Switzerland	47 00 N	8 00 E
Swains Island	American Samoa	11 03 S	171 15 W
Swan Islands	Honduras	17 25 S	83 56 W
Sydney (city)	Australia	33 53 S	151 13 E
T'bilisi (capital)	Georgia	41 43 N	44 49 E
Tadzhikistan (former name for Tajikistan)	Tajikistan	39 00 N	71 00 E
Tahiti (island)	French Polynesia	17 37 S	149 27 W
Taipei (capital)	Taiwan	25 03 N	121 30 E
Taiwan Strait	Pacific Ocean	24 00 N	119 00 E
Tallinn (capital)	Estonia	59 25 N	24 45 E
Tanganyika (former name for the mainland portion of Tanzania)	Tanzania	6 00 S	35 00 E
Tangier (city)	Morocco	35 48 N	5 45 W
Tannu-Tuva (region)	Russia	51 25 N	94 45 E
Tarawa (island)	Kiribati	1 25 N	173 00 E
Tartary, Gulf of	Pacific Ocean	50 00 N	141 00 E
Tashkent (capital)	Uzbekistan	41 20 N	69 18 E
Tasman Sea	Pacific Ocean	4 30 S	168 00 E
Tasmania (island)	Australia	43 00 S	147 00 E
Tatar Strait	Pacific Ocean	50 00 N	141 00 E
Taymyr Peninsula (Poluostrov Taymyr)	Russia	76 00 N	104 00 E
Tchad (local name for Chad)	Chad	15 00 N	19 00 E
Tegucigalpa (capital)	Honduras	14 06 N	87 13 W
Tehran (capital)	Iran	35 40 N	51 26 E
Tel Aviv (capital, de facto)	Israel	32 05 N	34 48 E
Teluk Bone (gulf)	Pacific Ocean	4 00 S	120 45 E
Teluk Tomini (gulf)	Pacific Ocean	0 30 S	121 00 E
Terre Adelie (claimed by France; also Adelie Land)	Antarctica	66 30 S	139 00 E
Terres Australes et Antarctiques Francaises (local name for the French Southern and Antarctic Lands)	French Southern and Antarctic Lands	43 00 S	67 00 E
Thailand, Gulf of	Pacific Ocean	10 00 N	101 00 E
The Former Yugoslav Republic of Macedonia	Macedonia	41 50 N	22 00 E
Thessaloniki (city; also Salonika)	Greece	40 38 N	22 57 E
Thimphu (capital)	Bhutan	27 28 N	89 39 E
Thuringia (region)	Germany	51 00 N	11 00 E
Thurston Island	Antarctica	72 20 S	99 00 W
Tiberias, Lake	Israel	32 48 N	35 35 E
Tibet (autonomous region; also Xizang)	China	32 00 N	90 00 E
Tibilisi (see T'bilisi)	Georgia	41 43 N	44 49 E
Tien Shan (mountains)	China, Kyrgyzstan	42 00 N	80 00 E
Tierra del Fuego (island, island group)	Argentina, Chile	54 00 S	69 00 W
Timor (island)	Timor-Leste, Indonesia	9 00 S	125 00 E
Timor Lorosa'e (local name for Timor-Leste)	Timor-Leste	9 00 N	126 00 E
Timor Sea	Pacific Ocean	11 00 S	128 00 E
Tinian (island)	Northern Mariana Islands	15 00 N	145 38 E

Name	Entry in *The World Factbook*	Latitude (deg min)	Longitude (deg min)
Tiran, Strait of	Indian Ocean	28 00 N	34 27 E
Tirana, Tirane (capital)	Albania	41 20 N	19 50 E
Tirol, Tyrol (region)	Austria, Italy	47 00 N	11 00 E
Tobago (island)	Trinidad and Tobago	11 15 N	60 40 W
Tokyo (capital)	Japan	35 42 N	139 46 E
Tonkin, Gulf of	Pacific Ocean	20 00 N	108 00 E
Toronto (city)	Canada	43 40 N	79 23 W
Torres Strait	Pacific Ocean	10 25 S	142 10 E
Torshavn (capital)	Faroe Islands	62 01 N	6 46 W
Toshkent (see Tashkent)	Uzbekistan	41 20 N	69 18 E
Transcarpathia (region; alternate name for Carpatho-Ukraine)	Ukraine	48 22 N	23 32 E
Transjordan (former name for Jordan)	Jordan	31 00 N	36 00 E
Transkei (enclave)	South Africa	32 15 S	28 15 E
Transvaal (region; former name for northeastern South Africa)	South Africa	25 10 S	29 25 E
Transylvania (region)	Romania	46 30 N	24 00 E
Trindade, Ilha de (island)	Brazil	20 31 S	29 20 W
Trinidad (island)	Trinidad and Tobago	10 22 N	61 15 W
Tripoli (capital)	Libya	32 54 N	13 11 E
Tripoli (city)	Lebanon	34 26 N	35 51 E
Tripolitania (region)	Libya	31 00 N	14 00 E
Tristan da Cunha Group (island group)	Saint Helena, Ascension, and Tristan da Cunha	37 15 S	12 30 W
Trobriand Islands	Papua New Guinea	8 38 S	151 04 E
Tromelin Island	Indian Ocean	15 52 S	54 25 E
Trucial Coast (former name for the United Arab Emirates)	United Arab Emirates	24 00 N	54 00 E
Trucial Oman (former name for the United Arab Emirates)	United Arab Emirates	24 00 N	54 00 E
Trucial States (former name for the United Arab Emirates)	United Arab Emirates	24 00 N	54 00 E
Truk Islands (former name for the Chuuk Islands)	Federated States of Micronesia	7 25 N	151 47 E
Tsugaru Strait	Pacific Ocean	41 35 N	141 00 E
Tuamotu Islands (Iles Tuamotu)	French Polynesia	19 00 S	142 00 W
Tubuai Islands (Iles Tubuai)	French Polynesia	23 00 S	150 00 W
Tunb al Kubra (island)	Iran	26 14 N	55 19 E
Tunb as Sughra (island)	Iran	26 14 N	55 09 E
Tunis (capital)	Tunisia	36 48 N	10 11 E
Turin (city)	Italy	45 04 N	7 40 E
Turkish Straits (see Bosporus and Dardenelles)	Atlantic Ocean	40 40 N	28 00 E
Turkiye (local name for Turkey)	Turkey	39 00 N	35 00 E
Turkmenia, Turkmeniya (former name for Turkmenistan)	Turkmenistan	40 00 N	60 00 E
Turks Island Passage	Atlantic Ocean	21 40 N	71 00 W
Tuscany (region)	Italy	43 25 N	11 00 E
Tutuila (island)	American Samoa	14 18 S	170 42 W
Tyrrhenian Sea	Atlantic Ocean	40 00 N	12 00 E
Ubangi-Shari (former name for the Central African Republic	Central African Republic	6 38 N	20 33 E
Ukrayina (local name for Ukraine)	Ukraine	49 00 N	32 00 E
Ulaanbaatar (capital)	Mongolia	47 55 N	106 53 E
Ullung-do (island)	South Korea	37 29 N	130 52 E

Name	Entry in *The World Factbook*	Latitude (deg min)	Longitude (deg min)
Ulster (region)	Ireland, United Kingdom	54 35 N	7 00 W
Uman (local name for Oman)	Oman	21 00 N	57 00 E
Unimak Pass (strait)	Pacific Ocean	54 20 N	164 50 W
Union of Soviet Socialist Republics or USSR (former name of a large Eurasian empire, roughly coequal with the former Russian Empire)	Armenia, Azerbaijan, Belarus, Estonia, Georgia, Kazakhstan, Kyrgyzstan, Latvia, Lithuania, Moldova, Russia, Tajikistan, Turkmenistan, Ukraine, Uzbekistan		
United Arab Republic or UAR (former name for a federation between Egypt and Syria)	Egypt, Syria		
Upper Volta (former name for Burkina Faso)	Burkina Faso	13 00 N	2 00 W
Ural Mountains	Kazakhstan, Russia	60 00 N	60 00 E
Urdunn (local name for Jordan)	Jordan	31 00 N	36 00 E
Urundi (former name for Burundi)	Burundi	3 30 S	30 00 E
Ussuri River	China, Russia	48 28 N	135 02 E
Vaduz (capital)	Liechtenstein	47 09 N	9 31 E
Vakhan (Wakhan Corridor)	Afghanistan	37 00 N	73 00 E
Valletta (capital)	Malta	35 54 N	14 31 E
Valley, The (capital)	Anguilla	18 13 N	63 04 W
Van Diemen Strait (Osumi Strait)	Pacific Ocean	31 00 N	131 00 E
Vancouver (city)	Canada	49 16 N	123 08 W
Vancouver Island	Canada	49 45 N	126 00 W
Vatican City (capital)	Holy See	41 54 N	12 27 E
Velez de la Gomera, Penon de (island)	Spain	35 11 N	4 18 W
Venda (enclave)	South Africa	23 00 S	31 00 E
Verde Island Passage	Pacific Ocean	13 34 N	120 51 E
Victoria (capital)	Seychelles	4 38 S	55 27 E
Victoria (island)	Canada	71 00 N	110 00 W
Victoria Land (region)	Antarctica	72 00 S	155 00 E
Vienna (capital)	Austria	48 12 N	16 22 E
Vientiane (capital)	Laos	17 58 N	102 36 E
Vilnius (capital)	Lithuania	54 41 N	25 19 E
Viti Levu (island)	Fiji	18 00 S	178 00 E
Vladivostok (city)	Russia	43 10 N	131 56 E
Vojvodina (region)	Serbia	45 35 N	20 00 E
Volcano Islands	Japan	25 00 N	141 00 E
Vostok Island	Kiribati	10 06 S	152 23 W
Wake Atoll	Wake Island	19 17 N	166 39 E
Wakhan Corridor (see Vakhan)	Afghanistan	37 00 N	73 00 E
Walachia (region)	Romania	44 45 N	26 05 E
Wales (region)	United Kingdom	52 30 N	3 30 W
Wallis Islands	Wallis and Futuna	13 17 S	176 10 W
Walvis Bay (city; former exclave)	Namibia	22 59 S	14 31 E
Warsaw (capital)	Poland	52 15 N	21 00 E
Washington, DC (capital)	United States	38 53 N	77 02 W
Weddell Sea	Southern Ocean	72 00 S	45 00 W
Wellington (capital)	New Zealand	41 28 S	174 51 E

Name	Entry in *The World Factbook*	Latitude (deg min)	Longitude (deg min)
West Frisian Islands	Netherlands	53 26 N	5 30 E
West Germany (Federal Republic of Germany; former name for western portion of Germany)	Germany	53 22 N	5 20 E
West Island (capital)	Cocos (Keeling) Islands	12 10 S	96 55 E
West Korea Strait (Western Channel)	Pacific Ocean	34 40 N	129 00 E
West Pakistan (former name for present-day Pakistan)	Pakistan	30 00 N	70 00 E
West Siberian Plain	Russia	60 00 N	75 00 E
Western Channel (West Korea Strait)	Pacific Ocean	34 40 N	129 00 E
Western Samoa (former name for Samoa)	Samoa	13 35 S	172 20 W
Wetar Strait	Pacific Ocean	8 20 S	126 30 E
White Sea	Arctic Ocean	65 30 N	38 00 E
Wilkes Land (region)	Antarctica	71 00 S	120 00 E
Willemstad (capital)	Curacao	12 06 N	68 56 W
Windhoek (capital)	Namibia	22 34 S	17 06 E
Windward Passage	Atlantic Ocean	20 00 N	73 50 W
Winnipeg (city)	Canada	49 53 N	97 10 W
Wrangel Island (Ostrov Vrangelya)	Russia	71 14 N	179 36 W
Xianggang (local name for Hong Kong)	Hong Kong	22 15 N	114 10 E
Y'israel (local name for Israel)	Israel	31 30 N	34 45 E
Yaitopya (local name for Ethiopia)	Ethiopia	8 00 N	38 00 E
Yalu River	China, North Korea	39 55 N	124 20 E
Yamoussoukro (capital)	Cote d'Ivoire	6 49 N	5 17 W
Yangon (see Rangoon)	Burma	16 47 N	96 10 E
Yaounde (capital)	Cameroon	3 52 N	11 31 E
Yap Islands	Federated States of Micronesia	9 30 N	138 00 E
Yaren (governmental center)	Nauru	0 32 S	166 55 E
Yekaterinburg (city; formerly Sverdlovsk)	Russia	56 50 N	60 39 E
Yellow Sea	Pacific Ocean	36 00 N	123 00 E
Yemen Arab Republic (also Yemen (Sanaa); former name for northern portion of Yemen)	Yemen	15 00 N	44 00 E
Yemen, People's Democratic Republic of (also Yemen (Aden); former name for southern portion of Yemen)	Yemen	14 00 N	46 00 E
Yerevan (capital)	Armenia	40 11 N	44 30 E
Yokohama (city)	Japan	35 26 N	139 37 E
Youth, Isle of (Isla de la Juventud)	Cuba	21 40 N	82 50 W
Yucatan Channel	Atlantic Ocean	21 45 N	85 45 W
Yucatan Peninsula	Mexico	19 30 N	89 00 W
Yugoslavia (former name for a federation of Serbia and Montenegro)	Montenegro, Serbia	43 00 N	21 00 E
Yugoslavia, Kingdom of (former name for a Balkan federation)	Bosnia and Herzegovina, Croatia, Macedonia, Montenegro, Serbia, Slovenia	43 00 N	19 00 E
Yugoslavia, Socialist Federal Republic of (former name for a Balkan federation)	Bosnia and Herzegovina, Croatia, Macedonia, Montenegro, Serbia, Slovenia	43 00 N	19 00 E
Zagreb (capital)	Croatia	45 48 N	15 58 E
Zaire (former name for the Democratic Republic of the Congo)	Democratic Republic of the Congo	15 00 S	30 00 E
Zakhalinskiy Zaliv (bay)	Pacific Ocean	54 00 N	142 00 E

Name	Entry in *The World Factbook*	Latitude (deg min)	Longitude (deg min)
Zaliv Shelikhova (bay)	Pacific Ocean	60 00 N	157 30 E
Zambezia (region)	Mozambique	16 00 S	37 00 E
Zanzibar (island)	Tanzania	6 10 S	39 11 E
Zhong Guo, Zhonghua (local name for China)	China	35 00 N	105 00 E
Zion, Mount (locale in Jerusalem)	Israel, West Bank	31 46 N	35 14 E
Zurich (city)	Switzerland	47 23 N	8 32 E

WEIGHTS AND MEASURES

Note: At this time, only three countries—Burma, Liberia, and the US—have not adopted the International System of Units (SI, or metric system) as their official system of weights and measures. Although use of the metric system has been sanctioned by law in the US since 1866, it has been slow in displacing the American adaptation of the British Imperial System known as the US Customary System. The US is the only industrialized nation that does not mainly use the metric system in its commercial and standards activities, but there is increasing acceptance in science, medicine, government, and many sectors of industry.

Mathematical Notation

Mathematical Power	Name
10^{18} or 1,000,000,000,000,000,000	one quintillion
10^{15} or 1,000,000,000,000,000	one quadrillion
10^{12} or 1,000,000,000,000	one trillion
10^{9} or 1,000,000,000	one billion
10^{6} or 1,000,000	one million
10^{3} or 1,000	one thousand
10^{2} or 100	one hundred
10^{1} or 10	ten
10^{0} or 1	one
10^{-1} or 0.1	one-tenth
10^{-2} or 0.01	one-hundredth
10^{-3} or 0.001	one-thousandth
10^{-6} or 0.000 001	one-millionth
10^{-9} or 0.000 000 001	one-billionth
10^{-12} or 0.000 000 000 001	one-trillionth
10^{-15} or 0.000 000 000 000 001	one-quadrillionth
10^{-18} or 0.000 000 000 000 000 001	one-quintillionth

Metric Interrelationships

Prefix	Symbol	Length, weight, or capacity
yotta	Y	10^{24}
zetta	Z	10^{21}
exa	E	10^{18}
peta	P	10^{15}
tera	T	10^{12}
giga	G	10^{9}
mega	M	10^{6}
kilo	k	10^{3}
hecto	h	10^{2}
deka	da	10^{1}
basic unit	–	1 meter, 1 gram, 1 liter
deci	d	10^{-1}
centi	c	10^{-2}

milli	m	10^{-3}
micro	u	10^{-6}
nano	n	10^{-9}
pico	p	10^{-12}
femto	f	10^{-15}
atto	a	10^{-18}
zepto	z	10^{-21}
yocto	y	10^{-24}

Conversion Factors

To Convert From	To	Multiply By
acres	ares	40.468 564 224
acres	hectares	0.404 685 642 24
acres	square feet	43,560
acres	square kilometers	0.004 046 856 422 4
acres	square meters	4,046.856 422 4
acres	square miles (statute)	0.001 562 50
acres	square yards	4,840
ares	square meters	100
ares	square yards	119.599
barrels, US beer	gallons	31
barrels, US beer	liters	117.347 77
barrels, US petroleum	gallons (British)	34.97
barrels, US petroleum	gallons (US)	42
barrels, US petroleum	liters	158.987 29
barrels, US proof spirits	gallons	40
barrels, US proof spirits	liters	151.416 47
bushels (US)	bushels (British)	0.968 9
bushels (US)	cubic feet	1.244 456
bushels (US)	cubic inches	2,150.42
bushels (US)	cubic meters	0.035 239 07
bushels (US)	cubic yards	0.046 090 96
bushels (US)	dekaliters	3.523 907
bushels (US)	dry pints	64
bushels (US)	dry quarts	32
bushels (US)	liters	35.239 070 17
bushels (US)	pecks	4
cables	fathoms	120
cables	meters	219.456
cables	yards	240
carat	milligrams	200
centimeters	feet	0.032 808 40
centimeters	inches	0.393 700 8
centimeters	meters	0.01
centimeters	yards	0.010 936 13
centimeters, cubic	cubic inches	0.061 023 744

Conversion Factors

To Convert From	To	Multiply By
centimeters, square	square feet	0.001 076 39
centimeters, square	square inches	0.155 000 31
centimeters, square	square meters	0.000 1
centimeters, square	square yards	0.000 119 599
chains, square surveyor's	ares	4.046 86
chains, square surveyor's	square feet	4,356
chains, surveyor's	feet	66
chains, surveyor's	meters	20.116 8
chains, surveyor's	rods	4
cords of wood	cubic feet	128
cords of wood	cubic meters	3.624 556
cords of wood	cubic yards	4.740 7
cups	liquid ounces (US)	8
cups	liters	0.236 588 2
degrees Celsius	degrees Fahrenheit	multiply by 1.8 and add 32
degrees Fahrenheit	degrees Celsius	subtract 32 and divide by 1.8
dekaliters	bushels	0.283 775 9
dekaliters	cubic feet	0.353 146 7
dekaliters	cubic inches	610.237 4
dekaliters	dry pints	18.161 66
dekaliters	dry quarts	9.080 829 8
dekaliters	liters	10
dekaliters	pecks	1.135 104
drams, avoirdupois	avoirdupois ounces	0.062 55
drams, avoirdupois	grains	27.344
drams, avoirdupois	grams	1.771 845 2
drams, troy	grains	60
drams, troy	grams	3.887 934 6
drams, troy	scruples	3
drams, troy	troy ounces	0.125
drams, liquid (US)	cubic inches	0.226
drams, liquid (US)	liquid drams (British)	1.041
drams, liquid (US)	liquid ounces	0.125
drams, liquid (US)	milliliters	3.696 69
drams, liquid (US)	minims	60
fathoms	feet	6
fathoms	meters	1.828 8
feet	centimeters	30.48
feet	inches	12
feet	kilometers	0.000 304 8
feet	meters	0.304 8
feet	statute miles	0.000 189 39
feet	yards	0.333 333 3
feet, cubic	bushels	0.803 563 95
feet, cubic	cubic decimeters	28.316 847
feet, cubic	cubic inches	1,728

Conversion Factors

To Convert From	To	Multiply By
feet, cubic	cubic meters	0.028 316 846 592
feet, cubic	cubic yards	0.037 037 04
feet, cubic	dry pints	51.428 09
feet, cubic	dry quarts	25.714 05
feet, cubic	gallons	7.480 519
feet, cubic	gills	239.376 6
feet, cubic	liquid ounces	957.506 5
feet, cubic	liquid pints	59.844 16
feet, cubic	liquid quarts	29.922 08
feet, cubic	liters	28.316 846 592
feet, cubic	pecks	3.214 256
feet, square	acres	0.000 022 956 8
feet, square	square centimeters	929.030 4
feet, square	square decimeters	9.290 304
feet, square	square inches	144
feet, square	square meters	0.092 903 04
feet, square	square yards	0.111 111 1
furlongs	feet	660
furlongs	inches	7,920
furlongs	meters	201.168
furlongs	statute miles	0.125
furlongs	yards	220
gallons, liquid (US)	cubic feet	0.133 680 6
gallons, liquid (US)	cubic inches	231
gallons, liquid (US)	cubic meters	0.003 785 411 784
gallons, liquid (US)	cubic yards	0.004 951 13
gallons, liquid (US)	gills (US)	32
gallons, liquid (US)	liquid gallons (British)	0.832 67
gallons, liquid (US)	liquid ounces	128
gallons, liquid (US)	liquid pints	8
gallons, liquid (US)	liquid quarts	4
gallons, liquid (US)	liters	3.785 411 784
gallons, liquid (US)	milliliters	3,785.411 784
gallons, liquid (US)	minims	61,440
gills (US)	centiliters	11.829 4
gills (US)	cubic feet	0.004 177 517
gills (US)	cubic inches	7.218 75
gills (US)	gallons	0.031 25
gills (US)	gills (British)	0.832 67
gills (US)	liquid ounces	4
gills (US)	liquid pints	0.25
gills (US)	liquid quarts	0.125
gills (US)	liters	0.118 294 118 25
gills (US)	milliliters	118.294 118 25
gills (US)	minims	1,920
grains	avoirdupois drams	0.036 571 43

Conversion Factors

To Convert From	To	Multiply By
grains	avoirdupois ounces	0.002 285 71
grains	avoirdupois pounds	0.000 142 86
grains	grams	0.064 798 91
grains	kilograms	0.000 064 798 91
grains	milligrams	64.798 910
grains	pennyweights	0.042
grains	scruples	0.05
grains	troy drams	0.016 6
grains	troy ounces	0.002 083 33
grains	troy pounds	0.000 173 61
grams	avoirdupois drams	0.564 383 39
grams	avoirdupois ounces	0.035 273 961
grams	avoirdupois pounds	0.002 204 622 6
grams	grains	15.432 361
grams	kilograms	0.001
grams	milligrams	1,000
grams	troy ounces	0.032 150 746 6
grams	troy pounds	0.002 679 23
hands (height of horse)	centimeters	10.16
hands (height of horse)	inches	4
hectares	acres	2.471 053 8
hectares	square feet	107,639.1
hectares	square kilometers	0.01
hectares	square meters	10,000
hectares	square miles	0.003 861 02
hectares	square yards	11,959.90
hundredweights, long	avoirdupois pounds	112
hundredweights, long	kilograms	50.802 345
hundredweights, long	long tons	0.05
hundredweights, long	metric tons	0.050 802 345
hundredweights, long	short tons	0.056
hundredweights, short	avoirdupois pounds	100
hundredweights, short	kilograms	45.359 237
hundredweights, short	long tons	0.044 642 86
hundredweights, short	metric tons	0.045 359 237
hundredweights, short	short tons	0.05
inches	centimeters	2.54
inches	feet	0.083 333 33
inches	meters	0.025 4
inches	millimeters	25.4
inches	yards	0.027 777 78
inches, cubic	bushels	0.000 465 025
inches, cubic	cubic centimeters	16.387 064
inches, cubic	cubic feet	0.000 578 703 7
inches, cubic	cubic meters	0.000 016 387 064
inches, cubic	cubic yards	0.000 021 433 47

Conversion Factors

To Convert From	To	Multiply By
inches, cubic	dry pints	0.029 761 6
inches, cubic	dry quarts	0.014 880 8
inches, cubic	gallons	0.004 329 0
inches, cubic	gills	0.138 528 1
inches, cubic	liquid ounces	0.554 112 6
inches, cubic	liquid pints	0.034 632 03
inches, cubic	liquid quarts	0.017 316 02
inches, cubic	liters	0.016 387 064
inches, cubic	milliliters	16.387 064
inches, cubic	minims (US)	265.974 0
inches, cubic	pecks	0.001 860 10
inches, square	square centimeters	6.451 600
inches, square	square feet	0.006 944 44
inches, square	square meters	0.000 645 16
inches, square	square yards	0.000 771 605
kilograms	avoirdupois drams	564.383 4
kilograms	avoirdupois ounces	35.273 962
kilograms	avoirdupois pounds	2.204 622 622
kilograms	grains	15,432.36
kilograms	grams	1,000
kilograms	long tons	0.000 984 2
kilograms	metric tons	0.001
kilograms	short hundredweights	0.022 046 23
kilograms	short tons	0.001 102 31
kilograms	troy ounces	32.150 75
kilograms	troy pounds	2.679 229
kilometers	meters	1,000
kilometers	statute miles	0.621 371 192
kilometers, square	acres	247.105 38
kilometers, square	hectares	100
kilometers, square	square meters	1,000,000
kilometers, square	statute miles	0.386 102 16
knots (nautical mi/hr)	kilometers/hour	1.852
knots (nautical mi/hr)	statute miles/hour	1.151
leagues, nautical	kilometers	5.556
leagues, nautical	nautical miles	3
leagues, statute	kilometers	4.828 032
leagues, statute	statute miles	3
links, square surveyor's	square centimeters	404.686
links, square surveyor's	square inches	62.726 4
links, surveyor's	centimeters	20.116 8
links, surveyor's	chains	0.01
links, surveyor's	inches	7.92
liters	bushels	0.028 377 59
liters	cubic feet	0.035 314 67
liters	cubic inches	61.023 74

Conversion Factors

To Convert From	To	Multiply By
liters	cubic meters	0.001
liters	cubic yards	0.001 307 95
liters	dekaliters	0.1
liters	dry pints	1.816 166
liters	dry quarts	0.908 082 98
liters	gallons	0.264 172 052
liters	gills (US)	8.453 506
liters	liquid ounces	33.814 02
liters	liquid pints	2.113 376
liters	liquid quarts	1.056 688 2
liters	milliliters	1,000
liters	pecks	0.113 510 4
meters	centimeters	100
meters	feet	3.280 839 895
meters	inches	39.370 079
meters	kilometers	0.001
meters	millimeters	1,000
meters	statute miles	0.000 621 371
meters	yards	1.093 613 298
meters, cubic	bushels	28.377 59
meters, cubic	cubic feet	35.314 666 7
meters, cubic	cubic inches	61,023.744
meters, cubic	cubic yards	1.307 950 619
meters, cubic	gallons	264.172 05
meters, cubic	liters	1,000
meters, cubic	pecks	113.510 4
meters, square	acres	0.000 247 105 38
meters, square	hectares	0.000 1
meters, square	square centimeters	10,000
meters, square	square feet	10.763 910 4
meters, square	square inches	1,550.003 1
meters, square	square yards	1.195 990 046
microns	meters	0.000 001
microns	inches	0.000 039 4
mils	inches	0.001
mils	millimeters	0.025 4
miles, nautical	kilometers	1.852 0
miles, nautical	statute miles	1.150 779 4
miles, statute	centimeters	160,934.4
miles, statute	feet	5,280
miles, statute	furlongs	8
miles, statute	inches	63,360
miles, statute	kilometers	1.609 344
miles, statute	meters	1,609.344
miles, statute	rods	320
miles, statute	yards	1,760

Conversion Factors

To Convert From	To	Multiply By
miles, square nautical	square kilometers	3.429 904
miles, square nautical	square statute miles	1.325
miles, square statute	acres	640
miles, square statute	hectares	258.998 811 033 6
miles, square statute	sections	1
miles, square statute	square kilometers	2.589 988 110 336
miles, square statute	square nautical miles	0.755 miles
miles, square statute	square rods	102,400
milligrams	grains	0.015 432 358 35
milliliters	cubic inches	0.061 023 744
milliliters	gallons	0.000 264 17
milliliters	gills (US)	0.008 453 5
milliliters	liquid ounces	0.033 814 02
milliliters	liquid pints	0.002 113 4
milliliters	liquid quarts	0.001 056 7
milliliters	liters	0.001
milliliters	minims	16.230 73
millimeters	inches	0.039 370 078 7
minims (US)	cubic inches	0.003 759 77
minims (US)	gills (US)	0.000 520 83
minims (US)	liquid ounces	0.002 083 33
minims (US)	milliliters	0.061 611 52
minims (US)	minims (British)	1.041
ounces, avoirdupois	avoirdupois drams	16
ounces, avoirdupois	avoirdupois pounds	0.062 5
ounces, avoirdupois	grains	437.5
ounces, avoirdupois	grams	28.349 523 125
ounces, avoirdupois	kilograms	0.028 349 523 125
ounces, avoirdupois	troy ounces	0.911 458 3
ounces, avoirdupois	troy pounds	0.075 954 86
ounces, liquid (US)	cubic feet	0.001 044 38
ounces, liquid (US)	centiliters	2.957 35
ounces, liquid (US)	cubic inches	1.804 687 5
ounces, liquid (US)	gallons	0.007 812 5
ounces, liquid (US)	gills (US)	0.25
ounces, liquid (US)	liquid drams	8
ounces, liquid (US)	liquid ounces (British)	1.041
ounces, liquid (US)	liquid pints	0.062 5
ounces, liquid (US)	liquid quarts	0.031 25
ounces, liquid (US)	liters	0.029 573 53
ounces, liquid (US)	milliliters	29.573 529 6
ounces, liquid (US)	minims	480
ounces, troy	avoirdupois drams	17.554 29
ounces, troy	avoirdupois ounces	1.097 143
ounces, troy	avoirdupois pounds	0.068 571 43
ounces, troy	grains	480

Conversion Factors

To Convert From	To	Multiply By
ounces, troy	grams	31.103 476 8
ounces, troy	pennyweights	20
ounces, troy	troy drams	8
ounces, troy	troy pounds	0.083 333 3
paces (US)	centimeters	76.2
paces (US)	inches	30
pecks (US)	bushels	0.25
pecks (US)	cubic feet	0.311 114
pecks (US)	cubic inches	537.605
pecks (US)	cubic meters	0.008 809 77
pecks (US)	cubic yards	0.011 522 74
pecks (US)	dekaliters	0.880 976 75
pecks (US)	dry pints	16
pecks (US)	dry quarts	8
pecks (US)	liters	8.809 767 5
pecks (US)	pecks (British)	0.968 9
pennyweights	grains	24
pennyweights	grams	1.555 173 84
pennyweights	troy ounces	0.05
pints, dry (US)	bushels	0.015 625
pints, dry (US)	cubic feet	0.019 444 63
pints, dry (US)	cubic inches	33.600 312 5
pints, dry (US)	dekaliters	0.055 061 05
pints, dry (US)	dry pints (British)	0.968 9
pints, dry (US)	dry quarts	0.5
pints, dry (US)	liters	0.550 610 47
pints, liquid (US)	cubic feet	0.016 710 07
pints, liquid (US)	cubic inches	28.875
pints, liquid (US)	deciliters	4.731 76
pints, liquid (US)	gallons	0.125
pints, liquid (US)	gills (US)	4
pints, liquid (US)	liquid ounces	16
pints, liquid (US)	liquid pints (British)	0.832 67
pints, liquid (US)	liquid quarts	0.5
pints, liquid (US)	liters	0.473 176 473
pints, liquid (US)	milliliters	473.176 473
pints, liquid (US)	minims	7,680
points (typographical)	inches	0.013 837
points (typographical)	millimeters	0.351 459 8
pounds, avoirdupois	avoirdupois drams	256
pounds, avoirdupois	avoirdupois ounces	16
pounds, avoirdupois	grains	7,000
pounds, avoirdupois	grams	453.592 37
pounds, avoirdupois	kilograms	0.453 592 37
pounds, avoirdupois	long tons	0.000 446 428 6
pounds, avoirdupois	metric tons	0.000 453 592 37

Conversion Factors

To Convert From	To	Multiply By
pounds, avoirdupois	quintals	0.004 535 92
pounds, avoirdupois	short tons	0.000 5
pounds, avoirdupois	troy ounces	14.583 33
pounds, avoirdupois	troy pounds	1.215 278
pounds, troy	avoirdupois drams	210.651 4
pounds, troy	avoirdupois ounces	13.165 71
pounds, troy	avoirdupois pounds	0.822 857 1
pounds, troy	grains	5,760
pounds, troy	grams	373.241 721 6
pounds, troy	kilograms	0.373 241 721 6
pounds, troy	pennyweights	240
pounds, troy	troy ounces	12
quarts, dry (US)	bushels	0.031 25
quarts, dry (US)	cubic feet	0.038 889 25
quarts, dry (US)	cubic inches	67.200 625
quarts, dry (US)	dekaliters	0.110 122 1
quarts, dry (US)	dry pints	2
quarts, dry (US)	dry quarts (British)	0.968 9
quarts, dry (US)	liters	1.101 221
quarts, dry (US)	pecks	0.125
quarts, dry (US)	pints, dry (US)	2
quarts, liquid (US)	cubic feet	0.033 420 14
quarts, liquid (US)	cubic inches	57.75
quarts, liquid (US)	deciliters	9.463 53
quarts, liquid (US)	gallons	0.25
quarts, liquid (US)	gills (US)	8
quarts, liquid (US)	liquid ounces	32
quarts, liquid (US)	liquid pints (US)	2
quarts, liquid (US)	liquid quarts (British)	0.832 67
quarts, liquid (US)	liters	0.946 352 946
quarts, liquid (US)	milliliters	946.352 946
quarts, liquid (US)	minims	15,360
quintals	avoirdupois pounds	220.462 26
quintals	kilograms	100
quintals	metric tons	0.1
rods	feet	16.5
rods	meters	5.029 2
rods	yards	5.5
rods, square	acres	0.006 25
rods, square	square meters	25.292 85
rods, square	square yards	30.25
scruples	grains	20
scruples	grams	1.295 978 2
scruples	troy drams	0.333
sections (US)	square kilometers	2.589 988 1
sections (US)	square statute miles	1

Conversion Factors

To Convert From	To	Multiply By
spans	centimeters	22.86
spans	inches	9
steres	cubic meters	1
steres	cubic yards	1.307 95
tablespoons	milliliters	14.786 76
tablespoons	teaspoons	3
teaspoons	milliliters	4.928 922
teaspoons	tablespoons	0.333 333
ton-miles, long	metric ton-kilometers	1.635 169
ton-miles, short	metric ton-kilometers	1.459 972
tons, gross register	cubic feet of permanently enclosed space	100
tons, gross register	cubic meters of permanently enclosed space	2.831 684 7
tons, long (deadweight)	avoirdupois ounces	35,840
tons, long (deadweight)	avoirdupois pounds	2,240
tons, long (deadweight)	kilograms	1,016.046 909 8
tons, long (deadweight)	long hundredweights	20
tons, long (deadweight)	metric tons	1.016 046 908 8
tons, long (deadweight)	short hundredweights	22.4
tons, long (deadweight)	short tons	1.12
tons, metric	avoirdupois pounds	2,204.623
tons, metric	kilograms	1,000
tons, metric	long hundredweights	19.684 130 3
tons, metric	long tons	0.984 206 5
tons, metric	quintals	10
tons, metric	short hundredweights	22.046 23
tons, metric	short tons	1.102 311 3
tons, metric	troy ounces	32,150.75
tons, net register	cubic feet of permanently enclosed space for cargo and passengers	100
tons, net register	cubic meters of permanently enclosed space for cargo and passengers	2.831 684 7
tons, shipping	cubic feet of permanently enclosed cargo space	42
tons, shipping	cubic meters of permanently enclosed cargo space	1.189 307 574
tons, short	avoirdupois pounds	2,000
tons, short	kilograms	907.184 74
tons, short	long hundredweights	17.857 14
tons, short	long tons	0.892 857 1
tons, short	metric tons	0.907 184 74
tons, short	short hundredweights	20
townships (US)	sections	36
townships (US)	square kilometers	93.239 572
townships (US)	square statute miles	36
miles, square statute	acres	640
miles, square statute	hectares	258.998 811 033 6
miles, square statute	square feet	27,878,400

Conversion Factors To Convert From	To	Multiply By
miles, square statute	square meters	2,589,988.110 336
miles, square statute	square yards	3,097,600
yards	centimeters	91.44
yards	feet	3
yards	inches	36
yards	meters	0.914 4
yards	miles	0.000 568 18
yards, cubic	bushels	21.696 227
yards, cubic	cubic feet	27
yards, cubic	cubic inches	46,656
yards, cubic	cubic meters	0.764 554 857 984
yards, cubic	gallons	201.974 0
yards, cubic	liters	764.554 857 984
yards, cubic	pecks	86.784 91
yards, square	acres	0.000 206 611 6
yards, square	hectares	0.000 083 612 736
yards, square	square centimeters	8,361.273 6
yards, square	square feet	9
yards, square	square inches	1,296
yards, square	square meters	0.836 127 36
yards, square	square miles	0.000 000 322 830 6

AFRICA

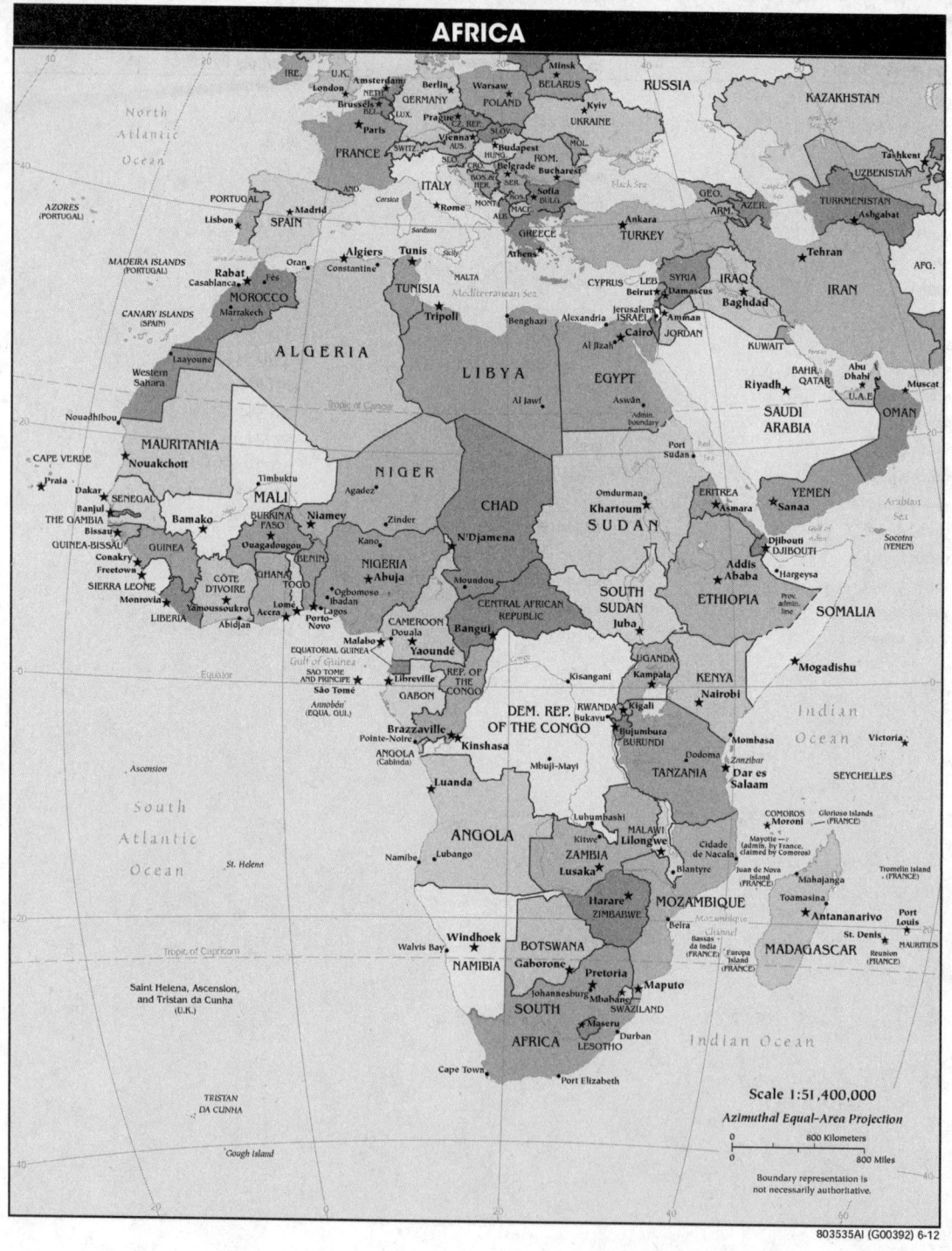

Scale 1:51,400,000

Azimuthal Equal-Area Projection

0   800 Kilometers

0   800 Miles

Boundary representation is
not necessarily authoritative.

803535AI (G00392) 6-12

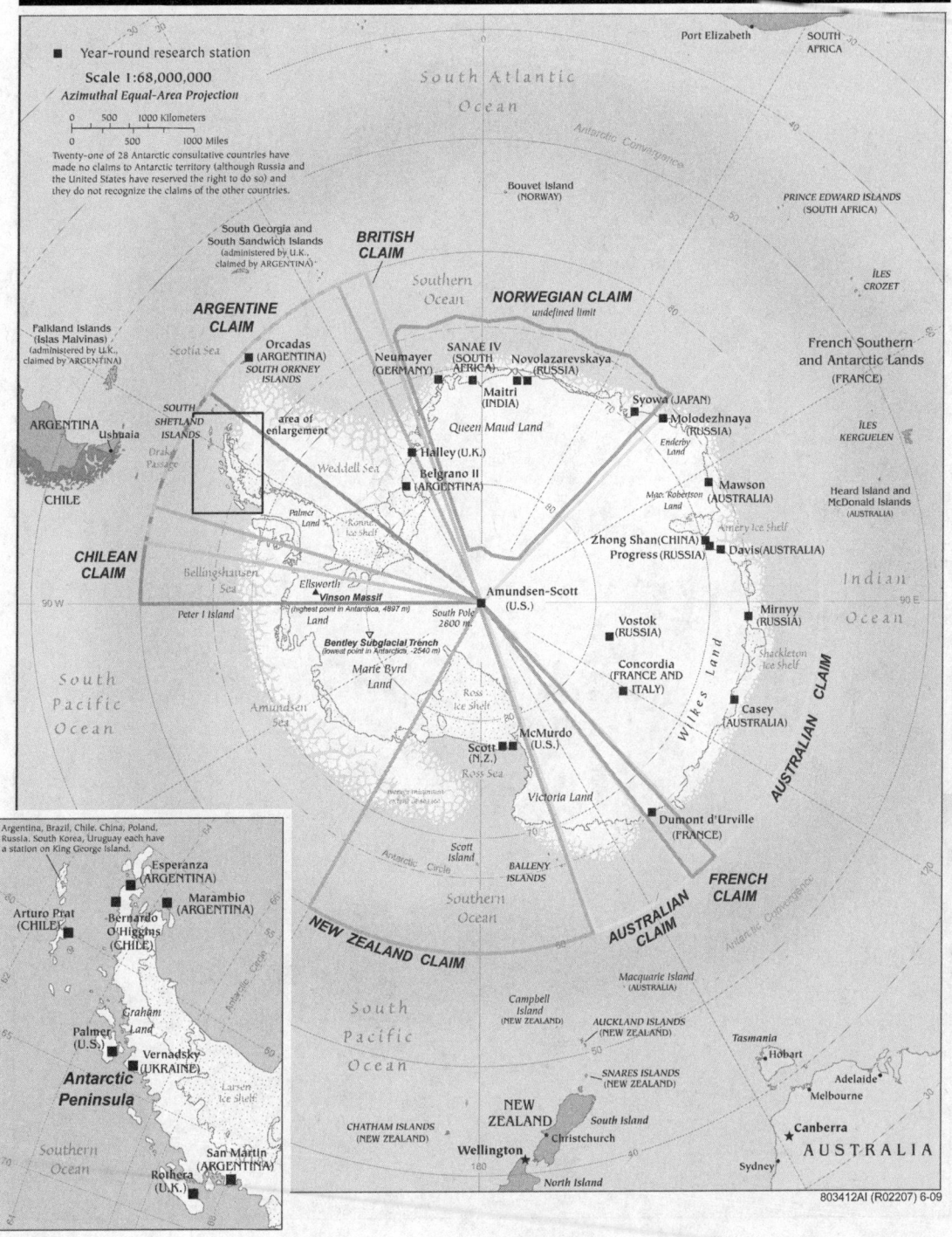

■ Year-round research station

Scale 1:68,000,000
Azimuthal Equal-Area Projection

Twenty-one of 28 Antarctic consultative countries have made no claims to Antarctic territory (although Russia and the United States have reserved the right to do so) and they do not recognize the claims of the other countries.

803412AI (R02207) 6-09

1117

ARCTIC REGION

North Pacific Ocean

ALEUTIAN ISLANDS

Bering Sea

KURIL ISLANDS

Petropavlovsk-Kamchatskiy

occupied by the Soviet Union in 1945;
administered by Russia; claimed by Japan.

JAPAN

Sea of Japan

Sea of Okhotsk

Khabarovsk

Kodiak

Bethel

Providniya

Anadyr'

Magadan

Okhotsk

Nome

Arctic Circle

Oymyakon

CHINA

Anchorage

Valdez

Juneau

UNITED STATES

Whitehorse

Fairbanks

Prince George

Dawson

Fort Nelson

Inuvik

Prudhoe Bay

Barrow

Chukchi Sea

Peyek

Cherskiy

Verkhoyansk

Yakutsk

Beaufort Sea

Banks Island

East Siberian Sea

Tiksi

NEW SIBERIAN ISLANDS

Fort McMurray

Yellowknife

Cambridge Bay

Victoria Island

QUEEN ELIZABETH ISLANDS

Arctic Ocean

Laptev Sea

Churchill

Arviat

Gjoa Haven

Resolute

Ellesmere Island

SEVERNAYA ZEMLYA

RUSSIA

Rankin Inlet

Repulse Bay

Pond Inlet

Alert

Nord

Noril'sk

Hudson Bay

Baffin Island

Qaanaaq (Thule)

FRANZ JOSEF LAND

Kara Sea

Dikson

Iqaluit

Baffin Bay

Davis Strait

Nuuk (Godthåb)

Sisimiut (Holsteinsborg)

Ilulissat (Jakobshavn)

Greenland (DENMARK)

Longyearbyen

Svalbard (NORWAY)

NOVAYA ZEMLYA

Barents Sea

Yekaterinburg

Perm'

Kuujjuaq

Labrador Sea

Qaqortoq (Julianehåb)

Tasiilaq

Ittoqqortoormiit (Scoresbysund)

Greenland Sea

Jan Mayen (NORWAY)

Bjørnøya (NORWAY)

Murmansk

Arkhangel'sk

Kazan'

Samara

Denmark Strait

Reykjavik

ICELAND

Arctic Circle

Norwegian Sea

NORWAY

FINLAND

Nizhniy Novgorod

KAZ.

North Atlantic Ocean

Tórshavn

Faroe Islands (DENMARK)

SHETLAND ISLANDS

SWEDEN

Helsinki

Oslo

Stockholm

Tallinn EST.

Saint Petersburg

Moscow

Saratov

Voronezh

Volgograd

Riga

LATVIA

LITH. Vilnius

RUS.

Minsk

BELARUS

Kharkiv

Rostov

Krasnodar

Scale 1:39,000,000

Lambert Azimuthal Equal-Area Projection

500 Kilometers

500 Miles

Copenhagen

DENMARK

Kaliningrad

Warsaw

POLAND

Kyiv

UKRAINE

Sochi

Belfast

Dublin

IRE.

U.K.

London

Amsterdam

NETH.

Berlin

GERMANY

Prague

CZECH REP.

SLOV.

HUNG.

ROMANIA

Chișinău

Black Sea

TURKEY

North Sea

Brussels BEL.

Scale 1:48,000,000

Azimuthal Equal-Area Projection

0 ——— 800 Kilometers

0 ——— 800 Miles

Boundary representation is
not necessarily authoritative.

803537AI (G00543) 6-12

EUROPE

Scale 1:19,300,000
Lambert Conformal Conic Projection,
standard parallels 40°N and 68°N

803539AI (G00772) 6-12

1121

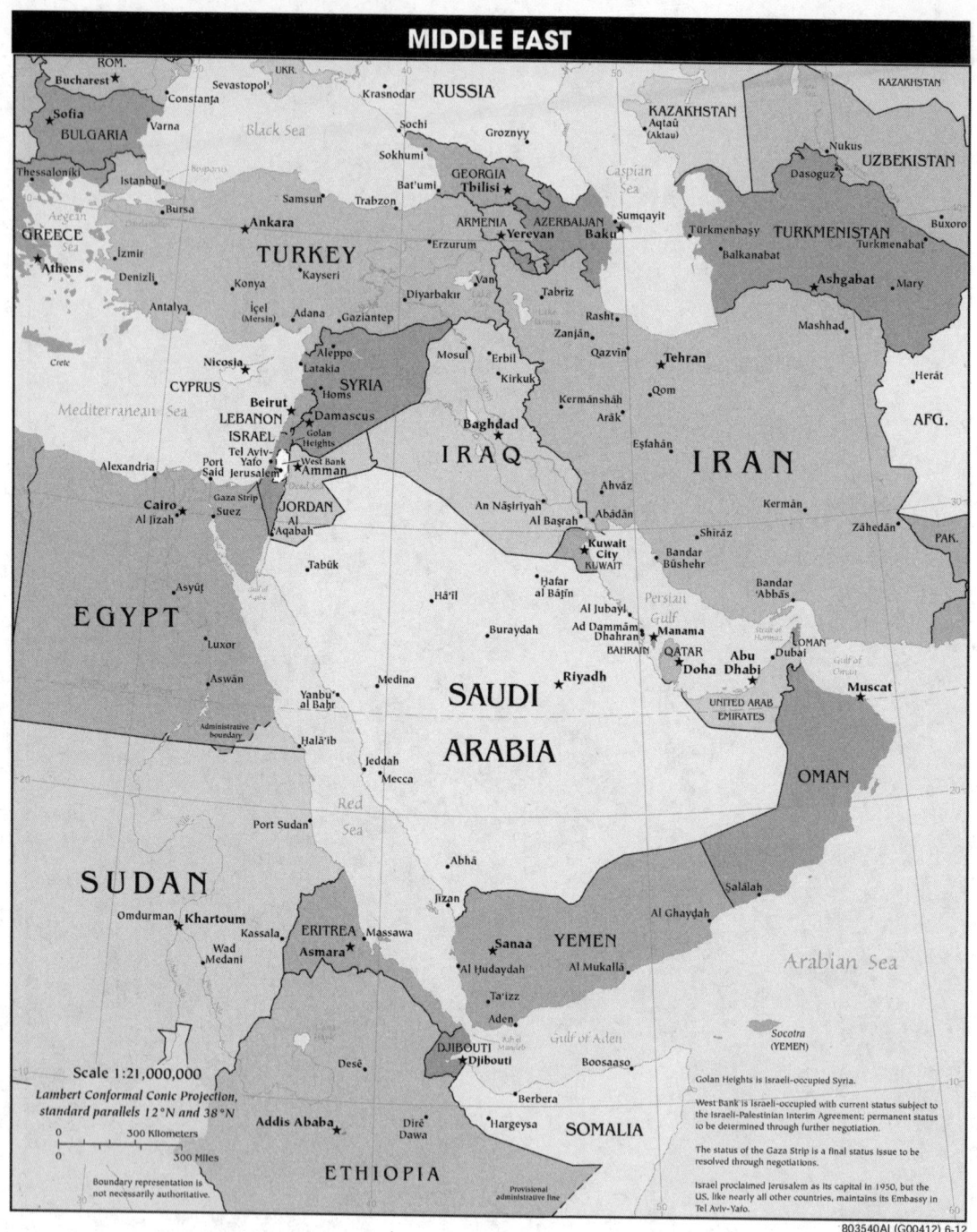

Golan Heights is Israeli-occupied Syria.

West Bank is Israeli-occupied with current status subject to the Israeli-Palestinian Interim Agreement; permanent status to be determined through further negotiation.

The status of the Gaza Strip is a final status issue to be resolved through negotiations.

Israel proclaimed Jerusalem as its capital in 1950, but the US, like nearly all other countries, maintains its Embassy in Tel Aviv-Yafo.

Scale 1:21,000,000

Lambert Conformal Conic Projection, standard parallels 12°N and 38°N

0   300 Kilometers

0   300 Miles

Boundary representation is not necessarily authoritative.

803540AI (G00412) 6-12

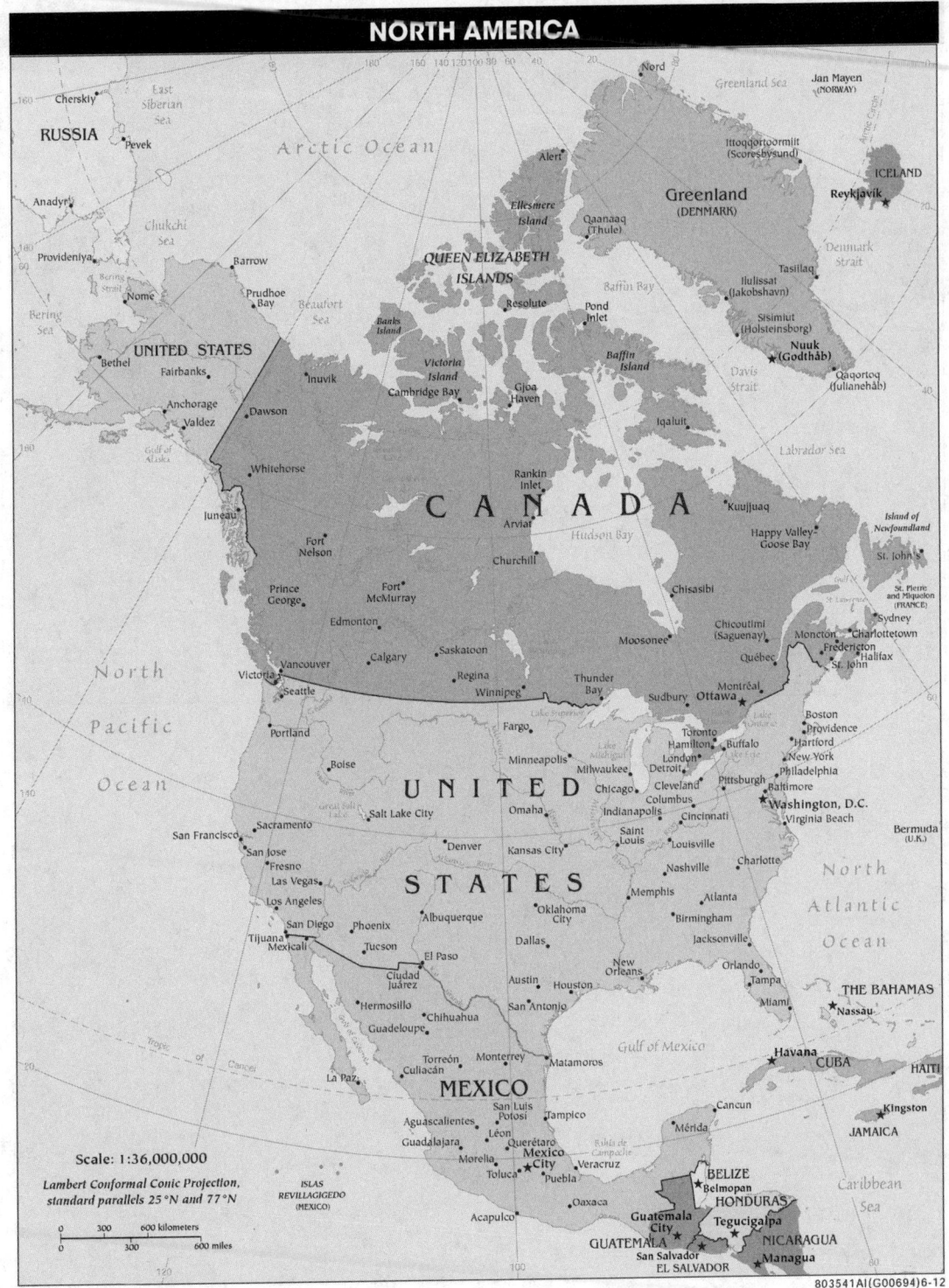

RUSSIA

Arctic Ocean

Nord

Greenland Sea

Jan Mayen
(NORWAY)

Cherskiy
Pevek

Anadyr

Providentya

Chukchi Sea

Barrow
Prudhoe Bay
Nome

Beaufort Sea

Alert

Ellesmere Island

Qaanaaq
(Thule)

Ittoqqortoormiit
(Scoresbysund)

Greenland
(DENMARK)

ICELAND

Reykjavík ★

Tasiilaq

Ilulissat
(Jakobshavn)

Sisimiut
(Holsteinsborg)

Nuuk
★ (Godthåb)

Qaqortoq
(Julianehåb)

Denmark Strait

UNITED STATES

Bethel

Fairbanks

Anchorage
Valdez

Dawson

Inuvik

Banks Island

Victoria Island

Cambridge Bay

Resolute

Gjoa Haven

QUEEN ELIZABETH ISLANDS

Baffin Bay

Pond Inlet

Baffin Island

Iqaluit

Davis Strait

Labrador Sea

Juneau

Whitehorse

Fort Nelson

Prince George

Fort McMurray

Edmonton

Calgary
Saskatoon

Rankin Inlet

Arviat

Churchill

Hudson Bay

CANADA

Kuujjuaq

Chisasibi

Moosonee

Happy Valley
Goose Bay

Island of Newfoundland

St. John's

St. Pierre
and Miquelon
(FRANCE)

Chicoutimi
(Saguenay)

Québec

Sydney

Moncton Charlottetown
Fredericton
St. John Halifax

North Pacific Ocean

Victoria
Seattle

Vancouver

Regina
Winnipeg

Thunder Bay

Sudbury Ottawa
Montréal

Boston
Providence
Hartford
New York
Philadelphia
Baltimore

Portland

Fargo

Lake Superior

Toronto
Hamilton
London
Detroit

Buffalo

Pittsburgh

Boise

Minneapolis
Milwaukee

Chicago

Cleveland
Columbus

UNITED

Salt Lake City

Omaha

Indianapolis
Cincinnati

Washington, D.C.
Virginia Beach

Bermuda
(U.K.)

San Francisco
San Jose
Fresno
Las Vegas
Los Angeles

Sacramento

Denver

Kansas City

Saint Louis
Louisville

Nashville

Charlotte

North Atlantic Ocean

STATES

San Diego
Tijuana
Mexicali

Phoenix
Tucson

Albuquerque

Oklahoma City

Memphis

Atlanta
Birmingham

El Paso

Dallas

Jacksonville

Ciudad Juárez

Austin
Houston

New Orleans

Orlando
Tampa

THE BAHAMAS

Nassau

Hermosillo
Chihuahua

San Antonio

Miami

Guadeloupe

Gulf of Mexico

Havana
CUBA

HAITI

La Paz

Torreón
Culiacán

Monterrey

Matamoros

MEXICO

Aguascalientes
Guadalajara

San Luis Potosí
León

Tampico

Cancún

Mérida

Kingston

JAMAICA

Morelia
Toluca

Querétaro
Mexico City
Puebla

Veracruz

Bahía de Campeche

BELIZE
Belmopan

HONDURAS

Caribbean Sea

Acapulco

Oaxaca

Guatemala City

Tegucigalpa

NICARAGUA

GUATEMALA

San Salvador
EL SALVADOR

Managua

Scale: 1:36,000,000

Lambert Conformal Conic Projection,
standard parallels 25°N and 77°N

ISLAS REVILLAGIGEDO
(MEXICO)

0   300   600 kilometers
0   300   600 miles

803541AI(G00694)6-12

OCEANIA

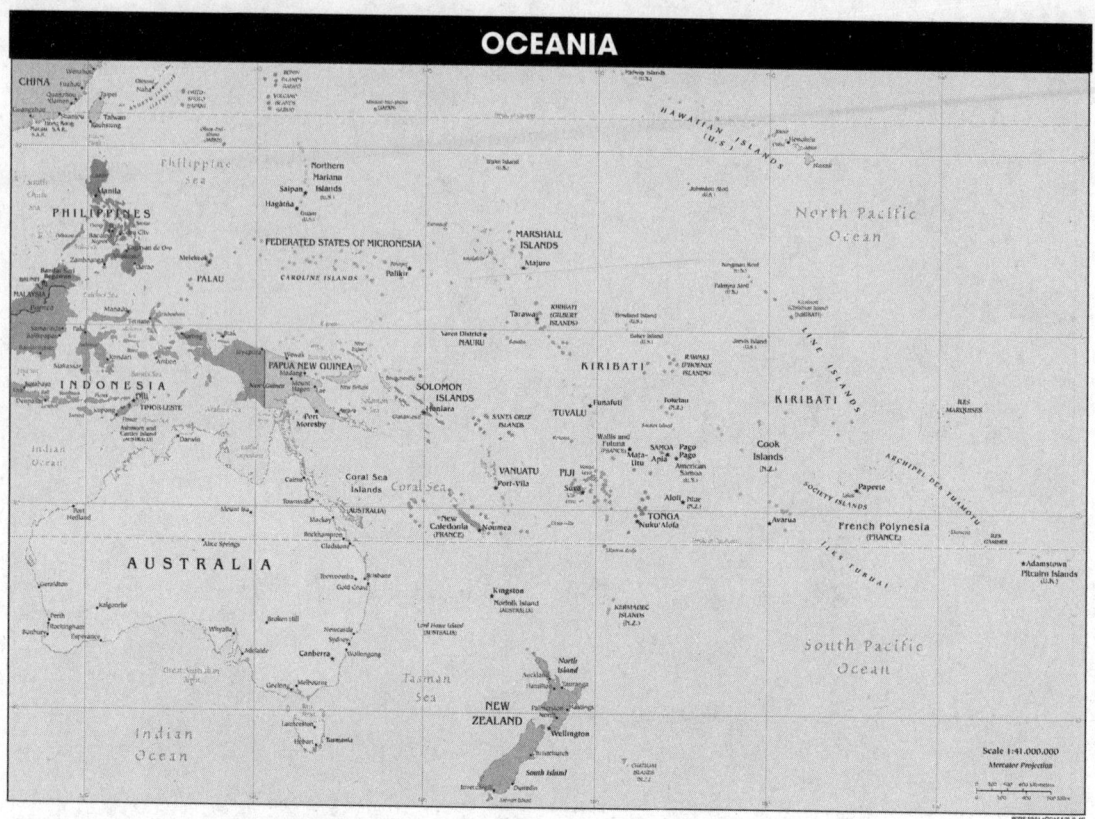

Scale 1:41,000,000
Mercator Projection

PHYSICAL MAP OF THE WORLD

Physical Map of the World, January 2015

POLITICAL MAP OF THE WORLD

Political Map of the World, January 2015

SOUTH AMERICA

SOUTHEAST ASIA

803620AI (G00834) 8-13

STANDARD TIME ZONE OF THE WORLD

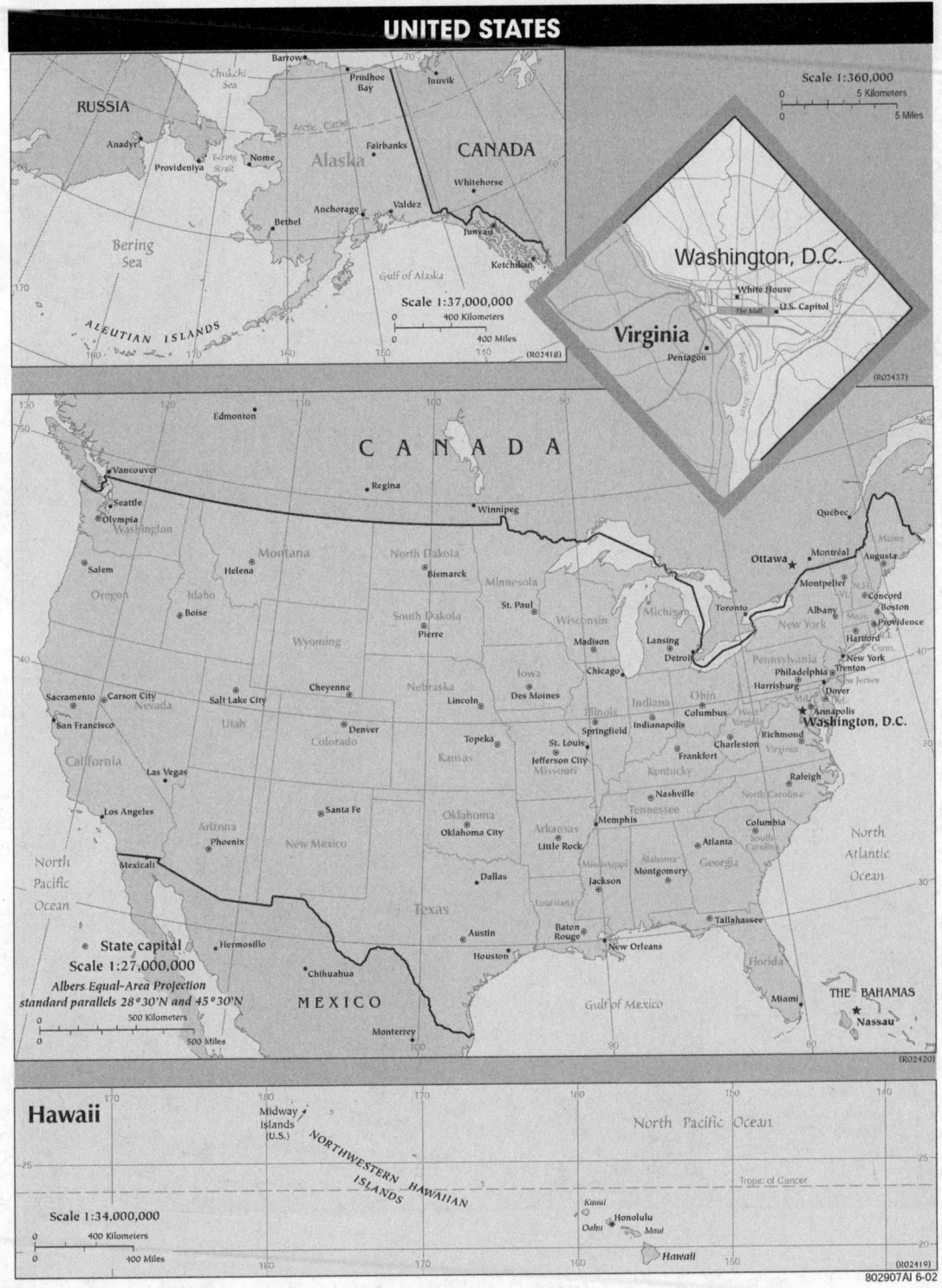

UNITED STATES

RUSSIA

Barrow
Prudhoe Bay
Inuvik
Chukchi Sea
Arctic Circle
Anadyr
Fairbanks
CANADA
Nome
Bering Strait
Provideniya
Alaska
Whitehorse
Bethel
Anchorage
Valdez
Juneau
Bering Sea
Gulf of Alaska
Ketchikan
ALEUTIAN ISLANDS

Scale 1:37,000,000
400 Kilometers
400 Miles
(R02418)

Scale 1:360,000
5 Kilometers
5 Miles

Washington, D.C.
White House
The Mall
U.S. Capitol
Virginia
Pentagon
(R02437)

CANADA

Edmonton
Vancouver
Regina
Winnipeg
Québec
Seattle
Olympia
Washington
Montana
North Dakota
Ottawa
Montréal
Maine
Augusta
Helena
Bismarck
Minnesota
Montpelier
Concord
Salem
Oregon
Idaho
Boise
South Dakota
Pierre
St. Paul
Wisconsin
Madison
Lansing
Michigan
Toronto
Detroit
New York
Albany
Hartford
Conn.
Boston
Providence
Sacramento
Carson City
Nevada
Salt Lake City
Cheyenne
Wyoming
Nebraska
Lincoln
Des Moines
Iowa
Chicago
Illinois
Indiana
Ohio
Columbus
Pennsylvania
Philadelphia
New York
Trenton
New Jersey
Dover
San Francisco
California
Las Vegas
Utah
Denver
Colorado
Topeka
Kansas
Springfield
St. Louis
Jefferson City
Missouri
Indianapolis
Frankfort
West Virginia
Charleston
Harrisburg
Md.
Annapolis
Washington, D.C.
Virginia
Richmond
Kentucky
Raleigh
Los Angeles
Arizona
Phoenix
Santa Fe
New Mexico
Oklahoma
Oklahoma City
Nashville
Tennessee
Memphis
Arkansas
Little Rock
North Carolina
Columbia
South Carolina
Atlanta
Georgia
North Atlantic Ocean
Mexicali
Dallas
Texas
Jackson
Mississippi
Alabama
Montgomery
North Pacific Ocean
Hermosillo
Austin
Houston
Baton Rouge
New Orleans
Louisiana
Tallahassee
Florida
Chihuahua
Monterrey
Miami
THE BAHAMAS
Nassau
Gulf of Mexico
MEXICO

⊙ State capital
Scale 1:27,000,000
Albers Equal-Area Projection
standard parallels 28°30'N and 45°30'N
500 Kilometers
500 Miles
(R02420)

Hawaii

Midway Islands (U.S.)
NORTHWESTERN HAWAIIAN ISLANDS
North Pacific Ocean
Tropic of Cancer
Kauai
Oahu
Honolulu
Maui
Hawaii
Scale 1:34,000,000
400 Kilometers
400 Miles
(R02419)

802907AI 6-02

1129